DICTIONARY
OF
INTERNATIONAL
BIOGRAPHY

2008

34th Edition

All communications to: International Biographical Centre
St Thomas' Place, ELY, CB7 4GG, GREAT BRITAIN

PUBLISHER
Nicholas S. Law

EDITOR IN CHIEF
Sara Rains

PRODUCTION/DESIGN
Scott Gwinnett

EDITORIAL ASSISTANTS
Rebecca Partner
Jenny Kirby

ISBN: 978 1903986 30 1

Printed and bound in the United Kingdom by:
CPI Antony Rowe, Bumper's Farm Industrial Estate,
Chippenham, Wiltshire, SN14 6LH, England

FOREWORD BY THE PUBLISHER

I am delighted to offer the Thirty Fourth Edition of the Dictionary of International Biography, the flagship publication of the International Biographical Centre of Cambridge, England, to its many readers or 'users' throughout the world.

The Dictionary of International Biography attempts to reflect contemporary achievement in every profession and field of interest within as many countries as possible. It is an ever growing reference source since very few biographical entries are repeated from one edition to the next and only then when they have been updated with relevant new material. In this way each new Edition adds thousands of new biographies to those already published in the series; to date more than 225,000 biographies have been presented from information supplied and checked by those individuals who are featured.

I am often asked how we select individuals for inclusion in the Dictionary of International Biography and for that matter other titles published by the IBC. Readers and researchers should know that we publish only information which has been provided by those listed and in every case we have had their permission to publish it. Selection is made on the grounds of achievement and contribution on a professional, occupational, national or international level, as well as interest to the reader. An additional intention is to provide librarians of major libraries with a cumulative reference work consisting of Volumes published annually.

It cannot be emphasised too strongly that there is no charge or fee of any kind for inclusion in the Dictionary. Every entrant was sent at least one typescript for approval before publication in order to eliminate errors and to ensure accuracy and relevance. While great care has been taken by our Editors it is always possible · that in a work of this size a few errors may have been made. If this is the case, my apologies in advance.

I would be grateful to hear from readers and researchers who feel that particular individuals should appear in future Volumes of the Dictionary of International Biography or any other relevant IBC works of reference. Such recommendations may be sent to the IBC's Research Department. Since our researchers have great difficulty in contacting some important figures it is always helpful to us to have addresses.

Nicholas S. Law
Director General
International Biographical Centre
Cambridge

November 2008

INTERNATIONAL BIOGRAPHICAL CENTRE
RANGE OF REFERENCE TITLES

From one of the widest ranges of contemporary biographical reference works published under any one imprint, some IBC titles date back to the 1930's. Each edition is compiled from information supplied by those listed, who include leading personalities of particular countries or professions. Information offered usually includes date and place of birth; family details; qualifications; career histories; awards and honours received; books published or other creative work; other relevant information including postal address. Naturally there is no charge or fee for inclusion. New editions are freshly compiled and contain on average 80-90% new information. New titles are regularly added to the IBC reference library.

Titles include:

2000 Eminent Scientists of Today
Dictionary of International Biography
Who's Who in Asia and the Pacific Nations
2000 Outstanding People
Who's Who in the 21st Century
2000 Outstanding Scientists of the 21st Century
2000 Outstanding Scholars of the 21st Century
2000 Outstanding Intellectuals of the 21st Century
Living Science
The Cambridge Blue Book

Enquires to:
Editorial Offices
International Biographical Centre
St Thomas' Place
ELY
CB7 4GG
GREAT BRITAIN

CONTENTS

CONTENTS

BIOGRAPHIES

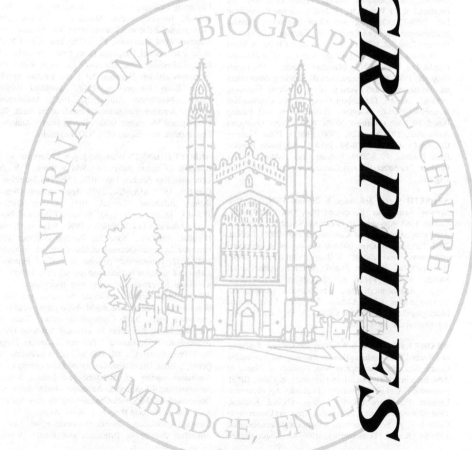

DICTIONARY OF INTERNATIONAL BIOGRAPHY

A

AAKER Everett, b. 20 April 1954, Wigan, Lancashire, England. Author. Education: HNC, Business Studies, Wirral College of Technology. 1982-86. Appointments: Professional career in business in England; Feature Writer, TV Scene Magazine, 1987-90. Publication: Television Western Players of the Fifties: A Biographical Encyclopaedia of All Regular Cast Members in Western Series, 1949-59, 1997; Encyclopaedia of Early Television Crime Fighters All Regular Cast Members in American Crime and Mystery Series 1948-1959, 2006. Honour: Associate, London Academy of Music and Dramatic Art, 1977. Membership: Institute of Purchasing and Supply, 1987. Address: c/o McFarland & Co, PO Box 611, Jefferson, North Carolina 28640, USA.

AARONSON Edward John (Jack), b. 16 August 1918. Company Director. m. Marian Davies, 2 sons. Education: CFS, London. Appointments: RA, Palestine to Tunisia, 1940-44, India, 1945-46, W/S Captain; Articled, Jackson Pixley & Co, 1946-49; Founder, General Secretary, The Anglo Israel Chamber of Commerce, 1950-53; Economic Advisor (Export), GEC, 1954-61, later General Manager Overseas Operations, 1961-63; Economic Advisor, Celmac Ltd, 1964-65; Deputy Chairman and part-time Chief Executive, The Steel Barrel Scammells & Associated Engineers Ltd, later Anthony Carrimore Ltd, 1965-68; Industrial Advisor, later Director, Armitage Industrial Holdings Ltd, 1965-68; Director, later Chairman, George Turton Platt, 1966-68; Director, E R & F Turner Ltd, 1967-68; Chairman Br Northrop Ltd, 1968-73; Chairman and Chief Executive, Scheme Manager and Creditors Committee Chairman, The G R A Property Trust Ltd, 1975-83; Non-Executive Chairman, Wand FC Bonham & Sons Ltd, 1981-89; Non-Executive Director, Camlab Ltd, 1982-89; Non-Executive Chairman, The Reject Shop plc, 1985-90. Memberships: FBI Standing Committees on overseas credit and overseas investment from inception, 1958-63; Council, The Export Group for the Construction Industries, 1960-63; Member, British Greyhound Racing Board, 1975-83; Chairman, NGRC Race Course Promoters Association, 1978-83; FCA, 1960; FInstD, 1980; Member General Committee, 1976-79, 1980-83, Chairman Pension Fund Trustees, 1985-2005, Reform Club. Address: 2 The Paddock, The Street, Bishops Cannings, Devizes SN10 2LD, England.

AARSETH Sverre Johannes, b. 20 July 1934, Steinkjer, Norway. Astronomer. Education: BSc, Oslo, 1959; PhD, Cantab, 1963. Appointments: Research Scientist, Institute of Astronomy, University of Cambridge, 1967-2001; Retired, 2001. Publications: Over 100 research papers in dynamical astronomy; Gravitational N-Body Simulations, 2003. Honours: Dirk Brouwer Award, American Astronomical Society; Asteroid #9836 named Aarseth. Memberships: Royal Astronomical Society; Royal Geographical Society; Alpine Club. Address: Institute of Astronomy, Madingley Road, Cambridge CB3 0HA, England. Website: www.ast.cam.ac.uk/~sverre

ABADIR Karim Maher, b. 6 January 1964, Egypt. Professor of Financial Econometrics; Head of Finance and Accounting Group. Education: Bachelor of Arts, Economics, Master of Arts, Economics, The American University in Cairo; DPhil, Economics, Oxford University, England. Appointments: Lecturer, Economics, Lincoln College, Oxford, England, 1988-92; Research Fellow, Economics, American University in Cairo, 1992-93; Senior Lecturer, Statistics and Econometrics, 1993-94, Reader, Econometrics, 1994-96, University of Exeter, England; Professor, Econometrics and Statistics, Departments of Mathematics and Economics, University of York, England, 1996-2005; Professor of Financial Econometrics, Imperial College London, 2005-. Publications: Numerous publications in professional journals and books; Numerous papers presented at national and international conferences. Honours: Invited lecturer at many conferences; ESRC Grants, 1996-98, 2001-04, 2003-06; Multa Scripsit Award, 1997; University of York Grant, 1998; Plura Scripsit Award, 2001. Memberships: Econometric Society; Institute of Mathematical Statistics; Fellow, Royal Statistical Society; European Science Foundation's Network on Econometric Methods for the Modelling of Nonstationary Data, Policy Analysis and Forecasting; Professional Association of Diving Instructors; Founder and Director, various undergraduate and graduate degrees; Editor of various journals. Address: Tanaka Business School, Imperial College London, London SW7 2AZ, England. E-mail: k.m.abadir@imperial.ac.uk

ABBOTT Gerry, b. 13 February 1935, Bow, London, England. University Teacher. m. Khin-Thant Han, 1 son, 2 daughters. Education: BA Honours, English, University College, London, 1958; PGCE with TEFL, Institute of Education, London, 1959; PhD, Education, University of Manchester, 1998. Appointments: National Service, 1953-55; Commissioned, 1955; Lecturer, College of Education, Bangkok, 1959-63; British Council Education Officer, Jordan, 1963-65; Lecturer, Teaching of English Overseas, Manchester University including numerous postings in Asia and Africa, 1965-92; Honorary Fellow, Manchester University, 1992-. Publications: Relative Clauses, 1969; Conditionals, 1970; Question-Word Questions, 1970; The Teaching of English as an International Language (with Peter Wingard), 1981; Back to Mandalay, 1990; Traveller's History of Burma, 1998; Numerous articles. Honours: 1st Prize, English Speaking Union Essay Competition, 1978; Appointed Honorary Fellow, Manchester University, 1992. Memberships: IATEFL; Amnesty International; Friends of the Earth; World Development Movement; Britain-Burma Society. Address: 16 Manor Drive, Manchester M21 7GQ, England.

ABBOTT-JOHNSON Winsome Joy, b. 17 September 1947, Australia. Dietician; Nutritionist. Widow, 1 son, 1 daughter. Education: Dip. Science, 1968; BSc, 1969; Dip. Nutrition and Dietetics, 1971; MApplSc, 1995. Appointments: Dietician, Sydney Adventist Hospital, 1971; Locum Dietician, 1979-81, Dietician, 1981-90, Senior Dietician, 1990-98, Senior Advanced Level Dietician, 1998-, Princess Alexandra Hospital, Brisbane, Australia; Private Practice, 1998-; Part-time Lecturer, Queensland University of Technology, 1988-2002. Publications: Articles in medical journals as author and co-author include most recently: Child-Pugh class, nutritional indicators and early liver transplant outcomes, 2001; Growth hormone treatment in adults with chronic liver disease: a randomized, double-blind placebo-controlled, cross-over study, 2002; Contributing author: Tomorrow's Nutrition Today, Australian Seventh-day Adventist Dietetic Association, 1975. Honours: Princess Alexandra Hospital Week Prize (jointly), 1994; Bob McMahon Scientific Prize (jointly), 1990, David Russell Clinical Prize (jointly), 1994, Australian Society of Parenteral and Enteral Nutrition. Memberships: Chairperson, Adventist Health Association, Queensland, 1994-95; Vice-Chairperson, Nutrition Society of Australia, Queensland Branch, 1996-97; American Overseas Dietetic Association; Dietetic Association of Australia; Australian Society of Parenteral and Enteral Nutrition;

Transplant Society of Australia and New Zealand. Address: 29 Brooke St, Crestmead, QLD 4132, Australia. E-mail: winsome@universal.net.au

ABBS Peter Francis, b. 22 February 1942, Cromer, Norfolk, England. Author; Lecturer. m. Barbara Beazeley, 10 June 1963, 1 son, 2 daughters. Education: BA, University of Bristol, England; DPhil, University of Sussex, England. Appointments: Lecturer, Senior Lecturer, Reader, Professor of Creative Writing, 1999-, University of Sussex, England. Publications: Poetry: For Man and Islands; Songs of a New Taliesin; Icons of Time; Personae; Love After Sappho, 2000; Viva la Vida, 2005; Non-Fiction: English for Diversity; Root and Blossom - The Philosophy, Practice and Politics of English Teaching; English Within the Arts; The Forms of Poetry; The Forms of Narrative; Autobiography in Education; Proposal for a New College (with Graham Carey); Reclamations - Essays on Culture, Mass-Culture and the Curriculum; A is for Aesthetic - Essays on Creative and Aesthetic Education; The Educational Imperative; The Polemics of Education; Editor, The Black Rainbow - Essays on the Present Breakdown of Culture; Living Powers - The Arts in Education; The Symbolic Order - A Contemporary Reader on the Arts Debate; The Polemics of Imagination: Essays on Art, Culture and Society; Against the Flow: Education, the Arts and Postmodern Culture, 2004; The Flowering of Flint: New edition selected poems, 2007. Contributions to: Times Higher Education Supplement; Agenda; Independent; Acumen; Stand; Daily Telegraph. Membership: Founding Member, New Metaphysical Art. Address: Graduate Research Centre in the Humanities, University of Sussex, Falmer, Brighton BN1 9RG, England.

ABD-ELMOTAAL Hussein, b. 7 October 1960, Cairo, Egypt. Professor. m. R Abd-Elkader, 1 son, 1 daughter. Education: BSc, Ain Shams University, Egypt, 1983; MSc, Ain Shams University, Egypt, 1987; PhD, Graz University of Technology, Austria, 1991. Appointments: Professor of Surveying and Geodesy, Head of Civil Engineering Department, Faculty of Engineering, Minia University. Honours: International Association of Geodesy, Best Paper Award, 1993; State Prize in Engineering Sciences, Egyptian Ministry for Scientific Research, 2003. Membership: Member, International Association of Geodesy. Address: Civil Engineering Department, Faculty of Engineering, Minia University, 61111 Minia, Egypt.

ABDEL SALAM Mohamed Soliman, b. 12 October 1944, Cairo, Egypt. Chairman; Managing Director. Education: MBA, Information Management System, American University, Cairo; Computer Science Diploma, Military Technical Academy. Appointments: Chairman, Cairo & Alexandria Stock Exchanges; Deputy Chairman, African Stock Exchanges Association; Consultant, Egyptian Stock Exchange Information Technology; Head, Egyptian-French project to establish the automated depository including the DVP system for the Egyptian market; Head, Capital Market Authority Information Technology Department; Chairman & Managing Director, Misr for Central Clearing, Depository & Registry (MCDR); Chairman, Nile Information Technology Company (NIT); President, Africa & Middle East Central Depositories Association (AMEDA); Deputy Chairman & Executive Director, Arab Stock Exchange (Arabex); Board Member, Cairo & Alexandria Stock Exchanges (CASE); Board Member, Information Technology Industry Development Authority (ITIDA); Chairman, Egyptian Securities Investor Protection Fund (EIPF). Honours: Man of the Year Award, 2007. Memberships: Egyptian Computers & Information Technology Association; Arab Computers & Information Technology Association; National Payment Council; American Chamber of Commerce. Address: 70 El-Gomhorya St, Cairo, Egypt. E-mail: m.abdsalam@mcsd.com.eg Website: www.mcsd.com.eg

ABDELMOTTLEP Mamdooh, b. 1 January 1955, Egypt. Professor of Criminal Justice. m. Enaam Eldosouki, 1 son, 1 daughter. Education: LLB (JD), BA, Police Sciences, Police University, Police College, Egypt, 1976; Diploma in Criminology, 1980, Diploma in Management & Organisation, 1983, MA, Police Sciences, 1983, PhD, Police Sciences, 1991, Graduate College of the Egypt Police University. Appointments: Police Officer, Egypt, 1976-91; Supervisor and Commander, Special Operations Regiment of 150 officers and 3,000 soldiers, 1986-93; Professor, Police Sciences & Criminal Justice, Police University, Egypt, Qatar and the United Arab Emirates, 1991-2004; Manager, Planning and Follow-up Office, Police Training Institute, Doha, Qatar, -1998; Head, Police Research Department, Police Research Center, General Police Headquarters, Sharjah, United Arab Emirates, 1998-2004; Expert and Legal Adviser, General Police Headquarters, Sharjah, 2000-; Security Training Expert, 2002-04; Visiting Professor, Sam Houston State University, Texas, USA, 2004-05; Adjunct Professor, Grambling State University, 2006. Publications: Numerous journal articles, presentations at conferences and meetings, books and monographs. Honours: Several monetary grants and certificates of appreciation and commendation. Memberships include: International Bar Association, USA; International Bar Association, UK; National Planning Institute of the Arab League, Kuwait; International Police Executive Symposium, USA; International Mediation & Arbitration Committee, USA. Address: 1905 Normal Park #806, Huntsville, TX 77340, USA. E-mail: drmamdooh@hotmail.com

ABDRAKHIMOV Ural Tutkabayevich, b. 22 September 1953, Republic of Kazakhstan. Professor; University Rector. 1 son, 3 daughters. Education: Graduate, Mechanics and Applied Mathematics, 1976, Post-graduate, 1978-81, Candidate of Science, 1983, S M Kirov Kazakh State University; Doctor's degree, 1993. Appointments: Assistant, 1976-78, Senior Teacher, 1982-88, Department of Structural Mechanics, Dzhambul Irrigation and Drainage Construction Institute; Leading Researcher, 1989-95; Head of Laboratory, Institute of Mechanics and Machinery, National Academy of Sciences, Republic of Kazakhstan, 1991; General Director, Republican Research and Production Engineering Centre of Mechanical Engineering, National Engineering Academy, Republic of Kazakhstan, 1993; Rector, Zhezkazgan Teacher's Training College (later O A Baikonurov Zhezkazgan University), 1995-2000; Professor, Dean, Almaty Technological University, 2000-04; Rector, Rudnyi Industrial Institute, Kazakhstan, 2004-. Publications: Over 100 articles and scientific works in the field of mechanical engineering. Honours: V G Shukhov Gold Medal, International Engineering Union, Russia, 1994; Honorary Worker of Education in the Republic of Kazakhstan Breastplate; Award for Active Labour Contribution, People's Democratic Party NurOtan, 2006. Memberships: National Engineering Academy, Republic of Kazakhstan. Address: 111500 50 let Oktyabrya Str 38, Rudnyi, Kostanai region, Kazakhstan.

ABDUL Paula, b. 19 June 1963, Los Angeles, California, USA. Singer; Dancer; Choreographer. Education: Television and Radio Studies, Cal State, Northridge College. Musical Education: Studied jazz and tap dance. Career: Choreographer, LA Laker basketball cheerleaders; Scenes in films: Bull Durham; Coming To America; The Waiting Game; Appeared in a Saturday Night Live sketch with David Duchovny. Choreographer, pop videos including: The Jacksons and Mick Jagger: Torture; George Michael: Monkey; with Janet Jackson: Nasty; When I Think Of You; What Have You Done For Me Lately; Fitness video, Cardio Dance. Worldwide performances as singer include: Tours throughout US, UK, Japan and Far East; Prince's Trust Rock Gala, London Palladium, 1989; America Has Heart (earthquake and hurricane benefit concert), 1989; LIFEbeat's Counteraid (AIDS benefit concert), 1993; Own dance company, Co Dance; Judge, American Idol, 2002-: The Search for a Superstar, 2002-. Recordings: Solo albums: Forever Your Girl (Number 1, US), 1989; Shut Up And Dance (The Dance Mixes), 1990; Spellbound (Number 1, US), 1991; Head Over Heels, 1995; Contributor, Disney charity album For Our Children, 1991; Greatest Hits, 2000; US Number 1 singles include: Straight Up; Forever Your Girl; Cold Hearted; Opposites Attract; Rush Rush; The Promise Of A New Day. Honours: MTV Video Award, Best Choreography, Janet Jackson's Nasty, 1987; Emmy, Best Choreography, for Tracey Ullman Show, 1989; Rolling Stone Awards, including Best Female Singer, 1989; American Music Awards include: Favourite Pop/Rock Female Vocalist, 1989, 1992; Billboard Magazine, Top Female Pop Album, 1990; Grammy, Best Music Video, Opposites Attract, 1991; Star on Hollywood Walk Of Fame, 1993; Humanitarian of the Year, Starlight Foundation, Los Angeles, 1992; Numerous Gold and Platinum discs. Address: Third Rail Entertainment, Tri-Star Bldg, 10202 W Washington Avenue, Suite 26, Culver City, CA 90232, USA.

ABDULLAH Ahmed, b. 26 September 1949, Malé, Maldives. Government Minister. m. Aminath Aboul Hakeem, 1 son, 3 daughters. Education: Secondary Education; English Language course, Australia; Certificate in General Administration; Certificate of Teaching: English Language, Maldivian Language Calligraphy, Art. Appointments: Secretary, Ministry of Health, 1969; Secretary, Ministry of Education, 1969; Secretary, Prime Ministers Office, 1972; Third Secretary, Embassy of Maldives, Sri Lanka, 1975; Secretary, Electricity Department, 1975; Secretary, Ministry of Transport, 1975; First Secretary, Permanent Mission of Maldives to the United Nations, New York, 1977; Under Secretary, Ministry of External Affairs, 1978; Senior under Secretary, Ministry of External Affairs, 1979; Counsellor Charge'de Affairs Embassy of Maldives, Sri Lanka (in charge of reopening the embassy), 1979; High Commissioner of Maldives to Sri Lanka Concurrently accredited to the member countries of South Asian Association for Regional Co-operation (SAARC), India, Pakistan, Bangladesh, Nepal, Bhutan, 1986; President of Colombo Plan, 1987; Dean of the Diplomatic Corps in Sri Lanka, 1991; Minister of Health, 1996, 1998; Minister of Information, Arts and Culture, 2004-05; Minister of Environment, Energy and Water, 2005-; Acting Chief of Galolhu Ward in Malé City, 1997-. Address: G.Mascot, Galolhu, Lonuziyaaraiy Magu, Malé, Maldives. E-mail: ahmed.mascot@gmail.com

ABDULLAH Mohd Azmuddin, b. 16 February 1970, Malaysia. Academician. Education: M Eng, Chemical Engineering and Biotechnology, University of Manchester Institute of Science and Technology, England, 1994; PhD, Bioprocess Engineering, Universiti Putra, Malaysia, 1999. Appointments: Research Assistant, 1994, Tutor, 1994-99, Universiti Putra, Malaysia; Visiting Scientist, Plant Tissue Culture and Plant Physiology Laboratory, Kinki University, Japan, 1997; Visiting Scientist, Biomaterials Science and Engineering Laboratory, Massachusetts Institute of Technology, USA, 2000-01; Associate Researcher,

Mathematical Sciences and Application Laboratory, Institute for Mathematical Research, 2003-, Associate Researcher, Natural Product Laboratory, Institute of Bioscience, 2003-, Lecturer, Department of Biotechnology, 1999-2004, Universiti Putra, Malaysia; Senior Lecturer, Department of Chemical Engineering, Universiti Teknologi PETRONAS, 2004-. Publications: Numerous articles in professional journals. Honours: Best Undergraduate project, 7th MSMBB Conference, 1996; Research Award, Japanese Society for the Promotion of Science, 1997; Research Award, Malaysia-MIT Biotechnology Partnership Programme, 2000-01; Gold Medal, Research & Design Exhibition, 2003; Silver Medal, Research & Design Exhibition, 2004; Silver Medal, Exhibition of Invention & Research, 2005; Bronze Medal, 16th International Exhibition on Invention, Innovation, Industrial Design & Technology, 2005; Overall Champion, EDX 15, 2005; Overall Champion, Engineering & Innovation Design Competition, 2006; Bronze Medal, 17th International Exhibition on Invention, Innovation, Industrial Design & Technology, 2006; Listed in international biographical dictionaries. Memberships: Subcommittee, Malaysian Society of Molecular Biology and Biotechnology; Academic Staff Association of UPM; Subcommittee, Society of Malaysian Chemical Engineers. Address: Department of Chemical Engineering, Universiti Teknologi Petronas, Bandar Sri Iskandar, 31750, Perak, Malaysia. E-mail: azmuddin@petronas.com.my

ABLE Graham George, b. 28 July 1947, Norwich, England. School Principal. m. Mary Susan Munro, 1 son, 1 daughter. Education: BA (later MA), Natural Sciences, 1968, PGCE, 1969, Trinity College, Cambridge; MA (by research and thesis), Social Sciences, Durham University, 1983. Appointments: Teacher of Chemistry, 1969-83, Housemaster (Boarding), 1976-83, Sutton Valence School; Second Master, Barnard Castle School, 1983-88; Headmaster, Hampton School, 1988-96; Master (Principal), Dulwich College, London, 1997-; Chairman, Dulwich College Enterprises Ltd, 1997-. Publications: MA Thesis on boarding education, 1983; Head to Head (co-author), 1992; Various newspaper and magazine articles. Memberships: Chairman, Academic Policy, 1998-2001, Chairman, 2003, Headmasters and Headmistresses Conference; Vice-President, 2004-, International Boy's School Coalition; Member of Council, Imperial College, 1999-2006; Member of Council, Roedean School, 2000-. Address: Dulwich College, London SE21 7LD, England. E-mail: the.master@dulwich.org.uk

ABRAMSKY Jennifer, b. 7 October 1946. Radio Producer and Editor. m. Alasdair Liddell, 1976, 1 son, 1 daughter. Education: BA, University of East Anglia. Appointments: Programme Operations Assistant, 1969, Producer, The World at One, 1973, Editor, PM, 1978, Producer, Radio Four Budget Programmes, 1979-86, Editor, Today Programme, 1986-87, Editor, News and Current Affairs Radio, 1987-93, established Radio Four News FM, 1991, Controller, Radio Five Live, 1993-96, Director, Continuous News, including Radio Five Live, BBC News 24, BBC World, BBC News Online, Ceefax, and Director, 1998-2000, BBC Radio and Music, 2000-, BBC Radio; News International Visiting Professor of Broadcast Media, 2002. Honours: Woman of Distinction, Jewish Care, 1990; Honorary Professor, Thames Valley University, 1994; Sony Radio Academy Award, 1995; Honorary MA, Salford University, 1997; Royal Academy Fellowship, 1998; Honorary RAM, 2002. Memberships: Member, Economic and Social Research Council, 1992-96; Editorial Board, British Journalism Review, 1993-; Member, Board of Governors, BFI, 2000-; Vice-Chair, Digital Radio Development Bureau, 2002-; News International Visiting Professor of Broadcast

Media, Exeter College, Oxford, 2002; Director, Hampstead Theatre, 2003-. Address: BBC, Room 2811, Broadcasting House, Portland Place, London W1A 1AA, England.

ABRAMSON Glenda Maureen, b. Johannesburg, South Africa. Academic. m. David Abramson, 2 sons. Education: University of the Witwatersrand, Johannesburg; Transvaal Teachers' Higher Diploma, Johannesburg College of Education. Appointments: Lecturer, 1965-73, Senior Lecturer, 1973-78, Department of Hebrew Studies, University of the Witwatersrand; Tutor, Department of Near and Middle East, School of African and Oriental Studies, London University, England, 1980-81; Visiting Lecturer, Oxford Centre for Postgraduate Hebrew Studies, 1980-81; Fellowship by Special Election, 1981-2004, Emeritus Fellowship, 2005, St Cross College, Oxford; Jacob and Shoshana Schreiber Fellowship in Modern Jewish Studies, Oxford Center for Hebrew and Jewish Studies, 1981-2000; Cowley Lecturer in Post-Biblical Hebrew, Oxford University, 2000-06; Professor of Hebrew and Jewish Studies, 2006. Publications include: Israeli Drama and the Bible: Kings on the Stage, 2004; Editor, The Encyclopedia of Modern Jewish Culture, 2005; Biblical Sources and the Literature of Catastrophe: Three Modern Hebrew Poems, 2005; Exile, Imprisonment and the Literary Imagination, 2006. Memberships: Association for Jewish Studies; British Association for Jewish Studies; European Association for Jewish Studies; Association for Israel Studies. Address: Oriental Institute, Pusey Lane, Oxford OX1 2LE, England. E-mail: glenda.abramson@stx.ox.ac.uk

ABRASZEWSKI Andrzej T, b. 4 January 1938, Paradyz, Poland. UN Official, Ambassador-at-large. m. Teresa Zagorska, 1 son. Education: MA, Central School for Foreign Service, Warsaw, 1961; LLD, Law School, Copernicus University, Torun, 1971; Senior Research Staff, Polish Institute of International Affairs; Postgraduate Research and Studies on International Organisations, The Hague, Geneva, Paris, Rome, Vienna and New York. Appointments: Researcher, Department of International Organisations, Polish Institute of International Affairs, Warsaw, 1961-71; Secretary, Polish National Committee on 25th Anniversary of the United Nations, 1970; Polish Delegate, 5th Committee of the General Assembly, 1971-90 and 2001-06; Member, Ad-hoc Working Group on United Nations Programme and Budget Machinery, 1975; Member, Advisory Committee on Administrative and Budgetary Questions, 1977-82; Vice Chairman, 5th Committee, 34th Session of the General Assembly, 1979; Chairman, 5th Committee, 37th Session of the General Assembly, 1982; Member, Committee on Contributions, 1983-88; Vice Chairman, Committee on Contributions, 1987, 1988; Vice Chairman, Committee for Programme and Co-ordination, 1989; Chairman, Committee for Programme and Co-ordination, 1990; Member, Joint Inspection Unit, 1991-2000; Vice Chairman, Joint Inspection Unit, 1993, 1998; Chairman, Joint Inspection Unit, United Nations and the specialised agencies, 1994; Member, Advisory Committee on Administrative and Budgetary Questions, United Nations, 2001-; Vice Chairman, 2006-. Publications: 3 books; Numerous articles on legal, political, administrative and financial problems of international organisations. Honours: Listed in Who's Who publications. Address: United Nations, ACABQ, Room CB-60, New York, NY 10016, USA. E-mail: abraszewski@un.org

ABSE Dannie, b. 22 September 1923, Cardiff, Glamorgan, Wales. Physician; Poet; Writer; Dramatist. m. Joan Mercer, 4 August 1951, 1 son, 2 daughters. Education: St Illtyd's College, Cardiff; University of South Wales and Monmouthshire,

Cardiff; King's College, London; MD, Westminster Hospital, London, 1950. Appointments: Manager, Chest Clinic, Central Medical Establishment, London, 1954-82; Senior Fellow in Humanities, Princeton University, New Jersey, 1973-74. Publications: Poetry: Funland and Other Poems, 1973; Lunchtime, 1974; Way Out in the Centre, 1981; White Coat, Purple Coat: Collected Poems, 1948-88, 1989; Remembrance of Crimes Past, 1990; On the Evening Road, 1994; Intermittent Journals, 1994; Twentieth-Century Anglo-Welsh Poetry, 1997; A Welsh Retrospective, 1997; Arcadia, One Mile, 1998; Goodbye Twentieth Century, 2001; New and Collected Poems, 2003; The Two Roads Taken, 2003, many others. Editor: The Music Lover's Literary Companion, 1988; The Hutchinson Book of Post-War British Poets, 1989. Fiction: Ash on a Young Man's Sleeve, 1954; Some Corner of an English Field, 1956; O Jones, O Jones, 1970; Voices in the Gallery, 1986; Ask the Bloody Horse, 1986; There was a Young Man from Cardiff, 2001; The Strange Case of Dr Simmonds and Dr Glas, 2002. Contributions to: BBC and various publications in UK and USA. Honours: Foyle Award, 1960; Welsh Arts Council Literature Prizes, 1971, 1987; Cholmondeley Award, 1985. Memberships: Poetry Society, President, 1979-92; Royal Society of Literature, Fellow, 1983; Welsh Academy, Fellow, 1990, President, 1995. Address: c/o PFD, Drury House, 34-43 Russell Street, London, WC2B 5HA, England.

ABUBAKAR Mohammed Kaoje, b. 19 October 1959, Zuru, Nigeria. University Lecturer. m. Rakkiya Aliyu-Carpenter, 1 son, 2 daughters. Education: BSc, 1982, MSc, 1989, Biochemistry, Ahmadu Bello University, Zaria; PhD, Biochemistry, University of Essex, England, 1994. Appointments: Graduate Assistant, 1983-84, Assistant Lecturer, 1984-89, Lecturer, II, 1989-92, Lecturer, 1992-95, Senior Lecturer, 1995-2000, Professor of Biochemistry, 2000-, Usman Danfodiyo University, Sokoto; Ag Head, Department of Biochemistry, 1989-91, 1995, 2000, Member, Senior Staff Disciplinary Committee, 1995-96, UDUS; Director General, 1996-98, Permanent Secretary, 1998, Honorable Commissioner, 2006-07, Kebbi State Ministry of Health; Permanent Secretary, 2000-03, Honorable Commissioner, 2003-06, Kebbi State Ministry of Education; Chairman, Implementation Committee, KBSUST, Aliero, 2006-07; Vice Chancellor, Kebbi State University of Science and Technology, Aliero, 2007-. Publications: 29 articles in professional journals. Honours: Best First Year Student of Biochemistry, 1980, Best Second Year Student of Biochemistry, 1981, Best Final Year Student of Biochemistry, 1982, Best Student in MSc Coursework, 1988, Ahmadu Bello University; Doctorate Fellowship, Institute of Administrative Management of Nigeria, 1998; Certified Distinguished Administrator, 1998; Certified Distinguished Health Administrator; Honours for Nutrition of the Child, FMOH and UNICEF, 1998; Elected Member, European Academy of Sciences; American Biographical Society Man of the Year, 2008. Memberships: Nigerian Society of Biochemistry and Molecular Biology; New York Academy of Sciences; European Academy of Sciences. Address: Kebbi State University of Science and Technology, Aliero, PMB 1144, Birnin Kebbi, Kebbi State, Nigeria. E-mail: professorkaoje@yahoo.com

ABUL-HAJ Suleiman Kahil, b. 20 April 1925, Palestine. Naturalised US Citizen, 1955. Pathologist. m. Elizabeth Abood, 11 February 1948, 3 sons. Education: BS, University of California at Berkeley, 1949; MS, 1951, MD, 1955, University of California at San Francisco. Appointments: Resident, University of California Hospital, San Francisco, 1949; Intern, Cook County Hospital, Chicago, 1955-56; Served to Major, US Army Medical Corps, 1956-62;

Resident, Brooke General Hospital, 1957-59; Chief, Clinical and Anatomical Pathology, Walter Reed Army Hospital, Washington, 1959-62; Consultant, Armed Forces Institute of Pathology, 1960-96, California Tumor Tissue Registry, 1962-96, Tripler General Hospital, Hawaii, 1963-67, Camarillo State Hospital, 1964-70; Senior Surgical Pathologist, Los Angeles County General Hospital, 1963; Associate Professor, University of Southern California School of Medicine, Los Angeles, 1963-96; Director, Department of Pathology, Community Memorial Hospital, Ventura, California, 1964-80, General Hospital, Ventura County, 1966-74; Director, Pathology Service Medical Group, 1970-. Publications: Articles in professional journals, on research in cardiovascular disease, endocrine, renal and skin diseases, also cancer. Honours: Borden Award, California Honor Society, 1949; Achievement Certificate, Surgeon General, US Army, 1962; Listed in numerous Who's Who publications and biographical dictionaries. Memberships: Fellow, American Society of Clinical Pathologists; Fellow, College of American Pathologists; Fellow, American Association for the Advancement of Science; International College of Surgeons; World Affairs Council; Board of Directors, Tri-Counties Blood Bank; Board of Directors, American Cancer Society. Address: 105 Encinal Way, Ventura, CA 93001-3317, USA.

ACKMAN Robert George, b. 27 September 1927, Dorchester, New Brunswick, Canada. Chemist. m. Catherine Isobel McKinnon, 2 daughters. Education: BA, University of Toronto, 1950; MSc, Dalhousie University, Halifax, Nova Scotia, Canada, 1952; PhD, University of London, DIC, Imperial College of Science and Technology, London, 1956; LLD Dalhousie University, 2000. Appointments: Fisheries Research Board of Canada, 1950, 1956, rose to Director, Marine Lipids, 1972-79; Full Professor, Nova Scotia Technical College, Department of Food Science and Technology, 1980-90; Research Professor, 1990-94, Professor Emeritus, 1995-, Dalhousie University/Canadian Institute of Fisheries Technology; Retired 2004. Publications: Over 600 on marine lipids, gas chromatography, thin-layer chromatography with FID readout; Low erucic acid rapeseed oil; Specialty long-chain omega-3 polyunsaturated fatty acids; Fish and marine invertebrate fatty acids; Editor: Marine Biogenic Lipids, 2 volumes. Honours: Fellow, Chemical Institute of Canada, 1972; H P Kaufman Medal International Society of Fat Research, 1980; Supelco-AOCS Award, 1994; Officer, Order of Canada, 2001; LLD honoris causa, Dalhousie University, 2003. Memberships: CIC; AOCS; AOAC; Nova Scotia Institute of Science; Original Member ISI Highly Cited Researcher's Database; Chemical Institute of Canada; American Oil Chemists Society; Canadian Society for Chemistry; International Society for the Study of Fatty Acids and Lipids. Address: Canadian Institute of Fisheries Technology, Dalhousie University, PO Box 1000, Halifax, NS, B3J 2X4 Canada. E-mail: robert.ackman@dal.ca

ADAM Gottfried W J, b. 1 December 1939, Treysa, Germany. Professor. 3 sons. Education: Dr Theol, University of Bonn, 1968; Dr Theol, Habil, University of Marburg, 1975. Appointments: Assistant, Theology Faculty, University of Bonn, 1966-67; Assistant, 1968-75, Lecturer, Professor, Practical Theology, 1976-78, 1980, University of Marburg; Professor, University of Goettingen, 1978-79; Professor, Protestant Theology, Chair, Philosophy Faculty, University of Wuerzburg, 1981-92; Professor, Religious Education, Chair, Faculty of Protestant Theology, Vienna, 1992; Dean, Faculty of Protestant Theology, University of Vienna, 1999-2006. Publications: Author: 6 books; Editor, Co-editor: 22 books; 3 periodicals; 3 book series; 430 articles on theological and religious educational questions. Honours: Diploma of Theology, honoris causa, Sibiu, Romania, 1996; Károli Gáspár Református University, Budapest, Hungary, 2000. Memberships: Wissenschaftliche Gesellschaft für Theologie; Rudolf-Bultmann-Gesellschaft für Hermeneutische Theologie; Arbeitskreis für Religionspaedagogik; Religious Education Association, USA. Address: Chair of Religious Education, Faculty of Protestant Theology, Schenkenstr 8-10, A-1010 Wien, Austria. E-mail: gottfried.adam@univie.ac.at

ADAM Robert, b. 10 April 1948, Bournemouth, England. Architect. m. Sarah, 1 son, 1 daughter. Education: Rome Scholarship, University of Westminster, 1973. Appointments: Director, Robert Adam Architects, 1977-; Chair, College of Chapters, INTBAU. Publications: Classical Architecture: A Complete Handbook, 1990; Buildings by Design, 1994; Editor, Tradition Today, 2008; Author of numerous articles and papers for publications including national and international newspapers, magazines and journals; Contributions to many TV and radio programmes. Honours: Commendation London Borough of Richmond-Upon-Thames Conservation and Design Awards Scheme, 1991; Winner, Copper Roofing Competition Copper Development Association, 1995; Elmbridge BC Design/Conservation Award, 1998; RIBA Southern Region National Housebuilder Design Award; Best Partnership Development Commendation for Roman Court, Rocester, 2000; Marsh Country Life Awards, 2001; Best Private Housing Development, Brick Awards, 2004; Award for a New Building in the Classical Tradition, The Georgian Group Awards, 2007; Award of Excellence for Masterplan for Western Harbour, Edinburgh, Congress for the New Urbanism Charter Awards, 2008. Memberships: RIBA; Brother, The Artworkers Guild; Fellow, Royal Society of Arts; Architecture Club Committee; Academy of Urbanism; Athenaeum and Home House. Address: Robert Adam Architects, 9 Upper High Street, Winchester, Hampshire SO23 8UT, England. E-mail: robert.adam@robertadamarchitects.com

ADAMS Anna Theresa, (Theresa Butt, Anna Butt as painter), b. 9 March 1926, London, England. Writer; Artist. m. Norman Adams, 18 January 1947, 2 sons. Education: NDD Painting, Harrow School of Art, 1945; NDD, Sculpture, Hornsey College of Art, 1950. Appointments: Teaching at various schools; Designer, Chelsea Pottery, 1953-55; Part-time Art Teacher, Manchester, 1966-86; Exhibited terracotta sculptures widely, various galleries in the North of England, 1969-86; Works in several public collections, including Rochdale Museum, Bradford University and Blackwell at Bowness; Art Teacher, Settle High School, 1971-74; Exhibited watercolours in RA Summer Show, 1986-2005; Poetry Editor, Green Book, 1989-92; Small retrospective, Peter Scott Gallery, Lancaster University, 2007. Publications: Journey Through Winter, 1969; Rainbow Plantation, 1971; Memorial Tree, 1972; A Reply to Intercepted Mail, 1979; Brother Fox, 1983; Trees in Sheep Country, 1986; Dear Vincent, 1986; Six Legs Good, 1987; Angels of Soho, 1988; Nobodies, 1990; Island Chapters, 1991; Life on Limestone, 1994; Green Resistance: Selected and New Poems, 1996; A Paper Ark, 1996; The Thames: Anthology of River Poems, 1999; London in Verse & Prose, 2002; Flying Underwater, 2004. Contributions to: Poetry Review; P N Review; The Countryman; 10th Muse; Country Life; Yorkshire Life; Dalesman; Pennine Platform; Western Mail; Stand; Sunday Telegraph; Poetry Durham; Poetry Canada; Poetry Nottingham; Poetry Matters; Encounter; Spokes; Meridian; Acumen; Aquarius; Orbis; Spectator; The North; Yorkshire Journal; Rialto; Scintilla; The Interpreter's House; The London Magazine; Magma; Temenos. Honours: 1st Prize, Yorkshire Poets, 1974, 1976, 1977; 1st Prize, Arnold

Vincent Bowen, 1976; Several Prizes, Lancaster Festival Poetry Competition; 1st Prize, Lincoln Open, 1984; 1st Prize, Rhyme International, 1986; 2nd Prize, Cardiff Festival Poetry Competition, 1987. Memberships: Poetry Society, London. Address: Butts Hill, Horton-in-Ribblesdale, Settle, North Yorkshire, BD24 0HD.

ADAMS Bryan, b. 5 November 1959, Kingston, Ontario, Canada. Singer; Songwriter; Musician. Career: International Recording Artist; Signed contract with A&M Records, 1979; 45 million albums sold world-wide, 1995; Numerous worldwide tours. Creative Works: Albums: Bryan Adams; Cuts Like A Knife, 1983; You Want It You Got It; Reckless, 1984; Into The Fire, 1987; Waking Up The Neighbours, 1991; Live! Live! Live!; 18 'Til I Die, 1996; The Best of Me, 2000. Singles: Kids Wanna Rock; Summer of 69; Heaven; Run To You; Can't Stop This Thing We've Started; It's Only Love; Everything I Do, I Do It For You; Have You Ever Really Loved A Woman; I Finally Found Someone; Soundtrack: Spirit: Stallion of the Cimarron, 2002; Room Service, 2004. Photography exhibitions: Toronto; Montreal; Saatchi Gallery, London; Royal Jubilee Exhibition, Windsor Castle, 2002. Publications: Bryan Adams: The Official Biography, 1995; Made in Canada; Photographs by Bryan Adams. Honours: Longest Standing No 1 in UK Singles Charts, 16 weeks, 1994; Diamond Sales Award; 12 Juno Awards; Recording Artist of the Decade; Order of Canada; Order of British Columbia. Address: c/o Press Department, A&M Records, 136-144 New King's Road, London, SW6 4LZ, England.

ADAMS Jad, b. 27 November 1954, London, England. Writer; TV Producer. Education: BA, University of Sussex, 1976; MA, University of London Birkbeck College, 1982; Fellow of the Royal Historical Society, 1997. Appointments: Television Professional, 1982-; Currently series producer; Councillor, London Borough of Lewisham, 1978-86; Chair, Nightwatch (homeless charity), 1992-; Research Fellow, Institute of English, School of Advanced Study, University of London, 2006. Publications: Tony Benn: A Biography, 1992; The Dynasty: The Nehru-Gandhi Story, 1997; Madder Music, Stranger Wine: The Life of Ernest Dowson, 2000; Pankhurst, 2003; Hideous Absinthe, 2004; Kipling, 2006. Honour: Young Journalist of the Year, British Press Awards, 1977; Best International Current Affairs Documentary, Royal Television Society, 1987. Membership: Institute of Historical Research. Address: 2 Kings Garth, 29 London Road, London SE23 3TT, England. E-mail: jadadams@btinternet.com Website: www.jadadams.co.uk

ADAMS Richard, b. 9 May 1920. Author. m. Barbara Elizabeth Acland, 26 September 1949, 2 daughters. Education: Bradfield College, Berkshire, 1938; Worcester College, Oxford, 1938; MA, Modern History, Oxford University, 1948. Appointments: Army service, 1940-46; Civil Servant, 1948-74; Assistant Secretary, Department of the Environment, 1974; Writer-in-Residence, University of Florida, 1975; Writer-in-Residence, Hollins College, VA, 1976. Publications: Watership Down, 1972, 2nd edition, 1982; Shardik, 1974; Nature Through the Seasons, co-author Max Hooper, 1975; The Tyger Voyage (narrative poem), 1976; The Ship's Cat (narrative poem), 1977; The Plague Dogs, 1977; Nature Day and Night, (co-author Max Hooper), 1978; The Girl in a Swing, 1980; The Iron Wolf (short stories), 1980; Voyage Through the Antarctic (co-author Ronald Lockley), 1982; Maia, 1984; The Bureaucats, 1985; A Nature Diary, 1985; Occasional Poets, anthology, 1986; The Legend of Te Tuna, narrative poem, 1986; Traveller, 1988; The Day Gone By, autobiography, 1990; Tales from Watership Down, 1996; The Outlandish Knight, 2000; Daniel, 2006. Honours: Carnegie Medal for Watership Down, 1972; Guardian Award for Children's Fiction for Watership Down, 1972. Memberships: President, RSPCA, 1980-82. Address: 26 Church Street, Whitchurch, Hampshire RG28 7AR, England.

ADAMSON Donald, b. 15 June 1943, Dumfries, Scotland. Writer; Poet; Editor. Education: MA, English Literature, 1965, MLitt, Applied Linguistics, 1975, Edinburgh University. Appointments: EFL posts in France, Finland, Iran and Kuwait; Longman EFL Division, Research and Development Unit; Freelance EFL Writer and Editor. Contributions to: Lines Review; Orbis; New Writing Scotland. Honours: Glasgow University/Radio Clyde Poetry Prize, 1985; 2nd Prize, Northwords Competition, 1995; Winner, Herald Millennium Poem Competition, 1999; Scottish Arts Council Writer's Bursary, 1995. Address: 1 St Peter's Court, Dalbeattie, Scotland.

ADAUKTUSSON Per Gustav Harry, b. 21 March 1962, Ljungby, Sweden. Systems Analyst. Education: Diploma in Mathematics and Applied Mathematics, Växjö University, Sweden, 1985; Diploma in Mathematics, 2001. Appointments: Senior System Analyst, Telub Inforum AB, Växjö, 1988-95; Senior System Analyst, Celsius Inforum AB, Växjö, 1995-96. Publications: Articles in professional journals. Address: Liedbergsgatan 43, 6 TR, Växjö 35232, Sweden. E-mail: per.adauktusson@netatonce.net

ADCOCK Fleur, b. 10 February 1934, Papakura, New Zealand. Poet. m. (1) Alistair Teariki Campbell, 1952, divorced, 1958, 1 son, (2) Barry Crump, 1962, divorced 1966. Education: MA Victoria University of Wellington, 1955. Appointments: Assistant Lecturer, 1958, Assistant Librarian, 1959-61, University of Otago; with Alexander Turnbull Library, 1962; with FCO, 1963-79; Freelance writer, 1979-; Northern Arts Fellowship in Literature, Universities of Newcastle-upon-Tyne and Durham, 1979-81; Eastern Arts Fellowship, University of East Anglia, 1986; Writer-in-Residence, University of Adelaide, 1986. Publications: The Eye of the Hurricane, 1964; Tigers, 1967; High Tide in the Garden, 1971; The Scenic Route, 1974; The Inner Harbour, 1979; Below Loughrigg, 1979; Selected Poems, 1983; The Virgin and the Nightingale, 1983; The Incident Book, 1986; Time Zones, 1991; Looking Back, 1997; Poems 1960-2000, 2000; Editor: The Oxford Book of Contemporary New Zealand Poetry, 1982; The Faber Book of 20th Century Women's Poetry, 1987; Translator and Editor, Hugh Primas and the Archpoet, 1994; Editor (with Jacqueline Simms), The Oxford Book of Creatures, 1995; Looking Back, 1997. Honours: Buckland Award, 1967, 1979; Jessie MacKay Award, 1968, 1972; Cholmondeley Award, 1976; New Zealand Book Award, 1984; Order of the British Empire, 1996; recipient of the prestigious Queen's Gold Medal for Poetry, 2006. Membership: Poetry Society. Address: 14 Lincoln Road, London N2 9DL, England.

ADELMAN Saul Joseph, b. 18 November 1944, Atlantic City, New York, USA. Astronomer; College Professor. m. Carol, 3 sons. Education: BS, Physics, University of Maryland, 1966; PhD, Astronomy, California Institute of Technology, 1972. Appointments: Postdoctorate, NASA Space Flight Center, 1972-74, 1984-86; Assistant Astronomer, Boston University, 1974-78; Assistant Professor, Associate Professor, Professor, The Citadel, 1978-. Publications: 325 papers; 7 articles; 1 book; 9 proceedings (co-editor). Honours: Phi Beta Kappa; Phi Kappa Phi; Sigma Pi Sigma; Sigma Xi. Memberships: International Astronomical Union; American Astronomical

Society; Astronomical Society of the Pacific; Canadian Astronomical Society. Address: The Citadel Department of Physics, 171 Moultrie St, Charleston, SC 29409, USA.

ADER Robert, b. 20 February 1932, New York, USA. Psychologist. m. Gayle Simon, 4 daughters. Education: BS, Tulane University, New Orleans, USA, 1953; PhD, Cornell University, Ithaca, New York, USA, 1957. Appointments: Teaching and Research Assistantships, Department of Psychology, Cornell University, 1953-57; Research Instructor, Psychiatry, University of Rochester School of Medicine and Dentistry, 1957-59; Research Senior Instructor, 1959-61; Research Assistant Professor, 1961-64; Associate Professor, 1964-68; Professor, Department of Psychiatry, University of Rochester, 1968-; Visiting Professor, Rudolf Magnus Institute for Pharmacology, University of Utrecht, The Netherlands, 1970-71; Dean's Professor, University of Rochester School of Medicine and Dentistry, 1982-83; Professor of Medicine, 1983-; George L Engel Professor, Psychosocial Medicine, 1983-2002; Distinguished University Professor, 2002-; Fellow, Centre for Advanced Study in the Behavioural Sciences, 1992-93. Publications: Behaviourally conditioned immunosuppression; Behaviour and the Immune System; Psychoneuroimmunology; The role of conditioning in pharmacotherapy; Many other publications. Honours: Research Scientist Award; Institutional Training Grant; Editor-in-Chief, Brain Behaviour and Immunity; Honorary MD; Honorary ScD; Many other honours. Memberships: Academy of Behavioural Medicine Research, President, 1984-85; American Psychosomatic Society, President, 1979-80; International Society for Developmental Psychobiology, President, 1981-82; Psychoneuroimmunology Research Society, Founding President, 1993-94; Many other memberships. Address: 7 Moss Creek Ct, Pittsford, NY 14534-1071, USA.

ADIE Kathryn (Kate) b. 19 September 1945, England. Television News Correspondent. Education: Newcastle University. Appointments: Technician and Producer, BBC Radio, 1969-76; Reporter, BBC TVS, 1977-79; BBC TV News, 1979-81; Correspondent, 1982-; Chief Correspondent, 1989-2003; Freelance Journalist, Broadcaster and TV Presenter, 2003-. Publications: The Kindness of Strangers, autobiography, 2002; Corsets to Camouflage: Women and War, 2003. Honours: RTS News Award, 1981, 1987; Monte Carlo International News Award, 1981, 1990; Honorary MA, Bath University, 1987; BAFTA Richard Dimbleby Award, 1989; Honorary DLitt, City University, 1989; Honorary MA, Newcastle University, 1990; Freeman of Sunderland, 1990; Honorary DLitt, Sunderland University, 1991; Loughborough University, 1991; Honorary Professor, Sunderland University, 1995; Order of the British Empire, 1993. Address: c/o BBC Television, Wood Lane, London W12 7RJ, England.

ADJANI Isabelle, b. 27 June 1955, France. Actress. 1 son with Bruno Nuytten and 1 son with Daniel Day-Lewis. Education: Lycée de Courbevoie. Appointment: President, Commission d'avances sur recettes, 1986-88. Career: Films include: Faustine et le bel été, 1972, Barocco, 1977; Nosferatu, 1978; Possession, 1980; Quartet, 1981; l'Eté Meurtrier, 1983; Camille Claudel, 1988; La Reine Margot, 1994; Diabolique, 1996; Paparazzi, 1998; La Repentie, 2002; Adolphe, 2002; Bon Voyage, 2003; Monsieur Ibrahim et les Fleurs du Coran, 2003. Theatre includes: La Maison de Bernada Alba, 1970; l'Avare, 1972-73 Port-Royal, 1973; Ondine, 1974; TV includes: Le Petit Bougnat, 1969; l'Ecole des Femmes, 1973; Top á Sacha Distel, 1974; Princesse aux Petit Pois, 1986. Honours: Best Actress, Cannes, Possession, 1981; Best Actress, Cannes,

Quartet, 1982; Best Actress César, Best Actress Award, Berlin Film Festival, Camille Claudel, 1989; Best Actress César, La Reine Margot, 1995. Address: c/o Phonogram, 89 Boulevard Auguste Blanqui, 75013 Paris, France.

ADLERSHTEYN Leon, b. 28 October 1925, St Petersburg, Russia. Naval Architect; Researcher; Educator. m. Irina Bereznaya. Education: MS, Shipbuilding Institute, St Petersburg, Russia 1945-51; DSc, Central Research Institute for Shipbuilding Technology, St Petersburg, Russia, 1970. Appointments: Private, Soviet Army, 1943-45; Foreman, Deputy Chief, Hull Shop, Baltic Shipyard, St Petersburg, Russia, 1951-63; Chief Technologist, Team Leader, 1963-74, Chief Researcher, 1993-94, Central Research Institute for Shipbuilding Technology; Head of the Chair, Professor, Shipbuilding Academy, 1974-94; Retired 1994. Publications: Author or co-author of 11 books which include: Accuracy in Ship Hull Manufacturing; Mechanisation and Automation of Ship Manufacturing; Modular Shipbuilding; Ship Examiner (2 editions); Handbook of Ship Marking and Examining Works and over 160 brochures and scientific articles; 9 Russian Patents. Honours: Order of the Patriotic War, 1st Class; 13 Russian Military Medals; 3 Medals of American Legion; 5 Medals of Russian Industrial Exhibition; Listed in numerous Who's Who and biographical publications. Memberships: Fellow, Institute of Marine Engineering, Science and Technology, UK; Society of Naval Architects and Marine Engineers, USA; American Association of Invalids and Veterans of WWII from the former Soviet Union. Address: 72 Montgomery Street, Apt 1510, Jersey City, NJ 07302-3827, USA. E-mail: bereznaya@gmail.com

ADVANI Chanderban Ghanshamdas, b. 23 July 1924, Hyderbad Sind, India. Businessman. m. Veena Chandru, 1 son, 1 daughter. Education: BA. Appointments: Manager, Narain Advani & Co, Karachi; Manager, French Drugs Co, Karachi; Manager, Indo-French Traders, Pondicherry; General Manager, L L Mohnani & Co, Yokohama, Japan; Chief Executive Officer, Nephews' International Inc. Yokohama, Japan; Proprietor, Nephews' Commercial Corporation, Karachi, India. Publications: Articles to various magazines and newspapers including Bharat Ratna, Hong Kong; Indian, Hong Kong. Honours: Medals, Citations, Mayors of Mumbai (India), Yokohama (Japan), Key to Yokohama from the Mayor of Yokohama. Memberships: Indian Chamber of Commerce, Japan; Indian Merchants Association of Yokohama; Foreign Correspondents Club of Japan; India International Centre, New Delhi; Yokohama Chamber of Commerce and Industry, Yokohama; Sinnim Lodge, Shriners Club, Tokyo. Address: 502, New Port Building, 25/16 Yamashita Cho, Naka Ku, Port PO Box 216, Yokohama 231-86-91, Japan. E-mail: nephewsjapan@yahoo.com

AFFLECK Ben, b. 15 August 1972, Berkeley, California, USA. Actor. m. Jennifer Garner, 2005. Career: Appeared in films including School Ties, 1992, Buffy the Vampire Slayer, Dazed and Confused, Mallrats, 1995, Glory Daze, Office Killer, Chasing Amy, Going All the Way, Good Will Hunting, film and screenplay, 1997, Phantoms, Armageddon, Shakespeare in Love, 1998; Reindeer Games, Forces of Nature, Dogma, Daddy and Them, The Boiler Room, 200 Cigarettes, 1999; Bounce, The Third Wheel (also producer), 2000; Pearl Harbor, 2001; The Sum of All Fear, Changing Lanes, 2002; Daredevil, Gigli, Paycheck, 2003; Jersey Girl, Surviving Christmas, 2004; Man About Town, 2005; Hollywoodland, 2006; Television appearances include: Voyage of the Mimi, Against the Grain, Lifetstories: Family in Crisis, Hands of a Stranger, Daddy. Honours: Academy Award for Good Will

Hunting, 1997; Golden Globe for Best Original Screenplay, 1997. Address: c/o Creative Artists Agency, 9830 Wilshire Boulevard, Beverly Hills, CA 90212, USA.

AFSHINNIA Farsad, b. 16 March 1970, Tehran, Iran. Physician. m. Parisa Jahanbani. Education: MD, Isfahan University of Medical Sciences, Iran, 1988-95; Speciality in Internal Medicine, Brookdale University Hospital and Medical Center, New York, USA, 2002-05. Appointments: Physician, VA Hospital of Janbazan Foundation, Iran, 1995-97; Physician, Private Practice, Iran, 1997-99; Researcher and Methodologist, Isfahan University of Medical Sciences, Iran, 1998-2000; Physician, Group Practice in Private Sector, Iran, 1999-2000; Physician, Resident of Internal Medicine, Brookdale Hospital, USA, 2002-05; Attending Physician, Memorial Medical Center, Modesto, California, USA, 2006-. Publications: Book: Applied Data Analysis, 2nd edition, 2005; Article: Relation of left ventricular geometry and renal function in hypertensive patients with diastolic heart failure, 2005. Honours: Best Researcher of Isfahan University of Medical Sciences, 1994; Certificates of Merit, American College of Physicians, 2003, 2004, 2005; Award Winner, American College of Physicians, 2005; Man of the Year, 2005. Memberships: American College of Physicians; American Medical Association; American Heart Association; American Diabetes Association. Address: 2200 Standiford Avenue, Apt 268, Modesto, CA 95350, USA.

AGARWAL Kishan Chandra, b. 15 March 1948, Agra, India. Medical Doctor. m. Sushma, 1 son, 1 daughter. Education: MS, Pediatrics, Mayo Graduate School of Medicine, University of Minnesota, USA, 1983; MBBS, G R Medical College, 1969, MD, Internal Medicine, 1973, Jiwaji University, India; Diploma in Complementary & Alternative Medicine/Homeopathy, British Institute of Homeopathy, England, 2001. Appointments: Clinical Instructor, Internal Medicine, Jiwaji University, India, 1972-74; Assistant Instructor, Pediatrics, State University of New York, USA, 1977-79; Lecturer, Pediatrics, Mount Sinai Medical School, USA, 1989-93; Assistant Professor, Pediatrics (Cardiology), 1983-86, Clinical Assistant Professor, 1986-89, Clinical Associate Professor, 1989-, Pediatrics, University of Medicine & Dentistry of NJ, USA; Invasive & Non-Invasive Pediatric Cardiology, Children's Hospital of New Jersey, 1982-86; Consulting private practice, Pediatric Cardiology, 1985-; Adjunct Associate Clinical Professor of Pediatrics, Mount Sinai School of Medicine, USA, 1994-; Clinical Associate Professor, 1991-2002, Clinical Professor, 2002-, Pediatrics, University of Medicine & Dentistry of NJ, Robert Wood Johnson Medical School; Consulting private practice, Complementary and Alternative Medicine, 1999-; Chief, Department of Pediatrics, Muhlenberg Regional Medical Center, Plainfield, New Jersey, 1999-2001. Publications: Numerous articles in professional journals. Honours: Listed in international biographical dictionaries. Memberships: Association of Indians in America. Address: 450 Plainfield Road, Edison, NJ 08820-2628, USA.

AGASSI Andre, b. 29 April 1970, Las Vegas, USA. Tennis Player. m. (1) Brooke Shields, 1997, divorced 1999; (2) Steffi Graf, 1 son, 1 daughter. Education: Coached from age of 13 by Nick Bolletieri; Strength coach Gil Reyes. Appointments: Semi Finalist, French Open, 1988; US Open, 1988, 1989; Member, US Team which defeated Australia in Davis Cup Final, 1990; Defeated Stefan Edberg to win inaugural ATP World Championships, Frankfurt, 1991; Finalist, French Open, 1990, 1991; US Open, 1990, 1995, 2002; Australian Open, 1994; Wimbledon, 1999; Men's Singles Wimbledon

Champion, 1992; Won, US Open, 1994; Canadian Open, 1995; Australian Open, 1995, 2000, 2001, 2003; Winner, Olympic Games Tennis Tournament, 1996; Association of Tennis Professionals World Champion, 1990. Cincinnati Masters, 2004. Retired from professional tennis 3 Sept 2006. Address: International Management Group, 1 Brieview Plaza, Suite 1300, Cleveland, OH 44114, USA.

AGEEV Alexander I, b. 12 July 1962, Russia. Economist. 3 sons. Education: Academician, Russian Academy of Natural Sciences; Doctor of Economics, Professor; MBA; Moscow State University, 1984; Institute of World Economy and International Relations, USSR Academy of Sciences, 1987; Kingston University, London, 2000; Academy of National Economy, 2001. Appointments: Senior Researcher, Head of Section, Institute of Economics, USSR Academy of Science, 1988-91; Director, Department for Strategic Analysis, Ministry of foreign Economic affairs, 1991-93; Adviser to the Director general, MIG organisation, 1994-1995; Director for Strategic Planning, MAPO Group, 1996-97; Founder, Director General, Institute for Economic Strategies, Russian academy of Science, 1990-92, 1998-; President, Akademia Prognozirovania (Russian Division, International Futures Research Academy), 2005-. Publications: 200 scientific and fiction publications; 9 monographs including: Enterprise at the end of the 20th Century, 1991; New Matrix or the Logic of Strategic Advantage, 2002; Co-author, Russia in the Space and the Time (the history of the future), 2004; Co-author, Value Chain, 2004. Honours: Man of the Year Award, 1993. Memberships: Member of the Board, Centre of Development of Informational Society; Academic Council, MEPHI; Interagency Task Force for Innovations under President RF; Journalists Union; Writers Union. Address: Institute for Economic Strategies, of 4, bld 1, 6, Sretenskii Boulevard, Moscow 505000, Russia. E-mail: ageev@inesnet.ru Website: www.inesnet.ru

AGIS Derya Fazila, b. 4 May 1977, Ankara, Turkey. Linguist; Philologist. Education: BA (honours), Italian Language and Literature, Ankara University, 1995-99; Graduate specialisation course in translation studies with literary emphasis: French/Italian, Italian/French, University of Bari, Italy, 2001-02;Middle East Technical University, Special Student, Department of Psychology, 2002-03; MA, Department of English Linguistics, Hacettepe University, 2007-. Appointments: Research Fellowship, Brown University, USA, 2000-01; Part-time work experience: Translator, Bilge, Candost, Efe and Gursoy Translation Offices, Ankara, Turkey, 1996-2005; Translator, Inlingua Translation Office, Bari, Italy, 2002; Private Teacher, English, French and Italian, 1999-2003; Internship training as a tourist guide, Cruise & Shipping Travel Agency, Bari, Italy, 2002; UNICEF, interpreter during a meeting on the Juvenile Justice System in Turkey, 2006; Senior Lecturer, Girne American University, 2007. Publications: Papers presented at symposia include: The Interlanguage Transitions Reinforcement Method for Teaching French to Turkish Children, 2004; Discovering the Kantian Origins of Cognitive Linguistics, 2005; Acquisition of the French Perception Verbs by Turkish French L2 Learners, 2006. Poems and articles. Honours: Global Citizenship, Finnish U N Association, 1995; Summer Course Fellowship, University of Milan, 1999; Kenyon Fellowship, Brown University, USA; Turkish and Italian Friendship Association, Fellowship, 2001; Leading Educators of the World, IBC, 2005; Encyclopedia of Women in Islamic Cultures, Women Gender and Religious Language, Use by Women in Turkey, Papers of the First International Conference of Sephardic Culture, Pragmatic Properties of the Judeo-Spanish Used in the Forum, An Approach to Politeness, A Cognitive Scientific Approach to Judeo-Spanish (Ladino) Songs, Emotions Hidden in the Linguistic Expressions Used in these Songs and their Perception by the Turks, 2006. Memberships: MLA, 2000-01; International Pragmatics Association, 2004, German Association of Cognitive Linguistics. Address: Ozveren Sokak No 38-7, Ulku Apt, TR-06570 Maltepe, Ankara, Turkey. E-mail: deryaagis@yahoo.com

AGIUS Marcus Ambrose Paul, b. 22 July 1946, Walton-on-Thames, England. Chairman of Barclays Bank PLC. m. Katherine Juliette de Rothschild, 2 daughters. Education: MA, Mechanical Sciences and Economics, Cambridge University, 1971; MBA, Harvard Business School, 1972; Vickers Scholarship, 1970. Appointments: Director, Exbury Gardens Limited, 1977-; Director. Exbury Gardens Retail Limited, 1998-; Deputy Chairman, Lazard LLC, 2002-; Chairman, The Foundation and Friends of the Royal Botanic Gardens, Kew, 2004-; Trustee to the Board of the Royal Botanic Gardens, Kew, 2006-; Chairman, BAA plc, 2002-2006; Chairman, Lazard London, 2001-06; Senior Independent Director, BBC New Executive Board, 2006-; Non-Executive Director, Barclays plc, 2006; Chairman, Barclays plc, 2007-. Memberships: Whites; Swinley Forest.

AGNEW Jonathan Geoffrey William, b. 30 July 1941, Windsor, England. Investment Banker. m. (1) Honourable Joanna Campbell, 1966, divorced 1985, 1 son, 2 daughters, (2) Marie-Claire Dreesmann, 1990, 1 son, 1 daughter. Education: MA Cantab, Trinity College, Cambridge. Appointments: with The Economist, 1964-65, IBRD, 1965-67; Various positions, 1967-73, Director, 1971, Hill Samuel and Co; Non-Executive Director, Thos Agnew and Sons Ltd, 1969-; Positions, 1973-82, Managing Director, 1977, Morgan Stanley and Co; with J G W Agnew and Co, 1983-86; Chief Executive, ISRO, 1986; Positions, 1987-93, Chief Executive, 1989-93, Kleinwort Benson Group plc; Chairman, Limit plc, 1993-2000; Member, Council, Lloyd's, 1995-98; Chairman, Henderson Geared Income and Growth Trust plc, 1995-2003; Non-Executive Director, 1997, Deputy Chairman, 1999-2002, Chair, 2002-, Nationwide Building Society; Chairman, Gerrard Group plc, 1998-2000; Non Executive Director, 2002-, Chair, 2003-, Beazley Group plc; Chairman, LMS Capital plc, 2006-; Chairman, The Cayenne Trust plc, 2006-; Non-Executive Director, Rightmove plc, 2006-. Address: Flat E, 51 Eaton Square, London SW1W 9BE, England. E-mail: jgwagnew@yahoo.co.uk

AGRAWAL Ajay, b. 15 February 1965, Agra, India. Consultant. m. Alpna Agrawal, 2 sons. Education: BSc, Combined Sciences, 1981-83, MSc, Chemistry, 1983-85, Agra University, India; PhD, Central Drug Research Institute, Lucknow, India, 1985-90. Appointments: Postdoctoral Fellow, Faculty of Medicine, University of Alberta, Canada, 1991-93; Senior Postdoctoral Fellow, Molecular Cell Pathology, Royal Free Hospital Medical School, London, 1993-95; Principal Scientist, polyMASC Pharmaceuticals plc, London, 1995-2001; Senior Consultant, numerous biotech and pharma companies worldwide, 2001-. Publications: Numerous research articles and reviews, including some pioneer work on infectious diseases documented in peer-reviewed journals and books; Several international presentations and invited lectures. Honours: Co-founder, polyMASC Pharmaceuticals, London, 1995; Member, Editorial Advisory Board of three international journals; Honorary Research Fellow, Royal Free and University College Medical School, London; National Merit Award and Research Fellowships, WHO and CSIR; Gold Medal, 1st place, Master's Exam. Memberships: London

Technology Network; London Biotechnology Network; Camden Badminton Club. Address: 12 Grange Avenue, Peterborough, Cambridgeshire PE1 4HH, England. E-mail: ajaymedpharm@aol.com

AGUTTER Jenny, b. 20 December 1952, Taunton, Somerset, England. Actress; Dancer. m. Johan Tham, 1990, 1 son. Education: Elmhurst Ballet School. Career: Film debut East of Sudan, 1964; Appeared in numerous films for both cinema and TV, dramas, plays and series on stage; Plays include: Spring Awakening; Tempest; Betrayal; Breaking the Code; Love's Labour's Lost; Peter Pan, 1997-98; Films include: Ballerina, 1964; The Railway Children, 1969; Logan's Run, 1975; Equus, 1975; The Eagle has Landed, Sweet William, 1980; An American Werewolf in London, 1981; Secret Places, 1983; Dark Tower, 1987; King of the Wind, 1989; Child's Play 2, 1991; Freddie as Fro 7, 1993; Blue Juice, 1995; English Places, English Faces, 1996; The Parole Officer, 2001; At Dawning, 2001; Number 1, Longing, Number 2, Regret, 2004; TV includes: Amy, 1980; Not a Penny More, Not a Penny Less, 1990; The Good Guys, 1991; Love Hurts, Heartbreak, 1994; The Buccaneers, 1995; And the Beat Goes On, 1996; A Respectable Trade, 1997; Bramwell, 1998; The Railway Children, 2000; Spooks, 2002; The Alan Clarke Diaries, 2004. Publication: Snap, 1983. Honour: Emmy Award for The Snow Goose, 1972; BAFTA Award for Equus, 1978. Address: c/o Marmont Management, Langham House, 308 Regent Street, London W1B 3AT, England.

AHEARN Geraldine, b. 14 August 1950, Brooklyn, New York, USA. Nursing; Author. m. James J Ahearn, divorced 2001, 2 daughters. Education: RN, CISH (SON), 3 year diploma, New York; AA degree, General Studies, SCCC, New York; Certified RN, CCRN, New York; CPR Instructor, New York; First Aid Instructors, New York. Appointments: Author, 6 books, 1995-; International Poet, Noble House Publishers. Publications: Chapbooks: Inspirations, Words to Live By; Books include: Life's Poetic Journey, 2001; The Nurse in the Purse, 2002, 2003; From America's Future Leaders, 2005. Honours: Fellow Poet Award, 2006; Published in several anthologies and Foreword Magazine, The NY Times, LA Times and USA Today; Listed in international biographical dictionaries. Memberships: AHA; ARC. Address: 10155 Val Vista Drive, #81 Mesa, AZ 85204, USA. E-mail: hrt4angel@aol.com

AHERN Bertie, b. 12 September 1951, Dublin, Ireland. Taoiseach (Prime Minister) of the Republic of Ireland. m. Miriam Patricia Kelly, 1975, separated, 2 daughters. Education: Rathmines College of Commerce, Dublin; University College, Dublin. Appointments: Elected to Dáil, constituency of Dublin-Finglas, 1977, represented Dublin Central, 1981-; Member, Dublin City Council, 1978-88, Lord Mayor, 1986-87; Assistant Government Whip, 1980-81; Fianna Fáil Front Bench spokesman on Youth, 1981-82; Minister of State, Department of the Taoiseach and at Department of Defence, and Government Chief Whip, 1982; Opposition Chief Whip, 1982-84; Fianna Fáil Front Bench spokesman on Labour, 1984-87; Minister for Labour, 1987-91; Chairman Dublin Millennium Committee, 1988; Chairman, European Investment Bank, 1991-92; Member, Board of Governors, World Bank, 1991-94; Member, Board of Governors, IMF, 1991-94; Minister for Finance, 1991-94; Minister for Industry and Commerce, 1993; Leader, Fianna Fáil Party, 1994-; Tánaiste (Deputy Prime Minister), 1994; Minister for Arts, Culture and the Gaeltacht, 1994; Taoiseach, 1997-2002, 2002-. Honours: Grand Cross, Order of Merit with Star and Sash, Germany, 1991; Thomas J Dodd Prize in International Justice and Human Rights (jointly awarded to Taoiseach and British Prime Minister Mr Tony Blair MP), 2003; European Voice Statesman of the Year, 2004; The Stara Planina, Bulgaria, 2005; American Lung Association Chairman's Award, 2005; Golden Statuette, Business Centre Club, Poland, 2005; Polio Eradication Champion Award, Rotary International, 2006; 7 honorary degrees. Memberships: Former Member, Board of Governors, University College Dublin, Dublin Port & Docks Board, Eastern Health Board, Dublin Chamber of Commerce; Chairman, Dublin Millennium Committee. Address: Department of the Taoiseach, Government Buildings, Merrion Street, Dublin 2, Republic of Ireland. E-mail: taoiseach@taoiseach.gov.ie

AHLSEN Leopold, b. 12 January 1927, Munich, Germany. Author. m. Ruth Gehwald, 1964, 1 son, 1 daughter. Publications: 13 plays, 23 radio plays, 68 television plays, 7 novels. Honours: Gerhart Hauptmann Prize; Schiller-Förderungspreis; Goldener Bildschirm; Hörspielpreis der Kriegsblinden; Silver Nymph of Monte Carlo; Bundesverdienstkreuz. Address: Waldschulstrasse 58, 81827 Munich, Germany.

AHLSKOG J Eric, b. 14 September 1945, Chicago, Illinois, USA. Neurologist. m. Faye Wayland, 3 sons. Education: BA, Michigan State University, 1967; PhD, Princeton University, 1973; MD, Dartmouth Medical School, 1976. Appointments: Instructor of Neurology, 1981-86, Assistant Professor of Neurology, 1986-93, Associate Professor of Neurology, 1993-98, Professor of Neurology, 1998-, Mayo Medical School, Rochester; Chair, Division of Movement Disorders, Department of Neurology, Rochester, 1992-2001; Consultant and Chair, Section of Movement Disorders, Mayo Clinic, Rochester, 2002-. Publications: Over 150 peer reviewed publications; Co-editor, Parkinson's Disease and Movement Disorders, 2000; Author: The Parkinson's Disease Treatment Book, 2005. Honours: Honors College, Michigan State University, 1967; Alpha Omega Alpha, Dartmouth Medical School, 1975. Memberships: American Academy of Neurology; Movement Disorder Society. Address: Department of Neurology, Mayo Clinic, 200 First St SW, Rochester, MN 55905, USA.

AHMAD Khalid, b. 22 August 1948, Kumpese, Ashanti, Ghana. Research Scientist. m. Khadija, 2 sons, 2 daughters. Education: BSc (Hons), Chemistry, University of Science and Technology, Kumasi, Ghana, 1974; MSc (Nuclear & Radiation Chemistry), Salford University, Greater Manchester, England, 1980; Certificate in Radioisotope Production, Institute of Isotope Production Co Ltd, Budapest, Hungary, 1995-96; PhD, University of Ghana, Legon, in progress. Appointments: Teacher, O and A level Chemistry and Physics, 1974-76; Trainee Scientific Officer, 1976-80, Scientific Officer, 1980-2002, Senior Scientific Officer, 2002-, Acting Head of Chemistry Department, 2005, Ghana Atomic Energy Commission. Publications: 10 technical papers; Numerous newspaper articles on science; Over 100 articles on Islam, 1982-; 9 refereed papers. Memberships: American Association of Science; Ghana Science Association. Address: Ghana Atomic Energy Commission, PO Box LG 80, Legon, Ghana.

AHMAD Mohammad Irfan, b. 29 August 1977, Karachi, Pakistan. Telecommunication Engineer. m. Midhat Riaz. Education: BE, Electronics Engineering, 2000; MS, Communication Engineering, 2003. Appointments: Telecom Engineer, Baud Telecom, Jeddah, 2000-01; Access Network Engineer, Huawi Technology, Riyadh, 2001-02; Project Engineers Transmission, Mobily-Riyadh, 2005-. Publications:

Modeling of Photonic Crystal Fiber, 2004; Finite Element of Photonic Device for Optical Comms, 2004; Modal Hybridism of Polarization of Photonic Fiber by Full Vectorial, 2004. Honours: Lan to Lan Wireless Communication Award, Pakistan Army, 2000. Memberships: MIEEE, USA; MIEE, UK; Life Member, Pakistan Engineering Council; Member, International Society for Optical Engineers, USA. E-mail: mirfan22@yahoo.com

AHMED Tarek, b. 7 August 1964, Dhaka, Bangladesh. University Teaching. m. Rubina Khan, 2 sons. Education: BSc, Electrical & Electronic Engineering, Bangladesh University of Engineering & Technology; M Eng, Electrical & Computer Engineering, Nagoya Institute of Technology, Japan; Doctor's Course & Research, Fukui University, Fukui City, USA; PhD, Computer Science, Texas Tech University, Lubbock, Texas, USA. Appointments: Graduate Assistant, Department of Computer Science, Texas Tech University, 2000-01; Assistant Professor, Computer Science, Eastern Kentucky University, Richmond, Kentucky, 2001-07; Associate Professor of Math & Computer Science, California University of Pennsylvania, 2007-; Adjunct Associate Professor, University of Maryland University College, 2007-. Publications: Forecasting business dynamics with predictive queue simulation, 2007; A generalized set theoretic approach for time and space complexity analysis of algorithms and functions, 2007. Honours: Japanese Government's Monbusho Scholarship in Open Merit Competitions; Listed in international biographical dictionaries. Memberships: Upsilon Pi Epsilon; Wode-Omen; International Institute of Informatics and Systemics; International Scientific Committee, CSECS, 2007, MATH, 2007. Address: 511 Payne Hill Road, #190-M, Jefferson Hills, PA 15025-4043, USA. E-mail: tarek@cup.edu

AHMEDOV Akmal Khurramovich, b. 13 January 1975, Samarkand, Uzbekistan. Historian. m. Rakhimova Saodat Abduakhatovna, 2 sons, 1 daughter. Education: Diploma in Linguistics, Tashkent Islamic Institute, 1999; Postgraduate Student, Social Economic Sciences Department, Samarkand branch, Academy of Sciences, Republic of Uzbekistan, 2001-. Appointments: Vice Chairman, Samarkand branch, Makhdumi A'zam Dahbedi Foundation, 1996-97; Historian, Social Economic Sciences Department, Samarkand branch, Academy of Sciences, Republic of Uzbekistan, 1998-2000; Chairman, Samarkand branch, International Charitable Foundation Golden Heritage, Samarkand, 2001-. Memberships: Central Eurasian Studies Society; Electronic Atlas Initiative. Address: Pulimugob kishlak, Uzbekistan kolkhoz, Samarkand tuman, Samarkand viloyat, Uzbekistan. E-mail: fuallanruz@yahoo.com

AHN Chang Wook, b. 6 March 1977, Haeje Muan, Jeolla Namdo, Republic of Korea. Computer Scientist. Education: BS, Applied Electrical Engineering, Korea University, Jochiwon, 1998; MS, Radio Sciences and Engineering, Korea University, Seoul, 2000; PhD, Information and Communications, Gwangju Institute of Science and Technology, 2005. Appointments: Leader, International Research Program, Gwangju Institute of Science and Technology, 2002-03; Visiting Scholar, Illinois Genetic Algorithms Laboratory, University of Illinois at Urbana-Champaign, USA, 2003; Research Staff Member, Samsung Advanced Institute of Technology, Giheung, Gyeonggi-do, Korea, 2005-07; Research Professor, Gwanju Institute of Science and Technology, Gwanju, Korea, 2007-. Publications: 1 book: Advances in Evolutionary Algorithms: Theory, Design and Practice; 1 book chapter; 17 international journal articles and lecture notes; 11 international conference proceedings; 1 international patent. Honours: Korean

Ministry of Science and Technology Scholarship, 2001-05; Visiting Scholar Fellowship, Korean Ministry of Education, 2003; Best Research Award, Gwangju Institute of Science and Technology, 2004 & 2005; Honour Prize, 11th Samsung Humantech Thesis Prize Awards, 2005; American Medal of Honor, ABI, 2005; Listed in numerous national and international biographical dictionaries; Committee Member for five international conferences, 2003-2007; Presentations to four national meetings; Reviewer of 10 international journals. Memberships: Institute of Electrical Electronics Engineers; IEEE Computational Intelligence Society; International Society for Genetic and Evolutionary Computation; Association for Computing Machinery. Address: Department of Information & Communications, Gwangju Institute of Science & Technology, 1 Oryong-dong, Buk-gu, Gwangju 500-712, Korea (South). E-mail: cwan@evolution.re.kr Website: http://www.evolution.re.kr

AHRENDS Peter, b. 30 April 1933, Berlin, Germany. Architect. m. Elizabeth Robertson, 1954, 2 daughters. Education: AA (Hons) School of Architecture; ARIBA. Appointments: Denys Lasdun and Partners, 1959-60; Teacher, Architectural Association School of Architecture, 1960-61; Partner, Director, Ahrends, Burton and Koralek architectural practice, London, 1961-; Professor, Bartlett School of Architecture and Planning, University College, London, 1987-90; Chair, Architects Support Group South Africa; Chair Camden Design Advisory Group; Member, RIBA Annual Awards Group; Principal projects include most recently New British Embassy, Moscow, 2000 Dublin Corporation Convent Lands Master Plan, 2000; Dublin Corporation/NEIC Civic Centre, 2001; Great Egyptian Museum Competition Entry, 2002; Whitworth Art Gallery Development Plan Review, 2002; Designs on Democracy Stockport winning competition entry, 2002; Riverside Building, London Docklands, 2003; Bexhill Town Centre, 2004. Publications: Ahrends, Burton and Koralek (monograph), 1991; Collaborations: The Architecture of ABK, August/Birkhäuser; Numerous articles in professional journals. Honours: Good Design in Housing Award, 1977, Architecture Awards, 1978, 1993, 1996, 1999, Structural Steel Design Award, 1980, Structural Steel Commendation, 1993; Gulbenkian Museum of the Year Award, 1999. Memberships: Royal Institute of British Architects; Design Council; Chairman, UK Architects Against Apartheid, 1988-93. Address: 16 Rochester Road, London NW1 9JH, England. E-mail: abk@abklondon.com Website: www.abk.co.uk

AHTIALA Pekka, b. 12 June 1935, Helsinki, Finland. Professor of Economics. m. Anna-Maija, 1 son, 2 daughters. Education: BBA, 1956, MBA, 1958, Helsinki School of Economics and Administration; PhD, Harvard University, USA, 1964. Appointments: Teaching Fellow, Instructor, Harvard, early 1960s; Professor of Economics, 1965-99, Dean, Faculty of Economics and Administration, 1969-71, University of Tampere; Minister of the Chancery responsible for Economic Policy, Finnish Government; Visiting Professor of Economics, Northwestern University and Princeton University. Publications: 4 books; Articles in several professional journals. Honours: Blue Cross of Finland; Earhart Prize, Harvard University; Knight Commander of the Order of the Lion of Finland; World Culture Prize: Statue of Victory, Centro Studi e Ricerche Delle Nazioni, Italy, 1985; Best Paper Award, Multinational Finance Journal, 1999; Honorary Member, Junior Chamber International; Honorary Member, Omicron Delta Epsilon. Memberships: Nomination College of the Nobel Prize Committee on Economics; Finnish

Economic Association; American Economic Association; European Economic Association. Address: Liutunkuja 3, 36240 Kangasala, Finland.

AICHINGER Ilse, b. 1 November 1921, Vienna, Austria. Novelist; Playwright. Education: University of Vienna, 1945-48. Appointment: Member of Grupe 47, 1951-. Publications: Die Grössere Hoffnung, 1948; Rede Unter dem Galgen, 1953; Eliza, Eliza, 1965; Selected Short Stories and Dialogue, 1966; Nachricht und Tag: Erzählungen, 1970; Schlechte Worter, 1976; Meine Sprache und Ich Erzählungen, 1978; Spiegelesichte: Erzählungen und Dialoge, 1979. Plays, Zu Keiner Stunde, 1957, 1980; Besuch im Pfarrhaus, 1961; Auckland: 4 Horspiele, 1969; Knopfe, 1978; Weisse Chrysanthemum, 1979; Radio Plays, Selected Poetry and Prose of Ilse Aichinger, 1983; Collected Works, 8 volumes, 1991. Honours: Belgian Europe Festival Prize, 1987; Town of Solothurn Prize, 1991. Address: c/o Fischer Verlag, Postfach 700480, 6000 Frankfurt, Germany.

AIELLO Danny, b. 20 May 1933, New York City, New York, USA. Actor. m. Sandy Cohen, 1955, 3 sons, 1 daughter. Career: Numerous film appearances including Bang the Drum Slowly, 1973; The Godfather II, 1976; Once Upon a Time in America, 1984; The Purple Rose of Cairo, 1985; Moonstruck, 1987; Do the Right Thing, Harlem Nights, 1989; Jacob's Ladder, 1990; Once Around, Hudson Hawk, The Closer, 29th Street, 1991; Mistress, Ruby, The Pickle, The Cemetery Club, 1992; The Professional, Prêt-à-Porter, Léon, 1994; City Hall, Power of Attorney, 1995; Two Days in the Valley, Mojave Moon, Two Much, 1996; A Brooklyn State of Mind, 1997; Bring Me the Head of Mavis Davis, 1998;Dust, 1999; Prince of Central Park, Dinner Rush, 2000; Off Key, 2001; The Russian Job, Marcus Timberwolf, The Last Request, 2002; Mail Order Bride, 2003; Zeyda and the Hit Man, 2004; Lobster Farm, 2005; Theatre appearances including Lamppost Reunion, 1975, Gemini, 1977, Hurlyburly, 1985; Appeared in TV films including The Preppie Murder, 1989; A Family of Strangers, 1993; The Last Don, mini-series, Dellaventura, series, 1997; The Last Don II, mini-series, 1998. Honours: Theatre World Award for Lamppost Reunion, 1975; Obie Award for Gemini, 1977; Boston Critics Award, Chicago Critics Award, Los Angeles Critics Award, all for Best Supporting Actor in Do the Right Thing, 1989; Emmy Award for A Family of Strangers, 1993. Address: William Morris Agency, 151 South El Camino Drive, Beverly Hills, CA 90212, USA.

AIMÉE Anouk, (Françoise Dreyfus), b. 27 April 1932, Paris, France. Actress. m. (2) Nico Papatakis, 1951, 1 daughter, (3) Pierre Barouh, 1966, (4) Albert Finney, 1970, divorced 1978. Education: Institut de Megève; Cours Bauer-Therond. Career: Theatre appearances include Sud, 1954, Love Letters, 1990, 1994; Appeared in films including Les mauvaises rencontres, 1955, Tous peuvent me tuer, Pot bouille and Montparnasse 19, 1957, La tête contre les murs, 1958, Les drageurs, 1959, La dolce vita, Le farceur, Lola, Les amours de Paris, L'imprévu, Quai Notre Dame, 1960, Le jugement dernier, Sodome et Gomorrhe, 1961; Les grands Chemins, Education sentimentale, Huit et demi, 1962, Un homme et une femme, 1966, Un soir un train, 1967, The Appointment Shop, Model Shop, Justine, 1968, Si c'était à refaire, 1976, Mon premier amour, 1978, Salto nel vuoto, 1979, La tragédie d'un homme ridicule, 1981, Qu'est-ce qui fait courir David?, 1982, Le Général de l'armée morte, 1983, Vive la Vie, Le succès à tout prix, 1984, Un homme et une femme: vingt ans déjà, 1986, Docteur Norman Bethune, 1992, Les Marmottes, 1993, Les Cents et Une Nuits, 1995, Prêt-à-porter, 1995; Une pour toutes, 2000; La Petite prairie aux bouleaux, 2003; Ils se mariérent et eurent beaucoup d'enfants, 2004; Margot, 2006; De particulier á particulier, 2006; Appeared on television in Une page d'amour, 1979, L'Île bleue, 2001; Des voix dans le jardin, Napoléon, 2002. Honours: Commandeur des Arts et des Lettres. Address: Bureau Georges Beaume, 3 Quai Malaquais, 75006 Paris, France.

AKCA Devrim, b. 27 May 1975, Gülnar, Turkey. Photogrammetrist; Researcher. Education: BSc, 1997, MSc, 2000, Geodesy and Photogrammetry Engineer, Karadeniz Technical University, Turkey; PhD, Photogrammetry, ETH Zurich, Switzerland, 2003-. Appointments: Surveying Engineer, General Directorate of Land Registry and Cadastre, Turkey, 1997-2000; Researcher, Ondokuz Mayis University, Turkey, 2000-01; Researcher, Istanbul Technical University, Turkey, 2001-02; Researcher, ETH Zurich, 2002-. Publications: A new algorithm for 3D surface matching, 2004; Fast correspondence search for 3D surface matching, 2005; Matching of 3D surfaces and their intensities, 2006. Honours: ISPRS Prize for Best Papers by Young Authors, 2004; Honorary degree in BSc graduation (first rank), Karadeniz Technical University, 1997. Memberships: Chambers of Mapping and Cadastre Engineers, Turkey; American Society for Photogrammetry and Remote Sensing. Address: Institute of Geodesy and Photogrammetry, ETH Honggerberg, CH-8093 Zurich, Switzerland. E-mail: akca@geod.baug.ethz.ch Website: www.photogrammetry.ethz.ch

AKINBODE Adeyemi, b. 29 July 1943, Ekiti State, Nigeria. Social Science Educator. m. Abimbola Rachael Akinleye, 1967, 2 children. Education: BA (Honours), 1967, PhD, 1974, Geography, Ibadan, Nigeria. Appointments: Lecturer II, 1971-74, Lecturer, I, 1974-75, College of Education of the University of Lagos; Lecturer I, 1975-77, Senior Lecturer, 1977-82, University of Benin, Benin City; Professor, Bendel/ Edo State/Ambrose Alli University, Ekpoma, 1982-2004; Professor of Geography, Delta State University, Abraka, 2005-07; Professor of Geography, Kogi State University, Anyigba, 2007-. Publications: Numerous articles in professional journals. Address: Department of Geography & Planning, Kogi State University, Anyigba, PMB 1008, Anyigba, Kogi State, Nigeria.

AKOMOLAFE Rufus Ojo Zacchaeus, b. 8 August 1959, Odo-Oro, Via Ikole, Nigeria. Banker; Lecturer; Accountant. m. 3 sons, 1 daughter. Education: Diploma in Accounting, 1981; BSc, Accounting, 1986; ACA, Nigeria, 1994; MSc, B & F, 1997; AMNIM, 1991, MNIM, 1995; ACTI, Nigeria, 1998; ACIB, Nigeria, 2003; FCA, Nigeria, 2003; FCTI, Nigeria, 2006. Appointments: Senior Manager, Inspection Skye Bank plc, 1995-96; Assistant Manager, 1995-97, Deputy Manager, 1997-2001, Manager, 2001-04, Senior Manager, 2004-, Co-operative Bank plc; Senior Lecturer, Lead City University, Nigeria, 2006-. Publication: Fraud Prevention and Control – Early Warning Signal. Honour: Best and Brightest For African Bankers, Mellon/Chase, USA in conjunction with IFESH and USAID. Memberships: Institute of Chartered Accountants, Nigeria; Nigerian Institute of Management; Chartered Institute of Bankers and Taxation, Nigeria. Address: Lead City University, GPO Box 37101, Dugbe, Ibadan, Nigeria.

AKŞIN I Sina, b. 1937. Professor. m. Tülin, 2 daughters. Education: Graduate, Robert College, 1955; Graduate, Law School, Istanbul University, 1959; MA, 1960, MALD, 1961, International Relations, Fletcher School of Law and Diplomacy, Boston, USA; PhD, Contemporary History, School of Literature, Istanbul University, 1968. Appointments: Instructor, History of Civilization, Robert College, School of Higher Education, 1961-67; Military Service, 1967-69; Teaching Assistant, Turkish Politics, School of Political Science, 1969, Associate Professor, 1975, Elected Chair, Turkish Politics, 1980, Assistant Director, Institute of Social Sciences, 1988, Full Professor, 1989, Chair, Department of Public Administration, 1991, Ankara University; Researcher, British State Archives, United Nations Fellowship, 1971-72; Researcher, 1978-79, 1989-90, French Foreign Ministry Archives. Publications: Numerous articles in professional journals; 5 books. Honours: Fulbright Award, 1960-61; Grand Prize, Türkiye İş Bankasi, 1994. Address: Siyasal Bilgiler Fakültesi, Cebeci, 06590 Ankara, Turkey.

AKYOL Ayla, b. 19 April 1940, Istanbul. Artist; Art Gallery Owner. m. Selahattin Akyol, 2 sons, 1 daughter. Education: English Literature, Istanbul University; Illumination and Miniature Course with Professor Dr Süheyl Ünver; Studied with artists including Deniz Orkuş, Dara Abadi, Hasan Taşdemir, Ümmet Karaca and Ildar Ahmet Veli. Appointments: Paintings Organiser, Love and Tolerance Train of Mevlana from Konya to Madrid, Turkish Ministry of Culture and Ministry of Foreign Affairs; Exhibitions of work at Akyol Art House, 2003-, and at Büyükada Anadolu Club for Prince Islands Resident Painters; Organiser, Jury Member, Children and Youth Paintings Competition, Anadolu Club. Publications: Subject of numerous articles in newspapers, magazines and books. Honours: One painting, The House of Atatürk in Trabzon, continuously exhibited in Beşiktaş Marine Museum. Memberships: Fine Arts Union; Artists Community; Anadolu Club of Ankara. Address: Nisantasi Ihlamur Yolu, Demir Palas, Apt No 36 D4, Topağaci, Istanbul.

AL DABBAGH Mahmoud, b. 14 August 1964, Damascus, Syria. Assistant Professor. m. Rana, 3 sons, 2 daughters. Education: BA, French Language, Civilization and Literature, University of Damascus, Syria; Master's, DEA, General and Applied Linguistics, Universite Rene Descartes, Paris V, France; PhD, Literary Transductology, Sorbonne, Nouvelle, Paris III, France. Appointments: Lecturer, French and Arabic, Curriculum Builder, Advisor, SUNY Brockport and Nazareth College, 2002-07; Head, BA Program in Arabic Studies (on line and on site, Curriculum Builder), Co-ordinator of General Education Requirements, Area G, Creation and Co-ordinating Placement and Waiver Tests for Foreign Language Programs (BA programs), Discussion Leader for Computer Language Courses in Area G Education, Assistant Professor and Lead Advisor, Arabic Studies, National University, 2007-. Publications: Numerous articles in professional journals. Honours: Listed in international biographical dictionaries. Memberships: SFT French National Association of Translators; American Translators' Association; Modern Language Association; Interfaith Organization of America; Southern Poverty Law Center; Sponsoring Founder, Wall of Tolerance Memorial, Washington, DC. Address: 9545 Genesee Ave, Apt A2, San Diego, CA 92121, USA. E-mail: mdabbagh@nu.edu

AL JUNAIBI Nasser Ahmed, b. 3 December 1972, Dubai, United Arab Emirates. Senior Electrical Engineer. Education: B Eng, Sultan Qaboos University, Oman, 1995; MSc (distinction), University of Bath, England, 1999. Appointments: Lecturer, Engineering, 1996-98; Engineering Researcher, 1999-2000; Power System Planning Engineer, 2001-03; Senior Electrical Engineer, 2004-. Publications: Numerous articles in professional journals; Several technical papers and conferences. Honours: MSc with distinction and Top Student, University of Bath; Research Grant, University of Manchester Institute of Science & Technology and

National Grid Company, England; Listed in international biographical dictionaries. Memberships: Chartered Engineer, Institute of Electrical Engineers, UK; Senior Member, Institute of Electrical and Electronics Engineers, USA; Senior Member, Power Engineering Society, USA. Address: PO Box 73626, Abu Dhabi, United Arab Emirates. E-mail: eemnaa16@hotmail.com

AL TAHER Mazen Nimr A, b. 20 December 1945, Nablus, Palestine. Dermato-Venereologist. m. Maha Kanan, 2 sons, 3 daughters. Education: MB BCh, Cairo University, 1971; Diploma, Plastic Surgery, Netherlands, 1974; MSc, Dermatology, Cairo, 1981; Diploma, Venereology, DVD, London, England, 1984. Appointments: In charge of Dermato-Venereology Centre, Military Hospital, Abu Dhabi, 1984-92; Owner, private clinic for dermatology, venereology and cosmotology of skin, 1992-. Publications: Clinical and Histo-Pathological Study Thesis of Adenoma-Sebaceum. Honours: Medal of Distinguished Services, Jordan University Hospital, 1976; Medal of Excellent Services, Armed Forces Medal Services, UAE, 1988; Dermatology Photographic Award, 1996; Dermatology Photographic Composition Award, 1998. Memberships: Jordan Medical Association for Dermatology; International Society of Dermatology; International Fellow, American Academy of Dermatology; Derma Club; Pan Arab League of Dermatology. Addresss: Hamdan St, PO Box 46467, Abu Dhabi, United Arab Emirates.

AL-ABDULLAH Her Majesty Queen Rania, b. 31 August 1970, Kuwait. Queen of Jordan. m. His Majesty King Abdullah bin Al-Hussein, 2 sons, 2 daughters. Education: Bachelor's degree, Business Administration, American University, Cairo, 1991. Appointments: Career in banking; Worked in field of information technology. Publications: The King's Gift, children's book. Memberships: Founder, Chairperson, Jordan River Foundation; Foundation Board Member, World Economic Forum; Board Member, GAVI Fund (Global Alliance for Vaccines and Immunization); Board Member, International Youth Foundation; Member, UNICEF Global Leadership Initiative for Children; Regional Ambassador of INJAZ (Junior Achievements World Wide). Address: Royal Hashemite Court, Amman, Jordan.

AL-ARRAYED Jalil Ebrahim, b. 26 January 1933. Emeritus Professor; University Administrator. Education: BA, Chemistry, American University, Beirut, Lebanon, 1954; MEd, Science Education, Leicester University, England, 1964; PhD, Comparative Science Education and Management of Curriculum Development, Bath University, England, 1974. Appointments: Teacher, Sciences, Maths, 1954-59, Science Inspector, 1959-66, Bahrain Government Department of Education; Principal, Bahrain Men's Teachers Training College, 1966-72; Under-Secretary, Bahrain Ministry of Education, 1974-82; Executive Council Member (Bahrain Rep), 1975-82, Deputy Chairman, 1978-79; Chairman, 1979-80, Arab Bureau of Education for the Gulf States; Member, Bahrain Representative, Council for Higher Education in the Gulf States, 1976-92; Member, Board of Trustees, Bahrain University College of Arts, Science and Education, 1979-86; Member Founding Committee, Arabian Gulf University, 1980-85; Member, IIEP Council of Consultant Fellows, Paris, 1984-92; Rector, Bahrain University College of Arts, Science and Education, 1982-87; Professor of Education, Vice President, Academic Affairs, University of Bahrain, 1987-91, Acting President, 1991; Participant, various regional and international conferences on education reform, and Chair, several committees.

Publications: Author of books: A Critical Analysis of Arab School Science Teaching, 1980, Development and Evaluation of University Faculty in Arab Gulf States, 1994, Some Aspects of Contemporary Management Thought, 1996; More than 50 articles on educational issues in general and science education in particular, 1956-78. Honours: Gold Medal for Academic Achievement, Bahrain Government Department of Education, 1969; Prize for Academic Achievement, Bahrain Ministry of Education, 1975; American Biographical Institute Commemorative Medal of Honour, 1988; State Award for Outstanding Citizens, Government of Bahrain, 1992; International Association of University Presidents Certificate for Outstanding Contributions, 1996. Memberships: Life Fellow, International Biographical Association; Life Member, Indian Institute of Public Administration; Various organizations including: Chartered Management Institute; Institute of Administrative Management, UK; International Association of University Presidents; Royal Society of Chemistry (UK); Listed in numerous biographical dictionaries. Address: PO Box 26165, Adlia, Manama, Bahrain.

AL-DUWAISAN Khaled Abdelaziz, b. 15 August 1947, Kuwait. Ambassador. m. Dalal Yacoub Al-Homaizi, 1 son, 1 daughter. Education: BA Commerce, Cairo University, Egypt; Postgraduate Diploma, Public Administration, University of Kuwait. Appointments: Diplomatic Attaché, Ministry of Foreign Affairs, 1970-74; Appointed Second Secretary, 1974; Joined Kuwait Embassy in Washington DC, USA, 1975; Appointed Ambassador to the Netherlands, 1984-90; Accredited Ambassador to Romania, 1988; Chairman, Kuwait Delegation for supervision of de-militarised zone between Iraq and Kuwait and Chief Co-ordinator for the return of stolen property, 1991; Ambassador to the United Kingdom, 1993 and accredited to Denmark, Norway and Sweden 1994-95, accredited to The Republic of Ireland, 1995; Joined Advisory Board, Centre of Near and Middle East Studies, School of Oriental and African Studies, 1998. Honours: GCVO (UK), 1995; Freedom of the City of London, 2001; Doyen of the Diplomatic Corps at the Court of St James, 2003; Honorary Certificate, Management of Public Sector Projects and Facilities (Executive Program for Kuwait), Harvard University, 2005; Participant in Workshop of International Diplomacy in the New Century, Kuwait Foundation for the Advancement of Sciences and John F Kennedy School of Government, Harvard University, Cambridge, Massachusetts, 2007. Address: Kuwait Embassy, 2 Albert Gate, Knightsbridge, London SW1X 7JU, England.

AL-HAJJAJI Najat-Mehdi, b. 26 July 1952, Tripoli, Libya. Ambassador; Permanent Representative of the Libyan Mission to the UN. 1 daughter. Education: Bachelor of Arts, Journalism, Cairo; Master of Arts, Mass Communications. Appointments: Editor, General Institution for Journalism, Tripoli, 1973-75; Correspondent, Libyan daily newspaper, Cairo, 1975-77; Minister Plenipotentiary, later Chargé d'Affaires, Permanent Mission of Libyan Arab Jamahiriya, Geneva, 1992-2000; Ambassador, Permanent Representative of the Libyan Arab Jamahiriya to the UN Office, Geneva, and international organisations in Switzerland, 2000-. Publications include: Obstacles facing sustainable development in Africa; Sale of children: what are the solutions?; The consequences of terrorism on human rights; How to promote human rights for disabilities; Trafficking in women: it's reasons and consequences; African NGO's: how to be more efficient?; The role of Libya in solving conflicts in Africa; Religious intolerance in Africa: to what extent?; Violence against women and children: how to eradicate it?; The UN and the international regional organisations; Towards African union;

The plight of the displaced persons in the third world; The image of Muslims in the western media; The mutual influence of politics and mass media. Honours: Award, Kuala Lumpur World Peace Conference, Malaysia, 2003; Medal, International Criminal Court on Rwanda, 2003; Member, Special Committee to select winner of UN Prize in field of Human Rights, 2003; Medal, General Head of Dubai Police, 2004; Award, Geneva Institute for Human Rights, 2004; Honorary Distinction, Arab Labour Organisations, Geneva, 2004; Honourable Representative, International Organisation for Peace, Care and Relief, Geneva; Reward, Arab Distinguished Woman, 3rd session, Arab Women Studies Centre, Dubai, 2006; International Socrates Award, Europea Business Assembly, Oxford, England, 2007; Listed in international biographical dictionaries. Memberships: United Nations Working Group on Mercenaries, 2005-08; Chair, Council of International Organisation for Migration, 2006-07. Address: 25 rue Richemont, 1202 Geneva, Switzerland. E-mail: n.alhajjaji@bluewin.ch

AL-HARMI Jehad, b. 6 December 1963, Kuwait City, Kuwait. Obstetrician; Gynecologist. Education: Bachelor, Medical Sciences, 1985, Bachelor, Medicine & Surgery, 1988, Kuwait University; Clinical Fellowship, Obstetrics and Gynecology, McGill University, 1997; Specialist Certificate, Royal College of Physicians and Surgeons of Canada, 1997. Appointments: Faculty Member, Kuwait Institute for Medical Specializations, 2001-; Co-Director, Postgraduate Training Program in Obstetrics and Gynecology, 2001-; Clinical Tutor in Obstetrics and Gynecology, 2000-05; Assistant Professor, Obstetrics and Gynecology, 2006-; Deputy Chairperson, Department of Obstetrics and Gynecology, Maternity Hospital, 2006-. Publications: 10 articles in professional medical journals including most recently: Increasing severity of hematuria with successive pregnancies in a woman with renal angiomyolipoma, 2007; Delivery after prior cesarean section in Kuwait, 2007; Maternal-fetal transport kinetics of methotrexate in perfused human placenta: in vitro study, 2007. Honours: Alice Benjamin Award for Excellence in Obstetrics, 1997. Memberships: Kuwait Medical Association; Society of Obstetrics and Gynecology of Canada; American College of Obstetrics and Gynecology; Royal College of Physician and Surgeons of Canada. E-mail: jalharmi@yahoo.com

AL-HARITHI Ibrahim Ahmad Mosallam, b. 21 November 1941, Idna-Hebron, Jordan. Educational Consultant. m. Fahima Murad, 5 sons, 7 daughters. Education: BSc, MSc, Physics, Tehran University, 1965; Diploma in Educational Technology, CETO Institute, London, UK, 1968; MEd, Diploma of Education, Jordan University, 1981; Diploma, Curriculum Planning for Developing Countries, Institute of Education, London University, UK, 1982; DEd, Ed M & MSc, Teachers College, Colombia University, New York, USA, 1985. Appointments: Physics Instructor, Al-Hussein College, Amman, Jordan, 1965-67; Physics Instructor, Royal Military College, Jordan, 1969-72; Head, Educational TV Division, 1968-69; Supervisor of Science Curriculum, 1972-75, Head of Science Division, 1978-81, Head of Curriculum and Supervision Division, 1981-83, General Director, Curriculum and Educational Technology, 1990-92, General Director, Cultural Relationships and Educational Information, 1992-93, Deputy General Secretary, 1993-96, Ministry of Education, Jordan; Supervisor, Teacher Training Center for Science, 1975-78; Director, Educational Technology and Computer Assisted Instruction, 1986-87; Educational Chancellor, Jordan Embassy, Kuwait, 1987-90; Chief of Experts, Educational Development in Educational Development Center, 1996-98, Executive Director, Educational Development Project,

1998-2000, Ministry of Education, Saudi Arabia; Consultant and Head, Development and Design Division, Saudi Pioneering Schools Project, 2001-03; General Supervisor, Project for Enhancing Thinking, Ministry of Education, Riyadh, Saudi Arabia, 2003-04; General Director of Academic Affairs, Al-Rowad Schools, Riyadh, Saudi Arabia, 2005-; Educational Consultant, Al-Rowad Educational Est, 2005-. Publications: Author and co-author of over 23 books; Numerous articles in professional journals. Honours: Many awards in Jordan and Saudi Arabia. Memberships: Association of Physics Teachers; Arab Network for Open & Distant Education, Amman, Jordan; Islamic Research and Study Society, Amman, Jordan; Jordanian Society for Preventing Pollution; Association for Supervision and Curriculum Development, USA; Arab Union for Science Clubs, Tunisia. Address: Al Rowad Schools, PO Box 87527, Riyadh 11652, Saudi Arabia.

AL-RABADI Anas N. Associate Professor. Education: BSc, Electrical Engineering, Jordan University of Science and Technology, 1995; MSc, 1998, PhD, 2002, Electrical and Computer Engineering, Portland State University, USA. Appointments: Post Doctoral and Research Fellow, Office of Graduate Studies and Research, and in Systems Science PhD Program, Adjunct Professor, Physics Department, and Research Assistant Faculty, Portland State University, 2002-04; Assistant Professor, 2004-07, Associate Professor, 2007-, Computer Engineering Department, University of Jordan; Interim Chairman (Head), JU Computer Engineering Department, 2005; Dean's Assistant for Computer Affairs, JU College of Graduate Studies, 2006-. Publications: Numerous articles and papers published in professional scientific journals worldwide. Honours: Kingdom of Jordan Scholarship, 1990-95; Academically Auxiliary Activities Fund Scholarships, 2001, 2002, 2003; Portland State University Marie Brown Graduate Student Travel Award, 2002; Portland State University Alumni Association Scholarship, 2002; Systems Science PhD Program Award, 2002; ACM/SIGDA Travel Grant, 2002; Office of Graduate Studies and Research, Portland State University Travel Awards, 2004; Honorary Doctorate in Engineering, The Yorker International University, USA, 2007. Listed in national and international biographical dictionaries. Memberships: Institute of Electrical and Electronics Engineers; Association for Computing Machinery; International Neural Network Society; Society for Industrial and Applied Mathematics; Sigma Xi The Scientific Research Honor Society; Tau Beta Pi; Eta Kappa Nu; Optical Society of America; American Physical Society; The International Society for Optical Engineering; American Society for Engineering Education. Address: Computer Engineering Department, The University of Jordan, Amman, JO 11942, Jordan. E-mail: alrabadi@yahoo.com Website: http://web.pdx.edu/~psu21829/

AL-RUZZEH Sharif, b. 2 April 1971. Physician. m. Kinda El-Borno, 1 son. Education: MBBS (1st Class Honours), Cairo University, Egypt, 1994; FRCSEd, 1999; FRCS (Eng), 2000; PhD, University of London, England, 2003. Publications: Numerous articles in professional journals, reviews, abstracts and reports. Honours: Listed in international biographical dictionaries; Award in Healthcare and Medicine, 2006. Memberships: International Society of Minimally Invasive Cardiac Surgery; European Association for Cardio-thoracic Surgeons. Address: 18 Fielding Way, Morley, Leeds LS27 9AB, England. E-mail: sharifalruzzeh@hotmail.com

AL-SABAH HRH Prince Mubarak Fahed Al-Salem, b. 8 September 1957, Kuwait. Deputy Undersecretary. Education: BA, European Culture Studies, American University of

Paris, France, 1982. Appointments: Deputy Undersecretary, Department of Protocol, Royal Palace of The Emir of Kuwait, 1982-; Official member of delegations accompanying High Highness The Emir of Kuwait worldwide. Honours: Chevalier dans l'Ordre des Arts et des Lettres, Paris, 1982; Officier dans l'Ordre des Arts et des Lettres, Paris, 1988; Suomen Leijoman RitariKunan, HE The President of the Republic of Finland, Helsinki, 1997. Memberships: Patron of many musical and charitable societies. Address: Salmya Palace, PO Box 8001, 22051 Kuwait. E-mail: royalmfs@hotmail.com

AL-SHAMMA' Khalil M H, b. 1935, Iraq. m. 1 son, 3 daughters. Education: BBA, 1957, MBA, 1959, American University, Beirut, Lebanon; PhD, Business Administration, University of California at Berkeley, USA, 1962; PhD, Business Management, World University, Benson, Arizona, USA, 1987. Appointments: Instructor, 1962, Assistant Professor, 1967, Associate Professor, 1972, Full Professor, 1975, University of Baghdad; Assistant Dean, College of Commerce, 1963; President, Economic and Administrative Research Centre, 1966-67; Dean, College of Administration and Economics, 1967-78; Chairman, Department of Business Administration, 1967-72; Chairman, PhD Committee, 1974-92; Teacher, Al-Bakr University for Postgraduate Military Studies, 1977-92; Teacher, Al-Mustansiriyah University, 1980-85; Chief, Research and Statistics Department, Central Bank of Iraq, 1963-65, Economic Advisor, State Economic Organisation, 1965-67, Chairman, Presidential Palace Committee, Reorganisation of State and Public Sector, 1970-77; Consultant, Arac Management Consultancy, 1967-72; Own consultancy, 1972-79; Assistant General Manager, 1992-95, First Deputy General Manager, 1995-96, Vice President, 1996-, Arab Academy for Banking and Financial Sciences; Supervision of thesis and dissertations: PhD: Business Management (27), Banking and Finance (1), Economics (5); High Diploma in Military Science (38); MSc: Business Administration (91), Accounting (83), Economics (14), Insurance (19). Publications: More than 100 articles in Arabic and English; Author of more than 50 books in the fields of: Banking, Financial Management, Financial Accounting, Cost Accounting, Management Accounting, Strategic Management, Housing, Credit, Savings Investments, Financial Markets, University Management, Management, Organisation Theory, Basel Committee on Banking Supervision, Feasibility Studies, Operations Management, Managerial Economics, Economic Development, Economic Planning; Chief Editor: Economic and Administrative Journal, University of Baghdad; Defence Review, Al-Bakr University for Postgraduate Military Sciences; Journal of Banking and Financial Studies, Arab Academy for Banking and Financial Sciences. Honours: Order of Distinctive National Service, 1975, Order of High Distinctive and National Service, 1977, President of Iraq; Prize, Minister of Defence, 1966; Prize, Central Bank of Iraq, 1985; Best University Professor, Minister of Higher Education, 1986; Best Professor, Al-Bakr University for Postgraduate Studies, 1991; Prize, National Insurance Company of Iraq, 1992; Best Professor, University of Baghdad, 1992. Memberships: Iraqi Economists Association; Iraqi Association of Accountants; Iraqi Teachers Association; Iraqi Management Association. Address: Arab Academy for Banking and Financial Sciences, PO Box 13190, Amman, Jordan.

AL-WALI Abdul Jaleel Kadhem, b. 1 July 1954, Thegar, Iraq. Professor of Philosophy. m. Hakema Kadhem Thahb, 1 son, 4 daughters. Education: BSc, 1975, MA, 1985, PhD, 1990, Philosophy, Baghdad University, Iraq. Appointments: Assistant Professor 1985-90, Associate Professor, 1990-94, Department of Philosophy, Faculty of Arts, Baghdad University; Associate Professor and Chairman, Department of Philosophy and Sociology, Faculty of Art and Science, Al-Tahaddi University, Libya, 1994-97; Associate Professor, 1997-2000, Professor, 2000-01, Department of Philosophy, Faculty of Arts, Sana'a University, Republic of Yemen; Professor, Department of Philosophy, Faculty of Humanities and Social Sciences, United Arab Emirates University, United Arab Emirates, 2001-. Publications: Books include: Theory of Ideas: The Construction of Plato and Aristotle's Criticism, 2002; Aristotle's Criticism of Pre-Socrates Natural Philosophy, 2004; Mind and Criticism, 2006; Greek Philosophy and Dialectical Globalization and Reading in Philosophy, in progress; Textbooks: Development of Philosophical Thought (co-author), 2003; Globalisation and Its Impact on the Arab World (co-author), 2003; Arabian Islamic Civilisation (co-author), 2004; Global Issues (co-author), 2005; Numerous research articles in academic journals and scientific essays in the media. Honours: International Conference on Poverty in the Muslim World & Communities, 2004; Islamic World and West, Bridges and Barriers conference, 2006. Memberships: Iraqi Philosophical Association; Arab Philosophical Association; Iraqi Writers and Authors Union. Address: United Arab Emirates University, Department of Philosophy, PO Box 17771, Al-Ain, United Arab Emirates. E-mail: jalilwali@hotmail.com

ALADEMIR Ayse Zeynep, b. 13 June 1976, Istanbul, Turkey. Medical Doctor; Biochemist. Education: Biochemistry and Clinical Biochemistry, 1999, English, 2004, University of Istanbul Cerrahpasa, Faculty of Medicine. Appointments: Volunteer Research Assistant, Turkish Heart Study, American Hospital, Gladstone Institute, 1995; Assistant, Biochemistry, University of Istanbul Cerrahpasa, Faculty of Medicine, 2000-04; Medical Doctor, Biochemistry Specialist and Director, Rize State Hospital Laboratory, 2005-. Publications include: Significance of the O_6-methylguanine-DNA methyltransferase and GST activity in the sera of the patients with malignant and benign ovarian tumors, 2005. Honours: Successful Researchers Award, University of Istanbul, 2002 and 2003. Memberships: Turkish Biochemical Society; Clinical Biochemistry Specialists Society (KBUD); TEMA. Address: Islampasa Mah, Diren apt B Blok no 3, Merkez/Rize 53000, Turkey. E-mail: azeynepalademir@yahoo.com

ALAGIAH George, b. 21 November 1955, Sri Lanka. Journalist; Television News Presenter. m. 2 sons. Education: Graduate, Durham University. Appointments: Journalist, South Magazine, 7 years; Contributed to The Guardian, the Daily Telegraph, The Independent, the Daily Express; Joined BBC, 1989; Foreign Correspondent and specialist on Africa and the developing world; Currently Co-Presenter BBC's Six O'Clock News, 2003-; Launched BBC4's international news programme, 2004; Presenter of a new programme on BBC World, World News Today, 2006; Has reported on: Trade in human organs in India; Murder of street children in Brazil; Civil war and famine in Somalia; Genocide in Rwanda and its aftermath; Plight of marsh Arabs in southern Iraq; Civil wars in Afghanistan, Liberia and Sierra Leone; Truth and Reconciliation Commission in South Africa; Fall of Mobuto Sese Seko in Zaire; Effects of Hurricane Mitch on Honduras; Kosovan refugee crisis; NATO liberation of Pristina; International intervention in East Timor; Farm invasions in Zimbabwe, Intifada in the West Bank; Aftermath of the terror attacks on New York; Documentaries and features include: Saddam Hussein's genocidal campaign against the Kurds of northern Iraq; The last reunion of the veterans of Dunkirk and a BBC 1 Special on the trial and conviction of Jill Dando's murderer. Publications: Book, A Passage to Africa, 2001;

Essay, Shaking the Foundations, in the BBC's book on the aftermath of September 11. Honours include: Critics Award and Golden Nymph Award, Monte Carlo Television Festival, 1992; Award for Best International Report, Royal Television Society, 1993; Commendation, BAFTA, 1993; Amnesty International's Best TV Journalist Award, 1994; One World Broadcasting Trust Award, 1994; James Cameron Memorial Trust Award, 1995; Bayeux Award for War Reporting, 1996; Media Personality of the Year, Ethnic Minority Media Award, 1998; BAFTA Award for coverage of the Kosovo conflict (BBC Team), 2000; Madoc Award, Hay Literary Festival, 2002. Memberships: Patron: The Presswise Trust; NAZ Project; Parenting, Education and Support Forum; Fairtrade Foundation. Address: British Broadcasting Corporation, BBC News Publicity, Television Centre, Wood Lane, London W12 7RJ, England.

ALAGNA Roberto, b. 7 June 1963, Clichy-sur-Bois, France. Singer (Tenor). m. (1) Florence Lancien, deceased 1994, 1 daughter , (2) Angela Gheorghiu, 1996. Education: Studied in France and Italy. Debut: Plymouth, 1988, as Alfredo in La Traviata for Glyndebourne Touring Opera. Career: Sang Rodolfo at Covent Garden (1990) and has returned for Gounod's Roméo and Don Carlos, 1994-96; sang Donizetti's Roberto Devereux at Monte Carlo (1992) and the Duke of Mantua at the Vienna Staatsoper (1995); Sang Don Carlos at the Théâtre du Châtelet, Paris, 1996; American appearances at Chicago and New York (debut at Met 1996, as Rodolfo); Alfredo at La Scala, Milan; Opened the 2006-07 season in Aida at La Scala, Milan. Recordings include: video of Gounod's Roméo et Juliette (Pioneer); La Traviata, from La Scala (Sony) and Don Carlos, Paris; Duets and Arias (with Angela Gheorghiu); La Boheme 1996, Don Carlos 1996, La Rondine 1997. Honours include: Winner, Pavarotti Competition, 1988; Chevalier des Arts et des Lettres; Personalite Musicale de l'Annee, 1994; Laurence Olivier Award for Outstanding Achievement in Opera, 1995; Victor Award for Best Singer, 1997. Address: c/o Lévon Sayan, 9 chemin de Plonjon, Geneva, Switzerland.

ALAGOA Ebiegberi Joe, b. 14 April 1933, Nembe, Nigeria. Historian. m. Mercy, 1 son, 1 daughter. Education: St Luke's School, 1943-48; Government College, Umuahia, 1948-54; University College, Ibadan, (London University) 1954-59; University of Wisconsin, Madison, Wisconsin, USA, 1962-65. Appointments: Deputy Vice-Chancellor, University of Port Harcourt, 1980-81; Pro-Chancellor, Niger Delta University, 2001-03; Chairman, Governing Board, Rev D O Ockiya College of Theology and Management Sciences, Emeyal, Bayesa State, 2004-. Publications: 29 books; 3 archival monographs; 49 contributors to books; 47 journal articles. Honours: Fellow, Historical Society of Nigeria, 1981; Officer of the Order of the Niger, 2000; Fellow, Nigerian Academy of Letters, 2001; Award of Excellence, Bayelsa State Government, 2004; Emeritus Professor of History, University of Port Harcourt, 2005; various research fellowships. Memberships: Historical Society of Nigeria; Diabetes Association of Nigeria; Diabetes UK. Address: 11 Orogbum Crescent, GRA Phase II, Port Harcourt, Rivers State, Nigeria. E-mail: kala_joe@yahoo.com

ALBARN Damon, b. 23 March 1968, Whitechapel, London, England. Singer; Songwriter. 1 daughter with partner Suzi Winstanley. Education: Drama School, Stratford East, 1 year. Musical Education: Part-time Music course, Goldsmith's College. Career: First solo concerts, Colchester Arts Centre; Member, Blur; Numerous television and radio appearances, include: Later With Jools Holland; Top Of The Pops; Loose Ends, Radio 4; Later With... Britpop Now; Extensive tours,

concerts include: Alexandra Palace, Reading Festival, 1993; Glastonbury, 1994; Mile End, 1995; V97, UK Arena Tour, 1997; Glastonbury, 1998; T in the Park, Reading and Leeds Festival, 1999; Actor, film, Face, 1997; Score for Ravenous, 1998; Score for Ordinary Decent Criminal, 1999; score for 101 Reykjavik (with Einar Benediktsson), 2000. Recordings: Albums: with Blur: Leisure, 1991; Modern Life Is Rubbish, 1993; Parklife, 1994; The Great Escape, 1995; Blur, 1997; 13, 1999; Best of Blur 2000; Think Tank, 2003; (with Gorillaz) Gorillaz, 2001; G-Slides, 2002; Phase One: Celebrity Take Down, 2002; We Are Happy Landfill, 2005; Singles: She's So High, 1990; There's No Other Way, Bang, 1991; Popscene, 1992; For Tomorrow, Chemical World, Sunday Sunday, 1993; Girls And Boys, To The End, Parklife, End Of A Century, 1994; Country House, The Universal, 1995; Stereotypes, 1996; Beetlebum, Song 2, On Your Own, MOR, 1997; Tender, Coffee and TV, No Distance Left To Run, 1999; Music is My Radar, (with Gorillaz) Clint Eastwood, 2000; 19-2000, Rock the House, 2001; Tomorrow Comes Today, 2002; Solo: Original score for film Ravenous, directed by Antonia Bird, with Michael Nyman, 1998; Score for film Ordinary Decent Criminal, directed by Thasseus O'Sullivan, 1999; Mali Music, various contributors, 2002; Democrazy, 2003. Honours: Mercury Prize Nomination; Platinum album, Parklife; BRIT Awards: Best Single, Video, Album and Band, 1995; Q Awards, Best Album, 1994, 1995; Mercury Music Prize nomination, 1999; Platinum albums. Current Management: CMO Management, Unit 32, Ransome Dock, 35-37 Parkgate Road, London SW11 4NP, England.

ALBEE Edward (Franklin III), b. 12 March 1928, Virginia, USA. Playwright. Education: Trinity College, Hartford, Connecticut, 1946-47. Appointments: Lecturer at various US colleges and universities. Publications: Plays: The Zoo Story, 1958; The Death of Bessie Smith, The Sandbox, 1959; The American Dream, 1960; Who's Afraid of Virginia Woolf?, 1962; Tiny Alice, 1963; A Delicate Balance, 1966; Box, Quotations from Chairman Mao, 1970; All Over, 1971; Seascape, 1975; Counting the Ways, 1976; Listening, 1977; The Lady from Dubuque, 1979; Finding the Sun, 1982; The Man Who Had Three Arms, 1983; Marriage Play, 1987; Three Tall Women, 1991; Fragments, 1993; The Play about the Baby, 1996; The Goat, or, Who is Sylvia? 2000; Occupant, 2001; Peter and Jerry (Act 1: Home Life, Act 2: The Zoo Story), 2004. Adaptions of: Carson McCuller's The Ballad of the Sad Café, 1963; James Purdy's Malcolm, 1965; Giles Cooper's Everything in the Garden, 1967; Vladimir Nabokov's Lolita, 1980. Honours: Tony Awards, 1963, 1965, 2002, 2005; Pulitzer Prizes in Drama, 1967, 1975, 1994; American Academy and Institute of Arts and Letters Gold Medal, 1980; Theater Hall of Fame, 1985. Memberships: Dramatists Guild Council; Edward F Albee Foundation, president. Address: 14 Harrison Street, New York, NY 10013, USA.

ALBERT II, b. 6 June 1934, Belgium. King of Belgium. m. Donna Paola Ruffo Di Calabria, 1959, 2 sons, 1 daughter. Appointments: Formerly Prince of Liege; Former Vice Admiral of Navy; President, Caisse d'Epargne et de Retraite, 1954-92; President, Belgian Red Cross, 1958-93; President, Belgian Office of Foreign Trade, 1962; Appointed by Council of Europe as President of Conference of European Ministers responsible for protection of Cultural and Architectural Heritage, 1969; Participant in Numerous Conferences on environment including UN Conference, Stockholm, 1972; Chair, Belgian Olympic and Interfed Committee; Succeeded to the throne 9 August 1993 following death of his brother King Baudouin I. Address: Cabinet of the King, The Royal Place, rue Bréderode, 1000 Brussels, Belgium.

ALBERT II, His Serene Highness Prince Albert Alexandre Louis Pierre, b. 14 March 1958. Sovereign Prince of Monaco and Marquis of Baux. Education: Albert I High School; Amherst College, Massachusetts, USA. Appointments: 1st Class Ensign (Sub-Captain); President, Monegasque Delegate to General Assembly, UN, 1993-; Chair, several sports federations and committees; Chair, Organisaing Committee, Monte Carlo International Television Festival, 1988-; Deputy Chair, Princess Grace Foundation of Monaco; named Sovereign Prince of Monaco, 2005; Honorary President, International Athletic Foundation, International Modern Pentathlon Union, World Beach Volleyball; Honorary Citizen of Fort Worth, 2000; Honorary Chair, Jeune Chambre Economique, Monaco Aide et Presence; Honorary Member, St Petersburg Naval Association; International Institute for Human Rights; Honorary Professor of International Studies, Tarrant County College, Fort Worth, 2000. Honours: Grand Cross, Order of Grimaldi, 1958; Grand Officier, National Order of the Lion of Senegal, 1977; Grand Cross, Order of Saint-Charles, 1979; Knight Grand Cross, Equestrian Order of the Holy Sepulchre of Jerusalem, 1983; Grand Officier, Legion of Honour, 1984; Colonel of the Carabineers, 1986; Chevalier, Order of Malta, 1989; Grand Officier, Merite International du Sang, 1994; Grand Cross, National Order of Merit, 1997; Grand Cross, National Order of Niger, 1998; Grand Cross of the Jordanian Renaissance (Nahdah Medal), 2000; Grand Cross, Order of the Sun of Peru, 2003; Grand Cross, Order Juan Mora Fernandez, Costa Rica, 2003; Order of Stara Planina, Bulgaria, 2004; Dr hc, Pontifical University, Maynooth, 1996. Address: Palais Princier, BP 518, MC 98015, Monaco. Website: www.palais.mc

ALBERTI Kurt George Matthew Mayer (Sir), b. 27 September 1937, Germany. Professor of Medicine. m.(1) 1964, 3 sons, (2) Stephanie Amiel, 1988. Education: Balliol College, Oxford; MA; DPhil; FRCP; FRCPath; FRCPEd; FRCPGlas; FRCPI. Appointments: Research Fellow, Harvard University, USA, 1966-69; Research Officer, Oxford University, England, 1969-73; Professor of Chemical Pathology, Southampton University, 1973-78; Professor of Clinical Biochemistry, 1978-85, Professor of Medicine, 1985-2002, Dean of Medicine, 1995-97, University of Newcastle; Director of Research and Development, Northern and Yorkshire Region, 1992-95; President, Royal College of Physicians, 1997-2002; Professor of Metabolic Medicine, Imperial College, London, 1999-2002; Senior Research Fellow, London, 2002-; National Director for Emergency Access, Department of Health, 2002-. Publications: International Textbook of Diabetes Mellitus, 1st and 2nd editions, co-editor; Diabetes Annual, volumes 1-6, co-editor; Over 1,000 papers, reviews and edited books. Honours: Honorary MD, University of Aarhus, Denmark, 1998; Honorary Fellow, Balliol College, Oxford, 1999; DMed hc (University of Aarhus), (Southampton), 2000; Fellow, Academy of Medicine, Singapore, Hong Kong; Fellow, College of Physicians, Sri Lanka, Thailand; Hon DMed (Århus), (Southampton) 2000, (Athens) 2002; Hon DSc (Cranfield) 2005, (Warwick) 2005. Address: Royal College of Physicians, 11 St Andrew's Place, Regents Park, London NW1 4LE, England. E-mail: professor.alberti@rcplondon.ac.uk

ALBRIGHT Carol Rausch, b. 20 March 1936, Evergreen Park, Illinois, USA. Writer; Editor; Retired Foundation Administrator. m. (1) Saul Gorski, 2 July 1961, deceased 22 June 1983, 2 sons ,(2) John Albright, 26 October 1991. Education: BA, Augustana College, Rock Island, Illinois, 1956; Graduate Study, Lutheran Schools of Theology, Chicago, Berkeley, Washington University, St Louis. Appointments: Director, Lutheran Campus Ministry, Oregon State University, 1958-61; Publishing Consultant, 1966-70; Assistant Editor, World Book Encyclopaedia, 1970-75; Publishing Consultant, 1975-98; Contributing Editor, Doctor I've Read...., 1983-93; Executive Editor, Zygon: Journal of Religion and Science, 1989-98; Managing Editor, Science and Religion South, 1995-99; Publisher, Bridge Building, 1999; Co-Director, John Templeton Foundation Science and Religion Course Programme, Southern US, 1995-99; Co-Director, CTNS Science and Religion course programme, Midwestern US,1999-2001; Visiting Professor of Religion and Science, Lutheran School of Theology at Chicago, 2006-. Publications: Beginning with the end: God, Science, and Wolfhart Pannenberg; The Humanizing Brain; Where God Lives in the Human Brain; Growing in the Image of God; NeuroTheology. Honours: Academic Achievement Award, Institute for Religion in an Age of Science; Phi Beta Kappa; Chicago Women in Publishing: Award for Excellence in Periodical Writing. Memberships: Treasurer, Centre for Advanced Study in Religion and Science; Executive Council, American Theological Society, Midwest Division; Vice President for Religion, Institute for Religion in an Age of Science; Augustana Lutheran Church of Hyde Park; European Society for the study of Science and Theology; Society of Midland Authors. Address: 5436 S Hyde Park Blvd, Chicago, IL 60615, USA.

ALBRIGHT Jack Lawrence, b. 14 March 1930, San Francisco, California. Educator, Professor Emeritus. m. Lorraine A Hughes, August 1957, 2 daughters. Education: BS, with honours, California Polytechnic State University, San Luis Obispo, 1952; MS, Dairy Science, Washington State University, 1954; PhD, Animal Science, Washington State University, 1957; Certificate in Animal Behaviour, Michigan State University, 1964. Appointments: Various positions including: Professor, Animal Science, Purdue University 1966-96; Professor of Animal Management and Behaviour, School of Veterinary Medicine, Purdue University 1974-96; Professor Emeritus of Animal Science and Veterinary Medicine, Purdue University, 1996-. Publications: Authored or co-authored 132 refereed research publications: 132 scientific abstracts; 91 books, books chapters, reviews and bound proceedings; 247 invited research lectures; 261 popular articles; 34 extension bulletins; 325 extension publications, talks, radio and TV interviews. Honours include: Fellow, American Association for the Advancement of Science, 1963; Fellow, Indiana Academy of Science, 1983; Fellow, American Dairy Science Association, 1997; Paso Robles High School, California First Inaugural Academic Hall of Fame 1998; Honorary Member of Los Lecheros Dairy Club, California Polytechnic State University, 1999; Tablet of Honor, Kiwanis International Foundation, 2000; Listed in Who's Who and biographical publications. Memberships: Life Member, American Dairy Science Association; Life Member, American Society of Animal Science; International Society for Applied Ethology; Universities Federation of Animal Welfare and Humane Slaughter Association, UK; Hoofed Animal Humane Association, USA; Council for Agriculture Science and Technology, USA. Address: Purdue University, West Lafayette, IN 47907, USA. E-mail: jackalbrig@aol.com

ALBRIGHT Joseph, b. 2 March 1954, Chillicothe, Ohio, USA. Military Support and Sustainment; Process Improvement. Divorced, 1 son, 1 daughter. Education: Bachelor of Mechanical Engineering, University of Dayton, Ohio, 1976; Master of Strategic Studies, US Army War College, Carlisle Barracks, Pennsylvania, USA, 2000; MSc, Industrial Engineering, University of Tennessee, Knoxville, 2001. Appointments: Commissioned Officer, US

Army Ordnance Corps, 1976-2004; Deputy Director, Army Enterprise Integration Oversight, 2004-07; Director for Sustainment, Office of the Deputy Under Secretary of the Army for Business Transformation, 2005-. Honours: Legion of Merit; National Defense Service Medal; Meritorious Service Medal; Army Commendation Medal; Tennessee Distinguished Service Medal; Alabama Commendation Medal; Honorable Order of St Barbara, Artillery Corps, US Army; Honorable Order of Samuel Sharpe, Ordnance Corps, US Army; Listed in international biographical dictionaries; Exceptional Performance Awards, 2005-07. Memberships: Life Member, United State Army, Ordnance Corps Association; Sons of the American Revolution; American Society of Mechanical Engineers. E-mail: joseph.albright@us.army.mil

ALBRIGHT Madeleine Korbel, b. 15 May 1937, Prague, Czechoslovakia (US citizen). Former Government Official; Diplomatist; International Affairs Adviser. m. Joseph Albright, 1959, divorced 1983, 3 daughters. Education: Wellesley College; Columbia University. Appointments: Professor, International Affairs, Georgetown University, 1982-83; Head, Centre for National Policy, 1985-93; Chief Legislative Assistant to Democratic Senator Edmund Muskie, 1976-78; Member, National Security Council Staff in Carter Administration, 1978-81; Advisor, Democratic candidates, Geraldine Ferraro, 1984, and Michael Dukakis, 1988; Permanent Representative to United Nations, 1993-97; Secretary of State, 1997-2001; Co-founder, Principal, The Albright Group LLC, 2001-; Chair, National Democratic Institute for International Affairs, Washington DC, 2001-; Chair, The PEW Global Attitudes Project; President, Truman Scholarship Foundation. Publications: Poland: the Role of the Press in Political Change, 1983; Madam Secretary: A Memoir, 2003; numerous articles. Memberships: Board, New York Stock Exchange; Council on Foreign Relations; American Political Science Association; American Association for Advancement of Slavic Studies. Address: 901 15th Street, NW, Suite 1000, Washington, DC 20005, USA.

ALCARAZ Jose Luis, b. 3 July 1963, Hellin, Albacete, Spain. Engineering University Professor. Education: Bachelor, Murcia, Spain, 1981; Graduated in Industrial Engineering, Valencia, Spain, 1988; Doctor in Industrial Engineering, San Sebastian, Spain, 1993. Assistant Lecturer, Valencia, Spain, 1988-89, San Sebastian, Spain, 1989-93; Bilbao, Spain, 1993-94; Full Professor, Bilbao, Spain, 1994-. Publications: Books: Theory of Plasticity and Applications, 1993; Elasticity and Strength of Materials, 1995; Elastic, Plastic and Viscous Behaviour of Materials, 2002; Contributed papers to international journals. Honour: Graduation Special Award, 1988. Memberships: European Mechanics Society; New York Academy of Sciences; Spanish Association for Mechanical Engineering. Address: Dep Ingenieria Mecánica, Escuela Superior de Ingenieros, Alameda Urquijo, s/n, 48013 Bilbao, Spain.

ALDA Alan, b. 28 January 1936, New York, USA. Actor. m. Arlene Weiss, 3 daughters. Education: Fordham University. Appointments: Performed with Second City, 1963; Broadway roles in The Owl and the Pussycat, Purlie Victorious, Fair Game of Lovers, The Apple Tree, Our Town, London, 1991, Jake's Women, 1992. Creative Works: Films include: Gone are the Days, 1963; Paper Lion, The Extraordinary Seaman, 1968; The Moonshine War, Jenny, 1970; The Mephisto Waltz, 1971; To Kill a Clown, 1972; California Suite, Same Time Next Year, 1978; The Seduction of Joe Tynan, also wrote screenplay, 1979; Four Seasons, 1981; Sweet Liberty, 1986; A New Life, 1987; Crimes and Misdemeanours, 1989; Betsy's

Wedding, 1990; Whispers in the Dark, 1992; And the Band Played On, Manhattan Murder Mystery, 1993; White Mile, 1994; Canadian Bacon, 1995; Everybody Says I Love You, 1996; Murder at 1600, Mad City, 1997; The Object of My Affection, 1998; What Women Want, 2000; The Aviator, 2004; The West Wing, 2004-06; Resurrecting the Champ, 2007; Numerous TV includes: The Glass House, 1972; MASH, 1972-83; The West Wing, 1999; Club Land, The Killing Yard, 2001. Honours: Theatre World Award; 5 Emmy Awards; 2 Directors Guild Awards; Writers Guild Award; 7 Peoples Choice Awards; Humanities Award for Writing; 5 Golden Globe Awards. Memberships: Trustee, Museum of TV and Radio; Rockefeller Foundation; President, National Commission for Observance of International Women's Year, 1976; Co-chair, National ERA Countdown Campaign, 1982. Address: c/o Martin Bregman Productions, 641 Lexington Avenue, NY 10022, USA.

ALDERMAN Minnis Amelia, b. 14 October 1928, Douglas, Georgia, USA. Counsellor; Psychologist, Business Woman, Executive. Education: AB, Music and Speech Dramatics, Georgia State College at Milledgeville, 1949; MA, Guidance, Counselling, Psychology, Supervision, Murray State University, Kentucky, 1960; PhD, Psychology and Performing Arts, ongoing. Appointments: Private music instructor, piano, violin, voice, organ 1981-; Band Director for Sacred Heart School 1982-98; Associate Dean, Professor and Head of Fine Arts Department, Wassuk College 1986-87; Academic Dean, Wassuk College 1987-90; Choir Director and Organist, Sacred Heart Church; Director, Ely Shoshone Tribal Child and Family Center and the Family and Community Center (ICWA and Social Services) 1988-93; Professor, Music Appreciation, General Psychology, Educational Psychology, Human Resource Management, Human Relations, Humanities, Great Basin College. Publications: Numerous articles, pamphlets, handbooks, journals and newsletters on guidance-counselling, functions and organisation in education, pupil personnel programs, music instruction and practice, social services programs, youth problems, mental health, problems of ageing and geriatrics, tribal law; news articles and feature stories for newspapers and state organisations' publications. Honours include: Fellowship recipient to University of Utah in geriatric psychology 1974; Fellowship, University of Utah, 1975; American Biographical Institute, nominee for Most Admired Woman of the Decade, 1994; Delta Kappa Gamma Rose of Recognition Award, 1994. Memberships include: Delta Kappa Gamma; International Platform Association; American Association of University Women; National Federation of Business and Professional Women; Eastern Nevada Child and Family Services Advisory Committee; Society of Descendants of Knights of the Most Noble Order of the Garter. Address: P O Box 150457, East Ely, NV 89315, USA.

ALDINGTON Peter John, b. 14 April 1933, Preston, Lancashire, England. Architect. m. Margaret, 2 daughters. Education: University of Manchester, School of Architecture. Appointments: Architect, London County Council Architects Housing Division, 1956-62; Timber Research and Development Association, 1962-63; Own Practice, Peter Aldington, 1963-70; Aldington & Craig, 1970-80; Aldington, Craig & Collinge, 1980-86; Visiting Critic, Sheffield University, 1975-95; Visiting lecturer at many Schools of Architecture; External Examiner, Birmingham, 1978-81, Newcastle, 1980-82, Leicester, 1982-85, London South Bank, 1983-87, Leeds, 1985-89; Lecturer, Vienna School of Architecture, 1979, and Cincinnati Centre for Urban Design, 1991; RIBA Council Member, 1976-79; Sat on seven RIBA committees (represented RIBA on others); Royal Gold Medal jury member, 1978, 1979; Assessor for many design awards and competitions; Retired, 1986; Garden Designer, 1986-; Practice archive (1963-86) donated to British Architectural Library; Formed Turn End Charitable Trust to ensure the future of Turn End and associated buildings 'to foster the integration of architecture and landscape thinking', 1999-; Member, English Heritage Post War Steering Group, 2000-03. Publications: Work published in 40 books in UK and Europe; 1 monograph in preparation, 2006; Work published over 300 times in 11 countries worldwide, 1963-88. Honours: Order of the British Empire, 1987; 14 Design Awards; 1 award for landscape; Two buildings listed as of Special Architectural or Historic Interest at Grade 2*, and four at Grade 2. Memberships: Associate, Royal Institute of British Architects; Member, Chartered Society of Designers. Address: Turn End, Townside, Haddenham, Aylesbury, Buckinghamshire HP17 8BG, England. E-mail: turnend.peter@macunlimited.net

ALDISS Brian Wilson, b. 18 August 1925, East Dereham, England. Literary Editor; Writer; Critic. m. (2) Margaret Manson, 11 December 1965, 2 sons, 2 daughters. Appointments: President, British Science Fiction Association, 1960-64; Guest of Honour at World Science Fiction Convention, London, 1965, World Science Fiction Convention Brighton, 1979; Chairman, Committee of Management, Society of Authors, 1977-78; Arts Council Literature Panel, 1978-80; Booker McConnell Prize Judge, 1981; Fellow, Royal Society of Literature, 1990; Prix Utopia, 1999; Grand Master of Science Fiction, 2000. Publications: Novels include: Hothouse, 1962; Frankenstein Unbound, 1973; The Malacia Tapestry, 1976; Life in the West, 1980; The Helliconia Trilogy, 1982, 1983, 1985, 1996; Forgotten Life, 1988; Dracula Unbound, 1991; Remembrance Day, 1993; Somewhere East of Life, 1994; Story collections include: Seasons in Flight, 1984; Best SF Stories of Brian W Aldiss, 1988; A Romance of the Equator, Best Fantasy Stories, 1989; A Tupolev Too Far, 1993; The Secret of This book, 1995; Non-Fiction includes: Cities and Stones: A Traveller's Jugoslavia, 1966; Bury My Heart at W H Smith's: A Writing Life, 1990; The Detached Retina (essays), 1995; At the Caligula Hotel (collected poems), 1995; Songs From the Steppes of Central Asia, 1996; The Twinkling of an Eye, My Life as a Englishman, 1998; When the Feast is Finished, 1998; White Mars (with Roger Penrose), 1999; Supertoys Last All Summer Long (made into Kubrick-Spielberg film, AI), 2001; The Cretan Teat, 2001; Super-State, 2002; Researches and Churches in Serbia, 2002; The Dark Sun Rises, poems, 2002; Affairs in Hampden Ferrers, 2004; Jocasta, 2005; Sanity and the Lady, 2005; Opera: Oedipus on Mars; Plays: SF Blues; Kindred Blood in Kensington Gore; Monsters of Every Day, Oxford Literary Festival, 2000; Drinks with the Spider King, Florida, 2000; Acted in own productions, 1985-2002; Contributions to: Times Literary Supplement; Nature. Honours: Hugo Awards, 1962, 1987; Nebula Award, 1965; various British Science Fiction Association awards; Ferara Cometa d'Argento, 1977; Prix Jules Verne, Sweden, 1977; Science Fiction Research Association Pilgrim Awards, 1978; First International Association of the Fantastic in the Arts Distinguished Scholarship Award, 1986; J Lloyd Eaton Award, 1988; World Science Fiction President's Award, 1988; Hugo Nomination, 1991; Order of the British Empire, 2005. Membership: Royal Society of Literature, fellow, honorary DLitt, 2000. Address: Hambleden, 39 St Andrews Road, Old Headington, Oxford OX3 9DL, England.

ALDRIDGE (Harold Edward) James, b. 10 July 1918, England. Author; Journalist. m. Dina Mitchnik, 1942, 2 sons. Appointments: with Herald and Sun, Melbourne, Australia, 1937-38; Daily Sketch and Sunday Dispatch, London, 1939;

Australian Newspaper Service, North American Newspaper Alliance (as war correspondent), Finland, Norway, Middle East, Greece, USSR, 1939-45; Correspondent, Time and Life, Tehran, 1944. Plays: 49th State, 1947; One Last Glimpse, 1981. Publications: Signed with Their Honour, 1942; The Sea Eagle, 1944; Of Many Men, 1946; The Diplomat. 1950; The Hunter, 1951; Heroes of the Empty View, 1954; Underwater Hunting for Inexperienced Englishmen, 1955; I Wish He Would Not Die, 1958; Gold and Sand, short stories, 1960; The Last Exile, 1961; A Captive in the Land, 1962; The Statesman's Game, 1966; My Brother Tom, 1966; The Flying 19, 1966; Living Egypt, with Paul Strand, 1969; Cairo: Biography of a City, 1970; A Sporting Proposition, 1973; The Marvellous Mongolian, 1974; Mockery in Arms, 1974; The Untouchable Juli, 1975; One Last Glimpse, 1977; Goodbye Un-America, 1979; The Broken Saddle, 1982; The True Story of Lilli Stubek, 1984; The True Story of Spit Mac Phee, 1985; The True Story of Lola MacKellar, 1993; The Girl from the Sea, 2003; The Wings of Kitty St Clair, 2006. Honours: Rhys Memorial Award, 1945; Lenin Peace Prize, 1972; Australian Childrens Book of the Year, 1985; Guardian Children's Fiction Prize. Address: c/o Curtis Brown, 28/29 Haymarket, London, SW1Y 4SP, England.

ALDRIN Buzz, b. 20 January 1930, Montclair, New Jersey. American Astronaut. m. (1) divorced 1978, (2) Lois Driggs-Cannon, 1988, 2 sons, 1 daughter. Education: US Military Academy; MA Institute of Technology. Appointments: Former Member, US Air Force; Completed Pilot Training, 1952; Flew Combat Mission during Korean War; Aerial Gunnery Instructor, Nellis Air Force Base, Nevada; Attended Squadron Officers School, Air University, Maswell Air Force Base, Alabama; Flight Commander, 36th Tectical Fighter Wing, Bitburg, Germany; Completed Astronautics Studies, MIT, 1963; Selected by NASA as Astronaut, 1963; Later assigned to Manned Spacecraft Centre, Houston, Texas; Pilot of Backup Crew for Gemini IX Mission, 1966; Pilot, Gemini XII, 1966; Backup Command module pilot for Apollo VIII; Lunar Module Pilot for Apollo XI; Landed on the moon, 20 July 1969; Commandant Aerospace Research Pilot School, 1971-72; Scientific Consultant, Beverly Hills Oil Co, Los Angeles; Chair, Starcraft Enterprises; Fellow, American Institute of Aeronautics and Astronautics; Retired from USAF, 1972; President, Research and Engineering Consultants Inc, 1972-; Consultant, JRW Jet Propulsion Laboratory. Publications: First on the Moon: A Voyage with Neil Armstrong, 1970; Return to Earth, 1973; Men from Earth, 1989; Encounter with the Tiber, 1996; Encounter with the Tiber – the Return, 2000. Honours: Honorary Member, Royal Astronautical Society; Several Honorary Degrees; Numerous Decorations and Awards. Address: 233 Emerald Bay, Laguna Beach, CA 92651, USA.

ALEINIKOV Gennady S, b. 10 November 1947, Minsk, Belarus. Banker. m. Olga Aleinikova, 3 sons. Education: Economy, Financing, Crediting, Belarussian State Institute of National Economy, 1977; International Economic Relations, Moscow Academy of Foreign Trade, 1985. Appointments: Chairman of the Board, Belvnesheconombank, Bank for Foreign Economic Affairs of the Republic of Belarus, 1992-97; Chairman, National Bank of the Republic of Belarus, 1997-98; Chairman, International Trade and Investment Bank (ITI Bank), Minsk, Belarus, 1999-. Publications: Several articles on banking and finance. Honours: "Birmingham Torch" for Leadership in Business and Management, International Academy and the International Institute for Finance and Economic Partnerships, 1995; Honour Certificate of the European Market Research Centre, Brussels, Belgium,

1996; Distinguished Economist of the Republic of Belarus. Memberships: International Academy for Finance and Economic Partnerships; Brussels International Banking Club. Address: ITI Bank, 12 Sovetskaya Street, 220030 Minsk, Belarus. E-mail: office@itibank.by

ALEKSANDROV Aleksandr Pavlovich, b. 20 February 1943, Moscow, Russia. Cosmonaut; Flight Engineer. m. Natalia Valentinovna Aleksandrova, 1 son, 1 daughter. Education: Baumann Technical Institute, Moscow; PhD. Appointments: Served in Soviet Army; Space Programme, 1964-; Participant, elaboration of control system of spacecraft, Cosmonaut, from 1978; Participant, Soyuz-T and Salyut programmes; Successful completion of 149-day flight to Salyut-T orbital station, 1983; Spacewalk, July 1987; Return to Earth, 1987; Completed 160-day flight on Mir Space Station; Chief, Department of Crew Training and Extra Vehicular Activity, Energya design and production firm; resigned from Cosmonaut team in 1993, became chief of NPOE Cosmonaut group; Chief flight test directorate of RKKE, 1996-. Member, Extra Vehicular Activity Committee, IAF, 1994-. Honours: Hero of Soviet Union, 1983, 1987; Hero of Syria. Memberships: Academician, International Informatization Academy, 1997. Address: Khovanskaya Str 3-27, 129515 Moscow, Russia.

ALEKSIN Anatoliy Georgievich, b. 3 August 1924, Moscow, Russia. Writer. m. Tatyana Alexina, 1 son, 1 daughter. Education: Moscow Institute of Oriental Studies, 1950. Career: Writer, 1951-; Playwright; Scriptwriter; Member, Russian Academy of Education, 1982-; Secretary, Union of the Writers of Russia, 1970-89; President of the Association, Peace to the Children of the World, 1986-90; Chairman, Council of Children's and Youth Literature of Russia, 1970-90; Host of monthly TV show, Friend's Faces, 1971-86; Writer of film, television scripts and numerous plays, staged in Russia and abroad. Publications: More than 220 books translated into 48 languages (over 120 million printed copies); More than 40 books published between 1998-2007; Translated into English, French, Dutch, Greek, Spanish, Japanese, Chinese, Korean, Finnish, Hebrew, Arabic, Hindi, Czech and others; Collected works published in 3 volumes, 1979-81, 5 volumes, 1998-99, 9 volumes, 2000-2001; More than 900 magazine articles; Editorial Board, Yunost Magazine, 1973-93. Honours: Mildred Batchelder Award Nomination for A Late Born Child, Association of American Libraries, USA, 1973; Russian Government Award, 1974; USSR Government Award, 1978; Two Orders of the Labour Banner; Included in Hans Christian Andersen Awards; IBBY Honor List; The International Board on Books for Young People for 'Deistvujuschtye Litsa I Ispolnitely'; Chosen as an Outstanding Example of Literature with International Importance, 1976; International European Maxim Gorky Award for Bezumnaya Evdokia (Crazy Evdokia), 1980; Award of Federation of Unions of Writers of Israel, 1999; Jubilee Medal, 200th Anniversary of A S Pushkin, 1999; Compassion Award for Assistance to People Suffering from Cancer, 1998, 2000; Title, Man of Legend, 2004; Gold Medal of Janush Korchik, 2005. Memberships: Writers Union of Moscow; International PEN Club; Russian Writers Union of Israel; Russian Academy of Education. Address: Rubinstein Street 39/17, Jaffo-Dalet 68212, Tel-Aviv, Israel.

ALESSENDRE Angelina, b. 3 November 1946, Beaconsfield, Buckinghamshire, England. Ballet Dancer; Dance Teacher. 1 son, 1 daughter. Education: Lycèe Français, London; French Institute, Budapest, 1959; Trained as a dancer under Miss Ballantyne, Betty Haines, Dr Ronald Heavey MBE. Career: Professional Ballet Dancer; Performances in England and Italy including The Scala and the Cambridge Theatres,

London; Became interested in teaching dance to children with learning difficulties in 1990; Founded the Alessendre Special Needs Dance School, 1992; Won international recognition for uncovering latent talents in people with special needs and helping them to develop into well adjusted and confident individuals more able to lead active, happy and fulfilled lives; Developed an innovative curriculum able to suit all sorts of learning difficulties including children with Down's Syndrome; The Larondina Dance Company (established in 1992) acts as a showcase for the School's work; Pupils have performed with great success in London's West End, also in Moscow, France, Germany and Guernsey; Performances in Ecuador and Nigeria are planned. Publications: Articles in Moscow Times, local papers and educational magazines. Membership: British Theatre Dance Association. Address: 17 Whistlers Avenue, Battersea, London SW11 3TS, England. E-mail: info@asneeds.org.uk Website: www.asneeds.org.uk

ALEXANDER Bill, b. 23 February 1948, Hunstanton, Norfolk, England. Theatre Director. m. Juliet Harmer, 1977, 2 daughters. Education: Keele University. Appointments: Directed Shakespeare and classical and contemporary drama, Bristol Old Vic; Joined, 1977, Associate Director, 1984-91, Artistic Director, 1991-, Royal Shakespeare Company, productions including Tartuffe, Richard III, 1984, Volpone, The Accrington Pals, Clay, Captain Swing, School of Night, A Midsummer Night's Dream, The Merry Wives of Windsor; Other theatre work, Nottingham Playhouse, Royal Court Theatre, Victory Theatre, New York and Shakespeare Theatre, Washington DC; Artistic Director, Birmingham Repertory Company, 1993-2000, productions including Othello, The Snowman, Macbeth, Dr Jekyll and Mr Hyde, The Alchemist, Awake and Sing, The Way of the World, Divine Right, The Merchant of Venice, Old Times, Frozen, Hamlet, The Tempest, The Four Alice Bakers, Jumpers, Nativity, 1999; Quarantine, 2000; Twelfth Night, 2000; An Enemy of the People, 2002; Frozen, 2002; Mappa Mundi, 2002; The Importance of Being Ernest, 2002; Titus Andronicus, RSC, 2003; King Lear, RSC, 2004. Publications: Film, The Snowman, 1998. Honours: Olivier Award for Director of the Year, 1986. Address: Rose Cottage, Tunley, Gloucestershire GL7 6LP, England.

ALEXANDER Rt Hon Douglas, b. 26 October 1967, Glasgow, Scotland. Secretary of State for International Development; Member of Parliament for Paisley and Renfrewshire South. m. Jacqueline Christian, 2 children. Education: Scholarship, Lester B Pearson College, Victoria, Canada, 1984; Scholarship, University of Pennsylvania, USA, 1988; LLB, Edinburgh University, Scotland, 1993. Appointments: Solicitor, Edinburgh, 1993-97; Member of Parliament for Paisley and Renfrewshire South, 1997-; Minister of State with responsibility for e-commerce and competitiveness, Department for Trade and Industry, 2001-02; Minister of State, Cabinet Office, 2002-03; Minister for the Cabinet Office and Chancellor of the Duchy of Lancaster, 2003; Minister for Trade, Department for Trade and Industry, and Foreign and Commonwealth Office; Minister of State for Europe during the UK Presidency, 2005; Member, Privy Council, 2005; Secretary of State for Transport, and Secretary of State for Scotland, 2006-07; Secretary of State for International Development, 2007-. Honours: Novice Moot Trophy, 1993.

ALEXANDER Michael Joseph, b. 21 May 1941, Wigan, Lancashire, England. Writer. m. (1) Eileen McCall, deceased, (2) Mary Sheahan, 1 son, 2 daughters. Education: Downside School; BA, 1962, MA, 1967, University of Oxford; University of Perugia; Princeton University. Appointments:

Lecturer d'anglais, Cahors; Editor, Wm Collins, 1963; English-Speaking Union Fellow, Princeton University, USA, 1965; Lecturer, University of California SB, 1966; Editor, André Deutsch, 1967; Lecturer, University of East Anglia, 1968; Lecturer, University of Stirling, 1969; Senior Lecturer, Reader; Berry Professor of English Literature, University of St Andrews, 1985-2003. Publications: The Earliest English Poems; Beowulf; The Poetic Achievement of Ezra Pound; A History of English Literature; Medievalism; and others. Honours: Ford Foundation Award to translate Beowulf; Arts Council Awards for translation of Old English Riddles and for critical book on the poetry of Ezra Pound. Memberships: The Athenaeum; Fellow, English Association. Address: 1 Lovers' Walk, Wells, Somerset BA5 2QL, England. E-mail: michael.alexander@mbzonline.net

ALEXANDER (Robert) McNeill, b. 7 July 1934, Lisburn, Northern Ireland. Emeritus Professor of Zoology. m. Ann Elizabeth Coulton, 1 son, 1 daughter. Education: BA, 1955, PhD, 1958, MA, 1959, Cambridge University; DSc, University of Wales, 1969. Appointments: Assistant Lecturer, 1958-61, Lecturer, 1961-68, Senior Lecturer, 1968-69, University College of North Wales; Professor of Zoology, 1969-99, Emeritus Professor and Research Professor, 1999-, University of Leeds; Editor: Proceedings of the Royal Society B, 1998-2004. Publications: Books: Functional Design in Fishes, 1967; Animal Mechanics, 1968, 1983; Size and Shape, 1971; The Chordates, 1975, 1981; Biomechanics, 1975; The Invertebrates, 1979; Locomotion of Animals, 1982; Optima for Animals, 1982, 1996; Elastic Mechanisms for Animal Movement, 1988; Dynamics of Dinosaurs and other Extinct Giants, 1989; Animals, 1990; The Human Machine, 1992; Exploring Biomechanics: Animals in Motion, 1992; Bones, 1994; How Animals Move (a multimedia CD-ROM), 1995; Energy for Animal Life, 1999; Principles of Animal Locomotion, 2003; Human Bones, 2004; About 270 scientific papers most of them on human and animal biomechanics. Honours include: Scientific Medal, Zoological Society of London, 1969; Linnean Medal for Zoology, Linnean Society of London, 1979; Fellow of the Royal Society, 1987; Muybridge Medal, International Society for Biomechanics, 1991; Member, Academia Europaea, 1996; CBE, 2000; Honorary DSc, University of Aberdeen, 2002; Honorary Doctor, University of Wageningen, 2003; Honorary Fellow, Zoological Society of London, 2003; Borelli Award, American Society of Biomechanics, 2004; Member, European Academy of Sciences, 2004. Memberships: Royal Society; Zoological Society of London, Secretary, 1992-99; Society for Experimental Biology, President, 1995-97; Honorary Member, Society for Integrative and Comparative Biology; International Society for Vertebrate Morphology, President, 1997-2001; Foreign Honorary Member, American Academy of Arts and Sciences; International Society for Biomechanics. Address: School of Biology, University of Leeds, Leeds LS2 9JT, England. E-mail: r.m.alexander@leeds.ac.uk

ALEXEEV Boris, b. 2 May 1938, Orechovo-Zuevo, Moscow Region. Physicist; Educator. Divorcee, 1 daughter. Education: Degree in Physics, Engineering, 1961, PhD, 1964, Moscow Institute of Physics and Technology; DSc, Computer Centre of USSR Academy of Sciences, 1973; Professor of Physics, Higher Attestation Commission of USSR, 1974. Appointments: Senior Research Scientist, Computer Centre, USSR Academy of Sciences, 1964-73; Head of Physics Department, Moscow Aviation Institute, 1973-83; Head of Physics Department, Moscow Fine Chemical Technology Institute, 1983-; Visiting Professor, University of Provence (Marseilles), 1992-95, University of Alabama (Huntsville, USA), 1995, 1997; Head,

Centre of the Theoretical Foundations in Nanotechnology, 2007-. Publications: Over 280 scientific works including 20 books including: Mathematical Kinetics of Reacting Gases (author), 1982; Transport Processes in Reacting Gases and Plasma (co-author), 1994, Generalized Boltzmann Physical Kinetics (author), Esevier, 2004. Honours: Meritorious Science and Technics Worker of Russia, USSR, 1989-; Presidents Stipend for Outstanding Russian Scientists, 1994-; Meritorious Worker, Higher Professional Education of Russia, 1998-; Man of the Year, Medal of Honor, ABI, 1999; Meritorious Science & Technics Worker of Russia, Russian Federation, 2008-. Memberships: Russian National Committee on Theoretical and Applied Mechanics, 1987-; Organising Committee, Russian Academy of Sciences and Head of the Moscow Regional Committee, Moscow, 1991; Academician of the International Higher Education Academy of Sciences (General Physics and Astronomy) 1993-; New York Academy of Sciences, 1995-. Address: 3rd Frunzenskaya h 9, ap 130 Moscow 119270, Russia.

ALI Hazrat, b. 17 February 1954, Jessore, Bangladesh. Writer; m. Hasina Begum, 3 sons, 1 daughter. Education: Bangali Literature, M M College, Jessore, 1976. Appointments: Writer. Publications: Dhoimo-o-Rastro (State and Religion); Samarpan; Proticchobi; Rokto Shidur; Paha Tieke Sagorey; Disillusioned Muslims and the Islamic Movements. Honours: Many local awards and independent awards of Bangladesh. Memberships: Founder Secretary, Jhikargacha Press Club; Member, Jhikargacha College, B M High School and Madrasha. Address: Kirtipur, Jhikargacha, Jessore, Bangladesh.

ALI Muhammad, b. 17 January 1942, Louisville, Kentucky, USA. Boxer. m. (1) Sonji Roi, divorced, (2) Belinda Boyd, divorced, (3) Veronica Porsche, 1977, divorced, (4) Yolanda Williams; 2 sons, 7 daughters. Education: Louisville. Appointments: Amateur Boxer, 1954-60; Olympic Games Light-Heavyweight Champion, 1960; Professional Boxer, 1960-; Won World heavyweight title, 1964; Stripped of title after refusing to be drafted into US Army, 1967; Returned to Professional Boxing, 1970; Regained World Heavyweight, 1974; Lost Title to Leon Spinks, 1978; Regained Title, Spinks, 1978; 56 victories in 61 fights, 1981; Lost to Larry Holmes, 1980; Acted in films, The Greatest; Freedom Road. Publications: The Greatest: My Own Story, 1975; Healing, 1996; More Than a Hero (with Hana Ali), 2000. Honours: Names Messenger of Peace, UN; Athlete of the Century, GQ Magazine; Lifetime Achievement Award, Amnesty International; Honorary Consul General for Bangladesh in Chicago; Named Messenger of Peace, UN, 1999; Presidential Medal of Freedom, 2005; Otto Hahn peace medal in Gold, 2005. Memberships: Black Muslim Movement; Peace Corps Advisory Council. Address: P O Box 160, Berrien Springs, MI 49103, USA.

ALIM Abdul, b. 4 September 1970, Jessore, Bangladesh. Journalist; Writer. m. Monira Sultana, 1 son. Education: M Ed, Analysis Group. Appointments: Author, History of Bangladesh. Publications: 4 books in Bengali literature. Honours: 2 local awards. Memberships: Local School and Social Institution. Address: Vill Shankarpur, Post Chanchara, Dist Jessore, Bangladesh.

ALLADIN Saleh Mohammed, b. 3 March 1931, Secunderabad, India. Retired Professor of Astronomy. m. Farhat Akhtar, 2 sons, 3 daughters. Education: St Patrick's High School Senior, Cambridge, 1948; BSc, Nizam College, 1953; MSc, Physics, Osmania University, 1955; PhD, Astronomy and Astrophysics, University of Chicago, 1963. Appointments: Research Scholar, Osmania University, 1955-59; Research Assistant, Yerkes Observatory, USA, 1960-63; Lecturer, 1964-65; Senior Research Fellow, 1965-68, Reader, 1968-78, Professor, 1978-91, Osmania University; Senior Associate Inter University Centre for Astronomy and Astrophysics, Pune, 1990-96. Publications: Articles on: The Dynamics of Colliding Galaxies, 1965; Gravitational Interactions between Galaxies, with Narasimhan, 1982; Views of Scientists on the Existence of God, 1991. Honours: Senior Visiting Fellow at the Universities of Oxford and Cambridge, 1980; Meghnad Saha Award for the Year 1981; University Grants Commission, India; Man of the Year, 2000; Bharat Excellence Award, 2006; Listed in several biographical publications. Memberships: International Astronomical Union; Astronomical Society of India. Address: Baitul Ehsan, Civil Lane Road, Mohalla Ahmadiyya, Qadian, Pin: 143516 Punjab, India.

ALLAM Salah El-Din, b. 30 December 1940, Cairo, Egypt. Professor. m. Kamilia Abdelmageed, 1 son, 1 daughter. Education: BSc, Mathematics and Education, 1960, Higher Diploma in Education, 1964, MEd, Educational Psychology, 1971, Ain Shams University, Egypt; PhD, Educational and Psychological Measurement, Evaluation and Statistics, University of Michigan, USA, 1980. Appointments: Professor, College of Education, Al-Azhar University, Cairo, 1991-; Consultant for UNESCO, Kuwait, Jordan, 1985-93; Visiting Professor, College of Education, Emirates University, United Arab Emirates, 1996; Head of Evaluation Department, National Center for Examinations and Educational Evaluation, Cairo, Egypt, 1999; Consultant, Ministry of Education, United Arab Emirates, 1999-2001; Visiting Professor, College of Education, Bahrain University, Bahrain, 2003. Publications: Data Analysis in Educational, Psychological and Social Research; Inferential Statistics Methods; Criterion-Referenced Diagnostic Tests; Educational Institutional Evaluation; Alternative Educational Assessment; The Design and Verification of a System Instructional Model for Psychological Statistics. Honours: Award for PhD dissertation, University of Michigan, 1981; Kuwait University Award, 1986; Ministry of Education Award, Quatar, 1995; NWL-Alhussein Association, Jordan, 1996; Dar Al-Fekr Alarabi Award, 2004; Listed in international biographical dictionaries. Memberships: American Educational Research Association; Egyptian Psychological Association; Arab Council for Gifted and Talented, Amman, Jordan; People to People Ambassador Programs, USA. Address: 52 Al-Nozha Street, Rabaa Bldgs, Madinet Nasr, Cairo, Egypt.

ALLAN Andrew Norman, b. 26 September 1943, Newcastle upon Tyne, England. Television Executive. m. (1) 2 daughters, (2) Joanna Forrest, 1978, 2 sons, 1 daughter. Education: BA, Birmingham University. Appointments: Presenter, ABC Television, 1965-66; Producer, Thames TV, 1966-69, 1971-75; Head of News, 1976-78; Producer, ITN, 1970; Director of Programmes, 1978-83, Deputy Managing Director, 1982-83, Managing Director, 1983-84, Tyne Tees TV; Director of Programmes, 1984-90, Managing Director, 1993-94, Central Independent TV; Managing Director, Central Broadcasting, 1990-93; Chief Executive, 1994-95, Director of Programmes, 1996-98, Carlton TV; Director, TV12, 1999-; Media Consultant, 1998-; Chair, Birmingham Repertory, 2000-; Chair, Route 4 PLC, 2001. Memberships: Fellow, Royal Television Society.

ALLEN Blair H, b. 2 July 1933, Los Angeles, California, USA. Writer; Poet; Editor; Artist. m. Juanita Aguilar Raya, 27 January 1968, 1 son, 1 daughter. Education: AA, San Diego City College, 1964; University of Washington, 1965-66; BA, San Diego State University, 1970. Appointments: Book Reviewer, Los Angeles Times, 1977-78; Special Feature Editor, Cerulean Press and Kent Publications, 1982-. Publications: Televisual Poems for Bloodshot Eyeballs, 1973; Malice in Blunderland, 1974; N/Z, 1979; The Atlantis Trilogy, 1982; Dreamwish of the Magician, 1983; Right Through the Silver Lined 1984 Looking Glass, 1984; The Magical World of David Cole (editor), 1984; Snow Summits in the Sun (anthology, editor), 1988; Trapped in a Cold War Travelogue, 1991; May Burning into August, 1992; The Subway Poems, 1993; Bonfire on the Beach, by John Brander (editor), 1993; The Cerulean Anthology of Sci-Fi/Outer Space/Fantasy/ Poetry and Prose Poems (anthology, editor), 1995; When the Ghost of Cassandra Whispers in My Ears, 1996; Ashes Ashes All Fall Down, 1997; Around the World in 56 Days, 1998; Thunderclouds from the Door, 1999; Jabberbunglemerkeltoy, 1999; The Athens Café, 2000; The Day of the Jamberee Call, 2001; Assembled I Stand, 2002; Wine of Starlight, 2002; Snow Birds in Cloud Hands (anthology, editor), 2003; Trek into Yellowstone's Cascade Corner Wilderness, 2003; Hour of Iced Wheels, 2003; Light in the Crossroads, 2004; Shot Doves, 2005; What Time Does: One Man Show (artbook retrospective), 2006; Moon Hiding in the Orange Tree, 2007; In the Face of Gateless High Walls, the Sound of Purple Horns, 2007; Opossom in the Fig Tree, 2008; When Morning is Still Night, 2008; Contributions to: Numerous periodicals and 18 anthologies. Honours: Nominated for "Pushcart Prize", for Poetry, 1982; 1st Prize for Poetry, Pacificus Foundation Competition, 1992; Pacificus Foundation Literary Prize for Lifetime Achievement in Poetry and Story Writing, 2003; Various other honours and awards. Memberships: The Academy of American Poets; Poets and Writers; Association for Applied Poetry; Beyond Baroque Foundation; California State Poetry Society; Medina Foundation. Address: PO Box 162, Colton, CA 92324, USA. Website: http://www.pw.org/ directory/writer-detail.php?writer_id=14154B

ALLEN Geoffrey (Sir), b. 29 October 1928, Clay Cross, Derbyshire, England. Polymer Scientist; Administrator. m. Valerie Frances Duckworth, 1972, 1 daughter. Education: PhD, University of Leeds. Appointments: Postdoctoral Fellow, National Research Council, Canada, 1952-54; Lecturer, 1955-65, Professor of Chemical Physics, 1965-75, University of Manchester Institute of Science and Technology; Professor of Polymer Science, 1975-76, Professor of Chemical Technology, 1976-81, Imperial College of Science and Technology, University of London; Chair, Science Research Council, 1977-81; Visiting Fellow, Robinson College, Cambridge, 1980-; Head of Research, 1981-90, Director for Research and Engineering, 1982-90; Unilever PLC, 1981-90; Non-Executive Director, Courtaulds, 1987-93; President, Society of Chemical Industry, Plastics and Rubber Institute, 1990-92, Institute of Materials, 1994-95; Executive Adviser, Kobe Steel Ltd, 1990-2000; Member, National Consumer Council, 1993-96; Chancellor, University of East Anglia, 1994-2003. Honours: Honorary MSc, Manchester; Dr Univ, Open University; Honorary DSc, Durham, East Anglia, 1984, Bath, Bradford, Keele, Loughborough, 1985, Essex, Leeds, 1986, Cranfield, 1988, Surrey, 1989, North London, 1999. Memberships: Fellow, Royal Society, Vice-President, 1991-93; Fellow, Institute of Physics; Fellow, Plastics and Rubber Institute; Honorary Fellow, Institute of Materials & Mining; Fellow, Royal Society of Chemistry; Honorary Fellow, Institute of Chemical Engineering. Address: 18 Oxford House, 52 Parkside, London SW19 5NE, England.

ALLEN Keith William, b. 9 April 1926, Reading, England. Retired University Don. m. Marguerite Florence Woods, 1 son, 4 daughters. Education: BSc, University of Reading, 1949; MSc, University of London, 1958; DSc, City University, 1994; Chartered Scientist, Chemist and Physicist. Appointments: Lecturer in Chemistry, 1949-83, Director of Adhesion Studies, 1982-92, City University; Visiting Professor, Oxford Brookes University, England, 1998-. Publications: Editor, Adhesion 1 – Adhesion 15 book series; Approximately 80 papers in refereed journals. Honours: Fulbright Scholar, 1961-62; Ellinger-Gardonyl and Wake Medals, 1999; Honorary Fellowship of the University, Oxford Brookes University, 2002. Memberships: Fellow, Royal Society of Chemistry; Fellow, Institute of Materials. Address: Ranworth, Tydehams, Newbury, RG14 6JT, England.

ALLEN Thomas (Sir), b. 10 September 1944, Seaham, County Durham, England. Opera Singer. m. (1) Margaret Holley, 1968, divorced 1986, 1 son, (2) Jeannie Gordon Lascelles, 1988, 1 stepson, 1 stepdaughter. Education: Royal College of Music. Appointments: Principal Baritone: Welsh National Opera, 1968-72; Royal Opera House, Covent Garden, 1972-78; Glyndebourne Opera, 1973; ENO, London Coliseum, 1986; La Scala, 1987; Chicago Lyric Opera, 1990; Royal Albert Hall, 2000; London Proms, 2002; Royal Opera House, Covent Garden, 2003. Performances include: Die Zauberflote, 1973; Le Nozze di Figaro, 1974; Cosi fan Tutte, 1975; Don Giovanni, 1977; The Cunning Little Vixen, 1977; Simon Boccanegra, Billy Budd, La Boheme, L'Elisir d'Amore, Faust, Albert Herring, Die Fledermaus, La Traviata, A Midsummer Night's Dream, Die Meistersinger von Nurnberg; as producer Albert Herring, 2002; Film: Mrs Henderson Presents, 2005. Publications: Foreign Parts: A Singer's Journal, 1993. Art Exhibitions: Chelsea Festival, 2001; Salisbury Playhouse, 2001. Honours: Honorary Fellow, University of Sunderland; Queen's Prize, 1967; Gulbenkian Fellow, 1968; MA Hon, Newcastle, 1984; RAM Hon, 1988; DMus Hon, Durham, 1988; Commander of the British Empire, 1989; Knight Bachelor, 1999; BBC Radio 3 Listeners' Award, 2004; Hon DMus, Birmingham, 2004. Address: c/o Askonas Holt Ltd, Lonsdale Chambers, 27 Chancery Lane, London WC2A 1PF, England.

ALLEN Tim, b. 13 June 1953, Denver, USA. m. (1) Laura Diebel,1984, divorced 2003, 1 daughter, (2) Jane Hajduk, 2006. Education: West Michigan University; University of Detroit. Career: Creative Director, advertising agency; Comedian, Showtime Comedy Club All Stars, 1988; TV series include: Tim Allen: Men are Pigs, 1990; Home Improvement, 1991-; Tim Allen Rewrites America; Showtime Comedy Club All-Stars II, 1988; Jimmy Neutron: Win, Lose and Kaboom (voice), 2004; Films include: Comedy's Dirtiest Dozen; The Santa Clause, 1994; Toy Story, 1995; Meet Wally Sparks, Jungle 2 Jungle, For Richer for Poorer, 1997; Galaxy Quest, 1999; Toy Story 2, Buzz Lightyear of Star Command: the Adventure Begins, 2000; Who is Cletis Tout?, Joe Somebody, 2001; Big Trouble, The Santa Clause 2, 2002; Christmas with the Kranks, 2004; The Shaggy Dog, Cars (voice), Zoom, The Santa Clause 3: The Escape Clause, Fired (documentary), 2006. Publications: Don't Stand Too Close to a Naked Man, 1994; I'm Not Really Here, 1996. Honours: Favourite Comedy Actor, People's Choice Award, 1995, 1997-99. Address: c/o Commercial Unlimited, 8883 Wilshire Boulevard, Suite 850, Beverly Hills, CA 90211, USA.

ALLEN Woody (Allen Stewart Konigsberg), b. 1 December 1935, Brooklyn, New York, USA. Actor; Writer. m. (1) Harlene Rosen, divorced, (2) Louise Lasser, divorced, 1 son

with Mia Farrow, (3) Soon-Yi Previn, 2 adopted daughters. Education: City College, New York; New York University. Career: Wrote for TV Performers: Herb Shriner, 1953; Sid Caesar, 1957; Art Carney, 1958-59; Jack Parr and Carol Channing; Also wrote for Tonight Show and the Gary Moore Show; Debut performance, Duplex, Greenwich Village, 1961; Performed in a variety of nightclubs across the US; Plays: Play It Again Sam; Don't Drink the Water, 1966; The Floating Light Bulb, 1981; Death Defying Acts, 1995; Films Include: What's New Pussycat?, 1965; Casino Royale, What's Up, Tiger Lily?, 1967; Take the Money and Run, 1969; Bananas, 1971; Everything You Always Wanted to Know About Sex, Play it Again Sam, 1972; Sleeper, 1973; Love and Death, 1976; The Front, 1976; Annie Hall, 1977; Interiors, 1978; Manhattan, 1979; Stardust Memories, 1980; A Midsummer Night's Sex Comedy, 1982; Zelig, 1983; Broadway Danny Rose, 1984; The Purple Rose of Cairo, Hannah and her Sister, 1985; Radio Days, September, 1987; Another Woman, 1988; Oedipus Wrecks, Crimes and Misdemeanors, 1989; Alice, 1990; Scenes from a Mall, Shadows and Fog, 1991; Husbands and Wives, 1992; Manhattan Murder Mystery, 1993; Bullets Over Broadway, Mighty Aphrodite, 1995; Everybody Says I Love You, Deconstructing Harry, 1997; Celebrity, Wild Man Blues, Stuck on You, 1998; Company Men, Sweet and Lowdown, 1999; Small Town Crooks, 2000; The Curse of the Jade Scorpion, Hail Sid Caesar! 2001; Hollywood Ending, 2002; Anything Else, 2003; Melinda and Melinda, 2004; Match Point, 2005; Scoop, 2006. Publications: Getting Even, 1971; Without Feathers, 1975; Side Effects, 1980; The Complete Prose, 1994; Telling Tales (contribution to charity anthology), 2004; Contributions to Playboy and New Yorker. Honours: Academy Award for Best Director; Best Writer; D W Griffith Award, 1996. Address: 930 Fifth Avenue, New York, NY 10021, USA.

ALLENDE Isabel, b. 2 August 1942, Lima, Peru. Writer. m. (1) Miguel Frias, 1962, 1 son, 1 daughter, (2) William C Gordon, 17 July 1988. Appointments: Journalist, Paula Magazine, 1967-74, Mampato Magazine, 1969-74; Channel 13 World Hunger Campaign, 1964; Channel 7, various humourous programmes, 1970-74; Maga-Cine-Ellas, 1973; Administrator, Marroco School, Caracas, 1978-82; Freelance journalist, El Nacional newspaper, Caracas, 1976-83; Visiting teacher, Montclair State College, New Jersey, 1985, University of Virginia, Charlottesville, 1988, University of California, Berkeley, 1989; Writer, 1981-; President, Chamber of Deputies, Chile, 2003-; Goodwill Ambassador for Hans Christian Andersen bicentennial, 2005. Publications: The House of the Spirits, 1982; Of Love and Shadows, 1984; La Gorda de Porcelana, 1984; Eva Luna, 1989; Tales of Eva Luna, 1990; The Infinite Plan, 1992; Paula, 1995; Aphrodite, a memoir of the senses, 1998; Daughter of Fortune, 1999; Portrait in Sepia, 2000; The Kingdom of the Golden Dragon, 2003; My Invented Country: A Nostalgic Journey Through Chile, 2003; Zorro, 2005, Plays: Paula; Stories of Eva Luna, 1989; The House of the Spirits ; Eva Luna, 1987; My Invented Country, 2003; Forest of the Pygmies, 2005; Ines of my Soul, 2006. Honours: Novel of the Year, Panorama Literario, Chile, 1983; Point de Mire, Belgium, 1985; Author of the Year and Book of the Year, Germany, 1984; Grand Priz d'Evasion, France, 1984; Colima for Best Novel, Mexico, 1985; Author of the Year, Germany, 1986; Mulheres Best Novel, Portugal, 1987; Dorothy and Jillian Gish Prize, 1998; Sara Lee Frontrunner Award, 1998; GEMS Women of the Year Award, 1999; Donna Dell'Anno Award, Italy, 1999; WILLA Literary Award, USA, 2000. Address: 116 Caledonia Street, Sausalito, CA 94965, USA.

ALLEY Kirstie, b. 12 January 1951,Wichita, Kansas, USA. Actress. m. Parker Stevenson, 1983-1997, 1 son, 1 daughter. Education: University of Kansas. Appointments: Stage appearances include: Cat on a Hot Tin Roof; Answers; Regular TV Show Cheers, 1987-93; Other appearances in TV films and series: Star Trek II, The Wrath of Khan, 1982; One More Chance, Blind Date, Champions, 1983; Runaway, 1984; Summer School, 1987; Look Who's Talking Too, Madhouse, 1990; Look Who's Talking Now, 1993; David's Mother (TV Film), 1994; Village of the Damned, It Takes Two, 1995; Sticks and Stones, Nevada, 1996; For Richer or Poorer, Victoria's Closet, Deconstructing Harry, Toothless, 1997; Drop Dead Gorgeous, The Mao Game, 1999; Blonde, 2001; Salem Witch Trials, Back By Midnight, 2002; Profoundly Normal, Family Sins, 2003; While I Was Gone, 2004; Fat Actress (series), 2005. Books: How To Lose Your Ass and Regain Your Life, 2005. Honours: 2 Emmy Awards. Address: Jason Weinberg and Associates, 122 East 25th Street, 2nd Floor, New York, NY 10010, USA.

ALLEYNE George (Sir), b. 7 October 1932, Barbados. Physician. m. Sylvan I Chen, 1958, 2 sons, 1 daughter. Education: MD, University of West Indies; Senior Resident, University Hospital of West Indies, 1963; FRCP. Appointments: Tropical Metabolism Research Unit, Jamaica, 1964-72; Professor of Medicine, 1972-81, Chair, Department of Medicine, 1976-81, Chancellor, 2003-, University of West Indies; Head of Research Unit, 1981-83, Director of Health Programmes, 1982-90, Assistant Director, 1990-95, Director, 1995-2003, Director Emeritus, 2003-, Pan American Health Organization, Washington DC, USA; Special Envoy, UN Secretary General for HIV/AIDS in the Caribbean, 2003-. Publications include: The Importance of Health: A Caribbean Perspective, 1989; Public Health for All, 1991; Health and Tourism, 1992; Over 100 articles in major scientific research journals. Honours: Honorary DSc, West Indies University, 1988; Order of the Caribbean Community, 2001. Address: Pan American Health Organization, 525 23rd Street NW, Washington, DC 20037, USA.

ALLI Waheed, Baron of Norbury in the London Borough of Croydon, b. 16 November 1964. Business Executive. Appointments: Co-Founder, Joint Managing Director, Planet 24 Productions Ltd, formerly 24 Hour Productions, 1992-99; Managing Director, Production, Carlton Productions, 1988-2000; Director, Carlton TV, 1998-2000; Director, 2002, Non-Executive Chair, 2003-, Chorion; Vice President, UNICEF UK, 2003-. Memberships: Member, Teacher Training Agency, 1997-98; Panel 2000, Creative Industry Taskforce; Board member, English National Ballet, 2001-; Director, Shine Entertainment Ltd; Shine M; Castaway TV; Digital Radio Group Ltd. Address: House of Lords, London SW1A 0PW, England.

ALLIANCE David (Baron Alliance), b. 15 June 1932, Kashan, Iran. Business Executive. Appointments: 1st acquisition, Thomas Hoghton, Oswaldtwistle, 1956; Chair, N Brown Group, 1968-; Acquired Spirella, 1968, Vantona Ltd to form Vantona Group, 1975; Group Chief Executive, 1975-90, Chair, 1989-99, Coats Viyella; Acquired Carrington Viyella to form Coats Viyella, 1983, Nottingham Manufacturing, 1985, Coats Patons to form Coats Viyella, 1986; Chair, Tootal Group PLC, 1991-99. Honours: Commander, Order of the British Empire; Honorary Fellow, University of Manchester Institute of Science and Technology; Honorary LLD, Manchester, 1989; Honorary FCGI, 1991; Honorary DSc, Heriot-Watt, 1991; Honorary LLD, Liverpool, 1996; Life Peer, 2004.

Memberships: Fellow, Royal Society of Arts; Companion, British Institute of Management. Address: N Brown Group, 53 Dale Street, Manchester M60 6ES, England.

ALLISON John Langsdale, b. 10 August 1930, Sutton Coldfield, Warwickshire, England. Mechanical Engineer; Naval Architect. m. Eunice Quick, 2 sons, 1 daughter. Education: King Edward's School, Birmingham; BSc, Engineering, University of Nottingham, 1954; Royal Naval Engineering College, Plymouth; Various university short courses. Appointments: Air Engineer Officer, Royal Naval Air Station Brawdy, Pembrokeshire, Wales, 1956; Senior Research Engineer, BSA Daimler Group, Research Center, Kitts Green, Birmingham, 1956-1958; Lecturer in Thermodynamics & Fluid Mechanics, Bromsgrove College of Further Education, Worcestershire, 1958-66; Senior Research Engineer, Bell Aerospace, New York, USA, 1966-71; Chief Engineer, Ship Technology, Textron Marine Systems, New Orleans, USA, 1971-87; Chief Engineer, CDI Marine Systems, 1987-2007. Publications: Numerous papers and articles in professional journals, including: Marine Waterjet Propulsion, Sname Transactions Vol 101, 1993 Centennial Year. Chapters for new edition of Ship Design and Construction, 2003-04; IMechE, International Conference Fans: Fan design for hovercraft and influence of new technology, 2004; The Influence of New Technology on the Design and Manufacture of High Speed Craft, 2004. Honours: Admiral Cochrane Award for Best Paper of the Year to a Section of the Society of Naval Architects and Marine Engineers, 1993; Listed in biographical dictionaries. Memberships: Fellow, Institution of Mechanical Engineers; Fellow, Royal Institution of Naval Architects; Member, Society of Naval Architects and Marine Engineers. Address: 4119 Hummingbird Court, Lebanon, OH 45036, USA.

ALLISON John William Francis, b. 31 March 1962, Durban, South Africa. Lecturer in Law. Education: BA, 1982, LLB, 1984, University of Stellenbosch; LLM, 1986, M Phil, 1987, PhD, 1992, Cambridge University. Appointments: Junior Lecturer, University of Stellenbosch, 1985; Bigelow Fellow and Lecturer in Law, University of Chicago Law School, USA, 1987-88; Lecturer, Queen Mary College, University of London, 1989-91; Research Fellow, Queens' College, University of Cambridge, 1991-94; Senior Lecturer, Department of Roman and Comparative Law, University of Cape Town, South Africa, 1994-95; University Lecturer, 1995-2001, University Senior Lecturer, 2001-, University of Cambridge. Publications include: The Procedural Reason for Judicial Restraint (journal article), 1994; A Continental Distinction in the Common Law: A Historical and Comparative Perspective on English Public Law (book), 1996; Parliamentary Sovereignty, Europe and the Economy of Common Law in M Andenas (editor), Liber Amicorum in Honour of Lord Slynn of Hadley: Judicial Review in International perspective, 2000; The English Historical Constitution: Continuity, Change and European Effects (book), forthcoming in October 2007. Honours: Jubilee Scholarship, Rondebosch Boys' High School, 1985-87; Elsie Ballot Scholarship, 1985-87; W M Tapp Studentship, Gonville and Caius College, Cambridge, 1988-89, 1990-91; Yorke Prize, Cambridge Law Faculty, 1993. Memberships: Fellow of Queens' College; European Group of Public Law. Address: Queens' College, Cambridge CB3 9ET, England.

ALLWOOD Michael John, b. 31 July 1925, Stoke-on-Trent, England. Medical Consultant. m. Rosemary Harrison, deceased 1983, 2 sons, 3 daughter. Education: MRCS, LRCP, 1948; MBBS, 1950, PhD, 1959, MD, 1970, King's College Hospital Medical School; AFOM, 1983, MA, Philosophy, 1990,

University of Wales. Appointments: Lecturer, St Thomas's Hospital Medical School, 1954-63; UK Space Group, RAF Farnborough, 1963-67; Consultant, Coventry NHS Group, 1967-90; Medical Officer, RNVR/RNR, 1949-82; Honorary Surgeon Captain, RNR, 1983; UK Representative, 1974-82, President, 1980-82, CIOMR (NATO). Publications: Articles on heart and circulation in medical journals. Honours: VRD, 1964; Clasp, 1974; Life Member, CIOMR (NATO), 1982; President, Sea Cadet Association (Midlands), 1988; Freeman City of London, 1992. Memberships: Ex-Council, Reserve Forces Association, 1974-82; Ex-Chairman, Midland Naval Officers Association, 1983-89; Faculty of Occupational Medicine, Royal College of Physicians; Physiological Society; Worshipful Society of Apothecaries; Naval Club, RNVR Officers Association. Address: 35 College House, High Street, Brackley, NN13 7NR, England.

ALMODÓVAR Pedro, b. 24 September 1949, La Mancha, Spain. Film Director. Career: Fronted a rock band; Worked at Telefónica, 10 years; Started film career with full-length super-8 films; Made 16mm short films, 1978-83, including Salome; Other films including Pepe, Luci, Bom y otras montón, Laberinto de pasiones, 1980, Dark Habits, 1983, What Have I Done to Deserve This?, 1985, Matador, 1986, Law of Desire, 1987, Women on the Verge of a Nervous Breakdown, 1988, Tie Me Up, Tie Me Down, 1990, Tacones Lejanos, 1991, Kika, 1993, The Flower of My Secret, 1996, Live Flesh, 1997, All About My Mother, 1991; Talk to Her, 2002; Bad Education, 2004; Volver, 2006. In 2006, Sony Pictures Classics re-released 8 of his greatest films. Publications: Fuego en las entrañas, 1982; The Patty Diphusa Stories and Other Writings, 1992. Honours: Felix Award, 1988; Academy Award for Best Foreign Language Film, 1999; BAFTA Award for Best Film not in the English Language, 2003; Academy Award for Best Original Screenplay, 2003. Address: c/o El Deseo SA, Ruiz Perelló 15, Madrid 28028, Spain.

ALNASER Waheeb Essa, b. 4 May 1959, Bahrain. Professor of Physics. m. Aneesa Agab, 2 sons. Education: BSc, Physics, 1978; MSc, Physics, 1982; PhD, Material Physics, 1986. Appointments: Chairman, Physics Dept., University of Bahrain; Dean, College of Deanship of Scientific Research; Dean, College of Science; Professor of Physics, University of Bahrain. Publications: Published more than 100 papers in Material Physics, Solar and Wind Energy, Environmental Physics, Astronomy, Astrophysics. Honours: ISESCO Prize, Physics; Showman Prize, Physics; Bahrain State Prize; University of Bahrain Prizes. Memberships: Institute of Physics; Chairman, Arab Section, ISES, Germany; Member, World Renewable Energy Council; Vice President and Ex-President, Bahrain Astronomical Society. Address: PO. Box 320389, Isa Town, University of Bahrain, Kingdom of Bahrain. E-mail: alnaserw@gmail.com

ALON Azaria, b. 15 November 1918, Wollodarsk, Ukraine. In Israel since 1925. Biologist. m. Ruth Diamant, 2 sons, 1 daughter. Appointments: Member of Kibbutz Beit-Hashitta, 1938-; Agricultural Worker; Youth Movement Leader; Educator; Teacher of Biology; One of Founders of Society for the Protection of Nature in Israel, 1951, General Secretary, 1969-77, Publication Editor; Played major part in campaign to save the wild flowers of Israel, 1964-; Created Governmental Nature Reserves Authority, Board Member, 1964-76; Mapping nature reserves and national parks of Israel, 1951-65; Numerous campaigns to save wildlife and environment; Created Field Study Centres; Took part in Stockholm Convention, 1972, IUCN and UNESCO Conference, Tbilisi, 1977, and IUCN conferences, 1963-90; Writer, Lecturer, Broadcaster on conservation of nature and the environment, 1951-; Senior Lecturer on Landscape, Technion, Haifa, Israel, 1992-. Publications: Hundreds of articles in daily papers, periodicals on nature, environment and conservation; 33 books: 8 books on flowers and trees; 3 books on Sinai and Israel's deserts; 5 books on landscape and animals; 3 books on environmental education; 7 books on plants and animals for children; 2 guidebooks to nature trails in Israel; 1 book on flower trails; 1 book on seven species in the Bible; Books in English, Russian and Arabic; Numerous booklets and brochures; Editor, Encyclopaedia of Plant and Animal Life of Israel, 12 volumes; Nature and landscape photographs: More than 1000 published in books and papers; Radio programme, The Landscape of Our Country, over 2,500 programmes broadcast. Honours: Kol Israel (Israel Radio) Prize, 1962; Zimerman Prize for Environmental Activity, 1977; Israel Prize, co-winner, 1980; Knesset (Israel Parliament) Prize for Environmental Activity, 1984; 500 Global Role of Honor, UNEP, 1987; Dr Honoris Causa, Weizman Institute, 1991; Yigal Alon Prize for Life Activity, 1994; Lions Israel Honour Roll for Life Activity, 2004. Memberships: Society for the Protection of Nature in Israel; Life & Environment. Address: Beit Hashitta, Israel 10801. E-mail: azaralon@bethashita.org.il

ALPERT Herb, b. 31 March 1935, Los Angeles, California, USA. Musician (trumpet); Songwriter; Arranger; Record Company Executive. m. Lani Hall, 1 son, 2 daughters. Education: University of Southern California. Career: 3 television specials; Leader, own group Tijuana Brass; Multiple world tours; Owner, Dore Records; Manager, Jan And Dean; Co-founder with Jerry Moss, A&M Records (formerly Carnival), 1962-89; Artists have included: The Carpenters; Captain And Tennille; Carole King; Cat Stevens; The Police; Squeeze; Joe Jackson; Bryan Adams. Compositions include: Wonderful World, Sam Cooke (co-writer with Lou Adler). Recordings: The Lonely Bull; A Taste Of Honey; Spanish Flea; Tijuana Taxi; Casino Royale; This Guy's In Love With You (Number 1, UK and US), 1968; Rise (Number 1, US), 1979; Albums include: The Lonely Bull, Tijuana Brass, 1963; Tijuana Brass Vol 2, 1964; South Of The Border, Whipped Cream And Other Delights, 1965; Going Places, 1966; SRO, Sounds Like Us, 1967; Herb Alpert's 9th, The Best Of The Brass, 1968; Warm, 1969; Rise, Keep Your Eyes On Me, 1979; Magic Man, 1981; My Abstract Heart, 1989; Midnight Sun, 1992; Second Wind, 1996; Passion Dance, 1997; Colors, 1999; Definitive Hits, 2001. Honours: Numerous Grammy Awards. Address: c/o Kip Cohen, La Brea Tours, Inc., 1414 Sixth Street, Santa Monica, CA 90401, USA.

ALSOP William Allen, b. 12 December 1947, Northamptom, England. Architect. m. Sheila Bean, 1972, 2 sons, 1 daughter. Education: Architectural Association. Career: Teacher of Sculpture, St Martin's College; Worked with Cedric Price; In practice with John Lyall; Designed ferry terminal, Hamburg; Design work on Cardiff barrage; Feasibility studies to recycle former De Lorean factory, Belfast; Designed government building, Marseilles; Established own practice, collaborates with Bruce Maclelan in producing architectural drawings; Principal, Alsop and Störmer Architects, 1979-2000; Principal, Director and Chair, Alsop Architects, 2001; Chair, Architecture Foundation, 2001-; Projects include: North Greenwich Station, 2000; Peckham Library and Media Centre, 2000; Commissioned to design Fourth Grace, Liverpool, 2002; Fawood Children's Centre, 2005; Alsop Toronto Sales Centre, 2006. Publications: City of Objects, 1992; William Alsop Buildings and Projects, 1992; William Alsop Architect: Four Projects, 1993; Will Alsop and Jan Störmer, Architects, 1993; Le Grand Bleu-Marseille, 1994;

SuperCity; Alsop and Störmer: Selected and Current Works. Honours: Officer, Order of the British Empire; Honorary LLD, Leicester; Stirling Prize, 2000. Memberships: Fellow, Royal Society of Arts. Address: 72 Pembroke Road, London W8 6NX, England. E-mail: walsop@alsopandstormer.co.uk Website: www.alsopandstormer.com

ALTARAC Silvio, b. 30 December 1958, Zagreb, Croatia. Urological Surgeon. m. Lidija Lopičić, 1 son, 1 daughter. Education: MD, 1983, PhD, 1989, School of Medicine, Zagreb. Appointments: Teaching Assistant, 1985-89, Scientific Associate, 1993, Scientific Adviser, 2007, Department of Physiology and Immunology, Zagreb; Clinical Research Fellow: University Hospital Pittsburgh, 1990, Royal Hallamshire Hospital, Sheffield, 1993-94, University Hospital Innsbruck, 1995, Brigham and Women's Hospital, Harvard University, Boston, 1995-96; Scientific Associate, 1993; Scientific Adviser, 2007. Publications: Numerous articles in professional journals; Expert columnist, Salud (i) Ciencia, Buenos Aires, Argentina; Citations, Campbell's Urology, Smith's General Urology; European Association of Urology: Guidelines on Urological Trauma; Reviewer, Liječnički Vjesnik, Croatian Medical Journal. Honours: Academician Drago Perović's Medal; Rector's Award for academic excellence; Listing in numerous biographical publications. Memberships: European Association of Urology; American Urological Association. Address: Bukovačka cesta 229C, 10 000 Zagreb, Croatia.

ALTHER Lisa, b. 23 July 1944, Tennessee, USA. Writer; Reviewer; University Professor. m. Richard Alther, 26 August 1966, divorced, 1 daughter. Education: BA, Wellesley College, 1966. Appointments: Staff Member, Atheneum Publishers, New York City, 1967-68; Freelance writer, 1968-; Lecturer, St Michael's College, Winooski, Vermont, 1980-81; Professor and Basler Chair, East Tennessee State University, 1999-2000. Publications: Kinflicks, 1975; Original Sins, 1980; Other Women, 1984; Bedrock, 1990; Birdman and the Dancer, 1993; Five Minutes in Heaven, 1995; Kinfolks: Falling Off the Family Tree, 2007. Contributions to: New York Times Magazine; New York Times Book Review; Natural History; New Society; Arts and Antiques; Boston Globe; Washington Post; Los Angeles Times; San Francisco Chronicle; Southern Living. Memberships: Authors Guild; National Writers Union; PEN; National Book Critics Circle. E-mail: lalther@aol.com

ALTON Roger Martin, b. 20 December 1947, Oxford, England. Journalist. Divorced, 1 daughter. Education: Exeter College, Oxford. Appointments: Graduate Trainee, then General Reporter and Deputy Features Editor, Liverpool Post, 1969-73; Sub-Editor, News, 1973-76, Chief Sub-Editor, News, 1976-81, Deputy Sports Editor, 1981-85, Arts Editor, 1985-90, Weekend Magazine Editor, 1990-93, Features Editor, 1993-96, Assistant Editor, 1996-98, The Guardian; Editor, The Observer, 1998-. Honours: Editor of the Year, What the Papers Say Awards, 2000; Editor of the Year, GQ Men of the Year Awards, 2005. Address: Office of the Editor, The Observer, 3-7 Herbal Hill, London EC1R 5EJ, England. E-mail: editor@observer.co.uk Website: www.observer.co.uk

AMADI Iwu Rowland, b. 14 June 1944, Avu, Owerri West LGA, Nigeria. Company Director; Sculptor. m. (1) Theresa, divorced, 1 son, 2 daughters, (2) Precious Adaku. Education: Higher Diploma in sculpture, Yaba College of Technology, Yaba, Lagos, 1976; Postgraduate Diploma in sculpture and Industrial Art, Portsmouth Polytechnic, England, 1978. Appointments: Art Instructor, Owerri Grammar School Imerienwe, States Schools Management Board, Enugu, 1970; Lecturer, Fine Art,

Institute of Management and Technology, Enugu, 1976-81; Senior Lecturer and Chief Instructor, Alvan Ikoku College of Education Owerri, 1981-92; Director, Blueprint Industrial Company 1992-. Creative Works: Exhibited works at several exhibitions in Nigeria and abroad; Inventor of Iwu Rubber Latex Mould and Unicast Cement Mould; Internationally accredited following demonstration at Leicester, England and at the GRP Mechanization 82, England; Built 2 aircraft models, "Spider 111 and Autodragon" as element of Biafran Aviation, 1969-70; Developed commemorative medals and medallions of honour on images of notable personalities; Developed the Standard African Figure mannequin; Improved the standards of the Nigeria Coat of Arms and first to sponsor bill at National Assembly, Abuja, for adoption of Uniform Standard Nigeria Coat of Arms, 2002; Commissioned by Imo State Government to sculpt 3 life size bronze statues of athletes, Dan Anyiam Stadium, Owerri, 1992 and 14ft bronze statue of the Unknown Soldier, 1991; Commissioned by Abia State Government, Nigeria to sculpt bronze statue of Dr M I Okpara and statue of Abia Woman, 1995. Honours include: Maiden Works Exhibited, Nigerian Independence Celebration Exhibition, 1960; Scholarship Award by Rotary International Club, Best Student at Yaba College of Technology, Yaba, 1974; Postgraduate Studies Scholarship Programme, British Council, 1978; Special Letter of Commendation, Nigerian Council for National Awareness, 1979; Nominated, Nigeria Merit Award, 1983; Honorary Cultural Doctorate, Industrial Art, World University in Benson, Arizona, USA, 1986; Invited to be Ennobled, Royal College of Heraldry, 1988; Commemorative Medal of Honor, ABI, 1991; Deputy Director General and Research Fellow, Nomination for World Intellectual of 1993, IBC, Cambridge, England; Millennium Award for Outstanding Achievement, Universal Intelligence Data Bank of America in collaboration with the Albert Einstein International Academy Foundation, 2000; Outstanding STAR Award, Imo State, Nigeria, 2000; Nomination for Top 100 Visual Artists, IBC, 2005; Living Legend, IBC; World Acclaimed Numismatic Medal of Dr Ernest Kay, Founder and First Director General, IBC Cambridge, England, IBA Newsletter, summer 2007; Genius Laureate of Nigeria Award, 500 Greatest Geniuses of the 21st Century, ABI, 2008; The Director General's Roll of Honour, IBC Cambridge, 2008. Memberships include: Vice-President, Nigeria Society for Education Through Art, Imo State Branch; Life Fellow, IBA; Research Committee, Institute of Management & Technology, Enugu, 1977-79; Avu Town Development Union, Owerri West LGA; Society of Nigerian Artists. Address: Blueprint Industrial Company Ltd, 90 Wetheral Road, Regional Secretariat Nigeria, PO Box 737, Owerri, Nigeria. E-mail: rblueprintind@yahoo.com

AMANPOUR Christiane, b. 12 January 1958, London, England. Broadcasting Correspondent. m. James Rubin, 1998, 1 son. Education: New Hall, Cambridge; University of Rhode Island, USA. Appointments: Radio Producer and Research Assistant, BBC Radio, London, 1980-82; Radio Reporter, WBRU, Brown University, USA, 1981-83; Electronic Graphics Designer, WJAR, Providence, Rhode Island, 1983; Assistant, CNN International Assignment Desk, Atlanta, Georgia, 1983; News Writer, CNN, Atlanta, 1984-86; Reporter, Producer, CNN, New York, 1987-90; International Correspondent, 1990, Senior International Correspondent, 1994, Chief International Correspondent, 1996, CNN; Assignments include Gulf War coverage, 1990-91, USSR break-up and subsequent war in Tbilisi, 1991, extensive reports on conflict in former Yugoslavia and civil unrest and crises coverage, Haiti, Algeria, Somalia and Rwanda; Contracted to CBS, 1996-2005. Honours: Dr hc, Rhode Island; 3 Dupont-Columbia Awards, 1986-96; 2

News and Documentary Emmy Awards, 1999; George Foster Peabody Award, 1999; George Polk Award, 1999; University of Missouri Award for Distinguished Service to Journalism, 1999. Memberships: Fellow, Society of Professional Journalists. Address: c/o CNN International, CNN House, 19-22 Rathbone Place, London W1P 1DF, England.

AMATO Giuliano, b. 13 May 1938, Turin, Italy. Politician; Professor. m. Diana Amato, 1 son, 1 daughter. Appointments: Joined Italian Socialist Party, 1958; Member, Central Committee, 1978-; Assistant Secretary; elected Deputy for Turin-Novara-Vercelli, 1983, 1987; Former Under-Secretary of State; President and Vice-President, Council of Ministers; Minister of the Treasury, 1987-89; Professor, Italian and Comparative Constitutional Law, University of Rome; National Deputy Secretary, Italian Socialist Party, 1988-92; Foreign debt negotiator for Albanian government, 1991-92, Prime Minister of Italy, 1992-93, 2000-01; Minister for Treasury, 1999-2001; Vice President, EU Special Convention on a Pan-European Constitution, 2001; Minister of the Interior in Romano Prodi's government, 2006-. Publications: Antitrust and the Bounds of Power, 1997; Tornare al Futuro, 2001. Honours: Foreign Honorary Member, American Academy of Arts and Sciences, 2001. Address: Special Convention on a European Constitution, European Union, 200 rue de la Loi, 1049 Brussels, Belgium.

AMER Ahmed Eissa, b. 27 April 1955, Cairo, Egypt. Consultant Engineer. m. Iman Kamal El-Ghor, 1 son, 1 daughter. Education: BSc, 1977, MSc, 1981, PhD, 1989, Mechanical Engineering. Appointments: Assistant Lecturer, Ain Shams University, 1978-89; Consultant Engineer, 1990-. Honours: Listed in international biographical dictionaries. Memberships: American Society of Heating R A/C Engineers; Past President, Rotary International. Address: 3 Almaza St, Heliopolis, Cairo 11341, Egypt. E-mail: codiacaea@yahoo.com

AMER Fahim Mohammed, b. 24 January 1935, El-Monofia, Egypt. Pharmacist. m. Soad, 2 sons, 1 daughter. Education: BSc, Pharmacy, 1956; Postgraduate Diploma, Drug Analysis, 1964; Postgraduate Diploma, Biochemical Analysis, 1969. Appointments: Chemical Drug Analyst, Quality Control Manager, QA/QC and R&D Director in some Egyptian and multinational pharmaceuticals companies, Egypt and Kuwait. Honours: Gold Medal, Egyptian Syndicate for Pharmacists; Listed in international biographical dictionaries. Memberships: American Chemical Society; American Association for Advancement of Science; AOAC International; FIP. Address: 6th October City, PO Box 43, SEDICO Pharmaceuticals, Giza 12566, Egypt.

AMETEMBUN Nikolaus Aloysius, b. 19 November 1933, Tanimbar, Indonesia. Educator. m. Pia Kelyombar, 1 son, 4 daughters. Education: Master, Educational Administration; PhD, Institute of Teacher Training & Education, Bandung, West Java, Indonesia. Appointments: Lecturer, 1967-98, Professor of Educational Administration, 1993-98, Professor Emeritus, 1999-, Institute of Teacher Training and Education, Bandung. Publications: The Role of Principal in Educational Reformation in Indonesia, 2004; Educational Supervision: A handbook, 8th edition, 2007. Honours: Medal of Honor, President of Republic of Indonesia, 1990. Memberships: Association for Supervision & Curriculum Development, USA; National Association of Indonesia Educators; Association of Indonesia Catholic Intelligentsia. Address: Jalan Melati Raya E22 No 9, Desa Melatiwangi-Ujung Berung, Bandung 40618, Indonesia.

AMIN Mohammed, b. 29 October 1950, Kalyanpur, Pakistan. Accountant. m. Tahara, 2 sons, 2 daughters. Education: Mathematical Tripos, Clare College, Cambridge, 1969-72; Graduate Certificate in Education, Leeds University, 1972-73; Associate (now Fellow), Institute of Chartered Accountant of England and Wales, 1977; Associate, 1978, Fellow, 2000, Institute of Taxation (now the Chartered Institute of Taxation); Associate Member, Association of Corporate Treasurers, 1995. Appointments: Teacher, Counthill School, Oldham, 1973-74; Trainee Accountant, Graham H Wood & Co, Ashton-under-Lyne and Hyde, 1974-77; Tax Senior, 1977-81, Tax Manager, 1981-84, Arthur Andersen, Manchester; Senior Tax Manager, 1984-85, Tax Partner, 1985-87, John Fairhurst & Co, Wigan; Senior Tax Manager, 1987-90, Partner, 1990-, Price Waterhouse, Manchester and London (now PricewaterhouseCoopers LLP). Publications: Articles in professional journals include most recently: Europe raises the taxing questions, Gordon Brown's Last Budget?, Treasury Tax: where are we now?, Treasury practice: should we hedge against translation risk?, Islamic Finance, 2005; Book chapters: UK Chapter in The Taxation of Equity Derivatives and Structured Products, 2002; Alternative Finance Arrangements in Butterworths' Finance Act 2005 Handbook, Alternative Finance Arrangements in Simons Direct Tax Service (loose-leaf reference service), 2005. Honours: Distinction in Final Examination, Institute of Taxation; Medal for the best fellowship thesis, Chartered Institute of Taxation, 1999; Finance Excellence Award, Northern region, Asian Jewel Awards, 2002; Included in The Asian Power 100, The Institute of Asian Professionals, 2005. Included in The Muslim Power 100, 2007. Memberships: Chartered Institute of Taxation; Institute of Chartered Accountants in England and Wales; Association of Corporate Treasurers; Muslim Jewish Forum of Greater Manchester; Conservative Muslim Forum; Manchester Chess Federation. Address: PricewaterhouseCoopers LLP, Hay's Galleria, 1 Hay's Lane, London SE1 2RD, England. E-mail: mohammed.amin@uk.pwc.com

AMINIGO Ebiokpo Rebecca, b. 25 January 1961, Koroama, Nigeria. Lecturer. m. Ibitamuno Mitchell Aminigo, 2 sons, 1 daughter. Education: BSc (2nd Class Upper), Microbiology, University of Port Harcourt, 1984; PGD, 1986, MSc, 1987, PhD, 1993, Food Technology, University of Ibadan. Appointments: Teaching/Research Assistant, University of Ibadan, 1988-90; Assistant Lecturer, 1992, Lecturer II, 1993, Lecturer I, 1997, Senior Lecturer, 2000, University of Port Harcourt; Part time Lecturer, University of Uyo, 2000-02. Publications: 4 book chapters; 13 articles in learned journals; 3 abstracts. Honours: Dean's List Scholar, University of Port Harcourt, 1980-84; Visiting Research Student, International Institute of Tropical Agriculture, 1991; Fulbright Scholar, 2003-04. Memberships: Nigerian Institute of Food Science and Technology; National Association of Women Academics; Third World Organization for Women in Science; Fulbright Alumni Association of Nigeria; American Society for Microbiology; National Registry of Environmental Professionals, USA. Address: Department of Microbiology, University of Port Harcourt, PMB 5323, Port Harcourt, Nigeria. E-mail: raminigo@yahoo.co.uk.

AMIRALI Evangelia-Lila, b. 28 November 1962. Medical Doctor; Psychiatrist. m. J Hadjinicolaou, 4 sons. Education: MD, University of Athens, Greece, 1986; Candidate, Canadian Institute of Psychoanalysis. Appointments: Research Fellow, McGill University, 1988-90, Clinical Fellow, 1990-92; Psychiatrist, Child Psychiatrist, Universite de Montreal, 2001; Assistant Professor, Universite de Montreal; Assistant Professor, McGill University. Honours: A S Onassis

Scholarship, 1990-92; Berta Mizne Award, 1988-90; Best Promising Clinician Prize, Department of Psychiatry, McGill University, 1999-2000; American Psychiatric Association Women Fellowship, 2001. Memberships: APA; CPA; QMA; AMPQ. Address: 2875 Douglas Avenue, Montreal, QC H3R 2C7, Canada.

AMIS Martin Louis, b. 25 August 1949, Oxford, England. Author. m. (1) Antonia Phillips, 2 sons (2) Isabel Fonseca, 3 daughters. Education: BA, Exeter College, Oxford. Appointments: Fiction and Poetry Editor, Times Literary Supplement, 1974; Literary Editor, New Statesman, 1977-79; Special Writer, Observer Newspaper, 1980-. Publications: The Rachel Papers, 1973; Dead Babies, 1975; Success, 1978; Other People: A Mystery Story, 1981; Invasion of the Space Invaders, 1982; Money: A Suicide Note, 1984; The Moronic Inferno and Other Visits to America, 1986; Einstein's Monsters: Five Stories, 1987; London Fields, 1989; Time's Arrow, 1991; Visiting Mrs Nabokov and Other Excursions,1993; The Information, 1995; Night Train, 1997; Heavy Water and Other Stories, 1999; Experience, 2000; The War Against Cliché, 2001; Koba the Dread: Laughter and the Twenty Million, 2002; Yellow Dog, 2003; House of Meetings, 2006; The Pregnant Widow, 2007. Honours: Somerset Maugham Award, 1974; James Tait Black Memorial Prize, 2000. Address: c/o Wylie Agency (UK), 17 Bedford Square, London WC1B 3JA, England. E-mail: mail: wylieagency.co.uk

AMLIE Jan Peder, b. 23 September 1940, Bøverbru, V Toten, Norway. Physician. m. May Lisbet, 1 son, 2 daughters. Education: C and Med, 1965, Dr Med, 1981, Oslo University; Speciality Internal Medicine and Cardiology, Sweden and Norway, 1973; Professor in Cardiology, 1991-. Appointments: Assistant Doctor, Sweden, 1966-73; University Lecturer, 1973-75, Research Fellow, 1975-80, Cardiologist, 1981-89, Professor, 1990-, Rikshospitalet, Oslo, Norway. Publications: 135 papers in medical journals and conference proceedings include: Prolonged Ventricular Repolarization, 1983; Books include: Dispension of Repolarization, 2000. Honour: President, UEMS, Cardiology Section, 2002-06. Memberships: Norwegian Society of Cardiology. Address: Risbakken 10, Oslo 0374, Norway.

AMOAKO Wilfred Yaw, b. 18 December 1949, Pakro, Ghana. Conference Translator; Interpreter. m. Christolite Amoako, 1 daughter. Education: Professional Diploma in Translation, English, French, Spanish, School of Translators, Accra, Ghana, 1972-76; Intensive Course in Translation, University of Madrid, Spain, 1975-76; Diplome Superieur D'Interprete & De Correspondancier, Commercial and the Advanced Diploma in Commercial Studies with special emphasis on English-French, French-English Commercial Translations,(Chamber of Commerce of London and Paris), Institut Superieur Universitaire D'Interpreteriat et de Traduction, Paris, France, 1976-77; Zertifikat Deutsche als Fremdsprache, Goethe Institute, Dakar, Senegal, 1995-99; MA, International Relations and Diplomacy, George Washington International University, Pennsylvania, USA, 2001-02. Appointments: Associate English Translator, United Nations Economic Commission for Africa, Addis Ababa, Ethiopia, 1979-80; English Translator, Organisation of African Unity Headquarters, 1980; Temporary English Translator, West African Rice Development Association, 1980; The Fund for Compensation and Development of the Economic Community of West African States, Lome, Togo, 1980-81; English Translator and Interpreter, United Nations African Institute for Economic Development and Planning, 1981-; Freelance Translator for UN System: UNESCO,

UNICEF, UNDP, UNFPA, WFP, ICAO, ILO and institutions including: AFCAC, CAEM, CODESRIA, CRAT, ENDA, Plan International, AAWORD, Union of African Population Studies, 1982-. Publications: Numerous published translations for the United Nations Include: Analysis of Gender Mainstreaming in National Plans for Education for All; Other published translations include those for the Association of African Women for Research and Development, Dakar, Senegal, CODESRIA, OAU, ICAO. Membership: International Association of Conference Translators and Interpreters, Geneva, Switzerland. Address: United Nations Economic Commission for Africa, BP 3186, Dakar, Senegal. E-mail: w.amoako@unidep.org

AMOROSO Santi, b. 17 June 1925, Italy. Physician. m. Gabriella Malanga, 3 sons, 1 daughter. Education: Graduate, 1949, Specialist in Pulmonary Diseases, 1951, Medical School, University "La Sapienza", Rome Italy; Licensed to practice medicine in Italy, Maryland, USA, Virginia, USA, 1959; Certified by ABFP, USA, 1978. Appointments: Internship and Residency, St Mary's Memorial Hospital, Knoxville, Tennessee, 1953-59; General Practitioner, Overlea Medical Group, Baltimore, Maryland, 1959-62; General Practitioner, Perry Hall Medical Group, Baltimore, Maryland, 1962-64; Private Practice, Rome, Italy, 1964-2005; Retired, 2005. Publications: 2 medical articles in an Italian medical journal; Book of poetry, Gocciole di Rugiada (Dewdrops). Honours: 2nd Place, Poetry Competition sponsored by Association of Italian Physicians Writers, 1996; Translator of English medical books and of "Treatment Guidelines" for CIS Publisher, Italy. Memberships: Former Member, AMA and AAFP; Member, Italian Medical Association. Address: Via Villa Belardi 24, 00154 Rome, Italy. E-mail: santi.amoroso@libero.it

AMOYAL Pierre Alain Wilfred, b. 22 June 1949, Paris, France. Violinist. Education: Studied at the Paris Conservatoire and with Jascha Heifetz between 1966 and 1971. Debut: Paris 1971, in the Berg Concerto, with the Orchestre de Paris. Career: Appearances with the BBC Symphony Orchestra, Hallé Orchestra, London Philharmonic, Philharmonia, Berlin Philharmonic, Boston Symphony, Cleveland Orchestra, Philadelphia Orchestra and Orchestras in Canada and France; Conductors include Karajan, Ozawa, Boulez, Dutoit, Sanderling, Maazel, Solti, Prêtre, Masur and Rozhdestvensky; Plays Concertos by Berg, Schoenberg and Dutilleux, in addition to the standard repertory; Played Brahms Concerto with the Royal Philharmonic Orchestra, 1995; Artist in Residence at Beaumaris Festival in Wales, 1995; Recitals at St John's Smith Square for the BBC; New York Carnegie Hall debut 1985; Professor at the Paris Conservatoire from 1977; Currently Professor at the Lausanne Conservatoire. Recordings: Concertos by Dutilleux, Respighi and Saint Saëns with the Orchestre National conducted by Charles Dutoit; Chamber music (sonatas by Brahms, Fauré and Franck) with Pascal Rogé; Schoenberg Concerto with the London Symphony Orchestra conducted by Boulez. Honours include: Ginette Neveu Prize, 1963; Paganini Prize, 1964; Enescu Prize, 1970. Address: c/o Jacques Thelen, 252 rue du Faubourg Saint-Honoré, 75008 Paris, France.

AN Beongku, b. 18 September 1960, Republic of Korea. Professor. m. Jeongran Baeck, 1 son. Education: BS, Kyungpook National Universitym, Korea, 1988; MS, Polytechnic University, USA, 1996; PhD, New Jersey Institute of Technology, USA, 2002. Appointments: Senior Researcher, RIST, Republic of Korea, 1989-94; Lecturer & RA, New Jersey Institute of Technology, USA, 1997-2002; Professor, Hongik University, Republic of Korea, 2003-.

Publications: 12 articles in professional international journals. Honours: Best Award Paper, KSEA, USA, 2001; Listed in international biographical dictionaries. Memberships: Institute of Electronics Engineering of Korea; Korea Information and Communications Society; Institute of Webcasting and Internet Television; Korea Multimedia Society; Korea Society of Transportation. Address: Department of Computer & Information Communications Engineering, Hongik University, Shinan-Ri, Jochiwon, Yeong-Gun, Chungnam, 339-701, Republic of Korea. E-mail: beongku@wow.hongik.ac.kr

ANANE Aomar, b. 1955, Figuig, Morocco. University Vice President. m. Zineb Benaissa, 2 sons, 1 daughter. Education: BA, Mathematics, University Mohammed V, Rabat, 1979; MA, Applied Mathematics, 1982, PhD, Mathematical Analysis, 1987, Université de Pau, France. Appointments: Professor, Mathematics, Director, Applied Mathematics and Parallel Computation doctorial programme, Head, Department of Mathematics and Computer Science, Vice President, University Mohammed I. Publications: More than 30 articles in professional journals. Honours: Man of the Year, 2007. Memberships: Morrocan Mathematical Society; Association Internationale de Pédagogie Universitaire. Address: 19 rue Sanawbar, Cite Bassatines, Soyahya, 60700, Oujda, Morroco. E-mail: anane@ump.mo

ANCRAM Earl of, Michael Andrew Foster Jude Kerr, 13th Marquis of Lothian, b. 7 July 1945. Politician. m. Lady Jane Fitzalan-Howard, 1975, 2 daughters. Education: Ampleforth; Christ Church College, Oxford; Edinburgh University. Appointments: Formerly in business; Columnist, Daily Telegraph (Manchester edition); Partner, Tenanted Arable Farm; Called to Scottish Bar, 1970; Practised Law, 1970-79; MP, Berwickshire and East Lothian, 1974; Edinburgh South, 1979-87; Devizes, 1992-; Parliamentary, Under-Secretary of State, Scottish Office, 1983-87; Parliamentary, Under-Secretary, Northern Ireland Office, 1993-94; Minister of State, 1994-96; Shadow Cabinet Spokesman for Constitutional Affairs, 1997-98; Chair, 1998-2001, Deputy Leader, 2001-, Conservative Party; Vice Chair, 1975-80, Chair, 1980-83, Conservative Party, Scotland; Chair, Northern Corporate Communications, 1989-91; Director, CSM Parliamentary Consultants, 1988-92; Member of Board Scottish Homes, 1988-90; D L Roxburgh, Ettrick and Lauderdale, 1990; Privy Counsellor, 1996; Queen's Counsel, 1996; Shadow Secretary of State for Foreign and Commonwealth Affairs, 2001-, for International Affairs, 2003-04, for International Development, 2004-. Memberships: House of Commons Energy Select Committee, 1979-83. Address: House of Commons, London, SW1A 0AA, England. Website: www.ancram.com

ANDERSLAND Orlando B, b. 15 August 1929, Albert Lea, Minnesota, USA. Civil Engineering Educator. m. Phyllis Burgess, 2 sons, 1 daughter. Education: BCE, University of Minnesota, Minneapolis, 1952; MSCE, 1956, PhD, 1960, Purdue University at West Lafayette, Indiana. Appointments: 1st Lieutenant, US Army Corps of Engineers, 1952-55; Staff Engineer, National Academy of Science, American Association of State Highway Officials Road Test, Ottawa, Illinois, 1956-57; Research Engineer, Purdue University, 1957-59; Faculty, 1960, Professor, 1968, Professor Emeritus, 1994-, Michigan State University. Publications: Co-author, Frozen Ground Engineering, 1994, 2nd edition, 2004; Co-editor, Contributor, Geotechnical Engineering for Cold Regions, 1978; Chapter in Ground Engineers Handbook, 1987; Numerous articles in professional journals; Co-author, Geotechnical Engineering and Soil Testing, 1992; Patentee in field. Honours: Distinguished Faculty Award, Michigan

State University, 1979; Norwegian Postdoctoral Fellowship, 1966; Best Paper Award, ASCE Journal of Cold Regions Engineering, 1991; Proceedings of the Association Asphalt Paving Technologists, 1956; National Defence Service Medal; United Nations Service Medal; Korean Service Medal. Memberships: Fellow, American Society of Civil Engineers; American Society for Testing Materials; International Society for Soil Mechanics and Foundation Engineering; American Society for Engineering Education; Chi Epsilon; Tau Beta Pi; Sigma Xi. Address: Department of Civil and Environmental Engineering, Michigan State University, East Lansing, MI 48824, USA.

ANDERSON Elizabeth Lang, b. 3 March 1960, Orange, New Jersey, USA. Composer; m. David S Baltuch. Education: BA, Music, Gettysburg College, Gettysburg, Pennsylvania, 1982; Master of Music in Composition, Peabody Institute, Baltimore, Maryland, 1987; Certificate, Composition, Royal Conservatory of Brussels, 1990; Diploma, Electronic Music Composition, Royal Conservatory, Antwerp, 1993; Premier Prix in Electroacoustic Music Composition, Royal Conservatory of Mons, 1997; Superior Diploma In Electroacoustic Music Composition, Royal Conservatory of Mons, 1998; PhD, Electroacoustic Music Composition, in progress, City University, London, 1998-. Appointments: Instructor of Musicianship (Creative Music Theory), Peabody Preparatory, Baltimore, Maryland, 1985-87; Professor, Electroacoustic Music Composition, Academy of Soignies, Belgium, 1994-2002; Lecturer in the Electroacoustic Music Department, Royal Conservatory of Mons, 2003-04. Publications: The following works are available on compact disc Mimoyecques, 1995, L'éveil,1997-98, Chat Noir, 2000, Neon, 2005, Les Forges de l'Invisible, 2004; Protopia/Tesseract, 2007. Honours: Music honoured in several competitions specialising in electroacoustic music including: Ascap/Seamus, Bourges, Città di Udine, Cimesp, Métamorphoses, Noroit, Stockholm; Commissions from Musiques & Recherches, Belgium and La Chambre d'Ecoute, Belgium; Numerous performances and conferences at international venues; Overseas Research Students Award Scheme Grant funded by the Committee of Vice-Chancellors and Principals of the Universities of the United Kingdom; Grant, British Federation of Women Graduates Charitable Foundation; Grant, Foundation SPES, Belgium. Memberships: Federation Belge de Musique Electroacoustique, International Computer Music Association, SACEM, Sonic Arts Network, Society for Electro-Acoustic Music in the United States. Address: Avenue de Monte Carlo, 11, 1190 Brussels, Belgium. E-mail: e.anderson@skynet.be

ANDERSON Gerry, b. 14 April 1929, England. Film Maker. m. (1) Betty Wrightman, 1952, 2 daughters, (2) Sylvia Thamm, 1961, divorced, 1 son, (3), Mary Robbins, 1981, 1 son. Appointments: Trainee, Colonial Film Unit, 1943; Assistant Editor, Gainsborough Pictures, 1945-47; Dubbing Editor, 1949-53; Film Director, Polytechnic Films, 1954-55; Co-founder: Pentagon Films, 1955, AP Films, 1956, AP Merchandising, 1961; Director of TV commercials, 1961, 1988-92; Chair, Century 21 Organisation, 1966-75. TV Series Include: Adventure of Twizzle (52 shows), 1956; Torchy the Battery Boy (26 shows), 1957; Four Feather Falls (52 shows), 1958; Supercar (39 shows), 1959; Fireball XL5 (39 shows), 1961; Stingray (39 shows), 1962-63; Thunderbirds (32 shows screened in 20 countries), 1964-66; Captain Scarlet (32 shows), 1967; Joe 90 (30 shows), 1968; The Secret Service (13 shows), 1968; UFO (26 shows), 1969-70; The Protectors (52 shows), 1971-72; Space 1999 (48 shows), 1973-76; Terrahawks (39 shows), 1982-83; Dick Spanner (26 shows), 1987; Space

Precinct, 1993-95; Lavender Castle, 1997; Firestorm, 2002; Gerry anderson's New Captain Scarlet, 2005; Numerous TV commercials; Films: Thunderbirds are Go, 1966; Thunderbird 6, 1968; Doppelganger, 1969. Honours: Honorary Fellow, British Kinematograph Sound and TV Society; President, Thames Valley and Chiltern Air Ambulance; Silver Arrow Award; Member of the Order of the British Empire, 2001.

ANDERSON Gillian, b. 9 August 1968, Chicago, USA. Actress. m. (1) Errol Clyde Klotz, divorced, 1 daughter; (2) Julian Ozanne, 2004-06; 1 son with Mark Griffiths, 2006. Education: DePaul University, Chicago; Goodman Theatre School, Chicago. Appointments: Worked at National Theatre, London; Appeared in two off-broadway productions; Best Known Role as Special Agent Dana Scully in TV Series, The X Files (Feature Film 1998); Film, The House of Mirth, 2000; Films include: Chicago Cab, 1995; The Turning, 1997; The X-Files, 1998; The Mighty, 1998; Playing By Heart, 1998; Princess Mononoke, 1999; House of Mirth, 2000; The Mighty Celt, 2005; Tristam Shandy: A cock and Bull Story, 2005; The Last King of Scotland, 2006; Straightheads, 2007. Plays include: Absent Friends, Manhattan Theater Club, 1991; The Philanthropist, Along Wharf Theater, 1992; What the Night is For, Comedy Theatre, London, 2002; The Sweetest Swing in Baseball, Royal Court Theatre, London, 2004; TV films include: Home Fire Burning, 1992; When Planes Go Down, 1996; Presenter, Future Fantastic, BBC TV; Bleak House, BBC TV, 2005. Honours: Theater World Award, 1991; Golden Globe Awards, 1995, 1997; Screen Actors' Guild Awards, 1996, 1997; Emmy Award, 1997. Address: William Morris Agency, 151 El Camino Drive, Beverly Hills, CA 90212, USA. Website: www.gilliananderson.ws

ANDERSON John Anthony (Sir), b. 2 August 1945, Wellington, New Zealand. Banker. m. Carol M Anderson, 1970, 2 sons, 1 daughter. Education: Christ's College; Victoria University of Wellington; FCA. Appointments: Deloitte Haskins and Sells chartered accountants, Wellington, 1962-69; Guest and Bell sharebrokers, Melbourne, Victoria, Australia, 1969-72; Joined, 1972, Chief Executive, Director, 1979, South Pacific Merchant Finance Ltd, Wellington; Deputy Chief Executive, 1988, Chief Executive, Director, 1990-2003, National Bank of New Zealand; Chair, Petroleum Corporation of New Zealand Ltd, 1986-88; Director, New Zealand Steel Ltd, 1986-87, Lloyds Merchant Bank, London, 1986-92, Lloyds Bank NZA, Australia, 1989-97; New Zealand Bankers' Association, 1991-92, 1999-2000; President, New Zealand Bankers Institute, 1990-2001; Chair, New Zealand Cricket Board, 1995-, New Zealand Sports Foundation Inc, 1999-2002; Managing Director, ANZ National Bank Ltd, 2003-; Other professional and public appointments. Honours: Knight Commander, Order of the British Empire; 1990 Commemoration Medal. Memberships: Chair, New Zealand Merchant Banks Association, 1982-89; Chair, New Zealand Bankers Association, 1992-. Address: 5 Fancourt Street, Karori, Wellington 5, New Zealand.

ANDERSON Katrina Marysia Tomaszewska, b. 7 December 1947, Springfield by Cupar, Fife, Scotland. Community Educator. m. William Anderson, 1 son, 2 daughters. Education: Master of Arts, English Literature (Honours), University of Dundee, 1999; Open University Postgraduate Diploma in Community Education, Northern College, Dundee, 2001. Appointments: Personal Assistant to husband in the family business, 1986-; Community Educator; Member, Volunteer, Tracing and Message Co-ordinator, Public Speaker, British Red Cross. Publications: Numerous poems published by International Society of Poets, 1998,

2000; Triumph House, 1997-2001; Brownstone Books, 1997. Honours: Cultural Relations Attache to Scotland, HRP (Title: The Hon); Medal, HRP, 1998; Honoured Poet, 1998; One of the Best Poets of the 20th Century; Woman of the Year, ABI, 2006; Member, ABI's Professional Women's Advisory Board; International Peace Prize; Nominated for Gold Medal, 2008; Listed in Who's Who publications and biographical dictionaries. Memberships: International Society of Poets; University of Dundee Alumni; British Red Cross; Lifetime Partronage, Hutt River Province, Australia. Address: 31 Clyde Court, Rimbleton, Glenrothes, Fife KY6 2BN, Scotland.

ANDERSON Michael, b. 30 January 1920, London, England. Film Director. m. (1) Betty Jordan, 1939, 5 children; (2) Vera Carlisle, 1969, 1 child; (3) Adrianne Ellis, 1977, 2 stepchildren. Education: France. Appointments: Co-Director with Peter Ustinov, film, Private Angelo, 1949; Director, films: Waterfront, 1950; Hell Is Sold Out, 1952; Night Was Our Friend; Dial 17; Will Any Gentleman?; The House of the Arrow, 1952; The Dam Busters, 1954; Around the World in Eighty Days, 1956; Yangtse Incident, 1957; Chase a Crooked Shadow, 1957; Shake Hands with the Devil, 1958; Wreck of the Mary Deare, 1959-60; All the Fine Young Cannibals, 1960; The Naked Edge, 1961; Flight from Ashiya, in Japan, 1962; Operation Crossbow, 1964; The Quiller Memorandum, 1966; Shoes of The Fisherman, 1969; Pope Joan, 1970-71; Doc Savage, in Hollywood, 1973; Conduct Unbecoming, 1974; Logan's Run, MGM Hollywood, 1975; Orca - Killer Whale, 1976; Dominique, 1977; The Martian Chronicles, 1978; Bells, 1979-80; Millennium; Murder by Phone; Second Time Lucky; Separate Vacations; Sword of Gideon; Jeweller's Shop; Young Catherine; Millennium; Summer of the Monkeys; The New Adventures of Pinocchio, 1999. Address: c/o Film Rights Ltd, 113-117 Wardour Street, London W1, England.

ANDERSON William Robert, b. 26 January 1929, Kittanning, Pennsylvania, USA. Physician; Pathologist. m. Carol J Tammen, 1 son, 1 daughter. Education: BA, University of Rochester, 1951; MD, University of Pennsylvania School of Medicine, 1958; Anatomic and Clinical Pathology Residencies, New York Hospital, Cornell Medical Centre, 1958-69, New York VA Hospital, 1960-62. Appointments: Neuropathology Fellowship, Duke University, 1962-64; Director, Anatomic Pathology, Hennepin County Medical Centre, 1967-97; Chief of Pathology, 1984-95; Professor, Department of Laboratory Medicine and Pathology, University of Minnesota School of Medicine, 1975-. Publications: Numerous scientific publications in national and international pathology journals. Honours: Phi Beta Kappa, University of Rochester, 1951; Sigma Xi, Duke University, 1963; Mentor Recognition, University of Minnesota, 1989. Memberships: College of American Pathologists; International Academy of Pathology; Society for Ultrastructural Pathology; President, Minnesota Society of Pathologists, 1980-81. Address: 5725 Merry Lane, Excelsior, MN 55331, USA.

ANDO Nisuke, b. 6 August 1935, Kyoto, Japan. Professor Emeritus of International Law. m. Noriko Fujimoto, 1 son, 2 daughters. Education: LLB, 1959, LLM, 1961, Kyoto University; PhD, Fletcher School of Law and Diplomacy, 1971. Appointments: Lecturer and Associate Professor, 1965-68, 1968-81, Kyoto University; Professor, 1981-90, Kobe University; Professor, Kyoto University, 1990-98; Professor, Doshisha University, 1998-2006; Director, Kyoto Human Rights Research Institute, 2001-. Publications: Surrender, Occupation and Private Property in International Law, 1991; Japan and International Law - Past, Present and Future, editor, 1999; Liber Amicorum Judge Shigeru Oda, co-editor, 2002; Towards Implementing Universal Human Rights, editor, 2004. Honours: Fulbright Graduate Student, 1962-64; Fulbright Research Fellow, 1969-70; British Council Fellow, 1976-78; Fulbright 50th Anniversary Distinguished Fellow, 1996. Memberships: Human Rights Committee under the International Covenant on Civil and Political Rights, 1987-2006; Judge, Administrative Tribunal of the International Monetary Fund, 1994-; Member, Permanent Court of Arbitration, 2001-. Address: 922-66 Kokubu 2-chome, Otsu-shi, Shiga-ken 520-0844, Japan.

ANDRADE Andres, b. 20 November, Tampa, Florida, USA. Vocal Instructor; Vocalist; Opera Producer. Education: Master of Music, New England Conservatory of Music, Boston, Massachusetts; Bachelor of Arts, University of South Florida, Tampa, Florida; Additional studies through or with faculty at Harvard University, Juilliard School of Music, Manhattan School of Music, University of Connecticut at Storrs. Appointments: New England Conservatory Teaching Fellowship; St Patrick's Old Cathedral, New York; LaGuardia Arts High School, New York; Citywide Youth Opera, New York City (Founder); Queens College, New York City. Publications: NYSTA Journal; Teacher Profile; Opera Workshop; Inside-Out. Honours: New England Conservatory Teaching Fellowship; Teacher Recognition Award, National Foundation for Advancement in the Arts; Marcia Van Dressler Scholarship Award, New England Conservatory; New England Conservatory Benevolent Society Scholarship Award. Memberships: Board Member, National Association of Teachers of Singing; New York Singing Teachers Association. Address: PO Box 20498, Columbus Circle Station, New York, NY 10023, USA. E-mail: andradeten@aol.com

ANDRÉ Maurice, b. 21 May 1933, Alès, Gard, France. Trumpeter. Education: Studied with his father and with Sabarich at the Paris Conservatoire. Career: Soloist with the Concerts Lamoureuz, 1953-60, L'Orchestre Philharmonique of ORTF (French Radio), 1953-62, and the orchestra of the Operé-Comique, Paris, 1962-67; Many concert performances in Europe; North American Professor at the Paris Conservatoire, 1967-78; Composers who have written for him include Boris Blacher (Concerto 1971), Charles Chaynes, Marcel Landowski, Jean-Claude Eloy, Harold Genzmer, Bernhard Krol, Jean Langlais (Chorals for trumpet and organ), Henri Tomasi and André Jolivet (Arioso barocco, 1968). Honours: Chevalier de la Légion d'honneur; Commandeur des Arts et des Lettres; First Prize, Geneva International Competition, 1955, Munich International Competition, 1963, Schallplattenpreis, Berlin, 1970, Victoire de la musique, 1987.

ANDREEV Rumen Dimov, b. 20 March 1955, Sofia, Bulgaria. Engineer. Education: Master of Science, 1980, PhD, 1987, Sofia Technical University, Sofia, Bulgaria. Appointments: Constructor, Institute of Computer Technique, 1980-82; Research Fellow, Central Institute of Computer Technique and Technology, 1982-88; Research Associate, Central Laboratory of Automation and Scientific Instrumentation, 1988-93; Associate Professor, Institute of Computer and Communication Systems, Bulgarian Academy of Sciences, 1994-. Publications: Monograph: Graphics Systems: Architecture and Realization, 1993; Articles in scientific journals including: Computer Graphics Forum; Computers and Graphics; Interacting with Computers. Honours: Medal, Ministry of Defence, Republic of Bulgaria, 1974; Nominated for International Scientist of the Year 2003, Diploma of Achievement in Science, IBC; Listed in Who's Who publications and biographical dictionaries. Memberships: Bulgarian Union of Automation and Informatics, British

Computer Society; New York Academy of Sciences. Address: Institute of Computer and Communication Systems, Bulgarian Academy of Sciences, str Acad. G Bonchev Bl 2, 1113 Sofia, Bulgaria. E-mail: rumen@isdip.bas.bg

ANDRES-BARQUIN Pedro Jose, b. 9 January 1964, Zaragoza, Spain. Neuroscientist; Veterinarian. m. Maria Clemencia Hernandez, 2 daughters. Education: DVM, 1987, PhD, 1992, University of Zaragoza, Spain; MPH, Spanish National School of Public Health, Spain, 1993. Appointments: Fellow: University of Zaragoza, 1982-92, INSERM, France, 1990-91, University of California, San Francisco, USA, 1994-98; Head of Laboratory, F Hoffmann-La Roche, Basel, Switzerland, 2000-2005; Director, VMC de l'Avenir, Delemont, Switzerland, 2007-. Publications: Contributor of articles to professional journals in the fields of biomedicine and education. Listed in Who's Who publications and biographical dictionaries. Honours: CAI Degree Prize, 1987, National Degree Prize, 1988, Spanish Ministry of Education and Science; Gold Medal, Veterinary Medicine, Official Association of Veterinary Surgeons of Malaga, 2004; Albeitar Gold Medal, Official Association of Veterinary Surgeons of Murcia, 2004; International Health Professional of the Year, IBC, Cambridge, England, 2004. Memberships: Society for Neuroscience; American Society for Cell Biology; Spanish Society for Biochemistry and Molecular Biology. Address: Claragraben 117, Basel 4057, Switzerland. E-mail: pjandres@datacomm.ch

ANDRETTI Mario Gabriele, b. 28 February 1940, Montona, Italy. Racing Driver. m. Dee Ann Hoch, 1961, 2 sons, 1 daughter. Appointments: Began midget car racing in US, graduating to US Auto Club National Formula; Indy Car National Champion, 1965, 1966, 1969, 1984; USAC Champion, 1965, 1966, 1969, 1974; Winner, Indianapolis 500 Miles, 1969; Winner, Daytona 500 Miles NASCAR Stock Car Race, 1967; Began Formula 1 Racing in 1968; World Champion, 1978; Third, 1977; Winner, International Race of Champions, 1979; President, MA 500 Inc, 1968-; Newman/Haas Racing, 1983; Honours: Driver of the Year, 1967, 1978, 1984; Driver of the Quarter Century, 1992; Driver of the Century, 1999-2000; All Time Indy Car Lap Leader (7587); Grand Prix Wins: South African (Ferrari); Japanese (Lotus Ford), 1976; US (Lotus Ford), 1977; Spanish (Lotus Ford), 1977; French (Lotus Ford), 1977; Italian (Lotus Ford), 1977; Argentine (Lotus Ford), 1978; Belgian (Lotus Ford), 1978; Spanish (Lotus Ford), 1978; French (Lotus Ford), 1978; German (Lotus Ford), 1978; Dutch (Lotus Ford), 1978; Commendatore dell'Ordine al Merito della Repubblica Italiana (known as the Commendatore), 2006. Address: 475 Rose Inn Avenue, Nazareth, PA 18064, USA.

ANDREW Christopher Robert, b. 18 February 1963, Richmond, Yorkshire, England. Rugby Football Player. m. Sara, 3 daughters. Education: Cambridge University. Appointments: Chartered Surveyor; Fly-half; Former Member, Middlesbrough, Cambridge University, Nottingham, Gordon, Sydney, Australia clubs; Member, 1987-91, 1992-96, Captain, 1989-90, Wasps Club; Toulouse, 1991-92; Barbarians, Newcastle, 1996-; International debut England versus Romania, 1985; Five nations debut, England Versus France, 1985; Captain, England Team, England versus Romania, Bucharest, 1989; Retired from International Rugby, 1995; Director of Rugby, Newcastle Rugby Football Club, 1995-2006; Elite Rugby Director, Rugby Football Union, 2006-. Publications: A Game and a Half, 1995. Honours: Record Holder for Drop

Goals in Internationals. Memberships: Grand Slam Winning Team. Address: c/o Rugby Football Union, Rugby House, Rugby Road, Twickenham TW1 1DS, England.

ANDREWS Anthony, b. 12 January 1948, Hampstead, London, England. Actor. m. Georgina Simpson, 1 son, 2 daughters. Career: Started acting, 1967; TV appearances include: Doomwatch, Woodstock, 1972, A Day Out, Follyfoot, Fortunes of Nigel, 1973, The Pallisers, David Copperfield, 1974, Upstairs Downstairs, 1975, French Without Tears, The Country Wife, Much Ado About Nothing, 1977, Danger UXB, 1978, Romeo and Juliet, 1979, Brideshead Revisited, 1980, Ivanhoe, 1982, The Scarlet Pimpernel, 1983, Colombo, 1988, The Strange Case of Dr Jekyll and Mr Hyde, 1989, Hands of a Murderer, 1990, Lost in Siberia, 1990, The Law Lord, 1991, Jewels, 1992, Ruth Rendell's Heartstones, Mothertime; David Copperfield, 2000; Love in a Cold Climate, 2001; Cambridge Spies, 2003; Marple: By the Pricking of my Thumbs, 2006. Films include: The Scarlet Pimpernel, Under the Volcano, A War of the Children, Take Me High, 1973, Operation Daybreak, 1975, Les Adolescents, 1976, The Holcroft Covenant, 1986, Second Victory, 1987, Woman He Loved, 1988, The Lighthorsemen, 1988, Hannah's War, 1988, Lost in Siberia, as actor and producer, 1990, Haunted, as actor and producer, 1995; Appeared in plays: 40 Years On, A Midsummer Night's Dream, Romeo and Juliet, One of Us, 1986, Coming into Land, 1986, Dragon Variation, Tima and the Conways; My Fair Lady, 2003. Address: c/o Peters Fraser and Dunlop Ltd, 503 The Chambers, Chelsea Harbour, London SW10 0XF, England.

ANDREWS Julie (Dame), b. 1 October 1935, Walton-on-Thames, Surrey, England. Singer; Actress. m. (1) Tony Walton, May 1959, divorced, 1 daughter; (2) Blake Edwards, 1969. Musical Education: Voice lessons with Lillian Stiles-Allen. Career: As actress: Debut, Starlight Roof, London Hippodrome, 1947; Appeared: Royal Command Performance, 1948; Broadway production, The Boy Friend, NYC, 1954; My Fair Lady, 1956-60; Camelot, 1960-62; Putting It Together, 1993; Film appearances include: Mary Poppins, The Americanization Of Emily, 1964; Torn Curtain, The Sound Of Music, Hawaii, 1966; Thoroughly Modern Millie, 1967; Stark, 1968; Darling Lili, 1970; The Tamarind Seed, 1973; 10, 1979; Little Miss Marker, 1980; S.O.B., 1981; Victor/Victoria, 1982; The Man Who Loved Women, 1983; That's Life!, Duet For One, 1986; The Sound of Christmas, TV, 1987; Relative Values, 1999; The Princess Diaries, 2001; Shrek 2 (voice), The Princess Diaries 2: Royal Engagement, 2004; Television debut, 1956; Host, The Julie Andrews Hour, 1972-73; Julie (comedy series), ABC-TV, 1992; Eloise at the Plaza, 2003; Eloise at Christmastime, 2003; Television films include Our Sons, 1991. Recordings: Albums: A Christmas Treasure, 1968; The Secret Of Christmas, 1977; Love Me Tender, 1983; Broadway's Fair, 1984; Love Julie, 1989; Broadway: The Music Of Richard Rogers, 1994; Here I'll Stay, Nobody Sings It Better, 1996; with Carol Burnett: Julie And Carol At Carnegie Hall, 1962; At The Lincoln Center, 1989; Cast and film soundtacks: My Fair Lady (Broadway cast), 1956; Camelot (Broadway cast), 1961; Mary Poppins (film soundtrack), 1964; The Sound Of Music (film soundtrack), 1965; The King And I (studio cast), 1992. Publications: Mandy (as Julie Edwards), 1971; The Last Of The Really Great Whangdoodles, 1974. Honours: Oscar, Mary Poppins, 1964; Golden Globe Awards, Hollywood Foreign Press Association, 1964, 1965; BAFTA Silver Mask, 1989; Kennedy Center Honor, 2001; SAG Life Achievement Award, 2007. Address: c/o Triad Artists, 10100 Santa Monica Boulevard, 16th Floor, Los Angeles, CA 90067, USA.

ANDSNES Leif Ove, b. 7 April 1970, Karmoy, Norway. Pianist. Education: Studied at the Music Conservatory of Bergen with Jiri Hlinka. Debut: Oslo, 1987; British debut, Edinburgh Festival with the Oslo Philharmonic, Mariss Jansons, 1989; US Debut, Cleveland Symphony, Neeme Järvi. Career: Appearances include: Schleswig-Holstein Festival and with orchestras such as Los Angeles Philharmonic, Japan Philharmonic, Berlin Philharmonic, London Philharmonic, Philharmonia, City of Birmingham Symphony Orchestra, Royal Scottish National Orchestra, BBC Philharmonic Orchestra for his debut at the Proms, 1992 and Chicago Symphony Orchestra; Soloist, Last Night of the Proms, 2002; Artistic Director, Risor Festival; Recitals at Teatro Communale, Bologna, Wigmore Hall, Barbican Hall, London, Herkulesaal, Munich, Concertgebouw, Amsterdam, Konzerthaus Vienna and Glasgow Royal Concert Hall. Recordings include: Grieg: A Minor and Liszt A Major concerti; Grieg: Lyric Pieces; Janacek, Solo Piano Music; Chopin, Sonatas and Grieg, Solo Piano Music; Brahmns and Schumann works for piano and viola with Lars Anders Tomter. Honours include: First Prize, Hindemith Competition, Frankfurt am Main; Levin Prize, Bergen, 1999; Norwegian Music Critics' Prize, 1988; Grieg Prize, Bergen, 1990; Dorothy B Chandler Performing Art Award, Los Angeles, 1992; Gilmore Prize, 1997; Instrumentalist Award, Royal Philharmonic Society, 2000; Gramophone Award, Best Concerto Recording, 2000; Best Instrumental Recording, 2002; Commander, Royal Norwegian Order of St Olav, 2002; Sibelius Prize, 2005; Spellemannpris, 2006. Address: c/o Kathryn Enticott, IMG Artists (Europe), Lovell House, 616 Chiswick High Road, London W4 5RX, England.

ANG Diing Shenp, b. 18 October 1969, Singapore. Professor. m. Foo Kwang Li (Evelyn), 1 son. Education: B Eng (Hons), 1994, PhD, Electrical Engineering, 1998, National University of Singapore. Appointments: Assistant Professor, National University of Singapore, 1998-2002; Assistant Professor, Nanyang Technological University, Singapore, 2002-. Publications: Numerous articles in professional journals. Honours: NTU Research Outstanding and Award Recognition, 2005, 2006; NUS Research Scholarship; Listed in international biographical dictionaries. Memberships: Institute of Electrical and Electronics Engineers. E-mail: edsang@ntu.edu.sg

ANG Hooi Hoon, b. 11 January 1964, Ipoh Perak, Malaysia. Lecturer; Researcher. Education: BPharm (Hons), 1988, PhD, 1993, University of Science, Malaysia; Admitted to PHP Institute, awarded Gold Medal, Doctoral Fellow, PHP Institute of Asia, Japan, 1995. Appointments: Graduate Assistant, School of Pharmaceutical Sciences, University of Science, Malaysia, 1988-90; Assistant Quality Control Manager, private pharmaceutical company, Ipoh Perak, 1992-93; Lecturer, 1994-2002, Associate Professor, 2002-, School of Pharmaceutical Sciences, University of Science, Malaysia. Publications: total of 300 publications. Honours: Awards from scientific institutions, fellowships, grants include: Third World Academy of Science, Trieste and Chinese Academy of Science Visiting Professorship, Beijing, February to April 1998; Awards: Young Investigator, European Societies of Chemotherapy, Stockholm, Sweden, 1998; Young Investigator, Science Council of Japan and Japanese Society of Parasitology, 1998; UNESCO Regional Office of Southeast Asia, Jakarta, 1998; Young Scientist and Technologist, ASEAN Committee of Science and Technology, Vietnam, 1998; Gold Star Award, Certificate of Achievement, International Woman of the Year Award, International Biographical Centre, England, 1998; International Woman of the Millennium, IBC, Cambridge, 1999; Postdoctoral Fellowship for Foreign

Researchers Awardee, Japan Society for the Promotion of Science, 1999-2000; American Medal of Honor, ABI, 2003. Memberships: Vice-Chairman, 1994-95, Honorary Secretary, 1995-, Malaysian Pharmaceutical Society, Penang; Malaysian Society of Parasitology and Tropical Medicine; Malaysian Microbiology Society; Japanese Society of Parasitology; Third World Academy of Science, Trieste; Institute of Biology, Queensberry, UK, 1998-. Address: School of Pharmaceutical Sciences, University of Science, Malaysia, Minden 11800, Penang, Malaysia.

ANG Peng Hwa, b. 20 November 1957, Singapore. Chair of School. m. Caroline Sai Lin Loy, 1 daughter. Education: Bachelor of Law, National University of Singapore, 1982; Postgraduate Practice Law Course, Board of Legal Education, Singapore, 1982; MA, Communication Management, University of Southern California, USA, 1988; PhD, Mass Media, Michigan State University, 1993. Appointments: Chair, School of Communication and Information; Associate Professor. Publications: 5 books; 18 book chapters; 9 peer reviewed publications; 11 invited publications; many others. Honours: Top Paper, 1993; Fellow, Harvard Information Infrastructure Project, 2000; Fulbright Award, 2000; Visiting Fellow, University of Oxford, 2001; Honorary Fellow, International University of Japan, 2001-07; Senior Fellow, Intellectual Property Academy, Singapore, 2003; Member, United Nation's Working Group on Internet Governance, 2004-05; Chairman, Inaugural Steering Committee, Global Internet Governance Academic Network, 2006; Listed in international biographical dictionaries. Memberships: International Communication Association, USA. Address: School of Communication and Information, Nanyang Technological University, 31 Nanyang Link, Singapore 637718. E-mail: tphang@ntu.edu.sg

ANGELOU Maya, b. 4 April 1928, St Louis, Missouri, USA. Author. Appointments: Associate editor, Arab Observer, 1961-62; Assistant administrator, teacher, School of Music and Drama, University of Ghana, 1963-66; Feature editor, African Review, Accra, 1964-66; Reynolds Professor of American Studies, Wake Forest University, 1981-; Teacher of modern dance, Rome Opera House, Hambina Theatre, Tel Aviv; Member, Board of Governors, Maya Angelou Institute for the Improvement of Child and Family Education, Winston-Salem State University, North Carolina, 1998-; Theatre appearances include: Porgy and Bess, 1954-55; Calypso, 1957; The Blacks, 1960; Mother Courage, 1964; Look Away, 1973; Roots, 1977; How to Make an American Quilt, 1995; Plays: Cabaret for Freedom, 1960; The Least of These, 1966; Getting' Up Stayed On My Mind, 1967; Ajax, 1974; And Still I Rise, 1976; Moon On a Rainbow Shawl (producer), 1988. Film: Down in the Delta (director), 1998. Publications include: I Know Why the Caged Bird Sings, 1970; Just Give Me A Cool Drink of Water 'Fore I Die, 1971; Georgia, Georgia (screenplay), 1972; Oh Pray My Wings Are Gonna Fit Me Well, 1975; Singin' and Swingin' and Gettin' Merry Like Christmas, 1976; And Still I Rise, 1976; The Heart of a Woman, 1981; Shaker, Why Don't You Sing, 1983; All God's Children Need Travelling Shoes, 1986; Now Sheba Sings the Song, 1987; I Shall Not Be Moved, 1990; Gathered Together in My Name, 1991; Wouldn't Take Nothing for my Journey Now, 1993; Life Doesn't Frighten Me, 1993; Collected Poems, 1994; My Painted House, My Friendly Chicken and Me, 1994; Phenomenal Woman, 1995; Kofi and His Magic, 1996; Even the Stars Look Lonesome, 1997; Making Magic in the World, 1998; A Song Flung up to Heaven, 2002. Honours: Horatios Alger Award, 1992; Grammy Award Best Spoken Word or Non-Traditional Album, 1994; Honorary Ambassador to

UNICEF, 1996-; Lifetime Achievement Award for Literature, 1999; National Medal of Arts; Distinguished visiting professor at several universities; Chubb Fellowship Award, Yale University; Nominated, National Book Award, I Know Why the Caged Bird Sings; Tony Award Nomination, Performances in Look Away; Honorary degrees, Smith College, Lawrence University; Golden Eagle Award; First Reynolds Professor; The Matrix Award; American Academy of Achievements Golden Plate Award; Distinguished Woman of North Carolina; Essence Woman of the Year; Many others. Memberships: The Directors Guild of America; Equity; AFTRA; Woman's Prison Association; Harlem Writers Guild; Horatio Alger Association of Distinguished Americans; National Society for the Prevention of Cruelty to Children. Address: Care Dave La Camera, Lordly and Dame Inc, 51 Church Street, Boston, MA 02116-5417, USA.

ANGUS Kenneth William, (Ken Angus), b. 13 August 1930, Rhu, Dunbartonshire, Scotland. Veterinary Pathologist. m. Marna Renwick Redpath, 4 November 1977, 1 son. Education: BVMS, Glasgow, 1955; FRCVS, 1976; DVM, Glasgow, 1985. Publications: Scotchpotch, 1995; Eechtie-Peechtie-Pandy, 1996; Wrack and Pinion, 1997; Breakfast with Kilroy, 2000; Only the Sound of Sparrows, 2001; Conversations with Hamsters, 2002; A Little Overnight Rain, 2004. Contributions to: New Writing Scotland; First Time; Cencrastus; Orbis; Poetry Scotland; Poetry Monthly; Poetry Life; Scarp (University of Wollongong, Berrima, Australia); Staple. Honours: Scottish International Poetry Competition, 1998. Memberships: Scottish Poetry Library; Poetry Association of Scotland. Address: 12 Temple Village, Gorebridge, Midlothian EH23 4SQ, Scotland.

ANIE Sylvia Josephine. Director of Policy Planning, Research, Monitoring and Evaluation. Education: BSc, 1st Class Honours, Applied Chemistry, University of Greenwich, England, 1982-86; PhD, Medical School, University of Manchester, England, 1986-90; Professional Certificate in Management, Open University Business School, England, 1995; Certificate, Principles and Practices of Behaviour Change Communication, Family Health International, 2001; Certificate, Strengthening Monitoring and Evaluation of National HIV/AIDS Programmes in the Context of the Expanded Response, MEASURE Evaluation, 2001; Certificate, Evaluation of AIDS Programmes, Makerere University, Uganda, 2002; Diploma: HIV and AIDS Prevention, College of Venereal Disease Prevention, London, 2004. Appointments: Junior Analyst, Drug Control and teaching Centre, Kings College, University of London, 1986; Teaching Assistant, Department of Pharmacy, University of Manchester, England, 1986-89; Postdoctoral Researcher, University College London/Institute of Neurology, University of London, 1990; Medical and Scientific Research Advisor, The Spastics Society, England, 1991-96; Deputy Chief Executive, Korle Bu Teaching Hospital, Ghana, 1997-2001; Director of Policy Planning, Research, Monitoring, Evaluation, Ghana AIDS Commission, Ghana, 2001-; Current Consultancies: World Bank; UNDP; Danida-Danish AID Programme; USAID Partners for Health Reformplus; UNDP-GOG; UNAIDS; IBIS NGO. Articles in scientific journals and reports as co-author include: Mutual health Organisations: A Quality Information Survey in Ghana, 2002; Contributor to: HIV/AIDS related knowledge, attitudes and behaviour. Demographic and Health Survey, Ghana, 2003; Balancing science, pragmatics and the need for collaboration in Ghana: How to be strategic in planning a national M/E system, 2004. Memberships: Fellow, Society of Medicine, UK; Professional Member and Chartered Chemist, Royal Society of Chemistry, UK; International Society of

Magnetic Resonance in Medicine. Address: Ghana AIDS Commission, PO Box CT 1836, Cantoments, Accra, Ghana. E-mail: sylviaanie@yahoo.com

ANISTON Jennifer, b. 11 February 1969, Sherman Oaks, California, USA. Actress. m. Brad Pitt, 2000, divorced 2005. Education: New York High School of the Performing Arts. Appointments: Theatre includes: For Dear Life; Dancing on Checker's Grave; Films include: Leprechaun, 1993; She's The One, Dream for an Insomniac, 'Til There Was You, 1996; Picture Perfect, 1997; The Object of My Affection, 1998; Office Space, The Iron Giant, 1999; Rock Star, 2001; The Good Girl, 2002; Bruce Almighty, 2003; Along Came Polly, 2004; Derailed, Rumor Has It, 2005; Room 10, Friends with Money, The Break-Up, 2006; The Senator's Wife, Diary, 2007; TV includes, Molloy (series), 1989; The Edge; Ferris Bueller; Herman's Head; Friends, 1994-2004. Honours: Emmy Award for Best Actress, 2002; Golden Globe for Best TV Actress in a Comedy, 2003. Address: c/o CAA, 9830 Wilshire Boulevard, Beverly Hills, CA 90212, USA.

ANN-MARGARET, b. 28 April 1941, Stockholm, Sweden. Actress; Singer; Dancer. m. Roger Smith, 1967. Appointments: Film Debut, Pocketful of Miracles, 1961; Films include: State Fair; Bye Bye Birdie; Once a Thief; The Cincinnati Kid; Stagecoach; Murderer's Row; C C & Co; Carnal Knowledge; RPM; Train Robbers; Tommy; The Twist; Joseph Andrews; Last Remark of Beau Geste; Magic; Middle Age Crazy; Return of the Soldier; I Ought to be in Pictures; Looking to Get Out; Twice in a Lifetime; 52 Pick-Up, 1987; New Life, 1988; Something More; Newsies, 1992; Grumpy Old Men, 1993; Grumpier Old Men, 1995; Any Given Sunday, 1999; The Last Producer, 2000; A Woman's a Helluva Thing, 2000; Interstate 60, 2002; Taxi, 2004; Mem-o-re, 2005; Tales of the Rat Fink (voice), The Break Up, The Santa Clause 3: The escape Clause, 2006; TV includes: Who Will Love My Children?, 1983; A Streetcar Named Desire, 1984; The Two Mrs Grenvilles, 1987; Our Sons, 1991; Nobody's Children, 1994; Following her Heart; Seduced by Madness; The Diana Borchardt Story, 1996; Blue Rodeo, 1996; Pamela Hanniman, 1999; Happy Face Murders, 1999; Perfect Murder, Perfect Town, 2000; The Tenth Kingdom, 2000; A Place Called Home, 2004; Also appears in cabaret. Publications: (with Todd Gold) Ann-Margaret: My Story, 1994. Honours: Five Golden Globe Awards; Three Female Star of the Year Awards. Address: William Morris Agency, 151 S, El Camino Drive, Beverly Hills, CA 90212, USA.

ANNAN Henry George, b. 23 October 1945, Accra, Ghana. Consultant Obstetrician and Gynaecologist. m. Zetha Melanie, 4 sons, 1 daughter. Education: Mfantsipim School, Ghana, 1959-65; Cambridge University and St Bartholomew's Hospital, 1966-73; MA (Cantab) MB B Chir, 1973; MRCOG, 1978; FRCOG, 1992; MEWI, 1996; FICS, 2003; FGCS, 2004; FFFP, 2005; DSc (Hon), 2005. Appointments: Consultant Obstetrician and Gynaecologist, Whipps Cross University Hospital, 1986-; Accredited Honorary Consultant to the Essex Fertility Centre; Recognised Clinical Teacher and Honorary Senior Lecturer, University of London, 1991-; Clinical Director, 1995-98; Examiner for RCOG, GMC (PLAB) and MBBS; RCOG College Tutor (1999-2005) and Preceptor in Minimal Access Surgery, 1997-; Council Member, Obstetrics and Gynaecology Section, RSM, 1987-90, 2005-08; RCOG Hospital Recognition Committee, 1997-2000; Member, International Editorial Advisory Board for Obstetrics and Gynaecology Today, 2001-; Trustee, London Consultants Association & Its Representative on HCSA; Trustee, Sudanese International Medical Academy; Course Organiser for MRCOG II in Sudan & Abu Dhabi, UAE, annually; Council Member, Selwyn College Association, 1989-91, 2005-2008; Honorary Treasurer, Section of Obstetrics and Gynaecology, Royal Society of Medicine, 2006-; Official Media Spokesperson for RCOG, 2006; External Examiner and Assessor, Fellowship of West African College of Surgeons (FWACS), 2006, 2007; External Examiner, MBBS Academy of Medical Sciences & Technology, Khartoum, 2007; Course Director, MRCOG Part II course, Madras Medical Mission, Chennai, India, 2007. Publications: Many publications in medical journals, 1980-; Presentations and lectures to healthcare professionals at local, regional, national and international meetings. Honours: Vice Chair, African Caribbean Medical Society, 1991-93; Justice of the Peace, 1996-2001; Governor, Epping Forest College, Freeman of the City of London, 1999; Professional Achievers Award for Medicine and for Innovation and Dedication, 2002; Gathering of Africa's Best Award for Achievement, 2003; DSc (Hon), Irish International University of Europe, 2005; Listed in Tatler's Best 150 Private Doctors in the UK, 2005-07. Memberships: British Society of Gynaecological Endoscopy; American Association of Gynecological Laparoscopists; International Continence Society; Royal Society of Medicine; Worshipful Society of Apothecaries of London; Founder Member, Expert Witness Institute; MCC; Guards Polo Club; ROSL; Oxford and Cambridge Club; Fellow, Atlantic Council of UK; Association of Medical Education for Africa, 2006. Address: Bachelors Hall, York Hill, Loughton, Essex IG10 1HZ, England. E-mail: henrygannan@ hotmail.com

ANNESLEY Hugh (Sir), b. 22 June 1939, Dublin, Ireland. Police Officer. m. Elizabeth Ann MacPherson, 1970, 1 son, 1 daughter. Appointments: Joined Metropolitan Police, 1958; Assistant Chief Constable of Sussex with special responsibility for personnel and training, 1976; Deputy Assistant Commissioner, Assistant Commissioner, 1985, Metropolitan Police; Head, Operations Department, Scotland Yard, 1987-89; Chief Constable, Royal Ulster Constabulary, 1989-96. Honours: Queen's Police Medal. Memberships: National Executive Institute, Federal Bureau of Investigation, 1986; Executive Committee, Interpol, British Representative, 1987-90, 1993-94; Member, 1997, Chair, 2000-, Board of Governors, Hill School for Girls. Address: c/o Brooklyn, Knock Road, Belfast BT5 6LE, Northern Ireland.

ANNIS Francesca, b. 14 May 1944, London, England. Actress. 1 son, 2 daughters. Appointments: with Royal Shakespeare Company, 1975-78; Plays include: The Tempest; The Passion Flower Hotel; Hamlet; Troilus and Cressida; Comedy of Errors; The Heretic; Mrs Klein; Rosmersholm; Lady Windermere's Fan; Hamlet; Films include: Cleopatra; Saturday Night Out; Murder Most Foul; The Pleasure Girls; Run With the Wind; The Sky Pirates; The Walking Stick; Penny Gold; Macbeth; Krull; Dune; Under the Cherry Moon; Golden River; El Rio de Oro; The Debt Collector; the End of the Affair; TV includes: Great Expectations; Children in Uniform; Love Story; Danger Man; The Human Jungle; Lily Langtry (role of Lily); Madam Bovary; Partners in Crime; Coming Out of Ice; Why Didn't They Ask Evans?; Magnum PI; Inside Story; Onassis - The Richest Man in the World, 1990; Parnell and the Englishwoman, 1991; Absolute Hell, 1991; The Gravy Train, 1991; Weep No More My Lady, 1991; Between the Lines, 1993; Reckless, 1997; Deadly Summer, 1997; Wives and Daughters, 1999; Milk, 1999; Deceit, 2000; Copenhagen, 2002; The Libertines, 2005. Address: c/o ICM, 76 Oxford Street, London, W1N 0AX, England.

ANOMOHANRAN Ochuko, b. 10 May 1967, Eku, Nigeria. Lecturer. m. Eguono Anomohanran, 2 daughters. Education: BSc, Physics, Bendel State University, Ekpoma, Nigeria, 1990; MSc, Geophysics, Ambrose Alli University, Ekpoma, Nigeria, 1996. Appointments: Physics Lecturer, Bauchi State Polytechnic, Nigeria, 1990-91; Physics and Mathematics Tutor, Ziks Grammar School, Sapele, Nigeria, 1991-92; Physics Lecturer, Delta State University, Abraka, Nigeria, 1992-. Publications: A survey of x-ray diagnostic services in Delta State Nigeria; The effect of gamma irradiation on the germination and growth of certain Nigerian agricultural crops; Comparative study of environmental noise in parts of Delta State, Nigeria; The use of 3rd degree polynomal for accurate conversion of time to depth; Energy generation, uses and distribution; The sky and its content. Honour: Outstanding Scientist of the 21st Century. Memberships: Institute of Physics, London; Science Association of Nigeria; Nigeria Institute of Physics. Address: Physics Department, Delta State University, PMB 1, Abraka, Delta State, Nigeria. E-mail: mrochuko@yahoo.com

ANONGBA Patrick Norbert B, b. 3 February 1960, Abidjan, Cote D'Ivoire. Physicist; Educator. m. Maria Teresa Varela, 2 sons, 1 daughter. Education: Physical Engineer, Department of Physics, 1985, DSc, 1989, Ecole Polytechnique Fédérale de Lausanne. Appointments: Assistant, Ecole Polytechnique Fédérale de Lausanne, 1985-90; Postdoctoral Research Associate, Institut de Physique Expérimentale, Université de Lausanne, 1990-92; Research Associate, Max-Planck-Institut für Metallforschung, Stuttgart, Germany, 1992-94; Assistant Professor, 1995-97, Associate Professor, 1997-, UFR Sciences des Structures de la Matière et de Technologie, Université de Cocody, Cote d'Ivoire. Publications: Several articles in professional journals. Honours include: Research Fellow, Max-Planck-Institut-Gesellschaft, 1992-94, Japan Society for the Promotion of Science, 1996-97; Fulbright Research Fellow, Department of Materials, Science and Engineering, University of Pennsylvania, 2000-01; Visiting Professor, Universidad Politécnica de Cataluña, Spain, 2002-03. Memberships: Swiss Physical Society; New York Academy of Sciences; Japan Society for the Promotion of Science. Address: UFR Sciences des Structures de la Matière et de Technologie, Université de Cocody, Cote d'Ivoire. E-mail: anongba@yahoo.fr

ANPUTHAS Markandu, b. 10 July 1970, Inuvil, Sri Lanka. Biometrician. Education: BS, Agriculture, Faculty of Agriculture, 1997, Master of Philosophy, Biostatistics, Postgraduate Institute of Agriculture, 2004, University of Peradeniya. Appointments: Research Assistant, Department of Economics, University of Peradeniya, 1997; National Data Collection Consultant, FAO and Department of Agriculture, Sri Lanka, 1998-99; Monitoring and Evaluation Co-ordinator, Care International, Sri Lanka, 1999-2001; Biometrician, International Water Management Institute, 2002-. Publications: Numerous papers and articles in professional journals; Conference, workshops and symposium proceedings. Honours: Merit, Higher Education Scholar, Ministry of Higher Education, Government of Sri Lanka, 1993; Best Presenter Award for Statistics, Postgraduate Institute of Agriculture, 2003. Memberships: Life Member, Applied Statistics Association of Sri Lanka; International Biometric Society. Address: KKS Road, Inuvil East, Maruthanarmadam, Jaffna, Sri Lanka. E-mail: m.anputhas@cgiar.org

ANSARI Naseem Akhtar, b. 8 January 1968, Muzaffarpur, India. Pathologist. m. Jihad Taiseer Al-Ratrout, 1 son. Education: BSc, Pharmacology, 1986-89, MBBS, 1986-92, St Bartholomew's Hospital Medical School, University of London; MRCPath, Royal College Pathologists, London, 2001; Certified Specialist, Training Authority, Medical Royal Colleges, UK, 2001; Specialist Registration, General Medical Council, London, 2001. Appointments: Pathologist, Centres for Disease Control & Prevention, Atlanta, Francistown, Botswana, 1997-98; Consultant, Histopathologist, Royal London Hospital, 2001-02; Associate Professor, Pathology, College of Medicine and Medical Sciences, Arabian Gulf University, Bahrain, 2002-; Consultant Histopathologist, Salmaniya Medical Complex, Bahrain, 2002-. Publications: Mortality and Pathology of HIV/AIDS in Botswana; RANTES expression in inflammatory bowel disease; Clinicopathological characteristics of malignant eccrine poroma; The use of immunohistochemistry for the differential diagnosis of malignant hepatic tumors in Bahrain; The importance of endothelins in canine physiology (work done with Nobel Prize winner, Professor Sir John Vane). Honours: Roxburgh Prize in Dermatology, St Bartholomew's Hospital Medical School, University of London, 1991; Neuropathology Prize, King's College Hospital, London, 1991; Grantee, Arabian Gulf University, 2004-05. Memberships: The Royal College of Pathologists; Association of Clinical Pathologists; International Academy of Pathology, British Division; Fellow, Royal Society of Medicine; Bahrain Association of Pathologists; Bahrain Medical Society; Advanced Board of Editors, Bahrain Medical Bulletin. Address: Arabian Gulf University, PO Box 22979, Manama, Bahrain. E-mail: ansarnas@hotmail.com

ANSARI S M Razaullah, b. 8 April 1932, Delhi, India. Physicist originally, presently Historian of Science. m. (1) Annemarie, (2) Shaukat Nihal, 1 son, 3 daughters. Education: BS (Honours), Physics, 1953, MSc, Physics, 1955, Delhi University; DSc (dr rer nat), Karl-Eberhardt University, Tübingen, Germany, 1966; Certificate in German, Goethe Institute, Munich, 1959; Certificate, Diploma in Russian Language, Aligarh Muslim University, 1981, 1982. Appointments: Retired Professor of Physics, Aligarh Muslim University, Aligarh; Historian of Science, especially History of Exact Science in Medieval India and Islamic Countries; Established Department of History of Medicine and Science, Hamdard Institute, New Delhi, Professor and Head, 1984-86; Editor, Studies in History of Medicine and Science, 1984-2000; President, IUHPS Commission for History of Ancient and Medieval Astronomy, 2001-05, re-elected, 2005-09; Present research fields: working on astronomical Zijes (tables) compiled in India and History of exact science in Medieval India. Publications: 1 monograph, Introduction of Modern Western Astronomy in India, 1985; 2 edited volumes: History of Oriental Astronomy, 2002; Science and Technology in the Islamic World, 2002; 80 papers in international and national journals; 25 conference reports; 3 research projects. Honours: Former Fellow, Alexander von Humboldt Foundation (Bonn), 1959-62; Former President, IAU-IUHPS Commission for History of Astronomy, 1997-2001; IUHPS Commission for Islamic Science & Technology, 1993-97; Former President, IAU Commission for History of Astronomy, 1994-97; President, IUHPS Commission for History of Ancient and Medieval Astronomy, 2005-09. Memberships: Editorial Board of Indian Journal of History of Science, New Delhi; International Academy of History of Science, Paris, 1997; International Astronomical Union (IAU), 1973-; Elected Fellow, Royal Astronomical Society, 1972; Life Member, Indian Astronomical Society; Life Member, Indian Society for History of Mathematics; IUHPS Council (Executive), elected 1989-93, 1994-97; Consultant on international project, Islamic Scientific Manuscripts Initiative, sponsored by Max Planck Institute of History of Science, Berlin and

MacGill University, Montreal; Secretary, Ibn Sina Academy of Medieval Medicine and Sciences, Aligarh, India. Address: Roshan Villa, Muzammil Manzil Compound, Dodhpur, Aligarh 202002, India. E-mail: raza.ansari@gmx.net

ANSELME Jean-Pierre Louis Marie, b. 22 September 1936, Port-au-Prince, Haiti. Professor. m. Marie-Céline Carrié, 3 daughters. Education: BA, Letters and Philosophy, St Martial College, Port-au-Prince, Haiti, 1955; BSc, Chemistry, Fordham University, Bronx, New York, 1959; PhD, Organic Chemistry, Polytechnic Institute of Brooklyn, New York, 1963. Appointments: Postdoctoral Fellow, 1963, 1965, Instructor, 1965, Polytechnic Institute of Brooklyn, New York; Assistant Professor, 1965-68, Associate Professor, 1968-70, Professor, 1970-, University of Massachusetts at Boston, Massachusetts; Visiting Professor, Kyushu University, Fukuoka, Japan, 1972; Visiting Professor, University of Miami, Florida, 1979. Publications: 117 publications as author and co-author in professional national and international journals; Co-author and editor of 2 books; Numerous invited lectures; Papers at international, national, regional and local meetings. Honours: 15 sponsored projects; Seymour Shapiro Award as Outstanding Graduate Student, Polytechnic Institute of Brooklyn, 1963; NSF Postdoctoral Fellow, Institut für Organische Chemie, Munich, Germany, 1964; Fellow, A P Sloan Foundation, 1969-71; Invited Lecturer, Fourth Cork Conference, Ireland, 1971; Invited Lecturer, Chemical Society of Japan, 1972; Fellow, Japan Society for the Promotion of Science, 1972; Honoree, Citizens' Committee for Immigration Reform, New York, 1982; Listed in numerous national and international biographical dictionaries and Who's Who publications. Memberships: Sigma Xi; Phi Lambda Upsilon; American Chemical Society; Royal Chemical Society, London. Address: Department of Chemistry, University of Massachusetts, Harbor Campus, Boston, MA 02125-3393, USA.

ANSTEE John Howard, b. 25 April 1943, Neyland, Milford Haven, England. Scientific Director. m. Angela J Young. Education: Milford Haven Grammar School; BSc, PhD, Nottingham University. Appointments: Senior Demonstrator, Zoology, 1968, Lecturer, Senior Lecturer, Professor, 1996-, Biological Sciences, Deputy Dean, Faculty of Science, 1991-94, Dean of Science, 1994-97, Pro Vice Chancellor, 1997-2000, Pro Vice Chancellor and Subwarden, 2000-04, Emeritus Professor of Biological Sciences, 2004-, University of Durham; Netpark Scientific Director, 2004-, County Durham Development Company; Directorships held in a number of companies involved in knowledge and technology transfer. Publications: Contributed chapters to books; Numerous articles to peer-reviewed scientific journals. Honours: Deputy Lieutenant for County Durham. Memberships: Fellow, Royal Entomological Society; Fellow, Zoological Society; Member, Society for Experimental Biology; Member, Company of Biologists. Address: 35 Albert Street, Western Hill, Durham DH1 4RJ, England. E-mail: john.anstee@durham.gov.uk

ANSTEE Margaret Joan (Dame), b. 25 June 1926, Writtle, Essex, England. United Nations Official; Lecturer; Consultant; Author. Education: Modern and Medieval Languages, Newnham College, Cambridge, 1944-47; MA, Newnham College, 1955; BSc, Economics, London University, 1964. Appointments: Lecturer in Spanish, Queen's University, Belfast, 1947-48; Third Secretary, Foreign Office, 1948-52; Administrative Officer, UN Technical Assistance Board, Manila, 1952-54; Spanish Supervisor, University of Cambridge, 1955-56; Officer-in-Charge, UN Technical Assistance Board, Bogota, 1956-57, Resident Representative, Uruguay, 1957-59, Bolivia, 1960-65; Resident Representative,

UNDP Ethiopia and UNDP Liaison Officer, ECA, 1965-67; Senior Economic Adviser, Office of Prime Minister, London, 1967-68; Senior Assistant to Commissioner in charge of study of Capacity of UN Development System, 1968-69; Resident Representative, UNDP, Morocco, 1969-72, Chile (also UNDP Liaison Officer with ECLA) 1972-74; Deputy to UN Under Secretary General in charge of UN Relief Operation to Bangladesh and Deputy Co-ordinator of UN Emergency Assistance to Zambia, 1973; Deputy Regional Director for Latin America, UNDP, New York, 1974-78; Deputy Assistant Administrator and Head, UNDP Administrator's Special Unit, 1975-77; Assistant Secretary-General of UN, Department of Technical Co-operation for Development), 1978-87; Special Representative of Secretary-General to Bolivia, 1982-92, for co-ordination of earthquake relief assistance to Mexico, 1985-87; Under Secretary-General, UN, 1987-93, Director-General of UN office at Vienna, Head of Centre for Social Development and Humanitarian Affairs, 1987-92, Special Representative of Secretary-General for Angola and Head of Angolan Verification Mission, 1992-93; Adviser to UN Secretary-General on peacekeeping, post-conflict peacebuilding and training troops for UN peacekeeping missions, 1994-; Chair, Advisory Group of Lessons Learned Unit, Department of Peacekeeping Operations, UN, 1996-2002; Co-ordinator of UN Drug Control Related Activities, 1987-90, of International Co-operation for Chernobyl, 1991-92; Secretary-General, 8th UN Congress on Prevention of Crime and Treatment of Offenders, August 1990; Writer, lecturer, consultant and adviser (ad honorem) to Bolivian Government, 1993-97, 2002-. Publications: The Administration of International Development Aid, 1969; Gate of the Sun: A Prospect of Bolivia, 1970; Africa and the World, 1970; Orphan of the Cold War: The Inside Story of the Collapse of the Angolan Peace Process, 1992-93, 1996; Never Learn to Type: A woman at the United Nations, 2003, 2nd edition, 2004. Memberships: Member, Advisory Board, UN Studies at Yale University, 1996-; Member, Advisory Council, Oxford Research Group, 1997-; Member, Advisory Board, UN Intellectual History Project, 1999-; Trustee, Helpage International, 1994-97; Patron and Board Member, British Angola Forum, 1998-; Member, President Carter's International Council for Conflict Resolution, 2001-; Vice President, UK UN Association, 2002-; Member, Editorial Board, Global Governance, 2004-. Honours: Honorary Fellow, Newnham College, Cambridge, 1991; Dr h c (Essex), 1994; Honorary LLD (Westminster), 1996; Honorary DSc (Economics) (London), 1998; Hon LLD, (Cambridge) 2004; Reves Peace Prize, William & Mary College, USA, 1993; Commander, Ouissam Alaouite, Morocco, 1972; Dama Gran Cruz Condor of the Andes, Bolivia, 1986; Grosse Goldene Ehrenzeichen am Bande, Austria, 1993; Dame Commander of the Most Distinguished Order of St Michael and St George, 1994; Gran Caballero, Orden de Bernardo O'Higgins, Chile, 2007. Address: c/o PNUD, Casilla 9072, La Paz, Bolivia; c/o The Walled Garden, Knill, Nr Presteigne, Powys LD8 2PR, United Kingdom.

ANTONSSON Haukur, b. 6 April 1947, Dalvik, Iceland. Education: Menntaskolinn A Akureyri, 1967. Career: Astrophysics; Cosmology; Mathematics. Publications: The Big Bang Paradox: Mathematics Changing with Time. Memberships: New York Academy of Sciences. Address: Lokastig 4 NH-TH, PO Box 33, IS-620 Dalvik, Iceland.

ANTWI-BOASIAKO Richmond, b. 18 March 1976, Effiduasi, Ashanti, Ghana. Broadcast Journalist. m. Barbara, 2 sons. Education: Certificate in Radio Broadcasting, Medianet Professional Radio Training School, Kumasi; Certificate in News and Feature Writing, London, 1998; Diploma in Journalism, Kumasi, 1999; Diploma in Integrated Missions Theology, Kumasi, 2001; Diploma, Travel and Tourism Management, Ghana Institute of Management and Aviation Studies, Ghana, 2006; Doctor of Administration, Yeshua International School of Theology, USA, 2007; Certificate in Broadcasting, Commonwealth Broadcasting Association, UK; Diploma in Newspaper Reporting, ICM, UK; Certificate in Broadcast Journalism, GIJ, Accra. Appointments: Feature journalist, The Pioneer, 1998-2000; Industrial Attachment, Luv FM, Kumasi, 1999-2000; Teacher, Perseverence Preparatory & JSS, Effiduasi, Ashanti, 1999-2001; Correspondent, Asante Tribune, 2000-01; Stringer, Ghanaian Chronicle, Golden Spear, 2000-02; Programmes Manager, Spirit FM, Kumasi, 2003-05; Hosted various radio programmes; Lecturer in Bible Study Methods, Heaven Life Theological College, Effiduasi, Ashanti; Co-founder, Heaven Life Ministries, Effiduasi, Ashanti; Currently, Broadcast Journalist, Solid FM. Publications: various newspaper articles, 1998-2000. Honours: Dedicated Statesman Committed to the welfare of Ghana; Best Gospel Presenter for the Ashanti Region of Ghana; Diploma, Certificate of Biblical Studies, International School of Ministry, USA. Membership: Heavenlife Ministries, Ghana. Address: PO Box 265, Effiduasi, Ashanti, Ghana, West Africa. E-mail: richboasko36@yahoo.com

ANTYPAS Spyridon, b. 29 August 1950, Athens, Greece. Paediatric Surgeon. m. Aneza Koytroypis, 1 son, 1 daughter. Education: Diploma of Medicine, University of Athens, 1976; Appointments: Assistant in Surgery, Kinderkrankenhaus, Koeln, Germany, 1977-79; Marine Hospital, Athens, 1980-81; Therapeutimion IKA, 1981-82; Assistant in Paediatric Surgery, Children's Hospital, Aghia Sophia, 1983-86; Lic, Paediatric Surgery, Nomarch's Office of Attica, Greece, 1986; Dr of Med, 1988. Appointments: Consultant, Paediatric Surgeon, 1986-; Associate Director, Academic and Research Activities, Tottori University, Urology Clinic, Yonago, Japan, 1992-93; University of Kentucky, Andrology Unit, Lexington, 1993; Gastarzt, Berlin Freie Universitat, 1989; Gastarzt, Children's Surgical Hospital, Koeln, Germany, 1993. Publications: Research in treatment of Mediastinal Tumours in childhood; Varicocele; Cryptochidism; Male Infertility; Elongating Spermatids for the treatment of Azoospermia; Relationship between Y chromasome micro deletions and testicular maldescent. Honours: Various awards, Greek Association of Pediatric Surgeons; Award, 10th Annual Meeting, ESHRE, 1994. Memberships: European Association of Pediatric Surgeons; General Secretary, Greek Association of Pediatric Surgeons; British Association of Paediatric Surgeons. Address: Children's Hospital, Aghia Sophia, 11573 Athens, Greece.

ANTZELEVITCH Charles, b. 25 March 1951, Israel. Executive Director. m. Brenda, 24 June 1973, 1 son, 1 daughter. Education: BA, Queens College, City University of New York, Flushing, 1973; PhD, University of New York at Syracuse, 1978. Appointments: Postdoctoral Fellow, Experimental Cardiology Department, Masonic Medical Research Laboratory, Utica, New York, 1977-80; Assistant Professor, Pharmacology Department, SUNY Health Science Centre, Syracuse, 1980-83; Research Scientist, Experimental Cardiology, Masonic Medical Research Laboratory, 1980-83; Associate Professor, Pharmacology Department, SUNY Health Science Centre, 1983-86; Senior Research Scientist, Experimental Cardiology, Masonic Medical Research Laboratory, 1984; Executive Director, Director of Research, 1984-, Gordon K Moe Scholar, 1987-, Masonic Medical Research Laboratory; Professor of Pharmacology, SUNY Health

Science Centre, 1995-. Publications: Numerous articles in professional journals. Honours include: Distinguished Service Award, RAM Medical Research Foundation, 1994; Charles Henry Johnson Medal, Grand Lodge F and AM, NYS, 1996; Distinguished Scientist Award, NASPE, 2002; Excellence in Cardiovascular Science Award, NE Affiliate AHA, 2003; Carl J Wiggers Lecturer, American Journal of Physiology, 2007; Gordon K Moe Lecturer, Cardiac Electrophysiology Society, 2006. Memberships: AHA; Association for the Advancement of Science; FASEB; APS; Cardiac Electrophysiology Society; Upstate New York Cardiac Electrophysiology Society; New York Academy of Sciences; Heart Rhythm Society; ISHR; ISCE. Address: Masonic Medical Research Laboratory, 2150 Bleecker Street, Utica, NY 13501, USA.

ANWYL Shirley Anne, b. 10 December 1940, Johannesburg, South Africa. Circuit Judge. m. Robin H C Anwyl, 2 sons. Education: BA, 1960, LLB, 1963, Rhodes University South Africa. Appointments: Called to South African Bar, 1963; Called to Bar of England and Wales by Inner Temple, 1966; Master of the Bench of Inner Temple, 1985; Recorder, 1981-95; Member of Criminal Injuries Compensation Board, 1980-95; President, Mental Health Review Tribunals, 1983-95; Deputy High Court Judge (Family Division), 1981-; Circuit Judge, 1995-; Resident Judge of Woolwich Crown Court, 1999-2007. Honours: Queen's Counsel, 1979; Freeman of the City of London, 1994. Memberships: Senate of Inns of Court and Bar, 1978-81; General Council of the Bar, 1987-88; Chairman, Barristers Benevolent Association, 1989-95; Royal Society of Arts, 1989-; Worshipful Company of Fruiterers, 1996-. Address: Snaresbrook Crown Court, 75 Hollybush Hill, London E11 1QW, England.

APASOV M Alexander, b. 13 June 1950, Gorno-Altaisk, Russia. Physicist; Educator. m. Galina Vasilyevna Yemets, 1 son. Education: Engineer-Physicist, Tomsk Polytechnical Institute, 1967-73; Postgraduate, 1981-85; Candidate of Science, 1991; Associate Professor, 2000; Doctor of Science, 2002. Appointments: Laboratory Assistant, Joint Institute for Nuclear Research, Dubna, USSR, 1971-73; Senior Laboratory Assistant, Physical Energetic Institute, Obninsk, 1973-75; Engineer-Designer, Bolshevik Works, Leningrad, 1975-77; Chief of the Laboratory, Machine Works, Yurga, 1977-92; Chief of the Office, Abrasive Works, Yurga, 1992-95; Vice Director, 1995-96, Department Head, Dean, 1995-2007, Tomsk Polytechnic University Branch, Yurga, Russia. Publications: Welding Destruction (monograph), 2002; Special Electometallurgy (textbook), 2003; Physical Foundation of Non-Destructive Testing During Welding (monograph), 2004; Materials Sciences (textbook), 2005; Introduction in the Theory and Technology of Manufacture Special Steels (textbook), 2006; Method to Analyse Failure of Welded Joints (Certificate); Method of Non-Melting Revealing (patent); Other patents and articles. Honours: Prize-Winner (Laureate) Nuclear Physics, Obninsk, 1974; Prize-Winner (Laureate) Technical Physics, Yurga, 1980; Tomsk Polytechnic University, Associate Professor of the Year Contest Winner, 2003; Contest Winner, The best textbook of the Kemerovo Region (Kuzbass), 2006; Honoured Scientist and Educator of Russian Federation, Moscow, 2007. Memberships: Deputy, Town Soviet of People's Deputies, 1990-95, 1997-99; First Lieutenant, Russian Military. Address: Moskovskay str. 26, Apart. 4, Yurga, Kemerovo Region, Russia 652050. E-mail: mchm@ud.tpu.edu.ru

APPIAH James Peter King, b. 16 February 1951, Baman, Kumasi, Ghana. Writer; Poet; Apostle. m. Angela Mabel Asare, 1 daughter. Education: Unesco Certificate in Writing and Publishing, 1972; Certificate of Completion, Morris Cerullo School of Ministry, San Diego, 1981; BA, Literary Studies, Pacific Western University, 1990; Diploma in Journalism, Story Writing, ICS Scranton, 1993; PhD, English Grade A, Washington International University, USA, 2001; Masters Degree in Biblical Studies, 2004, Grade A, Florida Christian University, Orlando, Florida. USA. Appointments: Library Assistant, Ghana Library, 1973-76; Founder, President, Followers of Christ International Church, FOCIC, 1974; Director, Adonten Literary Works, Kumasi, 1976-95; Ordained Bishop, Universal Ministries, 1980 President, Founder, Director, Editor in Chief, Appiah Esthermat Ltd, 1995; Feed the Poor and Preach the Gospel Ministries, 2002. Publications: The Lord of Praise, 1988; Prayer, The Key to a Triumphant Christian Living, 1992; Overcomers in the Blood, 1995; The Meaning of Pentecost, 1995; Ode to the Dead, Dedicated to the Princess of the People, 1998; Many other publications. Honours: Mondello Poetry International Award, First Prize, 1987; Honoured, City of Palermo (Unione Quartieri), 1988; Deputy Governor, ABI, 1999; Appointed to Research Board of Advisors, ABI, 2002; Selected among 500 Leading Intellectuals of the World and Great Minds of the Century, ABI, 2002; American Medal of Honor, ABI, 2003; Ambassador of Grand Eminence, ABI, 2004. Memberships: Morris Cerullo World Evangelism, Italy 1995-; United Christians Association in Italy, 1996; United Christians Association, 1998-; Ghana Young Pioneers; Ghana Youth Club; Ghana Association of Writers; United Christian Association; Christian Writers Forum; Member of the Adonten Royal Family of Asante, Mansa Nana. Address: Via Tignale del Garde 60, 41100 Modena, Italy.

APPLEBY Malcolm Arthur, b. 6 January 1946, West Wickham, Kent, England. Artist, Designer and Engraver. m. Philippa Swann, 1 daughter. Education: Beckenham School of Art; Ravensbourne College of Art; Central School of Arts and Crafts; Sir John Cass School of Art; Royal College of Art. Career: Held one-man art exhibition, Aberdeen Art Gallery, 1998: Is now the top gun engraver in the UK, famous for his Raven Gun which is housed in the Royal Armouries: the seal for the Victoria and Albert Museum and the silver centrepiece for the New Scottish Parliament. Honours: Littledale Scholar, 1969; Liveryman, Worshipful Company of Goldsmiths, 1991; Hon D Litt, Heriot-Watt, 2000. Memberships: Founder member and Chairman of the British Art Postage Stamp Society; Member of the British Art Medal Society and the Society for the Protection of Ancient Buildings. Address: Aultbeag, Grandtully, by Aberfeldy, Perthshire PH15 2QU, Scotland.

APTED Michael, b. 10 February 1941, Aylesbury, England. Film Director. Education: Cambridge University. Career: Researcher, Granada TV, 1963; Investigative Reporter, World in Action; Director debut as feature film director, The Triple Echo, 1972; Other films include Stardust, 1975; The Squeeze, 1977; Agatha, 1979; Coal Miner's Daughter, 1980; Continental Divide, 1981; Gorky Park, 1983; Firstborn, 1984; Critical Condition, Gorillas in the Mist, 1988; Class Action, 1991; Incident at Oglala, Thunderheart, 1992; Moving the Mountain, 1993; Nell, Blink, 1994; Extreme Measures, 1996; Enigma, 2001; Enough, 2002; Amazing Grace, 2006. Television films and direction: Coronation Street episodes; The Lovers comedy series; Folly Foot children's series; Another Sunday and Sweet F A, Kisses at Fifty, Poor Girl; Jack Point; P'tang Yang Kipperbang, 1984; New York News, 1994; Rome (mini-series), 2006; UP document series including 28 UP, 35 UP, 42 UP; Always Outnumbered. Honours: Several British Academy Awards including Best Dramatic Director.

Memberships: President of the Directors Guild of America. Address: Michael Apted Film Co, 1901 Avenue of the Stars, Suite 1245, Los Angeles, CA 90067, USA.

AQUINO Corazon (Cory), b. 25 January 1933, Manila, Philippines. Politician. m. Benigno S Aquino Jnr, 1954, assassinated 1983, 1 son, 4 daughters. Education: Mount St Vincent College, New York; Lived in USA in exile with husband, 1980-83. Appointments: President, Philippines, post-Marcos, 1986-92. Membership: United Nationalist Democratic Organization, 1985-; William Fulbright Prize for International Peace, 1996; Ramon Magsaysay Award for International Understanding, 1998. Address: 25 Times Street, Quezon City, Philippines.

ARAGALL GARRIGA Giacomo (Jaime), b. 6 June 1939, Barcelona, Spain. Tenor. Education: Studied with Francesco Puig in Barcelona and with Vladimir Badiali in Milan. Debut: La Fenice, Venice, 1963 in the first modern performance of Verdi's Jerusalem. Career: La Scala Milan in 1963 as Mascagni's Fritz; In 1965 sang in Haydn's Le Pescatrici with Netherlands Opera and at the Edinburgh Festival; Vienna Staatsoper debut in 1966 as Rodolfo in La Bohème; Covent Garden debut in 1966 as the Duke of Mantua; Metropolitan Opera debut in 1968; Guest appearances in Berlin, Italy, San Francisco and at the Lyric Opera Chicago; Sang at San Carlo Opera Naples in 1972 in a revival of Donizetti's Caterina Cornaro; Festival appearances at Bregenz and Orange in 1984 as Cavaradossi and Don Carlos; Sang Gabriele Adorno at Barcelona in 1990 and Don Carlos at the Orange Festival in 1990; Sang Rodolfo at Barcelona in 1991 and Don Carlos at the Deutsche Oper Berlin, 1992; Sang Cavaradossi at the Opéra Bastille, 1994. Other roles include Pinkerton, Romeo in I Capuleti e i Montecchi, Werther and Gennaro in Lucrezia Borgia. Recordings: La Traviata; Lucrezia Borgia; Faust; Rigoletto; Simon Boccanegra; Madama Butterfly. Address: c/o Stafford Law Associates, 6 Barham Close, Weybridge, Surrey KT13 9PR, England.

ARAI Asao, b. 10 January 1954, Chichibu, Saitama. Mathematician; Mathematical Physicist; University Professor. m. Sayoko Anada, 1 daughter. Education: BS, Chiba University, 1976; MS, University of Tokyo, 1979; DS, Gakushuin University, 1986. Appointments: Assistant Professor, Tokyo Institute of Technology, 1980-86; Lecturer, 1986-92, Associate Professor, 1992-95, Professor, 1995-, Hokkaido University. Publications: Mathematics of Symmetry, 1993, in Japanese; Hilbert Space and Quantum Mechanics, 1997, in Japanese; Quantum Field Theory and Statistical Mechanics, 1988, in Japanese; Mathematical Structures of Quantum Mechanics, 1999, in Japanese; Fock Spaces and Quantum Fields, 2000, in Japanese; Mathematical Principles of Physical Phenomena, 2003, in Japanese; Handbook of Modern Mathematical Physics, 2005, in Japanese; Mathematical Principles of Quantum Phenomena, 2006, in Japanese; Many articles in professional journals. Listed in: Biographical Publication. Memberships: New York Academy of Sciences; International Association of Mathematical Physics; The Mathematical Society of Japan. Address: Department of Mathematics, Hokkaido University, Sapporo 060 0810, Japan.

ARAI Hideo, b. 25 December 1931, Dalian, China. Microbiologist. m. Kiyoko Ninomiya, 2 sons, 1 daughter. Education: BS, Science University of Tokyo, Japan, 1957; PhD, University of Tsukuba, Japan, 1990. Appointments: Researcher, Laboratory of Taxonomy and Preservation of Micro-organisms, Institute of Applied Microbiology, University of Tokyo, 1962-70; Researcher, 1970-76, Head,

DICTIONARY OF INTERNATIONAL BIOGRAPHY

1977-91, Biology Research Section, Director, Department of Conservation Science, 1992-93, Emeritus Researcher, 1993-, Tokyo National Research Institute of Cultural Properties; Expert in biodeterioration of cultural property. Publications: Achievements include: Research in formation mechanism of foxing caused by fungi; ArP fumigation system using propylene oxide for cultural property; Blackening effects found in historical monuments and their countermeasures. Honours: Recipient Cultural Services Award, Board of Education, Chiba Prefecture, 1998; Recipient, National Cultural Services Award, The Order of the Sacred Treasure, Gold Rays with Rosette, Japan, 2003. Memberships: Conservation Council for Cultural Property, Board of education, Chiba Prefecture, 1984-2006; President, 1997-2000, Member Advisory Committee, 2000-, International Council for Biodeterioration of Cultural Property. Address: 6-34-3 Matsuba-cho, Kashiwa-shi, Chiba-ken 277-0827, Japan. E-mail: hharai@jcom.home.ne.jp

ARAKAWA Hiroaki, b. 18 August 1960, Akita, Japan. Medical Doctor; Radiologist. m. Kyoko Aoki, 2 daughters. Education: Bachelor of Science, Kyoko University, 1983; Graduate, Tohoku Medical School, 1989; Visiting Scholarship, Department of Radiology, University of California, San Francisco, 1996-97; Medical Doctor, St Marianna University School of Medicine, 1998. Appointments: Intern, Nakadori Hospital, 1989-91; Resident in Radiology, St Marianna University School of Medicine, 1991-96; Fellow, Department of Radiology, St Marianna University Hospital, 1997-2000; Assistant Professor, Department of Radiology, Dokkyo Medical School, 2000-. Publications: Books: Medical Radiology volume on Imaging of Occupational and Environmental Disorders; International Classification of HCRT for Occupational Lung Diseases, 2005; Articles in medical journals: Inhomogeneous lung attenuation at thin-section CT, 1998; Nonspecific Interstitial Pneumonia Associated with Polymyositis and Dermomyositis, 2003. Memberships: Japan Radiological Society; Radiologic Society of North America; Japanese Society of Thoracic Radiology. Address: 880 Kita-Kobayashi, Miba, Tochigi, 321-0293 Japan.

ARANEDA Jorgelina Elcira, b. 11 January 1962, Rosario, Argentina. Attorney. m. W Randall Stroud. Education: JD, University of North Carolina at Chapel Hill, 1989; LLM, International & Comparative Law, The National Law Center, George Washington University, 1992. Appointments: Admitted as Attorney and Counsellor at Law: North Carolina, 1990; District of Columbia, 1991; US District Court, Eastern District of North Carolina and US Court of Appeals, Fourth Circuit 1993; US Court of Appeals, Eleventh Circuit and US Supreme Court, 2003. Publications: Detention of Noncitizens, 2003; Immigration Legal Issues for Startups, 2004; H2B or Not H2B, That is the Crisis, 2005; How to Effectively Document Foreign Worker Employment, 2005; Handling Removal Proceedings in Immigration Court, 2006. Honours: Numerous appearances as an invited speaker on television; American Immigration Law Association Mentor; North Carolina Businesswoman of the Year Award, National Republican Congressional Committee Business Advisory Council, 2004; Member of Immigration Law Speciality Committee of the North Carolina State Bar, Board of Legal Specialization, 2005-08; Listed in international biographical dictionaries. Memberships: International Bar Association; American Bar Association; District of Columbia Bar; North Carolina State Bar; American Immigration Lawyers Association; Hispanic National Bar Association; Wake County Bar Association, North Carolina; North Carolina Bar Association Committee of

Hispanic/Latino Lawyers. Address: 4600 Marriott Drive, Suite 350, Raleigh, NC 27612, USA. E-mail: info@aranedalaw.com Website: www.aranedalaw.com

ARANOVICH Felix, b. 29 April 1930, Russia. Engineer. m. Svetlana, 1 son, 1 daughter. Education: Leningrad Military-Mechanical Institute, 1948-54; Doctoral Research, 2 years (not finished due to emigration to USA). Appointments: Design Engineer, Waterman Hydraulics; Senior Project Engineer Co-ordinator, Parker Hannifin. Publications: Articles: Throttling area in needle and poppet valves, 1983; Some thoughts on valve response time, 1992; The right way to calculate throttling area, 1999; Sizing up flow forces, 2005; 7 patents; Fiction: Nadgrobie Antokolskogo, 1982; Kali Nikta, 2005. Honours: Listed in international biographical dictionaries; 2 diplomas in amateur film festivals, St Petersburg, Russia. Memberships: National Fluid Power Association. Address: 5339 Lunt Ave, Skokie, IL 60077, USA.

ARBUTHNOTT Robert, b. 28 September 1936, Kuala Lumpur, Malaysia. British Council Officer. m. (Sophie) Robina Axford, 1 son, 2 daughters. Education: BA, MA, Modern Languages, Emmanuel College, Cambridge, 1957-60; Institute of Education, London and School of Oriental and African Studies, 1972-73; Royal College of Defence Studies, 1986. Appointments: Military Service, 2nd Lieutenant The Black Watch, 1955-57; British Council Service, 1960-94: Karachi, Lahore, 1960-64, London, 1964-67, Representative, Nepal, 1967-72, Representative, Malaysia, 1973-76, Director, Educational Contracts, 1977-78, Controller Personnel, 1978-81, Representative, Germany, 1981-85; RCDS, 1986; Minister (Cultural Affairs), British High Commission and Director British Council in India, 1988-93. Honours: Exhibitioner, Emmanuel College, Cambridge; CBE, 1991. Memberships: Fellow, Royal Asiatic Society; Council Member, Royal Society for Asian Affairs; Oxford-Cambridge Club. Address: Killicks, The Green, Mannings Heath, Horsham, West Sussex, RH13 6JX, England.

ARBUZ Joseph, b. 23 November 1949, New York, USA. Attorney. Divorced, 1 daughter. Education: Juris Doctor; Doctor of Divinity; Master of Public Administration; Master of Divinity; Bachelor of Arts. Appointments: Church Pastor; Assistant Attorney General; Assistant Staff Judge Advocate; American Express Financial Advisors; Joseph R Arbuz, PA. Publications: Commander's Guide; Many other airforce manuals and newspaper articles. Honours: JFK Teaching Scholarship; National Defence Service Medal; Air Force Service Medal; Listed in international biographical directories. Memberships: The Florida Bar; Federal District Court; Federal Court of Appeals; US Supreme Court; US Court of Military Appeals; DADE County Bar Association; Hispanic Chamber of Commerce. Address: 80 SW 8 St, Suite # 2000, Miami, FL 33130, USA. E-mail: joearbuz@aol.com

ARCHANGELSKY Sergio, b. 27 March 1931, Morocco. Palaeontologist. m. Jos Ballester, 1 son, 1 daughter. Education: PhD, Natural Sciences, Buenos Aires University, 1957. Appointments: Professor, La Plata University, 1961-78; Superior Researcher, National Research Council, Argentina, 1985-; Head, Paleobotany Division, Argentine Museum of Natural History, 1985-.2006. Publications: Fundamentals of Palaeobotany, 1970; Fossil Flora of the Baqueró Group, Cretaceous, Patagonia, 2003. Honours: Visiting Professor, Ohio State University, USA, 1984; Corresponding Member, Botanical Society America, 1975; Academician, National Academy Sciences, Cordoba, 1990; Honorary Vice-President,

XVI International Botanical Congress, St Louis, USA, 1999. Memberships: Argentine Geological Society; Argentine Palaeontological Society; British Palaeontological Association; Fellow, Paleobotanical Society, India. Address: Urquiza 1132 Vicente, Lopez B1638BWJ, Buenos Aires, Argentina.

ARCHER Richard Donald, b. 3 July 1947, Leicester, England. Teacher. Education: BA, University of Durham; PGCE, Christ's College of Education, University of Liverpool; MusB, Trinity College, Dublin; MMus, University of Sheffield; MPhil, University of East Anglia; FRCO; ADCM; FTCL; LRAM; ARCM. Appointments: Organist, Recitals Locally, Solo Organist at Concerts; Organist, Leicester Philharmonic Society; Radio Broadcasts, Conductor, Hinckley Choral Union and City of Leicester Singers; Guest Conductor, Accompanist, Director of Music, St John the Baptist, Leicester; Head of Modern Languages, Stoneygate School, Leicester. Publications: Works for Local Choirs in Manuscript, including 2 Sonnets, Fire of the Spirit; Recording, Fire of the Spirit. Honours: Prizes, organ playing competitions. Memberships: RCO; ATL; ISM; MU; Hymn Society of Great Britain and Ireland; Methodist Church Music Society; Leicester and District Organists' Association. Address: 11 Frampton Avenue, Leicester LE3 0SG, England.

ARCHER OF SANDWELL, Baron of Sandwell in the West Midlands; Peter Kingsley Archer, b. 20 November 1926, Wednesbury, England. Barrister; MP (Retired). m. Margaret Irene, 1 son. Education: London School of Economics, 1948-50; University College, London, 1950-52; LLB (External, London), 1947; LLM, London, 1950; BA, Philosophy, London, 1952. Appointments: Barrister, 1954; QC, 1971; Retired, 1994; Recorder, 1980-96; Member of Parliament, 1966; Solicitor General, 1974-79; Shadow Cabinet: Legal Affairs, 1979-82, Trade, 1982-83, Northern Ireland, 1983-87; Member House of Lords, 1992; Chairman, Council on Tribunals, 1992-99; Chairman, Enemy Property Compensation Assessment Panel, 1999-. Publications: The Queen's Courts, 1956; Social Welfare and the Citizen, 1957; Communism and the Law, 1963; Freedom at Stake, 1966; Human Rights, 1969; Purpose in Socialism (Symposium), 1973. Honours: Privy Councillor, 1977; Honorary Fellow, University College London, 1976; Honorary LLD, University of Wolverhampton, 1999. Memberships: President, Fabian Society; President, World Disarmament; President, One World Trust. Address: House of Lords, London, SW1 0PW, England.

ARCHER OF WESTON-SUPER-MARE, Baron of Mark in the County of Somerset; Jeffrey Howard Archer, b. 15 April 1940, Mark, Somerset, England. Author; Politician. m. Mary Weeden, 2 sons. Education: Brasenose College, Oxford. Appointments: Member, GLC for Havering, 1966-70; Member of Parliament for Louth (Conservative), 1969-74; Deputy Chair, Conservative Party, 1985-86; Served two years of a four year prison sentence for perjury and perverting the course of justice, 2001-03. Publications: Not a Penny More, Not a Penny Less, 1975; Shall We Tell the President?, 1977; Kane & Abel, 1979; A Quiver Full of Arrows (short stories), 1980; The Prodigal Daughter, 1982; First Among Equals, 1984; A Matter of Honour, 1986; A Twist in the Tale (short stories), 1988; As The Crow Flies, 1991; Honour Among Thieves, 1993; Twelve Red Herrings (short stories), 1994; The Fourth Estate, 1995; Collected Short Stories, 1997; The Eleventh Commandment, 1998; To Cut a Long Story Short (short stories), 2000; A Prison Diary, Volumes I and II, 2002; Sons of Fortune, 2003; A Prison Diary, Volume III, 2004; False Impression, Cat

O'Nine Tales, 2006. Plays: Beyond Reasonable Doubt, 1987; Exclusive, 1989; The Accused, 2000. Honours: Lord Archer of Weston super Mare, Queen's Birthday Honours, 1992. Address: Peninsula Heights, 93 Albert Embankment, London SE1 7TY, England.

ARCHER OF WESTON-SUPER-MARE, Lady Mary Doreen Archer, b. 22 December 1944, England. Scientist. m. Jeffrey Archer (Lord Archer of Weston-Super-Mare), 2 sons. Education: Cheltenham Ladies' College; St Anne's College, Oxford, Imperial College, London. Appointments: Junior Research Fellow, St Hilda's College, Oxford, 1968-71; Chemistry Lecturer, Somerville College, Oxford, temporary 1971-72; Research Fellow, Royal Institute of Great Britain, 1972-76; Chemistry Lecturer, Trinity College, Cambridge and Chemistry Fellow & Lecturer, Newnham College, Cambridge, 1976-86; Senior Academic Fellow, DeMontfort University, 1990-; Visiting Professor: Imperial College, London, 1991-2000; Centre for Energy Policy and Technology, 2001-03; University of Hertfordshire, 1993-; Director, 1992-, Vice Chair, 2000-02, Chair, 2002-, Addenbrooke's Hospital Trust, NHS Trust. Honours: Hon ScD (Herts), 1994; Energy Institute Melchett Medal, 2002. Publications: Rupert Brooke and the Old Vicarage, Grantchester, 1989; Clean Energy from Photovoltaics, 2001-; Molecular to Global Photosynthesis, 2004; Transformation and Change: the 1702 Chair of Chemistry at Cambridge, 2004; Contributes to various chemistry journals. Memberships: Council Member, Royal Institute, 1984-85, 1999-2001; Director, Anglia TV Group, 1987-95; Director, Mid Anglia Radio, 1988-94; Director, Q103 FM (formerly Cambridge and Newmarket Radio,) 1988-97; Member, Council of Lloyd's, 1989-92; President, Guild of Church Musicians, 1989-; Chair, 1990-2000, President, 2000-, National Energy Foundation; Trustee, Science Museum, 1990-2000; Cheltenham Ladies' College, 1991-2000; President, Solar Energy Society, 2001-; Chair, East of England Stem Cell Network, 2004-. Address: The Old Vicarage, Grantchester, Cambridge, CB3 9ND, England. Website: www.addenbrookes.org.uk

ARCHIBALD Roy McLellan, b. 9 July 1920, Huddersfield, Yorkshire, England. Consultant Physician. m. Mary McGowan Kerr Ross, 1 son, 2 daughters. Education: Glasgow University. Appointments: Medical Office, ICI Alkali Division, 1948-53; Area M O, North-Eastern Division, 1953-59, Divisional M O, Durham Division, 1959-67, Assistant Chief Medical Officer, 1969-72, Deputy Chief Medical Officer, 1972-79, National Coal Board, UK; Director, Medical Service, 1979-85; Independent Consultant, 1985-2000. Publications: Numerous papers and articles in public and professional journals. Honours: Mentioned in Dispatches, 1947; Knight of Grace, Order of St John. Memberships: Life Member, British Medical Association; Past Secretary, Past President, Honorary Member, Society of Occupational Medicine; Founder Fellow, 1978, Vice Dean, 1980-82, Faculty of Occupational Medicine; Honorary Fellow, Ergonomic Society. Address: D17 Oakwoods, 357 Queen Street, Richmond, Nelson, New Zealand. E-mail: royarchibald@xtra.co.nz

ARCULUS Ronald (Sir), b. 11 February 1923, Birmingham, England. Retired Diplomat and Company Director. Education: MA, Exeter College, Oxford, 1941, 1945-47. Appointments: 4th Queen's Own Hussars, 1942-45; HM Diplomatic Service, 1947-83; Ambassador to Italy, 1979-83; Director, Trustee and Consultant, Glaxo Holdings, 1983-92. Honours: KCMG; KCVO; Knight Grand Cross, Italian Order of Merit. Memberships: Army and Navy Club; Cowdray Park Polo Club; Hurlingham Club. Address: 20 Kensington Court Gardens, London W8 5QF, England.

ARDEN John, b. 26 October 1930, Barnsley, Yorkshire, England. Playwright. m. Margaretta Ruth D'Arcy, 4 sons, 1 deceased. Education: King's College, Cambridge; Edinburgh College of Art. Publications include: Fiction: Silence Among the Weapons, 1982; Books of Bale, 1988; Cogs Tyrannic, 1991; Jack Juggler and the Emperor's Whore, 1995; The Stealing Steps, 2003. Essays: To Present the Pretence, 1977; Awkward Corners (with M D'Arcy), 1988. Plays produced include: All Fall Down, 1955; The Life of Man, 1956; The Waters of Babylon, 1957; When Is A Door Not A Door?, Live Like Pigs, 1958; Serjeant Musgrave's Dance, 1959; Soldier Soldier, 1960; Wet Fish, 1961; The Workhouse Donkey, Ironhand, 1963; Armstrong's Last Goodnight, 1964; Left-Handed Liberty, 1965; Squire Jonathan, 1968; The Bagman, 1970; Pearl, 1978; Don Quixote, 1980; Garland for a Hoar Head, The Old Man Sleeps Alone, 1982; The Little Novels of Wilkie Collins, 1998; Woe alas, the Fatal Cashbox, 2000; Wild Ride to Dublin, Poor Tom, thy Horn is Dry, 2003; Scam, 2007. With M D'Arcy: The Happy Haven, The Business of Good Government, 1960; Ars Longa Vita Brevis, 1964; The Royal Pardon, Friday's Hiding, 1966; Harold Muggins is a Martyr, The Hero Rises Up, 1968; The Ballygombeen Bequest, The Island of the Mighty, 1972; The Non-Stop Connolly Show, 1975; Vandaleur's Folly, 1978; The Manchester Enthusiasts, 1984; Whose is the Kingdom?, 1988; A Suburban Suicide, 1994.

ARDEN-GRIFFITH Paul, b. 18 January 1952, Stockport, England. Opera, Oratorio and Concert Singer. Education: GRSM (Teachers), ARMCM (Teachers), pianoforte and singing, ARMCM (Performers), Singing, Royal Northern College of Music, Manchester. Career: A Midsummer Night's Dream, Sadlers Wells Theatre, 1973; The Merry Widow, English National Opera, 1975; Paul Bunyan, Aldeburgh Festival, 1976; We Come To the River, Royal Opera Covent Garden, 1976; Of Mice and Men, Wexford Festival Opera, Eire, 1980; Carmina Burana, Singapore Festival of the Arts, Singapore, 1984; Phantom of the Opera, Her Majesty's Theatre, 1986; The Duenna, Wexford Festival Opera, Eire, 1989; The Legendary Lanza, Wexford Festival Opera, Eire, 1989; The Barber of Seville, Opera East, UK Tour, 1992; Sunset Boulevard, Rhein-Main Theatre, Frankfurt, Germany, 1998; Sweeney Todd, Royal Opera Covent Garden, London, 2003; Die Fledermaus, Opera Holland Park, London, 2004; The Tales of Hoffman, White Horse Opera, UK, 2005; The Pocket Orchestra: The Unlikely Lives of the Great Composers, London, 2006. Recordings: Paul Arden-Griffith – The Song Is You, 1986; Phantom of the Opera (Original Cast Album), 1987; An Evening with Alan Jay Lerner, 1987; Minstrel Magic (Black & White Minstrel Cast Album), 1993; A Minstrel on Broadway, 1994; Encore! – Paul Arden Griffith in Concert, 1995; The Classic Collection, 1995; Accolade!, 1996. Honours: Gwilym, Gwalchmai Jones Scholarship for Singing; Listed in several Who's Who and biographical publications. Memberships: British Actors Equity Association; Musicians' Union; PAMRA; Concert Artistes' Association. Address: c/o Ken Spencer Personal Management, 138 Sandy Hill Road, London SE 18 7BA, England. E-mail: pagtenor@tesco.net

AREM Joel Edward, b. 28 December 1943, New York, USA. Mineralogist; Gemologist. m. Deborah, 1 son, 1 daughter. Education: BS, Geology, Brooklyn College, 1962; MA, Geology, Harvard University, 1967; PhD, Mineralogy, 1970. Appointments include: Consultant, US Department

of Commerce, 1975-76; Consultant, Encyclopaedia Britannica Educational Corp, 1975-76; Consultant, Jewellers Circular-Keystone, 1978-85; President, Accredited Gemologists Association, 1977-79; Co-Founder, Editorial Board, PreciouStones Newsletter, 1978-84. Publications: Crystal Chemistry and Structure of Idocrase, PhD Dissertation, 1970; Man-Made Crystals, 1973; Rocks and Minerals, 1973; Gems and Jewelry, 1975, 2nd edition, 1992; Color Encyclopedia of Gemstones, 1977, 2nd edition, 1987; Discovering Rocks and Minerals, 1991. Honours include: Harvard University Scholarships, 1964-66; National Science Foundation Scholarships, 1966-68; Sigma Xi; Phi Beta Kappa. Memberships: Fellow, Gemmological Association of Great Britain; Fellow, Canadian Gemmological Association; Mineralogical Society of America; American Association for Crystal Growth; Mineral Museums Advisory Council; Friends of Mineralogy. Address: PO 5056, Laytonsville, MD 20882, USA.

ARKHIPOV Andrei, b. 8 September 1946, Karaganda, Kazakhstan, USSR. Physicist. 2 sons. Education: Graduate, Leningrad State University, Russia, 1970; PhD, 1973, DSc, 1993, Institute of High Energy Physics, Russia. Appointments: Scientist of Theoretical Physics Division, 1973-1985, Senior Scientist, 1985-95, Principal Researcher, 1995-, Institute of High Energy Physics, Russia; Lecturer, Physics, Moscow State University, 1978-98. Publications: Articles in scientific journals including: Soviet Journal of Theoretical and Mathematical Physics, 1990; Nuclear Physics, 2001; Hadron Spectroscopy, 2002. Honours: Nominated for International Scientist of the Year, 2003; Inaugural Member, Leading Scientists of the World, 2005; Nominated as inaugural member of the Leading Scientist of the World 2005; Diploma of Achievement in Science Award, IBC, 2005; Nominated for Outstanding Scientists of the 21st Century, IBC, 2007; Nominated for Outstanding Scientists Worldwide, 2007. Address: Theoretical Physics Division, Institute for High Energy Physics, 142280 Protvino, Moscow Region, Russia. E-mail: Andrei.Arkhipov@ihep.ru

ARKIN Alan Wolf, b. 26 March 1934, USA. Actor; Director. m. (1) 2 sons, (2) Barbara Dana, 1 son. Education: Los Angeles City College; Los Angeles State Col; Bennington College. Appointments: Made professional theatre debut with the Compass Players, St Louis, 1959; Director, The Sunshine Boys, Eh?, 1972; Molly, 1973; Joan Lorraine, 1974; Films include: The Heart is a Lonely Hunter, 1968; Catch 22, 1970; Little Murders (also director), 1971; Last of the Red Hot Lovers, 1972; Freebie and the Bean, 1974; The In-laws, 1979; Simon, 1980; Chu Chu and the Philly Flash, 1981; The Last Unicorn, 1982; Joshua Then and Now (also director), 1985; Coupe de Ville, 1989; Havana, Edward Scissorhands, 1990; The Rocketeer, 1991; Glengarry Glen Ross, 1992; Indian Summer, 1993; So I Married an Axe Murderer, 1993; Mother Night, 1995; Grosse Point Blank, 1997; Gattaca, 1998; Slums of Beverly Hills, 1998; Jakob the Liar, 1999; Arigo, 2000; America's Sweethearts, 2001; Thirteen Conversations About One Thing, 2002; Noel, Eros, The Novice, 2004; Firewall, Little Miss Sunshine, The Santa Clause 3: The Escape Clause, 2006. Various TV appearances, including Escape from Sobibor, Necessary Parties; Cooperstown; Taking the Heat; Doomsday Gun; Varian's War, 2001; The Pentagon Papers, 2003; And Starring Pancho Villa as Himself, 2003. Publications: Tony's Hard Work Day; The Lemming Condition; Halfway Through the Door; The Clearing, 1986; Some Fine Grampha, 1995. Honours: Theatre World Award; Award Best Supporting Actor. Address: c/o William Morris Agency, 151 El Camino Drive, Beverly Hills, CA 90212, USA.

ARMANI Giorgio, b. 11 July 1934, Piacenza, Italy. Fashion Designer. Education: University of Milan. Appointments: Window dresser; Assistant buyer for La Rinascente, Milan, 1957-64; Designer and Product Developer, Hitman (menswear co of Cerruti Group), 1964-70; Freelance designer for several firms, 1970; founded Giorgio Armani SpA with Sergio Galeotti, 1975; Appeared on cover of Time, 1982. Honours: Dr hc (Royal College of Art), 1991; Numerous awards including Cutty Sark, 1980, 1981, 1984, 1986, 1987; First Designer Laureate, 1985; Ambrogino D'Oro, Milan, 1982; International Designer Award, Council of Fashion Designer of America, 1983; L'Pacchio D'Oro, 1984, 1986, 1987, 1988; L'Occhiolino D'Oro, 1984, 1986, 1987, 1988; Time-Life Achievement Award, 1987; Cristobal Balenciaga Award, 1988; Woolmark Award, New York, 1989, 1992; Senken Award, Japan, 1989; Award from People for the Ethical Treatment of Animals, USA, 1990; Fiorino d'Oro, Florence, for promoting Made in Italy image, 1992; Honorary Nomination from Brera Academy, Milan, 1993; Aguja de Oro Award, Spain, for best International Designer, 1993; Grand'Uffciale dell'ordine al merito, 1986; Gran Cavaliere, 1987. Address: Via Borgonuovo 21, 20121, Milan, Italy.

ARMATRADING Joan b. 9 December 1950, Basseterre, St Kitts, West Indies. Singer; Songwriter; Musician (guitar). Musical Education: Self-taught piano and guitar. Career: Songwriting, performing partnership, with Pam Nestor, 1969-73; Solo artiste, 1973-; Appearances include: Regular international tours; Concerts include: Prince's Trust Gala, Wembley Arena, 1986; Nelson Mandela's 70th Birthday Tribute, Wembley Stadium, 1988; Numerous world tours, 1973-96. Compositions include: Down To Zero; Willow, 1977. Recordings: Singles: Love And Affection, 1976; Rosie, 1980; Me Myself I, 1980; All The Way From America, 1980; I'm Lucky, 1981; Drop The Pilot, 1983; Perfect Day, 1997; Albums include: Whatever's For Us, 1973; Joan Armatrading, 1976; Show Some Emotion, 1977; Stepping Out, 1979; Me Myself I, 1980; Walk Under Ladders, 1981; The Key, 1983; Track Record, 1983; The Shouting Stage, 1988; The Very Best Of..., 1991; What's Inside, 1995; Living For You; Greatest Hits, 1996; Love And Affection, 1997; Lover Speak, 2003; DVD: All the Way from America, 2004; Also appears on: Listen To The Music: 70's Females, 1996; Carols Of Christmas Vol 2, 1997; Prince's Trust 10th Anniversary Birthday, 1997; Film soundtrack, The Wild Geese, 1978. Honour: BASCA Ivor Novello Award for Outstanding Contemporary Collection, 1996; MBE, 2001. Membership: President, Women of the Year, UK. Address: c/o F Winter and Co, Ramillies House, 2 Ramillies Street, London W1F 7LN, England.

ARMBRUESTER Thomas F, b. 18 February 1968, Bremen, Germany. Professor of Management. Education: Diploma, Management and Industrial Engineering, Berlin Technical University, Germany, 1994; PhD, London School of Economics and Political Science, England, 1999. Appointments: Assistant Professor of Management, University of Mannheim, Germany; Visiting Professor, Pompeu Fabra University, Barcelona, Spain; Professor of Business Administration, Witten/Herdecke University, Germany. Publications: Management and Organization in Germany, 2005; The Economics and Sociology of Management Consulting, 2006. Memberships: Academy of Management; European Group for Organizational Studies. Address: Witten/Herdecke University, 58448 Witten, Germany. E-mail: thomas.armbruester@uni-wh.de

ARMOUR Sir James, b. 17 September 1929, Basra, Iraq. Academic Veterinarian. m. Christine Strickland, 2 sons, 2 daughters. Education: MRCVS, PhD, University of Glasgow,

1947-52. Appointments: Veterinary Officer, Veterinary Research Officer, Colonial Service, Nigeria, 1952-60; Research Scientist, Cooper McDougall, Robertson, 1960-63; Lecturer, Senior Lecturer, Reader, Veterinary Parasitology, 1963-75, Professor in Veterinary Parasitology, 1975-96, Dean of the Veterinary School, 1986-91, Vice Principal, 1991-96, Dean of Faculties, 1996-99, Emeritus Professor, 1999-, University of Glasgow; Chairman Veterinary Products Committee (Part of Medicines Commission), 1988-97; Chairman, Glasgow Hospitals NHS Dental Trust, 1995-99; Chairman, Moredun Foundation, 2000-2004; Chairman, St Andrew's Clinics for Children in Africa; Vice-Chairman, Hannah Research. Publications: 150 articles on veterinary parasitology: Pathogenesis, immunology and control of internal parasites of livestock; Joint author of textbook on veterinary parasitology, translated into Spanish, Portuguese, Italian, Arabic and Russian. Honours: CBE, 1989; Kt, 1995; Honorary Degrees: Dr hc, Utrecht, DVM&S, Edinburgh, DU, Glasgow; DU, Stirling; Fellow, Royal Society of Edinburgh; Fellow, Academy of Medical Sciences; Honorary Fellow, Royal College of Veterinary Surgeons; Honorary Fellow, Institute of Biology; Honorary Doctorate, University of Stirling, 2005; Honorary Fellow, European Society for Veterinary Parasitology; Listed in biographical dictionaries. Memberships: Royal College of Veterinary Surgeons; British Veterinary Association; World Association for Advancement of Veterinary Parasitology; British Association for Veterinary Parasitology; Vice-Chairman, Hannah Trust. Address: 4b Towans Court, Prestwick, KA9 2AY, Scotland.

ARMSTRONG Isobel Mair, b. 25 March 1937, London, England. Emeritus Professor of English. m. John Michael Armstrong, 2 sons, 1 daughter. Education: BA, PhD, University of Leicester. Appointments: Assistant Lecturer then Lecturer, University College London, 1963-70; Lecturer then Senior Lecturer, University of Leicester, 1971-79; Professor of English, University of Southampton, 1979-89; Professor of English, Birkbeck College, University of London, 1989-2002. Publications: The Major Victorian Poets, 1969; Victorian Scrutinies, 1972; Language as Living Form in Nineteenth Century Poetry, 1982; Victorian Poetry: Poetry, Poetics and Politics, 1993; Nineteenth Century Women Poets (co-editor), 1996; The Radical Aesthetic, 2000; Victorian Glassworlds: Glass Culture and the Imagination 1830-1880, 2008. Honours: Fellow, British Academy, 2003; Hon DLitt, University of Leicester, 2004; Hinckley Visiting Professor, Johns Hopkins University, 2005. Memberships: President, British Association of Victorian Studies, 2003-06; Senior Research Fellow Institute of English Studies, 2002. Address: School of English and Humanities, Birkbeck College, Malet Street, London WC1E 7HX, England.

ARMSTRONG Neil A, b. 5 August 1930, Wapakoneta, Ohio, USA. Astronaut; Professor of Engineering. m. Janet Shearon, 2 sons. Education: Purdue University; University of South California. Appointments: Naval Aviator, 1949-52; Flew combat missions during Korean War; Joined NASA Lewis Flight Propulsion Laboratory, 1955; Transferred to NASA High Speed Flight Station, Edwards, California; Aeronautical Research Pilot, X-15 Project Pilot Flying to over 200,000 ft and at approximately 4,000 mph; Other Flight Test Work Including X-1 Rocket Research Plane; F-100, F-101, F-104, F5D, B-47 and the Paraglider; Selected as Astronaut by NASA, 1962; Backup Pilot for Gemini V, 1965; Command Pilot for Gemini VIII, 1966; Flew to moon, Apollo XI, 1969; First man to set foot on the moon, 1969; Chair, Peace Corps, National Advisory Council, 1969; Deputy Associate Administrator, Aeronautics, NASA, Washington, 1970-71;

Professor of Engineering, University of Cincinnati, 1971-79; Chair, Cardwell International Ltd, 1979-81; Chair, CTA Inc, 1982-92; AIL Systems Inc, 1989-2000; EDO Corporation, 2000-02; Director of numerous companies. Honours: Honorary Member, International Academy of Astronautics; Honorary Fellow, International Astronomical Federation; Numerous decorations and awards from 17 countries; Presidential Medal of Freedom, NASA Exceptional Service Award; Royal Geographic Society, Gold Medal and Harmon International Aviation Trophy, 1970; Rotary National Award for Space Achievement, 2004. Memberships: President's Commission on Space Shuttle, 1986; National Commission on Space, 1985-86; National Academy of Engineering; Fellow, Society of Experimental Test Pilots; American Institute of Aeronautics and Astronautics; Royal Astronautical Society. Address: EDO Corporation, 60 East 42nd Street, Suite 5010, New York, NY 10165, USA.

ARNAUDOV Boris, b. 16 August 1940, Sliven, Bulgaria. Physics. m. Svetla Evtimova, 1 son. Education: MS, Semiconductor Physics, Sofia University, 1966; PhD, Belorussian University, Minsk, 1979; DSci, Sofia University, Bulgaria, 2002. Appointments: Researcher, 1966-, Associate Professor, 1980-2004, Professor in Semiconductor Physics Department, Faculty of Physics, 2004-, Vice Dean, Faculty of Physics, 2000-04, Semiconductor Physics Department, Sofia University. Publications: Author, 2 books in three and one in two editions; Over 100 articles in international journals and conference proceedings; 6 patents. Memberships: Union of Physicists in Bulgaria. Address: University of Sofia Faculty of Physics, 5 James Bourchier Blvd, 1164 Sofia, Bulgaria. E-mail: arnaudov@phys.uni-sofia.bg

ARNOLD David Charles, b. 30 December 1941, Atlanta, Georgia, USA. Opera and Concert Singer. Education: BA, MA, Indiana University, Bloomington, Indiana; Artist's Diploma, New England Conservatory of Music, Boston, Massachusetts. Appointments: Metropolitan Opera, New York City Opera Company, English National Opera; Komische Oper, Berlin; International Festivals: Spoleto in Italy and USA; Concertgebouw, The Netherlands; Significant associations: Performing as soloist with Sir Georg Solti and the Chicago Symphony; Leonard Bernstein in premiere of David Diamond's 9th Symphony; André Previn and the Pittsburgh Symphony; James Levine with the Metropolitan Opera. Honours: National Opera Institute Career Grant; New York City Opera Gold Debut Award, Sullivan Foundation Award; Shoshana Foundation Award; Invited to sing at: White House on 2 occasions. Address: Grant House, 309 Wood Street, Burlington, NJ 08016, USA.

ARNOLD Thomas Richard (Sir), b. 25 January 1947, London, England. Theatre Producer; Publisher; Consultant, Middle East Affairs. m. Elizabeth Jane, dissolved 1993, 1 daughter. Education: MA, Pembroke College, Oxford. Appointments: Member of Parliament (Conservative), Hazel Grove, Manchester, 1974-97; Parliamentary Private Secretary to Secretary of State for Northern Ireland, 1979-81; Parliamentary Private Secretary to Lord Privy Seal, Foreign and Commonwealth Office, 1981-82; Vice-Chairman, Conservative Party, 1983-92; Member, 1992-94, Chairman, 1994-97, Treasury and Civil Service Select Committee. Honours: Freeman of the City of London (Baker's Company), 1969; Knighted, 1990. Address: No.1 Knightsbridge, London, SW1X 7LX, England.

ARPUTHARAJ Mariapragasam, b. 24 May 1944, Mullanvilai, Tamil Nadu. Worker in vineyard of Jesus. m. Boomadevi Maria Packiam, 3 sons, 1 daughter. Education: Diploma in Company Law; Diploma in Labour Law and Administrative Law; Diploma in Taxation Laws; Diploma in Theology; Diploma in D T P; P G Diploma in Personnel Management and Industrial Relations; BA; Bachelor of General Law; Bachelor of Law; Graduate in Theology; BTh, Master of Biblical Studies; Master of Religious Education; Doctor of Divinity; Doctor of Ministry; LLD; PhD; DLitt; ThD. Appointments: Catechist, Itinerant Evangelist; Cup-bearer in C.S.I; Assistant to Presbyter, Sunday Class Teacher; Vacation Bible School Teacher, Director; Preacher, Bible Teacher; Youth Leader; Christian Leader; Tracts and Bibles Distributor; Prayer Partner; Bible Hymns and Lyrics Composer; Writer in Christian Journals; Director of Bible Institute and Library. Publications: Biblical Essays; Christian Songs; Sermons; Biblical Poems; Publisher in many Christian journals. Honours: Divine Dazzle; Philanthropic Devotee; Man of Religious Education; Awards from Christian Arts and Literature League; Biblical Leader Award, Call Christian Society, Madras. Memberships: Associate Minister, Restoration Fellowship International; Association of Theologians; Amen Prayer Army; Indian Prayer Force; Prayer Partner of Evangelical Literature Service; Research Board of Advisors, American Biographical Institute. Address: 88/16 IKMME Complex, Post Box No 7, Sudamanipuram North Third Street, 100 Feet Road, Karaikudi-6330003, Tamil Nadu State, South India.

ARQUETTE Patricia, b. 8 April 1968, Chicago, Illinois. Actress. m. (1) Nicholas Cage, divorced, (2) Thomas Jane, 2006, 1 daughter, 1 son from a previous relationship. Appointments: Films Include: Pretty Smart, 1986; A Nightmare on Elm Street 3: Dream Warriors, 1987; Far North, 1988; The Indian Runner, Prayer of the Rollerboys, 1991; Trouble Bound, Inside Monkey Zetterland, 1992; True Romance, 1993; Ed Wood, 1994; Beyond Rangoon, 1995; Infinity, Flirting with Disaster, 1996; Lost Highway, Nightwatch, 1997; Goodbye Lover, Stigmata, Bringing Out the Dead, 1999; Little Nicky, 2000; Human Nature, 2001; Holes, Tiptoes, Deeper than Deep, 2003; Fast Food Nation, 2006. Films for TV Include: Daddy, 1987; Dillinger, 1991; Wildflower, 1991; Betrayed by Love, 1994; Toby's Story, 1998; The Hi -Lo Country, 1998; The Badge, 2002; Medium, 2005. Address: c/o UTA, 9560 Wilshire Blvd, 5th Floor, Beverley Hills, CA 90212, USA.

ARQUETTE Rosanna, b. 10 August 1959, New York, USA. Actress, Director, Producer. m. (1) divorced, (2) James N Howard, divorced, (3) John Sidel, 1993, divorced, 1 daughter. Appointments: Actress; Founder, Flower Child Productions; Films include: Gorp, 1980; SOB, 1981; Off The Wall, 1983; The Aviator, Desperately Seeking Susan, 1985; 8 Million Ways to Die, After Hours, Nobody's Fool, 1986; The Big Blue, 1988; Life Lessons, Black Rainbow, Wendy Cracked a Walnut, 1989; Sweet Revenge, Baby, It's You, Flight of the Intruder, 1990; The Linguini Incident, Fathers and Sons, 1992; Nowhere to Run, 1993; Pulp Fiction, 1994; Search and Destroy, 1995; Crash, 1996; Liar, Gone Fishin', Buffalo '66, 1997; Palmer's Pick Up, I'm Losing You, Homeslice, Floating Away, Hope Floats, Fait Accompli, 1998; Sugar Town, Palmer's Pick Up, Pigeonholed, Interview with a Dead Man, 1999; The Whole Nine Yards, Too Much Flesh, 2000; Things Behind the Sun, Big Bad Love, Good Advice, Diary of a Sex Addict, 2001; Gilded Stones, Dead Cool, 2004; Max and Grace, 2005; What About Brian, Grey's Anatomy, 2006. Directed and Produced: Searching for Debra Winger, 2002; All We Are Saying, 2005. TV Films include: Harvest

Home; The Wall; The Long Way Home; The Executioner's Song; One Cooks, the Other Doesn't; The Parade; Survival Guide; A Family Tree; Promised a Miracle; Sweet Revenge; Separation; The Wrong Man; Nowhere to Hide; I Know What You Did. Address: 8033 West Sunset Boulevard, #16, Los Angeles, CA 90046, USA.

ARRAND Geoffrey William, b. 24 July 1944. Archdeacon of Suffolk. Education: Scunthorpe Grammar School; KCL (BD, AKC); St Boniface College, Warminster. m. (1) Mary Marshall, dissolved 1986, 1 son, 2 daughters, (2) Margaret Elizabeth Frost, 2005. Appointments: Curate, Washington Diocese of Durham, 1967-70; South Ormsby Gp Dio of Lincoln, 1970-73; Team Vicar, Great Grimsby, Diocese of Lincoln, 1973-79; Team Rector, Halesworth Diocese of St Edmundsbury and Ipswich, 1979-85; Rector of Hadleigh, Layham and Shelley, 1985-94; Dean, Bocking, 1985-94; Rural Dean, Hadleigh, 1986-94; Canon of St Edmundsbury, 1992-, Archdeacon of Suffolk, 1994-. Honours: OstJ, 1994. Address: Glebe House, The Street, Ashfield-cum-Thorpe, Stowmarket, Suffolk IP14 6LX, England. E-mail: archdeacon.geoffrey@ stedmundsbury.anglican.org

ARSENJEV Serghey, b. 3 December 1937, Tiraspol Town, Moldova. Mechanical Engineer. m. Victoria Arsenjeva, deceased, 1 son, 1 daughter. Education: MEng for Lifting and Transporting Machines and Equipment, Polytechnic Institute of Odessa, USSR, 1958-63. Appointments: Principal Investigator, Leading Theorist, The Fundaments of Liquid and Gas Motion Physics, Organiser of Physical Technical Group, Informal Scientific Association, Pavlograd, Ukraine, 1990-. Publications: 28 articles, more than 200 of R&D accounts, reports, methods, 25 author's certificates and patent. Address: Physical Technical Group, Dobroljubova Street, 2, 29; Pavlograd Town, 51400 Ukraine. E-mail: usp777@ukr.net Website: www.lozik.h1.ru

ARTHUR Rasjid Arthur James, b. 7 June 1928, Stirling, Scotland. Journalist. Education: MA, Honours, English, Edinburgh University, 1950. Appointments: National Service, RAF, 1950-52; Local Reporter, Stirling, 1952-54; Sub Editor, 1954-55, Leader Writer, 1955-64, The Scotsman; Features Editor, News Editor and Writer, Central Office of Information, London, 1965-78; Freelance Writer on environment, development and related topics, 1978-. Publications: Many articles on environmental subjects for British and international magazines of the water industry and for the London Press Service of the Press Association. Membership: Chartered Institute of Journalists. Address: 32 Midway, Middleton Cheney, Banbury OX17 2QW, England. E-mail: rasjid_arthur@yahoo.co.uk

ARUKA Yuji, b. 16 December 1949, Bunkyo, Tokyo, Japan. Economics Professor. m. Miwako Kawamura. Education: Bachelor of Economics, 1972, MA, Economics, 1975, Waseda University, Tokyo, Japan; PhD, Economics, Kyoto University, 1999. Appointments: Senior Lecturer, 1980-83, Associate Professor, 1983-85, Chiba University of Commerce; Associate Professor, 1985-90, Professor, 1990-, Chuo University; Editor in Chief, Evolutionary and Institutional Economics Review, 2006-; Editor, Journal of Economic Interaction and Co-ordination, 2006-; Member, Foreign Service Examination Committee, Japanese Ministry of Foreign Affairs, 1997-2005. Publications: Generalised Goodwin's Theorems on general co-ordinates, SCED, 1991; How to measure social interaction via group selection, JEBO, 2004; Editor, Evolutionary Controversies in Economics, 2001. Memberships: Life Member, Cambridge Society,

England; Life Member, Clare Hall, Cambridge, England. E-mail: aruka@tamacc.chuo-u.ac.jp Website: http:// c-faculty.chuo-u.ac.jp/~aruka

AS-SALAAM Jamaal (William L Williams Jr), b. 20 April 1955, Albany, New York, USA. Actor; Writer; Poet; Director; Producer. m. (1) Veronica Foster, divorced, 1 son, 1 daughter, (2) Arlene Hooks, divorced, 1 son, (3) Terisita Ann Lopez, divorced, 1 daughter. Education: State University of New York, Film History, 1972-76; University of Northern Colorado, Accounting, 1984-86; National University, Encino, California, 1990-92; California Arts Partnership, 1995-98; MCSE, Ednet Career Institute, 1998. Appointments: Track Labourer, Burlington No RR, 1978-85; Computer Specialist, Denver Public School, 1980-86; Saks Consultant, Tom Hopkins Sales Training, Denver, 1984-86; Technical Support, Teleoptics, Los Angeles, 1988-94; Computer Technician, Los Angeles County Schools, California, 1987-94; Digital Video Editor, California Arts Community Partners, Los Angeles, 1994-99; Researcher, Sales Inc, Beverley Hills, California, 1996-97; Producer, Mile High Cable Co, Denver, 1983-86; Radio Announcer, Station KUVO, Denver, 1984-85; Actor; Director; Writer; Producer. Publications: Facing East, 1995; Portraits of Life, 1997. Memberships: Inner City Cultural Center; Denver Black Arts Theater Company; Win/Win Business Forum, Denver; Telepoetics; Los Angeles in Support of Gang Truce; Black Radical Congress. Honours: California Arts Community Project Award, California Institute of Arts; 1st prize, Upstate Photography, New York. Address: PO Box 815, Englewood, CO 80042-1072, USA. E-mail: jamaal21@hotmail.com

ASAWA Mitsuo, b. 15 October 1936, Matsumoto city, Nagano prefecture, Japan. Retired Materials Scientist; Retired Educator. m. Noriko Murayama, 1 son, 1 daughter. Education: Bachelor of Engineering, Metallurgy, Tohoku University, Sendai, 1959; Doctor of Engineering, Materials Science, University of Tokyo, 1982. Appointments: Engineer, Nittan Valve Co Ltd, Hadano, 1959-61; Associate Professor, Technology, 1971-83, Professor, Material Science, Faculty of Education, 1983-2002, Faculty of Education, Shinshu University; Independent Contractor, Translator and Summarist of Patent Specifications, Japan Patent Information Organisation, 2003-. Publications: Stress corrosion cracking of 18-8 austenitic stainless steel in sulfuric acid containing sodium chloride, 1971; Book, Stress Corrosion Cracking of Iron and Steel, 1983; Stress corrosion cracking regions on contour maps of dissolution rates for AISI 304 stainless steel in sulfuric acid solutions with chloride, bromide, or iodide, 1987; Book, Trends in Corrosion Research, 1993; Editor, NAVIX-Encyclopaedia of Current Knowledge, 1997; Effect of corrosion product layer on SCC susceptibility of copper containing type 304 steel in $1M\ H_2SO_4$, 2004. Honours: Third Yamaoka Award, The Iron and Steel Institute of Japan, 1983; Emeritus Professor, Shinshu University, 2003-. Memberships: Joint Research Council of The Iron and Steel Institute of Japan and The Japan Institute of Metals, 1977-79; Educational Activities Committee of The Iron and Steel Institute of Japan, 1995-2000. Address: Amori 7825-47, Nagano city, 380-0941, Japan. E-mail: teas@mx2.avis.ne.jp

ASCHERI Mario, b. 7 February 1944, Ventimiglia, Italy. Professor of Legal History. m. Cecilia Papi, 2 sons. Education: Law Degree, Siena, 1967. Appointments: Professor, University of Siena, 1971-; Professor, University of Sassari, 1972-76; Professor of Legal History, University of Rome 3 and Siena, 2002-. Publications include: Books: Istituzioni medievali, 1999; I diritti del Medioevo italiano (secoli XI-XV), 2000;

Siena nella storia, 2000; Lo spazio storico di Siena, 2001; Introduzione storica al diritto moderno e contemporaneo, 2003; Le città – Stato, Bologna, 2006. Honours: Doctor honoris causa, Université d'Auvergne, Clermont-Ferrand, France, 2001; Beirat Max-Planck-Institut für europäische Rechtsgeschichte, Frankfurt/Main, Germany; Consiglio Direttivo Deputazione di Storia patria per la Toscana, Florence; Direttore Sezione di Storia Accademia Senese degli Intronati, Siena; Premio della Città di Siena (Mangia d'oro), 2003; Premio della Città di Ventimiglia (San Segundin), 2003. Memberships: Editorial Member of historical periodicals published in Florence, Turin, Siena, Saragoza, Madrid. Address: Via G Duprè 99, I-53100 Siena, Italy. E-mail: ascheri@uniroma3.it

ASH William, b. 30 November 1917, Dallas, Texas, USA. Author; Radio Drama Script Editor. m. Ranjana, 1 son, 1 daughter. Education: University of Texas, Austin, Texas; MA, Modern Greats, Balliol College, Oxford. Appointments: Fighter Pilot, Royal Canadian Airforce, WWII; Prisoner of War, 1942-45; Representative, India and Pakistan, BBC, External Services; Script Editor, BBC Radio Drama Department; Literary Manager, Soho Poly Theatre; Chairman, Writers' Guild of Great Britain; Lecturer and Workshop Presenter. Publications: Fiction: The Lotus in the Sky, 1961; Choice of Arms, 1962; The Longest Way Round, 1963; Ride a Paper Tiger, 1968; Take-Off, 1969; Incorporated, 1980; Right Side Up, 1984; She? 1986; Bold Riot, 1992; What's the Big Idea, 1993; But My Fist Is Free, 1997; Rise Like Lions, 1998; Non-fiction: Marxism and Moral Concepts, 1964; Pickaxe and Rifle: The Story of the Albanian People, 1974; Morals and Politics: The Ethics of Revolution, 1977; A Red Square: The Autobiography of an Unconventional Revolutionary, 1978; The Way to Write Radio Drama, 1985; Marxist Morality, 1997. Honour: MBE (Military Division). Memberships: Writer's Guild; NATFHE. Address: Flat 9, 43 Moscow Road, London W2 4AH, England.

ASHDOWN OF NORTON SUB-HAMDON, Baron Ashdown of Norton Sub-Hamdon in the County of Somerset; Sir Jeremy John Durham (Paddy), b. 27 February 1941, New Delhi, India. Member of Parliament. m. Jane Courtenay, 1962, 1 son, 1 daughter. Appointments: Served RM and 42 Commando, 1959-71; Commanded 2 Special Boat Section; Captain, Royal Marines; HM Diplomatic Service, 1st Secretary, UK Mission to United Nations, Geneva, 1971-76; Commercial Managers Department, Westlands Group, 1976-78; Senior Manager, Morlands Ltd, 1978-81; Liberal Candidate, 1979; Dorset County Council, 1982-83; Spokesman for Trade and Industry, 1983-86; Liberal Member of Parliament for Yeovil, 1983-88; Liberal/SDP Alliance Spokesman on Education and Science, 1987; Liberal Democrat Member of Parliament for Yeovil, 1988-2001; Liberal Democrat Spokesman on Northern Ireland, 1988-; Leader, Liberal Democrats, 1988-99; Appointed Privy Counsellor, 1989; Appointed Non-Executive Director of Time Companies Ltd and Independent Newspapers Ltd, 1999; UN International High Representative to Bosnia and Herzegovina, 2002-06. Publications: Citizen's Britain: A Radical Agenda for the 1990s, 1989; Beyond Westminster, 1994; Making Change our Ally, 1994; The Ashdown Diaries 1988-97, 2000; The Ashdown Diaries Vol II, 1997-99, 2001. Honours: Knight Grand Cross of the Most Distinguished Order of Saint Michael and Saint George (GCMG), 2006. Address: c/o House of Lords, Westminster, London SW1A 0PW, England.

ASHE Geoffrey Thomas, b. 29 March 1923, London, England. Writer; Lecturer. m. (1) Dorothy Irene Train, 3 May 1946, deceased, 4 sons, 1 daughter, (2) Maxine Lefever, 8

December 1992, divorced, (3) Patricia Chandler, 3 April 1998. Education: BA, University of British Columbia, Canada, 1943; BA, Trinity College, Cambridge University, 1948. Appointment: Associate Editor, Arthurian Encyclopaedia, 1986. Publications: King Arthur's Avalon, 1957; From Caesar to Arthur, 1960; Land to the West, 1962; The Land and the Book, 1965; Gandhi, 1968; The Quest for Arthur's Britain, 1968; Camelot and the Vision of Albion, 1971; The Art of Writing Made Simple, 1972; The Finger and the Moon, 1973; The Virgin, 1976; The Ancient Wisdom, 1977; Miracles, 1978; Guidebook to Arthurian Britain, 1980; Kings and Queens of Early Britain, 1982; Avalonian Quest, 1982; The Discovery of King Arthur, 1985, re-issue 2003; Landscape of King Arthur, 1987; Mythology of the British Isles, 1990; King Arthur: The Dream of a Golden Age, 1990; Dawn Behind the Dawn, 1992; Atlantis, 1992; The Traveller's Guide to Arthurian Britain, 1997; The Book of Prophecy, 1999; The Hell-Fire Clubs, 2005; Merlin: The Prophet and His History, 2006; The Off-Beat Radicals, 2007. Contributions to: Numerous magazines and journals. Honour: Fellow, Royal Society of Literature, 1963. Memberships: Medieval Academy of America; Camelot Research Committee, secretary; International Arthurian Society. Address: Chalice Orchard, Well House Lane, Glastonbury, Somerset BA6 8BJ, England.

ASHE Rosemary, Soprano; Actress. Education: Royal Academy of Music; London Opera Centre; Vocal technique with Joy Mammen. Career: West End credits include: Carlotta, The Phantom Of The Opera, Her Majesty's; Miss Andrew, Mary Poppins, Prince Edward; Yum Yum, The Metropolitan Mikado, South Bank; Hortense, The Boyfriend, Albery; Manon, Bitter Sweet, Sadler's Wells; Forbidden Broadway, Fortune; Cunegonde, Candide, The Old Vic; Ellen, What About Luv?, Holland Park; Widow Corney, Oliver!, London Palladium; Other credits include: Side By Side By Sondheim, Manchester Library Theatre; Nickleby And Me, Chichester; Dear Ivor, Welsh National Opera; Janet, The Rocky Horror Show; Maria, West Side Story; Gianetta, The Gondoliers, Nottingham Playhouse; Julie Laverne, Showboat, Rsc/Opera North; The Witch, Into The Woods; Annie, Annie Get Your Gun; Lottie Grady, When We Are Married; Orinthia, The Applecart, Wolsey, Ipswich; Hermia, A Midsummer Nights Dream, Barbados Festival; The Old Bag, The Gingerbread Man, Birmingham Hippodrome; Asphynxia & Timothy's Mother, Salad Days; Mrs Darling, Peter Pan, Theatre Royal, Nottingham; Madame Spritzer, 13 Rue De Lamour, Theatre Royal, Northampton; Sister Mary Amnesia, Nunsense, Redgrave Theatre, Farnham; Viv Nicholson, Spend, Spend, Spend, West Yorkshire Playhouse; Lady Holyrood, Floradora, Finborough; Mrs Higgins, My Fair Lady, Larnaca Festival, Cyprus; Dottie Otley, Noises Off, Salisbury Playhouse; Together With Music, The Red Pear Theatre, Antibes; One-woman show, The Killer Soprano; Mad About The Boy, Algonquin Hotel, New York; Mrs Fraser, Stepping Out, Derby Playhouse; Operatic roles include: Esmeralda, The Bartered Bride; Venus, Orpheus, The Underworld; Papagena, The Magic Flute; Fiakermilli, Arabella; Zou Zou, La Belle Vivette; Helene, La Belle Helene, New Sadlers Wells Opera; Musetta, La Boheme, Opera Northern Ireland; Frasquita, Carmen, Earls Court And Japanese Tour; Josephine, HMS Pinafore, City Centre, New York; Clorinda, La Cenerentola, Garsington Festival; Dinah, Trouble, Tahiti, Belgian Tour; Suzanne, Robinson Crusoe, Iford Festival; Begger Woman, Sweeney Todd, The Royal Festival Hall; Ruth, The Pirates Of Penzance, Carl Rosa Opera Company, national tour of America and Canada; Mrs Lovett, Sweeney Todd, Gothernburg Opera; Numerous TV and radio appearances. Publications: Recordings include original cast albums of: Mary Poppins; The Witches Of Eastwick;

The Phantom Of The Opera; The Boyfriend; Bitter Sweet; Oliver; The Student Prince; Kismet; The 10th Anniversary Concert Of Les Miserables; The Killer Soprano; Serious Cabaret. Honours: Nominee, Laurence Olivier Award for Best Supporting Actress in a Musical. Address: c/o Hilary Gagan Associates, 187 Drury Lane, London, WC2B 5QD, England. www.rosemaryashe.com

ASHER Jane, b. 5 April 1946. Actress; Author; Businesswoman. m. Gerald Scarfe, 2 sons, 1 daughter. Career: As Cook: Owner Jane Asher's Party Cake Shop and Sugarcraft, 1990-; Cake Designer and Consultant for Sainsbury's, 1992-99; Spokesperson and Consultant, Heinz Frozen Desserts, 1999-2001; Cookware and Gift Food Designer, Debenhams, 1998-2005; Creator, Home Baking Mixes for Victoria Foods, 1999-; Actress: Films include: Greengage Summer; Masque of the Red Death; Alfie; Dreamchild; Tirant Lo Blanc, 2005; Death at a Funeral, 2006; TV Appearances include: Brideshead Revisited, 1981; Murder Most Horrid, 1991; The Choir, 1995; Good Living, 1997-99; Tricks Of The Trade, 1999; Crossroads, 2003; Murder at the Vicarage, 2004; New Tricks, 2005; A for Andromeda, 2006; Holby City, 2007; Stage Appearances include: Making it Better, Hampstead and Criterion Theatres, 1992; Things We Do for Love, Yvonne Arnaud and Gielgud Theatres, 1998; Is Everybody Happy, 2000; House and Garden, Royal National Theatre, 2000; What the Butler Saw, National Tour 2001; Festen, Almeida Theatre, 2004; Festen, Lyric Theatre, London, 2004-05; The World's Biggest Diamond, Royal Court Theatre. Publications include: The Moppy Stories, 1987, 2005; Calendar of Cakes, 1989; Eats for Treats, 1990; Time to Play, 1993; Jane Asher's Book of Cake Decorating Ideas, 1993; The Longing (novel), 1996; The Question (novel), 1998; Losing It (novel), 2002; Cakes for Fun, 2005; Beautiful Baking, 2007. Honour: Honorary LLD, Bristol University, 2001. Memberships: BAFTA; FORUM UK; Associate, RADA; Fellow, Royal Society of Arts; Charity Work: President: National Autistic Society, Arthritis Care, West London Family Service Unit; Vice-President: Child Accident Prevention Trust, Mobility Trust, National Deaf Children's Society. Address: c/o Actual Management, 7 Great Russell Street, London, WC1B 3NH, England.

ASHER Ronald E, b. 23 July 1926, Gringley-on-the-Hill, Nottinghamshire, England. University Professor. 2 sons. Education: BA, University of London, 1950; Certificate in Phonetics of French, University College London, 1951; PhD, University of London, 1955; DLitt, University of Edinburgh, 1993. Appointments: Lecturer, Linguistics, 1953-57, Lecturer in Tamil, 1957-65, School of Oriental and African Studies, University of London; Visiting Professor of Linguistics, University of Chicago, 1961-62; Senior Lecturer, 1965-70, Reader, 1970-77, Professor of Linguistics, 1977-93, Vice-Principal, 1990-93, Honorary Fellow, Faculty of Arts/ School of Humanities and Social Sciences, 1993-99, 2001-, University of Edinburgh; Visiting Professor of Linguistics and International Communication, International Christian University, Tokyo, 1994-95; First occupant of Vaikom Muhammad Basheer Chair, Mahatma Gandhi University, Kottayam, Kerala, India, 1995-96. Publications: Books include most recently: Critical essays on the novels and stories of Vaikom Muhammad Basheer, 1999; Colloquial Tamil (joint author), 2002; What the Sufi said (Translation from the Malayalam of novel by K P Ramanunni; joint translator), 2002; Wind Flowers: Contemporary Short Fiction from Kerala (joint editor and translator), 2004; Atlas of the World's Languages (joint editor), 2007. Honours: Listed in national and international biographical directories. Address: Linguistics

and English Language, The University of Edinburgh, Adam Ferguson Building, George Square, Edinburgh EH8 9LL, Scotland.

ASHIMOV Undassyn, b. 21 March 1951, Zerenda, Kokchetau oblast, Kazakhstan. Engineer; Electrician. m. Botagoz, 1 son, 1 daughter. Education: Specialist, Electrical Engineering, Kazakh Polytechnic Institute, 1973; Candidate of Technical Sciences, Kiev Polytechnic Institute, 1978; Doctor of Technical Sciences, Moscow Institute of Energetics, 1992. Appointments: Professor, First Vice Rector, Almaty Institute of Energetics, 1992-96; First Vice Rector, Kazakh National Technical University, 1996-2000; Senior Deputy Chairman, Higher Committee for Attestation, Republic of Kazakhstan, 2000-02; Rector, North Kazakhstan State University, 2002-. Publications: More than 160 scientific works; 2 monographs; 40 inventions. Honours: Dostyk State Medal of Kazakhstan; Academician, National Academy of Science; The United Europe, Kazakhstan International Award; Socrates, Kazakhstan International Award. Memberships: ICDE; CAMAN; EuroPACE; IAESTE; Consortium of Institutes of Kazakhstan and European Countries; Kazakhstan-American Social Financial Consortium. Address: 86 Pushkin St, North Kazakhstan State University, Petropavlovsk, 150000, Republic of Kazakhstan. E-mail: mail@nkzu.kz

ASHINO Makoto, b. 19 August 1965, Tsuruoka, Japan. Research Scientist. m. Chiemi Furuike, 2 sons. Education: BEng, Waseda University, Tokyo, 1990; MS, Materials Science, Tokyo Institute of Technology, 1992; PhD, Materials Engineering, Kanazawa Institute of Technology, Japan, 1995. Appointments: Assistant, Department of Electronic Engineering, Kanazawa Institute of Technology, Japan, 1992-95; Full time Researcher, Ohtsu Photon Control Project, Kanagawa Academy of Science and Technology, Kawasaki, Japan, 1995-97; Research Scientist, Bio Gr, Joint Research Center for Atom Technology, Tsukuba, Japan, 1997-2001; Research Scientist, Scanning Probe Method Gr, Institute of Applied Physics, University of Hamburg, Germany, 2001-. Publications: Fabrication and Evaluation of Localised Plasmon Resonance Probe for Near-field Optical Microscopy/ Spectroscopy, 1998; Atomic Resolution Noncontact Atomic Force and Scanning Tunneling Microscopy of $TiO_2(110)$-(1x1) and (1x2), 2001; Atomic Resolution Dynamic Force Microscopy and Spectroscopy of Single-Walled Carbon Nanotubes, 2004. Honours: Gold Medal, The Japan Society of Applied Physics, 1997; Outstanding Paper of the Year, Institute of Electrical Engineering, Japan, 1998; Most Outstanding Poster, Nano Scale II, International Conference, 2004; Listed in international biographical dictionaries. Memberships: The Physical Society of Japan; The Japan Society of Applied Physics.

ASHKENAZY Vladimir, b. 6 July 1937, Gorky, USSR. Musician. m. Thorunn Sofia Johannsdottir, 2 sons, 3 daughters. Education: Central School of Music, Moscow, 1945-55; Moscow Conservatory, 1955-62. Appointments: Conductor, Philharmonia Orchestra, Royal Philharmonic Orchestra, Cleveland Orchestra, Deutsches Symphonie-Orchester Berlin; Guest conductor, Berlin Philharmonic, Boston Symphony, Los Angeles Philharmonic, San Francisco Symphony, Philadelphia and Concertgebouw Orchestras; Chief Conductor of the Czech Philharmonic Orchestra, 1998-2003; Conductor Laureate, Philharmonia Orchestra; Music Director, NHK Symphony Orchestra, 2004-05; Music Director, European Union Youth Orchestra; Conductor Laureate, Iceland Symphony Orchestra. Honours: 2nd prize, Chopin Competition, Warsaw, 1955; 1st prize, Queen Elisabeth Competition, Brussels, 1956; 1st prize, Tchaikovsky Competition, Moscow, 1962; Six Grammy awards, -1999; Order of the Falcon, highest civil decoration of Iceland. Address: Savinka, Kappelistrasse 15, 6045 Meggen, Switzerland.

ASHLEY Bernard, b. 2 April 1935, London, England. Writer. Education: Teachers Certificate; Advanced Diploma, Cambridge Institute of Education. Publications: The Trouble with Donovan Croft, 1974; Terry on the Fence, 1975; All My Men, 1977; A Kind of Wild Justice, 1978; Break in the Sun, 1980; Dinner Ladies Don't Count, 1981; Dodgem, 1982; High Pavement Blues, 1983; Janey, 1985; Running Scared, 1986; Bad Blood, 1988; The Country Boy, The Secret of Theodore Brown, 1989; Clipper Street, 1990; Seeing off Uncle Jack, 1992; Cleversticks, Three Seven Eleven, 1993; Johnnie's Blitz, 1995; I Forgot, Said Troy, A Present for Paul, 1996; City Limits, 1997; Tiger Without Teeth, 1998; Growing Good, Little Soldier, 1999; Revenge House, 2002; Freedom Flight, 2003; Ten Days to Zero, 2005; Smokescreen, Down to the Wire, 2006; Flashpoint, Angel Boy, 2007; Solitaire, 2008. Contributions to: Guardian; Books for Your Children; Junior Education; Books for Keeps; Times Educational Supplement; School Librarian. Honours: The Other Award, 1976; Runner Up, Carnegie Medal, 1979, 1986, 1999; Royal TV Society Best Children's Entertainment Programme, 1993; Runner Up, Guardian Award, 2000; Honorary Doctorate in Education, Greenwich University, 2003; Honorary Doctorate in Letters, Leicester University, 2004. Memberships: Writers Guild. Address: 128 Heathwood Gardens, London SE7 8ER, England. Website: www.bashley.com

ASHLEY Leonard Raymond Nelligan, b. 5 December 1928, Miami, Florida, USA. Professor Emeritus of English; Author; Editor. Education: BA, 1949, MA, 1950, McGill University; AM, 1953, PhD, 1956, Princeton University. Appointments: Instructor, University of Utah, 1953-56; Assistant to the Air Historian, Royal Canadian Air Force, 1956-58; Instructor, University of Rochester, 1958-61; Faculty, New School for Social Research (part-time), 1962-72; Faculty, Brooklyn College of the City University, New York, 1961-95; Professor Emeritus, 1995-. Publications include: A Military History of Modern China (collaborator); Shakespeare's Jest Book (editor); Phantasms of the Living (editor); Ballad Poetry of Ireland (editor); Colley Cibber; George Peele: The Man and His Work; Relics of Irish Poetry (editor); Language in Contemporary Society (co-editor); Language in The Era of Globalization (co-editor); Language and Identity (co-editor); Eleven books on the occult; Geolinguistic Perspectives (co-editor); Language and Politics (co-editor); Phantasms of the Living (editor); Language in Modern Society; Animal Crackers, George Alfred Henty and the Victorian Mind, and others; Regular reviewer in Bibliotheque d'Humanisme et Renaissance, etc. Contributions to: Anthologies such as Modern American Drama: The Female Canon and Art, Glitter and Glitz, its Mainstream Playwrights... 1920s America; Reference books such as: Great Writers of the English Language; History of the Theater; Encyclopaedias (US and abroad); DLB; New DNB; Numerous works on names and naming including: Names of Places, Names in Literature, Names in Popular Culture, Art Attack: Essays on Names in Satire, Cornish Names; Over 160 articles in periodicals and scholarly journals; Poetry in over 60 publications; Co-editor of conference proceedings; Many other collaborations. Honours: Shakespeare Gold Medal, 1949; LHD (Columbia Theological) honoris causa, 1998; American Name Society Best Article Award; Fellowships and grants; American Name Society, president 1979, 1987, long-time member editorial board, executive board; American Name Society; International

Linguistic Association, Secretary, 1980-82; American Name Society, President, 1979, 1987; American Association of University Professors, former president, Brooklyn College Chapter; McGill Graduates Society of New York, President, 1970-75; American Society of Geolinguistics, president 1991-; Princeton Club of New York; New York Academy of Sciences; Modern Language Association. Address: Library Technical Services, Brooklyn College of the City University of New York, Brooklyn, NY 11210, USA.

ASHMOLE Michael Achille, b. 10 February 1939, Derby, England. Chartered Forester. m. Jean, 2 sons, 2 daughters. Education: Bemrose Grammar School, Derby; Fellow, Institute of Chartered Foresters. Appointments: Ex-Director, International Union of Societies of Foresters; Director & Chairman, Fountain International, 1989-; Chairman, AHG Group Ltd, 1989-; President, The Scottish Aero Club, 2003-. Memberships: Catenian Association; Royal Perth Golfing & Country Club; Flying Farmers Association; Scottish Aero Club. Address: Waterside, Isla Road, Perth, PH2 7HG, Scotland.

ASHTON Rt Hon Catherine Margaret, Baroness Ashton of Upholland, b. 20 March 1956. Leader of the House of Lords; Lord President of the Council. m. Peter Kellner, 1 son, 1 daughter. Appointments: Life peer, 1999; Parliamentary Under-Secretary of State, 2001, Minister for Sure Start, 2002, Department for Education and Skills; Parliamentary Under Secretary of State at the Department for Constitutional Affairs, 2004-; Parliamentary Under Secretary of State, Ministry of Justice, 2007-; Admitted to Privy Council, 2006; Leader of the House of Lords, 2007-; Lord President of the Council, 2007-.

ASHTON Robert, b. 21 July 1924, Chester, England. Retired University Professor. m. Margaret Alice Sedgwick, 30 August 1946, 2 daughters. Education: Magdalen College School, Oxford, 1938-40; University College, Southampton, 1946-49; BA, First Class Honours, London, 1949; PhD, London School of Economics, 1953. Appointments: Assistant Lecturer, Lecturer, Senior Lecturer, Nottingham University, 1952-63; Visiting Associate Professor, University of California, Berkeley, 1962-63; Professor, 1963-89, Emeritus Professor, 1989-, University of East Anglia; Visiting Fellow, All Souls College, Oxford, 1974-75, 1987; James Ford Special Lecturer in History, University of Oxford, 1982. Publications: The English Civil War: Conservatism and Revolution 1603-49, 1978, 2nd edition, 1989; The Crown and the Money Market 1603-40, 1960; James I by his Contemporaries, 1969; The City and the Court 1603-1643, 1979; Reformation and Revolution, 1558-1660, 1984; Counter Revolution: The Second Civil War and its Origins 1646-1648, 1994. Contributions to: Economic History Review; Bulletin of Institute of Historical Research; Past and Present; Historical Journal. Membership: Royal Historical Society, fellow 1961-, vice-president, 1983-84. Address: The Manor House, Brundall, Norwich NR13 5JY, England.

ASKEW Reginald James Albert, b. 16 May 1928, Aberdeen, Scotland. Clerk in Holy Orders. m. Kate Wigley, 1 son, 2 daughters. Education: BA, 1951, MA, 1956, Corpus Christi College, Cambridge; Scholae Cancelarii, Lincoln, 1955-57; King's College London, 1957-61. Appointments: Ordained Deacon, Church of England, 1957; Ordained Priest, 1958; Curate of Highgate, 1957-61; Lecturer and Vice-Principal, Wells Theological College, 1961-69; Priest Vicar, Wells Cathedral, 1961-69; Vicar, Christ Church, Lancaster Gate, 1969-73; Principal, Salisbury and Wells Theological College, 1973-87; Dean, King's College London, 1987-93; Retired,

1993. Publications: The Tree of Noah, 1971; Muskets and Altars, Jeremy Taylor and the Last of the Anglicans, 1997; Contributor: The Reality of God, 1986. Honours: Pilkington Prize, 1957, 1958; Canon, 1975-87, Canon Emeritus, 1988-, Salisbury Cathedral; Chaplain, Worshipful Company of Merchant Taylors, 1996-97. Memberships: Corrymeela Community, 1971-; President, Bath and Wells Clerical Society, 1996-. Address: Carters Cottage, North Wootton, Shepton Mallet, Somerset BA4 4AF, England. E-mail: reginald.askew@virgin.net

ASKEW Robert Wilson, b. 5 May 1964, Hertford, England. Chartered Scientist. m. Jacqueline Lisa, 2 daughters. Education: BSc (Hons), University of Brighton; MSc, Wye College, University of London. Appointments: Associate of Waterman CPM, 1995-2001; Associate of WSP Environmental Ltd, 2001-2005; Principal, Edafos, 2005-. Publications: Lowest Common Denominator (A review of the British Standard for topsoil), 1995. Memberships: Chartered Scientist, Science Council; President Elect, Institute of Professional Soil Scientists, 2006-2008; Registered Environmental Impact Assessment Practitioner, Institute of Environmental Management and Assessment. Address: The Old Stables, Upexe, Exeter, Devon, EX5 5ND, England. E-mail: robaskew@edafos.co.uk

ASLAM Muhammad, b. 1 June 1950, Dera Ghazi Khan, Pakistan. Medical Professor. m. 1 son, 1 daughter. Education: MBBS, M Phil (Physiology), University of Punjab, Lahore, Pakistan; PhD (Physiology), University of London, England. Appointments: Dean, Faculty of Medicine, NUST, Rawalpindi; Adviser in Basic Medical Sciences; Professor of Physiology, Head, Department of Physiology, Army Medical College, Rawalpindi; Managing Editor, Pakistan Armed Forces Medical Journal. Publications: 52 original articles; 16 review articles; 18 abstracts; 16 editorials; 2 books review; 2 case reports; Author of book, Laboratory Manual in Physiology, 1992. Honours: Pakistan Academy of Sciences Open Gold Medal in Medical Sciences, 1997; Conferred Fellowship, Pakistan Academy of Medical Sciences, 1998; Conferred Fellowship, College of Physicians & Surgeons, Pakistan, 1999; Man of the Year 2002, XIII Star Award; Conferred Hilal-i-Imtiaz (Military), Islamic Republic of Pakistan, 2004; Honorary Fellowship, Bangladesh College of Physicians & Surgeons, 2005. Memberships: Pakistan Physiological Society; Asia Pacific Scientific Editors Association, Singapore; Pakistan Army Representative for International Community of Military Medicine; Pakistan Medical Journalists Association; Academic Council of Foundation University, Pakistan. Address: Army Medical College, National University of Sciences & Technology, Abid Majid Road, Rawalpindi Cantt, Pakistan. E-mail: malsam@nust.edu.pk

ASNAFI Nader, b. 9 January 1960, Tehran, Iran. Manager. m. Maria Dahlberg, 2 sons. Education: MSc, 1987; Licentiate, 1990; PhD, 1997; Associate Professor, 2002. Appointments: Manufacturing Engineer, Esselte Dymo, Tore, Sweden, 1984-85; Research Engineer and Director of Studies, Department of Materials Science and Production Technology, Luleå University of Technology, Sweden, 1985-91; Senior Researcher and Research Group Leader, Swedish Institute for Metals Research, 1991-98; Project Leader, Industrial Development Centre, Olofström, Sweden, 1998-99; Manager, Sapa Technology, 1999-2001; Manager, Advanced Engineering, Product Design and Technology Development, Volvo Cars Body Components, Olofström, 2001-06; Senior Manager, Research and Advanced Engineering, Volvo Cars, Göteborg, 2006-. Memberships: Chair and National Technical Secretary, Swedish Deep Drawing Research Group. Address: Jupitervägen 5, 29170 Kristianstad, Sweden. E-mail: nasnafi@volvocars.com

ASPLUND Olle Olof Arne, b. 11 March 1943, Stockholm, Sweden. Consultant Plastic Surgeon. m. Franziska, 3 sons. Education: Medical Licentiate, Karolinska Hospital, Stockholm, Sweden, 1970; Specialisation in Plastic Surgery, Stockholm, 1978; Dr. Med. Scis. Korolinska Institute, Stockholm, 1984. Appointments: Danderyd Hospital, Stockholm, 1970-74; Karolinska Hospital, Stockholm, 1975-84; Charing Cross Hospital, 1991-2002; Consultant Plastic Surgeon, Charing Cross Hospital, 2002-. Publications: Numerous articles in medical journals include: Breast reconstruction after mastectomy (Dr. Med. Scis. Thesis), 1984; Vertical scar breast reduction, 1996. Honour: Barrons Prize, British Association of Plastic Surgeons, 1995. Memberships: British Association of Aesthetic Plastic Surgeons; British Association of Plastic Surgeons; Swedish and Nordic Association of Plastic Surgeons; European Section of International Confederation for Plastic, Reconstructive and Aesthetic Surgery. Address: Charing Cross Hospital, Department of Plastic Surgery, Fulham Place Road, London W6 8RF, England.

ASSUMPCÃO Francisco B Jr, b. 7 September 1951, São Paulo, Brazil. Psychiatrist. 2 daughters. Education: MD, Medical School FUABC, S Andre, Brazil, 1974; Doctor, Psychology PUC, São Paulo, Brazil, 1988; Professor, Child Psychiatry, Medicine School, Universidade De São Paulo, Brazil, 1993-2000. Appointments: Professor of Psychopathology, Psychology Institute, São Paulo University, 2005-. Publications: Child and Adolescent Psychiatry Handbook; Psychology and Comics; Psiquiatria Infantil Brasileira; Psiquiatria da Infância e Adolescência; Autismo; Adolescência Normal e Patologica; Semiologia em Psiquiatria da Infância e da Adolescência; Handbook of Child and Adolescent Psychiatry, 2003; Sexuality and Mental Retardation, 2005. Honour: Colar Gran Cruz Merito Da Medicina; Medal for Science and Peace. Memberships: Brazilian Psychiatry Society; APAL; Brazilian Child Psychiatry Association; President, Child Psychiatry Department, Brazilian Psychiatric Association, 2004-. Address: Al Lorena 105 ap 83, J Paulista, São Paulo, Brazil, CEP 01424-002. E-mail: cassiterides@bol.com.br

ASTROM Paul Fredrik Karl, b. 15 January 1929, Sundsvall, Vaesternld, Sweden. Archaeologist; Publisher. m. (1) Lena Soderhjelm, 1957, divorced 1974, 2 sons, (2) Inez Elisabet Mossberg, 1974, 1 son. Education: BA, University of Uppsala, Sweden, 1950; MA, 1951, BLic, 1957, University of Lund; PhD, University of Lund, 1958, University of Vienna, 1994, University of Athens, 1995, Joannina, 2001. Appointments: 1st amanuensis, Museum of Antiquities, University of Lund, 1951-55; Assistant Professor, University of Lund, 1957-69; Cultural Attaché, Royal Swedish Embassy, Athens, 1958-63; Director, Swedish Institute in Athens, 1958-63, Swedish Institute in Rome, 1967-69; Visiting Assistant Professor, University of Missouri, Columbia, 1963-64; Professor, Goteborg (Sweden) University, 1969-93; Publisher, Studies in Mediterranean Archaeology; others. Publications: Author: The Middle Cypriote Bronze Age, 1957; The Cuirass Tomb, Parts I and II, 1977, 1981; Gunnar Ekelof och antiken, 1992; others; Author/Editor: Hala Sultan Tekke 1-12, 1975-2007. Honours: Faxe Prize for Best Dissertation, University of Lund, 1958; Knight, Royal Order of the North Star, 1974; Prize, Swedish Academy, 1992; Grand Commander, Order of the Merit of Cyprus, 2005. Memberships: Fellow, Explorers Club; Member: Royal Society of Humanities and Sciences, Lund; Royal Society of Letters, Gothenburg; Society of Letters, Lund; Austrian Archaeological Institute; Royal Academy of Letters, Stockholm; Honorary Member: Archaeological Society, Athens; Society of Cypriote Studies; Ancient Fingerprint Society; Corresponding Member, Institut de France. Address: Mimersvaegen 44, SE-43364 Saevedalen, Sweden. E-mail: paul.astrom@bredband.net

ATALAR Cavit, b. 20 February 1948, Yagmuralan, Cyprus. Geotechnical Engineer. m. Ayse Ahmet, 1976, 3 children. Education: Diploma, Lefke Secondary, 1963, Turkish Lycee, 1966; MS, Ankara University, 1973; PhD, Geology, London University, 1980. Appointments: Faculty Member, 1994-, Associate Professor, 2001, Geotechnical Engineering, Near East University. Publications: Papers and articles in professional journals; Contributions to conference proceedings. Honours: First Class Honour, Ankara University, 1973; Fulbright Scholar, Cyprus Fulbright Commission, 2000. Memberships: Geotechnical Institute, Association of Engineering Geologists; Turkish National Committee of Soil Mechanics and Geotechnical Engineering. Address: Near East University, Near East Boulevard, Nicosia, TRNC, Mersin 10, Turkey.

ATHAWALE Vilas Dattatray, b. 3 November 1948, Mumbai, India. Professor. m. Vaishali, 1 son, 1 daughter. Education: BSc, Chemistry, Physics and Mathematics, 1969, MSc, Physical Chemistry, 1972, PhD, Chemistry, 1983, University of Mumbai. Appointments: Demonstrator, 1972-75, Lecturer, 1975-85, Reader, 1985-78, Professor, 1978-, Head of Department, 2002-, Department of Chemistry, University of Mumbai. Publications: Co-author, book: Experimental Physical Chemistry, 2001; Co-author of over 90 publications in the field of polymer chemistry in international journals include most recently: New interpenetrating polymer networks based on uralkyde/poly (methacrylate), 2001; Recent developments in polyurethanes and poly(acrylates) interpenetrating polymer networks, review, 2001; Lipase-catalyzed synthesis of geranyl methacrylate by transesterification: Study of reaction parameters, 2002; Effect of reaction parameters on synthesis of citronellyl methactylate by lipase-catalyzed transesterification, 2002; 4 review articles. Honours include: Member, Advisory Board, Journal of Polymer Materials; Member of Referee Panel of: Journal of Organic Chemistry; Organic Letters; Macromolecules; Journal of Applied Polymer Science; Journal of Chemical Engineering Data; Journal of Polymer Engineering and Science; Progress in Organic Coatings; Paint India; Journal of Polymer Materials; Biotechnology Progress; European Coatings Journal; Member, Research Board of Advisors, American Biographical Institute; Man of the Year 2002, American Biographical Institute; Listed In Who's Who publications and biographical dictionaries. Memberships: Membership offered by American Association for the Advancement of Science, American Association of Cereal Chemists, Oil and Colour Chemists Association, UK. Address: Department of Chemistry, University of Mumbai, Vidyanagari, Mumbai-400098, India. E-mail: vilasda@yahoo.com

ATHERTON David, Conductor. Education: Music, Cambridge University. Appointments: Joined music staff, 1967, Resident Conductor, 12 years, Royal Opera House, London; Guest Conductor, La Scala, Milan; Co-founder, Music Director, London Sinfonietta, 1967-; Music Director, San Diego Symphony Orchester, 1980-87; Titled positions with BBC Symphony, Royal Liverpool Philharmonic and BBC National Orchestra of Wales; Devised and conducted festivals in London with London Sinfonietta, London Symphony Orchestra, BBC Symphony Orchestra and the Royal Opera

House; Music Director, Hong Kong Philharmonic Orchestra, 1989-2000. Publications: Numerous recordings, including highly praised collections of works by Schoenberg, Janacek and Weill. Honours: Edison Award; Many Grammy Award nominations; Grand Prix du Disque; Serge Koussevitsky Critics' Award; Prix Caecilia; International Record Critics' Award; OBE, 2000; Conductor Laureate, Hong Kong Philharmonic Orchestra, 2000. Address: Lincoln House, 300 High Holborn, London WC1V 7JH, England. Website: askonasholt.co.uk

ATHERTON Richard, b. 15 February 1928, Liverpool, England. Catholic Priest. Education: St Francis de Sales School; St Francis Xavier Grammar School; Upholland College. Appointments: Assistant Priest, St Philip, St Cecilia's, 1954-60, Liverpool, 1960-65; RC Chaplain, HMP Walton, 1965-75; Senior RC Chaplain, HMP Appleton Thorn, 1975-77; Principal RC Chaplain, Prison Department, Home Office, 1977-89; Parish Priest, St Joseph's, Leigh, 1989-91; President, Ushaw College, Durham, 1991-96; Chaplain to Archbishop of Liverpool, 1996-2001; Retired. Publications: Summons to Serve, 1987; New Light, 1993; Praying the Prayer of the Church, 1998; Praying the Sunday Psalms (Year A) 2001, (Year B) 2002, (Year C) 2003. Honours: BA; MA; Dip Crim; OBE. Address: 8 Lindley Road, Elland, HX5 0TE, England. E-mail: r.atherton@rcaolp.co.uk

ATKINSON Rowan Sebastian, b. 6 January 1955, Newcastle-upon-Tyne, England. Actor; Author. m. Sunetra Sastry, 1990, 1 daughter, 1 son. Education: Universities of Newcastle and Oxford. Appointments: Stage Appearances include: Beyond a Joke, Hampstead, 1978; Oxford University, Revues at Edinburgh Fringe, One Man Show, London, 1981; The Nerd, 1985; The New Revue, 1986; The Sneeze, 1988; TV Appearances: Not the Nine O'Clock News, 1979-82; Blackadder, 1983; Blackadder II, 1985; Blackadder the Third, 1987; Blackadder Goes Forth, 1989; Mr Bean (13 episodes), 1990-96; Rowan Atkinson on Location in Boston, 1993; Full Throttle, 1994; The Thin Blue Line, 1995; Films Include: Never Say Never Again; The Tall Guy, The Appointments of Dennis Jennings, 1989; The Witches, 1990; Four Weddings and a Funeral, Hot Shots - Part Deux, 1994; Bean: The Ultimate Disaster Movie, 1997; Blackadder – Back and Forth, Maybe Baby, 2000; Rat Race, Scooby Doo, 2002; Johnny English, Love Actually, Mickey's PhilharMagic (voice), 2003; Keeping Mum, 2005; Mr. Bean's Holiday, 2007. Address: c/o PBJ Management Ltd, 7 Soho Street, London W1D 3DQ, England. E-mail: general@pbjmgt.co.uk

ATTENBOROUGH David Frederick, Sir, b. 8 May 1926, London, England. Naturalist; Film-Maker; Author. Education: Zoology, Clare College, Cambridge, England. Appointments: Military Service, Royal Navy, 1947-49; Editorial Assistant, educational publishing; Joined BBC Television, Trainee Producer, 1952; First expedition to West Africa, 1954; Many trips to study wildlife and human cultures, 1954-64; TV series, Zoo Quest; Controller, BBC2, 1965-68; Director of Television Programmes, BBC, 1969-72; Member, Board of Management; TV Series include: Life on Earth, 1979, The Living Planet, 1983, The Trials of Life, 1990; The Private Life of Plants, 1995; The Life of Birds, 1998; Life of Mammals, 2002; Life in the Undergrowth, The Life Collection, 2005; Planet Earth, 2007. Publications: Zoo Quest to Guiana, 1956; Zoo Quest for a Dragon, 1957; Zoo Quest in Paraguay, 1959; Quest in Paradise, 1960; Zoo Quest to Madagascar, 1961; Quest under Capricorn, 1963; The Tribal Eye, 1976; Life on Earth, 1979; The Living Planet, 1984; The First Eden, 1987; The Trials of Life, 1990; The Private Life of Plants,

1994; The Life of Birds, 1998; The Life of Mammals, 2002; Life on Air, autobiography, 2002; Life in the Undergrowth, 2005. Honours include: Silver Medal, Zoological Society of London, 1966; Gold Medal Royal Geographical Society; Kalinga Prize, UNESCO; Honorary Degrees: Leicester, London, Birmingham, Liverpool, Heriot-Watt, Sussex, Bath, Ulster, Durham, Bristol, Glasgow, Essex, Cambridge, Oxford; Knighted, 1985; Encyclopaedia Britannica Award, 1987; Edinburgh Medal, Edinburgh Science Festival, 1998; BP Natural World Book Prize, 1998; Faraday Prize, Royal Society, 2003; International Documentary Association Career Achievement Award, 2003; Raffles Medal, Zoological Society of London, 2004; Caird Medal, National Maritime Museum, 2004; British Book Awards Lifetime Achievement Award, 2004. Memberships include: Fellow, Royal Society, Honorary Fellow, British Academy of Film and Television Arts, The Culture Show British Icon Award, 2006. Address: 5 Park Road, Richmond, Surrey, England.

ATTENBOROUGH, Baron Attenborough of Richmond-upon-Thames, Sir Richard Samuel Attenborough, b. 29 August 1923, Cambridge, England. Actor; Producer; Director. m. Sheila Beryl Grant Sim, 1945, 1 son, 2 daughters. Education: Royal Academy of Dramatic Art, London. Appointments: First Stage Appearance as Richard Miller in Ah! Wilderness, Palmers Green 1941; West End Debut, Awake and Sing, 1942; First Film Appearance, In Which We Serve, 1942; Joined RAF, 1943; Seconded to RAF Film Unit for Journey Together, 1944; Demobilised, 1946; Returned to Stage, 1949; Formed Beaver Films, with Bryan Forbes, 1959; Allied Film Makers, 1960; Goodwill Ambassador for UNICEF, 1987-; Director, Chelsea Football Club, 1969-82; Many stage appearances; Film Appearances: School for Secrets; The Man Within; Dancing With Crime; Brighton Rock; London Belongs to Me; The Guinea Pig; The Lost People; Boys in Brown; Morning Departure; The Magic Box; The Great Escape; Dr Doolittle; David Copperfield; Jurassic Park; Miracle on 34th Street; The Lost World: Jurassic Park; Elizabeth; Puckoon; Snow Prince, 2006; Many others; Produced: Whistle Down the Wind, 1961; The L Shaped Room; Directed: Young Winston, 1972; A Bridge Too Far, 1976; Magic, 1978; A Chorus Line, 1985; Closing the Ring, 2004; Produced and Directed: Oh! What a Lovely War, 1968; Gandhi, 1981; Cry Freedom!, 1987; Chaplin, 1992; Shadowlands, 1993; In Love and War, 1997; Grey Owl, 1999; Closing the Ring, 2007. Publications: In Search of Gandhi, 1982; Richard Attenborough's Chorus Line, 1986; Cry Freedom, A Pictorial Record, 1987. Honours: 8 Oscars; 5 BAFTA Awards; 5 Hollywood Golden Globes; Directors Guild of America Award; others. Memberships: Tate Foundation; Royal Academy of Dramatic Arts; Help a London Child; President of RADA; President of BAFTA; Others. Address: Old Friars, Richmond Green, Surrey, TW9 1NQ, England.

ATWOOD Margaret (Eleanor), b. 18 November 1939, Ottawa, Ontario, Canada. Poet; Author; Critic. m. Graeme Gibson, 1 daughter. Education: BA, Victoria College, University of Toronto, 1961; AM, Radcliffe College, Cambridge, Massachusetts, 1962; Harvard University, 1962-63, 1965-67. Appointments: Teacher, University of British Columbia, 1964-65, Sir George Williams University, Montreal, 1967-68, University of Alberta, 1969-70, York University, 1971-72; Writer-in-Residence, University of Toronto, 1972-73, University of Alabama, Tuscaloosa, 1985, Macquarie University, Australia, 1987; Berg Chair, New York University, 1986. Publications: Poetry: Double Persephone, 1961; The Circle Game, 1964; Kaleidoscopes Baroque, 1965; Talismans for Children, 1965; Speeches for

Doctor Frankenstein, 1966; The Animals in That Country, 1968; The Journals of Susanna Moodie, 1970; Procedures for Underground, 1970; Oratorio for Sasquatch, Man and Two Androids, 1970; Power Politics, 1971; You Are Happy, 1974; Selected Poems, 1976; Marsh Hawk, 1977; Two-Headed Poems, 1978; True Stories, 1981; Notes Towards a Poem That Can Never Be Written, 1981; Snake Poems, 1983; Interlunar, 1984; Selected Poems II: Poems Selected and New, 1976-1986, 1986; Selected Poems 1966-1984, 1990; Margaret Atwood Poems 1965-1975, 1991; Morning in the Burned House, 1995; The Door, 2007; Fiction: The Edible Woman, 1969; Surfacing, 1972; Lady Oracle, 1976; Dancing Girls, 1977; Life Before Man, 1979; Bodily Harm, 1981; Encounters With the Element Man, 1982; Murder in the Dark, 1983; Bluebeard's Egg, 1983; Unearthing Suite, 1983; The Handmaid's Tale, 1985; Cat's Eye, 1988; Wilderness Tips, 1991; Good Bones, 1992; The Robber Bride, 1993; Alias Grace, 1996; The Blind Assassin, 2000; Oryx and Crake, 2003; Telling Tales (contribution to charity anthology), 2004; The Penelopiad, 2005; Juvenile: Up in the Tree, 1978; Anna's Pet, 1980; For the Birds, 1990; Princess Prunella and the Purple Peanut, 1995; Rude Ramsay and the Roaring Radishes, 2003; Bashful Bob & Doleful Dorinda, 2006; Non-Fiction: Survival: A Thematic Guide to Canadian Literature, 1972; Days of The Rebels 1815-1840, 1977; Second Words: Selected Critical Prose, 1982; The Oxford Book of Canadian Verse in English (editor), 1982; The Best American Short Stories (editor with Shannon Ravenel), 1989; Strange Things: The Malevolent North in Canadian Literature, 1995; Negotiating with the Dead: A Writer on Writing, 2002; Moving Targets: Writing with Intent 1982-2004, 2004; Curious Pursuits: Occasional Writings, 2005; Contributions to: Books in Canada; Canadian Literature; Globe and Mail; Harvard Educational Review; The Nation; New York Times Book Review; Washington Post. Honours: Guggenheim Fellowship, 1981; Companion of the Order of Canada, 1981; Fellow, Royal Society of Canada; Foreign Honorary Member, American Academy of Arts and Sciences, 1988; Order of Ontario, 1990; Centennial Medal, Harvard University, 1990; Commemorative Medal, 125th Anniversary of Canadian Confederation, 1992; Giller Prize, 1996; Author of the Year, Canadian Book Industry Award, 1997; Marian McFadden Memorial Lecturer, Indianapolis-Marion County Public Library Foundation, 1998; Booker Prize, 2000; International Crime Writers' Association Dashiell Hammett Award, 2001; Radcliffe Medal, 2003; Harold Washington Literary Award, 2003; Honorary degrees. Memberships: Writers Union of Canada, president, 1981-82; PEN International, president, 1985-86. Address: McClelland & Stewart, 481 University Ave, Suite 900, Toronto, Ontario, Canada M5G 2E9.

AUBERGER Bernard, b. 5 December 1937, Gennevilliers, France. Judge. m. Christine, 3 sons, 1 daughter. Education: Ingénieur Civil des Mines; Master in Law and Political Science; Diplômé de l'Ecole Nationale d'Administration; Inspecteur général des Finances. Appointments: Chief Executive Officer, Credit Agricole, 1986-98; Chief Executive Officer, Banque Cortal, 1991-98; Chief Executive Officer, Credit du Nord, 1993-95; Chief Executive Officer, Banque Directe, 1993-2001; Judge, Commercial Court, Paris, 1998-. Publications: La Reforme de l'Entreprise (en Collaboration), 1975. Honours: Officer de la Legion d'Honneur; Officer du Mérite National; Chevalier du Mérite Agricole. Memberships: Board, Musée Toulouse Lautrec. Address: 193 Boulevard St Germain, 75007 Paris, France. E-mail: auberger.bernard@wanadoo.fr

AUGSBACH Linda Jean Keller, b. 7 June 1951, Glendale, West Virginia, USA. Elementary School Teacher. m. Charles William Augsbach. Education: AA Degree, Minnesota Bible College; Postgraduate studies, Kentucky Christian College, 1973-74; BS Degree, Malone College, Canton, Ohio, 1975. Appointments: Grades 1-8 Tutor, Minerva Local School, Ohio, 1976-77; Grades 1 and 2 Teacher, Christian School of Cincinnati, Ohio, 1977-78; Substitute Teacher, Canton (Ohio) City School, 1978-82; Substitute Teacher, Pasco County School, Florida, 1982-83; Grade 6 Teacher, Dade City, Florida, 1983-87; Grade 4 Teacher, New Port Richey, Florida, 1987-88; Grade 6 Teacher, 1988-91, Grade 4 Teacher, 1991-96, alternately Grade 4 and Grade 5 Teacher, 1996-99, alternately Grade 4 and Grade 5 Teacher, 2000-, Mittye P. Locke Elementary, Elfers, Florida. Publications: Article in Learning Magazine, 1991; Copyright secured, 1999, for large curriculum: Learning: It's Just a Game – Science, History, Word Structure, Grammar, Writing and More, All Rolled Into One Exciting Unit, currently preparing for publication. Honours: The Best Teachers in America Selected by the Best Students, 1996; Selected attendee of Governor Bush's Second Annual Educators' Leadership Summit, 2002; Listed in Who's Who publications and biographical dictionaries. Membership: Christian Educators' Association International. Address: 1441 Wegman Drive, Tarpon Springs, FL 34689, USA.

AUGUSTYN Józef, b. 21 March 1950, Olpiny, Poland. Jesuit; Theologian. Education: BA Philosophical Studies, Jesuit School of Philosophy, Krakow, Poland, 1971-73; Theological Studies, Jesuit School of Theology, Warsaw, Poland, 1973-76; Graduate Studies, ThL, Religious Education, ATK University, Warsaw; Christian Spirituality, Gregorian University Rome, 1981-82; Research, The Center of Ignatian Spirituality, Quebec, Canada, 1989; PhD, Theology, Catholic University, Warsaw, 1994; Habilitation (qualification as a University Professor), 2002. Appointments: Professor, University School of Philosophy and Education "Ignatianum", Krakow, Poland; Editor, Pastores, 1996-2001; Currently Editor, Spiritual Life; Advisor, Polish Government, Department of Education, 1996-; Reviewer of Textbooks on sexual education and family values and public health and education, 1997-2000. Publications: 45 books and over 220 articles in the fields of spiritual life, Christian education, psychology and religion include: A Practice of Spiritual Direction, 1993; Sexual Integration. A Guidebook for discovering and maturing human sexuality, 1994; Homosexuality and Love, 1996; Sexual education in schools and families, 1997; Fatherhood: Pedagogical and spiritual dimensions, 1999; Know Yourself, 1999; Celibacy: Pedagogical and spiritual dimensions, 1999; Meditations based on the Spiritual Exercises of St Ignatius Loyola, 6 volumes, 2001; Deeply Shaken: The Church's Self-Cleaning, 2002, The Lustration of Priests, 2006, The Art of Confessing (editor), 2006, The Art of Spiritual Direction (editor), 2007. Honour: Award from the journal Powsciagliwosc I Praca, 1991. Memberships: Fellow of the State Committee, Department of Education, responsible for creating and implementing the school subject, Human Development and Sexuality, 1998; Advisor, Committee for Christian Education, Polish Conference of Catholic Bishops. Address: ul Kopernika 26, PL-31-501 Cracow, Poland.

AUKIN David, b. 12 February 1942, England. Producer. m. Nancy Meckler, 2 sons. Education: St Paul's; St Edmund Hall, Oxford. Appointments: President, Society of West End Theatres; Artistic Director, Hampstead Theatre; Artistic Director, Leicester Haymarket; Executive Director, Royal National Theatre; Head of Film, Channel 4;

Director, Daybreak Pictures. Address: Elsinore House, 77 Fulham Palace Road, London W6 8JA, England. E-mail: daukin@daybreakpictures.com

AUSTIN-COOPER Richard Arthur, b. 21 February 1932. International Banking Personnel Manager (Retired). m. (1) Sylvia Anne Shirley Berringer; (2) Valerie Georgina Drage, 1 son, 1 daughter; (3) Mariola Danuta Sikorska; (4) Rosemary Swaisland (née Gillespie). Education: Wellingborough Grammar School; Tottenham Grammar School. Appointments: Served RA, 1950-52 and TAVR in the RA, Intelligence Corps, 21 SAS Regt (Artist's Rifles), Essex ACF, 1952-68 and the Hon Artillery Co, 1978-79 (Commissioned 2 Lt TAVR 1968), OC ACF Canvey Island; Honorary Colonel Polish Militia, 1981; With Barclays Bank, 1948-60; Head Cashier, Bank of Baroda, 1960-63, Lloyd's Bank, 1963-69; Deputy Head, Stocks and Shares Department, Banque de Paris et des Pays Bas, 1969-74; Assistant Manager, Banking Division, Brook Street Bureau of Mayfair Ltd, 1974-75; Chief Custodian and London Registrar, Canadian Imperial Bank of Commerce and Registrar in Britain for Angostura Bitters Ltd, 1975-78; Personnel Officer, Deutsche Bank AG London Branch, 1978-85; Senior Manager, Head of Human Resources, Deutsche Bank Capital Markets Ltd, 1985-90; Partner Charsby Associates Recruitment Consultants, London, 1989-91; Retired, 1991. Publications: Books: Butterhill and Beyond, 1991; The Beavers of Barnack, 1995; The de Gidlow Family of Ince, 1996; The Peisley Family of Clifton Hampden, Oxon, 1996. Honours: Prizes for: Athletics, Operatic Singing (Tenor); Painting; Freeman, City of London, 1964; Hon LLD, Hon MA (USA), FHG, 1965; FRSA, 1974; FRSAIre, 1980, FCIB, 1987. Memberships: Founder Fellow, Institute of Heraldic and Genealogical Studies; Treasurer, Irish Genealogical Research Society; Irish Peers Association, 1964-; Life Governor Sherriff's and Recorder's Fund at the Old Bailey, 1979-; Vice-President, Bourne Lincs Family History Society, 1993-; Chairman, Arthritis Care, Stamford, Lincolnshire, 1993-94; Chairman, Eastbourne Branch, British Cardiac Patients Association, 2003-06; Vice-Chairman, Trustee and Member Executive Committee, Friends of Eastbourne Hospitals, 2003-06; Governor, American College in Oxford; Governor, City of London School for Girls; Governor, Freeman's School; Governor, Lansbury Adult Education Institute; Representative, City of London Corporation on the Greater London Arts Council; Trustee, City of London Imperial Volunteers; Member, City of London-TAVR Association; A Manager, Barbican School of Music and Drama; Member, City of London Mayor's Court of Common Council for Cripplegate Ward, 1978-81; President, Royal Artillery Association, Eastbourne, East Sussex, 2006-; SAS Regimental Association; Intelligence Corps OCA; Artists Rifles Association. Address: 2 Lea House, 1 Mill Road, Eastbourne, East Sussex BN21 2LY, England.

AVERY Charles Henry Francis, b. 26 December 1940, London, England. Fine Art Consultant. m. (Kathleen) Mary, 3 daughters (triplets). Education: MA, PhD, St John's College, Cambridge; Academic Diploma, Courtauld Institute of Art, London. Appointments: Deputy Keeper of Sculpture, Victoria and Albert Museum, 1965-69; Director, Sculpture Department, Christie's, 1979-90; Currently, Independent Fine Art Consultant. Publications: Books: Florentine Renaissance Sculpture, 1970; Studies in European Sculpture, 1981, 1987; Giambologna the Complete Sculpture, 1987; Renaissance and Baroque Bronzes in the Frick Art Museum, 1993; Donatello: An Introduction, 1994; David Le Marchand (1674-1726). An Ingenious Man for Carving in Ivory, 1996; Bernini, Genius of the Baroque, 1997; Studies in Italian Sculpture, 2001.

Honours: Cavaliere Dell'ordine Al Merito della Repubblica Italiana, 1979; Medal of the Ministry of Culture, Poland; FSA, 1985; Leverhulme Research Fellow, 1997-99; Honorary Life Member, Venice in Peril; Association Internationale des Critiques d'Art; Vetting Committee, Maastricht European Fine Art Fair. Memberships: United Oxford and Cambridge; Beckenham Tennis Club. Address: Holly Tree House, 20 Southend Road, Beckenham, Kent BR3 1SD, England.

AVTANDILOV Georgy Gerasimovitch, b. 21 September 1922, Kizljar, Dagestan, Russia. Professor. m. Lilya Osipova, 1 son, 1 daughter. Education: Graduate, State Medical Institute, North Osetiya, 1951, Candidate of Science, 1959, DSc, 1966, Professor, 1971. Appointments: Served in Army, 1940-45; Physician, Head of Pathological Anatomy Department, Republican Hospital, Karbardino-Balkaria, 1951-65; Head, Central Pathological Anatomy Laboratory, Institute of Human Morphology, USSR Academy of Medical Science, 1965-75; Professor, Head of Pathological Anatomy, Chairman, Russian Medical Academy for Postgraduate Education, Moscow, 1975. Publications include: Books: Vascular Plexuses of the Brain, 1962; Morphometry in Pathology, 1973; Systemic Stereometry in Studying the Pathological Process, 1982; Problems of Pathogenesis and Pathanatomical Diagnostics of Diseases in the Aspects of Morphometry, 1984; Medical Morphometry, 1990; Fundamentals of Pathologoanatomical Practice, 1994; The Computerised Microtelephotometry in Diagnostic Histocytopathology, 1996; Fundamentals of quantative Pathological Anatomy, 2002; Diagnosis registration, 2004; Conscience and Honour, 2005; Diagnostic Medical Ploidometry, 2006; Over 380 papers in professional journals; 13 inventions and 3 discoveries. Honours: Medal for Courage; 15 other medals; Patriotic War Order, 1941-45; Honour Scientist of Russian Federation, 1990. Memberships: Academy of Natural Science of Russian Federation; International Society of Stereologists; European Society of Pathologists. Address: Novopestschanaya, 16-150, 125252 Moscow, Russia.

AWBI Hazim Bashir, b. 1 July 1945, Mosul, Iraq. Academic Engineer. 4 daughters. Education: BSc, Mechanical Engineering, 1967, MSc, Heat Transfer, 1969, University of Manchester; PhD, Industrial Aerodynamics, Nottingham Trent University, 1974. Appointments: Engineer, Engineering Sciences Data Unit International, London, 1974-75; Lecturer, Mechanical Engineering Department, Baghdad University of Technology, Iraq, 1975-81; Head of the Air Distribution Section, Building Services Research and Information Association, Bracknell, England, 1981-83; Lecturer, Department of Mechanical, Manufacturing and Software Engineering, Napier University, Edinburgh, 1983-90; Senior Lecturer, School of Construction Management and Engineering, University of Reading, 1990-2007; Professor of Building Environmental Science, 2007-. Publications: Author of the computational fluid dynamics code VORTEX© for simulating the airflow and heat transfer in and around buildings; Book: Ventilation of Buildings (2 editions); Book (editor), Ventilation Systems – Design and Performance; Book (contributor), CFD in Ventilation Design; Contributor to 3 books; Over 120 scientific articles in journals and conference proceedings. Honours: Numerous research grants from UK and European funding agencies; Honorary Professor, Department of Architecture and Urban Planning, Chongqing University, China, 1994; Visiting Professor, Department of Civil Engineering, University of Technology, Lisbon, Portugal, 1999-2001; Listed in Who's Who publications. Memberships: Institution of Mechanical Engineers, London, 1977-; Royal Aeronautical Society, London, 1978-95;

Chartered Institute of Building Services Engineers, London, 1989-; American Society of Heating, Refrigeration and Air-Conditioning Engineers, 1998-; Board of Trustees, World Renewable Energy Network, 1992-2005; Editorial Board, 1995-2005, Associate Editor, 2005, International Journal of Renewable Energy; Editorial Board, International Journal of Ventilation, 2002-; Editorial Board, International Journal Human-Environment System, 2006-; Chairman and Organiser, Seventh International Conference on Air Distribution in Rooms (ROOMVENT 2000), Reading, 2000; Member, International Committees of numerous conferences in indoor environment and energy; Reviewer for many scientific journals; Assessor for research funding agencies in various countries;. Address: Indoor Environment and Energy Research Group, School of Construction Management and Engineering, University of Reading, Reading RG6 6AW, England. E-mail: h.b.awbi@reading.ac.uk

AYATOLLAHI Seyyed Mohammad Taghi, b. 6 January 1953, Shiraz, Iran. Professor. m. Sareh, 1 daughter. Education: BSc, Statistics, Shiraz University, School of Arts and Sciences, 1970-76; MSc, Biostatistics, School of Graduate Studies, 1976-78; MS, Biostatistics, Columbia University, School of Public Health, 1978-80; PhD, Medical Statistics, London University, School of Hygiene and Tropical Medicine, 1989-91; PDRA; FSS; CStat, Medical Statistics, Epidemiology, Newcastle University, The Medical School, UK, 1992-94. Appointments: Technician, 1975-76; Senior Teacher, High Schools of Shiraz; Statistician, Programmer, Shiraz University, 1976-78; Lecturer, Head, Department of Biostatistics, 1982-89; Associate Dean, School of Medicine, 1983-84; Chairman, Educational Planning Bureau, 1984-85; Vice Chancellor, Shiraz University, 1984-88; Chairman, Secretary, Cultural Council, Shiraz University of Medical Sciences, 1988-89; Visiting Lecturer, London School of Hygiene and Tropical Medicine, 1990-91; Computer Programmer, University College of London, 1990-91; Statistical Programmer, Oxford University, 1991-92; Research Associate, Newcastle University, 1992-94; Professor, Shiraz University of Medical Sciences, 1994-; Dean, School of Graduate Studies, Shiraz University of Medical Sciences, 1996-2000; Dean, School of Public Health, Shiraz University of Medical Sciences, 1998-2003. Publications: over 170 papers and 18 books published. Honours: Distinguished Graduate Student; Fellow, Royal Statistical Society; Chartered Statistician; International Man of the Year; Noble Prize Winner, 2001; many others. Memberships: New York Academy of Sciences; Society for the Study of Human Biology; Iran Statistical Society; others. Address: Department of Biostatistics and Epidemiology, P O Box 71345-1874, Shiraz, Islamic Republic, Iran.

AYAZ Iftikhar Ahmad, b. 18 January 1936, Tanzania. Educator. m. Amatul Basit, 5 daughters, 1 son. Education: BEd, University of Newcastle upon Tyne; Diploma of Comparative Education, Dip TEFL, MA, University of London; PhD, International University Foundation, USA. Appointments: Teacher, District Education Officer, Regional Inspector of Schools, Chairman, Teacher Education Panel, Head, Department of Education, Tanzania, 1960-78; Senior Curriculum Advisor, Institute of Education, University of Dar es Salaam, Tanzania, 1978-81; Publications Officer, Centre on Integrated Rural Development, Arusha, Tanzania, 1981-85; Education Advisor and Consultant, Commonwealth Secretariat, 1985-92; UNESCO Co-ordinator and Manager of Education For Life Programme, 1992-95; UN Human Rights Commission Workshop on Minority Group Rights, 1997-; Honorary Consul of Tuvalu in the UK, 1995-;

Attended numerous international conferences including most recently: World Conference against Racism, Racial Discrimination, Xenophobia and related Intolerance, Durban, South Africa, 2001; World Peace Summit in South Korea, 2003; Poverty Alleviation in SE Asia Conference, New Delhi, 2004; International Leadership Summit, South Korea, 2007; Broadcaster, Education programmes for teachers, Tanzania, 1979-81, Tuvalu, 1985-88; Co-ordinator, Language Support for Immigrant Workers, 1989. Publications: Numerous publications on education theory, philosophy and sociology, linguistics, literature, curriculum development, HR development, culture in education, peace education, education in small states. Honours: OBE, 1998; Alfred Nobel Medal, 1991; Hind Ratan and Hind Ratan Gold Medal, India, 2002; Nav Ratan and Nav Ratan Gold Medal, India, 2003; Federation for World Peace, USA, Ambassador for Peace Award; D Ed, Emeritus International University Foundation, USA; International Education Fellow, Commonwealth Institute, London, 1976-77; Commonwealth Fellowship for Higher Education; Vice-President, India's International Conference of Intellectuals, 2004; Great Minds of the 21st Century Medal, American Biographical Institute; Man of the Year, ABI, 2004; Senator, World Nations Congress, 2005. Memberships: The London Diplomatic Corps; The Commonwealth Association; The Royal Commonwealth Society; Commonwealth Education Council; Commonwealth Human Ecology Council; Universal Peace Federation; Pacific Peace Forum. Address: Tuvalu House, 230 Worple Road, London SW20 8RH, England. E-mail: tuvaluconsulate@netscape.net

AYCKBOURN Alan (Sir), b. 12 April 1939, London, England. Theatre Director; Playwright; Artistic Director. Career: Plays: Mr Whatnot, 1963; Relatively Speaking, 1965; How The Other Half Loves, 1969; Time And Time Again, 1971; Absurd Person Singular, 1972; The Norman Conquests, 1973; Absent Friends, Confusions, 1974; Bedroom Farce, 1975; Just Between Ourselves, 1976; Ten Times Table, 1977; Joking Apart, 1978; Sisterly Feelings, Taking Steps, 1979; Season's Greetings, 1980; Way Upstream, 1981; Intimate Exchanges, 1982; A Chorus Of Disapproval, 1984; Woman In Mind, 1985; A Small Family Business, Henceforward..., 1987; Man Of The Moment, Mr A's Amazing Maze Plays, 1988; The Revengers' Comedies, Invisible Friends, 1989; Body Language, 1990; Wildest Dreams, 1991; Time Of My Life, Dreams From A Summer House, (music by John Pattison), 1992; Communicating Doors, Haunting Julia, 1994; By Jeeves (with Andrew Lloyd Webber), The Champion Of Paribanou, 1996; Things We Do For Love, 1997; Comic Potential, The Boy Who Fell Into A Book, 1998; House & Garden, Callisto #7, 1999; Whenever, 2000; GamePlan, FlatSpin, RolePlay (aka Damsels In Distress Trilogy), 2001; Snake In The Grass, The Jollies, 2002; Sugar Daddies, Orvin – Champion Of Champions, My Sister Sadie, 2003; Drowning On Dry Land, Private Fears In Public Places, Miss Yesterday, 2004; Improbable Fiction, 2005; If I were you, 2006. Publications: Conversations with Ayckbourn, 1981; The Crafty Art of Playmaking, 2003; majority of plays have been published. Honours: Hon DLitt, Hull, 1981, Keele, 1987, Leeds, 1987, York, 1992, Bradford, 1994, Cardiff University of Wales, 1996, Open University, 1998, Manchester, 2003; Commander of the Order of the British Empire, 1987; Cameron Mackintosh Professor of Contemporary Theatre, 1992; Knighthood, 1997; Sunday Times Literary Award for Excellence, 2001. Memberships: Fellow, Royal Society of Arts. Address: c/o Casarotto Ramsay and Associates Ltd, National House, 60-66 Wardour Street, London W1V 4ND, England. Website: www.alanayckbourn.net

AYKROYD Dan (Daniel Edward), b. 1 July 1952, Ottawa, Canada. Actor. m. (1) Maureen Lewis, 1974, divorced, 3 sons, (2) Donna Dixon, 1983, 3 daughters. Education: Carleton University, Ottawa. Appointments: Started as stand up comedian and worked on Saturday Night Live, 1975-79; Created and performed as the Blues Brothers; Albums include: Made in America; Films include: 1941, 1979; Mr Mike's Mondo Video, 1979; The Blues Brothers, 1980; Neighbors, 1981; Doctor Detroit, Trading Places, Twilight Zone, 1983; Ghostbusters, Nothing Lasts for Ever, 1984; Into the Night, Spies Like Us, 1985; Dragnet, 1987; Caddyshack II, The Great Outdoors, My Stepmother is an Alien, 1988; Ghostbusters II, 1989; Driving Miss Daisy, 1990; My Girl; Loose Cannons; Valkemania; Nothing But Trouble, 1991; Coneheads, 1993; My Girl II, 1994; North; Casper, 1995; Sergeant Bilko, 1996; Grosse Point Blank, Blues Brothers 2000, The Arrow, 1997; Susan's Plan, 1998; Antz, Diamonds, 1999; The House of Mirth, Stardom, Dying to Get Rich, 2000; The Devil and Daniel Webster, Not A Girl, Pearl Harbour, Evolution, 2001; Crossroads, Who Shot Victor Fox, The Curse of the Jade Scorpion, Unconditional Love, 2002; Bright Young Things, 2003; 50 First Dates, Intern Academy, Christmas with the Kranks, 2004; Dan Aykroyd Unplugged on UFOs, 2005; I now Pronounce You Chuck and Larry, 2007 release. Honours: Emmy Award, 1976-77. Address: c/o CAA, 9830 Wilshire Boulevard, Beverly Hills, CA 90212, USA.

AZAB Hassan Ahmed, b. 16 June 1950, Ismailia, Egypt. Professor of Chemistry. m. Naima Fouad, 1 son, 1 daughter. Education: BSc, Chemistry, 1972; MSc, Chemistry, 1976; PhD, Chemistry, 1983. Appointments: Professor of Analytical and Inorganic Chemistry, Head of Chemistry Department, Vice-Dean, Faculty of Science, Suez Canal University, Ismailia, Egypt. Publications: More than 80 international publications in the field of analytical and inorganic chemistry; Recent publication on biologically important DNA-protein-metal ions systems; International Evaluator, FP7 and TEMPUS; Director, SFP982697 project in collaboration with Regensburg University, Germany. Honours: TWAS Award, 1989; Peaceful Fellowship, 1990 DAAD Award, 1996, 2003, 2006; DGF Award, 2000; EV (NATO) Award, 2004; Senior Visiting Award, WOU, 2005. Memberships: American Chemical Society; American Association for the Advancement of Science. Address: Faculty of Science, Chemistry Department, Suez Canal University, Ismailia, Egypt. E-mail: azab2@yahoo.com

AZAM Mohammad Ozair, b. 24 January 1940, Bhagalpur, India. Project and Finance Advisor. m. Education: MIE, UK, 1980; BSc Eng (Mech), 1982; Member, ASME, USA, 1982. Appointments: Senior Supervisor, Mechanical Engineering, Pakistan Industrial Technical Assistance Centre, Dacca, Lahore, 1965-69; Technical Officer, Engineering, Galfra Habib, Chittagong, 1969-70; DY Chief, Senior Mechanical Engineer, Charsadda Sugar Mills (PVT) Ltd, Charssada, Peshawar, 1970-76; Operation Head, DY Chief Engineer, Superintending Engineer, Executive Engineer, Pakistan Steel, Karachi, 1976-85; General Manager, Baluchistan Foundry Ltd, Hub Chawki, Lesbela, 1985-87; Executive Director (Project) Allied Engineering Services (PVT) Ltd, Karachi, General Manager, Polymer & Precision Engineers PVT Ltd, Karachi, 1987-94; Chief Executive, Azam Associates, 1994-; National/International Project Consultant and Project/Finance Advisor to various other companies. Publications: Technical paper entitled Material Failure published in Pakistan Steel. Honours: Arch of Europe for Quality & Technology, Business Initiative Directions, Spain; Gold Award, 2000. Memberships:

ASME, USA. Address: A-170, Block T, North Nazimabad, Karachi, Pakistan. E-mail: aassociates@cyber.net.pk Website: http://azamaa.8m.com

AZAM R M Ikram, b. Pakistan. Writer; Author. Education: BA, English, Gordon College, Rawalpindi; MA, English, Government College, Lahore; MA, Political Science, Punjab University, Lahore; MSc, Defence and Strategic Studies, Quaid-e-Azam University, Islamabad; MSc, Studies of the Future, University of Houston, Texas, USA; PhD, Futuristics: International Relations, D Litt, Futuristics, American University of London, England; Cultural Doctorate, Futuristics, World University (Roundtable), USA. Appointments: Income Tax Officer to Member of the Central Board of Revenue, Islamabad, 1961-95; Section Chief, Pakistan Council for National Integration, Federal Minisry of Information, 1964-67; Director, President's/PM's Inspection Team, 1972; Director, Finance & Administration, Programmes, Press, Publications & Public Relations: The Pakistan National Council of the Arts, Federal Ministry of Education, 1972-73; Deputy Education Advisor, Federal Ministry of Education, 1973-74; Secretary, Institute of Strategic Studies, Islamabad, 1974-76; Director, National Book Foundation of Pakistan, Director General, National Book Council, Federal Ministry of Education, 1991-94; Director, National Institute of Historical and Cultural Research, Federal Ministry of Culture, 1994. Publications: Several articles in professional journals; Author, 125 books; 3 plays; 22 books of poetry and verse; Editor, 25 books; 10 short novels; 4 stories. Honours: Distinguished Scholar and Speaker, USC-USA Trojan, 1984; Book of the Year Award, Pakistan Academy of Letters, Islamabad, 1987-88; First Dr Khurshid A Khan Memorial Honorary Triple Award, 1997; First Margalla Voices, Honorary Award, 1997; Warner Bloomberg Award, USA, 1998. Memberships: Board of Management, Rawalpindi Medical College and Allied Hospitals; Fellow, World Futures Studies Federation, USA; Life Member, International Advisory Council of the World Future Society; Founder, Futuristics in Pakistan; Honorary Chairman, Pakistan Futuristics Foundation and Institute. Address: 37, School/Bhitai Road, F-7/1, Islamabad, Pakistan. E-mail: pfi24@hotmail.com

AZAM Zohra, b. Pakistan. Educationist; Author; Social Welfare Worker. Education: FA/BA, St Anne's Convent College, Rawalpindi; BEd, The Lady Maclagan College, Lahore; MEd, Institute of Education and Research, Lahore; PhD, American University in London, England, 1993. Appointments: Education and Educational Administration; Teacher, local English medium schools including: Presentation Convent, Sir Syed Girls' Secondary School, and FG Girls' Public High School, Rawalpindi; Principl, City School, Islamabad; Principal, Federal Government Girls' Public Cantonment Garrison High School, Lalazar, Rawalpindi; Retired. Publications: 4 books. Honours: Elected as Women Teacher's Regional Representative, Noor Khan Education Council, 1970; 100 Heroines Award, USA, 1998; Army Education Directorate Merit Crest. Memberships: The Educator's Club, Rawalpindi; The Margalla Voices, Islamabad; Founder Member, PFI; Behbood Association; Shaukat Khannam Memorial Society; Sirat Ul Jannah; Representative, Pakistan Foundation Fighting Blindness; Rawalpindi-Islamabad Business and Professional Women's Club Organisation; Pakistan Federation of University Women, Islamabad; International University Women's Club; Educational Adviser to distinguished educational institutions; Life Member, Sir Syed Memorial Society; Zakir Shah's Madarsatal Zehra; Life Member, SOS. Address: 37 School Road, F-7/1, Islamabad, Pakistan. E-mail: pfi24@hotmail.com

AZINGER Paul William, b. 6 January 1960, Holyoke, Massachusetts, USA. Golfer. m. Toni, 2 daughters. Education: Florida State University. Appointments: Started playing golf aged 5; Turned professional, 1981; Won Phoenix Open, 1987; Herz Bay Hill Classic, 1988; Canon Greater Hartford Open, 1989; MONY Tournament of Champions, 1990; AT and T Pebble Beach National Pro Am, 1991; TOUR Championship, 1992; BMW International Open, 1990, 1992; Memorial Tournament, New England Classic, PGA Championship, Inverness, 1993; GWAA Ben Hogan Trophy, 1995; Member, US Ryder Cup Team, 1989, 1991, 1993, 2002, Named as the US Ryder Cup Captain for the 2008 event. Member, President's Cup, 1994, 2000; Broadcasting debut as reporter for NBC, Ryder Cup, 1995; Analyst, American Broadcasting Corporation (ABC) Sports, 2005-. Publications: Zinger. Honours: PGA Tour Player of the Year, 1987; Ben Hogan Award, 1995. Address: PGA Tour, 112 Tpc Boulevard, Ponte Vedra Beach, FL 33082, USA.

AZIZ Shaukat, b. 6 March 1949, Karachi, Pakistan. Politics; Banking. m. Rukhsana, 1 son, 2 daughters. Education: BSc, Gordon College, Rawalpini, Pakistan, 1967; Master, Business Administration, Institute of Business Administration, University of Karachi, Pakistan, 1969. Appointments: Citibank, Pakistan, 1969-75; Overseas designations, Citibank, 1975-92; Executive Vice President, Citibank, 1992-99; Finance Minister, Government of Pakistan, 1999-2004; Prime Minister of Pakistan, 2004-. Honours: Finance Minister of the Year, Euro Money and Bankers Magazine, 2001; Degree of Directorate Laws (Honoris Causa), Institute of Business Administration, University of Karachi, 2005; Congressional Medal of Achievement, House of Representative of the Philippines, 2006; Co-chair, Secretary-General's High-Level Panel, United Nations System-wide Coherence, 2006. Address: Prime Minister's House, Islamabad, Pakistan. E-mail: mhassan@apollo.net.pk

AZNAR LÓPEZ José María, b. 25 February 1953, Madrid, Spain. Lawyer; Politician. m. 3 children. Education: Licence in Law, Complutense University of Madrid. Appointments: State Finance Inspector; Secretary General, Logrono Popular Alliance Party, 1979; Secretary General, Popular Alliance Party, 1982-87; Avila Delegate, 1982-87; Castilla y León Regional President, Popular Alliance Party; National Vice-President, Popular Party, 1989; President, Autonomous Community of Castilla y León's Popular Alliance, 1987-89; Popular Party's Elected Candidate for Presidency of Government, 1989; National Delegate for Madrid in the 4th, 5th and 6th Legislature; President of the Popular Parliamentarian Group in the Congress of Delegates, 1991; Vice President, European Popular Party; Vice President, European Democratic Union; Invested President of Government of Spain (Prime Minister), 1996-2004; Vice President International Democratic Union, 2001; Distinguished Scholar in the Practice of Global Leadership, Georgetown University, Washington, DC, USA, 2004-. Publications: Ocho años de gobierno: una visión personal de España, 2004; Retratos y perfiles: de Fraga a Bush, 2005. Honours: President's Medal, Georgetown University, 2004. Address: Partido Popular, Genova 13, Madrid, Spain.

AZNAVOUR Charles (Varenagh Aznavourian), b. 22 May 1924, Paris, France. Singer; Actor. m. (1) Micheline Rugel, 1946, (2) Evelyene Plessis, 1955, (3) Ulla Thorsel, 1967, 5 children (1 deceased). Education: Ecole Centrale de TSF. Career: Centre de Spectacle, Paris; Jean Dasté Company, 1941; Les Fâcheux, Arlequin, 1944; Numerous film appearances, 1964-; Compositions include: Songs: Il Pleut; Le Feutre Tropez; Jezebel (all recorded by Edith

Piaf); Hier Encore (Yesterday When I Was Young); The Old Fashioned Way; She (theme for ITV series, The Seven Faces Of Woman); What Makes A Man; Happy Anniversary. Recordings: Albums include: Charles Aznavour Sings, 1963; Qui, 1964; Et Voici, 1964; Sings His Love Songs In English, 1965; Encore, 1966; De T'Avoir Aimée, 1966; Désormais, 1972; Chez Lui A Paris, 1973; A Tapestry Of Dreams, 1974; I Sing For You, 1975; In Times To Be, 1983; Aznavour, 1990; En Espanol, Vols I-III, 1991; The Old Fashioned Way, 1992; Jezabel, 1993; Toi Et Moi, 1994; Il Faut Savior, 1995; Paris Palais Des Congres, 1996; Jazznavour, 1999; Aznavour, 2000. He started his global farewell tour in late 2006. Honours: Chevalier Légion d'Honneur, Des Arts et Lettres; Grand Prix National de la Chanson, 1986; César d'honneur, 1997; Molière amical, 1999; Time Magazine Entertainer of the Century; Honorary President, Belgrade Film Festival, 2003; Commandeur, Légion d'honneur, 2004; Commandeur des Arts et des Lettres. Address: c/o Lévon Sayan, 76-78 Avenue des Champs Elysées, Bureau 322, 75008 Paris, France.

AZUMA Takehiro, b. 21 November 1976, Hokkaido, Japan. Physicist. Education: Graduate, Todaiji-Gakuen High School, 1995; BSc, 1999, MSc, 2001, PhD, 2004, Kyoto University. Appointments: JSPS DC2 Predoctoral Fellowship, Kyoto University, 2002-04; JSPS Postdoctoral Fellowship, High Energy Accelerator Research Organisation, 2004-06; Visiting Fellowship, Tata Institute of Fundamental Research, 2006-08; Full-time Instructor, Setsunan University, 2008-. Publications: Dynamical generation of gauge groups in the massive YMCS matrix model, 2005; Monte Carlo Studies of the GWW Phase Transition in Large N Gauge Theories, 2008. Honours: Listed in international biographical dictionaries. Memberships: Soryushiron Group. Address: Setsunan University, 17-8 Ikeda Nakamachi, Neyagawa, Osaka 572-8508, Japan. E-mail: azuma@mpg.setsunan.ac.jp Website: www2.yukawa.kyoto-u.ac.jp/~azuma/index.html

B

BABA Tatsuro, b. 6 February 1958, Shimonoseki, Yamaguchi, Japan. Engineer; Health Products Executive. m. Masako, 1 son. Education: BS, 1981, MS, 1983, Precision Engineering, Osaka University; D Eng, Mechanical System Engineering, Kobe University, 2006. Appointments: Engineer, Toshiba Medical System Corporation, Otawara, Japan, 1983-. Publications: Direction separation in Doppler audio of ultrasound diagnosis equipment, 2007; Evaluation of Post Wall Filter for Doppler Ultrasound systems, 2008. Honours: Doctor Engineering (Hons), Kobe University, 2006; Best Presentation Award, Society of Instrument and Control Engineering, 2006; Best Paper Award, Society of Signal Processing Applications and Technology of Japan, 2006. Memberships: Fellow, Japan Society of Ultrasonic Medicine; IEEE; Acoustical Society of Japan; Professional Engineers Association, Japan. E-mail: baba@us.nasu.toshiba.co.jp

BABAN Serwan M J, b. 23 April 1958, Kirkuk, Iraq. University Professor. m. Judith Anne, 2 daughters. Education: BSc, Geology, 1980, MSc, Geophysics, 1983, University of Baghdad, Iraq; PhD, Environmental Remote Sensing, University of East Anglia, UK, 1991. Appointments: Research Associate, Senior Research Associate, University of East Anglia, UK; Lecturer, Senior Lecturer, Coventry University, UK; Professor of Surveying and Land Information, 2000-, Chairman, School of Graduate Studies and Research, 2004-07, The University of the West Indies, Trinidad and Tobago; Professor, Environmental Geoinformatics and Head of School, Southern Cross University, Australia, 2007-. Publications: Over 80 articles in international and national journals, international conference proceedings, chapters in books as well as consultancy reports including most recently: Modelling Sites for Reservoirs in Tropical Environments, 2003; Responding to the Effects of Climate Change, 2003; Flooding and Landslides in the West Indies, 2004; Information Poverty and Decision-Making, 2004; Mapping Landslide Susceptibility in the Tropics, 2004, 2005; Examining land use changes due to irrigated agriculture in Jordan using Geoinformatics, 2005; Evaluating Water Circulation and Contaminant Transport Models for the Intra-American Seas, 2005; Accomplishing Sustainable Development in Southern Kurdistan Using Geoinformatics, 2005. Memberships: Fellow, Royal Geographical Society, 1999-; Remote Sensing Society Council, 1999-2001; Fellow, Geological Society, 2000-; Fellow, Remote Sensing and Photogrammetry Society, 2001; Visiting Fellow, School of Environmental Sciences, University of East Anglia, UK, 2002-; Member and National Representative, International Association of Hydrological Sciences. Address: Department of Surveying and Land Information, University of the West Indies, St Augustine, Trinidad and Tobago, West Indies.

BABICH Alexander, b. 12 November 1952, Donetsk, Ukraine. Metallurgist; Educator. m. Eugenia Goldstein, 1 son. Education: Metallurgy Engineering, Donetsk Polytechnic Institute, 1974; PhD (Tech), 1984; Associate Professor, 1989. Appointments: Furnace Worker, Foreman, Donetsk Steel Plant, 1974-76; Engineer, Scientific worker, Donetsk Polytechnic Institute, 1978-85; Associate Professor, Donetsk State University of Technology, 1985-96; Visiting Researcher, National Centre for Metallurgical Investigation, Madrid, 1997-98; Researcher, Aachen University of Technology, 1998-. Publications: Over 140 publications including a monograph, a textbook and 13 patents. Honours: Grant, Ministry of Education and Science, Spain; Who's Who in the World Diploma, 1999; Listed in several biographical publications, Address: Hauptstr 78, 52066 Aachen, Germany. E-mail: babich@iehk.rwth-aachen.de

BABITSKY Vladimir, b. 4 April 1938, Gomel, USSR. Mechanical Engineer. m. Eleonora Lublina, 1 son. Education: MSc Mechanical Engineering, Moscow State Technological University, 1960; PhD, 1964, DSc, 1973, USSR Academy of Sciences. Appointments: Engineer, 1960-61, Research Assistant, 1961-67, Senior Research Assistant and a Head of a research group, 1967-87, Founder and Head, Vibrations Systems Laboratory, 1987-91, Institute for Machine Studies, USSR Academy of Sciences; Guest Professor, Institute B for Mechanics, Munich, Germany, 1990; Consultant, HILTI AG, 1992-95; Professor of Dynamics, Loughborough University, England, 1995-. Publications: Books: Theory of vibro-impact systems and applications, 1998 (translation from Russian 1978); Vibration of strongly nonlinear discontinuous systems (co-author), 2001 (translation from Russian, 1985); Dynamics and Control of Machines (co-author), 2000; Resonant Robotic Systems (co-author), 2003; Ultrasonic Processes and Machines (co-author), 2007; Founder and Editor, Springer book series, Foundations of Engineering Mechanics, 1996-. Honours: President, International Centre of Vibro-Impact Systems, 2004-. Memberships: Euromech; FICoVIS; IFAC. Address: Wolfson School of Mechanical and Manufacturing Engineering, Loughborough University, Loughborough LE11 3TU, England. E-mail: v.i.babitsky@lboro.ac.uk

BABU Yallapragada Ramesh, b. 14 January 1952, Bhattiprolu, India. Engineer. Education: Graduate, Mechanical Department, College of Engineering, Jawaharlal Nehru Technological University, 1975; MEng, Industrial Engineering, College of Engineering, Sri Venkateswara University, 1979; PhD, Mechanical Department, College of Engineering, Andhra University, 1993. Appointments: Lecturer, Mechanical Department, Bapatla Engineering College, 1982-86; Faculty, College of Engineering, Gandhi Institute of Technology and Management, Visakhapatnam, 1986-. Publications: Several articles in professional journals. Honours: World Lifetime Achievement Award, 1997; 20th Century Award for Achievement, 1998; 2000 Millennium Medal of Honour, 1998; International Man of the Millennium, 1999; Outstanding Man of the 20th Century, 1999; International Personality of the Year 2001; International Scientist of the Year, 2001; International Man of the Year 2000-2001; Great Minds of the 21st Century; International Book of Honor; International Who's Who of Twentieth Century Achievement; 2000 Outstanding Scientists of the 20th Century; 2000 Outstanding Scientists of the 21st Century; Top 100 Scientists, 2005; Top 100 Engineers, 2006; IBC Salute to Greatness Award, 2005; The World Wide Honours List; 21st Century Award for Achievement; HE & The Honorable titles for Order of International Ambassadors; Global Year of Engineering, 2006; The Brunel Award. Memberships: Indian Institution of Industrial Engineering; Institution of Engineers, India; Research Board of Advisors, ABI, USA; Advisory Council IBC, England; Listed in numerous biographical publications including Five Hundred Leaders of Influence; Order of International Ambassadors. Address: Industrial Production Engineering, College of Engineering, Gandhi Institute of Technology and Management, Visakhapatnam 530 045, Andhra Pradesh, India.

BACALL Lauren, b. 16 September 1924, New York, USA. Actress. m. (1) Humphrey Bogart, 1945, died 1957, (2) Jason Robards, 1961, divorced, 2 sons, 1 daughter. Career: Films include: Two Guys from Milwaukee, 1946; The Big Sleep;

Young Man with a Horn; How to Marry a Millionaire; Blood Alley, Sex and the Single Girl; Murder on the Orient Express, 1974; Appointment with Death, 1988; Misery, 1990; All I Want for Christmas, 1991; The Field, 1993; Pret á Porter, 1995; Le Jour et la Nuit, 1996; The Mirror Has Two Faces, 1996; My Fellow Americans; Day and Night; Diamonds; The Venice Project; Presence of Mind; Dogville, 2003; The Limit, 2003; Birth, 2004; Manderlay, 2005; Those Foolish Things, 2006; The Walker, 2007. Publications: Lauren Bacall by Myself, 1978; Lauren Bacall Now, 1994; By Myself and Then Some, 2005. Honours: 2 Tony Awards, 1970, 1981; Woman of the Year Award, 1981; Golden Globe Award, 1996; Screen Actors' Guild Award, 1996. Address: c/o Johnnies Planco, William Morris Agency, 1325 Avenue of the Americas, New York, NY 10019, USA.

BACHTA Abdelkader, b. 5 July 1945, Tozeur, Tunisia. Professor of Philosophy and History of Science. m. Hafida, 3 sons. Education: Tunisian General Certificate of Education, 1966; French General Certificate of Education, 1968; Professorship of French Literature, 1968; Bachelor's Degree of Philosophy, Tunisia, 1972; Master of Philosophy, Tunisia, 1976; Highest grade of doctorate in France, Philosophy, Paris, 1983. Appointments: Professor of French in Secondary School; Professor of Philosophy in Secondary School, Tunisia; Seaker, at France, Philosophy, Paris X; Professor of Philosophy in University EAU; Professor of Philosophy in Tunis (the highest grade). Publications: Books include: (in French) L'espace et le temps chez Newton et Kant, 1991; (Arabic) What is the Epistemology?, 1995; Méthods in Islamic Science; Articles in journals on philosophy and history of science in Arabic and French. Honours: Memberships: Vice President, Arabic Society of Philosophy; CTHS French Section History of Science; Society of 18c S Grench; Society of History of Science, French. Address: BP 390 Pupliposte Nassr 1, Rianna 2037, Tunisia.

BACK Lloyd, b. 13 February 1933, San Francisco, USA. Mechanical Engineer. m. Carol Peterson, 1 son, 2 daughters. Education: BS, 1959, PhD, 1962, University of California at Berkeley. Appointments: Supervisor, Fluid Dynamics, Reactive Processes and Biomedical Research, Jet Propulsion Laboratory, California Institute of Technology, Pasadena, 1962-92; Clinical Assistant Professor of Medicine, University of Southern California, 1974-92; Volunteer Faculty Member, School of Medicine, University of Southern California, Los Angeles, 1992-. Publications: Over 150 experimental and analytical publications in technical journals including investigations in rocket propulsion and blood flow through diseased arteries. Honours: Exceptional Service Award, NASA, 1979; ASME Fellow, Heat Transfer Division; Distinguished Service Award, 1987; 50th Anniversary Award, 1988. Memberships: ASME; AIAA. Address: 16 Rushingwind, Irvine, CA 92614-7409, USA.

BACKLEY Steve, b. 12 February 1969, Sidcup, Kent, England. Athlete. m. Clare. Career: Specialist in Javelin; Coached by John Trower; Commonwealth record holder, 1992 (91,46m); Gold Medal European Junior Championships, 1987; Silver Medal, World Junior Championships, 1988; Gold Medal European Cup, 1989, 1997; Bronze Medal, 1995; Gold Medal World Student Games, 1989, 1991; Gold Medal World Cup, 1989, 1994, 1998; Gold Medal Commonwealth Games, 1990, 1994, 2002; Silver Medal, 1998; Gold Medal European Championships, 1990, 1994, 1998, 2002; Bronze Medal Olympic Games, 1992; Silver Medal, 1996, 2000; Silver Medal World Championships, 1995, 1997; Athlete of the Year, UK Athletics, 2000; MBE, 1995; OBE, 2003. Publication: The Winning Mind.

BACON Kevin, b. 8 July 1958, Philadelphia, USA. Actor. m. Kyra Sedgewick, 1 son, 1 daughter. Education: Manning St Actor's Theatre. Appointments: Stage appearances include: Getting On, 1978; Glad Tidings, 1979-80; Mary Barnes, Album, 1980; Forty-Deuce, 1981; Flux, Poor Little Lambs, 1982; Slab Boys, 1983; Men Without Dates, 1985; Loot, 1986; Road; Spike Heels; TV appearances include: The Gift, 1979; Enormous Changes at the Last Minute, 1982; The Demon Murder Case, 1983; Tender Age, Lemon Sky; Frasier; Happy Birthday Elizabeth: A Celebration of Life, 1997; Film appearances include: National Lampoon's Animal House, 1978; Starting Over, 1979; Hero at Large, Friday the 13th, 1980; Only When I Laugh, 1981; Diner, 1982; Footloose, 1984; Quicksilver, 1985; White Water Summer, Planes, Trains and Automobiles, 1987; End of the Line, She's Having A Baby, 1988; Criminal Law, The Big Picture, 1989; Tremors, Flatliners, 1990; Queens Logic, He Said/She Said, Pyrates, 1991; JFK, A Few Good Men, 1992; The Air Up There, The River Wild, 1994; Murder in the First, Apollo 13, 1995; Sleepers, 1996; Telling Lies in America, Picture Perfect, Digging to China, 1997; Wild Things, 1998; My Dog Skip, The Hollow Man, Stir of Echoes, 1999; Novocain, We Married Margo, 2000; 24 Hours, 2001; Trapped, 2002; In the Cut, Mystic River, 2003; The Woodsman, Cavedweller, 2004; Loverboy, Beauty ShopWhere the Truth Lies, 2005; Saving Angelo, The Air I Breathe, Black Water Transit, Will & Grace, 2006; Death Sentence, The 1 Second Film, 2007. Address: c/o Kevin Huvane, Creative Artists Agency, 9830 Wilshire Boulevard, Beverley Hills, CA 90212, USA.

BADAWI Mohamed Mustafa, b. 10 June 1925, Alexandria, Egypt. Lecturer; Writer. Education: BA, Alexandria University, 1946; BA, 1950, PhD, 1954, London University. Appointments: Research Fellow, 1947-54, Lecturer, 1954-60, Assistant Professor, 1960-64, Alexandria University, Egypt; Lecturer, Oxford University, and Brasenose College, 1964-92; Fellow, St Antony's College, Oxford, 1967-; Editor, Journal of Arabic Literature, Leiden, 1970; Advisory Board Member, Cambridge History of Arabic Literature. Publications: An Anthology of Modern Arabic Verse, 1970; Coleridge as Critic of Shakespeare, 1973; A Critical Introduction to Modern Arabic Poetry, 1975; Background to Shakespeare, 1981; Modern Arabic Literature and the West, 1985; Modern Arabic Drama in Egypt, 1987; Early Arabic Drama, 1988; Modern Arabic Literature: Cambridge History of Arabic literature (editor), 1992; A Short History of Modern Arabic Literature, 1993; Arabic translation and study of Selected Poems by Philip Larkin, 1998; Arabic translation of William Shakespeare's Macbeth, 2001, King Lear, 2003, Othello, 2004 and Hamlet, 2005; Several books and volumes of verse in Arabic. Honours: King Faisal International Prize for Arabic Literature, 1992; Egypt's Supreme Council of Culture Award for promoting Arabic Culture Worldwide, 2006. Memberships: Ministry of Culture, Egypt; UNESCO Expert on Modern Arabic Culture. Address: St Antony's College, Oxford, England.

BAE Chang Han, b. 26 August 1971, South Korea. Researcher. m. 1 son, 1 daughter. Education: BA, 1996, MD, 1998, PhD, 2002, Ajou University, Suwon, South Korea. Appointments: Senior Researcher, Korea Railroad Research Institute, 2002-; Lecturer, Korea National Railroad College, 2003-04. Publications: Numerous articles in professional journals: IEEE Transactions on Industry Applications; IEE proceedings on Electric Power Applications; IEE proceedings on Control

Theory Applications; Transactions on the KIEE; Transactions on the KIIEE; International Journal of Electronics. Honours: Full Scholarship, Korea Research Foundation, 1999; Paper Presentation Award, Korean Railway Society, 2004; Paper Award, Korean Institute of Illuminating & Electric Installation Engineering, 2006; Leading Engineers of the World, 2007. Memberships: IEEE; IEE; KIEE; KIIEE. Address: 612-804 Keukdong Apt, Yeongtong-Dong, Yeongtong-Gu, Suwon 443-470, South Korea. E-mail: chbae@krri.re.kr

BAE Imho, b. 13 April 1957, Seoul, Republic of Korea. Social Sciences Educator. m. Ilai Kim, 1986, 1 son. Education: BA, Social Work, 1981, MSW, 1986, Soongsil University, Seoul; PhD, Social Work, University of Minnesota, USA, 1991; Certificate, Victim Offender Mediator, California, USA. Appointments: Served with South Korean Armed Forces, 1991-92; Editorial Committee Member, Board of Directors, Korean Academy of Social Welfare, 1994-2001; Management Committee Member, US Association of Victim-Offender Mediation, 1995-98; Organising Committee Member, 12th International Congress on Criminology, Seoul, 1997-98; Committee Member, National Commission for Youth Protection, Office of Korean Vice President, 1997-2001; Consultant, Counselor, Crime Prevention Committee/ Ministry of Justice, Republic of Korea, 1997-; Adjunct Researcher, Korea Institute for Youth Development, 1998; Winner, Junior School Competition, International Society of Criminology, 1999-2000; Committee Member, National Committee for Korean Social Work Grade I License, 2004; Speaker in field; Visiting Scholar, University of California at Berkeley, 1998-99; Visiting Scholar, Harvard Law School, 2005-06; Asia Representative, International Prison Chaplains' Association, 1995-2005. Publications: Author: Social Work in Criminal Justice: Its Demand and Response, 1993; A Study on the Development of Anger Coping – Ability Training Program for the Juvenile Delinquent, 1998; Correctional Social Work, 2001; Introduction to Social Welfare, 2002; Social Work Around the World II, 2003; Associate Editor: Community Alternatives: International Journal of Family Care, 1993-96; The Contemporary Justice Review: Issues in Criminal, Social and Restorative Justice, 1997-99; Numerous articles in professional journals. Honours: Grantee, Samsung Welfare Foundation, 1992-94, 1997; Grantee, Korea Research Foundation, 1997-99; Grantee, Korean Institute for Youth Development, 1999-2000; Grantee, Asan (Hyundai) Welfare Foundation, 2002-04. Memberships: NASW; International Federation of Social Workers; American Correctional Association; International Prison Chaplains' Association; Association of Korean Juvenile Protection Studies; Korean Youth Research Association; Korea Association of Social Workers; Koran Academy of Social Welfare; Prison Fellowship International; US Association for Victim-Offender Mediation; Korean Society of Correction Services; Korean Society of Probation; Association of Korean Juvenile Protection Studies; Presbyterian. Address: Soongsil University, 511 Sangdo-dong, Dongjak-Gu, Seoul 156-743, Republic of Korea. E-mail: ihbae@ssu.ac.kr

BAE Kyung-Hoon, b. 10 May 1976, Seoul, Republic of Korea. Senior Engineer. Education: BS, 2001, MS, 2003, PhD, 2006, Department of Electronic Engineering, Kwangwon University, Seoul; MBA, Columbia Southern University, Alabama, USA, 2005; Stanford Advanced Project Management course, Stanford University, California, USA, 2006. Appointments: Senior Engineer, Samsung Thales Co Ltd, 2006-. Publications: Numerous articles in professional journals. Honours: Listed in international biographical dictionaries. Memberships: SPIE, The International Society for Optical Engineering. Address: Samsung Thales, San 14-1, Nongseo-dong, Giheung-gu, Yongin-city, Gyeonggi-do, 446-712, Korea. E-mail: khbae.bae@samsung.com

BAE Sun Hwan, b. 4 August 1964, Su Won, Korea. Professor. m. You Kyeong Jeong, 2 sons. Education: Graduate, College of Medicine, 1989, Resident, Paediatrics, Children's Hospital, 1994-98, PhD, Paediatrics, Medicine, 2002, Seoul National University; Clinical Fellowship, Paediatric Gastroenterology, Hepatology and Nutrition, 1998-99; Paediatric Gastrointestinal Endoscopist, Korean Society of Gastrointestinal Endoscopy, 2001. Appointments: Assistant Professor, Paediatrics, Eul Ji Medical College, Dae Jeon, Republic of Korea, 2001-03; Assistant Professor, 2004-07, Associate Professor, 2007-, Paediatrics, Konkuk University School of Medicine, Seoul. Publications: Two Paediatric cases of type I autoimmune hepatitis with normal immunoglobulin G level presenting as fulminant hepatitis, 2002; Risk of gastrointestinal bleeding associated with use of low dose Aspirin in Korean children, 2004; Deflazacort for type I autoimmune hepatitis in a Korean girl, 2006. Memberships: Korean Society of Paediatrics; Korean Society of Paediatric Gastroenterology, Hepatology and Nutrition; Korean Society of Gastrointestinal Endoscopy. Address: Paediatrics, Konkuk University Hospital 4-12, Hwa Yang Dong, Gwang Jin-Gu, Seoul 143-729, Korea. E-mail: baedori@hanafos.com

BAEDECKER Philip Ackerman, b. 19 December 1939, East Orange, New Jersey, USA. Research Chemist. m. Mary Jo LaFuze, 1 daughter. Education: BS, Chemistry, Ohio University, Athens, Ohio, 1957-61; MS, Chemistry, University of Kentucky, Lexington, Kentucky, 1964; PhD, Chemistry, 1967. Appointments: Research Associate, Massachusetts Institute of Technology, 1967-68; Assistant Professor, 1970-71, Assistant Research Chemist, 1968-73, University of California, Los Angeles; Research Chemist, Branch of Analytical Laboratories, 1974-81, Chief, 1981-86, Research Chemist,1986-96, Branch of Geochemistry, US Geological Survey. Publications: Published reports, abstracts. Honours: Haggin Fellow; Paul I Murrill Fellow; Tennessee Eastman Fellow; NSF Fellow; NASA Citatation; NAPAP Citation. Memberships: American Chemical Society; Meteoritical Society; American Association for the Advancement of Science; Sigma Xi; Geological Society of Washington. Address: 2221 Terra Ridge Drive, Vienna, VA 22181-3276, USA.

BAEKOVA Cholpon, b. 18 May 1947, Kurshab village, Osh region, Kyrgyzstan. Law. m. Sapar Baekov, 2 sons, 2 daughters. Education: Diploma, Law Faculty, Kyrgyz State University, Bishkek, 1969; Diploma, Political Science, Academy of Social Science, Central Committee of the CPSU, Moscow, 1990. Appointments: Public Prosecutor, Kyrgyz Soviet Republic, 1969-77; Member, Supreme Court of the Kyrgyz Soviet Republic, 1977-82; Chair, Issyk-Kul Regional Court, Kyrzyzstan, 1982-85; Chair, Issyk-Kul Regional Trade Union, Kyrgyzstan, 1985-88; First Substitute of the Minister of Justice, 1988-90; Public Deputy, Supreme Soviet of the Kyrgyz Republic, Chair of the Committee in the field of Legislation and Legality of the Supreme Soviet, 1990-91; Attorney General, Kyrgyz Republic, 1991-93; Chair, Constitutional Court of the Kyrgyz Republic, 1993-. Honours: Judge of High Qualification Class; Honoured Jurist, Kyrgyz Republic; Diploma of the Kyrgyz Republic, 1995; Manas Order of III Power, 1997; Femida Award, International Highest Legal Prize, 2000; Kurmanjan Datka international prize, Ruhanijat International Association. Memberships: European Commission for Democracy through

Law, Venice Commission; Moscow Lawyer Club. Address: 39 Erkindik Avenue, Bishkek 720040, Kyrgyzstan. E-mail: cckr@ktnet.kg

BAGG Charles, b. 7 May 1920, London, England. Physician (Retired). m. Diana Ovenden, deceased, 1980, 2 daughters. Education: MA (Camb), MRCS, LRCP, 1946; DPM, 1951; MRCPsych, 1971; FRCPsych, 1983; Cambridge University, Westminster Hospital Medical School; Postgraduate Courses, Neurology, Queen's Square, London; Electroencephalography, Maida Vale Hospital for Nervous Diseases; Child Psychiatry, Hill End Child Guidance Training Clinic. Appointments: RAF National Service, 1946-48; Various junior hospital appointments; Consultant Psychiatrist, Samaritans, Chilterns Branch, Buckinghamshire; Regional Tutor, Marriage Guidance Council, Hertfordshire; Lecturer in Psychiatry, High Wycombe and Amersham School of Midwifery; Talks to various lay organisations; Consultant Psychiatrist, St John's Hospital, Aylesbury, appointed by the Oxford Regional Health Board; Clinical Director, Amersham Child and Family Guidance Clinic; Consultant in Preventive Psychiatry, Buckinghamshire County Council; Deputy Director General, International Biographical Centre, 1987. Publications: Handbook of Psychiatry for Social Workers and Health Visitors; Palmar Digital Sweating in Women Suffering from Depression; Responses of Neonates to Noise in Relation to Personalities of their Parents; Senile Dementia and Psychiatric Problems of the Aged; Rare Pre-Senile Dementia Associated with Cortical Blindness; How Does Electoplexy Work?; Chapters in Samaritans books; Reviews of psychiatric books for Occupational Therapy: Current Themes in Psychiatry; Behaviour Modification for the Mentally Handicapped; Community Care for the Mentally Disabled; Use of Drugs in Psychiatry; Series of articles in British Medicine. Honours: DSc (Honoris Causa), MGS International University Foundation, 1988; IBC Inner Circle, (contribution to Health Education); Bronze Medal, Albert Einstein International Academy; Mitchell Memorial Prize, Council for Music in Hospitals (Jointly); Silver Medal, IBC; Gold Medal, ABI; Address to Samaritans National Conference; Listed in Who's Who publications: International Authors and Writers Who's Who, 1982; Who's Who in the Commonwealth, 1983; Who's Who in Western Europe, 1983; International Who's Who in Medicine, 1986. Memberships: Fellow, IBA; Fellow World Literary Academy; Member, Poetry Society supported by the Arts Council, England. Address: 20A Westgate, Chichester, West Sussex PO19 3EU, England.

BAGHEBO Michael, b. 23 March 1963, Foropa Town, Nigeria. Chartered Tax and Management Practitioner. m. Timipa Michael, 3 sons, 2 daughters. Education: NCE, Economics and Political Science, River State College of Education, Port Harcourt, 1985-88; BSc(Ed), Economics, 2nd Class Honours Upper Division, 1990-93, MSc, Economics, 1998-2001, University of Port Harcourt; Doctorate Degree, Public Administration, All Saints University of America, New York, 2003; PhD (Hons), Finance, Marlborough University, USA, 2003. Appointments: Accountant, Economic and Mathematics Teacher, Osalees International School, Effurun, Nigeria, 1989-90; Mathematics, Economics and Government Teacher, CSS Famgbe, Attissa, Nigeria, 1990-96; Teacher on transfer to St Judes Girls Secondary School, Amarata, Nigeria, 1996-98; Transport/Advances Officer, 1998-99, PRO/Information Officer, 1999-2001, National Orientation Agency; Lecturer in (then) Satellite University Campus of Futo, UNICAL and OAU, Yenagoa; Secretary/General Administration, Bayelsa State Board of Internal Revenue, 2001-02, Executive Chairman, 2002-03, Bayelsa State Board of Internal Revenue, Yenagoa, Nigeria. Publications: Poverty Alleviation and Economic Development in Nigeria (MSc thesis); BSc(Ed) Project on Problems and Prospects of 6-3-3-4 Education Policy in Nigeria; Multiplier Effect of Poverty; Dynamism in Governance; Stable Environment for Sustainable Development; Resource Wastage and Poverty in Nigeria; Effect of Multiplicity of Taxes in Nigeria. Honours include: DOC Degree in Public Administration; PhD, Finance; Distinguished Public Service Medal; Award for Excellence in Public Revenue Administration; Award for Excellence in Nigerian Public Service; Certified Distinguished Administrator; Chieftancy Title of Gbadero of Ifetedo Land, Osun State, Nigeria; Distinguished Leadership Award; National Vice President, Certified Institute of Management, Nigeria. Listed in Who's Who publications and biographical dictionaries. Memberships: Honorary Senior Fellowship, Institute of Internal Auditors of Nigeria; Fellow, Chartered Institute of Public Administrators of Nigeria; Fellow, Marlborough University Graduate Association; Fellow, Certified Institute of Management; Associate Member, Chartered Institute of Taxation of Nigeria; Member, Nigerian Institute of Public Relations; Member, Research Board of Advisors, ABI; Associate Member, Nigerian Institute of Management. Address: Edepie-Epie, PO Box 1147, Yenagoa, Bayelsa State, Nigeria.

BAHK Jaewan, b. 24 January 1955, Masan, Korea. Member of National Assembly of Korea. m. Moon Oak Oh, 1 son, 1 daughter. Education: BA, Economics, Seoul National University, 1977; MPP, 1988, PhD in Public Policy, 1992, Harvard University. Appointments: Assistant Director, National Security Council, 1980-83; Assistant Director, Board of Audit & Inspection, Korea, 1983-92; Deputy Director, Ministry of Finance, Korea, 1992-94; Assistant Chief Secretary, Office of the President of Korea, 1994-96; Professor, Sungkyunkwan University, 1996-2004; Chairman of National Council on Brain Korea 21 Project, 2002; Professor, University of California at San Diego, 2002-03; Chief Secretary to the Chairman of Grand National Party, 2006-. Publications: Numerous articles published in professional journals. Honours: Presidential Award for Best Academic Article, Seoul National University, 1974; Government Fellowship for Overseas Study, 1986; SBS Fellowship for Overseas Research, 2002. Memberships: International Institute of Public Finance; Many other associations. Address: #702 National Assembly Members Bldg, 1 Youido-dong, Seoul, Korea 150-702. E-mail: jbahk@assembly.go.kr Website: http://www.jll.org

BAI Daiseg, b. 25 May 1965, Daegu, Korea. Clinical Psychologist; Researcher. m. Younghee Seo, 1 son, 1 daughter. Education: BA, Department of Psychology, College of Social Science, 1991, MA, Clinical Psychology, 1993, PhD, Engineering, 2003, Graduate School, Kyungpook National University, Taegu. Appointments: Army Service, 1986-88; Trainee, Clinical Psychology on Mental Health, Ministry of Health and Welfare, Korea, 1993-98; Clinical Psychologist, Daedong Hospital, 1993-95; Clinical Psychologist, Kwak Ho Soon Neuropsychiatric Clinic, 1995-96; Clinical Psychologist, Division of Clinical Psychology, Pohang St Mary's Hospital, 1996-98; Consultant, Mental Health Project, Kyungju Health Center, 2001-02; Clinical Psychologist, Division of Clinical Psychology, Yeungnam University Medical Center, 1998-; Postdoctoral Researcher, Center for Healthcare Technology Department, Ministry of Science and Technology, 2004-06; Postdoctoral Researcher, Research Center for Biomedical Engineering, Yeungnam University, 2005-. Publications: 29 articles in professional scientific journals; Book: The Comprehension and Interpretation of Computerized Neurocognitive Function Test, 2005. Honours: Listed in international biographical dictionaries. Memberships: Korean Psychology Association; Korean Clinical Psychology Association; Koran Association of Health Psychology; American Psychological Association; APA, Div 40 Clinical Neuropsychology. Address: Division of Psychology, Department of Psychiatry, Yeungnam University Medical Center, 317-1, Daemyung-dong, Nam-gu, Daegu, 705-035, Korea. E-mail: dsbai@yumail.ac.kr

BAICA Malvina-Florica, b. 3 November 1942, Oravita, Banat, Romania (emigrated with political asylum to USA, 1968). University Professor; Mathematician; Researcher; Educator. m. Adrian Baica, 1963. Education: European Baccalaureate, Mathematics and Physics, Liceum General Drăgălina of Oravita, Romania, 1960; BS, Mathematics and Physics, 1964, MS, Mathematics (Projective and Differential Geometry), 1965, University of Timisoara, Romania; MS, Mathematics (Algebra & Number Theory), Illinois Institute of Technology, Chicago, Illinois, USA, 1974; PhD, Mathematics (Algebraic Number Theory & Universal Algebra), University of Houston, Texas, 1980. Appointments: Assistant Professor, Mathematics & Statistics, Western Illinois University, USA, 1978-80; Assistant Professor of Mathematics, Statistics & Computer Sciences, Marquette University, Milwaukee, Wisconsin, 1980-81; Assistant Professor of Mathematics & Computer Sciences, Marshall University, Huntington, West Virginia, 1981-83; Assistant Professor, Mathematics & Computer Sciences, Valparaiso University, Indiana, 1983-84; Lecturer, 1984-85, Assistant Professor, 1985-89, Associate Professor, 1989-91, Professor, 1991-, Mathematics & Computer Sciences, University of Wisconsin, Whitewater. Publications: Author of more than 60 papers and 3 books; Developed Baica's Generalised Euclidean Algorithm (BGEA) which is proved to be the Euler System for the Algebraic Number Theory (BGEA is used to prove long time unsolved problems in algebraic number theory and algebra, including the original Fermat's Last Theorem); Discovered Baica's Trigonometric Identities; In collaboration with M Cardu, introduced and developed for the first time the nonclassical trigonometries such as the infratrigonometry, ultratrigonometry, transtrigonometry, extratriganometry and paratrigonometry; Discovered Baica-Cardu Trigonometry Identities for these corresponding nonclassical trigonometries; Contributed significantly to the solution of Goldbach's problem and mathematical models for mechanical engineering applications. Honours: Pi Mu Epsilon, National Honorary Mathematics Fraternity Texas Theta, 1977; Excellence in Research Award, 1988, Certificate of Recognition Award for Outstanding Research, 1997, 1998, Certificate of Recognition Award for Research, 1999, Certificate of Excellence Award in Research, 2004, University of Wisconsin, Whitewater; Honorary Diploma, Romanian ASTRA Association, Timisoara, Romania, 2003. Memberships: American Mathematical Society; Mathematical Association of America; New York Academy of Sciences. Address: Department of Mathematical and Computer Sciences, University of Wisconsin, Whitewater, WI 53190, USA. E-mail: baicam@uww.edu

BAIKINA Nina Grigorievna, b. 18 July 1942, Altai region, Russia. Correctional Pedagogy Professor. m. Vitaliy Grigorievich Kulygin, 1 daughter. Education: MPC Doctor, Teacher of PE and Sport, Anatomy and Physiology, Uzbek State University of Physical Education, Tashkent, 1964; Doctor of Pedagogic Science, Correctional Pedagogy Institute, Moscow, 1992; Professor, Zaporizhzhya State University, 1994. Appointments: Teacher of Choreography, Republican Boarding School for Deaf Children, Tashkent,

1964-67; Teacher of PE and Sport, Tashkent State University, 1967-71; Lecturer, Chair of Sport, 1971-82, Head, Chair of Sport, 1983-87, Zaporizhzhya State University; Head, Chair of Correctional Pedagogy, 2003-06, Professor of Physical Education and Tourism Theory and Methods, 2007-08, Zaporizhzhya National University. Publications: 380 publications; Textbooks: Methods of Early Physical Training in Swimming for Children with Eyesight Deficiency; Special Methods of Adaptive Physical Education; Psycho-Motor Development Diagnosis and Correction of People with Eyesight Deficiency; Early Psycho-Motor Diagnosis and Correction of Children with Psycho-Motor Development Deficiency. Honours: Lecturer's Certificate, Moscow, 1992; Doctor of Pedagogical Science, Moscow, 1992; Professor, ZNU, Ukraine; Honour of Real Member of Academy, 2001. Memberships: Academy of Management in Education and Culture, Moscow. Address: Depovska Str 83, Flat 12, 69068, Zaporizhzhya, Ukraine.

BAILEY David, b. 2 January 1938, London, England. Photographer; Film Director. m. (1) Rosemary Bramble, 1960, (2) Catherine Deneuve, 1965; (3) Marie Helvin, divorced, (4) Catherine Dyer, 1986, 2 sons, 1 daughter. Appointments: Self taught photographer for Vogue, UK, USA, France, Italy; Advertising Photography, 1959-; Director, Commercials, 1966-; TV Documentaries, 1968-; Exhibition National Portrait Gallery, 1971; Photographers Gallery, 1973; Olympus Gallery, 1980, 1982, 1983; Victoria and Albert Museum, 1983; International Centre of Photography, New York, 1984; Hamilton Gallery, 1990, 1992; Director, Producer, TV Film Who Dealt?, 1993; Documentary: Models Close Up, 1998; Director, feature film, The Intruder, 1999. Publications: Box of Pinups, 1964; Goodbye Baby and Amen, 1969; Warhol, 1974; Beady Minces, 1974; Mixed Moments, 1976; Trouble and Strife, 1980; NW1, 1982; Black and White Memories, 1983; Nudes, 1981-84, 1984; Imagine, 1985; The Naked Eye: Great Photographers of the Nude (with Martin Harrison), 1988; If We Shadows, 1992; The Lady is a Tramp, 1995; Rock and Roll Heroes, 1997; Archive, 1999; Chasing Rainbows, 2001. Honours: Dr hc, Bradford University, 2001. Address: c/o Robert Montgomery and Partners, 3 Junction Mews, Sale Place, London, W2, England.

BAILYN Bernard, b. 10 September 1922, Hartford, Connecticut, USA. Professor Emeritus of History; Writer. m. Lotte Lazarsfeld, 18 June 1952, 2 sons. Education: AB, Williams College, 1945; MA, 1947, PhD, 1953, Harvard University. Appointments: Instructor, 1953-54, Assistant Professor, 1954-58, Associate Professor, 1958-61, Professor of History, 1961-66, Winthrop Professor of History, 1966-81, Adams University Professor, 1981-93, Director, Charles Warren Center for Studies in American History, 1983-94, James Duncan Phillips Professor of Early American History, 1991-93, Professor Emeritus, 1993-, Harvard University; Trevelyan Lecturer, 1971, Pitt Professor of American History, 1986-87, Cambridge University; Fellow, British Academy, and Christ's College, Cambridge, 1991. Publications: The New England Merchants in the Seventeenth Century, 1955; Massachusetts Shipping, 1697-1714: A Statistical Study (with Lotte Bailyn), 1959; Education in the Forming of American Society: Needs and Opportunities for Study, 1960; Pamphlets of the American Revolution, 1750-1776, Vol 1 (editor), 1965; The Apologia of Robert Keayne: The Self-Portrait of a Puritan Merchant (editor), 1965; The Ideological Origins of the American Revolution, 1967, new edition, 1992; The Origins of American Politics, 1968; The Intellectual Migration: Europe and America, 1930-1960 (editor with Donald Fleming), 1969; Religion and Revolution: Three Biographical

Studies, 1970; Law in American History (editor with Donald Fleming), 1972; The Ordeal of Thomas Hutchinson, 1974; The Great Republic: A History of the American People (with others), 1977, 4th edition, 1992; The Press and the American Revolution (editor with John B Hench), 1980; The Peopling of British North America: An Introduction, 1986; Voyagers to the West: A Passage in the Peopling of America on the Eve of the Revolution, 1986; Faces of Revolution: Personalities and Themes in the Struggle for American Independence, 1990; Strangers within the Realm: Cultural Margins of the First British Empire (editor with Philip B Morgan), 1991; The Debate on the Constitution: Federalist and Antifederalist Speeches, Articles and Letters during the Struggle over Ratification, 2 volumes, 1993;On the Teaching and Writing of History, 1994; To Begin the World Anew, 2003; Atlantic History: Concept and Contours, 2005. Contributions to: Scholarly journals. Honours: Bancroft Prize, 1968; Pulitzer Prizes in History, 1968, 1987; National Book Award in History, 1975; Thomas Jefferson Medal, American Philosophical Society, 1993; Honorary doctorates; Catton Prize, Society of American Historians, 2000. Memberships: American Academy of Arts and Sciences; American Historical Association, president, 1981; American Philosophical Society; National Academy of Education; Royal Historical Society. Address: 170 Clifton Street, Belmont, MA 02178, USA.

BAINBRIDGE Beryl Margaret (Dame), b. 21 November 1934, Liverpool, England. Author. Appointments: Actress, Repertory Theatres in UK, 1949-60; Clerk, Gerald Duckworth & Co Ltd, London, 1971-73. Publications: A Weekend with Claude, 1967; Another Part of the Wood, 1968; Harriet Said, 1972; The Dressmaker, 1973; The Bottle Factory Outing, 1974; Sweet William, 1975; A Quiet Life, Injury Time, 1976; Young Adolf, 1978; Winter Garden, 1980; English Journey or the Road to Milton Keynes, 1984; Watson's Apology, 1984; Mum & Mr Amitage, 1985; Forever England, 1986; Filthy Lucre, 1986; An Awfully Big Adventure, 1989; The Birthday Boys, 1991; Every Man For Himself, 1996; Master Georgie, 1998 According to Queeney, 2001. Honours: Guardian Fiction Award, 1974; Whitbread Award, 1977; Fellow, Royal Society of Literature, 1978; DLitt, University of Liverpool, 1986; Whitbread Award, 1997; James Tate Black Award, 1998; W H Smith Fiction Award, 1998; Dame Commander of the Order of the British Empire, 2000; David Cohen Prize, 2003; Heywood Hill Literary Prize, 2004. Address: 42 Albert Street, London NW1 7NU, England.

BAKER Alan, b. 19 August 1939, London, England. Mathematician. Education: BSc, Mathematics, University of London, 1961; PhD, Cambridge University, 1964. Appointments: Research Fellow, 1964-68, Director of Studies, Mathematics, 1968-74, Trinity College, Cambridge; Professor of Pure Mathematics, Cambridge University, 1974; Numerous Visiting Professorships in the USA and Europe; First Turán Lecturer, János Bolyai Mathematical Society, Hungary, 1978; Research into transcendental numbers. Publications: Numerous papers; Transcendental Number Theory, 1975; A Concise Introduction to the Theory of Numbers, 1984; New Advances in Transcendence Theory, as editor, 1988. Memberships: Fellow, Royal Society, 1973; Honorary Fellow, Indian National Science Academy, 1980; European Academy, 1998; Doctor Honoris Causa, University of Louis Pasteur, Strasbourg, 1998; Honorary Member, Hungarian Academy of Sciences, 2001. Address: Department of Pure Mathematics and Mathematical Statistics, 16 Mill Lane, Cambridge, CB2 1SB, England.

BAKER Carleton Harold, b. 2 August 1930, Utica, New York, USA. Physiology Educator. m. Sara Frances Johnson, 1963, 2 daughters. Education: BA, Utica College of Syracuse University, 1952; MA, 1954, PhD, 1955, Princeton University. Appointments: Assistant Instructor, 1952-54, Assistant in Research, 1954-55, Princeton University, New Jersey; Assistant Professor, 1955-61, Associate Professor, 1961-67, Professor, 1967, Medical College, Augusta, Georgia; Professor, Physiology and Biophysics, University of Louisville Health Sciences Center, 1967-71; Professor, Chairman, Department of Physiology and Biophysics, 1971-92, Deputy Dean for Research and Graduate Studies, 1980-82, Professor of Surgery, Physiology and Biophysics, Director of Surgical Research, 1992-95, University of South Florida, College of Medicine, Tampa; Professor Emeritus, University of South Florida, 1995-; Research Professor, Physiology, University of South Carolina, College of Medicine, Columbia, 1994-2001. Publications: Contributor of numerous articles in field. Honours: Service Awards, American Heart Association, 1977, 1977; Distinguished Scientist Award, University of South Florida, College of Medicine, 1981; Outstanding Artist/Scholar Award, Phi Kappa Phi, 1991; Dean's Citation, University of South Florida, College of Medicine, 1991; Founder Award, 1991. Memberships: Fellow, American Physiology Society; Member, Shock Society; European Microcirculatory Society; Microcirculatory Society; Torch Club International. Address: 4039 Old Waynesboro Road, Augusta, GA 30906, USA. E-mail: microves@bellsouth.net

BAKER Norman, b. 1957, Aberdeen, Scotland. Member of Parliament. Education: Degree in German, London University. Appointments include: Regional Executive Director, Our Price Records; Clerk, Hornsey Railway Station; Manager of a wine shop; Teacher of English as a Foreign Language; Liberal Democrats Environment Campaigner, House of Commons, 1989-90; Constituency Organiser, Liberal Democrat MP for Eastbourne, 1991; Member, Lewes District Council, 1987-99, Leader, 1991-97; East Sussex County Council, 1989-97; Chair, Economic Development and Public Transport sub-committees, Member of Parliament for Lewes Constituency, 1997-. Honours: Best Newcomer MP Award, 1997; Runner Up, Best Questioner, Runner Up, Best Opposition MP, Channel 4 Awards; Inquisitor of the Year, Zurich/Spectator Parliamentarian of the Year Awards, 2001; Winner, Opposition MP of the Year Award, Channel 4, 2002; RSPCA Lord Erskine Award, 2003. Address: House of Commons, London SW1A 0AA, England.

BAKER William, b. 6 July 1944, Shipston, Warwickshire, England. Professor. m. 16 November 1969, 2 daughters. Education: BA Hons, Sussex University, 1963-66; MPhil, London University, 1966-69; PhD, 1974; MLS, Loughborough, 1986. Appointments: Lecturer; Thurrock Technical College, 1969-71; Ben-Gurion University, 1971-77; University of Kent, 1977-78; West Midlands College, 1978-85; Professor, Pitzer College, Claremont, California, 1981-82; Housemaster, Clifton College, 1986-89; Professor, Northern Illinois University, 1989-; Presidential Research Professor (Distinguished Professor), Northern Illinois University, 2003-; Editor, The Year's Work in English Studies, 2000-; George Eliot – G.H. Lewes Studies, 1981-. Publications: Harold Pinter, 1973; George Eliot and Judaism, 1975; The Early History of the London Library, 1992; Literary Theories: A Case Study in Critical Performance, 1996; Nineteenth Century British Book Collectors and Bibliographers, 1997; Twentieth Century British Book Collectors and Bibliographers, 1999; Pre-Nineteenth Century British Book Collectors and Bibliographers, 1999; The Letters of Wilkie Collins, 1999;

Twentieth Century Bibliography and Textual Criticism, 2000; George Eliot: A Bibliographical History, 2002; Shakespeare: The Critical Tradition: The Merchant of Venice, 2005; Harold Pinter: A Bibliographical History, 2005; The Public Face of Wilkie Collins, 4 vols, 2005. Other: Editions of letters by George Henry Lewes, George Eliot, and Wilkie Collins, 2000-. Honours: Ball Brothers Foundation Fellowship, Lilly Library, Indiana University, 1993; Bibliographical Society of America, Fellowship, 1994-95; American Philosophical Society Grant, 1997; Choice Outstanding Academic Book of the Year Award, 2000; National Endowment for the Humanities Senior Fellowship, 2002-03. Memberships: Bibliographical Society of America; ALA; MLA; SHARP. Address: Department of English, Northern Illinois University, DeKalb, Illinois, USA.

BAKEWELL Joan Dawson, b. 16 April 1933, Stockport, England. Broadcaster; Writer. m. (1) Michael Bakewell, 1955, 1 son, 1 daughter, (2) Jack Emery, 1975. Education: Newnham College, Cambridge. Appointments: TV Critic, The Times, 1978-81; Columnist, Sunday Times, 1988-90; Associate, Newnham College, Cambridge, 1980-91; Associate Fellow, 1984-87; Gov BFI, 1994-99; Chair, 1999-2003; TV Includes: Sunday Break, 1962; Home at 4.30 (writer and producer), 1964; Meeting Point, The Second Sex, 1964; Late Night Line Up, 1965-72; The Youthful Eve, 1968; Moviemakers, National Film Theatre, 1971; Film 72; Film 73; Holiday, 74, 75, 76, 77, 78 (series); Reports Action (series) 1976-78; Arts UK: OK?, 1980; Heart of the Matter, 1988-2000; My Generation, 2000; One Foot in the Past, 2000; Taboo (series), 2001; Radio includes: Artist of the Week, 1998-99; The Brains Trust, 1999-; Belief, 2000. Publications; The New Priesthood: British Television Today, 1970; A Fine and Private Place, 1977; The Complete Traveller, 1977; The Heart of the Heart of the Matter, 1996; The Centre of the Bed: An Autobiography, 2003; Contributions to journals. Address: c/o Knight Ayton Management, 10 Argyll Street, London, W1V 1AB, England.

BALA'ZS András, b. 15 November 1949, Budapest, Hungary. Biophysicist. m. Mária Majoros, 1 son. Education: BA, Biology, 1974, MSc, Theoretical Chemistry, 1976, Eötvös L University; PhD (Candidate) Biology, Hungarian Academy of Sciences. Appointments: Research Assistant, 1974-81, Research Worker, 1981-95, Consultant, 1995-, Eötvös L University, Theoretical Chemistry Group, Departments of Atomic/Biological Physics. Publications: In professional journals. Honours: Listed in biographical publications. Memberships: European Cell Biology Organisation; Union of Hungarian Chemists; Hungarian Biochemical Society; Hungarian Theoretical Biological Society; Molecular Electronics and Biocomputing Society; Vienna Freud Museum; World Wild Fund. Address: Department of Biological Physics, Eötvös L University, Pa'zmány Sétány 1, H-1117 Budapest, Hungary.

BALALI-MOOD Mahdi, b. 6 September 1942, Birdjand, Iran. Professor of Medicine and Clinical Toxicology. m. Maryam Khordi-Mood, 1 son, 1 daughter. Education: BSc, Chemistry, Teacher Training University, Tehran, 1964; MD, Tehran University Medical School, 1970; Medical Army Certificate, 1971; Advanced Management Certificate, 1978; PhD, Clinical Pharmacology and Toxicology, Edinburgh University Medical School, 1981; Speciality in Therapeutics, 1981; Sub-Speciality in Poisonings, 1984. Appointments: Lecturer, Forensic and Clinical Toxicology, Faculty of Medicine, Ferdowsi University, Director, Poisons Treatment Centre, 1972-77; Research Fellow, Department of Clinical Pharmacology, Edinburgh University, 1978-81; Lecturer, Clinical Pharmacology, Edinburgh University, 1981-82;

Associate Professor, Clinical Toxicology, 1982-89, Professor of Medicine, Director, Medical Toxicology Centre, Imam Reza Hospital, Mashhad University of Medical Sciences (MUMS), 1989-; Regional Secretary of the World Federation of Clinical Toxicology and Poison Centre, 1994-; President, Asia Pacific Association of Medical Toxicology, 1993-2001; President, Iranian Society of Toxicology, 1990-98, 2001-03; Vice-Chairman, Scientific Advisory Board, OPCW, 2005-. Publications: 19 books and monographs, 3 chapters in international textbooks, 93 original papers and articles published in national and international journals, 225 short papers and abstracts published in journals, abstract books and proceedings of international conferences. Honours: Teaching Award in Chemistry, 1964; Research Award in Clinical Toxicology, Mashad University, 1983; Medical Care Award, Minister of Higher Education, 1986; Medical Management Award of Chemical War Gas Victims, 1987; Award of Medical Council of IR Iran, 2000; Research Awards, Ministry of Sciences, Research and Technology, Iran and Best Researcher, MUMS, 2005. Memberships: Medical Council of Iran, 1970-; European Association of Poisons Control Centres and Clinical Toxicologists, 1984-; Fellow, Academy of Sciences for Developing World (new name for the third World Academy of Science), 1997-; Iranian Academy of Medical Sciences, 1990-; Member of National Board for Toxicology, 1990-. Address: Medical Toxicology Centre, Imam Reza Hospital, Mashhad 91735-348, Iran. E-mail: mbalalimood@hotmail.com

BALANATHAN Kanthar Palany, b. 1 June 1943, Manipay, Ceylon. Electrical Engineer. m. Ranjini, 1 son, 1 daughter. Education: Electrical and Mechanical Engineering, Ceylon College of Technology; Diploma in Electrical Engineering, Staffordshire College of Technology, England; Graduate Certificate in Reliability Engineering, Monash University, Australia; Post Graduate Diploma in Business & Administration (Finance), Massey University, New Zealand. Appointments: Engineering Apprenticeship, Shift Charge Officer, Hydro Power Station, Department of Government Electrical Undertakings, Sri Lanka, 1965-67; Allan West EAC, St Albans, UK, 1968-69; Design Engineer, Colombo Engineers Ltd, Sri Lanka, 1969; Electrical Engineer, Works Engineer (Electrical), Ceylon Cement Corporation, 1969-77; Visiting Instructor, Lecturer, Polytechnic, Jaffna, 1969-73; Deputy Chief Engineer (Elect), Water Corporation of Oyo State, Nigeria, 1977-81; Chief Engineer, Gambill Builders (Nig) Ltd, Nigeria, 1981-84; Senior Electrical Design Engineer, Flembog Eng Systems & Research Co Ltd, Nigeria, 1984; Principal Engineer (Electrical Services), City Council of Harare, Zimbabwe, 1984-87; Senior Electrical Design Engineer, Beca Carter Hollings & Ferner Ltd, Consulting Engineers, Wellington, New Zealand, 1987; Senior Electrical Design Engineer, Northern Thermal Group, ECNZ, 1988-91; Technical Section Engineer, New Plymouth Thermal Group, ECNZ, 1991-96; Senior Electrical Engineer (Generation Services), Contact Energy Ltd, 1996-98; Senior Electrical Engineer, CS Energy Mica Creek Ltd, 1998-2000; Specialist Engineer Power & Control Systems, NRGGOS, Gladstone, 2000-03; Director, Principal Consultant, Power Engineering Solutions, Melbourne, 2004-. Publications: Life assessment of turbo generators at the New Plymouth Power Station, 1995; Condition Monitoring of Large Static & Rotating Machinery, 2003. Memberships: Chartered Electrical Engineer, Engineering Council, UK; Chartered Professional Engineer, NPER, Australia; Registered Professional Engineer of Queensland, Australia; Member, Institution of Engineering & Technology, UK; Member, Institution of Engineers, Australia;

Member, Association of Professional Engineers, Scientists & Managers, Australia. Address: 49 Cromwell Drive, Rowville, VIC 3178, Australia. E-mail: pengsol@bigpond.net.au

BALAS-WHITFIELD Susan, b. 29 April 1943, USA. Fine Artist. m. Marshall P Whitfield, 2 daughters. Education: BA, Rutgers University, 1964; New York University, 1961-64; Triune Brain studies, Mead Institute, New York. Appointments: Fine Artist; Lecturer on The Triune Brain, American University and Monmouth County, New Jersey high schools; Teacher of Russian, Spanish and English, New Jersey schools, 1964-89. Publications: Author, Into the Triangle: A Teacher's Trot. Honours: American Artists' Professional League Pastel Award for Excellence; Artist of the Year, Durango, Colorado, 2003. Memberships: Pastel Society of America; Colorado Pastel Society; Salmagundi Club of New York. Address: 22521 East Rowland Drive, Aurora, CO 80016, USA. E-mail: susan@balasart.com Website: www.balasart.com

BALASINGAM Manohari, b. 12 April 1965, Kuala Lumpur, Malaysia. Physician. Education: MBBS, Kasturba Medical College (University of Mangalore), Manipal, India, 1992; M Med, Master in Medicine, University of Malaya, 2000; Cardiovascular Medicine (Non Interventional) Certificate, National Heart Institute, Kuala Lumpur, 2006. Appointments: House Officer, Malacca Hospital, 1992-93; Medical Officer, Kuala Lipis Hospital, 1993-94; Medical Officer, Mentakab Hospital, 1994-95; Postgraduate in Internal Medicine, University Hospital, Kuala Lumpur, 1995-2000; Consultant Physician, Malacca Hospital, Clinical Lecturer in Medicine, Malacca Manipal Medical College, 2000-06; Senior Consultant and Head of Department of Medicine, Ampang Hospital Selangor, 2006-. Publications: Lipid profile in post menopausal women in Malacca, Malaysia; Determinants of left atrial size in hypertensive/non hypertensive patients in Malacca, Malaysia. Honours: Excellence in Service Award, University of Malaya, 2000; Outstanding Professional Award; Woman of the Year, ABI, 2006. Memberships: National Heart Foundation of Malaysia; Malaysian Medical Association; American Heart Association; Harvard Medical School Post Graduate Association. Address: No 4, Jalan Duku, Jalan Kasipillay, 51200 Kuala Lumpur, Malaysia. Address: manobm3@yahoo.com.sg

BALASKI Belinda L, b. 8 December 1947, Inglewood, California, USA. Actress; Teacher; Writer; Director; Photographer; Artist/Painter. 1 daughter. Education: Colorado Women's College, Denver, 1965-67; Parson's College, Fairfield, Iowa, 1967-69. Appointments: Actress appearing in theatre, television and movies; Founder, BB'S Kids Acting School, Los Angeles, 1989-. Publications: The T-Files, play, 1999; Shock Cinema, 2007. Honours: Los Angeles Drama Critics Circle Award, 1972; The Robbie Award, 1973, 1974; Emmy; Photography Awards, 2003-05. Memberships: SAG; AFTRA; EQUITY; Academy of Motion Pictures Arts & Sciences. Address: PO Box 461011, Los Angeles, CA 90046, USA. E-mail: bbs4kids@aol.com Website: www.bbskids.com

BALDRIGA Irene, b. 9 June 1970, Rome, Italy. Art History Scholar. Education: Degree in Modern Letters (with honours), 1993, PhD, Art History, 1999, Postdoctoral Fellowship, 1999-2001, University of Rome La Sapienza; Student, courses on the didactic of Art History, 2003-. Appointments: Art History Independent Scholar; Art History Teacher, Italian High School, 2001-; Art History Instructor, IES Rome, Luiss, 2003-; Postgraduate Art History Professor, University of Rome La Sapienza, 2007-. Publications: Numerous articles and papers in professional journals. Honours: Fellowship, Belgian Government, 1995; Intensive Course on The Culture of the Low Countries in the 17th Century, Internationale Vereniging voor Nederlandistiek, 1999; Teaching Award, IES Best Instructor of the Year, 2004. Memberships: Cultural Exchange 1400-1700; Giove Project. E-mail: irene@irenebaldriga.it

BALDWIN Alec (Alexander Rae Baldwin III), b. 3 April 1958, Masapequa, New York, USA. Actor. m. Kim Basinger, 1993, divorced, 1 daughter. Education: George Washington University; New York University; Lee Strasberg Theatre Institute; Studied with Mira Rostova and Elaine Aiken. Appointments: Stage Appearances Include: Loot, 1986; Serious Money, 1988; Prelude to a Kiss, 1990; A Streetcar named Desire, 1992; TV Appearances Include: The Doctors, 1980-82; Cutter to Houston, 1982; Knot's Landing, 1984-85; Love on the Run, 1985; A Dress Gray, The Alamo: 13 Days to Glory, 1986; Sweet Revenge, 1990; Nuremberg, Path to War, 2000; Second Nature, 2002; Dreams and Giants, 2003; Thomas and Friends: The Best of Gordon, 2004; Film Appearances Include: Forever Lulu, She's Having A baby, 1987; Beetlejuice, Married to the Mob, Talk Radio, Working Girl, 1988; Great Balls of Fire, 1989; The Hunt for Red October, Miami Blues, Alice, 1990; The Marrying Man, 1991; Prelude to a Kiss, Glengarry Glen Ross, 1992; Malice, 1993; The Getaway, The Shadow, 1994; Heaven's Prisoners, 1995; Looking for Richard, The Juror, Ghosts of Mississippi, 1996; Bookworm, The Edge, 1997; Thick as Thieves, Outside Providence, Mercury Rising (producer), 1998; The Confession, Notting Hill, 1999; Thomas and the Magic Railroad, State and Main, 2000; Pearl Harbor, Final Fantasy: The Spirit's Within, The Royal Tenenbaums, The Devil and Daniel Webster, 2001; Path to War, 2002; Dr Seuss' The Cat in the Hat, The Cooler, 2003; Along Came Polly, The Last Shot, The Aviator, 2004; Elizabethtown, Fun with Dick and Jane, 2005; The Good Shepherd, Brooklyn Rules, The Departed, Running with Scissors, Mini's First Time, 2006. Honours: The World Award, 1986. Memberships: Screen Actors Guild; American Federation of TV and Radio Artists; Actors Equity Association.

BALDWIN George Curriden, b. 5 May 1917, Denver, Colorado, USA. Physicist. m. Winifred M Gould, 2 sons, 1 daughter. Education: BA, magna cum laude, Kalamazoo College, 1939; MA, 1941, PhD, 1943, University of Illinois. Appointments: Research Associate, General Electric Research Laboratory, 1944-55; Nuclear Engineer, General Electric Aircraft Nuclear Propulsion Department, 1955-58; Loaned by General Electric to Argonne National Laboratory, 1957-59; Applied Physicist, General Electric General Engineering Laboratory, 1959-67; Professor, 1967-77, Emeritus, 1977-, Rensselaer Polytechnic Institute; Staff Member, Los Alamos National Laboratory, 1975-87; Retired, 1987. Publications: More than 100 articles in scientific journals; Books: An Introduction to Nonlinear Optics, 1967; The Science Was Fun, 2006. Honour: Fellowship, University of Illinois, 1942; Phi Beta Kappa, University of Illinois, 1943; Fellow, American Physical Society, 1958; Distinguished Alumnus, Kalamazoo College, 1987. Memberships: American Nuclear Society, 1956-85; American Physical Society; AAAS. Address: 1016 Calle Bajo, Santa Fe, NM 87501, USA. E-mail: geoc142857@msn.net

BALDWIN Mark, b. 29 July 1944, Simla, India. Publisher; Author. m. Myfanwy Dundas, 2 July 1977, 3 sons. Education: BA, MA, St Catharine's College, Cambridge, 1962-65; MSc, DIC, PhD, Imperial College, 1970-86. Appointments: Engineer with Mott Hay & Anderson, 1965-70; Lecturer,

Imperial College, London, England, 1971-86; Publisher & Bookseller, 1986-. Publications: British Freight Waterways Today and Tomorrow, 1980; Canals - A New Look, 1984; Canal Books, 1984; Simon Evans - His Life and Later Work, 1992; Cleobury 2000, 1999. Contributions to: Proc Institution Civil Engineers; Waterways World; Canal and Riverboat, Antiquarian Book Monthly Review, Book and Magazine Collector; Lecturer on Second World War Codebreaking. Address: 24 High Street, Cleobury Mortimer, Kidderminster DY14 8BY, England.

BALDWIN Michael, b. 1 May 1930, Gravesend, Kent, England. Author; Poet. Education: Open Scholar, 1949, Senior Scholar, 1953, St Edmund Hall, Oxford, 1950-55. Appointments: Assistant Master, St Clement Danes Grammar School, 1955-59; Lecturer, Senior Lecturer, Principal Lecturer, Head of English and Drama Department, Whitelands College, 1959-78; Writer and Presenter, 5 series of Thames TV's Writer's Workshop, 1970-77; Many BBC radio broadcasts, 1963-70. Publications: Poetry: The Silent Mirror, 1951; Voyage From Spring, 1956; Death on a Live Wire, 1962; How Chas Egget Lost His Way in a Creation Myth, 1967; Hob, 1972; Buried God, 1973; Snook, 1980; King Horn, 1983; Fiction includes: Grandad with Snails, 1960; Miraclejack, 1963; Sebastian, 1967; Underneath and Other Situations, 1968; There's a War On, 1970; The Gamecock, 1980; The Rape of Oc, 1993. The First Mrs Wordsworth, 1996; Dark Lady, 1998. Contributions to: Listener; Encounter; New Statesman; Texas Review; BBC Wildlife Magazine; Outposts. Honours: Rediffusion Prize, 1970; Cholmondeley Award, 1984; Fellow, Royal Society of Literature, 1985. Memberships: Vice Chairman, Arvon Foundation, 1974-90; Chairman, Arvon Foundation at Lumb Bank, 1980-89; Crime Writer's Association; The Colony Room; The Athenaeum. Address: 35 Gilbert Road, Bromley, Kent BR1 3QP, England.

BALDWIN William, b. 7 August 1948, Bolton, England. Clerk in Holy Orders. m. Sheila Margaret, 1 son, 1 daughter. Education: Bolton Technical College (part-time student), 1965-68; Nursing and Midwifery Council State Registration (General and Psychiatric Nursing), Bolton School of Nursing (Royal Bolton Hospital) and Whittingham Hospital, Preston, 1968-73; Further Education Teacher's Certificate/Registered Clinical Nurse Tutor, 1974-75; Examiners Qualification, Royal College of Nursing Study Centre, Birmingham, 1996; North West Ordination Course, General Ministry Examination, 1975-78; B Th (Hons), MA, Church History, PhD, Greenwich School of Theology (distance learning student), 1991-97. Appointments include: Various NHS appointments, 1968-78; Ordained Deacon, 1978; Ordained Priest, 1979; Assistant Curate, St Anne Royton, 1978-82; Vicar, St Thomas Halliwell, 1982-87; Rector of Atherton Team Ministry, 1987-2002; Team Vicar of Atherton and Hindsford with Howe Bridge St Michael, 2002-; Area Dean of Leigh, 2001-; Part-time Chaplain to: Oldham General Hospital/Kershaw's Cottage Hospital, 1978-82; Royal Bolton Hospital, 1983-87; Royal Naval Association/White Ensign Association, 1987-2002; Advisor on healing to the Lord Bishop of Manchester, 1991-2001; Tutor for distance learning students, Greenwich School of Theology, 1996-; Personal Tutor, Manchester, Ordained Local Ministry Course; Member, Manchester Diocesan Synod, 1982-97, 2001-06; Member, Wigan Metropolitan Borough Council's Faith Forum, 2001; Board Member SRB5 (single regeneration budget board) Atherton Building Communities Partnership, 2001-05; Board Member, Leigh Primary Care Group, 1998-2002; Non-Executive Director, 5 Boroughs NHS Trust, 2002-; Mental Health Act Manager, 2002-. Publications include: Booklets: Agape: A Devotion on 1 Corinthians

13, 1987; Christian Discipleship and the Created Order; Recognising Holiness in the Ordinary, 2000; Pastoral Letters of a Parish Priest, 2002; Poetry Address Book, 2003; Book: The Doctrine of Humanity Revisited, 2003; Several religious and secular poems published in anthologies. Honours: Elected Fellow of the Royal Society of Health, 1983; Awarded Serving Brother of the Order of St John of Jerusalem for service to humanity by H M the Queen, 1988; Elected Fellow, Royal Society of Medicine, 2006. Memberships: Associate, St George's House, Windsor Castle; Friend of St George's Chapel; Institute of Advanced Motorists. Address: Atherton Rectory, Bee Fold Lane, Atherton, Manchester M46 0BL, England. E-mail: frbill@fsmail.net

BALE Christian Charles Philip, b. 30 January 1974, Haverfordwest, Wales. Actor. m. Sibi Blazic, 2000, 1 daughter. Career: Empire of the Sun, 1987; Newsies, 1992; Swing Kids, 1993; Prince of Jutland, Little Women, 1994; Pocahontas (voice), 1995; The Secret Agent, The Portrait of a Lady, 1996; Metroland, 1997; Velvet Goldmine, All the Little Animals, 1998; A Midsummer Night's Dream, 1999; American Psycho, Shaft, 2000; Captain Corelli's Mandolin, 2001; Laurel Canyon, Reign of Fire, Equilibrium, 2002; El Maquinista, 2004; Howl's Moving Castle (voice), 2004; Batman Begins, Harsh Times, The New World, 2005; The Prestige, Rescue Dawn, Harsh Times, 2006; 3:10 to Yuma, 2007; I'm Not There, 2007; Dark Knight, 2008. Honours: Special Citation for Best Performance by a Juvenile Actor, National Board of Review, 1987.

BALI Professor Raj, b. 5 January 1952, Varanasi, India. Professor. m. C Mani Prajapati, 2 sons, 1 daughter. Education: BSc, Physics, Chemistry & Mathematics, 1972, MSc, 1974, PhD, Mathematics, 1978, BHU, Varanasi. Appointments: Assistant Professor, 1978-79, Associate Professor, 1992-2001, Professor, 2001-, Mathematics, Rector, Proctor and Warden of Hostel, University of Rajasthan, Jaipur; Collaborative research with Professor J V Narlikar; Organised 23rd IAGRG conference, 2004; Invited talk, ICGC conference, Pune, 2007. Publications: 2 books: Theory of Relativity; Advanced Tensor Analysis; 116 articles in professional journals. Honours: CSIR Fellowship, 1975-78; Senior Associate, IUAA, Pune, 1997-2000; Visiting Fellowship Research Award, INSA, New Delhi, 2007-08. Memberships: Life Member, IAGRG; Life Member, Rajasthan Academy of Physical Sciences; Life Member, Academy of Progress of Mathematics. Address: Department of Mathematics BHU, University of Rajasthan, Jaipur 302004, India. E-mail: balir5@yahoo.co.in

BALKAS Mustafa, b. 6 August 1957, Ankara, Turkey. Teacher. m. Burcin, 2 sons. Education: BS, Sports Academy, 1979; MA, Middle East Technical University, 1983. Appointments: Instructor, Exercise Physiology Training Theory, Middle East Technical University, 1981-88; IB Co-ordinator, HS Dean, CAS Co-ordinator, The Koc School, 1988-98; Director, Edirne College, 1998-2000; Director, Yuzyil ISIL, 2000-01; HS Principal, Enka Schools, 2001-. Honours: Established first community service project in schools in Turkey at Koc School which involved high school students teaching mathematics, computer studies and English in a very poor school. Memberships: Turkish Handball Federation Education Committee; Enka Sports Club Executive Committee; Turkish National Olympic Committee. Address: Enka Schools, Sadi Gulcelik Spor Sitesi, Istinye, Istanbul 80860, Turkey. E-mail: mustafabalkas@enkaschools.com

BALL Michael Ashley, b. 27 June 1962, Bromsgrove, England. Actor, Singer, Entertainer. Partner, Cathy McGowan. Education: Plymouth College. Musical Education: Guildford School of Acting, 1981-84. Career: The Pirates of Penzance, 1984; Les Miserables, West End, 1985; Phantom of the Opera, West End, 1987; Aspects of Love, West End & New York, 1989-1990; Passion, London, 1996; Alone Together, London, 2001; Chitty Chitty Bang Bang, London, 2002-04; The Woman in White, 2005-; Represented UK, Eurovision Song Contest, 1992; UK tours, 1992, 1993, 1994, 1996, 1999; Television appearances: Host, own series, Michael Ball, 1993, 1994; Soapstar Superstar, 2007. Film appearance, England My England, 1995. Recordings: Albums: Michael Ball, 1992; Always, 1993; West Side Story, 1993; One Careful Owner, 1994; The Best Of Michael Ball, 1994; First Love, 1996; Michael Ball: The Musicals, 1996; The Movies, 1998; Christmas, 1999; Live at the Royal Albert Hall, 1999; This Time It's Personal, 2000; Centre Stage, 2001; Music, 2005. Singles include: Love Changes Everything; The First Man You Remember; It's Still You; One Step Out of Time; Sunset Boulevard; From Here to Eternity; The Lovers We Were; Wherever You Are; Something Inside So Strong; Appears on cast albums: Les Miserables; Aspects of Love; Encore!, Andrew Lloyd Webber collection; West Side Story; Passion; Sang on Rugby World Cup album; Chitty Chitty Bang Bang, 2002. Honours: 6 Gold albums; 1 Platinum album. Current Management: James Sharkey Associates. Address: Phil Bowdery Management, 144 Wigmore Street, London W1H 9FF, England.

BALL Michael Thomas, b. 14 February 1932, Eastbourne, England. Retired Bishop. Education: Queens' College, Cambridge; Wells Theological College. Appointments: Schoolmaster, 1955-76; Co-founder, Community of the Glorious Ascension (religious community for men and women), 1960; Curate, Stroud, 1971-76; Senior Anglican Chaplain, Sussex University and Parish Priest of Stanmer with Falmer, 1976-80; Bishop of Jarrow, 1980-90; Bishop of Truro, 1990-97. Publications: So There We Are, 1996; The Foolish Risks of God, 2003; Articles to various magazines. Address: Manor Lodge, Aller, Langport, Somerset TA10 0QN, England.

BALLANTYNE Colin Kerr, b. 7 June 1951, Glasgow, Scotland. University Professor. m. Rebecca Trengove, 1 son, 1 daughter. Education: MA, University of Glasgow, 1973; MSc, McMaster University, Canada, 1975; PhD, University of Edinburgh; DSc, University of St Andrews, 2000. Appointments: Lecturer, Geography, 1980-89, Warden of McIntosh Hall, 1985-95, Senior Lecturer in Geography and Geology, 1989-94, Professor in Physical Geography, 1994-, University of St Andrews; Visiting Professor, UNIS, Svalbard, Norway, 1998-; Visiting Erskine Fellow, University of Christchurch, New Zealand, 2003. Publications: 145 scientific papers; Books include: The Quaternary of the Isle of Skye, 1991; The Periglaciation of Great Britain, 1994; Classic Landforms of the Isle of Skye, 2000; Paraglacial Geomorphology, 2002. Honours: Fellow, Royal Geographical Society, 1983; Warwick Award, British Geomorphological Research Group, 1987; President's Medal, Royal Scottish Geographical Society, 1991; Newbigin Prize, Royal Scottish Geographical Society, 1992; Fellow, Royal Society of Edinburgh, 1996; Scottish Science Award, Saltire Society, 1996; Fellow, Royal Society of Arts, 1996; Wiley Award, British Geomorphological Research Group, 1999. Memberships: Quaternary Research Association; British Geomorphological Research Group; Royal Scottish Geographical Society; International Permafrost Association;

Edinburgh Geological Society. Address: School of Geography and Geosciences, University of St Andrews, Fife KY16 9AL, Scotland. E-mail: ckb@St-and.ac.uk

BALLARD James Graham, b. 15 November 1930, Shanghai, China; British Novelist; Short Story Writer. m. Helen Mary Mathews, 1954, deceased 1964, 1 son, 2 daughters. Education: King's College, Cambridge. Publications: The Drowned World, 1963; The 4 Dimensional Nightmare, 1963; The Terminal Beach, 1964; The Drought, 1965; The Crystal World, 1966; The Disaster Area, 1967; The Atrocity Exhibition, 1970; Crash, 1973; Vermilion Sands, 1973; Concrete Island, 1974; High Rise, 1975; Low Flying Aircraft, 1976; The Unlimited Dream Company, 1979; Myths of the Near Future, 1982; Empire of the Sun, 1984; The Venus Hunters, 1986; The Day of Creation, 1987; Running Wild, 1988; Memories of the Space Age, 1988; War Fever, 1990; The Kindness of Women, 1991; The Terminal Beach (short stories), 1992; Rushing to Paradise, 1994; A User's Guide to the Millennium, 1996; Cocaine Nights, 1996; Super-Cannes, 2000; The Complete Short Stories, 2001; Millennium People, 2003; Kingdom Come, 2006. Address: 36 Old Charlton Road, Shepperton, Middlesex, TW17 8AT, England.

BALLESTEROS Severiano, b. 9 April 1957, Santander, Spain. Golfer. m. Carmen Botin, 1988, 2 sons, 1 daughter. Career: Professional Golfer, 1974-; Spanish Young Professional title, 1975, 1978; French Open, 1977, 1982, 1985, 1986; Japan Open, 1977, 1978; Swiss Open, 1977, 1978, 1989; German Open, 1978, 1988; Open Championship, Lytham St Anne's, 1979, 1988; St Andrews, 1984; US Masters, 1980, 1983; World Matchplay Championship, Wentworth, 1981, 1982, 1984, 1985; Australian PGA Championship, 1981; Spanish Open, 1985; Dutch Open, 1986; British Masters, 1991; PGA Championship, 1991; International Open, 1994; Numerous other titles in Europe, US, Australia; Member, Ryder Cup team 1979, 1983, 1985, 1987, 1989, 1995. Publication: Trouble Shooting, 1996. Honours: Prince of Asturias Prize for sport, 1989; Dr hc (St Andrews), 2000. Address: Fairway SA, Pasaje de Pena 2-4, 39008 Santander, Spain.

BALLIN Torben Bjarke, b. 21 August 1957, Frederikshavn, Denmark. Archaeologist. m. Beverley Smith. Education: Librarian, Danmarks Biblioteksskole, Denmark, 1981; Cand Phil Prehist Archaeology, 1991, PhD Prehist Archaeology, 1999, University of Aarhus, Denmark. Appointments: Project Manager, Specialist, 1992-98; Consultant Archaeologist, Specialist at Lithic Research, 1999-. Publications: Numerous articles in professional journals. Honours: Grants from: Historic Scotland, 2000-01, 2002-03, 2004-05, 2005-06, 2006-07; National Museum of Scotland, 2000-01, 2002-03, 2005-06; Society of Antiquaries Scotland, 2005-06, 2006-07; Russell Trust, 2001-02; Catherine Mackichan Bursary Trust, 2002-03; Shetland Amenity Trust, 2006-07. Memberships: Member, Institute of Field Archaeologists; Fellow, Society of Antiquarians of Scotland; Member and Vice Chair, Lithic Studies Society; Member, International Association for Obsidian Studies; Member, SKAM. Address: Banknock Cottage, Denny, Stirlingshire FK6 5NA, Scotland.

BALLS Edward Michael, b. 25 February 1967. Member of Parliament. m. Yvette Cooper, 1 son, 2 daughters. Education: BA, Economics, Keble College, Oxford University; MPA, Economics, Harvard University, USA. Appointments: Economics Leader Writer and Columnist, Financial Times, 1990-94; Economic Adviser to Gordon Brown as Shadow Chancellor of the Exchequer, 1994-97; Chancellor of the Exchequer's Economic Adviser, 1997-99; Chancellor's

Representative at the G20; Chief Economic Adviser to the Treasury, 1999-2004; Member of Parliament for Normanton, 2005-; Leading a Treasury Report with Jon Cunliffe, Supporting the Middle East Peace Process through economic development; Elected Vice Chair, Fabian Society Executive Committee, 2006; Economic Secretary to the Treasury, 2006-07; Secretary of State for Children, Schools and Families, 2007-. Publications: Principal Editor, 1995 World Banking Development Report – Workers in an Integrating World; Contributions to learned journals including: Scottish Journal of Political Economy; World Economics; Reports published by the Fabian Society, Social Justice Commission, Smith Institute; Reforming Britain's Macroeconomic Policy (co-editor), 2001; Towards a New Regional Policy (with John Healey MP), 2003; Microeconomic Reform in Britain (co-editor), 2004; Contributor, IPPR publication, Applying the Dismal Science: When Economists Given Advice to Governments; Regular articles for Tribune magazine, Building Magazine, national newspapers and the Wakefield Express. Honour: Honorary Doctorate of Law, Nottingham University, 2003. Memberships: Active member, TGWU, Unison and the Co-operative Party; Member, House Magazine Editorial Board; Northern Way Steering Group. Address: Dept of Children, Schools and Families, Sanctuary Buildings, Great Smith Street, London, SW1P 3BT, England.

BALNAVE Derick, b. 17 June 1941, Lisburn, Northern Ireland. Academic. m. Maureen Dawson, 1 son, 1 daughter. Education: BSc, 1963, PhD, 1966, DSc, 1983, Queen's University, Belfast, Northern Ireland. Appointments: Scientific, 1966-69, Senior Scientific, 1969-73, Principal Scientific, 1973-77, Officer, Department of Agriculture, Northern Ireland; Assistant Lecturer, 1967-71, Lecturer, 1971-75, Senior Lecturer, 1975-77, Reader, 1977, Queen's University, Belfast; Senior Lecturer, 1978-81, Associate Professor, 1981-2001, University of Sydney, Australia; Research Director, Poultry Research Foundation, University of Sydney, 1978-2001; Honorary Governor, Poultry Research Foundation, University of Sydney, 2001-; Adjunct Professor, North Carolina State University, 1995-2005; Visiting Fellow, Cornell University, 1989. Publications: Approximately 150 scientific papers in professional journals; Over 200 conference and trade publications. Honours: Recipient, World's Poultry Science Association Australia Poultry Award, 1998. Memberships: World's Poultry Science Association; Poultry Science Association Inc. Address: 26 Valley View Drive, Narellan, New South Wales, 2567 Australia. E-mail: derickbalnave@bigpond.com

BALTAS Nicholas Constantinos, b. 20 August 1946, Kastania, Evrytania, Greece. Professor of Economics. m. Maria (Tsamboula) Balta, 1 son, 1 daughter. Education: Athens School of Economics and Business Science, Department of Economics, 1965-70; MSoc Sc, 1970-72, PhD, 1972-74, University of Birmingham. Appointments: Research Assistant, Department of Econometrics and Social Statistics, University of Birmingham, 1972; Lecturer, Economics, British Institute of Marketing, 1975-76; Lecturer, Econometrics, Department of Economics, Aristotelion University of Thessaloniki, 1976-79; Senior Economist, Research and Planning Division, Agricultural Bank of Greece, 1976-1986; Associate Professor of Economics, 1985-90, Professor of Economics, 1990-, Head of Department, 1999-2003, Athens University of Economics and Business, Department of Economics; Expert, Ministry of Agriculture, Greece, 2002-03; Expert, European Commission (DGRTD and DG TREN), 2002-03; Expert, Economic and Social Committee, Greece, 2003 and 2004; Chairman of the Board of Directors and Managing Director, Hellenic Railways,

2004-07; Vice-President, Board of Directors, Centre of Greek Public Enterprises and Organisations, 2005-08; Chairman, Board of Directors of the Community Support Framework of Management Organisation Unit, 2007-. Publications include: Books and Research Monographs: Development Strategy and Investment in the Processing and Marketing of Agricultural Products, 2001; Numerous journals, book chapters and conference proceedings and articles including: Investment in the Greek Processing of Agricultural Products and Food: A Panel Data Approach, 2007; An Analysis of Investment Activity in the Greek Agricultural Products and Food Manufacturing Sector, 2008; Book review: The Greek Economy: Sources of Growth in the Postwar Era, 1993. Honours: Fulbright Scholarship, 1991; British Council Scholarship, 1993; Jean Monnet Chair: EU Institutions and Economic Policy, 1999. Memberships include: Hellenic University Association for European Studies, President, 1999-2000 and 2002-03; European Community Studies Association; The Agricultural Economics Society; Greek Agricultural Economic Society; Hellenic Economic Association, Hellenic Operational Research Society; Athenian Policy Forum; European Summer Academy. Address: Athens University of Economics and Business, 76 Patission Str, 104 34 Athens, Greece. E-mail: baltas@aueb.gr

BALTAY Charles, b. 15 April 1937, Budapest, Hungary. Professor. m. Virginia Rohan, 4 sons, 1 daughter. Education: BSc, Union College, 1958; MSc, Yale University, 1959; PhD, Yale University, 1963. Appointments: Professor of Physics, Columbia University, 1964-88; Higgins Professor of Physics, Yale University, 1988-. Publications: 3 books; 300 journal articles. Honours: Director, Nevis Laboratory, Columbia University, 1976-88; Chairman, Physics Department, Yale University, 1995-2001. Memberships: Fellow, American Physical Society Sigma Xi. Address: 86 Lower Road, Guilford, CT 06437, USA. E-mail: charles.baltay@yale.edu

BAMBER Juliette Madeleine, b. 21 August 1930, Tidworth, England. Occupational Therapist; Counsellor. m. Donald Liddle, 1957, divorced 1995, 2 sons. Education: Art School, Foundation Course, 1947-49 Psychology, Honours, Birkbeck College, 1957-60. Publications: Breathing Space, 1991; On the Edge, 1993; Altered States, 1996; Touch Paper, 1996; The Ring of Words, 1996; The Wasting Game, 1997; The Long Pale Corridor, 1998; Flying Blind, 2000; 5 collections of poetry. Honours: 1st Prize, London Writers; 1st Prize, National Poetry Foundation; A Blue Nose Poet of the Year, 1998; Commended in Houseman Prize, 2000. Address: 9 Western Road, East Finchley, London N2 9JB, England.

BANA Eric, b. 9 August 1968, Melbourne, Australia. Actor. m. Rebecca Gleeson, 1997, 1 son, 1 daughter. Education: National Institute of Dramatic Art, Sydney, Australia. Career: Barman; Comedian; Actor: TV: Full Frontal, 1993; Eric, 1996, 1997; Something in the Air, 2000; Films: The Castle, 1997; Chopper, 2000; Black Hawk Down, 2001; The Nugget, 2002; Finding Nemo (voice), 2003; Hulk, 2003; Troy, 2004; Munich, 2005; Romulus My Father, 2006; Lucky You, The Other Boleyn Girl, 2007.

BANARASI Das, b. 16 October 1955, Akorhi, Mirzapur, India. Teacher; Poet. m. Vimala Devi, 10 March 1972, 1 son. Education: Sahityacharya (Equivalent to MA in Sanskrit), 1982; BTC, 1988; MA, Hindi Literature, 1993. Appointments: Assistant Teacher, Government Basic School, Mirzapur, India. Publications: Srihanumadvandana, 1982; Srivindhyavasinicharitamrit, 1989; Sriashtabhujakathamanjari, 1991; Paryavarankaumudi in Sanskrit, Hindi, English,

1993; Utsarg, 1995; Hymn to Lord (Hanuman), 1995; Gandhari, 1996; Silver Poems, 1998. Contributions to: Poet International, Anthologised in Poems 96, World Poetry, 1996-2000. Honours: Sanskrit Literature Award, Uttar Pradesh Government Sanskrit Academy, 1995; Gram Ratna Award by Gram Panchayat Akorhi, Mirzapur, 1996; Winged Word Award, International Socio-Literary Foundation, 1997. Address: s/o Srimolai, Village-Post Akorhi, District, Mirzapur 231307, UP, India.

BANAT Mohamed, b. 15 July 1949, Algeria. Company Vice-President; Scientific Consultant; Professor. m. Yoko Matsuda, 2 sons. Education: Bachelor's Degree, Physics, University of Algiers, 1972; DEA's Degree, Physics, University of Toulouse, France, 1973; PhD, Physics, with special honours, University Paul Sabatier, Toulouse, France, 1975; DSc, with special honours, National Polytechnic Institute, Toulouse, France, 1985. Appointments: Researcher Scientist, IMFT/CNRS, Toulouse, France, 1980-85, Tokyo Institute of Technology, Japan, 1986-87; Consultant Scientist, Tokyo, Japan, 1987-88; Visiting Scientist, Tsukuba University, Japan, 1988-90; Senior Consultant Scientist, R&D Project Leader, Tokyo, 1990-99; R&D Project Supervisor, Riken/Science and Technology Agency, Japan, 1999-2000; Vice-President, Bell-Consulting Ltd, Tokyo, 1999-; R&D Consultant to numerous companies and institutions including: Mitsubishi-Atomic-Power-Industry, Japan Gasoline Corporation, Nuclear Fuel Industry. Publications include: Original Results related to the interfacial-turbulence physical phenomenon (in the physics of fluids), 1992; Discovery of the mechanism of the void-drift phenomena in thermalhydraulics with the down stream applications for the power and process industries, 1995. Honours: Special Honours PhD and DSc; Visiting Scientist, Long Term Invited Distinguished Scientists Programme, Tsukuba University, Japan, 1988-90; Listed in Who's Who publications and biographical dictionaries. Memberships: American Society of Mechanical Engineers; Japan Society of Mechanical Engineers.

BANATVALA Jangu, b. 7 January 1934, London, England. Doctor of Medicine. m. Roshan Mugaseth, 3 sons, 1 daughter, deceased. Education: Gonville and Caius College, Cambridge; The London Hospital Medical College; Fulbright Fellow, Department of Epidemiology and Health, Yale University, USA. Appointments: Polio Fund Research Fellow, Department of Pathology, University of Cambridge, 1961-64; Research Fellow, Department of Epidemiology and Health, University of Yale, 1964-65; Senior Lecturer and Reader, 1965-75, Professor, Clinical Virology, Honorary Consultant to the Hospitals (NHS trusts), 1975-99, St Thomas' Hospital Medical School later United Medical and Dental Schools of Guy's and St Thomas' Hospitals; Registrar, 1985-87, Vice President, 1987-90, Royal College of Pathologists; Honorary Consultant Microbiologist to the Army, 1992-97; Chairman, Department of Health Advisory Group on Hepatitis, 1990-98; Emeritus Professor, Clinical Virology, Guy's King's and St Thomas' School of Medicine and Dentistry, 1999-. Publications include: About 230 peer reviewed original papers published in General Medical journals and specialist Medical Journals; 50 Editorials for Lancet and BMJ; 30 Chapters in books; Editor, 3 books including Editions 1-5 of Principles and Practice of Clinical Virology (joint editor); Various reports on blood borne virus infections for Royal Colleges of Pathologists, Senate of Surgery, Cl Br Ireland and Royal College of Surgeons and Obstetrics in Gynaecology. Honours: Lionel Whitby Medal, University of Cambridge, 1964; Founder Member, Academy of Medical Sciences, 1998; CBE, 1999; Listed in biographical dictionary. Memberships: Council of

Governors, Forrest School, London, Mill Hill School, London; President, European Association Against Virus Diseases, 1981-83; Freeman, City of London, 1987; Council of the Medical Defence Union, 1987-2003; Liveryman, Society of Apothecaries, 1986; Athenaeum; MCC; Leander, Henley on Thames; Honorary member, Hawks, Cambridge. Address: Church End, Henham, Bishops Stortford, Hertfordshire, CM22 6AN, England. E-mail: jangu@btopenworld.co.uk

BANDERAS Antonio, b. 10 August 1960, Málaga, Spain. Film Actor. m. (1) Anna Leza, divorced, (2) Melanie Griffith, 1996, 1 child. Appointments: Began Acting aged 14; Performed with National Theatre, Madrid, 6 Years; Films Include: Labyrinth of Passion; El Senor Galindez; El Caso Almeria; The Stilts; 27 Hours; Law of Desire; Matador; Tie Me Up! Tie Me Down!; Woman on the Verge of a Nervous Breakdown; The House of Spirits; Interviews with the Vampire; Philadelphia; The Mambo King; Love and Shadow; Miami Rhapsody; Young Mussolini; Return of Mariaolu; Assassins; Desperado; Evita; Never Talk to Strangers; Crazy in Alabama (director); The 13th Warrior; Dancing in the Dark, 2000; The Body, 2000; Spy Kids, 2001; Femme Fatale, 2002; Frida, 2002; Spy Kids 2: Island of Lost Dreams, 2002; Spy Kids 3-D: Game Over, 2003; Once Upon a Time in Mexico, 2003; Imagining Argentina, 2003; Shrek II(voice), 2004; Legend of Zorro, 2005; Take the Lead, 2006; Bordertown, 2006; Shrek the Third, 2007; My Mom's New Boyfriend, 2008. Address: c/o CAA, 9830 Wilshire Boulevard, Beverley Hills, CA 90212, USA.

BANERJEE Pushan, b. 20 December 1975, Kolkata, India. Research Associate. Education: MSc, Physics, University of Calcutta (Kolkata), 1999; Master of Technology, Energy Science & Technology, Jadavpur University, Kolkata, 2002; PhD, Engineering, Jadavpur University, Kolkata, 2008. Appointments: UGC-Project Fellow, 2002-03; CSIR Senior Research Fellow, 2003-07; CSIR Research Associate, 2007-. Publications: 7 articles in international refereed journals. Honours: Listed in international biographical dictionaries; Many international honours and awards. Memberships: Life Member, Indian Association for the Cultivation of Science. Address: 85 PWD Road, Kolkata 700108, India. E-mail: b_pushan@rediffmail.com

BANGERTER Kate Isabel, b. 7 January 1981, Norfolk, England. Fine Arts Conservator. Education: BSc (Hons), Restoration and Conservation of Decorative Surfaces, London Guildhall University, 2002; MA, Fine Art Conservation, University of Northumbria, Newcastle, 2004. Appointments: Frame Conservation Department, National Portrait Gallery, London, 2001; Paintings Department, Victoria & Albert Museum, London, 2003; Paintings Department, Conservation Centre, Liverpool, 2003; Wallington Hall, Northumbria, 2004; Paintings Department, Belvedere Gallery, Vienna, Austria, 2006; Freelance in private practice, 2005-06. Address: Botriphnie Stables, Drummuir, Keith, Banffshire AB55 5JE, Scotland. E-mail: k_bangerter@hotmail.com

BANGERTER Michael, b. Brighton, England. Actor; Playwright; Lecturer; Freelance Tutor; Poet. m. Katya Wyeth, 8 May 1971, 1 son, 1 daughter. Education: Graduate Diploma, RADA, Teaching Certificate, Certificate in Advanced Writing; MA, Lancaster. Appointments: Actor in many television, film and theatre productions; Playwright in theatre and radio; Freelance Reviewer, Senior Tutor and Assessor, Open College of the Arts, 1999-2005. Publications: A Far Line of Hills, 1996; Freezing the Frame, 2001; Eyelines, 2002; Post Scripts, 2005; The Fat Lady Sings, 2006. Contributions to: Envoi;

Pause; Iota; Blithe Spirit; Pennine Platform; New Hope International Writing; Others; CDs: Dancing Bears, 2002 (Poetry and Music); Passions and Phantoms (Hardy Voice and Music), 2003. Honour: Award Winner, Kent and Sussex National Open Competition, 1991. Memberships: Union of University and College Teachers; British Haiku Society. Address: Botriphnie Stables, Drummuir, Keith, Banffshire AB55 5JE, England.

BANKS Iain, b. 16 February 1954, Fife, Scotland. Author. m. 1992. Education: Stirling University. Appointments: Technician, British Steel, 1976; IBM, Greenock, 1978. Publications: The Wasp Factory, 1984; Walking on Glass, 1985; The Bridge, 1986; Espedair Street, 1987; Canal Dreams, 1989; The Crow Road (adapted as TV series, 1996), 1992; Complicity, 1993; Whit, 1995; Science Fiction: Consider Phlebas, 1987; The Player of Games, 1988; Use of Weapons, 1990; The State of the Art, 1991; Against a Dark Background, 1993; Feersum Endjinn, 1994; Excession, 1996; A Song of Stone, 1998; Inversions, 1998; The Business, 1999; Windward, 2000; Dead Air, 2002; Raw Spirit: In Search of the Perfect Dram, 2003; The Algebraist, 2004; The Steep Approach to Goarbadale, 2007. Honours: British Science Fiction Association Best Novel, 1997; Hon DUniv, Stirling, 1997, St Andrews, 1997; Hon DLitt, Napier, 2003. Address: c/o Little, Brown, Brettenham House, Lancaster Place, London, WC2E 7EN, England.

BANKS Russell, b. 28 March 1940, Barnstead, USA. Author. m. (1) Darlene Bennett, divorced, 1962, 1 daughter, (2) Mary Gunst, divorced 1977, 3 daughters, (3) Kathy Walton, divorced 1988, (4) Chase Twichell. Education: Colgate University; University of North Carolina, Chapel Hill. Appointments: Teacher, Creative Writing, Emerson College, Boston; University of New Hampshire, Durham; University of Alabama; New England College; Teacher, Creative Writing, Princeton University, 1982-97; President, Parliament Internationale des Ecrivains, 2001-. Publications: Waiting to Freeze, 1967; 30/6, 1969; Snow; Meditation of a Cautious Man in Winter, 1974; Novels: Family Life, 1975; Hamilton Stark, 1978; The Book of Jamaica, 1980; The Relation of My Imprisonment, 1984; Continental Drift, 1985; Affliction, 1989; The Sweet Hereafter, 1991; Rule of the Bone, 1995; Cloudsplitter, 1998; The Angel on the Roof, 2000; The Darling, 2004; Collected Short Stories; Searching for Survivors, 1975; The New World, 1978; Trailerpark, 1981; Success Stories, 1986; Short Stories in literary magazines. Honours: Best American Short Stories Awards, 1971, 1985; Fels Award for Fiction, 1974; O Henry Awards, 1975; St Lawrence Award for Fiction, 1976; Guggenheim Fellowship, 1976; National Endowment for the Arts Fellowship, 1977, 1983; John Dos Passos Award, 1985; American Academy of Arts and Letters Award, 1985. Address: 1000 Park Avenue, New York, NY 10028, USA.

BANKS William McKerrell, b. 28 March 1943, Dreghorn, Ayrshire, Scotland. Professor of Engineering. m. Martha Ruthven Hair, 3 sons. Education: BSc (1st class honours), 1965, MSc, 1966, PhD, 1977, Mechanical Engineering, Strathclyde University; FIMechE, 1987; FIMMM, 1993; FRSA, 2000. Appointments: Indentured Senior Student Apprenticeship, Glacier Metal Co Ltd, 1961-65; Senior Research Engineer, G & J Weir Ltd, 1966; Teacher, Solid Mechanics; Teacher, specialist courses in Composite Materials and Structures for Industry in the context of Continuing Professional Development in the UK, Russia, Singapore, China, Greece and Norway; Research work on the structural exploitation of composites; Director, Centre for Advanced Structural

Materials. Publications: Over 175 research papers; 80 reports for industry; Numerous book reviews, invited lectures and seminar presentations. Memberships: Fellow, Royal Academy of Engineering; Fellow, Royal Society of Edinburgh. Address: 19 Dunure Drive, Hamilton, ML3 9EY, Scotland.

BANNISTER Roger G (Sir), b. 23 March 1929, London, England. Athlete; Consultant Physician; Neurologist; University Administrator. m. Moyra Elver Jacobsson, 2 sons, 2 daughters. Education: University College School Exeter; Merton College; Oxford St Mary's Hospital, Medical School, London. Appointments: Winner, Oxford and Cambridge Mile, 1947-50; President, Oxford University, Athletic Club, 1948; British Mile Champion, 1951, 1953, 1954; World Record One Mile, 1954; First Sub Four Minute Mile, 1954; Master Pembroke College, Oxford, 1985-93; Honorary Consultant Neurologist, St Mary's Hospital, Medical School, National Hospital for Neurology and Neurosurgery, London (non-executive director); London and Oxford District and Region; Chair, St Mary's Hospital Development Trust; Chair, Government Working Group on Sport in the Universities, 1995-97; Chair, Clinical Autonomic Research Society, 1982-84. Publications: First Four Minutes, 1955 (republished as 50th Anniversary Edition, 2004); Editor, Brain and Bannister's Clinical Neurology, 1992; Autonomic Failure (co-editor), 1993; Various Medical Articles on Physiology and Neurology. Honours: Honorary Fellow, Exeter College, Oxford, 1950; Merton College, Oxford, 1986; Honorary Fellow, UMIST, 1974; Honorary LLD, Liverpool, 1972; Honorary DSc, Sheffield, 1978; Grinnell, 1984; Bath, 1984; Rochester, 1986; Williams, 1987; Dr hc, Jvvaskyla, Finland; Honorary MD, Pavia, 1986; Honorary DL, University of Victoria, Canada, 1994; University of Wales, Cardiff, 1995; Loughborough, 1996; University of East Anglia, 1997; Hans-Heinrich Siegbert Prize, 1977. Memberships: Physiological Society; Medical Research Society; Association of British Neurologists; Fellow, Imperial College; Leeds Castle Foundation, 1988-; St Mary's Hospital Medical School Trust, 1994-; First Lifetime Award, American Academy of Neurology, 2005. Address: 21 Bardwell Road, Oxford, OX2 6SU, England.

BAR-COHEN Yoseph, b. 3 September 1947, Baghdad, Iraq. Physicist. m. Yardena, 1 son, 1 daughter. Education: BSc, Physics, 1971, MSc, Materials Science, 1973, PhD, Physics, 1979, Hebrew University, Jerusalem, Israel. Appointments: Senior NDE Specialist, Israel Aircraft Industry, 1971-79; Postdoctorate, National Research Council, 1979-80; Senior Physicist, Systems Research Laboratory, Dayton, Ohio, 1980-83; Principal Specialist, McDonnell Douglas Corporation, Long Beach, California, 1983-91; Senior Research Scientist and Group Supervisor, Advanced Technologies, Jet Propulsion Laboratory, Pasadena, California, 1991-. Publications: over 300 journals and proceedings papers and 4 edited books; 19 patents. Honours: National Research Council Fellowship Award, 1979; Nova Award, Outstanding Achievement in Technology, 1996; Nova Award, Technical Innovation and Leadership, 1998; Two SPIE Lifetime Achievement Award, 2001 and 2005; NASA Exceptional Engineering Achievement Medal, 2001; NASA Exceptional Technology Achievement Medal, 2006. Memberships: Fellow, American Society for Non-destructive Testing; Fellow, International Society for Optical Engineering. Address: Jet Propulsion Laboratory, MS-67-119, 4800 Oak Grove Drive, Pasadena, CA 91109-8099, USA.

BARAKA-LOKMANE Salima, b. 5 September 1964, Algiers, Algeria. Research Associate. m. Yahia, 2 daughters. Education: Engineer diploma, Hydrogeology, University of Algiers, Algeria, 1990; DEA, Water Resources and Management, University of Orsay, France, 1992; PhD, Hydrogeology, University of Tübingen, Germany, 1999. Appointments: Research Fellow, Edinburgh University, Scotland, 1999-2003; Research Associate, Heriot-Watt University, Scotland, 2003-. Publications: Numerous articles in professional scientific journals. Honours: DAAD Scholarship, 1990, KAAK Scholarship, 1994, University of Tübingen. Memberships: Society of Petroleum Engineers; European Geosciences Union. E-mail: salima.lokmane@pet.hw.ac.uk

BARAKZAI Shukria, b. 2 January 1972, Kabul, Afghanistan. Journalist; Human Rights Activist. m. Abdul Gaffar Dawi, 3 daughters. Education: BA, Geo-Physics, Kabul University. Appointments: MP, Parliament of Afghanistan; President, Third Line Political Group; President, Asia Women Organisation; Chief Editor, Women's Mirror. Publications: Numerous articles in professional journals. Honours: Editor of the Year, 2004; Young Global Year, 2006. Memberships: Young Global Leaders Forum. E-mail: shukria.barakzai@gmail.com

BARBA Harry, b. 17 June 1922, Bristol, USA. Writer. m. Marian, 1 son. Education: AB, Bates College, 1944; MA, Harvard University, 1951; MFA, 1960, PhD, honours, 1963, University of Iowa; Postgraduate, University of Middlebury, 1945, Boston University, 1950-51; New York University, 1955-56, CUNY, 1956-57, Columbia University, 1957-58. Appointments: Stringer, Feature Writer, Bristol Press, 1944-45; File Clerk, Supervisor, New Departure General Motors Corporation, 1944-45; Instructor, English and Writing, Wilkes College, 1947, University of Connecticut, Hartford, 1947-49; Teacher, English, Seward Park High School, New York City, 1955-59; Instructor, University of Iowa, 1959-63, Graduate Fellow, 1961-62; Assistant Professor, Skidmore College, 1963-68, Associate Professor, 1968; Fulbright Professor, Visiting American Specialist, Damascus University, 1963-64; Professor of English, Director of Writing, Marshall University, Huntington, West Virginia, 1968-70; Title I Writing Arts Director, West Virginia, 1969-70; Commercial and Public Services, Radio-TV Interviewee, Reader, Lecturer, Educator, 1961-. Publications include: For the Grape Season, 1960; 3 By Harry Barba, 1967, 3 x 3, 1969; The Case for Socially Functional Education, Art and Culture, 1970-74; One of a Kind (The Many Faces and Voices of America), 1976; The Day the World Went Sane, 1979; Round Trip to Byzantium, 1985; Mona Lisa Smiles, 1993. Honours: Creative awards for fiction, poetry, essays, music, compositions, photography and graphic arts; Pulitzer Nominee, 1985; Man of the Year, ABI, 1995; Man of the Year, IBC, 1996 International Hall of Fame, IBC, 1997; 100 Leaders of World Influence, ABI, 2000; Hall of Fame, World Leaders, American Biographical Centre, 2001. Address: 47 Hyde Boulevard, Ballston Spa, NY 12020-1607, USA.

BARBAKADZE Vladimir, b. 5 November 1940, Khashuri, Georgia. Industrial and Civil Engineer; Professor. 2 sons, 3 daughters. Education: Diploma, Georgian Polytechnic Institute, 1962; PhD, Moscow State University of Transporation, 1980; Professor, 1983. Appointments: Engineer, Coyusdorpoekt, Tbilisi, Georgia, 1962-64; Aspirant, 1965-68, Docent, 1969-81, Full time Professor, 1997-, Structural Division, Moscow State University of Transportation; Adjunct, Structural Mechanics, Dresdent Trancnortation University, Germany, 1967-68; Director, Science Department, Research and Development, Delta, Moscow, 1997-98; Professor, International University, Moscow, 1999-; President, Corporation, USA. Publications: Numerous articles in professional journals; 3 patents; Author, 20 books. Honours: MINVUZ, Russian Federation; Gold Medal, VDHH, 1978-79; Gold Medal, VVC, 1997. Memberships: Academician, Academy of Transport of Russian Federation; Honorary Member, Russia Academy of Architecture and Constructional Sciences; Active Member, New York Academy of Sciences; Member, Georgian Academy of Engineering Sciences. Address: 58 River Trail Drive, Palm Coast, FL 32137, USA. E-mail: vlbarba@juno.com

BARBARA John Anthony James, b. 2 April 1946, Cairo, Egypt (British). Transfusion Microbiologist. m. Gillian, 1 son, 1 daughter. Education: BA (Hons) Natural Sciences, Trinity College, Cambridge, 1968; MSc, Medical School, Birmingham University, 1969; MA, Cantab, PhD, Department of Microbiology, Reading University, 1972. Appointments: Lecturer, Department of Virology, Reading University, 1972-74; Examiner, Oxford University, GCE A Level Biology, 1974-85; Head of Microbiology, North London Blood Transfusion Centre, 1974-96; Honorary Associate Research Fellow, Brunel University, Middlesex, 1984-90; Open University Research Student Supervisor, 1988-99; Lead Scientist in Microbiology, London and South East Zone, 1996-2000; Principal, Transfusion Microbiology National Laboratories and Microbiology Consultant, 2000-06, Emeritus Consultant, 2006-, National Blood Authority; External Examiner, Bristol University, 2003-05; Visiting Professor, University of West of England, 2004. Publications: Over 300 papers, chapters, abstracts and reviews. Honours: Hong Kong Red Cross Foundation Lecturer, 1996; Kenneth Goldsmith memorial prize of the BBTS, 1991; Iain Cook Memorial Award of the SNBTS, 2002; Gold Medal of the BBTS, 2003; Oliver Memorial Award, 2003; International Society of Blood Transfusion Award, 2005; Medal, Polish Association of Haematology and Transfusion Medicine, 2005. Memberships: Institute of Biology; Past President, British Blood Transfusion Society; American Association of Blood Banks, -2006; Past Vice President, International Society of Blood Transfusion; Royal College of Pathologists; Association of Clinical Microbiologists. Address: National Transfusion Microbiology Laboratories, National Blood Service, North London, Colindale Avenue, London NW9 5BG, England. E-mail: john.barbara@nbs.nhs.uk Website: www.blood.co.uk

BARBER Francis, b. 13 May 1957, Wolverhampton, England. Actress. Education: Bangor University; Cardiff University. Appointments: Hull Truck Theatre Company; Glasgow Citizens Theatre; Tricycle Theatre; RSC; TV appearances include: Clem Jack Story; Home Sweet Home; Flame to the Phoenix; Reilly; Ace of Spies; Those Glory Glory Days; Hard Feelings; Behaving Badly; The Nightmare Year; Real Women; Just in Time; The Ice House; Dalziel & Pascoe; Plastic Man; Love in a Cold Climate; The Legend of the Tamworth Two, Trial and Retribution VIII, 2004; Marple: A Murder Is Announced, Funland, The IT Crowd, 2005. Film Appearances include: The Missionary, 1982; A Zed and Two Noughts; White City Castaway; Prick Up Your Ears; Sammy and Rosie Get Laid; We Think the World of You; The Grasscutter; Separate Bedrooms; Young Soul Rebels; Secret Friends; The Lake; Soft Top, Hard Shoulder; The Fish Tale; Three Steps to Heaven; Photographing Fairies; Shiner; Still Crazy; Esther Kahn; Mauvaise passe; 24 heures de la vie d'une femme, Flyfishing, 2002; Boudica, 2003; Evilenko, His Passionate Bride, 2004; Suzie Gold, 2004; Stage Appearances include: Night of the Iguana; Pygmalion; Closer; Uncle Vanya.

BARBOSA Pedro, b. 12 May 1948, Porto, Portugal. Writer; Professor; Researcher. 1 daughter. Education: BA, Romance Philology, Universidade de Coimbra, 1974; MA, Semiotics, Université Louis Pasteur, Strasbourg, France, 1988; PhD, Communication Sciences, Universidade Nova Lisboa, 1993. Appointments: Coordinator Professor, Instituto Politécnico do Porto; Visiting Scholar, PUC de São Paulo, Brazil; Researcher, Universidade Nova de Lisboa, Portugal; Researcher, Université Artois, France; Lecturer, University of Siena, Italy. Publications: Essay: Teoria do Teatro Moderno, 1982; Aspectos da Renovação Dramatúrgica na Trilogia do Teatro-no-Teatro de Pirandello, 1993; Metamorfoses do Real: arte, imaginário e conhecimento estético, 1995; A Ciberliteratura: criação literária e cumputador, 1996; Arte, Comunição & Semiótica, 2002; Theatre: Eróstrato, 1984; Anticleia ou os Chapéus-de-Chuva do Sonho, 1992; PortoMetropolitanoLento, 1993; PortoImaginárioLento, 2001; Alletsator – XPTO.Kosmos.2001, 2001; Fiction: O Guardador de Retretes, 1976, 1978, 1980; Histórias da Menina Minhó-Minhó, 1988; Prefácio para uma Personagem Só, 1993; Cyberliterature includes: Teoria do Homem Sentado, 1996; O Motor Textual, 2001. Honours: Essay Prize, Association of Portuguese Writers, 1982. Memberships: Association of Portuguese Authors; Association of Portuguese Writers. Address: Rua Andreas, 412 6 E, 4100, Porto, Portugal. E-mail: pedrobarbosa@netcabo.pt Website: www.pedrobarbosa.net

SOUSA Frederico Barbosa de, b. 24 December 1971, Joas Pessoa, Paraiba, Brazil. University Professor. m. Leila Cristiani de Freitas, 1 son. Education: Graduation in Dentistry, Federal University of Paraiba, 1993; Master's degree in Dentistry, Pedodontics, Federal University of Santa Catarina, Brazil, 1996; Doctorate in Biology, Federal University of Pernambuco Credlife, Brazil, 2005. Appointments: Private practice, Pediatric Dentistry, 1986-98; Senior Lecturer, Histology, Federal University of Paraiba, 1999-. Publications: Reported ultrastructural evidence that, during dental caries development, while some minerals leave the hard dental tissue other minerals are deposited on the surface of the hard tissue as tartar; Developed new mathematical approach that allowed, for the first time, to derive biochemical composition of dental enamel from it's birefringence. Memberships: Brazilian Society for Dental Research. Address: Department of Morphology, Health Sciences Center, Federal University of Paraiba, Joas Pessoa, 58051900, Paraiba, Brazil. E-mail: fredericosousa@hotmail.com

BARBULESCU Maria, b. 2 January 1941, Blaj-Veza, Romania. Professor. m. Haralambie Barbulescu. Education: History Department, Faculty of History, Babes-Bolyiai University, Cluj-Napoca, 1960-65; Study scholarships: Ravenna, Italy, 1974; University of Sofia, Bulgaria, 1973; Munich, Germany, 1981, 1990. Appointments: Lecturer, History, Pedagogical Institute of Constanta, 1965-73; Museologist, 1973-93, Scientific Researcher, 1993-2002, National Museum of Archaeology and History, Constanta; Reader Dr, Faculty of History, Constanta Ovidius University, 1993-. Publications: 2 monographs; Around 100 articles in specialised reviews. Honours: PhD, History, Babes-Bolyiai University, 1991; The Cultural Distinction for scientific research, President's Office, 2004. Memberships: Classical Studies Society of Romania; The Archaeologists of Romania; The Consultative International Commission for Promoting IndoEuropean and Thracian Studies. Address: Str Cpt Dobrila Eugeniu, Nr 2, Bl H, Sc A, Ap 19, Constanta, Code 900512, Romania. E-mail: mariabarbulescu@yahoo.fr

BARCLAY Linwood L, b. 20 March 1955, New Haven, Connecticut, USA. Journalist; Author. m. Neetha, 1 son, 1 daughter. Education: BA (Hons), English, Trent University, Peterborough, Ontario, Canada. Appointments: Journalist, 1981, Columnist, 1993-, Toronto Star, Toronto, Canada; Public Speaker. Publications: Father Knows Zilch, 1996; This House is Nuts, 1997; Mike Harris Made Me Eat My Dog, 1998; Last Resort, 2000; Bad Move, 2004; Bad Guys, 2005; Lone Wolf, 2006; Stone Rain, 2007; No Time For Goodbye, 2007. Honours: Best Columnist Award, Canadian Community Newspaper Association, 1981; Stephen Leacock Award of Merit (and Finalist for Stephen Leacock Award for Humour) for Book "Last Resort", 2001. Memberships: Writers Union of Canada; Canadian Journalists for Freedom of Expression; Southern Ontario Newspaper Guild; Crime Writers of Canada; Mystery Writers of America. Address: Burlington, Ontario, Canada. E-mail: lbarclay@thestar.ca

BARDOT Brigitte, b. 28 September 1934, Paris, France. Actress and Animal Rights Campaigner. m. (4) Bernard D'Ormale, 1992. Education: Paris Conservatoire. Career: Films include: Manina: La fille sans voile; Futures vedettes; Le grandes manouveures; En effueillent la marguerite; Une parisienne; En case de malheur; Voulez-vous danser avec moi?; Please not now?; Viva Maria; Les femmes, 1969; Don Juan, 1973. Publications: Initiales BB, 1996; Le Carré de Pluton, 1999; Un Cri Dans Le Silence, 2003. Memberships: President Fondation Brigitte Bardot. Honours: Etoile de Cristal, Academy of Cinema, 1966; Chevalier Légion d'honneur. Address: Fondation Brigitte Bardot, 45 rue Vineuse, 75016 Paris, France. E-mail: fbb@fondationbrigittebardot.fr

BARKAT Mourad, b. 6 January 1958, Constantine, Algeria. University Professor. m. Fatiha Hanani, 3 sons, 1 daughter. Education: BSc, 1981, MSc, 1983, PhD, 1987, Electrical Engineering, Syracuse University. Appointments: Teaching Assistant, Syracuse University, 1981-87; Assistant Professor, State University of New York at Stony Brook, 1987-91; Adjunct Professor, Ecole Militaire Polytechnique, 1996-2004; Rector (Chancellor), Badji Mokhtar-Annaba University, Algeria, 2000-02; Professor, 1997-2004, Associate Professor, 1991-97, Electrical Engineering, University of Constantine; Director of Signal Processing Laboratory, University of Constantine, 2000-04; Professor, American University of Sharjah, United Arab Emirates, 2005-. Publications: Signal Detection and Estimation, 2005; Many journal and conference papers. Honours: Listed in international biographical dictionaries; BSc magna cum laude; University Teaching Merit awards; Designated Member by the President of Algeria to study and reform the education system. Memberships: Senior Member, IEEE; Member, Tau Beta Pi; Engineering Honor Society, USA; Member, Eta Kappa Nu; Electrical Engineering Honor Society, USA. Address: Department of Electrical Engineering, American University of Sharjah, United Arab Emirates.

BARKER Dennis Malcolm, b. 21 June 1929, Lowestoft, England. Journalist; Novelist. m. Sarah Katherine Alwyn, 1 daughter. Education: National Diploma in Journalism, 1959. Appointments: Reporter and Sub-Editor, Suffolk Chronicle & Mercury, Ipswich, 1947-48; Reporter, Feature Writer, Theatre and Film Critic, 1948-58, East Anglian Daily Times; Estates and Property Editor 1958-63, also Theatre Critic, 1960-63, Express & Star, Wolverhampton; Midlands Correspondent, 1963-67, Reporter, Feature Writer, Columnist, The Guardian, 1967-91. Publications: Novels: Candidate of Promise, 1969; The Scandalisers, 1974; Winston Three Three Three, 1987; Games with The General, 2007; Non-fiction: The People of the Forces Trilogy (Soldiering On, 1981, Ruling the Waves,

1986, Guarding the Skies, 1989); One Man's Estate, 1983; Parian Ware, 1985; Fresh Start, 1990; The Craft of the Media Interview, 1998; How to Deal with the Media (2000); Seize the Day (contributor), 2001; The Guardian Book of Obituaries (contributor), 2003; Oxford Dictionary of National Biography (contributor), 2004; Tricks Journalists Play, 2007; Contributions to: BBC; Punch; East Anglian Architecture & Building Review (editor and editorial director, 1956-58); The Guardian, 1991-. Memberships: National Union of Journalists, Secretary, Suffolk Branch, 1953-58, Chairman 1958; Chairman, Home Counties District Council, 1956-57; Life Member, 1991; Life Member, Journalists' Charity; Writers Guild of Great Britain; Broadcasting Press Guild; Society of Authors. Address: 67 Speldhurst Road, London W4 1BY, England.

BARKER Elspeth, b. 16 November 1940, Edinburgh, Scotland. Writer. m. George Granville Barker, 29 July 1989, 3 sons, 2 daughters. Education: St Leonards School, Scotland, 1953-57; Oxford University, England, 1958-61. Publications: O Caledonia, 1991; Anthology of Loss, 1997. Contributions to: Independent on Sunday; Guardian; Harpers & Queen; TLS; Vogue; Big Issue; Sunday Times; Observer; Daily Mail. Honours: David Higham Award, Scottish Arts Council; Angel Literary Award; Royal Society of Literature Winifred Holtby Award. Address: Bintry House, Ittenigham, Aylsham, Norfolk NR11 7AT, England.

BARKER Ralph Hammond, b. 21 October 1917, Feltham, Middlesex, England. Author. m. (1) Joan Muriel Harris, deceased, (2) Diana Darvey, deceased, 1 adopted daughter. Education: Hounslow College, Hounslow, Middlesex, 1926-34. Career: Journalist, Sporting Life, London, 1935; Wartime Service RAF, 1940-46; Post-war Service RAF, 1949-61; Freelance contributor under contract to the Sunday Express, London, 1955-88; Full-time Author, 1961-. Publications: Books: Down in the Drink, 1955; The Ship-Busters, 1957; The Last Blue Mountain, 1959; Strike Hard, Strike Sure, 1963, 2003; Ten Great Innings, 1964; The Thousand Plan, 1965, 1975; Great Mysteries of the Air, 1966; Ten Great Bowlers, 1967; Aviator Extraordinary, 1969; Test Cricket, England v Australia (with Irving Rosenwater), 1969; Verdict on a Lost Flyer, 1969; The RAF at War, 1970; The Schneider Trophy Races, 1971, 1981; Against the Sea, 1972; One Man's Jungle, 1975; Survival in the Sky, 1975; The Blockade Busters, 1976; The Cricketing Family Edrich, 1976; The Hurricats, 1978, 2000; Not Here, But in Another Place, 1980; Innings of a Lifetime, 1982; Goodnight, Sorry for Sinking You, 1984; Purple Patches, 1987; That Eternal Summer, 1990; The Royal Flying Corps, Parts I and II, 1994, 1995; A Brief History of The Royal Flying Corps in World War I, 2002; Men of the Bombers, 2005; Bridging the Pond (The North Atlantic Ferry), in preparation, 2007; Articles: Over 250 main feature articles for the Sunday Express; Contributor to The Cricketer International and The Cricket Society Journal. Honour: Buchpreis des Deutschen Alpenvereins, 1982. Memberships: Society of Authors; Authors' Licensing and Collecting Society; NUJ; RAF Association; RAF Club; MCC; Savage Club; Cricket Society. Address: Old Timbers, 16 Aldercombe Lane, Caterham, Surrey CR3 6ED, England.

BARKIN Ellen, b. 16 April 1955, New York, USA. Actress. m. (1) Gabriel Byrne, 1988, 1 son, (2) Ronald Perelmar, 2000. Education: City University of New York; Hunter College, Indiana. Appointments: Stage Appearances include: Shout Across the River, Killings on the Last Line, 1980; Extremities, 1982; Eden Court; TV Appearances include: Search for Tomorrow, Kent State, We're Fighting Back, 1981; Terrible

Joe Moran, 1984; Before Women Has Wings, 1998. Films include: Diner, 1982; Daniel, Tender Mercies, Eddie and the Cruisers, 1983; The Adventures of Buckaroo Banzai, Harry and Son, 1984; Enormous Changes at the Last Minute, 1985; Down by Law, 1986; The Big Easy, Siesta, 1987; Sea of Love, 1989; Johnny Handsome; Switch; Man Trouble, 1992; Mac, This Boy's Life, Into the West, 1993; Bad Company, Wild Bill, 1995; Mad Dog Times, The Fan, 1996; Fear and Loathing in Las Vegas; Popcorn; Drop Dead Gorgeous; The White River Kid, 1999; Crime and Punishment in Suburbia, Mercy, 2000; Someone Like You, 2001; She Hate Me, 2004; Palindromes, 2005; Trust the Man, 2006; Ocean's Thirteen, 2007. Honour: Emmy Award. Address: c/o CAA, 9830 Wilshire Boulevard, Beverly Hills, CA 90212, USA.

BARKLEY Vada Lee, b. 28 September 1919, Union, Arkansas, USA. Teacher. m. Arthur E Barkley, deceased 2001. Education: Diploma, Salem High School, Salem, Arkansas, 1938; BA degree, Southern Nazarene University, Bethany, Oklahoma, 1942; MA degree, University of Oklahoma, Norman, Oklahoma, 1950. Appointments: English Teacher, Oklahoma public high schools; French and English Teacher, Southern Nazarene University; English Teacher, Redlands Community College; Chairman of Communicative Arts Division, Redlands Community College; Author. Publications: Smile - God Loves You; Inspirational Insights; Sanctify Them; The Pastor's Survival Kit; The Pastor's Sourcebook; God Bridged Death's Stream; How to Keep from Dying in Your Shell; A Cache of Gospel Jewels; Survive and Thrive after Fifty-Five; Old Time Gospel Preaching; My Awesome Journey with Jesus. Honours: Distinguished Alumni Award, SNU; Founding President, Academy of Senior Professionals at SNU; Fellow, International Biographical Association; International Educator of the Year, 2007; Lifetime Achievement Award, World Congress of Arts, Sciences and Communications; Listed in international biographical directories. Memberships: Academy of Senior Professionals at SNU; Church of the Nazarene, Bethany, Oklahoma; Oklahoma Teachers Retirement System of Oklahoma. Website: www.barkleybooks.com

BARNABY (Charles) Frank, b. 27 September 1927, Andover, Hampshire, England. Physicist; Author. m. 19 December 1972, 1 son, 1 daughter. Education: BSc, 1951, MSc, 1954, PhD, 1960, London University. Appointments: Physicist, UK Atomic Energy Authority, 1950-57; Member, Senior Scientific Staff, Medical Research Council, University College Medical School, 1957-68; Executive Secretary, Pugwash Conferences on Science and World Affairs, 1968-70; Director, Stockholm International Peace Research Institute (SIPRI), 1971-81; Professor of Peace Studies, Frei University, Amsterdam, 1981-85; Director, World Disarmament Campaign (UK), 1982-; Chair, Just Defence, 1982-; Consultant, Oxford Research Group, 1998-; Editor, International Journal of Human Rights. Publications: Man and the Atom, 1971; Disarmament and Arms Control, 1973; Nuclear Energy, 1975; The Nuclear Age, 1976; Prospects for Peace, 1980; Future Warfare, 1983; The Automated Battlefield, 1986; Star Wars Brought Down to Earth, 1986; The Invisible Bomb, 1989; The Gaia Peace Atlas, 1989; The Role and Control of Arms in the 1990's, 1992; How Nuclear Weapons Spread, 1993; Instruments of Terror, 1997; How to Build a Nuclear Bomb ad Other Weapons of Mass Destruction, 2003; The Future of Terror, 2007. Contributions to: Ambio; New Scientist; Technology Review. Honours: Honorary Doctorates: Frei University, Amsterdam, 1982; University of Southampton, 1996; University of Bradford, 2007. Address: Brandreth, Station Road, Chilbolton, Stockbridge, Hampshire SO20 6HW, England.

BARNARD Robert, b. 23 November 1936, Burnham on Crouch, Essex, England. Crime Writer. m. Mary Louise Tabor, 7 February 1963. Education: Balliol College, Oxford, 1956-59; Dr Phil, University of Bergen, Norway, 1972. Publications: Death of an Old Goat, 1974; Sheer Torture, 1981; A Corpse in a Gilded Cage, 1984; Out of the Blackout, 1985; Skeleton in the Grass, 1987; At Death's Door, 1988; Death and the Chaste Apprentice, 1989; Masters of the House, 1994; A Cry in the Dark, 2003. As Bernard Bastable: Dead, Mr Mozart, 1995; Too Many Notes, Mr Mozart, 1995; A Brontë Encyclopaedia (with M L Barnard), 2007. Honours: Seven Times Nominated for Edgar Awards; Recipient of Diamond Dagger for Lifetime's Achievement in Crime Fiction, 2003. Memberships: Crime Writers Association; Chairman, Brontë Society, 1996-99, 2002-2005; Society of Authors. Address: Hazeldene, Houghley Lane, Leeds LS13 2DT, England.

BARNES Richard John Black, b. 13 August 1950, Nyasaland, Malawi. Editor. m. Lucette Aylmer, 21 June 1975, 1 son, 1 daughter. Education: Stonyhurst College, 1959-68; Royal College of Agriculture, 1970-72; Polytechnic of Central London, 1972-75. Publications: The Sun in the East, 1983; Eye on the Hill - Horse Travels in Britain, 1987; John Bell, Sculptor, 1999; The Year of Public Sculpture, 2001; The Obelisk – A Monumental Feature in Britain, 2004; Memberships: Fellow of the Royal Geographical Society; Fellow of the Royal Society of Arts. Address: c/o Frontier Publishing, Windetts Farm, Long Lane, Kirstead, Norwich NR15 1EG, England.

BARNETT Correlli (Douglas), b. 28 June 1927, Norbury, Surrey, England. Author. m. Ruth Murby, 28 December 1950, 2 daughters. Education: BA, 1951, MA, 1955, Exeter College, Oxford. Appointments: Keeper of the Churchill Archives Centre, 1977-95; Fellow, Churchill College, 1977-; Development Fellow, Churchill College, 1997-99. Publications: The Hump Organisation, 1957; The Channel Tunnel (co-author), 1958; The Desert Generals, 1960, new enlarged edition 1984; The Swordbearers, 1963; Britain and Her Army, 1970; The Collapse of British Power, 1972; Marlborough, 1974; Strategy and Society, 1975; Bonaparte, 1978; The Great War, 1979; The Audit of War, 1986; Engage the Enemy More Closely: The Royal Navy in the Second World War, 1991; The Lost Victory: British Dreams, British Realities 1945-1950, 1995; The Verdict of Peace: Britain Between Her Yesterday and the Future, 2001; Television: The Great War (co-author), 1964; The Lost Peace (co-author), 1966; The Commanders, 1973. Honours: Best Television Documentary Script Award, Screenwriter's Guild, 1964; Royal Society of Literature Award, 1970; Chesney Gold Medal, Royal United Services Institute for Defence Studies, 1991; Yorkshire Post Book of the Year Award, 1991; DSc Honoris Causa, Cranfield University, 1993; CBE, 1997. Address: Catbridge House, East Carleton, Norwich NR14 8JX, England.

BARNIE John Edward, b. 27 March 1941, Abergavenny, Gwent, Wales. Editor; Writer; Poet. m. Helle Michelsen, 28 October 1980, 1 son. Education: BA, Honours, 1963, MA, 1966, PhD, 1971, Birmingham University; Dip Ed, Nottingham University, 1964. Appointments: Lecturer, English Literature, University of Copenhagen, 1969-82; Assistant, then Editor, Planet: The Welsh International, 1985-2006. Publications: Borderland, 1984; Lightning Country, 1987; Clay, 1989; The Confirmation, 1992; Y Felan a Finnau, 1992; The City, 1993; Heroes, 1996; No Hiding Place, 1996; The Wine Bird, 1998; Ice, 2001; At the Salt Hotel, 2003; The Green Buoy, 2006; Sea Lilies: Selected Poems 1984-2003, 2006; Trouble in Heaven, 2007; Contributions to: American Poetry Review; Critical Quarterly; Poetry Wales; New Welsh Review; Anglo-Welsh Review; Kunapipi; Juke Blues. Honour: Welsh Arts Council Prize for Literature, 1990. Memberships: Yr Academi Gymreig; Harry Martinson-Sällskapet. Address: Greenfields, Comins Coch, Aberystwyth, SY23 3BG, Ceredigion, Wales. E-mail: john.barnie@googlemail.com

BARR Geoffrey Samuel, b. 1 November 1952, Liverpool, England. Head and Neck Surgeon. m. Rowena M Bickerton, 5 May 1984, 2 sons, 1 daughter. Education: Queen's College, University of St Andrews, 1971-77. Appointments: Department of Head and Neck Surgery, University of Liverpool, 1980-84; Department of Head and Neck Surgery, University of Dundee, 1984-93; Department of Head and Neck Surgery, University of Birmingham, 1989-93; Consultant Otolaryngologist, Head and Neck Surgeon, Gwynedd Hospital, 1993-; Part time advisor to National Health Service Executive on Medical Research and Computing. Publications: Over 50 articles in peer reviewed medical and surgical journals. Honours: MBChB, University of Dundee, 1977; Fellow, Royal College of Surgeons, 1984; Master of Surgery, University of Dundee, 1989; Honorary Member, Oriole Society; Honorary Archivist, Schofield Statistical Society. Memberships: Royal Society of Medicine; Royal College of Surgeons; British Association of Otolaryngology, Head and Neck Surgery; British Association of Head and Neck Oncologists; Hospital Consultants and Specialists Association. Address: Department of Head and Neck Surgery, Gwynedd Hospital, Bangor, Gwynedd LL57 2PW, Wales, United Kingdom. E-mail: geoffrey.barr@nww-tr.wales.nhs.uk

BARR Patricia Miriam, b. 25 April 1934, Norwich, Norfolk, England. Writer. Education: BA, University of Birmingham; MA, University College, London. Publications: The Coming of the Barbarians, 1967; The Deer Cry Pavilion, 1968; A Curious Life for a Lady, 1970; To China with Love, 1972; The Memsahibs, 1976; Taming the Jungle, 1978; Chinese Alice, 1981; Uncut Jade, 1983; Kenjiro, 1985; Coromandel, 1988; The Dust in the Balance, 1989. Honour: Winston Churchill Fellowship for Historical Biography, 1972. Membership: Society of Authors. Address: 6 Mount Pleasant, Norwich NR2 2DG, England.

BARREIROS Jose Augusto Lima, b. 4 July 1951, Belém, Pará, Brazil. Electrical Engineer; Professor; Dean. m. Mária Cristina P M, 2 sons, 1 daughter. Education: Electrical Engineer, Federal University of Pará, Brazil, 1974; MSc, Electronic Engineering, University of Manchester Institute of Science and Technology, England, 1989; PhD, Doctor of Electrical Engineering, Federal University of Santa Catarina, Brazil, 1995; Post-doctorate, Faculty of Engineering, University of Porto, Portugal, 2003. Appointments: Assistant Professor, 1976, Full Professor, 1997, Vice Dean, 2001-05, Dean, 2006-2010, Institute of Technology, Chairman, Electrical and Computer Department, 1983-87, Co-ordinator, PDS Graduation Programme in Commercial Engineering with creation of Doctorate Course, Federal University of Para. Publications: Over 150 papers in conferences and periodical scientific journals in Brazil and around the world; More than a dozen research project reports; Editor of book on research projects and thesis of engineering in Amazon. Honours: Distinguished Engineer in Science, Club of Engineers of Pará, Brazil; Listed in international biographical dictionaries. Memberships: Institute of Electrical and Electronics Engineers; Power Engineering Society; Brazilian Society of Automatica; Regional Council of Engineers & Architects of the State of Pará, Brazil. Address: Ave Jeronimo Rimentel, 536, Ap 804, Belém, Pará, 66055-000, Brazil. E-mail: barreiro@ufpa.br

BARRETT Philip, b. 26 May 1925, Donoughmore, Co Cork, Eire. Roman Catholic Priest. Education: Diplomas with Honours in Arts, Philosophy, Theology and Canon Law, St Kieran's College, Kilkenny, Eire, 1950; BA, 1975, BA with Honours, 1993, Open University; MPhil Thesis, Crime and Punishment in a Lancashire Industrial Town: Law and Social Change in the Borough of Wigan 1800-1950, Polytechnic University, Liverpool, 1980; Ordained Priest, Roman Catholic Church, 1950. Appointments: Assistant Priest, St Oswald's, Ashton-in-Makerfield, near Wigan, England, 1950-58; Assistant Priest, St Benet's Netherton, Bootle, 1958-59; Assistant Priest, St Ambrose's, Speke, Liverpool, England, 1959-69; Assistant Priest, St Jude's, Wigan, England, 1969-76; Parish Priest, St Winefred's, Bootle, Liverpool, England, 1977-81; Parish Priest, Holy Family, Platt Bridge, Wigan, England, 1981-2003; Liverpool Archdiocesan Religious Inspector of Schools, 1950's. Publications: Unpublished M Phil Thesis available for reference purposes in Wigan Public Reference Library (History Shop). Honours: Numerous global awards and nominations; Listed in national and international biographical dictionaries. Address: Spring View Cottage, 244 Warrington Road, Spring View, Wigan, Lancashire WN3 4NH, England.

BARRON Christine Angela, b. 9 May 1949, Birmingham, England. Composer; Musician; Author; Adjudicator; Music Teacher. Education: Moseley School of Art, Birmingham. Musical Education: School of Contemporary Pop and Jazz; University of Leeds. Career: Began as freelance percussionist, including work with Birmingham Symphony Orchestra; Theatre, cabaret musician with top entertainers including: Bruce Forsyth; Des O'Connor; Leslie Crowther; Val Doonican. Part-time lecturer, percussion and composition; North Warwickshire and Hinkley College of Technology and Art, Nuneaton, Warwickshire; Well known in the UK for innovative percussion workshops and master classes featuring percussion; Presents new professional training packages for the Boosey & Hawkes and Schott Music Composer Workshop Scheme; Adjudicator and Member, British and International Federation of Festivals for Music, Dance and Speech. Compositions include: Television signature tunes: Shut That Door (also released as single); Where Are They Now; Commissioned by Chappell Music Library for album, short pieces as jingles, theme, incidental music for television, radio, films (distributed worldwide); Collaboration with Boosey and Hawkes Music Publishers on albums, including album recorded by Royal Philharmonic Orchestra; Also wrote for their educational catalogue under pseudonyms: Chris Barron, Christine Barron. Publications: 3 comprehensive tutors for Learn As You Play series: Learn As You Play Drums with cassette; Learn As You Play Tuned Percussion and Timpani; New edition of Learn As You Play Drums with CD. Memberships: The British Academy of Composers and Songwriters; British and International Federation of Festivals for Music, Dance and Speech. Address: 27 Madeira Croft, Coventry, Warwickshire CV5 8NX, England.

BARRY Essie Marilyn, b. 9 June 1913, Greenwood, Mississippi, USA. Educator; Writer; Inventor. m. Frank Barry, deceased, 3 daughters. Education: Licenced Practical Nurse, Brooklyn Hospital, New York, 1963-64; BA, CUNY, 1971; Doctor of Arts, Rochville University, 2005. Appointments: Hunter College, Social Work, 1971; Social Service Investigator, Department of Social Service, New York City, 1971-72; Teacher, State Education Department, New York, 1972-85; Webster College, 1973; Administrator, Intern P556 Brooklyn, 1974; Nursery-Grades K6 Teacher, Michigan State Department of Education, Licenced Teacher, New York

University and Columbia University, 1975; Educational Administrator, 1975-; Teacher, Kindergarten Workshop, Brooklyn, 1979; Co-ordination of P S 179 graduation exercises, 1985; Owner, CED, Information Express Group, Michigan, 1989-; Foster Care Certificate, Michigan, 1989; Licence for Care of Children, Michigan Department of Social Services, 1993; Certificate of Work with Foster Care Agency, Michigan, 1994; St Johns University, Proctor Home School, Farmington Hills, Michigan, 1995; Internet Consultant, American Association Online Agency Administration, San Francisco, 1996. Publications: Founder, Essie Barry Scholarship Fund, Steinhardt School, New York University, 2003; US Patent for scouring gloves, 2003; Author, Deep Dark Secrets, 2005; Preacher Daughter, 2005. Honours: Social Studies for High School, Brooklyn Education, 1972; 30 hours continuing certificate, Michigan State Education Department, 1975; New York State Education Department, District Administration and Supervision, 1975; Certificate of Appreciation, Brooklyn Education District 20, 1985; Certificate of Merit, New York, 1985; Teen Ranch Family Service, Michigan, 1993; Certificate of Achievement, Teen Ranch, Michigan, 1993; Jefferson Cup, Steinhardt School of Education, New York University, 2004; Listed in international biographical directories. Memberships: NYU Torchlight, 1975; NYU Alumni Group, 1978; UFT/Rtc, NY, 1985; NYU SUT; Wilderness Society; Wall of Tolerance, Alabama, 2003; BBB, 2004; United Negro College Fund, 2006; Defenders of Wildlife, Washington, DC, 2006. Address: 29606 Middlebelt Road #2801, Farmington Hills, MI 48334, USA. E-mail: E4115@aol.com

BARRYMORE Drew, b. 22 February 1975, Culver City, California, USA. Film Actress. m. (1) Jeremy Thomas, 1994, divorced, (2) Tom Green, 2001, divorced 2002. Appointments: Appeared in Dog Food Commercial, 1976; Film debut in TV Movie Suddenly Love, 1978; Films include: Altered States, 1980; ET, The Extra Terrestrial, 1982; Irreconcilable Differences, Firestarter, 1984; Cat's Eye, 1985; See You in the Morning, 1988; Guncrazy, Poison Ivy, Beyond Control: The Amy Fisher Story, 1992; Wayne's World 2, 1993; Bad Girls, 1994; Boys in the Side, Batman Forever, Mad Love, 1995; Scream, Everyone Says I Love you, 1996; All She Wanted, Best Men, 1997; Never Been Kissed, Home Fries, The Wedding Singer, Ever After, 1998; Charlie's Angels (also producer), 2000; Donnie Darko (also producer), Riding in Cars With Boys, 2001; Confessions of a Dangerous Mind, 2002; Duplex (also producer); So Love Returns (also producer); Charlie's Angels: Full Throttle (also producer), Duplex, 2003; 50 First Dates, 2004; Fever Pitch, 2005;Curious George, 2006; Music and Lyrics, Lucky You, 2007. Address: c/o EMA, 9025 Wilshire Boulevard, Suite 450, Beverly Hills, CA 90211, USA

BARSBOLD Rinchen, b. 21 December 1935, Ulaanbaatar, Mongolia. Vertebrate Paleontologist. m. Iliada Khabay, 2 sons. Education: Diploma, Geology Mining Institute, 1959; Candidate of Sciences, Geology and Geochronology Institute of Russian Academy of Science, 1969; Doctor of Biological Sciences, Institute of Paleontology, Russian Academy of Science, 1979. Appointments: Head of Paleontology-Stratigraphy Sector, Geological Institute, Mongolian Academy of Sciences, 1969-88; Director, Geological Institute, 1988-97; Member, Mongolian Parliament and Deputy Chairman, Mongolian Group in InterParliamentarian Association, 1990-92; Director, Paleontological Centre, Mongolian Academy of Sciences, 1997-. Publications: Carnivorous Dinosaurs from the Cretaceous of Mongolia, 1983; The Dinosauria, 1990, 2nd edition, 2004; Encyclopedia of Dinosaurs, 1992; 120 articles in journals. Honours: Mongolian Academy of Sciences

Award, 1986; Albert Einstein Diploma of World Science Council, 1989; Award of Government, 2002. Memberships: Mongolian Academy of Sciences, 1991; Academy for Developing Countries, 2002. Address: Enhtaivny Gudamj, BZD, Paleontological Centre, MAS, Ulaanbaatar 21351, Mongolia. E-mail: barsgeodin@magicnet.mn

BARTHOLD Kenneth van, b. 10 December 1927, Surabaya, Java, Indonesia. Concert Pianist; Teacher. m. (1) Prudence C M (2) Sarianne M C (3) Gillian R. 2 sons, 2 daughters. Education: Music Scholar, Bryanston School; British and French Government Scholar, Paris National Conservatoire of Music (class of Yves Nat), Laureat du Conservatoire National de Musique; LRAM. Career: Debut: Bournemouth Municipal Orchestra, 1944; Wigmore Hall, 1956; Frequent recitals in London Piano Series, Queen Elizabeth Hall and throughout the UK; Concerts in Canada, France, Israel and Eire including broadcasts; Concerto appearances with many orchestras including London Symphony Orchestra, British Concert Orchestra, English Chamber Orchestra, London Classical Players, Polyphonia under such conductors as: Sir Adrian Boult, Raymond Leppard, Sir Roger Norrington, Bryan Fairfax; Teaching: Director of Studies, Victoria College of Music, 1953-59; Professor of Piano, Trinity College of Music, 1959-65; Head of Music, City Literary Institute, 1960-83; Edinburgh University Annual Master Classes during the International Festival, 1968-; Senior Piano Tutor, ILEA, 1983-90; Lecturer on 19th and 20th Century Opera, Wimbledon College of Art, 1983-94; Master Classes in Israel, Canada and throughout the UK; International Juror in France and Canada; Wrote and presented 21 hour-long documentaries on television including the first ever full length studio documentary, BBC, 1964; Further frequent appearances interviewing, linking, profiling and performing on BBC and ITV. Recordings: Decca/Argo-Mozart Recital; Chopin Recital; Schumann Recital; Chopin Compilation; Darmo-Chopin/Liszt; Hommage à Pierre Max Dubois; Publications: Co-author, The Story of the Piano, 1976; Reviewer BBC Music Magazine; Various articles. Honour: Critics Award (television), 1972. Address: Arvensis, Stour Lane, Stour Row, Shaftesbury, Dorset SP7 0QJ, England. E-mail: kvanbarthold@aol.com

BARTHOLOMEW Debra Lee, b. 11 September 1958, New York, USA. Writer. m. Richard Ray Bartholomew, 1 son, 2 daughters. Education: Richmondville School, 1977. Appointments: Owner, Debi Lee Publishing, 2000. Publications: Author, Hope: Discovering the Power of No; Songwriter, Believing in Myself. Honours: Merit, Writer's Digest, 2001; Listed in international biographical dictionaries. Memberships: International Society of Poets. Address: 297 Main Street, Richmondville, New York, NY 12149-0150, USA. E-mail: rbartho1@nycap.rr.com

BARTLETT Neil, b. 15 September 1932, Newcastle upon Tyne, England. Chemist. m. Christina Isabel Cross, 1952, 3 sons, 1 daughter. Education: PhD, University of Durham, 1957. Appointments: University of British Columbia, Canada, 1958-66; Professor of Chemistry, Princeton University, USA, 1966-69; Scientist, Bell Telephone Laboratories, Murray Hill, New Jersey, 1966-69; Professor of Chemistry, University of California at Berkeley, 1969-94; Principal Investigator; Lawrence Berkeley Laboratory, 1969-; Professor Emeritus, 1994-; Carried out research on compounds of rare gases. Publications include: The Oxidation of Oxygen and Related Chemistry, 2001; Over 160 scientific papers and reports. Honours: Honorary doctorates from several universities; Research Corporation Award, 1965; Dannie Heineman Prize,

1971; Robert A Welch Award, 1976; W H Nichols Medal, USA, 1983; Moissan Fluorine Centennial Medal, Paris, 1986; Prix Moissan, 1988; American Chemical Society Award for Distinguished Service to Inorganic Chemistry, 1989; Pauling Medal, American Chemical Society, 1989; Award for Creative Work in Fluorine Chemistry, American Chemical Society, 1992; Bonner Chemiepreis, 1992; Foreign Fellow, Royal Society of Canada, 2001; Honorary FRSC, 2002; Royal Society (London) Davy Medal, 2002; Grand Prix de la Fondation Internationale de la Maison de la Chimie, Paris, 2004. Memberships: Leopoldina Academy, Halle, 1969; Corresponding member, Göttingen Academy, 1977; American Academy of Arts and Sciences, 1977; National Academy of Sciences, 1979; Associé Etranger, Academie des Sciences, France, 1989. Address: Department of Chemistry, University of California, Berkeley, CA 94720, USA.

BARTON Matthias, b. 6 August 1964, Wolfsburg, Germany. Physician. Education: MD, 1994, Dr. med., 1994, University of Hannover Medical School, Germany; PD (Associate Professor) in Cardiology, University of Zurich School of Medicine, Switzerland, 2001. Appointments: Intern, Internal Medicine/Cardiology, Hannover Medical School, 1994-95; Fellow, Cardiology, University Hospital, Bern, 1995-97; Fellow, Cardiology, 1997-99, Attending Physician, Internal Medicine, 2000-, Director of Research, Medical Policlinic, Internal Medicine, 2001-, University Hospital, Zurich. Publications: Book chapter: Estrogen and apoptosis in atherosclerosis, in Midlife Health – Current concepts and challenges for the future (editors, G Samsioe and S Skouby), 2002; Journal articles as author include: Angiotensin II increases vascular and renal endothelin converting enzyme activity in vivo: Role of ET_A-receptors for endothelin regulation, 1997; Salt Wars. On "The (Political) Science of Salt", 1998; Endothelin$_A$ receptor blockade restores NO-mediated endothelial dysfunction and inhibits atherosclerosis in apoE-deficient mice, 1998; Postmenopausal hormone-replacement therapy, 2002; Role of podocytes for reversal of glomerulosclerosis and proteinuria in the aging kidney after endothelin inhibition, 2004. Honours include: DAAD Scholarship for Clinical Training Abroad, 1993; Hannover Medical School, DFG Research Fellowship Award, 1995; Adumed Foundation Fellowship Award, 1997; Cardio-Vascular Biology Prize, Swiss Society of Cardiology, 1999; SCORE Career Development Award, Swiss National Science Foundation, 2000; Swiss Cardiology Fellowship Award, 2000; Finalist, Silver Medal of the Ludwig Heilmeyer Society, 2000; Young Investigator Award, 2000, 2001; Fellow, Council on Arteriosclerosis, Thrombosis and Vascular Biology, 2001, Fellow, Council for High Blood Pressure Research, 2002, American Heart Association. Memberships: German and Swiss Medical Associations; German and European Societies of Cardiology; American Heart Association; European Council for Blood Pressure and Cardiovascular Research; International and European Atherosclerosis Societies; North American Association for the Study of Obesity; American Diabetes Association. Address: Department of Internal Medicine, Medical Policlinic, University Hospital Zurich, Ramistrasse 100, 8091 Zurich, Switzerland. E-mail: barton@usz.ch

BARYSHNIKOV Mikhail, b. 28 January 1948, Riga, Latvia. Ballet Dancer. m. Lisa Rinehart, 2 daughters, 1 son; 1 daughter with Jessica Lange. Education: Riga Ballet School; Kirov Ballet School, Leningrad. Career: Member, Kirov Ballet Company, 1969-74; Guest Artist with many leading ballet companies, including American Ballet Theatre, National Ballet of Canada; Royal Ballet; Hamburg Ballet; Federal Republic of Germany; Ballet Victoria, Australia; Stuttgart

Ballet, Federal Republic of Germany; Alvin Ailey Co, USA, 1974-; Joined New York City Ballet Company, 1978, resigned 1979; Artistic Director, American Ballet Theatre, 1980-90; Co-Founder, White Oak Dance Project, 1990-2002; Stage debut in Metamorphosis, 1989; Launched perfume Misha, 1989; Founder, Baryshnikov Arts Center, New York, 2004; Ballets (world premieres) Vestris, 1969; Medea, 1975; Push Comes to Shove, 1976; Hamlet Connotations, 1976; Other Dances, 1976; Pas de Duke, 1976; La Dame de Pique, 1978' L'Apres-midi d'un Faune, 1978; Santa Fe Saga, 1978; Opus 19, 1979; Rhapsody, 1980; Films: The Turning Point, 1977; White Nights, 1985; Giselle, 1987; Dancers, 1987; Dinosaurs, 1991; Choreography: Nutcracker, 1976; Don Quixote, 1978; Cinderella, 1984; TV: Sex and the City, 2003-04. Publications: Baryshnikov at Work, 1977. Honours: Gold Medal, Varna Competition, Bulgaria, 1966; First International Ballet Competition, Moscow, USSR, 1968; Nijinsky Prize, First International Ballet Competition, Paris Academy de Danse, 1968; Kennedy Centre Honors, National Medal of Honour, Commonwealth Award. Address: c/o Vincent & Farrell Associates, 481 Eighth Avenue, Suite 740, New York, NY 10001, USA.

BASHKURTI Lisen, b. 21 September 1957, Shkodër, Albania. Diplomat. m. Majlinda, 1 son, 1 daughter. Education: Academy of Fine Arts, Tirana; Doctor of Sciences in Art (PhD); Minister Councelor. Appointments: Professor, History of Fine Arts, High School, Shkodër, 1981; First Secretary, Youth Organisation of Shkodër District, 1987; Secretary General, Youth Organisation of Albania, 1989; Secretary General, Social Democratic Party of Albania, 1991; Member, Albanian Parliament, 1992; Ambassador of Albania in the Republic of Hungary, 1992; Representative of Albania to the Council of Europe, Strasbourg, France, 1993; Expert in the State of Protocol, 1994, Head of UN Bureau, 1995, Director, Analyses and Prognosis, 2002, Dirctor of International Organisation, 2006, Head of Kosovo Division, 2006, Ministry of Foreign Affairs of Albania; Representative of Albania, UNGA, 49th Session, New York, 1995; Representative of Albania, UNGA, 50th Session, New York, 1996; President, Albanian Diplomatic Academy, 2001, 2006. Publications: 13 books; Numerous articles in professional journals. Honours: Gold Medal for article on Albanian-American friendships; 4 Silver Medals, Duna-Holding-Hungary, 1992-93. Memberships: International Forum on Diplomatic Training; Albanian Diplomatic Academy; Publishing Board, Diplomacy magazine; many others. Address: Akademia Diplomatke, Shqiptare, Str Rexhedjella, Tirana, Albania.

BASINGER Kim, b. 8 December 1953, Athens, Georgia, USA. Actress. m. (1) Ron Britton, divorced, (2) Alec Baldwin, divorced, 1 daughter. Career: Model, 1971-76; As actress, films include: Never Say Never Again, 1982; The Man Who Loved Women, 1983; 9 1/2 Weeks, 1985; Batman, 1989; Too Hot to Handle, 1991; The Real McCoy, 1993; Wayne's World, The Getaway, Prêt-à-Porter, 1994; LA Confidential, 1997; I Dreamed of Africa, Bless the Child, 2000; 8 Mile, People I Know, 2002; Elvis Has Left The Building, Cellular, The Door in the Floor, 2004; Jump Shot, 2005; The Sentinel, 2006; While She Was Out, 2007. Honours: Oscar, 1983; Academy Award and Golden Globe for Best Supporting Actress, 1997. Address: 3960 Laurel Canyon Boulevard, #414, Studio City, CA 91604, USA.

BASSEY Shirley, b. 8 January 1937, Tiger Bay, Cardiff, Wales. Singer; Entertainer. m. (1) Kenneth Hume, divorced 1965, deceased, (2) Sergio Novak, 1968, divorced 1977, 2 daughters, 1 deceased, 1 adopted son. Appointments: Variety and Revue Singer, 1950s; Concerts and TV appearances world-wide; Semi-Retired, 1981-; Artist for Peace, UNESCO, 2000; International Ambassador, Variety Club, 2001. Creative Works: I'm In the Mood For Love, 1981; Love Songs, 1982; All By Myself, 1984; I Am What I Am, 1984; Playing Solitaire, 1985; I've Got You Under My Skin, 1985; Sings The Songs From The Shows, 1986; Born To Sing the Blues, 1987; Let Me Sing And I'm Happy, 1988; Her Favourite Songs, 1988; Keep The Music Playing, 1991; Great Shirley Bassey (album), 1999; Thank You for the Years, 2003; The Columbia/EMI Singles Collection, 2006; Various compilations. Honours: CBE; 20 Gold Discs; 14 Silver Discs; TV Times Award, Best Female Singer, 1972; Britannia Award, Best Female Solo Singer in the Last 50 years, 1977; American Guild of Variety Artists Award, Best Female Entertainer, 1976; Britannia Award, Best Female Singer, 1977. Address: c/o CSS Stellar Management, Drury House, 34-43 Russell Street, London, WC2B 5HA, England.

BASSIL Andrea (Anna Nilsen), b. 16 September 1948, Manchester, England. Children's Book Author/Illustrator; Games Devisor. Education: Eastbourne School of Art, 1966-67; Dip AD, Edinburgh College of Art, 1967-72; SCSE, Moray House College of Education, 1972-73. Appointments: Full Time Assistant Teacher of Art, Mussleburgh Grammar School, 1973-74, St Margaret's School Edinburgh, 1974-85; ND and HND Course Director, Natural History Illustration, Bournemouth and Poole College of Art and Design, 1985-90; Head of Graphic Arts and Illustration, Anglia Polytechnic University, 1990-95; Children's Author/Illustrator, 1995-; Games Consultant, EFL CD Rom, Oxford University Press, 1996; Concept Designer and Illustrator, Falcon Games Ltd, 2004; Concept Devisor and Illustrator, Gibsons Amazeing Puzzles, 2004. Publications under pseudonym Anna Nilsen include: Terrormazia, 1995; Percy the Park Keeper Activity Book, Fairy Tales, Where is Percy's Dinner?, Ble Mae Cinio Bonso?, 1996; Follow the Kite, 1997; In the Jungle, On the Farm, People in My Neighborhood, Follow the Kite, I Can Spell Three Letter Words, Let's all Dig and Burrow, Let's all Hang and Dangle, Lego Puzzle Books: Spycatcher, Treasure Smuggler, Gold Robber, Jewel Thief, Insectoid Invasion, 1998; Let's all Swim and Dive, Let's all Leap and Jump, I Can Count from 1 – 10, I Can Count From 1 – 20, 1999; I Can Add, I Can Subtract, Art Fraud Detective, 2000; I Can Multiply, Magnificent Mazes (author and illustrator), 2001; The Great Art Scandal, 2003; Tip Truck! Tip!, Wave Baby! Wave!, Robotic Maths Games and Puzzles, My Best Dad, 2004; Bella's Mid-summer Secret, Peepers Jungle, Peepers People, Peepers, Art Auction Mystery, Famous Journeys, Australia, Magnificent Mazes, Dinosaur Trails, Ceiling Scenes (illustrations for Children's Hospital Operating Theatres), USA, 2005; Games: 3D Maths Maze Cube, 2004; Art Shark, Card Game, 2006; Multimedia: The Witches Academy, 1995; Piraten (CD Rom), Germany, 2004; Pirates, UK and Belgium, Breughel Art Fraud Puzzle, Inside-Out Museum, Inside-Out Cruise Ship, Renoir and Leonardo da Vinci Art Fraud Puzzles, Victorian Kitchen and Post-war Grocers, Walter's Wicked Jigsaw Puzzles, Ever so Edgey – Medieval Castle and Revelations – A Victorian Christmas (jigsaws), 2005; Jungle Safari, Counting Train, Little Helpers at the Garage, Little Helpers on the Farm, The AMAZEing Journey through Time, 3D Colour Maze Cube, It Shouldn't Happen to a Gardener, It Shouldn't Happen to a TV Chef, Cruising by Day & Night, A Pirates Fantasy, Wentworthworm, Christmas Conundrum, 2006; Baby Breezes, Pirates Galore, 2007. Honours: Goldsmith's Hall, Travelling Scholarship, 1981; Awards for Art Fraud Detective: Parent's Guide to Children's Media, 2001; Short-listed for BPF Book Design and Production Award, 2001; ABC Children's Booksellers Choices Awards,

2002; Department of the Ministry of Education in Mexico, 2003; Short-listed for Blue Peter Award, 2005; Short-listed for Toy of the Year Award, 2005. Memberships: Society of Authors; Cambridge Illustration Group; Authors Licensing and Collecting Society; Children's Book Circle. Address: 16, Emery Street, Cambridge, Cambridgeshire CB1 2AX, England.

BASSIOUNI Hischam, b. 13 April 1965, Cairo, Egypt. Physician. m. Sandra, 3 sons. Education: University of Cairo, Egypt, 1984-85; Georg-August University Göttingen, Germany, 1985-91. Appointments: Resident, Department of Neuroradiology, University of Göttingen, 1991-93; Resident, University of Aachen, Germany, 1993-96; Resident, Department of Neurosurgery, University of Essen, Germany, 1996-2000; Consultant Neurosurgeon, 2000-; Senior Consultant, 2000-07, Assistant Professor, Neurosurgery, 2007-, Department of Neurosurgery, Westpfalz-Klinikum, Kaiserslautern, Germany. Publications: 12 articles in professional medical journals. Honours: Listed in national and international biographical directories. Memberships: German Society of Neurosurgeons; European Association of Neurosurgical Societies; German Skullbase Society. Address: Department of Neurosurgery, Westpfalz-Klinikum GmbH, Hellmut-Hartert-Str 1, 67655 Kaiserslautern, Germany. E-mail: hibassiouni@yahoo.de

BASSO Maristela, b. 28 May 1960, Porto Alegre, Rio Grande do Sul, Brazil. Attorney in Law; Associate Professor; Researcher. Education: PhD, 1994, Postdoctoral studies in Law, 1997-2000, University of São Paulo. Appointments: Lawyer, University of Rio dos Sinos, 1982; Scholar Researcher, University of Rome I and II, Italy, 1987-90; Colegio de Mexico, 1996; Professor, Private International Law, Law School, Federal University, Rio Grande do Sul, Porto Alegre, Brazil, 1989-96; Associate Professor, International Law, Law School, University of São Paulo, 1996-; Invited Researcher, Max Planck Institute for Intellectual Property, Competition and Tax Law, Munich, Germany, 2004. Publications: Books: The Enforcement of Foreign Law by the National Judge – the Private International Law in Light of Jurisprudence, 1988; Mercosur – Legal Issues, Economic and Political Effects in the Member States, 1997; International Law of Intellectual Property, 2000; International Contracts in International Trade – From Negotiations, Closing and Practice, 2002; Joint Ventures – Handbook of the Company Associations, 2002; Intellectual property in the post TRIPS era, 2005; Mercosul/Mercosur, 2007. Memberships: Ordem dos Advogados de São Paulo; Ordem dos Advogados do Rio Grande do Sul; Member, Department of Conciliation and Arbitration of the Brazilian-Argentinean Chamber of Commerce; Permanent Board of Mediators and Arbitrators of Center for Mediation and Arbitration of Pernambuco State; Permanent Board of Arbitrators for Mediation and Arbitration of State of Rio Grande do Sul; Brazilian Arbitrators Board of the Dispute Settlement System of Mercosur; Brazilian Committee of Arbitration; Founder Brazilian Institute of International Trade Law & Development. Address: Rua Dr Gabriel dos Santos, 564/11, São Paulo, SP, 01231-010, Brazil. E-mail: mbasso@usp.br

BASU Subhajit, b. 10 August 1974, Calcutta, India. Lecturer. m. Baishakhi. Education: LLB, University College of Law, University of Calcutta, India, 1997; PhD, Liverpool John Moores University, 2000-03; PGCHET, Queen's University, Belfast, 2005-06. Appointments: Trainee under Senior Advocate, 1997-98; Solicitor and Advocate, L P Agarwalla & Co Solicitors and Advocates, 1998-2000; Ethnic Minority Law Network (UKCLE project), 2001-04; Lecturer (part time), Liverpool John Moores University, School of Law, Faculty of Business and Law, 2000-03; Lecturer, Information Technology Law, School of Law, Queen's University, Belfast, 2003-. Publications: 1 book; Several papers and articles in professional journals. Honours: Listed in international biographical dictionaries. Memberships: Executive Committee, British & Irish Law, Education and Technology Association; Bar Council of West Bengal, India; Tax Research Network (UK); Legal Network of E-Commerce Law Professionals; Member, LEFIS EU Project on IT and Legal Education; Society of Legal Scholars. Address: School of Law, Queen's University, Belfast, Northern Ireland.

BATABYAL Amitrajeet A, b. 6 September 1965, Chittaranjan, India. University Professor. m. Swapna B, 1 daughter. Education: BS, Cornell University, 1987; MS, University of Minnesota, 1990; PhD, University of California, Berkeley, 1994. Appointments: Visiting Assistant Professor, Economics, College of William & Mary, 1994-95; Assistant Professor, 1995-98, Associate Professor, 1998-2000, Utah State University; Arthur J Gosnell Professor of Economics, Rochester Institute of Technology, 2000-. Publications: 4 books; Numerous articles in professional journals. Honours include: Geoffrey J D Hewings Award, North American Regional Science Council, 2003; Moss Madden Memorial Medal, British and Irish Section of the Regional Science Association International, 2004; Outstanding Achievement in Research Award, Society for Range Management, 2006; Trustees Scholarship Award, Rochester Institute of Technology, 2007; Listed in international biographical dictionaries. Memberships: American Economic Association; American Agricultural Economics Association; Association of Environmental and Resource Economists; International Economics and Finance Society; Northeastern Agricultural and Resource Economics Association; Regional Science Association International. Address: 35 Crandon Way, Rochester, NY 14618, USA. E-mail: aabgsh@rit.edu

BATCHELOR John Barham, b. 15 March 1942, Farnborough, England. Professor of English Literature; Writer; Editor. m. Henrietta Jane Letts, 14 September 1968, 2 sons, 1 daughter. Education: MA, 1964, PhD, 1969, Magdalene College, Cambridge; MA, University of New Brunswick, 1965. Appointments: Lecturer in English, Birmingham University, 1968-76; Fellow and Tutor, New College, Oxford, 1976-90; Joseph Cowen Professor of English Literature, 1990-2007, Emeritus Professor and Senior Research Investigator, 2007-, University of Newcastle upon Tyne; Professor, University of Lancaster, 2001-. Publications: Mervyn Peake, 1974; Breathless Hush (novel), 1974; The Edwardian Novelists, 1982; H G Wells, 1985; Virginia Woolf, 1991; The Life of Joseph Conrad: A Critical Biography, 1994; The Art of Literary Biography (editor), 1995; Shakespearean Continuities (joint editor), 1997; John Ruskin: No Wealth But Life, 2000; Lady Trevelyan and the Pre-Raphaelite Brotherhood (book), 2006; Editor (English and American), Modern Language Review; General Editor, Yearbook of English Studies; Contributions to: Dictionary of National Biography; Times Literary Supplement; Observer; Economist; Articles in English, Yearbook of English Studies; Review of English Studies. Honours: Honorary Professor, University of Lancaster. Membership: International Association of Professors of English; English Association; MHRA. Address: School of English, Newcastle University, Newcastle upon Tyne NE1 7RU, England.

BATCHELOR Ronald Ernest, b. 15 July 1934, Southampton, England. Retired University Teacher. m. Patricia Anne, 1 son, 1 daughter. Education: Graduated French, Spanish, Latin (Hons), 1953-56, Certificate of Education, 1956-57, MA, thesis on the novels of Julian Green, 1958-61, University of Southampton; PhD Thesis, La Francophobie de Miguel de Unamuno, University of Nottingham, 1962-67. Appointments: Lecturer, University of Besançon, France, 1957-59; Teacher of English, S Sebastián, Spain, 1959-61; Teacher of French, Spanish, Southampton, 1961-62; Lecturer in French, 1962-67, Senior Lecturer in French, 1967-97, University of Nottingham. Publications: Unamuno Novelist A European Perspective, 1972; Using French A Guide to Contemporary Usage (co-author), 1982; Using Spanish A Guide to Contemporary Usage (co-author), 1992; Using French Synonyms (co-author), 1993; Using Spanish Synonyms, 1994; French for Marketing The Language of Media and Communications (co-author), 1997; Usage pratique et courant des synonymes anglais (co-author), 1998; Using Spanish Vocabulary (co-author), 2003; A Student Grammar of Spanish, 2006; Vocabulaire de la langue anglaise, ongoing; A Reference Grammar of the Spanish Language (including Spanish America), forthcoming (2009); Using Spanish Synonyms: L'Uso dei sinonimi SPAGNOLO, 2000; Usage Pratique et courant des synonymes anglais: L'Uso dei sinonimi INGLESE, 2001; 2nd and 3rd editions of some of the above; Numerous articles in learned journals on literary, philosophical and historical topics. Honours: Listed in several biographical dictionaries; Member, Research Board of Advisors, ABI; Member of advisory board of Anales de la Literatura Española Contemporánea, University of Colorado; Cambridge University Press Academic Best Seller. Address: 20 Moor Lane, Bramcote, Nottingham NG9 3FH, England. E-mail: ronaldbatchelor@btinternet.com

BATE (Andrew) Jonathan, b. 26 June 1958, Sevenoaks, Kent, England. Professor of English Literature; Critic; Novelist. m. (1) Hilary Gaskin, 1984, divorced 1995, (2) Paula Byrne, 1996, 1 son, 1 daughter. Education: MA, 1980, PhD, 1984, St Catharine's College, Cambridge. Appointments: Harkness Fellow, Harvard University, 1980-81; Research Fellow, St Catharine's College, Cambridge, 1983-85; Fellow, Trinity Hall, and Lecturer, Trinity Hall and Girton College, Cambridge, 1985-90; Visiting Associate Professor, University of California at Los Angeles, 1989; King Alfred Professor of English Literature, 1991-2003, Leverhulme Personal Research Professor, 1999-, University of Liverpool; Research Reader, British Academy, 1994-96; Professor of Shakespeare and Renaissance Literature, University of Warwick, 2003-. Publications: Shakespeare and the English Romantic Imagination, 1986; Charles Lamb: Essays of Elia (editor), 1987; Shakespearean Constitutions: Politics, Theatre, Criticism 1730-1830, 1989; Romantic Ecology: Wordsworth and the Environmental Tradition, 1991; The Romantics on Shakespeare (editor), 1992; Shakespeare and Ovid, 1993; The Arden Shakespeare: Titus Andronicus (editor), 1995; Shakespeare: An Illustrated Stage History (editor), 1996; The Genius of Shakespeare, 1997; The Cure for Love, 1998; The Song of the Earth, 2000; John Clare: A Biography, 2003; Editor, I Am: The Selected Poetry of John Clare, 2004. Contributions to: Scholarly publications. Honours: Calvin and Rose Hoffman Prize, 1996; FBA, 1999; Honorary Fellow, St Catherine's College, Cambridge, 2000; James Tait Black Memorial Prize, 2005; Commander of the British Empire, 2006. Address: c/o Department of English, University of Liverpool, PO Box 147, Liverpool L69 3BX, England.

BATEMAN Robert McLellan, b. 1930, Toronto, Canada. Artist. m. (1) Suzanne Bowerman, 1961, 2 sons, 1 daughter, (2) Birgit Freybe, 1975, 2 sons. Education: BA, University of Toronto, 1954; Ontario College of Education, 1955. Appointments: High School Art Teacher, Nelson High School, Burlington, Ontario, 1958-63, 1965-69, Government College, Umuahia, Nigeria, 1963-65, Lord Elgin High School, 1970-76; Lecturer, Resource Person in Art, Photography, Nature and Conservation. Creative Works: Major Exhibitions: Tryon Gallery, London, 1975, 1979; National Museum of Natural Sciences, Ottawa, 1981-82; Joslyn Art Museum, Omaha, Nebraska, 1987; Leigh Yawkey Woodson Art Museum, Wausau, Wisconsin, 1986-97; Smithsonian Institute, Museum of Natural History, Washington, 1987; Frye Art Museum, Seattle, Washington, 1988; Colorado Springs Fine Arts Museum, 1991; Carnegie Museum of Natural History, 1991; Canadian Embassy, Tokyo, 1992; Suntory Museum, Osaka and Tokyo, 1995-96; National Museum of Wildlife Art, 1997; Everard Read Gallery, Johannesburg, South Africa, 2000; Gerald Peters Gallery, Santa Fe, New Mexico, 2004; Masters Gallery, Calgary, Alberta, 2006; Several works in permanent collections. Publications: Books: The Art of Robert Bateman, 1981; The World of Robert Bateman, 1985; Robert Bateman: Artist in Nature, 1990; Robert Bateman,: Natural Worlds, 1996; Thinking Like a Mountain, 2000; Birds, 2002; Backyard Birds, 2005; Birds of Prey, 2007. Honours include: Queen Elizabeth Silver Jubilee Medal, 1977; Master Artist, Leigh Yawkey Woodson Art Museum, 1982; Officer of the Order of Canada, 1984; Governor General's Award for Conservation, Quebec City, 1987; Society of Animal Artists Award of Excellence, 1979, 1980, 1986, 1990; Rachel Carson Award, Society of Environmental Toxicology and Chemistry, 1996; Golden Plate Award, American Academy for Achievement, 1998; Order of British Columbia, 2001; Awards include 11 honorary doctorates; 3 Canadian schools named after him. Memberships include: Royal Canadian Academy of Arts; Sierra Club; Harmony Foundation, Ottawa; Jane Goodall Institute, Canada; Ecotrust; Kenya Wildlife Fund; Audubon Society; Sierra Legal Defense League. Address: PO Box 115, Fulford Harbour, Salt Spring Island, BC V8K 2P2, Canada. Website: www.robertbateman.ca

BATES Kathy, b. 28 June 1948, Memphis, Tennessee, USA. Actress. m. Tony Campisi, 1991, divorced 1997. Education: Southern Methodist University. Career: Various jobs before acting; Theatre includes: Varieties, 1976; Chocolate Cake, 1980; 'night Mother, 1983; Rain of Terror, 1985; Films include: Taking Off, 1971; Arthur 2: On the Rocks, 1988; High Stakes, 1989; Dick Tracy, Misery, 1990; Prelude to a Kiss, Fried Green Tomatoes at the Whistle Stop Café, 1991; North, 1994; Diabolique, The War at Home, 1996; Primary Colors, Titanic, 1998; A Civil Action, Dash and Lilly, My Life as a Dog, 1999; Bruno, 2000; Rat Race, American Outlaws, 2001; About Schmidt, Love Liza, 2002; Evelyn, The Tulse Luper Suitcases: The Moab Story, 2003; The Ingrate, Little Black Book, Around the World in 80 Days, The Bridge of San Luis Rey, 2004; Warm Springs, Relative Strangers, Rumor Has It, 2005; Failure to Launch, Charlotte's Web (voice), Christmas Is Here Again (voice), Bonneville, 2006; Bee Movie (voice), Have Mercy, 2007. TV Films and Appearances include: No Place Like Home; Murder Ordained; The Love Boat; St Elsewhere; LA Law; Cagney & Lacey; Annie, 1999; My Sister's Keeper, 2002. Honours: Pulitzer Prize, 1981; Outer Circle Critic's Award, 1983; Obie Award, 1987; Academy Award for Best Actress and Golden Globe, 1990. Address: c/o Susan Smith Associates, 121 N San Vincente Boulevard, Beverly Hills, CA 90211-2303, USA.

BATHAEE Soussan, b. 23 January 1953, Tehran, Iran. Engineer. Education: AS degree, Architecture, Riverside Community College, 1992; BSCE, 2003, MS-SE, 2007, California State University of Fullerton. Appointments: City Planning, Tehran, Iran, 1972-73; A/E Technician, National Iranian Oil Company, Tehran, Iran, 1973-75; Atomic Energy Organization, Tehran, Iran, 1975-80; Draftsperson, London, England, 1980-83; Draftsperson, Earl Walls Associates, San Diego, USA, 1984-85; Job Captain, Research Facilities Design, 1985-90; Engineering Service Technician, County of San Bernardino, 1991-2002; Computer Aided Engineer, LDIC – LSI Design & Integration Corp, 2002-. Honours: Certificate of Recognition, National Republican Party; America's Registry of Outstanding Professionals, 2003-04; 100 Top Scientists, 2005; Global Year of Engineering, 2006; Distinguished Service Award to Science & Engineering, 2007; Distinguished Order in Engineering; Listed in several Who's Who and biographical publications. Memberships: American Society of Civil Engineers; Architectural/Engineering Institute; The Riverside Greater Chambers of Commerce; The World Affair. Address: 42045 Kaffirboom Court, Temecula, CA 92591, USA. E-mail: soussanbathaee@yahoo.com

BATT Jürgen Otto Helmut, b. 18 August 1933, Gumbinnen, Germany. Professor of Mathematics. m. Hannelore Ulbricht, 2 daughters. Education: State Examination for Gymnasium Teachers, 1959; Dr. rer.nat. Technical College, Aachen, Germany, 1962; Habilitation, University of Munich, 1969. Appointments: Assistant, Nuclear Centre, Jülich, 1962-64; Assistant, Heidelberg University, 1964-66; Visiting Professor, 1967-68, Associate Professor, 1970-71, Kent State University, USA; Supernumerary Professor, 1974, Full Professor, Applied Mathematics, 1976-99, Dean of the Faculty of Mathematics, 1977-79, University of Munich. Publications: Many scientific articles in the area of differential equations and functional analysis in professional journals. Honours: Member of the University Senate, 1986-88; Member of the Assembly, 1988-98; Scholarly invitations to the following countries: Romania, USA, Switzerland, France, Austria, Italy, Netherlands, Australia, Brazil, India, Spain, Canada, China, Bulgaria, Czechoslovakia, Israel and Russia. Memberships: Deutsche Mathematiker-Vereinigung; American Mathematical Society; International Federation of Nonlinear Analysts. Address: Bauschneiderstrasse 11, 81241 Munich, Germany. E-mail: batt@rz.mathematik.uni-muenchen.de

BATTERHAM Robin John, b. 3 April 1941, Brighton, Victoria, Australia. Global Practice Leader – Innovation, Rio Tinto P/L. Education: BE, University of Melbourne; LLD (Hon), PhD, DSc (Hon), University of Technology, Sydney; AMusA, Post Nominals, AO, FAA, FTSE, FREng, CE, CPE, CSci, FNAE, FAusIMM, FISS, FIChemE; FIEAust; FICD; FAIM. Appointments: Chief, CSIRO Division of Mineral Engineering, 1984-88; Vice President, Resource & Processing Development CRA Ltd, 1988-94; President, International Mineral Processing Congress, 1989-; Deputy-Chair, Co-op Research Centres, 1992-2005; G K William Co-op Research Centre, 1993-99; Chair, Australian IMM Proceedings Committee, 1995-99; Deputy Director, Music, Scot's Church, Melbourne; Chairman, International Network for Acid Prevention, 1998-; Chief Scientist of Australia, 1999-2006; Australia Research Council Member, 1999-2006; Member, Major National Research Facilities Commission, 2001-06; President, Institution of Chemical Engineers, 2004-06; President, Academy of Technical Science, 2006-. Publications: 77 refereed papers in international journals and conferences. Honours: Officer of the Order of Australia; Presidents Medal, Australian Society of Sugar Cane Technologists; Fellow, Academy of Technology and Engineering Sciences; Fellow, Australian Academy of Science; Foreign Fellow, National Academy of Engineering, USA; Foreign Fellow, Swiss Academy of Engineering Sciences; CSIRO Postdoctorate Award; Esso Award of Excellence in Chemical Engineering, 1992; Distinguished Lecturer, University of British Columbia, University of Waterloo, University of California, Berkeley, University of Utah; Kernot Medal, University of Melbourne, 1996; Chemeca Medal, 2003; Centenary Medal of Australia, 2003; Australasian Institute of Mining and Metallurgy Medal, 2004. Memberships: Fellow, Iron Steel Society, America; Fellow, Australia Institute of Mining Metallurgy; Fellow, Institution of Chemical Engineers; Fellow, Institute of Australian Engineers; Fellow, Australian Institute of Management; Fellow, Australian Academy of Sciences; Fellow, Australian Academy of Technological Sciences and Engineering; Fellow, Royal Academy of Engineering. Address: 153 Park Drive, Parkville, Vic 3052, Australia.

BAUCH Efraim, b. 13 January 1934, Russia. Writer. m. Aura, 1 son, 1 daughter. Education: Geology Engineer, Faculty of Geology, University of Kishinev, 1953-58; High Literature Education, University of Literature in Framework of Union of Soviet Writers, 1971-74. Appointments: Editor-in-Chief, Zion literary journal, 1977-86; Chairman, Israeli Federation of Writer's Unions, 1994-; Editor-in-Chief, The Word of the Writer literary journal, 2000-06; President, PEN Centre, Israel, 2000-. Publications: The Dreams of Life cycle of novels: Kin and Orman, 1982; Mount Moria, 1982; Jakob's Ladder, 1987; Call, 1991; Sun of Suicides, 1994; The Desert Listens to God (in the Russian literature cycle, Masterpieces of Modern World Literature), 2002; The Screen of God – This cycle of seven novels is a unique in the literature of XX century – for the destiny of Jewish people in the modern time, 2006; Essays: Time of Confession, 1994; The Accusation of History, 2006; Poems: The Sides, 1963; Trams of Night, 1965; The Red Evening, 1968; The Transformations, 1972; The Spirit, 1978; The Shade and the Word (complete works of poem), 1999; In Hebrew: Dante in Moscow, novel, 1987; The Heritage from Far, poems, 2000; Numerous articles in newspapers and journals. Honours: Rafaely Prize, 1982; Zionist World Congress Prize, 1986; President of the State of Israel's Prize for Literature, 2001. Memberships: Union of Soviet Writers, 1964-77; Israel Federation of Writers' Union, 1977-; Union of Hebrew Writers, 1990-; International PEN Centre, 1980-. Address: Box 3461, Kiriat Ben-Gurion, Holon, 58133, Israel. E-mail: mail@efraimbauch.com

BAUGH Lisa Saunders, b. August 27 1969, Houston, Texas, USA. Research Chemist. m. Simon David Peter Baugh. Education: BS Chemistry (High Honours), University of Texas, 1991; PhD Polymer Chemistry, University of California at Berkeley, 1996. Appointments: Visiting Scholar, Polymer Science and Engineering Department, University of Massachusetts at Amherst, 1994-96; Senior Research Chemist, Air Products and Chemicals, Allentown, Pennsylvania, 1996-97; Senior Chemist, 1997-2005, Research Associate, 2005-, ExxonMobil Research and Engineering, Annandale, New Jersey; Guest Lecturer, Various Colleges and Universities, 1997-; College/High School Textbook Essayist, various publishers, 1990-; Owner, The Copy Chemist Scientific Editorial Service, Professional Classical Violinist and Violist, 1987-. Publications: Editor, Transition Metal Catalysts in Macromolecular Design, 2000; Editor, Late Transition Metal Polymerisation Catalysts, 2003; Author of articles in scientific journals including: Macromolecules, Chemical Reviews, Journal of the American Chemical Society; Patentee in the field of polymer chemistry. Honours: National Science

Foundation Predoctoral Fellow; National Merit Scholar, Deans Honoured Graduate, Merck Index Award, University of Texas. Memberships: American Chemical Society Catalysis and Surface Science Secretariat, Secretary General/Program Chair 2001, Polymeric Materials Science and Engineering Division, Member at Large, 2000-, Membership Chair, 2004-05, Women Chemists Committee, Committee Associate 2002-04; Editorial Advisory Board, Chemistry Magazine, 2003-; National Association of Science Writers; Alpha Chi Sigma Fraternity (Beta Theta Chapter); Phi Beta Kappa; Phi Kappa Phi. Address: ExxonMobil Research and Engineering, Route 22 East, Annandale, New Jersey, 08801, USA.

BAUM Carl Edward, b. 6 February 1940, Binghamton, New York, USA. Electromagnetic Theorist. Education: BS, honours, Engineering, 1962, MS, Electrical Engineering, 1963, PhD, Electrical Engineering, 1969, California Institute of Technology. Appointments: 2nd Lieutenant, USAF, 1962; Captain, Air Force Research Laboratory, 1963-67, 1968-71; Senior Scientist, Electromagnetics, Adviser, numerous US government agencies, 1971-2005; Distinguished Research Professor, Department of Electrical and Computer Engineering University of New Mexico, 2005-. Publications: Numerous articles in professional journals; 5 books as author or editor. Honours include: Air Force Commendation Medal, 1969; Air Force Research and Development Award, 1970; Air Force Nomination to Ten Outstanding Young Men of America, 1971; Fellow, IEEE, 1984; Richard R Stoddart Award, IEEE EMC Society, 1984; IEEE Harold Diamond Memorial Award, 1987; AFSC Harold Brown Award, 1990; Air Force Research Laboratory Fellow, 1996; Dr.-Ing. E.h. (equivalent to Doctor of Engineering honoris causa), Otto-von-Guericke University, Magdeburg, Germany, 2004; John Kraus Antenna Award, IEEE Antennas and Propagation Society, 2006; IEEE Electromagnetics Field Award, 2007; Listed in numerous international biographical dictionaries. Memberships include: SUMMA Foundation; URSI; IEEE. Address: 5116 Eastern Southeast Unit D, Albuquerque, NM 87108, USA.

BAUMAN Frank Anthony, b. 10 June 1921, Portland, Oregon, USA. Lawyer (Inactive). m. (1) Mildred Inez Packer, 9 September 1950, deceased 1997, 1 son, 2 daughters, (2) Divorced. Education: US Naval Japanese Language School, University of Colorado, 1943-44; AB, Stanford University, 1944; JD, Yale University, 1949; Postgraduate, International Law, University of London, 1951-52. Appointments: Member, Oregon US District Court; US Supreme Court; Private Practice, Portland, 1950-71: Wilbur Beckett Oppenheimer Mautz & Souther, Veatch Bauman Lovett, Keane Haessler Bauman & Harper; Lawyers Commission for Civil Rights Under Law, Mississippi, 1969; Representative, UN Australia and New Zealand, 1971-76, Papua New Guinea, 1971-73; Private Practice, Portland, 1978-91; Adjunct Professor of Law, Lewis and Clark Law School, 1978-80; Advisor Lillian Baumann Fund, 1985-; Co-Trustee Mildred P Bauman Trust, 1997-. Publications: The Prospects for International Law, 1973; Can a World Court be Made to Work, 1973; The Promise of the United Nations, 1973. Honours: Recipient, World Peace Award Assembly of the Bahais, Portland, 1985; E B MacNaughton Civil Liberties Award, ACLU, 1998; Co-Chairman Class of 1949 Reunion, Yale University, 2004; Co-chairman, Class of 1943 Reunion, Stanford University, 2008. Memberships include: Member and Past Trustee, President, World Affairs Council of Oregon, 1954-; Member and Past Chairman, Portland Committee on Foreign Relations, 1978-; Past Director and President, Oregon UN Association, 1977-92; Past Director and President, English Speaking Union, Portland, 1992-98; Director, Member, Executive Committee,

English Speaking Union, US, New York, 1997-2003; Member, American Bar Association, ABA; Patron, American Society of International Law; International Law Association, American branch; UN Association, USA; Arlington Club; Yale Club of New York City; Mason and Past Master; Member, Astoria Golf and Country Club, Oregon. Address: Suite 1507, Standard Plaza, 1100 SW Sixth Avenue, Portland, OR 97204-1016, USA. E-mail: FABEsquire@aol.com

BAUMAN Janina, b. 18 August 1926, Warsaw, Poland. Writer. m. Zygmunt Bauman, 18 August 1948, 3 daughters. Education: Academy of Social Sciences, 1951; University of Warsaw, 1959. Appointments: Script Editor, Polish Film, 1948-68. Publications: Winter in the Morning: A Dream of Belonging; Various other books and short stories published in Poland since 1990; Beyond These Walls; Contributions to: Jewish Quarterly; Oral History; Polin; British Journal of Holocaust Education; Thesis Eleven. Honour: Award by Polityka Weekly, Poland, 1991. Address: 1 Lawnswood Gardens, Leeds, Yorkshire LS16 6HF, England.

BAUMAN Zygmunt, b. 19 November 1925, Poznan, Poland. Sociologist. m. Janina Bauman, 18 August 1948, 3 daughters. Education: MA, 1954; PhD, 1956. Appointments: Warsaw University, 1953-68; Tel Aviv University, 1968-75; University of Leeds, 1971-91. Publications: Modernity and the Holocaust; Legislators and Interpreters; Intimations of Postinedermity; Thinking Sociologically; Modernity and Ambivalence; Freedom; Memories of Class; Culture as Praxis; Between Class and Elite; Mortality, Immortality and Other Life Strategies; Postmodernity and its Discontents, 1997; In Search of Politics, 1999; Liquid Modernity, 2000; Individualized Society, 2000; Community: Seeking Safety in an Uncertain World, 2001; Society Under Siege, 2002; Liquid Love: On the Frailty of Human Bonds, Wasted Lives: Modernity and its Outcasts, 2003; Europe: An Unfinished Adventure, Identity: Conversations with Benedetto Vecchi, 2004; Liquid Life, 2005; Liquid Fear, Liquid Times, 2006; Consuming Life, 2007. Contributions to: Times Literary Supplement; New Statesman; Professional Periodicals. Honour: Amalfi European Prize for Sociology; Theodor Adorno Prize, 1998; Dr honoris causa: Oslo, 1997, Lapland, 1999, Uppsala, 2000, West of England, 2001, London, 2002, Sofia, 2002, Charles University, Prague, 2002, Copenhagen, 2002, University of Leeds, 2004. Memberships: British Sociological Association; Polish Sociological Association. Address: 1 Lawnswood Gardens, Leeds LS16 6HF, England.

BAUMANN Herbert Karl Wilhelm, b. 31 July 1925, Berlin, Germany. Composer; Conductor. m. Marianne Brose, 2 sons. Education: Composing (with Paul Hoeffer and Boris Blacher) and Conducting (with Sergiu Celibidache), International Music Institute, Berlin. Appointments: Composer and Conductor, Deutsches Theater Berlin, 1947-53; Composer and Conductor, State Theatres Berlin, 1953-70; Musical Head Manager, Composer and Conductor, Bavarian State Theatre, 1970-79; Freelance Composer, 1979-. Publications: Music for more than 500 theatre plays and over 40 TV plays; Numerous CDs; Libretto for ballets, Alice in Wonderland and Rumpelstilzgen; Text for: Moritat vom eigensinnigen Eheweibe; Der unzufriedene Schneemann; Das blaue Kaninchen; Vom Millerburschen, dem ein Bauer das Pferd nahm; Der wohlfeile Gaensebraten; Numerous works for orchestra, for choir, and for chamber orchestra; Many chamber music works. Honours: Man of Achievement, 1973; Diploma of Honour, 1981; Bundesverdienstkreuz (Order of the Federal Republic of Germany); Member of Honour, Bund Deutscher Zupfmusiker, 1990; Diploma of Honour for 50 years' membership, GEMA, 1998. Memberships: GEMA; Bund Deutscher Zupfmusiker; Verband Muenchener Tonkuenstler. Address: Franziskanerstr 16, Aptm 1419, D-81669 Munich, Germany. Website: www.komponisten.net/baumann

BAUROV Yuriy Alexeevich, b. 14 March 1947, Russia. Physicist. m. 2 sons. Education: Moscow Aviation Institute, 1972; PhD, 1978. Appointments: Chief of Laboratory, Central Research Institute of Machine Building; Presidency of Council of Directors, Closed Joint-Stock Company, Research Institute of Cosmic Physics. Publications: Books: On the Structure of Physical Vacuum and a New Interaction in Nature (Theory, Experiment, Applications), 2000; Global Anisotropy of Physical Space, Experimental and Theoretical Basis, Nova Science, New York, 2004; Several articles in professional journals. Honour: Diplôme 26 Salon International des Inventions, Genève, 1998; Gold Award, Seoul International Invention Fair, 2004; Gold Award, Brussels Eureka! 2004. Membership: New York Academy of Sciences, 1994-98. Address: Central Research Institute for Machine Building, 141070, Koroloyov, Moscow Region, Pionerskaya 4, Russia.

BAUSER Nancy Perlmutter, b. 23 November 1950, Detroit, Michigan, USA. Social Worker/Disability Life Coach. m. William John Bauser. Education: BS, Education, University of Michigan, 1973; MSW, Social Work, University of Wisconsin-Madison, 1976. Appointments: Provided individual and group counselling to those having difficulty with social reintegration, personal interaction and substance abuse, 1985-87; Co-led psychotherapy group for brain injured substance abusers, 1990-97; Co-led brain injury/pain management peer group with neuropsychiatrist, 1993-99; Poster presentation, MAKING PROGRESS: RECOVERY THROUGH ACCEPTANCE, 2nd World Congress on Brain Injury, Seville, Spain, 1997; Led support group for brain injured addicts and for those with catastrophic injuries, 1997-2002; Life Coaching with persons having physical difficulties, 2001-. Publications: My Life Since My Head Injury, 1993, 2003; Acceptance Group for Head Injured Survivors, 1994; Acceptance Group for Survivors – A Guide for Facilitators, 2001, 2008. Honours: Listed in international biographical dictionaries; Board Certified Expert in Traumatic Stress with Board Certification in Disability Trauma, 2004-. Memberships: National Association of Social Workers; Academy of Certified Social Workers; Association of Traumatic Stress Specialists; American Academy of Experts in Traumatic Stress. Address: 4260 Wabeek Lake Drive-South, Bloomfields Hills, Michigan 48302, USA. E-mail: nancy@survivoracceptance.com Website: www.survivoracceptance.com

BAYAZID Hakam, b. 29 April 1941, Damascus, Syria. Civil Engineer. m. Hadba Sabbagh, 2 sons, 2 daughters. Education: BSCE, Purdue University, 1964; MSCE, University of Missouri, 1969; PhD, University of Missouri, 1972; MBA Work, Indiana University at South Bend, 1975-78. Appointments: Senior Civil Engineer, Ball Corporation, Broomfield, Colorado, USA, 1978-80; Assistant Professor of Civil Engineering, King Abdul Aziz University, Jeddah; Project Manager, Saud Consult, Riyadh, 1982-93; Senior Civil Engineer, Saudi Oger Ltd, 1993-. Publications: Author and co-author, Another Look at Buckling of Circular Arches, 1978. Honours: Charter Member, Structural Engineering Institute; Life Member, Society of Sigma Xi, Post Doctoral Fellowship, University of Missouri, 1972; Listed in biographical publications. Membership: Life Fellow, American Society of Civil Engineers. Address: GPC Division, Saudi Oger, P O Box 1449, Riyadh 11431, Saudi Arabia. E-mail: hbayazid@saudioger.com

BAYLEY Peter (Charles), b. 25 January 1921, Gloucester, England. Professor Emeritus; Writer. Education: Elementary school; The Crypt Grammar School, Gloucester; Exhibitioner, University College, Oxford, 1940-41; MA (first class), English Language and Literature, Oxford University, 1947. Appointments: War Service, Royal Artillery, Anti-Tank (later Intelligence Corps, India), Far East, 1941-46; Fellow, University College, 1947-72; Praelector in English, 1949-72, University Lecturer, 1952-72, Oxford University; First Founding Master, Collingwood College, University of Durham, 1972-78; Berry Professor and Head of English Department, 1978-85, Berry Professor Emeritus, 1985-, University of St Andrews, Fife. Publications: Edmund Spenser, Prince of Poets, 1971; Poems of Milton, 1982; An ABC of Shakespeare, 1985; Editor: The Faerie Queene, by Spenser, Book II, 1965, Book 1, 1966, 1970; Loves and Deaths, 1972. Contributions to: Patterns of Love and Courtesy, 1966; Oxford Bibliographical Guides, 1971; A Casebook on Spenser's The Faerie Queene, 1977; C S Lewis at the Breakfast Table, 1979; The Encyclopaedia of Oxford, 1988; Sir William Jones 1746-94, 1998; Editor, University College Record, 1949-71. Address: 63 Oxford Street, Woodstock, Oxford OX20 1TJ, England.

BAYLIS Robert Goodwin, b. 29 November 1925, Luton, Bedfordshire, England. Consulting Engineer. 2 sons, 1 daughter. Education: Highgate School; Trinity College, Cambridge. Appointments: Royal Navy; Director, Scientific Defence Management; Chairman, Nuffield Theatre; Director, BMT Reliability Consultants. Honours: CB; OBE. Memberships: Member, Royal Aeronautical Society. Address: Broadwaters, 4 Cliff Road, Hill Head, PO14 3JS, England. E-mail: gowith.theflow@ntlworld.com

BAYLISS Peter, b. 1 September 1936, Luton, England. Mineralogist. m. Daphne Phyllis Webb. Education: BE, 1959, MSc, 1962, PhD, 1967, University of New South Wales, Australia. Appointments: Professor, University of Calgary, Calgary, Alta, Canada, 1967-92; Professor Emeritus, 1992-; Research Associate, Australian Museum 1993-. Publications: 104 papers; 15 monographs; Over 38 book reviews; 61 X-ray powder diffraction data. Honours: University Soccer Blue, 1961; Commonwealth Scholarship, 1964; Fellow, Mineralogical Society of America, 1970; Killam Fellowship, 1981; New mineral named peterbaylissite, 1995; Fellow, International Centre Diffraction Data, 2000; Fellow, Mineralogical Society, Great Britain, 2000; Listed in national and international biographical dictionaries. Memberships: Mineralogical Association of Canada. Address: Department of Mineralogy, Australian Museum, 6 College Street, Sydney, NSW 2010, Australia.

BAZOPOULOU-KYRKANIDOU Euterpe, b. 4 August 1937, Florina, Greece. Emeritus Professor. m. Demetrios Kyrkanides, 1 son. Education: DDS, 1959, PhD, 1969, MD, 1972, University of Athens; MSc, 1977, Certificate of Oral Pathology and Genetics, 1977, University of Minnesota, USA; Fellow, American Academy of Oral Maxillofacial Pathology, 1977; Fellow, Medicine Department of Medical Genetics, Johns Hopkins University, 1980. Appointments: Research Fellow, 1965-72, Senior Instructor, 1972-82, Division of Oral Medicine, Lecturer, 1982-83, Assistant Professor, 1983-85, Associate Professor, 1985-2000, Head of Department, 1987-88, 2003-04, Professor, 2000-04, Professor Emeritus, 2004-, Department of Oral Pathology and Surgery, University of Athens; Invited Speaker and Visiting Professor, Graduate School, Eastman Dental Center, 1999. Publications: Papers and articles in international scientific journals. Honours: Eponym Syndrome; Bazopoulou-Kyrkanidou Syndrome;

Craniofaciocervical Osteoglyphic Dysplasia. Memberships: European Society of Human Genetics; Fellow, American Academy of Oral Maxillofacial Pathology. Address: 100 Makedonias St, Papagou, Athens, 15669, Greece. E-mail: ebazopou@dent.uoa.gr

BEALE Alfred James, b. 12 July 1935, Edinburgh, Scotland. Management Consultant. m. Kathleen, 1 son, 1 daughter. Education: George Heriot's School, Edinburgh, 1941-53; MA (Hons), University of Edinburgh, 1957. Appointments: Commissioned Officer, 1st Battalion The Royal Scots, 1957-59; Salesman, Brand Manager in Advertising Department, Procter & Gamble, 1959-64; Operating level, 1964-68, supervisor capacity, 1968-72, diagnostic survey work, 1972-77, Director, North East England, 1978-81, PA Consulting Group; Chief Executive, PA Cambridge Economic Consultants, -1993; Retired, 1993. Publications: Irish Salesmen Under the Microscope, 1971. Honours: OBE, 1997. Memberships: Honorary Fellow, Charted Institute of Marketing; Fellow, Chartered Management Institute; Fellow, Institute of Management Consultancy; Fellow, Institute of Directors; Fellow, Royal Society of Arts; Honorary President, European Marketing Confederation, 1997-. Address: Hallbankfield, Newcastle Road, Corbridge, Northumberland NE45 5LN, England.

BEALE Hugh Gurney, b. 4 May 1948. Professor of Law. m. Jane Wilson Cox, 2 sons, 1 daughter. Education: BA (Hons), Jurisprudence, Exeter College, Oxford. Appointments: Lecturer, Law, University of Connecticut, 1969-71; Lecturer, Law, University College of Wales, Aberystwyth, 1971-73; Lecturer, Law, 1973-86, Reader, Law, 1986-87, University of Bristol; Professor of Law, University of Warwick, 1987-; Law Commissioner, 2000-07. Publications: Remedies for Breach of Contract, 1980; Principles of European Contract Law: Parts I & II, joint editor with Ole Lando, 2000; Contract cases and materials, joint editor, 4th edition, 2001; Casebooks on the Common Law of Europe: Contract Law, joint editor, 2002; Chitty on Contracts, general editor, 29th edition, 2004. Honours: Honorary Bencher, Lincoln's Inn, 1999; Honorary QC, 2002; Fellow, British Academy, 2004. Membership: Study Group on a European Civil Code. Address: School of Law, University of Warwick, Coventry CV4 7AL, England. E-mail: hugh.beale@warwick.ac.uk

BEALE Peter John (Sir), b. 18 March 1934, Essex, England. Medical Practitioner. m. (1) Julia, deceased 2000, 4 sons, 2 daughters, 1 deceased; (2) Mary, 2 December 2001. Education: Gonville and Caius College, Cambridge, 1952-55; Westminster Hospital, 1955-58; BA; MB BChir, 1958; FRCP, 1979; FFCM, 1992; FFOM, 1993. Appointments: Army Doctor, 1960-94; Surgeon General, UK Armed Forces, 1991-94; Chief Medical Adviser, British Red Cross, 1994-2000; Governor, Yehudi Menuhin School. Publications: Medical articles on military matters Honour: KBE, 1991. Memberships: President, Tedworth Golf Club, 1999-2003; President, Army Officer's Golf Society, 2001-05. Address: The Old Bakery, Avebury, Wiltshire SN8 1RF, England. E-mail: peter.beale1@virgin.net

BEALES Derek (Edward Dawson), b. 12 June 1931, Felixstowe, England. Emeritus Professor of Modern History; Writer. Education: BA, 1953, MA, PhD, 1957, Sidney Sussex College, Cambridge University. Appointments: Research Fellow, 1955-58, Fellow, 1958-, Tutor, 1961-70, Vice Master, 1973-75, Sidney Sussex College, Cambridge University; Assistant Lecturer, 1962-65, Lecturer, 1965-80, Chairman, Faculty Board of History, 1979-81, Professor of

Modern History, 1980-97, Emeritus Professor, 1997-, Sidney Sussex College, Cambridge University; Editor, Historical Journal, 1971-75; Member of Council, Royal Historical Society, 1984-87; British Academy Representative, Standing Committee for Humanities, European Science Foundation, 1993-99; Recurring Visiting Professor, Central European University, Budapest, 1995-. Publications: England and Italy 1859-60, 1961; From Castlereagh to Gladstone 1815-85, 1969; The Risorgimento and the Unification of Italy, 1971, 2nd edition, with E F Biagini, 2002; History and Biography, 1981; History, Society and the Churches: Essays in Honour of Owen Chadwick (editor with G F A Best), 1985; Joseph II: In the Shadow of Maria Theresa 1741-80, 1987; Mozart and the Habsburgs, 1993; Sidney Sussex College Quatercentenary Essays, (editor with H B Nisbet), 1996; Prosperity and Plunder: European Catholic Monasteries in the Age of Revolution, 1650-1815, 2003; Enlightenment and Reform in the Eighteenth Century, 2005. Honours: Prince Consort Prize, 1960; Doctor of Letters, 1988; Fellow, British Academy, 1989; Stenton Lecturer, University of Reading, 1992; Birkbeck Lecturer, Trinity College, Cambridge, 1993; Leverhulme 2000 Emeritus Fellowship, 2001-2003; Paolucci/ Bagehot Prize, Intercollegiate Studies Institute, Wilmington, Delaware, USA, 2004. Memberships: Fellow, Royal Historical Society; Member, Athenaeum. Address: Sidney Sussex College, Cambridge CB2 3HU, England. E-mail: deb1000@cam.ac.uk

BEAN Sean, b. 17 April 1959, Sheffield, Yorkshire, England. Actor. m. (1) Debra James, 1981, divorced, (2) Melanie Hill, 1990, divorced 1997, 2 daughters, (3) Abigail Cruttenden, 1997, divorced 2000, 1 daughter. Education: Royal Academy of Dramatic Art. Creative Works: Appearances include: the Last Days of Mankind and Der Rosenkavalier at Citizen's Theatre, Glasgow, Who Knew Mackenzie? and Gone, Theatre Upstairs, Roy Court, Romeo in Romeo and Juliet, RSC, Stratford-upon-Avon, 1986, Captain Spencer in The Fair Maid of the West, RSC, London; TV Appearances include: Clarissa; Fool's Gold; Role of Mellors in BBC Dramatization of Lady Chatterley's Lover; Inspector Morse; Role Sharpe in TV Series; A Woman's Guide to Adultery; Jacob; Bravo Two Zero; Extremely Dangerous; Films: Caravaggio, Stormy Monday, War Requiem, The Field, Patriot Games, Gone With the Wind, Goldeneye, When Saturday Comes, Anna Karenina, Ronin; The Lord of the Rings: The Fellowship of the Ring; Don't Say a Word; Equilibrium; Tom and Thomas; The Big Empty; Windprints; Essex Boys; Troy, Pride (voice), National Treasure, 2004; The Island, North Country, Flightplan, 2005; The Dark, Silent Hill, The Elder Scrolls IV: Oblivion (video game), 2006; Outlaw, The Hitcher (remake), 2007. Address: c/o ICM Ltd, Oxford House, London W1R 1RB, England.

BEAR Isabel Joy, b. 4 January 1927, Camperdown, Victoria, Australia. Research Scientist. Education: Associate Diploma in Applied Chemistry, MTC, 1950; Associate Diploma in Applied Science, 1950; Fellowship Diploma Applied Chemistry, RMIT 1972; D App Sc, 1978. Appointments: Experimental Scientist, AERE Harwell, 1950-51; Research Assistant, University of Birmingham, UK, 1951-53; Experimental Scientist, CSIRO Division of Industrial Chemistry/Mineral Chemistry, 1953-67; Senior Research Scientist, CSIRO Division of Mineral Chemistry/Products, 1967-72; Principal Research Scientist, 1972-79; Senior Principal Research Scientist, 1979-92; Honorary Fellow, 1992-2006. Publications: More than 70 refereed papers in scientific journals; Co-author: Alumina to Zirconia – The History of the CSIRO Division of Mineral Chemistry, 2001. Honours: Appointed, Member of the Order of Australia for Services to Science; Leighton

Medallist, Royal Australian Chemical Institute; Listed on the Victorian Honour Roll of Women, 2005. Memberships: Royal Australian Chemical Institute; Australasian Institute of Mining and Metallurgy. Address: 2/750 Waverley Road, Glen Waverley, VIC 3150, Australia.

BEARD Jane Alida (Bryant), b. 22 August 1920, Belton, Bell County, Texas, USA. Accountant. m. Ledford F Beard, 2 sons. Education: Southwestern University (2 years), transferred to Texas College of Arts and Industry. Appointments: Accountant; Retired; Member, St Paul's Anglican Church. Publications: Births, Deaths & Marriages 1881-1899, 4 volumes; Waldo Williams, Southwest Artist; Footprints: of some Brown, Bryants, Cater, Holcomb Descendents. Honours: 1st place, Births, Deaths & Marriages vol 1, 1992; Outstanding Appreciation Volunteer Service, El Paso Public Library, 1993, 1995; RSVP Volunteer Honor for Service, 1994; Certificate for Contributions to Rio Grande Researcher, 1994; Star of Appreciation, Daughters of the Republic of Texas, 1996; 1st place, Births, Deaths & Marriages vol 3, 1996; 1st place, Births, Deaths & Marriages vol 4, 2000. Memberships: Colonial Dames of XVII Century; El Paso County Historical Society; United Daughters of the Confederacy; Daughters of the American Revolution; Daughters of the Republic of Texas; El Paso Genealogical Society; El Paso Mineral & Gem Society; Anthony Country Club; Anthony Ladies Golf & Bridge Association; Past Member, 20-30 Anns. Address: 931 Edgewood Road, Apt 110, Annapolis, MD 21403-3466, USA. E-mail: ledbird@aol.com

BEASLEY John David, (David Sellers), b. 26 October 1944, Hornsea, Yorkshire, England. Social Worker. m. Marian Ruth Orford, 1969, 1 son, 2 daughters. Education: London University Diploma in Sociology; Certificate of Qualification in Social Work, Polytechnic of North London, England. Appointments: United Kingdom Band of Hope Union, 1960-70; Social Worker, London Borough of Tower Hamlets, 1970-94. Publications: Who Was Who in Peckham, 1985; The Bitter Cry Heard and Heeded, 1989; 500 Quotes and Anecdotes, 1992; Origin of Names in Peckham and Nunhead, 1993; Peckham and Nunhead Churches, 1995; Peckham Rye Park Centenary, 1995; Peckham and Nunhead, 1995; Another 500 Quotes and Anecdotes, 1996; Transport in Peckham and Nunhead, 1997; East Dulwich, 1998; The Story of Peckham and Nunhead, 1999; Peckham and Nunhead Remembered, 2000; Southwark Remembered, 2001; East Dulwich Remembered, 2002; Southwark Revisited, 2004; Contributions to: Challenge; South London Press. Honour: Southwark Civic Award, 1997. Memberships: Society of Authors; Royal Historical Society. Address: South Riding, 6 Everthorpe Road, London SE15 4DA, England.

BEATRIX Wilhelmina Armgard (Queen of the Netherlands), b. 31 January 1938, Baarn, The Netherlands. m. Claus George Willem Otto Frederik Geert von Amsberg, March 1966, deceased 2002, 3 sons. Education: Leiden State University. Invested as Queen of the Netherlands, 30 April 1980-. Honour: Hon K.G. Address: c/o Government Information Service, Press & Publicity Department, Binnenhof 19, 2513 AA The Hague, The Netherlands.

BEATTIE Ann, b. 8 September 1947, Washington, District of Columbia, USA. Writer; Poet. m. Lincoln Perry. Education: BA, American University, Washington, DC, 1969; MA, University of Connecticut, 1970. Appointments: Visiting Assistant Professor, 1976-77, Visiting Writer, 1980, University of Virginia, Charlottesville; Briggs Copeland Lecturer in English, Harvard University, 1977; Guggenheim Fellow, 1977.

Publications: Secrets and Surprises, 1978; Where You'll Find the Other Stories, 1986; What Was Mine and Other Stories, 1991; With This Ring, 1997; My Life, Starring Dara Falcon, 1998; Park City: New and Selected Stories, 1998; New and Selected Poems, 1999; Perfect Recall, 2001; The Doctor's House, 2002; Follies: New Stories, 2005. Contributions to: Various publications. Memberships: American Academy and Institute of Arts and Letters; PEN; Authors' Guild. Honours: Award in literature, 1980; Hon LHD, American University. Address: c/o Janklow and Nesbit, 598 Madison Avenue, New York, NY 10022, USA.

BEATTY Warren, b. 30 March 1937, Richmond, Virginia, USA. Actor. m. Annette Bening, 1992, 4 children. Education: Stella Adler Theatre School. Creative Works: Film Appearances include: Splendor in the Grass, Roman Spring of Mrs Stone, 1961; All Fall Down, 1962; Lilith, Mickey One, 1965; Promise Her Anything, Kaleidoscope, 1966; Bonnie and Clyde, 1967; The Only Game in Town, 1969; McCabe and Mrs Miller, 1971; Dollars, 1972; The Parallax View, 1974; Shampoo, 1975; The Fortune, 1976; Heaven Can Wait, 1978; Reds, 1981; Ishtar, 1987; Dick Tracy, 1989; Bugsy, 1991; Love Affair, Bulworth, 1998; Town and Country, 2001; Dean Tavoularis: The Magician of Hollywood, 2003; One Bright Shining Moment, 2005. TV Appearances include: Studio One; Playhouse 90; A Salute to Dustin Hoffman, 1999. Theatre Roles include: A Loss of Roses, 1960. Honours include: Academy Award, Best Director, 1981; Commander, Ordre des Arts et des Lettres; Irving Thalberg Special Academy Award, 2000; Fellow, BAFTA, 2002; Honorary Chair, Stella Adler School of Acting, 2004; Kennedy Center Honors, 2004. Cecil B. Demille Award, 2007. Address: CAA, 9830 Wilshire Boulevard, Beverly Hills, CA 90212, USA.

BEAUMONT Mary Rose, b. 6 June 1932, Petersfield, Hampshire, England. Art Historian. m. Lord Beaumont of Whitley, 1 son, 2 daughters. Education: Prior's Field, Godalming, Surrey; Courtauld Institute of Art, University of London, 1975-78. Appointments: Founder, Centre for the Study of Modern Art, ICA, 1972; Lecturer, Modern Art Studies, Christie's Education, 1978-2001; Lecturer in Humanities, City & Guilds School of Art, 1996-. Publications include: Jean Macalpine-Intervals in Light, 1998; Carole Hodgson, London, 1999; George Kyriacou, London, 1999; Contributions include: Jock McFadyen, A Book about a Painter, 2000; New European Artists; an Annual of contemporary European artists introduced by prominent art critics, Amsterdam, 2001. Memberships: AICA, Association Internationale de Critiques d'Art; Arts Club; Chelsea Arts Club; Royal Overseas League. Address: 40 Elms Road, London, SW4 9EX, England.

BEAVEN Freda, b. 30 July 1923, Croydon, Surrey, England. Musician; Singer; Accompanist. m. C H J Beaven, 1945, 1 son. Education: Piano tuition from childhood; Private singing tuition, 1940-, later with Henry Cummings FRAM. Career: LRAM Teacher, 1967; LRAM Performer, 1968; Choral Experience at BBC, 1963-70; Recitals in London, 1968-; Director, The Lindsey Singers, Madrigals, 1970-74; Private Teaching, Singing, Piano and Theory, 1967-; Professional Choralist, London, 1970-74; Voice Tutor and Accompanist, Westwood Centre, Oldham, 1980-88; Singing and Theory Specialist; Voice and Language Tutor, Oldham Further Education College, 1980-88; Currently gives specialist voice training and advanced coaching to singers of the English Song, French Song, Italian and German Lieder repertoires, Southport. Publications: Music Theory Makes Sense, textbook, 1985; Established Roselle Publications, 1985; Contributions to: SINGING, publication of the Association of Teachers of

Singing. Memberships: Royal Society of Musicians; Emeritus Member Association of Teachers of Singing. Address: Southport, Merseyside PR8 2AF, England.

BEBB Prudence, b. 20 March 1939, Catterick, North Yorkshire, England. Writer. Education: BA, 1960, Diploma in Education, 1961, Sheffield University. Appointments: Teacher, Snaith School, 1961-63; History Teacher, Howden School, 1963-90. Publications: The Eleventh Emerald, 1981; The Ridgeway Ruby, 1983; The White Swan, 1984; The Nabob's Nephew, 1985; Life in Regency York, 1992; Butcher, Baker, Candlestick Maker, 1994; Georgian Poppleton, 1994; Life in Regency Harrogate, 1994; Life in Regency Scarborough, 1997; Life in Regency Whitby, 2000; Life in Regency Beverley, 2004; Life in Regency Bridlington, 2006. Contributions to: Impressions, the Journal of the Northern Branch of the Jane Austen Society. Membership: English Centre of International PEN. Address: 12 Bracken Hills, Upper Poppleton, York YO26 6DH, England.

BECK Matthias, b. 27 November 1956, Hannover, Germany. Assistant Professor of Medical Ethics and Interdisciplinary Research. Education: Mag. Pharm. University of Münster, Germany, 1982; MD, University of Munich, Germany, 1988; BA, Philosophy, Jesuit University of Philosophy, Munich, 1989; Dr. theol., University of Freiburg, Germany. Appointments: Current position: Assistant Professor of Medical Ethics and Interdisciplinary Research, University of Vienna, Austria; Scientific Research Projects: Medical College, Srinagar, India, 1985; Aims of Medicine, 1999-2000, Psychooncology: psychological, philosophical and theological aspects of cancer, 2000-2001, University of Vienna, Institute of Ethics and Law in Medicine; Lectures, 2000-: Anthropological background of psychosomatic medicine. "Soul" in psychology, philosophy and theology/body-mind-problem; Psychooncology: anthropological and ethical perspectives; Ethical questions concerning in-vitro-fertilisation, cloning (research and reproductive cloning), embryonic and adult stem cells; Euthanasia, brain-death-definition, organ transplantation; PGD, patentability of genes; gene-diagnosis and gene-therapy; Interpretation of sickness viewing aspects of science, psychosomatics, philosophy and theology; Medical ethics in different religions. Publications: Books: Hippokrates am Scheideweg. Medizin zwischen naturwissenschaftlichem Materialismus und ethischer Verantwortung, 2001; Seele und Krankheit. Psychosomatische Medizin und Theologische Anthropologie, 3rd edition, 2003; Der Krebs und die Seele. Gen-Geist-Gehirn-Gott, 2004; Many articles about preimplantation-genetic-diagnosis (PGD), pre-natal-diagnosis (PND), embryonic/adult stem cell research, euthanasia, body-mind-problem, interpretation of sickness viewing aspects of science, psychosomatics, philosophy and theology. Honours: Man of the Year 2005, American Biographical Institute; Man of Achievement, ABI, 2005; Order of International Ambassadors; Outstanding Professional Award, ABI; Listed in Who's Who publications and biographical dictionaries. Memberships: European Academy of Sciences and Arts; Academy of Ethics in Medicine, Göttingen, Germany; Life Fellowship, International Biographical Association, Cambridge, England; Member, ABI's Research Board of Advisors, USA; Scientific Advisory Board, Austria GenAu-Program. Address: Institute of Ethics and Law in Medicine, University of Vienna, Spitalgasse 2-4/Hof2.8, A-1090 Vienna, Austria. E-mail: matthias.beck@univie.ac.at

BECKER Boris, b. 22 November 1967, Leimen, Germany. Tennis Player. m. Barbara Feltus, divorced, 2001, 2 sons, 1 daughter by Angela Ermakova. Appointments: Started playing tennis at Blau-Weiss Club, Leimen; Won W German Junior Championship, 1983; Runner-up, US Junior Championship; Coached by Ion Tiriac, 1984-; Quarter Finalist, Australia Championship; Winner, Young Masters Tournament, Birmingham, England, 1985; Grand Prix Tournament, Queen's, 1985; Won Men's Singles Championship, Wimbledon, 1985, 1986, 1989, Finalist, 1988, 1990, 1991, 1995; Finalist, Benson & Hedges Championship, Wembley, London, 1985; Masters Champion, 1988, Finalist, 1989; US Open Champion, 1989; Semi Finalist, French Open, 1989; Winner, Davis Cup, 1989, Australian Open Championship, 1991, 1996, IBM/ATP Tour Championship, 1992, 1995, Grand Slam Cup, 1996. Publications: The Player (autobiography), 2004. Honours: Sportsman of the Year, 1985; Hon Citizen of Leimen, 1986; Named World Champion, 1991; 64 titles (49 singles). Memberships: Board member, Bayern Munich Football Club, 2001-; Chair, Laureus Sport for Good Foundation, 2002-.

BECKETT Kenneth Albert, b. 12 January 1929, Brighton, Sussex, England. Horticulturist; Technical Advisor; Editor. m. Gillian Tuck, 1 August 1973, 1 son. Education: Diploma, The Royal Horticultural Society. Appointments: Technical Editor, Gardener's Chronicle, Reader's Digest; Retired. Publications: The Love of Trees, 1975; Illustrated Dictionary of Botany, 1977; Concise Encyclopaedia of Garden Plants, 1978; Amateur Greenhouse Gardening, 1979; Growing Under Glass, 1981; Complete Book of Evergreens, 1981; Growing Hardy Perennials, 1981; Climbing Plants, 1983; The Garden Library, 4 volumes: Flowering House Plants, Annuals and Biennials, Roses, Herbs, 1984; The RHS Encyclopaedia of House Plants, 1987; Evergreens, 1990; Alpine Garden Society Encyclopaedia of Alpines, 2 volumes, 1993-94. Contributions to: The Garden; The Plantsman. Honours: Veitch Memorial Medal, Royal Horticultural Society, 1987; Lyttel Trophy, 1995 and Clarence Elliott Memorial Award, 1995, Alpine Garden Society. Memberships: The Royal Horticultural Society; The Wild Plant Conservation Charity; Botanical Society of the British Isles; The Plantsman; International Dendrology Society; Alpine Garden Society. Address: Bramley Cottage, Docking Road, Stanhoe, King's Lynn, Norfolk PE31 8QF, England.

BECKETT Lucy, b. 10 August 1942, Windsor, England. Writer; Teacher. m. John Warrack, 2 sons, 2 daughters. Education: Cranborne Chase School, 1955-59; MA, New Hall, Cambridge, University, 1960-63. Appointments: Teacher, Head of English, Head of VI Form, Monastic Tutor, Ampleforth Abbey and College, 1980-2001. Publications: Books: Wallace Stevens, 1974; Richard Wagner: Parsifal, 1981; York Minster, 1981; The Returning Wave, 1996; Rievaulx, Fountains, Byland and Jervaulx, 1998; The Time Before You Die, 1999; In the Light of Christ: Writings in the Western Tradition, 2006; Many articles, book reviews, etc. Address: Beck House, Rievaulx, York YO62 5LB, England. E-mail: lucy@aelred.demon.co.uk

BECKETT Margaret Mary, b. 15 January 1943, Ashton-under-Lyne, Lancashire, England. Politician. m. Leo Beckett, 2 step-sons. Education: Manchester College of Science and Technology, John Dalton Polytechnic. Appointments: Engineering Apprentice, Association of Electrical Industries, Manchester; Experimental Officer, University of Manchester; Researcher, Labour Party Headquarters; Special Adviser at ODA February-October 1974; Parliamentary Private Secretary, Minister for Overseas Development, 1974-75; Assistant Government Whip, 1975-76; Minister, Department of Education, 1976-79; Labour MP Lincoln, 1974-79; Sponsored by TGWU, 1977-; Principal Researcher, Granada

TV, 1979-83; Labour Party National Executive Committee, 1980-97; MP, Derby South, 1983-; Opposition Spokesperson, Social Security, 1984-89; Shadow Chief Secretary, 1989-92; Shadow Leader of the House, Campaigns Coordinator, Deputy Leader of the Opposition, 1992-94; Appointed to Privy Council, 1993; Leader of the Opposition, 1994; Shadow Secretary of State for Health, 1994-95; Shadow President, 1995-97, President, 1997-98, Board of Trade, President of Privy Council, Leader, House of Commons, 1998-2001; Secretary of State, Department of Environment, Food and Rural Affairs, 2001-06; Secretary of State for Foreign and Commonwealth Affairs, 2006-. Publications: The Need for Consumer Protection, 1972; The National Enterprise Board; The Nationalisation of Shipbuilding, Shiprepair and Marine Engineering; Relevant Sections of Labour's Programme, 1972, 1973; Renewing the NHS, 1995; Vision for Growth - A New Industrial Strategy for Britain, 1996. Memberships: Transport and General Workers' Union, Parliamentary Labour Party Group, National Executive Committee, 1988-98; National Union of Journalists; BECTU; Fabian Society; Tribune Group; Socialist Education Committee; Labour Women's Action Committee; Derby Co-op Party; Socialist Environment and Resources Association; Amnesty International; Council of St George's College, Windsor, 1976-1982. Address: House of Commons, London SW1A 0AA, England.

BECKHAM David Robert Joseph, b. 2 May 1975, Leytonstone, London, England. Footballer. m. Victoria Adams, 4 July 1999, 3 sons. Career: Player with Manchester United, trainee, 1991, team debut, 1992, League debut, 1995, 386 appearances, 80 goals, December 2002; 7 caps for England Under 21s, represented England 1996-, Captain, 2000-2006; Player with Real Madrid, 2003-07; Player with Los Angeles Galaxy, American Soccer League, 2007-. Publications: David Beckham: My World, 2001; David Beckham: My Side, 2003. Honours: Bobby Charlton Skills Award, 1987; Manchester United Player of the Year, 1996-97; Young Player of the Year Professional Football Association, 1996-97; Sky Football Personality of the Year, 1997; 5 Premiership Medals; 2 Football Association Medals; European Cup Medal; 2 Charity Shield Winner Medals.

BECKHAM Victoria, (Posh Spice), b. 17 April 1974, Cuffley, England. Vocalist. m. David Beckham, 4 July 1999, 3 sons. Career: Member, Spice Girls; Numerous TV and radio appearances, magazine interviews; Film, Spiceworld: The Movie, 1997; World tour including dates in UK, Europe, India and USA; Solo artist, 2000-. Recordings: Albums: The Spice Girls: Spice, 1996; Spiceworld, 1997; Forever, 2000; Singles: Wannabe, Say You'll Be There, 2 Become 1, 1996; Mama/ Who Do You Think You Are, Step To Me, Spice Up Your Life, Too Much, 1997; Stop, (How Does It Feel To Be) On Top of the World, with England United, Move Over/Generation Next, Viva Forever, Goodbye, 1998; Holler/Let Love Lead the Way, 2000. Solo: Out of Your Mind, 2000; Not Such an Innocent Girl, 2001; A Mind of Its Own, 2002; This Groove/ Let Your Head Go, 2003; Solo albums: Victoria Beckham, 2001; Not Such An Innocent Girl, 2004. Honours: Best Video (Say You'll Be There), Best Single (Wannabe), Brit Awards, 1997; 2 Ivor Novello song writing awards, 1997; Best Band, Smash Hits Award, 1997; 3 American Music Awards, 1998; Special Award for International Sales, Brit Awards, 1998. Publications: Learning to Fly, autobiography, 2001; That Extra Half an Inch: Hair, Heels and Everything In Between, 2006. Address: c/o Lee & Thompson, Green Garden House, 15-22 St Christopher's Place, London, W1M 5HE, England. Website: c3.vmg.co.uk/spicegirls

BECKINSALE Kate, b. 26 July 1973, London, England. Actress. m. Len Wiseman, 2004, 1 daughter with Michael Sheen. Education: French and Russian Literature, New College, Oxford University, 1991-94. Career: TV includes: One Against the Wind, 1991; Cold Comfort Farm, 1995; Emma, 1996; Alice Through the Looking Glass, 1998; Films include: Much Ado About Nothing, 1993; Haunted, 1995; Emma, Shooting Fish, 1997; The Golden Bowl, 2000; Pearl Harbor, Serendipity, 2001; Laurel Canyon, 2002; Underworld, Tiptoes, 2003; Van Helsing, The Aviator, 2004; Underworld: Evolution, Click, 2006; Play: The Seagull, 1995. Address: International Creative Management, Oxford House, 76 Oxford Street, London W1N 0AX, England.

BECKLES WILLSON Robina Elizabeth, b. 26 September 1930, London, England. Writer. m. Anthony Beckles Willson, 1 son, 1 daughter, Education: BA, 1948, MA, 1952, University of Liverpool. Appointments: Teacher, Liverpool School of Art, 1952-56; Ballet Rambert Educational School, London, 1956-58. Publications: Leopards on the Loire, 1961; A Time to Dance, 1962; Musical Instruments, 1964; A Reflection of Rachel, The Leader of the Band, 1967; Roundabout Ride, 1968; Dancing Day, 1971; The Last Harper, The Shell on Your Back, 1972; What a Noise, 1974; The Voice of Music, 1975; Musical Merry-go-Round, 1977; The Beaver Book of Ballet, 1979; Eyes Wide Open, Anna Pavlova: A Legend Among Dancers, 1981; Pocket Book of Ballet, Secret Witch, 1982; Square Bear, Merry Christmas, Holiday Witch, 1983; Sophie and Nicky series, 2 volumes, Hungry Witch, 1984; Music Maker, Sporty Witch, 1986; The Haunting Music, 1987; Mozart's Story, 1991; Just Imagine, 1993; Harry Stories in Animal World, Ambulance!, 1996; Very Best Friend, 1998; The King Who Had Dirty Feet, The Emperor's New Clothes, 2000. Address: 44 Popes Avenue, Twickenham, Middlesex TW2 5TL, England.

BEDDARD Nicholas Elliot, b. 26 April 1934, London, England. Barrister; Circuit Judge. m. Gillian Beddard, 2 sons, 1 daughter. Education: Eton College, 1947-52; Undergraduate, Essex University, 2005-. Appointments: National Service, commissioned in Royal Sussex Regiment, 1952-54; Management Trainee, United Africa Company, 1955-58; Assistant Public Policy Executive, Royal Automobile Club, 1958-68; Barrister, practising on South Eastern Circuit, 1968-86; Recorder, 1986; Circuit Judge, 1986-2003; Deputy Circuit Judge, 2003-2005. Memberships: Lansdowne Club; Aldeburgh Golf Club; Orford Sailing Club; Liveryman of Worshipful Company of Skinners. Address: The Old School, Sudbourne, Suffolk IP12 2BE, England.

BEDDINGTON John Richard, b. 15 September 1942, Haslemere, Surrey, England. Sports Manager. m. Roseann Madden, 11 July 1972, 2 sons. Education: Eton College, 1956-60; Goethe Institute, 1960-61; College of Law, 1962-65. Appointments: Articled Clerk, Birkbeck, Julius, Coburn and Broad, 1962-65; Marketing Department, BP Chemicals (UK) Ltd, 1966-72; European Director, Grand Prix Tennis Circuit, 1972-77; Vice President, International Management Group, 1977-82; Chairman, Chief Executive Officer, Beddington Sports Management Inc, Toronto, Canada, 1982-; Executive Vice President, Tennis Canada, 1983-95; Tournament Director, Chairman, Canadian Open Tennis Championships, Toronto and Montreal, 1979-95; Chairman, Canadian Open Squash Championships, 1985-95; Group Managing Director, Masters International Ltd, 1995-97; Consultant, Tennis Canada, 1995-98; Chairman, Chief Executive Officer, Beddington Sports Management Ltd, 1997-; Consultant, Squash Rackets Association, 1997-99;

Chairman, British Open Squash Championships, 2003-05; Tournament Director, The Masters Tennis at the Royal Albert Hall, 1997-2006; Chairman, Tennis World Cup, 2003-; Save the Children Tennis Tournament Advisory Board, 2007-; Chairman, Toronto Tennis Champions, 2007-. Publications include: Play Better Squash, 1974; Several articles in a wide variety of sports publications. Honours: Several organisation awards for sports events; Inducted into Hall of Fame of Canadian Tennis, 2006; Listed in several Who's Who publications. Memberships: Director, WTA Tour, 1993-98; Duke of Edinburgh Award, Toronto, 1990-95; Professional Squash Association, 1998-2000; Cambridge Club, Toronto; All England Lawn Tennis Club, Wimbledon; Fellow, Royal Geographical Society; Lambton Leisure; Mapledurham Golf & Country Club; The National Club, Toronto. Address: The Old School House, Hook End, Checkendon, Oxon RG8 0UL, England. E-mail: jrbeddington@btinternet.com.

BEDI Rohan, b. 2 February 1967, New Delhi, India. Anti-Money Laundering Specialist. m. Savita. Education: MA, Business Economics, Delhi University; BA (Hons), Economics, St Stephens College, Delhi University; Diploma in Systems Management, NIIT, Delhi. Appointments: Senior Implementation Manager, Standard Chartered Bank, Group AML Program, Singapore; Head of AML Services, PricewaterhouseCoopers, Singapore. Publications: Money Laundering – Controls and Prevention, 2004; Various articles published. Honours: Executive-in-Residence, NUS Business School, 2006-07; Book award, Chairman of PricewaterhouseCoopers, Singapore; Advisory Board Member, ICA, London; Listed in international biographical directories. Address: 42 Wan Tho Avenue, Sennett Estate, Singapore 347584. Website: www.rohanbedi.com

BEERBAUM Frederik, b. 1942, Hilversum, The Netherlands. Artist. m. Mary Byrde, 1995, 1 daughter. Education: Graduate, Gerrit Rietveld Academy, Amsterdam, 1969. Career: Artist living and working in The Netherlands and Portugal; Exhibitions from 1971 include more recently: SBK Leeuwarden, Internal Dialogue 65, improvisations, solo, 1990; Drents Museum, Assen, Goed Bekeken 3, Contemporary Art from Drenthe, 1991; NAM, Dutch Petroleum Company, organised by Arts Council, Drenthe, solo, 1992; 24 Drawings, Arti et Amicitiae, Amsterdam, solo, 1995; At Sea Everything is Possible, Arts Centre Zaanstad, Zaandam, solo, 1996; Arundel Festival, Arundel, West Sussex, England, 1997; Mirror Image, portraits, Arti et Amicitiae, Amsterdam, 1998; Drenthe by the Sea, Veere and Drents Museum, 1999; Millennium Exhibition Arts Centre (SBK), Amsterdam, solo, 2000; Where No Birds Sing, Town Hall, Aljezur, Portugal, solo, 2003; The Hogeschool Utrecht Faculty of Education, solo, 2003; The Observer Observed, the Fortaleza de Sagres, Portugal, 2004, 2005; Landscapes and city scenes of Amsterdam from the 70s and 80s, Jubilee Exhibition, SBK Amsterdam (50 years), Helmond, solo, 2005; "Eros and Thanatos" 733 drawings, slide show, DVD, Arti et Amicitiae, Amsterdam, 2005; Works in collections: Stedelijk Museum for Modern and Contemporary Art, Amsterdam; Amsterdam Council; Arts Council Drenthe; NAM (Dutch Petroleum Company); Ericsson Holland, Enschede, Amsterdam; Slotervaart Hospital, Amsterdam; Insurance Company "Het Groene Land", Lelystad; SBK: Amsterdam, Assen, Leeuwarden, Hilversum, Tilburg, Arnhem, Maastricht, Utrecht; Hogeschool Utrecht. Publications: Works featured in newspapers and magazines; Exhibition catalogues; Book cover, Children, Problems at School and Stress, 1991; Book cover and 24 drawings, Silent Terror, 1995; Book Cover, Stress theoretical aspects of remedial education, 1999; Book cover and 12 paintings commissioned by the Hogeschool Utrecht for a book (In the Teacher's Mind, 2003). Membership: Arti et Amicitiae, 1978-. Address: CP 1366 Azenha, 8670-115 Aljezur, Algarve, Portugal; Kerkstraat 167, 1017 GH Amsterdam, The Netherlands. Website: www.beerbaumart.com

BEERE Susan, b. 26 April 1951, Virginia, USA. Ceramic Tile Artist. m. Hugh L Wilkerson. Education: Palomar Junior College, 1970; Mesa College, 1987. Appointments: Taught children, Del Mar Shores Elementary, 1977-; Private Teacher, 1985-2001. Publications: Many articles in local papers and magazines. Commissions and Creative Works: Numerous commissions including, Nancy Hayward, 1975-2004, Candace Gietzen, 1978-2001; Dr A J Foster, Del Mar Medical Clinic, 1980-83; Richard Reilly, Curator Emeritus of the James S Copley Library, La Jolla, 1991; Del Mar Library, Historic Room, 1984-; When in Rome, 2004; Georgiana G Rodiger, 1986-2004; Shiela Cameron, 1979-99, Ron & Mimi Luker, 1982-2006; Joyce Klein, 1981. Honours: Superior Achievement, Art Competition, 1970; Second Prize, Sculptor, 1971; Competitive Bid Winner, Fine Arts Association, 1979; Award of Merit, San Angelo Museum of Art, 1991; Chosen for cover and in Handmade Tiles by Frank Giorgini, 2nd edition, 1995. Address: PO Box 670, Warner, NH 03278, USA. E-mail: susanbeere@earthlink.net Website: www.susanbeere.com

BEG Muhammad Abdul Jabbar, b. 10 October 1944, Dinajpur, East Bengal, India. Academic Scholar. m. S Nahar, 1 son, 1 daughter. Education: BA, Honours, Islamic History, 1965, MA, 1966, University of Rajshahi, East Pakistan; PhD, Middle Eastern History, Faculty of Oriental Studies, University of Cambridge, 1971. Appointments: Education Officer (temporary), Pakistan High Commission, London, 1971; Language Specialist (temporary), British Museum, 1972; Lecturer, Islamic History, Universiti Kebangsaan, Malaysia, 1974-76; Lecturer, History and Civilisation of Islam, National University of Malaysia, 1977-78; Associate Professor, National University of Malaysia, 1979-85; Associate Professor of History, University Brunei Darussalam, 1986-89; Professor, University of the Third Age, Cambridge, 1999-2005; Associate Professor, Markfield Institute of Higher Education, Leicester, UK, 2001. Publications: Books: Islamic and Western Concepts of Civilisation, 1980, 3rd edition, 1982; Social Mobility in Islamic Civilisation – the classical period, 1981; Fine Arts in Islamic Civilisation (edited), 1981; Arabic Loan-words in Malay: a comparative study, 1983; Historic Cities of Asia (edited), 1986; Brief Lives of the Companions of the Prophet Muhammad, 2003; A Short Encyclopaedia of the Companions of the Prophet Muhammad, 2007; The Image of Islamic Civilization, 2004-06; Articles to learned journals and the Encyclopaedia of Islam. Memberships: The Cambridge Society; Royal Asiatic Society of England and Ireland; Middle East Institute, Washington DC; MESA, USA. Address: 237 Coldhams Lane, Cambridge CB1 3HY, England. E-mail: muhammad_beg@yahoo.com

BEGOVIC Mirsada, b. 22 December 1956, Sarajevo, Bosnia and Herzegovina (naturalised, USA, 2001). Oncologist. Education: MD (summa cum laude), University of Sarajevo, 1979; Licensed Physician, Bosnia and Herzegovina, 1980; Postgraduate in Experimental Medicine, 1979-81; M of Medical Sciences – Immunology, 1985; Certificate of Internal Medicine, Bosnia and Herzegovina, 1986; DSc, 1991. Appointments: Lecturer, School of Nursing, Sarajevo, 1980-81; Resident, Internal Medicine, 1982-83, 1983-86, Attending Internist/Medical Oncologist, 1986-92, Bosnia and Herzegovina; Visiting Research Associate, 1992-98, 2004-05, Research Associate, 1998-2003, Health Science Professional

(Level III), 2003-04, University of Pittsburgh, USA. Publications: Numerous papers and articles in professional medical journals. Honours: Five Silver Medals and Hasan Brkic Gold Medal, special student annual awards, 1975-79, 1979, Four Awards for Best Scientific Paper, 1977, 1978, Award for Best Student, 1979, University of Sarajevo; DAAD Postdoctoral Fellowship, 1981-82; Postdoctoral Scholarship for research training in USA, Republic Research Council of Bosnia and Herzegovina, 1985; Fellowship, International Union of Immunological Societies, 1988; Fogarty International Center Postdoctoral Fellowship, 1989-90; Exchange Scientist, Oncology Research Faculty Development Program Award, 1993-96; Outstanding Citizen/Jefferson Award nomination, 1995; Listed in international biographical dictionaries. Memberships: University of Pittsburgh Cancer Institute; American Society of Clinical Oncology; Heidelberg Alumni International, University of Heidelberg, Germany; National Geographic Society. Address: University of Pittsburgh, Office of Senior Vice Chancellor for Health Sciences, Scaife Hall, Suite 401, 3550 Terrace Street, Pittsburgh, PA 15261-0001, USA. E-mail: begovicm@upmc.edu

BEHREND Louise, b. 3 October 1916, Washington, DC, USA. Violinist; Violin Teacher; Founder-Director of The School for Strings. Education: Violin studies with Louis Persinger, Juilliard Graduate School; Violin studies with Theodor Müller, 2 summers at The Mozarteum, Salzburg; Private violin studies with Herman Rakeman (a pupil of Joachim), Washington, DC. Appointments: Graduate Faculty and Pre-College Faculty, Juilliard, 1943-; Town Hall debut, 1950; Appearances in US as recitalist, soloist with orchestra, and in chamber ensembles; Far Eastern tour, 1965; Conferences with Shinichi Suzuki and observation of his work, Matsumoto, 1965; Director, The School for Strings, 1970-; Violin editor, American Suzuki Journal, 1984-88; Adjunct Professor, New York University, 1996-. Publications: Author, The Suzuki Approach, 1998; Many articles for the Suzuki Journal and The American String Teacher. Honours: ISO, 1989; ASTA, 1994; SAA, 1996; Ysaÿe Medal, Faculty, Henry Street Settlement Music School, 1941-70; NYU, 1967-70; 2nd Betty Allen Award for Contribution to Education in Chamber Music, Chamber Music Society of Lincoln Center, 2003. Address: 155 W 68th St, # 31F, New York City, NY 10023, USA.

BEIGI Bijan, b. 28 May 1958, Iran. Oculo-Plastic Surgeon. m. Donna, 3 sons. Education: Razi High School, Shiraz, 1973; MD, Tehran University, 1980. Appointments: Consultant Ophthalmic, Oculoplastic, Lacrimal & Orbital Surgeon, Norfolk & Norwich Hospital, 1999-; Lead of Ophthalmology, University of East Anglia, 2002-. Publications: 61 publications; 83 presentations; Numerous articles in professional journals. Honours: Maughan Gold Medal, University College, Dublin, 1993; European Oculoplastic Award, European Society of Ophthalmic Plastic, 1993; Barbara Knox Prize, Irish College of Ophthalmology, 1993; High Achievement Award, Iranian College of Ophthalmology, 2004. Memberships: Fellow, Royal College of Ophthalmologists; Fellow, Royal College of Surgeons of Glasgow; European Society of Ophthalmic Plastic & Reconstructive Surgery; American Society of Ophthalmic Plastic & Reconstructive Surgery; British Oculoplastic Surgery Society; The East Anglia Oculoplastic & Lacrimal Group; Institute for Learning and Teaching in Higher Education; and others. E-mail: clinic@ophthalmol.com

BELAFONTE Harry, b. 1 March 1927, New York, USA. Singer. m. (2) Julie Robinson, 1957, 1 son, 3 daughters. Education: Jamaica, 1935-39. Appointments: US Navy, 1943-45; American Negro Theatre; President, Belafonte Enterprises include; Goodwill Ambassador for UNICEF, 1987; Host, Nelson Mandela Birthday Concert, Wembley, 1988. Creative Works: European Tours, 1958, 1976, 1981, 1983, 1988; Broadway appearances: Three For Tonight; Almanac; Belafonte At The Palace; Films: Bright Road; Carmen Jones, 1952; Island in the Sun, 1957; The World, the Flesh and the Devil, 1958; Odds Against Tomorrow, 1959; The Angel Levine, 1969; Grambling's White Tiger, 1981; White Man's Burden; Buck and the Preacher, 1971; Uptown Saturday Night, 1974; White Man's Burden, 1995; Kansas City, 1996; Bobby, 2006: Concerts in USA, Europe, 1989, Canada, 1990, USA and Canada, 1991, North America, Europe and Far East, 1996. Honours include: Golden Acord Award, Bronx Community College, 1989; Mandela Courage Award, 1990; National Medal of the Arts, 1994; New York Arts and Business Council Award, 1997; Distinguished American Award, John F Kennedy Library, Boston, 2002; Several honorary doctorates. Membership: Board Member, New York State Martin Luther King JR Institute for Non-violence, 1989-.

BELEWU Moshood Adewale, b. 1960. Senior Lecturer. m. Education: OND, Agriculture, Lagos State College of Science and Technology, 1979; BSc, Agricultural Science, Marathwada Agricultural University, India, 1983; MSc, 1986, PhD, 1992, Animal Science, University of Ibadan; Certificate in Computer Science, Kwara State Polytechnic, 1994; MBA, University of Ilorin, 1998; NUCVIHEP Certificate, 2004. Appointments: Abstract Clerk, Leventis Stores Ltd, Iddo House, Lagos, 1977; Agriculture Assistant, Lagos State Ministry of Agriculture, 1977-85; Livestock Officer, Nigerian Institute for Oil Palm Research, Benin City, Nigeria, 1983-84; Teacher, Bethel Continuing Education Centre, Ibadan, 1985; Part time Lecturer, Lagos State Polytechnic, 1988-92; Part time Lecturer, Agricultural Open Learning Institute, 1996; Part time Lecturer, Kwara State College of Education, 1997-; Lecturer, 1993-, Sub-Dean, 2002-06, University of Ilorin, Nigeria; Consultant, FGN/EEC Middle Belt Programme, 1995; Part time Lecturer, Kwara State College of Education, 2000-; Part time Lecturer, University of Ilorin, 2000-; Resource Person, Kwara Agricultural Development Programme, 2003. Publications: Numerous articles and papers in professional scientific national and international journals. Honours: Silver Medal, Vyakatesh Seed Corporation, 1983; Late Shri S M Anviker Gold Medal, 1983; Distinction NUCVIHEP Certificate. Memberships: Nigerian Society for Animal Production; Animal Science Association of Nigeria; Nigerian Agricultural Science Teacher Association; Nigerian Institute of Management; Institute of Personnel Management of Nigeria; Nigerian Society for Experimental Biology; American Society of Microbiology, USA; American Association for the Advancement of Science, USA; International Goat Association, USA; Honorary Member, Editorial Board, Bulletin of Pure and Applied Science, India.

BELKIN Boris David, b. 26 January 1948, Sverdlovsk, Russia. Violinist. m. Dominique, 1 son, 1 daughter. Education: Began violin studies aged 6; Central Music School, Moscow; Moscow Conservatory with Yankelevitz and Andrievsky. Career: Public appearances from 1955; Debut in West, 1974 with Zubin Mehta and the Israel Philharmonic; Performances with Berlin Philharmonic, Concertgebouw, IPO, Los Angeles Philharmonic, Philadelphia, Cleveland, Season 1987-88, Pittsburgh, Royal Philharmonic and Tokyo Philharmonic Orchestras. Recordings: Paganini Concerto No 1 with the Israel Philharmonic; Tchaikovsky and Sibelius Concertos with the Philharmonia Orchestra; Prokofiev's Concertos with the Zurich Tonhalle Orchestra; Brahms Concerto with the London Symphony; Glazunov and Shostakovich Concerto No 1 with the Royal Philharmonic; Brahms Sonatas with Dalberto. Honour: Won Soviet National Competition for Violinists, 1972. Address: c/o Terry Harrison Artists Management, The Orchard, Market Street, Charlbury, Oxon OX7 3PJ, England.

BELL (Jared) Drake, b. 27 June 1986, Orange County, California, USA. Actor; Musician. Appointments: Actor in commercials from the age of 5 years; Several small roles in TV and film; Regular appearances on The Amanda Show, 1999-2002; Co-star, Drake & Josh, 2004-06; Films include: Jerry Maguire, 1996; The Jack Bull, 1999; High Fidelity, 2000; Singer, Composer and Musician. Publications: Albums: Telegraphy, 2005; It's On Time, 2006. Website: www.drakebell.com

BELL (John) Robin (Sinclair), b. 28 February 1933, Edinburgh, Scotland. Writer to the Signet. m. Patricia Upton, 4 sons, 1 deceased. Education: BA, Worcester College, Oxford; LLB, Edinburgh University. Appointments: National Service: Commissioned, The Royal Scots (Berlin), 1951-53; Captain, Territorial Army, 1953-63; Solicitor, Coward Chance, London, 1961-62; Solicitor, 1963-94, Partner, 1963, Senior Partner, 1987-94, Tods Murray WS, Edinburgh; Member, Company Law Committee of Council of Bars and Law Societies of European Union, 1976-94; Council Member, 1975-78, Member, Company Law Committee, 1975-91, Law Society of Scotland; Non-Executive Director: Edinburgh Financial Trust plc, 1983-87, Upton and Southern Holdings plc, 1984-93, Citizens Advice Scotland, 1997-99, East of Scotland Water Authority, 1995-2002; Scottish Charities Nominee, 1995-2001. Honour: MBE, 1999; Memberships: New Club, Edinburgh; The Royal Scots Club, Edinburgh. Address: 29 Saxe Coburg Place, Edinburgh EH3 5BP, Scotland.

BELL Martin, b. 31 August 1938. Broadcaster. m. (1) Nelly Gourdon, 1971, 2 daughters, (2) Rebecca Sobel, 1983, (3) Fiona Goddard, 1998. Education: King's College, Cambridge. Appointments: Joined BBC, 1962; News Assistant, Norwich, 1962-64; General Reporter, London and Overseas, 1964-76; Diplomatic Correspondent, 1976-77; Chief, North American Correspondent, 1977-89; Berlin Correspondent, BBC TV News, 1989-93; Vienna Correspondent, 1993-94; Foreign Affairs Correspondent, 1994-96; Special Correspondent, Nine O'Clock News, 1997; Reported in over 70 countries, covered wars in Vietnam, Middle East, 1967, 1973, Angola, Rhodesia, Biafra, El Salvadore, Gulf, 1991, Nicaragua, Croatia, Bosnia, Independent Member of Parliament for Tatton, 1997-2001; Humanitarian Ambassador for UNICEF, 2001-. Publication: In Harms Way, 1995; An Accidental MP, 2000; Through Gates of Fire, 2003. Honours include: Order of the British Empire, 1992; Royal TV Society Reporter of the Year, 1995; Institute of Public Relations President's Medal, 1996; Several honorary degrees. Address: 71 Denman Drive, London W11 6RA, England.

BELL BURNELL (Susan) Jocelyn, b. 15 July 1943, Belfast, Northern Ireland. Astrophysicist m. Martin Burnell, (dissolved), 1 son. Education: BSc, University of Glasgow, 1965; PhD, Cambridge University, 1968. Appointments: Worked with Gamma-Ray Astronomy, University of Southampton, 1968; X-Ray Astronomy, Mullard Space Science Laboratory, 1974-82; Senior Research Fellow, Royal Observatory, Edinburgh, Scotland, 1982; Head, James Clerk Maxwell Telescope Section; Professor of Physics, Open University, Milton Keynes, England, 1991-99; Visiting Professor for Distinguished Teaching, Princeton University, 1999-2000; Dean of Science, University of Bath, 2001-; President, Royal Astronomical Society, 2002-04; Visiting

Professor, University of Oxford, 2004-; Discovered first four pulsating radio stars (pulsars); Research contributions in the field of X-ray and gamma-ray astronomy; Frequent radio and TV broadcaster on science, on being a woman in science and on science and religion. Publications: 2 books; About 70 scientific papers and 35 Quaker publications. Honours: 14 honorary doctorates; Joseph Black Medal and Cowie Book Prize, Glasgow University, 1962; Michelson Medal, Franklin Institute, USA, 1973; J Robert Oppenheimer Memorial Prize, Center for Theoretical Studies, Florida, 1978; Beatrice M Tinsley Prize, American Astronomical Society, 1987; Herschel Medal, Royal Astronomical Society, 1989; Honorary Fellow, New Hall, Cambridge, 1996; CBE, 1999; Magellanic Premium, American Philosophical Society, 2000; Joseph Priestly Award, Dickinson College, Pennsylvania, 2002; Robinson Medal, Armagh Observatory, 2004. Memberships: FRAS, 1969; International Astronomical Union, 1979; FInstP, 1992; American Astronomical Society, 1992; FRSA, 1999; President, Royal Astronomical Society, 2002-04; Fellow, Royal Society of Edinburgh, 2004. Address: University of Oxford, Astrophysics, Denys Wilkinson Building, Keble Road, Oxford OX1 3RH, England. E-mail: jocelyn@astro.ox.ac.uk

BELLAMY David James, b. 18 January 1933, England. Botanist; Writer. m. Rosemary Froy, 1959, 2 sons, 3 daughters. Education: Chelsea College of Science and Technology; PhD, Bedford College, London University. Appointments: Lecturer, Botany, 1960-68, Senior Lecturer, Botany, 1968-82, Honorary Professor, Adult Education, 1982-, University of Durham; Television and radio presenter, scriptwriter of series including: Bellamy's New World, 1983; Seaside Safari, 1985; The End of the Rainbow Show, 1986; Bellamy on Top of the World, 1987; Turning the Tide, 1987; Bellamy's Bulge, 1987-88; Bellamy's Birds Eye View, 1988; Moa's Ark, 1989-90; Special Professor of Botany, University of Nottingham, 1987-; Visiting Professor, Natural Heritage Studies, Massey University, New Zealand, 1989-91; Director, Botanical Enterprises, David Bellamy Associates, National Heritage Conservation Fund, New Zealand, Conservation Foundation, London. Publications: The Great Seasons, 1981; Discovering the Countryside with David Bellamy, 4 volumes, 1982-83; The Mouse Book, 1983; The Queen's Hidden Garden, 1984; Bellamy's Ireland, 1986; Bellamy's Changing World, 4 volumes, 1988; England's Last Wilderness, 1989; How Green are You?, 1991; Tomorrow's Earth, 1991; World Medicine, 1992; Poo, You and the Poteroo's Loo, 1997; Bellamy's Changing Countryside, 1998; The Glorious Trees of Great Britain, 2002; Jolly Green Giant, autobiography, 2002; The Bellamy Herbal, 2003; Various books connected with television series. Honours: Officer of the Order of the British Empire; Dutch Order of the Golden Ark; UNEP Global 500 Award; Duke of Edinburgh's Award for Underwater Research; British Academy of Film and Television Arts; BSAC Diver of the Year; Richard Dimbleby Award; Chartered Institute of Water and Environmental Management, fellow. Memberships: Fellow, Linnaean Society; Founder-Director, Conservation Foundation; President, WATCH, 1982-83; President, Youth Hostels Association, 1983; President, Population Concern; President, National Association of Environmental Education. Address: Mill House, Bedburn, Bishop Auckland, County Durham DL13 3NW, England.

BELYAEVA Elena A, b. 31 January 1961, St Petersburg, Russia. Scientist. m. Alexander V Dubinin, 1 daughter. Education: MS, Biophysics, St Petersburg Polytechnic University, 1985; PhD, Biochemistry, Sechenov Institute, Russian Academy of Sciences, 1989. Appointments: Junior Scientific Researcher, Sechenov Institute of Evolutionary

Physiology and Biochemistry, Russian Academy of Sciences, St Petersburg, 1990-97; Scientific Researcher, 1997-2003; Senior Scientific Researcher, 2004-. Publications: 18 articles published in professional scientific journals. Honours: International Scientist of the Year, 2005; The Archimedes Award, IBC, 2006; Woman of the Year, American Biographical Institute, 2006. Memberships: Federation of European Biochemical Societies. Address: Nepokorennych pr 10/1-185, St Petersburg, 195220, Russia. E-mail: Belyaeva@iephb.ru

BELYAVSKIY Evgeniy Danilovich, b. 26 August 1940, Taganrog, USSR. Radio Physicist. m. Lyudmila, 2 sons. Education: Engineering Degree, USSR, 1964; PhD, Radiophysics, Saratov University, 1970; D of Physics, Maths Science, USSR, 1987. Appointments: Worker, Mechanical Plant, Poltava, USSR, 1957-59; Engineer, Orion Research Institute, Kiev, 1965-70; Researcher, 1970-71; Senior Researcher, 1971-89; Head of Laboratory, 1989-96; Professor, Physics, Kiev Politechnical Institute, Ukraine, 1996-. Publications: 107 articles to professional journals. Address: kv 212, Prospect Majokovskogo 79, 02232 Kiev, Ukraine.

BEN SAID Said, b. 11 July 1966, Tunis, Tunisia. Film Producer. m. Khadija Zeggai, 1 son, 2 daughters. Education: Ecole Saint Geneviève, Versailles, 1984-87; Ecole Supérieure des travaux publics, Paris, 1987-90. Appointments: Director of Acquisitions, M6 Metropole Television, 1995-96; Director of Acquisitions and Sales, Polygram France, 1996-99; Film Producer, UGC, 1999-; Founder and President, SBS Films; President, UGC International. Publications: Most important films: Loin, 2001; Tais-toi, 2002; The Witnesses, 2007; The Killer, 2008; Inju, 2008. Honours: Nomination for The Witnesses, Berlin Film Festival, 2007. Address: 46, Rue Madame, 75006 Paris, France.

BENAUD Richard, b. 6 October 1930. Cricketer. m. Daphne Elizabeth Surfleet, 1967, 2 sons. Appointments: Right-Hand Middle-Order Batsman and Right-Arm Leg-Break & Googly Bowler, Played for New South Wales, 1948-49 to 1963-64 (Captain, 1958-59, 1963); Played in 63 Tests for Australia, 1951-52 to 1963-64 as Captain, 28 as Captain, scoring 2,201 runs, including 3 hundreds, taking 248 wickets; First to score 2,000 runs and take 200 wickets in tests; Scored 11,719 runs and took 945 wickets in 1st Class Cricket; Toured England, 1953, 1956, 1961; International Sports Consultant; TV Commentator, BBC, 1960-99, Channel Nine, 1977-, Channel 4, 1999-2005. Publications: Way of Cricket, 1960; Tale of Two Tests, 1962; Spin Me A Spinner, 1963; The New Champions, 1965; Willow Patterns, 1972; Benaud on Reflection, 1984; The Appeal of Cricket, 1995; Anything But...An Autobiography, 1998. Honours: OBE; Wisden Cricketer of the Year, 1962; Inducted in the Australian Cricket Hall of Fame, 2007. Address: 19/178 Beach Street, Coogee, New South Wales 2034, Australia.

BENDON Christopher Graham (Chris), b. 27 March 1950, Leeds, Yorkshire, England. Freelance Writer; Critic. m. Sue Moules, 30 August 1979, 1 daughter. Education: BA, English, St David's University College, Lampeter, 1980. Appointments: Editor, Spectrum Magazine, 1983-88. Publications: Books: In Praise of Low Music, 1981; Software, 1984; Matter, 1986; Cork Memory, 1987; Ridings Writings - Scottish Gothic, 1990; Constructions, 1991; Perspective Lessons, Virtual Lines..., 1992; Jewry, 1995; Crossover, 1996; Novella, 1997. Chapbooks: Testaments, 1983; Quanta, 1984; Aetat 23, 1985; The Posthumous Poem, 1988; A Dyfed Quartet, 1992. Contributions to: Anthologies, magazines and journals. Honours: Hugh MacDiarmid Memorial Trophy, 1st

Prize, Scottish Open Poetry Competition, 1988; £1000 Prize, Guardian/WWF Poetry Competition, 1989; several awards, Royal Literary Fund. Membership: The Welsh Academy. Address: 14 Maesyderi, Lampeter, Ceredigion SA48 7EP, Wales.

BENEDICT Stewart Hurd, b. 27 December 1924, Mineola, New York, USA. Writer; Editor. Education: AB, summa cum laude, Drew University, 1944; MA, The Johns Hopkins University, 1945; Study at New York University, 1946-49, 1961-64. Appointments: Instructor in German New York University, 1946-49; Assistant Professor, Humanities, Michigan Technical University, 1951-54, 1955-61; Assistant Professor of English, New Jersey City University, 1961-64; Adjunct Professor of English: City College of New York, Rutgers University, Hudson County Community College, Essex County Community College, 1964-95; Drama Reviewer: Jersey Journal, 1964-71; Michael's Thing, 1990-2000, Stage Press Weekly, 2002-03; Book Reviewer for Publishers Weekly, 1970-98. Publications: Books include: Tales of Terror and Suspense, 1963; The Teacher's Guide to ..., several books in a series, 1966-73; The Literary Guide to the United States, 1981; Street Beat, 1982; Curtain Going Up, 2002 Numerous plays, 1967-2003, include most recently: The Robbery, Absolutely Fabulous Fairy Tales, Fancy Bread, Be Still My Liver, Yuletide Treasure, 1996; The Hero, 1999; Homicidal Murders, 2002; The Gap, 2003; Humanoids Using Goodness, 2003; Monody, 2004; Wow! 2005; Fox, Cinderella, Part II, 2007; Chapters in books; Periodical articles; Translations; Encyclopaedia articles. Honours: Various prizes, North Jersey Press Association. Memberships: Dramatists Guild; Communications Workers of America; Democratic Party. Address: Apt 4-A, 27 Washington Square N, New York, NY 10011-9165, USA.

BENEDICT XVI, His Holiness Pope, (Joseph Ratzinger), b. 16 April 1927, Bavaria, Germany. Head of the Roman Catholic Church. Education: University of Münich; Traunstein seminary; Ordained Priest, Freising, Southern Germany, 1951. Appointments: Professor of Theology, Freising, 1958, Bonn, 1959-63, Münster, 1963-66, Tübingen, 1966-69, Regensburg, 1969; Co-founder, Communio (theological journal), 1972; Archbishop, Munich-Freising, 1977-82; Created Cardinal of Munich by Pope Paul VI, 1977; Cardinal Bishop of the Episcopal See of Velletri-Segni, 1993; Former Chair, Bavarian Bishops' Conference; Prefect, Sacred Congregation for the Doctrine of the Faith, 1981-2005; Vice-Dean, 1998-2002, Dean, 2002-05, College of Cardinals; Titular Bishop of Ostia, 2002; Presided over funeral of Pope John Paul II, 2005; Elected Pope Benedict XVI, 2005-; President, International Theological Commission; Pontifical Biblical Commission. Honours: Dr hc (Navarra), 1998; Dr hc mult. Memberships: Congregations for the Oriental Churches, for the Divine Worship and the Discipline of the Sacrament, for the Bishops, for the Evangelization of Reapers, for Catholic Education; Member, Pontifical Council for the Promotion of Christian Unity. Address: Apostolic Palace, 00120 Vatican City, Rome, Italy.

BENEDIKTER Roland Anton Josef, b. 7 May 1965, Brunico-Brunek, Italy. Professor. m. Judith Hilber, 1 daughter. Education: Dott Dr Dr phil; Dr rer pol. Appointments: Contract Professor, Cultural Sciences; Former Speaker of the Cultural Minister, Autonomous Province of South Tyrol and Cultural Council of the European Regions; Scientific Staff, IPF Initiative for Practice Oriented Research group Solothurn, Switzerland; Permanent Fellow, Georgetown University, Washington, DC, USA; Visiting Professor, School of Globalism, RMIT

University Melbourne, Australia, 2008-09; Visiting Professor, School of Social Sciences, University of Northampton, England, 2007-09; External Adviser and Examiner, School of Social Sciences and School of Educational Sciences, University of Plymouth, England. Publications: Over 120 papers and articles; Co-author, Report to the Club of Rome, 2003. Honours: Research Fellowship, Damus Foundation, Mannheim, Future European Human Sciences, 2005-07; Dr Otto Siebert Prize for Scientific Publications, University of Innsbruck, 2005; Listed in international biographical dictionaries. E-mail: rbenedikter@unibz.it

BENGTSSON Erling Blöndal, b. 8 March 1932, Copenhagen, Denmark. Classical Cellist; Educator. m. Merete Bloch-Jørgensen, 2 sons. Education: Diploma, Curtis Institute of Music, Philadelphia, 1950. Career: Assistant Teacher of Cello, 1949-50, Teacher of Cello, 1950-53; Professor of Music, Royal Danish Conservatory, Copenhagen, 1953-90; Teacher of Cello, Swedish Radio's Institute of Advanced String Studies, Stockholm, 1958-78; Professor of Music, Staatliche Hochschule für Musik, Cologne, Germany, 1978-82; Professor of Cello, University of Michigan School of Music, Ann Arbor, 1990-2006; Teacher of cello masterclasses at conservatories and universities throughout Europe and the USA, 1953-; Appearances with most of the world's leading orchestras including: Royal Philharmonic, St Petersburg Philharmonic, English Chamber Orchestra, Salzburg's Mozarteum Orchestra, the Hague's Residentie Orchestra under the direction of many leading maestros including Yuri Temirkanov, Mariss Jansons, David Zinmann, Sixten Ehrling, Herbert Blomstedt, Sergiu Commissiona; Duo with the pianist Nina Kavtaradze, 1986-. Recordings: More than 50 albums include: Six Cello Suites of J S Bach, 1985; Zoltán Kodály Solo Sonata, 1998; The Cello and I, DVD, 2006. Honours: Grand Knight Order of Falcon, President of Iceland, 1970; Bronze statue of him erected in front of Reykjavik's University Concert Hall, 1970; Knight 1st Class, Order of Dannebrog, Queen of Denmark, 1972; Chevalier du Violoncello, Indiana University Eva Janzer Memorial Cello Centre, 1993; Award of Distinction, International Cello Festival, Manchester, England, 2001; English Hyam Morrison Gold Medal for Cello; Named Premier Master Cellist 2005, The Detroit Cello Society, USA; Honorary Award, International Federation of the Phonographic Industry, Denmark, 2006. Memberships: Royal Swedish Academy of Music; Board of Directors, Symphonicum Europae, New York, 1997. Address: 1217 Westmoorland, Ypsilanti, MI 48197, USA. E-mail: cellist@erlingbb.com

BENHAM Helen Wheaton, b. 4 December 1941, New York, New York, USA. Professor of Music. m. Samuel S Kim, 1 daughter. Education: Junior year abroad, Mozarteum, Salzburg, Austria, 1960-61; Mus.B, Piano, Oberlin Conservatory of Music, Oberlin, Ohio, 1962; BA, German, Oberlin College, Oberlin, Ohio, 1963; MS, Piano, The Juilliard School, New York City, 1965; Diploma in Teaching, The Diller-Quaile School of Music, New York City, 1966; PhD, Musicology and Theory, The Graduate Program in Music, Rutgers, The State University of New Jersey, 2001. Appointments: Faculty Member, The Diller-Quaile School of Music, 1964-75; Faculty Member, Preparatory School, Mannes College, 1966-82; Faculty Member, Monmouth Conservatory of Music, 1967-; Instructor, 1973-75, Assistant Professor, 1975-81, Associate Professor, 1981-89, Professor, 1989-, Brookdale Community College; Performances as pianist and harpsichordist in the United States, Canada, Europe and the Far East. Publications: Piano for the Adult Beginner, Book I, 1977; Piano for the Adult Beginner, Book II, 1977; The Life and Work of Anthony Louis Scarmolin (Dissertation), 2002. Honours: Phi Kappa Lambda,

Honour Society, Oberlin Conservatory of Music, 1962; Mu Phi Epsilon Professional Music Sorority, 1963; Outstanding Young Women of America Award, 1978; Included in 1989 edition of American Keyboard Artists; Outstanding Colleague Award, Brookdale Community College, 1991; Listed in Who's Who publications and biographical dictionaries. Memberships: Brookdale Community College Faculty Association; National Guild of Piano Teachers; Music Teachers National Association; The Piano Teachers Congress; The American Musicological Society; Trustee, Secretary, A Louis Scarmolin Trust. Address: 960 Elberon Avenue, Elberon, NJ 07740, USA.

BENIGNI Roberto, b. 27 October 1952, Misericordia, Tuscany, Italy. Actor; Director; Writer. Creative Works: Films include: Beliungua ti voglio bene, 1977; Down By Law, Tutto Benigni, 1986; Johnny Stecchino, Night on Earth, 1992; Son of the Pink Panther, 1993; Mostro, Life is Beautiful, 1998; Asterisk & Obelisk, 1999; Pinocchio, 2002; Coffee and Cigarettes, 2003 Tiger and the Snow, 2005. Honours include: Academy Award, Best Actor and Best Foreign Film, 1998; Dr hc (Bologna), 2002; Awarded the degree of Doctor Honoris Causa by the Katholieke Universiteit Leuven, Belgium, 2007.

BENING Annette, b. 29 May 1958, Topeka, USA. Actress. m. (1) Steven White, divorced, (2) Warren Beatty, 1992, 4 children. Creative Works: Stage appearances in works by Ibsen, Chekhov and Shakespeare in San Diego and San Francisco; Other roles in Coastal Disturbances, The Great Outdoors; Films: Valmont; The Grifters; Regarding Henry; Guilty By Suspicion; Bugsy; Love Affair; The American President; Richard III; Blue Vision; Mars Attacks!; Against All Enemies; The Siege; In Dreams; American Beauty; Forever Hollywood; What Planet Are You From?; Open Range, 2003; Being Julia, 2004; Diva, Mrs Harris, 2005; Running with scissors, 2006. Honours: European Achievement in World Cinema Award, 2000; Best Actress Award, National Board of Review, 2005; Best Actress in a Musical or Comedy, Golden Globe Awards, 2005. Address: c/o Kevin Huvane, CAA, 9830 Wilshire Boulevard, Beverly Hills, CA 90212, USA.

BENJAMIN Ellen, b. Boston, Massachusetts, USA. Private and Public Policy Analyst. Education: BA, Social Service Administration and Policy, Park College, Parkville, Missouri, USA, 1976; Graduate Credits, Political Science, Public Administration and Labour Market Analysis, University of New Hampshire; Urban Studies Graduate Level Public Administration and Policy, Portland State University, Portland, Oregon, 1991-93. Appointments: Director of Policy and Advisor to the President of the Council, New England Council Inc; Senior Policy Analyst for the Council of the State Government's Northeastern Committee on Human Service, New York City; Policy Advisor to the President of the New Hampshire State Senate, Director of Research for the entire Senate, Legislative Analyst for the Legislative Committee on Review of Agencies and Programs (Sunset Committee), Research Assistant in the Office of Legislative Services, Concord, New Hampshire; Research Associate for the Small Business Development Program, University of New Hampshire, Durham, New Hampshire; Committee Assistant, Maine Legislative Committee on Health and Institutional Services, Augusta, Maine; Assistant Director, Grant Writer, York County Employment and Training Agency, York County, Maine; Assistant Director of Adult Education, South Berwick, Maine; Sole Assistant to the Director of Planning and Research for all the programs administered by the Missouri Department of Social Services, Jefferson City Missouri; Currently, Public/Private Policy Analyst working in an independent consultant basis, Los Angeles, California. Publications: Human Capital: The Key to New England's Increased Productivity and Competitiveness, CSG Government News and ERC Conference Report Articles; Proceedings on productions of DC Seminar on Health Care Cost Containment in 1985, NYC, and 1986 Annual AIDS Sessions; The Benjamin Report, in publication. Honours most recently include: International Professional of the Year, 2005; Lifetime of Achievement One Hundred, 2005; Legion of Honour, United Cultural Convention, 2005; The World Medal of Freedom, 2005; American Hall of Fame, 2006; Woman of the Year, 2006; Secretary-General, United Cultural Convention, 2004-07; Lifetime Ambassador-General, United Cultural Convention, 2006; Salute to Greatness Award, 2006; The Excellence Award, 2006; IBC Awards Roster, 2005; Listed in national and international biographical directories. Website: www.benjaminreport.com

BENN Rt Hon Hilary, b. 26 November 1953, Hammersmith, London, England. Secretary of State for Environment, Food and Rural Affairs; Member of Parliament for Leeds Central. m. (1) Rosalind Retey, deceased, (2) Sally Christina Clark, 1982, 3 sons, 1 daughter. Education: Holland Park School; Russian and East European Studies, University of Sussex. Appointments: Research Officer, Head of Policy for Manufacturing Science and Finance, ASTMS; Elected Member, 1979, Council Deputy Leader, 1986-90, and Chair of Education, Ealing Borough Council; Special Advisor for David Blunkett, Secretary of State for Education and Employment, 1997-99; Member of Parliament for Leeds Central, 1999-; Parliamentary Under-Secretary of State for International Development, 2001-02; Minister for Prisons and Probation, Home Office, 2002-03; Secretary of State for International Development, 2003; Member, Privy Council, 2003; Secretary of State for Environment, Food and Rural Affairs, 2007-.

BENNETT Alan, b. 9 May 1934, Leeds, England. Dramatist. Education: BA, Modern History, Oxford, 1957. Career: Junior Lecturer, Modern History, Magdalen College, Oxford, 1960-62; Co-author and Actor, Beyond the Fringe, Edinburgh, 1960, London, 1961, New York, 1962; Fellow, Royal Academy; Author and Actor, On the Margin, TV series, 1966. Plays: Forty Years On, 1968; Getting On, 1971; Habeas Corpus, 1973; The Old Country, 1977; Enjoy, 1980; Kafka's Dick, 1986; Single Spies, 1988; The Wind in the Willows, 1990; The Madness of King George II, 1991, film, 1995; The Lady in the Van, 1999; The History Boys, 2004; Radio: The Last of the Sun, 2004; TV scripts: A Day Out, 1972; Sunset Across the Bay, 1975; A Little Outing, A Visit from Miss Prothero, 1977; Doris and Doreen, The Old Crowd, Me! I'm Afraid of Virginia Woolf, All Day on the Sands, Afternoon Off, One Fine Day, 1978-79; Intensive Care, Our Winnie, A Woman of No Importance, Rolling Home, Marks, Say Something Happened, An Englishman Abroad, 1982; The Insurance Man, 1986; 102 Boulevard Haussmann, A Question of Attribution, 1991; Talking Heads, 1992; Talking Heads 2, 1998; Films: A Private Function, 1984; Prick Up Your Ears, 1987; The Madness of King George, 1994; TV documentaries: Dinner at Noon, 1988; Poetry in Motion, 1990; Portrait or Bust, 1994; The Abbey, 1995; Telling Tales, 1999. Publications: Beyond the Fringe, 1962; Forty Years On, 1969; Getting On, 1972; Habeas Corpus, 1973; The Old Country, 1978; Enjoy, 1980; Office Suite, 1981; Objects of Affection, 1982; The Writer in Disguise, 1985; Two Kafka Plays, 1987; Talking Heads, 1988; Single Spies, 1989; The Lady in the Van, The Wind in the Willows, 1991; The Madness of King George III, 1992, screenplay, 1995; Writing Home, 1994; The Clothes They

Stood Up In, Talking Heads 2, The Complete Talking Heads, 1998; A Box of Alan Bennett, 2000; The Laying on of Hands, 2001; regular contributions to London Review of Books. Screenplays: A Private Function, 1984; Prick Up Your Ears, 1987; The Madness of King George, 1995; The History Boys, 2006. Honours: Honorary Fellow, Exeter College, Oxford; Honorary DLitt, Leeds; Evening Standard Award, 1961, 1969; Hawthornden Prize, 1988; 2 Olivier Awards, 1993; Evening Standard Award, 1996; Lifetime Achievement Award, British Book Awards, 2003; Evening Standard Award for Best Play, 2004; Critics Circle Theatre Award for Best New Play, 2005; Olivier Award for Best New Play, 2005; Olivier Award for outstanding contribution to British theatre, 2005. Address: Peter, Fraser and Dunlop, The Chambers, Chelsea Harbour, London, SW10 0XF, England.

BENNETT Hywel Thomas, b. 8 April 1944, Garnant, South Wales. Actor; Director. m. (1) Cathy McGowan, 1967, divorced 1988, 1 daughter, (2) Sandra Layne Fulford, 1998. Education: Henry Thornton Grammar School, London; Royal Academy of Dramatic Art. Career: Stage debut, Queen's Theatre, 1959; Repertory, Salisbury and Leatherhead, 1965; Stage: A Midsummer Night's Dream, 1967; Henry IV (I & II), 1970; Julius Caesar, 1972; The Birthday Party, 1973; Hamlet, 1974; Night Must Fall, 1974, 1975; Look Back in Anger, 1974; The Seagull, 1974; Otherwise Engaged, 1978; Terra Nova, 1979; The Case of the Oily Levantine, 1980; She Stoops to Conquer, 1984-85; The Three Sisters, 1987; Treasure Island, 1990; Director of several plays including: Rosencrantz and Guildenstern are Dead, 1975; A Man for All Seasons, 1976; I Have Been Here Before, 1976; Otherwise Engaged, 1978; What the Butler Saw, 1980; Fly Away Home (also producer), 1983; Films: The Family Way, 1966; Twisted Nerve, 1968; Virgin Soldiers, 1969; Loot, 1970; Percy, 1971; Alice in Wonderland, 1972; Endless Night, 1972; Murder Elite, War Zone, Frankie and Johnnie, 1985; The Twilight Zone, Checkpoint Chiswick, Age Unknown, Married to Malcolm, 1997; Misery Harbour, 1998; Nasty Neighbours, Vatel, Jesus and Mary, 2000; One for the Road, 2003; Radio: No Telegrams No Thunder; Dialogues on a Broken Sphere; Dracula; Witness for the Prosecution; Night Must Fall; TV: Romeo and Juliet; The Idiot; Unman; Wittering and Zigo; A Month in the Country; Malice Aforethought; Shelley; Tinker, Tailor, Soldier, Spy, 1979; Coming Out; Pennies from Heaven; Artemis '81; The Critic; The Consultant; Absent Friends; Checkpoint Chiswick; The Secret Agent; A Mind to Kill; Casualty; Virtual Murder; The Other Side of Paradise; Trust Me; Frontiers; Karaoke; Harpur and Isles; Hospital; Neverwhere; Dirty Work; Eastenders, 2003; The Second Quest, 2004; The Final Quest, 2004; Many voice overs and radio plays. Honours: Fellow, Welsh College of Music & Drama; Honorary Fellow, University of Wales, Cardiff, 1997. Address: c/o Gavin Barker, 2D Wimpole Street, London W1G 0EB, England.

BENNETT John Makepeace, b. 31 July 1921, Warwick, Queensland, Australia. Retired Computer Scientist. m. Rosalind Mary, 1 son, 3 daughters. Education: Southport CEGS; Universities of Queensland, Sydney, Melbourne and Cambridge. Appointments: 4 years RAAF Radar; 6 years Computer Department, Software and Computer Design Groups (Manchester and London), Ferranti Ltd; 31 years University of Sydney; Governor, ICCC, 1980-. Publications: Over 100 reports and papers in professional journals. Honours: IFIP Vice-President 1975-77; IFIP Silver Core Award, 1977; ACS Chips Award, 1981; Fulbright Award, 1981; ANCCAC Medal, 1984; AO (Officer of the Order of Australia), 1983; Fellow, Australian Academy of Technological Sciences and

Engineering; Centenary Medal, 2003. Memberships: Program and Organising Committees of 12 international conferences. Address: PO Box 22, 26 Beatty Street, Balgowlah, NSW 2093, Australia.

BENNETT Roger, b. 9 April 1948, Sheffield, England. Professor of Marketing. Education: BA (1st class honours), Business Studies, Kingston University, 1972; MSc (Econ), University College, London, 1973; PhD, University of Sussex, 1978. Appointments: Lecturer in Economics, Birkbeck College, London, 1975-82; Director, RHA Management Services, 1982-91; Senior Lecturer, 1991-95, Reader, Business Studies, 1995-2001, London Guildhall University; Professor of Marketing, London Metropolitan University, 2002-. Publications: 26 books (translated into 19 foreign languages); over 150 articles published in academic journals. Honours: Several best paper awards at academic conferences and for academic journals. Memberships: Chartered Marketer; MCIM. Address: London Metropolitan University, 84 Moorgate, London EC2M 6SQ, England. E-mail: r.bennett@londonmet.ac.uk

BENNETT Tony (Anthony Dominick Benedetto), b. 3 August 1926, Astoria, USA. Singer; Entertainer, Artist. m. (1) Patricia Beech, 1952, 2 children, (2) Sandra Grant, 1971, 2 daughters, (3) Susan Crow, 2007. Education: American Theatre Wing, New York; University Berkeley, California. Appointment: Owner, Improv Records. Creative Works: Paintings exhibited at Butler Institute of American Art, Youngstown, Ohio, 1994; Records include: The Art of Excellence, 1986; Bennett/Berlin, 1988; Astoria: Portrait of the Artist, 1990; Perfectly Frank, 1992; Steppin Out, 1993; The Essence of Tony Bennett, 1993; MTV Unplugged, 1994; Here's to the Ladies, 1995; The Playground, 1998; Cool, 1999; The Ultimate Tony, 2000; A Wonderful World (with kd lang), 2003. Publication: The Good Life: The Autobiography of Tony Bennett. Honours include: Grammy Awards: Best Traditional Pop Vocal, 1998; Best Traditional Vocal Performance, 1992; Album of the Year, 1994; Best Traditional Pop Vocal Album, 2004.

BENNETT Velma Jean, b. 29 September 1942, Jacksonville, Florida, USA. Teacher. m. Warren C Bennett, 1958, 1 son, 4 daughters. Education: BSc, Education, 1981; MEd, 1983; Graduate Course, Harvard University, 1996; Masters Degree, Educational Administration, Emmanuel College, 2004. Appointments: Kinderclass Teacher, Hamilton Elementary School, Massachusetts Board of Education; Teacher, various Boston public schools, 15 years. Publications: National Library of Poetry, 1994-98; Quill Books, Harlingen, Texas, 1996; Amherst Society, American Poetry Annual, 1996. Memberships: School-Based Management, 1993; Member, Boston Public Schools; Rollins Griffith Teacher Center, 1995-96; New England Regional Conference on Black Studies, 1979. Address: 80 Hyde Park Ave, Apt 1, Jamaica Plain, MA 02130-4132, USA.

BENOR Daniel J, b. 13 July 1941, New York, USA. Wholistic Psychiatric Psychotherapist; Author; Editor. Divorced, 2 daughters. Education: BA, Psychology, 1958-61, Medical School, 1961-63, MD, 1964-66, University of California, Los Angeles; Intern, University of Kansas Medical Centre, 1966-67; Psychiatric Resident, Cincinnati, Ohio and Denver, Colorado, 1967-72. Appointments include: Private practice (individual, marital, family and group therapy), 1973-; Founder, the Doctor-Healer Network UK and North America, 1988-; Psychiatrist, Northwest Human Services of Philadelphia, 1997-98; Psychiatrist, Northwest

Human Services of Bucks County, Pennsylvania, 1998-99; Psychiatrist, AtlantiCare Behavioral Health, Pleasantville and Seashore House, Atlantic City, 1998-; Adjunct Professor, Psychology, Spalding University, Kentucky, 1999; Editor, Publisher, Wholistic Healing Publications: 2001-; Adjunct Faculty, Institute for Transpersonal Psychology, California, 2002-; Professor, Wholistic Studies, Energy Medicine University, California, 2006-. Publications: Numerous papers and articles in professional medical journals, book reviews, lectures, interviews, conferences and workshops. Honours: Founding Diplomate, American Board of Holistic Medicine, 2001; International Health Professional of the Year, IBC, 2007. Memberships: American Holistic Medical Association; UK Scientific and Medical Network; Association for Comprehensive Energy Psychotherapy; Research Council for Complementary Medicine, UK; Council for Healing. Address: PO Box 76, Bellmawr, NJ 08099, USA. E-mail: db@wholistichealingresearch.com

BENSE László, b. 6 July 1941, Budapest, Hungary. Medical Doctor. m. Gyöngyi Temesi, 1 son. Education: MD, Semmelweis Medical University Budapest, 1965; Specialisation of Internal Medicine, Hungary, 1971; MD, Sweden, 1980; Specialisation of Internal Medicine, Sweden, 1981; Specialisation of Pulmonary Medicine, Sweden, 1983; PhD, Pathogenetic Mechanism and Treatment of Spontaneous Pneumothorax, 1987. Appointments: Postgraduate, Medical School, 1970; Department of Country Institute of Medical Experts, 1970; Medical Consultant, Hungarian Airlines, 1973; General Practitioner, Budapest, 1974; Medical Clinician, Södertälje Hospital, Sweden, 1977; Psychiatric Clinic, 1979, Department of Pulmonary Medicine, 1980, Occupational and Environmental Medicine, 1992, Huddinge University Hospital; Founder, Arno Nordic Co Ltd, 2001; Advisor, Gerson Lehrman Group, 2004. Publications: Numerous articles in professional medical journals; 2 patents. Listed in national and international biographical dictionaries. Honours: Leading Scientist of the World, 2005; Leading Educator of the World, 2005. Address: Postängsv 232, 14552 Norsborg, Sweden. E-mail: la.ben@swipnet.se

BENSINGER Lisa, b. 20 July 1964, Owosso, Michigan, USA. Rabbi; Chaplain; Expert in Traumatic Stress; Author; Poet. Education: Bachelor of Science, Indiana Wesleyan University, 1996; Graduate Studies, Columbia Theological Seminary, 1999; Master of Divinity, Christian Theological Seminary, 2000; Para-Rabbinic Fellows Program, Hebrew Union College, 2001; Smicha/Ordination, Rabbinical Seminary International, New York, 2002; Clinical Pastoral Education/Chaplaincy training (six units), 2002-03; PhD candidate, Department of Theological and Religious Studies, University of Wales, Lampeter, 2000-; Indiana University Mini-Medical School; Indiana Law Enforcement Chaplaincy Training. Appointments: Rabbi; Chaplain; Board Certified Expert in Traumatic Stress. Memberships: Diplomate, American Academy of Experts in Traumatic Stress. Address: 1826 North Dixie Highway, Apt #207, Fort Lauderdale, FL 33305, USA. E-mail: rabbilmbb@comcast.net

BENSON Noel Milton, b. 28 April 1930, Manitowoc, Wisconsin, USA. Communications Engineering. m. Kay, 1 son, 6 daughters. Education: Kansas State University; United States Air Force Engineer School Certificate. Appointments: Utility Data Corporation, 27 years, (rising to President and CEO last 10 years); Manager of Engineering, NISC, 1979-92; Retired, 1992; System Automation and Distribution Automation Services under contract with NRECA, Arlington, Virginia, 1992-; President, CEO, DSM

Consultants. Publications: Many articles for the NISC monthly journal. Honours: NRCC Award for Businessman of the Year, 2003, 2004; Gold medals, President's Business Advisory Council. Memberships: Life Member, American Society of Civil Engineers; American Institute of Aeronautics and Astronautics. Address: 6 Primgarden Court, St Peters, MO 63376, USA. E-mail: dsmcon@msn.com

BENTLEY George, b. 19 January 1936, Sheffield, England. Professor of Orthopaedic Surgery. m. Ann Hutchings, 2 sons, 1 daughter. Education: Rotherham Grammar School, 1943-54; MBChB, 1959, ChM, 1972, DSc, 2002, Sheffield University. Appointments: House Surgeon, House Physician and Senior House Officer in Orthopaedics, Sheffield Royal Infirmary, 1959-61; Lecturer in Anatomy, University of Birmingham, 1961-62; Senior House Officer in Surgery, Manchester Royal Infirmary, 1962-63; Rotating Surgical Registrar, Sheffield Royal Infirmary and Children's Hospital, 1963-65; Registrar in Orthopaedics, Orthopaedic Hospital, Oswestry, 1965-67; Senior Registrar in Orthopaedics, Nuffield Orthopaedic Centre, Oxford and Radcliffe Infirmary, Oxford, 1967-69; Instructor in Orthopaedics, University of Pittsburgh, USA, 1969-70; Lecturer, Senior Lecturer, Clinical Reader in Orthopaedics, Nuffield Orthopaedic Centre, University of Oxford, 1971-76; Professor of Orthopaedics and Trauma, University of Liverpool, 1976-82; Professor and Director, Institute of Orthopaedics, University College, London, 1982-2002; Honorary Consultant Orthopaedic Surgeon, Royal National Orthopaedic and Middlesex Hospital, 1982-2002; Emeritus Professor, UCL and Consultant Orthopaedic Surgeon, Royal National Orthopaedic Hospital, 2002-; Robert Jones Lecturer, Royal College of Surgeons of England and Orthopaedic Association, 2007. Publications: Over 300 publications on osteoarthritis, accident surgery, joint replacement, scoliosis, cartilage cell-engineering; 2 text books. Honours: President, British Orthopaedic Research Society, 1985-87, British Orthopaedic Association, 1991-92; Honorary Fellow, Romanian Orthopaedic Association, 1997; Membre d'Honneur, French Orthopaedic Association, 1999; Fellow, Medical Academy of Science, 1999; Honorary Fellow, Royal College of Surgeons of Edinburgh, 1999; Vice President, Royal College of Surgeons of England, 2002-04; Honorary Fellow, Argentinean Orthopaedic Association, 2000; Honorary Member, Royal Society of Medicine, 2004; Honorary Fellow, Czech Orthopaedic Association, 2004; Honorary Fellow, British Orthopaedic Association, 2004; President, EFORT (European Federation of National Associations of Orthopaedics and Traumatology), 2004-06; Visiting Professor at universities and orthopaedic associations in USA, South America, Australasia, Malaysia, Hong Kong, South Africa, India, Singapore, Japan and Scandinavia. Memberships: Royal College of Surgeons of England (Council, 1982-2004) and Edinburgh; British Orthopaedic Association; British Orthopaedic Research Society; SOFCOT – French Orthopaedic Society; SICOT, International Orthopaedic Society; Eastern Orthopaedic and Mid-Western Orthopaedic Associations, USA; Australian Orthopaedic Association; New Zealand Orthopaedic Association; South African Orthopaedic Association; Polish, Czech & Argentinean Orthopaedic Associations; Orthopaedic Research Society of USA; Oxford Medical Society; European Editor-in-Chief, Journal of Arthroplasty, 2001-. Address: 16 Park Street, Woodstock, Oxfordshire OX20 1SP, England. E-mail: profgbentley@aol.com

BENYON William Richard (Sir), b. 17 January 1930, London, England. Landowner. m. Elizabeth Hallifax, 2 sons, 3 daughters. Education: Royal Naval College Dartmouth.

Appointments: Served Royal Navy, 1947-57; Courtaulds Ltd, 1957-64; Landowner, 1964-; MP (Conservative), Buckingham, 1970-83, Milton Keynes, 1983-92; Parliamentary Private Secretary to Paul Channon as Minister for Housing, 1972-74; Opposition Whip, 1974-77; Member of the Executive, 1922 Committee, 1982-89. Honours: JP, Berkshire, 1962-77; DL, 1970; Knight, 1994; Vice-Lord Lieutenant of Berkshire, 1994-2005; High Sheriff of Berkshire, 1995. Memberships: Chairman: Peabody Trust, 1992-98; Chairman, Ernest Cook Trust, 1992-2004; Clubs: Boodle's; Pratt's; Beefsteak. Address: Englefield House, Englefield, Reading, Berkshire RG7 5EN, England. E-mail: benyuon@englefield.co.uk

BENZING Rosemary Anne, b. 18 September 1945, South India. Teacher; Counsellor; Freelance Journalist; Poet. m. Richard Benzing, 5 April 1969, 1 son, 1 daughter. Education: BA, Honours, English and Philosophy, University College of North Wales, Bangor, 1968; Diploma in Education, 1969; Diploma in Counselling, 1990. Appointments: Teacher, Edward Shelley High School, Walsall, 1968-71; Supply Teacher, Shropshire LEA, 1980-; Counsellor, SRCC, 1988-98. Contributions to: Hybrid; Foolscap; Folded Sheets; Smoke; Borderlines; Envoi; First Time; Purple Patch; Shropshire Magazine; Plowman; White Rose; Poetry Nottingham; Symphony; Psycho Poetica; Third Half; Krax; Bare Wires; Housewife Writers' Forum. Honour: Anglo Welsh Poetry Competition, 1986. Membership: Poetry Society. Address: Roden House, Shawbury, Shrewsbury, Shropshire, England.

BERECZ Endre, b. 10 January 1925, Csorna, Hungary. Professor Emeritus. m. Maria Illés, 1 son, 1 daughter. Education: Chemist, 1949; Candidate of Chemical Sciences, CSc, 1954; Dr rer nat, 1960; Doctor of Chemical Science, DSc, 1974; Doctor honoris causa, University of Miskolc, 1995. Appointments: Assistant, First Assistant, Assistant Professor, Eötvös L University, 1949-63; Full Professor, Head of Department of Physical Chemistry, Technical University of Heavy Industries, Miskolc, 1963-92; Dean of the Faculty of Metallurgy, 1965-68; University of Miskolc, 1990-. Publications: 283 science and professional articles; Monographs: 1 Hungarian, 1 English; 8 chapters in monographs; 13 textbooks for university students; 7 patents; 101 reports on research works sponsored by grants and state foundations. Honours: Outstanding Worker of Education, 1968, Metallurgy, 1972; Silver Class Medal of the Order of Labour, 1976; Medals for the Human Environment, 1982, 1989; A Szent-Györgyi Prize, 1995. Memberships: Science and Technology Advisory Committee, 1983-95; Board of Administration, European Federation of Corrosion 1995-2001; National Representative, 1.2 Committee of IUPAC, 1985-97; President, 1992-2004, Honorary President, 2005-, Hungarian Corrosion Association. Address: H-1025 Budapest, Zöldmáli lejtö 5, Hungary.

BEREDER Frédéric Laurent, b. 18 May 1960. Architect. m. Jin Wu, 1 son, 1 daughter. Education: Master in Architecture, France, 1986; Diploma, Tokyo Institute of Technology, Japan, 1991; First Class Architect and Building Engineer, Japan, 1997. Appointments: Director, Duct Sarl, 1986-89; Representative, Dumez Japan, 1991-93; Advisor, SE Corporation, 1993-96; President, Nichifutsu Sekkei KK, 1997-2003; Chairman, BEREDER Co Ltd (was Nichifutsu Sekkei KK), 2003-; Adviser, INGEROSEC, 2003-. Honours: 1st Prize Artificial Reefs, 1989; International Order of Merit, IBC; Listed in several biographical publications. Memberships: Ordre des Architects; College Architectural Expert; International College for Architect Experts; The Japan Institute of Architects; Tokyo Society of Architects and Building Engineers. Address: BEREDER Co Ltd, 2-25 Monmoku Miyabara Naka-ku, Yokohama 231-0804, Japan. Website: www.bereder.co.jp

BERENGER Tom, b. 31 May 1950, Chicago, USA. Actor. M. (1) Barbara Wilson, 1976-84, 2 children, (2) Lisa Williams, 1986-97, 3 children, (3) Patricia Alvaran, 1998, 1 child. Education: University of Missouri. Career: Stage: Regional theatre and off-Broadway including The Rose Tattoo; Electra; A Streetcar Named Desire; End as a Man; Films: Behind the Door, 1975; Sentinel; Looking for Mr Goodbar; In Praise of Older Women; Butch and Sundance: The Early Days; The Dogs of War; The Big Chill; Eddie and the Cruisers; Fear City; Firstborn; Rustler's Rhapsody; Platoon; Someone to Watch Over Me; Shoot to Kill; Betrayed; Last Rites; Major League; Love at Large; The Field; Shattered; Chasers; Sniper, Sliver, 1993; Major League 2, Last of the Dogmen, Gettysburg, 1994; The Substitute, An Occasional Hell, 1996; The Gingerbread Man, 1997; One Man's Hero (also producer), Diplomatic Siege, A Murder of Crows, 1999; Takedown, The Hollywood Sign, Fear of Flying, 2000; Training Day, Watchtower, Eye See You, 2001; Sniper 2, D-Tox, 2002; Sniper 3, 2004; Into the West, 2005; Nightmare & Dreamscapes, 2006; The Christmas Miracle of Jonathon Toomey, 2007. TV: One Life to Live (series); Johnny We Hardly Knew Ye; Flesh and Blood; If Tomorrow Comes; Johnson County War, Junction Boys, 2002; Peacemakers, 2003; Captial City, The Detective, 2004; October Road, 2007. Address: c/o CAA, 9830 Wilshire Boulevard, Beverly Hills, CA 90212, USA.

BEREZOWSKI Brian Mark, b. 17 October 1953, Cape Town, South Africa. Oral and Maxillo-Facial Surgeon. m. Cälilie, 2 sons. Education: BDS, 1975, M.Dent, 1985, University of the Witwatersrand; FFD(SA) (MFOS), College of Medicine of South Africa, 1986; FFD RCSI (Irel), Royal College of Surgeons in Ireland, 1987; Postgraduate Diploma in Dentistry (Forensic Dentistry), University of Stellenbosch, 1996; FDSRCS (Eng), Royal College of Surgeons of England, 1997. Appointments include: Specialist Consultant in Maxillo-Facial and Oral Surgery: University of Stellenbosch, 1986-, Tygerberg Hospital, 1986-, University of Western Cape and University of Cape Town, 1986-, Groote Schur Hospital, 1986-; Private Specialist Practice in Maxillo-Facial Surgery, Wynberg, Cape Town, South Africa, 1987-; Lecturer in Oral and Maxillo-Facial Surgery at undergraduate and post-graduate level at the Universities of Western Cape and Stellenbosch, 1986-; Examiner in Maxillo-Facial and Oral Surgery final qualifying examination in the Faculty of Maxillo-Facial and Oral Surgery of the College of Medicine of South Africa, 1986-; Consultant Maxillo-Facial Surgeon, South African National Defence Force, 2 Military Hospital, Wynberg, South Africa. 1995-. Publications include: Research projects: Comparison of Two Methods of Interior Alveolar Nerve Block (M.Dent Dissertation); Child Abuse in South Africa (DFO Course, Stellenbosch); Papers delivered at national and international meetings: Ankylosis of the Temporomandibular Joint (co-author), 1985; Irradiation and osteoradionecrosis, 1985; Review of Cysts of the Mouth, Head and Neck, 1988; Wisdom Teeth Hazards, 1994; The Le Fort I approach in base of skull surgery, 1996; 8 papers in medical journals. Honours: Life Member, American Association of Military Surgeons; FDSRCS (Eng) awarded Ad Eundem. Memberships include: South African Dental Association; American College of Oral and Maxillo-Facial Surgeons; International Association of Maxillo-Facial and Oral Surgeons, Geneva; General Dental Council of the United Kingdom; British Dental Association;

South African Association of Forensic Odonto-Stomatology. Address: 8 Mount Pleasant Road, Newlands, Cape Town 7700, South Africa.

BERG Adrian, b. 12 March 1929, London, England. Artist; Painter. Education: Gonville and Caius College, Cambridge; Trinity College, Dublin; St Martin's and Chelsea Schools of Art; Royal College of Art. Career: One-man exhibitions in London, Florence, Düsseldorf, Montreal, Toronto, Chicago; Arts Council, Serpentine Gallery; Paintings 1977-86, Piccadilly Gallery; Touring Exhibition, A Sense of Place, Barbican Centre, London, Bath, Plymouth, Gwent, Sheffield, Newcastle upon Tyne, Edinburgh, 1993-94; Royal Academy, 1992-94, watercolours, 1999; Work in Collections: Arts Council; British Museum; European Parliament; Government Picture Collection; Hiroshima City Museum of Contemporary Art; Tate Gallery, Tokyo Metropolitan Art Museum. Honours: Gold Medal, Florence Biennale, 1973; Major Prize, Tolly Cobbold Eastern Arts Association Exhibition, 1981; Third Prize, John Moores Liverpool Exhibition, 1982-83; First National Trust Foundation for Art Award, 1987; First Prize, RWS Open, 2001. Memberships: RA; Honorary Fellow RCA, 1994. Address: c/o Royal Academy of Arts, Burlington House, Piccadilly, London W1J 0BD, England.

BERG Paul, b. 30 June 1926, New York, New York, USA. Molecular Biologist. Education: Graduated, Pennsylvania State University, 1948; Doctorate, Western Reserve University, 1952. Appointments: American Cancer Society Research Fellow, Institute of Cytophysiology, Copenhagen, School of Medicine, Washington University, St Louis, 1952-54; Several positions, Washington University, 1955-74; Assistant Professor, Associate Professor, Microbiology Department, School of Medicine, 1955-59, Professor of Microbiology, 1959-69, Chairman, Microbiology Department, 1969-74; Wilson Professor of Biochemistry, Medical Centre, Stanford University, 1970-94; Director, Beckman Center for Molecular and Genetic Medicine, 1985-2001; Chair, National Advisory Committee, Human Genome Project, 1990-92; Robert W Cahill Professor of Cancer Research, 1994-2000; Director, National Foundation for Biomedical Research, 1994-; Research in genetic engineering, particularly DNA recumbent techniques; Advocated restrictions on genetic engineering research. Publications: Genes and Genomes, 1991; Dealing with Genes: The Language of Heredity, 1992; Exploring Genetic Mechanisms, 1997. Honour: Nobel Prize for Chemistry (with Walter Gilbert and Frederick Sanger), 1980. Address: Stanford University School of Medicine, Beckman Center, B-062, Stanford, CA 94305, USA.

BERGANT Boris, b 19 April 1948, Maribor, Slovenia. Journalist; Television Executive. m. Verena. Education: Studied at University in Ljubljana, Slovenia. Appointments: Journalist; Experience in Broadcasting: Editor, foreign affairs, Editor-in-Chief, news and current affairs, Deputy Director General RTV, Slovenia in charge of international relations and programme co-operation; President, Circom Regional, European Association of Regional Television 1990-92; Member Administrative Council, European Broadcasting Union (EBU), 1990-92, 1996-; Vice Chairman. TV Committee, EBU, EBU Radio Committee, 1993-98; Secretary-General, Circom Regional, 1995-2001; Vice President, European Broadcasting Union, 1998-; Representative of the Republic of Slovenia in different media committees of the Council of Europe. Publications: Several in the field of foreign politics and broadcasting. Honours: Tomšičeva nagrada for the Best Journalistic Achievement in Slovenija; Prizes at the TV Festivals at Monte Carlo, New York, Leipzig. Membership:

President, Slovenian Journalist Association, 1986-90; Member, International Academy of TV Arts & Sciences, New York; Member, World Standardisation Committee for ISAS. Address: RTV Slovenija, Kolodvorska 2, 1550 Ljubljana, Slovenia. E-mail: boris.bergant@rtvslo.si

BERGEN Candice Patricia, b. 9 May 1946, Beverly Hills, USA. Actress; Photojournalist. m. (1) Louis Malle, 1980, deceased, 1995, 1 daughter, (2) Marshall Rose. Education: Westlake School for Girls; University of Pennsylvania. Career: Photojournalist work has appeared in Vogue, Cosmopolitan, Life and Esquire; Films: The Group, The Sand Pebbles, 1966; The Day the Fish Came Out, Vivre Pour Vivre, 1967; The Magus, 1968; Getting Straight, Soldier Blue, The Adventurers, 1970; Carnal Knowledge, The Hunting Party, 1971; T R Baskin, 1972; 11 Harrowhouse, 1974; Bite the Bullet, 1975; The Wind and the Lion, 1976; The Domino Principle, A Night Full of Rain, 1977; Oliver's Story, 1978; Starting Over, 1979; Rich and Famous, 1981; Gandhi, 1982; Stick, 1985; Au Revoir les Enfants (co-director), 1987; Miss Congeniality, 2000; Sweet Home Alabama, 2002; View from the Top, The In-Laws, 2003. TV: Murphy Brown (series), 1989; Mary and Tim, 1996; Footsteps, 2003; Boston Legal (series), 2005; Law & Order: Trial by Jury, 2005. Publications: The Freezer, 1968; Knock Wood (autobiography), 1984. Honours: Best Short Plays, 1968; Emmy Award, 1989, 1990. Address: c/o William Morris Agency, 151 El Camino, Beverly Hills, CA 90212, USA.

BERGER André, b. 30 July 1942, Acoz, Belgium. Professor. m. M A Lallemand, 3 daughters. Education: MS, Meteorology, MIT, 1971; DSc, Catholic University Louvain, Belgium, 1973; Dr Honoris Causa, University Aix-Marseille, France, 1989; Docteur honoris causa de l'Université Paul Sabatier, Toulouse, 2000; Dr honoris causa, Faculté Polytechnique de Mons, 2004. Appointments: Assistant, University Catholic Louvain, 1965-73, Suppléant, 1973-76, Chargé de Cours, 1976-84, Head Institute of Astronomy and Geophysics, 1978-2001, Professor, 1984-89, Ordinary Professor, 1989-; Visiting Professor, Vrij Universiteit, Brussels, 1982-92, maitre de conference, University Liège, Belgium, 1985-93; Chaire Francqui, 1989; Chairman, Panel Special Program on Science of Global Environment Change NATO, 1992-93; Chairman, Special Program Panel in Air-Sea Interactions, 1981; Chairman International Commission Climate, 1987-93; Chairman, Paleoclimate Commission International Quaternary Association, 1987-95; President of European Geophysical Society, 2000-02; Member, Hearings Board European Parliament and Belgium Ministry of Research; Member, Science Council Gaz de France, 1994-99, Member Environment Council Electricité de France, 1998-; Member of the Scientific Committee of European Environment Agency, 2002-; Member, Scientific Council of Meteo-France, 2001-; Vice Chairman, 1998-99, Chairman, 2000-03, Expert Advisory Group on Global Change, Climate and Biodiversity of the European Commission; Member, Scientific Council of Centre National de le Recherche Scientifique, France, 2002-04; Member, Comité d'Orientation Scientifique et Stratégique du Collège de France, 2003-06. Publications: Le Climat de la Terre, un passé pour quel avenir?, 1992; Editor: Climatic Variations and Variability: Facts and Theories, 1981; Co-Editor: Milankovitch and Climate, Understanding the Response to Orbital Forcing, 1984; Understanding Climate Change, 1989; Contributor, research articles on climatic variations and climate modelling to professional journals. Honours: Recipient, Médaille d'Argent de Sa Sainteté, Pope Paul VI, Vatican, 1979; Prix de la première biennale Italian Society Physics, 1980; Prix Charles Lagrange, Classe des

Sciences Academie Royale des Sciences, des Lettres et des Beaux-Arts de Belgique, 1984; Norbert Gerbier-Mumm International Award, World Meteorological Society; Golden Award of European Geophysical Society, 1989; Milutin Milankovitch Medal, 1994; Prix quinquennial du Fonds National de la Recherche Scientifique de Belgique, 1995; European Latsis Prize, 2001; Knighted, 1996; Academia Europaea, 1989, Council Member, 1993-99; Koninklijke Nederlandse Akademie van Wetenschappen, Foreign Member, 1997; Fellow of American Geophysical Union, 1999; Associate Foreign Member, Académie des Sciences, Paris, 2000; Member of the Royal Academy of Sciences, Letters and Arts Belgium, 2002; Associate, The Royal Astronomical Society, 2003; Foreign Member, Serbian Academy of Sciences and Arts, 2006; Foreign Fellow, Royal Society of Canada, 2007. Honorary President of European Geo-Sciences Union; Chevalier de la Légion d'Honneur in France, 2004. Memberships: International Union of Geodesy and Geophysics, Lecturer, 1987; World Institute Science; American Geophysical Union; American Meteorological Society; Royal Meteorological Society, Foreign Member. Address: Catholic University Louvain, Institute Astronomy and Geophysics G Lemaitre, 2 Chemin du Cyclotron, B-1348 Louvain-la-Neuve, Belgium. E-mail: berger@astr.ucl.ac.be

BERGER John, b. 5 November 1926, London, England. Author; Art Critic. Education: Central School of Art; Chelsea School of Art, London. Appointments: Painter, Teacher of Drawing; Visiting Fellow, BFI, 1990-; Numerous TV appearances and exhibitions. Publications include: Fiction: A Painter of Our Time, 1958; The Foot of Clive, 1962; Corker's Freedom, 1964; Pig Earth, 1979; Once in Europa, 1989; Lilac and Flag, 1991; To The Wedding, 1995; Photocopies, 1996; King: A Street Story, 1999; Non-fiction includes: About Looking, 1980; Another Way of Telling, 1982; And Our Faces; My Heart; Brief as Photos, 1984; The White Bird, 1985; Keeping a Rendezvous (essays and poems), 1992; Titian: Nymph and Shepherd, 1996; Steps Towards a Small Theory of the Visible, 1996; The Shape of a Pocket, 2001; John Berger Selected Essays, 2001; Radio: Will It Be A Likeness? 1996; Poetry and translations. Honours include: New York Critics Prize, Best Scenario of Year, 1976; George Orwell Memorial Prize, 1977; Prize, Best Reportage, Union of Journalists and Writers, Paris, 1977. Address: Quincy, Mieussy, 74440 Taninges, France.

BERGER Thomas (Louis), b. 20 July 1924, Cincinnati, Ohio, USA. Author. m. Jeanne Redpath, 12 June 1950. Education: BA, University of Cincinnati, 1948; Postgraduate Studies, Columbia University, 1950-51. Appointments: Librarian, Rand School of Social Science, New York City, 1948-51; Staff, New York Times Index, 1951-52; Associate Editor, Popular Science Monthly, 1952-53; Distinguished Visiting Professor, Southampton College, 1975-76; Visiting Lecturer, Yale University, 1981, 1982; Regent's Lecturer, University of California at Davis, 1982. Publications: Crazy in Berlin, 1958; Reinhart in Love, 1962; Little Big Man, 1964; Killing Time, 1967; Vital Parts, 1970; Regiment of Women, 1973; Sneaky People, 1975; Who is Teddy Villanova?, 1977; Arthur Rex, 1978; Neighbors, 1980; Reinhart's Women, 1981; The Feud, 1983; Nowhere, 1985; Being Invisible, 1987; The Houseguest, 1988; Changing the Past, 1989; Orrie's Story, 1990; Meeting Evil, 1992; Robert Crews, 1994; Suspects, 1996; The Return of Little Big Man, 1999; Best Friends, 2003; Adventures of the Artificial Woman, 2004. Other: Plays and screenplays: Other People, Stockbridge Theatre festival, 1970. Honours: Dial Fellow, 1962; Rosenthal Award, National Institute of Arts and Letters, 1965; Western Heritage Award,

1965; Ohioana Book Award, 1982; Pulitzer Prize Nomination, The Feud, 1984; LittD, Long Island University, 1986; Listed in numerous Who's Who and biographical publications. Address: PO Box 11, Palisades, NY 10964, USA. E-mail: thosberg@earthlink.net

BERGKAMP Dennis, b. 10 May 1969, Amsterdam, Netherlands. Footballer. m. Henrita Ruizendaal, 1 son, 1 daughter. Appointments: Striker, played for Ajax Amsterdam, 1986-92, Holland, 1990-2000, Inter Milan, 1992-95, Arsenal, London, England, 1995-; Premiership Winner, 1998, 2002, 2004; Football Association Cup Winner, 1998, 2002, 2003; Former all-time leading scorer for Holland. Honours: Dutch Player of the Year, 1992, 1993; English Player of the Year, 1998; Football Writers' Player of the Year, 1998. Address: c/o Arsenal F C, Arsenal Stadium, Avenell Road, London N5 1BU, England. Website: www.arsenal.co.uk

BERGSJØ Per Bjarne, b. 17 March 1932, Baerum, Norway. Professor Emeritus. m. Jenny Benjaminsen, 2 sons, 1 daughter. Education: MD, Faculty of Medicine, Oslo University, 1956; Residencies in surgery, obstetrics, gynaecology, gynaecological oncology, pathology and anaesthesiology, 1956-1969; Dr Med, University of Oslo, 1968; Specialist, Obstetrics and Gynaecology, Norway, 1969; ECFMG, 1969. Appointments: Associate Professor, University of Bergen, Norway, 1971-72; Associate Professor, Faculty of Medicine, University of Oslo, 1973-80; Editor, 1979-, Editor-in-Chief, 1989-93, Acta Obstetricia et Gynecologica Scandinavica; Lectured, Johns Hopkins University, 1985; Head of Department, Gynaecology and Obstetrics, Akerhus Central Hospital, Norway, 1973-80; Professor I, Department of Obstetrics and Gynaecology, University of Bergen, Norway, 1980-1999; Consultant, The Norwegian System of Compensation to Patients, -2001. Guest scientist, Norwegian Institute of Public Health, Oslo, Norway, 2003-. Publications: 430 titles or articles in referred scientific journals, review and editorial articles, books and chapters in monographs and textbooks; Textbooks, monographs and special reports include: General plan of obstetrics and gynaecology in Norway, 3 volumes, 1976-78; Svangerskapsomsorg i allmennpraksis, 1985, revised 1991, 1998; Svangerskapsomsorg, 2006; Obstetrikk, 1987, revised 1993, 1998, 2000; Gynekologi, 1990, revised 1997, 2000; Obstetrikk og gynekologi, 2004. Author: Action against AIDS, The Mutan Report, 1996. Honours: The Schering Prize, Norwegian Gynaecological Society, 1992. Memberships include: The Norwegian Medical Association; The Federation of Scandinavian Societies of Obstetrics and Gynaecology; The Norwegian Gynaecological Society; The Norwegian Non-fiction Writers and Translators Association, 1989-; Society of Research Scientists, 1991-; Society of Senior Physicians, 2000-; Fellow, Royal Society of Medicine, UK. Address: Bergheimveien 11 C, N-1367 Snarøya, Norway. E-mail: p-bergsj@online.no. Office: Norwegian Institute of Public Health, Division of Epidemiology, PO BOX 4404 Nydalen, NO – 0403 Oslo, Norway. E-mail: Per.Bergsjo@fhi.no

BERGSTRÖM Lars, b. 17 July 1935, Stockholm, Sweden. Academic. m. Ulla von Heland, 1960, 1 son. Education: Stockholm University. Appointments: Associate Professor, Lecturer in Philosophy, Stockholm University, 1967-74; Professor of Practical Philosophy, Uppsala University, 1974-87; Professor of Practical Philosophy, 1987-2001, Professor Emeritus, 2001-, Stockholm University. Publications: The Alternatives and Consequences of Actions, 1966; Objektivitet, 1972; Grundbok I Värdeteori, 1990; Döden, Livet och Verkligheten, 2004. Memberships: Royal

Swedish Academy of Sciences, 1998-. Address: Department of Philosophy, Stockholm University, 106 91 Stockholm, Sweden.

BERISHA Sali, b. 15 October 1944, Tropoje, Albania. Professor of Medicine; Cardiologist; Prime Minister. m. Liri Rama, 1 son, 1 daughter. Education: Medical Doctor, 1967, Professor of Medicine, 1989, Tirana University Medical School; Graduate studies in Medicine, UNESCO Fellow, Paris, 1978. Appointments: Assistant Professor, Professor of Medicine, Tirana University Medical School, Cardiologist, Tirana General Hospital, 1967-90; Chairman, Democratic Party, 1991-; President, Republic of Albania, 1992-97; Leader, coalition of centre right wing parties, 2001-; Prime Minister of Albania, 2005-. Publications: Numerous works on cardiologist research studies in professional medical and scientific journals; Many articles and speeches published in Albanian and foreign magazines and journals. Memberships: European Medical Research Committee, WHO, Copenhagen, 1986. Address: Blv Dëshmorët e Kombit Nr 1, Council of Ministers, Tirana, Albania.

BERKOFF Steven, b. 3 August 1937, London, England. Writer; Director; Actor. m. (1) Alison Minto, 1970, (2) Shelley Lee, 1976, divorced. Education: Webber-Douglas Academy of Dramatic Art, London, 1958-59; École Jacques Lecoq, Paris, 1965. Appointments: Director of plays and actor in numerous plays, films and TV; Founding Director, London Theatre Group, 1973; Massage, performed at Edinburgh Festival, 1997; Shakespeare's Villains, Theatre Royal, Haymarket, UK and World Tour, 1998, 1999. Plays: In the Penal Colony, 1968; Metamorphosis, 1969; Agamemnon, 1973, 1984; The Fall of the House of Usher, 1974; The Trial, 1976; East, 1978; Hamlet, 1980, 2001; Greek, 1980; Decadence, 1981; West, 1983; Harry's Christmas, 1985; Kvetch and Acapulco, Sink the Belgrano!, 1986; With Massage, 1987; Lunch, Dog, actor, Brighton Beach Scumbags, Dahling You Were Marvellous, 1994; Coriolanus, Mermaid, 1996; Massage, 1997; Shakespeare's Villains, 1998; Messiah, 2000; Films include: Octopussy; First Blood 2; Beverley Hills Cop; Absolute Beginners; War and Remembrance; The Krays; Decadence, 1994; Rancid Aluminium, 2000; Head in the Clouds, Brides, 2004; Forest of the Gods, 2005. Publications: America, 1988; I am Hamlet, A Prisoner in Rio, 1989; The Theatre of Steven Berkoff: Photographic Record, Coriolanus in Deutschland, 1992; Overview, collected essays, 1994; Free Association, autobiography, 1996; Graft: Tales of an Actor, 1998; Shopping in the Santa Monica Mall, Ritual in Blood, Messiah, Oedipus, 2000; The Secret Love Life of Ophelia, 2001; Tough Acts, 2003. Honours: Los Angeles Drama Critics Circle Award, 1983; Comedy of the Year Award, Evening Standard, 1991. Address: c/o Joanna Marston, Rosica Colin Ltd, 1 Clareville Grove Mews, London SW7 5AH, England.

BERKOWITZ Diana Gale, Director. Education: BA (cum laude), Anthropology, Queens College, CUNY, 1972; MA, TESOL, 1976, MEd, Applied Linguistics, 1980, Teachers College, Columbia University; PhD, TESOL, Columbia University, 1986. Appointments: Teacher, ESL, 1973-76; Supervisor, Department of Language, Literature & Communication, Teachers College, Columbia University, 1979; Teacher, ESL, American Language Program, Columbia University, 1980-83; Teacher, TESOL Program, School of Education, Fairleigh Dickinson University, 1981-82; Teacher, English Language Institute & Linguistics Department, Queens College, CUNY, 1982-85; Teacher, Linguistics, TESOL Program, Hunter College, CUNY, 1984; Teacher, ESL, English Department, Hostos Community College,

CUNY, 1985-86; Director, English Language Program, Co-ordinator, MA in Applied Linguistics Program, Teacher, ESL, Hofstra University, 1986-91; Teacher, ESL, English and Communication Departments, Nassau Community College, SUNY, 1991-93; Co-ordinator, Teacher, ESL, Institute of ESL, St John's University, 1994-99; Director, CUNY Language Immersion Program, Queensborough Community College, CUNY, 1999-. Publications: 1 book; 1 book chapter; 6 refereed journal articles and selected papers in conference proceedings. Honours: Award, Women's League for Conservative Judaism. Memberships: Teachers of English to Speakers of Other Languages; New York State TESOL; CUNY ESL Council; American Association of Applied Linguistics; American Association of University Women. Address: CUNY Language Immersion Program, Queensborough Community College, The City University of New York, Bayside NY 11364, USA.

BERLIN Jeffrey B, b. 7 January 1946, Philadelphia, Pennsylvania, USA. Professor Emeritus. m. Anne F Levy, 1 son, 1 daughter. Appointments: Professor Emeritus of Comparative Literature. Publications: Books: An Annotated Arthur Schnitzler Bibliography, 1965-77 with an Essay on the Meaning of the Schnitzler-Renaissance, 1978; The Correspondence of Stefan Zweig with Raoul Auernheimer and with Richard Beer-Hofmann, 1983; Stefan Zweig. Briefwechsel mit Hermann Bahr, Sigmund Freud, Rainer Maria Rilke und Arthur Schnitzler, 1987 (also French (1994 and 2001) and Spanish (2004) translations); Approaches to Teaching Mann's Death in Venice and Other Short Fiction, 1992; Turn-of-the-Century Vienna and its Legacy: Essays in Honor of Donald G Daviau, 1993; Stefan Zweig: Briefe 1897-1942, 1995-2005 (also French (2000-06) and Spanish (in press) translations); Stefan Zweig-Friderike Zweig, Wenn einen Augenblick die Wolken weichen, Briefwechsel 1912-1942, 2006; Numerous articles in books, symposium proceedings and professional journals; 19 book reviews; Interviews and radio presentations. Address: 418 Fox Hollow Drive, Langhorne, PA 19053-2470, USA. E-mail: jbb106@aol.com

BERLUSCONI Silvio, b. 29 September 1936, Milan, Italy. Politician; Businessman. M. (1) Carla Dall'Oglio, 1965, (2) Veronica Lario, 1985. Education: University of Milan. Appointments: Owner, building and property development company, 1962-; Business interests include: Fininvest; Milan 2 Housing project, 1969; Canale 5 Network, 1980-; Owner, Italia 1 TV network, 1983; Owner, Rete 4 TV network, 1984; Stakeholder, La Cinq commercial TV network, 1985; Stakeholder, Chain, Cinema 5; Owner, Estudios Roma, 1986; Owner, Milan AC Football Club, 1986; Owner, La Standa department store, 1988; Chairman, Arnoldo Mondadori Editore SpA, 1990, half-share, 1991; Founder, President, Forza Italia political movement, 1993-; Full time political career, 1994-; Prime Minister of Italy, 1994-95, 2001-06, 2008-; MEP, 1999; Minister of Foreign Affairs, 2002; Stood trial on corruption charges; President, EU Council, 2003. Publications: Album, Meglio 'ne Canzone, 2003. Address: Office of the Prime Minister, Palazzo Chigi Piazza Colonna 370, 00187 Rome, Italy.

BERNE Stanley, b. Port Richmond, Staten Island, New York, USA. Research Professor; Writer. m. Arlene Zekowski, July 1952. Education: BS, Rutgers University, 1947; MA, New York University, 1950; Graduate Fellow, Louisiana State University, Baton Rouge, 1954-59; PhD, Marlborough University, 1990. Appointments: Associate Professor, English, 1960-80, Research Professor, English, 1980-, Eastern New Mexico University, Portales; Host, Co-Producer, TV series,

Future Writing Today, KENW-TV, PBS, 1984-85. Publications: A First Book of the Neo-Narrative, 1954; Cardinals and Saints: On the aims and purposes of the arts in our time, 1958; The Dialogues, 1962; The Multiple Modern Gods and Other Stories, 1969; The New Rubaiyat of Stanley Berne (poetry), 1973; Future Language, 1976; The Great American Empire, 1981; Every Person's Little Book of P-L-U-T-O-N-I-U-M (with Arlene Zekowski), 1992; Alphabet Soup: A Dictionary of Ideas, 1993; To Hell with Optimism, 1996; Dictionary of the Avant-Gardes, 1998; Gravity Drag, 1998; The Living Underground, 1999; Swimming to Significance, 1999; Extremely Urgent Messages, 2000; Empire Sweets - or How I Learned to Live and Love in the Greatest Empire on Earth!; Legal Tender - or It's All About Money!; You and Me - or How to Survive in the Greatest Empire on Earth! Contributions to: Anthologies and other publications. Honours: Literary research awards, Eastern New Mexico University, 1966-76. Memberships: PEN; New England Small Press Association; Rio Grande Writers Association; Santa Fe Writers. Address: Box 4595, Santa Fe, NM 87502, USA.

BERNSTEIN Carl, b. 14 February 1944, Washington, District of Columbia, USA. Journalist; Writer. m. Nora Ephron, 14 April 1976, divorced, 2 sons. Education: University of Maryland, 1961-64. Appointments: Copyboy to Reporter, Washington Star, 1960-65; Reporter, Elizabeth Journal, New Jersey, 1965-66, Washington Post, 1966-76; Washington Bureau Chief, 1979-81, Correspondent, 1981-84, ABC-TV; Correspondent, Contributor, Time magazine, 1990-91; Visiting Professor, New York University, 1992-93; Contributing Editor to Vanity Fair, 1997-; Executive Vice President and Executive Director, Voter.com, -2001. Publications: All the President's Men (with Bob Woodward), 1973; The Final Days (with Bob Woodward), 1976; Loyalties: A Son's Memoir, 1989; His Holiness (with Marco Politi), 1996; A Woman in Charge: The Life of Hillary Rodham Clinton, 2007. Honours: Drew Pearson Prize for Investigative Reporting, 1972; Pulitzer Prize Citation, 1972; Honorary LLD, Boston University, 1975. Address: c/o Janklow and Nesbit Associates, 598 Madison Avenue, New York, NY 10022, USA.

BERRADJA Abedenacer, b. 29 January 1972, Oran, Algeria. Research Scientist. Education: Secondary High School degree, 1990; Civil Engineer, Chemistry, 1997; Master's degree, Materials Science, 2000; PhD, Engineering, 2008. Appointments: Research Assistant, PCPM Lab, Université Catholique de Louvain, 2000-01; Research Assistant, 2002-07, Research Scientist, 2007-08, MTM Lab, Katholieke Universitat of Leuven. Publications: 4 articles in professional journals. Honours: Scholarship, K U Leuven, 2002-07; Special Scholarship, EGID-Paris (Ecole Centrale), 2004. Address: 148 Avenue Champ de Bataille, 7012 Jemappes, Belgium. E-mail: a.berradja@gmail.com

BERRY Chuck (Charles Edward Anderson Berry), b. 18 October 1926, Overland, Missouri, USA. Singer; Composer. m. Thermetta Suggs, 1948, 4 children. Appointments: TV Appearances, 1955-. Creative Works: Albums: After School Sessions, One Dozen Berry's, 1958; New Juke Box Hits, Chuck Berry, More Chuck Berry, On Stage, 1960; You Can Never Tell, Greatest Hits, Two Great Guitars, 1964; Chuck Berry in London, Fresh Berrys, 1965; St Louis to Liverpool, 1966; Golden Hist, At the Fillmore, Medley, 1967; Concerto in B Goods, 1969; Home Again, 1971; The London Sessions, Golden Decade, St Louis to Frisco to Memphis, In Memphis, 1972; Let the Good Times Roll, Golden Decade vol II, 1973, vol V, 1974; Bio, Back in the USA, 1973; I'm a Rocker, Chuck Berry 75, 1975; Motovatin, 1976; Rockit, 1979;

Chess Masters, 1983; The Chess Box, 1989; Missing Berries, Rarities, 1990; On the Blues Side, 1993; Anthology, 2000. Films: Go, Johnny Go, Rock, Rock, Rock, 1956; Jazz on a Summer's Day, 1960; Let the Good Times Roll, 1973; Hail! Hail! Rock 'n' Roll, 1987. Publication: Chuck Berry: The Autobiography, 1987. Honours include: Grammy Award for Life Achievement, 1984. Address: Berry Park, 691 Buckner Road, Wentzville, MO 63385, USA.

BERRY Halle, b. 14 August 1968, Cleveland, Ohio, USA. Actress; Model. m. (1) David Justice, 1993, divorced 1996, 1 daughter, (2) Eric Benet, 2001. Career: Numerous formal beauty contests in 1980s; TV and Film actress, 1989-; Films: Strictly Business, Jungle Fever, The Last Boy Scout, 1991; Boomerang, 1992; Father Hood, Alex Haley's Queen, The Program, 1993; The Flintstones, 1994; Losing Isaiah, 1995; The Rich Man's Wife, Executive Decision, Race the Sun, Girl 6, 1996; B.A.P.S, 1997; Why Do Fools Fall in Love, The Wedding, Bulworth, 1998; Victims of Fashion, Ringside, Introducing Dorothy Dandridge (also producer), 1999; X-Men, 2000; Swordfish, Monster's Ball, 2001; James Bond: Die Another Day, 2002; X-Men 2, Gothika, 2003; Catwoman, 2004; Robots (voice), 2005; X-Men: The Last Stand, 2006; Perfect Stranger, 2007. TV appearances: TV debut in sitcom Living Dolls, 1989; Knots Landing, 1991-92; Their Eyes Were Watching God, 2005. Honours: Harvard Foundation for Intercultural and Race Relations Award; Golden Globe for Best Actress, Screen Actor's Guild Award, 1999; Oscar, Actress in a Leading Role, 2001; Academy Award, 2002; NAACP Award for Best Supporting Actress, 2003. Membership: National Breast Cancer Coalition. Address: c/o William Morris Agency, 151 South El Camino Drive, Beverly Hills, LA 90212, USA.

BERRY Robert James, b. 26 October 1934, Preston, England. University Teacher. m. Caroline, 1 son, 2 daughters. Education: Gonville and Caius College Cambridge; University College London. Appointments: Professor of Genetics, University College London, 1978-2000; President: Linnean Society, 1982-85, British Ecological Society, 1987-89, European Ecological Federation, 1990-92, Mammal Society, 1995-98. Publications: Books: Teach Yourself Genetics, 1965; Adam and the Ape, 1972, 1975; Inheritance and Natural History, 1977; Natural History of Shetland, 1980; Neo-Darwinism, 1982; Free to Be Different, 1984; Natural History of Orkney, 1985; God and Evolution, 1988, 2000; God and the Biologist, 1996; Science, Life and Christian Belief, 1998; Orkney Nature, 2000; God's Stewards, 2002; God's Book of Works, 2003; Editor of 10 books; About 200 papers in scientific and other journals. Honours: UK Templeton Award for long and distinguished advocacy of the Christian faith among scientists, 1996; Marsh Award for Ecology, 2001. Memberships: Natural Environment Research Council, 1981-87; Human Fertilisation and Embryology Authority, 1990-96; Trustee, National Museums and Galleries on Merseyside, 1985-94; Chairman, 1968-87, President, 1993-95, Christians in Science; General Synod of the Church of England, 1970-90; Moderator, Environmental Issues Network of Churches Together in Britain and Ireland, 1989-. Address: Quarfseter, Sackville Close, Sevenoaks, Kent TN13 3QD, England.

BERRY Roger Julian, b. 6 April 1935, New York, USA. Physician. m. (Joseline) Valerie (Joan) Butler. Education: BA, New York University, 1954; BSc, 1957, MD, 1958, Duke University, Durham, North Carolina; DPhil, 1967, MA, Magdalen College, Oxford; MRCP, 1971; FRCP; 1978; FRCR, 1979; Honorary FACR, 1983; MFOM, 1988; FFOM, 1993. Appointments: Head, Radiobiology Laboratory, Churchill Hospital, Oxford, 1969-74; Royal Naval Reserve, 1971-92,

Principal Medical Officer (Reserves), 1987-88, Captain Medical Training (Reserves) on staff of Commander-in-Chief, Naval Home Command, 1988-90; Head, Neutrons and Therapeutic Effects Group, MRC Radiobiology Unit, Harwell, 1974-76; Sir Brian Windeyer Professor of Oncology, Middlesex Hospital School of Medicine (University of London), 1976-87; Director, Health Safety and Environmental Protection, British Nuclear Fuels plc, 1987-92; Director, Westlakes Research Institute, Cumbria, 1992-95; Commissioner, International Commission on Radiological Protection, 1985-89; Chairman, British Committee on Radiation Units and Measurements, 1995-2000; Visiting Professor, Institute of Environmental and Natural Sciences, Lancaster University, 1993-2003; Trustee, Bishop Barrow's Charity and Governor King William's College, 2000-; County Commander, St John Ambulance, 2005-. Publications: Book: Manual on Radiation Dosimetry (with N W Holm), 1970; Contributions to: Oxford Textbook of Medicine; Florey's Textbook of Pathology; Hunter's Diseases of Occupation; Over 190 scientific papers in medical journals. Honours include: Academic: Roentgen Prize, 1970, Silvanus Thompson Memorial Lecturer, 1991, British Institute of Radiology; Douglas Lea Memorial Lecturer, Institute of Physical Sciences in Medicine, 1993; Civil: Freeman of the City of London, 1982; Reserve Decoration, 1986; Honorary Physician to HM The Queen, 1987-90; CStJ. Memberships: President, 1986-87, British Institute of Radiology; Yeoman, 1981, Liveryman, 1984, Worshipful Society of Apothecaries of London; Fellow, Society for Radiological Protection, 1991-; Associate Member, The Nautical Institute, 1998-; Royal Overseas League; Royal Naval Sailing Association. Address: 109 Fairways Drive, Mount Murray, Santon, Douglas, Isle of Man IM4 2JE, United Kingdom. E-mail: r.j.b@advsys.co.uk

BERTA Melissa Rose, b. 29 April 1966, Van Nuys, California, USA. Professor. m. Bradley Braden Berta, 1 son, 1 daughter. Education: Associate in science, Mathematics, College of Canyons, 1989; BSc, Mathematics, California State University, Northridge, 1993; Masters, Mathematics & Statistics, University of Nebraska, Lincoln, 1996; Doctorate, Educational Leadership, Argosy University, 2007. Appointments: Military Police, US Army, 1984-87; MAERC Fellow, Minority Achievers in Science, California State University, Northridge, 1992-94; Teaching Assistant, University of Nebraska, Lincoln, 1994-96; Administrative and Founder, Berta Engineering, 1996-98; Professor of Mathematics, Orange Coast College, 1998-. Honours: MAREC Undergraduate Fellow, CSU Northridge, 1992-93; Minority Achievers in Science, Graduate of the Year, CSU, Northridge, 1992-93; Larson Minority Graduate of the Year, University of Nebraska, Lincoln, 1994-95; Graduate Teaching Assistantship (Fellow), University of Nebraska, Lincoln, 1994-96. Memberships: Faculty Association, California Community College; American Mathematical Association of 2 Year Colleges; American Mathematical Association; Association of California Community College Teacher Education Programs; National Association of Community College Teacher Education Programs. E-mail: mberta@occ.eecd.edu

BERTOLAMI Orfeu, b. 3 January 1959, São Paulo, Brazil. Physicist. m. M C Bento, October 1992, 1 daughter. Education: Graduate, Physics, São Paulo University, 1980; MSc, Inst Fís Teórica, São Paulo, 1983; Advanced Degree, Mathematics, University of Cambridge, England, 1984; PhD, Physics, University of Oxford, England, 1987. Appointments: Post-doctoral Positions: Institut für Theoretische Physik; University of Heidelberg, Germany, 1987-89; Instituto de Física and Mat, Lisbon, Portugal, 1989-91; Associate

Professor, Departmento Física, Instituto Superior Técnico, Lisbon, 1991-; Scientific Associate, Theory Division, CERN, 1993-95; Research Associate, Istituto Nazionale Fisica Nucleare, Turim, 1994-95; Visiting Scholar, Physics Department, New York University, 1999. Publications: Over 165 publications, over 100 of which in specialised international Physics Journals; 2 books. Honours: Honorary Mentions in the Essay Contest, Gravity Research Foundation, USA, 1995, 1997, 2001, 2003, 2007; Third Prize, 1999; Prémio União Latina (Latin America, Portugal), 2001; Prize, UTL/Santander Totta for scientific excellence in biophysics and physics, 2007; Listed in national and international biographical dictionaries. Memberships: Sociedade Portuguesa de Física; Sociedade Portuguesa de Astronomia. Address: Instituto Superior Técnico, Departmento de Física, Av Rovisco Pais, 1, 1049-001, Lisboa, Portugal. E-mail: orfeu@cosmos.ist.utl.pt Website: http://web.ist.utl.pt/orfeu.bertolami/homeorfeu.html

BERTOLINI Giancarlo, b. 9 January 1926, Riva (TN), Italy. Retired Physicist. m. Ester Bonfante, 5 sons. Education: Degree in Physics, Milan University, 1949; PhD, Radioactivity, 1958. Appointments: Assistant Professor, 1950-52, Associate Professor, 1952-58, Physics Institute, Polytechnic School, Milan; Head of Nuclear Chemistry, Laboratory of Ispra Nuclear Research Centre, CNEN – Italy, 1957-61; Head of Nuclear Chemistry, 1961-70, Head of Electronics Division, 1970-88, Head of Advanced Technologies Division, Institute of Remote Sensing Applications, 1989-91, CEE-JRC Ispra Establishment. Publications: Books: Co-editor of and contributor to, Semiconductor Detectors, 1968; Co-author of chapter in, Atomic Inner Shell Processes, 1975; 73 scientific papers as author or co-author include: Spontaneous Fission Rate Measurements by Means of Fast Time-of-Flight Multiplicity Analyser, 1986; Consideration on the Possibility of in Field RS of the Healthy State of Plants via Registration of the Chlorophyll Fluorescence, 1988; Problems related to tine-resolved fluorosensing of an extended aquatic medium, 1988; The Use of a Time-Resolved LIDAR to Study the Water Column, 1991; 7 review papers. Membership: American Physical Society. Address: 13, Via Scirello, 21020 Luvinate, Va, Italy.

BERTOLUCCI Bernardo, b. 16 March 1940, Parma, Italy. Film Director. m. (1) Adriana Asti, (2) Clare Peploe, 1978. Career: Director: La Commare Secca, 1962; Prima della Rivoluzione, 1964; Il Fico Infruttuoso in Vangelo 70, 1968; Partner, 1970; La Strategia del Ragno, 1970; Il Conformista, 1970; Last Tango in Paris, 1972; 1900, 1975; La Luna, 1979; Tragedy of a Ridiculous Man, 1981; The Last Emperor, 1986; The Sheltering Sky, 1989; Little Buddha, 1993; Stealing Beauty, 1995; I Dance Alone, 1996; Besieged, 1998; Ten Minutes Older: The Cello (segment), 2002; The Dreamers, 2003. Publications: In cerca del mistero (poems), 1962; Paradiso e inferno (poems), 1999. Honours: Viareggio Prize, 1962; European Film Award, 1988; Dr hc (Turin), 2000. Address: c/o Jeff Berg, ICM, 8942 Wilshire Boulevard, Beverly Hills, CA 90211, USA.

BESSON Luc, b. 18 March 1959, Paris, France. Film Director. M. (1) Anne Parillaud, (2) Milla Jovovich, 1997-99, (3) Virginia Silla, 2004. 1 daughter. Appointments: Assistant, Films in Hollywood and Paris; 1st Assistant for several advertising films. Creative Works: Films directed and produced: Le Dernier Combat, 1982; Subway, 1984; The Big Blue, 1988; Nikita, 1990; Atlantis, 1991; The Professional, Leon, 1994; The Fifth Element, 1996; The Messenger: the Story of Joan of Arc, 1999; The Dancer, Exit, 2000; Yamakasi, Baiser mortel du dragon, 2001; Le Transporteur, 2002; Taxi

3, Tristan, Cheeky, Vice & Versa, 2003; Crimson Rivers 2: Angels of the Apocalypse, 2004; Arthur and the Invisible, 2006. Address: Leeloo Productions, 53 rue Boissée, 91540 Mennecy, France.

BEST Keith Lander, b. 10 June 1949, Brighton, England. Chief Executive; Barrister. m. Elizabeth Gibson, 2 daughters. Education: BA (Hons) Jurisprudence, MA, Keble College, Oxford. Appointments: Called to the Bar, 1971; Lecturer in Law, Central London Polytechnic, 1973; General common law practice as barrister, 1973-87; Brighton Borough Councillor, 1976-80: Chairman of Lands Committee; Member of Parliament, Anglesey/Ynys Môn, 1979-87; Parliamentary Private Secretary to Secretary of State for Wales, 1981-84; Chairman (voluntary, unpaid), Executive Committee, World Federalist Movement/Institute for Global Policy, 1987-; Director, Prisoners Abroad (national charity), 1989-93; Chairman, Conservative Action for Electoral reforms, 1992-; Chief Executive Immigration Advisory Service (national charity), 1993-; Chairman, Electronic Immigration Network, 1996-2006; Chairman, Electoral Reform Society, 1997-2003; Chairman, Association of Registered Immigration Advisers, 2003-; Trustee, Gaustoun Drug Services, 2006-; Chairman, Electoral Reform International Services; Named on Society Guardian as one of the 100 Most Influential People in Public Services in the UK, September 2003; Served in airborne and commando forces leaving with the rank of Major, Territorial Army, 1967-87. Publications: Write Your Own Will, 1978; The Right Way to Prove a Will, 1981; Various articles in magazines, Wall Street Journal, newspapers; Former Deputy Editor District Council Revue. Honours: Territorial Decoration; Freeman of the City of London. Memberships include: management Committee, Brighton Housing Trust; Chairman, Vauxhall Conservative Association, 1997-98; Amnesty; FRSA. Address: 15 St Stephen's Terrace, London SW8 1DJ, England. E-mail: keith.best@iasuk.org

BEST Ronald O'Neal, b. 25 May 1957, London, England. Artist. Education: Byam Shaw School of Art; Croydon College of Art; RCA, London; Assistant to Winston Branch, painter. Career: Painter and printmaker, oils, etchings, watercolours; Teacher, Essendine Centre, 1989-91, Kensington and Chelsea College, 1994; Litho Teacher, Heatherley School of Fine Art, London, 1997-2001; Co-ordinator, Visual Arts, Portobello Festival; Founder, Chelsea Painters and Printmakers, 1999; Manager, Notting Hill Fine Art Gallery; Co-ordinator, Art for the Unemployed, Portobello Academy of Drawing. Exhibitions: Royal Institute of Oil Painters; New English Art Club; Pastel Society; Society of Graphic Art; Salon des National, Paris; Lynn Stern Young Artists, London; Eva Jekel Gallery; Twentieth Century British Art Fair; Royal College of Art, London; 1492-1992 Un Nouveau Regard sur les Caraibes, Paris; Art House, Amsterdam; Pall Mall Deposit Gallery; Chelsea Printmakers; The Portobello Group; Portobello Printmakers; W11 Gallery; Gallery Café; Portobello Printmakers; Notting Hill Fine Art. Work in collections: Royal College of Art; Croydon College; Grange Museum, London. Address: 50 Berkhamsted Avenue, Wembley, Middlesex, England.

BETHELL John, b. 9 April 1940, Salford, England. Musician; Administrator. Career: Music Librarian, BBC, 1956-90; Isle of Man Arts Council 1966-; General Administrator Erin Arts Centre 1971-; Founder and Director of Mananan International Festival of Music and the Arts, 1974-; Director and Chairman of the Lionel Tertis International Viola Competition and Workshop, 1980-; Conductor and Musical Director of Manx Festival Chorus, 1967-; Conductor and Musical Director of Oldham Choral Society, 1971-98; Conductor Emeritus, 1998-; Musical Director, Manchester University Gilbert and Sullivan Society, 1972-86; Musical Director, Philharmonic Choir of Manchester, 1989-2000; Founder and Director Latour International Festival of Music And The Arts (France), 1993-; Part-time Lecturer, The University of Liverpool, 1997, Vice President Gale Force – Music Theatre Group; Director and Chairman, Barbirolli International Oboe Festival and Competition, 2005-; Chairman, Manx Ballet Company, 2000; Director/Founder, Uzerche International Festival of Music (France), 2007-. Publications: Recordings: With Manx Festival Chorus, Manx Folk Songs, National Songs with Douglas Town Band; Contributions to: Manx Life; Manx Radio. Honours: Catenian Association Gold Medal. Honorary Doctorate of Music, Marquis Guiseppe International University, 1988; Albert Einstein International Academy Foundation Medal; Rotary Club International Ambassador Award, 1999, MBE, 2001. Memberships: Vice President of the Rushen Band; Royal Society of Musicians; Making Music/North West Council. Address: B House, Darrag Port Erin, Isle of Man IM9 6JB, British Isles.

BETTANY Paul, b. 27 May 1971, Harlesdon, London, England. Actor. m. Jennifer Connelly, 2003, 1 son, 1 stepson. Education: Drama Centre. Career: Films: Bent, 1997; The Land Girls, 1998; After the Rain, 1999; The Suicide Club, Kiss Kiss (Bang Bang), Gangster No 1, Dead Babies, 2000; A Knight's Tale, A Beautiful Mind, 2001; The Heart of Me, 2002; Dogville, The Reckoning, Master and Commander: The Far Side of the World, 2003; Euston Road, Wimbledon, 2004; Stories of Lost Souls, 2005; Firewall, The Da Vinci Code, 2006; Inkheart, 2007. TV: Sharpe's Waterloo, 1997; Coming Home, Killer Net, 1998; Every Woman Knows a Secret, 1999; David Copperfield, 2000. Honours: Nominated for Best Actor, London Film Critics Circle Awards, 2000; Best Supporting Actor, Evening Standard Film Award, 2001. Memberships: Academy of Motion Picture Arts and Sciences, 2004.

BEVINS Ann Bolton, b. 11 July 1936, Ashland, Kentucky, USA. Journalist; Historian. m. William B Bevins, 3 sons, 1 daughter. Education: Georgetown College, 1954-57. Appointments: Writer, Lexington Herald-Leader, 1955-80; Editor, Kentucky Heritage, Junior Historical Society, Frankfort, Kentucky, 1963-93; Consulting Architectual Historian, private practice, 1970-; Instructor, Historic Preservation Georgetown College, 1987-88; Columnist, Georgetown News-Graphic, 2003-. Publications: Author, A History of Scott County as told by Selected Buildings, 1981; That Troublesome Parish: St Francis/St Pius Church of White Sulphur, 1985; First Christian Church of Georgetown, Kentucky: The First Christian/Disciples Church, 1981; Editor/Author, Scott County, Kentucky: A History, 1993; Co-author, Images of America: Georgetown and Scott County, 1998; Bound context reports for Scott County Planning Commission: Slaves and Free Blacks in Scott County, Kentucky: 1774-1820; Agriculture in Scott County, Kentucky: 1865-1918; Blacks in Scott County Commerce, 1865-1918. Honours: Citizen of the Year, Scott County Chamber of Commerce, 1974; Citizen of the Year, Georgetown College, 1984; Founding President, Georgetown & Scott County Museum, 1990-95; Board Chair, Cane Ridge Preservation Project, Paris, Kentucky, 1996-2000; Clay Lancaster Award for Heritage Education, 2001, Lucy Graves Advocacy Award, 2006, Blue Grass Trust for Historic Preservation; Doug Cox Distinguished Citizen Award, 2006. Address: 1175 Lexington Road, Georgetown, KY 40324, USA. E-mail: abbevins@bellsouth.net

BEWES Richard Thomas, b. 1 December 1934, Nairobi, Kenya. Anglican Clergyman; Writer. m. Elisabeth Ingrid Jaques, deceased 2006, 2 sons, 1 daughter. Education: Marlborough School, 1948-53; MA, Emmanuel College, Cambridge, 1954-57; Ridley Hall Theological College, Cambridge, 1957-59. Publications include: The Church Reaches Out, 1981; The Church Marches On, When God Surprises, 1986; A New Beginning, The Resurrection, 1989; Speaking in Public - Effectively, 1998; The Lamb Wins, Talking About Prayer, The Bible Truth Treasury, 2000; The Stone That Became a Mountain, Wesley Country, 2001; The Top 100 Questions, Words That Circled the World, 2002; Beginning the Christian Life, 150 Pocket Thoughts, 2004. Contributions to: Decision Magazine. Honours: OBE, 2005. Membership: Guild of British Songwriters. Address: 50 Curzon Road, Ealing, London W5 1NF, England.

BEYONCÉ (Beyoncé Knowles), b. 4 September 1981, Houston, Texas, USA. Singer; Songwriter; Producer; Actress. m. Jay-Z, 4 April 2008. Career: Founding Member, GirlsTyme vocal group, 1989, renamed Something Fresh, then Dolls, and then Destiny's Child; Signed to Columbia Records, 1996; Live performances in USA and UK; Simultaneous solo career, 2001-; Established clothing label Touch of Couture. Recordings: Albums with Destiny's Child: Destiny's Child, 1998; The Writing's on the Wall, 1999; Survivor, Eight Days of Christmas, 2001; Destiny Fulfilled, 2004; Solo albums: Soul Survivors, 2002; Dangerously in Love, 2003; Live at Wembley, 2004; Singles with Destiny's Child: No No No, 1997; With Me, She's Gone, 1998; Get On The Bus, Bills Bills Bills, Bug-A-Boo, 1999; Say My Name, Jumpin' Jumpin' Independent Woman, 2000; Survivor, Bootylicious, Emotion, Eight Days of Christmas, 2001; Nasty Girl, This is the Remix, 2002; Lose My Breath, 2004; B'Day, 2006: Solo singles: Crazy in Love, The Closer I Get to You, Baby Boy, Check on it, 2003; Déjà vu, Irreplaceable, 2006; Beautiful Liar, 2007: Film appearances: Carmen: A Hip Hopera (TV), 2001; Austin Powers in Goldmember, 2002; The Fighting Temptations, 2003; Dreamgirls, 2007. Honours: Billboard Awards for Artist of the Year; Group of the Year; Hot 100 Singles Artist of the Year; New Female Artist of the Year; New R&B Artist; American Music Awards; Soul Train Award; Billboard R&B/ Hip Hop Awards for Top Female Artist; Grammy Award, Best R&B Song; NAACP Image Award; MTV Video Award; Grammy Award, Best R&B Song; Hot 100 Group of the Year, 2000; Favourite Soul/R&B Group, 2001; Sammy Davis Jr Award for Entertainer of the Year, 2001; American Music Award, Favorite Pop/Rock Album, 2001; Grammy Award, Best R&B Performance by a Duo or Group with Vocal, 2001; Outstanding Duo or Group, 2001; Best R&B Video, 2001; Favourite Pop/Rock Band, Duo or Group, 2002; BRIT Awards for Best International Group, 2002; Hot 200 Female Artist, 2003; Best International Female Solo Artist, 2004; Grammy Award for Best Contemporary R&B Album, 2004; New Artist, 2004; Best Rap/Sung Collaboration, 2004; Grammy Award for Best R&B performance by a Duo or Group, 2004; Grammy Award for Best Female R&B Vocal Performance, 2004.

BHARGAVA Pushpa Mittra, b. 22 February 1928, Rajasthan, India. Scientist; Writer; Consultant. m. Edith, 1958, 1 son, 1 daughter. Education: BSc, 1944; MSc, 1946; PhD, 1949. Appointments: Lecturer, Chemistry, Lucknow University; Research Fellow, National Institute of Sciences; Project Associate, McArdle Memorial Laboratory for Cancer Research, University of Wisconsin, USA; Special Wellcome Research Fellow, National Institute of Medical Research, London, UK, 1949-58; Appointed Scientist B, Regional

Research Laboratory, Hyderabad, India, 1958; Promoted to Scientist C, E and F; Scientist in Charge, Director, CCMB, Hyderabad, 1977-1990; CSIR Distinguished Fellow, 1990-93; Director, Anveshna Consultants, Hyderabad, 1993-. Publications: Over 125 major science publications; 400 articles; 4 books. Honours: Over 100 major national and international honours and awards; Padma Bhushan from the President of India; Chevalier de la Legion d'Honneur; Honorary DSc; National Citizen Award; Visiting Professorship, College de France; Life Fellow, Clare Hall, Cambridge; Wattumal Memorial Prize for Biochemistry; FICCI Award, Medical Sciences; Ranbaxy Award for Medical Sciences; SICO Award for Biotechnology; Goyal Prize; R D Birla Award for Medical Sciences; Lifetime Achievement Award for Biotechnology. Memberships: President or Past President: Society of Biological Chemicals of India; Indian Academy of Social Sciences; Association for Promotion of DNA Fingerprinting and Other DNA Technologies; Society for Scientific Values; Former Vice Chairman, National Knowledge Commission; Member, National Security Advisory Board, Government of India; 125 major national and international standing committees. Address: Anveshna, Furqan Cottage, 12-13-100, Lane #1, Street #3, Tarnaka, Hyderabad 500 017, India. E-mail: bhargava.pm@gmail.com

BHARGAVA Samir, b. 5 April 1965, Mumbai, India. Ear, Nose and Throat Surgeon. m. Shalini, 1 son, 1 daughter. Education: DORL, College of Physicians and Surgeons, 1990; Diplomate of National Board, Delhi, 1991; MS (ENT) University of Bombay, 1991; DLO, Royal College of Surgeons, London, UK, 1993. Appointments: Associate Professor, Ear, Nose and Throat, GS Medical College and KEM Hospital, -1997; Honorary Consultant, Sir Hurkisondas Hospital, Guru Nanak Hospital. Publications: Co-author: A Short Textbook of ENT Diseases; More than 20 articles in national and international journals and books. Honours: Homi Gandhi Research Scholarship; Dr Manubhai Mehta Prize, CPS, 1990; Seth Gagalbhai Nathubhai Prize, MS (ENT), 1991; Best Surgeon Award, All India Medical Professional, Delhi, 2001. Memberships: Association of Otolaryngologists of India; Indian Society of Otology; Indian Medical Association; Consultants' Association. Address: Bhargava Nursing Home, Gopal Bhuvan, Tagore Road, Santacruz (W), Mumbai 400 054, India. E-mail: bharsam@bom5.vsnl.net.in

BHATNAGAR Amit, b. 10 August 1976, Roorkee, India. Environmental Scientist; Researcher. m. Eva Kumar. Education: BSc, 1996, MSc, 1998, Ch Charan Singh University, Meerut; PhD, Indian Institute of Technology, Roorkee, 2003. Appointments: Research Fellow, Indian Institute of Technology, 1999-2003; Postdoctoral Researcher, EAWAG, Switzerland, 2004-05; Research Associate, CBRI, Roorkee, 2006; Postdoctoral Researcher, Yonsei University, South Korea, 2006-. Publications: Numerous articles in professional journals including most recently: Removal of bromophenols from water using industrial wastes as low-cost adsorbents, 2007; Adsorptive removal of cobalt from aqueous solutions by utilizing industrial waste and its cement fixation, 2007; Adsorption of orange G dye on paper mill sludge: Equilibrium and Kinetic Modeling, 2007; Observation of Difference in the Size and Distribution of Carbon and Major Inorganic Compounds of Atmospheric Aerosols after the Long-range Transport between the Selected Days of Winter and Summer, 2008; Vanadium Removal from Water by Waste Metal Sludge and Cement Immobilization, 2008; Removal of Nitrate from Water by Adsorption on Zinc Chloride Treated Activated Carbon, 2008. Honours: Research Fellowship, Ministry of Environment and Forests, Government of India,

1998-2002; Senior Research Fellowship, 2003, Research Associate Fellowship, 2006, Council of Scientific and Industrial Research, Government of India; World Laboratory Wilhelm Simon Scholarship, 2004; Brain Korea-21 Postdoctoral Fellowship, Yonsei University, South Korea, 2006-; Listed in international biographical dictionaries. Address: Department of Environmental Engineering, Yonsei University, Baekun Hall #332, 234 Maeji Heungup, Wonju, 220-710, South Korea. E-mail: amit_b10@yahoo.co.in

BHATTACHARYA Asim, b. 1 January 1949, Calcutta, India. Nuclear Engineer. m. Mitali Chakrabarti, 2 daughters. Education: Bachelor of Mechanical Engineering, Jadavpur University, 1969; PhD in Mechanical Engineering, University of Mumbai, 2005. Appointments: Engineer Trainee, Design Office of Metal Box, Calcutta, 1969; Joined Training School, 1970, completed postgraduate course in Nuclear and Reactor Engineering, Scientific Officer SC_2, 1971-77, Scientific Officer SD, 1977-87, Scientific Officer SE, 1987-95, Scientific Officer SF, 1995-2005, Scientific Officer SG, 2005-, Bhabha Atomic Research Centre. Publications: Articles in scientific journals as co-author: Determination of the Equivalent Properties of Perforated Plates by Numerical Experiment, 1994; Peak Stress Multipliers for Thin Perforated Plates with Square Arrays of Circular Holes, 2003; Yield Criterion for Thin Perforated Plates with Square Penetration Pattern, 2004; Yield surfaces for perforated plates with square arrays of holes, 2004. Honours: Gold Medal and Merit Scholarship, Board of Secondary Education, 1964; Prizes and Certificates in Mechanical Engineering, Jadavpur University, Calcutta; Special Awards and Certificates for proficiency in national language, Government of India. Listed in Who's Who publications and biographical dictionaries. Memberships: Life Member, Indian Nuclear Society, Mumbai, India; Life Member, Indian Society of Theoretical and Applied Mechanics and Mathematics, Indian Institute of Technology, Kharagpur, West Bengal, India. Address: 1/E Malayagiri, Anushakti Nagar, Mumbai 400094, India. E-mail: abhatta@magnum.barc.ernet.in

BHATTACHARYYA Sibaprosad, b. 2 March 1946, West Bengal, India. Contracting & Claim Administration Specialist. m. Mahashweta, 1 daughter. Education: MSc, Applied Mathematics, MSc, Operations Research, MSc, Business Finance. Appointments: Consultant to business, government and international organisations; Educator serving on cultural, educational and environmental boards. Publications: Author, The Dynamics of Competitor Analysis in Enterprise Management; Numerous articles in professional journals. Honours: Academic Excellence Awards. Memberships: Life Member, Indian Council of Arbitration; Indian Science Congress; Consultancy Development Centre; Indian Institute of Arbitration & Mediation; Indian Road Congress. Address: M-70 Saket, New Delhi, India. E-mail: sibaprosad5@hotmail.com

BHOPAL Rajinder S, b. 10 April 1953, British citizen. Professor of Public Health. m. 4 children. Education: BSc (Hons), Physiology, 1975, MBChB, 1978, MD, 1991, University of Edinburgh; MPH, Glasgow University, 1985. Appointments: Professor of Epidemiology and Public Health, Head of Department of Epidemiology and Public Health, University of Newcastle upon Tyne, 1991-99; Honorary Consultant, Public Health Medicine, 1991-99; Non-Executive Director, Newcastle and North Tyneside Health Authority, 1992-96; Visiting Professor, School of Public Health, North Carolina, USA, 1996-97; Non-Executive Director, Health Education Authority, 1996-99; Bruce and John Usher Chair of Public Health, University of Edinburgh, 1999-; Honorary

Consultant in Public Health Medicine, Lothian Health Board, 1999-; Head of Department, Division of Community Health Services, University of Edinburgh, 2000-03. Publications: Around 150 articles in peer reviewed journals and chapters in books; 2 textbooks, Concepts of Epidemiology, 2002 and Ethnicity, Race and Health in Multicultural Societies, 2007; and 2 edited volumes, Public Health: Past, Present and Future, and The Epidemic of Coronary Heart Disease in South Asian Populations. Honours: Littlejohn Gairdner Prize, 1985; John Maddison Research Prize, 1992; J T Neech Prize, 1994; J W Starkey Silver Medal, 2000; CBE, 2001; Honorary DSc, Queen Margaret University College, 2005. Memberships: Fellow, Royal College of Physicians (UK); Fellow, Faculty of Public Health. Address: Division of Community Health Sciences, University of Edinburgh Medical School, Teviot Place, Edinburgh EH8 9AG, Scotland. E-mail: raj.bhopal@ed.ac.uk

BHUIYAN Lutful Bari, b. 8 July 1951, Barisal, Bangladesh. Academic. m. Leena Ferdous Khan, 2 daughters. Education: BSc (Hons), 1972, MSc, 1974, University of Dhaka; DIC, 1975, PhD, 1977, Imperial College, London. Appointments: Assistant Professor, 1983-86, Associate Professor, 1986-91, Professor, 1991-, University of Puerto Rico. Publications: 94 articles in professional journals. Honours: Commonwealth Scholarship, 1974; Academic Excellence and Productivity Award, 1998; Numerous grants. Memberships: Life Member, Bangladesh Physical Society; Member, American Physical Society; Member, American Chemical Society. Address: Department of Physics, University of Puerto Rico, Box 23343, UPR Station, San Juan, Puerto Rico 00931-3343. E-mail: beena@beena.cnnet.clu.edu

BHUMIBOL ADULYADEJ (King of Thailand), b. 5 December 1927, Cambridge, Massachusetts, USA. m. Queen Sirikit, 28 April 1950, 1 son, 3 daughters. Education: Bangkok; Lausanne, Switzerland. Ascended to the Throne of Thailand 9 June 1946-. Address: Chitralada Villa, Bangkok, Thailand.

BIDDISS Michael Denis, b. 15 April 1942, Farnborough, Kent, England. Professor of History; Writer. m. Ruth Margaret Cartwright, 8 April 1967, 4 daughters. Education: MA, PhD, Queens' College, Cambridge, 1961-66; Centre des Hautes Etudes Européennes, University of Strasbourg, 1965-66. Appointments: Fellow in History, Downing College, Cambridge, 1966-73; Lecturer/Reader in History, University of Leicester, 1973-79; Professor of History, University of Reading, 1979-2004, Emeritus Professor, 2004-. Publications: Father of Racist Ideology, 1970; Gobineau: Selected Political Writings (editor), 1970; Disease and History (co-author), 1972, New Edition, 2000; The Age of the Masses, 1977; Images of Race (editor), 1979; Thatcherism: Personality and Politics (co-editor), 1987; The Nuremberg Trial and the Third Reich, 1992; The Uses and Abuses of Antiquity (co-editor), 1999; The Humanities in the New Millennium (co-editor), 2000. Memberships: Historical Association, President, 1991-94; Faculty, History and Philosophy of Medicine, Society of Apothecaries, London, President, 1994-98; Royal Historical Society, Joint Vice President, 1995-99. Address: c/o School of History, University of Reading, Whiteknights, Reading RG6 6AA, England.

BIDEL Siamak, b. 13 September 1962, Kermanshah, Iran. Medical Researcher. m. Giti Khalighi-Sikaroudi, 2 sons. Education: Diploma in Natural Sciences, Italian Don Bosco College, 1980; Medical Doctorate Degree, University of Medical Sciences, Iran, 1993; PhD, Medical Sciences, University of Helsinki, Finland, 2008. Appointments: Medical practice in different hospitals and health centres in Kurdistan, Iran; Medical Lecturer, Kurdistan University of Medical Sciences, Kurdistan; Co-ordinator of Pulmonary Disease Centre, Gilan University of Medical Sciences, Rasht; Medical Trainee, Medical Researcher, Radiology Department, Helsinki University Central Hospital; Medical Researcher, Department of Public Health, University of Helsinki, Helsinki, Finland; Medical Researcher, Department of Health Promotion and Chronic Disease Prevention, National Public Health Institute, Helsinki. Publications: Coffee consumption and risk of type 2 diabetes; Coffee consumption and Markers of glycemia; Coffee, gama glutamyl transfers and type 2 diabetes; Coffee and Parkinson's disease; The effects of the ulcergenic agents on actin cytoskeleton and cell motility in cultured rat gastric muscosal cells; Treatment of bleeding pseudoaneurysms in patients with chronic pancreatitis. Honours: Juho Vainio Foundation Research Grant. Memberships: Diabetes Society of Finland; Radiology Society of Finland; Intervention Radiology Society of Finland; Angiology Society of Finland; Cardiovascular and Interventional Radiology Society of Europe. Address: Pykälätie 5B, 00690 Helsinki, Finland. E-mail: siamak.bidel@ktl.fi

BIER Werner Philipp, b. 30 September 1956, Birkenfeld, Germany. Economist. m. Birgit Bier. Education: Studies in Economics and Business Administration, University of Saarland, 1975-80; Master's Degree in Economics, 1980. Appointments: Research Assistant and Lecturer, Economics, University of Saarland, 1980-89; Economist, Deutsche Bundesbank, 1989-90; Administrator of the European Commission, Statistical Office of the European Communities, 1991-94; Senior Economist Statistician and Head of Unit, General Economic and Financial Statistics, European Monetary Institute, 1995-98; Head of Division, Euro Area Accounts and Economic Statistics, 1998-2004, Deputy Director General, Statistics, 2004-, European Central Bank. Publications: Les critères de déficit et de dette publics dans le cadre de l'UEM: approche statistique, 1993; Measurement of Inflation: The Choice of the European Central Bank, 2001; Extended Statistics for the Support of the Stability and Growth Pact, 2004; Economic Statistics for a Single Monetary Policy – Objectives, Achievements, Important Gaps, 2005; Euro Area and European Union Accounts for Institutional Sectors, 2006; The HICP for Monetary Policy Purposes, 2007. Honours: Listed in Who's Who publications. Address: European Central Bank, Kaiserstrasse 29, D-60311 Frankfurt am Main, Germany. E-mail: werner.bier@ecb.int

BIESELE John Julius, b. 24 March 1918, Waco, Texas, USA. Biologist; Educator. m. (1) Marguerite McAfee, 3 daughters, (2) Esther Eakin. Education: BA, 1939, PhD, 1942, University of Texas, Austin. Appointments: Fellow, International Cancer Research Foundation, University of Texas, 1942-43; Barnard Skin and Cancer Hospital, St Louis, Missouri, 1943; Instructor, Zoology, University of Pennsylvania, 1943-44; Temporary Research Associate, Carnegie Institution of Washington, New York, 1945-46; Research Associate, Massachusetts Institute of Technology, 1946-47; Assistant to Associate Scientist of the Division of Experimental Chemotherapy, Sloan-Kettering Institute for Cancer Research, New York, 1946-78; Assistant Professor of Anatomy to Professor of Biology, Cornell University Medical School, New York, 1950-58; Professor of Zoology, Member of Graduate Faculty, University of Texas, Austin, 1958-78; Professor Emeritus of Zoology, University of Texas, 1978-99; Professor Emeritus, Section of Molecular Cell and Developmental Biology, University of Texas School of Biological Sciences, 1999-. Publications: 150 articles in journals and book chapters; Author, 1 book; 18 doctoral dissertations; 21 master's theses; 180 lectures, US and abroad. Honours include: Sigma Xi lecturer, 1957; Mendel lecturer, 1958, 1971; Research Career Awards, 1962, 1967, 1972, 1977; Fellow, New York Academy of Sciences; Fellow, Texas Academy of Science; Fellow, American Association for the Advancement of Science. Memberships: American Association for the Advancement of Science; American Association for Cancer Research; American Society for Cell Biology; American Institute of Biological Sciences; The Nature Conservancy; German-Texan Heritage Society. Address: 2500 Great Oaks Parkway, Austin, TX 78756-2908, USA.

BIKBULATOV Igor, b. 19 October 1941, Buribye, Bashkortostan, Russia. Scientist. m. Nina Muravyova, 3 daughters. Education: Bachelor of Technical Sciences, 1963, Doctor of Chemical Sciences, 1970, Professor of Faculty of General Chemical Technologies, 1985, Ufa Oil Institute; Member, Academic Council of Ufa Oil Institute; Head of Co-ordination Council on Ecology of Sterliamak. Appointments: Operator, chemical plant producing chemical rubber, Research Laboratory Engineer, Head of Laboratory, Head of the Sterlitamak Branch, Head of the Faculty of Ecology and Rational Use of Nature, Ufa Oil University, Sterlitamak, Bashkortostan, Russia. Publications: Wasteless production of chlorohydrins; Microwave radiation and intensification of chemical processes; Polymeric covering for isolating the surfaces of open reservoirs; Capsule of a pipeline; A building for placing chemical productions; Chrolohydrins I. Obtaining chloric acid in saturated chloride-ion solution. Honours: Inventor of the USSR; Honoured Higher School Worker of the Russian Federation; Honoured Worker of Science of Bashkortostan. Memberships: Academician, International Academy of Science of Pedagogical Education; Scientific Society of Ufa State Oil Technical University. Address: October Avenue 2, Sterlitamark, Bashkortostan, Russia. E-mail: sf@rusoil.net

BILIŪTĖ-ALEKNAVIČIENĖ Elvyra, b. 26 September 1948, Tolkūnai Village, Alytus District, Lithuania. Teacher of Lithuanian Language and Literature. m. Juozas Aleknavičius, 1 daughter. Education: Diploma of Philology, Lithuanian Literature and Language Teaching, Vilnius State University, 1967-72. Appointments: Methodologist, Alytus Evening Secondary School N1, 1973-79; Lecturer, Alytus Vocational School N54, 1979-95; Inspector, Alytus Municipality Education Department, 1996-. Publications: Books about Lithuanian education history, monographs about distinguished teachers and writers: Light of Kindness, 1996; Wings of Eternity, 1997; Love Song, 1999; Cradle of Life, 2000; Angel of Hope, 2002; Development of Primary School Teachers Training and Education System in Lithuania in 1940-57, 2004; Moving Away Echo, 2001; Son of Dawn, 2006; Co-author, Historic Development of Alytus, 2004; The Development of Primary School Teachers' Training in Lithuania in 1940-57, 2004; Articles on pedagogical topics. Honours: Honorary Diploma, Central Board of Lithuanian Catholic Science Academy, 1995; Gratitude Paper, Ministry of Education, 1996; Gratitude Paper, Lithuanian Parliament, 2001; Gratitude Papers, Mayor of Alytus, 2001, 2004; 21st Century Award for Achievement, 2004. Memberships: Chairwoman, Lithuanian Language and Literature Teachers' Union, Alytus Division; Lithuanian Beekeepers' Union; Lithuanian Florists' Union, Alytus Division. Address: Zuvinto Str 13-89, LT-62354 Alytus, Lithuania.

BILK Acker (Bernard Stanley), b. 28 January 1929, Pensford, Somerset, England. Musician (clarinet); Composer; Bandleader. m. Jean, 1 son, 1 daughter. Career: Began playing clarinet in Royal Engineers, 1948; Clarinet, Ken Colyer's Band; Formed Bristol Paramount Jazz Band; Currently freelance artiste; Guest musician on numerous records; Tours world-wide with Paramount Jazz Band; Played with Reunion Paramount Jazz Band, Isle of Bute Jazz Festival, 1995; Performed with Van Morrison, Prague, 2004, Oxford, 2005. Recordings with Van Morrison, 2001, 2001; 3B Concerts reuniting Acker and his Band with the Big Chris Barber Band and Kenny Ball and his Jazzmen, 2004; Giants of Jazz Concerts with Humphrey Lyttelton and George Melly, 2004; Owner of publishing company. Recordings: Singles include: Somerset; Aria; Stranger On The Shore (Number 1, US and UK, 1961); Albums include: The One For Me; Sheer Magic; Evergreen; Chalumeau-That's My Home; Three In The Morning (with Humphrey Lyttelton, John Barnes, Dave Green, Dave Cliff, Bobby Worth); Giants Of Jazz (with Paramount Jazz Band, Kenny Ball and his Jazzmen, Kenny Baker Don Lusher All Stars); Chris Barber and Acker Bilk, That's It Then!; Clarinet Moods, Acker Bilk, with string orchestra; Acker Bilk - The Oscars; Clarinet Moods with Acker Bilk; All the Hits and More; The Christmas Album; Acker Bilk And His Paramount Jazz Band; Acker Bilk In Holland; It Looks Like A Big Time Tonight; Hits Blues And Class; Great Moments; Best of Acker Bilk; As Time Goes By, 2004. Honour: MBE, 2001; BMI Award, London, 2004; Honorary Degree of Master of the Arts, University of Bristol, 2005. Address: c/o Acker's Agency, 53 Cambridge Mansions, Cambridge Road, London SW11 4RX, England.

BILLINGS Stephen Alec, b. 14 August 1951, Staffordshire, England. Professor of Signal Processing and Complex Systems. m. Catherine Grant Billings, 1 son, 1 daughter. Education: First Class Honours Degree, Electrical Engineering, Liverpool University, 1969-72; PhD, Control Systems, Sheffield University, 1972-75. Appointments: Lecturer, 1975-83, Senior Lecturer, 1983-85, Department of Control Engineering, Reader, 1985-90, Professor of Signal Processing and Complex Systems, 1990-, Department of Automatic Control and Systems Engineering, University of Sheffield. Publications: Over 250 journal articles and over 60 conference papers. Honours: Honoured by the Institute of Scientific Information (ISA), USA as one of the worlds most highly cited researchers in all branches of engineering, 1980-2000; Awarded D. Eng., Liverpool University, 1990. Memberships: Fellow, Institute of Electrical Engineers (UK); Chartered Engineer and Chartered Scientist; Fellow, Institute of Mathematics and its Applications; Chartered Mathematician. Address: Department of Automatic Control and Systems Engineering, University of Sheffield, Mappin Street, Sheffield S1 3JD, England. E-mail: s.billings@sheffield.ac.uk

BILLINGTON Rachel (Mary), b. 11 May 1942, Oxford, England. Writer. m. 16 December 1967, 2 sons, 2 daughters. Education: BA, English, London University. Publications: Over 20 books, including: Loving Attitudes, 1988; Theo and Matilda, 1990; The First Miracles, 1990; Bodily Harm, 1992; The Family Year, 1992; The Great Umbilical, 1994; Magic and Fate, 1996; The Life of Jesus (for children), 1996; Perfect Happiness, 1996; Tiger Sky, 1998; The Life of St Francis (for children), 1999; A Woman's Life, 2002; Far Out! (for children), 2002; The Space Between, 2004; One Summer, 2006; There's More to Life (for children), 2006. Contributions to: Reviewer, Columnist and short story writer for various publications; co-editor of Inside Time, the national newspaper for prisoners; 2 plays for BBC TV; 4 plays for

Radio. Memberships: Society of Authors; President, PEN, 1997-2000. Address: The Court House, Poyntington, Near Sherborne, Dorset DT9 4LF, England.

BILLINGTON Sandra, b. 10 September 1943, Eccles, England. Self-Employed Writer. Education: Guildhall School of Music and Drama, 1961-63; RADA, 1965-67; BA (Cantab), 1975, PhD (Cantab), 1980, Lucy Cavendish College, Cambridge. Appointments: Actress, BBC Radio Manchester, 1955-59; Theatre/Film, 1967-72; Lecturer, 1979-92, Reader, 1992-2003, Department of Theatre, Film and TV, University of Glasgow; Writer, 2003-. Publications: A Social History of the Fool, 1984; Mock Kings in Medieval Society and Renaissance Drama, 1991; The Concept of the Goddess (co-editor), 1996; Midsummer: A Cultural sub-text from Chrétien de Troyes to Jean Michel, 2000; Between Worlds, 2005; Early Pagan Midsummer Traditions in N-W Europe: fact or fiction? 2007. Honours: Katharine Briggs Prize for Folklore, 1984; Michaelis Jena Ratcliff Prize for Folklore, 1991; FRSE, 1998. Membership: Traditional Cosmology Society. Address: 4 Doune Quadrant, Glasgow, G20 6DL, England.

BINCHY Maeve, b. 28 May 1940, Dublin, Ireland. Writer. m. Gordon Thomas Snell, 29 January 1977. Education: BA, University College, Dublin, 1960. Appointments: Teacher, History and French, Pembroke School, Dublin, 1961-68; Columnist, Irish Times, London, 1968-2000; Writer. Publications: My First Book, 1976; The Central Line: Stories of Big City Life, 1978; Maeve's Diary, 1979; Victoria Line, 1980; Light a Penny Candle, 1982; Maeve Binchy's Dublin Four, 1982; The Lilac Bus, 1984; Echoes, 1985; Firefly Summer, 1987; Silver Wedding, 1988; Circle of Friends, 1991; The Copper Beech, 1992; The Glass Lake, 1995; Evening Class, 1996; Tara Road, 1999; Scarlet Feather, 2000; Aches and Pains, 2000; Quentins, 2002; Nights of Rain and Stars, 2004; Whitethorn Woods, 2006. Honours: International TV Festival Golden Prague Award, Czech TV, 1979; Jacobs Award, 1979; Hon DLit, National University of Ireland, 1990, Queen's Belfast, 1998; WHS Fiction Award, 2001. Address: PO Box 6737, Dun Laoghaire, Co Dublin, Ireland. Website: www.maevebinchy.com

BINGHAM Nicholas Hugh, b. 19 March 1945, York, England. Professor. m. Cecilie Anne Gabriel, 2 sons, 1 daughter. Education: Trinity College, Oxford, 1963-66; Churchill College, Cambridge, 1966-69. Appointments: Lecturer, 1969-80, Reader, 1980-84, Mathematics, Westfield College, London; Reader, 1984-85, Professor, 1985-95, Mathematics, Royal Holloway College, London; Professor, Statistics, Birkbeck College, London, 1995-99; Professor, Mathematics, Brunel University, 2000-03; Professor, Mathematics, University of Sheffield, 2003-06; Senior Research Associate, Imperial College, London, 2006-. Publications: Numerous articles in professional journals. Honours: DSc (Cantab); PhD (Cantab); MA (Oxon). Memberships: London Mathematical Society; Royal Statistical Society; Institute of Mathematical Statistics. Address: 13 Woodside Grange Road, London, N12 8SJ, England. E-mail: n.bingham@ic.ac.uk

BINJI Aishatu Muhammad, b. 2 March 1954, Kano, Nigeria. Accountant. m. H Binji, 2 sons, 2 daughters. Education: BSc, Accounting, 1st class honours, Institute of Administration ABU Zaria, 1974-77; Strathclyde University Glasgow, Scotland, 1987. Appointments: Accountant, Gwandu Rice Scheme, 1977-78; Accountant GII, Ministry of Finance, Treasury Division, Sokoto, 1978-79; Accountant in charge of store, 1979-80, Agricultural Chief Accountant, 1980-82, Gusau Agricultural Development Project; Chief Accountant,

SADP Headquarters, 1982-84; Head, Accounts Department, Sokoto Agricultural Development Project, 1984-88; Financial Controller, Farmers Agricultural Supply Company, 1988-95; Accountant General, 1995-2006, Commissioner of Finance, Sokoto State. Publications: Yara Mu Karanta; Simple Maths; Read and Write the Arabic Alphabets; My A B C D Writing Book. Honours: Member, Federal Republic of Nigeria, 2001; National Productivity Order of Merit Award, 2000; Merit Award, Madrasatul Ihyaul Islam Sokoto. Memberships: Member, Association of National Accountants of Nigeria; Institute of Corporate Executives of Nigeria. Address: Dada Books and System Ltd, No 9, Gawon Nama Area, Sokoto, Nigeria.

BINOCHE Juliette, b. 9 March 1964, Paris, France. Actress. 1 son, 1 daughter. Education: National Conservatory of Drama; Private Theatrical Studies. Creative Works: Films include: Les nanas; La vie de famille; Rouge Baiser; Rendez-Vous; Mon beau-frère a tué ma soeur; Mauvais Sang; Un tour de manège; Les amants du Pont-Neuf; The Unbearable Lightness of Being; Wuthering Heights, Damage, 1992; Trois Couleurs: Bleu, 1993; Le Hussard sur le Toit, 1995; The English Patient, 1996; Alice et Martin, Les Enfants du Siècle, 1999; La Veuve de Saint-Pierre, 2000; Chocolat, Code Unknown, 2001; Décalage horaire, 2002; Country of My Skull, 2004; Bee Season, Mary, Caché, 2005; Breaking and Entering, 2006; Le Voyage du Balloon Rouge, Dan in Real Life, Paris, 2007. Play: Naked, 1998. Honours: Academy Award, Best Supporting Actress, 1996; Berlin Film Festival Award, 1996; BAFTA Award, 1997. Address: c/o UTA, 9560 Wilshire Boulevard, Floor 5, Beverly Hills, CA 90212, USA.

BIRCH Clive Francis William, b. 22 December 1931, Edgware, Middlesex, England. Publisher; Author. Education: Uppingham School. Appointments: RAF National Service, 1950; Office Junior, Stretford Telegraph, 1952; Reporter, Stockport Express, 1954; Editor, Bucks Examiner, 1956; Public Relations Officer, Frigidaire Division, General Motors, 1958; Product Development, Metro-Cammell Weymann Ltd, 1959; Group Advertisement Manager, Modern Transport Publishing Company Ltd, 1965; Manager, Electrical Press Ltd, 1966; Director, Illustrated Newspapers Ltd, 1969 (including, Editor, Illustrated London News, 1970); Director, Northwood Publications Ltd, 1971; Managing Director designate, Textile Trade Publications Ltd, 1972; Publishing Director, Mercury House Ltd, 1973; Chairman, Barracuda Books Ltd, 1974-92; Managing Director, Quotes Ltd, 1985-97; Principal, Radmore Birch Associates (including Baron Books), 1991-; Visiting Tutor, RCA Vehicle Design Department, 2004-; Publishing Director, Boltneck Publications, 2006-. Publications: Book of Chesham; Book of Amersham (co-author) Book of Aylesbury; Book of Beaconsfield (co-author); Yesterday's Town : Chesham; Yesterday's Town: Amersham (co-author); Maps of Bucks (editor); Chesham Century (co-author); Remember Chesham; In Camera Series - Vale of Aylesbury; Buckingham; Chesham; Chiltern Thames; Milton Keynes (2); The Missendens; Chalfont St Giles; Chorleywood & Chenies; Wish you were here series – Buckingham; Chesham; The Freedom - City of London (co-author); On the Move - Road Haulage Association (co-author); Carr and Carman - London's Transport; A Decent Man (novel), 2006; Royal College of Art 2006 Vehicle Design (editor). Honours: Honorary Life Member, Chiltern Car Club, 1956; Fellow, Royal Society of Arts, 1980; Fellow, Society of Antiquaries of London, 1981; Honorary Life Member, Institution of the Royal Corps of Transport, 1985; MBE, 2000. Memberships include: Founder Chairman, Buckingham and District Chamber of Trade, Commerce and Industry, 1983-87; Founder and Chairman,

Buckingham Heritage Trust, 1985-97; Freeman City of London, 1960; Liveryman, Worshipful Company of Carmen, 1960, Court of Assistants, 1966, Master 1984-85; Founder Chairman, Carmen's Ball, 1985; Deputy Master, 1988-89; Chairman RSA Carmen Lectures, 1991-; Chairman, Carmen Marketing and Media, 1994-; Chairman, Carmen Awards Committee, 1999-; Founder Carmen Research Fellowship, 2001; Honorary Editor, 2002-; Chairman Carmen Past Masters, 2004-; Senior Past Master, Carmen, 2005-; Chevalier de la Confrerie des Chevaliers du Trou Normand, 1991. Address: King's Cote, Valley Road, Finmere, Oxon MK18 4AL, England.

BIRD Harold Dennis (Dickie), b. 19 April 1933, Barnsley, Yorkshire, England. Retired County Cricket, Test & World Cup Final Umpire. Education: Burton Road Primary School; Raley Secondary Modern School, Barnsley. Appointments: Played for Yorkshire & Leicestershire County Cricket Clubs; County Cricket, Test & World Cup Umpire, retired 1998; Fully Qualified MCC Advanced Cricket Coach; Umpired following: 4 World Cups; 3 World Cup Finals; West Indies v Australia, 1975; West Indies v England, 1979; India v West Indies, 1983; Both men's and women's World Cup Finals; International matches in Sharjah (UAE); Best Batsman in the World; World Double Wicket & Best All-Rounder competitions all over the world; The Rest of the World XI against a World XI, Wembley Stadium, 1983; Bi-Centenary Test Match World XI v The Rest of the World Lords, 1987; Asia v The Rest of the World, The Oval, 2000; The Princes Trust XI v The Rest of the World, Edgbaston, 1989; Brylcream Top of the World Cricket Tournament; 68 Test Matches; 93 one-day international matches; Test matches for 25 years; First Class County Matches for 30 years; All major cup finals in England including Gillette, Nat West, Benson & Hedges and Refuge Assurance Cup Finals; Queens Silver Jubilee Test Match, Trent Bridge, England v Australia, 1977; Centenary Test Match, Lords, England v Australia, 1980; 159 international matches; Other test matches and international matches including: Shell Shield Final, Christchurch, New Zealand, Wellington v Christchurch, 1981; National Grid Award, 60th Diamond test, Pakistan v Australia, Karachi, 1994; Asia Cub, Sri Lanka, 1984; Zimbabwe v New Zealand Test Series, 1993; New Zealand v Pakistan Test Series, 1994; Pakistan v Australia Test Series, 1994; India v West Indies Test Series, 1994; Australia v Pakistan Test Series, 1996; England U19s v South Africa U19s Test Series, 1995; England U19s v Pakistan U19s Test Series, 1998. Publications: Not Out; That's Out; From the Pavilion End; Dickie Bird, My Autobiography, 1997; White Cap and Bails, 1999; Dickie Bird's Britain, 2002. Honours: Voted Yorkshire Personality of Year, 1977; MBE, Queen's Birthday Honours List, 1986; Rose Bowl, Barnsley Council for 100th International Match, 1988; Variety Club of Great Britain Yorkshire Award, 1988; National Grid Award for 49th Test Zimbabwe v New Zealand, 1992; Honorary Doctorate, Hallam University, 1996; Yorkshire Man of the Year, 1996; People of the Year Award, 1996; EADAR National People of the Year Award, 1996; Variety Club of Great Britain Award, 1997; Honorary Doctorate in Law, Leeds University, 1997; Life Long Achievement Award, 1998; Special Merit Award, The Professional Cricketers Association, 1998; Services to Cricket Award, Yorkshire CC, 1998, Warwickshire CC, 1998; Freedom of the Borough of Barnsley, 2000; Commemorative Clock, Headingley, 2002; TCCB 25 years service; Barnsley Millennium Award of Merit, 2000; 30 Years of Service Award, ECB; Anglo American Sporting Club Award; Founder, The Dickie Bird Foundation for Underprivileged Children, 2004; Numerous appearances on radio and television. Memberships: MCC; Yorkshire County Cricket Club; Leicestershire County Cricket Club; Barnsley Football Club; Cambridge University Cricket Club. Address: White Rose Cottage, 40 Paddock Road, Staincross, Barnsley, South Yorkshire S75 6LE, England.

BIRKHEAD Timothy Robert, b. 28 February 1950, Leeds, England. Professor of Zoology. m. Miriam Enid, 1 son, 2 daughters. Education: BSc, University of Newcastle Upon Tyne, 1972; DPhil, Wolfson College, Oxford, 1976; DSc, University of Newcastle Upon Tyne, 1989. Appointments: Lecturer, 1976-86, Senior Lecturer, 1986-89; Reader, 1989-92, Nuffield Research Fellow, 1990-91; Personal Chair, 1992-, Leverhulme Research Fellow, 1995-96, Fellow of the Royal Society, 2004, University of Sheffield. Publications: Avain Ecology, 1983; The Survival Factor, 1989; The Magpies: the ecology and behaviour of black-billed and yellow-billed magpies, 1991; Sperm Competition in Birds; Evolutionary Causes and Consequences, 1992; Great Auk Islands, 1993; Sperm Competition and Sexual Selection, 1998; Promiscuity, 2000; The Red Canary, 2003; The Wisdom of Birds, 2008. Honours: FRS Royal Society, London, 2004; President, International Society for Behavioural Ecology; McColvin Medal for Best Reference Book; University of Sheffield Senate Award for Excellence in Teaching. Memberships: British Ornithologist's Union; International Society for Behavioural Ecology. Address: Animal & Plant Sciences, University of Sheffield, Western Bank, Sheffield, S10 2TN, England. E-mail: t.r.birkhead@sheffield.ac.uk

BIRT John, Baron of Liverpool, b. 10 December 1944, Liverpool, England. Broadcasting Executive. m. (1) Jane Frances Lake, 1965, divorced, 1 son, 1 daughter, (2) Eithne Wallis, 2006. Education: St Mary's College, Liverpool; St Catherine's College, Oxford. Appointments: TV Producer, Nice Time, 1968-69; Joint Editor, World in Action, 1969-70; Producer, The Frost Programme, 1971-72; Executive Producer, Weekend World, 1972-74; Head, Current Affairs, London Weekend TV, 1974-77; Co-Producer, The Nixon Interviews, 1977; Controller, Features and Current Affairs, LWT, 1977-81; Director of Programmes, 1982-87; Deputy Director General, 1987-92, Director General, 1992-2000, BBC; Vice President, Royal TV Society, 1994-2000; Adviser to Prime Minister on criminal justice, 2000-01; Strategy Adviser, 2001-; Adviser to McKinsey and Co Inc; Chair, Capital Ventures Fund, 2000. Publications: The Harder Path – The Autobiography. Honours: Visiting Fellow, Nuffield College, Oxford, 1991-99; Honorary Fellow: University of Wales, Cardiff, 1997; St Catherine's College, Oxford, 1992; Hon DLitt, Liverpool John Moores, 1992; City, 1998; Bradford, 1999; Emmy Award, US National Academy of Television, Arts and Sciences; Life Peerage, 2000. Memberships: Media Law Group, 1983-94; Working Party on New Technologies, 1981-83; Broadcasting Research Unit, Executive Committee, 1983-87; International Museum of TV and Radio, New York, 1994-2000; Opportunity 2000 Target Team, Business in the Community, 1991-98. Address: House of Lords, London SW1A 0PW, England.

BIRTS Peter William, b. 9 February 1946, Brighton, England. Circuit Judge. m. Angela, 1 son, 2 daughters. Education: Lancing College, Sussex; MA, St John's College, Cambridge. Appointments: Called to the Bar, 1968; Recorder, 1989; Queen's Counsel, 1990; Judicial Studies Board, 1992-96; Chairman, Mental Health Tribunals, 1994-; Queen's Counsel Northern Ireland, 1996; Deputy High Court Judge, 2000-05; Appointed Circuit Judge, 2005; Legal Member Parole Board, 2006. Publications: Trespass – Summary Procedure for Possession of Land, 1987; Remedies for Trespass, 1990; Contributor to Butterworths Costs Service, 2000-; Articles in various journals on legal costs, countryside law and civil procedure. Honours: Choral Scholarship to St John's College, Cambridge, 1964; MA (Cantab), 1973. Memberships: Hurlingham Club; Liveryman, Carpenters Company; Bencher of Gray's Inn, 1998-. Address: Snaresbrook Crown Court, 75 Hollybush Hill, Snaresbrook, London E11 1QW, England.

BIRTWISTLE Sir Harrison, b. 15 July 1934, Accrington, Lancashire, England. Composer. m. Sheila, 1958, 3 sons. Education: Royal Manchester College of Music; Royal Academy of Music, London. Career: Director of Music, Cranborne Chase School, 1962-65; Visiting Fellow (Harkness International Fellowship), Princeton, University, 1966; Cornell Visiting Professor of Music, Swarthmore College, Pennsylvania, 1973-74; Slee Visiting Professor, New York State University, Buffalo, New York, 1975; Associate Director, National Theatre, 1975-88; Composer-in-Residence, London Philharmonic Orchestra, 1993-98; Henry Purcell Professor of Composition, King's College, London University, 1994-2001; Visiting Professor, University of Alabama at Tuscaloosa, 2001-02; Director of Contemporary Music, RAM, 1996-2001; Works widely performed at major festivals in Europe; Formed (with Sir Peter Maxwell Davies), The Pierrot Players. Honours: Grawemeyer Award, University of Louisville, Kentucky, USA, 1987; Honorary Fellow, Royal Northern College of Music, 1990; Chevalier des Arts et Lettres; Siemens Prize, 1995. Allied Artists Agency, 42 Montpelier Square, London SW7 1JZ, England.

BISHOP James Drew, b. 18 June 1929, London, England. Journalist. m. 5 June 1959, 2 sons. Education: BA, History, Corpus Christi College, Cambridge, 1953. Appointments: Foreign Correspondent, 1957-64, Foreign News Editor, 1964-66, Features Editor, 1966-70, The Times; Editor, 1971-87, Editor-in-Chief, 1987-94, The Illustrated London News. Publications: Social History of Edwardian Britain, 1977; Social History of the First World War, 1982; The Story of The Times (with Oliver Woods), 1983; Illustrated Counties of England, editor, 1985; The Sedgwick Story, 1998. Contributions to: Books, newspapers and magazines. Membership: Association of British Editors, Chairman, 1987-96; Chairman, National Heritage, 1998-. Address: Black Fen, Stoke By Nayland, Suffolk, CO6 4QD, England.

BISSET Jacqueline, b. 13 September 1944, Weybridge, Surrey, England. Education: French Lycée, London. Career: Films include: The Knack, debut, 1965; Casino Royale, 1967; Bullitt, The Detective, 1968; Airport, 1970; Believe in Me, 1971; Stand Up and Be Counted, 1972; The Thief Who Came to Dinner, 1973; Murder on the Orient Express, 1974; The Deep, 1976; Le Manifique, 1977; Secrets, 1978; When Time Ran Out, 1980; Rich and Famous, 1981; Class, 1982; Forbidden, 1986; High Season, 1988; Wild Orchid, 1989; September, 1994; La Céremonie, End of Summer, 1995; Once You Meet a Stranger, Courtesan, 1996; Let the Devil Wear Black, Dangerous Beauty, 1998; Joan of Arc, 1999; In the Beginning, Jesus, Britannic, 2000; The Sleepy Time Gal, 2001; Sundance Holiday Gift Pack, Latter Days, 2003; Swing, Fascination, 2004; The Fine Art of Love: Mine Ha-Ha, Domino, 2005. Address: William Morris Agency, 151 El Camino Drive, Beverly Hills, CA 90212, USA.

BITAR Samir Antoun, b. 10 May 1961, Beirut, Lebanon. Senior Commercial Manager. m. Marina Nemr Chamoun, 1 son, 1 daughter. Education: MBA, Business Administration, 1985, PhD, Construction Management, 2006, Richmond University. Appointments: Senior Commercial Manager, Executive Project Management Team, Oil & Gas Projects with Saudi Aramco, Saudi Arabia. Honours: ISO 90011,

2000; Saudi Aramco Awards, 2001; Safety Awards, 2007. Memberships: Lebanese Culture Community, 1997; ISO, Lebanese Red Cross, 2005. Address: Kettaneh Construction Saudi Arabia Ltd, PO Box 383, Courniche Road, Jarir Book Store Bldg, 3rd Floor, Al Khobar 31952, Saudi Arabia. E-mail: bitar@kettaneh.kcs.com

BITTERLICH Joachim, b. 10 July 1948, Saarbrücken-Dudweiler, Germany. Reserve Officer. m. Martine, 3 children. Education: Studies in law, Economics and Politics, University of Saarbrücken; French National School of Administration, Paris, France, 1974-75; Second State Examination in Law, 1976. Appointments: Joined Federal Foreign Office, 1976, posted to Algiers, 1978-81, and Permanent Representation to the European Communities, Brussels, 1981-85; Advisor, Minister of Foreign Affairs, Hans-Dietrich Genscher, 1985-87; Head, European Policy Department, Federal Chancellor's Office, 1987-93; Director General of Foreign Policy, Economic Co-operation and External Security, Federal Chancellor's Office, and Foreign and Security Policy Advisor to Federal Chancellor, Helmut Kohl, 1993-98; Ambassador, Permanent Representative of the Federal Republic of Germany, North Atlantic Council, Brussels, 1998-99; Ambassador of the Federal Republic of Germany to the Kingdom of Spain and the Principality of Andorra, 1999-2002; Executive Vice President, International Affairs, Veolia Environment, Paris, 2003-; Professor, ESCP-EAP, Paris; Professor for Public Affairs and Political Communication, Member, Executive Board, European Institute for the Relationship Between the Economy and Politics, University of Management and Communication (FH), Potsdam, Germany. Publications: Author and co-author of 20 reports and articles in professional journals including most recently: Europe's Future, 2004; Europe – mission impossible, 2005; France – Germany: mission impossible? How to relaunch the European integration, 2005; EU and EC Treaties (juridical commentary), 4th edition, 2006. Honours: Comendador da Ordem du Mérito, 1991; Commendatore Ordine Merito de Republica Italiana, 1992; Honorary Commander of the British Empire, 1992; Gold Rays with Neck Ribbon, Order of the Rising Sun, 1993; Großes Goldenes Ehrenzeichen, 1993; Kommandeur m Stern-Kgl Norske Fortjenstorden, 1994; Encomienda de Numero de la Orden de Isabel la Católica, 1994; Suomen Valkoisen Ruusun ritarikunnan 1 luckan, 1994; Großes Silbernes Ehrenzeichen mit Stern, 1994; Grand officier de l'Ordre de Mérite, 1995; Grand Officier de l'Ordre de la Couronne, 1995; Grande Oficial do Ordem de Rio Branco, 1995; Officier de la Légión d'Honneur, 1996; Grand Commandeur de l'Ordre de l'Honneur, 1996; Grande ufficiale n'ell Ordine al Mérito della Repubblica Italiana, 1997; Encomienda de Número de la Orden de Isabel la Católica, 1997; Placa, Orden Mexicana del Aguila Azteca, 1997; Gran Cruz de la Orden del Mérito Civil, 1998; Orden de Mayo al Mérito – Gran Cruz, 1998; Orden do Infante Don Henrique, 1998; Comendador del Orden del Liberator Simon Bolivar, 1998; Cross of Commander of the Order of Grand Duke Gediminas of Lithuania, 2002. Memberships: Board of Directors: Veolia Environmental Services, Paris; Veolia Transport, Paris; DEKRA e V Stuttgart; Ecole Nationale d'Administration, Paris; MEDEF International, Paris; Notre Europe, Paris; Friends of Europe, Brussels; France-German Business Club, Paris; IISS; and others. Address: Veolia Environnement Head Office, 36-38 avenue Kleber, 75116, Paris, France. E-mail: joachim.bitterlich@veolia.com

BITTNER Wolfgang, b. 29 July 1941, Gleiwitz, Germany. Author. m. Renate Schoof, 2 sons, 1 daughter. Education: Law, Philosophy and Sociology, Universities of Goettingen and Munich, 1966-70; First Juridical Diploma, 1970, Dr Juridical, 1972, University of Goettingen; Second Juridical Diploma, Supreme Court, Braunschweig, 1973. Appointments: Government Official, Niedersachsen, 1963-1966; Lawyer, 1973; Professional author, 1974-; Member of Board of German Writers' Association, Verband deutscher Schriftsteller, 1997-2001; Member of Board, West German Radio, WDR, 1996-99. Publications: About 50 books including novels, poems, satire, children's literature, journalism, non-fiction, features, radio plays, scripts for tv, publications of literature, journalism and science in broadcasting, newspapers, journals and anthologies. Memberships; PEN; Verband deutscher Schriftsteller (German Writers' Association). Address: Gotenring 31, D-50679, Koeln, Germany. Website: http://www.wolfgangbittner.de

BJÖRK (Björk Godmunsdottir), b. 21 November 1965, Reykjavik, Iceland. Singer. 1 son, 1 daughter. Career: Solo release, aged 11; Singer, various Icelandic groups include: Exodus; Tappi Tikarras; Kukl; Singer, The Sugarcubes, 1987-92; Solo artiste, 1992-; Recent appearances include Reading Festival, 1995; Later.. with Jools Holland, Glastonbury Festival, 2007. Recordings: Albums: with the Sugarcubes: Life's Too Good, 1988; Here Today, Tomorrow, Next Week, 1989; Stick Around for Joy, 1992; It's It, 1992; Solo albums: Björk, 1977; Debut, 1993; Post, 1995; Telegram, 1996; Homogenic, 1997; Selmasongs, 2000; Vespertine, 2001; Dancer in the Dark, 2001; Greatest Hits, 2002; Family Tree, 2002; Medulla, 2004; Army of Me: Remixes and Covers (charity album), 2005; Hit singles: with The Sugarcubes: Birthday; Solo singles: Venus As A Boy; Violently Happy; Human Behaviour; Big Time Sensuality; Play Dead; Army Of Me; Isobel; It's Oh So Quiet; Possibly Maybe; I Miss You/Cover Me; Hyperballad; Hunter; Bachelorette; All Is Full Of Love; Alarm Call; Selmasongs, 2000; Triumph of a Heart, 2005; Other recordings: Gling-Go, Trio Gudmundar Ingolfssonar, 1990; Ex-El, Graham Massey, 1991; Tank Girl, 1995; Mission Impossible, 1996; Nearly God, 1996; Archive, 1997; Tibetan Freedom Concert, 1997; Not For Threes, 1998; Great Crossover Potential, 1998; Y2K Beat The Clock Version 1, 1999; Film: Dancer in the Dark, 2000. Honours: BRIT Award, Best International Female Artist, 1994,96,98; MOJO Award, 2007. Platinum and Gold records. Address: One Little Indian, 250 York Road, London SW11 3SJ, England.

BJØRKLI Leikny Annadotter, b. 22 June 1938, Balsfjord, Tromsø, Norway. Associate Professor; Institute for Human Potential Training Leader. m. Rolf Sjåvik, divorced, 2 sons, 1 deceased, 1 daughter. Education: Preliminary Examination, University of Oslo, Oslo, Norway, 1966; Teacher Training Education, Sagene Teachers' Training College, Oslo, 1967-69; Sociology (subsidiary subject, University of Oslo, 1974; School-Leader Education, Director of Education, Oslo/Akerhus, The National Council for Compulsory Education and The National Council for Innovations in Education, 1976-77; Cand. Mag., Sagene Teachers' Training College, 1987; Master of Arts, 1986, PhD, 1988, University of California, Santa Barbara, California, USA; Scholarship Recipient, The National Council for Leadership, Oslo, 1991-93; Product/Business Development, Østfold University College, Norway, 2001. Appointments: Teacher, 1969-75, Principal, 1975-89, Ullensaker Board of Education, Ullensaker, Norway; Researcher, Agder Research Association, Kristiansand, Norway, 1989-90; Associate Professor: Teachers' Training College, Oslo, Norway, 1992-95, Elverum, Norway, 1995-96, Notodden, Norway, 1996-2003; Leader, Owner of Independent Company, IHPT Institute for Human Potential Training, established in Norway, 1990-, Sweden, 2005-. Publications:

Books: How to Organise Your Teaching (co-author), 1976; The School System's Responsibility and Possibilities Concerning Equality Between the Sexes, 1980; Lifelong Learning. Architect for Your Own Destiny, 2002; Book Chapter: How to Establish Your Own Business in Women within Leadership, 1994; Author of several research reports and articles in journals and magazines. Honours: First Prize, Norwegian Association of Secondary School Teachers, 1976; Listed in many national and international biographical dictionaries; IBC Awards: The Order of International Fellowship, 2006; Hall of Fame, 2007; The Director General's Roll of Honour, 2007; Deputy Director General, 2007; International Order of Merit, 2007; Honorary Director General, 2007; Advisor to Director General, 2007; Lifetime Achievement Award, 2007; Vice President, Recognition Board, World Congress of Arts, Sciences and Communications, 2007; International Educator of Year, 2007; Salute to Greatness Award, 2007; Distinguished Service to Education Award, 2007; ABI Awards: Universal Award of Accomplishment and Award Statue, 2006; Order of International Ambassadors, 2006; Woman of the Year, 2006; Research Board of Advisors, 2007; Outstanding Female Executive Award, 2007; International Cultural Diploma of Honor, 2007; International Peace Prize, 2007; American Medal of Honor, 2007. Memberships: American Education and Research Association; Norwegian-American Association; Norwegian Research Association; Norwegian Teachers Association; Norwegian Association of Education; Norwegian Association of Professional Authors. Address: IHPT – Institute for Human Potential Training, Karleksstigen 10, 4448 Stenungsund, Sweden. E-mail: leik-bjo@frisurf.no Website: www.leiknyannadotter.com

BJÖRNSSON Helgi, b. 6 December 1942, Iceland. Research Professor. m. Thora Ellen Thorhallsdottir, 2 sons, 3 daughters. Education: Cand mag, 1967, Doctor of Science,1969, Doctor of Philosophy, 1988, University of Olso, Norway. Appointments: Hydrologist, Norwegian Water and Electricity Board, Oslo, 1970-71; Glaciologist, Science Institute, University of Iceland, 1971-73; Postdoctoral Fellow, H H Wills Physics Laboratory, University of Bristol, England, 1973-75; Research Scientist, 1975-82, Senior Research Scientist, 1982-90, Research Professor, 1990-, Head of the Division of Geophysics, 1991-95, Science Institute, University of Iceland; Adjunct Professor in Glaciology, University of Olso, Norway, 1994-2004; Visiting Scientist: Institute of Physical Geography, University of Stockholm, Sweden, 1980, Institute of Geography, University of Oslo, Norway, 1986-87, Institute of Arctic and Alpine Research, Boulder, Colorado, USA, 1996, Scott Polar Research Institute and British Antarctic Survey, Cambridge, England, 1997, University of British Columbia, Vancouver, Canada, 2005. Publications: Articles in scientific journals as co-author include most recently: Surges of glaciers in Iceland, 2003; New insights into the subglacial and periglacial hydrology of Vatnajökull, Iceland, from a distributed physical model, 2003; A coupled sheet-conduit model of jökulhlaup propagation, 2004; Sensitivity of Vatnajökull ice cap hydrology and dynamics to climate warming over the next 2 centuries, 2005; Simulation of Vatnajökull Ice Cap Dynamics, 2005. Honours: Member, Science Academy of Iceland, 1985; VISA Iceland Award for Science, 1999; Dr Honoris Causa, University of Stockholm, 2002; The University of Iceland Award for Research, 2003. Memberships: President, 1987-98, Iceland Glaciological Society; Editor of Jökull, 1977-85, 1989-98; Council Board Member, 1978-81, 1984, 1990-93, 1999-2001, Vice-President, 1999-2001, International Glaciological Society; International Polar Year Committee of Iceland, 2005-; Explorers Club,

2005. Address: Science Institute, University of Iceland, Dunhagi 3, 107 Reykjavik, Iceland. E-mail: hb@raunvis.hi.is Website: www.raunvis.hi.is

BJÖRNSSON Ólafur Grímur, b. 6 January 1944, Iceland. Senior Investigator; Physician. Education: Cand real, College of Reykjavík, 1964; Cand phil, 1965, Cand mag (part I of II), 1966, MD 1973, University of Iceland; PhD, University of London, England, 1982; Diploma in Clinical Biochemistry and Clinical Physiology, Iceland, 1984. Appointments: Intern at various hospitals affiliated with the University of Iceland, 1973-75; Medical Resident, Department of Clinical Biochemistry, University Hospital of Iceland, 1975-77; Research Fellow, Hammersmith Hospital, University of London, 1977-82; Senior Research Fellow, Medical Research Council Lipid Metabolic Unit, London, 1982-84; Research Associate, Department of Biochemistry and Biophysics, University of Pennsylvania, USA, 1984-89; Research Associate, Metabolic Research Laboratory, University of Oxford, England, 1989-94. Publications: Numerous articles in professional scientific medical journals; Editor of a Festschrift to Professor Emeritus David Davidsson, University of Iceland; Collaboration work, National Energy Authority, National Museum of Iceland, Department of Clinical Biochemistry, University Hospital of Iceland, University of Akureyri; Project Grantee, Icelandic Government, Icelandic Science Foundation and University Hospital of Iceland. Honour: Listed in Who's Who publications. Memberships: American Society of Biochemistry and Molecular Biology; Biophysical Society, USA; European Society for Clinical Investigation; The Icelandic Society London; Oxbridge, Iceland. Address: Department of Physiology, University of Iceland, Vatnsmýrarvegur 16, 101 Reykjavík, Iceland.

BLACK Jack, b. 28 August 1969, Hermosa Beach, California, USA. Actor, Musician. m. Tanya Haden, 2006, 1 son. Education: University of California at Los Angeles. Career: Films: Bob Roberts, 1992; Airborne, Demolition Man, 1993; Blind Justice, The NeverEnding Story III, 1994; Bye Bye, Love, Waterworld, Dead Man Walking, 1995; Crossworlds, Bio-Dome, The Cable Guy, Mars Attacks!, 1996; Bongwater, The Jackal, 1997; Johnny Skidmarks, Enemy of the State, 1998; Cradle Will Rock, Jesus' Son, 1999; High Fidelity, 2000; Saving Silverman, Frank's Book, Shallow Hal, 2001; Run Ronnie Run, Orange County, Ice Age (voice), 2002; The School of Rock, 2003; LaserFart, Envy, Shark Tale (voice), 2004; King Kong, 2005; Tenacious D in: The Pick of Destiny, Nacho Libre, The Holiday, 2006; Be Kind rewind, Margot at the wedding, 2007. TV: Our Shining Moment, 1991; Marked for Murder, 1993; The Innocent, 1994; Heat Vision and Jack, 1999; Tenacious D, 1999; Lord of the Piercing, 2002; Jack Black: Spider-Man, 2002; Bobobo-bo Bo-bobo, 2003; Computerman, 2003.

BLACK Peter Mclaren, b. 3 April 1944, Calgary, Canada. Neurosurgeon. m. Katharine, 2 sons, 3 daughters. Education: AB, Harvard College, 1966; MD, McGill University, 1970; PhD, Georgetown University, 1978. Appointments: Assistant Professor of Surgery, 1980-84, Associate Professor, 1984-87, Harvard Medical School; Franc D Ingraham Professor of Neurosurgery, Harvard Medical School, 1987-; Senior Surgeon the Active Staff, Brigham and Women's Hospital, Boston, Massachusetts, 1998-. Publications: Numerous articles in professional medical journals. Honours include: J Francis Williams Prize in Medicine, McGill University, 1970; Teacher-Investigator Award, NINDS, 1973-78; Distinguished Service Award, Joint Section on Tumors, American Association of Neurological Surgeons and Congress of

Neurological Surgeons, 1995; Pioneer Award, Children's Brain Tumor Foundation, 2004; ROFEH International Humanitarian Award, 2005; Honoured Guest of the Congress of Neurological Surgeons, 2006; Charles Wilson Award – AANS/CNS Section on Tumors, 2007. Memberships include: American Medical Association; Society for Health and Human Values; Research Society of Neurological Surgeons; Congress of Neurological Surgeons; New England Neurosurgical Society; New York Academy of Sciences; Society for Biological Psychiatry; Society of University Neurosurgeons; American Academy of Neurological Surgeons; American College of Surgeons; International Society of Pituitary Surgeons; Society of University Neurosurgeons; American Association of Neurological Surgeons; Congress of Neurological Surgeons; American Academy of Neurological Surgeons; International Society of Pituitary Surgeons; World Federation of Neurosurgical Societies. Address: Department of Neurosurgery, Brigham and Womens Hospital, 75 Francis Street, Boston, MA 02115, USA.

BLACK Shirley Temple, b. 23 April 1928, Santa Monica, California, USA. Actress; Diplomat. m. (1) John Agar Jr, 1945, divorced 1950, 1 daughter; m. (2) Charles A Black, 1950, deceased 2005, 1 son, 1 daughter. Education: Privately and Westlake School for Girls. Appointments: Career as film actress commenced at 3½ years; First full-length film was Stand Up and Cheer; Narrator/actress in TV series Shirley Temple Storybook, 1958; Hostess/Actress Shirley Temple Show, 1960; Delegation to UN New York, 1969-70; Ambassador to Ghana, 1974-76; White House Chief of Protocol, 1976-77; Ambassador to Czechoslovakia, 1989-92; Director, National Multiple Sclerosis Society. Publication: Child Star, 1988. Films include: Little Miss Marker; Baby Take a Bow; Bright Eyes; Our Little Girl; The Little Colonel; Curly Top; The Littlest Rebel; Captain January; Poor Little Rich Girl; Dimples; Stowaway; Wee Willie Winkie; Heidi; Rebecca of Sunnybrook Farm; Little Miss Broadway; Just Around the Corner; The Little Princess; Susannah of the Mounties; The Blue Bird; Kathleen; Miss Annie Rooney; Since You Went Away; Kiss and Tell; That Hagen Girl; War Party; The Bachelor and the Bobby-Soxer; Honeymoon. Honours: Dame Order of Knights of Malta - Paris - 1968; American Exemplar Medal, 1979; Gandhi Memorial International Foundation Award, 1988; Screen Actors guild, Lifetime Achievement Award, 2005: Numerous state decorations. Memberships: Member US Commission for UNESCO, 1973-; Member, US Delegation on African Refugee Problems Geneva, 1981. Address: c/o Academy of Motion Picture Arts and Sciences, 8949 Wilshire Blvd, Beverly Hills, CA 90211, USA.

BLACKBURN George Richard (Dick), b. 19 February 1917, Leeds, Yorkshire, England. Barrister-at-Law. m. Dulcie May Garrod, deceased 1989, 1 son, 1 daughter. Education: Sherborne School; MA, Christ's College, Cambridge, 1935-38; ALAM, London Academy of Music and Dramatic Art, 1951-52. Appointments: World War II: Private, QORWK, KOYLI, LRB Regiments, Army, 1940-41; Lt (A) RNVR (Pilot Fleet Air Arm), 1941-46; Flt Lt, RAFVR, 1949-52; Lt CDR, RNVR, 1952-58; RNR, 1958-; Bar, Inner Temple, 1948; Practised NE Circuit, 1950-56; Director, Legal Adviser, Tiltman Langley Laboratories Ltd, 1952-57; Lawyer with Shell-Mex & BP Ltd, 1956-63; Director of own company, Airfield, 1963-67; Legal Manager, Hotel & Catering Industry Training Board, 1967-71; Group Legal Officer, Calor Group, Slough, 1971-81; Consultancy work, 1981-; Company Secretary, Kings Park Management Co Ltd, Eastbourne, Sussex, 1986-. Honours: VRD, 1958. Memberships: Associate, Royal Aeronautical Society; Freemason/SLGR; Royal Aero

Club; RAF Historical Society; RAF Club; Naval Club; Bar Association Commerce, Finance, Industry; University of the Third Age; European Movement; Ashridge Circle. Address: 26 Pearl Court, Cornfield Terrace, Eastbourne, East Sussex BN21 4AA, England.

BLACKMAN Honor, b. 12 December 1927, London, England. Actress. M. (1) Bill Sankey, 1946-56; (2) Maurice Kaufmann, 1963, divorced 1975, 2 adopted children. Creative Works: Films include: Fame is the Spur, 1947; Green Grow the Rushes, 1951; Come Die My Love, 1952; The Rainbow Jacket, 1953; The Glass Cage, 1954; Dead Man's Evidence, 1955; A Matter of Who, 1961; Goldfinger, 1964; Life at the Top, 1965; Twist of Sand, 1967; The Virgin and the Gipsy, 1970; To the Devil a Daughter, 1975; Summer Rain, 1976; The Cat and the Canary, 1977; Talos - The Mummy; To Walk with Lions; Bridget Jones's Diary, 2001; Jack Brown and the Curse of the Crown, 2001; Plays include: Madamoiselle Colombe, 2000; Cabaret, 2007: TV appearances include: Four Just Men, 1959; Man of Honour, 1960; Ghost Squad, 1961; Top Secret, 1962; The Avengers, 1962-64; The Explorer, 1968; Visit From a Stranger, 1970; Out Damned Spot, 1972; Wind of Change, 1977; Robin's Nest, 1982; Never the Twain, 1982; The Secret Adversary, 1983; Lace, 1985; The First Modern Olympics, 1986; Minder on the Orient Express, 1986; Dr Who, 1986; William Tell, 1986; The Upper Hand (TV series); Jack and the Beanstalk: The Real Story, 2001; Revolver, 2001. Address: c/o Jean Diamond, London Management, 2-4 Noel Street, London W1V 3RB, England.

BLACKWELL Colin Roy, b. 4 September 1927, South Molton, Devon, England. Consulting Engineer. m. Susan Elizabeth Hunt. Education: BSc, Honours, Civil Engineering, University of Bristol, 1948-51. Appointments: Commissioned 83 LAA Regiment Royal Artillery, served Middle East, 1946-48; Joined, 1951, Site Engineer, Gold Coast (later Ghana), 1955-57, Senior Engineer, 1957-68, Principal Engineer, 1969-82, Freeman Fox & Partners, Consulting Engineers; Director, Freeman Fox Ltd, 1983-87; Consultant on telescopes and observatories to Hyder Consulting Ltd (formerly Acer Consultants Ltd, formerly Acer Freeman Fox), 1987-; Member, CIRIA Research Committee, 1976-79; Member, British Council Mission to Saudi Arabia, 1985; BSI CSB Committee, 1986-91. Publications: Das 64m Radioteleskop in Parkes (Australien), 1966; The reflector dishes of the 210 ft radio telescope at Parkes, Australia and the 150 ft diameter radio telescope at Lake Transverse, Ontario, 1966. Memberships: Fellow, Institution of Civil Engineers; Fellow, American Society of Civil Engineers; Fellow Royal Astronomical Society. Address: 14 St Mary's Court, Malthouse Square, Old Beaconsfield, Bucks HP9 2LG, England.

BLAINEY Geoffrey Norman, b. 11 March 1930, Melbourne, Victoria, Australia. Writer. Education: Ballarat High School; Wesley College, Melbourne; Queen's College, University of Melbourne. Publications: The Peaks of Lyell, 1954; A Centenary History of the University of Melbourne, 1957; Gold and Paper, 1958; Mines in the Spinifex, 1960; The Rush That Never Ended, 1963; A History of Camberwell, 1965; If I Remember Rightly: The Memoirs of W S Robinson, 1966; Wesley College: The First Hundred Years (co-author and editor), 1967; The Tyranny of Distance, 1966; Across a Red World, 1968; The Rise of Broken Hill, 1968; The Steel Master, 1971; The Causes of War, 1973; Triumph of the Nomads, 1975; A Land Half Won, 1980; The Blainey View, 1982; Our Side of the Country, 1984; All for Australia, 1984; The Great Seesaw, 1988; A Game of our Own: The Origins of Australian Football, 1990; Odd Fellows, 1991; Eye on

Australia, 1991; Jumping Over the Wheel, 1993; The Golden Mile, 1993; A Shorter History of Australia, 1994; White Gold, 1997; A History of the AMP, 1999; In Our Time, 1999; A History of the World, 2000; This Land is All Horizons, 2002; Black Kettle and Full Moon, 2003; A Very Short History of the World, 2004-; A Short History of the 20th Century, 2005. Honours: Gold Medal, Australian Literature Society, 1963; Encyclopaedia Britannica Gold Award, New York, 1988; Companion of the Order of Australia, 2000. Memberships: Australia Council, chairman, 1977-81; Commonwealth Literary Fund, chairman, 1971-73; Professor of Economic History and History, University of Melbourne, 1968-88; Professor of Australian Studies, Harvard, 1982-83; Inaugural Chancellor of University of Ballarat, 1994-98; Chairman, National Council for Centenary of Federation, 2001; Chairman, Australia-China Council, 1979-84. Address: PO Box 257, East Melbourne, Victoria 8002, Australia.

BLAIR Anna Dempster, b. 12 February 1927, Glasgow, Scotland. Author. m. Matthew Blair, 13 June 1952, 1 son, 1 daughter. Education: Dunfermline College, Graduated 1947. Appointment: Teacher, Glasgow Education Authority, 1947-52, 1965-75. Publications: A Tree in the West; The Rowan on the Ridge, 1980; Historical Novels: Tales of Ayrshire (Traditional Tales Retold), 1993; Tea at Miss Cranston's Reminiscences/ Social History, 1985; Croft and Creel, Scottish Tales, 1987; The Goose-Girl of Eriska, Seed Corn, 1989; Traditional Tales: More Tea at Miss Cranston's, 1991. Contributions to: Old Giffnock (local history); Various others. Address: 20 Barrland Drive, Giffnock, Glasgow G46 7QD, Scotland.

BLAIR Anthony Charles Lynton (Tony), b. 6 May 1953, Edinburgh, Scotland. Member of Parliament; Politician. m. Cherie Booth, 1980, 3 sons, 1 daughter. Education: Fettes College, Edinburgh; St Johns College, Oxford. Appointments: Barrister, Trade Union and Employment Law; MP, Sedgefield, 1983-; Shadow Treasury Spokesman, 1984-87; Trade and Industry Spokesman, 1987-88, Energy Spokesman, 1988-89; Employment Spokesman, 1989-92, Home Affairs Spokesman, 1992-94; Leader, Labour Party, 1994-, Prime Minister, First Lord of the Treasury and Minister for the Civil Service, 1997-2007; Middle East Envoy for the United Nations, United States, European Union and Russia, 2007. Publication: New Britain: My Vision of a Young Country, 1996; The Third Way, 1998. Honours: Honorary Bencher, Lincolns Inn, 1994; Honorary LLD, Northumbria; Charlemagne Prize, 1999. Address: 10 Downing Street, London SW1A 2AA, England.

BLAIR Claude, b. 30 November 1922, Manchester, England. Antiquary; Art Historian. Education: BA, 1950, MA, 1963, University of Manchester. Appointments: Assistant, Tower of London Armouries, 1951-56; Honorary Editor, Journal of Arms and Armour Society, 1953-77; Assistant Keeper, 1956-72, Deputy Keeper, 1966-72, Keeper, 1972-82, Metalwork, Victoria and Albert Museum, London; Consultant, Christie's, London, 1982-2004; Bonham's, London, 2005-. Publications: European Armour, 1958; European and American Arms, 1962; Pistols of the World, 1968; Three Presentation Swords in the Victoria and Albert Museum, 1972; The James A de Rothschild Collection at Waddesdon Manor: Arms, Armour and Base-Metalwork, 1974; Pollard's History of Firearms, 1983; A History of Silver, 1987; General Editor and contributor to The Crown Jewels, 1998. Honours: FSA, 1956; OBE, 1994; Gold Medal of the Society of Antiquaries, 1998; LittD (Honoris causa), Manchester University, 2004; CVO, 2005. Address: 90 Links Road, Ashtead, Surrey KT21 2HW, England.

BLAIR David Chalmers Leslie Jr, b. 8 April 1951, Long Beach, California, USA. Alternative Rock Artist; Composer; Artist; Author. Education: BA, French, ESL certificate, California State University at Long Beach, 1979; Postgraduate Studies, Université de Provence, Aix-en-Provence, France, 1979-80. Publications: Novels: Death of an Artist, 1982; Vive la France, 1993; Death of America, 1994; Mother, 1998; Evening in Wisconsin, 2001; The Girls (and Women) I Have Known, 2001; A Small Snack Shop in Stockholm, Sweden, 2002; Composer, Writer and Recorder of 108 albums including: Her Garden of Earthly Delights; Sir Blair of Rothes; Europe; St Luke Passion. Membership: Libertarian Party, USA. Address: 19331 105th Avenue, Cadott, WI 54727, USA.

BLAIR John Samuel Greene, b. 31 December 1928, Wormit, Fife, Scotland. Medical Historian; Former Surgeon. m. Ailsa Jean Bowes, 2 sons, 1 daughter. Education: High School of Dundee, Harris Gold Medal for Dux of School, Dux in English, 1946; Harkness Scholar, St Andrews University 1946-50; MB ChB, 1951; ChM, 1961; Clinical part of MD, St Andrews, 1953; D (Obst) RCOG, 1952; FRCS (Ed), 1958; FICS, 1983; BA (External), London, 1955. Appointments include: RAMC service 1952-55; Joined TA via St Andrews OTC (CO, 1967-71); Commanded RAMC and other Reserve Units, retired as Honorary Colonel, 225 (Highland) Field Ambulance, RAMC; Served at Musgrave Park Military Hospital as Consultant Surgeon on 2 tours during 1975-76, part of Security Forces Northern Ireland Command; Consultant Surgeon, Perth Royal Infirmary, 1965-90; Honorary Senior Lecturer in Surgery, Dundee University, Postgraduate Clinical Tutor, Perth, 1966-1971; Honorary Senior Lecturer, 1990-97, Reader, 1997-2001, History of Medicine, University of St Andrews; Current appointment: Honorary Senior Teaching Fellow, Medical History, Faculty of Medicine, University of Dundee. Publications: 14 articles in medical and surgical journals; 12 major historical articles; Books include: History of St Andrews OTC, 1982; History of Medicine in St Andrews University, 1987; Ten Tayside Doctors, 1988; History of the Bridge of Earn Hospital 1940-1990, 1990; History of the Royal Perth Golfing Society and County and City Club, 1997; In Arduis Fidelis. Definitive Centenary History of the Royal Army Medical Corps, 1989-1998, 1998, second edition, 2001; The Conscript Doctors: Memories of National Service, 2001; History of Tayforth Officers Training Corps, 2003; History of Medicine in Dundee University, 2007; Numerous invited lectures. Honours include: OBE (Military), 1974; Doctor of Letters, honoris causa, St Andrews, 1991; John Blair Fund set up by British Society for the History of Medicine, 1996; Honorary Fellow, Royal College of Physicians of Edinburgh, 2000; Fellow, Society of Antiquaries (Scotland), 1997; Captain, Royal Perth Golfing Society, 1997-99; Fellow Royal Historical Society, 2001; Honorary Member, SSHM, 2003. Memberships: Fellow BMA, 1993; Knight of St John - Hospitaller, Priory of Scotland, 1992-2000; President, Scottish Society of the History of Medicine, 1991-94; President, British Society for the History of Medicine, 1993-95; Apothecaries Lecturer, Worshipful Society of Apothecaries, London, 1994-; Ostler Club of London, 1996; Vice-President, International Society for the History of Medicine, 2000-; American Ostler Society, 2002. Address: "The Brae", 143 Glasgow Road, Perth PH2 0LX, Scotland. E-mail: jgb143@aol.com

BLAKE Quentin Saxby, b. 16 December 1932, Sidcup, Kent, England. Artist; Illustrator; Teacher. Education: Downing College, Cambridge; London Institute of Education; Chelsea School of Art. Appointments: Freelance Illustrator, 1957-; Tutor, Royal College of Art, 1965-86, Head, Illustration Department, 1978-86, Visiting Professor, 1989-, Senior Fellow, 1988; Children's Laureate, 1999-2001. Publications: Patrick, 1968; Mister Magnolia, 1980; Quentin Blake's Nursery Rhyme Book, 1983; Mrs Armitage on Wheels, 1987; Mrs Armitage Queen of the Road; Mrs Armitage and the Big Wave; The Story of the Dancing Frog; Quentin Blake's ABC, 1989; Angelo, 1990; All Join In, 1992; Cockatoos, 1992; Simpkin, 1993; La Vie de la Page, 1995; The Puffin Book of Nonsense Verse, 1996; The Green Ship, 1998; Clown, 1998; Drawing for the Artistically Undiscovered (with John Cassidy), 1999; Fantastic Daisy Artichoke, 1999; Words and Pictures, 2000; The Laureate's Party, 2000; Zagazoo, 2000; Tell Me a Picture, 2001; Loveykins, 2002; A Sailing Boat in the Sky, 2002; Laureate's Progress, 2002; Angel Pavement, 2004; Illustrations for over 250 works for children and adults, including collaborations with Roald Dahl, Russell Hoban, Joan Aiken, Michael Rosen, John Yeoman; Exhibitions: Quentin Blake – 50 Years of Illustration, The Gilbert Collection, Somerset House, London, 2003-04; Quentin Blake at Christmas, Dulwich Picture Gallery, London, 2004-05. Honours: Honorary Fellow: Brighton University, 1996; Downing College, Cambridge, 2000; Honorary RA; Chevalier des Arts et des Lettres, 2002; Dr hc: London Institute, 2000, Northumbria, 2001, RCA, 2001; Hon D Litt, Cambridge University, 2004; CBE, 2005. Address: Flat 8, 30 Bramham Gardens, London SW5 0HF, England.

BLAKELY Curt R, b. St Joseph, Missouri, USA. Assistant Professor. m. Mary Kathryn Johannsen, 2 sons, 2 daughters. Education: Baccalaureate, 1989, Masters, 1991, University of Nebraska; Education Specialist, Central Missouri State University, 1994; Doctorate, Southern Illinois University, 2003. Appointments: Graduate Teaching and Research Assistant, Department of Criminal Justice, University of Nebraska, 1989-91; Police Training Specialist, Union Pacific Railroad Police Department, 1991-92; Officer, Missouri Board of Probation/Parole, 1992-93; Graduate Research and Teaching Assistant, Office of Graduate Studies, Central Missouri State University, 1994; Job Development and Information Management Systems Co-ordinator and Classification Specialist, New Mexico Corrections Department, 1994-97; Police Training Specialist and Part-time Faculty, Department of Police Studies, Eastern Kentucky University, 1997-99; Graduate Teaching Assistant, Departments of Criminal Justice and Sociology, Southern Illinois University, 1999-2003; Assistant Professor, Department of Political Science & Criminal Justice, University of South Alabama, 2003-. Publications: 2 books; 5 chapters; Numerous articles in professional journals. Honours: 3 New Mexico Corrections Department Commendations, 1995-97; Undergraduate Special Population's Commission Award, 2001; Letters of Appreciation, American Correctional Association for Meritorious Service; Certificate of Appreciation, Academy of Criminal Justice Sciences, 2006; Top Professor, University of South Alabama, 2006. Memberships: American Society of Criminology; Southern Criminal Justice Association; Academy of Criminal Justice Sciences. Address: Department of Political Science & Criminal Justice, University of South Alabama, Humanities Bldg, Room 218-B, Mobile, AL 36688-0002, USA. E-mail: cblakely@usouthal.edu

BLAKEMORE Colin, b. 1 June 1944, Stratford-on-Avon, England. Neurophysiologist; Professor of Physiology. m. Andrée Elizabeth Washbourne, 1965, 3 daughters. Education: Natural Sciences, Corpus Christi College, Cambridge, 1965; PhD, Physiological Optics, Neurosensory Laboratory, University of California at Berkeley, 1968. Appointments: Demonstrator, Physiological Laboratory, Cambridge

University, 1968-72; Lecturer in Physiology, Cambridge, 1972-79; Fellow and Director of Medical Studies, Downing College, 1971-79; Professorial Fellow of Magdalen College, Oxford, 1979-; Wayneflete Professor of Physiology, Oxford University, 1979-; Chief Executive European Dana Alliance for the Brain, 1996-; President, 1997-98, Vice President, 1990-, British Association for the Advancement of Science; President, British Neuroscience Association, 1997-2000; President, Physiological Society, 2001-; Director, McDonnell-Pew Centre for Cognitive Neuroscience, Oxford, 1990-2003; Director, MRC Interdisciplinary Research Centre for Cognitive Neuroscience, Oxford, 1996-2003; Chief Executive Medical Research Council, 2003-; Associate Director, MRC Research Centre in Brain and Behaviour, Oxford, 1990-. Publications: Editor, Handbook of Psychobiology, 1975; Mechanics of the Mind, 1977; Editor, Mindwaves, 1987; The Mind Machine, 1988, Editor, Images and Understanding, Vision: Coding and Efficiency, 1990; Sex and Society, 1999; Oxford Companion to the Body, 2001; The Physiology of Cognitive Processes (co-editor), The Roots of Visual Awareness (co-editor), 2003; Contributions to: Constraints on Learning, Illusion in Art and Nature, 1973; The Neurosciences Third Study Program, 1974; and to professional journals. Honours: Robert Bing Prize, 1975; Man of the Year, 1978; Christmas Lectures for Young People, Royal Institute, 1982; John Locke Medal, 1983; Netter Prize, 1984; Bertram Louis Abrahams Lecture, Cairns Memorial Lecture and Medal, 1986; Norman McAllister Gregg Lecture and Medal, 1988; Royal Society Michael Faraday Medal, Robert Doyne Medal, 1989; John P McGovern Science and Society Lecture and Medal, 1990; Montgomery Medal, Sir Douglas Robb Lectures, 1991; Honorary DSc, Aston, 1992; Honorary Osler Medal, Ellison-Cliffe Medal, 1993; DSc, Salford, Charles F Prentice Award, 1994; Annual Review Prize Lecture, 1995; Century Lecture, Alcon Prize, 1996; Newton Lecture, Cockcroft Lecture, 1997; Memorial Medal, 1998; Alfred Meyer Award, British Neuroscience Association Outstanding Contribution to Neuroscience, Menzies Medal, Menzies Foundation, Melbourne, 2001; Bioindustry Association Award for Outstanding Personal Contribution to Bioscience, Lord Crook Gold Medal, Worshipful Company of Spectacle Makers, 2004; Edinburgh Medal, City of Edinburgh, Science Educator Award, 2005; Kenneth Myer Medal, 2006; Honorary Fellow: Cardiff University of Wales, 1998; Downing College, Cambridge, 1999-; Royal College of Physicians, 2004-; Institute of Biology, 2004-. Memberships: Editorial Board, Perception, 1971; Behavioural and Brain Sciences, 1977; Journal of Developmental Physiology, 1978-86; Experimental Brain Research, 1979-89; Language and Communication, 1979; Reviews in the Neurosciences, 1984-; News in Physiological Sciences, 1985; Clinical Vision Sciences, 1986; Chinese Journal of Physiological Sciences, 1988; Advances in Neuroscience, 1989-; Vision Research, 1993-; Honorary Member, Physiological Society, 1998; Associate Editor, NeuroReport, 1989-; Honorary Associate, Rationalist Press Association, 1986-; Editor-in-Chief, IBRO News, 1986-; Leverhulme Fellowship, 1974-75; BBC Reith Lecturer, 1976; Lethaby Professor, RCA, London, 1978; Storer Lecturer, University of California at Davis, 1980; Regents' Professor, 1995-96; Macallum Lecturer, University of Toronto, 1984; Fellow, World Economic Forum, 1994-98; Honorary Fellow, Corpus Christi College, Cambridge, 1994-; Founder, Fellow, Academy of Medical Sciences, 1998-; Foreign Member, Royal Netherlands Academy of Arts and Sciences, 1993; Member, Worshipful Company of Spectacle Makers and Freemen of the City of London, 1997; Member, Livery, 1998; Patron and Member, Professional Advisory Panel Headway (National Head Injuries Association), 1997-; Patron, Association for Art, Science, Engineering

and Technology, 1997-. Address: Medical Research Council, 20 Park Crescent, London W1B 1AL, England. E-mail: colin.blakemore@headoffice.mrc.ac.uk

BLANC Raymond Rene Alfred, b. 19 November 1949, Besançon, France. Chef, Restaurant Owner. 2 sons. Education: Besançon Technical College. Career: Various positions, 1968-76; Military Service, 1970-71; Manager and Chef de cuisine, Bleu, Blanc, Rouge, Oxford, 1976-77; Chef Proprietor, Les Quat'Saisons, Oxford, 1977; Director and Chair, 1978-88, Maison Blanc, 1978-; Le Manoir aux Quat'Saisons, 1984; Le Petit Blanc, in Oxford, 1996, in Cheltenham, 1998, in Birmingham, 1999, in Manchester, 2000; in Tunbridge Wells. Weekly recipe column in the Observer, 1988-90; TV series: Blanc Mange, 1994; Passion for Perfection, 2002. Publications: Recipes from Le Manoir aux Quat'Saisons, 1989; Cooking for Friends, 1991; Blanc Mange, 1994; Best A Blanc Christmas, 1996; Contributions to: Take Six Cooks, 1986; Taste of Health, 1987; Masterchefs of Europe, 1998; Blanc Vite, 1998; Restaurants of Great Britain, 1989; Gourmet Garden, 1990; European Chefs, 1990; Foolproof French Cooking, 2002. Honours: Representative of Great Britain at Grand Final of Wedgwood World Master of Culinary Arts, Paris, 2002; Hon DBA, Oxford Brookes University, 1999; European Chef of the Year, 1989; Personalité de l'Année, 1990; Craft Guild of Chefs Special Award, 2002; AA Restaurant Guide Chef of the Year, 2004; many other awards. Memberships: Academie Culinaire de France; British Gastronomic Academy; Restaurateurs Association of Great Britain. Address: Le Manoir aux Quat'Saisons, Church Road, Great Milton, Oxford OX44 7PD, England. Website: www.manoir.com

BLANCHETT Cate, b. 14 May 1969, Melbourne, Australia. Actress. m. Andrew Upton, 1997, 2 sons. Education: Melbourne University, National Institute of Dramatic Art. Appointments: Plays include: Top Girls; Kafka Dances; Oleanna; Hamlet; Sweet Phoebe; The Tempest; The Blind Giant is Dancing; Plenty. Films include: Parkland; Paradise Road, Thank God He Met Lizzie, Oscar and Lucinda, 1997; Elizabeth, 1998; Dreamtime Alice, also co-producer; The Talented Mr Ripley; An Ideal Husband; Pushing Tin, 1999; Bandit, The Man Who Cried, The Gift, Bandits, 2000; Heaven, The Lord of the Rings: The Fellowship of the Ring, Charlotte Gray, 2001; The Shipping News, The Lord of the Rings: The Two Towers, 2002; The Lord of the Rings: The Return of the King, Coffee and Cigarettes, 2003; The Life Aquatic, The Aviator, 2004; Stories of Lost Souls, Little Fish, 2005; Babel, The Good German, Notes on a Scandal, 2006; Hot Fuzz (cameo), The Golden Age, I'm Not There, 2007. TV includes: Heartland, 1994; GP Police Rescue. Honours: Newcomer Award, 1993; Rosemont Best Actress Award; Golden Globe Award, 1998; BAFTA Award for Best Actress, 1999; Best Actress, National Board of Review, 2001; Golden Camera Award, 2001; Oscar, Best Actress in a Supporting Role, 2004; Best Supporting Actress, Screen Actors Guild Awards, 2005; Best Actress in a Supporting Role, BAFTA Awards, 2005; Best Supporting Actress, Academy Awards, 2005. Address: c/o Robyn Gardiner, PO Box 128, Surry Hill, 2010 NSW, Australia.

BLANK Eugene, b. 8 May 1924, Baltimore, USA. Paediatrician; Radiologist; Educator. m. Esther Honikberg, 1958, 3 daughters. Education: BA, 1948, MD, 1954, Johns Hopkins University. Appointments: 2nd Lieutenant, USMC, South Pacific, 1942-45; Diplomate, American Board of Paediatrics, 1960; American Board Radiology, 1965; Professor Emeritus in Paediatrics and Radiology, Oregon

Health Sciences University, Portland, 1991. Publications: Paediatric Images Casebook of Differential Diagnosis, 1997; USMC457703, 2006. Address: 4940 SW Humphrey Park Road, Portland, OR 97221, USA.

BLASE Anthony Idomeneus, 30 July 1929, Chicago, USA. Retired Electronics Executive; Writer; Poet. m. Aspacia Mary Manos, 1952, 2 daughters. Education: BSBA, Loyola University, Chicago, 1955. Appointments: Corporal, US Army, 1948-50; Licensed general insurance broker, Illinois; Real Estate Broker, Illinois; Controller, Universal Wire and Cable Company, Chicago, 1958-64; Vice President, Controller, Rockola Manufacturing Corporation, Chicago, 1964-78; Executive Vice President, Treasurer, Board of Directors, Wells-Gardner Electronics, Chicago, 1978-88. Publications: In Search of Alexander, 1990; Contemplating Forms, 1989; Thus the Gods Taught Man, 1991; On Moral Purpose, Byzantium, 1992; Religious Paradigm?, 1993; Vessels Without Dimension, 1994; The Ultimate Comprehension, 1995; The History of Western Philosophy, 1996; The Universal Will, 1997; Historical Essays, Embracing the Universe, 1998; But Grain of Sand, The Etaireia, 1999; Uncompromising Nature, As I Understand Aristotle, 2000; Hellenism in the Post Classical World, 2001; Idomenian Ethics, 2002; From Acorn to Oak – Princip to Ground Zero, The Unloseable Wager, 2003; Unscripted Shadows, The Ideal Concept, 2004; Eternal Recurrence, 2004; Of Cardinal Virtues, 2004; Criterion of Truth, 2005; Analogous to Man, 2005; The Glow of Words in all their Prism, Philosophic Edits, Of Laurels Bright, Of Wreaths and Thorns, A Nation Keens, Unjeweled Crown, Twilight's Smold'ring Embers, A Lightning's Bolt, A Leapt Belief, A Depth Unknown, A Harvest's Glean, Ontology's Demand, Time in Space, Orphaned World, Affectation's Deceit, 2005; Credulity in Crept, Surgical Precision, A Mind Distilled, A Heart Fulfilled, A Fate's Unknown, In Meadow Lark, A Sourous Hark, A Book to Mark, Climatic Clime, Sieving Mind, Pandemic's Rise, Charting the Theogonies, The Whirlwind Creeps, Kinder, Gentler Thoughts, Realities Apprise, In Darkness Hid, A Promise Bid, A Horror's Rid, A Future's Hid, Of Ages Tolled, Beauty Compromised, 2006; Confounded World, A Martyr's Crown, Silver Lining Blurred, A Mount to Climb, A Sights Behold, 2007. Honours: Outstanding Contribution to Poetry Meritorious Decoration; Editor's Choice Award, 2006; 100 Top Writers, 2007; 2000 Outstanding Intellectuals of the 21st Century. Address: 3011 Applegate Ln, Glenview, IL 60025, USA. E-mail: tekanis5@aol.com

BLASHFORD-SNELL John Nicholas, b, 22 October 1936, Hereford, England. Colonel; Royal Engineers; Explorer; Author. m. Judith, 2 daughters. Education: Victoria College, Jersey, Channel Islands; RMA Sandhurst; The Staff College, Camberley. Appointments: Various military postings and commands, and leader of numerous scientific, military and youth development expeditions; Instructor and Adventure Training Officer, RMA Sandhurst, 1963-66; Leader, Great Abbai, Blue Nile Expedition, 1968; Chairman, Scientific Exploration Society, 1969-; Commander, Operation Drake, 1978-81; Director-General, Operation Raleigh, 1984-91; Lecturer, Ministry of Defence, 1991-; Chairman, The Starting Point Appeal, The Merseyside Youth Association, 1993-2001; Chairman, The Liverpool Construction Crafts Guild, 2001-; Appeal Director, The Trinity Sailing Trust, 2004-. Publications: Books, including Weapons and Tactics, (co-author), 1972; Where the Trails Run Out, 1974; In the Steps of Stanley, 1975; In the Wake of Drake, (co-author), 1980; Operation Drake, (co-author), 1981; 3 titles co-authored with Ann Tweedy, documenting the story of Operation Raleigh; Mammoth Hunt,

(co-author), 1996; Kota Mama, (co-author), 2000; East to the Amazon (with Richard Snailham), 2002; President, Just a Drop Charity, 2002-; Chair, The Liverpool Construction-Crafts Guild, 2003-. Honours: MBE; OBE; Selgrave Trophy, 1975; Freeman of the City of Hereford, 1984; Honorary DEng, University of Bournemouth, 1997; Honorary DSc, Durham University, 1986; Darien Medal, Colombia, 1972; Livingstone Medal, Royal Scottish Geographical Society, 1975; Patron's Medal, Royal Geographical Society, 1993; Paul Harris Fellow, Rotary International, 1981; Gold Medal, Institute of Royal Engineers, 1994; La Paz Medal, Bolivia, 2001. Memberships: President, Galley Hill Gun Club; President, The Centre for Fortean Zoology; The Vole Club; Trustee, Operation New World, 1996-. Address: Scientific Exploration Society, Expedition Base, Motcombe, Dorset, SP7 9PB, England. E-mail: jbs@ses-explore.org

BLATNÝ Pavel, b. 14 September 1931, Brno, Czech Republic. m. Danuse Spirková, 19 June 1982, 1 son, 1 daughter. Education: Studied Piano, Conducting and Composition; Musicology, University of Brno, 1958; Berklee School of Music, Boston, USA, 1968. Career: Composer; Conductor; Pianist; Chief, Music Department, Czech Television, to 1992; Professor, Janácek's Academy, Brno, to 1990. Compositions include: Concerto for Jazz Orchestra, 1962-64; Cantatas: Willow; Christmas Eve and Noonday Witch; Bells; Twelfth Night, based on Shakespeare's play, 1975; Full-length Musical for Children, Dilia, 1979; Two Movements for brasses, 1982; Signals for jazz orchestra, 1985; Prologue for mixed choir and jazz orchestra, 1984; Per organo e big band, 1983; Ring a Ring o' Roses, for solo piano, 1984; Symphony "Erbeniada" written for the festival "Prague Spring", world premier, 2004. Honours: Prize of Leos Jánácek, 1984; Antiteatro D'Argento for the Life's Work, Italy, 1988; Award for Life's Work, City of Brno, 2004. Honour: First place award, International Composer Composition, Prague Jazz Festival, 1966-67; Voted 5th place, 1967 and 3rd place, 1968, Composer category, Down Beat. Membership: President, Club of Moravian Composers. Address: Absolonova 35, 62400 Brno, Czech Republic.

BLAU Joseph Norman, b. 5 October 1928, Berlin, Germany. Consultant Neurological Physician. m. Jill Seligman, 2 sons, 1 daughter. Education: St Bartholomew's Medical College, London; Army (RAMC) Head Injury Hospital, Wheatley, Oxfordshire; Neurological Registrar to Sir Russell (later Lord) Brain, The London Hospital, Whitechapel; Research Fellow, Neurology Department (Immunology), Massachusetts General Hospital, USA; Degrees: MD, FRCP; FRCPath. Appointments: Formerly: Consultant Neurologist: Northwick Park Hospital and Research Centre, Harrow Middlesex, Royal National Throat, Nose and Ear Hospital, Gray's Inn Road, London, National Hospital for Neurology and Neurosurgery, Queen Square, London; Currently: Recognised Teacher in Neurology, University of London Institute of Neurology, Queen Square, London; Consultant Neurologist, St Luke's Hospital for the Clergy; Honorary Director and Honorary Consultant Neurologist, City of London Migraine Clinic, London. Publications: Books: The Headache and Migraine Handbook, 1986; Migraine - Clinical, Therapeutic, Conceptual and Research Aspects (editor and contributor), 1987; Understanding Headaches and Migraine, 1991; Book Chapter: Cervicogenetic Headache (with H Merskey), 2002; Articles: Life long migraine without headache (with SI Cohen), 2003; Harold G Woolf. The man and his migraine, 2004; Water deprivation headache (with Kell and Sperling), 2004; Ponytail Headache, 2004. Honours: Open Science Scholarship, St Bartholomew's Hospital Medical College; Nuffield Medical Research Fellowship; Research Fellow, Harvard University.

Memberships: Fellow and Past Councillor, Medical Society of London; Life Fellow, Royal Society of Medicine; Member and Past Chairman, British Association for the Study of Headache; Life Fellow, Past Councillor, Anglo-Dutch Migraine Association; Member, Association of British Neurologists; Member, International Headache Society; Honorary Medical Advisor, Migraine Action Association; Honorary Medical Advisor, British Society for Music Therapy; London Medical Orchestra (Cellist). Address: 5 Marlborough Hill, London NW8 0NN, England.

BLAŽIĆ Helena, b. 23 March 1966, Rijeka, Croatia. University Professor. 1 son, 1 daughter. Education: BA, Faculty of Economics, University of Rijeka, 1988; MA, Faculty of Economics, University of Ljubljana, 1989-93; Alpen-Adria Scholarship, University of Klagenfurt, Austria, 1994; Croatia Mentor Program, US Government Fellowship, Carol Martin Gatton College of Business and Economics, University of Kentucky, October 1997; PhD, Economics, University of Rijeka, 1999. Appointments: Research Assistant, 1989-93, Assistant, 1993-99, Senior Assistant, 1999-2000, Assistant Professor, 2000-2003, Associate Professor, 2003-08, Full Professor, 2008-, Director of Postgraduate Academic Study in Public Administration, 2004-, Faculty of Economics, University of Rijeka; Part-time Lecturer, University of Zagreb, 1996-97; Editorial Board Member of the Journal: Finacijska teorija i praksa, Institute of Public Finance, Zagreb, 2000-; President, Publishing Committee, Faculty of Economics, Member, Publishing Committee, 2000-07, Director, International Relations Office, Faculty of Economics, 2007-, University of Rijeka; Participant in numerous international conferences. Publications include most recently: Tax Compliance Costs of Companies in Croatia (journal article), 2004-07; Personal Income Tax Compliance Costs at an Individual Level in Croatia (journal article), 2004; The Investment Effects of PTAs in Southeast Europe (conference paper, co-author), 2004; Family Tax Treatment: A Comparative Analysis of Croatia and CEE (conference paper, co-author), 2005; Tax Compliance Costs for Companies in Slovenia and Croatia (journal article, co-author), 2005; Compliance Costs of Taxation in a Transition Country: The Example of Croatia (conference paper), 2005. Memberships: National Tax Association, USA; Croatian Society of Economists; Croatian Society of Accountants and Employees in Finance; Society for Development of High Education "Universitas" Croatia. Address: Faculty of Economics, University of Rijeka, Ivana Filipovića 4, 51000 Rijeka, Croatia. E-mail: helena@efri.hr

BLEARS Rt Hon Hazel Anne, b. 14 May 1956, Salford, England. Member of Parliament for Salford; Secretary of State for Communities and Local Government. m. Michael Halsall, 1989. Education: Wardley Grammar School; The Eccles (Sixth Form) College; BA (Hons), Law, Trent Polytechnic; Law Conversion Course, Chester College of Law, 1977. Appointments: Trainee Solicitor, Salford City Council, 1978-80; Private practice, 1980-81; Solicitor, Rossendale Borough Council, 1981; Elected Branch Secretary, NALGO, 1981; Solicitor, Wigan Metropolitan Borough Council, 1983; Education Solicitor, Manchester City Council; Councillor, Salford City Council, 1984-92; Chair, Salford Community Health Council; Member of Parliament for Salford. 1997-; Parliamentary Private Secretary to the Minister of State at the Department for Health, 1997-98; Parliamentary Private Secretary to the Chief Secretary to the Treasury, 1999; Member, later Deputy Head, Labour Party campaign team, General Election, 2001; Minister for Public Health and Parliamentary Under Secretary of State for Health. Department for Health, 2001-; Minister of State at the Home Office, 2003; Elected to National Executive Committee of the Labour Party, 2003; Member, Privy Council, 2005; Party Chair, 2006; Secretary of State for Communities and Local Government, 2007-.

BLEASDALE Alan, b. 23 March 1946. Playwright; Novelist. m. Julia Moses, 1970, 2 sons, 1 daughter. Education: Teachers Certificate, Padgate Teachers Training College. Publications: Scully, 1975; Who's Been Sleeping in My Bed, 1977; No More Sitting on the Old School Bench, 1979; Boys From the Blackstuff (televised), 1982; Are You Lonesome Tonight?, 1985; No Surrender, 1986; Having a Ball, 1986; It's A Madhouse, 1986; The Monocled Mutineer (televised), 1986; GBH (TV series), 1992; On the Ledge, 1993; Jake's Progress (TV), 1995; Oliver Twist, 1999. Honours: BAFTA Writer's Award, 1982; RTS Writer's Award, 1982; Broadcasting Press Guild TV Award for Best Series, 1982; Best Musical, London Stand Drama Awards, 1985; Hon DLitt, Liverpool Polytechnic, 1991; Best Writer, Monte Carlo International TV Festival, 1996; Best Drama Series, TV and Radio Industries Club, 2000. Address: c/o Harvey Unna and Stephen Durbridge Ltd, 24 Pottery Lane, Holland Park, London, W11 4LZ, England.

BLETHYN Brenda Anne, b. 20 February 1946, Ramsgate, Kent, England. Actress. Partner, Michael Mayhew, 1977. Education: Thanet Technical College; Guildford School of Acting. Creative Works: Theatre appearances include: Mysteries, 1979; Steaming, 1981; Double Dealer, 1982; Benefactors, 1984; Dalliance, A Doll's House, 1987; Born Yesterday, 1988; The Beaux' Stratagem, 1989; An Ideal Husband, 1992; Wildest Dreams, 1993; The Bed Before Yesterday, 1994; Habeas Corpus, Absent Friends, 1996; Mrs Warren's Profession, 2002-03. Films: The Witches, A River Runs Through It, 1992; Secrets and Lies, Remember Me, 1996; Music From Another Room, Girls' Night, 1997; Little Voice, Night Train, Daddy and Them, RKO 281, On the Nose, In the Winter Dark, 1999; The Sleeping Dictionary, Saving Grace, Yellow Bird, Pumpkin, Plots with a View, 2000; Anne Frank – The Whole Story, Lovely and Amazing, 2001; Sonny, Blizzard, 2002; Piccadilly Jim, Beyond the Sea, A Way of Life, 2004; On a Clear Day, Pooh's Heffalump Movie, Pride and Prejudice, 2005; Clubland, Atonement, 2007. TV includes: Henry VI (Part I), 1981; King Lear, 1983; Chance in a Million, 1983-85; The Labours of Erica, 1987; The Bullion Boys, 1993; The Buddah of Suburbia, 1993; Sleeping with Mickey, 1993; Outside Edge, 1994-96; First Signs of Madness, 1996; Between the Sheets, 2003; Belonging, 2004. Publications: Autobiography, Mixed Fancies, 2006. Honours include: Best Actress Award, Cannes Film Festival, 1996; Boston Film Critics Award, 1997; LA Film Critics Award, 1997; Golden Globe, 1997; London Film Critics Award, 1997; BAFTA, 1997; Honorary Dr of Letters, 1999. Membership: Poetry Society, 1976-. Address: c/o ICM, 76 Oxford Street, London W1N 0AX, England.

BLIGE Mary J, b. 11 January 1971, New York, USA. Singer. Actress. m. Martin Kendu Isaacs, 2003, 3 stepchildren. Career: Solo recording artiste; Support to Jodeci, UK tour, 1995. Recordings: Albums: What's The 411, 1992; My Life, 1994; Mary Jane, 1995; Share My World, 1997; The Tour, 1998; Mary, 1999; No More Drama, Ballads, 2001; Love & Life, 2003; Singles: What's The 411, 1992; Sweet Thing, 1993; My Love, 1994; You Bring Me Joy, All Night Long, 1995; Not Gon' Cry, 1996; Love Is All We Need, Everything, 1997; Seven Days, All That I Can Say, As, with George Michael, 1999; Also appears on: Father's Day, 1990; Changes, Close To You, 1992; Panther, Show, MTV Party To Go, Waiting To Exhale, 1995; Nutty Professor, Case, Ironman, 1996; Love And Consequences, Miseducation Of Lauryn Hill, Nu Nation

Project, 1998; Dance for Me, Rainy Dayz, 2002; Love @ 1st Sight, 2003; Be Without You, 2005; Runaway Love, 2006. Address: Steve Lucas Associates, 156 W 56th Street, New York, NY 10019, USA.

BLISH Kimberley, b. 6 November 1963, Kenosha, Wisconsin, USA. Entertainment. Education: Radio Announcing Diploma, National Broadcasting School, 1993; BSc, Business Administration Management, 2001; Payroll Skills (Primary), 2003, Paralegal Studies Program, 2004, Nevada Legal Secretary Certificate, 2004, CPA, in progress, University of Nevada, Las Vegas; State of Nevada Notary Public Training, 2004. Appointments: Label Copy Co-ordinator Assistant, 1989-92; Fundraising Co-ordinator Assistant (part time), 1993; Race Book Clerk, 1993-96, 1996, 1996-99; Race & Sports Clerk, 1999-2005; Entertainment Box Office Sales Agent, 2005-. Honours: Nominated by Sigma Iota Epsilon Honor Society, University of Nevada, Las Vegas; The National Dean's List, 1995-97; Certificate of Appreciation, Help of Southern Nevada, 2000; The Venetian Unmatched Service Standards Certification, 2000; Magnifico! Above and Beyond Employee of the Year 2001 Award, Venetian Resort, Hotel & Casino; University of Nevada, Las Vegas Alumni; Special Olympics Nevada Volunteer, 2003-; Paralegal Association of Southern Nevada Member, 2005-; The National Dean's List, 2004-05; Catch A Star Unmatched Guest Service Program Award, Venetian Resort, Hotel & Casino, 2005; National Academy of Recording Arts & Sciences Member, 2005-; Listed in national and international biographical dictionaries. Memberships: National Academy of Recording Arts and Sciences, 2005-; Paralegal Association of Southern Nevada, 2005-; Special Olympic Nevada; Fellow, ABI, 2006-; Professional Women's Advisory Board, ABI, 2007-. E-mail: kimdb.1@netzero.com

BLOOM Claire, b. 15 February 1931, London, England. Actress. m. (1) Rod Steiger, 1959, 1 daughter. (2) Hillard Elkins, 1969, (3) Philip Roth, 1990, divorced 1995. Education: London, Bristol and New York. Appointments: Oxford Repertory Theatre, 1946; Stratford-on-Avon, 1948. Creative Works: Performances include: Mary, Queen of Scots in Vivat, Vivat Regina!, New York, 1972; A Streetcare Named Desire, London, 1974; The Innocents, USA, 1976; Rosmersholm, London, 1977; The Cherry Orchard, Chichester Festival, 1981; When We Dead Awaken, 1990; The Cherry Orchard, USA, 1994; Long Day's Journey into Night, USA, 1996; Electra, New York, 1998; Conversations after a Burial, London, 2000; A Little Night Music, 2003; Six Dance Lessons in Six Weeks, 2006. Films include: A Doll's House, 1973; Islands in the Stream, 1975; The Clash of the Titans, 1979; Always, 1984; Sammy and Rosie Get Laid, 1987; Brothers, 1988; Crimes and Misdemeanours, 1989; Mighty Aphrodite, 1994; Daylight, 1995; Shakespeare's Women and Claire Bloom; The Book of Eve, 2001; Imagining Argentina, 2002; Daniel and the Superdogs, 2003; TV appreances include: A Shadow in the Sun, 1988; The Camomile Lawn, 1991; The Mirror Crack'd From Side to Side, 1992; Remember, 1993; A Village Affair, 1994; Family Money, 1996; The Lady in Question; Love and Murder; Yesterday's Children; One woman shows: Enter the Actress; These are the Women: A Portrait of Shakespeare's Heroines. Publications: Limelight and After, 1982; Leaving a Doll's House, 1996. Honours include: Evening Standard Drama Award for Best Actress, 1974. Address: c/o Jeremy Conway, 18-21 Jermyn Street, London SW1Y 6HB, England.

BLOOM Orlando, b. 13 January 1977, Canterbury, Kent, England. Actor. Education: National Youth Theatre, London; Scholarship, British American Drama Academy; Guildhall School of Music and Drama, 3 years. Career: Assistant, shooting club. Film appearances include: Wilde, 1997; The Lord of the Rings: The Fellowship of the Ring, 2001; The Lord of the Rings: The Two Towers, 2002; The Lord of the Rings: The Return of the King, Pirates of the Caribbean: Curse of the Black Pearl, 2003; Troy, The Calcium Kid, 2004; Kingdom of Heaven, Elizabethtown, 2005; Love and Other Disasters, Pirates of the Caribbean: Dead Man's Chest, Haven, 2006; Pirates of the Caribbean: At World's end, 2007. TV appearances include: TV series "Casualty"; Midsomer Murders, Smack The Pony, 2000; The Saturday Show, 2001; So Graham Norton, 2002; The Tonight Show with Jay Leno, Primetime Live, V Graham Norton, 2003; The Brendan Leanard Show, Access Hollywood, 2003; GMTV, T4, 2004. Honours: Internet Movie Awards, 2002; Best Debut, Empire Award, 2002; MTV Movie Awards, 2002; Hollywood Discovery Awards; MTV Movie Awards, 2004.

BLOOM Stephen, b. 24 October 1942, Maidstone, Kent, England. Professor of Medicine; Head of Division. m. Margaret Janet Sturrock, 2 sons, 2 daughters. Education: MB BChir, 1967; MA, 1968; FRCP, 1978; MD, 1979; DSc, 1982; FRCPath, 1993; FMedSci, 1997. Appointments: Professor of Medicine (Consultant Physician), Imperial College London and Hammersmith Hospital, 1982-; Director of Endocrinology, 1982-, Director, Chemical Pathology, 1994-, Clinical Director, Pathology and Therapy Services, 1996-, Hammersmith Hospital Trust; Head of Division of Investigative Science, Imperial College, 1997-; Chief Scientific Officer, Thiakis, 2006-. Publications: Co-edited books include: Gastrointestinal and Related Hormones, 1979; Radioimmunoassay of Gut Regulatory peptides, 1981; Basic Science in Gastroenterology, 1982; Gastrointestinal and Hepatobiliary Cancer, 1983; Systemic Role of Regulatory Peptides, 1982; Endocrine Tumours, 1985; Peptides: A Target for New Drug Development, 1991; Surgical Endocrinology, 1993; Numerous articles in major scientific and medical journals. Honours include: Walter Knox Chemistry Prize, 1962; Bacteriology Prize, 1965; Ophthalmology Prize, 1966; Radiotherapy and Radiology Prize, 1967; British Society of Gastroenterology Research Medal, 1977; Copp Lecturer, American Diabetic Association, 1978; Goulstonian Lecturer, Royal College of Physicians, 1979; Prossor White Oration, 1981; Eric-Sharpe Prize for Oncology, 1987; Arnold Bloom Lecture British Diabetic Association, 1995; Dale Medal, Society for Endocrinology, 2003; Keith Buchanan Memorial Lecture, Royal College of Surgeons, 2004; Lumleian Lecturer, Royal College of Physicians, 2005; Novo Nordisk Lecture, 2005; Moxon Trust Medal, Royal College of Physicians, 2005. Memberships: Association of Physicians; Physiological Society; British Diabetic Association; Endocrine Society (British and American); Society of Gastroenterology (British and American); Medical Research Society; Bayliss & Starling Society; Royal Society of Medicine; European Association for the Study of Diabetes; American Diabetic Association; European Neuroscience Association. Address: Department of Metabolic Medicine, Imperial College London, 6th Floor, Commonwealth Building; Hammersmith Campus, Du Cane Road, London W12 0NN, England. Website: www.imperial.ac.uk

BLOOMBERG Michael R, b. 14 February 1942, Medford, Massachusetts, USA. Mayor of the City of New York. Education: MBA, Harvard University. Appointments: Joined staff, 1966, Partner, 1972, Salmon Brothers, Wall Street; Established Bloomberg LP, 1982; Served on boards of 20 different civic, cultural, educational and medical institutions including: High School of Economics and Finance; Lincoln

Center for the Performing Arts; Metropolitan Museum of Art; Police & Fire Widows' & Children's Benefits Fund; SLE (Lupus) Foundation and Prep for Prep. Publications: Bloomberg by Bloomberg, 1997. Honours: School of Hygiene and Public Health renamed The Bloomberg School of Public Health. Memberships: Chairman, Board of Trustees, Johns Hopkins University, -2002. Address: The Mayor's Press Office, City Hall, New York, NY 10007, USA.

BLOW DARLINGTON Joyce, b. 4 May 1929, Morecambe, England. Retired. m. J A B Darlington. Education: MA, University of Edinburgh. Appointments: Council of Industrial Design, 1953-63; Publicity and Advertising Manager, Heal & Son Ltd, 1963-65; Board of Trade, 1965-67; Monopolies Commission, 1967-70; Assistant Secretary, Department of Trade & Industry, 1970-72; Assistant Secretary, Department of Prices and Consumer Protection, 1972-74; Under-Secretary, Office of Fair Trading, 1977-80; Under Secretary, Department of Trade and Industry, 1980-84; Vice-President, Trading Standard Institute, 1985-; Chairman, Mail Order Publishers Authority, 1985-92; Chairman, Direct Marketing Association Authority, 1992-97; Board Member, 1987-97, Chairman, Consumer Policy Committee, 1987-93, British Standards Institution; Trustee, University of Edinburgh Development Trust, 1990-94; Chairman, East Sussex Family Health Services Authority, 1990-96; President, Association for Quality in Healthcare, 1991-94; Chairman, Public Relations Education Trust, 1992-97; Chairman, Child Accident Prevention Trust, 1996-2002. Publication: Consumers and International Trade: A Handbook, 1987. Honours: Freeman City of London, 1984; OBE, 1994. Memberships: Hon FCIPR; FCMI; FRSA. Address: 17 Fentiman Road, London SW8 1LD, England

BLUM Igor Robert, b. 24 October 1969, Frankfurt am Main, Germany. Dentist; Researcher; Educator. Education: DDS, Dental Surgery, Semmelweis University, Budapest, Hungary, 1990-95; MSc, Oral Surgery, 1995-97, PhD, Restorative Dentistry, 1998-2002, University of Manchester, UK; Dr Med Dent, (Magna cum laude), Dental Medicine, Goethe University of Frankfurt, Germany, 2000-2002. Appointments: Associate Clinician in Dental Implantology, 1998-2001, Associate Clinician in Oral Medicine, 1998-2001, University of Manchester, UK; Founder and Chief Executive Officer, Globaldentistry, 2002-05; Clinical Teacher in Oral Surgery, 2004-05, Clinical Teacher in Prosthodontics, 2004-05, University of Manchester, UK; Lecturer at international conferences; Lecturer in Restorative Dentistry, University of Bristol, England, 2005-. Publications: Numerous articles in scientific dental journals as author, first author and co-author include most recently: Contemporary views on dry socket (alveolar osteitis): A clinical appraisal of standardisation, aetiopathogenesis and management: a critical review, 2002; The teaching of the repair of direct composite restorations, 2002; The repair of direct composite restorations: an international survey of the teaching of operative techniques and materials, 2003; Defective direct composite restorations – replace or repair? A Comparison of teaching between Scandinavian dental schools, 2003. Honours: First Class Achievement for Oral Health Sciences Thesis, National Institute of Dentistry, 1995; Achievement in introducing a standardised definition for alveolar osteitis (dry socket) to the dental profession. Listed in Who's Who publications and biographical dictionaries. Memberships: Postgraduate Membership in Oral Surgery; Postgraduate Membership in Prosthodontics; General Dental Council, England; Hessian Dental Chamber of Germany; British Dental Association; Royal College of Surgeons of England; Royal College of Surgeons of Edinburgh; European Association of Osseointegration; Association of Dental

Educators in Europe; International Association for Dental Research. Address: 109 Pinkers Mead, Emersons Green, Bristol BS16 7EJ, England.

BLUME Judy, b. 12 February 1938, Elizabeth, New Jersey, USA. Writer. m. (1) John M Blume, 1959, divorced 1975, 1 son, 1 daughter; (2) George Cooper, 1 stepdaughter. Education: New York University. Career: Founder and Trustee, The Kids Fund, 1981; Author of non-fiction and juvenile and adult fiction. Publications: Juvenile: The One in the Middle is the Green Kangaroo, 1969; Iggie's House, 1970; Are You There God? It's Me, Margaret, 1970; Then Again, Maybe I Won't, 1971; Freckle Juice, 1971; It's Not the End of the World, 1972; Tales of a Fourth Grade Nothing, 1972; Otherwise Known as Sheila the Great, 1972; Deenie, 1973; Blubber, 1974; Forever, 1975; Starring Sally J Freedman as Herself, 1977; Superfudge, 1980; Tiger Eyes, 1981; The Pain and the Great One, 1984; Just As Long As We're Together, 1987; Fudge-a-mania, 1990; Here's to You, Rachel Robinson, 1993; Summer Sisters, 1998; Places I Never Meant to Be (editor), 1999; Double Fudge, 2002; Adult: Wifey, 1978; Smart Women, 1983; Non-fiction: Letters to Judy: What Kids Wish They Could Tell You, 1986; The Judy Blue Memory Book, 1988. Honours: Honorary LHD, Kean College, 1987; Chicago Public Library Carl Sandburg Freedom to Read Award, 1984; American Civil Liberties Union Award, 1986; American Library Association Margaret A Edwards Award for Lifetime Achievement, 1996; National Book Foundation Medal for Distinguished Contribution to American Letters, 2004. Memberships: PEN Club; Authors' Guild; National Coalition Against Censorship; Society of Children's Book Writers. Address: Harold Ober Associates, 425 Madison Avenue, New York, NY 10017-1110, USA. Website: www.judyblume.com

BLUNKETT Rt Hon David, b. 6 June 1947, England. Politician. 3 sons. Education: Sheffield University. Appointments: Worker, East Midlands Gas Board; Teacher, Industrial Relations and Politics, Barnsley College of Technology; Joined Labour Party, 1963; Member, Sheffield City Council, 1970-87, Leader, 1980-87; Member, South Yorkshire County Council, 1973-77; MP for Sheffield Brightside, 1987-; National Executive Committee (NEC) of Labour Party, 1983; Chair, NEC Local Government Committee, 1984; Local Government Front Bench Spokesman in Opposition's Environment Team, 1988-92; Shadow Secretary of State for Health, 1992-94, for Education, 1994-95, for Education and Employment, 1995-97; Secretary of State for Education and Employment, 1997-2001, for the Home Department, 2001-04, for Work and Pensions, 2005 (resigned, 2005). Publications: Local Enterprise and Workers' Plans, 1981; Building From the Bottom: The Sheffield Experience, 1983; Democracy in Crisis: The Town Halls Respond, 1987; On a Clear Day (autobiography), 1995; Politics and Progress, 2001. Address: House of Commons, London SW1A 0AA, England.

BLYTHE Ronald George, b. 6 November 1922, Acton, Suffolk, England. Author. Appointments: Associate Editor, New Wessex Edition of the Works of Thomas Hardy, 1978. Publications: A Treasonable Growth, 1960; Immediate Possession, 1961; The Age of Illusion, 1963; Akenfield, 1969; William Hazlitt: Selected Writings, editor, 1970; The View in Winter, 1979; From the Headlands, 1982; The Stories of Ronald Blythe, 1985; Divine Landscapes, 1986; Each Returning Day, 1989; Private Words, 1991; Word from Wormingford, 1997; First Friends, 1998; Going to meet George, 1998; Talking About John Clare, 1999; Out of the Valley, 2000; The Circling Year, 2001; Talking to the Neighbours, 2002; The Assassin, 2004; Borderland, 2005; Field Work, 2007; Critical Studies of Jane Austen, Thomas Hardy, Leo Tolstoy, Literature of the Second World War, Henry James. Contributions to: Observer; Sunday Times; New York Times; Listener; Atlantic Monthly; London Magazine; Tablet; New Statesman; Bottegue Oscure; Guardian. Honours: Heinemann Award, 1969; Society of Authors Travel Scholarship, 1970; Angel Prize for Literature, 1986; Honorary MA, University of East Anglia, 1991; Hon DLitt, Anglia Polytechnic University, 2001; MLitt, Lambeth; Hon DLitt, University of Essex, 2002; Lay Canon, St Edmundsbury Cathedral, 2003; Benson Medal for Literature, 2006. Memberships: Royal Society of Literature, fellow; Society of Authors; The John Clare Society, president; Fabian Society. Address: Bottengoms Farm, Wormingford, Colchester, Essex, England.

BNINSKI Kazimierz Andrzej, b. 28 February 1939, Gdynia, Poland. Physician in General Practice. m. Teresa Maria de Gallen Bisping, 2 July 1988, 2 sons, 1 daughter. Education: MD, University of Gdansk, Poland, 1964. Appointments: Senior House Officer, Nelson Hospital, London, England, 1967; Senior House Officer, St Mary Abbots Hospital, London, England, 1968; Registrar in Medicine, St Mary's Hospital, 1972-77; Physician, 7th US Army, Germany, 1977-81; Junior Partner, General Practice, 1981-87; Senior Doctor, Director-in-Charge Polish Clinic, London, 1988-. Address: 131 Harley Street, London W1G 6BB, England.

BOARDMAN Christopher Miles, b. 26 August 1968, England. Former Professional Cyclist. m. Sally-Anne Edwards, 1988, 5 children. Education: Hilbre Secondary School; Withens College. Appointments: Competed in 9 World Championships; Holder of various national records and 20 national titles; Bronze Medal, Commonwealth Games, Edinburgh, 1986; 2 Bronze Medals, Commonwealth Games, Auckland, 1990; Gold Medal, 4,000m individual pursuit, Olympic Games, Barcelona, 1992; Double World Champion (pursuit and time trial), 1994; Winner, Tour de France Prologue and holder, Yellow Jersey, 1994, 1997, 1998; World Record for distance cycled in 1 hour, 1993, 1996; Winner, World 4,000m cycling championships, broke his own world record, 1996; Retired, 2001; Company director. Publications: Chris Boardman's Complete Book of Cycling. Honours include: Hon DSc, Brighton, 1997; Hon MSc, Liverpool; Man of the Year Award, Cheshire Life magazine, 1997. Memberships: English Sport Council, 1996-; Expert adviser to British cycling team 2004 Olympic Games.

BOATENG Paul (Yaw), b. 14 June 1951, Hackney, England. Diplomatist; Politician; Lawyer; Broadcaster. m. Janet Alleyne, 1980, 2 sons, 3 daughters. Education: Ghana International School; Accra Academy; Apsley Grammar School; University of Bristol. Appointments: Solicitor, Paddington Law Centre, 1976-79; Solicitor and Partner, B M Birnberg & Co, 1979-87; Called to the Bar, Gray's Inn, 1989; Legal Adviser, Scrap Sus Campaign, 1977-81; Member, GLC (Labour) for Walthamstow, 1981-86; Chair, Police Committee, 1981-86; Vice-Chair, Ethnic Minorities Committee, 1981-86; MP (Labour) for Brent South, 1987-2005; Home Office Member, House of Commons Environment Committee, 1987-89; Opposition Frontbench Spokesman on Treasury and Economic Affairs, 1989-92, on Legal Affairs, Lord Chancellor's Department, 1992-97; Parliamentary Under-Secretary of State, Department of Health, 1997-98; Minister of State, 1998-2001; Deputy Home Secretary, 1999-2001; Minister for Young People, 2000-01; Finanical Secretary to HM Treasury, 2001-02; Chief Secretary, 2002-05; High Commissioner to South Africa, 2005-. Publications: Reclaiming the Ground (contributor), 1993. Memberships: Chair, Afro-Caribbean

Education Resource Project, 1978-86, Westminster CRC, 1978-81; Govenor Police Staff College, Bramshill, 1981-84; Member, Home Secretary's Advisory Council on Race Relations, 1981-86; WCC Commission on Programme to Combat Racism, 1984-91; Police Training Council, 1981-85; Executive, National Council for Civil Liberties, 1980-86; Member, Court of University of Bristol, 1994-; Member, Board ENO, 1984-97. Address: High Commission of the United Kingdom, 255 Hill Street, Arcadia, Pretoria 0002, South Africa. Website: www.britain.org.za

BOBIER Claude-Abel, b. 18 March 1934, France. m. Manissier Arlette, 4 September 1959, 3 daughters. Education: BS, 1953; ENS St Cloud, 1956-60; Agreg SN, 1960; Doctor, 1971. Appointments: University of Paris VI, 1960-75; Professor, University of Tunis, 1975-86; MC University of Bordeaux I, 1986-99; Retired as Consultant, 1999. Publications include: Les éléments structuraux recents essentiels de la Tunisie nord-orientale, 1983; Morphologie de la marge Caraibe Colombienne: Relation avec la structure et la sedimentation, 1991; The Post-Triassic Sedimentary Cover of Tunisa: Seismic Sequences and Structure, 1991; Apports de l'analyse morphostructurale dans la connaissance de la physiographie du golfe de Tehuantepec (Mexique est-pacifique), 1993; Sequence stratigraphy, Basin dynamics and Petroleum geology of the Miocene from Eastern Tunisia, 1996; Recent tectonic activity in the South Barbados Prism. Deep towed side scan sonar imagery, 1998; Distribution des sédiments sur la marge du Golfe de Tehuantepec (Pacifique oriental). Example d'interaction tectonique-eustatisme, 2000; Rôle de l'halocinese dans l'evolution du Bassin d'Essaouira/Sud Ouest Morocain), 2004; Rôle du systeme de failles E-W dans l'evolution geódynamique de l'Avant Pays de la chaîne alpine de Tunisie. Example de l'accident de Sbiba-Cherishira Tunisie Centrale, 2003; The role of shearing on the sedimentary and morphostructural evolution of the southern part of the Barbados ridge at the Latitude of Trinidad. Honour: International Ambassador's Order, 1998. Memberships: Past Member, American Association of Petrololeum Geololgists; American Geophysical Union; Past Member, New York Academy of Sciences. Address: 6 Square du Gue, F-33170 Gradignan, France.

BOBKO Nataliya Andreyevna, b. 30 November 1960, Kiev, Ukraine. Psychophysiologist. Education: Biologist-Physiologist of Humans and Animals, Teacher of Biology and Chemistry (MSc equivalent), Biological Department, Kiev State University, 1982; Candidate of Biological Science, Hygiene (PhD equivalent), Kiev Research Institute of Labour Hygiene and Occupational Diseases, 1992. Appointments: Senior High-Educated Laboratory Assistant, 1982-84, Junior Research Scientist, 1984-85, Laboratory of Mental Labour Physiology, Junior Research Scientist, 1985-91, Research Scientist, Laboratory of Labour Physiology of Process Operators, 1991-92, Senior Research Scientist, Laboratory of Chronobiology Problems in Labour, 1992-95, Senior Research Scientist, Laboratory of Mental Labour Physiology, 1995-, Department of Labour Physiology, Institute for Occupational Health, Kiev, Ukraine (before 1992, Kiev Research Institute of Labour Hygiene and Occupational Diseases). Publications: Over 140 publications in national and international peer reviewed journals, collections and presented at conferences as author and co-author include most recently: Ageing and work in Ukraine, 2005; Effects of strain on cardiovascular system activity in human operators at different times of day and working week under round-the-clock industry, 2006; Effects of space related parameters on human caused accident rate in energetics, 2006; Effect of stress on the cardiovascular system activity in operators of predominantly mental work at different times of the day and the working week, 2007. Honours: 13 travel grants to attend international congresses, symposiums and conferences, 1995-2006; Title: Senior Research Scientist, Institute for Occupational Health, Kiev, Ukraine, 1994; International Scientist of the Year, 2002, 2007; Woman of the Year, 2005, 2006, 2007; International Peace Prize, 2005, 2006, 2007; American Medal of Honor, 2005, 2006; Woman of Achievement, 2006; Gold Medal for the Ukraine, 2006; Listed in many international biographical directories. Memberships: International Commission on Occupational Health, 2001-; National Secretary to Ukraine; Member, Joint Board of Shiftwork and Working Time Committee and Working Time Society; Member, Scientific Committee on Neurotoxicology and Psychophysiology; Member, Sigma Xi, The Scientific Research Society, USA, 2002-; Patents: 2001, 2003, 2004. Address: Institute for Occupational Health, Saksagansky St 75, Kiev, 01033 Ukraine. E-mail: nbobko@bigmir.net

BOCELLI Andrea, b. 22 September 1958, Lajatico, Pisa, Italy. Singer (tenor). m. Enrica, 2 children. Recordings: Albums: various music; Bocelli, Viaggio Italiano, 1995; Romanza, 1997; Aria, 1998; Sogno, Sacred Arias, 1999; Verdi, La Boheme, 2000; Cieli di Toscana, 2001; Cieli di Toscana, Verdi Requiem, 2001; Sentimento, 2002; Tosca, 2003; Il trovatore, Andrea, 2004; Werther, 2005; Amore, Leoncavallo: Pagliacci, 2006; numerous singles. Honours: Best Album, Classical BRIT Awards, 2003. Address: MT Opera and Blues Production and Management, via Irnerio 16, 40162 Bologna, Italy. Website: www.andreabocelli.org

BODO Michael, b. 10 September 1947, Debrecen, Hungary. Research Scientist. m. Janice Meer, 1 son, 4 daughters. Education: MD, Semmelweis University Medical School, Budapest, 1972; Student in Psychology, University of Eotvos L, Budapest, 1971-72; PhD, Biology, Sechenov's Institute of Evolutionary Physiology, Academy of Sciences of the USSR, 1990. Appointments: Fellow, Electroencephalographer, National Institute of Neurosurgery, Budapest, 1972-78; Research Associate, Department of Psychophysiology, Institute of Psychology, Hungarian Academy of Sciences, 1979-83; Research Associate, Department of Neurophysiology, 1984-92, Product Manager, Department of Strategic Marketing, 1993, Chemical Works of G Richter Ltd, Budapest; Visiting Scholar and Research Associate, Department of Neurology, University of Miami School of Medicine, Miami, Florida, USA, 1993-96; Consultant, Life Resuscitation Technologies Inc, Chicago, Illinois, USA, 1996-98; Consultant, National Naval Medical Center, NMRI, Bethesda, Maryland, USA, 1996-97; Director, Medical Research and Development, AHTC, Fairfax, Virginia, USA, 1997-99; Senior Research Associate, 2000-03, Senior Staff Scientist, 2004-, National Research Council, Walter Reed Army Institute of Research, Department of Resuscitative Medicine, Silver Spring, Maryland. Publications: 12 book chapters; 25 journal articles; 99 abstracts; 4 medical electronics patents; 27 chemical patents; 4 copyrights. Honours: President's Award, Hungarian Academy of Sciences, Budapest, 1980; Award, French Minister of Scientific Research, Concours Lepine, Paris, 1993; 2 Teaching Awards, Walter Reed Army Institute of Research, 2001 and 2002. Memberships: National Stroke Association; Phi Beta Delta Honor Society; International Society for Cerebral Blood Flow and Metabolism; Hungarian Pharmacological Society; Hungarian Psychological Society; Hungarian Physiological Society; Hungarian Society for EEG and Clinical Neurophysiology; Hungarian Stroke Society; Psychotherapeutical Association; etc. Address:

Walter Reed Army Institute of Research, Department of Resuscitative Medicine, 503 Robert Grant Avenue, Room 1N83, Silver Spring, MD 20910-7500, USA. E-mail: michael.bodo@us.army.mil

BOE Grethe, b. 11 March 1958, Oslo, Norway. Systems Engineer; Editor; Webmaster. m. Oyvind K Myhre, 1 son, 1 daughter. Education: BA, English (major), Political Science, Astronomy, University of Oslo, 1982. Appointments: Systems Engineer, IBM, Norway, 1983-92; Freelance Computer Consultant, 1992-; Administrator, Editor and Technical Advisor, Harrison Ford Media (http://www.hfm2.com), 2002-05; Co-administrator, Editor and Technical Advisor, Harrison Ford Web (http://www.harrisonfordweb.com), 2006-. Publications: Articles, Fact Collections and Research on website. Honours: IBM Professional Excellence Award, 1986; IBM Professional Marketing Award, 1988, 1990; LPIBA, 2005; MOIF, 2005; DO, 2005; DDG, 2005; AIOM, 2007; HonDG, 2006; AdVSci, 2006; Governor, IBA, 2006; Secretary General, United Cultural Convention, 2006; IBC Lifetime Achievement Award, 2005; Da Vinci Diamond, 2005; World Lifetime Award, ABI, 2006; Vice President, World Congress of Arts, Sciences and Communications; Scientist of the Year, IBA, 2006; Dame of Justice, Sovereign Order of the Knights of Justice, 2006; Vice President, World Congress of Arts, Sciences and Communication, 2007; Vice Chancellor, World Academy of Letters, 2008; Listed in various Who's Who publications and biographical dictionaries. Memberships: New York Academy of Sciences; American Film Institute. Address: Skolebakken 5, 2750 Gran, Norway. E-mail: gboee@online.no Website: www.harrisonfordweb.com

BOERSMA Lawrence Allan (Larry Allan), b. 24 April 1932, London, Ontario, Canada. Animal Advocate. m. June E Boersma, 3 sons, 1 daughter. Education: BA, 1953, MS, 1955, University of Nebraska, Omaha; PhD, Sussex, 1972; Postdoctoral Study, University of Oxford, 1996; ScD (hon), University of Berkeley. Appointments include: Advertising Executive, Better Homes and Gardens, 1959-63; Account Executive, This Week Magazine, 1963-66; Eastern Sales Director and Marketing Director, Ladies Home Journal, 1966-75; Vice-President, Publisher, The Country Gentleman, Vice-President, Associate Publisher, Saturday Evening Post, 1975; Vice-President, Director, Marketing and Advertising Sales, Photo World Magazine, 1975-77; Advertising Manager, La Jolla Light, 1977-80; Owner, Photographer, Allan-The Animal Photographers, San Diego and Sarasota, 1980-; President, Chief Executive Officer, The Photographic Institute International, 1982-86; Director of Development and Community Relations, San Diego Humane Society/Society for the Prevention of Cruelty to Animals, 1985-94; Associate Executive Director, The Centre for Humane Education for Southern California, 1994-98; Owner, Animal Art, San Diego and Sarasota, 1999-; Chairman and Chief Executive Officer, International Dolphin Project; Chairman, Chief Executive Officer & Advocate-General, Preserve Our Wildlife Organisation; California State Humane Officer. Publications: Numerous wildlife books include: Wildcats of North America Series – Bobcat, Cougar, Feral Cat, Lynx, 1998; Wild Canines of North America Series – Coyote, Foxes and Wolf, 2000; Creative Canine Photography, 2004; ASPCA Guide to Cats; Keep Wild Animals in Our Lives, 2005; The Dove Family Tale, 2008; ASPCA Guide to Dogs; Wildlife/Environmental Columnist Venice (FL) Gondolier Sun, 2005-; Photographs appear in numerous magazines, calendars, greeting cards and other printed media. Honours include: Fellow Royal Photographic Society of Great Britain; Award of Appreciation, Committee for a Cruelty Free California; Gold Mercury

Award, International Academy of Communication Arts and Sciences; Finalist, International Wildlife Photographer of the Year, British Natural History Museum and the BBC, 2003; Ansel Adams Award, Sierra Club, 2005; Lifetime Achievement Award, University of Nebraska/Omaha, 2007; Sierran of the Month, Sierra Club, 2007. Memberships include: Society of Animal Welfare Administrators; National Society of Fund Raising Executives; Public Relations Society of America; Defenders of Wildlife; Sierra Club; Masons; Wilderness Society; Natural Resources Defense Council; Union of Concerned Scientists; Environmental Defense Action Fund; Center for Biological Diversity. Address: 4238 65th Terrace East, Sarasota, FL 34243, USA.

BOEV Zlatozar Nikolaev, b. 20 October 1955, Sofia, Bulgaria. Zoologist; Ornithologist. m. Education: Graduate, Department of Zoology of the Vertebrate Animals, Faculty of Biology, University of Sofia, 1975-80; Postgraduate, Zoology Department, National Museum of Natural History, 1984-86. Appointments: Doctor of Philosophy, 1986; Associate Professor, 1992; Doctor of Sciences, 1999; Professor of Zoology, 2001. Publications: Over 230 papers in scientific journals chiefly on fossil and sub-fossil birds; Over 270 articles in popular science journals; 5 textbooks; 13 popular books; 16 countries in Europe, North America and Asia. Memberships include: Society of Avian Palaeontology and Evolution; International Council for Archaeology; Society of European Avian Curators; Association for Environmental Archaeology, Ethnoornithology Research and Study Group. Address: National Museum of Natural History, Bulgarian Academy of Sciences, 1 Blvd Tsar Osvoboditel, 1000 Sofia, Bulgaria. E-mail: boev@nmnh.bas.bg

BOGDANOFF Stewart R, b. 16 August 1940, London, England. Educator. m. Eileen Dolan, 1 son, 2 daughters. Education: BSc, Kings College, Briarcliff Manor, New York, 1963; MA and Professional Degree, New York University, 1965; Graduate Work NYU, SUNY New Platz, Harvard University, 1972-; Certificate in Administration and Supervision, 1988. Appointments: Coach, intramural director, curriculum writer, fundraiser Thomas Jefferson Elementary School, Lakeland School District, 1965-96; Physical Education Teacher, Lakeland School District, 1965-96; Head Teacher, Thomas Jefferson Elementary School, Lakeland School District, 1984-96; Acting Principal, Thomas Jefferson Elementary School, 1985-86; Educational Consultant, Speaker, Writer, 1996-. Honours include: New York State Teacher of Year, honoured at White House by President Reagan, 1983; Project Inspiration Award, National Association for Sport and Physical Education, 1992; Point of Light Award, President Bush, 1992; International Man of Year Award and Men of Achievement Award, International Biographical Centre, England, 1993; 1st teacher from NYS inducted into National Teachers Hall of Fame, Emporia, Kansas, honoured by President Clinton at Rose Garden Ceremony; Scholarship in name of Stewart Bogdanoff established by Servicemaster, 1993; Founders 2000 Award from American Alliance for Health, Physical Education Recreation and Dance with room dedicated in his honour, National Center in Reston, Virginia, 1995; J C Penny Golden Rule Award, Westchester County United Way Volunteer of Year, 1995; Inducted into Briarcliff High School Hall of Distinguished Alumni, 1995; Golden Years Award, New York State Association for Health, Physical Education, Recreation and Dance; Selected as one of the Fifty Most Influential People in Westchester and Putnam Counties during the 20th Century, Journal News; American Medal of Honor, ABI, 2003; Inducted into King's College Hall of Distinguished Alumni, 2005; Listed in numerous Who's Who and biographical publications including: Who's Who in American Education; Contemporary Who's Who, ABI, 2003; Great Minds of the 21st Century, ABI, 2003-04; Top 100 Teachers in the World, 2006. Memberships include: Kappa Delta Pi; New York State Teachers of the Year; Harvard Principals Center, others. Address: 588 Heritage Hills of Westchester, Unit A, Somers, NY 10589, USA.

BOGDANOV Faik Gasanovich, b. 28 November 1956, Tbilisi, Georgia. Radiophysicist; Scientist, Lecturer. m. Leila Z Gamidova, 2 sons. Education: MS, Radiophysics, Tbilisi State University, 1978; PhD, Physics and Mathematics, 1983; Doctor of Science, Physics and Mathematics, 1993. Appointments: Scientist, Senior Engineer, Senior Scientist, 1980-82, Senior Scientist, Laboratory of Applied Electrodynamics, 1996-2001, Tbilisi State University, Tbilisi; Senior Scientist, Institute of Space Construction, Tbilisi, 1983-90; Associate Professor, 1984-93, Professor, 1994-2003, Full Professor, 2003-, Georgian Technical University; Senior Scientist, TriD Team Manager, Acting Head of Development Department, EM Software and Consulting (EMCoS), Tbilisi, 2001-. Publications: 1 monograph; 7 textbooks; 2 book chapters; 60 referred journal papers; 30 conference proceeding papers; 20 conference abstracts. Honours: State Education Ministry's prize for best student scientific work, 1978; Georgian Republic Education Ministry's Special Prize for best scientific-methodical work, 1989; International Scientific Foundation personal scientific Grant, 1994; International Scientific Foundation personal educational Grants, 1996, 1997, 1998, 1999. Memberships: IEEE; ED/MTT/AP Societies; Dissertation Councils of Georgian Technical University. E-mail: faik.bogdanov@emcos.com

BOGDANOVICH Peter, b. 30 July 1939, Kingston, New York, USA. Film Director; Writer; Producer; Actor. m. (1) Polly Platt, 1962, divorced 1970, 2 daughters, (2) L B Straten, 1988, divorced 2001. Appointments: Film Feature-Writer, Esquire, New York Times, Village Voice, Cahiers du Cinema, Los Angeles Times, New York Magazine, Vogue, Variety and others, 1961-. Publications: The Cinema of Orson Welles, 1961; The Cinema of Howard Hawks, 1962; The Cinema of Alfred Hitchcock, 1963; John Ford, 1968; Fritz Lang in America, 1969; Allan Dwan: The Last Pioneer, 1971; Pieces of Time: Peter Bogdanovich on the Movies (in UK as Picture Shows), 1961, enlarged edition, 1985; The Killing of the Unicorn: Dorothy Stratten (1960-1980), 1984; A Year and a Day Calendar (editor), 1991; This is Orson Welles, 1992; Who the Devil Made It, 1997; Who the Hell's In It? 2004. Films: The Wild Angels, 1966; Targets, 1968; The Last Picture Show, 1971; What's Up Doc? 1972; Paper Moon, 1973; Daisy Miller, 1974; At Long Last Love, 1975; Nickelodeon, 1976; Saint Jack, 1979; They All Laughed, 1981; Mask, 1985; Illegally Yours, 1988; Texasville, 1990; Noises Off, 1992; The Thing Called Love, 1993; Who The Devil Made It (director), Mr Jealousy, Highball, 1997; Coming Soon, 1999; Rated X, The Independent, 2000; The Cat's Meow (director), Scene Stealer (actor), 2003; Hustle, 2004; The Sopranos, (1999-2007); Infamous, 2006. Honours: New York Film Critics' Award for Best Screenplay, British Academy Award for Best Screenplay, 1971; Writer's Guild of America Award for Best Screenplay, 1972; Silver Shell, Mar del Plata, Spain, 1973; Best Director, Brussels Festival, 1974; Pasinetti Award, Critic Prize, Venice Festival, 1979. Memberships: Directors Guild of America; Writer's Guild of America; Academy of Motion Picture Arts and Sciences. Address: c/o William Pfeiffer, 30 Lane of Acres, Haddonfield, NJ 08033, USA.

BOGLE Joanna Margaret, (Julia Blythe), b. 7 September 1952, Carshalton, Surrey, England. Author; Journalist. m. James Stewart Lockhart Bogle, 20 September 1980. Appointments: Local Borough Councillor, London Borough of Sutton, 1974-81; Governor, London Oratory School, 1976-86. Publications: A Book of Feasts and Seasons, 1986; When the Summer Ended (with Cecylia Wolkowinska), 1991; A Heart for Europe (with James Bogle), 1992; Caroline Chisholm, 1993; Come On In - It's Awful!, editor, 1994; We Didn't Mean to Start a School, 1998; The Pope Benedict Code, 2006; Contributions to: local newspapers, 1970-74; South London News, 1984-86; Catholic Times, 1994-; Various newspapers in Britain, the USA and Australia, 1980-. Address: Christian Projects, PO Box 44741, London SWIP 2XA, England.

BOHR Aage Niels, b. 19 June 1922, Copenhagen, Denmark. Physicist. m. (1) Marietta Bettina, deceased, 1978, 2 sons, 1 daughter, (2) Bente Scharff, 1981. Education: Graduated, University of Copenhagen. Appointments: Associate, Department of Science and Industrial Research, London, 1943-45; Research Assistant, Institute of Theoretical Physics, Copenhagen, 1946; Professor of Physics, University of Copenhagen, 1956-; Director, Niels Bohr Institute, 1963-70; Director, Nordita (Nordic Institute of Theoretical Physics), 1975-81. Memberships: Danish, Norwegian, Pontifical, Swedish, Polish, Finnish, Yugoslav Academies of Science; National Academy of Sciences, USA; American Academy of Arts and Sciences; American Philosophical Society; Royal Physiograph Society, Lund, Sweden; Academy of Technical Sciences, Copenhagen; Deutsche Academie der Naturforsche Lepoldina. Publications: Rotational States of Atomic Nuclei, 1954; Co-author, Nuclear Structure, Vol I, 1969, Vol II, 1975; Genuine Fortuitousness – Where Did That Click Come From? 2001; The Principle Underlying Quantum Mechanics, 2004. Honours: Honorary PhD, Oslo, Heidelberg, Trondheim, Manchester, Uppsala; Dannie Heineman Prize, 1960; Pius XI Medal, 1963; Atoms for Peace Award, 1969; Ørsted Medal, 1970; Rutherford Medal, 1972; John Price Wetherill Medal, 1974; Nobel Prize for Physics, 1975; Ole Rømer Medal, 1976. Address: c/o Niels Bohr Institute, Blegdamsvej 15-17, 2100 Copenhagen, Denmark.

BOICE Martha Hibbert, b. 1 October 1931, Toledo, Ohio, USA. Writer; Publisher. m. William V Boice, 1 son, 2 daughters. Education: BA, Ohio Wesleyan University, 1953; MSW, University of Michigan School of Social Work, 1955. Appointments: Caseworker, Travelers Aid, Toledo, Ohio, 1955-57; Publisher, Knot Garden Press, Dayton, Ohio, 1986-. Publications: Organiser, compiler, A Sense of Place, 1977; Author, compiler, Shaker Herbal Fare, 1985; The Wreath Maker, 1987; The Herbal Rosa, 1990; Maps of the Shaker West, 1997; Columnist, Centerville-Bellbrook Times, 1984. Honours: Distinguished Service Award, National Association of Monnett Clubs, Ohio Wesleyan University, 1974; Volunteer of the Year, Dayton-Montgomery County Park District, 1985; Centerville, Ohio' Mayor's Award for Community Service, 1988; Award of Excellence, OAHSM, 1998; Listed in biographical publications. Memberships: Phi Beta Kappa; Centerville-Washington Township Historical Society, Landmark Chair, 1972-78, 1980-84, 1997-2000; Landmarks Foundation of Centerville-Washington Township, Trustee, 1995-, Chair, 1997-2001; Herb Society of America, Library Committee Chair, 1988-1991; Western Shaker Study Group, Program Chair, 1988-91, 2003-04, Secretary, 1992-94, 2001, Chair, 2005-06; Dayton-Montgomery County Bicentennial Literature Committee Chair, 1994-96; Director, 2002-,

Secretary, 2002-04, Membership Chair, 2004-, Friends of White Water Shaker Village. Address: 7712 Eagle Creek Drive, Dayton, OH 45459, USA. E-mail: marthaboice@woh.rr.com

BOKSENBERG Alexander, b. 18 March 1936. Astronomer. m. Adella Coren, 1960, 1 son, 1 daughter. Education: BSc, Physics, University of London; PhD, 1961. Appointments: SRC Research Assistant, Department of Physics and Astronomy, University College London, 1960-65; Lecturer in Physics, 1965-75; Head of Optical and Ultraviolet Astronomy Research Group, 1969-81; Reader in Physics, 1975-78; SRC Senior Fellow, 1976-81; Professor of Physics and Astronomy, 1978-81; Sherman Fairchild Distinguished Scholar, California Institute of Technology, 1981-82; Director, Royal Greenwich Observatory, 1981-93; Royal Observatories, 1993-96; Research Professor, University of Cambridge and PPARC Senior Research Fellow, Universities of Cambridge and London, 1996-; Extraordinary Fellow, Churchill College, Cambridge, 1996-, member of Council, 1998-2003. Honours: Chair, New Industrial Concepts Ltd, 1969-81; President, West London Astronomical Society, 1978-; Chair, SRC Astronomy Committee, 1980-81; Numerous other committees on astronomy, 1980-; Visiting Professor, Department of Physics and Astronomy, University College, London, 1981-, Astronomy Center, University of Sussex, 1981-89; Honorary Doctorate, Paris Observatory, 1982; Asteroid (3205) named Boksenberg, 1988; Honorary Professor of Experimental Astronomy, University of Cambridge, 1991-; Hon DSc (Sussex), 1991; Executive Editor, Experimental Astronomy, 1995-; Honorary President, Astronomical Society of Glasgow; Hannah Jackson Medal, 1998; Glazebrook Medal and Prize, 2000. Membership: Past member of over 30 other councils, boards, committees, etc, 1970-; ESA Hubble Space Telescope Instrument Definition Team, 1973-; Fellow, Royal Society, 1978; SA Astronomical Observatory Advisory Committee, 1978-85; Freeman, Clockmakers Co, 1984; British Council Science Advisory Committee, 1987-91; Liveryman, 1989; Fachbeirat of Max Planck Institut für Astronomie, 1991-95; Fellow, University College, London, 1991-; Member of Court, 1994. Address: University of Cambridge, Institute of Astronomy, The Observatories, Madingley Road, Cambridge, CB3 0HA, England.

BOLDON Ato, b. 30 December 1973, Port of Spain, Trinidad (resident of USA, 1988-). Athlete. Education: University of California, Los Angeles. Appointments: Coached by John Smith; Central American and Caribbean Record Holder at 60m indoors (6.49 secs), 100m (9.86 secs) and 200m (19.77 secs). Honours: Gold Medal, World Junior Championships 100m and 200m, 1992; 4th, Commonwealth Games 100m, 1994; Bronze Medal, World Championships 100m, 1995; Gold Medal, NCAA Championships 100m, 1996; Bronze Medals, Olympic Games 100m and 200m, 1996; 100m World Champion, 1997, 1999; Gold Medal, World Championships 200m, 1997; Gold Medal, Goodwill Games, New York, 200m, 1998; Gold Medal, Commonwealth Games 100m, 1998; Silver Medal, 100m, Bronze Medal, 200m, Olympic Games, 2000; Youngest sprinter ever to run under 10 seconds in the 100m and under 20 seconds in the 200m (at end of 2001). Website: www.atoboldon.com

BOLDYREV Alexander Alexandrovitch, b. 5 September 1940, Arkhangelsk City, Russia. Biologist; Professor of Biochemistry. m. Valeria Maltseva, 28 September 1963, 2 daughters. Education: MSc, 1963, PhD, 1967, M V Lomonosov Moscow State University; DSc, Leningrad State University, 1977; Postdoctoral Fellow, University Aarhus, Denmark, 1973-74. Appointments; Senior Science

Researcher, Moscow State University, 1975-87; Visiting Professor, King's College London, England, 1982, 1986; Visiting Professor, Waseda University, Tokyo, Japan, 1990, 1993; Head, Laboratory of Clinical Neurochemistry, Institute of Neurology, Moscow, 1993-. Publications: More than 300 science articles and reviews in Russian and international journals; Several textbooks and monographs including: Carnosine and protection of tissues against oxidative stress, 1999; Ivanov-Kholodnyi biography. Honours: V S Gulevitch Prize, Russian Academy of Medical Sciences; Honorable Professor, International Albert Schweizer University; Honorable Professor, King's College, London; Meritorious Science Worker, Russia. Memberships include: International Society for Neurochemistry; Society for Neuroscience; The European Peptide Club; New York Academy of Sciences; London Diplomatic Academy, UK; International Academy of Scientific Discovers and Inventors, Russia; American Association for the Advancement of Sciences, USA; Pushkov Institute of Terrestrial Magnetizm, Ionosphere and Radio Wave Propagation. Address: Department of Biochemistry, M V Lomonosov Moscow State University, School of Biology, Room 141, Lenin's Hills 119992, Moscow, Russia. E-mail: aaboldyrev@mail.ru

BOLGER Dermot, b. 6 February 1959, Finglas, Ireland. Novelist; Dramatist; Poet; Editor. m. Bernadette Clifton, 1988, 2 sons. Education: Finglas and Benevin College, Finglas. Appointments: Factory hand, library assistant, professor author; Founder and Editor, Raven Arts Press, 1979-92; Founder and Executive Editor, New Island Books, Dublin, 1992-. Publications: Novels: Night Shift, 1985; The Woman's Daughter, 1987, augmented edition, 1991; The Journey Home, 1990; Emily's Shoes, 1992; A Second Life, 1994; Father's Music, Finbar's Hotel (collaborative novel), 1997; Ladies Night at Finbar's Hotel (collaborative novel), 1999; Temptation, 2000; The Valparaiso Voyage, 2001; The Family on Paradis Pier, 2005. Plays: The Lament for Arthur Cleary, 1989; Blinded by the Light, In High Germany, The Holy Ground, 1990; One Last White Horse, 1991; The Dublin Bloom, 1994; April Bright, 1995; The Passion of Jerome, 1999; Consenting Adults, 2000; From These Green Heights, 2005; The Townlands of Brazil, 2006; Walking the Toad, 2007. Poetry: The Habit of Flesh, 1979; Finglas Lilies, 1980; No Waiting America, 1981; Internal Exiles, 1986; Leinster Street Ghosts, 1989; Taking My Letters Back: New and Selected Poems, 1998; The chosen Moment, 2004. Editor: The Dolmen Book of Irish Christmas Stories, The Bright Wave: Poetry in Irish Now, 1986; 16 on 16: Irish Writers on the Easter Rising, Invisible Cities: The New Dubliners: A Journey through Unofficial Dublin, 1988; Invisible Dublin: A Journey through Its Writers, 1992; The Picador Book of Contemporary Irish Fiction, 12 Bar Blues (with Aidan Murphy), 1993; The New Picador Book of Contemporary Irish Fiction, 2000; Druids, Dudes and Beauty Queens: The Changing Face of Irish Theatre, 2001. Contributions to: Anthologies. Honours: A E Memorial Prize, 1986; Macauley Fellowship, 1987; A Z Whitehead Prize, 1987; Samuel Beckett Award, 1991; Edinburgh Fringe First Award, 1991, 1995; Stewart Parker BBC Award, 1991; Playwright in Association, Abbey Theatre, Dublin, 1998; Writer Fellow, Trinity College, Dublin, 2003. Address: c/o A P Watt, 20 John Street, London WC1N 2DR, England.

BOLGER Leslie, b. 11 August 1947, Liverpool, England. Musician (arranger); Lecturer. m. Claire Holland, 3 daughters. Education: Certificate in Education (with distinction), University of Manchester. Musical Education: Studied with world renowned jazz guitarist George Gola, Australia.

Career: Jazz performances with artistes including: Martin Taylor; Louis Stewart; Benn Clatworthy; Ike Isaacs; Gary Potter, etc; Many television and radio broadcasts; Arranger, Music Adviser, Granada Television; Session guitarist, Arranger, Piccadilly Radio; Backing guitarist for many top cabaret artists including: Tony Christy; The Nolans; Gerard Kenny; Joe Longthorne; Matt Monro; Bob Monkhouse, etc. Publications: Many publications in jazz/guitar magazines. Honours: Many first places with honours or distinction for Les Bolger Jazz Guitar Ensemble; Listed in international biographical directories. Membership: Musicians' Union. Address: 12 Firbank Close, Daresbury View, Runcorn, Cheshire WA7 6NR, England.

BOLKIAH MU'IZUDDIN WADDAULAH, HM Sultan Sir Muda Hassanal, b. 15 July 1946, Brunei. m. (1) Rajah Isteri Anak Saleha, 1965-, , (2) Pengiran Isteri Hajjah Mariam, divorced 2003, (3) Azrinaz Mazhar Hakim, 2005, altogether has 6 sons and 6 daughters. Education: Victoria Institute, Kuala Lumpur, Malaysia; Royal Military Academy, Sandhurst, England. Appointments: Crown Prince and Heir Apparent, 1961; Ruler of State of Brunei, 1967-; Prime Minister of Brunei, 1984-; Minister of Finance and Home Affairs, 1984-86, of Defence, 1986-, also Finance and Law. Honours include: Honorary Captain, Coldstream Guards, 1968; Honorary Marshall, RAF, 1992; Sovereign and Chief of Royal Orders, Sultans of Brunei. Address: Istana Darul Hana, Bandar Seri Begawan, BA 1000, Brunei. E-mail: pro@jpm.gov.bn

BOND (Thomas) Michael, b. 13 January 1926, Newbury, Berkshire, England. Author. m. (1) Brenda May Johnson, 29 June 1950, divorced 1981, 1 son, 1 daughter, (2) Susan Marfrey Rogers, 1981. Education: Presentation College, 1934-40. Publications: Children's Books: A Bear Called Paddington, 1958; More About Paddington, 1959; Paddington Helps Out, 1960; Paddington Abroad, 1961; Paddington at Large, 1962; Paddington Marches On, 1964; Paddington at Work, Here Comes Thursday, 1966; Thursday Rides Again, Paddington Goes to Town, 1968; Thursday Ahoy, Parsley's Tail, Parsley's Good Deed, 1969; Parsley's Problem Present, Parsley's Last Stand, Paddington Takes the Air, Thursday in Paris, 1970; Michael Bond's Book of Bears, Michael Bond's Book of Mice, 1971; The Day the Animals Went on Strike, Paddington Bear, Paddington's Garden, Parsley Parade, The Tales of Olga da Polga, 1972; Olga Meets Her Match, Paddington's Blue Peter Story Book, Paddington at the Circus, Paddington Goes Shopping, 1973; Paddington at the Seaside, Paddington at the Tower, Paddington on Top, 1974; Windmill, How to Make Flying Things, Eight Olga Readers, 1975; Paddington's Cartoon Book, 1979; J D Polson and the Dillogate Affair, Paddington on Screen, 1981; Olga Takes Charge, 1982; The Caravan Puppets, 1983; Paddington at the Zoo, 1984; Paddington's Painting Exhibition, Elephant, 1985; Paddington Minds the House, Paddington at the Palace, 1986; Paddington's Busy Day, Paddington and the Magical Maze, 1987; Paddington and the Christmas Surprise, 1997; Paddington at the Carnival, Paddington Bear, 1998; Olga Moves House, 2001; Olga Follows Her Nose, 2002; Paddington's Grand Tour, 2003. Adult Books: Monsieur Pamplemousse, 1983; Monsieur Pamplemousse and the Secret Mission, 1984; Monsieur Pamplemousse Takes the Cure, 1987; The Pleasures of Paris, Guide Book, 1987; Monsieur Pamplemousse Aloft, 1989; Monsieur Pamplemousse Investigates, 1990; Monsieur Pamplemousse Rests His Case, 1991; Monsieur Pamplemousse Stands Firm, Monsieur Pamplemousse on Location, 1992; Monsieur Pamplemousse Takes the Train, 1993; Bears and Forebears (autobiography), 1996; Monsieur

Pamplemousse Afloat, 1998; Monsieur Pamplemousse on Probation, 2000; Monsieur Pamplemousse on Vacation, 2002; Monsieur Pamplemousse Hits the Headlines, 2003; Monsieur Pamplemousse and The Militant Midwives, 2006. Honour: Officer of the Order of the British Empire, 1997. Address: The Agency, 24 Pottery Lane, Holland Park, London W11 4LZ, England.

BONDS Georgia Anna Arnett, b. 30 December 1917, New York, USA. Writer; Lecturer. m. Alfred Bryan Bonds, 2 sons, 2 daughters. Education: BA, University of North Carolina, 1938; MA, Louisiana State University, 1941; Post Graduate Work, University of North Carolina, 1941-42; Baldwin Wallace College, 1960-. Appointments: Editorial Assistant, The Southern Review; Editorial Assistant Public School Curriculum of Louisiana; Editor of English version of Wheat Growing In Egypt; First Lady of Baldwin Wallace College; Volunteer, World Association of Girl Guides And Girl Scouts; Worked world-wide for peace through international understanding. Publications: The Lake Erie Girl Scout Council, the First Seventy Five Years; First two chapters of A Promise Kept, 1912-2002, ninety years of helping girls succeed; Novel, Who Killed Bob Lawson?, 2003; Numerous articles in popular magazines. Honours: World Friendship and Understanding Through Girl Scouting; Thanks Badges, 1971, 1997. Memberships: Phi Beta Kappa; United Methodist Church; YWCA; AAUW; Eastern Star; AARP. Address: PO Box 768, Berea, OH, USA.

BONHAM CARTER Helena, b. 26 May 1966, Golders Green, London, England. Actress. 1 son with Tim Burton. Career: Films include: Lady Jane; A Room with a View; Maurice; Francesco; The Mask; Getting it Right; Hamlet; Where Angels Fear to Tread; Howard's End, 1991; A Dark Adapted Eye (TV), Mary Shelley's Frankenstein, The Glace Bay Miners' Museum, 1994; A Little Loving, Mighty Aphrodite, 1995; Twelfth Night, Margaret's Museum, 1996; Parti Chinois, 1996; The Theory of Flight, Keep the Aspidistra Flying, 1997; The Wings of the Dove, The Revengers' Comedies, 1998; Women Talking Dirty, Fight Club, 1999; Until Human Voices Wake Us, 2000; Planet of the Apes, The Heart of Me, Novocaine, 2002; Till Human Voices Wake Us, 2003; Charlie and the Chocolate Factory, Conversations with Other Women, Wallace & Gromit in The Curse of the Were-Rabbit (voice), The Corpse Bride (voice), Magnificent 7, 2005; Sixty Six, 2006; Sweeney Todd, Harry Potter and the Order of the Phoenix, 2007. Television appearances include: A Pattern of Roses; Miami Vice; A Hazard of Hearts; The Vision; Arms and the Man; Beatrix Potter; Live from Baghdad, 2002; Henry VIII, 2003. Address: c/o Conway van Gelder Limited, 18/21 Jermyn Street, London, SW1Y 6HP, England.

BONINGTON Sir Christian (John Storey), b. 6 August 1934. Mountaineer; Writer; Photographer. m. Muriel Wendy Marchant, 1962, 2 sons. Education: University College School, London. Appointments: RMA Sandhurst, 1955-56; Commissioned, Royal Tank Regiment, 1956-61; Unilever Management Trainee, 1961-62; Writer and Photographer, 1962-; Mountaineer of: Annapurna II, 1960, Central Pillar Freney, Mont Blanc, 1961, Nuptse, 1961, North Wall of Eiger, 1962, Central Tower of Paine, Patagonia, 1963; Member of Team, 1st descent of Blue Nile, 1968; Leader, Annapurna South Face Expedition, 1970; British Everest Expedition, 1972; Brammah Himalayas, 1973; Co-Leader, Changabang, Himalayas, 1974; British Everest Expedition, 1975; Ogre, 1977; Joint Leader, Kongur, North West China, 1981; Panch Chuli II, Kumaon, Himalayas, 1992; Mejslen, Greenland, 1993; Rang Rik Rank, Kinnaur, Himalayas, 1994,

Drangnag Ri, Nepal, 1995; Sepu Kangri Expedition, 1998; 1st ascent of Danga II, 2000. Publications: I Chose to Climb (autobiography), 1966; Annapurna South Face, 1971; The Next Horizon (autobiography), 1973; Everest, South West Face, 1973; Everest the Hard Way, 1976; Quest for Adventure, 1981; Kongur: China's Elusive Summit, 1982; Everest: The Unclimbed Ridge (co-author), 1983; The Everest Years, 1986; Mountaineer (autobiography), 1989; The Climbers, 1992; Sea, Ice and Rock (with Robin Knox-Johnston), 1992; Tibet's Secret Mountain, 1999; Quest for Adventure, 2000; Chris Bonington's Everest, 2002. Honours include: Founder Medal, Royal Geographical Society, 1971; Lawrence of Arabia Medal, 1986; Livingstone Medal, 1991; CBE; Honorary DSc, Sheffield; Honorary MA, Salford; Honorary DSc, Lancaster; Honorary DSc, Northumbria; Honorary Doctor of Letters, University of Bradford; Chancellor, Lancaster University, 2005-. Memberships include: Army Mountaineering Association; British Mountaineering Council; Council for National Parks; The Alpine Club. Address: Badger Hill, Nether Row, Hesket Newmarket, Wigton, Cumbria CA7 8LA, England.

BONO (Paul Hewson), 10 May 1960, Dublin, Ireland. Singer; Lyricist. m. Alison, 2 daughters, 2 sons. Career: Founder member, lead singer, rock group U2, 1978-; Regular national, international and worldwide tours; Major concerts include: US Festival, 1983; The Longest Day, Milton Keynes Bowl, Live Aid, Wembley, 1985; Self Aid, Ireland, A Conspiracy Of Hope (Amnesty International US tour), 1986; Smile Jamaica (hurricane relief concert), Very Special Arts Festival, White House, 1988; New Year's Eve Concert, Dublin (televised throughout Europe), 1989; Yankee Stadium, New York (second concert ever), 1992; Group established own record company, Mother Records. Compositions include: Co-writer, Jah Love, Neville Brothers; Lyrics, Misere, Zucchero and Pavarotti; Screenplay, Million Dollar Hotel. Recordings: Albums: with U2: Boy, 1980; October, 1981; War, Under A Blood Red Sky, 1983; The Unforgettable Fire, 1984; Wide Awake In America, 1985; The Joshua Tree, 1987; Rattle And Hum, also film, 1988; Achtung Baby, 1991; Zooropa, 1993; Passengers (film soundtrack), with Brian Eno, 1995; Pop, 1997; All Than You Can't Leave Behind, The Best of 1990-2000, 2000; How To Dismantle An Atomic Bomb, 2004; Hit singles include: Out Of Control, 1979; Another Day, 1980; New Year's Day, 1983; Two Hearts Beat As One, 1983; Pride (In The Name Of Love), 1984; The Unforgettable Fire, 1985; With Or Without You, I Still Haven't Found What I'm Looking For, Where The Streets Have No Name, 1987; Desire, Angel Of Harlem, 1988; When Love Comes To Town, with B B King, All I Want Is You, 1989; The Fly, 1991; Mysterious Ways, One, Even Better Than The Real Thing, Who's Gonna Ride Your Wild Horses, 1992; Stay, 1993; Hold Me, Thrill Me, Kiss Me (from film soundtrack Batman Forever), 1995; Discotheque, 1997; If God Will Send His Angels, Sweetest Thing, 1998; Beautiful Day, 2000; Stuck In A Moment You Can't Get Out Of, Walk On, Elevation, 2001; Electrical Storm, The Hands That Built America, 2002; Vertigo, 2004; Contributor, Do They Know It's Christmas?, Band Aid, Sun City, Little Steven, 1985; In A Lifetime, Clannad, 1986; Mystery Girl, Roy Orbison, 1988; Special Christmas, charity album, 1987; Folkways - A Vision Shared (Woody Guthrie tribute), 1988; Live For Ireland, 1989; Red Hot + Blue (Cole Porter tribute), 1990; Tower Of Song (Leonard Cohen tribute), 1995; Pavarotti And Friends, 1996; Forces Of Nature, 1999. Honours: Numerous Grammy Awards, BRIT Awards, Q Awards; Ivor Novello Award for Best Song Musically and Lyrically, 2002; Grammy, Album of the Year, 2006; Honorary Knight Commander of the Order of the British Empire, 2007; Many poll wins and awards, Billboard and Rolling Stone magazines; Gold and Platinum discs. Address: Principle Management, 30-32 Sir John Rogersons Quay, Dublin 2, Ireland.

BONSU Benjamin Daniel, b. 21 May 1933, Daaman, Mampon-Asante, Ghana. Catechist; Herbalist. m. 29 October 1956, 5 sons, 2 daughters. Education: Office Supervision, 1971; Office Management, 1972; Personnel Management, 1980. Appointments: Teacher, 1953-67; Mill Operator, Gihoc Fibre, 1968-78; Assistant Personnel Officer, Gihoc Fibre, 1979-83; Personnel Officer, Gihoc Farms, 1984; Service Manager, Gihoc Fibre, 1985-87; Catechist, PCG, 1956-67, 1975-; Herbalist, Federation of Traditional Healers, 1958-. Publications: Several articles in professional journals; Awaree Eye Onyankopon Nhyehee, 1986. Honours: Gihoc Fibre Products Co Ltd 10 years Service Award, 1968-78, 1986, 15 years Service Award, 1968-83, 1986. Memberships: Traditional Medicine Practitioners Association, Ghana; Ghana Institute of Personnel Management; Federation of Traditional Healers. Address: Sankofa Herbal Store & Clinic, PO Box 8224, Ahensan-Kumasi, Ghana.

BONTING Sjoerd Lieuwe, b. 6 October 1924, Amsterdam, The Netherlands. Biochemist; Anglican Priest-Theologian. m. (1) Susan Maarsen, deceased, 2 sons, 2 daughters, (2) Erica Schotman. Education: BSc, Chemistry, 1944, MSc, cum laude, Biochemistry, 1950, PhD, Biochemistry, 1952, University of Amsterdam; Ordained Priest, Episcopal Church, Washington, 1964. Appointments: Research Associate, University of Iowa, 1952-55; Assistant Professor, University of Minnesota, 1955-56; Assistant Professor, Biochemistry, University of Illinois, Chicago, USA, 1956-60; Section Chief, National Institutes of Health, Bethesda, Maryland, 1960-65; Professor, Head, Department of Biochemistry, University of Nymegen, Netherlands, 1965-85; Scientific Consultant, NASA-Ames Research Centre, Moffett Field, 1985-93; Assistant Priest, St Thomas Episcopal Church, Sunnyvale, USA, 1985-90; Assistant Priest, St Mark's Episcopal Church, Palo Alto, California, 1990-93; Anglican Chaplain, Church of England, Netherlands, 1965-85, 1993-. Publications: Scientific publications: 363 articles, 9 books including: Transmitters in the Visual Process, 1976; Membrane Transport, 1981; Advances in Space Biology and Medicine, vols 1-7, 1989-99; Theological publications: 92 articles, 7 books including: Evolution and Creation, 1978; Word and World, 1989; Creation and Evolution, 1996, 2nd edition, 1997; Humanity, Chaos, Reconciliation, 1998; Belief and Unbelief, 2000; Chaos Theology, a Revised Creation Theology, 2002; Creation and Double Chaos, 2005. Honours: Rudolf Lehmann Scholar, Amsterdam, 1941-46; Postdoctoral Fellowship, USPHS, Iowa City, USA, 1952-54; Fight for Sight Citation, National Council to Combat Blindness and Association for Research in Ophthalmology, 1961, 1962; Arthur S Flemming Award, Jaycees, Washington DC, USA, 1964; Prize for Enzymology on Leucocytes, Karger Foundation, Basel, Switzerland, 1964; Honorary Licentiate in Theology, St Mark's Institute of Theology, London, 1975; Citation by Archbishop of Canterbury for 20 years chaplaincy work in the Netherlands, 1985. Memberships: Sigma Xi, 1955-; American Society of Biology Chemists, 1958-; AAAS, 1960-; American Society of Cell Biology, 1960-; Netherlands Biochemical Society, 1965-; Board of Directors, Multidisciplinary Center for Church and Society, The Netherlands, 1981-85; Society of Ordained Scientists, 1989-. Address: Specreyse 12, 7471 TH Goor, The Netherlands. E-mail: s.l.bonting@wxs.nl Website: www.chaostheologie.nl

BONTRAGER Opal J, b. 22 June 1961, McMinnville, Oregon, USA. Accountant. Education: BA, Psychology and Social Work, 1983; MA, Business Administration in Accounting, 2005. Appointments: Trainer for Developmental Disabled, 1984-87; Office Worker, 1987-94; Accounting Clerk, 1994-99; Part time Tax Preparer, 1997-99; Tax Auditor, 1999-2001; Governmental Accountant, 2001-. Honours: Oregon Scholar, 1979; America's Outstanding Names & Places, 1979-80; Empire's Who's Who; Who's Who Professional of the Year in Governmental Accounting, 2006-07. Memberships: Licensed Tax Consultant; Oregon State Fiscal Association Member. Address: 2335 Saginaw St S, Salem, OR 97302, USA. E-mail: opal.bontrager@das.state.or.us

BOON Julia, b. 11 January 1916, Burgas, Bulgaria. Linguist. Widow, 1 son 1 daughter. Education: BA, Latin Philosophy, 1965; Certificate in Adult Education, 1973; Master of Arts, 1976; Incomplete PhD. Appointments: Founder, Director, language school teaching English as a second language, 1978-. Publications: Symbols and Words; Occupational English; Parlons francais c'est une des plus belles langues vivantes; Dialogues. Honours: Medal, Government of Canada; Plaque, Provincial Government; IBC Medal for Outstanding Intellectuals of the 21st Century. Memberships: UNESCO, Prairie Public TV; Sierra Legal; CNIB; Nature Canada; CWF; Care Cuso. Address: 34 Coleraine Crescent, Winnipeg, Manitoba R3P 0X4, Canada. E-mail: alcentre@alcentre.com

BOONRUANGRUTANA Samrerng, b. 23 February 1943, Ayutthaya, Thailand. m. Charweewon, 2 sons. Education: B Ed, Chemistry, 1966, M Ed, Test and Measurement, 1969, College of Education, Thailand; Certificate in Educational Innovation and Technology, INNOTECH Center, Singapore, 1972; PhD, Curriculum Research and Development, University of Illinois, USA, 1978; Certificate of National Defense, National Defense College, Thailand, 1993. Appointments: Teacher, Suravithayakarn School, 1966-67; Instructor, 1969-79, Assistant Professor, 1979-82, Associate Professor, 1982-87, Professor in Educational Measurement and Evaluation, 1987-2003, Director, Educational and Psychological Test Bureau, 1983-87, Vice President for Academic Affairs, 1987-93, Srinakharinwirot University, Thailand; Professor, Educational Measurement and Evaulation, Vongchavalitkul University, 2003-. Publications: Over 44 research papers and 155 articles in various national and international journals. Honours: Knight Grand Cordon (Special Class) of the Most Exalted Order of the White Elephant; Knight Grand Cordon (Special Class) of the Most Noble Order of the Crown of Thailand; Knight Grand Cross (First Class) of the Most Exalted of the White Elephant; Knight Grand Cross (First Class) of the Most Noble Order of the Crown of Thailand; Best Research in Education Award, 1986; Best Instructor of Srinakharinwirot University Award, 1997; Princess Prem Purachatra Award, 2001; Best University Instructor of the Nation Award, 2001; One of fifteen, Thai Wisdom in the Celebration of 400 years of the Death of King Naresuan the Great, 2005; Distinguished Alumni Award, College of Education, University of Illinois, 2007. Memberships: Kappa Delta Pi; American Educational Research Association. Address: 4/357 Soi 16 Sahakorn Village, Seri Thai Road, Klongkum, Bungkum, Bangkok 10240, Thailand.

BOOTH Betty Jean, b. 27 December 1944, St Louis Country, Missouri, USA. Author. m. Robert Lee Booth, 3 sons, 3 daughters. Education: Word Processing and Business, United Business College. Career: Author and poet. Publications: Traveling on the Wings of Life's Inner Circle, 2005. Honours: Listed in numerous national and international biographical directories. Memberships: International Society of Poets; The International Library of Poetry, Poetry.com. Address: 14503 Hazel Ridge, Detroit, MI 48205-3619, USA.

BOOTH Cherie, b. 23 September 1954, Bury, Lancashire, England. Barrister. m. A C L (Tony) Blair, 1980, 3 sons, 1 daughter. Education: London School of Economics. Appointments: Lincoln's Inn Bar, 1976; In Practice, 1976-77; New Court Chambers, 1977-91; Gray's Inn Square Chambers, 1991-2000; Queens Council, 1995; Assistant Recorder, 1996-99; Governor, London School of Economics, 1998-; Recorder, 1999-; Matrix Chambers, 2000-. Publication: Contributor, Education Law, 1997; The Goldfish Bowl, 2004. Honours: FJMU; FRSA; Fellow, John Moores University, Liverpool, Chancellor, 1998-; Patron, CLIC-Sargent Cancer Care for Children, 1998-; Patron, Breast Cancer Care, 1997-; Islington Music Centre, 1999-; Honorary Degree, Open University, 1999; Honorary LLD, Westminster University; Fellow of LSE; Fellow of International Society of Lawyers in Public Service; Hon Bencher, King's Inn, Dublin, 2002; Hon Fellow: LSE, 2003; Open University; Institute of Advanced Legal Studies; Hon President, Plater College, Hon Patron, Genesis Appeal; Hon DUniv, UMIST, 2003. Memberships: Fellow, Institute of Advisory Legal Studies. Address: Matrix Chambers, Griffin Building, Grays Inn, London WC1R 5LN, England.

BOOTH Paul L, b. 31 May 1931, Los Angeles, USA. Minister. m. Josephine. Education: BS, Business Administration, City University, Seattle, Washington, 1980; Diploma, Theological School of the Lord's New Church, Nova Hierosolyma, Bryn Athyn, Pennsylvania, 1991. Appointments: Priest, 1st degree, 1991, 2nd degree, 1994; Pastor, The Lord's New Church, Holland, 1992; President, The Swedenborg Society, Holland, 1992; Foundation, Nova Domini, 2004. Address: 16924 91st Avenue E, Puyallup, WA 98375, USA. E-mail: paul@laudsnewchapel.com

BOOTHROYD Christine, b. 31 March 1934, Batley, Yorkshire, England. Linguist; Poet. m. Don Brinkley, 10 April 1982, 1 stepson, 1 stepdaughter. Education: Leeds College of Commerce, 1951-52; Teachers Certificate, University College of Wales, Aberystwyth, 1966; Diplomas in Italian, Perugia and Florence. Appointments: Secretary, Harrogate, Paris, Rome, Vienna, 1952-63; Teacher of French/Italian, Leeds, 1963-65; Lecturer in charge of Modern Languages, North Oxfordshire Technical College, 1966-77; Part-time Lecturer, French/Italian, Banbury and Harrogate. Publications: The Floating World, 1975; The Snow Island, 1982; The Lost Moon, 1992; Spirit of Place, 2007. Contributions to: Arts Council Anthology 3; Workshop New Poetry; Orbis; Glasgow Magazine; Writers in Concert; Doors; Krax; Moorlands Review; Envoi; Penniless Press; Links; Dalesman; Poetry Nottingham; Yorkshire Journal; The Journal; Carillon; Quantum Leap; Poetry Monthly; Countryside Tales; Yorkshire History Quarterly; Cumbria. Membership: Harrogate Writers' Circle; Italian Cultural Institute. Address: 35 St George's Road, Harrogate, North Yorkshire HG2 9BP, England.

BORG Björn Rune, b. 6 June 1956, Sodertalje, Sweden. Tennis Player; Business Executive. m. (1) Mariana Simionescu, 1980, divorced 1984, 1 son by Jannike Bjorling, (2) Loredana Berte, 1989, divorced 1992. Appointments: Professional Player, 1972-; Italian Champion, 1974, 1978; French Champion, 1974, 1975, 1978, 1979, 1980, 1981; Wimbledon Champion, 1976, 1977, 1978, 1979, 1980 (runner-up 1981); WCT Champion, 1976; Grand Prix Masters Champion, 1980, 1981; World Champion, 1979, 1980; Winner,

Stockholm Open, 1980; Retired, 1983, returned, 1984, 1992; Founder, Björn Borg Enterprises Ltd. Publication: Björn Borg - My Life and Game (with Eugene Scott), 1980. Honours: Sweden's Sportsperson of the Century; Voted second-best tennis player ever, Sports Illustrated and l'Equipe newspaper; BBC Lifetime Achievement Award, 2006. Address: c/o International Management Group, The Pier House, Strand on the Green, Chiswick, London W4 3NN, England.

BORGNINE Ernest, b. 24 January 1917, Hamden, Connecticut, USA. Actor. m. (1) Rhoda Kemins, 1 daughter, (2) Katy Jurado, (3) Ethel Merman, (4) Donna Rancourt, 1 son, 1 daughter, (5)Tova Traesnaes, 1972-. Education: New Haven public schools; Randall School of Dramatic Arts, Hartford. Career: Actor: Films include: From Here to Eternity; Bad Day at Black Rock; Marty; Violent Saturday; Square Jungle; Three Brave Men; Hell Below; The Rabbit Trap; Man on String; Barabbas; Flight of the Phoenix, The Oscar, 1966; The Split; Ice Station Zebra; The Dirty Dozen, 1968; Willard, 1971; The Poseidon Adventure, Emperor of the North, 1972; Sunday in the Country, 1974; Law and Disorder, 1975; Convoy, 1978; Goin' South, 1979; The Black Hole, All Quiet on the Western Front, 1980; Last Days of Pompeii, 1984; Dirty Dozen: The Next Mission, 1985; Any Man's Death, 1990; Mistress, 1992; All Dogs Go To Heaven 2, 1996; McHale's Navy, Gattaca, 1997; BASEketball, 1998; Castlerock, Hoover, 2000; Crimebusters, 2003; Blueberry, 2004; 3 Below, Rail Kings, 2005; Chinaman's Chance, Cura del gorilla, La, 2006. TV includes: Little House on the Prairie; Love Boat; Murder She Wrote; The Blue Light, The Trail to Hope Rose, 2004; Bert & Becca, 2007. Address: 3055 Lake Glen Drive, Beverly Hills, CA 90210, USA.

BORN Gustav Victor Rudolf, b. 29 July 1921. Professor Emeritus. m. (1) Wilfreda Ann Plowden-Wardlaw 2 sons, 1 daughter, (2) Faith Elizabeth Maurice-Williams, 1 son, 1 daughter. Education: Vans Dunlop Scholar, MB, ChB, University of Edinburgh, 1943; DPhil (Oxford), 1951, MA, 1956. Appointments include: Medical Officer, RAMC, 1943-47; Member, Scientific Staff, Medical Research Council, 1952-53, Research Officer, Nuffield Institute for Medical Research, 1953-60, Departmental Demonstrator in Pharmacology, 1956-60, University of Oxford; Vandervell Professor of Pharmacology, RCS and University of London, 1960-73; Sheild Professor of Pharmacology, University of Cambridge and Fellow, Gonville and Caius College, Cambridge, 1973-78; Professor of Pharmacology, King's College, University of London, 1978-86, Professor Emeritus 1986-; Research Director, The William Harvey Research Institute, St Bartholomew's Hospital Medical College, 1989-; Visiting Professor in Chemistry, Northwestern University, Illinois, 1970; William S Creasey Visiting Professor in Clinical Pharmacology, Brown University, 1977; Professor of Fondation de France, Paris, 1982-84; Honorary Director, Medical Research Council Thrombosis Research Group, 1964-73; Scientific Advisor, Vandervell Foundation, 1967-2001; President, International Society on Thrombosis and Haemostasis, 1977-79; Adviser, Heineman Medical Research Center, Charlotte, North Carolina, USA, 1981-; Kuratorium, Shakespeare Prize, Hamburg, 1991-98; Forensic Science Advisory Group, Home Office; Numerous invited lectures. Publications: Articles in scientific journals and books. Honours include: FRS, 1972; FRCP, 1976; Hon FRCS, 2002; FKC, 1988; Honorary Fellow, St Peter's College, Oxford, 1972; Ten Honorary Degrees; Albrecht von Haller Medal, Göttingen University, 1979; Chevalier de l'Ordre National de Mérite, France, 1980; Auenbrugger Medal, Graz University, 1984; Royal Medal, Royal Society, 1987; Robert Pfleger

Prize, Bamberg, 1990; Alexander von Humboldt Award, 1995; Gold Medal for Medicine, Ernst Jung Foundation, Hamburg, 2001. Memberships include: Honorary Life Member, New York Academy of Sciences; Akademia Leopoldina; Honorary Member German Physiological Society; Corresponding Member, German Pharmacological Society; Royal Belgian Academy of Medicine. Address: 5 Walden Lodge, 48 Wood Lane, Highgate, London N6 5UU, England.

BOROVEČKI Ana, b. 9 October 1973, Zagreb, Croatia. Physician. m. Tomislav Borošak. Education: Medical Degree, 1998, Clinical Pharmacology and Toxicology degree, 2008, School of Medicine, Degree in Philosophy and Comparative Literature, School of Philosophy, 2000, University of Zagreb; European Master in Bioethics, University of Leuven, Belgium, 2004; PhD, University of Nijmegen, The Netherlands, 2007. Appointments: One Year Clerkship, passed Medical Bar Exam, 1998-99; Research Assistant, Department for the History of Medicine of The Croatian Academy of Sciences and Arts, 1999-2001; Research Assistant, Andrija Stampar School of Public Health, School of Medicine, University of Zagreb, 2001-. Publications: Numerous articles in professional journals. Honours: Dean's Prize, Zagreb University, 1998. Memberships: Croatian Medical Association; Croatian Philosophic Society. E-mail: abor@mef.hr

BORYSZEWSKI Ralph, b. 13 May 1918, Rochester, New York, USA. Author; Researcher; Police Officer. 1 son, 2 daughters. Education: Self educated in Law, The Constitution and Action Against Legislative, Executive and Judicial Decisions. Appointments: Sergeant, US Army, WW2; Police Officer, Rochester, New York, 27 years; Author of writings on Truth in Government; National Keynote Speaker. Publications: 2 books: The Constitution That Never Was; Treason; Articles and series of pamphlets on Government Reform and Redress, Powers of Grand Jury, Public Corruption and Public Rights. Honours: Officer of the Year, Montreal, Canada, 1968; Listed in international biographical dictionaries. Memberships: Foundation for Rights. Address: 26 Portland Ct, Apt 3, Rochester, NY 14621, USA.

BOSHELL VILLAMIZAR Francisco José, b. 22 September 1977, Colombia. Consultant in Sustainable Energy. Education; BSc, Mechanical Engineering, University of Los Andes, Colombia, 1994-99; Technology for Sustainable Development Certificate, 2004-06; MSc, Sustainable Energy Technology, Eindhoven University of Technology, 2004-06. Appointments: Maintenance Engineer, British Petroleum Exploration Company, Colombia, 1998; Project Engineer, General Motors Colmotres, Colombia, 2000-04; Commercial Director CDM Event, Andean Center for Economics in the Environment, 2006-07; Consultant in Sustainable Energy, KEMA Inc, 2007-. Honours: Best Graduated Student of the Year, 1993; Full Scholarship, Shell Centenary Scholarship Foundation, 2004; MSc Honourable Diploma with Great Appreciation, 2006. Address: Cra 7 B No 151-47, Bogotá, Colombia. E-mail: franciscoboshell@yahoo.com

BOSHOFF Carel Willem Hendrik, b. 9 November 1927, Nylstroom Transvaal, South Africa. m. Anna Verwoerd, 5 sons, 2 daughters. Education: BA, BD, MA, DD, University of Pretoria. Appointments: Missionary, Dutch Reformed Church, 1953-63; Secretary of Missions, Dutch Reformed Church, 1963-66; Professor and Head of Department, Science of Religion and Missiology, 1967-88, Dean of Faculty, 1978-80, Theological Faculty, University of Pretoria. Publications: Die Begin van die Evangelie van Jesus Christus, 1963; Uit God gebore, 1968; Die Nuwe Sendingsituasie,

1978; Swart Teologie van Amerika tot in Suid Africa, 1980; Numerous articles in various journals. Honours: Orde; Orde, Die Afrikaner Os; Honorary Member, Die Voortrekkers. Memberships: Chairman: SA Bureau of Racial Affairs, 1972-99; Die Afrikaner Broederbond, 1980-83; NG Kerkboekhandel, 1976-88; Council, SA College for Teachers Education, 1976-86; Afrikaner Volkswag Cultural Organisation, 1984-99; Council, Institute for Missiological Research, 1978-88; Member, SA Akademie vur Watenshaap en Kuas, 1979-; Leader, Die Voortrekker Beweging, 1981-89; Executive Chairman, Afrikaner Vryheidstigting, 1988-; Chairman, Director Orania Bestuursdienste Ltd, 1990-; Provincial Leader, Freedom Front NC, 1994-2003; Member, Legislative Province, Northern Cape, 1994-2003; President, Burger Council Afrikaner Vryheidstigting, 1994-. Address: PO Box 199, Orania 8752, South Africa.

BOSKOVIC Bojan Obrad, b. 27 March 1969, Belgrade, Serbia, Yugoslavia. Engineer; Physicist. m. Olivera Spasic-Boskovic, 2 daughters. Education: Dipl Ing, Faculty of Electrical Engineering, University of Belgrade, Yugoslavia, 1989-95; PhD, University of Surrey, England, 1998-2001. Appointments: Research and Teaching Assistant, Faculty of Electrical Engineering, 1995-97, Assistant Lecturer, Faculty of Mechanical Engineering, 1997-98, University of Belgrade, Yugoslavia; Senior Specialist, Morgan Group Technology, The Morgan Crucible plc, 2001-03; Research Associate, Department of Engineering, 2003-04, Research Associate & Visiting Scientist, Departments of Materials Science & Metallurgy, 2004-06, University of Cambridge; Principal Engineer, Carbon Scientist, Meggitt Aircraft Braking Systems, Meggitt plc, 2006-. Publications: Numerous articles in professional journals about carbon nanotechnology; 2 granted patents; Invited review articles and book chapters. Address: 14 Orchard Way, Cambourne, Cambridge, CB23 5BN, England. E-mail: boboskovic@yahoo.com

BOSTON Kenneth George, b. 9 September 1942, Melbourne, Australia. Chief Executive. m. Yvonne, 1 daughter. Education: MA, PhD, University of Melbourne, 1981. Appointments: Director General of Education, South Australia, 1988-91; Managing Director of Technical and Further Education; Director General of Education and Training, New South Wales, Australia, 1991-2002; Chief Executive, Qualifications and Curriculum Authority, London, 2002-. Honours: Officer of the Order of Australia, 2001. Memberships: Fellow Australian College of Education; Fellow Royal Geographical Society. Address: Qualifications and Curriculum Authority, 83 Piccadilly, London W1J 8QA, England.

BOTHAM Ian Terence, b. 24 November 1955, Heswall, Cheshire, England. Cricketer. m. Kathryn Waller, 1976 1 son, 2 daughters. Career: Debut for Somerset, 1974; Awarded County Cap, 1976; Test debut, 1977; Tours of Pakistan and New Zealand, 1977-78; Australia, 1978-79; Australia and India, 1979-80; West Indies, 1981; India and Sri Lanka, 1981-892; Australia, 1982-83; New Zealand and Pakistan, 1983-84; Captain, England, 1980-81; Captain, Somerset County Cricket Club, 1983-85; Worcestershire, 1987-91; Durham, 1992-93; Retired, 1993; Player for Queensland, Australia, and Worcestershire County Cricket Club, 1987; Became 1st player to score century and take 8 wickets in an innings in a Test Match v Pakistan, Lord's, 1978; Took 100th wicket in test cricket record time of 2 years 9 days, 1979 Achieved double of 1000 runs and 100 wickets in Tests to create world record of fewest Tests (21) and English records of shortest time (2 years 33 days) and at youngest age (23 years 279 days), 1979; Became 1st player to have scored 3000 runs and taken 250 wickets in Tests (55), 1982; 1st player to score century and take 10 wickets in Test Match v India; Scorer of over 1000 runs and taken more than 100 wickets in Tests gainst Australia; Won 100th Test cap for England, 1992; Has also played soccer for Scunthorpe Utd. Publications include: It Sort of Clicks, 1986; Cricket My Way, 1989; Botham: My Autobiography, 1994; The Botham Report, 1997. Honours: Hon MSc (UMIST); Wisden Cricketer of the Year, 1978; Lifetime Achievement Award, BBC Sports Personality of the Year, 2004; Knighted by the queen in 2007. Address: Mission Sports Management, Kirmington Vale, Barnetby, North Lincolnshire, DN38 6AF, England.

BOTTOMLEY OF NETTLESTONE Rt Hon Baroness, Virginia Hilda Brunette Maxwell, b. 12 March 1948. Politician. m. Peter Bottomley, 1967, 1 son, 2 daughters. Education: London School Economics. Appointments: Various positions before election as Conservative MP for Surrey South, 1984-2005; Parliamentary Private Secretary to Chris Patten, 1985-87; Parliamentary Private Secretary for Foreign and Commonwealth Affairs Sir Geoffrey Howe QC MP, 1987-88; Parliament Under-Secretary, Department of the Environment, 1988-89; Ministry for Health, 1989-92; Secretary of State, Department of Health, 1992-95, with responsibility for family policy, 1994-95; Chairman, Millennium Commission, 1995-97; Secretary of State, Department of National Heritage, 1995-97; Vice Chairman, British Council, 1997-2000; House of Commons Select Committee on Foreign Affairs, 1997-99; Supervisory Board, Akzo Nobel, NV; Executive Director, Odger Ray and Berndtson; President, Abbeyfield Society; Council Member, Ditchley Foundation; Governor, London School of Economics, London University of the Arts; UK Advisory Council; International Chamber of Commerce; Advisory Council, Cambridge University Judge School of Management Studies. Address: House of Lords, London SW1A 0PW, England.

BOULAUD Denis, b. 15 January 1947, Villeparisis, France. Research Director. m. Sophie Payet, 1 son, 1 daughter. Education: PhD, Geophysics, 1974, PhD, Physics (State Doctorate), University of Paris. Appointments: Assistant Professor, University of Paris, 1977-81; Assistant Head of Laboratory, 1981-84, Head of Laboratory, 1984-98, Research Director, 1996-, Head of Service, 1998-2003, Atomic Energy Commission, Scientific Director, 2003-2005, Deputy Director of the Environment Division, 2005-Institute for Radiological Protection and Nuclear Safety. Publications: Book: Aerosols: physics and measurement techniques; 8 book chapters; 55 papers in journals with reviewers; 185 communications in different conferences and congresses. Honour: Chevalier de l'ordre des Palmes Académiques, 2000; Award, International Aerosol Fellow, 2002. Memberships: President, French Association on Aerosol Research; General Secretary, European Aerosol Assembly, 1998-2000. Address: 20, allée de la ferme rose, F 91190 Gif/Yvette, France.

BOULIER Jean François, b. 14 March 1956, Caen, France. Executive. m. Marianne, 1 son, 2 daughters. Education: Ecole Polytechnique, 1977-80; ENGREF, 1980-82; Doctorate in Fluid Mechanics, Grenoble University, 1985. Appointments: Researcher, CNRS, 1985-87; Head of Quantative Analysis, Credit Commercial de France, 1987-89; Head of Research and Innovation, 89-99, Head of Market Risk Management, 1996-99, CCF; Chief Investment Officer, President, Sinopia Asset Management, 1999-2002; Professor of Finance, University Paris Dauphine, 2000-03; Head of Euro Fixed Income and Credits, Credit Aquicole Asset Management, 2004-; Associate Professor, Paris Dauphine University,

2000-06; Deputy Chief Investment Officer, Head of Fixed Income, Credit Lyonnais Asset Management, 2002-04; Head of Euro Fixed Income and Credit, Agricole Asset Management, 2004-. Publications: Numerous articles and reports in professional journals; Editor, Creator, Quants, quarterly journal of CCF; editor, Banque et Marchés, journal of the French Finance Association. Honour: Institute of Quantative Investment Research award, 1993; Banque & Marché Award, 2005; Listed in numerous publications. Memberships: Honorary Chairman, French Finance Association; Honorary Chairman, French Asset and Liability Managers' Association; Board Member, French Pension Fund Association; Chairman of the Asset Management Technical Committee of the French Fund Manager's Association, AFG; Secretary, Board of AMTE, the Euro Bond Market Association, 2004-. Address: 5 quai de l'Orme de Sully, 78230 Le Pecq, France. E-mail: jean-francois.boulier@ca-assetmanagement.fr

BOULTON James Thompson, b. 17 February 1924, Pickering, Yorkshire, England. Emeritus Professor of English Studies. m. Margaret Helen Leary, 6 August 1949, 1 son, 1 daughter. Education: BA, University College, University of Durham, 1948; BLitt, Lincoln College, University of Oxford, 1952; PhD, University of Nottingham, 1960. Appointments: Lecturer, Senior Lecturer, Reader in English Literature, 1951-63, Professor, 1964-75, Dean of Faculty of Arts, 1970-73, University of Nottingham; Professor of English Studies and Head of Department, 1975-88, Dean of Faculty of Arts, 1981-84, Public Orator, 1984-88, Director of Institute for Advanced Research in Arts and Social Sciences, 1987-99, Deputy Director, 1999-2006, Director Emeritus, 2006-, University of Birmingham. Publications: Edmund Burke: Sublime and Beautiful (editor), 1958, 3rd edition, 1987; The Language of Politics in the Age of Wilkes and Burke, 1963; Samuel Johnson: The Critical Heritage, 1971; Defoe: Memoirs of a Cavalier (editor), 1972; The Letters of D H Lawrence (editor), 8 volumes, 1979-00; Selected letters of D H Lawrence (editor), 1997; Volume I, The Early Writings: The Writings and Speeches of Edmund Burke (co-editor), 1997; D H Lawrence: Late Essays and Articles (editor), 2004; James Boswell: An Account of Corsica (co-editor), 2005; Further Letters of D H Lawrence, 2006. Honours: Fellow, Royal Society of Literature, 1968; Hon DLitt, Durham University, 1991, Nottingham University, 1993; Fellow, British Academy, 1994; Listed in Who's Who publications and biographical dictionaries. Address: Tyn y Ffynnon, Nant Peris, Caernarfon, LL55 4UH, Wales.

BOUND John Pascoe, b.13 November 1920, Redhill, Surrey, England. Paediatrician, Consultant (Retired). m. Gwendoline, deceased 1998, 2 daughters. Education: MB, BS, DCH, 1943, MD, 1950, University College, London and University College Hospital Medical School; MRCP (Lond), 1950; FRCP, 1971; FRCPCH, 1997. Appointments: House Physician, University College Hospital, 1943; Assistant Medical Officer, Alder Hey Children's Hospital, Liverpool, 1943-44; RAMC, 1944-47; Member, Sprue Research Team, Poona, India for 1 year; House Physician, North Middlesex Hospital, 1947; Paediatric Registrar and Senior Registrar, Hillingdon Hospital, Middlesex, 1948-53; Paediatric Registrar, 1953-54, First Assistant, Department of Paediatrics, 1954-56, University College Hospital, London; Consultant Paediatrician, Victoria Hospital, Blackpool, Lancashire, 1956-83. Publications: Articles on neonatal conditions and perinatal mortality; Articles on congenital malformations including: Incidence of congenital heart disease in the Fylde of Lancashire 1957-71; Seasonal prevalence of major congenital malformations, 1957-81; Neural tube defects, maternal cohorts and age: a pointer to aetiology; Down's Syndrome: prevalence and ionising radiation in an area of North West England, 1957-91; Involvement of deprivation and environmental lead in neural tube defects, 1957-81; Book, Borrowdale Beauty. Honours: International Medal of Honour, International Biographical Centre, Cambridge, 2003; American Medal of Honor, American Biographical Institute, Raleigh, North Carolina, USA, 2005; Order of International Ambassadors Medal, ABI, 2006; Legion of Honor Medal, United Cultural Convention, USA, 2006. Memberships: British Medical Association, 1943-; Expert Group on Special Care for Babies, Department of Health and Social Security, London, 1969-70; British Paediatric Association, 1960-97, Academic Board, 1972-75. Address: 48, St Annes Road East, Lytham St Annes, Lancs FY8 1UR, England.

BOUND Sally Anne, b. 7 September 1956, Hobart, Australia. Research Horticulturist. m. Chris White, 2 daughters. Education: BSc Botany and Zoology, University of Tasmania, 1979; Certificate in Horticulture, Hobart Technical College, 1981; Graduate Diploma of Science, University of Tasmania, 1993; PhD Agricultural Science, 2005. Appointments: Research Assistant, Botany Department, University of Tasmania, 1978-80; Part-time Teacher, Examiner and Moderator, Syllabus Writer, Education Department, Hobart Technical College, 1980-89; Technical Assistant, Research Clerk, Acting Senior Technical Officer, Technical Officer, Acting Manager, Senior Agricultural Research Officer, Department of Primary Industry and Fisheries, 1980-98; Senior Research Horticulturist, Acting Group Research Leader, Tasmanian Institute of Agricultural Research, 1998-. Publications: Numerous articles in refereed journals and popular press; Books and book chapters; Conference and Symposium papers and presentations. Honours: Nominated, Tasmanian Rural Woman of the Year, 1997; Listed in international biographical publications. Memberships: Australian Institute of Agricultural Science and Technology; International Society for Horticultural Science; American Society for Horticultural Science; Australia Pacific Extension Network; International Fruit Tree Association; Life Member, Scientific Faculty, IBC. Address: Tasmanian Institute of Agricultural Research, 13 St Johns Avenue, New Town, Tasmania 7008, Australia. E-mail: sally.bound@dpiw.tas.gov.au

BOURNE Malcolm Cornelius, b. 18 May 1926, Moonta, Australia. Professor of Food Science; Active Emeritus. m. Elizabeth Schumacher, 3 sons, 2 daughters. Education: BSc, Chemistry, University of Adelaide, 1950; MS, Food Science, 1961, PhD, Agricultural Chemistry, 1962, University of California, Davis, USA. Appointments: Chief Chemist, Brookers (Australia) Ltd, 1949-58; Research Assistant, University California, Davis, 1958-62; Professor, Food Science, 1962-95, Emeritus Professor, Food Science, 1995-, Cornell University. Publications: Many publications in refereed journals; 4 patents; Author, Food Texture and Viscosity, 1982, reprinted, 1994, second edition, 2002; Editor in Chief, Journal of Texture Studies, 1980-2006. Honours: Fellow, Institute of Food Science and Technology, UK, 1966; Fellow, Institute of Food Technologists, 1985 and International Award, 1992; Inaugural Fellow, 1998, Vice President, 2001-03, President, 2003-06, International Academy Food Science and Technology; Honorary Fellow, Australian Institute of Food Science and Technology, 1999; Fellow, Royal Australian Chemical Institute, 2003. Address: NYSAES, Cornell University, 630 West North Street, Geneva, NY 14456, USA.

BOUTROS-GHALI Boutros, b. 14 November 1922, Cairo, Egypt. Former Secretary General, United Nations. m. Maria Leia Nadler. Education: LLB, Cairo University, 1946; PhD, Paris University, 1949. Appointments: Professor, International Law and International Relations, Head, Department of Political Sciences, Cairo University, 1949-77; Founder, Editor, Al Ahram Iktisadi, 1960-75; Ministry of State, Foreign Affairs, Egypt, 1977-91; Member, UN Commission of International Law, 1979-92; Member, Secretariat, National Democratic Party, 1980-92; MP, 1987-92; Deputy PM, Foreign Affairs, 1991-92; Secretary-General, UN, 1992-96; Secretary-General, Organisations Internationales de la Francophonie. Publications: Contribution a l'étude des ententes régionales, 1949; Cours de diplomatie et de droit diplomatique et consulaire, 1951; Le problème du Canal de Suez (jtly), 1957; Egypt and the United Nations (jtly), 1957; Le principe d'égalité des états et les organisations internationales, 1961; Contribution a une théorie générale des Alliances, 1963; Foreign Policies in a World of Change, 1963; L'Organisation de l'unité africaine, 1969; Le mouvement Afro-Asiatique, 1969; Les difficultés institutionelles du panafricanisme, 1971; La ligue des états arabes, 1972; Les Conflits de frontières en Afrique, 1973; Numerous books in Arabic and contributions to periodicals. Address: 2 avenue Epnipgiza, Cairo, Egypt.

BOWER Neville, b. 3 October 1934, Allahabad, India. Composer. Widower. Education: Royal College of Music; ARCM, 1954; LRAM, 1956; BA, 1985; FTCL, 1987. Career: Pianist, Duo-Pianist, Ballet Rambert; Recitals in London, Oxford; Director of Music, Ealing Grammar School, 1967-74; Conductor Apollo Singers and semiprofessional orchestras; Music Examiner for London and East Anglian Council, 1987-94, University of London Examinations and Assessment Council, 1994-96, EDEXCEL Foundation, 1996-99. Compositions: 3 Choral Works; Our Lord and Our Lady; The Coming of Spring; Carillon, Carilla; Piano Sonata, Escapements, piano; Oboe Sonata; Concertante for oboe and orchestra; Evocation, clarinet; Glory, trumpet; Ecstasy, cello; The Dance of Life, viola; Eternal, organ; Fantasie Preludes for piano; Works for School Use; Processional March; Valse; Spring Dance; Song Cycles: The Dream Follower, The Path of Dreams, Songs of Innocence and Songs of Experience (words by Blake); Prelude and Threnody for strings; The Gardens of Villandry for full orchestra; Music for a While for piano Solo (3 series); Nightscape for soprano, baritone, clarinet, piano; Prism and Colour Studies, both for piano. Publications: Since 2002: Evocation; Dance of Life; The Dream Follower; Eternal; Prism; Music for a While; Songs of Innocence; Songs of Experience; Ghosts & Dreams; Greenscape; Night Music; The Bells of Rouen; Snowscape; Daydream; Songs for school choirs: Our Lord and Our Lady, The Coming of Spring, Carillon, Carilla; Essay on "Creativity" published on Nymet Music Internet Website, 2005 . Honours: Composition Prize, Waltham Forest Contemporary Music Society, 1966; Associate Member of Performing Right Society Ltd, 1994. Memberships: PRS; ISM; British Academy of Composers and Songwriters, 2006. Address: 1 Freeford Gardens, Lichfield, Staffs WS14 9RJ, England.

BOWLER John Vaughan, b. 22 March 1959. Education: King George V School, Hong Kong, 1971-75; Worksop College, Nottinghamshire, England, 1975-77; BSc (London) (1st Class Honours) in Basic Medical Sciences and Physiology, 1981, MB BS (London) (with Distinction) in Pathology, Medicine and Surgery, 1984, St Thomas' Hospital Medical School, University of London; MRCP (UK), 1987; MD (London), 1993; Certificate of Completion of Specialist Training, 1997; FRCP, 2001. Appointments: House Surgeon, St Helier

Hospital, Surrey, 1984-85; House Physician, Department of Medicine, 1985, Senior House Officer, Intensive Therapy, 1985-86, St Thomas' Hospital; Senior House Officer in Neurology, Hammersmith Hospital, 1986; Senior House Officer in Cardiology, National Heart Hospital, 1986-87; Registrar in General Medicine, Queen Mary's Hospital, Kent, 1987; Registrar in Neurology, Atkinson Morley's Hospital, 1987-88; Chest Heart and Stroke Association Research Fellow in Neurology, Charing Cross and Westminster Medical School, 1988-90; Registrar in Neurology, Charing Cross Hospital, 1991-92; Clinical Fellow in Neurology, University of Western Ontario, Canada, 1992-95; Lecturer (Honorary Senior Registrar) in Clinical Neurology, Charing Cross and Westminster Medical School, 1995-98; Consultant Neurologist and Honorary Senior Lecturer in Neurology, Royal Free Hospital, Royal Free and University College Medical School and the North Middlesex Hospital, 1998-. Publications: Numerous articles in professional scientific journals; Abstracts, posters and chapters in books. Honours: The Cochrane Prize, 1978; MRC Scholarship to read for the Intercalated BSc, 1980; The Third Beaney Prize, 1983; The Mead Medal and Perkins Prize, 1984. Memberships: Fellow, Royal College of Physicians; Member, Association of British Neurologists; Corresponding Associate Member, American Academy of Neurology; International Fellow, Stroke Council, American Stroke Association; Fellow, American Heart Association; Founder Member, The International Society for Vascular Behavioural and Cognitive Disorders. Address: Department of Neurology, Royal Free Hospital, Pond Street, London NW3 2QG, England. E-mail: john.bowler@ucl.ac.uk

BOYARSKY Victor, b. 16 September 1950, Rybinsk, USSR. Polar Explorer. m. Natalia, 1 son. Education: Radio Engineer, Electrotechnical University, 1973; PhD, Physics and Mathematics, 1983. Appointments: Scientist, Senior Scientist, Laboratory of Radiophysics, Arctic and Antarctic Research Institute, 1973-98; Director, Arctic and Antarctic Museum, 1998-. Publications: More than 25 scientific articles; 3 books: Seven Months of Infinity, 1992; Greenland's Meridian, 2001; Rhymes and Poems, 2002. Honours: Athlete of the Week, 1990; Honor Citizen, Lauzhou City; Several Russian medals. Memberships: Head, Polar Commission of Russian Geographical Society; Member, NGS, USA; Member, International Academy of Freeze. Address: 3 Mejozernoya ue, 194356StPetersburg,Russia.E-mail:boyarsky@norpolex.com Website: www.northpolextreme.com

BOYCOTT Geoffrey, b. 21 October 1940. Cricket Commentator. m. Rachael Swinglehurst, 2003, 1 daughter. Education: Hemsworth Grammar School. Appointments: Played Cricket for Yorkshire, 1962-86; County Captain, 1963; Played for England, 1964-74, 1977-82; Captain of Yorkshire, 1970-78; Cricket Commentator, BBC TV, TWI, Channel 9, SABC, Talk Radio; Channel 4 TV; ESPN/STAR TV; BBC Radio. Publications: Geoff Boycott's Book for Young Cricketers, 1976; Put to the Test: England in Australia 1978-79, 1979; Geoff Boycott's Cricket Quiz, 1979; On Batting, 1980; Opening Up, 1980; In the Fast Lane, 1981; Master Class, 1982; Boycott, The Autobiography, 1987; Boycott on Cricket, 1990; Geoffrey Boycott on Cricket, 1999; Geoff Boycott on Batting; Geoff Boycott Master Class; Articles in the Daily Telegraph. Honour: OBE. Membership: Honorary Life Member, Yorkshire County Cricket Club, 1984-93; Honorary Life Member, MCC. Address: c/o Yorkshire County Cricket Club, Headingley Cricket Ground, Leeds, Yorks LS6 3BY, England.

BOYD Della D, b. 21 January 1965, Warner Robbins, Georgia, USA. Principal Management Analyst. 1 son, 1 daughter. Education: Bachelor's degree, Management and Industrial Relations/Personnel (dual majors), 1988, Master's degree, Public Administration, 1996, University of Nevada, Las Vegas. Appointments: Clark County; McCarran International Airport Department of Aviation, 4 years; Office of the County Manager's Equal Opportunity/Office of Diversity Division, 9 years; Department of Real Property Management, 6 months; Department of Parks & Recreation, 4 years; Principal Management Analyst; Freelance Photographer. Publications: Americans with Disabilities Act Defined, 1995; The Challenge of Compliance, 1996; Equal Opportunity, 1999, 2000; Two photographs: Alaska's Outdoors Relaxing; Miss Dre in the Big Hat. Honours: Award for Service as President, American Society of Public Administration, Las Vegas Chapter, 2000-01; NOBCO Chairman's Award for Outstanding County Official of the National Organization of Black County Official, 2002; Outstanding Achievement in Amateur Photography Award, International Society of Photographers, 2006; Woman of the Year Award, 2006; Manchester Who's Who Award, 2006; Great Minds of the 21st Century Award, ABI, 2005-2006; Eminent Fellow, FABI, 2006; UCC's International Peace Prize, 2006. Memberships: Leadership Council, Wall of Tolerance Honoree, Southern Poverty Law Center; Alpha Kappa Psi, Business Fraternity; National Forum for Black Public Administrators, Las Vegas Chapter; Outstanding Female Executive Award, ABI, 2006; Professional Women's Advisory Board, ABI, 2006; Board of Governors Member, Deputy Governor, ABIRA, 2006; Vice President of the Recognition Board of the World Congress of Arts, Sciences and Communication; LFIBA, 2006; Director General's Roll of Honour; MOIF; The Order of International Fellowship, IBC, 2007; Medal of Honour, IBC; American Hall of Fame, 2007; Founding Member, American Order of Excellence, 2007; Director General's Roll of Honour, IBC; Di Vinci Diamond Life Achievement Award, 2007; IBC Hall of Fame, 2007; Honorary Director General, IBC, 2007; 2000 Outstanding Intellectuals of the 21st Century, 2007; The Cambridge Blue Book, 2007; Great Lives of the 21st Century, 1st edition, 2007; 500 Greatest Geniuses of the 21st Century, 2007; Pinnacle of Achievement Award, 2007; Top Two Hundred of the IBC, 2007; Dictionary of International Biography, 34th Edition; Decree of Excellence in Administration, USA, 2007; World Lifetime Achievement Award, 2007. Address: 6555 Lucky Boy Dr, Las Vegas, NV 89110, USA. E-mail: boydbstop@yahoo.com

BOYD Graham, b. 26 April 1928, Bristol, England. Artist. m. Pauline Lilian, 1 son, 1 daughter. Education: NDD, Watford School of Art, 1951; ATD, Institute of Education, London. Appointments: Army Service, 1946-48; Resident in Southern Rhodesia (Zimbabwe), 1953-55; Exchange Associate Professor, Plymouth State College, University of New Hampshire, USA, 1972-73; Visiting Artist, Reading University, 1975-83; Principal Lecturer in Fine Art, Head of Painting, Course Leader P/T BA/BA Honours Fine Art Degree Course, Herts College of Art & Design, St Albans/University of Hertfordshire, 1976-93; Participant in 2nd Triangle Workshop, New York, USA, 1983; Visiting Artist, Exeter College of Art and Design, 1983; Artists in Essex Exhibitions Selector, 1985; Guest Artist, Triangle Workshop, Barcelona, 1987; Anglo-Dutch Artists Workshop, Rounton, North Yorkshire, 1992; Guest Artist, International Multi-Media Symposium, Faial, Azores, 1995; Intuition and Reason Lecture to Tate Gallery Guides and Hertfordshire Visual Artists Forum, 2003; Exhibitions: Solo exhibitions, 1962 onwards include most recently: Colour Transactions, deli Art, Charterhouse Street, London, 1999; Graham Boyd – Disruptive Tendencies, University of Hertfordshire, 2001; The Energy of Colour, 2 person exhibition with Sheila Girling, Pilgrim Gallery, London, 2003; Striking Lights, Recent Painting, deli Art, 2004; The Long Haul, Bushey Museum and Art Gallery, 2004; The Alchemy of Colour, The Pavilion Gallery, Chenies Manor, Rickmansworth, 2004; Dancing with Colour, The Salt Gallery, Hayle, Cornwall, 2004; Group Exhibitions, 1950 onwards include most recently: Driven to Abstraction, Bell Gallery, Winchester, 2000; deli Art in Bristol, The Crypt Gallery, Summer Exhibition, Lemon Street Gallery, Truro, 2002; Confluence, The Pilgrim Gallery, London, 2004; Summer Exhibition, The Salt Gallery, Hayle, 2004 and 2006; Works in public and private collections. Publications: Works featured in numerous newspaper and journal articles and exhibition catalogues. Address: Blackapple, 54 Scatterdells Lane, Chipperfield, Herts WD4 9EX, England.

BOYD Robert David Hugh (Sir), b. 14 May 1938, Cambridge, England. Physician. m. Meriel Cornelia Boyd, 1 son, 2 daughters. Education: Cambridge University; University College Hospital Medical School. Appointments: MRC Fellow, University of Colorado, USA, 1971-72; Senior Lecturer, University College Hospital Medical School, 1973-80; Professor of Child Health, 1981-96, Dean of the Medical Faculty, 1989-93, University of Manchester; Chair Manchester Health Authority, 1994-96; Principal, St George's Hospital Medical School, 1996-2003; Pro-Vice Chancellor, Medicine, University of London, 2001-2003; Chair, Council of Heads of UK Medical Schools, 2001-2003; Chair, Lloyds TSB Foundation for England and Wales, 2003–; Chair, Council for Assisting Refugee Academics, 2004-. Publications: Paediatric Problems in General Practice (Joint), 3rd edition, 1996; Scientific articles on placenta, foetus, childhood illness, medical education. Honours: KB; Honorary DSc, Kingston University; Hon DSc, Keele University; Hon FRCPCH; Honorary Member, American Pediatric Society; Fellow, St George's University of London. Memberships: F Med Sci; FRCP (London); FFPH. Address: The Stone House, Adlington, Macclesfield, Cheshire, SK10 4NU, England.

BOYDE Andreas, b. 13 November 1967, Oschatz, Germany. Pianist. Education: Spezialschule and Musikhochschule, Dresden; Guildhall School of Music and Drama, London; Masterclasses, Musikfestwochen Luzern. Debut: With Berlin Symphony Orchestra, 1989. Career: Concerts with Dresden Philharmonic Orchestra, 1992, 1996; Recital, Munich Philharmonic Hall, Gasteig, 1992; Festival La Roque d'Antheron, France, 1993; Concert, Zurich Tonhalle with Zurich Chamber Orchestra, 1994; Concerts with Freiburg Philharmonic Orchestra, 1994, 1997, 1999; Dresden State Orchestra, 1994, 1995; Recitalist in Schumann Cycle Dusseldorf, 1995; South American debut, recital in Teatro Municipal Santiago, Chile, 1996; Concert, Munich Herkulessaal with Munich Symphony, Concert tour with Northwest German Philharmonic Orchestra, Recital, Munich Prinzregenten Theatre, Concert tour with Odessa Philharmonic Orchestra, including Cologne Philharmonic Hall and Stuttgart Liederhalle, 1997; Recital, Dresdner Musikfestspiele, Gave European premiere of Piano Concerto, Four Parables by Schoenfield with Dresdner Sinfoniker, 1998; Concerts with Halle Philharmonic, 1999, 2004; Schumann recital tour including own reconstruction of Schubert Variations in New York, Germany, London Wigmore Hall, World premiere of Piano Concerto by John Pickard with Dresdner Sinfoniker, Concerts, Konzertsaal KKL Lucerne with Lucerne Symphony Orchestra, 2000; Concerts with Bamberger Symphoniker, 2000, 2001; Concert tour with National Symphony Orchestra

of Ukraine in the United Kingdom, Concert with Bournemouth Symphony Orchestra, Recital tour in the United Kingdom, Concerts with Israel Northern Symphony Orchestra, Beethoven Fest Bonn, Concert tour with Bolshoi Symphony Orchestra in the United Kingdom, Recital, London Wigmore Hall, 2001; Concerts with Bucharest Philharmonic Orchestra, Concerts with Slovak Philharmonic Orchestra, Concerts, London Royal Festival Hall with London Philharmonic Orchestra, 2002; Concert, Manchester Bridgewater Hall with Hallé Orchestra, 2002, 2003, 2005; Concert tour with NYOS, including Birmingham Symphony Hall and Concertgebouw Amsterdam, 2002; Concert, Prague Autumn Festival with Prague Radio Orchestra in Prague Rudolfinum, Beethoven recital, Teatro Municipal Santiago, Chile, Concerts with Malaysian Philharmonic Orchestra, 2003; Concerts with London Mozart Players, Concert, Munich Prinzregenten Theatre, 2004; Concert, Cologne Philharmonic Hall with Weimar Staatskapelle, Masterclass, Concordia College, Minnesota, 2005; Concerts with Stuttgart Philharmonic Orchestra, Recitals, Schumann Fest Düsseldorf, Concerts with El Paso Symphony Orchestra, USA, Recital, Saint Louis, USA, Concert with Munich Symphony, 2006. Publications: Schumann, Variationen über ein Thema von Schubert, reconstructed score by Andreas Boyde, 2000. Recordings: CD releases including works by Schumann, Tchaikovsky, Mussorgsky, Ravel, Dvorak, Schoenfeld, Brahms, Skryabin and Rachmaninoff; Frequent broadcasts with most German Radio Stations and the BBC. Address: c/o Michael Kocyan Artists Management, Alt-Moabit 104a, 10559 Berlin, Germany.

BOYLE Danny, b. 20 October 1956, Radcliffe, Lancashire, England. Film Director. Appointments: Artistic Director, Royal Court Theatre, 1982-87; Producer, Elephant, TV film, 1989; Director, The Greater Good, TV series, 1991; Mr Wroe's Virgins, TV, Not Even God is Wise Enough, TV, 1993; Executive Producer, Twin Town, 1996. Creative Works: Films: Shallow Grave, 1994; Trainspotting, A Life Less Ordinary, 1996; The Beach, 1999; Vacuuming Completely Nude in Paradise, Strumpet, 2001; Alien Love Triangle, 28 Days Later, 2002; Millions, 2004; Sunshine, 28 Weeks Later (Producer), 2007. Honour: Golden Ephebe Award, 1997. Address: c/o ICM, 6th Floor, 76 Oxford Street, London W1N 0AX, England.

BRADFORD Barbara Taylor, b. Leeds, Yorkshire, England. Journalist; Novelist. m. Robert Bradford, 1963. Appointments: Editor, Columnist, UK and US periodicals. Publications: Complete Encyclopedia of Homemaking Ideas, 1968; How to Be the Perfect Wife, 1969; Easy Steps to Successful Decorating, 1971; Making Space Grow, 1979; A Woman of Substance, 1979; Voice of the Heart, 1983; Hold the Dream, 1985; Act of Will, 1986; To Be the Best, 1988; The Women in His Life, 1990; Remember, 1991; Angel, 1993; Everything to Gain, 1994; Dangerous to Know, 1995; Love in Another Town, 1995; Her Own Rules, 1996; A Secret Affair, 1996; Power of a Woman, 1997; A Sudden Change of Heart, 1998; Where You Belong, 2000; The Triumph of Katie Byrne, 2001; Three Weeks in Paris, 2002; Emma's Secret, 2003; Unexpected Blessings, 2004-05; Just Rewards, 2006; The Deravenel Triology – The Ravenscar Dynasty, 2006, Heirs of Ravenscar, 2007. Address: c/o Bradford Enterprises, 450 Park Avenue, Suite 1903, New York, NY 10022, USA.

BRADFORD Sarah Mary Malet, b. 3 September 1938, Bournemouth, England. Author; Journalist; Critic. m. (1) Anthony John Bradford, 31 April 1959, 1 son, 1 daughter (2) Viscount Bangor, 1 October 1976. Education: Lady Margaret

Hall, Oxford, England, 1956-59. Appointment: Manuscript Expert, Christie's, 1975-78. Publications: The Story of Port, 1978, 1983; Portugal and Madeira, 1969; Portugal, 1973; Cesare Borgia, 1976; Disraeli, 1982; Princess Grace, 1984; King George VI, 1989; Elizabeth: A Biography of Her Majesty The Queen, 1996; America's Queen, The Life of Jacqueline Kennedy Onassis, 2000; Lucrezia Borgia, Life, Love and Death in Renaissance Italy, 2004; Diana, 2006. Contributions to: Reviews in Daily Telegraph, Sunday Telegraph, The Times, Sunday Times, Times Literary Supplement, Literary Review; Mail on Sunday; Daily Mail; Spectator; Evening Standard. Address: c/o Aitken Alexander Associates, 18-21 Cavave Place, London SW10 9PT, England

BRADLEY Marjorie, b. 22 May 1916, Portsmouth, Hampshire, England. Retired Civil Servant; Poet. m. Reuben Stephen Bradley, 22 June 1938, 3 sons. Education: Municipal College, Portsmouth. Appointments: Junior Clerk, 1933-37; Tax Officer, 1937-38; Secretary, West Riding County Council, 1951-58; Clerical Officer, Department of Health and Social Security, 1958-73. Publication: Coffee Spoons. Contributions to: Envoi; Writer; London Calling; Purple Patch; Civil Service Author; Focus; Weyfarers; Success Magazine. Honours: Civil Service Authors, Herbert Spencer Competition; Open Poetry Competition; Envoi Magazine Open Competition; Salopian Poetry Competition; Success and Springboard Magazine Competitions. Memberships: Society of Civil Service Authors; Patchway Writers Group. Address: 88 Oak Close, Little Stoke, Bristol BS12 6RD, England.

BRADLEY Michael Carl, b. 17 February 1951, Birmingham, England. Trade Union Officer. m. Janice. Education: National Diploma, Business Studies, Brooklyn Technical College, Birmingham, 1968-70. Appointments: Executive Officer, Inland Revenue, 1971-74; Senior Payroll Administrator, Smedley H P Foods, 1974-80; Research Officer, Transport and General Workers Union, 1980-82; Staff Section Organiser, 1982-87, General Secretary, 1988-92, National Union of Lock and Metal Workers; General Secretary, General Federation of Trade Unions Educational Trust, 1993-. Honours: MBE. Address: Central House, Upper Woburn Place, London WC1H 0HY, England. E-mail: mike@gftu.org.uk

BRAGG Melvyn, b. 6 October 1939, Wigton, Cumbria, England. Author; Broadcaster. m. Cate Haste, 1 son, 2 daughters. Education: 2nd Class Honours, Modern History, Wadham College, Oxford, 1961. Appointments: General Trainee, BBC, 1961; Producer on Monitor, 1963; Director, films including portrait of Sir John Barbirolli, 1963; Writer, Debussy film for Ken Russell, 1963; Editor, for BBC2, New Release (Arts Magazine) which became Review, then Arena, 1964; Documentary, Writers World, 1964; Take It or Leave It (Literary Panel Game), 1964; Presenter, for Tyne Tees TV, In the Picture (local arts programme), 1971; Presenter/Producer, for BBC, Second House, 1974-8; Editor/Presenter, BBC, Read All About It, 1974-78; Interviewer for BBC, Tonight, 1974-78; Editor, Presenter, The South Bank Show, 1978; Head of Arts LWT, 1982-90; Programmes for Channel Four, 1982-90; Controller of Arts, LWT, 1990; Director, LWT Productions, 1992; Deputy Chairman, 1985-90, Chairman, 1990-95, Border TV, 1990-95; Governor LSE, 1997; Presenter, In Our Time, BBC Radio 4, 1998-. Publications: Books include: For Want of a Nail, 1965; The Second Inheritance, 1966; Without a City Wall, 1968; The Nerve, 1971; Josh Lawton, 1972; The Silken Net, 1974; Autumn Manoeuvres, 1978; The Cumbrian Trilogy, The Christmas Child, Love and Glory, 1984; A Time to Dance (BBC TV adaption 1992), 1991; Crystal Rooms, 1992; CREDO, 1996; The Sword and The Miracle (USA

publication), 1997; The Soldier's Return, 1999; A Son of War, 2001; The Adventure of English (executive producer/ presenter of television series), 2001; Crossing The Lines, 2003; Screenplays: Isadora; The Music Lovers; Jesus Christ Superstar; A Time to Dance, 1992; Musicals: Mardi Gras, 1976; The Hired Man, 1985; Play: King Lear In New York, 1992; Journalist in various newspapers. Honours include: Numerous for the South Bank Show, including 3 Prix Italias; Ivor Novello Award for Best Musical, 1985; Richard Dimbleby Award for Outstanding Contribution to TV, 1987; 2 TRIC Awards, 1990, 1994; VLV Award, 2000; WHSmith Literary Award, 2000; Numerous honorary degrees. Memberships: President, MIND; President, The National Campaign for the Arts (NCA). Address: 12 Hampstead Hill Gardens, London, NW3 2PL, England.

BRAIDOTTI Rosi, b. 28 September 1954 (dual citizenship Italian and Australian). Distinguished Professor in the Humanities. Education: Bachelor of Arts, 1st Class Honours, English Literature, 1976, Philosophy, 1977, The Australian National University, Canberra; Cum Laude Doctorate in Philosophy, University of Paris I (Panthéon-Sorbonne), 1981. Appointments: Professor and Foundation Chair, Department of Women's Studies, Arts Faculty, University of Utrecht, The Netherlands, 1988-2005; Director, Netherlands Research School of Women's Studies, 1995-2004; Distinguished Professor in The Humanities in the Globalised World, Arts Faculty, Utrecht University, 2005. Publications: Books: Patterns of Dissonance: an Essay on Women in Contemporary French Philosophy, 1991. 2nd edition, 1996; Women, the Environment and Sustainable Development Towards a Theoretical Synthesis (co-author), 1994; Nomadic Subjects: Embodiment and Sexual Difference in Contemporary Feminist Theory, 1994; Metamorphoses: Towards a Materialist Theory of Becoming, 2002; Baby Boomers: Vite parallele dagli anni Cinquanta ai cinquant'anni, 2003; Op doorreis: nomadisch denken in de 21ste eeuw, 2004; Feminismo, diferencia sexual y subjetividad nomade, 2004; Transpositions: on Nomadic Ethics, 2006; 4 edited books; Numerous book chapters and articles in journals. Translated in 17 languages. Honours: Knight in the Order of the Nederlandse Leeuw, awarded by HRM The Queen of the Netherlands, 2005; Recepient Golden Medal, Lodz University, Poland, 2006; Leverhulme Trust visiting Professorship, 2004-2006 at Birkbeck College, London University. Several visiting professorships and grants; Listed in Who's Who publications and biographical dictionaries. Memberships: International Association of University Women; Supporter of: Amnesty International, Greenpeace, Medecins sans Frontieres, Aids Fund, Foster Parents. Address: Muntstraat 2a, 3512 EV Utrecht, the Netherlands. Website: www.let.uu.nl/~rosi.braidotti/personal/

BRAMALL, Field Marshal Baron, Edwin Noel Westby, b. 18 December 1923, Tunbridge Wells, Kent. Army Officer; Lord Lieutenant of Greater London. m. Avril, The Lady Bramall, 1 son, 1 daughter. Education: Eton College, 1937-42; Student, Army Staff College, Camberley, 1952; Imperial Defence College, 1970. Appointments: Joined Army 1942; Commissioned into KRRC, 1943; Served in NW Europe, 1944-45; Occupation of Japan, 1946, War Office, 1947-48; Instructor, School of Infantry, 1949-51; PSC, 1952; Middle East, 1953-58; Instructor Staff College, 1958-61; Staff of Lord Mountbatten, Ministry of Defence, 1963-64; CO 2 Green Jackets, Malaysia, 1965-66; Command, 5 Airportable Brigade, 1967-69, IDC 1970; GOC, 1 Division BAOR, 1971-73; Lieutenant General, 1973; Commander, British Forces Hong Kong, 1973-76; General, 1976; Colonel Commandant 3 Battalion Royal Green Jackets, 1973-84; Colonel, 2 Gurkhas,

1976-86; Commander-in-Chief, UK Land Forces, 1976-78; Vice-Chief of Defence Staff, Personnel and Logistics, 1978-79; Chief of General Staff, 1979-82; ADC General to H M The Queen, 1979-82; Field Marshal, 1982; Chief of the Defence Staff, 1982-85. Publication: The Chiefs: The Story of the UK Chiefs of Staff (co-author). Honours: Lord Lieutenant of Greater London, 1986-98; KG; GCB; OBE; MC; JP. Memberships include: President, Gurkha Brigade Association, 1987-; President, Greater London Playing Fields Association, 1990-; President, MCC, 1988-89; Izingari Cricket Club; Free Foresters Cricket Club; Travellers; Army and Navy; Pratts. Address: House of Lords, Westminster, London SW1A 0PW, England.

BRAMWELL Fitzgerald, b. 16 May 1945, Brooklyn, New York, USA. Chemist. m. Charlott, 2 sons, 2 daughters. Education: BA, Chemistry, Columbia University, 1966; MS, 1967, PhD, 1970, Chemistry, University of Michigan. Appointments include: Dean, Graduate Studies and Research, Brooklyn College, CUNY, 1990-95; Executive Director, University of Kentucky Research Foundation, 1995-2001; Vice President for Research and Graduate Studies, University of Kentucky, 1995-2001; Manager Member, Empire Science Resources, LLC Lexington, KY, 2005-; Professor, Chemistry, University of Kentucky, 1995-. Publications include: Instructor's Guide for Investigations in General Chemistry Quantitative Techniques and Basic Principles, 1978; Instructor's Guide for Basic Laboratory Principles in General Chemistry with Quantitative Techniques, 1990. Honours include: Distinguished Service Award, Brooklyn College Graduate Students Organization, 1994, 1995; Brooklyn Subsection of American Chemical Society, 1995; Department of Chemistry Alumni Excellence Award, University of Michigan, 1996; Lyman T Johnson Alumni Association Award, University of Kentucky, 1996; CCNY LSAMP Founders Award, 2000; Kentucky Geological Survey Outstanding Leadership Award, 2000; Claude Fuess Award, Phillips Academy, Andover, 2000; Omicron Delta Kappa, Nu Chapter, 2001. Memberships include: Kentucky Academy of Sciences, 1996-; American Association for the Advancement of Science, 1996-; American Institute of Chemists and Chemical Engineers, 1996-; Sigma Xi, 1971-; American Physical Society, 1967-95; American Chemical Society, 1966-. Address: Chemistry Department, University of Kentucky, Lexington, KY 40506-0055, USA.

BRANAGH Kenneth, b. 10 December 1960, Belfast, Northern Ireland. Actor; Director. m. (1) Emma Thompson, divorced, (2) Lindsay Brunnock, 2003. Education: Royal Academy of Dramatic Art. Appointments: Numerous Theatre and Radio Work. Creative Works: Films: High Season; A Month in the Country; Henry V, 1989; Dead Again, 1991; Peter's Friends, Swing Kids, Swan Song, 1992; Much Ado About Nothing, 1993; Mary Shelley's Frankenstein; Othello, In the Bleak Midwinter, 1995; Hamlet, 1996; The Theory of Flight, The Proposition, The Gingerbread Man, 1997; Celebrity, Wild, Wild West, 1998; Love's Labour's Lost, 2000; How to Kill Your Neighbor's Dog, Rabbit Proof Fence, Harry Potter and the Chamber of Secrets, Alien Love Triangle, Shackleton, 2002; Five Children and It, 2004; Warm Springs, 2005; The Magic Flute (directed), As You Like It (directed), 2006; Sleuth (directed), 2007. Publications: Public Enemy (play), 1988; Beginning (memoirs), 1989; The Making of Mary Shelley's Frankenstein, 1994; In the Bleak Midwinter, 1995; Screenplays for Henry V, Much Ado About Nothing, Hamlet. Honours: Evening Standard Best Film Award; New York Film Critics Circle Best Director Award; Hon DLitt, Queens University, Belfast, 1990; BAFTA Award,

Best Director, 1990; Nominated, London Evening Standard Theatre Award for Best Actor, 2003; Nominated, Laurence Olivier Theatre Award for Best Actor, 2004. Memberships: RADA Council. Address: Shepperton Studios, Studio Road, Shepperton, Middlesex TW17 0QD, England.

BRANDON Peter Samuel, b. 4 June 1943, Writtle, Essex, England. Chartered Surveyor. m. Mary A E Canham, 1 son, 2 daughters. Education: MSc, Architecture, University of Bristol, 1978; DSc, Information Systems, University of Salford, 1996; DEng, Heriot-Watt University, 2006. Appointments: Surveyor, Surveying Practice, 1963-67; Surveyor, Local Government, 1968-70; Lecturer, 1969-73, Head of Surveying Department, 1981-85, Portsmouth Polytechnic; Principal Lecturer, Bristol Polytechnic, 1973-81; Head of Surveying Department, University of Salford 1985-93, Pro Vice Chancellor, 1993-2001, Director, Strategic Programmes and Public Orator, 2001-2003, University of Salford; Director of Strategic Programmes, School of the Built Environment, University of Salford, 2003-; Director, Salford University Think Lab & Centre for Virtual Environments, 2005-; Freelance Adviser on Research and Educational Matters, 2003-. Publications: Numerous articles including: Microcomputers in Building Appraisal (with G Moore), 1983; Computer Programs for Building Cost Appraisal (with G Moore and P Main), 1985; An Integrated Database for Quantity (with J Kirkham), 1989; Editor: Building, Cost Modelling and Computers, 1987; Quantity Surveying Techniques: New Direction, 1990; Investment, Procurement & Performance in Construction, 1991; Integrated Construction Information, 1995; Evaluation of the Built Environment for Sustainability, 1997; Cities & Sustainability: Sustaining Cultural Heritage, 2000; Evaluating Sustainable Development in the Built Environment (co-author Patrizia Lombardi), 2005; Over 150 publications in more than 30 countries worldwide. Honour: Honorary Member, South African Association of Quantity Surveyors for services to Quantity Surveying worldwide, 1994. Membership: Fellow, Royal Institute of Chartered Surveyors. Address: 3 Woodland Drive, Lymm, Cheshire, WA13 0BL, England. E-mail: p.s.brandon@salford.ac.uk

BRANDSTRUP Birgitte, b. 4 April 1965, Virum, Denmark. Surgeon; Researcher. m. Peter Starup, 1 son, 1 daughter. Education: Medical Doctor Certificate, 1992, PhD (Medicine), 2003, University of Copenhagen. Appointments: Junior Resident: Grindsted Hospital, 1992-94; Surgical Resident, Hvidovre University Hospital, 1994-95; Rigshospitalet, 1996; Glostrup University Hospital, 1996-98; Research Fellowship, Bispebjerg University Hospital, 1999-2002; Senior Resident: Glostrup University Hospital, 2002-04; Slagelse University Hospital, 2005-06; Bispebjerg University Hospital, 2006-. Publications: Thesis, Restricted Intravenous Fluid Therapy in Colorectal Surgery, 2003; Book, Rationel Fluid and Electrolyte Therapy and Nutrition, in Danish, 2004; Book chapters in Perioperative Fluid Therapy; Articles in Perioperative Fluid Management. Honours: 1st Prize, Best Research & Presentation, Danish Gastro-Enterological Society, 2001, 2002 and Danish Surgical Society, 2003. Memberships: The Danish Surgical Society; The Danish Gastro-Enterological Society; The European Society of Anaesthesiologists. Address: Farumgaards Alle 14, DK-3520 Farum, Denmark. E-mail: bbrandstrup@hotmail.com

BRANFIELD John Charles, b. 19 January 1931, Burrow Bridge, Somerset, England. Writer; Teacher. m. Kathleen Elizabeth Peplow, 2 sons, 2 daughters. Education: MA, Queens' College, Cambridge University; MEd, University of Exeter. Publications: Nancekuke,1972; Sugar Mouse,

1973; The Scillies Trip, 1975; Castle Minalto, 1979; The Fox in Winter, 1980; Brown Cow, 1983; Thin Ice, 1983; The Falklands Summer, 1987; The Day I Shot My Dad, 1989; Lanhydrock Days, 1991; A Breath of Fresh Air, 2001; Ella and Charles Naper: Life and Art at Lamorna, 2003; Charles Simpson: Painter of Animals and Birds, Coastline and Moorland, 2005; Tony Giles: Painter of Cornwall's Man-Made Landscape, 2005; Mingoose and Chapel Porth: The Story of a Cornish Valley, 2006. Address: Mingoose Villa, Mingoose, Mount Hawke, Truro, Cornwall TR4 8BX, England.

BRANSON Richard Charles Nicholas, b. 18 July 1950, Shamley Green, Surrey, England. Founder; Chairman; President. m. (1) Kristen Tomassi, 1972, divorced 1979, (2) Joan Templeman, 1989, 1 son, 1 daughter. Education: Stowe. Appointments: Editor, Student Magazine, 1968-69; Founder, Student Advisory Centre (now Help), 1970; Founder, Virgin Mail-Order Company, 1969, First Virgin record shop, 1971; Recording Company, 1973; Nightclub (The Venue), 1976; Virgin Atlantic Airways, 1984; Founder and Chairman, Virgin Retail Group, Virgin Communications, Virgin Travel Group, Voyager Group; Group also includes publishing, broadcasting, contraction, heating systems, holidays; Chairman, 1986-88, President, 1988-, UK 2000; Director, Intourist Moscow Ltd, 1988-90; Founder, The Healthcare Foundation, 1987; Founder, Virgin Radio, 1993; Founder, Virgin Rail Group Ltd, 1996; Launched Virgin Cola drink, 1994, Babylon Restaurant, 2001; Crossed Pacific in hot air balloon with Per Lindstrand, 1991; World Record for fastest crossing of the Channel in an Amphibious Vehicle, 2004. Honours: Blue Riband Title for Fastest Atlantic Crossing, 1986; Seagrave Trophy, 1987. Publication: Losing My Virginity, autobiography, 1998. Address: c/o Virgin Group PLC, 120 Campden Hill Road, London W8 7AR, England.

BRASSEAUX Carl Anthony, b. 19 August 1951, Opelousas, Louisiana, USA. Historian. m. Glenda, 21 July 1973, 2 sons, 1 daughter. Education: BA, Political Science, cum laude, University of Southwestern Louisiana, 1974; MA, History, 1975; Doctorat de 3e cycle, University of Paris, 1982. Appointments: Assistant Director, Center for Louisiana Studies, 1975-2000; Professor, History and Geography Department, University of Louisiana, Lafayette, 1998-; Director, Center for Louisiana Studies, 2003-; Director, Center for Cultural and Eco-Tourism, University of Louisiana at Lafayette, 2001-; Director, Center for Louisiana Studies, 2004-. Publications: 102 scholarly publications in journals in North America and Europe; 33 book length works. Honours: Kemper Williams Prize, 1979; Robert L Brown Prize, 1980; President's Memorial Award, Louisiana Historical Association, 1986; Book Prize, French Colonial Historical Society, 1987; Chevalier, L'Ordre des Palmes Academiques, 1994; University Distinguished Professor, History, 1995; National Daughters of the American Revolution Award, 1995; Fellow, Louisiana Historical Association, 2000-; Louisiana Writer of the Year, 2003; Louisiana Humanist of the Year, 2005-. Membership: Louisiana Historical Association. Address: 201 Parliament Drive, Lafayette, LA 70506, USA.

BRAZHNIKOV Andrey V, b. 28 October 1959, Kostroma, Russia. Scientist; Educator. m. Elena S Karpenko, 1 daughter. Education: BS, Electrical Engineering, major in Automatics and Telemechanics, Honours Degree, cum laude, 1982; PhD, Electromechanics 1985. Appointments: Chief of Laboratory, Research Institute, Krasnoyarsk, 1987-88; Deputy Director, Educational Institute, Director of Educational Centre, 1997-2002; Chief of several scientific projects among them 2 international projects, 1991-. Publications: More than 60 scientific works include: Additional Resources of Control of Multiphase Inverter Drives, 1993; Prospects for the Use of Multiphase Electric Drives in the Field of Mining Machines, 1995; Improvement of Technical and Economic Characteristics of Drilling Rigs Owing to the Use of Multiphase Electric Drives, 1996; Hydrodynamic Modelling of Force Fields, 1997. Honours: Annual Prizes for Scientific Work, Russian Research and Higher Educational Institutes, 1980-; Prizes for organising scientific work, Academy of Non-Ferrous Metals and Gold, Krasnoyarsk, Russia, 1997-; Listed in Who's Who publications and biographical dictionaries. Memberships: Institute of Electrical and Electronics Engineers; Research Board of Advisors, American Biographical Institute. Address: State University of Non-Ferrous Metals and Gold, 95 Krasnoyarsky Rabochy Avenue, 660025 Krasnoyarsk, Russia. E-mail: dnn@color.krasline.ru

BREAM Julian, b. 15 July 1933, London, England. Classical Guitarist and Lutenist. m. (1) Margaret Williamson, 1 adopted son, (2) Isobel Sanchez, 1980, divorced. Education: Royal College of Music. Career: Cheltenham, 1947; London debut, Wigmore Hall, 1950; Many transcriptions for guitar of Romantic and Baroque works; Commissioned new works from Britten, Walton, Henze and Arnold; Tours throughout the world; Recitals as soloist and with the Julian Bream Consort (formed 1960); Many recitals with Sir Peter Pears and Robert Tear; Guitar duo with John Williams; 60th Birthday Concert, Wigmore Hall, London, 1993. Honours: Fellow, Royal Northern College of Music, 1983; Honorary DUniv (Surrey), 1968; Honorary DMus (Leeds), 1984; Villa-Lobos Gold Medal, 1976; Numerous recording awards. Address: Hazard Chase, Norman House, Cambridge Place, Cambridge, CB2 1NS, England. Website: www.hazardchase.co.uk

BREEZE David John, b. 25 July 1944, Blackpool, England. Civil Servant. m. Pamela Diane Silvester, 2 sons. Education: BA, Honours, Modern History, 1965, PhD, 1970, University College, University of Durham. Appointments: Inspector of Ancient Monuments, 1969-89; Chief Inspector of Ancient Monuments, Scotland, 1989-2005. Publications: Books: The Northern Frontiers of Roman Britain, 1982; Roman Forts in Britain, 1983; A Queen's Progress, 1987; Roman Officers and Frontiers (with B Dobson), 1993; Roman Scotland: Frontier Country, 1996, 2nd edition, 2006; The Stone of Destiny (with G Munro), 1997; Historic Scotland, 1998; Hadrian's Wall, 4th edition (with B Dobson), 2000; Historic Scotland, People and Places, 2002; The Antonine Wall, 2006; Frontiers of the Roman Empire (with S Jilek and A Thiel), 2005; Handbook to the Roman Wall, 14th edition, 2006; Roman Frontiers in Britain, 2007; Papers in British and foreign journals. Honours: Trustee, Senhouse Roman Museum, Maryport, 1985-; President, Society of Antiquaries of Scotland, 1987-90; Chairman, Hadrian's Wall Pilgrimages, 1989, 1999; Chairman, British Archaeological Awards, 1993-; Visiting Professor of Archaeology, University of Durham, 1994-; Honorary Professor, University of Edinburgh, 1996-; Honorary Professor, University of Newcastle, 2003-; Vice-President, Royal Archaeological Institute, 2002-07; Vice-President, Cumberland and Westmorland Antiquarian and Archaeological Society, 2002-; Newcastle Society of Antiquaries, 2007-. Memberships: FRSA, 1975; Hon FSA Scot, 1970; FRSE, 1991; FRSA, 1999; Hon MIFA, 1990; Corresponding Member, German Archaeological Institute, 1979; UK Representative, International Committee on Archaeological Heritage Management, 1998-. Address: Historic Scotland, Longmore House, Salisbury Place, Edinburgh EH9 1SH, Scotland. E-mail: david.breeze@scotland.gsi.gov.uk

BREGU Eleonora (Lady of Soul), b. 8 April 1953, Erseka, Albania. Head of the Holy Mission Eleonore. Divorced, 1 son, 3 daughters. Education: Graduate, Faculty of Law, University of Tirana, 2000. Appointments: Lady, 20 July 1987; Founder and Head of the Holy Mission Eleonore, 1987-; Dervishe, 3 November 1992; Nigjar, 8 October 1993; Lady of Soul, 8 October 1996; Scientific sessions: What is religion?, Erseka; What is Equilibrium?, Tirana; Who was born first, man or his belief?; The Origin of Communication, Florida, USA; Holy Mission Eleonore, The Greatest Space and Civilisation of The New Millennium, Lisbon, Portugal; Meetings: All in the contribution for national peace, 30 January 1996; What does say the Divine Connection for Albanians, 18 April 1997. Publications: Poetry book: Rowing in no Returning, 1996; Philosophical books: Man in front of his being, 1995; Cosmos and we, 2000; Argument with the Philosophers, 2002; Sacred Messages: Spiritual Contact with Saint Marie, 1997; Sacred Message for the Bulgarian People from contact with her Holiness Vanga of Petrovic, Sofia, 1998; Sacred Message for the Albanian People, Tirana, 1997, 1998; Sacred Message for the Kosovo People, Tirana, 1999; Spiritual activity of The Lady of Soul in collaboration with The Heavenly Levels including activation of the Cosmic-Energetic Centres for protection of Equilibrium: Typhoon in Florida, 1997; Eclipse of the sun, 1999; Earthquake in India, 2001; Earthquakes in The Balkans and Asia, 2000, 2001; Civil conflict in Albania, 1997-98; War in Kosovo, 1999; Terrorist attack, USA, September 11 2001. Honours: Saintliness; The Title Lady of Soul; The nomination of Holy Mission named Eleonore; Diplomas from ABI, IBC; Devotion of 1,700,000 spiritual members; Lifetime Achievement Award; Woman of the Year, 1998; 2000 Millennium Medal of Honour; Gold Star Award. Memberships: Deputy Governor of the American Biographical Institute. International Order of Fellowship; Deputy Director General of the International Biographical Centre; IBC Millenium Time Capsule Commission; Member London Diplomatic Academy. Address: Holy Mission Eleonore, Ru. "Komuna e Parisit" #4, PO Box 7435, Tirana, Albania.

BREMNER Rory Keith Ogilvy, b. 6 April 1961, Edinburgh, Scotland. Impressionist; Satirist. m. (1) Susie Davies,1986, divorced 1994, (2)Tessa Campbell Fraser, 1999, 2 daughters. Education: BA (Hons), French and German, Kings College, London, 1984. Career: TV series, BBC, 1985-92; TV series, Channel 4, 1993-; Translation, The Silver Lake, Weill, 1998; Translation, Bizet's Carmen, Broomhill Opera, 2000. Honours: BAFTA, 1994, 1995; RTS, 1994, 1998, 1999; British Comedy Award, 1992; Channel 4 Political Humourist of the Year, 1999, 2001; Fellowship, Kings College London, 2005. Address: The Richard Stone Partnership, 2 Henrietta Street, London WC2E 8PS, England.

BRENNER Sydney, b. 13 January 1927, Germiston, South Africa (British Citizen). Molecular Biologist. m. May Woolf Balkind, 3 sons, 1 stepson, 2 daughters. Education: MSc, 1947, MB, BCh, 1951, University of Witwatersrand, Johannesburg; PhD, Oxford University, 1954. Appointments: Virus Laboratory, University of California at Berkeley, 1954; Lecturer in Physiology, University of Witwatersrand, 1955-57; Researcher, 1957-79, Director, Molecular Biology Laboratory, 1979-86, Director, Molecular Genetics Unit, 1986-92, Medical Research Council, Cambridge; Member, Scripps Institute, La Jolla, California, 1992-94; Director, Molecular Sciences Institute, Berkeley, California, 1996-2001; Distinguished Research Professor, Salk Institute, La Jolla, California, 2001-. Honours: Honorary DSc: Dublin, Witwatersrand, Chicago, London, Leicester, Oxford; Honorary LLD, Glasgow, Cambridge; Honorary DLitt, Singapore; Warren

Triennial Prize, 1968; William Bate Hardy Prize, Cambridge Philosophical Society, 1969; Gregor Mendel Medal of German Academy of Science Leopoldina, 1970; Albert Lasker Medical Research Award, 1971; Gairdner Foundation Annual Award, Canada, 1978; Royal Medal of Royal Society, 1974; Prix Charles Leopold Mayer, French Academy, 1975; Krebs Medal, Federation of European Biochemical Societies, 1980; Ciba Medal, Biochemical Society, 1981; Feldberg Foundation Prize, 1983; Neil Hamilton Fairley Medal, Royal College of Physicians, 1985; Croonian Lecturer, Royal Society of London, 1986; Rosenstiel Award, Brandeis University, 1986; Prix Louis Jeantet de Médecine, Switzerland, 1987; Genetics Society of America Medal, 1987; Harvey Prize, Israel Institute of Technology, 1987; Hughlings Jackson Medal, Royal Society of Medicine, 1987; Waterford Bio-Medical Science Award, The Research Institute of Scripps Clinic, 1988; Kyoto Prize, Inamori Foundation, 1990; Gairdner Foundation Award, Canada, 1991; Copley Medal, Royal Society, 1991; King Faisal International Prize for Science (King Faisal Foundation), 1992; Bristol-Myers Squibb Award for Distinguished Achievement in Neuroscience Research, 1992; Albert Lasker Award for Special Achievement, 2000; Nobel Prize for Physiology or Medicine, 2002. Memberships: Member, Medical Research Council, 1978-82, 1986-90; Fellow, King's College, Cambridge, 1959-; Honorary Professor of Genetic Medicine, University of Cambridge, Clinical School, 1989-; Foreign Associate, NAS, 1977; Foreign Member, American Philosophical Society, 1979; Foreign Member, Real Academia de Ciencias, 1985; External Scientific Member, Max Planck Society, 1988; Member, Academy Europea, 1989; Corresponding Scientifique Emerite de l'INSERM, Associe Etranger Academie des Sciences, France; Fellow, American Academy of Microbiology; Foreign Honorary Member, American Academy of Arts and Sciences, 1965; Honorary Member, Deutsche Akademie der Natursforsche Leopoldina, 1975; Society for Biological Chemists, 1975; Honorary FRSE; Honorary Fellow, Indian Academy of Sciences, 1989; Honorary Member, Chinese Society of Genetics, 1989; Honorary Fellow, Royal College of Pathologists, 1990; Honorary Member, Associate of Physicians of GB and Ireland, 1991. Address: Kings College, Cambridge, CB2 1ST, England.

BRENT William B, b. 28 June 1924, Kentucky, USA. Geologist. Education: BA, University of Virginia, 1949; MA, 1952, PhD, 1955, Cornell University; JD, University of Virginia, 1966. Appointments: Assistant Professor, Geology, Oklahoma State University; Associate Professor of Geology, Louisiana Tech University; Visiting Associate Professor of Geology, University of Virginia; Chief Geologist, Tennessee Division of Geology; Consulting Geologist. Publications: Texts and maps on the geologic structure and stratigraphy of the Appalachian Valley. Membership: Fellow, Geological Society of America; Sigma Xi. Address: 3100 Shore Drive, Apt 1048, Virginia Beach, VA 23451, USA.

BRERETON Richard Geoffrey, b. 5 January 1955, Westminster, London, England. University Professor. Education: BA, 1976, MA, 1980, PhD, 1981, Cambridge. Appointments: Researcher, Cambridge University, 1979-83; University Lecturer, Reader, Professor, 1983-, Director, Centre for Chemometrics, 2004-, Bristol University. Publications: 6 books; 13 book chapters; 130 journal papers; 9 conference contributions; 146 short articles including: Chemometrics: Applications of Maths and Statistics to Laboratory Systems, 1990 and 1993; Chemometrics: Data Analysis for the Laboratory and Chemical Plant, 2003, 2004 and 2006. Honours: Theophilus Redwood Lectureship,

2006; Royal Society of Chemistry; 76 invited and plenary conference lectures; Research Awards from 11 organisations. Memberships: Fellow, Royal Society of Chemistry; Fellow, Royal Statistical Society. Address: School of Chemistry, University of Bristol, Cantocks Close, Bristol BS8 1TS, England. E-mail: r.g.brereton@bris.ac.uk

BRESENHAM Jack E, b. USA. Chief Technical Officer; Emeritus Professor of Computer Science. Education: BSEE, University of New Mexico, 1959; MSIE, 1960, PhD, 1964, Stanford University. Appointments: Senior Technical Staff Member, Manager, Engineer, Planner, Programmer, Analyst, IBM, 1960-87; Teacher, Professor of Computer Science, Winthrop University, 1987-2003; Chief Technical Officer, Bresenham Consulting. Publications include: Algorithm for computer control of a digital plotter, 1965, reprinted, 1980, reprinted, 1998; Pixel processing fundamentals, 1996; Teaching the graphics processing pipeline: cosmetic and geometric attribute implications, 2001; The Analysis and Statistics of Line Distribution, 2002; 9 US Patents. Honours include: IBM Outstanding Contribution Award, 1967, 1984 and 1989; Distinguished Citizen Award, Wofford College National Alumni Association, 1993; Honorary Director and Invited Lecturer, University of Cantabria, Santander, Spain, July 2000; Jury Member of habilitation a diriger les recherches panel, University of Paris-8 for Jean Jaques Bourdin, 2000; Golden Quill Award in recognition of work to improve writing skills among computer science students, Winthrop University, 2001; Honorary Chair, The 11th International Conference in Central Europe on Computer Graphics, Visualization and Computer Vision, 2003; Named Distinguished Alumnus, School of Engineering, University of New Mexico, 2003. Address: 1166 Wendy Road, Rock Hill, SC 29732, USA.

BREWER Derek Stanley, b. 13 July 1923, Cardiff, Wales. Writer; Editor; Emeritus Professor. m. Lucie Elisabeth Hoole, 3 sons, 2 daughters. Education: Magdalen College, Oxford, 1941-42, 1945-48; BA, MA (Oxon), 1948; PhD, Birmingham University, 1956; LittD, Cambridge University, 1980. Appointments: include Professor, International Christian University, Tokyo, 1956-58; Senior Lecturer, Birmingham, 1958-65; Fellow, 1965-90, Master, 1977-90, Professor, 1983-90, Life Fellow, 1990-, Emeritus Professor, 1990-, Emmanuel College, Cambridge; Editor, The Cambridge Review, 1981-86; Corresponding Fellow, Medieval Society of America, 1987; Franqui Professor des Sciences Humaines, Belgium, 1998. Publications: Numerous contributions to specialist scholarly journals, and several books, mainly in the fields of medieval and later English literature, especially the works of Geoffrey Chaucer; Titles include, Chaucer, 1953; Proteus, 1958; The Parlement of Foulys, (editor), 1960; Chaucer: The Critical Heritage, 1978; Chaucer and his World, 1978, reprinted, 1992; Symbolic Stories, 1980, reprinted, 1988; English Gothic Literature, 1983; Chaucer: An Introduction, 1984; Medieval Comic Tales (editor), 1996; A Companion to the Gawain-Poet, 1996, (editor); A New Introduction to Chaucer, 1998; Seatonian Exercises and Other Verses, 2000; The World of Chaucer, 2000. Honours: Honorary Doctorates from 7 universities; 10 times winner, Seatonian Prize Poem, 1969-1999; Honorary Member, Japan Academy, 1981; Medal, Japan Academy, 1997; Medal des Sciences Humaines, Belgium, 1998; Honorary Fellow, English Association, 2001. Address: Emmanuel College, Cambridge, CB2 3AP, England. E-mail: dsb27@cam.ac.uk

BRIDGEMAN, Viscountess Victoria Harriet Lucy, b. 30 March 1942, Durham, England. Library Director; Writer. m. Viscount Bridgeman, 1966, 4 sons. Education: MA,

Trinity College, Dublin, 1964. Appointment: Executive Editor, The Masters, 1965-69; Editor, Discovering Antiques, 1970-72; Established own company producing books and articles on fine and decorative arts; Founder and Managing Director, Bridgeman Art Library, London, New York, Paris and Berlin. Publications: An Encyclopaedia of Victoriana, 1974; An Illustrated History, The British Eccentric, 1975; Society Scandals, 1976; Beside the Seaside, 1976; A Guide to Gardens of Europe, 1979; The Last Word, 1983; 8 titles in Connoisseur's Library series. Honours: European Woman of the Year Award, Arts Section, 1997; FRSA. Address: The Bridgeman Art Library, 17-19 Garway Road, London W2 4PH, England. Website: www.bridgeman.co.uk

BRIDGES Jeff, b. 4 December 1949, Los Angeles, USA. Actor. m. Susan Geston, 3 daughters. Creative Works: Films include: Halls of Anger, 1970; The Last Picture Show, Fat City, 1971; Bad Company, 1972; The Last American Hero, The Iceman Cometh, 1973; Thunderbolt and Lightfoot, 1974; Hearts of the West, Rancho Deluxe, 1975; King Kong, Stay Hungary, 1976; Somebody Killed Her Husband, 1978; Winter Kills, 1979; The American Success Company, Heaven's Gate, 1980; Cutter's Way, 1981; Tron, Kiss Me Goodbye, The Last Unicorn, 1982; Starman, Against All Odds, 1984; Jagged Edge, 1985; 8 Million Ways to Die, The Morning After, 1986; Nadine, 1987; Tucker, the Man and His Dream, 1988; See You in the Morning, Texasville, The Fabulous Baker Boys, 1990; The Fisher King, 1991; American Heart, The Vanishing, Blown Away, Fearless, 1994; Wild Bill, White Squall, 1995; The Mirror Has Two Faces, 1996; The Big Lebowski, 1997; Arlington Road, 1998; Simpatico, The Muse, 1999; The Contender, Raising the Hammoth (TV voice), 2000; K-Pax, 2002; Masked and Anonymous, Seabiscuit, 2003; The Door in the Floor, 2004; The Moguls, Tideland, 2005; Stick It, 2006; Surf's Up (voice), 2007. Address: c/o Creative Artists Agency, 9830 Wilshire Boulevard, Beverly Hills, CA 90212, USA.

BRIGGS, Baron of Lewes in the County of Sussex; Asa Briggs, b. 7 May 1921, Keighley, Yorkshire, England. Writer. m. Susan Anne Banwell, 1955, 2 sons, 2 daughters. Education: 1st Class History Tripos, Parts I and II, Sidney Sussex College, Cambridge, 1941; BSc, 1st Class (Economics), London, 1941. Publications: Victorian People, 1954; The Age of Improvement, 1959, new edition, 2000; History of Broadcasting in the United Kingdom, 5 volumes, 1961-95; Victorian Cities, 1963; A Social History of England, 1983, 3rd edition, 1999; Victorian Things, 1988. Honours: Marconi Medal for Communications History, 1975; Life Peerage, 1976; Medaille de Vermeil de la Formation, Foundation de l'Académie d'Architecture, 1979; Wolfson History Prize, 2000; 20 honorary degrees. Memberships: Fellow, British Academy; American Academy of Arts and Sciences; President, Social History Society; President, Victorian Society. Address: The Caprons, Keere Street, Lewes BN7 1TY, England.

BRIGGS Edward Samuel, b. 4 October 1926, St Paul, Minnesota, USA. Naval Officer. m. Nanette Parks, 1 son. Education: Graduate, US Naval Academy, 1949; Command and Staff School, US Naval War College, 1961; Joint Services Staff College, Latimer, England, 1965. Appointments: Midshipman to Vice Admiral, US Navy, 1945-84; Commanding Officer, USS Turner Joy (DD951), 1966-68; Commanding Officer, USS Jouett (DLG 29), 1971-72; Deputy Commander/ Chief of Staff, US Seventh Fleet, 1972-73; Rear Admiral, Commander, Cruiser-Destroyer Group Three, US Pacific Fleet, 1975-76; Commander, US Navy Recruiting Command, 1976-78; Commander, Naval District Pearl Harbor, 1978-79; Commander, Naval Logistics Command, US Pacific Fleet,

1978-79; Vice Admiral, Deputy Commander/Chief of Staff, US Pacific Fleet, 1980-82; Commander, US Naval Surface Forces, US Atlantic Fleet, 1982-84; Retired, 1984; Chairman, Escondido High School District Curriculum Review Council, 1994-98; Member, San Diego Unified School District History Curriculum and Instruction Advisory Committee, 1986-98. Publications: A Biography – Charles W Briggs; A Return to Liberal Education; The War We Are In, I/II, An Appraisal of the Iraq War and the Broader War Between Civilizations. Honours: Distinguished Service Medal; 5 Legion of Merits; 2 Air Medals; 3 Navy Commendation Medals; 2 Meritorious Unit Citations; 2 Bronze Stars. Memberships: US Naval Academy Alumni Association; Veterans of Foreign Wars; Navy League of the United States; San Diego Military Advisory Council.

BRIGGS Freda, b. 12 December 1930, Huddersfield, England. Emeritus Professor of Child Development. m. Kenneth, 1 son, 1 daughter, deceased. Appointments: Director, Early Childhood Education, State College, Victoria, 1976-80; Foundation Dean, de Lissa Institute of Early Childhood and Family Studies, University of South Australia, Adelaide, 1980; Senior Lecturer, Child Development; Early Childhood Teacher, Social Worker, (England); Board Member, Children's Education Assistance Department Veterans' Affairs, 1996-2002; Consultant, Department of Education, New South Wales, 1997; New Zealand Police and Education Ministry, 1985-; Consultant to Education authorities in Spain, Germany, Brazil; Avon & Somerset Police (Child-Safe); Police Consultant, States of Victoria, Queensland and Western Australia, 1985-93; Singapore, 2001; Save the Children, Australia; Professor, University of South Australia, 1991-2002; Co-investigator in handling of child sex abuse cases by the Anglican Diocese of Brisbane; Consultant to Rotary International for writing protocols and guidelines for safer student exchanges; Consultant to Federal Minister of Education for his Safe School Framework, 2003. Publications: 15 books and numerous papers and articles published in the fields of education, child development and child protection, including Teaching Children to Protect Themselves, Child Protection: A Guide for Teachers and Childcare Professionals; (with R Hawkins) The Early Years of School – Teaching and Learning (with GK Potter), 1990; Teaching Children to Protect Themselves, 2000. Honours: Citation for Research and Advice, New Zealand Police Authority, the first civilian recipient; Inaugural Australian Humanitarian Award, for services to children in developing countries, and pioneering, non-medical research and education for combating child abuse, 1998; University Chancellor's Community Service Award, 2000, 2001; Senior Australian of the Year Award, 2000; Centenary Medal for outstanding service to the nation in child protection, 2003. Memberships: Patron: Bravehearts; ASCA; Palliative Care Project, Adelaide Women & Children's Hospital; Several Government working parties and consultancies relating to child abuse and protection. Address: 17 Marola Avenue, Rostrevor, SA 5073, Australia. E-mail: freda.briggs@unisa.edu.au

BRIGGS Raymond Redvers, b. 18 January 1934, Wimbledon, London, England. Illustrator; Writer; Cartoonist. m. Jean T Clark, 1963, deceased 1973. Education: Wimbledon School of Art; Slade School of Fine Art, London, NDD; DFA (Lond); FSCD FRSL. Appointments: Freelance illustrator, 1957-; Children's author, 1961-. Publications: Midnight Adventure, 1961; Ring-a-Ring o'Roses, 1962; The Strange House, 1963; Sledges to the Rescue, 1963; The White Land, 1963; Fee Fi Fo Fum, 1964; The Mother Goose Treasury, 1966; Jim and the Beanstalk, 1970; The Fairy Tale Treasury, 1975; Fungus

the Bogeyman, 1977; The Snowman, 1978; Gentleman Jim, 1980; When the Wind Blows, 1982, stage and radio versions, 1983; The Tinpot Foreign General & the Old Iron Woman, 1984; Unlucky Wally, 1987; Unlucky Wally, Twenty Years On, 1989; The Man, 1992; The Bear 1994; Ethel and Ernest, 1998; UG, 2001; Blooming Books (with Nicolette Jones), 2003; The Puddleman, 2004; TV: Ivor the Invisible, 2001; Fungus the Bogeyman, 2004. Honours: Kate Greenaway Medals, 1966, 1973; British Academy of Film and Television Arts Award; Francis Williams Illustration Awards, V & A Museum, 1982; Broadcasting Press Guild Radio Award, 1983; British Book Awards: Childrens' Author of the Year, 1992; Kurt Maschler Award, 1992; British Book Awards, Illustrated Book of the Year, 1998; Smarties Silver Award, 2001. Memberships: Royal Society of Literature; Society of Authors. Address: Weston, Underhill Lane, Westmeston, Near Hassocks, Sussex BN6 8XG, England.

BRIGHOUSE OF BRIGHOUSE, David John (Lord Brighouse), b. 24 November 1931, Upton, Cheshire, England. Retired. m. Mary Irene Alice Barrett Arbasini-Bovary, Contessa della Torre dei Torti de San Pietro, 2 sons, 1 daughter. Education: ACMA, MBA, Oxbridge and Fundaçao Getulio Vargas, Brazil; IDOEF, Buenos Aires; RM (Retired). Appointments: Vestey Group, South American Division, 1958-91; Trustee and Treasurer, Kent Information Federation for the Disabled, 1996-2001; Councillor, Medway Council, 2000-2003; Member of the Kent Flood Defence Committee; School Governor, Gad's Hill School, Higham; Trustee, Foords Almshouses, Rochester. Honours: Order of St James, Spain; Environment Agency – Defenders of the South. Memberships: Catenian Association (Medway Circle); Gillingham Golf Club; Country Club UK. Address: Aurikberg, 130 Maidstone Road, Chatham, Kent ME4 6DX, England.

BRIGHOUSE Ronald John David, b. 19 May 1970, England. International Loss Adjuster; Historian. Education: St Paul's School, São Paulo, Brazil; Barker College, Argentina; Pbro Saenz School, Argentina; BA Hons, Cambridge University, England; MA, Birmingham University, England; Hispanic Studies, Universidad de Navarra, Pamplona, Spain; Linguistics & History, Heidelberg University. Appointments: International Loss Adjuster; Historian; Author; International Lecturer, Revolutionary & Napoleonic Wars. Publications: 2 books published in Spain about Peninsular Wars; Historical articles in Spain and UK. Honours: Sir John Moore Medal, La Coruña, Spain; Defence of Buenos Aires Commemorative Medal, Buenos Aires, Argentina. Memberships: Country Club UK; Trustee, Fort Amherst (Chatham); Chairman, Peninsula War Association. Address: Aurikberg, 130 Maidstone Road, Chatham, Kent ME4 6DX, England. Website: www.asche.org

BRIGHTMAN Sarah, Singer; Actress. Career: Dancer with Hot Gossip and Pan's People; Stage roles include: Cats; Requiem; the Phantom of the Opera; Aspects of Love (all music by Andrew Lloyd Webber); I and Albert; The Nightingale; The Merry Widow; Trelawney of the Wells; Relative Values; Dangerous Obsession; The Innocents. Concerts include: Barcelona Olympic Games, 1992; Concert for Diana, 2007; Live Earth, China, 2007. Recordings include: 5 Top Ten singles; Eden, album, 1999; La Luna, 2000. Address: c/o Sunhand Ltd, 63 Grosvenor Street, London W1X 9DA, England.

BRINDLEY Lynne J, b. 2 July 1950, United Kingdom. Librarian; Chief Executive. Education: BA, 1st Class Honours, Music, University of Reading, 1971; Diploma in Library and Information Studies, University College, London, 1975;

MA, Library and Information Studies, University of London, 1975; Degree Module in Computers and Computing, Open University, 1978; Diploma in Management, Open University Business School, 1984-84. Appointments include: Head of Marketing and Support Group, Bibliographic Services Division, 1979-83, Head of Chief Executives Office, 1983-85 British Library; Director of Library and Information Services, 1985-90, Pro-Vice-Chancellor for Information Technology, 1987-90, Aston University, Birmingham; Management Consultant, then Principal Consultant, KPMG Management Consulting, 1991-92; Librarian and Director of Information Services, London School of Economics, 1992-97; University Librarian, 1997-2000, Pro-Vice-Chancellor, 1998-2000, University of Leeds; Chief Executive Officer, The British Library, 2000-; Advisory Council for Libraries and Information Resources, Stanford University, California, USA, 1999-; Chair of IT Sub-Group, Conference of European National Libraries, 2000-; Research Libraries Support Group, 2001-; Executive Committee, National Museum Directors Conference, 2001-; Member Board of Trustees, Ithaka Horbors Inc, 2004-05. Publications: Numerous publications in the field of knowledge management, information industry and digital libraries. Honours: Honorary D.Letters: Nottingham Trent University, 2001, University of Leicester, 2002, Guildhall University, London, 2002, University of Sheffield, 2004, University of Reading, 2004; UCL Fellowship, 2002; Honorary D Litt, University of Oxford, 2002; Freeman of the City of London, 1989; Freeman of the Worshipful Company of Goldsmiths, 1989, Liveryman, 1993, Assistant to the Court, 2006-; Fellow, Royal Society of Arts; Companion Institute of Management, 2004; Doctor of Science, City University, 2006, University of Leeds, 2006, Open University, 2006; Honorary Fellow, University of Wales, Aberystwyth, 2007. Memberships: Fellow, Institute of Information Scientists; Fellow, Library Association. Address: The British Library, 96 Euston Road, London NW1 2DB, England. E-mail: chief-executive@bl.uk

BRINSMADE Akbar Fairchild, b. 31 May 1917, Puebla, State of Puebla, Mexico. Chemical Engineer Consultant, PE. m. Juanita Phillips, 1 son, 2 daughters. Education: BS, Chemistry, University of Wisconsin, Madison, 1935-39; MS, Chemical Engineering Practice, Massachusetts Institute of Technology, Cambridge, Massachusetts, 1940-42; Postgraduate studies: University of Houston, 1943-44, Polytechnic Institute, Brooklyn, New York, 1945-46, New York University, 1947-49, Tulane University, 1967-73; Registered Professional Engineer, North Carolina, 1958, Louisiana, 1979. Appointments: General Manager, Cia Minera San Francisco y Anex, San Luis Potosi, Mexico 1939-40; Senior Research Engineer, Shell Oil Company, Houston and New York City, 1942-48; Project Manager, International Industrial Consultants, New York City and Caracas, Venezuela, 1949-50; Managing Director, Promotora Nacional de Industrias, Caracas, Venezuela, 1952-57; Research and Development Engineer, Hercules Powder Co, Rocket Center, West Virginia, 1959-64; Research Engineering Specialist, Chrysler Space Division, New Orleans, Louisiana, 1966-69; Chemical Engineer Consultant to major US and foreign corporations, 1969-. Publications: Book Chapters in Solid Rocket Technology, 1967, and Author, Travel to the Stars, 1996; Author: The Expansion of the Universe - Revisited, 2000; US Patent: Gravity Habitat Module for Space Vehicle, 2001. Honours: Phi Eta Sigma; Military ROTC Bombardiers, University of Oklahoma, 1935; Phi Lambda Upsilon, University of Wisconsin, 1937. Memberships (current): Fellow, American Institute of Chemists; American Institute of Chemical Engineers; American Chemical Society; National

Society of Professional Engineers; Louisiana Engineering Society; Sigma Alpha Epsilon Fraternity. Address: 486 Channel Mark Drive, Biloxi, MS 39531, USA

BRISTOW Cynthia Lynn, b. 19 August 1951, Altus, Oklahoma, USA. Medical Immunology. 3 sons, 2 daughters. Education: BA (General Honors), Winthrop College, Rock Hill, South Carolina, 1972; MS, 1979, PhD, 1986, Medical University of South Carolina, Charleston; Medical Laboratory Immunology (CPEP), University of North Carolina, Chapel Hill, 2001. Appointments: Postdoctoral Associate, 1986-88, Medical University of South Carolina; Postdoctoral Associate, 1988-92, Research Associate, 1992-94, Assistant Professor, 1994-98, Clinical Fellow, 1999-2001, University of North Carolina, Chapel Hill; Research Associate, The Rockefeller University, 2001-02; Staff Scientist, Population Council, 2002-03; Investigator, Weill Cornell Medical College, 2003-; Director of Research, The Institute for Human Genetics and Biochemistry, 2003-; Assistant Professor, Mount Sinai School of Medicine, 2004-. Publications: 20 articles in professional scientific journals; 2 patents; 2 patents pending. Honours: Oral Presentation, XIII International AIDS Conference, Durban, South Africa, 2000; International Personality of the Year, IBC, 2001, 2002, 2006; Invited Speaker, NY/NJ Flow Cytometry Group, New York, 2002; Invited Speaker, The Institute of Human Virology, University of Maryland Biotechnology Institute, Baltimore, 2003; Invited Speaker, GU Cancer Immunotherapy Program, Duke University Medical Center, Durham, North Carolina, 2003; Invited Speaker, Brigham and Women's Hospital, Harvard Medical School, Boston, 2003; Invited Speaker, Duke University Medical Center, 2005; Oral Presentation, 2nd International Workshop on HIV Persistence during Therapy, St Martin, French West Indies, 2005; Listed in national and international biographical directories. Memberships: Association of Medical Laboratory Immunologists; American Association of Immunologists; American Chemical Society; American Diabetes Association; American Society for Microbiology; UNC Chapel Hill Center for AIDS Research; Committee for the Use of Human Subjects, UNC Chapel Hill; NY/NJ Flow Cytometry Users Group (METROFLOW); New York Academy of Sciences. Address: The Institute for Human Genetics and Biochemistry, 227 E 19th Street, Rm D477, New York, NY 10003, USA. E-mail: cynthia.bristow@rockefeller.edu

BRKIČ Slavko, b. 7 April 1948, Novo Mesto, Slovenia. Dental Technician. m. Alenka Slapšak, 1 daughter. Education: Dental Technician, Dental College, Ljubljana, Slovenia, 1967. Appointments: Head, Estetikdent Company; International professional lectures on aesthetic dentistry; Mentor and President, Section of Dental Technicians and Engineers of Dental Prosthetics, Chamber of Commerce and Industry, Slovenia. Publications: Modern Technologies of Dental Ceramics; Articles on dental work. Address: Iska 21 A 1292 IG, Ljubljana 1000, Slovenia. E-mail: slavko.brkic@siol.net

BROADBENT Dennis Elton, b. 6 February 1945, Price, Utah, USA. Psychologist; Director. m. Helen McRae, 1 son, 4 daughters. Education: BS, Psychology, Brigham Young University, 1972; MS, Education and Developmental Psychology, Florida State University, 1973; PhD, Clinical and Behaviour Therapy, School Psychology, Florida State University, 1979; Diplomate Forensic, Clinical Psychology, American Board of Psychological Specialties, 1999; Diplomate, Mental Health, 2001; Fellow, American Association of Integrative Medicine, 2001. Appointments include: Publisher, Psychological and Family Health Notes, 1983-; Director, Psychological and Family Health Associates,

1980-; Adjunct Professor, Glendale Community College, Glendale, Arizona, 1980-84; Private Clinical, Counselling, Consultant and School Psychologist, Psychological and Family Health Associates, Phoenix, Arizona, 1980-; Executive Director, Family Resource Center, 1980-; Director, Family Resource Center Charities, 1993-96; Director, The Southwest Institute for Behavioral Studies, 1986-; General Partner, The Family Resource Center, 1983-. Publications include: The Odyssey to Happiness, submitted for review; Teaching Values in Arizona Schools, 1990; Behavioral Marriage, Family, and Sexual Counseling: Principles and Techniques, submitted for publication. Honours include: Full University Scholarship, College of Eastern Utah, Brigham Young University; Forensics and Music Awards; Magna Cum Laude, Brigham Young University. Memberships: American Psychological Association; National Council on Family Relations; American College of Forensic Examiners; American Association of Integrative Medicine. Address: 3101 W Peoria Avenue Ste B309, Phoenix, AZ 85029-5210, USA.

BROADBENT Jim, b. 24 May 1949, Lincolnshire, England. Actor. m. Anastasia Lewis, 1987. Education: Graduate, London Academy of Music and Dramatic Arts, 1972. Career: Actor: Royal National Theatre; Royal Shakespeare Company; Co-founder, National Theatre of Brent; Films include: The Shout, 1978; The Hit, 1984; Time Bandits, 1981; Brazil, 1985; Life is Sweet, 1990; The Crying Game, Enchanted April, 1992; Bullets Over Broadway, Princess Caraboo, Widows' Peak, 1994; Little Voice, 1998; Topsy-Turvy, 1999; Bridget Jones's Diary, Moulin Rouge!, Iris, 2001; The Gangs of New York, 2002; Bright Young Things, 2003; Vanity Fair, Vera Drake, Bridget Jones: The Edge of Reason, 2004; The Magic Roundabout (voice), Robots (voice), Valiant (voice), The Chronicles of Narnia: The Lion, The Witch and The Wardrobe, 2005; Hot Fuzz, And When Did You Last See Your Father, 2007; TV includes: The Peter Principle, 1995; And Starring Pancho Villa as Himself, 2003; The Young Visiters, 2003; Pride (voice), 2004; Spider-Plant Man, 2005; The Street, Longford, 2006. Honours: Best Supporting Actor, BAFTA Award, 2001; Best Supporting Actor, Oscar, 2001; Nominated, Best Performance by an Actor, The Orange British Academy Film Awards, 2002; Nominated, Best Spoken Word Album for Children, Grammy Award, 2004. Memberships: Honorary President, Lindsey Rural Players.

BROADBENT John Michael (Mike), b. 24 November 1933. Freelance Journalist, Broadcasting Consultant and Lecturer. m. Sandra Elizabeth, 1961, 2 sons (1 deceased), 3 daughters (1 deceased). Education: Manchester Grammar. Appointments: National Service, Bombardier RA, 1953-55; Journalist, Kemsley Newspapers, 1950-57; Journalist, Star Newspaper, 1957-59; Scriptwriter, TV News, Producer (later Editor), Westminster (1968-72), Editor, Nine O'Clock News, News Editor, Sixty Minutes, Founding Editor, One O'Clock News, Editor, Commons TV, Assistant to Head, BBC Westminster, BBC TV, 1959-91; Freelance Journalist, Broadcasting Consultant and Lecturer, 1991-. Memberships: Accompanying Officer, FCO (OVIS), 1991-95; Founder and former Chairman, Whitehill Avenue Luton Residents Association; Member, Luton Town Supporters Club. Address: 1 Whitehill Avenue, Luton, Bedfordshire LU1 3SP, England. E-mail: mike_broadbent@yahoo.com

BROCKES Jeremy Patrick, b. 29 February 1948, Haslemere, Surrey, England. Academic Scientist. Education: BA, Cambridge University, 1969; PhD, Edinburgh University, 1972. Appointments: Department of Neurobiology Harvard Medical School, 1972-75; MRC Neuroimmunology Project,

University College London, 1976-77; Assistant Professor of Biology, 1978-80, Associate Professor of Biology, 1981-83, California Institute of Technology; Member, MRC Biophysics Unit, King's College London, 1983-88; Member, Ludwig Institute for Cancer Research, University College London Branch, 1988-97; MRC Non-Clinical Research Professor, Department of Biochemistry, University College London, 1997-. Publications: Numerous articles in scientific journals include: Appendage Regeneration in Adult Vertebrates and Implications for Regenerative Medicine (co-author), 2005. Honours: Scientific Medals: Zoological Society of London, 1986, Biological Council, 1990, Marcus Singer, 1990; FRS, 1994; Brookes Lecture, Harvard Medical School, 1997. Memberships: Fellow, European Molecular Biology Organisation, 1989; Academia Europaea, 1989. Address: Department of Biochemistry, University College London, Gower Street, London WC1E 6BT, England. E-mail: jbrockes@ucl.ac.uk

BROCKINGTON Ian Fraser, b. 12 December 1935, Chillington, Devon, England. Psychiatrist. m. Diana Pink, 2 sons, 2 daughters. Education: Winchester College; Gonville & Caius College, Cambridge. Appointments: Professor of Psychiatry, University of Birmingham, 1983-2001; Visiting Professorships: University of Chicago, 1980; Washington University of St Louis, 1981; University of Nagoya, 2002; University of Kumamoto, 2003. Publications: Articles on: African Cardiopathies; The Classification of the Psychoses; Methods of Clinical Psychiatric Observation; Puerperal Mental Disorders; Author: Motherhood and Mental Health, 1996; Eiliethyia's Mischief: the Organic Psychoses of Pregnancy, Parturition and the Puerperium, 2006; Editor: Motherhood and Mental Illness, 1982, 1988; The Closure of Mental Hospitals, 1990. Memberships: Founder, The Marcé Society; Founder, Section on Women's Mental Health, World Psychiatric Association; Fellow, European Psychiatric Association. Address: Lower Brockington Farm, Bredenbury, Bromyard, Herefordshire HR7 4TE, England. E-mail: i.f.brockington@bham.ac.uk

BRODERICK Matthew, b. 21 March 1962, New York, USA. Actor. m. Sarah Jessica Parker, 1997, 1 son. Theatre includes: Valentine's Day; Torch Song Trilogy; Bright Beach Memoirs; Biloxi Blues; The Widow Claire; How to Succeed in Business Without Really Trying; The Producers; Films include: War Games; Ladyhawke; 1918; On Valentine's Day; Ferris Bueller's Day Off; Project X; Biloxi Blues; Torch Song Trilogy; Glory; Family Business; The Freshman; Lay This Laurel; Out on a Limb; The Night We Never Met; The Lion King (voice); Road to Welville; Mrs Parker and the Vicious Circle; Infinity (also director); The Cable Guy; Addicted to Love; The Lion King II: Simba's Pride (voice); Godzilla; Election; Inspector Gadget, 1999; Walking to the Waterline, 1999; You Can Count on Me, 2000; Suspicious Minds, 2001; Good Boy! (voice), 2003; Marie and Bruce, 2004; Lion King 1 ½ (voice), 2004; Stepford Wives, 2004; Last Shot, 2004; Strangers with Candy, 2005; The Producers, 2005; Deck the Halls, 2006; Margaret, 2007; The She Found Me, 2007; Bee Movie, 2007; TV includes: Master Harold... and the Boys; Cinderella; Jazz, 2001; The Music Man, 2003. Honours: 2 Tony Awards. Address: c/o CAA, 9830 Wilshire Boulevard, Beverly Hills, CA 90212, USA.

BRODOV Yuri Myronovich, b. 15 April 1943, Sverdlovsk, Russian Federation. Engineer. m. Irina G Eidelstein, 2 daughters. Education: Diploma of Technician, College of Mining and Metallurgy, Sverdlovsk, 1957-61; Diploma of Engineer, Urals State Polytechnical Institute, Sverdlovsk,

1962-67; Candidate of Technical Sciences Diploma, 1972; Doctor of Technical Sciences Diploma, 1988. Appointments: Technician, Urals Thermoelectric Project Institute, 1961-62; Apprentice, Ural Turbo-Motor Works, 1962-65; Lecturer, 1967-70, Assistant Professor, 1970-74, Professor, 1974-89, Head of Turbines & Engines Department, 1989-, Urals State Polytechnical Institute. Publications: Books: Steam Turbine Condenser Units, 1994; Power Plant Heat Exchangers, 2003; Steam Turbine Heat Exchangers Improvement, 2004; Steam Turbine Heat Exchanger Maintenance and Repair, 2005; Encyclopaedia of Steam Turbine Heat Exchangers, 2006; Over 400 articles. Honours: Bronze Medal, 1987; Silver Medal, 1988; Higher Education Honoured Worker, 2000. Memberships: International Academy of Energetics; Academy of Engineering Sciences of Russian Federation. Address: 138 Bazhov Str Apt 6, 620026, Ekaterinburg, Russia. E-mail: turbine66@mail.ru

BRON Eleanor, b. 14 March 1938, Stanmore, England. Actress; Author. Education: North London Collegiate School; Newnham College, Cambridge. Career: Appeared at Establishment Night Club; Toured USA, 1961; TV satire, Not So Much a Programme, More a Way of Life; Co-writer and appeared in TV series, Where was Spring?, After That This, Beyond a Joke; Director, Actors' Centre, 1982-93; Director, Soho Theatre Co, 1993-2000; Stage appearances: Private Lives; Hedda Gabler; Antony and Cleopatra; Madwoman of Chaillot; Hamlet; Uncle Vanya, Heartbreak House, Oedipus; The Prime of Miss Jean Brodie; Present Laughter; The Duchess of Malfi; The Cherry Orchard; The Real Inspector Hound; The Miser; The White Devil; Desdemona – If You Had Only Spoken! (one woman show); Dona Rosita The Spinster; A Delicate Balance; Be My Baby; Making Noise Quietly; Twopence To Cross The Mersey, 2005; TV: Rumpole; Dr Who; French and Saunders; Absolutely Fabulous; Vanity Fair; BBC TV Play for Today: Nina; A Month in the Country; The Hour of the Lynx; The Blue Boy; Ted and Alice; Fat Friends; Films: Help!; Alfie; Two for the Road; Bedazzled; Women in Love; The National Health; Turtle Diary; Little Dorritt; The Attic; Deadly Advice, 1994; Black Beauty, 1993; A Little Princess, 1994; The House of Mirth, 2000; Iris, 2001; The Heart of Me, 2002; Love's Brother, 2003; Wimbledon, 2004; Concert appearance's as narrator include: Façade; Carnival des Animaux; Peter and the Wolf; Bernstein's Symphony No 3 with BBC Symphony Orchestra. Publications include: Song Cycle (with John Dankworth), 1973; Verses for Saint-Saëns Carnival of the Animals, 1975; Is Your Marriage Really Necessary? (with John Fortune), 1972; Life and Other Punctures, 1978; The Pillow Book of Eleanor Bron, 1985; Desdemona – If You Only Had Spoken! 1992; Double Take (novel), 1996. Address: c/o Rebecca Blond, 69A King's Road, London SW3 4NX, England.

BRONKAR Eunice Dunalee (Connor), b. 8 August 1934, New Lebanon, Ohio, USA. Visual Artist; Teacher. m. Charles William Bronkar, 1 daughter. Education: BFA, Wright State University, Dayton, Ohio, 1971; M Art Ed, with WSU and teacher certification, 1983; Additional studies, Dayton Art Institute, 1972, Wright State University, 1989; Participation in 12 workshops, 1972-93. Appointments: Part-time Teacher, Springfield Museum of Art, 1967-77; Education Chairman, 1973-74; Lead Teacher, Commercial Art Program, Clark State Community College, Springfield, Ohio, 1984-94; Assistant Professor Rank, 1989; Adjunct Instructor, 1974-84; Adjunct Assistant Professor, 1998-2000; Numerous solo exhibitions; Juried exhibitions: Over 100 national, regional, state and area shows; Cleaned and restored art collections: Seven public and numerous private collections; Advisory Board, Clark County Joint Vocational Commercial Art Program. Publications: Work featured in American Artist Renown, 1981; Catalogues and magazines. Honours: Teacher Excellence Award, Clark State community College, 1992; Over 50 art awards at exhibitions including 3 Best of Shows; 2 commissioned portraits, Continental Hall, Washington DC; Commissioned by Ohio 4H Foundation to paint portrait of the founder of the 4H movement, "A B Graham and granddaughter", 1976; Medal, SFLD, Ohio Bicentennial Celebration, 1976. Memberships include: Pastel Society of America; Allied Artists of America; Ohio Plein Aire Society; Ohio Watercolor Society; Portrait Society of America. Commissions and Creative Works: Work in public and private collections in Massachusetts, New Mexico, New York, Ohio and others, Athens, Greece, Jerusalem and Jaffa, Israel; Commissioned portraits and landscapes.

BROOKE Christopher Nugent Lawrence, b. 23 June 1927, United Kingdom. Historian. m. Rosalind Beckford Clark, 3 sons, 1 deceased. Education: BA, MA, DLitt, Gonville and Caius College, Cambridge. Appointments: National Service, 1948-50; Fellow, Gonville and Caius College, 1949-56 and 1977-, Assistant Lecturer in History, 1953-54, Lecturer in History, 1965-56; Dixie Professor of Ecclesiastical History, 1977-94, University of Cambridge; Professor of Medieval History, University of Liverpool, 1956-67; Professor of History, Westfield College London, 1967-77. Publications: Books include: From Alfred to Henry III, 1961; The Saxon and Norman Kings, 1963, 3rd edition, 2001; Europe in the Central Middle Ages, 1964, 3rd edition, 2000; The Monastic World 1000-1300 (with Wim Swaan), 1974, 2nd edition as The Age of the Cloister, 2003, 3rd edition as The Rise and Fall of the Medieval Monastery, 2006; A History of Gonville and Caius College, 1985; Oxford and Cambridge (with Roger Highfield and Wim Swaan), 1988; The Medieval Idea of Marriage, 1989; A History of the University of Cambridge IV, 1870-1990, 1993; Jane Austen, Illusion and Reality, 1999; A History of Emmanuel College, Cambridge (with S Bendall and P Collinson), 1999; Churches and Churchmen in Medieval Europe, 1999; The Monastic Constitutions of Lanfranc (with D Knowles), 2002. Honours include: FSA, 1964; FBA, 1970; FRHistS; Fellow, Società di Studi Francescani (Assisi); Honorary DUniv York. Memberships include: Royal Commission on Historical Monuments, 1977-84; President, Society of Antiquaries, 1981-84; Vice-President, Cumberland and Westmorland Antiquarian and Archaeological Society, 1985-89; Northamptonshire Record Society, 1987-; CBE, 1995. Address: Gonville and Caius College, Cambridge CB2 1TA, England.

BROOKE Rosalind Beckford, b. 5 November 1925, United Kingdom. Historian. m. Christopher N L Brooke, 3 sons. Education: BA, 1946, MA, PhD, 1950, Girton College, Cambridge. Appointments: Temporary Senior History Mistress, Mitcham County Grammar School for Girls, 1949-50; Regular Supervisor of Cambridge undergraduates for the History Tripos for various colleges, 1951-56; Part-time History Mistress, Birkenhead High School, 1958-59; Lecturer, Palaeography, 1963, Tutorial Teacher, part-time, 1964-66, University of Liverpool; Lecturer, part-time, Medieval History, 1968-73; Honorary Research Fellow, 1973-77, University College, London; Regular Supervisor of Cambridge Undergraduates for History Tripos and Theology Tripos for various colleges, 1977-94; Approved course of lectures for the History Faculty, Cambridge University, 1978-81. Publications: Books: Early Franciscan Government: From Elias to Bonaventure, 1959, reprinted 2004; The Writings of Leo, Rufino and Angelo, Companions of St Francis (editor and translator), 1970, reprinted 1990; The Coming of the Friars, 1975; Popular

Religion in the Middle Ages (with CNL Brooke), 1985; The Image of St Francis: Responses to Sainthood in the 13th Century, 2006; Contributions to learned journals and The Oxford Dictionary of National Biography, 2004. Honours: Exhibitioner, Girton College, Cambridge, 1943; Bryce-Tebb Scholarship, 1946-48; Old Girtonian's Studentship, 1948-49; Pennsylvania State International Fellowship (Paris and Normandy), International Federation of University Women, 1950-51; FRHistS, 1959; Fellow, Società Internazionale di Studi Francescani (Assisi), 1972; FSA, 1989. Memberships: Honorary Member, Lucy Cavendish College, 1977; Senior Member, Clare Hall, 1985. Address: The Old Vicarage, Ulpha, Broughton in Furness, Cumbria LA20 6DU, England.

BROOKING Barry Alfred, b. 2 February 1944. Chief Executive. Divorced. Education: Teacher's Certificate, University of Wales, 1962-65; Chartered Teacher's Certificate, College of Preceptors, 1970; BA, History and Education, Open University, 1974-76; Advanced Television Production Certificate, University of London, 1976; MA, Manpower Studies, University of London, 1978-80; Business Management Certificate, University of Westminster, 1981. Appointments: Commissioned Officer, retiring as Lieutenant Commander, 1965-81; Business Management Administrator, Medical Protection Society, 1981-92; Regional Director, St John Ambulance, 1992-95; Chief Executive, Parkinson's Disease Society of the United Kingdom, 1995-99; First Chief Executive, British Psychological Society, 2000-04. Honours: MBE. Memberships: Chartered Institute of Management; Royal Television Society; Chartered Institute of Personnel and Development. Address: 9 Hawkmoor Parke, Bovey Tracey, Devon TQ13 9NL, England.

BROOKNER Anita, b. 16 July 1928, London, England. Novelist; Art Historian. Education: BA, King's College, London; PhD, Courtauld Institute of Art, London. Appointments: Visiting Lecturer in Art History, University of Reading, 1959-64; Lecturer, 1964-77, Reader in Art History, 1977-88, Courtauld Institute of Art; Slade Professor of Art, Cambridge University, 1967-68. Publications: Fiction: A Start in Life, 1981; Providence, 1982; Look at Me, 1983; Hotel du Lac, 1984; Family and Friends, 1985; A Misalliance, 1986; A Friend from England, 1987; Latecomers, 1988; Lewis Percy, 1989; Brief Lives, 1990; A Closed Eye, 1991; Fraud, 1992; A Family Romance, 1993; A Private View, 1994; Incidents in the Rue Laugier, 1995; Visitors, 1998; Undue Influence, 1999; The Bay of Angels, 2000; The Next Big Thing, 2002; The Rules of Engagement, 2003; Leaving Home, 2005. Non-Fiction: An Iconography of Cecil Rhodes, 1956; J A Dominique Ingres, 1965; Watteau, 1968; The Genius of the Future: Studies in French Art Criticism, 1971; Greuze: The Rise and Fall of an Eighteenth-Century Phenomenon, 1972; Jacques-Louis David, a Personal Interpretation: Lecture on Aspects of Art, 1974; Jacques-Louis David, 1980, revised edition, 1987. Editor: The Stories of Edith Wharton, 2 volumes, 1988, 1989. Contributions to: Books and periodicals. Honours: Fellow, Royal Society of Literature, 1983; Booker McConnell Prize, National Book League, 1984; Commander of the Order of the British Empire, 1990. Address: 68 Elm Park Gardens, London SW10 9PB, England.

BROOKS James, b. 11 October 1938, West Cornforth, County Durham, UK. Consultant; Academic. m. Jan, 1 son, 1 daughter. Education: BTech(Hons), Applied Chemistry, 1964; MPhil, Analysis of wool wax and related products, 1966; PhD, chemical constituents of various plant spore walls, 1970; Fellow, Geological Society (FGS), 1974; Fellow, Royal Society of Chemistry, FRSC, 1976; Chartered Chemist

(CChem), 1976; DSc, research work in chemistry, geology, petroleum sciences and the origin of life, 2001; Chartered Geologist (CGeol), 2001; Chartered Scientist (CSci), 2004. Appointments: Research Geochemist, BP Research Centre, British Petroleum, 1969-75; Senior Research Fellow, University of Bradford, 1975-77; Visiting Scientist, Norwegian Continental Shelf Institute, 1975-78; Research Associate, Exploration Co-ordinator, Senior Scientist, Section Head of Production Geology, British National Oil Corporation/Britoil, 1977-86; Visiting Lecturer, University of Glasgow, 1978-99; Technical Director, Sutherland Oil and Gas Investments, 1996-98; Brooks Associates, 1986-; Chairman/Director, Petroleum Geology '86 Ltd, 1986-99; Executive Member, Scottish Baptist College, 2001-; Myron Spurgeon Visiting Professor in Geological Sciences, Ohio University, Athens, Ohio, USA, 2003; Collaborative research, teaching, professional and conference activities at numerous universities and research institutes throughout the USA, Canada, Europe, Russia, Australia and parts of Asia. Publications include: 15 books as author and editor and over 90 scientific research papers published in peer-refereed journals including: Chemical Structure of the Exine of Pollen Walls and a new function for carotenoids in nature, 1968; Chemistry and Morphology of Precambrian Microorganisms, 1973; Origin and Development of Living Systems, 1973; A Critical Assessment of the Origin of Life, 1978; Biological Relationships of Test Structure and Models for calcification and test formation in the Globigerinacea, 1979; The Chemistry of Fossils: biochemical stratigraphy of fossil plants, 1980; Organic Matter in Meteorites and Precambrian Rocks - clues about the origin of life, 1981; Origin of Life: from the first moments of the universe to the beginning of life on earth, 1985; Tectonic Controls on Oil & Gas occurrences in the Northern North Sea, 1989; Classic Petroleum Source Rocks, 1990; Cosmochemistry and Human Significance, 1999. Honours include: UK Government Exchange Scientist to USSR, 1971; Royal Society Visiting Scientist to India, 1977 and to USSR, 1991; Vice-President, Geological Society, 1984-89; Geological Society Christmas Lecture on Origin of Life, 1983; Golden Medallion and Order of Merit for book Origin of Life, 1985; Secretary, Geological Society, 1988-92; Life Member, American Association of Petroleum Geologists, 1993-; Distinguished Achievement Award, AAPG, 1993; Distinguished Service Award, The Geological Society, 1999; President of the Baptist Union of Scotland, 2002; First holder of Myron Sturgeon Visiting Professor in Geological Sciences, Ohio University, 2003; Man of Achievement, American Biographical Institute, 2005; Honorary Member, AAPG, 2006. Memberships: International IPU Committee, 1972-81; NERC Higher Degrees Research Committee, 1981-84; UK Consultative Committee on Geological Sciences, 1987-92; External Examiner, University of London, 1992-97; Series Editor, Geological Special Publications, 1989-93; International Editorial Board of Marine and Petroleum Geology, 1984-96; Council of Geological Society, 1984-92; Chairman, Shawlands Academy School Board, 1991-96; Board of Ministry of the Baptist Union of Scotland, 1998-; Member, Greater Glasgow NHS Board Research Ethics Committee; Chairman, SCORE - Scotland. Address: 10 Langside Drive, Newlands, Glasgow, G43 2EE, UK. E-mail: dr.jim.brooks@googlemail.com

BROOKS Mel (Melvin Kaminsky), b. 28 June 1926, New York, USA. Actor; Writer; Producer; Director. m. (1) Florence Baum, 2 sons, 1 daughter, (2) Anne Bancroft, 1964, deceased 2005, 1 son. Appointments: Script writer, TV Series, Your Show of Shows, 1951-54, Caesar's Hour, 1954-57, Get Smart, 1965; Founder, Feature Film Production Company, Brooksfilms. Creative Works: Films include: The Critic (cartoon), 1963; The

Producers, 1968; The Twelve Chairs, 1970; Blazing Saddles, 1974; Young Frankenstein, 1974; Silent Movie, 1976; High Anxiety, 1977; The Elephant Man (producer), 1980; History of the World Part I, 1981; My Favorite Year (producer), 1982; To Be or Not to Be (actor, producer), 1983; Fly I, 1986; Spaceballs, 1987; 84 Charing Cross Road, 1987; Fly II, 1989; Life Stinks (actor, director, producer), 1991; Robin Hood: Men in Tights, 1993; Dracula: Dead and Loving It, 1995; Svitati, 1999; It's A Very Merry Muppet Christmas Movie (voice), 2002; Jakers! The Adventures of Piggley Winks (TV series), 2003; Robots (voice), 2005; The Producers (voice), 2005. Musical: The Producers: The New Mel Brooks Musical (producer, co-writer, composer), 2001. Honours: Academy Awards, 1964, 1968; Emmy Awards for Outstanding Guest Actor in a Comedy Series, 1997, 1998, 1999; Tony Awards for Best Book, Best Score, Best Musical, 2001; Evening Standard Award for Best Musical, 2004; Critics Circle Theatre Award for Best Musical, 2005. Address: c/o The Culver Studios, 9336 West Washington Boulevard, Culver City, CA 90232, USA.

BROOKS (Troyal) Garth, b. 7 February 1962, Tulsa, Oklahoma, USA. Country Music Singer; Songwriter; Musician (guitar). m. (1) Sandra Mahl, 1986, 2 daughters, divorced, (2) Trisha Yearwood, 2005. Education: BS, Journalism and Advertising, Oklahoma State University, 1985. Career: Television specials include: This Is Garth Brooks, 1992; This Is Garth Brooks Too!, 1994; Garth Brooks - The Hits, 1995; Garth Brooks Live in Central Park, 1997; Best selling country album ever, No Fences (over 13 million copies). Recordings: Albums: Garth Brooks, 1989; No Fences, 1990; Ropin' The Wind, 1991; The Chase, 1992; Beyond The Season, 1992; In Pieces, 1993; The Hits, 1994; Fresh Horses, 1995; Sevens, 1997; In The Life Of Chris Gaines, 1999; The Colors Of Christmas, 1999; Scarcrow, 2001; Singles: If Tomorrow Never Comes, 1989; Tour EP, 1994; To Make You Feel My Love, 1998; One Heart At A Time, 1998; Lost In You, 1999; Call Me Claus, 2001; The Thunder Rolls; We Shall Be Free; Somewhere Other Than The Night; Learning to Live Again; TV Specials: This is Garth Brooks, 1992; This is Garth Brooks Too, 1994; Garth Brooks: The Hits, 1995; Garth Brooks Live in Central Park, 1997. Honours: Academy of Country Music Entertainer of the Year, 1991-94; Male Vocalist of the Year Award, 1991; Horizon Award, 1991; Country Music Association Entertainer of the Year Award, 1991, 1992; Academy of Country Music Album of the Year, 1991; CMA Award for Best Album, 1991; Academy of Country Music Song of Year, 1991; CMA Award for Best Single, 1991; Academy Country Music Single Record of the Year, 1991; American Music Country Song of the Year, 1991; Grammy Award for Best Male Country Vocalist, 1992; Best Male Country Music Performer, 1992, 1993; Best Male Musical Performer, People's Choice Awards, 1992-95; Country Music Award for Artist of the Decade, 1999; American Music Award for Favorite Country Artist, 2000; Special Award of Merit, 2002. Memberships: Inducted into Grand Ole Opry; ASCAP; CMA; ACM. Address: c/o Scott Stern, GB Management Inc, 1111 17th Avenue South, Nashville, TN 37212, USA.

BROSNAN Pierce, b. 16 May 1953, Navan, County Meath, Ireland. Actor. m. (1) Cassandra Harris, deceased, 1 son, 1 adopted son, 1 adopted daughter, (2) Keely Shaye Smith, 2001, 2 sons. Education: Drama Centre. Creative Works: Stage appearances include: Wait Until Dark; The Red Devil; Sign; Filumenia. TV: The Manions of America, 1981; Nancy Astor, 1982; Remington Steele, 1982-87; Noble House, 1988; Around the World in 80 Days, 1989; Murder 101, Victim of Love, 1991; Running Wilde, 1992; Death Train, The Broken Chain, 1993; Don't Talk to Strangers, 1994; Night Watch,

1995; Films: Resting Rough, 1979; The Carparthian Eagle, The Long Good Friday, 1980; Nomads, 1986; The Fourth Protocol, 1987; Taffin, The Deceivers, 1988; Mister Johnson, 1990; The Lawnmower Man, Live Wire, 1992; Mrs Doubtfire, Entangled, 1993; Goldeneye Love Affair, 1994; Mars Attacks!, The Mirror Has Two Faces, 1996; Dante's Peak, Robinson Crusoe, Tomorrow Never Dies 1997; The Nephew, 1998; The Thomas Crown Affair, The Match, Grey Owl, The World is Not Enough 1999; The Tailor of Panama, 2001; Die Another Day, Evelyn, 2002; Everything or Nothing, Laws of Attraction, After the Sunset, 2004; The Matador, 2005; Seraphim Falls, 2006; Butterfly on a Wheel, Married Life, 2007; Mamma Mia, 2008. Honours: Honorary OBE, 2003. Address: c/o Guttman Associates, 118 South Beverly Drive, Suite 201, Beverly Hills, CA 90212, USA.

BROUGHTON Peter, b. 8 September 1944, Keighley, Yorkshire, England. Civil Engineer. m. Jan, 2 sons. Education: BSc, Hons, Civil Engineering, 1963-66, PhD, Structural Engineering, 1966-70, Manchester University; FREng; FICE; FIStructE; FRINA; FIMarEST. Appointments: Research Student, Research Assistant, Department of Civil Engineering, University of Manchester, 1966-71; Structural Engineering Surveyor, Lloyds Register of Shipping, London, 1971-74; Partner, Subsidiary Practice, Campbell Reith and Partner, 1974-75; Structural Engineer, Burmah Oil Trading Ltd, 1975-77; Supervising Structural Engineer, British National Oil Corporation, 1977-79; Senior Structural Engineer, 1979-82, Civil Engineering Supervisor, 1982-86, Project Manager, 1990-94, Project Manager, 1998-2003, Phillips Petroleum UK Ltd; Project Engineer, 1986-90, Project Manager, 1994-98, Phillips Petroleum Company Norway; Visiting Professor, Department of Civil Engineering, Imperial College, University of London, 1991-2005; Royal Academy of Engineering Visiting Professor, Department of Engineering Science, University of Oxford, 2004-07; Consultant, Peter Fraenkel and Partners Ltd, 2003-. Publications include: Book: The Analysis of Cable and Catenary Structures, 1994; Numerous articles in journals including: The Ekofisk Protective Barrier, 1992; Cast Steel Nodes for the Ekofisk 2/4J Jacket, 1997; The Effects of Subsidence on the Steel Jacket and Piled Foundations Design for the Ekofisk 2/4X and 2/4J Platforms, 1996; Foundation Design for the Refloat of the Maureen Steel Gravity Platform, 2002; The Refloat of the Maureen Steel Gravity Platform, 2002; Deconstruction and Partial Re-Use of the Maureen Steel Gravity Platform and Loading Column, 2004. Honours include: Stanley Grey Award, The Institute of Marine Engineers, 1992; The George Stephenson Medal, 1993; Bill Curtin Medal, 1997; Overseas Premium, 1998; David Hislop Award, 1999, Certificate for Contribution to Institution Activity, 2002, The Institution of Civil Engineers; Phillips Petroleum Presidential Shield Award, 2002. Address: Peter Frankel & Partners Ltd, 21-37 South Street, Dorking, Surrey RH4 2JZ, England.

BROWN The Rt Hon (James) Gordon, b. 20 February 1951, Glasgow, Scotland. Prime Minister of the United Kingdom; Labour Party Leader; Member of Parliament. m. Sarah, 2000, 2 sons, 1 daughter (deceased). Education: MA, History (First Class honours), 1972, PhD, Edinburgh University. Appointments: Rector, Edinburgh University, 1972-75; Lecturer, Glasgow College of Technology, 1976-1980; Journalist and Producer for Scottish Television, 1980-1983; Member of Parliament, Dunfermline East, 1983-2005; Chairman, Scottish Labour Party, 1983-1984; Opposition Chief Secretary to the Treasury, 1987-89; Shadow Secretary of State for Trade and Industry, 1989-92; Shadow Chancellor of the Exchequer, 1992-97; Appointed to Labour's

National Executive Committee, 1992-; Chancellor of the Exchequer, 1997-2007; Member of Parliament, Kirkcaldy and Cowdenbeath, 2005-; Labour Party leader and Prime Minister of the United Kingdom, 2007-. Publications: Values, Visions and Voices; Co-author, The Real Divide; Moving Britain Forward. Address: 10 Downing Street, London, SW1A 2AA, England.

BROWN Olivia Parker, b. 29 January 1934, Maryland, USA. Teacher. m. Leonard L Brown, 1 son, 1 daughter. Education: Bachelor of Science, State Teachers' College, 1955; Master of Education, University of Maryland, 1962. Appointments: In Service Workshop Trainee; Special Drama and Speech Classes; Interim Building Supervisor; Curriculum Specialist; Use of Media (TV); Mentoring; Tutoring; Demonstration Lessons; English Department Head. Honours: Listed in Who's Who publications and biographical dictionaries. Memberships: AA County, Maryland Teachers Association; PC County, Maryland Teachers Association; United Federation of Teachers; Maryland State Teachers Association; Lutheran Church. Address: 4411 19th St NE, Washington, DC20019, USA.

BROWN Paul Ray Beck, b. 20 July 1944, Uxbridge, Middlesex, England. Journalist. m. Maureen McMillan, 1 daughter. Education: Churchers College, Petersfield, Hampshire. Appointments: Indentured Reporter: East Grinstead Courier, 1963-65, Lincolnshire Standard, 1965-66, Leicester Mercury, 1966-68, Birmingham Post, 1968-74; Post-Echo, Hemel Hempstead, 1974-81, News Editor, 1980-81; The Sun, 1981-82; The Guardian, 1982-2005, Environment Correspondent, 1989-2005; Teacher of Journalism, Guardian Foundation, 1998-; Freelance Journalist and Writer. Publications: The Last Wilderness, 80 Days in Antarctica, 1991; Greenpeace History, 1993; Global Warming, Can Civilisation Survive? 1996; Anita Roddick and the Body Shop, 1996; Energy and Resources, 1998; Just the Facts, Pollution, 2002; North South East West, 2005; Global Warming, Last Chance for Change, 2006, US edition 2007. Honours: Midlands Journalist of the Year, 1974; New York Library Prize, Best Childrens Book of the Year, 1994; Press Fellow, Wolfson College, Cambridge, 2007. Memberships: Fellow, Geologists Association; Fellow, Royal Geographical Society; Fellow and Member, Advisory Council, Royal Society of Arts, Manufacture and Commerce. E-mail: paulbrown5@mac.com

BROWN William Arthur, b. 22 April 1945, Oxford, England. University Professor. m. Kim Brown, 2 step daughters. Education: BA, Wadham College, Oxford. Appointments: Director, SSRC Industrial Relations Research Unit, University of Warwick, 1980-85; Montague Burton Professor of Industrial Relations, University of Cambridge, 1985-; Master of Darwin College, Cambridge, 2000-. Publications: Piecework Bargaining, 1973; The Changing Contours of British Industrial Relations, 1981; The Individualisation of Employment Contracts in Great Britain, 1998. Honour: CBE. Memberships: Low Pay Commission, 1997-; ACAS Council, 1998-2004. Address: Darwin College, Silver Street, Cambridge CB3 9EU, England.

BROWNE Rt Hon Des (Desmond Henry), b. 22 March 1952, Kilwinning, North Ayrshire, Scotland. m. Maura Taylor, 2 sons. Scottish Labour Party Politician; Member of Parliament for Kilmarnock and Loudoun; Secretary of State for Defence; Secretary of State for Scotland. Education: St Michael's Academy, Kilwinning; Law degree, University of Glasgow. Appointments: Apprentice Solicitor, James

Campbell & Co, 1974-76; Assistant Solicitor, 1976-80, Solicitor, 1980-85, Ross, Harper and Murphy; Partner, McCluskey Browne, 1985; Council Member, Law Society of Scotland, 1988-92; Elected to Faculty of Advocates, 1993; Practised at Scottish bar until 1997; Member of Parliament for Kilmarnock and Loudoun, 1997-; Parliamentary Private Secretary to the late Donald Dewar MP and Adam Ingram MP, 1998-2001; Parliamentary Under Secretary of State, Northern Ireland Office, 2001-03; Minister of State for Work at the Department for Work and Pensions, 2003-04; Minister with Responsibility for Immigration, Home Office, 2004-05; Chief Secretary to the Treasury, 2005-06; Member of Privy Council, 2005-; Secretary of State for Defence, 2006-; Secretary of State for Scotland, 2007-.

BROWNE Jackson, b. 9 October 1948, Heidelberg, Germany. Singer; Songwriter; Musician (guitar, piano). Career: Brief spell with Nitty Gritty Dirt Band, 1966; Solo singer, songwriter, musician, 1967-; Tours and concerts with Joni Mitchell; The Eagles; Bruce Springsteen; Neil Young; Major concerts include: Musicians United For Safe Energy (MUSE), Madison Square Garden (instigated by Browne and Bonnie Raitt), 1979; Glastonbury Festival, 1982; Montreux Jazz Festival, 1982; US Festival, 1982; Benefit concerts for: Amnesty International, Chile, 1990; Christie Institute, Los Angeles, 1990; Victims of Hurricane Inki, Hawaii, 1992; Various concerts for other environmental causes; Nelson Mandela Tributes, Wembley Stadium, 1988, 1990; Sang with Bonnie Raitt and Stevie Wonder, memorial service for Stevie Ray Vaughan, Dallas, Texas, 1990; Compositions: Songs recorded by Tom Rush; Nico; Linda Ronstadt; The Eagles; Co-writer with Glenn Frey, Take It Easy. Recordings: Albums: Jackson Browne, 1972; For Everyman, 1973; Late For The Sky, 1974; The Pretender, 1976; Running On Empty, 1978; Hold Out (Number 1, US), 1980; Lawyers In Love, 1983; Lives In The Balance, 1987; World In Motion, 1989; I'm Alive, 1993; Looking East, 1996; The Naked Ride Home, 2002; Sol Acoustic, Vol 1, 2005; Also featured on No Nukes album, 1980; Sun City, Artists United Against Apartheid, 1985; For Our Children, Disney AIDS benefit album, 1991; The Next Voice You Hear: The Best of Jackson Browne, 1997; Singles include: Doctor My Eyes, 1972; Here Come Those Tears Again, 1977; Running On Empty, 1978; Stay, 1978; That Girl Could Sing, 1980; Somebody's Baby, used in film Fast Times At Ridgemont High, 1982; Tender Is The Night, 1983; You're A Friend Of Mine, with Clarence Clemons, 1986; For America, 1987; World in Motion, 1989; Chasing You Into The Light, 1989; Anything Can Happen, 1989; I'm Alive, 1993; The Night Inside Me, 2002. Current Management: Donald Miller, 12746 Kling Street, Studio City, CA 91604, USA.

BROWNE Jimmie, b. 3 January 1953, Galway, Ireland. Engineer. m. Maeve, 4 sons. Education: BE, 1974, M Eng Sc, 1978, National University of Ireland, Galway, Ireland; PhD, 1988, DSc, 1990, University of Manchester. Appointments: Engineer, Nortel Networks, 1974-76; Research Assistant, National University of Ireland, Galway, 1976-78; Research Associate, UMIST, Manchester, England, 1978-80; Senior Lecturer, 1980-89, Professor, 1990-, Dean of Engineering, 1995-2000, Registrar and Deputy President, 2001-, National University of Ireland, Galway. Publications: 5 books as co-author include: Queuing Theory in Manufacturing Systems Analysis and Design, 1993; Production Management Systems - An Integrated Perspective, 2nd edition, 1997; IT and Manufacturing Partnerships - Delivering the Promise, 1998; CAD/CAM Principles, Practice and Manufacturing Management, 2nd edition, 1998; Strategic Decision Making in Modern Manufacturing, 2004; 8 edited and co-edited books; Numerous articles in peer reviewed academic journals. Honours: Fellow, Institution of Engineers in Ireland; Fellow, Irish Academy of Engineering; Member, Royal Irish Academy. Memberships: Institution of Engineers of Ireland, Royal Irish Academy. Address: 17 College Road, Galway, Ireland. E-mail: jimmie.browne@niugalway.ie

BROWNJOHN J(ohn Nevil) Maxwell, b. Rickmansworth, Hertfordshire, England. Literary Translator; Screenwriter. Education: MA, Lincoln College, Oxford. Publications: Night of the Generals, 1962; Memories of Teilhard de Chardin, Klemperer Recollections, 1964; Brothers in Arms, Goya, 1965; Rodin, The Interpreter, 1967; Alexander the Great, 1968; The Poisoned Stream, 1969; The Human Animal, 1971; Hero in the Tower, 1972; Strength Through Joy, Madam Kitty, 1973; A Time for Truth, The Boat, 1974; A Direct Flight to Allah, 1975; The Manipulation Game, 1976; The Hittites, 1977; Willy Brandt Memoirs, 1978; Canaris, Life with the Enemy, 1979; A German Love Story, 1980; Richard Wagner, The Middle Kingdom, 1983; Solo Run, 1984; Momo, The Last Spring in Paris, 1985; Invisible Walls, Mirror in the Mirror, 1986; The Battle of Wagram, Assassin, 1987; Daddy, The Marquis of Bolibar, 1989; Eunuchs for Heaven, Little Apple, Jaguar, 1990; Siberian Transfer, The Swedish Cavalier, Infanta, 1992; The Survivor, Acts, Love Letters From Cell 92, 1994; Turlupin, Nostradamus, 1995; The Karnau Tapes, 1997; Heroes Like Us, 1998; The Photographer's Wife, Carl Haffner's Love of the Draw, 1999; Birds of Passage, Eduard's Homecoming, The 13 ½ Lives of Captain Bluebear, 2000; The Stone Flood, Libidissi, Where do We Go From Here?, The Alexandria Semaphore, 2001; Headhunters, 2002; Berlin Blues, 2003; The Russian Passenger, Rumo, 2004; The City of Dreaming Books, Mimus, 2005; Ice Moon, Please, Mr Einstein, 2006; Screen Credits: Tess (with Roman Polanski), 1979; The Boat, 1981; Pirates, The Name of the Rose, 1986; The Bear, 1989; Bitter Moon (with Roman Polanski), 1992; The Ninth Gate (with Roman Polanski), 2000. Honours: Schlegel Tieck Special Award, 1979; US Pen Prize, 1981; Schlegel Tieck Prize, 1993, 1999; US Christopher Award, 1995; Helen and Kurt Wolff Award, US, 1998. Memberships: Translators Association; Society of Authors. Address: Bookend House, Hound Street, Sherborne, Dorset DT9 3AA, England.

BROWNLOW Bertrand (John), b. 13 January 1929, Nazeing, Essex, England. Aviation Consultant. m. Kathleen Shannon, 2 sons, 1 deceased, 1 daughter. Education: Beaufort Lodge School; Royal Air Force. Appointments: Group Captain, Defence and Air Attache, Sweden, 1969-71; Group Captain, Commanding Officer, Experimental Flying, RAF Farnborough, 1971-73; Air Commodore, Assistant Commandant, RAF College Cranwell, 1973-74; Air Commodore, Director of Flying (Research and Development), Ministry of Defence Procurement Executive, 1974-77; Air Commodore, Commandant, Aeroplane and Armament Experimental Establishment, 1977-80; Air Vice-Marshal, Commandant, RAF College Cranwell, 1980-82; Air Vice-Marshal, Director General, RAF Training, 1982-84; Director, Airport and Flight Operations, Marshall Aerospace, -1994; Non-Executive Director, Civil Aviation Authority Board, 1994-97; Aviation Consultant, 1994-. Publications: Articles in professional magazines and publications. Honours: Air Force Cross, 1961; OBE, 1966; CB, 1982; Royal Aero Club Silver Medal, 1983; Clark Trophy for Contribution to Air Safety, Popular Flying Association, 1996; Freeman of the City of London, 1997; Liveryman, The Guild of Air Pilots and Air Navigators, 1997; Sword of Honour, The Guild of Air Pilots and Air Navigators, 2000. Memberships: Fellow, Royal

Aeronautical Society; Empire Test Pilots' School Association; Liveryman, The Guild of Air Pilots and Air Navigators; Popular Flying Association; General Aviation Confidential Incident Reporting Programme Advisory Board; CAA, General Aviation Safety Review Working Group; Governor, Papworth Foundation Hospital Trust. Address: Woodside, Abbotsley Road, Croxton, St Neots, Cambridgeshire PE19 6SZ, England. E-mail: jbrownav@compuserve.com

BROWNLOW Kevin, b. 2 June 1938, Crowborough, Sussex, England. Author; Film Director; Film Historian. Publications: The Parade's Gone By, 1968; How It Happened Here, 1968, 2005; Adventures with D W Griffith, (editor), 1973; Hollywood: The Pioneers, 1979; The War, the West, and the Wilderness, 1979; Napoleon: Abel Gance's Classic Film, 1983, 2004; Behind the Mask of Innocence, 1990; David Lean - A Biography, 1996; Mary Pickford Rediscovered, 1999; The Search for Charlie Chaplin, 2005. Address: c/o Photoplay, 21 Princess Road, London NW1 8JR, England.

BRUDENELL Edmund Crispin Stephen James George, b. 24 October 1928, London, England. Landowner. m. Marian Manningham-Buller, 2 sons, 1 daughter. Education: Royal Agricultural College, Cirencester. Appointments: Conservative, contested Whitehaven, 1964; High Sheriff of Leicestershire, 1969; Deputy Lieutenant of Northamptonshire, 1977; High Sheriff of Northamptonshire, 1987. Membership: Liveryman Worshipful Company of Fishmongers. Address: Deene Park, Corby, Northamptonshire, England.

BRUDNER Harvey Jerome, b. 29 May 1931, Brooklyn, New York, USA. Scientist. m. Helen Gross, 2 sons, 1 daughter. Education: BS, 1952, MS, 1954, Engineering Physics, PhD, Physics, 1959, New York University. Appointments: Dean, Science and Technology, New York Institute of Technology, 1962-64; President, Westinghouse Learning Corporation, New York City, 1971-76; President, Joyce Kilmer Centennial Commission, New Brunswick, New Jersey, 1985-2008. Publications: Fermat and the Missing Numbers, 1994; How the Babylonians Solved Numbered Triangle Problems 3,600 Years Ago, 1998; How two even numbers can be used to produce three Pythagorean Numbers, 2005. Honours: Knight, Order of the Swan, 1996; Director, Raritan-Millstone Heritage Alliance Inc, 2006-08; Friends and Sponsors in the Guide Book. Memberships: The US House of Representatives; Commission of Science and Technology, 1977; Westinghouse SURE, Pittsburgh, 2004-08. Address: 812 Abbott Street, Highland Park, New Jersey, USA. E-mail: hjbe@aol.com

BRUDNER Helen G, b. New York City, USA. Professor. 2 sons, 1 daughter. Education: BS, 1959, MA, 1960, NYU; PhD, Fairleigh Dickinson University, 1973. Appointments: Teacher, NYC Board of Education, 1959-60; Instructor, Pratt Institute, Brooklyn, 1959-61; Assistant Professor, History, 1961-63, Director of Guidance, 1962-63, NY Institute of Technology, New York City; Associate Professor, Fairleigh Dickinson University, Rutherford, New Jersey, 1963-73; Vice President, HJB Enterprises, Highland Park, NJ, 1970-; Consultant, Auto Educational Systems, 1971-; Professor, History, Political Science, Teaneck, New Jersey, 1974-; Director, 1972-84, Chairman, Department of Social Science, 1980-88, President, University Senate, 1975-78, Assistant Provost, 1983-, Dean, 1984, Director of Graduate Programs, Associate Director, School of History, Politics and International Studies, 1995-, Director, Language Graduate Studies, President, Academy Senate, 1996-, Honors College, Rutherford, New Jersey; Vice Chairman, Board of Directors, WLC Inc, Highland Park, 1990-; Treasurer, Casitas De

Monte Corp, California, 2005; Vice Chairman, 2000-04, Treasurer, 2005, Casitas De Monte Associates, Palm Springs, California; Participant, Board of Trustees, FDU; Speaker, NJ Committee on Humanities. Publications: Numerous articles in professional journals. Honours: Woman of the Year Award; American Businesswomen's Association, 1980; Meritorious Service Award, NJ Credit Union League, 1997; Certificate of Special Congressional Recognition, 2000; NJ Division, Military and Veterans Affairs Award, 2004. Memberships: American Judicature Society; American Historical Society; Academy of Political Science; Phi Alpha Theta; Phi Sigma Alpha. E-mail: hhmts@att.net

BRUNDA Daniel Donald, b. 22 October 1930, Lansford, Pennsylvania, USA. Mechanical Engineer; Aerospace Engineer; Electromagnetics Scientist; Electromagnetic Powerline Radiation Engineer and Founder; Inventor; Author. Education: BSME, Lehigh University, 1952; MSME, 1953; Postgraduate, Johns Hopkins University, 1955, Princeton University, 1958-65, Drexel University, 1983. Appointments: Aerodynamicist, Bell Aircraft; Performance Engineer, Glenn L Martin, Baltimore; Aerospace Engineer, US Naval Air Propulsion Centre, Ewing, New Jersey, 1957-72; Local Manager, Independent Research and Development (IRAD), 1972-83; Consultant, Electromagnetic Radiation Engineer, Ewing, New Jersey, 1978-. Publications: Over 20 articles to professional journals; 1 patent; Powerline Radiation, Your Genes, copyrighted report, 2001, book published (by Xlibris) 2004; Control System for Adjusting the Amount of Low Frequency Electromagnetic Radiation of Power Transmission Lines, copyrighted report, 2001; The Design of Safe Electric Transmission and Distribution Lines, copyrighted book, 2001, published (by Xlibris), 2003. Honours: Lifetime Deputy Governor American Biographical Institute; Lifetime Deputy Director General in the Americas, International Biographical Centre; Member of Order of International Fellowship, 2001; Included in International Order of Merit, 2002; Certificate of Commendation for Services Rendered Since 1978, Mayor of Ewing Township, 2001; Work exhibited in IBA Gallery of Excellence, 2001; Scientific Faculty Member of the IBC, 2002; IBC On-Line Hall of Fame, 2002, (http://www.internationalbiographicalcentre.com); Scientific Advisor to the Director General, IBC, 2002; 2000 Outstanding Scientists of the 21st Century; The Lifetime of Achievement 100; IBC Ambassador of Goodwill and 1000 Greats, 2003; Living Science; Living Legends; Great Minds of the 21st Century, ABI, 2003; One Thousand Great Americans, 2003; Hall of Fame and Inner Circle, IBC, 2004; Order of Distinction, IBC, 2004; Da Vinci Diamond Award, IBC, 2004; Greatest Living Legends, IBC, 2004; Genius Elite in Engineering and Science, 2004; Einsteinian Chair of Science, World Academy of Letters, ABI, 2004; Top 100 Scientists of 2005, IBC, 2005; First Five Hundred, IBC, 2005; Expert in Electromagnetic Radiation Engineering, ABI, 2005; 21st Century Genius Medal, 2005; 500 Greatest Geniuses of the 21st Century, 2006; Genius Laureate, 2006; Man of Science, ABI, 2006; Archimedes Award, Global Year of Science Medal, IBC, 2006; President's Citation in Electromagnetic Radiation Science, ABI, 2007; World Record for Achievement in Electromagnetics, Radiation, Engineering and Science, ABI, 2007; Pinnacle of Achievement Award, IBC, 2007; Lifetime Achievement Award, IBC, 2008; Dedication, Great Minds of the 21st Century, 2007/08; ABI Medal for Distinguished Service Order and Cross, 2008. Memberships: Associate Fellow, Bioelectromagnetic Society; Life Member, ASME; Senior Member, AIAA; Ambassador of Grand Eminence, ABI, 2002; Founding Cabinet Member, World Peace and Diplomacy Forum, IBC, 2003; ABI President's Citation,

Electromagnetic Radiation Science, 17 August 2007; IBC Pinnacle of Achievement Award in Electromagnetic Radiation Engineering, 26 November 2007. Address: 106 West Upper Ferry Road, Ewing, NJ 08628, USA.

BRUNDIGE Kezzia Sue, b. 17 July 1956, Peru, Indiana, USA. Nursing Supervisor. Education: Emergency Medical Technician Diploma, 1981; Certificate in Homicide Investigation, 1982; Liberal Arts Degree, 1989; Nursing Associates Degree, 1989; Hospital/Freestanding Ambulatory Care Standards and Survey Process Certified, 1998. Appointments: Nurse Supervisor of Nephrology, Hypertension and Renal Transplant, Faculty for Advanced Clinical Training in Chronic Kidney Disease, 11 years; JCAHO Liaison on Henry Ford Hospital Safety Committee and CMS Regional Committee, Henry Ford Hospital Service Excellence Star Award, 2003. Publication: CKD – Advanced Clinical Training in: Constructing a Kidney Disease Clinic. Honours: Cum Laude Nursing Graduate Honours; Listed in Who's Who publications and biographical dictionaries. Memberships: American Nephrology Nurses' Association; Institute for Healthcare Improvements; International Transplant Nurse Society; Detroit Medical Center Emergency Sky Team; Nurse Supervisor Committee. Address: Henry Ford Hospital, Division of Nephrology, 2799 W Grand Blvd, Detroit, Michigan, USA. E-mail: kbrundi1@hfhs.org

BRUNO Franklin Roy (Frank), b. 16 November 1961, London, England. Boxer. m. Laura Frances Mooney, 1990, divorced, 2001, 1 son, 2 daughters. Education: Oak Hall School, Sussex. Appointments: Began boxing with Wandsworth Boys' Club, London, 1970; Member, Sir Philip Game Amateur Boxing Club, 1977-80; Won 20 out of 21 contests as amateur; Professional Career, 1982-96; Won 38 out of 42 contests as professional, 1982-89; European Heavyweight Champion, 1985-86 (relinquished title); World heavyweight title challenges against Tim Witherspoon, 1986, Mike Tyson, 1989; Staged comeback, won 1st contest, 1991; Lost 4th World Title Challenge against Lennox Lewis, 1993; World Heavyweight Boxing Champion, 1995-96, lost title to Mike Tyson, 1996; Appearances in Pantomimes, 1990, 1991, 1996, 1997, 1999; Former presenter, BBC TV. Publication: Personality: From Zero to Hero (with Norman Giller), 1996. Honours: SOS Sports Personality of the Year, 1990; TV Times Sports Personality of the Year, 1990; Lifetime Achievement Award, BBC Sports Personality of the Year Awards, 1996. Address: c/o PO Box 2266, Brentwood, Essex CM15 0AQ, England.

BRUSLOV Andrey Yurievich, b. 2 July 1954, Moscow, Russia. Reservoir Engineer. m. Irina, 1 daughter. Education: Diploma, Reservoir Engineer, 1976; PhD Diploma, Reservoir Engineering, 1986. Appointments: Scientist, Moscow Gubkin Oil & Gas Institute, 1977-88; Senior, Lead Scientist, Krylov All Russian Scientific Research Oil & Gas Institute, 1989-93; Chief Engineer, AGIO Oil & Gas Corp, 1994-97; Director, Business Development, ROSDI Corp, 1997-98; Co-ordinator, Sakhalin Energy Investment Co Ltd, 1998-2006; Advisor, Shell Exploration and Production Services RF (BV), 2006-. Publications: Over 50 articles and patents in the area of enhanced oil recovery methods, well stimulation, lettering group discussions, diversity & inclusiveness and business interaction, including original theory, approach and training on business focussed interactions. Honours: Honorable Diploma of SPE; Listed in international biographical dictionaries. Memberships: Society of Petroleum Engineers; American

Society for Training and Development. Address: Flat 187, Leninski prospekt, 45, Moscow 119334, Russia. Address: hibfi@gagarino.com

BRUTIAN Lilit, b. 7 August 1953, Yerevan, Armenia. Professor of Linguistics and English. m. Leonid Zilfugarian, 1 son, 1 daughter. Education: MA with distinction, English Language and Literature, 1970-75, PhD, Philology, 1975-80, Yerevan State University, Yerevan, Armenia; Certificate, International Summer Institute on Argumentation, University of Amsterdam, 1990; Doctor of Sciences in Philology, Institute of Linguistics, National Academy of Sciences, Yerevan, Armenia, 1984-92. Appointments: Assistant Professor, Chair of Foreign Languages, 1979-84, Associate Professor of English, Chair of English Philology and Chair of Foreign Languages, 1984-94, Professor of Linguistics and English, Chair of Linguistics, Chair of English Philology, 1994-2006, Yerevan State University; Senior Researcher, 1984-93, Principal Researcher, 1993-95, Institute of Linguistics, Head of Chair of Foreign Languages, 1994-96, National Academy of Sciences of Armenia; Visiting Professor, Institute for the Advancement of Philosophy for Children, Montclair State University, New Jersey, USA, 1994-95; Chairperson, Chair of Russian Linguistics, Typology and Theory of Communication, Yerevan State University, 2006-. Publications: 68 scientific publications, including 6 monographs include most recently: The Principles of the Theory of Implication, 2002; Teaching Place-Names as a Means of Intensification of Students' Knowledge, 2003; On David the Invincible's Linguistic Views, 2004; On the Pragmatics of Argumentative Discourse, 2005. Memberships include: International Society for the Study of Argumentation, The Netherlands; International Pragmatics Association, Belgium; Scientific Council Awarding Scientific Degrees, Yerevan State University and National Academy of Sciences of Armenia; Council, Department of Russian Philology, Yerevan State University; Scientific Council, V Brusov Yerevan State Linguistic University; Full member of the Armenian Philosophical Academy. Address: The 9th Street of Aigestan, 69, Apt 61, Yerevan 375025, Armenia. E-mail: lilit.brutian@gmail.com

BRUTUS Dennis, b. 28 November 1924, Salisbury, Rhodesia. Educationist; Poet; Writer. m. May Jaggers, 14 May 1950, 4 sons, 4 daughters. Education: BA, University of the Witwatersrand, Johannesburg, South Africa, 1947. Appointments: Director, World Campaign for Release of South African Political Prisons; International Defence and Aid Fund, formerly UN Representative; Director, Program on African and African-American Writing in Africa and the Diaspora, 1989-; Visiting Professor at universities in Amherst, Austin, Boston, Dartmouth, Denver, Evanstown, Pittsburgh. Publications: Sirens, Knuckles, Boots, 1963; Letters to Martha and Other Poems from a South African Prison, 1968; Poems from Algiers, 1970; Thoughts Abroad, 1970; A Simple Lust: Selected Poems, 1973; China Poems, 1975; Stubborn Hope, 1978; Strains, 1982; Salutes and Censures, 1984; Airs and Tributes, 1988; Still the Sirens, 1993; Remembering Soweto, 2004; Leafdrift, 2005; Poetry and Protest, 2006. Contributions to: Periodicals. Honours: Mbari Prize for Poetry in Africa; Freedom Writers' Award, Kenneth David Kaunda Humanism Award; Academic Excellence Award, National Council for Black Studies, 1982; UN Human Rights Day Award, 1983; Paul Robeson Award; Langston Hughes Award. Memberships: President, South African Non-Racial Olympic Committee (SAN-ROC); Chair, International Campaign Against Racism in Sport (ICARIS), Africa Network, 1984-; ARENA (Institute

for Study of Sport and Social Issues); African Literature Association; American Civil Liberties Union; Amnesty International; PEN; Union of Writers of African Peoples.

BRYDEN Alan, b. 27 August 1945, Folkestone, England. Ingenieur général du Corps des Mines. m. Laurence, 1 son, 2 daughters. Education: Ecole Polytechnique, Paris, France; Ecole des Mines, Paris; University d'Orsay, France; Diploma in Nuclear Physics. Appointments: Began working in Metrology, USA, National Bureau of Standards (now The National Institute of Standards and Technology); Chair, Laboratories Committee, ILAC (International Laboratory Accreditation Co-operation); Founder, Eurolab (European Federation of Measurement, Testing and Analytical Laboratories), President, 1990-96; Director General, French National Metrology and Testing Laboratory (LNE), 1981-99; Director General, French National Standards Body (AFNOR), 1999-2002; Secretary-General, International Organisation for Standardisation (ISO), 2003-. Honours: Chevalier de la Legion d'Honneur; Ordre National du Mérite, France. Address: International Organisation for Standardization, 1, Chemin de la Voie-Creuse, Case Postale 56, CH-1211 Genève 20, Switzerland. E-mail: central@iso.org Website: www.iso.org

BRYMER Timothy, b. 7 November 1951, London, England. Lawyer. m. Helen, 1 son, 1 daughter. Education: Dulwich College, London; Commercial Pilot, College of Air Training, 1970; Private Pilot's Licence and Instrument Rating; Solicitor, College of Law, Lancaster Gate, London, 1977. Appointments: Solicitor, Barlow Lyde & Gilbert, 1977-79; Director, International Insurance Services/Airclaims Ltd, 1979-85; Senior Partner, Brymer Marland & Co, 1986-90; Head of Aviation Department, Cameron McKenna, 1990-2004; Head of Aviation Group, Clyde & Co, 2004-. Publications: Numerous articles in professional journals. Memberships: Founder Member, Lawyers' Flying Association; Member, Guild of Pilots and Air Navigators. E-mail: tim.brymer@clydeco.com

BRYSON Bill, b. 1951, Des Moines, Iowa, USA. Writer. m. 4 children. Education: Drake University. Appointments: Orderly, mental hospital in England, 1973; Journalist, The Times and The Independent newspapers; Returned to USA, 1993; Author. Publications: Penguin Dictionary of Troublesome Words (Bryson's Dictionary of Troublesome Words), 1985; The Lost Continent, 1987; The Mother Tongue: English and How It Got That Way, 1994; Made in America, 1994; Neither Here Nor There: Travels in Europe, 1995; Notes from a Small Island, 1995; A Walk in the Woods, 1998; I'm a Stranger Here Myself (aka Notes from a Big Country), 1999; In a Sunburned Country (aka Down Under), 2000; The Best American Travel Writing, 2002; African Diary, 2002; A Short History of Nearly Everything, 2003; The Life and Times of the Thunderbolt Kid, 2006. Honours: Member of Selection Panel, Book of the Month Club, 2001; Commissioner for English Heritage; Chancellor, University of Durham, 2005-; Aventis Prize, 2004; Honorary DCL, Durham, 2004. Address: The Marsh Agency, 11 Dover Street, London W1S 4LJ, England. Website: www.marsh-agency.co.uk

BRYSON James Graeme, b. 4 February 1913, Caerleon, Monmouthshire, England (now Gwent, Wales). Judge (Retired). m. Jean Glendinning, 2 sons,1 deceased, 4 daughters. Education: LLM, Liverpool University, 1935; BSc, Open University, 1984. Appointments: Solicitor, 1935-47; Commissioned Officer to Royal Artillery, 1936; War Service, 1939-45, Lieutenant Colonel, now Colonel; Commanded Artillery Regiments, 1947-55; Registrar and Deputy Judge and District Judge to High Court of Justice and Admiralty

Registrar, 1947-79; Chairman, Medical Appeal Tribunal, 1978-86; Northwest Cancer Research Fund: Trustee, 1950-80, President, 1985-2001, Life President, 2001-. Publications: Books: Contributor to Halsbury's Laws of England, 1976; Shakespeare in Lancashire and the Gunpowder Plot, 1997; A Cathedral in my Time, 2003; A Century of Liverpool Lawyers, 2003; Poetry in My Veins, 2004, Contributor to New Oxford DNB, 2006. Honours: Territorial Decoration and two bars, 1952; OBE (Military), 1955; Queen's Commendation for Bravery, 1961; Her Majesty's Vice Lord Lieutenant of the County of Merseyside, 1979-89; County Life President, Royal British Legion; Fellow, Royal Society of Arts; Knight Commander, Order of St Gregory; Knight Commander, Knights of the Holy Sepulchre. Memberships: Life Member, Royal British Legion; Past President, Athenaeum (Liverpool); Honourable Society of Knights of the Round Table; Liverpool Law Society, President, 1970; Vice-Patron, Regular Forces Employment Association. Address: 36 Hillary Court, Formby, Merseyside L37 3PS, England.

BUBKA Sergey Nazarovich, b. 4 December 1963, Voroshilovgrad, Ukraine. Athlete. m. Lilya Tioutiounik, 1983, 2 sons. Appointments: World Champion Pole Vaulter, 1983; 16 World Records from 5-85m 1984 to 6.13m 1992, including world's first 6m jump, Paris, 1985; 18 World Indoor Records, from 5.81 1984 to 6.15 1993; Holder of indoors and outdoors world records, 2002; Now represents OSC Berlin. Honours include: Olympic Gold Medal, 1988. Memberships include: Member, IOC Executive Board, IOC Evaluation Commission for 2008; IOC Athletes' Commission; IAAF Council, 2001-; National Olympic Committee Board; Chairman, EOC Athletes; Commission; President, S Bubka Sports Club; Elected to Parliament, United Union Faction, 2002- Address: c/o State Committee of Physical Culture & Sport, 42 Esplanadnaya, 252023 Kiev, Ukraine.

BUCHAN Vivian Eileen Eaton, b. 19 May 1911, Eagle Grove, Iowa, USA. Freelance Writer; Poet. m. Warren Joseph Buchan, 4 September 1933. Education: BA, English, Coe College, 1933; MA, English, University of Illinois, 1958. Appointments: Teacher in Rhetoric Programme, University of Illinois, 1957-58; University of Iowa, 1959-67; Board of Directors, 1970-76, President, 1976, Iowa City Public Library. Publications: English Compositions, manual, 1960; Bibliography: Sara Teasdale, 1967-68; Sun Signs, 1979; Make Presentations with Confidence, 1991, translated into Portuguese, Indonesian, Chinese, Japanese, Arabic. Contributions to: Approximately 900 articles, essays, columns, poems in over 80 national and international publications. Honours: 2nd Place, Lyrical Iowa, 1964; 2nd Place, 1981, 3rd Place, 1987, 1st Place, 1995, 1996, editor: Iowa Poetry Association, 1970-84; International Woman of the Year, 1982-83; Merit Award, Coe College, 1983; Iowa City High School Hall of Fame, 1983; Friend of Education, Iowa City School Board, 1984; 4th Place, 1989, 2nd Place, 1989, 2 Grand Prizes, 1991, World of Poetry; President's Award for Highest Achievement in Liberal Arts Education, Coe College, 1992-93; Women's Inner Circle of Achievement, 1995; International Woman of the Year, 1995-96; Most Admired Woman of the Century, 1995-96; Most Admired Woman of the Decade, 1995-96; 20th Century Award of Achievement in Literature, Poetry and Art, 1997; Eaton-Buchan Art Gallery, Coe College, dedicated 1998; 1st place, Iowa Poetry Contest Sonnet Division (I Am the Wind), 2005; Listed in national and international biographical dictionaries. Address: 2423 Walden Road, #225, Iowa City, IA 52246-4104, USA.

BUCHANAN Colin Ogilvie, b. 9 August 1934, Croydon, Surrey, England. Church of England Clerk in Holy Orders. Education: BA, 1959, MA, 1962, Lincoln College, Oxford; Tyndale Hall, Bristol, 1959-61; DD, 1993. Appointments: Assistant Curate, Cheadle, Cheshire, 1961-64; Member of Staff, 1964-85, Principal, 1979-85, London College of Divinity (since 1970, St John's College, Nottingham); Bishop of Aston, Diocese of Birmingham, 1985-89; Assistant Bishop of Rochester, 1989-96; Bishop of Woolwich, Diocese of Southwark, 1996-2004; Retired, 2004; Honorary Assistant Bishop, Diocese of Bradford, 2004-. Publications: Modern Anglican Liturgies, 1958-68, 1968; Further Anglican Liturgies, 1968-75, 1975; Editor, News of Liturgy Monthly, 1975-2003; Latest Anglican Liturgies, 1976-84, 1985; Modern Anglican Ordination Rites, 1987; The Bishop in Liturgy, 1988; Joint Author: Growing into Union, 1970; Anglican Worship Today, 1980; Reforming Infant Baptism, 1990; Sole Author: Open to Others, 1992; Infant Baptism and the Gospel, 1993; Cut the Connection: Disestablishment and the Church of England, 1994; Is the Church of England Biblical? 1998; Consultant Editor: Common Worship Today, 2001; Consultant Editor, Oxford Guide to the Book of Common Prayer, 2006; Editor, Savoy Conference Revisited, 2002; Author, Historical Dictionary of Anglicanism, 2006; Taking the Long View: Three and a half decades of General Synod, 2006. Membership: Church of England Liturgical Commission, 1964-86; House of Clergy of General Synod of C/E, 1970-85; C/E Doctrine Commission, 1986-91; House of Bishops of General Synod of the Church of England, 1990-2004; Church of England General Synod Council for Christian Unity, 1991-2001; Vice President, President, 2005-, Electoral Reform Society. Address: c/o Bradford Diocesan Office, Kadugli House, Elmsley Street, Steeton, Keighley, BD20 6SE, England. E-mail: colinbuchanan101@btinternet.com

BUCHANAN Pat(rick Joseph), b. 2 November 1938, Washington, District of Columbia, USA. American Government Official; Journalist. m. Shelley Ann Scarney, 8 May 1971. Education: AB, English, cum laude, Georgetown University, 1961; MS, Journalism, Columbia University, 1962. Appointments: Editorial Writer, 1962-64, Assistant Editorial Editor, 1964-66, St Louis Globe Democrat; Executive Assistant to Richard M Nixon, 1966-69; Special Assistant to President Richard M Nixon, 1969-73; Consultant to Presidents Richard M Nixon and Gerald R Ford, 1973-74; Syndicated Columnist, 1975-; Various radio and television broadcasts as commentator, panellist, moderator, etc, 1978-; Assistant to President Ronald Reagan and Director of Communications, White House, Washington DC, 1985-87; Candidate for the Republican Party Nomination for President of the US, 1992, 1996; Chairman, The American Cause, 1993-95, 1997-; Chairman, Pat Buchanan & Co, Mutual Broadcasting System, 1993-95. Publications: The New Majority, 1973; Conservative Votes, Liberal Victories, 1975; Right from the Beginning, 1988; Barry Goldwater, The Conscience of A Conservative, 1990; The Great Betrayal, 1998; A Republic, Not an Empire, 2000; The Death of the West, 2002; Where the Right Went Wrong, 2004; State of Emergency: The Third World Invasion and Conquest of America, 2006. Contributions to: Newspapers and periodicals. Honour: Knight of Malta, 1987. Memberships: Republican Party; Roman Catholic Church. Address: 1017 Savile Lane, McLean, VA 22101, USA.

BUCK Karen, b. 30 August 1958. Member of Parliament. Partner: Barrie Taylor, 1 son. Education: BSc, MSc, MA, London School of Economics. Appointments: Charity specialising in employment for disabled people; London Borough of Hackney; Policy Officer specialising in health,

Labour Party Head Office; Labour Party's Campaigns Unit, 1992-97; Elected, Labour Member of Parliament for Regent's Park and Kensington North; Select Committee on Social Security, 1997-2001; Work and Pensions Select Committee, 2001-; Parliamentary Under Secretary of State, Department of Transport. Memberships: Chair, London Group of Labour MPs; Member, Mayor of London's Affordable Housing Commission; Board Member, Constituency SRB projects. Address: House of Commons, London SW1A 0AA, England. E-mail: k.buck@rpkn-labour.co.uk

BUCKINGHAMSHIRE Earl of, Sir (George) Miles Hobart-Hampden, b 15 December 1944, Madras, India. m. (1) Susan Jennifer Adams, dissolved, (2) Alison Wightman Wishart (nee Forrest), 2 stepsons. Education: Clifton College, Bristol, 1958-63; BA, Honours, History, Exeter University, 1963-67; MA, Area Studies, History and Politics of the Commonwealth, Birkbeck College, London University, 1967-68. Appointments: Noble Lowndes & Partners Ltd, latterly Director of Scottish Pension Trustees, 1970-81; Director, HSBC Gibbs, 1981-86; Wardley Investment Services International (subsidiary of HSBC), 1986-91, Marketing Director and Managing Director, 1988-91; The Wyatt Company, 1991-95; Partner, Watson Wyatt LLP, Watson Wyatt Worldwide, 1996-2004; BESTrustees Plc, 2004-, Director, 2005; Sat in House of Lords, 1984-99; Member All Party Groups on Occupational Pensions and on ageing issues; Member of Select Committee of EC sub-committees on Social and Consumer Affairs, 1985-90, on Finance, Trade and External Relations, 1990-92; Honorary Trustee, Illinois Wesleyan University, USA, 1991-; President, Old Cliftonian Society, 2000-2003 and Governor of Clifton College, 1994-; Member of Council, 2000- Buckinghamshire Chilterns University College; Director, Avnet Corporate Trustee Ltd, 2006. Memberships: Affiliated Member, Institute of Actuaries, 2001-; Director, Hatfield Real Tennis Club, 2001-06; Freeman, Cities of Glasgow and Geneva (Upper New York State USA); Director, 2004-, Deputy Chairman, 2006-, Britain-Australia Society; Chairman, The Cook Society, 2007; Patron: Sleep Apnoea Trust, Hobart Town (1804) Early Settlers Association (Tasmania), John Hampden Society; President, Friends of the Vale of Aylesbury; President, Downend Police and Community Amateur Boxing Club; Patron, Chilterns MS Centre, 2006. Address: The Old Rectory, Church Lane, Edgcott, Aylesbury, Bucks HP18 0TU, England.

BUCKLEY Richard Anthony, b. 16 April 1947, Leicester, England. Legal Scholar. m. Alison Jones, 1 daughter. Education: BA (Oxford), Jurisprudence, 1968, Doctor of Philosophy, 1973, Merton College, Oxford; Doctor of Civil Law, Oxford, 2006. Appointments: Lecturer in Law, King's College, London, 1970-75; Fellow and Tutor in Law, Mansfield College, Oxford, 1975-93; Professor of Law, University of Reading, 1993-. Publications: The Law of Nuisance, 1st edition, 1981, 2nd edition, 1996; The Modern Law of Negligence, 1st edition, 1988, 3rd edition, 1999; Illegality and Public Policy, 2002; The Law of Negligence, 2005; Articles in legal periodicals. Honours: Leverhulme Research Fellow, 2001. Address: School of Law, Foxhill House, University of Reading, Whiteknights Road, Reading RG6 7BA, England.

BUCKMAN James Cecil, b. 4 August 1923, Croydon, Surrey, England. Teacher. m. Peggy Taylor. Education: Stanley Technical School, 1936-39; City & Guilds Technical Electricity Grade 1, Borough Polytechnic, 1941; City & Guilds Telephony, Wimbledon Technical College, 1942; Course by correspondence with Wolsey Hall, Oxford, Royal Navy, 1945-46; Forces' Preliminary Exam, in lieu of London

Matriculation, 1946; BSc, Geography and Geology, Bristol University, 1950; PGCE, School of Education, 1951; MSc, by research, 1973. Appointments: Workshop experience, Ellis Optical Company, 1939-40; Apprenticed as Youth in Training, Post Office Telecommunications, 1940-42; Unestablished Skilled Workman, 1942-43; Rating, Air Branch of the Royal Navy, 1943-46; Recommended three months accelerated advancement to Air Mechanic Electrics First Class, served on Staff of Admiral (Air), 1945-46; In Education: Supply teaching, Surrey, 1952; Appointed by Air Service Training Ltd of Hamble as member of Team to set up the Pakistan Air Force Pre Cadet College at Sargodha in the Punjab, Head of Department, Housemaster, Deputy Headmaster, 1952-59; Housemaster and Head of Department, Aitchison College, Lahore, 1959-63; Master on Supply, Hampton School, 1963; Assistant Master, Brighton, Hove & Sussex Grammar School, 1963-69; Head of Geography, De la Salle College, Hove, 1969-71; Bristol Cathedral School part-time 6th Form, (while on Sabbatical at University completing MSc thesis), 1971-72; Head of Geography, Alleyn's School, Dulwich 1972-83; Retired, 1983; Part time teaching at Shoreham College, Hurstpierpoint College and on Supply in West Sussex, 1983-93. Publications: Article in Geography, Resources of Natural Gas in East Pakistan (now Bangladesh), 1968; Book, The Steyning Line and Its Closure, 2002. Honours: 12+ examination for entry to Stanley Technical School, 1936; 1st Class Award for Swimming; Royal Society of Arts Grouped Course Certificate and First Prize in Geography, 1938. Memberships: Scouting: Started Senior Scouts section of 7th Sanderstead Group, 1943; Elected Life Fellow, Royal Geographical Society, 1955; Bristol University Convocation and as an elected Representative on University Court – completed 3 four-year terms; University of Bristol Boat Club Alumni; currently Royal British Legion; Independent, Schools Committee, 1973-83 and Chairman, Inner London Branch, 1975-78 of Assistant Masters' Association (now Association of Teachers & Lecturers, ATL); Affiliated, Charted Institute of Transport (now Logistics and Transport), 1975; Probus; Steyning Society, Sussex Wildlife Trust; Steyning Parish Councillor, 1987-89; Life Member, Cyclists Touring Club; Life Member, Youth Hostels Association; Sometime Parochial Church Council of Steyning & Deanery Synod. Address: 38 King's Stone Avenue, Steyning, West Sussex BN44 3FJ, England.

BUCUR Constantin I, b. 19 March 1923, Gura Vaii, Racova, Bacau, Romania. m. Brigitte Iorgovan, 1 son. Education: Ferdinand Boarding College, Bacau; D A Sturza Military College for Officers, Craiova, Romania; Cavalry College for Officers, Targoviste, Romania; MSc with Distinction, ANEF Bucharest, 1947-51; PhD, Université Libre de Bruxelles, Belgium, 1968; Dr honoris causa, University of Craiova, 1998. Appointments: Higher Education Inspector, Bucharest, 1951-53; Assistant Lecturer, Part-time, IEFS, Bucharest, 1951-53; Lecturer, 1953, Consultant, 1962, Professor, 1984, Traian Vuia Polytechnic and University of Timisoara-Romania; Organiser, Principal Researcher, Physical Education Research Centre, 1953-84; Director, Sportforschung Zentrum, Mannheim, Germany, 1986-. Publications: 71 books and 400 booklets about sport research; Created own system in sport; Organised 70 conferences in field. Honours: Wounded, WWII, awarded medals for bravery, Retired General. Membership: Full Member, Professor Emeritus, American Romanian Academy of Arts and Sciences; Academia Românã, Filiala Timişoara. Address: Brandenburger Str 30, D-68309, Mannheim, Germany.

BUCUR Romulus Vasile, b. 19 March 1928, Padova, Italy. Chemistry Researcher (Retired). m. Doina Rodica Motiu, 1 daughter. Education: Graduate, Chemistry, University of Cluj, Romania, 1955; PhD, Electrochemistry, University of Bucharest, Romania, 1970. Appointments: Head Laboratory, Solvay Plant, Ocna Mures, Romania, 1955-56; Scientific Researcher, Institute of Atomic Physics, Cluj, Romania, 1956-58; Principal Scientific Researcher, 1958-87, Head Laboratory, 1974-87, Institute of Isotopic and Molecular Technology, Cluj, Romania; Scientific Researcher, Inorganic Chemistry, Uppsala University, Sweden, 1988-93; Scientific Research Associate, Materials Chemistry Department, Ångström Laboratory, Uppsala University, Sweden, 1993-98. Publications: About 120 scientific papers in the field of analysis and separation of heavy water, solid state electrochemistry (metallic hydrides and sulphides), materials for hydrogen storage, and piezoelectric quartz crystal microbalance. Membership: Honorary Member, The International Association for Hydrogen Energy, USA, 1983-. Address: Näktergalsv 5, SE-35242 Växjö, Sweden. E-mail: romulus.bucur@telia.com

BUDAEV Vladimir Michailovich, b. 25 October 1955, Moscow, Russia. Architect. 1 son, 1 daughter. Education: Diploma in Architecture, Moscow Architectural Institute, 1984. Appointments: Head of the Project and Chief-Architect, Park Pobedy (Park of Victory Over Fascism in the Second World War) with the Memorial, Poklonnaya Gora, Moscow, 1985-98; Chief Architect, Central Museum of the Great Patriotic War, 1941-45, Central Obelisk (150m high), Park Pokedy, Moscow, 1993-95; Chief Architect, Church of Georgiy Pobedonosetz (Church of Saint Georg, the first church built in Russia since 1917), 1993-95; Chief Architect, Synagogue-Memorial, with Museum of Holocaust in Park Pobedy, Moscow, 1996-98; Architect-constructor, Monument of Tsar Peter the Great, Moskva River, 1997; Architect-constructor, Zoo, Moscow, 1997; Architect of several multi-storey municipal buildings, 1998-2001; Head of Architectural and Artistic Planning Institute, Moscow, 1993-2001; Chief Architect, Central Scientific Kucherenko's Institute of Building Constructions, Moscow, 2003-. Publications: Several conceptual publications in professional journals. Honours: Winner, International Contest for the best project for Trinity Cathedral, Moscow, commemorating the Millennium of Christening of Russia, 1990; Medal of Holy Sergiy Radonezsky, from Russian Orthodox Church, 1995; Certificate of Honour from President of Russia, 1995; Honoured Architect of Russia, 1996; Medal and Diploma, IBC, 1999; Synagogue-Memorial with Museum of Holocaust in Park Pobedy, Moscow, qualified as one of the best in the world by the JOINT (International Jewish Congress); Listed in numerous international directories of biography. Membership: Union of Architects of Russia; Corresponding Member of International Academy of Investment and Economy of Building, 2000. Address: Petrovka 26-28, 103051 Moscow, Russia.

BUDENHOLZER Frank Edward, b. 21 August 1945. Catholic Priest; Educator; Chemist. Education: BA, Divine Word College, Epworth, Iowa, 1967; BS, DePaul University, Chicago, Illinois, 1969; MA, Catholic Theological Union, Chicago, Illinois, 1974; PhD, University of Illinois, Chicago, 1977. Appointments: Teaching Assistant, University of Illinois, Chicago, 1972-76; Chinese Language Training, Hsinchu, Taiwan, 1978-80; Associate Professor, Chemistry, Fu Jen University, 1978-83; Professor, Chemistry, 1983-; Director, Graduate Institute of Chemistry, 1980-84; Dean, College of Science and Engineering, 1984-90; Vice-President, 1990-97; Visiting Scholar, Center for Theolology and the Natural Sciences; 1997-98; Visiting Scholar, University of California, 1997-98; Member, Board of Trustees, Fu Jen University, 1999-; Resident Trustee, Fu Jen University, 2001-, Academic Co-ordinator, Centre for the Study of Religion and Science, 2002-; Publications: Religion and Science in Taiwan: Rethinking the Connection; Some Comments on the Problem of Reductionism; Classical Trajectory Study of the HFCO-HF+CO Reaction. Memberships: American Chemical Society; American Physical Society; Chinese Chemical Society; Chinese Physical Society; Institute for Religion in an Age of Science; Hastings Centre; Institute for Theoretical Encounter with Science and Technology. Address: Department of Chemistry, Fu Jen Catholic University, Hsinchuang 242, Taiwan. E-mail: 001898@mail.fju.edu.tw

BUDHOORAM Steve Ravindra, b. 24 July 1952, Trinidad & Tobago. Medical Doctor; Vascular Surgeon. m. Vashtie, 1 son. Education: Naparima College, 1964-70; MBBS, University of West Indies, 1977; Diploma, Fellow of Royal College of Surgeons (Edinburgh), 1983; Fellow, American College of Surgeons, 2001; Fellow, Caribbean College of Surgeons. Appointments: Consultant Surgeon and Medical Chief of Staff, San Grande Hospital; Consultant Vascular Surgeon, Chief of Surgery, San Fernando General Hospital; Chairman, South Branch, Trinidad/Tobago Medical Association; President, Society of Surgeons of Trinidad and Tobago; Associate Lecturer in Surgery, University of West Indies. Publications: Five year review of Aortic Aneurysms at San Fernando General Hospital; Primary repair of Acute Colonic injuries without colonoscopies; Cost effectiveness of anterior-venous shunts using native vessels; How to set up a vascular unit. Honours: Wall of Fame at Grant's Memorial School – primary education; Honoured by Naparima College for Achievements in Medicine. Memberships: Fellow, International College of Angiology; Member, American Association of Colon and Rectal Surgeons. Address: 30 Alexander Road, San Fernando, Trinidad & Tobago. E-mail: stevebud@tstt.net.tt

BUHR Juergen, b. 3 March 1943, Buetzow, Germany. Physician. m. Marion, 1 son, 1 daughter. Education: Physician, University of Rostock, 1968; Intern, 1969-73; Specialist training in Diabetology, 1973-76. Appointments: Director, Poliklinik Buetzow, 1984-90; External Research, Medical Academy, Dresden, 1984-90; Private Internist, Specialist for Diabetology, Buetzow, 1991-; Leader, Commission of Diabetes Organisation of Physicians, Mecklenburg. Publications: 25 articles in medical periodicals on physiology and diabetology. Memberships: German Diabetological Organisation. Address: Am Ausfall 43, D-18246, Buetzow, Germany. E-mail: dr.buhr1@freenet.de

BUJAUSKAS Algimantas V, b. 24 December 1932, Lithuania. Biologist. m. Janina Ivanauskaite, 6 March 1965, 1 son. Education: Diploma, Vilnius University, 1963; Dr.H, 1988; Professor, 1994. Appointments: Former Professor, Chief Scientific Worker, Lithuanian Institute of Agriculture. Publications: Several articles in professional journals; Memoirs, 1998; 4 books of poetry, 1998, 1999, 2000; Monograph: Potato Breeding for Resistance to Potato Cyst Nematode and Meristemic Seed Production, 2000; Selected Works: Aurora Borealis, Memoirs and Poetry of a Deportee, 2002. Honour: National Award, 1996. Memberships: Catholic Academy of Sciences, Lithuania. Address: Traku Voke, Tishkevich 13-3, LT-02231 Vilnius, Lithuania.

BUKHARAEV Rais Gatich, b. 24 April 1929, Tomsk, Siberia, Russia. Mathematician. m. Naira Khalitova, 2 sons. Education: Diploma with distinction, Faculty of Mathematics and Physics, Kazan State University, 1952; Candidate, Mathematical and Physical Sciences, 1956; Probationer, Computer Centre, Moscow State University, 1957; Doctor of Technical Sciences, 1968; Doctor of Mathematical and Physical Sciences, 1981; Academician. Academy of Non-Linear Sciences of Russia, 1995. Appointments: Assistant Professor, Chair of General Mathematics, 1955-57, Junior Research Worker, Mathematical Analysis Laboratory, 1957-60, Senior Lecturer, Computational Mathematics Chair, 1960, Head of the Section of Computation Theory, Mathematical Research Institute, 1960-70; Head of the Theoretical Cybernetics Chair, 1971-98, Full Professor, 1972, Kazan State University. Publications: About 130 published scientific works, including 9 monographs and 12 author's certificates; Main monographs and certificates: Foundations of probabilistic automata, 1985; Theorie der Stochstischen Automaten, 1995; Additional Device for Computers, 1967; The device for random process modelling (with co-author), 1985; The generator of random numbers (with co-authors), 1985. Honours include: Medal for Valiant Labour during the Great Patriotic War, 1949; Kazan University Prize for monograph: Probabilistic automata, 1977; Honoured Scientist of the Tatar Republic, 1979; Medal, Veteran of Labour, 1984; Breastplate, Honoured Worker of High Professional Education in the Russian Federation, 1999; Honoured Professor of Kazan State University, 2004; Medal "In Memory of the 1000th Anniversary of Kazan", 2005. Memberships include: Chairman, Tatar Republic Committee on Automation and Computation, 1972-88; Chairman, Council on Computer Science, Kazan Branch of the Russian Academy of Sciences, 1976-88; Editorial Board, Acta Cybernetica international scientific journal, 1989-95; AMS. Address: Kazan State University, Kremlevskaja Str 18, 420008 Kazan, Russia. E-mail: rais.bukharaev@ksu.ru

BULL Deborah Clare, b. 22 March 1963, Derby, England. Ballerina; Writer; Broadcaster; Artistic Director. Education: Royal Ballet School. Career: Dancer, 1981-, Principal Dancer, 1992-2001, Royal Ballet; Appearances with Royal Ballet include leading roles in La Bayadère, Swan Lake, The Sleeping Beauty, Don Quixote, Steptext; Appeared in Harrogate International Festival, 1993, 1995; An Evening of British Ballet, Sintra Festival, Portugal, 1994, 1995; Diamonds of World Ballet Gala, Kremlin Palace, Moscow, 1996; Rite of Spring, Teatro dell'Opera, Rome, 2001-02; Teacher of Nutrition, Royal Ballet School, 1996-99; Director, Clore Studio Upstairs, Royal Opera House, 1999-2001; Creative Director, ROH2, Royal Opera House, 2002-; Regular contributor to BBC Radio 4 including Breaking the Law, 2001; Law in Order, 2002; A Dance Through Time, 2002; TV: Writer and Presenter, Dance Ballerina Dance, 1998; Writer and Presenter, Travels with my Tutu, 2000; Coppelia, Royal Ballet (live broadcast); Rambert Dance Company, Sadler's Wells (live broadcast); Writer and Presenter, The Dancer's Body, 2002. Memberships: Dance Panel, Arts Council, 1996-98; Arts Council, 1998-; Governor, South Bank Centre, 1997-2003; BBC, 2003-; Columnist, The Telegraph, 1999-2002; Patron, National Osteoporosis Society; Patron, Foundation for Community Dance. Honours: Dr hc (Derby), 1998, (Sheffield), 2001; Prix de Lausanne, 1980; Dancer of the Year, Sunday Express and The Independent on Sunday, 1996; Overall Prize, Dancescreen Monaco, 2002. Publications: The Vitality Plan, 1998; Dancing Away, 1998; The Faber Guide to Classical Ballets (with Luke Jennings), 2004; numerous articles and reviews in newspapers and dance magazines. Address: Royal Opera House, Covent Garden, London WC2E 9DD, England. Website: www.deborahbull.com

BULL Sir George, b. 16 July 1936, London, England. Retired. m. J Fleur Therese, 4 sons, 1 daughter. Education: Ampleforth College, York. Appointments: Military Service with Coldstream Guards; Worked in advertising industry; Joined Wines & Spirits Trade, 1957; Joined International Distillers and Vintners (IDV), 1961; Chairman, Wines & Spirits Association of Great Britain, 1974-75; Deputy Managing Director, 1982, Chief Executive, 1984, Chairman, 1987, IDV Ltd; Appointed to the Board, Grand Metropolitan plc, 1985; Chairman and Chief Executive, GrandMet's Food Sector, 1992; Group Chief Executive, 1993, Chair, 1995-97, Grand Metropolitan plc; Joint Chair, Diageo plc, 1997, 1998; Retired, 1998; Chair, J Sainsbury plc, 1998-2004; Non-Executive Director, BNP Paribas UK Holdings Ltd, 2000-04; Non-Executive Director, The Maersk Company Ltd, 2001-2006; Member, Advisory Board of Marakon Associates, 2002-2006. Honours: Marketing Hall of Fame Award, 1998; Publicity Club of London Cup, 1999; Elected Grand Master of the Keeper of the Quaich, 1994-95, Patron, 1998; Vice President, Honorary Fellow, Chartered Institute of Marketing; Honorary Fellow, Marketing Society; Vice President, Marketing Council; President, Advertising Association, 1996-2000; Chevalier de l'Ordre National de la Legion d'Honneur, 1994; Freedom of the City of London, 1996; Knighted, 1998; Listed in national and international biographical dictionaries. Memberships: Chair, Mencap Jubilee Appeal, 1996-98; President, Wine & Spirit Trade Benevolent Society, 2000; Chair, Ampleforth Abbey & College Bi-Centenary Appeal, 2000,The Pilgrims, The Cavalry and Guards Club, The Royal Worlington Golf Club. Address: The Old Vicarage, Arkesden, Saffron Walden, Essex CB11 4HB, England.

BULL Peter, b. 24 April 1949, Exeter, Devon, England. University Lecturer. m. Ann Rose Gore, 1 son. Education: MA, Modern History, University of Oxford, 1970; BA, 1973, PhD, 1978, Psychology, University of Exeter. Appointments: Lecturer, 1977-93, Senior Lecturer, 1993-, Psychology, University of York. Publications: Numerous articles in professional journals; 5 books. Honours: Listed in international biographical dictionaries. Memberships: Elected Fellow, British Psychological Society; European Association of Experimental Social Psychology; International Association of Language and Social Psychology; International Society for Political Psychology. Address: Department of Psychology, University of York, Heslington, York YO10 5DD, England. Website: http://drbull.nfshost.com

BULLOCK Sandra, b. 26 July 1964, USA. Actress. m. Jesse James, 2005. Education: East Carolina University. Creative Works: Off-Broadway Productions include: No Time Flat (WPA Theatre). TV Roles: The Preppy Murder (film); Lucky Chances (mini series); Working Girl (NBC series). Films include: Love Potion 9, When The Party's Over, 1992; The Thing Called Love, The Vanishing, Demolition Man, Wrestling Ernest Hemingway, 1993; Speed, 1994; While You Were Sleeping, 1995; Two If By Sea, A Time To Kill, In Love and War, 1996; Speed 2: Cruise Control, 1997; Hope Floats, Making Sandwiches, Practical Magic, The Prince of Egypt (voice), 1998; Forces of Nature, 1999; Gun Shy, 28 Days, Miss Congeniality, 2000; Murder by Numbers, Divine Secrets of the Ya-Ya Sisterhood, Two Weeks' Notice, 2002; Crash, 2004; Loverboy, Miss Congeniality 2: Armed and Fabulous, 2005; The Lake House, Infamous, 2006; Premonition, 2007. Honours: Star on Hollywood Walk of Fame, 2005. Address: CAA, 9830 Wilshire Boulevard, Beverly Hills, CA 90212, USA.

DICTIONARY OF INTERNATIONAL BIOGRAPHY

BUNTON Emma Lee, (Baby Spice), b. 21 January 1978, London, England. Vocalist. Career: Actress, including appearances in Eastenders; Member, Spice Girls; Numerous TV and radio appearances, many magazine interviews; Films: Spiceworld: The Movie, 1997; Yes You Can, 2001; Chocolate, 2005; World tour including dates in UK, Europe, India and USA; Presenter on TV and radio including Radio 1 and satellite TV show; Solo date on Breast Cancer Awareness concert; Solo career, 1999-. Recordings: Albums with The Spice Girls: Spice, 1996; Spiceworld, 1997; Forever, 2000; Solo albums: A Girl Like Me, 2001; Free Me, 2004; Singles with The Spice Girls: Wannabe, Say You'll Be There, 2 Become 1, 1996; Mama/Who Do You Think You Are, Step To Me, Spice Up Your Life, Too Much, 1997; Stop, (How Does It Feel To Be) On Top Of The World, Move Over/Generation Next, Viva Forever, Goodbye, 1998; Holler/Let Love Lead The Way, 2000; Solo singles: What I Am, 1999; What Took You So Long?, Take My Breath Away, We're Not Gonna Sleep Tonight, 2001; Free Me, Maybe, 2003; Crickets For Anamaria, 2004; Downtown, 2006; All I Need to Know, 2007. Honours: BRIT Award, Best Single, 1997; BRIT Award, Best Video, 1997; 2 Ivor Novello songwriting awards, 1997; Smash Hits Award for Best Band, 1997; 3 American Music Awards, 1998; Special BRIT Award for International Sales, 1998. Address: c/o Virgin Records Ltd, 553-79 Harrow Road, London W10 4RH, England. Website: www.emmabuntonofficial.com

BURACAS Antanas, b. 17 June 1939, Kaunas, Lithuania. Political and Financial Economist. m. Marija Regina Jovaisaite, 2 sons, 1 daughter. Education: Magister of Political Economy, 1962; Dr Political Economy, Institute of World Economy and International Relations, USSR Academy of Sciences, 1967; Dr hab in Political Economy, 1971; Centre for Central Banking Studies, Bank of England, 1992. Appointments: Senior Researcher and Head, Departments of Social Infrastructure and Mathematical Modelling, Lithuanian Academy of Sciences 1967-91; Founding Vice Director, Scientific Center, Bank of Lithuania, 1991-92; Professor of Banking and Macroeconomics, Vytauti Magnus University 1991-2005; Intellectual Paradigmatics, 2000-2005; Professor of Banking and Macroeconomics, M Romeris Law University, 2005-; Head of Banking and Investment Department, 2006-; Chairman, State Nostrificat Commission in Social Sciences, 1994-; Associate Professor and Professor of Political Economy and Banking, Kaunas Polytechnic Institute and Vilnius University, 1962-75, 1995-99; Vice-Chairman, Editing Board, Lithuan Universal Encyclopedia – (now 12/22 vol). Publications: 32 books including: Reference Dictionary of Banking and Commerce in 7 volumes, 1997-2008; Dictionary of Statistical Terms (in 5 languages), 2007; Sacred Arts in Lithuania, 1999; The Old Types of the Grand Duchy of Lithuania, 2004; Finance & Investment Information DB on Web, 2006; Editor-in-Chief, Journal Intellectual Economics, 2007-. Honours: Elected Academician, Lithuanian Academy of Sciences, 1976-; Lithuanian Independence Medal, 2000; Honorary Chairman, Lithuanian Human Rights Association, 2000; Fellow, World Innovation Foundation, 2001; Listed in international, national biographical and encyclopedic publications. Memberships: Founding President, Lithuanian Association for Protection of Human Rights, 1989-94; Co-founding Member, Lithuanian Independence Movement Sajudis, 1988-94; Deputy of its I-II Seimas and Councils; President, Lithuanian Association of History and Philosophy of Science, 1986-92; International Sociological Association, 1982-86; Member of the Board and Presidium Lithuanian Cultural Foundation, 1995-. Address: Lūkescių 15, Vilnius 2043, Lithuania 04125. E-mail: antanas.buracas@gmail.com Website: www.buracas.com

BURBIDGE Geoffrey, b. 24 September 1925. Astrophysicist. m. Margaret Peachey, 1948, 1 daughter. Education: Graduated, Physics, Bristol University, 1946; PhD, University College, London; Agassiz Fellow, Harvard University. Appointments: Research Fellow, University of Chicago, 1952-53; Research Fellow, Cavendish Laboratories, Cambridge; Carnegie Fellow, Mount Wilson and Palomar University, Caltech, 1955-57; Assistant Professor, Department of Astronomy, University of Chicago, 1957; Associate Professor, 1962-63, Professor of Physics, 1963-88, Professor Emeritus, 1988, University of California at San Diego -; Director, Kitt Peak National Observatory, Arizona, 1978-84; Scientific editor, Astrophysics Journal, 1996-2002. Publications: Quasi-Stellar Objects, with Margaret Burbidge, 1967; A Different Approach to Cosmology, with F Moyle and J Narlikar, 2000; More than 400 astrophysics papers in scientific journals. Honours: Bruce Medal, 1999; Gold Medal, Royal Astronomical Society, 2005; National Academy of Sciences Award for Scientific Reviewing, 2007. Address: Department of Physics, Center for Astrophysics and Space Sciences, University of California, San Diego, La Jolla, CA 92093, USA.

BURDA Renate Margarete, b. 14 January 1960, Munich, Germany. Biologist. Education: Abitur, 1980; Diploma, Biology, Ludwig-Maximilian University, Munich, 1993. Appointments: Science Worker, Fluid Engineering, Technology University, Munich, 1985-2000; Laboratory Worker, Medical Care of Urology, Munich, 1995, 1998, 2000; Chief Assistant, Venomous Spider Working Group, Weissenburg, 1995-; Lector, Journal, Latrodecta, 1995-; Scientist, ABiTec, Munich, 2000-; Medical Information, Smith Kline Beecham, Munich, 1996-97, 2000; Medical Customer Care Center, GlaxoSmith Kline, 2001-; Medical Client Service, Bayer Diagnostics, Munich, 1999-2000. Publications: The Role of Web-Building Spiders; New Results Supporting the Theory that Cribra Orbitalia can be caused by iron deficiency anaemia; Electrophoresis of Scorpion Venoms; Die Rolle Radnetzbauender Spinnen in der Biologischen Schädlingsbekämpfung. Honours: Many exhibitions. Memberships: Judge of Trampoline Sports; Venomous Spider Working Group. Address: Eichenstr 17, 82054 Sauerlach, Germany.

BÜRGEL (Johann) Christoph, b. 16 September 1931, Germany. Professor of Islamic Studies. m. Magdalena Kluike, deceased 7 November 1997, 2 sons. Education: PhD, 1960, Habilitation, 1968, University of Göttingen, Germany. Appointment: Professor of Islamic Studies, Head of the Institute of Islamic Studies, University of Bern, Switzerland, 1970; Retired 1995. Publications: Die Hofkorrespondenz ʿAdud ad-Daulas, 1965; Arerroes contra Galenum, 1968; Steppe im Staubkorn. Texte aus der Urdu-Dichtung Muhammad Iqbals, 1982; The Feather of Simurgh, 1988; Allmacht und Mächtigkeit, 1991; Il discorso è nave, il significato un mare, 2006; Translations: 3 epics from Nizami (d. 1209), 1980, 1991, 1997; 2 anthologies from the Diwan of Rumi, 1974, reprinted 1992, 2003, 2005; Hafiz, 1976, reprinted 1977; Tausendundeine Welt-Klassische arabische Literatur vom Koran bis zu Ibn Chaldûn, 2007; Two volumes of poetry (lyrics): Im Lichtnetz, 1983; Im Sog Deutsche Ghaselen, 2003; Some 130 contributions to books and journals and some 140 book reviews. Honours: Medal, Government of Pakistan; Rückert Prize from the Town of Schweinfurt, 1983 Literature Prize from the Town of Bern, 1993 both for his lyrics and his translations of poetry from Arabic, Persian and Urdu. Memberships: UEAI; IASTAM; Humboldt Society; Institute for Advanced Study, Princeton, 2002-. Address: Eichholzweg 28, CH 3074 Muri/BE, Switzerland. E-mail: johann.buergel@islam.unibe.ch

BURGEN Arnold Stanley Vincent, b. 20 March 1922, London, England. Scientist. m. Olga Kennard, 2 sons, 1 daughter, Education: MB, BS 1945, MD, 1949, London; Member, 1949, Fellow, Royal College of Physicians; Fellow, Royal Society, 1964. Appointments: Demonstrator, Assistant Lecturer, Middlesex Hospital Medical School, 1945-49; Professor, Physiology, McGill University, Montreal, 1949-62; Deputy Director, McGill University Medical Clinic, 1957-62; Professor, Pharmacology, Cambridge University, 1962-71; Director, National Institute for Medical Research, 1971-82; Master, Darwin College, Cambridge, 1982-89; Foreign Secretary, Royal Society, 1981-86. Honours: Honorary DSc, McGill University, Liverpool and Leeds; Honorary MD, Utrecht, Zurich; Honorary Fellow, Downing College, Darwin College, Cambridge, Wolfson College, Oxford. Knight Bachelor, 1976; Wellcome Gold Medal, 1999. Publications: Papers in journals of pharmacology and physiology. Memberships: Academia Europaea; Academy of Finland; American Association of Physicians; Foreign Member, US Academy of Sciences. Address: Keelson, 8A Hills Avenue, Cambridge, CB1 7XA, England.

BURGER Wolfgang, b. 12 September 1954, Alberweiler, Germany. Chemist. m. Susanne Digel, 2 sons. Education: Diploma Chemistry, 1974-81, PhD, 1981-84, University of Tuebingen, Germany. Appointments: Scientific Assistant, Inorganic Chemistry, University of Tuebingen, 1981-85; Scientific Co-Worker, CeramTec AG, 1985-92; Head of Oxide Materials Development Department, 1992-2005; Independent Scientific Consultant and Head of Research, Process and Product Development, OxiMaTec ® GmbH, 2005-07; Shareholder and Managing Director, OxiMaTec® GmbH, 2007-. Publications: Numerous scientific publications on Y-TZP ceramics derived by coating methods; Description of ZPTA-mat, a new zirconia and platelet reinforced ceramic material; Publications on processing technologies with respect to colloidal chemistry. Honour: Listed in biographical and Who's Who publications. Memberships: Gesellschaft Deutscher Chemiker; Verein Alter Roigel e V. Address: Muehlhaldenweg 75, D-73207 Plochingen, Germany. E-mail: burger@oximatec.de

BURGIN Richard (Weston), b. 30 June 1947, Boston, Massachusetts, USA. Writer; Professor; Editor. m. Linda K Harris, divorced 1993, 1 son. Education: BA, Brandeis University, 1968; MA, 1969, MPhil, 1981, Columbia University. Appointments: Instructor, Tufts University, 1970-74; Critic-at-Large, Boston Globe Magazine, 1973-74; Founding Editor and Director, New Arts Journal, 1976-83; Visiting Lecturer, University of California at Santa Barbara, 1981-84; Associate Professor of Humanities, Drexel University, 1984-96; Founder-Editor, Boulevard, literary journal, 1985-; Professor of Communication and English, St Louis University, 1996-. Publications: Conservations with Jorge Luis Borges, 1969; The Man with Missing Parts (novella), 1974; Conversations with Isaac Bashevis Singer, 1985; Man Without Memory (short stories), 1989; Private Fame (short stories), 1991; Fear of Blue Skies (stories), 1998; Jorge Luis Burges: Conversations (editor), 1998; Ghost Quartet (novel), 1999; The Spirit Returns (short stories), 2001; Stories and Dreamboxes, 2002; The Identity Club: New and Selected Short Stories and Songs, 2005; The Conference on Beautiful Moments (short stories), 2007. Contributions to: Many anthologies and periodicals. Honours: Pushcart Prizes, 1983, 1986, 1999, 2002, 2007; Story included in The Best American Mystery Stories, 2005; Listed as one of the Best Books of 2005, The Times Literary Supplement; 2 books listed os Notable Books of the Year, Philadephia Enquirer;

Numerous city, state and national grants; Various honorable mentions and listings. Membership: National Book Critics Circle. Address: 7507 Byron Place, #1 Clayton, MO 63165, USA. E-mail: richardburgin@netzero.com

BURKE John Frederick, (Owen Burke, Harriet Esmond, Jonathan George, Joanna Jones, Robert Miall, Sara Morris, Martin Sands), b. 8 March 1922, Rye, England. Author. m. (1) Joan Morris, 13 September 1940, 5 daughters, (2) Jean Williams, 29 June 1963, 2 sons. Appointments: Production Manager, Museum Press; Editorial Manager, Paul Hamlyn Books for Pleasure Group; European Story Editor, 20th Century Fox Productions. Publications: Swift Summer, 1949; An Illustrated History of England, 1974; Dr Caspian Trilogy, 1976-78; Musical Landscapes, 1983; Illustrated Dictionary of Music, 1988; A Travellers History of Scotland, 1990; Bareback, 1998; Death by Marzipan, 1999; We've Been Waiting for You, 2000; Stalking Widow, 2000; The Second Strain, 2002; Wrong Turnings, 2004; Hang Time, 2007. Film and TV Novelisations. Contributions to: The Bookseller; Country Life; Denmark. Honour: Atlantic Award in Literature, 1948-49. Memberships: Society of Authors; Danish Club. Address: 5 Castle Gardens, Kirkcudbright, Dumfries & Galloway DG6 4JE, Scotland.

BURKE Kathy, b. London, England. Actress. Education: Anna Scher's Theatre School, London. Creative Works: TV include: Harry Enfield and Chums; Absolutely Fabulous; Common as Muck; Mr Wroes' Virgins; Tom Jones; Gimme Gimme Gimme; Ted & Ralph; The F-Word; Dawn French's Girls Who Do Comedy, 2006. Films: Scrubbers; Nil By Mouth; Elizabeth, 1998; This Year's Love, 1999; Love, Honour and Obey, 2000; The Martins, 2001; Once Upon a Time in the Midlands, 2002; Anita and Me, 2002; Flushed Away, (voice), 2006. Theatre includes: Mr Thomas, London; Boom Bang-a-Bang, London (director). Honours: Royal TV Society Award; Best Actress, Cannes Film Festival, 1997.

BURKE Philip George, b. 18 October 1932, London, England. Physicist. m. Valerie Mona Martin, 1959, 4 daughters. Education: BSc (1st Class Honours), Physics, University College, Exeter, 1953; PhD, Theoretical Nuclear Physics, University College, London, 1956. Appointments: Postdoctoral Research Fellow, UCL, 1956-57; Lecturer, University of London Computer Unit, 1957-59; Postdoctoral Research Physicist, Lawrence Berkeley Laboratory, California, USA, 1959-62; Research Fellow, Senior Principal Scientific Officer, Theory Division, AERE Harwell, 1962-67; Head, Theory & Computational Science Division, Daresbury Laboratory, joint app with QUB, 1977-82; Professor, Mathematical Physics, 1967-98, Emeritus Professor, 1998-, Queen's University, Belfast. Publications: Over 370 publications in research journals; 7 books. Honours: DSc, honoris causa, University of Exeter, 1981; Fellow, University College, London, 1986; CBE, 1993; DSs, honoris causa, Queen's University, Belfast, 1999; Guthrie Medal and Prize, Institute of Physics, 1994; David Bates Prize, Institute of Physics, 2000. Memberships: Fellow, Royal Society; Member, Royal Irish Academy; Fellow, Institute of Physics; Fellow, American Physical Society; Member, European Physical Society; Fellow, Royal Astronomical Society. E-mail: p.burke@qub.ac.uk

BURKERT Andreas Michael, b. 12 May 1959, Gangkofen, Germany. Astronomer. m. Inge C Burkert, 1 son. Education: Diploma in Physics, University of Munich, 1986; PhD, Astrophysics, 1989. Appointments: Research Associate, University of Illinois, 1989-90; Research Associate, University of California, 1990-91; Research Associate,

Max Planck Institute for Astrophysics, 1991-94; Head, Theoretical Research Group, Max Planck Institute for Astronomy, 1995-2003; Promotion for a BAT Ib Position to a BAT Ia Position, 1996; Promotion for a BAT Ia Position to a C3 Position, 1997; Full Professor at University of Munich, 2003-. Honours: Student Fellowship from the German Government, 1984; Feodor Lynen Postdoctoral Fellowship, Humboldt Foundation; Award for the best PhD in Physics, University of Munich; Feodor Lynen Postdoctoral Fellowship, Humboldt Foundation; Ludwig Biermann Prize, German Astronomical Society; Max-Planck-Fellow, 2006. Memberships: German Astronomical Society; American Astronomical Society; German Physical Society; International Astronomical Union. Address: University Observatory Munich, Scheinerstr 1, D-81679 Munich, Germany. E-mail: burkert@usm.uni-muenchen.de

BURKETT Mary Elizabeth, b. 7 October 1924, Northumberland, England. Teacher; Museum Director. Education: BA, University of Durham. Appointments: Art Teacher, The Laurels School, Wroxall Abbey, 1949-53; Teacher of Art and Craft, Charlotte Mason College, Ambleside, 1954-62; Assistant then Director, Abbot Hall Art Gallery and Museums, Kendal, 1962-86; Director, Border TV, 1982-93; Member: North Western Area Museums and Art Gallery Services Area Council, 1975-86; Arts Council Fine Arts Committee, 1978-80; National Trust North Western Region Executive Committee, 1978-85; Judge: Scottish Museum of the Year Award, 1977-2000, English Museum of the Year Award, 1986-2000; Member, British Tourist Authority Museums Mission to USA, 1981. Publications: The Art of the Felt Maker, 1979; Kurt Schwitters (in the Lake District), 1979; William Green of Ambleside (with David Sloss), 1984; Monograph on Christopher Steele, 1987; Read's Point of View (with David Sloss), 1995; Percy Kelly, A Cumbrian Artist (with V M Rickerby), 1996; Monograph of George Senhouse of Mayport, 1997; Christopher's Steele 1733-1767 of Acre Walls, Egremont: George Romney's Teacher, 2003; The Beckoning East (with Genette Malet de Carteret), Journey Through Persia & Turkey 1962, 2006; Jenny Cowern, A Softer Landscape, monograph (with V M Rickerby), 2007. Honours: OBE, 1978; FMA, 1980; Leverhulme Fellowship for studies in Cumbrian portrait painting, 1986; Honorary MA, Lancaster University, 1997; Honorary Fellow, Cumbria Institute of the Arts, 2005; Fellowship, Cumbria Institute of the Arts, 2005. Memberships: Friends of Abbot Hall Art Gallery Committee, 2000-; Trustee: Carlisle Cathedral Appeal, 1981-86, Armitt Trust, 1982-86, Senhouse Trust, 1985-; President: Feltmakers Association, 1984-, Executive Committee Lake District Art Gallery Trust, 1993-98, Carlisle Cathedral Fabric Committee, 1993-2001, Blencathra Appeal Committee, 1993-95; President Romney Society, 1999-; President, NADFAS, North Cumbria, 2003-. Address: Isel Hall, Cockermouth, Cumbria CA13 0QG, England. E-mail: m.e.burkett@amserve.net

BURNELL-NUGENT James Michael (Admiral Sir), b. 20 November 1949, Stutton, Nr Ipswich, Suffolk, England. Royal Navy Officer. m. Mary Woods, 1970-73, 3 sons, 1 daughter. Education: MA (Hons), Mathematics, Corpus Christi College, Cambridge, 1968-71. Appointments: Royal Navy: Joined 1971; Captain HMS Olympus (submarine), 1978; Captain, HMS Conqueror (submarine), 1984-86; Captain, 1990; Captain, Second Frigate Squadron and Captain HMS Brilliant (Bosnia), 1992-93; Commodore, 1994; Captain, HMS Invincible (Gulf, Kosovo), 1997-99; Rear Admiral, 1999; Assistant Chief of Naval Staff, 1999-2001; Member, Admiralty Board, 1999-2001 and 2003-07; Commander UK Maritime Forces and ASW Striking Force (Operation

Enduring Freedom), 2001-2002; Vice Admiral, 2003-05; Second Sea Lord and Commander-in-Chief Naval Home Command, 2003-05; Commander-in-Chief-Fleet, 2005-07; Vice Admiral of the United Kingdom, 2005-07. Honours: CBE, 1999; KCB, 2004; Queen's Gold Medal; Max Horton Prize; Freeman of the City of London, 1999; Younger Brother, Trinity House, 2004. Address: c/o The Naval Secretary, Leech Building, Whale Island, Portsmouth, England.

BURNET Sir James (William Alexander), (Sir Alastair Burnet), b. 12 July 1928, Sheffield, Yorkshire, England. Journalist. m. Maureen Campbell Sinclair, 1958. Education: Worcester College, Oxford. Appointments: Sub-Editor, Leader Writer, Glasgow Herald, 1951-58; Leader Writer, 1958-62; Editor, 1965-74, The Economist; Political Editor, 1963-64; Broadcaster, 1976-91, Associate Editor, 1982-91, Independent Television News; Editor, Daily Express, 1974-76; Director, Times Newspapers Holdings Ltd, 1982-, United Racecourses Holdings Ltd, 1985-94. Publications: The Time of Our Lives (with Willie Landels), 1981; The Queen Mother, 1985. Contributions to: Television programmes. Honours: Richard Dimbleby Awards, BAFTA, 1966, 1970, 1979; Judges' Award, Royal Television Society, 1981; Knighted, 1984. Membership: Institute of Journalists, honorary vice president, 1990-. Address: 33 Westbourne Gardens, Glasgow G12 9PF, Scotland.

BURNETT Alfred David, b. 15 August 1937, Edinburgh, Scotland. University Librarian; Poet. Education: MA, Honours, English Language and Literature, University of Edinburgh, 1959; ALA, University of Strathclyde, 1964. Appointments: Library Assistant, Glasgow University Library, 1959-64; Assistant Librarian, Durham University Library, England, 1964-90. Publications: Mandala, 1967; Diversities, 1968; A Ballad Upon a Wedding, 1969; Columbaria, 1971; Shimbara, 1972; Fescennines, 1973; Thirty Snow Poems, 1973; Hero and Leander, 1975; The True Vine, 1975; He and She, 1976; The Heart's Undesign, 1977; Figures and Spaces, 1978; Jackdaw, 1980; Thais, 1981; Romans, 1983; Vines, 1984; Autolycus, 1987; Kantharos, 1989; Lesbos, 1990; Root and Flower, 1990; Mirror and Pool, translations from Chinese (with John Cayley), 1992; Nine Poets, 1993; The Island, 1994, 2nd edition, 1996; Twelve Poems, 1994; Something of Myself, 1994; Six Poems, 1995; Transfusions, translations from French, 1995; Hokusai, 1996; Marina Tsvetaeva, 1997; Chesil Beach, 1997; Akhmatova, 1998; Cinara, 2001; Evergreens, 2002; Quoins for the Chase, 2003; Twelve Women, 2004; Despatches, 2006; Editor, anthologies. Contributions to: Poetry Durham; Numerous professional and critical periodical contributions and monographs. Honours: Essay Prize, 1956, Patterson Bursary in Anglo-Saxon, 1958, University of Edinburgh; Kelso Memorial Prize, University of Strathclyde, 1964; Essay Prize, Library Association, 1966; Sevensma Prize, International Federation of Library Associations, 1971; Hawthornden Fellowships, 1988, 1992 and 2002; Panizzi Medal, British Library, 1991; Fellow, British Centre for Literary Translation, Norwich, 1994. Memberships: Poetry Book Society; Fine Press Book Association; Private Libraries Association. Address: 33 Hastings Avenue, Merry Oaks, Durham DH1 3QG, England.

BURNHAM Rt Hon Andrew Murray, b. 7 January 1970, Liverpool, England. Member of Parliament for Leigh; Secretary of State for Culture, Media and Sport. Education: St Aelred's Roman Catholic High School; MA (Hons), English, Fitzwilliam College, Cambridge. Appointments: Researcher for Tessa Jowell MP, 1994-97; Researcher, NHS Confederation, 1997; Administrator, Football Task Force,

1997-98; Special Adviser to Secretary of State for Culture, Media and Sport, 1998-2001; Member of Parliament for Leigh, 2001-; Member of the Health Select Committee, 2001-03; Parliamentary Private Secretary to the Home Secretary, 2003-2004; Parliamentary Private Secretary to the Secretary of State for Education and Skills, 2004-05; Parliamentary Under Secretary of State at the Home Office for Immigration, Citizenship and Nationality, 2005-06; Minister of State for Quality and Patient Safety at the Department of Health, 2006-07; Chief Secretary to the Treasury, 2007-08; Secretary of State for Culture, Media and Sport, 2008-.

BURNS Jim, b. 19 February 1936, Preston, Lancashire, England. Writer; Part-time Teacher. Education: BA Honours, Bolton Institute of Technology, 1980. Appointments: Editor, Move, 1964-68; Editor, Palantir, 1976-83; Jazz Editor, Beat Scene, 1990-. Publications: A Single Flower, 1972; The Goldfish Speaks from beyond the Grave, 1976; Fred Engels bei Woolworth, 1977; Internal Memorandum, 1982; Out of the Past: Selected Poems 1961-1986, 1987; Confessions of an Old Believer, 1996; The Five Senses, 1999; As Good a Reason As Any, 1999; Beats, Bohemians and Intellectuals, 2000; Take it Easy, 2003; Bopper, 2003; Germany and all that Jazz, 2005; Short Statements, 2006; Laying Something Down, 2007. Contributions to: London Magazine; Stand; Ambit; Jazz Journal; Critical Survey; The Guardian; New Statesman; Tribune; New Society; Penniless Press; Prop; Verse; Others. Address: 11 Gatley Green, Gatley, Cheadle, Cheshire SK8 4NF, England.

BURNS William Joseph, b. 11 April 1956, North Carolina, USA. Diplomat. m. Lisa Carty, 2 daughters. Education: BA, History, LaSalle University; M Phil, D Phil, International Relations, Oxford University, England, 1981. Appointments: Served as Executive Secretary of the State Department and Special Assistant to the Secretary of State, Minister-Counselor for Political Affairs at US Embassy in Moscow, Acting Director and Principal Deputy Director for State Department's Policy Planning Staff, Special Assistant to the President and Senior Director for Near East and South Asian Affairs, National Security Council Staff, Foreign Service, Ambassador to Jordan, 1998-2001; Assistant Secretary of State for Near Eastern Affairs, 2001-05; Ambassador to the Russian Federation, 2005-. Publications: Author, Economic Aid and American Policy Toward Egypt 1955-1981, 1985. Honours: 3 honorary doctoral degrees; 2 Presidential Distinguished Service Awards; Numerous Department of State Awards; 2 Distinguished Honor Awards; James Clement Dunn Award; Robert C Frasure Memorial Award; 5 Superior Honor awards; Listed in 50 Most Promising American Leaders Under Age 40 and 100 Young Global Leaders, TIME magazine, 1994. Address: Embassy of the United States of America, Bolshoy Devyatinsky Pereulok, 8, 121099 Moscow, Russia.

BURNSTOCK Geoffrey, b. 10 May 1929, London, England. President, Autonomic Neuroscience Centre. m. Nomi, 3 daughters. Education: BSc (Special), King's College, University of London, 1953; PhD, King's College and University College London, University of London, 1957; MSc (Honorary), 1962, DSc, 1971, Melbourne University; MRCP (Hon) London, 1987; FRCS (Hon) England, 1999; FRCP (Hon) London, 2000. Appointments: Senior Lecturer, Department of Zoology, 1959, Reader in Physiological Zoology, 1962, Professor of Zoology and Chairman of Department, 1964-75, Associate Dean (Biological Sciences), 1969-72, University of Melbourne, Australia; Convenor, Centre for Neuroscience, UCL, 1979-, Vice Dean, Faculty of Medical Sciences, UCL, 1980-83, Head of Department, 1975-97,

Professor of Anatomy, 1975-2004, Department of Anatomy and Developmental Biology, University College London; Editor in Chief, Autonomic Neuroscience: Basic & Clinical, 1985-; Director, 1997-2004, President, 2004-, Autonomic Neuroscience Institute, Royal Free & University College Medical School; Editor in Chief, Purinergic Signalling, 2004-; Emeritus Professor, Department of Anatomy & Developmental Biology, University College London, 2004-. Publications: Over 1,200 papers; 68 invited reviews; 112 book chapters; 15 books. Honours: Vice President, Anatomical Society of Great Britain and Ireland, 1990; Honorary MSc Melbourne, 1962; Silver Medal, Royal Society of Victoria, 1970; Fellow, Australian Academy of Science, 1971; Fellow, Royal Society, 1986; Hon, MRCP, 1987; Special Award, NIH Conference, Bethesda, USA, 1989; Member: Academia Europaea, 1992; Russian Society of Neuropathology, 1993; Fellow, UCL, 1996-; Founder, FMedSci, 1998; Hon FRCS, 1999; Hon FRCP, 2000; Royal Gold Medal, Royal Society, 2000; Janssen Award, Gastroenterology, 2000; Dr Honoris Causa, University of Antwerp, 2002; Honorary Member, Physiological Society, 2003; Honorary Member, Pharmacological Society, 2004. Memberships: International Federation of Purine Clubs; International Pelvic Pain Society; International Brain Research Organisation; International Society for Developmental Neuroscience; European Neuroscience Association; Society of Neurogastroenterology. Address: Autonomic Neuroscience Centre, Royal Free & University College Medical School, Rowland Hill Street, London NW3 2PF, England. E-mail: g.burnstock@ucl.ac.uk

BURR Martin John, b. 19 February 1953, Amersham, Buckinghamshire, England. Barrister. Education: MA, 1978, Diploma in Comparative Philology, 1977, Pembroke College, Oxford. Appointments: Called to the Bar by Middle Temple, 1978; Practising Barrister, 1979-; Joint Head of Chambers at 2 Temple Gardens, 1989-93; Sole Head of Chambers at Eldon Chambers, 1993-; Associate of the Chartered Institute of Arbitrators, 1990; Member of the Society of Trusts and Estates Practitioners, 1992. Publications: Books include: The Law and Health Visitors, 1982; Chancery Practice, 1991-97; Taxation Recent Developments, 1999; Land Law, forthcoming. Numerous papers and poems published. Compositions: 43 Oratorios, 1981-2005. Honours: Freeman of the City of London; Secretary of the Guild Church Council at St Dunstan-in-the-West, Fleet Street, London; Member of the Council, Henry Bradshaw Society; Deputy Governor, American Biographical Institute; Lifetime Academy of Achievement, American Biographical Institute; Fellow, American Biographical Institute. Memberships: Middle Temple; Lincoln's Inn; Inner Temple; Sion College; Philological Society; Henry Sweet Society; International Arthurian Society; British Archaeological Association; Anglican and Eastern Churches Association; Henry Bradshaw Society; Society of Trust and Estate Practitioners; Ecclesiastical Law Society; Selden Society; Arthur Ransome Society. Address: First Floor, Temple Chambers, Temple Avenue, London, England EC4Y 0DA, England

BURR Michael Leslie, b. 20 October 1937, Barnet, England. Medical Epidemiologist. m. Sheila Martin, 4 daughters. Education: MBBS (Lond), University College London and UCH Medical School, 1960; D Obst RCOG, 1962; DPH (Lond), London School of Hygiene & Tropical Medicine, 1967; MD (Lond), 1976; FFPHM, 1992; DSc (Med) (Lond), 2001. Appointments: House appointments (Medicine, Surgery, Obstetrics), 1960; General Practitioner, 1962; Assistant Medical Officer, Staffordshire County Council, 1966; Medical Officer of Health, Stone Urban & Rural Districts, 1968;

Member of Scientific Staff, 1970, Consultant Epidemiologist, 1979, MRC Epidemiology Unit; Senior Lecturer, Public Health Medicine, University of Wales College of Medicine, 1993; Honorary Consultant in Public Health, South Glamorgan/Bro Taf Health Authority (now National Public Health Service), 1993; Reader, Epidemiology & Public Health Medicine, University of Wales College of Medicine, 2000. Publications: Numerous articles in professional journals. Memberships: British Medical Association; British Thoracic Society; British Society for Allergy and Clinical Immunology. Address: Department of Primary Care & Public Health, University of Wales, Neuadd Meirionnydd, Heath Park, Cardiff CF14 4YS, Wales. E-mail: mburr@doctors.org.uk

BURRELL Leroy, b. 21 February 1967, Landsdowne, Philadelphia, USA. Athlete. m. Michelle Finn, 2 sons. Education: University of Houston, Texas. Appointments: Established 'Clean' World Record, Running 100m in 9.9 seconds at US Championships, New York, 1991; Established World Record 100m, 1994; Head Track and Field Coach, University of Houston, 1998-. Honour: Olympic Gold Medal, 4x100m relay, Barcelona, 1992. Address: USA Track & Field Press Information Department, 1 RCA Dome, Suite 140, Indianapolis, IN 46225, USA.

BURRELL Mark William, b. 9 April 1937, London, England. Businessman. m. Margot, 2 sons, 1 daughter. Education: Pembroke College, Cambridge University, 1957-59, Harvard Business School, 1974. Appointments: A Managing Director, Lazard Brothers, 1970-86; Executive Director, Pearson plc, 1986-97; Chairman, Millbank Financial Services, 1986-; Non-Executive Director, Research Machines plc, 1997-2001; Non-Executive Director, Chairman, Merlin Communications International Ltd, 1997-2001; Chairman, Conafex SA, 1999-; Chairman, Margaret Pyke Memorial Trust, 1997; Member of Court, University of Sussex, 1997-; High Sheriff of West Sussex, 2002-2003; Governor, Northbrook College, Sussex, 2004-; Deputy Lieutenant, West Sussex, 2005-. Memberships: Whites; Boodles; Knepp Castle Polo Club. Address: Bakers House, Bakers Lane, Shipley, Horsham, West Sussex RH13 8GJ, England.

BURRELL Michael Philip, b. 12 May 1937, Harrow, England. Actor; Playwright. Education: BA, MA (Cantab), Peterhouse, Cambridge, 1958-61. Career: Freelance actor since 1961, appearing in major British companies including, the Royal Shakespeare Company, the Chichester Festival Company and Stratford East; Numerous TV appearances; Over 25 feature films; Directing career since 1964, posts include, Associate Director, Royal Lyceum Theatre, Edinburgh 1966-68; Director, Angles Theatre, Wisbech, 1995-2001; Serves on various arts boards, including the Drama Panel of the Eastern Arts Association, 1981-86; King's Lynn Festival and Arts Centre, 1992-95; Theatre Royal, Bury St Edmunds, 1994-2000; Company Secretary, Tiebreak Touring Theatre Ltd, 1987-2004; Chairman, Wisbech Events Forum, 1998-; Chairman, Huntingdon Branch Liberal Democrats, 2003-2006; Chairman, Natural High Experience Ltd, 2004-; Most recent London appearances in The Mousetrap, 2005-2006 and The Woman in Black, 2007. Publications: Over 17 plays including the multi-award winning Hess, 1978, 5 London productions, including one by the RSC at the Almeida; Borrowing Time; My Sister Next Door; The Man Who Lost America; Love Among the Butterflies; Lord of the Fens; Several articles; A current weekly column, In My View, in the Fenland Citizen newspaper. Honours: Obie Award, for Hess, 1980; Best Actor, Best Show, Edmonton Journal Awards, 1984, 1985; Capital Critics Award for Best Actor, Ottawa, 1986; Bronze Award,

New York Film Festival, 1988; Edmonton Journal Award for Best Show, for My Sister Next Door, 1989; Honorary President, Peterhouse Heywood Society, 2002-. Memberships: National Liberal Club, London. Address: c/o Richard Stone Partnership, 2 Henrietta Street, London WC2E 8PS, England. Website: www.michaelburrell.co.uk

BURRILL Timothy, b. 8 June 1931, St Asaph, North Wales, UK. m. (1) Philippa Hare, deceased, 1 daughter (2) Santa Raymond, divorced, 1 son, 2 daughters. Education: Eton College; Sorbonne, Paris, France. Appointments: Entered film industry 1956; Joined Brookfield Productions, 1965; Managing Director, Burrill Productions, 1966-; Director, World Film Services, 1967-69; First Production Administrator, National Film and TV School, 1972; Managing Director: Allied Stars, responsible for Chariots of Fire, 1980-81, Pathé Productions Ltd, 1994-99; Director: Artistry Ltd, responsible for Superman and Supergirl films, 1982, Central Casting, 1988-92; Consultant: National Film Development Fund, 1980-81, The Really Useful Group, 1989-90; UK Film Industry Representative on Eurimages, 1994-96; Vice-Chairman, 1979-81 Chairman, 1980-83, BAFTA, Film Asset Development plc, 1987-94, First Film Foundation, 1989-98, Production Training Fund, 1993-2001; Executive Committee, 1990-2001, Vice-Chairman, 1993-94, The Producers' Association; Director, British Film Commission, 1997-99; Producer Member: Cinematograph Films Council, 1980-83; General Council ACTT, 1975-76; Executive Committee, British Film and TV Producers' Association, 1981-90; Governor, National Film and TV School, 1981-92, Royal National Theatre, 1982-88; Member, UK Government's Middleton Committee on Film Finance, 1996; Le Club de Producteurs Européens; Board Member, International Federation of Film Producers Association, 1997-2001, UK Government's Film Policy Review, 1997-98, European Film Academy, 1997-. Films as Co-Producer include most recently: The Pianist, 2001-2002; Swimming Pool, 2002-2003; Two Brothers, 2002; Les Anges de l'Apocalypse, 2003; Double Zero, 2003; Oliver Twist, 2004; Renaissance, 2004; La Vie en Rose, 2006. Address: 19 Cranbury Road, London SW6 2NS, England. E-mail: timothy@timothyburrill.co.uk

BURRINGTON Ernest, Editor; Publisher. m. Nancy Crossley, 1 son, 1 daughter. Appointments: Army Service, 1944-47; Reporter, 1941-44, Sub-Editor, 1947-49, Oldham Chronicle; Sub-Editor, Bristol Evening World, 1950; Sub-Editor, Manchester, 1950, Night Editor, 1955, Night Editor, London, 1957, Daily Herald; Night Editor, 1964, Assistant Editor, 1965, The Sun (IPC); Assistant Editor and Night Editor, The Sun (News International), 1969; Deputy Night Editor, Daily Mirror, 1970, Editor, Sunday People, 1985-88, 1989-90; Assistant Publisher and Deputy Chairman, 1988-91, Managing Director, 1989-91, Chairman, 1991-92, Mirror Group Newpapers; Deputy Chairman, Mirror Publishing Company, 1988-91; Director: MGN Magazine and Newsday Ltd, 1989-91, Sunday Correspondent, 1990, Sygma Photo Agency, Paris, 1990-91, The European Ltd, 1990-91, IQ Newsgraphics Ltd, 1990-91; Chairman, Syndication International, 1989-92; Deputy Publisher, 1993-95, Vice-President Publishing, 1995, Globe Communications USA; President, Atlantic Media, 1996-98; Memberships: International Press Institute, British Executive, 1988-92; Foreign Press Association; Council, Newspaper Publishers' Association, 1988-92; Trustee, Institute of Child Studies, Youthscan, 1988-91; Life Member, NUJ. Address: South Hall, Dene Park, Shipbourne Road, Tonbridge, Kent TN11 9NS, England. E-mail: burringtone@aol.com

BURROUGHS Andrew, b. 5 April 1958, United Kingdom. Journalist. m. Jacqueline Margaret Wylson, divorced, 1 son, 1 daughter. Education: Exhibitioner, MA, St Catharine's College Cambridge; Guildhall School of Music and Drama. Appointments: News Trainee, Westminster Press, 1979-82; Far East Broadcasting, Seychelles, 1982-84; BBC World Service, 1985-85; BBC Radio 4, 1985-86; Producer, BBC News and Current Affairs, 1986-88; Religion, Arts and Community Affairs Correspondent, 1988-94, Social Affairs Correspondent and Videojournalist (features), 1994-98, Social Affairs Unit BBC TV; Videojournalism Features Correspondent, BBC News, 1998-2001; Videojournalist Features Correspondent, BBC Europe Direct, 2001-05; TV News Correspondent, BBC News 24 and BBC World, 2001-. Publication: Contributor: BBC Review of the Year, 1990, 1991. Honours: Highly Commended, BP Arts Journalism Award, 1991; TV Award Race in the Media, 1994. Membership: Wolfe Society (representative of descendant family General James Wolfe). Address: BBC Room 1634, Stage VI, Television Centre, Wood Lane, London W12 7RJ. E-mail: andrewburroughs@bbc.co.uk

BURROWAY Janet (Gay), b. 21 September 1936, Tucson, Arizona, USA. Professor; Writer; Poet. m. (1) Walter Eysselinck, 1961, divorced 1973, 2 sons, (2) William Dean Humphries, 1978, divorced 1981, (3) Peter Ruppert, 1993, 1 stepdaughter. Education: University of Arizona, 1954-55; AB, Barnard College, 1958; BA, 1960, MA, 1965, Cambridge University; Yale School of Drama, 1960-61. Appointments: Instructor, Harpur College, Binghamton, New York, 1961-62; Lecturer, University of Sussex, 1965-70; Associate Professor, 1972-77, Professor, 1977-, MacKenzie Professor of English, 1989-95, Robert O Lawson Distinguished Professor, 1995-2002, Emerita, 2002-, Florida State University; Fiction Reviewer, Philadelphia Enquirer, 1986-90; Reviewer, New York Times Book Review, 1991-; Essay-Columnist, New Letters: A Magazine of Writing and Art, 1994-. Publications: Fiction: Descend Again, 1960; The Dancer From the Dance, 1965; Eyes, 1966; The Buzzards, 1969; The Truck on the Track, children's book, 1970; The Giant Jam Sandwich, children's book, 1972; Raw Silk, 1977; Opening Nights, 1985; Cutting Stone, 1992; Bridge of Sand, 2009. Poetry: But to the Season, 1961; Material Goods, 1980; Essays: Embalming Mom, 2002. Other: Writing Fiction: A Guide to Narrative Craft, 1982, 7th edition, 2006; Imaginative Writing, 2nd edition, 2006; Editor, From Where You Dream: The Process of Writing Fiction, by Robert Olen Butler, 2005. Contributions to: Numerous journals and periodicals. Honours: National Endowment for the Arts Fellowship, 1976; Yaddo Residency Fellowships, 1985, 1987; Lila Wallace-Reader's Digest Fellow, 1993-94; Carolyn Benton Cockefaire Distinguished Writer-in-Residence, University of Missouri, 1995; Woodrow Wilson Visiting Fellow, Furman University, Greenville, South Carolina, 1995; Erskine College, Due West, South Carolina, 1997; Drury College, Springfield, Illinois, 1999. Memberships: Associated Writing Programs, vice president, 1988-89; Authors Guild; PEN. Address: N2484 Elgin Club Dr, Lake Geneva, WI 53147-3744, USA. E-mail: jburroway@fsu.edu

BURSHTEIN Sheldon, b. 13 March 1952, Montreal, Quebec, Canada. Lawyer. Education: B(Civ)Eng, 1974, BCL, 1977, LLB, 1978, McGill University. Appointments: Admitted to Law Society of Upper Canada, 1980; Registered Professional Engineer, Ontario, 1980; Registered Trademark Agent, Canada, 1980; Lawyer, Patent Agent and Trademark Agent; Registered Trademark Agent, US (Canadian Applicants), 1982; Partner, Blake Cassels & Graydon, LLP, Toronto, Ontario, 1986-; Registered Patent Agent, Canada, 1987, US

(Canadian Applicants), 1987; Certified Specialist, Intellectual Property (Patent, Trademark and Copyright) Law, Law Society of Upper Canada, 1994. Publications: Book, Patent Your Own Invention in Canada, 1991; Co-author, book, The Use of Another's Trademark, 1997; Author, book, Corporate Counsel Guide to Intellectual Property Law, 2000; Author, Domain Names and Trademark Issues on the Internet: Canadian Law & Practice, 2005; Author, numerous chapters in books on Intellectual Property, Licensing, Information Technology and related topics; Author of numerous contributions to journals, conferences on Patents, Trademarks, Copyright and Designs, Confidential Information, Information Technology, Electronic Commerce, Licensing and Franchising, Intellectual Property Aspects of Commercial Transactions, Intellectual Property and Free Trade, Intellectual Property Management, Engineering. Honours: Marie F Morency Memorial Prize, Intellectual Property Institute of Canada, Highest National Standing in Patent Drafting Exam, 1987; Selected as one of the World's Leading Patent Law Experts, Managing Intellectual Property; World's Five Leading Trademark Law Experts and World's Top 50 Trademark Lawyers Managing Intellectual Property; Canada's Leading Patent Lawyer; Selected to appear in: World's Leading Patent Law Experts; World's Leading Trade Mark and Copyright Law Experts; Who's Who Legal; and many others. Memberships: Editorial Advisory Board, The Licensing Journal; Advisory Board, Multimedia and Technology Licensing Law Report; Editorial Board, Laws of Com; Columnist, World Intellectual Property Report, Pharmaceutical, Canada; Chairman and Former Chairman, Various Committees, Intellectual Property Institute of Canada and other organisations. Address: c/o Blake Cassels & Graydon, LLP, PO Box 25, Commerce Court West, Toronto, Ontario M5L 1A9, Canada.

BURTON Anthony George Graham, b. 24 December 1934, Thornaby, England. Writer; Broadcaster. m. 28 March 1959, 2 sons, 1 daughter. Publications: A Programmed Guide to Office Warfare, 1969; The Jones Report, 1970; The Canal Builders, 1972, 4th edition, 2005; The Reluctant Musketeer, 1973; Canals in Colour, 1974; Remains of a Revolution, 1975, 2001; The Master Idol, 1975; The Miners, The Navigators, Josiah Wedgwood, Canal, 1976; Back Door Britain, A Place to Stand, Industrial Archaeological Sites of Britain, 1977; The Green Bag Travellers, 1978; The Past At Work, The Rainhill Story, 1980; The Past Afloat, The Changing River, The Shell Book of Curious Britain, 1982; The National Trust Guide to Our Industrial Past, The Waterways of Britain, 1983; The Rise and Fall of King Cotton, 1984; Walking the Line, Wilderness Britain, Britain's Light Railways, 1985; The Shell Book of Undiscovered Britain and Ireland, Britain Revisited, Landscape Detective, 1986; Opening Time, Steaming Through Britain, 1987; Walk the South Downs, Walking Through History, 1988; The Great Days of the Canals, 1989; Cityscapes, Astonishing Britain, 1990; Slow Roads, 1991; The Railway Builders, 1992; Canal Mania, The Grand Union Canal Walk, 1993; The Railway Empire, The Rise and Fall of British Shipbuilding, 1994; The Cotswold Way, The Dales Way, 1995; The West Highland Way, 1996; The Southern Upland Way, William Cobbett: Englishman, 1997; The Wye Valley Walk, The Caledonian Canal, Best Foot Forward, 1998; The Cumbria Way, The Wessex Ridgeway, Thomas Telford, 1999; Weekend Walks: Dartmoor and Exmoor, Weekend Walks: The Yorkshire Dales, Traction Engines, Richard Trevithick, 2000; The Orient Express, Weekend Walks: The Peak District, The Anatomy of Canals: The Early Years, The Daily Telegraph Guide to Britain's Working Past, 2001; The Anatomy of Canals: The Mania Years, 2002; Hadrian's Wall Path, The Daily Telegraph Guide to Britain's Maritime Past,

The Anatomy of Canals: Decline and Renewal, 2003; On the Rails, 2004; The Ridgeway, 2005; The Cotswold Way, 2007. Address: c/o Sara Menguc, 58 Thork Hill Road, Thames Ditton, Surrey, KT7 0UG, England.

BURTON George Martin, b. 11 May 1942, Bratislava, Slovakia. Civil Engineer. m. Edith, 3 daughters. Education: Technical College (with Honours), Czechoslovakia, 4 years; Degree in Civil & Traffic Engineering (with Honours), Technical University, Czechoslovakia, 5½ years. Appointments: Civil Engineer, The Research Institute of Civil Engineering, Bratislava, Czechoslovakia, 1965-68; Civil Engineer, Wargon, Chapman & Associates, Consulting Engineers, Sydney, Australia, 1968-69; Design Engineer, Metropolitan Water, Sewerage & Drainage Board, Sydney, 1969-70; Design Engineer, Department of Railways, New South Wales, 1970-71; Design and Consulting Manager, Kings Parking Group of Companies, 1971-85; General Manager, Kings Parking Company Pty Limited (NSW Operations), 1985-87; Company Director and General Manager, Consulting and Design Worldwide, 1987-88; Technical Director, Kings Parking Company Pty Limited, 1988-89; Technical Director, Kings Parking Limited, Technical and Development Executive, Kings Parking UK Ltd, 1989-91; Principal, G M Burton Consulting, later (PDS) Parking Design Specialists, 1991-. Publications: 10 articles in professional journals. Memberships: Institution of Engineers, Australia; Parking Association of Australia; Association of Professional Engineers, Scientists and Managers, Australia; Parking Consultants Council of America; National Parking Association of America. Address: 8 Walker Street, Blackheath, NSW 2785, Australia. E-mail: gmb@carparkingdesign.com

BURTON Gregory Keith, b. 12 February 1956, Sydney, New South Wales, Australia. Barrister-at-Law; Senior Counsel. m. Penelope Josephine Whitehead, 2004, 2 sons, 3 daughters. Education: BCL, Oxon; BA Honours, LLB Honours, University of Sydney; Graded Arbitrator, Accredited Mediator; Associate, Institute Arbitrators and Mediators, Australia; Barrister, New South Wales, High Court and Federal Courts, Queensland, Ireland; Barrister and Solicitor, Victoria, Western Australia, ACT, Northern Territory. Appointments: Solicitor, Freehill Hollingdale and Page, 1980-83; Associate to Sir William Deane, High Court of Australia, 1984-85; Senior Adviser to Federal MP, 1986; Lecturer, Law, Australian National University, 1987-88; Bar, 1989-; Senior Counsel, 2004-. Publications: Australian Financial Transactions Law, 1991; Chapters and articles in, and editor of, journals, book and legal encyclopaedias; Directions in Finance Law, 1990; Weaver and Craigie's Banker and Customer in Australia (co-author). Honours: Dux, Trinity Grammar School, Sydney, 1968-73; University Medal, History, University of Sydney, 1978; Prizes in Equity, Commercial Law, Public Law, English, History, Government; Editorial Committee, Sydney Law Review, 1978-79. Memberships: NSW Bar Association; Business Law Section, Law Council of Australia; Banking and Financial Services Law Association; Commercial Law Association; Australian Institute Administrative Law; Various ADR Organizations; Centre International Legal Studies, Vienna; Centre Independent Studies; Institute of Public Affairs; Sydney Institute; Director, Australian Elizabethan Theatre Trust; Procurator, Presbyterian Church of Australia. Address: 5th Floor, Wentworth Chambers, 180 Phillip Street, Sydney, NSW, Australia 2000.

BURTON, Hon Mr Justice; Hon Sir Michael John, b. 12 November 1946, Manchester, England. High Court Judge. m. Corinne Ruth Cowan, deceased, 1992, 4 daughters.

Education: Kings Scholar, Captain of School, Eton College, 1959-64; MA, Balliol College, Oxford, 1965-69 (JCR President of Balliol, First President, Oxford University Student Council). Appointments: Called to Bar, Gray's Inn, 1970; Barrister, 1970-98; Lecturer in Law, Balliol College, Oxford, 1970-73; Candidate (Labour), Kensington Council, 1971; Parliamentary Candidate (Labour), Stratford-on-Avon, 1974; Candidate (Social Democrat), GLC Putney, 1981; Queen's Counsel, 1984; Recorder of the Crown Court, 1989-98; Head of Chambers, 1991-98; Deputy Judge of the High Court, 1993-98; Judge of the High Court of Justice (Queen's Bench Division), 1998-; Judge of the Employment Appeal Tribunal, 2000-, President, 2002-05; Chairman, Central Arbitration Committee, 2000-; President, Interception of Communications Tribunal, 2000-2001; Vice-President, Investigatory Powers Tribunal, 2000-; Member, Bar Council Legal Services Commission, 1995; Publication: Civil Appeals (editor) 2002. Honours: Queen's Counsel, 1984; Bencher of Gray's Inn, 1993; Knighted, 1998. Memberships: Honorary Fellow, 1999-, Member of Council, 2003-05, Goldsmith's College London University; Fellow, Eton College, 2004-. Address: c/o Royal Courts of Justice, Strand, London WC2A 2RR, England.

BURTON Tim, b. 25 August 1958, Burbank, California, USA. Film Director. Partner, Helena Bonham-Carter, 1 son. Education: California Arts Institute. Appointments: Animator, Walt Disney Studios, projects include: The Fox and the Hound, The Black Cauldron; Animator, Director, Vincent (short length film). Creative Works: Films directed: Vincent (also animator), Luau, Hansel and Gretel (TV), 1982; Frankenweenie, 1984; Aladdin, Pee-wee's Big Adventure, Alfred Hitchcock Presents (TV episode, The Jar), 1985; Beetlejuice, 1988; Batman, 1989; Edward Scissorhands (also producer), 1991; Batman Returns (also producer), 1992; Ed Wood (also producer), 1994; Mars Attacks! (also producer), 1996; Sleepy Hollow, 1999; Planet of the Apes, 2001; Big Fish, 2003; Charlie and the Chocolate Factory, Corpse Bride (also producer), 2005; Inside the Two World's of The Corpse Bride, 2006; Producer: Beetlejuice (TV series), Family Dog (TV series), The Nightmare Before Christmas, 1993; Cabin Boy, 1994; Batman Forever, James and the Giant Peach, 1996; Lost in Oz (TV), 2000; Film screenplays: The Island of Dr Agor, 1971; Stalk of the Celery, 1979; Vincent, Luau, 1982; Beetlejuice (story), 1988; Edward Scissorhands (story), 1990; The Nightmare Before Christmas (story), 1993; Lost in Oz (TV pilot episode story), 2000; Point Blank (TV series), 2002. Publications: My Art and Films, 1993; The Melancholy Death of Oyster Boy and Other Stories, 1997; Burton on Burton, 2000; various film tie-in books. Honours include: 2 Awards, Chicago Film Festival. Address: Chapman, Bird & Grey, 1990 South Bundy Drive, Suite 200, Los Angeles, CA 90025, USA. Website: www.timburton.com

BURTON Verona Devine, b. 23 November 1922, Reading, Pennsylvania, USA. Botanist. m. Daniel F Burton, 1 son. Education: AB, Hunter College, New York City, 1944; MA, 1946, PhD, 1948, University of Iowa. Appointments: Assistant Professor, 1948-67, Compliance Officer, 1973-75, Minnesota State University; Associate Professor, 1967-70, Professor of Biology, 1970-86, Professor Emeritus, 1987-, Minnesota State University, Mankato. Publications: Several articles in professional journals. Honours: Community Leadership Award, YWCA, 1973; Women as Agent of Change, AAUW, 1985. Memberships: American Association for the Advancement of Science; American Association of University Women; Sigma Xi; Sigma Delta Epsilon. Address: 512 Hickory Street, Mankato, MN 56001, USA.

BUSAPATHUMRONG Pattamaporn, b. 8 January 1962, Bangkok, Thailand. Educator. Education: BA (Hons), Sociology and Anthropology, Thammasat University, Bangkok, 1982; AM, Anthropology, Stanford University, Palo Alto, USA, 1987; PhD, Social Work, University of Pennsylvania, USA, 1994. Appointments: Former Consultant to United Nations; Lecturer, Thammasat University, Thailand; Head, Department of Humanities and Social Sciences, Asian University, Chon Buri, Thailand; Associate Fellow, Academy of Moral and Political Sciences, Royal Institute of Thailand, Bangkok. Publications: 28 articles in professional scientific journals. Honours: King Anandha Mahidol Scholarship; International Peace Prize, UCC, USA, 2006; Listed in international biographical dictionaries. Memberships: International Consortium for Social Development. E-mail: pat_busapathumrong@mac.com

BUSCEMI Steve, b. 13 December 1957, Brooklyn, New York, USA. m. Jo Andres, 1987, 1 son. Education: Graduated, Valley Stream Central High School, Valley Stream, New York, 1975; Career: Bartender; Ice-cream truck driver; Stand-up comedian; Firefighter; Actor. Films include: The Way It Is, 1984; Tommy's, 1985; Sleepwalk, Parting Glances, 1986; Heart, 1987; Kiss Daddy Goodnight, Vibes, 1988; New York Stories, Slaves of New York, Mystery Train, Coffee & Cigarettes II, Borders, 1989; King of New York, 1990; Barton Fink, Zandalee, Billy Bathgate, 1991; In the Soup, CrissCross, Reservoir Dogs, Who Do I Gotta Kill? 1992; Claude, Rising Sun, Twenty Bucks, Ed and His Dead Mother, 1993; Floundering, The Hudsucker Proxy, Airheads, Somebody to Love, Pulp Fiction, 1994; Living in Oblivion, Dead Man, Things to Do in Denver When You're Dead, 1995; Fargo, Trees Lounge, Kansas City, Escape from LA, 1996; Con Air, The Real Blonde, 1997; The Wedding Singer, The Big Lebowski, The Imposters, Armageddon, Louis & Frank, 1998; Animal Factory, 28 Days, Ghost World, 2000; Final Fantasy: The Spirits Within, The Grey Zone, Monster Inc, 2001; The Laramie Project, Love in the Time of Money, 13 Moons, Mr Deeds, Spy Kids 2: Island of Lost Dreams, Deadrockstar, 2002; Spy-Kids 3-D: Game Over, Coffee and Cigarettes, Big Fish, 2003; Home on The Range, voice, The Sky is Green, Art School Confidential, 2004; Romance & Cigarettes, The Island, A Licence to Steel, Cordless, Delirious, 2005; Charlotte's Web, (Voice), 2006; Interview, I Think I Love My Wife, I Now Pronounce You Chuck and Larry, 2007; Director: What Happened to Pete? 1992; Trees Lounge, 1996; Animal Factory, 2000; Lonesome Jim, 2004; Interview, 2007; Producer: Animal Factory, 2000; Lonesome Jim, 2004; Writer: What Happened to Pete? 1992; Trees Lounge, 1996. TV includes: Saturday Night Live, 1975; Miami Vice, 1984; The Equaliser, 1985; Crossbow, 1986; The Simpsons, 1989; In The Life, 1992; Mad About You, 1992; The Drew Carey Show, 1995; The Sopranos, 2004. Honours include: Independent Spirit Award, Best Supporting Male, 1993; Chicago Film Critics Association Award, Best Supporting Actor, 2002; Independent Spirit Award, Best Supporting Male, 2002; Kansas City Film Critics Circle Award, Best Supporting Actor, 2002; Las Vegas Film Critics Society Award, Best Supporting Actor, 2002; San Diego Film Critics Society Award, 1997. Address: c/o Artists Management Group, 9465 Wilshire Blvd, #419, Beverly Hills, CA 90212, USA.

BUSH George W, b. 6 July 1946, USA. President of the United States of America. m. Laura Lane Welch, twin daughters. Education: Bachelor's Degree, History, Yale University; Master of Business Administration, Harvard University. Appointments: F-102 Pilot, Texas Air National Guard; Founder and Manager, Spectrum 7 Energy Corporation

(merged with Harken Energy Corporation, 1986), Midland Texas; Director, Harken Energy Corporation; Professional Baseball Team Executive with Texas Rangers, 1989-94; Elected Governor of Texas, 1994; Re-elected, 1998; Elected President of the United States, 2001-2004, re-elected 2004-. Address: The White House, Washington, DC 20500, USA.

BUSH Kate (Catherine), b. 30 July 1958, Bexleyheath, Kent, England. Singer; Songwriter. Partner, Danny McIntosh, 1 son. Education: Voice, dance and mime lessons. Career: Limited live performances include: Tour Of Life, Europe, 1979; Secret Policeman's Third Ball, London, 1987; Television appearances include: Bringing It All Back Home documentary, 1991; Writer, director, actress, film The Line, The Cross And The Curve, 1994. Recordings (mostly self-composed): Albums: The Kick Inside, 1978; Lionheart, 1978; Never For Ever (Number 1, UK), 1980; The Dreaming, 1982; Hounds Of Love (Number 1, UK), 1985; The Whole Story (Number 1, UK), 1987; The Sensual World (Number 2, UK), 1989; This Woman's Work, 1990; The Red Shoes (Number 2, UK), 1993; Aerial, 2005; Contributor, Games Without Frontiers, Peter Gabriel, 1980; Two Rooms - Celebrating The Songs Of Elton John And Bernie Taupin, 1991; Singles include: Wuthering Heights (Number 1, UK), 1978; The Man With The Child In His Eyes, 1978; Wow, 1979; Breathing, 1980; Babooshka, 1980; Army Dreamers, 1980; Sat In Your Lap, 1981; Running Up That Hill, 1985; Cloudbusting, 1985; Hounds Of Love, 1986; Experiment IV, 1986; Don't Give Up, duet with Peter Gabriel, 1986; This Woman's Work (from film soundtrack She's Having A Baby), 1988; The Sensual World, 1989; Moments Of Pleasure, 1993; Rubberband Girl, 1993; Man I Love, 1994; The Red Shoes, 1994. Honours: Ivor Novello Awards, Outstanding British Lyric, 1979; BRIT Award, Best British Female Artist, 1987; Q Magazine Award for Best Classic Songwriter, 2001; Ivor Novello Award for Outstanding Contribution to British Music by a Songwriter, 2002. Address: c/o KBC, PO Box 120, Welling, Kent DA16 3DS, England.

BUSH Laura Lane Welch, b. 4 November 1946, Midland, Texas, USA. m. George W Bush, 1977, twin daughters, 1981. Education: Bachelor's degree, Education, Southern Methodist University, 1968; Masters degree, Library Science, University of Texas, Austin, 1973. Career: School Teacher; Librarian; First Lady, Texas; First Lady, United States, 2001-. TV Appearences: A&E Biography: George W Bush - Son Also Rises, 2000; Express Yourself, 2001; Last Party, 2001; Intimate Portrait, 2003; Larry King Live, 2003; The Tonight Show with Jay Leno, 2004. Address: Office of the First Lady, 200 East Wing, The White House, 1600 Pennsylvania Avenue, NW, Washington, DC 20500, USA. Website: www.whitehouse.gov/firstlady

BUSH Ronald, b. 16 June 1946, Philadelphia, Pennsylvania, USA. Professor of American Literature; Writer. m. Marilyn Wolin, 1969, 1 son. Education: BA, University of Pennsylvania, 1968; BA, Cambridge University, 1970; PhD, Princeton University, 1974. Appointments: Assistant to Associate Professor, Harvard University, 1974-82; Associate Professor, 1982-85, Professor, 1985-97, California Institute of Technology; Visiting Fellow, Exeter College, Oxford, 1994-95; Drue Heinz Professor of American Literature, Oxford University, 1997-; Visiting Fellow, American Civilization Program, Harvard University, 2004. Publications: The Genesis of Ezra Pound's Cantos, 1976; T S Eliot: A Study in Character and Style, 1983; T S Eliot: The Modernist in History (editor), 1991; Prehistories of the Future: The Primitivist Project and the Culture of Modernism (co-editor), 1995; Claiming the Stones/Naming the Bones: Cultural Property and the

Negotiation of National and Ethnic Identity (co-editor), 2002. Contributions to: Scholarly books and journals. Honours: National Endowment for the Humanities fellowships, 1977-78, 1992-93; AHRB Research Grant, 2003-04. Address: St John's College, Oxford OX1 3JP, England.

BUSH Stephen Frederick, b. 6 May 1939, Bath, England. University Professor; Entrepreneur. m. Gillian Mary Layton, 1 son, 1 daughter. Education: Isleworth Grammar School, 1954-57; Trinity College Cambridge Senior Scholar, 1958, Starred First Class Honours in Engineering, 1960, Research Scholar, 1961, MA, PhD, 1965; NATO Research Studentship, 1960-63, SM, Control Engineering, Massachusetts Institute of Technology, USA, 1960-61; MSc, University of Manchester, 1979. Appointments: Successively, Technical Officer, Section Manager and Manager of Process Technology Group, ICI Corporate Laboratory, 1963-71; Head, Systems Technology Department, ICI Europa Ltd, 1971-79; Professor of Polymer Engineering, 1979-2003, Head of Centre for Manufacture, 2000-05, Professor of Process Manufacture, 2004-05, Professor Emeritus, 2006-, University of Manchester (Institute of Science and Technology) (UMIST); Consultant to many companies including: ICI, Cookson Group (USA), United Biscuits, Terrys-Suchard, Lucas, Camac Inc (USA), Ametex AG (Switzerland), Curver Ltd, Everite (Pty) Ltd (South Africa); Founder and Managing Director, Prosyma Research, 1987-; Executive Chairman and Co-founder, North of England Plastics Processing Consortium, 1990-2000; Chairman, NEPPCO Ltd, 2000-06; Director, Surgiplas Ltd, 2001-08; Advisory Board Member, Business Innovation Center, University of Massachusetts, USA, 2007-; Policy Advisor, UK Independence Party, 2007-. Publications: (Technical) Around 180 papers and 20 patents on the science and economics of process manufacture including: Measurement and Prediction of Temperature Oscillations in a Chemical Reactor, 1969; Long Glass Fibre Reinforcement of Thermoplastics, 1999; Technoeconomic Models for New Products and Processes, 2005; (Political) Around 90 articles and letters in the national press and 5 pamphlets including: Britain's Future – No Middle Way, 1990; The Importance of Manufacture to the Economy, 2000. Honours include: Sir George Nelson Prize for Applied Mechanics, Cambridge, 1960; Senior Moulton Medal, Institution of Chemical Engineers, 1969; Sir George Beilby Medal and Prize, Royal Society of Chemistry and the Institute of Materials, 1979; Fellowships: Institution of Mechanical Engineers, 1993 (Council, 1978-81); Institution of Chemical Engineers, 1993; Plastics and Rubber Institute, 1985 (Council, 1985-87); Institute of Materials, Minerals and Mining, 1993; Royal Society of Arts and Manufactures, 1998. Memberships: Council, Manchester Statistical Society, 2001-07; Editorial Board, International Journal Industrial Systems Engineering, 2005-; Royal Economic Society, 2006-. Address: Alfred House, Pokeriage Gardens, Thurston, Suffolk IP31 3TS, England.

BUSSELL Darcy, b. 27 April 1969, London, England. Ballerina. m. Angus Forbes, 1997, 1 daughter. Education: Royal Ballet School. Career: Birmingham Royal Ballet, then Sadlers Wells, 1987; Soloist; Royal Ballet, 1988, first solo, 1989; Principal, 1989-2006; Retired, 2007. Appearances include: The Spirit of Fugue, created for her by David Bintley; Swan Lake; The Nutcracker; The Prince of the Pagodas; Cinderella; Sleeping Beauty; Bloodlines; Romeo and Juliet; Giselle; Raymonda; Numerous appearances on TV; Guest with other ballet companies in Paris, St Petersburg and New York. Publications: My Life in Dance, 1998; Favourite Ballet Stories; The Young Dancer; Pilates for Life, 2005. Honours: Prix de Lausanne, 1989; Dancer of the Year, Dance and Dancers

Magazine, 1990; Sir James Garreras Award, Variety Club of Great Britain, 1991; Evening Standard Ballet Award, 1991; Joint winner, Cosmopolitan Achievement in the Performing Arts Award, 1991; Olivier Award, 1992; OBE, 1995.

BUTEVICH Anatol, b. 15 June 1948, Boyary, Republic of Belarus. Journalist. m. Taisa, 1 son, 2 daughters. Education: Philologist, Belorussian State University, 1966-71; PhD, Information Technologies, 1996. Appointments: Editor, Belorussian Telegraph Agency, 1971-73; Work at Youth Organisations, 1973-75, 1979-80; Deputy Editor-in-chief, Chyrvonaya Zmena newspaper, 1975-79; Work at Public Organisations, 1979-80, 1987-90; Director, Mastatskaya Litaratura Publishing House, 1986-87; Chairman, State Press Committee, BSSR, 1990-92; Minister of Information of the Republic of Belarus, 1992-94; Minister of Culture and Press of the Republic of Belarus, 1994-96; Consul General of the Republic of Belarus in Gdansk, Poland, 1996-98; Ambassador Extraordinary and Plenipotentiary of the Republic of Belarus in Romania, 1998-2001; Counsellor to the Chairman of the International Trade and Investment Bank, 2001-. Publications: Approximately 30 fiction books including books for children, historical prose, literary and critical stories; Numerous translations. Honours: Medal for Development of Virgin Lands, 1969; Charter of the Supreme Council of the Belorussian Soviet Socialist Republic, 1979; Honour Diploma, Council of Minister of the Republic of Belarus, 1998; Prize Winner, Golden Pen, Belorussian Union of Journalists, 2001; Award for Contribution to Polish Literature Translation, ZAiKS Association of Polish Writers, 2004; Order of the Holy Kiril Turovskiy, Belarusian Orthodox Church, Minsk, 2008. Memberships: Union of Belorussian Writers; Belorussian Union of Journalists; Deputy Chairman, Belarusian Fund of Culture. E-mail: anatolbut@mail.ru

BUTLER Manley Caldwell, b. 2 June 1925, Roanoke, Virginia, USA. Lawyer. m. June Parker Nolde, 4 sons. Education: Richmond College, The University of Richmond, Virginia, 1948; Law School, University of Virginia, 1950. Appointments: Private Practice of Law, Roanoke, Virginia, 1950-72; Member, Virginia House of Delegates, Richmond, Virginia, 1963-73; Member, United States House of Representatives, 1972-83; Partner, Wood Rogers Law Firm, Roanoke, Virginia, 1983-98; Retired, 1998. Publications: Co-Author, Abolition of Diversity Jurisdiction, 1983; University of Virginia Miller Center for Public Affairs: The 25th Amendment, 1988; Selection of Vice Presidents, 1992. Honours: Distinguished Eagle Scout Award of Blue Ridge Virginia Council of Boy Scouts of America, 1973; Phi Beta Kappa, Omicron Delta Kappa, Pi Delta Epsilon and Tau Kappa Alpha, University of Richmond; University of Virginia, Editorial Board, Virginia Law Review, Raven Society, Order of the Coif; Silver Hope Award of Multiple Sclerosis Society of Virginia, 1999; Business Hall of Fame Junior Achievement of Roanoke Valley, 1998; The Main United States Post Office Building, Roanoke, Virginia, named The M. Caldwell Butler Building, 2002; Commended for many years of service to the Commonwealth of Virginia, General Assembly of Virginia, 2001. Memberships: Roanoke Bar Association; Virginia State Bar Association; Virginia Bar Foundation;, District of Columbia Bar, American Bar Association; American Bar Foundation; American College of Bankruptcy; American Bankruptcy Institute; Board of Roanoke City Library Foundation; Board of Trustees of Virginia Theological Seminary; Board of Virginia Historical Society, Richmond, Virginia. Address: 200 The Glebe Blvd, unit 1024, Daleville, VA 24083, USA. E-mail: nuniepapa@gleberes.net

BUTLER Michael Gregory, b. 1 November 1935, Nottingham, England. Professor of Modern German Literature. m. Jean Mary Griffith, 31 December 1961, 1 son, 1 daughter. Education: BA, 1957, MA, 1960, Cambridge University; DipEd, Oxford University, 1958; FIL, 1967; PhD (CNAA), 1974; LittD, Cambridge University, 1999. Appointments: Assistant Master, King's School, Worcester, 1958-61, Reuchlin Gymnasium, Pforzheim, Germany, 1961-62; Head of German, Ipswich School, England, 1962-70; Lecturer in German, 1970-80, Senior Lecturer, 1980-86, Head, Department of German Studies, 1984-2001, Professor of Modern German Literature, 1986-, Head, School of Modern Languages, 1988-93, Public Orator, 1997-2005, Professorial Fellow, Institute for German Studies, 1997-2007, Fellow, Institute for Advanced Research in Arts and Social Sciences, 2004-, University of Birmingham; Visiting Fellow, Humanities Research Centre, Australian National University, 1979; Vice President, 1994-96, President, 1996-99, Conference of University Teachers of German in Great Britain and Ireland. Publications: Nails and Other Poems, 1967; Samphire (co-editor), 3 volumes, 1968-83; The Novels of Max Frisch, 1975; Englische Lyrik der Gegenwart (editor with Ilsabe Arnold Dielewicz), 1981; The Plays of Max Frisch, 1985; Frisch: 'Andorra', 1985, 2nd edition, 1994; Rejection and Emancipation - Writing in German-speaking Switzerland 1945-1991 (editor with Malcolm Pender), 1991; The Narrative Fiction of Heinrich Böll (ed), 1994; The Making of Modern Switzerland, 1848-1998 (ed) 2000; The Challenge of German Culture (editor with Robert Evans), 2000; General Editor (with William Paterson), New Perspectives in German Studies, 2000-, (Palgrave/Macmillan); Marks of Honour, Public Orations 1997-2005, 2007. Contributions to numerous learned journals; Migrant; Mica (California); Poetry Review; BBC; Sceptre Press; Vagabond (Munich); Universities Poetry; Many reviews in the Times Literary Supplement. Honour: Taras Schevchenko Memorial Prize, 1961; Knight's Cross of the Order of Merit, Federal Republic of Germany, 1999. Address: 45 Westfields, Catshill, Bromsgrove B61 9HJ, England.

BUTLER Sir Richard Clive, b. 12 January 1929, London, England. Retired Farmer and Company Director. m. Susan, 2 sons, 1 daughter. Education: Eton College; MA in Agriculture, Pembroke College, Cambridge. Appointments: Board Member, NFU Mutual Insurance Society, 1985-96; Main Board Non-Executive Director, NatWest Bank, 1986-96; Board Member, Avon Insurance, 1990-96. Honours: DL, Essex, 1972; KB, 1981; Master, Worshipful Company of Skinners, 1994-95; Master, Worshipful Company of Farmers, 1997-98; Trustee, The Butler Trust. Memberships: Life Member, Council of the National Farmers' Union for England and Wales; Chairman of the Trustees, Kennedy Institute for Rheumatology Trust. Address: Gladfen Hall, Halstead, Essex CO9 1RN, England.

BUTLER-SLOSS Rt Hon, Baroness (Ann) Elizabeth (Oldfield), b. 10 August 1933, England. Judge. m. Joseph William Alexander Butler-Sloss, 1958, 2 sons, 1 daughter. Education: Wycombe Abbey School. Appointments: Called to Bar, Inner Temple, 1955; Practising barrister, 1955-70; Contested Lambeth, Vauxhall as Conservative Candidate, 1959; Bencher, 1979; Registrar, Principal Registry of Probate, later Family Division, 1970-79; Judge, High Court of Justice, Family Division, 1979-87; Lord Justice of Appeal, 1988-99; President of Family Division, 1999-2005; Chair, Crown Appointments Commission, 2002-; Vice President, Medico-Legal Society; Chair, Cleveland Child Abuse Inquiry, 1987-88; Advisory Council, St Paul's Cathedral; President,

Honiton Agricultural Show, 1985-86; Treasurer, Inner Temple, 1998; Member, Judicial Studies Board, 1985-89; Honorary Fellow, St Hilda's College, Oxford, 1988; Visiting Fellow, 2001-; Fellow, Kings College, London, 1991; Member, Council, 1992-98; Chancellor, University of West of England, 1993-; Hon FRCP; Hon FRCPsych; Hon FRCPaed; Hon LLD (Hull) 1989, (Bristol) 1991, (Keele) 1991, (Brunel) 1992, (Exeter) 1992, (Manchester) 1995, (Cambridge) 2000, (Greenwich) 2000, (East Anglia) 2001, (Liverpool) 2001, (Ulster) 2004, (London) 2004; Hon DLit (Loughborough University of Technology) 1993; Hon DUniv (University of Central England) 1994. Publications: Joint editor, Phipson on Evidence (10th edition); Corpe on Road Haulage (2nd edition); Former editor, Supreme Court Practice 1976, 1976. Address: c/o Royal Courts of Justice, Strand, London WC2A 2LL, England.

BUTLIN Ron, b. 17 November 1949, Edinburgh, Scotland; Poet. Writer. m. Regula Staub (the writer Regi Claire), 1993. Education: MA, Dip CDAE, Edinburgh University. Appointments: Writer-in-Residence, Edinburgh University, 1983, 1985, Midlothian Region, 1990-91, Stirling University, 1993; Writer-in-Residence, The Craigmillar Literacy Trust, 1997-98; Examiner in Creative Writing, Stirling University, 1997-, University of Glasgow, 2004-; Writer in Residence, St Andrews University, 1998-. Publications: Creatures Tamed by Cruelty, 1979; The Exquisite Instrument, 1982; The Tilting Room, 1984; Ragtime in Unfamiliar Bars, 1985; The Sound of My Voice, 1987; Histories of Desire, 1995; Night Visits, 1997; When We Jump We Jump High! (editor), 1998; Faber Book of Twentieth Century Scottish Poetry; Our Piece of Good Fortune, 2003; Vivaldi and the Number 3, 2004; Without a Backward Glance: New and Selected Poems 2005; Good Angel, Bad Angel (opera), 2005; Coming on Strong, 2005; Belonging, 2006; No More Angels, 2007; The Perfect Woman (opera), 2008. Contributions to: Sunday Herald; Scotsman; Edinburgh Review; Poetry Review; Times Literary Supplement. Honours: Writing Bursaries, 1977, 1987, 1990, 1994, 2003; Scottish Arts Council Book Awards, 1982, 1984, 1985, 2007; Scottish Canadian Writing Fellow, 1984; Poetry Book Society Recommendation, 1985; Prix Millepages, 2004 (Best Foreign Novel); Prix Lucioles, 2005 (Best Foreign Novel). Membership: Scottish Arts Council Literature Committee, 1995-96; Society of Authors. Address: 7W Newington Place, Edinburgh EH9 1QT, Scotland.

BUTTERWORTH Arthur Eckersley, b. 4 August 1923, Manchester, England. Composer; Conductor. m. Diana Stewart, 2 daughters. Education: Royal Manchester College of Music. Career: Member Scottish National Orchestra, 1949-54; Member, Hallé Orchestra, 1955-61; Conductor, Huddersfield Philharmonic Orchestra, 1962-93; Teacher, Huddersfield School of Music. Compositions include: Symphony No 1 op 15, Cheltenham Festival, 1957 and BBC Proms, 1958; Symphony No 2 op 25, Bradford, 1965; Organ Concerto, 1973; Violin Concerto, 1978, Symphony No 3 op 52, Manchester, 1979; Piano Trio, Cheltenham Festival Commission, 1983; Symphony No 4 op 72, Manchester, 1986; Odin Symphony for Brass op 76, National Brass Band Festival London, 1989; Northern Light op 88, Leeds, 1991; Concerto alla Veneziana op 93, York, 1992; Viola Concerto op 82, Manchester, 1993; Mancunians op 96, Hallé Orchestra Commission, Manchester, 1995; 'Cello Concerto op 98, Huddersfield, 1994; Guitar Concerto op 109, Leeds, 2000; Symphony No 5 op 115, Manchester, 2003; Mill Town op 116, for large orchestra; Piano Trio No 2 in E flat op 121; Symphony No 6, 2006 op 124; Capriccio Pastorale op 125 – small orchestra. Honour:

MBE, 1995. Membership: Vice-President, British Music Society. Address: Pohjola, Dales Avenue, Embsay, Skipton, North Yorkshire, BD23 6PE, England.

BUZZONI Alberto, b. 4 November 1958, Ro di Ferrara, Italy. Astronomer. m. Claribel Garcia. Education: Doctor of Astronomy, University of Bologna, Italy, 1982. Appointments: Associate Professor, Bologna Astronomical Observatory, Italy; Tutor, 20 doctorate thesis in Astronomy, Physics and Philosophy of Science. Publications: 140 articles on international scientific reviews. Memberships: Italian Astronomical Society, 1985; International Astronomical Union, 1997; International Academic Evaluation Committee, National Institute of Astrophysics (INAOE), Mexico, 2004; Global Executive Forum (Intelligence Unit), The Economist, UK, 2005; Accredited International Referee for Mexican Conacyt (RCEA), 2006; Investigador Correspondiente, CONICET, Buenos Aires, Argentina, 2008. Address: Oss Astronomico di Bologna, Via Ranzani 1, I 40127 Bologna, Italy. Website: www.bo.astro.it/~eps/home.html

BYATT Dame Antonia Susan, b. 24 August 1936, England. Author. m. (1) Ian C R Byatt, 1959, dissolved 1969, 1 son (deceased), 1 daughter, (2) Peter J Duffy, 1969, 2 daughters. Education: The Mount School, York, Newnham College, Cambridge; Bryn Mawr College, USA; Somerville College, Oxford. Appointments: Westminster Tutors, 1962-65, Extra-Mural Lecturer, University of London, 1962-71; Part-time Lecturer, Department of Liberal Studies, Central School of Art and Design, 1965-69, Lecturer, 1972-81, Tutor of Admissions, 1980-82, Assistant Tutor, 1977-80, Senior Lecturer, 1981-83, Department of English, University College London; Associate, Newnham College, Cambridge, 1977-82; Full time writer, 1983-; External Assessor in Literature, Central School of Art and Design, External Examiner, UEA; Regular Reviewer and contributor to press, radio and TV. Publications: Shadow of the Sun, 1964, 1991; Degrees of Freedom, 1965, 1994; The Game, 1967; Wordsworth and Coleridge in Their Time, 1970; The Virgin in the Garden, 1978; Still Life, 1985; Sugar and Other Stories, 1987; Unruly Times, 1989; Possession: A Romance, George Eliot: The Mill on the Floss (editor), George Eliot: Selected Essays and Other Writings (editor), 1990; Passions of the Mind (essays), 1991; Angels and Insects, 1992; The Matisse Stories, 1993; The Djinn in the Nightingale's Eye: Five Fairy Stories, 1994; Imagining Characters (with Ignês Sodré), 1995; Babel Tower, 1996; The Oxford Book of English Short Stories (editor), Elementals: Stories of Fire and Ice, 1998; The Biographer's Tale, On Histories and Stories, 2000; Portraits in Fiction, Bird Hand Book (jointly), 2001; A Whistling Woman, 2002; Little Black Book of Stories (short stories), O Henry Prize Stories (contributed short story, The Thing in the Forest), 2003; Author of varied literary criticism, articles, reviews and broadcasts. Honours: PEN Macmillan Silver Pen of Fiction, 1985; Booker Prize for Fiction, 1990; Irish Times-Aer Lingus Literature Prize, 1990; CBE, 1990; Premio Malaparte Award, Capri, 1995; Mythopoeic Fantasy Award for Adult Literature, 1998; DBE, 1999; Toepfer Foundation Shakespeare Prize for contributions to British Culture, 2002; Chevalier de l'Ordre des Arts et des Lettres, France, 2003; Fellow, English Association, 2004; Hon DLitt: University of Bradford, 1987; University of Durham, 1991; University of York, 1991; University of Nottingham, 1992; University of Liverpool, 1993; University of Portsmouth, 1994; University of London, 1995; University of Cambridge, 1999; University of Sheffield, 2000; Honorary Fellow: Newnham College, Cambridge, 1999; London Institute, 2000; UCL, 2004; University of Kent, 2004. Memberships: Panel of Judges, Hawthornden

Prize, BBC's Social Effects of TV Advisory Group, 1974-77; Communications and Cultural Studies Board, CNAA, 1978-84; Committee of Management, Society of Authors, 1984-88 (Chair, 1986-88); Creative and Performing Arts Board, 1985-87; Kingman Committee on English Language, 1987-88; Advisory Board, Harold Hyam Wingate Fellowship, 1988-92; Member, Literary Advisory Panel British Council, 1990-98; London Library Committee, 1990-; Board British Council, 1993-98. Address: c/o Rogers, Coleridge & White, 20 Powis Mews, London W11 1JN, England. Website: www.asbyatt.com

BYE Erik, b. 13 September 1945, Oslo, Norway. Senior Scientist. m. Kirsten Offenberg, 2 daughters. Education: Cand real, Chemistry, 1972, Dr philos, 1976, University of Oslo. Appointments: Scientific Assistant in Chemistry, University of Oslo, 1972-78; Postdoctoral studies, ETH, Zurich, 1977; Scientist, Occupational Hygiene, National Institute of Occupational Health, 1979-; Guest Researcher, SINTEF, Oslo, 1987. Publications: Scientific publications in international journals of chemistry and occupational hygiene. Address: National Institute of Occupational Health, PO Box 8149 Dep, N-0033 Oslo, Norway. E-mail: erik.bye@stami.no

BYERS Rt Hon Stephen (John), b. 13 April 1953, Wolverhampton, England. Politician. Education: Chester City Grammar School; Chester College; Liverpool Polytechnic. Appointments: Senior Lecturer, Law, Newcastle Polytechnic, 1977-82; Labour Party MP for Wallsend, 1992-97, for Tyneside N, 1997-; Opposition Whip, 1994-95, frontbench spokesman on education and employment, 1995-97; Minister of State Department for Education and Employment, 1997-98; Chief Secretary to the Treasury, 1998-99; Secretary of State for Trade and Industry, 1999-2001, for Transport, Local Government and the Regions, 2001-02. Address: House of Commons, London SW1A 0AA, England.

BYRNE Gabriel, b. 1950, Dublin, Ireland. Actor. m. Ellen Barken, 1988, divorced, 1 son, 1 daughter. Education: University College, Dublin. Appointments: Archaeologist; Teacher; Actor. Creative Works: Films include: Hanna K Gothic; Julia and Julia; Siesta; Miller's Crossing; Hakon Hakenson; Dark Obsession; Cool World; A Dangerous Woman; Little Women; Usual Suspects; Frankie Starlight; Dead Man; Last of the High Kings; Mad Dog Time; Somebody is Waiting; The End of Violence (director); Tony's Story; Polish Wedding; This is the Dead; The Man in the Iron Mask; Quest for Camelot; An Ideal Husband; Enemy of the State; Stigmata; End of Days; Spider; Ghost Ship; Shade, 2003; Vanity Fair, 2004; PS, 2004; The Bridge of San Luis Rey, 2004; Assault on Precinct 13, 2005; Wah-Wah, 2005; Leningrad, 2006; Played, 2006; Jindabyne, 2006; Co-Producer, In the Name of the Father. Address: c/o ICM, 8942 Wilshire Boulevard, Beverly Hills, CA 96211, USA.

BYUN Jong Chul, b. 16 September 1953, Republic of Korea. Professor. m. Soon Ja Suk, 1 son, 1 daughter. Education: PhD, Department of Chemistry, Graduate School, Kyungpook National University, 1988. Appointments: Chairman, Department of Chemistry, 1993-97, Dean, College of Natural Sciences, 2007-, Cheju National University; Director, Korean Chemical Society, 2004. Publications: Synthesis and crystal structure of a new polymer built from a cyano nickel (II) oxa-azamacrocyclic complex, 2006; Synthesis and characterization of the first tetraazadiphenol macrocyclic dinickel (II) complex containing μ (O, O')-nitrito-nitro-aqua ligands, 2006; Synthesis and crystal structure of a mononuclear Ni(II) complex with tetraazadiphenol macrocycle bearing cyclohexanes, 2007. Memberships: The Korean Chemical Society. Address: Department of Chemistry, College of Natural Sciences, Cheju National University, Jeju 690-756, Republic of Korea.

C

CAAN James, b. 26 March 1940, Bronx, New York, USA. Actor; Director. m. (1) DeeJay Mathis, 1961, 1 daughter, (2) Sheila Ryan, 1976, 1 son, (3) Linda O'Gara, 1995, 2 children. Creative Works: Films include: Irma La Douce, 1963; Lady in a Cage, 1964; The Glory Guys, 1965; Countdown, Games, Eldorado, 1967; Journey to Shiloh, Submarine XI, 1968; Man Without Mercy, The Rain People, 1969; Rabbit Run, 1970; T R Baskin, 1971; The Godfather, 1972; Slither, 1973; Cinderella Liberty, Freebie and the Bean, The Gambler, Funny Lady, Rollerball, The Killer Elite, 1975; Harry and Walter Go to New York, Silent Movie, 1976; A Bridge Too Far, Another Man, Another Chance, 1977; Comes a Horseman, 1978; Chapter Two, 1980; Thief, 1982; Kiss Me Goodbye, Bolero, 1983; Gardens of Stone, 1988; Alien Nation, Dad, 1989; Dick Tracy, 1990; Misery, For the Boys, Dark Backward, 1991; Honeymoon in Vegas, 1992; Flesh and Bone, 1993; The Program, 1994; North Star, Boy Called Hate, 1995; Eraser, Bulletproof, Bottle Rocket, 1996; This Is My Father, Poodle Springs, 1997; Blue Eyes, 1998; The Yards, The Way of the Gun, 1999; In the Boom Boom Room, Luckytown, Viva Las Nowhere, 2000; In the Shadows, 2001; Night at the Golden Eagle, City of Ghosts, 2002; Dogville, Dallas 362, This Thing of Ours, Jericho Mansions, Elf, 2003; Director, Actor, Hide in Plain Sight, 1980; Director, Violent Streets, 1981; Starred in television movie, Brian's Song, 1971; The Warden, 2000; Numerous other TV appearances. Address: c/o Fred Specktor, Endeavor, 9701 Wilshire Boulevard, 10th Floor, Beverly Hills, CA 90212, USA.

CABALLÉ Monserrat, b. 12 April 1933, Barcelona, Spain. Soprano Opera Singer. m. Bernabé Marti, 1 son, 1 daughter. Education: Conservatorio del Liceo; Private studies. Appointments: North American Debut, Manon, Mexico City, 1964; US Debut, Carnegie Hall, 1965; Appearances in several opera houses and at numerous festivals. Creative Works: Lucrezia Borgia; La Traviata; Salomé; Aida. Honours: Most Excellent and Illustrious Dobna and Cross of Isabella the Catholic; Commandeur des Arts et des Lettres, 1986; UNESCO Goodwill Ambassador in her semi-retirement; Numerous honorary degrees, awards and medals. Address: c/o Columbia Artists Management Inc, 165 West 57th Street, New York, NY 10019, USA.

CABRIJAN Tomislav Viktor, b. 22 October 1934. Physician; Internist. m. Ivanka Tusek, 1 son, 1 daughter. Education: MD, Zagreb, Croatia, 1959; Internal Medicine Specialist, 1968, PhD, 1975, University of Zagreb; Full Professor, Internal Medicine, 1987. Appointments: Ward Internist, Endocrinologist, Sisters of Mercy, University Hospital, Zagreb, 1968-70; Head, Centre for Diabetes, Department of Endocrinology, 1970-90; Head, Department of Endocrinology Diabetes and Metabolic Diseases, 1990; Acting Director, Sisters of Mercy, University Hospital, Zagreb, Croatia, 1990. Publications: Editor (books): Obesity and Apnea Syndrome, 1993; How to Care About Your Diabetes (translation), 1995; Urgent States in Endocrinology, 1996; Rational diagnosis and therapy in Endocrinology, 2000; Scientific approach to hypoglycaemia, 2006; Contributor of articles to professional journals. Honour: Fellowship, Alexander von Humboldt Foundation, Bonn, Germany, 1972, 1975, 1978, 1982, 1989, 1998; Yearly award for science of the Parliament of Croatia, 2000. Memberships: German Diabetes Association, 1989-; Croatian Academy of Medical Sciences, 1990-; European Society for the Study of Diabetes, 1998; American Endocrine Society, 1998; European Federation of Endocrine Societies (EFES) 1999. Address: Petrova Street 110, 10000 Zagreb, Croatia.

CACKOVIC Hinko, b. Zagreb, Croatia. Resident in Berlin, Germany 1970-. Scientist; Research Physicist; Artist; Photoartist; Painter; Sculptor working in metal. m. Jasna Loboda-Cackovic. Education: Diploma in Science, Physics, University of Zagreb, Croatia, 1962; MSc, Solid State Physics, University of Zagreb, 1964; PhD, Fritz-Haber Institut der Max-Planck-Gesellschaft, Berlin-Dahlem, Germany, and University of Zagreb, 1970. Appointments: Scientist, Institute of Physics, University of Zagreb, 1962-65; Scientist, Atom Institute Ruder Boskovic, Zagreb, 1967-71; Postdoctoral, 1970-72, Scientist, 1965-67, 1970-80, Fritz-Haber Institut der Max-Planck-Gesellschaft, Berlin-Dahlem, Germany; Scientist, Technical University, Berlin, Germany, 1980-95; Freelance in multidisciplinary fields concerning new developments of art and new fields in science and technology, different aspects of human living and activity, 1995-; Always searching for new ways. Publications: Over 55 scientific articles to professional journals, including: Physics of polymers; Synthetic and biological molecules; Polymer liquid crystals; Memory in Nature, 1971; Self-ordering of the matter; Memory of solid and fluid matter; Order/disorder phenomena in the atomic, molecular and colloidal dimensions; Mutual dependence of order between atomic and colloidal entities; Theoretical and experimental development of small and wide angle x-rays scattering analysis, magnetic susceptibility and of broad line nuclear magnetic resonance analysis; Development of physical instruments; Works of Art in professional journals and books; Photoart-pictures cutting out parts of reality to change it; Photoart revealing hidden worlds; Creative activity in Photoart/sculpturing and science (physics, chemistry) is influenced by literature music, astrophysics; New aesthetic spaces are forming, through the fusion of art and science, in sculptures built up by physical instruments and machines; Developing of Universal Art including mentioned multidisciplinary fields; Intention to contribute: to synthesis of science, art and harmony, to the ethic and aesthetic part of human living and activity, to freedom in all its facets through culture in the widest sense; Photoart-pictures presented at numerous exhibitions in Germany, Austria, France, Switzerland, 1991- and in Internet galleries, 1998-; Innovative works, two-artist cooperation JASHIN, with Jasna Loboda-Cackovic from 1997; Permanent art representations: Gallery Kleiner Prinz, Baden-Baden, Germany, 1991-; Cyber Museum at wwwARTchannel, www.art-channel.net, 1999-; Virtual Gallery of Jean-Gebser-Akademie eV, Germany, www.artgala.de, 1999-. Honours: Awards for career achievements, accomplishments and contributions to society: Distinguished Leadership Award, 2000; 21st Century Achievement Awards, 2003; Gold Medal for Germany for Success, Passion, Courage, Spirit, Commitment, Excellence, Virtue, Germany, 2006; For outstanding contributions to the field of Physics: Hall of Fame, 1000 World Leaders of Scientific Influence, 2002; Distinguished Service to Science Award, for Various Aspects of Physical Science, 2007; Awards for Art, Science and their Creative Interaction: Da Vinci Diamond, 2004; IBC Lifetime Achievement Award, 2006; Dedication, Dictionary of International Biography, 33rd Edition, 2007; Salute to Greatness Award, 2007; The Roll of Honour, 2007-; Art awards include: Two Euro Art Prizes, Exhibitions, Germany: Dresden and Baden-Baden, 1994, 1995; Prize for Photoart, 5th Open Art Prize, Bad Nauheim, Germany, 1995 and prize Phoenix, International Virtual Internet Art Competitions, Forschungs-Instituts Bildender Kunste, Germany, 1998, 1999/2000, 2001; Prize and magna cum laude for the oeuvre, Virtual Internet Art Competitions, Jean-Gebser-Akademie, Germany, 2002-03, 2004-05; Grants: Technical University Berlin, Germany, 1965-67; Alexander von Humboldt Stiftung, Bad

Godesberg, Germany, 1970-72; Max-Planck-Gesellschaft, Fritz-Haber-Institut, Berlin-Dahlem, Germany, 1972-73. Memberships: Deutsche Physikalische Gesellschaft, 1972-95; Member, Cyber Museum Euro art channel, 1998-; Fellow, International Biographical Association, 1998-2001; Virtual Gallery artgala.de, Forschungs-Institut Bildender Künste and Jean-Gebser-Akademie eV, Germany, 1999-; Europäischer Kulturkreis Baden-Baden, 2002-; Active member, various organisations working against child poverty, sponsoring their education, 2006-; International Order of Merit, 2007-; Sovereign Ambassador, Order of American Ambassadors, 2007-; Vice President, Recognition Board, World Congress of Arts, Sciences and Communication, 2007-; Secretary-General, United Cultural Convention, 2007-09. Address: Im Dol 60, 14195 Berlin, Germany.

CADBURY (Nicholas) Dominic, Sir, b. 12 May 1940. Business Executive. m. Cecilia Sarah Symes, 1972, 3 daughters. Education: Eton College; Trinity College, Cambridge; Stanford University, USA. Appointments: Chief Executive, Cadbury Schweppes PLC, 1984-93, Chair, 1993-2000; Director, Economic Group, 1990-2003, Chair, 1994-2003; Joint Deputy Chair, Guinness, 1994-97, Deputy Chair, 1996-97; Joint Deputy Chair, EMI Group PLC, 1999-2004; President, Food and Drink Federation, 1999; Chair, Wellcome Trust, 2000-; Chair, Transense Techs, 2000-03; Non-Executive Director, Misys PLC, 2000-; Chancellor, University of Birmingham, 2002-. Memberships: Royal Mint Advisory Committee, 1986-94; President, Committee CBI, 1989-94; Food Association, 1989-2000; Stanford Advisory Council, 1989-95. Address: The Wellcome Trust, 183 Euston Road, London, NW1, England.

CAESAR Anthony Douglass, b. 3 April 1924, Southampton, England. Clerk in Holy Orders. Education: MA, MusB, FRCO, Magdalene College, Cambridge; St Stephen's House, Oxford. Appointments: RAF, 1943-46; Assistant Music Master, Eton College, 1948-51; Precentor, Radley College, 1952-59; Assistant Curate, St Mary Abbots, Kensington, 1961-65; Priest-in-Ordinary to The Queen, 1968-70; Chaplain, Royal School of Church Music, 1965-70; Assistant Secretary, Advisory Council for the Church's Ministry, 1965-70; Resident Priest, St Stephen's Church, Bournemouth, 1970-73; Precentor and Sacrist, 1974-79, Honorary Canon, 1975-76, 1979-91, Residentiary Canon, 1976-79, Winchester Cathedral; Sub-Dean of HM Chapels Royal, Deputy Clerk of The Closet, Sub-Almoner and Domestic Chaplain to The Queen, 1979-91; Chaplain, St Cross Hospital, Winchester, 1991-93. Publications: Co-Editor, New English Hymnal 1986, Church Music. Honours: John Stewart of Rannoch Scholar in Sacred Music, 1943; LVO, 1987; CVO, 1991; Extra Chaplain to The Queen, Canon Emeritus, Winchester Cathedral, 1991-. Address: 26 Capel Court, The Burgage, Prestbury, Cheltenham, Gloucestershire GL52 3EL, England.

CAGE Nicolas (Nicholas Coppola), b. 7 January 1964, Long Beach, California, USA. Actor. m. 1 son with Kristina Fulton, (1) Patricia Arquette, 1995, divorced 2000, (2) Lisa Marie Presley, 2002, divorced 2002, (3) Alice Kim, 2004, 1 son. Creative Works: Films include: Valley Girl, 1983; Rumble Fish; Racing With the Moon; The Cotton Club; Birdy; The Boy in Blue; Raising Arizona; Peggy Sue Got Married; Moonstruck; Vampire's Kiss; Killing Time; The Short Cut; Queens Logic; Wild of Heart; Wings of the Apache; Zandalee; Red Rock West; Guarding Tess; Honeymoon in Vegas; It Could Happen to You; Kiss of Death; Leaving Las Vegas; The Rock, The Funeral, 1996; Con Air, Face Off, 1997; Eight Millimeter, Bringing Out the Dead, 1999; Gone in 60

Seconds, 2000; The Family Man, Captain Corelli's Mandolin, Christmas Carol: The Movie (voice), 2001; Windtalkers, Sonny, Adaptation, 2002; Matchstick Men, Producer, The Life of David Gale, 2003; National Treasure, 2004; Lord of War, The Weather Man, 2005; The Ant Bull (voice), World Trade Center, The Wicker Man, 2006; Ghost Rider, Grindhouse, Next, Bangkok Dangerous, 2007. Honours include: Golden Globe Award, Best Actor, 1996; Academy Award, Best Actor, 1996; Lifetime Achievement Award, 1996; P J Owens Award, 1998; Charles A Crain Desert Palm Award, 2001. Address: Saturn Films, 9000 West Sunset Boulevard, Suite 911, West Hollywood, CA 90069, USA.

CAGLAR Mine, b. 14 November 1967, Turkey. Applied Probabilist. m. Mehmet Caglar, 1 son, 1 daughter. Education: BS, Middle East Technical University, 1989; MS, Bilkent University, 1991. Appointments: Assistant in Instruction, Princeton University, USA, 1992-97; Research Scientist, Bellcore, 1997-98; Assistant Professor of Mathematics, Koc University, Istanbul, Turkey, 1999-. Publications: Articles in scientific journals include: A Long Range-Dependent Workload Model for Packet Data Traffic, 2004. Honour: Mustafa Parlor Research Award, 2005. Memberships: Sigma Xi; Informs; Bernoulli Society. Address: Koc University, College of Arts and Sciences, Sariyer, Istanbul, Turkey 34450. Website: http://home.ku.edu.tr/~mcaglar

CAHILL George F, b. 7 July 1927, New York City, USA. Medical Science. m. Sarah duPont, 2 sons, 4 daughters. Education: BS, Yale University, 1949; MD, Columbia University, College of Physicians and Surgeons, 1953; MA, Harvard University, 1966. Appointments: Pharmacist Mate 2/c, USNR, American Theater, 1945-47; Research Fellow, National Science Foundation, Department of Biological Chemistry, Harvard Medical School, 1955-57; House Officer and Residencies, 1953-58; Director of Endocrine-Metabolic Unit, Peter Bent Brigham Hospital and Fellow to Director, Joslin Diabetes Research Laboratories, Boston, 1952-76; Member and Chairman, many committees of the National Institutes of Health, Veteran's Administration, National Commission on Diabetes, American Diabetes Association (President, 1975), Science Advisory Board (Merck, Sandoz, Johnson and Johnson); Investigator to Director of Research, 1962-89, Vice President, 1985-89, Howard Hughes Medical Institute; Instructor to Professor of Medicine, Emeritus, 1957-, Harvard Medical School; Professor of Biological Sciences, Dartmouth College, Hanover NH, 1990-96. Publications: Over 350 publications in professional journals, chapters in medical texts, etc. Honours: Oppenheimer Award, 1962; Lilly Award, 1965; Banting Award, 1974, 1976; JP Hoet Award, 1973; Joseph Mather Smith Award, 1975; Fellow, American Association for the Advancement of Science, 1975; President, American Diabetes Association, 1975; Charaka Award and Lecture, 1976; Goldberger Award in Nutrition, 1977; Banting Lecture, 1977; Gairdner International Award, 1979; Director's Award, 1989; Gold Medal, Columbia College of P&S, 1991; Medical Foundation, Boston, Annual Award, 1991; Hotchkiss School Outstanding Alumnus of the Year, 1995; Renold Award, 1996. Memberships: American Diabetes Association; American Academy of Arts and Sciences; American Physiological Society; Endocrine Society; Clinical and Climatological Association; American Society of Clinical Investigation; Association of American Physicians; Historical Society of Cheshire County, New Hampshire; Trustee, Village of Stoddard, NH; Trustee, Monadnock Conservancy; Member, New Hampshire US Agricultural Association; Various forestry state and national organisations.

CAIMBEUL Maoilios MacAonghais, b. 23 March 1944, Isle of Skye, Scotland. Writer; Poet. m. (1) Margaret Hutchison, 1971, divorced 1992, 1 son, (2) Margaret Goodall, 2002. Education: BA, Edinburgh University; Teaching Diploma, Jordanhill College, Glasgow, 1978. Appointments: Gaelic Teacher, Tobermory High School, 1978-84; Gaelic Development Officer, Highlands and Islands Development Board, 1984-87; Writer, 1987-. Publications: Eileanan, 1980; Bailtean, 1987; A Càradh an Rathaid, 1988; An Aghaidh na Sìorraidheachd, (anthology with 7 other Gaelic poets), 1991; Saoghal Ùr, 2003; Gràmar na Gàidhlig (workbook for schools), 2005; Inbhir Àsdal Nam Buadh (songs and poems by Iain Cameron), Editor with Roy Wentworth, 2006. Contributions to: Gairm; Lines Review; Chapman; Cencrastus; Orbis; Poetry Ireland Review; Comhar; Gairfish; Baragab; Weekend Scotsman; West Highland Free Press; An Guth; Gath; Northwords Now; Poetry Scotland; Contributor to Taking You Home, poems and conversations, 2006; Anthologies: Air Ghleus 2, 1989; Twenty of the Best, 1990; The Patched Fool, 1991; Somhairle, Dàin is Deilbh, 1991; An Tuil, 1999; An Leabhar Mòr, PNE, 2002; Scotlands, Poets and The Nation, 2004. Honours: Award, Gaelic Books Council Poetry Competition, 1978-79; Poetry/Fiction Prize, Gaelic Books Council, 1982-83; Poetry Prize Scottish Gaelic Section, Dunleary International Poetry Competition, 1998; Royal National Mod Bardic Crown, 2002; 2nd, BBC Alba Poetry Competition Prize, 2006. Membership: Scottish PEN. Address: 12 Flodigarry, Staffin, Isle of Skye, IV51 9HZ, Scotland.

CAIN Christopher Marden John, b. 24 September 1961, Adelaide, Australia. Orthopaedic Spinal Surgeon. m. Heather Jean, 1 son, 1 daughter. Education: University of Adelaide, 1979-84; Part I Surgical Fellowship, 1986; AO Basic Course, Adelaide, 1990; AO Spine Course, Brisbane, 1991; Fellow, Royal Australasian College of Surgery, 1993; Doctor of Medicine, University of Adelaide, 1993. Appointments: Intern, 1985, Basic Surgical Training, 1986, Neurosurgery Registrar, 1987, Advanced Trainee Orthopaedic Surgery, 1991, Queen Elizabeth Hospital; Orthopaedic Registrar, Royal Adelaide Hospital, Flinders Medical Centre, and Repatriation General Hospital, 1988; Trauma/Spinal Research Fellow, 1989, Advanced Trainee Orthopaedic Surgery, 1990, 1992, 1993, Royal Adelaide Hospital; Advanced Trainee Orthopaedic Surgery, Adelaide Children's Hospital, 1991, Flinders Medical Centre, 1992; Clinical Spinal Fellow to Mr John K Webb, University Hospital, Queen's Medical Centre, Nottingham, England, 1993-94; AO Spinal Fellow, Drs Fritz Margerl & Bernard Jeannerret, Kantonsspital St Gallen, Switzerland, 1994; Visiting Medical Specialist, 1994-97, Senior Visiting Medical Specialist, 1997-99, Flinder Medical Centre; Visiting Medical Specialist, 1994-98, Senior Visiting Medical Specialist, 1998-, Royal Adelaide Hospital; Senior Visiting Medical Specialist, Women's & Children's Hospital, 1999-; Director AMPCo, 2006-; Director, AMA Commercial Ltd, 2006-. Publications: 16 papers and articles in professional medical journals. Honours: Rob Johnston Award, 1990; Censor-in Chief's Prize, 1990, 1991; Smith & Nephew Richards Academic Prize, 1993; 3rd Prize, American Orthopaedic Residence Meeting, USA, 1993; President's Award, Australian Medical Association, 2003; Listed in international biographical dictionaries. Memberships: Australian Medical Association; Australian Society of Orthopaedic Surgeons; Australian Spine Society; Australian Doctors Fund; Asia Pacific Orthopaedic Association. Address: Adelaide Spine Clinic, 252 East Terrace, Adelaide, SA 5000, Australia. E-mail: drcmjcain@adelaide.on.net

CAINE Sir Michael (Maurice Joseph Micklewhite), b. 14 March 1933, London, England. m. (1) Patricia Haines, divorced, 1 daughter; (2) Shakira Khatoon Baksh, 1 daughter. Career: British Army service in Berlin and Korea, 1951-53; Repertory theatres, Horsham and Lowestoft, 1953-55; Theatre Workshop, London, 1955; Acted in: Over 100 TV plays 1957-63; Films include: A Hill in Korea, 1956; Zulu, 1964; The Ipcress File, 1965; Alfie, The Wrong Box, Gambit, 1966; Funeral in Berlin, 1966; Billion Dollar Brain, Woman Times Seven, Deadfall, 1967; The Magus, Battle of Britain, Play Dirty, 1968; The Italian Job, 1969; Too Late the Hero, The Last Valley, 1970; Kidnapped, Pulp, Get Carter, 1971; Zee and Co, 1972; Sleuth, 1973; The Wilby Conspiracy, 1974; The Eagle Has Landed, The Man Who Would be King, 1975; A Bridge Too Far, The Silver Bears, 1976; The Swarm, California Suite, 1977; Ashanti, 1978; Beyond the Poseidon Adventure, The Island, 1979; Deathtrap, The Hand, 1981; Educating Rita, Jigsaw Man, The Honorary Consul, 1982; Blame it on Rio, 1983; Water, The Holcroft Covenant, 1984; Sweet Liberty, Mona Lisa, The Whistle Blower, 1985; Half Moon Street, The Fourth Protocol, Hannah and her Sisters (Academy Award), 1986; Surrender, 1987; Without a Clue, Jack the Ripper (TV, Golden Globe Award), Dirty Rotten Scoundrels, 1988; A Shock to the System, Bullseye, 1989; Noises Off, 1991; Blue Ice, The Muppet Christmas Carol, 1992; On Deadly Ground, 1993; World War II Then There Were Giants, 1994; Bullet to Beijing, 1995; Blood and Wine, Mandela and de Klerk, 1996; 20,000 Leagues Under the Sea, Shadowrun, 1997; Little Voice, 1998; The Debtors, The Cider House Rules; Curtain Call, Quills, 1999; Get Carter, Shiner, 2000; Last Orders, Quick Sands, 2001; The Quiet American, 2002; The Actors, Secondhand Lions, The Statement, 2003; Around the Bend, 2004; The Weather Man, Batman Begins, Bewitched, The Weather Man, 2005; Children of Men, The Prestige, 2006; Flawless, 2007. Publications: Michael Caine's File of Facts, 1987; Not Many People Know This, 1988; What's It All About, 1992; Acting in Film, 1993. Honours: CBE, 1992; Oscar, Actor in a Supporting Role, 1999; Knighted by HM Queen Elizabeth II, 2000; Numerous awards, nominations and citations from film and TV industry institutes, including several Golden Globe and Academy awards. Address: International Creative Management, Oxford House, 76 Oxford Road, London W1R 1RB, England.

CAIRNS David (Adam), b. 8 June 1926, Loughton, Essex, England. Music Critic; Writer. m. Rosemary Goodwin, 19 December 1959, 3 sons. Education: Trinity College, Oxford. Appointments: Music Critic, Evening Standard, and Spectator, 1958-62, Financial Times, 1963-67, New Statesman, 1967-70, Sunday Times, 1973-; Classical Programme Co-ordinator, Philips Records, 1967-73; Distinguished Visiting Scholar, Getty Center for the History of Art and Humanities, 1992; Visiting Resident Fellow, Merton College, Oxford, 1993. Publications: The Memoirs of Hector Berlioz (editor and translator), 1969, 4th edition, 1990; Responses: Musical Essays and Reviews, 1973; The Magic Flute, 1980; Falstaff, 1982; Berlioz, 2 volumes, 1989, 2000; Berlioz Volume II: Servitude and Greatness, 1832-1869, 1999. Honours: Chevalier, 1975, Officier, 1991, de l'Ordre des Arts des Lettres, France; Derek Allen Memorial Prize, British Academy, 1990; Royal Philharmonic Society Award, 1990; Yorkshire Post Prize, 1990; Commander of the Order of the British Empire, 1997; Whitbread Biography Prize, 1999; Royal Philharmonic Society Award, 1999; Samuel Johnson Non-Fiction Prize, 2000. Address: 49 Amerland Road, London SW18 1QA, England.

CAIRNS Hugh John Forster, b. 21 November 1922. Professor of Microbiology. m. Elspeth Mary Forster, 1948, 2 sons, 1 daughter. Education: Medical Degree, Balliol College, Oxford, 1943. Appointments: Surgical Resident, Radcliffe Infirmary, Oxford, 1945; Various appointments in London, Newcastle, Oxford; Virologist, Hall Institute, Melbourne, Australia, 1950-51; Viruses Research Institute, Entebbe, Uganda, 1952-54; Director, Cold Spring Harbor Laboratory of Quantative Biology, New York, 1963-68; Professor, State University of New York, American Cancer Society; Head, Mill Hill Laboratories, Imperial Cancer Research Fund, London, 1973-81; Department of Microbiology, Harvard School of Public Health, Boston, 1982-91; Research work into penicillin-resistant staphylococci, influenza virus, E.coli and DNA replication in mammals. Address: Holly Grove House, Wilcote, Chipping Norton, Exon, OX7 3EA, England.

CAITHNESS Peter Westmacott, b. 25 May 1932. Cricklewood, London, England. Security Technologies Marketing Consultant. m. Claude-Noële Gauthier, divorced 1994, 1 son, 2 daughters. Appointments: National Service, 2nd Lieutenant, Royal Artillery, 1950-52; Overseas Management Trainee, Hong Kong & Shanghai Banking Corporation, 1953-54; Overseas Sales Manager, Bradbury Wilkinson, 1954-70; Sales and Marketing Director, Aeroprint, 1970-85; Consultant, British American Banknote Corporation, 1986-96; Director, SATS (UK) Ltd, 1996-. Publications: Numerous articles about security printing in popular and professional journals. Honours: National Marketing Award, 1972; Queen's Award for Export, 1980. Memberships: Institute of Marketing; Councillor, Wooburn and Bourne End Parish Council, 2001-; Wycombe Talking Newspaper Committee, 1997-. Address: Berriedale, 26 Baker's Orchard, Wooburn Green, Buckinghamshire, HP10 0LS, England.

CALDER Nigel (David Ritchie), b. 2 December 1931, London, England. Writer. m. Elisabeth Palmer, 22 May 1954, 2 sons, 3 daughters. Education: BA, 1954, MA, 1957, Sidney Sussex College, Cambridge. Appointments: Research Physicist, Mullard Research Laboratories, Redhill, Surrey, 1954-56; Staff Writer, 1956-60, Science Editor, 1960-62, Editor, 1962-66, New Scientist; Science Correspondent, New Statesman, 1959-62, 1966-71. Publications: The Environment Game, 1967, US edition as Eden Was No Garden: An Inquiry Into the Environment of Man, 1967; Technopolis: Social Control of the Uses of Science, 1969; Violent Universe: An Eyewitness Account of the New Astronomy, 1970; The Mind of Man: An Investigation into Current Research on the Brain and Human Nature, 1970; Restless Earth: A Report on the New Geology, 1972; The Life Game: Evolution and the New Biology, 1974; The Weather Machine: How Our Weather Works and Why It Is Changing, 1975; The Human Conspiracy, 1976; The Key to the Universe: A Report on the New Physics, 1977; Spaceships of the Mind, 1978; Einstein's Universe, 1979; Nuclear Nightmares: An Investigation into Possible Wars, 1980; The Comet is Coming!: The Feverish Legacy of Mr Halley, 1981; Timescale: An Atlas of the Fourth Dimension, 1984; 1984 and Beyond: Nigel Calder Talks to His Computer About the Future, 1984; The English Channel, 1986; The Green Machines, 1986; Future Earth: Exploring the Frontiers of Science (editor with John Newell), 1989; Scientific Europe, 1990; Spaceship Earth, 1991; Giotto to the Comets, 1992; Beyond this World, 1995; The Manic Sun, 1997; Magic Universe: The Oxford Guide to Modern Science, 2003; Einstein's Universe (updated), 2005; Einstein: Relativity (introduction), 2006; The Chilling Stars: A New Theory of Climate Change (co-author with Henrik Svensmark), 2007. Contributions to: Television documentaries; Numerous periodicals. Honours: UNESCO Kalinga Prize, 1972; AAAS, honorary fellow, 1986; Listed in national and international biographical dictionaries. Memberships: Association of British Science Writers, Chairman, 1960-62; Cruising Association, London, Vice President, 1982-85; Fellow, Royal Astronomical Society, Council, 2001-04; Thames Sailing Barge Trust; Fellow, American Association for the Advancement of Science. Address: 26 Boundary Road, Crawley, West Sussex RH10 8BT, England. E-mail: nc@windstream.demon.co.uk

CALDERWOOD James Henry, b. 25 January 1925, Liverpool, England. Engineer; Physicist. Education: St Francis Xavier's College, Liverpool; B Eng, 1946, M Eng, 1948, PhD, 1952, University of Liverpool; DSc, National University of Ireland, 1985. Appointments: Research Engineer, British Insulated Calendars Cables Ltd, 1946-49; Research Fellow, University of Liverpool, 1949-51; Lecturer, Electrical Engineering, University of Strathclyde, Glasgow, 1951-54; Research Associate, Physical Chemistry, Princeton University, 1954-55; Lecturer, Electrical Engineering, Imperial College, London, 1955-58; Head, Department of Electrical Engineering, Dean of Engineering, Pro-Vice-Chancellor, University of Salford, 1958-81; Dean, Faculty of Engineering, National University of Ireland at Galway, 1981-90; Professorial Research Fellow, University of Salford, 1990-93; Professor of Engineering Physics, 1993-, Chief Scientist, 2004-, University of Bolton. Publications: Numerous articles in research journals. Honours: Doctor of Science, honoris causa, University of Salford, 1973; Honorary Diplomate, Dublin Institute of Technology, 1975; Doctor in Science, honoris causa, University of Dublin (Trinity College), 1997; Foreign Member, Finnish Academy of Sciences and Letters, 1979; Permanent Honorary Professor, University of Xi'an Jiaotong, China, 1983; Volta Medallist of the University of Pavia, Italy, 1984; Honorary Fellow, Institution of Engineers of Ireland, 1989; Fellow, Irish Academy of Engineering, Member of Council, 1997-; Honorary Professor, University of Dublin, Trinity College, 2000-. Memberships: Adviser on senior staff appointments to universities around the world; Adviser, research applications to many grant giving bodies; Visiting professor to several universities worldwide; Founder Member, later Chairman, Dielectrics Society. Address: The University of Bolton, Bolton, Lancashire BL3 5AB, England. E-mail: jcl@bolton.ac.uk

CALLOW Simon Philip Hugh, b. 15 June 1949, England. Actor; Director; Writer. Education: Queen's University, Belfast; Drama Centre. Creative Works: Stage appearances include: Kiss of the Spider Woman, 1985; Faust, 1988; Single Spies, 1988, 1989; The Destiny of Me, 1993; The Alchemist, 1996; The Importance of Being Oscar, Chimes at Midnight, 1997; The Mystery of Charles Dickens, 2001-04; The Holy Terror, 2004; Films include: Four Weddings and A Funeral, 1994; Ace Ventura: When Nature Calls, 1995; James and the Giant Peach (voice), The Scarlet Tunic, 1996; Woman In White, Bedrooms and Hallways, Shakespeare in Love, Interview with a Dead Man, 1997; No Man's Land, 2000; Thunderpants, A Christmas Carol, 2001; Bright Young Things, 2003; George and the Dragon, 2004; Phantom of the Opera, Bob the Butler, Rag Tale, The Civilisation of Maxwell Bright, 2005; Surveillance, 2007; TV: Patriot Witness, 1989; Trial of Oz, 1991; Bye Bye Columbus, 1992; Femme Fatale, 1993; Little Napoleons, 1994; An Audience with Charles Dickens, 1996; A Christmas Dickens, 1997; The Woman in White, 1998; Trial-Retribution, 1999, 2000; Galileo's Daughter; The Mystery of Charles Dickens, 2002; Dr Who, Marple, Midsomer Murders, 2005; Director: Carmen Jones, 1994; Il Trittico, 1995; Les Enfants du Paradis, Stephen Oliver

Trilogy, La Calisto, 1996; Il Turco in Italia, HRH, 1997; The Pajama Game, 1998; The Consul, Tomorrow Week (play for radio), 1999; Le Roi Malgré Lui, 2003; Jus' Like That, 2004; Several other radio broadcasts. Publications: Being An Actor, 1984; A Difficult Actor: Charles Laughton, 1987; Shooting the Actor, or the Choreography of Confusion, 1990; Acting in Restoration Comedy, 1991; Orson Wells: The Road to Xanadu, 1995; Les Enfants du Paradis, Snowdon - On Stage, 1996; The National, 1997; Love is Where it Falls, 1999; Shakespeare on Love, Charles Laughton's the Night of the Hunter, Oscar Wilde and His Circle, 2000; The Nights of the Hunter, 2001; Dicken's Christmas, Henry IV Part One, 2002; Henry IV Part Two, 2003; Hello Americans, 2006; Several translations; Weekly columns in professional newspapers; Contributions to The Guardian, The Times, The Sunday Times, The Observer, Evening Standard and others. Honours: Laurence Olivier Theatre Award, 1992; Patricia Rothermere Award, 1999; CBE, 1999. Address: c/o BAT, 180 Wardour Street, London, W1V 3AA, England.

CALNE Roy (Yorke) (Sir), b. 30 December 1930. Professor of Surgery; Consultant Surgeon. m. Patricia Doreen Whelan, 1956, 2 sons, 4 daughters. Education: Guy's Hospital Medical School; MB, BS, Hons, London, 1953. Appointments: Guy's Hospital, 1953-54; RAMC, 1954-56; Departmental Anatomy Demonstrator, Oxford University, 1957-58; Senior House Officer, Nuffield Orthopaedic Centre, Oxford, 1958; Surgical Registrar, Royal Free Hospital, 1958-60; Harkness Fellow in Surgery, Peter Bent Brigham Hospital, Harvard Medical School, 1960-61; Lecturer in Surgery, St Mary's Hospital, London, 1961-62; Senior Lecturer and Consultant Surgeon, Westminster Hospital, 1962-65; Professor of Surgery, 1965-98, Emeritus Professor, 1998, University of Cambridge; Ghim Seng Professor of Surgery, National University of Singapore, 1998-. Publications include: Renal Transplantation, co-author, 1963; Lecture Notes in Surgery, 1965; A Gift of Life, 1970; Clinical Organ Transplantation, editor and contributor, 1971; Immunological Aspects of Transplantation Surgery, editor and contributor, 1973; Transplantation Immunology, 1984; Surgical Anatomy of the Abdomen in the Living Subject, 1988; Too Many People, 1994; Art Surgery and Transplantation, 1996; The Ultimate Gift, 1998; Numerous papers and book chapters. Honours include: Hallet Prize, 1957, Jacksonian Prize, 1961, Hunterian Professor, 1962, Cecil Joll Prize, 1966, Hunterian Orator, 1989, Royal College of Surgeons; Honorary MD, Oslo, 1986, Athens, 1990, Hanover, 1991, Thailand, 1993, Belfast, 1994, Edinburgh, 2001; Prix de la Société Internationale de Chirurgie, 1969; Fastin Medal, Finnish Surgical Society, 1977; Lister Medal, 1984; Knighted, 1986; Cameron Prize, Edinburgh University, 1990; Ellison-Cliffe Medal, 1990; The Medawar Prize, Transplantation Society, 1992; Honorary Fellow, Royal College of Surgeons of Thailand, 1992; Ernst Jung Prize, 1996; Gold Medal of the Catalan Transplantation Society, 1996; Grand Officer of the Republic of Italy, 2000; King Faisal International Prize for Medicine, 2001; Prince Mahidol Prize for Medicine, 2002; Thomas E Starzl Prize in Surgery & Immunology, 2002. Memberships include: Fellow, Royal College of Surgeons; Fellow, Royal Society; Fellow, Association of Surgeons of Great Britain; European Society for Organ Transplantation, 1983-84; Corresponding Fellow, American Surgical Association. Address: 22 Barrow Road, Cambridge CB2 2AS, England.

CALOGERO Francesco, b. 6 February 1935, Fiesole, Italy. University Professor. m. Luisa La Malfa. 1 son, 1 daughter. Education: Laurea in Fisica, cum laude, Rome University, 1958. Appointments: Various positions, Rome University, 1958-; Professor of Theoretical Physics, Rome University La

Sapienza, 1976-; Military service, 1959-60; two years in USA, 1961-63; three months in India, 1967; one year in Moscow, 1969-70; one year in London, 1979-80; Visiting Professor in Groningen, London, Montpellier, Hefei, Paris, Cuernavaca. Publications: Over 300 scientific papers published in international journals; 3 written books; 2 edited books; Over 400 publications on science and society (mainly arms control), including written and edited books and a regular column in the oldest popular science magazine in Italy; Member of several editorial boards. Honour: Accepted 1995 Nobel Peace Prize on behalf of the Pugwash Conferences on Science and World Affairs. Memberships: Member, 1987-90, Scientific Secretary, 1990-93, Chairman, 1993-96, Mathematical Physics Commission, International Union of Pure and Applied Physics; Secretary General, Pugwash Conferences, 1989-97; Chairman, Pugwash Council, 1997-2002; Scientific Council, Italian Union of Scientists for Disarmament; Committee on International Security and Arms Control of the Accademia dei Lincei. Address: Via Sant' Alberto Magno 1, 00153 Rome, Italy. E-mail: francesco.calogero@roma1.infn.it

CALVIN Wyn (Wyndham Calvin-Thomas), b. 28 August 1928, Narberth, Pembrokeshire, Wales. Actor. Education: Canton High School, Cardiff, Wales. Career: Non-stop career in Theatre, TV and Radio from 1945-. Publications: Numerous newspaper columns and magazine articles over many years. Honours: MBE; Officer of the Order of St John; Honorary Fellow, Royal Welsh College of Music and Drama; Liveryman, Wales Livery Guild; Freeman of the City of London; preceptor and past King Rat of the Grand Order of Water Rats (Britain's principle show-business fraternity and charity); Honorary Citizen , City of Macon, Georgia, USA. Memberships: Founder-Trustee Children's Hospital for Wales Appeal; Vice-president, London Welsh Male Choir; President, South Wales Massed Male Choirs; Executive Committee Member, Entertainment Artists Benevolent Fund; Producer, Presenter, Wales Annual Festival of Remembrance. Address: 121 Cathedral Road, Cardiff CF11 9PH, Wales.

CAMERON David, b. 9 October 1966. Member of Parliament; Conservative Party Leader. m. Samantha Gwendoline Sheffield, 2 sons, 1 daughter. Education: BA, Brasenose College, Oxford. Appointments: Conservative Research Department, 1988-92; Special Advisor, HM Treasury, then Home Office; MP (Conservative), Witney, 2001-; Member, Home Affairs Select Committee, 2001-; Shadow Deputy Leader, House of Commons, 2003; Deputy Chairman, Conservative Party, 2003; Front Bench Spokesman on Local Government Finance, 2004; Head of Policy Co-ordination (member of shadow cabinet), 2004-; Head, Corporate Affairs, Carlton Communications plc; Head of Policy Co-ordination, 2005; Shadow Secretary of State for Education and Skills, 2005; Leader, Conservative Party, 2005-. Address: House of Commons, London SW1A 0AA, England. Website: www.davidcameronmp.com

CAMERON James, b. 16 August 1954, Kapuskasing, Ontario, Canada. Director; Screenwriter. m. Linda Hamilton, 1 daughter. Education: Fullerton Junior College. Appointments: Founder, Lightstorm Entertainment, 1990, Head, 1992-; Chief Executive Officer, Digital Domain, 1993-. Creative Works: Films: Piranha II - The Spawning (director); The Terminator (director, and screenplay), 1984; The Abyss (director and screenplay), 1994; Terminator 2: Judgement Day (co-screenwriter, director, producer), 1994; Point Break (executive producer), 1994; True Lies; Strange Days; Titanic, 1996; Solaris (producer), 2002; Terminator 3: Rise of the Machines (writer), 2003; Ghosts of the Abyss (director and producer), 2003; Volcanoes of the Deep Sea (executive producer), 2003; Aliens of the Deep (director and producer), 2005. Honours include: Academy Award, Best Director; 11 Academy Awards. Address: Lightstorm Entertainment, 919 Santa Monica Boulevard, Santa Monica, CA 90401, USA.

CAMERY John William, b. 5 February 1951, Cincinnati, Ohio, USA. Computer Software Engineer. Education: BA (Honours) Mathematics, University of Cincinnati, 1972; MSc, Carnegie-Mellon University, 1974. Appointments: Mathematician, US Army Material Systems Analysis Agency, Maryland, 1973; Student Assistant Engineering, Spectrum Analysis Task Force, Federal Communications Commission, Park Ridge, Illinois, 1974; Mathematician, US Army Communications Electronics-Engineering Installation Agency, Washington DC, 1975-83; Mathematician, Defense Communications Agency, JDSSC, Washington DC, 1983-86; Programmer Analyst, General Sciences Corp, Laurel, Maryland, 1986-87; Software Engineer, Sygnetron Protection Systems, 1987-88; Consultant, Lockheed-Martin Ocean Systems, Operations, Glen Burnie, Maryland, 1988-89; Computer Software Engineer, RDA Logicon, Leavenworth, Kansas, 1989-2001; Lead Senior Systems Analyst, Anteon Corporation, a General Dynamics Company, Battle Command Training Center, Schofield Barracks, Hawaii, 2001-. Publications: Simulation Techniques for a Multiple CPU Military Communication System(co-author), 1976; Pentagon Consolidated Telecommunications Centers System (PCTCS), Video Subsystem Reference Manual, 1982; Tying Together New Technologies in Battle Simulation, 2003. Memberships: American Mathematical Society, 1974-; Christian Church; European Math Society; Greater Cincinnati Amateur Radio Association (WA8WNR), 1967; Imperial Hawaii Vacation Club, 1981-; IEEE Computer Society; Republican Party; Société Mathematique de France. Address: 94-647 Kauakapuu Loop, Mililani, HI 96789-1832, USA.

CAMPBELL Alastair John, b. 25 May 1957, England; Civil Servant; Journalist. Partner, Fiona Miller, 2 sons, 1 daughter. Education: Gonville & Caius College, Cambridge. Appointments: Trainee Reporter, Tavistock Times, Sunday Independent, 1980-82; Freelance Reporter, 1982-83; Reporter, Daily Mirror, 1982-86, Political Editor, 1989-93; News Editor, Sunday Today, 1985-86; Political Correspondent, Sunday Mirror, 1986-87, Political Editor, 1987-89, Columnist, 1989-91; Assistant Editor, Columnist, Today, 1993-95; Press Secretary to Leader of the Opposition, 1994-97; Press Secretary to Prime Minister, 1997-2001; Director of Communications and Strategy, 2001-03; Member, election campaign team, 2005-; Visiting Fellow, Institute of Politics, Harvard University, 2004. Publications: The Blair Years, 2007. Membership: President, Keighley Branch, Burnley Football Supporters' Club. Address: Prime Minister's Office, 10 Downing Street, London SW1A 2AA, England.

CAMPBELL Lynn Pamela, b. 11 January 1955, Bristol, England. Conservator. m. Hugh Campbell, 1985. Education: BA (Hons), Fine Art, Loughborough College of Art, 1977; Postgraduate qualification in Education, Liverpool, 1981; Postgraduate qualification in Conservation of Fine Art, Newcastle upon Tyne, 1983. Appointments: Practising Artist, numerous exhibitions throughout United Kingdom, 1977-83; Conservator, Royal Scottish Museum, Edinburgh, Scotland, 1983-84; Tutor, Zanzibar National Archives, Tanzania, East Africa, summer 1984, 1985; Lecturer, MA Conservation Course for Fine Art Conservation, Tyne & Wear, England, 1984-86; Conservator, Robert McDougall Art Gallery (now Christchurch Art Gallery), Christchurch, New Zealand,

1986-2007. Publications: IIC Conservation Studies; The effects of selected aqueous treatments on the properties of two papers. Memberships: ICON; AIC; AICCM; NZICCM. Address: 33 Locarno Street, Christchurch 2, New Zealand.

CAMPBELL Margaret, b. London, England. Author; Lecturer on Musical Subjects. m. Richard Barrington Beare, deceased, 2 sons, 1 daughter. Education: Art Scholarship, London. Career: Talks and Interviews on BBC Radio; Cleveland Radio; Voice of America; USA; CBC Canada; BBC and Southern Television; Lectures at Cornell; Oberlin; Indiana; Oklahoma and Southern Methodist Universities; Manhattan School of Music, New York; Rice University; University of Texas at Austin; University of Southern California USA; Cambridge, Guildford and Bath Universities; Guildhall School of Music and Drama; Purcell School, England; Festivals at Bergen and Utrecht, Holland; Editor, Journal of British Music Therapy, 1974-90; Member of Jury, International Cello Competition at Spring Festival, Prague, Czech Republic, 1994; Lectures at the Conservatoire and University of Sofia, Bulgaria, 1996; Member of Council (ESTA), 1996; Lectures at Sibelius Academy of Music, Helsinki, Finland, 1998 Publications: Dolmetsch: The Man and His Work, London and USA in 1975; The Great Violinists, London and USA in 1981, Germany 1982; Japan 1983 and China, 1999; The Great Cellists, 1988, Japan, 1996, China, 1999; Henry Purcell: Glory of His Age, London 1993, paperback 1995; Married to Music. A Biography of Julian Lloyd Webber, 2001; The Great Violinists and The Great Cellists revised 2nd editions, 2004. Contributions: The New Grove Dictionary of Music, 1980; The Independent; The Strad; Cambridge Companion to the Cello, 1999; The New Grove Dictionary of Music & Musicians, 2nd edition, 2000. Honours: Winston Churchill Memorial Travelling Fellowship, 1971; Fellow of the Royal Society of Arts, 1991; Board of Governors, The Dolmetsch Foundation; Freeman, Worshipful Company of Musicians, 2005; Freedom of the City of London, 2006. Memberships: Society of Authors; Royal Society of Literature; Royal Society of Arts; English Speaking Union. Address: 8 Kingfisher Court, Woodfield Road, Droitwich Spa, Worcs. WR9 8UU, England.

CAMPBELL Rt Hon Sir (Walter) Menzies, b. 22 May 1941. Member of Parliament; Leader of the Liberal Democrats. m. Elspeth Mary Grant-Suttie, 1970. Education: MA, LLB, University of Glasgow; Stanford University. Appointments: Competed in 1964 Olympic & 1966 Commonwealth Games; Captain, UK athletics team, 1965-66; Holder, UK 100 metres record, 1967-74; Called to Bar (Scotland), 1968; Chair, Scottish Liberals 1975-77; General Election Candidate 1974-83; Advocate Depute in the Crown Office, 1977-80; Appointed Queen's Counsel (Scotland), 1982; Elected to Parliament, North East Fife, 1987; Members' Interests Select Committee, 1988-90; Trade & Industry Select Committee, 1990-92; Chief Liberal Democrat Foreign Affairs & Defence Spokesperson 1992-97; Defence Select Committee, 1992-97 & 1997-99; Joint Cabinet Select Committee, 1997-2001; Liberal Democrat Shadow Foreign Secretary 1997-2003; Deputy Leader, Liberal Democrats, 2003-2006; Shadow Secretary of State for Foreign & Commonwealth Affairs, 2003-2006; Elected Leader of the Liberal Democrats, 2006-. Honours: QC (Scot), 1982; CBE, 1987; PC, 1999; Knight, 2004. Memberships: President, Glasgow University Union 1964-65; Scottish Sports Council 1971-81; Chair, Royal Lyceum Theatre Company, Edinburgh 1984-87; Broadcasting Council for Scotland 1984-87; Clayson Committee on Liquor Licensing Reform in Scotland; Trustee, Scottish International Education Trust; Part-time Chair, Medical Appeal Tribunal; Part-time Chair, VAT Tribunal (Scotland); Board of the British

Council; UK Delegation to the North Atlantic Assembly 1989-; UK Delegation to the Parliamentary Assembly of the CSCE 1992-. Address: House of Commons, London SW1A 0AA, England.

CAMPBELL Michael Gregory, b. 2 October 1941, Larne, Northern Ireland. Education: McKenna Memorial School, Larne; Campion House, Osterley; University College, Dublin; Gregorian University, Rome; Kings College, London. Appointments: Teacher, Chaplain, Assistant Priest, Christ the King School, Southport, 1972-75; Teacher, Chaplain, Bishop Challoner Girls' School, Tower Hamlets, 1976-85; Lecturer in Scripture, Jos, Nigeria, 1985-89; Secretary, Bishops' Conference E&W Theology Commission, 1991-2003; Prior, Austin Friars, Carlisle; Prior, Parish Priest, St Augustine's Hammersmith, 1999-. Publications: Translation of St Augustine's works: Faith & the Creed; Faith and the Unseen; Way of the Cross (meditations); A Root from the Staff of Jesse (Advent meditations); Mary, Woman of Prayer. Address: St Augustine's Priory, 55 Fulham Palace Road, Hammersmith, London W6 8AU, England.

CAMPBELL Neve, b. 3 October 1973, Guelph, Ontario, Canada. Actress. m. Jeff Colt, divorced 1998. Education: National Ballet School, Canada. Career: Dance: The Phantom of the Opera; The Nutcracker; Sleeping Beauty; Films include: Paint Cans, 1994; The Dark, 1994; Love Child, 1995; The Craft, 1996; Scream, 1996; A Time to Kill, 1996; Simba's Pride, 1997; Scream 2, 1997; Wild Things, 1998; Hairshirt, 1998; 54, 1998; Three to Tango, 1999; Scream 3, 2000; Investigating Sex, 2001; Last Call, 2002; The Company, 2003; Lost Junction, 2003; Blind Horizon, 2004; When Will I Be Loved, 2004; Churchill: The Hollywood Years, 2004; TV includes: Catwalk, 1992-93; Web of Deceit, 1993; Baree, 1994; The Forget-Me-Not Murders, 1994; Party of Five, 1994-98; The Canterville Ghost, 1996; Reefer Madness: The Movie Musical, 2005; Relative Strangers, 2006; Partition, 2007; I Really Hate My Job, 2007; Closing The Ring, 2007. Honours: Saturn Award for Best Actress, 1996; MTV Movie Award for Best Female Performance, 1996; Blockbuster Entertainment Award for Favourite Actress – Horror, 1997. Address: Creative Artists Agency, 9830 Wilshire Boulevard, Beverly Hills, CA 90212, USA.

CAMPBELL Ramsey, b. 4 January 1946, Liverpool, England. Writer; Film Reviewer. m. Jenny Chandler, 1 January 1971, 1 son, 1 daughter. Appointments: Film Reviewer, BBC Radio Merseyside, 1969-2007; Full-time Writer, 1973-. Publications: Novels: The Doll Who Ate His Mother, 1976; The Face That Must Die, 1979; The Parasite, 1980; The Nameless, 1981; Incarnate, 1983; The Claw, 1983, US edition as Night of the Claw; Obsession, 1985; The Hungry Moon, 1986; The Influence, 1988; Ancient Images, 1989; Midnight Sun, 1990; The Count of Eleven, 1991; The Long Lost, 1993; The One Safe Place, 1995; The House on Nazareth Hill, 1996; The Last Voice They Hear, 1998; Silent Children, 2000; Pact of the Fathers, 2001; The Darkest Part of the Woods, 2002; The Overnight, 2004; Secret Stories, 2005; The Grin of the Dark, 2007; Thieving Fear, 2008; Short stories: The Inhabitant of the Lake and Less Welcome Tenants, 1964; Demons by Daylight, 1973; The Height of the Scream, 1976; Dark Companions, 1982; Cold Print, 1985; Black Wine (with Charles L Grant), 1986; Night Visions 3 (with Clive Barker and Lisa Tuttle), 1986; Scared Stiff, 1987; Dark Feasts: The World of Ramsey Campbell, 1987; Waking Nightmares, 1991; Alone With The Horrors, 1993; Strange Things and Stranger Places, 1993; Ghosts and Grisly Things, 1998; Ramsey Campbell, Probably (non-fiction), 2002; Told by the Dead,

2003; Inconsequential Tales, 2008; Novella: Needing Ghosts, 1990. Honours: Liverpool Daily Post and Echo Award for Literature, 1993; World Fantasy Award, Bram Stoker Award, Best Collection, 1994; Best Novel, International Horror Guild, 1998; Grand Master, World Horror Convention, 1999; Lifetime Achievement Award, Horror Writers' Association, 1999; Many others. Memberships; British Fantasy Society, President; Society of Fantastic Films, President. Address: 31 Penkett Road, Wallasey CH45 7QF, Merseyside, England. Website: www.ramseycampbell.com

CAMPBELL OF ALLOWAY, Baron of Ayr in the District of Kyle and Carrick, Alan Robertson Campbell, b. 24 May 1917, United Kingdom. Queen's Counsel. m. Vivien de Kantzow. Education: Trinity Hall Cambridge; Ecole des Sciences Politiques, Paris. Appointments: Sits as Conservative Peer in the House of Lords; Commissioned 2 Lt RA Supplementary Reserve, 1939, served in BEF France and Belgium, 1939-40, POW, 1940-45; Called to the Bar, Inner Temple, 1939, Bencher, 1972; Western Circuit, Recorder, Crown Court, 1976-89; Head of Chambers; Consultant to Sub-Committee of Legal Committee of Council of Europe on Industrial Espionage, 1965-74; Chairman, Legal Research Committee, Society of Conservative Lawyers, 1968-80; Member of House of Lords Select Committees on: Murder and Life Imprisonment, 1988-89, Privileges, 1982-2000; Personal Bills, 1987-88, Joint Consolidation Bills, 2000; Member: House of Lords Ecclesiastical Committee, 2003-; Joint Committee on Human Rights; All Party Committees on Defence, and on Children. Honours: MA (Cantab); Emergency Reserve Decoration; QC, 1965. Memberships: Law Advisory Committee Bar Council, 1974-80; Management Committee, Association for European Law, 1975-90; Old Carlton Club Political Committee, 1967-79; Co-Patron, Inns of Court School of Law Conservatives, 1996-2000; President, Colditz Association, 1998-2004; Carlton; Pratt's; Beefsteak Clubs; Perennial Guest of Third Guards Club. Address: House of Lords, London SW1A 0PW, England.

CAMPESE David Ian, b. 21 October 1962, Queanbeyan, Australia. Rugby Football Player. m. Lara Berkenstein, 2003. Appointments: Partner, Campo's Sports Store; International Debut, Australia v New Zealand, 1982; Captain, Australian Team; Winner, World Cup, 1991; World's Leading Try Scorer with 64; Scored 310 points; Australian Most Capped Player (represented Australia 101 times); Director, David Campese Management Group, 1997-. Publication: On a Wing and a Prayer; My Game, Your Game, 1994; Still Entertaining, 2003. Honours: Australian Writers Player of the Year, 1991; English Rugby Writers Player of the Year, 1991; International Rugby Hall of Fame, 2001; Order of Australia Medal, 2002. Address: 13 Nicholas Avenue, Concord, Sydney, NSW 2137, Australia. Website: www.goosestep.com.au

CAMPION Jane, b. 30 April 1954, Wellington, New Zealand. Film Director; Writer. Education: BA, Anthropology, Victoria University, Wellington; Diploma of Fine Arts, Chelsea School of Arts, London, completed at Sydney College of the Arts; Diploma in Direction, Australian Film & TV School, 1981-84. Career: Writer/Director, films: Peel, 1981-82; Passionless Moments, 1984; Mishaps of Seduction and Conquest, 1984-85; Girls Own Story, 1983-84; After Hours, 1984; Producer: 1 episode ABC TV drama series, Dancing Daze, 1986; Director, Two Friends, for ABC TV Drama, 1985-86; An Angel at My Table, 1989-90; Sweetie, 1988; Writer/Director, The Piano, 1993; Director, The Portrait of a Lady, 1997; Holy Smoke, 1999; In the Cut, 2003; Executive Producer, Abduction: The Megumi Yokota Story, 2006; Bright Star, 2008. Honours:

Numerous awards include: for the Piano: Best Picture, 66th Academy Awards Nomination, Best Director, 66th Academy Awards Nomination, LA Film Critics Association, New York Film Critics Circle, Australia Film Critics, Director's Guild of America Nomination, BAFTA Nomination, AFI Awards, Producer, Producer's Guild of America, Best Screenplay, 66th Academy Awards, BAFTA Nomination, AFI Awards; For The Portrait of a Lady: Francesco Pasinetti Award, National Union of Film Journalists, 1996. Address: HLA Management Pty Ltd, 87 Pitt Street, Redfern, NSW 2016, Australia.

CAMROSE (Viscount), Sir Adrian Michael Berry. b. 15 June 1937, London, England. Writer; Journalist. Education: Christ Church, Oxford, 1959. Appointments: Correspondent, Time Magazine, New York City, 1965-67; Science Correspondent, 1977-96, Consulting Editor (Science), 1996-, Daily Telegraph, London. Publications: The Next Ten Thousand Years: A Vision of Man's Future in the Universe, 1974; The Iron Sun: Crossing the Universe Through Black Holes, 1977; From Apes to Astronauts, 1981; The Super Intelligent Machine, 1983; High Skies and Yellow Rain, 1983; Koyama's Diamond (fiction), 1984; Labyrinth of Lies (fiction), 1985; Ice With Your Evolution, 1986; Computer Software: The Kings and Queens of England, 1985; Harrap's Book of Scientific Anecdotes, 1989; The Next 500 Years, 1995; Galileo and the Dolphins, 1996; The Giant Leap, 1999. Honour: Royal Geographic Society, fellow, 1984-. Memberships: Royal Astronomical Society, London, Fellow, 1973-; British Interplanetary Society, Fellow, 1986-. Address: 11 Cottesmore Gardens, Kensington, London W8, England.

CANIVET Guy, b. 23 September 1943, Lons-le-Saunier, France. Judge. m. Françoise Beuzit, 2 sons, 2 daughters. Education: JD, Postgraduate studies, Civil and Criminal Laws, University of Dijon. Appointments: Judge, Trial Court of Chartres, 1972-75; Public Prosecutor, Paris, 1975-77; Secretary-General, Trial Court of Paris, 1977-83; Judge, Trial Court of Paris, 1983-86; Justice, Court of Appeal, 1986-94; Justice, Cour de cassation, 1994-96; Chief Justice, Paris Court of Appeal, 1996-99; Chief Justice, Cour de cassation, 1999-. Publications: Droit français de la concurrence, 1994; La déontologie des magistrats, 2004. Honours: Officier de la Légion d'Honneur; Officier de l'Ordre National du Mérite; Commandeur des Palmes Academiques; Docteur honoris causa: University of London, University of Laval and University St Kliment Ohridski de Sofia; Honorary Bencher of Grays' Inn; Member, British Academy. Memberships include: President, Network of the Supreme Judicial Courts of the European Union; President, Comité de coopération judiciaire franco-britannique; Co-president, l'Association Oxford-Sorbonne pour le droit comparé; Member, Comité consultatif de l'Academie de droit européen de Trèves; Member, Comité français de droit international privé; Member, l'Académie des privatistes européens; Vice President, l'Association des juristes européens; President, Forum des juges de l'Union européenne pour l'environnement; President, Groupement européen des magistrats pour la médiation; Secretary-General, l'Association des hautes juridictions de cassation des pays ayant en partage l'usage dur français; President, l'Association Louis Chatin pour la défense des droits de l'enfant; President, l'Association française d'étude de la concurrence; Member, l'Association Henri Capitant; Member, l'Institut des hautes études sur la justice; Member, l'Association française pour l'histoire de la Justice; Member, la Société de défense sociale nouvelle. Address: Cour de cassation, 5 quai de l'Horloge, 75055 Paris, Cedex 01, France. E-mail: pp.courdecassation@justice.fr

CANNON Jack Philip, b. 21 December 1929, Paris, France. Composer. m. Jane Dyson (Baroness Buijs van Schouwenburg). 1 daughter. Education: Dartington Hall, Devon; Royal College of Music, London. Appointments: Lecturer, Oxford Extramural Studies, 1950-58; Lecturer in Music, Sydney University, Australia, 1958-60; Deputy Professor of Composition, 1950-58, Professor of Composition, Royal College of Music, London, 1960-95. Publications: Many articles for music journals; 3 operas, chorus/orchestral works, orchestral works, choral works, chamber music, mostly commissioned by national and international bodies; Important historical commissions include: Symphony commissioned by the BBC to mark Britain's entry to the EC, 1972; Symphony commission by Radio France for première at a diplomatic occasion in Paris, 1972; Te Deum commissioned by and dedicated to H M The Queen of England for the Service of Thanksgiving at St George's Chapel, Windsor Castle, 1975. Honours: Grand Prix and Critics' Prize, Paris, 1965; Fellow of the Royal College of Music, 1971; Bard of Gorsedd Kernow, 1997. Memberships: Royal Philharmonic Society; British Academy of Composers and Songwriters; Savile; Chelsea Arts. Address: Elmdale Cottage, March, Aylesbury, Bucks HP17 8SP, England.

CANTER Jean Mary, b. 18 March 1943, Epsom, Surrey. Artist. Education: 13+ Art Award, Epsom School of Art, 1956-61; Major Art Award, Wimbledon School of Art, 1961-63. Career: Colourist, Baynton Williams Antique Prints; Part-time Tutor, Mid-Surrey Adult Education, 1972-2006; Freelance Artist; Exhibitions: London Royal Institute of Painters in Watercolours; Royal Watercolour Society; Society of Graphic Fine Art and many other society exhibitions; Medici Gallery; Llewellyn Alexander Gallery, London and many provincial galleries. Publications: Work reproduced in "How-to-do-it" Art Books; Several features for Artists and Illustrators Magazine; Regular contributor with The Drawing Class to Painting World Magazine, 1999-2001. Honours: Prizes: Society of Graphic Fine Art Exhibitions, Frisk Ltd, 1983, 1985, Rexel Ltd, 1984, 1996, Daler-Rowney, 1990, Liquitex, 1993, 1997, Winsor and Newton, 1996; Commendation of Excellence, Llewellyn Alexander Gallery, 2004, 2007. Society of Graphic Fine Art for work on Theme of 'Reflection' 2006; Faber-Castell Prize UK Coloured Pencil Society 2006. Listed in national and international biographical dictionaries. Memberships: Elected to the Society of Graphic Fine Art, 1977, Vice President, 1987-90, 1993-94, President, 1994-99; Signature Membership, UK Coloured Pencil Society, 2005. Address: 7 Cox Lane, Ewell, Epsom, Surrey KT19 9LR, England.

CANTLIFFE Daniel J, b. 31 October 1943, New York, USA. Professor of Horticulture. m. Elizabeth, 4 daughters. Education: BS, Delaware Valley College, 1965; MS, 1967, PhD, 1971, Purdue University. Appointments: Research Assistant, Purdue University, 1965-69; Research Associate, Cornell University, 1969-70; Research Scientist, Horticulture Research Institute of Ontario, 1970-74; Visiting Professor, Department of Horticulture, University of Hawaii, 1979-80; Assistant Professor, Assistant Horticulturist, 1974-76, Associate Professor, Associate Horticulturist, 1976-81, Professor, 1981-92, Vegetable Crops Department, Professor and Chairman, Horticultural Sciences Department, 1992-, University of Florida. Publications: 2 book editorships; 4 monographs; 1 bulletin; 18 book chapters; 622 publications. Honours include: Distinguished Agricultural Alumni Award, Purdue University, 1999; Best and Most Meritorious Paper, Vegetable Section, Florida State Horticultural Society, 1990, 1992, 1998, 2000-02, 2004; Honorary Membership,

Florida State Horticultural Society, 2006; Southern Region, American Society for Horticultural Science Leadership and Administration Award, 2000; Professorial Salary Adjustment Program Award, 2001 and University of Florida Research Foundation Professorship, 2005-07, Distinguished International Educator, 2005, UF/IFAS International Fellow, 2005, University of Florida; Outstanding Graduate Educator, 1991, Outstanding Researcher, 1997, Outstanding International Horticulturist, 2001, American Society for Horticultural Science; International Society for Horticultural Science Fellow Award, 2006. Memberships include: American Society for Horticultural Science; American Society of Plant Biology; American Society of Agronomy; Crop Science Society of America; Florida State Horticultural Society; International Seed Science Society; International Society for Horticultural Science; Listed in national and international biographical dictionaries. Address: Horticultural Sciences Department, University of Florida, IFAS, PO Box 110690, Gainesville, FL 32611-0690, USA. E-mail: djcant@ufl.edu

CANTOR Brian, b. 11 January 1948, Manchester, England. Vice-Chancellor. Widowed, 2 sons. Education: BA, MA, PhD, Christ's College, Cambridge, 1965-72. Appointments: Research Fellow then Lecturer, Sussex University, 1972-81; Lecturer, then Reader, then Professor, Oxford University, 1981-2002; Senior Research Fellow, Jesus College, Oxford, 1985-95; Professorial Fellow, St Catherine's College, Oxford, 1995-2002; Vice-Chancellor, University of York, 2002-; Consultancies: Alcan, 1986-94; Rolls-Royce, 1996-; Board Member: White Rose, Worldwide Universities Network, National Science Learning Centre, Yorkshire Science; Former Board Member: Isis Innovation, Kobe Institute; Amaethon, York Science Park; Adviser (at different times) to agencies including: EPSRC, NASA, the EU, Singapore-British Business Council, Dutch, Spanish and German Governments. Publications: Published over 300 papers, books and patents, given over 100 invited talks in more than 15 countries and on the ISI Most Cited Researchers list. Honours: Rosenhain Medal, Institute of Materials; Ismanam Prize, 1999; Platinum Medal, Institute of Metals, 2002. Memberships: Fellow, Royal Academy of Engineering; Fellow, Institute of Physics; Fellow, Institute of Materials; Member, Academia Europaea; World Technologies Forum. Address: Vice-Chancellor's Office, University of York, Heslington, York YO10 5DD, England. E-mail: vc@york.ac.uk Website: www.york.ac.uk

CANTRELL Joseph Sires, b. 31 July 1932, Parker, Kansas, USA. College Professor; Scientist. m. Margaret Joyce Herr, 3 sons. Education: AB, Emporia University, 1954; MS, 1957, PhD, 1961, Kansas State University. Appointments: Sargeant, Radar Section, US Army, 1954-56; Chief Corportion Scientist, Proctor and Gamble Co; Assistant Professor, 1965, Associate Professor, 1970, Professor, 1980, Section Head, 1980-85, Emeritus Professor, 2003-, Chemistry Department, Miami University; Corporation Scientist, Lockheed Martin (Butler), NASA Space Shuttle, 2005-. Publications: Over 250 scientific publications in refereed journals: American Chemical Society, Acta Crystallographica, Zeitschrift fur Krystallographie, Journal of Physical Chemistry, Review of Physics, Physics Rev F, Tetrahedron, Solid State Physics. Honours: Fellow, Ohio Academy of Science; Fellow, Institute of Environmental Science of Miami University. Memberships: American Chemical Society; American Society of Physics; Electrochemical Society; Ohio Academy of Science. Address: 206 Pearl River Trace, Pearl River, Louisiana 70452, USA. E-mail: joecantrell@bellsouth.net

CANTUNIARI-ADLER Adina Maria, b. 15 August 1948, Bucharest, Romania (Canadian citizen). Neurobiologist. m. Alfred Adler, 1 son. Education: BSc, Natural Sciences, 1972, MSc, Biology and Physiology, 1977, Bucharest University, Romania; PhD, Neurobiology, Stratford International University, USA, 2001. Appointments: Research Assistant, 1972-77; Biologist, 1977-81; Research Scientist, D Danielopolu Research Medical Institute for Normal and Pathological Physiology, Romanian Academy of Medical Sciences, Bucharest, 1981-84; Scientific Director of the Laboratory of Physiological Pharmacology, 1984-86; Laboratory Manager, Senior Research Assistant, McGill University, Montreal, Canada, 1988-94; Postdoctoral Faculty Research Associate, Morehouse School of Medicine, Atlanta, USA, 1994-96; Visiting Professor, Mahidol University, Bangkok, Thailand, 1998-2002; Research Director, ADCAN Laboratories, Vancouver, Canada, 1997-; Associate Professor of Neurobiology, Rutherford University, Canada/USA, 1999-. Publications: Articles in professional scientific and medical journals. Honours: D Danielopolu Institute Fellowship in Immunology and Immunopathology, V Babes Institute, 1980-81; Distinction List of Young Research Scientists, 1981; D Danielopolu Institute Fellowship in Hematology, I Cantacuzino Institute, Romanian Academy of Medical Sciences, 1985; Listed in national and international biographical dictionaries. Memberships: Canadian Association of Neuroscience; American Association for the Advancement of Science; Society for Neuroscience, USA; New York Academy of Science; ACFAS, Canada; International Brain Research Organisation. Address: ADCAN Laboratories, 8-2929 St John's St, PO Box 31116, Pt Moody, BC V3H 2C0, Canada. E-mail: cantuniari@adcanlaboratories.com

CAPORALE Guglielmo Maria, b. 25 January 1963, Naples, Italy. Professor. Education: Degree in Political Science, LUISS, Rome, Italy, 1984; MSc, 1987, PhD, 1990, Economics, LSE. Appointments: International Economist, Oxford Economic Forecasting, Oxford, 1990-91; Research Officer, National Institute of Economic and Social Research, London, 1991-93; Research Fellow, 1993-95, Senior Research Fellow, 1996-98, Centre for Economic Forecasting, London Business School; Professor of Economics, University of East London, 1998-2000; Professor of Economics and Finance, Director, Centre for Monetary and Financial Economics, currently Visiting Professor, London South Bank University, 2000-; Visiting Professor, London Metropolitan University, 2002-; Visiting Professor, Institute for Advanced Studies, Vienna, Austria, 2004; Professor of Economics and Finance, Brunel University, 2004-. Publications: Numerous articles in books and leading international academic journals. Honours: Foreign and Commonwealth Office and Economic and Social Research Council PhD Scholarships; ESRC and Leverhulme Trust research grants; Citation of Excellence, Highest Quality Rating, ANBAR Electronic Intelligence; Dae-Ying Prize for best publication, Journal of Economic Integration, 2005; Listed in national and international biographical dictionaries. Memberships: Royal Economic Society; Econometric Society; American Economic Association; European Economic Association; Latin American and Caribbean Economic Association; Money, Macro and Finance Research Group Committee; CESifo Research Network Fellow. Address: Department of Economics & Finance, Brunel University, Uxbridge, Middlesex, UB8 3PH, England. E-mail: guglielmo-maria.caporale@brunel.ac.uk

CARANI Dorothy Miriam Meyers, b. 6 April 1927, Pittsburgh, Pennsylvania, USA. Author; Poet; Lyricist. m. Lee Carani, 2 sons, 3 daughters. Education: Self-trained

Author. Appointments: Tenant Council President, Senior Apartment Building, College Park, Maryland, USA, 1998; Author. Publications: 15 Anthologies: Poetry Press, Yes Press, American Poetry, December Press, Illiad, Amherst, Sparrowgrass, National Library of Poetry, New Millennium, Famous Poets, Poetic Odyssey; 3 books in progress: Unto Me He Said (biblical); You Might Find it Here (humour); Great Men, Great Minds, Great Words (historical); Katrina Katrina (lyrics), Hurricane CD (proceeds to hurricane victims), 2006; You Made a Fool of Love (lyrics), 2008. Honours: American Presidential Eagle Award for contributions to literature, 1990; Silver Jubilee Album Award; England's White Rose Award; Lyndon B Weatherford Endowment; Homer Honor Society; International Poets; Gold Medal, ABI, 2006; Gold Medal Nomination, ABI, 2007; Rossi/Jacobs Endowment Award, 2007; Hirsh/Rothstein Group Assistance of the Year Award, 2008; Listed in national and international biographical directories. Memberships: ASCAP; Songwriters Club of America- Tin Pan Alley – Broadway Music; 100 Club; National Author's Registry; Manchester Who's Who, 2006-07. Address: 5320 Dorsey Hall Drive, Apt 321, Ellicott City, MD 21042-7867, USA.

CARDIN Pierre, b. 2 July 1922, San Biagio di Callatla, Italy. Couturier. Appointments: Worker, Christian Dior; Founder, Own Fashion Houses, 1949; Founder, Espace Pierre Cardin (Theatre Group); Director, Ambassadeurs-Pierre Cardin Theatre (now Espace Pierre Cardin Theatre), 1970-; Manager, Société Pierre Cardin, 1973; Chair, Maxims, 1982-; Honorary UNESCO Ambassador, 1991. Creative Works: Exhibition at Victoria & Albert Museum, 1990. Publications: Fernand Léger, Sa vie, Son oeuvre, Son reve, 1971; Le Conte du Ver a Soie, 1992. Honours include: Grand Officer of Merit, Italy, 1988; Order of the Sacred Treasure (Gold & Silver Star), 1991. Address: 27 Avenue Marigny, 75008 Paris, France.

CARDNELL Valerie Flora, b. 21 April 1928, Kent, England. Singer. Education: 4 year Nursing Course, Middlesex Hospital, London, England; 4 year Music Course, Trinity College of Music, London, England; Music Therapy Course with Juliette Alvin; Qualified Teacher. Appointments: Private Nursing Sister, England; Night Superintendent, St Luke's Hospital for Church of England Clergy, London, England; Professional Singer, oratorios, recitals, opera, concerts, recordings; Member, Vincian Trio; Radio and television programmes; Member Golden Age Singers; Many Educational Music Programmes for BBC including Andy Pandy; Professor of Singing; Music Examiner and Adjudicator. Honours: State Registered Nurse, England; Middlesex Hospital Certificate, London, England; Helen Trust Scholarship to Trinity College of Music; Music Degree FTCL; LTCL Singing; LTCL Piano; LRAM Singing; Winner, Elizabeth Schumann Lieder Competition, Trinity College of Music; Winner, Ricordi Opera Prize, Trinity College of Music; Winner, Silver Medal, Worshipful Company of Musicians; Winner, International Singing Competition, s'Hertogenbosch, Holland; Elected FRSA; Elected Honorary Fellow, Trinity College, London; Apostolic Blessing from His Holiness John Paul II. Memberships: Incorporated Society of Musicians, London, England; Trinity College of Music, London, England. Address: 20 Woodside Close, Surbiton, Surrey, England.

CAREY Mariah, b. 22 March 1970, Long Island, New York, USA. Singer; Songwriter. m. Tommy Mottola, divorced. Career: Backing singer, Brenda K Starr, New York, 1988; Solo recording artiste, 1988-; 80 million albums sold to date; Concerts worldwide; Founder, Crave record label, 1997; Founder, Camp Mariah holiday project for inner-city children; Recordings: Albums: Mariah Carey, 1990; Emotions, 1991; MTV Unplugged EP, 1992; Music Box, 1993; Merry Christmas, 1994; Daydream, 1995; Butterfly, 1997; #1s, 1998; Rainbow, 1999; Glitter, 2001; Greatest Hits, 2001; Charmbracelet, 2002; The Remixes, 2003; The Emancipation of Mimi, 2005; Singles: Vision Of Love, Love Takes Time, 1990; Someday, I Don't Wanna Cry, Emotions, 1991; Can't Let You Go, Make It Happen, I'll Be There, 1992; Dreamlover, Hero, 1993; Without You, Anytime You Need a Friend, Endless Love (with Luther Vandross), All I Want for Christmas Is You, 1994; Fantasy, One Sweet Day (with Boyz II Men), Always Be My Baby, 1995; Open Arms, 1996; Honey, Butterfly, Breakdown, 1997; My All, When You Believe (with Whitney Houston, in film The Prince of Egypt), 1998; I Still Believe, Heartbreaker, 1999; Thank God I Found You, Can't Take That Away, Against All Odds (with Westlife), 2000; Loverboy, Never Too Far, 2001; Through the Rain, Boy I Need You, 2002; Bringin' On The Heartbreak, 2003; Breaking All The Rules, 2004; Film: Glitter, 2001; Wise Girls, 2002; State Property 2, 2005. Honours include: Grammy Awards for Best New Artist, Best New Pop Vocal by a Female Artist, 1990; Soul Train Awards for Best New Artist, Best Single by a Female Artist, 1990; Rolling Stone Award for Best Female Singer, 1991; 8 World Music Awards, 1991-95; 7 Billboard Awards, 1991-96; 4 American Music Awards, 1991-95; International Dance Music Award for Best Solo Artist, 1996; American Music Awards Special Award for Achievement, 2000; World's Best Selling Female Artist of the Millennium. Address: The Agency Group Ltd, 361-373 City Road, London, EC1V 1PQ, England. Website: www.mariahcarey.com

CAREY Peter, b. 7 May 1943, Bacchus March, Victoria, Australia. Author. m. (2) Alison Summers, 1985, 2 sons. Education: Monash University. Appointments: Partner, McSpedden Carey Advertising Consultants, Sydney; Teacher, Columbia University, Princeton University. Publications: The Fat Man in History (short stories), 1974; War Crimes (short stories), 1979; Bliss (novel), 1981; Illywhacker (novel), 1985; Oscar and Lucinda, 1988; The Tax Inspector (novel), 1991; The Unusual Life of Tristan Smith (novel), 1994; Collected Stories, 1995; The Big Bazoohley (children's novel), 1995; Jack Maggs, 1997; The True History of the Kelly Gang, 2000; 30 Days in Sydney: A Wildly Distorted Account, 2001; My Life as a Fake, 2003; Wrong About Japan, 2005; Theft: A Love Story (novel), 2006; Screenplays: Bliss; Until the End of the World; Film: Oscar and Lucinda, 1998. Honours include: The Booker Prize (twice); Miles Franklin Award; National Council Award; Age Book of the Year Award. Address: c/o Amanda Urban, ICM, 40 West 57th Street, New York, NY 10019, USA.

CAREY OF CLIFTON Baron of Clifton in the City and County of Bristol (George Leonard Carey), b. 13 November 1935, London, England. Ecclesiastic; University chancellor. m. Eileen Harmsworth, 1960, 2 sons, 2 daughters. Education: Bifrons Secondary Modern School, Barking, Essex; King's College, London University; University studies and theological training, 1957-62. Appointments: National Service, RAF, 1954-56; Curate, St Mary's, Islington, 1962-66; Lecturer, Oak Hill Theological College, 1966-70; St John's College, Nottingham, 1970-75; Vicar, St Nicholas' Church, Durham, 1975-82; Principal, Trinity Theological College, Bristol, 1982-87; Bishop of Bath and Wells, 1987-91; Archbishop of Canterbury, 1991-2002; Chancellor, University of Gloucestershire, 2003-. Publications: I Believe in Man, 1978; The Great Acquittal, 1981; The Church in the Market Place, 1983; The Meeting of the Waters, 1985; The

Gate of Glory, 1986; The Great God Robbery, 1988; I Believe, 1991; Spiritual Journey, 1994; My Journey, Your Journey, 1996; Canterbury – Letters to the Future, 1998; Jesus, 2000; Know the Truth, 2004. Honours: Honorary Bencher, Inner Temple; Freeman, cities of London and of Wells, 1990; Hon DLitt, Polytechnic of East London, 1991; Hon DD (Kent) 1991, (Nottingham) 1992, (Bristol) 1992, (Durham) 1994; Hon LLD, (Bath) 1992; Several honorary degrees from American universities; Greek, Hebrew and theological prizes. Memberships: Patron or president of 300 organisations; Fellow, King's College, London. Address: House of Lords, Westminster, London SW1A 0PW, England.

CARINE James, b. 14 September 1934, Isle of Man, United Kingdom. Retired. m. Carolyn Sally Taylor, 5 sons, 2 deceased, 1 daughter. Education: Royal Naval College, Dartmouth, 1951-52; Qualified Company Secretary (FCIS), 1970. Appointments: Royal Navy, 1951-91; Captain, Executive Assistant to Deputy Supreme Allied Command Atlantic, 1982-95; Captain, Chief Staff Officer (Personnel and Logistics), 1985-88; Commodore in Command of HMS Drake, Devonport Naval Barracks, 1988-89; Rear Admiral, Chief of Staff to Commander-in-Chief, 1989-91; Chief Executive of The Arab Horse Society, 1992-2000; Member, Copyright Tribunal, 1999-; Chairman, Wiltshire Ambulance Service NHS Trust, 2002-06. Honours: Freedom of City of London, 1988; Master, Worshipful Company of Chartered Secretaries, 1997-98; Knight of the Order of St Gregory the Great, 1983. Memberships: Fellow Chartered Institute of Secretaries and Administrators, 1970; Admiralty Board nominated Trustee/Director and Executive and Investment Committees of the United Services Trustee (Quoted Unit Trusts), 1995-2005; Trustee/Director and Management and Financial Committees of the Ex-Services Mental Welfare Society (Combat Stress), 1997-2002; Governor St Antony's – Lewiston School, 1997-2005; Wiltshire Committee of the National Art Collections Fund, 2001-; Independent Chairman, Wiltshire and Swindon Fire Authority Standards Committee, 2001-; Independent Chairman, North Wiltshire District Council Standards Committee, 2002-; Chairman, Age Concern, Swindon, 2002-05; Chairman Royal United Hospital Bath, 2006-. Address: 5 Little Sands, Yatton Keynell, Chippenham, Wiltshire SN14 7BA, England. E-mail: j.carine@btinternet.com

CARL XVI GUSTAF, (King of Sweden), b. 30 April 1946. m. Silvia Sommerlath, 1976, 1 son, 2 daughters. Education: Sigtuna; University of Uppsala; University of Stockholm. Appointments: Created Duke of Jämtland; Became Crown Prince, 1950; Succeeded to the throne on death of his grandfather, King Gustaf VI Adolf, 1973. Honours: Dr hc, Swedish University of Agricultural Sciences, Stockholm Institute of Technology, Abo Academy, Finland. Memberships: Chair, Swedish Branch, World Wide Fund for Nature; Honorary President, World Scout Foundation. Address: Royal Palace, 111 30 Stockholm, Sweden.

CARLIER Willy-Paul, b. 25 July 1940, St-Trond, Belgium. International Travel Consultant. m. Odette de Cuyx, 1 son, 1 daughter. Education: Collège de Saint-Trond; Institut Saint Ferdinand, Jemappes, Mons, Belgium; MA, London University, England; Degree, Tourism, Cornell University, USA. Appointments: President of numerous tourism businesses and groups; Founder of Council, St-Trond Cultural Centre; President, Belgo-Albanaise Chamber of Commerce. Publications: Author, many books on Geotourism. Honours include most recently: Médaille d'Or de la Mérite Touristique Européen, 1982; Travel Counselor of the Year, Washington,

USA, 1987-88; Laureat National Geographic Society, New York, USA, 1989; Laureat, International Association of Travel Managers, Boston, 1990; Médaille d'Or de la Mérite Touristique. Belgium, 1992; Medaille Albert Schweitzer, Vienna, 1993; Man of the Year, American Institute of International Travel and Relations, 1998; Ereburger, Citoyen d'honneur de Lourdes, France, 2000; Officier Order Mérite Nationale, Charles de Gaulle, Paris, 2002; International Peace Medal, Tsunami Disaster, UNO, Washington, 2004-05 Oscar, Lifetime Achievement Award for Excellence in Tourism, UCC, 2006. Memberships: Order of American Ambassadors; Member of several French, Flemish and Belgian Brotherhoods and Commanderies. Address: Luikersteenweg 62, B-3800 Sint-Truiden, Flanders, Belgium.

CARLING William David Charles, b. 12 December 1965, Bradford-on-Avon, England. Rugby Player. m. (1) Julia Carling, 1994, divorced 1996, (2) Lisa Cooke, 1999, 1 son, 1 step-son, 1 step-daughter. Education: Durham University. Appointments: Owner, Inspirational Horizons Co, Insights Ltd; Former Member, Durham University Club; Member, Harlequins Club; International Debut, England v France, 1988; Captain, England Team, 1988-96; Retired, International Rugby, 1997; Played 72 times for England, Captain 59 times (world record); Rugby Football Commentator, ITV, 1997-. Publications: Captain's Diary, 1991; Will Carling (autobiography), 1994; The Way to Win, 1995; My Autobiography, 1998. Honours: OBE. Address: c/o Mike Burton Management, Bastian House, Brunswick House, Brunswick Road, Gloucester, GL1 1JJ, England. E-mail: will@willcarling.com

CARLYLE Robert, b. 14 April 1961, Glasgow, Scotland. Actor. m. Anastasia Shirley, 1997, 2 children. Education: Royal Scottish Academy of Music & Drama. Appointments: Director, Rain Dog Theatre Company. Creative Works: Productions include: Wasted; One Flew Over the Cuckoo's Nest; Conquest of the South Pole; Macbeth; Stage appearances include: Twelfth Night; Dead Dad Dog; Nae Problem; City; No Mean City; Cuttin' a Rug; Othello; TV includes: Face; Go on Byrne'; Taggart; The Bill; Looking After Jo Jo, 1998; Hitler: The Rise of Evil, 2003; Gunpowder, Treason and Plot, 2004; Films include: The Full Monty; Carla's Song; Trainspotting; Priest; Marooned; Being Human; Riff Raff; Silent Scream; Apprentices; Plunkett and Macleane, 1999; The World is Not Enough, 1999; Angela's Ashes, 2000; The Beach, 2000; There's Only One Jimmy Grimble, 2000; To End All Wars, 2000; 51st State, 2001; Once Upon a Time in the Midlands, 2002; Black and White, 2002; Dead Fish, 2004; Marilyn Hotchkiss' Ballroom Dancing and Charm School, 2005; The Mighty Celt, 2005; Flood, 2006; Eragon, 2006; 28 Weeks Later, 2007. Honours include: Paper Boat Award, 1992; BAFTA Award, Best Actor; Salerno Film Festival Award, 1997; Evening Standard Outstanding British Actor Award, 1998; Bowmore Whiskey/Scottish Screen Award for Best Actor, 2001; David Puttnam Patrons Award. Address: c/o ICM, Oxford House, 76 Oxford Street, London, W1D 1BS, England.

CARMEN Ira H, b. 3 December 1934, Boston, Massachusetts, USA. College Professor. m. Lawrence Lowell Putnam, 2 daughters. Education: BA, University of New Hampshire, 1957; MA, 1959, PhD, 1964, University of Michigan. Appointments: Member, Political Science Faculty, University of Illinois, 1968-; Member, Institute for Genomic Biology, University of Illinois, 2004-. Publications: Books, Movies, Censorship, and the Law, 1966; Power and Balance, 1978; Cloning and The Constitution, 1986; Politics in the Laboratory; The Constitution of Human Genomics, 2004. Honours: President George Bush's Educators Advisory Committee, 1989; Recipient of Seven Awards for Teaching Excellence, University of Illinois. Listed in biographical dictionary. Memberships: Recombinant DNA Advisory Committee, National Institutes of Health, 1990-1994; Human Genome Organisation, elected 1996. Address: Department of Political Science, 361 Lincoln Hall, University of Illinois, Urbana, IL 61801, USA.

CARON Leslie Claire Margaret, b. 1 July 1931, Boulogne-Billancourt, France. Actress; Ballet Dancer. m. (1) George Hormel, (2) Peter Reginald Frederick Hall, 1956, divorced 1965, 1 son, 1 daughter, (3) Michael Laughlin, 1969, divorced. Education: Convent of the Assumption, Paris; Conservatoire de Danse. Career: with Ballet des Champs Elysées, 1947-50; Ballet de Paris, 1954; Actress, films include: An American in Paris; Man with a Cloak; Glory Alley; Story of Three Loves; Lili; Glass Slipper; Daddy Long Legs; Gaby; Gigi; The Doctor's Dilemma; The Man Who Understood Women; The Subterranean; Fanny; Guns of Darkness; The L-Shaped Room; Father Goose; A Very Special Favor; Promise Her Anything; Is Paris Burning?, Head of the Family; Madron; The Contract; The Unapproachable, 1982; Deathly Moves, 1983; Génie du Faux, 1984; The Train, 1987; Guerriers et Captives, 1988; Courage Mountain, 1988; Damage, 1992; Funny Bones, 1995; Let It Be Me, 1995; The Reef, 1996; The Last of the Blonde Bombshells, 1999; Chocolat, 2000; Murder on the Orient Express, 2001; Le Divorce, 2003; Plays: Orvet; La Sauvage; Gigi; 13 rue de l'Amour; Ondine; Carola; La Répétition; On Your Toes; Apprends-moi Céline; Grand Hotel; George Sand; Le Martyre de Saint; Nocturne for Lovers; Babar the Elephant; stage appearances in Paris, London, USA, Germany and Australia. Honours: Chevalier Légion d'honneur; Officier Ordre nationale du Mérite. Address: PFD, Drury House, 34-43 Russell Street, London WC2B 5HA, England.

CARPINTERI Alberto, b. 23 December 1952, Bologna, Italy. Structural Engineer. Education: PhD, Nuclear Engineering cum laude, University of Bologna, Bologna, Italy, 1976; PhD, Mathematics cum laude, University of Bologna, 1981. Appointments include: Researcher, Consiglio Nazionale delle Ricerche, Bologna, Italy, 1978-80; Assistant Professor, University of Bologna, 1981-86; Professor of Structural Mechanics, Politecnico di Torino, Italy, 1986-; Founding Member and Director, Graduate School in Structural Engineering, Politecnico di Torino, Italy, 1990-; Director, Department Structural Engineering, Politecnico di Torino, 1989-95. Publications include: Localized Damage: Computer-Aided Assessment and Control, 1994; Advanced Technology for Design and Fabrication of Composite Materials and Structures, 1995; Structural Mechanics, 1997; Fractals and Fractional Calculus in Continuum Mechanics, 1998; Computational Fracture Mechanics in Concrete Technology, 1999. Honours include: Robert l'Hermite International Prize, 1982; JSME Medal, 1993; Doctor of Physics Honoris Causa, 1994; International Cultural Diploma of Honor, 1995; Honorary Professor, Nanjing Architectural and Civil Engineering Institute, Nanjing, China, 1996; Honorary Professor, Albert Schweitzer University, Geneva, Switzerland, 2000. Memberships: International Congress on Fracture, 1981-, Vice-President, 2005-2009; International Association of Fracture Mechanics for Concrete and Concrete Structures, 1992-, President, 2004-2007; Réunion Internationale des Laboratoires d'Essais et de Recherches sur les Matériaux et les Constructions, 1982-; American Society of Civil Engineers, 1985-; European Structural Integrity Society,

1991-, President, 2002-2006; European Mechanics Society, 1994-. Address: Chair of Structural Mechanics, Politecnico di Torino, 10129 Torino, Italy.

CARR Peter Derek, Sir, b. 12 July 1930, Mexborough, Yorkshire, England. Chairman. m. Geraldine Pamela, 1 son, 1 daughter. Education: Ruskin College, Oxford; Fircroft College, Birmingham; London University. Appointments: Director, Commission on Industrial Relations, 1969-74; Labour Social Affairs Counsellor, British Embassy, Washington, 1978-83; Regional Director, Department of Employment, 1984-89; Chairman, Occupational Pensions Board, 1993-98; Chairman and Founder, Northern Screen Commission, 1992-2000; Chairman, County Durham Development Company, 1990-99; Company Chairman, Durham County Waste Management, 1990-; Chairman, Northumberland and Tyne & Wear Strategic Health Authority, 2002-2006; Chairman, Northern Assembly Health Forum, 2003-; Chairman, Northern Advisory Committee on Clinical Excellence Awards, 2003-; Chairman, NHS North East SHA, 2006. Publications: Industrial Relations in the National Newspapers; Worker Participation in Europe; It Occurred To Me, 2004; Various articles on Management Issues in several journals. Honours: CBE, 1989; Knighthood, 2007; Deputy Lieutenant; Honorary Degree, University of Northumbria; Member of Council, University of Newcastle, 2005-. Membership: Royal Overseas League. Address: 4 Corchester Towers; Corbridge, Northumberland, NE45 5NP, England. E-mail: petercarr@aol.com

CARRERAS Christopher Michael, b. 22 December 1949, Maidenhead, England. 1st Assistant Film Director. m. Sally Turner, 2 daughters. Education: Lycee Francais De Londres. Appointments: Proof of Life; Harry Potter: Philosopher's Stone, Chamber of Secrets, Prisoner of Azkabahn, Goblet of Fire; United 93; Bourne Ultimatum. Honours: Production Guilds Individual Merit Award. Membership: Production Guild. E-mail: topherc@msn.com

CARRERAS Jose, b. 5 December 1946, Barcelona, Spain. Singer (Tenor). m. Ana Elisa, 1 son, 1 daughter. Appointments: Debut, Gennaro in Lucrezia Borgia, Liceo Opera House, Barcelona, 1970-71 Season; Appeared in La Boheme, Un Ballo in Maschera, I Lombardi alla Prima Crociata at Teatro Regio, Parm, Italy, 1972; US Debut as Pinkerton in Madame Butterfly with NYC Opera, 1972; Debut, Metro Opera as Cavaradossi, 1974; Debut, La Scala as Riccardo in Un Ballo in Maschera, 1975; Appeared in Film, Don Carlos, 1980, West Side Story (TV), 1985; Appeared at major opera houses and festivals including Teatro Colon, Buenos Aires, Covent Garden, London, Vienna Staatsoper, Easter Festival and Summer Festival, Salzburg, Lyric Opera of Chicago. Creative Works: Recordings include: Un Ballo in Maschera; La Battaglia di Legnano; Il Corsaro; Un Giorno di Regno; I Due Foscari; Simone Boccanegra; Macbeth; Don Carlos; Tosca; Thais; Aida; Cavalleria Rusticana; Pagliacci; Lucia di Lammermoor; Turandot; Elisabetta di Inghilterra; Otello (Rossini). Publication: Singing From the Soul, 1991. Honours: Grammy Award, 1991; Sir Lawrence Olivier Award, 1993; Gold Medal of City of Barcelona; Albert Schweizer Music Award, 1996; Commandeur des Arts et des Lettres; Chevalier Légion d'honneur and numerous other awards. Memberships: President, Jose Carreras International Leukaemia Foundation, 1988-; Honorary Member, Royal Academy of Music, 1990. Address: c/o FIJC, Muntaner 383, 2, 08021 Barcelona, Spain. E-mail: fundacio@fcarreras.es Website: www.fcarreras.es

CARREY Jim, b. 17 January 1962, Newmarket, Canada. Actor. m. (1) Melissa Worner, 1986, divorced 1995, 1 daughter, (2) Lauren Holly, 1995, divorced 1996. Appointments: Performed, Comedy Clubs, Toronto. Creative Works: Films include: Peggy Sue Got Married, 1986; The Dead Pool, 1988; Earth Girls Are Easy, 1989; Ace Ventura! Pet Detective; The Mask; Ace Ventura: When Nature Calls, 1995; Dumb and Dumber; Liar Liar, 1996; Batman Forever; The Cable Guy; The Truman Show, 1997; Man on the Moon; How the Grinch Stole Christmas, 2000; Me, Myself and Irene, 2000; The Majestic, 2001; Bruce Almighty, 2003; Pecan Pie, 2003; Eternal Sunshine of the Spotless Mind, 2004; Lemony Snicket's A Series of Unfortunate Events, 2004; Fun with Dick and Jane, 2005; The Number 23, 2007; Several TV appearances. Honours: 2 Golden Globe Awards; 9 MTV Awards; Star on Hollywood Walk of Fame, 2000; American Film Industry Star Award, 2005. Address: UTA, 9560 Wilshire Boulevard, 5th Floor, Beverly Hills, CA 90212, USA.

CARRICK Sir Roger John, b. 13 October 1937. Diplomat (Retired); International Consultant; Chairman, Strategy International Limited. m. Hilary Elizabeth Blinman, 1 September 1962, 2 sons. Education: Joint Services School for Linguists, London University School for Slavonic and East European Studies. Appointments: Royal Navy, 1956-58; Diplomatic Service, 1956-97: Foreign Office, 1958-61; Third Secretary British Legation (later Embassy), Sofia, Bulgaria, 1962-65; Foreign Office, 1965-67; Second, later First Secretary (Economic), British Embassy, Paris, 1967-71; Head of Chancery, British High Commission, Singapore, 1971-74; Foreign and Commonwealth Office, 1974-77; Visiting Fellow, University of California, Berkeley, 1977-78; Counsellor, British Embassy Washington, 1978-82; Head of Department, Foreign and Commonwealth Office, 1982-85; HM Consul-General, Chicago, 1985-88; Assistant Under-Secretary of State, Foreign and Commonwealth Office, 1988-90; HM Ambassador to Indonesia, 1990-94; British High Commissioner to Australia, 1994-97; Member, Board of Trustees, Chevening Estate, 1998-2003; Joint Founder, Worldwide Advice on Diplomatic Estates; Consultant, KPMG (Australia), 1998-2001; Deputy Chairman, the D Group, 1999-2006; NED, Strategy International Ltd, 2001-. Publications: East-West Technology Transfer in Perspective, 1978; RolleroundOz, 1998. Honours: Lieutenant of the Royal Victorian Order, 1972; Companion, Order of St Michael and St George (CMG), 1983; Knight Commander (KCMG), 1995; Freeman of the City of London, 2002. Memberships: Royal Overseas League; Cook Society, Chairman, 2002; Pilgrims; Royal Society for Asian Affairs; Anglo-Indonesian Society; Vice President, (President, West Country Branch), Britain-Australia Society; Churchill Fellow, Westminster College, Fulton, Missouri. Address: Windhover, Wootton Courtenay, Minehead, Somerset TA24 8RD, England.

CARRIERI Arthur H, b. 15 June 1953, Philadelphia, Pennsylvania, USA. Research Physicist. Education: BA, Physics, Temple University, Philadelphia, 1975; MSc, Physics, Pennsylvania State University, 1978; Continuing education, US Army RDECOM, Aberdeen Proving Ground, 1983-. Appointments: Research Physicist, US Army RDECOM, Aberdeen Proving Ground, 1983-. Publications: Numerous articles in professional journals; 10 US patents. Honours: DoD Research and Development Achievement Awards; Listed in international biographical dictionaries. Address: 3105 Cardinal Way, Unit K, Abingdon, MD 21009, USA. E-mail: ahcarrie@verizon.net

CARRINGTON 6th Baron (Peter Alexander Rupert Carrington), b. 6 June 1919. m. Iona, 1 son, 2 daughters. Education: Eton; RMC Sandhurst. Appointments: Major, Grenadier Guards, Northwest Europe; Justice of the Peace, Buckinghamshire, 1948, DL, 1951; Parliamentary Secretary, Ministry of Agriculture and Fisheries, 1951-54; MOD, 1954-56; High Commissioner, Australia, 1956-59; First Lord of Admiralty, 1959-63; Minister without portfolio and leader of House of Lords, 1963-64; Leader of Opposition, House of Lords, 1964-70, 1974-79; Secretary of State for Defence, 1970-74, Department of Energy, 1974; Minister of Aviation Supply, 1971-74; Secretary of State for Foreign and Commonwealth Affairs, and Minister of Overseas Development, 1979-82; Chairman, Conservative Party, 1972-74; Secretary General, NATO, 1984-88; Chariman, EC Peace Conference, Yugoslavia, 1991-92; Chairman, GEC, 1983-84 (director, 1982-84); Director, Christie's International plc, 1988-98 (chairman, 1988-93); Director, The Telegraph plc, 1990-2003; Non-Executive Director, Chime Communications, 1993-99; Non-Executive Director, Christie's Fine Art Ltd, 1998-. Publications: Reflect on Things Past: The Memoirs of Lord Carrington, 1988. Honours: Honorary Fellow, St Antony's College, Oxford, 1982; Honorary Bencher, Middle Temple, 1983; Honorary Elder, Brother Trinity House, 1984; Honorary LLD, universities of Leeds (1981), Cambridge (1981), Philippines (1982), South Carolina (1983), Aberdeen (1985), Harvard (1986), Sussex (1989), Reading (1989), Nottingham (1993), Birmingham (1993); Honorary DSc, Cranfield, 1983; Honorary DCL, Oxford, 2003; Honorary DUniv, Essex; Liveryman, Worshipful Company of Clothworkers. Memberships: Fellow, Eton, 1966-81; Member, International Board, United World Colleges, 1982-84; Chairman, Board of Trustees V&A Museum, 1983-88; Chancellor: Order of St Michael and St George (1984-94), University of Reading (1992-), Order of the Garter (1994-); President: Pilgrims (1983-2002), VSO (1993-98). Address: 32A Ovington Square, London SW3 1LR, England.

CARRINGTON Simon Robert, b. 23 October 1942, Salisbury, UK. Conductor; University Professor; Freelance Choral Consultant. m. Hilary Stott, 1 son, 1 daughter. Education: MA, Cantab; Choral Scholar, King's College, Cambridge; Teaching Certificate, New College, Oxford. Appointments: Founder and Co-Director, The King's Singers, 1968-2001; Director, Choral Activities, University of Kansas, Lawrence, 1994-2001; Director, Choral Activities, New England Conservatory, Boston, 2001-03; Professor of Choral Conducting, Conductor of the Yale Schola Cantorum, Yale School of Music, New Haven, 2005-; With the King's Singers: 3,000 concerts; 72 recordings, television and radio performances worldwide. Publications: Various choral arrangements. Honours: Grammy Nomination, 1986; Numerous awards and citations at choral festivals worldwide. Memberships: American Choral Directors Association; Association of British Choral Directors; Chorus America. Address: Yale School of Music, Yale Institute of Sacred Music, 409 Prospect Street, New Haven, CT 06511, USA. E-mail: simon.carrington@yale.edu Website: www.simoncarrington.com

CARSON Sol Kent, b. 6 July 1917, Philadelphia, Pennsylvania, USA. Professor of Fine Arts. m. Thelma Clearfield, 1 son. Education: BFA, Temple University Tyler School of Fine Arts, 1944; BSc (Honours), 1945, Education, MEd (Distinction), 1946, Fine Arts, Temple University Teachers College; PhD, Fine Arts, Minerva University Graduate School, Italy, 1960. Appointments: Assistantship, Temple University, 1940-45; Director, Department of Visual Education, Temple University,

1944-47; Museum Consultant, University of Pennsylvania, 1945-46; Director, Department of Art, Temple University, 1946-55; Art Teacher, Philadelphia Board of Education, 1947-58; Art Consultant, Bristol Township School District, Pennsylvania, 1956-66; Summer Faculty Art Department, Wisconsin State University, 1966-67; Associate Professor, Art Department, Millersville State College, Pennsylvania, 1966-68. Memberships: National Educational Association; Pennsylvania State Educational Association; Association for Higher Education; American Association of University Professors; Phi Delta Kappa; Artists' Equity; others. Address: 447 Alberto Way C128, Los Gatos, CA 95032, USA.

CARTER Jimmy (James Earl Jr), b. 1 October 1924, Plains, Georgia, USA. Politician; Farmer. m. Rosalynn Smith, 1946, 3 sons, 1 daughter. Education: Georgia Southwest College; Georgia Institute of Technology; US Naval Academy. Appointments: US Navy, 1946-53; Peanut Farmer, Warehouseman, 1953-77; Busman, Carter Farms, Carter Warehouses, Georgia; State Senator, Georgia, 1962-66; Governor of Georgia, 1971-74; President of USA, 1977-81; Distinguished Professor, Emory University, Atlanta, 1982-; Leader, International Observer Teams, Panama, 1989, Nicaragua, 1990, Dominican Republic, 1990, Haiti, 1990; Host, Peace Negotiations, Ethiopia, 1989; Visitor, Korea, 1994; Negotiator, Haitian Crisis, 1994; Visitor, Bosnia, 1994. Publications: Why Not The Best?, 1975; A Government as Good as its People, 1977; Keeping Faith: Memoirs of a President, 1982; The Blood of Abraham: Insights into the Middle East, 1985; Everything to Gain: Making the Most of the Rest of Your Life, 1987; An Outdoor Journal, 1988; Turning Point: A Candidate, a State and a Nation Come of Age, 1992; Always a Reckoning (poems), 1995; Sources of Strength, 1997; The Virtues of Ageing, 1998; An Hour Before Daylight, 2001; The Hornet's Nest, 2003; Sharing Good Times, 2004; Our Endangered Values: America's Moral Crisis, 2005; Faith and Freedom: The Christian Challenge for the World, 2005; Palestine Peace Not Apartheid, 2006. Honours include: Onassis Foundation Award, 1991; Notre Dame University Award, 1992; Matsunaga Medal of Peace, 1993; J William Fulbright Prize for International Understanding, 1994; Shared Houphouët Boigny Peace Prize, UNESCO, 1995; UNICEF International Child Survival Award (with Rosalynn Carter), 1999; Presidential Medal of Freedom, 1999; Eisenhower Medallion, 2000; Nobel Peace Prize, 2002. Address: The Carter Center, 453 Freedom Parkway, 1 Copenhill Avenue, North East Atlanta, GA 30307, USA.

CARVALHO Paulo de, b. 25 August 1960, Luanda, Angola. Sociologist. m. Anabela Cunha, 2 sons. Education: MA, Sociology, University of Warsaw, Poland, 1990; PhD, Sociology, ISCTE, Lisbon, Portugal, 2004. Appointments: Director of Press Centre, Luanda, Angola, 1991-92; Manager of Consulteste Ltd, 1994-; Lecturer in Sociology and Statistics, 1996-99, Assistant Professor, 1999-, University of Agostinho Neto, Luanda, Angola. Publications: Most important books: Social Structure in Colonial Angola, 1989; Students from Overseas in Poland, 1990; Media Audience in Luanda, Angola, How Much Time is Left until Tomorrow? 2002; Numerous newspaper articles about social and economic subjects, Luanda and Lisbon. Honours: Kianda Award on Economic Journalism, Luanda, Angola, 1998; Angolan Cultural Award on Social Research, 2002. Memberships: International Sociological Association; World Association for Public Opinion Research; American Sociological Association; British Sociological Association; American Statistical Association; Angolan Sociological Association. Address: Caixa Postal 420, Luanda, Angola. E-mail: pauldecarvlho@sociologist.com

CARVALHO Rui Pedro, b. 26 April 1969, Lisbon, Portugal. Senior Research Fellow. Education: Undergraduate Degree, Engineering Physics, 1992; MSc, Mechanical Engineering, 1996, PhD, Theoretical Physics, 2001, Technical University, Lisbon. Appointments: Research Fellow, Bartlett School of Graduate Studies, 2001-05, Senior Research Fellow, Centre for Advanced Spatial Analysis, 2005-, University College London. Publications: Numerous papers and articles in professional journals including: The Dynamics of the Linear Farmer Model, 2004; Environment and Planning, 2005. Honours: Listed in international biographical dictionaries. Address: Centre for Advanced Spatial Analysis, 1-19 Torrington Place, University College London, Gower Street, London WC1E 6BT, England. E-mail: rui.carvalho@ucl.ac.uk

CARWARDINE Richard John, b. 12 January 1947, Cardiff, Wales. University Professor. m. Linda Margaret Kirk, 17 May 1975. Education: BA, Oxford University, 1968; MA, 1972; DPhil, 1975. Appointments: Lecturer, Senior Lecturer, Reader, Professor, University of Sheffield, 1971-2002; Rhodes Professor of American History and Fellow of St Catherine's College, Oxford University, 2002-; Visiting Professor, Syracuse University, New York, 1974-75; Visiting Fellow, University of North Carolina, Chapel Hill, 1989. Publications: Transatlantic Revivalism: Popular Evangelicalism in Britain and America 1790-1865, 1978; Evangelicals and Politics in Antebellum America, 1993; Lincoln, 2003; Lincoln: A Life of Purpose and Power, 2006. Memberships: Fellow, British Academy, 2006-. Address: c/o St Catherine's College, Oxford OX1 3UJ, England.

CARY Phillip Scott, b. 10 June 1958, USA. Professor. m. Nancy Hazle, 3 sons. Education: BA, English Literature and Philosophy, Washington University, St Louis, 1980; MA, Philosophy, 1989, PhD, Philosophy and Religious Studies, 1994, Yale University. Appointments: Teaching Assistant, Philosophy Department, Yale University, 1988-92; Adjunct Faculty, Philosophy Department, University of Connecticut, 1993; Adjunct Faculty, Hillier College, University of Hartford, 1993-94; Arthur J Ennis Postdoctoral Fellow, 1994-97, Rocco A and Gloria C Postdoctoral Fellow, 1997-98, Core Humanities Programme, Villanova University; Assistant Professor of Philosophy, 1998-2001, Associate Professor of Philosophy, 2001-06, Professor of Philosophy, 2006-, Scholar in Residence, Templeton Honors College, 1999-, Eastern University, St Davids. Publications: 1 book; 13 articles in professional journals; 4 taped lecture series. Honours: University Fellowship, Yale University; Mylonas Scholarship, Phi Beta Kappa, Washington University; Lindbach Teaching Award, 2003; Listed in national and international biographical dictionaries. Memberships: APA; AAR; SCP; NAPS. Address: Eastern University, 1300 Eagle Road, St Davids, PA 19087-3696, USA. E-mail: pcary@eastern.edu

CASH Pat, b. 27 May 1965, Australia. Tennis Player. m. Emily, 1 son, 1 daughter. Education: Whitefriars College. Appointments: Coached by Ian Barclay; Trainer, Anne Quinn; Winner, US Open Junior, 1982 Brisbane and in winning Australian Davis Cup team, 1983; Quarter-finals, Wimbledon, 1985, Finalist, Australian Open, 1987, 1988; Wimbledon Champion, 1987; Retired, 1997; Co-Established a tennis training and coaching centre, Queensland; Sports Commentator. Honour: Australian Tennis Hall of Fame. Address: c/o Pat Cash and Associates, PO Box 2238, Footscray, Victoria 3011, Australia.

CASTLEDEN Rodney, b. 23 March 1945, Worthing, Sussex, England. Archaeologist; Geographer; Writer; Composer. m. Sarah Dee, 29 July 1987. Education: BA, Geography, Hertford College, 1967, Dip Ed, 1968, MA, 1972, MSc, Geomorphology, 1980, Oxford University. Appointments: Assistant Geography Teacher, Wellingborough High School, 1968-74 and Wellingborough School, 1974-75; Acting Head of Geography, Overstone School, 1975-76; Assistant Geography Teacher, North London Collegiate School, 1976-79; Head of Geography Department, 1979-90, Head of Humanities Faculty, 1990-2001, Head of Social Science Faculty, 2001-04, Roedean School; Freelance Writer, 2004-. Publications include: Classic Landforms of the Sussex Coast, 1982; The Wilmington Giant: The Quest for a Lost Myth, 1983; The Stonehenge People: An Exploration of Life in Neolithic Britain, 1987; The Knossos Labyrinth, 1989; Minoans: Life in Bronze Age Crete, 1990; Book of British Dates, 1991; Neolithic Britain, 1992; The Making of Stonehenge, 1993; World History: a Chronological Dictionary of Dates, 1994; British History: A Chronological Dictionary of Dates, 1994; The Cerne Giant, 1996; Classic Landforms of the Sussex Coast, 2nd edition, 1996; Knossos, Temple of the Goddess, 1997; Atlantis Destroyed, Out in the Cold, The English Lake District, 1998; King Arthur: the Truth Behind the Legend, The Little Book of Kings and Queens, 1999; Ancient British Hill Figures, 2000; The History of World Events, Britain 3000 BC, 2003; The World's Most Evil People, 2004; Infamous Murderers, Serial Killers, Mycenaeans, People Who Changed the World, Events That Changed the World, 2005; English Castles, Castles of the Celtic Lands, The Attack on Troy, The Book of Saints, Assassinations and Conspiracies, 2006; Natural Disasters that Changed the World, Inventions that Changed the World, Great Unsolved Crimes, 2007. Listed in national and international biographical dictionaries. Music: Cuckmere Suite, a suite for string orchestra, 1999; Winfrith, a chamber opera, 2000; String Sextet, 2007. Memberships: Society of Authors; Sussex Archaeological Society. Address: Rookery Cottage, Blatchington Hill, Seaford, East Sussex BN25 2AJ, England.

CASTONGUAY ROSATI Diane Claire, b. 27 November 1941, Brooklyn, New York, USA. Artist. m. Vincent S Rosati, 1 son, 1 daughter. Education: BS, cum laude, Wagner College, 1976; MPH, Columbia University School of Public Health, 1980. Appointments: Nurse Epidemiologist, Doctors Hospital of Staten Island, 1977-80; Infection Control Coordinator, Staten Island Hospital, 1980-; Professional Artist; Curator. Publications: Several articles in professional journals. Commissions and Creative Works: Numerous exhibitions including: 10 solo shows, 1992-; Pen and Brush Annual Pastel Exhibition, 1992; Mixed Media Shows; Moorings Gallery, Nova Scotia Sign of the Whale Art Gallery, Nova Scotia, Canada, 1992; Silvermine Guild Art Centre, International Print Biennial, 1994, 1996; International Miniprint Exhibition, Conn Graphics Art Centre, 1997; Acadia University Exhibition, invitational 4 person show, Nova Scotia; Curator, Coastline Gallery, Nova Scotia; Works in private collections. Honours include: Gerald Mennin Award for Graphics, National Art Club 97th Annual Exhibiting Members Show, 1995; Honorable Mention, Salmagundi Spring Auction, 1996; Robert Brockman Award, Pen and Brush 15th Pastel Exhibition, 1996; Solo Show Awards in Mixed Media and Pastel, Pen and Brush, 1997; Philip Isenburg Award in Graphics, Pen and Brush, 1997; Dorothy Koatz Myers Award, Salmagundi Non Juried Summer Exhibition, 1997; Silver Medal of Honour, 56th Annual Audubon Artists Show, 1998; Gene Alden Walker Memorial Award, Pen and Brush Graphics Show, 1999. Memberships include: National Art Club; Print Club of Albany; Society of American Graphic Artists; Visual Arts of Nova Scotia; National Association of Woman Artists; The Pen and Brush; Audubon Pastel Society of Canada; Salmagundi Club. Address: 1618 McLean Lake Road, RR#2 Sable River, NS B0T 1V0, Canada.

CATON-JONES Michael, b. 15 October 1957, Broxburn, Scotland. Film Director. Education: National Film School. Appointments: Stagehand, London West End Theatres. Creative Works: Films: Liebe Mutter; The Making of Absolute Beginners; Scandal, 1989; Memphis Belle, 1990; Doc Hollywood, 1991; This Boy's Life, 1993; Rob Roy, 1994; The Jackal, 1997; City By The Sea, 2002; Shooting Dogs, 2005; Basic Instinct 2, 2006. Honours: 1st Prize, European Film School Competition.

CATTO Sir Graeme Robertson Dawson, b. 24 April 1945. Professor of Medicine. m. Joan Sievewright, 1 son, 1 daughter. Education: MB ChB (Hons) , 1969, DSc, 1988, University of Aberdeen; MD (Hons), 1975. Appointments: House Officer, Honorary SHO, Registrar, Senior Registrar, Grampian Health Board Research Fellow, Lecturer in Medicine, University of Aberdeen, 1969-77; Harkness Fellow, Fellow in Medicine, Harvard University and Peter Bent Brigham Hospital, Boston, USA, 1975-77; Senior Lecturer, Reader, Professor of Medicine & Therapeutics, University of Aberdeen; Honorary Consultant Physician/Nephrologist, Aberdenn Royal Infirmary, 1977-2000; Dean, Faculty of Clinical Medicine, then Vice Principal, University of Aberdeen, 1992-2000; Medical Schools Council (now observer on Executive), 1992-; Chief Scientist, Scottish Office Department of Health, 1997-2000; Chairman, Education Committee, General Medical Council, 1999-2002; Founder Fellow, Member of Council & Treasurer, Academy of Medical Sciences, 1998-2002; Dean, Guy's, King's College & St Thomas' Hospitals' Medical & Dental School, Vice Principal, King's College London, Professor of Medicine, University of London, 2000-05; President, General Medical Council, 2002-; Pro Vice Chancellor (Medicine), University of London, 2003-; Member, Council for the Regulation of Healthcare Professionals, 2003-; Governor, Health Foundation (then PPP Healthcare Medical Trust), 2001-02; Professor of Medicine, University of Aberdeen, 2005-; Honorary Consultant Physician, NHS Grampian, 2005-; Chairman, Scottish Centre for Regenerative Medicine, then Member of Scottish Stem Cell Network, 2006-; Chairman, National Advisory Committee, Working in Health Access Network, 2006-. Publications: Numerous articles in professional journals. Honours: Honorary FRCGP, 2000; Knighted, 2002; Honorary FRCSE, 2002; Honorary Ll D, Aberdeen, 2002; Honorary DSc, St Andrews, 2003; Honorary MD, Southampton, 2004; Honorary DSc, Robert Gordon's College, 2004; Fellow, King's College London, 2005; Honorary DSc, Kent, 2007. Memberships include: Association of Physicians of Great Britain and Ireland; Royal Colleges of Physicians: London, Edinburgh, Glasgow; Scottish Society of Physicians; British Medical Association; Royal Society of Medicine; Royal Society of Edinburgh; Academy of Medical Sciences; and others. Address: General Medical Council, London, NW1 3JN, England. E-mail: gcatto@gmc-uk.org

CAULFIELD Patrick, b. 29 January 1936, London, England. Artist. m. (1) Pauline Jacobs, 1968, divorced, 3 sons, (2) Janet Nathan, 1999. Education: Chelsea School of Art; RCA. Appointments: Teacher, Chelsea College of Art. Creative Works: Exhibitions: FBA Galleries, 1961; Robert Fraser Gallery, London, 1965, 1967; Robert Elkon Gallery, New York, 1966, 1968; Waddington Galleries, 1969, 1971, 1973, 1975, 1979, 1981, 1985, 1997, 1998, 2002; Also in

France, Belgium, Italy, Australia, USA, Japan; Retrospective Exhibition, Tate Gallery, London, 1981; Serpentine Gallery, London, 1992; Hayward Gallery, London, 1999; Numerous group exhibitions in England, Europe, New York; Design, for Ballet Party Game, Covent Garden, 1984; Public Collections include: Tate Gallery; Victoria & Albert Museum; Manchester City Art Gallery and other museums and galleries in England, USA, Australia, Germany, Japan. Honours: Elected, Senior Fellowship, RCA, 1993; Honorary Fellow, London Institute, 1996; CBE, 1996; Honorary Fellowship, Bolton Institute, 1999; Honorary Doctorate, University of Surrey, 2000; Honorary Doctorate, University of Portsmouth, 2002. Address: 19 Belsize Square, London NW3 4HT, England.

CAVE Philip, b. 2 June 1949, Finedon, Northamptonshire, England. Landscape Architect. 1 son. Education: BSc, Honours, Plant Science, University of Newcastle upon Tyne, 1970; MA, Landscape Design, Sheffield University, 1973. Appointments: Landscape Architect, Nottinghamshire County Council, 1973-74; Landscape Architect, Norwich City Council, 1974-75; Study tour through Middle East, Asia, Far East and Japan, 1975-77; Landscape Architect, Mathews Ryan Partnership, 1978-79; Principal, Philip Cave Associates, Landscape Architects and Urban Designers, 1979-. Publications: Book: Creating Japanese Gardens, 1993; Section in book: Good Place Guide, 2003; Section in book: Garden UK 2003; Section in book: 1001 Gardens You Must See Before Your Die, 2007; Articles in Urban Design Quarterly, Landscape Design. Honours: Civic Trust Commendation, 2002; Bromley Environmental Award, 2002. Memberships: Landscape Institute, 1975; Urban Design Group, 1982. Address: 5 Dryden Street, Covent Garden, London WC2E 9NB, England. E-mail: principal@philipcave.com Website www.philipcave.com

CAWS Ian, b. 19 March 1945, Bramshott, Hants, England. Poet. m. Hilary Walsh, 20 June 1970, 3 sons, 2 daughters. Education: Churcher's College, Petersfield; North-Western Polytechnic. Publications: Looking for Bonfires, 1975; Bruised Madonna, 1979; Boy with a Kite, 1981; The Ragman Totts, 1990; Chamomile, 1994; The Feast of Fools, 1994; The Playing of the Easter Music (with Martin C Caseley and B L Pearce), 1996; Herrick's Women, 1996; Dialogues in Mask, 2000; Taro Fair, 2003; The Blind Fiddler, 2004; The Canterbury Road, 2007. Contributions to: Acumen Magazine; London Magazine; New Welsh Review; Observer; Poetry Review; Scotsman; Spectator; Stand Magazine; Swansea Review. Honours: Eric Gregory Award, 1973; Poetry Book Society Recommendation, 1990. Membership: Poetry Society. Address: 9 Tennyson Avenue, Rustington, West Sussex BN16 2PB, England.

CAZEAUX Isabelle Anne-Marie, b. 24 February 1926, New York, USA. Professor Emeritus of Musicology. Education: BA, magna cum laude, Hunter College, 1945; MA, Smith College, 1946; Ecole normale de musique, Paris, Licence d'enseignement, 1950; Première médaille, Conservatoire National de Musique, Paris, 1950; MS in Library Science, Columbia University, 1959, PhD, Musicology, 1961, Columbia University. Appointments: Music and phonorecords cataloguer, New York Public Library, 1957-63; Faculty of Musicology, Bryn Mawr College, 1963-92; Faculty of Musicology, Manhattan School of Music, 1969-82; A C Dickerman Professor and Chairman, Music Department, Bryn Mawr College; Visiting Professor, Douglass College, Rutgers University, 1978. Publications: Translations: The Memoirs of Philippe de Commynes, 2 vols, 1969-73; Editor: Claudin de Sermisy, Chansons, 2 vols, 1974; Author: French Music in the

Fifteenth and Sixteenth Centuries, 1975; Articles. Honours: Libby van Arsdale Prize for Music, Hunter College, 1945; Fellowships and scholarships from Smith College, Columbia University, Institute of International Education, 1941-59; Grants from Martha Baird Rockefeller Fund for Music, 1971-72, Herman Goldman Foundation, 1980; Listed in New Grove Dictionary of Music and Musicians, 1980; Festschrift, Liber amicorum Isabelle Cazeaux, 2005. Memberships: American Musicological Society; International Musicological Society; Société française de musicologie; National Opera Association. Address: 415 East 72nd Street, Apt 5FE, New York, NY 10021, USA.

CAZENOVE Christopher de Lerisson, b. 17 December 1943, Winchester, England. Actor. m. Angharad M Rees, 1974, divorced 1993, 2 sons. Education: Dragon School, Oxford; Eton College; Bristol Old Vic Theatre School. Career: Actor; Films include: Zulu Dawn; East of Elephant Rock; Eye of the Needle; Heat and Dust; Until September; Mata Hari; The Fantasist; Souvenir; Hold My Hand I'm Dying; Three Men and a Little Lady; Aces: Iron Eagle III; The Proprietor; Shadow Run; A Knight's Tale; Trance; Beginner's Luck; Lost and Found; Young Alexander the Great; Theatre includes: The Lionel Touch; My Darling Daisy; The Winslow Boy; Joking Apart; In Praise of Rattigan; The Life and Poetry of T S Eliot; The Sound of Music; An Ideal Husband; Goodbye Fidel; Brief Encounter; London Suite; Art; TV includes: The Regiment; The Duchess of Duke Street; Jennie: Lady Randolph Churchill; The Riverman; Jenny's War; Dynasty; Hammer's House of Mystery; Lace; Windmills of the Gods; Shades of Love; Souvenir; The Lady and the Highwayman; Tears in the Rain; Ticket to Ride (A Fine Romance); To be the Best; Judge John Deed; Johnson County War; La Femme Musketeer; Dalziel and Pascoe; Diamond Geezer. Address: c/o Lesley Duff, Diamond Management, 31 Percy Street, London W1T 2DD, England. E-mail: agent@diman.co.uk

CERCE Danica, b. 19 February 1953, Crna na Koroskem, Slovenia. Assistant Professor of American Literature. 1 son, 1 daughter. Education: BA, English and Italian Literatures, 1977; MA, Australian Literature, 1995, PhD, Literary Sciences, 2002, Faculty of Arts, University of Ljubljana, Slovenia; London Chamber of Commerce and Industry Certificate in Teaching English for Business, London Guildhall University, 1996. Appointments: Teacher, High School in Velenje, Slovenia, -1995; Assistant Professor of American Literature and English Teacher, Faculty of Economics, University of Ljubljana, 1995-. Publications: Several articles on American and Australian literature in various Slovene and American academic journals and literary magazines; Contributor to several papers on American and Australian literature at several international conferences in Europe, the United States, Japan and Australia; Book: Pripovednistvo Johna Steinbecka: druzbenokriticna misel v tradiciji mitov in legend, 2005. Memberships: New Steinbeck Society of America; Steinbeck Society; American Literature Association; Southern Comparative Literature Association; European Association of Australian Studies; International Association of Teachers of English as a Foreign Language. Address: Partizanska 3, 2380 Slovenj Gradec, Slovenia. E-mail: danica.cerce@ef.uni-lj.si

CERWENKA Herwig R, b. 18 June 1964, Leoben, Austria. Surgeon; Researcher. m. Wilma Zinke-Cerwenka, 1 son, 2 daughters. Education: Matura Examination, 1982; Doctor of Medicine, 1988; ECFMG/FMGEMS, 1989; Ius practicandi, 1993; Diploma in Emergency Medicine; Diploma in Surgery. Appointment: Professor of Surgery, Researcher, Department of Visceral Surgery, Medical University, Graz, Austria.

Publications: Numerous publications in scientific journals and contributions to books. Honours: Performance Grant, Karl-Franzens University; Numerous other grants and awards for congress contributions and publications. Memberships: International Society of Surgery; International Association of Surgeons and Gastroenterologists; Austrian Society of Surgery; Austrian Society of Surgical Research. Address: Department of Visceral Surgery, Medical University, Auenbruggerplatz 29, A-8036 Graz, Austria. E-mail: herwig.cerwenka@meduni-graz.at

CHA Kyung-Joon, b. 12 May 1958, Seoul, Korea. Professor. m. Young-Sun Suh, 1 son, 1 daughter. Education: BS, Hanyang University, 1980; MS, University of Wisconsin-Madison, 1985; PhD, Southern Methodist University, 1990. Appointments: Associate Director, Research Institute for Natural Sciences, 1995-98, Chairman, Department of Mathematics, 1997-99, Chair, Division of Natural Sciences, 2002-04, Director, Office of Admissions, 2005-, Hanyang University; Editor, Korean Statistical Society, 1995-97; Advisory Head, d2k Solutions Co Ltd, 2000-01; Advisory Committee, Korean Association of Risk Professionals, 2004-. Publications: 24 papers and articles in professional scientific journals. Honours: Best Paper of the Year, Korean Society of Perinatology, 2001; IJGO Prize Paper Award, International Journal of Obstetrics and Gynecology, 2002; Best Paper of the Year, Korean Society of Transportation, 2002. Memberships: American Statistical Association; Korean Statistical Society; Korean Society of Quality Management. Address: Hanyang University, Department of Mathematics, Seongdong-ku, Haengdang-dong, 17, 133-791 Seoul, Korea.

CHA Min Suk, b. 3 March 1970, Seoul, Republic of Korea. Researcher; Professor. m. Min Young Kim, 1 son, 1 daughter. Education: BS, Mechanical Engineering, POSTECH, Pohang, 1993; MS, 1995, PhD, 1999, Mechanical Engineering, Seoul National University, Seoul. Appointments: Part time Lecturer, Kookmin University, Seoul, 1999; Principal Researcher, Korea Institute of Machinery & Materials, Daejeon, 2000-; Visiting Scholar, University of Southern California, Los Angeles, 2004-05; Associate Professor, University of Science & Technology, Daejeon, 2005-; Associate Professor, KAIST, Daejeon, 2007-. Publications: Author, 29 peer-reviewed professional journal articles; Presenter, 80 presentations in professional conferences; Inventor, 34 patents in the field of plasma and combustion engineering. Honours: Listed in international biographical dictionaries; Jiseokyung Award, Korean Intellectual Property Office; Young Investigators Award, 3rd Asian Pacific Conference on Combustion, 2001. Memberships: Editorial Board, Korean Society of Combustion; Member, Combustion Institute; Korean Society of Automotive Engineers; Korean Society of Mechanical Engineers. E-mail: mscha@kimm.re.kr

CHADWICK Peter, b. 23 March 1931, Huddersfield, England. Retired. m. Sheila Salter, deceased 2004, 2 daughters. Education: Huddersfield College; BSc, University of Manchester, 1952; PhD, 1957, ScD, 1973, Pembroke College, Cambridge. Appointments: Scientific Officer, then Senior Scientific Officer, AWRE, Aldermaston, 1955-59; Lecturer, then Senior Lecturer in Applied Mathematics, University of Sheffield, 1959-65; Professor of Mathematics, 1965-91, Emeritus Professor of Mathematics, 1991-, Leverhulme Emeritus Fellow, 1991-93, University of East Anglia. Publications: Numerous papers and articles in learned journals and books; Continuum Mechanics, Concise Theory and Problems, 1976, 1999. Honours: FRS, 1977; Honorary DSc, University of Glasgow, 1991. Memberships: Fellow,

Cambridge Philosophical Society; Honorary Member, British Society of Rheology. Address: 8 Stratford Crescent, Cringleford, Norwich NR4 7SF, England.

CHADWICK Peter Kenneth, b. 10 July 1946, Manchester, England. Writer; Psychologist. m. Rosemary Jill McMahon, 1983. Education: BSc, Geology, University College of Wales, Aberystwyth, 1967; BSc, 1975, Psychology, University of Bristol; MSc, DIC, Structural Geology and Rock Mechanics, Imperial College, London University, 1968; PhD, Structural Geology, University of Liverpool, 1971; PhD, Cognitive and Abnormal Psychology, Royal Holloway and Bedford New College, University of London, 1989; DSc, Psychology, University of Bristol, 2007 (careers in geology, psychology and literature). Appointments: Royal Society European Programme Research Fellow, Geology and Psychology, University of Uppsala, Sweden, 1972-73; Senior Demonstrator in Psychology, University of Liverpool, 1975-76; Lecturer in Psychology, University of Strathclyde, 1976-78; Lecturer in Motivation Psychology, Goldsmiths College, University of London, 1984-85; Professor of Community Psychology, Boston University, 1991-94; Lecturer in Psychology, Birkbeck College, Faculty of Continuing Education, 1982-; Associate Lecturer in Psychology, Open University, London Region, 1982-98; Lecturer in Psychology, City Literary Institute, London, 1982-98; Associate Lecturer in Psychology, Open University, East of England Region, 1994-2006. Publications: The psychology of Geological Observations, 1975; Visual Illusions in Geology, 1976; Peak Preference and Waveform Perception, 1983; Borderline, 1992; Understanding Paranoia, 1995; Schizophrenia – The Positive Perspective, 1997; Personality as Art, 2001; Paranormal, Spiritual and Metaphysical Aspects of Psychosis, 2004; Beyond the Machine Metaphor, 2004; The psychology of Writing, 2005; The Playwright as psychologist, 2006; Freud meets Wilde: A playlet, 2007. Honours: Royal Society European Programme Research Fellowship, 1972-73; Bristol University Postgraduate Scholarship, 1975; British Medical Association Exhibition, 1985; Postdoctoral Award, British Gas Social Affairs Unit, 1991; Royal Literary Fund Award, 1995. Memberships: Fellow, Geological Society of London, 1972-77; Honorary Member, Mizar Society for Social Responsibility in Science, University of Mississippi, 1975-; Associate Fellow, British Psychological Society, 1989-2005; Member, Psychology and Psychotherapy Association, 1995-2005; Oscar Wilde Society, 2005-; Society for Psychical Research, 2005-; Society of Authors, 2005-; Royal Society of Literature, 2005-. Address: Psychology Division, Birkbeck College, Faculty of Continuing Education, University of London, School of Social and Natural Sciences, 26 Russell Square, Bloomsbury, London WC1B 5DQ, England.

CHAGOYA-CORTES Hector Elias, b. 8 October 1974, Mexico City, Mexico. Chemical Engineer. Education: Chemical Engineering, 1997, Diploma in College Teaching Skills, 2005, Universidad La Salle; Diploma in Management Skills, ITESM, 2000. Appointments: Manager of Technology Analysis and Transfer, Becerril, Coca & Becerril, S C, 1997-; Consultant in IP matters for Mexican and foreign companies in the fields of polymers, biotechnology, pharmaceuticals, chemical industry and electronics/communications, including trade secrets protection, patent strategies, patent litigation and licensing; Professor, Chemical Engineering program, La Salle University, 1999-; Teacher of diploma programs of Intellectual Property and Technology Transfer in several institutions, including the National Autonomous University of Mexico. Publications: Variety of articles in specialised international magazines of Intellectual Property and

Technology Licensing; Co-author of the chapter for Mexico in the publication Licensing Best Practices: Strategic, Territorial, and Technology Issues, 2006; Annual revision of the Chapter for Mexico for the manual, Trade Secrets Throughout the World, 2005-. Honours: Scholarship to Excellence, ULSA-P&G, 1995; Hermano Miguel Medal for best academic record; Expert in Engineering Economy (Industrial Property and Technology Transfer), National College of Chemical Engineers and Chemists; Listed in international biographical dictionaries. Memberships: Mexican Institute of Chemical Engineers; National College of Chemical Engineers and Chemists; Licensing Executives Society; Mexican Association for the Protection of Intellectual Property; International Trademark Association; Association of Graduates of the Chemical Sciences School of La Salle University. E-mail: hchagoya@bcb.com.mx

CHAI Sang-Hoon, b. 21 November 1958, Daegu, Korea. Professor. m. Ji-Hyun Cho, 1 son, 1 daughter. Education: BS, Electronic engineering, Kyungbuk National University, 1981; MS, 1983, PhD, 1992, Electronic Engineering, Busan National University; Professional Engineer, Electronics Application, 1989. Appointments: Project Leader, Semiconductor Division, Electronics & Telecommunications Research Institute, Korea, 1983-97; Professor, Electronic Engineering Department, Hoseo University, 1997-; Visiting Professor, ECE Department, University of Florida, USA, 2004-05. Publications: Numerous articles in professional journals. Honours: Excellent Design Award, Integrated Circuits Design & Education Centre, 2002; Excellent Design Award, Korea Electronics Company, 2008. Memberships: IEEE; Korean Institute of Electronic Engineering. Address: Electronic Engineering Department, Hoseo University, 165 Sechul-ri, Baebang-myun, Asan, Choongnam, 336-795, Korea. E-mail: shchai@hoseo.edu

CHAKRAPANI Anupam, b. 12 March 1965, New Delhi, India. Doctor. Education: MBBS, 1987, MD (Paediatrics), 1991, University of Bombay, India; DCH, College of Physicians and Surgeons, Bombay, 1990; MRCP (UK), Royal College of Physicians, London, England, 1995; MRCPCH, Royal College of Paediatricians and Child Health, London, 1998. Appointments: Consultant in Inherited Metabolic Disorders, Birmingham Children's Hospital, 2001-. Publications: Over 30 articles in professional medical journals. Honours: Best Healthcare Professional Well Child Award, 2005. Memberships: Society for the Study of Inborn Errors of Metabolism; Fellow, Royal College of Paediatrics & Child Health; Medical Advisory Panel, UK Galactosaemia Support Group; Executive Committee, British Inherited Metabolic Disease Group. Address: Birmingham Children's Hospital, Steelhouse Lane, Birmingham B4 6NH, England.

CHALFONT Baron, (Alun Arthur Gwynne Jones), b. 5 December 1919, Llantarnam, Wales. Member, House of Lords; Writer. m. Mona Mitchell, 6 November 1948, 1 daughter, deceased. Education: West Monmouth, Wales. Appointments: Regular Officer, British Army, 1940-61; Broadcaster and Consultant on Foreign Affairs, BBC, 1961-64; Minister of State, Foreign and Commonwealth Office, 1964-70; Minister for Disarmament, 1964-67, 1969-70; Minister in charge of day-to-day negotiations for Britain's entry into Common Market, 1967-69; Permanent Representative, Western European Union, 1969-70; Foreign Editor, New Statesman, 1970-71; Chairman, Industrial Cleaning Papers, 1979-86, All Party Defence Group of the House of Lords, 1980-96, Peter Hamilton Security Consultants Ltd, 1984-86, VSEL Consortium, later VSEL plc, 1987-95; Radio Authority, 1991-94, Marlborough Stirling Group, 1994-; Director, W

S Atkins International, 1979-83, IBM UK Ltd, 1973-90, Lazard Brothers & Company Ltd, 1983-90, Shandwick plc, 1985-95, Triangle Holdings, 1986-90, TV Corporation plc, 1996-201; President, Abington Corporation Ltd, 1981-, Nottingham Building Society, 1983-90; All Party Defence Group House of Lords, 1996-. Publications: The Sword and the Spirit, 1963; The Great Commanders (editor), 1973; Montgomery of Alamein, 1976; Waterloo: Battle of Three Armies (editor), 1979; Star Wars: Suicide or Survival, 1985; Defence of the Realm, 1987; By God's Will: A Portrait of the Sultan of Brunei, 1989; The Shadow of My Hand, 2000; Contributions to: Periodicals and journals. Honours: Officer of the Order of the British Empire, 1961; Created a Life Peer, 1964; Honorary Fellow, University College of Wales, 1974; Liveryman, Worshipful Company of Paviors; Freeman of the City of London. Memberships: International Institute for Strategic Studies; Royal Institute of International Affairs; Royal Society of the Arts, fellow; United Nations Association, chairman, 1972-73. Address: House of Lords, London SW1A 0PW, England.

CHALKLIN Christopher William, b. 3 April 1933, London, England. University Teacher (Retired). m. Mavis, 1 son, 2 daughters. Education: BA, University of New Zealand, 1953; BA, 1955, MA, University of Oxford; B Litt, University of Oxford, 1960; Litt D, University of Canterbury, 1986. Appointments: Assistant Archivist, Kent County Council, 1958-62; Senior Fellow, University of Wales, 1963-65; Lecturer in History, 1965-75, Reader in History, 1975-93, University of Reading. Publications: Seventeenth century Kent: A Social and Economic History, 1965; The Provincial Towns of Georgian England: A Study of the Building Process, 1974; English Counties and Public Building 1650-1830, 1998. Address: Grantley Lodge, Chinthurst Lane, Shalford, Surrey GU4 8JS, England.

CHAMBERS Aidan, b. 27 December 1934, Chester-le-Street, County Durham, England. Author; Publisher. m. Nancy Harris Lockwood, 30 March 1968. Education: Borough Road College, Isleworth, London University. Publications: The Reluctant Reader, 1969; Introducing Books to Children, 1973; Breaktime, 1978; Seal Secret, 1980; The Dream Cage, 1981; Dance on My Grave, 1982; The Present Takers, 1983; Booktalk, 1985; Now I Know, 1987; The Reading Environment, 1991; The Toll Bridge, 1992; Tell Me: Children, Reading and Talk, 1993; Only Once, 1998; Postcards from No Man's Land, 1999; Reading Talk, 2001; This Is All: The Pillow Book of Cordelia Kenn, 2005; Contributions to: Numerous magazines and journals. Honours: Children's Literature Award for Outstanding Criticism, 1978; Eleanor Farjeon Award, 1982; Silver Pencil Awards, 1985, 1986, 1994; Carnegie Medal, 1999; Stockport School Book Award KS4, 2000; Hans Christian Andersen Award, 2002; Michael L Printz Award, 2002; J Hunt Award, 2002; Honorary Doctorate, University of Umeå, Sweden, 2003; Honorary President, School Library Association, 2003-06. Membership: Society of Authors. Address: Lockwood, Station Road, Woodchester, Stroud, Gloucestershire, GL5 5EQ, England.

CHAMBERS Guy, b. 12 January 1963; Producer; Writer; Musician (Keyboards). Career: Jimmy Nail, Robbie Williams, World Party, The Waterboys, Julian Cope, Lemon Trees. Recordings: with Robbie Williams, Cathy Dennis, World Party, Holly Johnson: Blast; Julian Cope: Fried; Lemon Trees. Honours: Musicians' Union; PRS; 3 Ivor Novello Awards, 3 Brit Awards; Q Classic Songwriter Award; MMF Best Produced Record Award. Current Management: One Management, 43 St Alban's Avenue, London W4 5JS, England.

CHAMBERS Sarah, b. 8 November 1958, London. Civil Servant. m. Andrew Hearn, 3 sons. Education: BA (Hons) Philosophy, Politics, Economics, Oxford University, 1979. Appointments: Various appointments at DTI, 1979-94; Director of Licensing and International Affairs, OFTEL, 1994-98; Director, Strategy & Competitiveness Unit, DTI, 1999-2001; Director, Automotive Unit, DTI, 2001-04; Chief Executive, Postal Services Commission, November 2004-. Address: Hercules House, 6 Hercules Road, London, SE1 7DB. E-mail: sarah.chambers@psc.gov.uk

CHAMBERS William Edmond, b. 9 October 1943, Brooklyn, New York, USA. Mystery Writer. m. Marie A Kaczanowska. Education: High School Equivalency Diploma, Stevens Institute of Technology, Hoboken, New Jersey, 1961. Appointments: Truck Drivers Helper, M&M Transportation, Queens, New York, 1961-62; Construction Labourer, Roman Stone Construction Company, Brooklyn, New York, 1962-65; Telephone Technician, New York Tel/Verizon, 1965-91; Chief Steward in Verizon for Communications Workers of America, Local 1101, 1979-90; Entrepreneur, Owner of Bar Restaurant, Chambers' Pub, 1983-89; Member, National Board of Directors, 1970-74, New York Chapter President, 1995-97, Executive Vice-President, National Board of Directors, 2000-2002, Mystery Writers of America. Publications: Novels: Death Toll, 1976, reprinted as Print on Demand, 2001; The Redemption Factor, 1980, 2001; The Tormentress, 2005; Short Stories: Don't Kill a Karate Fighter, 1972, 2001, 2005; If I Quench Thee, 1976, London (required school curriculum reading), 1984, 1989; A Better Way, 1976; One Up, 1976; Daddy's Little Girl, 1977; Night Service, 1985; Above Reproach, 1999; The Rationalist, 2000, 2005; Another Night to Remember, 2003, 2004; Poem: An Ode to Freedom, 2000. Honours: Certificate of Merit United Way of Tri-State, 1980; Leadership Award, Communications Workers of America, City of Hope, 1986; Nominee Brooke Russell Astor Award, 2002; Couple of the Year Awards (with wife Marie), Seneca Club, Democratic Party, 1998, 2001, 2002, 2003, 2004, 2005; Listed in Who's Who publications and biographical dictionaries. Memberships: Mystery Writers of America; Private Eye Writers of America; Sisters in Crime; International Association of Crime Writers; International Thriller Writers, Inc; Honorary Life Member, Communication Workers of America. Address: 65 Meserole Avenue, Brooklyn, NY 11222, USA. E-mail: billchambers@verizon.net Website: www.williamechambers.com

CHAMPION Margrét Gunnarsdóttir, b. 30 January 1953, Reykjavik, Iceland. Senior Lecturer. Divorced. Education: English, Trinity College, Dublin, 1975-77; BA (magna cum laude), 1980, MA, 1985, PhD, 1991, English, University of Georgia. Appointments: Teaching Assistant, Department of English, University of Georgia, 1985-90; Lecturer, Department of Comparative Literature, University of Iceland, 1992-94; Research Fellow, 1995-98, Lecturer, 1999, Visiting Teacher, 2006-08, Part time Teacher, 2003-05, Department of English, University of Uppsala; Lecturer, Department of English, University of Stockholm, 1999; Senior Lecturer, Department of English, University of Gothenburg, 2000-. Publications: Numerous articles in professional journals. Honours: Exchange Scholarship, Trinity College, Dublin, 1975-76; Phi Beta Kappa (academic honours society), University of Georgia, 1980; Research Grant, University of Iceland, 1993; Research Grant, Icelandic Council of Sciences, 1993; Research Fellowship, University of Uppsala, 1995-98; Research Grant, Swedish Council of Sciences, 2000; Research Grant, Humanities Faculty, University of Gothenburg, 2002. Address: Geijersgatan 50A, 75231, Uppsala, Sweden. E-mail: margret.gunnarsdottir.champi@eng.gu.se

CHAN Alan Hoi Shou, b. 9 January 1960, Dongguan, Guandong, China. Ergonomics Educator. m Cindy Ip, 2 sons. Education: BSc, Industrial Engineering, 1982, MPhil, 1985, PhD, Ergonomics, 1995, University of Hong Kong. Appointments: Certified Engineer, Research Staff, Hong Kong University, 1982-85; Manager, Technical Services, YHY Food Products Ltd, 1988-89; Associate Professor, Ergonomics, City University of Hong Kong, 1989-; Council Member, Pan Pacific Council of Occupational Ergonomics, Japan, 1997-; Editor, Industrial and Occupational Ergonomics: Users Encyclopaedia, 1997; Member, Editorial Board, Asian Journal of Ergonomics, 1997-, and International Journal of Industrial Ergonomics, 1998-; Associate Editor, Industrial Engineering Research, 1997-; Regional Vice-President, Institute of Industrial Engineering, 2001-02. Publications: More than 120 papers in refereed journals and conference proceedings. Honour: Listed in Who's Who publications. Memberships: Institute of Electrical Engineering; Institute of Industrial Engineers; Ergonomics Society; Hong Kong Ergonomics Society; International Ergonomics Association. Address: MEEM Department, City University of Hong Kong, Tat Chee Avenue, Kowloon Tong, Hong Kong, China. E-mail: alan.chan@cityu.edu.hk

CHAN Jackie, b. 7 April 1954, Hong Kong. Actor; Producer; Director. m. Feng-Jiao Lin, 1 December 1982, 1 son; 1 daughter with Elaine Ng. Education: China Drama Academy. Career: Actor; Producer; Director; Films include: The Big Brawl, 1980; Cannonball Run, 1981, 1984; Project A, 1983 and 1987; Wheels on Wheels, 1984; The Protector, 1985; Armor of God, 1986, 1991; Police Story, 1987, 1989; Dragons Forever, 1988; Miracles, 1990; Twin Dragons, 1992; Policy Story 3 – Supercop, 1992; Crime Story, 1993; Rush Hour, 1998, Rush Hour 2, 2001; Shanghai Knights, 2003; Around the World in 80 Days, 2004; Enter the Phoenix, 2004; New Police Story, 2004; Rice Rhapsody, 2005; Rush Hour 3, 2007. Ambassador, Hong Kong Tourism Board, 2003-; Ambassador, Beijing Olympics, 2003-; UN Goodwill Ambassador, 2004-. Honours: Best Picture Award, Hong Kong Film, 1989; Best Actor, Golden Horse Awards, Taiwan, 1992, 1993; MTV Lifetime Achievement Award, 1995; Best Action Choreography, Hong Kong Film, 1996, 1999; Maverick Tribute Award Cinequest San Jose Film Festival, 1998; Third Hollywood Film Festival Actor of the Year, 1999; Silver Bauhinia Star, 1999; Indian Film Awards International Achievement Award, 2000; Montreal World Film Festival Grand Prix of the Americas, 2001; MTV Movie Awards Best Fight Scene, 2002; Golden Horse Best Action Choreography, Taiwan, 2004; Hong Kong Film Award for Professional Achievement, 2005; Member, Most Excellent Order of the British Empire, British Government for Hong Kong/Commonwealth; Chevalier des Arts et des Lettres, French Minister of Culture and Communication; Honorary Doctor of Social Science, Hong Kong Baptist University; Honorary Fellow, Hong Kong Academy of Performing Arts. Address: The Jackie Chan Group, 145 Waterloo Road, Kowloon-Tong, Kowloon, Hong Kong. E-mail: jcgroup@jackiechan.com Website: www.jackiechan.com

CHAN Keen Ian, b. 28 August 1972, Singapore. Assistant Principal Engineer. m. Serene, 1 daughter. Education: B Eng (1st class honours), 1997, M Eng, 2001, Nanyang Technological University, Singapore; SM (Aeronautics and Astronautics), Massachusetts Institute of Technology, USA,

2003. Appointments: Engineer, Chartered Ammunition Industries, 1997-99; Senior Engineer, 2003-07, Assistant Principal Engineer, 2007-, S T Aerospace. Publications: Numerous articles in professional journals. Honours: NTU Alumni Prize, 1997; Listed in international biographical dictionaries. Memberships: Senior Member, American Institute of Aeronautics and Astronautics; Member, Singapore Institute of Aerospace Engineers. Address: S T Aerospace Ltd, 540 Airport Road, Paya Lebar, S (539938), Singapore. E-mail: chanki@stengg.com

CHAN Raymond Chor Kiu, b. Hong Kong. Psychologist. Education: MPhil, 1996; PhD, 2001. Appointments: Full Professor, Deputy Head of Department of Psychology, Co-ordinator for Academic Research Collaboration and Development, Department of Psychology, Sun Yat-Sen University, China; Adjunct Associate Professor, Department of Psychiatry, The University of Hong Kong; Professor of Neuropsychology and Applied Cognitive Science Research Sciences, Institute of Psychology, Chinese Academy of Sciences, China. Publications: More than 41 articles; Editorial Boards of Clinical Rehabilitation, Neuropsychological Rehabilitation and Hong Kong Journal of Psychiatry. Honours: Rainbow Ambassador, Pok Oi Hospital, Hong Kong; One of the 10 recipients of Outstanding Staff, Hospital Authority of Hong Kong; Sir Edward York Memorial Fellowship; NARSAD Young Investigator Award; 100-Scholar, Sun Yat-Sen University; Senior Research Scientific Award for Schizophrenia; Regional Representative for Asia for the International Neuropsychological Society. Memberships: International Neuropsychological Society; National Academy of Neuropsychology; American Psychological Association; Schizophrenia International Research Society; British Neuropsychological Society. Address: Institute of Psychology, Chinese Academy of Sciences, Beijing 100101, China.

CHAN Siew Ling, b. 1963. Marketing Specialist; Entrepreneur. Education: BBA, National University of Singapore. Appointments: Account Manager, Leo Burnett Company (Advertising), 1986-90; Assistant Vice President, Citibank NA, 1990-93; Regional Marketing Manager, Visa International Asia Pacific, 1993-95; Correspondent, The Business Times, Singapore Press Holdings, 1995-96; Regional Vice President, ABN AMRO Bank NV Asia Pacific, 1996-99; Founder & Managing Partner, Red Square (S) Pte Ltd, creative & marketing agency, 1999-. Honours: Post Office Savings Bank Scholar, 1983-85; Singapore International Chamber of Commerce (SICC) City Commemorative Prize Fund Award, 1983; David B H Chew Meritorious Award, 1983; Listed in national and international biographical directories. Address: Red Square (S) Ptd Ltd, Red Square House, 125 Devonshire Road, Singapore 239884, Republic of Singapore.

CHANG Chen-Yu, b. 6 June 1969, Taipei, Taiwan. Lecturer. m. Hoi-Laam Karen Yu. Education: BSc, Civil Engineering, 1988-92, MSc, Construction Management, 1992-94, National Taiwan University; MPhil/PhD, Construction Economics and Management, University College London, University of London, England, 1997-2001. Appointments: Part-time Site Supervisor, construction project of NTU main library, 1992-94; Military Engineering Officer, construction project in Kaoshiung, 1994-96; Researcher, Century Development Corporation, 2002; Associate Researcher, Taiwan Construction Research Institute, 2002-04; Lecturer in Construction Economics and Management, Bartlett School of Construction and Project Management, 2003-. Publications: 15 papers in professional journals; 18 conference papers; 11 magazine articles; 8 completed research papers. Honours: Book Scroll Award,

National Taiwan University, 1988, 1989, 1990; Best Paper Award, Society of Chinese Engineers, 1991; Outstanding Compulsory Military Officer Certificate, Army of Taiwan, 1996; Ministry of Education Fellowship, Taiwan, 1996; Advanced Institute of Management Research (AIM) Scholar, 2004; Best Paper Award, Chinese Institute of Construction Management, 2007; Listed in national and international biographical dictionaries. Memberships: Associate Member, American Society of Civil Engineers; Member, Chinese Society of Civil and Hydraulic Engineers. Address: Wates House, The Bartlett, 22 Gordon Street, London WC1H 0QB, England. E-mail: chen-yu.chang@ucl.ac.uk

CHANG Chi-Cheng, b. 7 August 1959, Taipei, Taiwan. Professor of Learning Technology. m. Ting Hsu, 1 daughter. Education: M Ed, Industrial Education, National Taiwan Normal University, 1985; MS, Computer Science, University of Texas, USA, 1992; M Ed, Instructional Systems, 1995, PhD, Workforce Education and Development, 1996, Penn State University, USA. Appointments: Professor in Learning Technology, Institute of Technological and Vocational Education, 2000, Assistant Dean, College of Humanity and Science, 2001-2003, National Taipei University of Technology; Member of Evaluation Committee for Research Project, National Science Council, 2000-; Member of Evaluation Committee for Vocational-Technical High School, Ministry of Education, 2000-; Consultant, Division of Education and Training, Institute of Information Industry, 2000-2001; Member, Editorial Board, Global Chinese Journal on Computers in Education, 2003-; Member of Executive Committee, Global Chinese Society for Computers in Education, 2003-. Publications: Numerous articles in scientific journals and presented at conferences include most recently: An Electronic Performance Support System for performing and learning instructional designing tasks, 2003; A practical case, implications and issues of systematically building a university web-based learning community environment, 2003; The relationship between the usefulness of key components and the implementation benefits for Electronic Performance Support System, 2004. Honours include: Excellent Software of Information Management System, National Contest of Campus Software Creation, Ministry of Education, 2000; Outstanding Paper, Chinese Association of Video-Audio Education, 2001; Excellent Paper for Distance Education in Global Chinese Society, Open University, Taiwan, 2003; Listed in Who's Who publications and biographical dictionaries. Memberships: Association for the Advancement of Computing in Education; Asia-Pacific Society for Computers in Education; Global Chinese Society of Computers in Education; Chinese Association of e-Learning; Chinese Association of Educational and Telecommunication Technology; Chinese Association of Human Research Development; Chinese Association of Curriculum and Instruction. Address: Institute of Technological & Vocational Education, National Taipei University of Technology, No 1, Sec 3 Chung-Hsiao E Rd, Taipei 106, Taiwan. E-mail: f10980@ntut.edu.tw

CHANG Chip Hong, b. 7 September 1964, Singapore. Professor. m. Gek King Heng. Education: B Eng (Hons), National University of Singapore, 1989; M Eng, 1993, PhD, 1998, Postgraduate Diploma of Teaching in Higher Education, 2001, Nanyang Technological University, Singapore. Appointments: Supplier Quality Engineer, General Motor Singapore Ltd, 1989-90; Research Assistant, 1990-95, Assistant Professor, 1999-2005, Associate Professor, 2005-, Programme Director, Centre for Integrated Circuits and Systems, 2003-, Nanyang Technological University; Lecturer, French-Singapore Institute, 1994-98; Technical

Consultant, Flextech Electronics, 1989-99; Deputy Director, Centre for High Performance Embedded Systems, 2000-. Publications: 40 refereed international journals; 88 refereed international conference papers; 3 book chapters; 1 edited volume of lecture notes in computer science. Honours: Vista Research Society of Industry Leader; Listed in international biographical dictionaries. Memberships: Senior Member, Institute of Electrical and Electronics Engineers; Fellow, Institution of Engineering and Technology.

CHANG Jeong Ho, b. 18 November 1969, Cheong Ju City, Korea. m. Hye Eun Jang, 1 son, 1 daughter. Education: BS, 1995, MS, 1997, PhD, 2001, Chemistry, Chungbuk National University. Appointments: Pacific Northwest National Laboratory, US-DOE, 2000-02; Korean Institute of Ceramic Engineering and Technology, 2002-07. Publications: Papers and articles in professional scientific journals. Honours: NewTech Korea Awards, 2003, 2006; Best Research Award, KICET, 2005. Memberships: E-MRS; Biomaterials Society; International Sol-Gel Science. Address: 233-5 Gasan-dong, Guemcheon-gu, Seoul 153-801, South Korea. E-mail: jhchang@kicet.re.kr

CHANG Jun-Dong, b. 9 July 1955, Seoul, Korea. Medical Doctor; Professor. m. Kyung-Ok Joo, 1 son, 1 daughter. Education: MD, 1979; PhD, 1992. Appointments: President, Koran Hip Society; President, Korean Musculoskeletal Transplantation Society; Editorial Board, Journal of Arthroplasty; President, 12th International Biolox Symposium; Editorial Board, Journal of Korean Orthopaedic Association; Treasurer, Korean Fracture Society; Professor and Chief, Department of Orthopaedic Surgery, Hangang Sacred Heart Hospital, Hallyon University. Publications: Over 125 articles related to Arthroplasty. Honours: Academic Award, Korean Orthopaedic Association, 2003, 2005; Academic Award, Korean Hip Society, 2007; Listed in international biographical dictionaries. Memberships: Orthopaedic Research Society, USA; SICOT; Korean Orthopaedic Association; Korean Hip Society; Korean Knee Society. Address: #108-304 Mokdong e-pyeonhansesang Apt 950, Mok-2 Dong, Yangchun-ku, Seoul 158-052, Korea. E-mail: jdchangos@yahoo.com

CHANG Jung Hwan, b. 1 May 1968, Busan, Korea. Senior Researcher. m. Yu Min Sim, 2 sons. Education: Bachelor's degree, 1994, Master's degree, 1997, Electrical Engineering, Doctor's degree, 2001, Mechanical Engineering, Hanyang University. Appointments: Postdoctoral Brain Korea 21, Hanyang University, 2001-02; Research Fellow, University of California at Berkeley, 2002-03; Senior Research Engineer, Korea Electrotechnology Research Institute, 2003-. Publications: IEEE Transaction on Industry Applications; Transaction on Magnetics; IEE Proceedings Electric Power Applications; Journal on Magnetism and Magnetic Materials; Journal of Applied Physics. Honours: Baeck Nam Full Scholarship, Hanyang University, 1987-94; Outstanding Graduate Honor, 1994; Fellowship, Korea Science and Engineering Foundation, 2002-03. Memberships: IEEE; Korean Institution of Electrical Engineering. Address: TFM Research Group, KERI Seongu-Dong 28-1, Changwon City, 641-120, Korea. E-mail: cjhwan@keri.re.kr

CHANG Mao-Nan, b. 11 January 1968, Taipei, Taiwan. Researcher. m. Hsing-Yueh Ho, 1 son, 1 daughter. Education: BSc, 1990, MS, 1993, Physics, PhD, Electrical Engineering, 1999, National Central University, Taiwan. Appointments: Associate Researcher, 1999-2005, Deputy Manager, 2003-05, National Nano Device Laboratories; Associate Professor, Feng Chia University, 2004-05; Manager, 2005-,

Researcher, 2006-, Division of Nano Metrology, National Nano Device Laboratories; Program Chair, Symposium on Nano Device Technology, 2008. Honours: NARL Outstanding Research Award, 2007. Address: No 26, Prosperity Road I, Science-based Industrial Park, Hsinchu, 30078, Taiwan. E-mail: mnchang@mail.ndl.org.tw

CHANG Michael, b. 22 February 1972, Hoboken, New Jersey, USA. Former Tennis Player. Appointments: Aged 15 was youngest player since 1918 to compete in men's singles at US Open, 1987; Turned Professional, 1988; Played Wimbledon, 1988; Winner, French Open, 1989; Davis Cup Debut, 1989; Winner, Canadian Open, 1990; Semi-Finalist, US Open, 1992, Finalist, 1996; Finalist, French Open, 1995; Semi-Finalist, Australian Open, 1995, Finalist, 1996; Winner of 34 singles titles by end of 2002; Retired, 2003; USA Tennis High Performance Committee, US Tennis Association, 2005-06; Joined Jim Courier's Senior Tour, Naples, Florida, 2006. Address: Advantage International, 1751 Pinnacle Drive, Suite 1500, McLean, VA 22102, USA. Website: www.highperformance.usta.com/home.default.sps

CHANG Shih-Lin, b. 1 May 1946, Anhwei, China. Professor. m. Ling-Mei P Chang, 3 sons. Education: BS, Electrophysics, National Chiao Tung University, 1968; MS, Physics, Clemson University, USA, 1971; PhD, Physics, Polytechnic Institute of Brooklyn, USA, 1975. Appointments: Assistant Professor, 1975-78, Associate Professor, 1979-84, Professor, 1985, Solid State and Material Science, Universidade Estadual de Campinas, Brazil; Professor, Physics, 1985-, National Tsing Hua University, Taiwan; Head, Physics Department, National Tsing Hua University, 1987-90; Director General, Natural Science and Mathematics Department, National Science Council, Republic of China, 1993-94; Deputy Director, Synchrotron Radiation Research Centre, Republic of China, 1995; Dean of Research and Development, National Tsing Hua University, 1998-2004; Director, Joint Research Institute of ITRI/NTHU, 2003-2004; Dean, College of Science, National Tsing Hua University, 2004-; Chairman, National Crystallography Committee, Taiwan, Republic of China, 2004-. Publications: Over 130 scientific papers; 2 books; 1 monograph. Honours: Outstanding Research Award; Dr Sun Yat-Sen Academic Prize; Academic Prize in Natural Science; National Chair Professor in Natural Science (Ministry of Education); Tsing-Hua Chair Professor (Natural Science), 2004-06; Tsing Hua Distinguished Chair Professor, 2006-; Elected member, Asian-Pacific Academy of Materials Science; Teco Science & Technology Award, 2005. Memberships: American Crystallographic Association; Asian Crystallographic Association; Fellow, Physical Society of the Republic of China; Fellow, American Physical Society. Address: 101, Section 2, Kuang Fu Road, Hsinchu, Taiwan, 300, Republic of China. E-mail: slchang@phys.nthu.edu.tw

CHANG Shuenn-Yih, b. 12 June 1958, Taiwan. Professor. m. Chiu-Li Huang, 2 daughters. Education: BS, 1977-81, MS, 1981-83, National Taiwan University; M Eng, University of California, Berkeley, California, USA, 1988-92; PhD, University of Illinois, Urbana-Champaign, USA, 1992-94. Appointments: Engineer, Eastern International Engineers, 1985-87; Associate Research Fellow, National Center for Research on Earthquake Engineering, 1995-2002; Associate Professor, 2002-04, Professor, 2005-, National Taipei University of Technology. Publications: Application of the Momentum Equations of Motion to Pseudodynamic Testing, 2001; Explicit Pseudodynamic Algorithm with Unconditional Stability, 2002; Accuracy of Time History Analysis of Impulses, 2003; Nonlinear Error Propagation of Explicit Pseudodynamic

Algorithm, 2003; Experimental Study of Seismic Behaviors of As-Built and Repaired Reinforced Concrete Bridge Columns, 2004; Error Propagation in Implicit Pseudodynamic Testing of Nonlinear Systems, 2005; Accurate Representation of External Force in Time History Analysis, 2006; Development and Validation of Generalized Bi-axial Smooth Hysteresis Model, 2007. Honours: Research Award, National Science Council, Taiwan, Republic of China; Research Award, Chinese Institute of Civil and Hydraulic Engineering; Distinguished Research Award, National Taipei University of Technology, 2006. Memberships: Senior Member, Chinese Institute of Civil and Hydraulic Engineering; Chinese Institute of Earthquake Engineering. Address: National Taipei University of Technology, Department of Civil Engineering, #1 Section 3 Jungshiau East Road, Taipei, Taiwan, Republic of China. E-mail: changsy@ntut.edu.tw

CHANG Walter Tuck Sr, b. 16 February 1920, Honolulu, Hawaii. Machinist; Educator; Administrator; Sunday School Teacher; Realtor. m. Evelyn Show Chiao Haung Chang, 1 son, 1 daughter. Education: Scholastic Honours, Cadet First Lieutenant, The Kamehameha School for Boys, Military Academy, Trade and Religious School, 1934-39; BA, Industrial Arts with Honours and Teachers' Credentials, San Jose State Teachers College, 1939-45; Teachers Credentials, in Driver Education and Training, Vocational Education and Administration, University of California, 1948-55; MA, Education, Administration and Supervision Credentials of High School Teachers, San Francisco State University, 1955-59; Graduate Studies in Elementary School Administration, Supervision of Practice Teachers, University of Hawaii, 1959-64; Doctorate Dissertation, Maurice Kidjel Ratio Concept – Design and Drafting, University of Maryland, 1967-68; Taught Getting Started with the Cali-Pro, University of Maryland, 1967-68. Appointments: Drafting Apprenticeship, Hawaiian Electric Company, Engineering and Estimation Department, 1937-39; Machinist, Leadman, National War Manpower Job Instructor for Joshua Hendy Iron Works, Sunnyvale, California, 1942-45; Journeyman Machinist, Food Machinery Corporation, San Jose, California, 1946; Only Chinese-Hawaiian American Experimental Machinist, Tool Maker, helped to perfect the first guided missile in the world, Ames Aeronautical Laboratory, NASA, Moffett Field, California, 1946-51; Journeyman Machinist, Oliver United Filters Inc, Oakland, California, 1952-53; Vocational Instructor, San Jose State College, 1942-45; Adult Evening Vocational Instructor, Leland High School, San Jose, 1951; Vocational Instructor, John Swett Union High School, Crockett, California, 1951-59; Vocational Director, Evening High School Principal, 1952-59; Ad-hoc Chairman with 130 State Vocational Directors converted all Technical Schools into City, Community and Junior Colleges, 1956-58; Industrial Arts, English, World History Instructor, McKinley High School, Honolulu, Hawaii, 1959-62; Industrial Arts Instructor, New Industrial Arts Education Department, College of Education, University of Hawaii; Manoa Campus and Supervisor of Practice Teachers, Lab High School, University of Hawaii, 1962-64; Design, Drafting, Architecture, Engineering, Auto Cad, Electronic, Metals Technology, Instructor and Supervisor of Drivers Education and Training, Kamehameha Schools, 1964-90; Introduced Auto-Cad to the State of Hawaii Curriculum, 1985; Implemented Unified Phonics into curriculum making New Keola Elementary School first public school to have homogeneous classes, grades 2-6; Many other positions. Publications: Follow up study of graduates, 1953-58, of the trade and industry program, John Swett UHS, 1959 (thesis in Library of Congress); Getting started with the cali-pro, Maurice Kidjel Ratio Concept, 1965. Honours:

National Merit Honor Student; Epsilion Pi Tau; Kappa Delta Pi; Phi Delta Kappa; Most Outstanding Educator; Many others. Memberships: NEA; CTA; AVA; AIAA; HEA; OTA; OIATA; Vice President, President, 94 industrial arts teachers on O'ahu, 1961-62; PTA; Vice President, New Keola Elementary School, Kailua O'ahu, Hawaii, 1961-62. Address: 94-1015 Uke'e Place, Waipahu, HI 96797-4272, USA.

CHANG Yoon-Suk, b. 27 July 1965, Seoul, Republic of Korea. Research Professor. Education: BS, 1991, MS, 1993, PhD, 1996, Mechanical Engineering, Sungkyunkwan University, Republic of Korea. Appointments: Senior Researcher, 1996-99, Principal Researcher, 1999-2002, Power Engineering Research Institute, Korea Power Engineering Company, Republic of Korea; Fellow Researcher, Materialprufungsanstalt, University of Stuttgart, Germany, 2002; Fellow Researcher, Institute of Industrial Science, University of Tokyo, Japan, 2002-03; Research Professor, Department of Mechanical Engineering, Sungkyunkwan University, 2004-. Publications: Application of Grid-based Approach for Auto Mesh Generation of Vacuum Chamber, 2006; Assessment of Plastic Collapse Behavior for Tubes with Collinear Cracks, 2006; Failure Probability Assessment of Wall-thinned Nuclear Pipes Using PFM, 2006; Determination of Global Failure Pressure for Tubes with Two Parallel Cracks, 2006; Application of an Enhanced RBI Method for Petrochemical Equipments, 2006; Fluid-Structure Interaction Analysis on Wall-Thinned Pipes, 2006; Elastic-plastic Fracture Mechanics Assessment for Steam Generator Tubes with Through-wall Cracks, 2007; Determination of Failure Pressure for Tubes with Two Non-aligned Axial Through-wall Cracks, 2007; Fatigue Data Acquisition, Evaluation and Optimization of District Heating Pipes, 2007. Honours: President's Award, Korea Power Engineering Company, 2002; Co-author, 2nd Prize of Student Paper Competition on PVP Conference, ASME, 2005; Award for Best Research Team, Korean Ministry of Education and Human Resources Development, 2005. Memberships: Korean Society of Mechanical Engineers, 1992-; Korean Nuclear Society, 1996-; Korean Society for Precision Engineering, 2005-; Korean Society of Pressure Vessel and Piping, 2005-; ASME, 2005-. Address: 656-1041, Sungsu 1-Ga 2-Dong, Sungdong-Gu, Seoul, 133-823, Republic of Korea. E-mail: yschang7@skku.edu

CHANG Young Woon, b. 22 August 1954, Seoul, Korea. Medical Educator. m. Eun Hee Lee, 1 son, 1 daughter. Education: Graduate, Kyung Hee Medical School, Seoul, 1979. Appointments: Visiting Research Fellow, Southwestern Medical School, Dallas, Texas, USA, 1992-94; Assistant Professor, 1989-94, Associate Professor, 1994-99, Professor, 1999-, Director, 2005-, Gastroenterology Department, Kyung Hee Medical Hospital. Publications: Contribution of articles to professional journals: Role of Helicobacter pylori infection among gastric cancer family, 2002; Helicobacter pylori eradication in patients with functional dyspepsia, 2003; Interleukin-IB polymorphism in Gastric cancer, 2005. Honours: Medical Award, Korean Society of Gastroenterology, 1988, 2001; Listed in international biographical dictionaries. Memberships: Korean Society of Gastroenterology; Korean Society of Gastrointestinal Endoscopy; Korean Society of Biochemistry and Molecular Biology. Address: Department of Gastroenterology, Kyung Hee University College of Medicine, 1 Hoiki-Dong, Dongdaemoon-Gu, Seoul 130-702, Republic of Korea. E-mail: cywgi@chollian.net

CHANG Yu-Kaung, b. 2 December 1957, Taiwan. Professor. m. Chen Tsai-Chin, 2 sons, 1 daughter. Education: BS, Soochow University, 1981; MSc, Taiwan University, 1983;

PhD, Cambridge University, England, 1995. Appointments: Director, Center for Biochemical Engineering, Ming Chi University of Technology, 2003-; Professor, Graduate School of Biochemical Engineering, Ming Chi University; Dean, Student Affairs, 2006-. Publications: Direct recovery of proteins from unclarified feedstocks by expanded bed adsorption technique. Honours: 2nd prize, 2nd Creative Competition for College Student in Taiwan, 2001; Creativity Special Prize, 2001. Memberships: Phi Tau Phi; Administrator, Affairs of Biochemical Engineering Society of Taiwan, 2007-10. Address: 84 Gungjuan Road, Taishan, Taipei 24301, Taiwan. E-mail: ykchang@mail.mcut.edu.tw

CHANNAGIRI Ajit, b. 15 September 1950, Bangalore, India. Engineer. m. Sharada, 2 sons. Education: BSc, University of Mysore, 1969; B Eng, Indian Institute of Science, Bangalore, 1972; M Tech, 1974, Indian Institute of Technology, Bombay. Appointments: Assistant Executive Engineer to Chief Engineer, ITI Ltd, 1974-99; Programme Director, Centre for Development of Advanced Computing, 1999-2006; Technical Director, Instrument Research Associates Pvt Ltd, 2006-. Publications: Many papers/articles in national and international forums such as IEEE, IFIP, IFAC. Honours: Outstanding R&D Achievements, 1993; Excellence in Indigenous Development, 1996; Listed in international biographical directories. Memberships: Senior Member, Computer Society of India. Address: 100, 42 Cross, 8 Block, Jayanagar, Bangalore 560 082, India. E-mail: ajitcn@gmail.com

CHANNING Stockard, b. 13 February 1944, New York, USA. Actress. m. 4 times. Education: Harvard University. Career: Actress; Films include: Comforts of the Home, 1970; The Fortune, Sweet Revenge, 1975; The Big Bus, 1976; Grease, The Cheap Detective, Boys Life, 1978; Without A Trace, 1983; Heartburn, Men's Club, 1986; Staying Together, Meet the Applegates, 1987; Married to It, Six Degrees of Separation, 1993; Bitter Moon, 1994; Smoke, 1995; Up Close and Personal, Moll Flanders, Edie and Pen, The First Wives Club, 1996; Practical Magic, Twilight, Lulu on the Bridge (voice), 1998; The Red Door, Other Voices, 1999; The Business of Strangers, 2001; Life of Something Like IT, Behind the Red Door, 2002; Bright Young Things, Le Divorce, Anything Else, 2003; Red Mercury, Must Love Dogs, 3 Needles, 2005; Sparkle, 2007; Theatre includes: Two Gentlemen of Verona, 1972-73; No Hard Feelings, 1973; Vanities, 1976; As You Like It, 1978; They're Playing Out Song, Lady and the Clarinet, The Golden Age, 1983; A Day in the Death of Joe Egg, 1985; House of Blue Leaves, 1986; Woman in Mind, 1988; Love Letters, 1989; Six Degrees of Separation, 1990; Four Baboons Adoring the Sun, 1992; TV includes: The Stockard Channing Show, 1979-80; The West Wing, 1999-; Batman Beyond, 1999; The Truth About Jane, The Piano Man's Daughter, 2000; Confessions of an Ugly Stepsister, 2002; Hitler: The Rise of Evil, 2003; Jack, 2004; Out of Practice, 2005-06. Honours: Tony Award, Best Actress, 1985. Address: ICM, c/o Andrea Eastman, 40 W 57th Street, New York, NY 10019, USA.

CHANNON Merlin George Charles, b. 14 September 1924, St Johns Wood, London, England. Retired HM Inspector of Schools; Community Musician; Handelian. m. Ann Carew Robinson, 21 July 1951, 1 daughter. Education: Guildhall School of Music, College of St Mark and St John, 1943-45; BMus (London), Trinity College of Music, 1950-55; MA, Birmingham University, 1981-84; PhD, Open University, 1986-95. Appointments: Teacher, Middlesex and London schools, 1945-54; Director of Music, Woolverstone Hall School, Suffolk, 1955-62; Director of Music and Senior

Lecturer, St Paul's College, Cheltenham, 1962-65; HM Inspector of Schools, Department of Education and Science, Midland and Eastern Divisions successively, 1965-84; Conductor of various amateur orchestral and choral societies including: Ipswich Orchestral Society, 1956-62; Ipswich Bach Choir, 1957-62, 1975-87; Dudley Choral Society, 1966-72; Clent Hills Choral Society and Clent Cantata Choir, 1968-72; Kidderminster Choral Society, 1970-72; Suffolk Singers, 1972-78; Stowmarket Choral Society, 1973-75; Eye Bach Choir, 1974-94. Publications: Handel's 'Judas Maccabaeus' in Music and Letters and in the New Novello Choral Edition; Handel's 'Occasional Oratorio' for Halle Handel Edition, in preparation. Honours: Vice President, Ipswich Bach Choir; Hon FTCL; Conductor Emeritus, Eye Bach Choir. Memberships: Royal Music Association; Incorporated Society of Musicians; MCC; Royal Overseas League. Address: 42 Church Street, Eye, Suffolk, IP23 7BD, England.

CHAO Fu-Hou (Jacob), b. 8 March 1941 (citizen of Taiwan). Adviser. m. Man-Hsien Ho, 2 daughters. Education: BS, Accounting, National Cheng-Chi University, Taiwan, 1968; MBA, Marketing, Tulane University, USA, 1994. Appointments: Cost Management and Analysis Analyst, China Airlines, 1968-70; Senior Accountant, Metropolitan Bank, Taipei Branch, 1970-72; Senior Budget and Accounts Analyst, American Embassy AID, 1972; Supervisor of Financial Controls, Chase Manhattan Bank, Taipei Branch, 1972-77; Manager of Administrations, Arnhold Trading Co Ltd (Taiwan), 1977-79; Country Manager of APA/Taiwan-Card, 1979-82, Country Manager of APA/Taiwan-CFSG, 1982-83, Director and Country Manager of APA/Taiwan-CFSG, 1983, Acting General Manager of APA/Taiwan-TRS, 1983, General Manager of APA/Taiwan-TRS, 1984-87, Vice President and General Manager of APA/Taiwan-TRS, 1987-90, Vice President and Deputy Chairman of Japan, East Asia/Taiwan-TRS, 1990-91, American Express International (Taiwan) Inc; Attaining the ambition of making a breakthrough for many new, innovative consumer financial services and products notably launching the New Taiwan Dollar American Express Card in Taiwan market in 1989; Adviser, Mennonite, Christian Hospital, Taiwan, 1998-. Publication: Feasibility study for the card entry to Taiwanese market, 1981. Honours: President Award, G1 Rating, American Express International Inc, Asia, Pacific and Australia, 1986-88; Dean's Service Award, Tulane University, USA, 1994; Man of the Year, 2004; Great Minds of the 21st Century, ABI, 2004-05; World Lifetime Achievement Award in Business, ABI, 2005; 500 Greatest Geniuses Laureate of the 21st Century in Business, ABI, 2005; The Key Award, ABI, 2006; Greatest Minds of the Twenty First Century in Business, ABI, 2006; American Hall of Fame for Outstanding Commitment, Dedication and Inspirational Leadership, ABI; International Professional of the Year, IBC, 2005; 2000 Outstanding Intellectuals of the 21st Century, IBC, 2005; Top 100 Business Executives, IBC, 2006. Memberships: Ex-Bankers' Club; Deputy Chairman of the Board, Mennonite Christian Hospital, 2 terms; Council Chairman, Deacons' Council, Mennonite Sung-Chiang Christian Church, Taipei, 4 terms; Chairman of the Board, Mennonite Social Welfare and Charity Foundation. Address: 3rd Floor, No 21, Lane 46, Ching-Cheng Street, Taipei 105, Taiwan. E-mail: hellochao666@yahoo.com.tw

CHAO Kuei-Hsiang, b. 20 September 1962, Tainan, Taiwan. Associate Professor. m. Shih-Hua Yang, 2 daughters. Education: BEE, National Taiwan Institute of Technology, 1988; MEE, 1990, PhD, 2000, National Tsing Hua University, Taiwan. Appointments: Member, Buddhist Compassion Relief Tzu Chi Foundation, Hualien, Taiwan, 1990-2007; Rev

Commr, Photovoltaic sys Bur Energy, Ministry of Economic Affairs, Taipei, Taiwan, 2001; Head, Department of Electrical Engineering, 2001-04, Associate Professor, 2000-07, National Chin-Yi University of Technology. Publications: Design of soft-switching inverter for induction motor drive; Sensorless speed control of induction motor drive; Fault diagnosis of photovoltaic system; Solar energy driven car; A novel residual capacity estimation method based on extension neural network for lead-acid batteries. Honours: Excellent Paper Award, Symposium on Manufacture Technology, 1999; Industry and Academic Co-operation Award, Ministry of Education, Taiwan, 2000. Memberships: IEEE; Solar Energy and New Energy Association; Taiwan Power Electronics Association; CIEE. Address: National Chin-Yi University of Technology, No 35 Ln 215 Sec 1, Chung Shand Road, Taiping, Taichung 411, Taiwan. E-mail: chaokh@ncut.edu.tw

CHAPMAN Barry L W, b. 19 July 1953, Birmingham, England. Scientist; Inventor; Writer; Entrepreneur. Divorced, 1 daughter. Education: BSc, University of Nottingham, England, 1974; PhD, Victoria University, Manchester, England, 1981. Appointments: Computer Programmer, CAP/RAF Farnborough, 1974-76; Research Associate, Victoria University, Manchester, 1981-82; Research Assistant, Nottingham University, 1982-89, 1992-93; Assistant Professor, University of Alabama at Birmingham, USA, 1989-92; Freelance MR Consultant, Writer, 1993-94; Associate Professor, University of New York, USA, 1994-96; Freelance MR Consultant, Writer, Inventor and Entrepreneur, 1996-2001; Research Scientist, General Magnetic, Strelley, Nottingham, 2002-. Publications: 1 book; 39 articles and book chapters; 8 patents; 2 short stories. Address: General Magnetic, Strelley Hall, Strelley, Nottingham, England. E-mail: general-magnetic@fsmail.net

CHAPMAN Barry Lloyd, b. 6 June 1936, Werris Creek, New South Wales, Australia. Consultant Cardiologist; Educator; Military Officer (Retired). m. 1961, divorced 1988, 2 sons, 2 daughters. Education: MB, BS, Sydney University, 1960; Member, 1966, Fellow, 1972, Royal Australasian College of Physicians; Associate Member, 1980, Member 1981, Fellow, 2004, Cardiac Society of Australia and New Zealand. Appointments: Resident Medical Officer, 1960-62, Medical Registrar, 1963-66, Fellow in Medicine, 1967-70, Foundation Director of Coronary Care, 1968-70, Royal Newcastle Hospital, New South Wales, Australia; Research Fellow, Senior Registrar, West Middlesex Hospital, Isleworth, England, with attachment to Hammersmith Hospital, London, 1971-73; Staff Specialist in Medicine, 1973-91, Consultant Cardiologist, 1984-87, Senior Consultant Cardiologist, 1988-91, Royal Newcastle Hospital, New South Wales; Senior Consultant Cardiologist, John Hunter Hospital, Newcastle, New South Wales, 1991-2001; Clinical, and later Conjoint, Lecturer in Medicine, Faculty of Medicine and Health Sciences, University of Newcastle, New South Wales, 1979-2001; Retired, 2001. Publications: Numerous original papers on subjects including: Liver cirrhosis, peptic ulcer - particularly risk factors especially aspirin, coeliac disease, dermatitis herpetiformis, polymyalgia rheumatica, acute myocardial infarction - particularly prognostic factors, a new coronary prognostic index, effects of coronary care on myocardial infarction mortality, medical history (coronary artery disease in antiquity and prehistoric times), medical audit and quality control; Papers published in medical journals which include: Medical Journal of Australia; Australasian Annals of Medicine; Gut; Proceedings of the Third Asian Pacific Congress of Gastroenterology; Lancet; Proceedings of the Royal Society of Medicine; British Heart Journal; Papers

also read before learned societies. Honours: Australian Defence Medal; Efficiency Decoration; Medal, Anniversary of National Service, 1951-72; Award "in recognition of a long-term and substantive contribution to the Faculty of Medicine and Health Sciences", University of Newcastle, New South Wales, Australia, 2000; Testamur in "Sincere Appreciation for Support given in the Cause of Postgraduate and Continuing Education of Medical Practitioners in the Hunter Region", Board of the Hunter Postgraduate Medical Institute, Newcastle, New South Wales, 2008; Long Service Awards: Royal Newcastle Hospital, John Hunter Hospital, Hunter Area Health Service, New South Wales, Australia; American Medal of Honor, American Biographical Institute, Raleigh, North Carolina, USA; Da Vinci Diamond, IBC; Lifetime Achievement Award, World Congress of Arts, Sciences and Communications; Man of the Year, ABI, 2008. Memberships include: Retired Fellow, Cardiac Society of Australia and New Zealand; Life Fellow, Royal Australasian College of Physicians; Retired Member: World Federation for Ultrasound in Medicine and Biology; American Institute of Ultrasound in Medicine; Australian Society for Medical Research; International Society for Heart Research; Australasian Society of Ultrasound in Medicine; Gastroenterological Society of Australia; The Gut Foundation; Emeritus Member, American Association for the Advancement of Science; Emeritus Fellow, International College of Angiology; Life Member, New South Wales Society of the History of Medicine; Life Fellow, Royal Society of Medicine; Active Member, New York Academy of Sciences; Society Affiliate, American Chemical Society. Address: 31 Elbrook Drive, Rankin Park, NSW 2287, Australia.

CHAPMAN Jean, b. 30 October 1939, England. Writer. m. Lionel Alan Chapman, 1 son, 2 daughters. Education: BA (Hons), Open University, 1989. Appointments: Freelance Creative Writing Tutor and Speaker. Publications: The Unreasoning Earth, 1981; Tangled Dynasty, 1984; Forbidden Path, 1986; Savage Legacy, 1987; The Bellmakers, 1990; Fortune's Woman, 1992; A World Apart, 1993; The Red Pavilion, 1995; The Soldier's Girl, 1997; This Time Last Year, 1999; A New Beginning, 2001; And a Golden Pear, 2002; Danced Over The Sea, 2004. Other: Many short stories. Honours: Shortlisted, Romantic Novel of Year, 1982, 1996, and Kathleen Fidler Award, 1990. Memberships: Society of Authors; Chairman, Romantic Novelists Association, 2002-03. Address: 3 Arnesby Lane, Peatling Magna, Leicester LE8 5UN, England.

CHAPMAN Stanley D(avid), b. 31 January 1935, Nottingham, England. Professor; Writer. Education: BSc, London School of Economics and Political Science, 1956; MA, University of Nottingham, 1960; PhD, University of London, 1966. Appointments: Lecturer, 1968-73, Pasold Reader in Business History, 1973-, Professor, 1993-97, Emeritus Professor, 1997- University of Nottingham; Editor, Textile History Bi Annual, 1982-2002. Publications: The Early Factory Masters, 1967; The Beginnings of Industrial Britain, 1970; The History of Working Class Housing, 1971; The Cotton Industry in the Industrial Revolution, 1972, new edition, 1987; Jesse Boot of Boots the Chemists, 1974; The Devon Cloth Industry in the 18th Century, 1978; Stanton and Staveley, 1981; European Textile Printers in the 18th Century (with Serge Chassagne), 1981; The Rise of Merchant Banking, 1984; Merchant Enterprise in Britain from the Industrial Revolution to World War I, 1992; Hosiery and Knitwear: Four Centuries of Small-Scale Industry in Britain, 2002; Southwell Town and People (with Derek Walker), 2006. Address: Rochester House, Halam Road, Southwell, Nottinghamshire NG25 0AD, England.

CHAPPELL Gregory Stephen, b. 7 August 1948, Adelaide, Australia. Cricketer; Business Executive. m. Judith Elizabeth Donaldson, 1971, 2 sons, 1 daughter. Education: Adelaide College; Prince Alfred College, Adelaide. Appointments: Teams: South Australia, 1966-73, Somerset, 1968-69, Queensland, 1973-84 (Captain 1973-77, 1979-80); Tests for Australia, 1970-84, 48 as Captain, Scoring 7,100 runs (Average 53.8) including 24 Hundreds, and Holding 122 Catches; Scored 108 on Test Debut v England, Perth, 1970; Only Captain to have scored a Century in each innings of 1st Test as Captain (v West Indies, Brisbane 1975); Holds record for most catches in a Test Match (7, v England, Perth 1975); Scored 24,535 1st Class Runs (74 Hundreds); Toured England 1972, 1975, 1977, 1980; Managing Director, AD Sports Technologies, 1993-95, Greg Chappell Sports Marketing, 1995-98; Coach, South Australian Redbacks cricket team, 2002; Managing Director, Greg Chappell Promotions plc, 2003-; Contracted tours in Pakistan, 2005-07. Publication: Greg Chappell's Health and Fitness Repair Manual, 1998; Greg Chappell's Family Health and Fitness Manual, 1999. Honours include: Hon MBE, 1979; Wisden Cricketer of the Year, 1973; Australian Sportsman of the Year, 1976; Hon Life Member, MCC, 1985; Australian Team of the Century, 2000; Australian Cricket Hall of Fame, 2001. Memberships: MCC; South Australian Cricket Association, 2002; Patron, Leukaemia Foundation of SA, 1998-; Patron, Happi Foundation, 2001-03. Address: c/o South Australian Cricket Association, Adelaide Oval, North Adelaide, SA 5006, Australia.

CHARLIER Roger Henri Liévin Constance Louise, b. 10 November 1924, Antwerp, Belgium. University Professor. m. Patricia Simonet, 1 son, 1 daughter. Education: Certificate of Political and Adm Sci, Colonial University of Belgium, 1940; MPolSci, Brussels, 1942; MS (Earth and Oceans), Brussels, 1945; PhD, Erlangen (high honours), 1947; Postgraduate study, McGill University, 1953; LitD, Paris (high honours), 1956; Diploma, Industrial College of the Armed Forces, 1956; DSc (highest honours), Paris, 1958; Education Curriculum Diploma, Parsons College, 1962. Appointments include: Major (Intelligence), Major (Resistance Movement), 1941-45, Political Prisoner, 1943-44, World War II; Deputy Director, United Nations Relief & Rehabilitation Administration, 1945-46; Vice-Chair, id Belgian ORI-OIC Newspaper Correspondent, various US, Belgian, Swiss papers, 1945-60, 1983-99; Research Analyst, International War Crimes Tribunal, Nürnberg, 1946-47; Writer, Consultant, 20th Century Fox Corporation, Hollywood, California, USA, 1948; Professor, Polycultural University, Washington, DC, 1950-54; Professor, Finch College, USA, 1954-56; Special Lecturer, Chairman, Department of Geology and Geography, Hempstead NY, Hofstra University, USA, 1956-59; Visiting Professor, University of Minnesota, USA, 1959-61; Professor of Geology, Parsons College (now University), 1961-62; Professor of Geology, Geography and Oceanography, Northeastern Illinois University, Chicago, 1961-87, Special Research Scholar, 1962-64; Professor Extraordinary, 1970-86, Professor Emeritus, 1986-, Vrije Universiteit Brussels, Belgium; Professeur associé, 1970-74, hon, 1986-,Université de Bordeaux I, France; Fulbright Fellow, 1974-76; Kellogg Fellow, 1980-82; Scientific Advisor to CEO HAECON, 1984-88, 1989-2000; Scientific Advisor to CEO SOPEX, 1988-89; Professor Emeritus, Northeastern Illinois University, USA, 1988-; Chair, Task Force Environment and Sustainability, European Federation Consulting Engineers Association, 1998-2002; Research Professor, Florida Atlantic University, 2006-; Research Professor, Florida State University, Boca Raton, 2006-. Publications include: Books: I Was a Male War Bride, 1948; For the Love of Kate, 1958; Pensées, 1962;

Economic Oceanography, 1980; Study of Rocks, 1980; Tidal Power, 1982; Ocean Energies, 1993; Coastal Erosion, 1999; Tools for the Black Sea, 2000; Ocean Tidal Energy, 2007; Co-editor, Proc 6th Int Congr Hist Oceanog, [UNESCO] Ocean Sciences Bridging the Millennium, 2004; Black Sea Seminar, 2002; Ocean's Energies, 2007; Articles include: Small Sources of Methane; The Atmospheric Methane Cycle: Sources, Sinks, Distribution and Role in Global Change; Tourism and the Coastal Zone: The Case of Belgium: Ocean and Coastal Management; I was a Male War Bride. Honours include: Prix François Frank, 1939; Belgian Government Awards, 1939, 1975; Chicago Public Schools Award, 1975, 1987, 1992; Outstanding Achievement Presidential Award, 1980; Paul-Henri Spaak Memorial Lecture Award, 1992; Coastal Research and Education Foundation bursary, 2005, id 2006. Memberships include: Fellow, Geological Society of America; Charter Member, International Association for the History of Oceanography; Charter Member and Fellow, New Jersey Academy of Science, President, 1954-57, Past President, 1957-58; Fellow, American Association for the Advancement of Science; Fellow, Royal Belgian Society for Geographical Studies; Education Committee, Marine Technology Society; Association of American University Professors; Académie Nationale des Arts, Sciences et Belles-Lettres, France, 1970-; Romanian Society for Marine Studies. Address: 2 Ave du Congo, Box 23, Brussels 1050, Belgium.

CHARLTON John (Jack), b. 8 May 1935. Former Football Player; Broadcaster; Football Manager. m. Patricia, 1958, 2 sons, 1 daughter. Appointments: Professional footballer, Leeds Utd FC, 1952-73; Manager, Middlesborough FC, 1973-77, Sheffield Wednesday FC, 1977-83, Newcastle Utd FC, 1984-85, Republic of Ireland Football Team, 1986-95; Played with winning teams in League Championship, 1969, Football Association Cup, 1972, League Cup, 1968, Fairs Cup, 1968, 1971, World Cup (England v Germany), 1966. Publication: Jack Charlton's American World Cup Diary, 1994. Honours: Football Writers Association Footballer of the Year, 1967; OBE. Membership: Sports Council, 1977-82.

CHARLTON Robert (Bobby) (Sir), b. 11 October 1937. Former Football Player. m. Norma, 1961, 2 daughters. Career: Footballer with Manchester Utd, 1954-73; Played 751 games scoring 245 goals; FA Cup Winners' Medal, 1963; First Division Championship Medals, 1956-57, 1964-65, 1966-67; World Cup Winners' Medal (England team), 1966; European Cup Winners' Medal, 1968; 106 appearances for England, scoring 49 goals, 1957-73; Manager, Preston North End, 1973-75; Chairman, NW Council for Sport and Recreation, 1982-; Director, Manchester Utd Football Club, 1984-. Publications: My Soccer Life, 1965; Forward for England, 1967; This Game of Soccer, 1967; Book of European Football, Books 1-4, 1969-72. Honours: Honorary Fellow, Manchester Polytechnic, 1979; Honorary MA, Manchester University; Knighthood; CBE. Address: 17 The Square, Hale Barns, Cheshire WA15 8ST, England.

CHARNEY Lena London, b. 26 January 1919, Symiatycze, Poland. Retired Teacher; Historian; Poet, Business Woman. m. Roy L Charney, 1 son. Education: BA, cum laude, Hunter College, New York City, 1941; MA, Clark University, Worcester, Massachusetts, 1942; PhD. ABD, Columbia University, 1947-53. Contributions to: various anthologies, reviews, magazines, and journals. Appointments: Millinery designer, Sanjour Studio, 1937, 1939-41; Designer, Co-owner, Lenblac Millinery Store, 1938; Co-owner, Co-manager, Golden Dawn bungalow colony, 1939-46; Secretary to New York City Manager, Insurance Field, 1945; Assistant Editor, Insurance

Weekly, 1946; Saleslady, Bonwit-Teller, Arnold Constable and Lane Bryant, 1947-49; Director, Teacher, Workmen's Circle Yiddish School, Shrub Oak, New York; Sunday school teacher, Lakeland Jewish Centre and Temple Beth Am; Teacher, Principal, St Basil's Academy, Garisson, 1968-73; Substitute teacher, various districts, 1974-82; Co-manager, London's Studio Apartments, 1950-59; Owner, Manager, London's Studio Apartments, 1959-; Poet, 1984-. Honours: Finalist, Verve Poetry Competition, 1990; Honourable Mention, Nostalgia Poetry Contest, 1991; Finalist, Greenburgh Poetry Competition, 1993; Diamond Homer Award, Famous Poets Society, 1996, 1998 and 1999; Featured poet at "An Evening of Poetry", Mount Pleasant Public Library, Pleasantville, New York, 2001. Publications: Historical articles in: Wisconsin History, 1948; The Southwestern Historical Quarterly, 1954; Indiana Magazine of History, 1948; Iowa Journal of History, 1950; Military Affairs, 1951; Michigan History, 1952; Poetry in many publications and anthologies. Memberships: Association of American University Women; American Historical Association; Academy of Political Science; National Writers Union; Academy of American Poets; Hudson Valley Writers Centre; Poetry Society of America; Peregrine Poets. Address: 1833 East Main Street, Mohegan Lake, NY 10547, USA.

CHASE Chevy (Cornelius Crane), b. 8 October 1943, New York, USA. Comedian; Actor; Writer. m. (1) Jacqueline Carlin, 1976, divorced 1980, (2) Jayni Luke, 3 daughters. Education: Bar College; Institute of Audio Research, MIT. Career: Writer, Mad magazine, 1969; Actor: Channel One; The Great American Dream Machine; Lemmings; National Lampoon Radio Hour; Saturday Night Live; Films include: Tunnelvision, 1976; Foul Play, 1978; Oh Heavenly Dog, 1980; Caddyshack, 1980; Seems Like Old Times, Under the Rainbow, 1981; Modern Problems, 1981; Vacation, 1983; Deal of the Century, 1983; European Vacation, 1984; Fletch, 1985; Spies Like Us, 1985; Follow that Bird, 1985; The Three Amigos, 1986; Caddyshack II, 1988; Funny Farm, 1988; Christmas Vacation, 1989; Fletch Lives, 1989; Memoirs of an Invisible Man, 1992; Hero, 1992; Last Action Hero, 1993; Cops and Robbersons, 1994; Man of the House, 1995; National Lampoon's Vegas Vacation, 1997; Snow Day, 1999; Orange County, 2002; Bad Meat, 2003; Karate Dog (voice), 2004; Goose! 2004; Ellie Parker, 2005; Funny Money, 2005; Zoom, 2006; TV includes: The Great American Machine; Smothers Brothers Show; Saturday Night Live; The Secret Policeman's Ball, 2006; Law and Order, 2006. Honours: 3 Emmy Awards; Writers Guild of America Award; Man of the Year, Harvard University Theatrical Group, 1992. Memberships: American Federation of Musicians; Stage Actors Guild; Actors Equity; American Federation of TV and Radio Artists. Address: Cornelius Productions, Box 257, Bedford, NY 10506, USA.

CHATURVEDI Shailesh, b. 10 September 1950, Jaipur, India. Surgeon. m. Sujata, 2 sons, 1 daughter. Education: MB BS, 1974, MS, General Surgery, 1977, University of Rajasthan, Jaipur, India; FRCS, Royal College of Surgeons, 1980; MSc, Leeds, 1983; MD, Cambridge, 1985; FICS, International College of Surgeons, British Section, 1987; FRCSGen, Intercollegiate Speciality Board, 2000; FRCS (Edin) Honorary, Royal College of Surgeons of Edinburgh, 2004. Appointments: Consultant Surgeon (Armed Forces), 1986-89; Consultant Surgeon, West Wales General Hospital, 1989-92; Consultant Surgeon for Waiting List Initiative and Honorary Senior Lecturer in Surgery, Wrexham Maelor Hospital NHS Trust, 1992-93; Consultant Surgeon, RAF Hospital, Germany, 1993-97; Consultant Surgeon, Ministry of Defence Hospital Unit, Peterborough, 1997-2000; Consultant

General and Breast Surgeon, Clinical Senior Lecturer in Surgery, Aberdeen University & Grampian Hospitals NHS Trust, 2001-; Breast & Cosmetic Surgeon, Albyn Hospital, Aberdeen, 2001-. Publications: More than 25 articles in medical journals as author and co-author include most recently: Patterns of local and distant disease relapse in patients with breast cancer treated with primary chemotherapy: do patients with a complete pathological response differ from those with residual tumour in the breast? 2005; Guidelines, guidelines and more guidelines: And we still do not know how to follow up patients with breast cancer, 2005; Application of Nottingham prognostic index in patients with locally advanced breast cancer treated with primary chemotherapy, 2005; Numerous papers presented at conferences. Honours: Registrar's Prize for Best Oral Presentation, 1985; Professor Beterello Travelling Fellowship to Brazil, 1987; Commendation Award, World Organisation of Gastro-enterology, 1993; Meritorious Service Award, Royal Air Force, 1996; Innovative Surgical Technical Award, 2003; Outstanding Contribution to Art of Surgery Award, Delhi University, 2004, 2005; Honorary PhD, TIYU, New York, 2007. Listed in Who's Who publications and biographical dictionaries. Memberships: BASO, Breast Group; Association of Surgeons of Great Britain and Ireland; British Mensa; European Association of Surgical Oncology; World Philatelic and Numenistic Association. Address: Aberdeen Royal Infirmary, Fosterhill, Aberdeen AB32 6JG, Scotland. E-mail: s.chaturvedi@abdn.ac.uk

CHAUNY DE PORTURAS-HOYLE Gilbert, b. 8 March 1944, Lima, Peru. Diplomat. m. Carmen Loreto y Laos, 2 sons, 1 daughter. Education: Bachelor of Architecture, National University of Engineering, 1966; Bachelor in Arts & Humanities, Catholic University, Lima; Diplomat & Licenciate in International Relations, Diplomatic Academy of Peru. Appointments include: National Director for Frontier Development, 2002-03, Undersecretary for Cultural Affairs, 2003-05, Ministry of Foreign Affairs, Lima; Ambassador Extraordinary and Plenipotentiary of Peru to Hungary, 2005-06; Ambassador Extraordinary and Plenipotentiary of Peru to Croatia, 2005-06; Ambassador Extraordinary and Plenipotentiary of Peru to Bosnia-Herzegovina, 2005-06; Ambassador Extraordinary and Plenipotentiary of Peru to the Kingdom of the Netherlands, Permanent Representative of Peru to the Organisation for the Prohibition of Chemical Weapons, and Governor of Peru to the Common Fund for Commodities, 2007-. Publications: Numerous articles in professional journals. Honours: Knight of Magistral Grace of the Sovereign and Military Order of Malta; Ofical of the Orden de San Carlos, Colombia; Knight Commander of the Orden de Bogotá, Colombia; Oficial of the Orden de Isabel la Católica, Spain; Grand Cross of the Orden del Cóndor de los Andes, Bolivia; Gold Grand Cross with Badge of the Order Honour of Merit, Austria; Knight-Commander with Star of the Sacred Military Constantinian Order of St George; Grand Cross of the Order al Merito Melitense of the Sovereign and Military Order of Malta; Grand Cross of the Orden al Merito por Servicios Distinguidos, Peru. Memberships: Peruvian Institute for Genealogical Research; Peruvian Association of the Knights of the Sovereign and Military Order of Malta; Peruvian Institute for Aerospace Law. Address: Embassy of Peru, Nassauplein 4, 2585 EA, The Hague, Netherlands. E-mail: gilbertchauny@hotmail.com

CHAUSSY Christian Georg, b. 10 January 1945, Swinemuende, Germany. Medical Doctor; Professor of Urology. Education: Graduate, University of Munich Medical School, 1970. Appointments: Intern, Department of Internal Medicine, 1971; Department of Surgery, 1972, Researcher,

Institute for Surgical Research, 1972-74, Resident, Department of Urology, 1975-79, University of Munich; Teacher, Institute for Surgical Research, 1972-74, Transplantation Unit, 1975-84, Instructor in Urology, 1975-79, Assistant Professor, Urology, 1979-80, Associate Professor, Urology, 1981-, Director, Stone Center, Department of Urology, 1980-84, University of Munich; Worldwide first treatment of patient with kidney stone by Extracorporeal Shockwave Lithotripsy (ESWL), 1980; Director, Continuous ESWL and Endourology Training Program, Department of Urology, University of Munich; 1982-84, Professor of Urology, Director, Continuous ESWL and Endourology Training Program, UCLA Medical Center, Los Angeles, California, 1985-86; Chairman, Department of Urology, Municipal Hospital, Harlaching, 1986-; Full Professor and Member of Medical Faculty, University of Munich, Examiner, Medical Examinations, University of Munich, 1987-; Examiner, Board of Urology, Bavaria, FRG, 1987-. Publications: Author and co-author of more than 400 medical articles and publications; Over 600 lectures, presentations and appointments as visiting professor and invitational lectures. Honours: Numerous honours and awards including: Langenbeck Awar, Germany Surgical Society, 1975; Alken Award, German Urological Society, 1976 and 1983; Maximilian Nitze Award, 1981; Benjamin Franklin Literature and Medical Society Award, 1981; Motion Picture Award, German Urological Society, 1982; Motion Picture Award, American Urological Society, 1983; Distinguished Contribution Award, American Urological Association; International Lithotripsy Award, Dornier Medical Systems, 1994; Klinikfoerderpreis (First Prize) Landesbank, Munich, 2000; Lingen Award, 2001; Honorary Memberships Brazilian College of Surgeons, 1985; Gruene Rosette, European Science Award, 1985; Bay Urological Society, California, 1986; Urological Association, Republic of China, 1987; Permanent Visiting Professor, Medical University of Beijing, China, 1990; Honorary Fellowship, Royal College of Surgeons, Edinburgh, 1998; President, German Lithotripsy Society, 1990-.

CHEAH Phaik-Leng, b. 11 May 1955, Penang, Malaysia. Consultant Histopathologist. Education: MBBS, 1980; MRCPath, 1991; FRCPath, 1999; MD, 2001. Appointments: Professor of Pathology, Head of Electron Microscopy Unit, Faculty of Medicine, University of Malaya; Senior Consultant Histopathologist, Head of Laboratory Services, University of Malaya Medical Centre. Publications: Over 50 papers and articles on various cancers and renal diseases. Honours: Tun Abdul Razak Research Award, 2004. Memberships: Royal College of Pathologists, England; Academy of Medicine, Malaysia; International Academy of Cytology. Address: Department of Pathology, Faculty of Medicine, University of Malaya, 59100 Kuala Lumpur, Malaysia. E-mail: cheahpl@ummc.edu.my

CHEAL MaryLou, b. 5 November 1926, Michigan, USA. Research Psychologist. m. James Cheal, 2 sons, 1 daughter. Education: BA, Oakland University, Rochester, Michigan, USA, 1969; PhD, Psychology, University of Michigan, 1973. Appointments include: Assistant to Associate Psychologist, McLean Hospital, Harvard Medical School, 1977-83; Faculty Research Associate, Arizona State University, 1983-87; Visiting Professor, Air Force Systems Command University Resident Research Program Appointment, Williams Air Force Base, Arizona, USA, 1986-88; Research Psychologist, University of Dayton Research Institute at Williams Air Force Base, 1986-94; Adjunct Associate Professor, Professor, Department of Psychology, Arizona State University, USA, 1987-; Senior Research Psychologist, University of Dayton Research Institute at the Air Force Armstrong Laboratory,

Mesa, Arizona, USA, 1994-95. Publications: 70 publications including: Timing of facilitatory and inhibitory effects of visual attention, 2002; Inappropriate capture by diversionary dynamic elements, 2002; Efficiency of visual selective attention is related to the type of target, 2002. Honours include: Society of Sigma Xi, 1972; Fellow, American Association for Advancement of Science, 1987; Fellow, American Psychological Association, 1986; Charter Fellow, Association of Psychological Science, 1988; World Intellectual of 1993; Commemorative Medal of Honor, American Biographical Institute, 1993; Professional Women's Advisory Board, 1998; The C T Morgan Distinguished Service to Division 6 Award, American Psychological Association, 1999; Listed in national and international biographical dictionaries. Memberships include: American Association for Advancement of Science, 1969-87, Fellow, 1987-; Sigma Xi, 1972-; Society for Neuroscience, 1974-; American Psychological Association, member, 1980-86, fellow, 1986-; President, Division 6, 1997-98, Committee on Division/APA Relation, member, 1997-98, chair, 1999, Representative to Council, 2000-05, division 6; Committee on Structure and Function of Council Member, 2004-05, Chair, 2006, Membership Committee, Member, 2007-, Coalition for Academic Scientific and Applied Research; Member, 2000, Secretary, 2001-2004, President, 2005, Past President, 2006; The Psychonomic Society, 1988-; Association for Psychological Science, charter fellow, 1988-; International Brain Research Organization. Address: 127 Loma Vista Drive, Tempe, AZ 85282-3574, USA.

CHEATHAM Wallace McClain, b. 3 October 1945, Cleveland, Tennessee, USA. Musician. m. Willie Faye Watson, 2 daughters. Education: BS, Knoxville College, 1967; MS, University of Wisconsin-Milwaukee, 1972; PhD, Columbia Pacific University, 1982; DFA (honoris causa), University of Wisconsin-Milwaukee, 2002. Appointments: Music Teacher, Knoxville (Tennessee) City School System, 1967-68; Music Teacher, Unified School District, Racine, Wisconsin, 1968-71; Music Teacher, Milwaukee (Wisconsin) Public Schools, 1971-2003. Publications: Choral compositions and works for solo voice, piano, and organ; Contributing author, Challenges in Music Education, 1976; Just Tell the Story of Troubled Island, 2004; Editor, Dialogues on Opera and the African American Experience, 1997; Contributor of articles to professional journals. Honours: Listed in international biographical dictionaries. Memberships: Lyrica Society; National Association of Negro Musicians; Wisconsin Alliance of Composers; American Choral Directors Association; Music Educators National Conference; American Guild of Organists; African Methodist Episcopal Church; Phi Beta Sigma Fraternity. Address: 2961 North Fifth Street, Milwaukee, WI 53212, USA. E-mail: fchea44172@aol.com

CHEDID Andrée, b. 20 March 1920, Cairo, Egypt. Poet; Novelist; Dramatist. m. Louis A Chedid, 23 August 1942, 1 son, 1 daughter. Education: Graduated, American University of Cairo, 1942. Publications: Poetry Collections: Textes pour un poème (1949-1970), 1987; Poèmes pour un texte (1970-91), 1991; Par delà les mots, 1995; Fugitive Suns: Selected Poetry, 1999; Novels: Le Sommeil délivré, 1952, English translation as From Sleep Unbound, 1983; Jonathon, 1955; Le Sixième Jour, 1960, English translation as The Sixth Day, 1988; L'Autre, 1969; La Cité fertile, 1972; Nefertiti et le reve d'Akhnaton, 1974; Les Marches de sable, 1981; La Maison sans racines, 1985, English translation as The Return to Beirut, 1989; L'Enfant multiple, 1989; Lucy: La Femme Verticle, 1998; Le Message, 2000; Plays: Bérénice d'Egypte, Les Nombres, Les Montreur, 1981; Echec à la Reine, 1984; Les saisons de passage, 1996; Other: The Prose and Poetry of Andrée Chedid: Selected Poems, Short Stories, and Essays (Renée Linkhorn, translator), 1990; A la Mort, A la Vie, 1992; La Femme de Job, 1993; Les Saisons de passage, 1996; Le Jardin perdue, 1997; Territoires du Souffle, 1999; Le Cœur demeure, 1999; Essays; Children's books. Honours: Prix Louise Labe, 1966; Grand Prix des Lettres Francaise, l'Académie Royale de Belgique, 1975; Prix de l'Académie Mallarmé, 1976; Prix Goncourt de la nouvelle, 1979; Prix de Poèsie, Société des Gens de Lettres, 1991; Prix de PEN Club International, 1992; Prix Albert Camus, 1996; Prix Poésie de la SALEH, 1999; Légion d'honneur, Commandeur des Arts et des Lettres. Membership: PEN Club International. Address: c/o Flammarion, 26 rue Racine, Paris 75006, France.

CHEFFINS Richard Hamilton Alexander, b. 10 August 1941, Fulmer Chase, Buckinghamshire, England. Retired Librarian. Education: BA (Hons), History, University of Southampton, 1963; Dip.Lib., University of Sheffield, 1965. Appointments: Library Trainee, University of Southampton, 1963-64; Senior Assistant Librarian, National Central Library, 1965-73; Higher Scientific Officer, British Library Lending Division, 1973-80; Seconded to International Federation of Library Associations and Institutions, 1980-82; Senior Cataloguer, British Library Bibliographical Services Division, 1982-86; Curator, British Library Official Publications and Social Science Service, 1986-95; Deputy Head, British Library Social Policy Information Service, 1995-2001. Publications: Survey of existing national bibliographies, 1977; Commonwealth retrospective national bibliographies, 1981; Proceedings of the International Cataloguing-in-Publication Meeting, 1982 (Editor), 1983; Parliamentary Constituencies and their Registers since 1832, 1998; How to find information: official publications, 2004; Various articles. Honours: Knight of Justice, Sovereign Military and Hospitaller Order of St John of Jerusalem , of Rhodes and of Malta. Memberships: Various professional, historical, genealogical, local, amenity, religious and literary societies. Address: 19 Ashburnham Place, London SE10 8TZ, England.

CHELTSOV Vladislav, b. 24 June 1934, Moscow, Russia. Professor of Physics; Theorist in quantum electrodynamics of emission from microstructures. Divorced, 2 sons. Education: MS Diploma, Moscow Engineering Physical University, 1958; PhD, Kahzan University, 1969; Associate Professor of Physics, Textile Academy, 1972. Appointments: Assistant Professor, 1958-62, Researcher, 1962-69, Department of Theoretical Nuclear Physics of Moscow Engineering Physics University; Senior Instructor, Associate Professor, Higher School, 1969-88; Associate Professor, Department of Physics, Moscow State Mining University, 1988-. Publications: Effect of phase mixing of co-operative quantum states in the system of two level atoms and lasing without inversion, 1965, 1969, 1970, 1989; Theory of co-operative resonance fluorescence of two-level atoms, 1981-86; Theory of spontaneous and stimulated emission in semiconductor, Bose-Einstein distribution for photons with non-zero chemical potential, 1969 (thesis), 1971, 1997; New theory (without series expansions and intermediate virtual states but with using the novel algorithm in operating the causal functions) has been elaborated to describe spontaneous emission of resonance photons from atoms trapped in micro-cavities, 1993-95, 2003; Optical Mössbauer effect on the AC Stark-sublevels, 1998-99, 2001; Storage of light by two two-level atoms, 2001; New non-linear optical effects in emission and absorption of resonance photons by two-level atoms, trapped in damped microcavity, 2001; Cavity-controlled spontaneous emission spectral lineshape, 2003; Fundamentals of the theory of co-operative spontaneous emission from two level atoms

trapped in micro-cavity, 2006; Non-linear optical effects in spontaneous and stimulated emission from two band intrinsic semi-conductor, 2007; Spectral properties and non-linear dynamics of a spontaneous photon emitted by two level atoms trapped in a damped nanocavity with a single resonance mode, 2008. Honour: Nominee for the Peter Kahpitza Grant from the Royal Society, 1991. Memberships: Senior Member, IEEE/LEOS; Individual Member, European Physical Society; Member of the Institute of Physics, UK; Member, Optical Society of America. Address: Post Box 31, 119313 Moscow V313, Russia. E-mail: vcheltsov@stream.ru

CHEN Bing-Huei, b. 30 January 1954, Taichung, Taiwan. Professor. m. Wen-Huei Wang, 1 son, 1 daughter. Education: BS, Food Science, Fu Jen University, 1977; MS, Agricultural Chemistry, California State University, Fresno, 1983; PhD, Food Science, Texas A and M University, 1988. Appointments: Associate Professor, 1988-93, Professor and Chair, 1994-2001, Chair Professor in Food Science and Technology, 2004-, Department of Nutrition and Food Science, Fu Jen University, Taipei. Publications: More than 100 research articles have been published in internationally renowned journals. Honours: Outstanding Research Awards, National Science Council of Taiwan and Chinese Institute of Food Science and Technology. Memberships: Institute of Food Technologists; New York Academy of Science; AOAC International; American Chemical Society. Address: Department of Nutrition and Food Science, Fu Jen University, Taipei, Taiwan 242, ROC. E-mail: 002622@mail.fju.edu.tw

CHEN Chung-Hsuan, b. 1 April 1948, China. Scientist. m. Shan-Lan, 2 sons. Education: BS, Chemistry, National Taiwan University, 1969; MS, 1971, PhD, 1974, Chemistry, University of Chicago, USA. Appointments: Research Staff Member, 1974-89, Leader, Photophysics Group, 1989-2005, Senior Research Scientist, 1993-2005, Oak Ridge National Laboratory; Consultant, Atom Sciences inc, 1987-; Adjunct Professor, Vanderbilt University, 1990-2005; Consultant, Applied BioSystem Inc, 1993-2005; Adjunct Professor, University of Tennessee, Knoxville, 1993-2005; Research Fellow & Key Technology Division Head, 2005-, Deputy Director, 2006-, Distinguished Research Fellow and Acting Director, 2006-, Director, 2007-, Genomics Research Center, Chair, Mass Spectrometry Instrumentation Committee, 2005-, Adjunct Distinguished Research Fellow, Institute of Atomic & Molecular Sciences, 2006-, Academia Sinica; Consultant, Sci-Tec Inc, 2002-; Adjunct Professor, Chemistry Department, National Taiwan University, 2006-. Publications: 170 articles in referred journals; 140 presentations; 95 invited speeches; 7 patents. Honours: Three IR-100 (100 Most Important Inventions of the Year) Awards, 1984, 1987, 1992; Health and Safety Research Division Excellence in Research Award, 1991; Editorial Board, Rapid Communication of Mass Spectrometry, 1995; Honorary Professor, Tsing Hua University, Beijing, 1996; Outstanding Scholar Award, 2005; ASIA Award Recipient, Academia Sinica, 2006. Memberships: Fellow, American Physical Society; Department of Education Advisory Board; NSC Genome Research Advisory Board. E-mail: winschen@gate.sinica.edu.tw

CHEN Hung-Cheng, b. 1 March 1965, Chiayi, Taiwan. Electrical Engineering. m. Chiu-Yueh Yang, 1 son. Education: MS, 1989, PhD, 1993, National Taiwan University of Technology. Appointments: Electrical Engineer, Tongsiao Salt Plant, Miaoli, 1986-87; Lecturer, Oriental Institute of Technology, Taipei, 1989-93; Associate Professor, 1993-, Chair, Department of Electrical Engineering, 1993-96, Dean of Student Affairs Office, 1996-98, Secretary-General,

1999-2001, Chair, Institute of Information and Electrical Energy, 2003-04, National Chin-Yi University of Technology, Taichung. Honours: Design Competition Awards of Microcomputer Applications, 1999, 2001, Outstanding Education Officers, 2001, Practical Project Competition Awards of College Students, 2002, Ministry of Education. Memberships: IEEE; Professional Association. Address: 35, Lane 215, Sec 1, Chungshan Road, Taiping, Taichung 411, Taiwan. E-mail: hcchen@ncut.edu.tw

CHEN Jeng-Fung, b. 20 April 1958, Miaoli, Taiwan. Professor. m. Chien-Hui Chu, 1 son. Education: BS, Tunghai University, 1981; MS, Clemson University, 1987; PhD, Texas A&M University, 1991. Appointments: Associated Professor, 1992-2005, Professor, 2005-, Department of Industrial Engineering & Systems Management, Feng Chia University. Publications: Numerous articles in professional journals. Honours: Research Awards, 1995-98, 2003, 2007; Outstanding Research Award, 2004-06. Memberships: Phi Tau Phi. Address: Department of Industrial Engineering & Systems Management, Feng Chia University, No 100 Wenhwa Road, Seatwen, Taichung, Taiwan, 40724, ROC. E-mail: jfchen@fcu.edu.tw

CHEN Man-Ming, b. 4 March 1935, Miaoli, Taiwan. Professor of Chinese. m. Su-Chen Hsu, 1 son, 1 daughter. Education: BA, Department of Chinese, 1964, MA, Graduate School of Chinese Literature, 1967, National Taiwan Normal University. Appointments: Lecturer, 1967, Associate Professor, 1971, Professor, 1980-, Department of Chinese, National Taiwan Normal University. Publications: 24 books, more than 350 research articles include most recently: The Multiple, Binary and Unitary (Zero) Spiral Structure Concerning Images Based-Inference to Philosophy, Literature and Aesthetics, 2007; The Organization of Writing & the Multiple, Binary and Unitary (Zero) Spiral Structure, 2007; The Multiple, Binary and Unitary (Zero) Spiral Structure in Chinese Literary Works, 2007; Wang Shi-jei's View on The Organization of Writing – The Zero and Divagation, 2007; The Combination of Images – Continuation and Progressio, 2007; The Combination of Images – Study on The Artistic Theory of Poetry (Authored by Zhao Shanlin), 2007; Three–One Theory and Writing Instruction, 2007; The Interaction between Concept and Form – One Concept with Multiple Forms vs One Form with Multiple Concepts, 2007; The Divergence Theory and Writing Instruction, 2007. Honours include: International Excellent Thesis for research article, Association of Chinese Exchange Worldwide and Centre of Research on Literature and Arts Worldwide, 2003; First Prize of Outstanding Works for research article, Committee of China Innovation and Development Theories, 2004; Top Grade and Gold Prize for research article, Powerful China Dictionary, 2005; International Excellent Thesis for research article, Technological Forum, Technological Exchange Center, 2007; Listed in international biographical dictionaries. Memberships: Chinese Rhetoric Society, Taiwan; Chinese Characters Society, Taiwan; Consultant, The Art of Writing Society, China; General Director, Society of the Organization of Writing, Taiwan. Address: 5F-2, 28, Ln 265, Xinyi Rd, Section 4, Taipei 106, Taiwan, Republic of China. E-mail: t21004@ntnu.edu.tw.

CHEN Po-Han, b. 4 June 1972, Taipei, Taiwan. College Professor. m. Stella C Chia. Education: BSc, Engineering, National Taiwan University, 1994; MSc, Civil Engineering, 1999, PhD, 2001, Purdue University, USA. Appointments: Research Assistant, Hydrotech Research Institute, National Taiwan University, 1992-94; Assistant Researcher, Taiwan Construction Research Institute, 1996-97; Research Assistant, School of Civil Engineering, Purdue University, 1999-2001; Assistant Professor, 2001-, Program Director, MSc in Maritime Studies Program, 2006-, Nanyang Technological University, Singapore. Publications: More than 35 publications in refereed journals and conference proceedings, book chapters, reports, etc. Honours: Best Paper Award, 2007; Listed in international biographical dictionaries. Memberships: Associate Member, American Society of Civil Engineers; Member, Construction Institute, ASCE; Invited Member, Asian Institute of Intelligent Buildings, Singapore Chapter. Address: Block N1, #01a-14, 50 Nanyang Avenue, Singapore 639798, Singapore. E-mail: cphchen@ntu.edu.sg

CHEN Ruei-Ming, b. 16 December 1966, Kaoushung, Taiwan. Medical Research. m. Crystal L L Lin, 2 sons. Education: BS, Environmental Science, Tunghai University, Taichung, Taiwan, 1990; MS, 1994, PhD, 1998, Institute of Toxicology, College of Medicine, National Taiwan University, Taipei. Appointments: Assistant Professor, School of Medicine, 1992-2002, Associate Professor, 2002-06, Professor, 2006-, Graduate Institute of Medical Sciences, College of Medicine, Taipei Medical University, Taipei. Publications: Numerous articles in professional journals. Honours: Research Award, Wan-Fang Hospital, 2000-05; Research Award, 2004-07, Junior Research Award, 2006, Taipei Medical University. Memberships: Toxicology Society of Taiwan; Formosa Association of Regenerative Medicine. Address: Graduate Institute of Medical Sciences, Taipei Medical University, No 250, Wu-Hsing St, Taipei 110, Taiwan. E-mail: rmchen@tmu.edu.tw

CHEN Shen-Ming, b. 8 July 1957, Chunghua (Lukang), Taiwan. Professor. m. Mei-Lin Lu, 1 son, 1 daughter. Education: BSc, Chemistry, National Kaohsiung Normal University, Taiwan, 1980; MSc, 1983, PhD, 1991, National Taiwan University, Taiwan. Appointments: Associate Professor, Department of Chemical Engineering, 1991-97, Director of Extracurricular Activity, Office of Student Affairs, 1995-2000, Library Curator, 2000-06, National Taipei University of Technology, Taipei; Visiting Postdoctoral Fellow, Institute of Inorganic Chemistry, Friedrich-Alexander University, Erlangen-Nuremberg, Germany, 1997; Full Professor, Department of Chemical Engineering and Biotechnology, National Taipei University of Technology, Taipei, 1997-. Publications: Above 100 research papers in internationally peer-reviewed journals. Honours: Outstanding Research Award, National Taipei University of Technology, 2005; 3 Academic Honours, National Taipei University of Technology, 2005, 2006 & 2007; 3 Outstanding Research Awards, Engineering College, National Taipei University of Technology, 2004, 2005 & 2006. Memberships: International Society of Electrochemistry; Electrochemical Society; Chemical Society of Taipei. Address: Department of Chemical Engineering and Biotechnology, National Taipei University of Technology, No 1, Section 3, Chung-Hsiao East Road, Taipei, Taiwan 106 (ROC). E-mail: smchen78@ms15.hinet.net

CHEN Shi-Jay, b. 18 March 1972, Taipei, Taiwan, Republic of China. University Teacher. Education: PhD, Department of Computer Science and Information Engineering, National Taiwan University of Science and Technology, Taipei, 2004. Appointments: Assistant Professor, Department of Information Management. Publications: Fuzzy-number similarity measure; Fuzzy information retrieval; Fuzzy personal recommendation system; Fuzzy data mining; Fuzzy multi-criteria decision making. Honours: Winner, Outstanding Doctoral Dissertation Award, Chinese Fuzzy System Association, 2005; Winner,

Outstanding Doctoral Dissertation Award, Acer Dragon Thesis Award, 2005. Memberships: IEEE; Taiwanese Association for Artificial Intelligence. Address: No 1, Lien Da, Kung-Ching Li, Miao-Li 36003, Taiwan, Republic of China. E-mail: sjchen@nuu.edu.tw Website: web.nuu.edu.tw/~sjchen

CHEN Shilu, b. 24 September 1920, Dong Yang, Zhejiang, China. Professor. m. Xiaosu Gong, 2 sons, 1 daughter. Education: BSc, Aeronautics, Tsinghua University, China, 1945; PhD, Aeronautics, Moscow Aeronautical Institute, Russia, 1958. Appointments: Honorary Dean, College of Astronautics, Northwestern Polytechnical University, China, 1987-; Foreign Academician, Russian Academy of Astronautics, 1994-; Academician, Chinese Academy of Engineering, 1997-. Publications: Dynamic Stability Coupling and Active Control of Elastic Vehicles with Unsteady Aerodynamic Forces Considered; Longitudinal Stability of Elastic Vehicles; Progress and Development of Space Technology in China, 2000. Honours: Recipient of First Grade Award for Progress in Science and Technology on "Dynamics and Control of Elastic Vehicles", Chinese National Education Committee, 1991; Honoured as "Excellent Postgraduate Supervisor", "Distinguished Specialist", Ministry of Aeronautics and Astronautics, 1992. Memberships: Director, Chinese Society of Aeronautics and Astronautics, 1964-92; Chairman, Session of Aeronautics and Astronautics, China Advisory Committee for Academic Degrees, 1985-91; Honorary President, Shanxi Provincial Society of Astronautics, 1994-; Associate Fellow, AIAA, 1996-. Address: Northwestern Polytechnical University, South Apt 17-1-301, Xian 710072, People's Republic of China. E-mail: s.l.chen@nwpu.edu.cn

CHEN Shui-Bian, b. 18 February 1951, Taiwan. President of the Republic of China. m. Wu Shu-jen, 1 son, 1 daughter. Education: LLB, NTU, 1974; Honorary Dr Degree in Law, Kyungnam University, South Korea, 1995; Honorary Dr Degree in Economics, Plekhanov Russian Academy of Economics, Russia, 1995. Appointments: Chief Attorney-at-Law, Formosa International Marine & Commercial Law Office, 1976-89; Member, Taipei Ccoun, 1981-85; Publisher, Free Time serial magazine, 1984; Executive Member, Taiwan Association for Human Rights, 1984; Jailed for the Formosa Magazine of Taiwan Democratic Movement incident, 1986-87; Member, CSC, DPP, 1987-89 & 1996-2000; Member, CEC, 1987-89 and 1991-96; Member, Legislative Yuan, 1989-94; Executive Director, DPP Caucus, 1990-93, Convener, National Defence Committee, 1992-94; Convener, Rules Committee, 1993; Member, Judicial Committee, 1994; President of the Republic of China (Taiwan), 2000-04; Chairman, DPP, 2002-05; President of the Republic of China (Taiwan), 2004-. Publications: Series on Justice, 4 vols; Conflict, Compromise & Progress; National Defence Black Box & White Paper; Through the Line between Life & Death; The Son of Taiwan; The 1st Voyage of the Century. Honours: Man of the Taiwan Parliament, Newsweek magazine, 1993; Vice President, Rotary Club of Taipei North Gate, 1993; Global 100 Roster of Young Leaders for the New Millennium, Time magazine, 1994; Mayor, Taipei City, 1994-98; Asia's 20 Young Political Stars, Asiaweek magazine, 1999. Address: The Office of the President, No 122, Section 1, Chongcing South Road, Taipei 10048, Taiwan, Republic of China. E-mail: oop15@mail.oop.gov.tw Website: http://www.president.gov.tw

CHEN Willie, b. 15 February 1936, Muar Johore, Malaysia. Journalist; Photo-Journalist. m. Lee Geok Lan, deceased, 1 son, 2 daughters. Education: Diploma, Radio, Electronics, TV, National technical School, Los Angeles, California, USA, 1957; MBA, USA University, 1962; Diploma, Hotel/Motel Operations and Management Course, La Salle University, Chicago, 1987. Appointments: Hearst Metrotone News Inc; CBS News; Head, Hotels Chain Projects, PR China; Television News Provider World-Wide for television news coverage projected for 1000 stations; Regular Writer for American magazines; Real Estate Agent, Licensed by Malaysian Government. Publications: More than 2000 news reports written during the period of the Vietnam War. Honours: Various awards in journalism and services to newspapers and television, world-wide; Citation for the Best News Coverage; Award for Best Articles written on food. Memberships: American Society of Magazine Photographers in Communications; Pasir Pelangi Residents Association; Teochoew Association. Address: 120 Jalan Sultanah Aminah, Taman Iskandar, Johore Bahru, 80050, Malaysia. E-mail: colubia@tmnet.com.my

CHENG Fai Chut, b. 15 July 1933, Shanghai, China. Researcher in Electrical Engineering. Education: BSc, Electrical Engineering, Tsing Hua University, Beijing, 1957; MPhil, Electrical Engineering, University Hong Kong, 1990. Appointments: Engineer, NE Power Administration, Central Laboratory, Harbin, 1957-73; Technician, Tomoe Electrons Co, Hong Kong, 1973-76; Lecturer, School Science and Technology, Hong Kong, 1976-80; Part-time Demonstrator, University Hong Kong, 1980-88; Temporary Teacher, Haking Wong Technical Institute, Hong Kong, 1987-88; Evening Visiting Lecturer, 1988-89, 1990-93, Research Assistant, 1989-92, Teaching Assistant, 1992-93, Honorary Research Associate, 1993-94, Part-time Research Assistant, 1994-95, Hong Kong Polytechnic, now Hong Kong Polytechnic University; Part-time Research Assistant, 1995-97, Honorary Research Fellow, 1998-99, Honorary Fellow, 2000-02, Hong Kong Polytechnic University; Unemployed Researcher, 2003-. Publications: Insulation Thickness Determination of Polymeric Power Cables, 1994; Discussion on Insulation Thickness Determination of Polymeric Power Cables, in journal IEEE Transactions on Dielectrics and Electrical Insulation, 1995. Honours: Outstanding Achievement Medal, Gold Star Award, Silver Medal, IBC, 1997; Distinguished Leadership Award, 20th Century Achievement Award, Most Admired Man of the Decade, 1997 Man of Year Commemorative Medal, ABI, 1997; 2000 Millennium Medal of Honour, ABI, 1998. Memberships: IEEE, US; Institution of Engineering and Technology, UK. Address: 2-019 Lotus Tower 1, Garden Estate, 297 Ngau Tau Kok Rd, Kowloon, Hong Kong.

CHENG Wenyu, b. 28 June 1921, Chengdu, China. Professor of Economics. m. Helen Kuomei Huang, 2 sons, 2 daughters. Education: BA, Economics, National Wuhan University, 1943; Graduate Studies, Economics, Harvard University, 1945-46; MA, University of Chicago, 1950; PhD, 1954; University of Cambridge, 1982; UCLA Summer Course Work. Appointments: Professor of Economics, Marietta College, Ohio, 1948-95; Professor, 1960; Senior Distinguished Professor, 1985; Professor of Economics, Muskingum College, Ohio, 1987-91; Honorary Professor of Economics, Wuhan University, 1993-; Adjunct Professor of Economics, Ohio University, 1992-93; Emeritus, 1995. Publications: Survey of Economics; Co-author, Money and Banking; Principles of Economics; Many articles in professional journals. Honours: Scholarship Award, Overseas Dr Sun Yatsen Institute; Honorary Professorship, Wuhan University and Southwestern University of Finance and Economics, China; Omicron Delta Kappa Distinguished Service Key. Memberships: Association for Asian Studies; National Bureau for Asian Research. Address: 928 Glendale Road, Marietta, OH 45750, USA.

CHENG Yue, b. 23 August 1958, Wenzhou, Zhejing, China. Molecular Geneticist. m. Yuxing Xiong, 1 daughter. Education: BMed, Anhui Medical College, China, 1982; MMed, Sun Yatsen University of Medical Sciences, China, 1987; PhD, Hong Kong University of Science and Technology, 2002. Appointments: Teaching Assistant, Anhui Medical College, 1982-84; Assistant Professor, Sun Yatsen University of Medical Science, 1989-93; Visiting Assistant Researcher, University of California, Irvine, 1993-95; Visiting Scholar, Hong Kong University of Science and Technology, 1995-2002; Visiting Fellow, Genetics Branch, National Cancer Institute, National Naval Medical Center, USA, 2003-08; City of Hope Medical Center, Duarte, USA, 2008-. Publications: Articles in professional scientific journals. Honours: Grant, Sun Yatsen University of Medical Science, 1991; Scholarship, American Chinese Medical Board, 1993; Lifetime Achievement Award, Deputy Director General, IBC, 2001; Life Fellow, IBA, 2001; Vice Consul, IBC, 2002; Listed in Who's Who Publications; Fellowship Award, National Institutes of Health, USA, 2003-. Memberships: Chinese Medical Association, 1991-; Hong Kong Professional Teacher's Union, 1998-03; Member, American Association for the Advancement of Science, 2002-; American Association for Cancer Research, 2003-; American Society of Haematology, 2005-. E-mail: yuecheng@hotmail.com

CHER (Cherilyn LaPierre Sarkisian), b. 20 May 1946, El Centro, California, USA. Singer; Actress; Entertainer. m. (1) Sonny Bono, 1964, divorced, deceased, 1 daughter, (2) Gregg Allman, 1975, divorced, 1 son. Career: Worked with Sonny Bono in duo Sonny and Cher, 1964-74; Also solo artiste, 1964-; Performances include: Hollywood Bowl, 1966; Newport Pop Festival, 1968; Television includes: Sonny And Cher Comedy Hour, CBS, 1971; Cher, CBS, 1975-76; Sonny And Cher Show, CBS, 1976-77; Vocalist with rock group Black Rose, including US tour supporting Hall & Oates, 1980; Actress, films: Good Times, 1967; Chastity, 1969; Come Back To The Five And Dime, Jimmy Dean Jimmy Dean, 1982; Silkwood, 1984; Mask, 1985; The Witches Of Eastwick, Moonstruck, Suspect, 1987; Mermaids, 1989; Stuck on You, 2003; Lords of Dogtown, 2005; Love and Understanding; faithful; If these Walls could Talk; Pret-a-Porter; Tea with Mussolini. Recordings include: Singles: with Sonny And Cher: I Got You Babe (Number 1, UK and US), 1975; Baby Don't Go, Just You, But You're Mine, 1965; What Now My Love, Little Man, 1966; The Beat Goes On, 1967; All I Ever Need Is You, 1971; A Cowboy's Work Is Never Done, 1972; Solo hit singles include: All I Really Want To Do, 1965; Bang Bang, 1966; Gypsies Tramps And Thieves (Number 1, US), 1971; The Way Of Love, 1972; Half Breed (Number 1, US), 1973; Dark Lady (Number 1, US), 1974; Take Me Home, 1979; Dead Ringer For Love, duet with Meatloaf, 1982; I Found Someone, 1987; We All Sleep Alone, 1988; After All, duet with Peter Cetera (for film soundtrack Chances Are), If I Could Turn Back Time, Jesse James, 1989; Heart Of Stone, 1990; The Shoop Shoop Song (from film soundtrack Mermaids) (Number 1, UK), Love And Understanding, 1991; Oh No Not My Baby, 1992; Walking In Memphis, 1995; One By One, Paradise Is Here, 1996; Believe, 1998; Strong Enough, All Or Nothing, Dov'e l'Amore, 1999; The Music's No Good Without You, 2001; Alive Again, A Different Kind of Love, 2002; When the Money's Gone, 2003; Albums: with Sonny and Cher: Look At Us, All I Really Want To Do, 1965; The Wondrous World Of Sonny And Cher, 1966; Sonny And Cher Live, 1972; Solo albums include: All I Really Want To Do, 1965; The Sonny Side Of Cher, 1966; With Love, 1967; Backstage, 1968; Jackson Highway, 1969; Gypsies Tramps And Thieves, Foxy Lady, 1972; Greatest Hits, 1974; Stars,

1975; I'd Rather Believe In You, 1976; Take Me Home, 1979; I Paralyze, 1984; Cher, 1988; Heart Of Stone, 1989; Love Hurts, 1991; Cher's Greatest Hits 1965-1992, 1992; It's A Man's World, 1995; Believe, Black Rose, 1999; Living Proof, 2001; Live: The Farewell Tour, 2003. Honours include: Oscar, Best Actress, Moonstruck, 1988; Oscar Nomination, Best Supporting Actress, Silkwood, 1984; Grammy Award for Best Dance Recording, 2000; VH1 First Music Award for Achievements within the Music Industry, 2005. Address: Reprise Records, 3000 Warner Boulevard, Burbank, CA 19010, USA.

CHERPAK Evelyn, b. 3 April 1941, New Britain, Connecticut, USA. Archivist. Education: BA, Connecticut College; MA, University of Pennsylvania; PhD, University of the North Carolina. Appointments: Archivist, Naval War College, Newport, Rhode Island; Graduate Extension Studies, Adjunct Faculty, Salve Regina University, Newport. Publications: A Diplomat's Lady in Brazil: Selections from the Diary of Mary Robinson Hunter, 2001; The Memoirs of Admiral H K Hewitt, 2004; The Redwood Library, 2005; Timothy Murphy's Civil War: The Letters of a Bounty Solder and Sailor, 1864-1865, 2006. Honours: NDEA Fellowship in Latin American History; Lampadia Foundation Grant. Memberships: Newport Historical Society; Redwood Library; John Carter Brown Library; Association of Documentary Editors; New England Archivists; Manuscript Society; New England Council of Latin American Studies; Oral History Association; Academic & College Libraries, New England Chapter; Hakluyt Society; North American Society of Oceanic History; Nineteenth Studies Association. Address: 36D Glen Meade Drive, Portsmouth, RI 02871-3403, USA. E-mail: evelyn.cherpak@nwc.navy.mil

CHERRY Scott, b. 17 November 1951, Flint, Michigan, USA. Neuropsychologist. m. Nancy, 1 son. Education: BA, Psychology/Developmental Learning, Saginaw Valley State University, 1977; MA, Learning Disabilities/ Emotionally Impaired, Central Michigan University, 1980; MA, Clinical Psychology, 1989, PhD, Clinical Psychology/Neuropsychology, 1992, California School of Professional Psychology, Fresno. Appointments: Intern, Allen Park Veterans Administration Medical Center, Allen Park, Michigan, 1990-91; Adjunct Instructor, South Dakota State University, 1994-98; Neuropsychologist, Rapid City Regional Hospital, Rapid City, South Dakota. Publications: Psycholinguistic abilities of Reflective/Impulsive Learning in Disabled Children; Neuropsychological Considerations in Adult Learning Disabled; Comparison of the Boston Naming/ and Benton Naming Test. Honours: Advanced Practice Psychologist. Memberships: National Register of Psychology; International Health Professional, 2007. Address: Rapid City Regional Hospital, Regional Rehabilitation Institute, Neuropsychology Department, 2908 5th St, Rapid City, SD 57701, USA.

CHESHER Andrew Douglas, b. 21 December 1948, Croydon, England. Professor. m. Valérie Lechene, 2 sons, 2 daughters. Education: B Soc Sc, University of Birmingham, 1970. Appointments: Research Associate, The Acton Society, 1970-71; Lecturer, Econometrics, Department of Economics, University of Birmingham, 1971-83; Head, 1987-90, 1996-98, Professor of Econometrics, 1984-99, Department of Economics, Visiting Professor, 2000-, University of Bristol; Professor of Economics, Department of Economics, University College London, 1999-; Research Fellow, Institute for Fiscal Studies, 1999-; Director, Centre for Microdata Methods and Practice, 2001-. Publications: Numerous articles in professional journals. Honours: Elected Fellow, British Academy; Elected Fellow, Econometric Society, 1999. Memberships: Fellow, Royal Statistical Society; Fellow, Econometric Society. E-mail: andrew.chesher@ucl.ac.uk

CHESNAIS Jean Claude, b. 27 October 1948, France. Demographer. m. Diane Padureleanu, 2 sons. Education: PhD, Demography, University of Paris, 1975; PhD Economics, Institut d'Etudes Politiques, 1984. Appointments: Senior Research Fellow, Institut National d'Etudes; Professor, Ecole Nationale d'Administration and Ecole Polytechnique; Visiting Professor, School of Advanced International Studies, Johns Hopkins University. Publications: The Demographic Transition. its Stages, Patterns and Economic Implications; Demographic Transition Patterns and their Impact on the Age Structure; Worldwide Historical Trends in Murder and Suicide. Honours: La démographie, Que Sais-Je?, 6th edition, 2005; Academie Francaise Prize, 1996; Prize of the French Speaking Statistician. Memberships: International Statistical Institute; International Union for the Scientific Study of Population; World Humanity Action Trust. Address: INED 133 Boulevard, Davout 75020 Paris, France.

CHEVERESAN Constantin-Traian, b. 4 October 1947, Pecica, Arad, Romania. Teacher of English. m. Violeta Cristina Laura, 1 daughter. Education: Faculty of Philology, 1965-70, PhD, 1997, English-Romanian Department, Babes-Bolyai University, Romania; 10-week ESP course, Institute of English Language Education, University of Lancaster, England. 1994. Appointments: Assistant Lecturer, 1970-90, Senior Lecturer, 1990-98, Associate Professor (Reader), English and American Language and Literature, University of the West, Timisoara, 1998-. Publications: 8 books including: Voices and Languages, 1998; A Practical Handbook of Writing Conventions in English, 2000; Caregiving English for Social Work, 2003; English for Psychologists, 2005; College English; English Idioms: A Multilingual Students Approach; 100 articles; 15 translations (3 books); 7 textbooks. Honours: Diploma of Honour, Teachers' Day, Timisoara University, 1981; Certificate of Advanced Studies in Education, Lancaster University, 1994. Memberships: European Society for the Study of English; Romanian Society for Anglo-American Studies; Timisoara English Teachers' Association; Orizonturi Universitaire Association, Timisoara. Address: Str Aries, No 20, Sc C, Et 3, Ap 11, 300327 Timisoara, Romania. E-mail: ccheveresan@gmail.com

CHI Kuang-Hui, b. 27 May 1969, Chiayi, Taiwan. Computer Educator; Computer Scientist. m. Li-Ju Chen, 1 son, 2 daughters. Education: BS, Tatung University (formerly Tatung Institute of Technology), Taiwan, 1991; MS, 1993, PhD, 2001, National Chiao Tung University. Appointments: Exchange Academician (Visiting Scholar), University of Erlangen-Nuremberg, Germany, 2001; Engineer, Industrial Technology Research Institute, Taiwan, 2001-03; Assistant Professor, Department of Electrical Engineering, Taiwan, 2003-. Publications: 14 journal papers (10 international, 4 domestic); 11 conference papers (5 international, 6 domestic); 2 patents pending (USA and Taiwan). Honours: 3rd Place Award, Yearly Best Papers, Industrial Technology Research Institute, Taiwan, 2003; Best Paper Award, 12th Workshop on Mobile Computing, Taiwan, 2006. Memberships: ACM; IEEE. Address: Department of Electrical Engineering, National Yunlin University of Science and Technology, 123 University Road Section 3, Douliu 640, Taiwan. E-mail: chikh@yuntech.edu.tw

CHIA Su Hua, b. 19 February 1943, China. Teacher. m. Hung Hsin Liu, 1 son, 1 daughter. Education: Kung Chiu Chinese Medical College, China, 1993; British Institute of Homeopathy, 2006-09. Appointments: Assistant Professor of Training Course for Physicians, USA; Fellow, British Institute of Homeopathy; Lecturer, Society University of Song, Shan Chiu, Taipei City, Taiwan. Publications: Healthy Herb and Fruit Liquor; Sun Color Culture Publishing Co Ltd, Taiwan, 2002. Honours: Examplar Medal, National Youth Salvation Society. Memberships: Permanent Membership of Hong Chinese Medical Association; Naturopathic Association. E-mail: sowan@aptg.net

CHIANG Cheng-Wen, b. 24 October 1943, I-Lan, Taiwan. Cardiologist. m. Mei-Yu Yang, 2 sons. Education: Department of Medicine, College of Medicine, National Taiwan University, 1971. Appointments: Councilor, World Federation of Ultrasound in Medicine and Biology; President-Elect, Asian Federation of Societies of Ultrasound in Medicine and Biology; Secretary General, College of Asian Pacific Society of Cardiology; President-Elect, Asian Pacific Society of Cardiology; Executive Director, Taiwan Heart Foundation; President, Taiwan Society of Cardiology; Professor, Department of Internal Medicine, Cathay General Hospital, and Taipei Medical University. Publications: 130 articles in peer-reviewed medical journals. Honours: Best Medical Physician Award, Chang Gung Memorial Hospital, 1977; Cheng-Shin Medical Award, Medical Association of Taiwan, 1979; Long Ting Award, Taiwan Society of Cardiology, 2001. Memberships: Fellow, American College of Cardiology; Fellow, American College of Chest Physicians; American Society of Echocardiography; Asian Pacific Society of Cardiology; College of Asian Pacific Society of Cardiology; Taiwan Society of Internal Medicine; Taiwan Society of Cardiology; Taiwan Heart Foundation; Taiwan Society of Ultrasound in Medicine; Asian Federation of Society of Ultrasound in Medicine & Biology; World Federation of Society of Ultrasound in Medicine & Biology; Western Pacific Association of Critical Care Medicine, Taiwan; Formosan Medical Association. Address: 1st Fl, No 23, Lane 165, Kuang-Fu N Road, Taipei 10579, Taiwan. E-mail: cwchiang@cgh.org.tw

CHIBUNDU Victor Nwaozichi, b. 30 December 1930, Umuojima Ukwu, Abia State, Nigeria. Former Ambassador; Businessman. m. Catherine Ekpendu, 1 son, 4 daughters. Education: Postgraduate studies, International Relations, Cambridge University, Cambridge, England and New School for Social Research, New York, USA. Chartered Secretary (London). Appointments: Nigerian Foreign Service, 1961-90: Special Assistant to the First Minister of Foreign Affairs and Commonwealth Relations, Ministry of External Affairs; Charge d'Affairs, Embassy of the Federal Republic of Nigeria in Tehran, Iran; Director of several departments responsible for strategic areas including: Arab Affairs (now Middle East Affairs), Central and Southern Africa and Cultural Affairs; Ambassador Extraordinary and Plenipotentiary; Retired from Nigerian Foreign Service, 1990; Consultant, 1991-99, Retainer (Foreign Affairs), 1999-, Unipetrol Nigeria plc; Concurrently, Consultant (Foreign Affairs), Merchant Bank of Africa (now defunct); Co-Founder, City Savings and Investment Bank of Namibia (now merged with South West African Building Society), 1992; Founder, Chairman, Nigeria-China Friendship Association, 1994; Participant in events marking 30th Anniversary of the establishment of diplomatic relations between Nigeria and China, 2001; Leader of several official economic and cultural delegations to China and a participant in numerous visits by Chinese delegations to Nigeria. Publications: Books: Nigeria-China Foreign Relations: 1960-1999; Foreign Policy: With Particular Reference to Nigeria; NICAF Goes to Guangzhou, 2003. Honours: Traditional Chieftancy Title: Olu Oha 1 of Mbutu Ugwu Autonomous Community, 1984; Africa International Order of Merit, Intra-West Africa Communications, 2002; Hall of Fame, International Biographical Association, 2004. Memberships: Nigerian Institute of Management; Lagos Chamber of Commerce and Industry; Institute of Directors, Nigeria; Association of Retired Ambassadors of Nigeria. Address: PO Box 4346, 11 Badaru Street, Suru Lere, Lagos, Nigeria.

CHIKKALI Samir, b. 4 April 1978, Mangoli, India. Scientific Worker. Education: BSc, Chemistry, 1999, MSc, Polymer Chemistry, 2001, Shivaji University, Kolhapur, India; PhD, University of Stuttgart, Germany, in progress. Appointments: Project Assistant, 2001-03, Scientific Co-worker, 2003-, University of Stuttgart. Publications: 4 articles in professional scientific journals; Oral and poster presentations. Honours: Fellow, Indian Academy of Science, Bangalore. Memberships: German Chemical Society; American Chemical Society. E-mail: samir-chikkali@yahoo.com

CHIKURUNHE Innocent, b. 10 July 1973, Murewa, Zimbabwe. Polymer Engineer. m. Shongedzai Zisengwe, 1 son. Education: Certificate in Polyurethane Technology, Zimbabwe; LCCI Group Diploma in Marketing, London; NC, Plastics & Rubber Technology, ND, HND, Plastics Technology, Harare Polytechnic, Zimbabwe; MSc, Polymer Science and Engineering, London Metropolitan University, England. Appointments: Quality Controller, Megapak Plastics, Zimbabwe, 1996-97; Technical Manager, Prodorite Plastics, Zimbabwe, 1999-2001; Technical Director, Wisha Agencies, Zimbabwe, 1998-; Polymer Science Lecturer, Harare Polytechnic College, Zimbabwe, 2002-06; Managing Director, Goalsburg Engineering, Zimbabwe, 2004-; President & Founder, Cecilia Rosemary Chikurunhe Trust (an educational trust for HIV/AIDS orphans), 2005-; Process and Product Development Engineer, Arrow Plastics Ltd (Plastic Profile Extrusion Co), UK, 2007-. Publications: Re-designing, Re-formulating and Manufacturing of Snooker Balls; Research on making PET recycled plastics biodegradable for use in coffin manufacturing; Replacing rubber automotive suspension bushes with hard-wearing polyurethane elastomers. Honours: Zimbabwe's National Best Polymer Technologist Award, Saltrama Plastics, CMB and Pro-Plastics, 2005; London Metropolitan Graduate Scholarship, 2006-07; Guest Speaker, London Metropolitan University; Listed in international biographical dictionaries. Memberships: Society for Plastic Engineers (UK and Ireland); Plastics and Rubber Institute, Zimbabwe; Founder Member and Trustee, Cecilia Rosemary Chikurunhe Educational Trust; Plastics and Rubber Weekly, UK. Address: 5 Berrylands Road, 9 Meadowbank, Surbiton, Surrey, KT5 8RD, England.

CHILD Dennis, b. 10 July 1932, Ulverston, England. Emeritus Professor of Educational Psychology; Author. m. Eveline Barton, 1 son, 1 daughter. Education: teachers' Certificate, St John's College, York, 1957; BSc, London, 1962; M Ed, Leeds, 1968; PhD, Bradford, 1973. Appointments: Teacher of General Science, Easingwold Comprehensive School, near York, 1957-59; Teacher of Physics and Chemistry, Bootham School, York, 1959-62; Lecturer in Physics, 1962-65, Senior Lecturer in Education, 1965-67, City of Leeds College of Education; Lecturer, 1967-73, Senior Lecturer, 1973-76, Psychology of Education, Postgraduate School of Studies of Research on Education, University of Bradford; Visiting Professorships:

University of Illinois, USA, 1972, 1973; University of Yucatan, Merida, Mexico, (annually) 1979-89; Botswana and Malawi Teacher Training Colleges, 1980; University of Lisbon, Portugal, 1983; East China Normal University, Shanghai, 1987; Beijing Foreign Studies University, 1988; Professor and Head of School of Education, University of Newcastle upon Tyne, 1976-81; Professor of Educational Psychology, School of Education, 1981-92, Head of School, 1984-87, Emeritus Professor of Educational Psychology, School of Education, 1992-, University of Leeds; Author. Publications include: Some technical problems in the use of personality measures in occupational settings illustrated using the "Big Five" (book chapter), 1998; Painters of the Northern Counties of England and Wales, 1994, 2nd edition, 2002; The Yorkshire Union of Artists 1888-1922, 2001; Psychology and the Teacher, 7th edition (major revision), 2004, 8th edition, 2007; The Yorkshire Union of Artists 1888-1922 in Antique Collecting, 2004; Entry for James Lonsdale (1777-1839) in Dictionary of National Biography, 2004; Essentials of Factor Analysis, 3rd edition, 2006. Honours: OBE, 1997; Directions in Educational Psychology edited by Dianne Shorrocks-Taylor. An appreciation of the works of Dennis Child, 1998; Biography for Dennis Child in European Revue of Applied Psychology, 1999. Memberships: FBPsS; FCST; C Psychol; Past member of government and related bodies, as well as numerous organisations in the areas of medicine, education of the deaf and the performing arts. Address: The Cottage, Main Street, Scholes, Leeds LS15 4DP, England.

CHILD Mark Sheard, b. 17 August 1937, Stockton-on-Tees, England. University Professor. m. Daphne Hall, 1 son, 2 daughters. Education: BA (Cantab) Chemistry 1st class, 1959, PhD (Cantab), Theoretical Chemistry, 1962, Clare College, Cambridge. Appointments: Research Fellow, Lawrence Radiation Laboratory, University of California, Berkeley, USA, 1962-63; Lecturer, Theoretical Chemistry, University of Glasgow, 1963-66; Lecturer, Theoretical Chemistry, 1966-89, Aldrachian Praelector in Chemistry, 1989-92, Professor, Chemical Dynamics, 1992-94, Coulson Professor of Theoretical Chemistry, 1994-2004, University of Oxford; Visiting Fellow, University of Wisconsin, Madison, USA, 1963; Visiting Professor, Institute of Advanced Studies, Hebrew University of Jerusalem, 1978-79; Visiting Professor, University of Colorado, USA, 1988-89; Visiting Professor, Université de Paris-Sud, 1989; Visiting Professor, Joseph Fourier University, Grenoble, 1996. Publications: Author and Co-author of over 150 articles in scientific journals; Books: Molecular Collision Theory, 1974, reissued, 1996; Semiclassical mechanisms with molecular applications, 1991. Honour: Fellow of the Royal Society; William Draper Harkins Lecture, University of Chicago, 1985; Tilden Lecture, Royal Society of Chemistry, 1987-87; Condon Lecture, University of Colorado, 1987-88. Memberships: Royal Society; Royal Society of Chemistry.

CHIN Jacky, b. 2 April 1960, Ipoh, Perak, Malaysia. Corrosion Scientist. m. Ann Fong, 1 son. Education: Diploma in Technology, Materials Science, Tunku Abdul Rahman College, Malaysia, 1984; Bachelor of Science, Universiti Teknologi Malaysia, 1990; Doctorate, Southern Cross University, Australia, 1996. Appointments: Corrosion Scientist, Corrosion Science Research Centre, 1984-90; Director, Oriental Science Research Centre, 1990-; Visiting Professor, Zhongshan University, Guangzhou, China, 2000-. Publications: Book: Corrosion and Corrosion Protection of Building Materials; Article: Endothermic-based Atmospheres. Honours: The Outstanding Young Malaysian, 2000; Listed in Who's Who publications and biographical dictionaries.

Memberships: Institute of Metal Finishing, UK; Institution of Corrosion Science and Technology, UK. Address: PH131, 10 Persiaran Residen, Desa Parkcity, 52200, KL, Malaysia. E-mail: yschin@mailcity.com

CHIN Takaaki, b. 4 October 1960, Kobe, Japan. Medical Doctor. m. K Hayashi, 1 daughter. Education: Bachelor of Medicine, Tokushima University, Tokushima, Japan, 1986; Medical Diplomate, 1986; PhD, Kobe University. Appointments: Resident, University Hospital, Kobe, Japan, 1986-87; Doctor Course, Kobe University, Kobe, Japan, 1987-91; Research Fellow, McGill University, Montreal, Canada, 1990-92; Head Physician, Hyogo Rehabilitation Centre, Kobe, Japan, 1992-. Publications: Articles in medical journals including: Developmental Biology, 1996; Prosthetics and Orthotics International, 1997, 1999, 2002, 2006, 2007; Journal of Rehabilitation Research and Development, 2001; American Journal of Physical Medicine and rehabilitation, 2002, 2003; Journal of Bone and Joint Surgery (br), 2005; American Journal of Physical Medicine and Rehabilitation, 2006. Honour: Iida Prize, Japanese Society of Prosthetics and Orthotics, 2001. Memberships: Japanese Orthopaedic Association; Japanese Association of Rehabilitation Medicine; Councillor, 1998-, Japanese Society of Prosthetics and Orthotics; Vice-President, 2003-, President, 2008-, Japan Branch, International Society for Prosthetics and Orthotics; International Society of Orthopaedic Surgery and Traumatology; Councillor, The Japanese Association of Rehabilitation Medicine, 2006-; Visiting Associate Professor, Kobe University Graduate School of Medicine, 2007-; Councillor, The Japan Medical Society of Spinal Cord Lesion, 2007-. Address: Hyogo Rehabilitation Centre, 1070 Akebono-Cho, Nishi-Ku, Kobe, 651-2181 Japan.

CHIN Yoong Kheong, b. 13 April 1958, Ipoh, Perak, Malaysia. Accountant. m. Yap Siew Pin, 2 sons, 1 daughter. Education: BA Hons 1st Class, Economics/Accounting, University of Leeds, England, 1979; Doctor of Business Administration, American University of Hawaii, USA, 1996. Appointments: Auditor assistant/Audit Senior, KPMG Leeds, England, 1979-82; Auditor Assistant, KPMG Kuala Lumpur, 1983; Tax Consultant/Partner, KPMG Tax, Kuala Lumpur, 1983-97; Joint General Director, KPMG Vietnam, 1992-97; Partner-in-charge, KPMG Consulting, Malaysia, 1997-2004; Director, KPMG Business Advisory, Malaysia, 2004-. Publications: ASEAN: A Link in Your Global Strategy; Malaysian Taxation 4th Edition; Malaysian Taxation Practice. Honours: Crabtree Prize for Top Economic Students, University of Leeds, 1977; Gerald Veale Prize for Top Accounting Graduate, University of Leeds, 1979; Merit Award Winner, Professional Examination of the Institute of Chartered Accountants in England and Wales, 1980. Memberships: Fellow of Institute of Chartered Accountants in England and Wales; Member of Malaysian Institute of Certified Public Accountants; Malaysian Institute of Taxation; Malaysian Institute of Arbitrators; Institute of Financial Consultants. Address: 73 Jalan Semarak Api, Sierramas Resort Homes, 47000 Sungai Bhloh, Selangor, Malaysia. E-mail: cyk@kpmg.com.my

CHING Chiao-Liang Juliana, b. 23 February 1955, Hong Kong. Medicine; Business. Education: Bachelor of Science, Summa cum laude, Honours in Biology, Yale University, 1977; Doctor of Medicine, University of California, Davis School of Medicine, 1981. Appointments: Resident Doctor, UCLA Hospitals and Clinics, 1982-83; Resident Doctor, Harvard University Hospitals, 1983-85; Managing Director, Ideal Choice Development Limited, 1987-. Honours: Woman

of the Year, ABI, 1991-1998; International Order of Merit; Order of International Fellowship. Memberships: The New York Academy of Sciences; The Oxford Club; Eli Hu Yale Associates, Friends of the Cultural Centre of Hong Kong. Address: 4 Mount Butler Drive, Jardine's Lookout, Hong Kong.

CHIRAC Jacques René, b. 29 November 1932, Paris, France. Politician. m. Bernadette Chodron de Courcel, 1956, 2 children. Education: Lycée Carnot; Lycée Louis-le-Grand, Paris; Institute of Political Science, Paris; Harvard University Summer School, USA. Appointments: Military Service, Algeria; Auditor, Cour des Comptes, 1959-62; Special Assistant, Government Secretariat General, 1962 Counsellor, Cour des Comptes, 1965-94; Secretary of State for Employment Problems, 1967-68; Secretary of State for Economy and Finance, 1968-71; Minister for Parliamentary Relations, 1971-72, for Agriculture and Rural Development, 1972-74, of the Interior, 1974; Prime Minister of France, 1974-76, 1986-88; Secretary General, Union des Démocrates pour la République (UDR), 1975, Honorary Secretary General, 1975-76; President, Rassemblement pour la République (formerly UDR), 1976-94, Honorary Secretary General, 1977-80; Mayor of Paris, 1977-95; President of France, 1995-2002; Re-elected President of France, 2002-2007. Publications: Discours pour la France a l'heure du choix; La lueur de l'espérance: Réflexion du soir pour le matin, 1978; Une Nouvelle France, Reflexion 1, 1994; La France pour tous, 1995. Honours include: Prix Louis Michel, 1986; Grand-Croix de la Légion d'Honneur; Grand Croix de l'Ordre National du Mérite; Chevalier du Mérite. Address: Palais de l'Eysée, 55-57 rue du Faubourg Saint-Honoré, 75008 Paris, France.

CHITHAM Edward Harry Gordon, b. 16 May 1932, Harborne, Birmingham, England. Education Consultant. m. Mary Patricia Tilley, 29 December 1962, 1 son, 2 daughters. Education: BA, MA (Classics), Jesus College, Cambridge, 1952-55; PGCE, University of Birmingham, 1955-56; MA, English, University of Warwick, 1973-77; PhD, University of Sheffield, 1983. Publications: The Black Country, 1972; Ghost in the Water, 1973; The Poems of Anne Brontë, 1979; Brontë Facts and Brontë Problems (with T J Winnifrith), 1983; Selected Brontë Poems (with T J Winnifrith), 1985; The Brontës' Irish Background, 1986; A Life of Emily Brontë, 1987; Charlotte and Emily Brontë (with T J Winnifrith), 1989; A Life of Anne Brontë, 1991; A Bright Start, 1995; The Poems of Emily Brontë (with Derek Roper), 1996; The Birth of Wuthering Heights: Emily Brontë at work, 1998; A Brontë Family Chronology, 2003; Harborne: A History, 2004; Rowley Regis: A History, 2006. Contributions to: Byron Journal; Gaskell Society Journal; ISIS Magazine; Brontë Society Transactions. Memberships: Fellow, Royal Society of Arts, 1997. Joint Association of Classics Teachers; Gaskell Society; Brontë Society. Address: 25 Fugelmere Close, Harborne, Birmingham B17 8SE, England.

CHIU Dirk M, b. Malaysia. Engineering Educator. m. Lee H Lim, 1 son, 1 daughter. Education: BSc, Engineering, London, 1969; MSc, Edinburgh, 1976; PhD, Manchester, 1978. Appointments: Telecom Engineer, STC; Electronic Design Engineer, Control Systems Ltd; Electronic Senior Engineer, London University; Electronic Lecturer, Singapore Polytechnic; Microelectronic Lecturer, Paisley University; Course Co-ordinator in Electronics, Victoria University of Technology; Visiting Professor, Nankai University, and Dong Hwa University; Associate Professor, UPM. Publications: Electronic Science and Education (book); Over 100 articles on electronic sciences; Semiconductor Electronics; Power

Electronics; Microelectronics; Engineering Education. Honours: Taiwan SRC Research Professorship, 2000. Memberships: MIEE; CEng; PEng. Address: 71 Long Valley Way, Doncaster East, Victoria 3109, Australia.

CHIU Wan Cheng, b. 1 November 1919, Meihsien, Guangdong, China. Professor. m. Margaret C Y Liu, 3 daughters. Education: BS, National Central University, China, 1941; MS, 1947, PhD, Meteorology, 1951, New York University. Appointments: Technician, Fukien Weather Bureau, China, 1941-42; Teacher, Maths, Punshan Model School, Szechwan, China, 1942-43; Graduate Student, Assistant Teacher, Meteorology, National Central University, China, 1943-45; Graduate Student and Research Assistant, New York University, 1946-51; Research Associate, Research Scientist, New York University, 1951-61; Professor, Meteorology, University of Hawaii, 1961-87; Visiting Scientist, 1967-68, Senior Fellow, 1975, National Centre of Atmospheric Research. Publications: The relative importance of different heat-exchange process in the Lower Stratosphere; The spectrums of angular momentum transfer in the atmosphere; The Interpretation of the energy spectrum; The spectral equation of the statistical energy spectrum of atmospheric motion in the frequency domain; A study of the possible statistical relationship between the tropical sea surface temperature and atmospheric circulation. Honours: Fellow, New York University; Listed in numerous Who's Who and biographical publications. Memberships: American Meteorological Society; American Geophysical Union; Royal Meteorological Society of England. Address: 216 Kalalau Street, Honolulu, HI 96825, USA.

CHIZHOV Vladimir A, b. 3 December 1953, Moscow, Russia. Ambassador. m. Elena, 1 son, 1 daughter. Education: Graduated with honours, Moscow State Institute of International Relations, 1976. Appointments: Deputy Minister, Foreign Affairs, Moscow, 2002-05; Permanent Representative of the Russian Federation to the European Communities, Brussels, 2005-. Publications: Articles in several Russian and foreign magazines on European affairs, conflict management, Russia-EU and Russia-NATO relations, OSCE, and Balkans. Honours: Order of Friendship, Russia. E-mail: misrusce@coditel.net

CHKHAIDZE Ivane, b. 14 June 1958, Georgia. Paediatrician. m. Keti Gogvadze, 1 son, 1 daughter. Education: MD, Tbilisi State Medical University, 1980; Candidate of Medical Sciences, 1989; Doctor of Medical Sciences, 2001. Appointments: Clinical Co-ordinator, 1980-82, Postgraduate, 1982-86, Assistant professor, 1986-2002, Professor, 2002-, Department of Paediatrics, Tblisi State Medical University; Physician, 1982-86, Chief, 1989-92, Head of ICU Department, 1996-2007, Medical Director, 1998-2007, M Guramishvili Paediatric Clinic, Tblisi; Co-ordinator, National Paediatric Municipal Program, Ministry of Health, Georgia, 1998-2001; Chair, Quality Assurance Agency, Medical Faculty, Tblisi State Medical University, 2006-; Deputy Director, Tblisi Iashvili Central Childrens Hospital, 2007-. Publications: 153 publications including books, guidelines, book chapters, journal articles and abstracts. Memberships: Georgian Paediatric Society; International Paediatric Society; European Repiratory Society; Georgian Respiratory Association; Forum of Eurasia and Mediterranean Thoracic Societies; Global Alliance against Chronic Respiratory Diseases. Address: 8 Kutuzov str, Apt 4, 0194 Tblisi, Georgia.

CHO Chung-Hyun, b. 10 March 1940, Korea. Professor Emeritus. m. Hong Jong Duk, 2 daughters. Education: BA, Arts, 1963, MA, Ceramics, 1966, Ewha Womans University, Seoul; MFA, Ceramics, Southern Illinois University, Edwardsville, USA, 1976. Appointments: Professor, Department of Ceramic Art, College of Art and Design, 1971-2005, Director, Ewha Color and Design Research Institute, 1998-99, Dean, College of Art and Design, 1999-2003, Ewha Womans University, Seoul; Professor Emeritus, Ewha Womans University, Seoul. Publications: Korean Celadon of the Goryeo Period; Research on Onggi Wares; Architectural Ceramics; Over 37 publications and theses. Honours: Korean Prime Minister's Prize, Korean Arts Competition, 1969; Korean Minister of Tourism and Culture Prize, Korean Arts Competition, 1979. Memberships: Korean Contemporary Ceramics Association; Korean Crafts Association. Address: Yeungdeungpogu, Dangsandong 5 Ga 33-1, Hangang Posvil #1304, Seoul, Korea. E-mail: chcho@ewha.ac.kr

CHO Chungho, b. 27 December 1967, Namwon-gun, Jeonbuk, Republic of Korea. Mechanical Engineer; Researcher. m. Dongeun Lee, 1 daughter. Education: BS, 1992, MS, 1994, PhD, 2002, Chungnam National University, Daejeon, Republic of Korea. Appointments: Assistant Teacher, Chungnam National University, Daejeon, Republic of Korea, 1996-98; Lecturer, Cheongyang College, Chungnam, Republic of Korea, 1998-2002; Lecturer, Chungnam National University, Daejeon, Republic of Korea, 1999-2002; Postdoctoral Researcher, 2002-2004, Senior Researcher, 2004-, Korea Atomic Energy Research Institute, Daejeon, Republic of Korea. Publications: Articles in scientific journals. Honours: Listed in international biographical dictionaries. Memberships: Research Board of Advisors, ABI. Address: Korea Atomic Energy Research Institute, 150 Deokjin-dong, Yuseong-Gu, Daejeon 305-353, Republic of Korea. E-mail: chcho@kaeri.re.kr

CHO Dong Choon, b. 3 December 1947, Haeju, Korea. Professor. m. Yang Ho Kim, 1 son. Education: Bachelor of Economics, Kyunghee University; Master of Business Administration, Dongguk University; Doctor of Business Administration, Incheon University. Appointments: Executive, Korean Speech Culture Academy, 1971-; Member, Compilation Committee of Korean textbook, Ministry of Education, 1987-88; Professor, Donghae University, 1993-2002; President, Family First Society of Korea, 1993-; Lecturer, Incheon University, 1996-97; Honorary Professor, Liaoning University, 1996-; Lecturer on Happy Couples, Seoul Broadcasting System, 1997. Publications: How To Be a Happy Couple, 1980; Lovely Wife, 1984; Women, Go For It, 1984; To Be Loved, 1987; Women Who Have Vision Become Rich, 1998; Having a Happy Marriage is Hardwork, 2004. Honours: Award, Mayor of Seoul, 1963; Award, Minister of Home Affairs, 1964; Award, Prime Minister, 1996. Memberships: Boarding Member, Institute of Overseas Korean Affairs; Executive Member, Association of Promotion for Economy and Culture in Northeast Asia. Address: 101-1402 Hanshin Apt, Donam-dong, Seongbuk-gu, Seoul, Korea. E-mail: aterjo@dreamwiz.com Website: www.familya.or.kr

CHO Dong-Ho, b. 3 April 1956, JeonBuk, Republic of Korea. Professor. m. So-Ja Oh, 1982, 2 sons. Education: BS, Seoul National University, 1979; MS, 1981, PhD, 1985, Korea Advanced Institute of Science and Technology. Appointments: Professor, 1987-98, Chief, Computer Centre, 1989-95, Kyunghee University; Professor, KAIST, 1998-; Outside Director, KTF, 2002-04; Policy Advisor, 2003-06, Self Evaluation Member, 2007, Ministry of Information and Communication; Expert Member, National Council of Science and Technology, 2004-08; Self Evaluation Member, Ministry of Defense, 2006-; Director, KAIST Institute for Information Technology Convergence, 2007-. Publications: 5 international and 29 domestic patents; 19 international and 33 domestic patents pending; 108 international journals and 177 international conference papers; Numerous articles in professional journals. Honours: Best Professor for Academic Achievement, KAIST, 2001; National President Award, Korea Government, 2006; KAISTian of the Year, KAIST, 2007. Memberships: Editor, Journal of Communication and Networks, 2001-; Senior Member, IEEE, 2000-; Director, Korea Information and Communication Society, 1998-; Editor Board Member, Open Information System Journal, 2007-. Address: Division of Electric Engineering, KAIST, 335 Gwahangno Yuseonggu, Daejeon 305-701, Korea. E-mail: dhcho@ee.kaist.ac.kr Website: http://comis.kaist.ac.kr

CHO Mann-Ho, b. 25 March 1966, Gwang-Ju, Korea. Professor. m. Eunjoo Kim, 2 sons. Education: BS, 1992, MS, 1994, PhD, 1999, Physics. Appointments: Senior Researcher, Samsung Semiconductor R&D Center, Korea, 1994-2002; Postdoctoral studies, Stanford University, USA, 2002-03; Senior Researcher, Korea Research Institute of Standards and Science, Korea, 2003-07; Associate Professor, Yonsei University, Korea, 2007-. Publications: Over 80 articles in scientific journals. Honours: Samsung Representative Director Award, 1995; Outstanding Research Award, Korea Research Institute of Standards & Science, 2005. Memberships: Korean Physical Society; Korean Vacuum Society; Material Research Society. Address: #134 Department of Physics, Yonsei University, Seoul 120-749, Korea. E-mail: mh.cho@yonsei.ac.kr

CHO Myeong-Chan, b. 19 February, 1958, Kimhae, Republic of Korea. Cardiologist; Professor; Researcher. m. Kwang-Joo Kim, 1 son, 1 daughter. Education: MD, 1983, College of Medicine, PhD, 1992-96, Graduate School, Seoul National University, Seoul, Korea; Postdoctoral Fellow, University of California, San Diego, USA, 1996-97; Postdoctoral Fellow, University of North Carolina, USA, 1997-98. Appointments: Intern, 1983-84, Resident, Department of Internal Medicine, Clinical Fellow, Department of Cardiology, 1990-91, Seoul National University Hospital, Seoul, Korea; Chief in Cardiology, Capital Armed Forces General Hospital Seoul, Korea, 1987-90; Lecturer, 1991-93, Assistant Professor, 1993-98, Associate Professor, 1993-3003, Professor, 2003-, Chief in Cardiology and Director of Cardiovascular/Cath Laboratory, 1998-2004, Director of Department of Planning and Administration, 2003-2004, Chairman, Department of Internal Medicine, 2004-, Chungbuk National University Hospital, Cheongju, Korea; Visiting Professor, Department of Cardiology, Royal Infirmary, Glasgow, Scotland, 1994. Publications: Articles in international medical journals as co-author include most recently: Novel oral formulation of paclitaxel inhibits neointimal hyperplasia in a rat carotid artery injury model, 2004; Local delivery of green tea catchins inhibits neointimal formation in the rat carotid artery injury model, 2004; Implantation of bone marrow mononuclear cells using injectable fibrin matrix enhances neovascularization in infarcted myocardium, 2005. Honours: Cheongnam Scientific Award, Korean Society of Internal Medicine, 2001; Chungbuk Medical Scientific Award, Chungbuk National University, 2002; Best Editor, Korean Society of Circulation, 2003. Memberships include: Korean Medical Association, 1983-; Korean Society of Internal Medicine, 1987-; Associate Member: Korean Society of Hypertension, 1989-, Korean Society of Echocardiography, 1990, Korean Society of

Lipidology and Artherosclerosos, 1990-, Korean Society of Tissue Engineering, 1996-, Korean Society of Molecular Biochemistry and Molecular Biology. Address: Department of Cardiology, Chungbuk National University Hospital, 62 Gaeshin-Dong, Heungduk-Gu, Cheongju 361-711, Korea. E-mail: mccho@cbnu.ac.kr

CHO Seong Yun, b. 11 June 1974, Jinju, Republic of Korea. Researcher. m. Ju Hee Lee, 1 daughter. Education: B Eng, Department of Control and Instrumentation Engineering, 1997, M Eng, 1999, PhD, Navigation, 2003, Kwangwoon University, Republic of Korea. Appointments: Research Assistant, Automation and System Research Institute, 2003-04, Postdoctoral Fellow, School of Mechanical and Aerospace Engineering, 2004, Seoul National University; Senior Member Research Staff, ETRI, Daejeon, 2004-. Publications: Robust Positioning Technique in Low-Cost DR/GPS for Land Navigation; Performance Enhancement of Low-Cost Land Navigation for Location Based Service; Enhanced Tilt Compensation Method for Biaxial Magnetic Compass; A Calibration Technique for a Redundant IMU Containing Low-grade Inertial Sensors. Honours: Best Papers Award, ETRI, 2006; Listed in international biographical dictionaries. Memberships: IEEE; ICASE; KSAS. Address: ETRI 161 Gajeong-dong, Yuseong-gu, Daejeon 305-700, Republic of Korea. E-mail: sycho@etri.re.kr

CHOI Chul-Jin, b. 25 November 1961, Kyungnam, Korea. Researcher. m. Kang-ok, Bae, 2 sons. Education: BS, Seoul National University, 1984; ME, 1986, PhD, 1997, Korea Advanced Institute of Science and Technology. Appointments: Principal Researcher, Korea Institute of Machinery and Materials, 1986-. Publications: 55 scientific papers; 21 patents. Honours: Listed in international biographical dictionaries. Memberships: Mineral, Metallurgy and Materials Society; Materials Research Society. Address: 66 Sangnam-Dong, Changwon, Kyungnam, South Korea. E-mail: cjchoi@kmail.kimm.re.kr

CHOI Dong Ryong, b. 15 February 1945, Tokyo, Japan. Consulting Geologist. m. Chong-Ih Kim, 1 son, 1 daughter. Education: Doctor of Science, Hokkaido University, Japan, 1972. Appointments: Chief Engineer, Kokusai Kogyo Co Ltd, Tokyo, Japan, 1973-77; Postdoctoral Fellow, Assistant Professor, University of Miami, 1977-85; Senior Research Scientist, Bureau of Mineral Resources, Canberra, 1985-89; Consulting Geologist, Mineral Exploration and borehole imaging, 1989-. Publications: Surge Tectonics and Paleolands in the Pacific; Numerous contributions to professional journals. Honours: Research funds from US National Science Foundation; Listed in 500 Leaders of Influence; Editor-in-chief, New Concepts in Global Tectonics Newsletter; Invited Lectures: Japan National Oil Corporation and many others. Memberships: American Association of Petroleum Geology; Geological Society of Australia. Address: 6 Mann Place, Higgins, ACT 2615, Australia.

CHOI In-Sik, b. 30 October 1971, Seongju County, Republic of Korea. Professor. m. Kyung-Ok Park, 1 son. Education: BS, Kyungpook National University, 1998; MS, 2000, PhD, 2003, Pohang University of Science and Technology. Appointments: Senior Researcher, LG Electronics, 2003-04; Senior Researcher, Agency for Defense Development, 2004-07; Assistant Professor, Hannam University, 2007-. Publications: 11 articles in international professional journals and at international conference. Honours: Listed in international biographical dictionaries. Memberships: Korea Electromagnetic Engineering Society; Institute of

Electronics Engineers of Korea. Address: Department of Electronic Engineering, Hannam University, 133 Ojung-dong, Daeduk-gu, Daejeon 306-791, Republic of Korea. E-mail: recog@hannam.ac.kr

CHOI Jae-Hak, b. 7 April 1970, Seoul, Korea. Researcher. m. Ran-Sook Cho, 2 daughters. Education: BS, 1992, MS, 1994, Department of Polymer Science & Engineering, Chungnam National University; PhD, Department of Advanced Materials Engineering, Korea Advanced Institute of Science & Technology, 1998. Appointments: Senior Researcher, Hynix Semiconductor Industries, 1998-2002; Postdoctoral Studies, Korea Advanced Institute of Science & Technology, 2002-03, 2004-05; Postdoctoral Studies, University of North Carolina at Charlotte, USA, 2003-04; Senior Researcher, Project Manager, Korea Atomic Energy Research Institute, 2005-. Publications: 25 articles in professional journals; 15 foreign and domestic journal papers; 36 international conference papers; 12 US and domestic patents. Honours: Presidential Award, Chungnam National University, 1992; Listed in international biographical dictionaries. Memberships: The Polymer Society of Korea; The Korean Society of Industrial & Engineering Chemistry; The Membrane Society of Korea; Korean Society of Radiation Industry. Address: 1266 Sinjeong-dong, Jeongeup-si, Jeollabuk-do 580-185, Korea. E-mail: jaehakchoi@kaeri.re.kr

CHOI Jeong Ryeol, b. 21 March 1963, Kyeongju, Republic of Korea. Researcher in Mathematical Physics. Education: BS, Hankuk University of Foreign Studies, Yongin, Republic of Korea, 1989-93; MS, 1993-95, PhD, 1996-2001, Korea University, Seoul, Republic of Korea. Appointment: Professor, Department of Physics and Advanced Materials Science, Sun Moon University, Asan, Republic of Korea, 2003-08; Researcher, National Institute for Mathematical Sciences, Daejeon, Republic of Korea, 2008-. Publications: Articles in scientific journals: The dependency on the squeezing parameter for the uncertainty relation in the squeezed states of the time-dependent oscillator, 2004; Coherent and squeezed states of light in linear media with time-dependent parameters by Lewis-Riesenfeld invariant operator method, 2006; Quantum analysis for the evolution of the cosmological constant via unitary transformation, 2007. Address: National Institute for Mathematical Sciences, 628 Daedeokdaero, Yuseong-gu, Daejeon 305-340, Republic of Korea. E-mail: choiardor@hanmail.net

CHOI Kang-Seuk, b. 13 November 1967, Republic of Korea. Research Scientist. m. Sang-Ae Kim, 1 son, 1 daughter. Education: DVM, 1991, MSc, 1993, Seoul National University; PhD, Chung-buk National University, 2003. Appointments: Research Scientist, National Veterinary Research & Quarantine Service, South Korea, 1991-; Expert in Mongolia, Korean International Co-operation Agency, 2003; Visiting Professor, Seoul National University, Korea, 2005-. Publications: 15 articles in international scientific journals on highly transboundary infectious animal diseases. Honours: Best Researcher Award, NVRQS, 2004, 2006. Memberships: Microbiological Society of Korea; Korean Veterinary Medical Association. Address: National Veterinary Research & Quarantine Service, 480 Anyang-6, Anyang, Gyeonggi, 430-824, Republic of Korea.

CHOI Min-Ho, b. 23 May 1970, Busan, Republic of Korea. Plastic and Reconstructive Surgeon. m. Eun-joo Lee, 1 son. Education: Bachelor of Medicine, Medical Doctor, Medical College, In-Je University, 1990-96; Medical Specialist Course of Plastic and Reconstructive Surgeon, Dong-gang Hospital,

Ulsan, 1997-2002; Chief, Substation of Sangju Public Health Centre, Sangju, 2002-03; Staff, Department of Plastic and Reconstructive Surgery, Gyeong Sang Hospital, Kyungsan, Kyungbuk, 2003-. Publications: Treatment of Bone and Tendon-Exposed Wounds using Terudermis ®, 1999; Clinical Application of Single Hair Transplantation, 2000. Honours: Award, Korean Society for Public Health and Medicine, 2002; Mayor's Award, Sangju City, 2003. Memberships: Korean Medical Association; Kyungbuk Medical Association; Korean Society for Plastic and Reconstructive Surgeons; Oriental Society of Aesthetic and Plastic Surgery; Korean Society for Aesthetic Plastic Surgery; Korean Cleft Palate-Craniofacial Association; Korean Burn Society; Korean Society for Surgery of the Hand; Korean Microsurgical Society; Korean Society for Public Health and Medicine. Address: Noblesse Plastic Surgery, 3,4,5F 516-18 Bujeon2-dong, jin-gu, Busan, Korea, 614-847. E-mail: pscmh@hanmail.net

CHOI Sang Don, b. 20 January 1939, Daegu, Korea. Professor. m. Soo-Gyeon Lee, 1 son, 1 daughter. Education: BS, Kyungpook National University, Daegu, Korea, 1958; MS, 1962; PhD, State University of New York, Buffalo, USA, 1980. Appointments: Associate Professor, 1981-86, Professor, 1986-2004, Professor Emeritus, 2004-, Director, Basic Science Research Institute, 1993-96, Kyungpook National University. Publications: Theory of Cyclotron Resonance Line Shapes; Quantum-Statistical theory of high field transport phenomena. Honours: Outstanding Publication Award; Outstanding Research Award. Memberships: Korean Physical Society; Korean Society of Industrial and Applied Mathematics; Korean Society of Medical Physics. Address: Room 103-1108, Chung-gu Mansion, Wolsung-dong, Dalseogu, Daegu 704-767, Korea. E-mail: sdchoi@knu.ac.kr

CHOI Yong-soo, b. 7 June 1963, Gwangju, Korea. Medical Doctor. m. In-ok Cho, 2 sons. Education: Medical Doctor, 1988, PhD, 2004, Chonnam National University Medical School, Gwangju, Korea. Appointments: Medical Staff, Kwangju Christian Hospital, Gwangju, 1994-; Assistant Professor, Chonnam National University, Gwangju, 1995-99; Research Fellowship, Case Western Reserve University, Cleveland, USA, 2003-04; Chairman, Korean Orthopaedic Association Homam Branch, 2006; Professor, Kidok Nursing College, Gwangju, 2007. Publications: Combined instrumentation with soft & rigid stabilizer in Deg Lumbar disorders, 1994; Plate Augmentation leaving the nail in situ and bone grafting for nonunion of femur, 2005; Bridging Demineralized bone implant facilities posterolateral lumbar fusion, 2007; Electron microprobe analysis and tissue reaction around spinal implants, 2007. Memberships: Korean Orthopaedic Association; Korean Society of Spine Surgery; SICOT; Orthopaedic Research Society in USA. Address: Kumho Apartment 101-1003, 1072 Hwajung-dong Se-gu, Gwangju 502-842, Korea. E-mail: stemcellchoi@yahoo.co.kr

CHOI Young Hee, b. 8 February 1957, Seoul, South Korea. Psychiatrist. m. Hyo Sun Kim, 1 son, 1 daughter. Education: Doctor of Medicine, College of Medicine, 1983, Master of Medicine, Graduate School of Medicine, 1989, Korea University; PhD, Graduate School of Medicine, Inje University, 2000. Appointments: Military Service, 1983-86; Intern, Kangbuk Samsung Hospital, Seoul, 1986-87; Psychiatric Residency, Seoul National Mental Hospital, Seoul, 1987-90; Medical Manager, Keyo Hospital, Incheon, 1990-94; Clinical and Research Fellowship, UCLA Neuropsychiatric Institute and Hospital, California, USA, 1994-96; Associate Professor, 1996-2005, Clinical Professor of Psychiatry, 2005-, Paik Hospital of Inje University; Director, Mettaa Institute of

Cognitive Behaviour Therapy, Seoul, 2005-. Publications: 15 books; 54 articles. Memberships: International Association of Cognitive Psychotherapy; American Psychiatric Association; Association for the Advancement of Behavior Therapy; Fellow, Academy of Cognitive Therapy; President, Korean Association of Cognitive Behavior Therapy. Address: Mettaa Institute of Cognitive Behavioural Therapy, J Bldg 2F, #93-8, Nonhyun-Dong, Gangnam-Gu, Seoul 135-010, Republic of Korea. E-mail: lotha208@kornet.net Website: www.mettaa.com

CHOMSKY (Avram) Noam, b. 7 December 1928, Philadelphia, Pennsylvania, USA. Linguist; Philosopher; Professor; Author. m. Carol Doris Schatz, 24 December 1949, 1 son, 2 daughters. Education: BA, 1949, MA, 1951, PhD, 1955, University of Pennsylvania. Appointments: Assistant Professor, 1955-58, Associate Professor, 1958-61, Professor of Modern Languages, 1961-66, Ferrari P Ward Professor of Modern Languages and Linguistics, 1966-76, Institute Professor, 1976-, Massachusetts Institute of Technology; Visiting Professor, Columbia University, 1957-58; National Science Foundation Fellow, Institute for Advanced Study, Princeton, New Jersey, 1958-59; Resident Fellow, Harvard Cognitive Studies Center, 1964-65; Linguistics Society of America Professor, University of California at Los Angeles, 1966; Beckman Professor, University of California at Berkeley, 1966-67; John Locke Lecturer, Oxford University, 1969; Shearman Lecturer, University College, London, 1969; Bertrand Russell Memorial Lecturer, Cambridge University, 1971; Nehru Memorial Lecturer, University of New Delhi, 1972; Whidden Lecturer, McMaster University, 1975; Huizinga Memorial Lecturer, University of Leiden, 1977; Woodbridge Lecturer, Columbia University, 1978; Kant Lecturer, Stanford University, 1979; Jeanette K Watson Distinguished Visiting Professor, Syracuse University, 1982; Pauling Memorial Lecturer, Oregon State University, 1995. Publications: Syntactic Structures, 1957; Current Issues in Linguistic Theory, 1964; Aspects of the Theory of Syntax, 1965; Cartesian Linguistics, Topics in the Theory of Generative Grammar, 1966; Language and Mind, Sound Patterns of English (with Morris Halle), 1968; American Power and the New Mandarins, 1969; At War with Asia, 1970; Problems of Knowledge and Freedom, 1971; Studies on Semantics in Generative Grammar, 1972; For Reasons of State, The Backroom Boys, Counterrevolutionary Violence (with Edward Herman), 1973; Peace in the Middle East?, Bains de Sang (with Edward Herman), 1974; Reflections on Language, The Logical Structure of Linguistic Theory, 1975; Essays on Form and Interpretation, 1977; Human Rights and American Foreign Policy, 1978; Language and Responsibility, The Political Economy of Human Rights (with Edward Herman), 2 volumes, 1979; Rules and Representations, 1980; Radical Priorities, Lectures on Government and Binding, 1981; Towards a New Cold War, Some Concepts and Consequences of the Theory of Government and Binding, 1982; Fateful Triangle: The United States, Israel and the Palestinians, 1983; Modular Approaches to the Study of the Mind, 1984; Turning the Tide, 1985; Barriers, Pirates and Emperors, Knowledge of Language: Its Nature, Origin and Use, 1986; Generative Grammar: Its Basis, Development and Prospects, On Power and Ideology, Language in a Psychological Setting, Language and Problems of Knowledge, The Chomsky Reader, 1987; The Culture of Terrorism, Manufacturing Consent (with Edward Herman), Language and Politics, 1988; Necessary Illusions, 1989; Deterring Democracy, 1991; Chronicles of Dissent, What Uncle Sam Really Wants, 1992; Year 501: The Conquest Continues, Rethinking Camelot: JFK, the Vietnam War, and US Political Culture, Letters from Lexington:

Reflections on Propaganda, The Prosperous Few and the Restless Many, 1993; Language and Thought, World Orders, Old and New, 1994; The Minimalist Program, 1995; Powers and Prospects, 1996; The Common Good, Profit over People, 1998; The New Military Humanism, 1999; New Horizons in the Study of Language and Mind, Rogue States: The Rule of Force in World Affairs, A New Generation Draws the Line, Architecture of Language, 2000; 9-11, 2001; Understanding Power, On Nature and Language, 2002; Middle East Illusions, Hegemony or Survival: America's Quest for Global Dominance, 2003; Contributions to: Scholarly journals. Honours: Distinguished Scientific Contribution Award, American Psychological Association, 1984; George Orwell Awards, National Council of Teachers of English, 1987, 1989; Kyoto Prize in Basic Science, Inamori Foundation, 1988; James Killian Faculty Award, Massachusetts Institute of Technology, 1992; Lannan Literary Award, 1992; Joel Selden Peace Award, Psychologists for Social Responsibility, 1993; Homer Smith Award, New York University School of Medicine, 1994; Loyola Mellon Humanities Award, Loyola University, Chicago, 1994; Helmholtz Medal, Akademie der Wissenschaft, Berlin-Brandenburg, 1996; Benjamin Franklin Medal, Franklin Institute, Philadelphia, 1999; Rabinranath Tagore Centenary Award, Asiatic Society, 2000; Peace Award, Turkish Publishers Association, 2002; Many honorary doctorates. Memberships: American Academy of Arts and Sciences; American Association for the Advancement of Science, fellow; American Philosophical Association; Bertrand Russell Peace Foundation; British Academy, corresponding member; Deutsche Akademie der Naturforscher Leopoldina; Linguistics Society of America; National Academy of Sciences; Royal Anthropological Institute; Utrecht Society of Arts and Sciences. Address: 15 Suzanne Road, Lexington, MA 02420, USA.

CHONG Tae Hyong, b. 5 August 1946, Soonchun City, Korea. Professor. m. Young Sook Song, 2 sons, 1 daughter. Education: Bachelor of Engineering, Department of Mechanical Engineering, Hanyang University, Korea, 1970; Master of Engineering, 1977, Dr. Eng, 1983, Department of Precision Mechanics, Kyoto University, Japan. Appointments: Lieutenant, Korean Army, 1970-72; Assistant Professor, 1983-87, Associate Professor, 1987-92, Professor, 1992-, Hangyang University, Korea; Foreign Visiting Professor, Kyoto University, Japan, 1986-87; Foreign Visiting Professor, University of Tokyo, Japan, 1996-97. Publications: Simple Stress Formulae for a Thin-Rimmed Spur Gear; Development of a Computer-Aided Concurrent Design System of Mechanical Design; Multiobjective Optimal Design of Cylindrical Gear Pairs for Reduction of Gear Size and Meshing Vibration; A New and Generalised Methodology to Design Multi-Stage Gear Drives by Integrating the Dimensional and the Configuration Design Process. Honour: Dr. Eng, Kyoto University, Japan, 1983. Memberships: President, KSMTE; Member, KSME; JSME; KSPE; JSPE; AGMA; Vice President, KGMA. Address: #104-404, Daerim Apt, 501 Daebang-Dong, Dongjak-ku, Seoul, Korea 156-020. E-mail: thchong@hangyang.ac.kr Website: gearlab.hangyang.ac.kr

CHOPE John Norman, b. 27 June 1948, Birmingham, England. Dental Surgeon. m. Susan Mary Le Page, 1 daughter. Education: BSc (Hons), Physiology, 1969, BDS (Hons) Bristol University Faculty of Medicine, Department of Physiology and Dental School, 1966-72; LDS RCS Eng, Royal College of Surgeons of England, 1972; MFGDP (UK) RCS Eng, Royal College of Surgeons of England, 1992. Appointments include: Trainee Dental Technician, 1965, Dental Pathology Research Technician, University of Birmingham, 1966;

Neurophysiologist, USA, Sudan, 1969, 1973; Senior House Officer, Oral Surgery, United Bristol Hospitals, 1973; Associate Dental Surgeon, Backwell, Somerset, 1973, Stockwood, Bristol and Shepton Mallet, Somerset, 1973-74, Principal Dental Surgeon and Dental Practice Owner, Holsworthy, Devon, 1974-, Hartland, Devon, 1975-, Bude, Cornwall, 1981-90, Okehampton, Devon, 1983-98; Consultant, VDC plc (Veterinary Drug Company), 1996-98; Member, British Dental Association Research Foundation Committee, 1997-2000; National Council Member, 1989-2004, Chairman, 1995-2004, Confederation of Dental Employers; National Council Member, Dental Practitioners Association, 2004-; Elected Member, 1996-, Chairman of Standards Committee, 2005-, General Dental Council; Member, Dental Technicians Association Education Committee, 2003-; Editorial Board Member, Dentistry, 2000-; Justice of the Peace, 1993-; Expert Professional Panel Member, Family Health Services Appeal Authority, 2001-. Publications: Recording from taste receptors stimulated by vascular route, 1969; Dental Practice Guide to the Therapeutic Laser, 1995; A Look at Bodies Corporate, 1997; Numerous articles in dental journals, 1974-. Honours: Duke of Edinburgh's Gold Award; Associate Dental Company Scholarships, University of Bristol, 1966-67, 1969-72; Medical Research Council Award, Bristol University, 1967-69 L E Attenborough Medal, 1972, The George Fawn Prize, 1972, Bristol University. Memberships include: British Dental Association; British Medical and Dental Hypnosis Society; Dental Practitioners Association; Medical Protection Society; International Dental Federation; Magistrates Association; Country Landowners Association; Fellow, Royal Society of Medicine; Faculty of General Dental Practitioners(UK) Royal College of Surgeons of England. Address: Penroses Dental Practice, Bodmin Street, Holsworthy, Devon EX22 6BB, England.

CHOPRA Kiron, b. 1 July 1954, New Delhi, India. Business Professional. m. Neelam, 1 son, 1 daughter. Education: BSc, Diploma in Public Administration, University of Lucknow; Licentiate of the National College of Rubber Technology, London, England; Licentiate of the Plastics and Rubber Institute of UK; Graduate of the Plastics and Rubber Institute of UK. Appointments: Executive Director, Autoflex Private Limited; Managing Director, Autoflex Private Limited; Managing Director, Chopra Retec Rubber Products Ltd; Managing Director, Interlinks Distributors Ltd; Chairman, U.P. Council, Confederation of Indian Industry; Chairman, Chopra Retec Rubber Products Ltd. Publications: Strategies for Indian Companies For A Global Footprint; The Chinese Syndrome – Is A Syndrome; On Engineering – A Key Reason For High Cost; Growth Without Diversification. Honours: Governors Award, National College of Rubber Technology, London. Memberships: Amity Business College, Lucknow; Management Committee, Jaipuria School; Mahomed Bagh Club, Lucknow; Genesis Club, Lucknow; Golf Club, Lucknow; National Council, Confederation of Iman Industry. Address: 35-G Gokhle Marg, Lucknow 226001 (UP), India.

CHOPRA Ramesh, b. 8 April 1946, Lahore, Pakistan. Publishing Director. m. Neena, 1973, 2 sons. Education: BSc, Delhi University, 1966; B Tech, IIT, Madras, 1969. Appointments: Editor, Electronics For You, New Delhi, 1969-; Managing Director, EFY Enterprises Pvt Ltd, New Delhi, 1979-. Publications: Numerous articles in professional journals; Publisher of several magazines, books and directories. Honours: Udyog Ratna, 2003; Kohinoor of India Award, All India Achievers Conference, 2006. Memberships: Fellow,

Institute of Electronics and Telecommunication Engineers. Address: D 87/1, Okhla Industrial Area, Phase-I, New Delhi – 110020, India. E-mail: efymd@efyindia.com

CHOUDARY Alla Ditta Raza, b. 5 May 1951, Lahore, Pakistan. Professor of Mathematics. m. Valentina, 1 son, 1 daughter. Education: Bachelor of Sciences, Master of Sciences, Punjab University, Lahore; PhD, Mathematics, University of Bucharest, Romania, 1980. Appointments: Professor, Faculty of Science, 1981-82, 1984-86, General Co-ordinator, School of Mathematics, 1984-90, University of Guadalajara; Visiting Professor, Institute of Basic Sciences, University of Veracruz, 1983; Visiting Professor, Max Planck Institut für Mathematik, Bonn, Germany, 1989; Visiting Professor, Herzen University, St Petersburg, Russia, 1993; Visiting Professor, University of Sydney, Australia, 1994; Exchange Professor, Shimane Women's College, Japan, 1999-2000; Exchange Professor, Anhui University and China University of Science & Technology, 2002; Assistant Professor, 1986-91, Associate Professor, 1991-96, Professor, 1996-, Mathematics Department, Central Washington University; Director General (First), School of Mathematical Sciences, Government College University, Lahore, 2003-. Publications: Author of several books and numerous research papers in prestigious international journals. Honours: Most Inspirational Educator, 2002, Distinguished Professor of Research, 2003, Central Washington University. Memberships: American Mathematical Society. Address: School of Mathematical Sciences, 68-B, New Muslim Town, Lahore, Pakistan. E-mail: choudary@cwu.edu Website: www.sms.edu.pk

CHOUN Young-Sun, b. 4 September 1955, Seoul, Republic of Korea. Researcher. m. Seong-Hee Lee, 2 sons. Education: BS, 1978, MS, 1980, Department of Civil Engineering, School of Engineering, Yonsei University; PhD, Department of Civil Engineering, Korea Advanced Institute of Science and Technology, Daejeon, 1998. Appointments: Engineer, Korea Electric Power Company, 1979-81; Senior Engineer, Shinwha Engineering and Construction Co Ltd, 1981-86; Senior Research Engineer, 1987-95, Principal Research Engineer, 1995-, Korea Atomic Energy Research Institute. Publications: 8 articles in international journals; 26 papers at international conferences; 56 reports. Memberships: Korean Society of Civil Engineers; Earthquake Engineering Society of Korea; Korean Society of Hazard Mitigation; Korean Nuclear Society. Address: 1045 Daedeok-Daero, Yuseong-Gu, Daejeon 305-353, Korea. E-mail: sunchun@kaeri.re.kr

CHOW YUN-FAT, b. 18 May 1955, Lamma Island, China. Film Actor. m. Jasmine Chow. Appointments: Actor, TV Station, TVB, Hong Kong, 1973, appearing in over 1,000 TV series. Creative Works: Films include: The Story of Woo Viet; A Better Tomorrow, 1986; God of Gamblers, 1989; The Killer; Eighth Happiness; Once a Thief, 1991; Full Contact, 1992; Hard Boiled, 1992; Peace Hotel, 1995; Broken Arrow, 1999; Anna and the King, 1999; Crouching Tiger, Hidden Dragon, 2000; King's Ransom, 2001; Bulletproof Monk, 2003; Hua Mulan, 2004; Pirates of the Caribbean: At Worlds End, 2007; Stranglehold, 2007. Honours: 7 Awards, 15 nominations. Address: c/o William Morris Agency, 151 El Camino Drive, Beverly Hills, CA 90212, USA.

CHRISTENSEN Allan Robert, b. 5 January 1953, Newton, Kansas, USA. Electronics Engineer; Enrolled Agent; Social Services Advisor; Financial Services Advisor. Education: BSc, Electrical Engineering, Wichita State University, 1976; MSc, Electrical Engineering, Southern Methodist University, Texas, 1981; Texas Notarial Law, Notary Public, Eastfield College,

Mesquite, 1991; Special Agent Training Program, Enrolled Agent License, United States Department of Treasury, Dallas, 1992; Certificate of Completion, Montano Securities School, Dallas, 1995; Accreditation, Chartered Mutual Fund Counselor Program, 1998, Accredited Asset Management Specialist Program, 1999, College for Financial Planning, Denver; State Certification, Texas Agency on Aging, Dallas, 2005; State Certification, Texas Department of Insurance, Austin, 2005. Appointments include: Enrolled Agent/Tax Advisor, self employed, Garland, Texas, 1990-; Social Worker, Volunteer Co-ordinator, Board Member, Community Restoration Services, Dallas, 1998-2000; Senior Electrical Test Engineer, Montgomery Elevators Inc, Illinois, 2000-01; Senior Electrical Test Engineer, KONE Inc, Texas, 2001-; Social Worker/State Certified Benefits Counselor, Texas Department of Aging and Disability Services, and Texas Department of Insurance, Dallas, 2005-. Publications: Numerous articles in professional journals. Honours include: J C Penney Golden Rule Award, Dallas, 1995; Defense Systems and Deign Group Stretch Award, Defense Systems and Design Group Take a Shot Award, Texas Instruments Inc, Dallas, 1996; Defense Superior Management Award, United State Navy Group Award, Dallas, 1996-97; Silver Medalist Award, 2000, Gold Medalist Award, 2001, for Educational Achievement, NATP Inc, Wisconsin. Memberships: National Association of Tax Professionals; Eta Kappa Knu; Tau Beta Phi; American MENSA; Accreditation Council for Accountancy and Taxation; Mysterium Society, USA; Texas State Board of Registered Professional Engineers. Address: 2629 Emberwood Drive, Garland, TX 75043-6047, USA. E-mail: allanchris@yahoo.com

CHRISTENSEN Helena, b. 25 December 1968, Copenhagen, Denmark. Model. 1 son. Appointments: Former child model; Adult modelling career, 1988-99; Front cover model, major magazine covers; Major contracts with: Versace; Chanel; Lagerfeld; Revlon; Rykiel; Dior; Prada and others; Magazine Photographer, 1999-. Address: c/o Marilyn's Agency, 4 Rue de la Paix, 75003 Paris, France.

CHRISTIE Julie Frances, b. 14 April 1940, Assam, India. Actress. Education: Brighton Technical College; Central School of Speech & Drama. Creative Works: Films: Crooks Anonymous, 1962; The Fast Lady, 1962; Billy Liar, 1963; Young Cassidy, 1964; Darling, 1964; Doctor Zhivago, 1965; Fahrenheit 451, 1966; Far From the Madding Crowd, 1966; Petulia, 1967; In Search of Gregory, 1969; The Go-Between, 1971; McCabe & Mrs Miller, 1972; Don't Look Now, 1973; Shampoo, 1974; Demon Seed, Heaven Can Wait, 1978; Memoirs of a Survivor, 1980; Gold, 1980; The Return of the Soldier, 1981; Les Quarantiemes rugissants, 1981; Heat and Dust, 1982; The Gold Diggers, 1984; Miss Mary, 1986; The Tattooed Memory, 1986; Power, 1987; Fathers and Sons, 1988; Dadah is Death (tv), 1988; Fools of Fortune, 1989; McCabe and Mrs Miller, 1990; The Railway Station, 1992; Hamlet, 1995; Afterglow, 1998; The Miracle Maker (voice), 2000; No Such Thing, 2001; Snapshots, 2001; I'm With Lucy, 2002; Troy, 2004; Harry Potter and the Prisoner of Azkaban, 2004; Finding Neverland, 2004; The Secret Life of Words, 2005; Away From Her, 2006. Plays: Old Times, 1995; Suzanna Andler, 1997; Afterglow, 1998. Honours include: Motion Picture Laurel Award, Best Dramatic Actress, 1967; Motion Picture Herald Award, 1967. Address: c/o International Creative Management, 76 Oxford Street, London W1D 1BS, England.

CHRISTIE Linford, b. 2 April 1960, St Andrews, Jamaica. Athlete. 1 daughter. Appointments: Cashier, Wandsworth Co-op; Member, Thames Valley Harriers; Winner, UK 100m,

1985, 1987, 200m, 1985 (tie), 1988; Winner, Amateur Athletics Association 100m, 1986, 1988, 200m, 1988; Winner, European 100m Record; Silver Medallist, 100m, Seoul Olympic Games, 1988, Winner 100m Gold Medal, Commonwealth Games, 1990, Olympic Games, 1992; World Athletic Championships, 1993, Weltklasse Grand Prix Games, 1994, European Games, 1994; Winner 100m, Zurich, 1995; Co-Founder (with Colin Jackson), Managing Director, Nuff Respect sports man co, 1992-; Captain, British Athletics Team, 1995-97; Retired, 1997; Successful coach to several prominent UK athletes. Publications: Linford Christie (autobiography), 1989; To Be Honest With You, 1995; A Year in the Life of Linford Christie, 1996. Honours include: Male Athlete of the Year, 1988, 1992; BBC Sports Personality of the Year, 1993. Address: The Coach House, 107 Sherland Road, Twickenham, Middlesex TW9 4HB, England.

CHRISTODOULOU Christodoulos, b. 13 April 1939, Avgorou, Cyprus. Central Bank Governor. m. Maria, 1 daughter. Education: Bachelor's Degree in Political Sciences, Pantios High School of Political Sciences, Athens, Greece, 1968; Bachelor's Degree in Law, Aristotelian University of Salonica, Greece, 1972; PhD, Labour Law, University of Wales, Wales, UK, 1992. Appointments: Director of the Government Printing Office, 1972-85; Permanent Secretary at the Ministry of Labour and Social Insurance, 1985-89; Permanent Secretary at the Ministry of Agriculture and Natural Resources, 1989-94; Minister of Finance, 1994-99; Minister of Interior, 1999-2002; Governor of the Central Bank of Cyprus, 2002-07. Publications: Numerous studies and articles on legal, social and economic matters. Address: Ionos 20, Apt 501, 2406, Engomi, Nicosia, Cyprus. E-mail: christodoulou_c@cytanet.com.cy

CHRISTOPH Peter Richard, b. 25 April 1938, Albany, New York, USA. Editor; Librarian. m. Florence Anna Weaver, 2 sons, 2 daughter. Education: BA, Hartwick College, 1960; MA, 1964, Master of Library Science, 1968, State University of New York at Albany; Certificate, Institute of Archival Administration, University of Denver, 1969; Seminars in 17th and 18th century Dutch Language, Albany Institute of History and Art, 1978-79. Appointments: Student Librarian, 1965-67, Assistant Librarian, 1967-68, Cataloguing Section, Senior Librarian, 1968-72, Associate Librarian, 1972-77, Manuscripts and History, Associate Librarian, Manuscripts and Special Collections, 1977-88, Associate Librarian, New Netherland Project, 1988-91, New York State Library; Editor, New York Historical Manuscripts, 1974-. Publications: 12 books; Numerous articles in professional journals. Honours: Elected Fellow, Holland Society of New York, 1979; Grant, National Endowment for the Humanities for Historical Editing, 1992-94; Finalist, Jefferson Award for Public Service, 2005; Listed in international biographical dictionaries. Memberships: Town of Bethlehem Historical Association; Tombstone Territory Rendezvous; New Netherland Institute; Wild West Historical Association. Address: 181 Maple Ave, Selkirk, NY 12158, USA. E-mail: pchrist1@nycap.rr.com

CHRUŚCIEL Tadeusz Lesław, b. 30 January 1926, Lwów, Poland. Physician. 2 sons, 1 daughter. Education: MD, Faculty of Medicine, Medical Academy, Cracow, 1951; Postgraduate Fellow, Oxford, England, 1960; Affiliate Member, Royal Society of Medicine, London, 1960; Professorship, State Council, 1986; D hc (doctor honoris causa) Silesian Medical Academy, Katowice, 1998. Appointments: Academy of Medicine, Cracow, 1948-56; Professor, Chairman, Academy of Medicine, Zabrze, 1956-68; Senior Medical Officer, Drug Dependence, WHO, Geneva, 1968-75; Drug Research

DICTIONARY OF INTERNATIONAL BIOGRAPHY

Institute, Warsaw, 1976-85; Postgraduate Medical School, Warsaw, 1986-97; President of Board, Charity Foundation (J Wyzner) to treat cancer, 1992-; retired, 1997. Publications: Over 300 research papers and articles contributed to specialist journals. Honours: Polonia Restituta Commander's Cross, 2001; Distinction, Meritus pro Medicis, 2005; Numerous research awards. Memberships: International Narcotics Control Board, 1979-83; National Physicians' Council, President, 1989-93; WHO expert advisory panel on drug dependence, 1978-99; National Physicians & Dentist Chamber; Member of National Physician's Council, 1997-; NPC Member, 2001-; Commission of Social Response to Pharmacotherapy, Polish Academy of Sciences, 2004; Catholic Association of Polish Physicians GC Secretary, 2002-2006. Address: 6 Dzika Str, App 284, PL-00-172, Warsaw, Poland.

CHU Eui-Tak, b. 12 June 1960, Seoul, Korea. Medical Doctor. m. Sung-Shin Park, 2 sons. Education: Premedical, 1981, Bachelorship (Medicine), 1986, Mastership (Anatomy), 1994, College of Medicine, University of Chungang, Seoul. Appointments: Active Duty, Korean Army, 1986-89; Intern, 1989-90, Resident, 1990-94, Kangnam Sacred Heart Hospital, Seoul; Research Fellow, Severance Arthroscopy Surgery Unit, College of Medicine, University of Yonsei, Seoul, 1994-95; Instructor, 1994-95, Abroad Professor, 1995-, Department of Orthopaedic Surgery, Chunchon Sacred Heart Hospital, College of Medicine, University of Hallym, Kangwon; Research Fellow, Southern California Orthopedic Institute, USA, 1996; Research Fellow, Center for Sports Medicine & Rehabilitation, University of Pittsburgh, USA, 1995-96; Chief, Chu's Orthopaedic Surgery Clinic, Sports Medicine and Arthroscopy, Seoul, 1999-; Head Team Doctor, Doosan Bears Professional Baseball Club, Seoul, 1999-; Attending Doctor, SK Knights Professional Basketball Club, Seoul, 1999-; Attending Doctor, Samsung Thunders Professional Basketball Club, Seoul, 2000-04; Attending Doctor, Ulsan Mobis Phoebus Professional Basketball Club, Ulsan, 2000-. Publications: Books include: Backache, Arthritis, Osteoporosis, Obesity, Let's Overcome with Exercise, 1998; Dr Chu's Joint Clinic, 2002; Numerous articles in national and international journals including: Arthroscopic Posterior Cruciate Ligament Reconstruction, 1997; Arthoscopic Treatment for Localized Pigmented Villonodular Synovitis of the Knee, 2000. Honours: Excellent Medical Practice Award, Kangnam Sacred Heart Hospital, 1993; Failed Lumbar Disc Surgery, Korean Orthopaedic Association, 1994; Twice winner, Mahnrye Memorial Foundation, Korean Orthopaedic Association, 1998. Memberships: European Society of Sport Traumatology, Knee Surgery and Arthroscopy; Arthroscopy Association of North America; Seoul Seocho-District Medical Association; Korean Orthopaedic Society for Sports Medicine; Korean Shoulder and Elbow Society; Korean Arthroscopy Association; Korean Orthopaedic Practitioners Association; Korean Orthopaedic Association; Korean Medical Association.

CHU Kent-Man, b. 12 July 1963, Hong Kong. Doctor; Surgeon. Education: MB, BS, 1987; FRCS (Ed), 1992; FCSHK, 1992; FHKAM (Surgery), 1995; FACS, 1998; MS, 2001. Appointments: Professor, Chief of Division of Upper GI Surgery, Department of Surgery, University of Hong Kong Medical Centre; Director, Surgical Endoscopy Centre; Co-Director, Centre for Education and Training; Honorary Consultant and Deputy Chief of Service, Department of Surgery, Queen Mary Hospital; Honorary Consultant, Department of Surgery, Tung Wah Hospital; Director, Hong Kong Surgical Forum; Honorary Consultant in Surgery, Hong Kong Sanatorium & Hospital. Publications: 1 Master

of Surgery thesis; 139 Full Articles; 3 Book Chapters; 123 Abstracts; Invited speaker or faculty, 152 occasions; Listed in national and international biographical dictionaries. Honours: International Guest Scholar, The American College of Surgeons, 1999; Akita Award, Japanese Society of Gastroenterological Society, 2001; Faculty Teaching Medal, 2003. Memberships: 12 International or Local Associations and Colleges; Secretary General, Asian Surgical Association, 2005-. Address: Department of Surgery, University of Hong Kong Medical Centre, Queen Mary Hospital, Pokfulam, Hong Kong. Website: www.hku.hk/surgery/

CHU Tzong-Shinn, b. 1 September 1957, Keelung, Taiwan. Medicine. m. Guey-Shiun Huang, 1 son, 1 daughter. Education: MD, School of Medicine, 1982, PhD, Graduate Institute of Clinical Medicine, 1996, National Taiwan University. Appointments: Attending Physician, Department of Internal Medicine, National Taiwan University Hospital, 1989-; Associate Professor, Department of Primary Care Medicine, National Taiwan University College of Medicine, 2000-; Fellow in Nephrology, University of Texas, Southwestern Medical School at Dallas, 1993-95; Secretary General, Taiwan Association of Medical Education, 2004-. Publications: Numerous articles in international medical journals. Honours: Research Award, Taiwan Society of Nephrology, 1992, 1997, 2001; Research Award, National Science Council Taiwan, 1996, 1997, 2000; Teaching Award NTUH, 1998. Memberships: International Society of Nephrology; American Society of Nephrology; Society of General Internal Medicine. Address: 3-1, 3rd Floor, Lane 276, Rui-An Street, Taipei, Taiwan. E-mail: tschu@ntu.edu.tw

CHUANG Li-Yeh, b. 27 September 1958, Taiwan. Professor. m. Cheng-Hong Yang, 2 daughters. Education: MS, Department of Chemistry, UNC, USA, 1989; PhD, Department of Biochemistry, NDSU, USA, 1994. Appointments: Associate Professor, 1989-2007, Professor, 2007-, Department of Chemical Engineering, I-Shou University. Publications: BMC Bioinformatics/V-MitoSNP – Visualization of Human Mitochondrial SNPs. Honours: Listed in international biographical dictionaries. Memberships: Association of Chemical Engineering. E-mail: chuang@isu.edu.tw

CHUANG Yii-Der, b. 1 July 1934, Chekiang, China. Retired Business Executive and Diplomat. m. Chung-Hwa Lee, 2 sons, 1 daughter. Education: BS, Automotive Engineering, Chung-Cheng Institute of Science and Technology, 1957; MS, Metallurgical Engineering, Michigan State University, USA, 1966; PhD, Materials Science, New York University, USA, 1971. Appointments: Director, Hot Laboratory, Nuclear Energy Research Institute, Atomic Energy Council, Taiwan, 1972-82; Senior Scientist, Science and Technology Advisory Group, Executive Yuan, Taipei, Taiwan, 1980-84; Deputy Director, Preparation Office Materials Research Laboratory, Industrial Technology Research Institute, Taiwan, 1981-82; Deputy Director, Materials Research and Development Centre, Chung Shan Institute of Science and Technology, Taiwan, 1982-84; Director, Science Division, Taipei Economic and Cultural Office, Houston, 1984-86, San Francisco, 1986-92, Washington DC, USA, 1992-2000; President, H & Q Asia Pacific, Taiwan Office, 2000-2002; Senior Advisor, WI Harper Group, 2004-. Publications: 38 articles in scientific journals include: Beta Brass Bicrystal Stress-Strain Relations, 1973; Iodine-Induced Stress Corrosion Cracking of Cu-Barrier Zircaloy-4 Tubes, 1981; A New Processing System and Method for Examination of Irradiated Fuel Elements, 1981. Honours: A Hero Medal, President, Chiang Kai-Shek, Republic of China, 1963; Distinguished Scholar, New York

University, 1972; Listed in Who's Who publications and biographical dictionaries. Memberships: Founding Member, Monte Jade Science and Technology Association, West Coast, USA; Alpha Sigma Mu Honor Society; Founding Member, The Chinese Society for Materials Science. Address: 11F-5, No 70, Sec 2, An-He Road, Taipei 10680, Taiwan, Republic of China. E-mail: ydchuang@ms77.hinet.net

CHUN Dong Hyun, b. 23 March 1979, Mokpo, Jeonnam, Republic of Korea. Researcher. Education: BSc, 2001, MSc, 2003, PhD, 2007, Materials Science and Engineering, Korea Advanced Institute of Science and Technology. Appointments: Research Assistant, 2001-02, Research and Teaching Assistant, 2003-06, Department of Materials Science and Engineering, KAIST, Daejeon; Guest Scientist, Fuel Cell Materials Center, National Institute for Materials Science, Tsukuba, Ibaraki, Japan, 2004-05; Senior Researcher, Synfuel Research Center, Korea Institute of Energy Research, Daejeon, 2007-. Publications: Numerous articles in professional journals. Honours: Poster Presentation Award, Korean Institute of Metals and Materials; Grant, International Research Collaboration Program, Korea Research Foundation; Academic Paper Award, Korean Institute of Metals and Materials; PhD Thesis Award, Korea Advanced Institute of Science and Technology; Listed in international biographical dictionaries. Memberships: Korean Institute of Metals and Materials; Japanese Institute of Metals; American Institute of Chemical Engineers; Korean Institute of Chemical Engineers; Korean Electrochemical Society. Address: Synfuel Research Center, Korea Institute of Energy Research, 71-2 Jang-Dong, Yuseong-Gu, Daejeon 305-343, Republic of Korea. E-mail: cdhsl@kier.re.kr

CHUN Jae-Wook, b. 26 July 1939, Goseong, Gangwon-do, Korea. Educator. m. Hee-Jae Ko, 2 sons. Education: Graduate, Department of Laws, Sunkyunkwan University, 1962; Honorary Doctorate of Laws, Southern Weslayan University, USA, 1982; High-rank course, Educational Culture, Graduate School of Education, Yonsei University, 1996. Appointments: Dean, Dong-U College, 1989; Member, Central Edcuational Committee, Department of Education, 1990; Chairman, Council of Korean Colleges, 1990; Founder and Director, Kyung-Bok Educational Foundation, 1991-; Honorary President, Founder, Kyung Dong University, 2001-. Honours: Korean National Pomegranate Medallion, 1989. Memberships: 28th Central Chairman, Corporation Aggregate of Korean Junior Chamber, 1979; Head, Korean Federation for Libery, Seoul Branch, 1989. Address: Kyung Dong University, San 91-1, Bongpo-ri, Toseong-myeon, Goseong-gun, Gangwon Province, 219-832, Korea. Website: www.k1.ac.kr

CHUN Jang Ho, b. 23 November 1948, Koyang, Kyunggido, Korea. Professor; Researcher. m. Kyung Won Hong, 1 son, 1 daughter. Education: Bachelor of Electronic Engineering, Kwangwoon University, Seoul, Korea 1968-75; Master of Electronic Engineering, Yonsei University, Seoul, Korea, 1976-78; PhD, Electrophysics, Stevens Institute of Technology, New Jersey, USA, 1980-84; Professor and Researcher, Kwangwoon University, 1984-; Technical Advisor, Mission Telecom Company, Seoul, Korea, 2004-; Visiting Scientist, Princeton University, New Jersey, USA, 1988-89; Visiting Scientist, University of Tokyo, Tokyo, Japan, 1994. Publications include: The phase-shift method for determining adsorption isotherms of hydrogen at electrified interfaces; Methods for determining adsorption isotherms in electrochemical systems; Correlation constants between adsorption isotherms of intermediates in electrochemical systems. Honours: Commendation for Excellent Teaching

and Research, Korea Government, 1997, 2006; Fellowships for Visiting Scientists, Korea Science and Engineering Foundation, 1988-1989, 1994; Studying Abroad Scholarship, Korea Government, 1980-84; The Most Excellent Graduation, Kwangwoon University, 1979; Award of Excellent Papers, Korean Federation of Science and Technology Societies, 2006; Listed in Who's who publications and biographical dictionaries. Memberships: The Electrochemical Society; International Association for Hydrogen Energy; The Korean Electrochemical Society. Address: Department of Electronic Engineering, Kwangwoon University, Seoul 139-701, Korea. E-mail: jhchun@kw.ac.kr

CHUN Young Nam, b. 3 July 1961, Paju, Gyeonggi, Republic of Korea. Professor. m. Eum Mi Kang, 2 daughters. Education: BA, 1983, PhD, 1993, Inha University; Postdoctoral, University of Illinois at Chicago, 1999. Appointments: Visiting Researcher, Institute of IVD, Stuttgart University, Germany, 1990; Research, Development Institute of Korea Gas Corporation, 1990-92; Visiting Researcher, Institute of IVD, Stuttgart University, 1992-93; Visiting Researcher, Russian Academy of Sciences, 1993-94; Visiting Professor, McMaster University, 2004-05; Full Time Lecturer, 1994-96, Assistant Professor, 1996-2000, Associate Professor, 2000-05, Professor, 2005-, Chosun University, Korea; Head, Environmental Institute, Chosun University, 2007-; Technology Planning Committee Member, Korea Institute of Energy and Resources Technology Evaluation and Planning, 2008-. Publications: Air Pollution Engineering, 2000; Incineration and Air Pollution Control, 2002; Environmental Design and CAD, 2004; Environmental and Pollution, 2004. Honours: Best Teacher, Chosun University, 2001; Paper Award, Korea Society of Environmental Engineers; 2003; Listed in Who's Who publications and biographical dictionaries. Memberships: Korea Society of Environmental Engineers; Korean Society of Mechanical Engineers; Korean Society of Combustion. Address: Chosun University, #375 Seosuk-dong, Dong-gu, Gwangju 501-759, Republic of Korea. E-mail: ynchun@chosun.ac.kr

CHUNG Bum-Jin, b. 9 February 1965, Seoul, Korea. Professor. m. Il Sun, 1 son. Education: Bachelor's degree, 1987, Master's degree, 1989, PhD, 1994, Seoul National University, Korea. Appointments: Deputy Director, Ministry of Science and Technology, 1995-2002; Lecturer, Kyunghee University, 1996-99; Visiting Researcher, Manchester University, England, 1999-2001; Professor, Cheju National University, 2002-. Publications: Numerous articles in professional journals. Honours: Best Presentation Award, International Youth Nuclear Congress, 2004; Listed in international biographical directories. Memberships: Life Member, Korean Nuclear Society; Life Member, Korean Energy Engineering Society; Editor, Korean Radioactive Waste Society. Address: Cheju National University; Department of Nuclear & Energy Engineering, 66 Jejudaehakno, Jeju-Si, Jeju-Do, Korea. E-mail: bjchung@cheju.ac.kr

CHUNG Chan Kook, b. 8 September 1942, Seoul, Korea. Physician. m. Eun Hee, 1 son, 1 daughter. Education: MD, Yonsei University College of Medicine, 1967; Rotating Internship, Long Island College Hospital, Brooklyn, New York, 1971; Radiation Oncology Residency, Jefferson University Hospital, Philadephia, Pennsylvania, 1975. Appointments: Assistant Professor, University of Virginia Hospital, Charlottesville, Virginia, 1976-77; Associate Director, PA State University Hospital, Hershey, Pennsylvania, 1977-82; Chairman, Radiation Oncology Department, WA Hospital, Takoma Park, Maryland, 1982-; Director,

College Park Radiotherapy Center, College Park, Maryland, 1986-89; Director, Greenbelt Radiotherapy Center, Greenbelt, Maryland, 1997-2002. Publications: 38 publications including: Analysis & Factors Contributing to Treatment Failure in Stage IB IIA Carcinoma & Cancer, 1981; Evaluation and Adjacent Post-op Radiotherapy for Lung Cancer, 1982. Honours: Fellow, American College of Radiology, 1996; FACRO, 2002; Washingtonian Best Doctor, America's Top Physician, Consummer's Research Council of America, 2004-05. Memberships: ASTRO; ARS; ABS; ACRO; ACR. Address: 9810 Sorrel Avenue, Potomac, Maryland 20854, USA. E-mail: cchung@ahm.com

CHUNG Ihn Hwa, b. 24 September 1947, Kwangyang, Jeon nam, Korea. Doctor; Orthopaedic Specialist. m. Yoon Soo Lee, 2 sons. Education: Bachelor's degree, 1973, Orthopaedics Specialist Certification, 1981, 1981; Kyunghee University, Seoul; Master's degree, Graduate School of Medicine, Kyunghee University, 1980; Doctor's degree, Graduate School of Medicine, Korea University, 1983. Appointments: Professor Extrordinary, Kyunghee University, 1992; Professor Extrordinary, Korea University, 1993; Chairman of the Board, Kyunghee International Medical Co-operation Society, 1993-2006; Medical Consultant to the Public Prosecutor, 1997-; President, Seongnam Medical Association, 1997-2000; President, Sooncheon Foundation, Chung Hospital, 1998-; Committee Member of Insurance, Korean Orthopaedic Association, 1998-2003; Member of Standing Committee, Korean National Red Cross, Gyeonggi branch, 1999-2005; Chairman, Seongnam branch, Suwon District Public Prosecutor's Office, The Crime Prevention Committee members, Seongnam Area Conference, 2000-02; Chairman, Pavement Promotion Committee, Seongnam Pan-citizen Public Order Establishment, 2000-02; Chief Director, Enheangnamu Teenager Guidance Scholarship, 2004-; Governor, Korean Hospital Association and Gyeanggi-do Hospital Association; Board of Directors, Gyeonggi branch chairman, Korean Orthopaedic Association, 2005-; Chairman, Court of Justice Mediation Committee, Suwon District Court, Seongnam Lower Court, 2006-; President, Korean Small & Medium Hospital Association, 2006-. Publications: Papers and articles in professional medical journals; Joint Supervisor and Translator, Manual of Arthroscopic Surgery. Honours: Numerous awards including: Letter of Appreciation, President of the National Agricultural Co-operation Federation, 2001; Letter of Appreciation, President of Suwon District Court, 2001; Master Merchant Prince, Korean Medical Service, 2003; Seock-ru Prince, Ministry of Justice Crime Prevention Medal, 2004; Gold Prize, Korea National Red Cross, 2005; Letter of Appreciation, Director of National Police Agency, 2006. Memberships: Seongnam Medical Association; Korean Orthopaedic Association. Address: Chung Orthopaedic Hospital, 2968 Sujin2-dong, Sujong-gu, Seongnam 461-182, Korea.

CHUNG Ilyong, b. 14 October 1958, Gwangju, Korea, Professor. m. Haejeong Noh, 1 son, 1 daughter. Education: BE, Department of Metallurgical Engineering, Hanyang University, Korea, 1983; MS, 1987, PhD, 1991, Department of Computer Science, City University of New York, USA. Appointments: Senior Member of Technical Staff, ETRI Korea, 1991-94; Professor, 1994-, Associate Dean, College of Information Science, 1997-98, Director, University Information and Computing Centre, 1999-2000, Director, Information and Communications Security Research Centre, 2000-2001, Chosun University, Korea; Associate Editor, Journal of Korea Multimedia Society, 2004-. Publication: Design of an efficient load balancing algorithm on distributed

networks by employing a symmetric balanced incomplete block design (journal article), 2004. Honours: Listed in international biographical dictionaries. Memberships: IEEE; IEICE; KISS; KMMS; KICS. Address: Department of Computer Science, Chosun University, Gwangju 501-759, Korea. E-mail: iyc@chosun.ac.kr

CHUNG Inho, b. 20 December 1960, Jinhye, Korea. Professor. m. Yuko Takahashi, 2 sons. Education: Bachelor's degree, Education, Dankook University, 1987; Master's degree, 1990, Doctor's degree, 1993, Education, University of Tsukuba. Appointments: Solder in Korean Army, 1982-84; Research Student, University of Tsukuba, 1987-88; Lecturer, Special Education Department, Dankook University, 1993-94; Assistant, Humanities College, Tokyo Seitoku University, 1994-96; Assistant Professor, 1996-99, Associate Professor, 1999-, Institute of Disability Sciences, University of Tsukuba. Publications: Books: Reading Comprehension Process in the Deaf and Hard of Hearing, 1996; Education for Deaf and Hard of Hearing, 1998; Introduction to Special Education, 2000; Articles: Intra-Individual Variation in Reading at Different Levels of Interest; Analysis of Eye Movements of Children who are Hearing-Impaired, 2002. Honours: Listed in international biographical dictionaries. Memberships: Association of Disability Sciences; Japanese Reading Association; Korean Association for Children with Special Needs; Japanese Association of Special Education; Japanese Association for International Students Education. Address: #15-52 Nazukari, Nagareyama, Chiba 270-0145, Japan. E-mail: ichung@human.tsukuba.ac.jp

CHUNG Lan, b. 13 July 1952, Hampeong, Chonnam, Korea. Professor. m. Myong-Soon Kim, 2 sons, 1 daughter. Education: BS, 1976, MS, 1978, Architectural Engineering, Seoul National University; PhD, Civil Engineering, Northwestern University, 1988. Appointments: Assistant Professor, Associate Professor, Professor, 1980-, Dean, College of Architecture, 2005-, Dankook University; Director, Seismic Retrofitting & Remodeling Research Center, Dankook University, National Research Laboratory, 2002-. Publications: Author, Design of Concrete Structures, 2002; Author, Building Code and Commentary of Requirements of Concrete Structures, 2003; Editor, Journal of Seismic Retrofitting and Remodeling Research Center, 2002. Honours: Outstanding Paper Awards, Korea Concrete Institute, 1996; Award, Ministry of Construction and Transportation, 2006. Memberships: The National Academy of Engineering of Korea; Architectural Institute of Korea; Korea Concrete Institute; American Concrete Institute. Address: Department of Architectural Engineering, San 8, Hannam-dong, Yongsan-ku, Seoul 140-714, Republic of Korea. E-mail: lanchung@dku.edu Website: www.srrc.co.kr

CHUNG Sung Gyo, b. 19 May 1952, Hadong, South Korea. University Professor. Education: BS, Dong-A University, 1979; MSc, 1981, PhD, 1989, Seoul National University. Appointments: Geotechnical Engineer, Han-Yang Engineering Co Ltd, 1982-83; Lecturer, later Professor, Dong-A University, 1983-; Member of 34 advisory committees for government and others, 1985-; Visiting Scholar, University of Surrey, England, 1992-93. Publications: 5 books; 73 papers; 123 conference papers. Honours: Academic Award, Korean Geotechnical Society, 2002; Writing Award, 2003, Academic Award, 2006, Korean Society of Civil Engineers. Memberships: ASCE, US; ICE, UK; JGS, Japan; ISSMGE; KSCE, Korea; KGS, Korea; ATC-7, ISSMGE. Address: Dong-A University, School of Civil Engineering, 840 Hadan-dong, Saha-gu, Busan 604-714, Korea. E-mail: sgchung@dau.ac.kr

CHUNG Woojin, b. 20 November 1970, Seoul, Korea. Professor. Education: BS, Mechanical Engineering, Seoul National University, Korea, 1993; MS, 1995, PhD, 1998, Mechanical Engineering, University of Tokyo, Japan. Education: Senior Research Scientist, Korea Institute of Science and Technology, 1998-2005; Assistant Professor, Department of Mechanical Engineering, Korea University, 2005-. Publications: Non-holonomic Manipulators, 2004; Springer Handbook of Robotics, Chapter 13, 2008. Honours: Best Paper Award, Robotics Society of Japan, 1996; King-sun Fu Memorial Best Transaction Paper Award, IEEE Robotics and Automotion Society, 2002. Memberships: IEEE; Robotics Society of Japan; Korea Robotics Society. Address: Division of Mechanical Engineering, Korea University, Anam-dong, Sungbuk-ku, Seoul 136-701, Korea. E-mail: smartrobot@korea.ac.kr

CHUNG Woon Jin, b. 12 September 1972, Seoul, Republic of Korea. Assistant Professor. m. Hae Kyun Yoon. Education: BS, 1995, MS, 1997, PhD, 2001, Pohang University of Science and Technology (POSTECH). Appointments: Research Fellow, University of Leeds, England, 2002-03; Postdoctoral Research Fellow, Pohang University of Science and Technology (POSTECH), 2003; Senior Research Staff, Electronics & Telecommunications Research Institute (ETRI), 2003-06; Assistant Professor, Kongju National University, 2006-. Publications: 28 scientific and technical journal papers, including 24 SCI-rated. Honours: Listed in international biographical dictionaries. Memberships: Korean Ceramic Society. Address: 104-1202 Eunhasoo Apt, Dunsan-dong, Seo-gu, Daejeon, 302-733, Republic of Korea. E-mail: wjin@kongju.ac.kr

CHURCH Charlotte Maria, b. 21 February 1986, Llandaff, Cardiff, Wales. Singer. 1 daughter. Career: Albums include: Voice of an Angel, 1998; Charlotte Church, 1999; Christmas Offering, 2000; Dream a Dream, 2000; Enchantment, 2001; Tissues and Issues, 2005; Singles: Crazy Chick, 2005; Call My Name, 2005; Performances include: Charlotte Church: Voice of an Angel in Concert, 1999; Dream a Dream: Charlotte Church in the Holy Land, 2000; The Royal Variety Performance 2001, 2001; The 43rd Annual Grammy Awards, 2001; Concerts include: Hollywood Bowl; Hyde Park. Preludes include: Pie Jesu; Panis Anjulicus; Dream a Dream; The Prayer (duet with Josh Groban); It's the Heart that Matters; TV Appearances include: Heartbeat, 1999; Touched by an Angel, 1999; Have I Got News For You, 2002; The Kumars at No. 42, 2002; Parkinson, 2002, 2005; Friday Night with Jonathon Ross, 2003, 2005; This Morning, 2005; The Paul O'Grady Show, 2005, 2006; The Charlotte Church Show, 2006; Numerous others; Film: I'll Be There, 2003. Publications: Voice of An Angel – My Life (So Far), autobiography, 2001.

CHURCHILL Caryl, b. 3 September 1938, London, England. Dramatist. m. David Harter, 1961, 3 sons. Education: BA, Lady Margaret Hall, Oxford, 1960. Career: Playwright: Stage plays: Having a Wonderful Time, 1960; Owners, 1972; Objections to Sex and Violence, 1975; Vinegar Tom, 1976; Light Shining in Buckinghamshire, 1976; Traps, 1977; Cloud Nine, 1979; Top Girls, 1982; Fen, 1983; Softcops, 1984; A Mouthful of Birds, 1986; Serious Money, 1987; Ice Cream, 1989; Lives of the Great Poisoners, 1991; The Skriker, 1994; Thyestes, 1994; Hotel, 1997; This is a Chair, 1997; Blue Heart, 1997; Faraway, 2000; A Number, 2002; Drunk Enough to Say I Love You, 2006; Radio: The Ants; Not…not…not… not enough Oxygen; Abortive; Schreiber's Nervous Illness; Identical Twins; Perfect Happiness; Henry's Past; Television: The Judge's Wife; The After Dinner Joke; The Legion Hall

Bombing; Fugue. Publications: Owners, 1973; Light Shining, 1976; Traps, 1977; Vinegar Tom, 1978; Cloud Nine, 1979; Top Girls, 1982; Fen, 1983; Fen and Softcops, 1984; A Mouthful of Birds, 1986; Serious Money, 1987; Plays I, 1985; Plays II, 1988; Objections to Sex and Violence in Plays by Women Vol 4, 1985; Ice Cream, 1989; Mad Forest, 1990; Lives of the Great Poisoners, 1992; The Striker, 1994; Thyestes, 1994; Blue Heart, 1997; This is a Chair, 1999; Far Away, 2000; A Number, 2002; anthologies. Address: c/o Casarotto Ramsay Ltd, National House, 60-66 Wardour Street, London W1V 3HP, England.

CHUSHKIN Dmitry, b. 10 May 1969, Bashkiriya, USSR. Deputy Director of Federal Tax Service. m. Svetlana, 1 son, 1 daughter. Education: Ufa State Aviation Technical University. Appointments: Specialist of First Category, 1995-96, Chief Expert, 1996, Main Expert, 1996-97, Deputy Chief, 1997-98, Chief of Information Division, 1998-99, State Tax Inspection, Republic of Bashkortostan; Chief, Division of Information Support, Directorate of Taxation, Moscow, 1999-2000; Deputy Chief, Directorate of Taxation, Moscow, 2000-03; Deputy Minister, Russian Federation of Taxation, 2003-05; Deputy Chief, Fedaral Tax Service of Russia, 2005-. Publications: Business processes modeling in taxation inspections, 2006. Honours: Excellent Expert, Ministry of Taxation of Russian Federation.

CHVOJ Zdenek, b. 16 March 1948, Prague, Czechoslovakia. Scientist. m. Blanka Svobodova, 1 son, 1 daughter. Education: RNDr, Charles University, Prague, 1976; CSc, Charles University, 1977; DSc, 1990; Doctorate, Technical University, Prague, 1995. Appointments: Lecturer, Technical University Prague, 1969, 1992-; Researcher, Charles University, Prague, 1971-75; Institute of Physics ASCR, Prague, 1975-; Editor-in-Chief, Czechoslovak Journal of Physics. Publications: Co-author, Recent Trends in Crystal Growth, 1988; Kinetic Phase Diagrams, 1991; Co-editor, Collective Diffusion on Surfaces, 2001; More than 100 articles and papers contributed to professional journals. Honours: Honorary Appreciation Award, CSAV, 1982; Recipient, Czech Literature Foundation Award, 1986. Memberships: Czech Union of Mathematicians and Physicists; Editorial Board, Academia, Prague. Address: Institute of Physics, ASCR, vvi, Na Slovance 2, 18221 Prague 8, Czech Republic.

CHWESIUK Krzysztof, b. 23 February 1949, Biała Poldaslka, Poland. Communications Specialist. 1 daughter. Education: Engineering MSc, Communication, Technical University of Warsaw, 1973; PhD, Applied Informatics, System Analysis Institute, Polish Academy of Sciences, 1979; Full Professor, University of Szczecin, Poland, 1994. Appointments: Technical University of Warsaw, 1973-74; Institute of Systems Research, Polish Academy of Sciences, Warsaw, 1974-81; Technical University of Szczecin, 1981-95; Maritime University of Szczecin, 1995-. Publications: In the area of transport: 4 books; 7 monographs; 126 papers; 156 research papers. Honours: Man of the Year 2002, American Biographical Institute; American Medal of Honor, American Biographical Institute. Memberships: UN ECE WP4; UN ECE WP24. Address: 62 Zakole Str f.n. 7, 71-454 Szczecin, Poland. E-mail: chwesiuk@wsm.szczecin.pl

CIAMPI Sara, b. 24 January 1976, Genova, Italy. Writer; Journalist; Literary Critic. Education: Leaving Certificate, Linguistics School; Laurea Honoris Causa, Literature; Laurea Honoris Causa, Philosophy; Certificate, Ordre Docteurs Cee; Master Diploma, Literature and Philosophy. Career: Literary activity began at 14 years of age stimulated initially by significant health problems and later by serious illness (tuberculosis, malaria and scoliosis). Publications: Momenti, 1995; Malinconia di Un'anima, 1999; La Maschera Delle Illusioni, 1999; Rassegna di Novelle e Canti, 2000; Giacomo Leopardi, degree thesis, 2000; La Mia Vita, 2003; I Giorni dei Cristalli, 2006; L'Orizzonte e la Pietra (into Voci del Verso), 2008. Honours: Over 250 national and international honours and awards; Included in important anthologies and in prestigious Italian and foreign dictionaries and encyclopaedias; Premio della Cultura della Presidenza del Consiglio dei Ministri, 2001; Silver Medal, President of the Italian Republic, 2003; International Peace Prize, 2002; American Medal of Honor, 2002; International Writer of the Year, 2003; World Medal of Freedom, 2004; Legion of Honor, 2005; Gold Medal for Italy, 2006; Congressional Medal of Excellence, 2007; American Hall of Fame, 2007; Distinguished Service Order & Cross, 2008; Title of Countess of San Diego Tower, Baroness von Derneck and Dame St Lukas, with Royal Order; Candidate, Nobel Prize in Literature, 2001, 2002, 2007. Memberships: Pontzen Academy; Giosuè Carducci Academy; Micenei Academy; Paestum Academy; Costantiniana Academy; Gentium Pro Pace Academy; Etruscan Academy; Marzocco Academy; CONVIVIO Academy; Federico II Academy; International Biographical Centre; American Biographical Institute; International Writers and Artists Association. Address: Via San Fruttuoso 7/4, I 16143 Genova, Italy.

CIESZYŃSKI Tomasz Maria Tadeusz, b. 6 November 1920, Poznan, Poland. Professor. m. Maria Elzbieta, 1 son, 1 daughter. Education: Medical Faculty, John Casimir University, Lvov, 1938-44; Diploma, Jagellonian University, Cracow, 1945; Diploma, Faculty of Mathematics, Physics and Chemistry, University of Wroclaw, 1952; MD, 1947; Docent of Surgery, 1968. Appointments: Senior Assistant, Adjunct Chair of Crystallography, University of Wroclaw, 1950-52; Senior Assistant, Orthopaedic Clinic, Medical Academy of Warsaw, 1953; Senior Assistant, Adjunct, Docent, Extraordinary Professor, Second Surgical Clinic, Medical Academy, Wroclaw, 1953-91; Professor of Medical Sciences, 1992-; President and Founder: League of Descendants of Lvov's Professors Murdered by Gestapo in July 1941, 2001-07. Publications include: The Natural System of Foods, 1950; Ultrasonic Catheter for Heart Examination, 1956; The idea of quantum thermodynamics and the general function of physical density, 1968; Electrosynthetics, photosynthetics and thermosynthesis of melanin, 1969; About the Need to Protect Biological Increment in Poland, in Polish, 1971; Melting Point of Apatites as Bond Energy Property in Relation to Structure, 1974; Artifical heart propelled by respiratory muscles, 1977; Equalization of Asymmetric Extremities in Children, 1987; Anabolic and Catabolic Processes in Relation to the Polarity of Electric Fields, 1991; Electric Field inside Bone, in Polish, 1991; The Days Strong by Love, poem in Polish, 1999. Honours include: Golden Cross of Merit, 1975; Cross de Chevalier of the Order of Polonia Restituta, 1990; Medal, University of Tokyo, 1982; Medal, Medical Academy, Wroclaw, 1990. Address: Modrzewiowa 20, Oborniki Slaskie 55-120, Poland.

CILLIERS-BARNARD Bettie, b. 18 November 1914, Rustenburg, Transvaal. Artist. m. C H Cilliers, 1 son, 1 daughter. Education: BA, Pretoria University, 1937; Hon D Phil, Potchefstroom University, 1990; Hon DLitt et Phil, Rand Afrikaans University, 1999; Hon D Phil, University of Pretoria, 2002. Appointments: Art Teacher, Innesdale High School, 1938; Lecturer, Pretoria College of Education, 1938-43; Study and working sessions in Paris, 1948, 1956, 1964, 1971, 1981; 71 Solo Exhibitions in South Africa,

Paris, London, Taiwan; Graphic Art Exhibitions in Austria, Germany, Spain, Greece, Israel, USA, Australia; Two retrospective exhibitions of her work at Pretoria Art Museum, 1995 and SASOL Art Museum, 1996. Publications: A book on the life and work of Bettie Cilliers-Barnard, by Professor Muller Ballot, launched 1996. Honours: Artistic Award, 1966; Honorary Award for Painting, South African Academy for Science and Art, 1978; State Presidents Decoration for Meritorious Service, 1983; Chancellors Medal, University of Pretoria, 1985; Commemorative Medal of Honour, American Biographical Institute, 1988; Represented South Africa at a number of international exhibitions in Europe. Address: 4 Upper Terrace, Menlo Park, Pretoria 0081, South Africa.

CIMBALA Stephen Joseph, b. 4 November 1943, Pittsburgh, PA, USA. College Professor. m. Elizabeth Ann Harder, 2 sons. Education: BA, Pennsylvania State University, 1965; MA, 1967, PhD, 1969, University of Wisconsin, Madison. Appointments: Assistant Professor of Political Science, State University of New York, Stony Brook, New Brook, 1969-73; Associate Professor, 1973-86, Professor, 1986-, Distinguished Professor, 2000-, Political Science, Pennsylvania State University, Delaware County; Consultant to various US Government Agencies and Defense Contractors. Publications: Books include: The Past and Future of Nuclear Deterrence, 1998; Coercive Military Strategy, 1998; Nuclear Strategy in the Twenty-First Century, 2000; Clausewitz and Chaos, 2001; Through a Glass Darkly: Looking at Conflict Prevention, Management and Termination, 2001; Russian and Armed Persuasion, 2001; A New Nuclear Century: Strategic Stability and Arms Control, 2002; The Dead Volcano: The Background and Effects of Nuclear War Complacency, 2002; US National Security: Policymakers, Processes and Politics, 2002; Military Persuasion: The Power of Soft, 2002; The US, NATO and Military Burden Sharing, 2005; Nuclear Weapons and Strategy: US Nuclear Policy for the Twenty-First Century, 2005; Russia and Postmodern Deterrence, 2007; Contributing editor, various works; Numerous articles and chapters. Honours: Milton S Eisenhower Award for Distinguished Teaching, Pennsylvania State University, 1995; Distinguished Professor of Political Science, 2000. Address: 118 Vairo Library, Penn State Brandywine, 25 Yearsley Mill Road, Media, PA 19063-5596, USA. E-mail: chacal@psu.edu

CIMINO Lorenzo, b. 26 May 1938, Trani, Italy. Psychologist; Writer. m. Maria Peduzzi, 28 June 1975. Education: Piano Diploma, 1957; PhD, 1966. Appointment: Psychologist in public administration, 1972-92; Freelance Psychologist, 1992-2006; Writer; Musician. Publications: Scientific papers on: work psychology and family therapy, 1971-92; history of psychology and art psychology, 1993-2000; Music: Reviews in Magazines, 1979-91; A CD, 1998; Poetry: 5 books and numerous collective books, 1979-2006. Honours: Formal appreciation of paper from Psychological Service Director, Roma; Honours as a Piano Player, 1996-98; Literary Prizes in Roma, Firenze, Poppi, Prato, La Spezia, Genova, Leonforte and Buccino; Listed in Who's Who publications and biographical dictionaries. Memberships: Italian Society for Artistic and Literary Royalties; Italian Society of Psychology, Promoter of Italian Society of Arts Psychology; FWLA. Address: via Nosee 4, 22020 Schignano, Italy.

CLAIRE Regi, (Yvonne Regula Butlin-Staub), b. 8 June 1962, Münchwilen/TG, Switzerland. m. Ron Butlin. Fiction Writer; Translator. Education: Matura, Frauenfeld, Switzerland, 1981; lic. phil. 1, English and German, Zurich University, Switzerland, 1992. Appointment: Research Assistant, Department of English, Zurich University, 1992-93.

Publications: Inside-Outside (short stories), 1998; The Beauty Room (novel), 2002. Honours: Winner of Exchange Scholarship with Aberdeen University, 1983-84; Winner, Semester Prize, Zurich University, 1986; Winner, Edinburgh Review 10th Anniversary Short Story Competition, 1995; Scottish Arts Council Writer's Bursary, 1997; Inside-Outside shortlisted for Saltire First Book Award, 1999; Writer's Bursary from Thurgau Canton, Switzerland, 2002; The Beauty Room longlisted for Allen Lane/MIND Book of the Year Award, 2003; Writer's Bursary from Pro Helvetia (Swiss Arts Council), 2003; UBS Cultural Foundation Award, 2003. Memberships: Scottish PEN; Autorinnen und Autoren der Schweiz; Society of Authors. Address: 7 West Newington Place, Edinburgh EH9 1QT, Scotland.

CLAPTON Eric (Eric Patrick Clapp), b. 30 March 1945, Ripley, Surrey, England. Musician (guitar); Singer; Songwriter. m. (1) Patti Boyd, 1979, divorced; 1 son, deceased, 1 daughter, (2) Melia McEnery, 2002, 3 children. Career: Guitarist with groups: The Roosters, 1963; The Yardbirds, 1963-65; John Mayall's Bluesbreakers, 1965-66; Cream, 1966-68; Blind Faith, 1969; Derek and the Dominoes, 1970; Delaney And Bonnie, 1970-72; Solo artiste, 1972-; Concerts include: Concert for Bangla Desh, 1971; Last Waltz concert, The Band's farewell concert, 1976; Live Aid, 1985; Record series of 24 concerts, Royal Albert Hall, 1991; Japanese tour with George Harrison, 1991; Film appearance: Tommy, 1974; Blues Brothers 2000, 1998. Compositions include: Presence Of The Lord; Layla; Badge (with George Harrison). Recordings include: Albums: Disraeli Gears, 1967; Wheels Of Fire, 1968; Goodbye Cream, 1969; Layla, 1970; Blind Faith, 1971; Concert For Bangladesh, 1971; Eric Clapton's Rainbow Concert, 1973; 461 Ocean Boulevard, 1974; E C Was Here, 1975; No Reason To Cry, 1976; Slowhand, 1977; Backless, 1978; Just One Night, 1980; Money And Cigarettes, 1983; Behind The Sun, 1985; August, 1986; Journeyman, 1989; 24 Nights, 1992; MTV Unplugged, 1992; From The Cradle, 1994; Rainbow Concert, 1995; Crossroads 2, 1996; Live In Montreux, 1997; Pilgrim, 1998; One More Car One More Rider, 2002; Me and Mr Johnson, 2004; She's So Respectable, 2004; Sessions for Robert J, 2004; Soundtracks include: Tommy; The Color Of Money; Lethal Weapon; Rush; Starskey and Hutch; School of Rock; Friends; Hit singles include: I Shot The Sheriff; Layla; Lay Down Sally; Wonderful Tonight; Cocaine; Behind The Mask; Tears In Heaven; Contributed to numerous albums by artists including: Phil Collins; Bob Dylan; Aretha Franklin; Joe Cocker; Roger Daltrey; Dr John; Rick Danko; Ringo Starr; Roger Waters; Christine McVie; Howlin' Wolf; Sonny Boy Williamson; The Beatles: The White Album (listed as L'Angelo Mysterioso). Honours include: 6 Grammy Awards, 1993; Q Magazine Merit Award, 1995; Grammy Award for best pop instrumental performance, 2002. Address: c/o Michael Eaton, 22 Blades Court, Deodar Road, London, SW15 2NU, England.

CLARK David, Lord Clark of Windermere, b. 19 October 1939, Castle Douglas, Scotland. Member of Parliament. m. Christin, 1 daughter. Education: BA (Econ), MSc, 1963-65, University of Manchester; PhD, University of Sheffield, 1974-78. Appointments: House of Commons, 1970-2001; House of Lords, 2001-. Publications: Books: The Industrial Manager, 1966; Radicalism to Socialism, 1981; Labours Lost Leader, 1985; We Do Not Want The Earth, 1992. Honours: Privy Councillor, 1997; Freedom of South Tyneside, 1998. Address: House of Lords, London SW1A 0PW, England.

CLARK Douglas George Duncan, b. 3 October 1942, Darlington, England. Poet. Education: BSc, Honours, Mathematics, Glasgow University, 1966. Appointments: Actuarial Student, Scottish Widows Fund, Edinburgh, 1966-69; Research Investigator, British Steel, Teesside, 1971-73; Computer Officer, Bath University Computing Services, 1973-93. Publications: The Horseman Trilogy in 4 books: Troubador, 1985; Horsemen, 1988; Coatham, 1989; Disbanded, 1991; Dysholm, 1993; Selected Poems, 1995; Cat Poems, 1997; Wounds, 1997; Lynx: Poetry from Bath (editor), 1997-2000; Kitten Poems, 2002; Finality, 2005; Durham Poems, 2005. Contributions to: Lines Review; Cencrastus; Avon Literary Intelligencer; Outposts; Acumen; Sand Rivers Journal; Rialto; Completing the Picture: Exiles, Outsiders and Independents; Poet's Voice; Mount Holyoke News; Isibongo; Agnieszka's Dowry; Recursive Angel; Octavo; Perihelion; Autumn Leaves; Fulcrum; Scriberazone. Membership: Bath Writers' Workshop, 1982-1996. Address: 69 Hillcrest Drive, Bath, Somerset BA2 1HD, England.

CLARK Eric, b. 29 July 1937, Birmingham, England. Author; Journalist. m. Marcelle Bernstein, 12 April 1972, 1 son, 2 daughters. Appointments: Reporter, The Exchange Telegraph news agency, London, 1958-60; Reporter, The Daily Mail, 1960-62; Staff Writer, The Guardian, 1962-64; Home Affairs Correspondent, Investigations Editor, The Observer, London, 1964-72; Author and journalist, 1972-. Publications: Len Deighton's London Dossier, Part-author, 1967; Everybody's Guide to Survival, 1969; Corps Diplomatique, 1973, US edition as Diplomat, 1973; Black Gambit, 1978; The Sleeper, 1979; Send in the Lions, 1981; Chinese Burn, 1984, US edition as China Run, 1984; The Want Makers (Inside the Hidden World of Advertising), 1988; Hide and Seek, 1994; The Advertising Age Encyclopedia of Advertising, 2003; The Secret Enemy, in progress; Numerous newspaper articles. Honours: Fellow, English Centre, International PEN. Memberships: Society of Authors; Authors Guild; Mystery Writers of America; National Union of Journalist. Address: c/o A M Heath Agency, 6 Warwick Court, London WC1R 5DJ, England.

CLARK Graham Ronald, b. 10 November 1941, Littleborough, Lancashire, England. Opera Singer. m. Joan, 1 step-daughter. Education: Loughborough College of Education, Leicestershire, 1961-64; MSc, Recreation Management, Loughborough University, Leicestershire, 1969-70; Singing studies with Bruce Boyce in London. Career: Teacher, Head of Physical Education Departments in 3 schools, 1964-69; Senior Regional Officer, The Sports Council, 1971-75; Operatic début with Scottish Opera, 1975; Principal, English National Opera, 1978-85; Performances with Royal Opera Covent Garden, Opera North and Welsh National Opera in the UK; International performances include: 16 seasons and over 100 performances, Bayreuth Festspiele, 1981-2004; 14 seasons, Metropolitan Opera, New York, 1985-2006; Performances in Aix-en-Provence, Amsterdam, Barcelona, Berlin, Bilbao, Bonn, Brussels, Catania, Chicago, Dallas, Geneva, Hamburg, Los Angeles, Madrid, Matsumoto, Milan, Munich, Nice, Paris, Rome, Salzburg, San Francisco, Stockholm, Tokyo, Toronto, Toulouse, Turin, Vancouver, Vienna, Yokohama, Zurich, 1976-2007; Over 350 Wagner performances including over 250 performances of Der Ring des Nibelungen, 1977-2007; International festivals include, Amsterdam, Antwerp, Bamberg, Berlin, Brussels, Canaries, Chicago, Cologne, Copenhagen, Edinburgh, Lucerne, Milan, Paris, Rome, Tel Aviv, Washington and the London Proms. Recordings with the BBC, BMG, Chandos, Decca, Deutsche Grammophon, EMI, Erato, EuroArts, Opera Rara, Opus Arte, Philips, Sony, Teldec, The Met, WDR; Videos include: The

Makropulos Case, Canadian Opera, Toronto; The Ghosts of Versailles, The Met, New York; Die Meistersinger, Der fliegende Holländer, Der Ring des Nibelungen, Bayreuther Festspiele; Wozzeck, Deutsche Staatsoper, Berlin and The Met, New York; Ariadne auf Naxos, Opéra National de Paris; Der Ring des Nibelungen, Gran Teatre del Liceu, Barcelona; Der Ring des Nibelungen, De Nederlandse Opera, Amsterdam. Honours: 3 nominations for Outstanding Individual Achievement in Opera, including an American Emmy, 1983, 1986, 1993; Sir Laurence Olivier Award, 1986; Honorary Doctor of Letters, Loughborough University, 1999; Sir Reginald Goodall Prize, 2001. Membership: The Garrick Club. Address: c/o Ingpen & Williams, 7 St George's Court, 131 Putney Bridge Road, London, SW15 2PA, England.

CLARK Patricia Denise (Claire Lorrimer, Patricia Robins, Susan Patrick), b. 1921, England. Writer; Poet. Publications: As Claire Lorrimer: A Voice in the Dark, 1967; The Shadow Falls, 1974; Relentless Storm, 1975; The Secret of Quarry House, Mavreen, 1976; Tamarisk, 1978; Chantal, The Garden (a cameo), 1980; The Chatelaine, 1981; The Wilderling, 1982; Last Year's Nightingale, 1984; Frost in the Sun, 1986; House of Tomorrow (biography), 1987; Ortolans, 1990; The Spinning Wheel, Variations (short stories), 1991; The Silver Link, 1993; Fool's Curtain, 1994; Beneath the Sun, 1996; Connie's Daughter, The Reunion, 1997; The Woven Thread, The Reckoning, Second Chance, 1998; An Open Door, 1999; Never Say Goodbye, Search for Love, 2000; For Always, 2001; The Faithful Heart, 2002; Over My Dead Body, Deception, 2003; Troubled Waters, 2004; Dead Centre, 2005; Autobiography, You Never Know, 2006; Infatuation, 2007; Truth to Tell, 2008. As Patricia Robins: To the Stars, 1944; See No Evil, 1945; Three Loves, 1949; Awake My Heart, 1950; Beneath the Moon, Leave My Heart Alone, 1951; The Fair Deal, 1952; Heart's Desire, So This is Love, 1953; Heaven in Our Hearts, One Who Cares, 1954; Love Cannot Die, 1955; The Foolish Heart, Give All to Love, 1956; Where Duty Lies, He Is Mine, 1957; Love Must Wait, 1958; Lonely Quest, 1959; Lady Chatterley's Daughter, The Last Chance, 1961; The Long Wait, The Runaways, Seven Loves, 1962; With All My Love, 1963; The Constant Heart, Second Love, The Night is Thine, 1964; There Is But One, No More Loving, Topaz Island, 1965; Love Me Tomorrow, The Uncertain Joy, 1966; The Man Behind the Mask, Forbidden, 1967; Sapphire in the Sand, Return to Love, 1968; Laugh on Friday, No Stone Unturned, 1969; Cinnabar House, Under the Sky, 1970; The Crimson Tapestry, Play Fair with Love, 1972; None But He, 1973; Fulfilment, Forsaken, Forever, 1993; The Legend, 1997; Memberships: Society of Authors; Romantic Novelists Association. Address: Chiswell Barn, Marsh Green, Edenbridge, Kent TN8 5PR, England.

CLARK Petula (Sally Olwen), b. 15 November 1934, Epsom, Surrey, England. Singer; Actress. m. Claude Wolff, 1961, 1 son, 2 daughters. Musical Education: Taught to sing by mother. Career: Stage and screen actress, aged 7; Own radio programme, 1943; Numerous film appearances, 1944-; Films include: Medal For The General, 1944; Here Come The Huggetts, 1948; Finian's Rainbow, 1968; Goodbye Mr Chips, 1969; Stage appearances include: Sound Of Music, 1981; Someone Like You (also writer), 1989; Blood Brothers, Broadway, 1993; Sunset Boulevard, 1995-96; national tour 1994-95, Sunset Boulevard, 1995, 1996, New York, 1998, US tour, 1998-2000; Host, own BBC television series; US television special Petula, NBC, 1968; Solo singing career, 1964-; Sold over 30 million records to date. Recordings: Hit singles include: Ya-Ya Twist, 1960; Downtown (Number 1, US and throughout Europe), 1964; The Other Man's Grass;

My Love; I Know A Place; Downtown; Oxygen; Albums: Petula Clark Sings, A Date With Pet, 1956; You Are My Lucky Star, 1957; Pet Clark, Petula Clark In Hollywood, 1959; In Other Words, Petula, Les James Dean, 1962; Downtown, 1964; I Know A Place, The New Petula Clark Album, Uptown With Petula Clark, 1965; In Love, Hello Paris, Vols I and II, I Couldn't Live Without Your Love, 1966; Hit Parade, 1967; The Other Man's Grass Is Always Greener, Petula, 1968; Portrait Of Petula, Just Pet, 1969; Memphis, 1970; The Song Of My Life, Warm And Tender, 1971; Live At The Royal Albert Hall, Now, 1972; Live In London, Come On Home, 1974; I'm the Woman You Need, 1975; Don't Sleep on the Subway, 1995; Wind of Change, 1998; The Ultimate Collection, 2002. Honours include: 2 Grammy Awards; Grand Prix Du Disque, 1960; More Gold discs than any other UK female artist. Address: c/o John Ashby, PO Box 288, Woking, Surrey GU22 0YN, England.

CLARK Rodney Jeremy, b. 7 September 1944, Andover, England. Voluntary Sector Executive. Civil partnership: Peter Bailey. Education: University College, London. Appointments: Various posts, 1965-69; Administrative Assistant, Welfare Department, London Borough of Camden, 1969-71; Administrator, Capital Projects Manager, London Borough of Islington, then Camden and Islington Area Health Authority, 1971-78; Capital Projects Director, The Royal National Institute for the Deaf, 1978-81; Chief Executive, Sense, The National Deafblind & Rubella Association, 1981-2001; Consultant, Charities Aid Foundation; Chairman, Signhealth; Chairman, The Woodford Foundation; Chairman, Christopher Brock Trust; Co Secretary, Omega, The National Association for End of Life Care. Publications: Numerous articles in professional and popular journals. Honours: MBE. Address: 31 Sutton Road, Shrewsbury, Shropshire SY2 6DL, England.

CLARK Stanley, b. 16 April 1934, Sheffield, Yorkshire, England. Engineer. m. Audrey Limb, 1957, 1 daughter. Education: Carbrook C of E School, Rotherham College of Technology, Yorkshire. Appointments: National Service, Royal Air Force, 1952-54; Allied Peace Keeping Forces, Berlin, Germany, 1953-54; Head, Electronics Department, Thomas Electronics, 1964-66; Technical Production Co-ordinator, Hanimex Pty Ltd, 1967-77; Managing Director, Ligg Pty Ltd T/A Australian Bio Transducers, 1979-92; Technical Officer, Product Development Department, ResMed Limited, 1993-2000. Publications: Inventor of the world's first small and portable battery operated blood sugar glucose monitor. Honours: Inventor of the Year in Australia, 1978; Bronze Medal, 9th International Inventors' Convention, Geneva, 1980; Diabetes Australia Award for Distinguished Service to Diabetes, Channel 9 Programme, What'll They Think of Next, 1980; The Order of Australia medal, Small Business Award, 1981; Medal of the Order of Australia, 2001. Listed in international biographical dictionaries. Memberships: Manly Warringah Branch Diabetes Australia; Institute of Automotive Mechanical Engineers; Institution of Electronics, UK. Address: Post Office Box 5193, Erina Fair, NSW 2250, Australia.

CLARKE Ann Margaret, b. 3 November 1928, Madras, India. Psychologist. m. ADB Clarke, 2 sons. Education: BA, Psychology, University of Reading, 1948; PhD, Psychology, University of London, 1950. Appointments: Clinical Psychologist then Principal Psychologist, The Manor Hospital NHS, Epsom, 1951-62; Research Fellow, 1963-71; Lecturer, 1973-76; Reader,1976-85; Professor, 1985-87; Professor Emeritus, 1987-, Department of Educational

Studies, University of Hull. Publications with Alan Clarke: Mental Deficiency: the Changing Outlook, 1958, 1964, 1974, 1985; Early Experience: Myth and Evidence, 1976; Mental Retardation and Behavioural Research, 1973; Early Experience and the Life Path, 2000; Human Resilience: a Fifty Year Quest, 2003; numerous articles in Psychological and Medical journals. Honours: B A Priestly Prize as Best Female Undergraduate, University of Reading; Research Award, American Association on Mental Deficiency, 1977; Distinguished Achievement Award for Scientific Literature, International Association for Scientific Study of Mental Deficiency, 1982; Honorary Fellow, British Psychological Society, 2007. Membership: British Psychological Society. Address: 109 Meadway, Barnet, Hertfordshire EN5 5JZ, England.

CLARKE Sir Anthony Peter, b. 13 May 1943, Ayr, Scotland. Judge. m. Rosemary, 2 sons, 1 daughter. Education: MA, Economics Part I, Law Part II, King's College, Cambridge. Appointments: Called to Bar, Middle Temple, 1965; QC, 1979; Judge of the High Court QBD, 1993-8; Admiralty Judge, 1993-98; Lord Justice of Appeal, 1998-2005; Master of the Rolls, 2005-. Honours: Knight, 1993; PC, 1998. Memberships: Garrick Club; Rye Golf Club. Address: Royal Courts of Justice, Strand, London WC2A 2LL, England.

CLARKE Hilda Margery, b. 10 June 1926, Monton, Eccles, Manchester, England. Artist; Gallery Director. Widowed, 2 sons. Education: Studied privately in Manchester with L S Lowry, and in Hamburg; Drawing, Printmaking and Sculpture, Southampton College of Art, part-time, 1960-88; Ruskin School of Art Workshops under Tom Piper, Chris Orr and Norman Ackroyd, 4 weeks, 1975; BA (Honours), Open University, 1975-82. Career: Founder and Director, "The First" Gallery, Southampton, 1984-; Curator, long running national touring exhibitions, 1988-; Exhibitions: Southampton City Art Gallery; FPS Gallery, Buckingham Gate, London; Mall Galleries, London; Chalk Farm Gallery, London; Ditchling, Sussex; Bettles Gallery, Ringwood; New Ashgate Gallery, Farnham; Tib Lane Gallery, Manchester; John Martin of Chelsea, 2005; John Martin of London, Albemarle Street, 2006; One man exhibitions: Hamwic Gallery, Southampton, 1970; Westgate Gallery, Winchester, 1973; University of Southampton, 1975; Hiscock Gallery, Southsea, 1977; "The First" Gallery, Southampton, 1989, 1998, 2004; Turner Sims Concert Hall, Southampton (by invitation) for the Inauguration of the Foyer, 1994; Ramsgate Library Gallery, 2001; Southampton City Art Gallery, 2006; Works in public collections: Southampton University; Southern Arts Association; St Mary's Hospital, Isle of Wight; Works in private collections: Felder Fine Art, London; Michael Hurd, Liss; Mr and Mrs B Hunt, Southampton; Dr C Williams, Bristol; Lady Lucas. Publications: Catalogues: Two Memorable Men: Crispin Eurich (1936-76) photographs, LS Lowry (1887-1976) drawings; The Animated Eye; Paintings and Moving Machines by Peter Markey; Showman-Shaman-Showman: Paintings and Prints by Stephen Powell; Architect at Leisure: Watercolours and Drawings by Arthur Mattinson (1853-1932). Membership: FRSA, elected 1996. Address: "The First" Gallery, 1 Burnham Chase, Bitterne, Southampton SO18 5DG, England.

CLARKE Karen Ann, b. 21 January 1969, Freeport, Bahamas. Doctor of Medicine. Education: BSc Chemistry, 1989; MSc Microbiology and Immunology, 1993; Master of Public Health, Environmental Health, 1994; MD, 1996. Career: Internal Medicine Department, Catskill Regional Medical Center, Harris, New York, 2000-05; Internal Medicine Department, Tucson Medical Center, St Joseph's Hospital, and St Mary's Hospital, Tucson, Arizona, 2005-06; Internal Medicine Department, Christus St Michael Hospital, Texarkana, Texas, 2007-. Publications: Characterization of Anergy to the Superantigen SEB, 1993; A Stimulatory Mls-1 Superantigen is Destroyed by UV Light While Other MTV Antigens Remain Intact. Significance for Mls-1 Unresponsiveness, 1992; CD4 Engagement Induces Fas Antigen – Dependent Apoptosis of T Cells in vivo, Eur J Immunology, 1994. Honours: Outstanding Senior Chemistry Student, American Institute of Chemistry Foundation, 1989; Dean's List, NE Wesleyan University (twice). Memberships: Cardinal Key; American College of Physicians; Fellow, American Biographical Institute, 1995; Life Patron, IBA, 2001; Lifetime Achievement Award, IBC, 2001; America's Registry of Outstanding Professionals, 2002-; International Order of Merit, IBA, 2004. Listed in includes: Who's Who Among Students in American Universities and Colleges, 1988-89; The World Who's Who of Women 1994/5; 2000 Outstanding People of the 20th Century, 2001; Dictionary of International Biography. Address: 5911 Richmond Road, Apt. #6307, Texarkana, TX 75503, USA.

CLARKE Keith Edward, b. 1940, United Kingdom. Consultant. m. Barbara, 1 son, 1 daughter. Education: B Eng, Electrical Engineering, University of Bradford; Diploma, Computing Science, Imperial College of Science and Medicine; M Phil, Computing Science, University of London; Management, London Business School. Appointments: Adviser, Ministry of Technology, 1969-70; Various management posts, BT Research, 1972-83; Deputy Director of Research, BT, 1985-89; Director, Applications and Services Development, BT Laboratories, Martlesham, Suffolk, 1989-92; Senior Vice-President Engineering, BT North America, San Jose, California, 1992; Director, Group Systems Engineering, BT plc, 1992-95; Director of Engineering Collaboration and Business Planning, BT Global Engineering, 1995-97; Director, Technology External Affairs, BT plc, 1997-2000; Executive Director (part-time), British Approvals Board for Telecommunications; Consultant in ITC with clients in UK and Europe, 2000-; Company Directorships: BT (CBP) Limited, 1989-95; Cellnet Limited, 1989-92; British Approvals Board for telecommunications, 1992-2000; BPS Inc, 2000; BABT Holdings, 2000; Hermont (Holdings, 2000-2002. Publications: Over 60 publications in the field of telecommunications include: How Viewdata Works (editor, R Winsbury), 1981; The Immediate Past and Likely Future of Videotext Display Technology, 1982; On the Road to Worldwide Communication (jointly with J Chidley), 1987; Royal Academy of Engineering Seminar on the Public Perception of Risk-Lessons from the Mobile Phone Industry, 2000. Memberships: Guild of Freeman; The City Livery Yacht Club; The Little Ship Club; The Windsor Yacht Club (Past Commodore); Fellowships: Institution of Engineering and Technology, British Computer Society, Chartered Management Institute, Royal Academy of Engineering, RSA; Liveryman of the Worshipful Company of Information Technologists; Liveryman of the Worshipful Company of Engineers; Freeman of the City of London. E-mail: kclarke@totalonline.net

CLARKE Michael Gilbert, b. 21 May 1944, Halifax, England. Vice-Principal. m. Angela Mary Cook, 1 son, 2 daughters. Education: BA, Politics and Sociology, 1963-66, MA, Comparative Politics, 1966-67, University of Sussex. Appointments: Lecturer and Director of Studies, Politics, University of Edinburgh, 1969-75; Assistant, Director, 1975-76, Deputy Director, Policy Planning, Lothian Regional Council, 1976-81; Chief Executive, Local Government

Training Board, 1981-89; Chief Executive Local Government Management Board, 1989-93; Head School of Public Policy, Professor of Public Policy, 1993-98, Pro-Vice Chancellor, 1998-2002, Vice-Principal, 2002-, University of Birmingham. Publications: Articles and books on UK local governance and constitutional arrangements at sub-national level. Honours: Fellow, Royal Society of Arts, 1988; Honorary Member, Society of Local Authority Chief Executives, 1998; CBE, 2000; DL, 2000; Honorary MA, University College Worcester, 2003; Honorary Member, Chartered Institute of Public Finance and Accounting, 2004. Memberships: West Midlands Regional Assembly; Governor, The Kings School, Worcester; Governor, University of Worcester; Non-executive Director: Government Office for West Midlands, Birmingham Research Park, Malvern Hills Science Park; Chairman: Central Technology Belt, Worcestershire Strategic Partnership; Visit Worcester; Member, General Synod, Church of England; Lay Canon, Worcester Cathedral. Address: Millington House, Lansdowne Crescent, Worcester, WR3 8JE, England. E-mail: m.g.clarke@bham.ac.uk

CLARKE Robert Henry, b. 6 March 1919, London, England. Oceanographer. m. Obla Paliza de Clarke, 2 sons, 1 daughter. Education: Open Scholar, St Olave's and St Saviour's Grammar School, London, 1932-38; Open Scholar in Natural Science, New College Oxford, 1938-40, 1946-47; Bachelor of Arts and Master of Arts with honours in Zoology, Botany and Chemistry, University of Oxford, 1946; Doctor of Philosophy, University of Oslo, Norway, 1957. Appointments: Lieutenant (Sp), RNVR in British Navy, Admiralty Unexploded Bomb Department with operations in various seas, and Directorate of Admiralty Research and Development (India) with special operations in India, Burma and Ceylon, 1940-46; Biologist in the Discovery Investigations, British Colonial Office, 1947-49; Principal Scientific Officer, British National Institute of Oceanography, conducted oceanographical expeditions in all Oceans and in all Seas except the Caspian Sea and the Dead Sea, 1949-71; Lent to FAO of the United Nations in the grade P5 as a whale biologist in Chile, Ecuador and Peru, 1958-61; Fishing off the coast of Peru, 1971-77; Visiting Professor, Universities of Baja California and Yucatan, Mexico, 1977-82; Currently retired but continuing research. Publications: Author of more than 100 research publications, many of book length and mostly on whales (especially the sperm whale), whale conservation, whaling and on ambergris, squids and deep sea fishes. Honours: Honorary Member, Fundación Ecuatoriana para el Estudio de los Mamíferos Marinos; Honorary Member, Sociedad Geográfica de Lima; Included in the Encyclopaedia of the Azores. Memberships: Scientific Fellow, Zoological Society of London; Institute of Biology of Great Britain; Challenger Society; Marine Biological Association of the United Kingdom; Association of British Zoologists, Member of Council, 1962-65. Address: Apartado 40, Pisco, Peru. E-mail: robertclarke007@hotmail.com

CLARKE Ronald James, b. 1 January 1919, Huddersfield, Yorkshire, England. Chemist; Chemical Engineer. Education: Portsmouth Grammar School, 1929-32; Colfe's Grammar School, 1932-37; Keble College, Oxford, 1937-41. Appointments: Researcher, Unilever, 1941-52; Various posts and assignments, General Foods Research and Development, 1957-84; Chairman, ISO Coffee Standards Committee, 1990-96; Retired; Author; Editor. Publications: Author, Processing Engineering in the Food Industries, 1957; Author/ Co-Editor, Coffee, Vols 1-6, 1985-88; Recent Developments in Coffee, 2001; Wine Flavour Chemistry, 2004; Author, Down the Supermarket Aisles, 1999; Numerous articles and chapters in other books. Honours: MA in Chemistry (Oxon);

PhD (honorary), Marquis Scicluna Research Foundation, USA; Medal, Association Scientifique Internationale du Café, 1982; Distinguished Service Award, BSI London, 1993; Distinguished Service Award, Society of Chemical Industry, London, 2002. Memberships: Fellow, Institution of Chemical Engineers, 1967; Fellow, Institute of Food Science and Technology, London, 1972. Address: Ashby Cottage, Selsey Road, Donnington, Chichester, West Sussex PO20 7PW, England.

CLARKE William Malpas, b. 5 June 1922, Ashton-under-Lyne, England. Author. m. Faith Elizabeth Dawson, 2 daughters. Education: BA Hons, Econ, University of Manchester, England, 1948; Hon DLitt, London Guildhall University, 1992. Appointments: Financial Editor, The Times, 1956-66; Director-General, British Invisible Exports Council, 1967-87; Chairman, ANZ Merchant Bank, 1987-91; Chairman, Central Banking Publications, 1991-. Publications: City's Invisible Earnings, 1958; City in the World Economy, 1965; Private Enterprise in Developing Countries, 1966; The World's Money, 1970; Inside the City, 1979; How the City of London Works, 1986; Secret Life of Wilkie Collins, 1988; Planning for Europe, 1989; Lost Fortune of the Tsars, 1994; Letters of Wilkie Collins, 1999; The Golden Thread, 2000. Contributions to: The Banker; Central Banking; Euromoney; Wilkie Collins Society Journal. Honour: CBE, 1976. Memberships: Thackeray Society; Wilkie Collins Society; Reform Club. Address: 37 Park Vista, Greenwich, London SE10 9LZ, England.

CLAYTON Peter Arthur, b. 27 April 1937, London, England. Publishing Consultant; Archaeological Lecturer. m. Janet Frances Manning, 5 September 1964, 2 sons. Education: School of Librarianship; North West Polytechnic, London, 1958; Institute of Archaeology, London University, 1958-62; University College, London, 1968-72. Appointments: Librarian, 1953-63; Archaeological Editor, Thames & Hudson, 1963-73; Humanities Publisher, Longmans, 1973; Managing Editor, British Museum Publications, 1974-79; Publications Director, BA Seaby, 1980-87; Writer, Lecturer, 1987-; Consulting Editor, Minerva Magazine, 1990-; Expert Advisor (coins and antiquities), Department for Culture Media and Sport (Treasure Committee), 1992-2007; Member, The Treasure Valuation Committee, 2007-. Publications: The Rediscovery of Ancient Egypt; Archaeological Sites of Britain; Seven Wonders of the Ancient World; Treasures of Ancient Rome; Companion to Roman Britain; Great Figures of Mythology; Gods and Symbols of Ancient Egypt; Chronicle of the Pharaohs; Family Life in Ancient Egypt; The Valley of the Kings; Egyptian Mythology. Contributions to: Journal of Egyptian Archaeology; Numismatic Chronicle; Coin & Medal Bulletin; Minerva. Honours: Liveryman of the Honourable Company of Farriers of the City of London, 2000; Freeman of the City of London, 2000. Memberships: Chartered Institute of Library and Information Professionals, fellow; Society of Antiquaries of London, fellow; Royal Numismatic Society, fellow. Address: 41 Cardy Road, Boxmoor, Hemel Hempstead, Hertfordshire HP1 1RL, England.

CLEARE John Silvey, b. 2 May 1936, London, England. Photographer; Writer. m. (2) Jo Jackson, 12 May 1980, 1 daughter. Education: Wycliffe College, 1945-54; Guildford School of Photography, 1957-60. Appointments: Joint Editor, Mountain Life magazine, 1973-75; Editorial Board, Climber and Rambler magazine, 1975-85. Publications: Rock Climbers in Action in Snowdonia, 1966; Sea-Cliff Climbing in Britain, 1973; Mountains, 1975; World Guide to Mountains, 1979; Mountaineering, 1980; Scrambles Among the Alps, 1986;

John Cleare's Best 50 Hill Walks in Britain, 1988; Trekking: Great Walks in the World, 1988; Walking the Great Views, 1991; Discovering the English Lowlands, 1991; On Foot in the Pennines, 1994; On Foot in the Yorkshire Dales, 1996; Mountains of the World, 1997; Distant Mountains, 1999; Britain Then and Now, 2000; On Top of the World, 2000; Pembrokeshire – The Official National Park Guide, 2001; The Tao Te Ching, 2002; Moods of Pembrokeshire & its Coast, 2004; Portrait of Bath, 2004; Books of Songs, 2004; Tales from the Tao, 2005; Classic Haiku, 2007; Mountains – A Panoramic Vision, 2007; Contributions to: Times; Sunday Times; Independent; Observer; World; Country Living; Boat International; Intercontinental; Alpine Journal; High; Climber; Great Outdoors. Honour: 35mm Prize, Trento Film Festival, for film The Climbers (as Cameraman), 1971; Golden Eagle Award, Outdoor Writers Guild for Services to the Outdoors. Membership: Outdoor Writers Guild, executive committee; British Association of Picture Libraries; Alpine Club. Address: Hill Cottage, Fonthill Gifford, Salisbury, Wiltshire SP3 6QW, England.

CLEAVE Brian Elseley, b. 3 September 1939, Ilford, Essex, England. Barrister. m. Celia Valentine Williams. Education: LLB, Exeter University, 1961, 1958-61; Kansas University, 1961-62; Manchester University, 1962-63. Appointments: Admitted as a solicitor, 1966; Assistant Solicitor, 1978-86, Principal Assistant Solicitor, 1986-90, Solicitor, 1990-99, Inland Revenue; Called to the Bar, Gay's Inn, 1999; Senior Consultant, Tacis Tax Reform Project, Moscow, 2000-2002; Senior Consultant, Europeaid Tax Reform II Project, Moscow, 2003-05; Senior Consultant, Europe Aid Assistance to the Tax Administration of Ukraine Project, Kyiv, 2006-07. Honours: CB, 1995; QC, Honoris Causa, 1999. Memberships: FRSA; International Fiscal Association, British Branch; Institute for Fiscal Studies. Listed in biographical dictionaries. Address: Gray's Inn Tax Chambers, Third Floor, Gray's Inn Chambers, Gray's Inn, London WC1R 5JA, England. E-mail: bcleave@lawdraft.fsnet.co.uk

CLEESE John (Marwood), b. 27 October 1939, Weston-Super-Mare, Somerset, England. Author; Actor. m. (1) Connie Booth, 1968, dissolved 1978, 1 daughter, (2) Barbara Trentham, 1981, dissolved 1990, 1 daughter, (3) Alyce Faye Eichelberger, 1993. Education: MA, Downing College, Cambridge. Career: Began writing and making jokes professionally, 1963; Appeared in and co-wrote TV Series: The Frost Report; At Last the 1948 Show; Monty Python's Flying Circus; Fawlty Towers; The Human Face; Founder and Director, Video Arts Ltd, 1972-89; Films include: Interlude; The Magic Christian; And Now For Something Completely Different; Monty Python and the Holy Grail; Life of Brian; Yellowbeard, 1982; The Meaning of Life, 1983; Silverado, 1985; A Fish Called Wanda, 1988; Mary Shelley's Frankenstein, 1993; The Jungle Book, 1994; Fierce Creatures, 1996; The World Is Not Enough, 1999; The Quantum Project, Rat Race, Pluto Nash, 2000; Harry Potter and the Philosopher's Stone, 2001; Die Another Day, Harry Potter and the Chamber of Secrets, 2002; Charlie's Angels: Full Throttle, 2003; Around the World in 80 Days, 2004; Valiant (voice), Jade Empire (voice), 2005; Man About Town, Complete Guide to Guys', Entente cordiale, L̇, 2006; Charlotte's Webb (voice), 2006; Skrek the Third (voice), 2007. Publications: Families and How to Survive Them, (with Robin Skynner), 1983; The Golden Skits of Wing Commander Muriel Volestrangler FRHS and Bar, 1984; The Complete Fawlty Towers (with Connie Booth), 1989; Life and How to Survive It (with Robin Skynner), 1993; The Human Face (with Brian Bates), 2003; The Pythons Autobiography (co-author), 2003. Honour:

Honorary LLD, St Andrews; 7 Awards, 12 nominations. Address: c/o David Wilkinson, 115 Hazlebury Road, London SW6 2LX, England.

CLEGG Jerry S, b. 29 September 1933, Heber City, Utah, USA. Professor of Philosophy. m. Karen M, 3 daughters. Education: BA, 1955, MA, 1959, University of Utah, USA; PhD, University of Washington, USA, 1962. Appointment: Philosophy Department, Mills College, Oakland, California USA, 1962-, currently Professor of Philosophy. Publications: Books: The Structure of Plato's Philosophy; On Genius: From Schopenhauer to Wittgenstein; Articles in scientific journals: What Magellan's voyage didn't prove or why the Earth is flat; Symptoms; Self-Predication and Linguistic Reference in Plato's Theory of the Forms; Plato's Vision of Chaos; Wittgenstein on Verification and Private Languages; Faith; Some Artistic Uses of Truths and Lies; Nietzsche and the Ascent of Man in a Cyclical Cosmos; Nietzsche's Gods in the Birth of Tragedy; Freud and the Issue of Pessimism; Logical Mysticism and The Cultural Setting of Wittgenstein's Tractatus; Jung's Quarrel with Freud; Conrad's Reply to Kierkegaard; Mann contra Nietzsche; Freud and the "Homeric" Mind; Life in the Shadow of Christ: Nietzsche on Pistis versus Gnosis (in Nietzsche and the Gods). Address: 6636 Admiral Way SW, Seattle, WA 98116, USA.

CLEMENTS Christopher John, b. 21 January 1946, England. Medical Practitioner. m. Vivienne, 2 sons. Education: MB.BS, London Hospital, University of London, 1969; LRCP, MRCS, 1969; DObst, University of Auckland, 1972; DCH, Royal College of Physicians, London, 1973; MSc, University of Manchester, 1980; MCCM, 1980; MFPHM, 1980; FAFPHM, 1994. Appointments include: Registrar, Waikato Hospital, New Zealand, 1971; Medical Director, Hospital de Valle Apurimac, Peru, 1973-74; Chief Medical Officer, Save the Children Fund, Bangladesh Project, 1977, Afghanistan Project, 1977-78; Assistant Director, National Head of Disease Control, Department of Health, Head Office, Wellington, New Zealand, 1983-85; Medical Officer, Expanded Programme on Immunization, World Health Organisation, Geneva, 1985-2002; Honorary Associate Professor, Faculty of Medicine, Nursing and Health Services, Department of Epidemiology and Preventive Medicine, Monash University, Melbourne, Australia, 2003-; Associate Professor and Principal Fellow, School of Population Health, Faculty of Medicine and Dentistry, University of Melbourne, Australia, 2003-. Publications: Over 150 articles and chapters contributed to books on public health issues; Over 100 WHO publications. Memberships: Royal Australian College of Physicians. Address: 24 Millbank Drive, Mount Eliza, VIC 3930, Australia. E-mail: john@clem.com.au

CLEMENTS-CROOME Derek John, b. 5 May 1939, England. Architectural Engineering. Education: BSc; MSc; PhD; C Eng; C Phys; FICE; FCIBSE; FIOA; FRSA; FASHRAE; F Institute P. Appointments: Trainee Engineer, 1955-60, Research and Development Officer, 1960-66, Brightside Heating and Engineering Co Ltd, Birmingham; Research Fellow, Institute of Sound and Vibration, Southampton University, 1966-67; Lecturer/Senior Lecturer, Department of Ergonomics and Cybernetics, then Department of Civil Engineering, Loughborough University, 1967-78; Senior Lecturer/Reader, School of Architecture and Building Engineering, Bath University, 1978-88; Honorary Visiting Professor: Chongqing Jianzhu University, China, 1994; Tianjin University, 2000; Benxi University, 2002; Shenyang Jianzhu University, 2002; Shenyang Ligong University, 2002; Hong Kong Polytechnic University, 2006; Professor, Construction

Engineering, Department of Construction Management & Engineering, University of Reading, 1988-, and Director of Research, 2002-; Director, Intelligent Buildings Research Group, 2005-; Editor/Founder, Intelligent Buildings International Journal, 2006. Publications: Numerous papers and articles in professional journals. Honours: Bronze medallist, Chartered Institution of Building Services Engineers, 1970; Northcroft Silver medallist, Institute of Hospital Engineering, 1990; Ove Arup Partnership Award, 1993; Freedom of the City of London, 1996; Fellowship, American Society of Heating, Refrigeration and Air-conditioning Engineers, 1997; Lifetime Membership, International Academy of Indoor Air Sciences, 2000; UK Ambassador for Clima 2000, 7th World Congress, Naples, 2001; Silver Medal, Chartered Institution of Building Services Engineers, 2005; Commissioner for Ministry of Construction, Beijing and Member of Editorial Board for Proceedings for Conferences, 2005 and 2006; Appointed Member, Taiwan Government Science and Technology Advisor Group, 2005-; President, National Conference of University Professors, 2005-; Elected Vice President, CIBSE, 2007-. Memberships include: Board of British Council of Offices; Federation of European Heating and Air-conditioning Associations; Council of Building Services Research and Information Association; Executive Board Member, European Intelligent Building Group; Association of Parliamentary Engineering Group; Chairman, CIBSE; Intelligent Buildings Group; National Ventilation Group. E-mail: d.j.clements-croome@reading.ac.uk

CLEOBURY Stephen John, b. 31 December 1948, Bromley, Kent, England. Conductor. m. Emma Sian Disley, 3 daughters. Education: MA, Mus B, St John's College, Cambridge; FRCO; FRCM. Appointments: Director of Music, St Matthew's, Northampton. 1971-74; Sub-organist, Westminster Abbey, 1974-78; Master of Music, Westminster Cathedral, 1979-82; Director of Music, King's College, Cambridge, 1982-; Conductor, Cambridge University Music Society, 1983-; Chief Conductor, BBC Singers, 1995-. Publications: Sundry arrangements and short compositions. Honour: Hon D Mus, Anglia Polytechnic University, 2001. Memberships: ISM; Vice-President, RCO; Member of Advisory Board, RSCM. Address: King's College, Cambridge CB2 1ST, England. E-mail: sjc1001@cam.ac.uk

CLEVE Gunnel Inga-Lill, b. 13 May 1930, Helsinki, Finland. Professor Emerita. m. Johan Fredric Cleve, 1 son. Education: MS, 1960, Licentiate, 1978, University of Helsinki, Finland; Doctor of Philosophy, University of Turku, Finland, 1987. Appointments: Assistant in English Philology, University of Helsinki, 1966-71; Assistant in English, University of Tampere, 1972-73; Lecturer in English, The Swedish Business School, Helsinki, 1974-77; Lecturer in English, The Finnish Business School of Turku, 1977-79; lecturer in English, 1979-80, Assistant in English, 1981-83, University of Turku; Lecturer in English, Business School, 1983-90, Professor in the Didactics of Foreign Languages, 1989-93, Professor Emerita, 1993-, Åbo Akademi University, Turku. Publications: Elements of Mysticism in Three of William Golding's Novels (Dissertation Thesis), 1986; Mystic Themes in Walter Hilton's Scale of Perfection Book I, 1989; Basic Mystic Themes in Walter Hilton's Scale of Perfection Book II, 1994; Numerous articles in various publications. Honour: Memorial Medal, University of Turku. Address: Voudink 6 A 43, 20780 Kaarina, Finland.

CLIFF Ian Cameron, b. 11 September 1952, Twickenham, England. Diplomat. m. Caroline Redman, 1 son, 2 daughters. Education: 1st Class Honours, Modern History, Magdalen College, Oxford, 1971-74. Appointments: History Master, Dr Challoner's Grammar School, Amersham, 1975-79; 2nd Secretary, Foreign and Commonwealth Office, 1979-80; Arabic Language Training, Damascus and St Andrews University, 1980-82; 1st Secretary, British Embassy, Khartoum, 1982-85; 1st Secretary, Foreign and Commonwealth Office, 1985-89; 1st Secretary, UK Mission to UN, New York, 1989-93; Director, Exports to the Middle East, Near East and North Africa, Department of Trade and Industry, 1993-96; Deputy Head of Mission, British Embassy, Vienna, 1996-2001; HM Ambassador to Bosnia and Herzegovina, 2001-05; HM Ambassador to the Sudan, 2005-. Publications: Occasional articles in Railway Magazines. Honour: OBE, 1992. Address: c/o Foreign and Commonwealth Office, London SW1A 2AH, England.

CLIFFORD Max, b. April 1943, Kingston-upon-Thames, England. Public Relations Executive. m. Elizabeth, deceased, 1 daughter. Appointments: Worker, Department Store; Former Junior Reporter, Merton & Morden News; Former Press Officer, EMI Records (promoted the Beatles); Founder, Max Clifford Associates, clients have included Muhammad Ali, Marlon Brando, David Copperfield, O J Simpson, Frank Sinatra, Simon Cowell, SEAT, Laing Homes, Mohamed Al-Fayed, Michael Watson, Derek Hatton, Richard Tomlinson,Tony Martin, Rebecca Loos, Shilpa Shetty. Address: Max Clifford Associates Ltd, 109 New Bond Street, London, W1Y 9AA, England.

CLIFT Roland, b. 19 November 1942, Epsom, Surrey, England. Professor of Environmental Technology. m. Diana Helen Manning, 2 sons (1 deceased), 1 daughter. Education: BA, 1963, MA, 1966, Trinity College, Cambridge; PhD, McGill University, Montreal, Canada, 1970. Appointments: Head, Department of Chemical Engineering, 1981-91, Professor of Chemical Engineering, 1981-92, Professor of Environmental Technology, 1992-, University of Surrey; Editor-in-Chief, Powder Technology, 1987-95; Member, UK Ecolabelling Board, 1992-98; Director, Centre for Environmental Strategy, 1992-2005; Member, Royal Commission on Environmental Pollution, 1996-2005; Visiting Professor, Chalmers University, Göteborg, Sweden, 1999-; Director: ClifMar Associates Ltd, 1996-; Merrill Lynch New Energy Technologies Ltd, 1999-; Industrial Ecology Solutions Ltd, 2001-07; Member, Research Advisory Committee, Forest Research and Forestry Commission, 2004-; Member, Science Advisory Committee of Department of Environment, Food and Rural Affairs, 2006-. Publications: Bubble, Drops and Particles, 1978, reprint 2006; Slurry Transport using Centrifugal Pumps, 1996, 3rd edition 2005; Processing of Particulate Solids, 1997; Sustainable Development in Practice: Case Studies for Engineers and Scientists, 2004; Numerous edited books and articles in professional journals. Honours: Henry Marion Howe Medal, American Society for Metals, 1976; Frank Moulton Medal, Institution of Chemical Engineers, 1978; Officer of the Order of the British Empire, 1994; Sir Frank Whittle Medal, Royal Academy of Engineering, 2003; Commander of the Order of the British Empire, 2006. Memberships: Fellow, Royal Academy of Engineering; Fellow, Institution of Chemical Engineers; Honorary Fellow, Chartered Institute of Waste and Environmental Management; Fellow, Royal Society of Arts. Address: Centre for Environmental Strategy, University of Surrey, Guildford, Surrey GU2 7XH, England. E-mail: r.clift@surrey.ac.uk

CLINTON Hilary Rodham, b. 26 October 1947, Chicago, Illinois, USA. Lawyer and Former First Lady of USA. m. Bill Clinton, 1 daughter. Education: Wellesley College; Yale

University. Career: Rose Law Firm, 1977-, currently Senior Partner; Legal Counsel, Nixon Impeachment Staff, 1974; Assistant Professor of Law, Fayetteville and Director, Legal Aid Clinic, 1974-77; Lecturer in Law, University of Arkansas, Little Rock, 1979-80; Chair, Commission on Women in the Profession, ABA, 1987-91; Head, President's Task Force on National Health Reform, 1993-94; Newspaper Columnist, 1995-; Senator from New York, 2001-; Various teaching positions, committee places, public & private ventures. Publications include: It Takes a Village, 1996; Dear Socks, Dear Buddy, 1998; An Invitation to the White House, 2000; Living History (memoirs), 2003; numerous magazine articles. Honours include: Hon LLD (Little Rock, Arkansas) 1985, (Arkansas College) 1988, (Hendrix College) 1992; Hon DHL (Drew) 1996; One of Most Influential Lawyers in America, 1988, 1991; Outstanding Lawyer-Citizen Award, Arkansas Bar Association, 1992; Lewis Hine Award, National Child Labor Law Commission, 1993; Friend of Family Award, American Home Economics Foundation, 1993; Humanitarian Award, Alheimer's Association, 1994; Elie Wiesel Foundation, 1994; AIDS Awareness Award, 1994; Grammy Award, 1996; numerous other awards and prizes. Address: US Senate, 476 Russell Senate Office Building, Washington, DC 20510, USA. Website: www.clinton.senate.gov

CLINTON William Jefferson (Bill), b. 19 August 1946, Hope, Arizona, USA. Former President, USA. m. Hillary Rodham, 1975, 1 daughter. Education: BS, International Affairs, Georgetown University, 1964-68; Rhodes Scholar, University College, Oxford, 1968-70; JD, Yale University Law School, 1970-73. Appointments: Professor, University of Arizona Law School, 1974-76; Democrat Nominee, Arizona, 1974; Attorney-General, Arizona, 1977-79; State Governor of Arizona, 1979-81, 1983-92; Member, Wright, Lindsey & Jennings, law firm, 1981-83; Chairman, Southern Growth Policies Board, 1985-86; Chairman, Education Commissioner of the States, 1986-87; Chairman, National Governor's Association, 1986-87; Vice-Chairman, Democrat Governor's Association, 1987-88, Chairman elect, 1988-89, Chairman, 1989-90; Co-Chairman, Task Force on Education, 1990-91; Chairman, Democrat Leadership Council, 1990-91; President, USA, 1993-2001; Impeached by House of Representatives for perjury and obstruction of justice, 1988; Aquitted in the Senate on both counts, 1999; Suspended from practising law in Supreme Court, 2001-06; UN Special Envoy for Tsunami Relief, 2005-. Publications: Between Hope and History, 1996; My Life (memoir), 2004; Recordings: Peter and the Wolf: Wolf Tracks, 2003; My Life, 2005. Honours: National Council of State Human Service Administrators Association Award; Award, Leadership on Welfare Reform; National Energy Efficiency Advocate Award; Honorary Degree, Northeastern University, Boston, 1993; Honorary Fellow, University College, Oxford, 1993; Honorary DCL, Oxford, 1994; Honorary DLitt, Ulster University, 1995; Hon Co-Chair, Club of Madrid; Grammy Award, Best Spoken Word Album for Children, 2004, Best Spoken Word Album, 2005; British Book Award for Biography of the Year, 2005. Address: 55 West 125th Street, New York, NY 10027, USA. Website: www.clintonpresidentialcenter.org

CLOONEY George, b. 6 May 1961, Kentucky, USA. Actor. m. Talia Blasam, 1989, divorced 1993. Appointments: TV series: ER, 1984-85; The Facts of Life, 1985-86; Roseanne, 1988-89; Sunset Beat, 1990; Baby Talk, 1991; Sister, 1992-94; ER, 1994-. Films include: Return of the Killer Tomatoes, 1988; Red Surf, 1990; Unbecoming Age, 1993; From Dusk Till Dawn, 1996; Batman and Robin, The Peacemaker, 1997; Three Kings, 1999; O Brother, Where Art Thou?, Perfect Storm, 2000; Spy Kids, Ocean's Eleven, 2001; Welcome to Collinwood, Solaris, Confessions of a Dangerous Mind, 2002; Spy Kids 3-D: Game Over, Intolerable Cruelty, 2003; Ocean's Twelve, 2004; Good Night and Good Luck, Syriana, Good Night and Good Luck, 2005; The Good German, 2006; Ocean's Thirteen, Michael Clayton, 2007. Honours: Golden Globe Award, Best Supporting Actor, 2006; Oscar, Best Supporting Actor, 2006. Address: William Morris Agency, 151 El Camino, Beverly Hills, CA 90212, USA.

CLOSE Glenn, b. 19 March 1947, Greenwich, Connecticut, USA. Actress. m. (1) C Wade, divorced, (2) J Marlas, 1984, divorced, 1 daughter (with J Starke). Education: William and Mary College. Career: Co-owner, The Leaf and Bean Coffee House, 1991-; Films include: The World According to Garp, 1982; The Big Chill, 1983; The Stone Boy, 1984; Jagged Edge, 1985; Fatal Attraction, 1987; Dangerous Liaisons, Hamlet, 1989; The House of Spirits, Hamlet, 1990; 101 Dalmatians, Mars Attacks! 1996; Air Force One, Paradise Road, 1997; Tarzan, Cookie's Fortune, 1999; 102 Dalmatians, 2000; The Safety of Objects, 2001; Pinocchio (voice), 2002; Le Divorce, 2003; The Stepford Wives, Heights, 2004; Hoodwinked (voice), 2005; Nine Lives, The Chumscrubber, Tarzan II (voice), 2005; Evening, 2007; Theatre includes: The Rules of the Game; A Streetcar Named Desire; King Lear; The Rose Tattoo; Death and the Maiden; Sunset Boulevard; TV: The Lion in Winter, 2005. Honours: Golden Globe Award, Best Actress in a Miniseries or TV Movie, 2005; Screen Actors Guild Awards, 2005. Address: Creative Artists Agency, 9830 Wilshire Boulevard, Beverly Hills, CA 90212, USA.

CLOSSICK Peter, b. 18 May 1948, London. Artist. m. Joyce, 1 daughter. Education: Shoe Design, Leicester College of Art, 1969; BA, Fine Art, Camberwell College of Art, 1978; ATC, Goldsmiths London University, 1979. Appointments: Visiting Lecturer: Oxford-Brookes University; Open College of the Arts; Greenwich Community College; Ulster University; Art Consultant, Blackheath Conservatoire of Music and Art. Publications: Dictionary of Artists in Britain Since 1945, Art Dictionaries Ltd; Who's Who in Art Since 1927, Art Trade Press Ltd; Painting Without A Brush, Studio Vista; The London Group – 90th Anniversary, Tate Britain. Honour: Elected London Group President, 2000. Membership: President, The London Group, 2000-05. Address: 358 Lee High Road, Lee Green, London SE12 8RS, England. E-mail: j.clossick@ntlworld.com Website: www.thelondongroup.com/artists/clossick.html

CLOUDSLEY Anne, ((Jessie) Anne Cloudsley-Thompson), b. 20 March 1915, Reigate, Surrey, England. Physiotherapist. Artist. m. Professor JL Cloudsley-Thompson, 3 sons. Education: MCSP, ME, LET, 1937, University College Hospital, London, England; LCAD, 1976, DipBS Hons, 1977, Byam Shaw School of Art, University of the Arts, London. Appointments: Established Physiotherapy Department, Hatfield Military Hospital, Hertfordshire, England, 1940-42; Superintendent Physiotherapist, Peripheral Nerve Injuries Centre, Wingfield Orthopaedic Hospital, Oxford, England, 1942-44; Superintendent Physiotherapist, Omdurman General Hospital, Sudan, 1960-71; Founder and Honorary Gallery Curator, Africa Centre, London, 1978-82; Visiting Lecturer, Fine Art, University of Nigeria, Nsukka, 1981; Lecturer, Lithography, Working Men's College, London NW1, 1982-91. Publications: Women of Omdurman: life, love and the cult of virginity, 1983, reprinted 1983, 1984, 1987; Articles and reviews; Numerous exhibitions: Individual: AFD Gallery, 1977; Mandeer Gallery, 1981; Ecology Centre, 1990; Budapest, 1990; Walk Gallery, 2004; Little Known Aspects of Sudanese Life (throughout Europe 1982-84); SOAS and Brunei Gallery, 2006; Group: The Royal Academy Summer Exhibition, 1992, 1993; Fresh Art, 2001, 2002, 2003; Cork Street, 2003; Discerning Eye, Mall Galleries, 2004; Menier, 2004, 2007, 2008; Bankside, 2005, 2006; Pastel Society, Mall Galleries, 2006; Royal Society of British Artists, Mall Galleries, 2008. Honours: Listed in national and international biographical directories. Memberships: Chartered Society of Physiotherapy, 1935-; Print Makers Council, 1996-; Elected to The London Group, 2002-. Address: 10 Battishill Street, London N1 1TE, England.

CLOUDSLEY-THOMPSON John Leonard, b. 23 May 1921, Murree, India. Professor of Zoology. m. Jessie Anne Cloudsley, 3 sons. Education: BA, 1947, MA, 1949, PhD, 1950, Pembroke College, Cambridge; DSc, University of London, 1960. Appointments: War Service, 1940-44; Lecturer in Zoology, King's College, University of London, 1950-60; Professor of Zoology, University of Khartoum and Keeper, Sudan Natural History Museum, 1960-71; Professor of Zoology, Birkbeck College, University of London, 1972-86; Professor Emeritus, 1986-. Publications: Over 55 books, including: Ecophysiology of Desert Arthropods and Reptiles, 1991; The Nile Quest, novel, 1994; Biotic Interactions in Arid Lands, 1996; Teach Yourself Ecology, 1998; The Diversity of Amphibians and Reptiles, 1999; Ecology and Behaviour of Mesozoic Reptiles, 2005; Sharpshooter: Memories of Armoured Warfare 1939-45, 2006; Monographs, 11 Children's natural history books: Contributions to Encyclopaedia Britannica, Encyclopaedia Americana; Articles in professional journals. Honours: Honorary Captain, 1944; Royal African Society Medal, 1969; Institute of Biology KSS Charter Award, 1981; Honorary DSc, Khartoum and Silver Jubilee Gold Medal, 1981; Biological Council Medal, 1985; J H Grundy Memorial Medal, Royal Army Medical College, 1987; Peter Scott Memorial Award, British Naturalists' Association, 1993, Honorary Fellow, 2007; Fellow Honoris Causa, Linnean Society, 1997; Listed in national and international biographical publications. Memberships: Liveryman, Worshipful Company of Skinners; C Biol, FI Biol; FWAAS; FRES; FLS; FZS. Address: 10 Battishill Street, Islington, London N1 1TE, England.

CLUYSENAAR Anne, (Alice Andrée), b. 15 March 1936, Brussels, Belgium (Irish citizen). Retired Lecturer; Poet; Songwriter; Librettist; Painter. m. Walter Freeman Jackson, 30 October 1976. Education: BA, Trinity College, Dublin, 1957; University of Edinburgh, 1963; Huddersfield Polytechnic, 1972-73. Appointments: Lecturer, King's College, Aberdeen, 1963-65, University of Lancaster, England, 1965-71, University of Birmingham, England, 1973-76, Sheffield City Polytechnic, England, 1976-89; Part-time Lecturer, University of Wales, Cardiff, 1989-2002. Publications: A Fan of Shadows, 1967; Nodes, 1971; English Poetry Since 1960 (contributor), 1972; Aspects of Literary Stylistics, 1976; Selected Poems of James Burns Singers (editor), 1977; Poetry Introduction 4, 1978; Double Helix, 1982; Timeslips: New and Selected Poems, 1997; The Life of Metrical and Free Verse by Jon Silkin (contributor), 1997; Poets on Poets, Henry Vaughan (contributor), 1997; Henry Vaughan, Selected Poems (editor), 2004; The Hare That Hides Within, 2004; Scintilla (founding editor and present poetry editor); Batu-Angas, Envisioning Nature with Alfred Russel Wallace, 2008; Water to Breathe, 2008. Memberships: Usk Valley Vaughan Association; Second Light; Fellow, Welsh Academy. Address: Little Wentwood Farm, Llantrisant, Usk, Gwent NP15 1ND, Wales. E-mail: anne.cluysenaar@virgin.net

CO Le Cong, b. 28 November 1941, Quang Nam, Vietnam. Education. m. Nguyen Thi Loc, 1 son, 1 daughter. Education: Bachelor of Science. Appointments: Founder and President, Duy Tan University, Vietnam; Member, 8th Vietnam's National Assembly; Former General Secretary, Hue University, Vietnam. Publications: Years of Devotion; My School Fees Were Paid in Blood. Honours: Medal of Independence, Vietnam. Memberships: Association of Private Universities and Colleges in Vietnam; Vice President, Association of Private Universities and Colleges in Vietnam. Address: 64 Nguyen Thi Minh Khai St, Da Nang, Vietnam. E-mail: lecongco@yahoo.com

COBB David Jeffery, b. 12 March 1926, Harrow, Middlesex, England. Freelance Writer; Poet. Widowed, 2 sons, 3 daughters. Education: BA, Bristol, 1954; PGCE, 1955. Appointments: German Teacher, Nottinghamshire, 1955-58; Programme Officer, UNESCO Institute of Education, Hamburg, 1958-62; English Teacher, British Council, Bangkok, 1962-68; Assistant Professor, Asian Institute of Technology, Bangkok, 1968-72; Manager, RDU, Longman Group Ltd, 1972-84; Freelance, 1985-. Publications: A Leap in the Light; Mounting Shadows; Jumping From Kiyomizu; Chips off the Old Great Wall; The Spring Journey to the Saxon Shore; The Iron Book of British Haiku; A Bowl of Sloes; The Genius of Haiku, Readings From R H Blyth; Forefathers; Palm; The British Museum Haiku; The Dead Poets' Cabaret; Business in Eden; Im Zeichen des Janus; Veter se obrne (A Shift in the Wind); Contributions to: Rialto; Blithe Spirit; Modern Haiku; Frogpond; HQ; Snapshots; Chimera. Honours: 1st Prize, Cardiff International Haiku Competition, 1991; 2nd Prize, HSA Merit Book Awards, 1997 and 2002; The Sasakawa Prize for Innovation in the Field of Haikai, 2004; Takahama Kyoshi Prize, 2006. Memberships: British Haiku Society, president, 1997-2002; Haiku Society of America; John Clare Society; Robert Bloomfield Society; Royal Bangkok Sports Club. Address: Sinodun, Shalford, Braintree, Essex CM7 5HN, England. E-mail: davidcobb@beeb.net Website: http:// davidcobb.members.beeb.net/index.html

COCKCROFT John Anthony Eric, b. 9 August 1934, England. Freelance Consultant. m. Education: FTI, C Text, Burnley College of Science and Technology, 1954; BA, 1959, MA, 1963, Modern History and Economics, Cambridge University; MLitt, Politics/Strategic Studies, Aberdeen University, 1979; PhD, Strategy & Science & Technology Policy, Manchester University, 1982. Appointments: National Service, Commissioned, Sword of Honour, Army, 1954-56; Management Trainee, UK private industry including Ford Motor Co, 1959-65; Fellow, Ministry of Economic Co-ordination, Athens, Greece, OECD, Paris, 1965-67; Adviser, Inter-ministerial Investment Advisory Committee, Kabul, Afghanistan, FCO/ODA, 1970-71; Expert, Ministry of National Economy, Jordan, UNIDO, Vienna, 1971-72; Managing Director, Anglo-German Textile Manufacturing Co, UK, 1973-78; Fellow, Greece & Turkey, NATO, Brussels, 1979-80; Consultant, Dar Es Salaam, Tanzania, UNIDO, Vienna, 1980; Professor of Economics, University of Makurdi, Nigeria, 1982; Killam Research Fellow, Strategy, Centre for Foreign Policy Studies, Dalhousie University, Canada, 1983-84; Team Leader, Bangladesh, Cotton Industry, World Bank/IFC/PriceWaterhouse, 1985-86; Managing Director, private company spinning, weaving and making-up, UK, 1986-89; Manager, subsidiary of Allied Textiles plc, Bradford, UK, 1990-91; Consultant, Stoddard Sekers plc, Renfrew, Scotland, UK, 1991-94; Team Leader, Cotton Sector Assessment Project, Ethiopia, USAID, Washington, 1994; Team Leader, Cereal Seeds Project, Bangladesh, EU,

1994-97; Consultant, Agricultural Policy Reform Project, USAID/APRP, Cairo, 1997; Professor and Adviser in International Relations, Queen's University, Dhaka, 1997-98; Senior Management Consultant, Dhaka, Helen Keller, New York, 1998-99; Honorary Visiting Fellow, Centre for Defence Economics, University of York, UK, 2000-03; Consultant, Orissa, India, public sector, DFID/Adam Smith Institute, London, 2000; Consultant, W & E Africa, ITC/UN, Geneva, 2000; Consultant, Kosovo State Enterprise Conversion, EAR/UNMIK, EU, 2000; Product Development Consultant, London, 2001-; Private Consultant, Cairo, Egypt, 2001; Team Leader, EU Enterprise Restructuring Project, Bosnia, 2002; ITC Nominee, IF Mission to Malawi, World Bank, Washington/ ITC, Geneva, 2002; Specialist, Kosovo, Support for Economic & Institutional Reform, USAID Washington /SEGIR, 2003; Adviser, Haitian Economic Recovery and Opportunity Act, HERO, US Senate/USAID Washington, 2003; Adviser, Textiles/Trade, WTO & AGOA, East and Southern Africa, Regional Agricultural Trade Expansion Support, USAID Washington /RATES, 2003; Adviser, Southern African Global Competitiveness Hub, Regional Activity to promote Integration through Dialogue and Policy Implementation, USAID Washington/RAPID, 2003; Consultant in Mozambique, USAID, Washington/RAPID, 2004; Specialist, Paraguay Exports, USAID, Washington, DC, 2004; Team Leader, Africa Caribbean Pacific (ACP) sector study, EU, Brussels, 2003-04. Publications: Science & Technology in Economic Development: The Pilot Teams, Greece, OECD, Paris (Joint), 1968; BMD, NATO, Europe and UK to Y2K, private paper, 2005; An Exercise in Contemporary Strategy: A Study in Military Power, Influence and Science & Technology in Determining Plausibility of a New Soviet Limited War Strategy 1972-81, PhD thesis, 1981; Intra-Alliance Economic Co-operation & Military Assistance, Greece & Turkey, for NATO, Brussels, 1980; Glimpses into Star Wars: 1976-1982 & 2000-2007, Research Monograph; Over 25 reports for governments and international organisations; 3 letters to the editor on Global Security published in first place, The Times, 2001-02. Honours: Fellow, Textile Institute, Manchester; Textile Society, Bradford; Marksman, Army; Technical State Scholarship to Cambridge University. Memberships: Cavalry and Guards Club, London. Address: The Old Vicarage, Ledsham LS25 5LT, England. E-mail: cockcroftj@aol.com

COCKER Jarvis Branson, b. 19 September, 1963, England. Singer. m. Camille Bidault-Waddington, 1 son. Education: St Martin's College of Art & Design. Appointments: Singer with Pulp (formerly named Arabacus Pulp), 1981-; Made Videos for Pulp, Aphex Twin, Tindersticks; Co-Producer, Do You Remember The First Time? (TV). Creative Works: Singles include: My Legendary Girlfriend, 1991; Razzmatazz, 1992; O U, 1992; Babies, 1992; Common People, 1995; Disco 2000, 1996; Albums include: It; Freaks; Separations; PulpIntro: The Gift Recordings; His 'N' Hers; Different Class, 1995; This is Hardcore, 1998; We Love Life, 2001; Compositions for films: Do You Remember the First Time? 1994; Wild Side, 1995; Harry Potter and the Goblet of Fire, 2005; Children of Men, 2006. Address: Rough Trade Management, 66 Golborne Road, London W10 5PS, England. Website: www.pulponline.com

COCKER Joe, b. 20 May 1944, Sheffield, South Yorkshire, England. Singer; Songwriter. Appointments: Northern Club circuit, with group, The Grease Band, 1965-69; Solo Artist, 1968-; Regular worldwide tours and major concert appearances. Creative Works: With a Little Help from My Friends, 1969; Joe Cocker! 1969; Mad Dogs and Englishmen, 1970; Joe Cocker, 1973; I Can Stand a Little Rain, 1974; Jamaica Say You Will, 1975; Stingray, 1976; Live in LA,1976;

Luxury You Can Afford, 1978; Sheffield Steel, 1982; Civilized Man, 1984; Off the Record, 1984; Cocker, 1986; Unchain My Heart, 1987; One Night of Sin, 1989; Live! 1990; Night Calls, 1992; Have a Little Faith, 1994; Organic, 1996; Across from Midnight, 1997; Vance Arnold and the Avenge 1963, 2000; No Ordinary World, 2000; Respect Yourself, 2002; Definitive Collection, 2002; Sheffield Steel, 2002; Respect Yourself, 2002; Joe Cocker Greatest Love Songs; Heart and Soul. Honours: Grammy, Best Pop Vocal Performance, 1983; Academy Award, Best Film Song, 1983; Grammy Nomination, 1989. Address: c/o Roger Davies Management, 15030 Ventura Blvd #772, Sherman Oaks, CA 91403, USA.

COE, Baron of Ranmore in the County of Surrey, Sebastian Newbold, b. 29 September 1956. Athelete, Member of Parliament. m. Nicola Susan Elliott, 1990, 2 sons, 2 daughters. Education: BSc Hons, Economics, Social History, Loughborough University. Career: Winner, Gold Medal for running 1500m and silver medal for 800m, Moscow Olympics, 1980; Gold medal for 1500m and silver medal for 800m, Los Angeles Olympics, 1984; European 800m Champion, Stuttgart, 1986; World Record Holder at 800m, 1000m and mile, 1981; Research Assistant, Loughborough University, 1981-84; Member, 1983-89, Vice Chairman, 1986-89, Chairman, Olympic Review Group, 1984-85, Sports Council; Member, HEA, 1987-92; Olympic Committee, Medical Commission, 1987-; Conservative MP for Falmouth and Camborne, 1992-; PPS to Deputy PM, 1995-96; Assistant Government Whip, 1996-97; Private Secretary to Leader of the Opposition, The Rt Hon William Hague, MP, 1997-2001; Global Advisor, NIKE, 2000-; Council Member, International Association of Athletic Federations, 2003-; Vice Chair, 2003-04, Chair and President, 2004-, London 2012 Olympic and Paralympic Games Bid. Publications: Running Free, with David Miller, 1981; Running for Fitness, with Peter Coe, 1983; The Olympians, 1984, 1996; More Than a Game, 1992; Born to Run (autobiography), 1992. Honours: OBE, 1990, MBE, 1981, Life Peer, 2000, BBC Sports Personality of the Year, Special Award, 2005. Memberships: Associate Member, Academie des Sports, France; Athletes Commission, IOC; IOC Medical Commission, 1988-94; Member, Sport For All Commission, 1998-; IOC Commission 2000, 1999. Address: House of Lords, London SW1A 0PW, England.

COEN Ethan, b. 21 September 1958, St Louis Park, Minnesota, USA. Film Producer; Screenwriter. Education: Princeton University. Appointments: Screenwriter with Joel Coen, Crime Wave (formerly XYZ Murders); Producer, Screenplay, Editor, Blood Simple, 1984. Creative Works: Films: Raising Arizona, 1987; Miller's Crossing, 1990; Barton Fink, 1991; The Hudsucker Proxy, 1994; Fargo, 1996; The Naked Man; The Big Lebowski, 1998; O Brother, Where Art Thou? 2000; The Man Who Wasn't There, 2001; Fever in the Blood, 2002; Intolerable Cruelty, 2003; The Ladykillers, 2004; Paris I Love You, 2006; No Country for Old Men (Producer), 2007. Honours: 12 Awards, 32 nominations. Publication: Gates of Eden, 1998. Address: c/o UTA, 9560 Wilshire Boulevard, Beverly Hills, CA 90212, USA.

COEN Joel, b. 29 November 1955, St Louis Park, Minnesota, USA. Film Director; Screenwriter. Divorced. Education: Simon's Rock College; New York University. Appointments: Assistant Editor, Fear No Evil, Evil Dead; Worked with Rock Video Crews; Screenwriter with Ethan Coen, Crime Wave (formerly XYZ Murders). Creative Works: Films: Blood Simple, 1984; Raising Arizona, 1987; Miller's Crossing, 1990; Barton Fink, 1991; The Hudsucker Proxy, 1994; Fargo, 1996; The Big Lebowski; O Brother, Where Art Thou? 2000;

The Man Who Wasn't There, 2001; Intolerable Cruelty, 2003; The Ladykillers, 2004; Paris I Love You, 2006; No Country For Old Men, 2007. Honours include: Best Director Award, Cannes International Film Festival, 1996; 31 Awards, 44 Nominations. Address: c/o UTA, 9560 Wilshire Boulevard, Beverly Hills, CA 90212, USA.

COENEGRACHTS Kenneth, b. 28 September 1974, Tongeren, Belgium. Radiologist. m. Ilse Christine Vincent. Education: Resident, Catholic University of Leuven, 1999-2004; Management Training, Vlerick School, Ghent, 2005. Appointments: Staff Member, Department of Radiology, 2004-; President, Medical Audit; Secretary, International Management Planning; Member, Strategic Management Planning, AZ St-Jan AV, Bruges. Publications: 33 papers and articles in professional journals; 53 presentations. Memberships: Royal Belgian Society of Radiology; European Congress of Radiology; European Society of Gastrointestinal and Abdominal Radiologists; American Roentgen Ray Society; Société Francaise de Radiologie; International Society for Magnetic Resonance in Medicine. Address: AZ St-Jan AV, Bruges, Ruddershove 10, 8000 Bruges, Belgium. E-mail: kenneth.coenegrachts@azbrugge.be

COHEN Leonard, b. 21 September 1934, Montreal, Canada. Singer; Songwriter. 2 children. Education: McGill University. Creative Works: Recordings include: Songs of Leonard Cohen, 1967; Songs of Love and Hate, 1971; Live Songs, 1972; New Skin for the Old Ceremony, 1973; Best of Leonard Cohen, 1975; Death of a Ladies Man, 1977; Recent Songs, 1979; Songs From A Room, 1969; Various Positions, 1984; I'm Your Man, 1988; The Future, 1992; Cohen Live, 1994; Ten New Songs, 2001; Field Commander Cohen, 2002; The Essential Leonard Cohen, 2003; Dear Heather, 2004; Leonard Cohen, I'm Your Man, 2005. Publications: Let Us Compare Mythologies; The Favorite Game; Beautiful Losers; Energy of Slaves; Death of a Lady's Man; Book of Mercy; Stranger Music; The Favourite Game. Honours include: McGill Literature Award; Order of Canada. Address: c/o Macklam Feldman Management, 200-1505 W 2nd Ave, Vancouver, BC V6H 3Y4, Canada.

COHN Mildred, b. 12 July 1913, New York, USA. Biochemist. m. Henry Primakoff, 1 son, 2 daughters. Education: BA, Hunter College, 1931; MA, 1932, PhD, 1937, Columbia University. Appointments: Research Associate, Biochemistry, George Washington University, 1937-38; Research Associate, Biochemistry, Cornell Medical College, 1938-46; Research Associate, 1946-58; Associate Professor, 1958-1960, Biochemistry, Washington University, St Louis; Associate Professor of Biochemistry and Biophysics, 1960-61; Full Professor, 1961-1982, Benjamin Rush Professor, 1978-1982, University of Pennsylvania School of Medicine; Career Investigator, American Heart Association, 1964-1978; Senior Member, Fox Chase Cancer Center, 1982-85. Publications: More than 150 articles and chapters in professional journals and books. Honours include: 9 Honorary Degrees and Garvan Medal, American Chemical Society, 1963; Cresson Medal, Franklin Institute, 1975; Chandler Medal, Columbia University, 1986; National Medal of Science, 1982; Distinguished Service Award, College of Physicians, Philadelphia, 1987; PA Governor's Award for Excellence in Science, 1993; Stein-Moore Award, Protein Society, 1997; many others. Memberships: Phi Beta Kappa; Sigma Xi; American Chemical Society; American Society of Biochemistry and Molecular Biology; American Academy of Arts and Sciences; National Academy of Sciences; American Philosophical Society. Address: University of Pennsylvania School of Medicine, Department of Biochemistry and Biophysics, 242 Anat/Chem, Philadelphia, PA 19104-6059, USA.

COHN-SHERBOK Dan, b. 1 February 1945, Denver, Colorado, USA. Professor of Judaism. m. Lavinia Cohn-Sherbok. Education: BA, Williams College, 1962-66; BHL, MAHL, Hebrew Union College, 1966-71; PhD, Cambridge University, 1971-74. Appointments: Lecturer, Theology, University of Kent, Canterbury, 1975-97; Professor of Judaism, University of Wales, Lampeter, 1997-. Publications: The Jewish Heritage; Dictionary of Judaism and Christianity; Atlas of Jewish History; The Jewish Faith; The Hebrew Bible; Fifty Key Jewish Thinkers; Judaism; Judaism: History, Belief and Practice; Understanding the Holocaust; Holocaust Theology; Interfaith Theology; A Concise Encyclopaedia of Judaism; Jewish Mysticism: An Anthology; Judaism and Other Faiths; Jewish Petitionary Prayers; Modern Judaism; Dictionary of Jewish Biography; The Paradox of Antisemitism; Politics of Apocalypse. Honours: Honorary DD, Hebrew Union College; Listed in numerous Who's Who and biographical publications. Memberships: London Society for the Study of Religion; Cymmrodian Society; Athenaeum; Williams Club; Lansdowne Club. Address: Department of Theology and Religious Studies, University of Wales, Lampeter SA48 7ED, Wales.

COJOCARU Viorel, b. 7 August 1934, Cernãuti, Romania. Physicist; Scientist. m. Maria Cojocaru, 1 son, 1 daughter. Education: Graduate, Atomic Physics, Physics and Mathematics Faculty, Bucharest University, 1957; Fellow, Physics Institute, Uppsala University and Forskningsrådens Laboratorium, Studsvik, Sweden, 1967-68; Doctor in Physics, 1970. Appointments: Scientific Researcher, 1957-67, Senior Scientific Researcher, 1968-72, 1975-78, Atomic Institute of Physics, Mãgurele, Bucharest; Senior Scientific Researcher, Joint Institute for Nuclear Research, Dubna, USSR, 1972-75; Senior Scientific Researcher, National Institute for Physics and Nuclear Engineering "Horia Hulubei", Mãgurele, Bucharest, 1978-; Associate Professor, Faculty of Industrial Chemistry, University "Politehnica", Bucharest, 2000-2003. Publications: Co-author or author of over 140 scientific papers concerning nuclear spectroscopy in reactions with thermal neutrons, heavy ions and μ. mesons, atomic and nuclear archaeometry, atomic and nuclear analyses on the chemical composition including: Fission by radiationless transition in the μ mesonic atom ^{239}Pu, 1966; Internal conversion electrons from the reaction ^{168}Yb$(\eta,\gamma)^{169}$Yb, 1968; Fission of ^{232}Th,^{238}U and ^{235}U induced by negative muons, 1975; Fission probability of nucleus of ^{232}Th mesoatom, 1976; High –spin states in ^{70}As, 1991; Nuclear Analyses on Pietroasa gold hoard, 1999; EDXRF and PAA analyses of Dacian gold coins of KOSON Type, 2000; Micro-PIXE study of gold archaeological objects, 2003; Natural gold composition studies by proton activation analysis, 2003; A possible non-specific carrier for gold analysis in rocks, 2003; New Recommended Upper Limits for Dipole γ-Ray Strengths, 2004; Romanian ancient gold objects provenance studies using micro-beam methods: the Case of Pietroasa hoard, 2002; 1 monograph, 2006. Honours: Romanian Academy Award "D Hurmuzescu"; Man of the Year 2002; Member of Research Board of Advisors of ABI; American Medal of Honor; Leading Scientists of the World, 2005; Diploma of Expert in Nuclear Physics, 2005; Gold Medal for Romania, 2006; Da Vinci Diamond, 2006; Top 100 Scientists, 2006; Listed in Who's Who publications and biographical dictionaries. Address: National Institute for Physics and Nuclear Engineering, "Horia Hulubei", Mãgurele, Bucharest, Romania.

COLE B J, b. 17 June 1946, North London, England. Musician (pedal steel guitar); Producer. Career: Musician, Country Music circuit, London, 1964-; Pedal steel guitar player, Cochise; Founder member, producer, Hank Wangford Band; Leading exponent of instrument in UK; Currently prolific session musician and solo artiste; Leader, own group Transparent Music Ensemble; Replacement guitarist for the Verve, 1998-. Recordings: Solo albums: New Hovering Dog, 1972; Transparent Music, 1989; The Heart Of The Moment, 1995; As session musician: Tiny Dancer, Elton John, 1970; Wide Eyed And Legless, Andy Fairweather-Low, 1975; No Regrets, Walker Brothers, 1976; City To City, Gerry Rafferty, 1978; Everything Must Change, Paul Young, 1984; Silver Moon, David Sylvian, 1986; Diet Of Strange Places, k d lang, 1987; Montagne D'Or, The Orb, 1995; Possibly Maybe, Björk, 1995; with Hank Wangford: Hank Wangford, 1980; Live, 1982; Other recordings with: Johnny Nash; Deacon Blue; Level 42; Danny Thompson; Alan Parsons Project; Shakin' Stevens; Beautiful South; John Cale; Echobelly; Elton John, R.E.M, The Verve, Depeche Mode, David Gilmour.

COLE Natalie Maria, b. 6 February 1950, Los Angeles, California, USA. Singer. m. (1) Marvin J Yancy, 30 July 1976, divorced, (2) Andre Fischer, 17 September 1989, divorced. Education: BA, Child Psychology, University of Massachusetts, 1972. Career: Stage debut, 1962; Solo recording artist, 1975-; Major concerts worldwide include: Tokyo Music Festival, 1979; Nelson Mandela 70th Birthday Concert, Wembley, 1988; Nelson Mandela tribute, Wembley, 1990; John Lennon Tribute Concert, Liverpool, 1990; Homeless benefit concert with Quincy Jones, Pasadena, 1992; Rainforest benefit concert, Carnegie Hall, 1992; Commitment To Life VI, (AIDs benefit concert), Los Angeles, 1992; Television appearances include: Sinatra And Friends, 1977; Host, Big Break, 1990; Motown 30, 1990; Tonight Show, 1991; Entertainers '91, 1991; Recordings: Hit singles: This Will Be, 1975; Sophisticated Lady, 1976; I've Got Love On My Mind, 1977; Our Love (Number 1, US R&B chart), 1977; Gimme Some Time (duet with Peabo Bryson), 1980; What You Won't Do For Love (duet with Peabo Bryson), 1980; Jump Start, 1987; I Live For Your Love, 1988; Pink Cadillac, 1988; Miss You Like Crazy (Number 1, US R&B charts), 1989; Wild Women Do, from film Pretty Woman, 1990; Unforgettable (duet with father Nat "King" Cole), 1991; Smile Like Yours, 1997; Albums: Inseparable, 1975; Natalie, 1976; Unpredictable, 1977; Thankful, 1978; Natalie...Live!, 1978; I Love You So, 1979; Don't Look Back, 1980; Happy Love, 1981; Natalie Cole Collection, 1981; I'm Ready, 1982; Dangerous, 1985; Everlasting, 1987; Good To Be Back, 1989; Unforgettable...With Love (Number 1, US), 1991; The Soul Of Natalie Cole, 1991; Take A Look, 1993; Holly and Ivy, 1994; Stardust, 1996; This Will Be, 1997; Snowfall on the Sahara, 1999; Love Songs (compilation), 2000; with Peabo Bryson: We're The Best Of Friends, 1980. Honours: Numerous Grammy Awards include: Best New Artist, 1976; Best Female R&B Vocal Performance, 1976, 1977; 5 Grammy Awards for Unforgettable, including Best Song, Best Album, 1992; 5 NAACP Image Awards, 1976, 1988, 1992; American Music Awards: Favourite Female R&B Artist, 1978; Favourite Artist, Favourite Album, 1992; Soul Train Award, Best Single, 1988; Various Gold discs. Memberships: AFTRA; NARAS. Address: c/o Jennifer Allen, PMK, 8500 Wilshire Boulevard, Suite 700, Beverly Hills, CA 90211, USA.

CÖLFEN Helmut, b. 24 July 1965, Krefeld, Germany. Scientist; Chemist. m. Stefanie Sender, 2 daughters, 1 son. Education: Chemistry Studies, Gerhard-Mercator University, Duisburg, 1985-91; PhD, Chemistry, 1993; Postdoctoral Studies, National Centre for Macromolecular Hydrodynamics, Nottingham, England, 1993-95; Habilitation, Max-Planck-Institute for Colloids and Interfaces, 1995-2001. Appointments: Research Assistant, University of Duisburg, 1991-93; Postdoctoral Studies, 1993-95; Scientist, Head of Analytical Services in Colloid Chemistry, Head of Biomimetic Mineralisation Group, Max-Planck-Institute for Colloids and Interfaces, 1995-; Private Dozent, Potsdam University, 2004-. Publications: More than 130 papers as co-author and first author in scientific journals. Honours: Graduate Scholarship, University of Duisburg, 1991-93; Hochschulabsolventenpreis, University of Duisburg, 1991; Studienabschlussstipendium, Fonds der chemischen Industrie, 1993; Dr Hermann Schnell Award, German Chemical Society; Travel Award, Macromolecular Chemistry Division, German Chemical Society; Steinhofer Lecture, Steinhofer Foundation, University of Freiburg, 2006. Membership: German Chemical Society. Address: Max-Planck-Institute for Colloids and Interfaces, Colloid Chemistry, D-14424 Potsdam, Germany. E-mail: coelfen@mpikg.mpg.de

COLGAN Michael Anthony, b. 17 July 1950, Dublin, Ireland. Theatre, Film and TV Producer. Education: BA, Trinity College, Dublin. Appointments: Director, Abbey Theatre, Dublin, 1974-78; Co-Manager, Irish Theatre Company, 1977-78; Manger, 1978-81, Artistic Director, 1981-83, Member Board of Directors, 1983-, Dublin Theatre Festival; Artistic Director, Board Member, Gate Theatre Dublin, 1983-; Executive Director, Little Bird Films, 1986-; Co-Founder, Blue Angel Film Company, 1999 (producers of The Beckett Film Project 2000, commissioned by Channel 4 and RTÉ to film all 19 of Beckett's plays, and Celebration by Harold Pinter with Channel 4, 2006); Artistic Director Parma Film Festival, 1982; Chairman, St Patrick's Festival, 1996-99; Board Member: Millennium Festivals Ltd, Laura Pels Foundation, New York, 2000-04; Theatre productions include: Faith Healer, Dublin and New York; I'll Go On; Juno and the Paycock; Salomé; 5 Beckett Festivals (all 19 Samuel Beckett stage plays), Dublin, New York and London; 4 Pinter Festivals: Dublin and New York; World premieres include: Molly Sweeney, Afterplay, Shining City, The Home Place; Producer, Two Lives, TV drama, RTE, 1986. Honours: Sunday Independent Arts Awards, 1985, 1986; Eamonn Andrews Award for Excellence, 1996; People of the Year Award, 1999; Doctor in Laws Honoris Causa, Trinity College, Dublin, 2000; Peabody Award, 2002; Irish Times Theatre Lifetime Achievement Award, 2006; Chevalier dans l'Ordre des Arts et des Lettres, 2007. Memberships: Irish Arts Council, 1989-94; Governing Authority Dublin City University. Address: The Gate Theatre, 1 Cavendish Road, Dublin 1, Ireland. E-mail: info@gate-theatre.ie

COLLAZOS Julio, b. 11 March 1955, Tordehumos, Valladolid, Spain. Medical Doctor. Education: Medical Degree, Complutense University School of Medicine, Madrid, Spain, 1979; Doctor in Medicine, Autonoma University School of Medicine, Madrid, Spain, 1990. Appointments: Residency and Fellowship, Internal Medicine, Jimenez Díaz Foundation, Madrid, Spain, 1980-84; Attending Physician, Hospital Provincial, Alicante, Spain, 1984-87; Associate Professor, Alicante University School of Medicine, Alicante, Spain, 1984-87; Attending Physician, 1987-93, Chief Infectious Diseases Section, 1993-, Hospital de Galdakao, Vizcaya, Spain. Publications: Doctoral Thesis: The Tumor Makers in Benign Liver Disease; Many professional articles and book chapters. Honours: Medical Degree with honours, Complutense University School of Medicine; Doctor in Medicine cum laude, Autonoma University School of

Medicine; Nominated for numerous honours and awards from American Biographical Institute and International Biographical Centre, England. Memberships: President, Association of Infectious Diseases, Vizcaya, Spain; Fellow, American Biographical Institute, Raleigh, North Carolina, USA. Address: Section of Infectious Diseases, Hospital de Galdakao, 48960 Vizcaya, Spain.

COLLEDGE William Henry, b. 23 January 1962. Doctor. Education: Biochemistry, Imperial College of Science and Technology, University of London, 1980-83; PhD, National Institute for Medical Research, Laboratory of Eukaryotic Molecular Genetics, London, 1983-87. Appointments Research Associate, Faculty of Health Sciences, University of Ottawa, Ontario, Canada, 1987-88; Scientific Consultant for Animal Biotechnology, Cambridge, 1988-93; Senior Research Associate, University of Cambridge, Wellcome/CRC Institute, University of Cambridge, 1988-95; Technical Support Consultant for CAMBIO, 1990-2000; Lecturer, 1995-2000; Reader, Molecular Physiology, Physiological Laboratory, University of Cambridge, 2001-; Publications: 103 papers and articles for national and international professional journals; 60 refereed scientific journals; 40 assessed grant applications. Honours: Joint Medical Research Council/ICI Partnership Award; Lloyds of London Tercentenary Fellowship; Gunnar-Nilsson Cancer Research Trust Award; Senior Research Fellow, Churchill College, Cambridge; Sir Henry Wellcome Commemorative Award for Innovative Research; Royal Society Senior Research Fellowship, Leverhulme Trust; 22 research grants. Memberships: Scientific Advisory Board member, Paradigm Therapeutics, Cambridge; Scientific Advisory Member, TriStem, 2001-02; Member, Scientific Editorial Board, Professional Journal; Member, Faculty of 1000; Sub-committee Panel Member, external assessment, MRC Clinical Sciences, London; International Scientific Assessor, Georgian National Science Foundation. Address: Physiological Laboratory, University of Cambridge, Downing Site, Cambridge, CB2 3EG, England.

COLLETTE Toni, b. 1 November 1972, Sydney, Australia. Actor. m. Dave Galafassi, 2003. Education: National Institute of Dramatic Art, Sydney. Career: Actor: Theatre: Uncle Vanya; Away; Summer of the Aliens; King Lear; A Little Night Music; Blue Murder; The Wild Party; Films include: Muriel's Wedding, 1994; Emma, 1996; Velvet Goldmine, 1998; 8 ½ Women, The Sixth Sense, 1999; Shaft, 2000; Changing Lanes, About a Boy, The Hours, 2002; In Her Shoes, 2005; The Night Listener, Little Miss Sunshine, The Dead Girl, Tsunami: the Aftermath, 2006; Evening, Nothing is Private, 2007. Honours: Best Newcomer in a Play or Musical, 16th Annual Sydney Critic's Circle Award, 1992; Australian Film and Television Award for Best Actress, 1994; Australian Film Institute, Best Actress, 1994; Film Critic's Circle of Australia, Best Actress, 1994; Australian Film Institute, Best Supporting Actress, 1996; Australian Film Institute, Best Supporting Actress, 1998; The Blockbuster Film Awards, Best Supporting Actress (Suspense), 2000; Nominated, Broadway's Tony Award as Best Actress, 2000.

COLLINGBOURNE Stephen, b. 15 August 1943, Dartington, Devon, England. Artist. 1 son, 1 daughter. Appointments: Lecturer, Dartington College of Art, 1965-70; Worked at Serpentine Gallery, London, 1971; Assistant to Robert Adams, sculptor, 1972; Lived and worked in Malaya, 1972-73; Fellow in Sculpture, University College of Wales, 1974; Lecturer in Sculpture, Edinburgh College of Art, 1976-99; Early retirement, 1999-; One man exhibitions include: Bluecoat Gallery, Liverpool, 1972; British Council,

Kuala Lumpur, Malaysia, 1973; Plymouth City Art Gallery, 1977; Southampton City Art Gallery, 1977; Informal Works on Paper, Edinburgh Festival, 1990; High Cross House, Dartington, Devon, 1997; Galleri Viktor, Nykarleby, Finland, 1998; Group exhibitions include: Serpentine Gallery, London, 1972; Kettles Yard, Cambridge, 1973; Built in Scotland Touring Show, Camden Arts Centre, London, 1983; Renlands Konstmuseum, Karleby, Finland, 1998. Honours: Commissions include: Leicester University, 1974; Collections include: Welsh Arts Council; Leicester City Art Centre; Edinburgh City Art Gallery; Awards and prizes from: Arts Council of Great Britain, 1972; John Moore's Liverpool, 1972; The British Council, 1973; Welsh Arts Council, 1975; Arts Council of Great Britain, 1975; Welsh Arts Council, 1976; Royal Scottish Academy, 1977, 1978; Scottish Arts Council, 1985. Address: Tofts, Blyth Bridge, West Linton, EH46 7AJ, Scotland.

COLLINS Jackie, b. England. Novelist; Short Story Writer; Actress. m. Oscar Lerman, deceased, 3 children. Creative Works: Screenplays: Yesterday's Hero; The World in Full of Married Men; The Stud. Publications: The World is Full of Married Men, 1968; The Stud, 1969; Sunday Simmons and Charlie Brick, 1971; Sinners, 1981; Lovehead, 1974; The World is Full of Divorced Women, 1975; The Love Killers, Lovers & Gamblers, 1977; The Bitch, 1979; Chances, 1981; Hollywood Wives, 1983; Lucky, 1985; Hollywood Husbands, 1986; Rock Star, 1988; Lady Boss, 1990; American Star, The World is Full of Married Men, 1993; Hollywood Kids, 1994; Dangerous Kiss, 1999; Hollywood Wives: The New Generation, Lethal Seduction, 2001; Deadly Embrace, 2002; Hollywood Divorces, 2003; Drop Dead Beautiful – The Continuing Adventures of Lucky Santangelo, 2007; Married Lovers, 2008. Address: c/o Simon & Schuster, 1230 Avenue of the Americas, New York, NY 10020, USA.

COLLINS Joan, b. 23 May 1933, London, England. Actress. m. (1) Maxwell Reed, 1954, divorced, 1957, (2) Anthony Newley, 1963, divorced, 1970, 1 son, 1 daughter, (3) Ronald Kass, 1972, divorced, 1983, 1 daughter, (4) Peter Holm, 1985, divorced, 1987, (5) Percy Gibson, 2002. Career: Films include: I Believe in You, 1952; Girl in Red Velvet Swing, Land of the Pharaohs, 1955; The Opposite Sex, 1956; Rally Round Flag Boys, Sea Wife, 1957; Warning Shot, 1966; The Executioner, 1969; Revenge, 1971; The Big Sleep, Tales of the Unexpected, 1977; Stud, 1979; The Bitch, 1980; Nutcracker, 1982; Decadence, 1994; Hart to Hart, Annie: A Royal Adventure, In the Bleak Midwinter, 1995; The Clandestine Marriage, The Flintstones-Viva Rock Vegas, Joseph and the Amazing Technicolor Dreamcoat (voice), 1999; Ozzie, 2001; Alice in Glamourland, 2004; Plays include: The Last of Mrs Cheyne, 1979-80; Private Lives, 1990, 1991; Love Letters, 2000; Over the Moon, 2001; Full Circle, 2004; Numerous TV appearances include: Dynasty, 1981-89; Cartier Affair, 1984; Sins, 1986; Monte Carlo, 1986; Tonight at 8.30, 1991; Pacific Palisades (serial), 1997; These Old Broads, Will and Grace (USA), Guiding Light, 2002; Footballers' Wives, Hotel Babylon, 2006. Publications: J C Beauty Book, 1980; Katy: A Fight for Life, 1981; Past Imperfect, 1984; Prime Time, 1988; Love and Desire and Hate, 1990; My Secrets, 1994; Too Damn Famous, 1995; Second Act, 1996; My Friends' Secrets, 1999; Star Quality, 2002; Joan's Way, 2003; Misfortune's Daughters, 2004. Honours: Golden Globe, Best TV Actress, 1982; People's Choice, Favourite TV Performer, 1985; OBE, 1997; Lifetime Achievement Award, San Diego Film Festival, 2005. Address: c/o Paul Keylock, 16 Bulbecks Walk, South Woodham Ferrers, Essex, CM3 5ZN, England.

COLLINS Kenneth Darlington (Sir), b. 12 August 1939, United Kingdom. Environmentalist. m. Georgina Frances Pollard, 1 son, 1 daughter. Education: BSc (Hons), Glasgow University, 1965; MSc, Strathclyde University, 1973. Appointments: Steelworks Apprentice, 1956-59; Planning Officer, 1965-66; Tutor Organiser, Workers Educational Association, 1966-67; Lecturer: Glasgow College of Building, 1967-69, Paisley College of Technology, 1969-79; Member: East Kilbride Town and District Council, 1973-79, Lanark County Council, 1973-75, East Kilbride Development Corporation, 1976-79; European Parliament: Deputy Leader, Labour Group, 1979-84, Chairman Environment Committee, 1979-84, 1989-99, Vice-Chairman, 1984-87, Socialist Spokesman on Environment, Public Health and Consumer Protection, 1984-89; Chairman, Scottish Environment Protection Agency, 1999-2007. Publications: Contributed to European Parliament reports; Various articles on European environment policy. Honour: Knights Bachelor, 2003. Honours: Honorary Degree of Doctor, University of Paisley, 2004. Memberships: Fellow, Royal Scottish Geographical Society; Honorary Fellow, Chartered Institution of Water and Environment Management; Honorary Fellow, Chartered Institution of Wastes Management; Fellow, Industry and Parliament Trust; Former Board Member, Institute of European Environment Policy, 1999-2006; Former Board Member, Central Scotland Forest Trust; Board Member of Forward Scotland until 2003; Former Member, Management Board, European Environment Agency (nominated by the European Parliament); Honorary Vice-President, National Society for Clean Air; Vice-President: Royal Environmental Health Institute of Scotland, International Federation of Environmental Health, Town and Country Planning Association, Trading Standards Institute; Former Ambassador for Asthma UK, -2007; Former Board Member, Energy Action Scotland; Vice President, Association of Drainage Authorities; Former Chairman, Health Equality Europe, 2005-06; Member, Advisory Board, Euro Genomics Policy & Research Forum; European Public Affairs Consultancies Association (EAACA) Professional Practices Panel; European Commission's High Level Group on Competitiveness, Energy & The Environment. Address: 11 Stuarton Park, East Kilbride, G74 4LA, Scotland.

COLLINS Pauline, b. 3 September 1940, Exmouth, Devon, England. Actress. m. John Alderton, 2 sons, 1 daughter. Education: Central School of Speech & Drama. Creative Works: Stage Appearances: A Gazelle in Park Lane (stage debut, Windsor 1962); Passion Flower Hotel; The Erpingham Camp; The Happy Apple; The Importance of Being Ernest; The Night I Chased the Women with an Eel; Come as You Are; Judies; Engaged; Confusions; Romantic Comedy; Woman in Mind; Shirley Valentine; Films: Shirley Valentine, 1989; City of Joy, 1992; My Mother's Courage, 1997; Paradise Road, 1997; Mrs Caldicott's Cabbage War, 2002; TV appearances: Upstairs Downstairs; Thomas and Sarah; Forever Green; No-Honestly; Tales of the Unexpected; Knockback, 1984; Tropical Moon Over Dorking; The Ambassador, 1998; Man and Boy, 2002; Sparkling Cyanide, 2003; Bleak House, 2005; Doctor Who, 2006; What We Did on Our Holiday, 2006. Publication: Letter to Louise, 1992. Honours include: Olivier Award, Best Actress, London; BAFTA Award; Tony, Drama Desk & Outer Critics' Circle Awards, New York; OBE, 2001.

COLLINS Phil, b. 30 January 1951, Chiswick, London, England. Pop Singer; Drummer; Composer. m. (1) 1976, 1 son, 1 daughter, (2) Jill Tavelman, 1984, divorced, 1 daughter, (3) Orianne Cevey, 1999, divorced 2008, 2 sons. Education: Barbara Speake Stage School. Appointments: Former Actor,

Artful Dodger in London Production of Oliver; Joined Rock Group, Genesis as Drummer, 1970, Lead Singer, 1975-96. Creative Works: Albums with Genesis: Selling England by the Pound, 1973; Invisible Touch, 1986; We Can't Dance, 1991; Solo Albums include: Face Value, 1981; Hello I Must Be Going, 1982; No Jacket Required, 1985; 12"Ers, 1987; But Seriously, 1989; Serivous Hits Live, 1990; Dance into the Light, 1996; Hits, 1998; A Hot Night in Paris, 1999; Testify, 2002; The Platinum Collection, 2004; Love Songs: A Compilation ... Old and New, 2004; Solo Singles include: In the Air Tonight, 1981; You Can't Hurry Love, 1982; Against All Odds, 1984; One More Night, 1985; Easy Lover, 1985; Separate Lives, 1985; Groovy Kind of Love, 1988; Two Hearts, 1988; Another Day in Paradise, 1989; I Wish It Would Rain Down, 1990; Both Sides of the Story, 1993; Dance Into the Light, 1996; Soundtrack Albums: Against All Odds, 1984; White Nights, 1985; Buster, 1988; Tarzan, 1999; Brother Bear, 2003. Films include: Buster, 1988; Frauds, 1993. Honours include: 7 Grammy's; 6 Ivor Novello Awards; 4 Brits; 2 Awards, Variety Club of Great Britain; 2 Silver Clef's; 2 Elvis Awards; Academy Award for You'll be in my Heart from Tarzan film, 1999; Oscar for Best Original Song, You'll be in my Heart, 2000. Membership: Trustee, Prince of Wales Trust, 1983-97. Address: Hit and Run Music, 30 Ives Street, London SW3 2ND, England. Website: www.philcollins.co.uk

COLLIS Louise Edith, b. 29 January 1925, Arakan, Burma. Writer. Education: BA, History, Reading University, England, 1945. Publications: Without a Voice, 1951; A Year Passed, 1952; After the Holiday, 1954; The Angel's Name, 1955; Seven in the Tower, 1958; The Apprentice Saint, 1964; Solider in Paradise, 1965; The Great Flood, 1966; A Private View of Stanley Spencer, 1972; Maurice Collis Diaries (editor), 1976; Impetuous Heart: The story of Ethel Smyth, 1984. Contributions to: Books and Bookmen; Connoisseur; Art and Artists; Arts Review; Collectors Guide; Art and Antiques. Memberships: Society of Authors; International Association of Art Critics. Address: 65 Cornwall Gardens, London SW7 4BD, England.

COLSTON Freddie C, b. 28 March 1936, Gretna, Florida, USA. Professor of Political Science. m. Doris Suggs, 1 daughter. Education: BA, Morehouse College, 1959; MA, Atlanta University, 1966; PhD, Ohio State University, 1972. Appointments: Instructor, Social Studies, Attucks High School, Hollywood, Florida, 1959-65, The Fort Valley State College, Georgia, 1966-68; Teaching Associate, Political Science, Ohio State University, 1968-71; Lecturer, Political Science, Ohio Dominican College, 1970; Associate Professor, Political Science, Benedict College, Columbia, South Carolina, 1971-72; Lecturer, Black Politics, Franklin University. Colombus, Ohio, 1972; Associate Professor, Political Science, Southern University, Baton Rouge, 1972-73; Associate Professor, Political Science and Black Studies, University of Detroit, 1973-76; Associate Professor, Political Science, Chairman, Division of Social Science, Dillard University, New Orleans, 1976-78; Assistant Professor, Department of Political Science, Delta College, University Center, Michigan, 1978-79; Associate Director, Executive Seminar Center, US Office of Personnel Management, Oak Ridge, 1980-87; Professor of Public Administration and Coordinator of Graduate Studies, Institute of Government, Tennessee State University, 1987-88; Director, Public Administration Program, North Carolina Central University, Durham, 1988-91; Professor, Political Science, Georgia Southwestern State University, Americus, 1992-97. Publications: Articles in professional journals. Honours include: Scholarships, University of Illinois, Summer 1964, Atlanta University,

1965. Memberships: American Political Science Association; American Society for Public Administration; Center for the Study of Presidency. Address: 126 Hazleton Lane, Oak Ridge, TN 37830, USA.

COLTART John, b. 7 October 1943, Poole, Dorset, England. Consultant Cardiologist. 1 son, 3 daughters. Education: MD, MBBS, St Bartholomews Hospital, Medical College, 1962-72; MRCS; MRCP; FRCP, 1982; FACC, 1975; FESC, 1989. Appointments: Consultant, Cardiologist & Clinical Director, Guys & St Thomas Foundation Trust; Consultant Physician, Metropolitan Police; Civilian Consultant in Cardiology, Army & Royal Navy Federation; Consultant Cardiologist, King Edward VII & St Luke's Hospital for the Clergy. Publications: 2 books; Over 250 scientific papers in peer-reviewed journals. Honours: Buckston Browne Prize and Medal, Harveian Society; Paul Philip Reitlinger Prize, University of London. Memberships: FRCP; FACC; FESC; President, Cardiology Section, Royal Society of Medicine; Vice President, Postgraduate Medical Federation. Address: 47 Weymouth Street, London W16 8NS, England.

COLTRANE Robbie, b. 31 March 1950, Glasgow, Scotland. Actor. m. Rhona Irene Gemmel, 2000, 1 son, 1 daughter. Education: Glasgow School. Appointments: Director, Producer, Young Mental Health (documentary), 1973. Creative Works: Stage appearances include: Waiting for God; End Game; The Bug; Mr Joyce is Leaving; The Slab Boys; The Transfiguration of Benno Blimpie; The Loveliest Night of the Year; Snobs and Yobs; Your Obedient Servant (one-man show), 1987; Mistero Buffo; TV: The Comic Strip Presents...; Five Go Mad In Dorset; The Beat Generation; War; Summer School; Five Go Mad in Mescalin; Susie; Gino; Dirty Movie; The Miner's Strike; The Supergrass (feature film); The Ebb-tide; Alice in Wonderland; Guest Roles: The Yong Ones; Kick Up the Eighties; The Tube; Saturday Night Live; Lenny Henry Show; Blackadder; Tutti Frutti; Coltrane in a Cadillac; Cracker; The Plan Man, 2003; Frasier, 2005; TV film: Boswall and Johnson's Tour of the Western Isles; Films include: Mona Lisa; Subway Riders; Britannia Hospital; Defence of the Realm; Caravaggio; Eat The Rich; Absolute Beginners; The Fruit Machine; Slipstream; Nuns on the Run; Huckleberry Finn; Bert Rigby, You're A Fool; Danny Champion of the World; Henry V; Let It Ride; The Adventures of Huckleberry Finn; Goldeneye; Buddy; Montana; Frogs for Snakes; Message in a Bottle; The World is Not Enough, 1999; On the Nose, 2000; From Hell, 2000; Harry Potter and the Philosopher's Stone, 2001; Harry Potter and the Chamber of Secrets, 2002; Van Helsing, 2004; Harry Potter and the Prisoner of Azkaban, 2004; Ocean's 12, 2005; Harry Potter and the Goblet of Fire, 2005; Provoked: A True Story, 2006; Cracker, 2006; Stormbreaker, 2006; Harry Potter and the Order of the Pheonix, 2007. Publications: Coltrane in a Cadillac, 1992; Coltrane's Planes and Automobiles, 1999. Honours: OBE, 2006. Address: c/o CDA, 125 Gloucester Rd, London SW7 4TE, England.

COLUMBUS Chris, b. 10 September 1958, Spangler, Pennsylvania, USA. Film Director; Screenplay Writer. m. Monica Devereux, 1983, 2 daughters. Education: New York University Film School. Career: Wrote for and developed TV cartoon series, Galaxy High School; Founder of own production company, 1942 Productions; Screenplays include: Reckless, 1983; Gremlins, 1984; The Goonies, 1985; The Young Sherlock Holmes, 1985; Only the Lonely, 1991; Little Nemo: Adventures in Slumberland, 1992; Nine Months, 1995; Films directed include: Adventures in Babysitting, 1987; Heartbreak Hotel, 1988; Home Alone, 1990; Only the Lonely, 1991; Home Alone 2: Lost in New York, 1992; Mrs Doubtfire, 1993; Nine Months (also producer), 1995; Jingle All the Way (also producer), 1996; Stepmom (also producer), 1998; Monkey Bone (producer), 1999; Bicentennial Man (also producer), 1999; Harry Potter and the Philosopher's Stone (also producer), 2001; Harry Potter and the Chamber of Secrets (also producer), 2002; Harry Potter and the Prisoner of Azkaban (producer), 2004; Christmas wit the Kranks (producer), 2004; 3- D Rocks (producer), 2005; Fantastic Four (executive producer), 2005; Rent (producer), 2005; Night at the Mueeum (producer), 2006; 4: Rise of the Silver Surfer, 2007. TV directed includes: Amazing Stories; Twilight Zone; Alfred Hitchcock Presents (series). Address: c/o Beth Swofford, CAA, 9830 Wilshire Boulevard, Beverly Hills, CA 90212, USA.

COMANECI Nadia, b. 12 November 1961, Oneşti, Bacău County, Romania. Former Gymnast. m. Bart Connor, 1996. 1 son. Education: College of Physical Education and Sports, Bucharest. Career: Overall European Champion, Skien 1975, Prague 1977, Copenhagen 1979; Overall Olympic Champion, Montreal, 1976; First gymnast to be awarded a 10; Overall World Universal Games Champion, Bucharest, 1981; Gold medals: European Championships, Skien 1975 (vault, asymmetric bars, beam); Prague 1977 (bars); Copenhagen 1979 (vault, floor exercises); World Championships, Strasbourg 1978 (beam); Fort Worth 1979 (team title); Olympic Games, Montreal 1976 (bars, beam); Moscow (beam, floor); World Cup, Tokyo 1979 (vault, floor); World Universal Games, Bucharest 1981 (vault, bars, floor and team title); Silver medals: European Championships, Skien 1975 (floor); Prague 1977 (vault); World Championships, Strasbourg 1978 (vault); Olympic Games, Montreal 1976 (team title); Moscow (individual all-round, team title); World Cup, Tokyo 1979 (beam); Bronze medals: Olympic Games, Montreal 1976 (floor); Retired, May 1984; Junior Team Coach, 1984-89; Granted refugee status, USA, 1989; Currently with Bart Connor Gymnastics Academy, Oklahoma, USA; Performs as dancer, gymnastics entertainer and promotes commercial products; Contributing Editor, International Gymnast magazine; UN Spokesman for International Year of Volunteers, 2001; Founder, Nadia Comaneci Children's Clinic, Bucharest, 2004. Publications: Letters to a Young Gymnast, 2004. Honours: Sportswomen of the Century Prize, Athletic Sports Category, 1999; Government Excellence Diploma, 2001. Address: c/o Bart Conner Gymnastics Academy, 3206 Bart Conner Drive, POB 72017, Norman, OK 73070-4166, USA. Website: www.bartconnergymnastics.com

COMBS Sean (P Diddy), b. 1970, Harlem, New York, USA. Rap Artist; Producer; Fashion designer. Career: R&B label, Uptown; Talent spotter; Producer for Ma$e, Sting, MC Lyte, Faith Evans, The Lox, Mariah Carey, Aretha Franklin, Notorious BIG; Founder, Bad Boy Entertainment label, 1994-; Remixed and reworked songs by various artists; Co-producer, soundtrack to film Godzilla; Creator, fashion collection Sean John, 2001 (flagship stored opened 2002); Charged with gun possession, 1999; Acquitted of gun possession and bribery, 2001. Films: Made, 2001; Monster's Ball, 2001; Death of a Dynestry, 2003. Recordings include: I'll Be Missing You; Been Around the World, 1997; Roxanne, Can't Nobody Hold Me Down, 1997; Victory, 1998; Come With Me, 1998; It's All About the Benjamins, 1998; PE, 2000; Albums include: No Way Out, 1997; Forever, 1999; The Saga Continues, 2001; Albums produced include: Honey (Mariah Carey); Life After Death and Mo Money Mo Problems (Notorious BIG); Cold Rock a Party (MC Lyte); Cupid (112); Feel So Good (Ma$e); Plays: A Raisin in the Sun, 2004. Honours: Grammy Award,

Best Rap Performance by a Duo or Group, 1998; Grammy Award, Best Rap Album, 1998; Council of Fashion Designers of America menswear designer of the year award, 2004; Concert for Diana, 2007. Address: Sean John Clothing Inc, 525 Seventh Avenue, Suite 1009, New York, NY 10018, USA. Website: www.seanjohn.com

COMFORT Nicholas Alfred Fenner, b. 4 August 1946, London, England. Writer and Government Adviser. m. 2 sons, 1 daughter. Education: Scholar, Highgate School; MA (Exhibitioner), History, Trinity College, Cambridge. Appointments: Municipal Correspondent, Sheffield Morning Telegraph, 1968-74; Midlands Correspondent, Washington Bureau, Political Staff, Leader Writer, The Daily Telegraph, 1974-89; Political Editor, Independent on Sunday, 1989-90; Political Editor, The European, 1990-92; Political Editor, Daily Record, 1992-95; Obituarist, Daily Telegraph, 1995-; Consultant, Politics International, 1996-97; Freelance Lobby Correspondent, 1997-2000; Consultant on European Presentation, DTI, 2000-01; Special Adviser to Secretary of State for Scotland, 2001-02; Government Adviser, QinetiQ, 2003-06. Publications: Books: Olympic Report, 1976; The Tunnel: The Channel and Beyond, 1987; Brewer's Politics, 1993; The Lost City of Dunwich, 1994; The Mid-Suffolk Light Railway, 1997; How to Handle the Media, 2003; The Politics Book, 2005; The Channel Tunnel and its High Speed Links, 2006; Numerous articles. Memberships: The Athenaeum; Fellow, RGS; Essex CCC. Address: Flat 2, 39 Egerton Gardens, London SW3 2DD, England. E-mail: nc65464@yahoo.com

ČOMIĆ Irena, b. 29 March 1938, Subotica, Yugoslavia. Professor of Mathematics. m. Ljubomir, 2 daughters. Education: BSc, 1960; MA, 1966; PhD, 1974. Appointments: Faculty of Technical Sciences, University of Novi Sad, Yugoslavia. Publications include: Various papers on Finsler geometry and its generalisation appearing in mathematical journals and proceedings of conferences. Address: Department of Mathematics, Faculty of Technical Sciences, University of Novi Sad, 21000 Novi Sad, Yugoslavia. E-mail: comirena@uns.ns.ac.yu

COMPO-PRATT Paula Anita, b. 22 December 1950, Camden, New Jersey, USA. Teacher; Artist; Writer; Floral Designer. m. Thomas Calvin Pratt, 1 daughter. Education: BA, Rutgers University, 1973; Teacher of English, Permanent Teachers Certificate, State of New Jersey, 1973; Floral Designer Certification, The Branch Academy of Floral Design, 1984. Appointments: Teacher of English, Camden City Public Schools, 1973-; 8th Grade Adviser, Pyne Poynt Middle School, 10 years; Various positions, Morgan Village Middle School, 24 years. Publications: Russian Orthodox Journal; Sing Down The Moon, poetry; Published in Best Poets and Poems of 2005; Songs of Honor, poem in anthology; A Surrender to the Moon, poem in anthology; Poem in Anthology Centres of Expression; BooBoo's Story, children's book; 4 volumes of own poems. Honours: Junior National Honor Society, 1966; National Honor Society, 1967-69; Collegiate, Athenaeum Honor Society, 1972; Leaders in Elementary and Secondary Education, 1976; Creativity and Speed Awards, Branch Academy of Floral Design, 1984; Award for Cognetics, State of New Jersey, 1992-93; The Governor's Teacher Recognition Award, 1999; Deputy Director General, IBC, 2005; Lifetime Achievement Award, IBC, 2005; Universal Achievement Award of Accomplishment, ABI, 2005; Great Women of the 21st Century, 2004-05; Great Minds of the 21st Century, 2005; 2000 Outstanding Intellectuals of the 21st Century, 2005; Editor's Choice Award for Outstanding Achievement in Poetry, International Library of Poetry, 2005, 2006, 2007; Woman of the Year, World Medal of Freedom, Medal of Honor in Education, Lifetime Achievement Award, ABI, 2005; Leading Educators of the World, 2005; Outstanding Achievement in Poetry Awards, 2005, 2006; Lifetime Achievement Award for Excellence in Education, UCC, 2006; Plato Award, 2006; Sovereign Ambassador of the United States, ABI, 2006; International Educator of the Year, 2007; The Paula Anita Compo-Pratt Award Foundation, 2007; Secretary General, UCC, 2007-10; Listed in national and international biographical dictionaries. Memberships: New Jersey Education Association; Camden Education Association; New Jersey Council of Teachers of English; Research Board of Advisors, ABI. Address: 504 Almonesson Road, Westville, New Jersey, USA.

CONLON James, b. 18 March 1950, New York, USA. Conductor. m. Jennifer Ringo, 2 daughters. Education: Bachelor of Music, Juilliard School of Music, New York, 1972. Appointments: Professional conducting debut, Spoleto Festival, 1971; New York debut, La Boheme, Juilliard School of Music, 1972; Member of orchestral conducting faculty, Juilliard School of Music, 1972-75; Debuts: New York Philharmonic, 1974, Metropolitan Opera, 1976, Covent Garden, 1979, Paris Opera, 1982, Maggio Musicale, Florence, 1985, Lyric Opera of Chicago, 1988, La Scala, Milan, 1993, Kirov Opera, 1994; Music Director: Cincinnati May Festival, 1979-; Berlin Philharmonic Orchestra, 1979-; Rotterdam Philharmonic Orchestra, 1983-91; Ravinia Festival, 2005-; Musical Advisor to Director, 1995-, Principal Conductor, 1996-, Paris Opera; Conducted opening of Maggio Musicale, Florence, 1985; Chief Conductor, Cologne Opera, 1989; General Music Director, City of Cologne, Germany, 1990-; Frequent guest conductor at leading music festivals; Conducted virtually all leading orchestras in North America; Numerous television appearances. Honours: Grand Prix du Disque, Cannes Classical Award and ECHO Classical Award; Officier de l'Ordre des Arts et des Lettres, 1996; Zemlinsky Prize, 1999; Legion d'Honneur, 2001. Address: c/o Shuman Associates, 120 West 58th Street, 8D, New York, NY 10019, USA. E-mail: shumanpr@cs.com

CONNELLY Jennifer, b. 12 December 1970, Catskill Mountains, New York, USA. m. Paul Bettany, 1 son, 1 son with David Duggan. Education: Career: Actress; Films include: Once Upon a Time in America, 1984; Phenomena, Seven Minutes in Heaven, 1985; Labyrinth, 1986; Etoiler, Some Girls, 1988; The Hot Spot, 1990; The Rocketeer, 1991; Of Love and Shadows, 1994; Higher Learning, 1995; Mulholland Falls, Far Harbor, 1996; Inventing the Abbotts, 1997; Dark City, 1998; Waking the Dead, Requiem for a Dream, Pollock, 2000; A Beautiful Mind, 2001; Hulk, House of Sand and Fog, 2003; Dark Water, 2005; Little Children, Blood Diamond, 2006; Reservation Road, 2007. Honours: Golden Globe, 2001; BAFTA, 2001; AFI, 2001; Oscar for Best Supporting Actress, 2001. Address: c/o International Creative Management, 8942 Wilshire Boulevard, Beverly Hills, CA 90211, USA.

CONNERY Sean (Thomas Connery), b. 25 August 1930. Actor. m. (1) Diane Cilento, 1962, dissolved 1974, 1 son, (2) Micheline Roquebrune, 1975, 2 stepsons, 1 stepdaughter. Creative Works: Appeared in Films: No Road Back, 1956; Action of the Tiger, Another Time, Another Place, 1957; Hell Drivers, 1958; Tarzan's Greatest Adventure, Darby O'Gill and the Little People, 1959; On the Fiddle, 1961; The Longest Day, The Frightened City, 1962; Woman of Straw, 1964; The Hill, 1965; A Fine Madness, 1966; Shalako, The

Molly Maguires, 1968; The Red Tent, 1969; The Anderson Tapes, 1970; The Offence, Zardoz, 1973; Ransom, Murder on the Orient Express, 1974; The Wind and the Lion, The Man Who Would Be King, 1975; Robin and Marian, 1976; The First Great Train robbery, Cuba, 1978; Meteor, 1979; Outland, 1981; The Man with the Deadly Lens, Wrong is Right, Five Days One Summer, 1982; Highlander, 1986; The Name of the Rose, The Untouchables, 1987; The Presido, Indiana Jones and the Last Crusade, 1989; Family Business, the Hunt for Red October, 1990; The Russia House, Highlander II - The Quickening, 1991; Medicine Man, 1992; Rising Sun, 1993; A Good Man in Africa, 1994; First Knight, Just Cause, 1995; The Rock, Dragonheart, 1996; The Avengers, 1998; Entrapment, Playing By Heart, 1999; Finding Forrester, 2000; The League of Extraordinary Gentlemen, 2003; Sir Billi the Vet (voice), 2006; James Bond in: Dr No, 1963; From Russia with Love, 1964; Goldfinger, 1965; Thunderball, 1965; You Only Live Twice, 1967; Diamonds are Forever, 1971; Never Say Never Again, 1983. Publication: Neither Shaken Nor Stirred, 1994. Honours include: BAFTA Lifetime Achievement Award, 1990; Man of Culture Award, 1990; Rudolph Valentino Award, 1992; Golden Globe Cecil B De Mille Award, 1996 BAFTA Fellowship, 1998; AFI Life Achievement Award, 2006. Address: c/o Creative Artists Agency Inc, 9830 Wilshire Boulevard, Beverly Hills, CA 90212, USA.

CONNICK Harry Jr, b. 1968, New Orleans, USA. Jazz Musician; Actor; Singer. m. Jill Goodacre, 1994, 3 daughters. Education: New Orleans Centre for the Creative Arts; Hunter College; Manhattan School of Music; Studies with Ellis Marsalis. Creative Works: Band Leader, Harry Connick's Big Band; Albums include: Harry Connick Jr, 1987; 20, When Harry Met Sally, 1989; We Are In Love, Lofty's Roach Soufflé, Blue Light, Red Light, 1991; Eleven, 25, 1992; When My Heart Finds Christmas, 1994; She, 1994; Star Turtle, 1996; To See You, 1997; Come By Me, 1999; 30, Songs I Heard, 2001; Other Hours: Connick on Piano, Vol I, Harry for the Holidays, 2003; Only You, 2004; Contribution to music for films: Memphis Belle, 1990; Little Man Tate, 1991; Actor: Films: Memphis Belle, 1990; Little Man Tate, 1991; Copycat, 1995; Independence Day, 1996; Excess Baggage, Action League Now!! (voice), 1997; Hope Floats, 1998; The Iron Giant (voice), Wayward Son, 1999; My Dog Skip (voice), The Simian Line, 2000; Life Without Dick, 2001; Basic, 2003; Mickey, 2004; The Happy Elf (voice), 2005; Bug, 2006; TV includes: South Pacific, 2001; Will & Grace, 2002-; Theatre: Thou Shalt Not (composer), 2001; The Pajama Game (actor), 2005. Honours include: Grammy Award, Male Jazz Vocal Performance, 1990. Address: Columbia Records, 51/12, 550 Madison Avenue, PO Box 4450, New York, NY 10101, USA. Website: www.hconnickjr.com

CONNOLLY Billy, b. 24 November 1942. Comedian; Actor; Playwright; Presenter. m. (1) Iris Connolly, 1 son, 1 daughter, (2) Pamela Stephenson, 1990, 3 daughters. Appointments: Apprentice Welder; Performed originally with Gerry Rafferty and The Humblebums; 1st Play, The Red Runner, staged at Edinburgh fringe, 1979. Creative Works: Theatre: The Great Northern Welly Boot Show; The Beastly Beatitudes of Balthazar B, 1982; TV include: Androcles and the Lion, 1984; Return to Nose and Beak (Comic Relief); South Bank Show Special (25th Anniversary Commemoration), 1992; Billy; Billy Connolly's World Tour of Scotland (6 part documentary), 1994; The Big Picture, 1995; Billy Connolly's World Tour of Australia, 1996; Erect for 30 Years, 1998; Billy Connolly's World Tour of England, Ireland and Wales, 2002; Gentleman's Relish; World Tour of New Zealand, 2004; Films include: Absolution, 1979; Bullshot, Water,

1984; The Big Man, 1989; Pocahontas, 1995; Treasure Island (Muppet Movie), Deacon Brodie (BBC Film), 1996; Mrs Brown, Ship of Fools, 1997; Still Crazy, Debt Collector, 1998; Boon Docksaints, 1998; Beautiful Joe, An Everlasting Piece, 2000; The Man Who Sued God, White Oleander, Gabriel and Me, 2002; The Last Samurai, Timeline, 2003; Lemony Snicket's A Series of Unfortunate Events, 2004; Garfield: A Tail of Two Kitties, Fido, Open Season (voice), 2006; Numerous video releases of live performances include: Bite Your Bum, 1981; An Audience with Billy Connolly, 1982; Numerous albums include: The Great Northern Welly Boot Show (contains No 1 hit DIVORCE); Pick of Billy Connolly. Publications include: Gullible's Travels, 1982. Honours include: Gold Disc, 1982; CBE, 2003. Address: c/o Tickety-boo Ltd, 94 Charity Street, Victoria, Gozo VCT 105, Malta. E-mail: tickety-boo@tickety-boo.com Website: www.billyconnolly.com

CONNORS James Scott (Jimmy), b. 2 September 1952, Illinois, USA. Tennis Player. m. Patti McGuire, 1978, 1 son, 1 daughter. Education: University of California, Los Angeles. Appointments: Amateur Player, 1970-72; Professional, 1972-; Australian Champion, 1974; Wimbledon Champion, 1974, 1982; USA Champion, 1974, 1976, 1978, 1982, 1983; South Australian Champion, 1973, 1974; WCT Champion, 1977, 1980; Grand Prix Champion, 1978; Commentator, NBC; Played Davis Cup for USA, 1976, 1981. Honour: BBC Overseas Sports Personality, 1982. Address: Tennis Management Inc, 109 Red Fox Road, Belleville, IL 62223, USA.

CONRAN Jasper Alexander Thirlby, b. 12 December 1959, London, England. Fashion Designer. Education: Bryanston School, Dorset; Parsons School of Art & Design, New York. Appointments: Fashion Designer, Managing Director, Jasper Conran Ltd, 1978-. Creative Works: Theatre Costumes: Jean Anouilh's The Rehearsal, Almeida Theatre, 1990; My Fair Lady, 1992; Sleeping Beauty, Scottish Ballet, 1994; The Nutcracker Sweeties, Birmingham Royal Ballet, 1996; Edward II, 1997; Arthur, 2000; TV Costume Designer, Nutcracker Sweeties, 2006. Honours include: Fil d'Or (International Linen Award), 1982, 1983; British Fashion Council Designer of the Year Award, 1986-87; Fashion Group of America Award, 1987; Laurence Olivier Award for Costume Designer of the Year, 1991; British Collections Award (in British Fashions Awards), 1991. Address: Jasper Conran Ltd, 6 Burnsall Street, London SW3, England.

CONRAN Sir Terence (Orby), b. 4 October 1931, Esher, Surrey, England. Designer; Retail Executive. m. (1) Brenda Davison, divorced, (2) Shirley Conran, divorced 1962, 2 sons, (3) Caroline Herbert, 1963, divorced 1996, 2 sons, 1 daughter, (4) Vicki Davis, 2000. Education: Bryanston School, Dorset; Central School of Art and Design, London. Appointments include: Joint Chairman, Ryman Conran Ltd, 1968-71; Chairman, Habitat Group Ltd, 1971-88; RSCG Conran Design, 1971-92; Habitat France SA, 1973-88; Conran Stores Inc, 1977-88; J Hepworth & Son Ltd, 1981-83; Habitat Mothercare Ltd, 1982-88; Jasper Conran Ltd, 1982-; Heal & Sons Ltd, 1983-87; Richard Shops Ltd, 1983-87; Storehouse plc, 1986-90; Butlers Wharf Ltd, 1984-90; Bibendum Restaurant Ltd, 1986-; Benchmark Woodworking Ltd, 1989-; Blue Print Cafe Ltd, 1989-; Conran Shop Holdings Ltd, 1990-; Terence Conran Ltd, 1990-; Le Pont de La Tour Ltd, 1991-; Quaglino's Restaurant Ltd, 1991-; Conran Shop SA, 1991-; Cantina Del Ponte, 1992; Butlers Wharf Chop House Ltd, 1993-; Conran & Partners, 1993-; Chairman, Conran Holdings Ltd, 1993-; Bluebird Store Ltd,

1994-; Mezzo Ltd, 1995-; Conran Shop: Paris, 1992, 1999, Tokyo, 1994, (Marylebone) Ltd, 1995-, (Germany) Ltd, 1996, Fukuoka, 1996; Coq d'Argent Ltd, 1997-; Zinc Bar & Grill, 1997; Orrery, 1997; Sartoria Ltd, 1998; Accazar Ltd, (Paris), 1998; Conran Collection, 1998; Berns Ltd (Stockholm), 1999; Great Eastern Hotel, 1999; The Terence Conran Shop, (New York), 1999; Giastavino's (New York), 2000; Content by Conran, furniture for Christie Tyler, 2003. Publications: The House Book, 1974; The Kitchen Book, 1977; The Bedroom & Bathroom Book, 1978; The Cook Book (revised as The Conran Cookbook, 1996), 1980; The New House Book, 1985; Conran Directory of Design, 1985; Plants at Home, 1986; The Soft Furnishings Book, 1986; Terence Conran's France, 1987; Terence Conran's DIY by Design, 1989; Terence Conran's Garden DIY, 1990; Toys and Children's Furniture, 1992; Terence Conran's Kitchen Book, 1993; Terence Conran's DIY Book, 1994; The Essential House Book, 1994; Terence Conran on Design, 1996; The Essential Garden Book, 1998; Easy Living, 1999; Chef's Garden, 1999; Terence Conran on Restaurants, 1999; Terence Conran on London, 2000; Q and A: A Sort of Autobiography, 2001; Terence Conran on Small Spaces, 2001. Honours include: RSA Bicentenary Medal, 1982; Presidential Award, D&AD, 1989; Commandeur de l'Ordre des Arts et des Lettres, France, 1991. Memberships: Council, Royal College of Art, 1979-81, 1986-; Trustee, 1989-, Chair, 1992-, Design Museum; Creative Leaders' Network. Address: 22 Shad Thames, London SE1 2YU, England. Website: www.conran.com

CONROY (Donald) Pat(rick), b. 26 October 1945, Atlanta, Georgia, USA. Writer. m. (1) Barbara Bolling, 1969, divorced 1977, 3 daughters, (2) Lenore Guerewitz, 1981, divorced 1995, 1 son, 5 daughters. Education: BA in English, The Citadel, 1967. Publications: The Boo, 1970; The Water is Wide, 1972; The Great Santini, 1976; The Lords of Discipline, 1980; The Prince of Tides, 1986; Beach Music, 1995; My Losing Season, 2002; The Pat Conroy Cookbook: Recipes of My Life. Honours: Ford Foundation Leadership Development Grant, 1971; Anisfield-Wolf Award, Cleveland Foundation, 1972; National Endowment for the Arts Award for Achievement in Education, 1974; Governor's Award for the Arts, Georgia, 1978; Lillian Smith Award for Fiction, Southern Regional Council, 1981; SC Hall of Fame, Academy of Authors, 1988; Golden Plate Award, American Academy of Achievement, 1992; Georgia Commission on the Holocaust Humanitarian Award, 1996; Lotos Medal of Merit for Outstanding Literary Achievement, 1993; Many others. Memberships: Authors Guild of America; PEN; Writers Guild. Address: c/o Houghton Mifflin Co, 222 Berkeley Street, Boston, MA 02116, USA.

CONTI Tom, b. 22 November 1941, Paisley, Scotland. Actor; Director; Novelist. m. Kara Wilson, 1967, 1 daughter. Education: Royal Scottish Academy of Music. Creative Works: London Theatre include: Savages (Christopher Hampton), 1973; The Devil's Disciple (Shaw), 1976; Whose Life is it Anyway? (Brian Clarke), 1978; They're Playing Our Song (Neil Simon/Marvin Hamlisch), 1980; Romantic Comedy (Bernard Salde); An Italian Straw Hat, 1986; Two Into One; Treats, 1989; Jeffrey Bernard is Unwell, 1990; The Ride Down Mt Morgan, 1991; Present Laughter (also director), 1993; Chapter Two, 1996; Jesus My Boy, 1998; Barrymore, 2002; The Real Thing, 2005; Films include: Dreamer; Saving Grace; Miracles; Heavenly Pursuits; Beyond Therapy; Roman Holiday; Two Brothers Running; White Roses; Shirley Valentine; Chapter Two; Someone Else's America; Crush Depth; Something to Believe In, 1996; Out of Control, 1997; The Enemy, 2000; Derailed, 2005; Paid, 2006; Rabbit Fever, 2006; Almost Heaven, 2006; O Jerusalem, 2006; Dangerous

Parking, 2007; TV Works include: Madame Bovary; Treats; The Glittering Prizes; The Norman Conquests; The Beate Klarsfeld Story; Fatal Dosage; The Quick and the Dead; Blade on the Feather; The Wright Verdicts; Deadline; Donovan; Director: Last Licks; Broadway, 1979; Before the Party, 1980; The Housekeeper, 1982; Treats, 1989; Present Laughter, 1993; Last of the Red Hot Lovers, 1999. Publications: The Doctor, 2004. Honours: West End Theatre Managers Award; Royal TV Society Award; Variety Club of Great Britain Award, 1978; Tony Award, New York, 1979; Academy Award, Best Actor Nominee. Address: Finch & Partners, 4-8 Heddon Street, London W1B 4BS, England.

CONWAY Paul William Joseph, b. 28 May 1964, Crewe, England. Freelance Writer; Librarian. m. Kathryn, 1 son. Education: LLB Law Degree, University of Hull, 1986; PG Diploma, Librarianship, Birmingham Polytechnic, 1990; PG Diploma, Music, 1993, MPhil (submitted), 2006, University of Sheffield. Appointments: Library Assistant, History Faculty Library, University of Oxford, 1988-89; Assistant, Tax Librarian, Price Waterhouse, 1990; Assistant Librarian, Lovell White Durrant, 1991-92; Information Adviser, Sheffield Hallam University, 1995-. Publications: Karajan, The Music Not The Man, 1986/87; Exploring Hydriotaphia: William Alwyn's Fifth Symphony, 1993; The Influence of Gustav Mahler on the Symphonies of Egon Wellesz, 2000; Programme notes for The Proms (2001, 2004), The Spitalfields Festival (2002) and The Edinburgh Festival (2006); Chapter on John McCabe's Symphonies and Concertos in: Landscapes of the Mind (in progress), and A Moorland Symphony: An Introduction to the Music of Arthur Butterworth, in progress; Regular contributor to Tempo, 1997-; Regular concert reviewer, The Independent, 2000-. Memberships: British Music Society, 1996-. Address: 9 Blair Athol Road, Sheffield, S11 7GA, England. E-mail: paul@wjconway.fsnet.co.uk

COOK Colin Burford, b. 20 January 1927, London, England. Doctor of Medicine. Education: Stainsby Hall Boarding School, Derbyshire, England; St Aloyisius College, London, 1943; MBBS, London University, Middlesex Hospital, London, 1944-51; Rotating Internship, Bridgeport Hospital, Connecticut, USA, 1952-53; Ships Surgeon, British Navy, 1953-55; Resident, Psychiatry, Marquette School of Medicine, Milwaukee, Wisconsin; Resident, Psychiatry, Cornell University, White Plains, New York; Post Graduate Fellowship, National Hospital for Nervous Diseases, Queen Square, London, England. Appointments: Psychiatrist, Psycho-analytically orientated psychotherapy, private practice, Stamford, Connecticut, over 30 years; Professor, Psychiatry, Columbia University, New York City, 1992-95. Publications: Author (as Alan Phillips), Jazz Improvisation & Harmony, 1965, 4th edition, 1998. Honours: Diplomate, American Board of Psychiatry & Neurology, 1979. Memberships: American Medical Association; American Society of Psychoanalytic Physicians; Authors League; Masons 32°. Address: 373 Strawberry Hill Ave, Stamford, CT 06902, USA. E-mail: ccookie3210@aol.com

COOK John Barry, b. 9 May 1940, Gloucester, England. Educator. m. Vivien Lamb, 2 sons, 1 daughter. Education: BSc, Physics and Mathematics,1961, Associate, Diploma in Theology, 1961 King's College, University of London, 1958-61; PhD, Biophysics, 1965, Guy's Hospital Medical School, University of London, 1961-65. Appointments: Lecturer (part-time), Physics, Royal Veterinary College, 1962-64; Lecturer, Physics, Guy's Hospital Medical School, 1964-65; Physics Teacher, Senior Science Master, Head of Physics Department, Haileybury, Hertford, 1965-72;

Headmaster, Christ College, Brecon, 1973-82; Headmaster, Epsom College, 1982-92; Director, Inner Cities Young Peoples Project, 1992-95, Principal, King George VI and Queen Elizabeth Foundation of St Catharine's at Cumberland Lodge, 1995-2000, Educational Consultant, 2000-; OFSTED Inspector of Schools, 1993-2005; Inspecting, Consultancy and Advisory work for a wide range of schools in UK, Kenya, Egypt, Malaysia, Argentina, Abu Dhabi, France and Austria; Chairman, Academic Policy Committee, Headmasters' Conference; Chairman, South Wales Branch, Independent Schools' Information Service; Member, Curriculum Committee of the Schools' Council, the Council of the Midlands Examining Group, the Oxford and Cambridge Schools' Examination Board and of the Examination Committees of the Universities of Oxford and Cambridge; At various times Governor of 15 schools in Hertfordshire, Wales, Surrey, Staffordshire, Kent, Worcestershire; Chairman of Governors at The Royal School. Publications: Books as joint author: Solid State Biophysics; Multiple Choice Questions in A-level Physics; Multiple Choice Questions in O-level Physics; Papers and articles in: Nature, International Journal of Radiation Biology; Molecular Physics; Journal of Scientific Instruments; School Science Review. Memberships: College of Episcopal Electors and Governing Body of the Church in Wales; Chairman, Children's Hospice Association of the South East. Address: 6 Chantry Road, Bagshot, Surrey GU19 5DB, England.

COOK Manuela, b. 29 March 1941, Lisbon, Portugal. Professor. m. Ronald Cook, 1 daughter. Education: BA, Universidade Clássica de Lisboa, Portugal; MA, Universidade de Coimbra, Portugal; PhD, University of Birmingham, England; PGCE, University of Wolverhampton, England. Appointments: Teacher/Lecturer, Modern Languages, numerous institutions, 1960s-1970s; Portuguese Studies, School of Languages and European Studies, University of Wolverhampton, 1970s-1990s; Examiner, Principal, Chief Examiner, Moderator and Assessor for national and international boards, 1970s-; Book Reviewer for various publications including: The Times Higher Education Supplement, Contemporary Portuguese Politics & History Research Centre, Journal of the Association for Contemporary Iberian Studies, and Vida Hispánica, 1970s-; Committee chairmanships, course director, etc, 1990s-; Reviews Editor, International Journal of Iberian Studies, 1994-2004; Editor (by correspondence), Lusotopie, France, 2001-. Publications: Numerous papers and articles in scholarly journals. Honours: Fellowship, Linguist of Distinction, Institute of Linguistics, England, 1987-; Listed in international biographical dictionaries. Memberships: Society of Authors; Chartered Institute of Linguists; Association of Hispanists of Great Britain and Ireland; Association for Contemporary Iberian Studies; International Conference Group on Portugal; Women in Spanish, Portuguese and Latin American Studies; Anglo-Portuguese Society; Association for Language Learning; Associação Internacional de Lusitanistas; Founding Member, Association of British and Irish Lusitanists, 2006. E-mail: mcook.ac@btinternet.com

COOKE Fred C, b. 3 December 1915, Winchester, Tennessee, USA; Realtor Emeritus; Lt Col USAF (Ret). m. Pamela B Cooke, 4 children. Education: BA, 4 year pre-med; Realtor's Graduate Institute; Rated Senior Aerial Navigator, Kelly Field, 1942; Research and Development Engineer; Real Estate Counsellor and Exchanger, San Diego; Command School, USAF. Appointments: Realtor: Local Board President, 3 terms; State Director, 8 years; National Director, 4 years; Civitan International Club, Local President, District

Vice-President. Honours: Distinguished Flying Cross, 1942; Veteran, Battle of Midway, 1942; Air Medal with Oak Leaf Clusters, 1943; The first study from the air of Gulf Stream current velocities by Doeppler radar, 1952; Founder, Emerald Coast Sailing Association; Lincoln Memorial University Athletic Hall of Fame, 1980; Professional Hall of Fame, 1993. Memberships: Vestry Member, St Simon's on the Sound Episcopal Church, 1957; State of Florida Waterways Committee, 1976; Commander, Fort Walton, Power Squadron; Commodore, Fort Walton Yacht Club, 1990. Address: PO Drawer 4070, Ft Walton Beach, FL 32549, USA.

COOKE Jonathan Gervaise Fitzpatrick, b. 26 March 1943, London, England. Sailor; Administrator. m. Henrietta Chamier, 1 son, 2 daughters. Education: Marlborough College, 1956-61; Dartmouth 1961-64; Joint Services Defence College, 1984; Royal College of Defence Studies, 1993. Appointments: Royal Navy, 1961-96; Navigation and Submarine Specialist; Commanded HMS Rorqual, HMS Churchill, HMS Warspite, 1980-84; 3rd Submarine Squadron, 1988-89; Naval Attaché, Paris, 1990-93; Commodore, 1993; Director Intelligence, Ministry of Defence; Chief Executive to Leathersellers Company, 1996-; Director AngloSiberian Oil, 1998-2003. Honours: OBE; Commandeur de L'Ordre Nationale de Merité, France. Memberships: Naval and Military Club; Queen's Club. Address: Downstead House, Morestead, Winchester, Hampshire, SO21 1LF, England. E-mail: jcooke@leathersellers.co.uk

COOLAHAN Catherine Anne, b. 2 November 1929. Artist; Designer. m. Maxwell Dominic Coolahan, 5 March 1951. Education: Associate, Sydney Technical College, 1950. Appointments: Advertising and Publicity Design, Farmer and Co, Sydney, 1950-52; Advertising and Publicity Design, J Inglis Wright, New Zealand Ltd, 1952-53; Advertising and Publicity Design, Carlton Carruthers du Chateau and King, 1954-57; Assistant Education Officer, Dominion Museum, 1957-58; Fashion Illustrator, James Smith Ltd, 1959-60; Publicity Design, Carlton Carruthers, 1960-62; James Smith and Tutor, Wellington Polytechnic School of Design, 1962-64; Self-Employed Graphic Design, Fine Arts, Curriculum Development and Teaching for School of Design, 1964-66; Wellington Polytechnic, 1966-71, 1972-83, 1984, 1985, 1995; Travelling Scholarship, QE II Arts Council, 1971-72. Creative Works include: Flight, Fabric Sculpture, 1984; Predater, Predator, Paper Wood, Flax Ties, Sculpture, 1984; Hunter, Paper Sculpture, 1984; Appropriations, Aquatint, 1986; Lifeguard, 3 Dimensional Etching and Hand Made Paper, 1987; Map of the Sounds, Etching, 1988; Isis and Rangi, Lithograph, 1988; Art Sees, Etching, 1989; New Zealand Portraits, 1990; Winged Victories and Clipped Wings, 1992; Anima, Etching, 1994; Topiary, Multimedia Assemblage, 1998; Foxy, Artists' Book, 1999; Dawn, Artists' Book, 2000; Noah's Ark, Metal and Glass Diorama, 2000; Animus, Etching, 2000. Publications: New Zealand Dictionary of Biography, Vol. 5 (Contributor). Honours include: Represented New Zealand at 36th Venice Bienalle, 1972; Japanese cultural ex as Printmaker to learn papermaking, 1977; QE II Purchase Grant for Retrospective Exhibition at Dowse Art Museum, 1984; QE II Grant to attend National Paper Conference, Tasmanian University Research Co, Hobart, Australia, 1987; Appointed Life Member, New Zealand Crafts Council for work on Education Committee with Craft Design Courses, 1989; Funding Support/Sufferage Centennial Year Trust and QE II Arts Council, Dowse Art Museum, 1992; Doctor of Literature (honoris causa), Massey University, 2003; Listed in: Artists and Galleries of Australia and New Zealand, 1979; Numerous national and international biographical publications; Encyclopaedia of New Zealand,

1986; Concise Dictionary of New Zealand Artists, 2000; The Order of New Zealand – Merit, 2007. Memberships: Board, New Zealand Print Council, 1968-76; Board, New Zealand Design Council, 1977-84; Board, Queen Elizabeth II Arts Council, 1979; Board, Wellington Community Arts Council, 1981; Board, Central Region Arts Council, 1982-85; Design Council Representative, New Zealand Industrial Design Council, 1984; Board, New Zealand Craft Council, 1984-85; Board, Humanz, New Zealand Society of the Humanities, 1995-2002; Chair International Committee, Zonta International Wellington Club, 1998-99; Board, New Pacific Studios, Berkley, California and Masterton, New Zealand, 2000-01. Address: 3/5 Levy Street, Mount Victoria, Wellington 6011, New Zealand.

COOMBE Michael Ambrose Rew, b. 17 June 1930, Croydon, Surrey, England. Retired Judge. m. Anne Hull, deceased, 3 sons, 1 deceased, 1 daughter. Education: MA, English Language and Literature, New College Oxford, 1951-54; Called to Bar by Middle Temple, 1957. Appointments: Junior Prosecuting Counsel to the Crown, Inner London, 1971-74; Central Criminal Court, 1974-78; Senior Prosecuting Counsel to the Crown, 1978-85; Recorder of the Crown Court, 1976-85; Circuit Judge, 1985; Appointed to Central Criminal Court, 1986-2003. Honours: Middle Temple Harmsworth Scholar; Bencher, 1984; Reader of the Inn, Autumn 2001; Freeman of the City of London. Memberships: Garrick; Liveryman of the Worshipful Company of Stationers; Liveryman of the Worshipful Company of Fruiterers.

COOMBES Gaz (Gareth), b. 8th March 1976, Oxford. Singer; Musician (guitar). Career: Member, The Jennifers; Lead singer, guitarist, Supergrass, 1994-; Major concerts include: Support to Blur, Alexandra Palace, 1994; UK tour with Shed Seven, 1994; T In The Park Festival, Glasgow, 1995. Recordings: Albums: I Should Coco (Number 1, UK), 1995; In It for the Money, 1997; Supergrass, 1999; Singles: Caught By The Fuzz, 1994; Mansize Rooster, 1995; Lenny, 1995; Alright, 1995; Going Out, 1996; Sun Hits the Sky, 1997; Pumping On Your Stereo, 1999; Mary, 1999. Honours: Q Award, Best New Act, 1995; BRIT Award Nominations: Best British Newcomer, Best Single, Best Video, 1996. Address: c/o Courtyard Management, 22 The Nursery, Sutton Courtenay, Abingdon, Oxon OX14 4UA, England.

COONEY Anthony Paul, b. 3 July 1932, Liverpool, England. Schoolmaster; Poet. m. 12 April 1958, 2 daughters. Education: Gregg Commercial College, Liverpool, 1948-50; Ethel Wormald College of Education, 1968-70; Open University. Appointments: Assistant Master, 1971-91. Publications: Georgian Sequence; The Wheel of Fire; Germinal; Inflections; Mersey Poems; Personations; Land of My Dreams; Bread in the Wilderness; The Story of St George; St George – Knight of Lydda; The Rainbow Has Two Ends; Planet of the Shapes. Contributions to: Various small press magazines. Address: Rose Cottage, 17 Hadassah Grove, Lark Lane, Liverpool L17 8XH, England.

COONEY Muriel Sharon Taylor, b. 12 October 1947, Edenton, North Carolina, USA. Nurse. 2 sons. Education: BSN, East Carolina University, Greenville, North Carolina, 1969; MSN, St Louis University, St Louis, Missouri, USA, 1972; Orthopaedic Nurse Certificate. Appointments: Occupational: Staff Nurse, Johns Hopkins Hospital, Baltimore, Maryland, 1969-71; Staff Nurse, Barnes Hospital, St Louis, Missouri, 1971-72; Cardiovascular Clinical Nurse Specialist, Jackson Memorial Hospital, Miami, Florida, 1973-74; Home Healthcare Supervisor, Manager, Co-ordinator Council for

Senior Citizens, Durham, North Carolina, 1985; Person County Memorial Hospital, Roxboro, North Carolina, 1989-98; Teaching: Clinical Instructor, Shepherd College, Shepherdstown, West Virginia, 1983; Lecturer, Clinical Instructor, Shepherd College, 1984; Instructor, Piedmont Community College, Roxboro, North Carolina, 1989-90; Instructor, Watts School of Nursing, Durham, North Carolina, 1990-2004; Independent Education Consultant, 2005-; Instructor, North Carolina Central University, Durham, NC, 2006-2007; Instructor, Brunswick Community College, Supply, NC, 2007-. Publications: The Effects of Selected Teaching on the Recognition of Digitalis Toxicity, research thesis. Honours: Life Fellow, IBA; Distinguished Leadership Award for Service to Nursing Profession, 1994. Memberships: American Nurses Association; North Carolina Nurses Association; NCNA Council of Nurse Educators, Chairperson, 1994-97, Vice Chairperson, 1992-93; NCNA Council of Medical Surgical Nursing; NCNA Cabinet of Education and Resource Development; NCNA Council of Clinical Nurse Specialists; National League of Nursing; Academy of Medical Surgery Nursing, Bylaw Committee, 1994; Watts School of Nursing Association of Nursing, Student Advisors, 1993-2004; National Association of Orthopaedic Nurses, Parliamentarian, 2006; Triangle Chapter, Treasurer, 1995-, NAON; North Carolina Association of Nursing Students, Parliamentarian, 1997-2003; NCANS North Carolina Nurses Association Consultant, 2004-. Address: 6421 Ashton Court, Wilmington, North Carolina 28412, USA.

COONEY Thomas, b. 21 January 1942, Drogheda, Ireland. Catholic Priest; Augustinian. Education: Philosophical Studies, Good Counsel, House of Studies, Ballyboden, Dublin, Ireland, 1960-62; STB, Theological Studies, Gregorian University, Rome Italy, 1963-67; Dip.Catechtics, Corpus Christi College, London, 1968-69; MA, St Louis University, St Louis, Missouri, USA, 1973-75; Dip. Communications, Communication Centre, Hatch End, London, 1989; CPE, Holy Family Hospital and Medical Center, Methuen, Massachusetts, USA, 1990; Dip. Spiritual Direction, Center for Religious Development, Cambridge, Massachusetts, USA, 1990-91; Masters, Clinical Pastoral Counselling, Emmanuel College, Boston, Massachusetts, 1991-93. Appointments: Entered Augustinian Order, Dublin, 1959; Ordained, Rome, 1967; Teaching Chaplain, Vocational School, Dublin, 1967-68; Housemaster and Teacher, St Augustine's College, Dungarvan, 1969-72; Teacher, Good Counsel College, New Ross, 1972-73; Master of Students, Good Counsel, 1974-81; Provincial, Irish Province of the Augustinian Order, 1981-89; Executive, CMRS, 1983-89; President, Conference of Major Superiors of Ireland, 1986-89; Prior, St John's Priory, Dublin, 1993-95; Assistant General of the Augustinian Order, North West Europe and Canada, 1995-2001; Director of Pastoral Studies, Milltown Institute of Theology and Philosophy, Dublin, 2001-. Publications: Articles in religious and theological journals. Memberships: Honorary Treasurer and Member of the Executive, National Conference of Priests of Ireland, 1994-95; Theological Faculty, Milltown Institute, 2001-; Member of the Executive and Treasurer, All Ireland Spiritual Guidance Association, 2005; Honorary President, Seapoint, Pitch and Putt Golf Club, Termonfeckin, Ireland; Founding Member, Supervisors Association of Ireland. Address: St John's Priory, Thomas Street, Dublin 8, Ireland. E-mail: tcooney@milltown-intitute.ie

COOPER Alice (Vincent Furnier), b. 4 February 1948, Detroit, Michigan, USA. Singer. m Sheryl Goddard, 1 sons, 2 daughters. Career: First to stage theatrical rock concert tours; Among first to film conceptual rock promo videos (pre-MTV);

Considered among originators and greatest hard rock artists; Known as King of Shock Rock; Many film, television appearances including: Sextette, 1978; Sgt Pepper's Lonely Hearts Club Band, 1978; Leviatán, 1984; Prince of Darkness, 1987; Freddy's Dead: The Final Nightmare, 1991; The Attic Expeditions, 2001; Sound Off, 2005. Recordings: Singles include: I'm Eighteen; Poison; No More Mr Nice Guy; I Never Cry; Only Women Bleed; You And Me; Under My Wheels; Bed Of Nails; Albums include: School's Out, 1972; Billion Dollar Babies, 1973; Welcome To My Nightmare, 1976; From The Inside, 1978; Constrictor, 1986; Raise Your Fist And Yell, 1987; Trash, 1988; Hey Stoopid, 1991; Last Temptation, 1994; He's Back, 1997; Science Fictino, 2000; Brutal Planet, 2000; Alice Cooper Live, 2001; Take 2, 2001; Dragontown, 2001; Eyes of Alice Cooper, 2003; Hell Is, 2003. Publications: Wrote foreword to short story book: Shock Rock. Honour: Foundations Forum, Lifetime Achievement Award, 1994. Memberships: BMI; NARAS; SAG; AFTRA; AFofM. Address: Alive Enterprises, PO Box 5542, Beverly Hills, CA 90211, USA. Website: www.alicecooper.com

COOPER Barrington Spencer, b. 15 January 1923, Cardiff, Wales. Consulting Psychiatrist. m. Jane Eva Livermore Wallace, 1 daughter. Education: BA, Queens' College, Cambridge; MB BS, MRGCP, Bart's Medical School, London. Appointments include: House Physician, Whittington Hospital, 1946; House Physician, Ashford County Hospital, 1947; Medical Registrar, Oster House Hospital, 1947; Captain, Royal Army Medical Corps, Graded Psychiatrist, 1947-49; Chief Assistant, Academic Department of Psychological Medicine, St Bartholomew's Hospital, 1949-51; Clinical Assistant in Psychiatry: St Bartholomew's Hospital, 1951-53, London Jewish Hospital, 1951-53, National Hospital for Nervous Diseases, 1953-55; Elective Visiting Lecturer in Psychosomatic Medicine, University of Athens, University of Rome; Research Fellow, Sloane-Kettering Institute, New York City, 1951; Consulting Psychiatrist, Langham Clinic of Psychotherapy, London, 1970; Consulting Physician, Bowden House Clinic, London, 1974; Attending Physician, Foundation for Manic Depression, Columbia University, New York, 1974; Corresponding Associate, WHO Psychosocial Centre, Stockholm, 1977; Visiting Professor, Boston University Medical School, 1979-82; Consulting Physician, Clinic of Psychotherapy, London; Chairman and Consultant, Allied Medical Diagnostic Care; Currently: Medical Advisor: BACO Entertainment AG, Allied Medical Diagnostic Clinic, World Film Services, New Media Medical University, Fabyan Films Ltd, West One Productions Inc, Glesteams Ltd, Skyy Spirits Ltd, Caplin Cybernetic Ltd; Chairman and Consultant, Allied Medical Corporate Health Care; Private Practice, Devonshire Place, London; Independent Film Producer; The One Eyed Soldiers; The Doctor and the Devils; The Colonel's Children; Winner Takes All; Script Consultant; Director Fabyan Ltd and Fabyan Films Ltd. Publications: Author, Helix (ballet), 1982; Cockpits (novella), 1982; Contributing Editor, Kolokol Press UK, Kolokol Press US and Delos; Professional publications: Travel Medicine, 1982; Travel Sickness, 1982; Thomas Cook Health Passport, 4th edition, 1990; Consumer Guide to Over-the-Counter Medicines, 1996; Your Symptoms Diagnosed, 2nd edition, 1996; Consumer Guide to Prescription Medicines, 2001; Non-Allopathic Medication; Numerous articles in medical journals. Honours include: PhD, Cornell University; PhD, Columbia Pacific University. Memberships include: Member Royal College of General Practitioners, 1964; London Jewish Hospital Society; Life Fellow, Royal Society of Medicine; Fellow, Society of Clinical Psychiatrists; Foundation Member, Medical Section, British Psychological Society; British Association of Counselling; Fellow, American Academy of Arts and Sciences; British Medical Association; World Psychiatric Association; BAFTA; AIP; Founder and Patron, Salerno International Youth Orchestra Festival, Manhattan School of Music. Address: 10 Devonshire Place, London W1, England. E-mail: drbcooper@btclick.com

COOPER (Brenda) Clare, b. 21 January 1935, Falmouth, Cornwall, England. Writer. m. Bill Cooper, 6 April 1953, 2 sons, 1 daughter. Publications: David's Ghost; The Black Horn; Earthchange; Ashar of Qarius; The Skyrifters; Andrews and the Gargoyle; A Wizard Called Jones; Kings of the Mountain; Children of the Camps; The Settlement on Planet B; Miracles and Rubies; Timeloft; Marya's Emmets; Cat of Morfa, 1998; Stonehead, 2000; One Day on Morfa, 2001; Time Ball, 2003. Honour: Runner Up, Tir Na Nog Award. Memberships: PEN; Society of Authors; Welsh Academy. Address: Tyrhibin Newydd, Morfa, Newport, Pembrokeshire SA42 0NT, Wales.

COOPER Chris, b. 9 July 1951, Kansas City, Missouri, USA. Actor. m. Marianne Leone, 1983, 1 son. Education: University of Missouri; Ballet, Stephens College, Missouri. Career: US Coast Guard Reserves; Studied theatre acting, New York, 1976; Films include: Bad Timing, 1980; Matewan, Non date da mangiare agli animali, 1987; Guilty by Suspicion, Thousand Pieces of Gold, City of Hope, 1991; This Boy's Life, 1993; Money Train, Pharaoh's Army, 1995; Boys, Lone Star, A Time to Kill, 1996; Great Expectations, The Horse Whisperer, 1998; The 24 Hour Woman, October Sky, American Beauty, 1999; Me, Myself & Irene,The Patriot, 2000; Interstate 60, The Bourne Identity, Adaptation, 2002; Seabiscuit, 2003; Silver City, The Bourne Supremacy, 2004; Capote, Jarhead, Syriana, 2005; Beach, The Bourne Ultimatum, 2007; Stage appeareences include: Of the Fields Lately, 1980; The Ballad of Soapy Smith, A Different Moon, 1983; Cobb; The Grapes of Wrath; Sweet Bird of Youth; Love Letters. Honours: Best Actor Award, Cowboy Hall of Fame, 1991; Screen Actors Guild Award, 2000; Golden Globe Award, 2003; Best Supporting Actor: Academy Awards, 2004, National Board of Review, San Francisco Film Critics, Toronto Film Critics, San Diego Film Critics, Broadcast Film Association, LA Critics Association. Address: Paradigm Talent Agency, 10100 Santa Monica Boulevard, Suite 2500, Los Angeles, CA 90067, USA.

COOPER Jilly (Sallitt), b. 21 February 1937, Hornchurch, Essex, England. Writer; Journalist. m. Leo Cooper, 1961, 1 son, 1 daughter. Appointments: Reporter, Middlesex Independent Newspaper, Brentford, 1957-59; Columnist, The Sunday Times, 1969-85, The Mail on Sunday, 1985-. Publications: How to Stay Married, 1969; How to Survive from Nine to Five, 1970; Jolly Super, 1971; Men and Super Men, 1972; Jolly Super Too, 1973; Women and Super Women, 1974; Jolly Superlative, 1975; Emily (romance novel), 1975; Super Men and Super Women (omnibus), 1976; Bella (romance novel), 1976; Harriet (romance novel), 1976; Octavia (romance novel), 1977; Work and Wedlock (omnibus), 1977; Superjilly, 1977; Imogen (romance novel), 1978; Prudence (romance novel), 1978; Class: A View from Middle England, 1979; Supercooper, 1980; Little Mabel series, juvenile, 4 volumes, 1980-85; Violets and Vinegar: An Anthology of Women's Writings and Sayings (editor with Tom Hartman), 1980; The British in Love (editor), 1980; Love and Other Heartaches, 1981; Jolly Marsupial, 1982; Animals in War, 1983; The Common Years, 1984; Leo and Jilly Cooper on Rugby, 1984; Riders, 1985; Hotfoot to Zabriskie Point, 1985; Turn Right at The Spotted Dog, 1987; Rivals, 1988; Angels Rush In, 1990; Polo, 1991; The Man Who Made Husbands Jealous,

1993; Araminta's Wedding, 1993; Appassionata, 1996; How to Survive Christmas, 1996; Score! 1999; Pandora, 2002; Wicked, 2006. Honours: Publishing News Lifetime Achievement Award, 1998; OBE, 2004. Membership: NUJ. Address: c/o Vivienne Schuster, Curtis Brown, 4th Floor, Haymarket House, 28-29 Haymarket, London, SW1Y 4SP, England. E-mail: cb@curtisbrown.co.uk

COOPER Leon N, b. 28 February 1930, New York, USA. Physicist. m. Kay Anne Allard, 1969, 2 daughters. Education: BA, 1951, MA, 1953, PhD, 1954, Columbia University. Appointments: Institute for Advanced Study, Princeton, 1954-55; Research Associate, University of Illinois, 1955-57; Assistant Professor, Ohio State University, 157-58; Associate Professor, Brown University, Rhode Island, 1958-62; Professor, 1974, Thomas J Watson, Senior Professor of Science , 1974-, Director, Center for Neural Science, 1978-90, Institute for Brain and Neural Systems, 1991-, Brain Science Program, 2000-. Publications: An Introduction to the Meaning and Structure of Physics, 1968; Structure and Meaning, 1992; How We Learn, How We Remember, 1995. Honour: Comstock Prize, NAS, 1968; Joint Winner, Nobel Prize, Physics, 1972; Honorary DSc, Columbia, Sussex, 1973, Illinois, Brown, 1974, Gustavus Adolphus College, 1975, Ohio State University, 1976, Pierre and Marie Curie University, Paris, 1977; Award in Excellence, Columbia University, 1974; Descartes Medal, Academy de Paris, University Rene Descartes, 1977; John Jay Award, Columbia College, 1985. Memberships: National Science Foundation Post-doctoral Fellow, 1954-55; Alfred P Sloan Foundation Research Fellow, 1959-66; John Simon Guggenheim Memorial Foundation Fellow, 1965-66; Fellow, American Physical Society, American Academy of Arts and Sciences; American Federation of Scientists; Member, NAS, American Philosophical Society. Address: Box 1843, Physics Department, Brown University, Providence, RI 02912, USA.

COOPER Thomas Joshua, b. 19 December 1946, San Francisco, California, USA; Artist. m. Catherine Alice, 2 daughters. Education: BA cum laude, Special Studies – Art, Philosophy, Literature, Humboldt State University, California, 1969; MA, Art with Distinction in Photography, University of New Mexico, USA, 1972; California Lifetime Community College Teaching Credential, 1972. Appointments: Founding Head, Department of Photography, 1982-2000, Honorary Professor, 1998-, Elected Chair, School of Fine Art, 2000-2002, Senior Researcher and Professor of Fine Art, 2002-, Glasgow School of Art, Glasgow, Scotland. Publications: Solo publications include: Dialogue with Photography, 1979-2005; Between Dark and Park, 1985; Dreaming the Gokstadt, 1988; Simply Counting Waves, 1995; A Handful of Stones, 1996; wild, 2001; Some Rivers, Some Trees, Some Rocks, Some Seas, 2003; point of no return, 2004; true, 2009; Photographs included in numerous reference books and exhibition catalogues. Honours: John D Phelan Award in Art and Literature (first time ever awarded in photography) San Francisco, California, USA, 1970; Major Photography Bursary (joint award), Arts Council of Great Britain, 1976; Photography Fellow, National Endowment of the Arts, Washington DC, USA, 1978; Major Artists Award, Scottish Arts Council, Edinburgh, Scotland, 1994; Major Artists Award, Lannan Foundation, Santa Fe, New Mexico, USA, 1999-; Creakie, Scotland, 2005. Memberships: Society for Photographic Education; Founding Member, Scottish Society for the History of Photography; Royal Scottish Geographical Society. Address: The Glasgow School of Art, 167 Renfrew Street, Glasgow G3 6RQ, Scotland. E-mail: t.cooper@gsa.ac.uk

COOPER Rt Hon Yvette, b. 20 March 1969, Inverness, Scotland. Member of Parliament for Pontefract and Castleford; Chief Secretary to the Treasury. m. Ed Balls, 3 children. Education: Eggars Comprehensive; Alton Sixth Form College; BA, PEE, Balliol College, Oxford University; Kennedy Scholarship, Harvard University, 1991; MSc, Economics, London School of Economics. Appointments: Economics Researcher to Shadow Chancellor of the Exchequer, 1990; Domestic Policy Specialist, Arkansas, US Democratic Party presidential candidate, Bill Clinton, 1992; Policy Advisor to Labour's Treasury Team in Opposition, 1992-94; Research Associate, Centre for Economic Performance, 1994; Economic Columnist and Leader Writer on the Independent newspaper, 1995-97; Member of Parliament for Pontefract and Castleford, 1997-; Parliamentary Under Secretary of State for the Department of Health, 1999-2003; Parliamentary Under Secretary of State at the Office of the Deputy Prime Minister, 2003-05; Minister of State for Housing and Planning in the Department for Communities and Local Government, 2005-07; Minister for Housing, 2007-; Chief Secretary to the Treasury, 2008-.

COPE Jonathan, b. 1963, England. Ballet Dancer. m. Maria Almeida, 1 son, 1 daughter. Education: Royal Ballet School. Career: Dancer, 1982-, Soloist, 1985-86, Principal, 1987-90, 1992-, Royal Ballet; Property development business, 1990-92; Leading roles (with Royal Ballet): Swan Lake; The Sleeping Beauty; The Nutcracker; Romeo and Juliet; La Bayadère; Giselle; Le Baiser de la Fée; The Prince of the Pagodas; Cinderella; Ondine; Serenade; Agon; Apollo; Opus 19/The Dreamer; The Sons of Horus; Young Apollo; Galanteries; The Planets; Still Life at the Penguin Café; The Spirit of Fugue; Concerto; Gloria; Requiem; A Broken Set of Rules; Pursuit; Piano; Grand Pas Classique; Monotones; Mayerling; Different Drummer; The Judas Tree; A Month in the Country; Birthday Offering; La Valise; Air Monotones II; Renard; Fearful Symmetries; Symphony in C; Duo Concertant; If This Is Still A Problem; Manon; Illuminations. Address: The Royal Ballet, Royal Opera House, Covent Garden, London WC2E 9DD, England.

COPE Wendy Mary, b. 21 July 1945, Erith, Kent, England. Author. Education: Farringtons School, Chislehurst, Kent, 1957-62; BA, History, 1966, Diploma in Education, 1967, St Hilda's College, Oxford. Appointments: Teacher, Inner London Education Authority, 1967-86; Freelance Writer, 1986-. Publications: Making Cocoa for Kingsley Amis, 1986; Twiddling Your Thumbs, 1988; Is That the New Moon? (editor); The River Girl, 1990; Serious Concerns, 1992; The Orchard Book of Funny Poems (editor), 1993; The Funny Side (editor), 1998; The Faber Book of Bedtime Stories (editor), 2000; If I Don't Know, 2001; Heaven on Earth: 101 Happy Poems (editor), 2001; George Herbert: Verse and prose (a selection) (editor), 2002; Two Cures for Love: selected poems 1979-2006, 2008. Honours: Cholmondeley Award for Poetry, 1987; Michael Braude Award, American Academy of Arts and Letters, 1995; Fellow, Royal Society of Literature. Memberships: Society of Authors.

COPLEY Paul, b. 25 November 1944, Denby Dale, Yorkshire, England. Actor; Writer. m. Natasha Pyne, 1972. Education: Teachers Certificate, Northern Counties College of Education. Appointments: Freelance Actor/Writer; Extensive work in theatre, TV, radio and film: Theatre: For King and Country, Mermaid Theatre, 1976; Pillion, Bush Theatre, London, 1977; Viaduct, Bush Theatre, London, 1979; Tapster, Stephen Joseph Theatre, Scarborough, 1981; Fire-Eaters, Tricycle Theatre, London, 1984; Calling, Stephen Joseph

Theatre, Scarborough, 1986; Billy Liar, Ambassador Theatre Group National Tour; Ghosts Gate Theatre, 2007; Plays for children: Odysseus and the Cyclops, 1998; The Pardoner's Tale, 1999; Loki the Mischief Maker, 2000; Jennifer Jenks and Her Excellent Day Out, 2000; TV: Messiah 3: The Promise, BBC/Paramount TV; Best Friends, Granada TV series; Life on Mars, TV; The Street, TV; Waking the Dead. TV; Shameless, TV; Hornblower, TV; Dalziel and Pascoe, TV; The Lakes, TV; This Life, TV; Heartbeat, TV; Clocking Off, TV; Cracker, TV; Radio: On May-Day, BBC Radio 4 Sunday Play, 1986; repeated World Service, 1987, Radio 4, 1996; Tipperary Smith, BBC Radio 4, 1994; Words Alive, BBC Education Radio, 1996-2003; Radio 7, 2006; Serjeant Musgrave's Dance, BBC Radio 3; A Sunset Touch, BBC Radio 4; Film, The Remains of the Day; Jude; Blow Dry; A Bridge Too Far. Recorded over 200 hundred radio plays and TV works. Membership: Writers Guild. Address: Literary Agent, Casarotto Ramsey Ltd, 60 Wardour Street, London W1V 4ND, England.

COPPEDE` Fabio, b. 17 August 1975, Pietrasanta (LU), Italy. Research Scientist. Education: Doctor in Biological Sciences (cum laude), 2000, PhD, Microbiology and Genetics, 2005, University of Pisa, Italy. Appointments: Undergraduate Student, Researcher, 2000, PhD student, Department of Human Environmental Sciences, 2001-04, Contract Researcher, Department of Neuroscience, 2006-, University of Pisa; Academic Visitor, King's College, London, 2000; Visiting Researcher, School of Public Health, University of California, Berkeley, USA, 2002-03; Postdoctoral Researcher, Karolinska Institutet, Stockholm, Sweden, 2005-06. Publications: Author, over 20 scientific articles in peer-reviewed journals and scientific book chapters; Over 30 abstracts in proceedings of international meetings. Honours: Best Young Researcher Prize, Italian Society of Environmental Mutagenesis, 2006. Memberships: Italian Society of Environmental Mutagenesis; European Society of Environmental Mutagenesis. Address: Department of Neuroscience, via Roma 67, 56126 Pisa, Italy. E-mail: f.coppede@geog.unipi.it

COPPEN Luke Benjamin Edward, b. 8 February 1976, Basingstoke, Hampshire. Journalist. m. Marlena Marciniszyn, 1 daughter. Education: Testbourne Community School, Whitchurch, 1988-92; Cricklade Tertiary College, Andover, 1992-94; BA (1st class honours), Religion and Politics, School of Oriental and African Studies, London, 1997; Diploma, Journalism Studies, Cardiff, 1998. Appointments: Film Editor, The London Student, 1996-97; Reporter, 1998-2000, Deputy Editor, 2000-04, Editor, 2004-, The Catholic Herald. E-mail: editorial@catholicherald.co.uk

COPPOLA Francis Ford, b. 7 April 1939, Detroit, Michigan, USA. Film writer and director. m. Eleanor Neil, 2 sons (1 deceased), 1 daughter. Education: Hofstra University; University of California. Career: Films include: Dementia 13, 1963; This Property is Condemned, 1965; Is Paris Burning?, 1966; You're A Big Boy Now, 1967; Finian's Rainbow, 1968; The Rain People, 1969; Patton, 1971; The Great Gatsby, 1974; The Godfather Part II, 1975; The Black Stallion (produced), 1977; Apocalypse Now, 1979; One From the Heart, Hammett (produced), The Escape Artist, The Return of the Black Stallion, 1982; Rumble Fish, The Outsiders, 1983; The Cotton Club, 1984; Peggy Sue Got Married, Gardens of Stone, 1986; Life Without Zoe, Tucker: the Man and His Dream, 1988; The Godfather Part III, 1990; Dracula, 1991; My Family/ Mia Familia, Don Huan de Marco, 1995; Jack, 1996; The Rainmaker, 1997; The Florentine, The Virgin Suicides, 1999; Grapefruit Moon, 2000; Assassination Tango; Supernova;

Megalopolis; Executive producer: The Secret Garden, 1993; Mary Shelley's Frankenstein, 1994; Buddy, 1997; The Third Miracle, Goosed, Sleepy Hollow, 1999; Monster; Jeepers Creepers No Such Thing; Pumpkin; Lost in Translation, 2003; Kinsey, 2004; Marie Antoinette, The Good Shepherd, 2006; Youth Without Youth, 2007. Theatre direction includes: Private Lives, The Visit of the Old Lady (San Francisco Opera Co), 1972; Artistic Director, Zoetrope Studios, 1969-; Owner, Niebaum-Coppola Estate, Napa Valley. Honours: 5 Oscars, 36 awards including, Cannes Film Award for The Conversation, 1974; Director's Guild Award for The Godfather; Academy Award for Best Screenplay for Patton, Golden Palm (Cannes), for Apocalypse Now, 1979; Also awarded Best Screenplay, Best Director and Best Picture Oscars for the Godfather Part II; US Army Civilian Service Award; Commandeur, Ordre des Arts et des Lettres. Address: Zoetrope Studios, 916 Kearny Street, San Francisco, CA 94133, USA.

COPPOLA Sofia, b. 14 May 1971, New York, USA. Film Director; Screenwriter; Producer; Photographer. m. Spike Jonze, divorced, 2003; Partner, Thomas Mars, 1 daughter. Career: Creator, Pop-culture magazine show, Hi-Octane, 1994; Former designer, Milkfed fashon label; Photography work appeared in Interview, Paris Vogue and Allure; Films include: The Godfather: Part III, 1990; Lick the Star (director, producer and writer), 1998; Star Wars: Episode 1 – The Phantom Menace, 1999; The Virgin Suicides (director and writer); CQ, 2001; Lost in Translation (director, producer and writer), 2004; Cut Shorts, 2006; Marie Antoinette (producer), 2006; Honours: Academy Award, Best Original Screenplay, 2004; Golden Globe Award, Best Picture, and Best Screenplay, 2004; Independent Spirit Awards for Best Screenplay, Best Director, and Best Picture, 2004; Cesar Award for Best Foreign Feature, 2005. Memberships: Writers Guild of America. Address: c/o Focus Features, 65 Bleeker Street, Second Floor, New York, NY 10012, USA.

CORBET Philip Steven, b. 21 May 1929, Kuala Lumpur, West Malaysia. University Professor; Consultant Ecologist; Medical Entomologist. 1 daughter. Education: Dauntsey's School; BSc, First Class Honours, Botany, Geology, Zoology, 1949, BSc, First Class Honours, Zoology, 1950, University of Reading; PhD, Entomology, Gonville and Caius College, University of Cambridge, 1953; DSc, Zoology, University of Reading, 1962; ScD, Zoology, Gonville and Caius College, University of Cambridge, 1976; DSc, Zoology, University of Edinburgh, 2003; DSc, University of Dundee, 2005. Appointments: Entomologist, East African Freshwater Fisheries Research Institute, Jinja, Uganda, 1954-57; Entomologist, East African Virus Research Institute, Entebbe, Uganda, 1957-62; Research Scientist (Entomologist), Entomology Research Institute, Canada Department of Agriculture, Ottawa, Ontario, Canada, 1962-67; Director, Research Institute, Canada Department of Agriculture, Belleville, Ontario, Canada, 1967-71; Professor and Chairman, Department of Biology, University of Waterloo, Ontario, Canada, 1971-74; Professor and Director, Centre for Resource Management, University of Canterbury and Lincoln College, Christchurch, New Zealand, 1974-78; Professor of Zoology, Department of Zoology, University of Canterbury, Christchurch, New Zealand, 1978-80; Professor of Zoology, 1980-90, Head of Department, 1983-86, Department of Biological Sciences, Professor Emeritus of Zoology, 1990-, University of Dundee, Scotland; Honorary Professor, University of Edinburgh, Scotland, 1996-. Publications: Author or co-author of over 250 research reports on freshwater biology, medical entomology and conservation biology; 4 books: co-author, Dragonflies, 1960, reprinted 1985; A Biology of Dragonflies, 1962, reprinted

1983; co-author, The Odonata of Canada and Alaska, volume 3, 1975, revised edition, 1978, reprinted 1998; Dragonflies. Behaviour and Ecology of Odonata, 1999, reprinted 2001, 2004. Honours include: President, 1971-72 and Gold Medal for Outstanding Achievement, 1974, Entomological Society of Canada; Commonwealth Visiting Professor, University of Cambridge, 1979-80; President, British Dragonfly Society, 1983-91; President, Worldwide Dragonfly Association, 2001-2003; Neill Prize, Royal Society of Edinburgh, 2002; Elected Fellowships: Royal Entomological Society, 1951; Institute of Biology, 1967; Entomological Society of Canada, 1977, Royal Society of Tropical Medicine and Hygiene, 1985; Royal Society of Edinburgh, 1987; Royal Society of Arts, 1991; Honorary Memberships: British Dragonfly Society 1991; Société française d'odonatologie, 1997; Dragonfly Society of the Americas, 2000. Memberships: The Arctic Club.

CORBETT Peter George, b. 13 April 1952, Rossett, North Wales. Artist. Education: BA (Honours), Fine Art, Manchester Regional College of Art and Design, 1974. Career: Artist, oil on canvas; Speaker, Workers Educational Association, Liverpool, 1995; Life Drawing Tutor, Bluecoat Chambers, Liverpool, 1996; Originator "Liverpool European Capital of Culture 2008", 1996/1997; Exhibitions include: Centre Gallery Liverpool, 1979; Liverpool Playhouse, 1982; Acorn Gallery Liverpool, 1985; Major Merseyside Artists Exhibition, Port of Liverpool Building, 1988; Merseyside Contemporary Artists Exhibition, Albert Dock, Liverpool; Surreal Objects Exhibition, Tate Gallery, Liverpool, 1989; Unity Theatre, Liverpool, 1990; Royal Liver Building, Liverpool (two person), 1991; Senate House Gallery, Liverpool University (one man), 1993; Academy of Arts, Liverpool (two man), 1994; Grosvenor Museum Exhibition, Chester (open), 1995; Atkinson Gallery, Southport (one man), 1995; Liverpool Academy of Arts, 1998; Hanover Gallery, Liverpool (two man), 1999; Liverpool Biennial of Contemporary Art, 1999 Independent; DFN Gallery, New York (mixed), 2000; Influences and Innovations, Agora Gallery, New York (mixed), 2002; Retrospective Painting Exhibition, Senate House Gallery, University of Liverpool, 2004, included in Liverpool Biennial of Contemporary Art (independent); Design and Artists Copyright Society, 20th Anniversary Exhibition, Mall Gallery, London, 2004; Lexmark European Art Prize, London, Air Gallery, 2004; The Artcell Gallery, Barcelona, Spain, 2005; The Cornerstone Gallery, Hope University, Liverpool, 2005; Life and Image exhibition, Liverpool (mixed), 2006; Artfinder Gallery (mixed), Liverpool, 2007; Florence Biennale of Contemporary Art (mixed), Florence, Italy, 2007 . Works included in Liverpool University Art Collection; Atkinson Gallery, Southport; Hope University, Liverpool; Private Collections in America, Netherlands, Australia, Germany, Britain, Spain. Publications: Numerous poems in poetry anthologies including: A Celebration of Poets, 1999; Parnassus of World Poets, 2001; Tales of Erewhon (full collection of poems), 2001; The Best Poems and Poets of 2002; A Shield of Angels, 2002; The Sound of Poetry (Audio-cassette), 2002; Quantum Leap Magazine, 2003; The Pool of Life (full collection of own poems), 2003; The Hills are Alive, 2004; Images of Live, 2004; The Best Poems and Poets of 2004, 2004; The Inner Voice, 2005; Mixed Emotions, 2005; Celebrations, 2005; Poems from North and Northwest England, 2005; Aura of Life (single poem), 2006; Poetry from Northern England (Single poem), 2007; Restless Soul (single poem), 2007. Honours include: Honorary Professor of Fine Art, Institute of Co-ordinated Research, Victoria, Australia, 1994; Editor's Award for Outstanding Achievements in Poetry, International Library of Poets, USA, 1997; Nominated for Poet of the Year, International Society of Poets, USA, 1997; Diploma Winner, Scottish International Open Poetry Competition, 1998; International German Art Prize, 1998; Outstanding Achievement Award, Albert Einstein Academy, USA, 1998; Friedrich Holdrein Award and Gold Medal for Poetry, Germany, 2000; Prizewinner, International Library of Poetry, USA, 2000; International Peace Prize, United Cultural Convention, USA, 2002; World Lifetime Achievement Award, American Biographical Institute, 2002; International Poet of Merit Award, International Society of Poets, USA, 2002; Minister of Culture, American Biographical Institute, 2003; Poet of the Year, International Society of Poets, USA, 2003; Short listed for the Lexmark European Art Prize, exhibition of finalists in London, 2004; Genius Laureate for the United Kingdom (Art and Culture), ABI, 2006; Liverpool European Capital of Culture 08 Ambassador, 2006. Memberships: Design and Artists Copyright Society, London; Maison International des Intellectuels, Paris, France; Founder and Chairman, Merseyside Visual Arts Festival, 1989-90; Founding Member, American Order of Excellence, American Biographical Institute, 2002. Address: Flat 4, 7 Gambier Terrace, Hope Street, Liverpool L1 7BG, England. Website: www.axisweb.org/artist/petercorbett

CORBETT Robin, (Lord Corbett of Castle Vale), b. 22 December 1933, Fremantle, Australia. Parliamentarian. m. Valerie, 1 son, 2 daughters. Appointments: Trainee, Birmingham Evening Mail; Reporter, Daily Mirror; Deputy Editor, Farmer's Weekly; Editorial Staff Development Executive, IPC Magazines; Labour Relations Executive, IPC; National Executive Committee Member, Honorary Secretary Magazine and Book Branch, National Union of Journalists; Elected Member of Parliament for Hemel Hempstead, 1974-79; Elected Member of Parliament for Birmingham Erdington, 1983-2001; Opposition Front Bench Spokesman on Broadcasting and Media, 1987-94 and Disabled People's Rights, 1994-95; Chairman, House of Commons Home Affairs Select Committee, 1999-2001; Appointed to House of Lords, 2001; Member, Select Committee on the EU (SCF). Honours: Dr of Laws, Birmingham University, 2005. Memberships: Vice Chairman Indo-British Parliamentary Group; Chairman, Friends of Cyprus; Vice-Chairman, All Party Motor Group, sustainable development, renewable energy; Member, Wilton Park Academic Council, 1995-2005; Vice-President, Lotteries Council; Treasurer, ANZAC Group, 1946-2006; Member, Friends of Eden Project; Patron, Hope for Children; Director, RehabUK; Chairman, Castle Vale Neighbourhood Management Board, 2001-04; President, Josiah Mason College, Erdington, 2001-; Chairman, Castle Vale Neighbourhood Partnership, 2004-; Chairman, Parliamentary Labour Peers' Group, 2005-; Member, Lords PLP Co-ordination Committee, 2004-05. Address: House of Lords, London, SW1A 0PW, England. E-mail: castlevale@corbetts.plus.com

CORBIERE Stephane de, b. 13 September 1957, Saint-Sever, France. ENT Head and Neck Surgeon. m. Virginie Lecoquiere, 3 sons, 2 daughters. Education: Doctor of Medicine, 1987; Specialist Qualification in Otorhinolaryngology, 1989; Qualification in Head and Neck Surgery. Appointments: Head of ENT Department, 1998-, Head of Stomatology Department, American Hospital of Paris, Neuilly s/s, France. Publications: Use of Photodynamic therapy in the treatment of vocal chord carcinoma: Retrospective study on 41 cases, 1986-92; Use of photodynamic therapy in the treatment of vocal chord carcinoma (journal article), 1990. Honour: Award, Medical School of Paris René Descartes. Memberships: Fellow, American College of Surgeons, 1999; Life Member, French

Academy of Surgeons, 2001; Honorary Member, Science Academy of Romania, 2004. Address: 10 rue Greuze 75116, Paris France. E-mail: stephane.decorbiere@online.fr

CORBLUTH Elsa, b. 2 August 1928, Beckenham, Kent, England. Writer; Photographer. m. David Boadella, divorced 1987, 1 son, 1 daughter, deceased 1980. Education: BA, Combined Creative Arts, 1st Class Honours, Alsager College, 1982; MA, Creative Writing, Lancaster University, 1984. Publications: St Patrick's Night, poems on daughter's death in charity hostel fire while working there, 1988; The Planet Iceland, 2002; Various booklets; Wilds, travelling exhibition of poems illustrated by her photographs, accompanied by poetry readings; Group of 7 poems in SW Arts Proof Series of small books, 1998. Contributions to: Poetry Review; Outposts; The Rialto; Times Literary Supplement, etc; Anthologies: Green Book; Arts Council of Great Britain; PEN, etc. Honours: 1st Prizes, South-West Arts Competition, Bridport, 1979 and 1981; Joint 1st, Cheltenham Festival Competition, 1981; 1st, Sheffield Competition, 1981; 1st, ORBIS Rhyme Revival, 1986, 1993, 1995; 1st Prize Yorkshire Poetry Competition, 1997; and others. Membership: Harbour Poets Weymouth; CND. Address: Hawthorn Cottage, Rodden, Near Weymouth, Dorset DT3 4JE, England.

CORBY Peter John Siddons, b. 8 July 1924, Leamington Spa, England. Businessman. m. (1) Gail Susan Clifford-Marshall, 2 sons, (2) Inés Rosemary Mandow, 1 son. Education: Private Grammar School (Boarding). Appointments: Engineering Apprentice, Coventry Gauge & Tool Co Ltd, 1940-42; Wartime Service: Flight Engineer (Halifax and Lancaster), 78 Squadron, 4 Group, Bomber Command Royal Airforce, 1943-48; Managing Director of family business, Corbys Ltd and John Corby Ltd; Created manufactured and marketed the Corby Electric Trouser Press, also served on the boards of various other manufacturing and service companies, 1949-74; Sold Corby companies to Thomas Jourdan plc, 1974; Various non-executive directorships, including Thomas Jourdan plc, 1974-2006; Company Memberships: Cordeal Limited (family company); SaveTower Ltd (property company). Honours: Freeman of the City of London, 1977; Liveryman (Marketors), 1978. Memberships: Ocean Cruising Club; Island Sailing Club; Honorary Member, Yacht Club de France; Fellow of the Institute of Directors, 1955; Lloyd's of London, 1974. Address: The Sloop, 89 High Street, Cowes, Isle of Wight PO31 7AW, England.

CORDINGLY David, b. 5 December 1938, London, England. Writer. m. Shirley, 1 son, 1 daughter. Education: Honours Degree Modern History, MA, Oriel College, Oxford; D Phil, University of Sussex. Appointments: Graphic Designer with various design groups and publishing firms in London; Exhibition Designer, The British Museum; Keeper, Art Gallery and Museum, Brighton; Assistant Director, Museum of London; Keeper of Pictures and then Head of Exhibitions, National Maritime Museum, Greenwich. Publications: Books: Marine Painting in England 1700-1900, 1974; Painters of the Sea, 1979; Nicholas Pocock, Marine Artist, 1986; Life among the Pirates: the romance and the reality, 1995; Pirates: an illustrated history; Ships and Seascapes: an introduction to marine prints, drawings and watercolours, 1997; Heroines and Harlots: women at sea in the great age of sail, 2001; Billy Ruffian: the Bellerophon and the downfall of Napoleon, 2003. Address: 2 Vine Place, Brighton, Sussex BN1 3HE, England.

CORDOBA Gonzalo, Consulting Engineer. Education: BS, Civil Engineering, University of Panamá; BS, MsSc, PhD, Metallurgical Engineering, AD, Mechanical Engineering,

University of Tennessee, USA. Appointments: University Professor, Universidad Tecnológica de Panamá, 1970-; Assistant Project Manager, Catalytic Inc, Venezuela, 1974-75; Resident Manager, Northville Terminal Corporation, David, Republic of Panamá, 1981-82; Technical and Maintenance Manager, Petroterminales de Panamá, 1982-83; Construction Manager, Wickland Oil Aruba NV, San Nicolas, Aruba, 1989-91; General Manager, Instituto de Recursos Hidraulicos y Electrificación, 1991-94; Administrative Manager, Auto Partes Japanesas, Panama, 1994-95; Consulting Engineer, Ingenieria Gonzalo Córdoba, Panamá, 1994-; National Secretary, Secretaria Nacional de Ciencia, Tecnologia e Innovación, Clayton, Republic of Panamá, 1999-2004. Publications: Papers and articles in professional journals. Memberships: American Society of Civil Engineers; American Institute of Steel Construction; American Welding Society; National Association of Corrosion Engineers International; Institute of Electrical & Electronic Engineers; American Concrete Institute; Ciencia y Tecnologia Para el Desarrollo Iberoamericano; Rotary Club. Address: PO Box 0819-09135, El Dorado, Panamá, Republic of Panamá. E-mail: emacil@cwpanama.net

CORLUY Walter Josephus, b. 8 April 1938, Borgerhout, Belgium. Liquidator. Education: MA, Economics, PhD, Law, Catholic University, Louvain, Belgium. Appointments: Ex-Regional General Manager, Generale Bank (now Fortis Bank); Retired University Senior Teaching Professor, University of Antwerp; Liquidator, Corluy Management and Consulting EBVBA. Publications: Finance and Risk Management in International Trade, 1990, 2nd edition 1995; Co-author, Practical Guide for Financial Management, 1995; Different articles in professional papers. Honours: Knight, Order of Leopold, Belgium; Knight, Order of the Crown, Belgium; Senator, Jaycees International; Paul Harris Fellow, Sapphire, Rotary International; Diocesan Order of Merit with Silver (Diocese Antwerp); Honorary Inhabitant of Antwerp, 1993. Memberships: Rotary Club, Antwerpen Voorkempen; Formerly Chairman, Asociacion-Belgo-Ibero-Americana; Treasurer, Dante Alighieri; Director, NGO Trias; Chairman, Church Council, Saint Anthony, Antwerp. Address: Prins Albertlei, 5 Box 1, 2600 Antwerp, Belgium. E-mail: walter.corluy@skynet.be

CORNELL Cindy, Pain Management Nurse Practitioner. Education: BSN, Southern Illinois University, 1983; Certified Biofeedback Therapist, Stens Biofeedback, 1996; Certified Electro Acupuncturist/Instructor, Acumed Medical, 2000; LMT, Southwest Institute of Healing Arts, 2002; MSN-FNP, University of Phoenix, 2006. Appointments: Pediatric Pain Management Educator, Astra USA, New York, 1992-97; Nurse Clinician Pain Management/Co-ordinator, St Louis Children's Hospital, St Louis, 1984-97; Pain Management Nurse Educator/Consultant, CIGNA Healthcare, Phoenix, 1997-2005; Electro Acupuncture Instructor, Acumed Medical, Toronto, Canada, 2000-03; Student Family Nurse Practitioner, CIGNA Healthcare, Phoenix, 2005-; Pain Management Clinical Nurse, St Joseph's Hospital, Phoenix, 2005-; Student Family Nurse Practitioner, Valley Cancer Pain Treatment Center, Scottsdale, 2006; Student Family Nurse Practitioner, Arizona Pain Clinic, Scottsdale, 2006. Publications: Articles and papers in medical journals. Honours: National Dean's List, 1982-83; Nurse of the Year, St Louis Children's Hospital, 1989; CIGNA Healthcare Employee of the Month, 1997; Circle of Excellence Platinum Award, 2000, Circle of Excellence Gold Award, 2003, CIGNA Healthcare; Spirit of St Louis Half Marathon 5th Place Women's division, 2005; Sigma Theta Tau, International Honor Society of Nursing,

2006; Listed in international biographical dictionaries. Memberships: American Academy of Pain Management; American Society of Pain Educators; American Society of Pain Management Nurses; Cancer Counsel Committee, Catholic Healthcare West; International Association for the Study of Pain. Address: 4527 N 74th Place, Scottsdale, AZ 85251, USA. E-mail: craecornell1@cox.net

CORNWALL-JONES Mark Ralph, b. 14 February 1933, Quetta, Pakistan. Investment Manager. m. Priscilla Yeo, 3 sons, 1 daughter. Education: Jesus College, Cambridge. Appointments: National Service, Kings Royal Rifle Corps; Battersea Churches Housing Trust; The Debenture Corporation; John Govett & Co Ltd; Courage Ltd; Halifax Building Society; Govett Oriental Investment Trust; Ecclesiastical Insurance Group; Allchurches Trust; Treasurer, Corporation of the Church House. Honours: OBE, 2004. Address: Erin House, 3 Albert Bridge Road, Battersea, London SW11 4PX, England.

CORP Lester Desmond, b. 17 April 1946, London, England. Chartered Accountant; Finance Director. m. Mary Ann Robbins. Education: BSc, Economics, London School of Economics and Political Science, London University, 1967; Fellow, Institute of Chartered Accountants in England and Wales (FCA), 1970. Appointments: From Trainee to Manager, Coopers & Lybrand, London, 1967-75; Financial Accountant, Sun Life Assurance, London, 1975-78; Director of Finance and Resources, Conservative Party Central Office, 1978-84; Financial Controller, Leeds Castle Foundation, Maidstone, Kent, England, 1985-88; Director of Finance, Zoological Society of London, London, 1988-94; Finance Director, Grant Leisure Group Ltd, London, 1985-94; Director of Finance, Royal Albert Hall, London, 1994-2001; Director, Finance and Administration, Parkinson's Disease Society, London, 2002-. Memberships: Vice-Chairman, Conservative Party, Mid Sussex, England, 1975-84; Member, Chartered Management Institute, 1980-; Trustee, Brooke Hospital for Animals, 1994-. Address: 215 Vauxhall Bridge Road, London SW1V 3EJ, England.

CORP Ronald Geoffrey, b. 4 January 1951, Wells, Somerset, England. Musician; Cleric. Education: MA, Christ Church, Oxford; Dip. Theol., University of Southampton. Appointments: Librarian, Producer and Presenter, BBC Radio 3, 1973-87; Musical Director, Highgate Choral Society, 1984; Musical Director, The London Chorus, 1985; Founder, New London Orchestra, 1988; Founder, New London Children's Choir, 1991; Non-stipendiary Minister, St Mary's Kilburn with St James' West End Lane, 1998-2002; Non-stipendiary Assistant Curate, Christ Church, Hendon, 2002-07; Non-Stipendiary Assistant Curate, St Alban's, Holban; Compositions include: And All the Trumpets Sounded, 1989; Laudamus, 1994; Four Elizabethan Lyrics, 1994; Cornucopia, 1997; Piano Concerto, 1997; A New Song, 1999; Adonai Echad, 2001; Kaleidoscope, 2002; Missa San Marco, 2002; Dover Beach, 2003; Forever Child, 2004; Waters of Time, 2006. Publications: 18 recordings with New London Orchestra; CD of own choral music, Forever Child; Book: The Choral Singer's Companion, 1987, revised edition, 2000. Memberships: Trustee, 2000-, Chairman, Education Committee, Musician's Benevolent Fund; Vice-President, The Sullivan Society; President, Bracknell Choral Society. Address: Bulford Mill, Bulford Mill Lane, Cressing, Essex, CM77 8NS, England. E-mail: ronald.corp@btconnect.com

CORTES Joaquin, b. 1970, Madrid, Spain. Appointments: Joined Spanish National Ballet, 1985; Principal Dancer, 1987-90; Now appears in own shows, blending gypsy dancing, jazz blues and classical ballet; Films: Pedro Almodóvar's, The Flower Of My Secret; Gitano, 2000; Vaniglia e cioccolato, 2004.

CORTI Christopher Winston, b. 30 July 1940, London, England. Consultant. m. Shirley Anne Mack, 3 sons. Education: Bishopshalt School, Hillingdon, Middlesex, 1951-59; BSc, Metallurgy, Battersea College of Advanced Technology, London, 1959-63; PhD, Metallurgy, University of Surrey, Guildford, 1968-72. Appointments: Student, UK Atomic Energy Authority, Lancashire, 1961-62; Research Officer, Central Electricity Research Laboratories, Leatherhead, Surrey, 1963-68; Scientific Officer, Department of Materials Science & Engineering, University of Surrey, 1968-72; Project Leader, Brown Boveri Research Centre, Baden, Switzerland, 1973-77; Research Manager, Materials Technology, Johnston Matthey Technology Centre, Reading, 1978-88; Technical Director, Colour & Print Division, Johnson Matthey plc, Stoke on Trent, 1988-92; SPT Officer, Department of Trade & Industry, UK Government, 1993-94; Managing Director, International Technology, World Gold Council, London, 1994-2004; Managing Director, COReGOLD Technology Consultancy, 2004-. Publications: Over 70 scientific articles and conference papers in refereed scientific journals. Honours: Chartered Engineer; Chartered Scientist; Fellow, Institute of Materials, Minerals and Mining; Fellow, City & Guilds Institute, London. Memberships: Institute of Materials, Minerals and Mining, London; City & Guilds Institute, London; Engineering Council, UK; Science Council, UK; Royal Horticultural Society, UK; National Trust, UK. Address: 21 Marchwood Avenue, Emmer Green, Reading, Berkshire RG4 8UH, England. E-mail: chris@corti.force9.co.uk

COSBY Bill, b. 12 July 1937, Philadelphia, USA. Actor. m. Camille Hanks, 1964, 5 children (1 son deceased). Education: Temple University; University of Massachusetts. Appointments: Served USNR, 1959-60; President, Rhythm and Blues Hall of Fame, 1968-; TV appearances include: The Bill Cosby Show, 1969, 1972-73, I Spy, The Cosby Show, 1984-92, Cosby Mystery Series, "Cosby" 1996-2000; Touched by an Angel, 1997-99; Becker, 1999; Everybody Loves Raymond, 1999; Sylvia's Path (voice), 2002; Recitals include: Revenge, To Russell, My Brother With Whom I Slept, To Secret, 200 MPH, Why Is There Air, Wonderfulness, It's True, It's True, Bill Cosby is a Very Funny Fellow: Right, I Started Out as a Child, 8:15, 12:15, Hungry, Reunion 1982, Bill Cosby... Himself, 1983, Those of You With or Without Children, You'll Understand; Numerous night club appearances; Executive Producer: A Different Kind of World (TV series), 1987-; I Spy Returns (TV), 1994; "Cosby" (TV), 1996; Little Bill, 1999; Men of Honor, 2000; The Cosby Show: A Look Back (TV), 2002; Fatherhood (TV), 2004; Fat Albert, 2004; Films include: Hickey and Boggs, 1972; Man and Boy, 1972; Uptown Saturday Night, 1974; Let's Do It Again, 1975; Mother, Jugs and Speed, 1976; Aesop's Fables, A Piece of the Action, 1977; California Suite, 1978; Devil and Max Devlin, 1979; Leonard: Part IV, 1987; Ghost Dad, 1990; The Meteor Man, 1993; Jack, 1996; 4 Little Girls. Publications: The Wit and Wisdom of Fat Albert, 1973; Bill Cosby's Personal Guide to Power Tennis, Fatherhood, 1986; Time Flies, 1988; Love and Marriage, 1989; Childhood, 1991; Little Bill Series, 1999; Congratulations! Now What? 1999; Cosbyology: Essays and Observations from the Doctor of Comedy, 2001; I am what I Ate---and I'm Frightened!!!, 2003;

Friends of a Feather, 2003. Honours: 4 Emmy Awards and 8 Grammy Awards. Address: c/o The Brokaw Co, 9255 Sunset Boulevard, Los Angeles, CA 90069, USA.

COSH (Ethel Eleanor) Mary, b. Bristol, England. Historian. Education: MA, St Anne's College Oxford, 1946-49. Appointments: Employment Clerk/Officer, Ministry of Labour, 5 years; Worked for Design Review, Council of Industrial Design, 1951-52; Free-lance part-time employment includes: Transcriber for Hansard (for Standing Committees); Re-cataloguing Library, Order of St John; Artist's Model at leading London art schools. Publications: The Real World (fiction), 1961; Inveraray and the Dukes of Argyll (with the late Ian G Lindsay), 1973; Edinburgh: The Golden Age, 2003; A History of Islington, 2005; Numerous local publications including: The Squares of Islington (in 2 parts); Contributions to: The Times, Times Educational Supplement, The Spectator, Country Life. Honours: MA; FSA. Memberships: Conservation societies including: Society of Architectural Historians of Great Britain; National Trust; NACF; Georgian Group; Victorian Society; Architectural Heritage Society of Scotland; Cockburn Association. Address: 10 Albion Mews, Islington, London N1 1JX, England.

COSTA CABRAL E GIL Luis Manuel, b. 30 March 1960, Lisbon, Portugal. Researcher; Consultant; Translator. m. Maria Dulce, 1 son. Education: Graduate, Chemical Engineering, 1985; MSc, Technological Organic Chemistry, 1989; Specialisation, Science and Technology Management, 1994. Appointments: Research Engineer, ICTM, 1985-87; Researcher, INETI, 1987-2007; Patent Translator, AGCF, JPC, CM, RCF, 1990-2007; Technical Advisor, ART/Belgium, 1990-94; Researcher, ITIME, 1994-97; Consultant, ZILTCH, 1998-2005; Consultant, AIEC, BETACORK, JPC, 2004-2007. Publications: 101 technical and scientific papers in national and international journals; 97 presentations in international meetings; 7 technical books on cork; 2 chapters on books/ encyclopaedia; 12 patents. Honours: 5 patent awards, 4 national, 3 international; 1 international award (Europacork) for R & D work; 3 IBC awards; Listed in national and international biographical dictionaries. Memberships: Portuguese Engineer Association, 1987; New York Academy of Sciences, 1994; Creativity Portuguese Association, 1996; Portuguese Materials Society, 1997. Address: INETTI, Estrada Do Paço Do Lumiar, 1649-038 Lisboa, Portugal. E-mail: luis.gil@ineti.pt

COSTELLO Elvis (Declan McManus), b. 25 August 1955, London, England. Singer; Songwriter; Musician; Record Producer. m. (1) 1 child, (2) Cait O'Riordan, divorced, (3) Diana Krall, 2004, twin sons. Career: Lead singer, Elvis Costello And The Attractions, 1977-; Appearances include: UK tour, 1977; US tour, 1978; Grand Ole Opry, 1981; Royal Albert Hall, with Royal Philharmonic, 1982; Cambridge Folk Festival, 1995; Television includes: Appearance in Scully, ITV drama, 1985; Films: Americathon, 1979; No Surrender, 1985; Straight to Hell, 1987; Prison Song, 2001; De-Lovely, 2004; Also worked with The Specials; Paul McCartney; Aimee Mann; George Jones; Roy Orbison; Wendy James; Robert Wyatt; Jimmy Cliff; Co-organiser, annual Meltdown festival, South Bank Centre, London. Compositions include: Alison, Watching The Detectives, 1977; Crawling To The USA, Radio Radio, Stranger In The House, 1978; (I Don't Want To Go To) Chelsea, Girls Talk, Oliver's Army, 1979; Boy With A Problem, 1982; Every Day I Write The Book, 1983; Music for television series (with Richard Harvey): G.B.H., 1991; Jake's Progress, 1995; Other songs for artists including Johnny Cash; June Tabor. Recordings: Albums include: My Aim Is True, 1977; This Years Model, 1978; Armed Forces, 1979; Get Happy, Trust, 1980; Almost Blue, 1981; Taking Liberties, Imperial Bedroom, 1982; Goodbye Cruel World, Punch The Clock, 1984; The Best Of, 1985; Blood And Chocolate, King Of America, 1986; Spike, 1989; Mighty Like A Rose, My Aim Is True, 1991; The Juliet Letters, with the Brodksy Quartet, 1993; Brutal Youth, 1994; The Very Best Of Elvis Costello And The Attractions, Kojak Variety, Deep Dead Blue, Live At Meltdown (with Bill Frisell), 1995; All The Useless Beauty, 1996; Terror & Magnificence, 1997; Painted From Memory, 1998; The Sweetest Punch: The Songs of Costello, Best of Elvis Costello, 1999; For the Stars (with Anne Sofie von Otter), 2001; When I Was Cruel, 2002; North, Scarlet Tide, 2003, The Delivery Man, 2004; The River in Reverse, 2006. Honours include: BAFTA Award, Best Original Television Music, G.B.H., 1992; MTV Video, Best Male Video, 1989; Rolling Stone Award, Best Songwriter, 1990; 2 Ivor Novello Awards; Nordoff-Robbins Silver Clef Award; ASCAP Founders Award, 2003; Rock and Roll Hall of Fame, 2003.

COSTELLO R H Brian, Clinical, Educational and Forensic Psychologist; Teacher. Education: Victorian Education Department Certificate, 1964; FCP Thesis, The Psychology of Special Education, London, 1974; Fellow, Royal Chartered College of Teachers (College of Preceptors); South Australian Psychologists Board Certification, 1975; PhD, International College, Los Angeles, 1982; Victorian Psychologists Board Certification, 1984; ABPS Diplomas in Psychological Disabilities Evaluation and Rehabilitation, 1996; Diplomate, AAIM College of Pain Management, 2003-. Appointments include: Elementary Teacher, 1962; Junior Secondary Teacher, 1963-71; Secondary and Special Education Teacher, 1971-74; Lecturer and Senior Psychology Tutor, Victorian Institute of Social Welfare, SAIT, University of South Australia, Sturt CAE, Elizabeth CAE, Monash University, 1971-86; Research and Private Practice, 1975-; Director Cassel Research Centre (Publishing); Consultant, Management Psychologist, National Drugs Foundations, Government Departments and NGO's 1978-; National Faculty Member, United States Sports Academy, 1986-; Visiting Professor of Psychology, University of South Alabama, 1997-; Australian Postgraduate Distance Learning Co-ordinator; General Secondary and Swimming, Victorian State Teachers Institute. Publications: Author of numerous publications on pain control and mind-body medicine. Honours: Award of Merit as Examiner and Instructor, Royal Life Saving Society, 1968; US Golden Eagle Award of Excellence, 1997; Award of Distinction for International Forensics Education and Multinational Understanding, South Alabama University, 1997; Outstanding Service Award, American College of Forensic Examiners, 1999; Chairman, International Council of Integrative Medicine, 2000; Honorary Eminent Fellow of Wisdom and Award of Excellence for Education and Research, Wisdom Hall of Fame, 2001; Cambridge Who's Who Neuropsychology Professional of the Year in Mind Body Medicine, 2006; Listed in international biographical dictionaries. Memberships: Australian Chair, Director at Large, International Council of Psychologists, 1978; Fellow and Diplomate, American Board of Medical Psychotherapists, 1986; Chairman, American Board of Psychological Specialities and Chairman, Forensic Neuropsychology, ACFEI, 1999; Fellow, American Association of Integrative Medicine, 2002-; Ambassador, International Council of Psychologists; Diplomate, American Psychotherapy Association, 2006. Address: The Ibis Lodge, PO Box 1114, Pearcedale, Australia 3912. E-mail: bcos5371@aanet.com.au Website: www.cassel.edu.au

COSTNER Kevin, b. 18 January 1955. Actor. m. (1) Cindy Silva, 1978, divorced 1994, 1 son, 2 daughters, 1 son with Bridget Rooney (2) Christine Baumgartner, 2004. Education: California State University. Appointments: Directing debut in Dances With Wolves, 1990; Films include: Frances, 1982; The Big Chill, 1983; Testament, 1983; Silverado, 1985; The Untouchables, 1987; No Way Out, 1987; Bull Durham, 1988; Field of Dreams, 1989; Revenge, 1989; Robin Hood: Prince of Thieves, 1990; JFK, 1991; The Bodyguard, 1992; A Perfect World, 1993; Wyatt Earp, 1994; Waterworld, 1995; Tin Cup, 1996; Message in a Bottle, 1998; For Love of the Game, 1999; Thirteen Days, 2000; 3000 Miles to Graceland, 2001; Dragonfly, 2002; Open Range, 2003; Upside of Anger, 2005; Rumor Has It, 2005; The Guardian, 2006; Mr Brooks, 2007. Co-producer, Rapa Nui; Co-producer, China Moon. Honours include: Academy Award for Best Picture, 1991; 2 Oscars, 26 Awards, 30 nominations. Address: TIG Productions, Producers Building 5, 4000 Warner Boulevard, Burbank, CA 91523, USA.

COTTELL Michael Norman Tizard, b. 25 July 1931, Southampton, England. Retired Civil Engineer. m. Joan Florence, 2 sons. Education: Southampton University; Birmingham University. Appointments: Assistant County Surveyor, East Suffolk County Council, 1965-73; Deputy County Surveyor, East Sussex County Council, 1973-76; County Surveyor, Northants County Council, 1976-84; County Surveyor, Kent County Council, 1984-91; Executive Consultant, Travers Morgan Consultants, 1991-95; Chairman, Aspen Consultancy Group, 1995-2002. Honour: OBE, 1988.Memberships: F R ENG; FICE; F IHT; MCIM. Address: Salcey Lawn, Harrow Court, Stockbury, Sittingbourne, Kent, ME9 7UQ, England.

COTTRELL David Milton, b. 27 March 1969, Fort Dodge, Iowa, USA. Recording Engineer; Writer. Education: Bachelors Degree in Counseling, Almeda University; Consumer Electronics, Dick Grove Music Career Workshop. Appointments: FM Engineer; Songwriter; Recording Engineer/Producer; Music Publisher; Electronics Technician; Counselor; Personal Trainer. Honours: American Medal of Honor; Noble Laureate; Man of the Year, 2004, 2005, 2006, 2007; International Professional of the Year, 2005; Achievement in Science Award, 2005; Great Minds of the 21st Century; International Order of Merit; World's Most Respected Experts; IBC Hall of Fame; The Da Vinci Diamond; IBC Meritorious Decoration; Decree of Excellence; Pinnacle of Achievement, 2007; Listed in Who's Who publications and biographical dictionaries. Memberships: DeMolay; Natural Resources Defense Council. Address: 6232 Beck Avenue, North Hollywood, CA 91605, USA.

COULSON-THOMAS Colin Joseph, b. 26 April 1949, Mullion, Cornwall, England. Professor; Author; Chairman. 1 son, 2 daughters. Education: MSc, London Business School, 1975; DPA, 1977, MSc (Econ), 1980, LSE/London University; PCL, MA, CNAA, 1981, AM, 1982, University of Southern California; UNISA, MPA, 1985, PhD, 1988, University of Aston. Appointments: Consultant, Coopers & Lybrand, 1975-78; Editor, Publisher, Head of Public Relations, ICSA, 1978-81; Publishing Director, Longman Group, 1981-84; Corporate Affairs, Xerox, Rank Xerox, 1984-93; Founder, Chairman of companies including: Adaptation, ASK Europe, Cotoco, Policy Publications, 1987-; Willmot Dixon Professor, Dean of Faculty, Head of Patteridge Bury Campus, 1994-97, Visiting Professor, 1998-99 and 2006-, University of Luton; Professor, Head, Centre for Competitiveness, 2000-06; Professor of Direction and Leadership, University of Lincoln, 2005-;

Member, Institute of Directors, Board of Examiners, 1998-, Professional Accreditation Committee, 2003-. Publications: Author of over 30 books and reports including: The Future of the Organisation, 1997/98; Individuals and Enterprise, 1999; Shaping Things to Come, 2001; Transforming the Company, 2002, 2004; The Knowledge Entrepreneur, 2003; Winning Companies, Winning People, 2007; Developing Directors, 2007; Reports include: Pricing for Profit, 2002; Winning New Business, 2003. Honours: First place prizes in final examinations of these professions. Memberships: Chartered Accountant; FCA; FCCA; FCIS; FMS; FCIPR; FCIPD; FCIM; FCMI, Hon FAIA, FRGS; FSCA; Has served on regional and national public sector boards. Address: Mill Reach, Mill Lane, Water Newton, Cambridgeshire PE8 6LY, England. E-mail: colinct@tiscali.co.uk Website: www.coulson-thomas.com

COUPLES Fred, b. 3 October 1959, Seattle, Washington, USA. Professional Golfer. m. Thais, 1 son, 1 daughter. Education: University of Houston. Appointments: Member, Rider Cup Team, 1989, 1991, 1993; Named All-American, 1979, 1980; Winner, numerous tournaments including Kemper Open, 1983; Tournament Players Championship, 1984, Byron Nelson Golf Classic, 1987, French PGA, 1988, Nissan LA Open, 1990, 1992, Tournai Perrier de Paris, 1991, BC Open, 1991, Federal Express St Jude Classic, 1991, Johnnie Walker World Championship, 1991, 1995, Nestle Invitational, 1992, The Masters, 1992, with Jan Stephenson J C Penney Classic, 1983, with Mike Donald, Sazale Classic, 1990, with Raymond Floyd, RMCC Invitational, 1990, Buick Open, 1994, Dubai Desert Classic, 1995, Players Championship, 1996, Skins Game, 1996, Australian Skins Game, 1997; Member, US Team, Presidents Cup, 1997; Champion, Bob Hope Chrysler Classic, 1998; Champion, Memorial Tournament, 1998; Houston Open, 2004; Merrill Lynch Skins Game, 2004; ING Par-3 Shootout, 2006; Member, President Cup Team, 1998, 2005. Honours: Vardon Trophy, 1991, 1992; Named PGA Player of Year, Golf World magazine, 1991, 1992. Address: c/o PGA Tour, 100 Avenue of the Champions, PO Box 109601, Palm Beach Gardens, FL 33410, USA.

COURIER Jim (James Spencer), b. 17 August 1970, Sanford, Florida, USA. Tennis Player. Career: Professional Tennis Player, 1989-; Winner of tournaments including: Orange Bowl, 1986, 1987, Basel, 1989, French Open, 1991, 1992, Indian Wells, 1991, 1993, Key Biscayne, 1991, 1993, Australian Open, 1992-93, Italian Open, 93; Finalist US Open, 1991; Quarterfinalist, Wimbledon, 1991; Runner-up French Open, 1993, Wimbledon, 1993; Semifinalist, Australian Open, 1994, French Open, 1994; Winner of 23 singles titles and six doubles titles and over $16 million dollars in prize money; Retired, 2000; Founded InsideOut Sport and Entertainment, 2004; Now plays in the Outback Series was No 1, 2006. Address: IGM, Suite 300, 1 Erieview Place, Cleveland, OH 44114, USA. Website: www.atptennis.com/championstour/default.asp

COURTENAY Sir Thomas (Tom) Daniel, b. 25 February 1937. Actor. m. (1) Cheryl Kennedy, 1973, divorced 1982, (2) Isabel Crossley, 1988. Education: Kingston High School, Hull; University College, London; Royal Academy of Dramatic Art. Career: Actor, 1960-; Films include: The Loneliness of the Long Distance Runner, Private Potter, 1962; Billy Liar, 1963; King and Country, Operation Crossbow, King Rat, Doctor Zhivago, 1965; The Night of the Generals, The Day the Fish Came Out, 1967; A Dandy in Aspic, 1968; Otley, 1969; One Day in the Life of Ivan Denisovitch, 1970; Catch Me A Spy, 1971; The Dresser, 1983; The Last Butterfly, 1990; Redemption (TV), Let Him Have It, 1991; Old Curiosity Shop

(TV), 1995; The Boy from Mercury, 1996; A Rather English Marriage (TV), 1998; Whatever Happened to Harold Smith, 1999; Last Orders, Nicholas Nickleby, 2002; Ready When You Are Mr McGill (TV), 2003; Flood, 2006; Plays include: Billy Liar, 1961-62; The Cherry Orchard, Macbeth, 1966; Hamlet, 1968; She Stoops to Conquer, 1969; Charley's Aunt, 1971; Time and Time Again, 1972; Table Manners, 1974; The Norman Conquests, 1974-75; The Fool, 1975; The Rivals, 1976; Clouds, Crime and Punishment, 1978; The Dresser, 1980, 1983; The Misanthrope, 1981; Andy Capp, 1982; Jumpers, 1984; Rookery Nook, 1986; The Hypochondriac, 1987; Dealing with Clair, 1988; The Miser, 1992; Moscow Stations, Edinburgh, Poison Pen, Manchester 1993; London 1994, New York 1995; Uncle Vanya, New York 1995; Art, London 1996; King Lear, Manchester 1999. Publications: Dear Tom: Letters from Home (memoirs), 2000. Honours: Fellow, University College London; Hon DLitt (Hull); Best Actor Award, Prague Festival, 1968; TV Drama Award, 1968; Variety Club of Great Britain Stage Actor Award, 1972; Golden Globe Award, Best Actor, 1983; Drama Critics' Award and Evening Standard Award, 1980, 1983; BAFTA Award, Best Actor, 1999; KBE. Address: c/o Jonathan Altaras Associates, 13 Shorts Gardens, London WC2H 9AT, England.

COURTILLOT Vincent Emmanuel, b. 6 March 1948, Neuilly, France. Professor of Geophysics. m. Michèle Consolo, 1 son, 1 daughter. Education: Civil Engineer, Paris School of Mines, 1971; MS, Geophysics, Stanford University, 1972; PhD, Geophysics, University of Paris VI, 1974; DSc, Geophysics, University of Paris VII, 1977. Appointments: Assistant, University of Paris VII, 1973-77; Maitre-Assistant, 1977-78; Maitre de Conférences, 1978-83; Professor, 1983-89; Physicien classe exceptionnelle, 1989-94; Director, Ministry of Education, 1989-93; Professor classe exceptionelle, University of Paris VII, 1994-; Director, Graduate School of Earth Sciences, 1995-98; President, European Union of Geosciences, 1995-97; Professor, Institut Universitaire de France, 1996-; Director, Institut de Physique du Globe de Paris, 1996-98, 2004-; Special Adviser to the Minister of Education, Research and Technology, 1997-98; Director, Ministry of Research, 1999-2001; President, Scientific Council of the City of Paris, 2002-; Chief Editor, Earth and Planetary Science Letters, 2003-05; President, American Geophysical Union, Geomagnetism and Paleomagnetism section, 2006-. Publications: Several articles in professional journals, two books. Honours: Prix Gay, French Academy of Sciences, 1981; 1st Franco-British Prize, 1985; Fellow, AGU, 1990; Chevalier, Ordre national du Mérite, 1990, Officier, 1997; Silver Medal, Centre National de la Recherche Scientifique, 1993; Fairchild Distinguished Scholar, 1994; Chevalier, Legion of Honour, 1994; Member, Academia Europea, 1994; Gerald Stanton Ford Lecturer, University of Minnesota, 1996; Associate, Royal Astronomical Society; Commandeur, Ordre National des Palmes Académiques, 1997; Prix Dolomieu, French Academy of Sciences, Moore Distinguished Fellow, CalTech, 2002; Commencement Speaker, University of Lausanne; Member, Paris Academy of Sciences, 2003. Address: IPG, 4 Place Jussieu, 75230 Paris Cedex 5, France.

COWDREY Herbert Edward John, b. 29 November 1926, Basingstoke, Hampshire, England. University Teacher. m. Judith Watson Davis, 14 July 1959, deceased August 2004, 1 son, 2 daughters. Education: BA, 1949, MA, 1951, DD, 2000, Oxford University. Appointments: Chaplain and Tutor, St Stephen's House, Oxford, 1952-56; Fellow, 1956-94, Fellow Emeritus, 1994-, St Edmund Hall, Oxford; Honorary Fellow, St Stephen's House, Oxford, 2005. Publications: The Cluniacs and the Gregorian Reform; The Epistolae Vagantes

of Pope Gregory VII; Two Studies in Cluniac History; The Age of Abbot Desiderius; Popes, Monks and Crusaders; Pope Gregory VII, 1073-85; The Crusades and Latin Monasticism, 11th-12th Centuries; Popes and Church Reform in the 11th Century. Contributions to: Many articles. Honour: British Academy, fellow. Memberships: Royal Historical Society; Henry Bradshaw Society. Address: 19 Church Lane, Old Marston, OX3 0NZ, England.

COWEN Athol Ernest, b. 18 January 1942, Corbridge, Hexham, Northumberland, England. Writer; Poet; Publisher; Musician; Artist. Education: Queen Elizabeth Grammar School, Penrith. Career: Artist; Musician, Songwriter; Writer, Poet; Self-employed Publisher. Publications: Word Pictures (Brain Soup), 1989; Huh!, 1991; Work included in various anthologies published in Wales, England, India and the USA. Memberships: Publishers' Association; Poetry Society; Writers' Guild of Great Britain; Musicians' Union; Guild of International Songwriters and Composers; MRI; DG (ABIRA); IOA. Address: 40 Gibson Street, Wrexham, Wrexham County Borough LL13 7TS, Wales.

COX Brian, b. 1 June 1946, Dundee, Scotland. Actor. m. (1) Caroline Burt, 1 son, 1 daughter, (2) Nicole Ansari, 2 sons. Career: Actor; Films include: Braveheart; Rob Roy; The Long Kiss Goodnight; The Glimmer Man; Kiss The Girls; Strictly Sinatra; LIE; Bourne Identity; Adaption; The Rookie; The Ring; The 25th Hour; Sin; X-Men 2; Troy; The Bourne Supremacy; A Woman in Winter; Match Point; Red-Eye; The Ringer; Burns; Running With Scissors; Zodiac, 2007; The Escapist, 2007; The Bourne Ultimatum, 2007; Trick 'r Treat, 2007; The Secret of the Nutcracker, 2007; The Key Man, 2007; Theatre includes: As You Like It; Peer Gynt; Othello; Romeo and Juliet; Hedda Gabler; Julius Caesar; Macbeth; Rat in the Skull; Titus Andronicus; The Taming of the Shrew; Frankie and Johnny; Richard III; King Lear; The Master Builder; The Music Man; St Nicholas; Skylight; Art; Dublin Carol; Desire Under the Elms; Uncle Varick; Rock 'n Roll; TV includes: The Cloning of Joanna May; Inspector Morse; Sharpe's Rifles; The Negotiator; Picasso; Witness Against Hitler; Red Dwarf; Food For Ravens; Family Brood; Longitude; Nuremburg; The Cup; The Bench; Frasier; Blue/Orange; Deadwood; Producer: I Love My Love; The Philanderer; The Master Builder; Richard III; Oz. Publications: 2 books: The Lear Diaries; From Salem to Moscow. Honours: Winner, BSFC Award for Best Actor, 2001; Nominated AFI Film Award, Featured Actor of the Year (Male), 2002; Winner, Golden Satellite Award, Best Performance by an Actor in a Motion Picture (Drama), 2002; CBE, 2003. Address: c/o Conway Van Gelder, 18-21 Jermyn Street, London SW1Y 6HP, England.

COX Courtney, b. 15 June 1964, Birmingham, Alabama, USA. Actress. m. David Arquette, 1999, 1 daughter. Appointments: Modelling career, New York; Appeared in Bruce Springsteen music video, Dancing in the Dark, 1984; Films: Down Twisted, 1986; Masters of the Universe, 1987; Cocoon: The Return, 1988; Mr Destiny, Blue Desert, 1990; Shaking the Tree, 1992; The Opposite Sex, 1993; Ace Ventura, Pet Detective, 1994; Scream, Commandments, 1996; Scream 2, 1997; The Runner, Scream 3, 1999; The Shrink Is In, 2000; 3000 Miles to Graceland, Get Well Soon, 2001; Alien Love Triangle, 2002; November, 2004; The Longest Yard, 2005; Barnyard (voice), Zoom, The Ripper, 2006; TV series: Misfits of Science, 1985-86; Family Ties, 1987-88; The Trouble With Larry, 1993; Friends, 1994-2004; Dirt, 2007; TV films include: Roxanne: The Prize Pulitzer, 1989; Till We Meet Again, 1989; Curiosity Kills, 1990; Morton and

Hays, 1991, Tobber, 1992; Sketch Artist II: Hands That See, 1995. Address: c/o Creative Artists Agency, 9830 Wilshire Boulevard, Beverly Hills, CA 90212, USA.

COX Dennis William, b. 27 February 1957, Hornchurch, Essex, England. Director. m. Lisette Mermod, 1996, 2 stepdaughters. Education: Hornchurch Grammar School, 1965-75; BSc in Mathematics, Westfield College, London. Appointments: Various positions rising to Senior Manager of Banking and Finance, Arthur Young (now Ernst & Young), 1978-88; Senior Manager of Banking and Finance, BDO Binder Hamlyn, 1988-90; Audit Manager, Midland Bank, rising to Senior Audit Manager (Compliance) HSBC Holdings plc, 1991-97; Director of Risk Management, Prudential Portfolio Managers, 1997-2000; Director of Operational Risk, HSBC Operational Risk Consultancy Division, 2000-01; Chief Executive Officer, Risk Reward Limited, 2002-. Publications: Banks: Accounts, Audit & Practice, 1993; Mathematics of Banking and Finance, 2006; Frontiers of Risk Management: Key Issues and Solutions, 2007; Author of various articles in professional journals. Memberships: Institute of Chartered Accountants in England and Wales; Securities and Investments Institute; Financial Authorisation Committee of Institute of Actuaries; Council Member, ICAEW; MIFS, 1988; FCA, 1991; ACA, 1981; MSI, 1992; Chairman, Risk Forum Securities and Investments Institute, 2004-; Member, Treasury Select Committee, Money Laundry Deterrence, 2005-; FSI, 2005. Address: Risk Reward Limited, 46 Moorgate, London EC2R 6EH, England. E-mail: dwc@riskrewardlimited.com

COX Richard, b. 8 March 1931, Winchester, Hampshire, England. Writer. m. 1963, 2 sons, 1 daughter. MA degree in English, St Catherine's College, Oxford, 1955. Publications: Operation Sealion, 1974; Sam 7, 1976; Auction, 1978; The Time it Takes, 1980; KGB Directive, 1981; Ground Zero, 1985; The Columbus Option, 1986; An Agent of Influence, 1988; Park Plaza, 1991; Eclipse, 1996; Murder at Wittenham Park, 1998 (as R W Heber, 1997); How to Meet a Puffin (for children), 2005; Island of Ghosts, 2007. Contributions to: Daily Telegraph (Staff Correspondent, 1966-72); Travel & Leisure; Traveller; Orient Express Magazine. Honours: Territorial Decoration, 1966; General Service Medal, 1967. Membership: Army and Navy Club; CARE International UK Board, 1985-97, (Council of Patrons, 2006); Member, States of Alderney, 2001-; Representative States of Guernsey, 2003-06; Member, Guernsey Overseas Aid Commission, 2004-. Address: 18 Hauteville, Alderney, Channel Islands GY9 3UA.

COYLE Edward J, b. 22 April 1956, Philadelphia, Pennsylvania, USA. Professor. Education: BEE, University of Delaware, 1977; MA, 1980, MSE, 1980, PhD, 1982, Princeton University. Appointments: Assistant Professor, 1982-86, Associate Professor, 1986-94, School of Electrical Engineering, Professor, 1994-2007, School of Electrical and Computer Engineering, Co-Founder, Co-Director, Center for Engineering Projects in Community Service, 1995-2002, Assistant Vice Provost for Research in Computing and Communications, 2000-04, Co-Director, Center for Wireless Systems and Applications, College of Engineering, 2003-07, Purdue University; Visiting Professor, Department of Electrical Engineering, University of Delaware, 1990-91; Director, Motorola-Purdue Alliance, 1999-2000; Co-Founder, Co-Director, National Engineering Projects in Community Service Program, 1999-2002; Co-Founder, Director, EPICS Entrepreneurship Initiative, Burton Morgan Center, Purdue's Discovery Park, 2002-07; Kenan Trust Visiting Professor

for Distinguished Teaching, Princeton University, 2006-07; Arbutus Professor, Electrical and Computer Engineering and Georgia Research Alliance Eminent Scholar, 2008-. Publications: Numerous articles in professional journals; Research book contributions. Honours: Scott Paper Company Leadership Award, 1975-77; Delaware Bay Section Scholastic Achievement Award, 1978; ASSP Society's Best Paper Award for Authors under 30, 1986; Myril B Reed Best Paper Award, 1989; Chester F Carlson Award for Innovation in Engineering Education, 1997; Recognition of Excellence, Microsoft Research, 2002; Focus Award, 2002; First Annual Governor's Award for Outstanding Volunteerism, 2003; College of Engineering Team Excellence Award, 2003; Bernard M Gordon Prize for Innovation in Engineering and Technology Education, 2005; College of Engineering Faculty Award, 2005; Innovative Program Award, 2006. Memberships: IEEE Communications Society; IEEE Signal Proceessing Society; Association for Computing Machinery; American Society for Engineering Education. Address: School of Electrical and Computer Engineering, Purdue University, 318 MSEE Building, 465 Northwestern Avenue, West Lafayette, IN 47907-2035, USA. E-mail: coyle@purdue.edu Website: http://dynamo.ecn.purdue.edu/~coyle

CRACKNELL James, b. 5 May 1972, Sutton, Surrey, England. Oarsman. m. Beverley Turner, 2002, 1 son. Education: Kingston Grammar School. Career: International debut in coxed pair, 10th at Junior World Championships, 1989; Winner, gold medal in coxless four Junior World Championships, 1990; Senior international debut in coxless four, 7th in World Championships, 1991; Winner, silver medal in the Eight at World Student Games, 1993; Part of British coxless four tea, 1997-; Gold medals, World Championships, 1997-99; Gold medals, Federation Internationale des Societes d'Aviron World Cup, 1997, 1999, 2000; Gold medals, Olympic Games, Sydney, 2000, Athens, 2004; with Matthew Pinsent won gold medals in the pair at World Championships, 2001 and 2002, also gold medal in coxed pair; qualified geography teacher; took 12 month break from rowing, November 2004-; 2nd Pairs Division of the Atlantic Rowing Race with Ben Fogle, 2005-06; Retired from competitive rowing, 2006. Honours: MBE. Address: c/o British International Rowing Office, 6 Lower Mall, London W6 9DJ, England. Website: www.ara-rowing.org

CRAGGS Stewart Roger, b. 27 July 1943, Ilkley, West Yorkshire, England. Academic Librarian. m. Valerie J Gibson, 28 Sept 1968, 1 son, 1 daughter. Education: ALA, Leeds Polytechnic, 1968; FLA, 1974; MA, University of Strathclyde, Glasgow, 1978; PhD, University of Strathclyde, 1982. Appointments: Teesside Polytechnic, 1968-69; JA Jobling, 1970-72; Sunderland Polytechnic, later University, 1973-95; Consultant to the William Walton Edition, Oxford University Press, 1995-. Publications: William Walton: A Thematic Catalogue, 1977; Arthur Bliss: A Bio-Bibliography, 1988; Richard Rodney Bennett: A Bio-Bibliography, 1990; William Walton: A Catalogue, Second Edition, 1990; John McCabe: A Bio-Bibliography, 1991; William Walton: A Source Book, 1993; John Ireland: A Catalogue, Discography and Bibliography, 1993; Alun Hoddinott: A Bio-Bibliography, 1993; Edward Elgar: A Source Book, 1995; William Mathias: A Bio-Bibliography, 1995; Arthur Bliss: A Source Book, 1996; Soundtracks: An International Dictionary of Composers for Films, 1998; Malcolm Arnold: A Bio-Bibliography, 1998; William Walton: Music and Literature, 1999; Lennox Berkeley: A Source Book, 2000; Benjamin Britten: A Bio-Bibliography, 2001; Arthur Bliss: Music and Literature, 2002; Peter Maxwell Davies: A Source Book, 2002; Alan Bush: A Source Book,

2007; Alun Hoddinott: A Source Book, 2007; John Ireland: A Catalogue, Discography and Bibliography: Second Edition, 2007. Honour: Professor of Music Bibliography, University of Sunderland, 1993; Library Association McColvin Medal for Best Reference Book, 1990. Address: 106 Mount Road, High Barnes, Sunderland, SR4 7NN, England.

CRAIG Daniel, b. 2 March 1968, Chester, England. Actor. Divorced, 1 daughter. Education: National Youth Theatre; Guildhall School of Music and Drama. Career: Actor: TV includes: Between the Lines, 1993; Drop the Dead Donkey, 1993; Sharpe's Eagle, 1993; Our Friends in the North, 1996; The Fortunes and Misfortunes of Moll Flanders, 1996; The Ice House, 1997; Sword of Honour, 2001; Copenhagen, 2002; Archangel, 2005; Films include: The Power of One, 1992; Elizabeth, 1998; The Trench, 1999; I Dreamed of Africa, 2000; Some Voices, 2000; Hotel Splendide, 2000; Lara Croft: Tomb Raider, 2001; Road to Perdition, 2002; The Mother, 2003; Sylvia, 2003; Layer Cake, 2004; Casino Royale, 2006; The Invasion, 2007; His Dark Materials: The Golden Compass, 2007. Honours: One of European films Shooting Stars, European Film Promotion, 2000; Nominated London Evening Standard Theatre Award, 2002.

CRANHAM Kenneth Raymond, b. 12 December 1944, Dunfermline, Scotland. Actor. m. Fiona Victory, 2 daughters. Education: Tulse Hill School, London; Royal Academy of Dramatic Art; National Youth Theatre; Films: Two Men Went to War; Born Romantic; Shiner; Gangster No 1; Women Talking Dirty; The Last Yellow; Under Suspicion; Chocolat; The Clot; Oliver; Brother Sun Sister Moon; Joseph Andrews; The Rising; Layer Cake; Trauma; Mandancin; A Good Year; Hot Fuzz; Plays include: RSC: School for Scandal; Ivanov; The Iceman Cometh; National Theatre: Flight; An Inspector Calls; Kick for Touch; Cardiff East; From Kipling to Vietnam; The Caretaker; Strawberry Fields; Love Letters on Blue Paper; The Passion; The Country Wife; Old Movies; Madras House; Royal Court; Saved; Ruffian on the Stair; Samuel Beckett's Play; Cascando; The London Cuckolds; Tibetan in Roads; Magnificance; Cheek; Owners; Geography of a Horse Dreamer; West End: Loot; Comedians; Entertaining Mr Sloane; The Novice; Doctor's Dilemma; Paul Bunyan (Royal Opera House); Broadway: Loot; An Inspector Calls; Radio: The Barchester Chronicles; New Grub Street; Sons and Lovers; Hard Times; Answered Prayers; Earthly Powers; TV includes: Night Flight; Orange are Not the Only Fruit; Rules of Engagement; The Contractor; The Birthday Party; Lady Windemere's Fan; Thérèse Raquin; 'Tis Pity She's A Whore; Merchant of Venice; The Caretaker; The Dumb Waiter; La Ronde; The Sound of Guns; Sling Your Hook; Shine on Harvey Moon; The Genius of Mozart; Rome; The Party; Polyanna; Hustle; New Tricks; Afterlife; Doc Martin; Lilies; The Last Detective. Honours: Bancroft Gold Medal, RADA, 1966. Address: c/o Markham & Froggatt Ltd, 4 Windmill Street, London W1P 1HF, England.

CRAPON de CAPRONA Noël François Marie, (Comte), b. 23 May 1928, Chambéry, Savoie, France. Lawyer; UN Senior Official, retired. m. Barbro Sigrid Wenne, 2 sons. Education: Diploma, Institute of Comparative Law, 1951; LLB, University of Paris, 1952; Postgraduate Studies, School of Political Science, 1952-54. Appointments: Assistant Manager, Sta Catalina Estancias, Argentina, 1947-48; Editor, Food and Agriculture Organization of the United Nations, 1954-57; Liaison Officer, UN and Other Organisations, Director General's Office, 1957-65; Chief, Reports and Records, 1966-72; Chief, Conference Operations, 1972-74; Secretary General, Conference and Council, 1974-78; Director,

FAO Conference, Council and Protocol Affairs, 1974-83. Publication: The Longobards, a tentative explanation, 1995. Honours: FAO Silver Medal, 25 Years of Service; Medal of Honour, City of Salon de Provence, 1992; Who's Who Medal, 2000; World Medal of Honour, American Biographical Institute, 2003. Memberships: Society in France of the Sons of the American Revolution; Alumni Association College St Martin de France and Ecole des Sciences Politiques. Address: Lojovägen 73-75, S-18147 Lidingö, Sweden; Palais Hadrien, Place dei Tres Mast, 83600 Port-Frejus, France.

CRAVEN Wes, b. 2 August 1939, Cleveland, Ohio, USA. Director; Screenplay writer; Actor. m. (1) Bonnie Broecker, divorced, 2 children, (2) Mimi, divorced, (3) Iya Labunka, 2004. Education: Wheaton College, Johns Hopkins University. Career: Former Professor of Humanities; Assistant to Company President, film production house; Assistant Editor to Sena Cunningham; Screenplay writer; Editor; Writer; Films include: The Last House on the Left, 1972; The Hills Have Eyes, 1976; You've Got to Walk It Like You Talk It or You'll Lose That Beat, Deadly Blessing, 1979; Swamp Thing, 1980; The Hills Have Eyes II, 1983; Invitation to Hell, A Nightmare on Elm Street, 1984; Deadly Friend, A Nightmare on Elm Street III, 1986; The Serpent and the Rainbow, 1988; Shocker, 1989; The People Under the Stairs, 1991; Vampire in Brooklyn, 1995; The Fear, Scream, 1998; Scream 2, Music of the Heart, 1999; Scream 3; Carnival of Souls; Alice; Cursed, Red Eye, 2005; Paris, je t'aime, 2006; TV includes: A Stranger in our House, 1978; Invitation to Hell, 1982; Chiller, 1983; Casebusters, 1985; A Little Peace and Quiet, Wordplay, Chameleon, Her Pilgrim Soul, Shatterday, Dealer's Choice, 1987; The Road Not Taken, 1988; Night Vision, 1990; Nightmare Café, 1991; Laurel Canyon; Body Bags; Twilight Zone; Crimebusters. Memberships: Directors Guild of America. Address: c/o Joe Quenqua, PMK, 1775 Broadway, Suite 701, New York, NY 10019, USA.

CRAWFORD Alistair, b. 25 January 1945, Fraserburgh, Aberdeenshire, Scotland. Artist; Writer. m. Joan Martin. Education: Diploma in Art, Glasgow School of Art, 1966; Art Teachers Certificate, Aberdeen College of Education, 1968. Career: Painter; Printmaker; Photographer; Art Historian; Performer; Lecturer, Department of Textile Industries University of Leeds, 1968-71; Senior Lecturer, Graphic Design, Coventry Polytechnic, 1971-73; Lecturer in Graphic Art, 1974-83, Senior Lecturer, 1983, Reader, 1987, Head of Department, 1986-95; Professor of Art, 1990, Head of the new University of Wales, School of Art, Aberystwyth, 1994; Currently Research Professor of Art, University of Wales, Aberystwyth, 1995-; Balsdon Senior Fellow, 1995-96, First Archive Research Fellow, 1997-2001, British School at Rome; Exhibitions: 44 solo exhibitions and over 200 selected exhibitions in Britain and Europe and USA; 440 works represented in over 60 public and corporate collections and over 2,700 in private collections world-wide; Recent solo exhibitions include: A Return to Wales, Retrospective 1974-2000; New Paintings, National Library of Wales; Landscape Capriccios, the landscape of the mind, University of Wales, Aberystwyth, 2004-05; Martin's Gallery, Cheltenham, Denbighshire Arts Tour, North by Northwest, Jersey Arts Centre, 2006; Curator of several major exhibitions of photography in Europe and USA; Performances: An Evening with Eugene Strong, 1996-, Brief Exposure, 2001-; A Little Bit More Brief Exposure, 2004-. Publications: Over 120 publications; Books and catalogues include: John Thomas 1838-1905, Photographer (co-author), 1977; Mario Giacomelli, 1983, 1985; Elio Ciol, Italia Black and White, Carlo Bevilacqua, 1986; George Chapman, 1989;

Elio Ciol, Assisi, 1991; Will Roberts, 1993; Kyfflin Williams, Alistair Crawford Collected Photographs, 1995; The Welsh Lens, 1997; Robert MacPherson 1914-1872, 1999; Made of Wales, Father P P Mackey (1851-1935) Photographer, 2000; Mario Giacomelli, 2001, 2002, 2004, 2006; Erich Lessing Vom Festhalten der Zeit. Reportage – Fotografie 1948-73, 2002, 2003, 2005; Column "Brief Exposure", Inscape Magazine, 1999-; Co-editor, Photoresearcher, Vienna, 2004-. Honours include: Arts Council of Wales; British Council; British Academy; Goethe Institute; Winston Churchill Fellow, 1982; Gold Medal in Fine Art, Royal National Eisteddfod of Wales, 1985; Invited Fellow, Royal Photographic Society, 1991; Invited Academician, Royal Cambrian Academy, 1994; Elected Honorary Fellow, Royal Society of Painter-Printmakers, 2000. Memberships: Royal Cambrian Academy; Royal Society of Painter-Printmakers; European Society for the History of Photography. E-mail: alc@aber.ac.uk Website: www.alistaircrawford.co.uk

CRAWFORD Cindy, b. 1966, USA. Model. m. (1) Richard Gere, 1991, divorced, (2) Rande Gerber, 1998, 1 son, 1 daughter. Career: Major contracts with Revlon & Pepsi Cola; Presenter on own MTV fashion show; Appearances on numerous magazine covers, model for various designers; Face of Kelloggs Special K, 2000; Film: Fair Game, 1995; Released several exercise videos; Several TV appearances. Publications: Cindy Crawford's Basic Face, 1996; About Face (for children), 2001. Address: c/o Wolf-Kasteler, 231 South Rodeo Drive, Suite 300, Beverly Hills, CA 90212, USA.

CRAWFORD Michael, b. 19 January 1942. Actor; Singer. Appointments: Actor, 1955-; Films for Children's Film Foundation; 100's radio broadcasts; Appeared in original productions of Noyess Fludde and Let's Make an Opera, by Benjamin Britten; Tours, UK, USA, Australia. Stage roles include: Travelling Light, 1965; The Anniversary, 1966; No Sex Please, We're British, 1971; Billy, 1974; Same Time, Next Year, 1976; Flowers for Algernon, 1979; Barnum, 1981-83, 1984-86; Phantom of the Opera, London, 1986-87; Broadway, 1988, Los Angeles, 1989; The Music of Andrew Lloyd Webber (concert tour), USA, Australia, UK, 1992-92; EFX, Las Vegas, 1995-96; Dance of the Vampires, Broadway, 2003; The Woman in White, 2004-05; Performed at Harrah's Casino, Stateline, Nevada, 2007; Films include: Soap Box Derby, 1950; Blow Your Own Trumpet, 1954; Two Living One Dead, 1962; The War Lover, 1963; Two Left Feet, 1963; The Knack, 1965; A Funny Thing Happened on the Way to the Forum, 1966; The Jokers, 1966; How I Won the War, 1967; Hello Dolly, 1969; The Games, 1969; Hello Goodbye, 1970; Alice's Adventures in Wonderland, 1972; Condor Man, 1980; TV appearances include: Sir Francis Drake (series), 1962; Some Mothers Do 'Ave 'Em (several series); Chalk and Cheese (series), 1979; Sorry (play), 1979. Publication: Parcel Arrived Safely: Tied with String (autobiography), 2000. Honours: OBE; Tony Award, 1988. Address: c/o ICM Ltd, Oxford House, 76 Oxford Street, London W1D 1BS, England.

CRESSON Edith, b. 27 January 1934, Boulogne-sur-Seine, France. Politician. m. J Cresson, 1959, deceased 2001, 2 daughters. Education: Hautes Etudes Commerciales, Doctorat de Démographie. Appointments: Economist, Conventions des Institutions Republicanes, 1965; Socialist Party National Secretary, 1974; Mayor of Thure, 1977; Member, Eurpean Assembly, 1979; Ministry of Agriculture,1981-83; Mayor of Chatellerault, 1983-97; Adjoint au maire, 1997-; Minister, for Foreign Trade and Tourism, 1983-84, Minister, for Industrial Redeployment and Foreign Trade, 1984-86, Minister for European Affairs, 1988-90; PM, 1990-92; President of Schneider International Services Industries et Environnement, 1990-91, 1992-95; Commissaire européen chargé de la recherche et de l'éducation, 1995-99; Presidente de la Fondation pour les Ecoles de la Deuxième Chance. Publications: Avec le Soleil, 1976; Innover ou subir, 1998; Docteur Honoris Causa de l'Open University, UK and l'Institut Weisman, Israel, 1999; Présidente de la Fondation pour les Écoles de la Deuxième Chance, 2002-; President, Institut d'Etudes Européennes University de Seine St Denis; Chevalier de la Légion d'honneur; Dr hc, Weizmann Institute, and Open University, England. Address: 10 Av. George V, Paris, France.

CRICHTON John Michael, b. 23 October 1942, Chicago, Illinois, USA. Film Director; Author. Education: AB, summa cum laude, 1964, MD, 1969, Harvard University. Appointments: Visiting Lecturer in Anthropology, Cambridge University, 1965; Postdoctoral Fellow, Salk Institute for Biological Sciences, La Jolla, California 1969-70; Visiting Writer, Massachusetts Institute of Technology, 1988; Creator, Co-Executive Producer, ER, NBC, 1994-. Publications: The Andromeda Strain, 1969; Five Patients, 1970; The Terminal Man, 1972; The Great Train Robbery, 1975; Eaters of the Dead, 1976; Jasper Johns, 1977; Congo, 1980; Electronic Life, 1983; Sphere, 1987; Travels, 1988; Jurassic Park, 1990; Rising Sun, 1992; Disclosure, 1994; The Lost World, 1995; The Terminal Man, 1995; Airframe, 1996; Timeline, 1999; Prey, 2002; State of Fear, 2004; Non-fiction: Five Patients: The Hospital Explained, 1970; Jasper Johns, 1977, revised edition, 1994; Electronic Life, 1983; Travels, 1988; Screenplays: Westworld, 1975; Twister (with Anne-Marie Martin, 1996; Films include: Westworld, writer, director, 1973; Coma, writer, director, 1978; Jurassic Park, co-writer, 1993; Rising Sun, co-writer, 1993; Disclosure, co-producer, 1994; Twister, co-writer, co-producer, 1996; Sphere, co-producer, 1998; Eaters of the Dead, co-producer, 1998; 13th Warrior, co-producer 1999. Honours include: Edgar Awards, Mystery Writers of America, 1968, 1979; Academy of Motion Pictures Arts and Sciences technical Achievement Award, 1995; Emmy, Best Dramatic Series for "ER", 1996; Ankylosaur named Bienosaurus crichtoni, 2000. Memberships: Authors Guild Council, 1995-; PEN; Phi Beta Kappa; Writers Guild of America; Directors Guild; Academy of Motion Picture Arts and Sciences; Board of Directors, International Design Conference, Aspen, 1985-91; Board of Trustees, West Behavioural Sciences Institute, La Jolla, 1986-91; Board of Overseers, Harvard University, 1990-96. Address: Constant Productions, 2118 Wiltshire Blvd #433, Santa Monica, CA 90403, USA. Website: www.crichton-official.com

CRISP Adrian James, b. 21 November 1948, Harrow, Middlesex, England. Consultant Rheumatologist. 1 daughter. Education: University College School, London, 1962-66; Magdalene College, Cambridge, 1968-71; University College Hospital Medical School, London, 1971-74. Appointments: Consultant, Rheumatology and Metabolic Bone Diseases, Addenbrookes Hospital, Cambridge, 1985-; Associate Dean, University of Cambridge Clinical School and Eastern Deanery, 1997-2005; Director of Studies in Clinical Medicine and Fellow, Churchill College, Cambridge, 1991-. Honour: Listed in biographical publications. Memberships: Member of Council and Executive, and Chairman of Education Committee, British Society for Rheumatology. Address: The Old Forge, 83 High Street, Great Abington, Cambridge CB21 6AE, England.

CRISTEA Valentin Gabriel, b. 7 June 1968, Targoviste, Romania. Mathematician. Education: Bachelor Degree, Mathematics, University of Bucharest, Romania, 1987-91; Grant Holder, International Congress of Mathematicians, ICM '98, Technische Universität Berlin, Germany, 1998; Arbeitstagung, Max-Planck-Institut fuer Mathematik, Bonn Germany, 1999. Appointments: Assistant Professor of Mathematics "Valahia" University, Targoviste, Romania, 1995-; Assistant Professor of Mathematics, Politechnic University of Bucharest, 1995-96; Mathematician, Instituto de Fisica Aplicada, CSIC, Madrid, Spain, 1994-95 (6 months); Mathematician, CIMAT, Guanajuato, Mexico, 1998 (1 month); Mathematician Max-Planck-Institut fuer Mathematik, Bonn, Germany, 1999 (7 months). Publications: Considerations sur les paires de superconnexions sur des supervarietes, 1991; Remarks about the Supermanifolds, 1992; Totally geodesic graded Riemannian submanifolds of the (4,4)-dimensional graded Riemannian manifold, 1995; Existence and uniqueness theorem for Frenet frames supercurves, 1999; The reduced bundle of the principal superfibre bundle, 2001; Euler's superequations, 2001; Curvilinear Integral I(C) for problems of variations calculus on supermanifolds, 2002. Honours: Distinguished Leadership Award, American Biographical Institute; Nominated as inaugural member of the Leading Scientists of the World, 2005; Listed in biographical dictionaries. Membership: Romanian Society of Mathematical Sciences. Address: Str G-ral Matei Vladescu, BL 30 Sc A, Ap 6 Targoviste, 0200 Jud Dambovita, Romania. E-mail: valentin_cristea@yahoo.com

CRÓ Maria de Lurdes, b. 4 March 1950, Coimbra, Portugal. Teacher; Researcher. m. António Cró, 2 daughters. Education: Degree, Philosophy/Psychology, Coimbra University, 1972; Master, Educational Science, Aveiro University, 1987; PhD, Educational Science, Aveiro University and Catholic University, Leuven, Belgium, 1991; Aggregation exams for PhD, 1999. Appointments: Director, Pre-School Training Teachers, 1978-87; Co-ordinator, Pre- and Primary School Training Teachers, 1980-87; Vice President, Higher School of Education, Coimbra, 1985-97; European Co-ordinator Lingua, Arion, Socrates, Comenius, Brussels, 1992-98; Invited Teacher, 1992-95, Invited Researcher, 1992-2008, University of Aveiro; Invited Teacher, University of Coimbra, 1999-2008; Director, Regional Schools (Portugal Centre), 2002-06; Co-ordinator Teacher with Aggregation, Higher School of Education, Coimbra, 1999-2008. Publications: Books: Former and Continuous Training for Teachers, 1998; Activation of Psychological Development, 2001; Activities in Pre-School Education and Activation of Psychological Development, 2006; Book chapters: PDA Model in Teachers' Training, 2006; Implementing PDA Model in Children Socially and Culturally Handicapped in Brazil, 2006; Articles: Pupils' success versus Teachers' Training. Honours: Honoured by Brazilian school in Botucatu, São Paulo, 2007; Honoured by Jardim Escola João de Deus pre- and primary and secondary school, Brazil. Memberships: Association Internationale de Recherche sur la Personne de l'Enseignant (AIRPE); AIPELF; OMEP; SPCE; Portuguese Society of Education Science; GERFEC; College Universitaire Franco-Port. E-mail: mlurdescro@gmail.com

CRONENBERG David, b. 15 March 1943, Toronto, Canada. Film Director. Education: University of Toronto. Appointments: Directed fillers and short dramas for TV; Films include: Stereo, 1969; Crimes of the Future, 1970; The Parasite Murders/Shivers, 1974; Rabid, 1976; Fast Company, 1979; The Brood, 1979; Scanners, 1980; Videodrome, 1982; The Dead Zone, 1983; The Fly, 1986; Dead Ringers, 1988; The Naked Lunch, 1991; Crash, 1996; eXistenZ, 1998;

Camera, 2000; Spider, 2002; A History of Violence, 2005; To Each His Camera, 2007; Eastern Promises, 2007; Director: Transfer, 1966; From the Drain, 1967; Acted in: Nightbreed, 1990; The Naked Lunch (wrote screenplay); Trial by Jury; Henry and Verlin; To Die For, 1995; Extreme Measures, 1996; The Stupids, 1996; Director, writer, producer, actor, Crash, 1996. Publications: Crash 1996; Cronenberg on Cronenberg, 1996. Honours: Cannes Jury Special Prize, 1997; Silver Berlin Bear, 1999; 43 Awards, 25 nominations. Address: David Cronenberg Productions Ltd, 217 Avenue Road, Toronto, Ontario, M5R 2J3, Canada.

CRONIN James Watson, b. 29 September 1931, Chicago, Illinois, USA. Physicist. m. Annette Martin, 1954, 1 son, 2 daughters. Education: BS, Southern Methodist University, 1951; MS, 1953, PhD, Physics, 1955, University of Chicago. Appointments: National Science Foundation Fellow, 1952-55; Assistant Physicist, Brookhaven National Laboratory, 1955-58; Assistant Professor of Physics, 1958-62, Associate Professor, 1962-64, Professor, 1964-71, Princeton University; Professor of Physics, University of Chicago, 1971-; Loeb Lecturer in Physics, Harvard University, 1976. Honours: Research Corporation Award, 1968; Ernest O Lawrence Award, 1977; John Price Wetherill Medal, Franklin Institute, 1975; Joint Winner, Nobel Prize for Physics, 1980; Honorary DSc, Leeds, 1996; National Medal of Science, 1999. Memberships: NAS; American Academy of Arts and Sciences; American Physical Society. Address: Enrico Fermi Institute, University of Chicago, 5630 South Ellis Avenue, Chicago, IL 60637, USA.

CROSHAW Michael, b. 12 March 1943, Warwick, England. Poet. m. Theresa Belt, 6 June 1970, divorced 1976, 2 sons. Appointments: British Telecom, 1973-91; Associate Editor, Orbis Magazine, 1980-87. Publications: Alum Rock, 1992; A Harmony of Lights, 1993. Contributions to: Acumen; Babel; Bogg; Bradford Poetry Quarterly; Bull; Chapman; Completing the Picture; Core; Emotional Geology; Envoi; Envoi Book of Quotes on Poetry; The Interpreter's House; Jennings; Manhattan Poetry Review; Mercia Poets, 1980; The Month; Moorlands Review; New Hope International; Orbis; Ore; Other Poetry; Outposts Poetry Quarterly; Pennine Platform; Poetry Australia; Poetry Business Anthology, 1987-88; Poetry Nottingham; The Poet's Voice; Psychopoetica; Stride; Vigil; Weyfarers. Address: Queen's Road, Nuneaton, Warwickshire CV11 5ND, England.

CROSLAND Maurice Pierre, b. 19 March 1931, London, England. Emeritus Professor. m. Joan. Education: Stationers School, London; BSc, MSc, PhD, University of London. Appointments: Visiting Professor, University of Pennsylvania, Cornell University, and University of California, Berkeley, USA; Reader, History of Science, University of Leeds; Professor of History of Science, University of Kent. Publications: Books: Historical Studies in the Language of Chemistry; Gay-Lussac, Scientist and Bourgeois; Science under Control – The French Academy of Sciences 1795-1914; The Language of Science – From the Vernacular to the Technical; Scientific Institutions and Practice in France and Britain, circa 1700-1870, 2007. Honours: Dexter Award in the History of Chemistry; Former President, British Society for the History of Science. Memberships: Honorary Editor, British Journal for the History of Science; Member, International Academy of the History of Science. Address: School of History, Rutherford College, University of Kent, Canterbury CT2 7NX, England.

CROSLAND Neisha, b. 11 December 1960, London, England. Textile Designer. m. Stephane Perche, 2 sons. Education: Convent of the Sacred Heart, Woldingham; Hatfield Girls Grammar, Hertfordshire; BA, 1st Class Honours, Textile Design, Camberwell School of Arts and Crafts, 1984; MA, Printed Textiles, Royal College of Art, 1986. Career includes: Freelance textile designer; Teaching appointments: Glasgow School of Art; Winchester School of Art; Northbroke College, 1988-94; Freelance designer selling designs on paper for fabric and wallpaper; Designer, Romagna Collection for Osborne & Little,1990-94; Contributor, First Eleven portfolio, 1991; Founder, Neisha Crosland Scarves, 1994; Launched Neisha at Debenhams, 1998; Launched, Ginka ready to wear brand; Launched own Neisha Crosland wallpaper collection, 1999; Launched home decorative and stationary collection; Opened first retail outlet, London, 2000-01; Started licensed collection of scarves and fashion accessories for Hankyu, Japan, 2002; First collection of home furnishing fabrics; Opened Neisha Crosland flagship store, London, 2003; Designed a scarf and tie collection for Reed Employment, 2006; Collaborations: Mario Testino's Diana Princess of Wales at Kensington Palace; Bill Amberg; V&A Museum, London; The Rug Company; Veedon Fleece, 2005. Honours: Design & Decoration, 2004; Elle Decoration Award, 2005; Honoured with Royal Designer for Industry, 2006. Memberships: Chelsea Arts. Address: Unit 40, Battersea Business Centre, 99 Lavender Hill, London SW11 5QL, England. E-mail: info@neishacrosland.com

CROSSLAND Bernard, b. 20 October 1923, Sydenham, England. Mechanical Engineer. m. Audrey Elliott Birks, 2 daughters. Education: BSc, 1943, MSc, 1946, Engineering, Nottingham University College; PhD, University of Bristol, 1953; DSc, University of Nottingham, 1960. Appointments: Engineering Apprentice, 1940-44, Technical Assistant, 1943-45, Rolls Royce Ltd, Derby; Lecturer, Luton Regional Technical College, 1945-46; Assistant Lecturer, Lecturer, Senior Lecturer in Mechanical Engineering, University of Bristol, 1946-59; Professor of Mechanical Engineering, Head of Department of Mechanical and Manufacturing Engineering, 1959-84, Dean of the Faculty of Engineering, 1964-67, Senior Pro Vice Chancellor, 1978-82, Queen's University of Belfast; Engineering Consultant, 1984-; Involved in the investigations of several major disasters including: King's Cross Underground Fire, Bilsthorp Colliery Roof Fall, Southall Train Crash, Ladbroke Grove Rail Crash and numerous others. Publications: The Anatomy of an Engineer, Autobiography, 2006; Many articles in professional journals and books. Honours: 11 named lectures; 8 prizes; 3 Honorary DEng; 6 Honorary DSc; Honorary Fellowships: FWI, FIEI, Fellow of the University of Luton, FIMechE, FIStructE; CBE, 1980; Kt, 1990. Memberships: Royal Irish Academy; Fellowship: Royal Academy of Engineering; Royal Society; Irish Academy of Engineering. Address: 16 Malone Court, Belfast, BT9 6PA, Northern Ireland.

CROUCH Colin, b. 1 March 1944, Isleworth, Middlesex, England. University Professor. m. Joan Ann Freedman, 2 sons. Education: BA, first class, Sociology, London School of Economics, 1969; DPhil, Nuffield College, Oxford, 1975. Appointments: Temporary Lecturer in Sociology, London School of Economics, 1969-70; Research Student, Nuffield College, Oxford, 1970-72; Lecturer in Sociology, University of Bath, 1972-73; Lecturer, 1973-79, Senior Lecturer, 1979-80, Reader, 1980-85, Sociology, London School of Economics and Political Science; Professor of Sociology, Fellow of Trinity College, University of Oxford, 1985-95; Chairman, Department of Social and Political Sciences, Professor of Comparative Social Institutions, European University Institute, Florence, Italy; External Scientific Member, Max-Planck-Institut für Gesellschaftsforschung, Cologne, Germany; Chairman, The Political Quarterly Ltd. Publications: 8 books; Editor, 18 books; 108 other articles and chapters. Honours: Hobhouse Memorial Prize, 1969. Memberships: President of Society for the Advancement of Socio-Economics; Max-Planck-Gesellschaft. E-mail: colin.crouch@wbs.ac.uk

CROW Sheryl, b. 11 February 1962, Kennett, Missouri, USA. Singer; Songwriter; Musician (guitar). Musical Education: Classical Music degree, Missouri State University; Organ and piano lessons; Self-taught guitar. Career: Backing singer, Michael Jackson tour, 18 months; Also backing singer for Joe Cocker; Rod Stewart; Don Henley; Songwriter, solo performer, mid 1980s-; International concerts and tours with John Hiatt; Crowded House; Big Head Todd; Support tours to Bob Dylan; Eagles, 1994; Joe Cocker, Wembley Arena, 1994; Performed at Woodstock II, 1994. Recordings: Solo album: Tuesday Night Music Club, 1993; Sheryl Crow, 1996; The Globe Sessions, 1998; Sheryl Crow and Friends: Live in Central Park, 1999; C'mon C'mon, 2002; Sheryl Crow: Life At Budokan, 2003; The Very Best of Sheryl Crow, The Videos, 2004; Singles include: All I Wanna Do, 1994; Leaving Las Vegas, 1994; Strong Enough, 1994; Can't Cry Anymore, 1995; If It Makes You Happy, 1996; Everyday Is A Winding Road, 1996; My Favorite Mistake, 1998; There Goes The Neighbourhood, 1998; Anything But Down, 1999; Sweet Child O' Mine, 1999; Soak Up The Sun, 2002; Steve McQueen, 2002; First Cut is the Deepest, 2003; It's So Easy, 2004; Light In Your Eyes, 2004; Contributor, albums: The End Of Innocence, Don Henley, 1989; Late Night, Neal Schon, 1989; Other recordings by Eric Clapton; Wynnona Judd; Contributor, film soundtracks: Kalifornia, 1994; Leaving Las Vegas, 1995; Cars, 2006. Honours: 3 Grammy Awards, Tuesday Night Music Club, 1995; BRIT Award, Best International Female Artist, 1997; American Music Awards, Best Female Pop/Rock Artist, 2003, 2004. Address: Helter Skelter, The Plaza, 535 Kings Road, London SW10 0SZ, England. Website: www.sherylcrow.com

CROWE Russell, b. 7 April 1964, New Zealand. Actor. m. Danielle Spencer, 2003, 1 son. Career: Films include: The Crossing, 1993; The Quick and the Dead, Romper Stomper, Rough Magic, Virtuosity, Under the Gun, 1995; Heaven's Burning, Breaking Up, LA Confidential, 1997; Mystery Alaska, The Insider, 1999; Gladiator, Proof of Life, 2000; A Beautiful Mind, 2001; Master and Commander: The Far Side of the World, 2003; Cinderella Man, 2005; A Good Year, 2006; 3:10 to Yuma, Tenderness, American Gangster, 2007. Honours: Variety Club Award (Australia), 1993; Film Critics Circle Award, 1993; Best Actor, Seattle International Film Festival, 1993; Management Film and TV Awards, Motion Pictures Exhibitors Association, 1993; LA Film Critics Association, 1999; National Board of Review, 1999; National Society of Film Critics, 1999; Academy Award for Best Actor, 2000; Oscar, 2000; Golden Globe, 2001; BAFTA Award, 2001; Screen Actors' Guild Award for Best Actor, 2001. Address: ICM, 8942 Wilshire Blvd, Beverly Hills, CA, 90211, USA.

CROWTHER David E A, b. 6 April 1952. Professor. Education: MBA, Loughborough University, 1989; Postgraduate Diploma, Business Information Management, CNAA, 1992; BA, Psychology, 1993, M Ed, 2002, Open University; Certificate in Counselling, Nottingham University, 1994; PhD, 1999, Postgraduate Certificate in Education, 2000, Aston University. Appointments: Trainee Accountant,

1970-72, Assistant Accountant, 1972-74, Basford Rural District Council; Assistant Accountant, Mansfield District Council, 1974-75; Assistant Chief Accountant, 1975-76, Financial Planner, 1976-78, Newark District Council; Assistant Systems Accountant, 1978-81, Manager, Customer Accounts, 1981-85, Manager, Credit Services, 1985-92, Naafi; Independent Financial and Systems Consultant (self employment), 1992-94; ESRC Management Teaching Fellow, 1994-97, Lecturer in Accounting, 1997-2000, Aston University; Reader, Marketing, University of North London, 2000-01; Professor of Corporate Social Responsibility, University of North London/London Metropolitan University, 2001-05; Professor, Corporate Responsibility, De Montfort University, 2005-. Publications: 17 books, 6 in press; Over 250 articles in professional journals and magazines. Honours: Honorary Council Member, Ansted University, Malaysia, 2000; Honorary DSocSc, Ansted University, Malaysia, 2002; Fellow, North American Academy of Arts & Sciences, 2002; Diplome 'ad Honores', Académie Européenne des Arts, France, 2003; Académico de Mérito, Muy Ilustre Academia Mundial de Ciencias Tecnología Educación y Humanidades, Spain, 2003; Special Advisor to Vice-Rectorate, Honorary Doctor of Applied Science, Université Francophone Internationale, Belgium, 2003; Certificate of Registration as International Expert in Social Education, Association International pour l'Ecole de Promotion Collective, Togo, 2003; Ansted University Foundation Award, 2004; Highly Recommended Runner Up Educator, EABIS and Aspen Center for Business Education European Faculty Pioneer Awards, 2007; Listed in international biographical dictionaries. Memberships: Chartered Institute of Public Finance and Accountancy; Chartered Institute of Management Accountants; British Psychological Society; British Accounting Association; European Accounting Association; Fellow, Higher Education Academy; Standing Conference on Organizational Symbolism; Social Responsibility Research Network; Global Academy of Business & Economic Research; Knowledge Globalization Institute. Address: De Montfort University, Leicester Business School, The Gateway, Leicester LE1 9BH, England. E-mail: dcrowther@dmu.ac.uk Website: www.davideacrowther.com

CRUISE Tom (Thomas Cruise Mapother IV), b. 3 July 1962, Syracuse, New York, USA. Actor. m. (1) Mimi Rogers, 1987, divorced 1990, (2) Nicole Kidman, 1990, divorced 2001, 1 adopted son, 1 adopted daughter, (3) Katie Holmes, 2006, 1 daughter. Career: Actor, films include: Endless Love, Taps, 1981; All The Right Moves, Losin' It, The Outsiders, Risky Business, 1983; Legend, 1984; Top Gun, 1985; The Color of Money, 1986; Rain Man, 1988; Cocktail, Born on the Fourth of July, 1989; Daytona, Rush, Days of Thunder, 1990; Sure as the Moon, 1991; Far and Away, A Few Good Men, 1992; The Firm, 1993; Interview with the Vampire, 1994; Jerry Maguire, Mission Impossible, 1996; Eyes Wide Shut, 1997; Mission Impossible 2, Magnolia, 1999; Vanilla Sky, 2001; Minority Report, Space Station 3D, voice, 2002; The Last Samurai, 2003; Collateral, 2004; War of the Worlds, 2005; Mission Impossible 3, Lions for Lambs, 2007; Producer: Without Limits, Vanilla Sky, Narc, Hitting It Hard, Shattered Glass, The Last Samurai, Suspect Zero, Elizabeth Town, Ask the Dust, Elizabethtown, Ask the Dust, Mission Impossible 3. Honours: Golden Globe, 2000; David di Donatello lifetime achievement award, 2005. Address: Creative Artists Agency, 9830 Wilshire Boulevard, Beverly Hills, CA 90212-1825, USA. Website: www.caa.com

CRULL Jan Jr, b. The Netherlands. Lawyer. Education: Lake Forest Academy; Northwestern University; BA (Hons), Dalhousie University; MA, Purdue University; MA,

University of Chicago; JD, Tulane University. Appointments: Intern, GGvA, New York City, 1973-74; Teaching Assistant, Graduate Instructor, Purdue University, 1975-76; Assistant to OOTC, New York City, 1978; Assistant to Chapter President, Ramah Navajo Reservation, Pinehill New Mexico, 1979-80; Professional Staff Member, US House of Representatives, Washington DC, 1981; Assistant Money Manager, 1982, 1985-86, 1989, Counsel, Advisor, 1990-91, Gulf and Occidental Investment Co SA, Geneva; Counsel, Co-Principal, SandCru Inc, Chicago, 1992-; President, General Counsel, Vigil Film Production Co, Los Angeles and Sacramento, California, 1993-97; Director, Counsel, Von Quesar Holdings OHG, Vienna, 1994-98; Director, Counsel, Beeltsnijder KG, Berlin, 1994-97; Advisor, Infrastructure Bond Development, Cariocca Capital Partners, Rio de Janeiro, 1999; Advisor, LFFE Ltd, Heibei, China, 2004-08; Outside Director and Advisor, Shang Bat T&H, Shanghai, Luxembourg, and United Arab Emirates, 2004-. Publications: Provisions for First Reauthorization of Tribally Controlled Community College Assistance Act, 97th US Congress (author); Special Provisions for Native Americans in Library Services Construction Act, 97th-98th US Congress (author). Films: Developer: What About My Friend's Children, 1973; Not in Fiction Only: There and Here Also, 1974; A Free People, Free to Choose, 1992-93; AIDDS: American Indian's Devastating Dilemma Soon, 1993; To Mute Them Once Again, 1994; Indian Buckaroos, 1996. Honour: Nominee, Rockefeller Public Service Award, 1981. Memberships: American Bar Association; Chicago Council on Foreign Relations; Chicago Bar Association; Illinois State Bar Association; Calumet Country Club; Quadrangle Club, Chicago; 1781 Club, Netherlands Antilles; Phi Kappa Psi, Northwestern University. Address: c/o Shang Bat TZH, PO Box 0492, Chicago, IL 60690-0492, USA.

CRUYFF Johan, b. 25 April 1947, Amsterdam, Netherlands. Footballer. m. Danny Coster, 1968, 3 children. Appointments: Played for Ajax, 1964-73; Top scorer in Dutch league, with 33 goals, 1967; Moved to Barcelona, now Coach of Barcelona; Captained Netherlands, 1974 World Cup Final, 1974; Retired, 1978; Started playing again and signed for Los Angeles Aztecs; Played for Washington Diplomats, 1979-80; Levante, Spain, 1981; Ajax and Feyenoord, 1982; Manager, Ajax, 1987-87, winning European Cup-Winners Cup, 1987; Manager, Barcelona, winning Cup-Winners Cup, 1989, European Cup, 1992, Spanish League, 1991, 1992, 1993, Spanish Super Cup, 1992; Formed Cruyff Foundation for disabled sportspeople and Johan Cruyff University to assist retired sportspeople, 1998. Honour: European Footballer of the Year, 1971, 1973-74.

CRUZ Penelope, b. 28 April 1974, Madrid, Spain. Actor. Education: National Conservatory, Spain. Career: Actor: Several roles on Spanish TV and music videos; Films include: Live Flesh, Belle Epoque, Jamón Jamón, 1992; La Celestina, 1996; Open Your Eyes, 1997; The Hi-Lo Country, Talk of Angels, The Girl of Your Dreams, 1998; All About My Mother, 1999; Woman on Top, All the Pretty Horses, 2000; Captain Corelli's Mandolin, Blow, Vanilla Sky, 2001; Fanfan La Tulipe, Gothika, 2003; Noel, Head in the Clouds, Don't Move, 2004; Sahara, Chromophobia, 2005; Bandidas, Volver, 2006; The Good Night, Manolete, Elegy, 2007. Honours: Goya for Best Actress, 1998; 17 awards, 27 nominations. Address: c/o Kuranda Management International, 8626 Skyline Drive, Los Angeles, CA 90046, USA.

CRYSTAL Billy, b. 14 March 1947, Long Beach, NY, USA. Actor; Comedian. m. Janice Goldfinger, 2 daughters. Education: Marshall University. Appointments: Member of group, 3's Company; Solo appearances as stand-up comedian; TV appearances include: Soap, 1977-81; The Billy Crystal Hour, 1982; Saturday Night Live, 1984-85; The Love Boat; The Tonight Show; TV films include: Breaking Up is Hard to Do, 1979; Enola Gay; The Men; The Mission; The Atomic Bomb, 1980; Death Flight; Feature films include: The Rabbit Test, 1978; This is Spinal Tap, 1984; Running Scared, 1986; The Princess Bridge, Throw Momma From the Train, 1987; When Harry Met Sally..., 1989; City Slickers, 1991; Mr Saturday Night (Director, Producer, co-screenplay writer), 1993; City Slickers II: The Legend of Curly's Gold, 1994; Forget Paris, 1995; Hamlet; Father's Day; Deconstructing Harry; My Grant, Analyse This, 1998; The Adventures of Rocky and Bullwinkle, 2000; Monsters Inc (voice), 2001; America's Sweethearts, 2001; Mike's New Car (voice), 2002, 2006; Analyze That, 2002; Howl's Moving Castle (voice), 2004. Publication: Absolutely Mahvelous, 1986; My Giant, 1998; America's Sweethearts, 2001; I already Know I Love You, 2004; 700 Sundays, 2005; Grandpa's Little One, 2006..

CSABA György, b. 31 May 1929, Törökszentmiklos. Physician. m. (1) 1954, (2) Katalin Kallay, 1970, 2 sons, 2 daughters. Education: MD, 1953; PhD, 1957; DSc, 1969. Appointments: Assistant Professor, 1953-59, 1st Assistant, 1959-63, Associate Professor, 1963-70, Professor, 1970-, Director, Department of Biology, Semmelweis University of Medicine, 1971-94; Professor, 1970-99; Professor Emeritus, 2000-. Publications: 24 books, 24 chapters and over 800 scientific publications in peer-reviewed journals. Honours: Huzella Prize, 1983; Pal Bugat Award, Scientific Educational Society, 1989; Hung Higher Education Medal, Ministry of Education, 1994; Golden Signet, Semmelweis University of Medicine, 1994; 5 Prizes for High Level Books; Khwarizmi International Award; Comsats Award. Memberships: President, General and Theoretical Section, Hung Biological Society, 1978-87; Chairman, Book Committee, Scientific Press Council, Budapest, 1980-88; Chairman, Editorial Committee, Semmelweis Publisher, 1989-2001. Address: PO Box 370, H-1445 Budapest, Hungary.

CSIKAI Gyula, b. 31 October 1930, Tiszaladány, Hungary. Professor in Physics. m. Margit Buczkó, 2 sons. Education: University Diploma in Mathematics and Physics, 1953, Candidate, 1957, DSc, 1966, Corresponding, 1973, and Ordinary Member, 1985, Hungarian Academy of Sciences. Appointments: Head, Neutron Physics Department, ATOMKI, Debrecen, Hungary, 1956-67; Head Institute of Experimental Physics, Debrecen, 1967-95; Deputy Minister of Culture and Education of Hungary, 1987; Professor, 1967, Dean, 1972-75, Rector, 1981-86, Kossuth University, Debrecen, Hungary; Professor Emeritus, 2001-. Publications: More than 270 papers in scientific journals; Handbook of Fast Neutron Generators I-II, 1987; Handbook on Nuclear Data, 1987, 2003; 2 patents. Honours: Brody Prize, 1957; First Prize of Hungarian Academy of Sciences, 1967; Eötvös Medal, 1980, Golden Medal of Hungary, 1980; State Award, 1983; Named Honorary Freeman of Tiszaladány, 2000-; Honorary Doctor, Kiev National University, 2001; Leo Szilard Prize, 2004; Wigner Prize, 2005. Memberships: Expert UN-IAEA, Vienna, 1976; The New York Academy of Sciences, 1982; Hungarian Academy of Sciences, 1985; Academia Europea, 1991; Secretary, IUPAP Commission, Nuclear Physics, 1993-96; Editor of international journals. Address: Institute of Experimental Physics, University of Debrecen, H-4010 Debrecen-10, P O Box 105, Hungary.

CULKIN Macauley, b. 26 August 1980, New York, USA. Actor. m. Rachel Milner, 1998, divorced 2000. Education: George Balanchine's School of Ballet, NY. Appointments: Actor, films: Rocket Gibralter, 1988; Uncle Buck, 1989; See You in the Morning, 1989; Jacob's Ladder, 1990; Home Alone, 1990; My Girl, 1991; Only the Lonely, 1991; Home Alone 2: Lost in New York, 1992; The Nutcracker; The Good Son, 1993; The Pagemaster, 1995; Getting Even with Dad, 1995; Body Piercer, 1998; Party Monster, 2003; Saved! 2004; Richie Rich, 2004; Jerusalemski Sindrom, 2004; TV: Will & Grace, 2003; Frasier, 2004; Robot Chicken, 2005-06; Play: Madame Melville, Vaudeville Theatre, London, 2001. Address: c/o Brian Gersh, William Morris Agency, 151 S El Camino Drive, Beverley Hills, CA 90212, USA.

CULL-CANDY Stuart G, b. 2 November 1946. Professor of Neuroscience; Gaddum Professor of Pharmacology. m. Barbara Paterson Fulton, 1 daughter. Education: BSc (Hons), Biology, University of London, 1969; MSc, Physiology, University College London, 1970; PhD, Synaptic Physiology, University of Glasgow, 1974; Postdoctoral Fellow, Institute of Pharmacology, University of Lund, Sweden, 1974-75. Appointments: Beit Memorial Research Fellow and Associate Research Staff, Department of Biophysics, 1975-82, Wellcome Trust Senior Reader in Pharmacology, 1982-90, Professor of Neuroscience, Personal Chair, 1990-, Gaddum Chair of Pharmacology, Professor of Neuroscience, 2006-, University College London; Medical Research Council Neuroscience Committee, 1987-91; Wellcome Trust International Interest Group Grants Committee, 1991-97; International Research Scholar, Howard Hughes Medical Institute, 1993-98; Royal Society – Wolfson Position, 2003-; Royal Society University Research Fellow Grants Committee, 2003-; Leverhulme Trust Research Fellowship Committee, 2006; Royal Society Research Grants Board, 2007-. Publications: Numerous articles on synaptic transmission and glutamate receptors in the brain and peripheral nervous system in the scientific journals: Nature, Neuron, Nature Neurosciences, Journal of Neuroscience, Journal of Physiology; Various book chapters; Editor of scientific journals: Reviewing Editor, Journal of Neuroscience, 2000-; Editor, Neuron, 1994-98; External Editorial Adviser in Neuroscience, Nature, 1993-97; Editor, Journal of Physiology, 1987-95; European Journal of Neuroscience, 1988-; Guest Editor, Current Opinions in Neurobiology, 2007. Honours: Appointed International Scholar, Howard Hughes Medical Institute, USA, 1993-98; GL Brown Prize, Physiological Society, 1996; Elected Fellow of the Royal Society, 2002; Wolfson Award, Royal Society, 2003; Elected Fellow of the Academy of Medical Sciences, 2004; Elected Fellow, British Pharmacological Society, 2005; Listed in Who's Who and other biographical publications. Memberships: Royal Society; Academy of Medical Sciences; Society for Neuroscience, USA; Physiological Society, UK; British Neuroscience Association; International Brain Research Organisation; Pharmacological Society, UK. Address: Department of Pharmacology, University College London, Gower Street, London WC1E 6BT, England. E-mail: s.cull-candy@ucl.ac.uk

CURE Susan Carol, b. 18 August 1940, Los Angeles, USA. Biologist. m. Michel Y Cure, 1 son, 2 daughters. Education: BA, Biological Science, Stanford University, 1962; PhD, Medical Microbiology, Stanford University, 1967. Appointments: Postdoctoral Fellow, California Department of Health, 1966-1968; Researcher, Centre d'Études de la Biologie Prénatale, 1970-1974; Lecturer, Associate Professor, American University in Paris, 1971-1976, 1987-; Science Co-ordinator, Association Française Contre les Myopathies,

1989-; Researcher, Genethon, Genoscope, French Genome Centres, 1992-. Publications: Many articles in scientific journals: American Journal of Human Genetics; Nature; Journal of Investigative Dermatology. Memberships: AAAS; American Society of Microbiology; Club du Mt St Leger; Sigma Xi. Address: 3 av Robert Schuman, 75007, Paris, France.

CURIO Eberhard Otto Eugen, b. 22 October 1932, Berlin, Germany. Professor of Biology. m. Dorothea Curio, 1 son, 1 daughter. Education: Doctor rer. nat., Free University of Berlin, 1957; Professor of Biology, Ruhr University Bochum, 1970. Appointments: Research Associate, Max-Planck-Institute for Behavioural Physiology, 1957-64; Assistant Professor, 1964-68, Lecturer, 1968-70, Professor, 1970-, Ruhr University Bochum, Germany. Publications: The Ethology of Predation, 1976; Behavior as a Tool for Management Intervention in Birds (book chapter), 1998. Honours: Ornithologists Award, German Ornithologists' Society, 1994; Honorary Member, Ethological Society, 2000; Chair for Biodiversity, ASEAN Regional Center for Biodiversity Conservation, 2001-04. Memberships: Society for Conservation Biology; International Society for Behavioral Ecology; Ethological Society; Founding President, Philippine Association for Conservation and Development, 2005-07; Association for the Study of Animal Behaviour; Frankfurt Zoological Society; German Zoological Society; German Ornithologists' Society; American Society of Naturalists; Society for Conservation Biology. Address: Conservation Biology Unit, Faculty of Biology, Ruhr-University Bochum, Postfach 102148, 44780 Bochum, Germany. E-mail: eberhard.curio@rub.de Website: www.pescp.org

CURL James Stevens, b. 26 March 1937, Belfast, Northern Ireland. Architect; Architectural Historian. m. (1) 2 daughters, (2) Stanisława Dorota Iwaniec, 1993. Education: Queen's University, School of Architecture, Belfast, 1954-58; DiplArch, Oxford School of Architecture, 1961-63; Dip TP, Oxford Department of Land Use Studies, 1963-67; PhD, University College London, 1978-81. Appointment: Retired Professor Emeritus of Architectural History, having held Chairs at two British universities. Publications include: The Londonderry Plantation 1609-1914, 1986; English Architecture: An Illustrated Glossary, 1987; Encyclopaedia of Architectural Terms, 1993; A Celebration of Death, 1993; Egyptomania, 1994; Victorian Churches, 1995; The Oxford Dictionary of Architecture, 1999, 2000; The Honourable The Irish Society and the Plantation of Ulster 1608-2000: The City of London and the Colonisation of County Londonderry in the Province of Ulster in Ireland – A History and Critique, 2000; The Victorian Celebration of Death, 2000, 2004; The Art and Architecture of Freemasonry, 2002; Georgian Architecture, 2002; Classical Architecture, 2002; Death and Architecture, 2002; The Egyptian Revival, 2005; The Oxford Dictionary of Architecture and Landscape Architecture, 2006; Victorian Architecture; Diversity and Invention, 2007. Honours: British Academy Research Awards, 1982, 1983. 1992, 1994, 1998; Sir Banister Fletcher Award for Best Book of Year (1991) 1992; Building Centre Trust Award, 1992; Interbuild Fund Award, 1992 Royal Institute of British Architects Research Award, 1993; Marc Fitch Fund Award, 2003; Authors Foundation Fund Award, 2004. Memberships: Society of Authors; Royal Institute of British Architects; Royal Institute of the Architects of Ireland; Royal Incorporation of Architects in Scotland; Society of Antiquaries of Scotland; Society of Antiquaries of London; Oxford and Cambridge Club. Address: 15 Torgrange, Holywood, County Down BT18 0NG, Northern Ireland. E-mail: jscurl@btinternet.com

CURRIE JONES Edwina, b. 13 October 1946. Politician; Broadcaster; Writer. m. (1) R F Currie, 1972, dissolved 2001, 2 daughters, (2) John Jones, 2001. Education: St Anne's College, Oxford, London School of Economics. Appointments: Lecturer in Economics, Economics History and Business Studies, 1972-81; Elected: Birmingham City Council, 1975-86, Conservative MP Derbyshire South, 1983-97; Appointed: Junior Minister, Department of Health, 1985-86 and 1986-88; Chair, Conservative Group for Europe, 1995-97; Vice Chair, European Movement, 1995-99; Host of Radio Programme, Late Night Currie, BBC Radio 5 Live, 1998-2003; Presenter TV Programmes for BBC and others; Winner, Celebrity Mastermind, 2004; Appeared in numerous reality TV Programmes. Publications: Six novels, including, A Parliamentary Affair, 1994; A Woman's Place, 1996; She's Leaving Home, 1997; The Ambassador, 1999; Chasing Men, 2000; This Honourable House, 2001; Diaries (1987-92) 2002; Diaries (1992-97) 2004; Several non-fiction works, Life Lines, 1989; What Women Want, 1990; Three Line Quips, 1992. Honours: Speaker of the Year, 1990; Campaigner of the Year, Spectator, 1994. Address: c/o Little Brown, Brettenham House, Lancaster Place, London WC2E 7EN, England.

CURTIS David Roderick, b. 3 June 1927, Melbourne, Australia. Neuropharmacologist. m. Lauri Sewell, 1 son, 1 daughter. Education: MB BS, University of Melbourne, 1950; PhD, Australian National University, 1957. Appointments: Research Scholar, 1954-56, Research Fellow, 1956-57, Fellow, 1957-59, Senior Fellow, 1959-62, Professorial Fellow, 1962-66, Professor of Pharmacology, 1966-73, Department of Physiology, John Curtin School; Professor and Head, Department of Pharmacology, 1973-88, Chairman, Division of Physiological Sciences, 1988-89, Howard Florey Professor of Medical Research, Director of School, 1989-92, University Fellow, 1993-95, Emeritus Professor, 1993, John Curtin School of Medical Research, Australian National University. Publications: Numerous articles in professional journals; Co-author, The John Curtin School of Medical Research. The First Fifty Years, 1948-1998. Honours: FAA, 1965; FRS, 1974; Burnet Medal, Australian Academy of Science, 1983; President, Australian Academy of Science, 1986-92; FRACP, 1987; AC, 1992; Centenary Medal, 2003. Memberships: Honorary Fellow, The British Pharmacological Society; Honorary Member Emeritus, The Australian Association of Neurologists; Honorary Member: The Neurosurgical Society of Australasia; The Australian Neuroscience Society; The Australian Physiological and Pharmacological Society. Address: 7 Patey Street, Campbell, ACT 2612, Australia.

CURTIS Jamie Lee (Lady Haden-Guest), b. 22 November 1958, Los Angeles, California, USA. m. Christopher Guest, 1 son, 1 daughter. Education: University of the Pacific, California, USA. Career: Films include: Halloween; The Fog; Halloween 2; Prom Night; Trading Places; The Adventures of Buckaroo Banzai: Across the 8th Dimension; 8 Million Ways to Die; A Fish Called Wanda; Blue Steel; My Girl; Forever Young; My Girl 2; True Lies, 1994; House Arrest, 1996; Fierce Creatures, 1996; Halloween H20, 1998; Virus, 1999; The Tailor of Panama (also director), 2000; Daddy and Them; Halloween H2K: Evil Never Dies; True Lies 2, 2003; Freaky Friday, 2003; Christmas with the Kranks, 2004; Molly & Roni's Dance Party, 2005; The Kid & I, 2005; TV includes: Dorothy Stratten: Death of a Centrefold; The Love Boat; Columbo Quincy; Charlie's Angels; Mother's Boys; Drowning Mona (director), 2000; A Home for the Holidays, 2005. Publications: When I Was Little, 1993; Today I Feel Silly and Other Moods That Make My Day, 1999; Where Do Balloons Go? An Uplifting Mystery, 2000; I'm Gonna Like

Me Letting Off a Little Self-Esteem, 2002; It's Hard to be Five, Learning How to Work my Control Panel, 2004. Address: c/o Rick Kurtzmann, CAA, 9830 Wilshire Boulevard, Beverly Hills, CA 90212, USA.

CURTIS Tony (Bernard Schwarz), b. 3 June 1925, New York, USA. Film Actor. m. (1) Janet Leigh, divorced, 2 daughters, (2) Christine Kaufmann, divorced, 2 daughters, (3) Leslie Allen, divorced, 2 sons, (4) Lisa Deutsch, 1993, divorced, (5) Jill Vandenberg, 1998. Education: New School of Social Research. Appointments: Served in US Navy; Actor, films include: Houdini; Black Shield of Falworth; So This is Paris?; Six Bridges to Cross; Trapeze; Mister Cory; Sweet Smell of Success; Midnight Story; The Vikings; Defiant Ones; Perfect Furlough; Some Like It Hot, 1959; Spartacus, The Great Imposter, Pepe, 1960; The Outsider, 1961; Taras Bulba, 1962; Forty Pounds of Trouble, 1962; The List of Adrian Messenger, Captain Newman, 1963; Paris When It Sizzles, Wild and Wonderful, Sex and the Single Girl, Goodbye Charlie, 1964; The Great Race, Boeing, Boeing, 1965; Arriverderci, Baby, Not With My Wife You Don't, 1966; Don't Make Waves, 1967; Boston Strangler, 1968; Lepke, 1975; Casanova, The Last Tycoon, 1976; The Manitou, Sextette, 1978; The Mirror Crack'd, 1980; Venom, 1982; Insignificance, 1985; Club Life, 1986; The Last of Philip Banter, 1988; Balboa, Midnight, Lobster Man from Mars, The High-Flying Mermaid, Prime Target, Center of the Web, Naked in New York, The Reptile Man, The Immortals, The Celluloid Closet, 1995; Louis and Frank, Brittle Glory, 1997; Reflections of Evil (narrator), 2002; The Blacksmith and the Carpenter (voice), Funny Money, 2007; TV includes: Third Girl From the Left, 1973; The Persuaders, 1971-72; The Count of Monte Cristo, 1976; Vegas, 1978; Mafia Princess, 1986; Christmas in Connecticut, 1992; A Perry Mason Mystery: The Case of the Grimacing Governor; Elvis Meets Nixon; Hope & Faith, 2004; CSI: Crime Scene Investigation, 2005. Publications: Kid Andrew Cody and Julie Sparrow, 1977; The Autobiography, 1993. Honours include: Kt Order of the Republic of Hungary, 1966. Address: c/o William Morris Agency, 151 S El Camino Drive, Beverley Hills, CA 90212, USA.

CUSACK John, b. 28 June 1966, Evanston, Illinois, USA. Actor. Appointments: Piven Theatre Workshop, Evanston, from age 9-19; New Criminals Theatrical Company, Chicago; Films include: Class, 1983; Sixteen Candles, Grandview USA, 1984; The Sure Thing, 1985; One Crazy Summer, 1986; Broadcast News, Hot Pursuit, 1987; Eight Men Out, Tapeheads, 1988; Say Anything, Fatman and Little Boy, The Thin Red Line, 1989; The Grifters, 1990; True Colors, 1991; Shadows and Fog, Roadside Prophets, The Player, Map of the Human Heart, Bob Roberts, 1992; Money for Nothing, 1993; Bullets Over Broadway, The Road to Wellville, 1994; City Hall, 1995; Anastasia, Con Air, Hellcab, Midnight in the Garden of Good and Evil, 1997; This is My Father, Pushing Tin, 1998; Being John Malkovich, 1999; Live of the Party, 2000; America's Sweethearts, Serendipity, 2001; Max, Adaptation, 2002; Identity, Runaway Jury, 2003; Ice Harvest, 2005; The Ice Harvest: Alternate Endings, The Contract, 2006; 1408, Grace is Gone, Summerhood, Martian Child, War, Inc, 2007; Igor (voice), 2008; Actor, director, writer: Grosse Pointe Blank, 1997; Arigo (producer, actor), 1998; High Fidelity (actor, writer), 1997; The Cradle Will Rock, 1999. Address: 1325 Avenue of the Americas, New York, NY 10019, USA,

CUSACK Sinead Mary, b. 1948. Actress. m. Jeremy Irons, 1977, 2 sons. Appointments: Appearances with RSC include: Lady Amaranth in Wild Oats, Lisa in Children of the Sun,

Isabella in Measure for Measure, Celia in As You Like It, Evadne in the Maid's Tragedy, Lady Anne in Richard III, Portia in the Merchant of Venice, Ingrid in Peer Gynt, Kate in the Taming of the Shrew, Beatrice in Much Ado About Nothing, Lady MacBeth in MacBeth, Roxanne in Cyrano de Bergerac, Virago in A Lie of the Mind, 2001, The Mercy Seat, 2003; Other stage appearances at Oxford Festival, Gate Theatre, Dublin, Royal Court and others; numerous appearances in TV drama; Films include: Alfred the Great; Tamlyn; Hoffman; David Copperfield; Revenge; The Devil's Widow; Horowitz in Dublin Castle; The Last Remake of Beau Geste; Rocket Gibralter; Venus Peter; Waterland; God on the Rocks; Bad Behaviour; The Cement Garden; The Sparrow; Flemish Board; Stealing Beauty; I Capture the Castle; V for Vendetta, 2005; The Tiger's Tail, 2006; Eastern Promises, 2007. Address: c/o Curtis Brown Group, 4th Floor, Haymarket House, 28-29 Haymarket, London, SW1Y 4SP, England.

CUSSLER Clive (Eric), b. 15 July 1931, Aurora, Illinois, USA. Author; Advertising Executive. m. Barbara Knight, 28 August 1955, 3 children. Education: Pasadena City College, 1949-51; Orange Coast College; California State University. Appointments: Advertising Directorships; Author. Owner, Bestgen and Cussler Advertising, Newport Beach, California, 1961-65; Copy Director, Darcy Advertising, Hollywood, California and Instructor in Advertising Communications, Orange Coast College, 1965-67; Advertising Director, Aquatic Marine Corporation, Newport Beach, California, 1967-79; Vice President and Creative Director of Broadcast, Meffon, Wolff and Weir Advertising, Denver, Colorado, 1970-73; Chair, National Underwater and Marine Agency. Publications: The Mediterranean Caper, 1973; Iceberg, 1975; Raise the Titanic, 1976; Vixen O-Three, 1978; Night Probe, 1981; Pacific Vortex, 1982; Deep Six, 1984; Cyclops, 1986; Treasure, 1988; Dragon, 1990; Sahara, 1992; Inca Gold, 1994; Shock Wave, 1996; Flood Tide, 1997; Serpent, 1999; Atlantis Found, 1999; Blue Gold, 2000; Valhalla Rising, 2001; Fire Ice, 2002; Sea Hunters II, 2002; The Golden Buddha, 2003; White Death, 2003; Trojan Odyssey, 2003; Black Wind, 2004; Treasure of Khan, 2006. Honours: Numerous advertising awards; Lowell Thomas Award, New York Explorers Club. Memberships: Fellow, New York Explorers Club; Royal Geographical Society. Address: c/o Putnam Publishing Group, 2000 Madison Avenue, New York, NY 10016, USA.

CYWIŃSKI Zbigniew, b. 12 February 1929, Toruń, Poland. University Professor, Emeritus. m. Helena Wilczyńska, 11 April 1956, 1 son, 3 daughters. Education: Inż (BSc Eng), 1953; Mgr inż (MSc Eng), 1955; Dr inż (PhD Eng), 1964; Dr hab inż (DSc Eng), 1968; Professor, 1978. Appointments: Consulting Engineer, University of Baghdad, Iraq, 1965-66; Assistant Professor, University of Mosul, Iraq, 1970-73; UNESCO Expert, Ministry of Education, Mogadishu, Somalia, 1979-80; Professor, University of Tokyo, Japan, 1987-88; Vice Dean, 1975-78, Dean, 1984-87, 1993-99, Head, Structural Division, 1994-98, Faculty of Civil Engineering, Gdansk University of Technology. Publications: 3 textbooks, 2 books on structural mechanics; 2 monographs on bridges and on the TU Gdansk History; 363 published papers; 126 published reviews. Honours: Awards of the Minister of Education, 1964, 1976, 1978; Golden Cross of Merit, 1974; Cavalier Cross, 1980 and Officer's Cross, 1999, Poland's Rebirth Order; Medal, National Commission of Education, 1986; Gdańsk Millennium Medal, 1997. Memberships: Polish Society of Theoretical and Applied Mechanics, Regional Committee Head, 1990-92; International Association of Bridge and Structural Engineering, Alternate Delegate to

Permanent Committee, 1994-; Fellow, American Society of Civil Engineers; Polish Society of Bridge Engineers. Address: ul Mściwoja 50/32, 80-357, Gdańsk-Oliwa, Poland.

CZECZUGA-SEMENIUK Ewa, b. 13 April 1957, Mińsk, Belarus. Physician. m. Janusz Włodzimierz Semeniuk, 1 daughter. Education: PhD, Medicine, Medical University, Białystok, Poland, 1986. Appointments: Junior Researcher in Microbiology, 1982-83, Lecturer in Microbiology, 1983-85, Lecturer, 1985-2003, Senior Lecturer, Gynaecological Department, 2003-05, Senior Lecturer, Department of Reproduction and Gynaecological Endocrinology, 2005-, Medical University, Białystok, Poland. Publications: Numerous articles in professional scientific journals. Honours: Award I degree, 2000, Award II degree, 2005, Award I degree, 2006, Medical University, Białystok, Poland; Listed in national and international biographical dictionaries. Memberships: Polish Society of Gynaecology; Polish Society of Endocrinology; Polish Society of Menopause and Andropause. Address: Legionowa 9/54, 15-281, Białystok, Poland.

D

D'HEURLE Adma, b. 21 June 1924, Lebanon. Professor. m. Francois, 3 sons. Education: AB (distinction), University of Beirut, 1947; MA, Smith College, 1948; PhD, University of Chicago, 1953. Appointments: Lecturer, Social Thought, Slanford University, 1972-73; Adjunct Professor, Long Island University, 1975-80; Visiting Professor, University of Uppsala, Sweden, 1980-81; Visiting Adjunct Professor, University of Turku, Finland, 1987, 1989-96; Professor of Psychology, Mercy College, New York. Publications: Numerous articles in professional journals. Honours: Honoured Nominee for Professor of the Year, 1987; Fulbright Grant, 1987; Research Grant, Finnish Peace Institute, 1990; Outstanding Education of America, 1992; Special Recognition of Extraordinary Service to the Commission of Higher Education, 1994; Mercy College Teaching Excellence Award, 1995; Gold Medal for Distinguished Accomplishments in Psychology, Mercy College, 1998. Memberships: American Psychological Association; American Psychological Society; American Association of University Professors; Ibsen Association of America; Psychiatrists for Social Responsibility. Address: 1695 Spring Valley Road, Ossining, NY 10562, USA. E-mail: adamdh@gmail.com

D'AGUILAR Paul, b. 9 September 1924, London, England. Artist. Education: Educated privately in Spain, Italy and France; Trained by Professor Oscar Barblain, Sienna; Royal Academy Schools, 1949-54; Studied Conservation at the Courtauld Institute, London. Career: Artist in oil and watercolour; Critic and Reviewer, 1960-62; Travelled to Italy to restore pictures after the floods in Florence and Venice; Exhibitions: Leeds University, 1953; Daily Express Young Artists, 1953; Redfern and Leicester Galleries; National Society; Young Contemporaries; FPS; NEAC; RBA; Royal Academy; Biennal International de Cherbourg, France; Barcelona and Tarragona, Spain; St Ferme Abbey, Gironde, France, 1991; Retrospective Exhibition, Carlyle Gallery, Chelsea, London, 2003; Work in collections: Lord Rothermere; Wakefield and Bradford Educational Committees. Publication: Drawing Nudes (book), 1965. Honours: Bronze, Gold and Silver Medals, Royal Drawing Society; First Prize for drawing, Royal Academy; Leverhulme Scholarship. Address: 11 Sheen Gate Gardens, London SW14 7PD, England.

DA'LUZ VIEIRA-JONES Lorraine, b. 30 April 1955, London, England. Physician of Chinese Medicine; Lecturer; Chief Executive Officer. m. Schuyler Jones, 1 son, 1 daughter. Education: Lic. Ac. (Acupuncture, England), 1983; B Ac, 1986; M Ac, 1988; M St (Oxford), 1994; M Phil., distinction (Oxford), 1995; D Phil (Oxford), 1999; Dipl Ac (USA), 2002; DOM, Chelsea University, London, 2004; M Lett., 2005. Appointments: New Internationalist, 1979-80; World Information Service on Energy, 1980-83; Clinician and Consultant, Acupuncture Physician, 1982-; Lecturer, College of Traditional Acupuncture, England, 1984-97; Anthropology Adjunct Professor, Wichita State University, Kansas, USA, 1999-; Lecturer, Academy of 5 Element Acupuncture, Florida, USA, 2000-; Consultant and Lecturer Workshops, USA, 2000-; Chief Executive Officer, Healing Sanctuaries LLC, 2003-. Publication: The Credence Factor (book explaining placebo effect), forthcoming. Honours: Woman of the Year, 2004; International Peace Prize, 2004; Professional of the Year, 2005; Woman of Achievement, 2005. Memberships: Fellow, American Association of Integrative Medicine, 2002; Fellow, American Biographical Institute, 2003; American Association

of Oriental Medicine; Shakespeare Society, Wichita, USA. Address: The Prairie House, 1570 N Ridgewood Drive, Wichita, KS 67208, USA. E-mail: drlorijones@cs.com

DABBAGH Mohamed Aboul-Hay, b. 21 November 1937, Bethlehem, Palestine. Professor. m. Maha, 3 sons, 4 daughters. Education: AA, College of San Mateo, 1961; BA, San Jose State University, California, 1963; MA, University of California, Riverside, 1965; PhD, St Louis University, Missouri, 1974. Appointments: Adjunct Faculty, Florida Metropolitan University; Union College, Barbourville, Kentucky; Elmira College, Elmira, New York; Aba Dhabi Investment Authority, Abu Dhabi, United Arab Emirates; Economic advisor to different federal ministries. Publications: About 85 articles and book reviews. Honours: Listed in international biographical dictionaries. Memberships: American Economic Association; Southern Economic Association; Missouri Valley Economics Association; Global Awareness Society International. Address: 10309 Bloomfield Hills Dr, Seffner, FL 33584, USA. E-mail: ma_dabbagh@yahoo.com

DADIC Miroslav, b. 28 May 1932, Split, Croatia (Yugoslavia). Chemist (retired). Education: BSc, Chemistry, University of Zagreb, Croatia (Yugoslavia), 1955; PhD, Organic Chemistry, 1961; Postdoctoral work, MIT, Cambridge, Massachusetts, USA, 1964-67 and McGill University, Montreal, Canada, 1967-69. Appointments: Lecturer, University of Zagreb, 1956-64; External Associate, Institute Rudjer Boskovic, Zagreb, 1956-61; Research Associate, Department of Chemistry, MIT, Cambridge, Massachusetts, 1964-67; Postdoctoral Fellow, Chemical Department, McGill University, Montreal, Canada, 1967-69; Senior Research Chemist, R&D, Molson Co, Montreal & Toronto, 1969-90. Publications: 108 publications and patents since 1959, including: The Synthesis Of Oxygen Analogs Of Cepham. A New Bicyclic System, 1968; Phenolic Antioxidants as Potential Carcinostatic Agents, 1971; Beer Stability – A Key to Success in Brewing, 1984. Honours: Master Brewers Association of America Award of Merit, 1983. Past Memberships: American Chemical Society; Chemical Institute of Canada; Order of Chemists of Quebec; Association of Chemical Profession of Ontario; American Society of Brewing Chemists; New York Academy of Sciences. Address: 77 Gerard Street West #1204, Toronto, ON M5G 2A1, Canada.

DAEHNE Siegfried, b. 13 October 1929, Meissen, Saxony, Germany. Chemist. m. Anneliese Daehne Koelling, 2 sons, 1 daughter. Education: Study of Chemistry, 1949-57, Doctor's Degree, 1961, Habilitation, 1968, Humboldt University, Berlin; Venia Legendi, Technical University, Dresden, 1977. Appointments: Head of Laboratory, Institute of Optics and Spectroscopy, Berlin, 1957-62; Head of Department, 1963-84, Staff Member, 1985-87, Central Institute of Optics and Spectroscopy, Berlin; Head of Department, Analytical Centre, Academy of Sciences of the GDR, Berlin, 1988-91; Head of Laboratory, Federal Institute for Materials Research and Testing, Berlin, 1992-95; Head of Project, DFG Sonderforschungsbereich 337, Free University, Berlin, 1992-98; Consultant, Federal Institute for Materials Research and Testing, Berlin, 1996-2001. Publications: Over 260 research publications in professional journals; 9 patents in field of molecular spectroscopy, colour chemistry and supramolecular chemistry, with basic contributions to the mechanisms of spectral sensitization and desensitization in photography, 1965, 1967, theory of the ideal polymethine state, 1966, history of colour and constitution theories, 1970, 1978, structural principles of conjugated organic compounds (triad theory), 1977, 1985, 1990; Spontaneous and enantioselective generation of chiral J-aggregate helices from achiral cyanine dye molecules, 1996, 1997; Artificial light harvesting systems for photo-induced electron transfer reactions, 2003, 2006; Initiator, main author, Prognosis of Time-Resolved Spectroscopy, Berlin, 1968; Initiator and organiser, Annual Application Schools of Laser Pulse Spectrometry, Berlin, 1982-86; Fifth Symposium of Photochemistry, Reinhardsbrunn, 1986; NATO Advanced Research Workshop on Syntheses, Optical Properties and Applications of Near-Infrared Dyes in High Technology Fields, Trest, Czech Republic, 1997. Honours: Leibniz Medal of the Academy of Sciences of the GDR, 1976; Lieven Gevaert Medal, Society of Photographic Scientists and Engineers, USA, 1997. Memberships include: Society for German Chemists; European Photochemistry Association; German Bunsen Society of Physical Chemistry. Address: Kastanienallee 6, D-12587, Berlin, Germany.

DAESCU Constantin, b. 21 May 1943, Bucharest, Romania. Chemist; Professor. m. Ana-Elena, 25 November 1967, 1 son, 1 daughter. Education: Engineer, 1966, Doctorate Degree, 1977, Polytechnic University, Timisoara. Appointments: Assistant, 1966-77, Assistant Professor, 1977-89, Professor, 1990-, Polytech University, Timisoara. Publications include: Biosynthetic and Semisynthetic Products, 1982, 2006; Drugs Chemistry and Technology, 1994; Natural Fibrous Materials, 1996; Drug Industry, 1999, 2005; Print History, 2002; Dyeing and Printing, 2002. Honours: Listed in international biographical directories. Memberships: Romanian Chemical Society; New York Academy of Sciences, London Diplomatic Academy. Address: 11-13 Take Ionescu, 300062 Timisoara, Romania.

DAFINONE David Omueya, b. 12 March 1927. Senator; Chartered Accountant. Education: Diploma, Public Administration, University of Exeter, 1953; BSc, Economics, London University, 1958. Appointments: Numerous civil offices, including, Commissioner to investigate assets of public officers in Midwest State, Nigeria, 1967, 1968; Arbitrator, Federal Government of Nigeria under Ports Amendment Act, 1969; Appointment as Commissioner on Apapa Road Project Tribunal, Federal Government of Nigeria, 1970; Sole Commissioner to investigate Nigerian Pools Co. Ltd, 1971; Director, Central Bank of Nigeria, 1971-75; Chairman, D O Dafinone & Co (now Horwath Dafinone), 1966-97; Consultant, 1997-; Funding Consultant, Third Mainland Bridge Project, 1990-91; Numerous philanthropical and charitable roles. Honours: Elected Senator, Bendel South Senatorial Zone, Senator of the Federal Republic of Nigeria, 1979-83; Elected Fellow, National Geographical Society; Conferred with traditional title of Owhere I of Okpe Kingdom, for selfless service to the people, 1997; Certificate of Excellence for Professional Practice, Delta State Government, 1997; Entered in Guinness World Records as having the family with six practicing members of the Institute of Chartered Accountants in England and Wales, 2000; ICAN Certificate of Merit, Institute of Chartered Accountants of Nigeria, 2001; National Honour of the Officer of the Federal Republic of Nigeria OFR, 2003; Listed in: Who's Who in the Commonwealth; International Register of Profiles; Africa's Who's Who. Memberships: Numerous professional, charitable and political affiliations, including, Harvard Yale Centre for Cultural Studies, 2001; Secretary-General, United Cultural Convention, American Biographical Institute. Address: Ceddi Towers, 16 Wharf Road, Apapa, PO Box 2151, Marina, Lagos, Nigeria.

DAFOE Willem, b. 22 July 1955, Appleton, Wisconsin, USA. Actor. m. Giada Colagrande, 2005, 1 son from previous relationship. Education: Wisconsin University. Appointments: Actor, films include: The Loveless, New York Nights, 1981; The Hunger, 1982; Communists are Comfortable (and 3 other stories), Roadhouse 66, Streets of Fire, 1984; To Live and Die in LA, 1985; Platoon, 1986; The Last Temptation of Christ, Saigon, 1988; Mississippi Burning, Triumph of the Spirit, 1989; Born on the Fourth of July, Flight of the Intruder, Wild at Heart, 1990; The Light Sleeper, 1991; Body of Evidence, 1992; Far Away, So Close, Tom and Viv, The Night and the Moment, Clear and Present Danger, 1994; The English Patient, Basquiat, 1996; Speed 2: Cruise Control, Affliction, 1997; Lulu on the Bridge, Existenz, 1998; American Psycho, 1999; Shadow of the Vampire, Bullfighter, The Animal Factory, 2000; Edges of the Lord, 2001; Spider-Man, Auto Focus, 2002; Once Upon a Time in Mexico, 2003; The Clearing, The Reckoning, The Life Aquatic with Steve Zissou, The Aviator, 2004; xXx: State of the Union, Ripley Under Ground, Manderlay, Before It Had a Name, Ripley Under Ground, 2005; American Dreamz, Inside Man, Paris, je t'aime, 2006; The Walker, Mr Bean's Holiday, Spider-Man 3, Go Go Tales, Anamorph, 2007; Adam Resurrected, 2008; Fire Flies in the Garden, 2008. Address: c/o William Morris Agency, 1325 Avenue of the Americas, New York, NY 10019, USA.

DAHL Sophie, b. 1978. Fashion Model. Appointments: Discovered by Isabella Blow; Worked with fashion photographers: Nick Knight, David La Chapelle, Karl Lagerfeld, David Bailey, Enrique Badulescu, Herb Ritts and Ellen Von Unwerth; Appeared in: ID, The Face, Elle, Esquire, Scene magazines; Advertising campaigns for Lainey, Keogh, Bella Freud, Printemps, Nina Ricci, Karl Lagerfeld, Oil of Ulay, Hennes; Music videos for U2, Elton John, Duran Duran; Cameo appearances in films: Mad Cows, Best, 1999; Stage appearance in The Vagina Monologues, Old Vic Theatre, 1999; Judge, Orange Prize for Fiction, 2003. Publication: The Man with the Dancing Eyes, 2003. Address: c/o Storm Model Management, 5 Jubilee Place, London SW3 3TD, England.

DALAI LAMA The (Tenzin Gyatso), b. 6 July 1935, Taktser, Amdo Province, North East Tibet. Temporal and Spiritual Head of Tibet 14th Incarnation. Appointments: Enthroned at Lhasa, 1940; Rights exercised by regency, 1934-50; Assumed political power, 1950; Fled to Chumbi in South Tibet, 1950; Agreement with China, 1951; Vice-Chair, Standing Committee, Member, National Committee, CPPCC, 1951-59; Honorary Chairman, Chinese Buddhist Association, 1953-59; Delegate to National People's Congress, 1954-59; Chairman, Preparatory Committee for Autonomous Region of Tibet, 1955-59; Fled to India after suppression of Tibetan national uprising, 1959. Publications: My Land and People, 1962; The Opening of the Wisdom Eye, 1963; The Buddhism of Tibet and the Key to The Middle Way, 1975; Kindness, Charity and Insight, 1984; A Human Approach to World Peace, 1984; Freedom in Exile (autobiography), 1990; The Good Heart, 1996; Ethics for the New Millennium, 1998; Art of Happiness, (co-author), 1999; A Simple Path: basic Buddhist Teachings by His Holiness the Dalai Lama, 2000; Stages of Meditation: training the Mind for Wisdom, 2002; The Spirit of Peace, 2002. Honours: Dr Buddhist Philos (Monasteries of Sera, Drepung and Gaden, Lhasa), 1959; Supreme Head of all Buddhist sections in Tibet; Memory Prize, 1989; Congressional Human Rights Award, 1989; Nobel Prize, 1989; The Freedom Award (USA), 1991. Address: Thekchen Choeling, McLeod Ganj 176219, Dharamsala, Himachal Pradesh, India.

DALBY John Mark Meredith, b. 3 January 1938, Southport, Lancashire. Clergyman. Education: MA, Exeter College, Oxford; Ripon Hall, Oxford; PhD, University of Nottingham. Appointments: Ordained Deacon, 1963, Priest, 1964, Oxford;

Curate of the Hambledon Valley Group, 1963-68; Vicar of St Peter, Spring Hill, Birmingham, 1968-75; Rural Dean of Birmingham City, 1973-75; Secretary of the Committee for Theological Education, Advisory Council for the Church's Ministry, also Honorary Curate of All Hallows, Tottenham, 1975-80; Vicar, later Team Rector of Worsley, 1980-91; Rural Dean of Eccles, 1987-91; Archdeacon of Rochdale, 1991-2000; Chaplain of the Beauchamp Community, Newland, 2000-. Publications: Open Communion in the Church of England, 1959; The Gospel and the Priest, 1975; Tottenham: Church and Parish, 1979; The Cocker Connection, 1989; Open Baptism, 1989; Anglican Missals and their Canons, 1998; Infant Communion: The New Testament to the Reformation, 2003. Address: St Christopher's, The Beauchamp Community, Newland, Malvern, Worcestershire WR13 5AX, England. E-mail: jmmdalby@btinternet.com

DALE Jim (James Smith), b. 15 August 1935. Actor. m. 3 sons, 1 daughter. Education: Kettering Grammar School; Musical Hall Comedian, 1951; Singing, compering, directing, 1951-61; First film appearance, 1965; Theatre: The Card, 1973; The Taming of the Shrew, 1974; Scapino, 1974; Barnum, 1980; Joe Egg, 1985; Me and My Girl, 1987-88; Candide, 1997; Privates on Parade; Travels with My Aunt, 1995; Fagin in Oliver! 1995-97; Host, Sunday Night at the London Palladium, TV show, 1994; Lyricist for film, Georgy Girl; Films include: Lock Up Your Daughters; The Winter's Tale; The Biggest Dog in the World; National Health; Adolf Hitler – My Part in his Downfall; Joseph Andrews; Pete's Dragon; Hot Lead Cold Feet; Bloodshy; The Spaceman and King Arthur; Scandalous; Carry On Cabby; Carry On Cleo; Carry On Jack; Carry On Cowboy; Carry On Screaming; Carry On Spying; Carry On Constable; Carry On Doctor; Carry On Don't Lose Your Head; Carry On Follow That Camel; Carry On Columbus, 1992; Hunchback of Notre Dame, 1997. Honours: Tony Award, 1980. Address: c/o Sharon Bierut, CED, 257 Park Avenue South, New York, NY 10010, USA.

DALE Peter Grenville Hurst, b. 14 February 1935, Newcastle upon Tyne, England. Architect. 3 sons. Education: Diploma in Architecture, Durham University, 1961; MA, Architecture, Leeds Metropolitan University, 1994; Certificate in Construction,1958; Certificate in Town Planning, 1970. Appointments: County Architect, Humberside, 1977-85; Senior Lecturer, Leeds Metropolitan University; Professor of Architecture, University of Leeds, 1993-; Honorary Fellow, London College of Management/Information Technology. Publications: 4 Royal Institute of British Architects Training Manuals, 1991 (re-edited 1997); 10 archaeological magazine editorials. Honours: 33 national, regional and local awards; Chairman, Construction Industry Research, Department of the Environment, 1991/1997; Chairman, European Union, Construction Harmonisation Technology, 1997-. Memberships: Chairman, British Brick Association, 2004; Cordwainers Guild; Builders Guild; Freeman of England and Wales. Address: 19 Mile End Park, Pocklington, York YO42 2TH, England.

DALGLISH Kenneth (Kenny) Mathieson, b. 4 March 1951, Glasgow, Scotland. Football Manager. m. Marina, 4 children. Appointments: Played for Celtic, Scottish League Champions, 1972-74, 1977; Scottish Cup Winners, 1972, 1974, 1975, 1977; Scottish Cup Winners, 1972, 1974, 1975, 1977; Scottish league Cup winners, 1975; Played for Liverpool, European Cup Winners, 1978, 1981, 1984; FA Cup Winners, 1986, 1989; League Cup winners, 1981-84; Manager, 1986-91; Manager Blackburn Rovers, 1991-97; Newcastle United, 1997-98; Director of Football Operations, Celtic, 1999-2000; 102 full

caps for Scotland scoring 30 goals. Honours: Footballer of the Year, 1979, 1983; MBE; Freeman of Glasgow; 3 times Manager of the Year; Scottish Sports Hall of Fame, 2001; Scottish Football Hall of Fame, 2004. Address: c/o Celtic Football Club, Celtic Park, Glasgow, G40 3RE, Scotland.

DALLI Alex, b. 28 April 1958, Birkirkara, Malta. Painter. m. Anna, 2 sons. Education: Commenced art studies under George Fenech; Continued studies under Esprit Barthet and Harry Alden, School of Art, 1974-80; Studied History of Art/ Appreciation under Fr Marius Zerafa. Appointments: Personal Exhibitions: Nghinu bl-Arti, 1984; Fine Arts Museum, Valletta, 1989, 1992, 1994, 1996, 2006; New Dolmen Hotel, Qawra, 1998; Les Lapins, Ta Xbiex, 2000; German Maltese Circle, 2000; Galleria Complex, Fgura, 2000; Civic Centre, Zabbar, 2001; Gallerija il-Foyer, Hamrun, 2002; Vee Gee Bee Art Gallery (jointly with William Azzopardi), Valletta, 2004; Collective Exhibitions include: Art Exhibition, St James Cavalier, Valletta, 2000; De Kring Art Club, Amsterdam, 2004; Contemporary Maltese Art, Allard Pierson Museum, Amsterdam, 2004; Art Exhibition, Wine and Vineyards, Gallery G Lija, 2005; Collective Art Exhibition, The Holy Eucharist, Wignacourt Museum, Rabat, 2005; Six Generation of Maltese Contemporary Artists, Valletta Waterfront, 2005; Contemporary Art Exhibition, Museum of Archaeology, Valletta, 2005; The Arts Directory Malta Collective Exhibition, Phoenix Gallery, 2006. Publications: Works included in: Maltese Biographies of the 20th Century, 1997; The International Dictionary of Artists who painted Malta, 1988, 2nd edition 2002; Malta this month, 2000; Art in Malta Today, 2000; Numerous other reviews in local media. Honours: Works held in private collections around the world including Malta, Holland, UK, Brussels, USA and Australia. Address: 36 Guernica, Triq il Pellegrinagg tar-Ruti, Zabbar, Malta. E-mail: alexdalli@hotmail.com

DALRYMPLE William Benedict, b. 20 March 1965, Edinburgh, Scotland. Writer. m. Olivia Fraser, 2 sons, 1 daughter. Education: Exhibitioner, 1984, Senior History Scholar, 1986, MA, Honours, 1992, Trinity College, Cambridge; D Lit, St Andrews, 2006. Appointments: Author, 1989-. Publications: In Xanadu, 1989; City of Djinns, 1993; From the Holy Mountain, 1997; The Age of Kali, 1998; White Mughals, 2002; The Last Mughal, 2006. Contributions to: Times Literary Supplement; New Statesman; New Yorker; New York Review of Books; Guardian. Honours: Yorkshire Post, Best First Work Award, 1990; Scottish Arts Council, 1990; Thomas Cook, Travel Book Award, 1994; Sunday Times, Young British Writer of the Year, 1994; Scottish Arts Council Autumn Book Award, 1997; Grierson Award for Best Documentary, 2002; Wolfson Prize for History, 2003; Scottish Book of the Year, 2003; Mungo Park Medal (RSGS), 2003; Prix D'Astrolabe, 2005; Percy Sykes Medal (RSAA), 2005; FPA Media Award, Print Article of the Year, 2005. Memberships: FRSL, 1993; FRGS, 1993; FRAS, 1998; PEN, 1998. Address: 1 Pages' Yard, Church Street, London W4 2PA, England. E-mail: wdalrymple1@aol.com

DALTON Ann, b. 28 October 1933, East Sussex, England. Trainer in Broadcast Communications and Coloratura Soprano Soloist for classical, folk, cabaret and operatic concerts and recitals; BBC Programme Producer, Studio Manager and simultaneous Voluntary Radio and TV Communications Trainer to benefit mainly Third World Needs; Accredited Chaperone for children performing on stage (Glyndebourne Opera House and Talisman Film Company). Education: BBC Programme and Engineering Training Colleges, Evesham & Marylebone Road; Guildhall School of Music and Drama Performance Certificate (singing); Piano & Cello Grade V, Royal Academy of Music; City & Guilds Teaching Certificate. Appointments: Producer and Studio Manager, British Broadcasting Corporation, London, 1955-89; Seconded via BBC International Relations Department to be Head of Training and Operations (later Director, External Affairs) for the International Radio and TV Training Centre at Hatch End, Middlesex, to assist Third World and other communicators, 1972-89; Voluntary vocational assistance as Co-Founder and Manager of this centre (while off-duty from the BBC), 1955-72; Lecturer, Loyola University Summer Communications Courses, USA, 1973-76; Organiser, British Radio & TV UNDA Festivals and competitions to encourage the pursuit of excellence and to provide a forum for debate; Jury Member, Prix d'Italia UNDA-TV Awards, 1978; Jury Member, Sandford St Martin TV awards, 1987; Selected as Mass Media Commission Representative to present Loyal Address at Buckingham Palace, 1981; Broadcasters' Liaison Assistant, Rome, 1980-85; Various appearances on radio and television broadcasts; Selected singing candidate in the English National Opera TV series, "Operatunity", 2002; First solo singing broadcast live from BBC Concert Hall, accompanied by Dr George Thalben-Ball; Selected Classical Soloist for Gala Re-Opening of the De La Warr Pavilion, Bexhill, Sussex, 2005. Honours: Pro Ecclesia Cross, 1981; Woman of the Year Award, 1987; Seven Championship Awards from Sussex Singing Contests, 2000-2007; Two Gold Medals for Singing, Eastbourne, 2001, 2005; Listed in: Great Women of the 21st Century; Women of Achievement; International Peace Prize, United Cultural Convention; Great Minds of the 21st Century; UCC Legion of Honor; Hall of Fame; Dictionary of International Biography; Cambridge Blue Book, 2007; Order of International Ambassadors, ABI. Memberships: Fellow, Royal Society of Arts; Royal Television Society; Radio Academy; Association of Independent Producers; Advisory Council for Local Broadcasting; UNDA-World Association for Broadcast Communicators; Consultative Council for Animal Welfare; Associate, Institute of Qualified Private Secretaries; Environmental and Animal Carers. Address: 13 Warrior Square, St Leonards-on-Sea, East Sussex, TN37 6BA, England.

DALTON Timothy, b. 21 March 1946. Actor. Education: Royal Academy of Dramatic Art. Career includes: National Youth Theatre; Theatre includes: Toured with Prospect Theatre Company; Guest Artist, RSC; Co-starred with Vivien Merchant in Noel Coward's The Vortex; Anthony and Cleopatra, The Taming of the Shrew, 1986; A Touch of the Poet, Young Vic, 1988; Lord Asriel in Philip Pullman's His Dark Materials, National Theatre, 2003-04; Films include: The Lion in Winter, 1968; Cromwell, 1970; Wuthering Heights; Mary, Queen of Scots, 1972; Permission to Kill, 1975; The Man Who Knew Love; Sextette, 1977; Agatha, 1978; Flash Gordon, 1979; James Bond in The Living Daylights, 1987 and Licence to Kill, 1989; The Rocketeer, 1991; The Reef, The Beautician and the Beast, 1996; Made Men, Cleopatra, 1998; Possessed, 1999; American Outlaws, 2001; Looney Tunes – Back in Action, 2002; Hot Fuzz, 2007; TV roles include: Mr Rochester in Jane Eyre, BBC TV, 1983; Master of Ballentrae, HTV, 1983; Mistral's Daughter, TV mini-series, 1984; Florence Nightingale, TV mini-series; Sins, TV mini-series, 1985; Philip von Joel in Framed, mini-series, Anglia TV, 1992; Jack in Red Eagle; Rhett Butler in Scarlett, Sky, 1994; Salt Water Moose, comedy, 1995; The Informant, 1996; Cleopatra, 1998; Possessed, 1999; Time Share, 2000; Hercules, 2004; Dunkirk, 2005; Marple: The Sittaford Mystery, 2006. Membership: Actors' Equity. Address: c/o ICM, Oxford House, 76 Oxford Street, London W1D 1BS, England.

DALTREY David Joseph, b. 30 December 1951, London, England. Session Musician (guitar and piano); Guitar Tutor; Composer. Education: Guildhall School of Music and Drama; ALCM, London College of Music, 1969-72; City and Guilds, Adult Teacher Training, 1985-87. Appointments: Recording artist with EMI and DECCA; Worked for BBC, London; Composer; Producer; Session Musician; Tutor; Audio Consultant. Recordings: Tales of Justine-Albert/Monday Morning, UK, 1967; Joseph And The Amazing Technicolour Dreamcoat, UK 1969, USA 1971; Petals from a Sunflower, UK, 1998; The Wayfarer, UK, 2004. Honours: Gold Record, Scepter Records, USA, 1971. Memberships: Musicians' Union; Incorporated Society of Musicians; Audio Engineering Society; Institute of Acoustics, MIOA; Music Producer's Guild; Radio Academy; Institute of Sound and Communications Engineers, MISCE; Institute of Broadcast Sound, MIBS. Address: 76A Guildhall Street, Bury St Edmunds, Suffolk IP33 1QD, England. E-mail: yazzpeachey@aol.com Website: www.byor.com

DALY Peter Eugene, b. 21 July 1935. Company Director. m. Daphne Lilian, 1958, 1 son, 1 daughter. Appointments: Chairman, Ombudsman Service Ltd; Chairman, Financial Industry Complaints Service Ltd; Chairman, Aldersgale Finance Pty Ltd; Deputy Chairman, Gerling Australia Insurance Co Pty Ltd. Honour: AM. Address: Norwin, 2 Jacov Gardens, Templestowe, VIC 3106, Australia.

DALYELL Tam, b. 9 August 1932, Edinburgh, Scotland. Member of Parliament; Writer. m. Kathleen Wheatley, 26 December 1963, 1 son, 1 daughter. Education: Harecroft Hall, Eton; King's College, Cambridge, 1952-56. Appointments: Elected to House of Commons, 1962-2005; Father of the House of Commons, 2001-05. Publications: The Case for Ship Schools, 1958; Ship School Dunera, 1961; One Man's Falklands, 1982; A Science Policy for Britain, 1983; Misrule: How Mrs Thatcher Deceived Parliament, 1987; Dick Crossman: A Portrait, 1988. Contributions to: Weekly Columnist, New Scientist, 1967-; Many Obituaries, Independent Newspaper. Honours: Various Awards of Science; Honorary Doctor of Science, University of Edinburgh, 1994; Honorary Degree, City University, London, 1998; Trustee, History of Parliament, 1999-2005; Chairman, All-Party Latin America Group, 1999-2004; St Andrew's University, 2003; Napier University, Edinburgh, 2004; Northumbria University, 2005; Honorary Doctorate: Stirling University, 2006, Open University, 2006. Address: Binns, Linlithgow, EH44 7NA, Scotland.

DAMON Matt, b. 8 October 1970, Cambridge, Massachusetts, USA. Actor. Appointments: Film actor, Films include: Mystic Pizza, 1988; School Ties, 1992; Geronimo: An American Legend, 1993; Courage Under Fire, Glory Daze, 1996; Chasing Amy, The Rainmaker, Good Will Hunting (also co-writer), 1997; Saving Private Ryan, Rounders, 1998; Dogma, The Talented Mr Ripley (voice), All The Pretty Horses, 1999; The Legend of Bagger Vance, Finding Forrester, 2000; Ocean's Eleven, The Majestic (voice), 2001; Gerry (also writer), Spirit: Stallion of the Cimarron (voice), The Third Wheel, The Bourne Identity, 2002; Confessions of a Dangerous Mind, Stuck on You, 2003; Eurotrip, Jersey Girl, The Bourne Supremacy, Ocean's Twelve, 2004; The Brothers Grimm, Syriana, 2005; The Good Shepherd, 2006; Ocean's Thirteen, Margaret, The Bourne Ultimatum, Youth Without Youth, 2007; TV: Rising Son, 1990; The Good Old Boys, 1995. Honours: Empire Film Award for Best Actor, 2005. Address: Creative Artists Agency, 9830 Wilshire Boulevard, Beverly Hills, CA 90212, USA.

DANCE Charles, b. 10 October 1946, Rednal, Worcestershire, England. Actor. m. Joanna Haythorn, 1970, 1 son, 1 daughter. Appointments: Formerly employed in industry; with RSC, 1975-80, 1980-85; TV appearances include: The Fatal Spring; Nancy Astor; Frost in May; Saigon - The Last Day; Thunder Rock (drama); Rainy Day Women; The Jewel in the Crown (nominated for Best Actor BAFTA Award); The Secret Servant; The McGuffin; The Phantom of the Opera, 1989; Rebecca, 1996; In the Presence of Mine Enemies; The Ends of the Earth, Bleak House, 2004; Fingersmith, Last Rights, 2005; Consulting Adults, 2007; Films include: For Your Eyes Only; Plenty; The Golden Child; White Mischief; Good Morning Babylon; Hidden City; Pascali's Island, 1988; China Moon, 1990; Alien III, Limestone, 1991; Kabloonak; Century; Last Action Hero; Exquisite Tenderness, Short Cut to Paradise, 1993; Undertow; Michael Collins; Space Trucker, 1996; Goldeneye; The Blood Oranges; What Rats Won't Do; Hilary and Jackie, 1998; Don't Go Breaking My Heart, Jurij, 1999; Dark Blue World, 2000; Gosford Park, Ali G in da House, 2001; Black and White, 2002; Swimming Pool, Labyrinth, 2003; Ladies in Lavender (writer/director), 2005; Dolls, Scoop, Twice Upon a Time, 2006; Intervention, 2007; Theatre: Coriolanus (title role), RSC, 1989; Irma La Douce; Turning Over; Henry V; Three Sisters, 1998; Good, 1999; Long Day's Journey Into Night, Radio: The Heart of the Matter, The Charge of the Light Brigade, 2001; The Play What I Wrote, 2002; Address: c/o ICM, Oxford House, 76 Oxford Street, London, W1D 1BS, England.

DANDY Gillian Margaret (Gill), b. 17 August 1957, Ely, Cambridgeshire, England. Public Relations Consultant. Education: Birmingham College of Food and Domestic Arts, 1976-79. Appointments: Harrison Cowley Public Relations Ltd, Birmingham, 1980-83; Associate Director, Leslie Bishop Company, 1983-90; Director, Shandwick Communications, 1990-96; Director of Development and PR, London Bible College, 1990-2002; Communications Director, Evangelical Alliance, 2002-04; Non-Executive Director, Shared Interest Society Limited, 2004-. Memberships: Fellow, Chartered Institute of Public Relations; Fellow, Royal Society for the Encouragement of the Arts. Address: 56 Southerton Road, Hammersmith, London, W6 0PH, England. E-mail: gill.dandy@btinternet.com

DANES Claire, b. 12 April 1979, New York, USA. Film Actress. Education: Performing arts school, New York; Lee Strasburg Studio. Appointments: 1st acting roles in off-Broadway theatre productions: Happiness; Punk Ballet; Kids on Stage; Films: Dreams of Love (debut), 1992; Thirty (short), 1993; The Pesky Suitor (short); Little Women, 1994; Romeo and Juliet, To Gillian on Her 37th Birthday, 1996; Polish Wedding, U Turn, The Rainmaker, 1997; Les Misérables, 1998; The Mod Squad, Brokedown Place, 1999; Monteret Pop, Dr T and the Women, Flora Plum, 2000; The Cherry Orchard, Igby Goes Down, The Hours, 2002; Terminator 3: Rise of the Machines, 2003; Stage Beauty, 2004; Shopgirl, The Family Stone, 2005; Evening, The Flock, Stardust, 2007. TV: My So-Called Life (series); No Room for Opal (Film); The Coming Out of Heidi Leiter.

DANH Phan Thi, b. 17 December 1954, Kien Giang, Vietnam. Head of Clinical Biochemistry. m. Le Ngoc Thach, 2 sons. Education: BSc, Biochemistry, 1976; PhD, Clinical Biochemistry, 1990 University of Medicine, Prague; Certificate of Pharmacology, 1994; Certificate of Clinical Toxicology, 1999; Hospital Management Program, Singapore Management University, Singapore, 2006. Appointments: Head of Clinical Biochemistry, Pharmacology, Toxicology,

Immunology and Molecular Biology, Choray Hospital, Ho Chi Minh City, Vietnam. Publications: Articles in medical journals including: Monitoring the efficacy of erythropoietin in treatment of anemia in patients with chronic renal failures, 2006; Application of biochip technology in clinical biochemistry tests and the clinical values of cytokines, 2006; The role of biomarker of monoethylglycinexiylidide (MEGX) in diagnosis and prognosis in patients with liver cirrhosis or liver cancer, 2006; Case report: death due to injection of oil silicone for breast augmentation, 2006; Evaluation of the blood lipid concentrations in the vegetarian persons in Vietnam, 2006; Evaluation of the tumor marker, Cyfra 21-1, in patients with lung cancer, 2006. Honour: Regional Service Award for the abstract: Comparison of Serum Lipid Levels in People on Vegan and Non-Vegan Diets in Vietnam, 7th APCCB Congress News Bangkok, Thailand, 1995. Memberships: AACC; VNCC. Address: Choray Hospital, 201B Nguyen Chi Thanh St, District 5, Ho Chi Minh City, Vietnam. E-mail: danhpt03@yahoo.com

DANIEL Milan, b. 14 June 1931, Horazdovice, Czech Republic. Scientific Worker in Parasitology. m. Vlasta Pacakova, 1 son, 1 daughter. Education: RNDr, Charles University, Prague, 1956; PhD, 1959; DSc, 1987. Appointments: Assistant Professor, Charles University, Prague, 1954-55; Scientific Worker, Czech Academy of Sciences, Prague, 1956-86, Postgraduate Medical School, Prague, 1987-; Consultant, National Institute of Public Health, Prague, 2000-. Publications: Over 240 articles in scientific journals and 14 books including titles: Biomathematic Study on the Nest Environment of Susliks Citellus citellus, 1983; Small Mammals in Eastern Part of Nepal Himalaya, 1985; Mesostigmatid Mites in Nests of Small Terrestrial Mammals and Features of their Environment, 1988; Medical Entomology and Environment, 1989; Life and Death at the Summits of World; Secret Paths of Disease Vectors. Honours: Award, Czech Academy of Sciences, 1985; Award, Czech Literary Foundation, 1990. Memberships: Czech Society of Parasitology; New York Academy of Sciences. Address: Tomanova 64, CZ-169 00 Prague 6, Czech Republic.

DANIEL Reginald, b. 7 December 1939, London, England. Ophthalmic Surgeon. m. Carol Bjorck, 1 son, 1 daughter. Education: University of London, 1959-64; Westminster Hospital Medical School, 1961-64; MB BS, 1964; LRCP, 1964; FRCS, 1970; DO Eng, 1968; AKC, 1960; FRCOphth, 1988. Appointments: Chief Clinical Assistant, Moorfields Eye Hospital; Senior Registrar, Moorfields Eye Hospital; Teacher to University of London; Consultant Ophthalmic Surgeon, Guy's and St Thomas' Hospitals; Consultant Ophthalmic Surgeon, Private Practice, Harley Street, London. Publications: Author of many papers on retinal detachments, cataracts, corneal pathology and squints; Author of ophthalmic chapters in general surgical and medical reference books. Honour: Freeman of the City of London. Memberships: American Academy of Ophthalmology; Ophthalmic Society, UK; European Intraocular Implant Society; Contemporary Society of Ophthalmology in the USA; Moorfields Hospital Surgeons Society; Liveryman, Worshipful Company of Spectacle Makers; City of London Livery Club. Address: 144 Harley Street, London, W1G 7LD, England. E-mail: regandcarol@aol.com

DANIELS Jeff, b. 19 February 1955, Athens, Georgia, USA. Actor. m. Kathleen Treado, 1979, 3 children. Education: Central Michigan University. Appointments: Apprentice Circle Repertory Theatre, New York; Founder, Purple Rose Theatre Company, Chelsea, Michigan; Theatre: The Farm,

1976; Brontosaurus, My Life, Feedlot, 1977; Lulu, Slugger, The Fifth of July, 1978; Johnny Got His Gun (Obie Award), 1982; The Three Sisters, 1982-83; The Golden Age, 1984; Redwood Curtain, Short-Changed Review, 1993; Lemon Sky; Films: Ragtime, 1981; Terms of Endearment, 1983; The Purple Rose of Cairo, Marie, 1985; Heartburn, Something Wild, 1986; Radio Days, 1987; The House on Carroll Street, Sweet Hearts Dance, 1988; Grand Tour, Checking Out, 1989; Arachnophobia, Welcome Home, Roxy Carmichael, Love Hurts, 1990; The Butcher's Wife, 1992; Gettysburg, 1993; Speed, Dumb and Dumber, 1994; Fly Away Home, Two Days in the Valley, 101 Dalmatians, 1996; Trial and Error, 1997; Pleasantville, All the Rage, My Favourite Martian, 1999; Chasing Sleep, Escanaba in da Moonlight, 2000; Super Sucker, Blood Work, The Hours, Gods and Generals, 2002; I Witness, 2003; Imaginary Heroes, 2004; The Squid and the Whale, Because of Winn-Dixie, The Squid and the Whale, Good Night, and Good luck, 2005; RV, Infamous, 2006; The Lookout, Mama's Boy, A Plumm Summer, 2007; TV films: A Rumor of War, 1980; Invasion of Privacy, 1983; The Caine Mutiny Court Martial, 1988; No Place Like Home, 1989; Disaster in Time, 1992; Redwood Curtain, 1995; Teamster Boss: The Jackie Presser Story; (specials) Fifth of July; The Visit (Trying Times). Publications: Author, Plays: Shoeman, 1991; The Tropical Pickle, 1992; The Vast Difference, 1993; Thy Kingdom's Coming, 1994; Escanaba in da Moonlight, 1995; The Goodbye Girl, The Five People You Meet in Heaven, 2004. Address: Purple Rose Theatre, 137 Park Street, Chelsea, MI 48118, USA. Website: www.purplerosetheatre.org

DANILOV Gennady Stepanovich, b. 26 March 1935, St Petersburg, Russia. Physicist. m. Kotova Lidya Michajlovna, 1 son, 1 daughter. Education: PhD, 1964, DSc, 1976, Institute of Theoretical and Experimental Physics, Moscow. Appointments: Researcher, 1959-66, Senior Researcher, 1966-71, Physics Technical Institute, St Petersburg; Senior Researcher, 1971-86, Leading Researcher, 1986-, Head of Group, St Petersburg Nuclear Physics Institute. Publications: Several articles for professional journals. Address: St Petersburg Nuclear Physics Institute, 188350 Gatchina, Leningrad district, Russia. E-mail: danilov@thd.pnpi.spb.ru

DANN Colin Michael, b. 10 March 1943, Richmond, Surrey, England. Author. m. Janet Elizabeth Stratton, 4 June 1977. Publications: The Animals of Farthing Wood, 1979; In the Grip of Winter, 1981; Fox's Feud, 1982; The Fox Cub Bold, 1983; The Siege of White Deer Park, 1985; The Ram of Sweetriver, 1986; King of the Vagabonds, 1987; The Beach Dogs, 1988; The Flight from Farthing Wood, 1988; Just Nuffin, 1989; In the Path of the Storm, 1989; A Great Escape, 1990; A Legacy of Ghosts, 1991; The City Cats, 1991; Battle for the Park, 1992; The Adventure Begins, 1994; Copycat, 1997; Nobody's Dog, 1999; Journey to Freedom, 1999; Lion Country, 2000; Pride of The Plains, 2002. Honour: Arts Council National Award for Children's Literature, 1980. Membership: Society of Authors. Address: Castle Oast, Ewhurst Green, East Sussex, England.

DANNER Karl Heinz (né Roeckel von Huebner), b. 25 February 1940, Rodalben, Rhineland-Palatinate, Germany. Author; Poet; Cultural Mediator; Educator. m. Ingrid Karola Danner-Jekel, 1972. Education: German and Canadian Junior and Senior Matriculation, 1957, 1962, 1964, 1967 (Abitur), Pirmasens, Sudbury, Saarbruecken; BA, Laurentian University, Canada, 1964-65, 1981-82; Diplomas, Universities of Madrid and Salamanca, 1978 and 1981; Master of Arts, University of the Saarland, Germany, 1976; State Teaching Certificates, Universities of Mayence (Mainz) and Trèves (Trier), 1978, 1979, 1981, 1984; Licence/Maîtrise ès Lettres, University

of Toulouse-Le Mirail, France, 1984-86; Secondary School Honour Diploma, Diplôme d'études secondaires supérieures, Toronto, Canada, 1986; Master and Doctor of Education, Pacific Western University, Los Angeles, California, 1986, 1988; Doctor of Philosophy, Doctor of Literature, American University, 1990, 1994; Professor h.c; Doctor of Philosophy, University of London, 2007; Spiritual Education by Roberto Walser, Gabriel Marcel, Albert Schweitzer, Swami Ragagopalan, Doris Zoells; Willigis Jaeger, Clemens Kuby, Ernst Schoenwiese, Dalai Lama, Benedetto XVI, Martin Luther King. Appointments include: Teacher, Modern Languages and Literature, Canada and West Germany; Research Assistant, Associate and Lecturer, University of the Saarland, Germany, 1965-76; Lecturer and Senior Lecturer, Modern Languages, Education Authority, Regional Government of the Palatinate, Germany, 1978-2002; Student Exchange Organiser and Liaison Teacher, Exchanges in France and England; Adviser Partner for Cultural Exchange/Relations, 1989-; Founding Member, Member of the Board, General Secretary, International Robert Musil Society, Austria; Founder, President of German-Latin American Friendship Associations, 1989-; Member, Accademia Culturale d'Europa, Italy, 1989; Counsellor on German Culture in Europe and Overseas, 1991-; Extensive travelling and lecturing in Europe & the Americas, 1965-2005; Honorary Member, Societé de Philosophie, France, 1994; Member of Pontificia Academia, Vatican, Rome, 1996-; Member, Jury of National Foreign Language Competition; Curator of Literature exhibitions, 1965-77; Humanity Educator (Philogist). Publications: Poetry in English, French, German and German translations from Catalan, English, French, Portuguese, Spanish; Essays, reviews and studies on modern German, English, French, Portuguese/ Brazilian and Spanish literature; Over 1,300 articles in periodicals, Europe and the Americas; Research Publications; Didactics of Modern Languages; Emigration of German-speaking Europeans; 25 papers, dissertations, treatise in Humanities, documentations. Honours include: Prose Prize, Sudbury High School, Canada; Scholarship, University of Sudbury, Ontario, Canada, 1964; Poetry Prize, Laurentian University, Canada, 1965; Scholarship, Universidad de Salamanca, Spain, 1981; Medal of Merit of the Capital of Carinthia, Austria, 1984; Order of Carinthia, Austria, 1989; Festschrift/publication honouring K H Danner, When I Think Upon Friendship (in 5 modern European languages), 1990; National Citation Award, USA, 1999; Medaglia d'Oro, Instituto Europeo di Cultura, Italy, 1989; Medal and Plaque, Universidad de Salamanca, 1989 and 2003; Honorary President, German Federation of Folklore, 1993; Commander of the Order of National Merit, 1995; Doctor of Philosophy, honoris causa, International Christian University, 1999; Honorary Pin of Merit by the German Folklore Federation,2002; Certificates, diplomas and awards from IBC, UK and ABI, USA; Listed in national and international biographical directories. Memberships: German Schiller Society; German-Indian Children's Fund; Modern Language Association; Sponsor of Cultural, Literary & Academic Institutions in Austria, Brazil, Canada, Cuba, France, Germany, Spain, Israel and USA; Research Advisor, Cambridge, North & South America, Europe; German Folklore Federation. Address: Casa Carola, Burgstrasse 107, D 66955 Pirmasens, Germany.

DANSON Ted, b. 29 December 1947, San Diego, California, USA. Actor. m. (1) Randell L Gosch, divorced, (2) Cassandra Coates, 1977, divorced, 2 daughters, (3) Mary Steenburgen, 1995, 1 stepdaughter, 1 stepson. Education: Stanford University; Carnegie-Mellon University. Appointments: Teacher, The Actor's Institute, Los Angeles, 1978; Star, NBC-TV series Cheers, 1982-93; CEO Anasazi Productions

(Formerly Danson/Fauci Productions); Off-Broadway plays include: The Real Inspector Hound, 1972; Comedy of Errors; Actor, producer TV films including: When the Bough Breaks, 1986; We Are The Children, 1987; Executive Producer TV films: Walk Me to the Distance, 1989; Down Home, 1989; Mercy Mission: The Rescue of Flight 771, 1993; On Promised Land, 1994; Other appearances in TV drama; Films include: The Onion Field, 1979; Body Heat, 1981; Creepshow, 1983; A Little Treasure, 1985; A Fine Mess, 1986; Just Between Friends, 1986; Three Men and a Little Lady, 1990; Made in America, 1992; Getting Even With Dad, 1993; Pontiac Moon, 1993; Gulliver's Travels (TV), 1995; Loch Ness, 1996; Homegrown, 1998; Thanks of a Grateful Nation, 1998; Saving Private Ryan, 1998; Becker, 1998; Mumford, 1999; Fronterz, 2004; Our Fathers, 2005; The Moguls, 2005; Bye Bye Benjamin, 2006; Nobel Son, 2007; Mad Money, 2008. Address: c/o Josh Liberman, Creative Artists Agency, 9830 Wilshire Boulevard, Beverly Hills, CA 90212, USA.

DARLING Rt Hon Alistair, b. 28 November 1953, London, England. Chancellor of the Exchequer. m. Margaret Vaughan, 2 children. Education: Loretto School, Musselburgh; LLB, Aberdeen University. Appointments: Solicitor, Edinburgh, 1978; Called to Scottish Bar and admitted to the Faculty of Advocates, 1984; Member, Lothian Regional Council, 1982; Chairman, Council's Transport Committee; Elected to Parliament for Edinburgh Central, later Edinburgh South West, 1987-; Member, Opposition Home Affairs Team, 1988-92; Opposition Spokesman on the City and Financial Services, 1992-96; Shadow Chief Secretary to the Treasury, 1996-97; Chief Secretary to the Treasury, 1997-98; Secretary of State for Social Security, 1998-2001; Secretary of State for the Department of Work and Pensions, 2001-02; Secretary of State for Scotland, 2003-06; Secretary of State for Transport, 2002-06; Secretary of State for the Department of Trade and Industry, 2006-07; Chancellor of the Exchequer, 2007-.

DAS Sachi Nandan, b. 1 August 1944, Cuttack, Orissa, India. Hospital Consultant. m. Subha, 1 son 1 daughter. Education: MBBS (Utkal), Orissa, 1968; DMRT (RCP (Lond), RCS (Eng)), 1971; FRCR (UK), 1977. Appointments: Senior House Officer, Radiotherapy, Plymouth General Hospital, England, 1969-70; Registrar and Senior Registrar, Mersey Regional Centre for Radiotherapy, Liverpool, England, 1970-77; Consultant, Honorary Senior Lecturer, Radiotherapy and Oncology, Ninewells Hospital and Medical School, Dundee, Scotland, 1977-. Publications: Articles in various professional journals. Honours: Long Service Award, NHS Tayside; Listed in national and international biographical dictionaries. Memberships: Fellow, Royal College of Radiologists; Member, British Medical Association; Scottish Radiological Society. Address: Department of Radiotherapy & Oncology, Ninewells Hospital, Dundee DD1 9SY, Scotland.

DASHDONDOG Jamba, b. 1 March 1941, Buregkhangai Soum, Bulgan Province, Mongolia. Writer. m. Khandsuren, 1 son. Education: Graduate, Mongolian Language and Literature, National University of Mongolia. Appointments: Editor-in-Chief and Secretary, newspapers and magazines for children and youth for 26 years; Editor, Children's Literature Programme, Radio; Editor, Children's Film Studio; Chairman, Council for Children's Literature, Mongolian Writers' Union; Director General, Mongolian Children's Cultural Foundation. Publications: Over 60 books for children including: Mom, Dad and Me; The Tales on Horseback; The Stone Legends; The Seven-Humped Camel; 6 research books about children's literature; 16 operas, plays and films for children; 18 books published overseas; Translated 35 book by foreign writers into Mongolian; Over 60 critiques and interviews and over 30 research articles on his works published in Mongolian newspapers and magazines; Poems and fairy tales published in over 60 newspapers and magazines abroad. Honours: Award of the Mongolian Writers' Union; D Natsagdorj Prize; Honoured Cultural Worker of Mongolia; 18 awards for Best Book of Mongolia; 6 times winner, International Children's Literary prizes including: Golden Foal, International Association of Children's Writers of Mongolian Nationality; Gold Medal for Poetic Excellence, World Academy of Arts and Culture, IBBY Honour List, 2006; IBBY – Asahi Reading Promotion Award Winner, 2006. Memberships: Mongolian Writers' Union; Academy of Mongolian Literature; World Academy of Arts and Culture; Society of Children's Book Writers and Illustrators (SCBWI); Founder and Member, Mongolian section of the International Board on Books for Young People (IBBY). Address: PO Box 2106, 46/46, Ulaanbaatar, Mongolia. E-mail: jdondog@yahoo.com

DAŠIĆ Pedrag, b. 16 September 1958, Peć, Serbia. Professor of Information Scientific and Technical Systems. 1 son. Education: Graduate, Faculty of Mechanical Engineering, Priština, 1982; Master of Science, Faculty of Mechanical Engineering, Belgrade; ECDL Tester, 2005; ECDL Expert Tester, 2006. Appointments: Technological Designer of CNC Machines, 1982-1985, Research Assistant, 1985-88, Institute Industry "14 October", Kruševac, Serbia and Montenegro; Professor of Information Science and Technological Systems, High Mechanical School, Trstenik and High Technological School, Kruševac, Serbia and Montenegro 1988-; President of Organising Committee of the International Conference of RaDMI, 2001-2008. Publications: 300 scientific papers, 150 of them published abroad; 1 monograph; 7 books; 2 scripts; Editor of 18 proceedings; Over 10 scientific and research projects; 14 scientific software and 2 Web presentations. Honours: 2 innovations for improving production, Industry "14 October", Kruševac; 2nd Award, for scientific and technical creative work and innovations in Kruševac community, 1987; Editorial Board in 6 international journals. Memberships include: International Neural Network Society; European Neural Network Society; International Association for Statistic Computing; International Association for Management of Technology; European Association for Programming Languages and Systems; European Association of Software Science and Technology. Address: Ratka Pešića No 59, 37208 Čitluk-Kruševac, Serbia. E-mail: dasicp@yahoo.com Website: www.RaDMI.org/

DATTA Dipankar, b. 30 January 1933, India. Physician. m. Jean Bronwen, 1 son, 1 daughter. Education: MBBS, Calcutta University, 1958; MRCP (UK), 1970; FRCP, Royal College of Physicians and Surgeons of Glasgow, 1980; FRCP, Royal College of Physicians of London, 1996. Appointments: Consultant Physician with special interest in Gastroenterology, 1975-97; Honorary Senior Clinical Lecturer in Medicine, 1984-97, Honorary Clinical Sub-Dean, Faculty of Medicine, 1989-97, Member of the Faculty of Medicine, 1989-95, Member of the Senate, 1991-94, Glasgow University; Member of the Lanarkshire Health Board, 1983-87; President, BMA, Lanarkshire, 1993-95; Chairman, Overseas Doctor's Association, Scotland, 1989-95; Member, General Medical Council, UK, 1994-99; Chairman, South Asia Voluntary Enterprise, 1994-; Director, British Overseas NGO's for Development, 1993-96. Memberships: Royal College of Physicians and Surgeons of Glasgow; Royal College of Physicians of London. Address: 9 Kirkvale Crescent, Newton Mearns, Glasgow G77 5HB, Scotland.

DAUNTON Martin James, b. 7 February 1949, Cardiff, Wales. University Professor of History. m. Claire Gobbi, 7 January 1984. Education: BA, University of Nottingham, 1970; PhD, University of Kent, 1974; Litt D, Cambridge, 2005. Appointments: Lecturer, University of Durham, 1973-79; Lecturer, 1979-85, Reader, 1985-89, Professor of History, 1989-97, University College London; Convenor, Studies in History series, Royal Historical Society, 1995-2000; Professor Economic History, University of Cambridge, 1997-; Trustee, National Maritime Museum, 2002-; Master, Trinity Hall, Cambridge, 2004-; President, Royal Historical Society, 2004-; Syndic, Fitzwilliam Museum, 2006-. Publications: Coal Metropolis: Cardiff; House and Home in the Victorian City, 1850-1914; Royal Mail: The Post Office since 1840; A Property Owning Democracy?; Progress and Poverty; Trusting Leviathan; Just Taxes. Contributions to: Economic History Review; Past & Present; Business History; Historical Research; Charity, Self-Interest and Welfare in the English Past; English Historical Review; Twentieth Century British History; Empire and Others; Politics of Consumption; Organisation of Knowledge; Wealth and Welfare. Honour: Fellow of the British Academy, 1997; Honorary D. Lit (UCL), 2006. Membership: Royal Historical Society. Address: Trinity Hall, Cambridge, CB2 1TJ, England.

DAVE Ramesh Chhabilal, b. 3 April 1942. Retired Principal. m. Rekha, 18 August 1976, 1 son. Education: Kovid, 1960; STC, 1963; MEd, 1970; MA, 1972. Appointments: Teaching, 1958-; Headmaster, GVSS High School, Kachchh, Gujarat State, 1971-. Publications: Alpana, poems, 1972; Gagan Padechhe Nannun, short stories, 1972; Anant Ane Urmina Parakramo, stories for children, 1994; Educational articles: Dipdiksha 1, 1994; Dipdiksha 2, 1995; History of Gadhsisa, 2005; Ek Sapanun Kausualyanun (Life Skills), 2005; Tarunya Sapanan Ane Swashtya (Adolescence), 2005; English work book; Smaran Ane Sevano Setu, 2005; 2 prayer cassettes, Vandu Devi Sarswati. Honours: Best Teacher Award, Gujarat State, 1981; Best Teacher National Award, 1987; National Award, National Council for Child Education, 1988; Best Principal, Gujarat Madhyastha Parishad, 1992; Retirement honour from village people, 1999. Memberships: Member, Educational Committee, Gujarat Secondary Education Board, 1996; Gujarat State Text Book Committee, 1997; Adult Education; All-India Radio Broadcasting; Inspection Panel, Gujarat State; Gender Resource Centre; District Institute of Education and Training, 2004; Adolescent Reproductive Sexual Health, 2005. Address: GVSS High School, Gadhasisa 370 445, Gujarat State, India.

DAVEY-SMITH George, b. 9 May 1959. Professor of Clinical Epidemiology. Education: BA (Hons), Psychology, Philosophy, Physiology, 1981, MA, 1984, DSc, Epidemiology, 2000, Oxford University; MB BChir (distinction), 1983, MD, Epidemiology, 1991, Cambridge University; MSc (distinction), Epidemiology, London School of Hygiene & Tropical Medicine, 1988. Appointments: Clinical Research Fellow, Welsh Heart Programme, 1985-86; Wellcome Research Fellow, Clinical Epidemiology, University College and Middlesex School of Medicine, 1986-89; Lecturer, Epidemiology, London School of Hygiene & Tropical Medicine, 1989-92; Senior Lecturer, Public Health & Epidemiology, Honorary Senior Registrar, then Consultant in Public Health Medicine, Department of Public Health, University of Glasgow, 1992-94; Professor of Clinical Epidemiology, University of Bristol, Honorary Consultant, North Bristol NHS Trust, 1994-. Publications: Over 500 peer reviewed journal publications; Numerous editorials, commentaries, book chapters and reports, letters, abstracts and others. Honours: Honorary Professor, Department of Public Health, University of Glasgow; Visiting Professor, Department of Epidemiology and Population Health, London School of Hygiene & Tropical Medicine. Memberships: MFPHM, 1992, FFPHM, 1996, Faculty of Public Health Medicine; FRCP, Royal College of Physicians, 2005; FMedSci, Academy of Medical Sciences, 2006. E-mail: zetkin@bristol.ac.uk

DAVID Joanna Elizabeth, b. 17 January 1947, Lancaster, England. Actress. m. Edward Fox, 1 son, 1 daughter. Education: Elmhurst Ballet School; Royal Academy of Dance; Webber Douglas Academy of Dramatic Art. Career: Theatre includes: The Family Reunion, The Royal Exchange, 1973; Uncle Vanya, Royal Exchange Manchester, 1977; The Cherry Orchard, 1983 and Breaking the Code, 1986, Theatre Royal Haymarket; Stages, Royal National Theatre, 1992; The Deep Blue Sea, Royal Theatre Northampton, 1997; Ghost Train Tattoo, Royal Exchange Theatre, 2000; Copenhagen, Salisbury Playhouse, 2003; The Importance of Being Earnest, Royal Exchange Theatre, 2004; Television includes: War and Peace; Sense and Sensibility, Last of the Mohicans, Duchess of Duke Street, Rebecca, Carrington and Strachey; Fame is the Spur, First Among Equals; Paying Guests; Unexplained Laughter; Hannay; Children of the North; Secret Friends; Inspector Morse; Maigret; Rumpole of the Bailey; Darling Buds of May; The Good Guys; Sherlock Holmes; The Cardboard Box; Pride and Prejudice; A Touch of Frost; Bramwell; A Dance to the Music of Time; Midsummer Murders; Written in Blood; Dalziel and Pascoe; Blind Date; Heartbeat; The Mill on the Floss; The Dark Room; The Glass; The Way We Live Now; The Forsyte Saga; He Knew He Was Right; Brides in the Bath; Foyles War; Heartbeat; Monarch of the Glen; Falling; Bleak House; Films: Secret Friends; Rogue Trader; Cotton Mary, 1999; My Name was Sabina Spielrein; The Soul Keeper; The Tulse Hill Suitcase; These Foolish Things. Memberships: Trustee, Ralph and Meriel Richardson Foundation; Committee Member, The Theatrical Guild; Council Member, King George V Pension Fund; Board Member, Unicorn Children's Centre. Address: 25 Maida Avenue, London W2 1ST, England.

DAVID, Baroness of Romsey in the City of Cambridge, Nora Ratcliff David, b. 23 September 1913, Ashby-de-la-Zouch, Leicestershire. Member of House of Lords. m. Richard William David, 1935, deceased, 2 sons, 2 daughters. Education: MA, Newnham College Cambridge. Appointments: JP, Cambridge City, 1965-; Former Cambridge City Councillor; Cambridge County Councillor, 1974-78; Sits as Labour Peer in the House of Lords, 1978-; Opposition Whip, 1979-83, Deputy Chief Opposition Whip, 1983-87; Opposition Spokesman for Environment and Local Government in Lords, 1986-88; Opposition Spokesman for Education, 1979-83 and 1986-97; Member of the Board, Peterborough Development Corporation, 1976-78; EC Select Committee, 1991-94; EC Agriculture Committee, 1993-98. Honours: Baroness-in-Waiting to HM The Queen, 1978-79; Honorary Fellow: Newnham College, Cambridge, 1986, Anglia Higher Education College, 1989; Honorary DLitt, Staffordshire University, 1994. Memberships: CPRE; Save The Children; Howard League; All party Children's Group; All party Penal Group; All party Environment Group. Address: The House of Lords, London SW1, England. E-mail: davidn@parliament.uk

DAVIE Ronald, b. 25 November 1929, Birmingham, England. Child Psychologist. m. Kathleen, 1 son, 1 daughter. Education: BA Psychology (Hons), University of Reading, 1954; PGCE, University of Manchester, 1955; Diploma in Educational Psychology, University of Birmingham, 1961; PhD, University of London, 1970. Appointments: Various teaching, psychology and research posts, 1955-67; Co-Director, National Child Development Study and Deputy Director, National Children's Bureau, 1968-74; Director, NCB, 1982-90; Professor, Educational Psychology, University of Cardiff, 1974-81; Consulting and Forensic Psychologist, 1990-99; Member, SEN Tribunal, 1994-2003; Visiting Professor, University of Gloucestershire, 1997-2006. Publications include; Living With Handicap, 1970; From Birth to Seven, 1972; Children Appearing Before Juvenile Courts, 1977; The Home and The School, 1979; Street Violence and Schools, 1981; Children and Adversity, 1982; Understanding Behaviour Problems, 1986; Child Sexual Abuse, 1989; Childhood Disability and Parental Appeals, 2001; The Voice of the Child, 1996; Mobile Phone Usage in Pre-Adolescence, 2004. Honours: Hon DEd, CNAA, 1991; Hon Fellow, RCPCH, 1996; Hon DEd, University of West of England, 1998; Hon DLitt, University of Birmingham, 1999. Memberships: Fellow, British Psychological Society; Former President, National Association for SEN; Former Chairman, Association for Child Psychology and Psychiatry; Vice President, Young Minds. Address: Bridge House, Upton, Caldbeck, Wigton, Cumbria, CA7 8EU, England.

DAVIES (Hilary) Sarah (Ellis), b. 11 January 1962, Newcastle upon Tyne, England. Corporate Branding Consultant. m. Jeremy Fawcett Bourke, 1 son, 1 daughter. Education: Foundation, Wimbledon School of Art, 1980-81; Kingston Polytechnic, 1981-82. Appointments: Runner, 1982-84, TV Commercials Producer, 1984-85, Director, 1988; Head of Television, 1985-97, Managing Director and Shareholder, 1993-97, Lambie-Nairn Ltd; Commercial Director and Shareholder, The Brand Union Ltd incorporating Lambie-Nairn, Tutssels and The Clinic, 1997-99; The Brand Union sold to WPP Ltd, 1999; Corporate Branding Consultant, clients including: 3i, Pearson Television, Thames Television, 1999-2002; Consultant to Director of Business Development, Red Bee Media Ltd (formerly BBC Broadcast Ltd), 2002-. Publication: Building the Brand – Spectrum Magazine, 1995. Honours: Gold Lion, Cannes Advertising Festival, 1985; D&AD Silver, Most Outstanding Animation, 1985, 1986; Creative Circle Silver – Best Use of Videotape, 1986, 1987, Best Use of Computer Graphics, 1986; D&AD Silver – Most Outstanding Television Graphics, 1987; Lambie-Nairn awarded Queen's Award for Export, 1995. Memberships: Royal Television Society; Chelsea Arts Club; Trustee, Media Trust, 1994-, Director of the trust's television channel, The Community Channel; Trustee, TimeBank, 2000-. Address: 98 Bennerley Road, London SW11 6DU, England. E-mail: sarah@sarahdavies.demon.co.uk.

DAVIES Alan Roger, b. 6 March 1966, Chingford, Essex, England. Actor; Comedian; Writer. Education: BA (Hons), Drama, University of Kent, 1984-88. Career: Television: Jonathan Creek, BBC, 1996-; A Many Splintered Thing, BBC, 1998-2000; Bob and Rose, ITV, 2001; QI, BBC, 2003-; The Brief, ITV, 2004-; Roman Road, 2004; Marple: Towards Zero, 2006; The Good Housekeeping Guide, 2006; Radio: Alan's Big One, Radio 1, 1994-95; The Alan Davies Show, Radio 4, 1998. Publications: Regular contributor to The Times Sports Section; Urban Trauma, DVD/Audio Cassette; Live at the Lyric, DVD/Audio Cassette. Honours: Critics Award for Comedy, Edinburgh Festival, 1994; BAFTA Award for Best Drama for Jonathan Creek, 1997; Best Actor for Bob and Rose, Monte Carlo TV Festival, 2002; DLitt, University of

Kent, 2003. Membership: Arsenal Season Ticket Holder. Address: c/o ARG, 4 Great Portland Street, London W1W 8PA, England.

DAVIES James Atterbury, b. 25 February 1939, Llandeilo, Dyfed, Wales. Former Senior Lecturer; Writer. m. Jennifer Hicks, 1 January 1966, 1 son, 1 daughter. Education: BA, 1965; PhD, 1969. Appointments: Visiting Professor, Baylor University, Texas, 1981; Senior Lecturer, University College of Swansea, 1990-; Mellon Research Fellow, University of Texas, 1993; Senior Lecturer, UWS, 1990-98; Part-time Senior Lecturer, UWS, 1998-2001. Publications: John Forster: A Literary Life, 1983; Dylan Thomas's Places, 1987; The Textual Life of Dickens's Characters, 1989; Dannie Abse, The View from Row B: Three Plays (editor), 1990; Leslie Norris, 1991; The Heart of Wales (editor), 1995; A Swansea Anthology (editor), 1996; A Reference Companion to Dylan Thomas, 1998; Dylan Thomas's Swansea, 2000; A Swansea Anthology (editor) expanded edition 2006. Honours: Fellow, Welsh Academy, 1999. Address: 93, Rhyd-y-Defaid Drive, Sketty, Swansea SA2 8AW, Wales

DAVIES Jonathan, b. 24 October 1962. Rugby Player. m. (1) Karen Marie, 1984, deceased 1997, 2 sons, 1 daughter, (2) Helen Jones, 2002. Appointments: Rugby Union outside-half; Played for following rugby clubs: Trimsaran, Neath, Llanelli; Turned professional, 1989; with Cardiff, 1995-97; Played for Welsh national team (v England), 1985; World cup Squad (6 appearances), 1987; Triple Crown winning team, 1988; Tour New Zealand (2 test appearances), 1988; 29 caps, sometimes Captain; Also played for Barbarians Rugby Football Club; Rugby League career; Played at three-quarters; Widnes (world record transfer fee), 1989; Warrington (free transfer), 1993-95; Reverted to rugby union, 1995; Welsh national team; British national team; Tour New Zealand, 1990; 6 caps, former Captain; Hosts Rugby themed Chatshow, Jonathan, 2004. Publication: Jonathan, 1989. Address: C/o Cardiff Rugby Football Club, Cardiff Arms Park, Westgate Street, Cardiff, Wales.

DAVIES Josie Ennis, b. 8 December 1928, Coventry, Warwickshire, England. Retired School Teacher and College Lecturer; Poet. m. Harold Henry Davies, 26 December 1967. Education: Teaching Diploma, 1952, 1964; LGSM and LRAM Teaching Diplomas. Appointments: Tax Officer, Inland Revenue, 1946-50; School Teacher, 1952-62; Lecturer, Coventry Technical College, 1962-72; College Lecturer, Movement, Speech and Drama. Publications: Waiting for Hollyhocks; Shadows on the Lawn; The Tuning Tree; Marmalade and Mayhem; Miscellany; Understanding Stone, 1994; A Press of Nails, 1996; Grief Like A Tiger, 1996; Journey to Ride, 1997; Daisies in December, 1999; Alphabet Avenue and Other Tales, 2002; Going Places, 2002; Tunes from the Shopping Trolley, 2003; A Song in My Pocket, 2003; Walking Between Leaves, 2004; Poets on My Mind, 2005; The Review of Contemporary Poetry, 2005; For Bears and Other Animals, 2005; Selected Poems, 1980-2005; (Editor) Anthology of Poetry, From Airy Nothing, 2007. For children: Journey to Marble Mountain, 1986; Rag, Tag and Bobtail, 1993; Contributions to: Folio International; Pennine Platform; Iota; Periaktos; Poetry Nottingham; Spokes; Success; The Countryman; Weyfarers; The Writers Voice; The Lady; Vigil; Haiku Quarterly; Period Piece and Paperback; Envoi; Poetry Digest. Membership: National Poetry Foundation. Address: 349 Holyhead Road, Coventry, Warwickshire CV5 8LD, England.

DAVIES Laura, b. 5 October 1963, Coventry, England. Golfer. Appointments: Turned professional, 1985; Won Belgian Open, 1985; British Women's Open, 1986; US Women's Open, 1987; AGF Biarritz Open, 1990; Wilkinson Sword English Open, 1995; Irish Open, 1994, 1995; French Masters, 1995; LPGA Championship, 1996; Danish Open, 1997; Chrysler Open, 1998, 1999; WPGA Championship, 1999; Compaq Open, 1999; TSN Ladies World Cup of Golf (Individual), 2000; WPGA International Matchplay, 2001; Norwegian Masters, 2002; 2006. Represented, England, World Team Championship, Taiwan, 1992; Europe in Solheim Cup, 1990, 1992, 1994, 1996, 1998, 2000, 2002, 2003.; Women's World Cup of Golf, 2005, 2006, 2007. Publication: Carefree Golf, 1991. Honours: Rookie of the Year, 1985; Order of Merit Winner, 1985, 1986, 1992, 1996, 1999, 2004; MBE, 1988; Rolex Player of the Year, 1996; CBE, 2000. Address: c/o Women's Professional Golf European Tour, The Tytherington Club, Dorchester Way, Tytherington, Macclesfield, SK10 2JP, England.

DAVIES Mark Stephen, b. 16 March 1962, London, England. Foot and Ankle Surgeon. m. Claudia, 1 son, 1 daughter. Education: BA (oxon), Medicine, Hertford College, Oxford University, 1984; St Mary's Hospital, London, 1987. Appointments: Surgical trainee, London/Brisbane, 1987-1999; Consultant Orthopaedic and Trauma Surgeon, Guy's and St Thomas' Hospitals, London, 1999; Clinical Director and Founder of the London Foot and Ankle Centre, 2003-. Publications: Chapter in Aird's Companion in Surgical Studies; Chapter in Bailey and Love Surgical Text; Editor of 39th Ed Gray's Anatomy; Over 30 papers in peer-reviewed journals. Memberships: Fellow, Royal College of Surgeons, England; Fellow, British Orthopaedic Association; Fellow, British Foot and Ankle Society; MBBS, London; FRCS, England; FRCS (orth); RAC club member. Address: The London Foot and Ankle Centre, 60 Grove End Road, London, NW8 9NH, England.

DAVIES Noel, b. 18 December 1924, Buckley, Flintshire, North Wales. Musician (Clarinet, Saxophones); Music and Instrument Teacher. m. Edith Mary Edwards 16 July 1946, 2 sons. Education: Family professional and musical background; Graduate, Stanley Masters School of Music, Chester. Career: Played in stage bands, theatre orchestra (pit), concert and light orchestras, sound/vision dance, cabaret; Also in music business management both in UK and abroad, mid 1940's; Also Stars in Battledress, Central Pool of Artists, world tours; Forces Broadcasting, Radio SEAC and BFN, Germany; Currently, freelance musician, bandleader, conductor, music industry consultant. Memberships include: Elected Representative, Musicians Union; ACEA; Chartered Institute of Public Relations; Chartered Institute of Management. Address: Tamarak, 15 Landon Road, Herne Bay, Kent CT6 6HO, England.

DAVIES Ryland, b. 9 February 1943, Cwym, Ebbw Vale, Wales. Opera and Concert Singer (Tenor). m. (1) Anne Howells (divorced 1981); (2) Deborah Rees, 1983, 1 daughter. Education: FRMCM, Royal Manchester College of Music, 1971. Debut: Almaviva, Barber of Seville, Welsh National Opera, 1964. Career: Glyndebourne Chorus, 1964-66; Soloist and Freelance, Glyndebourne and Sadler's Wells, Royal Opera House, Covent Garden, Welsh National Opera; Scottish Opera, Opera North; Performances in Salzburg, San Francisco, Chicago, New York, Hollywood Bowl, Paris, Geneva, Brussels, Vienna, Lyon, Amsterdam, Mannheim, Rome, Israel, Buenos Aires, Stuttgart, Berlin, Hamburg, Nice, Nancy, Philadelphia; Sang Lysander in A Midsummer Night's

Dream at Glyndebourne, 1989, Tichon in Katya Kabanova at the 1990 Festival; Other roles have included Mozart's Ferrando and Don Ottavio, Ernesto, Fenton, Nemorino, Pelléas, (Berlin 1984), Oberon, (Montpellier, 1987); Tamino, Lensky, Belmonte and Enéas in Esclarmonde; Sang Podestà in Mozart's Finta Giardiniera for Welsh National Opera, 1994; Arbace in Idomeneo at Garsington, 1996; Season 1998 with Mozart's Basilio at Chicago; Concert appearances at home and abroad; Radio and TV Broadcasts; Appeared in films including: Capriccio, Entführung, A Midsummer Night's Dream; Trial by Jury, Don Pasquale; Die Entführung aus dem Serail; Love of Three Oranges; Katya Kabanova; Recordings include: Die Entführung; Les Troyens; Saul; Così fan tutte; Monteverdi Madrigals, Messiah, Idomeneo, Il Matrimonio Segreto, L'Oracolo (Leoni), Lucia di Lammermoor, Thérèse, Judas Maccabeus, Mozart Requiem, Credo Mass, Mozart Coronation Mass and Vêspres Solenelle; Oedipus Rex; Il Trovatore; Don Carlo; Le nozze di Figaro; Esclarmonde. Honours include: Boise and Mendelssohn Foundation Scholarship, 1964; Ricordi Prize, 1964; Imperial League of Opera Prize, 1964; John Christie Award, 1965; Honorary Fellow, Royal Manchester College of Music, 1971; Fellow, Welsh College of Music and Drama, 1996. Address: c/o Hazard Chase Ltd, 25 City Road, Cambridge CB1 1DP, England.

DAVIS Andrew (Frank) (Sir), b. 2 February 1944, Ashridge, Hertfordshire, England. Conductor. m. Gianna, 1 son. Education: DMusB (Organ Scholar), King's College, Cambridge; MA (Cantab), 1967; With Franco Ferrara, Rome, 1967-68; DLitt (Hons), York University, Toronto, 1984. Debut: BBC Symphony Orchestra, 1970. Career: Pianist, Harpsichordist, Organist, St Martin-in-the-Fields Academy, London, 1966-70; Assistant Conductor, BBC Scottish Symphony Orchestra, Glasgow, 1970-72; Appearances, major orchestras and festivals internationally including Berlin, Edinburgh, Flanders; Conductor, Glyndebourne Opera Festival, 1973-; Music Director, 1975-88, Conductor Laureate, 1988-, Toronto Symphony; Conductor, China, USA, Japan and Europe tours, 1983, 1986; Principal Guest Conductor, Royal Liverpool Philharmonic Orchestra, 1974-77; Associate Conductor, New Philharmonic Orchestra, London, 1973-77; Conducted: La Scala Milan, Metropolitan Opera, Covent Garden, Paris Opera; Music Director, Glyndebourne, 1988-; Chief Conductor, 1989-2000, Conductor Laureate, 2000-, BBC Symphony Orchestra; Musical Director, Chicago Lyric Opera, 2000-; Conducted La Clemenza di Tito, Chicago, Oct 1989; Szymanowski King Roger, Festival Hall, London, 1990; Katya Kabanova and Tippett's New Year, (1990) Glyndebourne Festival; Opened 1991 Promenade Concerts, London, with Dream of Gerontius; Glyndebourne, 1992, Gala and The Queen of Spades; Conducted Elektra, at First Night, 1993 London Proms; Berg's Lulu, Festival Hall, 1994, returned 1997, for Stravinsky's Oedipus Rex, Persephone and The Rakes's Progress; Hansel and Gretel, 1996-97, and Capriccio, 1997-98, for the Met; Philadelphia, Chicago and Boston Orchestras, New York Philharmonic, and other leading American and European orchestras; Contracted to become Music Director and Principal Conductor of the Chicago Lyric Opera, 2000; Season 1999 with a new production of Pelléas et Mélisande at Glyndebourne and Tippett's The Mask of Time at the London Prom concerts. Compositions: La Serenissima (Inventions on a Theme by Claudio Monteverdi); Chansons Innocentes. Recordings include: All Dvorák Symphonies, Mendelssohn Symphonies, Borodin Cycle; Enigma Variations, Falstaff, Elgar; Overtures: Coriolan, Leonore No 3, Egmont, Fidelio Beethoven; Symphony No 10, Shostakovich, and violin concertos; Canon and other digital delights, Pachelbel; Cinderella excerpts; The Young Person's Guide to the Orchestra; Concerto No 2, Rachmaninov; The Planets, Gustav Holst; Symphony No 5, Horn Concerto, Piano Concerto No 2, Hoddinott; Brahms piano concertos; Nielsen Symphonies nos 4 and 5; Currently working on The British Line series with the BBC SO including the Elgar Symphonies and Enigma Variations, Vaughan Williams, Delius, Britten and Tippett; Operatic releases including Glyndebourne productions of Katya Kabanova, Jenufa, Queen of Spades, Lulu and Le Comte Ory. Honours: 2 Grand Prix du Disque Awards, Duruflé's Requiem recording with Philharmonic Orchestra; Gramophone of Year Award, 1987, Grand Prix du Disque, 1988, Tippett's Mask of Time; Royal Philharmonic Society/Charles Heidsieck Award, 1991; CBE, 1992; Royal Phiharmonic Society Award, Best musical opera performance of 1994, Eugene Onegin, on behalf of Glyndebourne Festival Opera, 1995; Gramophone Award for Best Video for Lulu; 1998 Award for Best Contemporary recording of Birtwistle's Mask of Orpheus; Critics Choice Award for Elgar/Payne Symphony No 3; Knight Bachelor, New Years Honours List, 1999. Address: c/o Askonas Holt Ltd, Lonsdale Chambers, 27 Chancery Lane, London WC2A 1PF, England.

DAVIS Bryn Derby, b. 22 March 1938, Thurnscoe, Yorkshire, England. Professor Emeritus of Nursing Education. m. (1) Valerie, 1962, 2 sons, divorced, 1979, (2) Catherine, 1979,1 son, 1 daughter. Education: RMN, 1961; SRN, 1965; RNT, 1969; BSc (Hons), Psychology, 1973; PhD, Social Psychology, 1983. Appointments: Principal Tutor, Holloway Sanatorium, Virginia Water, Surrey, 1970-73; DHSS, Research Fellow, London School of Economics, 1973-76; Deputy Director, Nursing Research Unit, University of Edinburgh, 1976-84; Principal Lecturer, Head of Nursing Research, Brighton Polytechnic, 1984-89; Professor and Dean, School of Nursing, 1989-99, Professor Emeritus of Nursing Education, 1999-, University of Wales College of Medicine, Cardiff; Elected Member, UKCC, 1998-2003; Academic and Professional Nursing Consultant, 1999-; Editor, Journal of Psychiatric and Mental Health Nursing, 1998-2004; Non-Executive Director, Pontypridd and Rhondda NHS Trust, 2001-2003. Publications: Research into Nursing Education (editor), 1983; Nurse Education: research and developments (editor), 1987; Caring for People in Pain, 2000; Various articles in nursing journals and many chapters in books by others on pain, culture, relationships and mental health. Honours: Visiting Professor of Nursing, NEWI, Wrexham; Visiting Professor of Psychology, University of Wales, Bangor. Memberships: Royal College of Nursing; Fellow, Royal Astronomical Society. Address: 108 New Road, Brading, Sandown, Isle of Wight, PO36 0AB, England. E-mail: davisbryn3@aol.com

DAVIS Carl, b. 1936, New York, USA. Composer; Conductor. m. Jean Boht, 1971, 2 daughters. Education: Studied composition with Hugo Kauder and with Per Norgaard in Copenhagen. Career: Assistant Conductor, New York City Opera, 1958; Associate Conductor, London Philharmonic Orchestra, 1987-88; Principal Conductor, Bournemouth Pops, 1984-87; Principal Guest Conductor, Munich Symphony Orchestra, 1990-; Artistic Director and Conductor, Royal Liverpool Philharmonic Orchestra, Summer Pops, 1993-; Musical theatre: Diversions, 1958; Twists, 1962; The Projector and Cranford; Pilgrim; The Wind in the Willows, 1985; Alice in Wonderland, The Vackees, Incidental music for theatre includes: Prospect Theatre Co; The National Theatre; RSC. Ballet: A Simple Man, 1987; Lipizzaner, Liaisons Amoureuses, 1988; Madly, Badly, Sadly, Gladly; David and Goliath; Dances of Love and Death; The Picture of Dorian Grey; A Christmas Carol, 1992; The Savoy

Suite, 1993; Alice in Wonderland, 1995; Aladdin, 2000; Pride and Prejudice: First Impressions, 2002. Music for TV includes: The Snow Goose, 1971; The World at War, 1972; The Naked Civil Servant, 1975; Our Mutual Friend, 1978; Hollywood, 1980; Churchill: The Wilderness Years, 1981; Silas Marner, 1985; Hotel du Lac, 1986; The Accountant, The Secret Life of Ian Fleming, 1989; Separate But Equal, The Royal Collection, 1991; A Year in Provence, Fame in the 20th Century: Clive James, 1992; Ghengis Cohn, Thatcher: The Downing Street Years, 1993; Pride and Prejudice, Oliver's Travels, Eurocinema: The Other Hollywood, 1995; Cold War, 1998-99; Goodnight, Mr Tom, 1998; The Great Gatsby, 2000; The Queen's Nose; An Angel for May; Book of Eve, Promoted to Glory, 2003; Mothers and Daughters, 2004; Garbo, I'm King Kong! The Exploits of Merian C Cooper, 2005; The Understudy, 2008. Operas for TV: The Arrangement; Who Takes You to the Party?; Orpheus in the Underground; Peace. Film music: The Bofors Gun, 1969; The French Lieutenant's Woman, 1981; Champions, 1984; The Girl on a Swing, Rainbow, Scandal, 1988; Frankenstein Unbound, 1989; The Raft of the Medusa, 1991; The Trial, 1992; Voyage, 1993; Widow's Peak, 1994; Topsy Turvy, 2000; series of Thames Silents including Napoleon, 1980, 2000; The Wind; The Big Parade; Greed; The General; Ben Hur; Intolerance; Safety Last; The Four Horsemen of the Apocalypse, 1992; Wings, 1993; Waterloo, 1995; Phantom of the Opera, 1996; 6 Mutuals (Chaplin Shorts), 2004; Cranford Chronicles, 2007. Concert works: Music for the Royal Wedding; Variations on a Bus Route; Overture on Australian Themes, Clarinet Concerto, Lines on London Symphony, 1984; Fantasy for Flute and Harpsichord, 1985; The Searle Suite for Wind Ensemble; Fanfare for Jerusalem, 1987; The Glenlivet Fireworks Music, Norwegian Brass Music, Variations for a Polish Beggar's Theme, Pigeons Progress, 1988; Jazz Age Fanfare, Everest, 1989; Landscapes, The Town Fox, A Duck's Diary, 1990; Paul McCartney's Liverpool Oratorio, 1991. Recordings: Christmas with Kiri, Beautiful Dreamer, 1986; The Silents, 1987; Ben Hur, A Simple Man, 1989; The Town Fox and Other Musical Tales, 1990; Leeds Castle Classics, Liverpool Pops at Home, 1995. Honours: Obie Prize Best Review, 1958; Emmy Award, 1972; BAFTA Awards, 1981, 1989; Chevalier des Arts et des Lettres, 1983; Honorary Fellowship, Liverpool University, 1992; Honorary DA, Bard, New York, 1994; Honorary DMus, Liverpool, 2002; Special Achievement Award for Music for Television and Film, 2003; CBE, 2005. Address: c/o Paul Wing, 3 Deermead, Little Kings Hill, Great Missenden, Buckinghamshire, HP16 0EY, England.

DAVIS Colin (Rex) (Sir), b. 25 September 1927, Weybridge, Surrey, England. Conductor. m. (1) April Cantelo, 1949, 1 son, 1 daughter, (2) Ashraf Naini, 1964, 3 sons, 2 daughters. Education: Royal College of Music. Career: Conductor Associate, Kalmar Orchestra and Chelsea Opera Group; Assistant Conductor, BBC Scottish Orchestra, 1957-59; Conductor, Sadler's Wells Opera House (ENO), 1959, Principal Conductor, 1960-65, Musical Director, 1961-65; Artistic Director, Bath Festival, 1969; Chief Conductor, BBC Symphony Orchestra, 1967-71, Chief Guest Conductor, 1971-75; Musical Director, Royal Opera House, Covent Garden, 1971-86; Guest Conductor, Metropolitan Opera, New York, 1969 (Peter Grimes), 1970, 1972; Principal Guest Conductor, Boston Symphony Orchestra, 1972-84; Principal Guest Conductor, London Symphony Orchestra, 1975-95; Bayreuth Festival, first British conductor, 1977 (Tannhäuser); Vienna State Opera, debut, 1986; Music Director and Principal Conductor, Bavarian State Radio Orchestra, 1983-92; Honorary Conductor, Dresden Staatskapelle, 1990-; Principal Conductor, London Symphony Orchestra, 1995; Principal

Guest Conductor, New York Philharmonic Orchestra, 1998-2003; Has worked regularly with many orchestras in Europe and America; Season 1999 with the Choral Symphony at the London Prom concerts and Benvenuto Cellini and Les Troyens at the Barbican Hall, both with the London Symphony Orchestra. Recordings: Extensive recording with Boston Symphony Orchestra, London Symphony Orchestra, Dresden Staatskapelle, Bavarian Radio Symphony Orchestra. Honours: Officier dans L'Ordre National de Legion d'Honneur, 1999; Maximiliansorden, Bavaria, 2000; Best Classical Album and Best Opera Recording (for Les Troyens), Grammy Awards, 2002; Honorary DMus, Keele, 2002, RAM, 2002; South Bank Show Award, 2004. Address: c/o Alison Glaister, 39 Huntingdon Street, London N1 1BP, England.

DAVIS Geena, b. 21 January 1957, Wareham, Massachusetts, USA. Actress. m. (1) Richard Emmolo, 1981, divorced 1983, (2) Jeff Goldblum, divorced 1990, (3) Renny Harlin, 1993, divorced, (4) Reza Jarrahy, 2001, 2 sons, 1 daughter. Education: Boston University. Appointments: Member, Mt Washington Repertory Theatre Company; Worked as model; TV appearances incude: Buffalo Bill, 1983; Sara, 1985; The Hit List; Family Ties; Remington Steele; Secret Weapons, TV film; The Geena Davis Show, 2000; Commander in Chief, 2006; Films include: Tootsie, 1982; Fletch, 1984; Transylvania 6-5000, 1985; The Fly, 1986; The Accidental Tourist; Earth Girls Are Easy, 1989; Quick Change; The Grifters; Thelma and Louise; A League of Their Own; Hero; Angie; Speechless (also producer); Cutthroat Island; The Long Kiss Goodnight, 1996; Stuart Little, 1999; Stuart Little 2, 2002; Stuart Little 3: Call of the Wild (voice), 2005. Honours: Academy Award, Best Supporting Actress, 1989; Golden Globe Award, Best Actress in a TV Series, 2006. Address: C/o ICM, 8942 Wilshire Boulevard, Beverly Hills, CA 90211, USA.

DAVIS Steve, OBE, b. 22 August 1957, Plumstead, London, England. Snooker Player. m. Judith Lyn Greig, 1990, (divorced), 2 sons. Appointments: Professional snooker player, 1978; Has won 73 titles; In 99 tournament finals, as at 2002; Major titles include: UK Professional Champion, 1980, 1981, 1984, 1985, 1986, 1987; Masters Champion, 1981, 1982, 1988, 1997; International Champion, 1981, 1983, 1984; World Professional Champion, 1981, 1983, 1984, 1987, 1988, 1989; Winner, Asian Open, 1992, European Open, 1993, Welsh Open, 1994; Member, Board World Professional Billiards and Snooker Association, 1993-; TV: Steve Davis and Friends (chat show); They Think It's All Over (presenter), 2003-. Honours: BBC Sports Personality of Year, 1989; BBC TV Snooker Personality of Year, 1997; OBE, 2001. Publications: Steve Davis, World Champion, 1981; Frame and Fortune, 1982; Successful, 1982; How to Be Really Interesting, 1988; Steve Davis Plays Chess, 1996. Address: 10 Western Road, Romford, Essex, England.

DAWE (Donald) Bruce, b. 15 February 1930, Fitzroy, Victoria, Australia. Associate Professor; Poet; Writer. m. (1) Gloria Desley Blain, 27 January 1964, deceased 30 December 1997, 2 sons, 2 daughters, (2) Ann Elizabeth Qualtiough, 9 October 1999. Education: BA, 1969, MLitt, 1973, MA, 1975, PhD, 1980, University of Queensland; Hon. DLitt (USQ), 1995; Hon.DLitt (UNSW), 1997. Appointments: Lecturer, 1971-78, Senior Lecturer, 1978-83, DDIAE; Writer-in-Residence, University of Queensland, 1984; Senior Lecturer, 1985-90, Associate Professor, 1990-93, School of Arts, Darling Heights, Toowoomba. Publications: No Fixed Address, 1962; A Need of Similar Name, 1964; Beyond the Subdivisions, 1968; An Eye for a Tooth, 1969; Heat-Wave, 1970; Condolences of the Season: Selected Poems, 1971; Just

a Dugong at Twilight, 1974; Sometimes Gladness: Collected Poems, 1978, 5th edition, 1993; Over Here Harv! and Other Stories, 1983; Towards Sunrise, 1986; This Side of Silence, 1990; Bruce Dawe: Essays and Opinions, 1990; Mortal Instruments: Poems 1990-1995, 1995; A Poets' People, 1999; The Chewing-Gum Kid, 2002; No Cat – and That's That!, 2002; Show and Tell, 2003; Luke and Lulu, 2004. Contributions to: Various periodicals. Honours: Myer Poetry Prizes, 1966, 1969; Ampol Arts Award for Creative Literature, 1967; Dame Mary Gilmore Medal, Australian Literary Society, 1973; Braille Book of the Year, 1978; Grace Leven Prize for Poetry, 1978; Patrick White Literary Award, 1980; Christopher Brennan Award, 1984; Philip Hodgins Medal for Literary Excellence, 1997; Order of Australia, 1992; Distinguished Alumni Award, UNE, 1996; Australian Arts Council Emeritus Writers Award, 2000. Memberships: Australian Association for Teaching English, honorary life member; Centre for Australian Studies in Literature; Victorian Association for Teaching of English, honorary life member; Patron, Speech and Drama Teachers' Association of Queensland; Patron, PEN (Sydney). Address: c/o Pearson Education, 95 Coventry St, South Melbourne, Australia, 3205.

DAWIDS Richard Greene, b. 5 January 1941, Copenhagen, Denmark. Business Executive. Education: Davidson College, 1960-61; University of Grenoble, France, 1966-67; University of Copenhagen, 1968. Appointments: W Copenhagen Handelbank, 1968-85; Tokyo, 1985-89; Vice-President, Surongo SA, Brussels, 1987-90, President, 1991-2003; Board of Directors: Cie Bois Sauvage, Brussels, 1988-2006; Enterprises et Chemins de Fer en Chine, 1989-2006. Brussels Berenberg Bank, Hamburg, Germany; Phoenix Four Inc, Nassau, The Bahamas. Address: Groupe Surongo, 17 Rue du Bois Sauvage, 1000 Brussels, Belgium.

DAWKINS (Clinton) Richard, b. 26 March 1941, Nairobi, Kenya. Zoologist; Professor of the Public Understanding of Science. m. (1) Marian Stamp, 19 August 1967, divorced 1984, (2) Eve Barham, 1 June 1984, deceased, 1 daughter, (3) Lalla Ward, 15 September 1992. Education: BA, 1962, MA, 1966, DPhil, 1966, Balliol College, Oxford. Appointments: Assistant Professor of Zoology, University of California at Berkeley, 1967-69; Fellow, New College, Oxford, 1970-; Lecturer, 1970-89, Reader in Zoology, 1989-95, Charles Simonyi, Professor of the Public Understanding of Science, 1996-, Oxford University; Editor, Animal Behaviour, 1974-78, Oxford Surveys in Evolutionary Biology, 1983-86; Gifford Lecturer, University of Glasgow, 1988; Sidgwick Memorial Lecturer, Newnham College, Cambridge, 1988; Kovler Visiting Fellow, University of Chicago, 1990; Nelson Lecturer, University of California at Davis, 1990. Publications: The Selfish Gene, 1976, 2nd edition, 1989; The Extended Phenotype, 1982; The Blind Watchmaker, 1986; River Out of Eden, 1995; Climbing Mount Improbable, 1996; Unweaving the Rainbow, 1998; A Devil's Chaplain, 2003; The Ancestor's Tale: A Pilgrimage to the Dawn of Life, 2004. Contributions to: Scholarly journals. Honours: FRS; Royal Society of Literature Prize, 1987; Los Angeles Times Literature Prize, 1987; Honorary Fellow, Regent's College, London, 1988; Silver Medal, Zoological Society, 1989; Michael Faraday Award, Royal Society, 1990; Nakayama Prize, Nakayama Foundation for Human Sciences, 1994; Honorary DLitt, St Andrews University, 1995; Honorary DLitt, Canberra, 1996; International Cosmos Prize, 1997; Honorary DSc, University of Westminster, 1997; Honorary DSc, University of Hull, 2001; Kistler Prize, 2001; Honorary DUniv, Open University, 2003; Honorary DSc, Sussex, 2005; Honorary DSc, Durham,

2005; Honorary DSc, Brussels, 2005; Shakespeare Prize, 2005. Address: c/o Oxford University Museum, Parks Road, Oxford, OX1 3PW, England.

DAWKINS Wayne Jesse, b. 19 September 1955, New York, USA. Journalism. m. Allie Crump, 1 daughter. Education: BA, Long Island University, Brooklyn, New York, 1977; MS, Graduate School of Journalism, Columbia University, New York, 1980. Appointments: Reporter, Editorial Writer, Columnist, Courier-Post, Cherry Hill, New Jersey, 1984-96; Assistant Metro Editor, Post-Tribune, Gary, Indiana, 1996-98; Associate Editor, Daily Press, Newport News, Virginia, 1998-2003; Managing Editor/News, BlackAmericaWeb.com, 2003-05; Assistant Professor, Hampton University, Virginia, 2005 -. Publications: Black Journalists: The NABJ Story, 1997; Rugged Waters: Black Journalists Swim the Mainstream, 2003; Editor, Contributor to Black Voices in Commentary: The Trotter Group, 2006; Articles in Black Issues Book Review, 2003-07; Articles in NABJ Journal. Honours: Public Relations Society of America Award, New York, 1980; Robert Harron Award, Columbia University GSJ, 1980; Distinguished Journalism Alumni Award, Columbia University, 1990; T Thomas Fortune Lifetime Achievement Award GSABJ, 1994; Alumni Federation Medal, Columbia University, 2004. Memberships: National Association of Black Journalists; Publishers Marketing Association; Trotter Group; Association of Educators in Journalism and Mass Communications. Address: Hampton University, Scripps Howard School of Journalism and Communications, 546 East Queen Street, Room 114, Hampton, VA 23668, USA.

DAWN Indu, b. 18 September 1942, West Bengal, India. Author; Poet. Education: Science Graduate, Calcutta University. Appointments: Poet and Author. Publications: Over 11 novels; More than 19 books of poetry; 4 short stories; 2 books of rhymes; 1 book of songs; 1 drama; Contributions regularly published in national and local newspapers and magazines. Honours: Michael Madhusudan Puraskar, 1994; Jajan Sahitya Puraskar, 1995; Premendra Mitra Smriti Puraskar, 1995; Raigungakar Bharat Chandra Smriti Puraskar, 1996; Uttarbanga Natya Jagat Puraskar, 1996; Sayak Sahitya Samman, 1996; Dr B R Ambedkar Fellowship Award, 2000; Uttam Kumar Award, 2001; Sahitya Kala Shilpa Samaj Puraskar, 2002; Moni Kuntala Samman, 2003; Manab Seva Award, 2003; Searchlight Award, 2004. Address: c/o Sadhanendu Dawn, 58 Raja Ram Mohan Ray Sarani, PO Box Baidyabati, Dist: Hooghly, 712 222, India.

DAWNAY Charles James Payan, b. 7 November 1946, Glasgow, Scotland. Investment Trust Company Director. m. Sarah Stogdon, 1 son, 3 daughters. Education: MA (Hons), History, Trinity Hall, University of Cambridge, 1965-68; Investment Management Programme, London Business School, 1976. Appointments: Investment Manager, M & G Group, 1969-78; Export Sales Director, Alginate Industries Ltd, 1978-81; Managing Director, Vannick Products Ltd, 1981-83; SG Warburg & Co Ltd/Mercury Asset Management Group plc, 1983-92: Director SG Warburg & Co Ltd, 1984, Director, Mercury Asset Management Group plc, 1987, Chairman, Mercury Fund Managers Ltd, 1987; Business Development Director, 1992-99, Deputy Chairman, 1999-2000, Martin Currie Ltd; Currently: Chairman, Northern Aim VCT plc, 2000-; Chairman, Investec High Income Trust plc, 2001-; Director, Taiwan Opportunities Trust plc, 2001-; Chairman, Resources Investment Trust plc, 2001-; Chairman, CCLA Investment Management Ltd, 2004-; Investment Panel, The National Trust, 1991-; Chairman, Biggar Museum Trust, 1993-; Governor, Corporation of the Sons of Clergy, 1995-;

Member, Merchant Company of Edinburgh, 1995-; Chairman, Penicuik House Preservation Trust, 2001-; Member of the Board of Trustees, The National Galleries of Scotland, 2003. Memberships: Brooks; New Club (Edinburgh); Pratts. Address: Symington House, By Biggar, Lanarkshire ML12 6LW, Scotland.

DAWSON Earl Bliss, b. 1 February 1930, Perry, Florida, USA. Biochemist. m. Winnie Ruth Isbell, 1 son, 3 daughters. Education: BA, 1955; MA, 1960; PhD, 1964. Appointments: Instructor, University of Texas, Medical Branch (UTMB), 1963-64; Associate Professor, University of Texas Medical Branch, 1968. Publications: 7 books and manuals; 7 book chapters; 47 articles; 108 abstracts. Honours: Research Fellowships: in Cardiovascular Physiology, Bowman Gray School of Medicine, 1956; Renal Physiology, University of Missouri School of Medicine, 1958-59, Nutrition, Texas A&M University, 1960-61; National Science Foundation Pre-doctoral Scholarship Award (individual award), 1961-62; National Institute of Health Pre-doctoral Research Award (Individual Grant), 1962-63; Moody Foundation Research Award, 1964; Sigma Xi. Listed in national and international biographical dictionaries. Memberships: American Institute of Nutrition; American Society of Clinical Nutrition; American Society for Experimental Biology and Medicine; New York Academy of Science; American College of Nutrition; American Society for Reproductive Medicine. Address: 1610 Calico Canyon Lane, Pearland, TX 77581, USA.

DAWSON Patricia Vaughan, b. 23 January 1925, Liverpool, England. Artist; Poet. m. James N Dawson, 25 September 1948, 1 son, 2 daughters. Education: Croydon School of Art, 1941-45; Diploma, Industrial Design. Appointments: Ashfold School, 1947-48; Lecturer, Tate Gallery, London, 1963-66. Creative Works: Etchings in: La Bibliotheque Nationale, Paris, France; British Museum, and many UK museums. Publications: Poems and works represented in: New Education; Pictorial Knowledge; Still, New Knowledge; Observer; Guardian; Times Educational Supplement; The Artist Looks At Life; La Lanterne des Morts; The Kiln; The Forge; Reliquaries; Wet Leaves. Address: Flat 1, 3 Albion Villas Rd, London SE26 4DB, England.

DAY Doris, b. 3 April 1924, Cincinnati, Ohio, USA. Singer; Actress. m. (1) Al Jorden, March 1941, divorced 1943, m. (2) George Weilder divorced 1949, (3) Marty Melcher, 3 April 1951, deceased 1968. Career: Former dancer, Cincinnati; Singer, shows including: Karlin's Karnival, WCPO-Radio; Bob Hope NBC Radio Show, 1948-50; Doris Day CBS Show, 1952-53; Solo recording artist, 1950-; Actress, numerous films including: Tea For Two, 1950; Lullaby Of Broadway, 1951; April In Paris, 1952; Pajama Game, 1957; Teacher's Pet, 1958; Pillow Talk, 1959; Midnight Lace, 1960; Jumbo, 1962; That Touch Of Mink, 1962; The Thrill Of It All, 1963; Send Me No Flowers, 1964; Do Not Disturb, 1965; The Glass Bottom Boat, 1966; Caprice, 1967; The Ballad Of Josie, 1968; Where Were You When The Lights Went Out, 1968; Own television series, The Doris Day Show, 1970-73; Doris Day And Friends, 1985-86; Doris Day's Best, 1985-86; TV special, The Pet Set, 1972. Honours: Winner (with Jerry Doherty), Best Dance Team, Cincinnati; Laurel Award, Leading New Female Personality In Motion Picture Industry, 1950; Top audience attractor, 1962; American Comedy Lifetime Achievement Award, 1991. Address: c/o Doris Day Animal League, 227 Massachusetts Avenue NE, Washington, DC 20002, USA.

DAY Elaine, b. 30 June 1954, Hendon, North London, England. Freelance Writer. m. David John Day, 5 August 1994, 1 daughter. Publications include: Natural Tranquillity, Crystal Pillars/Fossil Seas Poetry Book, A Celebration of Poets, The Star-Laden Sky, anthology, 1997; Light of the World, anthology, 1997; Beyond the Horizon, anthology, 1997; Poetry Now East Anglia, Acorn Magazine, The Secret of Twilight, A Quiet Storm, anthology, 1998; A Celebration of Friendship (anthology), A Celebration of Poets (anthology), 1999; Prayer for Jesus and other poems, People Who Counted, Praying in Poems, Let's Shout About It, 2000; Praise Poetry Book, Praise the Lord, 2001; Heaven & Earth, 2003; History of Havering in Essex, Poetry Comes Like Waves, 2005; All Year Long, 2006. Contributions to: Dogs Monthly Magazine; Old Yorkshire Magazine; Acorn Magazine; One Magazine; Day By Day Magazine; Forward Press; Freehand Magazine; Poetic Hour Magazine; Citizen Newspaper; Faith in Focus anthology; Gentle Reader Magazine; Animal Crackers Magazine; Linkway Magazine; Science Friction anthology; Monomyth Magazine; Superfluity Magazine; The Snoring Cat Magazine; Linkway Magazine, International Poetry Institute of South Africa; BBC Children in Need Pamphlet, Rainstorms & Rainstorms Anthology, Small Press Poets Anthology, Roobooth Publications; Poetry Church, 2000; Book of Christian poetry, Knocking on Heaven's Door, Book of Christian poetry, Closer to Heaven, 2005. Honours: 7 Editors Choice Awards for Poetry; British Academy Certificate, 1983. Memberships: Imagine Writing Group; British Academy of Songwriters, Composers and Authors. Address: 141 Turpin Avenue, Collier Row, Romford, Essex RM5 2LU, England.

DAY Stephen Peter, b. 19 January 1938, Ilford, Essex. Consultant. m. Angela Waudby, 1 son, 2 daughters. Education: BA, MA, 1957-60, Visiting Fellow, 1987, Corpus Christi College, Cambridge. Appointments: Senior Political Officer in Aden Protectorate, Her Majesty's Overseas Civil Service, 1961-67; Foreign and Commonwealth Office, 1967-93: Ambassador to Qatar; Household of the Prince of Wales; Ambassador to Tunisia; Senior Trade Commissioner, Hong Kong; Currently, Chairman, British Tunisian Society. Honours: CMG; Commander of the Republic of Tunisia. Memberships: Hong Kong Club. E-mail: s.day@claremontassociates.net

DAY William, b. 28 August 1946, Hove, England. Music Teacher. m. Education: Bassoon and flute studies, Royal College of Music, London, 1963-66. Appointments: Part time flute and bassoon teacher, Drayton Manor Grammar School, 1964-66; Principal bassoon, D'Oyly Carte Opera Company, 1966-70; Principal bassoon, London Festival Ballet, 1968; Freelance engagements as principal and sub-principal bassoon, New Cantata Chamber Orchestra, 1966-70; Bassoon, BBC Training Orchestra, Bristol, 1970; Flute and bassoon teacher, Wolverhampton Education Authority, 1970-71; Woodwind teacher, Darlington Education Authority, 1971-73; Principal flute, Mid-Sussex Sinfonia, 1973-74; Woodwind coach, Brighton Youth Orchestra, 1973-75; Part time teacher of student teachers, Brighton Teacher Training College, 1973-77; Woodwind teacher, many schools and sixth form colleges, Brighton area, 1973-86; Solo flute, Music Room, Royal Pavilion, Brighton, 1974; Flute teacher, Roedean School, 1976; Various concerts, New Cantata Soloists, 1977-79; Solo flute and bassoon, Cantilena Soloists Ensemble, 1975; Teacher, Oriel School, Ludlow and Grange House School, Leominster, 1987-89; Woodwind tutor, Llandovery College, South Wales, 1999-2001; Education Network, 2001-; Unaccompanied Solo Flautist, 2004-. Memberships: Incorporated Society of Musicians. Address: 2 Prospect Place, Newton Street, Craven Arms, Shropshire, SY7 9PH, England.

DAY-LEWIS Daniel, b. 20 April 1957, London, England. Actor. m. Rebecca Miller, 1996; 2 sons (1 by Isabelle Adjani). Education: Bristol Old Vic Theatre School. Career: Plays: Class Enemy, Funny Peculiar, Bristol Old Vic; Look Back in Anger, Dracula, Little Theatre, Bristol and Half Moon Theatre, London; Another Country, Queen's Theatre; Futurists, National Theatre; Romeo, Thisbe, Royal Shakespeare Company Hamlet, 1989; TV: A Frost in May; How Many Miles to Babylon?; My Brother Jonathan; Insurance Man; Films: My Beautiful Launderette; A Room with a View; Stars and Bars; The Unbearable Lightness of Being; My Left Foot, 1989; The Last of the Mohicans, 1991; The Age of Innocence, 1992; In the Name of the Father, 1993; The Crucible, 1995; The Boxer, 1997; Gangs of New York, 2002; The Ballad of Jack and Rose, 2005; There Will Be Blood, 2007. Honours: Academy Award for Best Actor, BAFTA Award, Best Actor, (for My Left Foot) 1989; Screen Actors' Guild Award for Best Actor, 2003; BAFTA Award for Best Actor in a Leading Role, 2003. Address: c/o Julian Belfrage Associates, 46 Albemarle Street, London W1S 4DF, England.

DE Ashis Kumar, b. 3 December 1935, Calcutta, India. Medical Practitioner; Senior Consultant Physician. m. Nirmala. Education: MBBS, Calcutta University, 1959; MD (Medicine), Calcutta University, 1970; MRCP (UK), Royal College of Physician, 1978. Appointments: Resident House Officer, NRS Medical College, Kolkata, 1959-60; Medical Officer, E Railway, B R Singh Hospital, Kolkata, 1960-74, 1978-80; Senior House Officer and Registrar, various hospitals in England, 1974-78; Voluntary retirement from railways, 1981; Own practice as Physician and Cardiologist, 1981-88; Senior Consultant Cardiologist, KFS Hospital, Buraidah, Saudi Arabia, 1988-91; Senior Consultant Physician, General Medicine, Seven Hills Hospital, Visakhapatnam, India, 1992-. Publications: Several papers in different Indian medical journals. Memberships: Fellow, American College of Chest Physicians. Address: Flat 303, Kurupam Castle, Beach Road, Pedda Waltair, Visakhapatnam – 530 017, Andhra Pradesh, India.

DE ARAUJO Carlos José, b. 5 October 1967, Rio de Janeiro, Brazil. Professor. m. Gilmara B Da Silva Araujo. Education: Mechanical Engineer, 1991, Master of Science, Mechanical Engineering, 1994, Universidade Federal da Paraíba, Brazil; Doctor in Materials Science and Engineering, INSA of Lyon, France, 1999. Appointment: Associate Professor, Federal University of Campina Grande, Brazil, 1994-. Publications: More than 10 articles published in international journals and more than 40 papers presented in national and international conferences; Papers concerning shape memory alloys (fundamentals and applications). Honours: Listed in Who's Who publications and biographical dictionaries. Memberships: Brazilian Society of Mechanical Sciences. Address: DEM/CCT/UFCG, Caixa Postal: 10069, CEP: 58109-970, Campina Grande – PB, Brazil, Carlos@dem.ufcg.edu.br

DE BERNIÈRES Louis, b. 8 December 1954, Woolwich, London, England. Novelist. Education: Bradfield College, Berkshire; BA, Manchester University; MA, Leicester Polytechnic and University of London. Appointments: Landscape gardener, 1972-73; Teacher and rancher, Columbia, 1974; Philosophy tutor, 1977-79; Car mechanic, 1980; English teacher, 1981-84; Bookshop assistant, 1985-86; Supply teacher, 1986-93. Publications: The War of Don Emmanuel's Nether Parts, 1990; Señor Vivo and the Coca Lord, 1991; The Troublesome Offspring of Cardinal Guzman, 1992; Captain Corelli's Mandolin, 1994; Labels, 1997; The Book of Job, 1999; Gunter Weber's Confessino, 2001; Sunday Morning at the Centre of the World, 2001; Red Dog, 2001; Birds Without Wings, 2004. Contributions to: Second Thoughts and Granta. Honours: Commonwealth Writers Prizes, 1991, 1992, 1995; Best of Young British Novelists, 1993; Lannan Award, 1995. Membership: PEN. Address: c/o Secker and Warburg, Michelin House, 81 Fulham Road, London SW3 6RB, England.

DE BONO Edward (Francis Publius Charles), b. 19 May 1933, Malta. Author; Physician; Inventor; Lecturer. m. Josephine Hall-White, 1971, 2 sons. Education: St Edward's College, Malta; BSc, 1953, MD, 1955, Royal University of Malta; MA, 1957, DPhil, 1961, Oxford University; PhD, Cambridge University, 1963. Appointments: Research Assistant, 1957-60, Lecturer, 1960-61, Oxford University; Assistant Director of Research, 1963-76, Lecturer in Medicine, 1976-83, Cambridge University; Honorary Director and Founding Member, Cognitive Research Trust, 1971-; Secretary-General, Supranational Independent Thinking Organisation, 1983-; Lecturer. Publications: The Use of Lateral Thinking, The Five-Day Course in Thinking, 1967; The Mechanism of Mind, 1969; Lateral Thinking: A Textbook of Creativity, The Dog Exercising Machine, 1970; Lateral Thinking for Management: A Handbook of Creativity, Practical Thinking: Four Ways to Be Right, Five Ways to Be Wrong, 1971; Children Solve Problems, PO: A Device for Successful Thinking, 1972; Think Tank, 1973; Eureka: A History of Inventions (editor), 1974; Teaching Thinking, The Greatest Thinkers, 1976; Wordpower: An Illustrated Dictionary of Vital Words, 1977; Opportunities: A Handbook of Business Opportunity Search, The Happiness Purpose, 1978; Future Positive, 1979; Atlas of Management Thinking, 1981; De Bono's Thinking Course, Learn to Think, 1982; Tactics: The Art and Science of Success, 1984; Conflicts: A Better Way to Resolve Them, Six Thinking Hats: An Essential Approach to Business Management from the Creator of Lateral Thinking, 1985; CoRT Thinking Program: CoRT 1-Breadth, Letters to Thinkers: Further Thoughts on Lateral Thinking, 1987; Masterthinker II: Six Thinking Hats, 1988; Masterthinker, Masterthinker's Handbook, Thinking Skills for Success, I Am Right, You Are Wrong: From This to the New Renaissance: From Rock Logic to Water Logic, 1990; Handbook for the Positive Revolution, Six Action Shoes, 1991; Serious Creativity: Using the Power of Lateral Thinking to Create New Ideas, Surpetition: Creating Value Monopolies When Everyone Else is Merely Competing, 1992; Teach Your Child How to Think, Water Logic, 1993; Parallel Thinking, 1994; Teach Yourself to Think, Mind Pack, 1995; Edward do Bono's Textbook of Wisdom, 1996; How to be More Interesting, 1997; Simplicity, 1998; New Thinking for the New Millennium, Why I Want to be King of Australia, 1999; The Book of Wisdom, The de Bono Code, 2000; How to Have a Beautiful Mind, 2004; Six Value Medals, 2005; H+ (plus): A New Religion, 2006; How to Have Creative Ideas; 2007. Contributions to: Television series, professional journals, and periodicals. Honour: Rhodes Scholar; Honorary Registrar, St Thomas' Hospital Medical School, Harvard Medical School. Membership: Medical Research Society. Address: 12 Albany, Piccadilly, London W1V 9RR, England.

DE BONT Jan, b. 22 October 1943, Netherlands. Cinematographer and Director. Education: Amsterdam Film Academy. Appointments: Cinematographer: Turkish Delight; Keetje Tippel; Max Heulaar; Soldier of Orange; Private Lessons (American debut), 1981; Roar; I'm Dancing as Fast As I Can; Cujo; All The Right Moves; Bad Manners; The Fourth Man; Mischief; The Jewel of the Nile; Flesh and Blood; The Clan of the Cave Bear; Ruthless People; Who's That Girl;

Leonard Part 6; Die Hard, Bert Rigby - You're A Fool; Black Rain; The Hunt for Red October; Flatliners; Shining Through; Basic Instinct; Lethal Weapon 3, 1992; TV Photography: The Ray Mancini Story; Split Personality (episode of Tales From the Crypt); Director, films: Speed (debut), 1994; Twister; Speed 2: Cruise Control (also screenplay and story); The Haunting. Address: C/o David Gersh, The Gersh Agency, 232 North Canon Drive, Beverly Hills, CA 90210, USA.

DE BURGH Chris (Christopher Davison), b. 15 October 1948, Argentina. Singer; Songwriter. m. Diane Patricia Morley, 2 sons, 1 daughter. Education: Trinity College, Dublin. Career: Irish tour with Horslips, 1973; Solo artiste, 1974-; Album sales, 40 million to date; Sell-out concerts world-wide; Performances include: Carol Aid, London, 1985; The Simple Truth, benefit concert for Kurdish refugees, Wembley, 1991; Royal Albert Hall, London. Recordings: Singles include: Flying, 1975; Patricia The Stripper, 1976; A Spaceman Came Travelling, 1976; Don't Pay The Ferryman, 1982; High On Emotion, 1984; Lady In Red (Number 1, UK), 1984; Love Is My Decision, theme from film Arthur 2, 1988; Missing You, 1988; Albums: Far Beyond These Castle Walls, 1975; Spanish Train And Other Stories, 1975; At The End Of A Perfect Day, 1977; Crusader, 1979; Eastern Wind, 1980; Best Moves, 1981; The Getaway, 1982; Man On The Line, 1984; The Very Best Of Chris De Burgh, 1985; Into The Light, 1986; Flying Colours, 1988; From A Spark To A Flame - The Very Best Of Chris De Burgh, 1989; High On Emotion - Live From Dublin, 1990; Power Of Ten, 1992; This Way Up, 1994; Beautiful Dreams, 1995; The Love Songs, 1997; Quiet Revolution, 1999; Notes from Planet Earth – The Ultimate Collection, 2001; Timing is Everything, 2002; The Road to Freedom, 2004. Honours: ASCAP Award, The Lady In Red, 1985, 1987, 1988, 1990, 1991, 1997; IRMA Awards, Ireland, 1985-90; Beroliner Award, Germany; BAMBI Award, Germany; Midem Trophy, France. Current Management: Kenny Thomson, 754 Fulham Road, London SW6 5SH, England.

DE COURCY Anne Grey, b. London, England. Writer. m. Robert Armitage, deceased 1998, 1 son, 2 daughters. Education: Wroxall Abbey, Leamington, Warwickshire; Millfield, Street, Somerset. Appointments: Woman's Editor, London Evening News, 1973-80; Columnist and Section Editor, Evening Standard, 1980-91; Feature Writer, Daily Mail, 1991-2003. Publications: A Guide to Modern Manners, 1985; The English in Love, 1986; 1939, The Last Season, 1989; The Life of Edith, Lady Londonderry, 1992; The Viceroy's Daughters, 2000; Diana Mosley, 2003; Debs at War, 2005; Snowdon, The Biography, 2008. Memberships: Biographers' Club. Address: c/o Carole Blake, Blake Friedmann, 122 Arlington Road, London NW1 7HP, England. E-mail: anne@annedecourcy.co.uk

DE CRESPIGNY (Richard) Rafe (Champion), b. 16 March 1936, Adelaide, South Australia, Australia. m. Christa Charlotte Boltz, 1 son, 1 daughter. Education: BA, 1957, MA, 1961, Cambridge University; BA, University of Melbourne, 1961; BA, 1962, MA, 1964, PhD, 1968, Australian National University. Appointments: Lecturer, 1965-70, Senior Lecturer, 1970-73, Secretary-General, 28th International Congress of Orientalists, 1971, Reader in Chinese, 1973-1999, Dean of Asian Studies, 1979-1982, Australian National University, Canberra; Master, University House, 1991-2001; Adjunct Professor of Asian Studies, 1999-. Publications: The Biography of Sun Chien, 1966; Official Titles of the Former Han Dynasty (with H H Dubs), 1967; The Last of the Han, 1969; The Records of the Three Kingdoms, 1970; China: The Land and Its People, 1971; China This Century: A History of

Modern China, 1975, 2nd edition, 1992; Portents of Protest, 1976; Northern Frontier, 1984; Emperor Huan and Emperor Ling, 1989; Generals of the South, 1990; To Establish Peace, 1996; A Biographical Dictionary of Later Han to the Three Kingdoms, 2007. Membership: Australian Academy of the Humanities, fellow; Chinese Studies Association of Australia, President, 1999-2001. Address: Faculty of Asian Studies, Australian National University, Canberra 0200, Australia.

DE DUVE Christian René, b. 2 October 1917, Thames Ditton, Surrey, England (Belgian Citizen). Biochemist. m. Janine Herman, 1943, 1 son. Education: Graduated in Medicine, University of Louvain, Belgium, 1941. Appointments: Professor of Physiological Chemistry, 1947-85, Emeritus Professor, 1985-, University of Louvain Medical School, Belgium; Professor of Biochemical Cytology, 1962-88, Emeritus Professor, 1988-, Rockefeller University, New York City. Honours: Prix des Alumni, 1949; Prix Pfizer, 1957; Prix Francqui, 1960; Prix Quinquennal Belge des Sciences Médicales, 1967; Gairdner Foundation International Award of Merit, Canada, 1967; Dr H P Heineken Prijs, Netherlands, 1973; Nobel Prize for Medicine, 1974; Honorary DSc, Keele University, 1981; Doctor honoris causa, Rockefeller University, 1997; Numerous other honorary degrees. Memberships: Royal Academy of Medicine, Belgium; Royal Academy of Belgium; American Chemical Society, Biochemical Society; American Society of Biological Chemistry; Pontifical Academy of Sciences; American Society of Cell Biology; Deutsche Akademie der Naturforschung, Leopoldina; Koninklijke Akademie voor Geneeskunde van België; American Academy of Arts and Sciences; Royal Society, London; Royal Society of Canada. Address: c/o Rockefeller University, 1230 York Avenue, New York, NY 10021, USA.

DE FRANCIA Peter Laurent, b. 1921, Beaulieu, Alpes Maritimes, France. Artist; Professor. Education: Academy of Brussels, 1938-40; Slade School, University of London, 1945-48. Appointments: Canadian Government Exhibition Commission, Ottawa, 1949-50; Architects Department, American Museum, New York, USA, 1951; Head of Fine Art Programming, BBC Television, 1952-54; Department of Art History and Complementary Studies, St Martin's School of Art, 1954-61; Department of Art History and Complementary Studies, Royal College of Art, London, 1961-69; Principal, Department of Fine Art, Goldsmiths College, University of London, 1970-72; Professor of Painting (postgraduate), Royal College of Art, 1972-86; Exhibitions: 27 one-man exhibitions include most recently: Centre for Contemporary Art, New Delhi, India, 1991; Gloria Gallery, Nicosia, Cyprus, 1995; Austin Desmond Fine Art, London, 1996; The Place, London, 1999; Ruskin School of Drawing, Oxford, 1999; British Council, New Delhi, 2002; "The Bombing of Sakiet", Tate Modern, 2003-04; Royal West of England Academy, Bristol, 2004; The Gallery, Wimbledon School of Art, London, 2004; James Hyman Fine Art, London, 2005, 2006; Display Room, Tate Britain, 2006; Numerous group exhibitions. Work in collections: Ashmolean Museum, Oxford; British Museum, London; Graves Art Gallery, Sheffield; Imperial War Museum, London; Museum of Modern Art, New York; Museum of Modern Art, Prague; Tate Gallery, London; Victoria and Albert Museum, London; Arts Council of Great Britain; National Portrait Gallery, London; Scottish National Gallery of Modern Art, Edinburgh; Ulster Museum, Belfast; Pallant House, Chichester; British Council, New Delhi; Wimbledon School of Art, London; Works in private collections in the UK and overseas. Publications: Leger: The Great Parade, 1969;

The Life and Work of Fernand Leger, 1983; Untitled, 1989; Fables, 1990-2001, 2002. Address: 44 Surrey Square, London SE17 2JX, England.

DE GIOVANNI-DONNELLY Rosalie Frances, b. 22 November 1926, Brooklyn, New York, USA. m. Edward F, 2 sons. Education: BA, Brooklyn College, 1947; MA, 1953; PhD, Columbia University, 1961. Appointments: Chief, Microbial Genetics Laboratory, 1962-67; Research Biologist, Food and Drug Administration, 1968-88; Professor, George Washington University Medical School, 1968-. Publications: Articles to Scientific Journals. Honours: Food and Drug Award of Merit, 1970. Memberships: American Association for the Advancement of Science; American Society of Microbiology; Sigma Xi; Sigma Delta; Environmental Mutagen Society. Address: 1712 Strine Dr, McLean, VA 22101, USA.

DE HAMEL Christopher Francis Rivers, b. 20 November 1950. Fellow, Corpus Christi College, Cambridge. Education: BA, Otago University, New Zealand; DPhil, Oxford University. Appointments: Cataloguer, later Director, Western Manuscripts, Sotheby's, 1975-2000; Visiting Fellow, All Souls College, Oxford, 1999-2000; Donnelley Fellow Librarian, Corpus Christi College, Cambridge, 2000-. Publications include: A History of Illuminated Manuscripts, 1986, 2nd edition, 1994; Syon Abbey, The Library of the Bridgettine Nuns and their Peregrinations after the Reformation, 1991; Scribes and Illuminators, 1992; The Book: A History of the Bible, 2001. Honours: FSA; FRHistS; Hon LittD, St John's Minnesota, 1994; Hon LittD, Otago University, 2002; PhD, Cambridge, 2005. Membership: Roxburghe Club; Grolier Club; Chairman, Association for Manuscripts and Archives in Research Collections. Address: Corpus Christi College, Trumpington Street, Cambridge CB2 1RH, England.

DE HAVILLAND Olivia Mary, b. 1 July 1916, Tokyo, Japan. Actress. m. (1) Marcus Aurelius Goodrich, 1 sons, (2) Pierre Paul Galante, 1955, divorced 1979, 1 daughter. Appointments: Actress, films including: Captain Blood, 1935; Anthony Adverse, 1936; The Adventures of Robin Hood, 1938; Gone With The Wind, 1939; Hold Back the Dawn, 1941; Princess O'Rourke, 1942; To Each His Own (Academy Award), 1946; The Dark Mirror, 1946; The Snake Pit, 1947; The Heiress (Academy Award), 1949; My Cousin Rachel, 1952; Not as a Stranger, 1954; The Proud Rebel, 1957; The Light in the Piazza, 1961; Lady in a Cage, 1963; Hush Hush Sweet Charlotte, 1964; The Adventurers, 1968; Airport '77, 1976; The Swarm, 1978; The Fifth Musketeer; Plays: Romeo and Juliet, 1951; Candida, 1951-52; A Gift of Time, 1962; TV: Noon Wine, 1966; Screaming Women, 1972; Roots, The Next Generations, 1979; Murder is Easy, 1981; Charles and Diana: A Royal Romance, 1982; North and South II, 1986; Anastasia (Golden Globe award), 1986; The Woman He Loved, 1987. Publications: Every Frenchman Has One, 1962; Contributor, Mother and Child, 1975. Honours: Numerous awards include: Academy awards, 1946, 1949; New York Critics Award, 1948, 1949; Look Magazine Award, 1941, 1946, 1949; Venice Film Festival Award, 1948; Filmex Tribute, 1978; American Academy of Achievement Award, 1978; American Exemplar Medal, 1980; Golden Globe, 1988; DRhc, American University of Paris, 1994. Address: BP 156-16, 75764 Paris, Cedex 16 France.

DE JAGER Cornelis, b. 29 April 1921, Den Burg, Netherlands. Professor, Space Research and Astrophysics. m. Duotje Rienks, 2 sons, 2 daughters. Education: Doctoral Degree, 1945, Doctor Degree, cum laude, 1952, University of Utrecht. Appointments: Assistant, 1946, Senior Scientist,

1955, Lecturer, 1957, Professor, 1960, University of Utrecht; Professor, University of Brussels, 1961-86. Publications: 33 books, 400 scientific publications, 160 popular publications. Honours: Gold Medal, RAS, London; Hale Medal, AAS; Dr Hon Causa, Paris, Wroclaw. Memberships: Several. Address: Molenstraat 22, 1791 DL Den Burg, Texel, The Netherlands. E-mail: cdej@kpnplanet.nl

DE KLERK Frederik Willem, b. 18 March 1936, Johannesburg, South Africa. Politician. m. (1) Marike Willemse, 1959, 2 sons, 1 daughter, (2) Elita Georgiadis, 1998. Education: Potchefstrom University. Appointments: In law practice, 1961-72; Member, House of Assembly, 1972; Information Officer, National Party, Transvaal, 1975; Minister, Posts, Telecommunications and Social Welfare and Pensions, 1978; Minister, Posts, Telecommunications and Sport and Recreation, 1978-79; Minister, Mines, Energy and Environmental Planning, 1979-80; Mineral and Energy Affairs, 1980-82; Internal Affairs, 1982-85; National Education and Planning, 1984-89; Acting State President South Africa, August-September, 1989; State President, South Africa, 1989-94; Executive Deputy President, Government of National Party, 1994-96; Leader of Official Opposition, 1996-97; Founder, F W De Klerk Foundation, 2000; Founding Member of GLF, Global Leadership Foundation, 2004; Former, Chairman, Cabinet and Commander-in-Chief of the Armed Forces; Former, Chairman, Council of Ministers. Publications: The Last Trek: A New Beginning (autobiography), 1999; Various articles and brochures for the National Party Information Service. Honours: Joint winner, Houphouet Boigny Prize (UNESCO), 1991; Asturias Prize, 1992; Liberty Medal (SA), 1993; Shared Nobel Prize for Peace with Nelson Mandela, 1993; Order of Mapungubwe, Gold, 2000. Address: PO Box 15785, Panorama, 7506, Cape Town, South Africa.

DE LA BILLIÈRE Peter (Sir), b. 29 April 1934, Plymouth, Devon, England. Retired Army Officer. m. Bridget Constance Muriel Goode, 1965, 1 son, 2 daughters. Education: Royal College of Defence Studies, Staff College. Appointments: Joined King's Shropshire Light Infantry, 1952; Commissioned Durham Light Infantry; Served Japan, Korea, Malaya, Jordan, Borneo, Egypt, Aden, Gulf States, Sudan, Oman, Falklands; Commanding Officer 22 Special Air Service Regiment (SAS), 1972-74; General Staff Officer 1 (Directing Staff) Staff College, 1974-77; Commander, British Army Training Team, Sudan, 1977-78; Director, SAS, Commander, SAS Group, 1978-83; Commander, British Forces, Falklands and Military Commissioner, 1984-85; General Officer Commanding, Wales, 1985-87; General Officer Commanding South East District and Permanent Peace Time Commander, Joint Forces Operations Staff, 1987-90; Commander, British Forces, Middle East, 1990-91; Adviser to HM Government on Middle East Affairs; Current appointments: Director, Robert Fleming Holdings Ltd, 1977-99; Chairman, FARM Africa; Chairman, Meadowland Meats Ltd, 1994-2002; President, Army Cadet Force, 1992-99. Publications: Storm Command: A Personal Story, 1992; Looking For Trouble (autobiography), 1994; Supreme Courage: Heroic Stories from 150 Years of the Victoria Cross, 2004. Honours include: Several honorary doctorates; Order of Bahrain, 1st class, 1991; Chief Commander, Legion of Merit, USA, 1992; Meritorious Service Cross, Canada, 1992; Order of Abdul Aziz, 2nd class, Saudi Arabia, 1992; Kuwait Decoration, 1st class, 1992; Qatar Sash of Merit, 1992; KCB; KBE; DSO; MC and Bar; MSC DL. Address: c/o Naval and Military Club, 4 St James's Square, London SW1Y 4JU, England.

DE LA HOUSSAYE Brette Angelo-Pepe, b. 20 August 1960, Los Angeles, California, USA. Researcher; Engineer; Educator. Education: BSEET, DeVry Institute, City of Industry, California, 1989. Appointments: Engineer Researcher, private practice, 1990-2003; Calcgate (Software), 2003-; Mathematics Teacher, Los Angeles Unified School District, 2007-; Discovered alternate method for calculating energy using Newton's Second Law of Motion and Work Energy Theorem, applications also include integral calculus. Memberships: IEEE; American Physical Society; Institute of Nanotechnology; National Trust for Historic Preservation; American Museum of Natural History. Address: 7719 Goodland Ave, North Hollywood, CA 91605, USA. E-mail: brette@calcgate.com

DE LA MARE Walter Giles Ingpen, b. 21 October 1934, London, England. Publisher. m. Ursula Steward, 1 son, 1 daughter. Education: MA (Oxon), Trinity College, Oxford, 1955-59. Appointments: National Service, Royal Navy, 1953-55; Midshipman, RNVR, 1954, Sub-lieutenant, 1955; Director, Faber and Faber Ltd, 1969-98; Director, Faber Music Ltd, 1977-87; Director, Geoffrey Faber Holdings Ltd, 1990-; Chairman, Giles de la Mare Publishers Ltd, 1995-; Literary Trustee of Walter de la Mare, 1982-; Founder Walter de la Mare Society, 1997. Publications include: The Complete Poems of Walter de la Mare (editor), 1969; Motley and Other Poems by Walter de la Mare (editor with introduction for Folio Society), 1991; Publishing Now (contributor of general chapter), 1993; Short Stories 1895-1926 by Walter de la Mare (editor), 1996; Short Stories 1927-1956 by Walter de la Mare (editor), 2001; Richard de la Mare at 75 (editor with Tilly de la Mare), 2004; Short Stories for Children by Walter de la Mare (editor), 2006. Memberships: Publishers Association: Chairman, University, College and Professional Publishers Council, 1982-84, Member of PA Council, 1982-85, Chairman of Copyright Committee, 1988, Chairman, Freedom to Publish Committee, 1992-95, 1998-2000; International Publishers Association Freedom to Publish Committee, 1993-96; Stefan Zweig Committee, British Library, 1986-95; Executive Committee, Patrons of British Art, Tate Gallery, 1998-2001; Translation Advisory Group, Arts Council of England, 1995-98; Club: Garrick. Address: PO Box 25351, London NW5 1ZT, England. E-mail: gilesdelamare@dial.pipex.com; www.gilesdelamare.co.uk

DE LA RENTA Oscar, b. 22 July 1932, Santo Domingo. Fashion Designer. (1) Françoise de Langlade, 1967, deceased 1983, (2) Anne de la Renta, 1989. Education: Santo Domingo University; Academia de San Fernando, Madrid. Appointments: Staff designer, under Cristobel Balenciaga, AISA couture house, Madrid; Assistant to Antonio Castillo, Lanvin-Castillo, Paris, 1961-63; Designer, Elizabeth Arden couture and ready-to-wear collection, New York, 1963-65; Designer and partner, Jane Deby Inc, New York, 1965; After her retirement, firm became Oscar de la Renta Inc, purchased by Richton International, 1969; Chief Executive, Richton's Oscar de la Renta Couture, Oscar de la Renta II, Oscar de la Renta Furs, Oscar de la Renta Jewelry, Member of Board of Directors, Richton Inc, 1969-73; Oscar de la Renta Ltd, 1973; Chief Executive Officer, 1973--; Couturier for Balmain, Paris, Nov, 1992-; Producer, 80 different lines including high-fashion clothing, household linens, accessories and perfumes for shops in USA, Canada, Mexico and Japan; Owner, Oscar de la Renta Shop, Santo Domingo, 1968-. Honours: Recipient, numerous fashion awards; Caballero, Order of San Pablo Duarte, Order of Cristobal Colon. Address: Oscar de la Renta Ltd, 550 7th Avenue, 8th Floor, New York, NY 10018, USA.

DE LA TOUR Frances, b. 30 July 1944, Bovingdon, Hertfordshire, England. Actress. m. Tom Kempinski, 1972, divorced 1982, 1 son, 1 daughter. Education: Lycée français de Londres, Drama Centre, London; With the Royal Shakespeare Company, 1965-71. Appointments: Stage appearances include: As You Like It, 1967; The Relapse, 1969; A Midsummer Night's Dream, 1971; The Man of Mode, 1971; Small Craft Warnings, 1973; The Banana Box, 1973; The White Devil, 1976; Hamlet (title role), 1979; Duet for One, 1980; Skirmishes, 1981; Uncle Vanya, 1982; Moon for the Misbegotten , 1983; St Joan, 1984; Dance of Death, 1985; Brighton Beach Memoirs, 1986; Lillian, 1986; Facades, 1988; King Lear, 1989; When She Danced (Olivier Award), 1991; The Pope and the Witch, 1992; Greasepaint, 1993; Les Parents Terrible (Royal National Theatre), 1994; Three Tall Women, 1994-95; Blinded by the Sun (Royal National Theatre), 1996; The Play About the Baby (Almedia Theatre), 1998; The Forest (Royal National Theatre), 1998-99; Antony and Cleopatra (RSC), 1999; Fallen Angels (Apollo), 2000-01; The Good Hope and Sketches by Harold Pinter, (Royal National Theatre), 2001-02; Dance of Death (Lyric), 2003; Films include: Our Miss Fred, 1972; To The Devil a Daughter, 1976; Rising Damp, 1980; The Cherry Orchard, 1998; Harry Potter and the Goblet of Fire, 2005; The History Boys, 2006. TV appearances include: Crimes of Passion, 1973; Rising Damp, 1974, 1976; Cottage to Let, 1976; Flickers, 1980; Skirmishes, 1982; Duet for One, 1985; Partners, 1986; Clem, 1986; A Kind of Living (series), 1987, 1988; Downwardly Mobile (series), 1994; Cold Lazarus, 1996; Tom Jones, 1997; Heartbeat, 1998; Born & Bread, 2003; Poirot, 2004; Waking the Dead, 2004; Sensitive Skin, 2005; New Tricks, 2006. Honours: Best Supporting Actress Plays and Players Award, 1973; 3 Best Actress Awards, 1980; Best Actress Standard Film Award, 1980; Best Actress SWET Award, 1983; Honorary Fellow, Goldsmiths College, University of London, 1999; Best Actress, Royal Variety Club, 2000. Address: c/o Kate Feast Management, 10 Primrose Hill Studios, Fitzroy Road, London, NW1 8TR, England.

DE MORNAY Rebecca, b. 29 August 1959, Santa Rosa, California, USA. Actress. m. Bruce Wagner, 1989, divorced 1991. Patrick O'Neal, 2 daughters. Education: in Austria; Lee Strasberg Institute, Los Angeles. Appointments: Film and television actress: Theatre includes: Born Yesterday, 1988; Marat/Sade, 1990; Films include: One from the Heart, 1982; Risky Business, 1983; Testament, 1983; The Slugger's Wife, 1985; Runaway Train, 1985; The Trip to Bountiful, 1985; Beauty and The Beast, 1987; And God Created Woman, 1988; Feds, 1988; Dealers, 1989; Backdraft, 1991; The Hand that Rocks the Cradle, 1992; Guilty as Sin, 1993; The Three Musketeers, 1993; Never Talk to Strangers, 1995; The Winner, 1996; Thick as Thieves, 1998; Table for One, 1998; The Right Temptation, 2000; Identity, 2003; Raise Your Voice, 2004; Lords of Dogtown, 2005; Wedding Crashers, 2005; Music Within, 2007; American Venus, 2007. TV includes: The Murders in the Rue Morgue, 1986; By Dawn's Early Light, 1990; An Inconvenient Woman, 1992; Blind Side, 1993; Getting Out, 1994; The Shining, 1996; The Con, 1997; Night Ride Home, 1999; The Conversion (director), 1996; ER, 1999; Range of Motion, 2000; A Girl Thing, 2001; Salem Witch Trials, 2002; Manipulated, 2006; John from Cincinnati, 2007. Honours: Best Actress, Cognac Crime Film Festival, 1992.

DE NIRO Robert, b. 17th August 1943, New York, USA. Actor. m. Diahnne Abbott, 1976-88 (divorced) 1 son, 1 daughter, 2 children by Toukie Smith, Grace Hightower, 1997, 1 child. Career: Actor; Producer; Director; Films include: Trois

chambres à Manhattan, 1965; Greetings, 1968; The Wedding Party, 1969; Sam's Song, 1969; Bloody Mama, 1970; Jennifer On My Mind, Born To Win, The Gang That Couldn't Shoot Straight, 1971; Bang the Drum Slowly, Mean Streets, 1973; The Godfather Part II, 1974; The Last Tycoon, Taxi Driver, 1900, 1976; New York, New York, 1977; The Deer Hunter, 1978; Raging Bull, 1980; True Confessions, 1981; The King of Comedy, 1983; Once Upon a Time in America, 1984; Falling in Love, 1984; Brazil, 1985; The Mission, 1986; Angel Heart, The Untouchables, 1987; Midnight Run, 1988; We're No Angels, Jacknife, 1989; Stanley and Iris, Goodfellas, Awakenings, 1990; Backdraft, Cape Fear, Guilty of Suspicion, 1991; Mistress, Night and the City, Mistress, The Godfather Trilogy: 1901-1980, 1992; Mad Dog and Glory, This Boy's Life, A Bronx Tale, 1993; Mary Shelley's Frankenstein, 1994; Heat, Casino, Le Cent et une nuits de Simon Cinéma, 1995; The Fan, Marvin's Room, Sleepers, 1996; Jackie Brown, Wag The Dog, Cop Land, 1997; Great Expectations, Ronin, 1998; Analyze This, Flawless, 1999; Men of Honor, Meet the Parents, The Adventures of Rocky & Bullwinkle, 2000; 15 Minutes, The Score, 2001; Showtime, City by the Sea, Analyze That, 2002; Godsend, Shark Tale (voice), Meet the Fockers, The Bridge of San Luis Rey, 2004; Hide and Seek, 2005; The Good Shepherd, Chaos, King Arthur and the Invisibles (voice), 2006; Stardust, 2007; What Just Happened, 2008. Honours include: Commander, Ordre des Arts et des Lettres; Academy Award, Best Supporting Actor, 1974; Academy Award, Best Actor, 1980. Address: CAA, 9830 Wilshire Boulevard, Beverly Hills, CA 90212, USA.

DE PALMA Brian, b. 11 September 1940, Newark, New Jersey, USA. Film Director. m. Nancy Allan 1979 (divorced), Gale Ann Hurd, 1991, (divorced) 1 daughter, Darnell Gregoria De Palma, 1995 (divorced), 1 child. Education: Sarah Lawrence College, Bronxville; Columbia University. Appointments: Director: (short films) Icarus, 1960; 660124: The Story of an IBM Card, 1961; Wotan's Wake, 1962; (feature length) The Wedding Party, 1964; The Responsive Eye (documentary), 1966; Murder à la Mod, 1967; Greetings, 1968; Dionysus in '69 (co-director), 1969; Hi Mom!, 1970; Get to Know Your Rabbit, 1970; Sisters, 1972; Phantom of the Paradise, 1974; Obsession, 1975; Carrie, 1976; The Fury, 1978; Home Movies, 1979; Dressed to Kill, 1980; Blow Out, 1981; Scarface, 1983; Body Double, 1984; Wise Guys, 1985; The Untouchables, 1987; Casualties of War, 1989; Bonfire of the Vanities, 1990; Raising Cain, 1992; Carlito's Way, 1993; Mission Impossible, 1996; Snake Eyes, 1998; Mission to Mars, 2000; Femme Fatale, 2002; The Black Dahlia, 2006; Redacted, 2007; Capone Rising, 2008. Address: Paramount Pictures, Lubitsch Annex #119, 555 Melrose Avenue #119, W Hollywood, CA 90038, USA.

DE SARAM Rohan, b. Sheffield, Yorkshire, England. Cellist. m. Rosemary, 1 son, 1 daughter. Education: Studies with Gaspar Cassado and Andre Navarra, Chigiana Academy, Siena, Italy; Studies with Pablo Casals, Puerto Rico. Appointments: Solo international career with many leading orchestras of the world, since aged 12 years; Recitals with piano; Member, Arditti String Quartet and de Saram Clarinet Trio; Works written for him include works by Pousseur, Xenakis, Dillon and Berio (Sequenza XIV); Plays Kandyan drum from native Sri Lanka; Recitals and improvisations with various artists. Honours: Suggia Award to study with John Barbirolli and Pablo Casals, with academic studies in Oxford; Von Siemens Prize as a member of the Arditti String Quartet; Grammy Award for CD recording of works of Elliott Carter including cello sonata and solo cello piece, Figment I; Honorary PhD, Peradeniya University, Kandy, Sri

Lanka, 2004. Address: 20 St Georges Avenue, London N7 0HD, England. E-mail: rosiedesaram@hotmail.com Website: www.rohandesaram.co.uk

DE SAVORGNANI Adriane Aldrich, b. 17 December 1940, Boston, Massachusetts, USA. Nurse; Naval Medical Administrator. m. Luciano de Savorgnani, deceased, 1 son, 2 daughters. Education: AB, 1962, Radcliffe College, Cambridge, Massachusetts; Diploma, Coordinated Program, Radcliffe College and Massachusetts General Hospital General Hospital School of Nursing, Boston, Massachusetts, 1965; MPH, University of Hawaii School of Public Health, Honolulu, Hawaii, 1974; DBA, Nova University, Fort Lauderdale, Florida, USA, 1992. Appointments: Numerous nursing and executive medicine appointments in the USA and Europe, including, Charge Nurse Emergency Room, Outpatient Care Co-ordinator, Inpatient Care Co-ordinator, US Naval Hospital, Naples, Italy, 1979-83; Head, Health Care Plans, Special Projects, Head, Preventive Medicine and Health Promotion, Bureau of Medicine and Surgery, Washington, DC, 1989-92; Executive Officer, Naval Hospital, Lemoore, California, USA, 1995-98; Commanding Officer, US Naval Medical Clinics, United Kingdom, 1998-2001; Head, Clinical Plans and Management Division, and Assistant Deputy Chief, BUMED Medical Operations Support (Acting), Bureau of Medicine and Surgery, Washington, DC, 2001-03; Retired from Navy, 2003; Administrative Assistant, US Defense Attache Office, American Embassy, London. Publications: Numerous papers and articles in nursing and health care administration journals, such as Midwest Business Administration Association Proceedings; Military Medicine; Navy Medicine; The Nursing Spectrum; Caring; Journal of Nursing Administration; The Case Manager. Honours: Legion of Merit; Meritorious Service Medal (5 times awarded); Navy Commendation Medal (twice awarded); National Defense Service Medal (one star); Global War on Terrorism Service Medal; Volunteer Service Medal; Navy and Marine Corps Overseas Service Ribbon (7 stars). Memberships: Life Member, Association of Military Surgeons of the United States; Fellow, American College of Healthcare Executives; Member: American Nurses Association; American Public Health Association; Academy of Management; Sigma Theta Tau International; Recertified in Advanced Nursing Administration. Address: 14 Bardsley Lane, Greenwich, London SE10 9RF, United Kingdom.

DE SOUSA Alice, b. 11 January 1966, Portugal. Actress; Producer; Artistic Director. Education: BA, Honours, EEC Law, 1st Class, 1995; MA, Portuguese Studies, 1997. Career: Numerous roles in television, radio and film productions; Lead roles in over 30 productions, including Hermione, The Winter's Tale; Millamant, The Way of the World; Elvira, Blithe Spirit; Producer of more than 60 theatre productions, including: Never Nothing From No One, Hamlet, Company, Pymaglion, Richard III, You're Gonna Love Tomorrow, Hedda Gabler, Peep Show, Cousin Basillio; Shadows on the Sun; The Importance of Being Earnest, Three Sisters, The White Devil, 'Tis Pity She's a Whore, The Ruffian on the Stair and The Erpingham Camp, The Maias, Ines de Castro, King Lear, Absent Friends, A Doll's House, and The Heiress of the Cane Fields. Address: Greenwich Playhouse, 189 Greenwich High Road, London, SE10 8JA, England.

DE STACPOOLE Robert George Francis, b. 30 March 1924, London, England. Historian. m. Susan Mary Angela Trouncer, 1 son, 3 daughters. Education: BA, 1948, MA, 1963, Christ's College, Cambridge. Appointments: Active Academic Historian, 1948-2005; Working Member of

Lloyds, 1950-96; Insurer at Lloyds, 1956-93. Publications: Various historical articles relating to Europe, Ireland, USA and the Papacy. Memberships: 1900 Club, 1949-; St James' Club, 1947-75; Brooks Club, 1976-; Catholic Union, 1953-; Kensington Society, 2000-. Address: St Wilfrids Convent, 29 Tite Street, London, SW3 4JX, England.

DE VASCONCELOS Maria do Carmo, Full Professor. Education: Licenciatura, Germanic Philology and Postgraduation, Faculty of Letters, Classic University of Lisbon, 1974, 1975; Bacharelato, Film Studies, National Conservatory of Lisbon, Portugal, 1976; M Phil, English, 1994, PhD, English, 1995, Graduate Center, City University of New York, USA. Appointments: Instructor, 1974, Assistant Professor, 1975-80, English, Faculty of Letters, Classic University of Lisbon; Tutor and Instructor, English, New York Technical College, 1982; Instructor, English, The City College/The City University of New York, 1988-92; Adjunct Lecturer, 1990-94, Instructor, 1994-96, Assistant Professor, 1996-99, Associate Professor, 1999-2005, Full Professor, 2005-, English, Borough of Manhattan Community College/ The City University of New York. Publications: Translations as co-author from Portuguese into English including: Benamonte and Monique, 2006; Article on the poetry of Esther Phillips, a Barbadian poet; Translation of Luisa Coelho's poems on Angola. Honours: Professor of the Year, University of Lisbon several times, 1975-80; Wall of Tolerance Community Recognition; Article about her life and career, Luso American Newspaper; Conducted 36 Honor Projects, 1995-2007; Rosen Mentor Award, New Jersey College English Association, 2007; Listed in Who's Who publications and biographical dictionaries. Memberships: Modern Language Association; North East Modern Language Association; Past President, Women's Caucus; President, Academy for the Humanities and Sciences, City University of New York; League for Innovations; National Council of Teachers of English. Address: BMCC/CUNY, 199 Chambers Street, Department of English, New York, NY 10007, USA.

DE VILLIERS François Pierre Rousseau, b. 10 May 1950, Namibia. Professor of Paediatrics. m. (1) J Gai, deceased 2001, 1 son, 1 daughter (2) Mariana Catharina, 2004. Education: MBChB, 1974; BA, 1983; MMed, 1987; PhD, 1990; FACP, 2000; FCPaed (SA), 2001; FCFP (SA), 2007. Appointments: Professor and Chair, Paediatrics, 1994, Deputy Dean (Research), 1997-2001, Deputy Dean (Academic Matters), 2004-06, Medical University of South Africa. Publications: Book: Practical Management of Paediatric Emergencies, 4th Edition, 2004; Numerous articles in professional journals. Honour: Research Excellence Award, Medunsa, 1998; Research Excellence Award for Senior Researcher, Medunsa, 2001. Memberships: New York Academy of Sciences; International Society for the Study of Paediatric and Adolescent Diabetes; American College of Physicians. Address: PO Box 480, Medunsa 0204, South Africa.

DE VOS George, Anthropologist; Psychologist. Education: Japanese Language and Area Training, US Army, Yale University, University of Michigan, 1943-46; BA, Sociology, 1946, MA, Anthropology, 1948, PhD, Psychology, University of Chicago. Appointments: Academic Posts: Chief Psychologist, Director of Psychological Internship Training Program, Elgin State Hospital, Elgin, Illinois, 1951-53; Assistant Professor of Psychology, University of Michigan, 1955-57; Associate Professor of Social Welfare, 1957-65, Professor of Anthropology, 1965-91, Professor Emeritus, 1991-, University of California, Berkeley; Professional and Research Experience includes: Member, Japanese-American

Interdisciplinary Research Group affiliated with Chicago Institute for Psychoanalysis, 1947-51; Public Health Fellow, Illinois Neuropsychiatric Institute, University of Illinois, 1949-50; Research Associate in Psychology, Michael Reese Hospital, Chicago, 1950-51; Fulbright Act Research Senior Research Fellowship, Department of Neuropsychiatry, Nagoya National University, Nagoya, Japan; Director, Ford Foundation, Japanese Personality and Culture Research Project, University of Michigan, 1955-57; Chair, Center for Japanese and Korean Studies, 1965-68, Research Associate, Executive Committee Institute for Personality Assessment and Research, 1969-91, Associate, Institute for East Asian Studies, 1975-91 University of California, Berkeley; Numerous visiting and exchange professorships including University of Paris, University of Rome, Catholic University of Leuven (Belgium), University of Barcelona, University of Leningrad (now St Petersburg), Catholic University of Porto Allegro (Brazil, 1991-92). Publications: 22 books include most recently: Ethnic Identity: Creation, Conflict and Accommodation (co-editor), 5th edition 2006; Confucianism and the Family in an Interdisciplinary, Comparative Context (co-editor), 1998; Basic Dimensions in Conscious Thought. Volume I: The Psychocultural Research with the Thematic Apperception Test (co-author), 2004; Cross-Cultural Dimensions in Conscious Thought. Volume 2: Psychocultural Research with the Thematic Apperception Test (co-author), 2004; Numerous articles in professional journals, 1952-. Address: Department of Anthropology, University of California, Berkeley CA 94720, USA. E-mail: devos@berkeley.edu

DE WET Jacobus Anthony, b. 27 July 1929, Grahamstown, South Africa. Engineer; Mathematical Physicist. m. P A Van Reenen, 3 sons, 1 daughter. Education: BSc, 1950; MSc, 1952; PhD, 1970. Appointments: Principal Engineer, Department of Water Affairs; Senior Research Officer, Council of Scientific and Industrial Research. Publications: 15 papers on nuclear structure, recently making use of algebraic geometry. Memberships: South African Institute of Physics; South African Natural Scientist; Past Member, New York Academy of Sciences. Address: Box 514, 6600 Plettenberg Bay, South Africa.

DE WRACHIEN Daniele, b. 6 June 1938, Udine, Italy. Hydrologist; Educator; Consultant. 2 daughters. Education: Graduate, Geology, 1964, PhD degree, Advanced Engineering Geology, 1966, State University of Milan. Appointments: Graduate with technical functions, 1967-70, Lecturer of Geopedology, 1970-83, Associate Professor, 1983-86, Full Professor, 1986-, Irrigation and Drainage, Department Director, 2000-06, Department of Agricultural Hydraulics, State University of Milan. Publications: Author, Over 150 scientific papers, key-note lectures, books and technical reports; Co-author, Land Reclamation and Conservation, 1999; Author, Land Use Planning: A Key to Sustainable Agriculture, 2003; Co-organiser of over 50 international conferences, congresses, symposia and workshops in Africa, America, Asia and Europe; Co-editor: Water and Irrigation Development 2001; Crop Water Management for Food Production under Limited Water Supplies, 2002; Land Reclamation and Water Resources Development, 2003; Water Resources Management and Irrigation and Drainage Systems Development in the European Environment, 2007; Expert: Question 39, Irrigation and Drainage of Problem Soils, 1984; Question 48, Irrigation under Conditions of Water Scarcity, 1999; Co-leader of world-wide investigations: Conjunctive Use of Surface and Groundwater, 2002; Irrigation and Drainage Systems: Research and Development in the 21st Century, 2002; Global Warming and Drainage Development,

2004; Climate Variability Agriculture and Food Security: A World-wide View, 2004. Honours: Award for Truthful Support and Help in Organising and Improving Scientific Level of the Symposia, Actual Tasks on Agricultural Engineering, Croatian Agricultural Engineering Society, 2006; Award in Recognition of Services to the European Society of Agricultural Engineers, 2006. Memberships: International Commission on Irrigation and Drainage, 1988-; Past President, European Society of Agricultural Engineers, 1993-; International Commission of Agricultural Engineering, 1995-; Editorial Boards: Irrigation and Drainage; Progress in Agricultural Engineering Sciences; Journal of Agricultural Engineering; Listed in international biographical dictionaries. Address: Department of Agricultural Hydraulics, Via Giovanni Celoria 2, 20133 Milan, Italy. E-mail: daniele.dewrachien@unimi.it

DEAL Alicia Renee, b. 24 April 1982, Texas, USA. Student. Education: BA, Criminal Justice, 2003, MA, Criminology, 2006, PhD, in progress, Sam Houston State University, Huntsville, Texas. Appointments: First State Bank, Grapeland, 1999-2000, 2003-04; Student Assistant for Associate Dean Dr Wes Johnson, 2004-05; Teaching/Research Assistant to Dr Hee-Jong Joo, 2005-06; Texas Correctional Office on Offenders with Medical or Mental Impairments, 2006-. Honours: Dean's List, 2000, 2002, 2003; President's List, 2001, 2003; National Dean's List, 2002-03, 2003-04; SHSU Outstanding Writer Award, 2004; Chancellor's List, 2006-07; Listed in biographical directories. Memberships: Southwestern Association of Criminal Justice; American Society of Criminology; Academy of Criminal Justice Sciences. Address: PO Box 946, Grapeland, TX 75844, USA. E-mail: stdard11@shsu.edu

DEAN Christopher, OBE, b. 27 July 1958, Nottingham, England. Ice Skater. m. (1) Isabelle Duchesnay, 1991, divorced, 1993, (2) Jill Ann Trenary, 1994, 2 sons. Appointments: Police Constable, 1974-80; British Ice Dance Champion (with Jayne Torvill), 1978-83, 1993; European Ice Dance Champion (with Jayne Torvill), 1981, 1982, 1984, 1994; World Ice Dance Champion (with Jayne Torvill), 1981-84; World professional Champions, 1984-85, 1990, 1995-96; Choreographed Encounters for English National Ballet, 1996; Stars on Ice, USA, 1998-99, 1999-2000; Ice Dance: World tours with own and international companies of skaters, 1985, 1988, 1994, 1997, tours of Australia and New Zealand, 1984, 1991, UK, 1992, Japan, 1996, USA and Canada, 1997-98. Publications: Torvill and Dean's Face the Music and Dance (with Jayne Torvill), 1993; Torvill and Dean: An Autobiography (with Jayne Torvill), 1994; Facing the Music (with Jayne Torvill), 1996. Honours: BBC Sportsview Personality of the Year (with Jayne Torvill), 1983-84; Honorary MA, 1994; OBE, 1999. Address: c/o Sue Young, PO Box 32, Heathfield, East Sussex, TN21 0BW, England.

DEANE Seamus (Francis), b. 9 February 1940, Derry City, Northern Ireland. Professor of Irish Studies; Writer; Poet. m. Marion Treacy, 19 August 1963, 3 sons, 1 daughter. Education: BA, Honours, 1st Class, 1961, MA, 1st Class, 1963, Queen's University, Belfast; PhD, Cambridge University, 1968. Appointments: Visiting Fulbright and Woodrow Wilson Scholar, Reed College, Oregon, 1966-67; Visiting Lecturer, 1967-68, Visiting Professor, 1978, University of California at Berkeley; Professor of Modern English and American Literature, University College, Dublin, 1980-93; Walker Ames Professor, University of Washington, Seattle, 1987; Julius Benedict Distinguished Visiting Professor, Carleton College, Minnesota, 1988; Keough Professor of Irish Studies, University of Notre Dame, Indiana, 1993-. Publications:

Fiction: Reading in the Dark, 1996. Poetry: Gradual Wars, 1972; Rumours, 1977; History Lessons, 1983; Selected, 1988. Non-Fiction: Celtic Revivals: Essays in Modern Irish Literature, 1880-1980, 1985; A Short History of Irish Literature, 1986, reissued, 1994; The French Revolution and Enlightenment in England, 1789-1832, 1988; Strange Country: Ireland, Modernity and Nationhood, 1790-1970, 1997; Foreign Affections: Essays on Edmund Burke, 2005. Editor: The Adventures of Hugh Trevor by Thomas Holcroft, 1972; The Sale Catalogues of the Libraries of Eminent Persons, Vol IX, 1973; Nationalism, Colonialism and Literature, 1990; The Field Day Anthology of Irish Writing, 3 volumes, 1991; Penguin Twentieth Century Classics: James Joyce, 5 volumes, 1993; Field Day Review 1, 2005. Honours: AE Memorial for Literature, 1973; American-Irish Fund, Literature, 1989; Guardian Fiction Prize, 1997; Irish Times International Fiction Award, 1997; Irish Times Fiction Award, 1997; London Weekend Television South Bank Award for Literature, 1997; Ruffino Antico-Fattore International Literature Award, Florence, 1998; Honorary DLitt, Ulster, 1999. Memberships: Aosdana (Irish Artists' Council); Field Day Theatre and Publishing Company, director; Royal Irish Academy. Address: Institute of Irish Studies, 1145 Flanner Hall, University of Notre Dame, IN 46556, USA.

DEAR Nick, b. 11 June 1955, Portsmouth, England. Playwright. m. Penny Downie, 2 sons. Education: BA, Honours, European Literature, University of Essex, 1977. Appointments: Playwright-in-Residence, Essex University, 1985, Royal Exchange Theatre, 1987-88. Publications: Temptation, 1984; The Art of Success, 1986; Food of Love, 1988; A Family Affair (after Ostrovsky), 1988; In the Ruins, 1989; The Last Days of Don Juan (after Tirso), 1990; Le Bourgeois Gentilhomme (after Molière), 1992; Pure Science, 1994; Zenobia, 1995; Summerfolk (after Gorky), 1999; The Villains' Opera, 2000; Power, 2003; Lunch in Venice, 2005; The Turn of the Screw, 2005; The Miracle of Reason, 2005. Opera Libretti: A Family Affair, 1993; Siren Song, 1994; The Palace in the Sky, 2000; Other: Several radio plays. Films: The Monkey Parade, 1993; The Ranter, 1988; Persuasion, 1995; The Gambler, 1997; The Turn of the Screw, 1999; Cinderella, 2000; Byron, 2003; Eroica, 2003; The Hollow, 2004; Cards on the Table, 2006. Honours: John Whiting Award, 1987; Olivier Award nominations, 1987, 1988; BAFTA Award, 1996; Broadcasting Press Guild Award, 1996; South Bank Show Theatre Award, 1999; Prix Italia, 2003. Membership: Writer's Guild of Great Britain. Address: c/o Rosica Colin Ltd, 1 Clareville Grove Mews, London SW7 5AH, England.

DEARDEN James Shackley, b. 9 August 1931, Barrow-in-Furness, England. Appointment: Curator, Ruskin Galleries, Bembridge School, Isle of Wight and Brantwood Coniston, 1957-96. Publications: The Professor: Arthur Severn's Memoir of Ruskin, 1967; A Short History of Brantwood, 1967; Iteriad by John Ruskin (editor), 1969; Facets of Ruskin, 1970, Japanese edition, 2001; Ruskin and Coniston (with K G Thorne), 1971; John Ruskin, 1973, 2nd edition, 1981, Japanese edition, 1991, enlarged edition, 2004; Turner's Isle of Wight Sketch Book, 1979; John Ruskin and Les Alpi, 1989; John Ruskin's Camberwell, 1990; A Tour to the Lakes in Cumberland: John Ruskin's Diary for 1830 (editor), 1990; John Ruskin and Victorian Art, 1993; Ruskin, Bembridge and Brantwood, 1994; Hare Hunting on the Isle of Wight, 1996; John Ruskin, a life in pictures, 1999; King of the Golden River by John Ruskin (editor), 1999; Further Facets of Ruskin, 2007. Contributions to: Book Collector; Connoisseur; Apollo; Burlington; Bulletin of John Rylands Library; Country Life; Ruskin Newsletter (editor); Ruskin

Research Series (general editor); Journal of Pre-Raphaelite Studies; The Companion; Ruskin Programme Bulletin; Turner Society News; Whitehouse Edition of Ruskin's Works (joint general editor). Honour: Hon D Litt (Lancaster), 1998. Memberships: Ruskin Society; Turner Society; Companion of the Guild of St George, Master and Director for Ruskin Affairs; Old Bembridgians Association, past president; Isle of Wight Foot Beagles, former Master and President; Friends of Ruskin's Brantwood, vice president. Address: 4 Woodlands, Foreland Road, Bembridge, Isle of Wight, England.

DEARLOVE Richard Billing (Sir), b. 23 January 1945, Cornwall, England. Master, Pembroke College, Cambridge. m. Rosalind, 2 sons, 1 daughter. Education: MA, Queens' College Cambridge. Appointments: Entered Foreign Office, 1966; Nairobi, 1968-71; Prague, 1973-76; Foreign and Commonwealth Office, 1976-80; First Secretary Paris, 1980-84; Foreign and Commonwealth Office, 1984-87; Counsellor, UKMIS Geneva, 1987-91, Washington, 1991-93; Director, Personnel and Administration, 1993-94, Director, Operations, 1994-99, Assistant Chief, 1998-99, Chief, 1999-2004, Secret Intelligence Service; Master of Pembroke College, Cambridge, 2004-; Trustee, Kent School, Connecticut, USA, 2001-; Advisor to The Monitor Group, 2004-; International Advisory Board, AIG, 2005-; Chairman of Ascot Underwriting, 2006. Honours: OBE, 1984; KCMG, 2001; Honorary Fellow, Queens' College, Cambridge, 2004. Address: Master's Lodge, Pembroke College, Cambridge, CB2 1RF, England.

DEBAKEY Lois, b. Lake Charles, Louisiana, USA. Professor of Scientific Communication; Writer; Editor; Lecturer. Education: BA, Mathematics, Newcomb College, Tulane University; MA, PhD, Literature and Linguistics, Tulane University; Postgraduate Courses in Biostatistics, Medical School, Tulane University. Appointments include: Professor of Scientific Communications, Baylor College of Medicine, 1968-; Consultant, National Library of Medicine, Bethesda, Maryland, 1986-; Member, National Advisory Committee, University of Southern California Development and Demonstration Center in Continuing Education for Health Professionals; Consultant, American Bar Association Legal Writing Committee; Advisory Committee, Society for the Advancement of Good English; Trustee, DeBakey Medical Foundation; Member, Advisory Council, University of Texas at Austin School of Nursing Foundation, 1993-; Member, Usage Panel, American Heritage Dictionary; Team Leader Consultant, Health and Medical Data Base, Encyclopaedia Britannica; Current Editorial Board Member: Journal of the American Medical Association, Core Journals in Cardiology, International Angiology Network, CV Network; Internationally renowned course developer and authority in the field of medical writing; Acclaimed for use of cartoons and humour as teaching aids. Publications: Editor and author of numerous medical and scientific articles, chapters and books; Senior author, The Scientific Journal: Editorial Policies and Practices, 1976; Co-author, Medicine: Preserving the Passion, 1987; Co-author, Medicine: Preserving the Passion in the 21st Century, 2004. Honours include: Phi Beta Kappa; Golden Key National Honor Society; Distinguished Service Award, American Medical Writers Society, 1970; Inaugural John P McGovern Award, Medical Library Association, 1983; Member, Texas Hall of Fame; Life Honorary Member, Medical Library Association, 1989. Memberships include: Founding Board of Directors, Friends of the National Library of Medicine; Fellow, American College of Medical Informatics; Fellow, Royal Society for the Encouragement of Arts, Manufactures and Commerce, UK; Medical Library

Association; National Association of Science Writers; Foundation for Advanced Education in the Sciences; Plain English Forum. Address: Baylor College of Medicine, 1 Baylor Plaza, Houston TX 77030 3411, USA.

DEBAKEY Michael Ellis, b. 7 September 1908, Lake Charles, Louisiana, USA. Cardiovascular Surgeon. m. Katrin Fehlhaber, 4 sons, 1 daughter. Education: BS, 1930, MD, 1932, MS, 1935, Tulane University. Appointments: Chairman of Surgery, Baylor College of Medicine, 1948-93; Clinical Professor of Surgery, University of Texas Dental Branch, 1952-; President, The DeBakey Medical Foundation, Houston, 1961-; Distinguished Service Professor, Baylor College of Medicine, 1968-; Vice President for Medical Affairs and CEO, Baylor College of Medicine, 1968-69; President Baylor College of Medicine, 1969-79; Distinguished Professor of Surgery, Texas A&M University, 1972-; Chancellor, Baylor College of Medicine, 1978-96; Olga Keith Wiess Professor of Surgery, Baylor College of Medicine, 1981-; Director, The DeBakey Heart Center, Houston, 1985-; Chancellor Emeritus, Baylor College of Medicine, 1996-. Publications: Over 1,600 in books and professional journals. Honours include: More than 50 honorary degrees; US Army Legion of Merit, 1945; American Medical Association Distinguished Service Medal, 1959; Albert Lasker Award for Clinical Research, 1963; Presidential Medal of Freedom with Distinction, presented by Lyndon B Johnson, 1969; Eleanor Roosevelt Humanities Award, 1969; USSR Academy of Sciences 50th Anniversary Jubilee Medal, 1973; National Medal of Science, awarded by President Ronald Reagan, 1987; Academy of Athens induction, 1992; Thomas Jefferson Award, American Institute of Architects, 1993; Children Uniting Nations, Global Peace and Tolerance Lifetime Achievement Award for Science and Technology, 1999; John P McGovern Compleat Physician Award, 1999; Library of Congress Bicentennial Living Legend Award, 2000; Methodist DeBakey Heart Center, 2001; NASA Invention of the Year Award, 2001; Foundation for Biomedical Research Michael E DeBakey Journalism Award, 2002; Lindbergh-Carrell Prize, 2002; Golden Hippocrates International Prize for Excellency in Medicine, Laureate of the Year, 2003; Baylor College of Medicine, Michael E DeBakey Student Poetry Award, 2003; Russian Academy of Sciences, Lomonosov Gold Medal, 2004; American Heart Association National Chapter, Lifetime Achievement Award, 2004; Michael E DeBakey Veterans Affairs Medical Center, 2004; David E Rogers Award, Association of Medical Colleges and Robert Wood Johnson Foundation, 2004; Albert Lasker-Michael E DeBakey Clinical Medical Research Awards, 2005; American College of Surgeons Outstanding Surgical Patient Safety Award, 2005; Michael E DeBakey Chair in Cardiovascular Sciences, Balamand University Medical School, Beirut, Lebanon, 2005; New York Academy of Medicine 17th Annual Glorney-Raisbeck Lecture and Award in Cardiology, 2005; Russian Assembly of Health Charity Foundation Profession is Life International Prize Laureate, The Legend of the World Medicine, 2005; The Jonathan Club 2006 Reagan Distinguished American Award, 2006; National American Lebanese Medical Association Physician of the Century, 2006; Texas State History Museum Foundation History Making Texan Award, 2006; Covenant Health System, Michael E DeBakey Distinguished Lectureship Series, 2004; Baylor College of Medicine, Michael E DeBakey Library and Museum, 2004; Lake Charles City Council, Louisiana, Michael E DeBakey Aviation Complex, 2005; First recipient of the Castle Connolly Medical Ltd, and the Baylor Alumni Association Lifetime Achievement Awards, 2006; New Cardiovascular Horizons, Lifetime Achievement Award, 2006; Impact Player Partners Inc, Impact Player Hall of Fame,

2006; BioHouston, Michael E DeBakey Life Science Award, 2006; National Library of Medicine, Michael E DeBakey MD, Seminars in Medicine, 2006. Memberships include: World Medical Association; American Medical Association; International Cardiovascular Society; American College of Surgeons; American Surgical Association; Thoracic Surgery Directors Association; Texas Heart Association; Texas Academy of Science; Western Surgical Association. Address: Baylor College of Medicine, One Baylor Plaza, Houston, TX 77030, USA.

DEBAKEY Selma, b. Lake Charles, Louisiana, USA. Professor of Scientific Communication. Education: BA, Languages, Newcomb College; Postgraduate studies, French and Philosophy, Tulane University. Appointments: Director, Department of Medical Communications, Ochsner Clinic and Alton Ochsner Medical Foundation, New Orleans, 1942-68; Medical Writer and Editor; Consultant Editor; Internationally renowned course developer. Main professional interests: Internationally recognised authority in the field of medical writing and editing, most especially in the use of humour in the form of cartoons to depict faulty reasoning and language use; Ethics; Literacy; Publishing. Publications: A huge body of work, as writer, editor, consultant, course developer; Co-author, Current Concepts in Breast Cancer, 1967; Numerous articles and papers contributed to specialist peer-reviewed journals; Over 1000 articles as Editor; Judge for several prestigious medical writing awards, including Modern Medical Monographs Awards, AORN DuPuy Writer's Awards. Honours: Named in Texas Hall of Fame; Listed in numerous international and specialist biographical directories, including: Dictionary of International Biography; Outstanding People of the 21st Century; 2000 Outstanding Intellectuals of the 21st Century; 2000 Outstanding Scientists of the 21st Century; 2000 Outstanding Scholars of the 21st Century; 2000 Outstanding Women of the 20th Century; Who's Who in America; Who's Who in the World; Profiled in numerous newspapers and magazines. Memberships: American Association for the Advancement of Science; American Medical Writers' Association; Association of Teachers of Technical Writing; Council of Biology Editors; Society for Health and Human Values; Society for Technical Communication. Address: Baylor College of Medicine, 1 Baylor Plaza, Houston, TX 77030 3411, USA.

DECLERCQ Nico Felicien, b. 27 December 1975, Kortrijk, Belgium. Professor. m. Shirani de Silva, 1 son, 1 daughter. BSc, MSc (Hons), Physics, Catholic University of Leuven, Belgium, 2000; PhD, Engineering Physics (congratulations from the Jury), Ghent University, 2005. Appointments: Voluntary Researcher, Catholic University of Leuven, 2000-2001; PhD Researcher, Ghent University, Belgium, 2001-2005; Postdoctoral Researcher, Belgian National Science Foundation, 2005-2006; Assistant Professor, The Georgia Institute of Technology, USA, 2006-. Publications: Over 35 scientific papers; Over 60 congress presentations and proceedings; 2 papers in Nature News: Mexican Pyramid; Explanation of Acoustics of Hellenistic Theatre at Epidaurus. Honours: International Dennis Gabor Award, 2006; Various different awards and grants. Memberships include: Acoustical Society of America; British Institute of NDT; Société Française d'acoustique; Russian Acoustic Society; IEEE. Address: Woodruff School of Mechanical Engineering, The Georgia Institute of Technology, Atlanta, GA 30332-0405, USA. E-mail: nico.declerq@me.gatech.edu Website: www.me.gatech.edu\declerq

DEEGALLE Mahinda, b. 31 October 1961, Badulla, Sri Lanka. Academic; University Teacher. Education: BA (Hons) University of Peradeniya, 1985; MTS, Harvard University, 1989; PhD, University of Chicago, 1995. Appointments: Research Collaborator, Kyoto University, 1995-96; Research Fellow, Japan Society for the Promotion of Science, 1997-99; Research Fellow, International College for Advanced Buddhist Studies, 1999; Numata Visiting Professor, McGill University, 1999-2000; Instructor, Cornell University, 2000; Senior Lecturer, Study of Religions, Bath Spa University, 2005-. Publications: Pali Buddhism (co-editor), 1996; From Buddhology to Buddhist Theology, 2000; Is Violence Justified? Current Dialogue, 2002; Preacher as a Poet, 2003; Buddhist Prayer, 2003; Austerity as a Virtue, 2003; Sri Lankan Theravada Buddhism in London, 2004; Politics of the Jathika Hela Urumaya Monks, 2004; Buddhism, Conflict and Violence in Modern Sri Lanka (editor), 2006; Popularizing Buddhism: Preaching as Performance in Sri Lanka (author), 2006; Buddhist Monks as Foot Soldiers in Political Activisim in Sri Lanka, 2006. Honours: Honorary Title "Vimalakirti Sri; Fulbright Award, 1987-89; Valedictorian, Harvard University Divinity School, 1989; Bukkyo Dendo Kyokai Fellowship, 1995-96. Memberships: American Academy of Religion; International Association of Buddhist Studies; British Association for the Study of Religion; United Kingdom Association for Buddhist Studies; PTS. Address: Study of Religions, School of Historical and Cultural Studies, Bath Spa University, Newton Park, Bath BA2 9BN, England. E-mail: m.deegalle@bathspa.ac.uk

DEEKEN Alfons Theodor, b. 3 August 1932, Emstek, Niedersachsen, Germany. Philosopher; Educator; Writer. Education: MA, Berchmanskolleg, Munich, Germany, 1958; MA, Sophia University, Tokyo, 1966; PhD, Fordham University, New York, 1973. Appointments: Assistant Professor to Professor, 1973-82, Professor of Philosophy, 1982-2003, Professor Emeritus, 2003-, Sophia University, Tokyo, Japan; President, Japanese Association of Death Education & Grief Counselling, 1974-2003; President, Japanese Society of Clinical Thanatology, 2001-02. Publications: Growing Old and How to Cope With It, 1972; Process and Permanence in Ethics: Max Scheler's Moral Philosophy, 1974; Kirisutokyoo to Watakushi (Christianity), 1995; Humor wa Oi to Shi no Myooyaku (Humour), 1995; Confronting Death, 1996; Death Education, 2001; Hikari no dialogue (Words of the Bible), 2002; Yoku Iki, Yoku Warai, Yoki Shi to Deau (Good living, good humour, good death), 2003. Honours: Best Ethics Book of 1974, Catholic Press Association, America, 1975; Kikuchi Kan Literary Award, Literary Association of Japan, 1991; Cross of the Order of Merit of the German Federal Republic, President of Germany, 1998; Cultural Award, City of Tokyo, 1999. Memberships: Japanese Association for Clinical Research on Death and Dying; International Work Group on Death, Dying and Bereavement. Address: Sophia University, S J House, Kioicho 7-1, Chiyoda-ku, 102-8571 Tokyo, Japan.

DEERING Anne-Lise, b. Norway. Clay Artist; Medallic Sculptor; Former Potter. Education: Science Degree, Norway, 1954; Oil Painting, Southern Illinois University, Carbondale, Illinois, 1958; Ceramics, Foothill College, Los Altos, California, 1975; BA, Art, Penn State University, University Park, Pennsylvania, 1977; Computer Graphic Design and Medallic Art, Penn State University, 1990-91; Residential Real Estate Appraisal Courses, Marketing Strategy, Sales and Promotion Courses, PA Realtors Institute, 1994-96. Career: Middle Eastern Dance Teacher, 1975-80; Self-employed Clay Artist and Potter, 1977-98; Member, 1977-2000, Juried Member, 1981-2000, Board of Directors, 1984-97, Pennsylvania Guild of Craftsmen (PGC); Participant in PGC Craft Fairs for 10 years; Artist Member, Art Alliance of Central Pennsylvania, 1978-99; Participant in Art Alliance Gallery Shop, 1989-99; Licensed Real Estate Sales Person, 1991-99; Exhibits include: American Medallic Sculpture Association juried exhibit, Newark Museum, New Jersey, 1990; Invitational, Mountain Top Gallery, Cresson, Pennsylvania, 1998; The Pen and Brush Gallery juried exhibit, New York City, 1998, 1999, 2000, 2001; American Numismatic Association, Colorado Springs, 2001; Penn State University, 2002, Wroclav, Poland, 2002; AMSA juried exhibit, Ornamental Metal Museum, Memphis, Tennessee, 2003; Co-ordinator and chair of AMSA members juried exhibit, Nordic Heritage Museum, Seattle, Washington, 2004; In charge of AMSA medals displays at numerous libraries throughout the greater Seattle area, 2004; Participated in AMSA members exhibit, Forest Lawn Museum, Glendale, California, 2005; Medal in private collections and the permanent collection of the Museum of Medallic Art, Wroclav, Poland; Exhibited in FIDEM shows: Weimar, Germany, 2000; Paris, France, 2002; Seixal, Portugal, 2004; Colorado Springs, USA, 2007; AMSA members exhibit, Birmingham Museum, Birmingham, Michigan, 2007. Memberships: Pennsylvania Guild of Craftsmen and Central Pennsylvania Chapter, 1977-2000; Member of American Medallic Sculpture Association (AMSA), 1990-, Newsletter Editor, 2000-, Secretary, 2001-; Charter Member, National Museum of Women in the Arts, 1998-; Board of Directors, Washington Potters Association, 2000-; Member, Federation International de la Medaille (FIDEM); Member, Pacific Northwest Sculptors, 2006-; Listed in Who's Who publications and biographical dictionaries. Address: 24229 92nd Ave W, Edmonds, WA 98020, USA.

DEERING Richard John, b. 15 July 1947, London, England. Concert Pianist. m. Emma Caroline Budgen, 2 sons, 2 daughters. Education: Studied with Frank Merrick, Trinity College of Music, 1965-69; Private studies with Peter Wallfisch. Appointments: Senior Examiner, Trinity College, London; Concerts worldwide in over 90 countries, 1975-. Publications: Several recordings made in both UK and Japan; Numerous articles for Classical Music, Piano, Music Teacher and Business Traveller magazines. Honours: Award for Distinguished Service to British Music, Royal Philharmonic Society, 1981; Trinity College London Chairman's Award 2006. Memberships: Incorporated Society of Musicians; British Music Society; Royal Philharmonic Society; British & International Federation of Festivals; British MENSA. Address: 55 Dalmally Road, Croydon, Surrey CR0 6LW, England. E-mail: richard@malacca.demon.co.uk

DEGARMO Mark B, b. 2 November 1955, Connecticut, USA. Dancer; Choreographer; Arts Educator. Education: BFA, Dance, Juilliard School for the Performing Arts, 1982; PhD, Union Institute & University, 2007. Appointments: Founder & Executive Director, Mark DeGarmo Dancers/Dynamic Forms Inc, 1987-; Teaching Artist in Aesthetic Dance and Education, Lincoln Center Institute for the Arts in Education, 1986-2000. Publications: Windows on the Work, 6 volumes; 100 dances choreographed. Honours: Fulbright Senior Scholar Fellowship to Peru, 1998-99; American Cultural Specialist Award to Ecuador, 2000; Honorary Committee of the Martha Hill Award for Leadership in Dance, 2001. Memberships: Founding Board Member, A Room of Her Own Foundation, New Mexico; Board Member, Fulbright Association, Greater New York City; Board Member, Clemente Soto Vélez Cultural and Educational Center, New York. Address: 107 Suffolk Street, Suite 310, New York City, NY 10002, USA. Website: http://markdegarmoarts.org

DEGERFELT Kent, b. 28 March 1946, Gothenburg, Sweden. Ambassador. m. Brunella. Education includes: Interpreter in Russian, Military Interpreters' School, Uppsala, Sweden, 1969-70; BA, History of Economics, Political Sciences, International Development Co-operation, University of Gothenburg, Sweden, 1968-72; Master of Law, University of Lund, Sweden, 1968-73; Studies at Ecole National d'Administration, Paris, 1983-84. Appointments include: Attaché, Ministry for Foreign Affairs, Stockholm, 1973-74; Attaché, Permanent Mission of Sweden to the UN, Geneva, 1975; Second Secretary, Embassy of Sweden, Madrid, 1975-78; Deputy Head of Mission, Embassy of Sweden, Jakarta, Indonesia, 1978-80; First Secretary, Ministry for Foreign Affairs, Stockholm, 1981-82; Deputy Head of Mission, Embassy of Sweden in Guatemala City and Chargé d'Affairs in El Salvador, 1982-83; First Secretary, Embassy of Sweden, Paris, 1984-88; Deputy Head of Division/ Head of Section, Ministry for Foreign Affairs, Stockholm, 1988-90; Counsellor, Embassy of Sweden, Nairobi, Kenya, 1991; Deputy Head of Mission, Embassy of Sweden, Rabat, Morocco, 1991-95; Counsellor, 1995-96, Director, 1996, Ministry for Foreign Affairs, Stockholm; Ambassador, Head of Delegation, European Commission, Managua, Nicaragua, 1996-99; Adviser ad personam, Directorate General for External Relations, European Commission, Brussels, 2000-2002; Ambassador, Head of Delegation, European Commission, Khartoum, Sudan, 2002-. Honours: Knight of Isabela la Católica; Knight of Finland's Lion; Officier de L'Ordre du Mérite; Grand Cross of José Marcoleta. Address: Delegation Sudan, Service Valise Diplomatique, European Commission, B-1049 Brussels, Belgium. E-mail: kent.degerfelt@ec.europa.eu

DEIGHTON Len, b. 18 February 1929, London, England. Writer. m. Publications: The Ipcress File, 1962; Horse Under Water, 1963; Funeral in Berlin, 1964; Ou Est Le Garlic/ Basic French Cooking, 1965, 1979; Action Cook Book, 1965; Cookstrip Cook Book, Billion Dollar Brain, 1966; An Expensive Place to Die, Len Leighton's London Dossier, The Assassination of President Kennedy, co-author, 1967; Only When I Larf, 1968; Bomber, 1970; Declarations of War, 1971; Close-up, 1972; Spy Story, 1974; Eleven Declarations of War, Yesterday's Spy, 1975; Twinkle, Twinkle, Little Spy, Catch a Falling Spy, 1976; Fighter, 1977; SS-GB, Airshipwreck, co-author, 1978; Blitzkreig, 1979; Battle of Britain, co-author, 1980, 1990; XPD, 1981; Goodbye Mickey Mouse, 1982; Berlin Game, 1983; Mexico Set, 1984; London Match, 1985; Game, Set and Match, 13 part TV series; Winter: A Berlin Family 1899-1945, 1987; Spy Hook, 1988; Spy line, ABC of French Food, 1989; Spy Sinker, Basic French Cookery Course, 1990; Mamista, 1991; City of Gold, 1992; Violent Ward, Blood, Tears and Folly, 1993; Faith, 1994; Hope, 1995; Charity, Midnight in Saint Petersburg, 1996. Address: c/o Jonathan Clowes Ltd, 10 Iron Bridge House, Bridge House, Bridge Approach, London NW1 8BD, England.

DEL BENE Francesco M, b. 31 July 1964, Lecce, Italy. Lawyer; Professor of Civil Law. m. Ilaria Leo, 2 sons. Education: Diploma di Laurea in Giurisprudenza, University of Rome "La Sapienza", Law School, Rome, Italy, 1990; Master in Banking and Finance Law, University of Lecce, School of Economics and Banking, 1990-91; Master in Civil Law (Scholarship recipient), University of Toledo, School of Law, 1995. Appointments: Legal Intern, Studio Legale Avv Antonio del Bene, Lecce, 1990-91; Legal Intern, Avvocatura Distrettuale dello Stato, Lecce, 1991-93; Lawyer, Studio Legale Avv. Grand 'Uff. Franco Musco, Consulate General of Malawi, Rome, 1993-94; Lawyer, Prosperetti &

Associati, Rome, 1994-98; Lawyer, BBLP Pavia e Ansaldo Law Firm, Milan and Rome, 1998-99; Lawyer-Executive in charge, IntesaBCI SpA, Central Department, Milan, 2000-02; Lawyer, Eversheds International, PB Law Firm, Milan, 2002-04; Partner, Pirola Pennuto Zei & Associati, Milan, 2005-. Publications: 2 treatises; 4 books; 12 articles; 8 case notes; 7 presentations. Memberships: Istituto Studi Parlamentari-Coordinator of research and study of the Scientific Committee, Rome, 1993-94; Associazione Italiana Giuristi Europei, 1995-; International Bar Association, Banking Law Committee and Academics' Forum, 1997-; Subcommittee on Civil and Commercial Law of Centro Studi Giuridici Michele Di Pietro, 1995-98; Board of Directors, Law Periodical Giurisprudenza di Merito, 1997-; CERADI – Member of the Expert Committee on Banking and Financial Contracts, LUISS-Guido Carli University of Rome, Italy, 2001; Rome Bar Association, 1994-2001; Milan Bar Association, 2003-. Address: Via G Mercalli n 2, 20122 Milan, Italy. E-mail: francesco.del.bene@studiopirola.com

DELAHUNTY Ann Maree, b. 26 January 1963, Queensland, Australia. Neuropsychologist. m. Chris McDonagh, 1 son. Education: BA with honours, 1986; PhD, 1991. Appointments: Neuropsychologist, Hunter Area Mental Health Services, Newcastle, 1990-91; Senior Scientific Officer, 1991-92, Senior Scientific Officer, Private Practice, Greater Murray Health Service, Albury, New South Wales, 1995-98; Programme Director, Private Practice, 1992-95; Clinical Neuropsychologist and Private Practice, ACT Mental Health Services, Canberra, 1999-2000; Lecturer, University of Newcastle, 2001; Private Practice, Manager & Clinician, Clinical & Neuropsychological Services, 2001-. Publications: Author and editor, 2 book series (6 volumes each), child and adult versions of the Frontal/Executive Program; Contributor of articles to professional journals; Various other skills training programmes. Honours: Conjoint Senior Lecturer, University of Newcastle. Memberships: Australian Psychological Society; International Neuropsychological Society; Association for Study of Brain Impairment. Address: 6 Leo Close, Elermore Vale, NSW 2287, Australia. E-mail: annde@bigpond.com

DELBOURGO Roger, b. 21 February 1937, Alexandria, Egypt. Retired University Lecturer. m. (1) Françoise Valois, deceased, 1 son, (2) Maria Gloria Bernal. Education: BSc, Electrical Engineering, Battersea Polytechnic, London University, 1959; DIC, Imperial College, 1960; BSc, Pure Mathematics (part-time study), Birkbeck College, London University, 1974; MSc, Mathematics/Numerical Analysis (part-time study), 1980, PhD, Mathematics/Numerical Analysis (part-time study), 1984, Brunel University, Uxbridge. Appointments: Tutor in Mathematics, University Tutorial College, London, 1960-62; Teacher of Mathematics, Ealing Grammar School for Boys, 1963-64; Lecturer, Mathematics, Electrical Engineering Department, Hendon College of Technology, Hendon, London, 1964-72; Lecturer, then Senior Lecturer, Mathematics, Faculty of Engineering, Science and Mathematics, Middlesex Polytechnic (later University), Bounds Green, London, 1972-98, Retired, 1998. Publications: Pure Mathematics – A revision course for A-level (with R G Meadows), 1971; Articles published in the Journal of the Institute of Mathematics and Applications (jointly with J A Gregory), 1982-88; Articles in the Society for Industrial and Applied Mathematics, 1993. Honours: Certificate of Merit for Distinguished Service, 1996; Decree of Merit Plaque for an Outstanding Contribution to Mathematics, International Biographical Centre, 1996; American Medal of Honor, ABI, 2006; Honorary Member, Research Board of Advisors and Research Fellow, American Biographical Institute,

2005; Listed in Who's Who publications and biographical dictionaries. Memberships: New York Academy of Sciences, 1994-2003; Society for Industrial and Applied Mathematics, 1994-2002; American Association for the Advancement of Science, 1995-2002. Address: 10 Flanders Mansions, Flanders Road, Chiswick, London W4 1NE, England.

DELHANTY Joy Dorothy Ann, b. 16 March 1937, England. Human Geneticist. m. James Delhanty, 2 sons, 1 daughter. Education: BSc, Zoology, 1959, PhD, Human Genetics, 1962, University College London. Appointments: Honorary Research Assistant, Department of Human Genetics, UCL, 1960-65, Lecturer, Department of Genetics & Biometry, 1965-85, Senior Lecturer, Department of Genetics & Biometry, 1985-92, Reader, Genetics, 1992-97, Director, Clinical Cytogenetics Unit, UCL Hospitals, 1993-98, Professor, Human Genetics, 1997-2003, University College London; Emeritus Professor, Human Genetics, University of London, 2003-. Publications: Numerous book chapters and reviews; 160 refereed articles. Honours: Fellow, Royal College of Pathologists; Fellow, Royal College of Obstetricians and Gynaecologists. Memberships: Royal Society of Medicine; Genetical Society of the UK; British Society for Human Genetics; European Society for Human Genetics; American Society of Human Genetics; Cytogenetics and Genome Society. Address: Institute for Women's Health, Department of Obstetrics & Gynaecology, University College London, 86-96 Chenies Mews, London WC1E 6HX, England. E-mail: j.delhanty@ucl.ac.uk

DELILLO Don, b. 20 November 1936, New York, New York, USA. Author. Education: BA in Communication Arts, Fordham University, 1958. Publications: Americana, 1971; End Zone, 1972; Great Jones Street, 1973; Ratner's Star, 1976; Players, 1977; Running Dog, 1978; Amazons, 1980; The Names, 1982; White Noise, 1985; The Day Room, 1987; Libra, 1988; Mao II, 1991; Underworld, 1997; Valparaiso, 1999; The Body Artist, 2001; Cosmopolis, 2003; Game 6, 2005; The Rapture of the Athlete Assumed Into Heaven, 2007. Contributions to: Periodicals. Honours: National Book Award, 1985; Irish Times-Aer Lingus International Fiction Prize, 1989; PEN/Faulkner Award, 1992; Jerusalem Prize, 1999; William Dean Howells Medal, 2000. Address: c/o Wallace Literary Agency, 177 East 70th Street, New York, NY 10021, USA.

DELPY Julie, b. 21 December 1969, Paris, France. Film Actress. Education: New York University Film School. Appointments: Actress, films include: Detective, 1985; Mauvais Sang, 1986; La Passion Béatrice, 1987; L'Autre Nuit, 1988; La Noche Oscura, 1989; Europa Europa, Voyager, 1991; Warszawa, 1992; Young and Younger, The Three Musketeers, When Pigs Fly, 1993; The Myth of the White Wolf, Killing Zoe, Mesmer, Trois Couleurs Blanc, Trois Couleurs Rouge, 1994; Before Sunrise, 1995; An American Werewolf in Paris, 1997; The Treat; LA without a Map; Blah, Blah, Blah (director); The Passion of Ayn Rand, But I'm A Cheerleader, Beginner's Luck, 1999; Tell Me, Sand, 2000; Waking Life, MacArthur Park, 2001; Looking for Jimmy, Cinemagique, 2002; Notting Hill Anxiety Festival, 2003; Before Sunset, 2004; Broken Flowers, 3 & 3, 2005; The Legend of Lucy Keyes, The Hoax, The Air I Breathe, 2006; 2 Days in Paris, 2007. TV: ER, 2001; Frankenstein, 2004. Honours: Empire Film Award for Best Actress, 2005. Address: c/o William Morris Agency, 151 El Camino Drive, Beverley Hills, CA 90212, USA.

DELUISE Dom, b. 1 August 1933, Brooklyn, New York, USA. Comedian; Actor. m. Carol Arthur, 3 sons. Education: Tufts College. Career: 2 seasons with Cleveland Playhouse; TV debut, Garry Moore Show; Theatre includes; Little Shop of Horrors; Die Fledermause, New York; Peter and the Wolf; Films include: Fail Safe; Blazing Saddles; Hot Stuff; The Best Little Whorehouse in Texas; Always Greener, 2001; My X-Girlfriends Wedding Reception, 2001; It's All About You, 2002; Remembering Mario (voice), 2003; Girl Play, 2004; Breaking the Fifth, 2004; Bongee Bear and the Kingdom of Rhythm (voice), 2006; TV includes: The Entertainers; The Dean Martin Summer Show; Dom DeLuise Show; The Barrum-Bump Show; The Glenn Campbell Goodtime Show; The New Candid Camera; Fievel's American Tails (voice); Evil Roy Slade; Only With Married Men; Happy; Don't Drink the Water; The Tin Soldier; The Charlie Horse Music Pizza; All Dogs Go To Heaven. Address: The Artist Group, c/o Robert Malcolm, 10100 Santa Monica Boulevard, Los Angeles, CA 90067, USA. Website: www.domdeluise.com

DEMETRAKAKIS Chrishoula, b. 13 February 1955, Athens, Greece. Human Resource Manager. m. John Nittis, 1 son, 1 daughter. Education: Public Relations College of Management, Athens, 1980; Executive Diploma, Human Resource Management, College of Wells, 2006; MBA, Business Administration, Teeside University, 2006. Appointments: Executive of Technical Manager, graduate from Ellinik Pedia Elefsinas Shipyard, Elefsina Attiki, 1980; Human Resources Manager and Client Association, Expo Group of Companies, Athens, 1981-. Publications: Articles, essays and short stories in professional journals, magazines and anthologies; Books: Poetry (collection of poems), 2005; Fratzeska (novel), 2006. Honours: International Award Gold Medal, Literature 2006, M Madhusudan, M M Academy and Kolkata University; 1st Award (Ad Motion Poetry), 1st Award (Self-Knowledge Poetry), 22nd Symposium of Greek Poetry and Literature; Greek Novel Award (Fratzeska), 2006, 1st Award (Free Style Poetry), 2nd Award (Lyric Poetry), 21st symposium of Greek Poetry and Literature; Honor in Narrative, 3rd Award, Society of Greek Writers, 2004; Diploma of Poetry, Literature Greek Society, 2004; International Forum of Culture and Peace, 2005; Poem of the Week (The Dream), 2005; The World Poets Society (I Am Not Afraid), 2006. Memberships: Greek Literatures Society; Society of Cretans Journalist; Academy of American Poets; The World Poets Society; The Cretan Literature Society; International Forum of Culture and Peace; International Council of Dancing; World's Writers, Red Cross; The Runner's World; All Over the Greece Cretan's Society; Culture unions and alumnus unions. Address: 82a Aristidou str, Athens 17672, Greece. E-mail: info@chrishoulademetrakaki.com Website: www.chrishoulademetrakaki.com

DEMIDOV Vadim, b. 10 July 1954, Novosibirsk, Russia. Research Scientist; Freelance Writer/Editor. m. Inna Verba, 1 daughter. Education: MS, Physical/Chemical Engineering, Department of Molecular and Chemical Physics, Moscow Physical and Technical Institute, USSR, 1977; PhD, Biophysics, Institute of Molecular Genetics, Russian Academy of Sciences/Moscow Physical and Technical Institute, USSR, 1980. Appointments: Junior Research Scientist, Research Institute for Biological Testing of Chemical Compounds and Drugs, Moscow, 1980-85; Research Scientist, Moscow Institute of Biotechnology, 1985-87; Senior Research Scientist, Institute of Mineralogy, Geochemistry and Crystalochemistry of Rare Elements, Moscow, 1987-90; Senior Research Scientist, Institute of Molecular Genetics, Moscow, 1990-93; Visiting Assistant Research Professor, Department of Biology,

George Mason University, Fairfax, Virginia, USA, 1993; Visiting Research Professor, Department of Biochemistry and Medical Genetics, Copenhagen University, Denmark, 1993-94; Senior Research Associate, Center for Advanced Biotechnology, Boston University, USA, 1994-2007, Principal Investigator, Department of Biomedical Engineering, 2001-2007, Boston University, USA; Biotechnology Analyst, Global Prior Art Inc, Boston, USA, 2008-. Publications: Nearly 70 research and review papers; 40 news and feature articles in professional journals; Several patents; Contributing Editor, Drug Discovery and Development, 2004; Co-editor, DNA Amplification: Current Technologies and Applications, 2004. Honours: Silver Medal, All-Union National Exhibiton of Economic Achievements, Moscow, 1988; Senior Scientific Worker rank, USSR Superior Certifying Commission, 1990; Boston University Provost's Innovation Fund Award, 2001; Boston University Spring Award, 2002; Ten-Year Service Recognition Award, Boston University, 2006; Proposal Assessor for several international research foundations, 2002-06; Listed in international biographical directories. Memberships: New York Academy of Sciences; Society of Chemical Industry, London; The Planetary Society; Amnesty International. Address: Global Prior Art, Inc 21 Milk Street, 6th Fl., Boston, MA 02109, USA. E-mail: vvd@bu.edu Website: www.bu.edu/cab/Vadim%20Demidov.html

DEN ADEL Raymond Lee, b. 23 April 1932, Pella, Iowa, USA. Classics Professor. Education: BA, Central College, Pella, 1954; Army Intelligence School, 1956; MA, University of Iowa, Iowa City, 1959; PhD, University of Illinois, Urbana, 1971; Additional study: Drake University, USA, 1954; North Carolina State University, USA, 1956; American Academy, Rome, Italy, 1960; Vergilian School, Cumac, Italy, 1960; American School of Classical Studies, Athens, Greece, 1961. Appointments: High School, Pella, 1954-55; US Army Counterintelligence Corps, 1955-57; Teaching Assistant and Graduate Student, University of Iowa, 1957-58; Proviso West High School, Hillside, Illinois, 1958-62; Teaching Assistant, University of Iowa, 1962-63; Graduate Student and Instructor, University of Illinois, Urbana, 1963-67; Ass Professor, Associate Professor, Professor, Professor Emeritus of Classics, Rockford College, Rockford, Illinois, 1967-. Publications: Various articles in Classical Outlook, Classical Journal, Latin Vocabulary of Non Articulated Sounds, 1971. Honours: BA, magna cum laude, 1954; Fellowship and Assistantship, University of Iowa, 1957-58, 1962-63; Fulbright Grant, 1960; American Classical League Scholars Group, 1960; Field Scholarship, 1961; Fellowship and Assistantship, University of Illinois, 1963-67; Phi Beta Kappa, 1987; Distinguished Service Award, Archaeological Institute of America, 1997; District Government, Rotary District 6420, 1997-98; Inductee, Eta Sigma Phi (Classics); Inductee, Phi Sigma Iowa (Foreign Language); Preident, Illinois Classical Conference; President, Rockford Society of AIA; President, Rockford Chapter of AAUP; Trustee and Vice President, AIA; 1st Vice President, CAMUS; President, Chicago Classical Club; President, Rockford Chapter of OBK; President, Rockford Rotary Club; Secretary, Vergilian Society; Secretary, Classical Society of American Academy in Rome. Memberships: Life Member, Archaeological Institute of America; Life Member, American Philological Association; Rotary International, Rockford, Illinois Chapter; Life Member, American Classical League; Life Member, Classical Association of the Middle West and South (CAMUS); Phi Beta Kappa; United Presbyterian Church; Fulbright Alumni Association; Vergilian Society of America; Dutch International Society; Pella, Iowa Historical Society. Address: 701 Broadway St, Pella, IA 50219, USA.

DENCH Dame Judith (Judi), b. 9 December 1934, York, Yorkshire, England. Actress. m. Michael Williams, 1971, deceased, 1 daughter. Education: Central School of Speech Training and Dramatic Art. Career: Appeared Old Vic, leading roles, 1957-61; Royal Shakespeare Company, 1961-62; Leading roles include: Anya (The Cherry Tree); Titania (A Midsummer Dream); Isabella (Measure for Measure); West African Tour with Nottingham Playhouse, 1963; Subsequent roles include: Irina (The Three Sisters, Oxford Playhouse, 1964); Title role, St Joan and Barbara (Nottingham Playhouse, 1965); Lika (The Promise, 1967); Sally Bowles (Cabaret, 1968); Numerous appearances in lead roles and tours to Japan, 1970, 1972, and Australia, 1970 as Associate Member Royal Shakespeare Company, 1969-, these include: Viola (Twelfth Night); Beatrice (Much Ado About Nothing); Duchess (Duchess of Malfi); Other Performances include: Miss Trant (The Good Companions, 1974); Nurse (Too Good to Be True, 1975, 1976); Cymbeline, 1979; Lady Bracknell (The Importance of Being Ernest, 1982); Pack of Lies, 1983; Waste, 1985; Antony and Cleopatra, 1987; Hamlet, 1989; The Seagull (Royal National Theatre, 1994); The Convent, 1995; Absolute Hell, 1995; A Little Night Music, 1995; Amy's View, 1997, 1999; Filumena, 1998; The Royal Family, 2001; The Breath of Life, 2002; All's Well That Ends Well, 2003-04; Plays Directed: Much Ado About Nothing, 1988; Look Back in Anger, 1989; The Boys from Syracuse, 1991; Absolute Hell (Royal National Theatre, 1995); A Little Night Music, 1995; Amy's View, 1997; Filumena, 1998. Films include: A Study in Terror, 1965; Four in the Morning, 1966; A Midsummer Night's Dream (RSC, 1968); Dead Cert, Wetherby, 1985; A Room with a View, 1986; 84 Charing Cross Road, 1987; Henry V, 1989; Goldeneye, 1995; Tomorrow Never Dies, 1996; Mrs Brown, 1997, Shakespeare in Love, 1998; Tea with Mussolini, 1998; The World is Not Enough, 1999; Chocolat, 2000; Iris, 2001; The Shipping News, 2001; The Importance of Being Earnest, 2002; Die Another Day, 2002; Ladies in Lavender, 2004; The Chronicles of Riddick, 2004; Mrs Henderson Presents, 2005; Casino Royale, 2006; Notes on a Scandel, 2006; TV includes: Major Barbara; Talking to a Stranger; The Funambulists; Age of Kings; Jackanory; Neighbours; Marching Song; On Approval; Langrishe Go Down; Love in a Cold Climate; A Fine Romance; Going Gently; Saigon-Year of the Cat, 1982; Ghosts, 1986; Behaving Badly, 1989; Absolute Hell; Can You Hear Me Thinking?; As Time Goes By; Last of the Blonde Bombshells; Cranford Chronicles, 2007. Publications: Judi Dench: A Great Deal of Laughter (biography); Judi Dench - With a Crack in Her Voice (biography), 1998. Honours include: Numerous Honorary degrees and Honorary Fellowship (Royal Holloway College); Best Actress: Variety London Critic's (Lika, The Promise, 1967); Guild of Directors (Talking to a Stranger, 1967); Society West End Theatre (Lady MacBeth, 1977); New Standard Drama Awards: Juno and the Paycock, 1980; Lady Bracknell (The Importance of Being Ernest, 1983); Deborah (A Kind of Alaska, 1983); Variety Club Award for Best Actress, Filumena, 1998; Academy Award, Best Supporting Actress (Shakespeare in Love), 1999; BAFTA Award for Best Actress (Last of the Blonde Bombshells); BAFTA Award for Best Actress (Iris), 2002; BAFTA Tribute for Lifetime Achievement, 2002; Olivier Award for Lifetime Achievement, Society of London Theatres, 2004; The William Shakespeare Award, The Shakespeare Theatre in Washington, 2004; Evening Standard Special Award for Outstanding Contribution to British Theatre, 2004; Honorary Doctorate, Mary Baldwin College, Staunton, Virginia, 2004; Honorary Doctorate, The Juilliard Academy, New York, 2004; Theatregoers' Award for

Best Supporting Actress, 2005. Address: c/o Julian Belfrage Associates, 46 Albermarle Street, London, W1X 4PP, England.

DENEUVE Catherine (Catherine Dorléac), b. 22 October 1943, Paris, France. Actress. m. David Bailey (divorced), 1 son (by Roger Vadim), 1 daughter (by Marcello Mastroianni). Appointments: Film debut in: Les petitis chats, 1959; President, Director-General, Films de la Citrouille, 1971-79; Films include: Les portes claquent, 1960; L'homme à femmes, le Vice et la Vertu, Et Satan conduit le bal, 1962; Vacances portugaises, Les parapluies de Cherbourg (Palme D'Or, Cannes Festival), Les plus belles escroqueries du monde, 1963; La chasses à l'homme, Un monsieur de compagnie, La Costanza della Ragione, Repulsion, 1964; Le chant du monde, La Vie de chateau, Liebes Karusell, Les créatures, 1965; Les demoiselles de Rochfort, 1966; La chamade, 1966; Belle de jour (Golden Lion, Venice Festival), Benjamin, Manon 70, 1967; Mayerling, 1968; Folies d'avril, Belles d'un soir, La sirène du Mississippi, 1969; Tristana, 1970; Peau d'âne, Ça n'arrive qu'aux autres, Liza, 1971; Un flic, 1972; Touche pas la femme blanche, 1974; Hustle, 1976; March or Die, Coup de foudre, 1977; Ecoute voir... L'argent des autres, 1978; A nous deux, Ils sont grandes ces petits, 1979; Le dernier métro, Je vous aime, 1980; Hotel des Americaines, 1981; L'africain, The Hunger, 1983; Le bon plaisir, Paroles et musiques, 1984; Le lieu du crime, 1986; La reine blanche, 1991; Indochine (César Award), 1992; Ma saison préférée, 1993; La Partie d'Echecs, 1994; The Convent, Les cent et une nuits, Les Voleurs, 1995; Généalogie d'un crime, 1997; Le Vent de la nuit, Belle-Maman, Pola x, Time Regained, 1999; Dancer in the Dark, 2000; Je centre a la maison, Absolument fabuleux, 2001; 8 Femmes, Au plus près du paradis, 2002; Un film parle, 2003; Kings and Queen, Changing Times, 2004; Palais royal !, 2005; The Stone Council, Family Hero, 2006; After Him, Persepolis (voice), Je veux voir, 2007; Un conte de Noël, 2008. Honours: Honorary Golden Bear, Berlin Film Festival, Arts de l'Alliance française de New York Trophy, 1998. Memberships include: Co-Chairman, UNESCO Campaign to protect World's Film Heritage, 1994-. Address: c/o Artmedia, 20 avenue Rapp, 75007 Paris, France.

DENHAM Rt Hon John, b. 15 July 1953, Seaton, England. Member of Parliament for Southampton Itchen; Secretary of State for Innovation, Universities and Skills. Divorced, 3 children. Education: BSc, Chemistry, University of Southampton, 1977. Appointments: Advice Worker, Energy Advice Agency, Durham, 1977; Transport Campaigner, Friends of the Earth, 1978; Head of Youth Affairs, British Council, 1979-83; Public Education and Advocacy, War on Want, 1984-88; Worked for Christian Aid, Oxfam and other development agencies; Councillor, Southampton City Council, 1989-93; Member of Parliament for Southampton Itchen 1992-; Member, Environment Select Committee, 1993-95; Spokesman on Social Security, 1995-97; Parliamentary Under Secretary of State, 1997-98, Minister of State, 1998-99, Department for Social Security; Minister of State, Department of Health, 1999; Member of the Privy Council, 2000; Minister of State at the Home Office, 2001-03; Chairman, Home Affairs Select Committee, 2003; Secretary of State for Innovation, Universities and Skills 2007-. Memberships: Executive Committee, Fabian Society; AMICUS.

DENIZ Clare (Frances), b. 7 April 1945, England. Concert Cellist; Teacher. Education: Private piano study from age 5; Private cello study with Madeleine Mackenzie from age 11; Won Junior Exhibition to Royal Academy of Music after only one years tuition; Teachers: Lilley Phillips and Derek Simpson, gaining an LRAM; Further study with Christopher Bunting; Jacqueline du Pré and Antonia Butler; Masterclasses at Britten Pears School for Advanced Musical Studies, 1982; Personal invitation to masterclasses with Paul Tortelie then became a pupil (he remained a mentor until his death in 1990). Debut: Purcell Room, London, 1983. Career includes: Former Principal Cellist, Royal Ballet Orchestra; Sub-principal Cellist, English National Opera; Many recitals specialising in British and French music as well as standard repertoire; Appearances at Cambridge Festival and Oxford Festival to include Beautiful Music in Beautiful Places; Cheltenham Lunchtime Concerts; Fairfield Hall Centenary Concert for Arnold Bax; Elgar 'cello concerto, Wales, 1983; Unaccompanied inaugural concert, new Evesham Library; Concertgebouw Amsterdam debut, 1987; Life broadcast recital, Reading Festival, 1987; Unaccompanied Bach Suite recital, 1990; Haydn's C Major Concerto, 1990; 3 Concerts of first performances, Wessex Composers Group, 1990, conceived by Incorporated Society of Musicians; 11 recital series by Incorporated Society of Musicians, 1990; Unaccompanied recitals, Amsterdam, 1990 and 1992, and Paris, 1993; Recorded broadcast recital of French Music, BBC Radio Oxford, 1991; Invited to take part in Counterpoint; Children's concerts and workshops; Virtuoso Recital, Jacqueline du Pré Appeal Fund, 1992; Haydn D major concerto, Cornwall, 1993; Concert, EEC Brussels Commission, 1994; Language tuition, School of Slavonic and Eastern European Studies, London University, 1997-98; Performances at London South Bank Millennium Celebrations; Tours of Spain and Germany with small ensembles, 2001-; Founder, Belgravia Ensemble of London, 2001; Concerts (harp trio and string trio), Leominster Festival; Cheltenham Festival (unaccompanied Bach Suites), 2007; Cello/piano duo recitals: Reading University, Poole Art Centre, Cheltenham Town Hall, and Fairfield Hall, Croydon. Honours: Elected Fellow, Royal Society of Arts, 1990; Academic Awards, Post Graduate Diploma, Queens' University, Belfast, 1996; Masters Degree, London University, Goldsmiths College, 2000. Address: 31 Friday Street, Henley-on-Thames, Oxfordshire RG9 1AN, England.

DENNEHY Brian, b. 9 July 1939, Bridgeport, Connecticut, USA. Actor. m. (1) 3 children, (2) Jennifer. Education: Chaminade High School, Columbia; Yale University. Career: US Marine Corps, 5 years; Numerous stage appearances; Films include: Looking for Mr Goodbar, Semi-Tough, 1977; FIST, Foul Place, 1978; Butch and Sundance: the Early Days, 10, 1979; Little Miss Market, 1980; Split Image, First Blood, 1982; Never Cry Wolf, Gorky Park, 1983; Finders Keepers, The River Rat, 1984; Twice in a Lifetime, Silverado, Cocoon, 1985; The Check is in the Mail, F/X, Legal Eagles, 1986; Best Seller, The Belly of an Architect, 1987; Return to Snowy River, Miles from Home, Cocoon: The Return, 1988; Indio, Georg Elser – Einer aus Deutschland, 1989; The Last of the Finest, Presumed Innocent, 1990; FX2, 1991; Gladiator, 1992; Tommy Boy, The Stars Fell on Henrietta, 1995; Romeo + Juliet, 1996; Out of the Cold, Silicon Towers, 1999; Summer Catch, 2001; Stolen Summer, 2002; She Hate Me, 2004; Our Fathers, Assault on Precinct 13, 2005; 10th & Wolf, Everyone's Hero (voice), The Ultimate Gift, Welcome to Paradise, 2006; Ratatouille (voice), 2007; TV includes: Big Shamus, Little Shamus; Star of the Family, Birdland, The Exonerated; Our Fathers; Marco Polo. Honours: Tony Award, Best Actor in a Drama, 1999. Address: c/o Susan Smith & Associates, 121 North San Vicente Boulevard, Beverly Hills, CA 90211, USA.

DENNISTON Robin Alastair, b. 25 December 1926, London, England. Publisher; Anglican Minister. m. 1 son, 2 daughters. Education: MA, Oxon, 1949; MSc, Edinburgh, 1992; PhD, UCL, London, 1997. Appointments: 2nd Lieutenant, Airborne Artillery, National Service, 1948-50; Editor, Collins, 1950-58; Editor, Hodder & Stoughton, 1959-74; Deputy Chairman, George Weidenfeld and subsidiary companies, 1973-75; Chairman, Nelson & Michael Joseph Ltd; Chairman, Rainbird Ltd; Academic Publisher and Senior Deputy Secretary to the Delegates of the Press, Oxford University Press, 1978-89. Publications: Partly Living, 1967; Churchill's Secret War, 1997; Trevor Huddleston: A Life, 1998. Address: 25 Pyndar Court, Newland, Malvern, Worcestershire WR13 5AX, England.

DEPARDIEU Gerard, b. 27 December 1948, Chateauroux, France. Actor; Vineyard Owner. m. Elisabeth Guignot, 1970 (divorced), 1 son, 1 daughter. Education: Cours d'art dramatique de Charles Dullin and Ecole d'art dramatique de Jean Laurent Cochet. Appointments: President, Jury, 45th Cannes International Film Festival, 1992; Appeared in several short films. Creative Works: Feature Films include: Les gaspards, Les valseuses, 1973; Pas si mechant que ca, 1974; 1900, La derniere femme, Sept morts sur ordonnance, Maîtresse, 1975; Barocco, René la Canne, Les plages de l'Atlantique, Baxter vera Baxter, 1976; Dites-lui que je l'aime, Le camion, Reve de singe, 1977; Le sucre, 1978; Buffet froid, Loulou, 1979; Le dernier metro, 1980 (César award Best Actor, France); Le choix des armes, La femme d'à côté, La chèvre, Le retour de Martin Guerre, (Best Actor Award, American Society of Film Critics); Danton, 1981; Le grand frère, 1982 La lune dans le carniveau, Les compères, Fort Saganne, 1983; Tartuffe (also Director), Rive Droit, Rive Gauche, Police, 1984; One Woman or Two, Jean de Florette, Tenue de soirée, 1985; Rue de départ, Les fugitifs, 1986; Cyrano de Bergerac, 1989 (César award Best Actor); Uranus, 1990; Green Card (Golden Globe for Best Comedy Actor), Mon Pere Ce Heros, 1492: Conquest of Paradise, Tous les matins due monde, 1991; Germinal, 1992 A Pure Formality, Le Colonel Chabert, 1993; La Machine, Elisa, Les Cents et Une Nuits, Les Anges Gardiens, Le Garçui, all 1994; Bogus, Unhook the Stars, Secret Agent, 1995; Vatel, The Man in the Iron Mask, 1997; Les Portes du Ciel, Astérix et Obélix, Un pont entre deux rives (also Director), Vatel, 1999; Les Acteurs, Chicken Run, 2000; Le Placard, 102 Dalmatians, 2001; Astérix et Obélix: Mission Cleopatra, 2002; Nathalie, Tais-toi, Les Clefs de bagnole, 2003; San Antonio, Nouvelle France, 36 quai des orfevres, Bon Voyage, Changing Times, 2004; How Much Do You Love Me, 2005; Last Holiday, Paris, I Love You, The Singer, 2006; Bastardi, Disco, 2007; Asterix at the Olympic Games, Babylon A.D. 2008; Several plays and television productions. Publication: Lettres volées, 1988. Honours: Numerous national and international awards. Address: Art Media, 10 Avenue George V, 75008 Paris, France.

DEPP Johnny, b. 9 June 1963, Owensboro, Kentucky, USA. Actor. m. (1) Lori Anne Allison (divorced), (2) Vanessa Paradis, 1 son, 1 daughter. Appointments: Former rock musician; TV appearances include 21 Jump Street; Films include: A Nightmare on Elm Street; Platoon; Slow Burn; Cry Baby; Edward Scissorhands, 1990; Benny and Joon, 1993; What's Eating Gilbert Grape, 1991; Arizona Dream; Ed Wood; Don Juan de Marco, 1994; Dead Man; Nick of Time; Divine Rapture; The Brave (also writer and director), Donnie Brasco, 1997; Fear and Loathing in Las Vegas, The Astronaut's Wife, 1998; The Source, The Ninth Gate, The Libertine, Just to Be Together, Sleepy Hollow, 1999; Before Night Falls, The Man

Who Cried, Chocolat, 2000; Blow, From Hell, 2001; Lost in La Mancha, Once Upon a Time in Mexico, 2002; Pirates of the Caribbean: The Curse of the Black Pearl, 2003; Secret Window, Finding Neverland, 2004; The Corpse Bride, The Libertine, Charlie and the Chocolate Factory, 2005; Pirates of the Caribbean: Dead Man's Chest, 2006; Pirates of the Caribbean: At World's End, Sweeney Todd: The Demon Barber of Fleet Street, 2007. Honours: Screen Actors Guild Award, Best Actor, 2004.

DERANIYAGALA Ranjini S, b. 27 July 1939, Sri Lanka. Visiting Scholar. m. Prasadth Deraniyagala, 2 sons, 1 daughter. Education: BA, University of Peradeniya, Sri Lanka, 1965; DPA, University of London, 1970; MINST AM (Dip), Institute of Administrative Management, Orpington, Kent, 1995. Appointments: Administration Officer, Executive Officer, Manager, HM Customs & Excise, London, 1966-85; Various office assignments, Kelly Services, Manpower Services, Temp Livonia, Michigan, USA, 1990-98; Sales Advisor, Third Lead, 1998-99, Sales Advisor, First Lead, 1999-2000, Demonstration Supervisor, Manager, 2001-04, Club Demonstration Services Inc, Livonia; President, Jeanie-Derani, Canton, Michigan, 2004-. Publications: Managerial Problems of a Woman Executive - How Best to Resolve Them; Support for Teens in the 21st Century. Honour: Woman of the Year, 1996; Listed in international biographical dictionaries. Memberships: National Association for Female Executives, 1996; American Association of University Women; Research Board Advisor, Fellow, American Biographical Institute; Fellow, International Biographical Association, England. Address: 7016 Epping Court, Canton, MI 48187, USA.

DERBYSHIRE Eileen, b. 6 October 1931, Urmston, Manchester, England. Actress. m. Thomas Wilfrid Holt, 1 son. Education: Northern School of Music. Career: First broadcast, 1948; Appeared in numerous radio productions; First repertory appearance, 1952; Numerous repertory jobs including Manchester Library Theatre, Farnham, Harrogate Festival, Scarborough (Stephen Joseph Theatre in the Round); Touring with the Century Theatre; Played Emily Bishop in Coronation Street, 1961-2007. Honour: LRAM. Membership: Life Member, British Actors' Equity. Address: c/o Granada Television Ltd, Quay Street, Manchester, M60 9EA, England.

DERERA Nicholas F, b. 5 January 1919, Budapest, Hungary. Agricultural Scientist; Plant Breeder. m. Roza E Derera, 1 son. Education: Dip Agr Sc, 1942; Dip PB, 1943; CPAg, 1996. Appointments: Plant Breeder, Hungary, 1943-56; Process Worker, Laboratory Assistant, 1957-58; Research Agronomist, New South Wales Department of Agriculture 1958-61; Plant Breeder, Senior Plant Breeder, Officer-in-Charge, Director, Wheat Breeding, Plant Breeding Institute, North West Wheat Research Institute, Narrabri, 1961-81; Agricultural Science Consultant, 1981-; Adjunct Professor, University of Sydney, 1998-. Publications: Over 96 scientific, semi-popular and major conference papers. Honours: Fellow, Australian Institute of Agricultural Science, 1977; Certificate of Appreciation, RSL, 1979; Farrer Memorial Medal, 1981; Bronze Plaque and Citation, Canada, 1982; Rotary Award for Vocational Excellence, 1983; Member of the Order of Australia, 1994. Address: 5 Lister Street, Winston Hills, NSW 2153, Australia.

DERN Laura, b. 10 February 1967, Los Angeles, USA. Actor. 1 son, 1 daughter with Ben Harper. Appointments: Film debut aged 11 in Foxes, 1980; TV appearances include: Happy Endings; Three Wishes of Billy Greer; Afterburn;

Down Came a Blackbird; Director, The Gift, 1999; Within These Walls, 2001; Damaged Care, 2002; Films: Teachers; Mask; Smooth Talk; Blue Velvet; Haunted Summer; Wild of Heart; Rambling Rose; Jurassic Park; A Perfect World; Devil Inside; Citizen Ruth, Bastard Out of Carolina, Ruby Ridge, 1996; October Sky, 1999; Dr T and the Women, 2000; Daddy and Them, Focus, Novocaine, Jurassic Park III, I Am Sam, 2001; We Don't Live Here Anymore, 2004; Happy Endings, The Prize Winner of Defiance, Ohio, 2005; Lonely Hearts, Inland Empire, 2006; Year of the Dog, Tenderness, 2007.

DERSHOWITZ Alan (Morton), b. 1 September 1938, New York, New York, USA. Lawyer; Professor of Law; Writer. m. Carolyn Cohen, 2 sons, 1 daughter. Education: BA, Brooklyn College, 1959; LLB, Yale University, 1962. Appointments: Called to the Bar, Washington, DC, 1963, Massachusetts, 1968, US Supreme Court, 1968; Law Clerk to Chief Judge David L Bazelon, US Court of Appeals, 1962-63, to Justice Arthur J Goldberg, US Supreme Court; Faculty, 1964-, Professor of Law, 1967-, Fellow, Center for Advanced Study of Behavioural Sciences, 1971-72, Felix Frankfurter Professor of Law, 1993-, Harvard University. Publications: Psychoanalysis, Psychiatry and the Law (with others), 1967; Criminal Law: Theory and Process, 1974; The Best Defense, 1982; Reversal of Fortune: Inside the von Bulow Case, 1986; Taking Liberties: A Decade of Hard Cases, Bad Laws and Bum Raps, 1988; Chutzpah, 1991; Contrary to Popular Opinion, 1992; The Abuse Excuse, 1994; The Advocate's Devil, 1994; Reasonable Doubt, 1996; The Vanishing American Jew, 1997; Sexual McCarthyism, 1998; Just Revenge, 1999; The Genesis of Justice, 2000; Supreme Injustice, 2001; Letters to a Young Lawyer, 2001; Shouting Fire: Civil Liberties in a Turbulent Age, 2002; Why Terrorism Works, 2002; America Declares Independence, 2003; The Case for Israel, 2003; America on Trial, 2004; Rights from Wrongs: A Secular Theory of the Origins of Rights, 2004; The Case for Peace: How the Arab-Israeli Conflict Can be Resolved, 2005; Preemption: A Knife That Cuts Both Ways, 2006. Contributions to: Periodicals. Honours: Guggenheim Fellowship, 1978-79; Honorary doctorates. Memberships: Order of the Coif; Phi Beta Kappa. Address: c/o Harvard University Law School, Cambridge, MA 02138, USA.

DERWENT Richard Austin, b. 28 September 1953. Chartered Accountant. Education: BA Hons (1st Class), History, London University. Appointments: Chartered Accountant, Deloitte, Haskins and Sells, Southampton, 1972-81; Audit Manager, Brooking Knowles and Lawrence, 1981-82; Audit Manager, Rawlinson and Hunter, 1982-84; Senior Technical Manager, Pannell Kerr Forster, 1984-86; Senior Technical Manager, Clark Whitehill, 1986-91; Self-employed Consultant, 1991-. Publications: Charities: An Industry Accounting and Auditing Guide, 1995, 1997; Contributions to: Financial Reporting: A Survey of UK Published Accounts; The Times; Charity World; Accountancy; Certified Accountant; Corporate Money; True and Fair; The Small Practitioner. Memberships: Secretary and Chairman, London Society Financial Reporting Discussion Group, 1989-91; Financial Reporting Committee, ICAEW, 1990-97. Address: Flat 7, Foxlea, 70 Northlands Road, Southampton SO15 2LH, England.

DESAI Anita, b. 20 January 1972, Bangalore, India. Academician. m. Ajay R Desai, 1 son, 1 daughter. Education: B Tech, 1994, M Tech, 1996, Textiles, Government Shri Kirshnarajendra Silver Jubilee Technological Institute, Bangalore; Persuing PhD, Engineering Textiles, Central Silk Technological Research Institute, Ministry of Textiles, Government of India, Bangalore. Appointments:

Merchandising Officer, Welspun Terry Towels Ltd, Vapi, India, 1996-97; Senior Lecturer, Department of Textile Technology, Sarvajanik College of Engineering & Technology, 1997-. Publications: Over 31 articles in various national and international journals. Honours: Listed in international biographical dictionaries; Scholarship, Government of India, 1994. Memberships: Textile Association of India; Indian Society for Technical Education. Address: No C/7 Purnima Co-operative Society, Near Agricultural Farm, Ghoddod Road, Surat – 395 007, India. E-mail: aap_desai@yahoo.co.in

DESLIPPE Richard Joseph, b. 5 September 1962, Windsor, Ontario, Canada. Associate Professor of Ecology. Education: BSc, Biology, Department of Zoology, University of Guelph, 1981-85; MSc, Biology, Department of Biology, University of Windsor, 1987-1989; PhD, Zoology, Department of Zoology, University of Alberta, 1990-94. Appointments: Postdoctoral Fellow, Cornell University, 1994-96; Visiting Assistant Professor, Texas Tech University, 1996-97; Adjunct Professor, The Institute of Environmental and Human Health; Assistant Professor of Ecology, 1997-, Associate Professor, 2003-, Texas Tech University. Publications: Numerous papers and articles. Honours: Recipient of various awards. Address: Department of Biological Sciences, Texas Tech University, Lubbock, TX 79409-3131, USA. E-mail: richard.deslippe@ttu.edu

DETJEN David Wheeler, b. 25 January 1948, St Louis, Missouri, USA. Lawyer. m. Barbara Morgan Detjen, 2 daughters. Education: AB Magna Cum Laude, Washington University, 1970; History and Law, Eberhard-Karls Universität, Tübingen, Germany, 1969-70; JD with Honours, Washington University School of Law, 1973. Appointments: Law Clerk to the Honorable M C Matthes, Chief Judge and later Senior Judge of the United States Court of Appeals for the Eighth Circuit, St Louis, Missouri, 1973-1975; Adjunct Lecturer in Law, Washington University School of Law, 1975-80; Admitted to the Missouri Bar, 1973, the New York Bar, 1981; Associate, Lewis, Rice, Tucker, Allen and Chubb, St Louis, Missouri, 1975-80; Associate, 1980-82, Partner, 1983-2000, Walter, Conston, Alexander & Green, PC, New York, New York; Partner, Alston & Bird LLP, New York, New York, 2001-. Publications include: Distributorship Agreements in the United States, 1983, 2nd edition, 1989; The Germans in Missouri 1900-1918, Prohibition, Neutrality and Assimilation, 1985; Establishing a US Joint Venture with a Foreign Partner, 1988, 2nd edition, 1989, 3rd edition, 1993; Licensing Technology and Trademarks in the United States, 1988, 2nd edition, 1997; US Joint Ventures with International Partners, 2000; Executive Editor, 1988-, Editor-in-Chief, 2004-, International Law Practicum. Honours: Delta Phi Alpha (German Language Honorary); Order of the Coif (Law Honorary); Distinguished Alumnus, Washington University School of Law, 1998; Regional Distinguished Leadership Award, Washington University, 2003; Recipient, Knight's Cross of the Order of Merit of the Federal Republic of Germany, 2007; Political Offices: Member, Republican Central Committee of St Louis County, Missouri, 1976-83; Member, Representative Town Meeting (Municipal Legislature) of Greenwich, Connecticut, 2000-. Memberships: Atlantik-Bruecke, Berlin, Germany; American Council on Germany, New York City; Deutscher Verein (Board of Directors, 1994-97, 1999-2005, Vice President and Secretary, 2000-03), New York; Board of Trustees, Washington University, 2004-; Washington School of Law National Council, 1989-; Board of Trustees, Corporate Secretary, Vice-Chairman, American Institute for Contemporary German Studies, Johns Hopkins University, 1999-; Chairman German Forum, New York, 2005-; Board of Directors, Vice-Chairman, German American Chamber of

Commerce, New York, 2003-; Board of Directors, Friends of Goethe, New York Inc, 2005-; Board of Directors, Arthur M Burns Fellowship, 2006-American Bar Association; New York State Bar Association (Vice-Chairman, International Law and Practice Section, 2004-); Missouri Bar; Association of the Bar of the City of New York; Bar Association of Metropolitan St Louis; German American Law Association. Address: 90 Park Avenue, 14th Floor, New York, NY 10016, USA.

DETTORI Lanfranco (Frankie), b. 15 December 1970, Milan, Italy. Flat Race Jockey. m. Catherine Allen, 1997, 2 sons, 3 daughters. Appointments: Ridden races in England, France, Germany, Italy, USA, Dubai, Australia, Hong Kong and other countries in Far East, 1992-; 1000 rides and 215 wins in UK, 1995; Horses ridden include Lamtarra, Barathea, Vettori, Mark of Distinction, Balanchine, Moonshell, Lochsong, Classic Cliché, Dubai Millennium, Daylami; Sakhee; Authorized, Ouija Board; major race victories include: St Leger (twice), The Oaks (twice); The Breeders Cup Mile; Arc de Triomphe (three times); French 2000 Guineas (twice); English 1000 Guineas (twice); Queen Elizabeth II Stakes; Prix L'Abbaye; The Japan Cup (three time); The Dubai World Cup (three times); Rode winner of all 7 races at Ascot, 28 October 1996; Epsom Derby, 2007. Publication: A Year in the Life of Frankie Dettori, 1996; Frankie: The Autobiography, 2004. Honours: Jockey of the Year, 1994, 1995, 2004; BBC Sports Personality of the Year, 1996; International Sports Personality of the Year, Variety Club, 2000. Address: c/o Peter Burrell Classic Management, 53 Stewarts Grove, London, SW3 6PH, England. E-mail: pburrell@classicmanagement.com

DEUCHAR Stephen John, b. 11 March 1957, United Kingdom. Director, Tate Britain. m. Katie Scott, 1 son, 3 daughters. Education: BA, History 1st Class Honours, University of Southampton; PhD, History of Art, Westfield College, University of London, 1986; Andrew W Mellon Fellow in British Art, Yale University, 1981-82. Appointments: Curator of Paintings, 1985-87, Curator, Armada Exhibition, 1987-88, Corporate Planning Manager, 1988-90; Head of Exhibitions and Displays, 1990-95, Director, Neptune Court Project, 1995-97, National Maritime Museum; Director, Tate Britain, 1998-. Publications: Noble Exercise: the Sporting Ideal in 18th Century British Art, 1982; Paintings, Politics and Porter, Samuel Whitbread and British Art, 1984; Concise Catalogue of Oil Paintings in the National Maritime Museum (jointly), 1988; Sporting Art in 18th Century England: A Social and Political History, 1988; Nelson: An Illustrated History (jointly), 1995; Articles on British Art. Memberships: Visual Arts Committee, British Council; Advisory Council, Paul Mellon Centre for Studies in British Art; Council, University of Southampton; Trustee, Metropole Arts Centre Trust. Address: Tate Britain, Millbank, London SW1P 4RG, England.

DEUTSCH Claude, b. 20 July 1936, Paris, France. Professor of Physics. m. Nimet El Abed, 2 sons. Education: Engineer, ENSCP, Paris, 1959; Master of Theoretical Physics, Orsay, 1961; Doctor of Science, University Paris XI, 1969. Appointments: Visiting Scientist, Research Laboratory of Electronic, MIT, 1976-78; Visiting Physicist, Applied Physics Department, Stanford University, 1980; Director, Paris Sud Informatique, University Paris XI, Orsay, 1985-93; Director GDR-918, CNRS, Ion-plasma Interaction, 1989-96; Director, Physics Laboratory, University Paris XI, 1994-98; Invited Professor, Tokyo Institute of Technology, Japan, 1999-2000; Professor, Physics, Exceptional Class, 1995-. Publications: Numerous articles in professional journals; Co-editor, Laser Particle Beams. Honours: Bronze Medal, 1973, Silver Medal,

1980, CNRS; Bronze Medal, Madrid Polytechnic, 1995; Fellow, American Physical Society, 1996. Memberships: Societé Francaise de Physique; American Physical Society; Scientific Adviser, CEA-DAM; Scientific Adviser, CEA-Dam, France; Al Faroubi Reform Consultant, University Almaty, Kazakhstan. Address: Laboratoire de Physique des Gaz et Plasmas, Bat 210, UPS, 91405-Orsay, France. E-mail: claude.deutsch@lpgp.u-psud.fr

DEVANARAYANAN Sankaranarayanan, b. 11 November 1940, Thiruvananthapuram, India. University Professor; Physicist. m. Chitra, 1 son, 1 daughter. Education: BSc, University of Kerala, 1961; MSc, University of Kerala, 1963; PhD, Indian Institute of Science, Bangalore, 1969; Diploma, Uppsala University, Sweden, 1971; DSc, International University, USA, 1999. Appointments: Research Fellow, Indian Institute of Science, 1963-69; Senior Research Assistant, Indian Institute of Science, 1969-70; SIDA Fellow, Institute of Physics, Uppsala, Sweden, 1970-71; Lecturer, 1971-75, Reader, 1975-84, Professor, 1984-2000, Professor and Head, 1993-2000, Physics Department, University of Kerala; Professor, Physics, University of Puerto Rico, Rio Piedras, USA, 1989-91; Principal, KVVS Institute of Technology, Via Adur, 2003-; Computer Software Languages known: FORTRAN; JAVA; JAVASCRIPT; HTML; SERVELETS. Publications: Over 84 research articles in standard scientific journals in science in solid state physics, spectroscopy, crystal growth and atmospheric physics; Thermal Expansion of Crystals, monograph, 1979; Quantum Mechanics, book, 2005; Quantum Chemistry, book; in press; Physics in Nutshell for Competitive Tests, book, in press; A Course Book on Nuclear Physics, to be published. Honours: Merit Scholar, University of Kerala, 1961-63; SIDA Fellowship, Sweden, 1970-71; Associate Professor, University of Puerto Rico, 1989-91; Over 20 biographies in national and international publications. Memberships: American Physical Society, 1990-; Indian Physics Association, 1974-; Indian Meteorological Society, 1999-; United Writers' Association, 1998-; Indian Association Physics Teachers, 1974-; Senate, University of Kerala, 1998-2000; Academic Council, University of Kerala, 1991-2001; Chairman, PG Board of Studies in Physics, University of Kerala, 1993-2001; Commission of Enquiry, University of Kerala, 2000; Elite Indian, 2008, many others; Invited Scientist, Czech Academy of Sciences, Praha, Czech Republic, 2004. Address: TC 40/239, (G-9) PRS Enclave, Easwara Vilasom Road, Cotton Hill, Thiruvananthapuram – 695014, India. E-mail: sdevanarayanan@yahoo.com

DEVERALL Brian James, Education: BSc, Botany, Hons 1, Edinburgh, 1957; DIC, 1960, PhD, 1960, Plant Pathology, London. Appointments include: Harkness Fellow, Commonwealth Fund, New York, 1960-62; PostDoctoral Fellow, University of Wisconsin, 1960-61, University of Nebraska, USA, 1961-62; Lecturer, Imperial College, University of London, England, 1962-70; Principal Scientific Officer, Wye College, University of London, England, 1970-72; Professor of Plant Pathology, University of Sydney, Australia, 1973-2001; Emeritus Professor, University of Sydney, 2001-. Publications: 6 Monographs and edited books; Numerous research and review papers in leading international journals; 20 Review Chapters. Memberships: British Mycological Society, 1962-97; British Plant Pathology Society, since foundation in 1982-; Australasian Plant Pathology Society, 1972-, President, 1987-89; American Phytopathological Society, 1993-2002, Fellow, 1999; International Society for Plant Pathology, Vice President, 1993-98. Address: Faculty of Agriculture, Food and Natural Resources, University of Sydney, NSW 2006, Australia.

DEVINATZ Victor, b. 19 October 1957, St Louis, Missouri, USA. University Professor. Education: BSE, 1979, MS, 1980, Northwestern University; MS, University of Massachusetts, 1986; PhD, University of Minnesota, 1990. Appointments: Lecturer, Industrial Relations, University of Minnesota, 1990-91; Assistant Professor, 1991-94, Associate Professor, 1994-98, Professor, 1998-, Management, Illinois State University. Publications: Book, High-Tech Betrayal: Working and Organizing on the Shop Floor, 1999; Over 75 journal articles, essays and book chapters. Honours: Henry J Kaiser Family Foundation Grant, 1989; Caterpillar Faculty Scholar, 1999, 2004; Merl E Reed Research Fellowship in Southern Labor History, 2003; Listed in national and international biographical directories. Memberships: Labor and Employment Relations Association; United Association for Labor Education. Address: Department of Management and Quantitative Methods, College of Business, Illinois State University, Normal, IL 61790-5580, USA. E-mail: vgdevin@ilstu.edu

DEVINE Thomas Martin, b. 30 July 1945, Motherwell, Scotland. Professor; Writer. m. Catherine Mary Lynas, 1971, 2 sons, 3 daughters. Education:BA, University of Strathclyde, 1968; PhD, 1971; D Litt, 1991. Appointments: Assistant Lecturer, 1969-70, Lecturer, 1970-78, Senior Lecturer, 1978-83, Reader, 1983-88, Professor, 1988-88, Chairman, Department of History, 1990-93, Dean of Faculty of Arts and Social Sciences, 1993-94, Director, Research Centre in Scottish History, 1993-98, Vice Principal, Faculty of Education, 1994-98, University of Strathclyde; Adjunct Professor of History, Faculty of Graduate Studies, University of Guelph, Canada, 1989-; Adjunct Professor of History, University of North Carolina, USA, 1996-; Director, University Research Professor in Scottish History, Research Institute of Irish and Scottish Studies, University of Aberdeen, 1998-2004; Director, AHRC Centre of Irish and Scottish Studies, 2001-05; Glucksman Research Professor in Irish and Scottish Studies, 2004-06; Sir William Fraser Professor of Scottish History and Palaeography, University of Edinburgh, 2006-. Publications: The Tobacco Lords, Ireland and Scotland 1700-1850; The Great Highland Famine; People and Society in Scotland; Farm Servants and Labour in Lowland Scotland; Irish Immigrants and Scottish Society in the Eighteenth and Nineteenth Centuries; Scottish Emigration and Scottish Society; Clanship to Crofters' War: The Social Transformation of the Scottish Highlands; The Transformation of Rural Scotland: Agrarian and Social Change 1680-1815; Glasgow, Vol 1, Beginnings to 1930, 1995; Scotland in the Twentieth Century, 1996; Eighteenth Century Scotland: New Perspectives, 1998. Contributions to: Times Literary Supplement; Times Higher Education Supplement; Economic History Review; Social History; Scottish Historical Review; History Today; Scottish Economic and Social History. Honours: Fellow, Royal Society of Edinburgh; Fellow, British Academy, 1994; Henry Duncan Prize Lectureship, Royal Society of Edinburgh, 1995; OBE, 2005; Honorary Fellowship, Bell College of Higher Education, 2005; John Aitkenhead Inaugural Award for Education, 2005; Fellow of the Academy of Merit, 2005; Scot of the Year, Institute of Contemporary Scotland, 2005. Memberships: Economic and Social History Society of Scotland; Scottish Catholic Historical Association; Royal Society; Royal Historical Society; Trustee, National Museums of Scotland. Address: University of Strathclyde, 16 Richmond Street, Glasgow G1 1XQ, Scotland.

DEVLIN Dean, b. 27 August 1962. Actor; Screenplay Writer; Producer. Creative Works: Film produced: The Patriot, 2000; Eight Legged Freaks, 2002; Cellular, 2004; Who Killed the Electric Car? 2006; Fly Boys, 2006; Isobar, 2007; Films written and produced; Stargate, 1994; Independence Day, 1996; Godzilla, 1998; Universal Soldier: The Return, 1999; Isobar, 2007; Film screenplay: Universal Solider, 1992; Actor: My Bodyguard, 1980; The Wild Life, 1984; Real Genius, 1985; City Limits, 1985; Martians Go Home, 1990; Moon 44, 1990; Total Exposure, 1991; TV series: The Visitor (creator, executive producer), 1997; TV appearances in: North Beach, 1985; Rawhide, 1985; Hard Copy, 1987; Generations, 1989; Guest appearances in: LA Law; Happy Days; Misfits of Science. Address; c/o Creative Artists Agency, 9830 Wilshire Boulevard, Beverly Hills, CA 90212, USA.

DEWEY David Lewis, b. 17 November 1927, Scotland. Research Scientist. m. Jacqueline, 1 son, 2 daughters. Education: BA, 1948, MA, 1950, Cambridge; PhD, 1953, London. Appointments: Research Staff, University College Hospital Medical School, London, 1950; Research Staff, University College, London, 1953; Head of Biochemistry and Microbiology, The Gray Institute, 1956-90; Retired, 1990. Publications in the scientific journal, Nature, as author and co-author include: Diaminopimelic acid and lysine, 1952; Modification of the oxygen effect when bacteria are given large pulses of radiation, 1959; Effects of oxygen and nitric oxide on the radiosensitivity of human cells, 1960; X-ray inactivation of inducible enzyme synthesis, 1962; 6-Amino-nicotinamide and the radiosensitivity of human liver cells, 1963; Interconvertion of cystine and cysteine induced by X-rays, 1965; Action of atomic hydrogen on aqueous bacteriophage, 1968; Major publications in other journals include: The use of the Hersch Cell for the measurement of oxygen in biological material, 1961; Cell dynamics in the bean root tip, 1963; The X-ray sensitivity of Serratia marcescens, 1963; The mechanism of radiosensitisation by iodacetamide, 1965; The survival of Micrococcus radiodurans irradiated at high LET., 1969; The viability of bateriophage T4 after irradiation of only the head component or the tail component, 1973; Treatment of malignant melanoma by intravascular 4-hydroxyanisole, 1981. Honours: Rockefeller Fund Grant, 1950; Damon Runyon Memorial Fellowship, 1965. Memberships: Biochemical Society (Emeritus); British Association; Radiation Research Society (Emeritus); British Institution of Radiology. Address: Happs Edge, Box Lane, Bovingdon, Herts HP3 0DJ, England.

DEWHIRST Ian, b. 17 October 1936, Keighley, Yorkshire, England. Retired Librarian; Writer; Poet. Education: BA Honours, Victoria University of Manchester, 1958. Appointment: Staff, Keighley Public Library, 1960-91. Publications: The Handloom Weaver and Other Poems, 1965; Scar Top and Other Poems, 1968; Gleanings From Victorian Yorkshire, 1972; A History of Keighley, 1974; Yorkshire Through the Years, 1975; Gleanings from Edwardian Yorkshire, 1975; The Story of a Nobody, 1980; You Don't Remember Bananas, 1985; Keighley in Old Picture Postcards, 1987; In the Reign of the Peacemaker, 1993; Down Memory Lane, 1993; Images of Keighley, 1996; Co-editor, A Century of Yorkshire Dialect, 1997; Keighley in the Second World War, 2005. Contributions to: Yorkshire Ridings Magazine; Lancashire Magazine; Dalesman; Cumbria; Pennine Magazine; Transactions of the Yorkshire Dialect Society; Yorkshire Journal; Down Your Way. Honour: Honorary Doctor of Letters, University of Bradford, 1996; MBE, 1999. Memberships: Yorkshire Dialect Society; Edward Thomas Fellowship. Address: 14 Raglan Avenue, Fell Lane, Keighley, West Yorkshire BD22 6BJ, England.

DICTIONARY OF INTERNATIONAL BIOGRAPHY

DEXTER Colin, b. 29 September 1930, Stamford, Lincolnshire, England. Author; Educationist. m. Dorothy, 1 son, 1 daughter. Education: Christ's College, Cambridge; MA (Cantab); MA (Oxon). Appointments: National Service, Royal Signals, 1948-50; Assistant Classics Master, Wyggeston School for Boys, 1953-57; Sixth Form Classics Master, Loughborough Grammar School, 1957-59; Senior Classics Master, Corby Grammar School, 1959-66; Senior Assistant Secretary, Oxford University Delegacy of Local Examinations, 1966-88. Publications: Co-author, 3 General Studies textbooks, 1960s; Last Bus to Woodstock, 1975; Last Seen Wearing, 1976; The Silent World of Nicholas Quinn, 1977; Service of All the Dead, 1979; The Dead of Jericho, 1981; The Riddle of the Third Mile, 1983; The Secret of Annexe 3, 1986; The Wench is Dead, 1989; The Jewel That Was Ours, 1991; The Way Through the Woods, 1992; Morse's Greatest Mystery, 1993; The Daughters of Cain, 1994; Death is Now My Neighbour, 1996; The Remorseful Day, 1999; Chambers Book of Morse Crosswords, 2006. Honours: MA (Cantab); MA (Oxon); Hon MA (Leicester University); Hon D Litt (Oxford Brookes University); Crime Writers' Silver Dagger, 1979, 1981; Crime Writers' Gold Dagger, 1989, 1992; Crime Writers' Diamond Dagger, 1997; Officer of the Order of the British Empire, 2000; Freedom of the City of Oxford, 2001; Honorary Fellow, St Cross College, Oxford. Memberships: Housman Society; Crime Writers' Association; Detection Club. Address: 456 Banbury Road, Oxford OX2 7RG, England.

DHALL Dharam Pal, b. 8 December 1937, Kenya. Vascular Surgeon. m. Tehseen, 1 son, 1 daughter. Education: MBChB, 1961; FRCS, 1965; PhD, 1967; MD, 1968; FRACS, 1994, MACE, 2002. Appointments: Senior Registrar, Lecturer, Surgery, Aberdeen University; Professor of Surgery, University of Nairobi; Senior Consultant Surgeon, Canberra Hospital; Visiting Fellow, John Curtin School of Medical Research, Canberra; Director, Institute of Sathya Sai Education, Canberra, Director, Educare International Ltd; Academic Adviser, University of Central Queensland for Master of Learning Management in Human Values, University of Queensland; Adjunct Professor of Bioethics, University of Canberra. Publications: Approximately 200 articles in Scientific Medical Journals; 15 books on the teachings of Sri Sathya Sai Baba including Human Values, The Heart of Dynamic Parenting; Workshops on Dynamic Parenting; Stepping Stones to Peace; Dynamic Dharma; Over one hundred articles in professional journals. Honours include: Hallett Award, 1963; National Heart Foundation; NH and MRC, Australia; Pharmacia Uppsala, Sweden. Memberships: World Education Federation; Associate Member, Australian Counselling Association; Member, Australian College of Educators; Chairman, Education Committee, Prashanti Council, Puttaparthi, India; Member, Education Committee, Sr Sathya Sai World Foundation; Member, Expert's Panel in Education in Human Values, UN Habitat. Address: PO Box 697, Queanbeyan, NSW 2620, Australia. E-mail: paldhall@aol.com

DHAR Hirendra Lal, b. 2 October 1931, Chittagong, Bangladesh. Geriatrician; Medical Centre Director. m. Rikta Dhar, 1 son, 1 daughter. Education: BSc, 1950, MB BS, 1957, PhD, 1963, Calcutta University: DHA, University of Bombay, 1984; MD, Colombo, 1985; FRCP, Colombo, 2001. Appointments: Demonstrator, AIIMS, New Delhi, 1959; Lecturer, Maulana Azad Medical College, New Delhi, 1962; Reader, JIPMER, Pondicherry, 1967; Professor, Seth GS Medical College and Hospital, Mumbai, 1971; Professor and Head, 1972, Dean, 1985, Emeritus Scientist, 1989, LTM

Medical College and Hospital, Mumbai; Director, Medical Research Centre, Bombay Hospital Trust, Mumbai, 1991. Publications: Nearly 300 original works in national and international journals. Honours: Honorary, FCAI, 1964; Dr B C Roy National Award, 1991; Honorary DSc, 1992; The Ancient Royal Order of Physicians, Sri Lanka, 1993; Honorary FICG, 1998. Memberships: Member of many national and international research organisations; Fellow, Indian College of Allergy and Immunology, 1963; Fellow, Geriatrie Society of India, 2005; President, South Asia Chapter, International Association of Asthmology, 1975-90; President, ICAI, 1999. Address: Medical Research Centre, Bombay Hospital Trust, Bombay 400 020, India. E-mail: drdharmrc@hotmail.com

DHAR Omkar Nath, b. 22 February 1923, Srinagar, Kashmir, India. Hydrometerologist. m. Mohini, 1 daughter. Education: MSc, Physics, Lucknow University, 1944; Training in Meterology, India Met Department Training School, 1945; Training in Snow Surveying in the Himalayas, 1947; Training in Hydrometeorology, UN Fellowship programme, USA, 1966-67; PhD, Hydrometeorology, Jadavpur University, Calcutta, 1976. Appointments: Joined India Met Department, 1945; Deputed to Central Water Commission to undertake Snow Surveys in Himalayas and install observatories in the Himalayas, 1947-63; Deputy Director, Hydrometeorology, 1963-64; Senior Scientist, Hydrometeorology, Indian Institute of Tropical Meteorology, 1965-76; Assistant Director, Hydrometeorology In Charge, 1976-83; Consultant, Regional Office, World Bank, New Delhi, 1982-86; Retired, 1983; Honorary Emeritus Scientist, IITM, Pune, 1983-; Member, Dam Safety Panel, Karnataka Government, 1987-89; Member, Hydrology Team reviewing hydrology of river basins in India, World Bank, 1987. Publications: Around 284 scientific and review articles. Memberships: Regular member, American Geophysical Union, Washington, 1951; Fellow, Indian Meteorological Society, New Delhi. Address: Hydrometeorological Division, Indian Institute of Tropical Meteorology, Pashan, Pune 411-008, India. E-mail: nshobha@tropmet.res.in

DHARIWAL Kewal Singh, b. 17 March 1950, Chack Vendal, India. Mechanical Engineer. m. Balwinder Kaur. Education: HND, 1974, T Cert, 1984, University of Wolverhampton; BSc, University of Central England, 1981; MSc, University of Aston, 1983; DPTM, University of Greenwich, 1985; Fellowship, University of Sussex, 1990. Appointments: Various employment, 1968-70; Part-time Engineering Trainee, 1970-73; Designer, 1974-81; Education Officer (Technical), 1983-84; Employment Officer, 1984-87, late Chief Officer. Publications: Various research reports, educational and work related. Honours: Fellow, American Biographical Institute; Biographical Honour Award, IBC, 1993; Distinguished Leadership Award, ABI; World Lifetime Achievement Award, ABI, 1993; Gold Medal for England, ABI, 2007; The World Medal of Freedom, ABI, 2007; American Medal of Honor, ABI, 2007. Memberships: Member, Chartered Management Institute; Late Chartered Engineer; Late Member, Institute of Training and Development; Chairman and Executive Committee Member, Croydon Race E Council, 1987-93; Member, Croydon Ethnic Minority Forum, 1989-93; Croydon Police Consultative Committee, 1989-93; Croydon Career & Training Advice Committee, 1984-87; Served on various projects locally and internationally; Member, Siri Guru Singh Sabha and Sutton Race Equality Council. Address: 4 Clarice Way, Wallington, Surrey SM6 9LD, England.

DHOLAKIA Navnit, The Right Honourable Lord Navnit, Baron Dholakia of Waltham Brooks. m. 2 daughters. Appointments: Deputy Lieutenant, County of West Sussex, 1999; President, National Association for the Care and Resettlement of Offenders; Chair, NACRO Race Issues Advisory Committee; Vice President, Mental Health Foundation; Vice Chairman, Policy Research Institute on Ageing and Ethnicity; Sits on House of Lords Appointment Commission; Trustee, Pallant House Gallery, Chichester; Trustee, British Empire and Commonwealth Museum, Bristol; Previously with Commission for Racial Equality; Previously with Police Complaints Authority; Served on Council of Save the Children Fund; Served on Howard League of Penal Reform; Serves on Editorial Board of Howard Journal; Member, Ethnic Minority Advisory Committee of the Judicial Studies Board; Served on Lord Carlisle's Committee on Parole Systems Review; Magistrate and Member, Board of Visitors for HM Prison Lewes; Elected President, Liberal Democrats, 2000-04; Deputy Leader, Liberal Democrats, 2004. Honours: Asian of the Year, 2000; Pravasi Bharatiya Samman Award, 2003; OBE; Member of HGL Appointment Commission. Address: House of Lords, London SW1A 0PW, England.

DI FALCO Gerard Anthony, b. 26 September 1952, Camden, New Jersey, USA. Visual Artist; Independent Curator; Writer. Education: BA, Rutgers University, Camden, New Jersey, 1974; MS, Drexel University, Philadelphia, USA, 1985. Appointments: Self-employed Visual Artist, 1979-; Self-employed Curatorial Consultant, 1984-. Publications: Novel, Waiting for the Countdown, 2006; Over 250 solo and juried group exhibitions, 1984-. Honours: Alumni Association Award in Creative Writing, Rutgers University, 1974; Individual Artist's Grant, Pennsylvania Council on the Arts, 1992; Individual Artist's Grant, Pollock-Krasher Foundation, New York City, 2002; Resident Artist Award in Education, Philadelphia Museum of Art, 2003. Memberships: DaVinci Art Alliance, Philadelphia; Episcopal Church and Visual Artists. Address: 2201 Cherry Street, Unit 902, Philadelphia, PA 19103, USA. E-mail: gerarddifalco@msn.com

DI SCHINO Andrea, b. 23 February 1971, Terni, Italy. Researcher. m. Manola Mangoni. Education: Degree in Physics, University of Pisa, 1996; PhD, Materials Engineering, 2000. Appointments: Visiting Scientist, Aachen RWTH, Germany, 2000; Postdoctoral position, University of Perugia, 2000-2003; Researcher, Centro Sviluppo Materiali SpA, 2003-. Publications: Articles in scientific journals include: Advances in stainless steels: effect of grain size on the properties of austenitic stainless steels, 2002. Honours: Listed in Who's Who publications and biographical dictionaries. Membership: AIM. Address: via di Castel Romano 100, 00128 Rome, Italy. E-mail: a.dischino@c-s-m.it

DIAMA Benjamin, b. 23 September 1933, Hawaii, USA. Retired Public School Teacher. Education: BFA, School of the Art Institute, Chicago, 1956; State of Hawaii Government Teachers Certificate, 1962. Appointments: Art, Basketball Coach, Waimea High, 1963-67; Music, Art, Campbell High, 1967-68; Maths, Art, Waipahu High, 1968-69; Music, Art, Palisades Elementary, 1969-70; Art, Music, History, Typing, Honokaa High, 1970-73; Music, Kealakehe Elementary-Intermediate, 1973-74; Retired, 1974. Publications include: School One vs School Two on the Same Campus, 1983; The Calendar Clock Theory of the Universe with Faith - Above and Beyond, 1984-88; Inventor, Universal Calendar Clock and Double Washdeck Floating Boat; Benjamin Diama Calendar Clock Theory of the Universe, 1991, 1992, 1993. Honours: Hawaii Government Acquisition

Painting Collection Award, 1984; Medal of Honour, ABI, 1998. Memberships include: HEA; HSTA; NEA; ASCAP; New York Academy of Sciences; American Association for the Advancement of Science; American Geophysical Union; Smithsonian Society. Address: PO Box 2997, Kailua-Kona, Hawaii, HI 96745, USA.

DIAMOND Neil Leslie, b. 24 January 1941, Brooklyn, New York, USA. Pop Singer; Composer. m. (1) 2 children, (2) Marcia Murphey, 1975 (divorced), 2 children. Education: New York University. Appointments: Formerly with Bang Records, Uni, MCA Records, Los Angeles; Now recording artist with Columbia Records; Guest Artist, TV network shows. Publications: Songs include: Solitary Man; Cherry, Cherry; Kentucky Woman; I'm A Believer; September Morn; Sweet Caroline; Holly, Holy; A Little Bit Me, A Little Bit You; Longfellow Serenade; Song Sung Blue; America; I am I Said; Recordings: Numerous albums, 1966-; 19 Platinum albums; 28 Gold albums; Composer, film scores; Jonathan Livingston Seagull, 1973; Every Which Way But Loose, 1978; The Jazz Singer (also actor), 1980. Honours include: Grammy Award, Jonathan Livingston Seagull, 1973. Address: c/o Columbia Records, Sony BMG, 550 Madison Avenue, New York, NY 10022, USA. Website: www.neildiamond.com

DIAS Donaldo De Souza, b. 19 September 1936, Rio de Janeiro, Brazil. University Professor. m. Valéria, 2 daughters. Education: BSc, Engineering, University of Brazil, 1960; MSc, Catholic University of Rio de Janeiro, 1970; MSc, The University of Michigan, 1978; PhD, Federal University of Rio de Janeiro. Appointments: Managerial and Professional positions, IBM Brazil, 1961-91; Associate Professor, Graduate School of Business Administration, Federal University of Rio de Janeiro, 1991-, Dean, 1994-95. Publications: Author of 3 books (in Portuguese) and 2 book chapters (in English); 45 papers in international and Brazilian journals and conferences. Honours: Distinguished Professor, Data Processing Class of 86, Catholic University of Rio de Janeiro; Best Paper, Brazilian Computer Conference, 1986; Listed in several Who's Who publications and biographical dictionaries. Memberships: Information Resource Management Association; International Association for Computer Information Systems; Production and Operation Management Society. Address: Av General Felicissimo Cardoso 835, apto 1003, Bloco 2, CEP 22631-360, Rio de Janeiro, Brazil. E-mail: donaldo@ufrj.br

DIAZ Cameron, b. 30 August 1972, Long Beach, California, USA. Actress. Appointments: Films include: The Mask, 1994; The Last Supper, 1995; Feeling Minnesota, 1996; She's the One, 1996; A Life Less Ordinary, 1997; There's Something About Mary, 1998; Very Bad Things, 1998; Being John Malkovich, 1999; Invisible Circus, 1999; Any Given Sunday, 1999; Charlie's Angels, 2000; Things You Can Tell Just by Looking at Her, 2000; Shrek (voice), 2001; Vanilla Sky, 2001; The Sweetest Thing, 2002; Gangs of New York, 2002; Minority Report, 2002; Charlie's Angels: Full Throttle, 2003; Shrek 2 (voice), 2004; In Her Shoes, 2005. Honours: Boston Society of Film Critics Best Supporting Actress, 2001; Chicago Film Critics Best Supporting Actress, 2002; The Holiday, 2006; Skrek the Third (voice), 2007. Address: c/o International Creative Management, 8942 Wilshire Boulevard, Beverly Hills, CA 90211, USA.

DIAZ MAGGIOLI Gabriel, b. 7 October 1963, Montevideo, Uruguay. Educator. m. Gabriela Marcenaro, 4 sons, 1 daughter. Education: BA, Teaching English, National Teachers College, Uruguay; MA, Education, Doctoral Candidate, University of Bath, England. Appointments: Head of National Programme,

The British Schools, Uruguay; National Coordinator of Bilingual Education, Uruguay; National EFL Supervisor, Uruguay; Teacher Educator, National Teacher Education College, Uruguay. Publications: Teacher-centered Professional Development; National Curriculum Guides, Department of Education, Uruguay; Managing Learning Styles in the Language Classroom; Uruguay in Focus, 1, 2 and 3. Honours: Member, Board of Directors, TESOL International. Memberships: TESOL; ASCD. E-mail: gdiaz@british.edu.uy

DiCAPRIO Leonardo, b. 11 November 1974, Hollywood, USA. Actor. Films include: Critters III, 1991; Poison Ivy, 1992; This Boy's Life, 1993; What's Eating Gilbert Grape, 1993; The Quick and the Dead, 1995; The Basketball Diaries, 1995; William Shakespeare's Romeo and Juliet, 1996; Titanic, 1996; Man in the Iron Mask, 1997; The Beach, 1999; Don's Plum, 2001; Gangs of New York, 2002; Catch Me If You Can, 2002; The Aviator, 2004; TV series include: Parenthood, 1990; Growing Pains, 1991; The Departed, 2006; Blood Diamond, 2006. Honours: Commandeur de l'Ordre des Arts et Lettres; Platinum Award, Santa Barbara International Film Festival, 2005. Address: c/o Birken Productions Inc, PO Box 291958, Los Angeles, CA 90029, USA. Website: www.leonardodicaprio.com

DICKINSON Angie (pseudonym of Angeline Brown), b. 30 September 1931, Kulm, North Dakota, USA. Actress. Education: Glendale College. Appointments: Actress in films: Lucky Me, 1954; Man With the Gun; The Return of Jack Slade; Tennessee's Partner; The Black Whip; Hidden Guns; Tension at Table Rock; Gun the Man Down; Calypso Joe; China Gate; Shoot Out at Medicine Bend; Cry Terror; I Married a Woman; Rio Bravo; The Bramble Bush; Ocean's 11; A Fever in the Blood; The Sins of Rachel Cade; Jessica; Rome Adventure; Captain Newman MD; The Killers; The Art of Love; Cast a Giant Shadow; The Chase; Poppy is Also a Flower; The Last Challenge; Point Blank; Sam Whiskey; Some Kind of Nut; Young Billy Young; Pretty Maids All in A Row; The Resurrection of Zachery Wheeler; The Outside Man; Big Bad Mama; Klondike Fever; Dressed to Kill; Charlie Chan and the Curse of the Dragon Queen; Death Hunt; Big Bad Mama II; Even Cowgirls Get The Blues; The Maddening; Sabrina; The Sun - The Moon and the Stars; Sealed with a Kiss, 1999; The Last Producer, 2000; Duets, 2000; Pay It Forward, 2000; Big Bad Love, 2001; Ocean's Eleven, 2001; Elvis Has Left the Building, 2004; TV series: Police Woman; Cassie & Co; TV films: The Love War; Thief; See the Man Run; The Norliss Tapes; Pray for the Wildcats; A Sensitive Passionate Man; Overboard; The Suicide's Wife; Dial M for Murder; One Shoe Makes it Murder; Jealousy; A Touch of Scandal; Still Watch; Police Story: The Freeway Killings; Once Upon a Texas Train; Prime Target; Treacherous Crossing; Danielle Steel's Remembrance; Mini-series: Pearl; Hollywood Wives; Wild Palms. Address: 1715 Carla Ridge, Beverly Hills, CA 90120-1911, USA.

DICKINSON Clive Conrad, b. 16 April 1956, Gateshead, Tyne & Wear, England. Photographer. m. (1) divorced, 2 daughters; (2) Sylvia. Education: Newcastle College of Art. Appointments: Founder, Clive Dickinson Advertising Photography, 1980; Senior Studio Photographer, Photo Mayo, 1986-90; Senior Studio Photographer, North East Studios, 1990-92; Senior Studio Photographer, Image Visual Communications, 1992, 2002; MD, Aston Workshop, 2002-04, MD Designate, 2004-, Image Visual Communications; MD, Clive Dickinson Photography, 2007. Honours: British Institute of Professional Photography; Fellow of the Year, 1988 (Peter Grugeon Award Gold Medal). Memberships: Fellow, British Institute of Professional Photography. Address: 7 Station Road, Beamish, Co Durham, DH9 0QU, England. E-mail: shot@clivedickinson.com

DIDO (Dido Florian Cloud de Bounevialle Armstrong), b. 25 December 1971, London, England. Singer; Musician; Songwriter. Education: Guildhall School of Music, London. Career: Toured UK with classical music ensemble before joining pop groups aged 16; Toured with brother Rollo's band, Faithless; Signed solo deal with Arista Records, New York; Recordings: Albums: No Angel, 1999; Life for Rent, 2003; Singles: The Highbury Fields (EP), 1999; Here With Me, 2001; Thank You, 2001; Hunter, 2001; All You Want, 2002; Life for Rent, 2003; White Flag, 2003. TV: Numerous appearances. Honours: BRIT Award, Best Album, 2002; BRIT Award, Best Female Solo Artist, 2002, 2004; Ivor Novello Songwriter of the Year Award, 2002; BAMBI Award for Best International Pop Act, 2003; BRIT Award, Best British Single, 2004. Address: c/o Arista, 423 New King's Road, London SW6, England. Website: www.didomusic.com

DIEMER Emma Lou, b. 24 November 1927, Kansas City, Missouri, USA. Composer; Professor; Musician. Education: BM, 1949, MM, 1950, Yale School of Music; PhD, Eastman School of Music, 1960. Appointments: Composer-in-Residence, Arlington Virginia Schools; Professor of Composition, University of Maryland, 1965-70; Professor of Composition, 1971-91, Professor Emeritus, 1991-, University of California. Publications: Over 200 publications, 1957-2007; Orchestra, chamber works, choral works, vocal works and solo instrumental works; Several articles on music; Listed in national and international biographical dictionaries. Honours include: Fulbright Scholarship in composition and piano, 1952-53; NEA Fellowship in electronic music, 1980; ASCAP Award annually since 1962; AGO Composer of the Year, 1995; Honorary Doctorate, University of Central Missouri, 1999. Memberships: ASCAP; Mu Phi Epsilon; American Guild of Organists; American Music Center; International Alliance for Women in Music. Address: 2249 Vista del Campo, Santa Barbara, CA 93101, USA. E-mail: eldiemer@cox.net

DIERINGER Gregg, b. 18 October 1956, Athens, Ohio, USA. Plant Ecologist. m. Leticia Cabrera, 2 sons. Education: BS cum laude, 1979, MS, 1981, University of Akron; PhD, University of Texas at Austin, 1988. Appointments: Teaching Assistant, University of Akron, 1979-81; Teaching Assistant, 1983, Research Assistant, 1983-84, Teaching Assistant, 1984-88, Instructor, 1990-92, University of Texas at Austin; Instructor, Austin Community College, 1988, 1989-92; Assistant Professor, Southwest Texas State University, 1989; Visiting Professor, Instituto de Ecologia, Veracruz, Mexico, 1992-93; Assistant Professor, 1993-97, Associate Professor, 1997-99, Western Illinois University; Lecturer, University of Texas at Brownsville, 1999-2002; Associate Professor 2003-2006; Professor and Chair, 2006-, Department of Biological Sciences, Northwest Missouri State University. Publications: Numerous articles in professional journals; Presentations at scientific meetings; General reports and book reviews. Honours: Eagle Scout, 1973; Phi Sigma Alpha, University of Akron, 1978; Scholarship to attend Rocky Mountain Biological Station, 1983; Several research grants. Memberships: Botanical Society of America. Address: Department of Biological Sciences, Northwest Missouri State University, 800 University Dr, Maryville, MO 64468, USA. E-mail: greggd@nwmissouri.edu

DIETER Peter, b. 22 February 1952, Neustadt, Germany. Biochemist. m Kathrin Asman, 1 daughter. Education: PhD, 1981; Habilitation, 1991; Full Professor, 1997. Appointments: Canberra, Australia, 1986; NIH, Bethesda, USA, 1989; Freiburg, Germany, 1997; Full Professor, Dresden, Germany, 1997-. Publications: Many articles in journals; Impact factor N 300. Honour: Associate Professor, Thailand, 2004. Memberships: Many societies. Address: Briesnitzer Hoehe 42A, D-01157 Dresden, Germany.

DIGBY-BELL Christopher, b. 21 June 1948, Aberdeen, Scotland. Lawyer. m. Claire, 2 sons, 1 daughter. Education: Marlborough College, 1961-65; College of Law. Appointments: Articled at Taylor & Humbert, 1966-71; Taylor Garrett (now Taylor Wessing), 1972-89, Managing Partner, Taylor Garrett, 1987-89; Frere Cholmeley Bischoff, 1989-98, International Managing Partner, 1995-97; Chief Executive and General Counsel, Palmer Capital Partners, 1998-. Publications: Regular contributor to Times, Lawyer and other legal journals. Honours: Special Award, UNICEF Child Rights Lawyer of the Year Awards, 2002; Judges Award, Liberty/Justice Human Rights Lawyer of the Year Awards, 2002. Memberships: Law Society; Cambridgeshire and District Law Society; City of London Law Society; Honorary Legal Advisor, Down's Syndrome Association; City of London Member of Law Society Ruling Council, 2001-03; Bedfordshire & Cambridgeshire Member of Law Society Ruling Council, 2005. Address: Palmer Capital Partners, Time & Life Building, 1 Bruton Street, Mayfair, London W1J 6TL, England. E-mail: chdb@palmercapital.co.uk

DILLON Matt, b. 18 February 1964, New Rochelle, New York, USA. Actor. Appointments: Films include: Over the Edge, 1979; Little Darlings, 1980; My Bodyguard, 1980; Liar's Moon, 1982; Tex, 1982; The Outsiders, 1983; Rumble Fish, 1983; The Flamingo Kid, 1984; Target, 1985; Rebel, 1985; Native Son, 1986; The Big Town (The Arm), 1987; Kansas, 1988; Drugstore Cowboy, 1989; A Kiss Before Dying, 1991; Singles, 1992; The Saint of Fort Washington, 1993; Mr Wonderful, 1993; Golden Gate, 1994; To Die For; Frankie Starlight; Beautiful Girls; Grace of My Heart; Albino Alligator; In and Out, 1997; There's Something About Mary, 1998; One Night at McCool's, 2000; Deuces Wild, 2000; City of Ghosts, 2002; Employee of the Month, 2004; Loverboy, 2005; Factotum, 2005; Herbie Fully Loaded, 2005; You, Me and Dupree, 2006. Address: William Morris Agency, ICM 151 S El Camino Drive, Beverly Hills, CA 90212, USA.

DIMACOPOULOS Jordan E, b. 1 January 1940, Lebadeia, Boeotia, Central Greece. Retired High-Rank Civil Clerk. Education: Diploma, Athens Technical University, School of Architecture, 1964; PhD, Polytechnic School, Aristotle University of Thessaloniki, 1977; Diploma in Conservation Studies, University of York, UK, 1975. Appointments: Architect, IoannisDespotopoulos'ArchitecturalStudio, Athens, 1964-65; Architect, Directorate for Monument Restoration, 1965-76; Director, Directorate for Monument Restoration, 1976-80; Director, Directorate for the Restoration of Post 1830 Historic Monuments, 1980-82; Director, Directorate for the Restoration of Ancient Monuments, 1982-98; Director General, 1998-2000, Honorary Director General, 2001-, Directorate General for Monument Restoration, Museums and Construction Works; Member, Greek Central Archaeological Council, 1976-80, 1982-2000, 2002-05; Major works of tenure: Designed and built the museums of Poros, Kilkis, Lavrion and Setia, 1965-73; Much work on saving and restoring the Houses of Plaka, the area around the Acropolis, 1980-82; Conceived and supervised the erection of a tumulus-like shelter for the Vergina Royal Tombs, 1991-93; Constructed a system of walkways for visitors to the Knossos Minoan Palace, 1996-97. Publications: Books: The Houses of Rethymnon, 1977, reprinted 2001; An Anthology of Greek Architecture 15th –20th Centuries, 1981; George Whitmore on Corfu, 1994; Scripta Minora: Architectural Investigations and Monument-Conservation Projects, 2005; Articles in various learned periodicals and journals including: The Archaeologhikon Deltion; The Archaeologhike Ephemeris; Athens Annals of Archaeology; Bulletin of the Christian Archaeological Society; Castellum, Rome, The Architectural Review, London; Architectura, Berlin-Munich; Revue Archéologique, Paris; Arkos, Scienza e Restauro, Milan; ICOMOS Information, The Monumentum, Europa Nostra Bulletin. Honours: Athens Academy Award, 1982; Europa Nostra Medal, 1982; Greek State "Prize of Satisfaction", 1997. Memberships: Member of the Board, 2000, 2002-, Athens Archaeological Society; Korrespondierendes Mitglied des Deutschen Archäologischen Instituts, 1999. Address: 12 St George Karytsis Square, Athens 10561, Greece.

DIMBLEBY David, CBE, b. 28 October 1938, London, England. Broadcaster; Newspaper Proprietor. m. (1) Joceline Gaskell, 1967, dissolved, 1 son, 2 daughters, (2) Belinda Giles, 2000, 1 son. Education: Christ Church, Oxford; University of Paris; University of Perugia. Appointments: Presenter and interviewer, BBC Bristol, 1960-61; Broadcasts include: Quest; What's New?; People and Power, 1982-83; General Election Results Programmes, 1979, 1983, 1987; various programmes for the Budget, by-elections, local elections; Presenter, Question Time BBC, 1993-; Documentary films include: Ku-Klux-Klan; The Forgotten Million; Cyprus: The Thin Blue Line, 1964-65; South Africa: The White Tribe, 1979; The Struggle for South Africa, 1990; US-UK Relations: An Ocean Apart, 1988; David Dimbleby's India, 1997; Live commentary on many public occasions including: State Opening of Parliament; Trooping the Colour; Wedding of HRH Prince Andrew and Sarah Ferguson; H M The Queen Mother's 90th Birthday Parade; Funeral of Diana, Princess of Wales, 1997; Memorial Services including Lord Olivier. Publication: An Ocean Apart (with David Reynolds), 1988. Honours: Supreme Documentary Award, Royal TV Society; US Emmy Award, Monte Carlo Golden Nymph; Royal TV Society, Outstanding Documentary Award, 1990, 1997. Address: c/o Coutts & Co, 440 Strand, London WC1R 0QS, England.

DIMBLEBY Jonathan, b. 31 July 1944. Broadcaster; Journalist; Author. m. (1) Bel Mooney, 1968, divorced, 1 son, 1 daughter. (2) Jessica Ray, 2007, 1 daughter. Education: University College, London. Appointments: Reporter, BBC Bristol, 1969-70; BBC Radio, World at One, 1970-71; Reporter, This Week, Thames TV, 1972-78, 1986-88, TV Eye, 1979; Reporter, Yorkshire TV, Jonathan Dimbleby in Evidence: The Police (series); The Bomb, 1980; The Eagle and the Bear, 1981; The Cold War Game, 1982; The American Dream, 1984; Four Years On - The Bomb, 1984; Associate Ed/Presenter, First Tuesday, 1982-86; Presenter/Ed, Jonathan Dimbleby on Sunday, TV AM, 1985-86; On the Record, BBC TV, 1988-93; Charles: The Private Man, The Public Role, Central TV, 1994; Jonathan Dimbleby, London Weekend TV, 1995-; Presenter, Any Questions?, BBC Radio 4, 1987-; Any Answers?, 1989-; Writer/Presenter, The Last Governor, Central TV, 1997; An Ethiopian Journey, LWT, 1998; A Kosovo Journey, LWT, 2000; Michael Heseltine – A Life in the Political Jungle, LWT, 2000. Publications: Richard Dimbleby, 1975; The Palestinians, 1979; The Prince of Wales: A Biography, 1994; The Last Governor, 1997. Honours:

Richard Dimbleby Award, 1974. Memberships: VP, Council for Protection of Rural England, 1997-; Soil Association, 1997-; President, Voluntary Service Overseas, 1999-; Bath Festivals Trust, 2003. Address: c/o David Higham Associates Ltd, 5 Lower John Street, W1R 4HA, England.

DINI Luciana, b. 19 January 1955, Rome, Italy. Full Professor. Education: MD, Biology, University of Rome "La Sapienza", 1977. Appointments: Researcher, University of Rome "Tor Vergata", Department of Biology, 1982-92; Associate Professor of Comparative Anatomy and Cytology, Department of Biology, 1992-2000, Full Professor of Comparative Anatomy and Cytology, Department of Biological and Environmental Science Technology, 2000-, University of Lecce, Lecce, Italy. Publications: Articles in scientific journals including: Journal of Clinical Investigation, 1994; Blood, 1994; Hepatology, 1995; Microscopy Research Technology, 2002; Cell and Tissue Research, 2003. Honour: Award Winner for best work in the field of cellular biology, Societa Nazionale di Scienza, Lettere ed Arti, 1987. Memberships: European Microscopy Society; European Cell Death Organisation. Address: Department of Biological and Environmental Science Technology, University of Lecce, Via Per Monteroni, Lecce 73100, Italy. E-mail: luciana.dini@unile.it

DINSDALE Reece, b. 6 August 1959, Normanton, West Yorkshire, England. Actor. m. Zara Turner, 1 son, 1 daughter. Education: Normanton Grammar, 1970-77; Guildhall School of Music and Drama, 1977-80. Career: Films include: Rabbit on the Moon; Hamlet; Romance and Rejection; ID; A Private Function; Television includes: Conviction; Ahead of the Class; The Trouble with George; Spooks; Murder in Mind; Thief Takers; Young Catherine; Take Me Home; Coppers; Home to Roost; Threads; Winter Flight; Love Lies Bleeding; The Chase; Theatre includes: Visiting Mr Green; Love You Too; A Going Concern; Racing Demon; Wild Oats; Observe the Sons of Ulster Marching Towards the Somme. Honours: International Press Award for Best Actor at the Geneva Film Festival for the film ID, 1996; Honorary Vice-President of Huddersfield Town Football Club Patrons Association. Membership: Huddersfield Town Football Club. Address: c/o Jonathan Artaras Associates Ltd, 11 Garrick Street, London WC2E 9AR, England.

DINWIDDY Bruce Harry, b. 1 February 1946, Epsom, England. Diplomat. m. Emma Victoria Dinwiddy, 1 son, 1 daughter. Education: MA, Philosophy, Politics and Economics, New College, Oxford, 1964-67. Appointments: ODI Fellow, Swaziland, 1967-69; Research Officer, ODI, 1970-73; FCO, 1973; First Secretary, UK Delegation (MBFR) Vienna, 1975-77; FCO, 1977-81; Head of Chancery, British Embassy, Cairo, 1981-83; FCO, 1983-86, Cabinet Office, 1986-88; Counsellor, British Embassy, Bonn, 1989-91; Deputy High Commissioner, Ottawa, 1992-95; Head, African Department (Southern), FCO, 1995-98; Commissioner, British Indian Ocean Territory, 1996-98; High Commissioner, Dar Es Salaam, 1998-2001; Seconded to Standard Chartered Bank, 2001-2002; Governor, Cayman Islands, 2002-05; Trustee, Cayman Islands National Recovery Fund, 2004-; Council Member and Chairman, Wider Caribbean Working Group, UK Overseas Territories Conservation Forum, 2006-; Consultant, UK Trade and Investment, 2007-. Publication: Promoting African Enterprise, 1974. Honour: CMG, 2003. Memberships: Vincent's Club, Oxford; Aldeburgh Golf Club; Royal Wimbledon Golf Club. Address: 8 Connaught Avenue, London, SW14 7RH, England.

DION Celine, b. 30 March 1968, Charlemagne, Quebec, Canada. Singer. m. Rene Angelil, 17 December 1994, 1 son. Career: Recording Artiste, 1979-; Winner Eurovision Song Contest for Switzerland, 1988; Recorded in French, until, 1990; 35 million albums sold; Performed at opening ceremony of Olympic Games, Atlanta, 1996; Las Vegas show, A New Day, opened 2003 (200 shows a year for three years planned). Creative Works: Albums: Unison, 1990; Dion chante Plamondon, 1991; Sleepless in Seattle, 1993; The Colour of My Love, 1993; D'eux, 1995; Falling Into You, 1996; Let's Talk About Love, 1998; These are Special Times, 1998; All the Way, 1999; A New Day Has Come, 2002; One Heart, 2003; 1 Fille & 4 Types, 2003; Miracle, 2004; Singles include: Beauty and the Beast, 1992; If You Asked Me To; Nothing Broken But My Heart; Love Can Move Mountains; When I Fall In Love; The Power of Love; Misled; Think Twice; Because You Loved Me; My Heart Will Go On; Immortality, 1998; Treat Her Like a Lady, 1998; That's the Way, It Is, 1999; The First time I Ever Saw your Face, 2000; That's The Way It Is, 2000; A New Day Has Come, 2002; I'm Alive, 2002; I Want You To Need Me, 2003; Goodbye's The Saddest Word, 2003; I Drove All Night, 2003; One Heart, 2003; Tout l'Or des Hommes, 2003. Publications: All the Way, 2000; My Story, My Dreams, 2001; Miracle (with Anne Geddes), 2004. Honours: Pop Album of Year, 1983; Female Artist of Year, 1983-85, 1988; Discovery of the Year, 1983; Best Quebec Artist Outside Quebec, 1983, 1988; Best Selling Record, 1984, 1985; Best Selling Single, 1985; Pop Song of the Year, 1985, 1988; Journal de Quebec Trophy, 1985; Spectrel Video Award, Best Stage Performance, 1988; Album of the Year, 1991; Female Vocalist of the Year, 1991-93; Academy Award for Best Song written for a motion picture or TV, 1992; Grammy Award, 1993, 1999; Medal of Arts (France) 1996; American Music Award for Best Adult Contemporary Artist, 2003; World Music Diamond Award, 2004. Address: Les Productions Feeling, 2540 boulevard Daniel-Johnson, Porte 755, Laval, Quebec H7T 2S3, Canada. Website: www.celineonline.com

DIOUF Jacques, b. 1 August 1938, Saint-Louis, Senegal. m. Aïssatou Seye, 1963, 5 children. Education: Baccalaureate, Applied Sciences, Lycée Faidherbe, Saint-Louis, Senegal University; Bachelor of Science, Agriculture, Ecole national d'agriculture, Grignon-Paris, France; Master of Science, Tropical Agronomy, Ecole nationale d'application d'agronomie tropicale, Nogent-Paris, France; Doctor of Philosophy in Social Sciences of the Rural Sector (Agricultural Economics), Faculté de Droit et de Sciences économiques, Panthéon - Sorbonne, Paris, France; Certificate in Management, American Management Association, New York; United States Senior Programme Certificate in Management, American Management Association, New York. Appointments: Director, European Office and the Agricultural Programme of the Marketing Board, Paris/Dakar, France/Senegal, 1963-64; Executive Secretary, African Groundnut Council, Lagos, Nigeria, 1965-71; Executive Secretary, West Africa Rice Development Association, Monrovia, Liberia, 1971-77; Secretary of State for Science and Technology, Senegalese Government, Dakar, Senegal, 1978-83; Member of Parliament, Dakar, Senegal, 1983-84; Adviser to the President and Regional Director of the International Development Research Center, Ottawa, Canada, 1984-85; Secretary-General of the Central Bank for West African States, Dakar, Senegal, 1985-90; Special Adviser to the Governor, Central Bank for West African States, Dakar, Senegal, 1990-91; Ambassador, Senegalese Permanent Mission to the United Nations, New York, 1991-93; Director-General of FAO, 1994-. Publications: La détérioration du pouvoir d'achat de l'arachide, 1972; Le fondement du dialogue scientifique entre les civilisations euro-occidentales et négro-africaines, 1979; Intérêts et objectifs de l'Afrique dans les Sommets francophones, nouvel instrument des relations internationales, 1988; The Challenge of Agricultural Development in Africa, 1989; Eloges de Senghor, 1996; Ethique scientifique et problématique alimentaire, 1998. Honours include: Honorary Member, Academia de Stiinte Agricole si Silvice Gheorghe-Ionescu Sisesti, Romania, 1994; Honorary Professorship at the China Agricultural University, Beijing, China, 1995; Doctor ad honorem in Agricultural Science at Tuscia University, Italy, 1996; Doctor of Science, honoris causa, Laval University, Quebec, Canada, 1996; Medal of Honour, Tartu University, Estonia, 1996; Fellow of the National Academy of Agricultural Sciences, India, 1998; Founder Member and Honorary Member of the Academy of Technical Sciences of Senegal, Dakar, 2000; Foreign Member of the Academy of Agriculture of France, Paris, France, 2000; Diploma of Honorary Doctor of the University, National Agrarian University, Ukraine, 2003; Grand Master of the National Order (Republic of Madagascar), 2005; *Hilal I* Award (Pakistan), 2005; Commandeur de l'Ordre National du Mali (Mali), 2005; Order of Independence First Class, Jordan, 2005; Grand Cross of the National Order of the Southern Cross (Brazil), 2006; Grand Cross of the Order pro Merito Melitensi (Order of Malta), 2006; 10 Doctor *honoris causa* from around the world. Memberships: Representative for Africa, Consultative Group on International Agricultural Research, Washington, DC; Member of the Board of the International Agricultural Centers; Council Member, Islamic Foundation for Science and Technology for Development, Jeddah, Saudi Arabia; Advisory Committee on Medical Research; Committee on Transfer of Technology; Expert Advisory Panel on Public Health Administration and Medical Research, World Health Organization, Geneva, Switzerland; Council Member, African Advisers of the World Bank, Washington, DC; Adviser, International Conservation Financing Project of the World Resources Institute, Washington, DC; Board Member, United Nations University World Institute for Development Economics Research, Helsinki, Finland; Executive Board of the African Capacity Building Foundation, Harare, Zimbabwe; Chairman: Board of the African Regional Center for Technology (ARCT), Dakar, Senegal; the Industrial Company for the Uses of Solar Energy, Dakar, Senegal; and the Board of the Foundation for Development of Science and Technology, Dakar, Senegal. Address: Food and Agriculture Organisation of the United Nations, Viale delle Terme di Caracalla, 00100 Rome, Italy.

DIXON Alan (Michael), b. 15 July 1936, Waterloo, Lancashire, England. m. Josephine Stapleton, 13 August 1960. Education: Studied Art, Goldsmiths' College, University of London, 1956-63; University of London Diploma in Visual Arts. Appointment: Teacher of Art, Schools in London and Peterborough, England, 1959-87. Poetry collections: Snails and Reliquaries, 1964; The Upright Position, 1970; The Egotistical Decline, 1978; The Immaculate Magpies, 1982; The Hogweed Lass, 1991; A Far-Off Sound, 1994; Transports, 1996; The Ogling of Lady Luck, 2005. Contributions to: Poetry; Partisan Review; The Observer; The Times Literary Supplement; The Listener; New Statesman; London Review of Books; The Nation; London Magazine; Encounter; The Spectator; Prairie Schooner; Salmagundi; The Scotsman. Address: 51 Cherry Garden Road, Eastbourne, BN20 8HG, England.

DJUJIĆ Ivana, b. 23 February 1947, Belgrade, Serbia. Chemist. m. Borivoje Djujić. Education: BSc, Chemistry, 1970, MSc, Biochemistry, 1978, PhD, Veterinary Medicine, 1985, University of Belgrade. Appointments: Research Assistant,

1971-74, Research Fellow, 1974-79, Senior Researcher, 1979-84, Department of Chemistry, Senior Researcher, 1984-86, Department of Additives, Yugoslav Institute of Meat Technology, Belgrade; Lecturer, Meat Chemistry and Water Chemistry, School of Postgraduate Specialisation in Meat Technology, Belgrade, 1978-85; Research Associate, Institute of Nuclear Sciences, Department of Radiobiology and Radiation Medicine, Vinca, Belgrade, 1986-90; Lecturer, Radiation Protection, School of Postgraduate Specialisation in Radiology, Vinca, 1988-96; Group Leader, Serbian Academy of Sciences and Arts Project, Selenium and Magnesium Deficiency and Health, 1989-2006; Research Associate, 1990-95, Senior Research Associate, 1995-99, Research Professor, 1999-, Department of Chemistry, Institute of Chemistry, Technology and Metallurgy, University of Belgrade; Programme Leader for Serbia, FAO Regional Office for Europe, Research Network on Trace Elements, Natural Antioxidants and Contaminants in European Food and Diet, 1991-92, 1996-98; Programme Leader, Ecological Education in Serbia and Russia, 1995-; Member, Organising Committee and Jury, International Youth Bios-Olympics, 1996-; Scientific Leader, International Summer Bios-schools, Serbia, 1997-2000. Publications: Over 140 articles in professional scientific journals; 3 patents. Honours: 1st place, Inventors Association of Belgrade, 1998; 2nd place, Tesla-Fest, Novi Sad, 1998; 2nd place, International Women's Inventors Exposition, Subotica, 1998; 1st award, Serbian Trade Union, 1998; 1st award, Serbian Chamber of Agriculture, 2000; Honorary Member, Russian Society of Trace Elements in Medicine, 2001-; Ambassador of Good Will, Ecological Movements of Novi Sad, 2006; Special Recognition Award for Innovation, Belgrade Association of Inventors and Authors of Technical Improvements, 2006; Genius Medal and Diploma, 2006. Memberships: Serbian Chemical Society; Yugoslav Radiation Protection Society; Ecological Movements Society; Serbian Nutritionist Society; Serbian Society for Oncology; The Oxygen Society, USA; International Society of Elementology; International Selenium-Tellurium Association; International Organisation for Bio-politics in Bio-environment; Balkan Union of Oncology; Balkan Union of Chemistry; International Science Foundation; Mediterranean Radiation Protection Society; Russian Society of Trace Elements in Medicine. Address: Balkanska 47, 11000 Belgrade, Serbia. E-mail: ankivana@eunet.yu

DMITRIEV Andrey Nikolaevich, b. 11 September 1950, Elovo, Russia. Scientist. m. Olga Sapozhnikova, 2 daughters. Education: High School, Severouralsk, 1967; Ural Polytechnical Institute, Ekaterinburg, 1973; Scientific Degree of Candidate of Technical Sciences, Ekaterinburg, 1979; Scientific Degree of Doctor of Technical Sciences, Ekaterinburg, 1997. Appointments: Engineer, Younger Scientific Employee, Postgraduate Student, Ural Polytechnical Institute, Ekaterinburg, 1973-79; Senior Scientific Employee, Head of Laboratory for Pyrometallurgy of Reduction Processes, 1998, Institute of Metallurgy, Ural Branch of Russian Academy of Sciences, Ekaterinburg, 1979-; Professor, Chair of Iron and Alloys Metallurgy, Ural Polytechnical Institute, Ural State Technical University, Ekaterinburg, 2001-. Publications: Numerous articles in professional journals. Honours: Honourable Letter, Russian Academy of Sciences, 1999; Grum-Grzhimajlo Premium Medal, Academy of Engineering Sciences of Russia, 2004; Honourable Letter of Government of Sverdlovst Region. Memberships: Corresponding Member, Academy of Engineering Sciences of Russia Federation; Academician, Russian Academy of Natural Sciences. E-mail: redforest@r66.ru

DO Junghwan, b. 12 December 1968, Seoul, Korea. Professor. m. Hyunjung Kim, 2 daughters. Education: BS, 1993, MS, 1995, Ajou University, Korea; PhD, Chemistry, University of Houston, USA, 2000. Appointments: Postdoctoral Fellow, Department of Chemistry, Michigan State University, USA, 2001-03; Assistant Professor, 2003-07, Associate Professor, 2007-, Department of Chemistry, Konkuk University, Korea; Adjunct Professor, Department of Advanced Technology Fusion, Konkuk University, Korea, 2005-06. Publications: Numerous papers and articles in professional scientific journals. Memberships: Korean Chemical Society. Address: Department of Chemistry, Konkuk University, Hwayang-1Dong, Gwangjin-Gu, Seoul 143-701, Korea. E-mail: junghwan@konkuk.ac.kr Website: http://konkuk.ac.kr/~junghwan/jdo-home.htm

DO GIA Canh, b. 27 April 1954, Hanoi, Vietnam. Medical Doctor. m. Hoang Phuong Lan, 1 son, 1 daughter. Education: MD, Hanoi University of Medicine, 1978. Appointments: Chief, Division of Clinical Trial, NIHE; Clinical Review Expert, Vaccines & Biologic License Application, MOH, Vietnam; Member, IRB-MOH, Vietnam, 2008-12. Publications: Articles in internet. Honours: VIFOTEC Award, 1997; Award for great contribution to resolving flood disaster, 1999; Outstanding Doctor, 2003; Medal for dedication to people health, Minister of Health and Presidency, Vietnam, 2006. Memberships: Deputy General Secretary, Vietnam Preventive Medicine Association; Member, WFPHA; Member, APHA. Address: 1 Yersin Str, Haiba Dist, National Institute of Hygiene & Epidemiology (P308), Hanoi, Vietnam. E-mail: vncddp@hn.vnn.vn

DOBBS Michael John, b. 14 November 1948. Author. m. Amanda L Collingridge, 1981, 2 sons. Education: Christ Church, Oxford; Fletcher School of Law & Diplomacy, USA. Appointments: UK Special Adviser, 1981-87; Chief of Staff, UK Conservative Party, 1986-87; Joint Deputy Chairman, 1994-95; Deputy Chairman, Saatchi & Saatchi, 1983-91; Deputy Chairman, Conservative Party, 1994-95; Chairman, Spirit Advertising, 1998-; BBC TV Presenter, 1999-2001. Publications: House of Cards, 1989; Wall Ganes, 1990; Last Man to Die, 1991; To Play the King, 1993; The Touch of Innocents, 1994; The Final Cut, 1995; Goodfellowe MP, 1997; The Buddha of Brewer Street, 1998; Whispers of Betrayal, 2000; Winston's War, 2002; Never Surrender, 2003; Churchill's Hour, 2004; Saboteurs: The Nazi Raid on America, 2004; Churchill's Triumph, 2005; First Lady, 2006; The Lords Day, 2007. Address: Newton House, Wylye, Wiltshire BA12 0QS, England. E-mail: michldobbs@aol.com

DÖBEREINER Jürgen, b. 1 November 1923, Königsberg Pr, Germany. Veterinarian. m. Johanna Kubelka, deceased 2000, 2 sons, 1 deceased 1996, 1 daughter. Education: DMV, Rio de Janeiro, 1954; MSc, University Wisconsin-Madison, USA, 1963; Dr med vet hc, Justus-Liebig-University Giessen, Germany, 1977. Appointment: Research Worker in Animal Pathology, Ministry Agriculture-Embrapa, Rio de Janeiro, Brazil, 1955-. Publications: More than 170 scientific papers; Co-author, Plantas Tóxicas da Amazonia a Bovinos e outros Herbivoros, 1979; Co-author, Plantas Tóxicas do Brasil, 2000; Editor-in-Chief, Pesquisa Agropecuaria Brasileira (Brazilian Journal of Agricultural Research), 1966-76; Editor, Pesquisa Veterinária Brasileira (Brazilian Journal of Veterinary Research), 1981-. Honours: Frederico Menezes Veiga Prize, 2005. Membership: President, Brazilian College of Animal Pathology, 1978-; President, Brazilian Association of Science Editors, 2000-2004; President, The Johanna Döbereiner

Research Society, 2002-. Address: Embrapa-CNPAB/Sanidade Animal, Km 47, Seropédica, Rio de Janeiro 23890-000, Brazil.

DOBRESCU Mircea Virgil, b. 27 October 1952, Turnu-Magurele, Romania. (German citizen, arrived in Germany, 1983). Veterinary Surgeon; Veterinary Dentist and Periodontist; Consultant; Scientist; Researcher; Writer. Education: DVM, summa cum laude, 1976; PhD Veterinary Medicine, Dentistry Science and Periodontology, 1993, University of Bucharest; Master in Veterinary Dentistry and Periodontology, Munich, Germany, 1992; Studies throughout Europe and Israel. Appointments: Assistant Professor, Pathology, Diagnostics and Clinics, State Veterinary Institute, Beit-Dagan, Ministry of Agriculture of State of Israel, University of Tel Aviv, Weizmann Institute of Sciences, University of Jerusalem, 1978; Specialist in Microbiology, Virology, Pathology and Leukaemia, Central Laboratories for Diagnosis, Ministry of Agriculture, Bucharest, 1978-82; Studies in Germany for Specialist in Veterinary Dentistry and Periodontology, 1983-89; Private practice for Veterinary Dentistry and Peridontology for small animals, Augsburg, Germany, 1989-; Owner and Senior Lecturer, School of Veterinary Dentistry and Periodontology for medical postgraduate training in Europe, 1992-; Presenter, numerous animal and veterinary conferences, seminars and workshops. Publications include: Odonton Therapy: A new human and animal Periodontology therapy; First Periodontal Status and First Dentistry Reference Cards in Veterinary Medicine for Cat and Dog; Use of Periodontal Status in Veterinary Dentistry Science; First Vade-mecum stomatologicum in Veterinary Medicine; Cast crown restorative dentistry of canini in dogs and cats with gold and porcelain, two new methods; Corrective orthodontics of common malocclusions in dogs with acrylic intraorale plates with expansion screw; Corrective Protrusion (corrective orthodontic) of Incisivi in a Rottweiler with chrome-cobalt intraorale plate with expansion screw – a premiere; Books: Da grinst selbst das Pferd (Even the Horse Would Grin); Joyful Stories of a Veterinary Surgeon, edited in Germany, 1996; The Last Secret of the Red Stone, fiction-adventure-novel, forthcoming; 37 articles in professional journals on veterinary dentistry and Periodontology and on animal and human cancer. Honours: International Personality of the Year 2001 in recognition of service to Education; International Scientist of the Year 2001 and of the Year 2003; 2000 Eminent Scientists of Today, 2003; Great Minds of the 21st Century; Man of the Year, 2001-02; Living Legends; American Medal of Honor, 2002; World Medal of Honour, ABI, 2003; Nominated, International Peace Prize, United Cultural Convention, ABI, USA, 2003; Worldwide Honours List, IBC, 2003; Contemporary Hall of Fame, ABI, 2003; Leading Intellectuals of the World, ABI, 2004; The Contemporary Who's Who of Professionals, ABI, 2005; Listed in several international directories of biography. Memberships: Research Board of Advisors, American Biographical Institute; New York Academy of Sciences; American Association for the Advancement of Science; Federation of European Microbiological Societies; International Union of Microbiological Societies; Romanian Oncological Society. Address: Stettenstr 28, 86150 Augsburg, Bayern, Germany.

DOIG John, b. 2 August 1958, Helensburgh, Scotland. Violinist; Conductor. Education: First enrolled pupil, St Mary's Music School, Edinburgh, 1972. Appointments: BBC Symphony Orchestra, 1975-78; Principal Violin, BBC Philharmonic Orchestra, 1979-81; Co-Leader, Orchestra of Scottish Opera, 1981-83; Co-Leader and Guest Leader,

Scottish Chamber Orchestra, 1986-90; Leader, Orchestra of Scottish Opera, 1991-98; Founder and Artistic Director, Scottish Bach Consort, 1994-. Honour: Honorary President, Scottish Bach Society. Membership: Society of Musicians. Address: Endrick Mews, Killearn, Stirlingshire G63 9ND, Scotland.

DOJCINOVIC Uros, b. 15 May 1959, Belgrade, Yugoslavia. Guitarist; Composer; Pedagogue. m. Vesna Djukic-Dojcinovic, 1 son. Education: University of Philology, Belgrade, 1979; Music Academy, Zagreb, 1979-83; Graduated in Classical Guitar, 1984; Graduated, Music Pedagogy, Music University of Belgrade, 1985; Postgraduate work (Ph.d) in Musicology and Philology, University of Belgrade, 1988. Debut: Belgrade Concert Hall, Cultural Centre Stari Grad, 1976. Career: Over 2500 concerts worldwide; Over 500 radio and television appearances; Numerous masterclasses, lecturers and presentations; Professor of Classical Guitar, Chamber Music, various music schools in Belgrade and Zagreb. Compositions: Chamber Music with Guitar, opus 16, 26, 27, 31, 33, 34, 35, 36, 37, 39, 40, 48, includes 10 suites, themes with variations, fantasias, cycle-form compositions, some for different guitar orchestras and chamber groups including classical guitar; Music Works (published) include altogether 60 opus numbers. Recordings: South American Guitar; Exotic Guitar; Characteristic Guitar; Guitar Recital; Classical and Romantic Music for two guitars; Danza Caracteristica; Chamber Music for Guitar; Exotic Guitar Music. Publications: Magic World of the Guitar, 1984; Yugoslav Guitar History, 1992; The Guitar Triumph, 1994; The First Guitarist Steps, 1995; Anthology of Guitar Music in Serbia, 1996; Anthology of Guitar Music in Montenegro, 1996; Numerous articles in journals. Honours: Over 40 National and International medals, diplomas and prizes; First Republic and Federal Prizes in Guitar Composition, 1975, 1977; First Prize, Cultural Olympiad, Belgrade, 1978; Listed in national and international biographical dictionaries. Memberships: Society for Music Artists of Serbia; Society of Composers of Montenegro; Matica Srpska-Novi Sad; Founder, President, Yugoslav Guitar Society and Foundation, 2000-. Address: Solunska str 12, 11000 Belgrade, Serbia.

DOKULIL Milos, b. 23 July 1928, Brno, Czech Republic. University Professor. m. Anna Chudoba, 1 daughter. Education: BA, 1949, MA, 1951, University of Political and Social Sciences, Prague, 1947-51; Charles University, Faculty of Arts, 1948-50; MA, University of Russian Language and Literature, 1954-57; PhD, Czechoslovak Academy of Sciences, 1963; DSc, Charles University, 1993. Appointments: Lecturer, Senior Lecturer, Technical University, 1956-63; Senior Lecturer, Faculty of Pedagogy, 1963-69; For political reasons prevented from academic activity, including publishing of 3 books, 1970-89; Associate Professor, Department Head, 1990; Professor, Masaryk University, 1992-. Publications: A Primer of Logic for Teachers, 1967; Through the Philosophy of History to the History of Philosophy, 1970, enlarged, 1992; The Formation of a Philosopher: Through Toleration Towards the Epistemology of John Locke, 1972; On the Issue over Toleration: Lockean Contemplations, 1995; Ethics, 3 vols (Co-author, co-editor), 1998; Masaryk as a Rear-view Mirror? 2005; Masarykian Comebacks, 2006; Numerous professional articles. Honours: Nominations to Man of Year, International Biographical Centre, American Biographical Institute; Nomination for Ministry of Education Prize (Czech Republic), 1999; Nominations: IBC Top 100 Educators, 2006; International Educator, 2006; International Peace Prize, United Cultural Convention, 2005, 2006. Address: Faculty of Informatics, Masaryk University, Botanicka 68a, CZ 602 00 Brno, Czech Republic.

DOLE Elizabeth Hanford, b. 29 July 1936, Salisbury, North Carolina, USA. Administrator. m. Robert J Dole, 1975. Education: Duke University; Harvard University; University of Oxford. Appointments: Called to Bar, District of Columbia, 1966; Staff Assistant to Assistant Secretary for Education, Department of Health, Education & Welfare, 1966-67; Practising lawyer, Washington DC, 1967-68; Associate Director Legislative Affairs, then Executive Director Presidents Commission for Consumer Interests, 1968-71; Deputy Assistant, Office of Consumer Affairs, The White House, Washington DC, 1971-73; Commissioner, Federal Trade Commission, 1973-79; Assistant to President for Public Liaison, 1981-83; Secretary of Transport, 1983-87; Candidate for Republican presidential nomination, 1999; Senator from North Carolina, 2003-. Publications: A Leader in Washington, 1998; The Doles: Unlimited Partners, 1988; Hearts toughed by Fire: My 500 Most Inspirational Quotations, 2004. Memberships: Trustee, Duke University, 1974-88; Member, Visiting Committee, John F Kennedy School of Government, 1988-; Secretary of Labour, 1989-90; President, American Red Cross, 1991-98; Member, Commission, Harvard School of Public Health, 1992-; Board of Overseers, Harvard University, 1989-95. Address: Office of the Senator from North Carolina, Suite B34, Dirksen Building, US Senate, Washington, DC 20510, USA.

DOLE Bob (Robert J), b. 22 July 1923, Russell, Kansas, USA. Politician. m. (2) Elizabeth Hanford Dole, 1975, 1 daughter. Education: University of Kansas; Washburn Municipal University. Appointments: Member, Kansas Legislature, 1951-53; Russell County Attorney, 1953-61; Member, House of Representatives, 1960-68; US Senator from Kansas, 1969-96, Senate Majority Leader, 1995-96; Senate Republic Leader, 1987-96; House Majority Leader, 1985-87; Minority Leader, 1987; Chairman, Republic National Committee, 1971-72; Vice-Presidential Candidate, 1976; Presidential Candidate, 1996; Member of Counsel, Verner, Liipfert, Bernhard, McPherson and Hand, Alston and Bird, 2003-. Publications: Great Political Wit (co-ed), 1999; Great Presidential Wits, 2001. Memberships: Chairman, Senate Finance Committee, Dole Foundation, 1981-84; Director, Mainstream Inc; Advisor, US Delegate to FAO Conference, Rome, 1965, 1974, 1977; Member, Congressional delegate to India, 1966, Mid E, 1967; Member, US Helsinki Commission; Delegate to Belgrade Conference, 1977; Trustee, William Allen White Foundation, University of Kansas; Member, National Advisory Committee, The John Wesley Colleges; American Bar Association; National Advisory Committee, on Scouting for the Handicapped, Kansas Association for Retarded Children; Advisory Board of Utd Cerebral Plasy, Kansas; Honorary Member, Advisory Board of Kidney Patients Inc; Presidential Medal of Freedom, 1997; Distinguished Service Award, 1997. Address: Alston & Bird LLP, 10th Floor, North Building, 601 Pennsylvania Avenue, NW, Washington DC 20004-2601, USA. E-mail: bdole@alston.com Website: www.alston.com

DOLEZAL Urszula Marta, b. 8 September 1933, Krakow, Poland. Microbiologist, Scientific Worker. m. Marian Dolezal. Education: Manager, 1956, Doctor, PhD, 1959, Faculty Biology and Science of Earl Jagiellonian University; Associate Professor, Medical Academy in Cracow, 1965; Professor, sc.title, 1977; Professor ordinary Academy of Physical Education, 1990. Appointments: Head, Department of Mycology Medicine, Medical Academy Institute of Microbiology, 1970, Head of Chair, Department of Hygiene and Health Protection, later Health Promotion of Cracow Academy of Physical Education 1975; Retired, 2003-.

Publications: 243 publications of topics: mycological pollution of air, mycology of the human environment and the influence of fungi, mould, yeast on the health of the population, mycoflora of flats and buildings, hygiene and different topics of preventive medicine, new aspect of health promotion, HIV/AIDS. Honours: Zloty Krzyz Zaslugi, 1980; Medal Komisji Edukacji Narodowej, 1983; Krzyz kawalerski Orderu Odrodzenia Polski, 1987. Memberships: Polish Academy of Science Commission of Biology; Commission of Public Health; International Scientific Forum on Home Hygiene, delegate of Poland in ERNA/RECS; Inter. Red Cross and Red Crescent Societies. Address: Daszynskiego 32 app 6, 31534 Kracow, Poland.

DOLIN Lev Sergeevich, b. 16 May 1936, Gorky, USSR. Physicist. m. Irina Sergeevna Gryaznova, 1972, 1 son, 1 daughter. Education: Diploma of Physicist-Researcher, Gorky State University, 1959; Postgraduate Course, 1962; PhD, 1966. Appointments: Researcher, Senior Researcher, Gorky Radiophysical Institute, 1962-77; Head of Laboratory, Head of Department, Institute of Applied Physics, Russian Academy of Sciences, Nizhny Novgorod, 1977-2006. Publications: Author of more than 150 scientific articles; Co-author, 3 monographs. Honours: State prize, 1999. Address: Bykov st, 3-52, Nizhny Novgorod, 603136, Russia. E-mail: lev.dolin@hydro.appl.sci-nnov.ru

DOLLFUS Audouin Charles, b. 12 November 1924, Paris, France. Physicist; Astronomer. m. Catherine Browne, 1959, 4 children. Education: Doctor of Mathematics, Faculty of Sciences, University of Paris. Appointments: Astronomer, Astrophysical Section, Meudon Observatory, Paris, 1946-; Head of Laboratory for Physics of the Solar System; Astronomer, Observatoire de Paris, 1965; Discovered Janus, innermost moon of Saturn, 1966; Emeritus President, Observatoire de Triel, 1994-; Research into polarisation of light. Publications: 7 books; 350 scientific publications on astrophysics. Honours: Grand Prix of Academie des Sciences; International Award Galabert for Astronautics; Diploma Tissandier, International Federation of Astronautics. Memberships: International Academy of Astronautics; Société Astronomique de France; Aéro-club de France; French Association for the Advancement of Science; Royal Astronomical Society, London; Society of French Explorers; Explorers Club, USA; Société Philomatique de Paris; Honorary member, Royal Astronomical Society of Canada. Address: 77 rue Albert Perdreaux, 92370 Chaville, France.

DOMB Risa, b. 16 March 1937, Israel. Lecturer; Director of Studies. m. Richard Arnold, 3 sons, 1 daughter. Education: Teachers State Diploma, Levinsky State School for Teachers, Tel-Aviv, Israel, 1957; BA (2nd class honours), 1973, PhD, 1978, Hebrew, University of London, England. Appointments: Head, Hebrew Department, Hampstead Garden Suburb Institute, London, 1960-79; Lecturer, Modern Hebrew Literature, Faculty of Orient Studies, University of Cambridge, 1979-; Established (Director) Centre for Modern Hebrew Studies, University of Cambridge, 1993-; Director of Studies, Oriental Studies, 1995-, Tutorship, 1995-99, Supernumary Fellow, 1999, Life Fellow, 2004, Girton College; Director of Studies, Oriental Studies, 2001-03; Subject Examination Co-ordinator, Faculty of Oriental Studies, 2001, Subject Co-ordinator and Member of Faculty Board, 2001-05, Homerton College. Publications: 6 books; 14 essays in books; 20 articles and papers in professional journals; 3 translations; 19 book reviews; Numerous appearances on radio and television, and at public lectures and societies, etc. Memberships: Elected Member, Faculty of Oriental Studies,

University of Cambridge, 1982; Elected Bye Fellow, Girton College, 1988; Elected Affiliated Member, Newnham College, 1989; Life Fellow, Girton College, 2004. Address: Faculty of Oriental Studies, Sidgwick Avenue, Cambridge CB3 9DA, England.

DOMEIKA Povilas, b. 20 November 1938, Radviliskis Region, Lithuania. Economist; Professor. m. Audrone Zilnyte, 2 sons. Education: Economist, Lithuanian Academy of Agriculture (now University), 1963; Dr of Economics, Leningrad Institute of Agriculture (now St Petersburg State Agrarian University), 1970; Dr Habil of Economics, Lithuanian Institute of Agrarian Economics, 1991; Professor, Lithuanian Academy of Agriculture (now University), 1993. Appointments: Senior Assistant of Economics and Accounting Department, 1964-67, Dr Senior Assistant, 1970, Dr Associate Professor, 1976, Economical Cybernetics Department, Dr Associate Professor, Vice-Dean of Faculty of Economics, 1971-80; Dr Associate Professor, Head of Department of Economical Cybernetics, 1980-91, Dr Habil Professor, Department of Economical Cybernetics, 1993; Professor Dr Habil, Informatics Department, 1996-2005, Professor Dr Habil, Accounting and Finance Department, 2005-, Lithuanian University of Agriculture. Publications: Author of monographs: Mechanization of Accounting in Agricultural Enterprises, 1977, 1978; Co-author of textbooks: Accounting in Agriculture (with Essentials of Computerized Technology), 1974, 1980, 1987; Computerization of Accounting in Agricultural Enterprises, 1984; Author, over 100 published scientific articles. Honours include: Academician, International Academy of Informatization of the United Nations, 1999; Order of Merit, Lithuanian University of Agriculture, 2004. Memberships: Member of Senate, Lithuanian University of Agriculture; Council Board, Institute of Information Technologies; Member, Professors' Club "Scientia", Lithuanian University of Agriculture; Member, Lithuanian Scientific Society, 2006; Association of Lithuanian Agrarian Economists; Lithuanian Association of Ignotas Domeika. Address: Universiteto 10, Akademijos m, LT-53361 Kauno rajonas, Lithuania. E-mail: povilas.domeika@lzuu.lt

DOMIN Jan, b. 1 June 1947, Bzianka, dist Krosno, Poland. Physicist. m. Urszula, 1 daughter. Education: MS, Physics, Pedagogical College, Rzeszow, 1969; PhD, Physics, University of Gdansk, 1981. Appointments: Assistant, Pedagogical College, Rzeszow, 1970-80; Post-Doctoral Position, Pedagogical College, Rzeszow, 1981-84; Lecturer, Polish Institute of Science, Chicago, USA, 1985-88; Lecturer, Geodesy College, Rzeszow, 1989-93; Vice Director, Methodology Center, Rzeszow, 1994-96; Lecturer, University of Technology, Rzeszow, 1996-. Publications: Research work reports in professional international journals. Honours: Listed in international biographical dictionaries. Memberships: Polish Physical Association. E-mail: spjanusz@prz.edu.pl

DOMINGO Placido, b. 21 January 1941, Madrid, Spain. Singer; Conductor; Administrator. m. Marta Ornelas, 3 sons. Education: Studies in Piano, Conducting and Voice, National Conservatory of Music, Mexico City. Appointments: Operatic debut as Alfredo in La Traviata, Monterrey, Mexico, 1961; 12 roles, 280 performances, Israel National Opera, 2½ years; Title role, Ginastera's Don Rodrigo, New York City Opera, 1966; Debut as Maurizio in Adriana Lecouvreur, Metropolitan Opera, NY, 1968; 41 roles, over 400 performances, Metropolitan Opera, 36 years; Regularly appears at: Milan's La Scala, the Vienna State Opera, London's Covent Garden, Paris' Bastille Opera, the San Francisco Opera, Chicago's Lyric Opera, the Washington National Opera, the Los Angeles Opera, the Lyceo in Barcelona, the Colon in Buenos Aires, the Real in Madrid, and at the Bayreuth and Salzburg Festivals; Conductor of opera performances at the Metropolitan, London's Covent Garden and Vienna State Opera, etc; Conductor of symphonic concerts with the Berlin Philharmonic, London Symphony and Chicago Symphony, etc; Music Director, Seville World's Fair; General Director, Washington National Opera, 1994-; General Director, Los Angeles Opera, 2000-; Over 120 different roles including: Wagner's "Parsifal", "Lohengrin" and Seigmund in "Walkure"; "Meistersinger", "Tannhauser"; "Flying Dutchman"; Richard Strauss's "Die Frau Ohne Schattern"; Weber's "Oberon"; Beethoven's "Fidelio"; Gherman in Tchaikovsky's "Queen of Spades" (in Russian); the Spanish opera "Margarita la Tornera" by Roberto Chapi; Verdi's "La Battaglia di Legnano"; Anton Garcia Abril's "Divinas Palabras"; Rasputin in Deborah Drattell's "Nicholas and Alexandra"; Breton's "La Dolores"; Albeniz's "Merlin"; Founder, yearly competition for young singers, "Operalia"; Inaugurated Domingo Cafritz Young Artists Program of the Washington Opera, 2002; Special benefit concerts to help 1985 Mexican earthquake, AIDS charities, Armenian earthquake, mudslides in Acapulco, and others. Publications: Over 100 recordings; More than 50 videos; 3 theatrically released films; Double CD of every Verdi aria for the tenor voice; CD of excerpts from Wagner's "Siegfried" and "Gotterdaemmerung"; My First Forty Years (autobiography), 1983; My Operatic Roles, 2000. Honours: Dr hc, Royal College of Music, 1982; Dr hc, University Complutense de Madrid, 1989; Hon Dmus, University of Oxford, 2003; Commander, Legion d'honneur, 2002; Honorary KBE, 2002; Medal of Freedom; 9 Grammy Awards; European Culture Foundation Prize, 2003. Address: c/o Vincent and Farrell Associates, Suite 740, 481 8th Avenue, New York, NY 10001, USA.

DOMINIAN Jack, b. 25 August 1929, Athens, Greece. Doctor. m. Eddith Mary, 4 daughters. Education: MA; FRCPEd; FRCPsy; DSc (Hons); MBE. Appointments: Qualified as doctor, 1955; Qualified as psychiatrist, 1961; Consultant Psychiatrist, 1964-88; Private Practice, 1988-2003; Retired, 2003-. Publications: 32 books including: Christian Marriage, 1967; Marriage, Faith & Love, 1981; Marital Breakdown, 1968; Authority, 1976; Cycles of Affirmation, 1975; One Like Us, 1998; Let's Make Love, 2001; Living Love, 2004; Over 100 articles in leading Catholic journal, Tablet; Numerous articles in BMJ, Lancet and other scientific journals. Honours: DSc (Hon), Lancaster University, 1976; MBE, 1994. Memberships: Royal College of Psychiatry; Royal College of Physicians, Edinburgh; Fellow, Royal Society of Medicine, London. Address: 19 Clements Road, Chorleywood, Hertfordshire, England.

DOMINIK William John, b. 29 December 1953, Cleveland, Ohio, USA. Professor. Education: Cert IES, University of Durham, UK, 1974; BA, University of the Pacific, Stockton, California, USA, 1975; California Teaching Credential, 1975; MA, Texas Tech University, Lubbock, Texas 1982; PhD, Monash University, Melbourne, Australia, 1989. Appointments: Teacher, Administrator, Ministry of Education, Melbourne, Australia, 1976-90; Teaching and Research Assistant, 1981-82, Assistant Professor, 1990-91, Texas Tech University, Lubbock, USA; Tutor, Research Assistant, Monash University, 1985-88; Tutor, Council of Adult Education, Victoria, Australia, 1989; Lecturer, 1991-94, Associate Professor, 1994-97, 1998-2000, Professor, Chair, 2001, Classics, University of Natal, Durban, South Africa; Visiting Professor, Classics, University of Leeds, England, 1997-98; Visiting Teaching Fellow, Christ's College and Newnham College, University of Cambridge, England,

2000; Research Fellow, Clare Hall, University of Cambridge, England, 2000-01; Professor, Chair, Department of Classics, University of Otago, New Zealand, 2002-; Visiting Professor, Classics, Visiting Research Fellow, Institute for Advanced Studies in the Humanities, University of Edinburgh, Scotland, 2006-07. Publications: Over 160 publications, including 16 books. Honours: Recipient of 140 grants and awards including: Commonwealth Research Award, Australia, 1987-88; Commonwealth Fellowship, UK, 1997-98; Fellow and Life Member, Clare Hall, University of Cambridge, 2001-. Memberships: American Philological Association; Classical Association of South Africa; Australasian Society of Classical Studies; New Zealand Association of Classical Teachers; Classical Association of Otago. Address: Department of Classics, University of Otago, PO Box 56, Dunedin 9054, New Zealand. E-mail: william.dominik@stonebow.otago.ac.nz

DONG Yuning, b. 16 June 1955, Nanjing, China. Professor. Education: B Eng, 1982, M Eng, 1984, Nanjing University of Posts and Telecommunications; PhD, South East University, Nanjing, China, 1988; M Phil, Queen's University, Belfast, Northern Ireland, 1998. Appointments: Lecturer, 1988-92, Associate Professor, 1992-1999, Professor, Information Engineering Department, 1999-, Nanjing University of Posts and Telecommunications; Visiting Scholar, Imperial College, London, England, 1992-93; Postdoctoral Fellow, University of Texas, Galveston, Texas, 1993-95; Research Fellow, Queen's University, Belfast, Northern Ireland and University of Birmingham, England, 1995-98. Publications: 3D reconstruction of irregular shapes, 2001; Fast computation of various templates, 2003; Technical papers in Chinese Journal of Electronics, Chinese Journal of Computers and others, 2000-2003. Honours: Best University Teacher, Jiangsu Province, China, 1992; Best Researcher, Ministry of Posts and Telecommunications, China, 1993. Memberships: Senior Member, China Communications Institute; Senior Member, Chinese Institute of Electronics. Address: PO Box 166, Nanjing University of Posts and Telecommunications, Nanjing, Jiangsu 210003, China. E-mail: dongyn@njupt.edu.cn

DONIN Valery Il'yich, b. 11 March 1941, Nerchinsk, Eastern Siberia, Russia. Physicist. m. Tamara Kurtz, 1 daughter. Education: MSc, 1963, Tomsk State University; PhD (CPMSc), 1972; Doctorate in Phys and Math Sc, 1989, Russian Academy of Sciences. Appointments: Engineer, Research Scientist, Head of Laboratory, quantum electronics, Siberian Branch of Russian Academy of Sciences, 1963-. Publications: Over 100 research papers in field of laser and plasma physics; book, High-Power Gas Ion Lasers, 1991. Honours: First degree diploma, Siberian Branch of Russian Academy of Sciences, 1973; Honorary diplomas, Russian Academy of Sciences, 1974 and 1999; Medal, Exhibition of National Economic Achievements, USSR, 1979; Honorary professor, Albert Schweitzer International University, 2000; 21st Century Achievement Award and American Medal of Honor, ABI, 2001; Inducted into 500 Leaders of World Influence Hall of Fame, ABI, and 500 Founders of 21st Century Honours List, IBC, 2002. Memberships: Rozhdestvensky Optical Society, 1993; New York Academy of Sciences, 1997. Address: Institute of Automation and Electrometry, Siberian Branch of Russian Academy of Sciences, Acad Koptyuga pr. 1, Novosibirsk 630090, Russia. E-mail: donin@iae.nsk.su

DONNER Richard, b. 24th April 1930, New York, USA. Director; Producer. Appointments: Actor off-Broadway; Collaborated with director Martin Ritt on TV adaption of Somerset Maugham's Of Human Bondage; Moved to California and began commercials, industrial films and documentaries;

Films: X 15, 1961; Salt and Pepper, 1968; Twinky, 1969; The Omen, 1976; Superman, 1978; Inside Moves, 1981; The Toy, 1982 Ladyhawke, 1985; The Goonies, 1985; Lethal Weapon, 1987; Scrooged, 1988; Lethal Weapon 2, 1989; Radio Flyer, 1991; The Final Conflict (executive producer), 1991; Lethal Weapon 3, 1992; Free Willy (co-executive producer), 1993; Maverick, 1994; Assassins, 1995; Conspiracy Theory 1997; Free Willy 3: The Rescue; Lethal Weapon 4, 1998; Blackheart (producer), 1999; Timeline (producer), 2003; 16 Blocks, 2006. TV films: Portrait of a Teenage Alcoholic; Senior Year; A Shadow in the Streets; Tales From the Crypt presents Demon Knight (co-executive producer); Any Given Sunday, 1999; X-Men (executive producer), 2000; Series episodes of: Have Gun Will Travel; Perry Mason; Cannon; Get Smart; The Fugitive; Kojak; Bronk; Twilight Zone; The Banana Splits; Combat; Two Fisted Tales; Conspiracy Theory. Address: The Donners Company, 9465 Wilshire Boulevard, #420, Beverly Hills, CA 90212, USA.

DONOVAN Marie-Andrée, b. 1947, Timmins, Ontario, Canada. Writer. 1 daughter. Education: BA, University of Ottawa, Canada. Publications: Books: Nouvelles volantes (short stories), 1994; L'Envers de toi (novel), 1997, 2000; Mademoiselle Cassie (novel), 1999, 2003; L'Harmonica (novel), 2000; Les Bernaches en voyage (story for children), 2001; Les soleils incendiés (novel), 2004; Fantômier (short stories), 2005. Honours: Finalist, Prix littéraire Le Droit, 1998; Prix littéraire Le Droit, 2000; Finalist, Prix des lecteurs de Radio-Canada, 2001; Prix littéraire de la Fondation franco-ontarienne, 2002; Prix des lecteurs de Radio-Canada, 2005; Prix Émile-Ollivier, 2006; Prix Champlain, 2006; Listed in Who's Who publications and biographical dictionaries. E-mail: donovan@uottawa.ca

DOOSE Chris A Sr, b. 2 June 1951, San Angelo, Texas, USA. US Treasury Agent; Pilot (Retired). m. Cindy Lane, 1 son, 1 daughter. Education: BS, University of State of New York, 1987; MA, Austin Presbyterian Theological Seminary, 2000; Postgraduate studies, History and Government, Angelo State University, Texas. Appointments: CW3 US Army Attack Helicopter Pilot, Retired; GS-13 Treasury Agent, Pilot Retired; Airline Transport Pilot; MEL, Helicopter Instructor; MEL, Helicopter CFII Advanced Ground Instructor; Retired Federal Law Enforcement Officer, 32 years. Honours: US Customs Service Awards for Service and Duty in South America for Meritorious Duty in War on Drugs. Publications: All classified by Treasury Department. Memberships: FLEOA; Phi Kappa Psi Fraternity; Vietnam Veterans Association; VFW; DAV Association; Life Member MAFA. Address: 2732 A&M Avenue, San Angelo, TX 76904-5821, USA. E-mail: ccdoose@aol.com

DOOSE Cindy Lane, b. 16 October 1970, San Angelo, Texas, USA. Artist. m. Chris A Doose Sr, 1 son, 1 daughter. Education: Bachelor in Art History with honours summa cum laude, Architecture and Oil Painting, University of the State of New York, Albany, 1995-99. Career: Dancer; Homemaker; Working as an artist in oil on canvas from a studio at home, 1999-; Art Club Secretary, 1999; Junior League; Symphony Education Chair. Honours: 2nd Place, Young Artists Around the World, Museum, 1999; 1st Place for oil on canvas theme: Impressionistic Architecture and History, Showplacing Young Artists, hung for 8 days in each of 27 museums, 1998-2002. Memberships: Art Club of San Angelo; Symphony Chairman of Education; Junior League; Women's Republican Committee. Address: 2732 A&M Avenue, San Angelo, TX 76904-5821, USA. E-mail: ccdoose@aol.com

DORFF Stephen, b. 29 July 1973, Atlanta, Georgia, USA. Actor. Appointments: Started acting aged 9; Films: The Gate; The Power of One; An Ambush of Ghosts; Judgement Night; Rescue Me; Backbeat; SFW; Reckless; Innocent Lies; I Shot Andy Warhol; City of Industry, Blood and Wine, 1997; Blade, 1998; Entropy, 1999; Quantum Project, Cecil B Demented, 2000; The Last Minute, Zoolander, 2001; All For Nothin', Deuces Wild, Riders, FearDotCom, 2002; Den of Lions, Cold Creek Manor, 2003; Alone in the Dark, Tennis, Anyone?, Shadowboxer, 2005; World Trade Center, 45, 2006; Botched, The Passage, 2007. TV films: I Know My First Name is Steven, Always Remember I Love You, Do You Know the Muffin Man? 1989; A Son's Promise, 1990; Earthly Possessions, 1999; Skip Tracer, Covert One: The Hades Factor, 2007. TV series: What a Dummy, 1990. Address: 9350 Wilshire Boulevard, Suite 4, Beverly Hills, CA 90212, USA.

DORFMAN Ariel, b. 6 May 1942, Buenos Aires, Argentina (Chilean citizen). Research Professor of Literature and Latin; Author; Dramatist; Poet. Education: Graduated, University of Chile, Santiago, 1967. Appointment: Walter Hines Page Research Professor of Literature and Latin, Centre for International Studies, Duke University, Durham, North Carolina, 1984-. Publications: Fiction: Hard Rain, 1973; My House is On Fire, 1979; Widows, 1983; Dorando la pildora, 1985; Travesia, 1986; The Last Song of Manuel Sendero, 1986; Mascara, 1988; Konfidenz, 1996. Poetry: Last Waltz in Santiago and Other Poems of Exile and Disappearance, 1988. Plays: Widows, 1988; Death and the Maiden, 1991; Reader, 1992; Who's Who (with Rodrigo Dorfman), 1997. Films: Death and the Maiden, 1994; Prisoners in Time, 1995; My House is on Fire, 1997. Non-Fiction: How to Read Donald Duck (with Armand Mattelart), 1971; The Empire's Old Clothes, 1983; Some Write to the Future, 1991; Heading South, Looking North: A Bilingual Journey, 1998; The Nanny and Iceburg, 1999. Honours: Olivier Award, London 1991; Time Out Award, 1991; Literary Lion, New York Public Library, 1992; Dora Award, 1994; Charity Randall Citation, International Poetry Forum, 1994; Best Film for Television, Writers Guild of Great Britain, 1996. Address: c/o Centre for International Studies, Duke University, Durham, NC 27708, USA.

DOROFTEI Mugur Gideon, b. 11 October 1943, Bucharest, Romania. Music Educator; Conductor; Composer; Musician. m. Cornelia Mesinschi, 1969, 2 sons, 1 daughter. Education: MusM, Ciprian Porumbescu Conservatory of Music, Bucharest, 1970; PhD, Music Academy of Bucharest, 1994. Appointments: Violinist, Opera and Operetta, Constaniza, Romania, 1960-61; Violinist, Philharmonic Orchestra, Ploiesti, Romania, 1961-62; Violinist, Ciocirlia Opera Radio Orchestra Operetta, Bucharest, Romania, 1962-70; Violin Teacher, School of Arts No 1, Suceava, Romania, 1977-80; Artist in Residence, Strings & Orchestra, Southwestern University, Keene, Texas, USA, 1981-; Dallas Independent School District, 2001-04. Publications: Music Theory Made Clear; Music Theory Made Clear Workbook; Music Theory for the Young Musician; Music Theory for the Young Musician Workbook; Ear Trining Intervals & Chords; Solfeggio Sight Singing; Violin Method for Beginners Book One, with CD; Violin Method for Beginners Book Two, with CD. Honours: Personalities of the South, ABI, 1983; Presidential Citation of Excellence, 1987; Listed in international biographical dictionaries. Address: PO Box 711, Keene, TX 76059, USA.

DOTRICE Roy, b. 26 May 1925, Guernsey, Channel Islands. Actor. m. Kay Newman, 1946, 3 daughters. Education: Dayton and Intermediate Schools, Guernsey; Air Gunner, RAF, 1940;

POW, 1942-45; Acted in repertory, 1945-55; Formed and directed Guernsey Theatre Co, 1955; Films include: The Heroes of Telemark, 1965; A Twist of Sand, 1968; Lock up Your Daughters, 1969; Buttercup Chain; Tomorrow; One of Those Things, 1971; Nicholas and Alexandra, 1971; Amadeus; The Corsican Brothers, 1983; The Eliminators, 1985; Shaka Zulu, 1985; Young Harry Houdini, 1986; Camila; L-Dopa; The Lady Forgets; The Cutting Edge; The Scarlet Letter; Swimming with Sharks; Alien Hunter; These Foolish Things; Played; Go Go Tales; Stage appearances throughout England and tours of Canada and USA; TV includes: Dear Liar, Brief Lives; The Caretaker; Imperial Palace; Misleading Cases; Clochemerle; Dickens of London; Stargazy on Zummerdown; Life Begins; numerous appearances on US TV. Honours: TV Actor of the Year Award, 1968; Emmy Award; Tony Award, 2000. Address: 98 St Martin's Lane, London WC2, England.

DOUGLAS Brian David, b. 8 July 1948, Scotland. Painter. Education: York School of Art, 1963-67; Maidstone College of Art, 1967-70; Royal Academy Schools, London, 1970-73; Leeds Polytechnic, 1973-74. Career: Teacher, 1974-83; Technician, York University, 1984-89; Painter, 1970-2004. Honours: RAS (Painting and Engraving); NEAC; RBA. Memberships: Royal Society of British Artists; New English Art Club. Address: 26 Whitestone Drive, York YO31 9HZ, England.

DOUGLAS James, b. 4 July 1932, Dumbarton, Scotland. Composer. m. Helen Torrance Fairweather, 2 sons, 1 daughter. Education: Heriot Watt College, Edinburgh, Scotland; Paris Conservatoire, Paris, France; Mozarteum, Salzburg, Austria; Hochschule für Musik, Munich, Germany; LRAM, ARCM London. Appointments: Composer, Accompanist; Organist, International Recording Artist; Professor l'Académie des Sciences Universelles, Paris, 1992-; Managing Director: Eschenbach Editions, 1986-; Caritas Records, 1989-. Compositions include: 15 symphonies, 15 string quartets, 20 orchestral works, chamber music, piano music, organ music, choral music and over 200 songs; Operas: Mask, The King, Molière, Cuthbert, The Christ Church Sequence (75 Chamber works 2001-2006), The Glorious Sequence (33 works 2006-), Sing Unto the Lord (21 Choral pieces 2005); The Highlands and Islands Sequence (66 pieces) 1968-2007 and 17 recordings; Broadcasts on local and international stations; Performances in Edinburgh, Europe and America. Membership: Professional Member of the British Academy of Composers and Songwriters, London. Address: c/o Eschenbach Editions, Achmore, Moss Road, Ullapool, IV26 2TF, Scotland. E-mail: eschenbach@caritas-music.co.uk. Web: www.caritas-music.co.uk

DOUGLAS Kirk, b. 9 December 1916, Amsterdam, New York, USA. Actor. m. (1) Diana Dill, 2 sons, (2) Anne Buydens, 2 sons. Education: St Lawrence University; American Academy of Dramatic Arts. Appointments: President, Bryna Productions, 1955-; Director, Los Angeles Chapt, UN Association. Stage appearances: Spring Again; Three Sisters; Kiss and Tell; The Wind is Ninety; Alice in Arms; Man Bites Dog; The Boys of Autumn; Films include: The Strange Love of Martha Ivers; Letters to Three Wives; Ace in the Hole; The Bad and the Beautiful; 20,000 Leagues under the Sea; Ulysses; Lust for Life; Gunfight at Ok Corral; Paths of Glory; the Vikings; Last Train from Gun Hill; The Devil's Disciple; Spartacus; Strangers When We meet; Seven Days in May; Town Without Pity; The List of Adran Messenger; In Harms Way; Cast a Giant Shadow; The Way West; War Waggon; The Brotherhood; The Arrangement; There Was a Crooked Man; Gunfight, 1971; Light at the Edge

of the World; Catch Me a Spy; A Man to Respect, 1972; Cat and Mouse; Scalawag (director), 1973; Once is Not Enough, 1975; Posse (producer, actor), 1975; The Moneychangers (TV), 1976; Holocaust 2000, 1977; The Fury, 1977; Villain, 1978; Saturn 3, 1979; The Final Countdown, 1980; The Man From Snowy River, 1986; Tough Guys, 1986; Queenie (TV mini series), 1987; Oscar, Welcome to Veraz, Greedy, 1994; Diamonds, 1999; Family Jewels, 2002; Eddie Macon's Run; Tough Guys; Oscar; Greedy; Diamonds; It Runs in the Family; Illusion. Publications: The Ragman's Son: an Autobiography, 1988; Novels: Dance With The Devil, 1990; The Secret, 1992; The Gift, 1992; Last Tango in Brooklyn, 1994; Climbing the Mountain: My Search for Meaning, 1997; The Broken Mirror (novel), 1997; My Stroke of Luck, 2002. Honours: Academy awards, critics awards; Commandeur, Ordre des Arts et Lettres, 1979; Légion d'honneur, 1985; Presidential Medal of Freedom, 1981; American Film Industries Lifetime Achievement, 1991; Kennedy Center Honors, 1994; Lifetime Achievement Award, Screen Actors' Guild, 1999; Golden Bear, Berlin Film Festival, 2000; National Medal of Arts, 2002. Address: The Bryna Company, 141 S El Camino Drive, Beverly Hills, CA 90212, USA.

DOUGLAS Michael Kirk, b. 25 September 1944, New Brunswick, NJ, USA. m. (1) Diandra Mornell Luker (divorced), 1 son, (2) Catherine Zeta Jones, 2000, 1 son, 1 daughter. Appointments: Actor in films: It's My Turn; Hail Heroll, 1969; Summertime, 1971; Napoleon and Samantha, 1972; Coma, 1978; Running, 1979; Star Chamber, 1983; Romancing the Stone, 1984; A Chorus Line, 1985; Jewel of the Nile, 1985; Fatal Attraction, 1987; Wall Street, 1987; Heidi, 1989; Black Rain, 1989; The War of the Roses, 1990; Shining Through, 1990; Basic Instinct, 1992; Falling Down, 1993; The American President, 1995; The Ghost and the Darkness, 1996; The Game, 1997; A Perfect Murder, 1998; Traffic, 2000; Wonder Boys, 2000; One Night at McCool's, 2000; Don't Say a Word, 2001; A Few Good Years, 2002; It Runs in the Family, 2003; Monkeyface, 2003; The In-Laws, 2003; Producer, films including: One Flew Over the Cuckoo's Nest, 1975; The China Syndrome; Sarman (executive producer); Romancing the Stone; Jewel of the Nile, Flatliners, 1990; Made in America (co-executive, producer); Disclosure, 1994; A Perfect Murder, 1998; One Night at McCool's, 2000; Godspeed; Lawrence Mann, 2002; It Runs in the Family, 2003; The In-Laws, 2003; The Sentinel, 2006; You, Me and Dupree, 2006; Kings of California, 2007; Actor in TV series: Streets of San Francisco. Honours include: Academy Award for Best Actor for Wall Street, 1988; Spencer Tracey Award, 1999; UN Messenger of Peace, 2000. Address: C/o Creative Artists Agency Inc, 9830 Wilshire Boulevard, Beverly Hills, CA 90212, USA. Website: www.michaeldouglas.com

DOVE Ian William, b. 31 December 1963, Northampton, England. Barrister. m. Juliet Caroline, 2 sons. Education: Northampton School for Boys; St Catherine's College, Oxford; Inns of Court School of Law. Appointments: Immigration Judge, 2000; Recorder, 2003; QC, 2003. Honours: QC. Memberships: Inner Temple; Poetry Society. Address: 9 Clarendon Crescent, Leamington Spa, CV32 5NR, England. E-mail: id@no5.com

DOWD Lea Lewis, Businesswoman. Appointments: Animal Health Technician, 1977-82; Owner, Director, Equilab, Ft Lauderdale, Florida, 1982-88; Director, Vet Research Laboratories, Ft Lauderdale, 1988-91; Director, Technical Services, Research & Development, Vet Research Laboratories, Ft Valley, New York, 1991-92; Animal Health Specialist, Walt Disney World, Orlando, Florida, 1993-94;

President, CEO,1994-2001, Managing Director, 2001-, Immune Technologies (now Immune Modulators, 2001-), Cataula, Georgia. Publications: Papers and articles in professional journals; Book: Historic Linwood Cemetery of Columbus, Muscogee County, Georgia, 2006. Memberships: Association of Veterinary Microbiologists; Muscogee Genealogical Association; Historic Linwood Foundation. Address: 224 Ridgeway Drive, Cataula, GA 31804, USA. Email: leadowd@charter.net

DOWEL Terence, b. 7 April 1941, Kerang, Australia. Entrepreneur; Managing Director; Chief Executive Officer; Inventor. m. Kaye, 2 sons, 2 daughters. Education: Year 10; Dux Year 8; Dux Year 10. Appointments: Inventor and entrepreneur: Introduced Australia's first modern hair conditioner for retail sale, 1963; Built first aerosol filling machine in Australia, 1967; The first in Australia to commercially extract aloe vera juice, 1979; Formulated Australia's first two-in-one shampoo and conditioner, 1987; Built the first camera in wheel tyre test laboratory in the world, 2002; Discovered the cause of the mysterious scuff mark on tyres and rims, 2003; Formulated the world's first non-latex tyre puncture sealant to flow through the valve core, 2007; Owner/Managing Director, Trydel Research Pty Ltd; Owner, Chief Executive Officer, Natures Organics Pty Ltd. Honours: Outstanding Chapter Jaycee of the Year, 1976; Car Racing Hill Climb Vic (State) Champion (Historic Class), 2003; Car Racing Hill Climb Australian Champion (Historic Class), 2004. Memberships: Member, 1973-82, Chapter President, 1981, Jaycees; Art Deco Society; Classic and Historic Automobile Club; ACD (Auburn Cord Duesenburg) Club, Australia; ACD (Auburn Cord Duesenburg) Club, USA. Address: 31 Cornhill Street, Ferntree Gully, Victoria 3156, Australia. E-mail: info@naturesorganics.com.au

DOWER GOLD Catherine, b. 19 May 1924, South Hadley, Massachusetts, USA. Professor of Music History. m. Arthur Gold, 1994, deceased 1998. Education: Full Scholarship, Pius X School of Liturgical Music, Manhattanville College, 1945-46; Dean's Scholarship, AB, Music Composition, Hamline University, 1945; B. of Liturgical Music, University of Montreal & Gregorian Institute of America, 1948; MA, Musicology, Smith College, 1948; Musicology, Boston University School of Fine Arts, 1956-62; Visiting Scholar, University of Southern California, 1969; Dean's Scholarship, PhD, Catholic University of America, 1968; Public Speaking, Dale Carnegie, 1973; Poet Laureate Course, International Society of Poets, 2002. Career: Organist, St Theresa Church, South Hadley, Massachusetts, 1937-42; Organist, St Matthew, New York City, 1945-46; New England Representative, Gregorian Institute of America, 1948-49; School Music Teacher, Church Organist, Saint Rose School & Church, 1949-53; Elementary School Music Supervisor, Holyoke, Massachusetts, 1953-55; Instructor, University of Massachusetts, 1955; Visiting Associate Professor of Music, Herbert Lehman College, CUNY, 1970-71; Assistant Professor, 1956-68, Associate Professor, 1970, Professor, 1971-90, Westfield State College; Columnist & Feature Writer, Holyoke Daily Transcript, 1991-93. Publications: Books: 18th Century Sistina Capella Codices, 1968; Puerto Rican Music Following the Spanish American War, 1983; Alfred Einstein on Music, 1991; Yella Pessl, First Lady of the Harpsichord, 1993; Fifty Years of Marching Together, A Social History of the St Patrick's Committee of Holyoke, Massachusetts, Parade, 2001; Actividades Musicales en Puerto Rico, despues de la guerra hispanoamericana, 1898-1910, 2006; Monographs: And Suddenly It Is Evening, 1979; Yella Pessl, First Lady of the Harpsichord: A Life of Fire and Conviction, 1986;

Numerous articles in scholarly journals. Honours: Professor of the Year Award, Westfield State College, 1975; Installed as member of the Academia des Artes y Ciencias de Puerto Rico, 1977; Distinguished Service Awards, Westfield State College, 1979, 1981, 1983, 1985; Citation Academia Interamericana de Puerto Rico, 1979; Plaque, Springfield Symphony Orchestra, 1982; Citation, Holyoke Public Library, 1983; Human Relations Award, Massachusetts Teachers Association 1984; Invested in Papal Equestrian Order, 1984, Lady Commander, 1987, Lady Commander with Star, 1990, Order of the Holy Sepulchre of Jerusalem; Tolerance Medal, Council for Human Understanding, Holyoke, 1985; Career Woman of the Year, Quota International of Holyoke, 1988; Pride in Performance Award, Governor Michael Dukakis, 1988; US Congressional Certificate of Merit, 1990; Commonwealth of Massachusetts Citation, 1990; WSC concert series named Catherine A Dower Performing Arts Series, 1991; WSC seniors yearbook dedicated to Catherine Dower, 1991; Fellow, International Biographical Association, 1991; Professor Emerita conferred at WSC graduation, 1991; Award, Puerto Rican Revista Al Margen, 1992; Appointed to Westfield State College Foundation, 1994; Human Relations Award, Council for Human Understanding, Holyoke, 1994; Certificate of Honor, WSC, 1994; Honorary Member, Westfield State College Foundation & Scholarship in the name of Catherine Dower, 1994; First Prize, Survivors of the Holocaust: A Legacy of Hope, 1996; Phi Beta Kappa, Hamline University, 2000; Distinguished Member, International Society of Poets, 2002; Silver Bowl & Medal, International Poet of Merit Award, 2002; Outstanding Achievement in Poetry Award, 2003; Silver Bowl, Editor's Choice Award, 2004, 2005, 2006; Editor's Published Poet Ribbon Award Pin, 2007, 2008; Westfield State College Honorary Marshal, Holyoke St Patrick's Parade, 2007. Memberships: American Musicological Society; College Music Society; Church Music Association of America; Consociatio Internationalis Musicae Sacrae, Rome; Equestrian Order of the Holy Sepulchre of Jerusalem; National Society of Arts and Letters; Phi Beta Kappa; Life Member, Lifelong Learning Society Florida Atlantic University; University Club of Florida Atlantic University; American Friends of the Vatican Library; Life Member, Friends of the Conservatory of Music, Lynn University; International Society of Poetry; Board Member, Council for Human Understanding of Holyoke; St Patrick's Committee of Holyoke; Smith College Club of Hampshire County; Honorary Member, Westfield State College Foundation; Quota International of Holyoke; Irish Cultural Center at Elms College; Holyoke Public Library Corporator; Secretary, Parish Pastoral Council, Holy Cross Church, Holyoke; St Patrick's Committee of Holyoke; Board Member, Council for Human Understanding; Board Member, President, 2008-09, Friends of the Holyoke Public Library. Address: 60 Madison Avenue, Holyoke, Massachusetts 01040-2041, USA. E-mail: cdowergold@comcast.net

DOWLING Dame Ann Patricia, b. 15 July 1952. Professor of Mechanical Engineering. m. Thomas Paul Hynes, 1974. Education: Ursuline Convent School, Westgate, Kent; BA, 1973, MA, 1977, PhD, 1978, Girton College, Cambridge; CEng, FIMechE, 1990; FREng (FEng, 1996); FRAeS, 1997; Fellow, Royal Society, 2003; Fellow, Institute of Acoustics, 1989, ScD 2006. Appointments: Research Fellow, 1977-78, Director of Studies in Engineering, 1979-90, Sidney Sussex College, Assistant Lecturer in Engineering, 1979-82, Lecturer, 1982-86, Reader in Acoustics, 1986-93, Deputy Head, Engineering Department, 1990-93, 1996-99, Cambridge University; Jerome C Hunsaker Visiting Professor, MIT, 1999-2000; Moore Distinguished Scholar, CIT, 2001-02. Publications: Sound and Sources of Sound, with J E

Ffowes Williams), 1983; Modern Methods in Analytical Acoustics, with D G Crighton et al, 1992; Contributions to scientific and engineering journals. Honours: A B Wood Medal, Institute of Acoustics, 1990. Memberships: AIAA, 1990; Defence and Aerospace Technology Foresight Panel, 1994-97; Defence Scientific Advisory Council, 1998-2001; EPSRC, 2001-2006 (Member, 1998-2002, Chairman, 2003-06, Technical Opportunities Panel), Non-executive Director, DRA, 1995-97; Scientific Advisory Board, DERA, 1997-2001; Council, Royal Academy of Engineering, 1998-2002 (Vice President, 1999-2002); Trustee, Ford of Britain Trust, 1993-2002; Cambridge European Trust, 1994-; National Museum of Science and Industry, 1999-; Governor, Felsted School, 1994-99; Foreign Associate, French Academy of Sciences, 2002. Address: Engineering Department, Cambridge University, Trumpington Street, Cambridge CB2 1PZ, England.

DOWNES Andrew, b. 20 August 1950, Handsworth, Birmingham, England. Composer. m. Cynthia Cooper, 9 August 1975, 2 daughters. Education: Choral Scholar, 1969-72, BA Hons, 1972, St John's College, Cambridge; MA (Cantab), 1975; Royal College of Music, 1972-74; Singing with Gordon Clinton; Composition with Herbert Howells. Debut: Wigmore Hall, 1969. Career includes: Established Faculty of Composition, 1975, Head of School, 1990, Professor, School of Composition and Creative Studies, 1992-2005, Birmingham Conservatoire, England; Chaired Symposium on Music Criticism, Indian Music Congress, University of Burdwan, 1994; Performances of own works include: Berlin, Kaiser Willhelm Gedächtniskirche, 1980; Vienna, 1983, 1998, 2001, 2002; Israel Philharmonic Guest House, Tel Aviv, 1989; New York, 1993, 1996, 2003; Calcutta School of Music, 1994; Paris, 1995-2007; University of New Mexico, 1995, 1997, 1999; Bombay, Delhi, Calcutta, 1996; Barletta, Italy, 1996; Eugene, Oregon, 1996; Chicago, 1997; Caracas, Venezuela, 1997; Symphony Hall, Birmingham, 1997, 2003, 2004, 2005; Phoenix, Arizona, 1998, 2001; Rudolfinum, Prague, 1998, 2001, 2002, 2005; Lichtenstein Palace, Prague, 1999; James Madison University, Virginia, 2000; Boston, Massachusetts, 2000, 2005, 2006; Genoa, 2002; Washington, DC, 2002, 2003, 2004; Colorado, Michigan, Las Vegas, 2003; Dublin, 2003; North Carolina, California, Indiana, Columbia and Nashville, Tennessee, 2004; Mexico City, 2004; Mozarteum, Prague, 2005; Cambridge, Massachusetts, 2005; New Jersey, 2006; Harvard University, 2005, 2007; BBC Radio 2, 3 and 4; French Radio (France Musique); Austrian, Czech, Dutch and Beijing Radios; Italian TV. Compositions include: Sonata for 8 Horns Opus 54, University of New Mexico commission, 1994, performed by the horns of the Czech Philharmonic Orchestra, 1998, 2000, 2005; Sonata for 8 Flutes (premiered New York, 1996, subsequent performances worldwide); Songs From Spoon River, performed at Tanglewood Festival and on BBC Radio 3; Towards A New Age, premièred by the Royal Philharmonic Orchestra in Symphony Hall, Birmingham, 1997; New Dawn, oratorio based on American Indian texts, Adrian Boult Hall, Birmingham, 2000, King's College Chapel, Cambridge, 2001; Sonata for 8 Pianists, Birmingham, 2000, Genoa, 2002; Sonata for Horn and Piano for Roland Horvath of Vienna Philharmonic Orchestra; Concerto for 4 Horns and Orchestra for the Czech Philharmonic Orchestra, Prague, 2002, Czech radio, 2003; Songs of Autumn and Songs of the Skies, performed by massed children's choirs, Symphony Hall, Birmingham, 2003, 2004, 2005; Lichfield Cathedral, 2004; 5 dramatic pieces for 8 Wagner Tubas for Czech Philharmonic Horns, premiered Dvorak Hall, Prague, 2005; Opera, Far From The Madding Crowd for The Thomas Hardy Society, 2006. Recordings include: The Marshes of

Glynn, cantata, commission for Royal opening of Adrian Boult Hall, Birmingham, 1986; O Vos Omnes, motet, Cantamus commission (published by Faber Music in anthology, "30 Sacred Masterworks for Upper Voice Choir"); Sonata for 2 Pianos; Fanfare for a Ceremony, commission for Open University; Centenary Firedances, commissioned by City of Birmingham for its centenary celebrations; Shepherd's Carol; 3 Song Cycles on CD entitled "Old Loves Domain", 2000; The Souls of the Righteous, anthem, 1997; Sacred Choral Music on CD entitled "The Lord is My Shepherd", 2001; Sonata for Oboe and Piano, 1998; Sonata for 8 Horns by Horns of Czech Philharmonic Orchestra; Suite for 6 Horns, Sonata for Horn and Piano, Sontata for 4 Horns, Piano Sonata No 1 on 2 CDs on the Aricord label (Vienna); Concerto for 2 Guitars and Strings; Flute Choir Music by James Madison University Flute Choir and Massachusetts Flute Choir, 2000; Sonatina for Piano, Piano Sonatas 1 & 2 performed by Duncan Honeybourne, 2005. Publications (by Lynwood Music and Faber Music): 93 works including 5 symphonies, 4 large-scale choral works, 2 double concertos, 3 string quartets, 2 brass quintets, flute octet, Sonata for 8 pianists, horn octet, horn sextet and horn quartet, 9 song cycles, 2 operas and many sacred works. Honours include: Prizewinner, Stroud International Composers' Competition, 1980; Trees planted in Israel in name of Andrew Downes in recognition of composition, Sonata for 2 pianos, 1987; Invited by Crane Concert Choir, University of New York, to conduct his choral work A St Luke Passion, 1993; Leather bound presentation copy of Fanfare for a Ceremony given to HRH Prince Edward on his visit to Birmingham Conservatoire, 1995; Bound presentation copy of Fanfare for Madam Speaker given to Rt Hon Betty Boothroyd MP at her installation as Chancellor of Open University, 1995; Awarded Gold Medal by Institution of Mechanical Engineers for composition for their 150th Anniversary, 1997. Memberships include: Representing Birmingham Conservatoire, Indian Music Congress; President, Central Composers' Alliance; PRS; MCPS; Life Fellow, Royal Society of Arts. Address: c/o Lynwood Music, 2 Church Street, West Hagley, West Midlands DY9 0NA, England.

DOWNEY Robert Jr, b. 4 April 1965, New York, USA. Actor. m. Deborah Falconer, (divorced) 1 child. Susan, 2005. Career: Actor; Sentenced to probation for possession of cocaine; imprisoned for further drugs offence breaching terms of probation, 1997; released for rehabilitation, 1998; imprisoned again, 1999, freed, 2000, charged with drugs possession, 2000; Singing career, 2005-. Films include: Pound, 1970; Firstborn; Weird Science; To Live and Die in LA; Back to School; The Pick-Up Artist; Johnny B Good; True Believer; Chances Are; Air America; Soapdish; Chaplin; Heart and Souls; Short Cuts; The Last Party; Natural Born Killers; Only You; Restoration; Restoration; Danger Zone; Home for the Holidays; Richard III; Bliss Vision, The Gingerbread Man, 1997; Two Girls and a Guy, 1998; In Dreams, Friends and Lovers, 1999; Wonder Boys, Automotives, 2000; Lethargy, 2002; Whatever We Do, The Singing Detective, Gothika, 2003; Eros, 2004; Game 6, Kiss Kiss, Bang Bang, The Shaggy Dog, 2005; A Scanner Darkly, Good Night and Good Luck, 2006; Zodiac, Lucky You, Charlie Bartlett, 2007; Iron Man, 2008; Television includes: Mussolini: The Untold Story (TV mini-series), 1985; Mr Willoughby's Christmas Tree, 1995; Ally McBeal, 2000-01; Black and White, 2000. Honours: BAFTA Award. Address: c/o Sony Classical, 550 Madison Avenue, New York, NY 10022, USA. Website: www.robertdowneyjrmusic.com

DOWNING Richard, b. 8 February 1951, Stourbridge, West Midlands, England. Consultant Vascular Surgeon. m. Stella Elizabeth, 2 sons, 2 daughters. Education: BSc (Hons),

Physiology, 1972, MB ChB (Distinction in Pharmacology and Therapeutics), 1975, MD, 1983, University of Birmingham; Fellow, Royal College of Surgeons of England, 1980. Appointments: Lecturer in Anatomy, University of Birmingham, 1976-77; Research Associate, Washington University, St Louis, Missouri, USA, 1977-78; Registrar in Surgery, United Birmingham Hospitals, 1979-83; Lecturer in Surgery, 1983-86, Senior Lecturer in Surgery, 1986-90, University of Birmingham; Consultant Vascular Surgeon, 1990-, Director, Islet Research Laboratory, Worcestershire Royal Hospital. Publications: Publications on pancreatic islet transplantation, peripheral vascular disease. Honours: Examiner, Faculty of Dental Surgery, Royal College of Surgeons of England, 1989-95; Member of the Editorial Board: Journal of the Care of the Injured, 1989-96 and British Journal of Diabetes and Vascular Disease, 2002-. Memberships: Vascular Society of Great Britain and Ireland; European Society of Vascular and Endovascular Surgery; Association of Surgeons of Great Britain and Ireland; International Pancreas and Islet Transplant Society. Address: 46 Lark Hill, Worcester WR5 2EQ, England.

DOYEL David, b. 24 August 1946, Lindsay, California, USA. Archaeologist; Anthropologist. m. Sharon S Debowski. Education: BA, 1969, MA, 1972, California State University, Chico, USA; PhD, University of Arizona, Tucson, USA, 1977. Appointments: Director, Navajo Nation Archaeology and Museum Programme, Window Rock, Arizona, 1979-82; Director and Archaeologist, Pueblo Grande Museum, City of Phoenix, 1984-90; Owner, Estrella Cultural Research, Phoenix, Arizona, 1991-2005; Research Director, Archaeological Consulting Service, Tempe, Arizona, 1993-99; Principal Investigator, URS Corporation, 2000-2002; Principal Investigator, LBG Corporation, 2002-2004; Archaeologist, Luke Air Force Base, Glendale, Arizona, 2005-. Publications: 20 pages personal bibliography, including edited volumes, book reviews, monographs and articles in professional journals. Honour: Outstanding Supervisor, Navajo Nation; Sigma Xi. Membership: Society for American Archaeology. Address: PO Box 60474, Phoenix, AZ 85082-0474, USA.

DOYLE Roddy, b. 1958, Dublin Ireland. Writer. m. Bellinda, 2 sons. Publications: The Commitments, 1987, filmed 1991; The Snapper, 1990, filmed, 1992; The Van, 1991; Paddy Clarke Ha Ha Ha, 1993; The Women Who Walked Into Doors, 1996; Two Lives: Hell for Leather, 1999; A Star Called Henry, 1999; The Giggler Treatment, 2000; When Brendon Met Trudy, 2000; Rory and Ita, 2002; Oh, Play That Thing, 2004. Honour: Booker Prize for Paddy Clarke Ha Ha Ha, 1993. Address: c/o Patti Kelly, Viking Books, 375 Hudson Street, New York, NY 10014, USA.

DRABBLE Dame Margaret, b. 5 June 1939, Sheffield, England. Author. m. (1) Clive Swift, 2 sons, 1 daughter, (2) Michael Holroyd, 1982. Education; Newnham College, Cambridge. Appointments: Editor, The Oxford Companion to England Literature, 1979-84; Chairman, National Book League, 1980-82; Vice-Patron, Child Psychotherapy Trust, 1987-. Publications: A Summer Bird-Cage, 1963; The Garrick Year, 1964; The Millstone, 1965 Jerusalem the Golden, 1967; The Waterfall, 1969; The Needle's Eye, 1972; Arnold Bennett: A Biography, 1974; The Realms of Gold, 1975; The Genius of Thomas Hardy (editor), 1976; The Ice Age, 1977; For Queen and Country: Britain in the Victorian Age, 1978; A Writer's Britain, 1979; The Middle Ground (novel), 1980; The Oxford Companion to English Literature (editor), 1985; The Radiant Way (novel), 1987; A Natural Curiosity, 1989; Safe as Houses, 1990; The Gates of Ivory, 1991; Angus Wilson:

A Biography, 1995; The Witch of Exmoor (novel), 1996; The Peppered Moth (novel), 2001; The Seven Sisters (novel), 2002; The Red Queen, 2004; The Sea Lady, 2006. Honours include: John Llewelyn Rhys Memorial Prize, 1966; E M Forster Award, American Academy of Arts and Letters, 1973; Hon D Litt, Sheffield, 1976, Bradford, 1988, Hull, 1992; Honorary Fellow, Sheffield City Polytechnic, 1989; Honorary member, American Academy of Arts and Letters, 2002; St Louis Literary Award, 2003; Queen's Birthday Honours, 2008. Address: c/o PFD, Drury House, 34-43 Russell Street, London, WC2B 5HA, England.

DRAGOUN Otokar, b. 15 March 1937, Sedlec, Czech Republic. Physicist. m. Nadezda Novotná, 5 July 1961, 2 daughters. Education: Diploma in Engineering, Czech Technical University, Prague, 1962; PhD, Physics, 1967, DSc, Physics, 1985, Charles University, Prague. Appointments: Researcher, Nuclear Physics Institute, Czech Academy of Science, 1962-; Head of Research Group, 1971-2005; Postdoctoral Fellow, Max-Planck Institute for Nuclear Physics, Heidelberg, Germany, 1966-69; Visiting Professor, Faculty of Physics Technical University, Munich, Spring 1992, Summer 1994; External Lecturer, Charles University, Prague, 1986-2005; External Lecturer, Czech Technical University, Prague, 1999-2006; Member of the Karlsruhe Tritium Neutrino Experiment, 2001-. Publications: Contributor of reviews and science papers on nuclear, nuclear atomic and neutrino experimental physics in international journals; Patentee in field. Honours: Medal Science Achievement, Union Czech Mathematicians and Physicists, 1988. Membership: Czech Physical Society. Address: Nuclear Physics Institute of the Academy of Sciences of Czech Republic, CZ-25068, Rez near Prague, Czech Republic.

DRAŽANČIĆ Ante, b. 28 November 1928, Šibenik, Croatia. Physician. m. (1) Jakica, divorced, 1 son, 1 daughter, (2) Liliana, 1 daughter. Education: Medical Doctor, 1953; Specialist in Obstetrics & Gynaecology, 1961; PhD, University of Zagreb, 1966; Associate Professor, Obstetrics & Gynaecology, 1970; Professor of Obstetrics & Gynaecology, 1980. Appointments: Resident Physician, General Hospital Varaždin, 1953-57; Assistant Physician, Department of Obstetrics & Gynaecology, University Medical School of Zagreb, 1958-73; Head of Division of Perinatal Medicine, 1974-94; Retired, 1994. Publications: 4 books; 423 scientific and professional papers and reviews. Honours: Medal of Work, President of Yugoslavia; Past President, Croatian Medical Association; Past President, Croatian Society of Perinatal Medicine; Croatian Society of Obstetrics & Gynaecology. Address: Jakova Gotovca 7, 10000 Zagreb, Croatia. E-mail: ante.drazancic@zg.t-com.hr

DRCHAL Vaclav, b. 21 May 1945, Prague, Czech Republic. Physicist. m. Jaroslava, 2 sons. Education: Faculty of Mathematics and Physics, 1968, Doctorate, 1974, Charles University; Candidate of Science, 1974. Appointments: Academy of Sciences, Institute of Solid State Physics, 1968-80; Institute of Physics, 1980-. Publications: 211 original scientific articles, 1 monograph. Honours: State Prize, 1982; Prize, Academy of Sciences, 1989, 1998. Membership: Union of Czech Mathematicians and Physicists. Address: Academy of Sciences, Institute of Physics, Na Slovance 2, CZ-182 21, Prague 8, Czech Republic.

DREIMANIS Aleksis, b. 13 August 1914, Valmiera, Latvia. Geologist. m. Anita Kana, 2 daughters. Education: Mag.rer.nat, University of Latvia, 1938; Habilitation, 1941. Appointments: Assistant/Privatdocent, University of Latvia, 1937-44;

Military Geologist, Latvian Legion, 1944-45; Associate Professor, Baltic University, 1946-48; Lecturer/Professor Emeritus, University of Western Ontario, 1948-. Publications: Over 200 articles in professional journals. Honours include: Teaching Award, Ontario Confederation of University Faculty Associations, 1978; Fellow, Royal Society of Canada, 1979; Doctor honoris causa, University of Waterloo, 1969, University of Western Ontario, 1980; Distinguished Career Award, Quaternary Geology and Geomorphology Division of the Geological Society of America, 1987; Foreign Member, Latvian Academy of Sciences, 1990; Doctor geographiae honoris causa Univeritatis Latviensis, 1991; Distinguished Fellow, Geological Association of Canada, 1995; Three Star Order of Latvia, 2003. Address: 287 Neville Drive, London, Ontario, N6G 1C2, Canada.

DREW David Elliott, b. 13 April 1952, Gloucestershire, England. Member of Parliament. m. Anne, 2 sons, 2 daughter. Education: BA, University of Nottingham; PGCE, University of Birmingham; MA, Bristol Polytechnic; MEd, University of the West of England. Appointments: Teacher, 1976-86; Lecturer, University of the West of England, 1986-97; Member of Parliament, Labour/Co-operative Party, Stroud, 1997-; Chair, Parliamentary Labour Party Backbench Committee on Agriculture, 1997-2001; Chair, Parliamentary Labour Party Backbench Rural Affairs Group; Member, Select Committee, DEFRA; Town Councillor; Former District and County Councillor. Memberships: Co-operative Party; UNISON. Address: House of Commons, London SW1A 0AA, England. E-mail: drewd@parliament.uk

DREWS Gerhart, b. 30 May 1925, Berlin, Germany. Professor of Biology. m. Christiane May. Education: State Examination, 1951, Dr rer nat, 1953, Dr rer nat habil, 1960, University of Halle. Appointments: Scientific Assistant, University of Halle, 1953; Group Leader and Post Doctoral Studies, Institute of Microbiology and Experimental Therapy, Jena, 1954-60; Reader, 1961-63, Full Professor, 1964-93, University of Freiburg. Publications: 330 articles and books on structure, bioenergetics and morphogenesis of photosynthetic bacteria and history of microbiology. Honours: Dr hc, University of Buenos Aires; Werner-Heisenberg Medal, Alexander von Humboldt Foundation; Honorary Member, VAAM. Memberships: ASM; AAAS; SGM; DGHM; VAAM; GBM. Address: Schlossweg 27B, 79249 Merzhausen, Germany. E-mail: gerhart.drews@biologie.uni-freiburg.de

DREYFUSS Richard Stephen, b. 29 October 1947, New York, USA. Actor. m. Jeramie, 1983, 2 sons, 1 daughter. Education: San Fernando Valley State College. Appointments: Alternative military service, Los Angeles County General Hospital, 1969-71; Actor, stage appearances include: Julius Caesar, The Big Fix (also producer), 1978; Othello, 1979; Death and the Maiden, 1992; The Prison of Second Avenue, 1999; Films include: American Graffiti, 1972; Dillinger, 1973; The Apprenticeship of Duddy Kravitz, 1974; Jaws, Inserts, 1975; Close Encounters of the Third Kind, 1976; The Goodbye Girl, 1977; The Competition, 1980; Whose Life Is It Anyway?, 1981; Down and Out in Beverly Hills, 1986; Stakeout, 1988; Moon over Parador, Let It Ride, Always, 1989; Rosencrantz and Guildenstern are Dead, Postcards from the Edge, Once Around, Randall and Juliet, 1990; Prisoners of Honor, What About Bob?, 1991; Lost in Yonkers, Another Stakeout, 1993; The American President, Mr Holland's Opus, 1995; Mad Dog Time, James and the Giant Peach, 1996; Night Falls on Manhattan, The Call of the Wild, 1997; Krippendorf's Tribe, A Fine and Private Place, 1998; The Crew, The Old Man Who Read Love Stories, 2000;

Who is Cletis Tout? 2001; Silver City, 2004; Unsung (voice), Poseidon, 2006; Suburban Girl, 2007; TV includes: Oliver Twist, 1997; Fail Safe, 2000; Education of Max Bickford, Day Reagan Was Shot, 2001; Coast to Coast, Copshop, 2004; Tin Man, 2007; Director, producer, Nuts, 1987; Hamlet (Birmingham), 1994. Publication: The Two Georges (with Harry Turtledove), 1996. Honours: Golden Globe Award, 1978; Academy Award for Best Actor in the Goodbye Girl, 1978. Memberships: American Civil Liberties Union Screen Actors Guild; Equity Association; American Federation of TV and Radio Artists; Motion Picture Academy of Arts and Sciences. Address: William Morris Agency, 151 S El Camino Drive, Beverly Hills, CA 90212, USA.

DRIVER Minnie (Amelia), b. 21 January 1970. Actress. Appointments: Actress, TV appearances include: God on the Rocks; Mr Wroe's Virgins; The Politician's Wife; Film appearances include: Circle of Friends; Goldeneye; Baggage; Big Night; Sleepers; Grosse Point Blank; Good Will Hunting; The Governess; Hard Rain; An Ideal Husband, South Park: Bigger, Longer and Uncut, 1999; Slow Burn, Beautiful, Return to Me, The Upgrade, 2000; High Heels and Lowlifes, D.C. Smalls, 2001; Owning Mahoney, Hope Springs, 2003; The Phantom of the Opera, Ella Enchanted, Portrait, 2004; The Virgin of Juarez, Delirious, 2006; Ripple Efect, Take, The Simpsons Movie, (voice), 2007; Television appearances include: Will & Grace; The Riches; Mallory, 2007; Play: Sexual Perversity in Chicago, Comedy Theatre, London, 2003; Recording: Everything I've Got In My Pocket, 2004. Honours: Best Newcomer, 1997, Best Actress, 1988, London Circle of Film Critics. Address: c/o Lou Coulson, 1st Floor, 37 Berwick Street, London, W1V 3LF, England.

DRIVER Paul William, b. 14 August 1954, Manchester, England. Music Critic; Writer. Education: MA, Honours, Oxford University, 1979. Appointments: Music Critic, The Boston Globe, 1983-84; Sunday Times, 1985-; Member, Editorial Board, Contemporary Music Review; Patron, Manchester Musical Heritage Trust. Publications: A Diversity of Creatures (editor), 1987; Music and Text (editor), 1989; Manchester Pieces, 1996; Penguin Popular Poetry (editor), 1996; Ear to the Ground (series of conversations with British composers), BBC Radio 4, 2004. Contributions to: Sunday Times; Financial Times; Tempo; Gramophone; London Review of Books; New York Times; Numerous others; Frequent broadcaster. Membership: Critics Circle. Address: 15 Victoria Road, London NW6 6SX, England.

DRNOVŠEK Janez, b. 17 May 1950. President of the Republic of Slovenia. 1 son, 1 daughter. Education: Undergraduate studies, 1973, Master's degree, 1981, Boris Kidrič Faculty of Economics, Ljubljana; Doctoral dissertation, Maribor Faculty of Economics and Commerce, 1986. Appointments: Economist, Section of Development, IGM Zagorje; Head, Department of Economy, GIP Beton Zagorje; Economic Adviser, Embassy of the SFRY, Cairo; Director of Subsidiary, LB Trbovlje; Member, Credit and Monetary Committee of the Assembly of the SFRY; President, SFRY; Prime Minister, Government of the Republic of Slovenia. Publications: Books: Mednarodni denarni sklad in Jugoslavija, 1986; Moja resnica, 1996; Escape from Hell, 1996; Echappés de l'eufer, 1996; Meine Wahrheit, 1998; El laberinto de los Balcanes, 1999; The Thoughts of Life and Awareness, 2006; Numerous articles in professional and popular journals. Honours: Portuguese National Medal, 1990; Honorary Citizen of City of Lisbon, 1990; Cypriot National Medal, Order of Makarious, 1990; Golden Honorary Sign of Freedom, Republic of Slovenia, 1992; Honorary Doctorate, University of Boston, 1994; Chevalier du Tastevin, 1994; La Prix de la Méditerranée Award, 1995; Hubert H Humphrey Award, 1997; Award, American Studies Foundation, 1998; Honorary Citizen of Ciudad de Mexico, 1998; Dialogo Europeo Award, 1998; Honorary Texan, 1999; Honorary Doctorate, University of Illinois Weslayan University, 1999; Slovak National Medal, 2003; Ramon Trias Fargas Award, Foundation of Liberty and Democracy, 2003; Protector and Honorary Senator, European Academy of Sciences and Arts, Salzburg, 2004; Swedish Royal Order of the Seraphin, 2004; Cypriot National Order "Grand Collar of the Order of Makarios III, Nicosia, Cyprus, 2006. Memberships: Initiator of humanitarian action, World for Darfur, 2006. Address: Office of the President of the Republic of Slovenia, Erjavceva 17, Ljubljana 1000, Slovenia. E-mail: janez.drnovsek@up-rs.si Website: www.up-rs.si

DRUCE (Robert) Duncan, b. 23 May 1939, Nantwich, Cheshire, England. Musician. m. Clare Spalding, 15 September 1964, 2 daughters. Education: Royal College of Music, London, 1956; Kings College, Cambridge, 1957; BA, 1960; MusB, 1961; MA, York University, 1987. Appointments: Lecturer, Leeds University, 1964-65; BBC Radio Music Producer, 1965-68; Freelance Violinist and Composer, 1968-; Member, Fires of London and Academy of Ancient Music; Part-time Appointments at University of East Anglia, University of London Goldsmiths College, Lancaster University; Full time Senior Lecturer, Bretton Hall College, 1978-91, part-time, 1991-2002, Huddersfield University, 1993-. Compositions: Compositions commissioned by BBC, Huddersfield Contemporary Music Festival, Swaledale Festival, Yorkshire Bach Choir. Publications: New Completion, Mozart Requiem (Novello); Several articles in professional music magazines and journals; Regular contributor to Gramophone Magazine, 1996-. Memberships: Musicians Union; British Academy of Composers and Songwriters. Address: Hey Mount, 19a Back Lane, Holmfirth, HD9 1HG, England.

DRUYANOV Boris, b. 1 October 1930, Charkov, Ukraine. Lecturer; Scientific Worker. m. Yulia, 1 son, 1 daughter (deceased). Education: Candidate in Physics and Mathematics, 1961, Doctor in Physics and Mathematics, 1970, Professor of Theoretical Mechanics, 1971, Moscow State University. Appointments: Assistant, Docent, Professor, Head of the Department of Theoretical Mechanics, Moscow Institute for Industrial Devices, 1971-. Publications: Books: Technological Mechanics of Porous Bodies, 1993; Problems of Technological Plasticity, 1994; Direct Safe Design, in press. E-mail: borisu@bezeqint.net

DU Jia-Chong, b. 27 September 1962, Hou-Long Miao-Li, Taiwan. Civil Engineering Educator. m. Zhong-Chi Lou. Education: MSc, Civil Engineering, 1987-90; MS, Civil Engineering, 1994-97, PhD, Construction Engineering, 2000-2004. Appointments: Field Engineer, Pacific Engineers & Constructors Ltd, 1990-91; Structural Engineer, O'Hayo Group, 1991-93; Civil Engineer, Ebasco-CTIC Consultant Corporation, 1993-94; Graduate Research Assistant, University of Kansas, 1995-97; Civil Engineer, Neworks Bureau, Public Works Department, Taipei City Government, 1997-98; Lecturer, 1998-2004, Assistant Professor, 2004-, Tung-Nan Institute of Technology. Publications: Textbook: Construction Computer Drafting; Articles in professional journals including: ASCE, Journal of Materials in Civil Engineering, Civil Engineering and Environmental System; Construction and Building Materials; Journal of Grey System; ITSC; IEEE. Memberships: Chinese Pavement Association; Chinese Grey System Association. Address: 141-1 Station Street, Hou-Lung, Miao-Li, 356 Taiwan. E-mail: cctu@mail.tnit.edu.tw

DUBURS Gunars, b. 12 June 1934, Riga, Latvia. Chemist. m. Renate, 1 daughter. Education: Chemist, Latvian University, 1957; PhD, 1961; Dr chem habil, 1979; Professor, 1988. Appointments: Research Scientist, 1957-64, Head of Laboratory, 1964-, Scientific Director, 1980-2004, Institute of Organic Synthesis. Publications: 505 science papers, 169 patents. Honours include: D Grindel's Award, 1996; Award of the Latvian Cabinet of Ministers, 1999; Award of the Latvian Academy of Science and Patent Office, 2000; O Schmiedeberg's Medal, 2001; WIPO (World Intellectual Property Organization) Award, 2006; Diploma of Gratitude from the Prime Minister of Latvia, 2007; Listed in numerous biographical publications. Memberships: Latvian Academy of Science; International Society of Heterocyclic Chemistry; Albert Schweitzer International University; Latvian Chemical Society; UNESCO Molecular and Cell Biology Network. Address: 21 Aizkraukles Street, Latvian Institute of Organic Synthesis, Riga, LV 1006, Latvia.

DUBYCH Klavdiya Vasylivna, b. 6 June 1960, Rivne, Ukraine. Manager of Socio-Cultural Sphere. Widow, 1 daughter. Education: Diploma, Rivne National Institute of Culture, 1994. Appointments: Economist of Marketing Bureau, Commercial Department, OJSC RIVNELYON, 1996-99; Clerk on Social Issues, Rivne Regional Trade Union Council, 1999-2000; Vice-Rector on Teaching/ Educational Work, Associate Professor of Department of Social Work, Rivne Institute of Open International University of Human Development, Ukraina, 2000-. Publications: 3 textbooks: Basics of Telephone Consulting; Documenting in Management; Basics of the Theory of Administration and Management; 11 articles in professional journals. Honours: Honorable Diploma, President of Ukraina University, 2003; Honorable Educator of Ukraine, Ministry of Education and Science of Ukraine, 2004; Honorable Diploma, Department of Education and Science, 2004, Honorable Diploma, General Department of Labour and Social Protection, 2005, Rivne State Regional Administration. Memberships: Centre of Professional, Socio-Psychological and Physical Rehabilitation of Youth with Specific Needs; Rivne Steering Committee on Protection of Rights of Disabled People; Rivne Local Commission on Formation of Youth Policy; Charity fund for protection of orphans, Oberih. Address: 75 Gagarin St, app 10, 33022 Rivne, Ukraine. E-mail: kdubych@yahoo.com

DUCHOVNY David, b. 7 August 1960, New York, USA. Actor. m. Tea Leoni, 1997, 1 son, 1 daughter. Education: Yale University; Princeton University. Appointments: Stage appearances include: Off-Broadway plays, The Copulating Machine of Venice, California and Green Cuckatoo; TV series: The X Files; Films include: New Year's Day, 1989; Julia Has Two Lovers, 1990; The Rapture, 1991; Don't Tell Mom The Babysitter's Dead, 1991; Chaplin, 1992; Red Shoe Diaries, 1992; Ruby, 1992; Kalifornia, 1993; Venice, Venice, Apartment Zero; Close Enemy; Loan; Independence Day; Playing God; The X Files, 1998; Return To Me, 2000; Evolution, 2001; Zoolander, 2001; Full Frontal, 2002; XIII, 2003; Connie and Carla, 2004; House of D, 2004; The X Files: Resist or Serve (voice), 2004; Area 51 (voice), 2005; Trust the Man, 2005; The TV Set, 2006; The Secret, 2007; Things We Lost in the Fire, 2007; Television includes: Twin Peaks, 1990; The X-Files, 1993-; Life With Bonnie, 2002; Californication, 2007. Address: 20th Century Fox Film Corporation, PO Box 900, Beverly Hills, CA 90213, USA.

DUCORNET Erica Lynn, (Rikki Ducornet), b. 19 April 1943, New York, New York, USA. Writer; Artist; Teacher. 1 son. Education: Bard College, 1964. Appointments:

Novelist-in-Residence, University of Denver, 1988-; Visiting Professor, University of Trento, Italy, 1994. Publications: The Stain, 1984; Entering Fire, 1986; The Fountains of Neptune, 1989; Eben Demarst, 1990; The Jade Cabinet, 1993; The Butcher's Tales, 1994; Phosphor in Dreamland, 1995; The Word "Desire", 1997; The Fan-Maker's Inquisition, 1999. Contributions to: Periodicals. Honours: National Book Critics Circle Award Finalist, 1987, 1990, 1993; Critics Choice Award, 1995; Charles Flint Kellogg Award in Arts and Letters, 1998. Membership: PEN. Address: c/o Department of English, University of Denver, Denver, CO 80208, USA.

DUERDEN Brian Ion, b. 21 June 1948, Nelson, Lancashire, England. Medical Practitioner. m. Marjorie Hudson. Education: BSc, Honours, Medical Science, 1970, MB ChB, 1972, MD, 1979, Edinburgh University Medical School; MRCPath, 1978; FRCPath, 1990; FRCP Edin., 2005. Appointments: House Officer, Thoracic Surgery and Infectious Diseases, Edinburgh City Hospital, 1972-73; Lecturer in Bacteriology, Edinburgh University, 1973-76; Lecturer, 1976-79, Senior Lecturer, 1979-83, Professor, 1983-90, Medical Microbiology, Sheffield University; Honorary Consultant, Microbiology, Sheffield Children's Hospital, 1979-90; Professor of Medical Microbiology, University of Wales College of Medicine/Cardiff University, 1991-; Medical Director and Deputy Director of Service, 1995-2002, Director of Service, 2002-2003, Public Health Laboratory Service; Director for Clinical Governance and Quality, Health Protection Agency, 2003; Currently, Inspector of Microbiology and Infection Control, Department of Health. Publications: 140 articles in scientific journals; Contributions to text books for undergraduate and postgraduate use; Editor-in-Chief, Journal of Medical Microbiology, 1982-2002; Articles on anaerobic microbiology, antibiotics, healthcare associated infection and public health. Memberships: Society for Anaerobic Microbiology; Fellow, Infectious Diseases Society of America; Society for General Microbiology; Anaerobe Society of the Americas. Address: Department of Health, Wellington House, 133-155 Waterloo Road, London SE1 8UG, England. E-mail: brian.duerden@dh.gsi.gov.uk

DUFFY Lawrence Kevin, b. 1 February 1948, Brooklyn, New York, USA. Biochemist; Educator. m. Geraldine, 2 sons, 1 daughter. Education: BS, Chemistry, Fordham University, 1969; MS, Chemistry, University of Alaska, 1972; PhD, Biochemistry, 1977. Laboratory Instructor, University of Alaska, 1969-71; Research Assistant, University of Alaska Fairbanks, 1974-76; Post-doctoral Fellow, Boston University, 1977-78; Post-doctoral Fellow, Roche Institute of Molecular Biology, 1978-80; James W McLaughlin Fellow, University of Texas, 1980-81; Research Assistant Professor, University of Texas Medical Branch, 1982-83; Instructor, Middlesex Community College, 1983-84; Assistant Biochemist, McLean Hospital, Belmont, 1983-85; Assistant Professor, Biochemistry, Harvard Medical School, 1983-87; Science and Organic Chemistry Instructor, Roxbury Community College, 1984-87; Associate Biochemist, Brigham and Women's Hospital, 1985-87; Research Associate, Duke University Centre, 1986-87; Professor, Chemistry and Biochemistry, University of Alaska Fairbanks, 1987-; Co-ordinator, Program in Biochemistry and Molecular Biology, 1987-90, 1992-93; Adjunct Researcher, Brigham and Women's Hospital, 1987-90; Affiliate Professor, Centre for Alcohol Addiction Studies, 1995-98; Head, Department of Chemistry and Biochemistry, 1994-99; Co-ordinator, RSI Scientist in Residence Programme, 1996-2003; President, UAF Faculty Senate, 2000; President American Institute of Chemists 2005-2006; Associate Dean for Graduate Studies and Outreach, 2001-.

Member, Metals Working Groups. Arctic Monitoring and Assessment Program. Publications: 280 scientific papers and abstracts. Honours: Fiest Outstanding Advisor Award; ACS Analytical Chemistry Award; Phi Lambda Upsilon; NIDCD Minority Research Mentoring Award, 1996; University of Alaska Alumni Award for Professional Achievement, 1999; Usibelli Award for Research, 2002. Memberships: American Chemical Society; New York Academy of Sciences; Member of Editorial Board, The Science of the Total Environment, 1999; President, American Institute of Chemists, 2005-06. Address: 2712 Tall Spruce, Fairbanks, Box 80986, Alaska 99708-0986, USA.

DUKAKIS Olympia, b. 20 June 1931. Actress. m. Louis Zorich, 3 sons. Education: Boston University. Appointments: Teacher of Drama, New York University graduate programme for 15 years; Founding member, The Charles Playhouse, Boston, Whole Theatre, Montclair, New Jersey; Appeared in over 100 regional theatre productions; Off-Broadway shows including: Mann Ish Mann; The Marriage of Bette and Boo; Titus Andronicus; Peer Gynt; The Memorandum; The Curse of the Starving Class; Electra; Appearances in Broadway productions of Abraham Cochrane; The Aspern Papers; The Night of the Iguana; Who's Who in Hell; Mike Nichol's Social Security; Numerous TV appearances, TV include: Tales of the City (series); Films include: The Idolmaker; John Loves Mary; Death Wish; Rich Kids; Made for Each Other; Working Girl; Moonstruck; Dad; Look Who's Talking; Steel Magnolias; In the Spirit; Look Who's Talking Too; The Cemetery Club; Digger; Over the Hill; Look Who's Talking Now; Naked Gun 331/3; The Final Insult (Cameo); I Love Trouble; Jeffrey; Mighty Aphrodite; Mr Holland's Opus; Picture Perfect; My Beautiful Son, Ladies and The Champ, And Never Let Her Go, 2001; The Event, Charlie's War, 2003; The Intended, 2004; The Great New Wonderful, The Thing About My Folks, 3 Needles, Whiskey School, Jesus, Mary and Joey, 2005; Away fronm Her, Day on Fire, 2006; In the Land of Women, 2007. Honours: Academy Award for Best Supporting Actress for Moonstruck, 1988; 2 Obie awards. Membership: Board, National Museum of Women in the Arts, Washington DC. Address: William Morris Agency, 151 S El Camino Drive, Beverly Hills, CA 90212, USA.

DUKE Chris, b. 4 October 1938. London. England. Professor; Scholar. m. Elizabeth Sommerlad, 3 sons, 2 daughters. Education: BA, 1st Class Honours, 1960, PGCE, 1961, MA, 1963, Jesus College, Cambridge, England; PhD, King's College, London, England, 1966. Appointments: Woolwich Polytechnic, England, 1961-66; University of Leeds, 1966-69; Director (Founding), Continuing Education, Australian National University, 1969-85; Professor, Continuing Education, 1985-96, Pro-Vice-Chancellor, 1991-95, University of Warwick, England; President, UWS Nepean, Sydney, Australia and Professor of Lifelong Learning, 1996-2000; Director and Professor of Continuing Education, University of Auckland, New Zealand, 2000-2002; Professor and Director of Community and Regional Partnerships, RMIT University, Melbourne, Australia, 2002-. Publications: Many books, edited volumes, chapters and journal articles in the fields of higher education, adult, continuing and non-formal education and lifelong learning and in policy and management of higher education; Recent books include: The Learning University, 1992, reprinted 1996; The Adult University, 1999; Managing the Learning University, 2002. Honours: Hon. DLitt. Keimyung University, Republic of Korea; Fellow, Australian College of Education. Memberships: Leadership and membership of international and national professional bodies in the fields of adult and continuing education. Address: 26 Nepean Street, Emu Plains, NSW 2750, Australia. E-mail: chris.duke@rmit.edu.au

DULAMSUREN Samdan, b. 10 February 1946, Mongolia. Health Professional. m. Nyam Adiya, 1 son, 1 daughter. Education: Medical Doctor, 1969; PhD, Medicine, 1983; MPH, 1987. Appointments: Head, Department of Manpower & Medical Policy, Ministry of Health, Mongolia, 1990-96; Deputy Director, 1997-2003, Director, 2004-06, Deputy Director, 2006-, National Centre for Health Development. Publications: Human Resource Planning in Health Sector, 1998; Public Health textbook, 1999. Honours: Polar Star medal, 1992; Leading Professional of the Mongolian Health Sector, 1996. Memberships: President, New Public Health Association of Mongolia; Executive Board Member, Mongolian Family Doctors' Association. Address: National Centre for Health Development, Enkhtaivan Street 13-B, Ulaanbaatar, Mongolia – 48.

DUMAGUING Victor Romulo Gallardo, b. 21 May 1949, Naguilian, La Union, Philippines. Medical Doctor; College Professor. 1 son. Education: D Med, University of the East Ramon Magsaysay Memorial Medical Centre, 1977; Postgraduate studies, Clinical Biochemistry, UP College of Medicine. Appointments: Internal Medicine, St Louis University Hospital of the Sacred Heart, 4 years; Chairman, Biochemistry, SLU College of Medicine; Visiting Professor, University of Baguio, Pines City Colleges and Baguio Central University; Diplomate, Philippines Association of Academic Biochemists, 1995; Fellow, 2000, President, 2003-04, Physiology Society of the Philippines. Publications: Numerous articles in professional journals. Honours: Outstanding Teacher of the Philippines, 1999; Outstanding Citizen of Baguio City, 2001; Outstanding Physician of Baguio City, 2003; Dr Jose P Rizal Medal Award for Community Leadership, 2005; Outstanding Filipino Achiever in Medicine and Health Sciences, 2005; Outstanding Physician in Community Service Award, 2006; SLU Presidential Award for Community Service and Social Involvement Trophy, 2006, 2007. Memberships: Life Member, Philippine Medical Association and Baguio-Benguet Medical Society; American Heart Association; American Stroke Association. Address: College of Nursing, St Louis University, Baguio City, Philippines. E-mail: vrgdumaguing@slu.edu.ph

DUNAWAY (Dorothy) Faye, b. 14 January 1941, Bascom, Florida, USA. Actress. m. (1) Peter Wolf, 1974, (2) Terry O'Neill, 1981, (divorced), 1 son. Education: Florida University; Boston University. Appointments: Lincoln Center Repertory Company, New York, 3 years, appearances in: A Man For All Seasons; After the Fall; Tartuffe; Off-Broadway in Hogan's Goat, 1965; Old Times, Los Angeles; Blanche du Bois in A Streetcar Named Desire, 1973; The Curse of an Aching Heart, 1982; Films include: Hurry Sundown; The Happening; Bonnie and Clyde, 1967; The Thomas Crown Affair, 1968; A Place For Lovers, The Arrangement, 1969; Little Big Man, 1970, Doc, 1971; The Getaway, 1972; Oklahoma Crude, The Three Musketeers, 1973; Chinatown, 1974; Damned, Network, 1976; The Eyes of Laura Mars, 1978; The Camp, 1979; The First Deadly Sin, Mommie Dearest, 1981; The Wicked Lady, 1982; Supergirl, 1984; Barfly, 1987; Burning Secret, 1988; The Handmaid's Tale, On A Moonlit Night; Up to Date, 1989; Scorchers; Faithful; Three Weeks in Jerusalem; The Arrowtooth Waltz, 1991; Double Edge; Arizona Dream; The Temp; Dun Juan DeMarco, 1995; Drunks; Dunston Checks In; Albino Alligator; The Chamber; Fanny Hill, 1998; Love Lies Bleeding, The Yards, Joan of Arc, The Thomas Crown

Affair, 1999; The Yards, Stanley's Gig, 2000; Yellow Bird, 2001; Changing Hearts, Rules of Attraction, Mid-Century, The Calling, 2002; Blind Horizon, 2003; Last Goodbye, El Padrino, Jennifer's Shadow, 2004; Ghosts Never Sleep, Love Hollywood Style, 2005; Rain, 2006; Cougar Club, Say It in Russian, Dr Fugazzi, Flick, The Gene Generation, 2007; TV include: After the Fall, 1974; The Disappearance of Aimee, 1976; Hogan's Goat; Mommie Dearest, Evita! - First Lady, 1981; 13 at Dinner, 1985; Beverly Hills Madame, 1986; The Country Girl; Casanova; The Raspberry Ripple; Cold Sassy Tree; Silhouette; Rebecca; Gia, 1998; Running Mates, 2000; The Biographer, 2002; Anonymous Rex, Back When We Where Grownups, 2004; Pandemic, 2007. Publications: Looking for Gatsby (Autobiography with Betsy Sharkey), 1995. Honours include: Academy Award for Best Actress for Network. Address: c/o Ed Limato, ICM, 8942 Wilshire Boulevard, Beverly Hills, CA 90211, USA.

DUNBAR Adrian, b.1 August 1958, Enniskillen, Northern Ireland. Actor. m. Anna Nygh, 1 stepson, 1 daughter. Education: Guildhall School of Music and Drama, London, UK. Career: Films include: The Fear; A World Apart; Dealers; My Left Foot; Hear My Song, 1992; The Crying Game, 1993; Widow's Peak, 1994; Richard III, 1995; The Near Room, 1996; The General, 1998; Wild About Harry, 2000; Shooters, 2000; The Wedding Tackle, 2000; How Harry Became a Tree, 2001; Triggerman, 2002; Darkness, 2002; The Measure of My Days, 2003; Mickybo and Me, 2004; Tma, 2005; Against Nature, 2005; Eye of the Dolphin, 2006; Stage appearances include: Ourselves Alone, Royal Court Theatre, 1985; King Lear, Royal Court; TV appearances include: Reasonable Force; Cracker; Murphy's Law; Suspicion; Kidnapped; The Quatermass Experiment; Child of Mine.

DUNBAR Robert Everett, b. 24 November 1926, Quincy, Massachusetts, USA. Writer; Educator. m. Thelma Rose Arseneault, divorced, 1 son, 1 daughter. Education: BA, Marietta College, 1951; MS, Northwestern University, 1954. Appointments: With US Navy, 1944-45; Assistant Editor Publications, Continental Assurance Company Chicago, 1954-57; Director, Communications, Junior Achievement, Chicago, 1957-58; Editor, National Sporting Goods Association, Chicago, 1958-67; Director, Communications, American Society of Anesthesiologists, Park Ridge, Illinois, 1967-70; Director, Public Information Division, American Fund for Dental Health, Chicago, 1970-74; Owner, Dunbar Editorial, Nobleboro and Gardiner, Maine, 1974-; Designed two courses in scientific writing (1 basic, 1 advanced), School of Related Health Sciences, University of Life Sciences/The Chicago Medical School, 1973; Instructor, 1973-74, Adjunct Assistant Professor, 1974-75, University of Health Sciences, Chicago Medical School; Columnist, Maine Life Magazine, 1981-86; Performer, actor and singer, 1986-; Internet Bookseller, Christiesplus, Gardiner, Maine, 2004-. Publications: Learning How to Cope with Arthritis, Rheumatism and Gout, 1973; How to Debate, 1987; 15 books including: Homosexuality, 1996; Books for Musicals: Vaudeville Gold, 1986; Friends and Lovers, 1988; Folk and Fancy, 1991; Co-author, It's a Wonderful Life (stage adaptation). Honours: Beth Fonda Award for Excellence, Chicago Area Chapter American Medical Writers Association, 1974; "Homosexuality" named one of the Notable books of 1996, National Council for Social Studies and Children's Book Council, 1996. Memberships: Co-founder and first elected President, St Andrew's Society, Maine, 1980-81; First Selectman (mayor) of Nobleboro, Maine, 1977-78; Fellow, American Medical Writers Association (AMWA) (President, Chicago Area Chapter, 1970-71, General Chairman, Annual

Meeting, 1971, National Co-Chairman, Education Committee, 1971-75, Founder, Chairman, Organising Committee, New England Chapter, 1975-76, Treasurer, New England Chapter, 1976-77, Judith Linn Memorial Award Committee, 2001-; Judge, AMWA National Book Awards; Judge, New England Chapter, AMWA; Will Solemine Awards for Excellence in Medical Communication; Debate Judge, High School Tournaments, 1992-2003; Judge, National Tournament, 1995; Member: American Medical Writers Association; Thoreau Society, Authors Guild, New England Science Writers, Nobleboro Historical Society (President, 1978-79), Gaslight Theater. Address: 552 Water St, Gardiner, ME 04345, USA. E-mail: reddunbar@gmail.com

DUNCAN Doris Gottschalk, b. 19 November 1944, Seattle, Washington, USA. Professor of Computer Information Systems. Divorced. Education: BA 1967, MBA 1968, University of Washington, Seattle; PhD, Golden Gate University, San Francisco, 1978; Certified Data Processor, 1980; Certified Data Educator, 1984; Certified Systems Professional, 1985; Certified Computer Professional, 1994, 2003, 2006. Appointments: Marketing Supervisor and Communications Consultant, American Telephone (AT&T), Seattle and San Francisco, 1968-73; Director of Company Analysis and Monitoring programme, Input, Palo Alto, 1975-76; Lecturer, Associate Professor, Professor, Computer Information Systems, 1976-, co-ordinator, computer info systems, 1994-97, Co-adviser, grad programmes, computer info systems and electronic business, 1999-, Director of MBA Programs, 2006-present, California State University, East Bay, (formerly CSU Hayward); Independent Consultant, Computer Information Systems, part time, 1976-; Director, Information Systems Programme, Golden Gate University, San Francisco, 1982-83; Visiting Professor, Information Systems, University of Washington, Seattle, 1997-98. Publications: Computers and Remote Computing Services, 1983; Author of over 60 journal articles and papers in conference proceedings. Honours include: Computer Educator of the Year, International Association for Computer Information Systems, 1997; Distinguished research award for "Comicstand.com: an E-Commerce Start-Up", Allied Academics, 1999; Service awards from Association of Information Technology Professionals: bronze, silver, gold, emerald, diamond, double diamond, triple diamond, 2000; Meritorious service award as faculty advisor of student chapter, CSUH grant recipient; Winner of beautiful home awards and decorating, Foster City, 1994-96, 2003. Memberships include: Board member: Computer Repair Services, Institute for Certification of Computer Professionals, Education Foundation Board; AITP Special Interest Group in Education Board; Advisory Board, Ximnet Corp; Editorial Review Board member for 3 journals: Journal of Informatics and Education Research; Journal of Information Technology Education; Journal of Information Systems Education; Associate Editor, Journal of Informatics & Education Research; Member: Association of Information Technology Professionals (Past President, Vice President, Secretary and Committee Chair, San Francisco chapter); Association of Computing Machinery; International Academy of Information Management; International Association of Computer Information Systems; Association of Information Systems; Academy of Business Education; Decision Sciences Institute; Beta Gamma Sigma. Address: California State University, East Bay, Hayward, CA 94542, USA. E-mail: doris_duncan@hotmail.com

DUNCAN Norman Thomas, b. 5 August 1957, Goodwood, South Africa. Professor of Psychology. Education: BA, History & Psychology, 1979; BA (Honours), Psychology, 1981, D Phil, 1994, University of the Western Cape; Diplôme de la Langue Française, 1985, Certificat des Études Françaises, 1986, University of Bordeaux III, France; MA, Clinical Psychology, Université de Paul Valérie, Montpelier III, France, 1987. Appointments: Head, Department of Psychology, University of Western Cape, 1995-97; Associate Professor, Head of Department of Psychology, University of Venda, 1997-2002; Associate Professor, Institute for Social & Health Sciences, University of South Africa, Acting Director, ISHS and UNISA/MRC Crime, Violence and Injury Prevention Lead Programme, 2002-03; Chair/Professor, Discipline of Psychology, 2004-, Head, School of Human and Community Development, 2007, University of the Witwatersrand. Publications: Several articles, chapters and edited books; Co-edited volumes include: Contemporary issues in human development: A South African focus, 1997; Discourses on racism and cultural difference, 2002; Community Psychology. Theory, method and practice, 2001; Race, racism, knowledge production and psychology in South Africa, 2001. Honours: Elected to South African National Committee of the International Union of Psychological Science, 1999; Visiting Professor/ Researcher, Institute de Psychologie, University of Lyon, France, 2001; Editor, South African Journal of Psychology, 2002; Elected Member, Academy of Science of South Africa, 2003. Memberships: Academy of Science of South Africa; Psychological Association of South Africa; S A National Committee, International Union of Psychological Science. Address: School of Human and Community Development, University of the Witwatersrand, Private Bag X3, PO WITS, 2050, Johannesburg.

DUNN Charleta J, b. 18 January 1927, Clarendon, Texas, USA. Clinical Psychologist. m. Roy E Dunn Jr, 2 sons, 1 daughter. Education: BS, 1951, MEd, 1954, West Texas University at Canyon; EdD, University of Houston, Houston, Texas, 1966; Postdoctorate in Clinical Psychology, University of Texas Medical Branch, Galveston, Texas, 1971. Appointments: Teacher, Amarillo Public Schools, 1951-62; Assistant Professor, University of Houston, 1966-70; Director Pupil Appraisal, Goose Creek, ISD, Baytown, Texas, 1971-73, Full Professor, 1974-90, Professor Emeritus, 1990-, Texas Women's University. Publications: 6 research-based monographs (Funded Research Grants); Over 36 articles in professional journals; 4 books: World of Work, 1971; Sisk: Book of Ages, 1998; Burcham and Allied Families, 2000; For the Pearl Fisher, 2005. Honours: Woman of the Year, 1996-99, 2001. Memberships: National Registrar of Mental Health; American Medical Psycho-Therapy Association; American Psychological Association.

DUNN Douglas (Eaglesham), b. 23 October 1942, Inchinnan, Scotland. Professor of English; Writer; Poet. m. Lesley Jane Bathgate, 10 August 1985, 1 son, 1 daughter. Education: BA, University of Hull, 1969. Appointments: Writer-in-Residence, University of Hull, 1974-75, Duncan of Jordanstone College of Art, Dundee District Library, 1986-88; Writer-in-Residence, 1981-82, Honorary Visiting Professor, 1987-88, University of Dundee; Fellow in Creative Writing, 1989-91, Professor of English, 1991-, Head, School of English, 1994-99, University of St Andrews; Director, St Andrews Scottish Studies Institute, 1993-. Publications: Terry Street, 1969; The Happier Life, 1972; Love or Nothing, 1974; Barbarians, 1979; St Kilda's Parliament, 1981; Europea's Lover, 1982; Elegies, 1985; Secret Villages, 1985; Selected Poems, 1986; Northlight, 1988; New and Selected Poems, 1989; Poll Tax: The Fiscal Fake, 1990; Andromache, 1990; Scotland: An Anthology (editor), 1991; The Faber Book of 20th Century Scottish Poetry (editor), 1992; Dante's Drum-Kit, 1993; Boyfriends and Girlfriends, 1994; The Oxford Book of Scottish Short Stories (editor), 1995; Norman MacCaig: Selected Poems (editor), 1997; The Donkey's Ears, 2000; 20th Century Scottish Poems (editor), 2000; The Year's Afternoon, 2000; New Selected Poems, 2002; Contributions to: Newspapers, reviews, and journals. Honours: Somerset Maugham Award, 1972; Geoffrey Faber Memorial Prize, 1975; Hawthornden Prize, 1982; Whitbread Poetry Award, 1985; Whitbread Book of the Year Award, 1985; Honorary LLD, University of Dundee, 1987; Cholmondeley Award, 1989; Honorary DLitt, University of Hull, 1995. Membership: Scottish PEN. Address: c/o School of English, University of St Andrews, St Andrews, Fife KY16 9AL, Scotland.

DUNNING John Harry, b. 26 June 1927. Economist. m. Christine Mary Brown, 1975. Education: BSc (Econ), University College London; PhD, University of Southampton. Appointments: Sub Lieutenant, RNVR, 1945-48; Lecturer and Senior Lecturer, Economics, University of Southampton, 1952-64; Foundation Professor of Economics, 1964-75, Esmée Fairburn Professor of International Investment and Business Studies, 1975-88, ICI Research Professor in International Business, 1988-92, Emeritus Professor of International Business, 1992, University of Reading; Distinguished Professor of International Business, Rutgers University, 1989-2000; Past Chairman, Economists Advisory Group Ltd; Consultant to Government Departments, OEDC, UNCTAD and UNIDO. Publications: Books include most recently: Multinational Enterprises and the Global Economy, 1993, revised and extended edition (with Sarianna Lundan), 2007. The Globalization of Business, 1993; Foreign Direct Investment and Governments (with Rajneesh Narula), 1996; Globalization and Developing Countries (with Khalil Hamdani), 1997; Alliance Capitalism and Global Business, 1997; Governments, Globalization and International Business, 1997; Globalization, Trade and Foreign Direct Investment, 1998; Regions, Globalization and the Knowledge Based Economy, 2000; Global Capitalism at Bay? 2001; Theories and Paradigms of International Business Activity, 2002; Global Capitalism, FDI and Competitiveness, 2002; Making Globalization Good, 2003; Multinationals and Industrial Competitiveness (with Rajneesh Narula), 2004. Honours: Dr honoris causa, Universidad Autónoma Madrid, Spain, 1990; Honorary PhD: Uppsala University, Sweden, 1975; Antwerpen University, Belgium, 1997; Honorary Professor of International Economics and Business, Beijing, China, 1995; Honorary Dr in International Business, Chinese Cultural University, Taipei, Taiwan, 2007; Honorary Dr in Economics, Lund University, Sweden, 2007. Memberships: Royal Economic Society; Academy of International Business; President, 1987-88, Dean of Fellows, 1994-96, International Trade and Finance Association; President, 1994, Dean of Fellows, 2003-06, European Academy of International Business. Address: Holly Dell, Satwell Close, Rotherfield Greys, Henley-on-Thames, Oxon RG9 4QT, England.

DUNST Kirsten Caroline, b. 30 April 1982, Point Pleasant, New Jersey, USA. Actor. Career: Over 70 commercials, 1985-; Films include: New York Stories, 1989; Darkness Before Dawn, 1993; Greedy, 1994; Interview with the Vampire: The Vampire Chronicles, 1994; Little Women, 1994; Jumanji, 1995; Small Soldiers, 1998; Dick, 1999; Drop Dead Gorgeous, 1999; The Virgin Suicides, 1999; Deeply, 2000; Bring It On, 2000; Crazy/Beautiful, 2001; The Cat's Meow, 2001; Get Over It, 2001; Spider-Man, 2002; Levity, 2003; Mona Lisa Smile, 2003; Eternal Sunshine of the Spotless Mind, 2004; Spider-Man 2, 2004; Wimbledon, 2004; Elizabethtown, 2005; Marie Antoinette, 2006; Spider-Man 3, 2007; TV appearances

include: The Tonight Show with Jay Leno, 1992; Rank, 2001; Gun, 1997; Sisters, 1991. Honours include: Academy of Science Fiction, Fantasy & Horror Films, Best Performance by a Young Actor in Interview with the Vampire: The Vampire Chronicles, 1995; Boston Society of Film Critics Award, Supporting Actress, Interview with the Vampire: The Vampire Chronicles,1994; Empire Awards, Best Actress, Spider-Man, 2003; MTV Movie Awards, Best Female Performance, Spider-Man, 2003; MTV Movie Awards, Best Breakthrough Performance, Interview with the Vampire: The Vampire Chronicles, 1995; Young Star Award, Best Performance by a Young Actress in a Drama Film, 1995.

DUNWOODY Richard, b. 18 January 1964, Belfast, North Ireland. Jockey. Appointments: Rode winner of: Grand National (West Tip), 1986, (Minnehoma), 1994; Cheltenham Gold Cup (Charter Party), 1988; Champion Hurdle (Kribensis), 1990; Champion National Hunt Jockey, 1992-93, 1993-94, 1994-95; Held record for most wins at retirement in 1999; Group Manager, Partner, Dunwoody Sports Marketing, 2002. Publications: Hell For Leather (with Marcus Armytage); Dual (with Sean Magee); Hands and Heels (with Marcus Armytage); Obsessed. Honours: National Hunt Jockey of the Year 1990, 1992-95; Lester Award, Jump Jockey of the Year, 1990, 1992-95; Champion of Champions, 2001. Address: c/o Dunwoody Sports Marketing, The Litten, Newtown Road, Newbury, Berkshire, RG14 7BB, England. E-mail: richard.d@du-mc.co.uk

DURANDY Yves Dominique, b. 20 February 1947, Neuilly-sur-Seine, France. Medical Doctor. Education: Resident, 1973, Chief Resident, 1979, Paris hospitals; Medical Doctor, Paris University, 1979; Assistant in Paris hospitals; Specialisation, Intensive Care, 1983 and Internal Medicine, 1994. Appointments: Director, Intensive Care Unit, Pediatry (Post operative unit of cardiac surgery); Director, Perfusion (Cardio pulmonary bypass cardiac assistance and extracorporeal lung support). Publications: Numerous articles in professional journals. Honours: Silver Medal for Residency; Silver Medal for Medical Thesis. Memberships: French Society of Intensive Care; European Society of Intensive Care; American Society of Artificial Internal Organs. Address: Institut Hospitalier J Cartier, Avenue du Noyer Lambert, 91300 Massy, France. E-mail: iciprea@icip.org

DURDEN-SMITH Neil, b. 18 August 1933, Richmond, Surrey, England. Co-Director; Broadcaster. m. Judith Chalmers, 1 son, 1 daughter. Education: Aldenham and Royal Naval College. Appointments: Royal Navy, 1952-63; ADC to Governor General of New Zealand, 1957-59; Commanded HMS Rampart, 1960-62; Cricket and Hockey for Royal Navy and Combined Services; Producer, BBC Outside Broadcasts (special responsibility for 1966 World Cup), 1963-66; Radio and television broadcaster, Test Match and County Cricket, Olympic Games (1968 and 1972), International Hockey, Trooping the Colour, Royal Tournament, Money Matters, Sports Special, 1967-74; Director, The Anglo-American Sporting Clubs, 1969-74; Chairman and Managing Director, Durden-Smith Communications, 1974-81; Trustee, The Lord's Taverner's, 1976-2004; Chairman, The Lord's Taverners, 1980-82; Chairman, Sports Sponsorship International, 1982-87; Chairman, The Altro Group, 1982-94; Director, Ruben Sedgwick, 1987-95; Chairman, Woodside Communications, 1992-99; Director, BCM Grandstand, 1993-2006; President, Middlesex Region, The Lord's Taverners, 1993-; Chairman, Brian Johnston Memorial Trust, 1994-2000; Consultant, AON, 1995-2007; Trustee, Charlie Walker Memorial Trust, 1997-; Consultant, Tangible Securities, 2003-; Patron, Motor

Neurone Disease Association, 1993-; Aspire Trust, 2004-; Westminster Society for the Disabled, 2006-. Publications: Forward for England: Bobby Charlton's Life Story, 1967; World Cup '66, 1967. Honours: OBE, 1997; Freeman of the City of London. Memberships: MCC; The Lord's Taverners; Sparks; I Zingari; Cricket Writers; Free Foresters; Lords & Commons Cricket; County Cricketers Golf; Saints & Sinners; Home House; Ritz; 50 St James's; Highgate, Archerfield and Vale Do Lobo Golf Clubs; FAGS; Ladykillers and Surbiton Hockey Clubs. Address: 28 Hillway, Highgate, London N6 6HH, England.

DURKAN Mark, b. 26 June 1960, Derry, Northern Ireland. Social Democratic and Labour Party Member. m. Jackie, 1 daughter. Education: Politics at Queen's University Belfast; Public Policy Management at University of Ulster. Appointments: Managed Eddie McGrady's election as MP for South Down, 1987; Managed Seamus Mallon's successful by-election campaign, 1986; Assistant and Advisor to John Hume, 1984-1998; SDLP Chairperson, 1990-95; Elected to Northern Ireland Assembly for Foyle, 1998; Appointed Minister of Finance and Personnel, 1999; SDLP Leader, 2001; Deputy First Minister, 2001-2002; Elected to Northern Ireland Assembly for Foyle, 2003; Elected to Westminster as MP for Foyle, 2005; Re-Elected to Northern Ireland Assembly for Foyle, 2007. Address: 23 Bishop Street, Derry, BT48 6PR, UK. E-mail: m.durkan@sdlp.ie

DUROV Vladimir Alekseevich, b. 29 January 1950, Arkhangelsk, Russia. Chemist. m. Ol'ga Nikolaevna Durova, 1 daughter. Education: MSc, 1973, PhD, 1978, DSc, 1989, Lomonosov Moscow State University; Professor of Physical Chemistry, Academic Rank, Ministry of Higher Education of Russia, 1993. Appointments: Junior Researcher, 1977-82, Senior Researcher, 1982-90, Leading Researcher, 1990-92, Research Professor, 1993-95, Professor of Chemistry (Full Professor), 1995-, Department of Physical Chemistry, Moscow State University. Publications: Over 180 articles in refereed journals; 6 monographs; 12 textbooks. Honours: Grantee, Russian Foundation on Basic Research; Distinguished Professor of Chemistry; Award, International Soros Science Education Program, USA; Grantee, Moscow Government on Natural Sciences and Education. Memberships include: Bureau of Scientific Council on Chemical Thermodynamics and Thermochemistry, Russian Academy of Sciences, 1987-; Bureau of the Scientific and Methodical Council on Chemistry, Russian Ministry of Science and Education, 1992-; Joint Task Group of IUPAC and CODATA on Standardisation of Physico-Chemical Properties Electronic Datafile, 1998-; International Advisory Board of the International Conferences on Chemical Thermodynamics, 1999-; International Advisory Committee of the European-Japanese Molecular Liquids Group, 1999-; Editorial Board of the Journal of Molecular Liquids, 1999-; Academician, International Academy of Creative Endeavours, 2000-; Active member, Academician, Russian Section of the International Academy of Sciences, 2001. Address: Department of Physical Chemistry, Faculty of Chemistry, Lomonosov Moscow State University, W-234, Moscow 119899, Russia. E-mail: durov@phys.chem.msu.ru Website: www.chem.msu.ru/eng/people/durov.html

DURUP Jean, b. 8 July 1932, Paris, France. Professor Emeritus. m. Nicole Mathez, 1 son, 3 daughters. Baccalaureat, 1947, Licence, 1952, Doctorat, 1959, Paris, France. Appointments: Research Fellow, CNRS, Paris, 1952-61; Research Fellow, CNRS, Orsay, 1961-68; Professor, Université de Paris-Sud, Orsay, 1968-85; Professor, Université Paul Sabatier, Toulouse, 1985-97; Professor Emeritus, 1997-2005. Publications: Book,

Positive ion-molecule reactions in gas phase; Over 100 papers in high-level journals, on physics, biology and chemistry. Honours: Silver Medal of CNRS, 1968; Fellow, American Physical Society, 1980. Address: 16 rue Romain Rolland, F-34200 Sète, France.

DUTTA Shiva Brat (Shibu), b. 15 November 1931, Fyzabad, India. Architect; Urban Designer; Architectural Historian. m. Ruby, 2 daughters. Education: Diploma in Architecture, Sir J J School of Arts, Bombay, 1957; Royal Institute of British Architects, 1960; Master of Architecture, University of Liverpool, England, 1965. Appointments: Architect, Weightman & Bullen, Liverpool, 1967; Architect, Runcorn New Town Corporation, Runcorn, 1967; Senior Architect, Warrington New Town Corporation, Warrington, 1969; Senior Architect, Ministry of Works, Wellington, New Zealand, 1970; Senior Architect, National Capital Development Commission, Canberra, Australia, 1974; Senior Architect, Urban Designer, Interim Territory Planning Authority, Canberra, 1988; Senior Architect, Urban Designer, Urban Planner, ACT Planning Authority, Canberra, 1994; Director, Research and Design International, architectural design and concept consultancy, 1996. Publications: Author, joint author and major contributor to 15 books. Honours: Highly Commended, Japanese Cultural Centre Competition, Japanese Institute of Architects and RAIA; Highly Commended, Group entry for Urban Design Ideas Competition, UIA for Down Town Montreal; Commonwealth Scholarship for study in UK, 1963. Memberships: Fellow, Australian Institute of Architects; Member, Royal Institute of British Architects; Member, National Trust ACT, Australia; Member, Australia on the Map Committee. Address: 43 Booroondara Street, Reid, ACT 2612, Australia. E-mail: dutta@actewagl.net.au

DUURSMA Egbert Klaas, b. 27 March 1927, Smallingerland, Netherlands. Professor of Oceanology; Director. m. Caroline Bosch, 3 sons, 1 daughter. Education: Graduated, Organic Chemistry, Free University, Amsterdam; PhD, 1960. Appointments: Research Scientist, dairy industry, Leeuwarden, Netherlands, 1953-56; Senior Scientist, Marine Radioactivity, NIOZ, Den Helder, 1960-65; Chief of Section, Sedimentology, International Laboratory of Marine Radioactivity, IAEA, Monaco, 1965-76; Expert FAO, Jepara, Indonesia, 1975; Director, Delta Institute for Hydrobiological Research, Royal Netherlands Academy of Sciences, Yerseke, Netherlands, 1976-86; Chairman, Dutch Council for Ocean Research and Antarctic Commission, 1985-93; First Scientific, later General, Director, NIOZ, Texel, Netherlands, 1986-89; Professor of Oceanology, University of Groningen, 1986-91; Many Guest Professorships. Publications include: The dissolved organic constituents of sea water, chapter in Chemical Oceanography, 1965; Theoretical, experimental and field studies concerning reactions of radioisotopes with sediments and suspended particles of the sea, 1967; Geochemical aspects and applications of (all) radionuclides in the sea, chapter, 1972; Role of pollution and pesticides in brackish water aquaculture in Indonesia, 1976; Pollution of the North Sea, co-author, 1988; Are tropical estuaries environmental sinks or sources?, 1995; Environmental compartments, equilibria and assessment of processes (of radioactive, metal and organic contaminants), between air, sediments and water, 1996; Stratospheric ozone chemistry: A literature review and synthesis, 1997, 2000; Dumped chemical weapons in the sea, options, Synopsis on the state of the art, emergency actions, first aid and state responsibilities, Editor and co-author, 1999; Global and regional rainfall, river-flow and temperature profile records; consequences for water resources, 2002; Energy and environment; irreversible events, 2005; Numerous book chapters, articles in scientific journals and conference proceedings. Honour: Medal, Royal Netherlands Academy of Art and Sciences, 1986. Memberships: Academia Europaea. Address: 302 Av du Semaphore, 06190 Roquebrune/Cap Martin, France.

DUVALL Robert, b. 5 January 1931, San Diego, USA. Actor. m. (1) Barbara Benjamin, (2) Gail Youngs, divorced, (3) Sharon Brophy, 1991, divorced, (4) Luciana Pedraza, 2004. Education: Principia College, Illinois, USA; Student, Neighbourhood Playhouse, New York. Appointments: Actor, stage appearances include: A View From the Bridge (Obie Award), 1965; Wait Until Dark, 1966; American Buffalo; Films include: To Kill a Mockingbird, 1963; Captain Newman, MD, 1964; The Chase, 1965; Countdown, The Detective, Bullitt, 1968; True Grit, The Rain People, 1969; M*A*S*H, The Revolutionary, 1970; The Godfather, Tomorrow, The Great Northfield; Minnesota Raid, Joe Kidd, 1972; Lady Ice, 1973; The Outfit, The Conversation, The Godfather Part II, 1974; Breakout, The Killer Elite, 1975; Network, 1976; The Eagle Has Landed, The Greatest, 1977; The Betsy, 1978; Apocalypse Now, 1979; The Great Santini, 1980; True Confessions, 1981; Angelo My Love (actor and director), Tender Mercies, 1983; The Stone Boy, The Natural, 1984; The Lightship, Let's Get Harry, Belizaire the Cajun, 1986; Colors, 1988; Convicts; Roots in Parched Ground; The Handmaid's Tale, A Show of Force, Days of Thunder, 1990; Rambling Rose, 1991; Newsies, The New Boys, Stalin, 1992; The Plague; Geronimo; Falling Down, 1993; The Paper, Wrestling Ernest Hemingway, 1994; Something to Talk About: The Stars Fell On Henrietta; The Scarlet Letter; A Family Thing (also co-producer); Phenomenon, 1996; The Apostle, Gingerbread Man, 1997; A Civil Action, 1999; Gone In Sixty Seconds, A Shot at Glory (also producer), The 6th Day, 2000; Apocalypse Now: Redux, 2001; John Q, Assassination Tango (also producer), 2002; Secondhand Lions, Gods and Generals, Open Range, 2003; Kicking & Screaming, Thank You for Smoking, 2005; The Godfather: The Game, Broken Trail, 2006, (TV); Lucky You, We Own the Night, 2007; Glad All Over, 2008; Director, We're Not the Jet Set; Assassination Tango, 2002; Several TV films and appearances. Address: c/o William Morris Agency, 151 S El Camino Drive, Beverly Hills, CA 90212, USA.

DUVALL Shelley, b. 7 July 1949, Houston, Texas, USA. Actress; Producer. Appointments: Founder, TV production company, Think Entertainment; Actress in TV films: Brewster McCloud; Mccabe and Mrs Miller; Thieves Like Us; Nashville; Buffalo Bill and the Indians; Three Women (Cannes Festival Prize, 1977); Annie Hall; The Shining; Popeye; Time Bandits; Roxanne; Suburban Commando; The Underneath; Portrait of a Lady; Changing Habits; Alone, 1997; Home Fries, 1998; Space Cadet; Big Monster on Campus; The 4th Floor; Dreams in the Attic; Manna From Heaven, 2001; Tale of the Mummy; Twilight of the Ice Nymphs; The Portrait of a Lady; Television includes: Bernice Bobs Her Hair; Lily; Twilight Zone; Mother Goose Rock'n'Rhyme; Faerie Tale Theatre (Rumpelstiltskin, Rapunzel); Tall Tales and Legends (Darlin' Clementine); Executive producer: Faerie Tale Theatre; Tall Tales and Legends; Nightmare Classics; Dinner at Eight (film); Mother Goose Rock'n'Rhyme; Stories from Growing Up; Backfield in Motion (TV); Bedtime Stories; Mrs Piggle-Wiggle.

DVORETZKY Isaac, b. 24 January 1928, Houston, Texas, USA. Research Chemist; Research Manager (Retired); Consultant. m. Constance Alexandra Schwalbe, 1 son, 2 daughters. Education: BA, Hons, Chemistry, Rice University, 1948; MA, Chemistry, 1950; PhD, Chemistry, 1952. Appointments: Research Chemist, 1952-56, Research Group

Leader, 1956-58, 1959-62, Exchange Scientist, Amsterdam, 1958-59, Research Supervisor, 1962-67, 1968-70, Senior Research Liaison, 1967-68, Research Department Manager, 1970-72, Manager, PhD Recruitment and University Relations, 1972-93, Shell Oil Company. Publications: Numerous research papers in journals including Journal of the American Chemical Society, Journal of Organic Chemistry, Analytical Chemistry, Journal of Chromatography; Several papers delivered at conferences and symposia. Honours: Outstanding Volunteer of the Year, National Society of Fund Raising Executives, 1996; Meritorious Service Award, Association of Rice University Alumni, 2003; Honorary Fellowship, The Technion-Israel Institute of Technology, 2006. Memberships include: American Chemical Society; National Consortium for Graduate Degrees for Minorities in Science and Engineering; American Technion Society, President, Greater Houston Chapter; Member, National Board of Directors; International Board of Governors, The Technion-Israel Institute of Technology. Address: 2927 Rimrock Drive, Missouri City, Texas 77459, USA.

DYBKAER René, b. 7 February 1926, Copenhagen. Physician. m. Nanna Gjoel, deceased. Education: MD, 1951, Dr Med Sci, 2004, University of Copenhagen; Specialist Clinical Chemistry, 1957. Appointments: Various medical residencies, 1951-55; Reader, Copenhagen University Institute of Medical Microbiology, 1956-70; Head, Department of Medical Microbiology, Royal Dental School of Copenhagen, 1959-70; Head, Department of Clinical Chemistry at De Gamles By, 1970-77, at Frederiksberg Hospital, 1977-96, at Department of Standardization in Laboratory Medicine, H:S Kommunehositalet, 1997-99, H:S Frederiksberg Hospital, 2000-. Publications: Books: Quantities and units in clinical chemistry, 1967; Good practice in decentralised analytical clinical measurement, 1992; Continuous quality improvement in clinical laboratories, 1994; Compendium on terminology and nomenclature in clinical laboratory sciences, 1995; An Ontology on Property for physical, chemical and biological systems, thesis, 2004; numerous articles to professional journals. Honours: Commemorative Lecture Enrique Concustell Bas, 1988; Henry Wishinsky Distinguished International Services Award, 1993; Honorary member of various national clinical laboratory societies; Professor James D Westgard Quality Award, 1998. Memberships: Vice President, 1973-78, President, 1979-84, Past President, 1985-90, International Federation of Clinical Chemistry; President, European Confederation of Laboratory Medicine, 1994-97; Chairman, Danish Society of Clinical Chemistry, 1991-93. Address: Region H Frederiksberg Hospital, Department of Standardization in Laboratory Medicine, Nordre Fasanvej 57, DK-2000 Frederiksberg, Denmark.

DYER Charles, b. 17 July 1928, Shrewsbury, England. Playwright. m. Fiona, 20 February 1960, 3 sons. Publications: Turtle in the Soup, 1948; Who On Earth, 1950; Poison in Jest, 1952; Jovial Parasite, 1955; Red Cabbage and Kings, 1958; Rattle of a Simple Man, novel, play, film, 1962; Staircase, novel, play, film, 1966; Mother Adam, 1970; Lovers Dancing, 1982; Those Old Trombones, 2005; Various screenplays. Address: Old Wob, Gerrards Cross, Buckinghamshire SL9 8SF, England.

DYER James Frederick, b. 23 February 1934, Luton, England. Archaeological Writer. Education: MA, Leicester University, 1964. Appointment: Editor, Shire Archaeology, 1974-. Publications: Southern England: An Archaeological Guide, 1973; Penguin Guide to Prehistoric England and Wales, 1981; Discovering Archaeology in England and Wales,

1985, 6th enlarged edition, 1997; Ancient Britain, 1990; Discovering Prehistoric England, 1993, 2nd edition, 2001; The Stopsley Book, 1998; Luton Modern School History, 2004. Contributions to: Bedfordshire Magazine; Illustrated London News; Archaeological Journal. Honours: Honorary Doctor of Arts, University of Luton, 1999. Memberships: Society of Authors; Royal Archaeological Institute; Society of Antiquaries. Address: 6 Rogate Road, Luton, Bedfordshire LU2 8HR, England.

DYKE Greg, b. 20 May 1947. Television Executive. 1 son, 1 stepson, 1 daughter, 1 stepdaughter. Education: York University; Harvard Business School. Appointments: Management Trainee, Marks & Spencer; Reporter, local paper; Campaigner for Community Relations Council, Wandsworth; Researcher, The London Programme; London Weekend TV (LWT); Later, Founding Producer, The Six O'Clock Show; Joined TV-AM, 1983; Director of Programmes, LWT, 1987-91; Group Chief Executive, LWT (Holdings) PLC, 1991-94; Chairman, GMTV, 1993-94; Chairman, Chief Executive Officer, Pearson TV, 1995-99; Chairman, Channel 5 Broadcasting, 1997-99; Former TVB Hong Kong; Director, BSkyB, 1995; Phoenix Pictures Inc, New York, Pearson PLC, 1996-99 and others; Director (non-executive) Manchester Utd, 1997-99; Director General, BBC, 2000-04; Supervisory Board Member, ProSiebenSat.1 Media, 2004-. Publications: Memoirs, 2004. Honours: Royal TV Society Lifetime Achievement Award, Broadcasting Press Guild, 2004. Memberships: Trustee Science Museum, 1996-; English National Stadium Trust, 1997-99. Address: ProSiebenSat.1 Media AG, Medienhallee 7, 85774 Unterfoehring, Germany. Website: www.prosieben.com

DYKES David Wilmer, b. 18 December 1933, Swansea, Wales. Retired; Independent Scholar. m. Margaret Anne George, 2 daughters. Education: MA, Corpus Christi College, Oxford, 1952-55; PhD, University of Wales. Appointments: Commissioned Service, RN and RNR, 1955-62; Civil Servant, 1958-59; Administrative Appointments, University of Bristol and University College of Swansea, 1959-63; Deputy Registrar, University College of Swansea, 1963-69; Registrar, University of Warwick, 1969-72; Secretary, 1972-86, Acting Director, 1985-86, Director, 1986-89, National Museum of Wales. Publications: Anglo-Saxon Coins in the National Museum of Wales, 1977; Alan Sorrell: Early Wales Recreated, 1980; Wales in Vanity Fair, 1989; The University College of Swansea, 1992; The Eighteenth Century Token, forthcoming; Articles and reviews in numismatic, historical and other journals. Honours: Parkes-Weber Prize and Medal, Royal Numismatic Society, 1954; K St J, 1993; Honorary Member, President, 1998-2003, British Numismatic Society. Memberships: Liveryman, Worshipful Company of Tin Plate Workers; Freeman City of London; Foundation Member, Welsh Livery Guild, 1993; FSA; FRHistS; FRNS; FRSAI. Address: 3 Peverell Avenue East, Poundbury, Dorchester, Dorset, DT1 3RH, England.

DYLAN Bob (Robert Allen Zimmerman), b. 24 May 1941, Duluth, Minnesota, USA. Singer; Musician (guitar, piano, harmonica, autoharp); Poet; Composer. Musical Education: Self-taught. Career: Solo folk/rock artist, also performed with The Band; The Travelling Wilburys; Grateful Dead; Songs recorded by estimated 3000 artists, including U2, Bruce Springsteen, Rod Stewart, Jimi Hendrix, Eric Clapton, Neil Young; Numerous tours: USA, Europe, Australia, 1961-; Film appearances include: Pat Garrett and Billy The Kid; Concert For Bangladesh; Hearts Of Fire. Compositions include: Blowin' In The Wind; Like A Rolling Stone; Mr Tambourine

Man; Lay Lady Lay; Forever Young; Tangled Up In Blue; Gotta Serve Somebody; Don't Think Twice; It's Alright; A Hard Rain's Gonna Fall; The Times They Are A-Changin'; Just Like A Woman; I'll Be Your Baby Tonight; I Shall Be Released; Simple Twist Of Fate; Paths Of Victory; Dignity. Recordings: Over 40 albums include: The Freewheelin' Bob Dylan, 1964; Bringing It All Back Home, 1965; Highway 61 Revisited, 1965; Blonde On Blonde, 1966; John Wesley Harding, 1968; Nashville Skyline, 1969; Self Portrait, 1970; New Morning, 1970; Before The Flood, 1974; Hard Rain, 1976; Desire, 1976; Street Legal, 1978; Slow Train Coming, 1979; Infidels, 1983; Empire Burlesque, 1985; Knocked Out Loaded, 1986; Down In The Groove, 1988; Biograph (5 record set), 1988; Oh Mercy, 1989; Under The Red Sky, 1990; MTV Unplugged, 1995; Time Out of Mind, 1998; Love and Theft, 2001; with The Band: Planet Waves, 1974; Blood On The Tracks, 1975; with Travelling Wilburys: Travelling Wilburys, 1988; Vol 3, 1990; with Grateful Dead, Dylan And The Dead, 1989; No Direction Home: Bob Dylan, 2005; Singles include: One Too Many Mornings, 1965; Mr Tambourine Man, 1966; Love Sick, 1997. Publications: Tarantula, 1966; Writings And Drawings, 1973; The Songs Of Bob Dylan 1966-75, 1976; Lyrics 1962-85, 1986; Drawn Blank, 1994; Highway 61 Revisited (interactive CD-ROM). Honours include: Honorary D Mus, Princeton University, 1970; Inducted, Rock and Roll Hall of Fame, 1988; Grammy, 1990. Address: c/o Columbia Records, 550 Madison Avenue, New York, NY 10022, USA.

DYNAMITE Ms (Niomi McLean-Daley), b. 26 April 1981, London, England. Singer. 1 son. Education: Acland Burghley School. Career: Rap Artist and MC; Collaborations with Eminem, So Solid Crew; Human Rights and Anti-war campaigner; UK tour, 2002; Recordings: Albums: A Little Deeper, 2002; A Little Darker, 2003; Judgement Days, 2005. Singles: Booo! 2002; Dy-Na-Mi-Tee, 2002; It Takes More, 2002; Put Him Out, 2003; Father, 2005; Fall in Love Again, 2006. Honours: MOBO Awards: Best UK Act, Best Single, Best Newcomer, 2002; Mercury Music Prize, 2002; BRIT Awards: Best British Female, Best British Urban Artist, 2003; EMMA multi-cultural Award for Best British Music Act, 2003. Address: c/o Polydor (UK), 72 Black Lion Lane, London, W6 9BE, England. E-mail: msdynamite@deadlymedia.co.uk Website: www.msdynamite.co.uk

DYSON Freeman J(ohn), b. 15 December 1923, Crowthorne, England (US citizen, 1957). Professor of Physics Emeritus. m. (1) Verena Haefeli-Huber, 11 August 1950, divorced 1958, 1 son, 1 daughter, (2) Imme Jung, 21 November 1958, 4 daughters. Education: BA, Cambridge University, 1945; Graduate Studies, Cornell University, 1947-48, Institute for Advanced Study, Princeton, New Jersey, 1948-49. Appointments: Research Fellow, Trinity College, Cambridge, 1946-49; Warren Research Fellow, University of Birmingham, England, 1949-51; Professor of Physics, Cornell University, 1951-53; Professor of Physics, 1953-94, Professor Emeritus, 1994-, Institute for Advanced Study. Publications: Symmetry Groups in Nuclear and Particle Physics, 1966; Neutron Stars and Pulsars, 1971; Disturbing the Universe, 1979; Values at War, 1983; Weapons and Hope, 1984; Origins of Life, 1986; Infinite in All Directions, 1988; From Eros to Gaia, 1992; Imagined Worlds, 1997; The Sun The Genome and the Internet, 1999; The Scientist as Rebel, 2006; Advanced Quantum Mechanics, World Scientific, 2007. Honours: Heineman Prize, American Institute of Physics, 1966; Lorentz Medal, Royal Netherlands Academy of Sciences, 1966; Hughes Medal, Royal Society, 1968; Max Planck Medal, German Physical Society, 1969; J Robert Oppenheimer Memorial Prize, Center for Theoretical Studies, 1970; Harvey Prize, Israel

Institute of Technology, 1977; Wolf Prize, Wolf Foundation, 1981; National Book Critics Circle Award, 1984; Templeton Prize for Progress in Religion, 2000. Honorary doctorates. Memberships: American Physical Society; National Academy of Sciences; Royal Society, fellow. Address: 105 Battle Road Circle, Princeton, NJ 08540, USA.

DYSON James, b. 2 May 1947, Cromer, Norfolk, Designer. m. Deidre Hindmarsh, 1967, 2 sons, 1 daughter. Education: Royal College of Art. Appointments: Director, Rotork Marine, 1970-74; Managing Director, Kirk Dyson, 1974-79; Developed and designed, Dyson Dual Cyclone vacuum cleaner, 1979-93; Founder, Chairman Prototypes Ltd, 1979-; Dyson Appliances Ltd, 1992-; Hon DLitt (Staffordshire), 1996; Hon DSc, Oxford Brookes, 1997, Huddersfield, 1997, Bradford, 1998. Publications include: Doing a Dyson, 1996; Against the Odds (autobiography), 1997; History of Great Inventions, 2001. Honours: Numerous design awards and trophies; Knight Bachelor, 2006. Address: Dyson Ltd, Tetbury Hill, Malmesbury, Wiltshire SN16 0RP, England.

DZOKIC M Gjorgje b. 14 January 1957, Skopje, Macedonia. m Tatyana, 2 sons. Education: MD, 1980; General Surgeon, 1988; Plastic and Reconstructive Surgeon, 1991; PhD, Dr Sci, 1999; Docent of Surgery, 2000; Professor of Surgery, 2006. Appointments: University Clinic for Plastic and Reconstructive Surgery, 1983; Secretary of Macedonian Association of Plastic Surgeons, 1997-1999; Head of Clinic, 2000-2002; Head of Division for ambulance and daily hospital, medical educator, trainer and educator of medical students and nurses, mentor of post graduate and doctorate students, moderator of residents. Publications: author and co-author of over 80 articles in National and International Medical Journals and Congress book abstracts; author of scripta of Plastic Surgery for Students; author of chapters in forthcoming Macedonian Book of Surgery for Students. Honours: Executive Plaque of Macedonian Doctors Association, 2001; Certificate for Successful Completion of Second Workshop for Medical Education, 2002; numerous certificates as proof of inclusion in various well-known international biographies. Memberships: National and international associations of plastic surgeons, BAPRAS, ESPRAS, ISPRAS; Cathedra in Surgery, Faculty of Medicine; Skopje Educational-Scientific Council of the Faculty of Medicine; Skopje Board for Post Graduate Studies, Faculty of Medicine; Doctor Chamber of Macedonia; Macedonian Doctors' Association; National Commission for Doctors' Licence; National Commission for Specialist Examination for General and Plastic Surgeons. Address: University Sts Cyril and Methodius, Clinic for Plastic and Reconstructive Surgery, Medical Faculty, Str Vodnjanska No 17, Skopje 1000, Republic of Macedonia

E

EASTON Earnest Lee, b. 1 May 1943, South Bend, Indiana, USA. Scholar. Education: AA, Social Science, Chicago City College, Chicago, Illinois, 1968; BA, German, BA, Political Science, University of Illinois, Chicago, 1970; Master of Public Administration, Maxwell School of Citizenship and Affairs, 1971; MA, Department of Government, Cornell University, 1975; PhD, Government, Cornell University, 1978. Appointments: US Army, 1963-66, Communications Expert, Augsburg, Germany, 1964-65, Crypto Operator, Munich, Germany, 1965-66; Teaching Assistantships, Department of Government, Cornell University, Fall 1973-74, Spring, 1973-74, Summer, 1974, Fall, 1974-75, Spring, 1974-75, Fall, 1975-76; Honours: Decorated as sharpshooter, Fort Knox, Kentucky, 1963; US Most Distinguished Veteran; Student awards scholarships fellowships include: Oxford University Scholarship, 1970; Fellowships at Syracuse University, 1970-71, Cornell University, 1972-73, University of Michigan, 1973; Awards for Heroism, Board of Public Safety, South Bend, Indiana, 1994; Sheriffs Department, Saint Joseph County, Indiana, 1994, Mayors Office, Mishawaka, Indiana, 1995; EMS, Emergency Medical Services, Mishawaka, 1996; Chief of Fire, Mishawaka, 1998. Memberships: American Political Science Association; National Association of Scholars. Address: PO Box 533, South Bend, IN 46624, USA.

EASTON Sheena (Sheena Shirley Orr), b. 27 April 1959, Bellshill, Glasgow, Scotland. Singer; Actress. m. (1) Sandi Easton, 1979, divorced, (2) Rob Light, 1984, divorced, (3) Timothy Delarm, 1997 divorced, (4) John Minoli, 2002 divorced. 2 adopted children. Education: Speech and Drama, Royal Scottish Academy of Music and Drama. Career: Singer, Glasgow club circuit, 1979; Featured in television series; Concerts and tours worldwide; Television appearances include: TV special, Sheena Easton ...Act 1, NBC, 1983; Actress, Miami Vice, NBC, 1987; Stage debut, Man Of La Mancha, Chicago, then Broadway, 1991-92; Launched own Seven Minute Flat Stomach fitness video. Recordings: Albums: Sheena Easton, You Could Have Been With Me, 1981; Madness Money And Music, 1982; Best Kept Secret, 1983; A Private Heaven, Do You, 1985; The Lover In Me, For Your Eyes Only - The Best Of Sheena Easton, The Collection, 1989; What Comes Naturally, 1991; No Strings, 1993; My Cherie, 1995; Body and Soul, 1997; Freedom, Fabulous, 2000; Hit singles include: Modern Girl, 1980; Morning Train (9 To 5) (Number 1, US), One Man Woman, When He Shines, For Your Eyes Only, theme music to James Bond film, 1981; We've Got Tonight, duet with Kenny Rogers, Telefone, 1983; Strut, 1984; Sugar Walls, 1985; U Got The Look, duet with Prince, 1987; The Lover In Me (Number 2, US), 1989; What Comes Naturally, You Can Swing It, To Anyone, Contributor, Voices That Care charity record, 1991; Contributor, film soundtracks: Santa Claus - The Movie, 1985; About Last Night, 1986; Ferngully...The Last Rainforest, 1992. Honours include: Grammy Awards: Best New Artist, 1982; Best Mexican/American Performance, with Luis Miguel, 1985; First artist in history to have Top 5 hits in all major US charts (Pop, R&B, Country, Dance, Adult Contemporary), 1985; Emmy Award, Sheena Easton...Act 1, 1983. Current Management: Harriet Wasserman Management, 15250 Ventura Blvd, Suite 1215, Sherman Oaks, CA 91403-3201, USA.

EASTWOOD Clint, b. 31 May 1930, San Francisco, USA. Actor; Film Director. m. (1) Maggie Johnson, 1 son, 1 daughter; 1 daughter by Frances Fisher; m. (2) Dina Ruiz, 1996, 1 daughter. Education: Los Angeles City College.

Appointments: Lumberjack, Oregon; Army service; Actor, TV series, Rawhide, 1959-65; Owner, Malposo Productions, 1969-; Mayor, Carmel, 1986-88. Films include: The First Travelling Saleslady; Star in the Dust; Escapade in Japan; Ambush at Cimarron Pass; Lafayette Escadrille; A Fistful of Dollars, 1964; For a Few Dollars More, 1965; The Good, the Bad and the Ugly, 1966; The Witches, 1967; Hang 'Em High, Coogan's Bluff, Paint Your Wagon, 1968; Where Eagles Dare, 1969; Kelly's Heroes, Two Mules for Sister Sara, 1970; Dirty Harry, 1971; Joe Kidd, 1972; High Plains Drifter (also director), Magnum Force, 1973; Thunderbolt and Lightfoot, 1974; The Eiger Sanction (also director), 1975; The Outlaw Josey Wales (also director), The Enforcer, 1976; The Gauntlet (also director), Every Which Way But Loose, 1978; Escape From Alcatraz, 1979; Bronco Billy (also director), Any Which Way We Can, 1980; Firefox (also director), Honky Tonk Man (also director), 1982; Sudden Impact (also director), 1983; Tightrope, City Heat, 1984; Pale Rider (also director), 1985; Heartbreak Ridge (also director); Director, Breezy, 1973; Bird, The Dead Pool, 1988; Pink Cadillac, White Hunter, Black Heart (also director), 1989; The Rookie (also director), 1990; Unforgiven (also director), 1992; In the Line of Fire, A Perfect World (also director), 1993; The Bridges of Madison County (also director, producer), 1995; The Stars Fell on Henrietta (co-producer); Absolute Power (also director), Midnight in the Garden of Good and Evil, (director), 1997; True Crime, 1998; Space Cowboys (also director), 2000; Blood Work (also director, producer), 2002; Mystic River (director), 2003; Million Dollar Baby (also director, composer), 2004. Honours: Academy Awards, 1993; Fellow, BFI, 1993; Irving G Thalberg Award, 1995; Legion d'honneur, Commander, Ordre des Arts et Lettres, American Film Institute's Life Achievement Award, 1996; Screen Actors Guild, 2003; Special Filmmaking Achievement Award, National Board of Review, 2005; Best Director, Golden Globe Awards, 2005; Directors Guild of America Awards, 2005; Best Film, Best Director, Academy Awards, 2005. Address: c/o Leonard Hirshan, William Morris Agency, 151 S El Camino Drive, Beverly Hills, CA 90212, USA.

EBRÍ Bernardo Torné, b. 26 October 1949, Zaragoza, Spain. Internist; Medical Researcher. m. Immaculada, 3 sons, 2 daughter. Education: BSc, 1985, MD, 1972, PhD, 1978, University of Zaragoza; Studies in biological medicine and complementary therapies; Music Diploma, Specialist in Piano, 1984; Theological studies, Institute of Theological Studies, Zaragoza, 1989-92. Appointments: Research Fellow, Education & Science Ministry, Madrid, 1973-76; Assistant Professor, University of Zaragoza, 1973-86; Consultant, International Medicine, Miguel Servet Hospital, 1974; Director of Thesis and Advisor to Medical Residents, 1977-; Lecturer at Conferences of Bioethical and Medical-Social Issues, 1980-; Medical Resident, Miguel Servet Hospital, Zaragoza, 1986; Associate Professor, Faculty of Medicine, Zaragoza, 1987; Medical Homeopathic-Naturist, Zaragoza, 1993; Director and Professor of Post-graduate Courses in Biological Medicine, 1999-; National Group of Researchers of Cardiovascular Risk, Member of Spanish Society of Internal Medicine, 2002-. Publications: Author, 14 books on medical and humanities issues; More than 500 participations as lecturer and speaker in conferences on medical, ethical and humanities issues; More than 180 articles in professional journals. Honours: End of Degree Award, Zaragoza, 1971-72; Award of General Military Academy, Zaragoza, 1972; Award for Best Academy Record, Zaragoza City Council, 1973; Prince Ferdinand Award, 1973; Zaragoza City Hall Award, 1973; Extraordinary Degree Award, 1973; National Award Degree, 1975, PhD Award, 1979, Royal National Academy,

Madrid; Best Doctoral Thesis Award, Government of Aragon, 1976-77; First Award, Medical Surgical Research, Official College of Medicine Doctors, Zaragoza, 1988-89; Award for Best Communication of Internal Medical Resident, Semergen Congress of General Practitioners, Spain, 2004. Memberships: Life Protection Association, Zaragoza; Academic of Medicine, Zaragoza; Spanish Society of Internal Medicine; Association of Naturist Doctors, Zaragoza; New York Academy of Sciences; Hypertension Society of Aragon; Spanish and Aragon Federation of Homeopathic Doctors. Address: Viñedo Viejo 2, 13-1D, 50009, Zaragoza, Spain. E-mail: b.ebri@yahoo.es

ECCLESTON Christopher, b. 16 February 1964, Salford, England. Actor. Appointments: Actor, films: Let Him Have It, 1991; Shallow Grave, 1995; Jude, 1996; Elizabeth, 1998; A Price Above Rubies, 1998; Heart, 1999; Old New Borrowed Blue, 1999; Existenz, 1999; Gone in 60 Seconds, 2000; The Invisible Circus, 2001; The Others, 2001; I am Dina, 2002; 28 Days Later, 2002; The Dark Is Rising, 2007; New Orleans, Mon Amour, 2007; TV appearances: Cracker, 1993-94; Hearts and Minds, 1995; Our Friends in the North, 1996; Hillsborough, 1996; Strumpet, 2001; Flesh and Blood, 2002; Dr Who, 2005; Heroes, 2007. Theatre includes: Miss June, 2000. Address: Hamilton Asper Management, Ground Floor, 24 Hanway Street, London W1P 9DD, England.

ECCLESTONE Bernie, b. October 1930, Bungay, Suffolk, Business Executive. m. (1) 1 daughter, (2) Slavica, 2 daughters, 1 son. Education: Woolwich Polytechnic, London. Appointments: Established car and motorcycle dealership, Bexley, Kent; Racing-car driver for short period; Set up Brabham racing team, 1970; Owner, Formula One Holdings, now controls Formula One Constructors Association, representing all top racing-car teams; Vice-President in charge of Promotional Affairs, Federal Institute de l'Automobile (FIA), racing's international governing body. Address: Formula One Administration Limited, 6 Prince's Gate, London SW7 1QJ, England. Website: www.formula1.com

ECHAURREN Juan Carlos, b. 21 July 1966, Santiago, Chile. Mathematical Researcher. Education: Technician in Automation-Instrumentation, University of Santiago of Chile, 1988; Engineering Civil Systems Course, Mariscal Sucre University, 1995-97; Student, Industrial Engineering, Arturo Prat University. Appointments: Researcher, Mathematics Models and applications to analysis of risks; Researcher in quantum-mechanics, quantum cosmology and theory of solitons and harmonic analysis; Creation of risk maps in quantum formalism, applicated to space safety in NASA. Publications: Mathematical Aspects Associated to the Generation of Impact Craters on Mars, 2007; New Numerical Estimations for Both Impact Conditions and Hydrothermal Zones on Isidis Planitia, Mars, 2007; Numerical Estimations for Impact Conditions on Campo del Cielo, Crater Field, South America, 2007; Mathematical Models and Numerical Estimations for Tsunami Generated on Chicxulab, Mexico, 2007; New Calculations and Mathematical Refinements for Impact Conditions on Argyre Planitia, Mars, 2007. Honours: Award of Recognition, for Contribution to Analysis of Risks, Chuquicamata Division, Codelco, Chile, 1997; Grant, Max-Planck-Institut für Chemie, Germany, 2003. Memberships: American Mathematical Society; New York Academy of Sciences; Planetary Society; American Institute of Aeronautics and Astronautics. Address: Lince 976, Población Kamac Mayu 2, Calama, Chile. E-mail: jechaurren@hotmail.com Website: www.juanechaurren.blogspot.com

ECO Umberto, b. 5 January 1932, Alessandria, Italy. Professor of Semiotics; Author. m. Renate Ramge, 24 September 1962, 1 son, 1 daughter. Education: PhD, University of Turin, 1954. Appointments: Assistant Lecturer, 1956-63, Lecturer 1963-64, University of Turin; Lecturer, University of Milan, 1964-65; Professor, University of Florence, 1966-69; Visiting Professor, New York University, 1969-70, 1976, Northwestern University, 1972, Yale University, 1977, 1980, 1981, Columbia University, 1978, 1984; Professor of Semiotics, Milan Polytechnic, 1970-71, University of Bologna, 1971-. Publications: Il Problema Estetico in San Tommaso, 1956, English translation as The Aethetics of Thomas Aquinas, 1988; Sviluppo dell'Estetica Medioevale, 1959, English translation as Art and Beauty in the middle Ages, 1986; Diario Minimo, 1963; La Struttura Assente, 1968; Il Costume di Casa, 1973; Trattato di Semiotica Generale, 1976; Il Nome della Rosa (novel), 1981, English translation as The Name of the Rose; Sette anni di desiderio 1977-83, 1984; Il Pendolo di Foucault, 1988; L'isola del giorno prima (novel), 1995, English translation as The Island of the Day Before; The Search for the Perfect Language, 1995; Serendipities, 1997; Kant and the Platypus, 1999; Baudolino (novel), 2000; Experiences in Translation, 2000; Five Moral Pieces, 2001; Mouse or Rat?: Translation as Negotiation, 2003; On Beauty: A History of a Western Idea (editor), 2004; The Mysterious Flame of Queen Loana (novel), 2005; Contributions to: various publications. Honours: Medici Prize, 1982; McLuhan Teleglobe Prize, 1985; Honorary DLitt, University of Glasgow, 1990, University of Kent, 1992; Crystal Award, World Economic Forum, 2000; Prince of Asturias Prize for Communications and the Humanities, 2000. Membership: International Association for Semiotic Studies. Address: Scuola Superiore Studi Umanistici, Via Marsala 26, Bologna, Italy. E-mail: sssub@dsc.unibo.it

EDBERG Stefan, b. 19 January 1966, Vastervik, Sweden. Tennis Player. m. Annette, 1 son, 1 daughter. Appointments: Tennis player, winner of: Junior Grand Slam, 1983; Milan Open, 1984; San Francisco, Basle and Memphis Opens, 1985; Gstaad, Basle and Stockholm Opens, 1986; Australian Open, 1986, 1987; Wimbledon, 1988, 1990, finalist, 1989; US Open, 1991; Masters, 1989; German Open, 1992; US Open, 1992; Winner (with Anders Jarryd) Masters and French Open, 1986, Australian and US Opens, 1987; Member, Swedish Davis Cup Team, 1984, 1987; Semi-finalist, numerous tournaments; Retired in 1996 having won 60 professional titles and more than 20 million dollars in prize money; Founded the Stefan Edberg Foundation to assist young Swedish tennis players. Honour: Adidas Sportsmanship Award (four times); Inducted into International Tennis Hall of Fame, 2004. Address: c/o ATP Tour 200, ATP Tour Boulevard, Ponte Vedra Beach, FL 32082, USA.

EDER Andrew Howard Eric, b. 21 April 1964, London England. Dental Surgeon. m. Rosina Jayne Saideman, 2 sons, 1 daughter. Education: BDS (Hons), KCHMDS, University of London, 1986; LDS, Royal College of Surgeons of England; MSc, Conservative Dentistry, Eastman Dental Institute, University of London, 1990; Elected to MFGDP, Royal College of Surgeons of England; Membership in Restorative Dentistry, Royal College of Surgeons of England and Glasgow, 1994; Fellowship in Dental Surgery (Ad Eundum), Royal College of Surgeons of Edinburgh, 2003; Elected to FHEA, Higher Education Academy, 2002. Appointments: Professor of Restorative Dentistry and Dental Education, Honorary Consultant in Restorative Dentistry, UCL Eastman Dental Institute; Specialist in Restorative Dentistry and Prosthodontics, Director of London Tooth

Wear Centre ®, Private Practice; Currently: Chair, Division of Clinical Education and Director of Continuing Professional Development, UCL Eastman Dental Institute, Associate Dean, UCL School of Life and Medical Sciences. Publications: 40, single and multi-author papers, edited articles posters and abstracts; Textbook: Tooth Surface Loss (with R Ibbetson), 2000; Editorial Advisory Board: The European Journal of Restorative Dentistry, 1995-; Clinical Adviser, Editorial Advisory Board: Private Dentistry, 1997-; Board of Advisors, British Dental Journal, 2005-. Memberships: President, 1994-95, Chairman of Trustees, 2003-, Alpha Omega; Fellowship, 1997, President, 2005-2006, British Society for Restorative Dentistry; President, 2001-2002, Odontological Section, Royal Society of Medicine. Address: UCL Eastman CPD, 123 Gray's Inn Road, London WC1X 8WD, England. E-mail: aeder@eastman.ucl.ac.uk

EDGE (THE) (David Howell Evans), b. 8 August 1961, Barking, Essex, Musician. m. Aislinn O'Sullivan, 1983-96, (divorced), 3 daughters, Morleigh Steinberg, 2002, 1 daughter, 1 son. Appointments: Guitarist, Founder Member, U2, 1978-; Toured Australasia, Europe, USA, 1980-84; Live Aid Wembley, 1985; Self Aid Dublin, A Conspiracy of Hope (Amnesty International Tour), 1986; World tour, 100 performances, Europe and USA, 1987; Tour, Australia, 1989; New Year's Eve Concert Point Depot Dublin (Broadcast live to Europe and USSR, 1989; World tour, 1992-93; Dublin Concert, 1993. Recordings: Albums with U2: Boy, 1980; October, 1981; War, 1983; Under A Blood Red Sky, 1983; The Unforgettable Fire, 1984; The Joshua Tree, 1987; Rattle and Hum, 1988; Achtung Baby, 1991; Zooropa, 1993; Pop, 1997; All That You Can't Leave Behind, 2000; How to Dismantle an Atomic Bomb, 2004; Singles with U2 include: With Or Without You; I Still Haven't Found What I'm Looking For; Where the Streets Have No Name, 1988 (all 3 no 1 in US charts); Desire, 1988; Stay, 1993; Discotheque, 1997 (all 3 UK no 1); Sweetest Thing, 1998; Beautiful Day, 2000; Stuck in a Moment You Can's Get Out Of, 2001; Vertigo, 2004. Honours: BRIT Awards: Best International Act, 1988-90, 1992, 1998, 2001, Best Live Act, 1993, Outstanding Contribution to the British Music Industry, 2001; JUNO Award, 1993; World Music Award, 1993; American Music Award for Favorite Internet Artist of the Year, 2002; Grammy Awards: Album of the Year, 1987, Best Rock Performance by a Duo or Group with Vocal, 1987, 1988, 1992, 2000, 2001, 2005, Best Alternative Music Album, 1993, Best Rock Album, 2001, Song of the Year, 2000, Record of the Year, 2000, 2001, Ivor Novello Award for Best Song Musically and Lyrically, 2002, Best Rock Song, 2005, Best Short Form Music Video, 2005. Address: Principle Management, 30-32 Sir John Rogersons Quay, Dublin 2, Ireland. E-mail: candida@numb.ie Website: www.u2.com

EDGECOMBE Jean Marjorie, b. 28 February 1914, Bathurst, New South Wales, Australia. Author. m. Gordon Henry Edgecombe, 2 February 1945, 2 daughters, 2 sons. Education: BA, Honours, Sydney University, 1935. Publications: Discovering Lord Howe Island, (with Isobel Bennett), 1978; Discovering Norfolk Island, (with Isobel Bennett), 1983; Flinders Island, the Furneaux Group, 1985; Flinders Island and Eastern Bass Strait, 1986, 2nd edition, 1994, 3rd edition, 2007; Lord Howe Island, World Heritage Area, 1987; Phillip Island and Western Port, 1989; Norfolk Island, South Pacific: Island of History and Many Delights, 1991, revised 2nd edition, 1999; Discovering Flinders Island, 1992, revised 2nd edition, 1999; Discovering King Island, Western Bass Strait, 1993, revised 2nd edition, 2004. Contributions to: Articles and poems to various publications.

Honour: Medal of the Order of Australia, 1995. Membership: Australian Society of Authors; Hornsby Shire Historical Society; Australian Conservation Foundation; The Australian Museum Society; The National Trust of Australia (New South Wales); State Library of New South Wales Foundation. Address: 7 Oakleigh Avenue, Thornleigh, 2120 New South Wales, Australia.

EDMONDS Dean Stockett Jr, b. 24 December 1924. Professor of Physics. Education: BS, Physics, Massachusetts Institute of Technology (MIT), 1950; MA, Physics, Princeton University, 1952; PhD, MIT, 1958. Appointments: Co-founder, Vice President, Director, Nuclide Corporation, 1958-65; Research Fellow, Harvard University, Guest of Physics Department, MIT for work on Cambridge Electron Accelerator, 1959-61; Assistant Professor, 1961-67, Associate Professor, 1967-83, Physics, Boston University, College of Liberal Arts; Co-founder, Director, past President and past Chairman, Tachisto Laser Systems Inc, 1971-85; Visiting Professor of Physics, University of Western Ontario, Faculty of Science, London, Ontario, Canada, 1972-74; Director, Spectrametrics Inc, 1972-80; Honorary Professor of Physics, University of Western Ontario, Faculty of Science, Canada, 1974-; Director, Chief of Science Advisory Board, General Ionex Inc, 1974-85; Professor of Physics, Boston University, College of Liberal Arts, 1983-91; Professor of Physics Emeritus, Boston University, College of Arts and Sciences, 1991-. Publications; Numerous (as co-author) in professional journals and conferences. Honours: Special Merit Award, American Association of Physics Teachers, 1971; Sigma Xi, 1950-, President, Boston University Chapter, 1984-86. Memberships: American Physical Society, 1951-; American Association of Physics Teachers, 1962-; Institute of Electrical and Electronic Engineers (formerly Radio Engineers). Address: 1019 Spyglass Lane, Naples, FL 34102-7734, USA.

EDMONDS Philip Hanbury, b. 25 April 1940, Sydney, Australia. Real Estate and Business Valuer. m. Janet Gibson, 1 daughter. Education: BEcon (Hons), Sydney University. Appointments: Managing Director, Pacific Securities Pty Ltd, 1972-, Tasman Securities Pty Ltd, 1981-; Edmonds and Associates P/L, 1985. Memberships: Fellow, Australian Property Institute; Fellow, Chartered Institute of Secretaries; Certified Practising Accountant. Address: 44 Harbour Street, Mosman, NSW 2088, Australia.

EDWARDS Anthony, b. 19 July 1962, Santa Barbara, California, USA. Actor. m. Jeanine Lobell, 1994, 4 children. Education: RADA, London. Appointments: Member, Santa Barbara Youth Theatre in 30 productions, aged 12-17; Commercials aged 16; Stage appearance: Ten Below, New York, 1993. Actor, films: Fast Times at Ridgemont High, 1982; Heart Like a Wheel, 1982; Revenge of the Nerds, 1984; The Sure Thing, 1985; Gotcha!, 1985; Top Gun, 1985; Summer Heat, 1987; Revenge of the Nerds II, 1987; Mr North, 1988; Miracle Mile, 1989; How I Got Into College, 1989; Hawks, 1989; Downtown, 1990; Delta Heat, 1994; The Client, 1994; Us Begins with You, 1998; Don't Go Breaking My Heart, 1999; Jackpot, 2001; Northfork, 2003; Thunderbirds, 2004; The Forgotten, 2004; Zodiac, 2007. TV series: It Takes Two, 1982-83; Northern Exposure, 1992-93; ER, 1994-; Soul Man; TV films: The Killing of Randy Webster, 1981; High School USA, 1983; Going for Gold: The Bill Johnson Story, 1985; El Diablo, 1990; Hometown Boy Makes Good, 1990; In Cold Blood, 1996; TV specials: Unpublished Letters; Sexual Healing. Address: c/o United Talent Agency, 9560 Wilshire Boulevard, Suite 500, Beverly Hills, CA 90212, USA.

EDWARDS Blake, b. 26 July 1922, Tulsa, OK, USA. Film Director; Screen Writer. m. (1) Patricia Walker, 1953-67 (divorced), 2 children, (2) Julie Andrews, 1969, 2 children. Appointments: US Coast Guard Reserve WWII; Writer for radio shows: Johnny Dollar; Line-Up; Writer, Creator: Richard Diamond; Creator TV shows: Dante's Inferno; Peter Gunn; Mr Lucky; Co-producer and writer: Panhandle, 1947; Stampede, 1948; Writer on films: All Ashore, 1952; Sound Off, 1952; Cruisin' Down the River, 1953; Drive a Crooked Road, 1954; My Sister Eileen (musical version), 1955; Operation Mad Ball, 1957; Notorious Landlady, 1962; The Pink Panther, 2005; Director, writer, films include: Bring Your Smile Along, 1955; He Laughed Last, 1955; Mr Cory, 1956; This Happy Feeling, 1958; Director, films: Operation Petticoat, 1959; High Time, 1960; Breakfast at Tiffany's, 1961; Days of Wine and Roses, 1962; The Carey Treatment, 1972; Producer, co-writer, director: The Soldier in the Rain, 1963; The Pink Panther, 1964; A Shot in the Dark, 1964; What Did You Do in the War, Daddy, 1966; Peter Gunn, 1967; The Party, 1968; Darling Lili, 1969; Wild Rovers, 1971; The Tamarind Seed, 1974; The Return of the Pink Panther, 1975; The Pink Panther Strikes Again, 1976; Revenge of the Pink Panther, 1978; 10, 1979; SOB, 1980; Victor/Victoria, 1981; Trail of the Pink Panther, 1982; Curse of the Pink Panther, 1983; Blind Date, 1986; Sunset, 1988; Skin Deep, 1989; Switch, 1991; Son of the Pink Panther, 1993; The Pink Panther, 2006. Producer, writer: Experiment in Terror, 1962; Co-writer, director: The Great Race, 1964; Writer, director, co-producer: Victor/Victoria (stage musical), Broadway, 1995. Address: c/o Blake Edwards Company, Suite 501, 10520 Wilshire Boulevard, Apt 1002, Los Angeles, CA 90024, USA.

EDWARDS F Gary, b. 3 August 1943, Melbourne, Australia. Company Director; Architect; Health Facility Planner. m. Kathryn Winford, 1979, 1 stepson, 1 stepdaughter, 1 daughter. Education: Certificate in Architectural Draftsmanship, Royal Melbourne Institute of Technology, 1967; Diploma in Architectural Design, University of Melbourne, 1974; Architectural Registration, Architects' Registration Board of Victoria, 1975; Diploma in Architecture, Royal Melbourne Institute of Technology, 1976; Accreditation Certificate, Architects' Accreditation Council of Australia, 1991; Certificate, Computer Aided Drafting, Box Hill College of Technical and Further Education, Victoria, 1993. Appointments: Draftsman, then Architect, Stephenson and Turner Architects, Melbourne, 1961-83; Associate and Senior Health Facility Planner, Stephenson and Turner Architects, Australasia, 1983-91; Co-founding Principal, Health Facilities Consultant Architects, 1991-; Co-founding Director, Health Planners Australia Pty Ltd, 1993-98, Newpolis Pty Ltd, 1996-98, and ArcHealth Pty Ltd, 2000-; Honorary Practice Board Member, Lecturer, Awards Assessor, and Contracts, Fees and Complaints Committees Convenor, The Royal Australian Institute of Architects, 1978-; Honorary Councillor, RAIA Victorian Chapter, 1990-94; Architectural Practice Examiner, Architects' Registration Board of Victoria, 1980-; Honorary Committee Member, and Vice President, Bestchance-Child and Family Care, 1981-; Honorary Life Governor, Burwood Children's Homes-CFCN, 1986-; Senior Lecturer, Architectural Practice, RMIT University, 1995-97. Publications: Papers and articles in professional journals; Numerous architectural practice guidenotes, health facility planning guidelines and Standard Building Contracts. Honours: Applied Art Prize, Scotch College, Melbourne, 1960; Inaugural Art Prize, Stephenson and Turner, Melbourne, 1971; Recognition for Design Thesis (on Facilities for Care of Aged and Disabled), University of Melbourne, 1973; Honorary Life Governor, Burwood Children's Homes, 1986; Planning of

Freemason's Hospital Day Procedure and Women's Health Centre, Melbourne, which received the BOMA Award for Excellence, 1993; Certificate of Recognition for Contribution and Commitment to the Advancement of Architecture, Royal Australian Institute of Architects, 1994; Inaugural President's Award for Outstanding Contribution to the Profession of Architecture and the RAIA, RAIA, Victorian Chapter, 1995; Certificate of Appreciation for Voluntary Service to the Community, Premier of Victoria, 2001; Certificate of Appreciation in Recognition of over 35 years Voluntary Service to the Liberal Party of Australia and the Highfield Park Branch, 2005; Certificate of Appreciation for Generous Support to Upgrading of Camberwell Sportsground Pavilion, Old Scotch Football Club, Melbourne, 2006-07; International Health Professional of the Year for Innovative Health Facilities Architecture, IBC, 2007; Lifetime Achievement Award, for contributions to Health Architecture, Community and Business, The World Congress of Arts, Sciences and Communications, 2007. Memberships: Fellow, Royal Australian Institute of Architects; Chartered Member, Royal Institute of British Architects; Member, Association of Consulting Architects of Australia; Member, Institute of Hospital Engineering Australia; Member, Australian Institute of Company Directors; Associate Member, Royal Melbourne Institute of Technology; Member, Order of International Fellowship. Address: Health Facilities Consultant Architects, 10 Cochran Ave, Camberwell, VIC 3124, Australia. E-mail: hfca@bigpond.com

EDWARDS Gareth Owen, CBE, b. 12 July 1947. Rugby Union Player (retired); Businessman. m. Maureen Edwards, 1972, 2 sons. Education: Cardiff College of Education. Appointments: Welsh Secondary Schools Rugby international, 1965-66; English Schools 200 yards Champion (UK under 19 record holder), 1966; Welsh national team: 53 caps, 1967-78; Captain 13 times, youngest captain (aged 20), 1968; Played with clubs: Cardiff, 1966-78; Barbarians, 1967-78; British Lions, 1968, 1971, 1974; Joint Director, Euro-Commercials (South Wales) Ltd, 1982-; Players (UK) Ltd, 1983-889 Chairman, Hamdden Ltd, 1991-; Chairman, Regional Fisheries Advisory Committee, Welsh Water Authority, 1983-89; Commentator for BBC and S4C. Publications: Gareth - An Autobiography, 1978; Rugby Skills, 1979; Gareth Edwards on Rugby, 1986; Gareth Edwards' 100 Great Rugby Players, 1987. Address: Hamdden Ltd, Plas y Ffynnon, Cambrian Way, Brecon, Powys, LD3 7HP, Wales.

EDWARDS Harold (Harry) Raymond, b. 10 January 1927, Sydney, Australia. Economist. m. Elaine Lance, 18 August 1951, 1 son, 4 daughters. Education: BA, Honours, Sydney, 1948; DPhil, Oxford, 1957; Hon DLitt, Macquarie University, 1992. Appointments: Professor of Economics, University of Sydney, 1962-; Foundation Professor, Economics, Founder, Graduate School of Management, Macquarie University, 1966-72; Member of Parliament, Shadow Minister for Industry, Science, Finance, Leader of Australian Parliament Delegation and Member of International Executive, Inter-Parliamentary Union, Geneva, 1978-82, inaugurated National Prayer Breakfast, 1986, House of Representatives, Canberra, Parliament of Australia, 1972-93; Microfinance Consultant, Development Economics, Adviser 1985- and First Chairman of the Board, Opportunity International Australia Ltd, Overseas Aid Organisation; Emeritus Professor, Macquarie University, 1993-. Publications: Competition and Monopoly in the British Soap Industry, OUP, 1962; Articles in various journals. Honours: Queen Elizabeth Silver Jubilee Medal, 1977; Australia Centenary Medal, 2003; Member of the Order of Australia, AM, 2005. Memberships: Fellow,

Academy of the Social Sciences in Australia; Fellow, Australian Institute of Management; Layman, Uniting Church in Australia. Address: 12 John Savage Crescent, West Pennant Hills, NSW 2125, Australia.

EDWARDS Howell G M, b. 22 April 1943, Neath, Glamorgan, Wales. University Professor. m. Gillian Patricia, 1 daughter. Education: BA, 1966, D Phil, 1968, Chemistry, Oxford University; SERC Research Fellow, Cambridge University, 1968-69; Lecturer, Reader, Professor, University of Bradford, 1969-. Appointments: Reader, Molecular Spectroscopy, 1989; Personal Chair, Professor of Molecular Spectroscopy, 1996; Head, Division of Chemical & Forensic Sciences, University of Bradford, England, 2006. Publications: Over 750 publications in literature on applications of Raman spectroscopy to art/ archaeology, forensic science, astrobiology; Book, Handbook of Raman Spectroscopy: From Research Laboratory to Process Line, 2001; Book, Raman Spectroscopy in Archaeology & Art History, 2005. Honours: Sir Harold Thompson Award, Elsevier Science, 2005. Memberships: Fellow, Royal Society of Chemistry, London; Vice-Chair, Molecular Spectroscopy Group, RSC; Member, UK Astrobiology Society; ExoMARS, Raman/LIBS Team, European Space Agency. Address: Chemical & Forensic Sciences, School of Life Sciences, University of Bradford, Bradford BD7 1DP, England. E-mail: h.g.m.edwards@bradford.ac.uk

EDWARDS Jonathan, CBE, b. 10 May 1966, London, England. Athlete. m. Alison Joy Briggs, 2 sons. Career: Athlete, Bronze Medal, World Championships, 1993; Gold Medal, Fifth Athletics World Championships, Gothenburg, twice breaking own record for triple jump, clearing 18.29m, 1995, Edmonton, 2001; Silver Medal, Olympic Games, Atlanta, 1996; World Championships, 1997, 1999; Gold Medal, European Championships, 1998; European Indoor Championships, 1998; Goodwill Games, 1998; Sports Fellowship, University of Durham, 1999; Olympic Games, 2000; World Championships, 2001; Commonwealth Games, 2002; Retired from athletics after 2003 World Championships; Currently working mainly for the BBC as a sports commentator and presenter of programmes including Songs of Praise; Member London Organising Committee for the Olympic Games, 2012. Publication: A Time to Jump, 2000. Honours: BBC Sportsman of the Year, 1995; IAAF Athlete of the Year, 1995; BBC Sports Personality of the Year, 1995; British Male Athlete of the Year, 1995, 2000, 2001; CBE; Honorary Doctorate, University of Exeter, 2006; Duniv, University of Ulster, 2006. Address: c/o Jonathan Marks, MTC, 20 York Street, London W1U 6PU, England. E-mail: info@mtc-uk.com Website: www.mtc-uk.com

EDWARDS Philip Walter, b. 7 February 1923, Cumbria, England. Retired Professor of English; Writer. m. Sheila Mary Wilkes, 8 May 1952, 3 sons, 1 daughter. Education: BA, 1942, MA, 1946, PhD, 1960, University of Birmingham. Appointments: Lecturer, University of Birmingham, 1946-60; Professor, Trinity College, Dublin, 1960-66, University of Essex, 1966-74, University of Liverpool, 1974-90. Publications: Sir Walter Raleigh, 1953; Kyd, The Spanish Tragedy, 1959; Shakespeare and the Confines of Art, 1968; Massinger: Plays and Poems, 1976; Shakespeare's Pericles, 1976; Threshold of a Nation, 1979; Hamlet, 1985; Shakespeare: A Writers Progress, 1986; Last Voyages, 1988; The Story of the Voyage, 1994; Sea-Mark, 1997; The Journals of Captain Cook, 1999; Pilgrimage and Literary Tradition, 2005. Membership: British Academy, fellow, 1986-. Address: High Gillinggrove, Gillinggate, Kendal, Cumbria LA9 4JB, England.

EDWARDS Robert, b. 27 September 1925. Physiologist. m. Ruth E Fowler, 1956, 5 daughters. Education: University of Wales; University of Edinburgh. Appointments: Research Fellow, California Institute of Technology, 1957-58; Scientist, National Institute of Medical Research, Mill Hill, 1958-62; Glasgow University, 1962-63; Department of Physiology, University of Cambridge, 1963-89; Ford Foundation Reader in Physiology, 1969-85; Professor of Human Reproduction, 1985-89, Professor Emeritus, 1989-, University of Cambridge. Publications: A Matter of Life, with P C Steptoe, 1980; Conception in the Human Female, 1980; Mechanisms of Sex Differentiation in Animals and Man, with C R Austin, 1982; Human Conception in Vitro, with J M Purdy, 1982; Implantation of the Human Embryo, with J M Purdy and P C Steptoe, 1985; In Vitro Fertilisation and Embryo Transfer, with M Seppala, 1985; Life Before Birth, 1989; Numerous articles in scientific and medical journals. Honours: Honorary Member, French Society for Infertility; Honorary Citizen of Bordeaux; Hon FRCOG; Hon MRCP; Hon DSc (Hull, York, Free University Brussels); Gold Medal, Spanish Fertility Society, 1985; King Faisal Award, 1989. Memberships: Fellow, Churchill College, Cambridge, now Extraordinary Fellow; Scientific Director, Bourn Hall Clinics, Cambridge and London; Chair, European Society of Human Reproduction and Embryology, 1984-86; Visiting Scientist, Johns Hopkins University, 1965, University of North Carolina, 1966, Free University of Brussels, 1984; Honorary President, British Fertility Society, 1988-; Life Fellow, Australian Fertility Society; Chief Editor, Human Reproduction, 1986-. Address: Duck End Farm, Dry Drayton, Cambridge, CB3 8DB, England.

EDWARDS-NIXON Jennifer Veronica, b. 21 October 1956, Grenada. Certified Assistant Audiologist Speech Language Pathologist. m. Jude V Nixon, 2 sons, 1 daughter. Education: Cambridge University, England; Truett McConnell College, Cleveland, USA; Baylor University, Texas; California Colleges for Health Sciences, California. Appointments: Clinician, Laboratory Assistant, Electroneurodiagnostic & Intraoperative Monitoring; Assistant Audiologist Speech Language Pathologist, Immunopathology and Histology; Science Teacher/Supervisor Research Project Leader, Kiddy College; Co-ordinator Psychiatric Nursing. Publications: Composer, Move On (music lyrics on CD); 10 poems. Honours: Academic Rotary Scholarship; Principal's Prize, St George's University School of Medicine; Golden Key National Honor Society Academic Scholarship; William Beaumont Hospital Service Excellence Profession, WBH. Memberships: American Baptist Churches of Michigan Diversity Council; William Beaumont Hospital Center for Integrating Body, Mind & Spirit; American Journal of Electroneurodiagnostic Technology; Advance Medical Laboratory Professionals Interactive Communicating. Address: William Beaumont Hospitals, Suite #447, 3535 W 13th Mile Road, Royal Oak, MI 48073, USA. E-mail: jedwardsnixon@beaumonthospitals.com

EFIMOV Alexander Vasilievich, b. 12 May 1954, Lugovaya, Orenburg Region, Russia. Chemist. Widower, 1 daughter. Education: Bachelor's Degree, Moscow State University, 1976; Candidate of Science (PhD), 1983; Doctor of Science, Chemistry, 1995. Appointments: Probationer, 1976-79, Junior Researcher, 1979-87, Senior Researcher, 1987-96, Leading Researcher, 1996-1998, Principal Researcher, 1998-, Deputy Director, 2002-, Institute of Protein Research, Russian Academy of Sciences. Publications: Articles in scientific journals including: Journal of Molecular Biology, 1979, 1995; FEBS Letters, 1984, 1987, 1991, 1992, 1993, 1994, 1996, 1997, 1998, 2003; Structure, 1994; Proteins, 1997. Membership:

Scientific Secretary, 1989-2000; Deputy Director, 2002-, Institute of Protein Research. Address: Institute of Protein Research, RAS, 142290 Pushchino, Moscow Region, Russia. E-mail: efimov@protres.ru

EGON Nicholas, b. 15 November 1921, Brno, Czech Republic. Artist. m. Matti Xylas. Education: Private tutors; Birkbeck College, University of London; Magdalen College, Oxford. Appointments: Military Service: Official Czech War Artist in London, 1939-44; Joined British Army, served in Middle East, 1944-46; Senior Lecturer, Fine Art, Sir John Cass College, 1946-50; Artist, commissions included Greek War Memorial, portraits of Greek Royal Family including Queen Sophia of Spain aged 11 years, portraits of several royal families, heads of state, musicians, authors, actors and members of the international aristocracy for public and private collections, 1949-; Painted landscapes of Egypt as a guest of President Nasser of Egypt, 1964; 57 portraits for King Hussein of Jordan and his family, 1965-90; 37 landscapes of Arabia and many portraits for King Feisal of Saudi Arabia, 1966-79; Painted 120 landscapes of Jordan for King Hussein and Queen Noor, 1984-86; Painted landscapes of Iceland for President Vigdis Finbogadottir of Iceland, 1987; 10 solo exhibitions in London and Cambridge, England, 1950-90, also Nicholas Egon in Greece Exhibition, Benaki Museum, Greece, 2007. Publications: Some Beautiful Women (portraits), 1952; Paintings of Jordan (landscapes), 1986; Biography, Nicholas Egon by Fani-Maria Tsigakou, 2007; Collections: National Portrait Gallery, London; National Gallery of Fine Art, Amman, Jordan; Casa Toscanini, Parma; Royal collections: Windsor Castle; Royal Palaces of Saudi Arabia, Jordan, Spain, Oman, Morocco; Donation Francois Mitterand, Jarnac; Private collections: Palazzo Chigi in Siena (32 portraits of musicians); Villa Maser; Chatsworth; Longleat; other international collections. Memberships: Elected Fellow, Royal Society of Arts, 1947; Athenaeum; Annabels; Caryatid & Patron, British Museum; Chairman, Patrons of the Centre for Hellenic Studies, King College University of London; Patron, The Prince of Wales's School for Traditional Arts. Address: 34 Thurloe Square, London, SW7 2SR, England. E-mail: egon@faroship.com

EGTESADI Shahryar, b. 6 November 1952, Sanandaj, Iran. Professor of Clinical Nutrition. m. Akhtar Afshari, 3 daughters. Education: BS, Nutrition Science and Food Chemistry, Shahid Beheshti University, 1975, Tehran; MSPH, Nutrition Science, Tehran University, Teheran, 1977; PhD, Nutrition, University of California, Davis, USA, 1986. Appointments: Instructor, Tabriz University, Tabriz, Iran, 1978-86; Assistant Professor, 1986-90, Associate Professor, 1990-95, Professor, 1995-2002, Associate Dean for Education and Research Affairs, School of Public Health and Nutrition, 2002, Tabriz University of Medical Sciences; Chair, Department of Biochemistry and Nutrition, Tabriz, Iran, 1986-93; Visiting Scientist, Human Nutrition Research Center on Aging, Tufts University, USA, 1995; Chair, Department of Biochemistry and Clinical Nutrition, 1996-98; Head of Research Department, School of Public Health and Nutrition, Tabriz, Iran, 1996-2002; Professor, Iran University of Medical Sciences, School of Public Health, Tehran, 2002-; Chair, Department of Nutrition, Iran University of Medical Sciences, 2004-. Publications: Over 125 articles presented or published in Iranian and international journals and congresses mainly on the topics of regulation of metabolism, nutrition assessments of infants and children, growth pattern and nutrition status of adolescents, nutrition behaviour and food choice of adolescents, food insecurity, Trace Elements and antioxidants nutrition and metabolism, and issues of clinical nutrition. Honours: Distinguished Editor

of Article presented in the Iranian Research Forum, National Research Centre of Iran, Iranian Ministry of Science, 1999; Distinguished Scientist of Tabriz University of Medical Sciences, School of Public Health and Nutrition, 2000; Listed in Great Minds of 21st Century, ABI, 2001; Distinguished Scientist, Iran University of Medical Sciences, School of Public Health, 2002; Honoured Professor, Iranian Ministry of Health and Medical Education, 2006 and 2007. Memberships: Iranian Society of Nutrition; Iranian Society of Physiology and Pharmacology; Iranian Board of Nutrition; Ministry of Health and Medical Education of Iran, 2000-. Address: Iran University of Medical Sciences, School of Public Health, Dept of Nutrition, Argentina Square, Alvand Street, Tehran, Iran. E-mail: egtesadi@iums.ac.ir

EHLE Jennifer, b. 29 December 1969, Winston-Salem, North Carolina, USA. Actress. m. Michael Ryan, 2001, 1 son. Education: Central School of Speech and Drama. Career: Theatre includes: Summerfolk; The Relapse; The Painter of Dishonour; Richard III, 1996; Tartuffe; The Real Thing, 1999, 2000; The Philadelphia Story, 2005; TV includes: the Camomile Lawn, 1992; Micky Love, The Maitlands, 1993; Self Catering, Pleasure, La Récréation, 1994; Beyond Reason, Pride and Prejudice, 1995; Melissa, 1997; Films: Backbeat, 1994; Paradise Road, Wilde, 1997; Bedrooms and Hallways, 1998; This Year's Love, Sunshine, 1999; Possession, 2002; The River King, 2005; Alpha Male, 2006; Before the Rains, 2007; Pride and Glory, 2008. Honours: Tony Award, Best Actress, 2000; BAFTA Award, Best Actress, 1995. Address: c/o ICM, 76 Oxford Street, London W1N 0AX, England.

EHRENHAFT Peter D, b. 16 August 1933, Vienna, Austria (naturalised in USA, 1945). Law. m. Charlotte, 2 sons, 1 daughter. Education: AB (Honours), Columbia College, 1954; LLB and MIA (Honours), Columbia University Schools of Law and International Affairs, 1957; Bar Admissions: New York, 1958; District of Columbia, 1961; US Supreme Court, US Courts of Appeals for the DC, Federal, 2nd and 3rd Circuits, US Court of International Trade. Appointments: Government Service: Motions Law Clerk, US Court of Appeals for the DC Circuit, 1957-58; Senior Law Clerk to the Chief Justice of the United States, Earl Warren, 1961-62; Deputy Assistant Secretary and Special Counsel (Tariff Affairs), US Department of the Treasury, 1977-79; The Executive (Reserve), Office of the Judge Advocate General, USAF, 1980-85; Staff Judge Advocate (Reserve) HQ US Air Forces Europe, 1985-87; Judge (Reserve), Air Force Court of Military Review, 1987-88; Retired as Colonel; Private Employment: Associate, 1962-66, Partner, 1966-68, Cox, Lanford & Brown; Partner, Fried, Frank, Harris, Shriver & Kampelman, 1968-77; Partner, Hughes Hubbard & Reed, 1980-84; Partner, Bryan Cave, 1984-94, (Vice Chairman, International, Corporate and Business Department); Shareholder, Ablondi, Foster, Sobin & Davidow, pc, 1995-2001; Of Counsel, 2004-06, previously Member, Miller & Chevalier Chartered, 2001-03; Senior Counsel, Harkins Cunningham LLP, 2007-. Publications: Numerous articles in professional journals; 10 book reviews. Honours: Exceptional Service Award, Department of Treasury, 1979; Legion of Merit, US Air Force, 1988. Memberships: American Law Institute; American Bar Association; American Society of International Law; Washington Foreign Law Society; American Arbitration Association, Patent and International Arbitrators Panels; Advisory Board of Georgetown University International Law Journal; Advisory Board, Bureau of National Affairs; Patent, Copyright & Trademark Journal. Address: Harkins Cunningham, LLP, 1700 K Street, NW Suite 400, Washington, DC 20006-3804, USA. E-mail: pde@harkinscunningham.com

DICTIONARY OF INTERNATIONAL BIOGRAPHY

EHRNST Anneka Cecilia, b. 29 October 1945, Ostersund, Sweden. Physician, Scientist. m. Robert Grundin, 2 sons. Education: MD, 1972, PhD, 1978, Associate Professor 1980, Karolinska Institute; Specialist in Clinical Immunology, 1980; Specialist in Clinical Virology, 1983; Postdoctoral training at Harvard Medical School, 1981-82. Appointments: Laboratory Physician, 1973-82; Deputy Head, Polio Vaccine Development, National Bacterial Laboratory, 1982-83; Clinical Virologist: Stockholm Municipal Laboratory, 1983-93, Huddinge University Hospital, 1993-2003, Karolinska University Hospital, Huddinge, 2004-.; Deputy Head, Clinical Virology, 1992-95; Researcher Microbiology Tumorbiology Centre, Karolinska Institute, Stockholm, 1996-, Adjunct Professor 2004. Publications: Over 100 publications in international medical and scientific journals; approximately 100 presentations at scientific meetings; Scientific Secretary and Editor of Proceedings, V International CMV Conference. Memberships include: New York Academy of Science; European Society Clinical Virology; National Geographic Society; Others. Address: Microbiology and Tumorbiology Centre, Box 280, Karolinska Institute, SE 171 77 Stockholm, Sweden.

EIDERMAN Boris, b. 23 February 1934, Kharkov, Ukraine, USSR. Mechanics Researcher. m. Susanna Nuger, 1 son. Education: MSc, Engineer-Mechanic, Mining Institute, Kharkov, 1957; PhD, 1968, Dr Sci, 1986, Professorship, 1989, Academy, Mining Institute, Moscow. Appointments: Engineer and Designer of Mining Machinery, Machine Build Works, Kharkov, 1957-61; Head, Mechanics Section, Mining Institute, Kharkov, 1961-66; Senior Scientist, Leading Scientist, Professor, Mechanisation Section, Academy Mining Institute, Moscow, 1967-91; Scientist, Researcher, College of Technology, Jerusalem, Israel, 1992-93; Chief Scientist, Sortech Separation Technologies Ltd, Jerusalem, Israel, 1997-2003; Consultant, 2004-. Publications: Mechanisms for Formation of Traffic and Energy Expenditure of Conveyors, 1984; Parameters and Calculation Methods for Conveyors, 1987; Scraper Conveyors, 1993; Triboclassification Technology for Minerals and Fly Ash, 2000; Triboclassification Technology for Bulk Powder, 2001; Development of a high productivity Tribo-Classifier for mining 2003. Honours: Prize Winner, USSR Council of Ministers, 1983; Grantee, Ministry of Industry and Trade of Israel, 1992, 1997. Memberships: Forum for Bulk Solids Handling. Address: Home: Gvirtsman Moshe str 6/4, 97793 Jerusalem, Israel. E-mail: boris@eiderman.com

EIGEN Manfred, b. 9 May 1927, Ruhr, Germany. Physical Chemist. m. Elfriede Müller, 1 son, 1 daughter. Education: Doctorate, Göttingen University, 1951. Appointments: Assistant, Professor, Head of Department, 1953-, Director, 1964, Max-Planck Institute of Physical Chemistry, Göttingen; Honorary Professor, Technical University, Göttingen, 1971-; President, Studienstiftung des Deutschen Volkes, 1983-. Honours: Hon Dr, University of Washington, St Louis University, Harvard University, Cambridge University; Numerous other honorary degrees; Foreign Honorary Member, American Academy of Arts and Sciences; Otto Hahn Prize, 1967; Joint Winner, Nobel Prize for Chemistry, 1967. Memberships: Akademie der Wissenschaften, Göttingen; Foreign Associate Member, National Academy of Sciences, USA; Foreign Member, Royal Society, UK; Academie Française, 1978. Address: Georg-Dehio-Weg 14, 37075, Germany.

EISENREICH Günther, b. 12 April 1933, Leipzig, Germany. Retired Professor of Mathematics. m. Gisela Busse. Education: Studies in Mathematics, Physics and Biology, 1951-56; Degree in Mathematics, 1956; Doctor of Natural Sciences, 1963; Habilitation in Natural sciences, 1968. Appointments: Scientific Worker, Saxon Academy of Sciences, Leipzig, 1957-58; Scientific Assistant, 1959-67; Senior Assistant, 1967-69; University Docent, Mathematical Section, 1969-70, Professor of Theoretical Mathematics, 1970-98, (appointments delayed for political reasons), University of Leipzig. Publications: Books: Vorlesungen über Vektor–und Tensorrechnung; Lineare Algebra und Analytische Geometrie; Vorlesung über Funktionentheorie mehrerer Variabler; Lexikon der Algebra; Fachwörterbuch Mathematik Englisch/Deutsch/Französisch/Russisch; Fachwörterbuch Physik Englisch/Deutsch/ Französisch/Russisch; Articles on mathematics, biology, philosophy, linguistics and biographies which include: Untersuchungen über Ideale in Stellenringen; Eine Dualitätsbeziehung zwischen s-Moduln; Zur Syzygientheorie und Theorie des inversen Systems perfekter Ideale und Vektormoduln in Polynomringen und Stellenringen; Zum Wahrheitsproblem in der Mathematik; Numerous reviews, translations of Scientific books from the English, French, Russian and Hungarian. Honour: General Honouring for Scientific Success, Education of students and Democratizing the University. Memberships: Deutsche Mathematiker-Vereinigung, 1990-98; Mathematische Gesellschaft der DDR; Deutscher Hochschulverband, Speaker of the Saxons; Federation of Trade Unions. Address: Gartenbogen 7, D-04288 Leipzig, Germany.

EISERMANN Walter Friedrich, b. 5 April 1922, Hamburg, Germany. Professor of Educational Sciences. 2 sons. Education: Business Diploma, Hamburg, 1941; Teaching Certificate, Hamburg University, 1957; Doctor of Philosophy, Tuebingen University, 1958. Appointments: Teacher, Second Public Schools, Hamburg, 1958-60; Docent, Teachers Colleges, Stuttgart, Ludwigsburg, 1960-64; Professor, Low Saxony College of Education, Braunschweig, 1964-78; Vice Dean, 1965, Advanced Professor, 1970, Professor, Braunschweig Technical University, 1978-89; Professor Emeritus, 1989; Head, Eduard Spranger Archives, 1980-97. Publications include: 80 including: Ueber die Moeglichkeit einer Gewissenserziehung, 1958; Eduard Spranger: Psychologie und Menschenbildung, 1974; Zwischen Gewalt und Frieden in einem doppelgesichtigen Jahrhundert, 2008. Awards: Book of Honour, Zur Kritik und Neuorientierung der Paedagogik, 1987. Memberships: World Education Fellowship, 1950-; International Academy of Humanisation of Education, Russia, 1995-; New York Academy of Sciences, 1996-. Address: Tiergarten 95, D-38116 Braunschweig, Germany.

EISNER Michael Dammann, b. 7 March 1942, Mt Kisco, New York, USA. Entertainment Executive. m. Jane Breckenridge, 1967, 3 sons. Education: Denison University. Appointments: Senior Vice President, prime-time production and development, ABC Entertainment Corporation, 1973-76; President, COO, Paramount Pictures Corporation, 1976-84; Chairman and Chief Executive Officer, 1984-2004, CEO, 2004-05, Member of Board of Directors, 2005-06, The Walt Disney Company; Established Eisner Foundation.. Publications: The Keys to the Kingdom; Disney War. Honour: Légion d'honneur. Memberships: Board of Directors, California Institute of the Arts, Denison University; American Hospital of Paris Foundation; UCLA Executive Board for Medical Sciences; National Hockey League (ice hockey); Business Steering Committee of the Global Business

Dialogue on Electronic Commerce; The Business Council. Address: Walt Disney Company, 500 South Buena Vista Street, Burbank, CA 91521, USA.

EKLAND Elle, b. 6 March 1974, United Kingdom. Spokesmodel/Ambassador, World's Most Expensive Perfume; CEO President, Elle Ekland Enterprises. Education: BA (Hons), University of London. Appointments: St Jude Dedication Ceremony; Elton John White Tie & Tiara Ball, UK; Queen's 80th Anniversary Gift Presentation; V&A Museum, London; World's Most Expensive Perfume Launch, Dubai, New York City Los Angeles, Washington DC, Las Vegas. Publications: Town & Country; Avenue; New York Post; Vanity Fair; New York Observer; The Standard; GQ Magazine; The Times; The Guardian; New York Esquire; Tatler. Honours: St Jude Childrens Research Hospital Tribute. Memberships: Colony Club, New York. Address: 415 East 37th St, Apt 26D, New York, NY 10016, USA. E-mail: elleekland@aol.com

EL GAZAERLY Hanaa Mohamed, b. Egypt. Professor. m. Hassan Khalifa, 2 sons, 1 daughter. Education: BDS, MSc, PhD, Oral Pathology, Faculty of Dentistry, Alexandria University, 1977-87. Appointments: Lecturer, 1987, Associate Professor, 1992, Professor, 1997, Oral Pathology Department, Faculty of Dentistry, Tanta University. Publications: Numerous articles in professional journals. Honours: Certificate of Appreciation for Special Efforts in Dental Sciences, 1997-98; University Encouragement Award in Medical Sciences, Tanta University, 2000. Memberships: Oral Pathology Society; Egyptian Association of Dental Excellence; Quality Assurance Committee, Tanta University. Address: 4 Alayly Stre, From Eqbal Str, Louran, Alexandria, Egypt. E-mail: hanaa.gazaerly@gmail.com

EL HARIRI-HADDAD Khadîdja, b. 1 January 1932, Saida au Liban (French national). Doctor. m. Ghassan Haddad. Education: Diplômée d'un doctorat d'état en Sociologie. Appointments: Professor of Sociology; Participation in many seminars and scientific conferences. Publications: Many books and research projects on social aspects of Averroes. Address: 7 Allée du Bosquet, 92310 Sevres, France.

EL MIEDANY Yasser, b. 30 June 1961, Alexandria, Egypt. Professor of Rheumatology and Rehabilitation. m. Sally Sayed Youssef, 2 sons, 2 daughters. Education: MBChB, Ain Shams University, Cairo, Egypt, 1984; Diploma in Internal Medicine, 1987; MSc, Rheumatology and Rehabilitation, 1989; MD, Rheumatology and Rehabilitation, 1994; GMC Registration, 2001; FRCP (London). Appointments: House Officer, Ain Shams University Hospitals; Senior House Officer, General Medicine Department, 1986-87, General Medicine, Rheumatology and Rehabilitation Department, 1987-90, Registrar, Rheumatology and Rehabilitation Department, 1990-91, Registrar, Assistant Lecturer, 1992-94, Consultant, Lecturer, 1994-95, 1997-2001, Consultant, Associate Professor, 2001-, Ain Shams University Hospitals and Ain Shams University Specialist Hospital, Ain Sham University; Registrar, Glasgow Royal Infirmary, Centre for Rheumatic Diseases, 1991-92; Consultant Rheumatologist, Saudi German Hospital, Jeddah, Saudi Arabia, 1995-97; Consultant Rheumatologist (locum) Broomfield Hospital, Chelmsford, England, 2001-2002; Consultant Rheumatologist (locum), Princess Royal Hospital Haywards Heath, England, 2002; Consultant Rheumatologist (locum), North Hampshire Hospital Basingstoke, England, 2003; Consultant Rheumatologist, Darent Valley Hospital, Dartford, England, 2003-; Professor, Rheumatology & Rehabilitation, Ain Shams University, Cairo, Egypt, 2005-. Publications: Book: Basic Rheumatology for Postgraduates, 1995, 2001; Numerous articles as co-author in medical journals. Honour: Health Professional of the Year 2004. Memberships: Fellow, American College of Rheumatology; British Society for Rheumatology; Royal College of Physicians; Paediatric International Rheumatology Organisation; American Association for Diabetes Mellitus; Egyptian Society for Rheumatology and Rehabilitation. Address: 2 Italian Hospital Street, Abbassia, Cairo, Egypt 11381. E-mail: yasser_elmiedany@yahoo.com Website: www.dryasserelmiedany.egydoc.com

EL-BAZ Farouk, b. 1 January 1938, Zagazig, Egypt. Geologist; Educator; Researcher. m. Catherine Patricia O'Leary, 4 daughters. Education: BSc, Ain Shams University, Egypt, 1958; MS, Missouri School of Mines, 1961; PhD, University of Missouri, 1964. Appointments: Assiut University, 1958-69; Heidelberg University, Germany, 1964-66; Belcomm Inc, 1967-72; Smithsonian Institution, 1973-82; Itek Optical Systems, 1982-86; Director and Research Professor, Center for Remote Sensing, Boston University, Boston, Massachusetts, USA, 1986-. Publications: Say It In Arabic, 1968; The Moon as Viewed by Lunar Orbiter, 1970; Apollo Over the Moon, 1978; Astronaut Observations from the Apollo-Soyuz Mission, 1977; Egypt as Seen by Landsat, 1979; Apollo-Soyuz Test Project: Earth Observations and Photography, 1979; The Geology of Egypt: An Annotated Bibliography, 1984; Physics of Desertification, 1986; The Gulf War and the Environment, 1994; Atlas of Kuwait from Satellite Images, 2000; Wadis of Oman, 2002; Sultanate of Oman: Satellite Image Atlas, 2004. Honours: NASA Apollo Achievement Award; Order of Merit First Class, Egypt; Nevada Medal; Pioneer Award (Arab Thought Foundation); Golden Door Award, International Institute of Boston; Honorary Doctorates: New England College, New Hampshire, 1989; Mansoura University, Egypt, 2003; American University in Cairo, Egypt, 2004; University of Missouri-Rolla, 2004. Memberships: Royal Astronomical Society; US National Academy of Engineering; African Academy of Sciences; Arab Academy of Sciences; Academy of Sciences for the Developing World; Geological Society of America; American Association for the Advancement of Science; Explorers Club. Address: Center for Remote Sensing, 725 Commonwealth Avenue, Boston University, Boston, MA 02215, USA. E-mail: farouk@bu.edu

EL-RAYES Ehab, b. 20 December 1964, Egypt. Professor; Doctor. m. Rasha Gamal, 1 son, 1 daughter. Education: MD, MBCh, 1986; Master's degree, Ophthalmology, 1990; PhD, Ophthalmology, 1994; MD, Ophthalmology, 1992; Fellowship, Vitreo Retinal Surgery, 1995. Appointments: Professor, Ophthalmology Research Institute; Chief Consultant, Vitreo Retina Surgery, International Eye Hospital; Consultant, Speciality Eye Hospital, Cairo; Fellow, Associated Retinal Consultant, USA. Publications: Over 100 publications worldwide covering Ophthalmic Surgery and Ophthalmic Research. Honours: Pan Arab Amin Magraby Award, 2002. Memberships: American Academy of Ophthalmology; American Retina Specialist; Pan Arab Council of Ophthalmology. Address: 35 Salah Salem, #702, El-Borg, El-Obour Bldg, Cairo 11761, Egypt. E-mail: erayes1@hotmail.com

EL-SHARKAWY Mabrouk A, b. 7 April 1937, Shobratana, Gharbia Governate, Egypt. Scientist. m. Stella Navarro, 1 daughter. Education: BSc honours, Agriculture, Alexandria University, Egypt, 1958; Research Assistant, National Research Centre, Dokki, Cairo, 1958-60; Graduate Student, Louisiana State University and University of Arizona, 1960-65; MSc, Agronomy, Louisiana State University, 1962;

DICTIONARY OF INTERNATIONAL BIOGRAPHY

PhD, Agronomy, University of Arizona, 1965. Appointments: Associate Plant Physiologist, University of California at Davis, 1965-66; Crop Physiologist, Ministry of Agriculture, Cairo, 1966-68; Professor, University of Tripoli, Libya, 1968-78; Head, Agronomy Division, Faculty of Agriculture, 1972-75; Head, Plant Production, Arab Organization of Agricultural Development, 1978-80; Crop Physiologist, Centro Internacional de Agric Tropical, Cali, Colombia, 1980-97; Co-ordinator and Manager of Integrated Cassava Production Project, 1988-96; Discovered C3/C4 Syndrome in plant photosynthesis, farming sandy soil; Discovery leaf Kranz anatomy and photorespiration reassimilation in C4 photosynthesis species including maize, tropical grasses, amaranthus species; Physiological characteristics cassava productivity in tropics; Discovered mechanisms underlying resistance of cassava to atmospheric and edaphic water-stress; Selection of cassava cultivars drought and poor soils resistant; Integrated cassava production systems in hillside and marginal lands; Characterisation of cassava germ plasm for leaf photosynthesis in relation to crop productivity in humid, seasonally dry and semi-arid environment; Characterisation of cotton germ plasm for leaf photosynthesis; Genetic inheritance of fibre traits in upland cotton; Selection of wheat and barley cultivars for desert conditions; Research on cropping systems, irrigation and plant-soil relationships in Libyan Sahara Desert; Developed method to measure plant photorespiration in CO_2-free air now in use; Developed photosynthesis-based biochemical assay for drought tolerance in Cassava; Scientific advisor, centro de investigacion en Palma de Aceite, Cenipalma, Bogota, Colombia, 1997-2001. Publications: Over 150 in professional journals. Honours: University of Alexandria fellow, 1955-58; University of California fellow, 1965-66; Egyptian Government Scholar, 1959-65; Recipient, Citation Classic Award, Institute of Scientific Information, PA, USA, 1986; Over 1,000 citations in literature, Citation Index ISI; Recognition awards: Universidad Nacional, Palmira,Valle, Colombia, 2005; Universidad del Valle, Cali, Valle, Colombia, 2005; Centro Investigacion, Palmira CORPOICA, Valle, Cali, Colombia, 2005. Memberships: Sigma Xi; New York Academy of Sciences; American Society of Agronomy; Crop Science Society of America; AAAS; American Institute of Biological Sciences, Alpha Zeta. Address: A A 26360 Cali Valle, Colombia, South America. E-mail: elsharkawy@telesat.com.co

ELBERN Victor H, b. 9 June 1918, Düren, Germany. Art Historian. m. Theresia Schager, 2 sons, 1 daughter. Education: University of Bonn; Bacc Phil, Rome Gregorian University; Dr phil, Zurich University; Studies in Philosophy, History, Classical Archaeology, Roman Languages, History of Art. Appointments: Chief Curator, State Museums of Berlin, Early Christian and Byzantine Department; International Exhibitions: Essen, 1956, Brussels Expo, 1958; Honorary Professor, History of Art, Free University, Berlin, 1970; Chairman, Görres-Gesellschaft, 1982-93; Director, Jerusalem Institute Görres-Gesellschaft, 1987-93; Visiting Professor: Tel-Aviv University, 1979, Zurich University, 1983, Jerusalem Hebrew University, 1983. Publications: Der Goldaltar von Mailand, 1952; Das erste Jahrtausend, 3 volumes, 1962-64; Der eucharistische Kelch in frühen Mittelalter, 1964; St Liudger und die Abtei Werden, 1962; Dom und Domschatz in Hildesheim, 1979; Die Goldschmiedekunst in frühen Mittelalter, 1988; Fructus Operis, Gesammelte Aufsätze, 1998; Fructus Operis II, Beiträge liturgische Kunst, 2003; About 500 articles. Honours: Chevalier Couronne de Belgique, 1958; Cavaliere San Silvestro, 1958; Commendatore S Gregorio Magno, 1981; Bundesverdienstkreuz Deutschland, 1983; Grand Officer, Holy Sepulchre, 1990; Silver Palm of

Jerusalem, 1998. Memberships: Société des Antiquaires, Poitiers, 1961; Deutsches Archäologisches Institut, 1980; Braunschweig Wiss Gesellschaft, 1984; Accademia Nazionale dei Lincei Roma, 1988. Address: Ilsensteinweg 42, D-14129 Berlin, Germany.

ELDREDGE Jonathan DeForest, b. 10 March 1954, Boston, Massachusetts, USA. Medical Librarian, Informaticist; Educator. m. Regina Wolfe Eldredge, 1 son, 1 daughter. Education: BA, Cum Laude, Beloit College, Wisconsin, 1976; Master of Library Science, University of Michigan, 1978; MA, Political Science (State Politics), 1985, PhD, Public Policy Analysis, 1993, University of New Mexico. Appointments: Intern, Graduate Library, University of Michigan, 1978; Assistant Librarian for Public Services, Lake Forest College, Illinois, 1979-81; Chief of Outreach Programs, Medical Center Library, University of New Mexico, 1981-82; Library Director, Eastern New Mexico University, 1982-83; Chief Collection Development, Medical Center Library, 1986-96, Lecturer III, School of Medicine, 1986-90, Assistant Professor, School of Medicine, 1990-2004, Chief Collections and Information Resources Department, Health Science Center Library, 1996-2001, Academic and Clinical Services Co-ordinator, Health Sciences Library and Informatics Center, 2004-2004, Associate Professor, School of Medicine, 2004-, Library Knowledge Consultant, Health Sciences Library and Informatics Center, 2005-, University of New Mexico, Albuquerque, New Mexico. Publications: More than 20 articles as author and co-author in peer reviewed journals; 16 review articles and book chapters; 7 invited or contributed presentations at professional meetings; Numerous other writings and scholarly projects. Honours include: Certificate of Recognition, American Library Association/ Library Administration and Management Association, Public Relations Section, 1993; Louise Darling Medal for Distinguished Achievement in Collection Development in the Health Sciences, Medical Library Association, 1999; Staff Certificate of Service Award, Health Sciences Library and Informatics Center, University of New Mexico, 2000; Research Award, Medical Library Association, 2002; William D Postell Professional Development Award, South Central Chapter, Medical Library Association, 2003; Research Award, Medical Library Association, 2006; Hippo Award, University of New Mexico School of Medicine, 2007. Memberships: Medical Library Association including: Research Section, Collection Development Section, Public Health/Health Administration Section; American Library Association; Association of College and Research Libraries; Library Administration and Management Association; Medical Library Association/ South Central Chapter. Address: Health Sciences Library and Informatics Center, University of New Mexico, MSC09 5100, I University of New Mexico, Albuquerque, NM 87131-0001, USA. E-mail: jeldredge@salud.unm.edu

ELDRIDGE Colin Clifford, b. 16 May 1942, Walthamstow, England. Professor of History; Writer. m. Ruth Margaret Evans, 3 August 1970, deceased 2003, 1 daughter. Education: BA, 1963, PhD, 1966, Nottingham University. Appointments: Arts & Social Science Research Fellow, 1966-68, Lecturer, 1968-75, Senior Lecturer in History, 1975-92, Reader, 1992-98, Professor, 1998-, University of Wales. Publications: England's Mission: The Imperial Idea in the Age of Gladstone and Disraeli, 1973; Victorian Imperialism, 1978; Essays in Honour of C D Chandaman, 1980; British Imperialism in the 19th Century, 1984; Empire, Politics and Popular Culture, 1989; From Rebellion to Patriation: Canada & Britain in the Nineteenth & Twentieth Centuries, 1989; Disraeli and the Rise of a New Imperialism, 1996; The Imperial Experience:

From Carlyle to Forster, 1996; The Zulu War, 1879, 1996; Kith and Kin: Canada, Britain and the United States form the Revolution to the Cold War, 1997. Contributions to: Various learned journals. Honour: Fellow, Royal Historical Society. Memberships: Historical Association; Association of History Teachers in Wales; British Association of Canadian Studies; British Australian Studies Association. Address: Tanerdy, Ciliau Aeron, Lampeter, Ceredigion, SA48 8DL, Wales.

ELENAS Anaxagoras, b. 8 January 1960, Hrisoupolis, Greece. Assistant Professor in Civil Engineering. m. Areti Charissi, 1 son, 1 daughter. Education: Dipl-ing, University of Stuttgart, Germany, 1984; Dr-Ing, Ruhr-University of Bochum, Germany, 1990. Appointments: Researcher, Ruhr-University, Bochum, Germany, 1985-90; Greek Army, 1991; Lecturer, 1992-97, Assistant Professor, 1997-, Democritus University, Thrace, Greece. Publications: Over 60 in refereed international journals and conferences. Memberships: Technical Chamber of Greece; Seismological Society of America; Earthquake Engineering Research Institute; Council on Tall Buildings and Urban Habita. Address: Democritus University of Thrace, Institute of Structural Mechanics and Earthquake Engineering, vas Sofias 1, GR-67100 Xanthi, Greece.

ELFMAN Danny, b. 29 May 1953, USA. Composer; Musician (guitar); Vocalist. m. Bridget Fonda, 2003, 1 child. Career: Lead singer, songwriter, guitarist, band Oingo Boingo; Compositions: Films: Pee-Wee's Big Adventure; Beetlejuice; Batman; Batman Returns; Dick Tracy; Darkman; Edward Scissorhands; Sommersby; Weird Science; Ghostbusters II; Something Wild; Batman Returns, 1992; Dolores Claiborne, 1995; Mission Impossible, The Frighteners, Mars Attacks! 1996; Men In Black, 1997; Good Will Hunting; Scream 2; My Favorite Martian; Psycho; Sleepy Hollow, 1999; The Family Man, Proof of Life, 2000; Spy Kids, Planet of the Apes, Heartbreakers, Mazer World, Novocaine, 2001; Spider-Man, Men in Black II, Red Dragon, Chicago, 2002; Hulk, Big Fish, 2003; Spider-Man 2, 2004; Charlie and the Chocolate Factory, 2005; The Simpsons Movie, 2007. Recordings: Albums: with Oingo Boingo: Only A Lad, 1981; Nothing To Fear, 1982; Good For Your Soul, 1983; Dead Man's Party, 1985; Boingo, 1986; Skeletons In The Closet, 1989; Dark At The End Of The Tunnel, 1990; Article 99, 1992; Television series: The Simpsons, 1989-2007; Desperate Housewives, 2004-07. Honour: Emmy Nomination, The Simpsons. Current Management: L A Personal Development, 950 N. Kings Road, Suite 266, West Hollywood, CA 90069, USA.

ELIASSON Jan, b. 1940, Göteborg, Sweden. Ambassador; Minister for Foreign Affairs in Sweden; President of the 60th session by the General Assembly of the UN. m. Kerstin, 1 son, 2 daughters. Education: Exchange Student, Indiana, USA, 1957-58; Graduate, Swedish Naval Academy, 1962; Master's degree, Economics, 1965. Appointments: Part of UN mission mediating in the war between Iran and Iraq, 1980-86; Diplomatic Advisor to Swedish Prime Minister, 1982-83; Director General for Political Affairs, Ministry for Foreign Affairs, 1983-87; Secretary-General's Personal Representative on Iran/Iraq, 1988-92; Sweden's Ambassador ro the UN in New York, 1988-92; Chairman, UN Trust Fund for South Africa, 1988-92; Chairman, UN General Assembly's working group on emergency relief, 1991; Vice President of ECOSOC, 1991-92; Appointed first Under-Secretary-General for Humanitarian Affairs of the UN, 1992; Mediator, Nagorno Karabakh conflict for the OSCE; Visiting professor, Uppsala University, Sweden; State Secretary for Foreign Affairs, 1994-2000; Sweden's Ambassador to the US, 2000-05; Elected President of the 60th session by the General Assembly

of the UN, 2005; Minister for Foreign Affairs in Sweden, 2006-. Publications: Author and co-author of numerous books, articles and frequent lecturer on foreign policy and diplomacy. Honours: Honorary Doctorate degrees: American University of Washington DC; Göteborg University, Uppsala University, Sweden; Bethany College, Kansas; California Lutheran University, California; Decorated by numerous governments. Address: Stockbyvagen 15, 18278 Stocksund, Sweden. E-mail: jan.eliasson@yahoo.se

ELIOT John, b. 28 October 1933, Washington DC, USA. Professor. m. Sylvia Hewitt, 2 daughters. Education: AB, 1956; MAT, 1958, Harvard; EdD, Stanford, 1966; MTS, Washington Theological Union, 2006. Appointments: Professor, College of Education, College Park, Maryland, 1969-99. Publications: 7 books; several journal articles; 8 Spatial Ability tests. Honours: Fellow, APA. Memberships: APS; APA. Address: 2705 Silverdale Dr, Silver Spring, MD 20906, USA.

ELIZABETH II (Elizabeth Alexandra Mary), Queen of Great Britain and Northern Ireland and of Her other Realms and Territories, b. 21 April 1926, London, England. m. HRH The Prince Philip, Duke of Edinburgh, 3 sons, 1 daughter. Address: Buckingham Palace, London SW1A 1AA, England.

ELKADYM F, b. 28 January 1954, Cairo, Egypt. Businessman. Education: BBA, Business Administration; BSc, Economics and Political Science; MBA, Business Management and Administration; PhD, Business Administration. Appointments: Founder/Chairman, CEO and Managing Director, SGC Group, Saudi Arabia, 1976-; Chairman, CEO and Managing Director since 1996: Comerford Investments Ltd; MEK International Trade and Construction Services; Atlantic and Middle East Fidelity and Trust International Insurance Company Ltd; MEK Italia Srl; Sultan Aviation Millennium Services Srl; MEK International Aviation Services Ltd; MEK International Ltd; MEK International Group Ltd; MEK International Aviation Management, Ltd; Sultan for Food Security & Land Reclamation; Concorde for Tourism & Investments Co; International Company for Investment & Medical Projects; Sultan for General Construction & Development Group; The International Center for Studies & Integrated Works Consultations; New Concorde Tours; MEK Euro-Finance & Investments SA; MEK International Trade & Construction Services (USA) Ltd. Honours include: Year 2000 Universal Award for Accomplishment, 2000; American Order of Excellence, 2000; Man of the Year, 2000; Gold Record of Achievement, 2001; Degree of Merit, 2001; World Quality Commitment International Star Award, Paris, 2002; Century International Quality Era Award, Geneva, 2002; Presidential Seal of Honor, 2002; International Peace Prize, 2003; World Lifetime Achievement Award, 2003; Lifetime Achievement Award, 2003; International Quality Crown Award, 2004; Dedication of Leading Intellectuals of the World, 2004; Platinum Technology Award for Quality and Best Trade Name, Paris, 2005; Commemorative Medal, Man of the Year, 2005; American Medal of Honor Recipient, 2005; The Da Vinci Diamond, 2005; The Cambridge Blue Book Man of the Year, 2005; Genius Laureate of Saudi Arabia, 2005; International Professional of the Year, 2005. Memberships include: American Management Association; Union of Arab Banks; The Arab Academy for Banking & Financial Sciences; World Water Council; Arab Bankers Association; Royal United Services Institute for Defense Studies; Strategic Planning Society; American Economic Association; International Association for Energy Economics; Royal Institute of International Affairs; The Institute of

Petroleum; World Energy Council; International Institute for Strategic Studies; British Institute of Energy Economics; Research Institute for Peace and Security; Offshore Institute; International Public Relation Association; The Academy of Political Sciences; Hospitality Financial and Technology Professionals; Institute of Management Accounts; American Arab Chamber of Commerce. Address: MEK International Ltd, PO Box 6378, Jeddah 21442, Saudi Arabia.

ELLENS Jay Harold, b. 16 July 1932, McBain, Michigan, USA. Professor. m. Mary Jo, 3 sons, 4 daughters. Education: BA, 1953; BD, 1956; ThM, 1965; PhD, Psychology, 1970; MDiv, 1983; MA, 2000; PhD (cand), Greco Roman Studies, 2002. Appointments: Active Duty US Army, Colonel, 1955-62; Clergy, 1955-2006; Professor, 1965-85; Psychotherapist, 1970-2006; Executive Director, Christian Association for Psychological Studies International, 1974-89; Founder, Editor in Chief, The Journal of Psychology and Christianity, 1975-88. Publications: 165 books; 172 articles in professional journals. Honours: Numerous military medals; 4 MSM; 1 Legion of Merit; Numerous distinguished lectureships; Knighthood. Memberships: 26 invited professional and military officers societies. Address: 26705 Farmington Road, Farmington Hills, MI 48334-4329, USA.

ELLIOTT Sir John Huxtable, b. 23 June 1930, Reading, Berkshire, England. Historian. m. Oonah Sophia Butler. Education: BA, 1952, MA, 1955, PhD, 1955, Cambridge University. Appointments: Lecturer in History and Fellow, Trinity College, Cambridge, 1957-67; Professor of History, King's College, London, 1968-73; Professor, School of Historical Studies, Institute for Advanced Study, Princeton, USA, 1973-90; Regius Professor of Modern History and Fellow of Oriel College, Oxford University, 1990-97. Publications include: The Revolt of the Catalans, 1963; Imperial Spain, 1963; Europe Divided, 1968; The Old World and the New, 1970; A Palace for a King (with Jonathan Brown), 1980; Richelieu and Olivares, 1984; The Count-Duke of Olivares, 1986; Spain and Its World, 1989; Empires of the Atlantic World, 2006. Honours: Grand Cross Order of Alfonso X, 1988; FBA, 1992; Kt, 1994; Prince of Asturias Prize, 1996; Grand Cross Order of Isabel la Católica, 1996; Wolfson Prize, 1986; Balzan Prize for History, 1999; Francis Parkman Prize, 2007; Honorary Doctorates: Madrid (Autónoma); Madrid (Complutense); Genoa; Barcelona; Portsmouth; Valencia; Lleida; Warwick; Brown; College of William and Mary, London; Honorary Fellow: Trinity College, Cambridge; Oriel College, Oxford. Memberships: British Academy; American Philosophical Society; American Academy of Arts and Sciences; Accademia dei Lincei. Address: Oriel College, Oxford OX1 4EW, England.

ELLIS Harold, b. 13 January 1926, London, England. Professor of Surgery. m. Wendy Levine, 1 son, 1 daughter. Education: BM BCh, University of Oxford, 1948; FRCS, 1951; MCh, 1956; DM, 1962. Appointments: Resident appointments in: Oxford, Sheffield, Northampton and London, 1948-60; RAMC (Graded Surgical Specialist), 1950-51; Senior Lecturer in Surgery, 1960-62, Professor of Surgery, 1962-89, Westminster Medical School; Professor Emeritus, University of London, 1989; Clinical Anatomist, University of Cambridge, 1989-93; Clinical Anatomist, United Medical and Dental School, Guy's Campus (now School of Biomedical Sciences, King's College, Guy's Campus), 1993-. Publications: 25 books include most recently: Clinical Anatomy for Laparoscopic and Thoracoscopic Surgery, 1995; Gray's Anatomy (38th edition) Section Editor, 1995; Operations That Made History, 1996; Index to Differential Diagnosis, 1996; Index of Surgical Differential Diagnosis, 1999; Applied Radiological Anatomy, 1999; A History of Surgery, 2000; Numerous book chapters and articles in medical journals. Honours include: CBE, 1987; Honorary, FACS, 1989; Honorary Fellow, Royal Society of Medicine, 1996; Honorary Gold Medal, Royal College of Surgeons of England. Memberships: President, Armed Services Combined Assessment Board in Surgery; Honorary Freeman, Company of Barbers. Address: 16 Bancroft Avenue, London N2 0AS, England.

ELLIS John Norman, b. 22 February 1939, Leeds, England. Employment Law Consultant. m. 1 son, 2 stepsons, 1 daughter. Appointments: Civil Servant, 1954-68; Trade Union Full Time Officer, 1968-95; Deputy General Secretary, 1982-86, General Secretary, 1986-92, CPSA: Secretary General Council of Civil Service Unions, 1992-1995; Panel Member, Employment Tribunal, 1992; Associate Consultant, Talking People, an ACS Company. Publications: Published 36 editions of the National Whitley Bulletin, 1992-95: Articles in the Public Policy and Administration Journal. Honours: OBE for services to industrial relations, 1995. Memberships: Labour Party; Civil Service Pensioners' Alliance; Institute of Employment Right; Vice Chairman, Tandridge Leisure Ltd; Chairman, Cliff Crescent Management Ltd, 2001-. Address: 26 Harestone Valley Road, Caterham, Surrey CR3 6HD, England. E-mail: johnellis60@aol.com

ELLIS Richard Mackay, b. 9 July 1941, Chalfont St Peter, England. Consultant Physician. m. Gillian Ann Cole, 1 son, 1 daughter. Education: Wellington College; MB BChir, Clare College, Cambridge, 1965; St Thomas's Hospital Medical School, London; MD, New York, 1982. Appointments: Senior Lecturer in Rheumatology, University of Southampton, 1980; Consultant in Rheumatology and Rehabilitation, Salisbury District Hospital, 1980; Director, Wessex Rehabilitation Unit, Salisbury, 1989. Publications: Co-editor, Textbook of Musculoskeletal Medicine, 2005. Memberships: Fellow, Royal College of Surgeons, London, 1971; Editor, Journal of Orthopaedic Medicine, 1985; Fellow, Royal College of Physicians, London, 1988; Council Member, British Institute of Musculoskeletal Medicine, 1990; Convenor, Examining Board for Diploma in Musculoskeletal Medicine, Society of Apothecaries of London, 1998; Honorary President, Society of Orthopaedic Medicine, 2000. Address: 161 Bouverie Avenue, Salisbury, Wiltshire SP2 8EB, England.

ELLSAESSER Hugh Walter, b. 1 June 1920, USA. Atmospheric Scientist. m. Lois M McCaw, deceased, 1 adopted son, deceased, 1 son, 1 daughter. Education: AA, Bakersfield Junior College, 1941; MA, University of California, Los Angeles, 1947; PhD, University of Chicago, 1964. Appointments: 2nd Lieutenant, USAF, 1943, advanced to Lieutenant Colonel; Weather Officer, Antigua, San Juan, Florida, London, Washington, DC, Omaha; Physicist, Lawrence Livermore National Laboratory, 1963-86; Guest Scientist, 1986-97; Consultant Meteorologist, 1997-. Publications: Numerous articles in professional journals. Honour: Phi Beta Kappa Commendation Medal. Memberships: American Meteorological Society; American Geophysical Union; AAAS. Address: Samaritan Village, 7700 Fox Road, Apt F105, Hughson, CA 95326, USA. E-mail: hughel@svresidents.com

ELS Ernie, b. 17 October 1969, Johannesburg, South Africa. Professional Golfer. m. Leizl, 1 son, 1 daughter. Career: Professional, 1989-; Winner, US Open, 1994, 1997; Toyota World Matchplay Championships, 1994, 1995, 1996; South

Africa PGA Championship, 1995; Byron Nelson Classic, 1995; Buick Classic, 1996, 1997; Johnny Walker Classic, 1997; Bay Hill Invitational, 1998; Nissan Open, 1999; Int presented by Quest 2000; Standard Life Loch Lomond, 2000; Open Championship, 2002; Genuity Championship, 2002; British Open, 2002; Sixth World Match Play title, 2004; Mercedes Championship, 2003; Member, Dunhill Cup Team, 1992-2000; World Cup Team, 1992, 1993, 1996, 1997, 2001; Member, President's Cup, 1996, 1998, 2000; Founder, Ernie Els Foundation to help disadvantaged children, 1999. Honour: South African Sportsman of Year, 1995. Address: 46 Chapman Road, Klippoortjie 1401, South Africa.

ELSTEIN Cecile Hoberman, b. 8 February 1938, Cape Town, South Africa. Sculptor; Printmaker; Environmental Artist. m. Max Elstein, 1 son (deceased), 1 daughter. Education: 1961-69; Studied in London - ceramics with Catherine Yarrow, 1965-69; Drawing with Beatrice Lyssy; Sculpture, West Surrey College of Art, 1975-77, tutor Ian Walters; MA, Art as Environment, Manchester Metropolitan University, 1994-96. Career: Made constructed wood sculpture for landscape of Treloar School for physically disabled children, 1977; Invited to make sculpture for landscape of Wimpole Hall Gardens, Cambridge constructed in rope and metal, 1996; Commissions for Portrait Bronzes, 1959-2008; Latest commissions, 2005 – Michael Kennedy, author and music critic; Bronze portrait of Paul David Elstein MA, healer, 2008; 'Yellow/violet' screenprint editioned, 2008; Video direction and DVD production, 'Tangents, a mindscape in a landscape', co-production with Maureen Kendal, 1999-2004; Solo and group exhibitions of prints, drawing and sculpture in UK and abroad, 1965-2008. Publications: Co-production Cecile Elstein and Maureen Kendal "Tangents, a mindscape in a landscape" DVD with companion booklet, 2004; Included in 'Exhibiting Gender' by Sarah Hyde, Manchester University Press, 1997; Included in 'Manchester Memoirs', Manchester Literary and Philosophical Society, 2004-05; Including in A Colourful Canvas, 12 Women Artists in the North West, Judy Rose and Wendy J Levy, 2006. Awards: Bursary, North West Arts, 1984; Sericol Colour Prize, 9th British International Print Biennale, 1986. Memberships: Elected Member, MAFA; Elected Fellow, RSA, 1997; Member, Public Monument and Sculpture Association, Landscape and Arts Network. Address: 25 Spath Road, Didsbury, Manchester M20 2QT, England. E-mail: cecile@cecileelstein.com.Website: www.cecileelstein.com

ELTIS Walter (Alfred), b. 23 May 1933, Warnsdorf, Czechoslovakia. Economist. m. Shelagh Mary Owen, 5 September 1959, 1 son, 2 daughters. Education: Emmanuel College, Cambridge; BA, Cambridge University; MA, Nuffield College, 1960; DLitt, Oxford University, 1990. Appointments: Fellow, Tutor, Economics, 1963-88, Emeritus Fellow, 1988-, Exeter College, Oxford; Director General, National Economic Development Office, London, 1988-92; Chief Economic Adviser to the President of the Board of Trade, 1992-95; Visiting Professor, 1992-2004, University of Reading. Publications: Growth and Distribution, 1973; Britain's Economic Problem: Too Few Producers (with Robert Bacon), 1976; The Classical Theory of Economic Growth, 1984 (2nd Edition, Palgrave 2000); Keynes and Economic Policy (with Peter Sinclair), 1988; Classical Economics, Public Expenditure and Growth, 1993; Britain's Economic Problem Revisited, 1996; Condillac, Commerce and Government (editor, with Shelagh M Eltis), 1997; Britain, Europe and EMU, 2000. Contributions to: Economic journals and bank reviews. Memberships: Reform Club, chairman, 1994-95; Political Economy Club; Vice President, European

Society for the History of Economic Thought, 2000-04. Address: Danesway, Jarn Way, Boars Hill, Oxford OX1 5JF, England.

ELTON Ben(jamin Charles), b. 3 May 1959, England. Writer; Comedian. m. Sophie Gare, 3 children. Education: BA, Drama, University of Manchester. Appointments: Writer, TV series and for British Comedians; Stand-up Comedian: Tours, 1986, 1987, 1989, 1993, 1996, 1997; Host, Friday Night Live, TV Comedy Showcase, 1986-88; Co-writer, Presenter, South of Watford (documentary TV series), 1982; Writer/Director, Inconceivable, film, 2000. Publications: Bachelor Boys, 1984; Stark, 1989; Gridlock, 1991; This Other Eden, 1993; Popcorn, 1996; Blast from the Past, 1998; Inconceivable, 1999; Dead Famous, 2001; High Society, 2002; Past Mortem, 2004; The First Casualty, 2005; Chart Throb, 2006; Plays: Gasping, 1990; Silly Cow, 1991; Popcorn, 1996; Blast from the Past, 1998; The Beautiful Game, musical, book and lyrics, 2000; Maybe Baby, writer/director, feature film, 2000; High Society, 2002; We Will Rock You, musical, 2002; Tonight's the Night, 2003; Other: Recordings, The Young Ones, 1982; Happy Families, 1985; Blackadder, 1985, 1987, 1989; Filthy Rich and Catflap, 1986; Motormouth, 1987; Motovation (album), 1988; The Man From Auntie, 1990, 1994; The Very Best of Ben Elton Live, 1990; A Farties Guide to the Man From Auntie, 1990; Ben Elton Live, 1993; Stark, 1993; The Thin Blue Line (sitcom); 1995, 1996; Ben Elton Live, 1997; The Ben Elton Show, 1999. Honours: Best Comedy Show Awards, Brit Academy, 1984, 1987; Gold Dagger Award, 1996; TMA Award, 1997; Lawrence Olivier Award, 1998. Address: c/o Phil McIntyre, 2nd Floor, 35 Soho Square, London, W1D 3QX, England.

EMANUEL Elizabeth Florence, b. 5 July 1953, London, England. Fashion Designer. m. David Leslie Emanuel, 1975, separated 1990, 1 son, 1 daughter. Education: Harrow College of Art. Appointments: Opened London salon, 1978; Designer, wedding gown for HRH Princess of Wales, 1981; Costumes for Andrew Lloyd Webber's Song and dance, 1982; Sets and costumes for ballet, Frankenstein, The Modern Prometheus, Roy Opera House, London, La Scala Milan, 1985; Costumes for Stoll Moss production of Cinderella, 1985; Costumes for films: Diamond Skulls, 1990; The Changeling, 1995; Uniforms for Virgin Atlantic Airways, 1990; Britannia Airways, 1995; Launched international fashion label Elizabeth Emanuel, 1991; Launched Bridal Collection for Berkertex Brides UK Ltd, 1994; Launched bridal collection in Japan, 1994; Opened new shop and design studio, 1996; Launched own brand label (with Richard Thompson), 1999. Publications: Style for All Seasons (with David Emanuel), 1982. Address: Ground Floor Studio, 23 Warrington Crescent, London, W9 1ED, England.

EMBERSON Ian McDonald, b. 29 July 1936, Hove, Sussex, England. Retired Librarian; Writer and Artist. Publications: Doodles in the Margins of My Life, 1981; Swallows Return, 1986; Pirouette of Earth, a novel in verse, 1995; Natural Light, 1998; The Comet of 1811, 2001; The Snake and the Star, 2003; Pilgrims from Loneliness, an interpretation of Charlotte Brontë's Jane Eyre and Villette, 2005; Messages from Distant Shores, 2006; Yorkshire Lives and Landscapes, 2006. Contributions to: Pennine Platform; Envoi; Orbis; New Hope International; Bradford Poetry Quarterly; Dalesman; Countryman; Acumen; Poetry Scotland; Brontë Studies; IOTA; Poets Voice; Aireings; Pennine Ink. Honour: William Alwyn International Poetry Society Award, 1981. Memberships: Pennine Poets; Brontë Society; Gaskell Society. Address: Eastroyd, 1 Highcroft Road, Todmorden, Lancashire OL14 5LZ, England. Website: www.ianemberson.co.uk

EMEL'YANOV Vladimir, b. 1 June 1943, Moscow, Russia. Physicist. Divorced, 2 daughters. Education: Graduate, Faculty of Physics, 1966, Diploma of Physicist, postgraduate study, Diploma of Candidate of Science (PhD), 1973, Diploma of Doctor of Science, 1988, Moscow State University. Appointments: Research Fellow, 1973-75, Assistant Professor, 1975-89, Full Professor, 1989-, Physics Faculty, Moscow State University. Publications: 300 articles; 3 monographs: Co-operative effects in Optics, 1988; Interaction of strong laser radiation with solids, 1990; Co-operative effects in Optics, Superradiance and Phase Transitions, 1993. Honours: Prize Winner, International Publishing Company "Nauka", 1995; Lomonosov Prize Winner, highest award of Moscow State University, 1999; Listed in international biographical dictionary. Memberships: SPIE. Address: Physics Faculty, Moscow State University, 119899 Moscow, Russia. E-mail: emel@em.msk.ru

EMERY Alan E H, b. 21 August 1928, Manchester, England. Physician. m. Marcia Lynn Maler, 3 sons, 3 daughters. Education: University of Manchester, England; PhD, Johns Hopkins University, USA. Appointments: Reader, Medicine, Manchester University, 1964-68; Foundation Professor, Human Genetics, Edinburgh University, 1968-83; Research Professor and Fellow, Edinburgh University, 1983-90; Research Director, 1990-2000, Chief Scientific Adviser, 2000-, European Neuro-Muscular Centre; Visiting Professor, Peninsula Medical School, Exeter, 2002-. Publications: Around 300 medical science papers; 21 books. Honours: Various visiting professorships and named lectures; Honorary MD, University of Naples and University of Wurzburg; National Foundation USA, International Award; Gaetano Gold Medal; Honorary Membership or Fellowship: Dutch Society of Human Genetics; Association of British Neurologists; Royal Society of South Africa; Hon MD, Naples, Wurzburg; International Award for Genetic Research, USA; Gaetano Conte Prize for Clinical Research, 2000; Pro Finlandiae Gold Medal for contributions to Neuroscience, 2000; Lifetime Achievement Award, WFN, 2002. Memberships: FRCP; FRCPE; FLS; FRSE. Address: Peninsula Medical School, Department of Neurology, Royal Devon and Exeter Hospital, Exeter EX2 5DW, England.

EMERY Lin, b. New York, USA. Sculptor. m. S Braselman, deceased, 1 son. Education: Sorbonne: Cours de la civilisation française, 1949; Atelier of Ossip Zadkine, Paris, 1950; New York Sculpture Centre, 1952. Appointments: Solo Exhibitions: Retrospective, New Orleans Museum of Art, LA, 1996; Mitsuhashi Gallery & Honen-In Temple, Kyoto, Japan, 1999; Tour, Five Museums in Louisiana State, 2001-03; Arthur Roger Gallery, LA, 2005; Kouros Gallery, NY, 2006; Public Sculptures: G E, Wall Street, NY, 1994; Osaka Dome, Japan, 1997; Izumisano Hospital, Japan, 1997; Sterling Co, Dallas, TX, 1999; Schiffer Publishing, PA, 2000; Federal Aviation Authority, DC, 2001; Renaissance Arts Hotel, LA, 2004; Knight Oil Tool Co, LA, 2006. Publications: Articles in Museums and Art Centres worldwide. Honours include: Mayor's Award for Achievement in the Arts, 1980; Louisiana Women of Achievement Award, 1984; NOCCA Distinguished Louisiana Artist Award, 1988; YWCA Role Model Award, 1989; Lazlo Aranyi Award of Honour for Public Art, 1990; Delgado Society Award for Artistic Excellence, 1997; Osaka Prefecture, Japan, Grand Prix for Public Sculpture, 1998; Governor's Arts Award, 2001; Young Leadership Council, Role Model, New Orleans, 2003; Honorary Doctorate, Loyola University of the South, 2004. Memberships: Honorary Associations include: Century Association, New York; National Academy; Royal Society of British Sculptors (International

member) Sculptors Guild, New York; International Women's Forum. Address: 7520 Dominican Street, New Orleans, LA 70118-3738 USA. E-mail:lin@linemery.com

EMIN Tracey, b. 1964, Margate, England. Artist. Education: John Cass School of Art, London; Maidstone College of Art; Royal College of Art. Career: Founder, Tracey Emin Museum, London, 1996; Artist, exhibitions include: White Cube Gallery, London, 1992; Minky Manky, 1995; My Major Retrospective, Part of What Made Me What I Am, Loose Ends, 1998; Personal Effects, 1998; Made in London, 1998; Sweetie, 1999; Temple of Diana, 1999; Now It's My Turn to Scream, 1999; Art in Sacred Places, 2000; What Do You Know About Love, 2000; Commissions: The Roman Standard, BBC for Art05 Festival, London, 2005; Films: Why I Never Became a Dancer; Top Spot, 2004. Publications: Exploration of the Soul, 1995; Always Glad to See You, 1997; Tracey Emin: Holiday Inn, 1998; Tracey Emin on Pandaemonium, 1998; Absolute Tracey, 1998. Honours: International Award for Video Art, Baden-Baden, 1997; Video Art Prize, Suedwest Bank, Stuttgart, 1997; Royal Academician, Royal Academy of Arts, 2007. Address: The Tracey Emin Museum, 221 Waterloo Road, London SE1, England.

EMINEM (Slim Shady) (Marshall Bruce Mathers III), b. 17 October 1972, St Joseph, Missouri, USA. Rap Artist; Musician. m. Kim, 1999, divorced, 1 daughter. Career: Founder and Owner, Slim Shady record label, 1999-; Recordings: Albums: The Infinite, 1997; The Slim Shady LP, 1999; The Marshall Mathers LP, 2000; The Eminem Show, 2002; Eminem is Back, 2004; Encore, 2004; King Mathers, 2007; Singles: The Slim Shady EP, 1998; Just Don't Give a F***, 1999; My Name Is, 1999; Guilty Conscience, 1999; The Real Slim Shady, 2000; The Way I Am, 2000; Stan, 2000; Without Me, 2002; Lose Yourself, 2003; Business, 2003; Just Lose It, 2004. Honours: MTV Annual American Music Awards, Best Hip Hop Artist, 2000, 2002; MTV Award, Best Album, 2000; 3 Grammy Awards, 2001; Best Pop/Rock Male Artist, 2002; MTV Awards, Best Album, 2002; MTV Europe Music Awards, Best Male Act, Best Hip Hop Act, 2002; BRIT Award for Best International Male Solo Artist, 2002, 2005; Grammy Award, Best Rap Album, 2003; BRIT Award, Best International Album, 2003; American Music Awards for Best Male Pop/Rock Artist; Best Male Hip Hop/R&B Artist, 2003; Academy Award, Best Music (song in film, 8 Mile), 2004; Grammy Awards, Best Male Rap Solo Performance and Best Rap Song, 2004; Echo Award for Best International Hip Hop Artist, Germany, 2005. Address: c/o William Morris Agency, 1325 Avenue of the Americas, New York, NY 10019, USA. Website: www.eminem.com

EMMANUEL Rohinton, b. 22 May 1962, Jaffna, Sri Lanka. Architect. m. Melanie. Education: BS, Built Environment, 1984, MSc, Architecture, 1990, University of Moratuwa, Sri Lanka; MS, Architecture, Louisiana State University, USA, 1993; MS, Architecture, 1996, PhD, Architecture, 1997, University of Michigan. Appointments: Junior Assistant Architect, Architects Associated, Colombo, Sri Lanka, 1984-85; Junior Architect, Kahawita de Silva Associates, Colombo, 1986; Research Assistant, Construction Industry Indicators Project, 1988-89; Co-Investigator, Career Guidance Project, Rotary Club of Colombo, 1989-90; Lecturer, Faculty of Architecture, University of Moratuwa, Sri Lanka, 1990-97; Teaching Assistant, Louisiana State University, 1991-93; Research Assistant, Office of Community Preservation, Louisiana State University, 1992-93; Architectural Intern, Historic American Engineering Record, National Park Service, US Department of the Interior, 1993; Teaching Assistant,

College of Architecture & Urban Planning, University of Michigan, 1993-96; Architectural Intern, Facilities Planning & Design, University of Michigan, 1993-97; Senior Lecturer, 1998-2004, Professor, 2004-, Faculty of Architecture, University of Moratuwa, Architect, R Susil Weddikkara Associates, Dehiwala, 1998-2002. Publications: Papers and articles in professional journals including most recently: Architectural research: a short primer, 2005; An empirical study of human exposure and related health effects of transport-induced Respirable Particulate Matter in the Colombo Metropolitan Region, 2005; Urban development and climate change: Some mitigation options, 2005; Architectural education in contemporary Sri Lanka – a needs analysis for the developing world, 2006; The influence of urban morphology and sea breeze on hot, humid microclimate: the case of Colombo, Sri Lanka, 2006; The influence of urban design on the outdoor thermal comfort in the hot, humid city of Colombo, Sri Lanka, 2006. Honours: Numerous honours and awards including: United Nations University/Asian Institute of Technology Fellowship, Thailand, 1998; Swedish International Development Co-operation Agency Fellowship, Sweden, 1999; 2 Outstanding Research Performance Awards (3 Year Category), University of Moratuwa, 2000 and 2005; World Meteorological Organization Award, International Association for Urban Climate, 2006; Japan Prize for best paper, International Conference on Urban Climate, IAUC. Memberships: Corporate Member, Sri Lanka Institute of Architects; Registered Member, Architects' Registration Board, Sri Lanka; Life Member, Sri Lanka Association for the Advancement of Science; Member, Lighting Society of Sri Lanka. Address: Department of Architecture, University of Moratuwa, Moratuwa 10400, Sri Lanka.

EMMERICH Roland, b. 10 November 1955, Stuttgart, Germany. Director; Screenplay Writer; Executive Producer. Education: Film School in Munich. Appointments: Producer (as student) The Noah's Ark Principle, shown at Berlin Film Festival (sold to over 20 countries), 1984; Founder, Centropolis Film Productions; Films: Making Moon 44; Universal Soldier; Stargate; Independence Day; The Thirteenth Floor (producer); The Patriot; Eight Legged Freaks (executive producer), 2002; The Day After Tomorrow (producer), 2004; Trade (producer), 2007; Isobar (writer), 2007; 10,000 BC (producer), 2008; TV series: The Visitor (producer), 1997. Address: c/o Creative Artists Agency, 9830 Wilshire Boulevard, Beverly Hills, CA 90212, USA.

EMMS David Acfield, b. 16 February 1925, Lowestoft, Suffolk, England. Headmaster. m. Pamela Baker Speed, 3 sons, 1 daughter. Education: MA, Modern Languages, Diploma in Education, Brasenose College, Oxford, 1947-51. Appointments: War Service, Captain, Royal Indian Airborne Artillery, 1943-47; Assistant Master, Head, Modern Languages Department, OC, CCF, 1st XV Rugby Coach, Uppingham School, 1951-50; Headmaster, Cranleigh School, 1960-70; Headmaster, Sherborne School, 1970-74; The Master, Dulwich College, 1975-86; Vice-Chairman, The English Speaking Union, 1984-89; The Director, London House for Overseas Graduates, 1986-95. Publication: HMC Schools and British Industry, 1981. Honours: Rugby Football Blue, Oxford University, 1949, 1950; OBE, 1995. Memberships: FRSA, 1988; Master, Skinners' Company, 1987; Chairman, Headmasters' Conference, 1984; President, Independent Schools Careers Organisation, 2002-; President, Alleyn Club, 1985; Brasenose Society, 1987. Address: The Dove House, Church Lane, Birdham, nr Chichester, West Sussex PO20 7AT, England. Website: emms.dovehouse@tiscali.co.uk

ENDERBY Sir John Edwin, b. 16 January 1931, Grimsby, Lincolnshire, England. Physicist. m. Susan, 1 son, 3 daughters. Education: Westminster College, London; BSc, PhD, Birkbeck College, London. Appointments: Professor of Physics and Head of Department, University of Bristol, 1976-96; Vice President, Royal Society, 1999-2004; Chief Scientific Advisor, Institute of Physics Publishing, 2002-; Chairman, Melys Diagnostics Ltd, 2004-; President, Institute of Physics, 2004-06. Publications: Numerous papers and articles in professional journals. Honours: Westminster College Wright Prize, 1953; College Award, 1956; Guthrie Medal, 1995; Hon DSc, Loughborough University, 1996; CBE, 1997; Honorary Fellowship, Birkbeck College, 2000; Knight Bachelor, 2004. Memberships: Fellow, Institute of Physics; Fellow, Royal Society; Hon DSc, Leicester, 2006; Hon DSc, Bristol, 2006. Member, Academia Europaea; Atheneum Club. Address: 7 Cotham Lawn Road, Bristol, BS6 6DU, England.

ENDO Hiroshi, b. 29 September 1948, Tokyo, Japan. Professor. m. Seiko, 1 daughter. Education: Master Degree, Tokyo University of Science, 1974; PhD, Mathematics (Differential Geometry), Al I Cuza University, Iasi, 1997. Appointments: Senior High School Teacher, Chiba Prefecture, 1975-97; Associate Professor, Kurashiki City College, 1997-2000; Associate Professor, Tokoha Gakuen University, 2000-02; Professor, Utsunomiya University, 2002-. Publications: On invariant submanifolds of contact metric manifolds, 1985; The part of Bochner curvature tensors, Encyclopaedia of Mathematics, Supplement Vol I, 1997. Memberships: Mathematical Society of Japan; Tensor Society; Society of Finsler Geometry, Japan. E-mail: hsk-endo@cc.utsunomiya-u.ac.jp

ENFLO Bengt Olof, b. 8 March 1935, Falun, Sweden. Physicist. m. Anita Henriksson, 1 son, 2 daughters. Education: Matriculation, 1953; Master of Philosophy, 1957, Licentiate of Philosophy, 1959, Doctor of Philosophy, 1965, Stockholm University. Appointments: Instructor, 1962, Assistant Professor, 1965, Theoretical Physics, Stockholm University; Associate Professor, 1973, Professor, 1996, Mechanics, Royal Institute of Technology, Stockholm; Emeritus Professor, 2000-. Publications: Studies in strong interaction dynamics with application to the deuteron problem (doctoral thesis), 1965; Theory of Nonlinear Acoustics in Fluids (with C M Hedberg), 2002; Articles on quantum mechanics and theoretical acoustics in scientific journals. Memberships: Swedish Physical Society; Euromech. Address: Royal Institute of Technology (KTH), Department of Mechanics, Osquars Backe 18, S-10044 Stockholm, Sweden.

ENGELMANN Mads David Meding, b. 4 October 1958, Hillerød, Denmark. Head of Medical Affairs. m. Pernille, 2 sons. Education: MSc, Chemical Engineering, Technical University of Denmark, 1987; MD, Faculty of Health Sciences, 1993, PhD, Medicine, Research Department of Human Nutrition, 1996, University of Copenhagen; Specialist in Cardiovascular Diseases, 2005; Specialist in Internal Medicine, 2005. Appointments: House Officer, Department of Endocrinology, 1997, Staff Specialist, Department of Cardiology, 2006, Herlev University Hospital, Denmark; Senior House Officer, 2000, Senior Registrar, 2002, Department of Cardiology, University Hospital of Copenhagen, Rigshospitalet, Denmark; Medical Advisor, 2006-, Head of Medical Affairs, 2006-, GlaxoSmithKline Pharma, Denmark. Publications: Quality of Life in Atrial Fibrillation, 2003; Acute Medical Conditions, 2007; Several articles on cardiology in peer reviewed scientific journals. Memberships: European Society of Cardiology; Danish Society of Cardiology; European Society of Internal

Medicine; Danish Society of Internal Medicine; Danish Society of Medicine. Address: Furesøvej 36, DK 2830 Virum, Denmark. E-mail: engelmann@dadlnet.dk

ENGLISH Mary Phyllis, b. 10 April 1919, Kuala Lumpur, Malaya. Medical Mycologist. Education: St Stephen's College, Folkstone, 1932-36; Regent St Polytechnic, London, 1936-37; BSc in Botany, King's College, London, 1937-41; MSc in Mycology (London), 1941-43. Appointments: Agricultural Chemist, War Agricultural Advisory Centre, Bristol, 1941-43; Plant Pathologist, Mycology, East Malling Research Station, 1943-46; Mycologist, Messrs Science Films, London, 1946-48; Research Fellow, Mycology, Birmingham University, 1948-51; Mycologist, British Drug Houses Ltd, London, 1951-54; Medical Mycologist, United Bristol Hospitals, 1954-80; Retired, 1980-. Publications: 90 papers in scientific journals; 4 books: Medical Mycology, 1980; Mordecai Cubitt Cooke: Victorian Naturalist, Mycologist, Teacher and Eccentric, 1987; Victorian Values: The Life and Times of Dr Edwin Lankester, MD, FRS, 1990; Hospital Infection From Miasmas to MRSA, 2003 (with Graham A J Ayliffe). Honours: DSc (Bristol), Medical Mycology, 1970. Memberships: British Mycological Society; British Society for Mycopathology; International Society for Human & Animal Mycology; Institute of Biology; West of England Society for Dermatology; British Society for Dermatology. Address: 17 Blackstone's Court, St George's Avenue, Stamford, Lincolnshire, PE9 1UH, England.

ENGLISH Terence Alexander Hawthorne, b. 3 October 1932, Pietermaritzburg, South Africa. Cardiac Surgeon (Retired). m. (1) Ann Margaret Dicey, 2 sons, 2 daughters, (2) Judith Francis Milne. Education: BSc, Engineering, Witwatersrand University, South Africa, 1951-54; MB BS, Guy's Hospital Medical School, 1955-62; FRCS (England and Edinburgh), 1967. Appointments: Surgical training at Brompton and National Heart Hospitals, Senior Registrar; Consultant Cardiothoracic Surgeon, Papworth and Addenbrooke's Hospitals, 1972-95; Performed Britain's first successful heart transplant, 1979; President, Royal College of Surgeons of England, 1989-92; Master, St Catharine's College, Cambridge, 1993-2000; President, British Medical Association, 1995-96. Publications: Principles of Cardiac Diagnosis and Treatment, 2nd edition, 1992; 23 contributions to chapters in books; 118 peer-reviewed articles mainly on surgery and cardiac transplantation. Honours: KBE, 1991; Honorary DSc, Universities of Sussex and Hull; Honorary MD, Universities of Nantes and Mahidol, Thailand; Honorary Fellow, Worcester College, Oxford, St Catharine's College and Hughes Hall, Cambridge, King's College, London, American College of Surgeons, Royal College of Physicians and Surgeons of Canada, College of Medicine of South Africa, College of Physicians and Surgeons of Pakistan, Royal College of Anaesthetists, Royal College of Surgeons of Ireland. Memberships: 20 national and international professional societies; Clubs: The Athenaeum; The Hawk's Club, Cambridge, Chairman, 1997-2001. Address: 28 Tree Lane, Oxford, OX4 4EY, England. E-mail: tenglish@doctors.org.uk

ENO Brian Peter George, b. 15 May 1948, Melton, Suffolk, England. Recording Artist; Record Producer; Musician (keyboards). Career: Founder Member, Roxy Music, 1971-73; Invented Ambient Music, 1975; Visiting Professor, RCA, 1995-; Founder, Long Now Foundation, 1996; Co-founder (with Peter Gabriel), The Magnificent Union of Digitally Downloading Artists, 2004; Recordings: Solo Albums include: Here Come the Warmjets, 1973; Taking Tiger Mountain (by

Strategy), 1974; Another Green World, 1975; Music for Films, 1976; Before and After Science, 1977; Ambient 1/Music for Airports, 1978; Nerve Net, 1992; The Drop, 1996; Albums as producer include: with John Cale: Fear, 1974; with Robert Calvert, Lucky Lief And The Longships, 1975; with Michael Nyman: Decay Music, 1976; with Penguin Café Orchestra: Music From The Penguin Café, 1976; with Ultravox: Ultravox, 1977; with Talking Heads: More Songs About Buildings And Food, 1978; Remain In Light, 1980; with Devo: Q- Are We Not Men? A- We Are Devo, 1978; with U2: The Unforgettable Fire, 1984; The Joshua Tree, 1987; Achtung Baby, 1991; Zooropa, 1993; Passengers (film soundtrack), 1995; All That You Can't Leave Behind, 2000; with Carmel: The Falling, 1986; with Geoffrey Oryema: Exile, 1990; with James: Laid, 1993; Wah Wah, 1994; Pleased to Meet You, 2001; with Laurie Anderson: Bright Red, 1994; Collaborations include: with Roxy Music: Virginia Plain, 1972; Roxy Music, 1972; For Your Pleasure, 1973; Pyjamarama, 1973; with David Bowie: Low, 1977; Heroes, 1977; Lodger, 1979; with J Peter Schwalm: Music for Onmyo-ji, 2000; Drawn From Life, 2001; As guest musician: Captain Lockheed And The Starfighters, Robert Calvert, 1974; The End, Nico, 1974; The Lamb Lies Down On Broadway, Genesis, 1974; with Phil Mazanera: Diamond Head, 1975; Listen Now, 1977; with John Cale: Slow Dazzle, 1975; Helen Of Troy, 1975; Rain Dances, Camel, 1977; Exposure, Robert Fripp, 1979; Yellow Rain, The Neville Brothers, 1989; Rattle And Hum, U2, 1989; Mamouna, Bryan Ferry, 1994; with Jah Wobble: Spinner, 1995. Remix productions include: Unbelieveable, EMF, 1992; I Feel You, Depeche Mode, 1993; The River, Geoffrey Oryema, 1993; I'm Only Looking, INXS, 1993; In Your Room, Depeche Mode, 1993; Brian Eno: Box I & Box II, 1993; Introducing The Band, Suede, 1994; 39 Steps, Bryan Ferry, 1994; Protection, Massive Attack, 1994; Numerous film soundtracks. Honours: Doctor, Technology, University of Plymouth; Ivor Novello Award; 3 Grammy Awards; BRIT Awards: Best Producer, 1994, 1996; Q Magazine Awards: Best Producer (with Flood, The Edge), 1993; Inspiration Award (with David Bowie), 1995; Montblanc Arts Patronage Award, 2000; Grammy Award, Producer of Best Record of the Year, 2000. Memberships: PRS; BASCA; ICA; Long Now Foundation; Global Business Network. Current Management: Opal Ltd. Address: 4 Pembridge Mews, London W11 3EQ, England.

ENTEM David Rodriguez, b. 6 September 1971, Salamanca, Spain. Education; Research. m. Maria de los Dolores Alonso Alvarez, 1 son. Education: Diploma, 1994, PhD, 1999, Physics, University of Salamanca. Appointments: Ayudante de Escuela Universitaria, 1995-2001, Profesor Asociado, 2001-05, Profesor Contratado Doctor, 2005-, University of Salamanca; Fellow, Fundacion Ramon Areces, 2001-02, Postdoctoral Research Associate, 2002-03, University of Idaho. Publications: Contributed papers in professional journals. Honours: Premio Extraordinario de Graxo de Salamanca, 1995. Address: Universidad de Salamanca, P/Merced s/u, E-37008 Salamanca, Spain. E-mail: entem@usal.es Website: http://web.usal.es/entem

ENYA (Eithne Ni Bhraonain), b. 17 May 1961, Gweedore, County Donegal, Ireland. Singer; Musician (piano, keyboards); Composer. Musical Education: Clasical piano; Career: Member, folk group Clannad, 1980-82; Solo artiste, 1988-; 25 million albums sold to date. Compositions: Music for film and television scores: The Frog Prince, 1985; The Celts, BBC, 1987; LA Story, 1990; Green Card, 1990. Recordings: Albums: with Clannad: Crann Ull, 1980; Fuaim, 1982; Solo albums: Watermark, 1988; Shepherd's Moon, 1991; Enya,

1992; The Celts (reissued), 1992; The Book Of Trees, 1996; On My Way Home, 1998; Storms in Africa, 1998; Singles include: Orinoco Flow (Number 1, UK), 1988; Evening Falls, 1988; Storms In Africa (Part II), 1989; Caribbean Blue, 1991; How Can I Keep From Singing, 1991; Book Of Days, 1992; Anywhere Is, 1995; Only If, 1997; Oiche Chiun, 1998; Orinoco Flow, 1998. Honours: Grammy Award, Best New Age Album, Shepherd's Moon, 1993; IRMA Award, Best Irish Female Artist, 1993. Current Management: Aigle Music, 6 Danieli Drive, Artane, Dublin 5, Ireland.

EÖSZE László, b. 17 November 1923, Budapest, Hungary. Musicologist. m. (1) 1 son, 1 daughter, (2) Margit Szilléry, 1983. Education: PhD, Aesthetics and Literature. Appointments: Music Teacher and Pianist; Concerts in Hungary and Europe, 1946-51; Editor, 1955-57, Chief Editor, 1957-61, Art Director, 1961-87, Editio Musica, Budapest. Publications: 16 books including: Life and Work of Zoltán Kodály, 1956; Zoltán Kodály's Life in Pictures, 1957; History of Opera, 1960; Giuseppe Verdi, 1961, 2nd edition, 1966, enlarged, 1975; Zoltán Kodály, His Life and Work, in English, 1962, in German, 1965; Zoltán Kodály, 1967; Kodály, His Life in Pictures and Documents, in English and German, 1971; Richard Wagner, 1969; Richard Wagner, Eine Chronik seines Lebens und Schaffens, 1969; Zoltán Kodály, életének krónikája, 1977; 2nd , enlarged edition, 2007; 119 római Liszt dokumentum, 1980; Selected studies on Z Kodály, 2000; Essays and articles in various languages; Contributions to numerous professional publications. Honours: Erkel Prize, 1977; Gramma Award, 1978; Medium Cross of the Order of the Hungarian Republic, 1998; Medal for Merit of the President of the Republic, 2003; Grand Prize of the National Society of Creative Artists, 2003. Memberships: Honorary Co-president, F Liszt Society; Executive Secretary, 1975-95, International Kodály Society; Hungarian Musicological Society, 1996-. Address: Attila ut 133, 1012 Budapest, Hungary.

EPHRON Nora, b. 19 May 1941, New York, USA. Author; Scriptwriter. Education: BA, Wellesley College. m. (1) Dan Greenberg, (2) Carl Bernstein, 2 sons, (3) Nicholas Pileggi. Appointments: Reporter, New York Post, 1963-68; Freelance Writer, 1968-; Contributing Editor, New York Magazine, 1973-74; Film appearances: Crimes and Misdemeanours; Husband and Wives. Publications: Wallflower at the Orgy, 1970; Crazy Salad, 1975; Scribble, Scribble, 1978; Heartburn, 1983; Nora Ephron Collected, 1991; Screenplays: Silkwood (with Alice Arlen), 1983; Heartburn, 1986; When Harry Met Sally..., 1989; Cookie (co-executive producer, co-screenwriter with Delia Ephron); Sleepless in Seattle (also director), 1993; Mixed Nuts (also director); Michael (also director), 1996; You've Got Mail (also director), 1998; Red tails in Love: a Wildlife Drama in Central Park (also producer and director), 2000; Hanging Up (also producer), 2000; Lucky Numbers (director and screenwriter), 2000; Bewitched (director and screenwriter), 2005. Address: c/o Sam Cohm International Creative Management, 40 West 57th Street, New York, NY 10019, USA.

EPPERT Günter J, b. 2 August 1933, Friedland, Czechia, Germany. Chemist. m. Christa Traubach, 2 sons, 1 daughter. Education: Diploma, 1958; Dr rer nat, 1961; Dr habil, 1980. Appointments: University Lecturer in Analytical Chemistry, 1982; Collaborator of UNIDO, 1984-89; Founder of the firm SEPSERV Separation Service Berlin, Germany, 1990-. Publications: About 70 publications and patents; Books: Einführung in die Schnelle Flüssigchromatographie; Leitfaden ausgewählter Trennmethoden; HPLC Trouble Shooting; Flüssigchromatographie HPLC - Theorie und

Praxis. Membership: Gesellschaft Deutscher Chemiker. Address: Dovestr 1B, 10587 Berlin, Germany. E-mail: sepserv.berlin@t-online.de Website: www.sepserv.com

EPPSTEIN Ury, b. 3 February 1925, Saarbrücken, Germany. Israeli Musicologist. m. Kikue Iguchi, 2 sons. Education: MA, Hebrew University of Jerusalem, 1949; Diploma in Japanese Language, Tokyo University of Foreign Studies, 1959; Diploma in Japanese Music, Tokyo University of Fine Arts and Music, 1963; PhD, Tel Aviv University, 1984. Appointments: Academic Assistant, Music Research Centre, Hebrew University, 1966-1972; Lecturer, Musicology and Theatre Departments, Tel Aviv University, 1972-1977; Lecturer, Departments of Musicology, Theatre, East Asian St, Hebrew University, 1972-; Guest Lecturer, Copenhagen University; East Asian Institute and Musicology Department, Lund University, 1986; Guest Lecturer, Dokkyō University, Japan; Tokyo University of Fine Arts and Music, 1997. Publications: Kanjinchō, translation of Kabuki play from Japanese, 1993; The Beginnings of Western Music in Meiji Era Japan, 1994; Musical Means to Political Ends - Japanese School Songs in Manchuria, 1996; Governmental Policy and Controversy - The Beginnings of Western Music in Japan, 1998; Changing Western Attitudes to Japanese Music in: Collected Articles and Essays in Honour of His Imperial Highness Prince Mikasa on the Occasion of His 88th Birthday, 2004. Honours: Order of the Rising Sun conferred by the Emperor of Japan, 1989; Israel Ministry of Education and Culture Prize for translation of Kabuki drama from Japanese, 1996. Memberships: European Association for Japanese Studies, Israel Musicological Society. Address: 80 Tchernihovsky St, Jerusalem, Israel.

EPSTEIN (Michael) Anthony (Sir), b. 18 May 1921, London, England. Medical Scientist; University Teacher. 2 sons, 1 daughter. Education: Trinity College, Cambridge; Middlesex Hospital Medical School, London. Appointments: House Surgeon, Middlesex Hospital, London and Addenbrooke's Hospital, Cambridge, 1944; Lieutenant and Captain, Royal Army Medical Corps, 1945-47; Assistant Pathologist, Middlesex Hospital Medical School, 1948-65; Berkeley Travelling Fellow, 1952-53; French Government Scholar, Institut Pasteur, Paris, 1952-53; Visiting Investigator, Rockefeller Institute, New York, 1956; Honorary Consultant Virologist, Middlesex Hospital, 1965-68; Reader in Experimental Pathology, Middlesex Hospital Medical School, 1965-68; Honorary Consultant Pathologist, Bristol Hospitals, 1968-82; Professor of Pathology, 1968-85, Head of Department, 1968-82, University of Bristol; Emeritus Professor of Pathology, University of Bristol and Fellow, Wolfson College, Oxford, 1986-. Publications: Over 240 original contributions to major scientific journals; Joint Founder Editor, International Review of Experimental Pathology, volumes 1-28, 1962-86; Joint Editor, 5 scientific books including The Epstein-Barr Virus 1979; The Epstein-Barr Virus: Recent Advances, 1986; Oncogenic γ-herpesviruses: An Expanding Family, 2001. Honours include: Paul Ehrlich and Ludwig Darmstaedter Prize and Medal, West Germany, 1973; Fellow, Royal Society, 1979; Honorary Professor, Sun Yat Sen University, China, 1981; Bristol Myers Award for Cancer Research, USA, 1982; Honorary Fellow, Queensland Institute of Medical Research, 1983; CBE, 1985; Prix Grifuel, France, 1986; Honorary Fellow, Royal College of Physicians of London, 1986; Extraordinary Governing Body Fellow, Wolfson College, Oxford, 1986-2001; Honorary MD, University of Edinburgh, 1986; Honorary Professor, Chinese Academy of Preventive Medicine, 1988; Gairdner International Award, Canada, 1988; Honorary Fellow, Royal Medical Society of Edinburgh,

1988; Member, Academia Europea, 1988; Honorary Fellow, Royal Society of Edinburgh, 1991; Knight Bachelor, 1991; Royal Medal, The Royal Society of London, 1992; Fellow, University College London, 1992; Honorary Fellow, Royal College of Pathologists of Australasia, 1995; Honorary DSc, University of Birmingham, 1996; Honorary MD, Charles University of Prague, 1998; Founder Fellow, Academy of Medical Sciences, 1998; Honorary Fellow, Wolfson College Oxford, 2001. Address: Nuffield Department of Clinical Medicine, University of Oxford, John Radcliffe Hospital, Oxford, OX3 9DU, England.

EPSTEIN Trude Scarlett, b. 13 July 1922, Vienna, Austria. Development Anthropologist. m. A L Epstein, deceased, 2 daughters. Education: Diploma in Industrial Administration and Economics and Political Science, Oxford; BSc, Economics, PhD, Economics, Manchester. Appointments: Director, PEGS; SESAC & Intervention; Research Professor, Sussex University, England; Senior Fellow, Australian National University, Canberra, Australia; Visiting Professor: Australian National University, University of Minnesota, University of Minneapolis; Catholic Divine Wood University, Papua New Guinea; Adjunct Professor: Maryland University; Bengurion University of the Negev, Israel. Publications: Books: Southern India: Yesterday, Today and Tomorrow; Village Voices – Forty Years of Rural Transformation in South India; Capitalism: Primitive and Modern – A Manual for Culturally Adapted Social Marketing; Articles include: Development, There is Another Way – A Rural-Urban Paradigm. Honours: Sir Murdoch McDonald Award; Rockefeller Research Fellowship; Honorary Fellowship of the Indian Anthropological Association and the British Association of Social Anthropology; The Most Excellent Order of the British Empire (OBE). Memberships: Agricultural Development Council; UK-UNESCO Social Science Advisory Board; Council, Royal Anthropological Institute. Address: 5 Viceroy Lodge, Kingsway, Hove BN3 4RA, England. E-mail: scarlett@epstein.net Website: www.pegs.org

ERIKSON J Alden, b. 3 March 1926, Milwaukee, Wisconsin, USA. Chemist. m. Ruth L, 1 son, 1 daughter. Education: BS, Chemistry, University of Wisconsin, 1950; PhD, Chemistry, Massachusetts Institute of Technology, 1953. Appointments: Sargeant, T/4, United State Army, 1944-46; Senior Research Associate, PPG Industries Inc, 1953-88; Retired, 1988-. Publications: Book, "Models of Reality" for Static, Nuclei and Atoms; Approximately 30 US patents. Honours: Sigma Xi, Wisconsin; Strathmore's Professional of the Year, 2006; Man of the Year, ABI, 2007; Listed in international biographical dictionaries. Memberships: American Chemical Society; Alpha Chi Sigma Fraternity. Address: 4212 E Ewalt Road, Gibsonia, PA 15044-9538, USA.

ERITJA Ramon, b. 9 August 1955, Lleida, Spain. Chemist. m. Elisenda Olivella, 2 sons. Education: BSc, Chemistry, BSc Pharmacy, PhD, Chemistry, 1984, University of Barcelona, Spain. Appointments: Postdoctoral Fellow, Department of Molecular Genetics, Beckman Research Institute of the City of Hope, Duarte, California, USA, 1984-86; Research Associate, Department of Chemistry and Biochemistry, University of Colorado, Boulder, Colorado, USA, 1986-87; Postdoctoral Fellow, Department of Organic Chemistry, University of Barcelona, Spain, 1987-89; Research Associate, Group Leader, Centre for Research and Development, CSIC Barcelona, Spain, 1989-94; Group Leader, European Molecular Biology Laboratory, Heidelberg, Germany, 1994-99; Group Leader, Consejo Superior de Investigaciones Científicas, Barcelona, Spain, 1999-. Publications: 180 publications on synthesis and study of properties of oligonucleotides and peptides in scientific journals. Memberships: American Peptide Society; International Society for Nucleosides, Nucleotides and Nucleic Acids. Address: Tarragona 106, 1, 1, E-08015, Barcelona, Spain. E-mail: recgma@cid.csic.es

ERMENTINI Augusto Romolo, b. 16 November 1927, Genova, Italy. Psychiatrist. m. Graziella Pisa, 1 daughter. Education: Graduate, Medicine, 1952; Istituto Neuropsichiatrico San Lazzaro, Reggio Emilia, 1953-54; Psychiatry, Clinica delle Malattie Nervose e Mentali, University Milan, 1955-57; Clinica Psichiatrica University Milan, 1959-64; Psychoanalysis, Psychotherapeutic Relaxation, Child Psychotherapy, Rorschach Diagnostic Techniques, Clinique Psychiatrique de l'Universite Bel-Air, Geneve, Switzerland, 1961-62. Appointments: Counsellor, Child Psychiatry, Ente Comunale di Assistenza, Milan, 1958; Registrar, Psychiatry, Policlinico, Milan, 1968-75; Adjunct Professor of Psychometrics, Adjunct Professor of Psychodynamic Psychology, University Trento, 1970-71; Adjunct Professor, Criminal Anthropology, University Milan, 1972-73; Adjunct Professor, General Psychopathology, University Milan, 1977-78; Professor, General Psychiatry, University of Brescia, 1978-79; Professor, Psychiatry (3rd Chair), University Milan, 1979-80; Full Professor, Psychiatry, University of Brescia, 1982-2004; Chief, Department of Mental Health of Brescia, 1998-2002; Emeritus Professor, Psychiatry, University of Brescia, 2004-. Publications: Over 200 articles including: La depressione nell' epilessia, 1962; Il Thematic Apperception Test nella psiconevrosi ossessiva, 1967; Psicologia, Psicopatologia e Delitto, 1971; Piromania, 1973; Contributi allo studio del manierismo, 1975; La prevenzione della criminalità, 1975; Droga, famiglia e società, 1977; Psicopatologia generale e schizofreniz, 1979; Le depressioni e le parafrenie, 1980; Le nevrosi e le psicosi esogene, 1981; Edward Munch – arte e psicopatologia, 1989; Il transessualismo: un fenomeno antropologico, culturale e psichiatrico, 2003; Manuale Rorschach, 2008. Honours: Award of Excellence in Criminal Anthropology, University of Cagliari, 1970. Address: via Tosio 15/c, Brescia, Italy.

ERMIS Sitki Samet, b. 6 May 1969, Istanbul, Turkey. Ophthalmologist. m. Betul Ugur, 3 sons. Education: Medical Doctor, 1993, Ophthalmologist, 1997, University of Istanbul; Fellow, Kyoto Prefectural University of Medicine, Japan, 2003. Appointment: Assistant Professor of Ophthalmology, 2000-05, Associate Professor of Ophthalmology, 2005-, University of Afyon Kocatepe, Turkey. Publications: Articles to professional journals; Chapter in book, Progress in Glaucoma Research. Honour: Japanese Government Scholarship (Mombusho). Memberships: Turkish Ophthalmic Society; American Society of Cataract and Refractive Surgery; European Society of Cataract and Refractive Surgeons; Association for Research in Vision and Ophthalmology. Address: Seyhresmi mah, Yusufziyapasa sk, No:10/3 34240, Fatih, Istanbul, Turkey. E-mail: ssermis@yahoo.com

ESAKI Leo, b. 12 March 1925, Osaka, Japan. Physicist. m. (1) Masako Araki, 1959, 1 son, 2 daughters, (2) Masako Kondo, 1986. Education: Graduated, University of Tokyo, 1947, PhD. Appointments: With Sony Corporation, 1956-60; IBM Fellow, 1967-92, IBM T J Watson Research Center, New York, 1960-92, Manager, Device Research, 1962-92, IBM Corporation, USA; Director, IBM Japan, 1976-92, Yamada Science Foundation, 1976-; President, University of Tsukuba, Ibaraki, Japan, 1992-98; Chair, Science and Technology Promotion Foundation of Ibaraki, 1998-; Director General, Tsukuba International Congress Center, 1999-; President,

Shibaura Institute of Technology, 2000-. Publications: Numerous articles in professional journals. Honours: Nishina Memorial Award, 1959; Asahi Press Award, 1960; Toyo Rayon Foundation Award, 1961; Morris N Liebmann Memorial Prize, 1961; Stuart Ballantine Medal, Franklin Institute, 1961; Japan Academy Award, 1965; IBM Fellow, 1967; Joint Winner, Nobel Prize for Physics, 1973; Order of Culture, Japanese Government, 1974; Sir John Cass Senior Visiting Research Fellow, London Polytechnic, 1981; US-Asia Institute, Science Achievement Award, 1983; American Physical Society, Institute Prize for New Materials, 1985; IEEE Medal of Honour, 1991; Japan Prize, 1998; Grand Cordon Order of Rising Sun, First Class, 1998. Memberships: Japan Academy; American Philosophical Society; Max-Planck Gesellschaft; Foreign Associate, NAS; American National Academy of Engineering. Address: Shibaura Institute of Technology, 3-9-14 Shibaura, Minato-ku, Tokyo 108, Japan.

ESHAGHURSHAN Boburshan, b. 24 April 1952, Hamedan, Iran. Architect; Building Engineer; Urban Planner. m. Azam Sadechi, 2 daughters. Education: Doctorate in Architecture, Doctorate in Building Engineering, University of Rome; Certificate of CADD, SAIT. Appointments: Architect, University of Calgary, Canada; Architect, Architectural Engineering, Urban Planner, Robco Design & Consulting, Calgary; Architect, Architectural Engineer, Jasco Engineering Consulting, Calgary; Architect, Urban Planner, Armando Architect & Urban Planning; Architectural Engineer, Curtis Engineering, Calgary; Architect, Anfuso Architecture, Rome, Italy. Publications: Comprehensive Urban Development; South West Sprinkbank Development Proposals. Honours: Award for Excellence, American Concrete Institute. Memberships: Royal Architectural Institute of Canada; Alberta Architects Association; Italian Architects & Engineering Association; Iranian Architects Society. Address: 638 Diamond Court SE, Calgary, Alberta T2J 7C8, Canada. E-mail: robco@cia.com

ESSLEMONT Iain, b. 2 September 1932, Aberdeen, Scotland. General Medical Practitioner (Retired). m. Mary Gibb Mars, 1 son, 2 daughters. Education: MB ChB, 1956; D ObstRCOG, 1960; MRCGP, 1973; Dip Aust COG, 1980; FRACGP, 1981; MCGP (Malaysia), 1982; FAFP (Malaysia), 1997; FRCGP, 2006. Appointments: House Surgeon, Ayr County Hospital, Scotland, 1956-57; House Physician, Paediatrician, General Hospital, Dewsbury, England, 1957; RAMC, 1957-59; House Surgeon, Obstetrics, Ayrshire Central Hospital, Scotland, 1960; General Practitioner, Cha'ah, Johore, Malaya, 1960-62; General Practitioner, Drs Allan and Gunstensen, Penang, Malaysia, 1962-77; MO, Kununurra, Western Australia, 1977-78; Southside After-Hours Medical Service, Perth, Western Australia, 1978-82; General Practitioner, Huntingdale Family Medical Practice, Gosnells, Western Australia, 1979-99; General Practitioner, Gosnells Health Care Practice, Gosnells, Western Australia, 1999; Examiner, Royal Australian College of General Practitioners, 1985-2007; President, The Dalton Society, 1994; External Clinical Teacher, Royal Australian College of General Practitioners, 2001-02. Publications: Articles in the Australian Family Physician: Non surgical treatment for Meibomian Cysts, 1995; Sick doctors – a personal story, Why use soap?, What is a GP?, The clue was in the ingots, Birth, death and life, 2001; Where is general practice heading?, Dying, 2002. Honour: Paul Harris Fellowship (Rotary), 1998. Memberships: Royal College of General Practitioners; Royal Australian College of General Practitioners; Academy of Family Physicians Malaysia. Address: 2, Chardonnay Avenue, Margaret River, Western Australia, 6285 Australia. E-mail: esslemont@wn.com.au

ESTEFAN Gloria (Fajado), b. 1 September 1957, Havana, Cuba. Singer; Songwriter. m. Emilio Estefan, 1 September 1978. Education: BA, Psychology, University of Miami, 1978. Career: Singer, backed by Miami Sound Machine, 1974-; Billed as Gloria Estefan, 1989-; Appearances include: Tokyo Music Festival, Japan, 1985; World tour, The Simple Truth, benefit concert for Kurdish refugees, Wembley, White House State Dinner, for President of Brazil, 1991; South American tour, Royal Variety Performance, London, before Prince and Princess of Wales, Co-organiser, benefit concert for victims of Hurricane Andrew, Florida, 1992; 45 million albums sold to date. Compositions include: Anything For You; Don't Wanna Lose You; Oye Mi Canto (co-written with Jorge Casas and Clay Ostwald); Cuts Both Ways; Coming Out Of The Dark (co-written with Emilio Estefan and Jon Secada); Always Tomorrow; Christmas Through Their Eyes (co-written with Dianne Warren). Recordings: Albums: Renacer, 1976; Eyes Of Innocence, 1984; Primitive Love, 1986; Let It Loose, 1988; Anything For You (Number 1, UK), Cuts Both Ways, 1989; Exitos De Gloria Estefan, 1990; Into The Light, 1991; Greatest Hits, 1992; Mi Tierra, Christmas Through Your Eyes, 1993; Hold Me, Thrill Me, Kiss Me, 1994; Abriendo Puertas, 1995; Destiny, 1996; Gloria!; Santo Santo, 1999; Alma Caribeño: Caribbean Soul, 2000; Also featured on: Jon Secada, Jon Secada (also co-producer), 1991; Til Their Eyes Shine (The Lullaby Album), 1992; Hit singles include: Dr Beat, 1984; Conga, Hot Summer Nights, used in film soundtrack Top Gun, Bad Boy, Words Get In The Way, 1986; Rhythm Is Gonna Get You, 1987; Can't Stay Away From You, Anything For You (Number 1, US), 1-2-3, 1988; Oye Mi Canto (Hear My Voice), Here We Are, Don't Wanna Lose You, Get On Your Feet, 1989; Coming Out of The Dark (Number 1, US), Remember Me With Love, 1991; Always Tomorrow, 1992; Cuts Both Ways, Go Away, Mi Tierra, 1993; Turn the Beat Around, 1994; Abrienda Puertos; Tres Deseos; Mas Alla. Publications: The Magically Mysterious Adventures of Noelle the Bulldog, 2005; Noelle's Treasure Tale: A New Mysterious Adventure, 2006. Honours: Grand Prize, Tokyo Music Festival, 1985; Numerous Billboard awards, 1986-; American Music Award, Favourite Pop/Rock Duo or Group, 1989; Crystal Globe Award, 21 Club, New York, 1990; Latin Music Award, Crossover Artist Of Year, 1990; Humanitarian Award, B'Nai B'rith, 1992; Desi Entertainment Awards, Performer of Year, Song of Year, 1992; Humanitarian Award, National Music Foundation (for helping victims of Hurricane Andrew), 1993. Address: c/o Estefan Enterprises, 6205 Bird Road, Miami Beach, FL 33155, USA.

ESTEVE-COLL Elizabeth Anne Loosemore, b. 14 October 1938, Ripon, Yorkshire, England. Retired Academic; Freelance Arts Consultant. m. J Esteve-Coll, deceased. Education: Trinity College, Dublin; University of London. Appointments: Keeper, National Art Library, 1985-88; Director, Victoria & Albert Museum, 1988-2005; Vice-Chancellor, University of East Anglia, 2005-07; Chancellor, University of Lincoln, 2001-. Publications: Numerous articles. Honours: DBE, 1995; Hon FRIBA; CIMgt; Senior Fellow, Birkbeck College, University of London; Order of the Rising Sun, 2005; Honorary degrees: Teeside, Sussex, Hull, Kingston, East Anglia and Surrey Universities. Memberships: Institute of Management; Trustee, Sainsbury Institute for the Study of Japanese Arts & Culture. Address: Coldham Hall, Tuttington, Aylsham, Norfolk NR11 6TA, England.

ESTEVEZ Emilio, b. 12 May 1962, New York, USA. Actor. m. Paula Abdul, 1992, divorced 1994, 1 son, 1 daughter. Appointments: Actor, films include: Tex, 1982; Nightmares, 1983; The Outsiders, 1983; The Breakfast Club, 1984; Repo

Man, 1984; St Elmo's Fire, 1984; That Was Then...This is Now, 1985; Maximum Overdrive, 1986; Wisdom (also writer and director), 1986; Stakeout, 1987; Men at Work, 1989; Freejack, 1992; Loaded Weapon, 1993; Another Stakeout, 1993; Champions II, 1993; Judgement Night, 1993; D2: The Mighty Ducks, 1994; The Jerky Boys (co-executive, producer); Mighty Ducks 3; Mission Impossible, 1996; The War at Home, 1996; The Bang Bang Club, 1998; Killer's Head, 1999; Sand, 2000; Rated X, 2000; The LA Riot Spectacular, 2005; Bobby, 2006; Arthur and the Invisibles (voice), 2006. Address: c/o UTA, 5th Floor, 9560 Wilshire Boulevard, Beverly Hills, CA 90212, USA.

ESTÉVEZ RADÍO Hernán, b. 5 August 1950, Montevideo, Uruguay. Physicist. m. Eva Fernández Roqueiro, 1 daughter. Education: 2nd Class Deck Officer, 1972, 1st Class Deck Officer, 1974, Captain, 1978, Merchant Marine; BS, Physics, 1986; MS, Physics, 1987; PhD, Physics, 1992. Appointments: 3rd Officer, 2nd Officer, 1972, Chief Officer, 1973, Professor, 1978, Atlantic Polytechnic Institute; Professor, National University of Distance Education, Pontevedra, Spain, 1990-. Publications: IEEE Transactions on Microware Theory and Techniques; IEEE Transactions on Antennas and Propagation, Microwave and Optical Technology Letters; IJEEE; Anales de Fisica; Revisita Espanola de Fisica. Memberships: IEEE; Spanish Royal Society of Physics. Address: Torrente Ballester 4-1°F, 36204 Vigo, Pontevedra, Spain. E-mail: hernanestevezradio@hotmail.com

ETHERIDGE Melissa Lou, b. Leavenworth, Kansas, USA. Singer; Songwriter; Musician (guitar). 4 children. Musical Education: Berklee College of Music, Boston. Career: Musician, Los Angeles bars, 5 years; Recording artiste, 1988-. Recordings: Albums: Melissa Etheridge, 1988; Brave And Crazy, 1989; Never Enough, 1992; Yes I Am, 1993; Your Little Secret, 1995; Breakdown, 1999; Skin, 2001; Lucky, 2004; Greatest Hits: The Road Less Travelled, 2005; The Awakening, 2007; Singles: I'm the Only One, 1994; Come to My Window, 1994; If I Wanted To, 1995; Nowhere to Go, 1996; Angels Would Fall, 1999; Enough of Me, 2000; Breathe, 2004; This Moment, 2004; Cry Baby, 2005; Refugee, 2005; I Run for Life, 2005; I Need to Wake Up, 2006. Honours: Grammy Nomination, Bring Me Some Water, 1988. Current Management: Bill Leopold, W F Leopold Management, 4425 Riverside Drive, Ste 102, Burbank, CA 91505, USA.

ETIENNE Gilbert, b. 22 June 1928, Neuchâtel, Switzerland. Emeritus Professor. m. Annette Etienne, 2 sons, 1 daughter. Education: LLB, University of Neuchâtel, Switzerland, 1951; Diploma, Institute of Oriental Civilisation, Paris, France, 1954; PhD, India's Economy, University of Neuchâtel, Switzerland, 1955. Appointments: Lecturer, Hindu Art, Punjab University, Lahore, Pakistan, 1952-53; General Assistant, Favre-Leuba Company (Swiss Watch Company), Bombay, India, 1956-58; Professor of Development Economics, Graduate Institute of International Studies, 1959-96; Professor, Graduate Institute of Development Studies, 1964-96; Professor Emeritus at both institutes, 1996-; Visiting Professor, MIT, Cornell and Chicago Universities; Visiting Professor, EDI, World Bank, Collège de France, Paris. Publications: Numerous books include most recently; Chine-Inde, Chinese edition, 2000; Contribution to Le Pakistan (ed C Jaffrelot), 2002; Imprévisible Afghanistan, 2002; Le développement à contre-courant, 2003; Chine-Inde, la grade competition, 2007. Honour: Global Award for outstanding contribution to social and economic development studies, Priyadarshni Academy, Bombay, 2002. Memberships: International Committee of the Red Cross, 1973-85; Founding Member and Vice-chairman of the Board of African Institute (later Institute of Development Studies), 1961-64; Chairman, Geneva-Asia Society, 1997-. Address: 10 Chemin de Grange-Bonnet, 1224, Chene-Bougeries Genève, Switzerland.

ETTY Robert, b. 6 November 1949, Waltham, Lincolnshire, England. Schoolteacher. Education: BA. Publications: Hovendens Violets, 1989; New Pastorals, 1992; Marking Places, 1994; A Selection, 1997; Small Affairs on the Estate, 2000; The Blue Box, 2001; Half a Field's Distance, 2006. Contributions to: Poetry Review; The North; Spectator; Anon; Outposts; Rialto; Agenda; Stand; Verse; The Independent; Critical Survey. Address: Evenlode, Church Lane, Keddington, Louth, Lincolnshire LN11 7HG, England.

EUBANK Chris, b. 8 August 1966, Dulwich, England. Middleweight Boxer. m. 4 children. Career: WBC International Middleweight Boxing Champion, 2 defences, March-November, 1990; WBO Middleweight Boxing Champion, 3 defences, November 1990-August 1991; WBO World Super-Middleweight Boxing Champion, 14 defences, September 1991-March 1995; Lost title to Steve Collins, Cork, Sept 1995; Failed to regain title against Joe Calzaghe, Sheffield, October 1997; Unsuccessful fights for WBO Cruiserweight title against Carl Thompson, Manchester, April 1998, Sheffield, July 1998; Patron Breakthrough; Ambassador, International Fund for Animal Welfare; Spokesperson, National Society for the Prevention of Cruelty to Children. Address: 9 The Upper Drive, Hove, East Sussex, BN3 6GR, England.

EUN In-Ung, b. 6 May 1962, Jeonbuk, Republic of Korea. Professor. m. Yoo-Sook Lee, 1 son, 2 daughters. Education: BSc, Precision Mechanical Engineering, 1984, MSc, Mechanical Engineering, 1986, Chonbuk National University; Dr Ing, Mechanical Engineering, RWTH Aachen University, Germany, 1999. Appointments: Assistant, Department of Mechanical Design, Chonbuk National University, 1987-88; Researcher, Institute of Agricultural Engineering, University of Bonn, Germany, 1992-93; Researcher, Laboratory of Machine Tools and Production Engineering, RWTH Aachen University, 1993-94; Professor, Department of Mechatronics, Changwon National University, Republic of Korea, 2000-01; Professor, Department of Die and Mold Design, 2002-, Director of Planning and Co-ordination, 2005-06, Director of Academic Affairs, 2006-, Kyonggi Institute of Technology, Republic of Korea. Publications: Simulation of Run out caused by Imperfection of Ball Bearing for High-Speed Spindle Units, 2006; An Elastic Deformation Model of High-Speed Spindle Units, 2006. Honours: Highly Commended Paper Award, Korean Society for Precision Engineering. Memberships: Before Babel Brigade, Korea; Korean Society of Mechanical Engineers. Address: Baiksealmaeul Hyundai Apt 598-102, 870-1 Jeongjadong, Jangangu Suwonsi, Kyonggido, 440-300 Republic of Korea. E-mail: iueun@kinst.ac.kr

EUN Seok Chan, b. 15 January 1972, Jeon-Ju, Korea. Doctor. m. Hong Jae Hee, 1 son. Education: Graduate, College of Medicine, Hallym University, 1997. Appointments: Assistant Professor, Seoul National University, Bundang Hospital, 2007-. Memberships: Korea Society of Plastic and Reconstructive Surgeons. Address: Seoul National University, Bundang Hospital, 300 Gumi-Dong, Bundang-Gu, Seongnam-Si, Gyeonggi-do, 463-707, Korea. E-mail: sceun@snubb.org

EVAIGE Wanda Jo, b. Frederick, Oklahoma, USA. Store Owner; Retired Entrepreneur; Retired Teacher. Education: Huston-Tillotson College, Austin, Texas; Graduate Study,

University of Oklahoma, Norman, Oklahoma. Appointments: Legislative Commission, Oklahoma Education Association, 1974-83; Congressional Contact for 4th District, Oklahoma Education Association, 1980-83; City Council Member, elected 1983; Mayoral Representative for Tillman County, 1988-90, 1992-; Delegate, Democratic Convention, Atlanta, 1988; Oklahoma Constitution and Revision Committee, 1988-90; Minority Representative for Tillman County, 1990-91; Judicial Nominating Commission, 1993-99; Federal Judicial Commission, 1997-; Association of South Central Oklahoma Government, President, 2000-02; Huston-Tillotson University Alumni President, 2005-07; Mayor of Frederick (one term); Vice Mayor of Frederick (two terms); City Council Member (present); National President, Boyd Alumni Association; Past President, Frederick Association of Classroom Teachers; Past President, Theta Upsilon Omega Chapter of Alpha Kappa Alpha Sorority Inc; Tillman County 9-1-1 Board, Chairperson; Several committees, Oklahoma Municipal League; Affirmative Action Representative, Oklahoma's 4th Congressional District (two terms). Honours: Frederick Teacher of the Year, 1981; Frederick's Most Useful Female Citizen, 1990; O E Kennedy Humanitarian Award, Boyd Alumni, 1988; Oklahoma Human Rights Award Recipient, 1998; Beta Sigma Phi Frederick Woman of the Year, 2000-01; Frederick Chamber of Commerce Volunteer of the Year, 2004; Listed in international biographical dictionaries. Memberships: St Paul AME Church; Alpha Kappa Alpha Sorority Inc; Oklahoma Education Association/National Education Association; Frederick Chamber of Commerce; Board of Trustees, Shorter College, Little Rock, Arkansas; Affirmative Action Representative, Oklahoma's Fourth Congressional District; Member, Oklahoma Constitution Revision Commission; Huston-Tillotson University Alumni.

EVANGELISTA Linda, b. 10 May, 1965, St Catherines, Toronto, Ontario, Canada. Model. m. Gerald Marie (divorced 1993). 1 son previous relationship. Career: Face of Yardley Cosmetics; Numerous catwalk appearances. Address: c/o Elite Model Management, 40 Parker Street, London WC2B 5PH, England.

EVANS Chris, b. 1 April 1966, Warrington, England. Broadcaster. m. (1) Carol McGiffin, 1991, divorced, (2) Billie Piper, 2000, divorced, (3) Natasha Shishmanian, 2007. 1 daughter from previous girlfriend. Career: Numerous sundry jobs; Joined Piccadilly Radio, Manchester; Producer, GLR Radio, London; Presenter of numerous television programmes including Don't Forget Your Toothbrush, co-presenter, The Big Breakfast; Presenter, Radio 1 Breakfast Show, 1995-97; Virgin Radio Breakfast Show, 1997-2001; Established Ginger Productions, media production company; Presenter and Executive Producer, TFI Friday, Channel 4; Saturday Afternoon Show, 2005, Drive Time, 2006-, BBC Radio 2. Presenter BRIT Awards 2005, 2006. Honours: British Comedy Award Prizes, Best Entertainment Series, Top Channel 4 Entertainment Presenter, 1995; Sony music radio personality of the Year, 2006. Address: Ginger Productions, 131-151 Great Titchfield Street, London W1P 8DP, England.

EVANS (Daniel) John (Owen), b. 17 November 1953, Morriston, Swansea, South Wales. Broadcaster, Academic, Writer. Education: BMus, 1975; MA, 1976; PhD, University of Cardiff, Wales. Appointments: First Research Scholar, Britten-Pears Library and Archive, Aldeburgh, England, 1980-84; Music Producer, BBC Radio 3, 1985-89; Senior Producer, BBC Singers, 1989-92; Chief Producer, Series, BBC Radio 3, 1992-93; Head of Music Department, BBC Radio 3, 1993-97; Head of Classical Music, BBC Radio, 1997-2000;

Head of Music Programming, BBC Radio 3, 2000-2006; Executive Director, Oregon Bach Festival, 2007. Publications: Author with Donald Mitchell, Benjamin Britten: Pictures from a Life 1913-1976, 1978; Editor, Benjamin Britten: His Life and Operas, by Eric Walter White, revised 2nd edition, 1982; currently editing Benjamin Britten's private diaries for publication. Contributions include: A Britten Companion, 1984; A Britten Source Book, 1987; ENO, Royal Opera House and Cambridge Opera Guides on Britten's Peter Grimes, Gloriana, The Turn of the Screw, Death in Venice. Honours: Prix Italia Award and Charles Heidsieck Award, 1989; Royal Philharmonic Society Award, 1994; Sony Radio Award, 1997; Listed in Who's Who publications and biographical dictionaries. Memberships: Chair, Opera Jury for RPS Awards and Sony Radio Awards; Juror, BBC Singer of the World Competition; Tosti International Singing Competition, BBC Choir of the Year, Prix Italia 2005; Vice-President, Welsh Music Guild; Director, The Britten Estate Ltd; Trustee, The Britten-Pears Will Trust; Trustee, The Britten Family and Charitable Settlement. Address: Oregon Bach Festival, 1257 University of Oregon, Eugene OR97403-1257, USA. E-mail: bachfest@uoregon-edu

EVANS David, b. 27 August 1942, London, England. Professor of Logic and Metaphysics. Education: BA, MA, PhD, Classics, University of Cambridge. Appointments: Research Fellow, 1964-65, Official Fellow and Lecturer, 1965-78, Sidney Sussex College, Cambridge; Visiting Professor, Philosophy Department, Duke University, USA, 1972-73; Professor of Logic and Metaphysics, 1978, Head of Philosophy Department, 1978-92, Dean of the Faculty of Arts, 1986-89, Director of the School of Philosophical and Anthropological Studies, 1987-95, Chair, Postgraduate Research Committee, 1993-2003, Chair, University Research Ethics Committee, 2004-, Queen's University, Belfast. Publications: Books: Aristotle's Concept of Dialectic, 1977; Aristotle, 1987; Edited books: Moral Philosophy and Contemporary Problems, 1988; Teaching Philosophy on the Eve of the Twenty-First Century (with Ioanna Kuçuradi), 1998; Philosophy of Education, 2006. Honours: Craven Student, University of Cambridge, 1963-64; Member of the Royal Irish Academy, 1983. Memberships include: Steering Committee, International Federation of Philosophical Societies; British Philosophical Society; National Committee for Philosophy, Royal Irish Academy; Royal Institute of Philosophy; Aristotelian Society; Association Internationale des Professeurs de Philosophie; Arts Council of Northern Ireland; Governor, Strand Primary School, Belfast. Address: School of Philosophical Studies, Queen's University, Belfast BT7 1NN, Northern Ireland. E-mail: jdg.evans@qub.ac.uk

EVANS Donald, (Onwy), b. 12 June 1940, Cardiganshire, Wales. Retired Welsh Teacher. m. Pat Thomas, 29 December 1972, 1 son. Education: Honours Degree, Welsh, 1962, Diploma, Education, 1963, University College of Wales Aberystwyth; PhD, University of Wales Lampeter, 2006. Appointments: Welsh Master, Ardwyn Grammar School, Aberystwyth, 1963-73; Penglais Comprehensive School, Aberystwyth, 1973-84; Welsh Specialist, Cardigan Junior School, 1984-91; Welsh Supply Teacher in Ceredigion, Primary and Comprehensive Schools, 1991-2002. Publications: Egin (Shoots), 1976; Parsel Persain (Sweet Parcel) (editor), 1976; Haidd (Barley), 1977; Grawn (Seeds), 1979; Blodeugerdd o Gywyddau (Anthology of Alliterative Poems) (editor), 1981; Eden, 1981; Gwenoliaid (Swallows), 1982; Machlud Canrif (Century's Sunset), 1983; Eisiau Byw (Needing to Live), 1984; Cread Crist (Christ's Creation), 1986; O'r Bannau Duon (From the Black Hills), 1987; Iasau (Thrills), 1988;

Seren Poets 2 (with others), 1990; The Life and Work of Rhydwen Williams, 1991; Wrth Reddf (By Instinct), 1994; Asgwrn Cefen (Backbone), 1997; Y Cyntefig Cyfoes (The Contemporary Primitive), 2000; Contributions to: Several publications. Honours: National Eisteddfod Crown and Chair, 1977, 1980; Welsh Arts Council Literary Prizes, 1977, 1983, 1989; Welsh Academy Literary Award, 1989. Memberships: Welsh Academy; Welsh Poetry Society; Gorsedd of Bards, National Eisteddfod of Wales. Address: Y Plas, Talgarreg, Llandysul, Ceredigion SA44 4XA, West Wales.

EVANS Erin Dyan, b. 16 October 1970, Brisbane, Australia. Biotechnologist; Business Executive. m. Jason Edward Hilder, 1 daughter. Education: Bachelor of Applied Science, Biotechnology, First Class Honours, University of Queensland, 1988-92; Certificate, Barefoot Doctor, Chinese Medicine, 1994; Doctoral Studies, Biotechnology, University of Queensland and Agen Biomedical, 1993-96; Certificate in Clinical Research Associate Training, 1997, Certificate in Regulatory Affairs, 1997, IBAH Training Centre, Sydney; Master of Business Administration, Henley Management College, UK. Appointments: Scientist (PhD Studentship), Agen Biomedical Ltd and University of Queensland, 1993-96; Events and Publicity Manager for "Everyday Wonders" Conference, Australia, 1996-97; Clinical and Regulatory Affairs Manager, Vaccine Solutions, Australia, 1997-98; Senior Compliance Auditor, Corporate Quality Systems, Genzyme, The Netherlands, 2000-2003; Executive Director, Business Development, The Australian Lung Foundation, 2003; Director, Transcendence Consultants, 2003-; Voluntary Consultant work: Business Development and Communications, The Tube, Amsterdam; Strategy and Development Consultant, Kigoma Development Promotion Agency, Tanzania; Establishment of European NGO Office with 2 others, as Director of Strategy, 2004; Quality Services Executive, Head of Cardiovascular Division Quality, Quintiles, 2005; Strategy & Planning Advisor, Suncorp, 2008-. Publication: Patent: Development of a clot-targeted anticoagulant, 1994; 'Between the Covers: Revealing the State Library of Queensland's Collections', co-author and editor, 2006. Honours include: Australian Postgraduate Research Award, 1993-96; Finalist, Queensland Young Achiever of the Year Award, 1998; Finalist, Young Australian of the Year Award, Science and Technology Category, 1998; Award for Excellence, Allergan, 1999; Woman of the Year 2005, American Biographical Institute; Editor, Professional Women's Advisory Board, American Biographical Institute, 2005-; Listed in Who's Who publications and biographical dictionaries. Memberships: Catalyst Team Member, Evolutionary Leadership Action Network; The Centre for Human Emergence, The Netherlands; Findhorn Foundation Stewards; British Association of Research Quality Assurance; Toastmasters; Foundation Member of Genesis, 2006; Member of 'Be the Change' conference organising committee; Founder Member of Davies Park Protection Group, 2006; Member, Brisbane Integral Institute, 2007; Member, West End Community Association, 2007. Address: 36 Loch Street, West End, Brisbane, QLD 4101, Australia. E-mail: dr.erin.evans@gmail.com

EVANS Janet M, b. 16 September 1956, Raleigh, North Carolina, USA. Publisher. 2 sons. Education: Technical and Administrative Training. Appointments: Marketing assistant, Evans and Wade Advertising Ltd, 1977-78; Chief Executive Officer, American Biographical Institute: Chairman, ABI Research Association, 1979-97; Magazine and Newsletter Editor, 1979-; Director, Conference on Culture and Education, 1984; Executive Director, World Institute of Achievement,

1985-; President, American Biographical Institute, 1997-; General-in-Residence, United Cultural Convention, 2001-. Publications: Editor, Publisher, Biographical Reference. Honours: Honorary Life Fellow, International Biographical Association. Memberships: Foundation for International Meetings, Board Member 1992; Publishers' Association of the South; Raleigh Chamber of Commerce; American Society of Professional and Executive Women; National Association of Independent Publishers; Publishers Marketing Association. Address: American Biographical Institute, PO Box 31226, 5126 Bur Oak Circle, Raleigh, NC 27622, USA.

EVANS Louise, b. 6 September, San Antonio, Texas, USA. Investor; Clinical Psychologist (retired); Philanthropist. m. Thomas Ross Gambrell. Education: BS, Psychology, Northwestern University, 1949; MS, Clinical Psychology, Purdue University, 1952; Intern, Clinical Psychology, Menninger Foundation, 1953; PhD, Clinical Psychology, Purdue University, 1955; Post-doctoral Fellowship, Clinical Child Psychology, Department of Child Psychiatry, Menninger Clinic, 1956; Diploma, American Board of Examiners in Professional Psychology, 1966. Appointments: Teaching Assistant, Psychology Department, Purdue University, 1950-51; Intern, Menninger Foundation, 1952-53; Staff Psychologist, Kankakee State Hospital, Illinois, 1954-55; Postdoctoral Fellow Child Psychology, Menninger Clinic, US Public Health Service, 1955-56; Head Staff Psychologist, Child Guidance Clinic, Kings County Hospital, Brooklyn, New York, 1957-58; Clinical Research Consultant, Episcopal Diocese, St Louis, Missouri, 1959-60; Director, Psychology Clinic, Barnes-Renard Hospitals, Instructor, Medical Psychology, Washington University School of Medicine, St Louis, 1959-60; Private Practice, Fullerton, California, 1960-93. Publications: Articles in professional journals. Honours include: Citizenship Award for contributions to mental health (1 of first 5 ever given), Purdue University, 1975; Silver Goblet, World's Leading Biographee of 1987, IBC; World Biographical Hall of Fame, ABI, 1987; 25 Year Silver Achievement Award, ABI, 1993; World Lifetime Achievement Award, ABI, 1995; Distinguished Alumni Award, Purdue University, 1993; Old Master Award, Purdue University, 1993; Northwestern University College of Arts and Sciences, Merit Award (one of two given), 1997; International Woman of the Year, Medal of Honour, 1996-97; 2000 Outstanding Scientists of the 20th Century Medal; 2000 Outstanding Scientists of the 21st Century Medal, IBC; Scientific Achievement Award, ABI; American Psychological Association, International Division Award for Lifelong Contributions to the Advancement of Psychology Internationally, 2002; Plaque for Pioneering Leadership in International Psychology, 2003, Certificate as Ambassador in recognition of outstanding leadership and enduring commitment, 2003, International Council of Psychologists; Marie Curie Award and Gold Medal, IBC, 2006; ABI International Women's Review Board, Founding Member; Listed in numerous Who's Who publications and national and international biographical dictionaries. Memberships include Fellow of 15 professional organisations and societies, including: Life Fellow, IBA; Fellow: Academy of Clinical Psychology, American Psychological Association, Royal Society of Health, UK; Fellow, American Association for the Advancement of Science. Address: PO Box 6067, Beverly Hills, CA 90212-1067, USA.

EVANS William John, b. 23 July 1943, Bridgend, Wales. University Professor. m. Gillian Mary Phillips, 2 sons, 1 daughter. Education: BSc (Hons), PhD, 1969, DSc, 1996, University of Wales, Swansea. Appointments: Senior Scientific Officer, 1969-79, Principal Scientific Officer and

Head of Mechanical Design Research, 1979-85, (MOD(PE)) National Gas Turbine Establishment, Farnborough; Lecturer, Senior Lecturer, Reader, Interdisciplinary Research Centre and Materials Department, 1985-96, Professor and Director, Interdisciplinary Research Centre, 1997-2002, Director, Welsh Development Agency Centre of Excellence in Materials, 2002-2003, Director, Rolls Royce Technology Centre, 2001-, Head of Materials Research Centre, 2003-07, University of Wales Swansea. Publications: Over 200 scientific publications and numerous invitations to lecture at international events; Co-editor, Titanium 95 (3 volumes), 1996; Co-editor, Proceedings of the Component Optimisation Conference at Swansea (COMPASS 1999), 2000; Co-editor, COMPASS 2002, 2003. Honours: Elected Fellow, Royal Academy of Engineering; Visiting Professor, University of New South Wales, Australia; Listed in international biographical directories. Memberships: Fellow, Institute of Materials, Minerals and Mining (IOM³); Past President, South Wales Metallurgical Association; Chairman, Materials Network Wales (Welsh Development Agency sponsored); Editorial Board, Journal of Fatigue of Engineering Materials and Structures. Address: Materials Research Centre, School of Engineering, University of Wales Swansea, Singleton Park, Swansea SA2 8PP, Wales. E-mail: w.j.evans@swansea.ac.uk

EVANS Sir (William) Vincent (John), b. 20 October 1915, London, England. Barrister-at-Law. m. Joan Mary Symons, 1947, 1 son, 2 daughters. Education: Merchant Taylors' School, Northwood, 1925-34; BA, 1937, BCL, 1938, MA, 1941, Wadham College, Oxford; Called to the Bar, Lincoln's Inn, 1939; QC, 1973. Appointments: Served in HM Forces, 1939-46; Legal Adviser (Lieutenant Colonel), British Military Administration, Cyrenaica, 1945-46; Assistant Legal Adviser, Foreign Office, 1947-54; Legal Counsellor, UK Permanent Mission to United Nations, New York, 1954-59; Deputy Legal Adviser, Foreign Office, 1960-68; Legal Adviser, Foreign & Commonwealth Office, 1968-75; Director (Chairman), Bryant Symons & Co Ltd, London, 1964-85; UK Representative on European Committee on Legal Co-operation, 1965-75, Chair, 1969-71, Council of Europe; UK Representative on Council of Europe Steering Committee on Human Rights, 1976-80, Chair, 1979-80; Member, Human Rights Committee set up under the International Covenant on Civil & Political Rights, 1977-84; Judge, European Court of Human Rights, 1980-91; Member, Permanent Court of Arbitration, 1987-97. Honours: MBE (Military), 1945; CMG, 1959; KCMG, 1970; GCMG, 1976; QC, 1973; Honorary Fellow, Wadham College, Oxford, 1981; Honorary Bencher, Lincoln's Inn, 1983; Honorary Doctor, University of Essex, 1986. Memberships: Council of Management, British Institute of International and Comparative Law, 1969-2005; Board of Governors, British Institute of Human Rights, 1989-2004, Vice President, 1992-2004; Vice President, Honourable Society of Cymmrodorion, 1987-. Address: 4 Bedford Road, Moor Park, Northwood, Middlesex, HA6 2BB, England.

EVE Trevor, b. 1 July 1951. Actor. m. Sharon Patricia Maughn, 1980, 2 sons, 1 daughter. Education: Kingston Art College; RADA. Career: Actor, Theatre includes: Children of a Lesser God, 1981; The Genius, 1983; High Society, 1986; Man Beast and Virtue, 1989; The Winter's Tale, 1991; Inadmissible Evidence, 1993; Uncle Vanya, 1996; TV includes: Shoestring, 1980; Jamaica Inn, A Sense of Guilt, 1990; Parnell and the Englishwoman, A Doll's House, 1991; The Politician's Wife, Black Easter, 1995; Under the Sun, 1997; Evilstreak, David Copperfield, 1999; Waking The Dead, 2000-08; Films include: Hindle Wakes; Dracula; A Wreath of Roses; The Corsican Brothers; Aspen Extreme;

Psychotherapy; The Knight's Tale; The Tribe; Appetite; Possession; Troy; Producer for Projector Productions: Alice Through the Looking Glass, 1998; Cinderella; Twelfth Night, 2002. Honours include: Olivier Award for Best Supporting Actor, 1997. Address: c/o ICM Ltd, Oxford House, 76 Oxford Street, London, W1N 0AX, England.

EVERETT Rupert, b. 29 May 1960, Norfolk, England. Actor. Education: Central School for Speech and Drama, London. Appointments: Apprentice, Glasgow Citizen's Theatre, 1979-82; Model, Versace, Milan; Image of Opium perfume for Yves Saint Laurent; Stage appearances include: Another Country, 1982; The Vortex, 1989; Private Lives; The Milk Train Doesn't Stop Here Anymore; The Picture of Dorian Gray; The Importance of Being Earnest; Films include: Another Country, 1984; Dance With a Stranger, The Right Hand Man, 1985; Duet for One; Chronicle of Death Foretold, Hearts of Fire, 1987; Haunted Summer, 1988; The Comfort of Strangers, 1989; Inside Monkey Zetterland; Pret à Porter, The Madness of King George, 1995; Dunstan Checks In; My Best Friend's Wedding, 1997; A Midsummer's Night's Dream, B Monkey, 1998; An Ideal Husband, Inspector Gadget, 1999; The Next Best thing, 2000; Unconditional Love, The Importance of Being Earnest, The Wild Thornberrys Movie (voice), 2002; To Kill A King, 2003; Stage Beauty, People, Shrek 2 (voice), A Different Loyalty, 2004; Separate Lies, The Chronicles of Narnia: The Lion, the Witch and the Wardrobe (voice), 2005; Quiet Flows the Don, 2006; Shrek the Third (voice), Stardust, St Trinian's, 2007; TV includes: Arthur the King; The Far Pavilions, 1982; Princess Daisy, 1983. Publications: Hello Darling, Are You Working?, 1992; The Hairdressers of San Tropez, 1995. Address: c/o ICM, 8942 Wilshire Boulevard, Beverly Hills, CA 90211, USA.

EVERT Chris(tine) Marie, b. 21 December 1954, Fort Lauderdale, Florida, USA. Former Lawn Tennis Player. m. (1) J Lloyd, 1979, divorced 1987, (2) A Mill, 1988, divorced 2006, 3 sons, (3) Greg Norman. Education: High School, Ft Lauderdale. Career: Amateur, 1970-72; Professional, 1972-. Winner of: French Championship, 1974, 1975, 1979, 1980, 1982, 1985, 1986; Wimbledon Singles: 1974, 1976, 1981; Italian Championship: 1974, 1975, 1980; South African Championship: 1973; US Open: 1975, 1976, 1977, 1979, 1980, 1982 (record 100 victories); Colgate Series, 1977, 1978; World Championship, 1979; Played Wightman Cup, 1971-73; 1975-82; Federation Cup, 1977-82; Ranked No 1 in the world for seven years; Won 1309 matches in her career; Holds 157 singles titles and 18 Grand Slam titles. Appointments: President, Women's Tennis Association, 1975-76, 1983-91; Director, President's Council on Physical Fitness & Sports, 1991-; NBC TV sports commentator and host for numerous TV shows; Other: Established Chris Evert Charities, 1989; Owner, Evert Enterprises/IMG, 1989-; Chris Evert Pro-celebrity Tennis Classic, 1989-. Publications: Chrissie (autobiography), 1982; Lloyd on Lloyd (with J Lloyd) 1985. Honours include: International Tennis Hall of Fame, 1995; International Tennis Federation Chartrier Award, 1997; Named by ESPN as One of Top 50 Athletes of the 20th Century, 1999. Address: Evert Enterprises, 7200 W Camino Real, Suite 310 Boca Raton, FL 33433, USA.

EVTIMOVA Zdravka, b. 24 July 1959, Pernik, Bulgaria. Literary Translator; Author. m. Todor Georgiev, 2 sons, 1 daughter. Education: BA, American Studies, MA, English and American Studies, St Kiril and Methodius University, Bulgaria. Appointments: Translator, Interpreter, National Institute of Scientific Information, Sofia; Chief of Interpreters Section, Rare Earth Elements Institute, Bulgarian Academy of Sciences; Chief Expert, English and American Sector Translations, Ministry of Defence. Publications: Books published in Bulgaria: Your Shadow Was My Home (novel), 2000; Thursday (novel), 2003; 3 short story collections; Bitter Sky (short story collection) published in the UK, 2003. Honours: Chudomir Short Story National Award; Anna Kamenova National Literary Award, 1995; Gencho Stoev Short Story Award for a Short Story by a Balkan Author; Best Novel of the Year 2003 for the novel, Thursday; Best Short Story Collection by an established author; Award, MAG Press, San Diego, California; BBC Short Story Contest Award, 2005; Short Story Award, International Short Story Competition, Nantes, France, 2005; Golden Chain Short Story Award, Bulgaria, 2005. Membership: Bulgarian Writers' Union; Bulgarian PEN; International Organisation of Artists without Frontiers. Address: 36/61 Gagarin Street, 2304 Pernik, Bulgaria. E-mail: zevtimova@yahoo.com

EWINGTON John, b. 14 May 1936, Goodmayes, Essex, England. Lloyd's Broker; Church Musician. m. Helene Mary Leach, 2 sons. Education: County Technical School, Dagenham, South East Essex; ACertCM, 1968; Diploma, Church Music, Goldsmiths' College, 1988. Appointments: Administrative Assistant, Institute of London Underwriters, 1953-67; RN National Service, 1954-56; Underwriting Assistant, PCW Agencies, Lloyd's, 1967-86; Senior Broker, 1986-97, Consultant, 1997-2000, HSBC Gibbs; Director of Music and Organist: Blechingley Parish Church, 1966-97, St Mary Woolnoth, 1970-93 (also Senior Church Warden, 1973-93), St Katharine Cree, 1998-; Director, City Singers, 1976-; Vice Chairman of Governors, Oxted School, 1984-2005. Publications: Joint author (with Canon A Dobb), Landmarks in Christian Worship and Church Music; Articles on church music in professional journals. Honours: Knight, Order of St Lazarus of Jerusalem; Hon RSCM, 2002; MA, Lambeth Degree, 2003; Freeman, City of London, 1980; FGCM, 1988; Hon FCSM, 1990; Hon FFCM, 1998; OBE, 1996; Hon Fellow, University of Newcastle, NSW, 2004. Address: Hillbrow, Godstone Road, Blechingley, Surrey RH1 4PJ, England. E-mail: johnmusicsure@aol.com

EZE Prince Chukwumeka Uchenna, b. 29 June 1966, Nigeria. m. 3 children. Education: MBBS, College of Medicine, University of Benin, 1990. Appointments: Medical House Officer, University of Port Harcourt, 1991; Senior Medical Officer, St Jude Hospital & Medical Research Centre, Nigeria, 1992; Medical Director, Toronto Hospital Ltd, Nigeria, 1993; Chairman, Toronto Trade Centre Ltd, Nigeria, 1996; CEO, Adnoc FOD W/A (Adnoc Oil), Lagos, Nigeria, 1997; Secretary, Anambra State Oil and Gas Committee, 1999; Chairmanship candidate, Peoples' Democratic Party, 2002; Chairman, Co-ordinator, Anambra State, 2002; Chairman, PDP Presidential Flag-Off, Anambra State, 2003; Chairman, PDP Gubernatorial Flag-Off, Anambra State, 2003; Director of Mobilization, PPD Guber Elections Campaign, Anambra State, 2003; Director of Elections, PNP Senatorial Election, 2003; Secretary, Transition Committee, Anambra State Government, 2003; Anambra State Adviser, National Crime Prevention Campaign, 2003; State Co-ordinator, Anambra Delegation, 2005; Co-Chairman, PDP Membership Registration, 2006; Contestant, Senatorial Elections, Anambra North Senatorial Zone, 2007; Co-ordinator Health, New Partnership for Africa's Development and Africa Peer Review Mechanism, 2008. Honours: Jerusalem Pilgrim, 1985; Peoples' Warden, 1999-2001; Knight of St Christopher, 1999; Patron, Boys Brigade of Nigeria, 2000; Patron, Girls Guild, 2001; Peoples' Warden Emeritus, 2002; Patron, Nigeria Red Cross Society, 2006; Community Development Award, Rotary Club of

Nigeria, 2007. Memberships: Fellow, Royal Society for Arts, Manufactures and Commerce; Fellow, Institute of Journalism, Management and Continuing Education. Address: Toronto Hospital Ltd, 2 Upper Niger Bridge Road, PMB 1767, Onitsha, Anambra State, Nigeria. E-mail: ezenaukpo@yahoo.com

EZIN Jean-Pierre Onvêhoun, b. 7 December 1944, Guezin, Benin. University Professor. m. Victoire Akele, 3 sons, 1 daughter. Education: Doctorat de 3ᵉ cycle, 1972, Doctorat d'Etat, 1981, University of Lille I, France. Appointments: Lecturer, Catholic University of Lille, France, 1972-73; Lecturer, National University of Benin, 1973-77; Associate Professor, University of Lille I, France, 1978-81; Professor, National University of Benin, 1981-. Publications: At least 20 books, papers and articles on mathematics, mathematical physics and Riemannian geometry. Honours: Officier des Palmes Academiques Françaises; Vice-Chancellor of the National University of Benin, 1990-92. Memberships: American Mathematical Society; Société Mathématique de France; African Mathematical Union; Senior Associate, Abus Salam International Centre for Theoretical Physics; Lions Clubs International. Address: Institut de Mathématiques et des Sciences Physiques, IMSP, BP 613, Porto Novo, Benin. E-mail: jp.ezin@imsp-mac.org

ÉZSIÁS András (Andrew), b. 1 November 1953, Budapest, Hungary. Consultant Maxillofacial Surgeon. m. (1) Zsuzsanna Bártfai, divorced 1986, 1 son, (2) Edina Érsek, 1 son, 2 daughters. Education: Temesvári Pelbárt Franciscan College and Gymnasium, Esztergom, Hungary; DMD, Semmelweis University, Budapest, 1977; MD, 1981; Specialist Certificate in General Surgery, Postgraduate Institute of Budapest, 1986; Specialist Board Certificate in Oral and Maxillofacial Surgery, Royal College of Surgeons, England, Specialist Training Authority, UK, 1996; Diplomate, European Board of Oro-Maxillofacial Surgery, 2000; LLB, Cardiff Law School, 2006. Appointments: Postgraduate Trainee Surgeon, Janos Hospital, Budapest, Hungary, 1981-86; Sub-lieutenant, Hungarian Army Medical Corps, 1981-82; Senior House Officer, Liverpool Dental Hospital, England, 1988-90; St Lawrence Hospital, Chepstow, Wales, 1990-91; Registrar, Queen Alexandra Hospital, Portsmouth, England, 1991-92; St Lawrence Hospital and University Hospital of Wales, Cardiff, 1992-94; Senior Registrar, Cheltenham and Gloucester Hospitals, England, 1994-95; John Radcliffe Hospital, Oxford, England, 1995-98; Consultant, Prince Charles, Princess of Wales and Royal Glamorgan Hospitals, Wales, 1998-2005; Honorary Consultant, Welsh Regional Burns and Plastic Surgery Unit, Morriston Hospital, Wales, 2000-05. Publications: Contributor, articles to professional journals. Memberships: Fellow, Royal College of Surgeons, England; Fellow and Examiner, Royal College of Surgeons, Edinburgh; Fellow and Examiner, European Board of Oro-Maxillofacial Surgery; Fellow, International Association of Oral and Maxillofacial Surgeons; Fellow, British Association of Oral and Maxillofacial Surgeons; Member, European Association for Cranio-Maxillofacial Surgery; Member, British Association of Head and Neck Oncologists; Member, European Academy of Facial Plastic Surgery; Elected member, European Academy of Sciences and Arts. Address: 9 Gateside Close, Cardiff CF23 8PB, Wales. E-mail: ezsias@ntlworld.com

F

FAINLIGHT Ruth (Esther), b. 2 May 1931, New York, New York, USA. Writer; Poet; Translator; Librettist. m. Alan Sillitoe, 19 November 1959, 1 son, 1 daughter. Education: Colleges of Arts and Crafts, Birmingham, Brighton, UK. Appointment: Poet-in-Residence, Vanderbilt University, USA, 1985, 1990. Publications: Poetry: Cages, 1966; To See the Matter Clearly, 1968; The Region's Violence, 1973; Another Full Moon, 1976; Sibyls and Others, 1980, 2nd edition 2007; Climates, 1983; Fifteen to Infinity, 1983; Selected Poems, 1987, 2nd edition, revised, 1995; The Knot, 1990; Sibyls, 1991; This Time of Year, 1994; Sugar-Paper Blue, 1997; Burning Wire, 2002; Moon Wheels, 2006; Visitação: Selected Poems in Portuguese translation, 1995; Encore La Pleine Lune, Selected Poems in French translation, 1997; Poemas, translation of selected poems in Spanish, 2000; Bleue Papier-Sucre, 2000; La Verita Sulla Sibilla, selected poems in Italian translation, 2003; Plumas, selected poems in Spanish translation published in Mexico, 2005; Autoral la Rampă, selected poems in Romanian translation, 2007. Translations: All Citizens Are Soldiers, from Lope de Vega, 1969; Navigations, 1983; Marine Rose: Selected Poems of Sophia de Mello Breyner, 1988; currently Sophocles' Theban Plays (with Robert Littman). Short Stories: Daylife and Nightlife, 1971; Dr Clock's Last Case, 1994. Libretti: The Dancer Hotoke, 1991; The European Story, 1993; Bedlam Britannica, 1995. Contributions to: Atlantic Monthly; Critical Quarterly; English; Hudson Review; Lettre Internationale; London Magazine; London Review of Books; New Yorker; Poetry Review; Threepenny Review; Times Literary Supplement. Honours: Cholmondeley Award for Poetry, 1994; Hawthornden Award for Poetry, 1994. Memberships: Society of Authors; PEN Writers in Prison Committee. Address: 14 Ladbroke Terrace, London W11 3PG, England.

FAIRBRASS Graham John, b. 14 January 1953, Meopham, Kent, England. Traveller; Writer; Poet; Painter. Education: BA, Arts, Open University, 1991; Coleg Harlech, 1995-96; Diploma, University of Wales, 1996; Norwich School of Art and Design, 1996-99. Publication: Conquistadors Shuffle Moon, 1989; Moon on its Back, 2004; Ashes at the Moon, 2005; Twentyone Poems, 2006; Evolution, 2007; Contributions to: Poetry Now, 1994; Anthology South East; Parnassus of World Poets, 1994, 1995, 1997; Poetry Club Anthology, vol l, 1995; Birdsuit, 1997-99. Honours: BA Hons, Cultural Studies. Address: 6 Hornfield Cottages, Harvel, Gravesend, Kent DA13 0BU, England.

FAIRBROTHER Nicola Kim, b. 14 May 1970, Henley, England. Journalist. Education: Oaklands Infant and Junior Schools; Edgebarrow Comprehensive School. Appointments: Editor, Kokakids Judo Magazine, 2001-; Journalist, Costa Brava News, Alicante, Spain; Sports Writer, Reading Chronicle; BBC Commentator for Judo, Commonwealth Games, 2002, Olympic Games, Athens, 2004. Publications: Numerous sporting articles and some travel reports for variety of newspapers including The Times, Sunday Times, Telegraph and Guardian. Honours: 6th Dan, British Judo; Junior European Silver Medallist, 1986; Junior European Champion, 1987; European Bronze Medallist, 1990; World Bronze Medallist, 1991; European Champion, 1992; Olympic Silver Medallist, 1992; European Champion, 1993; World Champion, 1993; MBE, 1994; European Player of the Year, 1994; European Silver Medallist, 1994; European Champion, 1995; Olympic 5th Place, 1996. Address: 26 Broom Acres, Sandhurst, Berkshire GU47 8PW, England. E-mail: editor@kokakids.co.uk

FAIRBURN Eleanor M, (Catherine Carfax, Emma Gayle, Elena Lyons), b. 23 February 1928, Ireland. Author. m. Brian Fairburn, 1 daughter. Appointments: Past Member, Literary Panel for Northern Arts; Tutor, Practical Writing, University of Leeds Adult Education Centre. Publications: The Green Popinjays, 1962; New edition, 1998; The White Seahorse, 1964, 3rd edition, 1996; translated into German, 1997. The Golden Hive, 1966; Crowned Ermine, 1968; The Rose in Spring, 1971; White Rose, Dark Summer, 1972; The Sleeping Salamander, 1973, 3rd edition, 1986; The Rose at Harvest End, 1975; Winter's Rose, 1976. As Catherine Carfax: A Silence with Voices, 1969; The Semper Inheritance, 1972; To Die a Little, 1972; The Sleeping Salamander, 1973. As Emma Gayle: Cousin Caroline, 1980; Frenchman's Harvest, 1980. As Elena Lyons: The Haunting of Abbotsgarth, 1980; A Scent of Lilacs, 1982. Biographies (as Eleanor Fairburn): Edith Cavell, 1985; Mary Hornbeck Glyn, 1987; Grace Darling, 1988. Membership: Middlesbrough Writers Group, president, 1988, 1989, 1990. Address: 27 Minsterley Drive, Acklam, Middlesbrough, Cleveland TS5 8QU, England.

FAIRFAX John, b. 9 November 1930, London, England. Writer, Poet. 2 sons. Appointments: Co-Founder and Member of Council of Management, Arvon Foundation; Director, Phoenix Press, Arts Workshop, Newbury; Poetry Editor, Resurgence; Lectured at: Oriol College, Oxford; International Writing School, Philadelphia; Goldsmiths, London; Dulwich College. Publications: The Fifth Horseman of the Apocalypse, 1969; Double Image, 1971; Adrift on the Star Brow of Taliesin, 1974; Bone Harvest Done, 1980; ; The Way to Write, 1981; Wild Children, 1985; Creative Writing, 1989; Spindrift Lp, 1981; 100 Poems, 1992; Zuihitsu, 1996; Poem Sent to Satellite E2F3, 1997; Poem on Sculpture, 1998; Poem in Hologram, 1998; Commissioned poems: Boots Herbal Garden, engraved on glass for several institutes, 1999, 2000-05; Poems in Virtual Reality, 2003, 2004; Zero Zero, book of poems, 2007. Contributions to: Most major literary magazines. Honours: Numerous Royal Literary Awards, 2000-2006. Membership: The Arvon Foundation, co-founder, 1968. Address: The Thatched Cottage, Eling, Hermitage, Newbury, Berkshire RG16 9XR, England.

FAITHFULL Marianne, b. 29 December 1947, Hampstead, London, England. Singer. 1 son. Career: Recording artist, 1964-; Tours, appearances include: UK tour with Roy Orbison, 1965; US tour with Gene Pitney, 1965; Uxbridge Blues and Folk Festival, 1965; Montreux, Golden Rose Festival, 1966; Roger Water's The Wall, Berlin, 1990; Chieftains Music Festival, London, 1991; Acting roles include: I'll Never Forget Whatisname, 1967; Three Sisters, Chekkov, London, 1967; Hamlet, 1970; Kurt Weill's Seven Deadly Sins, St Ann's Cathedral, New York, 1990; Film appearance, Girl On A Motorcycle, 1968. Recordings: Singles include: As Tears Go By; Come And Stay With Me; This Little Bird; Summer Nights; Something Better/Sister Morphine; The Ballad Of Lucy Jordan; Dreaming My Dreams; Electra, 1999; Albums: Come My Way, 1965; Marianne Faithfull, 1965; Go Away From My World, 1966; Faithfull Forever, 1966; Marianne Faithfull's Greatest Hits, 1969; Faithless, with the Grease Band, 1978; Broken English, 1979; Dangerous Acquaintances, 1981; A Child's Adventure, 1983; Strange Weather, 1987; Blazing Away, 1990; A Secret Life, 1995; 20th Century Blues 1997; The Seven Deadly Sins, 1998; Vagabond Ways, 1999; Kissin' Time, 2002; Before the Prison, 2005. Contributor, Lost In The Stars - The Music Of Kurt Weill, 1984; The Bells Of Dublin, The Chieftains, 1992; Publications: Faithful (autobiography), 1994; Marian Faithfull Diaries, 2003; Memories, Dreams and Reflections (autobiography

2nd volume), 2007. Honours include: Grammy Nomination, Broken English, 1979. Address: c/o The Coalition Group Ltd, 12 Barley Mow Passage, London, W4 4PH, England. Website: pithuit.free.fr/FAITHFULL

FAKIOLAS Efstathios Tassos, b. 26 November 1971, Moscow, Russian Federation (Greek Citizen). Strategy Analyst. m. Eirini Tsoucala, 1 son. Education: BA, International Studies, 1989-93, Master of Arts, International Politics and Security, 1993-96, Athens Panteion University; Master of Arts, International Relations and Strategic Studies, Lancaster University, England, 1994-95; PhD, Department of War Studies, King's College, London, England, 2006. Appointments: Civil Servant, Finance Department, Social Insurance Fund Organisation for the Employees of the Hellenic Broadcasting Corporation and Tourism, September-November 2002; Strategy Analyst, Strategic Planning Department, Group Strategy Division, Agricultural Bank of Greece, 2002-. Publications: 20 peer-reviewed journal articles include most recently: Security, Strategy and Dialectic Realism: Ontological and Epistemological Issues in Constructing a New Approach to International Politics, 1999; Reflecting on the Relationship Between Security and Military Strategy, 2001; Theories of European Integration: A Neglected Dimension, 2002; Russia's Grand Strategic Alternatives at the Dawn of the New Century; Co-author, 1 book chapter; Numerous other articles in journals, periodicals and newspapers. Honours include: NATO Science Fellowships, 1994-95, 1996-99; Several scholarships and grants; 4 Distinctions, Athens Panteion University of Political and Social Sciences, 1989-93; Memorial Diploma, Public Benefit Foundation "Alexander S Onasis", 1995; British International Studies Association Research Award, 1998; CEU Summer Fellowship. Memberships include: International Institute for Strategic Studies; Royal United Services Institute for Defence Studies; International Studies Association; International Political Sciences Association; Academy of Political Science, USA; Hellenic Association of International Law and International Relations. Address: 86 Xanthipou Street, Papagou/Holargos, 155 61, Athens, Greece. E-mail: efakiolas@hotmail.com

FALCK (Adrian) Colin, b. 14 July 1934, London, England. Poet; Critic; Educator. (1) 1 daughter, (2) 2 sons. Education: BA, Philosophy, Politics and Economics, 1957, BA, Philosophy, Psychology and Physiology, 1959, MA, 1986, Magdalen College, Oxford; PhD, Literary Theory, University of London, 1988. Appointments: Military Service: British Army, Royal Artillery, 1952-54, Royal Air Force (Volunteer Reserve), 1954-65; Lecturer in Sociology, London School of Economics and Political Science, 1961-62; Part-time Lecturer in Philosophy and Education, University of Maryland, European Division, London, 1962-64; Lecturer in Modern Literature, Chelsea/King's College, University of London, 1964-84 Adjunct Professor in Literature, Syracuse University, London Program, Antioch University, London Program, 1985-89; Associate Professor in Literature, York College, Pennsylvania, 1989-99; Editorial: Co-Founder, 1962, Associate Editor, 1965-72, The Review; Poetry Editor, The New Review, 1974-78. Publications: The Garden in the Evening: Poems from the Spanish of Antonio Machado, 1964; Promises (poems), 1969; Backwards into the Smoke (poems), 1973; Poems Since 1900: An Anthology (editor with Ian Hamilton), 1975; In This Dark Light (poems), 1978; Robinson Jeffers: Selected Poems (editor), 1987; Myth, Truth and Literature: Towards a True Post-Modernism, 1989, 2nd edition, 1994; Edna St Vincent Millay: Selected Poems (editor), 1991; Memorabilia (poems), 1992; Post-Modern Love: An Unreliable Narration (poems), 1997; American

and British Verse in the Twentieth Century: The Poetry that Matters (critical history), 2003. Address: 20 Thurlow Road, London NW3 5PP, England.

FALCONE Frank Jr, b. 14 September 1964, Orange, New Jersey, USA. Oral and Maxillofacial Surgeon. m. Linda Rocanelli. Education: BA, Hamilton College, New York, 1986; Doctor of Dental Medicine, University of Medicine and Dentistry of New Jersey, 1990. Appointments: Clinical Assistant Instructor, State University of New York, Brooklyn, 1990-94; Chief Resident, Oral and Maxillofacial Surgery, Kings County Hospital Center, State University of New York Health Science Center at Brooklyn, Coney Island Hospital, and Maimonides Medical Center, Brooklyn, 1993-94; Senior Fellow, Oral and Maxillofacial Surgery, University of Medicine and Dentistry of New Jersey, Newark, 1994-95; Oral and Maxillofacial Surgeon: Overlook Hospital, New Jersey, 1995-98; Morristown Memorial Hospital, New Jersey, 1996-99; Kings County Hospital Center, 2000-05; Hazleton – St Joseph's Medical Center, 1996-2006; Hazleton General Hospital, Pennsylvania, 1996-; Clinical Instructor, Attending Staff Surgeon, Kings County Hospital Center, Brooklyn, 2000-05; Office Anesthesia Evaluator, Pennsylvania Society of Oral and Maxillofacial Surgeons/Pennsylvania State Board of Dentisry, 2005-. Numerous articles in professional journals. Honours: Employee Recognition Awards, Kings County Hospital Center, 1992, 1993; Mention of Honor, Republic of Columbia, State of Meta, 1994; Certificate of Recognition, American Cancer Society, 1999, 2000, 2001; Vice President, 1999, President, 2000, Past President, 2001, Hazleton Dental Society; Outstanding Service to Children, Big Brothers Big Sisters of America, 2004; Listed in America's Top Dentists/Oral & Maxillofacial Surgery, 2002-; Listed in The Best of the US, 2006-; Listed in international biographical dictionaries. Memberships: Fellow, American Association of Oral and Maxillofacial Surgeons; Fellow, American College of Oral and Maxillofacial Surgeons; Fellow, American Dental Society of Anesthesiology; Diplomate, National Dental Board of Anesthesiology; Member, Pennsylvania Society of Oral and Maxillofacial Surgeons; Member, Pennsylvania Dental Association; Member, International Congress of Oral Implantologists; Member, Hazleton Dental Society; Member, Pennsylvania 3rd District Dental Society; Member, American Dental Association. Address: Medical Arts Complex, 668 North Church Street, Suite 10, Hazleton, PA 18201, USA. E-mail: jawsurgn@epix.net

FALDO Nick, b. 18 July 1957, Welwyn Garden City, England. Professional Golfer. m. (1) Melanie, divorced, (2) Gill, divorced, 1 son, 2 daughters, (3) Valerie Bercher, 1 daughter. Career: Professional, 1976-; Winner numerous tournaments including: Skol Lager Individual, 1977; Colgate PGA Championship, 1978; Sun Alliance PGA Championship, 1980, 1981; Haig Whisky TPC, 1982; Paco Rabanne Open de France, 1983; Martini International, 1983; Car Care Plan International, 1983, 1984; Lawrence Batley International, 1983; Ebel Euro Masters Swiss Open, 1983; Heritage Classic, US, 1984; Peugeot Spanish Open, 1987; 116th Open Gold Championship, 1987; Peugeot Open de France, 1988, 1989; Volvo Masters, 1988; 2nd, US Open Championships, 1988; Masters Tournament, US, 1989; Volvo PGA Championship, 1989; Dunhill British Masters, 1989; Suntory World Match Play, 1989; 119th Open Golf Championship, 1990; Masters Tournament, US, 1991, 1996; Carroll's Irish Open, 1991, 1992, 1993; 121st Open Golf Championship, 1992; Scandinavian Masters, 1992; 2nd, USPGA Championship, 1992; GA European Masters, 1992; Toyota World Match Play, 1992; Volvo Bonus Pool, 1992; Johnnie Walker Classic, 1993;

2nd, 122nd Open Golf Championship, 1993; Alfred Dunhill Open, 1994; Doral-Ryder Open, US, 1995; Nissan Open, US, 1997; World Cup of Golf, 1998; 5th, US Open (including third round record 66), 2002; 8th 132nd Open Golf Championship, 2003; Team Member: Ryder Cup, 1977, 1979, 1981, 1983, 1985 (winners), 1987 (winners), 1989, 1991, 1993, 1995 (winners), 1997 (winners); Alfred Dunhill Cup, 1985, 1986, 1987 (winning team), 1988, 1991, 1993; World Cup of Golf, 1977, 1991, 1998 (winners). In 2006 signed with CBS as the networks leading golf analyst. Publications: In Search of Perfection, (with Bruce Critchley), 1995; Faldo - A Swing for Life, 1995. E-mail: nfdo@faldodesign.com

FALK Heinz, b. 29 April 1939, St Pölten. Professor Organic Chemistry. m. Rotraud, 1 son. Education: Dr Phil, University of Vienna. Appointments: Assistant, University Vienna, 1966; Post-Doctoral ETH, Zurich, 1971; Habilitation, University of Vienna, 1972; Assistant Professor, Physical Organic Chemistry, 1975; University Professor, Organic Chemistry, University Linz, 1979; Guest Professor, University of Barcelona, 1982; Dean, Science Technical Faculty, University of Linz, 1989-91. Publications: 300 papers in refereed journals; 2 books; Several patents. Honours include: Loschmidt Medal, 1998, and others. Memberships include: Austrian Academy of Science; Austrian Chemical Society; German Chemical Society; American Chemical Society; European Society of Photochemistry; American Society of Photochemistry Photobiology; New York Academy of Science; European Academy of Sciences. Address: Institute for Organic Chemistry, Johannes Kepler University Linz, Altenbergerstr 66, A 4040 Linz, Austria. E-mail: heinz@falk.net

FALKOWSKI Bogdan Jaroslaw, b. 21 January 1955, Warsaw, Poland. Professor; Researcher. m. Beata Olejnicka, 1 son. Education: Master of Electrical Engineering (Hons), Warsaw University of Technology, Warsaw, Poland, 1974-78; PhD, Electrical and Computer Engineering, Portland State University, Portland, USA, 1986-91. Appointments: Research and Development Engineer, Centre of Research in Information Systems, Blonie, Poland, 1978-80, Centre of Research in Computer Systems, Warsaw, Poland, 1981-86; Research Assistant, Department of Electrical and Computer Engineering, Portland, Oregon, USA, 1986-92; Professor, School of Electrical and Electronic Engineering, Nanyang Technological University, Singapore, 1992-. Publications: Articles in numerous scientific journals including: IEEE Transactions on Computers; IEEE Transactions on CAD of Integrated Circuits and Systems; IEEE Transactions on Circuits and Systems; IEE Proceedings, Circuits, Devices and Systems; IEE Proceedings, Digital Techniques and Computers; IEE Proceedings, Vision, Image and Signal Processing. Honours: IEEE/ACM Design Automation Conference Award, IEE Hartree Best Paper Award, 2002. Memberships: Senior Member, IEEE; Eta Kappa Nu Electrical Engineering Honor Society; Tau Beta Pi Engineering Honor Society. Address: Nanyang Technological University, School of EEE, Nanyang Avenue, 639798, Singapore, Singapore. E-mail: efalkowski@ntu.edu.sg

FALLOWELL Duncan Richard, b. 26 September 1948, London, England. Writer. Education: Magdalen College, Oxford. Publications: Drug Tales, 1979; April Ashley's Odyssey, 1982; Satyrday, 1986; The Underbelly, 1987; To Noto, 1989; Twentieth Century Characters, 1994; One Hot Summer in St Petersburg, 1994; Gormenghast (opera libretto), 1998; A History of Facelifting, 2003. Address: 44 Leamington Road Villas, London W11 1HT, England.

FANE Julian, b. 25 May 1927, London, England. Writer. m. Gillian Swire, 6 January 1976. Publications: Morning, 1956; A Letter; Memoir in the Middle of the Journey; Gabriel Young; Tug-of-War; Hounds of Spring; Happy Endings; Revolution Island; Gentleman's Gentleman; Memories of My Mother; Rules of Life; Cautionary Tales for Women; Hope Cottage; Best Friends; Small Change; Eleanor; The Duchess of Castile; His Christmas Box; Money Matters; The Social Comedy; Evening; Tales of Love and War; Byron's Diary; The Stepmother; The Sodbury Crucifix; The Collected Works of Julian Fane, Vols I, II, III, IV and V; The Harlequin Edition of Shorter Writings; Damnation, 2004; Games of Chance, 2005; The Time Diaries, 2005; According to Robin, 2006; Odd Woman Out, 2006; A Doctor's Notes; Meg and the Doodle Doo; The Fools of God; Sins of the Flesh, 2008. Honour: Fellow, Royal Society of Literature, 1974. Membership: Society of Authors. Address: Rotten Row House, Lewes, East Sussex BN7 1TN, England.

FANG Jin-Qing, b. 11 July 1939, Fu-jian, China. Scientific Researcher. m. 1 son, 1 daughter. Education: Graduate, Department of Physics, Tsing-Hua University, Beijing, China, 1958-64; Postdoctoral Fellow, Australian National University and University of Texas at Austin, USA, 1987-90. Appointments: Researcher into atomic energy science and technology, non-linear science, nonlinear complex networks and complexity science with applications including chaos control and synchronisation, China Institute of Atomic Energy, 1964; Research Professor (Fellow), 1987-; Head of the Key Program Projects of the National Natural Science Foundation of China, 2005- Visiting Professor in about 20 universities world-wide, 1990-. Publications include: More than 200 articles and more than 60 Science and EI recorded scientific papers; 10 monographs and textbooks from 1976 including most recently: Taming Chaos and Developing High Technology, 2002; Co-author: Chaos Control-Theory and Applications, 2003. Honours: 10 Awards and Prizes, China include: National Science Conference Prize, 1978; 2nd Prizes of Progress in Science and Technology in National Defence of China, 1998, 2000, 2002 and first prizes in 2005. Memberships: China Institute of Physics; Chinese Institute of System Science. Address: China Institute of Atomic Energy, PO Box 275-81, Beijing 102413, China. E-mail: fjq96@126.com

FANNING Fred, b. 8 December 1956, Valdosta, Georgia, USA. Public Administrator. m. Tammy Hanson, 2 sons. Education: BSc, Excelsior College, 1993; M Ed, National Louis University, 1996; MA, Webster University, 2005. Appointments: Safety Specialist, Fort Riley, Kansas, USA, 1986-89; Safety Specialist, 8th Infantry Division, Bad Kreuznach, Germany, 1989-90; Safety Manager, US Army Berlin, Germany, 1990-94; Safety Specialist, US Army Europe, Heidelberg, Germany, 1994-95; Safety Director, US Army V Corps, Heidelberg, Germany, 1995-98; Safety Director, Fort Leonard Wood, Missouri, USA, 1999-2004; Senior Safety Manager, Army Safety Office, Arlington, Virginia, USA, 2004-05; Safety Manager, Department of Commerce, Washington, DC, USA, 2005-06; Director for Administrative Services, Department of Commerce, Washington, DC, USA, 2005-. Publications: Basic Safety Administration: A Handbook for the New Safety Specialist, 2003. Honours: Appointed to Senior Executive Service; Department of Commerce Bronze Medal; NATO Medal. Memberships: American Society of Safety Engineers; Federal Administrative Managers Association; Federal Real Property Association; Missouri Writers Guild. Address: 3 Chandler Court, Fredericksburg, VA 22405, USA. E-mail: fanningf@netscape.com

FANTHORPE U(rsula) A(skham), b. 22 July 1929, Kent, England. Writer; Poet. Partner, Dr, R V Bailey. Education: BA, MA, Oxford University. Appointments: Assistant Mistress, 1954-62, Head of English, 1962-70, Cheltenham Ladies College; English Teacher, Howells School, Llandaff, 1972-73; Temporary Clerical Work, Bristol, 1973-74; Clerk, Receptionist, Burden Neurological Hospital, Bristol, 1974-89; Arts Council, Writer in Residence, St Martin's College, Lancaster, 1983-85; Northern Arts Literary Fellow, Universities of Durham and Newcastle, 1987-88; Freelance writer, 1989-. Publications: Side Effects, 1978; Standing To, 1982; Voices Off, 1984; Selected Poems, 1986; A Watching Brief, 1987; Neck Verse, 1992; Safe as Houses, 1995; Penguin Modern Poets 6, 1996; Double Act (audiobook with R V Bailey), 1997; Poetry Quartets 5 (audiobook), 1999; Consequences, 2000; Christmas Poems, 2002; Queueing for the Sun, 2003; Collected Poems, 2005; Homing In, 2006. Contributions to: A wide range of publications including BBC, newspapers etc. Honours: FRSL, 1988; The Queen's Gold Medal for Poetry, 2003; Travelling Scholarship, Society of Authors, 1983; Hawthornden Scholarships, 1987, 1997, 2002; Arts Council Writers Award, 1994; Chomondeley Award, Society of Authors, 1995; Honorary DLitt, the West of England, 1995; Honorary Fellow, University of Gloucestershire, 2000; CBE, 2001; Honorary Fellow, St Anne's College, Oxford, 2003; Honorary Fellow, Sarum College, Salisbury, 2004; Honorary Dlitt, University of Bath, 2006. Memberships: PEN.; Society of Authors. Address: Culverhay House, Wotton-under-Edge, Gloucestershire GL12 7LS, England.

FARAG Radwan Sedkey, b. 27 November 1941, Cairo, Egypt. Professor of Biochemistry. m. Fatma Mahmoud El-Shishi, 1 son. Education: BSc, 1963, MSc, 1967, Faculty of Agriculture, Cairo University, Egypt; PhD, St Bartholomew's Hospital Medical College, London University, 1974. Appointments: Demonstrator, 1963-67, Associate Lecturer, 1967-74, Lecturer, 1974-79, Associate Professor, 1979-84, Professor of Biochemistry, 1984-, Head of Biochemistry Department, 1988-94, Faculty of Agriculture, Cairo University; Director of Central Lab, 1975-95; Over 45 MSc and 53 PhD students obtained their degrees under his direct supervision. Publications: Author; Chromatographic Analysis, 1990; Lipids, 1991; Physical and Chemical Analysis of Fats and Oils, 1995; Principles of Biochemistry, 1999; Modern Methods of Amino Acid Analysis and Assessment of Protein Quality, 2003. Publications: Over 140 papers in prominent journals; Referee of some national and international journals. Honours: Egyptian State Award, Egyptian Academy of Scientific Research and Technology, 1978, 1984; 20th Century Award Achievement, IBC, 1997; Decree of Merit, Cairo University, 2008. Memberships: National Encyclopedia, Egypt; American Oil Chemists Society; International Association for Cereal Science and Technology; New York Academy of Sciences; American Association for the Advancement of Science; National Committee of Biochemistry and Molecular Biology; Advisory Board of J Drug Res. Address: Biochemistry Department, Faculty of Agriculture, Cairo University, PO 12613, El-Gamma St, Giza, Egypt.

FARHI Nicole, b. 25 July 1946. Fashion Designer. m. David Hare, 1992; 1 daughter with Stephen Marks. Education: Cours Berçot Art School, Paris. Appointments: Designer, Pierre d'Albi, 1968; Founder, French Connection with Stephen Marks, 1973; Former designer, Stephen Marks; Founder and designer, Nicole Farhi, 1983-; Nicole Farhi For Men, 1989-; Opened Nicole's Restaurant, 1994. Honours: British Fashion Award for Best Contemporary Design, 1995, 1996,

1997; FHM Awards Menswear Designer of the Year, 2000; Maxim Awards, British Designer of the Year, 2001. Address: 16 Foubert's Place, London W1F 7PJ, England.

FARMAN Allan George, b. 26 July 1949, Birmingham, England. Professor of Radiology and Imaging Sciences. m. Taeko Takemori. Education: BDS, 1971; LDSRCS, 1972; PhD, 1977; Dip ABOMR, 1982; EdS, 1983; MBA, 1987; DSc, 1996; Dip JBOMR, 1997. Appointments: Professor, Radiology and Imaging Science, School of Dentistry, University Louisville; Clinical Professor, Diagnostic Radiology, University Louisville School of Medicine, 1980-. Publications: 300 science articles, numerous texts and contributions to textbooks; Oral and Maxillofacial Diagnostic Imaging; Editor: Panoramic Imaging News, 2001-; Deputy Editor, International Journal of Computer Assisted Radiology and Surgery, 2006-. Honours: President of Honour, First Latin-American Regional Meeting on Dentomaxillofacial Radiology, 1996; Honoured Guest Professor, Peking University, 2006; Distinguished Service Medal, University of Louisville, 2006. Memberships: International Association of Dentomaxillofacial Radiology, President, 1994-97; American Academy of Oral and Maxillofacial Radiology, Editor, 1988-95 and 2005-; American Dental Association, Representative to International DICOM Committee, 2001-; Founder, Organiser, International Congress Computed Maxillofacial Imaging, 1995-. Address: c/o School of Dentistry, University of Louisville, Louisville, KY 40292, USA.

FARRELL Colin James, b. 31 May 1976, Castleknock, Dublin, Ireland. Actor. m. Amelia Warner, divorced, 1 son with Kim Bordenave. Education: Gaiety School of Drama. Career: TV: Ballykissangel, 1996; Falling for a Dancer, 1998; Scrubs, 2005; The War Zone, 1999; Ordinary Decent Criminal, 2000; Tigerland, 2000; Hart's War, 2002; Minority Report, 2002; Phone Booth, 2002; SWAT, 2003; The Recruit, 2003; Alexander, 2004; Miami Vice, 2006; Cassandra's Dream, 2007; In Bruges, 2008.

FARROW Mia Villiers, b. 9 February 1945, California, USA. Actress. m. (1) Frank Sinatra, 1966, divorced 1968, (2) André Previn, 1970, divorced 1979, 14 children, 1 deceased, including 1 son with Woody Allen. Career: Stage debut in The Importance of Being Ernest, New York, 1963; other stage appearances include: The Three Sisters, House of Bernard Alba, 1972-73; The Marrying of Ann Leete, Ivanov, RSC, London, 1976; Romantic Comedy, Broadway, 1979; Films include: Guns at Batasi, 1964; Rosemary's Baby, 1968; John and Mary, Secret Ceremony, 1969; The Great Gatsby, 1973; Full Circle, A Wedding, Death on the Nile, 1978; A Midsummer Night's Sex Comedy, 1982; Broadway Danny Rose, 1984; Hannah and Her Sisters, 1986; Radio Days, 1987; Another Woman, 1988; Oedipus Wrecks, 1989; Alice, Crimes and Misdemeanours, 1990; Husband and Wives, Shadows and Fog, 1992; Widow's Peak, 1994; Miami Rhapsody, 1995; Reckless, 1995; Private Parts, 1997; Coming Soon, 2000; Purpose, 2002; The Omen, 2006; Arthur and the Invisibles, 2006; Fast Track, 2006; Be Kind Rewind, 2007; TV appearances include: Peyton Place, 1964-66; Peter Pan, 1975. Publication: What Falls Away (autobiography), 1996. Honours: Academy Award; Best Actress, 1969; David Donatello, 1969; Film Festival Award, 1969; San Sebastian Award. Address: International Creative Management, c/o Sam Cohn, 40 West 57th Street, New York, NY 10019, USA. Website: www.mia-farrow.com

FAULKS Sebastian, b. 20 April 1953, Newbury, Berkshire, England. Author; Journalist. m. Veronica Youlten, 1989, 2 sons, 1 daughter. Education: Wellington College; Emmanuel

College, Cambridge. Appointments: Reporter, Daily Telegraph newspaper, 1979-83; Feature Writer, Sunday Telegraph, 1983-86; Literary Editor, The Independent, 1986-89; Deputy Editor, The Independent on Sunday, 1989-90, Associate Editor, 1990-91; Columnist, The Guardian, 1992-, Evening Standard, 1997-99; Mail on Sunday, 1999-2000. Television: Churchill's Secret Army, 2000. Publications: The Girl at the Lion d'Or, 1989; A Fool's Alphabet, 1992; Birdsong, 1993; The Fatal Englishman, 1996; Charlotte Gray, 1998; On Green Dolphin Street, 2001; Human Traces, 2005; The Footprints on Mount Low, 2005; Pistache (an essay collection), 2006; Engleby, 2007; Devil May Care, 2008. Address: c/o Aitken and Stone, 29 Fernshaw Road, London, SW10 0TG, England.

FAULL Margaret Lindsay, b. 4 April 1946, Sydney, Australia (British and Australian citizen). Chief Executive; Company Secretary. Education: BA (II, I), Archaeology, 1966, Diploma in Education, 1967, Sydney University; MA (Hons), England Language, Macquarie University, 1970; PhD, Archaeology, Leeds University, 1979; MA, Leisure Management, Sheffield University, 1990. Appointments: English/History Teacher, New South Wales, Australia, 1970-71; Sub-Warden, Oxley Hall, University of Leeds, 1972-75; Field Archaeologist, West Yorkshire MCC, 1975-83; Deputy County Archaeologist, West Yorkshire MCC, 1983-85; Project Manager, Thwaite Mills Industrial Museum, 1985-86; Director/Company Secretary, Yorkshire Mining Museum/National Coal Mining Museum for England, 1986-. Publications: Over 50 articles in professional and popular journals; Book, Domesday Book, 30: Yorkshire, 1986. Honours: ILAM Manager of the Year, 1996; Doctor of the University, Bradford University, 1997; Doctor of Civil Law, Huddersfield University, 2005. Memberships: Fellow, Royal Society of Arts, Manufactures and Commerce; Fellow, Institute of Directors; Affiliate, Institute of Mining, Materials and Metals; Fellow, Institute of Leisure and Amenity Management; Fellow, Society of Antiquaries; Member, Institute of Field Archaeologists. Address: National Coal Mining Museum for England, Caphouse Colliery, New Road, Overton, Wakefield WF4 4RH, England. E-mail: margaret.faull@ncm.org.uk

FAVRET Eduardo Alfredo, b. 5 May 1962, Moron, Argentina. Physicist. Education: Licentiate, Physical Sciences, University of Buenos Aires, 1992; PhD, Physical Sciences, Faculty of Sciences, University of Buenos Aires, 1998. Appointments: Researcher, Institute of Soils, INTA; Assistant Professor and Researcher, Institute of Technology, University of San Martin, National Commission on Atomic Energy; Researcher, Fellowships, National Council on Scientific and Technological Research, Argentina; Postdoctoral Fellowship, German Science Foundation, Saarland University, Germany, 2001-02; Researcher at Institute of Soils, National Institute of Agricultural Technology (INTA), 2005-. Publications: Materials Characterization, 1990, 1991, 2003; Practical Metallography, 1996, 1997, 1999, 2003; Optics and Laser Technology, 1997; Microstructural Science, 1999; Kerntechnik, 2000; Journal of Archaeological Science, 2001; Microscopy and Analysis, 2001, 2002; Microscopy Research and Technique, 2001; Microscopy and Microanalysis, 2002, 2003, 2004, 2006, 2007; Applied Surface Science, 2004; Microscopy Today, 2004, 2007; Microscopy Research and Technique, 2006; Microscopy and Analysis, 2007. Honours: 2nd Prize, International Metallographic Contest, 1995; Prize, Metallographic Photography, 1988; Honorable Mention Award, International Metallographic Contest, 2001. Memberships: Argentine Society of Microscopy; American

Society for Metals; International Metallographic Society; Microscopy Society of America. Address: Lincoln 831, (1712) Castelar, Argentina. E-mail: eafavret@cnia.inta.gov.ar

FEAST Michael William, b. 29 December 1926, Deal, Kent, England. Astronomer. m. Constance Elizabeth Maskew, 1 son, 2 daughters. Education: PhD, Physics, Imperial College, London, 1949. Appointments: NRC Postdoctoral Fellow, Ottawa, Canada, 1949-52; Astronomer, Radcliffe Observatory, Pretoria, 1952-74; South African Astronomical Observatory, 1974-92, Director, 1976-92; Royal Society Visiting Fellow, Cambridge University, 1992-93; Honorary Professor, University of Cape Town, 1983-. Publications: About 350 scientific publications. Honours: Vice-President International Astronomical Union, 1979-85; Associate (Honorary Fellow), Royal Astronomical Society, London, 1980; Gill Medal, Astronomical Association of South Africa, 1983; De Beer Gold Medal, South African Institute of Physics, 1992; DSc, honoris causa, University of Cape Town, 1993. Memberships: South African Academy; Fellow, Royal Society of South Africa; Royal Astronomical Society; Astronomical Society of South Africa. Address: Astronomy Department, University of Cape Town, Rondebosch 7701, South Africa. E-mail: mwf@artemisia.ast.uct.ac.za

FEBLAND Harriet, b. New York City, New York, USA. Artist. 2 sons. Education includes: Pratt Institute; New York University; The American Artists School; Art Students League; Studies abroad in England and France, 11 years. Career: Pioneer Constructionist Sculptor and Painter; Exhibitions in European art circles including Museé d'Art Moderne, Paris and Alwin Galleries, the Drian Gallery in London and the Lessedra Gallery in Sofia, Bulgaria; On return to USA opened a studio in New York and Westchester; Founded, 1962, Director until 1993, Harriet FeBland Art Workshop for advanced painters; Gave workshops in New York, Vermont, New Mexico and England; Lecturer and Instructor, New York University, 1960-61; Faculty Member, Westchester Art Workshop, 1965-72; Numerous group exhibitions; 51 solo exhibitions include most recently: Janer 81 Gallery New York City, 1998; Contemporary Illustrators Gallery, New York City, 1998; The National Space Society, New York City, 1996, Houston, Texas, 1999; UAHC Galleries, New York City, 1999-2000; The Donnell Library Center "Works on Paper", New York City, 2003; The Galleries of the Interchurch Center "Poetic Geometry", New York City, 2004; Berkeley College Gallery, New York City, 2006; National Association of Women Artists, 5th Ave Gallery, New York City, 2006-2007; Works in collections including: Pepsico, Somers, New York; Cincinnati Art Museum, Cincinnati, Ohio; Sealy Corp, Chicago, Illinois; Grounds for Sculpture Museum, Hamilton, New Jersey; Metromedia, Los Angeles, California; New School Art Center, New School for Social Research, New York City; Library of Congress, Washington, DC; Zimmerli Art Museum, Rutgers University, New Brunswick, New Jersey; Brainerd Art Museum, SUNY Potsdam, New York; The State of Hawaii Art and Cultural Foundation, Hilo, Hawaii; The Hudson River Museum, Yonkers, New York; Tweed Art Museum, University of Minnesota, Duluth, Minnesota. Publications: Works included in numerous books on art. Honours include: Various awards in painting, sculpture and printmaking, National Association of Women Artists, 1966-2002; Awards in painting and printmaking, American Society of Contemporary Artists, 1977-2005; Awards in painting and sculpture, Hudson River Museum, 1976-87; Robert Conover Memorial Award in Graphics, Society of American Graphic Artists, 1999; American Medal of Honor, ABI, 2002, 2005; Archives of American Art, Smithsonian Institution; International Art

Biography, Germany; Listed in Who's Who publications and biographical dictionaries. Memberships: Former President, New York Artists Equity Association, 1989-90; President, American Society of Contemporary Artists (ASCA), 1981-83, re-elected 2005-07; Editor, ASCA, 85th Year Book, 2003; Former Delegate, American Art Committee, United Nations. Address: 245 East 63rd Street, 1803, New York, NY 10021, USA. E-mail: harrietfebland@aol.com Website: www.harrietfebland.com

FEDERER Roger, b. 8 August 1981, Basel, Switzerland. Professional Tennis Player. Career: Started playing as junior in 1995, turned professional 1998. Career Titles/Finals: 12/8. Current ATP Rank: 1. Numerous television appearances and interviews. Honours: Winner of the Allianz Suisse Open Singles, Gstaad Singles, Halle Singles, Hamburg Singles, Australian Open Singles, Dubai Singles, Indian Wells Singles, 2004; Winner of the Marseille Singles, Dubai Singles, Munich Singles, Halle Singles, Wimbledon Singles (5 consecutive years, 2003-07), Vienna Singles, Tennis Masters Cup Singles, Miami Doubles (Max Mirny), Vienna Doubles (Yves Allegro), 2003. Address: Oberwil, Switzerland.

FEHR Manfred, b. 25 March 1936, Jena, Germany. Chemical Engineer. m. Giomar Yemaíl, 1 son, 1 daughter. Education: BS, Université Laval, Québec, 1967; MS, University of Alberta, Edmonton, 1969; PhD, Université Laval, Canada, 1978; Postdoctoral Fellow, Kungliga Tekniska Högskolan, Sweden, 1990; fluent in 5 languages. Appointments: Professional handball player, 2 clubs; International consultant, 33 clients; Marketing administrator 3 companies; Research and process engineer 4 companies; Lecturer and professor, 6 universities; Professional activities in 28 countries on 5 continents; Registered engineer, 2 countries; Citizen of 3 countries. Publications: 137 journal and newspaper articles; 104 research reports; 110 conference and symposium presentations; 52 invited speaking engagements; 3 books. Honours: 4 scholarships in Canada, 1963-75; 33 TV, radio and newspapers interviews in Argentina and Brazil, 1992-2008; Consular Warden in Brazil, 1991-2008; 76 citations in international biographical dictionaries, 1981-2008, 132 awards, 1963-2008; 286 honourable mentions. Memberships (past and present): 37 professional associations in various countries; Former President of Environmental Foundation; Former Local Chapter President, Engineering Association; Former President, University Staff Evaluation Commission. Address: PO Box 811, 38400974 Uberlândia, Brazil. E-mail: prosec22@yahoo.com Website: www.manfred.triang.net

FEILER Jo Alison, b. 16 April 1951, Los Angeles, California, USA. Artist-Photographer. Education: University of California, Los Angeles, California; Art Center College of Design, Los Angeles, California. BFA, 1973, MFA, 1975, California Institute of the Arts, Valencia, California. Career: Assistant Director, Frank Perls Gallery, Beverly Hills, California, 1969-70; Photography Editor, Coast Environment Magazine, Los Angeles, California, 1970-72; Art Director, Log/An Inc, Los Angeles, California, 1975-85; Special projects: De Paulo Health Plan, Los Angeles, Annual Report, 1971; Still Photographer, Hawk Films Ltd, Borehamwood, England, 1974; Still Photographer, Warner Brothers Films, London, England, 1974-75; Publicity Photographer, Warner Brothers Records Inc., Burbank, California, 1975; Still Photographer, CRM/McGraw-Hill Productions, Santa Monica California, 1977-79; Commissioned by MCA Inc., to create a photographic portfolio depicting behind the scenes operations at Universal Studios, 1983; Solo exhibitions: Institute of Contemporary Art, London, England, 1975; California Institute

of the Arts, Valencia, California, 1975; NUAGE, Los Angeles, California, 1978; Susan Harder Gallery, New York City, 1984; Group exhibitions, 1975-, include: The Museum of Fine Arts, Houston, Texas, 1983; Susan Harder Gallery, New York City, 1984, 1985; Musée de la Photographie, Port Sarrazine Mougins, France, 1993; Santa Barbara Museum of Art, Santa Barbara, California, 1993; Works in permanent collections including: National Portrait Gallery, London; Victoria and Albert Museum, London; The Metropolitan Museum of Art, New York; The Museum of Modern Art, New York City; Los Angeles Count Museum of Art; International Museum of Photography, Rochester, New York; Santa Barbara Museum of Art; Oakland Museum; Museum of Fine Arts, Houston; Smithsonian Institution, Washington, DC; Bioblioteque Nationale, Paris; Musée D'Art Moderne De La Ville de Paris; Fondation Vincent Van Gogh, Arles, France; Works in many private collections. Publications: Works featured in: Books: Portfolio One, Museum Edition Portfolio, 1976; Women on Women, 1978; The Nude 80 (France), 1980; Numerous articles in journals and magazines. Honours: Certificate of Art Excellence, Los Angeles County Museum of Art, 1968; Scholarship Grant (Photography), California Institute of the Arts, 1974; Cash Award, 2nd All California Photography Show, Laguna Beach Museum of Art, 1976. Memberships: Royal Photographic Society of Great Britain; The Friends of Photography, San Francisco, California.

FEILITZEN Maria Cecilia von, b. 26 September 1945, Stockholm, Sweden. Scientific Co-ordinator; Senior Researcher; Lecturer. Education: BA, 1969, PhD, 1971, Stockholm University. Appointments: Researcher, Swedish Broadcasting Corporation, 1964-96; Senior Researcher, Department of Journalism, Media and Communication, Stockholm University, 1981-2002; Senior Researcher and Lecturer, 2002-, Head of Department, 2003-06, Media and Communication Studies, University College of Södertörn; Scientific Co-Ordinator, The International Clearinghouse on Children, Youth and Media, Nordicom, Göteborg University, 1997-; President, Member Board of Directors, Association for Swedish Media and Communication Science; Examiner, Board of Films for Children and Young People, Swedish Film Institute, 1983-88; Head of Centre for Mass Communication Research, Stockholm University, 1990-93; Expert Member, The Media Council, The Swedish Ministry of Education and Culture, 1991-2006; Member, Board of Directors, Swedish National Board of Film Classifications, 2000-06; Co-Editor, several international journals on media and communication. Publications: About 225 scientific articles, reports and books in the field of media and communications. Memberships: International Association for Media and Communication Science; Association For Swedish Media And Communication Science; Amnesty International. Address: Media and Communication Studies, University College of Södertörn, 14189 Huddinge, Sweden.

FEKETE John, b. 7 August 1946, Budapest, Hungary. Professor of English and Cultural Studies; Writer. Education: BA, Honours, English Literature, 1968, MA, English Literature, 1969, McGill University; PhD, Cambridge University, 1973. Appointments: Visiting Assistant Professor, English, McGill University, Montreal, Quebec, 1973-74; Associate Editor, Telos, 1974-84; Visiting Assistant Professor, Humanities, York University, Toronto, Ontario, 1975-76; Assistant Professor, 1976-78, Associate Professor, 1978-84, Professor, English, Cultural Studies, 1984-, Trent University, Peterborough, Ontario. Publications: The Critical Twilight: Explorations in the Ideology of Anglo-American Literary Theory from Eliot to McLuhan, 1978; The Structural Allegory: Reconstructive

Encounters With the New French Thought, 1984; Life After Postmodernism: Essays on Culture and Value, 1987; Moral Panic: Biopolitics Rising, 1994. Contributions to: Canadian Journal of Political and Social Theory; Canadian Journal of Communications; Science-Fiction Studies. Address: 1818 Cherryhill Road, Peterborough, Ontario K9K 1S6, Canada.

FELBER Ewald, b. 24 March 1947, Vienna, Austria. Professor, Musician, Composer. m. Elfriede Halmschlager, 1 son. Education: Music Teacher, University of Music, Vienna, 1976; Primary School Teacher, State College, Vienna, 1983; Doctor Phil, Musicology, University of Vienna, 1993; Diploma, Summer Course, University of Santiago de Compostela, Spain, 1980. Appointments: Concert Activities, 1970-; Guitar Teacher, High School, Vienna, 1973-81; Professor, State College of Teacher Education, Vienna, 1981-2007; Professor, University of Education, Vienna, 2007-; Visiting Professor at various foreign universities. Publications: Book: Klangfarben zur Musik von Ewald Felber, 1998; Musical Notes (own compositions), 2004; Gesellschoftliche Standortbestimmung durch Analyse des gitarrebegleitoten Kunstliedes der Biedermeierzeit Journal fur Bildungsforschung, Wien, 2005; Records and CDs. Honours: Professor, 1983; Oberstudienrat, 1998; Winner, Composing Competition, 2003; Jury Member, European Doctorate, University of Granada, Spain, 2005. Memberships: Board Member, Vienna International Summer Course for New Music. Address: Rosentalgasse 5-7/2/6, A-1140 Vienna, Austria. E-mail: ewald.felber@ewaldfelber.com

FELDMAN Paula R, b. 4 July 1948, Washington, District of Columbia, USA. Professor of English; Writer. Education: BA, Bucknell University, 1970; MA, 1971, PhD, 1974, Northwestern University. Appointments: Assistant Professor, English, 1974-79, Associate Professor, English, 1979-89, Professor, English, 1989-, Director, Graduate Studies in English, 1991-93; C Wallace Martin Professor of English, 1999-, Louise Frye Scudder Professor of Liberal Arts, 2000-, University of South Carolina, Columbia. Publications: The Microcomputer and Business Writing (with David Byrd and Phyllis Fleishel), 1986; The Journals of Mary Shelley (editor with Diana Scott-Kilvert), 2 volumes, 1987; The Wordworthy Computer: Classroom and Research Applications in Language and Literature (with Buford Norman), 1987; Romantic Women Writers: Voices and Countervoices (editor with Theresa Kelley), 1995; British Women Poets of the Romantic Era, 1997; A Century of Sonnets: The Romantic Era Revival 1750-1850 (Editor with Daniel Robinson), 1999; Records of Woman, (Editor), 1999. Contributions to: Papers of the Bibliographical Society of America, 1978; Studies in English Literature, 1980; Manuscripts, 1980; Approaches to Teaching Shelley's Frankenstein, 1990; Blake: An Illustrated Quarterly, 1993; ADE Bulletin, 1995; Romanticism and Women Poets, 1999; Women's Poetry, Late Romantic to Late Victorian: Gender and Genre, 1999; Approaches to Teaching the Women Romantic Poets, 1997; New Literary History, 2002; Keats-Shelley Journal, 1997, 2006; Cambridge Guide to Women's Writing, 1999; Authorship, Commerce and the Public: Scenes of Writing, 2002; The Keepsake for 1829, 2006. Honours: Teacher of the Year, University of South Carolina, English Department,1986; Mortar Board Teaching Award, University of South Carolina, 1997; Distinguished Scholar Award, Keats-Shelley Association of America, 2007. Address: Department of English, University of South Carolina, Columbia, SC 29208, USA.

FELLGETT Peter Berners, b. 11 April 1922, Ipswich, Suffolk, England. University Research and Teaching. m. Janet Mary Briggs, 1 son, 2 daughters. Education: The Leys, Cambridge; Cambridge University. Appointments: Senior Assistant Observer, The Observatories, Cambridge University; PSO, Royal Observatory, Edinburgh; Professor of Cybernetics, University of Reading; Emeritus Professor. Publications: Around 100 articles in learned literature. Honours: Fellow, Royal Society. Memberships: FRS; FRSE; Fellow, Royal Astronomy Society; Fellow, IEEE. Address: Little Brightor, St Kew Highway, Bodmin PL30 3DU, England.

FELLS Ian, b. 5 September 1932, Sheffield, England. Professor of Energy Conversion. m. Hazel Denton Scott, 4 sons. Education: MA, PhD, Trinity College, Cambridge, 1952-58. Appointments: Lecturer, Chemical Engineering, Sheffield University, 1958-62; Reader, Fuel Science, Durham University, 1962-75; Professor of Energy Conversion, Newcastle University, 1975-88; Chairman, New and Renewable Energy Centre, Blyth, Northumberland, 2002-05; Former Science Adviser, World Energy Council; Special adviser to select committees in House of Lords and House of Commons; Served on several Cabinet and Research Council committees; Former Energy Adviser to the European Union and European Parliament; Principal, Fells Associates; Director and Trustee, International Centre for Life, Newcastle upon Tyne; Made over 500 radio and TV programmes including: The Great Egg Race, Take Nobody's World for It (with Carol Vorderman) and Murphy's Law; What If... The Lights Go Out? 2004. Publications include: UK Energy Policy Post Privatisation, 1991; World Energy 1923-1998 and beyond; Turning Point. Independent Review of UK Energy Policy; More than 200 articles. Honours: Royal Society Faraday Medal and Prize, 1993; Melchett Medal, Energy Institute, 1999; Collier Memorial Medal, Institute of Chemical Engineers and Royal Society, 1999; CBE, 2000; Kelvin Medal, 2002; Listed in national and international biographical directories. Memberships: Fellow, Royal Academy of Engineering; Fellow, Royal Society of Edinburgh; Fellow, Energy Institute; Fellow, Institution of Chemical Engineers. Address: 29 Rectory Terrace, Newcastle upon Tyne, NE3 1YB, England.

FENG Lanrui, b. 16 September 1920, Guiyang, Guizhou, China. Economics. m. Li Chang, 1946, 2 sons, 2 daughters. Education: Political Economy, Central Party School, Beijing, 1954-56. Appointments: Director of Propaganda Bureau, New Democratic Youth League, Municipal Committee of Shanghai; Director and Editor-in-Chief, Youth Daily; Standing Member, Editorial Committee, China Youth Daily; Editor-in-Chief, Harbin Daily; Director, Teaching and Research Department of Political Economy, Polytechnic University of Harbin; Deputy Director, Provincial Economic Institute of Heilongjiang; Deputy Director, Provincial Bureau of Statistics of Heilongjiang; Member, State Council's Political Research Department; Deputy Director, Party Secretary, Senior Research Fellow, and Advisor, Institute of Marxism-Leninism Mao Zedong Thought, Chinese Academy of Social Sciences; Professor, Postgraduate School, Chinese Academy of Social Sciences, -1986; Retired, 1986-. Publications include: How was the idea of the initial stage of socialism raised? – A historical retrospection, 2001; A suggestion for amending the PRC Constitution: Restore the citizen's freedom of residence and the freedom to change it, 2002; Improve the way to help the migrant laborers get their back pays through legal means, 2003; Memories Picked Up and Collected in the Study of Bamboos, 2003; Taking the Other Torturous Path in the World, 2005; Let democratic constitutionalism escort the reform, 2006; Five questions put to Mr Deng Liqun, 2006; Who is to supervise the supervisor? 2007; Friendship through half a story century – in memory of Liu Binyan, 2007. Honours: Sun Yefang Prize for Best Economic Articles, 1984; CASS Prize for Continuing Contributions from the Elderly, 1988; Marxism-Leninism Institute's Prize for Excellent Research Results, 1993; Xinhua Digest's Prize for Most Impressive Article of the Year, 1997. Memberships: Kaida Economist Consultation Center, Beijing; China Council of Economic Associations; Economics Weekly; Chinese People's Association for Friendship with Foreign Countries. E-mail: fenglanrui@sohu.com

FERGUSON Alexander Chapman (Sir), b. 31 December 1941, Glasgow, Scotland. Football Club Manager. m. Catherine Holding, 1966, 3 sons. Appointments: Footballer, Queen's Park, 1958-60, St Johnstone, 1960-64, Dunfermline Athletic, 1964-67, Glasgow Rangers, 1967-69, Falkirk, 1969-73, Ayr Utd, 1973-74; Manager, East Stirling, 1974, St Mirren, 1974-78, Aberdeen, 1978-86, Scottish National Team (assistant manager), 1985-86, Manchester Utd, 1986- (winners FA Cup 1990, 1994, 1996, 1999, 2004; European Cup Winners' Cup, Super Cup, 1991; FA Premier League Championship 1992/93, 1993/94, 1995/94, 1996/97, 1998/99, 1999/2000, 2000/01, 2002/03; 2006/07. League and FA Cup double 1994 and 1996 (new record); Champions League European Cup, 1999. Publications: A Light in the North, 1984; Six Years at United, 1992; Just Champion, 1993; A Year in the Life, 1995; A Will to Win, 1997; Managing My Life: My Autobiography, 1999; The Unique Treble, 2000. Honours include: KBE, 1999; CBE; Voted Best Coach in Europe, UEFA Football Gala, 1999; Freeman, Cities of Aberdeen, Glasgow and Manchester. Address: c/o Manchester United Football Club, Old Trafford, Manchester M16 0RA, England.

FERGUSON Ian Forster, b. 11 September 1931, Blundellsands, Crosby, Lancashire, England. Inorganic Chemist. m. Margot Y Scott, 2 daughters. Education: Andover Grammar School, 1942-45; King Edward VI School, Southampton, 1945-50; University of Southampton, 1950-53. Appointments: UKAEA, 1953-90; AERE, Harwell, 1953-59; Capenhurst, 1960; SNL, Springfields, 1960-1990. Publications: Scanning Auger Microprobe Analysis, Bristol, 1989; Numerous papers and articles for professional journals include Proc. Roy Soc; J Chem Soc; J Applied Cryst; La Vide; Computer Physics Communications. Honours: BSc (Special Chemistry) Southampton, 1953; BSc (Special Chemistry), 1954, MSc, 1956, PhD, 1961, External London; British Crystallographic Society Industrial Group Prize. Memberships: Member, Royal Society of Chemistry; Fellow, Institute of Physics; Chartered Physicist. Address: 1 Ingle Head, Fulwood, Preston, PR2 3NR, England. E-mail: Inglehead @aol.com

FERGUSON Kenneth Adie, b. 6 April 1921, Sydney, Australia. m. Helen Viner McVicar, 2 sons, 3 daughters. Education: BVSc, 1942; PhD, 1951. Appointments: Research Scientist, CSIRO, 1947-73; Chairman, Animal Research Laboratories, CSIRO, 1973-78; Director, Institute of Animal and Food Sciences, CSIRO, 1978-86; Consultant, Peptide Technology Ltd, Sydney, Copenhagen, Cambridge, 1986-93. Publications: Articles in professional journals including research on endocrinology and nutrition of wool growth, isolation and characterisation of pituitary hormones, foetal development of immunity to skin grafts, immunological enhancement of growth hormone action, protection of dietary nutrients against microbial degradation in rumen. Honours: Fellowships, Australian College of Veterinary Scientists, 1974, Australian Academy of Technological Sciences and Engineering, 1976. Memberships: Endocrine Society of Australia (President 1972-74); Society for Endocrinology, England; Australian Society of Animal Production; Australian Biochemical Society; Australian Physiological and Pharmacological Society; Australian Veterinary Association. Address: Compton, 595 Captain's Flat Road, Carwoola, NSW 2620, Australia.

FERNANDEZ Mary Joe, b. 19 August 1971, Dominican Republic. Tennis Player. m. Tony Godsick, 2000, 1 daughter, 1 son. Career: Ranked No 1 USA, 1984; Turned professional, 1986; Reached quarter-finals of French open, 1986, quarter-finals, Geneva, 1987, semi-finals Eastbourne, 1988, semi-finals, French Open, 1989, runner up to Graf in singles and runner up with Fendick in doubles, Australian Open, 1990; Reached semi-finals at Wimbledon and Australian Open, Italian Open, 1991; Runner-up Australian open, 1992; Won Bronze Medal in singles and Gold in doubles with G Fernandez, Olympic Games, 1992; Reached semi-finals US Open, 1992; Reached semi-finals Italian Open, quarter-finals Australian Open, 1993; Won singles title, Strasbourg, 1994; Winner, (with Davenport) French Open Doubles, 1996; Winner doubles, Hilton Head, Carolina, 1997, Madrid, 1997, won singles title German Open, 1997; Member, US Federal Cup Team, Atlantic City, 1991, 1994-99; Spokesperson for Will to Win Scholarship Programme, 1998; Retired, 2000. Publication: Mary Joe Fernandez (with Melanie Cole).

FERRARA Massimiliano, b. 8 June 1972, Pisa, Italy. Professor of Mathematical Economics. m. Marianna Foti. Education: Degree on Economics, 1995; PhD, Applied Mathematics, 2001. Appointments: Researcher, 2000-2002, Professor of Mathematical Economics, 2002-07, University of Messina, Italy; President of the Degree on Economics, Faculty of Law, University Mediterranea of Reggio Calabria, Italy. Publications: Author of 60 scientific articles in international journals; 4 scientific books; Fields of research: Mathematical economics, optimisation, differential geometry. Honours: Member, Accademia Peloritana dei Pericolanti; Balkan Society of Geometers. Memberships: Unione Matematica Italiana; AMASES; European Mathematical Society; SIMAI; Rotary International. Address: Faculty of Law, Via dei Bianchi, 2 Palazzo Zani, 89127 Reggio Calabria, Italy. E-mail: mferrara@unime.it Website: www.mferrara.it

FERRARIS Giovanni, b. 20 March 1937, Prarolo, Italy. Crystallographer. m. Margherita, 2 sons. Education: Laurea in Physics, 1960, Libera Docenza, DSc equivalent, in Crystallography, 1969, University of Turin. Appointments include: Currently Full Professor of Crystallography, Faculty of Sciences, University of Turin; Doctor Honoris Causa, University of Bucharest, Romania and Darmstadt, Germany. Publications: More than 200 articles in mineralogical crystallography and crystal chemistry; 2 monographs, 2004, 2005. Honours: Plinius Medal, SIMP; Tartufari Prize, Accademia dei Lincei. Membership: Russian Academy of Natural Sciences. Address: Dipartimento di Scienze Mineralogiche e Petrologiche, Università di Torino, Via Valperga Caluso 35, I-10125 Torino, Italy. E-mail: giovanni.ferraris@unito.it

FERREIRA Antonio Guilherme, b. 27 March 1937, Lisbon, Portugal. Medical Doctor. m. Maria do Rosário Vieira Coelho, 2 sons, 1 daughter. Education: MD, Lisbon University, Medicine Faculty, 1962. General Practice Resident, 1962-64, Psychiatry Resident, 1964-67, Santa Maria Hospital; Psychiatry Consultant, 1969-78, Head of Unit, 1978-, Head of Department, 1978-87, Head of Psychiatric Training, 1984-, Clinical Director, 1988-97, Director, 1987-98, Miguel

Bombarda Hospital; Professor, Superor Institute for Applied Psychology, 1978-; Professor, Modern University (License in Educative Psycho Pedagogy), 1998-. Publications: Co-author, Social Psychiatry and World accords, 1992; 122 articles in professional journals; 520 papers; Member of editorial board and contributor to 5 journals including: Grupanalise (Lisboa) (also director); Journal of the World Association for Social Psychiatry. Honours: Hon DSc, Psychiatry, Marquis G Seicluna University Foundation, 1987; Leonidas Finiffes Award, for work in social psychiatry in Mediterranean region; Plaque for services as WASP president, 1992. Memberships include: Fellow, Psychiatry Portuguese Association, President, General Assembly, 1980-84 Portuguese Group Analytic Society, President, 1982-95; World Association for Social Psychiatry, President, 1988-92; Mediterranean Sociopsychiatry Association, President, 2000-; International Association for Group Psychotherapy; Standing Committee of Presidents of International NGO Concerned with Mental Health Issues, 1991-94, New York Academy of Sciences. Address: Av Mousinho de Albuquerque - Lote B1-70, 1170-259 Lisboa, Portugal.

FERREIRA-COELHO Jose Manuel Martins, b. 7 May 1943, Lisbon, Portugal. Medical Doctor. m. Maria José Mayer Bleck da Silva, 1967, 1 son, 1 daughter. Education: MD, Classic Faculty of Medicine, Santa Maria Hospital, Lisbon, 1960-67; PhD, Classic Faculty of Medicine, Lisbon, 2000. Appointments: Resident, General Surgery, 1972-75, Urology, 1976-79, Hospitalar Assistant of Urology, 1980, Hospitalar Assistant of General Surgery, 1982, Graduation of Chief Service General Surgery, 1989, Hospitais Civis, Lisbon; Fellow, General Surgery, 1975, Urology College, 1982, Ordem dos Médicos, Lisbon; Specialist of General Surgery, 1982; Chief of Emergency Staff, Hospital Capuchos, Lisbon, 1991-98; Chief of Emergency Staff, Hospital S José, Lisbon, 1998-2002; Graduation of Chief Service of General Surgery, Hospital Desterro-Capuchos, Lisbon, 1991-2003; Retired, 2003-; Consultant, General Surgery and Urologist, Hospital Julio de Matos, Lisbon. Publications: Many papers and articles in professional medical journals; 3 books. Honours: Honoured by Mozambique Navy, 1970; Dr Bentes de Jesus Prize, 1997; Best Video Prize, 1998. Memberships: National Geographic Society; Association des Anatomistes, Paris; Sociedade Luso Brasileira de Anatomia; Sociedade Pan Americana de Anatomia; International Gastro-Surgical Club; Society of Laparoendoscopic Surgeons; European Association for Endoscopic Surgery and other International Techniques; Societe Internationale d'Urologie; Sociedade Brasileira de Urologia; International Society of Surgery; Fellow, American College of Surgeons; International Advisory Board of the Society of Laparoendoscopic Surgeons. Address (office): Rua das Picoas, no 4-2 Esq, 1050 Lisbon, Portugal. E-mail: fcoelho@hjmatos.min-saude.pt

FERRIGNO (Ferry) Pietro Camillo (John Bailey) (King Ferry of London), b. 10 December 1961, London, England (adopted 6 February 1962, Treviglio, Italy). Therapist. Education: Black belt of Karate, Milan, 1972; Diploma of Pianoforte, Bergamo, 1979; Diploma of mental Dynamics and Applied psychology, Rome, 1981; Diploma di Liceo Classico, Treviglio, 1982; Medical School, University of Milan; Studies in Parapsychology and Alchemy; Masseur's Certificate (Classical Massage-Shiatsu), Milan, 1995. Appointment: The Duke of Burlington; Chevalier, Order of Malta, 1989. Honours: Nominations for various awards, American Biographical Institute including The American Medal of Honor 2004-2005, 2006; The Da Vinci Diamond; International Medal of Honour; The Marie Curie Award, 2006; 21st Century Award for

Achievement, MM-MMC; Honorary Director General, IBC; Medical Advisor to the Director General, IBC; The Order of International Fellowship; IBC Lifetime Achievement Award; IBC Hall of Fame, 2007; Listed in Who's Who publications and biographical dictionaries. Memberships: International Order of Merit; Order of International Ambassadors; Sovereign Ambassador of the Order of American Ambassadors; IBC Leading Health Professionals of the World; Deputy Director General, IBC, 2006; Vice President, Recognition Board of the World Congress of Arts, Sciences and Communications; Legion of Honor, United Cultural Convention, 2006; Legion of Honour, 2008. Address: Via Ing Grossi 5, 24047 Treviglio (BG), Italy.

FERRY Bryan, b. 26 September 1945, Washington, County Durham, England. Singer; Songwriter; Musician. m. Lucy Helmore, 1982 (divorced 2003), 4 sons. Education: Fine Art, Newcastle University. Career: Formed Roxy Music, 1971; Solo artiste, 1973-; Worked with: Brian Eno; Phil Manzanera; Andy Mackay; Steve Ferrone; David Williams; Robin Trower; Pino Palladino; Nile Rodgers; Carleen Anderson; Shara Nelson; Jhelisa; Numerous worldwide tours; Major concerts include: Crystal Palace, 1972; Live Aid, Wembley, 1985; Radio City, New York, 1988; Wembley, 1989; Support tours, Alice Cooper, David Bowie; Television appearances include: Subject of Without Walls documentary, 1992; Videos: New Town (live), 1990; Total Recall (documentary), 1990. Recordings: Singles include: Love Is The Drug, 1975; Dance Away, 1979; Angel Eyes, 1979; Over You, 1980; Jealous Guy, 1981; Slave To Love, 1985; The Right Stuff, 1987; I Put A Spell On You, 1993; Albums: Solo: These Foolish Things, 1973; Another Time Another Place, 1974; Let's Stick Together, 1976; In Your Mind, 1977; The Bride Stripped Bare, 1978; Boys And Girls, 1985; Bete Noire, 1987; The Ultimate Collection, 1988; Taxi, 1993; Mamounia, 1994; As Time Goes By, 1999; Frantic, 2002; Dylanesque, 2007; with Roxy Music: Roxy Music, 1972; For Your Pleasure, 1973; Stranded, 1973; Country Life, 1974; Siren, 1975; Viva Roxy Music, 1976; Manifesto, 1979; Flesh And Blood (Number 1, UK), 1980; Avalon, (Number 1, UK), 1982; The High Road (live mini-album), 1983; The Atlantic Years, 1983; Street Life, 1987; Recent compilations include: The Thrill Of It All, 1995; More Than This - The Best Of Roxy Music and Bryan Ferry, 1995. Honours include: Grand Prix Du Disque, Best Album, Montreux Golden Rose Festival, 1973. Address: c/o Barry Dickins, ITB, 3rd Floor, 27A Floral Street, London, WC2E 9DQ, England.

FERZAK Franz Xaver, b. 27 October 1958, Neuenhinzenhausen, Germany. Publisher; Writer; Engineer. Education: Diploma of Mechanical Engineering, 1982. Appointments: Author, Publisher, 1986-; Translator, MVV Peiting, 1996-97, 2002. Publications: Nikola Tesla, 1986, Karl Freiherr von Reichenbach, 1987; Giordano Bruno, 1996; Wilhelm Reich, 1991; Jesus of Qumran, 1997; Viktor Schauberger, 2001; Nikola Tesla Photocollection, 2002; Nikola Tesla, der Erfinder des Radios (translation), 2004; Nikola Tesla, Colorado Springs Aufzeichnungen (translation), 2007; Etidorpha (translation), 2003; Technologie der bötter (translation), 2003; Nullpunktenergie (translation), 2003; Zeitreisen Handbuch (translation), 2003. Honours: Listed in Who's Who publications and biographical dictionaries. Address: Am Bachl 1, 93336 Altmannstein, Germany.

FETHERSTON Brian, b. 26 January 1955, Milwaukee, Wisconsin, USA. Artist; Sculptor; Painter. m. Marianne, 1 son. Education: Ontario College of Art, Canada. Appointments: Commissions and Creative Works: Solo exhibitions of

Fetherston & Fetherston (Brian & Marianne): Galerie Cluny, Geneva, Switzerland, 1986; Switzerland Gallery Jaime III, Palma de Mallorca, Spain, 1987; In permanence, Galerie Cluny, Geneva, 1989-90; Gallery Montserrat, New York, 1996; Six Tech SA, Geneva, Switzerland, 1997; Ballard-Fetherston Gallery, Seattle, Washington, 1998; DWT Gallery, Geneva, 2000-01; Fetherston Gallery Designer Work Team, 2005; Group exhibitions of Fetherston & Fetherston (Brian & Marianne) in Spain, Switzerland, Turkey, France, include: Gallery Ramko, Istanbul, Turkey, 1991; Gallerie du Vieux-Chène, Geneva, 1991; Museum International Art, Carnac, France, 1996; Finansbank SA, Geneva, 1991; United Nations, Geneva, 1995, 1996; Red Cross, Geneva, 1996; Biennale du Japon Grand Prix de Sapporo, Japan, 1997; Société Générale & Trust, Zurich, 1997; Art EXPO 99, New York, 1999; Barcelona Art Expo, 1999; Mural, Trompe l'Oeil, BPI Investments, Geneva; Mural, Gallay-Jufer, SA; Designer Work Team Gallery, Switzerland, 2000. Mural (Trompe L'Oeil BPI Investments, Geneva; Mural, Gallay-Jufer SA, Geneva. Publications: Gallery Guide Paris, 12th, 13th editions; Business Guide to Switzerland, 1992; Art News Magazine, USA, 1996; Gallery Guide, New York, 1996; Epoch Times Int, 2005-06. Honours: Accademical Knight, Greci Marino, Italy. Membership: Professor of Fine Arts, Greci Marino, Italy. Address: 8 rue de Fribourg, 1201 Geneva, Switzerland. Website: www.ffetherston.com

FETHERSTON Marianne, b. 14 August 1959, Alexandria, Egypt (Swiss citizen). Artist Painter. m. Brian, 1 son. Education: Ontario College of Art, Toronto, Canada. Honour: Gallery Art et Vie, Jury Prize, Paris, 1987. Commissions and Creative Works: Solo Exhibitions of Fetherston & Fetherston (Brian & Marianne): Galerie Cluny, Geneva, 1986; (permanent), Circulo Bellas Artes, Salon de Otono, Palma de Mallorca, Spain, 1987; Gallery Bearn, Palma de Mallorca, Spain, 1988; Galerie Cluny, Geneva, 1989-90; Gallery Montserrat, New York, 1996; Six Tech SA, Geneva, 1997; Ballard-Fetherston Gallery, Seattle, Washington, 1998; DWT Gallery, Geneva, 2000-01, 2005; Group exhibitions of Fetherston & Fetherston (Brian & Marianne) in Switzerland, Spain, France, Japan, USA, include: Finansbank SA, Geneva, 1991; Museum International Art, Carnac, France, 1996; United Nations, Switzerland, 1995-96; Red Cross, Geneva, 1996; Biennale du Japon Grand Prix de Sapporo, 1997; Société Générale & Trust, Zurich, 1997; Art Expo 99 New York, 1999; Barcelona Art Expo, 1999; Mural (Trompe l'oeil) BPI Investments, Geneva; Mural, Gallay-Jufer, SA; Solo exhibition of Fetherston & Fetherston Gallery Designer Work Team,Geneva, 2005. Publications: Gallery Guide, Paris, 12th, 13th edition; Art News Magazine, 1996; Gallery Guide, New York, 1996; Epoch Times International, 2005, 2006. Honours: Accademical Knight, Creamarino, Italy. Membership: Professor of Fine Arts, Greci Marino, Italy. Address: 8 rue de Fribourg, 1201 Geneva, Switzerland. Website: www.ffetherston.com

FETTWEIS Günter B L, b. 17 November 1924, Düsseldorf, Germany. Mining Engineer; University Professor Emeritus. m. Alice, 1 son, 3 daughters. Education: Diploma in Mining, Technical University of Aachen, 1950; Dr Jng, 1953, Assessor des Bergfachs (a of Mining), 1955. Appointments: Junior Mining Inspector, State of North Rhine-Westfalia, 1953-55; Mining Engineer, 1955-57, Production Manager, Mining Co Neue Hoffnung, Oberhausen, Germany, 1957-59; Professor of Mining, University of Leoben, Austria, 1959-93; Rector, 1968-70, Emeritus, 1993-. Publications: About 250 articles and 15 books about mining and mineral economics. Honours: Dr h C mult Aachen (D), 1980, Miskolc (H), 1987, Petrosani

(RO), 1996, Moscow (RG), 1999, Košice (SK), 2003; Several awards, Austria, Germany, Poland and the Vatican. Memberships: Austrian Academy of Sciences; Several other European academies of sciences; Indian National Academy of Engineering; Honorary Member, Austrian Mining Association (BVÖ); German Mining Association (GDMB); International Committee of World Mining Congress; Lions Club, Homburg, Germany; Board of the Austrian Mining Association, 1959-2000; Vice President, International Committee of World Mining Congress, 1976-2001; Explorers Club; Lions Club. Address: Gasteigergasse 5, A 8700 Leoben, Austria.

FEWEL John Gerrard, b. 20 August 1944, Chickasha, Oklahoma, USA. President, Miracle Wish Foundation. m. Vicki Ann, 2 sons. Education: BA, Microbiology, University of Texas, Austin; MS, Management, University of Texas, San Antonio. Appointments: Administrative Officer for Research & Development, Dallas VAMC, Boston VAMC, Boston Outpatient Clinic, 1983-2003; Executive Director, Dallas VA Research Corp, 1990-2002; President, Miracle Wish Foundation. Publications: Over 30 scientific publications in peer-reviewed journals. Honours: Congressional Medal of Distinction, 2006; Republican of the Year, National Republican Congressional Committee (NRCC), 2006; Businessman of the Year, NRCC, 2006; National Leadership Award, NRCC, 2006; Listed in international biographical dictionaries. Memberships: Member, Society of Research Administrators and President of the Government Division, 1997-98. Address: 1307 High Ridge Drive, Duncanville, TX 75137, USA. E-mail: feweljohn@aol.com

FIALOVÁ Daniela, b. 30 January 1975, Chrudim, Czech Republic. University Teacher; Researcher. m. Daniel Fiala, 1 daughter. Education: Graduate, 1998, Pharm D, PhD, Clinical Pharmacy, 2006, Faculty of Pharmacy, Charles University, Czech Republic; 1st Ward Certification in Clinical Pharmacy, Department of Clinical Pharmacy, Institute for Postgraduate Education and Training in Medicine and Pharmacy, Prague, 2001. Appointments: Clinical Pharmacist, Thomayer's Teaching Hospital, Prague, 1998-2001; Researcher, Academic Tutor, Geriatric Clinic, 1st Faculty of Medicine and General Teaching Hospital, Prague, 2001-; Member, European Aged in Home Care Research Group, 2001-; Researcher, Academic Tutor, Department of Social and Clinical Pharmacy, Faculty of Pharmacy, Charles University, 2003-. Publications: Papers and articles in professional scientific and medical journals. Honours: Award of the Dean of the Faculty of Pharmacy, Charles University, 1996, 1997, 1998; Merit, 1st Ward Certification Committee, Institute for Postgraduate Education and Training in Medicine and Pharmacy, Prague, 2001; French Award in Pharmacy, French Embassy and Sanofi-Aventis corp, Prague, 2005; Award, Czech Medical Society of J E Purkyne, 2005; Dr Paul Janssen's Scientific Award in Pharmacoeconomics and Drug Policy, 2006. Memberships: European Society of Clinical Pharmacy; Inter-Raj Corp; Czech Society of Clinical Pharmacists. E-mail: fialovad@faf.uni.cz

FIALOVA Ludmila, b. 20 February 1955, Prague, Czech Republic. Senior Lecturer. m. Antonin Fiala, 2 sons. Education: Student, Faculty of Physical Education and Sport, Faculty of Arts, 1974-79, Postgraduate Study, Paed Dr, 1988-89, Postgraduate Study, PhD, 1993-97, Associate Professor, 2001, Charles University, Prague. Appointments: Teacher, High School, Prague, 1979-83; Teacher, Basic School, Prague, 1988-89; Lecturer, Charles University, Prague, 1989-. Publications: A Body Image as a Part of Self Concept, 2001; Book chapter: Women and Sport in the Czech Republic in Sport and Women. Social Issues in International Perspective,

2003; Articles in professional journals: Health promoting behaviour and sport, 2004; The impact of physical activity on health and personal satisfaction, 2004. Honours: Woman of the Month, 2003; Listed in Who's Who publications and biographical dictionaries. Memberships: Research Agency of Charles University Commission of Psychology and Pedagogy; European Association for Sociology of Sport; Slovenska Vedecka Spolocnost Pre TV A Sport. Address: Faculty of Physical Education and Sport, Department of Psychology, Pedagogy and Didactics, J Martiho 31, 16252 Prague 6, Czech Republic. E-mail: fialova@ftvs.cuni.cz

FIECHTER Jean Jacques, b. 25 May 1927, Alexandria, Egypt. Historian; Novelist. 2 sons. Education: MA, History, 1950; PhD, History, Cum Laude, 1965. Appointments: CEO President, Blancpain Watches, 1950-80; General Manager, Swiss Watch Industrial Corporation, 1960-80; Independent Historian specialising in Egyptology, 1981-. Publications: More than 15 biographies and historical works including: Gouvernor Morris; Baron de Besenval; The Harvest of Gods; Mykerinos, le dieu englouti; Faux et Faussaires en Art Egyptien; 4 novels: Death by Publication; A Masterpiece of Revenge; A le Recherche du Sarcophage de Mykerinos; Immortelle. Honours: Grand Prize, Literature, Bern State; General History Prize, French Academy; French Grand Prize for detective novel. Memberships: Société de Belles-Lettres, Switzerland; PEN International (Swiss French Section). Address: 80 Rte Geneve, 1028 Preverenges, Switzerland.

FIELD Brian Orlando, b. 27 October 1932, Blackburn, Lancashire, England. University Senior Lecturer, retired. Education: Blackburn Technical High School and College, 1943-53; University of Durham, 1953-57. Appointments: Research Chemist, United Kingdom Atomic Energy Authority, Harwell, Berkshire, 1957-64; Lecturer in Inorganic Chemistry, Mid-Essex Technical College, Chelmsford, 1964-66; Senior Lecturer in Chemistry and Senior Halls Warden, City University, London, 1966-89; Publications: Numerous Research Papers in Professional Journals. Honours: The Gold Carrot Award from the Student Body of the City University. Membership: MRSC; FRSA. Address: 65 Woodnook Road, Appley Bridge, Wigan, Lancs WN6 9JR, UK. E-mail: brianfield@blueyonder.co.uk

FIENNES Ranulph (Twisleton-Wykeham), b. 7 March 1944, Windsor, England. Explorer; Writer. m. (1) Virginia Pepper, deceased 2004, (2) Louise Millington, 2005. Education: Eton College. Appointments: British Army, 1965-70; Special Air Service, 1966; Sultan of Muscat's Armed Forces, 1968-70; Led British Expeditions to White Nile, 1969, Jostedalsbre Glacier, 1970, Headless Valley, British Columbia, 1970; Transglobal expedition, first circumpolar journey round the world, 1979-82, North Pole (5 expeditions), 1985-90, Ubar Expedition (discovered the lost city of Ubar, Oman), 1992, First unsupported crossing of Antarctic continent, 1993; Land Rover 7x7x7 Challenge (7 marathons in 7 days on 7 continents), 2003; Climbed the Eiger by its North Face, 2007; Lectures; Television and film documentary appearances. Publications: A Talent for Trouble, 1970; Ice Fall on Norway, 1972; The Headless Valley, 1973; Where Soldiers Fear to Tread, 1975; Hell on Ice, 1979; To the Ends of the Earth: The Transglobe Expedition - The First Pole-to-Pole Circumnavigation of the Globe, 1983; Bothie the Polar Dog (with Virginia Fiennes), 1984; Living Dangerously (autobiography), 1988; The Feather Men, 1991; Atlantis of the Sands, 1992; Mind Over Matter: The Epic Crossing of the Antarctic Continent, 1994; The Sett, 1996; Ranulph Fiennes: Fit For Life, 1998; Beyond the Limits, 2000; The Secret Hunters, 2001; Captain Scott,

2003; . Honours: Dhofar Campaign Medal, 1969; Sultan of Muscat Bravery Medal, 1970; Krug Award for Excellence, 1980; Gold Medal and Honorary Life Membership, Explorer's Club of New York, 1983; Livingstone's Gold Medal, Royal Scottish Geographic Society, 1983; Founder's Medal, Royal Geographic Society, 1984; Hon DSc, Loughborough, 1986; Guinness Hall of Fame, 1987; Polar Medal and Bar, 1987, 1994; ITN Award, 1990; Officer of the Order of the British Empire, 1993; Hon DUniv, Birmingham, 1995; British Chapter, The Explorers' Club Millennium Award For Polar Exploration, 2000; Honorary DSc, Portsmouth University, 2000; Hon DLitt, Glasgow Caledonian, 2002. Membership: Honorary Membership, Royal Institute of Navigation, 1997. Address: Greenlands, Exford, Somerset TA24 7NU, England.

FIGES Eva, b. 15 April 1932, Berlin, Germany. Writer. 1 son, 1 daughter. Education: BA, Honours, English Language and Literature, University of London, 1953. Publications: Winter Journey, 1967; Patriarchal Attitudes, 1970; B, 1972; Nelly's Version, 1977; Little Eden, 1978; Waking, 1981; Sex and Subterfuge, 1982; Light, 1983; The Seven Ages, 1986; Ghosts, 1988; The Tree of Knowledge, 1990; The Tenancy, 1993; The Knot, 1996; Tales of Innocence and Experience, 2003. Honour: Guardian Fiction Prize, 1967. Membership: Society of Authors. Address: c/o Rogers, Coleridge & White Ltd, 20 Powis Mews, London W11 1JN, England.

FIGGIS Mike, b. 28 February 1949, Kenya. Film Director; Writer; Musician. Career: Came to England, 1957; Studied music, performing in band, Gas Board; Musician, experimental theatre group, The People Show, early 1970s; Maker of independent films including: Redheugh; Slow Fade; Animals of the City; TV film, The House, Channel 4; Films include: Stormy Monday (also screenplay and music), 1988; Internal Affairs (also music), 1990; Liebestraum (also screenplay and music), 1991; Mr Jones, 1993; The Browning Version, 1994; Leaving Las Vegas (also screenplay and music), 1995; One Night Stand, 1997; Flamenco Women, 1997; Miss Julie, 1999; The Loss of Sexual Innocence, 1999; Time Code, 1999; Hotel, 2001; The Battle of Orgreave, 2001; Ten Minutes Older: The Cello, 2002; Cold Creek Manor, 2003; Co/Ma, 2004. Honours: IFP Independent Spirit Award, 1996; National Society of Film Critics Award. Address: c/o ICM, 8942 Wilshire Boulevard, Beverly Hills, CA 90211, USA.

FILA John Charles, b. Boston, USA. Psychoanalyst. Education: AB, Harvard University, 1992; PhD, University of Berkeley, Michigan, 1995; Diplomate, American College of Professional Mental Health Practitioners. Appointments: Volunteer mentor of disadvantaged, 1995-; Private Practice, Wellesley, Massachusetts, 1997-2000; Santa Monica, California, 2000-; National Board of Directors, International Academy of Philosophy, North Hollywood, California. Publications: Contributed articles to professional journals. Honours: Affiliate: Sigma XI. Memberships: Ombudsman/Officer, The Prometheus Society International; Member, National Commission on American Foreign Policy, New York City; National Campaign for Tolerance, Montgomery, Alabama; AAAS; New York Academy of Sciences; Menninger Society; Harvard Club (Boston, South California and Palm Beach); The International Neuro-Psychoanalysis Society (London). Address: 2928 4th St, Apt 40, Santa Monica, CA 90405, USA. E-mail: psychdr721@hotmail.com

FILAR Marian Andrzej, b. 6 October 1942, Krosno, Poland. Lawyer; Professor of Law. m. Veronika Filar, 1 daughter. Education: Technical studies for miners, Cracow, Poland, 1960-62; MA, Legal Studies, Nicolaus Copernicus

University, Torun, 1962-67; Scholarships: Max Planck's Institute of International Criminal Law and Comparative Law, Freiburg, Germany, 1986; Institute of Criminal Law, University of Rome, 1972; PhD, 1972. Appointments: Assistant, 1967, Lecturer, 1972, Habilitated Doctor of Law, 1977, Vice Dean of the Faculty, 1985-87, Dean of the Faculty, 1987-90, Associate Professor, 1988, Professor, 1991-, Faculty of Law and Administration, Chair of Criminal Law and Criminal Policy, Vice-Rector for Student Affairs, 1990-93, University of Nicolaus Copernicus; Vice Chairman, State Tribunal (Poland), 1997-2001; Deputy to Sejm (Lower Chamber of Polish Parliament), 2007-. Publications include: Rape in Polish Criminal Law, 1974; Pornography. Studies in the Field of Criminal Policy, 1977; Sexual Offences in Polish Criminal Law, 1985; Criminal Justice Policies in the Crossnational Perspective, 1991; Medical Criminal Law, 2000; Commentary on Polish Act on Liability of Collective Bodies for Acts Forbidden under the Penalty, 2006; Criminal Law and Criminal Justice of the European Union Countries, 2007. Honours: Medal, Polish National Education Commission; Knight's Cross "Polonia Restituta". Memberships: International Association of Criminal Law; Former Vice-President, Member of the Board, Scientific Society of Criminal Law; Polish Medicine Academy; Polish Academy of Sexological Knowledge. Address: Suchatowka 73, 88-140 Gniewkowo, Poland.

FINE Anne, b. 7 December 1947, Leicester, England. Writer. m. Kit Fine, divorced, 2 daughters. Education: BA Honours, Politics and History, University of Warwick, 1965-68. Career, Novelist for both children and adults. Publications include: Novels: The Killjoy, 1986; Taking the Devil's Advice, 1990; In Cold Domain, 1994; Telling Liddy, 1998; All Bones and Lies, 2001; Raking the Ashes, 2005; Fly in the Ointment, 2008. For Older Children: The Summer House Loon, 1978; The Other Darker Ned, 1979; The Stone Menagerie, 1980; Round Behind the Ice House, 1981; The Granny Project, 1983; Madame Doubtfire, 1987; Goggle Eyes, 1989; The Book of the Banshee, 1991; Flour Babies, 1992; Step by Wicked Step, 1995; The Tulip Touch, 1996; Very Different (short stories), 2001; Up on Cloud Nine, 2002; The Road of Bones, 2006; Numerous books for younger children. Honours include: Guardian Children's Award, 1989; Carnegie Medals, 1989, 1993; Smarties Prize, 1990; Guardian Children's Literature Award, 1990; Publishing News, Children's Author of Year, 1990, 1993; Whitbread Children's Novel Awards, 1993, 1996; Children's Laureate, 2001-2003; Fellow, Royal Society of Literature, 2003; OBE, 2003. Membership: Society of Authors. Address: c/o David Higham Associates, 5-8 Lower John Street, Golden Square, London W1F 9HA, England. Website: www.annefine.co.uk

FINER Stephen Alan, b. 27 January 1949, London, England. Artist. Career: Solo Exhibitions: Four Vine Lane, London, 1981, 1982, 1985; Anthony Reynolds Gallery, London, 1986, 1988; Berkeley Square Gallery, London, 1989; Bernard Jacobson Gallery, London, 1992, 1995; Woodlands Art Gallery, 1994; Agnew's, London, 1998; Pallant House Gallery, Chichester, Sussex, 2001, Charleston, Sussex, 2002; Art Space Gallery, London, 2004; Selected Mixed Exhibitions: British Art, 1940-80, from the Arts Council Collection, Hayward Gallery, London, 1980; Collazione Inglese II, Venice Biennale, Italy, 1984; Academicians' Choice, Stephen Finer invited by Kitaj, Mall Galleries, London; The Portrait Now, National Portrait Gallery, London, 1993-94, 1990; The Discerning Eye, Stephen Finer invited by Martin Gayford, Mall Gallery, London, 1996; Men on Women, Touring Exhibition Stephen Finer invited by Peter Edwards, Wales,

1997-98; 50 Contemporary Self-Portraits, Six Chapel Row, Bath, 1998; British Art, 1900-98, Agnew's, London, 1998; About the Figure, Six Chapel Row, Bath, 1999; Painting the Century, 101 Portrait Masterpieces, 1900-2000, National Portrait Gallery, London, 2000-01; The National Portrait Gallery Collects, Bodelwyddan Castle, Wales, 2003; Fusion Gallery, Spain, 2005-07; Public Collections: Arts Council; Southport Art Gallery; The British Council; Contemporary Art Society; Los Angeles County Museum of Art; National Portrait Gallery, "David Bowie", London; Pallant House Gallery, "Sir Morris Finer", Chichester, Sussex. Selected publications: Allgemeines Kunstlerlexikon; Dictionary of British Artists Since 1945; Handbook of Modern British Painting and Printmaking, 1900-2000; The Portrait Now, Robin Gibson, National Portrait Gallery, 1993; Painting the Century 101 Portrait Masterpieces, 1900-2000, Robin Gibson, National Portrait Gallery, London, 2000; Stephen Finer: Presence and Identity, Martin Golding, Modern Painters, Spring, 2000; Intimacy and Mortality, Finer's People, Robin Gibson, Charleston Trust, 2002. Address: 20 Kipling Street, London SE1 3RU, England. Websites: www.stephenfiner.com

FINK Eloise Bradley, b. 13 March 1927, Decatur, Illinois, USA. Secondary School Educator; Writer; Educator. m. John Fink, divorced, 1 son, 2 daughters. Education: BA (Hons), English, University of Illinois, 1949; Student, Colorado College, 1951. Appointments: Certified Teacher, Illinois Teacher of English, Social Studies, Paxton, Decatur and Arlington Heights, Illinois, 1949-56; Freelance Scott Foresman, Encyclopaedia Britannica and SRA, 1956-80; Director, Public Relations Rehabilitation Institute, Chicago, 1980-82; Instructor, Creative Writing and Poetry, Loyola University, Water Tower Campus, Chicago, 1983-90; Artist-in-residence, Illinois Arts Council, 1984-93; Facilitator, workshops in poetry, fiction and nonfiction, New Trier Extension, 1974-; Founder, Editor, President, Thorntree Press, Winnetka, Illinois, 1985-. Publications: The Girl in the Empty Nightgown, 1986; Lincoln and the Prairie After, 1999. Honours: 2 awards, Friends of Literature; Gwendolyn Brooks award for Twenty Siginificant Illinois Poets; Breadloaf Writing Conference fellow, 1986; Poetry contest judge, USC Writers, 2005. Memberships: Academy of American Poets; Poetry Society of America. Address: 804 Kings Lake Court, Virginia Beach, VA 23452-4643, USA.

FINK Merton, (Matthew Finch, Merton Finch), b. 17 November 1921, Liverpool, England. Author. m. (1) 15 March 1953, 1 son, 1 daughter, (2) 24 November 1981. Education: School of Military Engineers, 1942; School of Military Intelligence, 1943; LDS, Liverpool University, 1952. Publications: Dentist in the Chair, 1953; Teething Troubles, 1954; The Third Set, 1955; Hang Your Hat on a Pension, 1956; The Empire Builder, 1957; Solo Fiddle, 1959; The Beauty Bazaar, 1960; Matchbreakers, 1961; Five Are the Symbols, 1962; Snakes and Ladders, 1963; Chew this Over, 1965; Eye with Mascara, 1966; Eye Spy, 1967; Jones is a Rainbow, 1968; Simon Bar Cochba, 1971; A Fox Called Flavius, 1973; Open Wide, 1976. Contributions to: Dental Practice, 1956-; Bath Chronicle, 1995. Honour: Richard Edwards Scholar, 1950. Memberships: Civil Service Writers; Deputy Chairman, Bath Literary Society; British Dental Association; Chairman, Service Committee, Bath British Legion. Address: 27 Harbutts, Bathampton, Bath BA2 6TA, England.

FINKELSTEIN Richard Alan, b. 5 March 1930, New York City, New York, USA. Microbiologist; Professor Emeritus. m. (1) Helen Rosenberg, 1 son, 2 daughters, (2) Mary Boesman, 1 daughter. Education: BS, University of Oklahoma, 1950; MA,

1952, PhD, 1955, University of Texas, Austin; Postdoctoral work, University of Texas Southwestern Medical School, Dallas, 1955-58. Appointments: Chief, Bioassay Section, Walter Reed Army Institute for Research, Washington DC, 1958-64; Deputy Chief, Chief, Department of Bacteriology and Mycology, US Army Medical Component, SEATO Medical Research Laboratory, Bangkok, Thailand, 1964-67; Associate Professor, Professor, Department of Microbiology, University of Texas Southwestern Medical School, 1967-79; Professor, Chairman, Department of Microbiology, 1979-93, Millsap Distinguished Professor, 1985-2000, Curators' Professor, 1990-2000, School of Medicine, University of Missouri, Columbia; Consultant, editorial boards, National Institutes of Health Study Sections. Publications: Over 230 including articles in scientific journals and texts on cholera, enterotoxins, gonorrhea, role of iron in host-parasite interactions. Honours include: Outstanding Achievement, 1964, Performance, 1965, US Army; Ciba-Geigy Lecturer, 1975; Visiting Scientist, Japanese Science Council, 1976; Robert Koch Prize, Science, Medicine, Bonn, Germany, 1976; Many lectureships, 1980-2000; Chancellor's Award for Outstanding Research, University of Missouri, 1985; Sigma Xi Research Award, 1986; Distinguished Service Award, American Society for Microbiology, 1998. Memberships: American Society for Microbiology, Texas, Missouri and National offices; American Academy of Microbiology, offices; American Association of Immunology; Infectious Diseases Society of America; Society of General Microbiology; Pathology Society of Great Britain and Ireland; Sigma Xi. Address: 3861 S Forest Acres, Columbia, MO 65203, USA.

FINN Neil, b. 27 May 1958, Te Awamutu, New Zealand. Singer; Musician (guitar); Songwriter. Career: Member, Split Enz, 1977-85; Founder member, Crowded House, 1985-; Duo with brother Tim, 1995; International concerts include: A Concert For Life, Centennial Park, Sydney, 1992; WOMAD Festival, 1993; Television appearances include: Late Night With David Letterman, NBC; The Tonight Show, NBC; In Concert '91, ABC; Return To The Dome, Ch4; MTV Unplugged; Top Of The Pops, BBC1. Recordings: Albums: with Split Enz: Frenzy, 1978; True Colours, 1979; Beginning Of The Enz, 1980; Waita, 1981; Time And Tide, 1982; Conflicting Emotions, 1984; See Ya Round, 1985; History Never Repeats Itself - The Best Of Split Enz, 1993; Oddz & Endz, 1993; Rear Enz, 1993; with Crowded House: Crowded House, 1986; Temple Of Low Men, 1988; Woodface, 1991; Together Alone, 1993; Seductive & Emotional, 1994; Unplugged in the Byrdhouse, 1995; Recurring Dream, 1996; Originals, 1998; with Tim Finn: Finn, 1995; Solo Albums: Try Whistling This, 1998; Encore!, 1999; Singles: with Split Enz include: I See Red; I Got You; History Never Repeats; Six Months In A Leaky Boat; with Crowded House include: Don't Dream It's Over; Something So Strong; Better Be Home Soon; Chocolate Cake; Fall At Your Feet; Four Seasons In One Day; Distant Sun; Nails In My Feet; Solo Singles: Sinner, 1998; She Will Have Her Way, 1998; Last One Standing, 1999; Can You Hear Us, 1999. Honours: Q Awards: Best Live Act (with Crowded House), 1992; Best Songwriter, 1993; OBE, for services to New Zealand, 1993. Current Management: Grant Thomas Management, 3 Mitchell Road, Rose Bay, NSW 2029, Australia.

FINNEY Albert, b. 9 May 1936. Actor. m. (1) Jane Wenham, divorced, 1 son; (2) Anouk Aimée, 1970, divorced, 1978. Education: Royal Academy of Dramatic Art. Appointments: Birmingham Repertory Company, 1956-58; Shakespeare Memorial Theatre Company, 1959; National Theatre, 1965, 1975; Formed Memorial Enterprises, 1966; Associate

Artistic Director, English Stage Company, 1972-75; Director, United British Artists, 1983-86; Plays include: Julius Caesar; Macbeth; Henry V; The Beaux Strategem; The Alchemist; The Lizard on the Rock; The Party, 1958; King Lear; Othello, 1959; A Midsummer Night's Dream; The Lily-White Boys, Billy Liar, 1960; Luther, 1961, 1963; Much Ado About About Nothing; Armstrong's Last Goodnight, Miss Julie, Black Comedy, Love for Love, 1965; A Flea in Her Ear, 1966; A Day in the Death of Joe Egg, 1968; Alpha Beta, 1972; Krapp's Last Tape, Cromwell, 1973; Chez Nous, 1974; Loot (Director), 1975; Hamlet, Tamburlaine the Great, 1976; Uncle Vanya, Present Laughter, 1977; The Country Wife, 1977-78; The Cherry Orchard, Macbeth, 1978; Has 'Washington' Legs?; The Biko Inquest (director), Sergeant Musgrave's Dance (director), 1984; Orphans, 1986; J J Farr, 1987; Another Time, 1989; Reflected Glory, 1992; Art, 1996; Films include: The Entertainer; Saturday Night and Sunday Morning, 1960; Tom Jones, Night Must Fall, 1963; Two For the Road, 1967; Scrooge, 1970; Gumshoe, 1971; Murder on the Orient Express, 1974; Wolfen, 1979; Looker, 1980; Shoot the Moon, 1981; Annie, 1982; Life of John Paul II, The Dresser, Under the Volcano, 1983; Miller's Crossing, The Image, 1989; The Run of the Country, 1995; Washington Square, Breakfast of Champions, Simpatico, Delivering Milo, 1999; Erin Brokovich, Traffic, 2000; Hemingway, The Hunter of Death, 2001; Big Fish, 2003; Corpse bride (voice), 2005; A Good Year, Amazing Grace, 2006; The Bourne Ultimatum, Before the Devil Knows You're Dead, 2007; TV appearances include: My Uncle Silas, 2001, 2003; The Gathering Storm, 2002. Honours: Hon DLitt (Sussex), 1966; Lawrence Olivier Award, 1986; London Standard Drama Award for Best Actor, 1986; Dilys Powell Award, London Film Critics Circle, 1999; BAFTA Fellowship, 2001; Emmy Award, 2002; BAFTA Award for Best Actor, 2003; Golden Globe, 2003. Address: c/o Michael Simkins, 45/51 Whitfield Street, London W1T 4HB, England.

FIORENTINO Linda, b. 9 March 1958, Philadelphia, Pennsylvania, USA. Actress. m. John Byrum, 1992, divorced, 1993. Education: Rosemont College; Circle in the Square Theatre School. Career: Member, Circle in the Square Performing Workshops; Films: Vision Quest, Gotcha, After Hours, 1985; The Moderns, 1988; Queens Logic, Shout, 1991; Wildfire, 1992; Chain of Desire, 1993; The Desperate Trail, The Last Seduction, 1994; Bodily Harm, Jade, 1995; Unforgettable, The Split, Men in Black, Kicked in the Head, 1997; Dogma, 1998; Ordinary Decent Criminal, Where the Money Is, 1999; What Planet Are You From? 2000; Liberty Stands Still, 2002; Films for TV include: The Neon Empire, 1989; The Last Game, 1992; Acting on Impulse, 1993; Beyond the Law, 1994; The Desperate Trail. Address: c/o United Talent Agency, 9560 Wilshire Boulevard, Floor 5, Beverly Hills, CA 90212, USA.

FIORINI Paul J, b. 7 July 1941, Jersey City, New Jersey, USA. Business Owner and President. Education: Bergen Community College, Paramus, New Jersey. Appointments: Owner, beauty salon; Movie extra, For Love of the Game, 1998; Driving School Instructor; Armed Escort/Limo Service for Corporate Clients and Celebrities; Fully Licensed and Bonded Detective Agency; Inventor, Sleeper Seat for Cars; Gun Appraiser; Notary Public; Licensed Hypnotist. Memberships: National Society of Inventors; National Council of Investigative and Security Services; World Association of Detectives; Society for Professional Investigators; Police Marksman Association; Private Detectives Association of New Jersey; International Narcotic Officers Association; International Cartridge Collectors Association; New England

Appraisers Association; National Rifle Association; National Association of Investigators and Special Police. Honours: Delegate, 3rd International Symposium on Middle Eastern Perspectives in Criminal Justice, 1993. Address: 142 Oakwood Avenue, Bogota, NJ 07603, USA.

FIRTH Colin, b. 10 September 1960. Actor. m. Livia Giuggioli, 1997, 3 children, 1 child from previous relationship. Education: Drama Center, London. Career: Theatre includes: Another Country, 1983; Doctor's Dilemma, 1984; The Lonely Road, 1985; Desire Under the Elms, 1987; The Caretaker, 1991; Chatsky, 1993; Three Days of Rain, 1999; TV appearances; Dutch Girls, 1984; Lost Empires (series), 1985-86; Robert Lawrence in Tumbledown, 1987; Out of the Blue, 1990; Hostages, 1992; Master of the Moor, 1993; The Deep Blue Sea, Pride and Prejudice (Mr Darcy), 1994; Nostromo, 1997; The Turn of the Screw, Donovan Quick, 1999; Radio: Richard II in Two Planks and a Passion, 1986; The One Before the Last (Rupert Brooke), 1987; Films: Another Country, 1983; Camille, 1984; A Month in the Country, 1986; Femme Fatale, 1990; The Hour of the Pig, 1992; Good Girls, 1994; Circle of Friends, 1995; The English Patient, Fever Pitch, 1996; Shakespeare in Love, 1998; The Secret Laughter of Women, My Life So Far, Relative Values, 1999; Londinium, Bridget Jones's Diary, 2000; The Importance of Being Earnest, 2002; Hope Springs, Girl With a Pearl Earring, Love Actually, 2003; Trauma, 2004; Where The Truth Lies, Nanny McPhee, 2005; The Last Legion, And When Did You Last See Your Father?, Then She Found Me, The Accidental Husband, St Trinian's, Genova, 2007; Mamma Mia! 2008. Honours: Radio Times Actor Award for Tumbledown, 1996; Best Actor Award, Broadcasting Press Guild for Pride and Prejudice. Address: c/o ICM Ltd, Oxford House, 76 Oxford Street, London, W1N 0AX, England.

FISCHER Ernst Otto, b. 10 November 1918, Munich, Germany. Inorganic Chemist. Education: Diploma in Chemistry, 1949, Doctorate, 1952, Munich Technical University. Appointments: Associate Professor, 1957, Professor, 1959, Professor and Director, Inorganic Chemistry, 1964, Munich Technical University; Research on Organometallic Compounds of Transition Metals. Publications: 500 scientific publications; $Fe(C_5H_5)_2$ Structure, 1952; $Cr(C_6H_6)_2$, 1955; Ubergansmetall-Carben-Komplexe, 1964; Metal-Complexes Vol I, with H Werner, 1966; Ubergansmetall-Carben-Komplexe, 1973. Honour: Gottinger Academy Prize for Chemistry, 1957; Alfred-Stock-Gedachtnis Prize, 1959; Hon Dr rer nat, Munich, 1972, Erlangen, 1977, Veszprem, 1983; Joint Winner, Nobel Prize for Chemistry, 1973; Hon DSc, Strathclyde, 1975; American Chemical Society Centennial Fellow, 1976. Memberships: Bayerische Akademie der Wissenschaften, 1964; Deutsche Akademie der Naturforscher Leopoldina, 1969; Corresponding Member, Austrian Academy of Sciences, 1976; Academy of Sciences, Gottingen, 1977; Foreign Member, Accademi Nazionale dei Lincei, 1976; Foreign Honorary Member, American Academy of Arts and Sciences, 1977. Address: Sohnckestrasse 16, 81479 Munich 71, Germany.

FISCHER-MÜNSTER Gerhard, b. 17 November 1952, Münster- Sarmsheim, Germany. Composer, Soloist, Lecturer, Conductor. m. Bettina, 1 son, 1 daughter. Education: Peter Cornelius Konservatorium Mainz, Staatliche Musikhochschule und Johannes-Gutenberg- Universität Mainz, Staatsexamen, 1974; Seminar for conducting, Bingen, Exam. Career: First Compositions in 1965. Concerts as Soloist, Piano and Clarinet; Concerts as Conductor of different orchestras and ensembles. TV records, Radio records/performances in Germany, Italy, Austria, Switzerland, France, Belgium, USA, Japan; Guest Conductor European Symphony Orchestra, Luxembourg 1993; Performances at International Festivals. Guest Lecturer at various Institutes; Founder of Symphonic Wind Orchestra of Conservatory Mainz 1991; Founder of Wind Chamber Ensemble 1981; Lecturer Peter-Cornelius Konservatorium, 1975-. Publications: Over 400 compositions (main: 5 Symphonies, Psalm 99, Schizophonie, Sonatas, Haiku-Lieder words by Sigrid Genzken-Dragendorff, Sonnet words by Shakespeare, Symphonic Lieder words by Brigitte Pulley-Grein, Piano Concertino, Daliphonie); Harmonie aus dem Einklang (historical/physical work)' Lehrplan Klarinette; Publications in Music Journals; Publications about Fischer-Münster at different Universities; Jury member at numerous music contests; Guest Lecturer, University Mainz. Honours: Award, Adv. Ministry of Culture 1984, 1989, 1992, 2000; Award, Adv. Management of International Music Festival of Switzerland, 1985; Honorary Member, IBC Advisory Council; St. Rochus Cup (Bingen) for cultural achievement; Honorary Member, ABI Research Board of Advisers and Research Fellow. Memberships: Deutscher Komponisten-Interessenverband; World Association for Symphonic Bands and Ensemble (WASBE), GEMA, Association for German Lecturers and Artists; Fördergesellschaft Peter-Cornelius-Konservatorium. Address: Auf den Zeilen 11, D-55424 Münster-Sarmsheim, Germany. E-mail: Fischer-Muenster@gmx.de Website: www.fischer-muenster.de

FISCHLER Ben-Zion, b. 24 May 1925, Vienna, Austria. Educator; Teacher; Lecturer. m. Bracha Dalmatzky, 2 sons. Appointments: Hebrew Teacher, detention camps in Cyprus, 1947-49; Teacher, Ulpanim in Pardess Chana & Motzkin, Haifa, 1949-58; Lecturer in Hebrew, Sir George Williams College (now Concordia University), Montreal, Canada, 1958-61; Lecturer in Hebrew, New School for Social Research (now New School University), New York, USA, 1961-64; Director, Hebrew Language Division, Department of Education & Culture, WZO, Jerusalem. Memberships: Founding Member, Executive Vice-President, Council on the Teaching of Hebrew (Hamoatza Lehanchalat Halashon); Founding Member, Acting Director, Committee on Hebrew Studies at Universities Abroad; Founding Member, Israel Association for Applied Linguistics; Member, Board of the (Hebrew University) Jerusalem Examination. Publications: Editor, Bulletins of The Council on the Teaching of Hebrew; Editor, From the Workshop (Studies & Research on Hebrew as a Second Language); Co-editor: Rosen Memorial Volume; Kodesh Jubilee Volume; Rabin Jubilee Volume; numerous other publications (see Bibliography in Studies in Hebrew, and Language Teaching in Honor of Ben-Zion Fischler, Israel 2001) & articles on Hebrew, Linguistics and (the) Sayings of the Sages (Talmud). Address: 5, Mendele St, Jerusalem 92147, Israel.

FISHBURNE Laurence, b. 30 July 1961, Augusta, Georgia, USA. Actor. m. (1) Hanja Moss, 1985, divorced 1 son, 1 daughter, (2) Gina Torres, 2002. Career: Stage appearances include: Short Eyes; Two Trains Running; Riff Raff (also writer and director); TV appearances include: One Life to Live (series, debut age 11); Pee-wee's Playhouse; Tribeca; A Rumour of War; I Take These Men; Father Clements Story; Decoration Day; The Tuskagee Airmen; Miss Ever's Boys; Always Outnumbered; Films include: Cornbread Earl and Me, 1975; Fast Break; Apocalypse Now; Willie and Phil; Death Wish II; Rumble Fish; The Cotton Club; The Colour Purple; Quicksilver; Band of the Hand; A Nightmare on Elm Street 3; Dream Warriors; Gardens of Stone; School Daze; Red Heat; King of New York; Cadence; Class Action; Boyz N the Hood;

Deep Cover; What's Love Got to Do With It?; Searching for Bobby Fischer; Higher Learning; Bad Company; Just Cause; Othello; Fled; Hoodlums (also exec producer); Event Horizon; Welcome to Hollywood; Once in the Life (also writer); The Matrix, 1999; Michael Jordan to the Max, Once in the Life, 2000; Osmosis Jones, 2001; The Matrix Reloaded, The Matrix Revolutions, Mystic River, 2003; Assault on Precinct 13, 2005; Akeelah and the Bee, Mission: Impossible III, Five Fingers, Bobby, 2006; The Death and Life of Bobby Z, 4: Rise of the Silver Surfer (voice), 2007; Days of Wrath, 21, 2008. Address: c/o Paradigm, 10100 Santa Monica Boulevard, 25th Floor, Los Angeles, CA 90067, USA.

FISHER Allen, b. 1 November 1944, Norbury, Surrey, England. Painter; Poet; Art Historian. Education: BA, University of London; MA, University of Essex. Appointment: Head of Contemporary Arts, Professor of Poetry and Art, Manchester Metropolitan University. Publications: Over 100 books including: Place Book One, 1974; Brixton Fractals, 1985; Unpolished Mirrors, 1985; Stepping Out, 1989; Future Exiles, 1991; Fizz, 1994; Civic Crime, 1994; Breadboard, 1994; Now's the Time, 1995; The Topological Shovel (essays), Canada, 1999; Gravity, 2004; Entanglement, 2004, Canada; Place (collected books), 2005. Contributions to: Various magazines and journals. Honour: Co-Winner, Alice Hunt Bartlett Award, 1975. Address: 14 Hopton Road, Hereford HR1 1BE, England.

FISHER Carrie, b. USA. Actress and Author. m. Paul Simon, 1983, divorced, 1984, 1 daughter with Bryan Lourd. Education: Central School of Speech & Drama, London. Career: First appearances: at a nightclub, with mother, aged 13, Broadway chorus in Irene, aged 15; Stage appearances: Censored Scenes from Hong Kong, Agnes of God, both Broadway; Films include: Star Wars; The Empire Strikes Back; Return of the Jedi; The Blues Brothers; Garbo Talks; The Man With One Red Shoe; When Harry Met Sally; Hannah and Her Sisters; The 'Burbs; Sibling Rivalry; Drop Dead Fred; Soapdish; This is My Life; Austin Powers: International Man of Mystery; Scream 3; Famous; Heartbreakers, 2001; Jay and Silent Bob Strike Back, 2001; A Midsummer Night's Rave, 2002; Charlie's Angels: Full Throttle, 2003; Wonderland, 2003; Stateside, 2004; Undiscovered, 2005; Suffering Man's Charity, 2007; Cougar Club, 2007; Fanboys, 2008; Several TV appearances. Publications: Postcards from the Edge, also screenplay, 1987; Surrender the Pink, 1990; Delusions of Grandma, 1994; Several short stories. Honours: Photoplay Best Newcomer of the Year, 1974; PEN for first novel (Postcards from the Edge, 1987). Address: Creative Artists Agency, 9830 Wilshire Boulevard, Beverly Hills, CA 90212, USA.

FISHER Charles Harold, b. 20 November 1906, Hiawatha, West Virginia, USA. Chemistry Researcher and Teacher. m. Elizabeth Snyder. Education: BS, Roanoke College, 1928; MS, 1929, PhD, 1932, University of Illinois, Urbana. Appointments: Instructor, Chemistry, Harvard University, 1932-35; Research Group Leader, US Bureau of Mines, Pittsburgh, Pennsylvania, 1935-40; Research Group Leader, USDA East Regional Research Center, Philadelphia, 1940-50; Director, USDA Southern Regional Research Center, New Orleans, Louisiana, 1950-72; Consultant, Textile Research, Republic of South Africa, 1967, Food Technology, Pan American Union, 1968; Research Associate, Roanoke College, Salem, Virginia, 1972-2006; Consultant, Paper Technology, Library of Congress, 1973-76; Established Lawrence D and Mary A Fisher Scholarship, Roanoke College, 1978. Publications: Over 200 including (co-author) book: Eminent

American Chemists, 1992; 72 patents include (co-inventor) Acrylic Rubber, 1992. Honours include: Honorary DSc, Tulane University, 1953, Roanoke College, 1963; Southern Chemists Award, 1956; Herty Medal, 1959; Chemical Pioneer Award, 1966; Polymer Science Pioneer, Polymer News, 1981; Distinguished Alumnus, Roanoke College, 1992; Hall of Fame, Salem Educational Foundation, 1996; Roanoke College established the Charles H Fisher Lectures; Roanoke College named laboratory 'Fisher Organic Chemistry Laboratory'. Memberships include: American Chemical Society, Board, 1969-71; American Institute of Chemists, President, 1962-63; Board Chairman, 1963, 1973-75; Roanoke College Alumni Association, President, 1978-79; Board Member, Salem Educational Foundation, 1990-99; Board Member, Salem Historical Society, 1991-93; American Institute of Chemical Engineers. Address: Brandon Oaks (352), 3804 Brandon Ave, SW, Roanoke, VA 24018, USA.

FISHER John William, b. 15 February 1931, Ancell, Missouri, USA. Professor Emeritus; Structural Engineer. m. Nelda Rae Adams, 3 sons, 1 daughter. Education: BScE, Washington University, St Louis, Missouri, USA, 1956; MS, 1958, PhD, 1964, Lehigh University, Bethlehem, Pennsylvania, USA. Appointments: US Army, 1951-53; Assistant Bridge Research Engineer, National Academy of Sciences, AASHO Road Test, Ottawa, Illinois, 1958-61; Research Instructor, 1961-64; Assistant and Associate Professor of Civil Engineering, 1966-69; Professor of Civil and Environmental Engineering, 1969-2002; Associate Director, Fritz Engineering Laboratory, 1971-85; Director, ATLSS, 1986-99; Joseph T Stuart Chair in Civil Engineering, 1988-2002; Co-Director, ATLSS Engineering Research Center (Center for Advanced Technology for Large Structural Systems), 1999-2001; Professor Emeritus, 2002. Publications: Co-author: 275 articles in professional journals; 4 books. Honours include: The John Fritz Medal awarded by the five engineering societies of the United Engineering Foundation, 2000; Roy W Crum Distinguished Service in 2000 Award by the Transportation Research Board, 2001; Achievement Educator Award, American Institute of Steel Construction, 2001; Laureate of the International Award of Merit in Structural Engineering, International Association for Bridge and Structural Engineering, 2001; Chairman's Lecture Award American Association of State Highway Officials Subcommittee on Bridges and Structures, 2004; Geerhard Haaijer Award for Excellence in Education, American Institute of Steel Construction, 2006; Outstanding Projects and Leaders (OPAL) Lifetime Achievement Award in Education, American Society of Civil Engineers, 2007; Listed in national and international biographical dictionaries. Memberships: National Academy of Engineers; Corresponding Member, Swiss Academy of Engineering Sciences; Transportation Research Board Executive Committee, 1997-2000; Committee A2CO2 Steel Bridge Committee; Specification Committee, American Institute of Steel Construction; Honorary Member of American Society of Civil Engineers; Specifications Committee, American Railroad Engineering and Maintenance-of-Way Association; American Welding Society; American Society for Engineering Education. Address: ATLSS Center, Lehigh University, 117 ATLSS Drive, Bethlehem, PA 18015, USA. E-mail: jwf2@lehigh.edu

FISHER Lynn Helen, b. 2 June 1943, Red Wing, Minnesota, USA. Writer; Poet; Editor; Inventor. Education: College Studies; Doctor of Genius Degree, 1986. Appointments: Editor, Genius Newsletter, 1990-98, A Welcome Neighbor Newsletter, 1995-2000, Genius Newsletter Renewed, 2003-. Publications: The 1, 2, 4 Theory: A Synthesis, Sexual

Equations of Electricity, Magnetism and Gravitation, Human Sexual Evolution, 1971; Middle Concept Theory, A Revised Meaning of Paradox, 1972; Unitary Theory, 1973; An Introduction to Circular or Fischerian Geometry, Two Four Eight Theory, 1976; Fischer's Brief Dictionary of Sound Meanings, 1977; Introducing the Magnetic Sleeve: A Novel Sexual Organ, 1983; The Expansion of Duality, 1984; The Inger Poems, 1985; Circular Geometry, The Four Inventions, The Expansion of Dualism: A 2 4 8 System, The Early Poems of Musical Lynn, 1990; The Musical Lynn Song Lyrics, 1991; The Musical Lynn Essays, Caveman Talk, The Three in One Ring (and) The Magnetic Woman, 1992; Music that Sings, Apple Skies, 1993; Math of Poetry, 1994; A Triversal Woman, 1997; Feature: Theory Construction of 8.4.2 Unified Theory on Website; A Visit to a Friend, 2006. Membership: The Loft Literary Center. Address: 2728 East Franklin Avenue, Apt 1907, Minneapolis, MN 55406-1164, USA. E-mail: lynnatmn42@juno.com Website: mnartists.org/ Lynn_H_Fisher

FITCH Val Lodgson, b. 10 March 1923, Nebraska, USA. Physicist. m. (1) Elise Cunningham, 1949, died 1972, 2 sons, 1 deceased, (2) Daisy Harper Sharp, 1976. Education: BEng, McGill University, 1948; PhD, Physics, Columbia University, 1954. Appointments: US Army, 1943-46; Instructor, Columbia University, 1953-54; Instructor, 1954-60, Professor of Physics, 1960-, Chair, Department of Physics, 1976, Cyrus Fogg Bracket Professor of Physics, 1976-84, Princeton University; James S McDonald Distinguished University Professor of Physics, 1984-. Honour: Research Corporation Award, 1968; Ernest Orlando Laurence Award, 1968; John Witherill Medal, Franklin Institute, 1976; Joint Winner, Nobel Prize for Physics, 1980. Membership: Sloan Fellow, 1960-64; Member, NAS, American Academy of Arts and Sciences, President's Science Advisory Committee, 1970-73; American Philosophical Society. Address: PO Box 708, Princeton University, Department of Physics, Princeton, NJ 08544, USA.

FITZGERALD Elizabeth Alyssam, b. 1 August 1922, Akyab, Burma (English citizen). Architect. m. (1) William Denny, deceased, (2) Desmond FitzGerald, deceased, 1 son, deceased. Education: St Mary & St Anne's, Abbots Bromley, Staffordshire; Cheltenham Ladies College, Gloucestershire; Served in Armed Forces, 1939-45; MA, Cambridge University; Architectural Association, Beford Square, London. Appointments: Architect, own practice, Kenya; Retired due to ill health, 1982; Lecturer, G A University; Founder, now President, Family Crisis Anonymous, Perth, Australia, 1980-. Publications: (as Buff Denny): Orphan of the British Raj; How Did Religion Start?. Honours: Mention in Despatches; OBE; Associate, Royal Institute of British Architects; Architectural Association, London; Active Member, Australian Red Cross. Address: Unit 427, 118 Monash Avenue, Nedlands, Perth, WA 6009, Australia.

FITZGERALD Tara, b. 18 September 1967, Cuckfield, Sussex. Actress. m. John Sharian, 2001 (separated). Career: Stage debut in Our Song, London; Ophelia in Hamlet, London, 1995; Antigone, 1999; TV appearances include: The Black Candle; The Camomile Lawn; Anglo-Saxon Attitudes; Six Characters in Search of An Author; Fall From Grace; The Tenant of Wildfell Hall; The Student Prince; Women in White; Frenchman's Creek; In the Name of Love; Like Father Like Son; The Virgin Queen; Jane Eyre; Waking the Dead; Theatre includes: Our Song (London); Hamlet (New York); Films: Sirens, 1994; The Englishman Who Went up a Hill but Came Down a Mountain, 1995; Brassed Off, 1996;

Childhood, 1997; Conquest, 1998; New World Disorder, 1998; The Cherry Orchard, 1999; Rancid Aluminium, 1999; Dark Blue World, 2000; I Capture the Castle, 2003; Secret Passage, 2004; Five Children and It, 2004; In A Dark Place, 2006. Address: c/o Caroline Dawson Associates, 19 Sydney Mews, London, SW3 6HL, England.

FITZPATRICK Nicholas David, b. 23 January 1947, Leicester, England. Consulting Actuary. m. Jill Brotherton, 1 son, 1 daughter. Education: Industrial Economics, Nottingham University. Appointments: Investment Analyst, Friends Provident, 1969-72; Portfolio Manager, Abbey Life, 1972-76; Equity Manager and Director of Investments, British Rail Pension Fund, 1976-86; Partner, 1986-92, Head of Investment Consulting, 1992-2001, Bacon & Woodrow; Head of Global Investment Consulting, Hewitt, 2001-05; Associate, BESTrustees plc. Memberships: UKSIP; FIA; FRSA. Address: Sommarlek, Woodhurst Park, Oxted, Surrey, RH8 9HA, England. E-mail: ndfitz@gmail.com

FJERDINGSTAD Erik, b. 4 October 1940. Physical Chemist. Education: Student, 1959, Filosoficum, 1960, BSc, 1962, Magister Scientiarum, 1966, BEd, 1967, Diploma of Public Health, 1972. Appointments: Instructor, University of Copenhagen, 1962-66; Adjunct Virum Gymnasium, 1966-72; Assistant Professor, University of Copenhagen, 1972-76; Associate Professor, 1976-80; Now retired. Publications: Articles in international journals about the environment, heavy metals; Compendia for university students in biology and hygiene, seminar reports. Honours: Scholarship to Nordic School of Public Health, Affiliation Gothenburg University. Memberships: AAS; NYAS; LFIBA; Dan-Soc Mater Res; Danish Magister Organizations. Address: Bredebovej 23 mf, DK-2800 Kgs Lyngby, Denmark.

FLEGEL Kenneth M, Professor of Medicine. Education: BSc, 1968, MDCM, 1972, McGill University, Canada; MSc, London University, England, 1986. Appointments: Rural Medical Officer-in-Charge, Cottage Hospital, Nigeria, 1974-76; Consultant Internist, Private Practice, Montreal, Canada, 1979-82; Associate Director, Division of Internal Medicine, 1979-81, Consultant Internist, 1979-97, Founder and Director, Residents' Group Practice, 1981-82, Director, Division of Ambulatory Services, Department of Medicine, 1982-87, Senior Physician, 1982-97, Founder and Director, Division of General Internal Medicine, 1984-93, Royal Victoria Hospital, Montreal; Chief of Service, 6 Medial CTU, 1997; Associate Professor of Medicine, 1983-98, Associate Member, Department of Epidemiology & Biostatistics, 1986-97, Director, Inter-Division Affairs, General Internal Medicine, 1987-93, Tenure granted, 1997, Full Professor of Medicine, 1999-, McGill University. Publications: Over 80 papers and articles in professional medical journals. Honours: University Scholar, 1966-67, McConnell Scholar, 1967-68, University Scholar, 1969-72, McGill University; Osler Gold Medal Essayist, American Association for the History of Medicine, 1972; Allan Aitken Memorial Trust Fellowship, 1978; Travers-Allan Travelling Fellowship, 1984; W H Philip Hill Award, 1994. Memberships: Fellow, American College of Physicians; Fellow, Royal College of Physicians of Canada. Address: Division of General Internal Medicine, Royal Victoria Hospital, Rm A4.21, 687 Pine Avenue West, Montreal, Quebec H3A 1A1, Canada. E-mail: ken.flegel@muhc.mcgill.ca

FLEISCHMANN Ernest (Martin), b. 7 December 1924, Frankfurt, Germany. Music Administrator. Divorced, 1 son, 2 daughters. Education: Bachelor of Commerce,

Chartered Accountant, University of the Witwatersrand, South Africa, 1950; Bachelor of Music, University of Cape Town, 1954; Postgraduate work, South African College of Music, 1954-56. Debut: Conductor with Johannesburg Symphony Orchestra, 1942. Career: Conductor of various symphony orchestras and operas, 1942-55; Music Organiser, Van Riebeeck Festival, Cape Town, 1952; Director of Music and Drama, Johannesburg Festival, 1956; General Manager, London Symphony Orchestra, 1959-67; Director for Europe, CBS Records, 1967-69; Managing Director, Los Angeles Philharmonic and General Director, Hollywood Bowl, 1969-98; Artistic Director, Ojai Festival, 1998-2003; President, Fleischmann Arts, International Arts Management and Consulting Services, (consultant to orchestras, festivals and government bodies in USA and Europe), 1998-. Publications: Commencement address, The Orchestra is Dead, Long Live the Community of Musicians, Cleveland Institute of Music, 1987; The Recession, Cultural Change, and a Glut of Orchestras, paper for Economics of The Arts, Salzburg Seminar, 1993; The Community of Musicians, Musicians for the Community (Royal Philharmonic Society, London), 2000. Honours include: Doctor of Music (honoris causa), Cleveland Institute of Music, 1987; Grand Cross of the Order of Merit, Germany, 1996; First Living Cultural Treasure of the City of Los Angeles, 1998; Officer, Ordre des Arts et Lettres, France, 1998; Knight First Class, Order of the White Rose, Finland, 1999; Gold Baton Award, American Symphony Orchestra League, 1999; Life Achievement Award, American Youth Symphony, 2006. Memberships: Board of Councillors, USC Thornton School of Music; Board of Directors, Los Angeles Philharmonic Association. Address: 2225 Maravilla Drive, Los Angeles, CA 90068, USA.

FLESSEL Klaus, b. 5 December 1940, Recklinghausen, Germany. University Professor. m. Michiko Flessel-Takayanagi, 2 daughters. Education: PhD, Sinology, 1971, Habilitation, Sinology, 1983, Tübingen University, Germany. Appointments: Assistant Professor, 1971, Lecturer, 1979-84, Tübingen University; Professor, Erlangen-Nürnberg University, 1984-. Publications: Der Huang-Ho und die Historische Hydrotechnik in China (author); Lexikon Alte Kulturen, 3 volumes (author/editor), 1990-93; Frühe Hochkulturen in Fernost – Brockhaus Weltgeschichte Volume 1, 3, (author) 1997-98. Address: Ringstr 5, 91475 Lonnerstadt, Germany. E-mail: kflessel@phil.uni-erlangen.de

FLETCHER Philip, b. 2 May 1946. Director General of OFWAT. m. Margaret Anne Boys, 2 daughters, 1 deceased. Education: MA, Trinity College, Oxford. Appointments: Joined Civil Service, 1968, Director, Central Finance, 1986-89, Director (grade 3), Planning & Development Control, 1990-93, Chief Executive, PSA Services and Property Holdings, 1993-94, Deputy Secretary (grade 2), Cities and Countryside, 1994-95, Department of Environment; Receiver, Metropolitan Police District, 1996-2000; Director General, Water Services, 2000-. Address: OFWAT, Centre City Tower, 7 Hill Street, Birmingham B5 4UA, England. E-mail: philip.fletcher@ofwat.gsi.gov.uk

FLETCHER Robin, b. 11 February 1966. Education: NCTJ National Certificate in Journalism, South Glamorgan Institute, Cardiff, 1987; MBA, University of Glamorgan, 1999; MPhil (Journalism), Cardiff University, 2002. Appointments: Trainee Reporter, 1984-87, Senior Reporter, 1987-89, Birmingham Evening Mail/Birmingham Post; Deputy Editor/Acting Editor, Bromsgrove Weekly Mail Series, 1989; News Editor, Focus Newspapers, Birmingham, 1989-90; Senior Editor, Midland Weekly Media & Editor, Solihull News, 1990-92;

Editor/Director, Northampton Chronicle & Echo, 1992-94; Editor/Director, Evening Gazette, Blackpool, 1994-95; Editor, Wales on Sunday, Western Mail and Echo, Cardiff, 1996-97; Editor, South Wales Echo, Western Mail and Echo, Cardiff, 1997-2001; Change Development Manager, 2001-02, Communications Director, 2002-03, Trinity Mirror Regionals, London; Founding Director, Reflex Business Services Ltd, Stonehouse, Gloucestershire, 2003-; Non-Executive Director, Williams Ross Ltd, Cardiff, 2006-; Director, Five Valleys Business Network Ltd, 2007-. Honours: Highly Commended, Regional Editor of Year Awards, 1994; Honorary Fellow, Royal Society of Arts, 1999; Honorary Fellow, University of Wales Institute, Cardiff, 2002; Joint Winner, Best Consultancy, Communicators in Business South West Awards, 2004. Memberships: Member, Communicators in Business; Institute of Directors. Address: Reflex Business Services Ltd, Solstar House, 11 Blackwell Close, Stonehouse, Gloucestershire GL10 2HF, England. E-mail: robinfletcher@reflexservices.com Website: www.reflexservices.com

FLINT Willis (Wolfschmidt), b. 27 December 1936, Kenton, Ohio, USA. Artist; Musician. Education: Diploma in Commercial Art, Art Career School, New York City, 1957-60; Fine Art Studies, Instituto Allende, San Miguel de Allende, Gto Mexico, 1961; Mural studies under assistant to Jose Clemente Orosco, Mexico, 1962. Appointments: Kossak Advertising, Arizona, 1961; Mithoff Advertising, Texas, 1962-63; Technical Illustrator, Volt Technical Corporation, New York City, 1967; General Illustrator, Salesvertising Advertising, Colorado, 1967; General Boardman, Consultant, Burr-Brown Research Corporation, Arizona, 1969-71; Muralist, private practice, San Diego, Tucson, New York City, 1976-80; Originator, Fantasy-expressionism/painting concept, 1981; Musician, The Wild Ones, Tucson, 1982-83; Musician, Comic, Paul Baron's Harmonica Rascals, 1965-85; Art Instructor, Private Practice, Tucson, 1981-85; Consulting Muralist, Yaqui Indian Center, Tucson, 1989; Freelancer of Commercial & Fine Art; Easel Painter, Tucson, 1985-; Sculptor, Tucson, 1996-2003; Musician, Comic, Desert Rats, 1999; Harmonicist, Stand-Up Comic, Northwest Senior Ct, 2003-. Publications: Author, The Treatise of Psyche-objectivism, 1972; Poetry published in several books, 1994-2002; The Fantasy Expressionism of Wolfschmidt; Articles in several small town newspapers. Honours: Letters of Commendation, Department of the Navy, San Diego, California, 1979; University of Arizona, Family Practice, Tucson, 1978; Certificate of Appreciation, Vietnam, 1971; Eighth Army, Korea, 1970; United States Department of Defense, Vietnam, 1969; Two Silver Cup Awards, Army, Vietnam; Plaque of Appreciation, Army and Navy (2), Philippines, 1971; Scholarship, Award of Merit, Latham Foundation, 1967; Listed in national and international biographical directories; Several awards for poetry, 1994-2002. Memberships: International Platform Association, 1994-95; Arizona Association of Former Foster Children, 1989; Maverick Artists, Tucson, 1967-2003; Society for the Preservation of the Harmonica, Michigan, 1967. Address: 707 W Calle Progreso, Tucson, AZ 85705, USA.

FLINTOFF Freddie (Andrew), b. 6 December 1977, Preston, England. Cricketer. m. Rachael Wools, 2005, 2 sons, 1 daughter. Career: Played in Lancashire Leagues for Preston; Played for Lancashire County Cricket Club; International debut, played for England against South Africa, 1998; Played for England, Ashes, 2005. Honours: Man of Series, 2005 England Ashes.

FLÖCKINGER Gerda, b. 8 December 1927, Innsbruck, Austria (naturalised British citizen, 1946). Designer Maker Jewellery; Photographer; Lecturer. Education: Painting, St Martin's School of Art, 1945-50; Etching, Jewellery Techniques and Enamelling, Central School of Arts and Crafts, 1950-56. Appointments: Creator and Teacher, Modern Jewellery Course, Hornsey College of Art, 1962-68; Invited to be first living woman to have a solo show at the V&A, 1971; Seven solo shows and numerous group shows throughout the UK and internationally. Honours: CBE, 1991; Freeman of the Goldsmiths' Company, 1998; Honorary Fellow, University of the Arts, 2006; Entries in many biographical dictionaries and in numerous books and magazines. Address: c/o Catherine Williams, The Crafts Council, 44a Pentonville Road, London N1 1BY, England. Goldsmiths' Company Website: www.whoswhoingoldandsilver.com

FLOOD Thomas, b. 21 May 1947, Dublin, Ireland (British Citizen). Chief Executive. Education: BA, English, Metaphysics and Politics, 1967-69, University College, Dublin. Appointments: Market Research Team, A E Herbert Ltd (Machine Tools), Coventry, 1969-70; Secondment to Research Team, W S Atkins Consulting Engineers, Epsom, Surrey, 1970-72; Market Research Department, 1972-73, Marketing Manager, Industrial Product Division, 1973-75, Marketing Manager, Packaging Systems Group, 1975-77, Sales Manager, Strapping Systems Unit, 1977-79, Sales and Marketing Director, Decorative Materials Unit, 1979-82, Group Marketing Manager, Packaging Systems Division, 1982-86, 3M United Kingdom PLC, Bracknell, Berkshire; Marketing Director, Wallingford, 1986-90, Deputy Chief Executive, Wallingford, 1990-92, Charity Chief Executive, Wallingford, 1992-2001, Group Chief Executive, London, 2001-, BTCV (British Trust for Conservation Volunteers). Honours: Fellow, Royal Society of Arts, 1995; Fellow, British Institute of Management, 1995; Commander of the British Empire (CBE), 2004. Memberships: Chair of Trustees, 1994-99, Red Admiral Aids Charity; Board Member, 1996-98, Tree Council; Board Member, 1997-99, Age Resource; Trustee, BTCV Pension Scheme, 1997-; Member, UK Biodiversity Steering Group, 1998-; Member, 1999-2001, New Deal Task Force; Member, Home Office Volunteering Group, 2000-01; Co-opted to Board, ACEVO, 2002; ODPM, Cleaner, Safer, Greener Communities Board, 2005-; Treasury revisory group on role of Third Sector in delivering public services. Address: c/o BTCV, 80 York Way, London N1 9AG, England.

FLOROS Constantin, b. 4 January 1930, Salonica, Greece. Professor of Musicology. Education: Composition and Conducting, Vienna Music Academy, 1953; Doctorate, Musicology, Art History, Philosophy and Psychology, Vienna University, 1955. Appointments: Habilitation, Musicology, Hamburg University, 1961; Supernumerary Professor, 1967, Professor of Musicology, 1972, Professor Emeritus, 1995, University of Hamburg. Publications: 25 books; Numerous papers; Monographs on Mozart, Beethoven, Joh Brahms, Bruckner, Mahler (4 volumes), Alban Berg, G Ligeti and Tchaikovsky; Translated oldest Byzantine and Slavic notations and developed new method of semantic analysis. Honours: President, Gustav Mahler Vereinigung, Hamburg, 1988; Honorary Doctorate, University of Athens, 1999; Member, European Academy of Sciences and Arts, 2002; Honorary Doctorate, University of Salonica, 2004; Golden Honorary Diploma, University of Vienna, 2005. Address: Schlangenkoppel 18, 22117 Hamburg, Germany.

FLOUD Sir Roderick Castle, b. 1 April 1942, Barnes, England. University Professor. m. Cynthia Anne, 2 daughters. Education: BA, 1961, MA, D Phil, 1970, Oxford University. Appointments: Lecturer, Economic History, University College London, 1966-69; Lecturer in Economic History and Fellow of Emmanuel College, Cambridge, 1969-75; Professor of Modern History, Birkbeck College, London, 1975-88; Visiting Professor of History and Economics, Stanford University, California, 1980-81; Provost of City of London Polytechnic (later London Guildhall University), 1988-2002; Vice-Chancellor, 2002-2004, President, 2004-06, President Emeritus, 2006-, London Metropolitan University; Acting Dean, School of Advanced Study, University of London, 2007-. Publications include: An Introduction to Quantitative Methods for Historians, 1973-80; The British Machine Tool Industry 1850-1914, 1976; Height, Health and History (with K Wachter and A Gregory), 1990; The Cambridge Economic History of Modern Britain (editor with P Johnson), 2004. Honours: Honorary DLitt, City University; Honorary Fellow, Birkbeck College, Wadham College, Emmanuel College; Fellow British Academy; Fellow of City and Guilds of London Institute; Knight Bachelor, 2005; Honorary DLitt, University of Westminster. Memberships: Athenaeum; Board, European University Association (Vice-President, 2005-09); Board of Trustees, The Samaritans, 2006-07; Chair, Standing Committee for Social Sciences, European Science Foundation, 2007-. Address: London Metropolitan University 31 Jewry St, London EC3N 2EY, England. E-mail: r.floud@londonmet.ac.uk

FLOURNOY Dayl Jean II, b. 17 December 1944, San Antonio, Texas, USA. Clinical Microbiologist. m. 2 sons, 1 daughter. Education: BS, Southwest Texas State University, San Marcos, Texas, 1965; AS, San Antonio College, Texas, 1966; MT, ASCP, Santa Rosa Medical Center, Texas, 1966; MA, Incarnate Word College, San Antonio, Texas, 1968; PhD, University of Houston, Texas, 1973; Postdoctoral, St Luke's Episcopal Hospital, Houston Texas, 1975; Fellow, Oklahoma Geriatric Education Center, Oklahoma City, 1991. Appointments: Director of Clinical Microbiology/Serology, Veterans Affairs Medical Center, Oklahoma City, 1975-; Professor of Pathology, OUHSC, 1987-. Publications: Over 200 articles in peer reviewed journals. Honours: Fellowships, awards include: Charlotte S Leebron Memorial Trust Award, Oklahoma State Medical Association, 1993; Advanced Toastmaster Silver Certification, Toastmasters International, 2000; Fellow, American Academy of Microbiology, 1986-; Fellow, Society for Hospital Epidemiology of America, 2004. Listed in national and international biographical dictionaries. Memberships include: American Society of Microbiology; Society for Hospital Epidemiology of America; Southwestern Association of Clinical Microbiology; Editorial Board, American Journal of Infection Control, 2000-2003. Address: Dir Micro, VAMC (113) 921 13th Street, Oklahoma City, OK 73104, USA.

FLOWER David John Colin, b. 7 June 1956, London, England. Occupational Physician. m. Harriett Ann Sinclair, 1 son, 1 daughter. Education: BSc (Eng), Chemical Engineering, 1977; MB BS, 1982; MD, 1996; Diploma, Royal College of Obstetricians & Gynaecologists, 1986; Member, Royal College of General Practitioners, 1987; Associate, 1993, Member, 1996, Fellow, 2002, Faculty of Occupational Medicine RCP; Diploma in Aviation Medicine, 1999; Fellow, American College of Occupational and Environmental Medicine, 2007. Appointments: House Surgeon, Professorial Surgical Unit, University College Hospital, London; Principal in General Practice, Wantage, Oxfordshire; Occupational Physician, UK

Atomic Energy Authority; Consultant and Senior Consultant, Occupational Physician, British Airways plc; Chief Health Officer, Centrica plc; Director Health, Refining and Marketing, BP plc; Part-time Consultant, Adviser, UK Sport. Publications: Scientific and popular articles on alertness, performance and the management of jet lag; Contributing author, British Olympic Association Athlete Publications, Sydney 2000, Athens 2004; Battelle, US Department of Transportation, Handbook on Fatigue in Transportation; Kushida Editor, Sleep Deprivation: Clinical Issues, Pharmacology and Sleep Loss Effects. Memberships: Past President, Section of Occupational Medicine; Royal Society of Medicine; Member, Society of Occupational Medicine. Address: Nethercote Barn, Cote, Bampton, Oxfordshire OX18 2EG, England.

FLOWER Roderick John, b. 29 November 1945, Southampton, England. Pharmacologist. m. Lindsay Joyce Riddell. Education: BSc, University of Sheffield, 1971; PhD, University of London, 1974; DSc, 1985. Appointments: Senior Scientist, Wellcome Foundation, 1973-84; Professor of Pharmacology, University of Bath, 1984-89; Lilly Professor, Biochemical Pharmacology, St Bart's Hospital Medical School, London, 1989-94; Wellcome Trust Principal Fellow, Professor of Pharmacology, 1994-; Head of William Harvey Research Institute, 1998-2002; Consultant in field; Co-editor, Glucocorticoids, 2000. Publications: More than 200 peer reviewed papers; More than 200 other publications including reviews, books, book chapters, abstracts, conference proceedings, editorials and published correspondence. Honours: Sandoz Prize,1978, Gaddum Medal, 1986, William Withering Prize, 2003, British Pharmacological Society; Fellow Academy of Medical Sciences; Fellow, Royal Society. Memberships: British Pharmacological Society; Academia Europea, 2002

FLOYD Edward Jeffrey (Ted), b. 18 August 1946, Sydney, Australia. Soil Science. Education: BSc Agr, Sydney University, 1968. Appointments: Investigation Officer, Soil Conservation Service, Wagga Wagga, 1969-73; Analytical Chemist, NSW Department of Mines, 1974-80; Analytical Chemist, Sydney University, 1981-83; Analytical Chemist, University of New South Wales, 1984-91; Convenor, Friends of the Earth, Sydney, 1992-98. Publications: Forestry, Agriculture, Soils and the Greenhouse Problem, 1990; Soil Water Infiltration, 1996; Transpiration Benefits for Urban Catchment Management, 2001; Suburban Water Harvesting, 2005; Soils, Catchments and Creeks, 2007; Creekcare, 2008. Honours: International Scientist of the Year, 2007. Memberships: Australian Soil Science Society; Stormwater Industry Association. Address: PO Box 83, Balmain, NSW 2041, Australia. E-mail: floydej@gmail.com Website: www.ramin.com.au/creekcare

FO Dario, b. 24 March 1926, Leggiuno-Sangiamo, Italy. Dramatist; Actor. m. Franca Rame, 1954, 1 child. Education: Academy of Fine Arts, Milan. Appointments: Dramatist and Actor in agitprog theatre and television; Co-Founder (with Franca Rame), Dramatist, Actor, Nuova Scena acting groupe, 1968, Collettivo Teatrale la Comune, 1970. Publications: Numerous plays, including: Le commedie, I-IX, 1966-91, 1992; Morte accidentale di un anarchico (Accidental Death of an Anarchist), 1974; Non si paga, non si paga! (We Can't Pay? We Won't Pay!), 1974; Tutta casa, letto e chiesa (Adult Orgasm Escapes From the Zoo), 1978; Female Parts (with Franca Rame), 1981; Manuale et minimo dell attore, 1987; Mistero Buffo, 1977; Coming Home; History of Masks; Archangels Don't Play Pinball; Hooters, Trumpets and Raspberries; The Tricks of the Trade, 1991; Il papa e la stega (The Pope and the

Witch), 1989; L'Eroina-Grassa e'Bello, 1991; Johan Padan a la Descoverta de le Americhe, 1991; Dario Fo Recita Ruzzante, 1993; Il diavolo con le zinne, 1997; Pareja abierta Una, 2002; Matka Reimsiin, 2003. Honour: Hon DLitt, Westminster, 1997; Nobel Prize for Literature, 1997.

FODOR László, b. 25 November 1961, Budapest, Hungary. Geologist. m. Judit Fodor, 1 daughter. Education: Master of Geology, Eötvös University, Budapest, Hungary, 1987; PhD, Université P et M Curie, Paris, France, 1991. Appointments: Assistant Lecturer, Department of Applied and Environmental Geology, 1993-98, Assistant Professor, Department of Applied Geology, 1998-2000, Eötvös University; Senior Scientist, Geological Institute of Hungary, 2000-. Publications: Articles in scientific journals as co-author include: Miocene-Pliocene tectonic evolution of the Slovenian Periadriatic line and surrounding area, 1998; Tectonics 17, 690-709; Tertiary tectonic evolution of the Pannonian basin system and neighbouring origins: a new sythesis of paleostress data, Geol Soc, London, Spec Publ. 156, 1999; An outline of neotectonic structures and morphotectonics of the western and central Pannonian basin, 2005. Honours include: Széchenyi Professorial Scholarship, Ministry of Education of Hungary, 1997-2000; Bolyai Janos Scholarship for Research, Hungarian Academy of Sciences, 2001-04, 2006-. Memberships: American Geophysical Union; Geological Society of America; International Association of Sedimentologists; Hungarian Geological Society. Address: Geological Institute of Hungary; Stefania ut 14, H-1143 Budapest, Hungary. E-mail: fodor@mafi.hu

FOK Kathy Kamun, b. Hong Kong. Music Director. m. Carl Choi, 1 daughter. Education: Master's degree, Music (Choral Conducting), Moores School of Music, University of Houston, 1992. Appointment Music Director and Principal Conductor, The Hong Kong Children's Choir, 1997-. Publications: 4 CDs; 1 VCD; 2 DVDs; 8 songbooks. Honours: Ten Outstanding Young Persons HK Award, 2001; Persons with Outstanding Contributions to the Development of Arts & Culture Award, 2007. E-mail: kathy@hkcchoir.org

FOMENKO Piotr Naumovich, b. 13 July 1932. Theatre Director. m. Maya Andreyevna Tupikova, 1 son. Education: Moscow State Pedagogical Institute, Philological Faculty, 1955; The Russian Academy of Theatre Arts (GITIS), Moscow, Faculty of Directing, 1961. Appointments: Stage Director, 1972-78, Chief Stage Director, 1978-82, Akimov State Academic Comedy Theatre, Leningrad (St Petersburg), Russia; Professor, Head of the Department of Directing, Dramatic Theatre, 1982-2003, The Russian Academy of Theatre Arts (GITIS), Moscow; Founder, Artistic Director, Theatre "Masterskaya P Fomenko" (Theatre Workshop of Piotr Fomenko), Moscow, 1993-. Guest Director of various productions in Moscow, Leningrad, Georgia and many European cities; Masterclasses at theatre schools in Europe and Russia; Films include: To the Rest of the Lifetime, 1975; Almost Funny Story, 1977; About a Ride in An Old Car, 1985; Over 80 productions for theatre, television and cinematography. Honours: within Russia, include various awards worldwide. Member: The Theatre Union of the Russian Federation. Address: Pobedy Pl, 1 korp A, Apt 75, 121293, Moscow, Russia. Website: http://fomenko.theatre.ru

FONDA Bridget, b. 27 January 1964, Los Angeles, CA, USA. Actress. m. Danny Elfman, 2003. Education: NY University theatre programme; Studied acting at Lee Strasburg Institute and with Harold Guskin. Career: Workshop stage performances include Confession and Pastels; Films: Aria (Tristan and Isolde sequence), 1987; You Can't Hurry Love,

Shag, 1988; Scandal, Strapless, 1989; Frankenstein Unbound, The Godfather: Part III, 1990; Doc Hollywood, Out of the Rain, 1991; Single White Female, Singles, 1992; Bodies Rest and Motion, Point of No Return, 1993; Little Buddha, It Could Happen To You, Camilla, The Road to Welville, 1994; Rough Magic, Balto (voice), 1995; Grace of My Heart, City Hall, 1996; Drop Dead Fred; Light Years (voice); Iron Maze; Army of Darkness; Little Buddha; Touch; Jackie Brown; Finding Graceland; The Break Up; South of Heaven West of Hell; Monkey Bone; Lake Placid; Delivering Milo; Monkeybone; Kiss of the Dragon; The Whole Shebang. TV series: 21 Jump Street; Jacob Have I Loved; WonderWorks (episode), 1989; The Edge (The Professional Man); After Amy; The Chris Isaak Show; Snow Queen. TV film: Leather Jackets, 1991; In the Gloaming, 1997. Address: c/o IFA, 8730 West Sunset Boulevard, Suite 490, Los Angeles, CA 90069, USA.

FONDA Jane, b. 21 December 1937. Actress. m. (1) Roger Vadim, 1967, divorced 1973, deceased 2000, 1 daughter, (2) Tom Hayden, 1973, divorced 1989, 1 son, (3) Ted Turner, 1991, divorced. Education: Vassar College. Films include: Tall Story, 1960; A Walk on the Wild Side, 1962; Sunday in New York, 1963; La Ronde, 1964; Barbarella, 1968; They Shoot Horses Don't They? 1969; Steelyard Blues, Tout va Bien, 1972; The Blue Bird, 1975; Fun with Dick and Jane, 1976; Coming Home, California Suite, 1978; The China Syndrome, 1979; Nine to Five, 1980; On Golden Pond, 1981; Agnes of God, 1985; Stanley and Iris, 1990; Lakota Woman, Producer, 1994; Monster-in-Law, 2005; Georgia Rule, 2007; Stage Work includes: Invitation to a March; The Fun Couple; Strange Interlude; TV: The Dollmaker, 1984. Publications: Jane Fonda's Workout Book, 1982; Women Coming of Age, 1984; Jane Fonda's Workout and Weightloss Program, 1986; Jane Fonda's New Pregnancy Workout and Total Birth Program, 1989; Jane Fonda Workout Video; Jane Fonda Cooking for Healthy Living, 1996. Honours: Academy Award Best Actress, 1972, 1979; Emmy Award, The Dollmaker, 1984. Address: c/o Kim Hodgert, CAA, 9830 Wilshire Boulevard, Beverly Hills, CA 90212, USA.

FONDA Peter, b. 23 February 1940, NY, USA. Film Actor, Director and Producer. m. Susan Brewer, divorced 1974, 2 children. Education: University of Omaha. Career: Tammy and the Doctor, The Victors, 1963; Lilith, The Young Lovers, 1964; The Wild Angels, 1966; The Trip, 1967; Easy Rider (also co-screenplay writer, co-producer), 1969; The Last Movie, The Hired Hand (also director), 1971; Two People (also director), 1973; Dirty Mary, Crazy Harry, 1974; Race With the Devil, 92 in the Shade, Killer Force, 1975; Fighting Mad, Future World, 1976; Outlaw Blues, 1977; High Ballin', 1978; Wanda Nevada (also director), 1979; Open Season; Smokey and the Bandit II, 1980; Split Image, 1982; Certain Fury, 1985; Dead Fall, 1993; Nadja, Love and a 45, 1994; Painted Hero, Escape From LA, 1996; Idaho Transfer (also director); Ulee's Gold, 1997; Spasm; Fatal Mission; Reckless; Cannonball Run (cameo); Dance of the Dwarfs; Mercenary Fighters; Jungle Heat; Diajobu My Friend; Peppermint Frieden; The Rose Garden; Family Spirit; South Beach; Bodies Rest and Motion; Deadfall; Molly and Gina; South of Heaven West of Hell; The Limey; South of Heaven, West of Hell; Thomas and the Magic Railroad; Second Skin; Wooly Boys; The Laramie Project; El Cobrador: In God We Trust; Ghost Rider, Wild Hogs; Japan; 3:10 to Yuma; TV films: The Hostage Tower, 1980; Don't Look Back, 1996; A Reason to Live; A Time of Indifference; Sound; Certain Honorable Men; Montana; The Maldonado Miracle; Capital City. Address: IFA Talent Agency, 8730 West Sunset Boulevard, Suite 490, Los Angeles, CA 90069, USA.

FONF Vladimir, b. 13 August 1949, Michurinsk, Russia. Mathematician. Divorced, 1 daughter. Education: MSc, Mathematics, 1971; PhD, Mathematics, 1979; DSc, Mathematics, 1991. Appointments: Docent, Professor, Kharkov Railroad Institute, Ukraine, 1983-93; Associate Professor, Ben-Gurion University, Israel, 1993-97, Professor, Ben-Gurion University of the Negev, 1997-. Publications: More than 60 articles in mathematical journals in: Bulgaria, Canada, England, Germany, Israel, Poland, Spain, USA, USSR; Co-author, Handbook of Banach Spaces, 2001. Honour: Guastella Fellowship, 1993-96. Membership: Israel Mathematical Union. Address: Department of Mathematics, Ben-Gurion University of the Negev, PO Box 653, Beer-Sheva 84105, Israel. E-mail: fonf@math.bgu.ac.il

FONG Eileen Peksiew, b. 1 April 1964, Malaysia. Plastic Surgeon. m. Andreas Kompa. Education: MBBS, Malaya, 1989; FRCS, Edinburgh, 1993; Dipl Plastic Surgery, British Association of Plastic Surgeons, RCS, England, 1997; FAM, Singapore, Plastic Surgery, 2000. Appointments: Residency in General Surgery, UK, 1991; Residency in Plastic Surgery, UK, 1993-97; Registrar in Plastic Surgery, Singapore, 1997-2000; Consultant Plastic Surgeon, University Hospital Kuala Lumpur, Malaysia, 2000-2004; Consultant Plastic Surgeon, Gleneagles Intan Medical Centre, Kuala Lumpur, Malaysia, 2004-, Sunway Medical Centre, Selangor, Malaysia, 2004-. Publications: Articles in medical journals: Immediate Autogenous Breast Reconstruction in Stage 1 to Stage 3 Breast Cancer, 2001; Keloids – The Sebum Hypothesis Revised, 2002. Honour: Excellence in Service Award, University of Malaya, 2003. Memberships: Malaysian Association of Plastic, Aesthetic and Cranomaxillofacial Surgeons; Oriental Society of Aesthetic Plastic Surgeons; Fellow, Academy of Medicine of Singapore; Fellow of the Royal College of Surgeons of Edinburgh. Address: Suite #06-09, Sunway Hospital, 5, Jalan Lagoon Selatan, Bandar Sunway, 46150, Selangor, West Malaysia. E-mail: dreileenfong@yahoo.com

FONG Maryanne Tam-Po, Public Sector Researcher. Education: BA, USA; MBA, USA; MSc, UK; Doctoral Candidate, UK. Honours: BA (USA); MBA (USA); MSc (UK); Doctorals Candidate (UK); Researcher; American Hall of Fame Induction (USA); Deputy Director General, IBC; Honorary Director General, IBC; Honorary ABI Ambassador; IBC Hall of Fame Induction; Leading Scientists of the World Award, IBC, 2005; Deputy Governor, ABI; Great Minds of the 21st Century Award, ABI; American Medal of Honor, ABI; International Peace Prize, UCC; Lifetime Senator of the World Nations Congress, WNC; International Order of Merit; 2000 Outstanding Intellectuals of the 21st Century Award with Reference Inclusion; Woman of the Year 2006 Award, International Research Board; Personal Advisor to the Director General of IBC in the field of Business Management; Honorary Director General for the Americas, IBC; World Congress and Communications Lifetime Achievement Award; Fellow, ABI; International Order of Fellowship; Member, Order of International Ambassadors; Woman of the Year Award, 2007; Fellow, IBA; Fellow, ABI; Gold Medal for Canada, 2007; Da Vinci Diamond Award; Distinguished Service to Humankind Award, 2007; Lifetime Achievement Award, IBC; Decree of Excellence in Business; Key Award; Salute to Greatness Award; Presidential Seal of Honor, ABI; many others. Memberships include: Institute of Directors; Institute of Health Promotion and Education; Royal Society of Health; Institute of Direct Marketing; Institute of Sales & Marketing; Institute of Travel & Tourism; Professional Business & Technical Management; Chartered Management Institute; Institute of Leadership & Management; Chartered Institute of Logistics & Transport;

City & Guilds Institute; Association of Project Management; Institute of Commercial Management; Institute of Public Sector Management; Institute of Administrative Management; Institute of Professional Business & Technology Management; Institute of Management Specialists; Academy of Executives & Administrators; The Institution of Occupational Safety & Health; The Irish Institute of Training and Development; The Australian Institute of Management; Certified Professional Manager; Chartered Institute of Marketing; Certified Environmental Inspector, Member of the Environmental Assessment Association; Certified Environmental Consultant, Member of the Environmental Assessment Association; British Occupational & Hygiene Society; Adult Learning Australia; Institute of Financial Services/Institute of Bankers; The Chartered Institute of Insurers; Richmond Hill Chamber of Commerce; American Sociological Association; Ohio Arts & Crafts Guild; Chinese Music Society of North America; Competitive Scotland.com; Information Systems Audit & Control Association; European Association for Sport Management; American Society of International Law; Fellow, Royal Society of Arts, London, UK. Address: Suite 1221, 12th Floor, 32 Clarissa Drive, Richmond Hill, Ontario L4C 9R7, Canada. E-mail: mfongc575@rogers.com

FORBES Bryan, b. 22 July 1926, Stratford, London, England. Film Executive; Director; Screenwriter; Author. m. Nanette Newman, 1955, 2 daughters. Education: West Ham Secondary School; Royal Academy of Dramatic Art. Appointments: Writer, Producer, Director of numerous films and TV programmes. Publications: Truth Lies Sleeping, 1951; The Distant Laughter, 1972; Notes for a Life, 1974; The Slipper and the Rose, 1976; Ned's Girl, 1977; International Velvet, 1978; Familiar Strangers, 1979; That Despicable Race, 1980; The Rewrite Man, 1983; The Endless Game, 1986; A Song at Twilight, 1989; A Divided Life, 1992; The Twisted Playground, 1993; Partly Cloudy, 1995; Quicksand, 1996; The Memory of all That, 1999. Honours: Best Screenplay Awards; UN Award; Many Film Festival Prizes; Honorary DL, London, 1987; Honorary Doctor of Literature, Sussex University, 1999; CBE. Memberships: Ex-President, Writers Guild of Great Britain; Ex-President, Beatrix Potter Society; President, National Youth Theatre of Great Britain. Address: Pinewood Studios, Iver Heath, Buckinghamshire, England.

FORD Anna, b. 2 October 1943, Tewkesbury, Gloucestershire. Broadcaster. m. (1) Alan Holland Bittles, (2) Charles Mark Edward Boxer, deceased 1988, 2 daughters. Education: Manchester University. Appointments: Work for student interests, Manchester University, 1966-69; Lecturer, Rupert Stanley College of Further Education, Belfast, 1970-72; Staff Tutor, Social sciences, North Ireland Region, Open University, 1972-74; Presenter and Reporter, Granada TV, 1974-76, Man Alive, BBC, 1976-77, Tomorrow's World, BBC, 1977-78; Newscaster, ITN, 1978-80; W TV am, 1980-82; Freelance broadcasting and writing, 1982-86; BBC news and current affairs, 1989-; Non-executive director, J Sainsbury plc, 2006. Publication: Men: A Documentary, 1985. Honour: Hon LLD (Manchester), 1998; Honourable Bencher Middle Temple, 2002. Membership: Trustee, Royal Botanic Gardens, Kew. Address: BBC Television Centre, Wood Lane, London, W12 7RJ, England.

FORD Harrison, b. 13 July 1942, Chicago, USA. Actor. m. (1) Mary Marquardt, 2 sons, (2) Melissa Mathison, divorced 2004, 1 son, 1 daughter. Education: Ripon College. Career: Numerous TV appearances; Films include: Dead Heat on a Merry-Go-Round, 1966; Luv, The Long Ride Home, 1967; Getting Straight, Zabriskie Point, 1970; The Conversation,

American Graffiti, 1974; Star Wars, Heroes, 1977; Force 10 from Navarone, 1978; Hanover Street, Frisco Kid, 1979; The Empire Strikes Back, 1980; Raiders of the Lost Ark, 1981; Blade Runner; Return of the Jedi, 1983; Indiana Jones and the Temple of Doom; Witness; The Mosquito Coast, 1986; Working Girl, Frantic, 1988; Indiana Jones and the Last Crusade, 1989; Presumed Innocent, 1990; Regarding Henry, 1991; The Fugitive, Patriot Games, 1992; Clear and Present Danger, 1994; Sabrina, 1995; Air Force One, 1996; Six Days and Seven Nights, 1998; Random Hearts, 1999; What Lies Beneath, 2000; K-19: The Widowmaker (also executive producer), 2002; Hollywood Homocide, 2003; Firewall, 2006; Crossing Over, 2007. Address: 10279 Century Woods Drive, Los Angeles, CA 90067, USA.

FORD-JONES Elizabeth Lee (Pearson), b. 25 July 1950, Portland, Oregon, USA. Paediatrician. m. Anthony Eric Andre Ford-Jones, 2 daughters. Education: MD, Queens' University, Kingston, Ontario, Canada, 1974. Appointments: Lecturer, 1979-80, Assistant Professor, 1980-81, Department of Paediatrics, McGill University, Montreal; Assistant Professor, 1981-90, Associate Professor, 1990-2002, Department of Paediatrics, University of Toronto, Faculty of Medicine, Toronto; Professor of Paediatrics, 2002-, Training Program Director, Paediatric Infectious Diseases, 2002-, The Hospital for Sick Children, Toronto and University of Toronto. Publications: Over 130 articles in peer-reviewed journals; 34 books, chapters in books and proceedings; Numerous reports, reviews and articles. Honours: Co-editor, Paediatrics and Child Health, official journal of Canadian Paediatric Society. Memberships: Canadian Paediatric Society; Infectious Diseases Society of America; Association of Medical Microbiology and Infectious Diseases, Canada. Address: The Hospital for Sick Children, 555 University Ave, Toronto, Ontario, Canada. E-mail: lee.ford-jones@sickkids.ca

FORDE Walter Patrick, b. 17 June 1943, Bunclody, County Wexford, Ireland. Roman Catholic Priest. Education: Maynooth College, Ireland, BA, 1964; BD, 1967; H Dip Ed, 1969; Diploma in Social Science, 1972; Ordained, 1968. Appointments: Teacher, St Peter's College, Wexford, 1969-73; General Secretary, National Youth Federation, 1973-74; Director of Social Services and Press Officer, The Diocese of Ferns, 1974-96; Parish Priest, Castlebridge, Co Wexford. Publications: Books include: Adventuring in Priesthood, 1993; The Christian in the Market Place, 1994; Changing Social Needs, 1995; Changing Christian Concerns, 1999; Joan's People, 2003. Honours: County Wexford Person of the Year, 1988; Honorary Life Member, National Youth Federation; Lifetime Achievement Award, Religious Press Association of Ireland, 1998. Address: The Presbytery, Castlebridge, Co Wexford, Ireland.

FOREMAN Alfred G, b. 19 March 1960, Sulfur, Louisiana, USA. Theologian; Philosopher. Education: BA, University of Louisiana, Layfayette, Louisiana, 1987; MA, Liberty University, Lynchburg, Virginia, 1991. Appointments: Pastor, Church of God, 1986-2002; Al-Ruh-Al-Amin Mosque (Spirit of Faith and Truth Mosque); Louisiana Philosophical Institute of Humanities; Lecturer, Islamic Center of Lafayette, Louisiana; Founder, South Louisiana Weather Station. Publications: Exposition of Islamic Philosophy I: Book of Philosophy, Prophetic Wisdom and Directive, Exposition of Islamic Philosophy II: Book of Islamic Thesis in History; Dialectic of Islam: Doctrine of Comprehensive, Exposition of Islamic Philosophy III: Book of Christian Thesis in History; Ecclesiastic Order: Apology; The Eclectic, Cosmological Constant and Formula. Honours: Listed in Who's Who

Publications. Membership: International Palm Society; Center for Islam and Science. Address: 130 Palms Road, Crowley, LA 70526, USA.

FORGHANI-ABKENARI Bagher, b. 10 March 1936, Bandar-Anzali, Iran. Scientist. m. Nikoo Alavi, 1969, 2 daughters. Education: MS, 1961, PhD, 1965, Justus Liebig University, Giessen, Germany. Appointments: Postdoctoral Fellow, 1965-67, Research Associate, 1969-70, Utah State University, Logan, Utah; Assistant Professor, National University of Iran (now Beheshti University), Tehran, Iran, 1967-69; Postdoctoral trainee, 1970-72, Research Specialist, 1972-82, Research Scientist and Chief of Immuno-Serology Section, 1982-, California State Department of Health Service. Publications: Over 80 research papers in virology and immunology in national and international scientific and professional journals; Chapters in several professional books in virology. Honours: Scientific Advisory Board of Varicella-Zoster Foundation, New York, 1991. Memberships: American Society for Microbiology; American Academy of Microbiology; American Society for Clinical Pathology. Address: California Department of Public Health, 850 Marina Bay Parkway, Richmond, CA 94804, USA. E-mail: bagher.forghani@cdph.ca.gov

FORMAN Milos, b. 18 February 1932, Caslav. Producer, Director. m. (1) Jane Brejchova, divorced, (2) Vera Kresadlova, divorced, 2 children, (3) Martina Zhorilova, 1999, 2 children. Education: Film Faculty, Academy of Music and Dramatic Art, Prague. Appointments: Director, Film presentations, Czech TV, 1954-56; of Laterna Magika, Prague, 1958-62; Member, artistic committee, Sebor-Bor Film Producing Group; Director, films including: Talent Competition; Peter and Pavla, 1964; The Knave of Spades; A Blonde in Love, 1965; Episode in Zruc; Like a House on Fire (A Fireman's Ball), 1968; Taking Off, 1971; Co-Director, Visions of Eight, 1973; One Flew Over the Cuckoo's Nest, 1975; Hair, 1979; Ragtime, 1980; Amadeus, 1983; Valmont, 1988; The People Vs Larry Flint, 1995; Man on the Moon, 1999; Goya's Ghosts, 2006; Appeared in New Year's Day, 1989; Keeping the Faith, 2000. Publications: Turnaround: A Memoir (with Jan Novak), 1993. Honours: Czech Film Critics' award for Peter and Pavla, 1963, Grand Prix 17th International Film Festival, Locarno, for Peter and Pavla, 1964; Prize Venice Festival, 1965; Grand Prix, French Film Academy for a Blonde in Love, 1966; Klement Gottwald State Prize, 1967; Academy Award (Best Director) for One Flew Over the Cuckoo's Nest, 1976; Academy Award, César Award, 1985; Golden Globe for Best Director, 1996; Silver Bear for Best Director, Berlin Film Festival, 2000.

FORREST Sir (Andrew) Patrick (McEwen), b. 25 March 1923, Mount Vernon, Lanarkshire, Scotland. Surgeon (retired). m. (1) Margaret Beryl Hall, 1955, deceased 1961, (2) Margaret Anne Steward, 1964, 1 son, 2 daughters. Education: BSc, 1942, MB ChB, 1945, University of St Andrews; ChM (Honours), 1954; MD (Honours), 1958; Fellow, Royal Colleges of Surgeons of Edinburgh, 1948, London, 1950, and Glasgow, 1962; Fellow, Royal Society of Edinburgh, 1976; Fellow, Institute of Biology, 1986; Fellow, Royal College of Physicians of Edinburgh, 2000. Appointments: House Surgeon, Dundee Royal Infirmary, 1945; Service with Royal Navy, 1946-48; House Physician, North General Hospital, Edinburgh, 1948; Junior surgical training posts, Dundee, 1948-54; Mayo Foundation Fellow, Mayo Clinic, Rochester, Minnesota, USA, 1951-52; Lecturer, Senior Lecturer in Surgery, University of Glasgow, 1954-62; Professor of Surgery, Welsh National School of Medicine, University of Wales, 1962-71; Regius Professor of Clinical Surgery, 1971-88, Honorary Fellow, Faculty of Medicine, 1988-93, Professor Emeritus, 1988-, University of Edinburgh; Civil Consultant to Royal Navy for Surgical Research, 1977-88; Chief Scientist (part time), Department of Home and Health, Scotland, 1981-87; Visiting Scientist, National Cancer Institute, Bethesda, Maryland, USA, 1989-90; Associate Dean of Clinical Studies, International Medical University, Kuala Lumpur, 1993-95. Publications: 5 books; Numerous articles in professional medical journals. Honours: Knight Bachelor, 1986; University Gold Medal, 1954; Rutherford Gold Medal, 1988; Hon DSc: University of Wales, 1981, Chinese University of Hong Kong, 1986; Hon LLD, University of Dundee, 1986; Hon MD, International Medical University, 2007. Memberships: Honorary Fellow: American Surgical Association; Royal Australian College of Surgeons; Royal College of Radiologists; Royal College of Physicians and Surgeons of Canada; Faculty of Public Health Medicine; Member: Scottish Society of Experimental Medicine; Surgical Research Society; Association of Surgeons of Great Britain and Ireland; British Breast Group; James IV Association of Surgeons; International Surgical Group; British Society of Gastroenterology; British Association of Surgical Association; European Surgical Association. Address: 19 St Thomas Road, Edinburgh EH9 2LR, Scotland. E-mail: patrickforrest@blueyonder.co.uk

FORSLING Mary Louise, b. 25 March 1942, Rugby, England. University Professor. m. Jonathan Townley-Smith, 2 daughters. Education: BSc, 1963, PhD, 1967, Bedford College, University of London. Appointments: Research Lecturer, Chemical Pathology, St Bartholomew's Hospital, 1969-73; Lecturer, 1975-78, Senior Lecturer, 1979-88, Department of Physiology, Middlesex Hospital Medical School; Reader, Physiology, University College of Middlesex School of Medicine, 1988-89; Reader, Reproductive Physiology, United Medical & Dental School of Guys & St Thomas Hospitals (UMDS), 1989-95; Professor, Neuroendocrinology, GKT School of Medicine (formerly UMDS), 1995-. Publications: 16 books; 300 papers and reviews in professional medical journals. Honours: DSc, 1995; Edkins Memorial Prize; Numerous other awards for research. Memberships: Physiological Society; Society for Endocrinology; Honorary Member, British Society Neuroendocrinology; Trustee, British Society for Neuroendocrinology; Trustee, Martyn Jones Memorial Fund. Address: Department of Women's Health, 10th Floor, North Wing, St Thomas' Hospital, Lambeth Palace Road, London SE1 7EH, England.

FORSTER Gordon Colin Fawcett, b. 30 August 1928, Tadcaster, Yorkshire, England. Academic. m. Judith Mary Duffus Passey. Education: BA, University of Leeds, 1949; Institute of Historical Research, University of London, 1950-52. Appointments: Douglas Knoop Research Fellow, University of Sheffield, 1952-55; Assistant Lecturer, Lecturer, Senior Lecturer, School of History, 1955-93; Chairman, School of History, 1982-85, Life Fellow, 1993-, University of Leeds. Publications: Chapters in Victoria County History volumes: York; Hull; Beverley; Chester; The East Riding Justices of the Peace in the Seventeenth Century; Catalogue of the Records of the Borough of Scarborough; Articles in Northern History and county historical journals; Founder-Editor, Northern History, 1966-. Honours: Fellow of the Royal Historical Society; Fellow of the Society of Antiquaries; Silver Medal, Yorkshire Archaeological Society. Memberships: Committee, Historic Towns Atlas, 1968-; President, Yorkshire Archaeological Society, 1974-79; Chairman, Yorkshire Archaeological Society Record Series, 1978-; President, Thoresby Society, 1983-87;

President, Conference of Regional and Local Historians; Vice President, Surtees Society, 1986-; Council, Chetham Society, 1988-. Address: School of History, University of Leeds, Leeds LS2 9JT, England.

FORSYTH Frederick, b. 25 August 1938, Ashford, Kent, England. Writer. m. (1) Carole Cunningham, 1973, 2 sons, (2) Sandy Molloy. Education: University of Granada. Appointments: Reporter, Eastern Daily Press, 1958-61, Reuters News Agency, 1961-65; Reporter, 1965-67, Assistant Diplomatic Correspondent, BBC, 1967-68; Freelance journalist, Nigeria and Biafra, 1968-69; Narrated Soldiers (TV), 1985; Several TV appearances. Publications: Novels: The Day of the Jackal, 1971; The Odessa File, 1972; The Dogs of War, 1974; The Shepherd, 1975; The Devil's Alternative, 1979; The Fourth Protocol, 1984; The Negotiator, 1989; The Deceiver, 1991; Great Flying Stories, 1991; The Fist of God, 1993; Icon, 1996; The Phantom of Manhattan, 1999; Quintet, 2000; The Veteran and Other Stories, 2001; Avenger, 2003; The Afghan, 2006. Other: The Biafra Story, 1969, revised edition as The Making of an African Legend: The Biafra Story, 1977; Emeka, 1982; No Comebacks: Collected Short Stories, 1982; The Fourth Protocol (screenplay), 1987. Honour: Edgar Allan Poetry Award, Mystery Writers of America, 1971; CBE. Address: c/o Bantam Books, 62-63 Uxbridge Road, London, W5 5SA, England.

FOSTER Brendan, MBE, b. 12 January 1948, Hebburn, County Durham, England. Athlete. m. Susan Margaret Foster, 1972, 1 son, 1 daughter. Education: Sussex University; Carnegie College, Leeds. Career: Competed: Olympic Games, Munich, 5th in 1500 m, 1972; Montreal, bronze medal in 10,000m, 5th in 5000m, 1976; Moscow, 11th in 10, 000m, 1980; Commonwealth Games, Edinburgh, bronze medal at 1500m, 1970; Christchurch, silver medal at 5,000m, 1974; Edmonton, gold medal at 10,000m, bronze medal at 5000m, 1978; European champion at 5000m, 1974 and bronze medallist at 1500m, 1974; World record holder at 3000m and 2 miles; European record holder at 10,000m Olympic record holder at 5000m; Director, Recreation, Gateshead, March, 1982; Managing Director, Nike International, 1982-86; Vice President, Marketing (Worldwide), Vice President (Europe), 1986-87; Chairman and Managing Director, Nova International; BBC TV Commentator, 1980-. Publications: Brendan Foster with Cliff Temple, 1978; Olympic Heroes 1896-1984, 1984. Honours: Hon MEd, Newcastle University; Hon DLitt, Sussex University, 1982; BBC Sports Personality of the Year, 1974; MBE, 1976. Address: Nova International, Newcastle House, Albany Court, Monarch Road, Newcastle upon Tyne, NE4 7YB, England.

FOSTER David (Manning), b. 15 May 1944, Sydney, New South Wales, Australia. Novelist. Education: BSc, Chemistry, University of Sydney, 1967; PhD, Australian National University, Canberra, 1970. Publications: The Pure Land, 1974; The Empathy Experiment, 1977; Moonlite, 1981; Plumbum, 1983; Dog Rock: A Postal Pastoral, 1985; The Adventures of Christian Rosy Cross, 1986; Testostero, 1987; The Pale Blue Crochet Coathanger Cover, 1988; Mates of Mars, 1991; Self Portraits (editor), 1991; A Slab of Fosters, 1994; The Glade Within the Grove, 1996; The Ballad of Erinungarah, 1997; Crossing the Blue Mountain (contributor), 1997; In the New Country, 1999; The Land Where Stories End, 2001. Short Stories: North South West: Three Novellas, 1973; Escape to Reality, 1977; Hitting the Wall: Two Novellas, 1989. Honours: The Age Award, 1974; Australian National Book Council Award, 1981; New South Wales Premier's Fellowship, 1986; Keating Fellowship, 1991-94; James

Joyce Foundation Award, 1996; Miles Franklin Award, 1997; Courier Mail Award, 1999; Shortlisted, International Dublin IMPAC Award, 1998. Address: PO Box 57, Bundanoon, New South Wales 2578, Australia.

FOSTER Giles Henry, b. 30 June 1948, Winchester, England. Film and TV Director. m. Nicole Anne Coates, 2 sons. Education: BA Honours, English, University of York, 1969-72; MA (RCA), Film and TV, Royal College of Art, 1972-75. Career: Film and Television Director and Writer; TV include: Summer Solstice; Foyle's War; Bertie and Elizabeth; The Prince and the Pauper; Coming Home; Oliver's Travels; The Rector's Wife; Adam Bede; Monster Maker; Northanger Abbey; Dutch Girls; The Aerodrome; The Obelisk; 5 Alan Bennett scripts; Hotel du Lac; Silas Marner; A Lady of Letters; Devices and Desires; Films: Consuming Passions; Tree of Hands (Innocent Victim, USA); The Lilac Bus. Honours: BAFTA Nominations for: Silas Marner, A Lady of Letters, BAFTA Award for: Hotel du Lac; Grierson Award for Best Short Film for: Devices and Desires. Memberships: British Academy of Film and Television Arts; Groucho Club. Address: c/o ICM, Laura Burn, 76 Oxord Street, London, W1D 1BS. E-mail: ghf@clara.co.uk

FOSTER Jodie (Alicia Christian), b. 19 November 1962, Los Angeles, USA. Actress; Film Director and Producer. 2 sons. Education: Yale University. Career: Acting debut in TV programme, Mayberry, 1969; Films include: Napoleon and Samantha, Kansas City Bomber, 1972; Menace of the Mountain; One Little Indian, Tom Sawyer, 1973; Alice Doesn't Live Here Any More, 1975; Taxi Driver, Echoes of a Summer, Bugsy Malone, Freaky Friday, 1976; The Girl Who Lives Down the Lane, Candleshoe, 1977; Foxes, Carny, 1980; Hotel New Hampshire, The Blood of Others, 1984; Siesta, Five Corners, 1986; The Accused, Stealing Home, 1988; Catchfire, The Silence of the Lambs, 1990; Little Man Tate (also director), 1991; Shadows and Fog, 1992; Sommersby, 1993; Maverick, Nell, 1994; Home for the Holidays (director, co-producer only), 1996; Contact, The Baby Dance (executive producer only), 1997; Waking the Dead (executive producer only), Contact, 1998; Anna and the King, 1999; Panic Room, The Dangerous Lives of Altar Boys (also producer), 2002; Flightplan, 2005; Inside Man, 2006; The Brave One, 2007. Honours: Academy Award for Best Actress, 1989, 1992; Hon DFA, Yale, 1997. Address: E G G Pictures Production Co, 7920 Sunset Boulevard, Suite 200, Los Angeles, CA 90046, USA.

FOTOPOULOS Takis, b. 14 October 1940, Greece. Political Philosopher; Writer; Editor; Senior Lecturer. m. Sia Mamareli, 28 July 1966, 1 son. Education: LLB, 1962, BA, Economics & Politics, 1965, University of Athens; MSc, Economics, London School of Economics, 1968. Appointments: Lecturer Grade I, Economics, 1969-70, Lecturer, Grade II, 1970-72, North Western Polytechnic; Senior Lecturer, Economics, University of North London, 1973-89; Editor, Society and Nature, 1992-98, Democracy and Nature, 1999-2003; Editor, International Journal of Inclusive Democracy, 2004-. Publications: Towards An Inclusive Democracy, 1997; Per Una Democrazia Globale, 1999; Vers une democratie generale, 2002; Hacia Una Democracia Inclusiva, 2002; Umfassende Demokratie, 2003; The multi-dimensional crisis and Inclusive Democracy (in Chinese), 2007; Published in Athens: Dependent Development, 1985; The War in the Gulf, 1991; The Neoliberal Consensus, 1993; The New World Order and Greece, 1997; Inclusive Democracy, 1999; Drugs, liberalisation vs penalisation, 1999; The New Order in the Balkans, 1999; Religion, Autonomy and Democracy,

2000; From Athenian Democracy to Inclusive Democracy, 2000; Globalisation, Left and Inclusive Democracy, 2002; The war against "terrorism", 2003; Chomsky's capitalism, Albert's post-capitalism and inclusive democracy, 2004; Critical Perspectives on Globalisation, 2006. Contributions to: Education, Culture and Modernization, 1995; Routledge Encyclopedia of International Political Economy, 2001; Defending Public Schools, 2004; Complessita sistemica e sviluppo eco-sostenibile, 2001; Studies on the contemporary Greek Economy, 1978; Environment, Growth and Quality of Life, 1983; Globalisation and Social Economy, 2001; Psyche, Logos Polis – in memory of Castoriadis, 2007. Over 600 articles to English, American, French, Hungarian, German, Spanish, Dutch, Chinese, Norwegian, Arabic, Turkish and Greek scholarly journals, magazines and newspapers. Memberships: Theomai Editorial Board; Alternatives Journal Editorial Board; Inclusive Democracy (in Greek) Advisory Board. Address: 20 Woodberry Way, London N12 OHG, England. Website: www.inclusivedemocracy.org/fotopoulos/

FOULKES OF CUMNOCK George (Rt Hon Lord Foulkes of Cumnock), b. 21 January 1942, Oswestry, England. Director of Voluntary Organisations; Former Member of Parliament. m. Elizabeth Anna Hope, 1970, 2 sons, 1 daughter. Education: BSc, Psychology, Edinburgh University, 1964. Appointments: President, Scottish Union of Students, 1964-66; Director, ELEC, 1966-68; Scottish Organiser, European Movement, 1968-69; Director, Enterprise Youth, 1969-73; Director, Age Concern Scotland, 1973-79; Member of Parliament for Carrick Cumnock & Doon Valley, 1979-2005; Parliamentary Under-Secretary of State, Department of International Development, 1997-2001; Minister of State, Scotland Office, 2001-02; Elected, Member of Scottish Parliament, 2007 Publications: Editor, 80 Years On (History of Edinburgh University SRC); Chapters in: Scotland – A Claim of Right and Football and the Commons People. Honours: Privy Counsellor, 2000; Justice of the Peace; Wilberforce Medal, 1998. Memberships: Commonweath Parliamentary Association; President, Caribbean Britain Business Council; Chair, Dominican Republic and Belize All-Party Parliamentary Group; Vice Chair, Trinidad & Tobago and British – Central American All Party Parliamentary Group. Address: House of Lords, London SW1A 0WP, England. E-mail: foulkesg@parliament.uk

FOWLER Sandra, b. West Columbia, West Virginia, USA. Poet. Education: Studied poetry with Lilith Lorraine, Founder Director of Avalon; Cultural Doctorate in Literature, World Roundtable, 1981; Honorary Doctorate, Literature, The World Academy of Arts and Culture, 2002. Career: Associate Editor, Ocarina, 1978-89; Guest Editor, Friendship Bridge, India, 1979. Publications: Book of Poetry: In the Shape of the Sun, 1972-73, 1975; The Colors Cry in Rain, 1983; Ever Sunset, 1992; Poetry on Websites: Able Muse, Poetry.Com, Poetry Depth Quarterly, Sandra Fowler Poetry Exhibit, International Poetry Hall of Fame Museum; Works in: The World Anthology of Haiku; Cyber Literature; The Chinese Poetry International Quarterly; The World Poetry Quarterly, China; Work posted on internet at poetry.com and poemhunter.com; Poems recorded on cassette and CD. Honours include: Medal of Honor for Lifetime Achievement, American Biographical Institute, 1980; Honorary Member, Steering Committee, Clinton-Gore Campaign, 1995 and Gore-Lieberman Campaign, 1999; Inducted into International Poetry Hall of Fame, 1997; Nominated for the Pushcart Prize, 1998; Commemorative Coin for work in human rights, Amnesty International, 1998; Named on Wall of Tolerance, 2001; Back cover photograph, bio-data and poems, The World Poet's Quarterly, May 2005;

Article: Ageless Poetry, The World Poet's Quarterly, 2005. Memberships: Distinguished Member, International Society of Poets; World Academy of Arts and Culture; Founding Member, The United States Holocaust Memorial Museum; Southern Poverty Law Center; World Renaissance for Classical Poetry; Charter Member, National Women's History Museum, first ever Women's History Museum, Washington, DC. Address: Rt 1, Box 50, West Columbia, WV 25287, USA.

FOX Edward, b. 13 April 1937. Actor. m. (1) Tracy Pelissier, 1958, divorced 1961, 1 daughter, (2) Joanna David, 2 children. Education: Royal Academy of Dramatic Art. Career: Actor, 1957-; Provincial repertory theatre, 1958; Worked widely in films, stage plays and TV; Stage appearances include: Knuckle, 1973; The Family Reunion, 1979; Anyone for Denis, 1981; Quartermaine's Terms, 1981; Hamlet, 1982; The Dance of Death, 1983; Interpreters, 1986; The Admirable Crichton, 1988; Another Love Story, 1990; The Philanthropist, 1991; My Fair Lady; Father, 1995; A Letter of Resignation, 1997; The Chiltern Hundreds, 1999; The Browning Version, 2000; The Twelve Pound Look, 2000; Films include: The Go-Between, 1971; The Day of the Jackal; A Doll's House, 1973; Galileo, 1976; A Bridge Too far; The Duellists; The Cat and the Canary, 1977; Force Ten from Navarone, 1978; The Mirror Crack'd, 1980; Gandhi, 1982; Never Say Never Again, 1983; Wild Geese; The Bounty, 1984; The Shooting Party; Return from the River Kwai, 1989; Circles of Deceit (TV), 1989; Prince of Thieves, 1990; They Never Slept, 1991; A Month by the Lake, 1996; Prince Valiant, 1997; Lost in Space, 1998; All the Queen's Men, 2001; The Importance of Being Earnest, 2002; Nicholas Nickleby, 2002; The Republic of Love, 2003; Stage Beauty, 2004; Lassie, 2005; Television includes: I Was a Rat, 2001; Daniel Deronda, 2002; Foyle's War, 2002; Poirot, 2004; Oliver Twist, 2007. Honours: Several awards for TV performance as Edward VIII in Edward and Mrs Simpson.

FOX James, b. 19 May 1939, London, England. Actor. m. Mary Elizabeth Piper, 1973, 4 sons, 1 daughter. Career: Actor, films include: Mrs Miniver, 1952; The Servant, 1963; King Rat, 1965; Those Magnificent Man in Their Flying Machines, 1965; Thoroughly Modern Millie, 1966; Isadora, 1967; Performance, 1969; Passage to India, 1984; Runners, 1984; Farewell to the King, 1987; Finding Mawbee (video film as the Mighty Quinn), 1988; She's Been Away, 1989; The Russia House, 1990; Afraid of the Dark, 1991; Patriot Games, 1991; As You Like It, 1992; The Remains of the Day, 1993; The Old Curiosity Shop, 1994; Gulliver's Travels, 1995; Elgar's Tenth Muse, 1995; Uncle Vanya, 1995; Anna Karenina, 1997; Mickey Blue Eyes, 1998; Jinnah, 1998; Up at the Villa, 1998; The Golden Bowl, 1999; Sexy Beast, 2000; The Lost World, 2001; The Prince and Me, 2004; The Freediver, 2004; Charlie and the Chocolate Factory, 2005; Goodbye Mr Snuggles, 2006; Wide Blue Yonder, 2008. Publication: Comeback: An Actor's Direction, 1983. Address: c/o ICM Oxford House, 76 Oxford Street, London, W1D 1BS, England.

FOX Matthew, b. 14 July 1966, Wyoming, USA. Actor; Former Model. m. Margherita Ronchi, 1991, 1 son, 1 daughter. Education: Economics, Columbia University; The School for Film and Television, New York City. Career: TV: Freshman Dorm, 1992; Party of Five, 1994; Haunted, 2002; Lost, 2004-; Film: A Token for Your Thoughts, 2003; We Are Marshall, 2006; Vantage Point, 2008.

FOX Michael J, b. 9 June 1961, Edmonton, Alberta, Canada. Actor. m. Tracy Pollan, 1988, 1 son, 2 daughters. Career: TV appearances include: Leo and Me, 1976; Palmerstown USA, 1980; Family Ties, 1982-89; Spin City, 1996-2000; Scrubs,

2004; Boston Legal, 2006; The Magic 7 (voice), 2008; TV films include: Letters from Frank, 1979; Poison Ivy, 1985; High School USA, 1985; Films include: Midnight Madness, 1980; Class of '84, 1981; Back to the Future, 1985; Teen Wolf, 1985; Light of Day, 1986; The Secret of My Success, 1987; Bright Lights, Big City, 1988; Back to the Future II, 1989; Back to the Future III, 1989; The Hard Way, 1991; Doc Hollywood, 1991; The Concierge, 1993; Give Me a Break, 1994; Greedy, 1994; The American President, 1995; Mars Attacks!, 1996; The Frighteners, 1996; Stuart Little (voice), 1999; Atlantis: The Lost Empire (voice), 2001; Interstate 60, 2002; Stuart Little 2 (voice), 2002; Stuart Little 3: Call of the Wild (voice), 2005. Address: c/o Kevin Huvane, CAA, 9830 Wilshire Blvd, Beverly Hills, CA 90212, USA.

FOXALL Gordon Robert, b. 16 July 1949, Birmingham, England. Research Professor. m. Jean, 1 daughter. Education: BSc, Honours, Social Studies, 1970, MSc, Management, 1972, University of Salford; PhD, University of Birmingham, 1983; PhD, University of Strathclyde, 1990; D Soc Sc, University of Birmingham, 1995. Appointments: Lecturer, University of Newcastle upon Tyne, 1972-79; Lecturer, Birmingham University, 1980-83; Reader, Cranfield University, 1983-86; Professor, Strathclyde University, 1987-90; Professor, Birmingham University, 1990-97; Distinguished Research Professor, Cardiff University, 1997-. Publications: Books include: Corporate Innovation; Marketing Psychology; Consumer Psychology for Marketing; Understanding Consumer Choice; Context and Cognition; Consumer Behaviour Analysis. Honours: Fellow, British Psychological Society; Fellow, British Academy of Management; Academician of the Academy of Social Science. Address: Cardiff Business School, Cardiff University, Colum Drive, Cardiff CF10 3EU, Wales.

FOXX Jamie, b. 13 December, 1967, Texas, USA. Actor; Singer; Standup Comic. Career: TV: Roc, 1991; In Living Color, 1991; The Jamie Foxx Show, 1996; Film: Any Given Sunday, 1999; Ali, 2001; Collateral, 2004; Ray, 2004; Jarhead, 2005; Miami Vice, 2006; Dreamgirls, 2006; The Kingdom, 2007; Album: Peep This, 1994; Featured on Slow Jamz, 2004; Featured on Gold Digger, 2004; Featured on Georgia, 2005; Unpredictable, 2005. Honours: Academy Award for Best Actor, 2004; Academy of Motion Picture Arts and Sciences, 2005; Best Duet/Collaboration, BET Awards, 2006; Video of the Year, 2006; Hollywood Walk of Fame, 2007.

FRAGOMENI James Mark, b. 24 September 1962, Columbus Ohio, USA. Engineer; Educator. Education: Bachelor of Science (BS) in Metallurgical Engineering, University of Pittsburgh, Pennsylvania, 1981-85; Master of Science in Engineering (MSE), 1987-89, Doctor of Philosophy (PhD), Mechanical Engineering, 1990-94, Purdue University, College of Engineering, West Lafayette, Indiana. Appointments: Purdue Engineering Research Center, 1987-94; Purdue CINDAS, 1995; Assistant Professor, University of Alabama, 1995-97; NASA Faculty Research Fellow, summers, 1996, 1997; AFOSR/Airforce Faculty Research Fellow, summer, 1998; Assistant Professor, Ohio University, 1997-2000; Assistant Professor, University of Detroit Mercy, 2000-2005; Instructor at Ford Training Center, 2001-2005; Instructor at Focus Hope (part-time), Detroit, Michigan, 2001-2003. Publications: Over 60 technical articles in conference proceedings and scientific journals including: Acta Mechanica, 1999; Aluminum Transactions, 2000; Journal of Advanced Materials, 2001, 2002, 2005; Acta Astronautica, 2002, 2004; Aerospace Science and Technology, 2002; Computer Assisted Mechanics and Engineering Sciences,

2004; Journal of Materials Engineering and Performance, 2005. Honours: University of Pittsburgh Merit Scholarship, 1981-85; Carpenter Technology Scholarship, 1982; Order of Engineer, 1989; Tau Beta Pi; Phi Eta Sigma; Omicron Delta Kappa; Sigma Xi The Scientific Research Society, 1996-; Pi Tau Sigma, Mechanical Engineering Honor Society, 1998-; Certified Quality Technician, 2005; ABI: Lifetime Deputy Governor, 2005; Life Fellow, 2005; Ambassador of Grand Eminence, AGE, 2005; International Directory of Experts and Expertise, 2006; American Hall of Fame, 2006; Great Minds of the 21st Century, 2006; 500 Greatest Geniuses of the 21st Century, 2006; Great Minds of the 21st Century Hall of Fame, 2006; Outstanding Professional Award, 2006; Man of the Year, 2005, 2006; International Peace Prize, 2006; Ambassador-General of the United Cultural Convention, 2006. Memberships: The Materials Society; The American Society for Engineering Education; The American Society for Mechanical Engineers; The American Society for Quality; The American Society for Materials; Michigan Education Association, 2001-; Engineering Society of Detroit, 2002-; Society of Manufacturing Engineers, 2002-; Motown Writers Network, 2006. Address: 25105 Biarritz Circle, #C Oak Park, MI 48237, USA. E-mail: jamesfrag@yahoo.com Website: www.jamesmatsci.org, www.jamesfrag.net

FRAILE Medardo, b. 21 March 1925, Madrid, Spain. Writer; Emeritus Professor in Spanish. Education: DPh, DLitt, University of Madrid, 1968. Publications: Cuentos con Algun Amor, 1954; A La Luz Cambian las Cosas, 1959; Cuentos de Verdad, 1964; Descubridor de Nada y Otros Cuentos, 1970; Con Los Dias Contados, 1972; Samuel Ros Hacia una Generacion Sin Critica, 1972; La Penultima Inglaterra, 1973; Poesia y Teatro Espanoles Contemporaneos, 1974; Ejemplario, 1979; Autobiografia, 1986; Cuento Espanol de Posguerra, 1986; El gallo puesto en hora, 1987; Entre parentesis, 1988; Santa Engracia, numero dos o tres, 1989; Teatro Espanol en un Acto, 1989; El rey y el pais con granos, 1991; Cuentos Completos, 1991; Claudina y los cacos, 1992; La Familia irreal inglesa, 1993; Los brazos invisibles, 1994; Documento Nacional, 1997; Contrasombras, 1998; Ladrones del Paraiso, 1999; Cuentos de Verdad (anthology), 2000; Descontar y Contar, 2000; Años de Aprendizaje, 2001; Escritura y Verdad, 2004; Palabra en el tiempo, 2005; En Madrid Tambien Se Vive En Oruro, 2007. Translation: El Weir de Hermiston by R L Stevenson, 1995; Contributions to: Many publications. Honours: Sesamo Prize, 1956; Literary Grant, Fundacion Juan March, 1960; Critics Book of the Year, 1965; La Estafeta literaria Prize, 1970; Hucha de Oro Prize, 1971; Research Grant, Carnegie Trust for Universities of Scotland, 1975; Colegiado de Honor del Colegio heraldico de España y de las Indias, 1995; Comendador con Placa de la Orden Civil de Alfonso X El Sabio, 1999; Orden venezolana de Primera Clase de Don Balthazar de Leon. Memberships: General Society of Spanish Authors; Working Community of Book Writers, Spain; Association of University Teachers. Address: 24 Etive Crescent, Bishopbriggs, Glasgow G64 1ES, Scotland.

FRANCHI Giuseppe, b. 16 November 1924, Siena, Italy. University Professor. m. Rampazzo Rosana, 1 son. Education: Laurea Pharmacy, University of Siena, 1948; Libera Docenza, Pharmaceutical Technology and Legislation, 1958; Libera Docenza, Pharmaceutical Chemistry, 1962. Appointments: Lecturer and Professor, Pharmaceutical Technology and Legislation, 1958-75; Dean Faculty of Pharmacy, University of Siena, Italy, 1976-88; Pharmaceutical Chemistry Department, University of Siena, Director, 1976-81, 1995-97; Retired, 1997. Publications: 92 papers on pharmaceutical

DICTIONARY OF INTERNATIONAL BIOGRAPHY

chemistry and pharmaceutical techniques, 1951-97; 1 book on analytical chemistry; 2 patents on pharmaceutical technological equipment. Honours: Gold Medal for services to school, culture and art, 1984; Commendatore al merito della Repubblica Italiana, 1997. Memberships: Accademia delle Scienze di Siena, detta dei Fisiocritici, 1954, President, 1990-98; Association of Italian Teachers and Researchers in Pharmaceutical Technology and Legislation, 1971, President, 1981-97; Italian Society of Pharmaceutical Sciences, 1966-2004; Pharmaceutical Society of Latin Mediterranean Countries, 1963; Rotary Club 2070 District, 1980. Address: Via della Sapienza 39, 53100 Siena, Italy.

FRANIN Dina, b. 29 March 1959, Zagreb, Croatia. Author; Poet; Lawyer. Education: Graduate, Law Faculty, Zagreb University, 1987. Publications: Poetry: Primal Scream (collection of poems), 1995; Woman's Pride is a Hard Stone (collection of poems), 1996; The Last Juices of Summer (collection of poems), 1999; The Sheltered Moon (collection of haiku), 1999; Blue Nature (collection of poems), 2002; In The Breath of The Wind (collection of haiku), 2006; Short stories: Here Beside Me, 1996; The Pair of Scales, 1999; Numerous poems published in anthologies and magazines nationally and internationally. Honours: Honourable Mention, 6th Annual Haiku Competition, Croatian Haiku Association, 1998; 3rd Prize, International Kumamoto Kusamakura Haiku Competition, Japan, 1999; 3rd Honourable Mention, International Competition, Hawaii Education Association, 1999; Editor's Award, International Library of Poetry, Owing Mills, USA, 1999; 1st Prize, 8th Annual Haiku Competition, Croatian Haiku Association, 2000; Commended Haiku, International Yellow Moon Literary Competition, Australia, 2000; Highly Commended Poem, International Yellow Moon Literary Competition, Australia, 2000. Memberships: Matica Hrvatska; The Association of Croatian Haiku Poets; The Association of Artists August Šenoa; The Association of Artists Vjekoslav Majer; The Association of Artists Tin Ujević; Editor's Board of miscellany Naša riječ; Distinguished Member of the International Society of Poets. Address: Republike Austrije 21, 10000 Zagreb, Croatia. E-mail: dinafranin@yahoo.com Website: http://www.webramba.com/dinafranin/index.html

FRANKLAND (Anthony) Noble, b. 4 July 1922, Ravenstonedale, England. Historian; Biographer. m. (1) Diana Madeline Fovargue Tavernor, 28 February 1944, deceased 1981, 1 son, 1 daughter, (2) Sarah Katharine Davies, 7 May 1982. Education: Open Scholar, MA, 1948, DPhil, 1951, Trinity College, Oxford. Appointments: Served Royal Air Force, 1941-45, Bomber Command, 1943-45; DFC, 1944; Official British Military Historian, 1951-60; Deputy Director of Studies, Royal Institute of International Affairs, 1956-60; Director, Imperial War Museum, 1960-82. Publications: Crown of Tragedy: Nicholas II, 1960; The Strategic Air Offensive Against Germany (co-author), 4 volumes, 1961; The Bombing Offensive Against Germany: Outlines and Perspectives, 1965; Bomber Offensive: The Devastation of Europe, 1970; Prince Henry, Duke of Gloucester, 1980; Witness of a Century: Prince Arthur, Duke of Connaught, 1850-1942, 1993; History at War: The Campaigns of an Historian, 1998; The Unseen War (novel), 2007; Encyclopaedia of Twentieth Century Warfare (general editor and contributor), 1989; The Politics and Strategy of the Second World War (joint editor), 9 volumes. Contributions to: Encyclopaedia Britannica; Times Literary Supplement; The Times; Daily Telegraph; Observer; Spectator; Military journals. Honours: Companion of the Order of the Bath; Commander of the Order of the British Empire; Holder of the Distinguished Flying Cross. Address: 26/27 River View Terrace, Abingdon, Oxon, OX14 5AE, England.

FRANKLIN Aretha, b. 25 March 1942, Memphis, TN, USA. Singer. m. (1) Ted White, divorced, (2) Glynn Turman, 1978, divorced. Career: First recordings, father's Baptist church, Detroit; Tours as gospel singer; Moved to New York, signed with Columbia Records, 1960, Atlantic, 1966, Arista, 1980. Publications: Recordings include: Aretha, 1961; The Electrifying Aretha Franklin, 1962; Laughing on the Outside, The Tender, the Moving, the Swinging Aretha Franklin, 1963; Running Out of Fools, The Gospel Sound of Aretha Franklin, 1964; Soul Sister, 1966; I Never Loved a Man the Way I Love You, 1967; Lady Soul, Aretha Now, Aretha in Paris, 1968; Aretha's Gold, 1969; This Girl's in Love With You, Spirit in the Dark, 1970; Live at Fillmore West, 1971; Young Gifted and Black, Amazing Grace, 1972; Hey Now Hey, The Best of Aretha Franklin, The First Twelve Sides, 1973; Let Me in Your Life, With Everything I Feel in Me, 1974; You, 1975; Sparkle, Ten Years of Gold, 1976; Sweet Passion, 1977; Almighty Fire, 1978; La Diva, 1979; Aretha, 1980; Love All the Hurt Away, 1981; Jump to It, 1982; Get It Right, 1983; One Lord, One Faith, 1988; Through the Storm, 1989; What You Can See is What You Sweat, 1991; Jazz to Soul, 1992; Aretha After Hours, Chain of Fools, 1993; Unforgettable: A Tribute to Dinah Washington, 1995; Love Songs, 1997; The Delta Meets Detroit, 1998; A Rose is Still a Rose, 1998; Amazing Grace, 1999; So Damn Happy, 2003; A Woman Falling Out of Love, 2007. Publications: Aretha: From these Roots (with David Rib). Honours: Numerous Grammy Awards, 1967-87; American Music Award, 1984; John F Kennedy Centre Award, 1994; Rock and Roll Hall of Fame, 1987; Honorary Doctor of Music degree, Berklee College of Music, 2006; University of Pennsylvania, 2007. Address: 8450 Linwood Street, Detroit, MI 48206, USA.

FRANKLIN H Bruce, b. 28 February 1934, Brooklyn, New York, USA. Professor. m. 3 children. Education: BA, Amherst College, Massachusetts, 1955; Doctor of Philosophy, English and American Literature, Stanford University, 1961; Certificate of Environmental Horticulture, College of San Mateo, California, 1974. Appointments: Batch Worker, Mayfair Photofinishing Company, New York, 1951, 1952; Upholster, Carb Manufacturing Company, 1953; Foreman, Shipping Department, 1954; Tugboat Deckhand; Mate; Pennsylvania RR Marine Department, Pier H, Jersey City, New Jersey, 1955-56; Navigator; Intelligence Officer, Strategic Air Command, United States Air Force, 1956-59; Lecturer, Department of Adult Education, San Jose, California, 1963-64; Assistant Professor, English and American Literature, Stanford University, 1961-64; Assistant Professor, English and American Literature, The Johns Hopkins University, 1964-65; Lecturer, Free University of Paris, France, 1967; Lecturer, Venceremos College, Redwood City, California, 1971; Associate Professor, English and American Literature, Stanford University, 1965-72; Visiting Lecturer, American Studies, Yale University, 1974-75; Professor, English, Rutgers University, 1975-80; Professor II, English, 1980-87; John Cotton Dana Professor, English and American Studies, Rutgers, The State University, 1987-. Publications: The Wake of the Gods; Future Perfect; War Stars; Prison Literature in America; Vietnam and other American Fantasies; TheMost Important Fish in the Sea, 2007; Many others. Honours: Stanford Willson Fellow; The Alexander Cappon Prize; Many others. Address: English Department, Rutgers University, Newark, NJ 07102, USA. E-mail: hbf@andromeda.rutgers.edu

FRANKS Michael, b. 6 May 1928, Kingsclere, Hampshire, England. Strategic Consultant. m. (1) Anne Home, 2 daughters, (2) Nicola Stewart Heath (née Balmain). Education: Epsom College, 1942-46; MA, Classics and Law, Merton College, Oxford, 1946-50; Called to the Bar, Gray's Inn, 1953. Appointments: Sub-Lieutenant, RNVR, National Service, 1951-53; Chancery Bar, 1953-58; Financial and Commercial Management, Royal Dutch/Shell Group, UK, Netherlands, Carribean, Venezuela, 1959-69; Director, Beaverbrook Newspapers, 1969-73; Chairman, Clyde Paper plc, 1971-76; Manager, First National Holdings, 1973-74; Since 1976 involved as Chairman, Director, Consultant or Trouble-Shooter with numerous quoted and private companies; Currently, Strategic Consultant, South & West Investments. Publications: Limitation of Actions, 1959; The Clerk of Basingstoke, A Life of Walter de Merton, 2003; The Basingstoke Admiral, A Life of Sir James Lancaster, 2006. Membership: Royal Thames Yacht Club. Address: South & West Investments, Field House, Mapledurwell, Basingstoke, Hants RG25 2LU, England.

FRASER Lady Antonia, (Lady Antonia Pinter), b. 27 August 1932, London, England. Author. m. (1) Sir Hugh Fraser, 1956, dissolved 1977, 3 sons, 3 daughters, (2) Harold Pinter, 1980. Education: MA, Lady Margaret Hall, Oxford. Appointment: General Editor, Kings and Queens of England series. Publications: King Arthur and the Knights of the Round Table, 1954; Robin Hood, 1955; Dolls, 1963; A History of Toys, 1966; Mary Queen of Scots, 1969; Cromwell, Our Chief of Men, 1973; King James: VI of Scotland, I of England, 1974; Kings and Queens of England (editor), 1975; Scottish Love Poems: A Personal Anthology (editor), 1975; Love Letters: An Anthology (editor), 1976, revised edition, 1989; Quiet as a Nun, 1977; The Wild Island, 1978; King Charles II, 1979; Heroes and Heroines (editor), 1980; A Splash of Red, 1981; Mary Queen of Scots: Poetry Anthology (editor), 1981; Oxford and Oxfordshire in Verse: An Anthology (editor), 1982; Cool Repentance, 1982; The Weaker Vessel: Woman's Lot in Seventeenth Century England, 1984; Oxford Blood, 1985; Jemima Shore's First Case, 1986; Your Royal Hostage, 1987; Boadicea's Chariot: The Warrior Queens, 1988; The Cavalier Case, 1990; Jemima Shore at the Sunny Grave, 1991; The Six Wives of Henry VIII, 1992; The Pleasure of Reading (editor), 1992; Political Death, 1994; The Gunpowder Plot, 1996; The Lives of the Kings and Queens of England, 1998; Marie Antoinette: the Journey, 2001; Love and Louis XIV: The Women in the Life of the Sun King, 2006; Other: Several books adapted for television. Contributions to: Anthologies. Honours: James Tait Black Memorial Prize, 1969; Wolfson History Award, 1984; Prix Caumont-La Force, 1985; Honorary DLitt, Universities of Hull, 1986, Sussex, 1990, Nottingham, 1993 and St Andrews, 1994; St Louis Literary Award, 1996; CWA Non Fiction Gold Dagger, 1996; Shortlisted for NCR Award, 1997; Norten Medlicott Medal, Historical Association, 2000. Memberships: Society of Authors, chairman, 1974-75; Crimewriters' Association, chairman, 1985-86; Writers in Prison Committee, chairman, 1985-88, 1990; English PEN, vice president, 1990-. Address: c/o Curtis Brown Ltd, 162-168 Regent Street, London W1R 5TB, England.

FRASER Ian Masson, b. 15 December 1917, Forres, Moray, Scotland. Ordained Minister. m. Margaret D D Stewart, deceased, 2 sons, 1 daughter. Education: MA, BD (New College for Theology), with distinction in Systematic Theology, 1936-42; PhD, 1955, Edinburgh University, Scotland. Appointments: Manual Working Industrial Chaplain, Fife, Scotland, 1942-44; Interim appointment, Hopemouth Church, Arbroath, Scotland, 1944-45; Scottish Secretary,

Student Christian Movement, 1945-48; Parish Minister, Rosyth, Fife, Scotland, 1948-60; Warden of Scottish Churches House, Dunblane, Scotland, 1960-69; Executive Secretary, Consultant and Programme Co-ordinator, 1969-75, World Council of Churches; Dean and Head of the Department of Mission, Selly Oak Colleges, Birmingham, England, 1973-82; Voluntary Research Consultant, Scottish Churches' Council, 1982-90, Action of Churches Together in Scotland, 1990-. Publications: Numerous articles and books including: Strange Fire, a book of life stories and prayers, 1994; A Celebration of Saints, 1997; Signs of Fire (audio cassette), 1998; Salted with Fire, more stories, reflections, prayers, 1999; Caring for Planet Earth, children's stories and prayers, 2002; R B Cunninghame Graham – Fighter for Justice, 2002; ACTS, Ecumenical Adventure, beginnings in the 1960s of the work of Scottish Churches House and Council, 2002; Many Cells One Body, 2003; The Way Ahead – grown-up Christians in integrated community serving the world God loves, 2006. Honours: Cobb Scholarship, Cunningham Fellowship, Gunning Prize, New College, Edinburgh. Address: Ferndale, Gargunnock, by Stirling FK8 3BW, Scotland.

FRASER Malcolm, b. 20 October 1952, Troy, New York, USA. Professor. m. Tresa S, 3 sons. Education: BSc, Biological Sciences, Wheeling College, Wheeling, West Virginia, 1975; MSc, 1979, PhD, 1981, Entomology, Invertebrate Pathology, The Ohio State University. Appointments: Postdoctoral Research Associate, Pennsylvania State University, 1980-81; Postdoctoral Research Associate, Texas A&M University, 1981-83; Assistant Professor, 1983-89, Associate Professor, 1989-2000, Professor, 2000-, University of Notre Dame. Publications: Numerous articles in professional journals. Honours: NIH Research Career Development Award, American Association for the Advancement of Science Fellows. Memberships: AAAS; American Society for Virology; Entomological Society of America; American Chemical Society; American Society for Tropical Medicine and Hygiene. Address: Department of Biological Sciences, University of Notre Dame, Notre Dame, IN 46556-0369, USA. E-mail: fraser.1@nd.edu

FREASIER Aileen W, b. 12 November 1924, Edcouch, Texas, USA. Educator. m. Ben C Freasier, deceased, 3 sons, 1 son deceased, 2 daughters. Education: BS, Home Economics, Texas A&I University, 1944; M Ed, Special Education, 1966, 90 hours above the Master's level, Louisiana Tech University. Appointments: Fourth Grade Teacher, Robstown Elementary School, Robstown, Texas, 1948-49; EMR Class teacher, San Antonio Independent School District, San Antonio, Texas, 1961-62; TMR Day Care Program Teacher, Lincoln Parish Association for Retarded Children, Ruston, Louisiana, 1965-71; Teacher, Lincoln Parish Association for Retarded Children's Summer Program, Ruston, Louisiana, 1969; EMR, TMR Class Teacher, Lincoln Parish Schools, I A Lewis, Lincoln Center, Ruston, Louisiana, 1971-77; EMR Resource Room Teacher, Hico Elementary, Lincoln Parish Schools, Hico Louisiana, 1977-80; Co-ordinating Teacher, Early Childhood Program, Lincoln Parish Schools, Ruston, Louisiana, 1980-81; IEP Facilitator/Educational Diagnostician, Special Schools District #1, Louisiana Training Institute, Monroe, Louisiana, 1981-95; Retired Senior Program Volunteer PreGED Class Tutor, Lincoln Parish Detention Center, Ruston, Louisiana, 1995-. Publications: 20 publications in professional special education, correctional education, and technology education journals; 11 commercial workbooks/duplicating masters books for special education students; 3 international, 46 national, 24 state presentations to special education, correctional and technology-using educators. Honours include: Mary C Wilson

Award, Lincoln Parish Schools, 1978; State Named Bolivar L Hait Research and Projects Endowment Honouree, American Association of University Women, Louisiana Division, 1982; Special Schools District # 1, Teacher of the Year, 1988; Phi Delta Kappa Service Award, 1991; J E Wallace Wallin Education of the Handicapped Children Award, Louisiana Federation of the Council for Exceptional Children, 1994; President's Award for Outstanding Service, Louisiana Council for Exceptional Children, Technology and Media, 1997; Lifetime Achievement Award, ABI, 2005; Listed in Who's Who publications and biographical dictionaries. Memberships include: American Association of University Women; Council for Exceptional Children, Correctional Education Association; Daughters of the American Revolution; Delta Kappa Gamma; Kappa Kappa Iota; Lincoln Parish Retired Teachers; Louisiana Reading Association; Phi Delta Kappa; Ruston Mayor's Commission for Women. Address: PO Box 1595, Ruston, LA 71273-1595, USA. E-mail: aileenwf@bayou.com

FREEMAN Cathy, b. 16 February 1973, Mackay, Australia. Athlete. m. Alexander Bodecker, separated, 2003. Career: Public Relations Adviser; Winner, Australian 200m, 1990-91, 1994, 1996; Australian 100m, 1996; Amateur Athletics Federation 400m, 1992, 200m, 1993; Gold Medallist 4x100m, Commonwealth Games, 1990; Gold Medallist 200m, 400m, Silver Medallist 4x100m, Commonwealth Games, 1994; Silver Medallist 400m, Olympic Games, Atlanta, 1996; Winner, World Championships 400m, Athens (first Aboriginal winner at World Championships), 1997; Set 2 Australian 200m records, 5 Australian 400m records, 1994-96; 1st, World Championships, Seville, 400m, 1999; Gold Medallist, Sydney Olympic Games 400m, 2000; took break from athletics in 2001; returned to international competition, Gold Medal 4x400m relay, Commonwealth Games, Manchester, 2002; Retired from competition, 2003; Media and Communications Officer, Australia Post. Honours: Numerous national awards include: Australian of the Year, 1998; OAM, 2001. Address: c/o Melbourne International Track Club, 43 Fletcher Street, Essendon, Vic 3040, Australia.

FREEMAN David Franklin, b. 13 April 1925, Raleigh, North Carolina, USA. Adult and Child Psychiatrist and Psychoanalyst. m. Constance Covell Freeman, 1 son, 2 daughters. Education: BS, Wake Forest College, North Carolina, 1948; MD, Bowman Gray School of Medicine, Winston-Salem, 1951; Internship, Philadelphia General Hospital, 1951-52; Resident, Adult and Child Psychiatry, Boston Psychopathic Hospital, Massachusetts, 1952-55; Research Fellow, Psychiatry, Harvard University, 1952-55; 2nd Year Child Psychiatry, Worcester Youth Guidance Center, Massachusetts, 1955-56; Candidate, Adult and Child Psychoanalysis, Boston, Washington, UNC-Duke University Psychoanalytic Institutes, 1955-66. Appointments: Private Practice, Adult and Child Psychiatry, Lincoln, Massachusetts, 1956-61; Director, North Central Mental Health Consultation Service, Fitchburg, Massachusetts, 1956-57; Staff Psychiatrist, Douglas A Thom Clinic for Children, Boston, Massachusetts, 1957-61; Assistant in Child Psychiatry, Boston University School of Medicine, 1960-61; Consultant, several child psychiatry clinics, 1956-66; Clinical Faculty, Assistant Professor to Clinical Professor, University of North Carolina, 1961-95; Adjunct Professor, University of North Carolina at Chapel Hill, 1995-; Training and Supervising Psychoanalyst, UNC-Duke University Psychoanalytic Education Program, 1972-; Psychiatric Consultant, NE Home for Little Wanderers, Boston, Massachusetts, 1959-61; Director, Child Psychiatry Outpatient Clinic, North Carolina Memorial Hospital, Chapel Hill, 1961-63; Private Practice, Adult and Child Psychiatry

and Psychoanalysis, Chapel Hill, North Carolina, 1963-. Publications: Several articles in professional medical journals. Honours include: Alpha Omega Alpha, 1950; Herman Lineberger Award, 1997; NC Psychoanalytic Foundation, 2003. Memberships include: Life member: American Psychiatric Association; International Psychoanalytical Association; North Carolina Psychiatric Association; American Academy of Child and Adolescent Psychiatry; North Carolina Medical Society; American Psychoanalytic Association; Association for Child Psychoanalysis; Life Member and Past President: North Carolina Psychoanalytic Society; North Carolina Council of Child Psychiatry; Founder and Chair: North Carolina Psychoanalytic Foundation, 1995-2000. Address: 374 Carolina Meadows Villa, Chapel Hill, NC 27517, USA.

FREEMAN Jennifer Margaret, b. 28 October 1944, Sale, Cheshire, England. Architectural Writer; Director; Chairman. m. Rt Hon Lord Freeman, 1 son, 1 daughter. Education: BA (Honours), University of Manchester, 1963-66; Postgraduate Diploma in Building Conservation, Architectural Association, London, 1979-81. Appointments: Economic Intelligence Department, Bank of England, London, 1966-68; Eurobond Dealer, N H Rothschild & Sons, London, 1967-68; International Banking Department, Bankers Trust Company, New York City, 1969-70; Consultant Researcher, New York City Landmarks Preservation Commission, 1970-72; Assistant to Architect, European Architectural Heritage Year 1975, Civic Trust, 1972-74; Co-author, Project Co-ordinator, Save the City: A Conservation Study of the City of London, 1974-80; Secretary, The Victorian Society, 1982-85; Founding Member, London Advisory Committee, English Heritage, 1986-2001; Member, Council for the Care of Churches, 1991-2001; Leading organiser of national efforts to save and refurbish 23 historic buildings in the City of London including Mansion House/No 1 Poultry, 1980's and 1990's; Chairman, Freeman Historic Properties Ltd, 1991-; First Director, Historic Chapels Trust, 1993-. Publications include: Save the City: a Conservation Study of the City of London (co-author), 1976, reprinted, 1977, revised, 1979; Billingsgate Market (co-author) 1981; W D Caroe: His Architectural Achievement, 1991; Kensal Green Cemetery (co-author), 2001; Don't Butcher Smithfield (contributor), 2004; Numerous articles in architectural and conservation journals. Honour: Honorary Doctorate of Arts, De Montfort University, 1997; Freedom of the City of London, 1998; FRSA, 2003; FSA, 2005. Memberships include: Institute of Historic Buildings and Conservation; President, Friends of Kensal Green Cemetery; Vice-President, Friends of the City Churches; Committee Member, Save Britain's Heritage, 1977-; Founding Trustee, Heritage Link, 2002-; Trustee, Constable Trust, 2004; Trustee, Building Crafts and Conservation Trust, 2002; Bodleian Library Development Board, 2003; President, Kettering Civic Society, 2004. E-mail: freemanr@parliament.uk

FRENCH Arthur Edmund, b. 10 January 1933, Blechingley, Surrey, England. Barrister. m. Charlotte Towneley, 1 son, 1 daughter. Education: Ampleforth College, York; Trinity College, Cambridge. Appointments: Practiced at Criminal Bar, 1962-92; Retired. Memberships: Chairman, North of England Branch, Irish Guards Association. Address: Old School House, Nunnington, Yorkshire YO62 5UX, England.

FREUD Anthony Peter, b. 30 October 1957, London, England; Opera Administrator; Barrister. Education: LLB (Hons), King's College, London, 1975-78; Inns of Court School of Law, 1978-79. Appointments: Trained as Barrister; Theatre Manager, Sadler's Wells Theatre, 1980-84; Company Secretary, Director of Opera Planning, Welsh National

Opera, 1984-91; Executive Producer Opera, Philips Classics, 1992-94; General Director, Welsh National Opera, 1994-. Honour: Honorary Fellowship of Cardiff University, 2002. Memberships: Member, Honorary Secretary of Gray's Inn, 1979; Chairman of Jury, Cardiff Singer of the World, 1995-; Chairman, Opera Europa, 2002-; Trustee, National Endowment for Science, Technology and the Arts (NESTA), 2004-. Address: Welsh National Opera, Wales Millennium Centre, Bute Place, Cardiff Bay CF10 5AL, Wales. E-mail: anthony.freud@wno.org.uk

FREUD Bella, b. 17 April 1961, London, England. Fashion Designer. Education: Accademia di Costuma e di Moda, Rome; Institutto Mariotti, Rome. Appointments: Assistant to Vivienne Westwood on her designer collections, 1986-89; Launched own label presenting autumn/winter collection of tailored knitwear and accessories, 1990; Exhibited, London Designer Show, 1991, London Fashion Week, 1993. Honours: Winner, Innovative Design - the New Generation Category (British Fashion Awards), 1991. Address: 21 St Charles Square, London, W10 6EF, England.

FREUD Lucian, b. 8 December 1922. Painter. m. (1) Kathleen Epstein, 1948, divorced 1952, 2 daughters, (2) Lady Caroline Maureen Blackwood, 1953, divorced 1957, deceased 1996. Education: Central School of Art, East Anglian School of Painting and Drawing. Appointments: Teacher, Slade School of Art, London, 1948-58; First one-man exhibition, 1944; Exhibitions, 1946, 1950, 1952, 1958, 1963, 1972, 1978, 1979, 1982, 1983, 1988, 1990-96; Retrospectives: Hayward Gallery, 1974, 1988, 1989; Tate Gallery, Liverpool, 1992; Works included in public collections: Tate Gallery, National Portrait Gallery, Victoria and Albert Museum, Arts Council of Great Britain, British Council, British Museum, Fitzwilliam Museum (Cambridge), National Museum of Wales (Cardiff), Scottish National Gallery of Modern Art (Edinburgh), Walker Art Gallery (Liverpool), Ashmolean Museum of Art, Oxford, in Brisbane, Adelaide, Perth (Australia), Musée National d'Art Moderne (Paris, France), Art Institute of Chicago, Museum of Modern Art (NY), Cleveland Museum of Art (OH), Museum of Art Carnegie Institute (Pittsburgh), Achenbaach Foundation for Graphic Arts and Fine Arts (San Fran), The St Louis Art Museum, Hirshborn Museum and Sculpture Garden, Smithsonian Institute (Wash), Rubenspeis, City of Siegen, 1997. Address: c/o Diana Rawstron, Goodman-Derrick, 90 Fetter Lane, London, EC4A 1EQ, England.

FREWER Glyn Mervyn Louis, (Mervyn Lewis), b. 4 September 1931, Oxford, England. Author; Scriptwriter. m. Lorna Townsend, 11 August 1956, 2 sons, 1 daughter. Education: MA, English Language and Literature, St Catherine's College, Oxford, 1952-1955. Appointments: Student Officer, British Council, Oxford, 1955; Copywriter, various agencies, 1955-64; Advertising Agency Associate Director, 1974-85; Retired; Proprietor antiquarian/secondhand bookshop, 1985-2001. Publications: Scripts: The Hitch-Hikers (BBC Radio Play), 1957; also scripts for children's television series, industrial films, etc; Children's books: Adventure in Forgotten Valley, 1962; Adventure in the Barren Lands, 1964; The Last of the Wispies, 1965; The Token of Elkin, 1970; Crossroad, 1970; The Square Peg, 1972; The Raid, 1976; The Trackers, 1976; Adult fiction: Death of Gold (as Mervyn Lewis), 1970; Wildlife fiction: Tyto: The Odyssey of an Owl, 1978; Bryn of Brockle Hanger, 1980; Fox, 1984; The Call of the Raven, 1987; Poetry: Shout to the Sky, 2007. Contributions to: Birds; Imagery; The Countryman. Honours:

Junior Literary Guild of America Choice, for Adventure in Forgotten Valley, 1964; Freeman of the City of Oxford, 1967. Address: Cottage Farm, Taston, Oxford OX7 3JN, England.

FRIEDLANDER John B, b. 4 October 1941, Toronto, Canada. Mathematician. m. Cherryl, 2 sons, 2 daughters. Education: BSc, University of Toronto, 1965; MA, University of Waterloo, 1966; PhD, The Pennsylvania State University, 1972. Appointments: Assistant to A Selberg, 1972-73, Member, 1973-74, Institute for Advanced Study, Princeton, New Jersey; Lecturer, Massachusetts Institute of Technology, 1974-76; Visiting Professor, Scuola Normale Superiore, Pisa, Italy, 1976-77; Assistant Professor, 1977-79, Associate Professor, 1980-82, Scarborough College, University of Toronto; Lecturer, University of Illinois, Urbana, 1979-80; Appointed to School of Graduate Studies, 1980; Professor, 1982-; Member, School of Mathematics, Institute for Advanced Study, 1983-84; Chair, Department of Mathematics, University of Toronto, 1987-91; Visitor, 1990-91, Member, 1995-96, 1999-2000, 2004, School of Mathematics, Institute for Advanced Study, Princeton; Research Professor, Mathematical Science Research Institute, Berkeley, California, 1991-92; Visiting Professor, Macquarie University, Sydney, 1996. Publications: Over 100 articles and papers in professional journals; Numerous lectures at conferences and workshops. Honours: Fellow, Royal Society of Canada, 1988; Invited Lecture, ICM Zurich, 1994; Participant, Taniguchi Symposium in Analytic Number Theory, Kyoto, 1996; Jeffery-Williams Prize Lecturer, Canadian Mathematical Society, 1999; Principal's Research Award, University of Toronto at Scarborough, 1999-2000; CRM-Fields Prize, 2002; University Professor, University of Toronto, 2002-; Killam Research Fellowship, 2003-05. Memberships: Royal Society of Canada; Canadian Mathematical Society; American Mathematical Society. Address: Computer and Mathematical Sciences, University of Toronto at Scarborough, Toronto ON M1C 1A4, Canada.

FRIEDMAN (Eve) Rosemary, (Robert Tibber, Rosemary Tibber, Rosemary Friedman), b. 5 February 1929, London, England. Writer. m. Dennis Friedman, 2 February 1949, 4 daughters. Education: Queen's College, Harley Street, London; Law Faculty, University College, London University. Publications: No White Coat, 1957; Love on My List, 1959; We All Fall Down, 1960; Patients of a Saint, 1961; The Fraternity, 1963; The Commonplace Day, 1964; Aristide, 1966; The General Practice, 1967; Practice Makes Perfect, 1969; The Life Situation, 1977; The Long Hot Summer, 1980; Proofs of Affection, 1982; A Loving Mistress, 1983; Rose of Jericho, 1984; A Second Wife, 1986; Aristide in Paris, 1987; An Eligible Man, 1989; Golden Boy, 1994; Vintage, 1996; The Writing Game, 1999; Intensive Care, 2001; Paris Summer, 2004; A Writer's Commonplace Book, 2006; Others: Home Truths, (stage play), 1997; Change of Heart (stage play), 2004; Commissioned screenplays and television drama; Contributions to and reviewer for: Sunday Times; Times Literary Supplement; Guardian; Jewish Quarterly. Memberships: Royal Society of Literature; Society of Authors; Writers' Guild of Great Britain; British Academy of Film and Television Arts; Fellow, English PEN. Address: Apt 5, 3 Cambridge Gate, London NW1 4JX, England. E-mail: rosemaryfriedman@hotmail.com Website: www.rosemaryfriedman.co.uk

FRIEDMAN Isaiah, b. 28 April 1921, Luck, Poland. University Professor Emeritus; Historian. m. Barbara Joan Braham, 1 son. Education: BA, 1945, MA, 1945, Jewish History, Hebrew University, Jerusalem; PhD, International History, London School of Economics and Political Science,

University of London, 1964. Appointments: Research Fellow, Hebrew University, 1965-68; Fellow, Deutsche Forschungsgemeinschaft, 1968-71; Associate Professor, Modern Jewish History and Political Science, Dropsie University, Philadelphia, 1971-77; Professor of History, Ben-Gurion University, Beersheba, Israel, 1977-91; Professor Emeritus of History, 1991-. Publications: Books: The Question of Palestine, 1914-1918, British-Jewish-Arab Relations, 1973, 2nd and expanded edition, 1992 (also in Hebrew); Germany, Turkey and Zionism, 1897-1918, 1977, 2nd edition, 1998 (also in Hebrew); The Rise of Israel: A Documentary Record, 12 volumes, 1987; Palestine: A Twice Promised Land? (also in Hebrew), 2000; Editor, Sefer Luck (Hebrew), 2007; Co-editor, Encyclopaedia Judaica, 2007; Contributed numerous articles and entries. Honour: Recipient Theodor Körner Foundation Prize, University of Vienna, 1964. Memberships: Fellow, American Philosophical Society, 1971-76; Fellow, American Council Learned Society, 1972; Fellow, The Lucius Littauer Foundation, 1972; Fellow, American Academy for Jewish Research, 1975; Member, World Jewish Studies; Oriental Society of Israel. Address: 39 Sigalon Street, Omer 84-965, Beersheba, Israel.

FRIEDRICH Fabian, b. 2 May 1965, Blumenau, Santa Catarina, Brazil. Biochemist; Molecular Biologist. Education: Graduation, Biochemistry, Universidade Federal de Santa Catarina, Brazil, 1988; Postgraduate Specialisation, Biotechnology, Universidade Federal do Rio Grande do Sul, Brazil, 1988; Master Degree, Parasitology, Molecular Biology, Institute Oswaldo Cruz, Fiocruz, Brazil, 1993; Doctorate (PhD), Cell and Molecular Biology, Instituto Oswaldo Cruz, Fiocruz, Brazil, 1996. Appointments: Working with molecular biology and biotechnology, for past 16 years. Publications: Images of UFOs; UFOs: The Search for Unidentified Flying Objects and Unknown Civilizations Continues ... (exobiology and ufology); Articles in professional biomedical journals and nucleotide sequences published in the gene bank. Honours: Listed in numerous biographical directories. Membership: Brazilian Society of Virology, 1993-2000. Address: Rua Vasco da Gama, 69, Blumenau- Santa Catarina, Cep 89.065-080, Brazil.

FRIER Brian Murray, Consultant Physician; Honorary Professor of Diabetes. m. Isobel Wilson, 1 daughter. Education: BSc (Honours Class 1), Physiology, 1969, MB ChB, 1972, MD, 1981, University of Edinburgh. Appointments: Junior medical appointments in Edinburgh and Dundee, 1972-76; Clinical Research Fellow, Cornell University Medical Center, The New York Hospital, New York, USA, 1976-77; Senior Medical Registrar, Edinburgh, 1978-82; Consultant Physician, Western Infirmary and Gartnavel General Hospital, Glasgow, 1982-87; Consultant Physician, Royal Infirmary of Edinburgh, 1987-, and Honorary Professor of Diabetes, University of Edinburgh, 2001-. Publications: Books co-edited with B M Fisher: Hypoglycaemia and Diabetes, Clinical and Physiological Aspects, 1993; Hypoglycaemia in Clinical Diabetes, 1999; Hypoglycaemia and Clinical Diabetes, Second Edition, 2007; Original publications in peer reviewed journals, review articles, editorials and book chapters on hypoglycaemia, insulin therapy, complications of diabetes, driving and diabetes etc. Honours: R D Lawrence Lecturer of British Diabetic Association, 1986; Somogyi Award of the Hungarian Diabetes Association for hypoglycaemia research, 2004. Memberships: MRCP (UK), 1974; FRCP (Edin), 1984; FRCP (Glas), 1986; Chairman of Honorary Medical Advisory Committee on Driving and Diabetes to Secretary of State for Transport; Council Member 2002-, Royal College of Physicians of Edinburgh; Chairman, Chief Scientist Office committee on Diabetes Research in Scotland 2003-2006. Address: Department of Diabetes, Royal Infirmary, Edinburgh EH16 4SA, Scotland.

FRIGGIERI Oliver, b. 27 March 1947, Furjana, Malta. Professor; Poet; Novelist; Critic. m. Eileen, 1 daughter. Education: BA, cum laude, 1968; MA, 1975; PhD, 1978. Appointments: Full Professor; Ex-Head of Department of Maltese, University of Malta, 1987-2005; Presenter of radio programmes; Guest Speaker at numerous academic and literary international congresses in Europe. Publications: Numerous books in Maltese, most of which have been translated and published in numerous languages; History of Maltese Literature; Dictionary of Literary Terms; Numerous scholarly articles in Maltese, English, Italian, published in major international magazines; Translator, various works from Latin, English, Italian into Maltese; Guest Poet in various international poetry recitals throughout Europe; Books: Storia della Letteratura Maltese; Rituel du Crepuscule; Nous Sommes un Desir; La Menzogna; Storie per una Sera; La cultura italiana a Malta – Dun Karm; It-Tfal Jigu Bil-Vapuri; Fil-Parlament ma Jikbrux Fjuri; Koranta and other Short Stories from Malta; A Mentira; Author of various oratorios and cantatas. Honours: Holder of various international literary awards including Premio Mediterraneo Internazionale, Palermo and Premio Internazionale Trieste Poesia, 2002; Holder of the Maltese Government Prize for Literature; Guest Lecturer in various foreign Universities; Member of the Order of Merit, Maltese Government, 1999. Memberships: Association International des Critiques Litteraire, Paris; Member PEN Club Switzerland. Address: Department of Maltese, University of Malta, Msida, Malta.

FRITZE Lothar, b. 5 April 1954, Karl-Marx-Stadt. Researcher; Political analyst. m. Ulrike Fritze Otto, 2 sons. Education: Dipl-Ing oec, Betriebswirtschaft, 1978; Dr phil, Promotion in Philosophie, 1988; Dr phil habil, Habilitation in Politikwissenschaft, 1998. Appointments: Scientific collaborator, Forschungsinstitut fuer Textiltechnologie, Karl-Marx-Stadt, 1978-90; Institut fuer Wirtschafts u Sozialforschung, Chemnitz, 1992-93; Hannah-Arendt-Institut fuer Totalitarismusforschung, Dresden, 1993-. Publications: Books: Innenansicht eines Ruins: Gedanken zum Untergang der DDR, 1993; Panoptikum DDR-Wirtschaft: Machtverhaeltnisse, Organisationsstrukturen, Funktionsmechanismen, 1993; Die Gegenwart des Vergangenen: Ueber das Weiterleben der DDR nach ihrem Ende, 1997; Taeter mit gutem Gewissen: Ueber menschliches Versagen im diktatorischen Sozialismus, 1998; Die Toetung Unschuldiger. Ein Dogma auf dem Pruefstand, 2004; Verfuehrung und Anpassung. Zur Logik der Weltanschauungsdiktatur, 2004; Die Moral des Bombenterrors. Alliierte Flaechenbombardements im Zweiten Weltkrieg; Numerous articles to professional journals. Honours: Außerplanmaßiger Professor, Technical University, Chemnitz; Award, Gesellschaft fuer Deutschlandforschung, 1998. Address: Georgistrasse 2, D-09127 Chemnitz, Germany.

FROLOV Sergei Vladimirovich, b. 14 August 1967, Leningrad, USSR. Mathematician; Physicist; Engineer; Educator. Education: Bachelor's Degree, Physics, 1989, Master's Degree, Mathematical Physics, 1993, St Petersburg State University; Doctor, Processes and Apparatus of Food Technology, St Petersburg State University of Refrigeration and Food Technologies, 1998. Appointments: Scientific Advisor, St Petersburg State University, 1991-95; Associate Professor, 1995-2000, Professor, 2000-, St Petersburg State University of Refrigeration and Food Technologies. Publications: Articles in scientific journals including: Physical Review, Theoretical and Mathematical Physics, Russia; Engineering Physical Journal, Russia; Journal of Applied Chemistry, Russia. Address: Flat 27, Italyanskaya St. 6, 191011, St Petersburg, Russia. E-mail: frol@sf1251.spb.edu

FROST Christopher Peter, b. 9 July 1950, Carlisle, England. Journalist; Academic. m. Vanessa, 3 daughters. Education: Postgraduate Diploma (Distinction), Higher Education, 1997; MA, Education, 1999. Appointments: Editor and Journalist, Bedfordshire Journal, 1970-80; Journalist, Blackpool Gazette, 1980-90; Senior Lecturer in Journalism, University of Central Lancashire, 1990-2002; Head of Journalism, 2002, Professor of Journalism, 2004-, Liverpool John Moores University. Publications: Media Ethics and Self Regulation, 2000; Reporting for Journalists, 2001; Designing for Newspapers and Magazines, 2003; Journalism Ethics and Regulation, 2007; Various academic papers; Various popular reports. Memberships: National Union of Journalists; Higher Education Academy; Association for Journalism Education. Address: Liverpool John Moores University, Dean Walters Building, St James Road, Liverpool L1 7BR, England. E-mail: c.p.frost@livjm.ac.uk

FROST David (Paradine) (Sir), b. 7 April 1939, Tenterden, Kent, England. Television Personality; Author. m. (1) Lynn Frederick, 1981, divorced 1982, (2) Lady Carina Fitzalan-Howard, 1983, 3 sons. Education: MA, Gonville and Caius College, Cambridge. Appointments: Various BBC TV series, 1962-; Many ITV series, 1966-; Chairman and Chief Executive, David Paradine Ltd, 1966-; Joint Founder and Director, TV-am, 1981-93; Regular appearances on US television. Publications: That Was the Week That Was, 1963; How to Live Under Labour, 1964; Talking with Frost, 1967; To England With Love, 1967; The Presidential Debate 1968, 1968; The Americans, 1970; Whitlam and Frost, 1974; I Gave Them a Sword, 1978; I Could Have Kicked Myself, 1982; Who Wants to be a Millionaire?, 1983; The Mid-Atlantic Companion (jointly), 1986; The Rich Tide (jointly), 1986; The World's Shortest Books, 1987; David Frost: An Autobiography, Part I: From Congregations to Audiences, 1993. Honours: Golden Rose Award, Montreux, 1967; Richard Dimbleby Award, 1967; Silver Medal, Royal Television Society, 1967; Officer of the Order of the British Empire, 1970; Religious Heritage of America Award, 1970; Emmy Awards, 1970, 1971; Albert Einstein Award, 1971; Knighted, 1993. Address: c/o David Paradine Ltd, 5 St Mary Abbots Place, London W8 6LS, England.

FRY Charles George, b. 15 August 1936, Piqua, Ohio, USA. Minister; Educator. m. Amy Euw, 3 sons, 1 daughter. Education: BA, Capital University; MA, PhD, Ohio State University; BD, M Div, Evangelical Lutheran Theological Seminary; DD (hc), Cranmer Seminary; D Ministry, Winebrenner Theological Seminary; STM, MRE, DRE, Holy Trinity; D Litt (hc), North Tennessee Bible Institute and Seminary. Appointments: Teacher, Texas A&M University, Texas, 1960-61; Teacher, Wittenberg University, Ohio, 1962-63; Ordained Lutheran Minister, 1963; Instructor, Assistant, Associate Professor, Capital University, Ohio, 1963-75; Adjunct Teaching (summer), Brock University, Ontario, 1964-; Adjunct Teaching, Reformed Bible College, Michigan, 1975-80; Director, Missions Education, Associate Professor, Concordia Theological Seminary, Indiana, 1975-83; Head, Social Studies department, Protestant Chaplain, Associate Professor, University of St Francis, Indiana, 1982-92; Adjunct Teaching, Indiana-Purdue University, Indiana, 1982-98; Chair, Professor, Philosophy and Theology,

Lutheran College of Health Professions, Indiana, 1992-98; Ordained Deacon, Priest, 1995, Bishop, 1996, Southern Episcopal Church; Professor, English Bible and Church History, Winebrenner Theological Seminary, Ohio, 1999-; Teaching Theologian: North Community Lutheran Church, Ohio, 3 years; First Community Church, Ohio, 2 years; Pahlavi Avenue Presbyterian Church, Iran, 2 years; American Church, Istanbul, 1969; Queenstown Lutheran Church, Singapore, 7 years; Broad Street Presbyterian Church, Pennsylvania, 3 times in residence; St George's Anglican Church, Singapore; Parish Priest, local churches in Texas, Ohio, Indiana, Michigan, Tennessee and overseas. Honours: Praestantia Award, Capital University, 1970; Citation, Concordia Historical Institute, St Louis, Missouri, 1977, 2005; Charles A Trentham Homiletics Award, 2003; Postdoctoral Fellow, Regional Council for International Education, 1969; Postdoctoral Fellowship, Ankara University, 1969; Joseph j Malone Postdoctoral Fellow, Egypt, 1986, United Arab Emirates, 1987; Chaplain, Military Order of St Lazarus of Jerusalem; Chaplain General, General Society of the War of 1812; Ohio State Chaplain; President, Ohio Society, 2005-08. Publications: 60 books; Hundreds of magazine and journal articles. Memberships: American College of Counselors; American Psychotherapy Association; American Board of Certified Chaplains; Society for the Cure of Souls; College of Pastoral Counseling, American Association of Integrative Medicine; British Interplanetary Association. Address: 158 West Union Street, Circleville, OH 43113, USA. E-mail: gfry@winebrenner.edu

FRY Stephen John, b. 24 August 1957. Actor; Writer. Education: Queen's College, Cambridge, England. Appointments: Columnist, The Listener, 1988-89, Daily Telegraph, 1990-; Appeared with Cambridge Footlights in revue, The Cellar Tapes, Edinburgh Festival, 1981; Re-wrote script: Me and My Girl, London, Broadway, Sydney, 1984; Plays: Forty Years On, Chichester Festival and London, 1984; The Common Pursuit, London, 1988 (TV, 1992); TV series: Alfresco, 1982-84; The Young Ones, 1983; Happy Families, 1984; Saturday Night Live, 1986-87; A Bit of Fry and Laurie, 1989-95; Blackadder's Christmas Carol, 1988; Blackadder Goes Forth, 1989; Jeeves and Wooster, 1990-92; Stalag Luft, 1993; Laughter and Loathing, 1995; Gormenghast, 2000; Fortysomething, 2003; A Bear Named Winnie, 2004; Tom Brown's Schooldays, 2005; Absolute Power, 2003-05; Bones, 2007; Kingdom, 2007; Radio: Loose Ends, 1986-87; Whose Line Is It Anyway?, 1987; Saturday Night Fry, 1987; Harry Potter and the Chamber of Secrets (Narrator, CD), 2002; Harry Potter and the Prisoner of Azkaban (Narrator, CD), 2004; Films: The Good Father; A Fish Called Wanda; A Handful of Dust; Peter's Friends, 1992; IQ, 1995; Wind in the Willows, 1997; Wilde, 1997; A Civil Action, 1997; Whatever Happened to Harold Smith? 2000; Relatives Values, 2000; Discovery of Heaven, 2001; Gosford Park, 2001; Thunderpants, 2002; Bright Young Things, 2003; Tooth, 2004; The Life and Death of Peter Sellers, 2004; MirrorMask, 2005; The Hitchhiker's Guide to the Galaxy (voice), 2005; A Cock and Bull Story, 2005; V for Vendetta, 2005; Stormbreaker, 2006; Eichmann, 2007; St Trinian's, 2007. Publications: Paperweight (collected essays), 1992; The Liar (novel); The Hippopotamus, 1994; Fry and Laurie 4 (with Hugh Laurie), 1994; Paperweight, 1995; Making History, 1996; Moab is My Washpot (autobiography), 1997; The Star's Tennis Balls (novel), 2000. Honour: Hon LLD (Dundee), 1995. Memberships: Patron, Studio 3 (arts for young people); Freeze (nuclear disarmament charity); Amnesty International; Comic Relief. Address: c/o Hamilton Asper Management, Ground Floor, 24 Hanway Street, London, W1P 9DD, England.

FRYBA Ladislav, b. 30 May 1929, Studenec. Professor. m. Dagmar Frybova. Education: Ing, 1953, DSc, 1959, Docent, 1966, Professor, 1993, Czech Technical University; Doctor honoris causa, University of Pardubice, 2004. Appointments: Head, Bridge Department, Railway Research Institute, 1972-84; Professor, Institute of Theoretical and Applied Mechanics, Academy of Sciences of the Czech Republic, 1984-. Publications: 6 books, co-author 6 books, 201 papers in 9 world languages; Best known world-wide: Dynamics of Railway Bridges, 3rd edition, 1996; Vibration of Solids and Structures Under Moving Loads, 3rd edition, 1999. Honours: Medals, Czechoslovak Academy of Sciences, Czech Society for Mechanics; 5 medals from Japanese Universities and Society of Japanese Association of Mechanical Engineering; Diploma, European Association for Structural Dynamics; Listed in international biographical dictionaries. Memberships: Chairman, Committees of Experts of the European Rail Research Institute, Utrecht, 1967-2001; President, Czech Society for Mechanics, 1991-2007; President, European Association for Structural Dynamics, 1996-99; Member, Engineering Academy of the Czech Republic, 1996-; Research Board of Advisors, American Biographical Institute, 1999; Member, Editorial Board of the Journal of Sound and Vibration, 2001-.

FUENTES Carlos, b. 11 November 1928, Panama City, Panama. Professor of Latin American Studies; Writer. m. (1) Rita Macedo, 1957, 1 daughter, (2) Sylvia Lemus, 1973, 1 son, 1 daughter. Education: Law School, National University of Mexico; Institute de Hautes Études Internationales, Geneva. Appointments: Head, Cultural Relations Department, Ministry of Foreign Affairs, Mexico, 1955-58; Mexican Ambassador to France, 1975-77; Professor of English and Romance Languages, University of Pennsylvania, 1978-83; Professor of Comparative Literature, 1984-86, Robert F Kennedy Professor of Latin American Studies, 1987-, Harvard University; Simon Bolivar Professor, Cambridge University, 1986-87; Professor-at-Large, Brown University, 1995-. Publications: La Region Mas Transparente, 1958; Las Buenas Conciencias, 1959; Aura, 1962; La Muerte de Artemio Cruz, 1962; Cantar de Ciegos, 1964; Cambio de Piel, 1967; Zona Sagrada, 1967; Terra Nostra, 1975; Una Familia Lejana, 1980; Agua Quemada, 1983; Gringo Viejo, 1985; Cristóbal Nonato, 1987; Myself with Others (essays), 1987; Orchids in the Moonlight (play), 1987; The Campaign, 1991; The Buried Mirror, 1992; El Naranjo, 1993; Geography of the Novel: Essays, 1993; La frontera de cristal (stories), 1995; Los Años con Laura Diaz (novel), 1999; Los Cincosoles de Mexico (anthology), 2000; Inez, 2000; Ce que je crois, 2002; La Silla de Aguila, 2003; Contra Bush, 2004; Todas las Familias Felices, 2006. Contributions to: Periodicals. Honours: Biblioteca Breva Prize, Barcelona, 1967; Rómulo Gallegos Prize, Caracas, 1975; National Prize for Literature, Mexico, 1984; Miguel de Cervantes Prize for Literature, Madrid, 1988; Légion d'Honneur, France, 1992; Principe de Asturias Prize, 1992; Latin Civilisation Prize, French and Brazilian Academies, 1999; DLL, Ghent, 2000, Madrid, 2000; Mexican Senate Medal, 2000; Los Angeles Public Library Award, 2001; Commonwealth Award Delaware, 2002. Memberships: American Academy and Institute of Arts and Letters; El Colegio Nacional, Mexico; Mexican National Commission on Human Rights. Address: c/o Brandt & Brandt, 1501 Park Avenue, New York, NY 10036, USA.

FUENTES Martha Ayers, b. 21 December 1923, Ashland, Alabama, USA. m. Manuel Solomon Fuentes, 11 April 1943. Education: BA, Education University of South Florida, USA, 1969. Appointments: Playwright/Author, at present; Jewellery Sales, Tampa, Florida, 1940; Later served in various business positions; Author, 1953. Publications: Pleasure Button, full length play, 1995-96; Jordan's End, 1998. Honours: Iona Lester Scholarship, Creative Writing, University Southern Florida, George Sergel Drama Award, University of Chicago, Southeastern Writers Conference; Instructor, Playwriting and TV; Feature Writer for national magazines. Memberships: Dramatist Guild; Authors Guild; Florida Theatre Conference; North Carolina Writers' Network; Florida Studio Theatre, Sarasota, Florida; United Daughters of the Confederacy; Southern Heritage Society. Address: 102 Third Street, Belleair Beach, FL 33786-3211, USA.

FUJIMAKI Norio, b. 15 February 1953, Niigata, Japan. Researcher. m. 10 July 1988, 2 daughters. Education: BSc, 1975, MSc, 1977, PhD, 1980, Electronic Engineering, University of Tokyo. Appointments: Fujitsu Laboratories Ltd, 1980-99; National Institute of Information and Communications Technology (previous name, Communications Research Laboratories), 1999-. Publications: Neuromagnetism (co-author), 1997; Handbook of Quantum Engineering (co-author), 1999; Encyclopedia of Linguistic Sciences, 2006; Several articles in professional journals including: IEEE Transactions; Journal of Applied Physics; Neuroscience Research; Human Brain Mapping; Neuro Image; Co-author, Encyclopedia of Linguistic Sciences, 2006. Memberships: Institute of Electrical and Electronics Engineers; Institute of Electronics, Information and Communications Engineers; Japan Society of Applied Physics; Japan Biomagnetism and Biomagnetics Society; Japan Society of Medical Electronics and Biological Engineering; Society for Neuroscience; Japan Neuroscience Society. Address: Brain Information Group, National Institute of Information and Communications Technology, 588-2, Iwaoka, Iwaoka-cho, Nishi-ku, Kobe 651-2492, Japan. E-mail: fujimaki@po.nict.go.jp

FUJINO Kazuo, b. 22 September 1925, Tokyo, Japan. Emeritus Professor. m. Junko Suzuki, 1 son, 1 daughter. Education: Bachelor's degree, 1950, PhD, 1962, Tokyo University. Appointments: Research Worker, The Whales Research Institute, Tokyo, 1950-64; Programme Chief, US Department of Interior, Department of Commerce, Honolulu, Hawaii, USA, 1964-71; Affiliate Faculty, University of Hawaii, Genetics, Honolulu, 1965-71; Professor, 1972-91, Dean, 1982-86, Emeritus Professor, 1991-, Kitasato University, Sanriku, Japan. Publications: Over 100 original and reviewing scientific papers and books in genetics on marine animals, 1953-97; Genetically Distinct Skipjack Tuna Subpopulations Appeared in the Central and the Western Pacific Ocean, 1996; Population Genetic Studies on Marine Fish - Seeking Way to Explore New Order in International Fisheries, 1999. Honour: Superior Performance Award, US Department of Interior, 1969. Membership: Honorary Member, President, 1980-90, Japanese Society of Fish Genetics and Breeding Science. Address: 2-28-22 Shakujiidai, Nerima, Tokyo 177-0045, Japan. Email: katsabal@sepia.ocn.ne.jp

FUJITA Masayuki, b. 15 August 1956, Takamatsu, Kagawa, Japan. Biologist; Educator. m. Tomoko, 1 son. Education: BS, Chemistry, Shizuoka University, Faculty of Science, 1975-79; Doctor of Agriculture, Biochemistry, Nagoya University, Graduate School of Bioagricultural Sciences, 1979-83. Appointments: Assistant Professor, 1983-91, Associate Professor, 1991-99, Professor, 1999-, Kagawa University; Serving concurrently as Professor, Ehime University and The United Graduate School of Agricultural Sciences, 1999-; Researcher, Institute of Biological Chemistry, Washington State University, USA, 1996-97. Publications: Plant Infection,

1982; Handbook of Phytoalexin Metabolism and Action, 1995; Lignin and Lignan Biosynthesis, 1998; Biochemistry and Molecular Biology of Plant Stress, 2001; Floriculture, Ornamental and Plant Biotechnology, Vol III, 2006. Honour: Fellow, Co-operative Research Programme: Biological Resource Management for Sustainable Agricultural Systems, Organisation for Economic Co-operation and Development (OECD). Memberships: American Society of Plant Biologists; Phytochemical Society of North America; International Society for Horticultural Science. Address: Kagawa University; 2393 Ikenobe Miki-cho, Kagawa 761-0795, Japan. E-mail: fujita@ag.kagawa-u.ac.jp

FUKASAWA Ryoko, b. 22 June 1938, Togane City, Chiba Prefecture, Japan. Pianist. m. Tomoyuki Fukasawa, 2 October 1967, deceased. Education: Hochschule für Musik und darstellende Kunst, Vienna, 1956-59. Debut: Recital in Tokyo with Tokyo Symphonia Orchestra, 1953; Recital in Vienna, 1959. Career: Regular concerts with Tonkünstler Orchester conducted by E Märzendorfer and others, Musikverein, since 1960; NHK Symphony Orchestra conducted by S Ozawa in Tokyo, 1963; Wiener Kammer Orchester conducted by A Quadri, 1965; NHK Symphony Orchestra, conducted by L von Matačić, 1966; Concert tours of Western Europe, Hungary and Japan, 1965-68; Concert tours in Central Europe (as a Cultural Envoy for Music) in 1992, and in South America and Asia in the 1980s; Television and radio appearances in Japan and Europe; Numerous premieres of contemporary music in Japan and Europe. Recordings: Encore Album, 1988; Piano Recital, 1989; Beethoven Violin Sonata, 1991; Schubert and Beethoven, 1992; Trout Quintet with Wiener Kammer Ensemble, 1992; Moments Musicaux, 1997; Mozart Recital, 1999; W A Mozart, 12 variations on the French song, "Ah, vous dirai-je, Maman", 2005. Publications: Diary for the Piano, 1955; Diary from Vienna, 1957; Schubert and Vienna, pocketbook on music, 1980; The Piano and Me, 1991. Honours: 1st Prize at the Student Music Competition in Japan, 1950; 1st Prize, Japan Music Competition organised by NHK and Mainichi Newspaper, 1953; Top Prize, Geneva International Music Competition, 1961; Osaka Theatre Incentive Award, 1963, Distinguished Service in the field of culture, 1995. Memberships: Japan Piano Teachers Association; Japanese Federation of Musicians; Committee for Music and Dance in Japan. Address: 2-18-1 Chome, Tamagawa Denenchofu, Setagaya-ku, Tokyo 158-0085, Japan.

FULLER Betty Stamps, b. 19 February 1938, Prentiss, Mississippi, USA. Music Educator. m. Allan R Fuller, 2 daughers. Education: Prentiss High School, 1953-56; Attended Mississippi College, Clinton, Mississippi, 1958; Bachelor of Liberal Arts, McNeese State University, Lake Charles, Louisiana; Postgraduate, Loyola University, New Orleans, Louisiana. Appointments: Director, Youth String Orchestra Program, Mississippi College, 1967-72; Music Educator, Episcopal Day School, Lake Charles, 1975-85; Music Educator, Our Lady's Catholic School, Sulphur, 1985-2005; Mentor Teacher for Student Teachers, Catholic Education University, Notre Dame, South Bank, Indiana, 2000-01. Honours: Board member, Lake Charles Symphony Orchestra, 1975-77; Citizen of the Day, Radio Station KLOU (for work with Lake Charles Symphony); Teacher of the Year, Episcopal Day School, Lake Charles, 1980; Teacher of the Year, Our Lady's Catholic School, Sulphur, 1995. Memberships: Calcasieu Parish, Lake Charles; Vocal Music Teachers' Association. Address: 2715 Roxton Street, Sulphur, LA 70663, USA.

FULLER Cynthia Dorothy, b. 13 February 1948, Isle of Sheppey, England. Poet; Adult Education Tutor. Divorced, 2 sons. Education: BA Honours, English, Sheffield University, 1969; Postgraduate Certificate of Education, Oxford University, 1970; MLitt, Aberdeen University, 1979. Appointments: Teacher of English, Redborne School, 1970-72; Freelance in Adult Education, University Departments at Durham and Newcastle Universities, also Open University and Workers Education Association. Publications: Moving towards Light, 1992; Instructions for the Desert, 1996; Only a Small Boat, 2001; Jack's Letters Home 1917-18, 2006. Contributions to: Poems in various magazines including: Other Poetry; Iron; Poetry Durham; Literary Review. Honour: Northern Arts Financial Assistance. Address: 28 South Terrace, Esh Winning, Co Durham DH7 9PR, England.

FUNABASHI Yochi, b. 15 December 1944, Beijing, China. Journalist. m. Reiko, 1 son, 1 daughter. Education: BA, University of Tokyo, 1968; Neiman Fellowship, Harvard University, 1975-76; PhD, Keio University, 1992. Appointments: Beijing Correspondent, 1980-81, Washington Correspondent, 1984-87, American General Bureau Chief, 1993-97, Columnist and Chief Diplomatic Correspondent, 1997-2007, Editor-in-Chief, 2007-, Asahi Shimbun; Visiting Fellow, Institute for International Economics, 1987; Donald Keene Fellow, Columbia University, 2003; Distinguished Guest Scholar, Brookings Institution, Washington, DC, 2005-06. Publications: Numerous book including most recently, The Peninsula Question: A Chronicle of the Second Korean Nuclear Crisis, 2007; Many articles and papers in professional journals. Honours: Vaughn-Ueda Prize, 1985; Yoshino Sakuzo Prize, 1988; Ishibashi Tanzan Prize, 1992; Japan Press Award, 1994; Mainichi Shimbun Asia Pacific Grand Prix Award, 1995; Shincho Arts and Sciences Award, 1998. Memberships: International Crisis Group; Trilateral Commission; Asia Society; Brookings Institution's Center for Northeast Asian Policy Studies; The Washington Quarterly; The Prime Minister's Commission on Japan's Goals in the 21st Century; Government Commission for Reform of the Foreign Ministry. E-mail: ja6868@sepia.ocn.ne.jp

FUNDAMENSKI Wojciech Robert, b. 1969, Poland (Polish and Canadian citizen). Plasma Physicist; Nuclear Engineer. Education: Bachelor's degree, Engineering Science, 1992, PhD, Plasma Physics and Nuclear Fusion, 1999, University of Toronto, Canada; Master's degree, Nuclear Fusion Engineering, McMaster University, 1994. Appointments: Leading expert, edge plasma transport, power exhaust and plasma-surface interactions; Boundary Plasma Expert, Euratom/UKAEA Fusion Association, Abington, England, 1999-; Deputy Leader, EFDA-JET Task Force Exhaust EFDA-JET, Abington, 2004-; EU representative, Divertor and SOL International Tokamak Physics Activity; Visiting Lecturer in Plasma Physics, Imperial College London, 2007-. Publications: Author or co-author of over 100 articles in professional scientific journals; Book, Power Exhaust in Fusion Plasmas, in progress; Numerous talks at over 30 international conferences and workshops. Honours: Dean's Honour List, University of Toronto, 1988-92; Canada Scholarship, Government of Canada, 1988-92; Wilfred McCleary Scholarship, University of Toronto, 1989-90; The Association of Professional Engineers of Ontario Scholarship, 1990; Centennial Scholarship, McMaster University, 1992-93; Graduate Fellowship, Canadian Fusion Fuels Technology Project, 1992-97; Open Fellowship, University of Toronto, 1996-98; NSERC Post-Doctoral Fellowship, Government of Canada, 2000-01; G N Paterson Millennium Award, UTIAS, 2000; Nominated for NSERC Doctorate Award, University of Toronto, 2000. Memberships: Institute of Physics; Plasma Physics Committee. Address: Euratom/UKAEA Fusion Association, Culham Science Centre, Abingdon, Oxfordshire OX14 3DB, England. E-mail: wfund@jet.uk

FUNG Wye-Poh, b. 9 January 1937, Telok-Anson, Malaysia. Consultant Physician; Gastroenterologist. m. Saw-Lin Fung, 1 son, 1 daughter. Education: MB, BS, University of Malaya, Singapore, 1961; MRACP, Melbourne, 1965; FRACP, 1972; FACG, 1972; MD, University of Singapore, 1972; FAMS, 1978. Appointments: Assistant Lecturer, Clinical Medicine, University of Singapore, 1964-65; Research Fellow, Gastroenterology, A W Morrow, Department of Gastroenterology, Royal Prince Alfred Hospital, Camperdown, Sydney, 1965-66; Lecturer, Clinical Medicine, 1965-70, Senior Lecturer, Medicine, 1970-74, Associate Professor, Medicine, 1975, University of Singapore, Singapore General Hospital; Associate Physician, Department of General Medicine, Royal Perth Hospital, 1975-76; Senior Lecturer, Medicine, University of Western Australia, Royal Perth Hospital, 1976-85; Visiting Associate Professor, Department of Medicine and GI Unit, University of California, San Francisco, 1981-82; Consultant Physician, Gastroenterologist, Private Practice, 1985-; Gastroenterologist, Swan District Hospital, 1985-; St John of God Hospital, Wembly, Australia, 1986-; Osborne Park Hospital, 1986-; Armadale-Kelmscott Hospital, 1987-, Perth, Western Australia. Publications: Numerous articles in professional journals. Memberships: Foundation Secretary, Treasurer, Gastroenterological Society of Singapore, 1967-75; Gastroenterological Society of Australia, 1975-. Address: Mount Claremont, WA 6010, Australia.

FURUKUBO-TOKUNAGA Katsuo, b. 24 September 1954, Nagoya, Japan. Professor. m. Midori Furukubo, 1 daughter. Education: BSc, Kyoto University, 1978; MSc, 1980, Doctorate, Science, 1983, Nagoya University, Japan; Advanced Graduate Course, National Institute of Basic Biology, Okazaki, Japan, 1983. Appointments: Research Fellow, National Institute of Basic Biology, Okazaki, 1983; Senior Researcher, Chiba Cancer Center, Chiba, Japan, 1983-88; Senior Research Associate, 1988-92, Assistant Professor, 1992-95, University of Basle, Switzerland; Associate Professor, University of Tsukuba, Ibaraki, Japan, 1995; Project Leader, Tsukuba Advanced Research Alliance, Ibaraki, Japan, 2000-2006; Chief research achievement: Discovery of Cross-phylum conservation of genetic programs of brain development between fruitflies and human. Publications: Numerous research papers and articles in specialist peer-reviewed journals such as Cell Press; Proceedings of the National Academy of Sciences, USA; Genes and Development; Development. Honours: Research grant, Roche Research Foundation, 1993-95; Research grant, Swiss National Science Foundation, 1994-97; Research grant, The Yamaha Science Foundation, 1996-97; Research grant, Tsukuba Advanced Research Alliance, 2000-2006. Memberships: Numerous scientific and professional affiliations including, The Genetical Society, UK; The Genetics Society of America; Society for Neuroscience; The Japanese Society of Developmental Biologists; The Molecular Biology Society of Japan; Japan Neuroscience Society. Address: Institute of Biological Sciences, University of Tsukuba, Tennodai 1-1-1-, Tsukuba, Ibaraki, Japan.

FURUTA Satoshi, b. 15 August 1969, Kyoto, Japan. Reaction Chemistry. Education: Graduate, Tokyo University, 1992; Doctorate, 2008. Appointments: Researcher, Nippon Mining Corporation, 1992; Researcher, 1994, 2005, Senior Researcher, 2007, Japan Energy Corporation; External Researcher, Total SA, France, 2004. Honours: Thesis prize, Society of Automotive Engineers of Japan, 2006; Noguchi Memorial awards for Encouragement of R&D, Japan Petroleum Institute, 2007. Memberships: Japan Petroleum Institute; Society of Chemical Engineers, Japan; Combustion Society of Japan. E-mail: s.furuta@j-energy.co.jp

FURUYAMA Masaaki, b. 20 January 1961, Tokyo, Japan. Professor. m. Masako Kita, 2 sons. Education: LLB, Waseda University, 1983; LLM, Hitotsubashi University, 1985. Appointments: Assistant Professor, 1988-91, Associate Professor, 1991-2001, Professor, 2001-, Faculty of Economics, Nagasaki University; Member, Disciplinary Committee, Nagasaki Bar Association, 1992-; Research Member of Committee Authorising Textbooks for the Ministry of Education, 1994. Publications: M&A and Law, A Study on the Takeover Bid Regulation, 2005. Memberships: Japan Association of Economic Law; Japan Association of Private Law. Address: Faculty of Economics Nagasaki University, 4-2-1 Katafuchi Nagasaki, 850-8506, Japan.

FUSCHETTO Brian M, b. 12 February 1976. Business and Computer Studies Teacher. Education: ASEd (honours), Bergen Community College, 1996; BSEd (summa cum laude), Montclair State University, 1999; Masters in Business Administration, in progress; Masters in Educational Leadership, in progress. Appointments: Accounts Payable Controller, Video Services Corp, 1994-99; Northern Highlands Regional High School, Allendale, New Jersey, 1999-2002; Bogota High School, Bogota, New Jersey, 2002-03; Lyndhurst High School, Lyndhurst, New Jersey, 2003-. Honours: Bergen Community College Dean's List, 1994, 1995, 1996; Montclair State University Dean's List, 1996, 1997, 1998, 1999; National Dean's List, 1995, 1996, 1997, 1998, 1999; Pi Omega Pi National Honor Society, President 1998-99; Dean's Award, Outstanding Academic Achievement, Montclair State University, 1999; Dean's Award, Outstanding Service, Montclair State University, 1999; Outstanding Teacher Candidate Award, New Jersey Association of Teachers, 1999; Student of the Year, National Business Education Association, 1999; Student of the Year, New Jersey Business Education Association, 1999; Phi Kappa Phi International Honor Society; Alpha Lambda International Honor Society of Graduate Students; Golden Key National Honor Society; Who's Who Among America's Teachers, 2002, 2003, 2004-2005, 2006; Leading Educators of the World, 2005, 2006; American Medal of Honor, 2006; Great Minds of the 21st Century, 2006. Memberships: DECA New Jersey State Advisory Board; Montclair State University Master's Program Advisory Board; National Education Association; National Business Education Association; SASI Administration Software Consultant; Association of Curriculum Development; Computer Science Teacher's Association; Intervention and Referral Services Child Crisis Team, Lyndhurst High School. Address: 321 Prospect Avenue, Apt C6, Hackensack, NJ 07601, USA. E-mail: fuschettob@aol.com

FUSHIMI Masahito, b. 4 May 1964, Hokkaido, Japan. Psychiatrist. m. Hiromi, 1 son, 2 daughters. Education: MD, 1990, PhD, 1997, Akita University School of Medicine, Japan. Appointments: Medical Staff, Department of Neuropsychiatry, Akita University School of Medicine, 1990-91, 2000-03; Director, Akita Prefectural Mental Health & Welfare Centre, Daisen city, 2003-. Publications: PLEDs in Creutzfeldt-Jakob disease following a cadaveric dural graft, 2002; Benign bilateral independent periodic lateralized epileptiform discharges, 2003; Progression of P300 in a patient with bilateral hippocampal lesions, 2005;

Suicide patterns and characteristics in Akita, Japan, 2005. Memberships: Japan Medical Association; Japanese Society of Psychiatry and Neurology; Japanese Society of Clinical Neurophysiology; Japanese Society of Biofeedback Research; International Association for Suicide Prevention. Address: 352 Gohyakukarita, Kyowa-kamiyodokawa, Daisen city, Akita prefecture, 019-2413, Japan.

FUTKO Sergey Ivanovich, b. 11 June 1968, Minsk, Belarus. Research Scientist; Physicist. Education: MSc, Honours, Moscow Physico-Technical Institute, 1991; Internship, University of Illinois at Chicago, USA, 1997; PhD, Honours, Byelorussian Academy of Sciences, 2003. Appointments: Junior Research Scientist, 1994-2001, Research Scientist, 2001-2004, Senior Research Scientist, 2004-, Heat and Mass Transfer Institute, NAS, Minsk, Belarus. Publications: Articles in scientific journals: Models of FCG with Allowance for Flame Turbulence, 2002; Effect of Kinetic Properties of a Mixture on Wave Macrocharacteristics of Filtration Combustion of Gases, 2003; Mechanism of Upper Temperature Limits in a Wave of FCG, 2003; Kinetic Analysis of the Chemical Structure of Waves of FCG in Fuel-Rich Compositions, 2003; Analysis of NOx Formation in FC of methane-air mixtures, 2003; Book: Chemistry of Filtration Combustion of Gases, 2004. Honours: Listed in Who's Who publications and biographical dictionaries; International Scientist of the Year, 2005. Address: Institute of Heat and Mass Transfer, P Brovki 15, Minsk, 220072, Belarus. E-mail: foutko@itmo.by

FYODOROV Nikolai Vasilyevich, b. 9 May 1958, Chuvash Republic. Politician. m. Svetlana Yuryevna Fyodorova, 1 son, 1 daughter. Education: Graduate, Law Faculty, Kazan State University, 1980; Cand. Sc. (Law), Moscow Institute of State and Law, 1985; Appointments: Teacher, Chuvash State University, 1980-82, 1986-89; Member, USSR Supreme Soviet, 1989-91; Minister of Justice of Russia, 1990-93; President of Chuvash Republic, 1994-, re-elected, 1997 and 2001; Member, Council of Federation, 1996-2002; Representative of Russia in the Parliamentary Assembly of Council of Europe. Publications: More than 100 books and articles in economy, law and national relations. Honours: State Counsellor of Justice of Russia; The Russian Federation State Prize in the field of science and technology for restoration of the historical part of Cheboxary, 1999; Order, For Merits in Fatherland IV class; The highest All-Russian Femida Prize, 1997; Peter the Great National Prize; Honorary Construction Worker of Russia; Order of the Saint Duke Daniil Moskovskii 1 class and Order of Reverend Sergii Radonezhskii, Russian Orthodox Church. Address: 1 Republic Square, House of Government, 428004 Cheboxary, Chuvash Republic, Russia. E-mail: president@cap.ru

G

GABRIEL Peter, b. 13 February 1950, Cobham, Surrey, England. Singer; Composer. m. (1) Jill Moore, 1971, divorced, 1987, 2 children, (2) Meabh Flynn, 2002, 1 child. Appointments: Co-Founder, Genesis, 1966; Solo Artiste, 1975-; Appearances worldwide in concerts; Founder, World of Music, Arts and Dance (WOMAD), music from around the world, 1982; Founder, Real World Group, 1985; Real World Studios, 1986; Real World Records, 1989; Real World Multimedia, 1994; Launched Witness Human Rights Programme, 1992. Creative Works: Singles: Solsbury Hill; Games Without Frontiers; Shock The Monkey; Sledgehammer; In Your Eyes; Don't Give Up; Biko; Big Time; Red Rain; Digging in the Dirt; Steam; Blood of Eden; Kiss That Frog; Solo albums: PG I-IV, PG Plays Live, 1983; So, 1986; Shaking the Tree (compilation), 1990; Us, 1992; Ovo, 2000; Up, 2002; Big Blue Ball, 2007; Soundtrack albums: Birdy; Passion (Last Temptation of Christ). Honours: Ivor Novello Awards, 1983, 1987; Brit Awards, 1987, 1993; 9 Music Video Awards; Video Vanguard Trophy, 1987; Grammy Awards, 1990, 1993; Q Magazine Lifetime Achievement Award, 2006; Ivor Novello Award for Lifetime Achievement, 2007. Address: c/o Real World, Box Mill, Box, Wiltshire, SN14 9PL, England.

GABRIEL Vincent Albert, b. 30 August 1942, Singapore. Management Consultant. m. Chua Lim Neo, 2 sons. Education: BSc (Hons) Economics, University of London, England; Certificate in Education, Singapore; Diploma in Marketing, UK; Certificate in Non-Formal Education; Certificate in Urban Education. Appointments: Secondary School Educator, 1961-72; Supervisor in Advanced Training Techniques, 1973-79; Curriculum Advisor, 1979-80; Management Consultant, 1980-. Publications: Management; A Guide to Management of Business; Management of Business; At Your Finger Tips: Physical Geography, Economic Geography, Elective Geography; Success in the Retail Business; Success in Franchising; Success as an Education Provider. Honours: Best in the World in English (LCCI); Second Prize, National Banking Essay Competition; Joint First in Asian Productivity Organisation; Joint First, Institute of Administration Management Essay Competition; Prize Winner, Switch Sounds of the Century; Long Service Award; Chinese Chamber of Commerce. Website: www.foodweath.com

GADA Manilal Talakshi, b. 12 January 1947, Gujarat, India. Psychiatrist. m. Manjula, 2 daughters. Education: MBBS, University of Bombay, 1971; DPM, College of Physicians and Surgeons of Bombay, 1975; MD, University of Bombay, 1976. Appointments: Professor of Psychiatry, Padamashree Dr D Y Patil Medical College (deemed University); Head, Department of Psychiatry and Psychiatrist, Rajawadi Municipal General Hospital; Retired; Senior Specialist (Psychiatrist), Panel Consultant, Oil and Natural Gas Commission, Bombay Region; Honorary Psychiatrist, Sulabha School for Mentally Retarded Children; Post Graduate Teacher and Examiner for DPM, DNB; Psychiatrist, Dr L H Hiranandani Hospital, Powai, Bombay; Conducts continuing medical education programmes for family physicians. Publications include: Defeat Depression: A Guide for Patients and Their Family Members, 1994, 2nd edition, 1998; Mansik Hatasha Hatao (book in local Gujarati language), 1998; Defeat Depression, 4th edition, 2000, reprint 2001, reprint 2005; Stress Management: Holistic Approach, 2001, reprint 2002, revised 2nd edition, 2006; Khinnata Nakoj (Defeat Depression, book in local Marathi language), 2003; Co-editor, Essentials of Post-graduate Psychiatry, 2005; Chitabraham, book on schizophrenia in local Gujarati language, 2005; Essential information on

schizophrenia, 2004, reprint 2006; 8 book chapters; More than 60 papers in scientific journals, newspaper article on Psychiatry every fortnight. Honours include: Invited by WHO Mental Health Division to participate in a Multicentric Study on Depressive Disease; Tilak Venkoba Rao Oration Award, Indian Psychiatric Society, 1987; President, Lions Club of Bombay Pantnagar, 1994-95; Late Dr R K Menda Oration Award, Indian Medical Association, Nagpur Branch, 1995; Late Dr S M Lulla Oration Award, Bombay Psychiatric Society, 2000; West Zone President's Award, 1984, 1997; District Committee Chairman, Lions District 323A2 of Lions Club International, 1998-; Lions International President's Appreciation Certificate, 2003; Essential Information on Schizophrenia, 2004, reprint 2006; Chitabraham (book on schizophrenia in local Gujarati language), 2005; Dr L P Shah Oration Award, Indian Psychiatric Society West Zone, 2006. Memberships include: Life Fellow, Indian Psychiatric Society; Chair, Biological Psychiatry Section, 1997-99; Chair, Ethics Committee, 2001-03, 2003-05; Chairman, Organising Committee of 58th Annual Conference of Indian Psychiatric Society, 2006; Life Fellow, Indian Psychiatric Society - West Zone, President, 1994-95; Life Fellow, Bombay Psychiatric Society, President, 1989-90; Life Fellow, Indian Association of Private Psychiatry; Founder Life Fellow, Indian Association for Child and Adolescent Mental Health; Life Member, Kutchi Medicos Association, President, 1992-94; Life Member Indian Medical Association; Member, Editorial Board of Archives of Indian Psychiatry, journal of Indian Psychiatric Society West Zone. Address: 201 Kumudini, Above Andhra Bank, 7th Road, Rajawadi, Ghatkopar (East), Bombay 400 077, India.

GADDAFI Colonel Mu'ammar Muhammad al, b. 1942, Serte, Libya. Libyan Army Officer; Political Leader. m. 1970, 8 children. Education: University of Libya, Benghazi. Appointments: Served, Libyan Army, 1965-; Chair, Revolutionary Command Council, 1969-; Commander-in-Chief of Armed Forces, 1969; Prime Minister, 1970-72; Minister of Defence, 1970-72; Secretary General of General Secretariat of General Peoples Congress, 1977-79; Chair, OAU, 1982-83. Publications: The Green Book, 3 vols; Military Strategy and Mobilization; The Story of the Revolution. Honours: Title, Colonel; Rank of Major-General, 1976. Membership: President, Council, Federation of Arab Republics, 1972. Address: Office of the President, Tripoli, Libya.

GADSBY Roger, b. 2 March 1950, Coventry, England. General Practitioner. m. Pamela Joy, 1 son, 1 daughter. Education: BSc (Hons), Medical Biochemical Studies, 1971, MB ChB (Hons), Obstetrics and Gynaecology, 1974, Birmingham University Medical School; Post qualification experience in hospitals in Birmingham and Stoke-on-Trent, GP training in Stoke. Appointments: Full-time General Practitioner, now Senior Partner, Redroofs Practice, Nuneaton Warwickshire, 1979-; Part-time Associate Clinical Professor, University of Warwick, 1992-; Co-Founder, Warwick Diabetes Care, 2000. Publications: Over 150 papers and articles on diabetes and pregnancy sickness symptoms; 2 textbooks on diabetes; 2 chapters on diabetes issues in primary care in major diabetes textbooks. Honours: DCH, 1978; DRCOG, 1978; MRCGP (by examination), 1978; FRCGP (by election), 1992. Memberships: Fellow, Royal College of General Practitioners; Diabetes (UK); Primary Care Diabetes Society; American Diabetes Association; British Medical Association; Chairman of Trustees, Pregnancy Sickness Support Charity. Address: Rivendell, School Lane, Exhall, Coventry, CV7 9GF, England. E-mail: rgadsby@doctors.org.uk

GAFUROV Ravil Gabdrakhmanovich, b. 18 April 1930, Chistopol, Republic of Tatarstan, Russia. Chemist; Investigator. m. Margarita Pavlovna, 1 son. Education: Engineer, Chemist-Technologist, Technology Organic Synthesis (1st class honours), 1948-53, Candidate of Chemical Science (the first higher science degree in USSR and Russia), 1964, Kazan State Technological University, Kazan, Republic of Tatarstan, Russia; PhD, Chemical Science, Zelinski Institute of Organic Chemistry, Russian Academy of Science (RAS), Moscow, 1978, Professor on Organic Chemistry, 1982, and Bioorganic Chemistry, 1990, Institute of Physiologically Active Compounds RAS, Chernoglovka, Moscow, Russia; Engineer, Telecomputer Science, Moscow Aviation Institute, Moscow, 1989-90. Appointments: Student, 1948-53, Senior Laboratory Assistant, 1953-56, Post Graduate Student, 1956-59, Assistant Lecturer, 1959-65, Kazan State Technological University, Kazan, Republic of Tartarstan, Russia; Senior Scientific Worker, Institute of Chemical Physics Problems RAS, Chernogolovka, Moscow area, Russia, 1965-80; Scientific Deputy Director, 1980-86, Head of Laboratory of Chemistry of Low-Molecular Bioregulators, 1986-93, Chief Scientific Worker, 1993-, Institute of Physiologically Active Compounds RAS, Chernogolovka; Director and Supervisor of Studies, Innovation Centre, Chernogolovka, 1993-. Publications: Numerous articles in professional journals. Honours: Medal, for valorous work in commemoration of the 100th anniversary of V I Lenin's birthday, 1970; Medal, Veteran of Labour, 1988; Medal of Order for merits before Fatherland II degrees, 1999; Listed in international biographical dictionaries. Memberships: Russian Academy of Natural Sciences. Address: Centralnaya, 4-A, Apartment 24, Chernogolovka, Moscow, 142432, Russia. E-mail: ravig@icp.ac.ru

GAGARINA Elena, b. 17 April 1959, Murmansk, Russia. Museum Director. 1 daughter. Education: Master's degree, 1981, PhD, 1990, Art History, Moscow State University. Appointments: Curator, Deputy Head, Department of Works on Paper, State Pushkin Museum of Fine Arts, 1981-2001; Director General, State Moscow Kremlin Museums, 2001-. Publications: Essays on English XVIIth – XVIIIth Century engravings and English art; Major accomplishment, Restoration of the Architectural Complex of the Moscow Kremlin; Organisation of the 200 year anniversary of the Moscow Kremlin Museums; Organisation of special exhibitions. Honours: Honorary Degree, Distinguished Worker of Culture of the Russian Federation; Special Sign for Merits in Culture; Order of Karl Faberge. Memberships: International Council of the Museum of Modern Art, New York.

GAGRAT Rustam Jehangir, b. 5 November 1959, Bombay, India. Lawyer. m. Lia Gagrat, 1 son. Education: BA (Hons) Politics, Elphinstone College, Bombay, 1979; BA (Hons) Law, 1981, MA, 1985, Downing College, Cambridge University; Solicitor, Bombay, 1984; Solicitor, England and Wales, 1987; PIL, Harvard University Law School, 1993. Appointments: Advocate Supreme, Court of India; Solicitor, Supreme Court of England; Notary, Union of India; Senior Partner, Gagrat and Co, Advocates and Solicitors, Bombay; Partner, Gagrat and Co, Supreme Court Advocates, Delhi; Company Director of Public and Private Companies; Trustee of Public and Private Trusts; Member, Committees of Chambers of Commerce. Publications: Presented and published papers at international and domestic law conferences. Honours: Tata Scholar, Cambridge University; Rustomji Mulla Prize, Bombay Law Society. Memberships: Supreme Court of India Bar Association; Bombay Bar Association; Bombay Law Society; Law Society of England; International Law Association; International Bar Association; Oxford and Cambridge Society. Address: Gagrats, Advocates, Solicitors & Notaries, Nirmal, Nariman Point, Mumbai 400 021, India. E-mail: rjgagrat@gagrats.com

GAILLARD Mary K, b. 1 April 1939, New Brunswick, New Jersey, USA. m. Bruno Zumino, 2 sons, 1 daughter. Education: BA, Hollins University, 1960; MA, Columbia University, 1961; Doctorat de Troisième Cycle, 1964, Doctorat d'Etat, 1968, University of Paris, Orsay. Appointments: Attaché de research, 1964-66, Chargé de research, 1968-73, Maître de research, 1973-79 CNRS; Visiting Scientist, Fermilab, 1973-74, 1983; Scientific Associate, Theory Division, CERN, 1964-81; Theory Group Leader, LAPP; Directeur de research, CNRS, 1980-81; Professor of Physics, University of California, Berkeley, Faculty Senior Staff, Lawrence Berkeley Laboratory, 1981-. Publications: 180 articles in scientific journals and conference proceedings; Co-editor: Weak Interactions, 1977; Gauge Theories in High Energy Physics, 1982. Honours: Woodrow Wilson Scholarship, 1960; Prix Thibaud, 1977; Loeb Lecturer in Physics, Harvard University, 1980; Chancellor's Distinguished Lecturer, University of California, Berkeley, 1981; Warner-Lambert Lecturer, University of Michigan, 1984; Fellow, American Physical Society, 1985; Miller Research Professorship, University of California, Berkeley, 1987-88, Fall 1996; E O Lawrence Memorial Award, 1988; Guggenheim Fellow, 1989-90; Fellow, American Academy of Arts and Sciences, 1989; Member, National Academy of Arts and Sciences, 1991; J J Sakurai Prize, 1993; Trustee, Council of Penn Women Lecturers, University of Pennsylvania, 1994; APS Centennial Lecturer, 1998-99; Member, American Philosophical Society, 2000. Memberships: American Physical Society; French Physical Society; European Physical Society; American Association for the Advancement of Science; American Civil Liberties Union; Arms Control Association; Union of Concerned Scientists. Address: Department of Physics, University of California, Berkeley, CA 94720, USA

GAKHRAMANOV Nadir Farroukh, b. 24 May 1945, Sisyan, Azerbaijan. Physicist. m. Yetar Hamid Musayeva, 1 son, 1 daughter. Education: MSc, 1967, PhD, 1976, Baki State University; Dr Sc, Professor, Moscow Radio Electronics Research Institute, Russia, 1986. Appointments: Teacher, Trainer, Associate Professor, Dr Sc Professor, Head of Department of Physics, Baki State University, 1968-2000; Rector, Sumgayit State University, 2000-. Publications: 220 scientific articles; 3 monographs; 16 textbooks; 20 inventions and patents. Memberships: Association of Caspian States Universities. Address: Matbuat Ave, House 2A, Flat 2, Baki, AZ1073, Azerbaijan.

GALASKO Charles Samuel Bernard, b. 29 June 1939, Johannesburg, South Africa. Orthopaedic Surgeon. m. Carol Freyda Lapinsky, 29 October 1967, 1 son, 1 daughter. Education: MB, BCh, 1st Class Honours, 1962, ChM, 1970, Witwatersrand; FRCS, Edinburgh, 1966; FRCS, England, 1966; Honorary MSc, Manchester, 1980; FCMSA (Honorary Fellow, College of Medicine of South Africa), 2003; FFSEM, Ireland, 2002; (UK), 2006. F Med Sci. Appointments include: House positions, Johannesburg and London; Nuffield Scholar, Nuffield Orthopaedic Centre, Oxford, 1969; Registrar, 1970, Senior Orthopaedic Registrar, 1970-73, Radcliffe Infirmary and Nuffield Orthopaedic Centre, Oxford; Director, Orthopaedic Surgery, Assistant Director, Division of Surgery, Royal Postgraduate Medical School, Director, Orthopaedic Surgery, Consultant, Hammersmith Hospital, 1973-76; Member, Unit Management, Royal Manchester Children's

Hospital, Clinical Director, Department of Orthopaedic Surgery, Salford General Hospitals, 1989-92; Member, Unit Management Board, 1989-96, Medical Director, 1993-96, Salford Royal Hospitals NHS Trust; Professor, Orthopaedic Surgery, University of Manchester, 1976-2004; Consultant Orthopaedic Surgeon, Hope Hospital and Royal Manchester Children's Hospital, 1976-2004; Director of Education and Training, Salford Royal Hospitals NHS Trust, 2002-05. Publications: Numerous articles and papers in the field of orthopaedics; 9 books include: Skeletal Metatases, author, 1986; Competing for the Disabled, co-author, 1989; Editor: Principles of Fracture Management, 1984; Neuromuscular Problems in Orthopaedics, 1987. Honours include: Moynihan Prize, Association of Surgeons of Great Britain and Ireland, 1969; Hunterian Professor, Royal College of Surgeons of England, 1971; AO Fellowship; Australian Commonwealth Fellowship, 1982; Sir Arthur Sims Commonwealth Professor, 1998; Scholarships; Academic prizes; Numerous lectureships, UK and abroad. Memberships include: International Orthopaedic Research Society, Programme Chairman, 1984-87, Membership Committee Chairman, 1987-90, President, 1990-93; International Association Olympic Medical Officers, Treasurer, 1988-2000; British Orthopaedic Association, Council, 1988-91, 1998-2003, Vice President, 1999-2000, President, 2000-2001; Royal College of Surgeons, England, Council, 1991-2003, Vice-President, 1999-2001, Chairman, Training Board, 1995-99, Chairman, Head Injury Working Party, 1997-99; Chairman, Joint Committee on Higher Surgical Training of the United Kingdom and Ireland, 1997-2000; Chairman, Intercollegiate Academic Board for Sport and Exercise Medicine, 2002-05; President, Faculty of Sport and Exercise Medicine, 2006-. Address: 72 Gatley Road, Gatley, Cheshire, SK8 4AA, England.

GALL Henderson Alexander (Sandy), b. 1 October 1927, Penang, Malaysia. Writer; Broadcaster. m. Eleanor Mary Patricia Anne, 1 son, 3 daughters. Education: MA, Aberdeen University, Scotland, 1952. Appointments: National Service, RAF, 1945-48; Foreign Correspondent: Reuters, 1953-63, Independent Television News, 1963-92; Co-presenter, News At Ten, 1970-90; Writer, Presenter, Producer of numerous documentaries including: Cresta Run, 1970, 1985; King Hussein, 1972; Afghanistan, 1982, 1984, 1986; George Adamson, 1989; Richard Leakey, 1995; Empty Quarter, 1996; Imran's Final Test, 1997; Afghanistan: War Without End, 2004. Publications: Books: Gold Scoop, 1977; Chasing the Dragon, 1981; Don't Worry about the Money Now, 1983; Behind Russian Lines: An Afghan Journal, 1983; Afghanistan: Agony of a Nation, 1988; Salang, 1989; George Adamson: Lord of the Lions, 1991; News From the Front: The Life of a Television Reporter, 1994; The Bushmen of Southern Africa: Slaughter of the Innocent, 2001. Honours: Rector, 1978-81, Honorary LLD, 1981, Aberdeen University; Sitara-i-Pakistan, 1986; Chairman, Sandy Gall's Afghanistan Appeal, 1986-; Lawrence of Arabia Memorial Medal; RSAA, 1987; Commander of the Order of the British Empire, 1988. Memberships: Turf; Travellers, Saints & Sinners; Special Forces; Royal St George's Golf Club; Rye Golf Club; Honorary Member, St Moritz Tobogganing. Address: Doubleton Oast House, Penshurst, Tonbridge, Kent TN11 8JA, England. E-mail: sgaa@btinternet.com Website: www.sandygallsafghanistanappeal.org

GALLAGHER Liam, b. 21 September 1972, Burnage, Manchester, England. Singer; Musician; Producer. m. Patsy Kensit, 1997, divorced 2000, 1 son; 1 son with partner Nicole Appleton. Career: Singer with Oasis, 1991-; Tours in USA and Britain; Founder and recorded for Big Brother records, 2000-.

Publications: Singles: Supersonic, Shakermaker, Live Forever, Cigarettes & Alcohol, Whatever, 1994; Some Might Say, Roll With It, Morning Glory, Wonderwall, 1995; Don't Look Back In Anger, Champagne Supernova, 1996; D'You Know What I Mean? Stand By Me, 1997; All Around The World, Don't Go Away, 1998; Go Let It Out, Who Feels Love? Sunday Morning Call, 2000; The Hindu Times, Stop Crying Your Heart Out, Little By Little/She Is Love, 2002; Songbird, 2003; Lyla, The Importance Of Being Idle, Let There Be Love, 2005. Albums: Definitely Maybe, 1994; (What's The Story) Morning Glory? 1995; Be Here Now, 1997; The Masterplan, 1998; Standing on the Shoulder of Giants, Familiar To Millions (Double CD), 2000; Familiar To Millions (Single CD), 2001; Heathen Chemistry, 2002; Don't Believe The Truth, 2005. Honours: 4 platinum discs for Definitely Maybe, 8 platinum discs for (What's the Story) Morning Glory, 1996; 3 Brit Awards, 1996; Outstanding Contribution to Music Award at the BRIT Awards, 2007. Address: C/o Ignition Management, 54 Linhope Street, London, NW1 6HL, England. Website: www.oasisnet.com

GALLOWAY Janice, b. 2 December 1955, Ayrshire, Scotland. Writer. 1 son. Education: MA, University of Glasgow, 1974-78; Postgraduate Diploma, Secondary Education, Hamilton College of Education, 1979. Appointments: Teacher of English, Garnock Academy, Ayrshire, Scotland, 1980-90; SAC Teacher of Creative Writing HMPs Barlinnie, Cornton Vale and Dungavel, 1994; Times Literary Supplement Research Fellow, The British Library, 1999; Affiliate Tutor, Creative Writing, Glasgow University, 2002-04. Publications: Novels and Short Stories: The Trick is to keep Breathing, 1990; Blood, 1991; Foreign Parts, 1994; Where You Find It, 1996; Clara, 2002; Editor (with Hamish Whyte): The Day I Met the Queen Mother, 1990; Scream if you want to go Faster, 1991; Pig Squealing, 1992; Meantime, 1993; How Would You Feel? An anthology of prisoners' writings, 1995; Pipelines (with Anne Bevan), 2001; Boy Book See (poetry), 2002; Rosengreen (with Anne Bevan), 2004; A wide variety of anthologised work including short stories, novel extracts, poems, prose-poetry and visual arts collaborations. Honours: The Trick is to keep Breathing: Shortlisted, Whitbread First Novel, Scottish First Book, Aer Lingus Awards, Winner, MIND/Allan Lane Prize; Scottish Arts Council Award; Blood: Shortlisted, Guardian Fiction Prize, People's Prize, Satire Award, Winner, Scottish Arts Council Award, Perrier/ Cosmopolitan Prize, New York Times Notable Book of the Year 1992; Foreign Parts: Shortlisted, Saltire Award, Winner, McVitie's Prize, Scottish Arts Council Award; American Academy of Arts and Letters, EM Forster Award, 1995; Creative Scotland Award, 2001, granted by the Scottish Arts Council; Clara: Shortlisted, SAC Book of the Year, nominated for the Dublin IMPAC Award, Winner Saltire Award, 2002. Address: c/o Derek Johns, AP Watt Literary Agency, 20 John Street, London, WC1N 2DR. E-mail: djohns@apwatt.co.uk

GALLOWAY Peter, b. 19 July 1954, United Kingdom. Area Dean, Church of England. Education: BA, Goldsmiths College, University of London, 1976; Certificate in Theology, St Stephen's House, Oxford, 1983; PhD, King's College, University of London, 1987. Appointments include: Ordained Deacon, 1984, Ordained Priest, 1984, Church of England; Curate, St John's Wood Church, London, 1986-86; Assistant Master, Arnold House School, 1983-85; Chaplain, Hospital of St John and St Elizabeth, 1983-86; Curate, St Giles-in-the-Fields, London, 1986-90; Chaplain: Moorfields Eye Hospital, 1986-88, St Paul's Hospital and the Shaftesbury Hospital, 1986-90, Cambridge Theatre, 1988-90; Governor, Soho Parish School, 1989-91; Justice of the Peace, City of London, 1989-; Priest-in-Charge, 1990-95, Vicar, 1995-,

Emmanuel, West Hampstead, London; Chairman of Governors, Emmanuel School, West Hampstead, 1990-; Joint Chairman, Hampstead Council of Christians and Jews, 1992-99; Member: Goldsmiths College Council, 1993-1999. London Borough of Camden Education Committee, 1997-2001, London Borough of Camden, Schools Organisation Committee, 1999-2004, West End Green Conservation Area Advisory Committee, 1996-2000, Committee of the Friends of Hampstead Cemetery, 2000-2005; Area Dean of North Camden, 2002-2007; Member, Edmonton Episcopal Area Bishop's Council, 2002-2007; University of London Council, 1999-; Heythrop College Council, 2006-. Publications: The Order of St Patrick, 1983; Henry Mackay, 1983; Good and faithful servants, 1988; The Cathedrals of Ireland, 1992; The Order of the British Empire, 1996; Royal Service Vol 1 (with others), 1996; The Most Illustrious Order, 1999; A Passionate Humility, Frederick Oakley and the Oxford Movement, 1999; The Cathedrals of Scotland, 2000; The Order of St Michael and St George, 2000; Companions of Honour, 2002; The Order of the Bath, 2006. Honours: OBE, 1996; Service Medal of the Order of St John, 1996; KStJ, 1997; Honorary Fellow, Goldsmiths College, 1999; Memberships: Order and Medals Research Society, 1977-, Nikaean Club, 1988-, The Athenaeum, 1990-; Freeman, City of London, 1995-; Fellow, Society of Antiquaries, 2000-; Liveryman, Worshipful Company of Glaziers, 1998-; Sub-Dean, The Order of St John (Priory of England), 1999-2007; Registrar, 2007-. Member, Board of Directors, St John Ambulance, 1999-2005. Address: The Vicarage, Lyncroft Gardens, London NW6 1JU, England.

GAMAL M Nour Abdalla, b. 9 April 1934, Cairo, Egypt. Pharmacist. m. Aida M Elbadry, 2 sons, 1 daughter. Education: B Pharm, 1956, Higher Diploma of Drug Analysis & Biological Standardisation, 1961, MSc, Pharmaceutical Sciences (Pharmacognosy), 1970, Cairo University. Appointments: Expert on Drug Analysis and Director of Central Labs, General Pharmaceutical Industry Co, Samaraa, Iraq, 1971-74; Director, Research & Control, Misr Pharmaceutical Co, 1980-86; Chairman, CEO, Kahira Pharmaceutical Co, 1986-89; Deputy Chairman, Egyptian Drug Organisation, 1989-92; Deputy Chairman, Member of the Board, 1992-96, Counsellor, Member of the Board, 1996-2000, Egyptian Drug Holding Co; Member of the Board, Egyptian Drug Holding Co, 2000-. Publications: More than 18 original research papers and survey studies in international and local pharmaceutical periodicals; Main contributor to Case Study of Egyptian Pharma Industry in the Nineties. Honours: Several medals and awards. Memberships: Egyptian Pharmaceutical Society; Drug Research Section, Medical Research Assembly; Academy of Scientific Research and Technology. E-mail: mgnour2005@yahoo.com

GAMBLE Cynthia Joan, b. 20 December 1941, Much Wenlock, Shropshire, England. University Lecturer. Education: L ès L, Université de Grenoble, Grenoble, France, 1971; BA (Hons), 1971, Diploma in Education, 1974, PhD, 1997, Birkbeck College, University of London; Appointments: Assistante d'Anglais, Lycée de Jeunes Filles, Quimperlé, 1963-64; Assistante d'Anglais, Lycée Stendhal, Grenoble, 1964-65; Head of French Department, Lanfranc School, Croydon, 1965-69; Teacher of French, Ealing Girls' Grammar School, London, 1969-71; Lecturer in French, City of Leeds and Carnegie College of Education, Leeds, 1971-76; Senior Lecturer in French, Director of International Exchanges, Department of International Relations, 1976-86, Head of European Secretariat, Senior Lecturer in French, Leeds Metropolitan University 1986-89; Head of European

Relations, University of East London, 1989-97; Honorary Research Fellow, The Ruskin Programme, Lancaster University, 1997-2001; Honorary Research Fellow, Birkbeck College, London University, 2001-2002; Visiting Fellow, The Ruskin Programme, Lancaster University, 2001-. Publications: Author, Proust as Interpreter of Ruskin: The Seven Lamps of Translation, 2002; Insights into Ruskin's Northern French Gothic: Abbeville, Amiens and Rouen, 2002; A Perpetual Paradise: Ruskin's Northern France (co-author with S Wildman), 2002; Ruskin-Turner: Dessins et Voyages en Picardie romantique (co-author with M Pinette and S Wildman), 2003; Contributor, Dictionnaire Marcel Proust, 2004; Numerous conference papers and invited lectures. Honours: Honorary Secretary and Founder, Ruskin Society, 1997. Memberships: Société des Amis de Marcel Proust et de Combray; Franco-British Society. Address: Flat 89, 49 Hallam Street, London W1W 6JP, England.

GAMBLING William Alexander, b. 11 October 1926, Port Talbot, UK. Electrical Engineer. m. (1) Margaret Pooley, 1952, dissolved 1994, 1 son, 2 daughters, (2) Barbara Colleen O'Neil, 1994. Education: BS (1st Class Hons), Electrical Engineering, University of Bristol, 1947; PhD, Electrical Engineering, University of Liverpool, 1955; DSc, University of Bristol, 1968. Appointments: Lecturer, Electrical Power Engineering, University of Liverpool, 1950-55; National Research Council Fellow, University of BC, 1955-57; Lecturer, Senior Lecturer, Reader, 1957-64, Dean of Engineering and Applied Science, 1972-75; Professor, Electrons, 1964-80, Head of Department, 1974-79, Professor, Optical Communications, 1980-95, Director, Optoelectrons Research Centre, 1989-95, University of Southampton; Director, York Ltd, 1990-97; Royal Society Kan Tang Po Professor and Director, Optoelectrons Research Centre, City University, Hong Kong, 1996-; Industrial consultant; Visiting Professor, Universities including: CO, USA, 1966-67; Bhabha Atomic Research Centre, India, 1970; Osaka University, Japan, 1977; City University, Hong Kong, 1995. Publications: 300 papers on electrons and optical fibre communications. Honours include: Academy Enterprise Award, 1982; J J Thomson Medal, IEE, 1982; Faraday Medal, IEE, 1983; Churchill Medal, Society of Engineers, 1984 and Simms Medal, Society of Engineers, 1989, for Research innovation and leadership; Honorary Professor, Huazhung University Science and Technology, 1986-, Beijing University Posts & Telecommunications, 1987-, Shanghai University, 1991-. Micro-optics Award, Japan, 1989; Freeman, City of London, 1987; Dennis Gabor Award, International Society for Optical Engineering, USA, 1990; Rank Prize for Optoelectronics, 1991; Medal and Prize, Foundation for Computer and Communications Promotion, Japan, 1993; Mountbatten Medal, National Electrons Council, 1993; Dr hc University Politèchnic of Madrid, 1994, Aston University, 1995, Bristol University, 1999. Memberships include: FIERE; CEng, FIEE; President, Honorary Fellow, IERE; FEng; FRS. Address: Optoelectronics Research Centre, City University of Hong Kong, 83 Tat Chee Avenue, Kowloon, Hong Kong, China.

GAMBON Sir Michael John, b. 19 October 1940, Dublin, Ireland. Actor. m. Anne Miller, 1962, 1 son. Appointments: Former, Mechanical Engineer; Actor with Edwards/ Macliammoir Co, Dublin, 1962, National Theatre, Old Vic, 1963-67, Birmingham Repertory and other provincial theatres, 1967-69; Title roles include: Othello; Macbeth, Coriolanus, King Lear, Anthony and Cleopatra, Old Times; RSC, Aldwych, 1970-71; The Norman Conquests, 1974; Otherwise Engaged, 1976; Just Between Ourselves, 1977; Alice's Boys, 1978; with National Theatre, 1980; with RSC,

Stratford and London, 1982-83; TV appearances include: Ghosts; Oscar Wilde; The Holy Experiment; Absurd Person Singular; The Borderers; The Singing Detective; The Heat of the Day; Maigret; The Entertainer, Truth; Joe's Palace. Films: The Beast Must Die; Turtle Diary; Paris by Night; The Cook, the thief, his wife and her lover; A Dry White Season; The Rachel Papers; State of Grace; The Heat of the Day; Mobsters; Toys; Clean Slate; Indian Warrior; The Browning Version; Mary Reilly; Two Deaths; Midnight in Moscow; A Man of No Importance; The Innocent Sleep; All Our Fault; Two Deaths; Nothing Personal; The Gambler; Dancing at Lughnasa; Plunket and McClean; The Last September; Sleepy Hollow; The Insider, End Game; Charlotte Gray; Gosford Park; Ali G Indahouse; Path to War; The Actors; Open Range; Harry Potter, The Prisoner of Azkaban; Being Julia; Sky Captain and the World of Tomorrow; Layer Cake; The Life Aquatic with Steve Zissou; Stories of Lost Souls; Harry Potter and the Goblet of Fire; Celebration; The Omen; Amazing Grace; John Duffy's Brother; The Good Shepherd; Cranford Chronicles; The Good Night; The Baker; The Alps; Harry Potter and the Order of the Phoenix. Honours include: London Theatre Critics Award for Best Actor; Olivier Award for Best Comedy Performance; Evening Stand Drama Award. Membership: Trustee, Roy Armouries, 1995-. Address: c/o ICM, Oxford House, 76 Oxford Street, London, W1N 0AX, England.

GAMMON Philip Greenway, b. 17 May 1940, Chippenham, Wiltshire, England. Pianist; Conductor. m. Floretta Volovini, 2 sons. Education: Royal Academy of London, London, 1956-61; Badische Müsikhochschule, Karlsruhe, Germany, 1961-64. Appointments: Deputy Piano Teacher, RAM and RASM, 1964; Pianist, Royal Ballet, Covent Garden, 1964-68; Principal Pianist, Ballet for All, 1968-71; Pianist, Royal Ballet, 1971-99; Principal Pianist, Royal Ballet, 1999-2005; Also Conductor with Royal Ballet and as Guest Conductor with the English National Ballet, Hong Kong Ballet and National Ballet of Portugal; Guest Pianist, Royal Ballet, 2005-. Honours: The Recital Diploma, 1960; MacFarren Gold Medal, 1961; Karlsruhe Kultür Preis, 1962; ARCM, 1968; ARAM, 1991; FRAM, 2002. Membership: Musician's Union. Address: 19 Downs Avenue, Pinner, Middlesex HA5 5AQ, England.

GAN John Qiang, b. 10 October 1962, Pingxiang, China. Reader. Education: B Eng, Department of Electronic Engineering, Northwestern Polytechnical University, Xi'an, China, 1978-82; MSc, Department of Automatic Control, Southeast University, Nanjing, China, 1982-85; PhD, Department of Biomedical Engineering, Southeast University, Nanjing, China, 1988-91. Appointments: Assistant Lecturer, 1985-87, Lecturer, 1987-88, Department of Electronic Engineering and Automatic Control, East China University of Science and Technology, Shanghai, China; Lecturer, 1991, Associate Professor, 1992-94, Professor, 1995-96, Research Institute for Bio-computing and Machine Intelligence, Department of Biomedical Engineering, Southeast University, Nanjing, China; Visiting Associate Professor, Centre for Pattern Recognition and Machine Intelligence, Concordia University, Montreal, Canada, 1993-94; Research Fellow, School of Electrical and Electronic Engineering, Nanyang Technological University, Singapore, 1996-98; Research Fellow, Department of Electronics and Computer Science, University of Southampton, 1998-2000; Senior Lecturer, 2000-06, Reader, 2006-, Department of Computer Science, University of Essex, Colchester, England. Publications: One monograph and over 100 research papers. Honours: Elite Young Professor Award, 1993, Outstanding Research Award, 1995, Southeast University; Third Prize of Science

and Technology Advancement, Ministry of Education, China, 1996; 17 funded projects; Listed in national and international biographical dictionaries. Memberships: Council member, Chinese Institution of Biophysics, 1994-96; Council member, Chinese Institution of Electronics, 1996-98; Senior member, IEEE, 2001-; Member, over 20 Program Committees for international conferences and symposia; Associate Editor, IEEE Transactions on Systems, Man and Cybernetics, Part B, 2006-; Associate Editor, Neurocomputing, 2005-; Member, 3 Editorial Boards of international journals. Address: Department of Computer Science, University of Essex, Colchester, CO4 3SQ, Essex, England. E-mail: JQGAN@essex.ac.uk

GANCHEV Ivan, b. 30 June 1964, Shumen, Bulgaria. University Lecturer. m. Petya, 2 sons. Education: Dip Eng, Leningrad Electro-technical Institute of Telecommunications, 1989; PhD, St Petersburg State University of Telecommunications, 1994. Appointments: Telecom Expert, Bulgarian Telecom, 1995; Visiting Lecturer, ECE Department, University of Limerick, 1997, 1998, 1999; Part-time Senior Lecturer, Department of Informatics, University of Shumen, 1999-2000; Junior Lecturer, 1996, Lecturer, 1997, Senior Lecturer, 1998, Associate Professor, 2004, Department of Computer Systems, Plovdiv University, Bulgaria; Lecturer, Department of Electronic and Computer Engineering, University of Limerick, 2000-; Deputy Director, Telecommunications Research Centre, University of Limerick, 2004-. Publications: 2 books; 9 chapters and contributions to books; 12 papers in refereed journals; 85 papers published in international conferences and workshops proceedings; 20 technical reports. Honours: Research Seed Funding Award, University of Limerick, 2001; Grant Award, Teaching & Research Innovation Programme Funding, General Electric & University of Limerick Foundation, 2001-04; Grant Award, Targeted Funding for Strategic Initiatives, Higher Education Authority, Ireland, 2002-06; Basic Research Grant Award, Science Foundation, Ireland, 2004-07; Travel Grant Award, Higher Education Authority/Department of Education and Science, Ireland, 2005; Best Research Paper Award, 2005. Memberships: IEEE; IEEE Communication Society. Address: TRC, ECE Department, University of Limerick, Ireland. E-mail: ivan.ganchev@ul.ie

GANDOLFO Francois Gerard Georges, b. 25 September 1970, Marseille, France. Chemist. m. Carmen Hortensia Reinoso Becerra, 1 son, 1 daughter. Education: Chemical Engineer degree, Ecole Nationale Superieure de Chimie de Paris, France, 1994; PhD, Chemistry, The City University of New York, USA, 1998. Appointments: Technical Project Leader, Unilever Bestfoods, Brazil, 2006; Global Technical Project Leader, Unilever R&D, Vlaardingen, 2006-08; R&D Manager, Oils and Fats, Unipro NV, 2008-. Honours: Marie Curie Fellowship, European Community, 2000-02; Listed in international biographical dictionaries. Memberships: American Chemical Society.

GANELLIN Charon Robin, b. 25 January 1934, London, England. Medicinal Chemist. m. Tamara Green, deceased, 1 son, 1 daughter. Education: BSc, 1955, PhD, 1958, Queen Mary College, London University; Fellow of the Royal Society of Chemistry, 1968; Chartered Chemist, 1976; DSc, London University, 1986; FRS, 1986. Appointments: Medicinal Chemist, Smith Kline & French, 1958; Research Associate, Massachusetts Institute of Technology, 1960; Medicinal Chemist, 1961-62, Head of Chemistry, 1962-78, Director, 1978-86, Vice-President Research, 1980-84, Vice-President, 1984-86, Smith Kline & French Research Ltd; Smith Kline & French Professor of Medicinal Chemistry, 1986-2002, Emeritus

Professor of Medicinal Chemistry, 2002-, University College London. Publications: Books as co-editor: Pharmacology of Histamine Receptors, 1982; Frontiers in Histamine Research (a tribute to Heinz Schild), 1985; Dictionary of Drugs, 1990; Medicinal Chemistry, 1993; Dictionary of Pharmaceutical Agents, 1997; Practical Studies in Medicinal Chemistry, 2007; 250 papers and articles as author or co-author in learned scientific journals or books. Honours include: UK Chemical Society Medallion in Medicinal Chemistry, 1977; Prix Charles Mentzer, 1978; Medicinal Chemistry Award, American Chemical Society, 1980; RSC Tilden Medal and Lecture, 1982; SCI Messel Medal and Lecture, 1988; Society for Drug Research Award for Drug Discovery (jointly), 1989; USA National Inventors Hall of Fame, 1990; Fellow, Queen Mary and Westfield College, London, 1992; DSc, Honoris Causa, Aston University, 1995; RSC Adrien Albert Lectureship and Medal, 1999; Nauta Prize for Medicinal Chemistry, European Federation for Medicinal Chemistry, 2004; Foreign Corresponding Academician of the Spanish Rpyal Academy of Pharmacy, 2006; Pratest Medal from the Medicinal Chemistry Division of the Italian Chemical Society, 2006. Memberships: American Chemical Society; British Pharmacological Society; European Histamine Research Society; International Union of Pure and Applied Chemistry; The Royal Society; The Royal Society of Chemistry; Save British Science Society; Society of Chemical Industry; Society for Medicines Research. Address: Department of Chemistry, University College London, 20 Gordon Street, London WC1H 0AJ, England. E-mail: c-r.ganellin@ucl.ac.uk

GANS-LARTEY Joseph Kojo, b. 28 August 1951, Accra-Ghana. Barrister. m. Rosmarie Ramrattan, 1 son, 1 daughter. Education: HNC, Business Studies, 1979; LLB, Honours, 1982; Called to the Bar, 1983; LLM, London, 1986. Appointments: Senior Legal Assistant, 1984-86, Crown Prosecutor, 1986-88; Senior Crown Prosecutor, 1988-90; Principal Crown Prosecutor, 1990-92; Prosecution Team Leader, 1992-; Borough Crown Prosecutor, 2005. Publications: The Challenge Ahead Parts I, II, III. An Analysis of Political and Legal History of Ghana Since Independence. Honour: Times Lawyer of the Week, 2000. Membership: Honorary Member, Society of Lincoln's Inn. Address: Crown Prosecution Service, Prospect West 9th Floor, 81 Station Road, Croydon, Surrey CRO 2RD, England. E-mail: ganslartey@aol.com

GANTI Prasada Rao, b. 25 August 1942, Seethanagaram (AP), India. Educator. m. Meenakshi Vedula, 1 son, 2 daughters. Education: BE, (Hons), Electrical Engineering, Andhra University, Waltair, India, 1963; M Tech, Control Systems Engineering, 1965, PhD, Electrical Engineering, 1970, Indian Institute of Technology, Kharagpur, India. Appointments: Assistant Professor, Department of Electrical Engineering, PSG College of Technology, Coimbatore, India, 1969-71; Assistant Professor, 1971-78, Professor, 1978-97, Chairman, Curriculum Development Cell, Electrical Engineering, 1978-80, Indian Institute of Technology, Kharagpur, India; Commonwealth Postdoctoral Research Fellow, Control Systems Centre, University of Manchester Institute of Science and Technology, Manchester, England, 1975-76; Alexander von Humboldt Foundation Research Fellow, Ruhr University, Bochum, Germany, 1981-83, 1985, 1991, 2003, 2004, 2007; Scientific Advisor, Directorate of Power and Desalination Plants, Water and Electricity Department, Government of Abu Dhabi, 1992-; Visiting Professor, Henri Poincare University, Nancy, France, 2003; Fraunhofer Institute für Rechnerarchitektur und Software Technik (FIRST), Berlin, 2007, 2007; Royal Society Visiting Professor, Brunel

University, England, 2007; Member, UNESCO-EOLSS Joint Committee. Publications: Author and Co-author of 4 books and over 150 research papers; Co-editor of 1 book. Honours include: IIT Kharagpur Silver Jubilee Research Award, 1985; The Systems Society of India Award, 1989; International Desalination Association Best Paper award, 1995; Honorary Professor, East China University for Science and Technology. Memberships: Life Fellow, Institution of Engineers, India; Fellow, Institution of Electronic and Telecommunications Engineers, India; Fellow, IEEE, USA; Fellow Indian National Academy of Engineering; Member of numerous editorial boards. Address: PO Box 2623, Abu Dhabi, United Arab Emirates. E-mail: gantirao@emi.ae

GARAB Gyözö, b. 1 January 1948, Szomód, Hungary. Research Scientist. m. Anikó, 27 October 1979, 2 sons, 2 daughters. Education: Physics, University of Szeged, 1971; PhD, Biophysics, 1974; DSc, 1992. Appointments: Research Scientist, Head of Laboratory, 1987-, Deputy Director, 1999-2000, Biology Research Centre, Szeged; Visiting Scientist, University of Illinois, University of New Mexico, CEA Saclay, Brookhaven National Laboratory; Director, Biofotonika Ltd, 2004-. Publications: Photosynthesis: Mechanisms and Effects; More than 100 articles in professional journals. Honours: J Ernst Award, Hungarian Biophysical Society, 1994; Straub Medal, Biology Research Centre, 2001. Memberships: Hungarian Biophysical Society; International Society of Photosynthesis Research. Address: Dózsa György u 7, H-6720 Szeged, Hungary.

GARAYEV Abulfas, b. 13 November 1956, Baku, Azerbaijan. Minister of Culture and Tourism. m. Lala Kazimova, 1 daughter. Education: University of Foreign Languages and Pedagogic, Baku, Azerbaijan, 1973-78; Academy of Social Sciences, Moscow, 1989-92. Appointments: Teacher, University of Politology and State Administration, 1992-93; Director General, Improtex Commers company, 1993-94; Minister of Youth and Sport, 1994-2001, Minister of Youth, Sport and Tourism, 2001-06, Minister of Culture and Tourism, 2006-, Republic of Azerbaijan. Publications: Cultural Aspects of Azerbaijan Diaspora in the years 1918-1930; Analysis of Space as a means of Consolidation in the World; Methodological basis for the analysis of the socialization of youth. Memberships: Safari International Life Membership; National Olympic Committee; National Geographic Society. E-mail: minister@met.gov.az

GARCIA Y GARCIA Ernesto Luis, b. 23 August 1946, Cogolludo, Spain. Doctor in Medicine and Surgery; Rehabilitation and Physical Medicine Specialist; Phoniatry. m. María Soledad Vicente, 1971, 2 sons, 1 daughter. Education: Degree in Medicine and Surgery, Medical Faculty Zaragoza, Spain, 1970; Certified in Puericulture, 1975; Certified in Medicine of the Work, 1976; Resident in Rehabilitation and Physical Medicine Specialist, University Hospital Miguel Servet, 1974-77; Doctor in Medicine and Surgery, 1991. Appointments: General Physician and General Health Management in autonomous communities of Guadalajara, Aragon and Catalonia, Spain, 1970-73; Emergency in Medicine Officer, Royal and Provincial Hospital, Saragossa, Spain, 1973-88; Specialist, Rehabilitation Department, Chief of Unit of Phoniatry and Logotherapy, University Hospital Miguel Servet, Saragossa, 1977-; Vicarial-Consultant, Company Derfonia SL, 1997-; Director, Centre of Phoniatric and Logotherapy Aragon; Specialist, Rehabilitation, Cerebral Palsy Centre, ASPACE, Aragon 1980-92; Lecturer on medical rehabilitation, phoniatry and the handicapped at scientific sessions and congresses; Lecturer tutor, MIR of Rehabilitation,

1992-2003, Co-ordinator, Improvement of Assistance Quality, Department of Rehabilitation, 2003-, Chief of Service, Physical Medicine and Rehabilitation, 2004-, University Hospital Miguel Servet. Publications: Articles in professional journals on human communication disorders; Editor of book chapters and magazines. Honours include: Premium FAMI Aragon, 1995; Aragon Man of 2002; Recognition as team member for Choclear Implant, School of Doctors of Zaragoza, 2002. Memberships: President, Founding Manager, Spanish Phoniatry Magazine; Chairman, Spanish Medical Society of Phoniatry, 1992-97; Aragon Society of Rehabilitation and Physical Medicine; Spanish Society of Medical Physicians and rehabilitation; Aragon Society of Otorinolaryngology; Member numerous investigative commissions; Collaborative Associate, NGO's and humanitarian associations; First Vice-Cairman, Civil International Committee. Address: University Hospital Miguel Servet, Physical Medicine and Rehabilitation Service, Isabel la Catolica 1-3, 50007 Saragossa, Spain. E-mail: elgarcia@salud.aragob.es

GARDARSDÓTTIR Hólmfrídur, b. 18 July 1957, Iceland. Associate Professor. Education: BA, University of Iceland, 1993; MA, 1996, PhD, 2001, University of Texas at Austin, USA. Appointments: News Correspondent, Icelandic National Broadcasting Service, Buenos Aires, Argentina, 1987-88; Managing Director, Association of Icelandic Students Abroad, Reykjavik, Iceland, 1988-90; Spanish Instructor, Hamrahlid College, Reykjavik, 1988-92; Special Assistant, Executive Director, Consul General for Spain, Reykjavik, 1990-94; Spanish Instructor, Reykjavik Adult Education Center, 1993-94; Assistant Instructor of Spanish, University of Texas at Austin, 1995-98; Instructor of Spanish, 1998-2003, Visiting Assistant Professor, 1998-2003, Planner and Instructor, Spanish Program, 1999-2003, Instructor of Spanish as a Foreign Language, 2000-04, Assistant Professor, 2003-04, Faculty of Humanities, Elected Chair, 2004-07, Associate Professor, 2004-, Department of Romance and Classical Languages, University of Iceland. Publications: Books: La Reformulación de la Identidad Genérica en la Narrativa de Mujeres Argentina de Fin de Siglo XX, 2005; Mujeres latinoamericanas en movimiento, 2006; Gustur úr djúpi nætur: Ljóðasaga Lorca á Íslandi, 2007; Lærdómsleitandinn: Ljóðasaga Jorge Luis Borges á Íslandi, 2007; Numerous book chapters and articles in professional journals. Honours: Research Grants, University of Iceland; Fulbright Scholar, 1994-98. Memberships: Society of LA Studies; NOLAN; Red Haina. Address: University of Iceland, Nyja Gardi, 101 Reykjavik, Iceland. E-mail: holmfr@hi.is Website: www.hi.is

GARDNER Mariana Carmen Zavati, b. 20 January 1952, Bacau, Romania. Writer. m. John Edward Gardner, 8 August 1980, 1 son, 1 daughter. Education: Baccalauréat with distinction, Vasile Alecsandri Boarding College for Girls, 1971; MSc, Philology, 1st class hons, Alexandru Ioan Cuza University of Iasi, 1975; PGCE, University of Leeds, 1987; Postgraduate Courses: Goethe Institut Rosenheim, Germany, 1991; L'Ecole Normale Supérieure, Auxerre, France, 1991. Appointments: English Teacher, various schools, Part-time Assistant Lecturer, University "Al I Cuza", Iasi, Full-time Assistant Lecturer, University of Bacau, 1975-80; Teacher, Latin, French, German, Spanish and Italian, various schools in England, 1980-2000; Bilingual writer, 2000-. Publications: Translations of poetry by Fleur Adcock, Al Florin Tene, Eugen Evu, Valeriu Bargau, Ozana Budau, Magdalena Constantinescu, Nicolae Szekely, Katrina Porteous and Denise Riley; Poems in 70 anthologies in UK, USA and Romania; Short stories included in: The Unexplained; Mysteries of the World; Tales with a Twist; The Unforgettable; Echoes on the Wind; Life's Scribes Dawn; Novel, Miss Mariana in Black and White; Numerous journalistic contributions around the world. Honours: 4 Editor's Choice Awards, UK and USA; Bronze Medal, North American Poetry Competition, USA, 1998; The American Romanian Academy Award, Canada, 2001; The Ionel Jianu Award for Arts, Canada, 2001. Memberships: American Romanian Academy of Arts and Sciences, USA; LiterArt XXI, International Association of Romanian Writers and Artists, USA; National Geographic Society; Poetry Society, UK; Uniunea Scriitorilor, Romania. Address: 14 Andrew Goodall Close, East Dereham, Norfolk NR19 1SR, England.

GARDNER-THORPE Christopher, b. 22 August 1941. Consultant Neurologist. Education: St Philip's School, London, 1948-54; Beaumont College, Old Windsor, Berkshire, 1954-59; MB BS, 1964, MD, 1973, University of London, St Thomas' Hospital; FRCP; FACP. Appointments: House Surgeon, Peace Memorial, Watford, 1964; House Physician, Royal South Hants Hospital, Southampton, 1964-65; Senior House Officer in Neurology, 1965-66, Registrar in Neurology, 1967-69, Wessex Neurological Centre, Southampton General Hospital; Medical Registrar, North Staffordshire Infirmary and City General Hospital, Stoke on Trent, 1966-67; Registrar in Neurology, Southampton General Hospital, 1969; Neurological Research Registrar, 1969-71, Neurological Registrar, Special Centre for Epilepsy, 1969-71, Bootham Park Hospital, York and General Infirmary, Leeds; Senior Registrar in Neurology, Newcastle General Hospital and Royal Victoria Infirmary, Newcastle-upon-Tyne, 1971-74; Physician in Charge, Newcourt Hospital, Exeter, 1974-88; Consultant Neurologist, South Western Regional Health Authority, 1974-93; Consultant Neurologist, North Devon District Hospital, Barnstable, 1974-95; Consultant Neurologist, Mardon House Neurorehabilitation Centre, 1997-2006; Consultant Neurologist, Royal Devon and Exeter Hospital, Exeter and Plymouth General Hospital, 1993-2006, Lead Clinician in Neurology, 1997-2006, Exeter Healthcare NHS Trust; Independent Consultant Neurologist, 2006-. Publications: Numerous articles in professional and popular journals; Editor, Journal of Medical Biography. Honours: Freeman of the City of London, 1979; Her Majesty's Lieutenant for the City of London, 1981-; Freeman, 1979-, Liveryman, 1980-, Worshipful Company of Barbers; Esquire, Order of St John, 1980-; Invited Fellow, Royal Society of Arts, 1997. Memberships include: World Federation of Neurology; European Federation of Neurological Societies; Association of British Neurologists; International League Against Epilepsy; British Epilepsy Association; Irish Neurological Association; British Medical Association; Royal Society of Medicine; Royal College of Physicians; Society of Expert Witnesses; Institute for Learning and Teaching; Fellow, Linnaean Society. Address: The Coach House, 1a College Road, Exeter, Devon, EX1 1TE, England. E-mail: cgardnerthorpe@doctors.org.uk

GAREGNANI Pierangelo, b. 9 August 1930, Milan, Italy. Professor of Economics. Education: Scholarship student, Collegio Ghislieri, University of Pavia; Degree in Political Sciences (cum laude), 1949-53; Foreign Bursar, Trinity College Cambridge, PhD, Economics, Faculty of Economics, Cambridge University, 1953-58; Libera docenza, 1960. Appointments: Assistant, Economics, Faculty of Economics and Commerce, University of Rome "La Sapienza", 1959-61; Researcher, Associazióne per lo Sviluppo del Mezzogiorno, Rome, 1959-61; Rockefeller Fellow, MIT, Cambridge, Massachusetts, USA, 1961-62; Lecturer, Economics, University of Sassari, 1962-63; Full Chair in Economics, University of Sassari, 1963-66, University of Pavia, 1966-69,

University of Florence, 1969-74, University of Rome "La Sapienza", 1974-92, University of Rome Three, 1992-; Visiting Professor, Cambridge University, 1973-74, Fellow, Trinity College Cambridge, 1973-74, 1990-91; Director of Research, Research Doctorates, University of Rome; Visiting Professor, Stanford University, USA, 1985-86, New School for Social Research, New York, 1987-91; Participant in numerous international conferences and seminars. Publications include: Il capitale nelle teorie della distribuzione, 1960, 1972, 1974, 1976, 1982; Notes on Consumption Investment and Effective Demand, 1978, 1979 (reprinted in Keynes's Economics and the Theory of Value and Distribution, editors J Eatwell and M Milgate, 1983); Value and Distribution in the Classical Economists and Marx, 1984; Savings, Investment and the Quantity of Capital in General Intemporal Equilibrium, 2000. Memberships: Academia Europaea, Cambridge, 1988-; Corresponding Member, Accademia Nazionale dei Lincei, 2001-. Address: Viale Gorizia 33, 00198 Rome, Italy.

GARMANOV Maksim E, b. 29 May 1961, Moscow, Russia. Chemist; Electrochemist; Researcher; Scientist. Education: Highest Degree with honours, Chemical Faculty, Moscow State University, Russia, 1983; Postgraduate Course, The Karpov's Physico-Chemical Research Institute, Moscow, Russia, 1990. Appointments: Special Researcher, Institute of Physical Chemistry, Academy of Sciences, Moscow, 1983-86; Junior Scientist, 1986-87, Postgraduate Student, 1987-90, The Karpov's Physico-Chemical Research Institute, Moscow; Junior Scientist, 1990-92, Scientist, 1992-, Institute of Physical Chemistry, Academy of Sciences, Moscow. Publications: Numerous articles in professional scientific journals. Honours: Highest degree with honours, Moscow State University, 1983; All-Russia Exhibition Centre Award, Moscow, 2003; Listed in national and international biographical honours and grand editions. Memberships: Trade Union of Scientific Workers; New York Academy of Sciences, 1995-2004; Honorary Research Consultant, IBC, 2002-; Distinguished Research Board of Advisors, ABI, USA, 2005-. Address: The Institute of Physical Chemistry and Electrochemistry of RAS, Leninsky Prospect 31, Moscow 119991, Russia. E-mail: maxsuperrrr@rambler.ru Website: http:// maxsuper.boom.ru/index.html

GARNER Alan, b. 17 October 1934, Cheshire, England. Author. m. (1) Ann Cook, 1956, divorced, 1 son, 2 daughters, (2) Griselda Greaves, 1972, 1 son, 1 daughter. Education: Magdalen College, Oxford, 1955-56. Appointment: Member, International Editorial Board, Detskaya Literatura Publishers, Moscow, 1991-. Publications: The Weirdstone of Brisingamen, 1960; The Moon of Gomrath, 1963; Elidor, 1965; Holly from the Bongs, 1966; The Owl Service, 1967; The Book of Goblins, 1969; Red Shift, 1973; The Guizer, 1975; The Stone Book Quartet, 1976-78; Fairy Tales of Gold, 1979; The Lad of the Gad, 1980; British Fairy Tales, 1984; A Bag of Moonshine, 1986; Jack and the Beanstalk, 1992; Once Upon a Time, 1993; Strandloper, 1996; The Voice that Thunders, 1997; The Well of the Wind, 1998; Thursbitch, 2003. Honours: Carnegie Medal, 1967; Guardian Award, 1968; Lewis Carroll Shelf Award, USA, 1970; Gold Plaque, Chicago International Film Festival, 1981; Children's Literature Association International Phoenix Award, 1996; OBE, 2001; FSA, 2007. Membership: Portico Library, Manchester. Address: Blackden, Holmes Chapel, Crewe, Cheshire CW4 8BY, England.

GARNER James (James Baumgardner), b. 7 April 1928, Norman, Oklahoma, USA. Actor. m. Lois Clarke, 1995, 1 son, 2 daughters. Appointments: Former travelling salesman, oil field worker, carpet layer, bathing suit model; Toured with road companies; Actor, TV appearances include: Cheyenne, Maverick, 1957-62; Nichols, 1971-72; The Rockford Files, 1974-79; Space, 1985; The New Maverick; The Long Summer of George Adams; The Glitter Dome; Heartsounds; Promise (also executive producer); Obsessive Love; My Name is Bill (also executive producer); Decoration Day; Barbarians at the Gate; The Rockford Files; A Blessing in Disguise; Dead Silence; First Monday (series), 2002; Films include: Toward the Unknown; Shoot-Out at Medicine Bend, 1957; Darby's Rangers, 1958; Sayonara; Up Periscope, 1959; The Americanization of Emily, 1964; 36 Hours; The Art Of Love, 1965; A Man Could Get Killed, 1966; Duel at Diablo, 1966; Master Buddwing, 1966; Grand Prix, 1966; Hour of the Gun, 1967; Marlowe, 1969; Support Your Local Sheriff, 1971; Support Your Local Gunfighter, 1971; Skin Game, 1971; They Only Kill Their Masters, 1972; One Little Indian, 1973; Health, 1979; The Fan, 1980; Victor/Victoria, 1982; Murphy's Romance, 1985; Promise (made for TV), 1986; Sunset, 1987; Decoration Day (TV film), 1990; Fire in the Sky, 1993; Maverick (TV), 1994; My Fellow Americans, 1996; Twilight, 1998; Space Cowboys, 2000; Atlantis: The Lost Empire, 2001; Roughing It (TV), 2002; Divine Secrets of the Ya-Ya Sisterhood, 2002; First Monday (TV), 2002; The Land Before Time X: The Great Longneck Migration, 2003; The Notebook, 2004; Al Roach: Private Insectigator, 2004; 8 Simple Rules...for Dating My Teenage Daughter (TV), 2003/05; The Ultimate Gift, 2006; Terra, 2008. Honours: Emmy Award; Purple Heart.

GARNER Lydia M, b. 25 February 1937, Santos, São Paulo, Brazil. Professor. m. Stanton Garner, 1 son. Education: BA, History, University of Texas, Arlington, 1979; MA, 1982, PhD, 1987,History, Johns Hopkins University. Appointments: Assistant Student, 1982, Invited Professor, 1982-88, Johns Hopkins; Visiting Professor, University of Delaware, 1988, 1991-92; Professor, Texas State University, 1992-. Publications: Isabel of Brazil, Biographical Encyclopedia, 2000; Journal of Borderlands Studies: Settling the Brazilian Frontiers, 1998; The Two Bodies of the King: The Several Bodies of Pedro II, 1999, RIHGB; Justiça Administrativa no Brazil do Segundo Reinado, Revista de História, 2002. Honours: Fellow, School of Advanced International Studies, Johns Hopkins, 1982-83; Shell Education Fellowship, Latin America, 1982; Elected Correspondent Member, Instituto Histórico e geográfico Brasileiro, 2005. Memberships: American Historical Association; World History Association; World History Association of Texas; Latin American Studies Association. Address: 111 East Sierra Circle, San Marcos, Texas 78666, USA. E-mail: lg11@txstate.edu

GARNETT Richard (Duncan Carey), b. 8 January 1923, London, England. Writer; Publisher; Translator. Education: BA, King's College, Cambridge, 1948; MA, 1987. Appointments: Production Manager, 1955-59, Director, 1957-66, Rupert Hart-Davis Ltd; Director, Adlard Coles Ltd, 1963-66; Editor, 1966-82, Director, 1972-82, Macmillan London; Director, Macmillan Publishers, 1982-87. Publications: Goldsmith: Selected Works (editor), 1950; Robert Gruss: The Art of the Aqualung (translator), 1955; The Silver Kingdom (in US as The Undersea Treasure), 1956; Bernard Heuvelmans: On the Track of Unknown Animals (translator), 1958; The White Dragon, 1963; Jack of Dover, 1966; Bernard Heuvelmans: In the Wake of the Sea-Serpents (translator), 1968; Joyce (editor with Reggie Grenfell), 1980; Constance Garnett: A Heroic Life, 1991; Sylvia and David, The Townsend Warner/Garnett Letters (editor), 1994; Rupert Hart-Davis Limited: A Brief History, 2004. Address: Hilton Hall, Hilton, Huntingdon, Cambridgeshire PE28 9NE, England.

GARRETT Godfrey John, b. 24 July 1937, Beckenham, Kent, England. Former Diplomat; Consultant. m. Elisabeth Margaret Hall, 4 sons, 1 daughter. Education: Degree in Modern Languages, Sidney Sussex College, Cambridge, 1958-61. Appointments: Foreign and Commonwealth Office, 1961-93; Head of International Peace Keeping Missions in Croatia and Ukraine, 1993-95; Consultant to Control Risk Company, 1996-98; Consultant on Eastern Europe, 1998-2006; Consultant for HMG in Global Conflict Prevention Policy, 2004-06. Honours: OBE, 1982; Swedish Order of the North Star, 1983. Address: White Cottage, Henley, Haslemere, Surrey GU27 3HQ, England.

GARRETT Lesley, b. 10 April 1955. Opera Singer. m. 1991, 1 son, 1 daughter. Education: Royal Academy of Music; National Opera Studio. Career: Winner, Kathleen Ferrier Memorial Competition, 1979; Performed with Welsh National Opera; Opera North; At Wexford and Buxton Festivals and at Glyndebourne; Joined ENO (Principal Soprano), 1984; Major roles includes: Susanna, Marriage of Figaro; Despina, Cosi Fan Tutte; Musetta, La Bohème; Jenny, Rise and Fall of the City of Mahaggony; Atalanta, Xerxes; Zerlinda, Don Giovanni; Yum-Yum, The Mikado; Adèle, Die Fledermaus; Oscar, A Masked Ball; Dalinda, Ariodante; Rose, Street Scene; Bella, A Midsummer Marriage; Eurydice, Orpheus and Eurydice; Title roles in the The Cunning Little Vixen and La Belle Vivette; Numerous concert hall performances in UK and abroad (including Last Night of the Proms); TV and radio appearances. CDs include: Prima Donna; Soprano in Red; Travelling Night; The Best of Lesley Garrett; When I Fall In Love. Honours: Hon DArts (Plymouth), 1995; Best selling Classical Artist, Gramophone Award, 1996. Address: The Music Partnership Ltd, 41 Aldebert Terrace, London, SW8 1BH, England.

GARTON George Alan, b. 4 June 1922, Scarborough, England. Retired Biochemist. m. Gladys F Davison, 2 daughters. Education: BSc, PhD, DSc, University of Liverpool. Appointments: Service with Ministry of Supply during WWII; Johnston Research and Teaching Fellow, University of Liverpool, 1949-50; Biochemist, 1950-63, Head, Lipid Biochemistry Department, 1963-83, Deputy Director, 1968-83, Honorary Research Associate, 1984-92, Honorary Professorial Fellow, 1992-, Rowett Research Institute; Member, Council, British Nutrition Foundation, 1982-2004; President, International Conferences on Biochemistry of Lipids, 1982-89; Chairman, British National Committee for Nutritional and Food Sciences, 1985-87. Publications: Numerous articles and papers on biochemistry and nutrition. Honours: FRSE, 1966; Visiting Professor of Biochemistry, University of North Carolina, 1967; FRS, 1978; SBStJ, 1986; Honorary Research Fellow, University of Aberdeen, 1987-. Memberships: Farmers Club, London; Fellow, Royal Society, London; Fellow, Royal Society of Edinburgh. Address: 2 St Devenicks Mews, Cults, Aberdeen, AB15 9LH, Scotland.

GASCOIGNE (Arthur) Bamber, b. 24 January 1935, London, England. Author; TV Presenter. m. Christina Ditchburn. Education: Eton College; Magdalene College, Cambridge. Appointments: Freelance Author; Chairman, University Challenge TV series, 1962-87; Author and Presenter of numerous TV documentaries including: The Christians, 1977; Man and Music, 1987-89; The Great Moghuls, 1990; Creator and Editor-in-Chief, HistoryWorld, 1994-. Publications: Novels and children's books; History books include: World Theatre, 1968; The Great Moghuls, 1971; Treasures and Dynasties of China, 1975; The Christians, 1977; Encyclopaedia of Britain, 1993. Address:

HistoryWorld, 1 St Helena Terrace, Richmond, London TW9 1NR, England. E-mail: bamber@historyworld.net Website: www.historyworld.net

GASCOIGNE Paul John, b. 26 May 1967, Gateshead, England. Footballer. m. Sheryl Failes, divorced, 1 son. Career: Played for Newcastle United, 1985-88; Tottenham Hotspur, 1988-92, Lazio, Italy, 1992-95, Glasgow Rangers, 1995-98; Middlesbrough, 1998-2000; Everton, 2000-02; Burnley, 2002; Signed as player/coach, Gansu Tianma (Gansu Sky Horses), Chinese B-League, 2003; Played for England, 13 under 21 caps, 57 full caps, World Cup Italy, 1990. Publication: Paul Gascoigne, autobiography with Paul Simpson, 2001; Gazza: My Story, 2004; Gazza: Tackling My Demons, 2006. Honours: BBC Sports Personality of the Year, 1990; FA Cup Winners Medal, 1991. Address: c/o Robertson Craig & Co, Clairmont Gardens, Glasgow, G3 7LW, Scotland.

GASKIN Catherine Marjella, b. 2 April 1929, County Louth, Dundalk, Ireland. Novelist. m. Sol Cornberg, 1 December 1955, deceased, 1999. Education: Holy Cross College, Sydney, Australia; Conservatorium of Music, Sydney. Publications: This Other Eden, 1946; With Every Year, 1947; Dust in Sunlight, 1950; All Else is Folly, 1951; Daughter of the House, 1952; Sara Dane, 1955; Blake's Reach, 1958; Corporation Wife, 1960; I Know My Love, 1962; The Tilsit Inheritance, 1963; The File on Devlin, 1965; Edge of Glass, 1967; Fiona, 1970; A Falcon for a Queen, 1972; The Property of a Gentleman, 1974; The Lynmara Legacy, 1975; The Summer of the Spanish Woman, 1977; Family Affairs, 1980; Promises, 1982; The Ambassador's Women, 1985; The Charmed Circle, 1988. Memberships: Society of Authors; Author's Guild of America. Address: Villa 139, The Manors, 15 Hale Road, Mosman, NSW 2088, Australia.

GATES William Henry (Bill), b. 8 October 1955, Seattle, USA. Computer Software Executive. m. Melinda French, 1994, 1 son, 2 daughters. Education: Harvard University. Appointments: Joined MITS, 1975; Programmer, Honeywell, 1975; Founder, Chairman, Board, Microsoft Corporation, 1976-, CEO, 1976-99; Software Architect, 1999-. Publications: The Future, 1994; The Road Ahead, 1996; Business at the Speed of Thought, 1999. Honours: Howard Vollum Award, Reed College, Portland, Oregon, 1984; Named CEO of Year, Chief Executive Magazine. Address: Microsoft Corporation, 1 Microsoft Way, Redmond, WA 98052, USA.

GATHERCOLE Peter William, b. 27 March 1929, Tilney St Lawrence, Norfolk, England. Anthropologist. 3 sons, 1 daughter. Education: Downshall Council School, Ilford, Essex, 1934-38; St Paul's Cathedral Choir School, London, 1939-43; Clifton College, Bristol, 1943-46; BA, 1952, MA, 1964, Cambridge; PostGraduate Diploma, Institute of Archaeology, London University, 1954. Appointments: Trainee Assistant, Birmingham Museum, England, 1954-56; Curator, Scunthorpe Museum, Scunthorpe, Lincolnshire, England, 1956-58; Head, Department of Anthropology, Otago University, Dunedin, New Zealand, 1958-68; Lecturer in Ethnology, Oxford University, England, 1968-70; Curator, University Museum of Archaeology and Anthropology, Cambridge, England, 1970-81; Official Fellow, (sometime Dean), 1977-96, Emeritus Fellow, 1996-, Darwin College, Cambridge, England. Publications: Pacific Anthropology, the history of Archaeology (especially on the life and works of V Gordon Childe), Museology and Cultural Politics. Honours: Honorary Member, New Zealand Archaeological Association; Honorary Member, Museum Ethnographers Group; Honorary Fellow, Department of Anthropology, Otago

University, Dunedin, New Zealand, 2003. Memberships: Royal Anthropological Institute; Polynesian Society, Cornwall Archaeological Society (Past President). Address: Roseland Cottage, Veryan Green, Truro, Cornwall, TR2 5QQ, England. E-mail: p.gathercole@virgin.net

GATHORNE-HARDY Jonathan, b. 17 May 1933, Edinburgh, Scotland. Author. m. (1) Sabrina Tennant, 1962, 1 son, 1 daughter, (2) Nicolette Sinclair-Loutit, 12 September 1985. Education: BA, Arts, Trinity College, Cambridge, 1957. Publications: One Foot in the Clouds (novel), 1961; Chameleon (novel), 1967; The Office (novel), 1970; The Rise and Fall of the British Nanny, 1972; The Public School Phenomenon, 1977; Love, Sex, Marriage and Divorce, 1981; Doctors, 1983; The Centre of the Universe is 18 Baedeker Strasse (short stories), 1985; The City Beneath the Skin (novel), 1986; The Interior Castle: A Life of Gerald Brenan (biography), 1992; Particle Theory (novel), 1996; Alfred C. Kinsey - Sex The Measure of All Things, A Biography, 1998; Half An Arch (autobiographical memoir), 2004. Other: 12 novels for children. Contributions to: Numerous magazines and journals. Honours: J R Ackerley Prize for Autobiography, 2005. Address: 31 Blacksmith's Yard, Binham, Fakenham, Norfolk NR21 0AL, England.

GATTING Michael William (Mike), b. 6 June 1957, Kingsbury, Middlesex, England. Cricketer. m. Elaine Mabbott, 1980, 2 sons. Career: Right-hand batsman and right-arm medium bowler, played for Middlesex, 1975-98, Captain, 1983-97; 79 Tests for England, 1977-95, 23 as Captain; Scoring 4,409 runs (average 35.5) including 10 hundreds; Scored 36,549 first-class runs (94 hundreds); Toured Australia (Captain), 1986-87; Captain, rebel cricket tour to South Africa, 1989-90; 92 limited-overs internationals, 37 as Captain; Member, England Selection Committee, 1997-; Director of Coaching, Middlesex Cricket Club, 1999-2000; Director, Ashwell Leisure, 2001-. Publications: Limited Overs, 1986; Triumph in Australia, 1987; Leading From the Front (autobiography), 1988. Honour: OBE; Wisden Cricketer of The Year, 1984; President, Lord's Taverners, 2005/2006. Address: c/o Middlesex County Cricket Club, Lord's Cricket Ground, St John's Wood Road, London, NW8 8QN, England.

GAUDRON Alfred W(asserman), b. 11 October 1947, Sydney, Australia. Retired Librarian. Education: BA (Hons), 1972, MA (Hons), 1977, Sydney University; Diploma in Librarianship (Dip.Lib), University of New South Wales, 1973. Appointments: Assistant Auditor, Auditor General's Department of New South Wales, 1966-67; Trainee Librarian, State Library of New South Wales, 1968-71; Commonwealth Scholar/Academic, University of Sydney, 1972-77; Professional Medical Librarian, 1978-99. Publications: Is there a future for Libraries (articles), 1976; For Lord Mountbatten (sonnet), Anthology of Australian Poetry, 1987; No Blunt Invention (poems), 1989; Narrabeen North Public School: Fiftieth Anniversary, 1989; A Model Library (articles), 1988; Narrabeen and Other Places: Poems drawn from the Northern Beaches, 1974-1991; Concision and Precision: Poems for Fred, 1993; Sydney Qumran Verse: Sydney Tales and Lore Illustrated by the Author, 1993; Israel and Egypt: A Poet's Journey Illustrated by the Author, 1995; Miscellanies: Being Essays, Plays and Poems on Peace, Society, Psychiatry and Librarianship, 1995; 12 Thought Stories (or Kiss a Wizard Today), 1995; The Honeyed Muse: Love Sonnets, 1996; Locked Ward: 13 Short Stories, 1996; Some Temporal Words (Poems), 2001; Reflections: Old Poems and New Sonnets, 2003; Essay on World Peace, 2003; Dead Sea Scrolls and Other Poems, 2004; Sir Thomas Browne: Doctor of Faith and

Science, 2005; Love's Pauper (poem), China; Various Poems of Love and Nature, 2006. Honours: Doctor of Literature (Litt D), World Academy of Arts and Culture; Honorary Degree, World Congress of Poets, Haifa University, Israel, 1992. Memberships: Voltaire Foundation; Schizophrenia Foundation of New South Wales; Jewish Board of Deputies; Benjamin Short Society; Mission Australia; New South Wales Chess Association; Voices Israel: Group of Poets in English; Affiliated with World Peace and Diplomacy Forum; Full Member, Australian Society of Authors. Address: 14 Oak Street, North Narrabeen, NSW 2101, Australia.

GAUGHAN John Anthony, b. 19 August 1932, Listowel, Co Kerry, Ireland. Catholic Priest. Education: BA, University College, Dublin, 1953; BD, St Patrick's College, Maynouth, Ireland, 1956; MA, University College, Dublin, 1965; PhD, 1992; DLitt, 1996. Appointments: Chaplain and Vocational School Teacher, Presentation College, Bray, 1957-60; Reader, Most Precious Blood, Cabra West, 1960-62; Curate, Most Sacred Heart: Aughrim-Greenane, 1962-64; Chaplain and University Tutor, University College Dublin, St Mary's Convent, Donnybrook, 1964-65; Curate, St Joseph's, Eastwall, 1965-67, Our Lady of Good Counsel, Drimnagh, 1967-70, St Patrick's, Monkstown, 1970-77, St Thérèse, Mount Merrion, 1977-83, University Church, St Stephen's Green, 1983-88; Parish Priest, Guardian Angels, Blackrock, 1988-. Publications: Contributor of over 95 articles to professional journals; Author of 25 books including most recently: Olivia Mary Taaffe (1832-1918): Foundress of St Joseph's Young Priests Society, 1995; Memoirs of Senator Joseph Connolly: A Founder of Modern Ireland (editor), 1996; Newmans's University Church: A History and Guide, 1997; Memoirs of Senator James G Douglas: Concerned Citizen (editor), 1998; At the Coal Face: Recollections of a City & Country Priest 1950-2000, 2000; Scouting in Ireland, 2006; Articles and book reviews to various periodicals and newspapers. Memberships: National Library of Ireland Society, Chairman, 2000-; Kerry Archaeological and History Society, Committee Member, 1976-89; Writers Week, Founding Member, 1971, President, 1983-90, Vice-President, 1991-; Irish PEN, Committee Member, 1976-, Chairman, 1981-2004. Address: 56 Newtownpark Ave, Blackrock, Co Dublin, Ireland.

GAULTIER Jean-Paul, b. 24 April 1952, Arcueil, Paris. Fashion Designer. Career: Launched first collection with his Japanese partner, 1978; Since then known on international scale for his men's and women's collections; First junior collection, 1988; Costume designs for film The Cook, The Thief, His Wife and Her Lover, 1989, for ballet le Défilé de Régine Chopinot, 1985; Madonna's World Tour, 1990; My Life Is Hell, 1991; The City of Lost Children, 1995; The Fifth Element, 1997; Absolutely Fabulous, 2001; Dangerous Liaisons, 2003; Bad Education, 2004; Madonna: The Confessions Tour Live from London (TV), 2006; Released record, How to Do That (in collaboration with Tony Mansfield), 1989; Launched own perfume, 1993; Designer of costume for Victoria Abril in Pedro Almodóvar's film Koka, 1994. Launched perfume brands Jean-Paul Gaultier, 1993, La Mâle, 1995, Fragile, 1999. Honours: Fashion Oscar, 1987; Progetto Leonardo Award for How to Do That, 1989; Chevalier des Arts et des Lettres. Address: Jean-Paul Gaultier SA, 30 rue du Faubourg-Saint-Antoine, 75012 Paris, France.

GAVAYEVA Nadezhda N, b. 7 February 1951, Saransk, Russia. Professor of English. Education: Diploma, Mordovian State University, 1973; Candidate of Philological Sciences, 1985; Associate Professor, 1991. Appointments: Postgraduate, Leningrade State University, 1973-77; Assistant, English

Language Department, 1978-86, Teacher of English, 1978-86, Senior Teacher, 1986-89, Associate Professor, 1989-, Mordovian State University. Publications: 51 publications on text linguistics, ways of teaching English as a foreign language, cultural aspects of teaching English. Honours: Gold Medal, high school, 1968; Honoured Doctor, Udmurt State University, Russia, 1995. Address: 52-15 Demokraticheskaya Street, Saransk, Mordovia 430000, Russia.

GAYDUK Sergey A, b. 3 May 1974, Minsk, Belarus. Professor. m. Alena, 1 daughter. Education: Byelorussian Academy of Physical Culture, 1991-95; Postgraduate student, Belarusian State University of Physical Culture, 2000-04; Doctor of Pedagogy, 2005. Appointments: Professor, Ministry of Internal Affairs, Academy of the Republic of Belarus. Publications: 55 papers and articles in professional journals. Honours: Corresponding Member, International Academy of Information Technologies, 2006. Address: 108-96 Kropotkina St, Minsk 220 123, Belarus. E-mail: gsa.4791@mail.ru

GEBAUER Phyllis, b. 17 October 1928, Chicago, Illinois, USA. Novelist; Writer; Teacher. m. Frederick A Gebauer, 1950, deceased. Education: BS, Northwestern University, 1950; MA, University of Houston, 1966; Postgraduate, several universities. Appointments: Workshop Leader, Santa Barbara Writers' Conference, 1980-2005; Instructor, University of California at Los Angeles Extension Writers' Program, 1989-; Lecturer, San Diego State University Writers Conference, 1995-. Publications: The Pagan Blessing, 1979; The Cottage, 1985; The Final Murder of Monica Marlowe, 1986; Criticism, The Art of Give and Take, 1987; Hot Widow, 2008. Honours: 1st Prize for Fiction, Santa Barbara City College, 1972; 1st and 2nd Prizes for Fiction, Santa Barbara City College, 1973. Memberships: PEN Center, USA, West; Dorothy L Sayers Society; Mystery Writers of America; Sisters in Crim, Author's Guild. Address: 515 West Scenic Drive, Monrovia, CA 91016-1511, USA.

GÉBLER Carlo, b. 21 August 1954, Dublin, Ireland. Writer; Film-Maker. m. Tyga Thomason, 23 August 1990, 3 sons, 2 daughters. Education: BA, English and Related Literature, University of York, 1976; Graduate, National Film and Television School, 1979. Appointments: Part-time Teacher, Creative Writing, HMP Maze, Co Antrim, 1993-95; Appointed Writer-in-Residence, HMP Maghaberry, Co Antrim, 1997; International Writing Fellow, 2004, Arts Council Writing Fellow, 2006, Trinity College, Dublin.; Temporary Lectureship in Creative Writing, Queen's University, Belfast, 2007. Publications: The Eleventh Summer, 1985; August in July, 1986; Work & Play, 1987; Driving through Cuba, 1988; Malachy and His Family, 1990; The Glass Curtain: Inside an Ulster Community, 1991; Life of a Drum, 1991; The Cure, 1994; W9 and Other Lives, 1998; How to Murder a Man, 1998; Frozen Out, 1998; The Base, 1999; Father & I, 2000; Dance of Death, 2000; Caught on a Train, 2001; 10 Rounds, 2002; August' 44, 2003; The Siege of Derry, A History, 2005; The Bull Raid, 2005; Silhouette, 2007. Membership: Elected to Aosdána, Ireland, 1990. Address: c/o Antony Harwood, 103 Walton Street, Oxford, OX2 6EB, England.

GEDDES Gary, b. 9 June 1940, Vancouver, British Columbia, Canada. Professor of English; Writer; Poet. m. (1) Norma Joan Fugler, 1963, divorced 1969, 1 daughter, (2) Jan Macht, 1973, divorced 1999, 2 daughters. Education: BA, University of British Columbia, 1962; Diploma in Education, University of Reading, 1964; MA, 1966, PhD, 1975, University of Toronto. Appointments: Lecturer, Carleton University, Ottawa, Ontario, 1971-72; University of Victoria, British Columbia,

1972-74; Writer-in-Residence, 1976-77, Visiting Associate Professor, 1977-78, University of Alberta, Edmonton; Visiting Associate Professor, 1978-79, Professor of English, 1979-98, Concordia University, Montreal, Quebec; Distinguished Professor of Canadian Culture, Western Washington University, 1999-2001; Writer-in-Residence, University of Ottawa, 2004; Adjunct Professor and Writer-in-Residence, University of British Columbia, 2005; Writer-in-Residence, Vancouver Public Library, 2006. Publications: 20th Century Poetry and Poets, 1969, 4th edition, 1996, 5th edition, 2006; 15 Canadian Poets (editor with Phyllis Bruce), 1970, 4th edition, 1999; Poems, 1970; The Inner Ear: An Anthology of New Canadian Poets (editor), 1983; The Unsettling of the West (stories), 1986; Letters from Managua: Meditations on Politics or Art (essays), 1990; The Art of Short Fiction: An International Anthology, 1992; Active Trading: Selected Poems, 1970-95, 1996; Sailing Home: A Journey Through Time, Place and Memory (non-fiction), 2001; Kingdom of Ten Thousand Things: An Impossible Journey from Kabul to Chiapas (non-fiction), 2005; Verse: Rivers Inlet, 1972; Snakeroot, 1973; Letter of the Master of Horse, 1973; The Acid Test, 1981; The Terracotta Army, 1984; Changes of State, 1986; Hong Kong, 1987; Light of Burning Towers, 1990; Girl By the Water, 1994; The Perfect Cold Warrior, 1995; Flying Blind, 1998; Skaldance, 2004, Italian translation, 2006; Falsework, 2007. Honours: E J Pratt Medal; National Poetry Prize, Canadian Authors Association; America's Best Book Award, Commonwealth Poetry Competition, 1985; Writers Choice Award; National Magazine Gold Award; Archibald Lampman Prize; Silver Medal, Milton Acorn Competition; Poetry Book Society Recommendation; Gabriela Mistral Prize, 1996. Memberships: League of Canadian Poets; Writers' Union of Canada; Playwright's Guild of Canada. Address: 2750 Seaside Drive, RR 2, Sooke, British Columbia, V0S 1N0, Canada.

GEDEONOV Andrei, b. 10 September 1949, Leningrad, USSR. Radiochemist. m. Iulia Basova, 1 daughter. Education: Chemist, Leningrad State University, Leningrad, USSR, 1966-71, Postgraduate Student, 1971-74; PhD, Postgraduate Study V G Khlopin Radium Institute, Leningrad, 1977; Junior Research Worker, 1974-79, Senior Research Worker, 1979-91, Head of Laboratory, 1991-, V G Khlopin Radium Institute, Saint Petersburg, Russia. Publications: Articles as co-author in scientific journals and conference proceedings including: Journal of Environmental Radioactivity, 2002; Proceedings of the 5th International Conference on Environmental Radioactivity in the Arctic and Antarctic, St Petersburg, Russia, 2002; 3 USSR Patents. Honours: Medal, Exhibition of National Economic Achievement, 1978; Honorary Title, Inventor of the USSR, 1983; Honorary Title Veteran of Atomic Industry, 1998. Membership: Fellow, House of Scientists, Saint Petersburg, Russia. Address: Dzeleznovodskaja St 27-72, 199155 Saint Petersburg, Russia. E-mail: gedeonov@pop3.rcom.ru

GEE Arthur, b. 10 January 1934, Latchford, Warrington, Lancashire, England. Artist. m. Margaret Ray Robinson, 1 son, 1 daughter. Education: St Helens College of Art and Design, 1983-84. Appointments: Trainee, Wire Industry, 1949-52; RAF, 1952-55; Mechanical Engineering Draughtsman, 1956-83; Full Time Artist, 1983-94; Semi-Retired, 1994-; Artist in Residence, 2003 and 2006; Nature in Art, Wallsworth Hall, Twigworth, Gloucestershire; Co-founder, National Exhibition of Wildlife Art, North West England. Creative works: 2 illustrations for Flights of Imagination edited by Mike Mockler; Works in collections: Acrylic titled Mallard in the Sere Wood; Collection at Nature in Art, Twigworth,

Gloucester, 2004; Printmaker, originator of the Green Man Press, 2004; Etchings, Lithographs, Mezzotints, Artists Books, 2006; latest production The Bird Alphabet. Honours: Certificate of Merit, Italian Academy of Art, Salsomaggiore; Drawing Prize, National Exhibition of Wildlife Art, Liverpool; Highly commended acrylic, Welsh Snow, NAPA Show, St Ives, Cornwall, 2003; Best British Painting Award, National Acrylic Painters Association Annual Exhibition, St Ives, Cornwall, 2004; Purchase Prize, Mini Print International, Barcelona, Spain. Listed in national and international biographical directories. Memberships: Society of Wildlife Artists, 1969-99; National Acrylic Painters Association, 1992-; Sefton Guild of Artists, 1996-; Warrington Visual Artists Forum, 1998-. Address: 31 Karen Close, Burtonwood, Warrington, Cheshire, WA5 4LL, England.

GEERTZ Clifford (James), b. 23 August 1926, San Francisco, California, USA. Professor of Social Science; Writer. m. (1) Hildred Storey, 30 October 1948, divorced 1982, 1 son, 1 daughter, (2) Karen Blu, 1987. Education: AB, Antioch College, 1950; PhD, Harvard University, 1956. Appointments: Research Assistant, 1952-56, Research Associate, 1957-58, Massachusetts Institute of Technology; Instructor and Research Associate, Harvard University, 1956-57; Fellow, Center for Advanced Study in the Behavioral Sciences, Stanford, 1958-59; Assistant Professor of Anthropology, University of California at Berkeley, 1958-60; Assistant Professor, 1960-61, Associate Professor, 1962-64, Professor, 1964-68, Divisional Professor, 1968-70, University of Chicago; Senior Research Career Fellow, National Institute for Mental Health, 1964-70; Professor of Social Science, 1970-, Harold F Linder Professor of Social Science, 1982-, Professor Emeritus, 2000-, Institute for Advanced Study, Princeton, New Jersey; Visiting Lecturer with Rank of Professor, Princeton University, 1975-2000; Various guest lectureships. Publications: The Religion of Java, 1960; Old Societies and New States (editor), Agricultural Involution: The Processes of Ecological Change in Indonesia, Peddlers and Princes, 1963; The Social History of an Indonesian Town, 1965; Person, Time and Conduct in Bali: An Essay in Cultural Analysis, 1966; Islam Observed: Religious Development in Morocco and Indonesia, 1968; The Interpretation of Cultures: Selected Essays, Kinship in Bali (with Hildred Geertz), 1973; Myth, Symbol and Culture (editor), 1974; Meaning and Order in Moroccan Society (with Hildred Geertz and Lawrence Rosen), 1979; Negara: The Theatre State in Nineteenth Century Bali, 1980; Local Knowledge: Further Essays in Interpretive Anthropology, Bali, interprétation d'une culture, 1983; Works and Lives: The Anthropologist as Author, 1988; After the Fact: Two Countries, Four Decades, One Anthropologist, 1995; Available Light: Anthropological Reflections on Philosophical Topics, 2000. Contributions to: Scholarly books and journals. Honours: Talcott Parsons Prize, American Academy of Arts and Sciences, 1974; Sorokin Prize, American Sociological Association, 1974; Distinguished Lecturer, American Anthropological Association, 1983; Huxley Memorial Lecturer and Medallist, Royal Anthropological Institute, 1983; Distinguished Scholar Award, Association for Asian Studies, 1987; National Book Critics Circle Prize in Criticism, 1988; Horace Mann Distinguished Alumnus Award, Antioch College, 1992; Fukuoka Asian Cultural Prize, 1992. Memberships: American Academy of Arts and Sciences, fellow; American Association for the Advancement of Science, fellow; American Philosophical Society, fellow; British Academy, corresponding fellow; Council on Foreign Relations, fellow; National Academy of Sciences, fellow;

Royal Anthropological Institute, honorary fellow. Address: c/o School of Social Science, Institute for Advanced Study, Princeton, NJ 08540, USA.

GEFFEN David, b. 21 February 1943, Brooklyn, New York, USA. Film, Recording and Theatre Executive. Appointments: William Morris Talent Agency, 1964; Launched new film studio with Steven Spielberg and Jeffrey Katzenberg; Founder, Music Publishing Company Tunafish Music with Laura Nyro; Joined Ashley Famous Agency; Appointed Vice President, Creative Man (now International Creative Man), 1968; Founder, Asylum Records and Geffen-Roberts Management Company with Elliot Roberts, 1970; Sold Asylum to Warner Communications, but remained President, 1971, merged it with Elektra, signed up Bob Dylan and Joni Mitchell; Vice-Chairman, Warner Bros Pictures, 1975-76; Founder, Geffen Records, President, 1980-, signed up Elton John, John Lennon and Yoko Ono and many others, sold label to Music Corporation of America Inc, 1990; Founder, Geffen Film Company, Producer: Personal Best, 1982; Little Shop of Horrors,1986; Beetlejuice, 1988; Men Don't Leave; Defending Your Life; Interview with the Vampire: The Vampire Chronicles, 1994. Co-producer, musical, Dreamgirls, 1981-85; Cats, 1982; Madame Butterfly, 1986; Social Security; Chess, 1990; Miss Saigon; Founder, DGC record label; Co-founder, Dreamworks, SKG, 1995-. Address: Dreamworks SKG, 100 Universal Plaza, Building 477, Universal City, CA 91608, USA.

GELLER Scott Allen, b. 14 January 1964, Oaklawn, Illinois, USA. Executive Business Consultant. m. Deborah Ruth Shuman, 2 sons, 1 daughter. Education: BA, Law, Business, Theatre, Carthage College, 1986; MS, Clinical Psychology, Long Island University, 1990; M Div, Religion, Trinity International; Staff Placement, US Chaplain's School, West Point Military Academy, 3 years. Appointments: Advanced Manager Recruit, Pepsi Co; Assistant Chaplain, Staff, West Point Military Academy; Field Associate, College Liaison, General Motors; Executive Director, Sunrise Assisted Living; Marketing Consultant, Salem Communications Corp; Administrator, General Manager, The Harbor Campus; Regional/National Healthcare Administrator, Sunwest Management Company; President, CEO, Sterling Country International Consultancy. Publications: Numerous articles in professional journals. Honours: Army Commendation Medal with Oakleaf Cluster; Southwest Asian Service Medal with attached Bronze Star; Army Achievement Medal; National Defense Medal; Overseas Service Ribbon; Army Service Ribbon; Presidential Commendation Notes; Gamma Kappa Alpha; Listed in international biographical dictionaries. Memberships: American Legion; PBS Television; Salvation Army; Mosquito Hill Educational Nature Center; Elena's Hope Mito Research Foundation; Habitat for Humanity; Community Benefit Tree; Republican National Party; The Cancer Lymphoma Society; Youth Educated in Safety; Community Hospice Foundation; West Point Military Academy; Maritime Museum; Memorial Fireman's Fund. Address: PO Box 151, Appleton, WI 54912, USA. E-mail: sgeller@new.rr.com

GENEL (Guenel) Leonid Samooilovitch, b. 11 August 1946, Moscow, Russia. Materials Scientist. m. Galkina Valentina Vassilyevna. 2 sons. Education: Moscow Steels and Alloys Institute, 1964-69; Magistre Diploma, 1969; Moscow D I Mendeleev Chemical Processing Institute; Postgraduate Studies, 1976-79; DrPhil, 1980. Appointments: Engineer, Institute for Sources of Electrical Energy, 1972; Senior Engineer, Research Worker, Institute for Metal Protection from

Corrosion, 1982; Chief of Sector, Chief of Department, NPO Polymerbyt, 1991; General Director, Spectroplast Ltd, 1991-. Publications: More than 90 publications including patents and author's certificates in the following fields: Mechanochemistry of gluing, treatment of surface, development of polymer based materials with new properties; Wave approach to the control strength and durability of solids and making new materials; Secondary coolants; Concentrates of additives: anti-corrosion, anti-scaling, controlling viscosity, decreasing foaming and freezing point; Philosophy and physico-chemistry of live matter as doctrines concerning: bioquanta and biozones, explaining some aspects of behaviour of living organisms' associations, including people's; origin of the olive from the lifeless; interdependence mass and space through acceleration of the Universe's expansion; language, creating the Universe, in which explanation of possibility of effect of expressions, including prayers, being emitted by human, on cosmic vacuum has been given. All main kinds of sounds (and corresponding to them letters) form 5 positions of tongue in larynx. Each position generates signal of excitation in a concrete area of cerebral cortex. The excited area of cerebral cortex consists of hundreds of millions of cells with 46 (45) the same chromosomes in each cell. At the excitation they sound as orchestra with electromagnetic (but not acoustic) instruments – DNA-quantum generators. Such electromagnetic waves as 'electromagnetic symphonies' being coherent and chiral are capable to go out into the cosmic space and in certain way to structure it; Analogously sounds and the accumulation of nerve cells near the heart. Honours: The Outstanding Scholar of the 20th Century Medal, IBC, 2000; The Leading Intellectual of the World Medal, IBC, 2004; The Top 100 Scientists Medal, IBC, 2005; The World Medal of Freedom, ABI, USA, 2005; The Laureate of All-Russian Exhibition Centre Medal; Title of Honorary Chemical Industry Worker, Russia. Memberships: D I Mendeleev Chemical Society; Academician of Russian Academy of Sciences and Arts; Academician of International Academy of Refrigeration Address: Spectroplast Ltd, 11, 2nd Vladimirskaya str, Moscow 111123, Russia. E-mail: lg@splast.ru

GEORGE Andrew Robert, b. 3 July 1955, Haslemere, Surrey, England. University Professor. m. Junko, 3 sons. Education: BA (1st Class Honours), University of Birmingham, 1976; PhD, 1985. Appointments: Teaching Assistant, 1983-85, Lecturer, Ancient Near Eastern Studies, 1985-94, Reader, Assyriology, 1994-2000, Professor, Babylonian, 2000-, Head, Department of Near and Middle East, 2001-04, School of Oriental and African Studies (SOAS), London; Honorary Research Fellow, Institute of Archaeology, University College, London, 1995-98; Honorary Lecturer, Institute of Archaeology, University College, London, 1998-2002; Visiting Professor, Seminar für Sprachen und Kulturen des vorderen Orients, Ruprecht-Karls-Universität, Heidelberg, Germany, 2000; Honorary Professor, Institute of Archaeology, University College, London, 2002-; Visiting Scholar, School of Historical Studies, Institute for Advanced Study, Princeton, New Jersey, 2004-05; Fellow, British Academy, 2006-. Publications: Babylonian Topographical Texts, 1992; House Most High. The Temples of Ancient Mesopotamia, 1993; The Epic of Gilgamesh, A Concise Dictionary of Akkadian, Wisdom, Gods and Literature. Studies in Assyriology in Honour of W G Lambert, 2000; The Babylonian Gilgamesh Epic. Introduction, Critical Edition and Cuneiform Texts, 2003; La epopeya de Gilgamesh (Spanish translation), 2004; Nineveh: Papers of the 49e Recontre Assyriologique Internationale, London, 7-11 July 2003, 2005; Many articles in academic journals. Honours: Kuwait-British Fellowship Society Prize for Middle Eastern Studies, 2000.

Memberships: Vice Chair, Treasurer, London Centre for the Ancient Near East, 2001-; Board, Norwegian Institute for Palaeography and Historical Philology, Oslo, 2003-; Patron, Enhednanna Society, 2003-; Kommission für das Akademie prokjekt Edition der Literarischen Keilschriftexte aus Assur, Heidelberger Akademie der Wissenschaften, 2004-. Address: SOAS, University of London, Russell Square, London WC1H 0XG, England. E-mail: ag5@soas.ac.uk

GEORGIEV Viden, b. 1 February 1925, Gintsi, Sofia Region, Bulgaria. Physician. m. Elena Kisselkova, 1 son, 1 daughter. Education: Doctor of Medicine, Medical University, Sofia, Bulgaria, 1954; Doctor of Philosophy, Institute of Experimental Medicine, Saint Petersburg, Russia, 1962. Appointments: Assistant, 1955-58, Senior Assistant, 1959-63, Associate Professor, 1967-75, Professor of Physiology, 1975-, National Sports Academy, Sofia, Bulgaria; Researcher, Sorbonne, Paris, France, 1964-66. Publications: Author: Proprioceptors and Circulation, (monograph), 1965; Vascular Reactions in Sportsmen after Physical Efforts (monograph), 1973; Nervous System and Sport (book), 1975; Peripheral and Brain Circulation at Physical Efforts (monograph), 1991. Memberships: Bulgarian Society of Physiological Sciences; Bulgarian Society of Sports Medicine; New York Academy of Sciences; National movement for development and protections of the science and higher education. Address: 14 Tsar Peter Street, Sofia 1463, Bulgaria.

GEORGIEVA Milena, b. 22 August 1957, Sofia, Bulgaria. Barrister. m. Todor Tabakov, 1 son, 1 daughter. Education: German Language College, Sofia; MSc, Law, Sofia Law University. Appointments: Assistant Judge, 1980-82, Legal Advisor, 1982-84, Bulgarian Chamber of Commerce and Industry; Legal Advisor, Ministry of Foreign Affairs; Counsel to the Prime Minister of Bulgaria, 1992-; Head, Legal Department, Ministry of Foreign Affairs, 1997-; Chief of the Office of the Minister of Foreign Affairs, 1998-2000; Barrister, Partner in Interlex; President, Association of Patent Attorneys. Publications: Agreements on Mutual Encouragement and Protection of Investments; Enforcement of Industrial Property Rights. Memberships: Sofia Bar Association; European Patent Institute; American Bar Association; Bulgarian Association of Patent Attorneys. E-mail: m.tabakova@interlex-bg.com

GERSTER Richard, b. 29 May 1946, Winterthur, Switzerland. Economist. m. Doris Gerster, 1 son, 2 daughters. Education: PhD Econ, University of St Gall, Switzerland, 1973. Appointments: Programme Co-ordinator, Helvetas, 1972-81; Director, Alliance Sud (Swiss Coalition of Development Organisations), 1981-98; Director, Gerster Consulting (www.gersterconsulting.ch), for public policy and international development, 1998-. Publications: Switzerland as a Developing Country, 1998; Alternative Approaches to Poverty Reduction Strategies (SDC working paper), 2000; Patents and Development, Third World Network, 2001; Globalisation and Equity, 2nd edition 2005. Honour: Christoph Eckenstein Award for the Relations Switzerland-Third World, 1987; Blue Planet Award, 2002. Memberships: Member of Parliament in the Canton of Zürich, 1987-92; Member, Governing Board of State Bank of Zürich, 1988-2003; Member, Development Advisory Council to the Government of Austria, 2000-. Address: Goldistrasse 1, CH-8805 Richterswil, Switzerland.

GHAFOOR Abdul, b. 10 February 1928, Mansehra, Pakistan. m. Tahera, 1 son, 1 daughter, deceased. Education: BA, Honours, Urdu Language and Literature, 1955; PhD, Honours, Engineering, USA, 1995; Master with Hons: English, Urdu,

Hindi Literature (USA), 2006. Appointments: Lt Colonel and Acting Brigadier, Engineer Corps, Pakistan Army, 1952-77; Chief Engineer, Government of Punjab, Provincial Government of Pakistan, 1977-79; Director of Works and Chief Engineer, Private Limited Construction Company, 1979-81; General Manager and Chief Engineer, Saudi Development Company, Jeddah, 1981-82; Chief Resident Engineer, private Consulting Engineers firm, Pakistan, 1982-85; Project Director, Riyadh, Saudi Arabia consultant engineers company, 1985-86; Chief Engineer, consulting engineers firm, Pakistan, 1987; Chief Engineer, construction company, Pakistan, 1988-90; Director of Works in Pakistan, private trading and finance company, 1990; Chairman, Chief Executive, Private Ltd Consulting Engineers, 1990-98; Director General Al-Beruni Group for Education, 1998-. Publications: Anne Frank – Diary of a Young Girl, Urdu Edition; Silver Spoon Guide for Quality English Writing; Numerous articles in professional magazines and newspapers. Honours: Several medals and letters of appreciation; International Peace Prize, UCC; Legion of Honor, ABI; Listed in Who's Who publications and biographical dictionaries. Memberships: Life Fellow, American Society of Civil Engineers, USA; Fellow, Institution of Engineers, Pakistan, Structure Institute of Engineers, USA; PE of Pakistan Engineering Council; Member, Advisory Council, IBC; Deputy Governor, ABIRA, USA. Address: House no 36, Street 5, F-8/3, Islamabad, Pakistan.

GHANI Abdul Ghani A, b. 10 April 1956. New Zealand Citizen. Education: BSc, Physics, 1978, MSc, Physics, 1981, Baghdad, Iraq; PhD, Chemical Engineering, Food Engineering, The University of Auckland, New Zealand, 2001. Appointments: Research Associate, Iraqi Atomic Energy Agency, Baghdad, Iraq, 1978-81; Physicist, Private Factory, Iraq, 1981-83; Research Fellow, Solar Energy Research Centre, Iraqi Scientific Research Council, Baghdad, Iraq, 1983-90; Lecturer, Numerical Analysis and Computer Programming, Department of Physics, University of Baghdad, Iraq, 1985-86; Lecturer, Mathematics, Numerical Analysis and Computer Programming, University of Tikrit, Iraq, 1990-91; Technical Manager, Private Factory, Baghdad, Iraq, 1991-95; PhD Student, 1997-2001, Research Fellow, Department of Chemical and Materials Engineering 2001-, The University of Auckland, New Zealand; Consultant, Software Design Ltd, Auckland. Publications: Book: Sterilization of Food in Retort Pouches, 2005; Book chapter: Numerical simulation of transient two-dimensional profiles of temperature, concentration and flow of liquid food in a can during sterilization (co-author), 2003; Over 75 articles in professional international journals and presented at conferences as co-author include: A computational and experimental study of heating and cooling cycles during thermal sterilization of liquid foods in pouches using CFD, 2003; Analysis of thermal sterilization of solid-liquid food mixture in cans, 2003; 2 chapters in area of computational Fluid Dynamics. Honours: 2 Scholarships, 1998-2000, Research Fellowship, Department of Chemical and Materials Engineering, University of Auckland, New Zealand; Best Doctoral Thesis in the Faculty of Engineering, 2001; Post Doctoral Fellowship and Senior Research Scientist, 2002-2005, New Zealand Foundation of Research Science and Technology; Listed in Who's Who publications and biographical dictionaries. Memberships include: Food Science and Process Engineering Group, Department of Chemical and Materials Engineering, The University of Auckland; Australian New Zealand Solar Energy Society; International Solar Energy Society; Institute of Professional Engineers of New Zealand; Society of Chemical Engineering New Zealand. Address: 5-238 St Heliers Bay Road, Auckland, New Zealand. E-mail: ghanialbaali@hotmail.com

GHARIBI Wajeb, b. 14 October 1961, Idleb, Syria. Associate Professor. m. Mariana Pereu, 2 sons. Education: BSc, Mathematics, Aleppo University, Syria, 1983; M Inf, University of the State of Moldova, Kishineve, Moldova, 1987; PhD, Computer Science & Operations Research, Minsk, Belarus, 1990. Appointments: Assistant Professor, 1990-94, Associate Professor, 1998-2001, Aleppo University, Syria; Associate Professor, Taiz University, Yemen, 1994-98; Associate Professor, King Khalid University, Abha, Saudi Arabia, 2001-. Publications: Numerous articles in professional journals. Honours: Third World Academy of Science Prize, Supreme Council of Sciences, Syria, 2001; Listed in international biographical dictionaries. Memberships: Active Member, New York Academy of Science; Member, Indian Society for Technical Education: Member, National Syrian Computer Society. Address: PO Box 394, College of Computer Science, King Khalid University, Abha 61411, Kingdom of Saudi Arabia. E-mail: gharibiw@hotmail.com

GHISTA Dhanjoo Noshir, b. 10 January 1940, Bombay, India. Professor. m. Garda Kirsten, 1 son, 2 daughters. Education: PhD, Stanford University, California, 1964. Appointments: Post-Doctoral Research Associate, National Academy of Sciences, National Research Council, Washington DC, 1964-66; Aerospace Engineering and Medical Engineering Scientist, National Academy of Sciences, (NRC) and NASA, Ames Research Centre, 1966-69; Associate Professor, Washington University, St Louis, USA, 1969-71; Professor and Head, Biomedical Engineering Division, Indian Institute of Technology, 1971-75; Senior Scientist, NASA, Ames Research Centre, and Stanford VA Medical Centre, 1975-78; Professor of Biomechanics and Engineering Mechanics, Michigan Technological University, 1979-81; Head, Biomedical Engineering Department, Chedoke-McMasters Hospitals, Ontario, Canada, 1981-84; Professor of Medicine and Engineering Physics, Chairman, Biomedical Engineering, McMaster University, 1981-87; Vice President, Board of Directors, Corporation for Medical Devices and Industry Development, Ontario, 1988-89; Founding Professor and Chairman, Department of Biophysics, Faculty of Medicine and Health Sciences, United Arab Emirates University, Al Ain, United Arab Emirates, 1989-95; Professor and Head, Biomedical Engineering Department, Osmania University, Hyderabad, India, 1995-2000; Professor, Nanyang Technological University, Singapore, 1998-99, 2000-; Vice-chancellor designate, Ananda Marga Gurukula University and Neohumanistic University System, 2000-. Pioneered: Biomedical Engineering, Healthcare Engineering and Management Science, Community-development Engineering of Sustainable Townships (for rural development and urban transformation) and advancement of Third-world countries. Prime Interests: Neo Global Political-Economic Order: Economic democracy, Political (Party-less) Governance based on elected representatives from Soceital/Community sectors, and World Government; Biomedical and Healthcare Sciences and Engineering; Socio-Economic-Political Science and Engineering; Neohumanistic Education System (for liberating the intellect); Consciousness and Cognitive Science; Psychological and Behavioural Science; Sports Science and Medicine; Role of University in Society. Publications: Over 20 books in Biomedical Engineering and Social Sciences: Biomechanics, Engineering-physiology, Cardiovascular physics, Orthopaedic mechanics, Osteo-arthro mechanics, Medical and life physics, Human-body dynamics, Spinal-injury biomedical engineering and African development; Author, Socio-Economic Democracy and the World Government, 2004; Over 300 journal, professional and academic articles; Editor in Chief: Renaissance Universal Journal, 1980-89,

Automedica Journal, 1995-. Honours: Rotary Prize, 1959; Bhabha Endowed Professorship, ITT, Madras, 1973-75; Teaching Award, Faculty of Medicine and Health Sciences, UAE University, 1994-95; Kenneth H Clarke Prize, Best Paper, 1994. Memberships: Founding Member, Conference on Mechanics in Medicine and Biology, 1978-; Co-founder and Board Member, Gauss Institute, 1987; Co-Founder, Al Khaleej Institute of Advanced Studies, 1991. Address: School of Chemical and Biomedical Engineering, Nanyang Technological University, 50 Nanyang Avenue, Singapore, 639798. E-mail: mdnghista@ntu.edu.sg

GHOSH Narendra Nath, b. 1 January 1970, Bankura, India. Scientist. m. Swayang Probha Ghosh. Education: BSc (Hons), Chemistry; MSc, Chemistry; PhD, Chemistry. Appointments: Post-Doctoral Fellow, University of Delaware, USA, 1998-2000; Faculty, Chemistry Department, Birla Institute of Technology and Science, Pilani, 2000-2002; Post-Doctoral Fellow, University of Tennessee, 2002-2004; Postdoctoral Research Scientist, University of Kentucky, Lexington, USA, 2004; Faculty, Birla Institute of Technology and Science, Pilani, Goa, India, 2005-. Publications: Papers published in Journal of Nanostructured Materials; British Ceramic Transactions; Journal of Materials Science and Engineering; British Journal of Materials Science and Engineering; Bulletin of Materials Science; Ceramic Transactions; European Journal of Solid State and Inorganic Chemistry; Chemical Communications. Honours: Invited as Chairperson in the Conference, Materials for New Millennium; Eminent Scientist of Today Medal, International Biographical Association. Reviewer of papers for many international journals; Listed in Who's Who publications and biographical dictionaries. Address: Department of Chemistry, Birla Institute of Technology and Science – Pilani (Goa Campus), Zuarinagar, Goa-403726, India. E-mail: naren70@yahoo.com

GIACCONI Riccardo, b. 6 October 1931, Genoa, Italy (US Citizen). Astrophysicist. m. Mirella Manaira, 1957, 1 son, 2 daughters. Education: Doctorate, University of Milan, 1954. Appointments: Assistant Professor of Physics, University of Milan, 1954-56; Research Associate, Indiana University, 1956-58; Research Associate, Princeton University, 1958-59; American Science and Engineering Inc, 1958-73; Associate, Harvard College Observatory, 1970-72; Associate Director, Center for Astrophysics, 1973-81; Professor of Astrophysics, Harvard University, 1973-81; Professor of Astrophysics, 1981-99, Research Professor, 1999-, Johns Hopkins University; Director, Space Telescope Science Institute, Baltimore, 1981-92; Professor of Astrophysics, Milan University, Italy, 1991-99; Director General, European Southern Observatory, Garching, Germany, 1993-99; President, Associated Universities Inc, 1999-; Carried out fundamental investigations in the development of x-ray astronomy. Publications X-Ray Astronomy (co-editor), 1974; Physics and Astrophysics of Neutron Stars and Black Holes (co-editor), 1978; A Face of Extremes; The X-ray Universe (co-editor), 1985; Numerous articles in professional journals. Honours: Space Science Award, AIAA, 1976; NASA Medal for Exceptional Scientific Achievement, 1980; Gold Medal, Royal Astronomical Society, 1982; A Cressy Morrison Award in Natural Sciences, New York Academy of Sciences, 1982; Wolf Prize, 1987; Laurea hc in Physics, Rome, 1998; Nobel Prize in Physics, 2002; National Medal of Science, 2003; Numerous other awards. Memberships: American Academy of Arts and Sciences; American Astronomical Society; American Physical Society; Italian Physical Society; International Astronomical Union; Max Planck Society;

Foreign member, Accademia Nazionale dei Lincei. Address: Associated Universities Inc, 1400 16th Street, NW, Suite 730, Washington, DC 20036, USA.

GIBB Barry, b. 1 September 1947, Isle of Man, emigrated to Australia, 1958, returned to UK, 1967. Singer and Songwriter. m. Linda Gray, 6 children. Career: Formed Bee Gees with brothers Robin and the late Maurice and Andy. Publications: Albums with BeeGees include: Bee Gees 1st; Odessa; Main Course; Children of the World; Saturday Night Fever; Spirits Having Flown; High Civilisation; Size Isn't Everything; Still Waters; One Night Only; This Is Where I Came In; Their Greatest Hits – The Record; Singles include; NY Mining Disaster 1941; Massachusetts; To Love Somebody; Holiday; I've Gotta Get a Message to You; I Started a Joke; Lonely Days; How Can You Mend a Broken Heart; Jive Talkin'; Staying Alive; Night Fever; How Deep Is Your Love; Too Much Heaven; Tragedy; Love You Inside Out; One; You Win Again; First of May; Writer of songs for other artists including: Elvis Presley (Words); Sarah Vaughn (Run To Me); Al Green, Janis Joplin, Barbara Streisand (Guilty album); Diana Ross (Chain Reaction); Dionne Warwick (Heartbreaker); Dolly Parton and Kenny Rogers (Island in the Stream); Ntrance (staying Alive)Take That (How Deep is Your Love); Boyzone (Words); Yvonne Elliman (If I Can't Have You). Honours: 7 Grammy Awards; elected to Rock and Roll Hall of Fame, 1996; International Achievement, 1997; 5th most successful recording artists ever, have sold over 100 million records worldwide. Address: c/o Middle Ear, Studio, 1801 Bay Road, Miami Beach, FL 33139, USA.

GIBB Robin, b. 22 December 1949, Isle of Man, emigrated to Australia, 1958, returned to UK 1967. Singer and Songwriter. m. Dwina Murphy, 1 son. Career: Formed Bee Gees with brothers Barry, and the late Maurice and Andy. Publications: Albums with the Bee Gees include: Bee Gees 1st; Odessa; Main Course; Children of the World; Saturday Night Fever; Spirits Having Flown; High Civilisation; Size Isn't Everything; Still Waters; One Night Only; Their Greatest Hits – The Record; Solo album: Magnet, 2003; Singles include: NY Mining Disaster 1941; Massachusetts; To Love Somebody; Holiday; I've Gotta Get a Message to You; I Started a Joke; Lonely Days; How Can You Mend a Broken Heart; Jive Talkin'; Stayin' Alive; Night Fever; How Deep Is Your Love; Too Much Heaven; Tragedy; Love You Inside Out; One; You Win Again; First of May; Writer, songs for other artists including: Elvis Presley (Words); Sarah Vaughn (Run to Me); Al Green, Janis Joplin, Ntrance (Stayin' Alive); Take That (How Deep is Your Love); Boyzone (Words); Yvonne Elliman (If I Can't Have You). Honours: 7 Grammy awards; Elected to Rock and Roll Hall of Fame, 1996; International Achievement Award, American Music Awards, 1997; Brit Award for Outstanding Contribution to Music, 1997; World Music Award for Lifetime Achievement, 1997; 5th most successful recording artists ever, have sold 100 million records worldwide. Address: Middle Ear, 1801 Bay Road, Miami, FL 33139, USA.

GIBSON Mel, b. 3 January 1956, Peekshill, New York, USA. Actor; Producer. m. Robyn Moore, 5 sons, 1 daughter. Education: National Institute for Dramatic Art, Sydney. Career: Founder, ICONS Productions; Actor, films include: Summer City; Mad Max, Tim, 1979; Attack Force Z; Gallipoli, 1981; The Road Warrior (Mad Max II), 1982; The Year of Living Dangerously, 1983; The Bounty, The River, Mrs Soffel, 1984; Mad Max Beyond the Thunderdome, 1985; Lethal Weapon; Tequila Sunrise; Lethal Weapon II; Bird on a Wire, 1989; Hamlet, 1990; Air America, 1990; Lethal Weapon III, 1991; Man Without a Face (also director), 1992; Maverick,

1994; Braveheart (also director, co-producer), 1995; Ransom, 1996; Conspiracy Theory, Playback, 1997; Lethal Weapon 4, 1998; The Million Dollar Hotel, 1999; The Patriot, What Women Want, 2000; We Were Soldiers, Signs, 2002; The Singing Detective, 2003; Paparazzi, 2004; Payback: Straight Up – The Director's Cut, 2006; Plays include: Romeo and Juliet; Waiting for Godot; No Names No Pack Drill; Death of a Salesman. Honours include: Commandeur, Ordre des Arts et des Lettres. Address: c/o ICONS Productions, 4000 Warner Boulevard, Room 17, Burbank, CA 91522, USA.

GIBSON OF MARKET RASEN, Baroness of Market Rasen in the County of Lincolnshire, Anne Gibson, b. 10 December 1940, United Kingdom. m. (1) John Donald Gibson, 1 daughter, (2) John Bartell, 1 stepdaughter. Education: BA, University of Essex. Appointments: Full-time Organiser, Labour Party, Saffron Walden, 1965-70; Researcher, House Magazine (journal of Houses of Parliament), 1975-77; Party Candidate, Labour, Bury St Edmunds, 1979; Assistant, Assistant Secretary and Deputy Head of Organisation and Industrial Relations Department, TUC, 1977-87; National Officer Amicus, with special responsibility for voluntary sector and equal rights sections, 1987-96, policy and political work, 1996-2000; Member: General Council, TUC, 1989-2000; Trade Union Sustainable Development Committee; Department of Employment Advisory Group on Older Workers, 1993-96; Board, Bilbao Agency, 1996-2000; Parliamentary and Scientific Committee; Labour Party: NEC Women's Committee, 1990-98, National Constitutional Committee, 1997-2000, Labour Party Policy Reform, 1998-2000; Subcommittees in the House of Lords: Foreign and Commonwealth Affairs Group, Home Affairs Group, Defence Group; Member, BBC Charter Review Group; Equal Opportunities Commissioner, 1991-98, Health and Safety Commissioner, 1996-2000; Member All-Party Parliamentary Groups: Adoption, Brazil, Bullying at Work, Arts and Heritage, Asbestos Sub-Committee, Asthma, BBC, Breast Cancer, Children, Countryside, Fibromualgia, Insurance and Financial Services, Latin America, Rail Freight, Safety and Health, Sex Equality, TU(nion) Group of MP's, Wildlife Protection, World Government. Publications: Numerous TUC and MSF equal opportunities booklets including: Disability and Employer – A Trade Union Guide, 1989; Charter of Equal Opportunities for 1990's, 1990; Lesbian and gay Rights in Employment, 1990; recruitment of Women Workers, 1990; Part-time Workers Rights, 1991; Sexual Harassment at Work, 1993; Caring – A Union Issue, 1993; Women in MSF, 1991. Honours: OBE, 1998; Life Peer, 2000. Memberships: Chair, Andrea Adams Trust, 2002-2004; President, RoSPA; Chair, DTI Dignity at Work Group; Fawcett Society; Fabian Society. Address: House of Lords, London SW1A 0PW, England.

GIDDENS Anthony, Baron Giddens of Southgate in the London Borough of Enfield, b. 18 January 1938. University Administrator; Sociologist. m. Jane M Ellwood, 1963. Education: Hull University; London School of Economics; Cambridge University. Appointments: Lecturer, late Reader, Sociology, University of Cambridge, 1969-85; Professor of Sociology, 1985-97; Fellow, King's College, 1969-96; Director, London School of Education, 1997-2003. Publications: Over 34 books and 200 articles including; Capitalism and Modern Social Theory, 1971; Ed, Sociology of Suicide, 1972; Politics and Sociology in the Thought of Max Weber, 1972; Editor and translator, Emile Durkheim: Selected Writings, 1972; Ed, Positivism and Sociology, 1974; New Rules of Sociological Method, 1976; Studies in Social and Political Theory, 1976; Central Problems in Social Theory, 1979; Class Structure of the Advanced Societies (2nd editor),

1981; Contemporary Critique of Historical Materialism (vol 1), Power, Property and State, 1981, (vol 2), Nation, State and Violence, 1985; Jointly, Classes, Power and Conflict, 1982; Profiles and Critiques in Social Theory, 1983; Joint editor, Social Class and the Division of Labour, 1983; Constitution of Society, 1984; Social Theory and Modern Sociology, 1987; Joint editor, Social Theory Today, 1987; Sociology, 1989; The Consequences of Modernity, 1990; Modernity and Self-Identity, 1991; The Transformation of Intimacy, 1992; Beyond Right and Left, 1994; In Defence of Sociology, 1996; Third Way, 1998; Over to You, Mr Brown – How Labour Can Win Again, 2007. Honours include: Prince of Asturias Award, Spain, 2002; Life Peerage, 2004; Member, House of Lords. Address: London School of Economics, Houghton Street, London, WC2A 2AE, England.

GIELEN Uwe Peter, b. 15 August 1940, Berlin, Germany. Professor of Psychology. Education: MA, Psychology, Wake Forest University, 1968; PhD, Social Psychology, Harvard University, USA, 1976. Appointments: Assistant Professor of Psychology, City University of New York, 1977-80; Associate Professor, 1980-87, Professor, 1987-, Chairman, 1980-90, Director, Institute for International and Cross-Cultural Psychology, 1998-, St Francis College, New York, USA. Publications: 16 books; 120 other publications; Editor-in-Chief, World Psychology, 1995-97, International Journal of Group Tensions, 1997-2002; Co-editor, Psychology in the Arab Countries; International Perspectives on Human Development; The Family and Family Therapy in International Perspective; Cross-Cultural Topics in Psychology; Migration: Immigration and Emigration in International Perspective; Handbook of Culture, Therapy and Healing; Families in Global Perspective; Childhood and Adolescence; Violence in Schools: Cross-National and Cross-Cultural Perspectives, 2005; Toward a Global Psychology: Theory, Research, Intervention and Pedagogy, 2007. Honours: Kurt Lewin Award, 1993, Wilhelm Wundt Award, 1999, New York State Psychological Association; Distinguished International Psychologist Award, International Psychology Division, American Psychological Association, 2005. Memberships: Fellow, American Psychological Association; Fellow, American Psychological Society; Fellow, New York Academy of Sciences; President, International Council of Psychologists, 1994-95; President, Society for Cross-Cultural Research, 1998-99; Fellow New York Academy of Sciences. Address: Department of Psychology, St Francis College, Brooklyn, NY 11201, USA. E-mail: ugielen@hotmail.com

GIESY John Paul, b. 9 August 1948, Youngstown, Ohio, USA. Professor. m. Susan Elaine Damerell, 1 daughter. Education: BS, Summa Cum Laude, Honours, Biology, Alma College, 1970; MS, Limnology, 1971, PhD, Limnology, 1974, Michigan State University. Appointments include: Adjunct Assistant Professor, Zoology, 1976-80, Graduate Faculty, 1976-80, Ecology Faculty, 1978-80, University of South Carolina, Aitken Campus; Adjunct Assistant Professor of Biology, 1978-81; Adjunct Assistant Professor of Environmental Engineering, 1978-81; Pesticide Research Center, 1981-87; Professor of Fisheries and Wildlife, 1985-97, Distinguished Professor of Zoology, Professor of Veterinary Medicine, Michigan State University; Professor and Canada Research Chair in Environmental Toxicology, University of Sakatchewan, Canada, 1997-2006; Concurrent appointments include: Center for Integrative Toxicology, 1981-, Center for Hazardous Waste Management, 1990-, National Food Safety and Toxicology Center, 1997-; Visiting Scientist: Office of Water, Soil and Air Hygiene, Federal Republic of Germany, Berlin, 1989, Italian Hydrobiological Institute,

Italian National Research Council, Pallanza, Italy, 1989-90, Biological Research Station of Helgoland, List/Sylt, Germany, 1993; Visiting Professor, Chair of Ecological Chemistry and Geochemistry, University of Bayreuth, Germany, 1987-88; Chair Professor at Large of Biology and Chemistry, City University of Hong Kong; Professor of Environmental Science, Nanjing University, China. Publications: 5 books include: Microcosms in Ecological Research; Sediments: The Chemistry and Toxicology of In-Place Pollutants; Editor, 6 books; 649 peer reviewed articles in scientific journals as author and co-author; 1067 lectures world-wide. Honours include: Chevron Distinguished Lecture, University of California-Davis, 1989; Sigma Xi Meritorious Research Award, 1990; CIBA GEIGY Agricultural Recognition Award, 1990; Willard F Shepard Award, Michigan Water Pollution Control Association, 1992; Distinguished Professor Award, Michigan State University, 1993; Quintessence Award, 1994; Vollenweider Environmental science Award, 1994; Numerous awards for papers; Founders Award, Society of Environmental Toxicology and Chemistry, 1995; SETAC/ Menzie-Curra Environmental Education Award, 2002; 2nd most cited author in the field of Ecology/Enviromental Science, 1996-2006; Listed in Who's Who Publications and biographical dictionaries. Memberships include: International Association for Sediment and Water Science; International Association of Great Lakes Research; Sigma Xi; Society of Environmental Toxicology and Chemistry; SETAC Foundation for Environmental Education; American Association for the Advancement of Science; American Chemical Society; American College of Toxicology; American Fisheries Society; American Institute of Biological Sciences; International Water Association. Address: Department of Veterinary Biomedical Sciences, Toxicology Centre, 44 Campus Dr, University of Saskatchewan, Saskatoon, SK S7N 5B3, Canada. E-mail: jgiesy@aol.com

GIFFORD Zerbanoo, b. 11 May 1950, India. Foundation Director. m. Richard Gifford, 2 sons. Education: Roedean School; Watford College of Technology; London School of Journalism; BA Honours, Open University. Appointments: Director ASHA Foundation; National Endowment of Science, Technology and Arts Fellowship; Adviser to Rt. Hon. Jack Straw on Community Relations at the Home Office; Director Anti-Slavery International. Publications: The Golden Thread – Asian Experiences in Post Raj Britain; Thomas Clarkson and the Campaign Against Slavery; Dadabhai Naoroji – The 1st Asian MP; Celebrating India; Asian Presence in Europe; Confessions to a Serial Womaniser – the Secrets of the World's Inspirational Women. Honours: Nehru Centenary Award for international work championing the cause of women and children; Freedom of City of Lincoln, Nebraska for work against all forms of slavery and racism; International Woman of the Year for Humanitarian Work , 2006. Address: 4 Dean Rise, Dean Road, Newnham on Severn, Gloucestershire, GL17 0EA, England. E-mail: zerbanoogifford@hotmail.com www.zerbanoogifford.org

GIGENA SEEBER Carlos Julio, b. 4 September 1942, Buenos Aires, Argentina. Chief Executive Officer. m. Paulina O Delgado, 1 son, 2 daughters. Education: School of Engineering, 3 years, School of Physics, 3 years, School of Philosophy, University of Buenos Aires. Appointments: Central Laboratory, School of Physics, 1961-66; Alson SA, 1966-72; Founder, President and Chief Executive Officer, AADEE SA, 1973-. Publications: Researcher, LSC, Teaching about Reliability, 1972; Blood Gas Analysis, Conference over Cosmology; Techno Entrepreneur, Argentine Credit Bank, 1994. Honours: Techno Entrepreneur, 1994. Memberships:

Senior Member, IEEE; Member, AYAS; Member, AAAS; Titular Member, UAPE. Address: Alte Blanco Encalada 3882, 1430 Buenos Aires, Argentina. E-mail: carlos@gigenaseeber.com.ar

GIL David Georg, b. 16 March 1924, Vienna, Austria. Professor of Social Policy; Author. m. Eva Breslauer, 2 August 1947, 2 sons. Education: Certificate in Psychotherapy with Children, Israeli Society for Child Psychiatry, 1952; Diploma in Social Work, School of Social Work, BA, 1957, Hebrew University, Jerusalem, Israel; MSW, 1958, DSW, 1963, University of Pennsylvania. Appointment: Professor of Social Policy, Brandeis University. Publications: Violence Against Children, 1970; Unravelling Social Policy, 1973, 5th edition, 1992; The Challenge of Social Equality, 1976; Beyond the Jungle, 1979; Child Abuse and Violence (editor), 1979; Toward Social and Economic Justice (editor with Eva Gil), 1985; The Future of Work (editor with Eva Gil), 1987; Confronting Injustice and Oppression, 1998; Confronting Injustice and Oppression (German translation), 2006. Contributions to: Over 50 articles to professional journals, book chapters, book reviews. Honours: Leadership in Human Services, Brandeis University, Heller School, 1999; Social Worker of the Year, National Association of Social Workers, Massachusetts, 2000; Mentoring Award, Brandeis University, Heller School, 2005; Presidential Award, Council on Social Work Education, 2006. Memberships: National Association of Social Workers; American Orthopsychiatric Association; Association of Humanist Sociology. Address: Heller School for Social Policy & Management, Brandeis University, MS 035, Waltham, MA 02454-9110, USA.

GIL Kyehwan, b. 22 December 1963, Daejeon, Korea. Researcher. m. Hyeonju Lee, 1 son. Education: BS, Mechanical Engineering, Seoul National University, Seoul, 1986; MS, Mechanical Engineering, KAIST, Daejeon, 1988; PhD, Mechanical Engineering, POSTECH, Pohang, 2001. Appointments: Researcher, 1989-91, Senior Researcher, 1991-2004, Staff Researcher, 2004-, Pohang Accelerator Laboratory. Publications: Sensors and Actuators A, Vol 93, 2001; Nuclear Instruments and Methods A, Vol 470, 2001, Vol 467-468, 2001; Microsystem Technologies, Vol 7, 2001. Memberships: Council Member, Korean Vacuum Society; Member, Korean Society for New and Renewable Energy; Member, Korean Physical Society. Address: Nakwon Apt 8-1301, Jigok-Dong, Nam-Gu, Pohang, Gyeongbuk 790-751, Republic of Korea. E-mail: khgil@postech.ac.kr

GILBERT Anthony, b. 26 July 1934, London, England. 2 sons, 1 daughter. Composer. Education: MA, DMus, University of Leeds; Composition with Anthony Milner, Matyas Seiber, Alexander Goehr and Gunther Schuller; Conducting with Lawrence Leonard, Morley College, London. Career: Lecturer in Composition, Goldsmiths College, 1968-73; Composer in Residence, University of Lancaster, 1970-71; Lecturer in Composition, Morley College, 1972-75; Senior Lecturer in Composition, Sydney Conservatorium, Australia, 1978-79; Composer in Residence, City of Bendigo, Victoria, 1981; Senior Tutor in Composition, Royal Northern College of Music, 1973-96; Head of School of Composition and Contemporary Music, Royal Northern College of Music, 1996-99. Compositions: Operas: The Scene-Machine, The Chakravaka-Bird; Orchestra: Symphony; Sinfonia; Ghost and Dream Dancing; Crow Cry; Towards Asavari; On Beholding a Rainbow; Sheer; Groove, Perchants; Wind orchestra: Dream Carousels; Chamber: 4 string quartets; Saxophone Quartet; Quartet of Beasts; Nine or Ten Osannas; Vasanta With Dancing; Palace of the Winds; Instrumental: Ziggurat;

Reflexions, Rose Nord; Moonfaring; Dawnfaring; 3 Piano Sonatas; Spell Respell; The Incredible Flute Music; Treatment of Silence; Osanna for Lady O; Farings; Stars; Rose luisante; Vocal: Certain Lights Reflecting; Love Poems; Inscapes; Long White Moonlight; Beastly Jingles; Vers de Lune; Encantos; Music Theatre: Upstream River Rewa. Recordings: Os; Moonfaring; Beastly Jingles; Nine or Ten Osannas; Towards Asavari; Dream Carousels; Igorochki; Quartet of Beasts; Six of the Bestiary; Another Dream Carousel; Quartets Number 3 and 4; Farings; On Beholding a Rainbow; Certain Lights Reflecting; ... into the Gyre of a Madder Dance; Unrise. Honours: Fellow of Royal Northern College of Music, 1981; Listed in national and international biographical dictionaries. Memberships: Society for the Promotion of New Music; Performing Right Society; Mechanical Copyright Protection Society; British Academy of Composers and Songwriters. Address: 4 Oak Brow Cottages, Altrincham Road, Styal, Wilmslow, Cheshire SK9 4JE, England.

GILBERT Robert Andrew, b. 6 October 1942, Bristol, England. Antiquarian Bookseller; Editor; Writer. m. Patricia Kathleen Linnell, 20 June 1970, 3 sons, 2 daughters. Education: BA, Honours, Philosophy, Psychology, University of Bristol, 1964. Appointment: Editor, Ars Quatuor Coronatorum, 1994-2000. Publications: The Golden Dawn: Twilight of the Magicians, 1983; A E Waite: A Bibliography, 1983; The Golden Dawn Companion, 1986; A E Waite: Magician of Many Parts, 1987; The Treasure of Montsegur (with W N Birks), 1987; Elements of Mysticism, 1991; World Freemasonry: An Illustrated History, 1992; Freemasonry: A Celebration of the Craft (J M Hamill), 1992; Casting the First Stone, 1993; Editor with M A Cox: The Oxford Book of English Ghost Stories, 1986; Victorian Ghost Stories: An Oxford Anthology, 1991; The Golden Dawn Scrapbook, 1997; Editor, The House of the Hidden Light, 2003. Contributions to: Ars Quatuor Coronatorum; Avallaunius; Christian Parapsychologist; Dictionary of National Biography; Dictionary of 19th Century British Scientists; Dictionary of Gnosis and Western Esotericism; Gnosis; Hermetic Journal; Cauda Pavonis; Yeats Annual. Memberships: Society of Authors; Arthurian, Supreme Council for England and Wales (A&A Rite); Prestonian Lecturer, United Grand Lodge of England, 1997. Address: 215 Clevedon Road, Tickenham, Clevedon, North Somerset, BS21 6RX.

GILBERT Walter, b. 21 March 1932, Boston, Massachusetts, USA. Molecular Biologist. m. Celia Stone, 1953, 1 son, 1 daughter. Education: Graduated, Physics, Harvard University, 1954; Doctorate in Mathematics, Cambridge University, 1957. Appointments: National Science Foundation Fellow, 1957-58; Lecturer, Research Fellow, 1958-59, Professor of Biophysics, 1964-68, Professor of Molecular Biology, 1969-72, American Cancer Society Professor of Molecular Biology, 1972, Harvard University; Devised techniques for determining the sequence of bases in DNA. Honours: US Steel Foundation Award in Molecular Biology (NAS), 1968; Joint Winner, Ledlie Prize, Harvard University, 1969; Joint winner, Warren Triennial Prize, Massachusetts General Hospital, 1977; Louis and Bert Freedman Award, New York Academy of Sciences, 1977; Joint winner, Prix Charles-Léopold Mayer, Académie des Sciences, Institute de France, 1977; Harrison Howe Award of the Rochester branch of the American Chemical Society, 1978; Joint winner, Louisa Gross Horowitz Prize, Columbia University, 1979; Gairdner Foundation Annual Award 1979; Joint winner, Albert Lasker Basic Medical Research Award, 1979; Joint winner, Prize for Biochemical Analysis, German Society for Clinical Chemistry, 1980; Sober Award, American Society of Biological Chemists, 1980; Joint Winner, Nobel

Prize for Chemistry, 1980; New England Entrepreneur of the Year Award, 1991; Ninth National Biotechnology Ventures Award, 1997. Memberships: Foreign member, Royal Society; NAS; American Physical Society; American Society of Biological Chemists; American Academy of Arts and Sciences. Address: Biological Laboratories, 16 Divinity Avenue, Cambridge, MA 02138, USA.

GILFANOV Marat, b. 18 July 1962, Kazan, USSR. Astrophysicist. m. Marina Gilfanova, 1 daughter. Education: Diploma Physics, Moscow Physical-Technical Institute, 1985; PhD, Physics, Space Research Institute, Moscow, 1989; Doctor of Physics and Mathematics, Space Research Institute, Moscow, 1996. Appointments: Junior Scientist, Space Research Institute, Moscow, 1985-88; Scientist, 1988-91; Senior Scientist, 1991-; Leading Scientist, 1996-; Max-Planck-Institut für Astrophysik, Garching, Germany, 1996-. Publications: Over 300 in international scientific journals. Honours: COSPAR, Commission E Zeldovich medal, 1992. Memberships: COSPAR, Commission E; International Astronomical Union, 1994-; Scientific Council of Space Research Institute, 1997-; Wissenschaftlicher Institutsrat, Max-Planck-Institut für Astrophysik. Address: Max-Planck-Institut für Astrophysik, Karl-Schwarzschild-Str 1, 85741 Garching, Germany.

GILL Sir Ben, b. 1 January 1950. Company Director. m. Carolyn Davis, 4 sons. Education: Barnard Castle School, Co Durham, 1960-67; General Agriculture degree, St John's College, Cambridge, 1968-71. Appointments: Worked on family farm, North Yorkshire, 1971; Teacher of science and agriculture, Namasagali College, Uganda, East Africa, 1972-75; Ran 200 sow pig unit, Holderness, East Yorkshire, 1975-77; Family farming business, North Yorkshire, 1978-; Chairman, English Apples & Pears Ltd, 2007-; Non-Executive Director, One Planet Ltd, 2007-; Managing Director, The Hawk Creative Business Park Ltd, 2007-. Honours: CBE, 1996; Visiting Professorship, Department of Biology, Leeds University, 1996; Fellow, Royal Agriculture Society, 1997; Honorary DSc, Leeds University, 1997; Fellow, Institute of Grocery Distribution, 1998; Honorary DSc, Cranfield University, 2000; Honorary DSc, University of West England, 2002; Honorary D, Civil Law University of East Anglia, 2003. Memberships: Parent Governor, Easingwold County Primary School, 1982-88; Member, Vice Chairman, 1985-86, NFU National Marketing Committee, 1984-87; Member, NFU National Council, 1985-2004; Member, Vice Chairman, 1986-87, Chairman, 1987-2001, National Livestock and Wool Committee, 1985-1991; Vice President, NFU, 1991-92; Deputy President, NFU, 1992-98; President, NFU, 1998-2004; Member, Agriculture and Food Research Council, 1991-94; Member, Chairman of Agricultural Systems Directorate, Biotechnology and Biological Sciences Research Council, 1994-97; Founder and Chairman, Alternative Crops Technology Interaction Network, 1994-2004; OST Technology Foresight, 1994-99; Director of FARM Africa, 1991-98; Executive Member, International Federation of Agricultural Producers, 1998-2004; Member, Council of Food from Britain, 1999-2005; Vice President, Comitee des Organisations Professionelles des Agriculteurs, 1999-2003; President, Confederation of European Agriculture, 2000-04; Non-Executive Director, Countrywide Farmers plc, 2004-; Governor, University of Lincoln, 2004-; President, Cambridge University Potato Growers Research Association, 2004-; Director, Hawkhills Consultancy Ltd, 2004-; Member, Governing Council of the John Innes Centre, Norwich, 2002-; Patron: Pentalk, Farmers Overseas Action Group, Plants & Us, Rural Stress Information Network, St John's Ambulance

Bricks and Wheels Appeal. Address: Prospect Farm, Upper Dormington, Hereford, HR1 4ED, England. E-mail: sirbengill@hawkcreative.com

GILL Christopher J F, b. 28 October 1936, Wolverhampton, England. m. Patricia M, 1 son, 2 daughters. Education: Birchfield Preparatory School, 1944-50; Shrewsbury School, 1950-54. Appointments: Ordinary Seaman, Royal Naval Volunteer Reserve, 1952-54; RN, 1955-57; Joined family meat processing and wholesaling business, F A Gill Ltd, 1959, retired as Chairman of the company, 2007; Member, Wolverhampton Borough Council, 1965-72; Chairman, Public Works Committee, 1967-69; Chairman, Local Education Authority, 1969-70; Retired as Lieutenant Commander, RNR, 1979; Active member, West Midlands Conservative Associations; Past President, Midlands West European Conservative Council; Member of Parliament for Ludlow, 1987-2001; Former Vice-Chairman, Conservative European Affairs Committee; Vice-Chairman, Conservative Agriculture Committee, 1991-94; Member, Agriculture Select Committee, 1989-94; Member, Welsh Affairs Select Committee, 1995-97; Member, Council of Europe, 1997-99; Past President, Meat Training Council; Past President, British Pig Association. Publications: Whips' Nightmare – Diary of a Maastricht Rebel, 2003. Memberships: Honorary President, The Freedom Association. Honours: Reserve Decoration, 1971; Liveryman, Worshipful Company of Butchers; Freeman of the City of London. Address: Billingsley Hall Farm, Bridgnorth, Shropshire, WV16 6PJ, England.

GILL Devinder Singh, b. 4 February 1955, Ludhiana, Punjab, India. Senior Plant Physiologist. m. Sudeep Kaur Gill, 1 son, 1 daughter. Education: BSc (Hons), Botany; MSc (Hons), Botany; PhD Botany, Crop Physiology; Diploma in Computer Science, NIIT, 2006. Appointments: Research Associate, 1980, Assistant Plant Physiologist, 1984, Plant Physiologist, 1992, Senior Plant Physiologist, 2000, Punjab Agricultural University, Ludhiana, Punjab, India. Publications: 75 research papers; 4 review articles; 3 book chapters; 35 papers at conference. Honours include: Glory of India Gold Medal, International Institute of Success Awareness, 2007; Rajiv Gandhi Shiromani Award, India International Friendship Society, 2007; Vikras Rattan Award, International Institute of Success Awareness, 2007; Best Citizen of India Award, India International Friendship Society, 2007; International Order of Merit, IBC, 2007; IBC Medal of Honour for Intellectual and Vocational Excellence, 2007. Memberships include: New York Academy of Sciences; American Chemical Society; Canadian Society of Plant Physiologists; Chivalric Order of the Knights of Justice, UK; Scientific American, India; Punjab Academy of Science; Indian Science New Association, Calcutta; Plant Physiological Society of India; Ecological Society of India; India International Friendship Society; Agricultural Research Communication Society of India. Address: 90-A, Model Town Ext-II, Ludhiana-141002, Punjab, India. E-mail: dsgill90@sify.com

GILL-SHARMA Manjeet Kaur, b. 20 July 1949, Faridkot, Punjab, India. Scientist. m. Pradeep Sharma, 1 son, 1 daughter. Education: BSc (Hons), 1969, MSc (Hons), 1971, Biochemistry, Language Certificate, French, 1971, Panjab University, Chandigarh; Language Certificate, Université de Poitiers, France, 1973; Doctorat d'Université, Université Louis Pasteur, Strasbourg, France, 1978; Language Certificate (2nd degree), Language Certificate (3rd degree), Université des Sciences Humaines, Strasbourg, 1977. Appointments: Pool Officer, 1979-80, Assistant Research Officer, 1980-91, Research Officer, 1991-96, Senior Research Officer,

1996-2001, Assistant Director, 2001-06, Deputy Director, 2006-, Head of Department, 2007-, Neuroendocrinology Department, National Institute for Research in Reproductive Health, Mumbai. Publications: Numerous articles in professional journals. Honours: National Merit Scholarship, 1969-71; UGC Fellowship, 1971-72; Registered PhD Guide, Mumbai University, 1998-; French Government Fellowship for higher studies, 1972-78; Fogarty Fellowship, NIH, 2004-05; Department of Science & Technology Project, 2007-10. Memberships: National Sports Club of India. Address: D-9, ICMR Staff Quarters, R G Thadani Marg, Worli, Parel, Mumbai 400 025, India. E-mail: manjitgill_sharma@hotmail.com

GILLAM Beatrice, b. 25 January 1920, Carlisle, England. Retired Teacher and Occupational Therapist. Education: Certificate of Education, Bedford Froebel Training College, 1941; First year of BSc Course in Zoology and Botany, Bristol University, 1963-64; Certificate of Proficiency in Natural History, London University Extra-mural, 1966. Appointments: Teacher, Hall School, Bratton Seymour, Wincanton; Occupational Therapist, Bristol Mental Hospital; Occupational Therapist, St James's Hospital Devizes; Peripatetic Occupational Therapist, Wiltshire Welfare Service; Occupational Therapist, Cheshire Home; Botanical Surveyor on chalk downland for English Nature. Publications: Breeding Birds of Sunnyhill Farm, Pewsey, 1962-83, Breeding Birds of Home Covert, Roundway, Devizes, 1981-86 (both of these in "Hobby", annual publication of Wiltshire Ornithological Society); Breeding Birds of Tiree in "Scottish Birds"; The Wiltshire Flora, 1993; The Butterflies of Wiltshire, 1995; Birds of Wiltshire, 2007. Honours: MBE for services to wildlife conservation in Wiltshire, 1983; Voluntary Warden's Award, English Nature, 1991. Memberships: Founder Member, now Vice-President, Wiltshire Wildlife Trust; Founder Member, now Honorary Member, Wiltshire Ornithological Society; Founder Member, Wiltshire FWAG; Ministry of Defence Salisbury Plain Conservation Groups; BTO; RSPB; Mammal Society; Butterfly Conservation; British Entomological and Natural History Society; British Dragonfly Society; MS Society. Address: 19 Roundway Gardens, Devizes, Wiltshire SN10 2EF, England.

GILLARD David Owen, b. 8 February 1947, Croydon, Surrey, England. Writer; Critic. m. Valerie Ann. Education: Tavistock School, Croydon, Surrey. Appointments: Scriptwriter and Assistant Director, Associated British Pathé, 1967-70; Film and Theatre Critic, Daily Sketch, 1970-71; Ballet Critic, Daily Mail, 1971-88; Instituted drama preview pages, The Listener, 1982; Founder-Editor, English National Opera Friends Magazine, 1983-92; Radio Correspondent, Radio Times, 1984-91; Classical Music Editor, Radio Times, 2001-2003; Opera Critic, Daily Mail, 1971-. Publications: Play: Oh Brothers! 1971; Beryl Grey: A Biography, 1977. Memberships: National Union of Journalists; Critics Circle; Broadcasting Press Guild. Address: 1 Hambledon Court, 18 Arundel Way, Highcliffe, Christchurch, Dorset, BH23 5DX, England.

GILLES Herbert Michael, b. 10 September 1921. Emeritus Professor of Tropical Medicine. m. (1) Wilhelmina Caruana, 1955, deceased, 3 sons, 1 daughter; (2) Mejra Kacic-Dimitri, 1979. Education: St Edward's College, Malta; Royal University of Malta, Rhodes Scholar, 1943; MSc Oxon; MD (Malta); FRCP; FFPH; FMCPH (Nig); DTM&H. Appointments: Alfred Jones and Warrington Yorke Professor of Tropical Medicine, 1972-86, Emeritus Professor, 1986-, University of Liverpool; Served in World War II, 1939-45; Member of Scientific Staff, MRC Laboratory, Gambia, 1954-58; University of Ibadan Lecturer, Tropical Medicine, 1958-63; Professor of Preventive and Social Medicine, 1963-65; Senior Lecturer, Tropical Medicine, Liverpool University, 1965-70; Professor of Tropical Medicine (Personal Chair), 1970; Visiting Professor, University of Lagos, 1965-68; Royal Society Overseas Visiting Professor, University of Khartoum, Sudan, 1979-80; Honorary Professor of Tropical Medicine, Sun-Yat-Sen Medical College, Guangzhou, People's Republic of China, 1984; Visiting Professor of Public Health, University of Malta, 1989-; Consultant in Malariology to the Army, 1974-86; Consultant in Tropical Medicine to the RAF, 1978-86, to the DHSS, 1980-86; President, RSTM&H, 1985-87; Vice President, International Federation of Tropical Medicine, 1988-92; Liverpool School of Tropical Medicine, 1991-; Visiting Professor of Tropical Medicine, Royal College of Surgeons in Ireland, Dublin, 1994-; Visiting Professor of Tropical Medicine, Mahidol University, Bangkok, 1980-; Member, Malta Association of Physicians, 2000-; Honorary President, Malta Association of Public Health Physicians, 2003-. Publications: Over 150 papers in peer-reviewed journals including: Tropical Medicine for Nurses, 1955, 4th edition, 1975; Pathology in the Tropics, 1969, 2nd edition, 1976; Management and Treatment of Tropical Diseases, 1971; A Short Textbook of Public Health Medicine for the Tropics, 1973, 4th edition, 2003; Atlas of Tropical Medicine and Parasitology, 1976, 4th edition, 1996; First Prize, BMA Medical Book Competition, 1996; Recent Advances in Tropical Medicine, 1984; Human Antiparasitic Drugs, Pharmacology and Usage, 1985; The Epidemiology and Control of Tropical Diseases, 1987; Management of Severe and Complicated Malaria, 1991; Hookworm Infections, 1991; Editor, Essential Malariology, 4th edition, 2002; Highly Commended, BMA Medical Book Competition, 2003; Tropical Medicine: A Clinical Text, 5th edition, 2006; Protozoal Diseases, 2001. Honours: 1939-45 Star; Africa Star; VM; Honorary MD, Karolinska Institute, 1979; Honorary DSc, Malta, 1984; Darling Foundation Medal and Prize, WHO, 1990; Mary Kingsley Medal, 1996; Officer of the Order of Merit (Malta), 2003; CMG, 2005; Manson Medal, Royal Society of Tropical Medicine & Hygiene, 2007; Knight of Justice, Sovereign Order of St John of Jerusalem, 2007. Memberships: Royal Society of Tropical Medicine & Hygiene; Royal Society of Medicine; International Epidemiological Association. Address: 3 Conyers Avenue, Birkdale, Southport PR8 4SZ, England.

GILLHAM Paul Maurice, b. 26 November 1931, Carshalton, Surrey, England. Company Director. m. Jane Pickering, 2 sons, 1 daughter. Education: Royal College of Music, 1950-52; Guildhall School of Music, 1954-55; BA, MA, Christ's College, Cambridge. Appointments: Chairman, St Giles Properties Ltd; 1984: Chairman, Patent Developments International Ltd; 1986; Chairman, AccuSphyg LLC, New York, USA; Chairman, Gillham Hayward Ltd, 1994; Chairman, London Philharmonic Orchestra Council, 1994-1999; Director, Cathedral Capital Plc, 1997-2007. Honours: MA (Cantab); LGSM. Address: Edmonds Farmhouse, Gomshall, Guildford, Surrey GU5 9LO, England.

GILLIAM Terry Vance, b. 22 November 1940, Minnesota, USA. Animator; Film Director; Actor; Illustrator; Writer. m. Margaret Weston, 1 son, 2 daughters. Education: BA, Occidental College. Appointments: Associate Editor, HELP! magazine, 1962-64; Freelance illustrator, 1964-65; Advertising copywriter/art director, 1966-67; with Monty Python's Flying Circus (UK), 1969-76; Animator: And Now For Something Completely Different (film); Co-director, actor, Monty Python and the Holy Grail; Director, Jabberwocky; Designer,

actor, animator, Monty Python's Meaning of Life (film), 1983; Co-writer, director, Brazil, 1985; The Adventures of Baron Munchausen, 1988; Director, The Fisher King (film), 1991; Twelve Monkeys, 1996; Presenter, TV series: The Last Machine, 1995; Executive Producer, Monty Python's Complete Waste of Time, 1995; Director and co-writer, Fear and Loathing in Las Vegas, 1998; Executive Producer, Monty Python's Complete Waste of time (CD-Rom), 1995; Appeared in Lost in La Mancha, documentary, 2002; Director and co-writer, The Brothers Grimm (film), 2005; Director and co-writer, Tideland (film), 2005. Publications: Monty Python's Big Red Book; Monty Python's Paperback, 1977; Monty Python's Scrapbook, 1979; Animations of Mortality, 1979; Monty Python's The Meaning of Life; Monty Python's Flying Circus - Just the Words (co-ed), 1989; DFA (hon), Occidental College, 1987; The Adventures of Baron Munchausen, 1989; Not the Screenplay or Fear and Loathing in Las Vegas, 1998; Gilliam on Gilliam, 1999; Dark Knights and Holy Fools, 1999; The Pythons Autobiography by the Pythons, 2003. Honour: Hon DFA, Occidental College, 1987; Hon DFA, Royal College of Art, London, 1988; Honorary Dr of Arts, Wimbledon School of Art, 2004. Address: c/o Jenne Casarotto, National House, 60-66 Wardour Street, London, W1V 4ND, England.

GILLIS Richard, b. 22 April 1950, Dundee, Scotland. Solicitor; Managing Director. m. Ruth J P Garden. Education: Admitted as a Solicitor, 1975; Kenya Advocate, 1978. Appointments: Solicitor, Greater London Council, 1975-77; Solicitor, Archer & Wilcock, Nairobi, Kenya, 1977-80; Shoosmiths, 1980-81; Assistant to the Secretary, TI Group plc, 1981-85; Secretary, ABB Transportation Holdings Ltd (British Rail Engineering Ltd until privatisation), Trustee, Company Pension Scheme, 1985-95; Clerk to the Council and Company Secretary, University of Derby, 1995-2002; Managing Director, family investment companies, 2001-; Secretary, Justice report on perjury; Director then Vice-Chairman, Crewe Development Agency, 1992-95; The Order of St John: Chairman, Property Committee, Derbyshire Council of the Order of St John, 1994-2003; Trustee, Priory of England and the Islands of the Order of St John and Trustee, St John Ambulance, 1999-2003; Chairman, Audit Committee and Priory Regulations Committee, Regional Member of Priory Chapter, 1999-2005; Court of Assistants, Worshipful Company of Basketmakers, 2004-; Court, City University, 2007-. Honours: OStJ, 1999; Honorary Life Member, Court of the University of Derby, 2003. Memberships: CBI East Midlands Regional Council, 1993-95; Stakeholders' Forum, Derby City Challenge, 1993-98; Guild of Freemen of the City of London; Provincial Grand Lodge of Warwickshire; Maccabæans; FRSA; Clubs: Athenæum; City Livery; New (Edinburgh); New Golf (St Andrews). Address: Nether Kinfauns, Church Road, Kinfauns, Perth, PH2 7LD, Scotland.

GILLY François-Noel, b. 1 May 1955, Lyon, France. University Surgeon. 2 daughters. Education: Medical Doctor, 1984; Digestive Surgeon, 1986. Appointments: Surgeon, civil hospitals in Lyon, 1986-; University Professor, 1995; Dean of Medical Faculty, Lyon University, 1999-. Publications: Articles in professional medical journals. Honours: Officier des Palmes Academiques; Prix Patey Mathieu; Prix A Ponet. Memberships: Academie Nationale de Chirugie; ICHS; ISIORT; IAGS; AFC. Address: Department of Surgery, Lyon University CHLS, 69495 Pierre Benite Cedex, France. E-mail: francogi@lyon-sud.univ-lyon1.fr

GILMOUR Pat (McGuire), b. 19 March 1932, Woodford, Essex, England. Art Historian; Curator. m. Alexander Tate Gilmour, 2 daughters. Education: Sculpture, Glasgow School of Art, 1956-58; Distinction in Art and in Theory of Education, Sidney Webb College, London, 1962-65; Diploma in Design Education, Hornsey College of Art, 1968-70; BA (Hons), History of Art and English Literature, London University, 1971-73. Appointments: Journalist, West Essex Gazette, 1949-55; Assistant to Editor, Percival Marshall Publishers, London, 1959-62; Lecturer II, in charge of Art and Design, Southwark College for Further Education, 1965-74; Founding Curator of Prints, Tate Gallery, London, 1974-77; Senior Lecturer in charge of Contextual Studies, North East London Polytechnic, 1977-79; Head of Art History and Liberal Studies, Central School of Art & Design, London, 1979-81; Senior and Founding Curator in charge of the Department of International Prints & Illustrated Books, National Gallery of Australia, Canberra, 1981-89; Free-lance Art Historian and Curator, 1990-; Expert Witness on Picasso: Kornfeld v Tunick, 1993; Member of Editorial Board, Print Quarterly, 1996-; Selector and Cataloguer of numerous exhibitions in Great Britain and Australia, 1972-99; Member of many Print Biennale Juries and President of the Ljubljana Jury, 1993. Publications include: Modern Prints, 1970; Henry Moore, Graphics in the Making, 1975; Artists at Curwen, 1977; Artists in Print, BBC TV series, 1981; Ken Tyler: Master Printer, 1986; Lasting Impressions: Lithography as Art, editor and contributor, 1988; The Life and Work of Shikō Munakata, captions and essay, 1991; Innovation in Collaborative Printmaking: Kenneth Tyler 1963-1992, 1993; Numerous entries for the Macmillan Dictionary of Art. Honours: Ken Tyler gift of prints presented to the Tate Gallery in her honour, 2004. Memberships include: Committee, Institute of Contemporary Arts, London, 1979-81; Committee, Print Council of Australia, 1983-89; Guest Editor, The Tamarind Papers, 1990; Contributor and member, Editorial Board, Print Quarterly, 1986-. Address: 3 Christchurch Square, Victoria Park, London E9 7HU, England.

GINAT Rami, b. 5 February 1958, Israel. Historian. m. Nicola, 2 sons, 1 daughter. Education: BA, Middle Eastern Studies, 1984, MA, Middle Eastern and Soviet Studies, 1987, Tel-Aviv University, Israel; PhD, London School of Economics, England, 1991. Appointments: Research Associate, Cummings Centre for Russian and East European Studies, Tel-Aviv University, 1991-96; Senior Lecturer, Middle Eastern Studies, Hebrew University, Jerusalem, 1994-2006; Senior Lecturer, Middle Eastern Studies, Bar-Ilan University, Ramat-Gan, 1995-. Publications: The Soviet Union and Egypt 1945-1955, 1993; Egypt's Incomplete Revolution, 1997; Gaza and Jericho First: Security and Military Aspects 1993-1995, 2004; Syria and the Doctrine of Arab Neutralism, 2005; Numerous articles in various journals. Honours: Research grants from the Israel Science Foundation and The British Academy. Memberships: The Middle East and Islamic Studies; Association of Israel. Address: 13 Pinsker Street, Rehovot, 76308, Israel. E-mail: ginatr@mail.biu.ac.il

GINGRICH Newt (Newton Leroy), b. 17 June 1943, Harrisburg, USA. American Politician. m.(1) Jackie Battley, 2 daughters (divorced), (2) Marianne Ginther, 1981-99 (divorced), Callista Bisek, 2000. Education: Emory and Tulane Universities. Appointments: Member, Faculty, West Georgia College, Carrollton, 1970-78, Professor of History, 1978; Member, 96-103rd Congresses from 6th District of Georgia, 1979-92; Chair, GOPAC, now Chair Emeritus; House Republican Whip, 1989; Speaker, House of Representatives, 1994-99; Adjunct Professor, Reinhardt College, Waleska,

Georgia, 1994-95; Co-founder, Congressional Military Reform Caucus, Congressional Space Caucus; Chief Executive Officer, The Gingrich Group, Atlanta, 1999-; Board of Directors, Internet Policy Institute; Advisory Board, Museum of the Rockies. Publications: Window of Opportunity, 1945, 1995; To Renew America, 1995; Winning the Future, 2005; Rediscovering God in America, 2006; A Contract with the Earth, 2007. Honour: Distinguished Visiting Scholar, National Defense University, 2001. Membership: AAAS. Address: The Committee for New American Leadership, 1800 K Street #714, Washington, DC 20006, USA.

GINOLA David, b. 25 January 1967, Gassin, Var, France. Professional Footballer; Sportsman. m. Coraline Delphin, 1990, 2 daughters. Career: Football clubs: 1st division Toulon clubs, 1986-87; Matraracing, Paris, 1987-88; Racing Paris 1, 1988-89; Brest-Armorique, 1989-90; Paris-Saint-Germain (French national champions, 1993-94, winners Coupe de France, 1993, 1995, winners coupe de la ligue, 1995) 1991-95; Newcastle Utd, England, 1995-97, Tottenham Hotspur, 1997-2000; Aston Villa, 2000-02; Everton, 2002; 17 International caps; Anti-landmine campaigner for Red Cross, 1998-. Honours: Football Writers' Association, Player of the Year, 1999; Professional Football Association Player of the Year, 1999. Publication: David Ginola: The Autobiography (with Niel Silver), 2000. Website: www.ginola14.com

GINZBURG Vitaly, b. 4 October 1916, Moscow, Russia. Physicist. m. Nina Ginzburg, 1946, 1 daughter. Education: Graduated, Physics, Moscow University, 1938, Postgraduate, Physics Institute, Academy of Sciences. Appointments: P N Lebedev Physical Institute, USSR (now Russian) Academy of Sciences, 1940-; Professor, Gorky University, 1945-68; Moscow Institute of Physics, 1968-. Publications: The Physics of a Lifetime, 2001. Honours include: Honorary DSc, Sussex, 1970; Mandelstam Prize, 1947; Lomonosov Prize, 1962; USSR State Prize, 1953; Order of Lenin, 1966; Gold Medal, Royal Astronomical Society; 1991; Bardeen Prize, 1991; Wolf Prize, 1994, 1995; Varilov Gold Medal, Russian Academy of Sciences, 1995; Lomonsov Gold Medal, Russian Academy of Sciences, 1995; UNESCO Nils Bohr Gold Medal, 1998; APS Nicholson Medal, 1998; IUPAP O'Ceallaigh Medal, 2001; Order of Lenin; Nobel Prize in Physics, 2003; many others. Memberships: Foreign Member, Royal Danish Academy of Sciences and Letters; Foreign Honorary Member, American Academy of Arts and Science; Honorary Fellow, Indian Academy of Science; Foreign Fellow, Indian National Science Academy; Foreign Associate, NAS, USA; Foreign Member, Royal Society, London; Academia Europaea. Address: P N Lebedev Physical Institute, Russian Academy of Sciences, Leninsky Prospect 53, 117924 GSP, Moscow B-333, Russia.

GIVENCHY Hubert de, b. 21 February 1927, Beauvais, France. Fashion Designer. Education: Ecole Nat Supérieure des Beaux-Arts, Paris; Faculté de Droit, Univ de Paris. Appointments: Apprentice, Paris fashion houses of Lucien Lelong, 1945-46, Robert Piguet, 1946-48, Jacques Fath, 1948-49, Elsa Shiaparelli, 1949-51; Established own fashion house in Parc Morceau, Paris, 1952-56, Avenue George V, 1956; President, Director-General Society Givenchy-Couture and Society des Parfums Givenchy, Paris, 1954; Honorary President, Administrative Council Givenchy SA, 1988-; President, Christie's France, 1997-; Work included in Fashion: An Anthology, Victoria & Albert Museum, London, 1971; Costume designer for films: Breakfast at Tiffany's, 1961; Charade, 1963; The VIPs, 1963; Paris When It Sizzles, 1964;

How to Steal a Million, 1966; Love Among Thieves, 1987. Honour: Chevalier, Légion d'honneur. Address: 3 Avenue George V, 75008 Paris, France.

GJESSING Ketil, b. 18 February 1934, Oslo, Norway. Education: Magister Artium and Candidatus Philologae, majoring in Literature, University of Oslo, 1965. Appointments: Teacher, Atlantic College, now United World College of the Atlantic, 1965-66; Dramaturge, Radio Drama Department of Norwegian Broadcasting Corporation, 1966-99, Retired, 2000-; Adviser, Klassisk Musikkmagasin, 2001-. Publications: Collections of poetry: Kransen om et møte, 1962; Frostjern, 1968; Private steiner bl a, 1970; Utgående post, 1975; Snøen som faller i fjor, 1977; Bjelle, malm, 1979; Vinger, røtter, 1982; Slik pila synger i lufta, 1985; Nådefrist, 1988; Dans på roser og glass, 1996; Represented in a Slovak language anthology of Norwegian poetry, German language selection of 60 poems was published in 2000; Short story published in Danish, Japanese and Swedish translation. Honours: Gyldendals legat, 1978; Språklig Samlings Literary Prize, 1995. Memberships: Norwegian Association of Writers; Norwegian Writers' Centre; Norwegian Association of Translators. Address: Dannevigsvn 12, 0463 Oslo, Norway.

GLANDORF Debora, b. 2 April 1962, Cincinnati, Ohio, USA. Educator; Teacher. Education: BA, Miami University, 1985; MEd, Xavier University, 1992. Appointments: Mathematics Teacher, Oaks Hill High School, 1985-; Mathematics Teacher, Bridgetown Junior High, 1 year. Honours: Listed in international biographical directories. Memberships: NCTM; OCTM; Association for Supervision & Curriculum. Address: 3000 Wardall Ave, Apt #11, Cincinnati, OH 45211, USA.

GLASSMAN George M, b. 7 September 1935, New York City, USA. Physician; Dermatologist. m. Carol Frankford, 1 son, 1 daughter. Education: BA, Brown University, Providence, Rhode Island, 1957; MD, New York University School of Medicine, New York, 1962; Rotating Internship, Greenwich Hospital, Greenwich, Connecticut, 1962-63; Dermatology Residency, New York University Medical Centre (including Bellevue Hospital, University Hospital, Skin and Cancer Unit and Manhattan VA Hospital), 1963-66. Appointments: Chief of Dermatology, LCDR, MC, US Naval Hospital, St Albans, New York, 1966-68; Private Practice in Dermatology, White Plains, New York, 1968-96; Clinical Assistant Professor, Albert Einstein College of Medicine, 1970-75; Clinical Assistant Professor, New York Medical College, 1975-87; Associate Attending, Westchester County Medical Centre, 1974-87; Attending, White Plains Hospital, 1969-96 (Associate attending, 1969-77) (Honorary, 1996-); Associate Attending, St Agnes Hospital, White Plains, 1978-96 (Assistant attending, 1969-78) (Honorary, 1996-). Publications: 1 article, New York State Journal of Medicine. Honours: Continuing Medical Education Award of American Academy of Dermatology 1980-; Physician's Recognition Award of the American Medical Association, 1980-; Who's Who in Science and Engineering; Who's Who in the World; Who's Who in America; Who's Who in the East. Memberships: American Academy of Dermatology; New York State Society of Dermatology; Westchester County Medical Society; Westchester Academy of Medicine; AMA; Society for Paediatric Dermatology. Address: 268 Stuart Dr, New Rochelle, NY 10804-1423, USA.

GLATTRE Eystein Junker, b. 16 April 1934, Kristiansand, Norway. Epidemiologist. m. Ruth Lillian Jordal, 3 daughters. Education: MD, University of Oslo, 1962; Fellowship in Medical Statistics, Medical Statistics Institute, Oslo, 1965-67,

Mayo Graduate School of Medicine, Rochester, USA, 1967-68; PhD, History of Ideas (Bio-temporal Structures), University of Aarhus, Denmark, 1980. Appointments: Assistant Professor, Nordic School of Public Health, Sweden, 1968-69; Consultant, Statistics Norway, 1969-70, Amanuensis, Institute of Preventive Medicine, University of Oslo, 1970-79; Senior Epidemiologist, 1980-91, Head of Department, 1992-2002, Cancer Registry of Norway; Leader of Norwegian Thyroid Cancer Project, 1985-; Board Member, Norwegian Canine Cancer Registry, 1990-2000; Professor in Epidemiology, Norwegian Veterinary College, 1992-2002; Main project since 1997 has been the development of fractal epidemiology. Publications: Around 160 papers and books on cancer research, trace element research, disease classification, cartography, vital statistics, theory of science and mathematics including: A Temporal Quantum Model, 1972; (co-author) Atlas of Cancer Incidence in Norway 1970-79, 1985; Prediagnostic s-Selenium in a Case-Control Study of Thyroid Cancer, 1989; Case-control study testing the hypothesis that seafood increases the risk of thyroid cancer, 1993; Human papillomavirus infection as a risk factor for squamous cell carcinoma of the head and neck, 2001; Fractal Analysis of a case-control study, 2002; The Norwegian Thyroid Cancer Project: History, achievements and present view on carcinogenesis, 2003; Fractal meta-analysis and causality embedded in complexity: Advanced understanding of disease aetiology, 2004. Honour: H M King Olav's Award for Young Mathematicians, 1953. Memberships: Norwegian Medical Association; Norwegian Epidemiological Association; European Thyroid Association; Czech Society for Experimental and Clinical Pharmacology and Toxicology; Society for Chaos Theory in Psychology and Life Sciences. Address: Dron Ingeborgs v 14 N-3530 Royse, Norway.

GLEESON Thomas Alexander, b. 11 August 1920, New York City, New York, USA. Meteorologist. m. Jeanette Lucas, 1 son. 1 daughter. Education: Massachusetts Institute of Technology, US Army, 1942; BS, Harvard University, 1946; MS, 1947, PhD, 1950, New York University. Appointments: First Lieutenant, US Army, US and Middle East, 1942-45; Professor, Florida State University, Tallahassee, 1949-94; Consultant to US Navy, Norfolk, Virginia, 1962-67; Consultant to NASA, Huntsville, Alabama, 1964-73; State Climatologist, US Weather Service, Tallahassee, 1984-94. Publications: Articles in the journals of the American Meteorological Society. Honours: Sigma Xi Research Society; Listed in Who's Who publications and biographical dictionaries. Memberships: Fellow, American Meteorological Society; Member, American Geophysical Union. Address: 2106 Old Bainbridge Road, Tallahassee, FL 32303, USA. E-mail: tomgleeson@aol.com

GLENDINNING Victoria, b. 23 April 1937, Sheffield, England. Author; Journalist. m. (1) O N V Glendinning, 1958, 4 sons, (2) Terence de Vere White, 1981, (3) K P O'Sullivan O.B.E. 1996. Education: BA, Honours, Modern Languages, Somerville College, Oxford, 1959; Diploma, Social Administration, 1969. Appointment: Editorial Assistant, Times Literary Supplement, 1970-74. Publications: A Suppressed Cry: Life and Death of a Quaker Daughter, 1969; Elizabeth Bowen: Portrait of a Writer, 1977; Edith Sitwell: A Unicorn Among Lions, 1981; Vita: The Life of Victoria Sackville-West, 1983; Rebecca West: A Life, 1987; The Grown-ups (novel), 1989; Hertfordshire, 1989; Trollope, 1992; Electricity (novel), 1995; Sons and Mothers (co-editor), 1996; Jonathan Swift, 1998; Flight (novel), 2002; Leonard Woolf: A Life, 2006. Contributions to: Various journals, newspapers and magazines. Honours: Duff Cooper Memorial

Award, 1981; James Tait Black Prize, 1981; Whitbread Awards, 1983, 1992; Whitbread Award, Trollope, 1992; Honorary DLitt, Southampton University, 1994, University of Ulster, 1995, Trinity College, Dublin, 1995, University of York, 2000; Commander of the Order of the British Empire, 1998; Honorary Fellow, Somerville College, Oxford, 2004. Memberships: Royal Society of Literature, Vice-President; English PEN, President, 2001-03; Vice-President, English PEN, 2004. Address: David Higham Associates, 5/8 Lower John Street, Golden Square, London W1, England.

GLENN John Herschel, b. 18 July 1921, Cambridge, Ohio, USA. US Senator. m. Anna Margaret Castor, 1943, 1 son, 1 daughter. Education: Muskingum College; Naval Aviation Cadet program. Appointments: Marine Corps, 1943; Test Pilot, USN and Marine Corps; 1 of 1st 7 Astronauts in US Space Program, 1959; 1st American to orbit Earth, 1962; Resigned, US Marine Corps, 1965; Director, Roy Crown Cola Company, 1965-74; Consultant, NASA; US Senator, Ohio, 1975-99; Announced return as astronaut, 1997, on board Discovery shuttle, 1998. Publications: We Seven, co-author, 1962; P.S., I Listened to Your Heart Beat. Honours include: DFC 6 times; Air Medal with 18 Clusters; Set environmental speed record for 1st flight to average supersonic speeds from Los Angeles to New York, 1957; Space Congressional Medal of Honour; 1st Senator to win 4 consecutive terms in office. Address: Ohio State University, John Glenn Institute, 100 Bricker Hall, 190 North Oval Mall, Columbus, OH 43210, USA.

GLENNIE Evelyn, b. 19 July 1965, Aberdeen, Scotland. Musician. m. Gregorio Malcangi, 1993, (divorced). Education: Ellon Academy, Aberdeenshire; Royal Academy of Music; Furthered studies in Japan on a Munster Trust Scholarship, 1986. Appointments: Solo debut Wigmore Hall, 1986; Concerts with major orchestras world-wide; Tours UK, Europe, USA, Canada, Australia, New Zealand, Far East, Japan, Middle East, South America, China; Performs many works written for her including Bennett, Bourgeois, Heath, Macmillan, McLeod, Muldowney and Musgrave; First solo percussionist to perform at the Proms, London, 1989, subsequent appearances, 1992, 1994, 1996, 1997. Creative work: Recordings include: Rebounds; Light in Darkness; Dancin'; Rhythm Song; Veni, Veni, Emmanuel; Wind in the Bamboo Grove; Drumming; Sonata for two pianos and percussion – Bela Bartok; Last Night of the Proms – 100th Season; Her Greatest Hits; The Music of Joseph Schwantner; Street Songs, Reflected in Brass; Shadow Behind the Iron Sun. Publications: Good Vibrations (autobiography), 1990; Great Journeys of the World, Beat It! Honours: Honorary Doctorates include: Honorary DMus from the Universities of Aberdeen, 1991, Bristol, 1995, Portsmouth, 1995, Surrey, 1997; Queens University, Belfast, 1998, Exeter, Southampton, 2000; Hon DLitt from Universities of Warwick, 1993, Loughborough, 1995; Numerous prizes include Queen's Commendation Prize (RAM); Gold Medal Shell/LSO Music Scholarship, 1984; Charles Heidsieck Soloist of the Year Award, Royal Philharmonic Society, 1991; OBE, 1993; Personality of the Year, International Classical Music Awards, 1993; Young Deaf Achievers Special Award, 1993; Best studio percussionist, Rhythm Magazine, 1998, 2000, 2002, 2003, 2004; Best Live Percussionist, Rhythm Magazine, 2000; Classic FM Outstanding Contribution to Classical Music, 2002; Walpole Medal of Excellence, 2002; Musical America, 2003; 2 Grammy Awards. Address: IMG Artists Europe, Lovell House, 616 Chiswick High Road, London W4 5RX, England. Website: www.evelyn.co.uk

GLOAG Julian, b. 2 July 1930, London, England. Novelist. 1 son, 1 daughter. Education: Exhibitioner, BA, 1953, MA, 1957, Magdalene College, Cambridge. Publications: Our Mother's House, 1963; A Sentence of Life, 1966; Maundy, 1969; A Woman of Character, 1973; Sleeping Dogs Lie, 1980; Lost and Found, 1981; Blood for Blood, 1985; Only Yesterday, 1986; Love as a Foreign Language, 1991; Le passeur de la nuit, 1996; Chambre d'ombre, 1996. Teleplays: Only Yesterday, 1986; The Dark Room, 1988. Memberships: Royal Society of Literature, fellow; Authors Guild. Address: 36 rue Gabrielle, 75018 Paris, France

GLOVER Danny, b. 22 July 1946, Georgia, USA. Actor. m. Asake Bomani, 1 daughter. Education: San Francisco State University. Appointments: Researcher, Office of Mayor, San Francisco, 1971-75; Member, American Conservatory Theatre's Black Actor Workshop; Broadway debut, Master Harold...and the Boys, 1982; Other stage appearances include: The Blood Knot, 1982; The Island; Sizwe Banzi is Dead; Macbeth; Suicide in B Flat; Nevis Mountain Dew; Jukebox; Appearances in TV films and series; Founder, with wife, Bomani Gallery, San Francisco; Actor films: Escape From Alacatraz, 1979; Chu Chu and the Philly Flash, 1981; Out, 1982; Iceman, Places in the Heart, Birdy, The Color Purple, 1984; Silverado, Witness, 1985; Lethal Weapon, 1987; Bat 21, 1988; Lethal Weapon II, 1989; To Sleep With Anger, Predator 2, 1990; Flight of the Intruder, A Rage in Harlem, Pure Luck, 1991; Grand Canyon, Lethal Weapon II, 1992; The Saint of Fort Washington, Bopha, 1993; Angles in the Outfield, 1994; Operation Dumbo Drop, 1995; America's Dream, 1996; The Rainmaker, 1997; Wings Against the Wind, Beloved, Lethal Weapon IV, Prince of Egypt (voice), Antz (voice), 1998; The Monster, 1999; Bàttu, Boseman and Lena, Wings Against the Wind, Freedom Song, 2000; 3 A M, The Royal Tenebaums, 2001; The Real Eve (TV series), 2002; Good Fences (TV), The Henry Lee Project (TV), 2003; Saw, The Cookout, Legend of Earthsea (TV), 2004; The Exonerated (TV), Missing in America, Manderlay, 2005; The Shaggy Dog, The Adventures of Brer Rabbit, Bamako, Dreamgirls, 2006; Poor Boy's Game, Shooter, Honeydripper, Be Kind Rewind, 2007; Terra, 2008. Honours: Chair's Award, National Association for the Advancement of Colored People, 2003. Address: c/o Cary Productions Inc, PMB 352, 6114 LaSalle Avenue, Oakland, CA 9461, USA.

GLOVER Judith, b. 31 March 1943, Wolverhampton, England. Author. 2 daughters. Education: Wolverhampton High School for Girls, 1954-59; Aston Polytechnic, 1960. Publications: Place Names of Sussex (non-fiction), 1975; Place Names of Kent (non-fiction), 1976. Drink Your Own Garden (non-fiction), 1979; The Sussex Quartet: The Stallion Man, 1982, Sisters and Brothers, 1984, To Everything a Season, 1986; Birds in a Gilded Cage, 1987; The Imagination of the Heart, 1989; Tiger Lilies, 1991; Mirabelle, 1992; Minerva Lane, 1994; Pride of Place, 1995; Sussex Place-Names (non-fiction), 1997. Address: c/o Artellus Ltd, 30 Dorset House, Gloucester Place, London NW1 5AD, England.

GOCH Vasyl, b. 3 August 1953. Professor; Doctor of Sciences. Appointments: Professor; Doctor of Sciences, Technical and Biology; Honorary Professor, Department of Biology, Azerbaijan International University; Honorary Doctor, University Francophone International, Brussels and Geneva. Publications: 262 scientific works; 54 monographs; 4 Russian patents; 7 Ukrainian patents. Memberships: Academician: European Academy of Natural Sciences, Hanover; International Academy of Energertic-Information Sciences, Moscow; M Nostrodamus International Academy of Proskopy Sciences, Moscow, Minsk; Russian Academy of Medical-Technical Sciences, Moscow. Address: Skalistaya 5, Selo Rezervnoe, Sevastopol, 99811, Ukraine.

GODDARD Douglas George (Major), b. 4 November 1920. Retired. m. Eve (deceased), 1 son, 1 daughter. Education: Roan School, Blackheath; Brighton Technical College. Appointments: Territorial Army, 1938; Emergency Commission, Royal Artillery, joined 112th (Wessex) Field Regiment RA, 43rd Wessex Division, 1942; Normandy and NW Europe campaigns, 1944-45; Adjutant, 112th Regiment; Adjutant, 40th Field Regiment RA, Germany, 1945-47; Regular Commission, 1946; Staff Captain, 1 AA Group RA, London, 1947-50; Battery Captain, 80th LAA Regiment RA, Egypt and Jordan, 1950-53; Staff College Examination, 1952; Field Artillery Long Gunnery Staff Course then Instructor of Gunnery, Royal School of Artillery, 1953-58; Resigned Commission, 1959; Divisional Secretary, Sulzer Brothers Ltd, London, then Assistant Secretary/Chief Accountant, Mallory Batteries Ltd, Crawley, 1959-64; Secretary then Deputy Chief Executive, The Chartered Institute of Building, 1964-85; Organiser, 'Year of Building', Chartered Institute of Building and Royal Institute of British Architects, 1984; Berkshire County Honorary Secretary then Chairman of the National 'Industry Year' campaigns, 1986-87; Elected Member, 1978-92, and Council Chairman, 1988-90, Workingham District Council; President, Museum of Berkshire Aviation; Branch President, Royal British Legion; Syndicate Speaker on Joint Services Command and Staff College Advanced Course, 1994-; Speaker on Normandy, NW Europe and Arnhem Battlefield Tours; Chief Author and Publisher of '112th (Wessex) Field Regiment RA TA, 1938-46' history. Honours: Liveryman and Freeman, City of London, 1978; BAOR Commander in Chief Certificate, 1946; Queen's Silver Jubilee Medal, 1977; MBE, 1996; RBL/MOD TV advertisement for 'WW2 Veterans' Awareness Week', 2005. Memberships include: Fellow, Chartered Institute of Secretaries and Administrators; Army Benevolent Fund; Constitutional Monarchy Association; St Mary's Church Council, Wargrave; Custodian Trustee, Lady Elizabeth Age Concern Centre, Twyford; Trustee, Honorary Secretary, Woodclyffe Almshouses Trust, Wargrave; Normandy, Market Garden and Suez Veterans Associations; Royal Artillery Institution and Historical Trust; MCC; Phyllis Court Club, Henley; many others. Address: Quinnells, 38 Ridgeway, Wargrave-on-Thames, Berkshire, RG10 8AS, England.

GODFREY Peter David Hensman, b. 3 April 1922, Bluntisham, Huntingdonshire (now Cambridgeshire), England. Musician. m. (1) Sheila McNeile, deceased, 1993, 4 daughters (2) Jane Barnett, 1994. Education: Chorister, King's College Choir, Cambridge, 1931-36; Music Scholar, Denstone College, 1937-40; Choral Scholar, King' College, 1941-42, 1945-46; John Stewart of Rannoch Scholar in Sacred Music, MusB, 1942, BA, 1946, MA, King's College Cambridge; ARCM, Royal College of Music, 1947; ARCO, 1947; FRCO, 1951. Appointments: Assistant, Felsted School, 1946-47, Assistant, Uppingham School, 1947-49, Assistant, Marlborough College, 1949-54, Director of Music, 1954-58, Marlborough College; Organist, Marlborough Parish Church, 1949-54; Lecturer in Music, 1958-73, Professor of Music, 1974-82, University of Auckland, New Zealand; Director of Music, Auckland Cathedral, 1958-74; Conductor, Auckland String Players, 1959-64; Founder, Symphonia of Auckland, 1964-68, Conductor, Auckland Dorian Singers, 1961-82; Conductor, New Zealand National Youth Choir, 1979-88; Director of Music, Wellington Cathedral, 1983-89; Conductor, Wellington Orpheus Choir, 1984-89; Acting Director of

Music, King's College Chapel, 1978; Director of Music, Trinity College, Melbourne University, 1989-91; Conductor, Kapiti Chamber Choir, 1992-2006; Conductor, Kapiti Chorale, 1994-2003; Director of Music, St Michael's Church Choir, 2003-; Founder, President, now Patron, New Zealand Choral Federation, 1985-; In late 1960's and early 70's directed 7 summer schools for the Royal College of Church Music in Australia, USA and England. Recordings include: Festival of Nine Lessons and Carols, Music of the Church's Year, Devotions in Music for the Holy Communion, Carols, Psalms and Anthems, The Way of the Cross, O Sing unto the Lord a New Song with St Mary's Cathedral, Auckland; Faure Requiem, Auckland Dorian Singers and Symphonia, 1969; World Tour, University of Auckland Festival Choir, 1972; Five Centuries of Sacred Music, Auckland Dorian Singers, 1985; On Tour, The National Youth Choir of New Zealand, 1982; A Royal Occasion, National Youth Choir with Kiri Te Kananwa, 1982; Carols, Psalms & Anthems, Trinity College Chapel Choir, Melbourne, Australia, 1990; CDs: New Zealand Choral Music, Auckland University Festival Choir, 1998; The Dorians Sing, Dorian Choir (Auckland), 1998. Honours: FRSCM, 1974; MBE, 1978; CBE, 1988; Icon for Music, New Zealand Arts Foundation, 2005. Membership: Patron, East Anglian Society, New Zealand. Address: 11 Karaka Grove, Waikanae 5036, New Zealand. E-mail: pjgodfrey@paradise.net.nz

GODFREY Sylvia Ann, b. 3 July 1937, Washington, DC, USA. Real Estate Mortgage Broker. m. Lynn, deceased, 1 son, 3 daughters. Education: Degree, University of Maryland School of Law, 1960; Business, University of Florida, 1963, 1975; Business, St Leo Jr College, 1973; Environmental Studies, Florida Keys Jr College, 1975; College studies in applied and art history, music and music industry. Appointments: President, Founder, Florida Keys Juvenile Services Inc; President, Founder, God Free Music Ministries Inc; Business Owner, Licensed Real Estate Broker; Business Owner, Licensed Mortgage Broker; President, God Free Music Co; Author; Composer; Publisher; Producer; Administrator, Island Home for Abused and At Risk Youths; Grant Writer; Administrator of Island Home for Florida Keys Juvenile Services, Inc. Publications: Legislation to provide housing and supportive services for America's homeless; Numerous articles concerning Youth Services, Health Issues, etc; Subject of numerous articles and honours; Numerous songs and recorded works. Honours: Honorary Conch Status for 20 years service to the underprivileged children of Monroe County, Florida; Annual Doing Good Award, 3 years in a row; Good Citizenship Award, 6 times; Honoured by President Bush and Governor Pataki, New York; United Cultural Convention International Peace Prize, 2005; Woman of the Year, International Biographical Centre; Listed in Who's Who publications and biographical dictionaries. Memberships: South Florida Center for the Arts; American Red Cross; Chamber of Commerce, Key Largo, Florida; Irish American Club. Address: 216 Orange Blossom Road, Tavernier, FL 33070, USA. E-mail: fkjs_island@earthlink.net Website: www.islandhome.org

GODWIN-AUSTEN Richard Bertram, b. 4 October 1935, London, England. Neurologist. m. (1) Jennifer Jane Himely, 1 son, 1 daughter, (2) Dierdre (Sally) Toller. Education: Charterhouse; MB BS, St Thomas's Hospital, London, 1959; Training in Neurology, St Thomas's Hospital, Middlesex Hospital and the National Hospitals for Neurology and Neurosurgery, Queen Square; MRCP (Lond) 1963; FRCP (Lond) 1976; MD (Lond), 1969. Appointments: Senior Consultant Neurologist to the Departments of Neurology, Nottingham, Derby and South Lincolnshire Hospitals,

1970-97; Consultant Emeritus, 1997-; Clinical Teacher in Neurology, Faculty of Medicine, University of Nottingham, 1970-97; Clinical Director, University Hospital Nottingham, 1990-93; Vice-President, European Federation of Neurological Societies, 1996-2000; Secretary, Treasurer General, World Federation of Neurology, 1999-. Publications: Approximately 100 articles published in peer-reviewed journals the majority relating to Parkinson's Disease and related disorders; Also: Ethics and Law on Brain Implants, 1988; Fitness for Work – Neurological Disorders, 1988; The Neurology of the Elderly (text book) 1999, currently under revision; Standards of Care for Patients with Neurological Disease, 1990; The Organisation of Neurological Services in the United Kingdom, for the WHO Symposium, Marseilles, 1995. Honours: Fellowship of the Royal College of Physicians, 1976; President, Association of British Neurologists, 1997-99; High Sheriff of Nottinghamshire, 1994-95. Memberships include: Medical Advisory Panel, Parkinson's Disease Society, 1970-99; UK Delegate, World Federation of Neurology, 1989-93; Chairman, Sheffield Regional Advisory Committee on Neurology and Neurosurgery, 1990-93; European Board of Neurology, 1996-2000; Church Warden, Papplewick and Linby PCC, 1994-2005; Council of the Academy of Experts. Address: 15 Westgate, Southwell, Nottinghamshire NG25 0JN, England.

GOH Eui-Kyung, b. 16 July 1953, Jeju City, Korea. Professor; Physician. m. Mie Lee, 1 son, 1 daughter. Education: MD, Pusan National University Medical School, 1978; PhD, Pusan National University, 1989; Korean Board of Otolaryngology, 1983. Appointments: Army Surgeon of Republic of Korea, 1983-86; Professor, 1986-, Vice Dean, 1999-2001, Pusan National University Medical School; Chairman, Department of Otolaryngology, Pusan National University Hospital, 2001-07; President Elect, Korean Equilibrium Society, 2005-. Publications: Dizziness, 1999; Otolaryngology – Head and Neck Surgery, 2002; Equilibrium and Disequilibrium, 2005. Memberships: Korean Otolaryngological Society; Korean Equilibrium Society; American Academy of Otolaryngology; Politzer Society. Address: Department of ENT, Pusan National University Hospital, #1-10, Ami-dong, Seo-gu, Busan 602-739, Korea.

GOKTEPE Ahmet Burak, b. 15 October 1970, Trabzon, Turkey. Civil Engineer. m. E Zeynep, 1 son, 1 daughter. Education: BSc, 1993, MSc, 1995, PhD, 2004, Civil Engineering, Istanbul Technical University. Appointments: Site Engineer, Bakacak Dam Construction, Canakkale, 1993-95; Project Manager, Derebucak Dam Construction, Konya, 1995; Software Engineer, Focus Computer Ltd, Istanbul, 1995-96; Project Manager, Bakacak Dam Construction, Canakkale, 1996-2000; Chief Engineer, Dim Dam & HEPP Construction, Antalya, 2000-03; Visitor, 2001, Research Assistant, 2001-02, Department of Mechanical Engineering, Lehigh University, USA; Assistant Professor, Department of Civil Engineering, Ege University, Izmir, 2003-05; Research Associate, University of Texas at Austin, USA, 2005; Project Manager, Akkoy Day & HEPP Construction, Kurtun, 2005-08; Project Manager, Construction, Kurtun, 2005-08. Publications: Numerous articles in professional journals and at international conferences; 3 books; 9 citations in scientific journals. Honours: NSF Fellowship, National Science Foundation, USA, 2001; Scientific Paper Award, Turkish Road Association, 2004 and 2005; Listed in international biographical dictionaries. Memberships: Turkish Chamber of Civil Engineers; American Society of Civil Engineers; ASCE Transporation & Development Institute; Turkish Road Association; International Neural Network Society;

International Computational Intelligence Society; British Council Science Hub; National Geographic Society. Address: Vedat Dalokay Cad, 5 Sok, 37/10, GOP, Ankara, Turkey. E-mail: burak.goktepe@ege.edu.tr

GOLAN Shammai, b. 5 April 1933, Poland. Emigrated to Israel, 1947. Holocaust Survivor; Hebrew Writer; Diplomat. m. Arna Ben-Dror, 2 sons, 2 daughters. Education: BA, Literature and History, Hebrew University of Jerusalem, 1961. Appointments: Director, Writers' House, Jerusalem, 1971-78; Head, Department of Jewish Education and Culture for the Diaspora, Buenos Aires, Argentina, 1978-81; Chairman, Hebrew Writers' Association, 1981-84, 1989-91; Counsellor, Cultural Affairs, Embassy of Israel, Mexico, 1984-87, Moscow, 1994-99; Director and Secretary, Board of Directors, Society of Authors, Composers and Music Publishers in Israel, 2000-. Publications: Novels and short stories: The Last Watch; Guilt Offerings; The Death of Uri Peled; Escape for Short Distances; Canopy: The Ambush; Holocaust: Anthology; My Travels with Books: Essays; And If You Must Love, novel, 2008; Scenarios; Radio plays; Numerous articles. Honours: Literary Awards: Barash, 1962; Acum, 1965; Ramat-Gan, 1973; The Agnon Jerusalem, 1976; Walenrod Prize, 1979; Prime Minister's Prize, 1992; Laureate of Light (Khattan Haor), Zionist Council, Israel, Jerusalem, 2006. Memberships: Hebrew Writers' Association; PEN Centre; ACUM; Cultural Academy of Mexico; Council, Yad Vashem Museum Memorial. Address: 1 Haamoraim Str, Tel Aviv 69207, Israel. E-mail: golan-sa@barak.net.il

GOLDBERG Abraham (Sir), b. 7 December 1923, Edinburgh, Scotland. Professor of Medicine. m. Clarice Cussin, 2 sons, 1 daughter. Education: MBChB, University of Edinburgh, 1941-46; MD (Gold Medal), Edinburgh, 1956; FRCP, Glasgow, 1964; FRCP, Edinburgh, 1965; DSc, University of Glasgow, 1966; FRCP, London, 1967; FRSE, 1971; FFPM, 1989. Appointments include: Nuffield Research Fellow, University College Hospital Medical School, 1952-54; Medical Research Council Travelling Fellow in Medicine, University of Utah, USA, 1954-56; Regius Professor of Materia Medica, University of Glasgow, 1970-78; Chairman, Medical Research Council Grants Committee, 1973-77; Regius Professor of the Practice of Medicine, now Emeritus, University of Glasgow, 1978-89; Chairman, Committee on the Safety of Medicines, 1980-86; Honorary Professorial Research Fellow, Department of Modern History, University of Glasgow, 1996-2003. Publications: Diseases of Porphyrin Metabolism (co-author), 1962; Recent Advances in Haematology (co-editor), 1971; Disorders of Porphyrin Metabolism (co-author), 1987; Pharmaceutical Medicine and the Law (co-editor), 1991; Papers on clinical and investigative medicine, 1951-. Honours: Editor, Scottish Medical Journal, 1962-63; Sydney Watson Smith Lecturer, Royal College of Physicians, Edinburgh, 1964; Henry Cohen Lecturer, University of Jerusalem, 1973; Knighted (KB), 1983; Fitzpatrick Lecturer, Royal College of Physicians, London, 1988; Goodall Memorial Lecturer, Royal College of Physicians and Surgeons of Glasgow, 1989; Lord Provost Award for Public Service, City of Glasgow, 1988; Foundation President, Faculty of Pharmaceutical Medicine of the Royal Colleges of Physicians, 1989. Membership: Association of Physicians of Great Britain and Ireland. Address: 16 Birnam Crescent, Bearsden, Glasgow, G61 2AU, Scotland.

GOLDBERG Whoopi, b. 13 November 1949, New York, USA. Actress. m.(1) Alvin Martin 1973-79, divorced, 1 daughter, (2) David Claessen, 1986-88, divorced, (3) Lyle Trachtenberg, 1994-95 divorced. Career: First appearance aged 8, Hudson Guild Theatre, New York; Helen Rubenstein Children's Theatre, San Diego, moved 1974; Co-founder, San Diego Repertory Theatre, appeared in 2 productions, Brecht's Mother Courage and Marsha Norman's Getting Out; Moved to San Francisco, Jointed Blake Street Hawkeyes Theatre, appeared in The Spook Show and Moms, co-wrote, a one-woman show in US Tours, debut, The Lyceum Theatre, Broadway, 1984; Films include: The Color Purple, 1985; Jumpin' Jack Flash, Ghost, 1990; Sister Act; Made in America, 1992; Sister Act II; Corrina Corrina, 1993; Star Trek Generation 5; Moonlight and Valentino; Bogus; Eddie; The Associate, The Ghost of Mississippi, 1996; How Stella Got Her Groove Back, 1998; Deep End of the Ocean, Jackie's Back! Girl Interrupted, 1999; Rat Race, Call Me Claus, Kingdom Come, Monkeybone, Golden Dreams, 2001; Star Trek: Nemesis, Blizzard (voice), More Dogs Than Bones, 2002; Good Fences, 2003; Pinocchio 2000 (voice), Jiminy Glick in La La Wood, 2004; Racing Stripes (voice), The Magic Roundabout (voice), 2005; Farce of the Penguins (voice), Doogal (voice), 2006; If I Had Known I Was a Genius, Homie Spumoni, 2007. TV: Moonlighting, 1985-86; own TV show, 1992-93; What Makes a Family, 2001; It's a Very Merry Muppet Christmas Movie, 2002; Whoopi (series), 2003; Littleburg (series), 2004. Honours: Several nominations as best actress for The Color Purple including Academy Award, Golden Globe; Emmy Nomination for Moonlighting; Grammy for Best Comedy Album, 1985; Hans Christian Andersen Award for Outstanding Achievement by a Dyslexic; Mark Twain Prize for Humor, Kennedy Centre of Arts, 2001. Address: 4000 Warner Boulevard, #404, Burbank, CA 90068, USA.

GOLDBLUM Jeff, b. 22 October 1952, Pittsburgh, USA. Actor. m. (2) Geena Davis, divorced. Education: Studied at New York Neighbourhood Playhouse. Career: Actor, films include: California Split, Death Wish, 1974; Nashville, 1975; Next Stop Greenwich Village, 1976; Annie Hall, Between the Lines, The Sentinel, 1977; Invasion of the Body Snatchers, Remember My Name, Thank God it's Friday, 1978; Escape From Athena, 1979; The Big Chill, The Right Stuff, Threshold, 1983; The Adventures of Buckaroo Banzai, 1984; Silverado, Into the Night, Transylvania 6-5000, 1985; The Fly, 1986; Beyond Therapy, 1987; The Tall Guy, Earth Girls Are Easy, First Born (TV), 1989; The Mad Monkey, 1990; Mister Frost, 1991; Deep Cover, The Favour, The Watch and the Very Big Fish, 1992; Father and Sons, Jurassic Park, 1993; Lushlife (TV), Future Quest (TV), 1994; Hideaway, Nine Months, 1995; Independence Day, 1996; The Lost World, 1997; Holy Man, 1998; Popcorn, 1999; Chain of Fools, Angie Rose, 2000; Cats and Dogs, 2001; Igby Goes Down, 2002; Dallas 362, Spinning Boris, 2003; Incident at Loch Ness, The Life Aquatic with Steve Zissou, 2004; Mini's First Time, Fay Grim, Man of the Year, 2006; Raines (TV), 2007; Adam Resurrected, 2008. Producer: Little Surprises, 1995; Holy Man, 1999. Address: c/o Peter Lemie, William Morris Agency, 151 El Camino Drive, Beverly Hills, CA 90212, USA.

GOLDENBERG Iosif Sukharovich, b. 1 May 1927, Ukraine. School Teacher. Education: PhD, Philology Department, Kharkov State University, 1949. Publications: Tavolga, English translation as Meadow-sweet; Nad Propast'yu v Tishi, English translation as On the Verge of Abyss in the Silence; Zalozhniki Zaveta, English translation as Hostages of Behest; Izbrannoe, English translation as Selected Rhymes; Stikhi dlya Detei (Rhymes for Children); Serdoliki (Sards); Kashtanovye Svechi (Chestnut Candlelights); Na Kazhdyi Den' (Everyday Reading); Ten' I Svet (Shade and Light); 1996 God (The Year of 1996); Iz Pushchino s Lyubov'yu

(From Pushchino with Love); Sto Stikhotvorenyi (A Hundred Rhymes); Predvaritelnye Itogi (Preliminary Outcomes). Contributions to: Periodicals. Address: Building AB-1, Apt 43, 142292 Pushchino, Moscow Region, Russia.

GOLDING Allan Peter, b. 26 March 1960, Jamestown, South Australia. Physician. m. Dymphna, 2 sons, 1 daughter. Education: MBBS, University of Adelaide, Australia, 1984; Diploma in Obstetrics, Gynaecology and Neonatal Care, Royal Australian and New Zealand College of Obstetrics and Gynaecology, 1987; Registered Medical Board of South Australia; Certificate, Civil Aviation Medicine, Australia, 2001. Appointments include: Intern, Royal Adelaide Hospital, Adelaide, 1984; Resident Medical Officer, Lyell McEwin Health Service, Elizabeth Vale, 1985-86; Resident Medical Officer, Modbury Hospital, Modbury, South Australia, 1987; Rural General Practice, Medicine, Surgery and Obstetrics, Port Pirie, South Australia, 1988-; Clinical Lecturer, University of Adelaide, Department of General Practice, 1993-; Designated Aviation Medical Examiner, 2000-06; Steering Committee, Mid-North Rural South Australia Division General Practice, 1994-; Chairman, Drug and Therapeutics Committee, Port Pirie Regional Health Service Inc, 1994-2000; Mental Health Advisory Committee, Mid-North Regional Health Service Inc, 1996-2000; Medical Officer, Port Pirie Abattoir, 1991-; Club Surgeon, Port Pirie Racing and Harness Club, 1993-95; Club Doctor, Port Pirie Power Boat Club, 1990-2003. Publications: Articles in medical journals as co-author: South Australian Hypertension Survey. General Practitioner Knowledge and Reported Management Practices – A Cause for Concern? 1992; A Comparison of Outcomes with Angiotensin-Converting Enzyme Inhibitors and Diuretics for Hypertension in the Elderly. Honours: Order of International Fellowship, 2004; International Health Professional of the Year, 2004, 2005; Fellow, ABI, 2005; ABI, Man of the Year, 2004, 2005; Legion of Honour, UCC, 2005; International Peace Prize, UCC, 2006. Memberships include: Fellow, Royal Australian College of General Practitioners; Fellow, Australian College of Rural and Remote Medicine; Port Pirie Medical Practitioners Society; Australian Medical Association; Sports Medicine Australia; International Federation of Sports Medicine; Arthritis Foundation of Australia; Rural Doctors Association of Australia; Australasian Society of Aerospace Medicine; Port Pirie Asthma Support Group; Life Member, Asthma Foundation; Leader Member, Lord Baden-Powell Society; Patron, Member of Lord Baden Powell Society, 2005. Address: Central Clinic, 101 Florence Street, Port Pirie, SA 5540, Australia. E-mail: supadocs@westnet.com.au

GOLDMAN William, b. 12 August 1931, Chicago, Illinois, USA. Author. m. Ilene Jones, 1961-91 (divorced), 2 daughters. Education: Columbia University. Publications: Novels: The Temple of Gold, 1957; Your Turn to Curtsey, My Turn to Bow, 1958; Soldier in the Rain, 1960; Boys and Girls Together, 1964; The Thing of It Is, 1964; No Way to Treat a Lady (as Harry Longbaugh); Father's Day, 1971; Marathon Man, 1974; Wigger, 1974; Magic, 1976; Tinsel, 1979; Control, 1982; The Silent Gondoliers, 1983; The Color of Light, 1984; Play: Blood Sweat and Stanley Poole (with James Goldman), 1961; Musical comedy: A Family Affair (with James Goldman and John Kander), 1962; Non-fiction: Adventures in the Screen Trade, 1983; Hype and Glory, 1990; Four Screenplays, 1995; Five Screenplays, 1997; Screenplays: Harper, 1966; Butch Cassidy and the Sundance Kid, 1969; The Princess Bride, 1973; Marathon Man, 1976; All the President's Men, 1976; A Bridge Too Far, 1977; Magic, 1978; Heat, 1985; Brothers, 1987; Year of the Comet, 1992; Memoirs of an Invisible Man, 1992; Chaplin, 1992; Indecent Proposal, 1993; Maverick,

1994; Ghost and the Darkness, 1996; Absolute Power, 1997; Hearts in Atlantis, 2001; Dreamcatcher, 2003; The Monkey Wrench Gang, 2008. Honours: Academy Awards, 1970, 1977. Address: c/o William Morris, 151 El Camino Drive, Beverly Hills, CA 90212, USA.

GOLDSCHEIDER Gabriele Maria (Gaby), b. 7 March 1929, Vienna, Austria. Independent Bookseller; Writer; Publisher. Education: Ruskin School of Art, Oxford University, 1949-53. Appointments: International Media Buyer, Foote, Cone and Belding; Librarian, Advertising Association; Editor, Hamlyn Publishing. Publications: Articles in Antiquarian Book Monthly Review; Dolls; Bibliography of Arthur Conan Doyle; Publisher of Holmesiana (Sherlock Holmes); Richard Jeffries: A Modern Appraisal; General Editor of Medallion Collectors' series for Constable Publishers. Honour: Certificate of Merit for conservation of Charles Dickens Bookshop, Isle of Wight Society, 1987. Memberships: Antiquarian Booksellers Association, 1978-2002; Committee Member, Windsor Literary Society; Private Libraries Association; Ex-member, Authors' Society. Address: Deep Dene, 5 Baring Road, Cowes, Isle of Wight PO31 8DB, England.

GOLDSHMIDT Vladimir Y, b. 26 December 1928, Kirovograd, Ukraine, USSR. Engineer-Geophysicist. m. 1 daughter. Education: MSc, Geophysics, Kazakh Mining-Metallurgical Institute, 1955; PhD, Academy of Sciences of Kazakhstan, 1965; DSc, Moscow State University, 1977; Professor, USSR Supreme Certification Commission, 1989. Appointments: Chief Engineer, Geologic-Geophysical expedition in Kazakhstan, 1955-65; Head of the Department of Interpretation of Geological Data, Institute of Mining Geophysics, Almaty, 1966-1991, Concurrently, Professor-Lecturer, Institute of Qualification Updating of the USSR, Almaty, 1968-91; Professor-Researcher-Geophysicist, 1992-2000, Professor Consultant, 2001-2004, The Geophysical Institute of Israel. Publications: USSR, 1958-92: 20 books, teaching aids, methodical recommendations: 4 author, 7 co-author, 9 participant, Certificates for Inventions; 120 articles, abstracts in Russian;1 book translated from Russian into Chinese; Israel, USA, Europe, 1992-2005: 60 articles, abstracts and reports; 2002-2003, scientific and other publications in newspapers. Honours: Prospector Award, Ministry of Geology of the USSR, 1978; USSR Inventor, State Committee of Inventions and Discoveries of the USSR, 1984; Honoured Scientist (Meritorious Science Worker) of Kazakhstan, 1989; Medals from USSR and Kazakhstan; Biography and main scientific works published in book: Russian Applied Geophysics of the XXth Century by Biographies, Academy of Sciences, Moscow, 1998; Listed in Encyclopaedia of Kazakhstan. Membership: Israel Geology Society, Jerusalem; Scientists of the South Association. Address: Abarbanel Street 22/11, Beer-Sheva 84759, Israel.

GOLDSMITH David Julian Alexander, b. 29 August 1959, Salford, England. Medical Consultant. m. Deborah Mary Gillatt, 1 son, 1 daughter. Education: BA, 1980; MBB Chir, 1983; MA, 1984; MRCP, 1985; FRCP, 1999; Diploma of Teaching, South Thames Deanery, 2001. Appointments include: Surgical House Officer, Warwick Hospital, 1983-84; Medical House Officer, 1984, Senior HP, 1984-85, Renal Registrar, 1987-88, Renal Research Registrar, 1988-91, St Thomas' Hospital; Senior HP, Professorial Renal Unit, Hammersmith Hospital, 1985; Senior HP, Thoracic Medicine, Brompton Hospital, 1985-86; Senior HP, National Hospital for Nervous Diseases, 1986; Registrar, General Medicine, Kingston Hospital, 1986-87; Senior Registrar (Locum), Endocrine Unit, Guy's Hospital, 1991; Senior Registrar, Nephrology, Withington

Hospital, 1991-94; Senior Registrar, Nephrology, Manchester Royal Infirmary, 1994-95; Consultant in Nephrology, General Medicine, Brighton, 1995-98; Consultant, Nephrology, Guy's and St Thomas' NHS Trust, 1998-. Publications include: 10 books/chapters; Over 200 publications; 22 letters; 140 abstracts presented at National and International Meetings; Core-reviewer, contributor, Medical Masterclasses; Editor, Journal of Nephrology, 2003-; Educational, 2003-; Editor, Neprology, Dialysis, Transplantation, 2004-; ABC of Kidney Disease, 2007. Honours: Bronze Clinical Excellence Award, 2006. Memberships include: Royal College Committee on Renal Diseases, 1995-2000; South Thames Regional Monospeciality Training Committee, 1998-; Royal College of Physicians, 2000-; UK Renal Association Executive Committee, 2002-; External Grant Review Member, National Kidney Research Fund, 2003-; Honorary Secretary, UK Renal Association, 2004-; Member, Executive Council, European Renal Association, 2004-; Royal Society of Medicine; London Hypertension Society; Medical Society of London; UK Renal Association; International Society of Nephrology; Chairman, Paper Selection Committee, ERA, 2005-. E-mail: goldsmith@london.com Website: www.dgoldsmith.co.uk

GOLDSMITH Harvey, CBE, b. 4 March 1946, London, England. Chief Executive; Impresario. m. Diana Gorman, 1971, 1 son. Education: Christ's College; Brighton College of Technology. Appointments: Partner, Big O Posters, 1966-67; Organised first free open-air concert, Parliament Hill Fields, with Michael Alfandary, 1968; Opened Round House, Camden Town, 1968, Crystal Palace Garden Party series concerts, 1969-72; Merged with John Smith Entertainment, 1970; Formed Harvey Goldsmith Entertainment (rock tours promotion co), 1976; Acquired Allied Entertainment Group (rock concert promotions co), 1984; Formed Classical Productions with Mark McCormack, 1986; Promoter and Producer, pop rock, classical musical events including: Concerts: Bruce Springsteen; The Rolling Stones; Elton John; The Who; Pink Floyd; Live Aid, 1985; Pavarotti at Wembley, 1986; Opera: Aïda, 1988, Carmen, 1989, Tosca, Earls Court; Pavarotti in the Park, 1991; The Three Tenors, Mastercard Masters of Music, 1996; Music for Monserrat, 1997; The Bee Gees, Ozzfest, Paul Weller, 1998; Live 8, 2005. Honour: CBE, 1996. Memberships include: Chairman, Concert Promoters Association, 1986; Chairman, National Music Festival, 1991; Co-Chairman, President's Club, 1994; Vice Chairman, Prince's Trust Action Management Board, 1993; VP, REACT, 1989; VP, Music Users Council, 1994; Trustee, Band Aid, 1985; Trustee, Live Aid Foundation, 1985; Trustee, Royal Opera House, 1995; Trustee, CST, 1995; British Red Cross Coms Panel, 1992; Prague Heritage Fund, 1994; London Tourist Board, 1994. Address: Harvey Goldsmith Entertainment Ltd., Greenland Place, 115-123 Bayham Street, London NW1 0AG, England.

GOLDSTEIN Myrna, b. 5 August 1948, Rochester, New York, USA. Professor; Journalist; Writer; Businesswoman. Education: Master's Degree, Teaching English as a Second/Foreign Language, St Michael's College, Vermont, USA; BSJ, Journalism, Northwestern University, Illinois, USA; Diploma, Italian Language and Culture; Certification to Teach Italian, University for Foreigners, Perguia, Italy; Owner, Euroglobal Communications® Snc and Are You in Your English File?® Second Language Learning Research Center, Loiri/Porto San Paolo, Sardinia, Italy. Appointments: Journalism: Business Market Editor/Reporter, Fairchild Publications, New York City, 1971-73; Contributing Journalist, Publicist, New York City, 1973-74; Venice Italy, 1981-86; Syndicated Feature Writer and Food Editor promoted to Editorial Board Member,

Writer Columnist Opinion Pages; Feature Writer, Gannett Co, Rochester New York and Harrison, Westchester County, New York, 1974-81, 1986-89; Cross-Cultural Journalist, Editor, Copywriter, Publicist, Perugia, Italy, 1990-; Teaching Appointments: Journalism and Mass Communications, State University of New York, 1974; Instructor, Italian Language for Foreigners, Elizabeth Seton College, Yonkers, New York and Manhattan Community College, New York City, 1987-88; Conversation Instructor, Perugia Board of Education, 1995-2004; Professor and Creator "Greatest Hits" Experimental Linguistic Laboratory, Perugia, 1996-98; Professor, Tourism English, 1997-98, Professor, Business Communications and International Marketing, 1997-98, Institute for Commercial Services, Gualdo Tadino; Professor of Journalism, Spoleto and Norcia, 2000; Professor, Italian Army Officers Language Training Centre (SLEE), Perugia, 1998-2003; Lecturer, 2001-2002, Professor, 2002-04, Program for Interpreters and Translators, Faculty of Philosophy and Letters, University of Perugia; Director, Chief Researcher, Are You in Your English File?®, Second Language Learning Research Center, Division Euroglobal Communications® Snc; Professor TESOL, Politecnico, Milan, Italy 2006-; Professor North American English, Catholic University of the Sacred Heart, Milan 2007-. Unpublished works: Are You in Your English File? Decoding Listening Comprehension Through Pre-Listening Strategies: A Pilot Case Study, 2002; Sensing Worlds of Worlds – Poem-Songs on Loving and the World, 2004; Stealing Vesuvius, 2004. Honours: Pulitzer Prize Nominee; Reader's Digest Magazine Writing Award; Summer Intern, Magazine Publishers Association, 1969. Memberships: European Society for the Study of English (ESSE); International Women's Media Foundation, Washington DC, USA; Italian Association for English Professionals (AIA); SIETAR; TESOL Italy; TESOL, USA; Italian Association of Applied Linguists; Linguistic Society of America; FAI; Italian Chamber of Commerce. Address: Casella Postale No 1865, Agenzia Poste Italiane di, 20101 Milano, Italy. E-mail: goldzec@euroglobalcomm.com

GOLDSTEIN-JACKSON Kevin Grierson, b. 2 November 1946, Windsor, Berkshire, England. Writer; Artist; Poet. m. Mei Leng Ng, 6 September 1975, 2 daughters. Education: BA, Reading University; MPhil, Southampton University; FRSA. Appointments: Programme Organizer, Southern TV, 1970-73; Assistant Producer, HK-TVB, Hong Kong, 1973; Freelance Writer, TV Producer, 1974-75; Head of Film, Dhofar Region TV Service, Sultanate of Oman, 1975-76; Assistant to Head of Drama, Anglia TV, 1977-81; Founder, Chief Executive and Programme Controller, Television South West, 1981-85; Freelance Writer, 1985-. Contributions to numerous magazines and newspapers including: Sunday Times; Financial Times; Author of 19 published books; Writer of film and TV screen plays; Poetry published in US, UK, Australia, Canada, etc. Memberships: Writers' Guild; Society of Authors; Poetry Society. Address: c/o Alcazar, 18 Martello Road, Branksome Park, Poole, Dorset BH13 7DH, England.

GOLDTHORPE (John) Michael, b. 7 February 1942, York, England. Singer (Tenor). Education: MA, Trinity College, Cambridge, 1964; Certificate of Education, King's College, London, 1965; Guildhall School of Music and Drama, London, 1966-67. Debut: Purcell Room, London, January 1970. Career includes: Paris debut, 1972; Opera Royal, Versailles, 1977; Royal Opera, Covent Garden and BBC Television, 1980; Regular Broadcaster, BBC Radio; US debut, Miami Festival, 1986; Appearances in Singapore, Iceland, most countries Western Europe; Concertgebouw, Amsterdam, 1986, Directed Medieval Concert in Rome, 1987; Noted Bach Evangelist

and exponent of French Baroquer; Lucerne Festival's performance of Frank Martin's Golgotha, 1990; Series of concerts for the Sorbonne, Paris, 1992; London performances Verdi Requiem, Janácek's Glagolitic Mass, Britten's Cantata Misericordium Beethoven's Missa Solemnis; Former Teacher, Royal Holloway College, Egham, London College of Music, Great Marlborough Street, Trinity College of Music, London; Lecturer and Adjudicator; Currently Singing Tutor at Roehampton University, London; Founder and Artistic Director of the specialist Victorian music group and charity, The Bold Balladiers, 1995; Musical Director, Lymington Choral Society, 2006. Recordings include: Rameau: Hippolyte et Aricie, La Princesse de Navarre and Pygmalion; Charpentier Missa Assumpta est Maria; Mondonville Motets; Cavalli Ercole Amante; 100 Years of Italian Opera; Delius Irmelin; L'Incoronazione di Poppea; Monteverdi Madrigali Libri Primo, Secondo, Sesto; Blanchard Cantatas; The Snowy Breasted Pearl (Victorian and Edwardian Ballads); St Cuthbert of Lindisfarne and other Songs by Stuart Ward. Honours: Lieder Prize GSM, 1967; Choral Exhibition, Cambridge, 1961; GLAA Young Musicians Award, ISM Young Musicians Award, Park Lane Group's Young Musician Award, early 1970's; Wingate Scholarship, 1994. Memberships: Hon Fellow, Cambridge Society of Musicians, 1993; Member of the Royal Society of Musicians of Great Britain, 1999. Address: 77 Southampton Road, Lymington, Hants, SO41 9GH, England.

GOLOVACHENKO Klara Kondelevna, b. 26 March 1962, Verkhnij-Alenuj settlement, Chita region, Russia. Psychologist; Sociologist. 1 daughter. Education: Irkutsk State Technical University. Appointments: President, Interregional Centre of Cause and Consequence Relations and Causative Psychology, Azorel, 1999-; Consultant on questions of causality. Honours: Acknowledged Healer Certificate; Certificate for Outstanding Achievements in Complementary Medicine and Renaissance Statuette; Great Women of the 21st Century Award; Sign of Distinction of Scientific Causality School; Certificate for Developing and Introducing New Ways and Methods of Improving Quality of Life; Certificate for Novelty and Practical Usefulness. Address: 1 Microrajon, 8-56, Shelekov, Irkutsk Region, Russia.

GOLU Mihai, b. 4 March 1934, Poienari, Gorj, Romania. Psychologist; University Professor. m. Elena, 2 sons. Education: Diploma, Primary School Teacher, Educational College, 1952; Psychologist's Diploma, Master of Arts, Psychology, University of Moscow, 1958; Doctoral Studies, 1962-66, PhD, 1968, University of Bucharest; Postdoctoral Advanced Research in Human Information Processing, Carnegie-Mellon University, Pittsburgh, USA, 1973-74. Appointments: Assistant, 1958-62, Lecturer, 1962-70, Assistant Professor, 1970-82, Full Professor, 1990-2001, Department of Psychology, Senior Researcher, Anthropological Center, 1982-90, University of Bucharest; Minister of Education, Minister of Culture, 1991-93; Professor and Head, Department of Psychology, University Spini Havet, Bucharest, 2001-. Publications: Over 150 articles; Books: Sensory Processes, 1970; Introduction to Psychology, 1972; Psychophysiology, 1976; Principles of Psychocybernetics, 1978; Handbook of General Psychology, 2003; Dynamics of Personality, 2005; Handbook of Neuropsychology, 2006. Honours: National Order for Merit; UNESCO Medal, Pablo Picasso; Medal Ian Amos Comeius, Iokeck Academy. Memberships: Romanian Academy of Scientists; Romania Association of Psychologists; International Association of Cybernetics. Address: Bd Libertatii 22, bloc 102, sc 5, apt 89, sector 5, Bucharest, Romania.

GOMES Luis Daniel Teia dos Santos Mendes, b. 31 December 1980, Aradas, Aveiro, Portugal. PhD Researcher. Education: Master's degree, Physics Engineering, Faculty of Science and Technology, University Nova of Lisbon, Monte da Caparica, Almada, Portugal, 1998-2000; Master's degree (1st class honours), Aerospace Engineering, 2000-04, Airbus sponsored PhD, Aerospace Engineering, 2004-, University of Manchester, England. Appointments: Designer, Rocket Recovery System, UK Aspire Space, Manchester, England, 2000-01; Co-ordinator, Satellite Power Control Subsystem, 7th EUROAVIA design workshop, Carlo Gavazzi Space Co, Milan, Italy, 2001; Co-ordinator, Zero Gravity Flight Campaign, European Space Agency (ESA), Bordeaux, France, 2001-02; Main Co-ordinator, Satellite Thermal Control Subsystem, Student Space Exploration & Technology Initiative (SSETI), European Space Agency, 2001-03; Project Investigator, Athens 2004 Olympia Sailing Campaign, University of Manchester, England, 2002-03; Project Manager, Component Rig Tests, Rolls-Royce, Dhalewitz, Berlin, Germany, 2003-04; Researcher, Airbus funded research workshop, 2nd European Forum on Flow Control, University of Poitiers, France, 2006. Publications: Mast Device for Aerodynamic Improvement of Sail Boats, 2004; Towards a Practical Piezoceramic Diaphragm-based Synthetic Jet Actuator for High Subsonic Applications – Effect of Chamber and Orifice Depth on Actuator Peak Velocity, 2006; Towards a Practical Synthetic Jet Actuator for Industrial Scale Flow Control Applications, 2006; An Evaluation of the Mass and Power Scaling of SJA Flow Control Technology for Civil Transport Aircraft Applications, 2007. Honours: Winner, EUROAVIA European Design Contest, 2001; Project Poster Prize, Athens 2004 Olympics Project, University of Manchester, 2002-03; Grantee, Leonardo da Vinci Grant, European Union Leonardo da Vinci Mobility Programme, 2003-04; Silver Award for Extraordinary Involvement, SSETI Project, European Space Agency, 2003; Educational Award, Royal Aeronautical Society, 2004; Listed in international biographical dictionaries. Memberships: American Institute of Aeronautics & Astronautics (AIAA); Royal Aeronautical Society (RAeS); Institution of Mechanical Engineers (IMechE). Address: Flat C2 Room 3, Daisybank Villas, 5-7 Anson Road, Manchester, M14 5BR, England. E-mail: tcs_luis@yahoo.co.uk

GOMES DE MATOS Francisco Cardoso, b. 3 September 1933, Crato, Brazil. University Professor. m. Helen Herta Bruning, 1 son, 2 daughters. Education: Bachelor in Law and Languages, Federal University, Pernambuco, 1958; Master's in Linguistics, University of Michigan, 1960; PhD in Applied Linguistics, Catholic University of Sao Paulo, 1973. Appointments: Visiting Professor, Catholic University of Sao Paulo, 1966-79; Fulbright Visiting Professor, University of Georgia, Athens Georgia, USA, 1985-1986; Professor, Federal University of Pernambuco, 1980-; Co-founder, Brazil-America Association; Retired 2003 from the Federal University of Pernambuco, Consultant (Language & Culture) to Brazil America Association, Recife. Publications: Plea for Universal Declaration of Linguistic Rights, 1984; Plea for Communicative Peace, 1993; Chapter on Using Peaceful Language, from Principles to Practices in EOLSS, 2005; Chapter on Language, Peace and Conflict Resolution in the Handbook of Conflict Resolution (2nd Edition), 2006. Honours: Benefactor Member, International Society for the Teaching of Portuguese as a Foreign Language; Received Tribute at the 30th Anniversary of the Graduate Program in Letters/ Linguistics, Federal University of Pernambuco, 2006; Listed in biographical publications. Memberships: Brazilian Linguistics Association; Brazilian Academy of Philology;

Brazilian Association for Applied Linguistics; Columbia University-based research group www.humiliationstudies.org. Address: Rua Setubal 860-B, Apto 604, 51030-010 Recife, Brazil. E-mail: fcgm@hotlink.com.br

GOMEZ Rajan Gaetan, b. 21 November 1938, Kalutara, Sri Lanka. Consultant and Researcher in Parliamentary and Commonwealth Affairs. m. Rosanne Pinto, 2 daughters. Education: BSc (Hons), University of Sri Lanka, 1961; DIC (Diploma of Imperial College), 1973, MSc, Management Studies (with Distinction) Imperial College, 1973. Appointments: Directorates in the Commonwealth Secretariat and the Sri Lanka Administrative Service; Director of Development and Planning, Commonwealth Parliamentary Association, 1992-2003; Senior Research Fellow, University College London. Publications: Several publications in management operations research, human resource development, parliamentary and public administration; Member of Editorial Boards including Journal of Public Administration and Development. Honours: Nominee for Smith-Mundt Fulbright Award, 1961-62; Kluwer-Harrap Award, University of London, 1973. Memberships include: Fellow Royal Society of Chemistry; Fellow Royal Society of Arts; Member, Institute of Management Services; Trustee, Emmaus UK. Address: 51 Linkway, London SW20 9AT, England.

GÖNCZ Árpád, b. 10 February 1922, Budapest, Hungary. Politician; Writer; Dramatist; Translator. m. Maria Zsuzsanna Göntér, 1947, 2 sons, 2 daughters. Education: DJ, Pázmány Péter University, 1944; University of Agricultural Sciences. Appointments: Active with Independent Smallholders' Party, 1947-48; Imprisoned for political activities, 1957-63; Founding Member, Free Initiative Network, Free Democratic Federation, Historic Justice Committee; Member and Speaker of Parliament, 1990; Acting President, 1990, President, 1990-2000, Republic of Hungary. Publications: Men of God (novel), 1974; Hungarian Medea (play), 1979; Iron Bars (play), 1979; Encounters (short stories), 1980; 6 plays, 1990; Homecoming (short stories), 1991; Shavings (essays), 1991. Honours: Honorary Knight Commander of the Order of St Michael and St George, England, 1991; Dr hc, Butler, 1990, Connecticut, 1991, Oxford, 1995, Sorbonne, 1996, Bologna, 1997; George Washington Prize, 2000; Pro Humanitate Award, 2001; Polish Business Oscar Award, 2002. Membership: Hungarian Writers' Union, President, 1989-90.

GONG Shih-Chin, b. 26 August 1968, Taipei, Taiwan. R&D Senior Manager. Education: Freshman, Department of Geophysics, 1988, BE (formal diploma), Department of Mechanical Engineering, 1991, Master courses, 1991-92, PhD, 1996, Institute of Mechanical Engineering, National Central University. Appointments: Ensign (Military Service), Navy 812 Hospital, Keelung, Taiwan, 1996-98; Project Manager, Metrodyne Microsystems Corp, Hsinchu, 1998-2001, Department Manager, Intelligent Sensor Systems Division, Asia Pacific Microsystems Inc, Hsinchu, 2001-03; Visiting Scientist, University of Michigan, Ann Arbor, Michigan, USA, 2003-04; R&D Senior Manager, Merry Electronics Co Ltd, Taicung, Taiwan, 2004-. Publications: Author, over 20 journal and conference papers; Inventor of 14 patents and 14 patents pending. Honours: Consultant, Department of Automatic Control Engineering, Feng Chia University, 2006-08; Paper Reviewer, Sensors and Actuators A, 2004; Project Reviewer, Industrial Technical Research Institute, Hsinchu, Tainan, 2003; Listed in international biographical dictionaries. Memberships: American Society of Mechanical Engineers; Institute of Electrical and Electronics

Engineers; International Society for Optical Engineering; Chinese Society of Mechanical Engineers. Address: 3F, No 14, Lane 133, Min-Quan W Road, Taipei 103, Taiwan. E-mail: shinchingong@yahoo.com.tw

GONZALES Theresa Sullivan, b. 20 January 1959, Walhalla, South Carolina, USA. Dentist; Oral and Maxillofacial Pathologist. 1 son. Education: BS, College of Charleston, 1979; DMD, Medical University of South Carolina, 1984; MS, George Washington University, 2006. Appointments: Chief, Oral Pathology, Walter Reed Army Medical Center, Washington, DC, 2000-02; Chief, Oral and Maxillofacial Pathology, William Beaumont Army Medical Center, El Paso, Texas, 2002-04; Fellow, Orofacial Pain, Naval Postgraduate Dental School, Bethesda, Maryland, 2002-04; Director, Orofacial Pain Management, Tripler Army Medical Center, Honolulu, Hawaii, 2006-. Publications: Over 30 articles in peer-reviewed journals. Honours: Teacher of the Year, International College of Dentists, 1998; Award for Excellence in Research; Variety of military awards for distinguished service. Memberships: American Dental Association; American College of Dentists; International College of Dentists; American Pain Society; American Academy of Orofacial Pain. Address: 4666 Fairfax Avenue, Dallas, TX 75209, USA.

GONZALEZ Luis Alberto, b. 2 June 1943, Santa Fe, Argentina. Teacher of English; Translator. Education: Public Translator and Teacher of English, National University of Córdoba, 1973; Grade Twelve with distinction, Trinity College, London, England, 1997; MA TEFL, University of Reading, England, 2003. Appointments: English Teacher, Córazon de Maria Secondary School, Córdoba, 1964-96; English Teacher, Liceo Militar Gral Paz, 1977-87; Teacher, British Culture Association, 1974-; Lecturer, National Technological University, Córdoba, 1977-79; Co-ordinator of International Examinations, Oral Examiner, International Cambridge Examinations; Lecturer, Villa Maria, 1998-99; Lecturer, Catholic University of Salta, 1999-2001; Member, Executive Board, Faculty of Languages, National University of Córdoba, 2002-03; Currently, Senior Lecturer, Language and Grammar, Faculty of Languages, National University of Córdoba. Publications: Numerous short stories, proceedings, journal articles and contributions to anthologies. Honours: Scholarship, Gonzaga University, Washington, 1965; Grantee, Experiment in International Living, 1974; Grantee, British Council; Certificate, New Latin American Writer, 2003; Listed in national and international biographical dictionaries; Lectured in many countries around the world. Memberships: Argentine Linguistics Association; Linguistics Research Centre of Córdoba. Address: La Habana 1686, Barrio América Residencial 5012, Córdoba, Argentina. E-mail: clpgonzl@onenet.com.ar

GONZALEZ CASTILLO Jose, b. 25 December 1942, León Gto., Mexíco. Educator. Education: Certificate, 1969, MSc, 1970, Industrial Chemical Engineering, Superior School, Engineering, Chemistry and Extractive Industries, National Polytechnic Institute, México City; Doctor of Technical Sciences, University of Tuzla, Yugoslavia, 1982. Appointment: Educator, Electrochemistry and Corrosion, Superior School, Engineering, Chemistry and Extractive Industries, National Polytechnic Institute, México City, México, 1969-. Publications: Electrochemical Kinetics of cl^-, Br, I, and Free Energy Diagram ($\Delta G°$) for Fe^+, Fe^-, 1971; Nitration by Electrocatalysis to obtain (TNB) Trinitrobenzene, (TNT) Trinitrotoluene, (MNM) Monitromethane, 1969-79; The Equilibrium E_H(pH; log a_i) Diagram for $C-H_2O$ System

and the Thermodynamic Consideration of Mechanisms on Carbon., 1981-82; The Equilibrium E_H(pH; log a_i) Diagram for Fe- H_2O System, 1984-2000; Book: Notes of Electrochemistry and Corrosion, 1980; Conference Paper, A possible introduction to the thermodynamic electrochemistry of cancer, 1992. Honours: Distinguished Professor, 1971; President, 1989, currently, Member of Honour Association of Residents of Acueducto de Gpe. Address: Arrecifes 57, Acueducto de Gpe, G A Madero, 07279 Mexico DF.

GONZALEZ-GONZALEZ Jesus Maria, b. 25 January 1961, Herreros de Suso, Avila, Spain. Stomatologist. m. Maria Teresa Rubio Hortells, separated 2003, 2 children. Education: BMed, University of Salamanca, 1985; Programmer Basic, Pontificia University of Salamanca, 1988; Specialist in Stomatology, University of Murcia, 1992; DMed, University of Alicante, 1992. Appointments: Medical Practitioner, State Health Service, Salamanca and Provence, 1987-88; La Manga, Murcia, 1990; Dentist, State Health Service, Cartagena, Murcia, 1990, 1991, Bejar and Ciudad Rodrigo, Salamanca, 1992; Private Practice in Stomatology, Murcia, 1991, Salamanca, 1991-; Speaker in field, 13 reports in congress. Publications: Several books in Spanish; Articles in professional journals and magazines; 2 patents. Honours: Honorable Mention, Children's Meeting of Painting, Town House of Salamanca, 1974 and Military Service, Lerida, 1986; Listed in numerous Who's Who publications and biographical dictionaries. Memberships: Professional Association of Dentists, Spain; Ski Club of Salamanca; New York Academy of Sciences; Founder President, Asociacion de Padres de Familia Separados de Salamanca y Pro-Derechos de Nuestros Hijos. Address: c/ Avila, No 4, lo A, 37004 Salamanca, Spain.

GONZALEZ-MARINA Jacqueline, b. 19 February 1935, Madrid, Spain. Lecturer; Translator and Official Interpreter in 7 Languages; Poet; Writer; Publisher; Journalist; Editor; Artist. m. (1) 2 sons, 1 daughter, (2) Desmond Savage, 22 December 1982. Education: BA, Modern Philology, 1959, MA, Modern Philology, 1962, University of Barcelona. Appointments: Lecturer, University of Barcelona, 1960-68, St Godrics College, London, 1970-91; Founder, Editor, Dandelion Magazine, 1979-; Editor, Fern Publications, 1979-; Editor, The Student Magazine (International), 2000- Lecturer in Modern Languages, American Intercontinental University, London, 1994-2000; More than 60 art exhibitions, one person and collective in England and Spain. Publications: Dieciocho Segundos, 1953; Tijeras Sin Filo, 1955; Antología de Temas, 1961; Short Stories, 1972; Brian Patten, 1975; A Survival Course, 1975; Once Poemas a Malaga, 1977; Poesía Andaluza, 1977; Adrian Henri, 1980; Historias y Conversaciones, 1995; Mediterranean Poetry, bilingual anthology, 1997; Conversaciones en Español, 1998; Drawing and Painting for Fun, 1998; The Millennium Anthology, poetry and prose, Vol 1, 1999, Vol II, 2000; The International Book of Short Stories, 2002; Cats in the Palm Tree and Other Stories (co-writer), 2002; Dali & I, poems, 2003; Contributions to: Countless anthologies and international magazines; Writer and broadcaster for the BBC, London, 1975-78. Honours: Royal Academician, Royal Academy of St Telmo, Malaga, Spain, 1975; Honorary Member of the Atheneum in Alicante, Spain, 1999. Memberships: Society of Women Writers and Journalists, London, 1980-; The Historical Association Saxoferreo, Cordoba, Spain, 1997-; Listed in national and international biographical dictionaries. Address: "Casa Alba", 24 Frosty Hollow, East Hunsbury, Northants NN4 0SY, England.

GOO Byeong Choon, b. 16 January 1962, Sacheonsi, Korea. Researcher; Engineer. m. Sang-Jung Byun, 1 son, 1 daughter. Education: BS, Ajou University, Soowon, Korea, 1984; MS, Korea Advanced Institute of Science & Technology, 1989; DEA, 1993, PhD, 1996, University of Frache-Comte, Besancon, France; BS, Korea Open University, Seoul, Korea, 2006. Appointments: Engineer, Ssangyong Motors, 1989-1992; Adjunct Professor, Seoul National University of Technology, 2002-; Adjunct Professor, University of Science and Technology, 2004-. Honours: Top Researcher of the Year, Korean Railroad Research Institute, 2004; Scientific Award, The Korean Society of Railway, 2005. Membership: Korea Red Cross. Address: 360-1 Woulamdong, Uiwangsi, Gyeonggido 427-757, Republic of Korea.

GOOCH Graham Alan, OBE, b. 23 July 1953, Leytonstone, London. Cricketer. m. Brenda Daniels, 3 daughters. Career: Right-hand opening batsman, right-arm medium bowler; Played for Essex 1973-97, (captain, 1986-87, 1989-94), West Prov, 1982-83,1983-84; Played in 118 tests for England, 1975 to 1994-95, 34 as captain, scoring 8900 runs (England record, average 42.5) including 20 hundreds (highest score 333 and Test match aggregate of 456 v India, Lord's 1990, becoming only batsman to score triple century and century in a first-class match and holding 103 catches; scored 44,841 runs (128 hundreds) and held 555 catches in first-class cricket; Toured Australia 1978-79, 1979-80, 1990-91 (captain) and 1994-95; 125 limited-overs internationals, including 50 as captain (both England records); Member, England Selection Committee, 1996-; Manager, England Tour to Australia, 1998-99; Head Coach, Essex, 2001-2005. Publications: Testing Times, 1991; Gooch: My Autobiography, 1995. Honours include: OBE; Wisden Cricketer of the Year, 1980. Address: c/o Essex County Cricket Club, The County Ground, New Writtle Street, Chelmsford, Essex, CM2 0PG, England.

GOOD-BLACK Edith Elissa, b. 10 January 1945, Hollywood, California, USA. Writer. m. Michael Lawrence Black, deceased. Education: BA, English, California State University, Northridge, 1974; Student, University of California, Los Angeles and University of California, Berkeley, 1962-92; Explorer, Mayan ruins, Mexico, 1963; Music student, Ballet Folklorico, Mexico, 1963. Appointments: Participant, numerous dance, art, music, literature, mathematics and science classes; Dancer, Hajde Dance Troop, Berkeley, California, 1962-66; One-woman art shows, Los Angeles, 1962-95; Singer in various languages, coffee houses, cafés, nightclubs, half-way houses, libraries, churches, temples and others, Los Angeles, 1986-; Sole Proprietor, Gull Press. Publications include: (pseudonym, Pearl Williams) The Trickster of Tarzana, 1992; Short Stories, 1995; Mad in Craft, 1995; Missives, 1995; Dictionary of Erudition, 1995. Contributed poetry to CDs, radio and ipod broadcasts, internet broadcasts, publications. Honours: Summa Cum Laude, California State University; Writing chosen by a jury of experts for permanent collection in the Library of Congress, USA; Leonardo da Vinci Prize, International Biographical Centre; 25 Years Award, MENSA; Listed in numerous Who's Who and biographical publications. Memberships: MENSA; American Society of Composers, Authors and Publishers; Plummer Park Writers; Westside Writers; Democratic clubs, California and Mexico, 1962-; Supporter, mental health organisations, 1962-; Delegate to local Democratic conventions, fundraiser, canvasser, office worker, driver and participant in consciousness raising groups in support of civil rights; CORE, San Francisco, Berkeley, Los Angeles, and Oakland, 1965; Peace in Alliance for Survival, Berkeley, Oakland, Los Angeles, 1964-80; Women's rights, Westside Women's Center, Woman's Building, Los Angeles, 1974-80; Environment in Earth Day, Los Angeles, 1977; Literary Consultant, tutor and book reviewer; Supporter of Residential Collective, 1985-; Member, Advisory Board, American Biographical Institute; Member, Research Academy, IBC. Address: 1470 South Robertson Blvd, Apt B, Los Angeles, CA 90035-3402, USA.

GOODALL Sir (Arthur) David (Saunders), b. 9 October 1931, Blackpool, England. Diplomatist (retired). m. Morwenna Peecock, 1962, 2 sons, 1 daughter. Education: Ampleforth College; Trinity College, Oxford. Appointments: Army service in Kenya, Aden, Cyprus, 1954-56; Joined Foreign (now Diplomatic) Service, 1956, served at Nicosia, Jakarta, Bonn, Nairobi, Vienna, 1956-75; Head, Western European Department, FCO, 1975-79; Minister, Bonn, 1979-82, Deputy Secretary, Cabinet Office, 1982-84, Deputy Under-Secretary of State, FCO, 1984-87; High Commissioner in India, 1987-91; Joint Chair, Anglo-Irish Encounter, 1992-97; President, Irish Genealogical Research Society, 1992-; Chair, Leonard Cheshire Foundation, 1995-2000 (Chair International Committee, 1992-95); Chair, British-Irish Association, 1997-2002; Chair, Advisory Governors, Ampleforth College, 2004-; Chair, Governing Body, Heythrop College, University of London, 2000-06, Honorary Fellow, 2006; Visiting Professor in Irish Studies, University of Liverpool, 1996-; Member of Council, University of Durham, 1992-2000 (Vice Chair, 1997-2000); One-man exhibitions: (watercolours): Berlin, 1979; Bonn, 1982; London, 1987, 1994; New Delhi, 1991; Durham, 1996; Hull, 1998; Helmsley (York), 2004, 2006. Publications: Remembering India, 1997; Rydale Pilgramage, 2000; Contributions to The Tablet, The Ampleforth Journal; The Past; The Irish Genealogist. Honours: GCMG 1991 (KCMG 1987); KSG, 2006; Honorary Fellow, Trinity College, Oxford; Distinguished Friend of the University of Oxford, 2001; Honorary Fellow, Heythrop College, 2006; Honorary LLD (Hull), 1994. Address: Greystones, Ampleforth, North Yorkshire, YO62 4DU, England.

GOODBODY Michael Ivan Andrew, b. 23 January 1942, Wicklow, Ireland. m. Susannah Elizabeth Pearce, 1 son, 2 daughters. Education: Kingstown School, Dublin, Ireland. Appointments: J & L F Goodbody Ltd, Jute Manufacturers, 1960-62; Member of the Stock Exchange, 1968-87; Member of the Securities Institute, 1987-2006; Stockbroker, Smith Rice & Hill, 1962-74; Stockbroker, 1974-82, Partner/Director, 1982-89, Divisional Director, 1989-2000, Capel-Cure Myers Ltd; Private Client Fund Manager, Carr Sheppards Crosthwaite, 2000-06-. Publications: The Goodbody Family of Ireland, 1979; A Quaker Wedding at Lisburn; Occasional articles on family history. Memberships: Territorial Army – 289 Parachute Regiment RHA, 1964-75; Society of Genealogists; Treasurer, Colne and Stour Countryside Association; Member, Irish Genealogical Research Society; Quaker Family History Society. Address: The Old Rectory, Wickham St Paul's, Essex CO9 2PJ, England.

GOODENOUGH Frederick Roger, b. 21 December 1927, Broadwell, Oxfordshire, England. Retired Director; Farmer. m. Marguerite June, 1 son, 2 daughters. Education: MA (Cantab), 1955; MA (Oxon), 1975; FCIB; FLS; FRSA. Appointments: RN, 1946-48; Joined Barclays Bank Ltd, 1950; Local Director, Birmingham, 1958-60, Reading, 1960-69, Oxford, 1969-87, Director Barclays, Bank UK, Ltd, 1971-87, Barclays Bank International Ltd, 1977-87, Barclays PLC, 1985-89, Barclays Bank PLC, 1979-89; Advisory Director, Barclays Bank Thames Valley Region, 1988-89; Member, London Committee Barclays Bank DCO, 1966-71,

Barclays Bank International Ltd, 1971-80; Senior Partner, Broadwell Manor Farm, 1968-; Curator, Oxford University Chest, 1974-93; President, Oxfordshire Rural Community Council, 1993-98; Trustee: Nuffield Medical Benefaction, 1968-2002 (Chairman, 1987-2002), Nuffield Dominions Trust, 1968-2002 (Chairman, 1987-2002); Nuffield Oxford Hospitals Fund, 1968-2003 (Chairman, 1982-88), Nuffield Orthopaedic Centre Trust, 1978-2003 (Chairman, 1981-2003), Oxford Preservation Trust, 1980-89, Radcliffe Medical Foundation, 1987-98; Governor: Shiplake College, 1963-74 (Chairman, 1966-70),Wellington College, 1968-74, Goodenough College, 1985-2006; Patron, Anglo Ghanaian Society, 1991-. Publication: Co-author, Britain's Future in Farming (edited by Sir Frank Engledow and Leonard Amey, 1980. Honours: High Sheriff, Oxfordshire, 1987-88; Deputy Lieutenant, Oxfordshire, 1989-; Supernumerary Fellow, 1989-95, Honorary Fellow, 1995, Wolfson College, Oxford. Memberships: Fellow, Linnean Society (Member of Council 1968-75, Treasurer, 1970-75, Finance Committee, 1968-); Brooks's, London. Address: Broadwell Manor, Nr Lechlade, Gloucestershire, GL7 3QS, England. E-mail: f.r.goodenough@broadwellmanor.co.uk

GOODING Cuba Jr, b. 2 September 1968, Bronx, New York, USA. Actor. m. Sara Kapfer, 1994, 3 children. Career: TV appearances include: Kill or Be Killed, 1990; Murder with Motive: The Edmund Perry Story, 1992; Daybreak, 1993; The Tuskagee Airmen; Film appearances include: Coming to America, 1988; Sing, 1989; Boyz N the Hood, 1991; Gladiator, A Few Good Men, Hitz, 1992; Judgement Night, 1993; Lightning Jack, 1994; Losing Isiah, Outbreak, 1995; Jerry Maguire, The Audition, 1996; Old Friends, As Good As It Gets, 1997; What Dreams May Come, 1998; A Murder of Crows, Instinct, Chill Factor, 1999; Men of Honor, 2000; Pearl Harbor, Rat Race, In the Shadows, 2001; Snow Dogs, Boat Trip, 2002; Psychic, The Fighting Temptations, Radio, 2003; Home on the Range (voice), A Dairy Tale (voice), 2004; Shadowboxer, Dirty, 2005; Lightfield's Home Videos, End Game, 2006; Norbit, What Love Is; Daddy Day Camp, American Gangster, Hero Wanted, 2007. Honours: 2 NAACP Awards; Academy Award; Best Supporting Actor (for Jerry Maguire), 1997; Chicago Film Critics Award; Screen Actor Guild Award. Address: c/o Rogers and Cowan, 1888 Century Park East, Suite 500, Los Angeles, CA 90067, USA.

GOODISON Sir Nicholas, b. 16 May 1934, Radlett, England. Former Chairman, London Stock Exchange. m. Judith Abel Smith, 1960, 1 son, 2 daughters. Education: BA Classics, 1958, MA, PhD, Architecture and History of Art, 1981, King's College, Cambridge. Appointments: H E Goodison & Co (now Citigroup, Quilter & Co Ltd), 1958-86, Chairman, 1975-86; Member of Council, 1968-88, Chairman, 1976-88, Stock Exchange, London; President, International Federation of Stock Exchanges, 1985-86; Member, Panel on Takeovers and Mergers, 1976-88; Member, Council for the Securities Industry, 1978-85; Member, Securities Association, 1986-88; Director, Ottoman Bank, 1986-92; Director, Banque Paribas Capital Markets, 1986-88; Director, General Accident plc, 1987-95; Director, 1989-2002, Deputy Chairman, 1993-99, British Steel plc (from 1999, Corus plc); Chairman, TSB Group plc, 1989-95; Deputy Chairman, Lloyds TSB Group plc, 1995-2000; President, British Bankers' Association, 1991-96; Member, Executive Committee, 1976-2002, Chairman, 1986-2002 National Art Collections Fund; Director, 1975-, Chairman, 2002-07, Burlington Magazine; Director, 1977-98, Vice-Chairman, 1980-88, English National Opera; Chairman, 1982-2002, Member of Governing Board, 2002-, Courtauld Institute of Art, London University; Trustee, Kathleen

Ferrier Memorial Scholarship Fund, 1987-; Trustee, National Heritage Memorial Fund, 1988-97; Member of Council ABSA (now Arts and Business), 1990-99; Chairman, Crafts Council, 1997-2005; Member of Council, 1965-, President, 1990-, Furniture History Society; Trustee, 2001-, Chairman, 2003-, National Life Story Collection; Governor Marlborough College, 1981-97; Trustee, Harewood House Trust; Chairman of Review Steering Group, National Record of Achievement, (Department for Education and Science) 1996-97; Member, Royal Commission on Long Term Care for the Elderly, 1997-99; Chairman, Goodison Group on Lifelong Learning, 1999-2006; Member, Further Education Funding Council, 2000-2001; Leader and author, Goodison Review "Securing the Best for our Museums: Private Giving and Government Support" (HM Treasury), 2003. Publications: English Barometers 1680-1860, 1968, 2nd edition, 1977; Ormolu: the Work of Matthew Boulton, 1974, revised as Matthew Boulton: Ormolu, 2003; Hotspur, Eighty Years of Antiques dealing (with Robin Kern), 2004; These Fragments, 2005; Articles and lectures on stock exchange, banking, financial regulation, etc; Articles and lectures on arts, history of decorative arts, museums, etc. Honours: KB, 1982; Chevalier, Legion d'Honneur, 1990; Hon DLitt, City University, 1985; Hon LLD, Exeter University, 1989; Hon DSc, Aston University, 1994; Hon DArt, deMontfort University, 1998; Hon DCL, University of Northumbria, 1999; Hon DLitt, University of London, 2003; Honorary Fellow, King's College, Cambridge, 2002; Honorary Fellow, Courtauld Institute of Art, 2003; Honorary Fellow, British Academy, 2004; Honorary Fellow, Royal Academy of Arts; Senior Fellow, Royal College of Art; Honorary Fellow, RIBA. Memberships: Fellow, Society of Antiquaries; Fellow, Royal Society of Arts. Address: PO Box 2512, London W1A 5ZP, England.

GOODMAN Anthony Eric, b. 21 July 1936, London, England. Academic. m. Jacqueline, 1 daughter. Education: BLitt, MA (Oxon), Oxford University, 1965. Appointments: Member of Academic Staff, 1961-2001, Professor of Medieval and Renaissance History, 1993-2001; Professor Emeritus, 2001-, History Department, University of Edinburgh. Publications: The Loyal Conspiracy, 1971; A History of England from Edward II to James I, 1977; The Wars of the Roses, 1981; The New Monarchy, 1988; John of Gaunt, 1992; Margery Kempe and her World, 2002; The Wars of the Roses. The Soldiers' Experience, 2005. Honour: Fellow of the Royal Historical Society. Address: 23 Kirkhill Gardens, Edinburgh EH16 5DF, Scotland.

GOODMAN D Wayne, b. 14 December 1945, Glen Allen, Mississippi, USA. Professor. m. Sandra Faye Hewitt, 1 son. Education: BS, Mississippi College, 1968; PhD, University of Texas, 1974; NATO Postdoctoral Fellow, Technische Hochschule, Germany, 1975-76. Appointments: National Research Council Research Fellow, 1976-78, Staff Member, 1978-80, National Bureau of Standards; Staff Member, 1980-84, Supervisor, Surface Science Division, 1985-88, Sandia National Laboratories; Adjunct Professor, Department of Chemistry, University of Texas, 1985; Professor of Chemistry, 1988-94, Head, Physical and Nuclear Division, 1991-93, Robert A Welch Professor of Chemistry, 1994-, Robert A Welch Chair of Chemistry, 1998-, Distinguished Professor of Chemistry, 2000-, Texas A&M University. Publications: Over 500 reviewed papers and book chapters, mainly on chemisorption and catalytic reactions on atomically clean and chemically modified metal single crystal surfaces, also fundamental chemistry of processes occurring at the solid-gas/solid-liquid interface relating to coatings and corrosion. Honours: NATO Fellowship, 1975, National

Research Council Fellowship, 1976; Distinguished Visiting Lecturer, University of Texas, Austin, 1982; Ipatieff Prize, American Chemical Society, 1983; 1 of 100 Outstanding Young Scientists in America, Science Digest, 1985; Frontiers in Chemistry, Lecturer, Texas A&M University, 1987; Procter and Gamble Lecturer, University of Cincinnati, 1990; Langmuir Lecturer, American Chemical Society, 1991; Ipatieff Lecturer, Northwestern University, 1992; Colloid and Surface Chemistry Award, American Chemical Society, 1993; Yarwood Medal, British Vacuum Society, 1994; Humboldt Research Prize, 1995; Texas A&M University Distinguished Research Award, 1997; Robert Burwell Lecturer, North American Catalysis Society, 1997; Fellow, American Vacuum Society, 1998; Elected Fellow, Institute of Physics, 1999; Giuseppe Parravano Award, 2001; ACS Arthur W Adamson Award for Distinguished Service in the Advancement of Surface Chemistry, 2002; ACS Gabor Somorjai Award, 2005. Memberships: American Chemical Society, Division of Colloid and Surface Chemistry Treasurer, 1979, Division Vice-Chairman, 1984, Division Chairman, 1985, Speaker's Tour, 1984, 1991, Member, Joint Board-Council Committee on Publications, 1998; American Vacuum Society, Executive Committee, Surface Science Division, 1980, 1985; Southwest Catalysis Society, President, 1993. Address: Texas A&M University, Department of Chemistry, PO Box 30012, College Station, TX 77842-3012, USA. E-mail: goodman@mail.chem.tamu.edu

GOODMAN John, b. 20 June 1952, St Louis, USA. Film Actor. m. Annabeth Hartzog, 1989, 1 daughter. Education: South West Missouri State University. Career: Broadway appearances in: Loose Ends, 1979; Big River, 1985; TV appearances include: The Mystery of Moro Castle; The Face of Rage; Heart of Steel; Moonlighting, Chiefs (min-series); The Paper Chase; Murder Ordained; The Equalizer; Roseanne (series); Normal, Ohio, Pigs Next Door, 2000; Films include: The Survivors, Eddie Macon's Run, 1983; Revenge of the Nerds, CHUD, 1984; Maria's Lovers, Sweet Dreams, 1985; True Stories, 1986; The Big Easy, Burglar, Raising Arizona, 1987; The Wrong Guys, Everybody's All-American, Punchline, 1988; Sea of Love, Always, 1989; Stella, Arachnophobia, King Ralph, 1990; Barton Fink, 1991; The Babe, 1992; Born Yesterday, 1993; The Flintstones, 1994; Kingfish: A Story of Huey P Long, 1995; Pie in the Sky, Mother Night, 1996; Fallen, Combat!, The Borrowers, 1997; The Big Lebowski, Blues Brothers 2000, Dirty Work, 1998; The Runner, 1999; Coyote Ugly, One Night at McCool's, 2000; Happy Birthday, My First Mister, Storytelling, Monsters Inc (voice), 2001; Dirty Deeds, 2002; Masked and Anonymous, The Jungle Book 2 (voice), 2003; Home of Phobia, Clifford's Really Big Movie (voice), Beyond the Sea, 2004; Marilyn Hotchkiss Ballroom Dancing & Charm School, The Emperor's New Groove 2: Kronk's New Groove (voice), 2005; Cars (voice), 2006; Evan Almighty, Drunkboat, Death Sentence, Bee Movie, In the Electric Mist, 2007; Speed Racer, 2008. Address: c/o Fred Spektor, CAA 9830 Wilshire Boulevard, Beverly Hills, CA 90212, USA.

GOODSON Ivor, b. 30 September 1943, Reading, England. Professor of Learning Theory. m. Mary Nuttall, 1 son. Education: BSc (Econ), University College, London, 1965; Teachers Certificate (Distinction), 1970, Academic Diploma, 1974, London Institute of Education; DPhil, University of Sussex, 1979. Appointments: Lecturer, BA General, University of Kingston, 1966-69; Specialist in History and Social Studies, Countesthorpe College, Leicestershire, 1970-73; Head of Humanities Faculty, Stantonbury Campus, Milton Keynes, 1973-75; Research Fellow, 1975-78, Director, The Schools Unit, 1978-85, University of Sussex; Full Professor, Faculty of Education, Faculty of Graduate Studies and Centre for Theory and Criticism, 1986-96, Director of Educational Research Unit, 1989-96, Honorary Professor of Sociology, 1993-98, University of Western Ontario, Canada; Frederica Warner Scholar, Scholar in Residence and Professor of Education, Margaret Warner Graduate School, University of Rochester, 1996-2002; Chair of Education, Centre for Applied Research in Education, School of Education and Professional Development, University of East Anglia, England, 1996-2004; Professor of Learning Theory, Education Research Centre, University of Brighton, 2004-; Research Associate, Von Hugel Institute, St Edmunds College, University of Cambridge, 2004-. Publications: Numerous books, and articles published in professional journals. Honours: Visiting Professor, University of Sussex, University of Exeter, Institute of Political Science in Paris, France; Stint Foundation Professor, Sweden, 2003-08; Catalan Research Professor, Spain, 2005; Michael Huberman Award, USA, 2006; Laureate Chapter of Kappa Delta Pi, USA, 2007; Listed in international biographical dictionaries. Memberships: Executive Member, Centre for Theory and Criticism. E-mail: i.f.goodson@brighton.ac.uk

GOODSON-WICKES, Dr Charles, b. 7 November 1945, London, England. Consulting Physician; Company Director; Business Consultant; Charity Executive. m. Judith Hopkinson, 2 sons. Education: MB BS, St Bartholomew's Hospital, 1970; Barrister-at-Law, Inner Temple, 1972. Appointments: House Physician, Cambridge and London, 1971-72; Surgeon Captain The Life Guards, served BAOR, Northern Ireland, Cyprus, 1973-77; Clinical Assistant and Locum Consultant, St Bartholomew's Hospital, London, 1976-80; Consulting Physician, BUPA Medical Centre, 1976-86; Regular Army Reserve of Officers, 1977-2000; Special Liaison and Research, Conservative Central Office, 1979-87; Principal, Private Occupational Health Practices, London, 1980-94; Member of Parliament for Wimbledon, 1987-97; Re-enlisted as Lieutenant Colonel for Gulf Campaign, on Active Service in advance from Saudi Arabia through Iraq to Kuwait, 1990-91; Parliamentary Private Secretary to: The Department of the Environment, The Treasury, The Department of Transport, 1992-96; Non-Executive Director, Merton Enterprise Agency Ltd, 1988-97; Non-Executive Director, Nestor Healthcare Group plc, 1993-99; Chief Executive, Medarc Ltd, 1982-; Director, Thomas Greg & Sons Ltd, 1992-; Non-Executive Director, Property Reversions I, II, III, 1993-; Non-Executive Director, Gyrus Group plc, 1997-2007; Chairman, British Field Sports Society, 1994-97; Founder Chairman, The Countryside Alliance, 1997-99; Chairman, The Rural Trust, 1999-; Chief Executive, London Playing Fields Foundation, 1998-; London Sports Board, 1999-2003. Publications: The New Corruption, 1984; Another Country (contributor), 1999. Honour: Deputy Lieutenant of Greater London, 1999-. Memberships: Clubs: Boodle's; Pratt's; MCC. Address: Watergate House, Bulford, Wiltshire, SP4 9DY, England.

GOODWIN Timothy Alan, b. 3 May 1961, New Albany, Mississippi, USA. Information Technologist. Education: Bachelor of Business Administration in Computer Information Systems (BBA-CIS), Delta State University, 1985; Associate of Applied Science in Information Technology (AAS-IT), State Technical Institute, 1999; Master of Information Systems (HonMIS) and Master of Information Technology (HonMIT), World Academy of Letters, 2005; Certifications: ASP.NET, HTML, and Javascript from the International Webmasters Association and Brainbench; NCSA Certified Computer Hardware Technician. Appointments: Computer Analyst, Tyler Computers and Office Supplies, 1986-88;

Programmer/Analyst, 1988-2002, Web Analyst, 2002, Commercial Data Corporation. Publications: Co-authored systems: CDC Shopping Card and Order Management System, ASP.NET Edition, 2002-06; Profitline Solutions Human Resources and Payroll System, Windows Edition, 1999-2002; Profitline Solutions Accounting System, Unix Edition, 1989-93, 1997-98; Paul Tyler and Associates: Authored: Ambulatory Billing System, 1986-87, Charged-off Loans System, 1986, and Financial Customer Profiling System, 1986; Co-authored: Automotive Finance Loans System, 1987-88 and Retail Accounting System, 1987-88. Honours: IBC Honorary Director General; Governor, IBC Board of Governors; IBC Deputy Directors General; ABI Deputy Governor; ABI World Laureate; ABI World Lifetime Achievement Award; IBC Lifetime Achievement Award; IBC Companion of Honour; ABI Congressional Medal of Excellence; ABI World Medal of Freedom; IBC International Medal of Honour; ABI American Medal of Honor; NRA National Patriot's Medal; ABI International Medal of Vision; UCC Legion of Honor; NRA Legion of Honor; NRA-ILA Defender of the Second Amendment Award; The DaVinci Diamond Award; 21st Century Award for Achievement; IBC Hall of Fame; American Hall of Fame; Leading Intellectuals of the World Hall of Fame; Great Minds of the 21st Century Hall of Fame; Commercial Data Corporation Service Awards; International Who's Who of Information Technology; Empire Who's Who; Madison Who's Who. Memberships: American Order of Excellence Founder Member; Life Fellow, American Biographical Institute; International High IQ Society; Life Patron, International Biographical Association; International Order of Merit; International Order of Distinction; Order of International Fellowship; Order of International Ambassadors; World Peace and Diplomacy Forum; Association for Computing Machinery; International Webmaster's Association; HTML Writers Guild; IEEE Computer Society; Phi Theta Kappa; Delta Mu Delta; World Black Belt Bureau; NRA Golden Eagles; NRA Endowment Member; 51st Tennessee Infantry Regiment; Mid-America Dharma; Background Acting/Historical Films: Battlefield Detectives: Civil War –Shiloh, 2006. Address: 10307 Riggan Drive, Olive Branch, MS 38654, USA. E-mail: timgoodwin@ieee.org

GOOS Roger, b. 29 October 1924, Beaman, Iowa, USA. Botanist; Mycologist. m. Mary Lee Engel, 2 daughters. Education: BA, 1950, MS, Botany, 1955, PhD, Botany, Mycology, 1958, University of Iowa. Appointments: Research, United Fruit Co, 1958-62; Medical Mycology, National Institute of Health, 1962-64; American Type Culture Collection, Rockville, Maryland, 1964-68; Scientist, Department of Botany, University of Hawaii, 1968-70; Associate Professor, Professor, 1970-95, Chair, Department of Botany, 1972-87, University of Rhode Island; Retired, 1995. Publications: Approximately 100 articles in professional scientific journals. Honours: Indo-American Fellowship, University of Madras, 1981; President, Mycological Society of America, 1985-86; Fulbright Fellow, University of Lisbon, 1993. Memberships: Mycological Society of America; British Mycological Society; Mycological Society of Japan; Botanical Society of America; AAAS.

GOPAL Madhuban, b. 17 October 1951, Allahabad, India. Scientist. m. Manjari, 1 son, 1 daughter. Education: BSc, 1970, MSc, 1972, D Phil, 1977, University of Allahabad; PhD, University of Ottawa, Canada, 1982. Appointments: Lecturer, Kanpur University, 1973-76; Scientist S-1, 1976-82, Scientist S-2 1982-84, NIRJAFT (JTRL), Calcutta, Scientist S-2, IARI, 1984-85, Senior Scientist, 1986-98, Principal Scientist, 1998-, National Fellow, IARI, New Delhi, 1999-,

ICAR. Publications: 91 articles in professional journals; 114 research papers; 16 book chapters; 2 books. Honours: I Prize in GK of Chemistry, 1972, Empress Victoria Scholarship, 1973, University of Allahabad; Prize for Novel Research Ideas, 1980; Best Teaching Assistant, University of Ottawa, 1982; Hindi Awards, 1999, 2000, 2003; Fellowship Award, Bioved Research & Communication Centre, Allahabad, 2003; Living Science Award, 2004; APSI Best Research Paper, Gold Medal, Academy of Plant Sciences, 2004; Best Poster Presentation, SPS India, 2005; Listed in international biographical dictionaries. Memberships: Fellow, Society of Plant Protection Sciences; Fellow, Plant Protection Association of India. Address: Division of Agricultural Chemicals, LBS Building, Room No 243, Indian Agricultural Research Institute, New Delhi 110012, India. E-mail: madhubangopal@hotmail.com

GOPHEN Moshe, b. 18 December 1936, Israel. Professor. m. Eva, 1 son, 3 daughters. Education: BSc, 1960-63, MSc, 1964-67, PhD, 1971-76, Hebrew University, Jerusalem. Appointments: Senior Scientist, 1969-2001, Director, 1980-86, Kinneret Limnological Laboratory, Israel; Visiting Professor, University of Oklahoma, USA, 1992-95; Consultant for Reservoir Management, Brazil, on behalf of Tahal, Israel, 1995; Scientific Co-ordinator, Hula Project, Israel, 1995-; External Full Professor, Tel Hai Academic College, Israel, 1996-; Chairman, Hula Committee, Israel, 1997; Senior Scientist, Migal, Israel, 2002-; Consultant for Reservoir Management, China, on behalf of Tahal, Israel, 2005. Publications: Lake Kinneret, Jerusalem, 1992; 70 Research reports; 160 papers in reviewed international journals; 50 articles in non-reviewed magazines. Honours: Fellowship, Eshkol Foundation, Ministry of Science, Israel, 1969-; Fellowship, Limnology, UNESCO, Israel, 1970; Fellowship, Carlsberg Institute, Denmark, Ministry of Science, Israel, 1974; Fellowship, Oceanographic Institute, Plymouth, England, 1978; Fellowship, DAAD, Germany, Konstanz; Fellowship, MINERVA, Konstanz, Germany; Fellowship, University of Western Australia, Perth, Australia. Memberships: International Association of Theoretical and Applied Limnology, SIL; American Society of Limnology and Oceanography, ASLO; Israel Zoological Society; Israel Malacological Society, Chairman, 1977-8; Israel Ecological Society, ISEEQ; Freshwater Biological Association, FBA, England, Life Member; North American Lake Management Society, NALMS; The National Geographic Society. Address: Migal-Galilee Technology Center, POB 831 Kiryat Schmone, Israel, 11016. E-mail: Gophen@Migal.Org.IL

GORBACHEV Mikhail Sergeyevich, b. 2 March 1931, Privolnoye, Krasnogvardeisky, Stavropol, Russia. Politician. m. Raisa Titarenko, 25 September 1953, 1 daughter. Education: Faculty of Law, Moscow State University, 1955; Stavropol Agricultural Institute, 1967. Appointments: Machine Operator, 1946; Joined CPSU, 1952; Deputy Head, Department of Propaganda Stavropol Komsomol Territorial Committee, 1955-56; First Secretary, Stavropol Komsomol City Committee, 1956-58; Second, then First Secretary Komsomol Territorial Committee, 1958-62; Party Organizer, Stavropol Territorial Production Board of Collective and State Farms, 1962; Head Department of Party Bodies of CPSU Territorial Committee, 1963-66; First Secretary, Stavropol City Party Committee, 1966-68; Second Secretary, Stavropol Territorial CPSU Committee, 1968-70, First Secretary, 1970-78; CPSU Central Secretary for Agricultural, 1978-85; General Secretary, CPSU Central Committee, 1985-91; Chairman, Supreme Soviet, 1989-90; President, USSR, 1990-91; Head, International Foundation for Socio-Econ and Political Studies, 1992-; Head, International Green Cross, 1993-; Co-founder,

Social Democratic Party of Russia, 2000-04. Publications: A Time for Peace, 1985; The Coming Century of Peace, 1986; Speeches and Writings, 1986-90; Peace Has No Alternative, 1986; Moratorium, 1986; Perestroika: New Thinking for Our Country and the World, 1987; The August Coup (Its Cause and Results), 1991; December-91, My Stand, 1992; The Years of Hard Decisions, 1993; Life and Reforms, 1995. Honours: Indira Gandhi Award, 1987; Nobel Peace Prize, 1990; Peace Award World Methodist Council, 1990; Albert Schweitzer Leadership Award, Ronald Reagan Freedom Award, 1992; Honorary Citizen, Berlin, 1992; Freeman of Aberdeen, 1993; Urania-Medaille, Berlin, 1996; Honorary Degrees: University of Alaska, 1990; University of Bristol, 1993; University of Durnham, 1995; Order of Lenin, 3 times; Orders of Red Banner of Labour, Badge of Honour and other medals. Address: International Foundation for Socio-Economic and Political Studies, Leningradsky Prosp 49, 125468 Moscow, Russia.

GORBACHEV Mikhail Yurievich, b. 14 October 1959, Kishinev, Moldova. Chemist. m. V V Gorbacheva, 3 sons, 1 daughter. Education: MSc, Chemistry, Kishinev State University, 1981; PhD, Chemistry, Rostov-on-Don State University, 1986. Appointments: Post Graduate, 1982-85, Scientific Researcher, 1986-95, Senior Scientific Researcher, 1995-, Institute of Chemistry, Academy of Sciences of Moldova. Publications: 58 scientific publications including articles in the journal Physics and Chemistry of Liquids, 2000, 2001, 2002, 2003, 2004, 2006. Honour: Diploma, Russian Mendeleev's Society of Chemistry, Odessa, 1983. Memberships: Russian Mendeleev's Society of Chemistry; International Association of Water Quality; Moldavian Chemical Society. Address: Drumul Viilor Str. 42, Ap 77, Kishinev MD-2021, Republic of Moldova. E-mail: myugorbachev@yahoo.com

GORDON John William, b. 19 November 1925, Jarrow-on-Tyne, England. Writer. m. Sylvia Young, 9 January 1954, 1 son, 1 daughter. Publications: The Giant Under the Snow, 1968, reissue, 2006, sequel, Ride the Wind, 1989; The House on the Brink, 1970; The Ghost on the Hill, 1976; The Waterfall Box, 1978; The Spitfire Grave, 1979; The Edge of the World, 1983; Catch Your Death, 1984; The Quelling Eye, 1986; The Grasshopper, 1987; Secret Corridor, 1990; Blood Brothers, 1991; Ordinary Seaman (autobiography), 1992; The Burning Baby, 1992; Gilray's Ghost, 1995; The Flesh Eater, 1998; The Midwinter Watch, 1998; Skinners, 1999; The Ghosts of Blacklode, 2002; Left in the Dark (short story collection) 2006. Contributions to: Beginnings (Signal 1989); Ghosts & Scholars 21. Membership: Society of Authors. Address: 99 George Borrow Road, Norwich, NR4 7HU, England.

GORDON Lyndall, b. 1941, Capetown, South Africa. Biographer. m. Siamon, 2 daughters. Education: BA (Hons), University of Cape Town, 1960-63; PhD (distinction), Columbia University, New York, 1973. Appointments: Assistant Professor, Columbia University, 1975-76; Lecturer, Jesus College, Oxford, 1977-84; CUF Lecturer in English, Oxford University and Tutorial Fellow (Dame Helen Gardner Fellow), St Hilda's College, 1984-95; Senior Research Fellow, St Hilda's College, 1995-. Publications: Books: Charlotte Bronte: A Passionate Life, 1994; T S Eliot: An Imperfect Life, 1998; A Private Life of Henry James, 1998; Shared Lives, 1992; Vindication: A Life of Mary Wollstonecraft, 2005; Revised edition of Virginia Woolf: A Writers Life, 2006. Honours: British Academy's Rose Mary Crawshaw prize; James Tait Black prize for biography; Cheltenham prize for literature. Memberships: Fellow, Royal Society of Literature; PEN. Address: St Hilda's College, Oxford, OX4 1DY, England.

GORDON Philip H, b. 13 September 1942, Saskatoon, Saskatchewan, Canada. Physician. m. Rosalie, 1 son, 1 daughter. Education: MD, University of Saskatchewan, 1966; LMCC, 1966; Diplomate, National Board of Medical Examiners, 1968; Certifications: Royal College of Surgeons of Canada, 1972, General Surgery, Province of Quebec, 1972; Diplomate, American Board of Surgery, 1973; Diplomate, American Board of Colon and Rectal Surgery, 1974, Recertification, 1994; Training in medicine and surgery, Jewish General Hospital, Montreal, Canada, 1966-74; McGill University, Montreal, Montefiore Hospital Pittsburgh, USA, University of Minnesota, USA, St Mark's Hospital, London, England. Appointments: Clinical Assistant, 1974-77, Assistant Surgeon, 1977-79, Associate Surgeon, 1979-87, Senior Surgeon, Director, Division of Colon and Rectal Surgery, 1987-, Director Clinical Teaching Unit II, 1989-, Vice-Chairman, Department of Surgery, 1993-, Department of Surgery, Sir Mortimer B Davis, Jewish General Hospital, Montreal, Canada; Lecturer, 1978-79, Assistant Professor of Surgery, 1979-84, Associate Professor of Surgery, 1984-89, Professor of Surgery, 1989-, Director, Section of Colorectal Surgery, 1996-, Department of Surgery, Professor of Oncology, Department of Oncology, 1992-, McGill University, Montreal, Canada; Advisory Council, American Board of Colon and Rectal Surgery, 2001-. Publications: Author and co-author of over 133 articles in medical journals; 5 textbooks; 37 textbook chapters; numerous abstracts, editorials, book reviews and papers presented at national and international conferences and symposia. Honours include: William & Mary Diefenbaker Fellowship, 1962; Agora Award "Ambassador by Appointment", Palais de Congress, City of Montreal, 1988; American Medical Illustrators Best Illustrated Medical Textbook of the Year 1992; Award of Appreciation, American Society of Colon and Rectal Surgeons, 1999; Dr Carl Arthur Goresky Memorial Award, McGill Inflammatory Bowel Disease Research Group, 2002; Listed in numerous Who's Who publications and biographical dictionaries. Memberships include: Fellow, Royal College of Surgeons of Canada, Royal Society of Medicine, American College of Surgeons, American and Canadian Society of Colon and Rectal Surgeons; Founding President, Canadian Society of Colon and Rectal Surgeons; Past President, American Society of Colon and Rectal Surgeons; Past President, American Board of Colon and Rectal Surgery. Address: 3755 Cote Ste, Catherine Road, Suite G-314, Montreal, Quebec, Canada H3T 1E2. E-mail: philip.gordon@mcgill.ca

GORDON Robert Patterson, b. 9 November 1945, Belfast, Northern Ireland. University Teacher. m. Helen Ruth, 2 sons, 1 daughter. Education: St Catharine's College, Cambridge, 1964-69: BA, 1968, MA, 1972, PhD, 1973, Litt. D, 2001 (all Cambridge). Appointments: Assistant Lecturer, Hebrew and the Old Testament, 1969-70, Lecturer in Hebrew and Semitic Languages, 1970-79, University of Glasgow; Lecturer in Divinity, 1979-95, Regius Professor of Hebrew, 1995-, University of Cambridge. Publications: 1 and 2 Samuel: Introduction, 1984; 1 and 2 Samuel: A Commentary, 1986; The Targum of the Minor Prophets (jointly), 1989; Studies in the Targum to the Twelve Prophets, 1994; The Old Testament in Syriac: Chronicles, 1998; Hebrews: Commentary, 2000; Holy Land, Holy City, 2004; The Old Testament in its World (jointly), 2005; Hebrew Bible and Ancient Versions, 2006; The God of Israel (editor), 2007. Honours: Jarrett Scholarship, 1966; Rannoch Hebrew Scholarship, 1966; Senior Scholarship,

1968; Bender Prize, 1968; Tyrwhitt Scholarship, 1969; Mason Prize, 1969. Memberships: Society for Old Testament Studies; British Association of Jewish Studies; National Club. Address: 85 Barrons Way, Comberton, Cambridge CB23 7DR, England.

GORDONOVA Polina, b. 22 April 1957, Leningrad, Russia. Civil Engineer; Researcher. Divorced, 1 son, 1 daughter. Education: MS, Civil Engineering (with honours), Leningrad's Building University, USSR, 1979; Licentiate in Engineering, University of Technology, Lund, Sweden, 1998. Appointments: Head of Business Services Group, Leading Civil Engineer, Design and Research Institute, Leningrad, 1979-91; Research Scientist, University of Technology, Lund, Sweden, 1993-2005; Senior Consultant, Carl Bro AB, Malmoe, Sweden, 2001-. Publications: Spread of Smoke and Fire Gases via Ventilation System (scientific report); Smoke Ventilation in Large Industrial Spaces (paper); Fire in the Hole – Nuclear Engineering International (paper); New principles and methods for prevention of smoke and fire gases spread via the ventilation systems in the Swedish underground storage facility for spent nuclear fuel (scientific paper). Honours: Who's Who in the World, 2006; Who's Who in Science and Engineering, 2006-07. Address: Carl Bro AB, Carl Gustafs vag 4, 20509 Malmoe, Sweden. E-mail: polina.gordonova@carlbro.se

GORE Albert Jr, b. 31 March 1948. Politician. m. Mary E Aitcheson, 1970, 1 son, 3 daughters. Education: Harvard University; Vanderbilt University. Appointments: Investigative reporter, editorial writer, The Tennessean, 1971-76; Home-builder and land developer, Tanglewood Home Builders Co, 1971-76; Livestock and tobacco farmer, 1973-; Head, Community Enterprise Board, 1993-; Member, House of Representatives, 1977-79; Senator, from Tennessee, 1985-93; Vice President, USA, 1993-2001; Democrat candidate in Presidential Elections, 2000; Lecturer, Middle Tennessee State, Fisk, Columbia Universities, 2001-; Vice-Chairman, Metropolitan West Financial, 2001-; Senior Advisor, Google Inc, 2001-; Chair, Newsworld International network, 2004-; Co-founder and Chair, Generation Investment Management, Washington, DC and London, England, 2004-; President, Current TV; Director, Apple Inc; Chairman, Alliance for Climate Protection. Publications include: Earth in the Balance, 1992; The Spirit of Family, 2002; Joined at the Heart: The Transformation of the American Family, 2002; An Inconvenient Truth, 2006; The Assault on Reason, 2007. Honours include: Dr hc, Harvard 1994, New York, 1998. Address: Metwest Financial, 11440 San Vicente Boulevard, 3rd Floor, Los Angeles, CA 90049, USA.

GORMLEY Antony Mark David, b. 30 August 1950, London, England. Sculptor. m. Vicken Parsons, 2 sons, 1 daughter. Education: BA, Archaeology, Anthropology and History of Art, Trinity College, Cambridge, 1968-71; Central School of Art, London, 1974-75; BA, Fine Art, Goldsmiths School of Art, London, 1975-77; Postgraduate Studies, Slade School of Fine Art, London, 1977-79. Career: Artist and Sculptor; Solo exhibitions include: Whitechapel Art Gallery, London, 1981; Coracle Press, London, 1983; Riverside Studios, Cardiff, Wales, 1984; Drawings, 1981-1985; Salvatore Ala Gallery, New York, USA, 1985; Five Works, Serpentine Gallery, London, England, 1987; The Holbeck Sculpture, Leeds City Art Gallery, Leeds, England, 1988; Drawings, Mcquarrie Gallery, Sydney, Australia, 1989; Bearing Light, Burnett Miller Gallery, Los Angeles, USA, 1990; Drawings and Etchings, Frith Street Gallery, London, England, 1991; American Field (touring), USA, 1992;

Antony Gormley (touring), Konsthall, Malmo, Sweden, Tate Gallery, Liverpool, England, Irish Museum of Modern Art, Ireland, 1993; Field for the British Isles (touring) UK, 1994; Critical Mass, Remise, Vienna, Austria, 1995; Total Strangers, Koelnischer Kunstverein, Cologne, Germany, 1997; Angel of the North, The Gallery, Central Library, Gateshead, England, 1998; Quantum Cloud (part of North Meadow Sculpture Project), Millennium Dome, London, England, 2000; New Works, Galerie Nordenhake, Berlin, Germany, 2001; Gormley Drawing, The British Museum, London, England, 2003; Asian Field (touring) China, 2003; Domain Field, The Great Hall, Winchester, England, 2004; Antony Gormley Display, Tate Britain, London, England, 2004; Antony Gormley: New Works, Sean Gallery, New York, USA, 2005; Antony Gormley, Glyndebourne Opera House, England, 2005; Another Place, Crosby Beach, Merseyside, England; Field for the British Isles, Longside Gallery, Yorkshire Sculpture Park, England, 2005; Certain Made Places, Koyanagi Gallery, Tokyo, Japan, 2005; Asian Field, ICA, Singapore, 2005; Inside Australia, Anna Schwartz Gallery, Melbourne, Australia, 2005; Numerous group exhibitions, including: British Sculpture in the Twentieth Century, Whitechapel Art Gallery, London, England, 1982; Aperto '82, Biennale de Venezia, Venice, Italy; An International Survey of Recent Painting and Sculpture, The Museum of Modern Art, New York, USA, 1984; Turner Prize, Tate Gallery, London, England, 1994; A Secret History of Clay: From Gauguin to Gormley, Tate Liverpool, Liverpool, England, 2004; Space: Now and Then, Art and Architecture, Fundament Foundation, AaBé Fabrieken, Tilburg, Netherlands, 2005; Works in collections including: Arts Council of Great Britain; Tate Gallery; British Council; Walker Arts Center Minneapolis; Leeds City Art Gallery; Irish Museum of Modern Art; Major commissions include: The Angel of the North, Gateshead, 1998; Quantum Cloud, London, 2000. Honours: Turner Prize, 1994; OBE, 1998; South Bank Art Award, 1999; Civic trust Award (for The Angel of the North), 2000; Honorary Fellow, RIBA, 2001; Honorary Doctorates: University of Sunderland, 1998, University of Central England, Birmingham, 1998, Open University, 2001, Cambridge University, 2003, Newcastle University, 2004, Teeside University, 2004; Honorary Fellowships: Goldsmith's College, University of London, 1998, Jesus College, Cambridge, 2003, Trinity College, Cambridge, 2003; Fellow, RSA, 2000; RA, 2003; Trustee, Baltic Centre for Contemporary Art; Trustee, British Museum, 2007. Address: 15-23 Vale Royal, London N7 9AP, England. Website: www.antonygormley.com

GORNIK Christian Josef, b. 31 May 1974, Eisenstadt, Austria. Process Engineer. Education: College for Aeronautical Engineering, 1988-93; Plastics Engineering, University of Leoben, 1993-98; Dipl Ing Degree, 1998; Dr Degree, University of Leoben, 2007. Appointments: Director, Special Technologies, Battenfeld Kunststoffmaschinen GmBH, 2000-; Part time Lecturer, University of Applied Sciences, Wels, Austria, 2006-. Publications: 25 articles in professional journals; 27 presentations; 6 patents. Honours: Rektor Platzer Ring; Honoring Award of the Education Minister; Pro Sciencia Scholar. Memberships: Board of Polymer Competence Centre, Leoben; Verein Deutsche Ingenieure; Verband Leonbener Kunststoff Techniker. Address: Wr Neustaedter str 81, A-2542 Kottingbrunn, Austria. E-mail: christian.gornik@battenfeld-imt.com

GOROKHOV Igor M, b. 6 April 1932, Leningrad, Russia. Professor of Geochemistry. m. Irina A Ostrovskaya, 1 daughter. Education: Certificate of Research Chemist (honours), Leningrad State University, 1954; PhD, Chemical

Sciences, Leningrad Technology Institute, 1965; Senior Research Officer, Geochemistry, Higher Education Board of the USSR, Moscow, 1979; DSc, Geology and Mineralogical Sciences, Institute of Geochemistry, Kiev, Ukraine, 1981. Appointments: Junior Research Fellow, USSR Academy of Science, V G Khlopin Radium Institute, Leningrad, 1954-61; Junior Research Fellow, USSR Academy of Science, Laboratory of Precambrian Geology, Leningrad, 1961-67; Junior Research Fellow to Head of Laboratory, Russian Academy of Science, Institute of Precambrian Geology and Geochronology, St Petersburg, 1967-. Publications: 2 books; Over 100 articles in scientific journals. Honours: Medal for scientific service, Geological Survey, Prague, 1986; Medal for scientific service, Geological Survey, Bratislava, 1986; State Scientific Grants, 1994, 1997, 2000; Awards, Nauka/Interperiodica Publishing House, 1996, 2003; Academician A.P. Karpinsky medal for scientific achievements, Russian Academy of Sciences and St Petersburg City Administration, 2007. Memberships: Board, Council on Isotope Geology and Geochronology, USSR Academy of Sciences, 1973-91, 1999-, Commission on the Upper Precambrian, Moscow, 1988-; Editorial Board, Chemical Geology, 1987-99; New York Academy of Sciences, 1995. Address: Institute of Precambrian Geology and Geochronology, Russian Academy of Sciences, nab Makarova 2, 199034 St Petersburg, Russia. E-mail: gorokhov@ig1405.spb.edu

GORRARA Sir Richard, b. 29 May 1964, Metz, France. Magistrate. Education: MA, English, 2004; PhD, Political Science, 2005; LLM, Criminal Justice, 2006; LLD (Doctorate), Law, 2006; Professor of Law, 2006; Doctor of Music, 2006. Appointments: Investment Advisor; Business Consultant; Magistrate; Judge. Honours: Knighthood; Lord of the Manor; Baron; Chevalier Legion d'honneur; Sir (Knight), Order of St John. Memberships: Labour Party; Conservative Party; European Bar Association. Address: CP44, Centro Posta, Via Zani, 43036 Fidenza, Parma, Italy. E-mail: mailcom1000@yahoo.co.uk

GORRIE Donald Cameron Easterbrook, b. 2 April 1933, Dehra Dun, India. m. Astrid Salvesen, 2 sons. Education: MA, Modern History, Corpus Christi College, Oxford, 1953-57. Appointments: School Master: Gordonstoun School, 1957-60, Marlborough College, 1960-66; Director of Research then Administration, Scottish Liberal Party, 1968-75; Liberal Councillor, Edinburgh Town Council, 1971-75, Councillor and Liberal Democrat Group Leader, Lothian Regional Council, 1974-96, City of Edinburgh District Council, 1980-96, City of Edinburgh Council, 1995-97; MP, Liberal Democrat, Edinburgh West, 1997-2001; Member Liberal Democrat Scotland Team, 1997-99; MSP, Liberal Democrat, Central Scotland, 1999-2007; Spokesman on Local Government, 1999-2000, Finance, 2000-01; Justice, 2001-03; Procedures, 1999-2003, 2005-2007; Communities, Culture, Sport, Voluntary Sector, Older People, 2003-05; Convenor, Procedures Committee, 2005-2007. Honours: Former holder of Scottish Native Record 880 yards, 1955; OBE; DL; Backbencher of the Year, 1999; Free Spirit of the Year, 2001. Publications: Party manifestos and political pamphlets including Planning: Beyond the White Paper. Memberships: Former Chairman, Edinburgh Youth Orchestra; Sometime Board/Committee: Royal Lyceum Theatre; Queen's Hall, Edinburgh; Edinburgh Festival; Scottish Chamber Orchestra; Castle Rock Housing Association; Lothian Association of Youth Clubs; Edinburgh City Youth Café; Diverse Attractions; Edinburgh Zoo; Corstorphine Dementia Project, Friends of Corstorphine Hill; President, Lothian Association of Youth

Clubs, Edinburgh City Youth Café; Edinburgh Athletic Club, Corstorphine AAC; Vice President, Achilles Club. Address: 9 Garscube Terrace, Edinburgh EH12 6BW, Scotland.

GORSHKOV Oleg, b. 8 December 1959, Permskaya Region, Russia. Physicist; Educator. m. Elena Rolandovna, 1 son. Education: Honorary School Certificate, 1977; Honorary Engineer's Diploma, Moscow Aviation Institute, 1983; PhD, 1990, DSc, 2006, Keldysh Research Center. Appointments: Engineer, 1983-88, Section Manager, 1988-89, Research Assistant, 1989-90, Senior Staff Scientist, 1990-91, Head, Department of Electrophysics, 1991-, Chief Designer, Electric Propulsion, 2000-, Keldysh Research Centre, Moscow; Lecturer, 1997-2000, Assistant Professor, 2000-, Institute of Physics and Technology, Moscow. Publications: Numerous articles in professional journals. Honours: Prize, Russian Academy of Sciences, 2001; Honoured Worker, Rocket-Space Industry of the Russian Federation, 2003; Grants, ISTC, 1997, 1999, 2000, 2002, 2003 and 2004. Memberships: Scientific Council, Russian Academy of Sciences; International Astronautical Federation. Address: Keldysh Research Centre, 8 Onezhskaya, Moscow 125438, Russia. E-mail: kercgor@dol.ru

GORYAEVA Elena Mikhailovna, b. 11 November 1944, Leningrad, Russia. Research Scientist; Physicist. m. Mikhail Alexandrovich Goryaev, 1976, 1 daughter. Education: MS, Opto-Electronics, Leningrad Institute of Optics and Exact Mechanics, 1967. Appointments: Engineer, 1967-72, Junior Research Specialist, 1972-82, Research Specialist, 1982-2008, Retired 2008, Laboratory of Luminescence and Photochemistry, S I Vavilov State Optical Institute, St Petersburg. Publications: Over 40 scientific publications, patents and reports presented. Honours: Labour Veteran Medal, Leningrad City Council of People's Deps, 1988; Listed in national and international biographical dictionaries. Memberships: Member, All Russian Inventors Society. Address: S I Vavilov State Optical Institute, Birzhevaya liniya 12, 199034 St Petersburg, Russia. E-mail: goryaeva@yahoo.com or ogoryaev@og2172.spb.edu

GOSLING-HARE Paula Louise, (Ainslie Skinner, Holly Baxter), b. 12 October 1939, Michigan, USA. Author; Crime and Suspense Fiction. m. (1) Christopher Gosling, September 1968, divorced 1978, 2 daughters, (2) John Hare, 1982. Education: BA, Wayne State University. Appointments: Copywriter, Campbell Ewald, USA; Copywriter, Mitchell & Co, London; Copywriter, Pritchard Wood, London: Freelance Copywriter, 1974-. Publications: A Running Duck, 1976; Zero Trap, 1978; The Woman in Red, 1979; Losers Blues, 1980; Minds Eye (as Ainslie Skinner), 1980; Monkey Puzzle, 1982; The Wychford Murders, 1983; Hoodwink, 1985; Backlash, 1987; Death Penalties, 1990; The Body in Blackwater Bay, 1992; A Few Dying Words, 1994; The Dead of Winter, 1995; Death and Shadows, 1999; Underneath Every Stone, 2000; Ricochet, 2002; Tears of the Dragon, 2004. Honours: Gold Dagger, Crime Writers' Association; Arts Achievement Award, Wayne State University. Memberships: Crimewriters' Association, chairman, 1982; Society of Authors. Address: c/o Greene & Heaton Ltd, 37 Goldhawk Road, London W12 8QQ, England.

GOTO Hiroyuki, b. 28 June 1971, Kanagawa, Japan. Associate Professor. m. Wakako Obata. Education: BS, 1995, MS, 1997, University of Tokyo; DEng, Tokyo Metropolitan Institute of Technology, 2004. Appointments: Researcher, Mitsubishi Research Institute Inc, Tokyo, 1997-99; Systems Engineer, Hakusan Corporation, Fuchu-shi, Japan, 1999-2001; Senior Researcher, The Japan Research Institute Ltd, Tokyo,

2001-2005; Associate Professor, Nagaoka University of Technology, 2005-. Publications: Contributor of articles to professional journals in the fields of discrete event systems and management science; Patents for time series analysis, controller design for discrete event systems and management science including demand prediction and inventory management. Honour: Best Paper Award, The Institute of System Control and Information Engineers, Japan, 2004. Institute of Electronics, Information and Communication Engineers; Japan Industrial Management Association; Society of Plant Engineers. Address: Nagaoka University of Technology, 1603-1 Kamitomiokamachi, Nagaoka Niigata, 940-2188 Japan. E-mail: hgoto@kjs.nagaokaut.ac.jp

GOTO Noboru, b. 4 January 1940, Tokyo, Japan. Professor of Anatomy. m. Naoe Sekine, 1 son. Education: MD, Nihon University School of Medicine, 1966; Assistant, Department of Anatomy, 1967-72; PhD, 1972; Senior Lecturer, 1972; Postgraduate Fellow, National Hospital, Queen Square, London, 1973-75. Appointments: Associate Professor of Neuroanatomy, Department of Anatomy, Nihon University School of Medicine, 1977-91; Professor and Chairman, Department of Anatomy, Showa University School of Medicine, 1991-2005; Professional Member of American Heart Association and American Stroke Association, 2003 (FAHA, 1981); Honorary President, Koriyama Professional Training College of Health Sciences, 2005-. Publications: Monographs: Anatomy of the blood vessels of the central nervous system, 1971; Atlas of the human brainstem and cerebellum, 1989; Articles: Primary pontine hemorrhage, 1980; Olivary enlargement: Chronological and morphometric analyses, 1981. Memberships: Professional Member, AHA & ASA; Registered Neurologist, JNA; Registered Stroke Specialist, JSA; Life Member, Japanese Society of Anatomists. Address: 28-10 Soshigaya 6, Setagaya-ku, Tokyo 157-0072, Japan. E-mail: goto@sea.plala.or.jp

GOTO Yukio, b. 20 August 1928, Aichi Prefecture, Japan. Professor. m. 1956, 2 sons, 1 daughter. Education: Bachelor of Economics, Nagoya University, Aichi, 1951; Doctor of Business Administration, Kobe University, Hyogo, 1968. Appointments: Lecturer, 1954-57, Professor, 1959-65, President, 1986-89, Emeritus Professor, 1989-, Kobe University of Commerce, Kobe, Hyogo; Professor and Trustee, 1989-92, Emeritus Professor, 1998-, Emeritus Trustee, 2006-, Otemon-Gakuin University, Ibaraki, Osaka; President, Otemon-Gakuin Judicial Person, Ibaraki, 1992-1998, re-elected, 2002-06. Publications: Author, 3 books: Theory of the Investment of the Corporation, 1965; The Corporate Planning and Management Analysis, 1979; The Financial Management of Corporation, 1983. Honours: Order of the Sacred Treasure, Gold Rays with Neck Ribbon, Prime Minister of Japan, 2006. Memberships: Fellow, Science Council of Japan, 1985-94; Councillor, Japan Society for the Promotion of Science, 1986-94. Address: 30-3, Asahigaoka, Ashiya, Hyogo Prefecture, 659-0012, Japan.

GOUGH Douglas Owen, b. 8 February 1941, Stourport, Worcestershire, England. Astrophysicist. m. Rosanne Penelope, 2 sons, 2 daughters. Education: BA, 1962, MA, PhD, 1966, St John's College, University of Cambridge; DSc, University of Sydney, 1987. Appointments: Research Associate, Joint Institute for Laboratory Astrophysics, and Department of Physics and Astrophysics, University of Colorado, 1966-67; Visiting Member, Courant Institute of Mathematical Sciences, New York University, 1967-69; National Academy of Sciences Senior Postdoctoral Resident/ Research Associate, Goddard Institute for Space Studies,

New York, 1967-69; Member, Graduate Staff, Institute of Theoretical Astronomy, 1969-73; Lecturer, Astronomy and Applied Mathematics, 1973-85, Reader in Astrophysics, 1985-93 Institute of Astronomy and Department of Applied Mathematics and Theoretical Physics, Professor of Theoretical Astrophysics, 1993-, Deputy Director, 1993-99, Director, 1999-2004, Institute of Astronomy, University of Cambridge; Associate Professor, University of Toulouse, 1984-85; Honorary Professor of Astronomy, Queen Mary and Westfield College, University of London, 1986-2005; Fellow Adjoint, Joint Institute for Laboratory Astrophysics, Boulder, Colorado, 1986-; Scientific Co-ordinator, Institute for Theoretical Physics, University of California, Santa Barbara, 1990; Visiting Professor, Department of Physics, Stanford University; Visiting Fellow, South African Astronomical Observatory, 2004; Visiting Fellow, Japan Society for the Promotion of Science, 2005; Chercher Associé du Centre National de la Recherche Scientifique, Observatoire de Paris-Meudon, France, 2005-06; Visiting Professor, Department of Physics and Astronomy, Aarhus University, 2006. Publications: About 300 papers in scientific literature; Books edited include: Problems of solar and stellar oscillations, 1983; Seismology of the Sun and the distant stars, 1986; Challenges to theories of the structure of moderate-mass stars, 1991; Equation-of-state and phase-transition issues in models of ordinary astrophysical matter, 2004; The Scientific Legacy of Fred Hoyle, 2005. Honours: Gravity Research Foundation Prize (shared with F W W Dilke), 1973; James Arthur Prize, Harvard University, 1982; William Hopkins Prize, Cambridge Philosophical Society, 1984; George Ellery Hale Prize, American Astronomical Society, 1994; Mousquetaire d'Armagnac, 2001; Eddington Medal, Royal Astronomical Society, 2002. Memberships: Fellow, Royal Astronomical Society; American Astronomical Society; International Astronomical Union; Astronomical Society of India; Fellow, Royal Society; Fellow, Institute of Physics; Foreign Member, Royal Danish Academy of Sciences and Letters. Address: Institute of Astronomy, Madingley Road, Cambridge CB3 0HA, England. E-mail: douglas@ast.cam.ac.uk

GOULD Elliott, b. 29 August 1938, Brooklyn, New York, USA. Actor. m. (1) Barbra Streisand, 1963, divorced 1971, 1 son, (2) Jenny Bogart, divorced, 1 son, 1 daughter. Career: Actor, theatre appearances include: Say Darling, 1958; Irma La Douce, 1960; I Can Get It For You Wholesale, 1962; Drat! The Cat, 1965; Alfred in Little Murders, 1967; Toured in the Fantastiks with Liza Minelli; National tour with Deathtrap; Films include: The Confession, 1966; The Night They Raided Minsky's, 1968; Bob and Carol and Ted and Alice, 1969; Getting Straight, 1970; M*A*S*H, 1970; The Touch, 1971; Little Murders, 1971; The Long Good-Bye, 1972; Nashville, 1974; I Will...I Will...For Now, 1976; Harry and Walter Go to New York, 1976; A Bridge Too Far, 1977; The Silent Partner, 1979; The Lady Vanishes, 1979; Escape to Athens, 1979; The Muppet Movie, 1979; Falling in Love Again, 1980; The Devil and Max Devlin, 1981; Over the Brooklyn Bridge, 1984; The Naked Face, 1984; Act of Betrayal, 1988; Dead Men Don't Die, 1989; Secret Scandal, 1990; Strawanser, The Player, Exchange Lifeguards, Wet and Wild Summer, Naked Gun 331/3, the Final Insult (cameo), White Man's Burden, The Glass Shield, Kicking and Screaming, A Boy Called Hate, Johns, The Big Hit, American History, X, Bugsy, Hoffman's Hunger, Capricorn One; Boys Life 3, 2000; Ocean's Eleven, 2001; Puckoon, 2002; The Cat Returns (voice), 2002; Ocean's Twelve, 2004; Open Window, 2006; Ocean's Thirteen, 2007; Little Hercules in 3-D, 2007; The Ten Commandments (voice),

2007; The Redemption of Sarah Cain, 2007; Numerous TV appearances including Doggin' Around; Once Upon a Mattress; Friends; Kim Possible. Website: www.elliottgould.net

GOURLAY Caroline, b. 10 August 1939, London, England. Poet. m. Simon Gourlay, 17 May 1967, 3 sons. Education: Royal Academy of Music, 1957-60; LRAM, 1960. Appointment: Editor, Blithe Spirit, Journal of the British Haiku Society, 1998-2000. Publications: Crossing the Field, 1995; Through the Café Door, 1999; Reading All Night, 1999; Against the Odds, 2000; This Country, 2005; Lull Before Dark, 2005. Contributions to: Envoi; Poetry Wales; New Welsh Review; Iron; Haiku Quarterly; Outposts; Blithe Spirit; Journal of the British Haiku Society; Planet; Modern Haiku; Frogpond; Tanka Splendor; American Tanka; Presence. Honour: James Hackett Award, 1996. Address: Hill House Farm, Knighton, Powys LD7 1NA, Wales.

GOVES Andrew, b. 10 November 1951, High Wycombe, Buckinghamshire, England. Chief Fire Officer. m. Nikki, 1 daughter. Education: LLB (Hons), Law, University of Buckingham, 1998; MA, Management, Coventry University, 2001; MSc, Fire Command and Management, 2001; MCGI, Management, City and Guilds Institute, 2002. Appointments: Firefighter to Senior Divisional Officer, 1974-98, Assistant Chief Fire Officer, 1998-2000, Deputy Chief Fire Officer, 2000-03, Buckinghamshire Fire and Rescue Service; Member of Directing Staff, Fire Service College, 1986-88; Chief Fire Officer, Wiltshire Fire and Rescue Service, 2003-. Publications: Numerous articles in professional journals. Honours: Fire Brigade Long Service and Good Conduct Medal, 1994; Gore Technology Scholarship Award, Brigade Command Course, 2001; Queen Elizabeth II Golden Jubilee Medal, 2002. Memberships: Member, 1981-, Fellow, 2006, Institution of Fire Engineers; Member, Institute of Management; Member, Institute of Leadership and Management.

GOVRIN Nurit, b. 6 November 1935, Israel. Educationist; Researcher; Writer. m. Shlomo Govrin, 3 sons. Education: BA, Hebrew Literature, Bible Studies; MA, Hebrew Literature; PhD, Hebrew Literature; Tel-Aviv University; Harvard University, USA; University of Oxford, England. Appointments: Administrative positions, Tel-Aviv University; Teaching, University of California at Los Angeles, Columbia University, New York, Hebrew Union College; Assistant, 1965-68, Teacher, 1968-72, Lecturer, 1972-74, Senior Lecturer, 1974-78, Associate Professor 1978-90, Full Professor, 1990-, Tel-Aviv University; Public Council for Culture and Art, Ministry of Education; Judge, Selection Committees for many literary prizes. Publications: 14 books including: G Shoffman: His Life and Work, 2 volumes, 1982; The Brenner Affair - The Fight for Free Speech, 1985; The Literature of Eretz - Israel in the Early Days of the Settlements, 1985; The First Half - The Life and Work of Dvora Baron 1888-1923, 1988; Honey from the Rock, 1989; Brenner - Nonplussed and Mentor, 1991; Burning - Poetry About Brenner, 1995; Literary Geography - Lands and Landmarks on the Map of Hebrew Literature, 1998; Reading the Generations – Contextual Studies in Hebrew Literature, 2 Volumes, 2002; Nurit Govrin: Bibliography: 1950-2004 by Joseph Galrom-Goldshlayer; Nurit Govrin: The Forgotten Traveler: Shlomith F Flaum – Her Life and Work, 2005; Prescriptives on Modern Hebrew Literature – In Honor of Professor Nurit Govrin, edited by Avner Holzman, 2005; Editor of 14 books. Honours: Postgraduate Scholarship, Rothschild Fund, 1973-74; Research Grants: Israel National Academy for Sciences, 1975-78, Jewish Memorial Fund, 1982, Israel Matz Fund, 1982, 1984-86, 1989, American Academy for Jewish Studies, 1984-85, 1989; Haifa Municipality Prize,

1993; Shalom Aleichem Prize, 1996; Creative Woman Prize, Wizo Prize, 1998; Bialik Prize, 1998; Israel Efros Prize, 2001. Memberships: Katz Institute for Research of Hebrew Literature; Literature Committee, Israel National Academy of Sciences and Humanities. Address: 149 Jobotinsky St, Tel-Aviv 62150, Israel.

GOWANS James, b. 7 May 1924, Sheffield, England. Medical Scientist. m. Moyra, 1 son, 2 daughters. Education: Kings College, London; Kings College Medical School, London; Lincoln College, Oxford. Appointments: Research Professor, Royal Society, Oxford University, 1962-77; Secretary, UK Medical Research Council, 1977-87; Secretary General, Human Frontier Science Program, Strasbourg, France, 1989-93. Publications: Numerous articles in scientific journals. Honours: FRS; FRCP; Kt; CBE; Royal Medal, Royal Society; Foreign Associate, US National Academy of Sciences; Gairdner Foundation Award, Toronto; Wolf Prize in Medicine, Israel; Honorary Degrees at Yale, Chicago, Rochester, New York, Birmingham, Edinburgh, Glasgow, Southampton. Memberships: Honorary Fellow at Lincoln, Exeter and St Catherine's Colleges, Oxford. Address: 75 Cumnor Hill, Oxford, OX2 9HX, England.

GOWER David Ivon, b. 1 April 1957, Tunbridge Wells, Kent, England. Cricketer. m. Thorunn Ruth Nash, 1992, 2 daughters. Education: University College, London. Career: Left-hand batsman; Played for Leicestershire, 1975-89, captain, 1984-86, Hampshire, 1990-93; Played in 117 Tests for England, 1978-92, 32 as captain, scoring then England record 8,231 runs (average 44.2) with 18 hundreds; Toured Australia, 1978-79, 1979-80, 1982-83, 1986-87, 1990-91; Scored 26,339 first-class runs with 53 hundreds; 114 limited-overs internationals; Sunday Express Cricket Correspondent, 1993-95; Public Relations Consultant for cricket sponsorship National Westminster Bank, 1993-; Commentator, Sky TV, 1993-; Commentator and presenter, BBC TV, 1994-99; Columnist, Sunday Telegraph, 1995-98; Presenter, Sky TV cricket, 1999-; Columnist, The Sun, 2000-04; Colmunist, The Sunday Times, 2004-; Television: They Think It's All Over, 1995-2003. Publications: A Right Ambition, 1986; On The Rack, 1990; The Autobiography, 1992; Articles in Wisden Cricket Monthly. Address: SFX Sports Group, 35/36 Grosvenor Street, London W1K 4QX, England.

GRABOVSHCHINER Albert, b. 7 July 1940, Russia. Quantum Medicine. m. Galina, 1 son, 1 daughter. Education: Moscow Power Energy Institute, 1964; Postgraduate Residency, 1974; Special Traineeship in Microprocessors and Programming, Moscow Institute of Electronics Mathematics, 1981; Traineeship in Marketing, Aboveboard Britain University, 1995. Appointments: Engineer, Chief Engineer, Senior Researcher, 1963-91; General Director, ISC MILTA-PKP GIT, 1991-; President, Quantum Medicine Association, 1997-; Rector, Quantum Medicine Institute, 1998-. Publications: 18 patents for inventions and industrial samples; Over 100 scientific issues and publications in Quantum Medicine methodology. Honours: Russian State Awards: Order of Honour; 4 medals; Gold Medal, Russia Academy of Natural Sic; Order of Fatherland Merit, International Science Academy. Memberships: Russia Academy of Quality; International Academy of Real Economy; World Academy of Biomedical Technologies; Moscow Chamber of Commerce & Industry. Address: 151 Lublinsky str, Moscow 109341, Russia. E-mail: info@kvantmed.ru Website: www:quantmed.ru

GRACE Sherrill Elizabeth, b. Ormstown, Quebec, Canada. University Professor. 2 children. Education: BA, University of Western Ontario, 1962-65; MA, 1968-70, PhD, 1970-74, McGill University. Appointments: Teacher, Netherhall Secondary Girls School, Cambridge, England, 1967-68; Teaching Assistant, 1970-73, Special Lecturer, 1974-75, Assistant Professor, 1975-77, McGill University; Assistant Professor, 1977, Associate Professor, 1981, Professor, 1987-, Departmental Head, 1997-2002, University of British Columbia. Publications include: Violent Duality: A Study of Margaret Atwood, 1980; The Voyage That Never Ends: Malcolm Lowry's Fiction, 1982; Regression and Apocalypse: Studies in North American Literary Expressionism, 1989; Sursum Corda: The Collected Letters of Malcolm Lowry, 1995, 1996; Staging the North: 12 Canadian Plays, 1999; Canada and the Idea of North, 2002; Performing National Identities: Essays on contemporary Canadian Theatre, 2003; New annotated edition, A Woman's Way Through Unknown Labrador, 2004; Inventing Tom Thomson: From Biographical Fictions to Fictional Autobiographies, 2004. Honours include: University of British Columbia President Killam Research Prize, 1990; FEL Priestley Award, 1993; University of British Columbia Jacob Biely Research Prize, 1998; Fellow, Royal Society of Canada; Richard Plant Prize, 2003; Canada Council Killam Fellowship, 2003-05; Brenda and David McLean Chair in Canadian Studies, 2003-05; UBC Distinguished University Scholar, 2003-. Memberships: International Association of University Professors of English; Modern Language Association; Association of Canadian University Teachers of English. Address: Department of English, University of British Columbia, #397-1873 East Mall, BC V6T 1Z1, Canada.

GRADE Michael Ian, b. 8 March 1943, London, England. Broadcasting Executive. m. (1) Penelope Jane Levinson, 1967, divorced 1981, 1 son, 1 daughter, (2) Hon Sarah Lawson, 1982, divorced, (3) Francesca Mary Leahy, 1998, 1 son. Education: St Dunstan's College, London, UK. Appointments: Trainee Journalist, Daily Mirror, 1960, Sports Columnist, 1964-66; Theatrical Agent, Grade Organisation, 1966; Joint Managing Director, London Management and Representation, 1969-73; Deputy Controller of Programmes (Entertainment), London Weekend TV, 1973-77; Director of Programmes and Member Board, 1977-81; President, Embassy TV, 1981-84; Controller, BBC 1, 1984-86; Director of Programmes BBC TV, 1986-87; Chief Executive Officer, Channel Four, 1988-87; Chairman, VCI PLC, 1995-98; Director, 1991-2000, non-executive Chairman, 1995-97, Chairman, 1997-98, First Leisure Corp; Vice President, Children's Film Unit, 1993-; Delfont Macintosh Theatres Ltd, 1994-99; Entertainment Charities Fund, 1994-; Deputy Chairman, Society of Stars, 1995-; RADA, 1996-; Royal Albert Hall, 1997-; Charlton Athletic Football Club, 1997-; Camelot Group, 2000-04; Digitaloctopus, 2000-; Chair, Octopus, 2000-; Pinewood Studio Ltd, 2000-; Hemscott.NET, 2000-; BBC, 2004-06; ITV, 2007-. Publications: It Seemed Like a Good Idea at the Time, 1999. Honours: Honorary Professor, Thames Valley University, 1994; Honorary Treasurer, Stars Organisation for Spastics, 1986-92; CBE, Hon LLD (Nottingham), 1997; Royal TV Society Gold Medal, 1997. Memberships: International Council National Academy of TV Arts and Sciences, 1991-97; Council, London Academy of Music and Dramatic Art, 1981-93; BAFTA, 1981-82, 1986-88 (Fellow, 1994); Gate Theatre, Dublin, 1990-; Cities in Schools, 1991-95; Cinema and TV Benevolent Fund, 1993-; Royal Academy of Dramatic Art, 1996-; Royal Albert Hall, 1997; 300 Group; Milton Committee; British Screen Advisory Council, 1986-97; National Commission of Inquiry into Prevention of Child Abuse, 1994-96; Board of Governors, BANFF TV Festival, 1997-; Trustee, Band Aid; National Film

and TV School; Virgin Health Care Foundation. Address: BBC, Broadcasting House, London W1A 1AA, England. Website: www.bbc.co.uk

GRAF Steffi, b. 14 June 1969, Bruehl, Germany. Tennis Player. m. Andre Agassi, 2001, 1 son, 1 daughter. Career: Won Orange Bowl 12s, 1981; European 14 and under and European Circuit Masters, 1982, Olympic demonstration event, Los Angeles; Winner, German Open, 1986, French Open, 1987, 1988, 1993, 1995, 1996; Australian open, 1988, 1989, 1990, 1994; Wimbledon, 1988, 1989, 1991, 1992, 1993, 1995, 1996, US Open, 1988, 1989, 1993, 1995, 1996; Ranked No 1, 1987; Official World Champion, 1988; Grand Slam winner, 1988, 1989; Olympic Champion, 1988; German Open, 1989; Youngest player to win 500 Singles victories as professional, 1991; 118 tournament wins, 23 Grand Slam titles, 1996; Won ATP Tour World Championship, 1996; Numerous Women's Doubles Championships with Gabriela Sabatini, Federation Cup, 1992; Retired, 1999. Publication: Wege Zum Erfolg, 1999. Honours: Olympic Order, 1999; German Medal of Honour, 2002; International Tennis Hall of Fame, 2004. Memberships: Ambassador, World Wildlife Fund, 1984-; Founder and Chair, Children for Tomorrow; Ambassador, EXPO 2000. Address: Stefanie Graf Marketing GmbH, Mallaustrasse 75, 68219 Mannheim, Germany. E-mail: kontakt@stefanie-graf.com Website: stefanie.graf.com

GRAFTON Rupert Quentin, b. 14 July 1962, Kaduna, Nigeria. Professor. m. Carol-Anne Kubanek, 1 son, 1 daughter. Education: BAg Econ, Massey University, 1981; MS, Iowa State University, 1985; PhD, University of British Columbia, 1992. Appointments: Assistant Professor, 1992-96, Associate Professor, 1996-2001, Director, Institute of the Environment, 1999-2001, University of Ottawa; Senior Fellow, Australian National University, 2001-04; Professor of Economics, Australian National University, 2004-. Publications: Numerous books include: Dictionary of Environmental Economics, Science and Policy, 2001; The Economics of the Environment and National Resources, 2004; Understanding the Environment: Bridging the Disciplinary Divides, 2005; Articles in professional journals. Honours: Young Researcher of the Year, University of Ottawa, 1998; William Evans Visiting Fellow, 1998, Honorary Professor, University of Otago; Premier's Research Excellence Award, Ontario, 2000. Memberships: American Economics Association; Association of Environmental and Resource Economists; European Association of Environmental & Resource Economists.; Australian Agricultural and resource Economics Society; Economics Society of Australia Address: Crawford School of Economics and Government, J G Crawford Building (13), The ANU, Canberra, ACT 0200, Australia. E-mail: quentin.grafton@anu.edu.au Website: http://apseg.anu.edu.au/staff/qgrafton.php

GRAHAM Henry, b. 1 December 1930, Liverpool, England. Lecturer; Poet. Education: Liverpool College of Art, 1950-52. Appointment: Poetry Editor, Ambit, London, 1969-. Publications: Good Luck to You Kafka/You'll Need It Boss, 1969; Soup City Zoo, 1969; Passport to Earth, 1971; Poker in Paradise Lost, 1977; Europe After Rain, 1981; Bomb, 1985; The Very Fragrant Death of Paul Gauguin, 1987; Jardin Gobe Avions, 1991; The Eye of the Beholder, 1997; Bar Room Ballads, 1999; Kafka in Liverpool, 2002. Contributions to: Ambit; Transatlantic Review; Prism International Review; Evergreen Review; Numerous anthologies worldwide. Honours: Arts Council Literature Awards, 1969, 1971, 1975;

Award, The Royal Literary Fund, 2003, 2004, 2005, 2006, 2007. Address: Flat 5, 23 Marmion Road, Liverpool L17 8TT, England.

GRAHAM Tony, b. 23 November 1951, London, England. Artistic Director. Education: BA Hons, University of Kent, 1971-74; Didsbury College of Education, Manchester University, 1974-75. Appointments: Drama Teacher, Head of Drama and Dance, numerous inner-city ILEA secondary schools, 1975-85; ILEA Drama Advisory Team, Inner London Education Authority, 1986-88; Associate Director, 1989-92, Artistic Director, 1992-97, TAG Theatre; Artistic Director, Unicorn Theatre for Children, 1997-. Memberships: Action for Children's Arts; ASSITEJ. Address: c/o Unicorn Theatre, 147 Tooley Street, London, SE1 2HZ, England. E-mail: artistic@unicorntheatre.com

GRAHAM-DIXON Anthony Philip, b. 5 November 1929, Woodford, England. Retired Queen's Counsel. m. Suzanne Villar, 1 son, 1 daughter. Education: Westminster School; MA, Christ Church, Oxford, 1948-52; CS Russian Interpreter Examination, 1955. Appointments: Lieutenant, Special Branch RNVR, 1955; Called to the Bar, Inner Temple, 1956, Bencher, 1982; QC, 1973; Retired from the Bar, 1986; Governor, Bedales School, 1988-96; Deputy Chairman, Public Health Laboratory Service, 1988-95; Chairman of the Trustees, London Jupiter Orchestra, 1999-2003; Chairman of the Trustees, Society for the Promotion of New Music, 1990-95. Publications: Consulting Editor, Competition Law in Western Europe and the USA, 1973. Honours: Scholar, Westminster School and Christ Church Oxford; QC, 1973. Membership: Member of the Livery, Goldsmiths Company. Address: Masketts Manor, Nutley, East Sussex TN22 3HD, England. E-mail: anthony@graham-dixon.com

GRAHAM-SMITH Francis (Sir), b. 25 April 1923, Roehampton, Surrey, England. Astronomer. m. Elizabeth Palmer, 3 sons, 1 daughter. Education: Natural Sciences Tripos, Downing College Cambridge, 1941-43, 1946-47; PhD (Cantab), 1952. Appointments: Telecommunications Research Establishment, Malvern, 1943-46; Research into Radio Astronomy Cavendish Laboratory, Cambridge, 1946-64, Jodrell Bank, 1964-74 and 1981-; Director, Royal Greenwich Observatory, 1976-81; Responsible for establishing the Isaac Newton Group of telescopes on La Palma, Canary Islands; Professor of Radio Astronomy, 1964-74, 1981-90, Langworthy Professor of Physics, 1987-90, Pro-Vice-Chancellor, 1988-90, Emeritus Professor, 1990-, University of Manchester; Director, Nuffield Radio Astronomy Laboratories, Jodrell Bank, 1981-88; 13th Astronomer Royal, 1982-90. Publications: Books: Radio Astronomy, 1960; Optics (with J H Thomson), 1971, 2nd edition, 1988; Pulsars, 1977; Pathways to the Universe (with Sir ACB Lovell), 1988; Pulsar Astronomy (with A G Lyne), 1989, 2nd edition, 1998; Optics and Photonics (with T King), 2000; Introduction to Radio Astronomy (with B F Burke), 1997, 2nd edition, 2002. Honours: Fellow, 1953-64, Honorary Fellow, 1970, Downing College, Cambridge; Kt Bachelor, 1986; Royal Medal, Royal Society, 1987; DSc: Queens University Belfast, 1986, Keele University 1987, Birmingham University, 1989, Dublin University, 1990; Nottingham University, 1990, Manchester University, 1993; Salford University, 2003, Liverpool, 2003; Glazebrook Medal, Institute of Physics, 1991. Memberships: Fellow of the Royal Society, Physical Secretary and Vice-President, 1988-94; Fellow of the Royal Astronomical Society, Secretary, 1964-71, President, 1975-77; Foreign Associate, Royal Society of South Africa, 1988; Chairman

of the Governors, Manchester Grammar School, 1987-98. Address: Old School House, Henbury, Macclesfield, Cheshire SK11 9PH, England. E-mail: fgsegs@ukonline.co.uk

GRANIK Alex T, b. 19 August 1939, Tadzhikistan. Physicist. m. Rita Visitei. Education: MS, Engineering, Odessa Institute of Technology, Odessa, USSR, 1956-61; PhD, Theoretical Physics and Mathematical Physics, Physics Department, Odessa University and Institute of Thermal Physics, Academy of Sciences, Novosibirsk, USSR, 1963-66. Appointments: Assistant Professor, Associate Professor, Department of Physics, Odessa Institute of Technology, 1966-76; Application Programmer, PBL Associates, Pt Richmond California, USA, 1978; Associate Professor Physics Department, Kentucky State University, USA, 1979-82; Scientific Consultant, Lawrence Livermore National Laboratory, USA, 1984-88; Associate Professor, Physics Department, University of the Pacific, California, USA, 1982-2005; Professor Emeritus, 2005-. Publications: More than 50 publications in refereed journals including: Foundations of Physics, Physics of Fluids, Journal of Fluid Mechanics, Astrophysical Journal, Astrophysics and Space Science, Physics Essays; Numerous presentations at national and international conferences. Address: Physics Department, University of the Pacific, Stockton, CA 95211, USA. E-mail: agranik@pacific.edu

GRANOV Anatoly Mikhaylovich, b. 21 April 1932, Donetsk, Russia. Surgeon; Physician. m. Svetlana Vashetina, 1 son. Education: Diploma, Donetsk Medical Institute, 1956; PhD, 1963; Doctoral thesis, 1970; Professor of Medical Sciences, 1974. Appointments: Physician, Department Head, Donetsk Medical Institute, 1956-69; Assistant Faculty Head, Donetsk Medical Institute, 1964-65; Junior Researcher, N N Petrov Institute of Oncology, Leningrad, 1965-66; Assistant Professor, N I Pavlov First Medical Institute, Leningrad, 1966-77; Faculty Head, Odessa Medical Institute, 1977-80; Head of Operative Surgery Department, 1980-93, Director, 1993-, Central Research Institute of Roentgenology and Radiology. Publications: Author, 7 books; Over 350 articles published in domestic and western medical journals. Honours: Medal "For Labour Activity", 1984; State Prize Winner, 1993; Order "For Services to Motherland", 2001; Medal "For Services to Domestic Health Care", 2001; Pirogov Gold Medal, IV grade, 2003; N N Blokhin Gold Medal "For Development in Domestic Oncology", 2003; Order of Andrey Pervozvanny, 2004; Russian Federation Government Prizewinner, 2006. Memberships: Member, Russian Academy of Medical Sciences; Honoured Member of N N Pirogov Association of Surgeons; Member, Association of Oncologists; Member, Association of Radiologists. Address: 197758 Leningradskaya st, 70/, Pesochny, St Petersburg, Russia.

GRANT Hugh John Mungo, b. 9 September 1960, London, England. Actor. Education: BA, New College, Oxford. Career: Actor in theatre, TV and films, producer for Simian Films; Began career in the Jockeys of Norfolk (writer with Chris Lang and Andy Taylor); Films include: White Mischief, Maurice, 1987; Lair of the White Worm, La Nuit Bengali, 1988; Impromptu, 1989; Bitter Moon, 1992; Remains of the Day, 1993; Four Weddings and a Funeral, Sirens, 1994; The Englishman who went up a hill but came down a mountain, Nine Months, An Awfully Big Adventure, Sense and Sensibility, 1995; Restoration, Extreme Measures, 1996; Mickey Blue Eyes, Notting Hill, 1998; Small Time Crooks, 2000; Bridget Jones' Diary, 2001; About a Boy, Two Weeks' Notice, 2002; Love Actually, 2003; Bridget Jones: The Edge of Reason, 2004; Travaux, on sait quand ça commence..., 2005; American Dreamz, 2006; Music and Lyrics, 2007.

Honours include: Golden Globe Award, BAFTA Award for Best Actor, Four Weddings and a Funeral, 1995; Peter Sellers Award for Comedy; Evening Standard British Film Awards, 2002; London Critics Circle Film Awards, Best British Actor, 2003; BAFTA/LA Stanley Kubrick Britannia Awad, 2003. Address: c/o Simian Films, 3 Cromwell Place, London SW7 2JE, England.

GRANT James Russell, b. 14 December 1924, Bellshill, Scotland. Physician; Poet. m. (1) Olga Zarb, 23 March 1955, divorced, 1 son, (2) Susan Tierney, 22 April 1994. Education: Medal in English, Hamilton Academy, 1941; MB CHb, University of Glasgow, 1951; Institute of Psychiatry, University of London, 1954-55. Appointments: Various medical posts. Publications: Hyphens, 1959; Poems, 1959; The Excitement of Being Sam, 1977; Myths of My Age, 1985; In the 4 Cats, 1997; Jigsaw and the Art of Poetry, 2001; Essays on Anxiety, 2001; London Poems, 2006; Contributions to: Glasgow University Magazine; Botteghe Oscure; Saltire Review; Prism International; Fiddlehead; Chapman; Ambit; BBC; CBC; Agenda; Edinburgh Review; Anthologies: Oxford Book of Travel Verse, 1985; Christian Poetry, 1988; Book of Machars, 1991. Honours: Scottish Open Poetry Competition, 1976; UK National Poetry Competition. Memberships: British Medical Association. Address: 255 Creighton Avenue, London N2 9BP, England.

GRANT Richard E, b.5 May 1957, Mbabane, Switzerland. Actor. m. Joan Washington, 1 daughter. Career: Actor, Theatre appearances include: Man of Mode, 1988; The Importance of Being Earnest, 1993; A Midsummer Night's Dream, 1994; TV appearances include: Honest, Decent, Legal and True, 1986; Here is the News, 1989; Suddenly Last Summer, 1992; Hard Times, 1993; Karaoke, A Royal Scandal, 1996; The Scarlet Pimpernel, 1998; Hound of the Baskervilles, 2002; Posh Nosh, 2003; Patrick Hamilton: Words, Whisky and Women, 2005; Films: Withnail and I, 1986; How to Get Ahead in Advertising, Warlock, 1989; Henry and June, Mountains of the Moon, 1990; LA Story, Hudson Hawk, 1991; Bram Stoker's Dracula, 1992; The Player, The Age of Innocence, 1993; Prêt à Porter, Jack and Sarah, Portrait of a Lady, Twelfth Night, 1995; The Serpent's Kiss, 1996; The Match, 1998; A Christmas Carol, Trial and Retribution, Little Vampires, 1999; Hildegarde, 2000; Gosford Park, 2001; Monsieur 'N', 2002; Bright Young Things, 2003; Tooth, 2004; The Story of an African Farm, Corpse Bride (voice), Colour Me Kubrick: A True…ish Story, 2005; Garfield: A Tail of Two Kitties (voice), Penelope, 2006; Always Crashing in the Same Car; 2007; Jackboots on Whitehall, The Garden of Eden, 2008. Publications: With Nails: The Film Diaries of Richard E Grant, 1995; Twelfth Night, 1996; By Design - A Hollywood Novel. Address: c/o ICM, Oxford House, 76 Oxford Street, London W1N 0AX, England. Website: www.richard-e-grant.com

GRAPSA Eirini, b. 6 November 1956, Exanthia, Greece. Nephrologist. Education: Faculty of Medicine, University of Ferrara, Italy, 1975-81; Degree in Nephrology, University of Athens, 1990; Doctorate, University of Athens, 1992; Certificate of Competency in English, Michigan; Certificate of Competency in Italian, Perugia. Appointments: Rural Doctor, Milea, Greece, 1982-83; Lef kada Hospital, 1983-84; Internal Medicine, St Andrews General Hospital, 1984-86; Nephrology training, Ippocration Hospital, 1986-90; Staff, Alexandra Hospital, Athens, 1990-93; Toronto General Hospital, Canada, 1993-94; Associate Director, Alexandra Hospital, Athens, Greece, 1994-2006. Publications: 15 articles; Book chapters include: Dialysis in the elderly; Replacement of renal function by dialysis, 1996, 2004; Textbook of Peritoneal dialysis, 2000,

2008. Honours: Award in Poetry, 1990-93; Award, European Accreditation Council, 2002. Memberships: EDTA; ASFA; ISFA; PDI; HSH; HSN. Address: Kousidou 97, Zografou, Athens 15772, Greece. E-mail: egrapsa@teledomenet.gr

GRATTON Guy Brian, b. 16 July 1970, Kirkcaldy, Scotland. Engineer; Writer; Test Pilot. Education: BEng (Hons), Aeronautics and Astronautics, 1992, PhD, Aerospace Engineering, 2005, University of Southampton. Appointments: Flight Test Engineer, 1993-96, Manager, Environmental Test Facilities, 1996-97, Ministry of Defence, Boscombe Down; Chief Technical Officer, British Microlight Aircraft Association, 1997-2005; Lecturer, Aeronautics, Brunel University, 2005-. Publications: Articles in professional journals including: International Journal of Aerospace Management, 2002; Journal of Aerospace Engineering, 2003; Aeronautical Journal, 2006; SETP Cockpit, 2003, 2006. Honours: D G Astridge Prize for Aerospace Safety, 2003; Safety in Mechanical Engineering Award, 2003; Herman R Salmon Technical Publications Award, 2006. Memberships: Institution of Mechanical Engineers; Fellow, Royal Aeronautical Society; Society of Experimental Test Pilots. Address: School of Engineering Design, Brunel University, Uxbridge, Middlesex UB8 3PH, England. E-mail: guy@gratton.org

GRATWICK John, b. 2 March 1923, Langley, Buckinghamshire, England. Operational Research. m. (1) Dorothy Shirley Vincent, 1945-57, 1 son, 1 daughter, (2) Gwendoline Sybil Johnston, 1957, 1 son. Education: Radio-Physics Certificate, 1942, BSc, Mathematics, Psychology, Physics, 1948, King's College, London; Royal Statistical Society Certificate, 1952; Management Planning and Control Systems, MIT, 1965; Advanced Transportation Management Program, Northwestern University, 1968; Fellow, Chartered Institute of Transport, 1984. Appointments: RAF Radar Branch, 1942-46; Scientific Officer, UK Colonial Office, Gambia, 1948-50; Scientific Officer, Air Ministry, UK, 1950-57; Technical Officer, DND, Canada, 1957-60; Senior Operational Research Analyst, CN, 1960-63; Senior Technical Adviser, Express Department, CN, 1963-69; Co-Chairman, Departmental Task Force, Transport Canada, 1969; Chairman, Transportation Development Agency, Transport Canada, 1970-72; Vice President, 1972-82, R&D, 1972-78, Corporate Affairs, 1978-80, Executive, 1981-82, CN; President, CN Marine, 1979-81; Professor, School of Business Administration, Executive Director, Canadian Marine Transportation Centre, Dalhousie University, 1983-87; Partner, 1983-, Director, 1983-2007, Hickling Corporation; Executive Director, International Institute for Transportation and Ocean Policy Studies, 1987-88; Associate and Director, Oceans Institute of Canada, 1988-96; Chairman, Halifax-Dartmouth Port Development Commission, 1991-96; Commissioner, National Transportation Act Review Commission, 1992-93; Director, CPCS Transcom Inc, 1996-2007. Honours: Award of Merit, Canadian Operational Research Society, 1985; Award of Achievement, National Transportation Week, 1990; Service Award, Canadian Operational Research Society, 1991; Honorary Life Member, Canadian Transportation Research Forum, 1993; Anniversary Award, Mount Saint Vincent University, 2000. Memberships: Canadian Operational Research Society; Canadian Transportation Research Forum; Royal Statistical Society; Chartered Institute of Transport; International Association of Marine Economists. Address: 984 Bellevue Avenue, Halifax, Nova Scotia, B3H 3L7, Canada.

GRAVES Rupert, b. 30 June 1963, Weston-Super-Mare, England. Actor. m. Susie Lewis, 2 children. Career: Theatre: Killing Mr Toad; Sufficient Carbohydrates; Torch Song Trilogy; The Importance of Being Earnest; A Midsummer Night's Dream; Madhouse in Goa; The Elephant Man, 2002; Films: A Room With a View, 1986; Maurice, 1987; A Handful of Dust, 1988; The Children, The Plot to Kill Hitler, 1990; Where Angels Fear to Tread, 1991; Damage, 1992; Royal Celebration, 1993; The Madness of King George, Sheltering Desert, 1994; The Innocent Sleep, 1995; Intimate Relations, Different for Girls, 1996; The Revenger's Comedies, Mrs Dalloway, 1997; Dreaming of Joseph Lees, 1998; Room to Rent, 2000; The Extremists, 2002; Rag Tale, V for Vendetta, 2005; Death at a Funeral, The Waiting Room, Intervention, 2007. TV: Fortunes of War, 1987; Open Fire, Doomsday Gun, 1994; The Tenant of Wildfell Hall, 1996; Blonde Bombshell, Cleopatra, 1999; The Forsyte Saga, 2002; Charles II: The Power and the Passion, 2003; Pride (voice), 2004; Son of the Dragon, 2006; To Be First, Clapham Junction, 2007. Honours: Best Actor, Montreal Film Festival, 1996. Website: www.rupert-graves.com

GRAVITIS Janis, b. 11 February 1948, Aluksne, Latvia. Physical Chemist. m. Daina Barone Gravite, 1 son, 1 daughter. Education: Chemist (certified diploma), University of Latvia, 1970. Appointments: Head, Wood Materials Department, Latvian State Institute of Wood Chemistry, Riga, Latvia, 1993-96; Visiting Professor, Institute of Advanced Studies in the UN University, Tokyo, Japan, 1996-2000; Head, Biomass Eco-Efficient Conversion Laboratory, Latvian State Institute of Wood Chemistry, Riga, Latvia, 2001-. Publications: Lignin Structure and Properties from the Viewpoint of General Disordered Systems Theory, 1992; Global Prospects Substituting Oil by Biomass, 2001; Green Biobased Chemistry Platform for Sustainability, 2006. Honours: First Prize, Latvian Academy of Science, Presidium of Latvian Academy of Science, 1979, 1982, 1984. Memberships: Fellow, International Academy of Wood Science; Member, International Centre for Sustainable Materials, Tokyo, Japan; Member, ACS; Member, Japan Wood Research Society; Member, International Lignin Institute; Member, International Editorial Board, Journal of Environmental Engineering and Landscape Management. Address: Laboratory of Eco-efficient Biomass Conversion, Latvian State Institute of Wood Chemistry, Dzerbenes St 27, Riga, LV1006, Latvia. E-mail: jgravit@edi.lv

GRAY (Edna) Eileen Mary, b. 25 April 1920, United Kingdom. Cyclist. m. Walter Herbert Gray, deceased 2001, 1 son. Education: St Saviour's; St Olave's Grammar School for Girls, London. Appointments: Inspectorate, Fighting Vehicles, 1940-45; Invited to ride abroad, British Women's Cycling Team, 1946; International Delegation, Paris, 1957; Organiser first international competition for women in UK, 1957; Campaigner for international recognition of women in cycling; Team Manager, inaugural women's world championship, 1958; Member, Executive Committee, 1958-87, President, 1976, British Cycling Federation; Elected to Federation International Amateur de Cyclism, 1977; Vice-President, British Olympic Association, 1992-, Vice-Chairman, 1988-92; Chairman, British Sports Forum, 1991; Member, Manchester & Birmingham Olympic Bid Committee, 1991; Deputy Commandant, British Olympic Team, 1992; International Official, Commonwealth Games, Edmonton and Brisbane; Trustee, London Marathon Trust. Councillor, 1982-98, President, Kingston Sport Council, Mayor, 1990-91, Royal Borough of Kingston upon Thames. Honours: Special Gold Award, Ministry of Education, Taiwan; OBE, 1978; Freeman of the City of London, 1987; Olympic Order, International Olympic Committee, 1993; Grandmaster, Hon Fraternity of Ancient Freemasons (women); CBE, 1997. Memberships: Chairman, 1990-2007, President, 2007-, London Youth Games; Vice-President: Cyclists Touring Club, 2000; British School Cycling Association, 2001. Address: 129 Grand Avenue, Surbiton, Surrey KT5 9HY, England.

GRAY Douglas, b. 17 February 1930, Melbourne, Victoria, Australia. Professor of English; Writer. m. 3 September 1959, 1 son. Education: MA, Victoria University of Wellington, New Zealand, 1952; BA, 1956, MA, 1960, Merton College, Oxford. Appointment: J R R Tolkien Professor of English, Oxford, 1980-97, Emeritus, 1997-. Publications: Themes and Images in the Medieval English Religious Lyric, 1972; Robert Henryson, 1979; The Oxford Book of Late Medieval Verse and Prose (editor), 1985; Selected Poems of Robert Henryson and William Dunbar (editor), 1998; The Oxford Companion to Chaucer (editor), 2003. Contributions to: Scholarly journals. Honours: British Academy, fellow, 1989; Honorary LitD, Victoria University of Wellington, 1995. Memberships: Early English Text Society; Society for the Study of Medieval Languages and Literatures, president, 1982-86. Address: Lady Margaret Hall, Oxford OX2 6QA, England.

GRAY Dulcie (Winifred Catherine), CBE, b. 20 November 1919, Kuala Lumper, Malaya. Actress; Dramatist; Writer. m. Michael Denison, 29 April 1939-98, (deceased). Education: England and Malaysia. Appointments: Numerous stage, film, radio, and television appearances. Publications: Murder on the Stairs, 1957; Baby Face, 1959; For Richer, for Richer, 1970; Ride on a Tiger, 1975; Butterflies on My Mind, 1978; Dark Calypso, 1979; The Glanville Women, 1982; Mirror Image, 1987; Looking Forward, Looking Backward (autobiography), 1991; J B Priestley, biography, 2000. Contributions to: Periodicals. Honours: Queen's Silver Jubilee Medal, 1977; Times Educational Supplement Senior Information Book Prize, 1978; Commander of the Order of the British Empire, 1983. Memberships: British Actors Equity; Linnean Society, fellow; Royal Society of Arts, fellow; Society of Authors. Address: Shardeloes, Amersham, Buckinghamshire HP7 0RL, England.

GRAY John Clinton, b. 9 April 1946, Ripon, Yorkshire, England. University Professor. m. Julia Hodgetts, 1 son, 1 daughter. Education: BSc, Biochemistry, 1967, PhD, 1970, University of Birmingham; MA, University of Cambridge, 1977. Appointments: University Research Fellow, University of Birmingham, 1970-73; Research Biochemist, University of California, Los Angeles, 1973-75; Science Research Council Research Fellow, 1975-76, University Demonstrator, 1976-80, University Lecturer, 1980-90, Reader in Plant Molecular Biology, 1990-96, Professor of Plant Molecular Biology, 1996-, Head of Department of Plant Sciences, 2003-, University of Cambridge. Publications: Numerous articles in scientific journals; Ribulose Bisphosphate Carboxylase-Oxygenase (editor with R J Ellis), 1986; Plant Trichomes (editor with D L Hallahan), 2000. Honours: Nuffield Foundation Science Research Fellowship, 1984-85; Royal Society Leverhulme Trust Senior Research Fellowship, 1990-91; European Molecular Biology Organisation Member, 1994; Listed in national and international biographical dictionaries. Membership: Midlands Association of Mountaineers. Address: 47 Barrons Way, Comberton, Cambridge CB3 7EQ, England. E-mail: jcg2@mole.bio.cam.ac.uk

GRAY Thomas Cecil, b. 11 March 1913, Liverpool, England. Retired Professor. m. (1) Marjorie Kathleen Hely, deceased, 1 son, 1 daughter, (2) Pamela Mary Corning, 1

son. Education: MB, ChB, University of Liverpool Medical School, 1937; DA, (RCP & RCS Eng), 1941; MD, 1947. Appointments: General Practice, Liverpool and Wallasey, 1937-41; Consultant Anaesthetist: David Lewis Northern Hospital, Royal Southern Hospital, Liverpool Royal Infirmary, Liverpool Thoracic Surgical Centre at Broadgreen Hospital, Sefton General Hospital, Plastic Surgical Centre at Whiston Hospital, 1941-47; Active Service (invalided out), RAMC, 1942-44; Elected Senior Honorary Consultant Anaesthetist to Royal United Hospital by former RLUVHB, 1946; Part time Demonstrator in Anaesthesia, 1942, 1944-46, Full time Reader and Head of Department of Anaesthesia, 1947-59, Awarded Personal Chair in Anaesthesia, 1959-76, Postgraduate Dean, 1966-70, Dean, 1970-76, Faculty of Medicine, University of Liverpool; Sims Commonwealth Travelling Professor, 1961; Institution of Cecil Gray Prize, Australian and New Zealand College of Anaesthetists, 1961. Publications: Numerous articles in professional journals and proceedings; 4 editorships. Honours: Numerous awards and honours including: Clover Lecturer and Medal, Royal College of Surgeons of England, 1954; Liveryman, Society of Apothecaries, 1956; Sir James Young Simpson Lecture and Gold Medal, Royal College of Surgeons, Edinburgh, Scotland, 1957; Honorary Civilian Consultant in Anaesthetics to the Army at Home, 1960-78; JP (retired), Liverpool, 1966; Henry Hill Hickman Medal, 1972; CBE, 1976; Emeritus Professor, 1976; Awarded George James Guthrie Medal, RAMC, 1977; George James Guthrie Medal, 1977; Honorary Gold Medal, Royal College of Surgeons, England, 1978; Ralph M Waters Medal and Award, 1978; Honorary Fellow, Royal Society of Medicine, London, 1979; O St J, 1979; Emeritus Consultant to the Army, 1979-; Kirkpatrick Lecture and Silver Medal, 1981; John Snow Silver Medal, 1982; Papal Gold Medal, 1982; KCSG, 1982; Freeman, City of London, 1984; Cecil Gray Eponymous Lecture inaugurated by the Tri-Service Anaesthetic Society, 1993-; Magill Gold Medal, 2003; Visiting Professor and Lecturer. Memberships: Liverpool Medical Institution; Association of Anaesthetists of Great Britain and Ireland; Royal Society of Medicine; Order of St John; University of Liverpool Heritage Group; Society of Ancient Brethren; Guild of Catholic Doctors; History of Anaesthesia Society; Liverpool Medical History Society; Liverpool Society of Anaesthetists; Association Medicine Internationale N D de Lourdes; General Medical Council; Merseyside Benevolent Fund; Royal Medical Benevolent Fund; Retired Members Club, Liverpool Medical Institution; Senior Fellows Club, Royal College of Anaesthetists; Twenty Club; The Medical Defence Union; British Medical Association; World Federation of Societies of Anaesthesiologists; Medical Research Council; Liverpool Regional Hospital Board; Merseyside Area Health Authority; Board of Governors, United Liverpool Hospitals; Linacre Centre for the Study of the Ethics of Health Care; Association of Liverpool Medical School. Address: 6 Ravenmeols Lane, Formby, Liverpool, L37 4DF, England.

GRECHISHKIN Vadim Sergeevich, b. 31 October 1933, St Petersburg, Russia. Physicist; Researcher. m. Rufina Vasiljevna Ershova, 1956, 1 daughter. Education: Candidate of Science, Leningrad University, 1960; Dr of Science, Moscow University, 1968. Appointments: Docent, 1960-63, Head of Chair, 1963-72, Perm University; Vice Rector, 1972-75, Head of Chair, 1975-, Dean of Faculty, 1991-94, Kaliningrad University. Publications: Book: Quadrupole Interaction in Solids, 1973; Introduction to Radiofrequency Spectroscopy, Perm, 1969; Nuclear Spin Resonans, 1990; Theory of Waves, 2001; Contributions to over 585 articles to professional journals; 32 patents in field. Honours: Medal of Peking University, 1990; Honoured Scientist of Russia,

1992; Soros Professor, 1994; Medal of Poznan University, 1997; 4 medals of Russia. Memberships: New York Academy of Sciences; Russian Academy of Science and Art; Vice President of RUAN, 2003; President of Baltic RUAN, 2003. Address: Kaliningrad State University, A Nevsky 14, 236041 Kaliningrad, Russia. E-mail: grechishkin@kern.ru

GREEN Bryn(mor) Hugh, b. 14 January 1941, Mountain Ash, South Wales. Academic. m. Jean Armstrong, 1965, 2 sons. Education: Dartford Grammar School; BSc, Botany, 1962, PhD, Plant Ecology, 1965, The University of Nottingham. Appointments: Lecturer, Department of Botany, University of Manchester, 1965-67; Regional Officer for SE England, Nature Conservancy Council, 1967-74; Lecturer and Senior Lecturer, Wye College, 1974-87; Professor and Head of the Environment Sub-Department, Wye College, University of London, 1987-96; Emeritus Professor of Countryside Management, University of London, 1996-. Publications: Countryside Conservation: landscape ecology, planning and management, 1981, 1985, 1996; Co-author, The Diversion of Land: conservation in a period of farming contraction, 1991; The Changing Role of the Common Agricultural Policy: the future of farming in Europe, 1991; Threatened Landscapes: conserving cultural environments, 2001; Numerous chapters in books and papers in scientific journals. Memberships: Vice President, Kent Wildlife Trust; Vice President, Kent and Sussex Farming and Wildlife Advisory Group; Former Countryside Commissioner; England Committee Member, Nature Conservancy Council; Chairman, Landscape Conservation Working Group of IUCN; Chairman, Kent White Cliffs Heritage Coast Countryside Management Project; Deputy Chairman, The Kent Trust for Nature Conservation; Member, Editorial Advisory Boards of Landscape and Urban Planning; Journal of Environmental Planning and The International Journal of Sustainable Development and World Ecology. Honours: OBE, 1995; Churchill Fellow, 1999. Address: Heatherbank, 49 Brockhill Road, Saltwood, Hythe, Kent CT21 4AF, England.

GREEN Charles, Arthur. Educator. m. Carol. Education: BS, Industrial Technology, Central State University, Wilberforce, Ohio, 1957-61; MA, Management and Supervision, Central Michigan University, Mt Pleasant, Michigan, 1973-74; PhD, Education Administration, University of Texas at Austin, 1977-80; Institute for Educational Management, Harvard University, Cambridge, Massachusetts, 1984; American Association of Community and Junior College Presidents Academy, Vail, 1988, Breckenridge, 1994, Colorado. Appointments: United States Army, 1961-76; Professor, Business and Management, American Technological University, Killeen, Texas, 1975-79; Administrative Intern, Odessa College, Texas, 1978; Dean of Continuing Education, Inver Hills Community College, Inver Grove Heights, Minnesota, 1979-81; President, Maricopa Technical Community College, Phoenix, Arizona, 1981-85; President, Rio Salado Community College, Phoenix, 1985-90; Chancellor, Houston Community College System, Houston, Texas, 1990-95; Consultant, Kennedy-King College and the Chicago Public Schools, Chicago, Illinois, 1996-98; Manager, Offsite Programs, Chicago Public Schools, Chicago, 1998-99; Assistant Director, Education-to-Careers Program, Chicago Public Schools, Chicago, 1999-2002; Vice President for Student Services, 2000-02, Interim President, 2002-03, Vice President for Student Services, 2003-04, Olive-Harvey College, Chicago; Retired, 2004; President, Bermuda College, Bermuda, 2004-. Honours: Distinguished Graduate, Community College Leadership Program, University of Texas at Austin, 1988; One of 200 Community College Presidents,

The Transformational Leadership Study – Year 2000, 1989; Inaugural Inductee, Central State University Achievement Hall of Fame, 1989; Distinguished Alumni, National Association for Equal Opportunity in Higher Education, Historically and Predominantly Black Colleges and Universities, 1989; Master Teacher, National Institute for Staff and Organisational Development, University of Texas, 1991; Doctor of Technical Letters, Cincinnati Technical College, 1993; Honorary Professor, Universidad Autonoma de Guadalajara, Mexico, 1993. Memberships: National Association for the Advancement of Colored People; Life Member, Alpha Phi Alpha Fraternity; Life Member, Phi Kappa Phi Honor Society; Member, Prince Hall Masonic Lodge, 33rd Degree; Founding Co-ordinator, Presidents' Round Table, Affiliate of the National Council on Black American Affairs. Address: 3831 S Braeswood Blvd, Houston, TX 77025, USA. E-mail: chagreen@aol.com

GREEN Michael Frederick, b. 2 January 1927, Leicester, England. Writer. Education: BA, Honours, Open University. Publications: The Art of Coarse Rugby, 1960; The Art of Coarse Sailing, 1962; Even Coarser Rugby, 1963; Don't Print my Name Upside Down, 1963; The Art of Coarse Acting, 1964; The Art of Coarse Golf, 1967; The Art of Coarse Moving, 1969 (TV serial, 1977); The Art of Coarse Drinking, 1973; Squire Haggard's Journal, 1976 (TV serial, 1990 and 1992); Four Plays For Coarse Actors, 1978; The Coarse Acting Show Two, 1980; Tonight Josephine, 1981; The Art of Coarse Sex, 1981; Don't Swing from the Balcony Romeo, 1983; The Art of Coarse Office Life, 1985; The Third Great Coarse Acting Show, 1985; The Boy Who Shot Down an Airship, 1988; Nobody Hurt in Small Earthquake, 1990; Coarse Acting Strikes Back, 2000. Memberships: Society of Authors; Equity; National Union of Journalists. Address: 31 Clive Road, Twickenham, Middlesex, TW1 4SQ, England.

GREEN Paul John, b. 27 July 1936, Seattle, Washington, USA. Scholar. Education: BA, Seattle Pacific College, 1957; MA, University of Washington, 1958; MLS, University of California at Berkeley, 1968; PhD, Washington State University, 1981; Further part-time language study, University of Oregon, 2003-05. Appointments: Teaching Assistant, English, University of Washington, 1963-66; Instructor in English, Central Washington University, 1966-67; Research Assistant in Librarianship, University of California, Berkeley, 1967-68; Assistant Serials Librarian, University of Oregon, 1968-69; Teaching Assistant in English, Washington State University, 1974-76; Bibliographic Searching Assistant, Washington State University, 1984-2001. Publications: Contributor of numerous articles, reviews, notes and translations, bibliographies, poems, letters and an abstract; Editor, Student Writing, 1966-67, 1967; Novel: The Life of Jack Gray, (privately printed), 1991, new expanded edition, 2002; Previously unpublished literary reviews, 1997-99, 2001; Previously unpublished literary essays, 1992-2000, 2001; From Russia with Love and a Literary Potpourri, 2003; Collected Writings on the Fiction of Franz Kafka, with a Germanics Supplement, 2003; Eighteenth Century Salad with French and Italian Dressing: Swift-Voltaire, Fielding-Manzoni and Reviews Franco-Italian, and Italian, 2003; On Our Mutual Friend and Other Dickensiana, 2003; The Song of Eugene, with expanded introductory materials and nine Heinrich Heine translated poems, 2004; The Song of Eugene with Translations from the Poetry of Heinrich Heine and René Char, 2006; Studies in European Fiction: Swift-Voltaire, Fielding-Manzoni, Dickens, a Dostoevsky Duo, and Kafka, 2006; In and Against in This, Our Century of the Living Dead (play), 2006; Ye Olde XerOxenford Annuaire (collection of essays), 2006. Honours: Freshman Scholarship,

Seattle Pacific College, 1954-55; Non-resident Tuition Waiver, University of California, Berkeley, 1967-68; Editorial Board Member, Works and Days, 1984-94; Editorial Board Member, Recovering Literature, 1994-2000; Phi Sigma Iota Consultant, Language Pedagogy, China, 1997; Cavalier, World Order of Science, Education and Culture; Legion of Honor, United Cultural Convention. Memberships: MLA; American Comparative Literature Association; Order of International Ambassadors; Academy of American Poets; International Comparative Literature Association; LFIBA; DGABIRA; Life Member, London Diplomatic Academy; Arnold Bennett Hall Society, University of Oregon; Industrial Workers of the World; Sierra Club; People to People International; Oregon Shakespeare Festival; American Civil Liberties Union; Benjamin Ide Wheeler Society, University of California, Berkeley; Henry Suzzallo Society, University of Washington; Bowmer Society, Oregon Shakespeare Festival; American Library Association; Fine Arts Museums, San Francisco; United Nations Association of the USA; Life Member, University of California Alumni Association; Life Member, University of Washington Alumni Association; American Association for the Advancement of Science. Address: 825 Washington St #20, Eugene, OR 97401-2845, USA.

GREEN Philip Nevill, b. 12 May 1953, Walsall, England. Chief Executive. m. Judy Green, 2 daughters. Education: BA (Hons) Economics and Politics, University of Wales; MBA, London Business School. Appointments: Vice-President, Marketing, Crayonne (USA) Inc, 1977-80; Managing Director, Home Furnishing Division, 1980-85, Group Development Director, 1985-89, Group Managing Director, 1989-90, Coloroll Group plc; Regional Director, Northern Europe and Anglophone Africa, 1990-94, Chief Operating Officer, Europe and Asia, 1994-99, DHL Worldwide Network NV/SA; Chief Executive Officer, Trading Solutions Division, 1999-2001, Chief Operating Officer, Reuters Group, 2001-2003, Reuters Group PLC; Chief Executive Officer, Royal P&O Nedlloyd BV, 2003-; Chief Executive, United Utilities plc. Memberships: Advisory Board, London Business School, 2000-; Trustee, Philharmonia Orchestra, London, 2002-; Trustee, Mission Aviation Fellowship, MAF Europe, 2005-06; NED, Lloyds, TSB Plc, 2007-. Address: United Utilities plc, Haweswater House, Lingley Mere Business Park, Great Sankey, Warrington, Cheshire WA5 3LP, England. E-mail: philip.green@uuplc.co.uk

GREEN Timothy (Seton), b. 29 May 1936, Beccles, England. Writer. m. Maureen Snowball, October 1959, 1 daughter. Education: BA, Christ's College, Cambridge, 1957; Graduate Diploma in Journalism, University of Western Ontario, 1958. Appointments: London Correspondent, Horizon, and American Heritage, 1959-62; Life, 1962-64; Editor, Illustrated London News, 1964-66. Publications: The World of God, 1968; The Smugglers, 1969; Restless Spirit, UK edition as The Adventurers, 1970; The Universal Eye, 1972; World of Gold Today, 1973; How to Buy Gold, 1975; The Smuggling Business, 1977; The World of Diamonds, 1981; The New World of Gold, 1982, 2nd edition, 1985; The Prospect for Gold, 1987; The World of Gold, 1993; The Good Water Guide, 1994; New Frontiers in Diamonds: The Mining Revolution, 1996; The Gold Companion, 1997; The Millennium in Gold, 1999; The Millennium in Silver, 1999; The Ages of Gold, 2007. Address: 8 Ponsonby Place, London, SW1P 4PT, England.

GREEN-CREWS Freda Voncille, b. 17 March 1936, Oleustee, Florida, USA. Christian Psychotherapist; Educator; TV Host. m. William R Crews Sr, 1 son, 2 daughters.

Education: MA, Counseling, North American Baptist Seminary, Souix Falls, South Dakota; Doctor of Ministry, Trinity Evangelical/Divinity School, Deerfield, Illinois; PhD, International University for Graduate Studies, St Kitts-Nevis, West Indies. Appointments: Director/Dean of International University for Graduate Studies, School of Christian Counseling and Religious Education; Licensed Professional Counselor; Certified Clinical Mental Health Counselor; Director, Time for Hope Ministries, and Host of Time for Hope TV, internationally syndicated, faith-based mental health TV talk show; Administrator and COO, Bible Study Time Inc, 1974-. Publications: Author, several books and booklets related to mental health and personal and spiritual formation and development; Counseling From the Book of Job, 1980; A Comprehensive Introduction to Lay Counseling, 1983; Get Off Your Own Back: Confront Your Myths With Reality, 1997. Honours: Businesswoman of the Year, National Republican Congressional Committee, 2005; Listed in international biographical dictionaries. Memberships: AACC; ACA; AMHCA; NBCC; SC Counseling Association; SCMHCA. E-mail: drfvc@charter.net Website: www.drfredacrews.com

GREENSTOCK Sir Jeremy Quentin, b. 27 July 1943, Harrow, Middlesex, England. Diplomat. m. Anne Ashford Hodges, 1 son, 2 daughters. Education: Worcester College, Oxford. Appointments: Assistant Master, Eton College, 1966-69; Diplomatic Postings in Lebanon, Dubai, Washington, Saudi Arabia, Paris, 1969-90; Assistant Under Secretary for Western and Southern Europe, 1990-93; Minister, Washington, 1994-95; Political Director, Foreign and Commonwealth Office, 1996-98; UK Permanent Representative at the United Nations, 1998-2003; UK Special Representative for Iraq, 2003-2004; Director, The Ditchley Foundation, 2004-. Honours: CMG, 1991; KCMG, 1998; GCMG, 2003. Membership: Oxford and Cambridge Club. Address: Ditchley Park, Enstone, Chipping Norton, Oxon OX7 4ER, England. E-mail: director@ditchley.co.uk

GREENWOOD Duncan Joseph, b. 16 October 1932, New Barnet, Hertfordshire, England. Research Scientist. Education: Hutton Grammar School; BSc, Liverpool University, 1954; PhD, 1957, DSc, 1972, Aberdeen University. Appointments: Research Fellow, Aberdeen University, 1957-59; Research Leader, National Vegetable Research Station, 1959-66; Head of Soils and Crop Nutrition, Horticultural Research International (formerly National Vegetable Research Station), 1966-92; Emeritus Research Fellow, 1992-2004; Associate Fellow, Warwick University, Warwick HRI, 2004-; Visiting Professor, Leeds University, 1985-93; Honorary Professor, Birmingham University, 1986-93. Publications: 180 scientific publications mostly on soil science, plant nutrition and agronomy. Honours: Sir Gilbert Morgan Medal, Society of Chemical Industry, 1962; Research Medal, Royal Agricultural Society of England, 1979; President's Medal, Institute of Horticulture, 2004; President, International Committee, Plant Nutrition, 1978-82; Elected FRS, 1985; Individual Merit Promotion DCSO (UG5), 1986; President, British Society of Soil Science, 1991-92; CBE, 1993; Inaugural Lifetime Achievement Award, Grower of the Year, 2000; Honorary Life Member, Association of Applied Biologists, 2004; Named Lectures; Blackman, Oxford, 1982; Distinguished Scholars, Belfast, 1982; Hannaford, Adelaide, 1985; Shell, Kent, 1988; Amos, Wye, 1989. Memberships: Elected FRCS, 1977; F.Inst.Hort, 1986; FRS, 1985; British Society of Soil Science; Society of Chemical Industry. Address: 23 Shelley Road, Stratford-upon-Avon CV37 7JR, England.

GREENWOOD Norman Neill, b. 19 January 1925, Melbourne, Australia. Emeritus Professor of Chemistry. m. Kirsten Rydland, 3 daughters. Education: BSc, 1st Class, 1946, MSc, 1st Class, 1948, DSc, 1966, University of Melbourne, Australia; PhD, 1951, ScD, 1961, Cambridge University. Appointments: Laboratory Cadet, CSIR(O), Melbourne, 1942-46; Resident Tutor and Lecturer in Chemistry, Trinity College, Melbourne, 1946-48; Exhibition of 1851 Overseas Scholar, 1948-51; Senior Harwell Research Fellow, Atomic Energy Research Establishment, Harwell, 1951-53; Lecturer, then Senior Lecturer, Inorganic Chemistry, University of Nottingham, 1953-61; Professor and Head of Department of Inorganic Chemistry, University of Newcastle upon Tyne, 1961-71; Professor and Head of Department of Inorganic and Structural Chemistry, 1971-90, Head of the School of Chemistry, 1971-74, 1983-86, Dean of the Faculty of Science, 1986-88, Emeritus Professor of Chemistry, 1990-, University of Leeds; Numerous visiting professorships, 1966-93. Publications: Some 480 research papers and reviews; 10 books. Honours include: Tilden Lectureship and Medal, Chemical Society, London, 1966; Main Group Element Chemistry Award and Medal, 1974, Liversidge Lectureship and Medal, 1984, Ludwig Mond Lectureship and Medal, 1991, Tertiary Education Award and Medal, 1993, Royal Society of Chemistry; A W von Hofmann, Lectureship, Gesellschaft Deutscher Chemiker, 1983; Foreign Member, l'Académie des Sciences, Institut de France, 1992; Fellow of the Royal Society, 1987; Royal Society Humphry Davy Lectureship, 2000; D de l'Université, honoris causa, Université de Nancy I, France, 1997; Gold Medal and Honorary Citizenship of the City of Nancy, France, 1977; DSc, honoris causa, Toho University, Tokyo, Japan, 2000. Memberships: FRSC; MRI; FRS. Address: University of Leeds School of Chemistry, Leeds, LS2 9JT, England.

GREER Germaine, b. 29 January 1939, Melbourne, Victoria, Australia. Writer; Broadcaster. Education: BA, Honours, Melbourne University, 1959; MA, Honours, Sydney University, 1962; PhD, Cambridge University, 1967. Appointments: Senior English Tutor, Sydney University, 1963-64; Assistant Lecturer and Lecturer, English, University of Warwick, 1967-72; Broadcaster, journalist, columnist and reviewer, 1972-; Lecturer, American Program Bureau, 1973-78; Visiting Professor, Graduate Faculty of Modern Letters, 1979, Professor of Modern Letters, 1980-83, University of Tulsa; Founder-Director, Tulsa Centre for Studies in Women's Literature, 1981; Proprietor, Stump Cross Books, 1988-; Special Lecturer and Unofficial Fellow, Newnham College, Cambridge, 1989-98. Publications: The Female Eunuch, 1969; The Obstacle Race: The Fortunes of Women Painters and Their Work, 1979; Sex and Destiny: The Politics of Human Fertility, 1984; Shakespeare (editor), 1986; The Madwoman's Underclothes (selected journalism), 1986; Daddy, We Hardly Knew You, 1989; The Change: Women, Ageing and the Menopause, 1991; Slip-Shod Sybils: Recognition, Rejection and the Woman Poet, 1995; The Whole Woman, 1999. Editor: The Uncollected Verse of Aphra Behn, 1989. Co-Editor: Kissing the Rod: An Anthology of Seventeenth Century Verse, 1988; Surviving Works of Anne Wharton (co-editor), 1997; The Whole Woman, 1999; John Wilmot, Earl of Rochester, 1999; 101 Poems by 101 Women (editor), 2001; The Boy, 2003; Poems for Gardeners (editor), 2003; Whitefella Jump Up, 2004. Contributions to: Numerous articles in Listener, Spectator, Esquire, Harper's Magazine, Playboy, Private Eye and other journals. Honours: Scholarships, 1952, 1956; Commonwealth Scholarship, 1964;

J R Ackerly Prize and Premio Internazionale Mondello, 1989. Address: c/o Aitken and Stone Associates Ltd, 29 Fernshaw Road, London SW10 0TG, England.

GREIG Geordie, b. 16 December 1960. Editor. m. Kathryn, 1 son, 2 daughters. Education: Eton College; MA English, Lang & Lit, St Peter's College, Oxford University. Appointments: Reporter, South-East London & Kentish Mercury 1981-83; Daily Mail, 1984-85; Today, 1985-87; Reporter, Sunday Times, 1987-89; Arts Correspondent, 1989-91; NY Correspondent, 1991-95; Literary Editor, 1995-99; Editor, Tatler, 1999-. Publications: Louis and the Prince, 1999. Memberships: Fellow of the Royal Society of Arts.

GRENVILLE Hugo, b. 5 August 1958, London, England. Painter. m. Sophia, 2 sons. Education: Life Classes, Chelsea School of Art, 1978; Open Studio, Heatherley's School of Art, 1988-89. Career: H M Armed Forces, Coldstream Guards, served in Northern Ireland, Rhodesia, UK, West Africa, Germany and NATO HQ, 1977-83; J Walter Thompson Advertising Agency, 1983-84; Founder and Director of company dealing in contemporary art, 1984-89; Became full-time painter, 1989; Visiting Tutor to the Gorhambury Art Group as well as teaching one day a week from London Studio, 1990-94; Course Director of Red House Studios, 2001-2006; Group Exhibitions include: The Chelsea Art Society, 1975, 1993; The Arts Club, London, 1990; Royal Institute of Oil Painters, 1991, 1993, 1996; Royal Institute of Painters in Watercolours, 1992; The Burlington Gallery, London, 1993; Royal Society of British Artists, 1996, 1997, 1998; Fosse Gallery Summer Exhibition, 1998, 1999, 2000; The Tresco Gallery, Tresco, 2002; Summer Exhibition Fraser Fine Art, San Francisco, USA, 2005; Summer Exhibition, Richmond Hill Gallery, 2005; One-Man Shows: New King's Road Gallery, London, 1991; The Newbury Museum, featured artist of the Newbury Festival, 1992; Smith's Gallery, London, 1992; Oliver Swann Galleries, London, 1994; Tryon & Swann Gallery, London, 1995; China Club, Hong Kong, 1995; David Messum Gallery, London, 1997, 1999, 2000, 2001, 2003, 2004, 2005; Wally Findlay Gallery, New York, 2006-2007; Wally Findlay Galleries, Palm Beach, 2007-. Works in collections in UK, USA, Canada, France, Hong Kong and Australia include: Edinburgh City Council; The Worshipful Company of Ironmongers; The Ministry of Defence, The China Club, Hong Kong, The Tresco Estate; The Late Duke of Devonshire. Publications: Songs of Light: Illustrations to Philip Wells' poems, 2006; Regular contributor to The Artist and The Literary Review. Membership: The Chelsea Arts Club. Address: 157 Mount View Road, London, N4 4JT, England. E-mail: hugo@hugogrenville.com Website: www.hugogrenville.com

GRESSER Sy, b. 9 May 1926, Baltimore, Maryland, USA. Stone Sculptor; Writer; Poet. 5 sons, 1 daughter. Education: BS, 1949, MA, 1972, Zoological Sciences, English and American Literature, University of Maryland; Institute of Contemporary Arts, Washington, DC, 1949-50. Appointments: Publications Consultant for various firms, 1960-; Teacher, 1965-70; Private Students. Publications: Stone Elegies, 1955; Coming of the Atom, 1957; Poems From Mexico, 1964; Voyages, 1969; A Garland for Stephen, 1971; A Departure for Sons, 1973; Fragments and Others, 1982; Hagar and Her Elders, 1989; Stone, Wood and Words, 2006. Contributions to: Poetry Quarterly; Stand; Antioch Review; Western Humanities Review; Johns Hopkins Review; Atavist Magazine; New York Times Book Review. Address: 1015 Ruatan Street, Silver Spring, MD 20903, USA.

GRETZKY Wayne, b. 26 January 1961, Brantford, Canada. Ice Hockey Player. m. Janet Jones, 1988, 2 sons, 1 daughter. Career: Former player with Edmonton; Played with Los Angeles Kings, 1988-96, St Louis Blues, 1996, New York Rangers, 1996-99; Retired, 1999; Director Canadian National Men's Hockey Team, 2002. Part-owner Phoenix Coyotes, 2000; Head Coach Peoenix Coyotes, 2005-. Most prolific scorer in National Hockey League history; Most Valuable Player (9 times). Publication: Gretzky: An Autobiography (with Rick Reilly). Honour: Hockey Hall of Fame, 1999. Address: New York Rangers, Madison Square Garden, 2 Pennsylvania Plaza, New York, NY 10121, USA.

GREY-THOMPSON Dame Tanni (Carys Davina), b. 26 July 1969, Cardiff, Wales. Athlete. m. Ian Thompson, 1999, 1 daughter. Education: Loughborough University of Technology. Career: Bronze Medal, 400m wheelchair races, Seoul Paralympics, 1988; Gold Medals, 100m, 200m, 400m and 800m wheelchair races, Barcelona Paralympics, 1992; Gold Medal, 800m, Silver Medals for 100m, 200m and 400m wheelchair races, Atlanta Paralympics, 1996; Gold Medals, 100m, 200m, 400m and 800m wheelchair races, Sydney Paralympics, 2000; Gold Medals, 100m and 400m wheelchair races, Athens Paralympics, 2004; Gold Medals, women's wheelchair race, London Marathon, 1992, 1994, 1996, 1998, 2001, 2002, Bronze Medal, 1993, Silver Medals, 1997, 1999, 2000, 2003; 3 Gold Medals and 1 Silver Medal, European Championships, 2003; Broke over 20 world records; Development Officer, UK Athletics, 1996-2001; TV and radio presenter, conference and motivational speaker, numerous guest appearances; President, Welsh Association of Cricketers with a Disability; Vice-president, Women's Sports Foundation, South Wales Region of Riding for the Disabled, Get Kids Going; Deputy Chair, UK Lottery Awards Panel (Sport). Publications: Seize the Day: My Autobiography, 2001; Articles in popular press. Honours: Hon Fellow: University of Wales College, Cardiff, 1997; University of Wales Institute, Cardiff, 2001; University of Swansea, 2001; College of Ripon and York St John, 2001; Institute of Leisure and Amenity, Manchester, 2001; University of Wales College, Newport, 2003; Freeman, City of Cardiff, 2003; Hon DUniv (Staffordshire) 1998, (Southampton) 1998; Hon LLD (Exeter) 2003; Dr hc (Surrey) 2000, (Leeds Metropolitan) 2001, (Wales) 2002, (Loughborough) 2002, (Heriot-Watt) 2004; Hon Masters degree (Loughborough) 1994, (Teeside) 2001; Hon MSc (Manchester Metropolitan) 1998; BBC Wales Sports Personality of the Year; Sunday Times Sportswoman of the Year 1992, 2000, (3rd place) 2004; Royal Mail Best Female Performance of the Paralympic Games, 1992; Panasonic Special Award, 1992; Variety Club Disabled Sportwoman of the Year, 1992; Welsh Sports Hall of Fame, 1993; Sports Writers' Association Female Disabled Athlete of the Year, 1994; Sporting Ambassador, 1998; Sportswriters Award, 2000; 3rd place, BBC Sports Personality of the Year, 2000; Helen Rollason Award for Inspiration, BBC Sports Personality of the Year, 2000; Helen Rollason Award, Sunday Times Sports Woman of the Year, 2000; Welsh Woman of the Year, 2001; Pride of Britain Special Award, 2001; UK Sporting Hero, Sport UK, 2001; Chancellor's Medal, University of Glamorgan, 2001; Appears in 50 British Sporting Greats, 2002; Walpole Best British Sporting Achievement Award, 2002; Commonwealth Games Sports Award for Best Female Disabled Athlete, 2002; 3rd Greatest Briton of all time; 47th, 100 Greatest Sporting Moments, 2002; BBC Ouch disability website, 2003; UK Sport Fair Play Award, 2004; Sports Journalist UK Sport Award, 2004; Numerous appearances on radio and TV. Memberships: The Sports Council for Wales's National Excellence Panel; Sports Council for Wales

Sportlot Panel; Minister of Sport Implementation Group for the Development of Sport; Welsh Hall of Fame Roll of Honour, 1992-; English Sports Council Lottery Awards Panel, 1995-99; Sports Council for Wales, 1996-2002, for UK Sport, 1998-2003; National Disability Council, 1997-2000; Manchester Commonwealth Games Organising Council Association, 2002; Member Elect, 2001, Member, 2002-, Laureus World Sports Academy; Patron: British Sports Leaders; British Sport Trust; Durham Sport Millennium Youth Games; Regain; Youth Sport Trust; The National Sports Medicine Institute of the United Kingdom; Shelter Cymru; 2003 London Marathon; Lady Taverners; The National Blood Service; Vice-patron, The Helen Rollason Cancer Care Appeal; The Jubilee Sailing Trust, 2002-. Address: c/o Helen Williams, Creating Excellence, Equity House, 1st Floor, Knight Street, South Woodham Ferrers, Chelmsford, Essex CM3 5ZL, England. Website: www.creatingexcellence.co.uk

GRIEVES John Kerr, b. 7 November 1935, England. Business Consultant. m. Ann, 1 son, 1 daughter. Education: MA, Keble College, Oxford, 1955-58; Harvard Business School, USA, 1979. Appointments: Joined, 1963, Partner, 1964-74, Departmental Managing Partner, Company Department, 1974-78, Managing Partner, 1979-85, Head of Corporate Finance Group, 1985-89, Senior Partner, 1990-96, Freshfields; Subsequently Non-Executive Director: Northern Electric, Enterprise Oil, Hillsdown Holdings, First Leisure Corporation plc (Chairman), New Look Group plc, (Chairman), Esporta plc (Chairman). Membership: The Athenaeum. Address: 7 Putney Park Avenue, London SW15 5QN, England.

GRIFFIN James Patrick, b. 8 July 1933, Wallingford, Connecticut, USA. White's Emeritus Professor of Moral Philosophy. m. Catherine Maulde Von Halban, deceased, 1 son, 1 daughter. Education: BA, Yale University, USA, 1955; D Phil, 1960, MA, 1963, University of Oxford, England. Appointments: Tutorial Lecturer, Christ Church, Oxford, 1960-66; Lecturer in Philosophy, University of Oxford, 1964-90; Fellow and Tutor in Philosophy, Keble College, University of Oxford, 1966-96; Reader in Philosophy, 1990-96, White's Professor of Moral Philosophy, 1996-2000, University of Oxford; Fellow, 1996-2000, Emeritus Fellow, 2000-, Corpus Christi College, Oxford; Adjunct Professor, Centre for Applied Philosophy and Public Ethics, Canberra, Australia, 2002-; Distinguished Visiting Professor, Rutgers University, USA, 2002-. Publications: Books: Wittgenstein's Logical Atomism, 1964; Well-Being, 1986; Value Judgement, 1996; Values, Conflict and the Environment (with others), 1996. Honours: Medal, National Education Commission, Poland; Order of Diego de Lusada Venezuela; Doctor, honoris causa, University of Santiago de Compostela, Spain. Memberships: Brooks's; Oxford and Cambridge Club; Honorary Fellow, Keble College, Oxford, 2002-. Address: 10 Northmoor Road, Oxford OX2 6UP, England.

GRIFFITH Melanie, b. 9 August 1957, New York, USA. Actress. m. (1) Don Johnson, 1975, divorced 1976, remarried 1989, divorced 1993, 1 daughter, (2) Steve Bauer, divorced, 1 daughter (3) Antonio Banderas, 1996, 1 daughter. Education: Hollywood Professional School. Career: Films include: Night Moves, 1975; One On One, 1977; Roar, Body Double, 1984; Stormy Monday, 1987; Working Girl, 1988; Bonfire of the Vanities, 1991; Close to Eden, 1993; Nobody's Fool, 1994; Mulholland Falls, 1996; Lolita, 1996; Shadow of Doubt, 1998; Celebrity, 1998; Another Day in Paradise, 1998; Crazy in Alabama, 1999; Cecil B. Demented, 2000; Forever Lulu, 2000; Life with Big Cats, 2000; Tart, 2001; Stuart Little 2

(voice), 2002; The Night We Called It a Day, 2003; Shade, 2003; Tempo, 2003; Have Mercy, 2006; TV Includes: Once an Eagle (mini-series); Carter Country (series); Steel Cowboy; She's in the Army Now; Heartless; Twins. Address: Creative Artists Agency, 9830 Wilshire Boulevard, Beverly Hills, CA 90212, USA.

GRIGGS Ian Macdonald, b. 17 May 1928, Essex, England. Church of England Priest. m. Patricia Margaret Vernon-Browne, 3 sons, 1 deceased, 3 daughters. Education: MA, Trinity Hall, Cambridge, 1949-52; Westcott House, Cambridge, 1952-54. Appointments: Curate of St Cuthbert, Portsmouth, 1954-59; Domestic Chaplain to Bishop of Sheffield (half-time), Diocesan Youth Chaplain (half-time), 1959-64; Vicar of St Cuthbert, Fir Vale, Sheffield, 1964-71; Vicar of Kidderminster, Honorary Canon of Worcester, 1971-83; Archdeacon of Ludlow, 1983-87; Bishop of Ludlow, Diocese of Hereford, 1987-94; Honorary Assistant Bishop, Diocese of Carlisle, 1994-. Memberships: Governor, Atlantic College, 1990-2004; Chairman, Churches Council for Health and Healing, 1990-99; Member, Patterdale Mountain Rescue Team, 1996-. Address: Rookings, Patterdale, Cumbria CA11 0NP, England.

GRIGORYAN Karen Kevin, b. 18 August 1965, Armenia, Yerevan. Economist; Attorney at International Law. m. Sona Arustamyan, 3 sons, 1 daughter. Education: Master Degree, Economics, 1988, Master Degree, International Attorney at Law, 1992, Armenian State University; PhD, Free Market Economy, 1995. Appointments: Adviser to Armenian President, 1987; Adviser to Armenian Armeconobank, 1988; Economic Adviser to Academy of Science of Armenia, 1995; Professor, Armenian State University, 1996; Economist, GK Consulting, 1998. Publications: Listed in international biographical dictionaries. Honours: Republican Senatorial American Spirit Award, 2006 and 2007; Patriot of the Year, 2006 and 2007; Congressional Order of Merit, 2006 and 2007. Memberships: US Presidential Club; National Republican Congressional Committee; Republican Senatorial Inner Circle; Republican Presidential Task Force; Citizen United; Ronald Regan Presidential Foundation; George Bush Senior Presidential Foundation. Address: 211 S State College Blvd, Suite #190, Anaheim, CA 92806, USA. E-mail: gkconsultingusa@aol.com Website: www.mrkarengrigorian.gop.com

GRIMES Diane, b. 18 March 1960, Philadelphia, USA. Professor. m. Ken Grimes, 3 sons, 1 daughter. Education: BS, 1983, Graphic Design Certification, 2002, Moore College of Art; MA, The University of the Arts, 1994; MFA, Marywood University, 2003-05. Appointments: Art Director, YMCA Camp Ockanickon, Medford, 1995-96; Instructor, University of the Arts, 1996; Instructor, Jewish Community Center, 1996; Art Instructor, Perkins Center for the Arts, 1995-96; Adjunct Art Professor, Camden County College, 1994-96; Art Lecturer, Burlington County College, 1994-2000; Adjunct Art Professor, Farleigh Dickenson University, 2003; Adjunct Art Professor, Richard Stockton College, 2003-04; Co-ordinator, Fine and Graphic Design Programs, Assistant Professor, Cumberland County College, 2000-05; Chair, Art Department, Fine Arts and Graphic Design, Immaculata University, 2005-. Publications: Numerous articles in professional journals. Honours: Dr Albert N Lalli Memorial Award, 1985; Samuel S Fleshier Art Memorial, 1986; Meyer E Maurer Award, 1986; Graduate Scholarship, University of the Arts, 1994; Merion Reproduction Co Award, PAFA Fellowship, 1994; American College of Sculpture Award, 1995; Permanent Collection/ Purchase Award, Pennsylvania Academy of Fine Arts, 1997; Maxim B Gottlieb Memorial, 1997; Listed in international biographical dictionaries. Memberships: CAA. Address: 52 Neeta Trail, Medford Lakes, NJ 08055, USA. E-mail: dgrimes@immaculata.edu

GRIMSBY Bishop of, The Rt Rev David Douglas James Rossdale, b. 22 May 1953, London, England. Bishop. m. Karen, 2 sons. Education: Westminster College, Oxford; Roehampton Institute. Appointments: Curate of Upminster, 1981-86; Vicar of St Luke's Moulsham, 1986-90; Vicar of Cookham, 1990-2000; Area Dean of Maidenhead, 1994-2000; Honorary Canon, Christ Church, Oxford, 1990-2000; Canon and Prebendary, Lincoln Cathedral, 2000-; Suffragan Bishop of Grimsby, 2000-. Honours: Diploma in Applied Theology, 1990; MA in Applied Theology, 1991; MSc, Management of Ministry, 2001. Memberships: Chairman of the Board of Education for the Diocese of Lincoln; Commissioner on the Churches Regional Commission for Yorkshire and the Humber Region; Governor, Wellington College, 2004-. Address: Bishop's House, Church Lane, Irby, Grimsby, North East Lincolnshire DN37 7JR, England. E-mail: rossdale@btinternet.com

GRINDE Kjell, b. 1 August 1929, Bergen, Norway. Civil and Structural Engineer. m. (1) Heidi, divorced, 1 son, 1 daughter, (2) Anneliv, 2 step-daughters. Education: BSc, 1954, MSc, 1956, Technical University of Norway; Diploma, Total Quality Management, Lausanne, Switzerland. Appointments: Scientific Assistant to Professor, Technical University of Norway, 1954-56; Site Engineer, Snowy Mountains Hydro-Electric Authority, Australia, 1956-58; Site Engineer, Norconsult Ethiopia, Koka Power Plant, 1958-60; Site Engineer, Assab Harbour and Water Supply, 1960-62; Chief Engineer and Resident Manager, Norconsult Nigeria, 1962-64; Marketing Director, 1964-68, Managing Director, 1968-81, Norconsult International, Oslo; Projects for World Bank, UN Agencies, Regional Banks, Developing Countries' Governments; Saga Petroleum, Oslo; Corporate Management Technical Director, projects in North Sea, Benin, Caribia, USA, 1981-91; Working Chairman, Senior Expert Group, 1991-. Publications: Professional articles; Conference papers. Honours: Honours Award for Technical Assistance to Developing Countries, Norwegian Natural Sciences Research Council, 1976. Memberships: Director, President, Federation International des Ingenieurs Conseil, 1973-80; Chairman of the Board, Norwegian Petroleum Consultants, 1975-80; Member, Executive Committee Royal Polytechnical Society, 1979-84; Director, Norwegian Export Council, 1975-80; Elected Member, The Norwegian Academy of Technological Sciences, 1976-; Chairman, Drammen Technical Society, 1996-2004. Address: Hanna Winsnesgate 1, 3014 Drammen, Norway. E-mail: annh-gr@online.no

GRISEZ Germain, b. 30 September 1929, University Heights, Ohio, USA. Professor of Christian Ethics; Writer. m. Jeannette Selby, 9 June 1951, 4 sons. Education: BA, John Carroll University, University Heights, Ohio, 1951; MA and PhL, Dominican College of St Thomas Aquinas, River Forest, Illinois, 1951; PhD, University of Chicago, 1959. Appointments: Assistant Professor to Professor, Georgetown University, 1957-72; Lecturer in Medieval Philosophy, University of Virginia at Charlottesville, 1961-62; Special Assistant to Patrick Cardinal O'Boyle, Archbishop of Washington, DC, 1968-69; Consultant, Archdiocese of Washington, DC, 1969-72; Professor of Philosophy, Campion College, University of Regina, Saskatchewan, Canada, 1972-79; Archbishop Harry J Flynn Professor of Christian Ethics, Mount Saint Mary's College, Emmitsburg, Maryland, 1979-. Publications: Contraception and the Natural Law, 1964;

Abortion: The Myths, the Realities, and the Arguments, 1970; Beyond the New Morality: The Responsibilities of Freedom (with Russell Shaw), 1974, 3rd edition, 1988; Beyond the New Theism: A Philosophy of Religion, 1975; Free Choice: A Self-Referential Argument (with Joseph M Boyle Jr and Olaf Tollefsen), 1976; Life and Death with Liberty and Justice: A Contribution to the Euthanasia Debate (with Joseph M Boyle Jr), 1979; The Way of the Lord Jesus, Vol I, Christian Moral Principles (with others), 1983, Vol II, Living a Christian Life (with others), 1993, Vol III, Difficult Moral Questions (with others), 1997; Nuclear Deterrence, Morality and Realism (with John Finnis and Joseph M Boyle Jr), 1987; Fulfilment in Christ: A Summary of Christian Moral Principles (with Russell Shaw), 1991; Personal Vocation: God Calls Everyone by Name (with Russell Shaw), 2003. Contributions to: Many scholarly journals. Honours: Pro ecclesia et pontifice Medal, 1972; Special Award for Scholarly Work, 1981, Cardinal Wright Award for Service to the Church, 1983, Fellowship of Catholic Scholars; Various other fellowships and grants. Memberships: American Catholic Philosophical Association, president, 1983-84; Catholic Theological Society of America. Address: Mount Saint Mary's College, Emmitsburg, MD 21727, USA.

GRISHAM John, b. 8 February 1955, Jonesboro, Arkansas, USA. Author; Lawyer. m. Renée Grisham, 1 son, 1 daughter. Education: Mississippi State University; University of Mississippi Law School. Appointment: Ran one-man criminal defence practice in Southaven, Mississippi, 1981-90. Publications: The Pelican Brief; A Time to Kill; Stand in Line at a Super Crown; The Firm; The Client; The Chamber; The Rainmaker; The Runaway Jury; The Partner; The Street Lawyer; The Testament; The Brethren; A Painted House, 2001; Skipping Christmas, 2001; The Summons, 2002; The King of Torts, 2003; Bleachers, 2003; The Last Juror, 2004; The Broker, 2005; The Innocent Man, 2006; Playing For Pizza, 2007. Address: Doubleday & Co Inc, 1540 Broadway, New York, NY 10036, USA.

GROENING Matthew, b. 15 February 1954, Portland, Oregon, USA. Writer; Cartoonist. m. Deborah Lee Caplan (divorced), 2 children. Education: Evergreen State College. Appointments: Cartoonist, Life in Hell syndicated weekly comic strip, Sheridan, Oregon, 1980-; President, Matt Groening Productions Inc, Los Angeles, 1988-; Bongo Entertainment Inc, Los Angeles, 1993-; Creator, The Simpsons interludes, The Tracey Ullman Show, 1987-89; Creator, Executive Producer, The Simpsons TV show, 1989-; Founder and Publisher, Bongo Comics Group; Founder and Publisher, Zongo Comics, including Jimbo, 1995, Fleener, 1996. Publications: Love is Hell, 1985; Work is Hell, 1986; School is Hell, 1987; Childhood is Hell, 1988; Akbar and Jeff's Guide to Life, Greetings From Hell, 1989; The Postcards That Ate My Brain, The Big Book of Hell, The Simpsons Xmas Book, Greetings From the Simpsons, 1990; With Love From Hell, The Simpsons' Rainy Day Fun Book, The Simpsons' Uncensored Family Album, The Alphabet Book, Maggie Simpson's Counting Book, Maggie Simpson's Book of Colors and Shapes, Maggie Simpson's Book of Animals, 1991; The Road to Hell, The Simpson's Fun in Sun Book, Making Faces with the Simpsons, 1992; Bart Simpson's Guide to Life, The Simpsons Ultra-Jumbo Rain-Or-Shine Fun Book, 1993; Binky's Guide to Love, Love is Hell 10th Anniversary Edition, Simpsons Comics Extravaganza, Simpsons Comic Spectacular, Bartman: The Best of the Best, 1994; Simpson Comics Simps-O-Rama, Simpsons Comics Strike Back, 1995; Simpsons Comics Wing Ding, The Huge Book of Hell, 1997; Bongo Comics.

GROSSMAN Margaret Rosso, b. 17 October 1947, Illinois, USA. Professor. m. Michael, 2 sons. Education: BMus, highest honours, University of Illinois, 1969; AM, Stanford University, 1970; PhD, Musicology, 1977, JD, summa cum laude, 1979, University of Illinois. Appointments: Bock Chair and Professor, Agricultural Law, Department of Agricultural and Consumer Economics, University of Illinois at Urbana-Champaign; Frequent Visiting Professor, Wageningen University, The Netherlands. Publications: Numerous law review articles, book chapters, books. Honours: Fulbright Research Fellow (3 awards); German Marshall Fund Research Fellow; Distinguished Service Award, American Agricultural Law Association, 1993; Silver Medal, European Council for Agricultural Law, 1999; Professional Scholarship Award, American Agricultural Law Association, 2006. Memberships: American Agricultural Law Association; American Veterinary Medical Law Association; European Council for Agricultural Law; Dutch Society for Agrarian Law; Unione Mondiale degli Agraristi Universitari; European Union Studies Association. Address: 333 Mumford Hall, 1301 W Gregory Dr, Urbana, IL 61801, USA.

GROSSMANN Friedrich Karl Wilhelm, b. 16 March 1927, Stuttgart, Germany. Phytopathology Educator; Researcher. m. Hannelore Müller, 1955, 2 sons. Education: Diplom-Landwirt, 1950, DrAgr, 1953, University of Hohenheim in Stuttgart. Appointments: Served with the German Air Force 1944-45; Scientific Assistant, University of Göttingen; Ordinary Professor, 1963-70, Dean, Faculty of Agriculture, University of Giessen; Professor of Phytopathology and Plant Protection, 1970-90, Dean, Faculty of Agricultural Sciences I, 1979-81, University of Hohenheim; Retired, 1990. Publications: More than 150 articles in scientific journals and handbooks; Editor, Zeitschrift für Pflanzenkrankheiten und Pflanzenschutz, 1973-88. Honours: Dr-Fritz-Merck-Preis, 1963; Adventurers in Agricultural Science award of distinction, Washington, 1979; Bundesverdienstkreuz (Order of Merit of the Federal Republic), President of the Federal Republic of Germany, 1990; Otto-Appel-Denkmünze Foundation grantee, 1990; Anton-de-Bary Medal, Deutsche Phytomedizinische Gesellschaft, 1997. Memberships: Honorary Member, Deutsche Phytomedizinische Gesellschaft; American Phytopathological Society; Deutsche Botanische Gesellschaft; International Society for Plant Pathology (President, 1978-83). Address: Tiefer Weg 63, 70599 Stuttgart, Germany.

GROVES Paul Raymond, b. 28 July 1947, Gloucester, England. m. Annette Rushton Kelsall, 1 June 1972, 2 daughters. Education: Teaching Certificate, Caerleon College of Education, 1969. Appointments: Assistant Master in various state schools; evening class lecturer in Creative Writing; visiting poet in schools, Poetry Society. Publications: Poetry Introduction 3, 1975; Green Horse, 1978; Academe, 1988; The Bright Field, 1991; Ménage à Trois, 1995; Eros and Thanatos, 1999; Wowsers, 2002. Honours: Eric Gregory Award, 1976. 1st Prizes: The Times Literary Supplement/ Cheltenham Festival, 1986; Green Book, 1986; Yeats Club, 1987; Surrey Poetry Group, 1987, 1988, 1991; Charterhouse International, 1989, 1990; Rainforest Trust, 1991; Orbis International, 1992; Bournemouth Festival, 1994; Cotswold Writers, 1995; Wilkins Memorial, 1997. Address: 4 Cornford Close, Osbaston, Monmouth NP25 3NT, Wales.

GROVES Philip Denys Baker, b. 9 January 1928, Watford, Hertfordshire, England. Architect. m. Yvonne Joyce Chapman, 2 sons, 1 daughter. Education: Watford Grammar School, 1939-44; Regent Street Polytechnic School of Architecture, 1948-55. Appointments: RAF, 1945-48: Served in UK,

Palestine, Egypt; Architects Co-Partnership: Joined 1955, Partner, 1965, Chairman, 1983-95; Architect for education and health projects, UK, Middle East, Far East and Caribbean; Royal Institute of British Architects; Member of Council, 1962-81, Vice President, 1972-75, 1978-80, Chairman, Board of Education, 1974-75, 1979-80; ARCUK Council, 1962-80; Chairman, 1971-74; Chairman, University of York Centre for Continuing Education, 1978-81; Chairman, CPD in Construction Gp, 1990-96; Construction Industry Council, 1993-96; Comité de Liaison des Architects du Marché Commun, 1986-92; Examiner at Schools of Architecture UK and overseas; Chairman, HCCI, 1985-88; President, 1989, Herts Community Foundation; Chairman, 1988-97, Vice President, 1998-; Chairman, Herts TEC, 1992-97; Business Link Herts, 1993-2003, TEC National Council, 1996-99. Publications: Design for Health Care (jointly); Hospitals and Health Care Facilities (jointly); Various articles in professional journals. Honours: Associate, 1955, Fellow, 1968, Royal Institute of British Architects; FRSA, 1989; Deputy Lieutenant of Hertfordshire, 1988-. Memberships: Fellow, Royal Institute of British Architects; Registered Architect ARB; Fellow Royal Society of Arts. Address: The Dingle, Whisper Wood, Loudwater, Rickmansworth, Hertfordshire WD3 4JU, England.

GRUBERG Martin, b. 28 January 1935, New York, USA. Professor. 1 son, 1 daughter. Education: BA, City College, New York City, 1955; PhD, Columbia University, New York City, 1963. Appointments: Agent Adjudicator, US State Department, NY Passport Agency, 1960-61; Social Studies Instructor, Pelham, New York and New York City High Schools, 1961-63, Hunter College, 1961-62, Wisconsin State University, 1965; Professor, Political Science Department, University of Wisconsin, Oshkosh, 1963-. Publications: Around over 30 articles in professional journals; 4 book chapters; Books: Women in American Politics, 1968; A Case Study in US Urban Leadership: The Incumbancy of Milwaukee Mayor Henry Maier, 1996; A History of Winnebago County Government, 1998; Introduction to Law, 2003. Honours: Book, Women in American Politics, twice cited by US Supreme Court; Senior Editor, Encyclopedia of American Government. Memberships: American Political Science Association; International Political Science Association; Midwest Political Science Association; Wisconsin Political Science Association; Academy of Criminal Justice Sciences; American Civil Liberties Union. Address: 2121 Oregon Street, Oshkosh, WI 54902, USA. E-mail: gruberg@uwosh.edu

GRUSZKA Barbara Maria, b. 10 September 1936, Toncza, Poland. Academic Teacher of Economy. Education: Master of Arts, 1965, Doctor, 1971, Post doctoral degree, 1986, Main School of Planning and Statistics, Warsaw; Scientific degree of the Professor of Economy, President of the Republic of Poland, 2000. Appointments: Junior Lecturer, 1965, Senior Lecturer, 1967, Assistant Professor, 1971, Docent, 1987, Department of Finance, Associate Professor, Department of Banking, 1993, Professor of Economy, 2004-, Warsaw School of Economics (previously Main School of Planning and Statistics); Advisor to President, Team of Experts, Headquarters of National Bank of Poland, 1982-88; Secretary, Program Council and Editorial Committee, Finance and Banking Encyclopaedic Dictionary 1991, 1987-90; Docent, Office of Money and Banking, Institute of Finance, Ministry of Finance, 1988-91; Deputy Director, Department of Finance and Banking, Private College of Business and Administration, 1992-93; Research Projects Expert, State Committee for Scientific Research, Ministry of Education and Science, 1997-. Publications: Book, Optimal financial result in industrial enterprises, 1977; Co-author,

Internal conformity of the financial policy as a condition for the credit policy effectiveness, 1985; Book, Economic-financial mechanism of industrial enterprises, 1986; Co-author, book, Risk in banking activity: System guarantees, 1992; Book, Efficiency and investment risk in commercial banks during system transformation, 1999; Author of chapter, Liquidity risk, in Banking – Academic Handbook, 2004; Author of chapter, Role of a credit in financing newly established economic entities introducing new technologies, in Retail Banking, 2005. Honours: 2nd degree, President of the Main School of Planning and Statistics, 1986, 1989; Golden Cross of Merit, Council of State, 1987; Medal, National Education Commission, Ministry of National Education, 1996. Address: ul Juliana Bruna 30 m8, 02-594 Warszawa, Poland. E-mail: barbara.gruszka@gmail.com

GRYNING Sven-Erik, b. 9 June 1948, Naestved, Denmark. Scientist. m. Susanne, 2 sons. Education: MS, Technical University of Denmark, 1972; PhD, 1982; D Sc, 2006. Appointments: Scientific Staff, Health Physics Department, Riso National Laboratory, 1974-77; Scientific Staff, Physics Department, 1977-84; Scientific Staff, Meteorology and Wind Energy, 1984-; Senior Scientist, 1992-; Adjoint Director, Research, Swedish Defence Research Establishment, 1992-96; Chairman, Convenor, NATO/CCMS International Technical Conference Series on Air Pollution Modelling and its Application, 1992-2000; Project Leader, Oresund Experiment, 1982-90; Chairman, Executive Committee, NOPEX, 1992-; Member, Scientific Panel on Atmospheric Chemistry European Commission, 1995-2000. Publications: Editor, Air Pollution Modeling and Its Application. X, XI, XII, XIII, XIV; Guest Editor, Atmospheric Environment, Theoretical and Applied Climatology, Agricultural and Forest Meteorology; Associate Editor, Quarterly Journal of the Royal Meteorological Society, 2002-. Honours: ITM Scientific Committee Award, 2000; Grantee, Nordic Council of Ministry. Memberships: Danish Meteorological Society; European Association for the Science of Air Pollution. Address: Haraldsborgvej 120, DK-4000 Roskilde, Denmark.

GUARRACINO Fabio, b. 26 February 1964, Naples, Italy. Medical Doctor. m. Liberata, 2 sons, 2 daughters. Education: Undergraduate training, Postgraduate training in Anaesthesia, Intensive Care Medicine and Cardiology, Padua Medical School, Italy. Appointments: Director, Perioperative Echocardiography, Venice Hospital, Italy, 2001; Director, Cardiothoracic Anaesthesia and Intensive Care Medicine, Pisa University Hospital, 2002-; Teaching Professor, Pisa Medical School, 2003-. Publications: Numerous articles in professional journals. Honours: First Award, Best Research Study, Italian Society of Anaesthesia and Intensive Care Medicine, 2001, 2002, 2005; President, Italian Association of Cardiothoracic Anaesthesiologists. Memberships: ASE; ESA; EACTA; SIAARTI; ESA Subcommittee on Circulation Research; EACTA TOE Committee; ESC/EACTA TOE Accreditation Committee.

GUERIN Orla, b.15 May 1966, Dublin, Ireland. Journalist. Education: Certificate in Journalism, College of Commerce, Rathmines, Dublin, 1985; Masters Degree, Film Studies, University College, Dublin, 1999. Appointments: News Reporter, 1987-1990, Eastern European Correspondent, 1990-94, RTE, Irish Broadcasting Service; BBC News Correspondent, 1995; BBC Southern Europe Correspondent, 1996-2000; BBC Middle East Correspondent, 2001-05; BBC Africa Correspondent, 2006-. Honours: London Press Club Broadcaster of the Year Award, 2002; Honorary Degree, University of Essex, 2002; News and Factual Award from

Women in Film and Television, 2003; MBE Hons, Services to Broadcasting, 2004; Honorary Doctorate, Dublin Institute of Technology, 2005.

GUESGEN Hans Werner, b. 24 April 1959, Bonn, Germany. Professor. m. Gaby, 11 August 1984, 3 daughters. Education: Dipl-Inform, University of Bonn, 1983; Dr rer nat, University of Kaiserlautern, 1988; Dr habil, University of Hamburg, 1993. Appointments: Post Doctoral Fellow, ICSI, Berkeley, California, 1989-90; Scientific Researcher, GMD St Augustin, Germany, 1983-92; Associate Professor, Computer Science Department, University of Auckland, 1992-2007; Professor, Institute of Information Sciences and Technology, Massey University, Palmerston North, New Zealand, 2007-. Publications: 2 monographs; 8 edited books, journals and reports; Over 100 refereed articles in journals, books, conference proceedings and workshop notes; Over 30 technical reports. Memberships: Association for the Advancement of Artificial Intelligence. Address: Institute of Information Sciences and Technology, Massey University, Private Bag 11222, Palmerston North, New Zealand. E-mail: h.w.guesgen@massey.ac.nz

GUEST Harry, (Henry Bayly Guest), b. 6 October 1932, Glamorganshire, Wales. Poet; Writer. m. Lynn Doremus Dunbar, 28 December 1963, 1 son, 1 daughter. Education: BA, Trinity Hall, Cambridge, 1954, DES, Sorbonne, University of Paris, 1955. Appointments: Lecturer, Yokohama National University, 1966-72; Head of Modern Languages, Exeter School, 1972-91; Teacher of Japanese, Exeter University, 1979-96. Publications: Arrangements, 1968; The Cutting-Room, 1970; Post-War Japanese Poetry, (editor and translator), 1972; A House Against the Night, 1976; Days, 1978; The Distance, the Shadows, 1981; Lost and Found, 1983; The Emperor of Outer Space (radio play), 1983; Mastering Japanese, 1989; Lost Pictures, 1991; Coming to Terms, 1994; Traveller's Literary Companion to Japan, 1994; So Far, 1998; The Artist on the Artist, 2000; A Puzzling Harvest, Collected Poems, 2002; Time After Time, 2005. Contributions to: Reviews, quarterlies, and journals. Honours: Hawthornden Fellow, 1993; Honorary Research Fellow, Exeter University, 1994-; Honorary Doctor of Letters, Plymouth University, 1998; Elected to the Welsh Academy, 2001. Membership: Poetry Society, General Council, 1972-76. Address: 1 Alexandra Terrace, Exeter, Devon EX4 6SY, England.

GUEUDET Edouard Philippe, b. 20 January 1976, Paris, France. Banker. Education: JD, Université Paris II Panthéon – Assas, 1999; MS, Institut Supérieur du Commerce de Paris, 2000; LLM, American University, Washington, DC, 2002; MBA, Kogod School of Business, American University, Washington DC, 2006. Appointments: Project Manager, Procar SA, 2000-01; Compagnie Financière d'Organisation et de Gestion (CFOG), 2002-05; Gueudet Frères SA, 2004-05; Consultant, 2006-07; Banker, Associate, Hottinger & Cie Geneva, 2007-; Assistant Vice President, Hottinger Bank & Trust Limited, Nassau, The Bahamas, 2008. Memberships: Lyford Cay Club; Old Fort Bay Club, Bahamas; Automobile Club de France; The Travellers, Paris; Cercle MBC; France-Amériques; Cercle Saint-Germain-des-Près; American International Club of Geneva; French-American Foundation. Address: Hottinger & Cie Bankers, 3 Place des Bergues, CH-1201, Geneva.

GUFFANTI Fabio Paolo, b. 31 July 1965, Milan, Italy. Consultant; Director. Education: Degree, Political Science, University of Milan, 1990; Certificate in EU International Affairs, SIOI, Milan, 1991; Diploma in EU Law and Politics,

SIOI, Rome, 1993; Certificate of International Trade, IUIL Luxembourg, 1994; Certificate in Human Rights and International Humanitarian Law, Strasbourg Institute R Cassin, 1995; Certificate in Political Affairs, Milan, 1998; ISPI – The Enlargement of the European Union, 2000; ASERI, Postgraduate Course on International relations, High School of International Relations, 2001; ASERI, Equilibri.net Course in Political Analysis of International Politics/Relations, Milan, 2005. Appointments: Military service in the secretariat of the General Commander of the Italian First Air Region, Milan, 1991-92; Consultant of the Vice President, European Parliament, 1996-; Consultant, Nyrae Group, 1997-99; Consultant, Electoral Committee of Mr Pecorella, MP of Italian Parliament; Consultant, ETCETERA Ltd, Milan, Nairobi, 1999-; Private Brokerage of Commodities, 2000-; Consultant, Electoral Campaign of Mrs C Muscardini for re-election at EU Parliament, 2004; UN Volunteer Service (on-line) Consulting Service, 2005-. Publications: Some publications written for the Vice President of the European Parliament. Honours: Distinguished Deputy Governor and Continental Governor, American Biographical Institute; Life Fellow, International Biographical Institute; Order of International Merit, IBC, 2001; Knight of the World Order of Education, Science and Culture, Euro-Academy, Brussels, 2000; Researcher of the Year, ABI, 2001; Eminent Personalities of India, 2005. Memberships: Experts Board, EU Consultants Affairs; Press and Publicity International; Secretary General, United Cultural Convention; International Directory and Distinguished Leadership; 2000 Leaders of Influence; Outstanding People of the 20th Century; International Diplomatic Academy; World Council for Peace and Diplomacy, 2003; International Association of Business Leaders, 2003; Federation of UN Associations, 2004; IBRF Governor, Nagpur, India, 2005. Address: Viale Umbria 109, I-20135, Milan, Italy.

GUGUSHVILI Sergo, b. 14 April 1950, Tbilisi, Georgia. Veterinarian. m. Mary Saladze, 1 son, 1 daughter. Education: Doctors degree, 1976. Appointment: Veterinarian, University of Zoovet, 1980-. Publications: 193 works and articles including, Georgian's Rubit. Address: St Depo N19, Tbilisi, Georgia. E-mail: ninomeskhi@yahoo.com

GUHA Kamal Kumar, b. 25 September 1928, Dhaka, Bangladesh. Writer and Retired Banker. m. Sujaya Basu, deceased, 1970. Education: BA (Hons); MA; LLB. Appointments: Management Staff, Anz Grindlays Bank, Retired; Editor, Himavanta: Mountaineering Journal. Publications: Co author of best Bengali Film Story, Bigolito Koruna, 1972; Editor, Himavanta: India's only Mountaineering Monthly for 39 Years Since 1968, judged as one of four World's Best Mountaineering Journals by UIAA. Honours: Civic Reception by Kolkata Corporation for promotion of mountaineering in 1969. Memberships: Himalayan Mountaineering Institute, Darjeeling, Nehru Institute of Mountaineering; Jawahar Institute of Mountaineering; Himalayan Club, Mumbai. Address: 63E Mahanirban Road, Kolkata 700 029, India.

GUI Gerald P H, b. 8 June 1962, Kuala Lumpur, Malaysia. Consultant Surgeon. m. Corina Espinosa, 2 sons. Education: MB BS, University College and Middlesex Hospital Medical School, London, 1981-86; FRCS Edinburgh, 1990; FRCS England, 1991; Master of Surgery, University of London, 1996. Appointments: Previously: Senior Registrar and Lecturer in Surgery, St George's Hospital Medical School; Registrar in Surgery, St Bartholomew's Hospital, London; Currently: Consultant Surgeon, Royal Marsden NHS Trust and Honorary Senior Lecturer, Institute of Cancer Research, London.

Publications: Many peer-reviewed original manuscripts in surgery and breast cancer management, tumour biology of breast cancer. Honours: University of London Laurels, 1986; Royal College of Surgeons of England Travelling Fellowship, 1997; Surgeon in Training Medal, Royal College of Surgeons, Edinburgh, 1994. Memberships: British Association of Surgical Oncology; British Breast Group; British Oncological Association; Society of Academic and Research Surgeons; Fellow, Association of Surgeons of Great Britain and Ireland. Address: Academic Surgery (Breast Unit), Royal Marsden NHS Trust, Fulham Road, London SW3 6JJ, England. E-mail: gerald.gui@rmh.nhs.uk

GUILLEMIN Roger Charles Louis, b. 11 January 1924, Dijon, France (US Citizen). Endocrinologist. m. Lucienne Jeanne Billard, 1951, 1 son, 5 daughters. Education: BA, 1941, BSc, 1942, University of Dijon; Medicine, University of Lyons, medical degree, 1949; PhD, Institute of Experimental Medicine and Surgery, Montreal, 1950. Appointments: Resident Intern, University Hospital, Dijon, 1949-51; Professor, Institute of Experimental Medicine and Surgery, Montreal; Baylor College of Medicine, Houston, Texas, 1953; Associate Director, Department of Experimental Endocrinology, Collège de France, Paris, 1960-63; Resident Fellow and Research Professor, 1970-89, Dean, 1972-73, 1976-77, Distinguished Professor, 1997-, The Salk Institute for Biological Studies, San Diego, California; Distinguished Scientist, 1989-93, Medical and Scientific Director, Director, 1993-94, 1995-97, Whittier Institute for Diabetes and Endocrinology, La Jolla; Adjunct Professor of Medicine, University of California, San Diego, 1995-97. Honours: Bonneau and La Caze Awards in Physiology, 1957, 1960; Gairdner Award, 1974; Officier, Legion d'honneur, Lasker Foundation Award, 1975; Nobel Prize for Physiology or Medicine, 1977; National Medal of Science, 1977; Barren Gold Medal, 1979; Dale Medallist, UK Society for Endocrinology, 1980. Memberships: NAS; American Academy of Arts and Sciences; American Physiological Society; Society for Experimental Biology and Medicine; International Brain Research Organisation; International Society for Research in Biology and Reproduction; Swedish Society of Medical Sciences; Academie Nacionale de Medecine; Academie des Sciences; Academie Royale de Medecine de Belgique; The Endocrine Society. Address: The Salk Institute, 10010 North Torrey Pines Road, La Jolla, CA 92037, USA.

GUIMARAES Romeu Cardoso, b. 29 July 1943, Belo Horizonte MG, Brazil. m. Alexandrina M Guimaraes. Education: MD, 1965; PhD, Pathology, 1970; Full Professor, Genetics, 1987. Appointments: University Federal Minas Gerais, 1966-75, 1993-; University Estadual Paulista, 1976-93; Currently working on: Origin of Life, Philosophy of Biology. Honour: Illustrious Son of Belo Horizonte. Memberships: Sao Paulo Academy of Sciences; Minas Gerais Academy of Medicine. Address: Dpto Biologia Geral, Instituto Ciencias Biologicas, UFMG, 31270-901 Belo Horizonte MG, Brazil. E-mail: romeucg@icb.ufmg.br

GUINNESS (Cecil) Edward, b. 1924, Great Britain. Brewery Director. m. Elizabeth Mary Fossett Thompson, 3 daughters, 1 deceased. Education: Stowe School, 1938-42; Army Course, University of Belfast, 1942-43; Ex-Serviceman's Course, School of Brewing, Birmingham, 1946-47. Appointments: WWII: Officer Cadet, Royal Artillery (invalided out due to Battle Course injury), 1942-45; Former Vice-Chairman, Guinness Brewing Worldwide; Joined Guinness as Junior Brewer, 1945; Director: Wolverhampton and Dudley Breweries, 1964-87, Guinness plc, 1971-89;

Chairman and Managing Director, Harp Lager Consortium, 1971-87; Chairman: Brewer's Society, 1985-86, Fulmer Parish Council, 1973-81, UK Trustees Duke of Edinburgh's Commonwealth Study Conferences, 1972-86; Licensed Trade Charities Trust, 1981-92, Governing Body, Dame Alice Owen's School, Potters Bar, 1981-92, Scottish Licensed Trade Association, 1972, Wine and Spirit Trade Benevolent Society, 1989-90, Chairman, Executive Committee, Fulmer Sports and Community Association, 2003-2004; President, 2004-, Chairman, Development Trust, 1993-96, Governor and Member of Executive Committee, 1996-, Queen Elizabeth Foundation for Disabled People; President: Performing Arts Centre Campaign, Dame Alice Owen's School, 1997-2002, Fulmer Recreation Ground Campaign, 2000-2003; Former President and Vice-President, 1980 and 1991, Licensed Victuallers National Homes; Member, Governing Body, Lister Institute of Preventive Medicine, 1968-2001, Gerrards Cross with Fulmer Parochial Church Council, 2002-2005. Publication: The Guinness Book of Guinness, 1988. Honours: CVO, 1986; Master, Worshipful Company of Brewers, 1977-78. Membership: Life Member, Industrial Society. Address: Huyton Fold, Fulmer Village, Buckinghamshire SL3 6HD, England.

GULBENKIAN Boghos Parsegh (Basil Paul), b. 23 March 1940, London, England. Solicitor; Judge. m. Jacqueline Gulbenkian, 2 daughters. Education: LLB, London School of Economics, London University, 1958-61; Qualified as a Solicitor, 1984. Appointments: Senior Partner, Gulbenkian Andonian Solicitors; Immigration Judge; Honorary Consul, Armenian Embassy; Assistant Commissioner to the Boundary Commission. Publications: Editor: Entry and Residence in Europe; Immigration Law and Business in Europe. Honours: Encyclicals from His Holiness Vasken I; St Mesrob Medal; Freeman of the City of London. Memberships: Founder, Solicitors Family Law Association; Immigration Law Practitioners Association; President, European Immigration Lawyers Group; Council of Immigration Judges; International Association of Refugee Law Judges. Address: Sicilian House, Sicilian Avenue, London WC1A 2QH, England. E-mail: paulg@gulbenkian.co.uk

GULIK Elisabeth Thecla Maria van der, b. 19 December 1947, Amsterdam, Netherlands. Occupational Health Physician. Education: Analytical Chemist, Westeinde Hospital, The Hague, 1967-69; MD, Catholic University, Nijmegen, 1969-80; Course in General and Experimental Oncology, Institute ARC, Villejuif, France, 1985-86; Assessment Medicine, SMI course, School of Public Health, Utrecht, 1999; Counseling and Coaching, Benelux University Centre, Eindhoven, 2002-05. Appointments: Assurance Physician, General Administration Office, GAK, Amsterdam, 1992-96; Assurance Physician, Joint Executive Organization GUO, Zoetermeer, Netherlands, 1996-98; Cure Supplies, Netherlands, ZVN BV, Amsterdam, 1998-99; Occupational Health Physician, AGG Arbo Service, Amstelveen, 1999, 2000; Arbo Unie, Delft, 2001, Commit Arbo, De Meern, 2001, 2002; Arbo Unie BV 21731, 2002-04; AGW, 2005-06, Hoorn; Maetis, Amsterdam, 2006-. Honours: Grantee, Association Naturalia et Biologia, 1985; Decree of Merit, The World Who's Who of Women, IBC, 1997; Achievement Award, Five Hundred Leaders of Influence, ABI, 1997; International Woman of the Year, 1997-98, IBC; Award of Excellence, ABI-IBC International Congress, 1998; World Laureate, ABI, 1999; Continental Governor and Member of the International Governors Club, ABI Research Association, 1999; Lifetime Deputy Governor, ABI Research Association, 1999; Member, Research Board of Advisors, ABI, 1999;

2000 Millennium Medal of Honor, 1999; Hall of Fame, International Who's Who of Professional and Business Women, 6th edition, ABI, 1999; International Book of Honor, 6th world edition, ABI, 1999; Research Council Member, IBC, 2000; Award for Outstanding Artistic Performance, ABI-IBC International Congress, 2000, 2001, 2002, 2004, 2005, 2006, 2007; ABI-IBC Congress Medal, 2000; Life Patron, IBA, 2001; Medical Advisor to the Director General, IBC, 2001; Secretary General, United Cultural Convention, 2001; Diploma of the Greatest Minds of the 21st Century, 2001; International Directory of Distinguished Leadership, 10th Edition, 2001; Hall of Fame, IBC, 2007; American Medal of Honor, ABI, 2007. Memberships: Dutch Royal Academy of Medicine, Utrecht, 1979; General Association for Counselling, The Netherlands, Koog aande Zaan, 2005. Address: Smedemanstraat 2, NL 1182 HT Amstelveen, Netherlands. E-mail: etm.vander.gulik@12move.nl

GÜLSOY Tanses Yasemin, b. Verdun, France.Manager. Education: BA, Pomona College, Claremont, California, USA, 1985; MA, Journalism and Mass Communication, New York University, New York, New York, 1988; PhD, Contemporary Management Studies, Isik University, Istanbul, Turkey, 2006. Appointments: Fellow, Harry Frank Guggenheim Foundation and Research Assistant, New York University, New York, 1986-88; Advertising Copywriter, 1989-97, International Advertising Director, 1997-2001, Manajans/Thompson, Istanbul, Turkey; Founder and Owner, Tans Communications Consultancy, Istanbul, Turkey, 2001-2003; General Manager, Gültan Elektrik Tic ve San A S, Istanbul, Turkey, 2003-. Publications: Why the Fight over Peace Studies, 1988; An English-Turkish Dictionary of Advertising with Turkish-English Index, 1999; 38 newspaper articles in American newspapers. Honours: Bogazici University, Business Administration Department Dean's List, 1982; Pomona College Academic Scholarship, 1982-85; Pomona College Honnold Fellowship for Graduate Study, 1985; Harry Frank Guggenheim Foundation Fellowship, 1986-88; Profiled by weekly news magazine Aktüel as one of Turkey's brightest young minds, 2002; Honours Award, Turkey's Association of Advertising Creatives, 2002; Listed in Who's Who 2003, 2004, 2005, 2006 and 2007 publications and biographical dictionaries. Memberships: American Marketing Association; Turkish Society for Opinion and Marketing Research; Turkish Association of Advertising Creatives; New York University European Alumni Group; Pomona College Alumni Volunteers; Member of Board of Directors, 1994-96, Robert College Alumni Association. Address: Adnan Saygun Cad, Dag Apt 54/10, I.Ulus, 34360 Istanbul, Turkey.

GUMBS Pamela Yancy, b. 6 August 1946, Andover, Massachusetts, USA. Clinical Pharmacy. m. John J Gumbs. Education: Doctorate-in-Pharmacy, UCSF School of Pharmacy, 1975; Geriatric Residency, UCSF Geriatric Institute, 1991. Appointments: CEO Clinical Affairs, Clinical Pharmacist, Royal Medical Inc United Pharmacy, 1996-. Publications: Editor, Pills & Potions Newsletter Alameda Country Pharmacists Association. Honours: Pharmacy Leader, Presidential Tour, 1987; Northern California Forensics Association Award for Communication Excellence, 1987. Memberships: California Pharmacists' Association; American Society of Consultant Pharmacists'; Christian Pharmacists Fellowship International; American Pharmacists association; National Association of Female Executives. Address: Royal Medical Ltd, 2929 Telegraph Ave, Berkeley, CA 94705, USA. E-mail: drpam@consultwithdrpam.com

DICTIONARY OF INTERNATIONAL BIOGRAPHY

GUMLEY-MASON Frances Jane Miriah Katrina, b. 28 January 1955, London, England. Headmistress. m. Andrew Samuel Mason, 1 son, 1 daughter. Education: MA, Newnham College, Cambridge. Appointments: Parliamentary Researcher, 1974; Braille Transcriber, 1975; Editorial Assistant, 1975-76, Staff Reporter and Literary Editor, 1976-79, Editor, 1979-81, Catholic Herald; Senior Producer, Religious Broadcasting, BBC, 1981-88; Series Editor, Channel 4, 1988-89; Acting Executive Producer, Religion, BBC World Service, 1989; Guest Producer and Scriptwriter, BBC Radio 4, 1989-95; Headmistress, St Augustine's Priory, Ealing, 1995-. Publications: Books (with Brian Redhead): The Good Book; The Christian Centuries; The Pillars of Islam; Protestors for Paradise; Discovering Turkey (jointly). Honour: MA, Newnham College, Cambridge. Membership: Mistress of the Keys, Catholic Writers' Guild, 1982-87. Address: St Augustine's Priory, Hillcrest Road, Ealing, London W5 2JL, England. E-mail: admin@saintaugustinespriory.org.uk

GUMPERTZ Werner H, b. 26 December 1917, Berlin, Germany. Consulting Engineer. Education: BCE Swiss Federal Institute of Technology, 1939; Sanitary Engineering, New York University, 1941; SB in Civil Engineering, MIT, 1948; SM in Building Engineering and Construction, MIT, 1950; Advanced Professional degree of Building Engineer, MIT, 1954; Appointments: Office and Field Engineer, United Engineers and Constructors, 1948-49; Assistant Professor of Building Technology, Massachusetts Institute of Technology, 1949-1957; Senior Principal, Simpson Gumpertz & Heger Inc, 1956-. Publications: Numerous publications, presentations and lectures on field of building and building materials, 1948-. Honours: Sigma Xi; 1st Prize, paper contest, American Society of Civil Engineers, 1948; Citation for Good Citizenship, Freedom Inc, 1957; Award of Merit, Boston Arts Festival, 1958; Commendation for Public Service, member of Engineering Board, City of Newton, Massachusetts, 1961; Honour Award for Design in Urban Transportation, US Department of Housing and Urban Development, 1968; Award of Appreciation, American Society for Testing and Materials, 1980-85; Award of Merit, American Society for Testing and Materials, 1986; ASTM Walter C Voss Award to Engineer for Outstanding Contribution to Advancement of Building Technology, 1987; William C Cullen Award, ASTM, 2005. Memberships: Fellow, ASCE; Fellow, ASTM; ACI; AAA; NFPA; Midwest Roofing Contractors Association. Address: c/o Simpson Gumpertz & Heger Inc, 41 Seyon Street, Waltham, MA 02453, USA.

GUNAJI S P, b. 11 July 1927, Satana, District Nasik, Maharashtra, India. Ophthalmologist. Education: MBBS (BOM), 1951; DO, Baroda University, 1962; MS (OPHTH), Jabalpur, 1975; FICS; FICA. Appointments: Army Medical Corps, 1953-82; Classified Specialist, Ophthalmology Command Hospital, Armed Forces Medical College, Pune, 1976-82; Assistant Professor of Ophthalmology, Goa Medical College, Panaji, 1982-84; Low cost consultations of ophthalmic patients, Goa State, 1985-98; Instituted Late Dr P R Gunaji Gold Medal (in commemoration of father), 1996; Charitable (free) work in ophthalmic practice on humanitarian grounds, Goa State, 2004-. Honours: 8 military medals and stars; Bhartiya Chikitsak Ratna Award with Gold Medal, Trophy & Certificate of Excellence, 2004; Jankalyan Sadbhavana Award with Gold Medal, 2004. Address: 54, Defence Colony, Alto Porvorim, Bardez (Goa) 403521, India.

GUNAWAN Benny, b. 1 March 1948, Bogor, Indonesia. Senior Lecturer. m. Sri Saptaningsih, 1 son, 2 daughters. Education: BSc, University of Pajajaran, Bandung, 1975;

MSc, Department of Animal Husbandry, University of Sydney, Australia, 1980; PhD, School of Fibre Science and Technology, University of New South Wales, Sydney, Australia, 1986; Professor, Postgraduate Studies in Management, University of Satyagama, Jakarta, Indonesia, 1999. Appointments: Director of Research Institute, Department of Agriculture, 1987-90; Director of Postgraduate Studies, University of Satyagama, 1997-2006; Director of Postgraduate Studies in Business Administration, Stiami, 2001-2006; Chairman of Foundation for Regional Community Development, 2001-; Dean of Faculty for Political and Social Science, University of Pramita Indonesia, 2005-; Director, Postgraduate Studies in Political and Social Science, University of Pramita Indonesia, 2007-. Publications: More than 200 articles published in local and international journals since 1976. Honours: Listed in Who's Who publications and biographical dictionaries. Membership: National Geographic Society. Address: Komp MG Cempaka Mas Blok A5, JI Letjend Suprapto, Cempaka Putih, Jakarta Pusat 10640, Indonesia. E-mail: bgunawan@cbn.net.id

GUNDEM BRANDTZAEG Bjoerg Signy, b. 25 August 1927, Aalesund, Norway. Professor Emeritus. m. Thorleif Gundem, 2 sons. Education: Diploma, English as a Foreign Language, College of Education, 1949; BA (Hons), English, 1969, Academic Degree (Hons), Education, Cand Paed, 1976, Dr Philos, 1987, University of Oslo. Appointments: Advisor, Teaching of English as a Foreign Language, Oslo Teachers' Centre, 1965-71; Expert, Nordic Cultural Secretariat, Harmonization of the School System of the Nordic Countries, 1971-74; Lecturer and Senior Lecturer in Education, Oslo Post Graduate Institute for Teacher Training, 1976-79; Assistant Professor, 1976-79, Associate Professor, 1979-83, Professor of Education, 1983-97, Professor Emeritus, 1997-, Institute for Educational Research, University of Oslo. Publications: 5 books; 32 research monographs; 35 articles in Nordic and international scientific journals; 44 articles in books and encyclopaedia. Honours: Comenius Medal, 1992; Honorary publication in honour of 70th birthday, 1997; Honorary seminar/lecture in honour of 80th birthday, University of Oslo, 2007. Memberships: American Educational Research Association; Society for the Study of Curriculum History; The International Standing Conference for the History of Education; The John Dewey Society; Professors of Curriculum; US Society for Distinguished Curriculum Professors. Address: Kastellveien 13, N-1170 Oslo, Norway. E-mail: bjorg.gundem@ped.uio.no

GUNNELL Sally, b. 29 July 1966, Chigwell, Essex, England. Sport Commentator; Former Professional Athlete. m. Jonathan Bigg, 1992, 3 sons. Education: Chigwell High School; Trained by Bruce Longdon. Career: Specialised in hurdles; 400m hurdles, Olympic Games, Seoul, 1988; 2nd, 400m hurdles World Championship, Tokyo, 1991; Bronze Medal, 400m relay, Olympic Games, Barcelona, 1992; Women's Team Captain, Olympic Games, 1992-97; Gold Medal, 400m hurdles, Olympic Games, Barcelona, 1992; Gold Medal (world record), 400m hurdles, World Championships, 1993; Gold Medal, 400m hurdles, European Championships, Helsinki, 1994; Gold Medal, 400m hurdles, Commonwealth Games, Canada, 1994; Retired, 1997; Sport Commentator, BBC, 1999-2006; Fitness Consultant, Crown Sports, 2001-. Publication: Running Tall (with Christopher Priest), 1994; Be Your Best, 2001. Honour: OBE, 1999; Only woman in history to have held four gold medals concurrently as at end of 2002. Membership: Essex Ladies Athletic Club. Address: Old School Cottage, School Lane, Pyecombe, West Sussex, BN45 7FQ, England.

GUNSTON Bill, (William Tudor Gunston), b. 1 March 1927, London, England. Author. m. Margaret Anne, 10 October 1964, 2 daughters. Education: University College, Durham, 1945-46; City University, London, 1948-51. Appointments: Pilot, Royal Air Force, 1946-48; Editorial Staff, 1951-55, Technical Editor, 1955-64, Flight; Technology Editor, Science Journal, 1964-70; Compiler, Jane's All the World's Aircraft, 1968-; Compiler/Editor, Jane's Aero-Engines, 1996-; Freelance author, 1970-; Director, So Few Ltd. Publications: Over 370 books including: Aircraft of The Soviet Union, 1983; Jane's Aerospace Dictionary, 1980, 4th edition, 1998; Encyclopaedia of World Aero Engines, 1986, 3rd edition, 1995; 5th edition, 2006; Encyclopaedia of Aircraft Armament, 1987; Airbus, 1988; Avionics, 1990; Giants of the Sky, 1991; Faster Than Sound, 1992; Jet Bombers, 1993; Piston Aero Engines, 1994, 2nd edition, 1998; Encyclopaedia of Russian Aircraft, 1995; Jet and Turbine Aero Engines, 1995, 2nd edition, 1997, 4th edition, 2006; Night Fighters, 2nd edition, 2004; The Cambridge Aerospace Dictionary, 2004; World Encyclopaedia of Aircraft Manufacturers, 2nd edition, 2005; Contributions to: 188 periodicals; 18 partworks; 75 video scripts; Member Association of British Science Writers. Honours: Fellow, Royal Aeronautical Society; Officer of the Order of the British Empire. Address: High Beech, Kingsley Green, Haslemere, Surrey GU27 3LL, England.

GUO George Xuezhi, b. 22 January 1956, Sichuan, China. Professor. m. Yanqing Sun, 1 son, 1 daughter. Education: BS, Management of Ocean Engineering, South China University of Technology, 1982; MPA, Master of Public Administration, University of North Florida, 1993; PhD, Foreign Affairs, University of Virginia, 1999. Appointments: Associate Professor, Political Science and East Asian Studies, Guilford College, Greensboro, North Carolina, 2002-. Publications: Dimensions of Guanxi in Chinese Elite Politics, 2001; The Ideal Chinese Political Leader: A Historical and Cultural Perspective, 2002. Honours: Phi Kappa Phi; Listed in international biographical directories. Memberships: American Political Science Association. Address: Political Science Department, Guilford College, 5800 W Friendly Ave, Greensboro, NC 27410, USA. E-mail: gguo@guilford.edu

GUO Gong-Yi, b. 16 June 1940, Shanghai, China. Professor. m. Yu-Li Chen, 2 daughters. Education: BS, Rare Metals, East China University of Science and Technology, 1963. Appointments: Associate Professor, Shanghai Jiao Tong University, 1988-96, Professor, Shanghai Jiao Tong University, 1996-. Publications: Book, Fuel Cells, 1984; New Research on Solid State Chemistry, Chapter 3, 2007; Numerous articles in national and international scientific journals include most recently: Optical and Thermal Properties of Some Chemically Durable Lead Phosphate Glasses, 1998; Structural Study of a Lead-Barium-Aluminium Phosphate Glass by MAS-NMR Spectroscopy, 1998; ^{31}P-and ^{27}Al-MAS-NMR Investigations of Some Lead Phosphate Glasses, 1999; Achieving Practically Zero Discharge for an Acrylic Acid Plant by a Metalorganic Precipitation Process, 2000; High-Quality Zirconia Powder Resulting from the Attempted Separation of Acetic Acid from Acrylic Acid with Zirconium Oxychloride, 2001. Honours: Progress in Science and Technology on Extraction and Purification of Scandium Oxide, State Ministry of Education, 1991; Shanghai Excellent Invention on Yttria-stabilised Zirconia Ultrafine Powder, Shanghai Scientific and Technological Commission, 1996. Memberships: TMS, USA; The American Ceramic Society; The Chinese Society of Rare Earth. Address: Department of Materials Science Engineering, Shanghai Jiao Tong University, 1954 Hua Shan Road, 200030 Shanghai, China. E-mail: guo_gongyi@hotmail.com

GUO Wei Dong, b. 17 May 1963, Anhui, People's Republic of China. Geotechnical Engineering. m. Xiao Chun Tang, 2 daughters. Education: Bachelor, Civil Engineering, Hohai University, Nanjing, 1984; Master, Engineering, Xian University of Architecture & Technology, 1987; PhD, University of Western Australia, 1997. Appointments: Assistant Lecturer, Department of Construct Engineering, Xian University of Architecture & Technology, 1987-89; Researcher (Lecturer), Department of Irrigation & Drainage, Hohai University, 1989-92; Senior Geotechnical Engineer, APG Geosystem Sdn Bhd, Kuala Lumpur, 1997-98; Post-doctoral Research Fellow, Department of Civil Engineering, National University of Singapore, 1998-99; Lecturer/Senior Lecturer, Griffith University, 2002-05. Publications: Numerous articles on new solutions on soils and foundations. Honours: Fellowship, Singapore Science & Technology Board; Monash Logan Research Fellowship; Australian Research Council Post-doctoral Fellowship; Magnolia Talent Foundation, Shanghai, China; John Henry Garrood King Medal, Institute of Civil Engineers, UK. Memberships: Institute of Engineers, Australia; Australian Geomechanics Society; International Society of Soil Mechanics & Geotechnical Engineering; American Society of Civil Engineers. E-mail: w.guo@griffith.edu.au

GUPTA Rajendra Kumar, b. 18 February 1946, Alwar, Rajasthan. Remote Sensing Technologist Educator. m. Sashi, 2 children. Education: BSc, University of Rajasthan, Jaipur, India, 1965; MSc, Physics, 1967; PhD, Physics, Jawaharlal Nehru Technological University, Hyderabad, 1991. Appointments: Lecturer, Government of Rajasthan, 1967-70; Senior Scientific Assistant, Indian Institute of Tropical Meteorology, Pune, 1970-72; Junior Scientific Officer, 1972-79; Head, Systems Engineering and Meteorology Cell, National Remote Sensing Agency, Hyderabad, 1979-82; Head, Satellite Meteorology Section, 1982-88; Head, Training Group, 1988-2002; Group Director, Training, 2002-, Vice-Chair, COSPAR Sub-Commission A3, Paris, 2002-; Chairman, National Symposium on Advanced Technologies in Meteorology, 1995; Editor, International Journal of Remote Sensing, UK; Organiser, UN/ESCAP Workshop on GIS and remote sensing and sustainable development, 1996; Scientist 'G' and Group Director, Training and Education, Chaired sessions of COSPAR Symposiums, USA, 1992, UK, 1996, Japan, 1998, Poland, 2000, USA, 2002, Main Scientific Organiser and Editor, COSPAR Symposium, USA, 1992, USA, Japan, 1998, Paris, 2004, Beijing, 2006, Dy Organiser and Editor, one COSPAR Symposium, Warsaw, 2002, Houston, 2002; Presenter of numerous conferences. Publications: 145 publications: 52 refereed journals of which 30 are international. Memberships: Fellow: Andhra Pradesh Academy of Sciences; Institute of Electronics and Telecommunication Engineers; Indian Geophysical Union; Member, Expert Panel for Academic Research of Indian Society of Geomatics; Life Membership: Indian Meteorological Society; Indian Society of Remote Sensing; Indian National Cartographic Association; Associate, COSPAR, France. Address: E-8, NRSA Housing Complex, Manovikasnagar, Hashmatpet, Secunderabad, 500 009, India.

GUPTA Suman, b. 4 October 1975, Allahabad (UP), India. Research Fellow. Education: BSc, 1996, MSc, 2000, D Phil/PhD, 2005, University of Allahabad; Certificate, Computer Application course, University of Allahabad, 2002. Appointments: Post Doctorate Research Fellow, Scientist, University Grant's Commission project on Viability and Reproduction of Algae facing periodic Water Stress, University of Allahabad, Lecturer in Government

Post-Graduate College. Publications: Vegetative Survival and Reproduction under Submerged and Air-Exposed Conditions and Vegetative Survival as Affected by Salts, Pesticides and Metals in Aerial Green Alga 'Trentepohlia aurea', 2004; Zoosporangia survival, dehiscence and zoospore Formation, and motility in the green alga 'Rhizoclonium hieroglyphicum' as affected by different factors, 2004; Motility and survival of 'Euglena ignobilis' as affected by different factors, 2005; Survival of blue-green and green algae under stress conditions, 2006; Motility in 'Oscillatoria salina' as affected by different factors Folia Mitrobio, 2006; Survival and Motility of Diatoms Navicula grimmei and Nitzschia palea addected by some physical and chemical factors, 2007, Folia Microbiol, 52 (1). Honours: National Scholarship Holder; Merit Award in Master of Science; Abstract of papers also published in "Current content" and "Biological Abstract"; Participated, National Symposium on Science and Ethics of Environmental Care and Sustainability, 2002; Presented paper, National Symposium on Biology and Biodiversity of Freshwater Algae, 2004; Presented paper, International Conference on Sustainable Development and Resource Utilisation Current Trends and Perspectives, Department of Chemistry, University of Rajasthan, Jaipur, 2005; Participated and presented paper in National Seminar on Sustainable Water Management, 2005; National Seminar on Intellectual Property Rights: Plant Varieties and Genome Conservation, 2006. Memberships: Life Member, Association of Microbiologists of India, IARI, New Delhi; Member of Research Advisory Board, 2005-2006 by American Biographical Institute, Raleigh, USA. Address: 369-A/140-A, Tula Ram Bagh, P O Daraganj, Allahabad (UP), 211006, India.

GUPTA Surya Mohan, b. 20 June 1966, Agra (UP), India. m. Deepali, 2 daughters. Education: BSc (Hons), 1986, MSc, 198, Chemistry, University of Delhi; M Tech, Materials Science, 1990, PhD, 1995, IIT, Bombay. Appointments: Postdoctoral Research Associate, University of Illinois at Urbana Champaign, USA, 1994-98; Technical Consultant, EIPRO International Limited, Pune, 1998; Research Officer, SIMS, Cranfield University, Bedfordshire, UK, 1999; Scientific Officer E, 1999-2004, Scientific Officer, 2004-, Raja Ramanna Center for Advanced Technology, Indore. Publications: 25 papers in refereed journals; 35 papers in national and international conferences. Honours: Merit Award, Ramjon College; MSc (1st position), University of Delhi; Junior and Senior Research fellowship during M Tech and PhD; Best Paper Award, 1994. Memberships: Life Member, Materials Research Society of India; Life Member, Indian Physics Association. Address: 122 Sudarsham Nagar, Indore 452009, MP, India. E-mail: surya@cat.emet.in

GUPTA Vinod Kumar, b. 23 March 1954, Jaipur, India. Internist; Researcher; Poet; Ethicist. m. Anjali Dhankani, 10 May 1979, 1 son. Education: MB, BS, 1976, MD, 1980, University of Rajastan, Jaipur, India; MRCP (UK) Part 1, 1988; ECFMG (USA), 1989. Appointments: Junior Resident in Medicine, All India Institute for Medical Sciences, New Delhi, India, 1977-78; Registrar in General Medicine, 1978-79, Senior Registrar in General Medicine, 1979-80, JLN Medical College, Ajmer, India; Consultant Physician, Panacea Medical Clinic, Delhi, 1980-85; General Physician and Medical Doctor, Emirates Diagnostic Clinic, Dubai, United Arab Emirates, 1985-87; Specialist Physician, Al-Rasheed Medical Clinic, Dubai, 1988-89; Physician, Dubai Police, 1989-2007; Consultant Physician & Neuroscientist, Holy Family Hospital, New Delhi, 2007-. Publications: Spirit of Enterprise, 1990; Contributed articles to professor journals. Honours include: Rolex Award, 1990; Certificate of Merit

Ministry of Education and Youth Services, Government of India, 1970-71; Lala Ramchander Memorial Award, 1970-71; Merit Scholarship, Board of Secondary Education, 1970-71, University of Rajastan, 1973-75; Prize for Courteous Behavior and Service to Community, Rotary International, 1985; New Century Award, Barons 500, 1999; Leaders for the New Century; Editors Choice Award, 2002; Best Poets of 2002; 3rd place medal, Poetry.com; Nominated for: International Man of the Year 2003; Great Minds of the 21st Century, 2004; American Medal of Honor, 2005; World Medal of Freedom, 2005; Leading Health Professionals of the World, 2005; Man of the Year, 2005; Man of Achievement, 2005; International Peace Prize, 2005. Memberships: American Association for the Advancement of Science; New York Academy of Science; American Headache Society. Address: Holy Family Hospital, Okhla Road, Jamia Nagar, New Delhi, DL 110025, India. E-mail: dr_vkgupta@yahoo.com

GURDON John Bertrand, b. 2 October 1933, Dippenhall, Hampshire, England. Molecular Biologist. m. Jean Elizabeth Margaret Curtis, 1964, 1 son, 1 daughter. Education: Graduated, Zoology, Christ Church College, Oxford, 1956; Doctorate, Embryology, Zoology Department, 1960. Appointments: Beit Memorial Fellow, 1958-61; Gosney Research Fellow, California Institute of Technology, 1961-62; Research Fellow, Christ Church, Oxford, 1962-72, Departmental Demonstrator, 1963-64, Lecturer, Department of Zoology, 1966-72; Visiting Research Fellow, Carnegie Institute, Baltimore, 1965; Scientific Staff, 1973-83, Head of Cell Biology Division, 1979-83, John Humphrey Plummer Professor of Cell Biology, 1983-2001, Medical Research Council, Molecular Biology Laboratory, University of Cambridge; Master, Magdalene College, Cambridge, 1995-2002; Fellow, Churchill College, Cambridge, 1973-95; Croonian Lecturer, Royal Society, 1976; Dunham Lecturer, Harvard Medical School, 1974; Carter-Wallace Lecturer, Princeton University, 1978; Fellow, Eton College, 1978-93. Publications: Control of Gene Expression in Animal Development, 1974. Honours: Hon DSc, 1978, 1988, 1998, 2000; Hon Dr, 1982; Albert Brachet Prize, 1968; Scientific Medal of Zoological Society, 1968; Feldberg Foundation Award, 1975; Paul Ehrlich Award, 1977; Nessim Habif Prize, 1979; CIBA Medal, Biochemical Society, 1981; Comfort Crookshank Award for Cancer Research, 1983; William Bate Hardy Triennial Prize, 1983; Charles Leopold Mayer Prize, 1984; Ross Harrison Prize, 1985; Royal Medal, 1985; Emperor Hirohito International Biology Prize, 1987; Wolf Prize for Medicine, jointly, 1989; Distinguished Service Award, Miami, 1992; Knight Bachelor, June 1995; Jean Brachet Memorial Prize, International Society for Differentiation, 2000; Conklin Medal, Society of Developmental Biology, 2001; Copley Medal Royal Society, 2003. Memberships: Honorary Foreign Member, American Academy of Arts and Sciences, 1978; Honorary Student, Christ Church, Oxford, 1985; Fullerian Professor of Physiology and Comparative Anatomy, Royal Institute, 1985-91; President, International Society for Developmental Biology, 1990-94; Foreign Associate, NAS, 1980, Belgian Royal Academy of Science, Letters and Fine Arts, 1984, French Academy of Science, 1990; Foreign Member, American Philosophical Society, 1983; Chair, Wellcome Cancer Campaign Institute, University of Cambridge, 1990-2001; Governor, The Wellcome Trust, 1995-2000; Chair, Company of Biologists, 2001-. Address: Whittlesford Grove, Whittlesford, Cambridge CB2 4NZ, England.

GURNEY A(lbert) R(amsdell), b. 1 November 1930, Buffalo, New York, USA. Professor of Literature; Dramatist; Writer. m. Mary Goodyear, 1957, 2 sons, 2 daughters. Education:

BA, Williams College, 1952; MFA, Yale University School of Drama, 1958. Appointments: Faculty, 1960-, Professor of Literature, 1970-, Massachusetts Institute of Technology. Publications: Plays: Children, 1974; The Dining Room, 1982; The Perfect Party, Another Antigone, Sweet Sue, 1986; The Cocktail Hour, 1988; Love Letters, 1989; The Old Boy, 1991; The Fourth Wall, 1992; Later Life, 1993; A Cheever Evening, 1994; Sylvia, Overtime, 1995; Labor Day, 1998; The Guest Lecturer, Far East, Ancestral Voices, 1999; Human Events, 2000; Buffalo Gal, 2001; O Jerusalem, Big Bill, 2003; Mrs Farnsworth, 2004; Screen Play, 2005; Novels: The Gospel According to Joe, 1974; The Snow Ball, 1985. Screenplay: The House of Mirth, 1972. Television: O Youth and Beauty (from a story by John Cheever), 1979; Kinder; The Dining Room; My Brother's Wife; Love Letters; Far East; Silvija. Opera libretto: Strawberry Fields. Honours: Drama Desk Award, 1971; Rockefeller Foundation Grant, 1977; National Endowment for the Arts Award, 1982; Theatre Award, American Academy of Arts and Sciences, 1990; Lucille Lortel Award, 1992; William Inge Award, 2000; Theatre Hall of Fame, 2005; Honorary doctorates. Address: 40 Wellers Bridge Road, Roxbury, CT 06783, USA.

GUSEV Vladimir Aleksandrovich, b. 25 April 1945, Kalinin, Russia. Art Administrator. m. Mukhina Xenia Vladimirovna, 1 daughter. Education: I Repin Leningrad Academy of Painting, Sculpture and Architecture. Appointments: Scholarly Secretary, Leningrad Branch of the Union of Painters, 1974-78; Scientific Researcher, Head of Department, Deputy Director, 1978-88, Director, 1988-, State Russian Museum; Head of Reconstruction of Michailovsky Palace and Marble Palace, St Petersburg; Member, Presidential Committee for State Awards in the field of literature and art; Corresponding Member, Russian Academy of Arts. Publications: Over 60 articles in Russian, English, German, French, Italian and Spanish. Honours: Medal for Valorous Work, 1971; Honourable Worker of Arts of the Russian Federation, 1996; Active Member, Russian Academy of Arts, 2001; State Award, Russian Federation for Literature and Arts, 2003; Medal in Memory of the 300th Anniversary of St Petersburg, 2003. Memberships: Chairman, Scientific Council, State Russian Museum; Scientific Council, Hermitage; Board of international charitable foundation for St Petersburg Revival; Russian Branch, UNESCO Committee for Culture; St Petersburg Branch, Union of Painters; Board of the Union of Art and Museum Workers, St Petersburg; Board of the Russian Committee, International Museum Council (ICOM); Committee for the State Awards for Literature and Arts, Russian Federation President's Administration. Address: 22 Bolshaya Monetnaya str, apartment 9, 197101 Saint Petersburg, Russia. E-mail: info@rusmuseum.ru Website: www.rusmuseum.ru

GUSEV Vladimir Georgiyevich, b. 20 April 1939, Novosibirsk, Russia. Physicist. m. Nikulina N G, 1 daughter. Education: Tomsk State University, 1963. Appointment: Vice-Professor, Tomsk State University. Publications include: Articles in journals: Russian Physics Journal, 2000-03, 2005-08; Optics of Atmosphere and Ocean, 2001-03, 2005-08. Many articles to other professional journals; Listed in national and international biographical dictionaries. Memberships: New York Academy of Sciences. Address: Tomsk State University, Lenina 36, 634050 Tomsk, Russia.

GUSTAFSON Mardel Emma, b. 10 June 1922, Waukesha, Wisconsin, USA. Author. m. Wayne C Gustafson, 1950, 4 sons, 2 daughters. Education: BSc, Education, University of Wisconsin-Madison, 1946; MA (9 credits), University of Madison, 1947-48. Appointments: Science Teacher, Hannibal High School, Hannibal, Wisconsin, 1946-49; Science Teacher, St Johns, North Dakota, 1949-50; Stay-at-home mother. Publications: What is Happening to our Children? How to Raise Them Right, 1993; All My Love - Letters from the Korean War, 2001 (as Hope Gustav); Why a Role Mother, 2001; Don't Do It: Sex: If You Are Not Married; various editorials in Waukesha Freeman. Honour: Timeline on My Life, Waukesha County Museum, 2005. Memberships: include Wisconsin Alumni Association; National Honor Society. Address: W289 S2915 County Road, DT, Waukesha, WI 53188-9581, USA. E-mail: waynemardel@aol.com

GUTERSON David, b. 4 May 1956, Seattle, Washington, USA. Writer. m. Robin Ann Radwick, 1979, 5 children. Education: BA, 1978, MA, 1982, University of Washington. Appointment: High School Teacher of English, Bainbridge Island, Washington, 1984-94. Publications: The Country Ahead of Us, The Country Behind, 1989; Family Matters: Why Home Schooling Makes Sense, 1992; Snow Falling on Cedars, 1994; The Drowned Son, 1996; East of the Mountains, 1999; Our Lady of the Forest, 2003. Honour: PEN/Faulkner Award for Fiction, 1995; Barnes and Noble Discovery Award, 1995; Pacific NW Booksellers Award, 1995. Address: c/o Georges Borchardt Inc, 136 East 57th Street, New York, NY 10022, USA.

GUTHRIE Robin (Robert Isles Loftus), b. 27 June 1937, Retired Public Servant. m. Sarah Julia, 2 sons, 1 daughter. Education: MA, Classics, Trinity College, Cambridge, 1958-61; Certificate of Education, Liverpool University, 1961-62; MSc , Economics, London School of Economics, 1966-68. Appointments: Head, Cambridge House, Founder Cambridge House, Literacy Scheme, Teacher at a Brixton Comprehensive School, 1963-69; Social Development Officer, Peterborough Development Corporation, 1969-75; Assistant Director, Social Work Service, DHSS, 1975-79; Director, Joseph Rowntree Memorial Trust (now the Joseph Rowntree Foundation), 1979-88; Chief Charity Commissioner for England and Wales, 1988-92; Director of Economic and Social Affairs, Council of Europe, 1992-98. Publications: Numerous articles and papers in journals including: New Society; The Good European's Dilemma, 2000; New Europe, a graceless trudge – analysis of EU Enlargement; Lectures: First Geraldine Aves Memorial Lecture; First Wynford Vaughan Thomas Memorial Lecture; Fourth Arnold Goodman Charity Lecture; Henri de Koster Memorial Lecture, Strasbourg, 1994. Honour: Honorary DLitt, Bradford University, 1991. Memberships include currently: Chair and Founder, York Museums and Gallery Trust; Chair of Governors, University of York St John; Chair, Jessie's Fund; Chair, Rodolphus Choir; Trustee, The Thalidomide Trust UK; Member of Court, University of York; Vice-President, Cambridge House; Chair, Hans Gal Society; President, York Anglo-German Society. Address: Braeside House, Acomb Road, York, YO24 4EZ, England. E-mail: robin@theguthries.co.uk

GUTHRIE OF CRAIGIEBANK, Gen. Charles Ronald Llewelyn Guthrie, b. 17 November 1938, London, England. Company Director. m. Catherine Worrall, 2 sons. Education: Royal Military Academy, Sandhurst. Appointments: Command, Welsh Guards, 1979; Served BAOR and Aden 22 SAS Regiment, 1965-69; Staff College Graduate, 1972; Military Assistant to Chief of General Staff, Ministry of Defence, 1973-74; Brigade Major, Household Division, 1976-77; Commanding Officer, 1 Battalion Welsh Guards, served Berlin and Northern Ireland, 1977-80; Colonel General Staff Military Operations, Ministry of Defence, 1980-82;

Command British Forces New Hebrides, 1980, 4 Armed Brigade, 1982-84; Chief of Staff, 1 (British) Corps, 1984-86; General Officer Commanding, North East District Command 2 Infantry Division, 1986-87; Assistant Chief to the General Staff, Ministry of Defence, 1987-89; Command 1 British Corps, 1990-91; Commander in Chief, BAOR, 1992-94; Command, Northern Army Group, 1992-93 (now disbanded); Chief of the General Staff, 1994-97; Chief of the Defence Staff, 1997-2001; Colonel Commandant, Intelligence Corps, 1986-95; Colonel Life Guards (Gold Stick; ADC General to HM The Queen, 1993-2001; Colonel Commandant, SAS Regiment, 2000-; Non-Executive Director: N M Rothschild & Sons; Advanced Interactive Systems Inc; Ashley Gardens Block 2 Limited; BICE Chileconsult; Colt Defence LLC; N M Rothschild & Sons (Brazil) Limitada; N M Rothschild & Sons (Mexico) SA de CV; Rothschilds Continuation Holding AG; Member of Council, Institute of International Strategic Studies. Honours: LVO, 1977, OBE, 1980; KCB, 1990; GCB, 1994; Kt SMO Malta, 1999; Commander, Legion of Merit, USA, 2001; Life Peer, 2001; Freeman City of London, 1988; Liveryman, Painter Stainers Co, 1989. Memberships include: President: Federation of London Youth Clubs, Action Research, Army Benevolent Fund; Chairman of the Advisory Board, King's Centre for Military Health Research; Patron: Canning House Library Appeal, Cardinal Hume Centre, Household Cavalry Museum Appeal, Order of Malta's Care Trust, Second World War Experience Centre, UK Defence Forum. Address: New Court, St Swithin's Lane, London EC4P 4DU, England. E-mail: lordguthrie@rothschild.co.uk

GUTIN Gregory, b. 17 January 1957, Novozibkov, Russia. University Professor. m. Irina Gutin, 2 sons. Education: MSc, Mathematics, Gomel University, Belarussia, 1979; PhD, Mathematics, Tel Aviv University, Israel, 1993. Appointments: Research Assistant, Lecturer, Odense University, Denmark, 1993-96; Lecturer, Brunel University, UK, 1996-2000; Professor of Computer Science, Royal Holloway, University of London, 2000-. Publications: Digraphs (monograph with J Bang-Jenson), 2000; Traveling Salesman Problem (editor with A Punnen), 2002; More than 100 research papers. Honour: Kirkman Medal, Institute of Combinatorics and Its Applications, 1996. Address: Department of Computer Science, Royal Holloway, University of London. E-mail: gutin@cs.rhul.ac.uk

GWYNN-JONES Peter Llewellyn, b. 1940. Garter Principal King of Arms. Education: Wellington College; MA, Trinity College, Cambridge. Appointments: Assistant to Sir Anthony Richard Wagner (Garter Principal King of Arms), 1970, appointed Bluemantle Pursuivant of Arms in Ordinary, 1973, promoted to Herald, 1982, served as Lancaster Herald of Arms in Ordinary, and House Comptroller, -1975, Garter Principal King of Arms, 1995-, College of Arms. Honours: Secretary, Harleian Society, 1981-94; Lieutenant of the Royal Victorian Order, 1994; Inspector of Regimental Colours, 1995-; Genealogist to the Order of Bath, Hon Genealogist of the Order of St Michael and St George, and Genealogist of the Most Venerable Order of the Hospital of Saint John of Jerusalem, 1995-; Knight of Justice of the Most Venerable Order of the Hospital of Saint John of Jerusalem, 1995; Non-Executive Vice-President, The Heraldry Society, 1996-; Inspector of Royal Air Force Badges, 1996-; Fellow, Society of Antiquaries, 1997; Commander of the Royal Victorian Order, 1998. Address: The College of Arms, Queen Victoria Street, London EC4V 4BT, England. E-mail: garter@college-of-arms.gov.uk

H

HA Heung Yong, b. 3 October 1960, Jeungpyong, Korea. Research Scientist. m. Mee-Kyung Joh, 1 son, 2 daughters. Education: BS, Department of Chemical Engineering, Seoul National University, 1984; MS, 1986, PhD, 1993, Department of Chemical Engineering, KAIST, Korea. Appointments: Senior Research Scientist, 1993, Principal Research Scientist, Korea Institute of Science and Technology; Postdoctoral studies, University of Wisconsin-Madison, USA, 1993-94; Visiting Scholar, University of Utah, 2004. Publications: More than 60 academic papers; More than 40 patents on fuel cells, catalysts and electrochemistry. Honours: Listed in international biographical dictionaries. Memberships: Korea Membrane Society; Electrochemical Society, USA; Korea Chemical Engineering Society. Address: KIST, 39-1 Hawolgok-dong, Seongbuk-gu, Seoul 136-791, South Korea. E-mail: hyha88@hotmail.com

HA Sang Jun, b. 18 September 1962, Masan City, Korea. Nuclear Engineer. m. Yoon Kyung Yoo, 1 son, 1 daughter. Education: BS, Han Yang University, Seoul, Korea, 1985; MS, 1987, PhD, 1998, Korea Advanced Institute of Science and Technology, Daejeon, Korea. Appointment: Principal Researcher, Korea Electric Power Research Institute, 1985-. Publications: 9 articles in international journals and papers presented at conferences, include most recently: A Dry-Spot Model for Transition Boiling Heat Transfer in Pool Boiling, 1998; A Dry-Spot Model of Critical Heat Flux Applicable to both Pool Boiling and Subcooled Forced Convection, 2000; An Integral Effects Test of Loss of Residual Heat Removal during Mid-loop Operation, 2002; Perspective and Technology Policy of Korean Power Industry for the Hydrogen Economy Era, 2006. Honours: Listed in Who's Who publications and biographical dictionaries. Membership: Korea Nuclear Society, Daejeon, 1987-. Address: Korea Electric Power Research Institute, 103-16, Munji-Dong, Yusong-Gu, Daejeon 305-380, Republic of Korea. E-mail: hsj@kepri.re.kr

HA Seoyong, b. 30 January 1969, Seoul, Korea. Material Scientist. m. Jungeun Kim. Education: BSc, 1991, MSc, 1993, Seoul National University, South Korea; MSc, 1998, PhD, 2002, Carnegie Mellon University, Pittsburgh, Pennsylvania, USA. Appointments: Senior Researcher, LG Cable and Machinery, 1994-97; Research Associate, Carnegie Mellon University, 2002-04; Senior Research Engineer, Samsung Corning Precision Glass, 2004-07; Principal Research Engineer, Samsung Corning Precision Glass, 2007-. Publications: Contributed articles to professional journals. Honours: Sejong Institute Scholarship, Seongnam, 1997-2001; Graduate Seminar Award for Excellence, Carnegie Mellon University, 2002. E-mail: seoyong@gmail.com

HA Sung Ho, b. 5 January 1965, Deagu, Korea. Professor. m. Soo Jeong Son, 1 son, 1 daughter. Education: Bachelor of Business Administration, Yonsei University, Korea, 1990; MS, 1998, PhD, 2001, Management Information Systems, Korea Advanced Institute of Science and Technology (KAIST), Korea. Appointments: Office Worker, Yugong Corporation (Oil Company), 1990-91; System Analyst, LG-EDS Corporation (System Integration), 1991-98; Assistant Professor, Kyungpook National University, 2002-. Publications: Articles in international journals: IEEE Intelligent Systems; Expert Systems with Applications; Computers and Industrial Engineering; Several Korean articles; Several international conference proceedings; Several edited book chapters. Honours: Listed in Who's Who publications and biographical dictionaries. Memberships: IEEE Computer Society; ACM; Decision Sciences Institute; IEEE Computational Intelligence Society; Several Korean academic societies. Address: School of Business Administration, Kyungpook National University, 1370 Sangyeok-dong, Buk-gu, Daegu, Korea 702-701. E-mail: hsh@mail.knu.ac.kr Website: http://database.knu.ac.kr

HA Tae-Sun, b. 6 February 1962, Seoul, Korea. Medical Doctor; Professor. m. Sun-Min Kim, 1 son, 1 daughter. Education: MD, Bachelor of Science, 1987, Master of Medical Science, 1992; Medical Doctorship of Medicinal Science, 1995, Seoul National University, Seoul, Korea. Appointments: Residency, Seoul National University Hospital, 1988-91, Instructor, 1992-94, Assistant Professor, 1994-98, Associate Professor, 1998-2003, Professor, 2003-, Chungbuk National University, Korea. Publications: Articles in scientific journals as author and first author include most recently: Regulation of glomerular endothelial cell proteoglycans by glucose, 2004; Effects of advanced glycosylation end products on perlecan core protein of glomerular epithelium, 2004; The role of tumour necrosis factor-a in Henoch-Schönlein purpura, 2005. Honour: Research Award, Chungbuk National University College of Medicine, 2005; AGE inhibition can improve orthostatic proteinuria associated with nutcracker syndrome, 2006; High glucose and AGE affect the expression of a-actinin-4 in glomerular epithelial cells, 2006; Scrotal involvement in childhood Henoch-Schonlein purpura, 2007. Honours: Research Award, Korean Paediatric Society, 2006. Memberships: Korean Society of Nephrology; Korean Paediatric Society; Korean Society of Paediatric Nephrology; International Paediatric Nephrology Association; American Society of Nephrology; European Renal Association; International Society of Nephrology. Address: Yongam Hyundai Apt 103-805; Sangdang-gu, Cheongju, Chungbuk, Republic of Korea. E-mail: tsha@chungbuk.ac.kr

HAAS Gordon Lewis, b. 18 June 1940, Casper, Wyoming, USA (deceased 2 July 2007). Sandpainter. Education: Engineering, Lockheed, UCLA Extension. Appointments: US Army, 1963-69; Engineer, Lockheed Martin Co, 1963-95; Support to Rockwell International and NASA; Member, Space Shuttle Orbiter Structural Test Team; Sandpainter. Honours: Knight, Order of the Golden Eagle of Poland.

HAAS Russell Luciene, b. 18 June 1940, Casper, Wyoming, USA. Director; CEO; President. Education: Engineering, Scranton, Pennsylvania; Engineering, Lockheed, UCLA Extension; Doctor of Religious Humanities, Phoenix, Arizona; Doctor of Divinity, Modesto, California. Appointments: US Army, 1963-69; Engineer, Lockheed Martin Corporation, 1963-95; Support to Rockwell International and NASA; Member, The Space Shuttle Orbiter Structural Test Team; Director, CEO and President, RL Haas Corporation; Postmaster General of The Principality of Saint Michael de Claremont and Elbasan King of Arms of the Elbasan College of Arms. Memberships: Americans for Change, The Presidential Task Force, 1993-2001; Life Member, The New York Academy of Sciences; Life Member, The US Archaeological Conservancy; Citizen of The Kingdom of Belize (British Honduras), The Hutt River Province, Kingdom of Australia and The United States of America. Honours: Order of Merit, USA; Order of Merit, UK; Diplomatic Service Medal, James Earl Carter, William Jefferson Clinton, Queen Elizabeth II; The Knight Commander of the Order of the Star of the Nile; The Knight Commander of the Order of Saint Andrew of Jerusalem; The Knight of the Order of Saint Victor; The Knight Commander of the Patriarchal Order of the Holy Cross of Jerusalem. Address: 36633 North, 94th Street East, Littlerock, CA 93543, USA.

HABER Harvey M, Lawyer. m. 4 children. Education: BA, University of Toronto, 1957; LLB, Osgoode Hall Law School, 1960; Called to Bar of Ontario, 1962; Queen's Counsel, 1978. Appointments: Partner, Greening & Haber, 1962-63; Corporate Counsel, Trizec Equities Ltd, 1963-67; Corporate Counsel, Jiger Corporation Ltd, 1967-68; Corporate Counsel, Dylex Ltd, 1968-70; Corporate Secretary, The Greater York Group, 1970-74; Corporate Counsel, Courtot Investments Ltd, 1974-75; Senior Leasing Counsel, The Cadillac Fairview Corporation Ltd, 1975-81; Associate, Perry, Farley & Onyshuk, 1981-84; Partner, Goldman, Litwack, Nash & Haber, 1984-87; Partner, Lilly, Goldman, 1987-90; Senior Partner, Goldman Sloan Nash & Haber LLP, 1990-. Publications: Author: The Commercial Lease: A Practical Guide, 1989; Landlord's Rights and Remedies in a Commercial Lease: A Practical Guide, 1996; Understanding the Commercial Agreement to Lease, 1990; Editor: Distress: A Commercial Landlord's Remedy, 2001; Tenant's Rights and Remedies in a Commercial Lease: A Practical Guide, 1998; Distress: A Commercial Landlord's Remedy, 2001; Assignment, Subletting and Change of Control in a Commercial Lease: A Practical Guide, 2002; Editor-in-Chief: Shopping Centre Leases, 1976; Co-Author, Giving Thanks – Graces for Every Occasion, 1994; Numerous papers and articles in professional journals. Honours: Listed in Canadian Legal Lexpert Directory, 1997-2004; Ontario Bar Association Award, 2000; Law Society Medal, 2002; Alumni Gold Key Award, Osgoode Hall Law School, 2005; Mediator, Arbitrator and Expert Witness. Memberships: Director and Member, The Metropolitan Toronto Lawyers Association; Vice President, Canadian Bar Associations; Member, Canadian Law Conference Program Committee, International Council of Shopping Centers; Member, Board of Editors, Commercial Leasing Law & Strategy; Member, Editorial Board, National Real Property Law Review; Member, Board of Advisors, Commercial Lease Law Insider's Commercial Property Law Digest; Member, Editorial Advisory Board, Law Times; Member, Board of Advisors, Commercial Lease Law Insider; Member, Volunteer Lawyers Service; Member, Advisory Council of Second Harvest; Member, Board of Editors, Retail Law Strategist; Member, Editorial Board, The Jewish Tribune; Director, Board of Directors, Metropolitan Toronto Condominium Corporation No 1093. Address: 250 Dundas Street West, Suite 700, Toronto, Ontario M5T 2Z5, Canada. E-mail: haber@gsnh.com Website: www.gsnh.com/lawyers/haber.html

HABERMAN Mandy Nicola, b. 19 October 1954, United Kingdom. Inventor; Entrepreneur. m. Steven Haberman, 1 son, 2 daughters. Education: BA (Hons), Graphic Design, St Martin's School of Art, London, 1976. Career: Freelance design contract, ILEA adult literacy project, 1976-78; Career change to become inventor and entrepreneur, invented Haberman Feeder, 1982, Founder and Manager, Haberman Feeders Ltd (to establish product in hospitals and mail order), 1984; Invented the Anywayup Cup, 1990, Founder, The Haberman Company, 1995; Principal, Haberman Associates, 1998-; Director, CafeBabe Ltd, 2003-; Founded independent on-line forum: www.makesparksfly.com to promote awareness and debate in intellectual property rights issues, 2002; Member: Intellectual Property Strategic IT Committee, Patent Office, 2001, Chartered Institute of Patents Agents Disciplinary Board, 2001-, Intellectual Property Advisory Committee, 2002-2005, Advisory Council for European Commission's Information Society Technologies Programme, 2002, Simfonec Advisory Committee, CASS Business School, 2003; Editorial Board of Patent World, Informa Law; Speaker on innovation, design and intellectual property rights at numerous national and international events. Honours: Anywayup® Cup is a Millennium Product, 2000; 3M Award for Innovation, 2000, Nokia Award for Consumer Product Design, 2000, Design in Business Association; Female Inventor of the Year, 2000; Gold Medal, Geneva Salon des Inventions, 2000; Horners Award for Innovation, British Plastics Federation, 2002; Tommy Award (St Thomas' Hospital) for Most Parent Friendly Innovative Product, 2000 and 2001; Honorary Doctorate in Design and Honorary Fellow, University of Bournemouth, 2002; Special Recognition Award, Global Woman Inventors and Innovators Network, 2003; Special Achievement Award, IOD Suffolk, 2003; Recognised as "Pioneer to the Life of the Nation" by HM Queen Elizabeth, 2003; Finalist in Veuve Clicquot Business Woman of the Year Award, 2004. Memberships: Fellow, Royal Society of Arts; Ideas 21. Address: 44 Watford Road, Radlett, Hertfordshire WD7 8LR, England. E-mail: mandy.haberman@virgin.net Website: www.mandyhaberman.com

HABGOOD Anthony John, b. 8 November 1946, Woodbastwick, England. Company Director. m. Nancy Atkinson, 2 sons, 1 daughter. Education: BA, Economics, Gonville and Caius College, Cambridge University, 1968; MS, Industrial Administration, Carnegie-Mellon University, Pittsburgh, USA, 1970; MA, Economics, Gonville and Caius College, 1972. Appointments: Director, 1976-86; Member, Management Committee, 1979, Member, Executive Committee, 1981, Boston Consulting Group Inc; Director, 1986-91, Chief Executive Officer, 1991, Tootal Group plc; Non-Executive Director, Geest plc, 1988-93; Chief Executive, 1991-96, Chairman, 1996-, BUNZL plc; Non-Executive Director, Powergen plc, 1993-2001; Non-Executive Director, SVG Capital plc, 1995-; Non-Executive Director, National Westminster Bank plc, 1998-2001; Non-Executive Director, Marks and Spencer plc, 2004-5; Chairman, Whitbread Plc, 2005-. Address: 110 Park Street, London W1K 6NX, England.

HABGOOD John Stapylton, Baron of Habgood Calverton, b. 23 June 1927. Retired Archbishop of York; Author. m. Rosalie Mary Ann Boston, 7 June 1961, 2 sons, 2 daughters. Education: BA, 1948, MA, 1951, PhD, 1952, King's College, Cambridge; Cuddesdon College, Oxford. Appointments: Demonstrator in Pharmacology, Cambridge, 1950-53; Fellow, King's College, Cambridge, 1952-55; Curate, St Mary Abbots, Kensington, 1954-56; Vice Principal, Westcott House, Cambridge, 1956-62; Rector, St John's Church, Jedburgh, 1962-67; Principal, Queen's College, Birmingham, 1967-73; Bishop of Durham, 1973-83; Archbishop of York, 1983-95; Pro Chancellor, University of York, 1985-90; Hulsean Preacher, University of Cambridge, 1987-88; Bampton Lecturer, University of Oxford, 1999; Gifford Lecturer, University of Aberdeen, 2000. Publications: Religion and Science, 1964; A Working Faith: Essays and Addresses on Science, Medicine and Ethics, 1980; Church and Nation in a Secular Age, 1983; Confessions of a Conservative Liberal, 1988; Making Sense, 1993; Faith and Uncertainty, 1997; Being a Person: Where Faith and Science Meet, 1998; Varieties of Unbelief, 2000; The Concept of Nature, 2002. Contributions: Theology and the Sciences, Interdisciplinary Science Reviews, 2000. Honours: Honorary DD, Universities of Durham, 1975, Cambridge, 1984, Aberdeen, 1988, Huron, 1990, Hull, 1991, Oxford, 1996, Manchester, 1996; Honorary DU, York, 1996; Privy Counsellor, 1983; Honorary Fellow, King's College, Cambridge, 1986; Life Peer, 1995. Address: 18 The Mount, Malton, North Yorkshire YO17 7ND, England.

HACKMAN Gene, b. 30 January 1930, San Bernardino, California, USA. Actor. m. 1. Fay Maltese 1956, divorced 1985, 1 son, 2 daughters; 2. Betsy Arakawa, 1991. Education: Studied Acting, Pasadena Playhouse. Career: Films include: Lilith, 1964; Hawaii, 1966; Banning, 1967; Lucky Lady, 1975; Night Moves, 1976; Domino Principle, 1977; Superman, 1978; Superman II, 1980; Bat 21, 1987; The Package, The Von Metz Incident, Loose Connections, Full Moon in Blue Water, Postcards From the Edge, Cass Action, 1989; Loose Canons, Narrow Margin, 1990; Necessary Roughness, The William Munny Killings, 1991; The Unforgiven, The Firm, 1992; Geronimo, Wyatt Earp, 1994; Crimson Tide, The Quick and the Dead, 1995; Get Shorty, Birds of a Feather, Extreme Measures, The Chamber, Absolute Power, 1996; Twilight, Enemy of the State, 1998; Under Suspicion, 2000; Heist, The Royal Tenenbaums, 2001; Runaway Jury, 2003; Welcome to Mooseport, 2004; Numerous TV appearances and stage plays. Publication: Co-author, Wake of the Perdido Star, 2000. Honours: Academy Award, Best Actor; New York Film Critics Award; Golden Globe Award; British Academy Awards; Cannes Film Festival Award; National Review Board Award; Berlin Film Award; Golden Globe for Best Actor in a Musical or Comedy, 2001; Cecil B DeMille Award, Golden Globes, 2003. Address: c/o Barry Haldeman, 1900 Avenue of the Stars, 2000 Los Angeles, CA 90067, USA.

HADDAD Ghassan, b. 1926, Lattaquia, Syria. Educationist; Academic. Education: Bachelor and Master in Military Sciences, Military Academy, Damascus, Syria; PhD in Economic Sciences, DSc in International Economic Sciences, University of Humboldt-Berlin, Germany. Appointments: Several important military positions before reaching the rank of Staff Major General, Syria, 1963; Planning Minister, Syria, 1963-66; Researcher then Visiting Professor, Germany, 1866-75; Economic Advisor and Chief of Experts, Ministry of Planning, Baghdad, Iraq, 1975-85; Professor of Postgraduate Studies in Economic Science, Baghdad University, 1975-85; Professor of Postgraduate Studies in Economic Science, Al Mustansyriah, Iraq, 1985-2002; Researcher and Visiting Professor of Postgraduate Studies in Economic Science, Paris, France, 2002-. Publications: Books and researches in Arabic, French and German. Honours: Many distinguished medals and honours include: Syrian Medal of Merit (Excellent Degree); Syrian Medal of Fidelity; Certificate of Honour, Iraqi Union of Writers; Listed in Who's Who publications and biographical dictionaries; Participation in many regional, national and international conferences. Memberships: Union of Arab Writers; Union of Arab Historians; Union of Arab Economists; Editorial committees of several academic periodicals. Address: 7 Allée du Bosquet, 92310 Sèvres, France. E-mail: ghassanmrhaddad@yahoo.com

HADFIELD Andrew David, b. 25 April 1962, Kendal, Cumbria, England. Professor of English. m. Alison Sarah Yarnold, 1 son, 2 daughters. Education: BA, 1st Class Honours, University of Leeds, England, 1984; DPhil, University of Ulster, Northern Ireland, 1988. Appointments: British Academy Postdoctoral Fellow, University of Leeds, 1989-92; Lecturer in English, 1992-96, Senior Lecturer in English, 1996-98, Professor of English, 1998-2003, University of Wales, Aberystwyth; Visiting Professor in English, Columbia University, New York, USA, 2002-2003; Professor of English, University of Sussex, England, 2003-. Publications: Literature, Politics and National Identity, 1994; Spenser's Irish Experience, 1997; Literature Travel and Colonial Writing, 1998; The English Renaissance, 2000; Shakespeare, Spenser and the Matter of Britain, 2003; Shakespeare and Renaissance Politics, 2003; Shakespeare and Republicanism, 2005.

Honours: Fellow of the English Association; Leverhulme Major Award, 2001-2004; Chatterton Lecture at the British Academy, 2003. Memberships: English Association; Spenser Society of America. Address: Department of English, University of Sussex, Falmer, Brighton BN1 9QN, England.

HAFI Aurangzeb, b. 19 December 1972, Gujranwala, Pakistan. Research Scholar. Education: BSc, Colombo South Government, General University and Teaching Hospital, Sri Lanka, 1992; MSc, University of Alma Ata, 1994; PhD, Academia Sinica, Republic of China, 1997; D Litt, University of la PAIX, Russia, 2001. Appointments include: Visiting Professor, Colombo South Government General University & Teachin Hospital, 1995-2000; Chief Research Methodologist, Academia Sinica, Beijing, Republic of China, 1997-99; Adjunct Professor, Institute de Korte, Amsterdam, Netherland, 1999-2000; Keynote Speaker, World Congress on Integration of Medicines, WHO, 1999-2000; Senior Research Advisor, United Nations SMOKHM International University, 1999-2000; Chief Research Methodologist, Commonwealth Sovereign Military Hospitallers' International Institute of Higher Studies & Research, 1999-; Post Doctoral Professorial Fellow, Commonwealth Institute UK, 2001; Professorial Fellow, Advisory Committee on Biomagnetics, The Commonwealth Institute; Doctoral and Post Doctoral Research Analyst, MAVSO International Lahore, Pakistan, 2003-; All Universities Steering Task Force for the Asian Earth Quake Management, 2005-06; Principal Investigator, Tsunami Child Retardation Risk Assessment Project, Sri Lanka & Maldives, 2005; Prime Executory Head & Chief Task Executor, Tsunami Child Retardation Risk Management Program, Sri Lanka; Chief Researcher & Principal Assessor, Post Earth Quake Child Retardation Risk Assessment Program, Kashmir, Pakistan; Professor Emeritus, University of la PAIX; Adjunct Professor, United Nation Ecumenical International Institute of Humanities, Ethics, Legislation & Integrated Sciences; Adjunct Professor, The Commonwealth Institute, UK; Senior Research Advisor, United Nations University, Belgium; Chief Research Methodologist, Senior Research Advisor, Oxford Steering Committee on Humanitarianism and Research Methodology; BRT Research Advisor; Keynote Speaker, Chief Theme Speaker, Tsunami International Summit, 2006-07. Publications: Over 335 scientific research papers; Supervision of 27 doctoral and 2 post-doctoral thesis; Presented over 115 research papers at national and international conferences. Honours include: Grand Chevalier Officer, Royal Order of the Knights of Peace and Justice; Meritorious Royal Knight Supreme of the Roll of Honour & Chevalier of Merit; Meritorious Royal Knight Supreme, 20th Century Person of Exceptional Merits, Protector & Grand Bailiff for Asia & Oceania, Sovereign Military Order of the Knights Hospitallers of Malta; Man of the Year 2003; Dag Hammarskjöld UN Scholarship, 1997-2001; Pax Mundi Research Scholarship, 1999-2002; Professional Excellence Award, Royal Assyrian Order of Merit; Yellow Emperor's Award, Chinese Academy of Sciences; Universal Recognition Award, Ancient Royal Order of Physicians; Ambassador of World Peace & Humanitarianism, 2005-06; Commendary Head in Asia, The Ancient Assyrian Order of Knights, Knights of the Djuna Academy of Science, Royal Order of the Knights of Peace and Justice. Address: 21-T-St, Z-Block, Peoples Colony, Gujranwala, Pakistan. E-mail: chancellor@siraurangzeb.org Website: www.siraurangzeb.org

HAGA Tatsuya, b. 14 February 1941, Tokyo, Japan. Scientist. m. Kazuko Tsutsumi. Education: Bachelor Degree, Faculty of Science, Tokyo University, 1963; PhD, Department of Biochemistry, Graduate School of Science, Tokyo

University, 1970. Appointments: Instructor, Tokyo University, 1969-74; Associate Professor, Hamamatsu University School of Medicine, 1974-88; Professor, Tokyo University, 1988-2001; Director and Professor Gakushuin University, Institute for Biomolecular Science, 2001-. Publications: Solubilization, purification and molecular characterization of receptors: Principles and strategy (Chapter in Receptor Biochemistry), 1990; G Protein-coupled receptors, Structure, Function and Ligand Screening, (editor), 2006. Membership: International Society of Neurochemistry. Address: Institute for Biomolecular Science, Gakushuin University, 1-5-1 Mejiro, Toshima-ku, Tokyo 171-8588, Japan. E-mail: tatsuya.haga@gakushuin.ac.jp

HAGER Hermann Amadeus, b. 1 February 1955, Vienna, Austria. Artist; Painter. Education: Bachelor of Medicine, University of Norway, 1980; Doctor of Psychology and Philosophy, University of Italy, 1990. Career: Painter; Musician; Composer; Journalist; Educator; Consultant; Soul-Doctor; Reformer of Psycho-Methods; Inventor of the "Cromo-School" to help people suffering from Crom-anomolies; Advocates the company of cats as a therapy for people suffering from mental illness (and the purring of cats helps also against hypertension, the purring is the fact which enables cats to help patients); Created the painting style "Colourmetry"; Created the music composition style "musimetry"; Created the architectural style "Archimetry" Currently working on the design of his T-Shirt Collection. Publications: Books: How to Communicate Successfully with Austrians; 100 Logical Puzzles; Geometric Colouring Book; 100 Mathematical Puzzles; Train Your Brain; Introduction to Musimetry; Many articles in different magazines. Honours: Numerous honours and awards include: Nominated for Man of the Year 2004, 2005, 2006 and 2007, American Biographical Institute; Listed in Who's Who publications and biographical dictionaries. Memberships: American Association for the Advancement of Science; New York Academy of Sciences. Address: Piaristengasse 5-7, 1080 Vienna, Austria.

HAGGER Nicholas Osborne, b. 22 May 1939, London, England. British Poet; Verse Dramatist; Short Story Writer; Lecturer; Author; Man of Letters; Philosopher; Cultural Historian. m. (1) Caroline Virginia Mary Nixon, 16 September 1961, 1 daughter, (2) Madeline Ann Johnson, 22 February 1974, 2 sons. Education: MA English Literature, Worcester College, Oxford, 1958-61. Appointments: Lecturer in English, University of Baghdad, 1961-62; Professor of English Literature, Tokyo University of Education and Keio University, Tokyo, 1963-67; Tokyo University, 1964-65; Lecturer in English, University of Libya, Tripoli, 1968-70; Freelance Features for Times, 1970-72. Publications: The Fire and the Stones: A Grand Unified Theory of World History and Religion, 1991; Selected Poems: A Metaphysical's Way of Fire, 1991; The Universe and the Light: A New View of the Universe and Reality, 1993; A White Radiance: The Collected Poems 1958-93, 1994; A Mystic Way: A Spiritual Autobiography, 1994; Awakening to the Light: Diaries, Vol 1, 1958-67, 1994; A Spade Fresh with Mud: Collected Stories, Vol 1, 1995; The Warlords: From D-Day to Berlin, A Verse Drama, 1995; A Smell of Leaves and Summer: Collected Stories, Vol 2, 1995; Overlord, The Triumph of Light 1944-1945: An Epic Poem, Books 1 & 2, 1995, Books 3-6, 1996, Books 7-9, 10-12, 1997; The One and the Many, 1999; Wheeling Bats and a Harvest Moon: Collected Stories, Vol 3, 1999; Prince Tudor, A Verse Drama, 1999; The Warm Glow of the Monastery Courtyard: Collected Stories, Vol 4, 1999; The Syndicate: The Story of the Coming World Government, 2004; The Secret History of the West: The

Influence of Secret Organisations on Western History from the Renaissance to the 20th Century, 2005; Classical Odes: Poems on England, Europe and a Global Theme, and of Everyday Life in the One, 2006; The Light of Civilization, 2006; Overlord, one-volume edition, 2006; Collected Poems, 1958-2005, 2006; Collected Verse Plays, 2007; Collected Short Stories: A Thousand and One Mini-Stories or Verbal Paintings, 2007; The Secret Founding of America, 2007; The Rise and Fall of Civilizations: Why Civilizations Rise and Fall and What Happens When They End, 2007; The Last Tourist in Iran, 2007; Universalism, 2008. Membership: Society of Authors. E-mail: info @nicholashagger.co.uk Website: www.nicholashagger.co.uk

HAGUE William Jefferson, b. 26 March 1961, Rotherham, Yorkshire, England. Politician; Management Consultant. m. Ffion Jenkins, 1997, 1 son. Education: BA, Honours, Magdalen College, Oxford, England; MBA, Insead Business School, France, 1986. Appointments: Management Consultant, McKinsey & Co, 1983-88; Elected to Parliament, Richmond, Yorkshire, England, 1989; Parliamentary Private Secretary to Chancellor of Exchequer, 1990-93; Parliamentary Under-Secretary of State, Department Social Security, 1993-94; Ministry of State, Department of Social Security, 1994-95; Secretary of State for Wales, 1995-97; Leader, Conservative Party, 1997-2001; Chair, International Democratic Union, 1999-2001; Political Adviser, JCB PLC, 2001-; Non-Executive Director, AES Eng PLC, 2001-; Member, Political Council of Terra Firma Capital Partners, 2001-; Shadow Foreign Secretary, 2005-. Publications: William Pitt the Young, 2004. Honours: British Book Award for History Book of the Year, 2005. Honour: Privy Councillor, 1995. Address: House of Commons, London SW1A 0AA, England.

HAHN Frank Horace, b. 26 April 1925, Berlin, Germany. Emeritus Professor of Economics. m. Dorothy Salter. Education: Bournemouth Grammar School; BSc (Econ), 1945, PhD, 1951, London School of Economics; MA, University of Cambridge, 1960. Appointments: Lecturer in Economics, University of Birmingham, 1948-58; Reader in Mathematical Economics, University of Birmingham, 1958-60; Fellow, Churchill College, Cambridge, 1960-; Lecturer in Economics, University of Cambridge, 1960-66; Professor of Economics, London School of Economics, 1967-72; Professor of Economics, 1972-92, Professor Emeritus, 1992-, University of Cambridge; Professor Ordinario, 1989-2000, Emeritus Professor, 2000-, University of Siena. Publications: 135 publications including books written and edited. Honours: D Soc Sci, Birmingham, 1981; Doctor Honoris Causa, Strasbourg, 1984; D Litt, East Anglia, 1984; DSc (Econ), London, 1985; Doctor of the University, York, 1991; Doctor of Letters, Leicester, 1993; Doctor of Philosophy, Athens, 1993; Docteur Honoris Causa de l'Universite Paris X, Nanterre, 1999. Memberships: Fellow, British Academy; Corresponding Fellow, American Academy of Arts and Sciences; Foreign Associate, US National Academy of Sciences; Honorary Member, American Economic Association; Honorary Fellow, London School of Economics; Member, Academia Europaea; Palacky Gold Medal, Czechoslovak Academy of Sciences; Honorary Member, Italian Association for the History of Political Economy; President, Econometric Society, 1968-69; President, Royal Economic Society, 1986-89; President, Section F, British Association for the Advancement of Science, 1990. Address: Churchill College, Cambridge, CB3 0DS, England.

HAIN Peter Gerald, b. 16 February 1950, Nairobi, Kenya. Member of Parliament. m. Elizabeth Haywood, 2 sons. Education: BSc, Economics and Political Science, Queen Mary College, University of London, 1973; MPhil, Sussex University, 1976. Appointments: Chairman, Stop the Seventy Tour Campaign, 1969-70; Chairman, Young Liberals, 1971-73; Press Officer, Anti-Nazi League, 1977-80; Assistant Research Officer, Union of Communication Workers, 1976-87; Head of Research, Union of Communication Workers, 1987-91; Opposition Whip, 1995; Opposition Spokesman on Employment, 1995-96; Parliamentary Under-Secretary of State, Wales Officer, 1997-99; Minister of State, Foreign and Commonwealth Office, 1999-2001; Minister of State, Department of Trade and Industry, 2001; Ministry of State (Europe), Foreign and Commonwealth Officer, 2001-02; Secretary of State for Wales, 2002-; Leader of the House of Commons and Lord Privy Seal, 2003-05; Secretary of State for Northern Ireland, 2005-06; Secretary State for Work and Pensions, 2007. Publications: Don't Play with Apartheid, 1971; Community Politics, 1976; Mistaken Identity, 1976; Editor, Policing the Police, vol 1, 1978, vol 2, 1980; Neighbourhood Participation, 1980; Crisis and Future of the Left, 1980; Political Strikes, 1986; A Putney Plot, 1987; The Peking Connection, 1995; Ayes to the Left, 1995; Sing The Beloved Country, 1996.; The Future Party, 2004. Memberships: GMB; Neath Workingmen's Club; Neath Rugby Club; Resolven Rugby Club; Resolven Royal British Legion Institute. Address: House of Commons, London SW1A 1AA, England.

HAINES John Francis, b. 30 November 1947, Chelmsford, Essex, England. Government Official; Poet. m. Margaret Rosemary Davies, 19 March 1977. Education: Padgate College of Education, 1966-69; ONC in Public Administration, Millbank College of Commerce, 1972. Appointments: General Assistant; Payments Assistant. Publications: Other Places, Other Times, 1981; Spacewain, 1989; After the Android Wars, 1992; Orders from the Bridge, 1996; Pennine Triangle (with Steve Sneyd & J C Hartley), 2002; A Case Without Gravity (translation), 2005; The Bards 14: Overdrawn at the Memory Bank, 2006; Bus Stop (with Dainis Bisenieks 'The Long Trip') 2006. Contributions to: Dark Horizons; Fantasy Commentator; First Time; Folio; Idomo; Iota; Macabre; New Hope International; Not To Be Named; Overspace; Purple Patch; Sandor; The Scanner; Simply Thrilled Honey; Spokes; Star Line; Stride; Third Half; Yellow Dwarf; A Child's Garden of Olaf; A Northern Chorus; Ammonite; Boggers All; Eldritch Science; Foolscap; Heliocentric Net; Lines of Light; Ore; Pablo Lennis; Pleiade; Premonitions; Mentor; Rampant Guinea Pig; Zone; Positively Poetry; What Poets Eat; Mexicon 6 - The Party; Terrible Work; Xenophilia; Literae; XUENSē; Dreaming Scryers True Deceivers; Yesterday & Today, Tomorrow. Memberships: Science Fiction Poetry Association; British Fantasy Society; The Eight Hand Gang, founder-member. Address: 5 Cross Farm, Station Road, Padgate, Warrington WA2 0QG, England.

HAINS Gaétan Joseph Daniel Robert, b. 9 May 1963, Montreal, Canada. Computer Scientist. Education: BSc, honours, Concordia University, 1985; MSc, 1987, DPhil, 1990, Oxford University. Appointments: Researcher, CRIM Montreal, 1989; Assistant Professor, Associate Professor, University of Montreal, 1989-95; Visiting Professor, ENS Lyon, 1994; Visiting Researcher, Fujitsu-ISIS, Japan, 1994-95; Professor, 1995-, Director, 2000-05, 1st Class Professor, 2004-, Laboratoire d'informatique fondamentale d'Orleans, University of Orleans; Program Officer, Software Research Programs at Agence Nationale de la Recherche (ANR),

2005-06; Professor, 2006-, Director, 2007-, Laboratoire d'Algorithmique Complexité et Logique, Université Paris 12. Honours: Commonwealth Scholar, 1986-89; IISF Visiting Scholarship, Japan, 1992. Address: LACL, Université Paris 12, 94000 Créteil, France. Website: http://hains.org

HAKIM Alan James, b. 4 March 1968, London, England. Doctor. Education: MB BChir, MA, Fitzwilliam College, Cambridge University, 1991. Appointments: House Officer, 1992-93, Senior House Officer, 1993-94, Addenbrooke's Hospital, Cambridge; Specialist Registrar, North Thames Deanery, 1994-2000; Clinical Research Fellow, Arthritis Research Campaign, St Thomas' Hospital, London, 2000-03; Consultant Rheumatologist and Physician, Whipps Cross University Hospital, 2001-; Honorary Consultant Rheumatologist, University College London Hospitals, 2003-. Publications: 56 papers, reviews, chapters and abstracts; Text book, The Oxford Handbook of Rheumatology, 2003, 2nd edition, 2006. Honours: Highly Commended, British Medical Association Book Competition, 2003. Memberships: Fellow, Royal College of Physicians, London; Vice President, Section for Rheumatology and Rehabilitation, The Royal Society of Medicine; British Society of Rheumatology; British Medical Association; Hunterian Society; Advanced Medical Leader, British Association of Medical Managers, 2007. Address: Department of Rheumatology, Whipps Cross University Hospital NHS Trust, Leytonstone, London E11 1NR, England.

HAKKINEN Mika, b. 28 September 1968, Helsinki, Finland. Racing Driver. m. Erja Honkanen, 1 son, 1 daughter. Appointments: Formerly, go-kart driver, Formula Ford 1600 driver, Finnish, Swedish and Nordic Champion, 1987; Formula 3 driver, British Champion with West Surrey racing, 1990; Formula 1 driver Lotus, 1991-93, McLaren, 1993-2001; Grand Prix wins: European, 1997, Australia, 1998, Brazil, 1998, 1999, Spain, 1998, 1999, 2000, Monaco, 1998, Austria, 1998, 2000, Germany, 1998, Luxembourg, 1998, Japan, 1998, 1999, Malaysia, 1999, Hungary, 1999, 2000, Belgium, 2000; Formula One Driver's Championship Winner, 1998, 1999; Sabbatical, 2001; Retirement from Formula One, 2002; FIA European Rally Championship, Finland, 2003. Publication: Mika Hakkinen: Doing What Comes Naturally.

HAKOBYAN Hrant, b. 17 December 1927, Sarukhan, Gegharkunik, Armenia. Philologist; Historian; Philosopher. m. Tereza Ohanyan, 1 son, 3 daughters. Education: Historian, Higher Education Diploma, 1950; Philologist, Higher Education Diploma, 1956; Candidate of Sciences, Philosophy, 1973; Doctor of Sciences, Philosophy, 1990. Appointments: History Teacher, 1947-50; School Headmaster, 1950-62; Administrator, Propaganda Section of CPSU, Kamo, 1962-63; Headmaster, boarding school, Kamo, 1963-64; Professor, Yerevan Polytechnical Institute, 1964-85; Chairman, Department of Religious Studies, Yerevan State University, 1985-2005; Founder, Gavar State University, 1993; Rector, 1993-2006, Chairman, 2006-, Gavar State University Administration Council. Publications: 6 books; 60 papers; 200 conference talks. Honours: Supreme Council Medal & Diploma, Labour Braveness; Honoured Citizen of Gavar, Diploma; Fridtjof Nansen Gold Medal. Memberships: Knowledge Association; Yerevan State University Scientific Council; Gavar State University Scientific Council; Commission for Awarding Scientific Degrees in Philosophy.

HALE-BARRETT Lori, b. 15 February 1960, St Louis, Missouri. Realtor. Education: Degrees in Psychology, Education and Business, Washington University, St Louis,

1982. Appointments: Optical Specialist, Marketing, Trans America Optical Co Inc, 1991-92; Realtor, 1992- Research Advisor, IBC, ABI., 1991-. Publications: Several professional publications including: Tips on a Good Direct Mail Marketing Program, 1990. Honours: Participant in Miss Missouri Pageant and Judge, 1980's; First Place Ribbons in Public Speaking; First Place regional Awards in Marketing and Sales; The Key of Success Award, 1991; The Most Admired Woman of the Decade, ABI; International Woman of the Year, 1991-98; Delta Gamma Sorority; Outstanding Woman of the 20th Century; Outstanding Woman of the 21st Century; International Woman of the Millennium, 2000; International Ambassador of Goodwill to England, IBC, 2003; 100 of the Most Intriguing People, IBA, 2003; Inducted into Hall of Fame for Real Estate, IBC, 2004; International Peace Prize, IBA, 2004. Address: PO Box 491, Chesterfield, MO 63006, USA.

HALILI Antonio Marquez, b. 9 January 1951, Coloocan City, Philippines. Facilities Maintenance Mechanic. m. Brenda Gotay Ferrer, 2 sons, 3 daughters. Education: Diploma, National Technical School, Los Angeles, California; Attended, El Camino Community College, Torrance, California. Appointments: Salesman, Manila, Philippines, 1966-70; Seafarer, Merchant Marine International (Q/M, A/B, O/S, Wifer), 1970-76; Head Bussboy, Denny's Restaurant, Sunset Boulevard, Hollywood, California, 1976-77; Class A Wireman, Strand Century Lighting, Inglewood, California, 1977-79; Production Electrician Mechanic, 1979-86, Production Electrician, Technical Engineer, 1986-89, Todd Pacific Shipyard, San Pedro, California; Facilities Maintenance Mechanic, American Airline Los Angeles International Airport, California, 1989-. Publications: Biographer, The Cry of the Dying Medicine Man; Inventor: Liquid Hose Clean Up Attachment. Honours: YMCA Certificate, Beginners Swimming Course, 1967; Domain of Neptunus Rex, 1974; Citation USS Antietam CG-54, 1987; National Management Association of California, 1987; Certificate of Appreciation and Recognition, Magat Salamat Elementary School, Tondo, Manila, Philippines, 2003; Oath of Office, City of Carson, California (Adviser/Tondo Association USA, 2004; Certificate of Recognition, Tondo Association, USA, 2004; Certificate of Appreciation WWII Memorial, Washington DC, 2004; Listed in Who's Who publications and biographical dictionaries. Memberships: Knight of Columbus, Carson, California Chapter, 1987; National Management Association, California, 1987; March of Dimes/Saving Babies, 2001-2002; Vice-Chairperson, Asian Pacific Islanders Employee Resource Group, American Airlines, 2003; Go for Broke Foundation (WWII Japanese/American Soldiers); WWII Filipino Veterans Advocate, 1997-; WWII Memorial Lifetime Charter Member; Adviser, Tondo Association, USA, Lakewood, California, 2004-2006. 1318 East 55th Street, Long Beach, CA 90805, USA. E-mail: tbhalili@hotmail.com

HALL Christopher Sandford, b. 9 March 1936, Tunbridge Wells, Kent, England. Solicitor. m. Susanna Bott, 3 sons. Education: MA, Trinity College, Cambridge. Appointments: National Service and Reserve TAVR, 5 Royal Inniskilling Dragoon Guards, 1954-56, 1956-70; Solicitor, 1963, Partner, Senior Partner, 1964-96, Cripps, Harries, Hall, Tunbridge Wells; Consultant, Knights Solicitors; Chairman, A Burslem & Son Ltd, Stonemasons; Director, Brighton Race Course Ltd; Chairman, International League for the Protection of Horses; Racing Welfare, retired 2006. Honours: Territorial Decoration (TD), 1970; Deputy Lieutenant, East Sussex, 1986. Memberships: Tunbridge Wells and Tonbridge District Law Society, President, 1987; Jockey Club, 1990-, Chairman

Disciplinary Committee and Steward, 1996-2000; Member, Jockey Club Appeal Board; Chairman, Jockey Club Arab Horse Racing Committee; South of England Agricultural Society, Chairman, 1984-90; Worshipful Company of Broderers, Master, 1980; Member County Committee for Sussex, Country Landowners Association (retired 2007); Southdown and Eridge Hunt, Chairman, 1978-84; Olympia Show Jumping, Chairman, 2000; Hackney Horse Society, President, 2007-2009. Address: Great Danegate, Eridge, Tunbridge Wells TN3 9HU, England. E-mail: cshall.danegate@virgin.net

HALL Jerry, b. 2 July 1956, Texas, USA. Model; Actress. m. Mick Jagger, 1990, divorced 1999, 2 sons, 2 daughters. Education: Trained at the Actors Studio in New York and the National Theatre, London; 2 years Humanities, Open University. Career: Began modelling, Paris, 1970s; Numerous TV appearances including David Letterman Show, USA; Own TV series, Jerry Hall's Gurus, BBC, 2003; Contributing editor, Tatler, 1999-; Stage debut in William Inge's Bus Stop, Lyric Theatre, London, 1990; Films: Merci Docteur Rey, Willie and Phil, 1980; Urban Cowboy, 1980; Topo Galileo, 1987; Let's Spend the Night Together, Running Out of Luck, 1987; Hysteria! 2 (TV), 1989; The Emperor and the Nightingale, Batman, 1989; 25 x 5: The Continuing Adventures of the Rolling Stones, 1989; The Wall: Live in Berlin (TV), 1990; Bejewelled (TV), 1991; Freejack, 1992; Princess Caraboo, 1994; Savage Hearts, 1995; Vampire in Brooklyn, 1995; Diana and Me, 1997; RPM, 1997; Being Mick (TV), 2001; Comic Relief, 2001; Tooth, 2004; Plays: The Graduate, 2000, 2003; Picasso's Women, 2001; The Play What I Wrote, 2002; The Vagina Monologues, 2002, 2003; Benchmark, 2003; Bus Stop. Publications: Tell Tales, 1985; Jerry Hall's Gurus, 2004. Address: c/o Artists International Network, 32 Tavistock Street, London WC2E 7PB, England.

HALL J(ohn) C(live), b. 12 September 1920, London, England. Poet. Education: Oriel College, Oxford. Appointments: Staff, Encounter Magazine, 1955-91; Editor, Literary Executor of Keith Douglas. Publications: Poetry: Selected Poems, 1943; The Summer Dance and Other Poems, 1951; The Burning Hare, 1966; A House of Voices, 1973; Selected and New Poems 1939-84, 1985; Long Shadows: Poems 1938-2002, 2003. Other: Collected Poems of Edwin Muir, 1921-51 (editor), 1952; New Poems (co-editor), 1955; Edwin Muir, 1956. Address: 9 Warwick Road, Mount Sion, Tunbridge Wells, Kent TN1 1YL, England.

HALL Nigel John, b. 30 August 1943, Bristol, England. Sculptor. m. Manijeh Yadegar. Education: NDD, West of England College of Art; MA, Royal College of Art; Harkness Fellowship to USA, 1967-69. Career: Tutor, Royal College of Art, 1971-74; Principal Lecturer, Chelsea School of Art, 1974-81; Solo exhibitions include: Robert Elkon Gallery, New York, 1974, 1977, 1979, 1983; Annely Juda Fine Art, London, 1978, 1981, 1985, 1987, 1991, 1996, 2000, 2003, 2005; Galerie Maeght, Paris, 1981, 1983; Staatliche Kunsthalle, Baden-Baden, 1982; Nishimura Gallery, Tokyo, 1980, 1984, 1988; Garry Anderson Gallery, Sydney, 1987, 1990; Gallery Hans Mayer, Dusseldorf, 1989, 1999; Galerie Scheffel, Bad Homburg, 2004, 2007; Kunsthalle, Mannheim, 2004; Park Ryu Sook Gallery, Seoul, 1997, 2000, 2005; Galerie Lutz und Thalman, Zurich, 2006; Group Exhibitions include: Documenta Kassel, 1977; Whitechapel Gallery, 1981; Tokyo Metropolitan Museum, 1982; Le Havre Museum of Fine Art, 1988; MOMA, New York, 1993; Fogg Art Museum, Harvard University, 1994; Schloss Ambras, Innsbruck, 1998; British Council Touring Exhibition, Pakistan, South Africa, Zimbabwe, 1997-99; Bad Homburg, 2001, 2003; Work in public collections include: Tate Gallery; National Museum of Modern Art, Paris; National Gallery, Berlin; MOMA, New York; Australian National Gallery, Canberra; Art Institute of Chicago; Kunsthaus, Zurich; Tokyo Metropolitan Museum; Museum of Modern Art, Brussels; Louisiana Museum, Denmark; National Museum of Art, Osaka; Museum of Contemporary Art, Sydney; Dallas Museum of Fine Art; Tel Aviv Museum; Los Angeles County Museum; National Museum of Contemporary Art, Seoul; Commissions include: Australian National Gallery, Canberra, 1982; IBM London, 1983; Airbus Industries, Toulouse, 1984; Museum of Contemporary Art, Hiroshima, 1985; Olympic Park, Seoul, 1988; Clifford Chance, London, 1992; Glaxo Wellcome Research, Stevenage, 1994; NTT, Tokyo, 1996; Bank of America, London, 2003; Said Business School, University of Oxford, 2005; Bank for International Settlements, Basel; Sparkasse, Lörrach. Honour: Elected, Royal Academy, 2003. Address: 11 Kensington Park Gardens, London, W11 3HD, England.

HALL Peter (Geoffrey), b. 19 March 1932, London, England. Professor of Planning; Writer. m. (1) Carla Maria Wartenberg, 1962, divorced 1966, (2) Magdalena Mróz, 1967. Education: MA, PhD, St Catharine's College, Cambridge. Appointments: Assistant Lecturer, 1957-60, Lecturer, 1960-66, Birkbeck College, University of London; Reader in Geography, London School of Economics and Political Science, 1966-68; Professor of Geography, 1968-89, Professor Emeritus, 1989-, University of Reading; Professor of City and Regional Planning, 1980-92, Professor Emeritus, 1992-, University of California at Berkeley; Professor of Planning, 1992-, Director, School of Public Policy, 1995-96, University College, London. Publications: The Industries of London, 1962; London 2000, 1963, revised edition, 1969; Labour's New Frontiers, 1964; Land Values (editor), 1965; The World Cities, 1966, 3rd edition, 1984; Von Thunen's Isolated State (editor), 1966; An Advanced Geography of North West Europe (co-author), 1967; Theory and Practice of Regional Planning, 1970; Containment of Urban England: Urban and Metropolitan Growth Processes or Megapolis Denied (co-author), 1973; Containment of Urban England: The Planning System: Objectives, Operations, Impacts (co-author), 1973; Planning and Urban Growth: An Anglo-American Comparison (with M Clawson), 1973; Urban and Regional Planning: An Introduction, 1974, 2nd edition, 1982; Europe 2000, 1977; Great Planning Disasters, 1980; Growth Centres in the European Urban System, 1980; Transport and Public Policy Planning (editor with D Banister), 1980; The Inner City in Context (editor), 1981; Silicon Landscapes (editor), 1985; Can Rail Save the City? (co-author), 1985; High-Tech America (co-author), 1986; Western Sunrise (co-author), 1987; The Carrier Wave (co-author), 1988; Cities of Tomorrow, 1988; London 2001, 1989; The Rise of the Gunbelt, 1991; Technoples of the World, 1994; Sociable Cities (co-author), 1998; Cities in Civilisation, 1998; Urban Future 21 (co-author), 2000; Working Capital, 2002. Honours: Honorary Fellow, St Catharine's College, Cambridge, 1988; British Academy, fellow, 1983; Member of the Academia Europea, 1989; Knight Bachelor, 1998; Prix Vautrin Lud, 2001; Gold Medal, Royal Town Planning Institute, 2003. Memberships: Fabian Society, chairman, 1971-72; Tawney Society, chairman, 1983-85. Literary Agent: Peters, Fraser, Dunlap. Address: c/o Bartlett School, University College, London, Wates House, 22 Gordon Street, London WC1H 0QB, England.

HALL Sir Peter (Reginald Frederick), b. 22 November 1930, Bury St Edmunds, Suffolk, England. Director and Producer for Stage, Film, Television, and Opera; Associate Professor of Drama. m. 1) Leslie Caron, 1956, divorced 1965, 1 son, 1 daughter, (2) Jacqueline Taylor, 1965, divorced 1981, 1 son, 1 daughter, (3) Maria Ewing, 1982, divorced 1990, 1 daughter, (4) Nicola Frei, 1990, 1 daughter. Education: BA, Honours, St Catharine's College, Cambridge. Appointments: Director, Arts Theatre, London, 1955-56, Royal Shakespeare Theatre, 1960, National Theatre, 1973-88; Founder-Director-Producer, International Playwright's Theatre, 1957, Peter Hall Co, 1988; Managing Director, Stratford-on-Avon and Aldwych Theatre, London, 1960-68; Associate Professor of Drama, Warwick University, 1966-; Co-Director, Royal Shakespeare Co, 1968-73; Artistic Director, Glyndebourne Festival, 1984-90; Artistic Director, Old Vic, 1997; Wortham Chair in Performing Arts, Houston University, Texas, 1999; Chancellor, Kingston University, 2000-; Theatre, opera and film productions. Publications: The Wars of the Roses, adaptation after Shakespeare (with John Barton), 1970; John Gabriel Borkman, by Ibsen (translator with Inga-Stina Ewbank), 1975; Peter Hall's Diaries: The Story of a Dramatic Battle (edited by John Goodwin), 1983; Animal Farm, adaptation after Orwell, 1986; The Wild Duck, by Ibsen (translator with Inga-Stina Ewbank), 1990; Making an Exhibition of Myself (autobiography), 1993; An Absolute Turkey, by Feydeau (translator with Nicola Frei), 1994; The Master Builder (with Inga-Stina Ewbank), 1995; Mind Millie For Me (new translation of Feydeau's Occupe-toi d'Amélie, with Nicola Frei), 1999; Cities in Civilization, 1999; The Necessary Theatre, 1999; Exposed by the Mask, 2000; Shakespeare's Advice to the Players, 2003. Honours: Commander of the Order of the British Empire, 1963; Honorary Fellow, St Catharine's College, Cambridge, 1964; Chevalier de l'Ordre des Arts et Des Lettres, France, 1965; Tony Award, USA, 1966; Shakespeare Prize, University of Hamburg, 1967; Knighted, 1977; Standard Special Award, 1979; Special Award for Outstanding Achievement in Opera, 1981, and Awards for Best Director, 1981, 1987; Several honorary doctorates. Membership: Theatre Directors' Guild of Great Britain, founder-member, 1983-.

HALLETT Christine Margaret, b. 4 May 1949, Barnet, Hertfordshire, England. Vice-Chancellor. MA, University of Cambridge; PhD, Loughborough University. Appointments: Civil Servant, 1970-74; Teaching and research posts in Social Policy, Universities of Oxford, Leicester, Western Australia, Keele and Stirling; Principal and Vice-Chancellor, University of Stirling, 2004-. Publications include: Interagency Co-operation in Child Protection, 1995; Women and Social Policy: An Introduction (editor), 1996; Hearing the Voices of Children: Social Policy for a New Century (co-author), 2003. Honour: Fellow of the Royal Society of Edinburgh, 2002. Address: The Principal's Office, University of Stirling, Stirling FK9 4LA, Scotland.

HALLIWELL Geri Estelle, b. 7 August 1972, Watford, England. Singer. 1 daughter. Career: Member, Spice Girls, -1998; Started as Touch, renamed as Spice Girls; Found manager and obtained major label recording deal; Numerous TV appearances, radio play and press interviews; UK, European and US tours; Nominated United Nations Ambassador, 1998; Solo career, 1998-; Video and book releases. Recordings: Singles with Spice Girls: Wannabe, 1996; Say You'll Be There, 1996; 2 Become 1, 1996; Mama/Who Do You Think You Are, 1993; Spice Up Your Life, 1997; Too Much, 1997; Stop, 1998; (How Does It Feel to Be) On Top of the World, as part of England United, 1998; Move Over/Generation Next, 1998; Viva Forever, 1998; Albums: Spice, 1996; Spiceworld, 1997; Solo Singles: Look At Me, 1999; Mi Chico Latino, 1999; Lift Me Up, 1999; Bag It Up, 2000; It's Raining Men, 2001; Scream If You Want to Go Faster, 2001; Calling, 2002;

Ride It, 2004; Desire, 2005. Albums: Schizophonic, 1999; Scream If You Want to Go Faster, 2001;Passion, 2005. Films: Spiceworld The Movie, 1997; Fat Slags, 2004. Publications: If Only, 1999; Just for the Record, 2002. Honours: With Spice Girls, numerous music awards in polls. Address: Hackford Jones PR, Third Floor, 16 Manette Street, London W1D 4AR, England. Website: www.geri-halliwell.com

HALLWORTH Grace Norma Leonie Byam, b. 4 January 1928, Trinidad, West Indies. Ex-Librarian; Author; Storyteller. m. Trevor David Hallworth, 31 October 1964. Education: Exemptions from Matriculation, 1946; Associate of Library Association, 1956; Diploma in Education, London University, 1976; Editorial Board Member, Institute of Education, University of London, 1995. Publications: Listen to this Story, 1977; Mouth Open Story Jump Out, 1984; Web of Stories, 1990; Cric Crac, 1990; Buy a Penny Ginger, 1994; Poor-Me-One, 1995; Rhythm and Rhyme, 1995; Down By The River, 1997 Contributions to: Books and journals. Honours: Runner-up for Greenaway Medal. 1997. Membership: Society for Storytelling, patron, 1993-94. Address: Tranquillity, 36 Lighthouse Road, Bacolet Point, Scarborough, Tobago, West Indies.

HALPERN Daniel, b. 11 September 1945, Syracuse, New York, USA. Associate Professor; Poet; Writer; Editor. m. Jeanne Catherine Carter, 31 December 1982, 1 daughter. Education: San Francisco State College, 1963-64; BA, California State University at Northridge, 1969; MFA, Columbia University, 1972. Appointments: Founder-Editor, Antaeus literary magazine, 1969-95; Instructor, New School for Social Research, New York City, 1971-76; Editor-in-Chief, Ecco Press, 1971-; Visiting Professor, Princeton University, 1975-76, 1987-88, 1995-96; Associate Professor, Columbia University, 1976-. Publications: Poetry: Traveling on Credit, 1978; Seasonal Rights, 1982; Tango, 1987; Foreign Neon, 1991; Selected Poems, 1994. Other: The Keeper of Height, 1974; Treble Poets, 1975; Our Private Lives: Journals, Notebooks and Diaries, 1990; Not for Bread Alone: Writers on Food, Wine, and the Art of Eating, 1993; The Autobiographical Eye, 1993; Holy Fire: Nine Visionary Poets and the Quest for Enlightenment, 1994; Something Shining, 1998. Editor: Borges on Writing (co-editor), 1973; The American Poetry Anthology, 1975; The Antaeus Anthology, 1986; The Art of the Tale: An International Anthology of Short Stories, 1986; On Nature, 1987; Writers on Artists, 1988; Reading the Fights (with Joyce Carol Oates), 1988; Plays in One Act, 1990; The Sophisticated Cat (with Joyce Carol Oates), 1992; On Music (co-editor), 1994. Contributions to: Various anthologies, reviews, journals, and magazines. Honours: Jesse Rehder Poetry Award, Southern Poetry Review, 1971; YMHA Discovery Award, 1971; Great Lakes Colleges National Book Award, 1973; Borestone Mountain Poetry Award, 1974; Robert Frost Fellowship, Bread Loaf, 1974; National Endowment for the Arts Fellowships, 1974, 1975, 1987; Pushcaft Press Prizes, 1980, 1987, 1988; Carey Thomas Award for Creative Publishing, Publishers Weekly, 1987; Guggenheim Fellowship, 1988; PEN Publisher Citation, 1993. Address: c/o The Ecco Press, 100 West Broad Street, Hopewell, NJ 08525, USA.

HALSEY Alan, b. 22 September 1949, Croydon, Surrey, England. Bookseller; Poet. Education: BA, Honours, London. Publications: Yearspace, 1979; Another Loop in Our Days, 1980; Present State, 1981; Perspectives on the Reach, 1981; The Book of Coming Forth in Official Secrecy, 1981; Auto Dada Cafe, 1987; A Book of Changes, 1988; Five Years Out, 1989; Reasonable Distance, 1992; The Text of Shelley's

Death, 1995; A Robin Hood Book, 1996; Fit to Print (with Karen McCormack), 1998; Days of '49 , with Gavin Selerie, 1999; Wittgenstein's Devil: Selected Writing 1978-98, 2000; Sonatas and Preliminary Sketches, 2000; Marginalien (Poems, Prose & Graphics 1988-2004), 2005; Not Everything Remotely: Selected Poems 1978-2005, 2006. Contributions to: Critical Quarterly; Conjunctions; North Dakota Quarterly; Writing; Ninth Decade; Poetica; South West Review; Poetry Wales; Poesie Europe; O Ars; Figs; Interstate; Prospice; Reality Studios; Fragmente; Screens and Tasted Parallels; Avec; Purge; Grille; Acumen; Shearsman; Oasis; New American Writing; Agenda; Colorado Review; Talisman; PN Review; Resurgence; West Coast Line; The Gig; Boxkite. Membership: Thomas Lovell Beddoes Society; David Jones Society. Address: 40 Crescent Road, Nether Edge, Sheffield S7 1HN, England.

HAM Ok Kyung, b. 19 January 1966, Incheon, Korea. Assistant Professor. m. Jin Bae Kim, 1 son. Education: BSc, Nursing, College of Nursing, Yonsei University, 1988; MPH, Yonsei University Graduate School of Public Health, 1997; PhD, Health Studies, Texas Woman's University, 2002. Appointments: Nurse, Severance Hospital, 1988-96; Researcher, Nursing Policy Research Institute, Yonsei University, 2000-03; Assistant Professor, Lecturer, College of Nursing, Kyungpook National University, 2003-06; Assistant Professor, Department of Nursing, Inha University, 2006-. Publications: The intention of future mammography screening among Korean women; Factors affecting mammography behavior and intention among Korean women; Stages and process of smoking cessation among adolescents. Honours: Certified Health Education Specialist, 2005; Listed in international biographical directories. Memberships: International Member, Society for Public Health Education; Life Member, Korean Society of Nursing Science. Address: #253 Yonghyun-dong, Nam-gu, Incheon, 402-751, Korea. E-mail: okkyung@inha.ac.kr

HAMBURGER Michael, (Peter Leopold), b. 22 March 1924, Berlin, Germany (British Citizen). Poet; Writer; Translator; Editor. m. Anne Ellen File, 1951, 1 son, 2 daughters. Education: MA, Christ Church, Oxford, England. Appointments: Assistant Lecturer in German, University College, London, 1952-55; Lecturer, then Reader in German, University of Reading, 1955-64; Florence Purington Lecturer, Mount Holyoke College, South Hadley, Massachusetts, 1966-67; Visiting Professor, State University of New York at Buffalo, 1969, and at Stony Brook, 1971, University of South Carolina, 1973, Boston University, 1975-77; Visiting Fellow, Wesleyan University, Middletown, Connecticut, 1970; Regent's Lecturer, University of California at San Diego, 1973; Professor (part-time), University of Essex, 1978. Publications: Poetry: Flowering Cactus, 1950; Poems 1950-51, 1952; The Dual Site, 1958; Weather and Season, 1963; Feeding the Chickadees, 1968; Penguin Modern Poets (with A Brownjohn and C Tomlinson), 1969; Travelling, 1969; Travelling I-V, 1973; Ownerless Earth, 1973; Travelling VI, 1975; Real Estate, 1977; Moralities, 1977; Variations, 1981; Collected Poems, 1984; Trees, 1988; Selected Poems, 1988; Roots in the Air, 1991; Collected Poems, 1941-94, 1995, paperback, 1998; Late, 1997; Intersections, 2000; The Take-Over (story), 2000; From a Diary of Non-Events, 2002; Wild and Wounded, 2004; Circling the Square, 2007. Prose: Reason and Energy, 1957; From Prophecy to Exorcism, 1965; The Truth of Poetry, 1970, new edition, 1996; A Mug's Game (memoirs), 1973, revised edition as String of Beginnings, 1991; Hugo von Hofmannsthal, 1973; Art as a Second Nature, 1975; A Proliferation of Prophets, 1983; After the Second Flood: Essays in Modern

German Literature, 1986; Testimonies: Selected Shorter Prose 1950-1987, 1989; Philip Larkin: A Retrospect, 2002; Michael Hamburger in Conversation with Peter Dale, 1998. Translator: Many books, including: Poems of Hölderlin, 1943, revised edition as Hölderlin: Poems, 1952; J C F Hölderlin: Selected Verse, 1961; H von Hofmannsthal: Poems and Verse Plays (with others), 1961; H von Hofmannsthal: Selected Plays and Libretti (with others), 1964; J C F Hölderlin: Poems and Fragments, 1967, new edition, enlarged, 1994, 2004; The Poems of Hans Magnus Enzenberger (with others), 1968; The Poems of Günter Grass (with C Middleton), 1969; Paul Celan: Poems, 1972, new edition, enlarged as Poems of Paul Celan, 1988, 3rd edition, 1995; Selected Poems, 1994; Kiosk, 1997; Günter Grass: Selected Poems and Fragments, 1998; W G Sebald: After Nature, 2002; Unrecounted, 2004. Contributions to: Numerous publications. Honours: Bollingen Foundation Fellow, 1959-61, 1965-66; Translation Prizes, Deutsche Akademie für Sprache und Dichtung, Darmstadt, 1964; Arts Council of Great Britain, 1969; Medal, Institute of Linguistics, 1977; Wilhelm-Heinse Prize, 1978; Schlegel-Tieck Prizes, 1978, 1981; Goethe Medal, 1986; Austrian State Prize for Literary Translation, 1988; Honorary LittD, University of East Anglia, 1988; European Translation Prize, 1990; Hölderlin Prize, Tübingen, 1991; Petrarca Prize, 1992; Officer of the Order of the British Empire, 1992; Honorary DPhil, Technical University, Berlin, 1995; Cholmondeley Award for Poetry, 2000; Horst-Bienek Prize, Munich, 2001. Address: c/o John Johnson Ltd, Clerkenwell House, 45-47 Clerkenwell Green, London EC1 0HT, England.

HAMILTON Linda, b. 26 September 1956, Salisbury, Maryland, USA. Actress. m. (1) Bruce Abbott, divorced, (2) James Cameron, 1996, divorced, 1 daughter. Career: Stage appearances: Looice, 1975; Richard III, 1977; Films include: TAG: The Assassination Game, 1982; Children of the Corn, 1984; The Stone Boy, 1984; The Terminator, 1984; Black Moon Rising, 1986; King Kong Lives! 1986; Mr Destiny, 1990; Terminator 2: Judgement Day, 1991; Silent Fall, 1994; The Shadow Conspiracy, 1997; Dante's Peak, 1997; Skeletons in the Closet, 2001; Wholey Moses, 2003; Jonah, 2004; Smile, 2005; Missing in America, 2005; The Kid and I, 2005; In Your Dreams, 2006; Broken, 2006. TV: The Secrets of Midland Heights, 1980-81; King's Crossing, 1982; Beauty and the Beast, 1987-90; Country Gold, 1982; Secrets of a Mother and Daughter, 1983; Secret Weapons, 1985; Club Med, 1986; Go Toward the Light, 1988; On the Line, 1998; Point Last Seen, 1998; The Color of Courage, 1999; The Secret Life of Girls, 1999; Sex & Mrs X, 2000; A Girl Thing, 2001; Bailey's Mistake, 2001; Silent Night, 2004; According to Jim, 2005; Thief, 2006; Home by Christmas, 2006. Address: United Talent Agency, 5th Floor, 9560 Wilshire Boulevard, Beverly Hills, CA 90212, USA.

HAMLAT Abderrahmane, b. 4 June 1952, Tizi Ouzou, Algeria. Neurosurgeon. Education: Bachelor lycée Technique, Algiers, 1972; MD, University-Faculty of Medecine, Algiers, 1979; Doctorat en Medecine Specialisee, Neurochirurgie, Faculte Medecine, Algiers, 1983; Admis, Concours Praticien Adjoint Contractuel, France, 1998; Admis au Concours Praticien Hospital, France, 2006. Appointments: Resident, Neurosurgery, Algiers, 1979-83; Maitre Assistant, CHU AIT IDIR, 1983-88; Assistant Associe, CHU Pont Chaillou, 1988-93; Chef de Clinique Associe, CHU Pont Chaillou, 1993-95; Assistant Associe, 1995-98; Praticien Adjoint Contractuel, 1998-2006; Praticien Hospitalier, 2006-. Publications: 33 articles in professional medical journals. Honours: Grand Diplome de Neurochirurgie, Societe Française de Neurochirurgie; Listed in biographical directories.

Memberships: Society of Algerian Neurosurgery; Societe Francaise de Neurochirurgie; Societe de Neuro Oncology, Bretonne. Address: Service de Neurochirurgie, CHU Pont Chaillou, 2 Rue Henri le Guilloux, 35000 Rennes, Cedex 2, France. E-mail: abdhamlat@yahoo.fr

HAMMETT Louise B (Biddy), b. 18 September 1929, Columbus, Georgia, USA. Community Service Volunteer; Artist; Writer; Playwright; Historian; Publisher. m. Paul Lane Hammett Jr (deceased), 2 daughters. Education: BA, Auburn University, Alabama, 1950; Postgraduate Studies, Audited Art Studies, LaGrange College, Georgia, 1962-69; Certified equivalent MA in Art, University of Georgia, 1982. Appointments: School Teacher, LaGrange Public Schools, Georgia, 1950-51; Founder of Art Division, 1970, Volunteer, 1970-71, LaGrange Academy; Co-founder and Art Instructor, Chattahoochee Valley Art Museum Association, LaGrange; Founder and Chair, Chattahoochee Valley Art Association's Sidewalk Art Show; Artist in Residence, Instructor, Chattahoochee Valley Community College; Private Studio Art Instructor, LaGrange, 1963-80; Exhibited Power Crossroads, Coweta Counter, Georgia, 1971; Private Studio Art Instructor, Columbus, 1980-; Oil painting demonstrations; Represented in group shows and in permanent art collections. Publications: Articles in professional and popular journals and magazines; Oil painting, Georgia to Georgia, gifted to Zugdidi, Republic of Georgia; Oil painting, Peach Trees, gifted to Kiryu City, Japan; I Must Sing! The Era with Carrie Fall Bunson, 2007. Honours: Selected for the Vincent Price Contemporary Southern Art Festival, 1964; Selected for Gardens Festival Eight; Award of Excellence, LaGrange Academy Art Program; Award of Appreciation, Ocfuskee Historical Society Inc, 1974; Appreciation Award, Regional Historic Preservation Advisory Council, Chattahoochee Flint Area, 1980; Historic Columbus Foundation Award for Outstanding Contributions in the Field of Historic Preservation in Columbus, Georgia, 1986; 1st place award, Commemorative Events Category, NSDAR; Award for Excellence in Community Service, NSDAR, 1990; Award for Outstanding Support, NSSAR, 1993; Chattahoochee Valley Art Museum, 1994; 6 separate awards under the Seals of two Mayors and Councils of Columbus, Georgia for Meritorious Civic Service. Memberships: National Daughers of the American Revolution, Home Chapter Oglethorpe, Associate Chapters, Kettle Creek and La Grange; United Daughters of the Confedracy; Georgia Poetry Society; Friends of Columbus State University Swobe Library; American Author's Guild. Address: Cherith Creek Designs, P O Box 123, Columbus, GA 31902-0123, USA.

HAMMOND Jane Dominica, b. 6 April 1934, London, England. Public Relations Management Training Consultant. m. Rudolph Samuel Brown, deceased, 1 daughter. Education: CAM Diploma in Public Relations (Communication, Advertising and Marketing) with Distinction, 1974; National Vocational Qualification Assessor in Public Relations, Institute of Personnel and Development, 1998. Appointments: Press Office Assistant, Swissair, 1959-61; Assistant Editor, Dairy Industries, 1961-63; Reporter, Public Service Newspaper, NALGO (now UNISON), 1964-65; Health Service Public Relations Officer, NALGO, 1965-68; Public Relations Officer, St Teresa's Hospital, 1968-70; Senior Information Officer: London Borough of Hammersmith, 1971-73, and Community Relations Commission, 1973-77 and its successor, Commission for Racial Equality, 1977-78; Editor, Hollis Public Relations Weekly, 1978-80; Consultant, Trident Public Relations Ltd, 1980-2002; Trident Training Services, 1986-; Independent; Course Director, London Corporate Training Courses, 1998-; Lecturer, Westminster Kingsway

College, 1991-; Lecturer, Birkbeck College, 1999-2002. Publications: Chapter on non-commercial public relations in Public Relations Practice, 1995; Report for DFID on Romanian Government Relations with Public, 1997; Articles in professional journals; Papers: A Public Relations Training Decade, Public Relations Education Forum, 1998; How Media Measurement Helps Public Relations, International Symposium on Research for Public Relations, Tehran, Iran, 2005. Memberships: NUJ, 1962; Associate, 1965, Member, 1968, Fellow, 1981, Chartered Institute of Public Relations; Member, 1974, Fellow, 2000, CAM Foundation: Millennium Founder Member, Guild of Public Relations Practitioners, 2000; Member and past-President, Rotary Club of Putney, 1998. Address: Trident Training Services, Suite 5, 155 Fawe Park Road, London SW15 2EG, England. E-mail: trident@btconnect.com Website: www.tridenttraining.com

HAMMOND Peter, b. 13 July 1942. Mining Supervisor. m. Diane Ivy, 12 August 1989. Education: Modules Diploma of Higher Education, 1985. Appointments: Environmental and Mining Supervisor; Public Speaker on Poetry and Literature Black Country in Colleges and Universities, Schools and Art Societies nationwide. Publications: Two in Staffordshire with Graham Metcalf, 1979; Love Poems, 1982. Contributions to: New Age Poetry; Outposts; Charter Poetry; Chase Post; Swansea Festival, 1982. Honour: School Poetry Prize, 1956. Memberships: Rugeley Literary Society; Co-Founder, Cannock Poetry Group; Poetry Society Readings. Address: 6 Gorstey Lea, Burntwood, Staffordshire WS7 9BG, England.

HAMMONS Thomas James, b. England. Chartered Engineer; Power Engineer; Consultant, University Teacher. Education: BSc, 1957; PhD, Imperial College, London University, 1961; ACGI, 1957; DIC, 1961. Appointments: Engineer, System Engineering Department, AEI, 1961-62; Fc Engineering, Glasgow University, 1962-2002; Professor, Electrical and Computer Engineering, McMaster University, 1978-79; Visiting Professor, Silesian Polytechnic University, 1978; Visiting Scientist, University Saskatchewan, Canada, 1979; Visiting Academic, Czechoslovak Academic Science, 1982, 1985, 1988; Visiting Professor, Polytechnic University Grenoble, 1984; Consultant, Mawdsleys, 1965-78; NSHEB, 1965-70; GEC, 1975-84. Publications: Over 350 Scientific Papers and Articles. Memberships: Universities Power Engineering Conf; Eur Ing, CEng Institution Mechanical Engineering, CIGRE Institute of Diagnostic Engineers; Institute of Electrical and Electronic Engineers, Energy Development and Power Generation Committee, Synchronous Machinery Subcommittee, Chair, International Practices Subcommittee, Past Chair, Station Control Subcommittee, PES, Standards Voting Committee, Standards committees, Chair, UKRI Power Engineering Chapter, 1994-2004. Honours: Chairman, Institute of Electrical and Electronic Engineers (IEEE) UKRI Section, 2000-2002; Deputy Director General, Life Patron, International Biographic Society; Permanent Secretary, International Universities Power Engineering Conference (UPEC), 2005-; Fellow, Institute of Electrical and Electronic Engineers, 1996; Distinguished Service Award, IEEE/PES, 1996; IEEE PES Outstanding Large Chapter Award, UKRI Chapter, 2003; IEEE Region 8 Chapter of the Year Award, 2001 and 2004; IEEE UKRI Chapter, Outstanding Engineer Award, 2004; State Scholar; Cultural Doctorate, World University. Address: Clairmont, 11c Winton Drive, Kelvinside, Glasgow G12 0PZ, Scotland. E-mail: T.Hammons@ieee.org

HAMNETT Katharine, b. 16 August 1948. Designer. 2 sons. Education: St Martin's School of Art. Appointments: Tuttabankem, 1969-74; Designed freelance in New York, Paris, Rome and London, 1974-76; Founder, Katherine Hamnett Ltd, 1979; Launched Choose Life T-shirt collection, 1983; Involved in Fashion Aid, 1985; Opened first Katherine Hamnett shop, London, 1986, 2 more shops, 1988; Production moved to Italy, 1989; Visiting Professor, London Institute, 1997-; International Institute of Cotton Designer of the Year, 1982; British Fashion Industry Designer of the Year, 1984; Bath Costume Museum Menswear Designer of the Year Award, 1984; British Knitting and Clothing Export Council Award for Export, 1988. Publications: Various publications in major fashion magazines and newspapers. Address: Katherine Hamnett Ltd, 202 New North Road, London N1 7BJ, England.

HAMPE Michael H, b. 3 June 1935, Heidelberg, Germany. Stage Director. m. Sibylle, 1 daughter. Education: Studied Literature, Musicology, Philosophy, D Phil, Universities of Munch, Heidelberg and Vienna. Appointments: Deputy Director, Schauspielhaus, Zurich, 1965-70; Intendant, National Theatre, Mannheim, 1972-75; Intendant, Cologne Opera and Ballet, 1975-95; approximately 250 productions in opera and drama. Member, Board of Directors, Salzberg Festival, 1984-90; Intendant, Dresden Music Festival, 1992-2000; Stage Director, opera, drama, television, 2000-. Publications: Articles, books, features on various subjects concerning opera and theatre, theatre administration, theatre construction. Honours: Großes Bundesverdienstkreuz, Germany; Commendatore della Repubblica Italiana; Goldenes Ehrenzeichen des Landes, Salzburg; Olivier Award, London. Membership: Board member, European Music Theatre Academy, Vienna. Address: Carl Spitteler Straße 105, CH 8053 Zurich, Switzerland. E-mail: mhampe@bluewin.ch

HAMPSHIRE Susan, b. 12 May 1942, England. Actress. m. (1) 1 son, (2) Eddie Kulukundis, 1981. Education: Hampshire School, Knightsbridge. Career: Theatre work includes: Expresso Bongo, 1972; Follow That Girl; Fairy Tales of New York; The Ginger Man; A Doll's House; The Taming of the Shrew; Peter Pan, 1974; As You Like It; Arms and the Man; Miss Julie; Man and Superman; The Circle, 1976; Crucifer of Blood; Night and Day, 1979; Tribades; The Revolt, 1980; House Guest, 1981; Blithe Spirit, 1986; Married Love, 1989; A Little Night Music; The King and I, 1990; Relative Values, 1993; Susanna Andler, 1995; Black Chiffon, 1996; Relatively Speaking, 2000-2001; Relative Values, 2002; The Lady in the Van, 2004-05; Films include: During One Night, 1961; Three Lives of Thomasina; Night Must Fall and Wonderful Life, 1964; Monte Carlo or Bust, 1969; David Copperfield, Paris in August, Living Free, Malpertius and A Time for Loving, 1972; Bang; TV appearances include: Andromeda; The Forsyte Saga, 1970; Sarah Churchill; The First Churchills, 1971; Vanity Fair, 1973; Going to Pot, 1985; The Barchester Chronicles, 1982; Leaving, Series I and II, 1984-85; Don't Tell Father, 1992; The Grand, 1997, series 2, 1998; Monarch of the Glen, 1999-2005; Sparkling Cyanide, 2003. Publications include: Susan's Story, 1981; Lucy Jane at the Ballet; The Materal Instinct, 1985; Every Letter Counts, 1990; Lucy Jane on Television; Lucy Jane and the Dancing Competition, 1991; Lucy Jane and the Russian Ballet, 1993; Rosie's First Ballet Lesson, 1997. Honours: Best Actress Awards: Emmys for: The Forsyte Saga, 1970; The First Churchills, 1971; Vanity Fair, 1973; E Poe Prizes du Film Fantastique, 1972; Hon DLit City University, London, 1984; Hon DLit, St Andrews University,

Scotland; Hon DEd, Kingston University, Surrey, 1994; Hon DArts, Boston, USA, 1994; OBE, 1995. Address: c/o Chatto & Linnit Ltd, 123A King Road, London SW3 4PL, England.

HAMPSON Norman, b. 8 April 1922, Leyland, Lancashire, England. Retired University Professor. m. Jacqueline Gardin, 22 April 1948, 2 daughters. Education: University College Oxford, 1940-41, 1945-47. Publications: La Marine de l'An ll, 1959; A Social History of The French Revolution, 1963; The First European Revolution, 1963; The Enlightenment, 1968; The Life and Opinions of Maximilien Robespierre, 1974; A Concise History of the French Revolution, 1975; Danton, 1978; Will and Circumstance: Montesquieu, Rousseau and The French Revolution, 1983; Prelude to Terror, 1988; Saint-Just, 1991; The Perfidy of Albion, 1998; Not Really What You'd Call a War, 2001. Contributions to: Numerous magazines and journals. Honour: D Litt (Edinburgh), 1989. Memberships: Fellow, British Academy; Fellow, Royal Historical Society. Address: 305 Hull Road, York, YO10 3LU, England.

HAMPTON Christopher (James), b. 26 January 1946, Fayal, The Azores. Playwright. m. Laura de Holesch, 1971, 2 daughters. Education: Lancing College, Sussex, 1959-63; BA, Modern Languages, 1968, MA, New College, Oxford. Career: Resident Dramatist, Royal Court Theatre, London, 1968-70; Freelance Writer, 1970-. Publications: Tales from Hollywood, 1983; Tartuffe or The Imposter (adaptation of Molière's play), 1984; Les Liaisons Dangereuses (adaptation of C de Laclos's novel), 1985; Hedda Gabler and A Doll's House (translations of Ibsen's plays), 1989; Faith, Hope and Charity (translator), 1989; The Ginger Tree (adaptation of Oscar Wynd's novel), 1989; White Chameleon, 1991; The Philanthropist and Other Plays, 1991; Sunset Boulevard, 1993; Alice's Adventures Underground, 1994; Carrington, 1995; Mary Reilly, 1996; The Secret Agent, 1996; Art (translator), 1996; Nostromo, 1997; An Enemy of the People (translator), 1997; The Unexpected Man (translator), 1998; Conversations After a Burial (translator), 2000; Life x Three, 2001; Three Sisters, 2003. Screenwriter: The Quiet American, 2002; Imagining Argentina, 2003; Atonement, 2007; Tokyo Rose, 2008. Other: Screenplays, radio and television plays. Honours: Evening Standard Award, 1970, 1983, 1986; Plays and Players London Critics' Award, 1970, 1973, 1985; Los Angeles Drama Critics Circle Award, 1974; Laurence Olivier Award, 1986; New York Drama Critics' Award, 1987; Prix Italia, 1988; Writers Guild of America Screenplay Award, 1989; Oscar, 1989; BAFTA, 1990; Special Jury Award, Cannes Film Festival, 1995; 2 Tony Awards, 1995; Scott Moncrieff Prize, 1997; Officier, Ordre des Arts et des Lettres, 1998. Membership: Royal Society of Literature, fellow. Address: National House, 60-66 Wardour Street, London W1V 3HP, England.

HAN Il-Song, b. 1 February 1956, Seoul, Korea. Professor. m. In-Sung Kim, 2 sons. Education: BSc, Electronic Engineering, Seoul National University, 1979; MSc, 1981, PhD, 1984, Electrical Engineering, Korea Advanced Institute of Science & Technology; MBA, School of Management, Cranford University, England, 1999. Appointments: Postdoctoral Research Fellow, KAIST, 1984-85; Principal Member of Technical Staff, Korea Telecom (R&D Group), Korea, 1985-99; Research Fellow, Department of Electronic Engineering, Imperial College, London, England, 2000; Senior Engineer, Jennic Ltd, Milton Keynes, England, 2001-02; Lecturer, Department of Electronic and Electrical Engineering, University of Sheffield, England, 2002-07; Honorary Visiting Fellow, Department of Electronic and Electrical Engineering, University College London, England, 2007; Research Professor, Institute for Information

Technology Convergence, KAIST, 2007-. Publications: A novel tunable transconductance amplifier based on voltage-controlled resistance by MOS Transistors, 2006; Mixed-signal neuron-synapse implementation for large scale neural networks, 2006; Biologically inspired hardware implementation of neural networks with programmable conductance, 2007; Biologically inspired neurocomputing hardware implementation with programmable conductance and spike operation, 2008. Honours: Award for Distinguished Contribution by Minister of Information and Communication, 1992; Award for Distinguished Contribution by the Committee of EXPO, 1993; Korea Telecom Best Researcher Award, 1995. Memberships: IEEE. Address: 45 The Paragon, Searles Road, London, SE1 4YL, England. E-mail: ishan@netsgo.com

HAN Jae-Kil, b. 25 May 1968, Daecheon-city, South Korea. Researcher. m. Soon-Hyun Jung, 2 sons. Education: BS, Chemistry, 1990, MS, Analytical Chemistry, 1993, Chungnam National University, Daejeon, Korea; PhD, Ecomaterial Design & Process, Tohoku University, Sendai, Japan, 2005. Appointments: Senior Researcher, Korea Institute of Machinery & Materials, 1993-2000; Senior Researcher, Korea Research Institute of Analytical Technology, 2000-02; Research Professor, Kongju National University, 2002-05; Senior Researcher, Sondo Techno Park, 2005-. Publications: Microstructures and material properties of fibrous Al_2O_3-ZrO_2(m)/t-ZrO_2 composite by fibrous monolithic process, 2004; Synthesis of high purity nano-sized hydroxyapatite powder by microwave-hydrothermal method, 2006; TEM microstructure characterization of nano TiO_2 coated on nano ZrO_2 powders and their photocatalytic activity, 2006. Honours: Outstanding Scientific Poster, 2004, Best Articles Prize, 2005, Archives of Bioceramics Research. Memberships: Korean Institute of Metals & Materials; Korean Ceramic Society; Korean Society of Analytical Science; Institute of Asian Culture & Development. Address: Poonglim i-want, Apt 402-502, Songdo-dong, Yeonsu-gu Incheon, 406-730, South Korea.

HAN Man-Soo, b. 4 September 1969, Jindo, Jeonnam, Republic of Korea. Professor. Education: BE, 1992, ME, 1994, PhD, 1999, Electrical Engineering, Korean Advanced Institute of Science and Technology. Appointments: Senior Researcher, Electronics and Telecommunications Research Institute, 1999-2003; Full time Lecturer, Mokpo National University, 2003-05; Assistant Professor, Mokpo National University, 2005-. Publications: Author, 45 papers in the field of electrical engineering; 3 patents. Honours: Scholarship, Korea Advanced Institute of Science and Technology, 1988-94; Scholarship, Samsung Electronics, 1995-99. Memberships: Korean Institute of Communication and Sciences; Institute of Electronics Information and Communications Engineers; IEEE. Address: Information Engineering Division, Mokpo National University, 61 Dorim-ri, Chonggyu-myun, Muan-gun, Jeonnam, 534-729, Republic of Korea. E-mail: mindtyphoon@yahoo.co.kr

HAN Min Ho, b. 15 June 1974, Daejon, Republic of Korea. Researcher. m. Eun Young Kim, 1 daughter. Education: BS, 1999, MS, 2001, Computer Engineering, Chungnam National University. Appointments: Senior Member of Engineering Staff, Electronics and Telecommunications Research Institute, 2000-. Publications: Several articles in professional journals include: A security system for preventing an intrusion on network; A dynamic routing method for active packets; Tracing and response against Attacker in VPN; Network Processor Architecture for IPSec; The Design of IPSec Application in IXDP2400; The Security Mechanism in VPN. Honours: Cisco

Career Certification, 2002; Listed in national and international biographical dictionaries. Memberships: Advanced Computing System Association; Korean Information Science Society. Address: ETRI, 161 Gajeong-dong, Yuseong-gu, Daejon 305-350, Republic of Korea. E-mail: mhhan@etri.re.kr Website: www.etri.re.kr

HAN Myeong-Sook, b. 24 March 1944. Prime Minister of the Republic of Korea. Education: BA, French Literature & Language, 1967, MA, Women's Studies, 1986, Ewha Womans University. Appointments: Member of Staff, Korea Christian Academy, 1974-79; Jailed as a prisoner of conscience, Christian Academy Case, 1979-81; Lecturer, Department of Women's Studies, Ewha Womans University, 1986-87; Lecturer, Department of Women's Studies, Sungsim Womans University, 1988-94; Chair, Special Committee on Revision of Family Law, Korea Women's Associations United (KWAU), 1989; President, Korean Womenlink, 1990-94; Chief Director, Korea Institute for Environmental and Social Policies, 1992; Member of Executive Committee, Seoul and Pyungyang Symposium, Peace of Asian and Women's Role, 1992-96; Co-representative, Viewers Alliance for Fair Broadcasting Policy Advisor, Committee for Interchange and Co-operation, Ministry of Unification, 1993-94; Member, Environmental Reservation Committee, Ministry of Environment, Member of Anti-Corruption Committee, The Board of Audit and Inspection of the Republic of Korea, 1993-95; Co-Representative, KWAU, 1993-96; Co-Representative, Citizens Association for Broadcasting Reform, 1994-95; Visiting Researcher, Asian Center for Women's Studies, Ewha Womans University, 1996-2003; Member, 16th National Assembly, Republic of Korea, 2000-01; Minister of Gender Equality, 2001-03; Minister of Environment, 2003-04; Elected Member, 17th National Assembly, Republic of Korea, 2004; Member, National Assembly, Unification, Foreign Affairs and Trade Committee, 2004-; President, Korean Parliamentary League on Children, Population and Environment, 2004-06; President, Executive Committee, Asia-Pacific Parliamentarians Conference on Environment and Development, 2004-06; Member, Central Standing Committee, Uri Party, 2005; President, Korea-Singapore Parliamentarians' Friendship Association, 2004-; Vice President, Korea-Japan Parliamentary League, 2006-; Member, National Assembly, Environment and Labor Committee, 2006-; 37th Prime Minister of the Republic of Korea, 2006-. Honours: Civil Merit Medal, 1998; Order of Service Merit Medal (Blue Stripes), 2005. Address: Prime Minister's Office, Seoul, Republic of Korea.

HAN Youngmo, b. 22 June 1969, Republic of Korea. Professor. Education: BSc, Department of Physics Education, Seoul National University, 1992; BE, Department of Control and Instrumentation, Seoul National University, 1995; ME, Department of Electric Engineering, Seoul National University, 1998; PhD, Department of Mechanical and Aerospace Engineering, Seoul National University, Seoul, Republic of Korea, 2002. Appointments: Researcher, 2002-03; Research Professor, 2003, UAV group of Sejong-Rockheed Martin Aerospace Research Center, Seoul; Part time Lecturer, Department of Mechanical Engineering, Dankook University, Seoul, 2002-04; Full time Research Lecturer, 2004-05, Research Professor, 2005-06, Department of Information Electronics, Ewha Womans University, Seoul; Full time Lecturer, Assistant Professor, Department of Computer Engineering, Hanyang Cyber University, Seoul, 2006-; Deputy Director General and Honorary Director General, IBC, 2007-; Vice President, World Congress of Arts, Science and Communications, 2007-. Publications: 9 papers and articles in professional journals. Honours: Graduated 2nd, 1995, Department Control and Instrumentation, Graduated 4th, Department of Physics Education, 1992, Seoul National University; Listed in international biographical directories. Memberships: IEE; Korean Information Science Society; Institute of Electronics Engineers. Address: Department of Computer Engineering, Hanyang Cyber University, HIT 2F, 17 Haengdang-Dong, Seongdong-Gu, Seoul 133-791, Republic of Korea. E-mail: ymhan123@hanmail.net

HAN Yung Keun, b. 21 November 1956, Jeonju, Korea. Professor. m. Mikyung Lee, 2 sons. Education: BS, 1981, MS, 1985, Sungkyunkwan University; Dr Sci Tech, Swiss Federal Institute of Technology, Zurich, Switzerland, 1991; Diploma, Feed Manufacturing Technology, Uzwil, Switzerland, 1994. Appointments: Chief Researcher, National Agricultural Co-operatives Federation, 1992-2005; Committee Member, Korean Society of Animal Science and Technology, 1997-; Research Professor, SungKyunKwan University, Suwon, Korea, 2005-; Editorial Board Member, Asian-Australasian Journal of Animal Sciences, 2006-; Head of Hazard Analysis Critical Point Research Center, SKKU, 2006-. Publications: 62 scientific journal publications; 38 conference presentations; 2 books (author and co-author); 1 book chapter; 1 patent; 76 popular press articles; 51 technical research papers. Honours: Minister's Prize, Ministry of Agriculture & Forestry, Korea, 1998, 2004; Science Prize, Korean Society of Animal Science and Technology, 2001. Memberships: Korean Society of Animal Science and Technology; 4 science societies. Address: 101-805, Hyundai-2-cha Apt, Dunchon-2-dong, Gangdong-gu, Seoul 134-708, Korea. E-mail: swisshan@paran.com

HANDOO Surrinder Kumar, b. 15 January 1950, Srinagar, Kashmir. Scientist. m. Kiran Handoo, 3 daughters. Education: MSc, Physics, 1971; PhD, Physics, 1977. Appointments: Scientist E-1, Cement Research Institute of India, 1977, Scientist E-2, 1981, Scientist E-3, 1983, Programme Leader, Newer Materials and Processes, 1988, Group Manager, Newer Materials and Cements, 1994; General Manager, Marketing, Quality Management, Testing, 2001-, General Manager, Head, Centre for Quality Management, Standards and Calibration Services, 2003, National Council for Cement and Building Materials, Ballabgarh, India. Publications: 55 in national and international journals; 3 patents. Membership: Life Member, Indian Thermal Analysis Society; Subcommittee, Bureau of Standards, New Delhi. Address: National Council for Cement and Building Materials, Ballabgarh-121 004, Haryana, India. E-mail: skhandoo@rediffmail.com

HANDRICH Klaus Dieter, b. 7 September 1939, Hoyerswerda, Germany. Physicist. 2 sons, 1 daughter. Education: Diploma in Physics, 1962, PhD, Physics, 1967, University of Leipzig; Habilitation, Technical University of Dresden, Germany, 1973. Appointments: Assistant Lecturer, Technical University of Dresden, 1967-75; University Lecturer, 1975-89, Vice-Director, Department of Physics, 1980-86, Technical University of Merseburg; Professor of Theoretical Physics, 1989-, Director Institute of Physics, 1990-92, Head of Department of Theoretical Physics, 1989-2004, Technical University of Ilmenau. Publications: Monograph (with S Kobe): Amorphe Ferro- und Ferrimagnetika, 1980 (Russian edition, 1982); Articles in scientific journals include: General behaviour of the quenched averaged spectral density with a change in the ensemble probability distribution (with M Schulz), 1993; Energy Renormalization and Damping of Long-Wavelength Phonons in Amorphous Solids (with R Öttking), 2001. Honour: Award, Technical University of Merseburg, 1983. Membership: Deutsche Physikalische

Gesellschaft, Bad Honnef. Address: Technical University of Ilmenau, Institute of Physics, PF 100565, D98684 Ilmenau, Germany. E-mail: klaus.handrich@tu-ilmenau.de

HANKS Tom, b. 9 July 1956, California, USA. Actor. m. (1) Samantha Lewes, 2 children, (2) Rita Wilson, 1988, 2 sons. Career: Began acting with Great Lakes Shakespeare Festival; Appeared in Bosom Buddies, ABC TV, 1980; Films include: Splash; Bachelor Party; The Man with One Red Shoe; Volunteers; The Money Pit; Dragnet; Big; Punch Line; The Burbs; Nothing in Common; Every Time We Say Goodbye; Joe Versus the Volcano, The Bonfire of the Vanities, 1990; A League of Their Own, 1991; Sleepless in Seattle, Philadelphia, 1993; Forrest Gump, 1994; Apollo 13, 1995; That Thing You Do (also directed), Turner & Hooch, 1997; Saving Private Ryan, You've Got Mail, 1998; Cast Away, The Green Mile, Toy Story 2 (voice), From the Earth to the Moon, 1999; Road to Perdition, 2002; Catch Me If You Can, 2003; The Ladykillers, The Terminal, Elvis Has Left the Building, The Polar Express, 2004; The Da Vinci Code, 2006; The Great Buck Howard, 2007. Honours: Academy Award, 1994, 1995. Membership: Board of Governors, Academy of Motion Picture Arts and Sciences, 2001-. Address: c/o CAA, 9830 Wilshire Boulevard, Beverly Hills, CA 90212, USA.

HANLI Hakan, b. 6 March 1967, Hekimhan, Malatya. Attorney at Law. m. Petra Leonard, 1 son. Education: LLB, University of Ankara, Law School, 1989; LLM, University of Catholic Leuven, Law School, 1993; LLB (equivalent), 1994, PhD, 2003, University of Free Brussels. Appointments: Trainee, EC Directorate General, Telecommunications, Information Industries & Innovation, 1992-93; Senior Associate, Akin, Gump, Strauss, Hauer & Feld LLP, Brussels, 1994-96; Partner, Smit & Partners, Brussels, 1996-99; Partner, Stanbrook & Hooper, Brussels, 2002-04; Partner, Rawling Giles, Brussels, 2004-; Senior Partner, Pekin & Pekin, Istanbul, 2004-07: Senior Partner, Çağa & Çağa Law Firm, Istanbul 2007-. Publications: Numerous papers and articles in scientific and research articles on international, European and Turkish laws. Honours: Distinguished prizes and awards from various international, European and national institutions; 1st Prize, Outstanding Young Person in the World, 1999. Memberships: Ankara Bar Association; Brussels Bar Association; International & European Bar Councils. Address: Çağa & Çağa Law Firm, Süleyman Seba Caddesi, No. 48 BJK Plaza A/88, Beşiktaş 34357 Istanbul, Turkey. E-mail: hakan@caga.gen.tr

HANNAH Daryl, b. 1960, Chicago, Illinois, USA. Actress. Education: University of California at Los Angeles; Professional Training: Ballet tuition with Marjorie Tallchief, also studied with Stella Adler. Career: Film appearances include: The Fury; The Final Terror; Hard Country; Blade Runner; Summer Lovers; Splash; The Pope of Greenwich Village; Reckless; Clan of the Cave Bear; Legal Eagles; Roxanne; Wall Street; High Spirits; Steel Magnolias; Crazy People; At Play in the Fields of the Lord; Memoirs of an Invisible Man; Grumpy Old Men; Attack of the 50ft Woman; The Tie That Binds; Grumpier Old Men; Two Much; The Last Days of Frankie the Fly; Wild Flowers, My Favorite Martian, 1999; Dancing at the Blue Iguana, Cord, 2000; Speedway Junky, Jackpot, 2001; A Walk to Remember, Hard Cash, 2002; Northfork, Kill Bill Vol 1, Casa de Los Babys, 2003; Yo puta, Kill Bill Vol 2, Silver City, Careful What You Wish For, 2004; Lucky 13, Supercross, 2005; Love Is The Drug, Keeping up with the Steins, Olé, 2006; The Poet, Vice, Dark Honeymoon, 2007. Play: The Seven Year Itch, 2000; Directed: The Last

Supper, 1994; A Hundred and One Nights, 1995. Address: Columbia Plaza Producers, Building 8-153, Burbank, CA 91505, USA.

HANNAH John, b. 23 April 1962, Glasgow, Scotland. Actor. m. Joanna Roth, 2 children. Education: Royal Scottish Academy of Music and Drama. Career: Formerly electrician, formerly with Worker's Theatre Company; TV appearances include: McCallum; Joan; Faith; Rebus; Dr Jekyll and Mr Hyde, MDs, Amnesia, Marple: 4.50 from Paddington; Sea of Souls; Cold Blood; New Street Law. Film appearances include: Four Weddings and a Funeral, 1994; Sliding Doors, 1998; The James Gang, 1999; The Mummy, 1999; The Mummy Returns, 2001; Pandaemonium, 2001; Before You Go, 2002; I'm with Lucy, 2002; I Accuse, 2003; Male Mail, 2004; Ghost Son, 2006; The Last Legion, 2007.

HANRAHAN Brian, b. 22 March 1949, London, England. Journalist. m. 1 daughter. Education: BA, Essex University. Appointments: Far East Correspondent, Hong Kong, 1983-85; Moscow Correspondent, 1986-88; Foreign Affairs Correspondent, working in Middle East, Balkans and Eastern Europe, 1987-97; Diplomatic Editor, BBC TV News, 1997-. Publications: "I counted them all out and I counted them all back": The Battle for the Falklands (with Robert Fox), 1982; The Day That Shook the World (Essays on 9/11 by BBC journalists), 2002. Honours: Reporter of the Year, Royal Television Society, 1982; Richard Dimbleby Award, British Academy of Film and Television Arts (BAFTA), 1982; Honorary Doctorates, Essex University, Middlesex University. Memberships: Chicken Shed Theatre Trust; Royal Institute of International Affairs; Royal United Services Institute; Frontline Club. Address: c/o BBC TV News, Television Centre, Wood Lane, London W12 7RJ, England.

HANS-ADAM II (His Serene Highness Prince Hans-Adam II of Liechtenstein), b. 14 February 1945, Vaduz, Liechtenstein. m. Marie Kinsky von Wchinitz und Tettau, 3 sons, 1 daughter. Education: Advanced Level Diploma and Abitur Certificate, Grammar School, Zuoz, 1960-65; Licentiate Degree, Management and Economics, University of St Gallen, 1965-69. Appointments: Bank trainee, London, England; Undertook reorganisation of management and administration of assets belonging to the Princely House, 1970; Appointed permanent deputy to Prince Franz Joseph II, 1984; Assumed regency, 1989; Transferred executive power to Hereditary Prince Alois, 2004. Address: Schloss Vaduz, FL-9490 Vaduz, Fürstentum, Liechtenstein.

HANSON Albert L, b. 9 July 1952, Gainesville, Florida, USA. Physicist; Engineer. m. Anta LoPiccolo, 2 sons. Education: BS with Honors, Engineering Honors Program, North Carolina State University, 1974; MSE, 1976, PhD, 1979, University of Michigan. Appointments: Research Associate, 1979-81, from Assistant Physicist to Physicist, 1981-, Brookhaven National Laboratory, Upton, New York, USA. Publications: Contributed more than 55 articles to professional journals; 7 Reports for the US Government. Honour: Co-recipient, Research and Development 100 Award, 1988. Memberships: American Nuclear Society; American Association for the Advancement of Science; International Radiation Physics Society. Address: Brookhaven National Laboratory, Department of Energy Sciences and Technology, Building 475, Upton, NY 11973, USA. E-mail: alh@bnl.gov

HANSON Curtis, b. 24 March 1945, Los Angeles, USA. Film Director; Screenplay Writer. Partner: Rebecca Yeldham, 1 son. Career: Editor, Cinema magazine; Began film career as screenplay writer; Director, films: The Arousers, 1970; Sweet Kill (also screenplay), 1972; Little Dragons (also co-producer), 1977; Losin' It, 1983; The Bedroom Window (also screenplay), 1988; Bad Influence, 1990; The Hand That Rocks the Cradle, 1992; The River Wild, 1994; LA Confidential, 1998; The Children of Times Square (TV film); Wonder Boys, 1999; 8 Mile, 2002; In Her Shoes, 2005; Lucky You, 2007. Screenplays: The Dunwich Horror, 1970; The Silent Partner, 1978; White Dog, 1982; Never Cry Wolf, 1983; Television: Hitchcock: Shadow of A Genius, 1999. Address: United Talent Agency, 9560 Wilshire Boulevard, Floor 5, Beverly Hills, CA 90212, USA.

HARADA Masaaki, b. 15 August 1974, Japan. Information Electronics Engineer. Education: BE, 1998, ME, 2000, PhD, 2004, Information Electronics Engineering, Nagoya University. Appointments: Research Associate, Kyoto Institute of Technology, 2004-. Honours: Distinguished Contribution Award, IEICE, 2006; Lifetime Achievement Award, IBC, 2008; The Pinnacle of Achievement Award, IBC, 2008. Memberships: IEEE; IEICE; Life Fellow, IBA; Order of International Fellowship, IBC; Listed in international biographical dictionaries. E-mail: m.harada@m.ieice.org

HARARY Keith, b. 9 February 1953, New York, USA. Research Scientist; Writer; Science Journalist. Education: BA, Psychology, Duke University, 1975; PhD, Union Institute, 1986. Appointments: Research Consultant, American Society for Psychical Research, 1971-72; Crisis Counselor, Durham Mental Health Centre, 1972-76; Research Associate, Psychical Research Foundation, 1972-76; Research Associate, Department of Psychiatry, Maimonides Medical Centre, Brooklyn, 1976-79; Director of Counseling, Human Freedom Center, Berkeley, California, 1979; Research Consultant, SRI International, Menlo Park, California, 1980-82; Visiting Researcher, USSR Academy of Sciences, 1983; Design Consultant, Atari Corp, Sunnyvale, California, 1983-85; Lecturer in field; Adjunct Professor, Antioch University, San Francisco, 1985-86; Guest Lecturer, Lyceum School for Gifted Children, 1985-89; President, Research/Executive Director, Institute for Advanced Psychology, 1986-; Freelance Science Journalist, 1988-; Science Applications International Corp, 1991-93; Invited Lecturer, Duke University, 1995; Editor at Large, Omni Magazine, 1996-98; Senior Vice President, Research Director, Capital Access, 1996-2001; Psychological Consultant, National Media Spokesperson for Budget Rent A Car Corp, 1997-99; Psychological Consultant, Microsoft Corp, 1998-99; Executive Vice President, Owl's Pals, 2003-; Editorial Director, Netsplorer, 2004-. Publications: Author: Owl Pals Children's Book Series 2007-; Co-author, The Mind Race, 1984, 1985; 30-Day Altered States of Consciousness Series, 1989-91, revised edition 1999; Co-author, Who Do You Think You Are? Explore Your Many Sided Self with the Berkeley Personality Profile, 1994, revised edition, 2005, CD-ROM edition 1996; Monthly Columnist, Omni Mind Brain Lab in Omni Magazine, 1995-98; Contributor of over 100 articles to professional journals and other publications. Memberships: American Psychological Association; Association for Media Psychology; American Society for Psychical Research. Address: PO Box 4601, Portland, OR 97208, USA.

HARBOUR Malcolm John Charles, b. 19 February 1947, Woking, Surrey, England. Member of the European Parliament. m. Penny Johnson, 2 daughters. Education: MA, Mechanical Engineering, Trinity College, Cambridge; Diploma in Management Studies, University of Aston in Birmingham. Appointments: Engineering Apprentice, 1967; Designer and

Development Engineer, 1969-72, Product Planning Manager, Rover-Triumph, 1972-76, Project Manager, Medium Cars, 1976-80, Director, Business Planning, Austin Rover, 1980-82, Director Marketing, 1982-84, Director, Sales UK and Ireland, 1984-86, Director, Overseas Sales, 1986-89, BMC, Longbridge; Established Harbour Wade Brown, Motor Industry Consultants, 1989-; Jointly founded ICDP (International Car Distribution Programme), 1993; Co-Founder and Project Director, 3 Day Car Programme, 1998-99; Member of the European Parliament for the West Midlands, 1999-, Re-elected 2004-; Committee Member: Internal Market and Consumer Protection; Industry, Technology Research and Energy; Co-Chairman, European Forum for the Automobile and Society; Chairman, European Ceramics Industry Forum; Governor, European Internet Foundation; Chairman, Conservative Technology Forum; Leader of European Parliament Delegation to the World Summit on the Information Society, 2003; Member, EP delegation, 2005; Global Internet Governance Forums, 2006-07; EPP-ED Group Co-ordinator, International Market and Consumer Protection Committee; Vice President, Science and Technology Options Assessment (STOA); Member, Lisbon Strategy Co-ordinating Committee; Member, High Level Working Group on the Car Industry. Publications: Winning Tomorrow's Customers, 1997; Many car industry reports. Memberships: CEng; MIMechE; FIMI; Solihull Conservative Association, 1972-, Former Chairman, Solihull Constituency; International Policy Committee, Royal Society; Guardian, Birmingham Assay Office. Address: Manor Cottage, Manor Road, Solihull, West Midlands B91 2BL, England. E-mail: malcolm.harbour@europal.europa.eu

HARCOURT Geoffrey (Colin), b. 27 June 1931, Melbourne, Australia. Academic; Professor Emeritus; Economist; Writer. m. Joan Margaret Bartrop, 30 July 1955, 2 sons, 2 daughters. Education: BCom, Honours, 1954, MCom, 1956, University of Melbourne; PhD, 1960, LittD, 1988, Cambridge University. Appointments: Professor Emeritus, University of Adelaide, 1988; President, Jesus College, Cambridge, 1988-89, 1990-92; Reader in the History of Economic Theory, Cambridge University, 1990-98; Emeritus Reader, History of Economic Theory, Cambridge, 1998-; Emeritus Fellow, Jesus College, Cambridge, 1998-. Publications: Economic Activity (with P H Karmel and R H Wallace), 1967; Readings in the Concept and Measurement of Income (editor with R H Parker), 1969; Some Cambridge Controversies in the Theory of Capital, 1972; Theoretical Controversy and Social Significance: An Evaluation of the Cambridge Controversies, 1975; The Microeconomic Foundations of Macroeconomics (editor), 1977; The Social Science Imperialists (selected essays), 1982; Keynes and His Contemporaries: The Sixth and Centennial Keynes Seminar Held in the University of Kent at Canterbury (editor), 1985; Controversies in Political Economy (selected essays), 1986; International Monetary Problems and Supply-Side Economics: Essays in Honour of Lorie Tarshis (editor with Jon S Cohen), 1986; On Political Economists and Modern Political Economy (selected essays), 1992; The Dynamics of the Wealth of Nations. Growth, Distribution and Structural Change. Essays in Honour of Luigi Pasinetti (co-editor with Mauro Baranzini), 1993; Post-Keynesian Essays in Biography: Portraits of Twentieth Century Political Economists, 1993; Income and Employment in Theory and Practice (editor with Alessandro Roncaglia and Robin Rowley), 1994; Capitalism, Socialism and Post-Keynesianism: Selected Essays, 1995; A "Second Edition" of The General Theory (editor, with P A Riach), 2 volumes, 1997; 50 Years a Keynesian and Other Essays, 2001; Selected Essays on Economic Policy, 2001; L'Economie rebelle de Joan Robinson, editor, 2001; Joan Robinson: Critical Assessments of Leading

Economists, 5 volumes (editor with Prue Kerr), 2002; Editing Economics: Essays in Honour of Mark Perlman (co-editor), 2002. Contributions to: Many books and scholarly journals. Honours: Fellow, Academy of the Social Sciences in Australia (FASSA), 1971; President, Economic Society of Australia and New Zealand, 1974-77; Officer in the General Division of the Order of Australia (AO), 1994; Economic Society of Australia, Distinguished Fellow, 1996; Honorary DLitt, De Montfort University, 1997; Honorary Fellow, Queen's College, University of Melbourne, 1998; Honorary DComm, Melbourne, 2003; Hon D.h.c.rer.pol., University of Fribourg, Switzerland, 2003; Academician of the Academy of Learned Societies for the Social Sciences (AcSS), 2003; Distinguished Fellow, History of Economics Society, USA, 2004; Honorary Member, European Society for the History of Economic Thought, 2004. Memberships: Royal Economic Society. Address: Jesus College, Cambridge CB5 8BL, England.

HARCOURT Richard David, b. 17 September 1931, Melbourne, Australia. Quantum Chemist. m. Alison Grant Doig, 1 son, 1 daughter. Education: Ripponlea State School, 1938-42; Wesley College, Melbourne, 1943-48; BSc, 1949-51, Dip Ed, 1952, MSc, 1958-60, Melbourne University; PhD, Monash University, 1961-62. Appointments: Victorian Education Department, Box Hill and Sale Technical Schools, 1953-55; Overseas Travel, 1957; Postdoctoral Research Fellow, 1963-64, Lecturer/Senior Lecturer, 1965-93, Research Fellow, 1994-96, Honorary Research Fellow, 1997-2008, School of Chemistry, University of Melbourne. Publications: Book: Qualitative Valence Bond Descriptions of Electron-Rich Molecules: Pauling "3-Electron Bonds" and "Increased-Valence" Theory, 1982; Over 160 papers and articles including: Bohr Circular Orbit Diagrams for some Fluorine Containing Molecules, 2006; Atomic Shell Structure People Identity: Pauli + Schrödinger = Heisenberg + Bohr, (online comment) 2007; Increased-Valence or Electronic Hypervalence for Symmetrical Three-Centre Molecular Orbital Configurations, 2007; Pauling Three-Electron Bonds and Increased-Valence Structures as Components of the "Intellectual Heritage" of Qualitative Valence Bond Theory, 2008; Quantum Chemistry Formulae for Atomic Shell Structure, Separation of Variables, Valence, Hartree-Fock/Hückel Orbitals and Electron Transfer Matrix Element, 2008. Memberships: Royal Australian Chemical Institute. Address: School of Chemistry, The University of Melbourne, Victoria 3010, Australia. E-mail: r.harcourt@unimelb.edu.au

HARDCASTLE Michael, (David Clark), b. 6 February 1933, Huddersfield, England. Author. m. Barbara Ellis Shepherd, 30 August 1979, 4 daughters. Appointment: Literary Editor, Bristol Evening Post, 1960-65. Publications: Author of over 140 children's books, 1966-; One Kick, 1986; James and the TV Star, 1986; Mascot, 1987; Quake, 1988; The Green Machine, 1989; Walking the Goldfish, 1990; Penalty, 1990; Advantage Miss Jackson, 1991; Dog Bites Goalie, 1993; One Good Horse, 1993; Soccer Captain, 1994; Puzzle, 1995; Please Come Home, 1995; Matthew's Goals, 1997; Carole's Camel, 1997; The Price of Football, 1998; Shoot-Out, 1998; Eye for a Goal, 1998; Goal-Getter, 1999; Injury Time, 1999; Rivals United, 1999; Danny's Great Goal, 1999; My Brother's a Keeper, 2000; Mine's a Winner, 2000; Sam's Dream, 2000; The Striker's Revenge, 2000; The Most Dangerous Score, 2001; Archie's Amazing Game, 2002. Contributions to: Numerous articles in magazines and journals. Honour; Member of the Order of the British Empire, 1988. Memberships: Federation of Children's Book Groups, national chair, 1989-90. Address: 17 Molescroft Park, Beverley, East Yorkshire HU17 7EB, England.

HARDING Anthony Filmer, b. 20 November 1946, Bromley, Kent, England. Professor of Archaeology. m. Lesley Eleanor, 2 sons. Education: BA, 1968, MA, 1973, PhD, 1973, Cambridge University. Appointments: Lecturer in Archaeology, 1973-87, Senior Lecturer in Archaeology, 1987-90, Professor of Archaeology, 1990-2004, University of Durham; Professor of Archaeology, University of Exeter, 2004-. Publications: The Bronze Age in Europe (with J M Coles), 1979; The Mycenaeans and Europe, 1984; European Societies in the Bronze Age, 2000; Warriors and Weapons in Bronze Age Europe, 2007. Honours: FBA, 2001; President, European Association of Archaeologists, 2003-2006 and 2006-2009. Address: Department of Archaeology, Laver Building, North Park Road, Exeter EX4 4QE, England. Website: www.ex.ac.uk/sogaer/archaeology/staff-harding.html

HARDISH Patrick, b. Perth Amboy, New Jersey, USA. Librarian; Composer. Education: BA, Queens College, CUNY, 1976; MS, Pratt Institute, 1981; Juilliard School, 1969-72; Columbia University, graduate work, 1978-80; Bennington College composition seminar, 1980. Appointments: Library Assistant V, Columbia University, 1978-84; Co-Director and Co-Founder, Composers Concordance and its New Music Now Series, 1983-; Senior Librarian, New York Public Library, 1984-; Editorial Board, New Music Connoisseur, 1994-; Virginia Center for Creative Arts: Fellowships, 1981, 1982, 1986, 1988; Guest Composer Lectures, New York University, 2000. Publications: Reviews in music journal, Notes, 1985, 1994; Accordioclusterville (for Accordian), 1985; Article on-line, 1999; Music: Sonorities VI (for Vibraphone), 2004; Sonorities VII (for Clarinet), 2004; Duo (for Piano and Percussion), 2005; 2 recordings; . Honours: Meet the Composer awards, 1978, 1982 (2x), 1983, 1991, 1997; Margaret Fairbank-Jory Copying Assistance Program from the American Music Center; lectures; many radio and television interviews. Memberships: St Ansgar's Scandinavian Catholic League; American Music Center; Music Library Association (and its New York Chapter); Kosciuszko Foundation; International Big Band Society; New York Library Club; North American Guild of Change Ringers. Address: PO Box 36-20548, PABT, New York, NY 10129, USA. E-mail: pathardish@hotmail.com

HARDWICK David Francis, b. 24 January 1934, Vancouver, Canada. Pathologist; Professor. m. Margaret M, 1 son, 2 daughters. Education: MD, University of British Columbia, 1950-57. Appointments: Research Associate, Paediatrics, University of Southern California, 1960-62; Clinical Instructor, Pathology, 1963-65, Assistant Professor, Pathology, 1965-69, Associate Professor, Pathology, 1969-74, Professor, Pathology, 1974-99, Professor and Head, Pathology, 1976-90, Honorary Associate Professor, Paediatrics, 1972-87, Honorary Professor, Paediatrics, 1974-99, Special Advisor Planning, Medicine, 1997-, Professor Emeritus, Pathology and Paediatrics, 1999-, University of British Columbia; Secretary, International Academy of Pathology, 2006. Publications: Author and co-author of numerous refereed journals; books; chapters; abstracts; reports. Honours include: Certificate of Merit, Master Teacher Awards; University of British Columbia Teaching Excellence Award; Canadian Silver Jubilee Medal, 1978; President's Award for service to the University of British Columbia; LLD honoris causa, University of British Columbia, 2001; Senior Member, Canadian Medical Association, 2002; Gold Medal, International Academy of Pathology, 2002; President's Award, US and Canadian Academy of Pathology, 2004; Bartholomew Mosse Memorial Lecturer, Dublin, 2004. Memberships include: BC Association of Pathologists; Canadian Association of Pathologists; Society for Paediatric Pathology; Secretary, International Academy of Pathology, 2006. Address: Dean's Office, Faculty of Medicine, University of British Columbia, #317-2194 Health Sciences Mall, Vancouver, British Columbia, Canada V6T 1Z3. E-mail: david.f.hardwick@ubc.ca

HARDWICK Elizabeth, b. 27 July 1916, Lexington, Kentucky, USA. Writer; Critic; Teacher. m. Robert Lowell, 28 July 1949, divorced 1972, 1 daughter. Education: AB, 1938, MA, 1939, University of Kentucky; Columbia University. Appointments: Co-Founder and Advisory Editor, New York Review of Books, 1963-; Adjunct Associate Professor of English, Barnard College. Publications: Fiction: The Ghostly Lover, 1945; The Simple Truth, 1955; Sleepless Nights, 1979. Non-fiction: The Selected Letters of William James (editor), 1960; A View of My Own: Essays on Literature and Society, 1962; Seduction and Betrayal: Women and Literature, 1974; Rediscovered Fiction by American Women: A Personal Selection (editor), 18 volumes, 1977; Bartleby in Manhattan (essays), 1984; The Best American Essays 1986 (editor), 1986; Sight Readings: American Fictions (essays), 1998; Herman Melville, A Life, 2000. Contributions to: Periodicals. Honour: Gold Medal, American Academy and Institute of Arts and Letters, 1993. Address: 15 West 67th Street, New York, NY 10023, USA.

HARDWIG Nancy Sue, b. 29 September 1942, Marion, Illinois, USA. Business Education. m. Ronald B Hardwig, 1 son, 3 daughters. Education: BS, Education, Southern Illinois University, 1964; IBM Corporation Degree, Technology – Business Partner, 1985. Appointments: Business Education Teacher, secondary education, Illinois, 1965-70; AS/400 Systems Manager, Illinois State University, Normal, Illinois, 1991-94; Business Partner, IBM Corporation, 1985-2000; President, R&S Data Systems Inc, 1985-2000; President, R&S Designs Inc, 2001-. Publications: Author, Dare to be Happy: Ten Golden Commandments for a Joy-Filled Life, 2006; Author, Celebrating Chamness Roots, 2008. Honours: IBM Marketing Awards, 1988, 1989, 1990 and 1991. Memberships: Life Member, National Association of Professional & Executive Women. Address: 2213 Windsor Court, Bloomington, IL 61705, USA. E-mail: rsdesignsinc@comcast.net Website: www.rseasycount.com

HARDY Alan William, b. 10 March 1951, Luton, Bedfordshire, England. Teacher; Poet. m. Sibylle Mory, 24 August 1985, 1 daughter. Education: BA, English and Italian Literature, 1973, MA, Comparative Literature, 1976, Warwick University; Dip TEFL, Christ Church College, Kent University, 1983. Appointments: English Teacher, Sir Joseph Williamson's Mathematical School, Rochester, Kent; English Language Teacher, Whitehill Estate School of English, Flamstead, Hertfordshire. Publications: Wasted Leaves, 1996; I Went With Her, 2007. Contributions to: Orbis; Envoi; Iota; Poetry Nottingham; The Interpreter's House; South; Poetic Licence; Braquemard; Fire; Borderlines. Honour: 2nd Prize, Hastings National Poetry Competition, 1994. Address: Whitehill Estate School of English, Flamstead, St Albans, Hertfordshire AL3 8EY, England.

HARDY Geraldine, b. 24 January 1929, Greenville, South Carolina, USA. Private Medical Practice and Osteoporosis Centre. Education: BS degree, Winthrop College, South Carolina, 1950; MD, Wayne State University College of Medicine, Michigan, 1955. Memberships: American Board of Internal Medicine; American Thoracic Society; American Diabetics Society; American College of Physicians. Address: 19707 Mack Ave, Grosse Pointe Woods, MI 48236, USA.

HARDY Robert, b. 29 October 1925. Actor; Author. m. (1) Elizabeth Fox, 1 son, (2) Sally Pearson (divorced), 2 daughters. Career: Theatre appearances include: 4 seasons of Shakespeare, Stratford-on-Avon, 2 at Old Vic; World tours include Henry V and Hamlet, USA; Numerous appearances London and Broadway theatres, 1952-; Winston Churchill in Celui qui a dit Non, Palais des Congres, Paris, 1999-2000; Writer and/or presenter numerous TV programmes including The Picardy Affair, The History of the Longbow, Heritage, Horses in Our Blood, Gordon of Khartoum; Other TV appearances include; Prince Hal and Henry V in Age of Kings; Prince Albert in Edward VII; Malcolm Campbell in Speed King; Winston Churchill in the Wilderness Years; Siegfried Farnon in All Creatures Great and Small; Twiggy Rathbone and Russell Spam in Hot Metal; The Commandant in the Far Pavilions; Sherlock Holmes; Inspector Morse; Middlemarch; Castle Ghosts; Gulliver's Travels; Grand Charles, Le; Murder on the Orient Express, 2008. Films include: How I Won the War; Yellow Dog; Dark Places; Young Winston; Ten Rillington Place; Le Silencieux; Gawain and the Green Knight; The Spy Who Came in From the Cold; La Gifle; Robin Hood; The Shooting Party; Paris By Night; War and Remembrance; Mary Shelley's Frankenstein; Sense and Sensibility; Mrs Dalloway; The Tichborne Claimant, 1998; An Ideal Husband, 1999; The Gathering, 2001; Harry Potter and the Chamber of Secrets, 2002; Harry Potter and the Prisoner of Azkaban, 2004; Harry Potter and the Goblet of Fire, 2005; Lassie, 2005; Grand Charles. Le, 2005; Goodbye Mr Snuggles, 2006; Harry Potter and the Order of the Phoenix, 2007. Publications: Longbow, 1976; The Great War Bow, 2005. Honours: Hon DLitt (Reading), 1990; CBE; FSA. Memberships: Consultant, Mary Rose Trust, 1979-, Trustee, WWF, 1991-; Trustee, Royal Armouries, 1984-96; Master of Worshipful Company of Bowyers, 1988-90. Address: c/o Chatto & Linnit, 123A King's Road, London, SW3 4PL, England.

HARE David, b. 5 June 1947, St Leonards, Sussex, England. Dramatist; Director. m. (1) Margaret Matheson, 1970, divorced 1980, 2 sons, 1 daughter, (2) Nicole Farhi, 1992. Education: Lancing College; MA, Honours, Jesus College, Cambridge. Appointments: Founder, Portable Theatre, 1968, Joint Stock Theatre Group, 1975, Greenpoint Films, 1982; Literary Manager and Resident Dramatist, Royal Court, 1969-71; Resident Dramatist, Nottingham Playhouse, 1973; Associate Director, National Theatre, 1984-88, 1989-. Plays: Slag, 1970; The Great Exhibition, 1972; Knuckle, Brassneck, 1974; Fanshen, Teeth 'n' Smiles, 1976; Plenty, Licking Hitler, 1978; Dreams of Leaving, 1980; A Map of the World, 1982; Saigon, 1983; The History Plays, 1984; Pravda, Wetherby, 1985; The Asian Plays, The Bay at Nice and Wrecked Eggs, 1986; The Secret Rapture, 1988; Paris by Night, 1989; Straples, Racing Demon, 1990; Writing Lefthanded, Heading Home, The Early Plays, Murmuring Judges, 1991; The Absence of War, Asking Around, 1993; Skylight, Mother Courage, Skylight, 1995; Ivanov, 1996; Amy's View, 1997; The Judas Kiss, The Blue Room, Via Dolorosa, 1998; My Zinc Bed, Royal Court, Via Dolorosa, 2000; The Hours, Lee Miller, 2001; The Breath of Life, 2002; The Permanent Way, 2003; Stuff Happens, 2004; The Corrections, 2005; My Zinc Bed, 2008. Honours: John Llewellyn Rhys Award, 1974; BAFTA Award, 1978; New York Drama Critics' Circle Award, 1983; London Standard Award, 1985; Plays and Players Awards, 1985, 1990; Drama Award, 1988; Olivier Award, 1990; Critic's Circle Best Play of the Year, 1990; Time Out Award, 1990. Membership: Royal Society of Literature, fellow.

HARE John Neville, b. 11 December 1934, Bexhill, England. Explorer; Writer. m. Philippa, 3 daughters. Education: ABU, University of Zaria, Nigeria, 1957; Diploma, Administration/ Law. Appointments: District Officer, Colonial Service, Northern Nigeria, 1957-64; Director, Macmillan Publishers, 1965-75; Consultant, Hodder and Stoughton Publishers, 1975-89; United National Environment Programme, 1989-96; Founder, Wild Camel Protection Foundation, 1996-. Publications: The Lost Camels of Tartary, 1998; Shadows Across the Sahara, 2003; 32 books for children on environmental issues; Over 50 articles on the wild Bactrian camel and expeditions in the Gobi and Saharan Deserts. Honours: Ness Award, Royal Geographical Society, 2004; Lawrence of Arabia Memorial Medal, Royal Society of Asian Affairs, 2004; Mungo Park Medal, Royal Scottish Geographical Society, 2006. Memberships: Reform Club. Address: School Farm, Benenden, Kent TN17 4EU, England. E-mail: harecamel@aol.com Website: www.wildcamels.com

HARJO Joy, b. 9 May 1951, Tulsa, Oklahoma, USA. 1 son, 1 daughter. Education: BA, University of New Mexico 1976; MFA, University of Iowa, 1978; Non-degree, Film-making, Anthropology, Film Centre, 1982; Native Screenwriters Workshop, Sundance Institute, 1998; Summer Songwriting Workshop, Berklee School of Music, 1998. Appointments: Assistant Professor, Department of English, University of Colorado, 1985-88; Associate Professor, Department of English, University of Arizona, 1988-90; Professor, Department of English, University of New Mexico, 1991-97; President, Mekko Production Inc, 1992-; Visiting Writer, UCLA Department of English, 1998; Professor, UCLA, 2001-; Joseph M Russo Professor of Creative Writing, University of New Mexico, 2005-. Publications: She Had Some Horses, 1985; Secrets from the Centre of the World, 1989; In Mad Love & War, 1990; The Woman Who Fell From the Sky, 1994; Reinventing the Enemy's Language; A Map To The Next World, poems and tales, 2000; The Good Luck Cat, children's book, 2000; How We Became Human, New and Selected Poems, W W Norton, 2002; Co-author, A Thousand Roads (signature film of The National Museum of The American Indian), 2005; CDs: Native Joy for Real, Joy Harjo, Mekko Prod; Letter from the End of the 20th Century, music and poetry with her band Joy Harjo and Poetic Justice, 1997; Native Joy for Real, 2006; She Had Some Horses, 2006. Honours: National Council on the Arts; The London Observer Best Book of 1997 (Reinventing the Enemy's Language); Lila Wallace Reader's Digest Writers Award, 1998-2000; Honorary Doctorate, St Mary-in-the-Woods College, 1998; First American in the Arts, Outstanding Medal of Achievement, 1998; Lifetime Achievement in the Arts, National Writers Circle of America; Western Literature Distinguished Achievement Award, 2000; Oklahoma Book Arts Lifetime Achievement, 2002. Membership: Board of Directors, Russell Moore Foundation; Board of Directors, Arts Research. Address: Mekko Productions Inc, 1140 D Alewa Drive, Honolulu, HI 96817, USA.

HARMAN Rt Hon Harriet, b. 30 July 1950, London, England. Queen's Counsel; Deputy Leader and Party Chair of the Labour Party; Leader of the House of Commons; Lord Privy Seal; Minister for Women and Equality; Member of Parliament for Camberwell and Peckham. Education: St Paul's Girls' School; University of York. Appointments: Legal Officer, National Council for Civil Liberties, 1978-82; Member of Parliament for Camberwell and Peckham, 1982-; Labour's front-bench spokesperson for Social Services, 1984, and then Health, 1987; Shadow Chief Secretary to the Treasury, later Shadow Secretary for Health, 1992-; Secretary

of State for Social Security, 1997-; Solicitor General, 2001-; Minister of State, Department for Constitutional Affairs, 2005-; Minister of State, Ministry of Justice, 2007-; Deputy Leader and Party Chair of the Labour Party, 2007-. Honours: Honorary Silk (QC), 2005.

HARMAN Nigel, b. 11 August 1973, Purley, England. Actor. Education: Dulwich College, London; Rosslyn School of Drama, London. Career: Theatre: Mamma Mia; Three Sisters; A Midsummer Night's Dream; Guys and Dolls; The Caretaker; TV: Eastenders, 2003-05; The Outsiders, 2006; Blood Diamond, 2006; City of Vice, 2008; Lark Rise to Candleford, 2008. Honours: Best Newcomer at the National Television Awards, 2003.

HARNICK Sheldon Mayer, b. 30 April 1924, Chicago, Illinois, USA. Lyricist. m. (1) Mary Boatner, 1950, (2) Elaine May, 1962, (3) Margery Gray, 1965, 1 son, 1 daughter. Education: Northwestern University. Career: Contributor to revues: New Faces of 1952; Two's Company, 1953; John Murray Anderson's Almanac, 1954; The Shoestring Revue, 1955; The Littlest Revue, 1956; Shoestring 1957, 1957; with composer Jerry Bock: Body Beautiful, 1958; Fiorello, 1959; Tenderloin, 1960; Smiling The Boy Fell Dead (with David Baker), 1961; She Loves Me, 1963; Fiddler On The Roof, 1964; The Apple Tree, 1966; The Rothschilds, 1970; Captain Jinks Of The Horse Marines (opera with Jack Beeson), 1975; Rex (with Richard Rodgers), 1976; Dr Heidegger's Fountain Of Youth (opera with Jack Beeson), 1978; Gold (cantata with Joe Raposo), 1980; Translations: The Merry Widow, 1977; The Umbrellas Of Cherbourg, 1979; Carmen, 1981; A Christmas Carol, 1981; Songs Of The Auvergne (musical; book; lyrics), 1982; The Appeasement of Aeolus, 1990; Cyrano, 1994. Address: Kraft, Haiken & Bell, 551 Fifth Avenue, 9th Floor, New York, NY 10176, USA.

HARRELSON Woody, b. 23 July 1961, Midland, Texas, USA. Actor. m. Laura Louie, 1997, 3 children. Education: Hanover College. Career: Theatre includes: The Boys Next Door; 2 on 2 (author, producer, actor); The Zoo Story (author, actor); Brooklyn Laundry; Furthest from the Sun; On An Average Day; TV includes: Cheers; Bay Coven; Killer Instinct; Films include: Wildcats; Cool Blue; LA Story; Doc Hollywood; Ted and Venus; White Men Can't Jump; Indecent Proposal; I'll Do Anything; The Cowboy Way; Natural Born Killers; Money Train; The Sunchaser; The People vs Larry Flint; Kingpin; Wag the Dog; The Thin Red Line; After the Sunset; The Big White; North Country; The Prize Winner of Defiance, Ohio; A Prairie Home Companion; Free Jimmy (voice); A Scanner Darkly; The Walker; No Country for Old Men; The Grand; Transsiberian; Sleepwalking; Battle in Seattle; Semi-Pro. EdTV, 1999; Play It to the Bone, 2000; American Saint, 2000; Scorched, 2002; Anger Management, 2003; She Hate Me, 2004. Address: c/o Creative Artists Agency, 9830 Wilshire Boulevard, Beverly Hills, CA 90212, USA.

HARRIES The Rt Revd Richard Douglas, Lord Harries of Pentregarth, b. 2 June 1936. Ecclesiastic. m. Josephine Bottomley, 1963, 1 son, 1 daughter. Education: Wellington College; Royal Military Academy, Sandhurst; Selwyn College, Cambridge; Cuddesdon College, Oxford. Appointments: Lieutenant, Royal Corps of Signals, 1955-58; Curate, Hampstead Parish Church, 1963-69; Chaplain, Westfield College, 1966-69; Lecturer, Wells Theological College, 1969-72; Warden of Wells, Salisbury and Wells Theological College, 1971-72; Vicar, All Saints, Fulham, London, 1972-81; Dean, King's College, London, 1981-87; Bishop of Oxford, 1987-2006; Vice-chair, Council of Christian Action, 1979-87;

Council for Arms Control, 1982-87; Chair, Southwark Ordination Course, 1982-87, Shalom, End Loans to South Africa (ELSTA), 1982-87; Christian Evidence Society; Chair, Church of England Board of Social Responsibility, 1996-2001; Consultant to Archbishops on Jewish-Christian Relations, 1986-92; Chair, Council of Christians and Jews, 1993-2001; House of Lords Select Committee on Stem Cell Research, 2001-02; Visiting Professor, Liverpool Hope College, 2002; Member, Home Office Advisory Committee for Reform of Law on Sexual Offences, 1981-85; Board of Christian Aid, 1994-2001; Royal Commission on Lords Reform, 1999-; Nuffield Council of Bioethics, 2002-; Human Fertilisation and Embryology Authority, 2003-. Publications: Prayers of Hope, 1975; Turning to Prayer, 1978; Prayers of Grief and Glory, 1979; Being a Christian, 1981; Should Christians Support Guerrillas?, 1982; The Authority of Divine Love, 1983; Praying Around the Clock, 1983; Seasons of the Spirit (co-editor), 1984; Prayers and the Pursuit of Happiness, 1985; Reinhold Niebuhr and the Issues of Our Time (editor), 1986; Morning has Broken, 1985; Christianity and War in a Nuclear Age, 1986; C S Lewis: The Man and his God, 1987; Christ is Risen, 1988; Is There a Gospel for the Rich? 1992; Art and the Beauty of God, 1993; The Value of Business and its Values (co-author), 1993; The Read God, 1994; Questioning Faith, 1995; The Gallery of Reflections, 1995; In the Gladness of Today, 2000; Christianity: Two Thousand Years (co-editor), 2000; God Outside the Box: Why Spiritual People Object to Christianity, 2002; After the Evil: Christianity and Judaism in the Shadow of the Holocaust, 2003; Praying the Eucharist, 2004; The Passion in Art, 2004; Abraham's Children, 2005. Contributions to several books; Numerous articles. Honours: Fellow, Kings College, London, 1983; Sir Sigmund Sternberg Award, 1989; Honorary Fellow, Selwyn College, Cambridge; St Annes College, Oxford; Honorary Fellow, Academy of Medical Sciences, 2004; Fellow, Royal Society of Literature, 1996; Hon DD (London), 1996; Hon DUniv (Oxford Brookes), 2001; Hon DUniv, Open University; Life Peer, 2006; Honorary Professor of Theology, Kings College, London, 2006-. Address: The House of Lords, London SW1A 0PW, England.

HARRIS Alfred, b. 21 July 1930, London, England. Artist. m. Carmel, 1 son, 2 daughters. Education: Intermediate Arts, Willesden School of Art, 1947-49, 1950-52; ARCA, Royal College of Art, 1952-55. Appointments: Senior Lecturer (retired), University of London, Institute of Education; Chairman, Department of Art and Design; Exhibitions include: New Art Centre London; Beaux Arts Gallery, London; Grosvenor Gallery, London; Ben Uri Gallery, London; Falum Museum, Sweden; Orerro Museum, Sweden; Dalarnas Museum, Sweden; Royal College of Art, London; Tate Gallery, London. Honours: Elected Member, The London Group; Elected Member, Royal West of England Academy; Elected Fellow, Royal Society of Arts. Address: 70 Camden Mews, London NW1 9BX, England.

HARRIS Angela Felicity (Baroness Harris of Richmond), b. 4 January 1944, St Annes-on-Sea, Lancashire, England. Member of the House of Lords. m. John Philip Roger Harris, 1 son from previous marriage. Education: Ealing Hotel and Catering College. Appointments: Member, Richmond Town Council, 1978-81, 1991-99, Mayor of Richmond, 1993-94; Member, 1979-89, Chairman, 1987-88, Richmondshire District Council; Member, 1981-2001, First Woman Chair, 1991-92, North Yorkshire County Council; Deputy Chair, Association of Police Authorities, 1997-2001; Chair, North Yorkshire Police Authority, 1994-2001; Appointed to House of Lords, 1999; Member, Refreshment Select Committee,

2000-, Member, EU Select Committee, 2000-04, Chair, EU Select Sub-Committee, 2000-04, House of Lords. Honours: Deputy Lieutenant of North Yorkshire, 1994; Created Liberal Democrat Life Peer, 1999. Memberships: Member, Court of the University of York, 1996-; Former Member: Service Authority, national Crime Squad, 1997-2000, Police Negotiating Board, 1995-2001; Former Justice of the Peace, 1982-98; Former, NHS Trust Non-Executive Director, 1990-97; President, National Association of Chaplains to the Police. Address: House of Lords, London, SW1A 0PW. E-mail: harrisa@parliament.uk

HARRIS Edward Allen (Ed), b. 28 November 1950, Englewood, New Jersey, USA. Actor. m. Amy Madigan, 1 child. Education: Columbia University; University of Oklahoma, Norman; California Institute of Arts. Career: Stage appearances include: A Streetcar Named Desire; Sweetbird of Youth; Julius Caesar; Hamlet; Camelot; Time of Your Life; Grapes of Wrath; Present Laughter; Fool for Love; Prairie Avenue; Scar, 1985; Precious Sons, 1986; Simpatico, 1994; Taking Sides, 1996; Films include: Come, Borderline, 1978; Knightriders, 1980; Creepshow, 1981; The Right Stuff, Swing Shift, Under Fire, 1982; A Flash of Green, Places in the Heart, 1983; Alamo Bay, 1984; Sweet Dreams, Code Name: Emerald, 1985; Walker, 1987; To Kill a Priest, 1988; Jacknife, The Abyss, 1989; State of Grace, 1990; Paris Trout, 1991; Glengarry Glen Ross, 1992; Needful Things, The Firm, 1993; China Moon, Milk Money, 1994; Apollo 13, Just Cause, Eye for an Eye, 1995; The Rock, Riders of the Purple Sage, 1996; Absolute Power, 1997; Stepmom, The Truman Show, 1998; The Third Miracles, 1999; Enemy at the Gates, A Beautiful Mind, 2001; The Hours, 2002; Buffalo Soldiers, Masked and Anonymous, The Human Stain, Radio, 2003; Winter Passing, 2005; Dirt Nap, Copying Beethoven, 2006; Gone Baby Gone, Cleaner, Winston, National Treasure: Book of Secrets, 2007. TV films include: The Amazing Howard Hughes, 1977; The Seekers, 1979; The Aliens are Coming, 1980; The Last Innocent Man, 1987; Running Mates, 1992; The Stand, 1994. Address: 22031 Carbon Mesa Road, Malibu, CA 90265, USA.

HARRIS Emmylou, b. 2 April 1947, Birmingham, Alabama, USA. Singer. m. Tom Slocum, 1969 (divorced) 1 daughter, Brian Ahern, 1977-84 (divorced) 1 daughter, Paul Kennerley, 1985 (divorced). Education: UNC, Greensboro. Career: Toured with Fallen Angel Band; Performed across Europe, USA; Recording artist; Appeared in rock documentary, The Last Waltz. Compositions: Songs; Co-writer, co-producer, Ballad Of Sally Rose with Paul Kennerley, 1985. Recordings: Singles include: Together Again, 1975; Two More Bottles of Wine, 1978; Beneath Still Waters, 1979; (Lost His Love) On Our Last date, 1982; To Know Him is to Love Him (Trio), 1987; We believe in Happy Endings (duet with Earl Thomas Conley), 1988; Wheels of Love, 1990; Never Be Anyone, 1990; High Powered Love, 1993; Albums include: Gliding Bird, 1969; Pieces Of The Sky, 1975; Elite Hotel, 1976; Luxury Liner, 1977; Quarter Moon In A Ten-Cent Town, 1978; Blue Kentucky Girl, 1979; Roses in the Snow, 1980; Evangeline, 1981; Cimarron, 1981; Last Date, 1982; White Shoes, 1983; Profile: Best Of Emmylou Harris, 1984; The Ballad Of Sally Rose, 1985; Thirteen, 1986; Trio (with Dolly Parton, Linda Ronstadt), 1987; Angel Band, 1987; Bluebird, 1989; Brand New Dance, 1990; Duets (with Nash Ramblers), 1990; At The Ryman, 1992; Cowgirls Prayer, 1993; Wrecking Ball, 1995; Portraits, 1996; Nashville, 1996; Spyboy, 1998; Light of the Stable, 1999; Red Dirt Girl, 2000; Singin' with Emmylou Harris, 2000; Anthology, 2001; Stumble into Grace, 2003; Assisted Gram Parsons on album GP, Grievous Angel,

1973. Honours: 7 Grammy Awards, 1976-95; 27 Grammy Nominations; Female Vocalist of the Year, Country Music Association, 1980; Academy Country Music Award, Album of the Year, 1987. Membership: President, Country Music Foundation, 1983. Address: Monty Hitchcock Management, PO Box 159007, Nashville, TN 37215, USA.

HARRIS Robert Sidney, b. 30 March 1951, London, England. Engineer. m. Beverley, 1 son, 2 daughters. Education: BSc (Eng) 1st Class Honours, Electrical Engineering, Imperial College, London, 1969-72. Appointments include: Spacecraft AOCS Designer, 1972-74, Project Leader on ESTEC AOCS Contracts, 1975-79, BAC Bristol, UK; AOCS Group Leader on ESTEC AOCS Contracts, 1980, AOCS Systems Engineer responsible for design and analysis of L-SAT AOCS, 1981-82, Design Manager for HIPPARCOS power subsystem, harness subsystem and AOCS, 1982-87, Proposal preparation for STSP missions, 1987-89, Design Manager for STSP activities (SOHO AOCS, CLUSTER AOCS, CLUSTER reaction control subsystem), 1989-94, BAe, Bristol, UK; Design Manager for INTEGRAL AOCS, 1997-99, Design Manager of XMM AOCS, 1994-99, Member of SOHO recovery team following the temporary loss of the spacecraft, 1998, Member of SOHO "tiger team", 1998, part of recovery team at NASA leading to a successful transition back to full operations, 1998-99, MMS Bristol, UK; Senior Principal Consultant, working on systems, AOCMS, RCS and operations activities for the Rosetta spacecraft, 1999-2003, supporting launch campaign and post-launch activities for the Rosetta spacecraft at ESOC, design and operations for the drag-free attitude control system of the GOCE spacecraft, Phase A design for the GAIA spacecraft, proposal preparation for the BepiColombo spacecraft, AOCS architect responsible for the design and development of the AOCS for the BepiColombo spacecraft, 2003-, RHEA Systems SA, Louvain-La-Neuve, Belgium (located at Astrium GmbH, Friedrichshafen, Germany). Publications: Numerous technical reports supporting the design development and operations of the various spacecraft attitude and orbit control systems. Honours: Sylvanus P Thompson Award for achieving the top degree in electrical engineering and electronics, 1972; MBE for contribution to the recovery of the SOHO spacecraft, 2000; Laurels for Team Achievement Award (jointly), International Academy of Astronautics, 2003. Memberships: Associate, City and Guilds Institute; Institution of Engineering and Technology. Address: Hoher Weg 60, 88048 Friedrichshafen, Germany. E-mail: family.harris@t-online.de

HARRIS Rolf, b. 30 March 1930, Perth, Australia. TV Entertainer; Singer; Musician; Artist. m. Alwen Myfanwy Wiseman Hughes, 1 March 1958, 1 daughter. Education: University of Washington; Claremount Teachers College, Washington. Appointments: TV Entertainer, Australia and England; Host of English TV programmes including, Hey Presto, It's Rolf, Rolf Harris Show, Rolf on Saturday OK!, Rolf's Walkabout, Cartoon Time, Rolf's Amazing World of Animals, Animal Hospital; Rolf On Art; Rolf Harris Star Portraits. Appearances include, Opening Ceremony, Commonwealth Games, Brisbane, 1982, Olympic Gala, Los Angeles, 1984, Bicentennial Command Performance, Sydney, 1988. Creative Works: Numerous hit recordings include: Tie Me Kangaroo Down Sport; Sun Arise; Jake the Peg; Two Little Boys; Stairway to Heaven. Publications: How to Write Your Own Pop Song, 1968; Rolf Goes Bush, 1975; Your Cartoon Time, 1986; Catalogue of Comic Verse, 1988; Every Picture Tells a Story, 1989; Win or Die: The Making of a King, 1989; Your Animation Time, 1991; Personality Cats, 1992; Me and You and Poems Too, 1993; Beastly Behaviour, 1997;

Draw Your Own Cartoons with Rolf Harris, 1998; Can You Tell What It Is Yet? (autobiography), 2001; Rolf on Art, 2002. Honours: MBE, 1968; OBE, 1978; AM, 1989; 3 times winner, National TV Awards; 2 times winner, TV Quick Award; CBE, 2006. Memberships: President, PHAB; Equity. Address: c/o Jan Kennedy, Billy Marsh Associates, 174-178 North Gower Street, London NW1 2NB, England.

HARRIS Rosemary, b. Ashby, Suffolk, England. Actor. m. John Ehle, 1 daughter. Education: Bancroft Gold Medal, Royal Academy of Dramatic Art, 1952. Career: Bristol Old Vic; London Old Vic; Chichester Festival Theatre; National Theatre at the Old Vic; West End: Seven Year Itch; Plaza Suite; All My Sons; Heartbreak House; The Petition; Best of Friends; Steel Magnolias; National Theatre: Women of Troy; Broadway: Lion in Winter; A Street Car Named Desire; Hay Fever; An Inspector Calls; A Delicate Balance; Films: Tom & Viv; Sunshine; Spiderman; Spiderman Two; Spiderman Three; When the Devil Knows You Are Dead. Honours: Evening Standard Award; Golden Globe Award; Emmy Award; Tony Award; Academy Award Nomination. Address: c/o ICM Ltd; 76 Oxford Street, London W1N 0AX, England.

HARRIS Thomas, b. 1940, Jackson, Tennessee, USA. Writer. m. divorced, 1 daughter. Education: Baylor University, Texas, USA. Appointments: Worked on newsdesk Waco News-Tribune; Member, Staff, Associated Press, New York. Publications: Black Sunday; Red Dragon (filmed as Manhunter); The Silence of the Lambs (filmed); Hannibal; Hannibal Rising. Address: St Martin's Press, 175 Fifth Avenue, New York, NY 10010, USA.

HARRISON Sir David, b. 3 May 1930, Clacton-on-Sea, Essex, England. Retired University Vice-Chancellor. m. Sheila Rachel Debes, 2 sons, 1 deceased, 1 daughter. Education: BA, 1953, PhD, 1956, MA, 1957, ScD, 1979, FREng, FRSC, FIChemE, FRSA, FRSCM, CIMgt, Selwyn College, Cambridge. Appointments: Senior Tutor, 1967-79, Master, 1994-2000, Fellow, Selwyn College, Cambridge; Vice-Chancellor, University of Keele, 1979-84; Vice-Chancellor, University of Exeter, 1984-94; President, IChemE, 1991-92; Chairman, Committee of Vice-Chancellors and Principals, 1991-93; Deputy Vice-Chancellor, University of Cambridge, 1995-2000; Chairman, Board of Trustees, Homerton College, Cambridge; Chairman, Governing Body, Shrewsbury School, 1989-2003; Director, Salters Institute of Industrial Chemistry; Liveryman, Salters' Company; Chairman, Ely Cathedral Council; Chairman, Council Royal School of Church Music, 1996-2005. Publications: Fluidised Particles (with J F Davidson), 1963; Fluidization (with J F Davidson and R Clift), 1971, 1985. Honours: CBE, 1990; Hon DUniv, Keele University, 1992; Hon DSc, Exeter University, 1995; Kt, 1997; George E Davis Medal, IChemE, 2001. Memberships: Athenaeum; Oxford and Cambridge; Federation House, Stoke-on-Trent. Address: 7 Gough Way, Cambridge, CB3 9LN, England. E-mail: sirdavidharrison@yahoo.co.uk

HARRISON Derek, b. 5 January 1929, Oswaldtwistle, Lancashire, England. Retired Personal Care Industry Executive; Inventor; Journalist. m. Joyce (Joy) Alice Whitaker, 1955, 1 son, 1 daughter. Education: Regional College of Art, Department of Architecture, Manchester University, 1947-52. Appointments: Territorial Army, 1948-1953; Military Service, 1948-53; National Service, Royal Engineers, 1953-55; Assistant Manager, 1955-57, Manager, 1957-71, Principal, 1971-, Retired, 1986, Consultant, 1986-, Moorside Laundry, Swinton, Manchester; Chairman, 1996-99, Manchester Branch, British Institute of Management; Member, Trafford

Park Quality Forum, 1994; Laundry Wages Council, 1972-88; National Executive Council, Association of British Laundry, Cleaning and Rental Services, 1984-87; Chairman, British Diabetic Association (Salford), 1995-2000; Life Member, Diabetes UK; Member, Executive Council, Manchester Chamber of Trade and Industry (Salford), 1996; Governor, Registrar, Bridgewater School, Worsley, 1971-74; Liveryman, Worshipful Company of Launderers, London; Senior Lecturer, Head of Department, Laundry Technology, Hollings College, 1962; Member, Chapel Street Regeneration and Business Group, Salford City Council, 2000; Member, Salford Coronary Heart and Diabetes Update Club, NHS Primary Care Trust; University of Manchester Teaching Hospital (Salford Royal Hospital), 2002. Publications: Patentee in field. Honours: Drummond Cup, University of Manchester, 1947, 1948; Recipient, Freedom of the City of London, 1979; The Ernest and Nan Albinson Award for journalism, 1999, 2002, Honorary Life Member, 2003, National President, 2007, Guild of Cleaners and Launderers. Memberships: Manchester University Motor Club, Vice-President, 1969-70; President, Manchester Society of Architects Students Association, 1953; Award of Merit, Institute of Professional Designers, 1985; Branch Honorary Officer Award, Institute of Management, 2001; Honorary Vice-President, Guild of Cleaners and Launderers, 1978, 2003; Deputy Master, College of Fellows Guild of Cleaners and Launderers, 1998-2005; Master of the College, 2005; Senior Vice President, GCL, 2005; Northern Centre Chairman, GCL, 1979-; Honorary Life Member, Automobile Association; Honorary Life Member, City Livery Club, London; Listed in national and international biographical dictionaries. Address: 5 Woodlands Avenue, Swinton, Manchester M27 0DJ, England.

HARRISON John, b. 12 November 1944, Stockton-on-Tees, England. Chartered Accountant. m. Patricia Alice Bridget, 1 son, 2 daughters. Education: BA Honours, Economics, Sheffield University; FCA. Appointments: Articled Clerk, Coopers & Lybrand, 1963-67; Corporate Planner, Tillotson, 1967-70; Partner, DeLoitte & Touche, 1970-2001; Chairman, Portal Ltd, 2001-; Chairman, Spring Grove plc, 2002-07; Non-executive Director, Dere Holdings plc, 2005-; Non-executive Director, Crown Northcorp Inc, 2007-. Membership: FRSA. Address: Goodwin Manor, Swaffham Prior, Cambridge CB25 0LG, England. E-mail: john.harrison@swaffham.demon.co.uk

HARRISS-WHITE Barbara, b. 4 February 1946, Westminster, England. Academic. 2 daughters. Education: BA, MA, Geography, 1968, Diploma, Agricultural Science, 1969, University of Cambridge; PhD, Development Studies, University of East Anglia, 1977. Appointments: Research Officer, Centre of South Asia Studies, Cambridge, 1972-77; Research Associate, Overseas Development Institute, London, 1977-81; Research Fellow, London School of Hygiene and Tropical Medicine, 1981-97; University Lecturer in Agricultural Economics, 1987-96, Reader in Development Studies, 1996, Professor of Development Studies, 1998, Director, Queen Elizabeth House International Development Centre, 2004-, University of Oxford, UK Chair, HEFCE RAE Sub-Panel for Development Studies. Publications: 15 authored books, 10 edited books, 11 research reports and 174 papers and chapters; Illfare in India, 1999; Outcast from Social Welfare: Adult Disability in Rural South India, 2002; India Working, 2003; Rural India Facing the 21st Century, 2004; India's Market Society, 2005; Coming to Terms with Nature, 2006; Trade Liberalisation and India's Informal Economy, 2007. Honours: Cambridge University Smuts Memorial Commonwealth Lecturer, 1998-99; Asian Development Research Institute Foundation Lecturer,

2002; Radhakamal Mukherjee Lecturer, Indian Society of Labour Economics, 2003; Honorary Research Fellow, Ecole des Hautes Etudes en Sciences Sociales, Paris, 2004. Memberships: Development Studies Association; British Association of South Asian Studies; Alpine Club. Address: Department of International Development, Queen Elizabeth House, 3 Mansfield Road, Oxford OX1 3TB, England. E-mail: barbara.harriss-white@qeh.ox.ac.uk Website: www.qeh.ox.ac.uk/

HARRY Deborah Ann, b. 1 July 1945, Miami, Florida, USA. Singer; Songwriter; Actress. Career: Former Playboy bunny waitress; Singer, groups: Wind In The Willows; The Stilettos; Founder, Blondie, 1974-83; Appearances include: New York punk club, CBGBs, 1974; Support to Iggy Pop, US, 1977; Solo recording career, 1981-; Actress, films including: Blank Generation, 1978; The Foreigner, 1978; Union City, 1979; Roadie, 1980; Videodrome; Hairspray; The Killbillies; Tales from the Darkside: The Movie, 1990; Intimate Stranger, 1991; Joe's Day, 1999; 200, 1999; Six Ways to Sunday, 1999; Ghost Light, 2000; Dueces Wild, 2000; Red Lipstick, 2000; The Curse of Blondie, 2003; Honey Trap; 2005; Patch, 2005; I Remember You Now; 2005; Full Grown Men; 2006; Anamorph, 2007; Elegy, 2007. TV appearances: Saturday Night Life; The Muppet Show; Tales from the Darkside; Wiseguys; Theatre: Teaneck Tanzi; The Venus Flytrap; Recordings: Hit singles: with Blondie: Denis (Denee), 1978; (I'm Always Touched By Your) Presence Dear, 1978; Picture This, 1978; Hanging On The Telephone, 1978; Heart Of Glass, 1979; Sunday Girl, 1979; Dreaming, 1979; Union City Blue, 1979; Call Me, 1980; Atomic, 1980; The Tide Is High (Number 1, UK and US), 1980; Rapture (Number 1, US), 1981; Island Of Lost Souls, 1982; Solo: Backfired, 1981; French Kissin' (In The USA), 1986; I Want That Man, 1989; I Can See Clearly, 1993; Albums with Blondie: Blondie, 1976; Plastic Letters, 1978; Parallel Lines, 1978; Eat To The Beat, 1979; Autoamerican, 1980; The Best Of Blondie, 1981; The Hunter, 1982; Solo albums: Koo Koo, 1981; Rockbird, 1986; Def, Dumb And Blonde, 1989; Debravation, 1993; Compilations: Once More Into The Bleach, 1988; The Complete Picture, 1991; Blonde And Beyond, 1993; Rapture, 1994; Virtuosity, 1995; Rockbird, 1996; Der Einziger Weg, 1999; No Exit, 1999; Livid, 2000; Contributor, film soundtracks: American Gigolo, 1980; Roadie, 1980; Scarface; Krush Groove, 1984. Publications: Making Tracks - The Rise Of Blondie (co-written with Chris Stein), 1982. Memberships: ASCAP; AFTRA; Equity; Screen Actors Guild. Current Management: Overland Productions, 156 W 56th Street, 5th Floor, New York, NY 10019, USA.

HART David, b. 6 September 1950, Darlington, England. Radiation Protection Scientist. m. Doreen Carter. Education: BSc, University College London; PhD, University of Edinburgh. Appointments: Research Fellow, Imperial College London, 1978-80; Lecturer, University of East Anglia, Norwich, 1980-87; Principal Radiation Scientist, Health Protection Agency and National Radiological Protection Board, 1987-. Publications: The Volta River Project, 1980; Nuclear Power in India, 1983; Articles in Nature, New Scientist, British Journal of Radiology, Nuclear Medicine Communications, European Journal of Radiology. Membership: Institute of Physics and Engineering in Medicine. Address: Radiation Protection Division, Health Protection Agency, Chilton, Didcot, Oxfordshire OX11 0RQ, England.

HART Pamela Walker, b. Jacksonville, Florida, USA. Artist; Writer; Educator. m. Donald Hart. Education: BA, Fashion Merchandising, Florida State University; BS, Art Education, University of Nebraska at Omaha; MS Education, Elmira

College, New York. Appointments: Department Manager, Maas Brothers Department Stores, Florida, 1965-68; Office Manager, Cole of California, Regional Office, Atlanta, Georgia, 1968-70; Human Resources Management Officer, United States Air Force, 1970-74; Visual Arts Educator, K-12 Public Schools, Nebraska, Wisconsin, New York, 1978-89; Professional Artist, Speaker, Writer, Westernville, New York, 1989-; Commissioner, Commission of the Arts, Rome, New York, 2005. Publications: The Best of Sketching and Drawing, 1999; Cover Art: Fearless Through Fire "Women in Motion", 2004; Artwork and article, Inspiration in snow country "Women in Motion", 2004; The Art of Layering: Making Connections, 2004; Artist and author, Mother Wisdom, 2004; Speaker Presentations: Landscape-based abstractions, 2001; Inner Voice/Artistic Choice, 2001; Represented in: Library of the National Museum of Women in the Arts, Washington DC; Numerous private and public collections, United States and Canada. Honours include: Master's Award, Watercolour, Utica Art Association, Tri-County Regional, Marcy, New York, 1995; First Prize, Watercolour, State University of New York, Utica/Rome Campus, New York, 1995; Special Recognition Award, Rome Art Association Regional, Rome, New York, 1997; First Prize, Acrylic, Mohawk Valley Centre for the Arts, Little Falls, New York, 1997; First Prize, Acrylic, State University of New York, Utica/Rome Campus, 1999; Merit Award, Watermedia, East Washington Watercolor Society National, Richland, Washington, 1999; Adolph and Clara Obrig Prize for a watercolour by and American artist, National Academy of Design, New York, 2000; Prize for Watermedia, 66th National Exhibition, Art Association Galleries, Cooperstown, New York, 2001. Memberships: Elected Member: National Association of Women Artists, Society of Layerists in Multimedia, Central New York Watercolor Society; National League of American Pen Women; Charter Member: National Museum of Women in the Arts, National Women's History Museum.

HART Raymond Kenneth, b. 15 February 1928, Newcastle, New South Wales, Australia. Forensic Metallurgist. m. Betty Joyce Hart, 1 son, 1 daughter. Education: ASTC, Sydney Technical College, 1949; DIC, Imperial College, London, 1952; PhD, Metallurgy, University of Cambridge, 1955; JD, Kennedy Western University, 1991. Appointments: Scientific Officer, Aeronautical Research Laboratories, Melbourne, Victoria, 1955-58; Senior Scientist, Argonne National Laboratory, Illinois, USA, 1958-70; Manager, ANL-AMU High Voltage Program, 1966-70; Principal Research Scientist, Georgia Institute of Technology, 1970-74; President, Pasat Research Association Inc, 1974-90; Contracted with California Institute of Technology/Jet Propulsion Laboratory to design/build a space vehicle compatible Scanning Electron Microprobe Analyzer (SEMPA), 1976-82; Consultant Metallurgist, Raymond K Hart Ltd, Atlanta, Georgia, 1991. Publications: 22 refereed scientific texts; 5 chapters in technical books; 41 presentations at professional meetings; 400 sworn depositions; 100 trial testimonies. Honours include: NASA Certificate of Recognition, 1976; President's Award, Midwest Society of Electronic Microscopy, 1986; Distinguished Scientist Award, Southeastern Microscopy Society, 1993; Morton D Maser Distinguished Service Award, Microscopy Society of America, 1995; Elected to Guild of Benefactors, Corpus Christi College, Cambridge, 1996; International Order of Merit, IBC, 2000; IBC Millennium Time Capsule Book, 2000; American Medal of Honor, ABI, 2001; Engineering Sciences Section's Founders Award, American Academy of Forensic Sciences, 2002; Companion of the 1209 Society, University of Cambridge, 2003; Founding Member, 1352 Foundation Society, Corpus Christi College, Cambridge, 2005;

Eminent Fellow, ABI, 2006. Memberships: Fellow, American Academy of Forensic Science; Honorary Life Fellow, Royal Australian Chemistry Institute; American Society of Metals, International Branch; American Physical Society; Microscopy Society of America; Sigma Xi; Diplomate, International Institute of Forensic Engineering Sciences, 2002-. Address: 145 Grogan's Lake Dr, Sandy Springs, GA 30350-3115, USA. E-mail: rayhart@comcast.net

HART-DAVIS Duff, b. 3 June 1936, London, England. Author. Education: BA, Oxford University, 1960. Appointments: Feature Writer, 1972-76, Literary Editor, 1976-77, Assistant Editor, 1977-78, Sunday Telegraph, London; Country Columnist, Independent, 1986-2001. Publications: The Megacull, 1968; The Gold of St Matthew (in USA as The Gold Trackers), 1968; Spider in the Morning, 1972; Ascension: The Story of a South Atlantic Island, 1972; Peter Fleming (biography), 1974; Monarchs of the Glen, 1978; The Heights of Rimring, 1980; Fighter Pilot (with C Strong), 1981; Level Five, 1982; Fire Falcon, 1984; The Man-Eater of Jassapur, 1985; Hitler's Games, 1986; Armada, 1988; The House the Berrys Built, 1990; Horses of War, 1991; Country Matters, 1991; Wildings: The Secret Garden of Eileen Soper, 1992; Further Country Matters, 1993; When the Country Went to Town, 1997; Raoul Millais, 1998; Fauna Britannica, 2003; Audubon's Elephant, 2004; Honorary Tiger, 2005. Address: Owlpen Farm, Uley, Dursley, Gloucestershire GL11 5BZ, England.

HART-DYKE David, b. 3 October 1938, Havant, Hampshire, England. Retired Naval Officer. m. Diana Luce, 1967, 2 daughters. Education: St Lawrence College, Ramsgate, 1952-57; Britannia Royal Naval College, Dartmouth, 1959-61; Staff Course, Royal Naval College, Greenwich, 1974-75. Appointments: Royal Navy, 1958-90; National Service, Commissioned Midshipman RNVR, 1958-59; Sub-Lieutenant RN, HMS Eastbourne, Far East Fleet, 1961-62; Lieutenant, HM Coastal Forces, 1962; Served in HM Ships Lanton, Palliser and Gurkha; Specialist Navigation Course, HMS Dryad, 1967; Navigating Officer, Promoted to Lieutenant Commander, Frigates HMS Tenby, HMS Scylla, 1968-71; Divisional Officer and Head of Navigation, Britannia Royal Naval College, Dartmouth, 1971-73; Promoted to Commander, 1974, Executive Officer, Guided Missile Destroyer, HMS Hampshire, 1974; Staff, Royal Naval Staff College, Greenwich, 1976; Commander of the Royal Yacht Britannia, 1978; Captain, 1980; Captain, HMS Coventry, 1981-82 when sunk by enemy action in the Falklands War; Assistant Chief of Staff to the Commander of the Chief Fleet, Northwood, 1982-84; Assistant Naval Attaché and Chief of Staff to the Commander British Naval Staff, Washington DC, 1985-87; Director of Naval Recruiting, Ministry of Defence, 1987; Retired from Royal Navy, 1990; Clerk to the Worshipful Company of Skinners, City of London, 1990-2003. Publications: Four Weeks In May (The story of HMS Coventry in the Falklands War 1982) 2007. Articles on experiences in the Falklands War and on Combat Stress published in Naval Review and other related journals. Honours: LVO, 1979; ADC to Her Majesty the Queen, 1988-90; CBE, 1990. Address: Hambledon House, Hambledon, Hants PO7 4RU, England. E-mail: dhartdyke@tiscali.co.uk

HARTCUP Adeline, b. 26 April 1918, Isle of Wight, England. Writer. m. John Hartcup, 11 February 1950, 2 sons. Education: MA, Classics and English Literature, Oxon. Appointments: Editorial Staff, Times Educational Supplement; Honorary Press Officer, Kent Voluntary Service Council. Publications: Angelica, 1954; Morning Faces, 1963; Below Stairs in the

Great Country Houses, 1980; Children of the Great Country Houses, 1982, 2000; Love and Marriage in the Great Country Houses, 1984; Spello: Life Today in Ancient Umbria, 1985. Contributions to: Times Educational Supplement; Harper's; Queen; Times Higher Educational Supplement. Address: 8F Compton Road, London N1, England.

HARTER John J, b. 31 January 1926, Canyon, Texas, USA. Diplomat; Economic Analyst. m. Irene T Harter, 2 sons, 1 daughter. Education: BA, 1948, MA, 1953, University of Southern California; MA, Economics, Harvard University, 1963. Appointments: Lecturer, History, University of Southern California, 1948-53; Foreign Service Officer, US Department of State with assignments in South Africa, Chile, Thailand, Geneva, Washington, 1954-83; Oral Historian, 1983-; Declassifier, Agency for International Development, 1998-. Publications: Views on Global Economic Development, 1979; The Language of Trade, 1984; Numerous articles in Foreign Service Journal and State Magazine. Memberships: American Foreign Service Association; Diplomatic and Consular Officers Retired. Address: 12109 Kershaw Place, Glen Allen, VA 23059-6978, USA. E-mail: jjitharter@aol.com

HARTILL Edward Theodore, b. 23 January 1943, United Kingdom. Consultant. m. Gillian Ruth Todd, 2 sons, 2 sons from previous marriage. Education: BSc, Estate Management, College of Estate Management, London University; FRICS. Appointments: Joined Burd and Evans, Land Agents, Shrewsbury, 1963; Estates Department, Legal and General Assurance Company, 1964-73; Visiting Lecturer in Law of Town Planning and Compulsory Purchase, Hammersmith and West London College of Advanced Business Studies, 1968-78; Property Investment Department, Guardian Royal Exchange Assurance Group, 1973-85, Head Office Manager, 1980-85; City Surveyor, City of London Corporation, 1985-2008; Member, 1985-2007, National Council, 1988-2007, President, 1996-97, Association of Chief Estates Surveyors and Property Managers in Local Government (formerly Local Authority Valuers' Association); Member, General Practice Divisional Council, 1989-97, President, 1992-93, General Council, 1990-2004, Honorary Treasurer, 2000-04, Royal Institution of Chartered Surveyors; Member, Steering Group, 1992-99, Chairman Property Services Sub-Group, 1992-99, Construction Industry Standing Conference; Founder Member, Chairman, Property Services NTO, 1999-2005; Chair, 2003, Vice Chair, 2004-2007, Assets Skills (a sector Skills Council); Member of Council, 2004-, Deputy Chairman Estates Committee, 2006-, University of London; Governor and Trustee, Coram Family, 2006-, Vice Chairman 2007-; Consultant, Corderoy (International Chartered Quantity Surveyors and Cost Consultants), 2008-. Publications: Occasional lectures and articles on professional topics. Honours: Honorary Associate, Czech Chamber of Appraisers, 1992; Honorary Member Investment Property Forum, 1995; OBE, 2004. Memberships: British Schools Exploring Society; FRSA, 1993; Liveryman, 1985-, Court of Assistants, 1991-, Master, 2003-2004, Worshipful Company of Chartered Surveyors. Address: 215 Sheen Lane, East Sheen, London SW14 8LE, England.

HARTLAND Michael, b. 7 February 1941. Writer and Broadcaster. m. 1975, 2 daughters. Education: Christ's College, Cambridge, 1960-63. Appointments: British Diplomatic and Civil Service, 1963-78; United Nations, 1978-83; Full-time Writer, 1983-; Book Reviewer and Feature Writer, The Sunday Times, The Times, Guardian and Daily Telegraph; Thriller Critic, The Times, 1989-90; Daily Telegraph, 1993-2003; Travel Correspondent: The Times, 1993-2003; Television and Radio include: Sonia's Report, ITV documentary, 1990;

Masterspy, interviews with KGB defector Oleg Gordievsky, Radio 4, 1991. Publications: Down Among the Dead Men; Seven Steps to Treason (dramatised for BBC Radio 4, 1990); The Third Betrayal; Frontier of Fear; The Year of the Scorpion; The Verdict of Us All (jointly, short stories); Masters of Crime: Lionel Davidson & Dick Francis; As Ruth Carrington: Dead Fish. Honours: Fellow, Royal Society of Arts; Honorary Fellow, University of Exeter; South West Arts Literary Award. Memberships: Executive Committee of PEN, 1997-2001; Detection Club; Mystery Writers of America. Address: Cotte Barton, Branscombe, Devon, EX12 3BH, England.

HARTMANN Reinhard R K, b. 8 April 1938. Education: Translator's Diploma, University of Vienna, 1956-60; BSc, Economics, 1956-60, Doctorate, 1960-65, Vienna School of Economics; MA, International Economics, Southern Illinois University, USA, 1961-62. Appointments: Lecturer, Modern Languages, University of Manchester Institute of Science and Technology, 1964-68; Lecturer, Applied Linguistics, University of Nottingham, 1968-74; Director, Language Centre and Head of Linguistics, University of Exeter, 1974-92; Reader, Applied Linguistics, 1991-, Head, Department of Applied Linguistics, 1992-96, in School of English, 1996-2001, University of Exeter; Honorary Professor of Lexicography, Department of English, University of Birmingham, 2000-; Honorary University Fellow, School of English, University of Exeter, 2001-. Publications: Author/editor of 18 books; Articles in national and international scholarly journals; Papers presented at conferences; Numerous invited contributions. Honours: Fellow, Royal Society of Arts; Fellow, Chartered Institute of Linguists (London); Honorary Life Member, European Association for Lexicography; MCB UP/Literati Club award for best specialist reference work, 1998. Memberships include: British Association for Applied Linguistics; European Association for Lexicography. Address: 40 Velwell Road, Exeter, Devon EX4 4LD, England. E-mail: r.r.k.hartmann@exeter.ac.uk

HARTMANN Vladimir, b. 21 February 1947, Khabarovsk, Russia. Education: Physics Engineer, Moscow Institute of Physics and Technology, 1971; PhD, Russian Chemical Engineering University, Moscow, 2000. Appointments: Junior Researcher, 1971-76, Senior Researcher, 1976-2003, Chief of Department, 2004-, Novomoskovsk Institute of Nitrogen Industry. Publications: Long-term behaviour of commercial sulphur removal unit, 2004; Effect of sulphur removal catalyst granule properties on the commercial scale bed macrokinetics, 2005. Address: Moskovskaya 1-42, Novomoskovsk, Tula Region, 301664, Russia. E-mail: vl.hartmann@gmail.com

HARUTYUNIAN Gagik, b. 23 March 1948, Geghashen, Kotayk Region, Armenia. President of the Constitutional Court of the Republic of Armenia. Education: Graduate, Faculty of Economics, 1970, Postgraduate Student, Yerevan State University. Appointments: Lecturer, Yerevan State University, 1973; Chief Lecturer, Institute of National Economics; Economist-Lecturer, Central Committee of Communistic Party of the Armenian Republic, 1982-87; Head, Social-Economic Department, Central Committee, 1987; Elected Deputy, Supreme Council of the Republic of Armenia, 1990; Elected Vice Chairman, Supreme Council of the Republic of Armenia, 1990; Elected Vice President, Republic of Armenia 1991-1996; Prime Minister of the Republic of Armenia, 1991-92; President, Constitutional Court of the Republic of Armenia, 1996; President, Center of Constitutional Law, Republic of Armenia, 1996-. Publications: Author: 20 monographs; 125 scientific works. Honours: High Judicial Qualification of Judge, Decree of the President of the

Republic of Armenia, 1998; Scientific Degree of Doctor of Law, 1999. Memberships: Member, International Academy of Information, 1997; Member, Council of International Association of Constitutional Law, 1998; Co-ordinator of Mandatory Acting, Conference on Constitutional Review bodies of New Independent Countries and President of Editorial Council of International Bulletin on Constitutional Justice (published in 2 languages), 1997; Member, European Commission for Democracy through Law, Council of Europe, 1997; Head of Project, Almanac; Constitutional Justice in the New Millennium (published in 4 languages), 2002. Address: The Constitutional Court of the Republic of Armenia, 10 Marshal Bagramyan Avenue, Yerevan 0019, Republic of Armenia 375019. E-mail: mma@athgo.org

HARVEY Barbara Fitzgerald, b. 21 January 1928, Teignmouth, Devon, England. University Teacher. Education: BA (Oxon) 1949, MA (Oxon), 1953, B Litt (Oxon), 1953, Somerville College, Oxford. Appointments: Assistant, Department of Scottish History, University of Edinburgh, 1951-52; Assistant Lecturer then Lecturer, Department of History, Queen Mary College, University of London, 1952-55; Tutor in Medieval History, 1955-56, Fellow and Tutor in Medieval History, 1956-93, Emeritus Fellow, 1993-, Somerville College, Oxford. Publications: Books: Westminster Abbey and its Estates in the Middle Ages, 1977; The Westminster Chronicle, 1381-94 (editor with L C Hector), 1982; Living and Dying in England 1100-1540: The monastic experience, 1993; The Twelfth and Thirteenth Centuries, 1066-c.1280 (editor) in Short Oxford History of the British Isles, 2001; Articles in: Transactions of the Royal Historical Society; Bulletin of the Institute of Historical Research; Economic History Review; Journal of Ecclesiastical History and other learned journals and similar works. Honours: FBA, 1982; Ford's Lecturer in English History, University of Oxford, 1989; Joint Winner, Wolfson Foundation Prize for History, 1993; CBE, 1997. Memberships: Fellow, Society of Antiquaries, London, 1964-; President, Henry Bradshaw Society, 1997-2007; Honorary Vice-President, Royal Historical Society, 2003-. Address: 66 Cranham Street, Oxford OX2 6DD, England. E-mail: barbara.harvey@some.ox.ac.uk

HARVEY John Robert, b. 25 June 1942, Bishops Stortford, Hertfordshire, England. University Lecturer; Writer. m. Julietta Chloe Papadopoulou, 1968, 1 daughter. Education: BA, Honours Class 1, English, 1964, MA, 1967, PhD, 1969, University of Cambridge. Appointments: English Faculty, Emmanuel College, Cambridge; Editor, Cambridge Quarterly, 1978-86; University Reader, Cambridge; Vice-Master, Emmanuel College, Cambridge. Publications: Victorian Novelists and Their Illustrators, 1970; Men in Black, 1995. Novels: The Plate Shop, 1979; Coup d'Etat, 1985; The Legend of Captain Space, 1990. Contributions to: London Review of Books; Sunday Times; Sunday Telegraph; Listener; Encounter; Cambridge Quarterley; Essays in Criticism. Honour: David Higham Prize, 1979. Address: Emmanuel College, Cambridge, England.

HARVEY Jonathan Dean, b. 3 May 1939, Sutton Coldfield, England. Composer. m. Rosaleen Marie Harvey, 1 son, 1 daughter. Education: Major Scholar, MA, St John's College Cambridge, 1957-61; PhD, Glasgow University, 1961-63; DMus, Cambridge University, 1970. Appointments: Lecturer, Senior Lecturer, Southampton University, 1964-77; Senior Lecturer, Professor, Sussex University, 1977-92; Full Professor, Stanford University, 1995-2000; Visiting Professor, Imperial College, 1999-2002; About 200 performances per annum. Publications: Books: The Music of

Stockhausen, 1975; Music and Inspiration, 1999; In Quest of Spirit, 1999; About 40 articles; About 200 compositions for orchestra, choir, chamber and electronic combinations; 3 operas. Honours: Britten Award, 1993; 2 Koussevitsky Awards; British Academy Composer Award, 2004; Honorary Doctorates: Bristol, Southampton and Sussex Universities; FRCM; Honorary RAM; FRSCM; Honorary Fellow, St John's College, Cambridge. Memberships: British Academy; European Academy. Address: c/o Faber Music, 3 Queen Square, London WC1N 3AU, England.

HARVEY Pamela Ann, b. 15 October 1934, Bush Hill Park, Edmonton, London, England. Writer; Poet. Education: 6 GCEs, Edmonton County Grammar; RSA Diploma. Appointments: Secretarial Work, London; Library Work, Southgate Library. Publications: Poetry, 1994; Quiet Lines, 1996; The Wellspring (co-author with Anna Franklin), 2000; Children's Fun Fiction (story), 2006; The Jovian System (booklet), 1990. Contributions to: The People's Poetry; Romantic Heir; Rubies in the Darkness; Cadmium Blue Literary Journal; Pendragon (stories, articles, poems); Keltria, USA; Celtic Connections; Silver Wheel (articles and poems); Sharkti Laureate; Time Haiku; Azami, Japan; The Lady magazine (short story); Avalon magazine (articles); Poetry Now (new fiction) included: Hold That Thought (story), Timeless Tales (story) and Share Our Worlds Anthology (poem); Contributor to poems on an All About War theme; Littoral magazine (articles and poems), 2005-2006; Celebrations (Poetry Now), 2006. Honours: 1st prize Poetry (Rubies in Darkness Award, editor Peter G P Thompson), 2004; 3rd prize, Poetry (Rubies in Darkness), 2005. Memberships: Enfield Writers Group; New Renaissance Poets Society; Metverse Muse (poetry magazine).

HARVEY William Graeme, b. 15 January 1947, Watford, England. Naturalist. m. (1) 1 son, 2 daughters, (2) Pauline. Education: University College, Oxford, 1966-69. Appointments: British Council appointments in London, Tanzania, Indonesia and India, 1969-86; Director, British Council, Bangladesh, 1986-93; General Manager, Technical Co-operation Training, British Council, 1990-93; Regional Director, Eastern and Central Africa, British Council, Nairobi, 1993-98; Director, International Partnerships, British Council, London, 1998-2000; Naturalist, Writer, 2000-. Publications: Articles and papers on birds and conservation in UK, Africa and Asia, 1967-; Birds in Bangladesh, 1990; Photographic Guide to the Birds of India, 2002; Tails of Dilli (Animal Stories for Children), 2004; Atlas of the Birds of Delhi and Haryana, 2006. Memberships include: British Ornithologists Union; British Ornithologists Club; Life Member: Bombay Natural History Society; East African Wildlife Society; Madras Club, Chennai, India. Address: Pound Farm, Blackham, Tunbridge Wells, TN3 9TY, England. E-mail: billharvey08@googlemail.com

HASELHURST Alan Gordon Barraclough (Rt Hon Sir), b. 23 June 1937, South Elmsall, Yorkshire, England. Member of Parliament. m. Angela Margaret Bailey, 2 sons, 1 daughter. Education: Oriel College, Oxford, 1956-60. Appointments: Member of Parliament for Middleton and Prestwich, 1970-74; MP for Saffron Walden, 1977-; Parliamentary Private Secretary to the Home Secretary, 1973-74; Parliamentary Private Secretary to Education Secretary, 1979-81; Chairman of Ways and Means and Deputy Speaker, 1997-; Member of Committee of Essex County Cricket Club, 1996-. Publications: Occasionally Cricket, 1999; Eventually Cricket, 2001; Incidentally Cricket, 2003. Honours: Knight Bachelor, 1995; Privy Counsellor, 1999. Memberships: MCC; Essex County Cricket Club; Yorkshire County Cricket

Club. Address: House of Commons, London SW1A 0AA, England. E-mail: haselhursta@parliament.uk Website: www.siralanhaselhurst.net

HASHIGUCHI Yasuo, b. 31 July 1924, Sasebo, Japan. Professor of English (retired). m. Eiko Uchida, 1 son, 1 daughter. Education: BA, University of Tokyo, 1948; MEd, Ohio University, USA, 1951. Appointments: Associate Professor, English, Kagoshima University, 1951-64, 1964-68, Professor, 1968-82, Kyushu University; Fukuoka University, 1982-88; President, Fukuoka Jo Gakuin Junior College, 1988-93; Professor, Yasuda Women's University, 1993-96. Publications: Editor, Complete Works of John Steinbeck, 20 vols, 1985. Honours: Dick A Renner Prize, 1977; Special Recognition for Outstanding Publication, 1988; Recognition for Many Years of Outstanding Leadership in American Literature & Steinbeck Studies, 1991; Richard W and Dorothy Burkhardt Award, 1994; John J and Angeline Pruis Award, 1996; John J and Angeline R Pruis Award for the Outstanding Steinbeck Translator in Honour of John Steinbeck's Centennial, 2002. Memberships: President, 1977-89, Advisor 1989-, Kyushu American Literature Society; President, 1977-91, Honorary President, 1991-, Steinbeck Society of Japan; International Association of University Professors of English, 1999-. Address: 7-29-31-105 Iikura, Sawara-ku, Fukuoka 814-0161 Japan.

HASKINS Christopher (The Rt Hon The Lord Haskins), b. 1937, Dublin, Ireland. Businessman; Member of House of Lords. m. Gilda Horsley, 5 children. Education: History (Hons), Trinity College, Dublin. Appointments: De La Rue Trainee, 1959-60; Ford Motors Dagenham Personnel, 1960-62; Manager, Belfast, 1962-68, Pioneered foods in Marks & Spencer, 1968-2002; Director, 1974, Deputy Chair, 1974, Chairman, 1980, Northern Dairies (later Northern Foods); Chairman, Express Dairies (merged with Northern Foods), 1998-2002; Member, MAFF Review of CAP, 1995; Chairman, Better Regulation Task Force, 1997-2002; Member, New Deal Task Force, 1998-2001; Member, Britain in Europe Campaign, 1998-; Non Executive Director, Yorkshire Regional Development Agency, 1998-; Advisor to the Prime Minister on Foot and Mouth "Recovery", 2001; Heading Review of Defra, 2002-2003; Chair, Selby Coalfields Task Force (Managing the impact of closure), 2002-2003; Member, CBI President's Committee, 1995-98; Member, Hampel Committee on Corporate Governance, 1996-98; Member, Irish Economic Policy Review Group, 1998; Member, Commission for Social Justice, 1992-94; Member, UK Round Table on Sustainable Development. 1995-98; Trustee, Runnymede Trust, 1989-98; Chairman, Demos Trustees, 1993-2000; Trustee, Civil Liberties, 1997-99; Trustee, Legal Assistance Trust, 1998-2004; Trustee, Lawes Agricultural Trust, 1999-; Director, Yorkshire TV, 2002-; Trustee, Business Dynamics, 2002; Chair, DEFRA Review Group, 2002-03; Chair, European Movement, 2004-; Chair of Council and Pro-Chancellor, Open University, 2005-; Regular speaker and writer about Europe, agriculture, regulation, corporate governance. Honours: Labour Peer, 1998; Honorary Degrees: Dublin, Hull, Essex, Nottingham, Leeds, Metropolitan, Cranfield, Huddersfield. Address: Quarryside Farm, Main Street, Skidby, Nr Cottingham, East Yorkshire HU16 5SG, England.

HASLAM Michael Trevor, b. 7 February 1934, Leeds, England. Retired Medical Director. m. Shirley Dunstan, 1 son, 2 daughters. Education: Exhibitioner to St John's College, Cambridge, MA, MD, BChir, 1947-52; LMSSA, LRCP, MRCS, St Bartholomew's Hospital, London, 1955-59; MRCP

(G), 1967, F, 1979; MA, Theology, St John's College, York, 2003; Diploma in Psychological Medicine, 1962; Diploma in Medical Jurisprudence, 1972; MRCPsych, 1972, F, 1980; Certificate in Hypnotherapy, BSMDH, 1982. Appointments: Captain, RAMC, Military Service, 1960-62; Senior Registrar to Sir Martin Roth, Newcastle upon Tyne, 1964-67; Consultant in Psychological Medicine, Doncaster, 1967-70; Consultant in Psychological Medicine, York, 1970-89; Medical Director, Harrogate Clinic, 1989-91; Medical Director, South Durham, NHS Trust, 1994-98; Retired 1999. Publications: Books: Psychiatric Illness in Adolescence, 1975; Sexual Disorders, 1978; Psychosexual Disorders, 1979; Psychiatry Made Simple, 1982; Clifton Hospital an era, 1996; Close to the Wind, 2006; Editor: Transvestism, 1996; Psychiatry in the New Millennium, 2002; Editor of the Celtic Times, 1953-56. Honours: TD (Territorial National Service Decoration); Retired Fellow, Royal College of Physicians, Glasgow, 2001-; Retired Fellow, Royal College of Psychiatrists, 2001; Freeman of London; Liveryman of the Society of Apothecaries; Retired, Warden of North, Association of Freeman of England and Wales; Listed in national and international biographical dictionaries. Memberships: Chairman retired, Society of Clinical Psychiatrists; Author's Club to 1999; Royal Society of Medicine to 2004. Address: Chapel Garth, Crayke, York, YO61 4TE, England.

HASSAN IBN TALAL H R H, b. 20 March 1947, Amman, Jordan. Crown Prince of Jordan. m. Sarrath Khujista Akhter Banu, 1968, 1 son, 3 daughters. Education: Christ Church, Oxford University. Appointments: Regent to the throne of Jordan in absence of King Hussein; Ombudsman for National Development, 1971-; Founder, Royal Science Society of Jordan, 1970; Royal Academy of Islamic Civilization Research (AlAlbait), 1980; Arab Thought Forum, 1981; Forum Humanum (now Arab Youth Forum), 1982; Co-Chairman, Independent Commission on International Council for Science and Technology; Honorary General of Jordan Armed Forces. Publications: A Study on Jerusalem, 1979; Palestinian Self-Determination, 1981; Search for Peace, 1984; Christianity in the Arab World, 1994; Continuity, Innovation and Change, 2001; To be a Muslim, 2003; In Memory of Faisal I: The Iraqi Question, 2003. Honours: Honorary degrees from universities of Yarmouk, 1980, Bogazici (Turkey), 1982, Jordan, 1987, Durham, 1990, Ulster, 1996; Medal, President, Italian Republic, 1982; Knight of Grand Cross of Order of Self-Merit (Italy), 1983. Address: The Royal Palace, Amman, Jordan.

HASSAN Syed Tajuddin Bin Syed, b. 11 October 1948, Perak, Malaysia. Professor. m. Husna Jamaludin, 2 sons, 1 daughter. Education: Royal Military College, Kuala Lumpur, HSC, Cambridge University, 1964-67; BSc, First Class Honours, University of New England, Australia, 1968-71; MSc, 1972-74, PhD, 1976-80, University of Queensland, Australia. Appointments: Tutor, 1974, Lecturer, 1980-, Head of Department of Biology, 1987-88, Associate Professor, 1988-98, Professor, 1998-, Director, Rainforest Academy, 2002-2004, Universiti Putra, Malaysia. Publications: 34 in professional research journals; 85 in proceedings; 4 translated books; 5 original books and booklets; 8 articles in books. Honours: Fulbright Scholar; US Environmental Fellowship; International Editor, Conservation Ecology; London Times Fellowship; UNESCO Travel Award; Colombo Plan Scholar; Excellence Award for Teaching and Research, Universiti Putra, Malaysia; Asia Foundation Advisory Consultant; Australian Government, Ecosystem-Modelling Course Grant; Malaysian Government Research Grant; Putrajaya Environmental Management Consultant. Memberships: System Dynamics Society; Ecological Association of

Malaysia; Malaysian Applied Biology; Malaysian Plant Protection Society; Entomological Society of Queensland. Address: 41 Jalan USJ 5/1J, 47610 Subang Jaya, Selangor, Malaysia. E-mail: stsh@streamyx.com Website: www.fsas.upm.edu.my/~stshasan/

HASTE Cate (Catherine Mary), b. 6 August 1945, Leeds, England. Writer; Television Documentary Producer/Director. m. Melvyn Bragg (Rt Hon The Lord Bragg), 18 December 1973, 1 son, 1 daughter. Education: BA Honours, English, University of Sussex, 1963-66; Postgraduate Diploma Adult Education, Manchester University, 1967. Appointments: Television: The Secret War (BBC); End of Empire (Granada TV); Writing on the Wall (Channel 4) Munich – The Peace of Paper (Thames); Secret History – Death of a Democrat (Channel 4); The Churchills (ITV); Cold War (Jeremy Isaacs Productions/BBC/CNN); Millennium (Jeremy Isaacs Productions/BBC/CNN); Hitler's Brides (Flashback TV/ Channel 4); Married to the Prime Minister (Flashback TV/ Channel 4). Publications: Keep the Home Fires Burning: Propaganda to the Home Front in the First World War, 1977; Rules of Desire: Sex in Britain World War I to the Present, 1992; Nazi Women – Hitler's Seduction of a Nation, 2001; The Goldfish Bowl – Married to the Prime Minister 1955-97, co-authored with Cherie Booth, 2004; Editor, Clarissa Eden: A Memoir from Churchill to Eden, 2007. Memberships: British PEN; British Academy of Film and Television Arts. Address: 12 Hampstead Hill Gardens, London NW3 2PL, England. E-mail: cate.haste@virgin.net

HASTINGS Max Macdonald, (Sir) b. 28 December 1945, London, England. Author; Broadcaster; Journalist. m. (1) Patricia Edmondson, 1972, dissolved, 1994, 2 sons, 1 deceased, 1 daughter, (2) Penny Grade, 1999. Education: Exhibitioner, University College, Oxford, 1964-65; Fellow, World Press Institute, St Paul, Minnesota, USA, 1967-68. Appointments: Researcher, BBC TV, 1963-64; Reporter, London Evening Standard, 1965-67, BBC TV Current Affairs, 1970-73; Editor, Evening Standard Londoner's Diary, 1976-77; Editor, Daily Telegraph, 1986-95; Editor, Evening Standard, 1996-2002; Columnist, Daily Express, 1981-83, Sunday Times, 1985-86; Editor-in-Chief and a Director, Daily Telegraph Plc, 1989-96. Publications: The Fire This Time, 1968; Ulster, 1969; The Struggle for Civil Rights in Northern Ireland, 1970; Montrose: The King's Champion, 1977; Yoni: The Hero of Entebbe, 1979; Bomber Command, 1979; The Battle of Britain (with Lee Deighton), 1980; Das Reich, 1981; Battle for the Falklands (with Simon Jenkins), 1983; Overlord: D-Day and the Battle for Normandy, 1984; Oxford Book of Military Anecdotes (editor), 1985; Victory in Europe, 1985; The Korean War, 1987; Outside Days, 1989; Outside Days, 1989; Scattered Shots, 1999; Going to the Wars, 2000; Editor, 2002; Armageddon, 2004; Warriors, 2005; Country Fair, 2005; Nemesis, 2007. Honours: Somerset Maugham Prize, 1979; British Press Awards, Journalist of the Year, 1982; Granada TV Reporter of the Year, 1982; Yorkshire Post Book of the Year Award, 1983, 1984; Editor of the Year, 1988; Honorary DLitt. Leicester University, 1992; Royal Society of Literature, Fellow, 1996; KBE, 2002; Honorary Fellow of King's College, London; Doctorate, Nottingham University, Nottingham; Knighthood. Address: c/o PFD, Drury House, 34-43 Russell Street, London WC2B 5HA, England.

HASTINGS Lady Selina, b. 5 March 1945, Oxford, England. Writer. Education: St Hugh's College, Oxford, England. Appointments: Daily Telegraph, books page, 1968-82; Harper's & Queen Literary Editor, 1986-94. Publications: Nancy Mitford, biography, 1985; Evelyn Waugh, 1994;

Rosamond Lehmann, 2002; various children's books. Contributions to: Daily & Sunday Telegraph; Spectator; TLS; New Yorker; Harper's & Queen. Honour: Marsh Biography Award, 1993-96. Memberships: Royal Society of Literature Committee, 1994-99. Address: c/o Rogers Coleridge & White, 20 Powis Mews, London W11, England.

HASUNUMA Keisuke, b. 24 October 1946, Kiryu, Gumna, Japan. Law Professor. m. Akiko Yune. Education: BA, Law, Tokyo University, 1969. Appointments: Civil Officer, Finance Ministry, Tokyo, 1969; Research Fellow, Law Faculty, Tokyo University, 1971; Assistant Professor, Law Faculty, Kobe University, 1974; Professor, Law Faculty, 1983; Professor, Graduate School of Law, Kobe, 2000. Publications: The Philosophy of Kant and the Epistemology of Norms, 1985; A Study on the Philosophy of NISHI Amane before the Meiji Restoration, 1987; Is Meiji Ishin a Revolution of Restoration? 1990; A Critique of the Communicative Reason, 2007. Address: 2-19-5-501 Nakacho, Musasino, Tokyo, Japan.

HATADA Kazuyuki, b. 23 December 1951, Maebashi City, Gunma, Japan. Mathematician; Educator. m. Kumiko Yoshikawa, 1 son. Education: BSc, 1974, MSc, 1976, DSc, 1979, The University of Tokyo. Appointments: Research Fellow, Faculty of Science, The University of Tokyo, 1979-80; Associate Professor (Algebra and Geometry), 1981-99, Professor (Algebra), 1999-, Department of Mathematics, Faculty of Education, Gifu University; Visiting Professor, Université Paris XI (France), 1993. Publications: Articles for professional mathematical journals, including: Eigenvalues of Hecke operators on $SL(2,Z)$, 1979; Congruences for eigenvalues of Hecke operators on $SL\_2(Z)$, 1981; Siegel cusp forms as holomorphic differential forms on certain compact varieties, 1983; Homology groups, differential forms and Hecke rings on Siegel modular varieties, 1989; Correspondences for Hecke rings and (co-)homology groups on smooth compactifications of Siegel modular varieties, 1990; On the action of Hecke rings on homology groups of smooth compactifications of Siegel modular varieties and Siegel cusp forms, 1990; Estimates for eigenvalues of Hecke operators on Siegel cusp forms, 1996; Problems on elliptic modular forms, 1985; On the rationality of periods of primitive forms, 1981; Multiplicity one theorem and modular symbols, 1981; Mod 1 distribution of Fermat and Fibonacci quotients and values of zeta functions at 2-p, 1987; On the local zeta functions of compactified Hilbert modular schemes and action of the Hecke rings, 1994; Hecke correspondences and Betty cohomology groups for smooth compactifications of Hilbert modular varieties of dimension<=3, 1996; On classical and l-adic modular forms of levels Nl**m and N, 2001; How big a simplex do the excentres of a simplex form?, 1986; Problems on the n dimensional simplex, 1994; On the reason why the product of two negative integers must be positive, 1994; Isochronism of the cycloidal pendulum, 2006; Hecke operators and p-parameters on Siegel cusp forms (preprint). Honours: Gold Medal for the first 500, 1990; The International Order of Merit, 1990; Albert Einstein International Academy Foundation Honoree, 1998; International Scientist of the Year, 2002; American Medal of Honor, 2002; Lifetime Achievement Award for contributions to Number Theory, 2002; Certificate of Greatest Lives, 2005; Top 100 Scientists, 2005; The World Congress of Arts, Sciences and Communications Lifetime Achievement Award for contributions to the Generalized Ramanujan Conjecture, 2005; The Archimedes Award for significant contributions to Hecke Operators, p-Parameters and the Generalized Ramanujan Conjecture on Siegel Cusp Forms, 2006. Memberships: World Institute of Achievement; Mathematical Society of Japan; The American Mathematical

Society (reviewer); The Mathematical Association of America. Address: Department of Mathematics, Faculty of Education, Gifu University, 1-1, Yanagido, Gifu City, GIFU 501-1193, Japan.

HATEGAN Cornel, b. 17 August 1940, Ohaba-Matnic Romania. Physicist. m. Dora, 9 October 1965, 1 daughter. Education: University Diplomat Physics, University Bucharest, 1964; Dr, Physics, Institute of Atomic Physics, Bucharest, 1973. Appointments: Assistant Researcher, Researcher, Senior Researcher, Institute of Atomic Physics, 1964-70, 1972-; Humboldt Researcher, University Erlangen Nuernberg, 1970-71; Humboldt Researcher, University Munich (Summer Semesters 2002, 2004, 2006). Publications: Science Papers on Atomic and Nuclear Physics. Honours: Urkunde of Humboldt Foundation; Physics Prize of Romanian Academy; Corresponding Member Romanian Academy, elected, 1992; Fellow, Institute Physics, London, elected 2000. Memberships: Humboldt Club; Nuclear Physics Division of Romanian Physical Society. Address: Institute of Atomic Physics, CP MG 6, 76900 Bucharest, Magurele, Romania.

HATOMBWE Innocent, b. 25 May 1970, Choma, Zambia. Chief Accountant. m. Felistan Switzzy, 1 son, 1 daughter. Education: Bachelor, Business Administration; Fellow, ACCA. Appointments: Accountancy, 1995-96; Senior Accountant, 1996-97; Principal Accountant, 1998-2000; Chief Accountant, 2001-. Memberships: Fellow, Chartered Institute of Certified Accountants; Fellow, Zambia Institute of Certified Accountants. Address: PO Box 70153, Ndola, Zambia.

HATTERSLEY OF SPARKBROOK, Baron Roy Sydney George, b. 28 December 1932, Sheffield, England. Politician; Writer. m. Molly Loughran, 1956. Education: BSc, Economics, University of Hull. Appointments: Journalist and Health Service Executive, 1956-64; Member, City Council, Sheffield, 1957-65; Member of Parliament, Labour Party, Sparkbrook Division, Birmingham, 1964-97; Parliamentary Private Secretary, Minister of Pensions and National Insurance, 1964-67; Director, Campaign for a European Political Community, 1966-67; Joint Parliamentary Secretary, Ministry of Labour, 1967-69, Minister of Defence for Administration, 1969-70; Visiting Fellow, Harvard University, 1971, 1972, Nuffield College, Oxford, 1984-; Labour Party Spokesman on Defence, 1972, and on Education and Science, 1972-74; Minister of State, Foreign and Commonwealth Office, 1974-76; Secretary of State for Prices and Consumer Protection, 1976-79; Principal Opposition Spokesman on the Environment, 1979-80, Home Affairs, 1980-83, Treasury and Economics Affairs, 1983-87, Home Affairs, 1987-92; Deputy Leader, Labour Party, 1983-92. Publications: Nelson: A Biography, 1974; Goodbye to Yorkshire (essays), 1976; Politics Apart, 1982; Press Gang, 1983; A Yorkshire Boyhood, 1983; Choose Freedom: The Future for Democratic Socialism, 1987; Economic Priorities for a Labour Government, 1987; The Maker's Mark (novel), 1990; In That Quiet Earth (novel), 1991; Skylark Song (novel), 1994; Between Ourselves (novel), 1994; Who Goes Home? 1995; 50 Years On, 1997; Buster's Diaries: As Told to Roy Hattersley, 1998; Blood and Fire: The Story of William and Catherine Booth and their Salvation Army, 1999; A Brand from the Burning: The Life of John Wesley, 2002; The Edwardians, 2004. Contributions to: Newspapers and journals. Honours: Privy Counsellor, 1975; Columnist of the Year, Granada, 1982; Honorary doctorates; Life Peer, 1997. Address: House of Lords, London SW1A 0PW, England.

HAUER Rutger, b. 23 January 1944, Amsterdam, Holland. Actor. m. (1) Heidi Merz (divorced), 1 child, (2) Ieneke, 1985, 1 child. Career: Turkish Delight, 1973; The Wilby Conspiracy, Keetje Tippel, 1975; Max Havelaar, 1976; Mysteries, Solider of Orange, 1978; Woman Between Dog and Wolf, 1979; Spetters, 1980; Nighthawks, Chanel Solitaire, 1981; Blade Runner, Eureka, 1982; Outsider in Amsterdam, The Osterman Weekend, 1983; A Breed Apart, Ladyhawke, 1984; Flesh and Blood, 1985; The Hitcher, Wanted Dead or Alive, 1986; The Legend of the Holy Drinker, 1988; Salute of the Juggler, Ocean Point, On a Moonlit Night, Split Second, Buffy the Vampire Slayer, Past Midnight, Nostradamus, Surviving the Game, The Beans of Egypt Maine, Angel of Death, New World Disorder, 1999; Wilder, Lying in Wait, Partners in Crime, 2000; Jungle Juice, Flying Virus, 2001; I Banchieri di Dio, Scorcher, Warrior Angels, Confessions of a Dangerous Mind, 2002; In the Shadow of the Cobra, Tempesta, Camera ascunsa, 2004; Sin City, Batman Begins, 2005; Minotaur, Mentor, 2006; Goal II: Living the Dream, 7eventy 5ive, Moving McAllister, Magic Flute Diaries, Tonight at Noon, Spoon, 2007. TV: commercials for Guinness, 1989; TV films: Angel of Death, 1994; Menin, 1998; The 10th Kingdom, 2000. Address: c/o William Morris Agency, 151 El Camino Drive, Beverly Hills, CA 90212, USA.

HAWK Tony, b. 12 May 1968, San Diego, California, USA. Professional Skateboarder. m.(1) Cindy Dunbar, 1990-95 (divorced) 1 son (2) Erin Lee, 1996-2004 (divorced), 2 sons, (3) Lhotse Merriam, 2006. Career: Started skateboarding 1978; Turned Professional for Dogtown, 1982; Created own company, Birdhouse skateboards, 1992; Film appearances including: Police Academy 4, 1987; Sight Unseen, Transworld skateboarding, 2001; Tony Hawk's Gigantic Skatepark Tour, 2001; Haggard, 2002; End, 2002; Tony Hawk's Boom Boom Huck Jam, 2004; TV Appearances including: Tony Hawk's Gigantic Skatepark Tour; Various "X-Games" Vert Competitions (televised); Various "Gravity Games" Vert Competitions (televised); Jackass, 2000; Max Steel, 2000; Viva la Bam, 2003. Publications: Tony Hawk, Occupation: Skateboarder, autobiography, 2002; The Tony Hawk Pro Skater series, 1999-2004. Honours include: 16 X Games Medals, all Gold, 1995-2004; Various awards for his games, including best game, 2000; Best sports game, 2003; Transworld, best Vert skater, 2000; Slam City Jam, Best Vert trick, 2003. Address: Carlsbad, California, USA.

HAWKE Ethan, b. 6 November 1970, Austin, Texas, USA. Actor. m. Uma Thurman, 1998-2004 (divorced) 2 children. Career: Co-founder, Malaparte Theatre Company; Theatre appearances include: Casanova, 1991; A Joke, The Seagull, 1992; Sophistry; Films include: Explorers, 1985; Dead Poets Society, Dad, 1989; White Fang, Mystery Date, 1991; A Midnight Clear, Waterland, 1992; Alive, Rich in Love, Straight to One (director), 1993; Reality Bites, Quiz Show, Floundering, 1994; Before Sunrise, 1995; Great Expectations, Gattaca, Joe the King, 1999; Hamlet, 2000; Tape, Waking Life, Training Day, The Jimmy Show, 2001; Before Sunset, Taking Lives, 2004; Assault on Precinct 13, Lord of War, 2005; Fast Food Nation, The Hottest State, 2006; Tonight at Noon, Before the Devil Knows You're Dead, 2007; Staten Island, 2008. Publications: Ash Wednesday, 2002. Address: Creative Artists Agency, 9830 Wilshire Boulevard, Beverly Hills, CA 90212, USA.

HAWKESWORTH Pauline Mary, b. 28 April 1943, Portsmouth, England. Secretary. m. Rex Hawkesworth, 25 October 1961, 2 daughters. Appointments: Secretarial Manager, Administrator, Ladies Athletic Club; Track and

Field Judge. Publications: 2 books, 82 poems. Anthologies: Parents Enitharmon, 2000; Spirit of Wilfred Owen, 2001. Contributions to: Envoi; South; Interpreters House; Script; Iota; Poetry Nottingham International; Frogmore Press; Others. Honours: 1st Prize, Short Story, Portsmouth Polytechnic, 1981; 1st Prize, South Wales Miners Eisteddfod, 1990; 1st Prize, Hastings Open Poetry Competition, 1993; Runner-Up, Redbeck Competition, 1996; 1st Prize Tavistock and North Dartmoor, 2000; 1st Prize Newark and Sherwood Millennium Project, 2001; 2nd Prize Richmond Adult CC. Membership: President, Portsmouth Poetry Society. Address: 4 Rampart Gardens, Hilsea, Portsmouth PO3 5LR, England.

HAWKING Stephen (William), b. 8 January 1942, Oxford, England. Professor of Mathematics; Writer. m. (1) Jane Wilde, 1965, divorced, 2 sons, 1 daughter, (2) Elaine Mason, 1995. Education: BA, University College, Oxford; PhD, Trinity Hall, Cambridge. Appointments: Research Fellow, 1965-69, Fellow for Distinction in Science, 1969-, Gonville and Caius College, Cambridge; Member, Institute of Theoretical Astronomy, Cambridge, 1968-72; Research Assistant, Institute of Astronomy, Cambridge, 1972-73; Research Assistant, Department of Applied Mathematics and Theoretical Physics, 1973-75, Reader in Gravitational Physics, 1975-77, Professor, 1977-79, Lucasian Professor of Mathematics, 1979-, Cambridge University. Publications: The Large Scale Structure of Space-Time (with G F R Ellis), 1973; General Relativity: An Einstein Centenary Survey (editor with W W Israel), 1979; Is the End in Sight for Theoretical Physics?: An Inaugural Lecture, 1980; Superspace and Supergravity: Proceedings of the Nuffield Workshop (editor with M Rocek), 1981; The Very Early Universe: Proceedings of the Nuffield Workshop (co-editor), 1983; Three Hundred Years of Gravitation (with W W Israel), 1987; A Brief History of Time: From the Big Bang to Black Holes, 1988; Black Holes and Baby Universes and Other Essays, 1993; The Nature of Space and Time (with Roger Penrose), 1996 and other essays; The Universe in a Nutshell, 2001; The Theory of Everything: The Origin and Fate of the Universe, 2002; The Future of Space Time, co-editor, 2001; On the Shoulders of Giants, 2002; Information Loss in Black Holes, 2005; A Briefer History of Time, 2005. Contributions to: Scholarly journals. Honours: Eddington Medal, 1975, Gold Medal, 1985, Royal Academy of Science; Pius XI Gold Medal, Pontifical Academy of Sciences, 1975; William Hopkins Prize, Cambridge Philosophical Society, 1976; Maxwell Medal, Institute of Physics, 1976; Dannie Heinemann Prize for Mathematical Physics, American Physical Society and American Institute of Physics, 1976; Honorary fellow, University College, Oxford, 1977; Trinity Hall, Cambridge, 1984; Commander of the Order of the British Empire, 1982; Paul Dirac Medal and Prize, Institute of Physics, 1987; Wolf Foundation Prize for Physics, 1988; Companion of Honour, 1989; Britannica Award, 1989; Albert Medal, Royal Society of Arts, 1999; Honorary doctorates. Memberships: American Academy of Arts and Sciences; American Philosophical Society; Pontifical Academy of Sciences; Royal Society, fellow. Address: c/o Department of Applied Mathematics and Theoretical Physics, Cambridge University, Silver Street, Cambridge CB3 9EW, England.

HAWKINS Angus Brian, b. 12 April 1953, Portsmouth, England. Historian. m. Esther Armstrong, 20 May 1980, 2 daughters. Education: BA Hons, Reading University, 1975; PhD, London School of Economics, 1980. Publications: Parliament, Party and the Art of Politics in Britain, 1987; Victorian Britain: An Encyclopaedia, 1989; British Party Politics, 1852-1886, 1998; The Political Journals of the First Earl of Kimberley, 1862-1902, 1998. Contributions to: English Historical Review, Parliamentary History, Journal of British Studies, Victorian Studies; Nineteenth Century Prose, Archive. Honours: McCann Award, 1972; Gladstone Memorial Prize, 1978. Memberships: Reform Club; Fellow, Royal Historical Society. Address: Rewley House, University of Oxford, 1 Wellington Square, Oxford, England.

HAWKINS Peter John, b. 20 June 1944, Old Welwyn, Hertfordshire, England. Art and Antiques Consultant. Education: Eton; MA, Modern Languages, Oxford University. Appointments: Director of Christie's (Auctioneers), 1973-2003; Managing Director of Christie's, Monte Carlo, 1987-89. Publication: The Price Guide to Antique Guns and Pistols, 1973. Honours: Freedom of the City of London; Liveryman of the Worshipful Company of Gunmakers, 1978-; Memberships: Turf Club, 1973-. Address: 20 Ennismore Gardens, London SW7 1AA, England.

HAWN Goldie, b. 21 November 1945, Washington, USA. Actress. Divorced, 3 children. Career: debut, Good Morning, World, 1967-68; TV includes: Rowan and Martin's Laugh-In, 1968-70; Pure Goldie, Natural history documentary, 1996; Films include: Cactus Flower; There's a Girl in my Soup; Dollars; The Sugarland Express; The Girl from Petrovka; Shampoo; The Duchess and the Dirtwater Fox; Foul Play; Seems Like Old Times; Private Benjamin; Best Friends; Protocol; Swing Shift; Overboard; Bird on a Wire; Housesitter; Deceived; Death Becomes Her; The First Wives Club, 1996; Everybody Says I Love You, 1996; The Out of Towners, 1999; Town and Country, 2001; The Banger Sisters, 2003; Star and Executive Producer: Goldie Hawn Special, 1978, Private Benjamin, 1980; Executive Producer, Something To Talk About; Co-Executive Producer, My Blue Heaven, 1990. Address: Creative Artists Agency, 9830 Wilshire Boulevard, Beverly Hills, CA 90212, USA.

HAWORTH John, b. 13 April 1942, Bury, Lancashire, England. Medical Practitioner. m. W Eleanor Roan, 1 daughter. Education: University of St Andrews (Queen's College, Dundee), 1960-66; MB, ChB, 1966; D Obst RCOG, 1970; MRCGP, 1974; FRCGP, 1991; DFFP, 1993; MFSEM (UK), 2007. Appointments: House Physician, Maryfield Hospital, Dundee, 1966-67, House Surgeon, Perth Royal Infirmary, 1967; Senior House Officer: Medicine, Cumberland Infirmary, Carlisle, 1968, Obstetrics and Gynaecology, City Maternity Hospital, Carlisle, 1968-69, Accident and Emergency Department, Cumberland Infirmary, Carlisle, 1969; Trainee General Practitioner, 1969-70; Principal in General Practice, Carlisle, 1970-97; Member, Faculty Board, Cumbria Faculty, 1977-, Treasurer, 1980-90, Vice-Chairman, 1992-93, Chairman, 1993-96, Provost, 2004-, Royal College of General Practitioners; Honorary Secretary, East Cumbria Division, 1976-, Member, Representative Body, 1984-, Member, Retired Members Forum, 2004-, British Medical Association; Medical Officer, Carlisle United Association Football Club, 1991-; Medical Officer, Aotearoa Maori Rugby League Team, Rugby League World Cup, 2000; Justice of the Peace, 1997-. Publications: Many serious and humorous articles and papers in: The Practitioner, Trainee Supplement to Update, Pulse, Update, The Physician, Prescriber, GP; Chapters in Alimentary, My Dear Doctor and in Nervous Laughter; Author, Deeply Darkly Beautifully Blue, 2005. Memberships include: Royal College of General Practitioners; British Medical Association; Vice-Chairman, Carlisle District Crime Prevention Panel, 2000-; Director, Carlisle Rugby League Football Club, 1983-92; Secretary, 1973-76, President,

1988-89, Carlisle Medical Society; President, Carlisle Branch, Multiple Sclerosis Society, 1989-. Address: 40 Brampton Road, Carlisle, Cumbria CA3 9AT, England.

HAWRYLYSHYN Bohdan, b. 19 October 1926, Koropec, Ukraine. Professor. m. Leonida Haydiuska, 1 son, 2 daughters. Education: BA Sc, Mechanical Engineering, University of Toronto; MBA, IMI (now IMD), Geneva, Switzerland; PhD, Social and Economic Studies, University of Geneva, Switzerland. Appointments: Adviser to 3 prime ministers, 4 chairmen of Parliament and 1st President of Ukraine; Chairman, International Center for Policy Studies, Kyiv; Chairman, International Renaissance Foundation, Ukraine; Chairman, International Management Institute (IMI), Kyiv. Publications: 2 books; Over 100 articles in professional journals. Honours: Honorary Doctorates: University of York, Toronto; University of Alberta, Edmonton; Ternopil Academy of National Economy; V Stefanyk University; Y Fedlovsky University, Ukraine. Memberships: 2 medals from two Presidents of Ukraine; Gold Medal, President of the Republic of Italy; Club of Rome; International Management Academy; Jean Monet Foundation; World Academy of Art and Science; National Academy of Science of Ukraine; Baden Powell Fellowship.

HAY Jocelyn, b. 30 July 1927, Wales, United Kingdom. Writer. m. Andrew Hay, 2 daughters. Education BA (Hons), Open University. Appointments: Freelance Writer and Broadcaster, 1954-83; Work included: Forces Broadcasting Service, Woman's Hour, BBC Radio 2 and 4, World Service; Head, Press and PR Department, Girl Guides Association, Commonwealth Headquarters, 1973-78; Founder and Director, London Media Workshops (training agency), 1978-94; Founder and Honorary Chairman, Voice of the Listener and Viewer(the leading advocate of the citizen and consumer in broadcasting in the UK), 1983-; Honorary Trustee, The Voice of the Listener Trust, 1987-; Honorary Trustee, Presswise, 2003-; President Emeritus, The European Association of Listeners' and Viewers' Associations, Euralva. Publications: Numerous articles, speeches and broadcasts on broadcasting and cultural issues. Honours: MBE, 1999; Commonwealth Broadcasting Association's Elizabeth R Award for services to public service broadcasting, 1999; CBE, 2005; European Woman of Achievement Award (Humanitarian Category), European Union of Women, British Section, 2007. Memberships: Fellow, Royal Society of Arts; Society of Authors. Address: 101 King's Drive, Gravesend, Kent DA12 5BQ, England.

HAYASHI Nobuhiko, b. 23 August 1971, Okayama, Japan. Theoretical Condensed Matter Physicist. Education: BS, 1994, MS, 1996, PhD, 1999, Okayama University. Appointments: Research Fellow, Japan Society for the Promotion of Science, Okayama University, 1998-99; Research Associate, Okayama University, 1999-2004; Research Fellow, Japan Society for the Promotion of Science, ETH Zurich, 2004-06; Postdoctoral Researcher, ETH Zurich, 2006-07; Postdoctoral Researcher, Japan Atomic Energy Agency, 2007-. Publications: Numerous articles in professional journals. Memberships: Physical Society of Japan; American Physical Society. Address: CCSE, Japan Atomic Energy Agency, 6-9-3 Higashi-Ueno, Tokyo 110-0015, Japan. E-mail: nbse22@gmail.com Website: http://mp.okayama-u.ac.jp/~hayashi

HAYEK Selma, b. 2 September 1966, Coatzacoalcos, Veracruz, Mexico. Actress. 1 daughter. Career: Films: Mi vida loca, 1993; Desparado, Four Rooms, Fair Game, 1995; From Dusk Till Dawn, Fled, 1996; Fools Rush In, Breaking

Up, Follow Me Home, 1997; The Velocity of Gary, 54, 1998; Wild Wild West, Dogma, 1999; Frida, Death to Smoochy, 2002; Once Upon A Time in Mexico, Hotel, 2003; After the Sunset, 2004; Sian Ka'an (voice), 2005; Bandidas, Ask the Dust, Lonely Hearts, 2006; Across the Universe, 2007. TV: NYPD Blue; Dream On; Nurses; Action; Ugly Betty. Address: c/o William Morris Agency, 1325 Avenue of the Americas, New York, NY 10019-4701, USA.

HAYMAN, Rt Hon Baroness Helene Valerie, b. 26 March 1949, Wolverhampton, England. Peer. m. Martin Hayman, 4 sons. Education: BA Law, Newnham College, Cambridge, 1969. Appointments: MP, Labour, Welwyn and Hatfield, 1974-79; Founder Member, Maternity Alliance, Broadcaster, 1979-85; Vice-Chairman, Bloomsbury Health Authority, 1985-92; Chairman, Bloomsbury and Islington District Health Authority, 1992; Chairman, Whittington Hospital National Health Trust, 1992-97; Sits as Labour Peer in The House of Lords, 1995-; Parliamentary Under Secretary for State, Department of Environment, Transport and the Regions, 1997; Parliamentary Under Secretary of State, Department of Health, 1998; Minister of State, Ministry of Agriculture Fisheries and Food, 1999-2001; Chair, Cancer Research UK, 2001-2004; Lord Speaker, House of Lords, 2006. Member, Committee of Privy Counsellors reviewing the Anti-Terrorism, Crime and Security Act, 2001; Trustee, Royal Botanic Gardens, Kew, 2002; Member, Board of Road Safe, 2003; Chair, Specialised Health Care Alliance, Member, Select Committee on the Assisted Dying for the Terminally Ill Bill, 2004; Member, Constitution Committee, 2004; Chair, Human Tissue Authority, 2005; Member, Human Fertilisation and Embryology Authority. Honours: Life Peerage, 1995; Privy Counsellor, 2000. Address: The House of Lords, Westminster, London SW1A 0PW, England.

HAYMAN Walter Kurt, b. 6 January 1926, Cologne, Germany. Mathematician. m. (1) Margaret Riley Crann, 1947, deceased 1994, 3 daughters, (2) Waficka Katifi, 1995, deceased 2001; (3) Marie Jennings, MBE, 2007. Education: St John's College, Cambridge, 1943-46; MA ScD Fellow, 1947-50. Appointments: Lecturer, King's College, Newcastle, 1947, Exeter, 1947-53; Reader, 1953-56; Professor of Pure Mathematics, Imperial College, University of London, 1956-85; Dean of RCS, 1978-81; FIC, 1989; Part time Professor, University of York, 1985-93; Professor Emeritus, Universities of London and York, Senior Research Fellow, Imperial College, 1995-. Publications: Multivalent Functions, Cambridge, 1958, 2nd edition, 1994; Meromorphic Functions, Oxford, 1964; Research Problems in Function Theory, 1967; Subharmonic Functions, Vol I 1976, Vol II 1989; Papers in various journals. Honours: 1st Smith's Prize, 1948, shared Adam's Prize, 1949, Cambridge University; Junior Berwick Prize, 1955, Senior Berwick Prize, 1964, de Morgan Medal, 1995, Vice President, 1982-84, London Mathematical Society; Co-founder with Mrs Hayman, British Mathematical Olympiad. Memberships: London Mathematics Society, 1947-; Visiting Lecturer, Brown University, USA, 1949-50; American Mathematics Society, 1961; Fellow, 1956-, Council, 1962-63, Royal Society; Foreign Member, Finnish Academy of Science and Letters; Accademia Nazionale dei Lincei (Rome); Corresponding Member, Bavarian Academy of Science; Hon DSc, Exeter, 1981, Birmingham, 1985, University of Ireland, 1997; Hon Dr rer nat, Giessen, 1992; Hon DPhil, Uppsala, 1992. Address: Department of Mathematics, Imperial College London, London SW7 2AZ, England.

HE Ji-Fan, b. 30 June 1937, Shanghai, China. Mechanical Educator; Researcher. m. Bang-An Ma, 1972. Education: Master Tsinghua University, Beijing, 1959. Appointments: Assistant, 1959-79, Lecturer, 1979-86, Associate Professor, 1986-96, Professor, 1996-, Tsinghua University, Beijing. Publications: A refined shear deformation theory of laminated plates and shells, 1989; A twelfth-order theory of bending of isotropic plates, 1996. Honour: Achievements in basic research, Tsinghua University, 1996. Memberships: Chinese Society of Theoretical and Applied Mechanics; Chinese Society of Composite Materials; Chinese Society of Vibration Engineering. Address: Department of Engineering Mechanics, School of Aerospace, Tsinghua University, Beijing 100084, China.

HEALD Tim(othy Villiers), (David Lancaster), b. 28 January 1944, Dorset, England. Journalist; Writer. m. (1) Alison Martina Leslie, 30 March 1968, dissolved, 2 sons, 2 daughters, (2) Penelope Byrne, 1999. Education: MA, Honours, Balliol College, Oxford, 1965. Appointments: Reporter, Sunday Times, 1965-67; Feature Editor, Town magazine, 1967; Feature Writer, Daily Express, 1967-72; Associate Editor, Weekend Magazine, Toronto, 1977-78; Columnist, Observer, 1990; Visiting Fellow, Jane Franklin Hall, University of Tasmania, 1997, 1999; University Tutor, Creative Writing, 1999, 2000; FRSL, 2000; Writer-in-Residence, University of South Australia, 2001. Publications: It's a Dog's Life, 1971; Unbecoming Habits, 1973; Blue Book Will Out, 1974; Deadline, 1975; Let Sleeping Dogs Die, 1976; The Making of Space, 1999, 1976; John Steed: An Authorised Biography, 1977; Just Desserts, 1977; H.R.H: The Man Who Will be King, with M Mohs, 1977; Murder at Moose Jaw, 1981; Caroline R, 1981; Masterstroke, 1982; Networks, 1983; Class Distinctions, 1984; Red Herrings, 1985; The Character of Cricket, 1986; Brought to Book, 1988; Editor, The Newest London Spy, 1988; Business Unusual, 1989; By Appointments: 150 Years of the Royal Warrant, 1989; Editor, A Classic English Crime, 1990; Editor, My Lord's, 1990; The Duke: A Portrait of Prince Philip, 1991; Honourable Estates, 1992; Barbara Cartland: A Life of Love, 1994; Denis: The Authorised Biography of the Incomparable Compton, 1994; Brian Johnston: The Authorised Biography, 1995; Editor, A Classic Christmas Crime, 1995; Beating Retreat: Hong Kong Under the Last Governor, 1997; Stop Press, 1998; A Peerage for Trade, 2001; Village Cricket, 2004; Death and the Visiting Fellow, 2004; Death and the d'Urbervilles, 2005; Princess Margaret – A Life Unravelled, 2007. Contributions: Short stories: EQMM; Strand magazine; Tatler; Mail on Sunday. Memberships: Crime Writers Association, Chairman, 1987-88; PEN; Society of Authors. Address: 66 The Esplanade, Fowey, Cornwall PL23 1JA, England. E-mail: timheald@compuserve.com

HEALEY Denis (Lord Healey of Riddlesden), b. 30 August 1917, Keighley, Yorkshire, England. Politician; Writer. m. Edna May Edmunds, 1945, 1 son, 2 daughters. Education: BA, 1940, MA, 1945, Balliol College, Oxford. Appointments include: Served, World War II, 1939-45; Contested, (Labour) Pudsey and Otley Division, 1945; Secretary, International Department, Labour Party, 1945-52; Member of Parliament, South East Leeds, 1952-55, Leeds East, 1955-92; Shadow Cabinet, 1959-64, 1970-74, 1979-87; Secretary of State for Defence, 1964-70; Chancellor of the Exchequer, 1974-79; Opposition Spokesman on Foreign and Commonwealth Affairs, 1980-87; Deputy Leader, Labour Party, 1980-83; Member House of Lords. Publications: The Curtain Falls, 1951; New Fabian Essays, 1952; Neutralism, 1955; Fabian International Essays, 1956; A Neutral Belt in Europe, 1958; NATO and American Security, 1959; The Race Against the H

Bomb, 1960; Labour Britain and the World, 1964; Healey's Eye, 1980; Labour and a World Society, 1985; Beyond Nuclear Deterrence, 1986; The Time of My Life (autobiography), 1989; When Shrimps Learn to Whistle (essays), 1990; My Secret Planet, 1992; Denis Healey's Yorkshire Dales, 1995; Healey's World, photographs, 2002. Honours include: Grand Cross of Order of Merit, Germany, 1979; Freeman, City of Leeds, 1992; FRSL, 1993. Membership: President, Birkbeck College, 1992-98. Address: House of Lords, London SW1A 0PQ, England.

HEALEY Robin Michael, b. 16 February 1952, London, England. Historian; Biographer. Education: BA, 1974, MA, 1976, University of Birmingham. Appointments: Documentation Officer, Tamworth Castle and Cambridge Museum of Archaeology and Anthropology, 1977-80; Museum Assistant, Saffron Walden Museum, 1983-84; Research Assistant, History of Parliament, 1985-92; Visiting Research Fellow, Manchester University, 1997-2003, Editor, Lewisletter, 2000-; Judge, HASSRA Literary Competition, 2003-; Co-editor, Also, 2006-. Publications: Books: Hertfordshire (A Shell County Guide), 1982; Diary of George Mushet (1805-13), 1982; Grigson at Eighty, 1985; A History of Barley School, 1995; My Rebellious and Imperfect Eye: Observing Geoffrey Grigson, 2002; Contributions to: Biographical Dictionary of Modern British Radicals, 1984; Domesday Book, 1985; Secret Britain, 1986; Dictionary of Literary Biography, 1991; Encyclopaedia of Romanticism, 1992; Consumer Magazines of the British Isles, 1993; Postwar Literatures in English, 1998-; I Remember When I Was Young, 2003; Oxford Dictionary of National Biography, 2004. Also: Country Life; Hertfordshire Countryside; Guardian; Literary Review; Private Eye; Book and Magazine Collector; Rare Book Review; Independent; Times Literary Supplement; Bristol Review of Books; Local History Magazine; Art Newspaper; B M Insight; Mensa Magazine; Wyndham Lewis Annual; Charles Lamb Bulletin; Cobbett's New Political Register. Honour: 1st Prize, Birmingham Post Poetry Contest, 1974. Memberships: Executive, Charles Lamb Society, 1987-; Press Officer, Alliance of Literary Societies, 1997-2005; Wyndham Lewis Society, 2000-. Address: 80 Hall Lane, Great Chishill, Royston, Herts SG8 8SH, England.

HEANEY Seamus (Justin), b. 13 April 1939, County Londonderry, Northern Ireland. Poet; Writer; Professor. m. Marie Devlin, 1965, 2 sons, 1 daughter. Education: St Columb's College, Derry; BA 1st Class, Queen's University, Belfast, 1961. Appointments: Teacher, St Thomas's Secondary School, Belfast, 1962-63; Lecturer, St Joseph's College of Education, Belfast, 1963-66; Queen's University, Belfast, 1966-72, Carysfort College, 1975-81; Senior Visiting Lecturer, 1982-85, Boylston Professor of Rhetoric and Oratory, 1985-97, Harvard University; Professor of Poetry, Oxford University, 1989-94. Publications: Eleven Poems, 1965; Death of a Naturalist, 1966; Door Into the Dark, 1969; Wintering Out, 1972; North, 1975; Field Work, 1979; Selected Poems, 1965-1975, 1980; Sweeney Astray, 1984, revised edition as Sweeney's Flight, 1992; Station Island, 1984; The Haw Lantern, 1987; New Selected Poems, 1966-1987, 1990; Seeing Things, 1991; The Spirit Level, 1996; Opened Ground: Selected Poems, 1966-1996, 1998; Electric Light, 2000; The Testament of Cresseid, 2005; District & Circle, 2006. Prose: Preoccupations: Selected Prose, 1968-1978, 1980; The Government of the Tongue, 1988; The Place of Writing, 1989; The Redress of Poetry: Oxford Lectures, 1995; Beowulf: A New Verse Translation and Introduction, 1999; Finders Keepers: Selected Prose, 1971-2001. Honours: Somerset Maugham Award, 1967; Cholmondeley Award, 1968; W H

Smith Award, 1975; Duff Cooper Prize, 1975; Whitbread Awards, 1987, 1996; Nobel Prize for Literature, 1995; Whitbread Book of the Year Award, 1997, 1999; Honorary DLitt, Oxford, 1997, Birmingham, 2000. Memberships: Royal Irish Academy; British Academy, American Academy of Arts and Letters. Address: c/o Faber & Faber, 3 Queen Square, London WC1N 3RU, England.

HEAP Sir Peter William, b. 13 April 1935, Dunchurch, Warwickshire, England. Former Diplomat; Consultant. m. Ann, 1 son, 1 stepson, 2 daughters, 1 stepdaughter. Appointments: Foreign and Commonwealth Office, 1959-95; Diplomatic assignments to New York, Venezuela, Sri Lanka, Irish Republic, Canada; Head, Energy Science and Space Department, Foreign Office, 1980-83; High Commissioner to the Bahamas, 1983-86; Deputy High Commissioner, Nigeria, 1986-89; Trade Commissioner to Hong Kong and Consul General, Macau, 1989-92; HM Ambassador to Brazil, 1992-95; Adviser to the Board, HSBC Investment Bank Ltd, 1995-98; Chairman, Brazil Chamber of Commerce in Great Britain, 1996-; Chairman, Brazil Britain Business Forum, 1998-2003; Former Non-Executive Director, DS Wolf International Ltd; Former Adviser to the BOC Group plc; Adviser Amerada Hess Ltd, 1996-2005; Deputy Chairman and Director, RCM Group, 2002-05; Chairman, Labour Finance & Industry Group, 2003-; Chairman, Regal Petroleum plc, 2005-06; Chairman, Maria Nobreiga Foundation (UK), 2005-. Honours: KCMG; CMG. Address: 6 Carlisle Mansions, Carlisle Place, London SW1P 1HX, England. E-mail: pwheap@aol.com

HEBB Bernard Dean Jr, b. 22 February 1941, Ludlow, Massachusetts, USA. Professor of Guitar. m. Ingrid Beschnidt. Education: Guitar Studies under Francis La Pierre; Music Major, St Petersburg Junior College and the University of South Florida, 1961-63; Student of and Assistant to Professor Karl Scheit, University of Music, Vienna, Austria, 1965-69; Masters Degree with Honours, University of Music Vienna, 1969. Career: Guitar Instructor, Conservatories of Hamburg, Germany, 1969-76 and Bremen, Germany, 1977-80; Professor of Guitar, University of the Arts, Bremen, Germany, 1980-; Guest Professor, Escuela de Musica de la Universidad de Guanajuanto, Mexico, 2005- Concerts and Masterclasses given in Australia, Austria, Bulgaria, Denmark, France, Germany, Greece, Mexico, The Netherlands, Poland, Thailand, Venezuela, Yugoslavia and the USA; Jury Member at international festivals; Radio and television appearances in Australia, Germany, Bulgaria, France, Venezuela; Founding Member and Artistic Director, Zevener Guitar Festival, Germany. Publications: Series of music for the guitar published in Germany; Interviews and articles in music. Recordings include: Interlockings (with Karsten Behrmann), 1977; Recordings for oboe and guitar with Helmut Schaarschmidt as Duo Geminiani include: Music for Oboe and Guitar, Music at the Court of Ludwig the XIV, Serenade; Founding member and director, International Guitar Competition, 1985-98; Guitar Impressions (with Finn Svit), 2001; Twilight (with Gabriel Guillén), 2006; Musical Advisor, active performer and teacher, Grotniki Guitar Festival, Poland, 2006-; Dedications, new solo guitar recording, 2007. Honours: Gold Medal of Honour, Federation of the Worker's Music Association of Austria, 1973; Pack House Prize, Denmark, 2002; Silver Medal, City of Zeven, Germany, 2005; Listed in Who's Who publications 2006-2009 and other biographical dictionaries. Memberships: Order of International Ambassadors, 2007. Address: Landauerweg 29, 28279 Bremen, Germany. Website: www.bernardhebb-guitar.de

HECHE Anne, b. 25 May 1969, Aurora, Ohio, USA. Actress. m. Coleman Lafoon, 1 son. Career: Films: An Ambush of Ghosts, 1993; The Adventures of Huck Finn, 1993; A Simple Twist of Fate, 1994; Milk Money, 1994; I'll Do Anything, 1994; The Wild Side, 1995; Pie in the Sky, 1995; The Juror, 1996; Walking and Talking, 1996; Donnie Brasco, 1997; Volcano, 1997; Subway Stories, Wag the Dog, 1997; Six Days and Seven Nights, 1998; A Cool Dry Place, 1998; Psycho, 1998; The Third Miracle, 1999; Auggie Rose, 2001; John Q, 2002; Prozac Nation, 2003; Birth, 2004; Sexual Life, 2005; Suffering Man's Charity, 2007; What Is Love, 2007. TV: Another World; O Pioneers! 1992; Against the Wall, 1994; Girls in Prison, 1994; Kingfish: A Story of Huey P Long, 1995; If These Walls Could Talk, 1996; If These Walls Could Talk 2, One Kill, 2000; Gracie's Choice, 2004; The Dead Will Tell, 2004; Silver Bells, 2006; Fatal Desire, 2006; Men in Trees, 2006-07. Address: c/o CAA, 9830 Wilshire Boulevard, Beverly Hills, CA 90212, USA.

HEFNER Hugh Marston, b. 9 April 1926, Chicago, Illinois, USA. Publisher. m. (1) Mildred Williams, 1 son, 1 daughter, (2) Kimberley Conrad, 1989, 2 daughters. Education: BS, University of Illinois. Appointments: Editor-in-Chief, Playboy magazine, 1953-, Oui magazine, 1972-81; Chairman Emeritus, Playboy Enterprises, 1988-; President, Playboy Club International Inc, 1959-86. Honour: International Press Directory International Publisher Award, 1997. Address: Playboy Enterprises Inc, 9242 Beverly Boulevard, Beverly Hills, CA 90210, USA.

HEGEDÜS Lóránt, b. 11 November 1930, Hajdunánás, Hungary. Professor of Philosophy of Religion; Bishop of Reformed Church. m. Dr Med Zsuzsa Illés, 2 sons, 2 daughters. Education: Ref, Theological Academy, 1954; Diploma of Theology, 1955; Budapest, Dr of Systematic Theology, Basel University, 1979; Visiting Fellow of Habil, Princeton Theological Seminary, 1985-; Professor H C Ref University Budapest, 1992; Professor H C Veszprém, 1993; Dr H C Theology, Klausenburg, 1955; PhD, Budapest, 1997. Appointments: Ref Assistant Pastor Budapest Calvin Sqare, 1956; Ref Pastor, Hidas, 1965; Ref Pastor, Budapest, Szabadság Tér, 1983-96; Ref Pastor, Budapest, Calvin Tér, 1996-2005, Ref Bishop and President of the Hungarian Reformed Synod, 1991-96; Ref Bishop, 1991-2002; Professor of Religious Philosophy, 1993; M Bishop, General Synod of Hungarian Reformed Churches, 1994-2007; President. Publications: Nyitás a Végtelenre (Opening to Infinity), BP, 1989, 2003; Aspekte der Gottesfrage, Basel, 1979, Klausenburg, 1998; The Concept of Transcendence, Princeton, 1986, Edinburgh, 1991; Isten és Ember Titka (The Secret of God and Man), 1992; Kálvin Theologiája (The Theology of Calvin) Kolozsvár, 1995; Újkantiánus és Értékteológia (New-Kantian and Value-Theology), Budapest, 1996; Jézus és Európa (Jesus and Europe), 1998; Mai soskérdéseink (The Questions of our Life Today), 2001; 1 Mózes 22, 2001; Evangéliumot Prédikál a Prédikátor (The Book of Ecclesiastes, 2005), 2005; Apokalypszis Most és Mindörökké (The Revelation both Now and Ever), 2005; Zakariás Könyvének Magyarázata (The Book of Zachariah), 2006; Püspöki Jelentések, 1991-2002, (Accounts of the Bishop 1991-2002), 2007; 35 books; Over 1000 articles. Honours: Hüség Diploma, Budapest, 1995; Bocskai Dij, Kolozsvár, 1996; Árpád Díj, Bpest, 2007; Diploma of City of Perth Amboy and Los Angeles. Address: Szabadság tér 2 V 1, H-1054 Budapest, Hungary.

HEGELER Sten, b. 28 April 1923, Frederiksberg, Denmark. Psychologist. 1 son, 1 daughter. Education: Candidate for Psychology, University of Copenhagen, 1953. Publications:

Peter and Caroline; Men Only; Choosing Toys for Children; What Everybody Should Know About AIDS; On Selenium; An ABZ of Love (with I Hegeler); Ask Inge and Sten; World's Best Slimming Diet; On Being Lonesome; XYZ of Love; Living is Loving. Contributions to: Aktuelt; Info; Editor, Taenk magazine. Honour: Ph-Fund and Honorary member of Danish Psychologists Association. Memberships: Danish Psychological Association; Danish Journalist Association; Danish Authors Association. Address: Frederiksberg Alle 25, DK-1820 Frederiksberg, Denmark.

HEGGLAND Roar, b. 25 May 1954, Vikebygd, Norway. Geoscientist. m. Lindis Åslid, 2 daughters. Education: Cand Real (MSc), Physics, University of Bergen, Norway, 1982. Appointment: Geophysicist, Statoil, 1984-. Publications include as author and co-author most recently: Chimneys in the Gulf of Mexico, 2000; Detection of Seismic Chimneys by Neural Networks a New Prospect Evaluation Tool, 2000; Detection of Seismic Objects, the Fastest Way to do Prospect and Geohazard Evaluations, 2001; Identifying gas chimneys and associated features in 3D seismic data by the use of various attributes and special processing, 2001; Mud volcanoes and gas hydrates on the Niger Delta front, 2001; Seismic Evidence of Vertical Fluid Migration Through Faults, Applications of Chimney and Fault Detection, 2002; Method of Seismic Signal Processing including Detection of objects in seismic data like gas chimneys and faults; More than 7 invited papers and articles including Using gas chimneys in seal integrity analysis, 2005. Address: Statoil ASA, N-4035 Stavanger, Norway. E-mail: rohe@statoil.com

HEINE Susanna L, b. 17 January 1942, Prague, Czechoslovakia. University Professor. m. Peter Pawlowsky. Education: Arbitur, 1960; Mag theol, University of Vienna, 1966; Ordained Pastor, Lutheran Church, 1968; Dr theol, University of Vienna, 1973; Habilitation, University of Vienna, 1979. Appointments: Assistant, New Testament Studies, 1968-79; Dozent (Lecturer) Religious Education, 1979-82; Professor, Religious Education, 1982-90; Professor of Pastoral Theology and Psychology of Religion, University of Zurich, 1990-96; Professor of Pastoral Theology and Psychology of Religion, University of Vienna, 1996-. Publications: Leibhafter Glaube, 1976; Biblische Fachdidaktik, 1976; Women and Early Christianity, 1987, 1990; Christianity and the Goddesses, 1988, 1990; Keines Religiöses Wörterbuch, (editor) 1984; Europa in der Krise der Neuzeit (editor), 1986; Islam Zwischen Selbstbild und Klischee (editor), 1995; Frauenbilder – Menschenrechte, 2000; Gedanken für den Tag, 2001; About 200 articles on education, psychology, feminism, history of ideas, interreligious dialogue. Memberships: European Academic Society of Theology, 1988-, Vice Chairman, 1996-2002, Science Board, Sigmund Freud Society, 1995-; World Conference, Religions and Peace, 1996-; Contact Committee for Questions concerning Islam, 1996-; Abrahamitic Friends, 1996-; Austrian Research Community on Social Ethics, 1997-; Board, International Society of Psychology of Religion, 1998-. Address: Protestant Faculty, University of Vienna, Schenkenstrasse 8-10, A-1010 Vienna, Austria.

HELD Gerhard, b. 5 March 1944, Vienna, Austria. Meteorologist. 2 sons, 1 daughter. Education: Studies in Meteorology, Geophysics, Physics, Mathematics, University of Vienna, 1962-67; PhD, 1968. Appointments include: In Charge, Bioclimatol Division, Zentralanstalt für Meteorologie und Geodynamik, Vienna, 1969-70; Radar Meteorologist (Research Officer, 1970-84, Special Researcher, 1984-), Atmospheric Physics Division, National Physics Research Laboratory, CSIR, Pretoria, South Africa, 1970-; Research Area Leader, Atmospheric Processes, in new programme for Atmospheric Processes and Management Advice for Division of Earth, Marine and Atmospheric Science and Technology (former National Physics Research Laboratory), CSIR, 1990-; Senior Environment Consultant, 1992, Chief Consultant, 1999--, Technology Research & Investigations (now called Technology Services International), Eskom, Johannesburg; Visiting Professor, 2000, Consultant, 2001, Senior Researcher, 2002, Radar Meteorology, Co-ordinator of Operations and Co-ordinator of Informatics, 2007-, Instituto de Pesquisas Meteorologicas (IPMet), Universidade Estadual Paulista, Brazil. Publications: Numerous papers in refereed journals, conference proceedings, research or contract reports; 1 book; 3 book chapters; 2 book reviews. Memberships: South African Council for Science Professions; National Association for Clean Air; South African Society for Atmospheric Sciences (council member, 1983-, President, 1998-); Founder Member, Environmental Science Association, Chairman, 1997-; Board of Trustees, International Life Sciences Institute, South Africa, 1997-. Address: 1171 Dormer Avenue, Queenswood 0186, South Africa.

HELLAWELL Keith, b. 18 May 1942, Yorkshire, England. Anti-Drugs Co-ordinator; Police Officer. m. Brenda Hey, 1963, 1 son, 2 daughters. Education: Dewsbury Technology College; Cranfield Institute of Technology; London University. Appointments: Miner, 5 years; Joined Huddersfield Borough Police, progressed through every rank within West Yorkshire Police to Assistant Chief Constable; Deputy Chief Constable of Humberside, 1985-90; Chief Constable of Cleveland Police, 1990-93; Chief Constable of West Yorkshire Police, 1993-98; First UK Anti Drugs Co-ordinator, 1998-2001; Adviser to Home Secretary on International Drug Issues, 2001-. Publications: The Outsider, autobiography, 2002. Memberships include: Association of Police Officers Spokesman on Drugs; Advisory Council on the Misuse of Drugs; Board, Community Action Trust; Trustee, National Society for the Prevention of Cruelty to Children; Editorial Advisory Board, Journal of Forensic Medicine. Address: Government Offices, George Street, London SW1A 2AL, England.

HELLWIG Birgitta Öman, b. 11 June 1932, Borås, Sweden. Mathematician. m. Professor Günter Hellwig, 1 son, 3 daughters. Education: Filosofie Kandidat, Uppsala University, Sweden, 1954. Appointments: Technical Officer, Imperial Chemical Industries Ltd, Birmingham, England, 1957; Assistant, Mathematics Department, Uppsala University, 1958; Teaching Fellow, Harvard University Cambridge, Massachusetts, 1959; Senior Mathematician, Republic Aviation, Farmingdale, New York, 1960; Member, Research Staff, Systems Research Center, Lockheed Electrons Co, Bedminster, New Jersey, 1960-61; Translator Maths Textbooks, Addison-Wesley Publishing Co, Reading, Massachusetts, 1964; Reviewer Mathematics Reviews, Ann Arbor, Michigan, 1968-; Assistant to applicants' lawyers by proceedings European Court Human Rights, Strasbourg, France, 1989-. Publications: Contribution articles on differential equations in scientific journals: Math Zeitschrift 86, 1964; Math Zeitschrift 89, 1965; Journal of Mathematical Analysis and Applications 26, 1969; Wissenschaftliche Zeitschrift der Technischen Hochschule Karl-Marx-Stadt, 1969. Honour: Grantee, University Zürich, Switzerland, 1955-56. Memberships: President, Foreign Students Association, Zürich, 1955-56; Secretary, Swedish Students Association, Zürich, 1955-56;

Nordiska Komitten för Mänskliga Rättigheter, 1998-. Listed in: Several Biographical Publications. Address: Pommerotter Weg 37, D-52076 Aachen, Germany.

HELYAR Jane Penelope Josephine, (Josephine Poole), b. 12 February 1933, London, England. Writer. m. (1) T R Poole, 1956, (2) V J H Helyar, 1975, 1 son, 5 daughters. Publications: A Dream in the House, 1961; Moon Eyes, 1965; The Lilywhite Boys, 1967; Catch as Catch Can, 1969; Yokeham, 1970; Billy Buck, 1972; Touch and Go, 1976; When Fishes Flew, 1978; The Open Grave, The Forbidden Room (remedial readers), 1979; Hannah Chance, 1980; Diamond Jack, 1983; The Country Diary Companion (to accompany Central TV series), 1983; Three For Luck, 1985; Wildlife Tales, 1986; The Loving Ghosts, 1988; Angel, 1989; This is Me Speaking, 1990; Paul Loves Amy Loves Christo, 1992; Scared to Death, 1994; Deadly Inheritance, 1995; Hero, 1997; Run Rabbit, 1999; Fair Game, 2000; Scorched, 2003. Television scripts: The Harbourer, 1975; The Sabbatical, 1981; The Breakdown, 1981; Miss Constantine, 1981; Ring a Ring a Rosie, 1983; With Love, Belinda, 1983; The Wit to Woo, 1983; Fox, 1984; Buzzard, 1984; Dartmoor Pony, 1984; Snow White (picture book), 1991; Pinocchio (re-written), 1994; Joan of Arc (picture book), 1998; The Water Babies (re-written), 1996; Anne Frank (picture book), 2005. Address: Poundisford Lodge, Poundisford, Taunton, Somerset TA3 7AE, England.

HEMINGWAY Wayne, b. 19 January 1961, England. Designer. m. Gerardine, 2 sons, 2 daughters. Education: BSc, Honours, Geography and Town Planning, 1979-82, University College, London; MA, Surrey. Appointments: Joint business, market stall, Camden, London; Creator and Co-founder with Geraldine Hemingway of footwear, clothing and accessory label, Red or Dead, 1992; Collection retailed through 8 Red or Dead shops in England, 3 Red or Dead shops in Japan and wholesaled to international network of retailers; Business sold, 1999; Joint venture with Pentland Group PLC, 1996-; Founder, Hemingway Design, 1999; Designer, new wing for Institute of Directors, Pall Mall, 2001; Current design and consultancy projects include Staiths South Bank, Tyneside (800-unit housing estate), carpet design, wall covering and menswear; Projects with local councils including: Lancashire, Copeland Borough Council and the North West Development Agency, Newcastle and Gateshead; Chair, Prince's Trust Fashion Initiative; Patron, Morecambe Winter Gardens; Judge, Stirling Prize; Professor, Development and Planning Department, Northumbria University, Newcastle upon Tyne. Publications: The Good, the Bad and the Ugly, with Geraldine Hemingway, 1998; Kitsch Icons, 1999; Just Above the Mantelpiece, 2000; Mass Market Classics The Home, 2003. Honours: Second Place, Young Business Person of the Year, 1990; Street Designers of the Year, British Fashion Awards, 1995, 1996, 1997, 1998; MBE, 2006. Address: Hemingway Design, 15 Wembley Park Drive, Wembley, Middlesex HA9 8HD, England.

HEMMERT Martin, b. 5 March 1964, Oberhausen, Germany. Professor. m. Mi Jung, 1 son. Education: Diploma, 1989, Doctoral Degree, 1993, Business Administration, University of Cologne; Habilitation (professorial qualification), Business Administration, University of Essen, 2001. Appointments: Research Assistant, University of Cologne, 1989-90; Visiting Research Fellow, Hitotsubashi University, 1990-93; Research Associate, DIJ Tokyo, 1993-98; Assistant Professor, 1998-2001, Associate Professor, 2001-04, University of Essen; Associate Professor, Korea University Business School, 2004-. Publications: 5 books including: Technology and Innovation in Japan: Policy and Management for the 21st Century, 1998;

Over 50 articles in peer reviewed journals and book chapters. Honours: First Foreign Business Professor appointed for a permanent position in Korea; DFG Research Fellowship, 1998-2001. Memberships: Academy of Management; Academy of International Business; Euro-Asia Management Studies Association. E-mail: mhemmert@korea.ac.kr

HEMMING John Henry, b. 5 January 1935, Vancouver, British Columbia, Canada. Author; Publisher. m. Sukie Babington-Smith, 1979, 1 son, 1 daughter. Education: McGill and Oxford Universities; MA; D.Litt. Appointments: Explorations in Peru and Brazil, 1960, 1961, 1971, 1972, 1986-87; Director and Secretary, Royal Geographical Society, 1975-96; Joint Chairman, Hemming Group Ltd, 1976-; Chair, Brintex Ltd., Newman Books Ltd. Publications: The Conquest of the Incas, 1970; Tribes of the Amazon Basin in Brazil (with others), 1973; Red Gold: The Conquest of the Brazilian Indians, 1978; The Search for El Dorado, 1978; Machu Picchu, 1982; Monuments of the Incas, 1983; Change in the Amazon Basin, (editor), 2 volumes, 1985; Amazon Frontier: The Defeat of the Brazilian Indians, 1987; Maracá, 1988; Roraima: Brazil's Northernmost Frontier, 1990; The Rainforest Edge (editor), 1994; The Golden Age of Discovery, 1998; Die If You Must, Brazilian Indians in the 20th Century, 2003. Honours: CMG; Pitman Literary Prize, 1970; Christopher Award, New York, 1971; Order of Merit (Peru) 1991; Order of the Southern Cross (Brazil), 1998; Honorary doctorates, University of Warwick, University of Stirling; Honorary Fellow, Magdalen College, Oxford; Medals from Royal Geographical Society, Boston Museum of Science, Royal Scottish Geographical Society; Citation of Merit, New York Explorers' Club. Address: Hemming Group Ltd, 32 Vauxhall Bridge Road, London SW1V 2SS, England. E-mail: j.hemming@hgluk.com

HENDERICKX Willem F M R, b. 17 March 1962, Lier, Belgium. Composer; Professor. m. Beatrice Steylaerts, 3 sons. Education: First Prizes in Percussion, Harmony, Counterpoint, Fugue, Musical Analysis, Composition, Royal Antwerp Conservatory, 1984-92; Composition Courses in Darmstadt, Germany, 1988; Courses in Electronics, The Hague, The Netherlands, 2001. Appointments: Timpanist, Beethoven Academy, Antwerp, Belgium, 1985-95; Professor of Composition and Musical Analysis: Royal Antwerp Conservatory of Music, 1996-, Lemmensinstitut, Louvain, Belgium, 1989-, Royal Conservatory of Amsterdam, The Netherlands, 2002-; Composer of opera, symphonic works and chamber music; House Composer, Music Theatre Transparant, Antwerp, 2005-. Publications: Ons Erfdeel: Wim Henderickx by H Heughebaert, 1995; Mens en melodie: The Composer Wim Henderickx by Y Knockaert, 1998; Matrix, Flemish Composers by J Vandenhauwe: Wim Henderickx, 2001; Wim Henderickx, Levisioni Dipaura,1990 by M Beirens, 2006, Contemporary Music in Flanders III, Matrix. Honours: Prize of Contemporary Music, Quebec, Canada, 1993; Prize of the Province of Antwerp, 1999; Prize of the Royal Flemish Academy, Flanders, Belgium, 2002; Nominated for the Flanders Culture Prizes, Music, 2006.Memberships: SABAM (Belgian Copyright); CEBEDEM (Belgian Music Publisher). Address: Florisstraat 8, B-2018 Antwerp, Belgium. Website: www.wimhenderickx.com

HENDERSON Douglas James, b. 28 July 1934, Calgary, Alberta, Canada. Theoretical Physicist. m. Rose-Marie Steen-Nielssen, 3 daughters. Education: BA, 1st Class Honours, 1st place, Mathematics, University of British Columbia, 1956; PhD, Physics, University of Utah, USA, 1961. Appointments include: Assistant Professor, Associate Professor, Professor, Physics, Arizona State University, USA, 1962-69; Associate

Professor, Physics, 1964-67, Professor, Applied Mathematics, Physics, 1967-69, Adjunct Professor, Applied Mathematics, 1969-85, University of Waterloo, Canada; Research Scientist, 1969-90, Research Scientist Emeritus, 1992-, IBM Almaden Research Center, San Jose, California; Research Scientist, IBM Corporation, Salt Lake City, Utah, 1990-92; Adjunct Professor, Physics, 1990-93, Adjunct Professor, Chemistry, Mathematics, 1990-95, Research Scientist, Center for High Performance Computing, 1990-95, University of Utah; Manuel Sandoral Vallarta Professor, Physics, 1988; Juan de Oyarzabal Professor, Physics, 1993-95, Juan de Oyarzabal Honorary Professor, 1996-, Universidad Autonoma Metropolitana, Mexico; Honorary Professor of Chemistry, University of Hong Kong, 1993-, Rush Medical University, 2002-; Professor, Chemistry, Brigham Young University, 1995-; Many visiting positions. Publications: Over 450 research papers in scientific journals; Co-author, Statistical Mechanics and Dynamics, 1964, 2nd edition, 1982; Co-editor, Physical Chemistry: An Advanced Treatise, 15 volumes, 1966-75; Co-author, Chemical Dynamics, 1971; Co-editor, Advances and Perspectives, 6 volumes, 1973-81; Editor, Fundamentals of Inhomogeneous Fluids, 1992; Co-author, Stochastic Differential Equations in Science and Engineering, 2006. Honours include: Alfred P Sloan Foundation Fellowship, 1964, 1966; Ian Potter Foundation Fellowship, 1966; Outstanding Research Contribution Award, 1973, Outstanding Innovation Award, 1987, IBM; Corresponding Member, National Academy of Sciences of Mexico, 1990; Catedra Patrimoniales de Excelencia, Mexico, 1993-95; Premio a las Areas de Investigacion, Universidad Autonoma Metropolitana, 1996; John Simon Guggenheim Memorial Foundation Fellow, 1997; Joel Henry Hildebrand National American Chemical Society Award in Theoretical and Experimental Chemistry of Liquids, 1999; American Chemical Society Utah Award, 2005; Listed in Who's Who publications and biographical dictionaries. Memberships include: Fellow, American Physical Society, 1963-; Fellow, Institute of Physics, UK, 1965-; Fellow, American Institute of Chemists, 1971-; American Chemical Society; Biophysical Society; Canadian Association of Physicists; Mathematical Association of America; New York Academy of Sciences; Phi Kappa Phi; Sigma Xi; Sigma Pi Sigma. Address: Department of Chemistry, Brigham Young University, Provo, UT 84602, USA. E-mail: doug@chem.byu.edu

HENDERSON Michael John Glidden, b. 19 August 1938, Calcutta, India. Chartered Accountant. m. Stephanie Maria Dyer, 1965, 4 sons. Education: St Benedict's School, Ealing, 1948-56; Qualified as Chartered Accountant (FCA), 1961. Appointments: Williams Dyson Jones (Chartered Accountants), 1956-62; Whinney, Smith & Whinney (Chartered Accountants), 1962-65; Joined, 1965, Director, 1975, Managing Director, 1978, Chief Executive, 1984-89, Chairman, Chief Executive Officer, 1989-91, Goodlass, Wall & Lead Industries, renamed Cookson Group Plc; Chairman, Henderson Crossthwaite Holdings, 1995-2000; Director, Guiness Mahon Holdings plc, 1988-2000; Director, Quexco Inc (Vice-Chairman), 1999-2007; Director, Cyril Sweett Group plc, 1998-; Director, Wisley Golf Club Plc, 2002-07, and Deputy Chairman, 2004-07; Governor, 1990-, and Deputy Chairman, 2002-, Chairman, Finance & General Purposes, Committee, 1992-, St George's College, Weybridge; Governor, 1992-, and Deputy Chairman, 1999-, Chairman, Finance and General Purposes Committee, 1992-, Cranmore School, West Horsely; Governor, 2002-, and Chairman, Finance and General Purposes Committee, 2003-, St Teresa's School, Effingham; Chairman, QUEXO Inc Advisory Board, 2007-. Memberships: Innovation and Advisory Board, DTI,

1988-93; Trustee, Natural History Museum Development Trust, 1990-2000; FRSA, 1989; Knight of the Holy Sepulchre (KHS), 2005; MCC; Queens Club; The Wisley Golf Club; Salcombe Yacht Club; Thurlestone Golf Club; Kingsbridge Tennis; Horsley Sports. Address: "Langdale" Woodland Drive, East Horsley, Surrey KT24 5AN, England.

HENDERSON Neil Keir, b. 7 March 1956, Glasgow, Scotland. Education: MA, English Language, English Literature and Scottish Literature, Glasgow University, 1977. Publications: Maldehyde's Discomfiture, or A Lady Churned, 1997; Fish-Worshipping – As We Know It, 2001; An English Summer In Scotland and other Unlikely Events, 2005. Contributions to: Mystery of the City, poetry anthology, 1997; Loveable Warts: A Defence of Self-Indulgence, Chapman 87, 1997; Mightier Than the Sword: The Punch-Up of the Poses, Chapman 91, 1998; The Red Candle Treasury, 1998; Labyrinths 6 (written in entirety), 2002; Electric Sheep, 2004; Spiders and Flies, 2005. Address: 46 Revoch Drive, Knightswood, Glasgow G13 4SB, Scotland.

HENDERSON William James Carlaw, b. 26 September 1948, Galashiels, Selkirkshire, Scotland. Lawyer; Writer to the Signet. Education: George Heriot's School, Edinburgh; Old College, Faculty of Law, University of Edinburgh. Appointments: Trainee Solicitor, Patrick and James WS, 1971-73; Solicitor, Wallace and Guthrie, 1973-74; Solicitor, 1974-76, Partner, 1976-83, Allan McDougall and Co; Partner, Brodies WS, 1983-2003. Publications: 2 seminar papers, Moscow School of Political Studies, 1996, 1997; 1 monograph, 2001. Honours: Bachelor of Laws, LLB, 1971; Notary Public, 1975; Writer to the Signet, 1981. Memberships: Society of HM Writers to the Signet; Fellow, Royal Geographical Society; Royal Scottish Geographical Society; Secretary, 1980-83, Society of Scottish Artists, Honorary Life Member, 2005; Governor, Edinburgh College of Art, 1996-99; Director, Edinburgh Printmakers Workshop, 2001-; Trustee, Mendelssohn on Mull Music Festival, 2003-; Director, Family Mediation, Lothian, 2005-; Member, Royal Highland Yacht Club; Member, Edinburgh Sports Club. Address: 11 Inverleith Place, Edinburgh EH3 5QE, Scotland. E-mail: wjchenderson@suhamet.com

HENDRY Diana (Lois), b. 2 October 1941, Meols, Wirral, Cheshire, England. Poet; Children's Writer. Divorced, 1 son, 1 daughter. Education: BA, Honours, 1984, MLitt, 1986, University of Bristol, England. Appointments: Reporter and Feature Writer, Western Mail, Cardiff, 1960-65; Scriptwriter/ broadcaster, Radio Merseyside, 1965-67; Freelance journalist, 1967-80; Tutor, University of Bristol, 1984-87; Part-time English Teacher, Clifton College, 1984-87; Part-time Lecturer, University of the West of England, Bristol, 1987-93; Tutor, Open University, 1991-92; Tutor, Creative Writing, University of Bristol, 1995-97; Tutor, Creative Writing, North Cornwall, 1996; Writer-in-Residence, Dumfries and Galloway Royal Infirmary, 1997-98; Tutor, University of Bristol, 1999; Writer-in-Residence, Edinburgh Royal Infirmary, 2000; Book Reviewer, The Spectator, 2000-; Tutor, Poetry Course, Ty Newydd, 2001; Tutor, Poetry, Fiction and Children's Writing, 2001, Pushkin Prize Students, 2005, 2006, Moniack Mhor; Assistant Editor, Mariscat Press, 2004-. Publications: Children's books include: The Crazy Collector, 2001; You Can't Kiss It Better, 2003; No Homework Tomorrow, 2003; Swan Boy, 2004; The Very Snowy Christmas, 2005; Catch a Gran, 2006; Poetry books: Making Blue, 1995; Strange Goings-on, 1995; Borderers, 2001; Twelve Lilts: Psalms & Responses, 2003; No Homework Tomorrow, 2003; Sparks! 2005; Numerous contributions to anthologies and periodicals;

Poems and books broadcast on radio and television. Honours: Stroud Festival International Poetry Competition, 1976; 3rd Prize, 1991, 2nd Prize, 1993, Peterloo Poetry Competition; Whitbread Award, 1991; 1st Prize, Housman Poetry Society, 1996; Commended, Phras Open Poetry Competition, 1997, 1998; Commended, Blue Nose Rivers Competition, 2000; Scottish Arts Council Children's Book Award, 2001. Memberships: Society of Authors; PEN; The Poetry Society; Shore Poets, Edinburgh. Address: 23 Dunrobin Place, Stockbridge, Edinburgh EH3 5HZ, Scotland.

HENDRY Stephen Gordon, b. 13 January 1969, Edinburgh, Scotland. Snooker Player. m. Amanda Elizabeth Teresa Tart, 1995, 2 sons. Appointments: Professional Player, 1985; Scottish Champion, 1986, 1987, 1988; Winner, Rothmans Grand Prix, 1987; World Doubles Champion, 1987; Australian Masters Champion, 1987; British Open Champion, 1988, 1991, 1999; New Zealand Masters Champion, 1988; Benson and Hedges Master Champion, 1989, 1990, 1991, 1992, 1993, 1996; UK Professional Champion, 1989, 1990, 1994, 1995, 1996; Asian Champion, 1989; Regal Masters Champion, 1989; Dubai Classic Champion, 1989; Embassy World Champion, 1990, 1992, 1993, 1994, 1995, 1996, 1999; 2006. Irish Masters, 1992; International Open, 1993; Malta Cup, 2004. Publication: Snooker Masterclass, 1994. Honours: MBE, 1994; Dr hc (Stirling), 2000; MacRoberts Trophy, 2001. Address: Stephen Hendry Snooker Ltd, Kerse Road, Stirling FK7 7SG, Scotland.

HENLEY Elizabeth Becker, b. 8 May 1952, Jackson, Mississippi, USA. Playwright. Education: BFA, Southern Methodist University. Publications: Crimes of the Heart, 1981; The Wake of Jamey Foster, 1982; Am I Blue, 1982; The Miss Firecracker Contest, 1984; The Debutante Ball, 1985, 1991; The Lucky Spot, 1987; Abundance, 1989; Beth Henley: Monologues for Women, 1992; Screenplays: Nobody's Fool, 1986; Crimes of the Heart, 1986; Miss Firecracker, 1989; Signatures, 1990; Control Freaks, 1993; Revelers, 1994; L-Play, 1996; Impossible Marriage, 1998; Family Week, 2000; Ridiculous Fraud, 2006. Honours: Pulitzer Prize for Drama, 1981; New York Drama Critics Circle Best Play Award, 1981; George Oppenheimer/Newsday Playwriting Award, 1981. Address: c/o The William Morris Agency, 1350 Avenue of the Americas, New York, NY 10019, USA.

HENNING JOCELYN Ann Margareta Maria (Countess of Roden), b. 5 August 1948, Göteborg, Sweden. Author; Playwright; Translator; Broadcaster. m. Earl of Roden, 13 February 1986, 1 son. Education: BA, Lund University, Sweden, 1975. Publications include: The Connemara Whirlwind Trilogy, 1990-95; Keylines, 2000-06; Keylines for Living, 2007. Plays: Smile, Göteborg, 1972; Baptism of Fire, Galway, 1997; Pernik, 1999; The Alternative, Galway, 1998. Contributions to: Swedish and Irish Radio and Television. Memberships: Irish Writer's Union; Irish Playwrights' and Scriptwriters' Guild. Address: 4 The Boltons, London SW10 9TB, England.

HENRIQUEZ Jorge M, b. 4 June 1973, Mexico. Civil Engineering. m. Rosa Esperanza Pineda Magaña. Education: Civil Engineering, Economic Planning; Graduate in Corporate Finance and Macroeconomic Development; Economic Perspectives; Financial Management; Corporate Leadership and Planning; Financial Regulation; Integral Negotiations; Statistic Analysis. Appointments: Corporate Sales Manager, Promotora Profisa, SA de CV, 1995-96; Corporate General Manager, Grupo Corporativo Trescom, 1996-2001; Operations Manager, ARS Impresos, SA de CV, 2001-02; General Manager,

Mexico and Latin America, Clayton de Mexico, SA de CV. Publications: US Industry Today; Process Heating, 2007. Honours: Listed in international biographical dictionaries. Memberships: AMERIC; American Chamber of Mexico. Address: Manuel L Stampa 54, Col Nva Industrial Vallejo, DF CP 07700, Mexico. E-mail: jmhenr@clayton.com.mx Website: www.claytonmexico.com.mx

HENRY Lenny, b. 29 August 1958, England. m. Dawn French, 1 daughter. Appointments: Numerous tours including Loud!, 1994; Australia, 1995. Creative Works: TV includes: New Faces (debut), Tiswas, Three of a Kind, 1981-83; The Lenny Henry Show, Alive and Kicking, 1991; Bernard and the Genie, 1991; In Dreams, 1992; The Real McCoy, 1992; Chef (title role) (3 series), Lenny Hunts the Funk, New Soul Nation, White Goods, 1994; Funky Black Shorts, 1994; Comic Relief, Lenny Go Home, 1996; Lenny's Big Amazon Adventure, 1997; Lenny Goes to Town, 1998; The Man, 1998; Hope and Glory, 1999, 2000; Lenny's Big Atlantic Adventure, 2000; Lenny in Pieces, 2000, 2001; Lenny Henry – This is My Life, 2003; The Lenny Henry Show, 2004; Films include: True Identity, 1991; Video: Lenny Henry Live and Unleashed, 1989; Lenny Henry Live and Loud, 1994; Toured Australia with Large! Show, 1998; Live performances: Have You Seen This Man tour, 2001; So Many Things to Say, 2003, tour 2004. Publications: The Quest for the Big Woof (autobiography), 1991; Charlie and the Big Chill (childrens book), 1995; Berry's Way, 2006. Honours include: Monaco Red Cross Award; The Golden Nymph Award; BBC personality of the Year, Radio and TV Industry Club, 1993; Golden Rose of Montreux Award for Lenny in Pieces, 2000; CBE, 1999; Lifetime Achievement Award for Ongoing Performance, UK Comedy Awards, 2003. Address: c/o PBJ Management Ltd, 5 Soho Square, London W1V 5DE, England.

HENSEL Robert Michael, b. 8 May 1969, Rota, Spain. Disabled Advocate; Poet; Guinness & Ripley's World Record Holder. m. Amy Beth. Honours: Nominee, Best Poet of the 20th Century; Nominee, PushCart Prize for Poetry; Editor's Choice Award, 2000; New York State Assembly Excelsior Award for Excellence; New York Senate Certificate of Merit; State of New York Executive Chamber Certificate of Commendation; Guinness World Record Holder & Ripley's World Record Holder for the longest non-stop wheelie in a wheelchair at 6.178 miles; VIP invitation to carry torch for 2006 Asian Games. Address: 138 East Bridge Street, Apt #A, Oswego, NY 13126, USA. E-mail: wheelierecord@yahoo.com

HENSON Gavin Lloyd, b. 1 February 1982, Bridgend, Wales. Rugby Player. 1 daughter with Charlotte Church. Education: Brynteg Comprehensive, Bridgend, South Wales. Career: Joined Swansea RFC, 2000; International debut for Wales against Japan, 2001; Joined Ospreys, 2003; Grand Slam in the Six Nations Championship, 2005. Publications: My Grand Slam Year, 2005. Honours: International Rugby Board's Young Player Of The Year award, 2001; Named Man of the Match, EDF cup Semi Final, 2008.

HENSON Ray David, b. 24 July 1924, Johnston City, Illinois, USA. Lawyer; Professor of Law. Education: BS, 1947, JD, 1949, University of Illinois. Appointments: Counsel, Continental Assurance Co, and Continental Casualty Co, 1952-70; Professor of Law, Wayne State University, 1970-75; Professor of Law, 1975-95, Professor Emeritus, 1995-, University of California, Hastings College of Law. Publications: Landmarks of Law, 1960; Secured Transactions, 1973, 2nd edition, 1977; The Law of Sales, 1985; Documents of Title, 1983, 2nd edition, 1990; Various other books and numerous articles in American law reviews. Honours: Chairman, Business Law Section, American Bar Association, 1969-70; Chairman, Uniform Commercial Code Committee, American Bar Association, Illinois State Bar Association and Chicago Bar Association at various times; Member, Legal Advisory Committee, New York Stock Exchange, 1970-75. Memberships: American Bar Association; Illinois State Bar Association; Chicago Bar Association; American Law Institute; University Club, San Francisco. Address: 1400 Geary Blvd, II 2303, San Francisco, CA 94109-6561, USA.

HERBERT (Edward) Ivor (Montgomery), b. 20 August 1925, Johannesburg, South Africa. Author; Journalist; Scriptwriter. Education: MA, Trinity College, Cambridge, 1949. Appointments: Travel Editor, Racing Editor, The Mail on Sunday, 1982-2002. Publications: Eastern Windows, 1953; Point to Point, 1964; Arkle: The Story of a Champion, 1966, further editions, 1975, 2003; The Great St Trinian's Train Robbery (screenplay), 1966; The Queen Mother's Horses, 1967; The Winter Kings (co- author), 1968, enlarged edition, 1989; The Way to the Top, 1969; Night of the Blue Demands, play (co-author), 1971; Over Our Dead Bodies, 1972; The Diamond Diggers, 1972; Scarlet Fever (co-author), 1972; Winter's Tale, 1974; Red Rum: Story of a Horse of Courage, 1974, further editions, 1974, 1977, 1995, 2005; The Filly (n, 1977; Six at the Top, 1977; Classic Touch (TV documentary), 1985; Spot the Winner, 1978, updated, 1990; Longacre, 1978; Horse Racing, 1980; Vincent O'Brien's Great Horses, 1984; Revolting Behaviour, 1987; Herbert's Travels, 1987; Reflections on Racing (co-author), 1990; Riding Through My Life (with HRH The Princess Royal), 1991; Vincent O'Brien (official biography), 2005. Memberships: Society of Authors; Writers' Guild: Turf Club. Address: The Old Rectory, Bradenham, Buckinghamshire HP14 4HD, England.

HERBERT James (John), b. 8 April 1943, London, England. Author. Education: Hornsey College of Art, 1959. Publications: The Rats, 1974; The Fog, 1975; The Survivor, 1976; Fluke, 1977; The Spear, 1978; Lair, 1979; The Dark, 1980; The Jonah, 1981; Shrine, 1983; Domain, 1984; Moon, 1985; The Magic Cottage, 1986; Sepulchre, 1987; Haunted, 1988; Creed, 1990; Portent, 1992; James Herbert: By Horror Haunted, 1992; James Herbert's Dark Places, 1993; The City, 1994; The Ghosts of Sleath, 1994; '48, 1996; Others, 1999; Once, 2001; Devil in the Dark, Craig Cabell, 2003; Nobody True, 2003; The Secret of Crickley Hall, 2006. Films: The Rats, 1982; The Survivor, 1986; Fluke, 1995; Haunted, 1995. Address: c/o Bruce Hunter, David Higham Associates, 5-8 Lower John Street, London W1R 4HA, England.

HERDMAN John Macmillan, b. 20 July 1941, Edinburgh, Scotland. Writer. m. (1) Dolina Maclennan, divorced, (2) Mary Ellen Watson, 17 August 2002. Education: BA, 1963, MA, 1967, PhD, 1988, Magdalene College, Cambridge, England. Appointments: Creative Writing Fellow, Edinburgh University, Scotland, 1977-79; William Soutar Fellow, Perth, Scotland, 1990-91. Publications: Descent, 1968; A Truth Lover, 1973; Memoirs of My Aunt Minnie/Clapperton, 1974; Pagan's Pilgrimage, 1978; Stories Short and Tall, 1979; Voice Without Restraint: Bob Dylan's Lyrics, 1982; Three Novellas, 1987; The Double in Nineteenth-Century Fiction, 1990; Imelda and Other Stories, 1993; Ghostwriting, 1996; Cruising (play), 1997; Poets, Pubs, Polls and Pillarboxes, 1999; Four Tales, 2000; The Sinister Cabaret, 2001; Triptych, 2004; My Wife's Lovers, 2007. Honours: Scottish Arts Council Book Awards, 1978, 1993. Listed in national biographical dictionaries. Address: Roselea, Bridge of Tilt, Pitlochry, Perthshire PH18 5SX, Scotland.

HERLEA Alexandre, b. 11 October 1942, Brasov, Romania (French and Romanian Citizen). Professor. Married, 1 daughter. Education: Mechanical Engineer, Institutul Politechnic, Brasov, Romania, 1965; PhD, History of Science and Technology, Ecole des Hautes Etudes en Sciences Sociales and Conservatoire National des Arts et Métiers (CNAM), 1977; Habilitation, Sciences, Université de Paris Sud – Orsay, Sorbonne, France, 1993. Appointments: Engineer, IRGU Company, Bucharest, Romania, 1966-69; Lecturer, Scoala Technica "23 August", Bucharest, Romania, 1969-72; University Researcher, History of Technology, CNAM, Paris, 1972-77; Visiting Researcher, Smithsonian Institution and Harvard, Princeton and Pennsylvania Universities, 1978-79; Research Engineer, CNAM, Paris, 1980-88; Associated Professor, Ecole Centrale des Arts et Manufactures, 1980-88; Senior Lecturer, History of Technology, 1988-94, Member of Teaching Staff, PhD Programmes, 1988-2000, CNAM, Paris; Visiting Professor, Michigan Technological University, USA, 1990, Universitatea Bucuresti, Romania, 1994; Professor with tenure, History of Technology, 1995-, Director of Social Science Department, 1995-97, Director of International Relations, 2001-, Université de Technologie, Belfort-Montbeliard, France; Minister for European Integration, Romanian Government, 1996-99; Ambassador, Head of the Romanian Mission to the European Union, 2000-2001. Publications: Author, co-author and editor of 12 books published in France, Italy, United States, United Kingdom including: Histoire générale des techniques. Les techniques de la civilisation industrielle, 1978; Les moteurs, 1985; Over 40 scientific studies and numerous political articles. Honours: Silver Medal, Société d'Encouragement au Progrés, France; The Prize "Soziale Marktwirtschaft, Wirtschaftspolitischer Club, Berlin, Germany; Chevalier du Merite de l'Invention, Chambre Belge des Inventeurs, Belgium; Commandeur de la Légion d'Honneur, France; Mare Ofiter (High Officer) Serviciul Credincios, Romania; Doctor Honoris Causa, University Transilvania Brasov, Romania. Memberships include: Comité das Traveaux Historiques et Scientifiques, France; International Committee for the History of Technology (Member of the Executive Committee, former President); International Academy of the History of Science; Romanian Christian Democrat Party (PNT-CD – former Vice-President); Christian Democratic International (Member of the Executive Committee, former Vice-President). Address: 4, rue H. Fragonard, 92130 Issy-les-Moulineaux, France. E-mail: alexandre.herlea@wanadoo.fr

HERMANN Armin Daniel, b. 26 November 1937, Neu-Sarata, Moldavia. Nuclear Chemistry Engineer. m. Christine Seidel Hermann, 1970, divorced 1981, 1 son. Education: Diploma in Engineering, 1961, DSc, 1984, Technical University Dresden; PhD, Lomonossow University, Moscow, 1965. Appointments: Scientist, 1965-66, Group Leader, 1966-75, Head of Department, 1975-87, German Academy of Sciences; Project Manager, Paul Scherrer Institute, Switzerland, 1990-2005; Adviser, Nuclear Fuel Industry Research Group, Palo Alto, 1994-2004; Member, Co-ordination Council, Council of Mutual Economic Aid, Moscow, 1971-87; Nuclear Chemistry Educator, German Academy of Sciences, Technical High School, Zittau, Technical University, Dresden. Publications: Radiochemical Methods, textbook; 100 articles in scientific publications; Patentee in field of nuclear reactors. Honour: Recipient, Order Banner of Labour, governmental award. Memberships: German Chemical Society; Working Group, Nuclear Chemistry; German Society of Nuclear Technology; Swiss Nuclear Forum; Christian Parish Control Commission. Address: Sommerhaldenstr 5A, 5200 Brugg, Aargau, Switzerland. E-mail: armin.hermann@bluewin.ch.

DICTIONARY OF INTERNATIONAL BIOGRAPHY

HERMANN Edward Robert, b. 9 October 1920, Newport, Kentucky, USA. Professor Emeritus; Consultant. m. Eleanor Hill Hermann, 3 sons, 4 daughters. Education: BSCE, University of Kentucky, 1942; SM, Sanitary Engineering, MIT, 1949; CE, University of Kentucky, 1953; PhD, University of Texas, 1957. Appointments: Director of Industrial Hygiene Graduate Programmes, University of Illinois Medical Centre; Professor of Environmental and Occupational Health Sciences, School of Public Health, University of Illinois at Chicago; Professor, Acting Director, Occupational and Environmental Medicine, University of Illinois School of Public Health; Professor, Environmental Engineering, Department of Civil Engineering, Mechanics and Metallurgy, University of Illinois at Chicago; Professor, Environmental Health Engineering, Northwestern University; Industrial Health Engineer, Humble Oil and Refining Company, (now Exxon Mobil); Chief Sanitary Engineer and Chief of Public Health, US Atomic Energy Commission, Los Alamos, New Mexico; Consultant to various industries, government agencies, law offices and universities. Publications: Over 100 articles, monographs and book chapters in reviewed scientific, engineering and medical journals. Honours: Harrison Prescott Eddy Medal, 1959; Resources Division Award, American Water Works Association, 1960; Michigan Industrial Hygiene Society Award, 1964; Radebaugh Award, 1976; Award of Merit, Chicago Technical Societies Council, 1978; Borden Foundation Award, 1988; Outstanding Civil Engineering Alumnus Award, University of Kentucky, 1995; Donald Eddy Cummings Memorial Award, 1999; Outstanding Publications Award, American Industrial Hygiene Association, 2000. Memberships include: Fellow, American Association for the Advancement of Science; American Academy of Environmental Engineers; Fellow, American Public Health Association; Fellow, Life Member, American Society of Civil Engineers. Address: 117 Church Road, Winnetka, IL 60093, USA.

HERRING Horace Jean-Pierre, b. 13 July 1950, London, England. Freelance Writer; Researcher. Divorced, 1 son, 1 daughter. Education: BSc (Hons), Engineering with Social Studies, Sussex University, 1971-74; PhD, Open University, 1994-2003. Appointments: Conservation Officer, National Union of Students, London, 1974-75; Editor, Whole Earth magazine, Brighton, 1975-78; Senior Research Associate, Energy Analysis Group, Lawrence Berkeley Lab, University of California at Berkeley, USA, 1980-81; Principal Energy Conservation Officer, Department of Energy, Government of Fiji, 1982-84; Research Fellow, Chief Scientist's Group, Energy Technology Support Unit, Harwell Lab, Oxfordshire, 1985-88; Energy Economist, Business Planning Branch, PowerGen plc, 1988-92; Research Fellow, Faculty of Technology, Open University, 1999-2001; Freelance Consultant, Writer, specialising in energy economics, energy efficiency policy and environmental history, 1992-. Publications: Alternative Technology Directory, 1978; Energy Use in UK Commercial and Public Buildings, 1988; Energy Use in the UK Domestic Sector up to Year 2010, 1990; Energy Savings in Domestic Electrical Appliances, 1992; Is Britain a Third World Country? The case of German refrigerators, 1994; Electricity Use in Minor Appliances in the UK, 1995; Is Energy Efficiency Good for the Environment: some conflicts and confusions, 1996; Does energy efficiency save energy? The debate and its consequences, 1999; Editorial: How Green is Energy Efficiency?, 2000; The Conservation Society: harbinger of the 1970s environment movement in the UK, 2001; The Rebound Effect, Sustainable Consumption and electronic appliances, 2001; Sustainable Services, Electronic Education and the Rebound Effect, 2002; The Rebound

Effect and Energy Conservation, 2004; Energy Efficiency and Consumption, 2004; Energy Efficiency: A Critical View?, 2005; From Energy Dreams to Nuclear Nightmares: Lessons for the 21st century from a previous nuclear era, 2005. Honours: Best Paper Award, 15th International Symposium, Informatics for Environmental Protection, Zurich, 2001. Memberships: Chair, Interdisciplinary Research Network of Environmental Researchers, UK, 2000-05; Referee, Energy – the International Journal, and Ecological Economics; Member, Editorial Board, Energy and Environment Journal. Address: EERU, The Open University, Milton Keynes, MK7 6AA, England. E-mail: h.herring@open.ac.uk

HERSCHAN Otto, b. 31 May 1927, Vienna, Austria. Retired Company Director. 1 son. Education: Higher School Certificate, Belmont Abbey School, Hereford. Appointments: Manager, the Boltons Theatre, London, 1948-51, The Embassy Theatre, London, 1952-53; Managing Director, Catholic Herald, Scottish Catholic Observer, 1953-98, Retired, 1998; Managing Director, The Irish Catholic, 1982-2005; Director, The Irish Catholic, 2005-08. Publications: Numerous articles in professional and popular journals. Honours: Knight of St Gregory, 1978. Memberships: St Stephen's Green-Hibernian Club, Dublin. Address: 28 Corrig Avenue, Dun Laoghaire, Co Dublin, Ireland.

HERSHEY Barbara, b. 5 February 1948, Hollywood, California, USA. Actress. m. (1) 1 son, (2) Stephen Douglas, 1992, divorced 1995. Career: Films: With Six You Get Eggroll, 1968; Heaven with a Gun, The Last Summer, 1969; The Liberation of L B Jones, The Baby Maker, 1970; The Pursuit of Happiness, 1971; Dealing: Or the Berkeley-to-Boston Forty-Brick Lost-Bag Blues, Boxcar Bertha, 1972; Love Comes Quietly, 1973; The Crazy World of Julius Vrooder, 1974; You and Me, Diamonds, 1975; Trial by Combat, The Last Hard Men, 1976; The Stuntman, 1980; The Entity, Americana, Take This Job and Shove It, 1981; The Right Stuff, 1983; The Natural, 1984; Hoosiers, 1986; Tin Men, Shy People, 1987; T Hannah and Her Sisters, The Last Temptation of Christ, A World Apart, Beaches, 1988; Tune in Tomorrow..., Paris Trout, 1990; The Public Eye, Defenseless, 1991; Swing Kids, Splitting Heirs, Falling Down, 1993; A Dangerous Woman, 1994; Last of the Dogmen, 1995; Portrait of a Lady, The Pallbearer, 1996; A Soldier's Daughter Never Cries, 1998; Frogs for Snakes, Drowning on Dry Land, Breakfast of Champions, 1999; Lantana, 2001; 11:14, 2003; Riding the Bullet, 2004; The Bird Can't Fly, Love Comes Lately, Childless, 2007; Vacuuming the Cat, 2008; Many TV shows and series. Honours: Best Actress, Cannes Film Festival, 1987, 1988; Emmy and Golden Globe Awards, 1990. Address: c/o Suzan Bymel, Bymel O'Neill Management, N Vista, Los Angeles, CA 90046, USA.

HERTFORD, 9th Marquess of, Henry Jocelyn Seymour, b. 6 July 1958, Birmingham, England. Landowner. m. Beatriz Karam, 2 sons, 2 daughters. Education: Royal Agricultural College, Cirencester. Appointments: Estate Owner; Farm Manager; Flock Master; Shepherd. Memberships: Country Land and Business Association; National Farmers Union. Address: Ragley Hall, Alcester, Warwickshire B49 5NJ, England. E-mail: info@ragleyhall.com

HERVAS Francisco Ignacio, b. 9 August 1951, Madrid, Spain. Doctor. m. Maria Francisca. Education: MD, University of Granada, Spain, 1976; Specialist, Pathology, 1981; Specialist, Clinical Microbiology, 1982; Master in Sanitary Designs, University Politechnica, Madrid, 1993; PhD, University of Complutense, Madrid, 1994.

Appointments: Lt Col, Medical Corps, Spanish Army, Spain; Associate Professor, Clinical Microbiology, Department of Microbiology I, School of Medicine, University of Complutense, Madrid, -1987; Responsible for Clinical Microbiology Teaching Unit, Spanish Armed Forces; Chief, Microbiology Department, Hospital Central de la Defensa, Madrid. Publications: Over 100 papers in scientific magazines; Books include: Procedimientos de inteligencia artificial en el studio de las enfermedades infecciosas, 1999; Modelos de gestión para médicos de familia, 2004; Calidad y rentabilidad en las empresas sanitarias, 2006. Honours: Excellence in Health Care Prize, 2005; Doctor Honoris Causa in Health Sciences, 2005; Listed in international biographical dictionaries. Memberships: ESCMID; SEIMC; SEMC; VIP's; AMYS. E-mail: fhermal@oc.mde.es

HERZENBERG Arvid, b. 16 April 1925, Vienna, Austria. Theoretical Physicist. m. Marjorie, 1 son, 2 daughters. Education: BSc, 1st Class Honours Physics, 1946-49, PhD, Physics, 1952, DSc, 1964, University of Manchester, England. Appointments: Assistant Lecturer to Reader in Theoretical Physics, University of Manchester, England, 1952-69; Faculty, 1970-, Emeritus Professor in Physics and Applied Physics, 1995-, Yale University, New Haven, Connecticut, USA. Publications: Articles in scientific journals: Geomagnetic Dynamos, 1958; Anomalous Scattering and the Phase Problem (with H S M Lau), 1967; Core Polarization Corrections to Oscillator Strengths in Alkali Atoms, 1968; Oscillatory Energy Dependence of Resonant Electron-Molecule Scattering, 1968 (Boomerang Model). Memberships: Fellow, British Physical Society; Fellow, American Physical Society. Address: 6 Legrand Road, North Haven, CT 06473, USA. E-mail: arvid.herzenberg@yale.edu

HESELTINE Michael (Rt Hon Michael Ray Dibdin Heseltine), b. 21 March 1933, Swansea, Wales. Politician. m. Anne Edna Harding Williams, 1962, 1 son, 2 daughters. Education: Pembroke College, Oxford. Appointments: Chair, Haymarket Press, 1965-70, 1999-; MP for Tavistock, 1966-74, for Henley, 1974-2001; Parliamentary Sectretary, Ministry of Transport, 1970; Parliamentary Under Secretary of State, Department of the Environment, 1970-72; Minister of Aerospace and Shipping, 1972-74; Opposition Spokesman for Industry, 1974-76, for the Environment, 1976-79; Secretary of State for the Environment, 1979-83, 1990-92, for Defence, 1983-86; Secretary of State for Industry and President of the Board of Trade, 1992-95; Deputy Prime Minister and First Secretary of State, 1995-97; Director, Haymarket Publishing Group, 1997-, Chair, 2001-; President, Association of Conservative Clubs, 1982-83, Chair, Conservative Mainstream, 1998-; President, Quoted Companies Alliance International Advisory Council, 2000-, Federation of Korean Industries, Anglo-China Forum, 1998-; President, Conservative Group for Europe, 2001-; Development Patron, Trinity College of Music, Institute of Marketing. Publications: Reviving the Inner Cities, 1983; Where There's A Will, 1987; The Challenge of Europe: Can Britain Win? 1988; Life in the Jungle (memoirs), 2000. Honorary Fellow, Pembroke College, Oxford, 1986, University of Wales (Swansea); Bentinck Prize, 1989; Honorary Fellow, Chartered Institute of Management, 1998; Hon FRIBA; Hon LLD (Liverpool) 1990; Hon DBA (Luton), 2003. Address: House of Lords, London SW1A 0PW, England.

HESKETH Ronald David, b. 16 June 1947, Broughty Ferry, Angus, Scotland. Chaplain. m. Vera, 1 son, 1 daughter. Education: BA Hons, Geography, University of Durham, 1968; Theology, University of Cambridge, 1969; Diploma,

Pastoral Studies, St Michael's College, Cardiff, 1971; Diploma, Reformation Studies, Open University, 1977. Appointments: Ordained Deacon, 1971; Priest, 1972; Curate, Holy Trinity Church, Southport, 1971-73; Assistant Chaplain, Mersey Mission to Seamen, 1973-75; RAF Chaplain, 1975-98; Command Chaplain, 1998-2001; Chaplain-in-Chief, 2001-2006; Vocations Officer Diocese of Worcester, 2006-. Honours: Honorary Chaplain to HM The Queen, 2001-2006; Fellow, Royal Geographical Society; Companion of the Most Honourable Order of the Bath; CB; BA; DPS; RAF; Listed in national biographical dictionaries. Membership: Royal Air Force Club; Fellow of the Chartered Management Institute, 2006-; Chairman of the Naval, Military and Airforce Bible Society, 2006-. Address: The Old Police Station, Bredon Road, Tewkesbury Gloucestershire, GL20 5BZ, England. E-mail: vera&ron.hesketh@dunelm.org.ok

HESSE Axel, b. 16 July 1935, Berlin, Germany. Ethnomusicologist. m. Flora, 29 February 1964, 1 son, 1 daughter. Education: studied University of Berlin, Institute of Musicology, 1955; PhD, 1970, Postgraduate, Academy Sciences, Cuba, Doctorate 1971. Appointments: Translator; Member, International Folk Music Council, 1967; Lecturer, Ethnomusicology, Humboldt University, Germany, 1970-; Visiting Professor, National Music School, Peru; posts in various organisations, including: Academy Sciences of Germany, Committee of GDR-Portugal, International Council Traditional Music; Director of the 1254 founded Extraordinary Music Chair Francisco Salinas, Salamanca University; Research work: Collection of German folk songs and Latin American Music; Book on Music Life in Latin America 1492-1969 (with Flora Pérez); Organisation and Chairman, Fink-Folklore Initiativkomitee; Documentary, musical field work, 1983; Founder, Ciplice Folk Sound Archives, Freyburg/Unstrut, 1989; The Multidisciplinary Salinas Colloquium on Rhythm, 1991-94; Street Musician, 1994, Arcos en Compañía, 1995; Retired, 1998, Música Peatonal 2000; Steps to scientifical come-back to save his 12000 items of collected ethnic music; Folía en Compañia, 2002. Publications: The Little A-Y-O of Western Music History; 200 Years of Music in the Jesuit republic and It's Echo; Football Polychorality and Research, 2004. Honours: Order of International Ambassadors, 1995; Listed in biographical publications. Address: Fürstenwalder Allee 366, D-12589 Berlin, Germany. E-mail: harpviol@hotmail.de

HESTERWERTH Kathleen Ann (Kathy), b. 8 June 1948, McCook, Nebraska, USA. Business Owner. Education: Associate of Arts Degree, McCook University, 1968; BSc, Home Economics/Business Administration, University of Nebraska, Kearney, 1971. Appointments: Federal Service Career: Washington DC Area – HQ COMD USAF; US Army Military Personnel Center; Naval Telecommunications Unit; HQ US Army Computer Systems Command; HQ Military Traffic Management Command; US Government Printing Office; US Small Business Administration, Jacksonville, Florida; US National Park Service, Yellowstone National Park, Wyoming; Air Force Flight Test Center, Edwards Air Force Base, California; Established Flat Rock Oil, LLC, 2001. Honours: Cambridge Who's Who Empowering Executives, Professionals and Entrepreneurs Executive of the Year, 2006-2007 representing Crude Oil Production; Eminent Fellow, ABI; International Peace Prize and Ambassador General, United Cultural Convention. Memberships: American Home Economics Association; Appaloosa Horse Club; American Paint Horse Association; Arabian Horse Association. E-mail: flatrockoil@earthlink.net

HETZEL Basil Stuart, b. 13 June 1922, London, England. Medical Scientist. m. Anne Gilmour Fisher, 3 sons, 2 daughters. Education: MBBS, University of Adelaide, 1944; Registrar, Royal Adelaide Hospital, 1946-49; MD, 1949; Member, Royal Australasian College of Physicians, 1949; Research Fellowships, Adelaide, New York, London, 1949-55. Appointments: Reader, Professor of Medicine, Adelaide University, 1956-68; Honorary Physician, Royal Adelaide Hospital and Queen Elizabeth Hospital; Foundation Professor, Social & Preventive Medicine, Monash University, Melbourne, 1968-75; Visiting Commonwealth Professor, University of Glasgow, 1972-73; First Chief, CSIRO Division of Human Nutrition, Adelaide, 1976-85; Executive Director, Chairman, International Council for Control of Iodine Deficiency Disorders, 1985-95, Chairman, 1986-2001; Lieutenant Governor of South Australia, 1992-2000. Publications include: Health & Australian Society, 1974; Lifestyle & Health, 1987; The Story of Iodine Deficiency, 1989; SOS for a Billion, 1994; Towards the Global Elimination of Brain Damage due to Iodine Deficiency, 2004; Chance and Commitment, Memoirs of a Medical Scientist, 2005. Honours: Companion of Order of Australia, 1990; Honorary Professor, Tianjin Medical University, China, 1989; Alwyn Smith Medal, Royal Colleges of Physicians, UK, 1993; Anzac Peace Prize, Australia, 1997. Memberships: President, Endocrine Society of Australia, 1964-66; Life Member, Public Health Association of Australia; Fellow, Nutrition Society, Australia, 1991; Honorary Member, International Epidemiology Association, 1993; Chancellor, University of South Australia, 1992-98. E-mail: iccidd@a011.aone.net.au

HEWISH Antony, b. 11 May 1924, Fowey, Cornwall, England. Astronomer; Physicist. m. Marjorie E C Richards, 1950, 1 son and 1 daughter. Education: Graduated, Gonville and Caius College, Cambridge, 1948. Appointments: War Service, 1943-46; Research Fellow, Gonville and Caius College, 1951-54; Supernumerary Fellow, 1956-61; University Assistant Director of Research, 1953-61, Lecturer, 1961-69; Fellow, Churchill College, Cambridge, 1962-; Reader in Radio Astronomy, University of Cambridge, 1969-71, Professor, 1971-89, Professor Emeritus, 1989; Professor, Royal Institute, 1977; Director, Mullard Radio Astronomy Observatory, Cambridge, 1982-88; Vikram Sarabhai Professor, Ahmedabad, 1988. Publications: The First, Second, Third and Fourth Cambridge Catalogues; Seeing Beyond the Invisible, Pulsars and physics laboratories. Honours: Hamilton Prize, 1951; Eddington Medal, Royal Astronomical Society, 1968; Boys Prize, Institute of Physics, 1970; Dellinger Medal, International Union of Radio Science, Hopkins Prize, Cambridge Medal and Prize, Society Francaise de Physique, 1974; Nobel Prize for Physics, 1974; Hughes Medal, Royal Society, 1977; Vainu Bappu Prize, Indian National Science Academy, 1998. Memberships: Foreign Member, American Academy of Arts and Sciences, 1970; Member, Belgian Royal Academy of Arts and Sciences, 1989; Member, Emeritus Academia Europea, 1996; Foreign Fellow, Indian National Science Academy; 6 Honorary ScD. Address: Cavendish Laboratory, Madingley Road, Cambridge, CB3 7NQ, England.

HEWITT Patricia Hope, b. 2 December 1948. Politician. m. William Birtles, 1981, 1 son, 1 daughter. Education: Cambridge University. Appointments: Public Relations Officer, Age Concern, 1971-73; Women's Rights Officer, 1973-74, General Secretary, 1974-83, National Council for Civil Liberties (now Liberty); Labour Party candidate, Leicester East general election, 1983; Press and Broadcasting Secretary to Leader of Opposition, 1983-88; Policy Co-ordinator, 1988-89;

Senior Research Fellow, 1989, Deputy Director, 1989-94, Institute for Public Policy Research; Visiting Fellow, Nuffield College, Oxford, 1992-; Head, then Director of Research, Andersen Consulting (now Accenture), 1994-97; Labour MP for Leicester West, 1997-; Member, Select Committee on Social Security, 1997-98; Economic Secretary to the Treasury, 1998-99; Minister of State, Department of Trade and Industry, 1999-2001; Secretary of State for Trade and Industry, 2001-05; Minister for Women, 2001-05; Secretary of State for Health, 2005-07. Publications: Civil Liberties, the NCCL Guide, 1977; The Privacy Report, 1977; Your Rights at Work, 1981; The Abuse of Power, 1981; Your Second Baby, 1990; About Time: The Revolution in Work and Family Life, 1993; Pebbles in the Sand, 1998; Unfinished Business, 2004. Honours: Hon Fellow, London Business School, 2004. Address: Department of Health, Richmond House, 79 Whitehall, London SW1A 2NS, England. Website: www.doh.gov.uk

HIBBARD B Pearl, b. 4 January 1940, Pittsfield, Massachusetts, USA. Psychotherapist. m. John L Laughlin, 2 sons. Education: PhD, 1997. Appointments: Partner, Living Toward Wholeness; Psychotherapist. Publications: Quantum Physics and Psychospiritual Healing. Honours: Listed in international biographical dictionaries. Memberships: American Psychotherapy Association; American Counseling Association; National Board of Addiction Examiners; American College of Professional Mental Health Practitioners; Academy of Domestic Violence Counselors. Address: 9918 Locust Street, Glenn Dale, MD 20769, USA. E-mail: dr.pearl@verizon.net

HIBBERD Alan Ronald, b. 25 October 1931, Bendigo, Australia. Clinical Ecologist; Toxicologist. m. (1) Doreen Imilda Collier, 2 sons, 2 daughters, (2) Lois Stratton. Education: Ridley College, Melbourne; PhC, Victorian College of Pharmacy; DCC, PhD, Chelsea College, University of London. Appointments: Community Pharmacy Practice, Melbourne, 1953-73; Director: ARH Pharmaceuticals, 1959-74, Pressels Laboratories, 1959-74; Part-time Demonstrator, Practical Pharmaceutics, Victorian College of Pharmacy, 1961-64; Lecturer to Postgraduate Students in Pharmacology and Therapeutics and Consultant in Dental Therapeutics and Prescribing, Victorian Branch, Australian Dental Association, 1966-74; In Charge of Drug Information Department and Ward Pharmacy Services, Hackney Hospital, London, 1975; Research Fellow, Pharmacy Department, Chelsea College, University of London, 1976-79; Lecturer, School of Pharmacy, University of London, 1980-81; Tutor in Clinical Pharmacy, Northwick Park Hospital, Harrow, 1980-81; First Course Organiser and Supervisor MSc Course in Clinical Pharmacy, University of London, 1980-81; Director, Hibbro Research, Hereford, 1981-84; Private Practice in Clinical Ecology, London, 1985-; Consultant, Clinical Pharmacology and Toxicology, Biocare Ltd, 1989-; Consultant in Clinical Biochemistry/Pharmacology, Society for Promotion of Nutritional Therapy (UK), 1992-97; Scientific Adviser to Register of Nutritional Therapists (UK), 1993-. Publications: Author of numerous articles and scientific papers on drug metabolism and relating to specialist field; Contributor to numerous learned publications. Memberships: Vice-president, International Academy of Oral Medicine and Toxicology (UK), 1994; Fellow (by examination), Pharmaceutical Society of Victoria, 1961; Royal Society of Victoria, 1968; British Dental Society for Clinical Nutrition, 1985; Nutrition Association, 1987; Environmental Dental Association, USA, 1991; British Society for Allergy, Environmental and Nutritional Medicine, 1993; FRSH, 1971; MRPharmS, 1974; Life Fellow, Pharmaceutical Society of Australia, 1991;

British Association for Nutritional Therapy, 2001; Fellow, The Royal Society of Medicine, 2003; The British Society for Ecological Medicine, 2005. Address: Bayswater Clinic, 25B Clanricarde Gardens, London W2 4JL, England.

HIBBERT Christopher, b. 5 March 1924, Enderby, Leicestershire, England. Author. m. Susan Piggford, 1948, 2 sons, 1 daughter. Education: MA, Oriel College, Oxford. Appointments: Served in Italy, 1944-45; Captain, London Irish Rifles; Military Cross; Partner, firm of land agents, auctioneers and surveyors, 1948-59. Publications: The Road to Tyburn, 1957; King Mob, 1958; Wolfe at Quebec, 1959; The Destruction of Lord Raglan, 1961; Corunna, 1961; Benito Mussolini, 1962; The Battle of Arnhem, 1962; The Roots of Evil, 1963; The Court at Windsor, 1964; Agincourt, 1964; The Wheatley Diary (editor), 1964; Garibaldi and His Enemies, 1965; The Making of Charles Dickens, 1967; Waterloo: Napoleon's Last Campaign (editor), 1967; An American in Regency England: The Journal of Louis Simond (editor), 1968; Charles I, 1968; The Grand Tour, 1969; London: Biography of a City, 1969; The Search for King Arthur, 1970; Anzio: The Bid for Rome, 1970; The Dragon Wakes: China and the West, 1793-1911, 1970; The Personal History of Samuel Johnson, 1971; George IV, Prince of Wales 1762-1811, 1972; George IV, Regent and King 1812-1830, 1973; The Rise and Fall of the House of Medici, 1974; Edward VII: A Portrait, 1976; The Great Mutiny: India, 1857, 1978; The French Revolution, 1981; Africa Explored: Europeans in the Dark Continent, 1796-1889, 1982; The London Encyclopaedia (editor), 1983; Queen Victoria in Her Letters and Journals, 1984; Rome: The Biography of a City, 1985; Cities and Civilizations, 1985; The English: A Social History, 1987; Venice: Biography of a City, 1988; The Encyclopaedia of Oxford (editor), 1988; Redcoats and Rebels: The War for America 1760-1781, 1990; The Virgin Queen: The Personal History of Elizabeth I, 1990; Captain Gronow: His Reminiscences of Regency and Victorian Life (editor), 1991; Cavaliers and Roundheads: The English at War 1642-1649, 1993; Florence: Biography of a City, 1993; Nelson: A Personal History, 1994; Wellington: A Personal History, 1997; George III: A Personal History, 1998; Queen Victoria: A Personal History, 2000; The Marlboroughs: John and Sarah Churchill, 2001; Napoleon: His Wives and Women, 2002; Disraeli: A Personal History, 2004. Honours: Heinemann Award for Literature, 1962; McColvin Medal, 1989; Honorary DLitt, Leicester University, 1996. Address: Albion Place, 6 West Street, Henley-on-Thames, Oxfordshire RG9 2DT, England.

HICK Graeme Ashley, b. 23 May 1966, Salisbury, Zimbabwe. Cricketer. Appointments: Right-Hand Batsman, Off-Break Bowler, Slip Fielder; Teams: Zimbabwe, 1983-86, Worcestershire, 1984-, Northern Districts, 1987-89, Queensland, 1990-91; Scored 100 aged 6 years; Youngest player to appear in 1983 World Cup and youngest to represent Zimbabwe; 65 tests for England, 1991-97, scoring 3,383 runs (average 31.32), including 6 hundreds; Scored 30,189 1st class runs (average 55.2), with 104 hundreds (including 9 doubles, 1 triple, 1 quadruple (405 not out) to 1 April 1999); Youngest to score 2,000 1st class runs in a season, 1986; Scored 1,019 runs before June 1988, including a record 410 runs in April; Fewest innings for 10,000 runs in county cricket (179); Youngest (24) to score 50 1st class hundreds; Toured Australia, 1994-95; 120 limited-overs ints for 3,846 runs (average 37.33) by December 2002; Scored 315 not out v Durham, June 2002- (highest championship innings of the season); Played 65 tests and 120 one-day Internationals for England. Publication: My Early Life (autobiography), 1992. Honours: Wisden Cricketer of the Year, 1987. Membership: England World Cup Squad, 1996. Address: c/o Worcestershire County Cricket Club, New Road, Worcester WR2 4QQ, England.

HICKS Philip, b. 11 October 1928, Leamington Spa, England. Artist; Painter. m. Jill Doreen Tweed, 1 son, 1 daughter. Education: Royal Military Academy, Sandhurst; Chelsea School of Art and Royal Academy Schools, 1949-54. Career: Part-time teacher, various schools of art, London area, 1960-86; Full-time painting, over 40 solo exhibitions, UK and abroad; Work appears in many public and corporate collections, including Tate Britain, Victoria and Albert Museum, Imperial War Museum, Contemporary Art Society, Royal College of Music, Nuffield Foundation; Represented by Messum's Fine Art, Cork Street, London. Publications: Mentioned in numerous journals, magazines and newspapers. Honours: British Council Award, 1977. Memberships: Royal Overseas League, St James's, London; Chelsea Arts Club, London; Past Chairman and Vice President, The Artists General Benevolent Institution. Address: Radcot House, Buckland Road, Bampton, Oxfordshire OX18 2AA, England.

HIDDLESTON James Andrew, b. 20 October 1935, Edinburgh, Scotland. Professor of French. Widower, 2 daughters. Education: MA, 1957, PhD, 1961, Edinburgh University; D Litt (Oxon), 2006. Appointments: Lecturer in French, University of Leeds, 1960-66; Fellow, Exeter College, Oxford, 1966-, Professor of French, University of Oxford, 1996-2003; Retired, 2003. Publications: Books: L'Univers de Jules Supervielle, 1965; Malraux: "La Condition humaine", 1973; Poems: Jules Laforgue, edition with introduction and notes, 1975; Essai sur Laforgue et les derniers vers, suivi de Laforgue et Baudelaire, 1980; Baudelaire and "Le Spleen de Paris", 1987, Japanese translation, 1989; Laforgue aujourd'hui (contributing editor), 1988; Collaboration with Michel Collot in edition of Jules Supervielle, Oeuvres poétiques complètes, 1996; Baudelaire and the Art of Memory, 1999; Victor Hugo, romancier de l'abîme (contributing editor), 2002; A wide variety of articles. Honour: Officier de l'ordre des arts et des lettres. Memberships: Society of French Studies; Nineteenth-Century French Studies. Address: 16 Dean Terrace, Edinburgh EH4 1NL, Scotland. E-mail: james.hiddleston@exeter.ox.ac.uk

HIGGINBOTHAM Prieur Jay, b. 16 July 1937, Pascagoula, Mississippi, USA. Author; Archivist. m. Alice Louisa Martin, 27 June 1970, 2 sons, 1 daughter. Education: BA, University Mississippi, 1961; Graduate study, City College of New York; American University, Washington DC. Appointments: Assistant Clerk, MS House of Representatives, 1955-58; Teacher, Mobile City Public Schools, 1962-73; Head, Local History Department, 1973-83; Director, Mobile Municipal Archives, 1983-. Publications include: Old Mobile, 1977; Fast Train Russia, 1983; Autumn in Petrisheva, 1987; Man, Nature and the Infinite, 1998; Mauvila, 2000; Alma, 2002; One Man in the Universe, 2003; Narrow is the Way, 2004. Honours: Gilbert Chinard Prize, 1978; Alabama Library Literature Award, 1979; Mississippi Historical Society Award, 1979; Louisiana Historical Society Award, 1979; Elizabeth Gould Award, 1980. Alabama Library Association, Humanitarian Award, 1999. Listed in: Several Who's Who Publications. Memberships: Society Mobile-Rostov-on-Don; Society Mobile-La Habana; President, Friends of Freedom; Founder and First President, The Mobile Tricentennial, Inc. Address: 60 North Monterey Street, Mobile, AL 36604, USA.

HIGGS Peter Ware, b. 29 May 1929, Newcastle upon Tyne, England. University Teacher (retired). m. JoAnn Williamson, 2 sons. Education: Halesowen Grammar School, 1940-41;

Cotham Grammar School, Bristol, 1941-46; City of London School, 1946-47; BSc, 1950, MSc, 1951, PhD, 1954, King's College London. Appointments: Senior Student, Royal Commission for the Exhibition of 1851, King's College London, 1953-54, University of Edinburgh, 1954-55; Senior Research Fellow, University of Edinburgh, 1955-56; ICI Fellow, University of London, 1956-58; Lecturer in Mathematics, University College London, 1959-60; Sabbatical Leave, University of North Carolina, USA, 1965-66; Lecturer in Mathematical Physics, 1960-70, Reader in Mathematical Physics, 1970-80, Professor of Theoretical Physics, 1980-96, University of Edinburgh. Publications: Papers in professional journals. Honours: Hughes Medal, Royal Society, 1981; Rutherford Medal, Institute of Physics, 1984; Scottish Science Award, Saltire Society, 1990; James Scott Prize Lectureship, Royal Society of Edinburgh, 1993; Paul Dirac Medal & Prize, Institute of Physics, 1994; Hon DSc, Bristol, 1997; High Energy & Particle Physics Prize, European Physical Society, 1997; Hon DSc, Edinburgh, 1998; Honorary Fellow, Institute of Physics, 1998; Fellow, King's College London, 1998; Royal Medal, Royal Society of Edinburgh, 2000; Hon DSc, Glasgow, 2002; Wolf Prize in Physics, 2004. Memberships: Fellow, Royal Society of Edinburgh, 1974; Fellow, Royal Society, 1983. Address: 2 Darnaway Street, Edinburgh EH3 6BG, Scotland.

HIGHMORE Freddie, b. 14 February 1992, London, England. Actor. Education: Currently studying for GCSE's. Appointments: Lead roles in the following, Finding Neverland, 2004; Two Brothers, 2004; Five Children and IT, 2004; Charlie and the Chocolate Factory, 2005; A Good Year, 2006; Arthur and the Invisibles, 2006; The Golden Compass (voice), 2007; Spiderwick Chronicles, 2008; August Rush, 2008; Honours: BFCAA, Best Young Actor, 2005, 2006; Empire Award, Best Newcomer, 2005; Golden Satellite Award, Outstanding New Talent, 2005; Young Artist Award, Best Leading Young Actor, 2005; Nominated for Screen Actors Guild, Outstanding Supportive Male Actor and Outstanding Cast, 2005. Membership: Screen Actors Guild. Address: C/o Artists Rights Group Limited, 4 Great Portland Street, London W1W 8PA, England.

HIGSON Philip (Willoughby-), b. 21 February 1933, Newcastle-under-Lyme, Staffordshire, England. Poet; Translator; Editor; Historian; Art Historian; Playwright. Education: BA, Honours, and Charles Beard Research Studentship in Medieval History, 1956, MA, 1959, Research Fellowship in Modern History, 1963, PhD, 1971, Liverpool University; PGCE, Keele University, 1972. Appointments: Lecturer, Senior Lecturer in History, 1972-89, Visiting Lecturer, 1989-90, the now University of Chester; Chairman, President, Anthology Editor, Chester Poets, 1974-92; President, The Baudelaire Society, Chester and Paris, 1992-. Publications: The Bizarre Barons of Rivington, 1965; The Riposte and Other Poems, 1971; A Warning to Europe: The Testimony of Limouse (co-author), 1992; The Complete Poems of Baudelaire with Selected Illustrations by Limouse (editor and principal translator), 1992; Limouse Nudes, 1994; Childhood in Wartime Keele: Poems of Reminiscence, 1995; Poems on the Dee, 1997; Inner City Love-Revolt: Footage from a Fifties Affair, 2000; A Poet's Pilgrimage: The Shaping of a Creative Life, 2000; The Jewelled Nude: A Play about Baudelaire and Queen Pomaré, 2002; Sonnets to My Goddess in This Life and The Next: The Prize-winning Volume Expanded, 2002; Poems of Sauce and Satire: A Humorous Selection, 2002; Maurice Rollinat: A Hundred Poems from Les Névroses (translated and introduced), 2003; Ut Pictura Poesis: Pictorial Poems, 2004; Manichaean Contrasts: a Late

Selection of Poetry, 2004; Souvenir of a Triple Launch: play, translations, sonnets, 2004; D'Annunzio: selected poems translated and introduced, 2005; Baudelaire and Limouse: Their Ennobling Mission for Art, 2006; The Singular Lords Willoughby: a Lancashire Family Saga, 2007; Contributions: historical articles to Oxford DNB and to journals including: Antiquaries Journal, Genealogists' Magazine, Coat of Arms, Northern History, 2 Lancashire and Cheshire journals; Poems to: Making Love: the Picador Book of Erotic Verse, 1978; Rhyme Revival, 1982; Poets England: Staffordshire, 1987; Red Candle Treasury, 1998 and to journals including: Critical Quarterly, Collegian, Chester Poets Anthologies, Candelabrum, The Eclectic Muse, Mandrake Poetry Review, Cadmium Blue Literary Journal, Lexikon, Rebirth, Solar Flame, Romantic Renaissance, Rubies in the Darkness, Metverse Muse, Poet Tree, A Bard Hair Day, Quantum Leap; Contemporary Rhyme; Bulletin de la Société "Les Amis de Maurice Rollinat". Honours: 1st Prize for an Established Poet, The Eclectic Muse, Vancouver, 1990; David St John Thomas Poetry Publication Prize, 1996; Prize-winner, Lexikon Poetry Competition, 1996; 1st Prize (Gold Award) Rubies in the Darkness Poetry Competition, 2003. Memberships: FSA; FRHistS; FRSA; Society of Authors. Address: 1 Westlands Avenue, Newcastle-under-Lyme, Staffordshire, ST5 2PU, England.

HIGUCHI Takayoshi, b. 29 October 1927, Agematsu, Nagano, Japan. Professor Emeritus. m. Sachiko, 1 daughter. Education: BSc, Nagoya University, 1950; D Agric Science, University of Tokyo, 1959; Dr honoris causa, University of Science, Technology & Medicine, Grenoble, France, 1987. Appointments: Instructor, 1950-53, Lecturer, 1953-59, Associate Professor, 1960-67, Professor, 1967-68, Faculty of Agriculture, Gifu University, Japan; Professor, 1968-91, Director, 1978-84, 1988-91, Wood Research Institute, Professor Emeritus, 1991-, Kyoto University, Japan; Professor, Nihon University, College of Agriculture and Veterinary Medicine, Tokyo, 1991-94; Research Fellow, Prairie Regional Laboratory, Saskatoon, Canada, 1960-62; Associate Professor, Faculty of Science, Grenoble University, France, 1963-64; Concurrent Professor, Beijing Institute of Forestry, and Nanjing Institute of Forestry, People's Republic of China, 1985-86. Publications: Biosynthesis and Biodegradation of Wood Components, Academic Press, 1985; Biochemistry and Molecular Biology of Wood, Springer, 1997; Over 300 scientific papers. Honours: Japan Forestry Prize, 1959; Japan TAPPI Prize, 1959; Japan Forestry Science & Technology Prize, 1968; Japan Agricultural Science Prize, 1985; Anselme Payen Award, American Chemical Society, 1987; International Academy of Wood Science Award, 1988; Purple Ribbon Medal for outstanding contribution, 1990; Foreign Associate, US National Academy of Science, 1991; Fujiwara Award, 1992; The Second Order of the Sacred Treasure, 2000; Japan Academy Award, 2001. Memberships: Editorial Board Member, Cellulose Chemistry and Technology, Romania; Editorial Advisory Board Member, Journal of Wood Chemistry and Technology, USA; Holzforschung, Federal Republic of Germany. Address: Fushimiku, Momoyamacho, Yosai 22-8, Kyoto-shi 612-8016, Japan.

HILFIGER Tommy, b. 24 March 1951, Elmira, New York, USA. Men's Fashion Designer. m. Susie 1980-2000 (divorced), 4 children. Appointments: Opened 1st store, People's Place, Elmira, 1969; Owned 10 clothes shops, New York State, 1978; Full-time Designer, 1979; Launched own sportswear label, 1984; Acquired fashion business from Mohan Muranji; Founder, Tommy Hilfiger Corporation, 1989. Honours include: Winner, From the Catwalk to the Sidewalk

Award, VH-1 Fashion and Music Awards, 1995; Menswear Designer of the Year, Council of Fashion Designers of America, 1995. Memberships: Board, Fresh Air Fund, Race to Erase Multiple Sclerosis.

HILL (Anthony) Edward, b. 30 December 1959, Coventry, England. Oceanographer. m. Jacqueline Patricia Caukwell, 2 sons. Education: BSc, 1st Class Special Honours, Applied Mathematics, University of Sheffield, 1981; MSc, Physical Oceanography, 1983, PhD, Oceanography, 1987, University of Wales, Bangor (formerly University College of North Wales, Bangor). Appointments: Lecturer, 1986-95, Senior Lecturer, 1995-99, University of Wales, Bangor; Director, Proudman Oceanographic Laboratory, Bidston (relocated to Liverpool, 2004), University of Earth Sciences, University of Liverpool, 1999-2005; Director National Oceanography Centre, Southampton (formerly Southampton Oceanography Centre) (joint centre Natural Environment Research Council and the University of Southampton), Professor of Oceanography, University of Southampton, 2005-. Publications: Numerous articles in learned journals mostly relating to the physical oceanography of continental shelf seas. Honours: Listed in national biographical dictionaries. Memberships: Challenger Society for Marine Science; Oceanography Society; Fellow of the Institute of Marine Engineering Science and Technology (FIMarEST) 2006-. Address: National Oceanography Centre, Southampton, University of Southampton, Waterfront Campus, Empress Dock, Southampton, SO14 3ZH, England.

HILL Christina Bernadette Thérèse, b. England. Deputy Lieutenant, Royal County of Berkshire; Environmental and Educational Consultant. Education: BA (Hons), University of Wales; MA, PhD, University of Birmingham. Appointments: Field Officer, Midlands Director, Director of Development and Training, Head of Research and Legislation, Tidy Britain Group, 1977-88; National Director, School and Group Travel Association (SAGTA), 1988-94; Director of Public Affairs, Aviation Environment Federation and Trust, 1988-89; Chair, YWCA Steering Group for Major Appeal Committee, Open the Door Appeal Committee and Special Events Committee, 1993-96; General Secretary, UK Environmental Law Association, 1996-2006; General Commissioner of Income Tax, 1998-; Chairman, Berkshire General Commissioners of Income Tax, 2004-; Member, Lord Chancellor's Advisory Committee on JPs, 1998-; Non-Executive Director, Berkshire Healthcare NHS Trust, 2001-07; Lead Governor, Berkshire Healthcare NHS Foundation Trust, 2007-. Publications: Litter Law - Is It Working? 1988; Editor: School and Group Travel Association (SAGTA) Conference Papers: Safety During School Travel, 1989; Editor, SAGTA Education Reform Act 1988: Charging for School Activities, 1989; Editor, SAGTA Safety Rules, 1990 and SAGTA Code of Conduct, 1990; Editor, SAGTA Conference Papers, Safety and Good Practice During School and Group Travel, 1991; Editor SAGTA Conference Papers, EU Directive on Package Travel, 1994; Numerous articles in environmental and educational press. Memberships: Fellow, Royal Geographical Society, 1989-; Fellow, Royal Society of Arts, 1989-; Affiliate Member, Institute of Wastes Management, 1994-; Associate Member, Chartered Institution of Environmental Health, 1988-; Fellow Institute of Personnel and Development, 1985-96. Address: Honeycroft House, Pangbourne Road, Upper Basildon, Berkshire RG8 8LP, England.

HILL Colin Arnold Clifford, b. 13 February 1929, Cambridge, England. Clerk in Holy Orders. m. (1) Shirley Randall, deceased 1963, (2) Irene Florence Chamberlain, 1 son, 1 stepson. Education: Bristol University, 1955; Ripon

Hall Theological College, Oxford, 1957; M Phil, University of Wales, Bangor, 2003; Ordained, Sheffield Cathedral, 1957. Appointments: Curate, Rotherham Parish Church, 1957; Vicar of Brightside, 1961; Rector of Easthampstead, 1964; Chaplain, RAF Staff College, Bracknell Berkshire, 1968-73; Vicar of Croydon, 1973-94; Honorary Canon, Canterbury Cathedral, Canterbury, 1974; Honorary Canon, Southwark Cathedral, 1984; Chaplain to The Queen, 1990-99. Publication: Unpublished thesis: Archbishop John Whitgift: Free School and Hospital 1596-1604. Honour: OBE, 1995. Memberships: General Synod and Convocation of Canterbury, 1969-73, 1984-86; Leander Club. Address: Silver Birches, Preston Crowmarsh, Wallingford, Oxfordshire OX10 6SL, England. E-mail: colinatSB@clara.co.uk

HILL Damon Graham Devereux, b. 17 September 1960, Hamstead, London, England. Motor Racing Driver. m. Georgie Hill, 1988, 2 sons, 2 daughters. Appointments: Began motorcycle racing, 1979; Driver, Canon Williams Team, 1993; Driver, Rothmans Williams Renault Team, 1994-96; Driver, Arrows Yamaha Team, 1997; Benson and Hedges Jordan Team, 1998-99. Honours: First motor racing victory in Formula Ford 1600, Brands Hatch, 1984; First Formula One Grand Prix, Silverstone, 1992; Winner, Hungarian Grand Prix, 1993; Winner, Belgian and Italian Grand Prix, 1993, 1994; 3rd Place, Drivers' World Championship, 1993; Winner, Spanish Grand Prix, Barcelona, 1994; Winner, British Grand Prix , Silverstone, 1994; Winner, Portuguese Grand Prix, 1994; Winner, Japanese Grand Prix, 1994, 1996; French Grand Prix, 1996; Spanish Grand Prix, 1995, 1996; San Marino Grand Prix, 1995, 1996; Hungarian Grand Prix, 1995; Brazilian Grand Prix, 1996; German Grand Prix, 1996; Australian Grand Prix, 1995, 1996; Canadian Grand Prix, 1998; Belgian Grand Prix, 1998; 2nd place, Drivers' World Championship, 1994-95; World Champion, 1996; British Competition Driver of the Year, Autosport Awards, 1995; 122 Grand Prix starts; 22 wins; 20 pole positions; 19 fastest laps; 42 podium finishes; numerous racing and sports personality awards; OBE; President, British Racing Driver's Club, 2006. Publications: Damon Hill Grand Prix Year, 1994; Damon Hill: My Championship Year, 1996; F1 Through the Eyes of Damon Hill.

HILL Debora Elizabeth, b. 10 July 1961, San Francisco, California, USA. Author; Journalist; Screenwriter. Education: BA, Journalism/Creative Writing, 1983; Graduate work in Ancient History, 1983-85. Appointments: Host, Rock Journal, television show, Viacom Cablevision, 1981; Journalist, national and international newspapers, 1990-2000; Worked on concept development team for Star Trek: Deep Space Nine and Star Trek: Voyager (on Alan Seligman's team), 1997-98; Began work as an online journalist, 1999; Northern California correspondent for Neighborhood America, 2000-01; Feature columnist on Elder Care for Access Life, 2000-01; Member, Board of United Film Productions International, 2005-06; Contracted to Vision Angels Film Financing, 2007. Publications: Non-fiction: The San Francisco Rock Experience, 1979; CUTS From a San Francisco Rock Journal, 1982; PUNK RETRO: The Music of the No-Future Generation, 1988; Novels: A Ghost Among Us, 2002; Jerome's Quest, 2003; A Wizard by Any Other Name, 2005; with Sandra Brandenburg: The Land of the Wand, 2006; The Crystal Chalice, 2007; The Sword and the Scabbard, 2008; Included in poetry anthologies: Between Darkness and Light, 2000; The Best Poets of 2000, 2001, 2002, 2003, 2004 and 2006; Eyes of the World, 2001; The Silence Within, 2002; Hidden Frontiers, 2002; Labours of Love, UK, 2005; The International Who's Who of Poetry, 2004 and 2005;

Co-writer, The Lost Myths Ink Film Fund, 2007. Honours: Included in Who's Who of American Women; Who's Who in the US; Who's Who in the World; Who's Who in the West; White House Millennium Time Capsule. Memberships: Film Gravity; Associated Content. Address: PO Box 1181, Santa Rosa, CA 95404, USA. E-mail: debhill@att.net

HILL Jennifer Louise, b. 10 May 1969, Leicester, England. University Lecturer; Military Officer (retired). Education: BA Honours, Geography, 1990, MA, Geography, 1996, St Anne's College, University of Oxford; PhD, Geography, University of Wales Swansea, 1995; Post Graduate Certificate (Teaching & Learning) in Higher Education, 2005, Faculty of Education, University of the West of England Bristol, 2005. Appointments: Research Assistant, Department of Geography, Oxford University, 1990-91; Lieutenant, Royal Monmouthshire Royal Engineers (Militia), 1994-2006; Lecturer, Department of Geography, University of Worcester, 1995-96; Tutor, Department of Geography, University of Exeter, 1996-97; Lecturer, 1997-2001, Senior Lecturer, 2001-, School of Geography & Environmental Management, UWE, Bristol. Publications: Numerous articles in professional journals; Contributions to edited books, book chapters and conference presentations. Honours: Queen's Golden Jubilee Medal; Iraq Medal; Volunteer Reserves Services Medal; TA Cane of Honour, Royal Military Academy, Sandhurst, 1997. Memberships: Fellow, Higher Education Academy; Chartered Geographer; Fellow, Royal Geographical Society; Member, British Ecological Society; Member, Association for Tropical Biology and Conservation. Address: Department of Geography & Environmental Management, University of the West of England (UWE), Bristol, Frenchay Campus, Bristol BS16 1QY, England. E-mail: jennifer.hill@uwe.ac.uk

HILL Shaun Donovan, b. 11 April 1947, London, England. Restaurateur. m. Anja, 1 son, 2 daughters. Education: St Marylebone Grammar School; The London Oratory. Appointments: Chef, Capital Hotel, Knightsbridge, London; Chef, Lygon Arms, Broadway, Worcester; Owner, Hill's Restaurant, Stratford upon Avon; Chef, Gidleigh Park, Chagford, Devon; Owner, Merchant House, Ludlow, Shropshire; Owner, The Glasshouse, Worcester. Publications: Gidleigh Park Cookery Book, 1990; Quick & Easy Vegetables, 1993; Archestratus – Life of Luxury (translation and commentary), 1994; Cooking at the Merchant House, 2000; How to Cook Better, 2004; Food in the Ancient World, 2006. Honours: Egon Ronay Guide Chef of the Year, 1993; Caterer & Hotelkeeper Chef Award, 1993; Caterer & Hotelkeeper Independent Restaurateur Award, 2001; A A Guide, Chef's Chef Award, 2003; Entrepreneur Award, Carlton Television Midlander of the Year 2004. Memberships: Research Fellow, Department of Classics, Exeter University; Consultant to British Airways and Fortnum & Mason. Address: 24 Droitwich Road, Worcester, WR3 7HL, England. E-mail: shaunhill@merchanthouse.co.uk

HILL Sonia Geraldine, b. 26 September 1939, London, England. Artist in Oils. Partner, G H Clarke, deceased 1997. Education: Maidenhead Art College, Berkshire, England, 1955-57; Studied perspective composition with A Hayward, Zambia, 1957-62. Career: Architectural Assistant, contract work, London, 1982-1990; Architectural Assistant, Victoria, London, 1991; Exhibitions: Royal Academy, 1993, 2 oil paintings sold and 3 further works accepted by the selection committee; Royal Academy, 2000, oil painting of Quentin Crisp sold, now hanging in Vancouver; Christies, 2001-2002, 2003, 3 works in oils sold (Art for Life); Exhibitions at Richmond and Paris. Publication: Painting "Jack the Lad"

illustrated in Royal Academy Magazine, 1993. Honour: Fine Art, Maidenhead College, 1957; Who's Who Book of Art, 1993-2007. Memberships: Friend: Royal Academy, London, 1993-2007, The Royal Overseas League, London, 2004, The Mall Galleries, London, 2007. Address: 6a Warfield Road, Hampton TW12 2AY, England.

HILLION Pierre, b. 31 January 1926, Saint-Brieuc, France. Senior Physicist. m. Jeanne Garde, deceased, 2 sons, 2 daughters. Education: Engineer, Ecole Supérieure d'Electricité, 1952; Licencié ès Sciences, 1955; Docteur ès Sciences, 1957. Appointments: Engineer, Le Materiel Electrique S-W, 1950-55; Mathematical Physicist, Army Technical Section, 1955-64; Head, Mathematical Physics Department, Laboratoire Central de l'Armement, 1964-83; Maître de Conférences, Ecole Nationale Supérieure des Techniques Avancées, 1976-88; Scientific Adviser, Centre d'Analyse de Défense, 1983-91; Senior Physicist, Institut Henri Poincaré, 1991-. Publications: About 200 papers on mathematical physics and electromagnetism in various scientific journals and several books, including: Relativité et Quanta, 1968; Essay on formal aspect of electromagnetism, 1993; Electromagnetic Waves, PIER 18, 1998. Honours: Merit for Research and Invention; Officier, Palmes Académiques; Chevalier, Ordre National du Mérite; Chevalier, Légion d'Honneur. Memberships: Société Mathématique de France; Société Internationale de Physique Mathématique; Member, New York Academy of Sciences; Académie d'Electromagnetisme. Address: 86 bis, Route de Croissy, 78110 Le Vésinet, France.

HILMOLA Olli-Pekka Kristian, b. 15 February 1975, Seinäjoki, Finland. Researcher. Education: MSc, 1998, DSc, 2001, Economics and Business Administration, University of Vaasa, Finland. Appointments: Assistant Professor, International Business (Logistics), 2002-03, Professor, Logistics, 2003-04, Part time Research Fellow of Logistics, 2004-05, Department of Marketing, Turku School of Economics and Business Administration, Turku, Finland; Part time Supply Chain Manager, Rotatek Finland, Lappeenranta, Finland, 2004-05; Professor of Logistics, Department of Industrial Engineering and Management, Lappeenranta University of Technology, 2005-; Visiting Professor of Logistics, University of Skövde, Sweden, 2006-. Publications: 40 articles in professional scientific journals. Honours: Listed in national and international biographical directories. Memberships: Editorial board member: International Journal of Industrial Management and Data Systems; International Journal of Integrated Supply Management; International Journal of Services and Operations Management; International Journal of Services and Standards; Baltic Journal of Management; World Review of Intermodal Transportation Research. Address: Prikaatintie 9, FIN-45100, Kouvola, Finland.

HIMMELFARB Gertrude, b. 8 August 1922, New York, USA. Professor of History Emerita; Writer. m. Irving Kristol, 18 January 1942, 1 son, 1 daughter. Education: Jewish Theological Seminary, 1939-42; BA, Brooklyn College, 1942; MA, 1944, PhD, 1950, University of Chicago; Girton College, Cambridge, 1946-47. Appointments: Professor, 1965-78, Distinguished Professor of History, 1978-88, Professor Emerita, 1988-, Graduate School of the City University of New York. Publications: Lord Acton: A Study in Conscience and Politics, 1952; Darwin and the Darwinian Revolution, 1959, revised edition, 1968; Victorian Minds: Essays on Nineteenth Century Intellectuals, 1968; On Liberty and Liberalism: The Case of John Stuart Mill, 1974; The Idea of Poverty: England in the Industrial Age, 1984; Marriage and

Morals Among the Victorians and Other Essays, 1986; The New History and the Old, 1987; Poverty and Compassion: The Moral Imagination of the Late Victorians, 1991; On Looking Into the Abyss: Untimely Thoughts on Culture and Society, 1994; The De-Moralization of Society: From Victorian Virtues to Modern Values, 1995; One Nation, Two Cultures, 1999; The Roads to Modernity: The British, French and American Enlightenments, 2004; The Moral Imagination: From Edmund Burke to Lionel Trilling, 2006; Contributions to: Scholarly books and journals. Honours: American Association of University Women Fellowship, 1951-52; American Philosophical Society Fellowship, 1953-54; Guggenheim Fellowships, 1955-56, 1957-58; National Endowment for the Humanities Senior Fellowship, 1968-69; American Council of Learned Societies Fellowship, 1972-73; Phi Beta Kappa Visiting Scholarship, 1972-73; Woodrow Wilson Center Fellowship, 1976-77; Rockefeller Humanities Fellowship, 1980-81; Jefferson Lectureship, National Endowment for the Humanities, 1991; Templeton Foundation Award, 1997; Professional Achievement Citation, University of Chicago Alumni Association, 1998; National Humanities Medal, 2004. Memberships: American Academy of Arts and Sciences; American Historical Association; American Philosophical Society; British Academy, fellow; Royal Historical Society, fellow; Society of American Historians. Address: 2510 Virginia Avenue, NW, Washington, DC 20037, USA.

HINDE Robert Aubrey, b. 26 October 1923, Norwich, England. Biologist; Psychologist. m. (1) Hester Cecily Coutts, dissolved 1971, 2 sons, 2 daughters, (2) Joan Stevenson, 2 daughters. Education: BA, 1948, St John's College, University of Cambridge; BSc, London University, 1948; DPhil, Oxford University, 1950; ScD, University of Cambridge, 1961. Appointments: RAF Pilot, Coastal Command, 1940-45; Research Assistant, Edward Grey Institute, Oxford University, 1948-50; Curator, Ornithological Field Station, University of Cambridge, 1950-64; Research Fellow, 1951-54, Steward, 1956-58, Fellow, 1958-89, 1994-, Tutor, 1958-63, St John's College, Cambridge; Royal Society Research Professor, 1963-89; Honorary Director, Medical Research Council Unit on the Development and Integration of Behaviour, 1970-89; Master, St John's College, Cambridge, 1989-94; Chair, British Pugwash Group, 2001; President, Movement for the Abolition of War, 2005. Publications: Over 300 journal articles and book chapters; 8 books. Honours: Fellow, Royal Society; Foreign Honorary Member, American Academy of Arts & Science; Honorary Foreign Associate, US National Academy of Sciences; Honorary Fellow, Royal College of Psychiatry; Zoological Society's Scientific Medal; Osman Hill Medal; Leonard Cammer Award; Albert Einstein Award for Psychiatry; Commander of the British Empire; Huxley Medal; Distinguished Scientific Contribution Award, Society for Research in Child Development; Frink Medal; Distinguished Career Award; G Stanley Hall Medal; Royal Society Medal; Association for the Study of Animal Behaviour Society's Medal; Honorary DSc, Oxford University; Numerous honorary doctorates, memberships and fellowships committees. Memberships: British Psychological Society; British Trust for Ornithology; Chair, British Pugwash Group; St John's College; Movement for the Abolition of War. Address: St John's College, Cambridge, CB2 1TP, England. E-mail: rah15@hermes.cam.ac.uk

HINDIE Elif, b. 2 August 1959, Aleppo, Syria. Medical Educator; Physician; Researcher. m. Maya Khoury, 1 son, 1 daughter. Education: MD, Faculty of Medicine, Aleppo, 1981; Specialist in Endocrinology, French Board, University of Paris V, 1984; Specialist in Nuclear Medicine, French

Board, University of Paris XII, 1987; PhD in Biology and Medical Engineering, University of Paris XII, 1990. Appointments: Assistant Professor, 1989-92, Associate Professor, 1993-99, Faculty of Medicine, Paris XII, Hospital Henri Mondor; Associate Professor, Hopital Saint-Antoine, University of Paris VI, 2000-05; Medical Educator, Board of Nuclear Medicine, Saclay, 2002-; Medical Educator, Board of Endocrinology, Paris, 2003-; Associate Professor, Hôpital Saint-Louis, University of Paris VII, Saint Antoine, 2005-. Publications: Ion Microscopy: A new approach for subcellular localization of labelled molecules, 1988; Pre-operative imaging of the parathyoid glands, 1999; Non-medical exposure to radioiodines and thyroid cancer, 2002; and others. Honours: PhD Award, VIIth International Conference on Spectrometry SIMS VII, Monterey, USA, 1989; Award from Electricitie de France, 2001. Memberships: Fellow, French Society of Nuclear Medicine; French Society of Endocrinology; French Society of Microscopy; President, MEDALE. Address: Service de Médicine Nucléaire, Hôpital Saint-Louis, 1 Avenue Claude Vellefaux, 75475 Paris, France. E-mail: elif.hindie@sat.aphp.fr

HINE Patrick, b. 14 July 1932, Chandlers Ford, Hampshire, England. Air Force Officer. m. Jill Adèle Gardner, 1956, 3 sons. Career: Fighter Pilot and Member, RAF Black Arrows and Blue Diamonds Formation Aerobatic Teams, 1957-62; Commander, No 92 Squadron, 1962-64 and 17 Squadron, 1970-71; RAF Germany Harrier Force, 1974-75; Director, RAF Public Relations, 1975-77; Assistant Chief of Air Staff for Policy, 1979-83; Commander in Chief, RAF Germany and Commander, NATO's 2nd Allied Tactical Air Force, 1983-85; Vice Chief of the Defence Staff, 1985-87; Air Member for Supply and Organisation, Air Force Board, 1987-88; Air Officer Commanding in Chief, Strike Command, Commander in Chief, UK Air Forces, 1988-91; Joint Commander, British Forces in Gulf Conflict, 1990-91; with reserve force, rank of Flying Officer, 1991-; Military Adviser to British Aerospace, 1992-99. Honours: King of Arms, Order of the British Empire, 1997.

HINGIS Martina, b. 30 September 1980, Košice, Czech Republic. Tennis Player. Appointments: 1st Tennis Tournament, 1985; Winner, French Open Junior Championship, 1993, Wimbledon Junior Championship, 1994; Competed in the Italian Open, US Open, Chase Championship (New York) and Wimbledon; Won 1st Professional Tournament, Filderstadt, Germany, 1996; Winner, Australian Open, 1997 (youngest winner of a Grand Slam title in 20th Century), 1998, 1999; Beaten Finalist, Australian Open, 2000, 2001, 2002; Winner, US Open, 1997; Beaten Finalist, US Open, 1998, 1999; Wimbledon Singles Champion, 1997; Winner, Australian Open, 1998; Won US Open, 1997, beaten finalist, 1998, 1999; Wimbledon singles champion, 1997; Swiss Federation Cup Team, 1996-98; Semi-finalist, US Open, 2001; By end of 2002 had won 76 tournament titles including five Grand Slam singles and nine doubles titles; Elected to WTA Tour Players' Council, 2002; After injury returned to WTA tour, 2005. Honours: WTA Tour Most Impressive Newcomer, 1995; Most Improved Player, 1996; Player of the Year, 1997. Address: c/o AM Seidenbaum 17, 9377 Truebbach, Switzerland.

HINTON Alistair, b. Dunfermline, Scotland. Composer; Archivist. m. Terry Piers-Smith. Education: Royal College of Music, London; Composition with Humphrey Searle, Piano with Stephen Savage. Career: Numerous performances worldwide; Founder and Curator of The Sorabji Archive. Compositions include: String Quintet, 1969-77; Violin Concerto, 1980; Pansophiæ for John Ogdon (organ), 1990;

Sequentia Claviensis, 1993-94; Vocalise-Reminiscenza (piano), 1994; 5 Piano Sonatas, 1962-95; Variations for piano and orchestra, 1996; Szymanowski-Étude (18 wind instruments), 1992-96; In Solitude, In Plenitude (bass, piano), 1996; Sinfonietta, 1997; Cadenza to Medtner's Piano Concerto No 3, 1998; Conte Fantastique (euphonium, piano), 1999; Sonata for 'cello and piano, 1999, String quartet, 1999. Recordings: Variations and Fugue on a Theme of Grieg, 1970-78; Pansophiæ for John Ogdon, 1990; String Quintet, 1999. Publications: Sorabji: A Critical Celebration, 1992, reprinted, 1994. Contributions to: Grove's Dictionary of Music and Musicians; Tempo; The Organ; The Godowsky Society Newsletter; Notes (USA). Address: The Sorabji Archive, Easton Dene, Bailbrook Lane, Bath BA1 7AA, England.

HIRSCH Judd, b. 15 March 1935, New York, USA. Actor. m. Elissa 1956-58 (divorced), Bonni Chalkin, 1992-2005 (divorced), 2 children. Career: Theatre: Barefoot in the Park, 1966; Knock Knock, 1976; Scuba Duba, 1967-69; King of the United States, 1972; Mystery Play, 1972; Hot L Baltimore, 1972-73; Prodigal, 1973; Chapter Two, 1977-78; Talley's Folly, 1979; The Seagul, 1983; I'm Not Rappaport, 1985-86, revival 2002; Conversations with My Father, 1992; A Thousand Clowns, 1996; Below the Belt, 1996; Death of a Salesman, 1997; Art, 1998; Sixteen Wounded, 2004; TV: Devecchio, 1976-77; Taxi, 1978-83; Dear John, 1988-92; George and Leo, 1997; Welcome to New York, 2000; The Law, 2001; Philly, 2001; Law and Order, 2002; Regular Joe, 2003; NUMB3RS, 2005-07; many TV movies; Films: King of the Gypsies, 1978; Ordinary People, 1980; Without A Trace, 1983; Teachers, 1984; The Goodbye People, 1984; Running on Empty, 1988; Independence Day, 1996; Man on the Moon, 1999; A Beautiful Mind, 2002; Zeyda and the Hitman, 2004; Brother's Shadow, 2006. Honours: Drama Desk Award, 1976; Obie Award, 1979; Tony Award, 1986, 1992; Emmy Award; Golden Globe Award. Memberships: Screen Actors Guild; AEA; AFTRA. Address: c/o J Wolfe Provident Financial Management, POB 4084, Santa Monica, CA 90411-9910, USA.

HIRST Damien, b. 1965, Bristol, England. Artist. 2 sons. Education: Goldsmiths College, London. Creative Works: One-man exhibitions include: Institute of Contemporary Arts (ICA), London, 1991; Emmanuel Perrotin, Paris, 1991; Cohen Gallery, New York, 1992; Regen Projects, Los Angeles, 1993; Galerie Jablonka, Cologne, 1993; Milwaukee Art Museum, 1994; Dallas Museum, 1994; Kukje Gallery, Seoul, 1995; White Cube/Jay Jopling, London, 1995; Prix Eliette von Karajan, 1995; Max Gandolph-Bibliothek, Salzburg, Germany, Gasogian Gallery, New York, 1996; Bruno Bischofberger, Zurich, 1997; Astrup Fearnley, Oslo, 1997; Southampton City Art Gallery, 1998; Pharmacy, Tate Gallery, London, 1999; Sadler's Wells, London, 2000; Damian Hurst, The Saatchi Gallery, 2003; The Agony and The Ecstasy: Selected Works from 1989-2004, Archaeological Museum, Naples, 2004; MFA, Boston, 2005; Numerous group exhibitions world-wide. Television: Channel 4 documentary about Damien Hirst and exhibition at Gagosian Gallery, directed by Roger Pomphrey, 2000. Publications: I Want to Spend the Rest of My Life Everywhere, One to One, Always, Forever, 1997; Theories, Models, Methods, Approaches, Assumptions, Results and Findings, 2000. Honour: Turner Prize, 1995.

HIRST Paul Heywood, b. 10 November 1927, Huddersfield, England. Academic. Education: BA, 1958, MA, Trinity College, Cambridge, 1945-48, 1951-52; Academic Diploma in Education, University of London, 1954; MA, Christ Church Oxford, 1955. Appointments: Lecturer and Tutor, University

of Oxford, Department of Education, 1955-59; Lecturer in Philosophy of Education, London University, Institute of Education, 1959-65; Professor of Education, King's College, University of London, 1965-71; Professor of Education and Head, Department of Education, University of Cambridge, Fellow of Wolfson College, Cambridge, 1971-88; Emeritus Professor of Education, University of Cambridge, 1988-; Emeritus Fellow of Wolfson College, Cambridge, 1988-; Visiting Professor, Universities of British Columbia, Malawi, Otago, Melbourne, Puerto Rico, Alberta, Sydney; Visiting Professor, Kingston Polytechnic; Visiting Professor or Visiting Professorial Fellow, University of London, Institute of Education; Member, Swann Committee on Education of Children of Ethnic Minorities, 1981-85; Chair, Universities Council for the Education of Teachers, 1985-88; Chair, Committee for Research, CNAA, 1988-92. Publications: Logic of Education (with R S Peters), 1970; Knowledge and the Curriculum, 1974; Moral Education in a Secular Society, 1974; Educational Theory and Its Foundation Disciplines (editor), 1983; Initial Teacher Training and the Role of the School (with others), 1988; Philosophy of Education: Major Themes in the Analytic Tradition, 4 volumes (co-editor), 1998; 87 papers published in collections and philosophical and educational journals. Honours: Member, Royal Norwegian Society of Sciences and Letters; Honorary DEd, CNAA; Honorary DPhil, Cheltenham and Gloucester College of Higher Education, now University of Gloucestershire; Honorary DLitt, University of Huddersfield. Listed in national and international biographical dictionaries. Memberships: Honorary Vice-President, Philosophy of Education Society; Athenaeum Club. Address: Flat 3, 6 Royal Crescent, Brighton BN2 1AL, England.

HISASHIGE Tadao, b. 6 April 1936, Tokyo, Japan. Professor Emeritus. m. Sayoko. Education: BA, 1959, MA, 1961, Tokyo University; Docteur d'Etat ès Lettres, Université de Paris, 1982. Appointments: Full time Lecturer, 1966, Assistant Professor, 1971, Professor, 1977-2003, Chief of Research Institute of Humanities, 1986-90, Chief Librarian, 1998-2002, Senshu University. Publications: Phénoménologie de la conscience de culpabilité, 1983; Ethics of A-symmetry, 2002. Honours: Watsuji Prize, Japanese Association of Ethics, 1967. Memberships: Société Franco-Japonaise de Philosophie. Address: 1598-15 Nohgaya, Machida, Tokyo, Japan.

HISLOP Ian David, b. 13 July 1960. Writer; Broadcaster. m. Victoria Hamson, 1988, 1 son, 1 daughter. Education: Ardingly College; BA Honours, English Language and Literature, Magdalen College, Oxford. Appointments: Joined staff, 1981-, Deputy Editor, 1985-86, Editor, 1986-, Private Eye, satirical magazine; Columnist, The Listener magazine, 1985-89; TV Critic, The Spectator magazine, 1994-96; Columnist, Sunday Telegraph, 1996-2003; Radio: Newsquiz, 1985-90; Fourth Column, 1992-96; Lent Talk, 1994; Gush (with Nicholas Newman), 1994; Words on Words, 1999; The Hislop Vote, 2000; A Revolution in 5 Acts, 2001; The Patron Saints, 2002; A Brief History of Tax, 2003; The Choir Invisible, 2003; There'll be Bluebirds Over the White Cliffs of Dover, 2004; Are We Being Offensive Enough? 2004; Television scriptwriting: Spitting Image, 1984-89 (with Nick Newman) The Stone Age, 1989; Briefcase Encounter, 1990; The Case of the Missing, 1991; He Died a Death, 1991; Harry Enfield's Television Programme, 1990-92; Harry Enfield and Chums, 1994-97; Mangez Merveillac, 1994; Dead on Time, 1995; Gobble, 1996; Sermon from St Albion's, 1998; Confessions of a Murderer, BBC2, 1999; My Dad is the Prime Minister, 2003, 2004; Performer: Have I Got News For You, 1990-; Great Railway Journeys, 1999; Documentaries:

Canterbury Tales, 1996; School Rules, 1997; Pennies from Bevan, 1998; East to West, 1999; Who Do You Think You Are? 2004. Publications: various Private Eye collections, 1985-; Contributor to newspapers and magazines on books, current affairs, arts and entertainment. Honours: BAFTA Award for Have I Got News for You, 1991; Editors' Editor, British Society of Magazine Editors, 1991; Magazine of the Year, What the Papers Say, 1991; Editor of the Year, British Society of Magazine Editors, 1998; Award for Political Satire, Channel 4 Political Awards, 2004. Address: c/o Private Eye, 6 Carlisle Street, London W1V 5RG, England.

HLAVÁČ Libor Metoděj, b. 19 January 1958, Karviná 4, Czech Republic. Professor. m. Irena, 3 sons, 4 daughters. Education: Physical Engineer Diploma, Physical Electronics, Faculty of Nuclear and Physical Engineering, Czech Technical University, Prague, 1982; PhD degree, Automation of Technological Processes, Faculty of Mining and Geology, VŠB Technical University, Ostrava, 2001; Inception at Applied Physics, Palacki University, Olomouc, 2003. Appointments: Research Worker, Electronics and Optics, Research Institute of Civil Engineering, Ostrava, 1982-86; Research Worker, Problem of Liquid Jets, Mining Institute of Czechoslovak Academy of Sciences, Ostrava, 1986-93; Scientific Worker, Physical Problems of Liquid Jet Interactions with Materials, Institute of Geonics, Czech Academy of Sciences, Ostrava, 1993-97; Lecturer of Physics, Scientific Worker on Interactions of Liquid and Laser Jets with Solid-State Materials, Institute of Physics, VŠB-Technical University, Ostrava, 1997-2003; Assistant Professor, Professor 2006, Scientific Worker in Physical Problems of Liquid and Laser Jet Interactions, Institute of Physics, VŠB-Technical University, Ostrava, 2006-. Publications: Over 140 publications including: Physical analysis of the energy balance of the high energy liquid jet collision with brittle non-homogeneous material, 1995; Interaction of grains with water jet – the base of the physical derivation of complex equation for jet cutting of rock materials, 1996; JETCUT – software for prediction of high-energy waterjet efficiency, 1998; Theoretical model of abrasive liquid jet, 2001; Listed in national and international biographical publications. Memberships: Union of Czech Mathematicians and Physicists; Waterjet Technology Association; Czech Engineering Association. Address: Proskovická 37/679, 70030 Ostrava-Výškovice, Czech Republic. E-mail: libor.hlavac@vsb.cz

HO Feng-Chi (Frank), b. 10 December 1942, Taiwan. Clinical Oncology. m. 2 sons. Education: PhD, Cytalogical Study of Genetics, Tokyo University of Agriculture, 1988; Postdoctoral Course, Clinical Oncology, Institute of Oriental Medicine, 1991. Appointments: President, International Canceriatry Academy of Chinese Medicine, Canada, 2001-; Leadership, AACR-Foundation for the Prevention and Care of Cancer, USA, 2003-07; UICC-Global Cancer Control Community, 2007. Publications: 3-prenylindoles from Murraya paniculata and their biogenetic significance, 1989; Chemical studies on Sophora tomentosa: The Isolation of a new class of flavonid, 1990; Tannins and Related Compounds, 1990; New Flavoid Compounds in the Roots of Euchresta formosana, in press. Honours: National Science Council Grant, 1970-80; International Plant Taxonomist, Carnegie-Mellon University, 1980; Recognised by Pacific Science Association, 1983; Merit Award of Scientific Research, Research Society of Chinese Medicine, Japan, 1983. Memberships: American Chemical Society; American Association of Oriental Medicine; Director, Institute for Botanical Resources, Taiwan; Life

Member, International Dendrology Society, UK; International Association for Plant Taxonomy, Netherlands. E-mail: sinocan@hotmail.com

HO George Van Hoa, b. 20 April 1940, Vietnam. Retired. m. Thi Ngoc Minh Chau, 2 sons, 2 daughters. Education: Graduation, 1962, Faculty of Pedagogy, Bachelor of Mathematics, 1965, Doctorat du 3ème Cycle, 1969, Doctorat d'État ès Sciences Physiques (with honour), 1975, University of Saigon, Vietnam. Appointments: Teacher, Mathematics, High School, 1962; Assistant Lecturer, Faculty of Sciences, University of Saigon, 1970; Certified Quality Analyst, Quality Assurance Institute, Orlando, USA, 1994; Application Programmer, Project Leader, Development Consultant, Baycorp Advantage Limited (now Veda Advantage Limited), 1987-2006. Publications: Numerous articles in professional journals; Books: Sudoku Training, 2007; Explained Sudoku, 2007; Game: Mathematical Chess, 2008. Honours: Appreciations and Award, Baycorp Advantage, 1987, 1990, 2002, 2004, 2006. Memberships: Former Member: Australian Computer Society; Australian Mathematical Society; Australian Software Metrics Association. Address: 7 Croydon Road, Croydon, NSW 2132, Australia. E-mail: hvhoa@tpg.com.au

HOAGLAND Edward, b. 21 December 1932, New York, USA. Author; Teacher. m. (1) Amy J Ferrara, 1961, divorced 1964, (2) Marion Magid, 28 March 1968, died 1993, 1 daughter. Education: AB, Harvard University, 1954. Appointments: Faculty: New School for Social Research, New York City, 1963-64, Rutgers University, 1966, Sarah Lawrence College, 1967, 1971, City University of New York, 1967, 1968, University of Iowa, 1978, 1982, Columbia University, 1980, 1981, Bennington College, 1987-2001, Brown University, 1988, University of California at Davis, 1990, 1992, Beloit College, Wisconsin, 1995; General Editor, Penguin Nature Library, 1985-2004. Publications: Cat Man, 1956; The Circle Home, 1960; The Peacock's Tail, 1965; Notes from the Century Before: A Journal from British Columbia, 1969; The Courage of Turtles, 1971; Walking the Dead Diamond River, 1973; The Moose on the Wall: Field Notes from the Vermont Wilderness, 1974; Red Wolves and Black Bears, 1976; African Calliope: A Journey to the Sudan, 1979; The Edward Hoagland Reader, 1979; The Tugman's Passage, 1982; City Tales, 1986; Seven Rivers West, 1986; Heart's Desire, 1988; The Final Fate of the Alligators, 1992; Balancing Acts, 1992; Tigers and Ice, 1999; Compass Points, 2000; Hoagland on Nature, 2003; Numerous essays and short stories. Honours: Houghton Mifflin Literary Fellowship, 1954; Longview Foundation Award, 1961; Prix de Rome, 1964; Guggenheim Fellowships, 1964, 1975; O Henry Award, 1971; New York State Council on the Arts Award, 1972; National Book Critics Circle Award, 1980; Harold D Vursell Award, 1981; National Endowment for the Arts Award, 1982; Literary Lion Award, New York Public Library, 1988; National Magazine Award, 1989; Lannon Foundation Literary Award, 1993; Literary Lights Award, Boston Public Library, 1995; American Academy of Arts and Letters, 1982. Address: PO Box 51, Barton, VT 05822, USA.

HOANG-NGOC Minh, b. 29 July 1929, Vietnam. Doctor of Medicine. m. Nguyen Thi Long, 2 sons, 2 daughters. Education: MD, 1958, Postgraduate Training Residency, Johns Hopkins, MD, USA, 1958-60. Appointments: Chief, Department Gynaeco-Surgical Tu Du Hospital, Saigon, Vietnam, 1965; Assistant Professor, Saigon Faculty of Medicine, 1968; Associated Professor, CHU Amiens, France, 1971. Publications: 280 publications. Memberships: President, French Society of Gynaecology, 1996-98; General Secretary of French Society of Gynaeco-Pathology; Vice President, European Society of Gynaecology, 2001-2003; Life Member, American Society for Reproductive Medicine, Senior Member: ICGS, ISGYP, New York Academy of Sciences. Address: 4 Rue Eugene Delacroix, 94410 Saint Maurice, France.

HOBBS Lewis Mankin, b. 16 May 1937, Upper Darby, Pennsylvania, USA. Astronomer. m. Jo Ann Hagele Hobbs, 2 sons, 1 daughter. Education: BEP, Engineering Physics, Cornell University, Ithaca, New York, 1960; MS, Physics, 1962, PhD, Physics, 1966, University of Wisconsin, Madison, Wisconsin. Appointments: Junior Astronomer, Lick Observatory, University of California, 1965-66; Assistant Professor, 1966-72, Associate Professor, 1972-76, University of Chicago; Director, Yerkes Observatory, University of Chicago, 1974-82; Professor of Astronomy and Astrophysics, University of Chicago, 1976-; Emeritus Professor, 2002. Publications: About 150 articles in professional journals. Honours: Alfred P Sloan Scholar, 1956-60. Memberships: International Astronomical Union; American Astronomical Society; American Physical Society. Address: University of Chicago, Yerkes Observatory, Williams Bay, WI 53191, USA.

HOBBS Peter Thomas Goddard, b. 19 March 1938, Gloucester, England. Director. m. Victoria Christabel Matheson, 1 daughter. Education: Waugh Scholar, MA, Exeter College, Oxford; CCIPD, 1988; F Inst D, 1989; FRSA, 1992. Appointments: Manager, ICI Ltd, 1962-79; Director, Wellcome Foundation and Wellcome plc, 1979-92; Founder Chairman, Employers Forum on Disability, 1986-93; HM First Non-Police Inspector of Constabulary, 1993-98; Non-Executive Director, Forensic Science Service, 1996-2006; Chairman, Learning From Experience Trust, 1992-93, 1998-. Publications: Miscellaneous human resource and organisation matters; Old St Albans Court Archaeologia Cantia, 2005. Honour: Dr hc, IMC, 2000. Memberships: Confederation of British Industry, Education and Training Committee, 1990-94; Institute of Directors, Employment Committee, 1989-93; Chemical Industries Association, Training Committee, Employment Board, Council, 1979-92. Address: Blenheim Crescent, London W11 2EQ, England.

HOBHOUSE Penelope, (Penelope Malins), b. 20 November 1929, Castledawson, Northern Ireland. Writer; Designer. m. (1) Paul Hobhouse, 1952, 2 sons, 1 daughter, (2) John Malins, 1 November 1983. Education: Honours, Economics, University of Cambridge, 1951. Publications: The Country Gardener; Colour in Your Garden; Garden Style; Flower Gardens; Guide to the Gardens of Europe; The Smaller Garden; Painted Gardens; Private Gardens of England; Borders; Flower Gardens; Plants in Garden History; Garden Style; The Story of Gardening; The Gardens of Persia. Contributions to: The Garden; Horticulture; Vogue; Antiques; Plants and Gardens. Honour: Awarded Royal Horticultural Society Victoria Medal of Honour, 1996; Lifetime Achievement Award, Guild of Garden Writers, 1999; MA; Hon DLitt. Address: The Coach House, Bettiscombe, Bridport, Dorset DT6 5NT, England.

HOBSBAWM Eric John Ernest, b. 9 June 1917, Alexandria, Egypt (British citizen). Professor of Economic and Social History Emeritus; Writer. m. Marlene Schwarz, 1962, 1 son, 1 daughter. Education: BA, 1939, MA, 1943, PhD, 1951, University of Cambridge. Appointments: Lecturer in History, 1947-59, Reader in History, 1959-70, Professor of Economic and Social History, 1970-82, Professor Emeritus, 1982-, Birkbeck College, University of London; Fellow, King's College, Cambridge, 1949-55 (Honorary Fellow, 1971).

Publications: Labour's Turning Point, 1880-1900 (editor), 1948; Primitive Rebels, 1959, US edition as Social Bandits and Primitive Rebels, 1959; The Jazz Scene, 1959, revised edition, 1993; The Age of Revolution, 1789-1848, 1962; Labouring Men, 1964; Industry and Empire: An Economic History of Britain since 1750, 1968, 1999, US edition as Industry and Empire: The Making of Modern English Society, 1968; Captain Swing (with George Rudé), 1969; Bandits, 1969, revised edition, 1981, 2000; Revolutionaries, 1973; The Age of Capital, 1848-1875, 1975; Marxism in Marx's Day (editor), 1982; The Invention of Tradition (editor with Terence Ranger), 1983; Worlds of Labour: Further Studies in the History of Labour, 1984, US edition as Workers: Worlds of Labor, 1984; The Age of Empire, 1875-1914, 1987; Politics for a Rational Left: Political Writing, 1977-1988, 1989; Echoes of the Marseillaise: Two Centuries Look Back on the French Revolution, 1990; Nations and Nationalism since 1780: Programme, Myth, Reality, 1990, 2nd edition, 1992; Age of Extremes: The Short Twentieth Century, 1914-1991, 1994; US edition as The Age of Extremes: A History of the World, 1914-1991, 1994; On History (essays), 1997; Uncommon People: Resistance, Rebellion and Jazz, 1998; On the Edge of the New Century, 2000; Interesting Times, 2002; Globalisation, Democracy and Terrorism, 2007; Contributions to: Scholarly journals and general publications. Honours: Palmes Académiques, France, 1993; Commander, Order of the Southern Cross, Brazil, 1996; Companion of Honour, 1998; Numerous honorary degrees. Memberships: British Academy, fellow; American Academy of Arts and Sciences, honorary foreign member; Hungarian Academy of Sciences, foreign member; Academy of Sciences, Turin; The Japan Academy, honorary foreign member. Address: School of History, Birkbeck College, University of London, Malet Street, London WC1E 7HX, England.

HOBSON Fred Colby Jr, b. 23 April 1943, Winston-Salem, North Carolina, USA. Professor of Literature; Writer. m. 17 June 1967, divorced, 1 daughter. Education: AB, English, University of North Carolina, 1965; MA, History, Duke University, 1967; PhD, English, University of North Carolina, 1972. Appointments: Professor of English, University of Alabama, 1972-86; Professor of English and Co-Editor, Southern Review, Louisiana State University, 1986-89; Professor of English, Lineberger Professor in the Humanities and Co-Editor, Southern Literary Journal, University of North Carolina at Chapel Hill, 1989-. Publications: Serpent in Eden: H L Mencken and the South, 1974; Literature at the Barricades: The American Writer in the 1930's (co-editor), 1983; Tell About the South: The Southern Rage to Explain, 1984; South-Watching: Selected Essays of Gerald W Johnson (editor), 1984; The Southern Writer in the Post-Modern World, 1990; Mencken: A Life, 1994; Thirty-Five Years of Newspaper Work by H L Mencken (co-editor), 1994; The Literature of the American South: A Norton Anthology (co-editor), 1998; But Now I See: The Southern White Racial Conversion Narrative, 1999; Faulkner's Absalom, Absalom!: Selected Essays (editor), 2002; South to the Future: An American Region in the Twenty-First Century (editor), 2002; The Silencing of Emily Mullen and Other Essays, 2005; Off the Rim: Basketball and Other Religions in a Carolina Childhood, 2006. Contributions to: Virginia Quarterly Review; Sewanee Review; Atlantic Monthly; Kenyon Review; New York Times Book Review; American Literature; Times Literary Supplement. Honours: Lillian Smith Award, 1984; Jules F Landry Award, 1994, 1999. Address: Department of English, University of North Carolina at Chapel Hill, NC 27599-3520, USA.

HOCKNEY David, b. 9 July 1937, Bradford, England. Artist. Education: Bradford College of Art; Royal College of Art. Appointments: Teacher, Maidstone College of Art, 1962, University of Iowa, 1964, University of Colorado, 1965, University of California, Los Angeles, 1966, University of California, Berkeley, 1967. Creative Works: First one-man exhibition, Kasmin Galley, London, 1963; Subsequent one-man exhibitions include: Nicholas Wilder, Los Angeles, 1976; Galerie Neundorf, Hamburg, 1977; Warehouse Gallery, 1979; Knoedler Gallery, 1979, 1981, 1982, 1983, 1984, 1986; Tate Gallery, 1980, 1986, 1988; Hayward Gallery, 1983, 1985; Los Angeles County Museum, 1988; The Metro Museum of Art, New York, 1988; Knoedler Gallery, London, 1988; A Emmerich Gallery, New York, 1988, 1989; Los Angeles Louvre Gallery, Venice, 1982, 1983, 1985, 1988; Nishimura Gallery, Tokyo, Japan, 1988; Manchester City Art Galleries, 1996; National Museum of American Art, Washington DC, 1997, 1998; Museum Ludwig, Cologne, 1997; Museum of Fine Arts, Boston, 1998; Centre Georges Pompidou, Paris, 1999; Musee Picasso, Paris, 1999; Annely Juda Fine Art, 2003; National Portrait Gallery, 2003. Publications: Hockney by Hockney, 1976; David Hockney, Travel with Pen, Pencil and Ink, 1978; Photographs, 1982; China Diary (with Stephen Spender), 1982; Hockney Paints the Stage, 1983; David Hockney: Cameraworks, 1984; Hockney on Photography: Conversations with Paul Joyce, 1988; David Hockney: A Retrospective, 1988; Hockney's Alphabet, 1991; That's the Way I See It, 1993; Off the Wall: Hockney Posters, 1994; David Hockney's Dog Days, 1998; Hockney on Art: Photography, Painting and Perspective, 1998; Hockney on "Art": Conversation with Paul Joyce, 2000; Secret Knowledge: Rediscovering the Lost Techniques of the Old Masters, 2001; Hockney's Pictures, 2004. Honours: Numerous; Companion of Honour, 1997. Memberships include: Royal Academy, 1985. Address: c/o 7508 Santa Monica Boulevard, Los Angeles, CA 90046, USA.

HODDINOTT Dudley Stuart, b. 2 April 1944, Kilmington, Wiltshire, England. Metallurgical Engineer. m. Brenda, 1 daughter. Education: MA, Engineering and Metallurgy, PhD, Metallurgy, Churchill College, University of Cambridge; Postgraduate Diploma, Occupational Health and Safety, Aston University. Appointments: Team Leader, Mechanical Engineering Section, British Rail Research, Derby, 1969-77; Head, Railway Product Development Centre, British Steel/ Corus Research Laboratories, Rotherham, 1977-81; Manager, Materials Engineering, AEA Technology, Harwell, Oxon, 1981-91; Systems Safety Assurance Manager, British Rail/ Railtrack, London, 1991-97; Technology Foresight and Metallurgy Manager, HM Railway Inspectorate, London, 1997-2006; Research Manager, Office of Rail Regulation, London, 2006-. Publications: Author: Railway Safety Critical Work: Guidance on the Definition of Activities Regarded as Safety Critical under the Railways (Safety Critical Work) Regulations 1994, 1999; Developing and Maintaining Staff Competence, 2002; Railway axle failure investigations and fatigue crack growth monitoring of an axle, 2004; 3 patents. Memberships: Industry Research Strategy Group, Newrail Centre for Railway Research, University of Newcastle upon Tyne; Licensing Committee, Institute of Railway Signal Engineers, London; Institution of Mechanical Engineers; Institute of Materials, Minerals and Mining; Association for Project Management. Address: 17 Clover Close, Cumnor Hill, Oxford OX2 9JH, England. E-mail: bhoddinott@clara.co.uk

HODDLE Glenn, b. 27 October 1957, England. Footballer; Football Manager. m. Christine Anne Stirling, divorced, 1 son, 2 daughters. Appointments: Player with Tottenham Hotspur, 1976-86, AS Monaco, France, 1986; (12 under 21 caps, 53 full caps on England National Team 1980-88, played in World Cup 1982, 1986); Player/Manager, Swindon Town, 1991-93 (promoted to FA Premier League 1993); Player/Manager, Chelsea, 1993-96; Coach, English National Team, 1996-99; Manager, Southampton, 2000-01; Manager, Tottenham Hotspur, 2001-03; Wolverhampton Wanderers, 2004-06; Skysports, 2006-. Publication: Spurred to Success (autobiography); Glenn Hoddle: The 1998 World Cup Story, 1998. Honours: FA Cup Winners Medal (Tottenham Hotspur), 1984; French Championship Winners Medal (Monaco), 1988.

HODGE Ian David, b. 15 February 1952, Chelmsford, Essex, England. Professor of Rural Economy. m. Bridget Anne, 1 son, 3 daughters. Education: BSc, Agricultural Economics, University of Reading, 1973; PhD, Countryside Planning Unit, Wye College, University of London, 1977. Appointments: Temporary Lecturer and Research Associate in Agricultural Economics, University of Newcastle upon Tyne, 1976-78; Visiting Research Associate, Department of Agricultural Economics, University of Idaho, USA, 1982; Lecturer in Agricultural Economics, University of Queensland, Australia, 1979-83; Gilbey Lecturer in the History and Economics of Agriculture, 1983-2000, Acting Head, Department of Land Economy, 1998, University Senior Lecturer, 2000-2001, University Reader in Rural Economy, 2001-05, Head of Department of Land Economy, 2002-, Professor of Rural Economy, 2005-, University of Cambridge; Visiting Professor, Department of Agricultural Economics, University of Wisconsin, 1994; Governor: Macaulay Land Use Research Institute, 1998-2003, Cambridge International Land Institute, 2003-. Publications include: Rural Employment: Trends, Options, Choices (with Martin Whitby), 1981; Environmental Economics: Individual Incentives and Public Choices, 1995; Countryside in Trust, Land management by Conservation, Amenity and recreation Organisations (with Janet Dwyer), 1996; Numerous article in academic journals. Honours: BSc, University of Reading, 1973; PhD, University of London, 1977; Fellow Royal Institution of Chartered Surveyors, 2004; President, Agricultural Economics Society, 2007-08. Memberships include: Fellow Hughes Hall Cambridge, 2004; Socio Economic Advisory Group, English Nature, 1994-2006, Broads Research Advisory Panel, 1999-2003, MAFF/DEFRA Academic Economist Panel, 1999-; MAFF Task Force for the Hills, 2000-2001; Resource Policy Research Consortium, 1989-. Address: Department of Land Economy, University of Cambridge, 19 Silver Street, Cambridge CB3 9EP, England. E-mail: idh3@cam.ac.uk

HODGE Patricia, b. Grimsby, England. Actress. m. Peter Owen, 2 sons. Education: London Academy of Music and Dramatic Art. Creative Works: Stage appearances include: No-one Was Saved; All My Sons; Say Who You Are; The Birthday Party; The Anniversary; Popkiss; Two Gentlemen of Verona; Pippin; Maudie; Hair; The Beggar's Opera; Pal Joey; Look Back in Anger; Dick Whittington; Happy Yellow; The Brian Cant Children's Show; Then and Now; The Mitford Girls; As You Like It; Benefactors; Noel and Gertie; Separate Tables; The Prime of Miss Jean Brodie; A Little Night Music; Heartbreak House, 1997; Money, 1999; Noises Off, 2000-01; His Dark Materials, 2004. Film appearances: The Disappearance; Rose Dixon - Night Nurse; The Waterloo Bridge Handicap; The Elephant Man; Heavy Metal; Betrayal; Sunset; Just Ask for Diamond; The Secret Life of Ian Fleming; The Leading Man, 1996; Prague Duet, 1996; Jilting Joe, 1997; Before You Go, 2002. TV appearances: Valentine; The Girls of Slender Means; Night of the Father; Great Big Groovy

Horse; The Naked Civil Servant; Softly, Softly; Jackanory Playhouse; Act of Rape; Crimewriters; Target; Rumpole of the Bailey; The One and Only Mrs Phyllis Dixey; Edward and Mrs Simpson; Disraeli; The Professionals; Holding the Fort; The Other 'Arf; Jemima Shore Investigates; Hayfever; The Death of the Heart; Robin of Sherwood; OSS; Sherlock Holmes; Time for Murder; Hotel du Lac; The Life and Loves of a She Devil; Rich Tea and Sympathy, 1991; The Cloning of Joanna May, 1991; The Legacy of Reginald Perrin, 1996; The Moonstone, 1996; The Falklands Play, 2002; Sweet Medicine, 2003; Maxwell. 2007. Honours: Eveline Evans Award for Best Acrtress; Olivier Award for Best Supporting Actress, 1999; Hon D Litt (Hull) 1996, (Brunel) 2001, (Leicester) 2003; The Olivier Award, 2000. Address: c/o ICM, Oxford House, 76 Oxford Street, London W1R 1RB, England.

HODGSON Kenneth Jonah, b. 2 August 1936, Liverpool, England. Clergyman; Social Worker; Artist. 2 daughters. Education: Ponsbourne Pre-Ordination College, Hertfordshire, 1964-66; Oak Hill College, London, 1966-69; Ordained, 1969; The Open University, 1976-79; North East Wales Institute, Wrexham, Cymru, 1987-89. Appointments: Clerical Work, 1952-54; Royal Air Force, 1954-57; Clerical Work, 1957-60; Family Business, 1960-61; School Welfare Officer, 1961-64; Anglican Clergyman, 1969-78; Social Worker, 1978-96; Chaplain, TAVR, 1979-82; Chaplain, Regular Army Reserve, 1982-91; Anglican Clergyman, NSM, 2001-06; Diocesan licence, 2006-; Artist in acrylic, oil and water-colour; Collective exhibitions: Royal Cambrian Arts; Williamson Art Gallery, Wirral; Various Liverpool and Chester galleries; Newcastle, Staffordshire; Ludlow; RBSA Gallery Birmingham; Durham; Flintshire; St Ives, Cornwall, St David's Hall, Cardiff, Cymru and USA venues; Individual exhibitions on Merseyside and Wirral; Associated with Daylight Group – a joint Tate Liverpool and Metropolitan Borough of Wirral SSD Arts Project, Art Forum, 1993; Paintings in private and public collections in UK and other countries. Memberships: Member, Merseyside Artist's Association; Member, 1983, Secretary, 1983-87, Committee Member, 2005-, Wirral Society of Arts; Steering Committee Secretary, Merseyside Contemporary Artists, 1988-89; Director, Founder, National Acrylic Painters' Association, 1985; Instigator and Co-founder, NAPA USA, 1995 (evolved into ISAP, 2005), Honorary Vice-President, International Society of Acrylic Painters, USA, 2005. Address: 134 Rake Lane, Wallasey, Wirral, Merseyside CH45 1JW, England.

HODGSON Peter Barrie, b. 12 March 1942, Gosforth, England. Market Research Director. m. Audrone Grudzinskas, 1 son. Education: BA, St Peter's College, Oxford, England. Appointments: Senior Research Executive, Marplan Ltd, 1967-69; Senior Research Planner, Garland Compton Ltd, 1970-72; Director, Opinion Research Centre Ltd, 1973-75; Managing Director, Professional Studies Ltd, 1975-77; Director, Professional Studies Ireland Ltd, 1977-78; Managing Director, Action Research Ltd, 1977-78; Director, City Research Associates, Ltd, 1981-89; Managing Director, Travel and Tourism Research Ltd, 1978-. Publications: Articles published in: Espaces (Paris); Marketing; Journal of the Market Research Society; Journal of the Professional Marketing Research Society of Canada; Tourism Management; Journal of Travel Research; BMRA Bulletin; Synergie. Honours: Fellow, Tourism Society; Fellow, Institute of Travel and Tourism. Memberships: Council Member, Market Research Society, 1978-81; Council Member Tourism Society, 1981-84; Chairman, Association of British Market Research Companies, 1987-89; Chairman, Association of European Market Research Institutes, 1991-93; Deputy Chairman/

Honorary Secretary, British Market Research Association, 1998-2004. Address: Travel and Tourism Research Ltd, 4 Cochrane House, Admirals Way, London E14 9UD, England. E-mail: pb.hodgson@virgin.net

HOE Susanna Leonie, b. 14 April 1945, Southampton, England. Writer. m. Derek Roebuck, 18 August 1981. Education: London School of Economics, 1980-82; BA, University of Papua New Guinea, 1983-84. Appointments: Campaign Co-ordinator, British Section Amnesty International, 1977-80; TEFL Teacher, Women's Centre, Hong Kong, 1991-97. Publications: Lady in the Chamber, 1971; God Save the Tsar, 1978; The Man Who Gave His Company Away, 1978; The Private Life of Old Hong Kong, 1991; Chinese Footprints, 1996; Stories for Eva: A Reader for Chinese Women Learning English, 1997; The Taking of Hong Kong, with Derek Roebuck, 1999; Women at the Siege, Peking 1900 (history), 2000; At Home in Paradise (Papua New Guinea, travel), 2003; Madeira: Women, History, Books & Places, 2004; Crete: Women, History, Books and Places, 2005. Contributions to: Times (Papua New Guinea); Liverpool Post; Women's Feature Service. Honours: Te Rangi Hiroa Pacific History Prize, 1984. Membership: Honorary Research Fellow, Centre of Asian Studies, University of Hong Kong, 1991-. Address: 20A Plantation Road, Oxford OX2 6JD, England.

HOFFMAN Dustin Lee, b. 8 August 1937, Los Angeles, California, USA. Actor. m. (1) Anne Byrne, 1969, divorced, 2 daughters, (2) Lisa Gottsegen, 1980, 2 sons, 2 daughters. Education: Santa Monica City College. Appointments: Attendant, Psychiatric Institute; Demonstrator, Macy's Toy Department. Creative Works: Stage appearances include: Harry, Noon and Night, 1964; Journey of the Fifth Horse, Star Wagon, Fragments, 1966; Eh?, 1967; Jimmy Shine, 1968; Death of a Salesman, 1984; The Merchant of Venice, 1989; Films include: The Tiger Makes Out, Madigan's Millions, 1966; The Graduate, 1967; Midnight Cowboy, John and Mary, 1969; Little Big Man, 1970; Who is Harry Kellerman..?, Straw Dogs, 1971; Alfredo Alfredo, Papillon, 1973; Lenny, 1974; All the President's Men, 1975; Marathon Man, 1976; Straight Time, 1978; Agatha, Kramer vs Kramer, 1979; Tootsie, 1982; Ishtar, 1987; Rain Man, 1988; Family Business, 1989; Dick Tracy, 1990; Hook, Billy Bathgate, 1991; Hero, 1992; Outbreak, 1995; American Buffalo, Sleeper, 1996; Wag the Dog, Mad City, Sphere, 1997; Joan of Arc, The Messenger: the Story of Joan of Arc, Being John Malkovich, 1999; Moonlight Mile, 2002; Confidence, Runaway Jury, 2003; Finding Neverland, I Heart Huckabees, Meet the Fockers, 2004; Racing Stripes (voice), The Lost City, 2005; Prefume: The Story of a Murderer, Stranger Than Fiction, 2006; Mr Magorium's Wonder Emporium, 2007; Kung Fu Panda, 2008. TV appearances in: Death of a Salesman, 1985. Honours include: Obie Award, 1966; Vernon Rice Award, 1967; Academy Award, 1980; New York Film Critics Award, 1980, 1988; Golden Globe Award, 1988; BAFTA Award, 1997. Address: Punch Productions, 1926 Broadway, Suite 305, NY 10023, USA.

HOGWOOD Christopher (Jarvis Haley), b. 10 September 1941, Nottingham, England. Harpischordist; Conductor; Musicologist; Writer; Editor; Broadcaster. Education: BA, Pembroke College, Cambridge, 1964; Charles University, Prague; Academy of Music, Prague. Appointments: Founder-Member, Early Music Consort of London, 1967-76; Founder-Director, The Academy of Ancient Music, 1973-; Faculty, Cambridge University, 1975-; Artistic Director, 1986-2001, Conductor Laureate, 2001-, Handel and Haydn

Society, Boston; Honorary Professor of Music, University of Keele, 1986-89; Music Director, 1988-92, Principal Guest Conductor, 1992-98, St Paul Chamber Orchestra, Minnesota; International Professor of Early Music Performance, Royal Academy of Music, London, 1992-; Visiting Professor, King's College, London, 1992-96; Principal Guest Conductor, Kammerorchester Basel, 2000-; Principal Guest Conductor, Orquesta Ciudad de Granada, 2001-04. Publications: Music at Court, 1977; The Trio Sonata, 1979; Haydn's Visits to England, 1980; Music in Eighteenth-Century England (editor), 1983; Handel, 1984; Holme's Life of Mozart (editor), 1991; The Keyboard in Baroque Europe, 2003. Contributions to: The New Grove Dictionary of Music and Musicians, 1980, 2000. Honours: Walter Wilson Cobbett Medal, 1986; Commander of the Order of the British Empire, 1989; Honorary Fellow, Jesus College, Cambridge, 1989, Pembroke College, Cambridge, 1992; Freeman, Worshipful Company of Musicians, 1989; Incorporated Society of Musicians Distinguished Musician Award, 1997; Martinu Medal, Bohuslav Martinu Foundation, Prague, 1999; Honorary Professor of Music, Cambridge University, 2002-. Membership: Royal Society of Authors, fellow. Address: 10 Brookside, Cambridge CB2 1JE, England.

HOLBROOK David (Kenneth), b. 9 January 1923, Norwich, England. Author. m. 23 April 1949, 2 sons, 2 daughters. Education: BA, Honours, English, 1946, MA, 1951, Downing College, Cambridge. Appointments: Fellow, King's College, Cambridge, 1961-65; Senior Leverhulme Research Fellow, 1965, Leverhulme Emeritus Research Fellow, 1988-90; Writer-in-Residence, Dartington Hall, 1972-73; Fellow and Director of English Studies, 1981-88, Emeritus Fellow, 1988, Downing College; Publications: English for Maturity, 1961; Imaginings, 1961; Against the Cruel Frost, 1963; English for the Rejected, 1964; The Secret Places, 1964; Flesh Wounds, 1966; Children's Writing, 1967; The Exploring Word, 1967; Object Relations, 1967; Old World New World, 1969; English in Australia Now, 1972; Gustav Mahler and the Courage to Be, 1975; Chance of a Lifetime, 1978; A Play of Passion, 1978, 2004; English for Meaning, 1980; Selected Poems, 1980; Nothing Larger than Life, 1987; The Novel and Authenticity, 1987; A Little Athens, 1990; Edith Wharton and the Unsatisfactory Man, 1991; Jennifer, 1991; The Gold in Father's Heart, 1992; Where D H Lawrence Was Wrong About Women, 1992; Creativity and Popular Culture, 1994; Even If They Fail, 1994; Tolstoy, Women and Death, 1996; Wuthering Heights: a Drama of Being, 1997; Getting it Wrong with Uncle Tom, 1998; Bringing Everything Home (poems), 1999; A Study of George MacDonald and the Image of Woman, 2000; Lewis Carroll: Nonsense Against Sorrow, 2001; Going Off The Rails, 2003. Contributions to: Numerous professional journals. Honour: Festschrift, 1996. Honours: Founding Fellow, English Association, 2000. Membership: Society of Authors. Address: 1 Tennis Court Terrace, Cambridge CB2 1QX, England.

HOLBROOKE Richard C, b. 24 April 1941, New York, USA. Diplomat. m. (1) 2 sons, (2) Kati Morton, 1995. Education: Brown University; Woodrow Wilson School; Princeton University. Appointments: Foreign Service Officer, Vietnam and Related Posts, 1962-66; White House Vietnam Staff, 1966-67; Special Assistant to Under-Secretaries of State, Katzenbac and Richardson, Member, US Delegate to Paris Peace Talks on Vietnam, 1967-69; Director, Peace Corporations, Morocco, 1970-72; Managing Director, Foreign Policy (quarterly magazine), 1972-76; Consultant, President's Commission on Organisation of Government for Conduct of Foreign Policy, Contributing Editor, Newsweek, 1974-75;

Co-ordinator, National Security Affairs, Carter-Mondale Campaign, 1976; Assistant Secretary of State for East Asian and Pacific Affairs, 1977-81; Vice President of Public Strategies, 1981-85; Managing Director, Lehman Brothers, 1985-93; Ambassador to Germany, 1993-94; Assistant Secretary of State for European and Canadian Affairs, 1994-96; Vice Chair, Credit Suisse First Boston Corporation, 1996-98; Adviser, Baltic Sea Council, 1996-98; Special Presidential Envoy for Cyprus, 1997-98, to Yugoslavia (on Kosovo crisis); Permanent Representative to UN, 1999-2000; Ambassador to UN, 1999-2001; Director, Human Sciences Inc, 2001-04; Chairman, Asia Society, 2002-. Publications: Counsel to the President, 1991; To End a War, 1998; Several articles and essays. Honours: 12 honorary degrees; Distinguished Public Service Award, Department of Defense, 1994, 1996; Humanitarian of the Year Award, American Jewish Congress, 1998; Dr Bernard Heller, Prize, Hebrew Union College, 1999; Grand Cross of the Order of Merit (Germany), 2002. Address: c/o Department of State, 2201 C Street NW, Washington, DC 20520, USA.

HOLDER Stanley John, b. 21 September 1928, London, England. Nursing Educator. Education: South East Essex Technical College and School of Art Day School; Battersea College (University of Surrey); Sister Tutor Diploma, Advanced Diploma in Education, Master's Level, Adult Education, London University; Institute of Education; Registered General Nurse, Oldchurch Hospital, Romford, Essex. Appointments include: Charge Nurse, Surgical Unit, 1950-54, Tutor, 1956-60, Oldchurch Hospital; Principal Tutor, Hackney Hospital, London, 1960-65; Assistant Editor, Nursing Times, 1965-67; Principal Tutor, St Mary's Hospital, London, 1967-70; Director of Education, St Mary's Hospital and Parkside Health Authority, 1970-90; Chief Nursing Advisor, BRCS, 1988-93; Consultant: Curriculum Design, Middlesex University, 1991, BBC Nursing Education Series, 1991, Tayside Health Board, Scotland, 1991; Government and Official Appointments: Secretary of State appointments: East London Hospital Management Committee, 1966-74, Tower Hamlets Health Authority, 1980-90; Education Consultant, Rampton Inquiry, 1979; DHSS Working Party, Extended Role of the Nurse, 1974-77; Chairman, King's Fund Working Party overseas recruitment, The Language Barrier, 1973-74; Chairman, Member of Council Royal College of Nursing Representative Body, 1969-74; Chief Assessor, University of London Extra Mural Department, 1965-89; Founding Member, 1978-83, Vice-Chairman, 1981-83, Linacre Centre for Health Care Ethics; Vice-Chairman, Mildmay Mission Hospital (HIV/AIDS), 1983-91; Chairman, Mental Health Managers, Tower Hamlets, 1980-98; Elected Member, Chairman, Adult Nursing Committee, English National Board for Nursing, Midwifery and Health Visiting, 1983-90; Member, UK Council for Nursing and Midwifery, 1983-90. Publications: Founding Editor, Nurse Education Today; UK Editor, Nursing Series, McGraw Hill; Co-author, Programmed Learning text of Physiology of Respiration; Numerous articles on health matters and nursing education. Honours: OBE; Fellow, Royal College of Nursing; Florence Nightingale Scholar, USA and Canada, Florence Nightingale Foundation; Freeman City of London; Badge of Honour for Distinguished Service, BRC Society. Memberships: Freeman of City of London, Freeman's Guild; Rotary International, President, Epping, 2003-2004; University of the Third Age. Address: 155 Theydon Grove, Epping, Essex CM16 4QB, England.

HOLE Derek Norman, b. 5 December 1933, Plymouth, Devon, England. Provost Emeritus of Leicester. Education: Public Central School, Plymouth; Lincoln Theological

College, 1957-60. Appointments include: National Service Royal Air Force, 1952-54; Assistant Librarian, Codrington Library, Oxford, 1954-56; Ordained Deacon, 1960, Ordained Priest, 1961, Leicester Cathedral; Assistant Curate, St Mary Magdalene, Knighton, Leicester, 1960-62; Domestic Chaplain to the Archbishop of Cape Town, 1962-64; Assistant Curate, St Nicholas, Kenilworth, Warwickshire, 1964-67; Rector of St Mary the Virgin, Burton Latimer, Kettering, Northants, 1967-73; Independent Member, Burton Latimer Urban District Council, 1971-73; Vicar of St James the Greater, Leicester, 1973-92; Chaplain, Lord Mayor of Leicester, 1976-77, 1994-95, 1996-97; Chaplain, Leicester Branch of the Royal Air Forces Association, 1978-92; Chaplain, Haymarket Theatre, Leicester, 1980-83, 1993-95; Member, Actors' Church Union, 1980-95; Chaplain, High Sheriffs' of Leicestershire, 1980-85, 1987-88, 1999-2000, 2001-02; Honorary Canon, Leicester Cathedral, 1983-92; Rural Dean of Christianity South in the City of Leicester, 1983-92; Chaplain, Leicester High School, 1983-92; Chaplain to the Queen, 1985-92; Chairman, House of Clergy for the Diocese of Leicester, 1986-94; Vice-President, Leicester Diocesan Synod, 1986-94; President, Leicester Rotary Club, 1987-88; Member, Association of English Cathedrals, 1992-99; Provost of Leicester, 1992-99; Governor, Leicester Grammar School, 1992-99; Governor, Leicester High School, 1992-2004; Vice-President, The English Clergy Association, 1993-; Priest Associate, Actors' Church Union, 1995-; Chaplain, Merchant Taylors' Company, 1995-96; Chaplain, Guild of Freemen of the City of Leicester, 1996-99; Commissary to the Bishop of Wellington, New Zealand, 1998-; Senior Fellow, De Montford University, Leicester, 1998-; Trustee Leicester Grammar School, 1999-2007, Patron, 2007-; Provost Emeritus of Leicester, 1999-; Chairman of the Leicestershire Branch of the Britain-Australia Society, 2000-05; Chaplain, The Royal Society of St George, 2000-2006; Chaplain to the Master of the Worshipful Company of Framework Knitters, 2004-08; Chaplain to the Mayor of Oadby & Wigston Borough Council, 2005-06; Chaplain, Leicestershire Branch, Royal Society of St George, 2006-; Chaplain, British Korean Veterans Association, Leicestershire Branch, 2006-. Publications: Contributions to: The History of St James The Greater, Leicester, edited by Dr Alan C McWhirr; Century to Millennium St James the Greater Leicester 1899-1999. Honours: Honorary D Litt, De Montfort University, 1999; Freeman of the City of London, 2003-; Liveryman of the Worshipful Company of Framework Knitters, 2003-; Honorary LLD, Leicester University, 2005. Memberships: Leicestershire Club; The Royal Western Yacht Club of England; Leicestershire Golf Club. Address: 25 Southernhay Close, Leicester LE2 3TW, England. E-mail: dnhole@leicester.anglican.org

HOLLAND Jools (Julian), b. 24 January 1958, London, England. Musician (keyboards); Television Presenter. 1 son, 2 daughters. Career: Founder member, pianist, Squeeze, 1974-81, 1985-90; Solo artiste and bandleader: Jools Holland and his Big Band, 1982-84; Jools Holland and his Rhythm And Blues Orchestra, 1991-; Television presenter, music shows: The Tube, C4, 1981-86; Juke Box Jury, 1989; Sunday Night (with David Sanborn), 1990; The Happening, 1990; Hootenanny, 1992-; Later With Jools Holland, BBC2, 1993-; Various other television specials, including Sunday Night, NBC, 1989; Beat Route, BBC2, 1998-99; Jools Meets the Saint, 1999. Recordings: Albums: with Squeeze: Squeeze, 1978; Cool For Cats, 1979; Argy Bargy, 1980; Cosi Fan Tutti Frutti, 1985; Babylon And On, 1987; Frank, 1989; Solo albums: A World Of His Own, 1990; The Full Complement, 1991; A To Z Of The Piano, 1992; Live Performance, 1994; Solo Piano, 1994; Sex and Jazz and Rock and Roll, 1996; Lift

up the Lid, 1997; The Best of Jools Holland, 1998; Sunset Over London, 1999; Hop the Wag, 2000; Small World Big Band – Friends, 2001; Small World Big Band Vol 2 – More Friends, 2002; Small World, Big Band Vol 3, 2003; Beatroute, 2005; Swinging the Blues, Dancing the Ska, 2005; Moving Out To The Country, 2006. Hit singles include: with Squeeze: Take Me I'm Yours, 1978; Cool For Cats, 1979; Up The Junction, 1979; Slap And Tickle, 1979; Another Nail In My Heart, 1980; Pulling Mussels From A Shell, 1980; Hourglass, 1987; 853 5937, 1988. Honours: OBE, 2003; Deputy Lieutenant for Kent, 2006. Memberships: Musicians' Union; Equity; Writer's Guild.

HOLLINGHURST Alan, b. 26 May 1954, Stroud, Gloucestershire, England. Novelist. Education: BA, 1975, MLitt, 1979, Magdalen College, Oxford. Appointments: Assistant Editor, 1982-84, Deputy Editor, 1985-90, Poetry Editor, 1991-95, Times Literary Supplement, London; Old Dominion Fellow, Princeton University, 2004. Publications: Novels: The Swimming-Pool Library, 1988; The Folding Star, 1994; The Spell, 1998; The Line of Beauty, 2004. Translator: Bajazet, by Jean Racine, 1991. Honours: Somerset Maugham Award, 1988, E M Forster Award of the American Academy of Arts and Letters, 1989; James Tait Black Memorial Prize, 1995; Man Booker Prize, 2004. Memberships: Fellow, The Royal Society of Literature. Address: c/o Antony Harwood, 103 Walton Street, Oxford, OX2 6EB, England.

HOLLOWAY James, b. 24 November 1948. Gallery Director. Education: Courtauld Institute of Art, London University, 1969-71. Appointments: Research Assistant, National Gallery of Scotland, 1972-80; Assistant Keeper of Art, National Museum of Wales, 1980-83; Deputy Keeper, Scottish National Portrait Gallery, 1983-97; Director, Scottish National Portrait Gallery, 1997-. Publications: Editor, Scottish Masters booklets for National Gallery of Scotland; Several articles; Frequent lectures on Scottish art and collections. Memberships: Curatorial Committee, National Trust for Scotland; Committee Member, Scottish Sculpture Trust; Committee Member, Scottish-Indian Arts Forum. Address: Scottish National Portrait Gallery, 1 Queen Street, Edinburgh, EH2 1JD, Scotland.

HOLLOWAY Julian Robert Stanley, b. 24 June 1944, Watlington, Oxford, England. Actor; Director; Writer; Producer. m. (1) Zena Cecilia Walker, dissolved 1977, 1 daughter, (2) Deborah Jane Wheeler, dissolved 1996. Education: Ludgrove Preparatory School; Harrow School; Royal Academy of Dramatic Art. Career: Actor: Theatre includes: My Fair Lady; Arsenic & Old Lace; The Norman Conquests; Charley's Aunt; Pygmalion; Spitting Image; Films include: Ryan's Daughter; Carry on Up The Khyber; Carry on Loving; Carry on Henry; Carry on Camping; Carry on England; Carry on Doctor; Hostile Witness; Rough Cut; TV includes: The Importance of Being Earnest; An Adventure in Bed; Rebecca; The Scarlet and The Black; Ellis Island; The Endless Game; Michelangelo; Grass Roots; Torch Song; The Vet; Dan Dare; Remember Wenn; My Uncle Silas; Doctor Who; The Chief; Where's Wally (voice); My Uncle Silas II; Father of the Pride; Director: Play It Again Sam; When Did You Last See My Mother; Actor/Producer: Carry on Films; The Spy's Wife; The Chairman's Wife; Loophole. Address: c/o Michelle Braidman Associates, Suite 10, 11 Lower John Street, London W1R 3PE, England.

HOLLOWAY Laurence, b. 31 March 1938, Oldham, Lancashire, England. Musician (Piano); Composer; Musical Director. m. Marion Montgomery, deceased, 2 daughters.

Career: Touring Dance Band Pianist, 1950s; Cyril Stapleton Showband; Joe Daniels Hotshots, 1950s; Cunard Line, 1956-57; London Weekend Television, regular pianist, 1967-80; Musical Director, Engelbert Humperdinck, 1970-75; Played at studios in London, 1975-85; Musical Director for many top artistes such as Judy Garland, Cleo Lane, Sacha Distel, Dame Edna Everage, Liza Minelli, Rolf Harris, Frankie Howerd, Mel Torme, Elaine Paige in "Piaf"; Featured pianist on Dame Kiri Te Kanawa's popular music albums; Musical Director for Michael Parkinson on the "Parkinson" series; Musical Director of Strictly Come Dancing, BBC, 2004. Compositions: several saxophone quartets, clarinet quartets, pieces for flute and piano and clarinet and piano; Numerous TV signature tunes including Blind Date, Beadle's About; Walking Fingers selected by Associated Board of the Royal Schools of Music for 2001/2002 Grade 1 Examinations;. Recordings: Solo albums: Blue Skies; Showtime; Cumulus; About Time; Laurie Holloway, Live at Abbey Road, 2000; The Piano Player, 2004; Also recorded with many artists including Kiri Te Kanawa, Marion Montgomery, Robert Farnon, Rolf Harris. Honour: Gold Badge of Merit, BASCA. Membership: Temple Golf Club. Address: Elgin, Fishery Road, Bray, Nr Maidenhead, Berkshire SL6 1UP, England.

HOLLOWAY Patricia, (Patricia Pogson), b. 8 March 1944, Rosyth, Scotland. Yoga Teacher; Poet. m. (1) 1 son, 1 daughter, (2) Geoffrey Holloway, 27 August 1977. Education: National Diploma in Design, 1964; Teaching Certificate, 1971; Diploma, British Wheel of Yoga, 1987. Appointments: Draughtswoman Restorer, Ashmolean Museum, Oxford, 1964-66; Part-time Yoga Teacher; Poetry Tutor, Schools and Writing Centres, Libraries. Publications: Before the Road Show, 1983; Snakeskin, Belladonna, 1986; Rattling the Handle, 1991; A Crackle from the Larder, 1991; The Tides in the Basin, 1994; Holding, 2002. Contributions to: Anthologies, journals, reviews and magazines. Honours: 1st Prize, York Open Competition, 1985; 3rd Prize, Manchester Open Competition, 1989; 2nd Prize, National Poetry Competition, 1989; 1st Prize, BBC Kaleidoscope Competition, 1990. Memberships: Brewery Poets, Brewery Arts Centre, Kendal; Keswick Poetry Group. Address: 4 Gowan Crescent, Staveley, nr Kendal, Cumbria LA8 9NF, England.

HOLM Ian, Sir, b. 12 September 1931, Ilford, England. Actor. m. (1) Lynn Mary Shaw, 1955, 2 daughters, (2) Bee Gilbert, 1 son, 1 daughter, (3) Sophie Baker, 1982, 1 son, (4) Penelope Wilton, 1991, 1 step-daughter, (5) Sophie de Stempel, 2003-. Education: Royal Academy of Dramatic Arts. Creative Works: Roles include: Lennie in The Homecoming; Moonlight, 1993;Puck, Ariel, Lorenzo, Henry V, Richard III, the Fool (in King Lear), King Lear, 1997; Max in The Homecoming, 2001; Films include: Young Winston; Oh!; What a Lovely War; Alien; All Quiet on the Western Front; Chariots of Fire; The Return of the Soldier; Greystoke, Laughterhouse, 1984; Brazil, Wetherby, Dance with a Stranger, Dreamchild, 1985; Henry V, Another Woman, 1989; Hamlet, 1990; Kafka, 1991; The Hour of the Pig, Blue Ice, The Naked Lunch, 1992; Frankenstein, 1993; The Madness of King George, Loch Ness, 1994; Big Night, Night Falls on Manhattan, 1995; The Fifth Element, A Life Less Ordinary, 1996; The Sweet Hereafter, 1997; Existence, Simon Magus, 1998; Esther Kahn, Joe Gould's Secret, Beautiful Joe, 1999; From Hell, The Emperor's New Clothes, 2000; The Lord of the Rings: The Fellowship of the Ring, 2001; The Lord of the Ring: The Return of the King, 2003; Garden State, The Day After Tomorrow, The Aviator, 2004; Strangers with Candy, Chromophobia, Lord of War, 2005; Renaissance, The Treatment, O Jerusalem, Ratatouille (voice), 2006. TV

appearances include: The Lost Boys, 1979; We, the Accused, 1980; The Bell, Strike, 1981; Inside the Third Reich, 1982; Mr and Mrs Edgehill, 1985; The Browning Version, 1986; Game, Set and Match, 1988; The Endless Game, 1989; The Last Romantics, 1992; The Borrowers, 1993; The Deep Blue Sea, 1994; Landscape, 1995; Little Red Riding Hood, 1996; King Lear, 1997; Alice Through the Looking Glass, 1998; Animal Farm (voice), The Miracle Maker (voice), The Last of the Blonde Bombshells, 2000; D-Day 6.6.1944 (voice), 2004. Publications: Acting My Life, 2004. Honour: CBE, 1990; Laurence Olivier Award, 1998; Knighted, 1998. Address: c/o Julian Belfrage Associates, 46 Albemarle Street, London W1X 4PP, England.

HOLMES Bryan John, (Charles Langley Hayes, Ethan Wall, Jack Darby, Sean Kennedy), b. 18 May 1939, Birmingham, England. Lecturer (retired); Writer. m. 1962, 2 sons. Education: BA, University of Keele, 1968. Publications: The Avenging Four, 1978; Hazard, 1979; Blood, Sweat and Gold, Gunfall, 1980; A Noose for Yanqui, 1981; Shard, Bad Times at Backwheel, 1982; Guns of the Reaper, On the Spin of a Dollar, 1983; Another Day, Another Dollar, 1984; Dark Rider, 1987; I Rode with Wyatt, 1989; Dollars for the Reaper, A Legend Called Shatterhand, 1990; Loco, 1991; Shatterhand and the People, The Last Days of Billy Patch, Blood on the Reaper, 1992; All Trails Leads to Dodge, Montana Hit, 1993; A Coffin for the Reaper, 1994; Comes the Reaper, Utah Hit, Dakota Hit, 1995; Viva Reaper, The Shard Brand, 1996; High Plains Death, Smoking Star, 1997; Crowfeeders, 1999; North of the Bravo, 2000; Pocket Crossword Dictionary, 2001; The Guide to Solving Crosswords, Jake's Women, 2002; Solving Cryptic Crosswords, 2003; Rio Grande Shoot-Out, Trail of the Reaper, Three Graves to Fargo, The Expediter, 2004; Trouble in Tucson, Shotgun, 2005; Pocket Crossword Dictionary, 2006; Short stories, contributions to professional journals and peer-reviewed papers in academic journals. Address: c/o Robert Hale Ltd, Clerkenwell Green, London EC1R 0HT, England.

HOLMES James Christopher (Jim), b. 21 November 1948, London, England. Musician; Opera Conductor and Coach. m. Jean Wilkinson, 2 sons. Education: BA (Hons), University of Sheffield; Repetiteurs Diploma, London Opera Centre. Appointments: Principal Coach, Conductor, English National Opera, 1973-96; Numerous productions including: Pacific Overtures, London premiere; Street Scene, also BBC TV; La Belle Vivette, premiere of new version with Michael Frayn; Dr Ox's Experiment, world premiere; Arranger, National Youth Orchestra, BBC Proms; Musical Assistant to Simon Rattle, Glyndebourne Festival Opera, 1986-94; Associate Music Director, Carousel, Royal National Theatre; Conductor, BBC Concert Orchestra, London Sinfonietta, Montreal Symphony Orchestra, City of Birmingham Symphony Orchestra, Sinfonia Viva; Head of Music, Opera North, 1996-; Conductor: Gloriana, Tannhäuser, Sweeney Todd, Of Thee I Sing, Katya Kabanova, Pélléas and Melisande, Genoveva, Paradise Moscow, Cunning Little Vixen, Albert Herring; Arranger: Something Wonderful and If Ever I Would Leave You for Bryn Terfel; Guest Lecturer/Coach: National Opera Studio, Royal Northern College of Music. Publications: Numerous articles for programmes especially relating to American musical theatre; Arrangements of American musical songs for singers including: Bryn Terfel, Sally Burgess, Lesley Garrett; TV Programmes: I'm a Stranger Here Myself, Kurt Weill in America, BBC/HR; Street Scene BBC and WDR. Honours: USA Grammy Nomination for recording of Pacific Overtures; Gramophone Award for recording of Lesley Garrett, Soprano in Red. Memberships: Member, Advisory Board, Kurt Weill

Complete Edition; Joint Artistic Advisor, Kurt Weill Festival, Dessau. Address: c/o Opera North, Grand Theatre, New Briggate, Leeds, W Yorkshire LS1 6NU, England.

HOLMES John Eaton (Sir), b. 29 April 1951, Preston, England. Diplomat. m. Margaret Penelope Morris, 3 daughters. Education: BA, 1st Class Honours, Literae Humaniores (Greats), 1973, MA, 1975, Balliol College, Oxford. Appointments: Joined Foreign and Commonwealth Office, 1973: Second Secretary, British Embassy, Moscow, 1976-78; Near East and North Africa Department, 1978-82; Assistant Private Secretary to the Foreign Secretary, 1982-84; First Secretary (Economic), British Embassy, Paris, 1984-87; Deputy Head, Soviet Department, Foreign and Commonwealth Office, 1987-89; Seconded to Thomas de la Rue & Co, 1989-91; Economic and Commercial Counsellor, New Delhi, 1991-95; Head of the European Union Department, Foreign and Commonwealth Office, 1995; Private Secretary then Principal Private Secretary to the Prime Minister, 1996-99; British Ambassador to Portugal, 1999-2001; British Ambassador to France, 2001-. Honours: CMG, 1997; CVO, 1998; KBE, 1999; GCVO, 2004. Address: 35 rue du Faubourg St-Honoré, 75383 Paris Cedex 08, France. Website: www.amb-grandebretagne.fr

HOLMES-WALKER William Anthony, b. 26 January 1926, Horwich, Lancashire, England. Scientist. m. Marie-Anne Russ, 2 daughters. Education: BSc (Hons) Chemistry, 1950, PhD, Chemistry, 1953, Queen's University, Belfast, Northern Ireland; DIC, Chemical Engineering, Imperial College, London, 1954. Appointments: Technical Officer, ICI Limited, 1954-59; Head of Plastics R&D, The Metal Box Company, 1959-66; Professor of Polymer Science and Technology, Chairman of School of Materials, Brunel University, 1966-74; Director, The British Plastics Federation, 1974-81; Visiting Professor, The City University, 1981-83; Secretary General, European Brewers' Trade Association, CBMC, Brussels, 1983-87; Director, Industrial Liaison, University of Reading, 1987-90; Director, International Technology and Innovation, 1990-94; Chairman of Working Group, The Executive Committee, 1995-96; Chairman, BioInteractions Ltd, 1991-. Publications: Many articles in scientific journals and business publications; Chapter in Thermoplastics, 1969; Polymer Conversion, 1975; Best Foote Forward, 1995; Life-Enhancing Plastics, forthcoming. Honours: ERD, 1972, TD, 1980; Member, Army Emergency Reserve and TAVR, with rank of Lieutenant Colonel. Memberships: Royal Institution, 1953; FRSC, 1966; FPRI, 1969; FIM, 1972; FSA, 1989; Past Master, Skinners' Company. Address: 7 Alston Road, Boxmoor, Herts HP1 1QT, England. E-mail: anthonyhw@ntl.com.uk

HOLROYD Michael (de Courcy Fraser), Sir, b. 27 August 1935, London, England. Biographer; Writer. m. Margaret Drabble, 17 September 1982. Appointment: Visiting Fellow, Pennsylvania State University, 1979. Publications: Hugh Kingsmill: A Critical Biography, 1964; Lytton Strachey: A Critical Biography, 2 volumes, 1967, 1968, revised edition, 1994; A Dog's Life (novel), 1969; The Best of Hugh Kingsmill (editor), 1970; Lytton Strachey by Himself: A Self-Portrait (editor), 1971, new edition, 1994; Unreceived Opinions (essays), 1973; Augustus John, 2 volumes, 1974, 1975, revised edition, 1996; The Art of Augustus John (with Malcolm Easton), 1974; The Genius of Shaw (editor), 1979; The Shorter Strachey (editor with Paul Levy), 1980; William Gerhardie's God Fifth Column (editor with Robert Skidelsky), 1981; Essays by Diverse Hands (editor), Vol XLII, 1982; Peterley Harvest: The Private Diary of David Peterley (editor), 1985; Bernard Shaw: Vol I, The Search for Love

1856-1898, 1988, Vol II, The Pursuit of Power 1898-1918, 1989, Vol III, The Lure of Fantasy 1918-1950, 1991, Vol IV, The Last Laugh 1950-1991, 1992, Vol V, The Shaw Companion, 1992, one-volume abridged edition, 1997; Basil Street Blues, 1999; Works on Paper, 2002; Mosaic, 2004. Contributions to: Radio, television, and periodicals. Honours: Saxton Memorial Fellowship, 1964; Bollingen Fellowship, 1966; Winston Churchill Fellowship, 1971; Irish Life Arts Award, 1988; Commander of the Order of the British Empire, 1989; Prix du Meilleur Live Etranger, 1995; Heywood Hill Prize, 2001; Companion of Literature, 2004; David Cohen British Literature Prize, 2005; Golden Pen Award, 2006; Kt. 2007; Honorary DLitts, Universities of Ulster, 1992, Sheffield, 1993, Warwick, 1994, and East Anglia, 1994, London School of Economics, 1998. Memberships: Arts Council, chairman, literature panel, 1992-95; National Book League, chairman, 1976-78; PEN, president, British branch, 1985-88; Royal Historical Society, fellow; Royal Society of Literature, chairman, 1998-2001, President, 2003-; Society of Authors, chairman, 1973-74; Royal Society of Arts, fellow; Strachey Trust, chairman, 1990-95; Public Lending Right Advisory Committee, chairman, 1997-2000; Royal Literary Fund, vice-president, 1997-. Address: c/o A P Watt Ltd, 20 John Street, London WC1N 2DR, England.

HOLSTEIN-BECK Maria Danuta, b. 9 September 1923, Warsaw, Poland. Sociologist. m. Marian, 1 son, 3 daughters, 1 deceased. Education: Master of Sociology, University of Warsaw, 1968; Dr of Humanistic Science, Praxeology Department, Polish Academy of Science, 1973; Dr Hab of Economy in Social Policy, Main School of Planning and Statistics, Warsaw, 1979; Professor of Humanistic Science, 1990. Appointments: Social Inspector, Institute of Mathematical Machines, Polish Academy of Science, 1959-63; Sociologist, Warsaw Mechanical Works DELTA, 1967-71; Economist, 1971-73; Adjunct, 1974-80, Docent, 1981-90, Chief of Department of Management Technics, 1982-90, Administration and Management Institute, 1971-90; Lecturer, R Łazarski First Business College, Warsaw, 1994-96; Full-time Professor, P Włodkowic Academy, Płock, 1996-2001; Full-time Professor, L Koźminski Academy of Management, Warsaw, 2001-05; Full-time Professor, Chief of Cathedra of Social-Economical Globalization, First Private School of Business and Administration, Warsaw, 2004-08. Publications: Over 160 reports for conferences, articles, papers, handbooks, monographs; Books: Conflicts, 1978-83; Study on the Work, 1987; To Be or Not To Be a Manager, 1997; Manager Wanted, 2001; Managerial Functions, 2004; The Brilliant Gateway to Heaven, 2000; Studies and Materials of Social Policy, 2007. Honours: The Cavalry Cross, Polonia Restituta, 1987; Medal of 55th Anniversary of Married Life, 1998; Listed in international biographical dictionaries. Memberships: ISA, 1973-90; PTS, 1968-; TNOIK, 1973-. Address: ul Boya-Żeleńskiego str No 4/55, 00-621 Warsaw, Poland. E-mail: maria.hosteinbeck@neostrada.pl

HOLT Derek Francis, b. 21 March 1949, Wembley, England. Professor of Mathematics. m. Catherine Wattebot, 2 sons. Education: Undergraduate, 1967-70, Postgraduate, 1970-74, University College, Oxford. Appointments: Assistant, University of Tübingen, Germany, 1973-75; Research Fellow, Brasenose College, Oxford, 1975-78; Lecturer, Mathematics, 1978-87, Reader, Mathematics, 1987-2001, Professor of Mathematics, University of Warwick, 2001-. Publications: 80 articles in mathematical journals; Books: Perfect Groups (with W Plesken), 1989; Handbook of Computational Group Theory (with B Eick and E A O'Brien), 2005. Honour: London Mathematical Society Junior Whitehead Prize, 1981.

Membership: London Mathematical Society, 1979. Address: Mathematics Institute, University of Warwick, Coventry CV 4 7AL, England. E-mail: d.f.holt@warwick.ac.uk

HOLUB Karel, b. 9 November 1933, Prague, Czech Republic. Seismologist. m. (1) Maria, 1954, divorced 1982, (2) Olga, 1984, 3 sons, 1 daughter. Education: Diploma in Applied Geophysics, 1959, Dr rer nat (MA) 1982, PhD, Mathematics and Physics, 1991, Charles University, Prague; DSc, Geology, Czech Academy of Sciences, Prague, 2001. Appointments: Geophysical Institute, AS CR, Prague, 1959-78; Research Mining Institute, Ostrava, 1979-93; Research Worker, Project Leader, Senior Research Worker, Institute of Geonics AS CR, Ostrava; Principal Research Worker, 1994-. Publications: More than 170 papers in different journals, more than 110 research and technical reports. Honour: Award of Czechoslovakia Academy of Sciences, 1963. Memberships: Czech Association of Applied Geophysicists; Czech Society for Mechanics; New York Academy of Sciences; Advisory Council IBC; Research Board of Advisors ABI. Address: Horymírova 110, CZ 700 30 Ostrava-Za'břeh, Czech Republic.

HOLYFIELD Evander, b. 19 October 1962, Atlanta, Georgia, USA. Boxer. Career: Founder, Real Deal Record Label, 1999; Founder, Holyfield Foundation to help inner-city youth; Bronze Medal, Olympic Games, 1984; World Boxing Association Cruiserweight Title, 1986; International Boxing Federation Cruiserweight Title, 1987; World Boxing Council Cruiserweight Title, 1988; World Heavyweight Champion, 1990-92, 1993-94, 1996- (following defeat of Mike Tyson, 1996); Defended title against Mike Tyson 1997 (Tyson disqualified for biting off part of Holyfield's ear); Defended IBF Heavyweight Title against Michael Moorer, 1997; Defended WBA and IBF Titles, and Contested WBC Title, against Lennox Lewis, 1999, bout declared a draw; Lost to Lennox Lewis, November 1999; WBA heavyweight champion, 2000-01; career record 42 wins, 8 defeats, 2 draws; Suspended by NY State Boxing Commission after defeat by Larry Donald, 2004. Honours: Epsy Boxer of the Decade, 1990-2000. Address: Main Events, 390 Murray Hill Parkway, East Rutherford, NJ 07073, USA.

HOMAN Roger Edward, b. 25 June 1944, Brighton, England. University Professor. m. Caroline Baker. Education: BA, Religious Studies, University of Sussex, 1969; MSc, Government, London School of Economics, 1979; PhD, Sociology, University of Lancaster, 1979. Appointments: School teaching posts, 1966-67, 1969-71; Lecturer, Brighton College of Education, 1971-76; Senior Lecturer in Education, Brighton Polytechnic, 1976-92; Principal Lecturer, 1992-98; Professor of Religious Studies, 1998-, University of Brighton. Publications: 90 articles published in academic and professional journals. Honours: Fellow, Victoria College of Music, 1994. Memberships: Victorian Society; National Vice President, Prayer Book Society; Anglo-Catholic Research Society; Ecclesiological Society. Address: University of Brighton, Falmer, East Sussex, BN1 9PH, England. E-mail: r.homan@bton.ac.uk

HOME, Earl of, David Alexander Cospatrick Douglas-Home, b. 20 November 1943, Coldstream, Scotland. Banker. m. Jane Margaret Williams-Wynne, 1 son, 2 daughters. Education: MA, Christ Church, Oxford. Appointments: Director, Morgan Grenfell & Co Ltd, 1974-99; Chairman, Coutts & Co, 1999-; Chairman, Committee for Middle East Trade, 1986-92; Trade Industry and Finance

Spokesman, House of Lords, 1997-98. Honours: CVO; CBE; FCIB. Membership: Turf. Address: Coutts & Co, 440 Strand, London WC2R 0QS, England.

HONEYBOURNE Duncan, b. 27 October 1977, Weymouth, Dorset, England. Concert Pianist. Education: Junior Academy, Royal Academy of Music, 1992-96; Birmingham Conservatoire 1996-2000; Studied with Rosemarie Wright, John York, Philip Martin; Leeds with Fanny Waterman and London with Mikhail Kazakevich; BMus, First Class Honours, 2000; HonBC, 2006. Debut: Symphony Hall, Birmingham, and National Concert Hall, Dublin, 1998. Career: Concertos and Recitals throughout UK and Ireland; Has recorded for BBC Radio 3 and RTE, Dublin, Radio and TV; Piano Teacher: Bryanston School, 2003-; Lecturer in Piano and Performance Tutor University of Chichester, 2005-; Dedicatee and first performer of Sonatas by Andrew Downes and John Joubert. Publications: Articles contributed to The Times, The Western Mail, The Birmingham Post, and BMI Insight. Honours include: Sheila Mossman Memorial Prize and Silver Medal, AB London; Iris Dyer Piano Prize, Royal Academy of Music, 1995; Several solo piano and chamber music prizes at Birmingham Conservatoire; Goldenweiser Scholarship; John Ireland Prize, 1999; Honorary Member, Birmingham Conservatoire. Membership: ISM Solo Performers' and Musicians' in Education sections. Address: 77 Monmouth Avenue, Weymouth, Dorset, DT3 5JR, England. E-mail: duncan.honeybourne@btopenworld.com

HONG Ikpyo, b. 4 August 1962, Yeongi-gun, Korea. Researcher; Chemical Engineer. m. Seonmi Park, 1 son, 1 daughter. Education: Bachelor, 1984, Master, 1986, Chemical Engineering, Chungnam National University; PhD, Chemical Engineering, Hanyang University, 2003. Appointments: Researcher, Shinwha Chemical Industry Co Ltd, Korea, 1986-88; Researcher, Samchully Co Ltd, Korea, 1988-91; Senior Researcher, Research Institute of Industrial Science and Technology, Korea, 1991-. Publications: Metal dispersed activated carbon fibers and their application, 2002; Performance of tin oxide-graphite composite anode for lithium ion battery, 2007; Adsorption properties of activated carbon filters by electrical decomposition, 2007. Memberships: Korea Carbon Society; Korea Institute of Chemical Engineers; Korean Society of Environmental Engineers; Korean Hydrogen & New Energy Society. Address: RIST, San 32 Hyoja-Dong, Nam-Gu, Pohang 790-600, Republic of Korea. E-mail: iphong@rist.re.kr Website: www.rist.re.kr/

HONG In Pyo, b. 3 May 1960, Gwangju, South Korea. Researcher. m. Yung Gyun Kim, 1 son, 1 daughter. Education: BS, Yonsei University, Seoul, South Korea, 1982; MS, Chungbuk National University, South Korea, 1997; PhD, Yonsei University, Seoul, South Korea, 2004. Appointments: Principal Researcher, Agency for Defence Development, Daejeon, South Korea, 1984-; Senior Researcher, Matra Marconi Space UK Ltd, Portsmouth, England, 1997-99; Senior Researcher, Korea-Russia Science and Technological Co-operation Centre of Korea Institute of Science and Technology, 2001; Principal Researcher, Member of Security Management Commission, Daejeon, South Korea, 2005-. Publications: many papers in scientific journals including: Institute of Electronics, Information and Communication Engineers Transactions on Communications; Signal Processing; The Journal of Korea Electromagnetic Engineering Society; The Journal of Korea Institute of Communication and Sciences; Journal of Defence Technical Research; Paper, 5th World Wireless Congress, San Francisco, USA; Technical Report, Agency for Defence Development.

Honours: National Defence and Science Prize, 1989 and 2006, Medal for Distinguished Services, 2004, Agency for Defence Development; Research Bounty on National Defence and Science (special grade), Ministry of National Defence, Seoul, South Korea, 1993; Man of the Year, 2006; American Order of Excellence; American Hall of Fame; Great Minds of the 21st Century; Universal Awards of Accomplishment, 2006; Deputy Governor, ABI; Listed in Who's Who in the World, 23rd edition, 2006; Who's Who in Science and Engineering, 9th edition, 2006-07; Who's Who in Asia, 1st edition, 2006-07. Memberships: Korea Electromagnetic Engineering Society; Korea Institute of Communication and Science; Institute of Electronics, Information and Communication Engineers; Korean Council on Systems Engineering; Husband and Wife Anthem Chorus of Centralgate Baptist Church, Daejeon, South Korea; Chairman, Beautiful People Committee, Centralgate Baptist Church, Daejeon, South Korea. Address: 215 Sunam-dong, #317-101, Yuseong-gu, Daejeon 305-152, South Korea. E-mail: hip7777@naver.com

HONG Jung-Jin, b. 11 April 1969, Seoul, Korea. Orthodontist. m. Song Yi Kim, 2 daughters. Education: DDS, 1994, MD, 2001, PhD, 2005, KyungHee University. Appointments: Orthodontic Residency, 1997-2001, Clinical Assistant Professor, 2006-, Department of Orthodontics, KyungHee University. Publications: Cephalometric evaluation of effect of cervical pull head ger to mandibular molars in Class III malocclusion, 2001; Effects of IL-1β, TNF-α, INF-γ on production of nitric oxide in mouse calvarial osteoblast, 2005. Memberships: Fellow, World Federation of Orthodontics; International Member, American Association of Orthodontics. Address: Yangchun-gu, Shinjung 5-dong, Izung Bd Well-dental Clinic, Seoul 158-857, Korea. E-mail: orthojj@hotmail.com

HONG Kyung Pyo, b. 17 February 1954, Busan, South Korea. Physician; Educator. m. Hyoun Tae Kim, deceased, 2 sons. Education: MD, Seoul National University College of Medicine, 1978; PhD, Chung-Ang University Medical School, Seoul, Korea, 1990; Fellow, University of Alberta Hospital, Edmonton, Canada, 1988; Fellow, Westminster Hospital, London, England, 1990-91. Appointments: House Officer, Seoul National University Hospital, 1978-83; Professor, Hallym University College of Medicine, 1986-94; Physician, 1994-, Vice Chairman, Cardiac and Vascular Centre, 1999-2001, Chief, Division of Cardiology, 2001-2002, Samsung Medical Centre; Professor, 1997-, Director, Office of Medical Education, 2003-2007, Associate Dean, 2005-2007, Sungkyunkwan University School of Medicine; Editor-in-Chief, Korean Circulation Journal, 2000-2002. Publications: Clinical Cardiology (co-author), 2nd edition 2007; Textbook of Cardiovascular Medicine (co-author), 2001; Contributor of articles to professional journals. Honour: President, Korean Society of Cardiovascular Rehabilitation and Prevention, 1997-2000; Chair, Problem-based Learning Working Group, 2007-. Memberships: Fellow, American Association of Cardiovascular and Pulmonary Rehabilitation; Fellow, Korean Society of Circulation; Member of Editorial Board, 1998-2001, Korean Association of Internal Medicine; Korean Society of Cardiovascular Rehabilitation and Prevention; Korean Society of Medical Education. Address: Samsung Medical Centre, 50 Irwon-Dong, Gangnam-Gu, 135-710 Seoul, Korea. E-mail: kphong@skku.edu

HONG Seok Min, b. 1 November 1957, Seoul, South Korea. Principal Researcher. m. Young Hee Hong Lee, 1 son, 1 daughter. Education: Bachelor degree, Kwang Woon University, Seoul, 1979; Master degree, 1991, PhD, 1995,

Chung Nam National University, Dae Jeon City. Appointments: Researcher/Senior Researcher, 1979-97; Principal Researcher, 1998-, Agency for Defense Development, Dae Jeon, South Korea. Publications: Articles in professional journals. Honours: Minister of National Defense, South Korea, 1999, 2005; Prime Minister's Award, South Korea, 2001. Address: Agency for Defense Development (3rd R&D Institute-1), Yuseong PO Box 35-3, Dae Jeon City, 305-600, South Korea. E-mail: hongsm@add.re.kr

HONG Seok-In, b. 12 August 1967, Seoul, Republic of Korea. Research Scientist. m. Kyu-Hei Song, 1 son, 1 daughter. Education: BS, 1990, MS, 1992, Food Engineering, PhD, Food and Biotechnology, 1997, Yonsei University. Appointments: Research Scientist, 1992-99, Senior Research Scientist, 1999-2007, Principal Research Scientist, 2007-, Korea Food Research Institute; Visiting Research Fellow, UC Davis, USA, 2000-01. Publications: Papers and articles in professional scientific journals. Honours: MAF Minister Award for Outstanding Activity, 1998, 2006; KoSFoST Award for Academic Progress, 2002; KFRI Merit Award for Creative Research, 2002, 2005. Memberships: Korean Society of Food Science and Technology; Korean Society for Food Engineering; Institute of Food Technologists. Address: Korea Food Research Institute, 516, Baekhyun, Bundang, Seongnam, Kyonggi 463-746, Republic of Korea. E-mail: sihong@kfri.re.kr

HONG Seong Pyo, b. 10 September 1944, Seoul, Korea. Professor. 2 sons. Education: BA, 1968, MA, 1974, Seoul National University. Appointments: Researcher, Korean Educational Institute, 1977-78; Lecturer, Han Yang University, 1978-79; Junior Lecturer, Kwan Dong University, 1979-80; Professor, Chungbuk National University, 1980-; Dean, College of Education, 1999-2001. Publications: 4 books including Crime and Society in Medieval Society, 2006; Translations: 5 books including Food and Feast in Medieval England, 2003; 40 History papers including Implication of Edward I's Politics to Scotland, 2007. Membership: Editorial Board, The Korean Society of Western History, 1984-86; Editor, The Korean History Education Society, 1990-94; President, The Chungbuk Historical Society, 1993; President, The Korean Society for Western Medieval History, 1998-2000; Fellow, Royal Historical Society. Address: Department of History Education, Chungbuk National University, Cheongju, Chungbuk 361-763, Korea. E-mail: sphong@chungbuk.ac.kr

HONG Sinpyo, b. 10 April 1959, Busan, Republic of Korea. Research Professor. Education: BA, Pusan National University, Busan, Korea, 1982; MS, Korea Advanced Institute of Science and Technology, Seoul, 1985; PhD, University of California, Los Angeles, USA, 1993. Appointments: Design Engineer, Korea Heavy Industries and Constructions Co, 1985-86; Research Engineer, Development of a Robot at Samsung Advanced Institute of Technology, Giheung, Korea, 1986-90; Postdoctoral Fellow, Development of Navigation Systems at UCLA, 1993-97; Postdoctoral Fellow, 2000-03, Research Professor, Development of Navigation Systems, 2003-, Pusan National University. Publications: A Car Test for the Estimation of GPS/INS Alignment Errors, 2004; Experimental Study on the Estimation of Lever Arm in GPS/INS, 2006. Memberships: Institute of Navigation. Address: Pusan National University, Advanced Ship Engineering Center, San 30, Kumjeong-gu, Jangjeon-dong, Busan 609-735, Republic of Korea. E-mail: sinpyo@pusan.ac.kr

HONG Sung Jei, b. 11 July 1968, Seoul, Korea. Researcher. Education: BA, 1991, MA, 1993, Sungkyunkwan University; PhD, Tohoku University, 2006. Appointments: Principal Researcher, Korea Electronics Technology Institute, 1993-. Publications: Articles in professional scientific journals: Fabrication of Indium Tin Oxide (ITO) Thin Film with Pre-Treated Sol Coating; Quantum Confined Y_2O_3:Eu^{3+} Nanophosphor Fabricated with Pre-dissipation Treatment; Improvement in the Long-Term Stability of SnO_2 Nanoparticle Surface Modification with Additives; Low Temperature Catalyst Adding (LTCA) for Tin Oxide Nanostructure Gas Sensors; Indium tin oxide (ITO) thin film fabricated by indium-tin-organic sol including ITO nanoparticle; Optimization of solvent condition for highly luminescent Y_2O_3: Eu^{3+} nanophospor. Honours: Best Oral Presentation Award; Best Poster Presentation Award, 2002. Address: 1122-903, Bakhap LG APT, Sanbon 2 Dong, Gunposi, Gyeonggido, 435-743, Republic of Korea.

HONG Wei-Chiang, b. 14 November 1972, Taichung, Taiwan. Assistant Professor. m. Su-Mei Tsai, 1 son. Education: Bachelor's degree, Applied Mathematics, 1994; Master's degree, Traffic & Transportation, 1996; PhD, Management, 2008. Appointments: Project Manager, Asian Pacific Consultant Ltd, Taiwan, 1996-97; Finance Manager, Mutual Group, Taiwan, 1997-98; Senior Specialist, Newa Insurance Co Ltd, Taiwan, 1999-2000; Marketing Manager, Taiwan Electronic Co Ltd, Taiwan, 2001-02; Adjunct Lecturer, Da-Yeh University, Changhua, Taiwan, 2002-06; Senior Lecturer, 2006-07, Assistant Professor, 2007-, Oriental Institute of Technology, Panchiao, Taiwan. Publications: Numerous articles in professional journals. Honours: Best Paper Award, Chinese Road Federation, 1997; Best Paper Award, International Conference on New Global Management Environment, 2006; Best Presentation Award, Joint 2nd International Conference on Soft Computing and Intelligent Systems and 5th International Symposium on Advanced Intelligent Systems, Japan, 2004. Memberships: Institute for Operations Research and Management Sciences; IEEE; Senior Member, Institute of Industrial Engineers, USA. Address: No 58, Sec 2, Sichuan Road, Yuanlin, Changhua, 51065, Taiwan. E-mail: samuelhong@ieee.org

HONG Yang-Pyo, b. 27 September 1936, Kangwon-Do, Korea. Professor Emeritus. m. Dung-Ja Hwang, 2 sons. Education: BA, Department of Political Science, Tong-Ah University, Busan, Korea, 1970; MA, 1975, PhD, 1984, Department of Political Science, Graduate School, Kyungpook National University (KNU), Daegu. Appointments: Army Officer, 1960-73, Retired as captain, 1973; Military Training, Huntsville Alabama US for HAWK Maintenance, 1965-66, 1970-71; Councillor, Kyungpook National University Chorus, 1978-; Director, Korean Association of Middle East Studies, 1980-2002; Full Instructor, Teachers College, 1977-80, Assistant Professor, 1980-84, Associate Professor, 1984-90, Professor, 1990-2003, Kyungpook National University; Board Member, Daegu YMCA, 1985-2002; Fulbright Senior Scholar for Research, Lecturing and Exchanging Course, Hoover Institute, Stanford University, USA, 1985; Standing Committee of Daegu Citizens Activity for Economy Justice, 1990-96; Vice President, Korean Ethics Association, 1993-; Director, Korean Political Science Association, 1997-; Director, Peace House for Runaway Adolescence, Daegu, 1997-; President, KNU Political Science Association, 2001-02. Publications: Numerous papers and articles in professional scientific journals; 5 books. Honours: Outstanding Contribution, 80th Anniversary of Daegu YMCA, 1977; Professor Hong's Tenor Concert with Chorus commemoration

of 60th birthday, 1986; Yellow Bird Medal, President of Korea, 2002; Another Hong's Concert commemoration of Retirement, KNU University Chorus, 2002; Listed in Who's Who in the World, 1999-2006; Diploma of Achievement in Education, IBC, 2005; International Peace Prize, United Cultural Convention; International Professional of the Year, IBC, 2005. Memberships: Korean Ethics Studies Association; Korean Political Science Association; International Political Science Association; Korean Association of Middle East Studies; KNU Political Science Association; Bibliotheque World Wide Society; Daegu Christian Elders' Choir. Address: 257-23 Sinam-Dong, Dong-Gu, Daegu 701-812, Korea. E-mail: yphong45@hotmail.com

HONIG Edwin, b. 3 September 1919, New York, New York, USA. Retired Professor of English and of Comparative Literature; Poet; Writer; Dramatist; Translator. m. (1) Charlotte Gilchrist, 1 April 1940, deceased 1963, (2) Margot Dennes, 15 December 1963, divorced 1978, 2 sons. Education: BA, 1939, MA, 1947, University of Wisconsin at Madison. Appointments: Poetry Editor, New Mexico Quarterly, 1948-52; Instructor, Claremont College, California, 1949; Faculty, 1949-57, Assistant Professor of English, Harvard University; Faculty, 1957-60, Professor of English, 1960-82, Professor of Comparative Literature, 1962-82, Professor Emeritus, 1983-, Brown University; Visiting Professor, University of California at Davis, 1964-65; Mellon Professor, Boston University, 1977. Publications: Poetry: The Moral Circus, 1955; The Gazabos: 41 Poems, 1959; Survivals, 1964; Spring Journal, 1968; Four Springs, 1972; At Sixes, 1974; Shake a Spear with Me, John Berryman, 1974; Selected Poems 1955-1976, 1979; Interrupted Praise, 1983; Gifts of Light, 1983; The Imminence of Love: Poems 1962-1992, 1993; Time and Again: Poems 1940-97, 2000. Stories: Foibles and Fables of an Abstract Man, 1979. Non-Fiction: García Lorca, 1944, revised edition, 1963; Dark Conceit: The Making of Allegory, 1959; Calderón and the Seizures of Honor, 1972; The Poet's Other Voice: Conversations on Literary Translation, 1986. Plays: Ends of the World and Other Plays, 1984. Translations: Over 10 books, 1961-93. Contributions to: books, anthologies, reviews, journals, and periodicals. Honours: Guggenheim Fellowships, 1948, 1962; National Academy of Arts and Letters Grant, 1966; Amy Lowell Traveling Poetry Fellowship, 1968; Rhode Island Governor's Award for Excellence in the Arts, 1970; National Endowment for the Humanities Fellowship, 1975, and Grants, 1977-80; National Endowment for the Arts Fellowship, 1977; Translation Award, Poetry Society of America, 1984; National Award, Columbia University Translation Center, 1985; Decorated by the Portuguese President for translation of Pessoa, 1989; Decorated by the King of Spain for translation of Calderón, 1996. Memberships: Dante Society of America; Poetry Society of America. Address: 229 Medway Street, Apt 305, Providence, RI 02906, USA.

HOOGENBOOM Carol, Clinical Psychologist. Education: BS, 1985, MA, 1987, Western Michigan University, Kalamazoo, Michigan; Psy D, Forest Institute of Professional Psychology, Missouri, 1993. Appointments: Child Counselor, 1983, Child Researcher, 1984, Child Development Center, Kalamazoo; Child Counselor, Children's Learning Village, Kalamazoo, 1984-85; Psychotherapist, Center for Counselling & Psychological Services, Kalamazoo, 1985-87; Neuropsychometrian, Neuropsychology, Kalamazoo, 1987; Clinical Therapist/Psychometrican, Comprehenisve Psychological Services, Chicago, 1989; Psychological Internship/Residency, Cermak Hospital, Chicago, 1991-92; Clinical Therapist/Psychometrician, Behavioral Associates,

Oak Park, Illinois, 1993-94; Psychologist/President, National Neuropsychological & Psychological Services Inc, Glenview, Illinois, 1995-98; Clinical Psychologist, CAH Psychological Services, Chicago, Illinois, 1999-. Publications: Author, How to Start a Domestic Abuse Shelter, 2004; Articles in popular journals; 2 research projects. Honours: Society of Distinguished Americans; American Indian Scholarship, Albuquerque, New Mexico, 1982-87; United States American Indian Scholarship, Washington DC, 1987-93; President Elect, Student Council, Forest Institute of Professional Psychology, 1988-89; Lifetime Member, Psi Chi Honor Society; 1st female American Indian to obtain a Doctoral degree in Psychology in the US, 1993; Listed in international biographical dictionaries; Many athletic awards, ribbons & trophies. Memberships: American Psychological Association. Address: 28 E Jackson Bldg, #10-H580, Chicago, IL 60604, USA. E-mail: carolhoogenboom@yahoo.com

HOOK Andrew Dunnet, b. 21 December 1932, Wick, Caithness, Scotland. m. Judith Ann Hibberd, deceased, 1984, 2 sons, 1 daughter, deceased, 1995. Education: MA, University of Edinburgh, Scotland, 1954; PhD, Princeton University, USA, 1960. Appointments: Assistant Lecturer, 1961-63, Lecturer in American Literature, 1963-71, University of Edinburgh; Senior Lecturer in English, University of Aberdeen, 1971-79; Bradley Professor of English Literature, University of Glasgow, 1979-98; Visiting Fellow, English Department, Princeton University, 1999-2000; Gillespie Visiting Professor, The College of Wooster, Wooster, Ohio, 2001-2002; Visiting Professor, Dartmouth College, Hanover, New Hampshire, 2003. Publications: Scott's Waverley (editor), 1972; Charlotte Brontë's Shirley (co-editor), 1974; John Dos Passos, Twentieth Century Views (editor), 1974; Scotland and America 1750-1835, 1975; American Literature in Context 1865-1900, 1983; History of Scottish Literature, Vol II 1660-1800 (editor), 1987; Scott Fitzgerald, 1992; The Glasgow Enlightenment (co-editor), 1995; From Goosecreek to Gandercleugh: Studies in Scottish-American Literary and Cultural History, 1999; Scott's The Fair Maid of Perth (co-editor), 1999; F Scott Fitzgerald: A Literary Life, 2002. Honours: Fellow, Royal Society of Edinburgh, 2000-; Fellow, British Academy, 2002. Memberships: British Association for American Studies; Eighteenth Century Scottish Studies Society; Modern Languages Association; Institute of Contemporary Scotland. Address: 5 Rosslyn Terrace, Glasgow G12 9NB, Scotland.

HOOKWAY Harry Thurston (Sir), b. 23 July 1921, London, England. Administrator. m. Barbara Butler, deceased, 1 son, 1 daughter. Education: BSc, PhD, London University. Appointments: Assistant Director, National Chemical Laboratory, 1959; Director, United Kingdom Scientific Mission to North America, Scientific Attaché, British Embassy, Washington, Scientific Advisor, High Commission, Ottawa, 1960-64; Head, Information Division, DSIR, 1964-65; Chief Scientific Officer, Department of Education and Science, 1966-69; Under Secretary, Department of Education and Science, 1969-73; Deputy Chairman and Chief Executive, British Library Board, 1973-84; Pro-Chancellor, Loughborough University, 1987-93. Publications: Papers in learned and professional journals. Honours: Hon LLD; Hon D Litt; HON FLA; Hon F I Inst Sci; Gold Medal, International Federation of Library Associations; Knight Bachelor, 1978; President, Institute of Information Scientists, 1973-76; President Library Association, 1985. Memberships: Royal Commission on Historical Monuments (England), 1981-87; Fellow, Royal Society of Arts. Address: 3 St James Green, Thirsk, North Yorkshire YO7 1AF, England.

HOON Rt Hon Geoffrey William, b. 6 December 1953, Derby, England. Parliamentary Secretary to the Treasury and Chief Whip. m. Elaine Dumelow, 1981, 1 son; 2 daughters. Education: Nottingham High School; BA, Law, 1974, MA, Jesus College, Cambridge. Appointments: Lecturer in Law, Leeds University, 1976-82; Called to the Bar, Gray's Inn, 1978; Visiting Professor of Law, University of Louisville, Kentucky, 1980-81; Barrister in Nottingham, 1982-84; Member of the European Parliament for Derbyshire and Ashfield, 1984-94; Member of the European Parliament's Legal Affairs Committee, 1984-94; Member of Parliament for Ashfield, 1992-; Parliamentary Secretary, 1997-98, Minister of State, 1998-99, Lord Chancellor's Department; Minister of State with responsibility for Asia and the Pacific, the Middle East and North Africa, Foreign and Commonwealth Office, 1999; Secretary of State for Defence, 1999-2005; Lord Privy Seal and Leader of the House of Commons, 2005-06; Minister for Europe, 2006-; Parliamentary Secretary to the Treasury and Chief Whip, 2007.

HOOPER Michael Wrenford, b. 2 May 1941, Gloucester, England. Cleric. m. Rosemary, 2 sons, 2 daughters. Education: St David's College, Lampeter, Dyfed; St Stephen's House, Oxford. Appointments: Curate, Bridgnorth, Shropshire, 1965; Victor of Minsterley, Rural Dean, Pontesbury, 1970; Rector and Rural Dean, Leonminster, 1981; Archdeacon of Hereford, 1997; Suffragan Bishop of Ludlow, Archdeacon of Ludlow, 2002.

HOPE Christopher David Tully, b. 26 February 1944, Johannesburg, South Africa. Writer. m. Eleanor Marilyn Margaret Klein, 1967, 2 sons. Education: BA, Natal University, 1969; MA, University of the Witwatersrand, 1972. Publications: Cape Drives, 1974; A Separate Development, 1981; The Country of the Black Pig, 1981; The King, the Cat and the Fiddle, 1983; Kruger's Alp, 1984; The Dragon Wore Pink, 1985; White Boy Running, 1988; My Chocolate Redeemer, 1989; Serenity House, 1992; The Love Songs of Nathan J Swirsky, 1993; Darkest England, 1996; Me, The Moon and Elvis Presley, 1997; Signs of the Heart, 1999; Heaven Forbid, 2001; Brothers Under The Skin (Travels in Tyranny), 2003; My Mother's Lovers, 2006; The Garden of Bad Dreams, 2008. Contributions to: Times Literary Supplement; London Magazine; Les Temps Modernes. Honours: Cholmondeley Award, 1974; David Higham Prize, 1981; International PEN Award, 1983; Whitbread Prize, 1985. Memberships: Royal Society of Literature, fellow; Society of Authors. Address: c/o Rogers, Coleridge & White Ltd, 20 Powis Mews, London W11 1JN, England.

HOPE Ronald Anthony, b. 16 March 1951, London, England. Professor of Medical Ethics. m. Sally Hirsh, 2 daughters. Education: MA, New College, Oxford, 1970-73; PhD, National Institute for Medical Research, 1973-76; BM BCh, University of Oxford Clinical School, 1977-80. Appointments: House Surgeon, Royal United Hospital, Bath, 1980-81; House Physician, John Radcliffe Hospital, Oxford, 1981; Senior House Officer, Registrar rotation in Psychiatry, Oxford Hospital, 1981-85; Wellcome Trust Training Fellow in Psychiatry, 1985-87; Clinical Lecturer in Psychiatry, University of Oxford, 1987-90; Leader, Oxford Practice Skills Project, 1990-95; University Lecturer in Practice Skills, 1995-2000; Reader in Medicine, 1996-2000, Professor of Medical Ethics, 2000-, University of Oxford; Delegate, Oxford University Press; Chairman, Wellcome Trust Medical Humanities Strategy Committee; Chairman, Working Party on Ethics and Dementia, Nuffield Council on Bioethics. Publications: Books: Oxford Handbook of Clinical Medicine, editions, 1,

2, 3, 4 (9 translations), 1985-98; Essential Practice in Patient Centred Care, 1995; Manage Your Mind (4 translations), 1995; Medical Ethics and Law, 2003; A Very Short Introduction to Medical Ethics, 2004; Numerous articles and chapters mainly in fields of medical ethics and behavioural disturbance in Alzheimer's Disease. Honours: Rhodes Travel Scholarship, 1969; Bosanquet Open Scholarship, New College, 1970; Wellcome Trust Training Fellowship, 1985-87; Research Prize and Medal, Royal College of Psychiatrists, 1997; Member, through distinction, Faculty of Public Health, 2003. Memberships: Fellow, St Cross College, Oxford; Fellow, Royal College of Psychiatrists; Member, Faculty of Public Health. Address: Departments of Public Health and Primary Care, University of Oxford, Old Road Campus, Oxford OX3 7LF, England. E-mail: admin@ethox.ox.ac.uk

HOPE Ronald (Sidney), b. 4 April 1921, London, England. Writer. Education: BA, 1941, MA, 1946, DPhil, New College, Oxford. Appointments: Fellow, Brasenose College, Oxford, 1945-47, Director, Seafarers' Education Service, London, 1947-76; Director, The Marine Society, 1976-86. Publications: Spare Time at Sea, 1954; Economic Geography, 1956; Dick Small in the Half Deck, Ships, 1958; The British Shipping Industry, 1959; The Shoregoer's Guide to World Ports, 1963; Seamen and the Sea, 1965; Introduction to the Merchant Navy, 1965; Retirement from the Sea, 1967; In Cabined Ships at Sea, 1969; Twenty Singing Seamen, 1979; The Seamen's World, 1982; A New History of British Shipping, 1990; Poor Jack, 2001. Address: 2 Park Place, Dollar, FK14 7AA, Scotland.

HOPKINS Anthony (Philip), b. 31 December 1937, Port Talbot, South Wales. Actor. m. (1) Petronella Barker, 1967, divorced 1972, 1 daughter, (2) Jennifer Lynton, 1973, divorced 2002, (3) Stella Arroyave, 2003. Education: Welsh College of Music and Drama. Career: Assistant Stage Manager, Manchester Library Theatre, 1960; Joined Nottingham Repertory Company; Royal Academy of Dramatic Art; Phoenix Theatre, Leicester; Liverpool Playhouse and Hornchurch Repertory Company. Films include: The Lion in Winter, 1967; The Looking Glass War, 1968; Hamlet, 1969; Young Winston, 1971; A Doll's House, 1972; The Girl from Petrovka, 1973; Juggernaut, 1974; Audrey Rose, A Bridge Too Far, 1976; International Velvet, 1977; Magic, 1978; The Elephant Man, 1979; A Change of Seasons, 1980; The Bounty, 1983; The Good Father, 1985; 84 Charing Cross Road, 1986; The Dawning, 1987; A Chorus of Disapproval, 1988; Desperate Hours, 1989; The Silence of the Lambs, Free Jack, One Man's War, Spotswood, 1990; Howard's End, Bram Stoker's Dracula, 1991; Chaplin, The Trial, The Innocent, Remains of the Day, 1992; Shadowlands, Legends of the Fall, The Road to Wellville, 1993; August, 1994; Nixon, Surviving Picasso, 1995; The Edge, 1996; The Mask of Zorro, Amistad, Meet Joe Black, 1997; Instinct, 1998; Titus, 1999; Hannibal, Hearts of Atlantis, 2000; Mission Impossible 2, Hannibal, The Devil and Daniel Webster, 2001; Bad Company, Red Dragon, 2002; Human Stain, 2003; Alexander, 2004; Proof, The World's Fastest Indian, 2005; Bobby, 2006; Slipstream, Fracture, City of Your Final Destination, Beowulf, 2007. Theatre includes: A Flea in Her Ear, 1967; A Woman Killed with Kindness, 1971; Macbeth, 1972; Equus, 1974; The Tempest, USA, 1979; Old Times, USA, 1984; The Lonely Road, 1985; King Lear, 1986. TV includes: A Company of Five, 1968; The Poet Game, 1970; War and Peace, 1971; Lloyd George, 1972; All Creatures Great and Small, 1974; Kean, 1978; The Bunker, 1980; Othello, BBC, 1981; A Married Man, 1982; Blunt, 1985; Across the Lake, Heartland, 1988; To Be the Best, 1990; A Few Selected Exits, Big Cats, 1993. Honours include: Variety Club Film and Stage Actor Awards, 1984, 1985, 1993;

BAFTA Best Actor Awards, 1973, 1991, 1994, 1995; Emmy Awards, 1976, 1981; Oscar, 1991; Laurence Olivier Awards 1985; CBE, 1987; KB, 1993; Commandeur dans l'Ordre des Arts et des Lettres, France, 1996; Honorary DLit, University of Wales, 1988; Honorary Fellowship, St David's College, Wales, 1992; 2 Los Angeles Film Critics Association, Best Actor Awards, 1993; Donesta, 1998; Cecil B DeMille Award, 2006; Numerous other awards. Address: c/o CAA, 9830 Wilshire Blvd, Beverly Hills, CA 90212, USA.

HOPKINS Antony, b. 21 March 1921, London, England. Musician; Author. m. Alison Purves, 1947, deceased 1991. Education: Royal College of Music with Cyril Smith and Gordon Jacob. Career: Lecturer, Royal College of Music, 15 years; Director, Intimate Opera Company, 1952-64; Series of radio broadcasts, Talking About Music, 1954-92. Compositions include: Operas: Lady Rohesia; Three's Company; Hands Across the Sky; Dr Musikus; Ten o'Clock Call; The Man from Tuscany; Ballets: Etude; Cafe des Sports; 3 Piano Sonatas; Numerous scores of incidental music including: Oedipus; The Love of Four Colonels; Cast a Dark Shadow; Pickwick Papers; Billy Budd; Decameron Nights. Publications include: Understanding Music, 1979; The Nine Symphonies of Beethoven, 1980; The Concertgoer's Companion, 2 volumes, 1984, 1986. Honours: Gold Medal, Royal College of Music, 1943; Italia Prize for Radio Programme, 1951, 1957; Medal, City of Tokyo for Services to Music, 1973; Commander of the British Empire, 1976. Address: Woodyard, Ashridge, Berkhamsted, Hertfordshire HP4 1PS, England.

HOPKINS Timothy John, b. 7 March 1967, Manchester, England. Roman Catholic Priest. Education: MA, Classics, Christ's College, Cambridge, 1985-88; STL, PhB, Venerable English College and Pontifical Gregorian University, Rome, 1988-94. Appointments: Assistant Priest, St Willibrord's, Clayton, 1994-95; Chaplain, St Gregory's RC High School, Openshaw, 1994-99; Diocesan Chaplain to Italian Community, 1994-; Parish Priest, St Brigid's, Beswick and St Vincent's, Openshaw, 1995-2003; Governor, St Brigid's RC Primary Beacon School, 1995-; Secretary, Diocesan Council of Priests, 1997-2003; Chair, East Manchester Education Action Zone, 1999-2004; Vice Chair, University of Manchester Settlement, 1999-; Governor, Corpus Christi with St Anne RC Primary School, 1999-; Chaplain, Lord Mayor of Manchester, 2001-02; Governor, St Bede's College, Manchester, 2001-; Founder and Chair, East Manchester E-Learning Foundation, 2001-; Chaplain, Commonwealth Games, Manchester, 2002; Manchester LEA Joint Consultative Committee, 2002-; Manchester City Council Children and Young People Scrutiny Committee, 2002-; Greater Manchester Area Officer, Salford Diocese Boundaries & Sites Board, 2003-; Parish Priest of St Anne, St Brigid, St Michael and St Vincent, East Manchester, 2003-; Education Team, New East Manchester Urban Regeneration Company, 2004-. Publications: The Power of the Holy Spirit in the Sacrament of Reconciliation, 1994; Commonwealth Games Chaplaincy: Going for Gold in Manchester, 2002; Education Action Zone and Microsoft Work Together for a Prosperous Future in East Manchester, 2003. Address: St Anne's Roman Catholic Church, Carruthers Street, Ancoats, Manchester, M4 7EQ, England. E-mail: tim@vincents.fslife.co.uk

HOPKINSON Betty Constance, b. 11 March 1920, Coventry, England. Portrait Painter; Art Teacher. m. George S Hopkinson, deceased, 1 son, 2 daughters. Education: Part-time studies in portrait painting with Bernard Hailstone, Maidstone College of Art, 1952-57 and Goldsmiths College of Art, 1957-63 and life drawing with Sam Rabin; Certificate in Fine and Applied

Art (Printmaking), Sir John Cass College, City of London Polytechnic, 1984-86. Career: Professional Portrait Painter, 1964-; Teacher of Art, Portrait Painting, St Alban's College of Further Education, 1967; Teacher of Art, Portrait Painting, Hendon College of Further Education 1984-; Teacher of Art, Harpenden Further Education Centre (renamed Oaklands College, Harpenden Campus); Exhibitions: One Man Shows: North and East Finchley Libraries, 1966; Woodstock Galleries, 1972; Upstairs Gallery, Stamford, 1974; The Crest Gallery, Totteridge, 1978; Camden Arts Centre, 1979; Royal Free Hospital, 1980; Old Bull Gallery, Barnet, 1984; Bow House Gallery, Barnet, 1989; Crypt Gallery, St Martins-in-the-Field, London, 1990; Group Exhibitions: La Société des Artists Française, Paris Salon, 1964, 1967, 1971; Royal Society of Portrait Painters, 1960-; Royal Society of British Artists, 1960-; Royal Society of Oil Painters, 1960-; National Society of Painters, Sculptors and Printmakers; Contemporary Portrait Society; Hampstead Arts Council; Printmakers Council; National Open Print Competition Scarborough; Medici Gallery, London; Royal Festival Hall Printmakers Council Exhibitions; Royal Festival Hall GLC Spirit of London; John Laing Landscape Exhibitions; Works in private collections in USA, Canada, Australia, France, Germany, Belgium, Holland, Zimbabwe and UK. Publication: Birthday Cards, The Medici Society Ltd. Honours: Honourable Mention for "Mr Mears", 1964, Medaille d'Argent for "Homage to Bonnard", 1967; Medaille d'Or for "Someone in the Kitchen", 1971, Société des Artistes Française, Paris Salon. Memberships: Founder and Honorary Member, Harpenden Arts Club; National Society of Painters, Sculptors and Printmakers, 1986; Hampstead Arts Council. Address: 2 Lyndhurst Avenue, Mill Hill, London NW7 2AB, England.

HOPPER Dennis, b. 17 May 1936, Dodge City, USA. Actor; Author; Photographer; Film Director. m. (1) Brooke Hayward, 1 daughter, (2) Doria Halprin, one daughter, (3) Katherine La Nasa, 1989, 1 son, (4) Victoria Duffy, 1996, 1 child. Creative Works: Film appearances include: Rebel Without a Cause, I Died a Thousand Times, 1955; Giant, 1956; Story of Mankind, Gunfight at the O.K. Corral, 1957; Night Tide, Key Witness, From Hell to Texas, 1958; Glory Stompers, 1959; The Trip, 1961; The Sons of Katie Elder, 1962; Hang 'Em High, 1966; Cool Hand Luke, 1967; True Grit, 1968; The American Dreamer, 1971; Kid Blue, 1973; The Sky is Falling, 1975; James Dean – The First American Teenager, Mad Dog Morgan, 1976; American Friend, 1978; Tracks, Apocalypse Now, 1979; Wild Times, 1980; King of the Mountain, Human Highway, 1981; Rumble Fish, 1983; The Osterman Weekend, 1984; Black Widow, Blue Velvet, 1986; River's Edge, 1987; Blood Red, Flashback, The American Wars, 1989; Chattahoochie, Motion and Emotion, Superstar: The Life and Times of Andy Warhol, Hot Spot, 1990; True Romance, Boiling Point, Super Mario Bros, 1993; Chasers, Speed, 1994; Waterworld, Search and Destroy, 1995; Basquiat, Carried Away, 1996; Star Truckers, Blackout, 1997; Tycus, 1998; Sources, Lured Innocence, Justice, Straight Shooter, Jesus' Son, Venice Project, Bad City Blues, Prophet's Game, 1999; Spreading Ground, Luck of the Draw, Held for Ransom, Choke, 2000; Ticker, Knockaround Guys, LAPD: To Protect and Serve, 2001; Unspeakable, Leo, 2002; Night We Call It A Day, Keeper, 2003; Out of Season, House of 9, 2004; Americano, The Crow: Wicked Prayer, Land of the Dead, 2005; Tainted Love, 10th & Wolf, Memory, 2006; Sleepwalking, Elegy, 2007; Hell Ride, 2008. Actor, Writer, Director: Easy Rider, 1969; The Last Movie, 1971; Paris Trout, 1990; The Indian Runner, 1991; Actor, Director: Out of the Blue, 1980; Director: Colors, 1988; The Hot Spot, 1990; Catchfire, 1991; Nails, 1991; Several public exhibitions of photographs. Publication: Out of the Sixties (photographs), 1988. Honours include: Best New Director, Cannes, 1969; Best Film Award, Venice, 1971, Cannes, 1980. Address: c/o Creative Artists Agency, 9830 Wilshire Boulevard, Beverly Hills, CA 90212, USA.

HOPWOOD David Alan (Sir), b. 19 August 1933, Kinver, Staffordshire, England. Scientist. m. Joyce Lilian Bloom, 2 sons, 1 daughter. Education: BA 1st class honours, Natural Sciences, 1954, PhD, 1958, University of Cambridge; DSc, University of Glasgow, 1974. Appointments: John Stothert Bye-Fellow, Magdalene College, Cambridge, 1956-58; University Demonstrator, Assistant Lecturer in Botany, University of Cambridge, 1957-61; Research Fellow, St John's College, Cambridge, 1958-61; Lecturer in Genetics, University of Glasgow, 1961-68; John Innes Professor of Genetics, University of East Anglia, Norwich and Head of the Genetics Department, John Innes Institute, 1968-98; John Innes Emeritus Fellow, John Innes Centre, Emeritus Professor of Genetics, University of Eat Anglia, Norwich, 1998-; Visiting Research Fellow, Kosan Biosciences, Inc, 1998-. Publications: Over 270 articles on genetics, microbiology and genetic engineering in scientific publications. Honours: 3 honorary memberships; 4 honorary fellowships; Fellow, Royal Society of London; Foreign Fellowship, Indian National Science Academy; 2 honorary Doctorates of Science; Medal of the Kitasato Institute for Research in New Bioactive Compounds; Hoechst-Roussel Award for Research in Antimicrobial Chemotherapy; Chiron Biotechnology Award; Knight Bachelor; Mendel Medal of the Czech Academy of Sciences; Gabor Medal of the Royal Society; Stuart Mudd Prize, International Union of Microbiological Societies; Ernst Chain Prize, Imperial College, London; Andre Lwoff Prize, Federation of European Microbiological Societies. Memberships: Genetical Society of Great Britain; Society for General Microbiology; American Society for Microbiology; European Molecular Biology Organisation; Academia Europaea. Address: John Innes Centre, Norwich, Norfolk NR4 7UH, England. E-mail: david.hopwood@bbsrc.ac.uk

HORBELT Carlton Vincent, b. 27 November 1954, Galveston, Texas, USA. Dentist. m. Carol, 1 son, 2 daughters. Education: Doctor of Dental Surgery, 1981; Fellow, Academy of Dentistry for Persons with Disabilities, 2001; Diplomate, American Board of Special Care Dentistry, 2004. Appointments: Dental Director, Richmond State School, Richmond, Texas, 1986-2001; President, SAID, 1999; Dental Director, Arlington Developmental Center, Arlington, Tennessee, 2001-; Associate Professor, Department of Paediatric Dentistry & Community Oral Health, University of Tennessee College of Dentistry, 2001-; President, Academy of Dentistry for Persons with Disabilities, 2002-03; President, American Board of Special Care Dentistry, 2006-07; President Elect, Special Care Dentistry Association, 2006-. Publications: Numerous papers and peer reviewed articles in professional journals. Honours: Harold Berk Award, 2005; International Award for Exemplary Leadership and Contributions to the Advancement of Oral Health for Persons with Disabilities; Omicron Kappa Upsilon, National Dental Honor Society; Distinguished Practitioner, Dental Academy, National Academies of Practice. Memberships: Special Care Dentistry Association; Academy of Dentistry for Persons with Disabilities; American Association of Hospital Dentists; American Society for Geriatric Dentistry; American Dental Association; International Association for Disabilities and Oral Health. Address: Arlington Developmental Center, PO Box 586, Arlington, TN 38002-0586, USA. E-mail: carlton.horbelt@state.tn.us

HORDER John Plaistowe, b. 9 December 1919, Ealing, London, England. Physician; General practitioner. m. Elizabeth June Wilson, 2 sons, 2 daughters. Education: Classical Scholarship, University College Oxford, 1938-40; Army war service; Medical Student, Oxford and London Hospital, 1943-48; Intern Appointments, London Hospital, 1948-51. Appointments: General Practitioner, North West London, 1951-81; Foundation Member, 1952, various offices including President, 1979-82, Royal College of General Practitioners; Vice-President, Royal Society of Medicine, 1987-89; Visiting Professor, Royal Free Hospital Medical School, 1983-92; Founder, 1st President, Centre for the Advancement of Inter-professional Education, 1983-2003. Publications include: Articles in medical journals: Illness in General Practice, 1954; Physicians and Family Doctors, A New Relationship, 1977; Book: The Future General Practitioner. Learning and Teaching, (editor and contributor), 1972; Book: General Practice under the National Health Service 1948-1997, (joint editor and contributor), 1998. Honours: OBE, 1971; CBE, 1981; Honorary MD, 1985; Honorary DSc, 2000; FRCGP, 1970; FRCP, 1972; FRCP (Ed), 1981; FRCPsych, 1980; Honorary Fellow, Green College, Oxford, 1985; Honorary Fellow, Queen Mary College University of London, 1997. Memberships: Medical Royal Colleges; Royal Society of Medicine; Past President, Medical Art Society. Address: 98 Regents Park Road, London NW1 8UG, England.

HORLOCK John Harold (Sir), b. 19 April 1928, Edmonton, England. University Administrator and Engineer. m Sheila J Stutely, 1 son, 2 daughters. Education: MA, Mechanical Sciences, 1953, PhD, Mechanical Engineering, 1955, ScD, Mechanical Engineering, 1975, Cambridge University. Appointments: Design and Development Engineer, Rolls-Royce Ltd, 1948-51, Research Fellow, St John's College Cambridge, 1954-57; Lecturer, Engineering, 1956-58, Professor of Engineering, Cambridge University, 1967-74; Harrison Professor of Mechanical Engineering, University of Liverpool, 1958-67; Vice-Chancellor, University of Salford, 1974-80; Vice-Chancellor, 1981-90, Fellow, 1991-, Open University; Treasurer and Vice-President, Royal Society, 1992-97; Pro-Chancellor UMIST, 1995-2001; President, Association for Science Education, 1999. Publications: Books: Axial Flow Compressors, 1958; Axial Flow Turbines, 1973; Actuator Disc Theory, 1978; The Thermodynamics and Gas Dynamics of Internal Combustion Engines (co-editor), Volume I, 1982, Volume II, 1986; Cogeneration, Combined Heat and Power, 1987; Combined Power Plants, 1992; Energy for the Future (co-editor), 1995; Advanced Gas Turbine Cycles, 2003. Honours include: James Clayton Prize, 1962, Thomas Hawksley Gold Medal, 1969, Arthur Charles Main Prize, 1997, Institution of Mechanical Engineers; Honorary Doctorates: Heriot-Watt University, 1980, University of Salford, 1981, University of East Asia, 1987, University of Liverpool, 1987, Open University, 1991, CNAA, 1991, De Montford University, 1995, Cranfield University, 1997; Honorary Fellowships: St John's College, Cambridge, 1989, UMIST, 1991, Royal Aeronautical Society, 2003; Knighthood, 1996; R Tom Sawyer Award, ASME, 1997; Sir James Ewing Medal, ICE, 2002; ISABE Achievement Award, 2003. Memberships: Fellow, Royal Society; Fellow, Royal Academy of Engineering; Fellow, Institution of Mechanical Engineers; Fellow, American Society of Mechanical Engineers; Foreign Associate, National Academy of Engineering, USA. Address: 2 The Avenue, Ampthill, Bedford MK45 2NR, England. E-mail: john.horlock1@btinternet.com

HORNBY Nick, b. 17 April 1957, London, England. Freelance Journalist; Novelist. m. Virginia Bovell (divorced), 1 son. Publications: Contemporary American Fiction, 1992; Fever Pitch, 1992; My Favourite Year: A Collection of New Football Writing, 1993; High Fidelity, 1995; Speaking With the Angel, 2000; About a Boy, 2000; How to be Good, 2001; 31 Songs, 2003; A Long Way Down, 2005;The Polysyllabic Spree, 2004; Housekeeping vs. the Dirt, 2006; Slam, 2007. Screenplay: Fever Pitch, 1997; About a Boy. Contributions to: Sunday Times; Times Literary Supplement; Literary Review; New Yorker; New York Times. Honours: William Hill Sports Book of the Year Award, 1992; Writers' Guild Best Fiction Book Award, 1995; American Academy of Arts and Letters E M Forster Award, 1999; WHSmith Fiction Award, 2002; London Award, 2003. Address: c/o Peters Fraser and Dunlop, Drury House, 34-43 Russell Street, London WC2B 5HA, England.

HORNE Alistair Allan (Sir), b. 9 November 1925, London, England. Author; Journalist; Lecturer. m. (1) Renira Margaret Hawkins, 3 daughters, (2) The Hon Mrs Sheelin Eccles, 1987. Education: MA, Jesus College, Cambridge. Appointments: Served WWII: RAF, 1943-44; Coldstream Guards, 1944-47; Captain attached Intelligence Service MI-5; Director Ropley Trust Ltd, 1948-77; Foreign Correspondent, Daily Telegraph, 1952-55; Founded Alistair Horne Research Fellowship in Modern History, 1969, Honorary Fellow, 1988-, St Antony's College, Oxford, 1969; Honorary Fellow, Jesus College Cambridge, 1996-; Fellow Woodrow Wilson Center, Washington DC, 1980-81; Member: Management Committee, Royal Literary Fund, 1969-91; Franco-British Council, 1979-93; Committee of Management, Society of Authors, 1979-82; Trustee, Imperial War Museum, 1975-82. Publications: Back into Power, 1955; The Land is Bright, 1958; Canada and the Canadians, 1961; The Price of Glory: Verdun 1916, 1962; The Fall of Paris 1870-1871, 1965; To Lose a Battle: France 1940, 1969; Death of a Generation, 1970; The Terrible Year: The Paris Commune, 1971, 2005; A Savage War of Peace: Algeria, 1954-62, 1977, new edition 2006; Small Earthquake in Chile, 1972; Napoleon, Master of Europe 1805-1807, 1979; The French Army and Politics 1870-1970, 1984; Macmillan, Vol I, 1894-1956, 1985; Vol II, 1957-1986, 1989; A Bundle from Britain, 1993; The Lonely Leader: Monty 1944-45, 1994; How Far From Austerlitz: Napoleon 1805-1815, 1996; Telling Lives (editor), 2000; Seven Ages of Paris, 2002; The Age of Napoleon, 2004; Friend or Foe: An Anglo-Saxon History of France, 2004; La Belle France, 2005; Numerous contributions to books and periodicals. Honours: Hawthornden Prize, 1963; Yorkshire Post Book of Year Prize, 1978; Wolfson Literary Award, 1978; Enid Macleod Prize, 1985; Commander of the Order of the British Empire, 1992; Chevalier, Legion d'Honneur, 1993; LittD, Cambridge, 1993; Kt, 2003. Memberships: Society of Authors; Fellow, Royal Society of Literature. Address: The Old Vicarage, Turville, Nr Henley on Thames, Oxon RG9 6QU, England.

HORNE ROBERTS Jennifer, b. 15 February 1949, Harrow, London, England. Barrister; Writer. m. Keith M P Roberts, 1 son, 1 daughter. Education: Diploma, Italian, University of Perugia, Italy, 1966; BA, Honours, London University, 1969; Law Diploma CLLE, 1974; Bar Finals, Council of Legal Education, Middle Temple, 1976; Ad eundem Member, Inner Temple. Appointments: In practice at Bar 1976-; Currently, Civil Law, Goldsmith Chambers, Temple, London. Publications: Trade Unionists and Law, 1984; New Frontiers in Family Law (co-author), 1994; Labour's True Way Forward, 1998; Labour's Agenda, 2000; Selected Poems, 2002; The MMR10 −Access to Justice (co-author)

2006, The MMR10-Justice in Europe (co-author) 2006. Memberships: Executive Committee Member, Chair, Family Law Committee; Society of Labour Lawyers; Founder and First Chair, Association of Women Barristers; Family Law Bar Association; Tate; Royal Academy; Highgate Literary and Scientific Society; Fabian Society; Executive Member Human Rights Lawyers Association; Member Society of Labor Lawyers. Address: Goldsmith Chambers, Temple, London EC4Y 7BL, England. E-mail: keith@horne-roberts.co.uk. Website: www.Horne-Roberts.co.uk

HORNER Ronald, Assistant Professor. Education: BSEd, Music Education, Indiana University of Pennsylvania, 1978; MM, Performance, 1988, Artist Diploma, Timpani, 1992, Duquesne University; DMA, Performance, West Virginia University, USA. Appointments: Performed with many world reknowned conductors and soloists, 1978-2007; Numerous featured solo performances and premiers; Percussionist, Israel Philharmonic Orchestra, Tel-Aviv, Israel, 1978-80; Principal Percussionist, 1980-90, Principal Timpanist, 1990-, Johnstown Symphony Orchestra, Johnstown; Director of Vocal Music, Somerset Area School District, 1981-82; Principal Percussionist, Bedford Springs Music Festival, Bedford, 1982-89; Principal Timpanist, 1982-2001, 2001-, Westmoreland Symphony Orchestra, Greenburg; Percussion Instructor, Seton Hill College, Greensburg, Pennsylvania, 1983-85; Senior Lecturer of Music, Frostburg State University, Maryland, 1983-; Instructor of Music, University of Pittsburgh, Pennsylvania, 1985-96; Staff Percussionist, Allegheny Highlands Regional Theatre, Ebensburg, 1986-87; Principal Percussionist, River City Brass Band, Pittsburgh, 1987; Timpanist, Somerset Music Festival, 1987-89; Adjunct Percussionist, Pittsburgh Symphony Orchestra, Pittsburgh, 1989-96; Assistant Professor of Percussion, West Virginia University, Washington, 1998-99; Assistant Professor of Music (Adjunct), Indiana University of Pennsylvania, 1996-; Timpanist and Percussionist, Keystone Wind Ensemble, Indiana, 1997-. Publications: Numerous articles in professional journals; Many recordings around the world. Honours: Listed in international biographical dictionaries; National Collegiate Music Award, United States Achievement Academy 1988; National Dean's List, 1988; National Music Honor Society, Pi Kappa Lambda, 1988; Governor's Citation, State of Maryland, 2002; Faculty Development Grant, Frostburg State University, 2004. Memberships: American Federation of Musicians; American Society of Composers, Authors and Publishers; Delta Omicron; Percussive Arts Society; Phi Mu Alpha Sinfonia; Pi Kappa Lambda. Address: Division of Performing Arts – Music, Frostburg State University, Frostburg, MD 21532, USA. E-mail: rhorner@frostburg.edu

HOROVITZ Michael, b. 4 April 1935, Frankfurt am Main, Germany. Writer; Poet; Editor; Publisher; Literary and Arts Journalist; Songwriter; Singer; Musician; Visual Artist; Impresario. Education: BA, 1959, MA, 1964, Brasenose, College, Oxford. Appointments: Editor and Publisher, New Departures International Review, 1959-; Founder, singer-player, director, Jazz Poetry SuperJam bandwagons, 1969-; Founder, Co-ordinator and Torchbearer, Poetry Olympics Festivals, 1980-. Publications: Europa (translator), 1961; Alan Davie, 1963; Declaration, 1963; Strangers: Poems, 1965; Poetry for the People: An Essay in Bop Prosody, 1966; Bank Holiday: A New Testament for the Love Generation, 1967; Children of Albion (editor), 1969; The Wolverhampton Wanderer: An Epic of Football, Fate and Fun, 1971; Love Poems, 1971; A Contemplation, 1978; Growing Up: Selected Poems and Pictures 1951-1979, 1979; The Egghead Republic (translator), 1983; A Celebration of and for Frances Horovitz

(editor), 1984; Midsummer Morning Jog Log, 1986; Bop Paintings, Collages and Drawings, 1989; Grandchildren of Albion (editor), 1992; Wordsounds and Sightlines: New and Selected Poems, 1994; Grandchildren of Albion Live (on cassette and CD) (editor), 1996; The POW! Anthology, 1996; The POP! Anthology, 2000; The POM! Anthology, 2001; Jeff Nuttall's Wake on Paper, 2004; Jeff Nuttall's Wake on CD, 2004; Lost Office Campaign Poem, 2005; The POT! Anthology, 2005; A New Waste Land: Timeship Earth at Nillennium, 2007. Honours: Arts Council of Great Britain Writers Award, 1976; Arts Council Translator's Award, 1983; Poetry Book Society Recommendation, 1986; Creative Britons Award, 2000; Officer of the Order of the British Empire, 2002. Address: PO Box 9819, London, W11 2GQ, England.

HOROWITZ Irving (Louis), b. 25 September 1929, New York, USA. Editor; Publisher. m. (1) Ruth Lenore Horowitz, 1950, divorced 1964, 2 sons, (2) Mary Curtis Horowitz, 1979. Education: BSS, City College, New York City, 1951; MA, Columbia University, 1952; PhD, University of Buenos Aires, 1957; Postgraduate Fellow, Brandeis University, 1958-59. Appointments: Associate Professor, University of Buenos Aires, 1955-58; Assistant Professor, Bard College, 1960; Chairman, Department of Sociology, Hobart and William Smith Colleges, 1960-63; Editor-in-Chief, Transaction Society, 1962-94; Associate Professor to Professor of Sociology, Washington University, St Louis, 1963-69; President, Transaction Books, 1966-94; Chairman, Department of Sociology, Rutgers, The State University of New Jersey, 1969-73; Professor of Sociology, Graduate Faculty, 1969-, Hannah Arendt Professor of Social and Political Theory, 1979-, Rutgers University; Bacardi Chair of Cuban Studies, Miami University, 1992-94; Editorial Chairman and President Emeritus, Transaction/USA and Transaction/UK. Publications: Numerous articles in professional journals; Books include: Daydreams and Nightmares: Reflections of a Harlem Childhood, 1990; The Decomposition of Sociology, 1993; Behemoth: Main Currents in the History and Theory of Political Sociology, 1999; Veblen's Century: A Collective Portrait, 2002; Tributes: An Informal History of Twentieth Century Social Science, 2004; The Long Night of Dark Intent: A Half-Century of Cuban Communism, 2008. Honours: Best Biography, National Jewish Book Award, 1990; Harold D Lasswell Award; Festschrift, 1994; Lifetime Achievement Award, Inter-University Seminar on Armed Forces and Sco; Gerhart Neimeyer Award, Intercollegiate Studies Association, 2003; International Humanist Award, 2004; Thomas S Szasz Award, Centre for Industrial Thought, 2004; Distinguished Scholarly Lifetime Achievement Award, American Sociological Association, 2006. Memberships: AAAS; AAAS Science and Human Rights Program; AAUP; USIA; American Political Science Association; National Association of Scholars; Authors Guild; Center for Study of the Presidency; Council on Foreign Relations; International Society of Political Psychology; Society for International Development; US General Accounting Office; US Information Agency; National Association of Scholars; Institute for a Free Cuba; Raymond Aron Society. Address: Rutgers University, Transaction Pubs Bldg, 4051 New Brunswick, NJ 08903, USA. E-mail: ihorowitz@transactionpub.com

HORRIDGE G Adrian, b. 12 December 1927. Professor. m. Audrey Lightburne, 1 son, 3 daughters. Education: First Class Honours, Natural Sciences Tripos, St John's College, Cambridge, England. Appointments: Scientific Officer, Senior Scientific Officer, Department of Structures, Royal Aircraft Establishment, Farnborough, England, 1953-54; Research Fellowship, St John's College, Cambridge. 1954-56; Lecturer,

Reader in Zoology, St Andrews University, Scotland, 1956-59; Visiting Associate Professor, University of California, Los Angeles, USA, 1959-60; Fellow, Center for Advanced Study in the Behavioural Sciences, Stanford, California, USA, 1959-60; Director, Marine Laboratory, St Andrews University, Scotland, 1960-69; Visiting Full Professor, Yale University, USA, 1965; Fellow, Royal Society of London, 1969; Professor of Behavioural Biology, Australian National University, Canberra, Australia, 1969; Fellow, Australian Academy of Science, 1971; Examiner in Biology, University Sains, Penang and University of Malaya, Kuala Lumpar, Malaysia, 1972, 1976, 1980, 1984; Visiting Fellowship, Balliol College, Oxford, England, 1973-74; Chief Scientist, US Research Ship, Alpha Helix, in the Moluccas, East Indonesia, 1975; Visiting Fellow, Churchill College, Cambridge, England, 1976-77; Executive Director, Centre for Visual Sciences, Australian National University, 1987-1990; Royal Society Visiting Professorship, St Andrews, Scotland, 1992; Visiting Fellow, Churchill College, Cambridge, 1993-94; Appointed University Fellow, Australian National University, 1993. Publications: 230 papers on Sciences; 20 titles on Indonesian traditional boats; 10 titles on other topics, including: The Structure and Function of the Nervous Systems of Invertebrates (co-author), 1965; Interneurons, 1968; The Compound Eye of Insects (editor), 1975; The Prahu, Traditional Sailing Boat of Indonesia, 2nd edition, 1985; Sailing Craft of Indonesia, 1986; Outrigger Canoes of Bali and Madura, Indonesia, 1987; Natural and low-level seeing systems (co-editor), 1993. Memberships: Fellow, Royal Society of England; Society for Nautical Research; Fellow, Australian Academy of Science. Address: 76 Mueller Street, Yarralumla, ACT, Australia 2600. E-mail: horridge@rsbs.anu.edu.au

HORROCKS Jane, b. 18 January 1964, Lancashire, England. Actress. Partner Nick Vivian, 1 son, 1 daughter. Education: Royal Academy of Dramatic Art. Creative Works: Stage appearances include: The Rise and Fall of Little Voice; TV appearances include: Hunting Venus (film); Red Dwarf (series); Absolutely Fabulous; The Flint Street Nativity; Little Princess; The Amazing Mrs Pritchard. Film appearances: The Dressmaker, 1989; Life is Sweet, 1991; Little Voice, 1998; Born Romantic, 2001; Chicken Run (voice), 2002; Last Rumba in Rochdale (voice), 2003; Wheeling Dealing, 2004; Corpse Bride (voice), 2005; Brothers of the Head, 2005; Garfield: A Tail of Two Kitties (voice), 2006; No One Gets Off in this Town, 2008. Honour: Best Supporting Actress Los Angeles Critics Award, 1992. Address: ICM, Oxford House, 76 Oxford Street, London W1D 1BS, England.

HORROCKS Rod, b. 11 December 1950, Liverpool, England. Chartered Engineer. Education: Bachelor's degree, Mechanical Engineering, Sheffield; MSc, Machine Tools, Birmingham. Appointments: Graduate Engineer, Staveley Industries, 1974-76; Graduate Engineer, Froude Consine, 1976; Industrial Engineer, BNFL, 1977-80; Consultant, PE Consulting, 1980-84; Consultant, OD Consulting, 1984-87; Consultant, Ingersoll Engineering, 1987-89; Consultant, Ernst & Young. Address: Procertis Ltd, 3 Charles Court, Budbrooke Road, Warwick, CV34 5LZ, England. E-mail: rod.horrocks@procertis.com Website: www.procertis.com

HORSBRUGH Oliver Bethune, b. 13 November 1937, London, England. Freelance Television Director. m. Josephine Elsa Hall, 1 son, 1 daughter. Education: St Paul's School, Hammersmith, London, 1949-54. Appointments: BBC Director, 1968-71; Freelance Director, 1971-; Drama: BBC: Bergerac; Juliet Bravo; Z Cars; 30 Minute Theatres; Granada: Kind of Loving; Cribb; Fallen Hero; Strangers; Coronation Street (over 200 episodes); Crown Court; YTV: Emmerdale (over 250 episodes); Kate; LWT: New Scotland Yard; Channel 4: Scott Inquiry; Birmingham 6 Appeal; Gibraltar Inquest; Other: Corporate productions: Many for Visage, Wardlow Grosvenor, Aspen, CTN, Evolution; Training programmes; Interactive videos; ITN: Numerous News At Ten, Channel 4 and other live news bulletins and outside broadcasts; World This Week (3 series), live political programme for ITN. Honours: GSM (Near East), RN, National Service, 1958; BAFTA for Emmerdale, 2000. Memberships: BAFTA; MCC; Press Officer, Cinema Theatre Association. Address: 23 Bishops mansions, Bishops Park Road, London SW6 6DZ, England

HORST Frank, b. 3 January 1966, Muenster, Germany. Orthopaedic Surgeon. m. Heike, 1 son, 1 daughter. Education: Rheinische Friedrich-Wilhelms-University of Bonn, 1986-92; Scholarship, Konrad0-Adenauer-Foundation for graduate studies, 1988; Scholarship, Konrad-Adenauer-Foundation for US university rotation, 1992. Appointments: Intern, PGY 1 and 2, Berufsgenossenschaftliche Unfallklinik University, 1993-95; PGY 2-5, Department of Orthopaedic Surgery, 1996-98, Faculty, Attending in Orthopaedic Surgery, 1998-, 2002-04, Krankenhaus der Augustinerinnen, Cologne; Fellow, Foot & Ankle Surgery, 2001-02, Visiting Fellowship Sportsmedicine, 2003, Visiting Fellow, Adult Reconstruction, 2006, Duke University Medical Center, Durham; Chief, Hospital of Special Orthopaedic Surgery and Trauma, St Josef-Stift Sendenhorst, 2004-; Visiting Fellow, Department for Orthopaedic Surgery, Duke University, 2005; Visiting Fellow, University of California San Francisco, 2007. Publications: 3 book chapters; Numerous articles in professional journals. Memberships: American Orthpaedic Foot and Ankle Society; German Association of Foot & Ankle Surgery; German Association of Orthopaedic Surgery; German Association of Chiropractic Medicine; European Academy of Acupuncture; German Association of Sportsmedicine; Piedmont Society; American Field Service; and many others. Address: St Josef-Stift Sendenhorst, Westtor 7, 48324 Sendenhorst, Germany.

HORVAT Vashti, b. 22 March, Rochester, USA. Audit & Compliance Executive. Education: BS, Computer Science for Information Systems, DeVry University, UCLA. Appointments: Project Manager, Information Technology Auditor, 1996-2001; E-mail: Marketing/Sweepstakes Manager, Travelocity.com, 2001-03; Managing Principal, Orr Consulting, Texas, 2003-. Publications: Listed in international biographical dictionaries. Honours: Certified Information Systems Auditor. Memberships: ASUG; ISACA.org; Gerson Lehrman Group Council; IT Compliance Institute. Address: 8409 Pickwick Lane Suite 180, Dallas, TX 75225, USA. E-mail: info@orrconsulting.us

HORWITZ Angela Joan, b. 14 October 1934, London, England. Sculptress; Painter; Professor. 2 sons, 1 daughter. Education: Lycée Francais de Londres; Studied art, Marylebone Institute, 1978-90; Sir John Cass College, 1983-85; Hampstead Institute, 1990-92. Career: Fashion Designer, owner of own company, 1960-80; Exhibitions: Grand Palais, Paris, 1985, 1986; RBA, NS, RAS, SWA, Mall Galleries, Civic Centre, Southend, SEFAS, Guildhall, Ridley Society, City of Westminster Arts Council, Alpine Gallery, Smiths Gallery Covent Garden, Wintershall Gallery; The Orangery Hyde Park Gallery, London (Winchester Cathedral, 1992); Exhibition with City of London Polytechnic, Whitechapel, London, 1985; Salon International du Livre et de la Presse à Geneva, 1997; Miramar Hotel, 1998 and Beaux Arts, Cannes,

France, 1999; Raymond Gallery, Beaux Arts, 2000; The Atrium Gallery, London, 2000; Gallery le Carre d'or, Paris, 2000; Le Cannet, St Sauveur, 2005; Lansdowne Club, Mayfair, 2005; Plaister's Hall in aid of the Red Cross, 2005 Work in permanent collections: Sculpture in stone for Winchester Cathedral; Well Woman Centre, The United Elizabeth Garrett Anderson Hospital for Women, London; Private collection: Zurich, Switzerland; National Society Ridley Arts Society. Honours: Academical Knight, Arts, Academia Internazionale Greci-Marino, 1999; Academical Knight, Department of Arts, Ordine Accademico Internatzionale, Italy; Fellow, American Biographical Institute. Memberships: NS, 1982; RAS, 1983; FABI, 2005; Beaux Arts, Cannes, France, 1997-2007; Landsdown Club; British Red Cross. Address: 6 Wellington House, Aylmer Drive, Stanmore, Middlesex HA7 3ES, England.

HOSEIN Tajmool, b. 14 November 1921. Barrister; Attorney at Law. m. Shalimar Mohammed, 1952, 3 sons, 2 daughters. Education: BA, London, 1944; LLB, honours, London, 1946; Bar, 1st class Final Exam, Inns of Court Law School, London, 1946. Appointments: Queens Counsel of Trinidad, 1947-; Delegate to Trinidad Independence Constitutional Conference, London, 1962; Member, Trinidad Parliament, 1961-66; Barrister, West Indian Islands, St Lucia, Grenada, St Vincent, Barbados, 1965-; Director, several companies, including: Chairman, Trinidad Express Newspapers, 1969-82; Colonial Life Insurance, Co Ltd, 1969-92; Bank of Nova Scotia, 1972-95; Member, Judicial and Legal Service Commission, 1973-88, Law Reform Commission, 1973-88, Campus Council, University of West Indies, 1986-88. Publications: Editor, Trinidad Law Reports, 1952-55; Vice Chairman, Committee of Revising Supreme Court Rules, 1975; Editor, 6 volumes of Discourses by Spiritual Teacher Sathya Sai Baba, 1984-98; Editor, Teachers Handbook, Education in Human Values. Honours: Buchanan and Certificate of Honour Prizes, Lincoln's Inn, London, 1947; QC, Trinidad, 1964; QC, Eastern Caribbean Associated States, 1982; Trinity Cross, Trinidad, 1982; Hon LLD, UWI, 2005. Memberships: Law Association, Trinidad; Chairman, Education in Human Values Society, 1987-; Chairman, Sathya Sai Baba Organisation of West Indies, 1988-2005; Union Club; Queen's Park Cricket Club. Address: Juris Chambers, 39 Richmond Street, Port of Spain, Trinidad, West Indies.

HOSKING Geoffrey Alan, b. 28 April 1942, Troon, Scotland. University Teacher. m. Anne Lloyd Hirst, 2 daughters. Education: Kings College, Cambridge, 1960-64; Moscow State University, 1964-65; St Antony's College, Oxford, 1965-66. Appointments: Lecturer in History, University of Essex, 1966-71, 1972-76; Visiting Professor, Department of Political Science, University of Wisconsin-Madison, 1971-72; Gastprofessor, Slavisches Institut, University of Cologne, 1980-81; Senior Lecturer, Reader in Russian History, University of Essex, 1976-80, 1981-84; Professor of Russian History, 1984-99, 2004-07, Emeritus Professor, 2007-, SSEES, University of London; Leverhulme Personal Research Professor in Russian History, SSEES-UCL, 1999-2004. Publications: Author: The Russian Constitutional Experiment, 1973; Beyond Socialist Realism, 1980; The First Socialist Society: A History of the Soviet Union from Within, 1985, 1990, 1992; The Awakening of the Soviet Union, 1990; The Road to Post-Communism: Independent Political Movements in the Soviet Union 1985-91, 1992; Russia: People and Empire (1552-1917), 1997; Russia and the Russians: A History from Rus to Russian Federation, 2001; Rulers and Victims: the Russians in the Soviet Union, 2006; Editor: Myths and Nationhood, 1997; Russian Nationalism Past and Present, 1998; Reinterpreting Russia, 1999. Honours: Los Angeles Times History Book Prize, 1986; US Independent Publishers History Book Award, 2002; Alec Nove Prize, 2008; Fellow, British Academy, 1993; Fellow, Royal Historical Society; Honorary Doctorate, Russian Academy of Sciences, 2000; Member, Council of the Royal Historical Society, 2002-06. Memberships: Writers and Scholars Educational Trust; Museum of Contemporary History, Moscow; Moscow School of Political Studies. Address: School of Slavonic and East European Studies, University College London, Gower Street, London WC1E 6BT, England. E-mail: geoffreyhosking@mac.com

HOSKINS Bob (Robert William), b. 26 October 1942, Bury St Edmunds, Suffolk. Actor. m. (1) Jane Livesey, 1970, 1 son, 1 daughter: (2) Linda Barnwell, 1984, 1 son, 1 daughter. Career: Several stage roles at the National Theatre; Films include: National Health, 1973; Royal Flash, 1974; Zulu Dawn, The Long Good Friday, 1980; The Wall, 1982; The Honorary Consul, 1983; Lassiter, The Cotton Club, 1984; Brazil, The Woman Who Married Clark Gable, Sweet Liberty, 1985; Mona Lisa, 1986; A Prayer for the Dying, The Lonely Passion of Judith Hearne, Who Framed Roger Rabbit?, 1987; The Raggedy Rawney (director, actor and writer), 1988; Mermaids, 1989; Shattered, Heart Condition, The Projectionist, The Favour, The Watch and the Very Big Fish, 1990; Hook, 1991, The Inner Circle, Super Mario Brothers, 1992; Nixon, 1995, The Rainbow (also director), Michael, Cousin Bette, 1996; Twenty-four-seven, The Secret Agent, 1998; Felicia's Journey, Parting Shots, 1999; Enemy at the Gates, Last Orders, 2001; Where Eskimos Live, Maid in Manhattan, 2002; Sleeping Dictionary, Den of Lions, 2003; Vanity Fair, Beyond the Sea, 2004; Unleashed, Son of the Mask, Mrs Henderson Presents, Stay, 2005; Paris, I Love You, Garfield: A Tail of Two Kitties (voice), Hollywoodland, 2006; Sparkle, Outlaw, Ruby Blue, Go Go Tales, Doomsday, 2007. TV appearances include: Omnibus – It Must be Something in the Water, 1971; Villains, Thick as Thieves, 1972; Schmoedipus, Shoulder to Shoulder, 1974; Pennies From Heaven, Peninsular, 1975; Sheppey, Flickers, 1980; Othello, 1981; The Beggers' Opera, 1983; Mussolini and I, 1984; The Changeling, World War Two: Then There Were Giants, 1993; David Copperfield, 1999; The Lost World (film), 2001; The Wind in the Willows, 2006; The Englishman's Boy, 2007. Stage: Old Wicked Songs, 1996. Honours: For Mona Lisa, New York Critics Award, Golden Globe Award, Best Actor Award, Cannes Festival, 1986; Variety Club Best Actor Award, 1997; Richard Harris Award for Outstanding Contribution by an Actor to British Film, British Film Awards, 2004.

HOSKINS Donald, b. 9 June 1932, Abertillery, Wales. Pianist; Conductor. m. Dinah Patricia Stanton, 1972. Education: BMus, including piano studies, Cardiff University, 1950-54; MA, University of Wales, 1974; PhD, University of Wales, 1990. Career: National Service, 1954-56; Directed choral groups, gave lectures and recitals and performed on television; Teacher, Tudor Grange Grammar School, Solihull, 1956-60; Presented music concerts; Adjudicated at school festivals; Founded local arts orchestra; Performed as soloist with Birmingham Philharmonic Orchestra, 1956-60; Guest Conductor on a visit to Wales, 1962; Director of Music, Hayes Grammar School, Middlesex, 1960-64; Founded and conducted local chamber orchestras and ensembles for concerts at major London venues; Solo recital, Paris, 1962; Lecturer, Eastbourne College of Education, East Sussex, 1964-67; Piano Soloist, Hillingdon Festival, 1964; Senior Lecturer, Department of Education, Barking Regional College of Technology, 1967; Song Recital Accompanist, Purcell

Room, South Bank, 1972; Researcher, English musical theatre during 18th and early 19th centuries (MA and PhD degrees); Head, North East London Polytechnic Music Centre, 1978; Created wide range of musical teaching, training courses, and conducted many prestigious concerts with international artists; Established annual band courses and festivals by the University of East London concert band, 1980; Guest Conductor, London Mozart Players, 1983; Piano recital, Athens, 1984; Founded and Directed Aminta Chamber Orchestra (of London), 1985; Guest Piano Soloist with combined Desford Dowty, Fodens and Coventry brass bands conducted by Harry Mortimer, 1989; Soloist, inaugural concert, Zweibrucken University, Germany, 1994; Presented concert band performances in Witten, Germany, 1995, University of Kaiserslautern, 1997 and Royal Star and Garter Home, Richmond, 1998-2002; President, Redbridge Music Society; Visiting Professor, University of Provo, Salt Lake City, and Music Conservatorium, University of Cincinnati, 1994; Guest Conductor, Royal Philharmonic Concert Orchestra, 1995 and 1996, BBC Concert Orchestra, 1997 and 1998, London Philharmonic Choir, 1999, 2000 and 2002 (latter two concerts at Queen Elizabeth Hall, South Bank London); Retired, 1996; Continued as Consultant and Director of Concerts, University of East London; Presented 26th annual concert band performance at UEL and 22nd annual concert given by Aminta Chamber Orchestra, Church of St Martin-in-the-Fields, London, 2006; Directed children's concerts and open-air symphony concerts including 10th annual event at Barking Abbey, Essex. Honours: Honorary Degree, Doctor of Music, University of East London, Barbican Theatre, London, 2003; Guest Conductor, Cantus Firmus Chamber Orchestra, Moscow, 2004; Freedom of the Borough, London Borough of Barking and Dagenham, 2005; MBE, 2007; Conducted Aminta Concert Orchestra in 75th birthday concert at Queen Elizabeth Hall, London; Piano soloist, chamber music concert, Moscow Conservatoire, and Conductor, Cantus Firmus chamber orchestra of Moscow, Bulgarian Cultural Centre, 2007. Address: Aminta, 12 Hurst Park, Midhurst, West Sussex GU29 0BP, England.

HOSSAIN Mohammad Samir, b. 28 November 1976, Dhaka, Bangladesh. Teacher of Psychiatry; Physician; Psychotherapist. m. Tahmina Rahman Chowdhury, 2 sons. Education: CME, Harvard Medical School and Johns Hopkins University School of Medicine, USA; PhD, Psychotherapy, Bircham International University, Spain; MS, Abnormal Psychology, UGA, California, USA; Diploma in Psychology, Free-ed Ltd, Ohio, USA; MBBS – SSMC, University of Dhaka, Bangladesh. Appointments: Assistant Professor of Psychiatry and Psychotherapist; Registrar of Psychiatry; Honorary (trainee) Medical Officer in Psychiatry; General Physician (practitioner). Publications: Articles in professional journals. Honours: Full Scholarships; Leading Health Professionals of the World, 2006; Listed in international biographical directories; Fellow, Bircham International University, Spain; Honorary Professional Member, AFSP, New York, USA. Memberships: Faculty, Bircham International University, Spain; American Psychiatric Association; American Psychological Association; AFSP; IAAP; Schizophrenia Research Forum; MGH Post Graduate Psychiatry. Address: Shimla House, 1st Floor, 60/11 West Mothertek, Dhaka 1214, Bangladesh. E-mail: hmanjur@bttb.net.bd

HOTTA Masashi, b. 19 August 1965, Niihama, Ehime, Japan. Engineer; Educator. Education: BE, Electronics, 1988; ME, Electronics, 1990; Dr Eng, 1995. Appointments: Assistant Professor, Department of Electrical & Electronic Engineering, Ehime University, 1990-99; Part-time Lecturer, Department of Education, 1995-96; Visiting Research Fellow,

Electrical Engineering Department, University of California, Los Angeles, 1997-98; Lecturer, 1999-2002, Associate Professor, 2002-, Department of Electrical and Electronic Engineering; Associate Professor, Division of Information and Design Engineering, Graduate School of Science and Engineering, Yamaguchi University; Associate Editor, IEICE Transactions on Electronics in Japan, 2005-08; Vice Chairman, IEEE Hiroshima Section, 2007-08. Publications: Technical papers and journal papers. Honours: Fellow, ABI; Listed in biographical dictionaries. Memberships: Institute of Electrical and Electronics Engineers; United Union of Radio Science; The International Society for Optical Engineering; American Institute of Physics; Optical Society of America; American Association for the Advancement of Science; Institute of Electronics Information and Communication Engineers in Japan; The Planetary Society. Address: Division of Information and Design Engineering, Graduate School of Science and Engineering, Yamaguchi University, 2-16-1 Tokiwadai, Ube, Yamaguchi 755-8611, Japan. E-mail: hotta@yamaguchi-u.ac.jp

HOU Wanqiu, b. 16 August 1974, Shandong Province, China. Immunologist. Education: PhD, Chinese Academy of Sciences, China, 2004; Research Scientist. Publications: Numerous articles in professional journals. Honours: Scholarship, Shanghai-Unilever Research and Development Fund, 2003; Diao Scholarship, Chinese Academy of Sciences, 2003; Scholarship, 6th Conference Asia-Pacific International Molecular Biology Network, 2003; Best Presentation Award, Research Poster Session, Annual Microbiology-Immunology Department Retreat, 2007. Memberships: Sigma Xi, American Association of Immunologists; American Society for Virology; American Society for Microbiology; International Society of Neuroimmunology; Inflammation Research Association. Address: 244 E Pearson St, Apt 1814, Chicago, IL 60611, USA. E-mail: w-hou@northwestern.edu

HOUGHTON Eric, b. 4 January 1930, West Yorkshire, England. Teacher; Author. m. Cecile Wolffe, 4 June 1954, 1 son, 1 daughter. Education: Sheffield City College of Education, 1952. Publications: The White Wall, 1961; Summer Silver, 1963; They Marched with Spartacus, 1963; A Giant Can Do Anything, 1975; The Mouse and the Magician, 1976; The Remarkable Feat of King Caboodle, 1978; Steps Out of Time, 1979; Gates of Glass, 1987; Walter's Wand, 1989; The Magic Cheese, 1991; The Backwards Watch, 1991; Vincent the Invisible, 1993; Rosie and the Robbers, 1997; The Crooked Apple Tree, 1999. Honour: American Junior Book Award, 1964. Memberships: Society of Authors; Childrens Writers Group. Address: The Crest, 42 Collier Road, Hastings, East Sussex TN34 3JR, England.

HOUGHTON Ivan Timothy, b. 23 February 1942, Royal Leamington Spa, England. Physician. m. Teresa Wan. Education: St John's College, Cambridge, 1960-63; St Thomas's Hospital Medical School, 1963-1966, BA (Cantab), 1963; LMSSA (Lond), 1966; BChir (Cantab), 1966; MB (Cantab), 1966; MA (Cantab), 1967; FFARCS (Eng), 1970; LLB (Lond), 1987; MD, Chinese University of Hong Kong, 1993; DMCC, 1995; Dip Med Ed (Dundee), 1996; LLM (Wales), 2000; BSc (Lond Met) 1st Class Honours, 2005. Appointments include: Various positions as House Surgeon, House Officer and Registrar, 1966-72; RAMC, 1972-2002, Brigadier L/RAMC, 1996-2002; Senior Specialist, Anaesthesia, 23 Parachute Field Ambulance, 1973-75; Regimental Medical Officer, 22 Special Air Service Regiment, 1975-76; Second in Command, 19 Airportable Field Ambulance, 1976-77; Consultant Anaesthetist, 6 Field Ambulance, 1977-78; Second in Command, 5 Field Force Ambulance, Münster, 1978-80; Consultant Anaesthetist and Second in Command, Military Wing, Musgrave Park Hospital, Belfast, 1981-82; Consultant Anaesthetist, British Military Hospital, Hong Kong, 1982-85; Senior Consultant Anaesthetist, British Military Hospital, Münster, 1985-87; Senior Consultant Anaesthetist, British Military Hospital, Hong Kong, 1987-94; Honorary Lecturer, Anaesthesia, 1982-85, Honorary Lecturer, Anaesthesia and Intensive Care, 1987-94, Chinese University of Hong Kong; Senior Consultant Anaesthetist, 1994-97, Commanding Officer, 1996-97, British Military Hospital, Rinteln; Clinical Director of Clinical Care, Royal Hospital Haslar, 1997-98; Regional Educational Adviser (Armed Forces), Royal College of Anaesthetists, 1998-2001; Consultant Adviser in Anaesthesia and Resuscitation to the Surgeon General, 1998-2001; Queen's Honorary Surgeon, 1999-2002; Editor, European Journal of Anaesthesiology, 2002-05; Currently: Restoration and Conservation, Sir John Cass Department of Art, Media and Design, London Metropolitan University. Publications: Papers on field anaesthesia, ethnic differences in anaesthesia, history of anaesthesia and conservation. Memberships: Liveryman, Society of Apothecaries; Fellow, Royal Society of Medicine; Army and Navy Club; Hong Kong Jockey Club; British Medical Association; Association of Anaesthetists of Great Britain and Ireland; Medico-Legal Society; The Institute of Conservation; British Antiques Furniture Restorers Society. Address: Canary Riverside, Canary Wharf, London E14, England. E-mail: ivanhoughton@doctors.org.uk

HOUSE Michael Charles Clutterbuck, b. 31 May 1927, Weston-super-Mare, Somerset, England. Catholic Priest. Education: Officers Training School, Bangalore, 1946; Kings College, London, 1948-51; Campion College, Osterley, 1952-53; St Mary's College, Oscott, Birmingham, 1954-60. Appointments: 2nd Battalion Queen's Royal Regiment, 1945-48; Ordained Priest, 1960; Assistant Priest: St Joseph's, Bristol, 1960-64, St Gerard Majella, Bristol, 1964-69, St Patrick's, Bristol, 1968-69; Financial Secretary to the Bishop of Clifton and Diocesan Trustees, 1969-80; Parish Priest: St George's, Warminster, 1980-87, St Mary's, Bath, 1987-91, St Thomas More, Marlborough, 1991-98; Religious Advisor to HTV West, 1966-98; Chairman of Governors, St Augustine's School, Trowbridge, 1985-87 and St Edward's School, Romsey, 1969-98; Catholic Chaplain to Marlborough College, 1991-98; National Conference of Priests, 1992-98. Publications: Articles in local papers and magazines. Honours: British Empire War Medal, 1939-45; Associateship of Kings College, London, 1951. Membership: Honorary Member, Portishead Cruising Club, Commodore, 1978-79. Address: Mirthios, Finikas 74060, Rethymnon, Crete, Greece.

HOUSE William C, b. 2 June 1933, Eastland, Texas, USA. Professor. m. Rose Adrian Musselwhite, 1 daughter. Education: BBA, Accounting, University of Texas at Austin, 1954; MBA, 1958, PhD, 1965, University of Texas; DPMA, Certificate of Data Processing, 1966; Mathematical Analysis of Voting Behavior; Simulation and Model Building, University of Missouri at Kansas City, 1975-76. Appointments: Budget Analyst, Texas Eastern Transmission Corporation, 1958-60; Summer Research Fellow, Travelers Insurance Company, Hartford, Connecticut, 1960; Instructor, Accounting and Finance, University of Texas, 1960-62; Assistant Professor, Business Administration, Texas A&M University, 1962-69; Project Group Leader and Guest Lecturer, Texas A&M Executive Development Program, 1966-69; Associate Professor, Management, Texas A&M University, 1966-69; Professor, Quantitative Management Science and Co-ordinator, 1969-71, Professor, Management,

1972-78, Professor, Business Analysis and Data Processing, 1978-98, University of Arkansas at Fayetteville; Professor, Management, University of Arkansas Program in Europe, 1971-72. Publication: 11 books on information technology and quantitative analysis; Articles in casebooks, professional journals and in professional proceedings. Honours: NATO Advanced Study Institute on Computer Science, 1976; Outstanding Educators of America, 1973; Best Management Paper, SW Business Symposium, 1986. Memberships: Institute of Management Science; Society for Case Research; International Association for Computer Information Systems. Address: College of Business, University of Arkansas, Fayetteville, AR 72702, USA.

HOUSTON Whitney, b. 9 August 1963, Newark, New Jersey, USA. Singer. m. Bobby Brown, 18 July 1992 (divorced), 1 daughter. Musical Education: Singing lessons with mother, Cissy Houston. Career: New Hope Baptist Junior Choir, age 8; Nightclub performances with mother, 1978; Backing vocalist, Chaka Khan and Lou Rawls, 1978; Model, Glamour and Seventeen magazines; Actress, television shows, USA; Solo artiste, 1985-; First US and European tours, 1986; Montreux Rock Festival, 1987; Nelson Mandela Tribute concert, Wembley, 1988; National anthem, Super Bowl XXV, Miami, 1991; Speaker, HIV/AIDs rally, London, 1991; Television specials include: Welcome Home Heroes (return of Gulf troops), 1991; Whitney Houston - This Is My Life, ABC, 1992; Actress, film The Bodyguard, 1992; 87 million albums sold to date. Recordings: Singles include: You Give Good Love, Saving All My Love For You (Number 1, UK and US), 1985; How Will I Know, Greatest Love Of All (Number 1, US), 1986; I Wanna Dance With Somebody (Number 1, US and UK), Didn't We Almost Have It All (Number 1, US), So Emotional (Number 1, US), 1987; Where Do Broken Hearts Go (Number 1, US), Love Will Save The Day, One Moment In Time (Number 1, UK), 1988; I'm Your Baby Tonight (Number 1, US), 1990; All The Man That I Need (Number 1, US), Miracle, 1991; My Name Is Not Susan, 1991; I Will Always Love You (Number 1 in 11 countries), 1992; I'm Every Woman, I Have Nothing, Run To You, 1993; Queen of the Night, 1994; Why Does It Hurt So Bad, 1996; Step by Step, 1997; When You Believe, 1998; It's Not Right But It's Okay, I Learned from the Best, 1999; If I Told You That, Could I Have This Kiss Forever, Heartbreak Hotel, 2000; Whatchlookinat, One of Those Days, 2002; Albums: Whitney Houston, 1985; Whitney, 1987; I'm Your Baby Tonight, 1990; My Love Is Your Love, 1998; Whitney: The Greatest Hits, 2000; Love Whitney, 2001; Just Whitney, 2002; Film soundtrack: The Bodyguard (Number 1 in 20 countries), 1992. Also featured on: Life's A Party, Michael Zager Band; Duet with Teddy Pendergrass, Hold Me, 1984; Duet with Aretha Franklin, It Isn't, It Wasn't, It Ain't Ever Gonna Be, 1989. Honours include: 2 Grammy Awards; 7 American Music Awards; Emmy, 1986; Songwriter's Hall Of Fame, 1990; Longest-ever US Number 1 record (14 weeks), highest-ever US 1-week sales total, second best seller in US ever, all for I Will Always Love You, 1992; Numerous Gold and Platinum discs. Current Management: Nippy Inc., 2160 N Central Road, Fort Lee, NJ 07024, USA.

HOWARD Anthony Michell, b. 12 February 1934, London, England. Biographer; Reviewer; Writer. m. Carol Anne Gaynor, 26 May 1965. Education: BA, Christ Church, Oxford, 1955. Appointments: Called to the Bar, Inner Temple, 1956; Political Correspondent, Reynolds News, 1958-59; Editorial Staff, Manchester Guardian, 1959-61; Political Correspondent, 1961-64, Assistant Editor, 1970-72, Editor, 1972-78, New Statesman; Whitehall Correspondent, 1965,

Sunday Times; Washington Correspondent, 1966-69, Deputy Editor, 1981-88, Observer; Editor, The Listener, 1979-81; Reporter, BBC TV News and Current Affairs, 1989-92; Obituaries Editor, The Times, 1993-99. Publications: The Making of the Prime Minister (with Richard West), 1965; The Crossman Diaries: Selections from the Diaries of a Cabinet Minister (editor), 1979; Rab: The Life of R A Butler, 1987; Crossman: The Pursuit of Power, 1990; The Times Lives Remembered (editor with David Heaton), 1993; Basil Hume: The Monk Cardinal, 2005. Contributions to: Books, newspapers, and journals. Honours: Harkness Fellowship, USA, 1960; Commander of the Order of the British Empire, 1997; Hon LLD, Nottingham, 2001; Hon DLitt, Leicester, 2003. Address: 11 Campden House Court, 42 Gloucester Walk, London W8 4HU, England.

HOWARD Catherine Audrey, b. 5 February 1953, Huddersfield, England. Retired Government Officer. m. Leslie Howard, 3 April 1987. Education: Harold Pitchforth School of Commerce; Ashlar and Spen Valley Further Education Institute; Royal Society of Arts Diplomas. Appointments: Clerk, Treasury Department, 1969-70, Clerk, Housing Department, 1970-74, Elland Urban District Council; Clerk, Telephonist, Housing Department, Calderdale Metropolitan Borough Council, 1974-83; Social Work Assistant; Social Services Department, Calderdale, 1983-88. Publications: Elland in Old Picture Postcards, 1983; Poetry: Down By the Old Mill Stream, 1993; The Flamborough Longsword Dance, 1994; Sacrifice for Christianity, 1994; My Pennine Roots, 1994; The Old and the New, 1994; Having Faith, 1994; The Might of the Meek, 1995; Tough as Old Boots, 1995; Portrait of All Hallows, 1996; Childhood Memories, 1996; Old Ways in Modern Days, 1996; Northern Cornucopia, 1996; A Glimpse of Spring, 1998; Poetry From Yorkshire, 1999. Contributions to: Mercedes-Benz Gazette, 1996; Commemorative Poem presented to Bridlington Public Library on the centenary of Amy Johnson, titled Wonderful Amy, 2003. Honours: National Poet of the Year Commendations, 1996 (3 times); National Open Competition Commendations, 1996, 1997; Robert Bloomfield Memorial Awards Commendation, 1998. Address: 17 Woodlands Close, Bradley Grange, Bradley, Huddersfield, West Yorkshire HD2 1QS, England.

HOWARD Deborah (Janet), b. 26 February 1946, London, England. Architectural Historian; Writer. m. Malcolm S Longair, 26 September 1975, 1 son, 1 daughter. Education: BA, Honours, 1968, MA, 1972, Newnham College, Cambridge; MA, 1969, PhD, 1973, University of London. Appointments: Professor of Architectural History, University of Cambridge, 2001-; Fellow, St John's College, Cambridge; Head of Department of History of Art, University of Cambridge. Publications: Jacopo Sansovino: Architecture and Patronage in Renaissance Venice, 1975, 2nd edition, 1987; The Architectural History of Venice, 1980, 3rd edition, 1987, revised and enlarged edition, 2002; Scottish Architecture from the Reformation to the Restoration, 1560-1660, 1995; Venice and the East: The Impact on the Islamic World on Venetian Architecture 1100-1500, 2000. Contributions to: Professional journals. Honour: Honorary Fellow, Royal Incorporation of Architects of Scotland; Fellow, Royal Society of Edinburgh. Memberships: Fellow, Society of Antiquarians of Scotland; Fellow, Society of Antiquaries. Address: St John's College, Cambridge CB2 1TP, England.

HOWARD Grahame Charles William, b. 15 May 1953, London, England. Consultant Clinical Oncologist. 3 sons. Education: St Thomas Hospital Medical School, London, 1970-76; London University Degrees: BSc, MBBS, MD.

Appointments: Registrar, The Royal Free Hospital, London; Senior Registrar and Research Fellow, Addenbrooke's Hospital Cambridge; Honorary Senior Lecturer, University of Edinburgh; Consultant Clinical Oncologist, 1987-, Clinical Director, The Edinburgh Cancer Centre, 1999-2005; Clinical Director, Cancer Services, 2005-. Publications: Author of over 100 publications in scientific journals on various topics related to cancer; several book chapters including oncology chapter in Davidson's Principles and Practice of Medicine; Co-author of several evidence based guidelines for various cancers. Professional qualifications: MRCP; FRCP (Ed); FRCR; Assistant Editor, Clinical Oncology; Chair, Scottish Intercollegiate Guideline Network, Cancer Speciality Subgroup; Chair, South East Scotland Urology Oncology Group. Address: 4 Ormelie Terrace, Edinburgh, EH15 2EX, Scotland.

HOWARD John Winston (The Honourable), b. 26 July 1939, Earlwood, New South Wales, Australia. Prime Minister of Australia. m. Alison Janette Parker, 4 April 1971, 2 sons, 1 daughter. Education: LLB, University of Sydney, 1961. Appointments: Solicitor, Supreme Court, New South Wales, 1962; Partner, solicitors' firm, 1968-74; MP for Bennelong, New South Wales, Federal Parliament, 1974-; Minister for Business and Consumer Affairs, 1975-77; Minister Assisting Prime Minister, 1977; Minister of State for Special Trade Negotiations, 1977; Federal Treasurer, 1977-83; Minister for Finance, 1979; Deputy Leader of the Opposition, 1983-85; Leader of the Opposition, 1985-89, 1995-96; Leader, Liberal Party, 1985-89; Prime Minister, Government of Australia, 1996-. Memberships: Member State Executive, New South Wales Liberal Party, 1963-74; Vice President, New South Wales Division, Liberal Party, 1972-74. Honours: Centenary Medal, 2001; Named one of the most influential people, TIME magazine, 2005; Star of the Soloman Islands, 2005. Address: St MG8 Parliament House, Canberra, ACT 2600, Australia.

HOWARD Michael, b. 7 July 1941. Member of Parliament. m. Sandra, 1 son, 1 stepson, 1 daughter. Education: Llanelli Grammar School; Peterhouse, Cambridge. Appointments: Called to the Bar, 1964; Appointed QC, 1982; Elected Member of Parliament, Folkestone and Hythe, 1983; Parliamentary Private Secretary to the Solicitor General, 1984; Parliamentary Under Secretary of State, Department of Trade and Industry, 1985; Minister of State for Local Government, Minister of State for Water and Planning, Department of Environment, 1987-90; Secretary of State for Employment, Member of Cabinet, 1990-92; Secretary of State for the Environment, 1992-93; Home Secretary, 1993-97; Shadow Foreign Secretary, 1997-99; Shadow Chancellor, 2001-03; Leader of the Conservative Party, 2003-05; Deputy Chairman, Entre Gold Inc; Non-Executive Director, Northern Racing Limited; Non-Executive Director, Amteus plc; Member, International Advisory Board, Thorium Inc. Address: House of Commons, London, SW1A 0AA, England. E-mail: howardm@parliament.uk

HOWARD Michael Newman, b. 10 June 1947, London, England. Barrister; Arbitrator. Education: Clifton College; MA, BCL, Magdalen College, Oxford. Appointments: Queens Counsel, 1986-; Recorder of Crown Court, 1993; Visiting Professor, Maritime Law, University College, London, 1996-99; Bencher, Gray's Inn, 1996-; Leader of Admiralty Bar, 2000-. Publications: Phipson on Evidence, 1983, 2000; Force Majeure and Frustration of Contract, 1991, 1995; Halsbury's Laws of England: Title – Damages; Articles, notes, reviews, etc in legal journals. Memberships: Oxford

& Cambridge Club; RAC; Garrick Club. Address: Quadrant Chambers, 10 Fleet Street, London EC4Y 1AU, England. E-mail: michael.howard@quadrantchambers.com

HOWARD Norman, b. 25 November 1926, London, England. Medical Practitioner; Consultant Clinical Oncologist. m. Anita, deceased, 2 sons. Education: BM BCh, MA, 1952; DM, 1965, Oxford University; FFR, 1958; FRCR, 1975. Appointments: House Physician and Surgeon, 1953-54, Registrar, 1954-56, University College Hospital; Registrar and Senior Registrar, Royal Marsden Hospital, 1956-63; Consultant, Radiotherapy and Oncology, Charing Cross Hospital, 1963-91, Wembley Hospital, 1964-91; Honorary Consultant, Royal Marsden Hospital, 1970-; Consultant in Clinical Oncology, Cromwell Hospital, 1982-2001; Chairman: Royal College of Radiologists Research Appeal, 1993-2003, Gunnar Nilsson Cancer Research Trust Fund, Medical Staff Committee, Charing Cross Hospital, 1974-79. Publications: Mediastinal Obstruction in Lung Cancer, 1967; Numerous chapters and articles concerning cancer, radiotherapy and radioisotopes. Honour: Commendatore Order of Merit Republic of Italy, 1976. Memberships: Royal College of Radiologists; Royal Society of Medicine; British Medical Association. Address: 5A Clarendon Road, London W11 4JA, England. E-mail: norman.anita@btinternet.com

HOWARD Ron, b. 1 March 1954, Duncan, Oklahoma, USA. Film Actor; Director; Producer. m. Cheryl Alley, 1975, 2 sons, 2 daughters. Education: University of Southern California; Los Angeles Valley College. Appointments: Director, Co-Author, Star, Grand Theft Auto, 1977; Regular TV series The Andy Griffith Show, 1960-68, The Smith Family, 1971-72, Happy Days, 1974, and many other TV appearances. Creative Works: Films directed include: Night Shift, 1982; Splash, 1984; Cocoon, 1985; Gung Ho, 1986; Return to Mayberry, 1986; Willow, 1988; Parenthood, 1989; Backdraft, 1991; Far and Away (also co-producer), 1992; The Paper, 1994; Apollo 13, 1995; A Beautiful Mind, 2001; The Missing, 2003; Cinderella Man, 2005; Film appearances include: The Journey, 1959; Five Minutes to Live, 1959; Music Man, 1962; The Courtship of Eddie's Father, 1963; Village of the Giants, 1965; Wild Country, 1971; Mother's Day, 1974; American Graffiti, 1974; The Spikes Gang, 1976; Eat My Dust, 1976; The Shootist, 1976; More American Graffiti, 1979; Leo and Loree (TV), 1980; Act of Love, 1980; Skyward, 1981; Through the Magic Pyramid (director, executive producer), 1981; When Your Lover Leaves (co-executive producer), 1983; Return to Mayberry, 1986; Ransom, 1996; Osmosis Jones (voice), 2001; Arrested Development (TV) 2003-06. Ed TV, 1999. Honours include: Outstanding Directorial Achievement in Motion Picture Award, Directors Guild of America, 1996; Academy Awards for Best Director and Best Film (producer), 2002; DGA Best Director Award, 2002; National Medal of Arts, 2003. Address: c/o Peter Dekom, Bloom Dekom & Hergott, 150 South Rodeo Drive, Beverly Hills, CA 90212, USA.

HOWARTH Nigel John Graham, b. 12 December 1936, Manchester, England. Circuit Judge. m. Janice Mary Hooper, 2 sons, 1 daughter. Education: LLB, 1957, LLM, 1959, University of Manchester; Bar Finals, 1st class honours, Inns of Court Law School, 1960; Macaskie Scholar, 1960, Atkin Scholar, 1961, Grays Inn. Appointments: Called to the Bar, Grays Inn, 1960; Private practice, Chancery Bar, Manchester, 1961-92; Assistant Recorder, 1983-89; Acting Deemster, Isle of Man, 1985, 1989; Recorder of Crown Court, 1989-92; Circuit Judge, 1992-. Memberships: Vice President, Disabled Living; Manchester Pedestrian Club; Northern Chancery Bar Association, Chairman, 1990-92.

Address: c/o Circuit Administrator, Northern Circuit Office, 15 Quay Street, Manchester, M60 9FD, England. E-mail: nhowarth@lix.compulink.co.uk

HOWE Elspeth Rosamund Morton (Baroness Howe of Idlicote), b. 8 February 1932. Member of the House of Lords. m. Lord Howe of Aberavon, 1953, 1 son, 2 daughters. Education: BSc, London School of Economics, 1985. Appointments: Secretary to Principal, A A School of Architecture, 1952-55; Deputy Chairman, Equal Opportunities Commission, Manchester, 1975-79; President, Federation of Recruitment and Employment Services, 1980-94; Non-Executive Director, United Biscuits plc, 1988-94; Non-Executive Director, Kingfisher plc, 1986-2000; Non-Executive Director, Legal and General, 1989-97; Chairman, The BOC Foundation for the Environment, 1990-2003; Chairman, The Broadcasting Standards Commission, 1993-99. Publications: 2 pamphlets; Co-author, Women on the Board, 1990; Articles for newspapers; Lectures, speeches, television and radio broadcasts. Honours: Honorary Doctorates: London University, 1990; The Open University, 1993; Bradford University, 1993; Aberdeen University, 1994; Liverpool University, 1994; Sunderland University, 1995; South Bank University, 1995; Honorary Fellow, London School of Economics, 2001. Memberships: President, the UK Committee of UNICEF, 1993-2002; Vice Chairman, The Open University, 2001-03; Trustee, The Architectural Association; Trustee, The Ann Driver Trust; Institute of Business Ethics; President, The Peckham Settlement; NCVO Advisory Council. Address: House of Lords, London SW1A 0PW, England. E-mail: howee@parliament.uk

HOWE, 7th Earl, Frederick Richard Curzon, b. 29 January 1951, London, England. Parliamentarian. m. Elizabeth Helen, 1 son, 3 daughters. Education: BA, 1973, MA, 1977, Christ Church College, Oxford. Appointments: Barclays Bank plc, 1973-87; Director, Adam & Co plc, 1987-90; Government Whip, 1991-92; Parliamentary Secretary, Ministry of Agriculture and Fisheries, 1992-95; Parliamentary Under Secretary of State for Defence, 1995-97; Opposition Spokesman for Health and Social Services, 1997-; Chairman, LAPADA, 1999-. Address: House of Lords, London SW1A 0PW, England.

HOWE Geoffrey (Lord Howe of Aberavon), b. 20 December 1926. Politician; Lawyer m. Elspeth Rosamund Morton Shand, 1953, 1 son, 2 daughters. Education: MA, LLB, Trinity Hall, Cambridge. Appointments: Lieutenant, Royal Signals, 1945-48; Chairman, Cambridge University Conservative Association, 1951; Chairman, Bow Group, 1955; Contested Aberavon, 1955, 1959; Managing Director, Crossbow, 1957-60; Editor, 1960-62; Called to the Bar, Middle Temple, 1952, QC, 1965, Bencher, 1969, Reader, 1993; Member, General Council of the Bar, 1957-61; Member, Council of Justice, 1963-70; MP, Bebington, 1964-66, Reigate, 1970-74, Surrey East, 1974-92; Secretary, Conservative Parliamentary Health and Social Security Committee, 1964-65; Opposition Front Bench Spokesman on labour and social services, 1965-66; (Latey) Interdepartmental Committee on Age of Majority, 1965-67; Deputy Chairman, Glamorgan Quarter Sessions, 1966-70; (Street) Committee on Racial Discrimination, 1967; (Cripps) Conservative Committee on Discrimination Against Women, 1968-69; Chair, Ely Hospital, Cardiff, Inquiry, 1969; Solicitor-General, 1970-72; Minister for Trade and Consumer Affairs, Department of Trade and Industry, 1972-74; Opposition front bench spokesman on social services, 1974-75, on Treasury and Economic Affairs, 1975-79; Director, Sun Alliance & London

Insurance Co Ltd, 1974-79; AGB Research Ltd, 1974-79; EMI Ltd, 1976-79; Chancellor of the Exchequer, 1979-83; Chair, Interim Committee, IMF, 1982-83; Secretary of State, Foreign and Commonwealth Affairs, 1983-89; Lord President of the Council, Leader of House of Commons, Deputy Prime Minister, 1989-90; Visiting Fellow, John F Kennedy School of Government, Harvard University, 1991-92; Glaxo Holdings, 1991-95; Herman Phleger Visiting Professor, Stanford Law School, California, 1993; Glaxo Wellcome plc, 1995-96; BICC plc, 1991-97; Visitor, SOAS, University of London, 1991-2001; Special Adviser, International Affairs, Jones, Day, Reavis & Pogue, 1991-2001; Advisory Council, Bertelsmann Foundation, 1992-97; J P Morgan International Advisory Council, 1992-2001; Chair, Framlington Russian Investment Fund, 1994-2003; Chair, Steering Committee, Tax Law Rewrite Project, Inland Revenue, 1996-; Fuji Wolfensohn International European Advisory Board, 1996-98; Carlyle Group, European Advisory Board, 1997-2001; Fuji Bank International Advisory Council, 1999-. Publications: Conflict of Loyalty (memoirs), 1994; Various political pamphlets. Honours include: Grand Cross, Order of Merit (Portugal), 1987; Hon LLD, Wales, 1988; Honorary Freeman, Port Talbot, 1992; Grand Cross, Order of Merit, Germany, 1992; Life Peer, 1992; Hon DCL, City, 1993; Joseph Bech Prize, FVS Stifting, Hamburg, 1993; Companion of Honour, 1996; Order of Public Service, Ukraine, 2001. Memberships: International Advisory Council; Member, Council of Management, Private Patients' Plan, 1969-70; Honorary Vice President, 1974-92, President, 1992-, Association for Consumer Research; National Union of Conservative and Unionist Associations, 1983-84; Institute of International Studies, Stanford University, California, 1990-; Patron, Enterprise Europe, 1990-2004; Vice President: RUSI, 1991-; Joint President, Wealth of Nations Foundation, 1991-; Member, Advisory Council, Presidium of Supreme Rada of Ukraine, 1991-97; Member, Steering Committee, Project Liberty, 1991-97; Chair, Advisory Board, English Centre for Legal Studies, Warsaw University, 1992-99; Centre for European Policy Studies, 1992-; English College Foundation in Prague, 1992-; GB China Centre, 1992-; Trustee: Cambridge Commonwealth Trust, 1993-; Cambridge Overseas Trust, 1993-; Paul Harris Fellow, Rotary International, 1995; Thomson Foundation, 1995-, Chair, 2004-; President, Academy of Experts, 1996-; Honorary Fellow: UCW, Swansea, 1996; President: Conservative Political Centre National Advisory Committee, 1997-79; Patron, UK Metric Association, 1999-; UCW, Cardiff, 1999; American Bar Foundation, 2000; Chartered Institute of Taxation, 2000; SOAS, 2003. Address: House of Lords, London SW1A 0PW, England.

HOWELL David Arthur Russell (Lord Howell of Guildford), b. 18 January 1936, London, England. Economist; Journalist; Author. m. Davina Wallace, 1 son, 2 daughters. Education: King's College, Foundation Scholar. Appointments: Member of Parliament for Guildford, 1966-97; Parliamentary Secretary, Civil Service Department, 1970-72; Minister of State, Northern Ireland, 1972-74; Secretary of State for Energy, 1979-81; Secretary of State for Transport, 1981-83; Chairman, House of Commons Foreign Affairs Select Committee, 1987-97; Chairman, UK-Japan 21st Century Group, 1989-2001; Visiting Fellow, Nuffield College, Oxford, 1991-99; Director, Monks Investment Trust, 1993-; Advisory Director, UBS Warburg, 1996-2000; Chairman, Lords European Committee, Sub-Committee, 1998-2000; Director, John Laing plc, 1999-2002; Trustee, Shakespeare Globe Theatre, 2000-; Chief Opposition Spokesman on Foreign Affairs, House of Lords, 2000-. Publications: Columnist: The Japan Times; Wall Street Journal; International Herald Tribune; Books: Freedom and Capital, 1979; Blind Victory,

1986; The Edge of Now, 2000; Numerous pamphlets and articles. Honours: Privy Counsellor, 1979; Created Peer of the Realm, 1997; Grand Cordon of the Order of the Sacred Treasure, Japan, 2001. Memberships: Beefsteak Club; County Club, Guildford. Address: House of Lords, London SW1A 0PW, England. E-mail: howelld@parliament.uk

HOWELL Sister Veronica (formerly known as Sister Mary Aidan), b. 23 May 1924, Woolwich, London, England. Educator. Education: Mount Pleasant Training College, Liverpool; Corpus Christi Theological College, London; Heythrop Theological College, London University; Licentiate of the Royal College of Music. Appointments: Became a member of the Congregation of the Daughters of Jesus, 1944; Teacher, Our Lady of Lourdes Convent School and Sacred Heart Infants School, Colne, Lancashire, 1946-51; Teacher, St Teresa's, Princes Risborough, Buckinghamshire, 1951-56; Teacher, St Stephen's Primary School, Welling, Kent, 1956-60; Teacher, Sts Thomas More and John Fisher Secondary School, Colne, Lancashire, 1960-63; Head Mistress, St Stephen's Primary School, Welling, Kent, 1963-75; Assistant to National Director and Training Officer of Catholic Information Services of England and Wales also helping to produce audio-visual material for spiritual retreats, 1975-79; Vocation's Director for the English Province of the Daughters of Jesus (Religious Congregation), 1979-84; Communications and Press Officer for female and male religious of England and Wales for the Pope's visit to England and Wales, 1982; Parish Assistant of Our Lady of Grace Parish, Governor of St Augustine's First and Middle School, Sister in Charge of Religious Community, High Wycombe, Buckinghamshire, Co-ordinator of Communications for Diocese of Northampton, Co-Editor of Diocesan newspaper, Member of Steering Committee winning the charter for a Christian radio station, 1986-92; Sister in Charge of Community and Parish Sister, Our Lady Help of Christians Parish, Rickmansworth, Hertfordshire, 1993-99; Parish Sister to Sacred Heart Church, Colne, Lancashire, 2000-; Governor of St Thomas More Catholic Humanities College, 2001-. Publication: Founder and Co-editor, The Vine newspaper, Northampton Diocese. Memberships: Congregation of the Daughters of Jesus; Founder and Chairperson, Association of Christian Education, Welling, Kent, 1970-75; Co-Founder, Day Centre for Elderly Mentally Infirm, High Wycombe, Buckinghamshire, 1988-92; Caring Church Week Groups, 1979-84; Association of Head Teachers, 1963-75. Address: Southworth, 6 Netherheys Close, Colne, Lancashire, BB8 9QY, England. E-mail: vghowell@yahoo.uk.com

HOWIE Kelli Ann Bennett, b. 23 November 1956, Dallas, Texas, USA. Artist. Education: BA, Theatre and Art, University of Dallas, 1980; Master of Fine Arts and Design, Southern Methodist University, 1983. Appointments: Head Designer, Technical Theatre Department, Blue Ribbon High School, Dallas; Costume Designer, University of Dallas; Costume Professor, Dallas Baptist University; Chairman, Art Department, Wade College, Dallas; Owner, Kelli's Blue Mesa Studies Inc. Publications: Articles in Dallas Morning News and Today Newspapers. Honours: Executive Female Professional of the Year, Artist/Designer of Visual Arts Theatre Production and Design, 2006-07; Bronze Medal, Sons of the American Revolution. Memberships: Cedar Hill Association of the Cultural Arts; Visual Arts Guild of Frisco; Texas Visual Arts Association; National Museum of Women in the Arts; Duncanville Chamber of Commerce; Visual Artists of Cedar Hill. Address: 1055 Lansdale, Duncanville, TX 75116, USA. E-mail: kelliannhowie@yahoo.com Website: www.kelliehowiestudios.com

HOWLETT Neville Stanley, b. 17 April 1927, Prestatyn, Wales. Retired Air Vice-Marshal. m. Sylvia, 1 son, 1 daughter. Education: Liverpool Institute High School and Peterhouse, Cambridge, England. Appointments: Pilot Training, Royal Air Force, 1945-48; 32 and 64 Fighter Squadrons, 1948-56; RAF Staff College, 1957; Squadron Commander, 224 (Fighter) OCU, 1958-59; OC Flying Wing, RAF Coltishall, 1961-63; Directing staff, RAF Staff College, 1967-69; Station Commander, RAF Leuchars, 1970-72; Royal College of Defence Studies, 1973; Director of Operations, Air Defence and Overseas, 1973-74; Air Attaché, Washington DC, USA, 1975-77; Director, Management Support of Intelligence, 1978-80; Director General, Personal Services, 1980-82; Retired, 1982; Member, Lord Chancellors Panel of Independent Inquiry Inspectors, 1982-95; Member, Pensions Appeal Tribunal, 1988-2001. Honour: CB. Memberships: Royal Air Force Club; Royal Air Forces Association, Vice-President, 1984-, Chairman Executive Committee, 1990-97, Chairman Central Council, 1999-2001; Royal Air Force Benevolent Fund; Officers Association; Phyllis Court Club, Henley; Huntercombe Golf Club. Address: Milverton, Bolney Trevor Drive, Lower Shiplake, Oxon RG9 3PG, England.

HOZUMI Motoo, b. 12 March 1933, Fukushima, Japan. Cancer Research. m. Sakiko Wakabayashi, 1 son, 2 daughters. Education: BSc, 1956, MSc, 1958, DSc, 1961, Tokyo University of Education. Appointments: Research Member, National Cancer Center Research Institute, Tokyo, 1962-64; Chief, Central Laboratory, National Cancer Center Research Institute, Tokyo, 1964-75; Research Member, Roswell Park Memorial Institute, Buffalo, New York, 1965-67; Director, Department of Chemotherapy, Saitama Cancer Center Research Institute, Japan, 1975-93; Visiting Professor, Showa University School of Medicine, Tokyo, 1988-2001; Director, Saitama Cancer Center Research Institute, 1990-93. Publications: Over 300 papers and books on cancer research. Honours: Princess Takamatsu Cancer Research Foundation Prize, Tokyo, 1974. Memberships: Japanese Cancer Association; Japanese Haematological Society; American Cancer Association; American Association for the Advancement of Science. Address: 12-288 Fukasaku, Minuma, Saitama, Saitama 337, Japan.

HŘIB Jiři Emil, b. 16 September 1942, Frýdek-Místek, Czech Republic. Plant Physiologist. m. Marie Malá, 16 January 1970, 1 daughter. Education: Engineer, 1966, PhD, 1973, University of Agriculture, Brno (now Mendel University of Agriculture and Forestry, Brno). Appointments: Scientist Aspirant, Scientific Film Laboratory, Institute of Scientific Instruments, 1967-73, Scientist, Institute of Vertebrate Zoology, 1973-74, Scientist, Institute of Botany, 1974-83, Scientist, Institute of Experimental Phytotechnics, 1984-87, Scientist, Institute of Systematic and Ecological Biology, 1987-91, Czechoslovak Academy of Sciences, Brno; Scientist, Institute of Plant Genetics, 1991-97, Principal Scientist, Institute of Plant Genetics and Biotechnology, 1997-98, External Scientific Co-worker, Institute of Plant Genetics and Biotechnology, 1999-, Slovak Academy of Sciences, Nitra. Publications: Over 100 articles in professional scientific journals; The Co-Cultivation of Wood-Rotting Fungi with Tissue Cultures of Forest Tree Species, 1990; Research films: (author) Ontogeny of the Alga Scenedesmus quadricauda, 1973; Co-author, Regeneration of the Cap in the Alga Acetabularia mediterranea, 1980. Honours: Research Board of Advisors, American Biographical Institute, 1999; Consulting Editor, Contemporary Who's Who, 2003; FABI, 2005; Consulting Editor, International Directory of Experts and Expertise, 2006. Memberships: Czech Society for Scientific Cinematography,

Brno, 1965; Czech Botanical Society, Prague, 1967; International Association for Plant Tissue Culture and Biotechnology, 1990; International Association of Sexual Plant Reproduction Research, 1993; New York Academy of Sciences, 2001; Czechoslovak Biological Society, Brno, 2001; Czech Algological Society, Prague, 2002. Address: Ukrajinská 17, 625 00 Brno, Czech Republic.

HSIEH Ching-Hua, b.14 November 1967, Kaohsiung, Taiwan. Plastic Surgeon. m. Hui-Hong Tsai, 2 sons. Education: Doctor of Medicine, National Taiwan University, Taipei, Taiwan, 1985-92; Postgraduate, Graduate Institute of Clinical Medical Science, PhD Program, Chang Gung University, Taiwan, 2005-. Appointments: Residency in General Surgery, 1994-96, Residency in Plastic Surgery, 1996-2000, National Taiwan University Hospital; Attending in Department of Traumatic Surgery, Chang Gung Memorial Hospital, Kaohsiung, 2001-. Publications: More than 20 articles in international medical journals include most recently: Anterolateral thigh adipofascial perforator flap, 2003; Traumatic optic neuropathy, 2004, 2005; Biblobed flap for radial forearm flap donor defect, 2004; Teleconsultation with mobile camera-phone in remote evaluation of replantation potential, 2005. Honour: International Guest Scholarship, American College of Surgeons, 2005. Memberships: Taiwan Society of Surgery; Taiwan Society of Plastic Surgery; Taiwan Society of Surgery of the Hand; Taiwan Society of Critical Care Medicine; Taiwan Society of Trauma. Address: No 123 Ta-Pei Road, Niao-Sung Hsiang, Kaohsiung Hsien, 833 Taiwan. E-mail: m93chinghua@yahoo.com.tw

HSU Tien-Pen, b. 30 August 1958, Tainan County, Taiwan. Traffic Engineering Researcher; Educator. m. Swee Kiang Ng, 1 son, 1 daughter. Education: BS, Department of Transportation Engineering, National Chiao-Tung University, 1980; MS, Institute of Civil Engineering, National Taiwan University, 1982; Doctor Engineer, Department of Civil Engineering, Universitat Karlsruhe, Germany, 1991. Appointments: Associate Professor, National Taiwan University, 1991-; Mayor Advisor, Taipei Capital City, Taipei, 1996-99; Municipal Advisor, Taipei County, 1998-2005; Secretary General, Chinese Institute of Transportation, Taipei, 2001-03; President, Taipei Society for Traffic Safety, Taipei, Taiwan, 2002-04; National Councillor of National Sustainable Development Council, Executive Yuan, Taiwan, 2005-07. Publications: Research report of development of a segregated motorcycle traffic signal, 1999; The Level of Sustainability for Urban Transport, chapter in book, Sustainable Planning & Development, 2003. Honours: Outstanding Paper Award, 1999; Excellent Teaching Award, 2001, Outstanding Teaching Award, 2004, National Taiwan University; Grant of International Co-operative Research Activity, 2002-03, 2004-05. Memberships: Honorary Board Member, Taipei Society for Traffic Safety; Standing Board Member, Chinese Institute of Transportation; Member, Deutsche Verkhrswissenshaftliche Gesellschaft ev. Address: Taipei Roosevelt Road, Sec 4, No 1, Taipei, Taiwan. E-mail: hsutp@ntu.edu.tw

HSU Wen-Ping, b. 13 August 1963, Kaohsiung, Taiwan. Professor. m. Pei-Hua Tsai, 2 daughters. Education: Bachelor, Chemical Engineering, National Taiwan University, Taipei, Taiwan, 1985; Master, Chemical Engineering, 1990, PhD, Chemical Engineering, 1992, Polytechnic University, New York, USA. Appointments: Associate Professor, 1993-99, Professor, 1999-2004, Chairman, 2002-04, Department of Applied Chemistry, Chia-Nan University of Pharmacy & Science, Tainan, Taiwan; Professor, Department of Chemical

Engineering, 2004-, Curator of Library, 2007, Dean of Research and Development, 2007-, National United University, Miao-Li, Taiwan. Publications: About 37 scientific papers. Honours: Listed in national and international biographical directories. Memberships: Polymer Society, Taiwan, Republic of China; Taiwan Institute of Chemical Engineers. E-mail: wenping@nuu.edu.tw

HSU Zuey-Shin, b. 13 December 1930, Shining, Taiwan. Professor of Physiology. Education: MD, National Taiwan University, 1956. Appointments: Physician, Department of Internal Medicine, National Taiwan University Hospital; Educator, Department of Legal Medicine, Kaohsiung Medical College; Part-time Forensic Pathologist, Taipei Regional Court; Physiologist, Professor, Department of Physiology, Kaohsiung Medical College; Professor, High School of Research, Alliance Universelle pour la Paix. Membership: Fellow, Institute of Medical Science, Tokyo University, 1967-; World Institute of Achievement, 1989-; International Parliament for Safety and Peace, 1991-; Academy MIDI, 1992-; London Diplomatic Academy, 2000-. Address: 8F-1, No 153 Min-Tsu Road, Taichung, Taiwan.

HU Bingkun, b. 15 July 1935, Shanghai, China. Qigong Therapist; Qigong Master. m. Linda Susan Weems-Hu, 1 daughter. Education: BA, English and Linguistics, Fudan University, China, 1956; MA, Folklore and Cultural Anthropology, University of California in Berkeley, USA, 1985; PhD, Psychology, Sierra University, Costa Mesa, USA, 1987. Appointments: Associate Professor, Shanghai Science and Technology Institute and Fudan University, 1964-80; Instructor, Monterey Institute of International Study, 1980-84; Qigong therapist, Private practice, San Francisco Bay, 1988-; Adviser, East-West Academy of Healing Arts; Adviser, Qigong Institute; Instructor, San Francisco State University. Publications: Articles on Qigong in magazines and journals; Qigong workshops and lectures, 1997-2007; 11 Qigong DVDs (9 of which are devoted to Wild Goose Qigong). Honours: Listed in Who's Who publications and biographical dictionaries. Memberships: American Qigong Association; World Qigong Federation. Address: 2114 Sacramento Street, Berkeley, CA 94702, USA.

HUANG Chiang Cheng, b. 6 August 1946, Miao-Li County, Taiwan. Business. m. King Ying Hong, 3 daughters. Education: Graduate, SMB Elite Camp, Graduate, Training Camp for Top Management at Operation Headquarter, Industrial Development Bureau, Graduate, Advanced Research Camp for 21st Century Entrepreneurs, Department of Commerce, Graduate, SMB Top Manager Training Camp, Taiwan Ministry of Economy Affairs; Graduate, Finance Management Study, Small and Medium Business Administration, Ministry of Economy Affairs; Graduate, 2nd Advanced Business Development Study, US MSC. Appointments: Factory Chief, Sankyo Electric and Machinery Ltd Co, 1967-80; Vice President & Co-Founder, Chief Engineer of R&D Department, Factory Chief, Director of Procurement Department, Sunonwealth Electric and Machinery Industrial Ltd Co, 1980-2003; President/Founder, Risun Expance Corp, 1999-. Publications: Numerous articles in professional journals. Honours: Good Samaritan Awards, 2003, 2005, 2006; Industrial Contribution Award, 2005, Accomplished Research Award, 2006, Taiwan Association for Magnetic Technology; Golden Root Award, Taiwan Industrial Technology Association, 2006; Golden Role Model for Outstanding Entrepreneurs of Small and Medium Business, 2006; Golden Quality Award for Customer Satisfaction, 21st Century Economy and Trading Development Association; Industry Innovation Award, Leaders in Creativity,

2006; Outstanding Asian-Pacific Role Model for Business Operation, 2007. Memberships: Motor Industry Association of Northern Taiwan; Council of Chinese Qiji Daoyin Research; Taiwan Association for Magnetic Technology; 21st Century Economy and Trading Development Association. E-mail: c.c.huang@ms.risun.com.tw

HUANG Christopher, b. 28 December 1951, Singapore. Professor of Cell Physiology. Education: BA (Oxford), The Queen's College, Oxford, 1971-74; BM BCh (Oxford), Oxford University Clinical School, 1974-76; Medical Research Council Scholar, Physiological Laboratory and Gonville and Caius College, Cambridge, 1978-79; PhD (Cambridge), 1980; DM (Oxford), 1985; MD (Cambridge), 1986; DSc (Oxford), 1995; ScD (Cambridge), 1995. Appointments: Pre-registration appointments, Nuffield Department of Medicine, University of Oxford, 1977-78; University Demonstrator in Physiology, 1979-84; Fellow and College Lecturer in Physiology, 1979-2002, Director of Studies in Medical Sciences, 1981-, Professional Fellow, 2002-, New Hall, Cambridge; University Lecturer in Physiology, 1984-96, University Reader in Cellular Physiology, 1996-2002, University Professor of Cell Physiology, 2002-, Cambridge; Several visiting professorships, 1984-2004. Publications: Monographs and books: Intramembrane charge movements in striated muscle, 1993; Applied Physiology for Surgery and Critical Care (co-editor), 1995; Research in medicine. A guide to writing a thesis in the medical sciences (co-author), 1999; Molecular and cellular biology of bone (co-editor), 1998; Over 200 scientific papers in medical journals. Honours: Florence Heale Open Scholar, The Queen's College, Oxford, 1971-76; President's Scholar, Republic of Singapore, 1971-76; Benefactor's Prize, The Queen's College, Oxford, 1973; Brian Johnson Prize in Pathology, University of Oxford, 1976; LEPRA Award, British Leprosy Relief Association, 1977; Rolleston Memorial Prize for Physiological Research, University of Oxford, 1980; Gedge Prize in Physiology, University of Cambridge, 1981. Memberships: Physiological Society, UK; Research Defence Society, UK; American Society of General Physiologists, USA; Biophysical Society, USA; Association of Bone and Mineral Research, USA; Ordinary Member of Council, 1994-, Biological Secretary, 2000-08, Adjudicator and Convenor, William Bate Handy Prize, 2008, Cambridge Philosophical Society; Director, AW Boon Haw Foundation, 2004-; Independent Non-Executive Director, Hutchison China Meditech, 2006-. Address: New Hall, Huntingdon Road, Cambridge CB3 0DF, England.

HUANG Dongzhou, b. 5 November 1949, Ruijin, China. Scientist; Educator, Civil Engineer. m. Yingying Shu, 1 son. Education: BS, Civil Engineering, 1974; MS, Civil Engineering, 1985; PhD, Structural Engineering, 1989. Appointment: Professor, Civil Engineering, Fuzhou University; President, BSD Engineering Inc, USA; Associate Editor, Journal of Bridge Engineering, ASCE; Developed finite element methods for analyzing elastic and inelastic lateral buckling of trussed-arch bridges; Developed methods for analyzing dynamic/impact factors of various types of bridges due to moving vehicles; Found basic relationships between static and dynamic responses as well as between impact factor and lateral distribution factor; Developed a practical method for determining lateral load distribution factors of arch and beam bridges, a load capacity rating method of bridges through field test and a shear reinforcement design method for prestressed concrete beam anchorage zones; Developed a finite element method for static and dynamic analysis of curved box girder bridges. Publications: Over 50 papers in professional journals, 2 books. Honour: 1st Prize,

Best Publications. Memberships: ASCE; AISC; IABSZ; New York Academy of Sciences; American Association for the Advancement of Science. Address: 2408 Tea Olive Terrace, Valrico, FL 33594, USA.

HUANG Her-Hsiung, b. 10 October 1964, Taiwan. Educator and Researcher. m. Wei-Ho Lo, 1 son, 1 daughter. Education: BS, Mechanical Engineering, 1987, MS, Mechanical Engineering, 1989, National Central University; PhD, Materials Science, National Cheng Kung University, Taiwan, 1995. Appointments: Assistant Professor, Institute of Dental Materials, 1999-2002, Associate Professor, Institute of Oral Materials Science, 2002-05, Chung Shan Medical University, Taiwan; Associate Professor, Department of Chemical and Materials Engineering, National University of Kaohsiung, Kaohsiung, Taiwan, 2005-06; Professor, School of Dentistry, National Yang-Ming University, Taipei, Taiwan, 2006-. Publications: More than 80 articles published in related journals and conference proceedings. Honours: Scholar, Industry of Science and Technology, Ministry of Education, Taiwan, 1989-92; Scholar, Sandwich Programme of NSC, Taiwan/DAAD, Germany, 1991-92; Listed in Who's Who publications and biographical dictionaries. Memberships: National Association of Corrosion Engineers; International Association for Dental Research; Chinese Society for Materials Science; Association for Dental Sciences of the ROC; Corrosion Engineering Society of the ROC. Address: National Yang-Ming University, School of Dentistry, No 155, Sec 2, Li-Nong Street, Bei-Tou District, Taipei City 112, Taiwan. E-mail: hhhuang@ym.edu.tw Website: http://home.educities.edu.tw/biomaterials

HUANG Hung-Chia, b. 5 August 1924, (Beijing) Peking. Microwave Photonics Researcher; Educator. m. Shen Jin-Ying, 2 sons. Education: BS, National Southwest Associated University, 1944; MS, University of Michigan, 1949; Hon DSc, University Eurotech, 1992. Appointments: War service, Major-ranked interpreter, China-US-UK Allied Force, Yunan-Burma Route War Area, 1944-45; Assistant, Peking University, 1946-47; Assistant, Shanghai Jiao Tong University, 1947-48; Associate Professor, Professor, North Jiao Tong University, 1950-64; Research Professor, Academia Sinica, 1964-79; Professor, Honorary President, Shanghai University, 1979-; Academician, Academia Sinica, 1980-; Guest Professor, University of Karlsruhe, West Germany, 1984; Guest Professor, Chinese University of Hong Kong, 1989; Guest Professor, University of Leuven, 1992; Currently Principal Scientist, Joint Project with Shanghai Electric Power. Publications: Microwave Principles; Microwave Approach to Highly Irregular Fibre Optics; Over 100 papers in diverse national and international journals; 6 US patents; 7 Chinese patents. Memberships: Fellow, Chinese Institute of Electronics, 1964-; Chairman, Committee of Science and Technology, Europe China Association, 1983-85; Member and Chairman for PRC, Union Radio Science International, 1984-; Fellow, The Electromagnetics Academy, MIT, 1989-. Address: Shanghai University, Shanghai 201800, China.

HUANG Joshua Zhexue, b. 19 July 1959, Heilongjiang, China. Research and Education. m. Margaret Hua Song, 1 son, 1 daughter. Education: BS, Harbin Institute of Technology, China; Master's degree, Northeast Forestry University, Harbin, China; PhD, Royal Institute of Technology, Sweden. Appointments: Lecturer, Northeast Forestry University, Harbin, 1982-88; Visiting Scientist, PhD Student, Royal Institute of Technology, Sweden, 1988-94; Research Scientist, CSIRO, Australia, 1994-98; Senior Consultant, MIP, Australia, 1998-2000; Assistant Director, ETI, The University of Hong

Kong, 2000-. Publications: Extensions to the K-means Algorithm for clustering large Data Sets with Categorical Values, 1998; A Fuzzy K-modes Algorithm for clustering categorical data, 1999; Automated variable weighting in K-means type clustering on pattern analysis and machine intelligence, 2005. Honours: Most Influential Paper Award, The Pacific Conference on Knowledge Discovery and Data Mining. Memberships: IEEE; ACM; SIGKDD.

HUANG Kuohsiu, b. 13 February 1960, Taoyuan City, Taiwan. University Professor. m. Yazu Young, 2 sons, 1 daughter. Education: BS, National Taiwan University, 1982; MS, Iowa State University, USA, 1987; PhD, University of Michigan, USA, 1992. Appointments: Project Engineer, Ford Motor Co, USA, 1991-93; Technical Specialist, CASE Corporation, USA, 1993-97; Assistant Professor, Associate Professor, Professor, Department of Mechanical Engineering, Dayeh University, 1997-2006; Professor, Department of Vehicular Engineering, National Taipei University of Technology, Taiwan, 2006-. Publications: Optimization of Size of Vehicle and Flow Domain for Underhood Airflow Simulation, 2004; Hybrid Pneumatic Power System which Recycles Exhaust Gas of an Internal-combustion Engine, 2005; Air-conditioning System of an Intelligent Vehicle Cabin, 2006. Honours: Grantee, National Science Council; Listed in international biographical dictionaries. Memberships: Society of Automotive Engineers; American Society of Mechanical Engineers; Society of Electric Motorcycle Development. Address: 4F-1, 299 Fu-Shing Rd, Taoyuan City, Taiwan 330. E-mail: kdavidh@ntut.edu.tw

HUANG Pai-Tsang, b. 28 April 1960, Taipei, Taiwan. Physician. m. Shu-Ru Chen, 2 sons. Education: Doctor of Medicine, Taipei Medical College, 1978-85; MSc, Department of Environmental Health, University of Cincinnati, USA, 1991-93. Appointments: Resident Physician, Internal Medicine, Chang Gung Memorial Hospital, Taoyuan, Taiwan, 1987-91; Assistant Physician, Instituet für Arbeitsmedizin Freie Unversität Berlin, Germany, 1993-95; Attending Physician, Department of Occupational Medicine & Department of Health Screening, Changhua Christian Hospital, Changhua, Taiwan, 1995-2005; Physician, Dr Lin's Clinic, Taipei, 2005-; Consultant, Taiwan Semi-conductor Manufacturing Company, Hsinchu, 2005-; Company Physician, Grand Hyatt, Taipei, Taiwan, 2005-. Publications: Body lead stores and urate excretion in men with chronic renal disease, 1994; Persistent leukocyte abnormalities in children years after previous long-term low-dose radiation exposure, 1999; The peculiarities of occupational diseases and work injuries in Taiwan – a reflection from the German point of view, 2002. Honours: Public Health Contribution Award, Changhua Precinct, Taiwan, 2000; Listed in international biographical dictionaries. Memberships: Taiwan Environmental & Occupational Medicine Association; Taiwan Society of Internal Medicine. Address: 7F No 3 Lane 323, Jia-Hsin Street (106), Taipei, Taiwan. E-mail: ptsr2.huang@msa.hinet.net

HUANG Yung-Sheng, b. 1 June 1966, Cheng-Hua, Taiwan. Professor. m. Fang-Ling Chang, 2 daughters. Education: BS, Department of Physics, National Cheng-Kung University, 1994; MS, Institute of Physics, National Chung-Hsiung University, 1996; PhD, Institute of Electro-Physics, National Chiao-Tung University, 2000. Appointments: Assistant/Associate Technician, Department of Transportation and Communication, National Center Weather Bureau, Electronic Communication Center, 1991-93; Associate Researcher, National Space Organisation, EE Sections, 2001; Assistant Professor, 2001-05, Associate Professor, 2006-, EE

Department, I-Shou University. Publications: Thermo-Optic effects affecting the high pump power end pumped solid state lasers: Modeling and analysis, 2007; Optical Parametric Oscillation Processes based on Quantum Optics Theory, 2008. Honours: Listed in international biographical dictionaries. Memberships: IEEE; American Physical Society. Address: I-Shou University EE Department, No 1, Sec 1, Syuecheng Road, Dashu Twp Kaohsiung 840, Taiwan. E-mail: yshuang@isu.edu.tw

HUANG Zheng-Bo, b. 26 December 1949, Xiamen, China. Physician. m. Liya He, 1 daughter. Education: MD, Fujian Medical College, Fujian, 1976; Internal Medicine Residency, 1st Teaching Hospital of Fujian Medical College, 1977-79; Fellowship, Internal Medicine, Peking Union Medical College, Beijing, 1979-82; Resident, Internal Medicine, St Luke's-Roosevelt Hospital Center, USA, 1993-96; Geriatrics Fellowship, Mt Sinai Medical Center, New York, 1996-98. Appointments: Attending Physician, Peking Union Medical College Hospital, Beijing, China, 1982-84; Physician and Medical Consultant, The Chinese Mission to the United Nations, New York, 1984-86; Research Associate, St Luke's-Roosevelt Hospital Center, New York, 1986-93; Assistant Professor of Medicine, New York Medical College, 1998-2003; Director, Geriatrics Consult Service, 1999-2002, Director, Geriatric Medical Education & Research, 2002-03, Department of Medicine, St Vincent's Hospital and Medical Centre, New York; Assistant Professor of Clinical Medicine, Weill Medical College of Cornell University, New York, 2003-; Director, Inpatient Geriatrics, 2003-, Director, Geriatric Fellowship Program, 2005-, New York Hospital Medical Center of Queens, New York. Publications: 15 articles in professional journals; 17 presentations or posters. Memberships: Association of Chinese American Physicians; Geriatrics Research Institute of Fujian Province; American Geriatrics Society; American Society of Internal Medicine; Metropolitan Area Geriatrics Society; Chinese American Medical Society; American Chinese Medical Association. Address: 142-18 38th Ave, #1C, Flushing, NY 11354, USA. E-mail: zhuang@nyc.rr.com

HUBALEK Zdenek, b. 22 August 1942, Brno, Czech Republic. Research Microbiologist. m. Dagmar, 2 daughters. Education: MS, Biology, 1964, RNDr, 1970, University of Brno; PhD, 1972, DSc, 1987, Academy of Sciences, Prague. Appointments: Research Assistant, Institute of Fodder Research, 1964-66; Research Assistant, Institute of Parasitology, Academy of Sciences, Prague, 1966-83; Principal Research Worker, Institute of Systematic and Ecological Biology, Institute of Landscape Ecology, Institute of Vetrebrate Biology, Academy of Sciences, Brno, 1984-; Associate Professor, Masaryk University, Brno, 1999-2006; Professor, Veterinary Microbiology, Immunology and Parasitology, Veterinary and Pharmaceutical University of Brno, 2007-. Publications: 250 scientific articles on the ecology of pathogenic microorganisms which are arthropod-borne, numerical classifications, medical zoology and ornithology; 1 book: Cryopreservation of Microorganisms, 1996. Honours: J E Purkyne Medal for Achievements in Biology, Czech Academy of Sciences, Prague; Award, Czech Academy of Sciences, Prague, 2004. Memberships: Czech Scientific Societies of: Biology; Microbiology; Mycology; Zoology; International Society of Vector Ecology. Address: Medical Zoology Laboratory, Institute of Vertebrate Biology, Academy of Sciences, Klasterni 2, CZ-69142 Valtice, Czech Republic. E-mail: zhubalek@brno.cas.cz

HUBEL David Hunter, b. 27 February 1926, Ontario, Canada. Neurophysiologist. m. S Ruth Izzard, 1953, 3 sons. Education: Graduated, Medicine, McGill University, Montreal, Canada. Appointments: Professor of Neurophysiology, Harvard Medical School, 1965-67; George Packer Berry Professor of Physiology and Chairman, Department of Physiology, 1967-68; George Packer Berry Professor of Neurobiology, 1968-92; John Franklin Enders University Professor, 1982-; George Eastman Professor, University of Oxford, 1991-92; First Annual George A Miller Lecture, Cognitive Neuroscience Society, 1995; Worked on the physiology of vision and the way in which the brain processes visual information. Publications: Eye, Brain and Vision, 1987; Articles in scientific journals. Honours: Lewis S Rosenstiel Award for Basic Medical Research, 1972; Friedenwald Award, 1975; Karl Spencer Lashley Prize, 1977; Louisa Gross Horwitz Prize, 1978; Dickson Prize in Medicine, 1979; Society of Scholars, Johns Hopkins University, 1980; Ledlie Prize, 1980; Joint Winner, Nobel Prize for Physiology or Medicine, 1981; New England Ophthalmological Society Award, 1983; Paul Kayser International Award of Merit in Retina Research, 1989; City of Medicine Award, 1990; Gerald Award, 1993; Charles F Prentice Medal, 1993; Helen Keller Prize, 1995. Memberships: NAS; Leopoldina Academy, Board of Syndics, Harvard University Press; Foreign Member, Royal Society, London; Senior Fellow, Harvard Society of Fellows; Fellow, American Academy of Arts and Sciences. Address: Department of Neurobiology, Harvard Medical School, 220 Longwood Avenue, Boston, MA 02115, USA.

HUČÍN Bohumil, b. 30 March 1934 Velké Popovice, Czech Republic. Cardiac Surgeon. m. Jana Hučínová-Vrbská. 3 sons, 1 daughter. Education: Graduate, Medical School, Charles University, Prague, Czech Republic, 1958; Specialist in General Surgery, 1962; Specialist in Paediatric Surgery, 1967; PhD, 1967; Doctor of Medical Sciences, 1987; Professor of Surgery, 1990; Specialist in Cardiac Surgery, 1998. Appointments: Resident, Department of General Surgery, Regional Hospital Vlašim, Czech Republic, 1958-61; Clinical Assistant in Paediatric Surgery, Prague, 1962-67; Head of Division of Paediatric Cardiac Surgery, Department of Paediatric Surgery, Children's University Hospital, Prague, 1968-76; Surgeon in Chief, Paediatric Cardiac Centre, University Hospital Motol, Prague, Czech Republic, 1977-2004; Retired Professor Emeritus of Paediatric Cardiac Surgery, 2004. Publications: Cardiac Surgery in Newborns and Infants; Cardiac Surgery in Deep Hypothermia and Circulatory Arrest in Infants; Cardiac Surgery in Adults with Congenital Heart Defects; Paediatric Cardiac Surgery (monograph), 2002. Honours: National Prize of Czechoslovak Republic, 1984; Prize of City of Prague; Medal of Charles University Prague; Medal of Czech Medical Society; Medal of Faculty of Paediatrics; Medal of University of Padua, Italy. Memberships: Czech Medical Society; British Association of Paediatric Surgeons; European Association for Cardio-thoracic Surgery; European Society of Cardiovascular Surgery; Society of Cardiac Surgeons (USA), International Society of Cardio-thoracic Surgeons (Japan); Association of Cardiovascular Surgery of Ukraine. Address: Hodkovická 10/64, Prague 4, 142 00 Czech Republic. E-mail: bohumil.hucin@volny.cz

HUCKNALL Mick, 8 June 1960, Manchester, England. Singer; Songwriter. Partner: Gabriella Wesberry, 1 daughter. Career: Formed early band, Frantic Elevators, 1979; Formed Simply Red, essentially a solo career with changing band members; Numerous hit singles, television appearances; Numerous tours and festival dates worldwide; Founder, Blood and Fire label, dedicated to vintage reggae tracks. Recordings:

Singles: Money's Too Tight to Mention; Come To My Aid; Holding Back the Years; Jericho; Open Up The Red Box; Ev'ry Time We Say Goodbye; The Right Thing; Infidelity; Maybe Some Day; Ev'ry Time We say Goodbye; I Won't Feel Bad; It's Only Love; If You Don't Know Me By Now; A New Flame; You've Got It; Something Got Me Started; Stars; For Your Babies; Thrill Me; Your Mirror; Fairground; Remembering The First Time; Never Never Love; We're In This Together; Angel; Nightnurse; Say You Love Me; The Air That I Breathe; Ghetto Girl; Ain't That a Lot of Love; Your Eyes; Sunrise; Albums: Picture Book, 1985; Early Years, 1987; Men and Women, 1987; A New Flame, 1989; Stars, 1991; 12"ers, 1995; Life, 1995; Fairground, 1995; Greatest Hits, 1996; Blue, 1998; Love and the Russian Winter, 1999; It's Only Love (greatest hits), 2000; Home, 2003. Address: PO Box 20197, London, W10 6YQ, England.

HUDÁK Ondrej, b. 23 April 1953, Michalovce, Slovak Republic. Lecturer; Physicist; Capital Market Consultant. m. Tatianna Hudáková, 1 son, 1 daughter. Education: Theoretical Physics, 1971-76, RNDr, Theoretical Physics, 1981, DrSc, Physics, 1985, Charles University, Prague; Bratislava International Commodity Exchange and The International Financial Services Institute, 1994. Appointments: Scientist, Safarik University, Kosice, 1978-79; Postgraduate, Institute of Physics, Academy of Sciences, Prague, 1979-82; Scientist, Solid State Physics, Institute of Experimental Physics, Kosice, 1982-90; Scientist, Institute of Physics, Czech Academy of Sciences, Prague, 1990-96; Lecturer, Faculty of Finance, Mate, Bel's University, 1997-2005; Scientist, Faculty of Mathematics and Physics, Comenius University, Bratislava, 1998; Scientist, Faculty of Materials and Technologies, Slovak Technical University, Bratislava, 1999-2000; Capital Market Consultant, 1994-2005. Publications include: Technical Analysis and Our Capital Markets, Brno, 1994; Technical Analysis, Banskà Bystrica, 1999; Portfolio Analysis, Banskà Bystrica, 2004; Various scientific papers on physics; Various capital market papers. Honours: Award from Czechoslovak Academy of Science, 1981; Alexander von Humboldt-Stifftung Stipendium, 1992; Who's Who in the World, 1998, 1999, 2000, 2001. Memberships: Slovak Genealogical Heraldic Society; Society of Saint Vojtech; CS TUG Society. Address: Stierova 23, SK-04011 Košice, Slovak Republic. E-mail: hudako@mail.pvt.sk

HUDSON Anthony Bruce Edward, b. 11 October 1938, London, England. Schoolmaster. m. Elizabeth Clare Willis, 1 son, 2 daughters. Education: Grenoble University, 1958-59; MA, Modern History, Lincoln College, Oxford, 1959-62; Dip. Ed., Institute of Education, London University, 1962-63. Appointments: Head of English, La Roseraie, Dieulefit, France, 1963-64; Radley College, 1964-88, Housemaster, 1970-84, Sub-Warden, 1980-88, Acting Warden, 1986; Headmaster, Pangbourne College, 1988-2000. Publication: Just to See His Name, 2002. Honour: MBE. Memberships: Skinners' Company, Master 2004-2005; Vincents; Harlequins Rugby Football Club; MCC; Huntercombe Golf Club. Address: Howgate Boathouse, Cleeve Road, Goring on Thames RG8 9BT, England.

HUDSON Harry Robinson, b. 18 November 1929, Kingston-upon-Hull, England. Emeritus Professor of Chemistry. m. Jacqueline Ruth Feeney, 2 sons, 2 daughters. Education: BSc (Special) Honours, Chemistry, External Student of London University at Hull Municipal Technical College, 1949; ARIC by Examination; PhD, Organic Chemistry, London University, 1960; DSc (London), 1976. Appointments: National Service, Education Branch, Technical

Training Command, Royal Air Force, 1949-51; Research and Development Chemist, Distillers Company Ltd, Chemical Division, Hull, 1951-58; Research Assistant, 1958-60, Full-time Member of Academic Staff, 1961-94, Reader in Chemistry, 1969, Professor, 1990-94, Emeritus Professor, 1995-, Northern Polytechnic (subsequently The Polytechnic of North London, University of North London, London Metropolitan University); Consultant: Dermal Laboratories Ltd, 1977-87; KenoGard AB, Stockholm, 1987-91; British Technology Group, 1989-92. Publications: Book: Aminophosphonic and Aminophosphinic Acids: Chemistry and Biological Activity (co-editor), 2000; Author or co-author of 6 book chapters and over 100 research publications and review articles. Honours: Fellow Royal Society of Chemistry, 1964; Honorary Research Fellow, University College, London, 1979-80; Visiting Lecturer, Royal Holloway College, University of London, 1979-82; Medal, Organophosphorus Chemistry, University of Lódz, Poland, 1996. Membership: Royal Society of Chemistry. Address: Department of Health and Human Sciences, London Metropolitan University, 166-220 Holloway Road, London N7 8DB, England. E-mail: harryrhudson@aol.com

HUET Denise, b. 2 February 1931, Nancy, France. Professor Emeritus. Education: Agregation de Mathematiques, 1954; Doctorat d'etat en Mathematiques, Paris, 1959. Appointments: Attachee de Recherche, Centre National de la Recherche Scientifique, Paris, 1955-59; Professor, Faculty of Sciences, Dijon, 1959-66; Visiting Professor, Georgetown University, USA, 1966-67; Visiting Professor, Professor, University of Maryland, USA, 1967-72; Professeur à la l'Université de Nancy I, France, 1972-94; Professor Emeritus, 1994-. Publications: Many publications. Honours: Woman of the Year, American Biographical Institute, 1996; 2000 Millennium Medal of Honor; Legion of Honor, United Cultural Convention, 2005. Memberships: American Mathematical Society; Societe Mathematique de France. Address: 86 Rue Felix Faure, 54000 Nancy, France.

HUFFMAN Felicity, b. 9 December 1962, New York, USA. Actress. m. William H Macy, 2 daughters. Education: BFA in Drama, New York University, Tisch School of the Arts, 1988. Career: Films include: Raising Helen, 2004; Christmas with the Kranks, 2004; Transamerica, 2005; Georgia Rule, 2007; Phoebe in Wonderland, 2009. TV includes: The DA; Frasier; Desperate Housewives.

HUGHES Barry Peter, b. 29 August 1932, Wolverhampton, England. Professor. m. Pamela Anne Barker, 1 son, 2 daughters. Education: BSc honours, 1953, PhD, 1956, Civil Engineering, University of Birmingham. Appointments: Assistant Civil Engineer, Concrete Engineer, Berkeley Power Station, 1956-59; Civil Engineer, Planning Engineer, John Laing Construction Ltd, 1959-62; Lecturer, 1962-68, Senior Lecturer, 1968-73, Professor of Civil Engineering, 1974-95, Emeritus Professor, 1995-, University of Birmingham; Private Consulting, Concrete and Concrete Structures, 1989-; Visiting Professor, University of Coventry, 1999-. Publications: Numerous research and technical papers on concrete and concrete structures; 2 books. Honours: Reader in Concrete Technology, 1971, DSc, 1972, DEng, 1990, Emeritus Professor, 1995, University of Birmingham. Memberships: Institution of Civil Engineers; Institution of Structural Engineers; Concrete Society. Address: Long Barn, 8 Parkfields, Arden Drive, Dorridge, Solihull, West Midlands, B93 8LL, England. E-mail: bphughes@onetel.net.uk

HUGHES Christopher Wyndham, b. 22 November 1941, Ipswich, Suffolk. Solicitor. m. Gail, 3 sons. Education: LL.B. Honours, University College, London, 1960-63; College of Law, London, 1963-64. Appointments: Solicitor then Partner, 1970, Wragge & Co; Managing Partner, Wragge & Co, 1993-95; Head of International Wragge & Co LLP, 2004-; Notary Public; Non-executive roles: Board Member, Severn Trent Water Authority, 1982-84; Chairman, Newman Tonks Group PLC, 1995-97; Member, Board of the Pension Protection Fund, 2004-. Publications: Former Member, Editorial Board, The Guide to Professional Conduct of Solicitors. Honour: LL.B. (London), 1963. Membership: Warwickshire County Cricket Club. Address: Cuttle Pool Farm, Cuttle Pool Lane, Knowle, Solihull, West Midlands B93 0AP, England. Website: www.wragge.com

HUGHES Henry Goronwy Alun (Alun Gwenffrwd), b. 15 July 1921, Pontlotyn, Glamorgan, Wales. Writer; Editor; Reviewer; Translator. m. (1) Alison M Mair, (2) Brenda Cross (née Stenning), 2 adopted sons, (3) Zuzana Dvořáková (née Kot'átková) 1964, deceased 1996, 1 daughter, deceased. Education: BA (Hons II); LI B; MA; D Phil; CSc; D Ed; D Anthrop; prom fil; Meyricke Exhibitioner in Modern Languages, Jesus College, Oxford, 1939-40, 1944-46; University of London; University of Liverpool; Charles University, Prague; Oriental Institute, Czechoslovak Academy of Sciences, Prague. Appointments: Merchant Seaman in Norwegian, Swedish, Panamanian and British ships, and Naval Counter-intelligence agent, 1940-44; Research Assistant, Tropical Education, I of E, London, 1947-49; Lecturer, Oceanic Languages, SOAS, London, 1949-53; Lecturer, London Co-operative Society, 1953-56; Freelance journalist, international conference interpreter, film critic; International Librarian, Liverpool, 1956-59; Lecturer, Liverpool College of Commerce, 1956-59; Head of Department/Vice Principal, Colwyn Bay Technical College, 1959-63; Editor, ČTK Praha, 1963-66; Senior Lecturer, KU Praha and U 17. eho listopadů, Praha, 1963-66; Krátký Film, Praha, 1963-66; Borough Librarian/Chief Officer, Flint MB, 1966-74; Counsellor, Open University, Wales, 1972-75; Retired, 1975; National Secretary, Cyngres Gweithwyr Cymru (Congress of Welsh Workers); Financial Administrator and Hospital Secretary, St Clare's Convent, Pantasaph; Associate, Swayne, Johnson and Wight Solicitors, Denbigh; Trade Union Representative (MSF), Writer, Editor, Reviewer, Translator; Bookdealer, Bronant Books; Publisher, Gwasg Gwenffrwd; Proprietor, ASTIC Research Associates, A&Z Hughes Ltd, Bronant Books, Gwasg Gwenffrwd, Translations Wales, 1947-2007; Adult Education and Extra-mural Lecturer, Film Critic, Scriptwriter and Commentator, Trade Union Representative, Political Militant and Anti-war Activist, 1947-. Publications: Numerous articles, bibliographies, poems, reviews and translations; 60 books, monographs, pamphlets and CDs. Memberships: Institute of Polynesian Languages and Literatures; Polynesian Society; North Wales Racial Equality Network; Friends of the Clwyd Archives; Friends of the National Library of Wales, Cefnogwyr Y Byd; Friends of the Welsh Books Council; Denbighshire Voluntary Services Council; Institute of Welsh Affairs; Bevan Foundation; Friends of the Earth; CND Cymru; Movement for the Abolition of War; VES/ Dignity in Dying; Woodland Trust; Socialist History Society; Cymru Rydd; Senedd '04; Communist Party of Scotland; Connolly Association; UNISON; AMICUS; Cynon Valley History Society; Glamorgan History Society; Pentyrch and District Local History Society; Cymdeithas Hanes Gweithwyr Cymru; Friends of the National Museums and Galleries of Wales; Denbighshire Historical Society; Red Poets Society; All 6 family history societies in Wales; Royal British Legion;

National Secretary, PGC/CPW (Communist Party of Wales). Address: Hendre Bach, Cerrigydrudion, Corwen LL21 9TB, Wales.

HUGHES John W, b. 18 February 1950, Detroit, Michigan, USA. Film Producer; Screenplay Writer; Director. m. Nancy Ludwig, 2 sons. Education: University AZ. Appointments: Copywriter, Creative Director, Leo Burnett Co; Editor, National Lampoon Magazine; Founder, President, Hughes Entertainment, 1985-. Creative Works: Films: National Lampoon's Class Reunion, 1982; National Lampoons Vacation, 1983; Mr Mon, 1983; Nate and Hayes, 1983; Sixteen Candles, 1984; National Lampoons European Vacation, 1985; Weird Science, 1985; The Breakfast Club, 1985; Ferris Bueller's Day Off, 1986; Pretty in Pink, 1986; Some Kind of Wonderful, 1987; Planes, Trains and Automobiles, 1987; The Great Outdoors, 1988; She's Having a Baby, 1988; National Lampoons Christmas Vacation, 1989; Uncle Buck, 1989; Home Alone, 1990; Career Opportunities, 1990; Dutch, 1991; Curly Sue, 1991; Only the Lonely, 1991; Beethoven, 1992; Home Alone 2: Lost in New York, 1992; Dennis the Menace, 1993; Baby's Day Out, 1993; Miracle on 34th Street, 1994; 101 Dalmations, 1996; Reach the Rock, 1998; New Port South, 1999; 102 Dalmations, 2000; Just Visiting, 2001; Maid in Manhatten; 2002; Drillbit Taylor, 2008. Honours include: Commitment to Chicago Award, 1990; NATO/Sho West Producer of the Year, 1990. Address: c/o Jacob Bloom, Bloom & Dekom, 150 South Rodeo Drive, Beverly Hills, CA 90212, USA.

HUGHES Lee Terence, b. 16 January 1951, Epsom, Surrey, England. Government Servant. Education: BA (Hons) Business Studies, Middlesex Polytechnic, 1979-82; Postgraduate Certificate, Public Service Management, University of Birmingham, 2000-2001. Appointments: Various posts in Criminal Justice and Police Department, Home Office, 1977-98; Head of Freedom of Information/Data Protection, 1998-2003; Secretary, Hutton Inquiry, 2003-2004; Head Judicial Appointments (Courts), 2004-07; Secretary, Inquests into the deaths of Diana, Princess of Wales and Mr Dodi Al Fayed, 2007-. Honour, CBE, 2004. Address: Room E200, Royal Courts of Justice, Strand, London WC2A 2LL, England. E-mail: lee.hughes@scottbaker-inquests.gsi.gov.uk

HUGHES Shirley, b. 16 July 1927, Hoylake, England. Children's Fiction Writer and Illustrator. Education: Liverpool Art School; Ruskin School of Drawing and Fine Arts, Oxford. Appointments: Public Lending Right Registrars Advisory Committee, 1984-88; Library and Information Services Council, 1989-92. Publications: Lucy & Tom Series, 6 volumes, 1960-87; The Trouble with Jack, 1970; Sally's Secret, 1973; It's too Frightening for Me, 1977; Moving Molly, 1978; Up and Up, 1979; Charlie Moon and the Big Bonanza Bust Up, 1982; An Evening at Alfies, 1984; The Nursery Collection, 6 volumes, 1985-86; Another Helping of Chips, 1986; The Big Alfie and Annie Rose Story Book, 1988; Out and About, 1989; The Big Alfie Out of Doors Story Book, 1992; Giving, 1993; Bouncing, 1993; Stories by Firelight, 1993; Chatting Hiding, 1994; Rhymes for Annie Rose, 1995; Enchantment in the Garden, 1996; Alfie and the Birthday Surprise, 1997; The Lion and the Unicorn, 1998; Abel's Moon, 1999; Shirley Hughes Collection, 2000; Alfie Weather, 2001; A Life Drawing (autobiography), 2002; Olly and Me, 2003; Ella's Big Chance, 2003; Alfie Wins a Prize, 2004; A Brush with the Past, 2005; Alfie's World, 2006; Alfie and the Big Boys, 2007; Jonodab and Rita, 2008. Honours: Kate Greenaway Medal for Dogger, 1977; Kate Greenaway Medal for Ella's Big Chance, 2004. Eleanor Farjeon Award, 1984;

Honorary Fellow, Library Association, 1997; OBE, 1999; Doctor of Letters, University of East Anglia, 2004; Doctor of Letters, University of Liverpool, 2004; Hon. Fellowship Liverpool John Moores University, 2004. Membership: Society of Authors; Fellow, Royal Society of Literature, 2000; Greenaway Picture Book of All Time for Dogger, 2007. Address: c/o Bodley Head, Random House Children's Books, 61-63 Uxbridge Road, London W5 5SA, England.

HUH Kyu Chan, b. 30 July 1963, Daegu, Korea. Medical Professor. m. Mi Jung Lee, 1 son, 1 daughter. Education: Bachelor's degree, 1990, MS, 1997, PhD, 2000, Graduate School, Keimyung University, Daegu. Appointments: Instructor, Keimyung University Hospital, 1999-2001; Assistant Professor, 2001-04, Associate Professor, 2004-, Konyang University Hospital, Daejeon. Publications include: Numerous papers and articles in professional journals including: Inflammation in Functional Gastrointestinal Disorder, 2005; Pugatives, 2005; CT colonography using 16-MDCT in evaluation of colorectal cancer, 2005; Intussuscepted sigmoid colonic lipoma mimicking carcinoma, 2006; Radiologic Findings of Gastrointestinal Complications in an Adult Patient with Henoch-Scholein Purpura, 2006; Techniques of Colonoscopy, 2006. Honours: Listed in international biographical dictionaries. Memberships: Korean Medical Association; Korean Association of Internal Medicine; Korean Society of Gastroenterology; Korean Society of Gastronintestinal Endoscopy; Korean Association for the Study of Intestinal Diseases; Korean Society of Neurogastroenterology and Motility; American Gastroenterological Association; American Society of Gastrointestinal Endoscopy; Neurogastroenterology and Motility. Address: Division of Gastroenterology, Konyang University Hospital, #685 Gasuwon-dong, Seo-gu, Daejeon 302-718, Korea. E-mail: kchuh2020@hanmail.net

HUH Moo Ryang, b. 11 May 1951, Pusan, Korea. Doctor. m. Sook Mi Kim, 1 son, 1 daughter. Education: Pusan National University College of Medicine, 1969-75; Graduate School, Pusan National University, 1976-82, PhD, 1979-89. Appointments: Director, Proctology Centre, Jae Hae Hospital, 1980-87; Clinical Professor, Department of Surgery, Pusan National University, College of Medicine, 1983-; Solo Practice, Dr Huh's Proctological Clinic, 1987-; Clinical Professor, Dong-A University College of Medicine, 1990-. Publications: Complete Treatment for Anal Diseases, 1987; Memberships: Japanese Society of Coloproctology, 1984-; International Society of Surgery, 1987; American Society of Colon and Rectal Surgeons, 1993-; The Association of Coloproctology of Great Britain and Ireland, 2001-. Address: 377-13 Kwangan 4-Dong, Suyoung-Zu, Nam-Ku, Pusan, Korea.

HUI-BON-HOA Max Lin, b. 3 August 1954, Hong Kong, China. University Teacher. Education: BA, 1978, MA, 1981, MA, 1982, Stanford University, USA; Certificate of Advanced Studies, Harvard University, 1991; PhD, University of London, 1997. Appointments: Language Instructor, 1985-2003, Senior Language Instructor, Acting Director, 2004-, English Centre, University of Hong Kong. Publications: Translator, 17 books from English to Chinese. E-mail: maxhuibonhoa@hku.hk

HULCE Tom, b. 6 December 1953, Detroit, Michigan, USA. Actor. m. Cecilia Ermini, 1 child. Education: North Carolina School of Arts. Career: Plays: The Rise and Rise of Daniel Rocket, 1982; Eastern Standard, 1988; A Few Good Men, 1990; Films: September 30th 1955; National Lampoon's Animal House; Those Lips Those Eyes; Amadeus, 1985;

Echo Park, 1985; Slam Dance, 1987; Nicky and Gino, 1988; Parenthood, 1989; Shadowman; The Inner Circle; Fearless; Mary Shelley's Frankenstein, 1994; Wings of Courage, 1995; The Hunchback of Notre Dame (voice), 1996; Home at the End of the World (producer), 2004; Stranger Than Fiction, 2006; Jumper, 2008. TV: Emily Emily; St Elsewhere; Murder in Mississippi, 1990; Black Rainbow; The Heidi Chronicles, 1995. Address: c/o CAA, 9830 Wilshire Boulevard, Beverly Hills, CA 90212, USA.

HULL Robin (Frank Martin), b. 21 October 1931, Harpenden, England. Retired Doctor; Freelance Writer. m. Gillian, 3 daughters. Education: Christ's Hospital; St Mary's Hospital Medical School. Appointments: Professor of General Practice, Free University, Amsterdam; Senior Lecturer, General Practice and MacMillan Senior Lecturer, Palliative Care, Birmingham Medical School. Publications: Just a GP, 1994; A Schoolboys War, 1994; Scottish Birds: Culture and Tradition, 2001; Ravens Over the Hill: The History of Dun Coillich, 2004; The Healing Island, 2004; The Silver Sea, 2005; Black Sand, Gold Sand, in progress; Scottish Mammals, 2007; Over 600 articles in medical journals and newspapers. Honours: FRCGP; Fellow, Society of Medical Writers. Memberships: Past President, Society of Medical Writers. Address: West Carliath, Strathtay, Perth, PH9 0PG, Scotland. E-mail: robin@carnliath.fsnet.co.uk

HULMES Edward Dominic Antony, b. 13 June 1932, Urmston, Manchester, England. Theologian. m. Shirley Dorothy Mary Lester-Taylor, 3 daughters. Education: Oriel College, Oxford; Victoria University of Manchester; MA, BD, DPhil. Appointments: Eaton Hall Officer Cadet School and Commissioned Army Service in the Intelligence Corps, 1956-59; Commercial Administration, West Africa, 1960-66; Various teaching posts, Manchester, 1966-72; Director, Farmington Institute, Oxford, 1972-80; Spalding Professorial Fellow in Comparative Theology, University of Durham, 1981-94; Member of the Center of Theological Inquiry, Princeton, USA, 1986-. Publications: Commitment and Neutrality, 1979; The Religious Dimension of Islam (with Riadh El-Droubie), 1980; Education and Cultural Diversity, 1989; Islam: The Straight Path, 2001; The Ecumenical Imperative, 2001; The Spalding Trust and the Union for the Study of the Great Religions, 2002; Catholic Belief and Inter-Faith Encounter, 2004; Over 200 articles in Encyclopaedia of Islamic Civilisation and Religion, 2007; Numerous contributions to symposia, articles and book-reviews on comparative theological studies and religious education. Honours: William Belden Noble Lecturer, Harvard University, 1981-82; Lecturer on Missions, Princeton Theological Seminary, USA, 1984; Appointed Knight of the Equestrian Order of the Holy Sepulchre of Jerusalem, 1985, Knight Commander, 2000; Trustee and Archivist of the Spalding Trust for the Study of the Great Religions, 1985-2002; Fellow, Maryvale Institute, Birmingham. Address: Rock House, Cressbrook, Monsal Dale, via Buxton, Derbyshire SK17 8SY, England.

HULTQVIST Bengt K G, b. 21 August 1927, Hemmesjo, Sweden. Professor; Director. m. Gurli Gustafsson, 2 sons, 1 daughter. Education: Dr Sci Degree, Physics, University of Stockholm, 1956. Appointments: Director, Swedish Institute of Space Physics (and its predecessors). 1957-94; Director, International Space Science Institute, 1995-99; Chairman, Space Science Advisory Committee of ESA, 1998-2000; Secretary General of IAGA, 2001-. Publications: Some 200 articles in scientific journals and books; 3 books; Editor of 6 scientific books. Honours include: Grand Gold Medal, Royal

Swedish Academy of Engineering Science, 1988; Cospar Prize for International Co-operation, 1990; King's Medal, 1991; Bartel's Medal, 1998; Hannes Alfvén Medal, 2002. Memberships include: Royal Astronomical Society (UK); International Academy of Astronautics; Academia Europaea; Royal Swedish Academy of Sciences; Royal Swedish Academy of Engineering Science; Academy of Finland; Royal Norwegian Academy of Sciences. Address: Gronstensv 2, S-98140, Kiruna, Sweden. E-mail: hultqv@irf.se

HUME John, b. 18 January 1937, Londonderry, Northern Ireland. Politician. m. Patricia Hone, 1960, 2 sons, 3 daughters. Education: St Colomb's College, Londonderry; St Patrick's College, Maynooth; National University of Ireland. Appointments: Research Fellow, Trinity College; Associate Fellow, Centre for International Affairs, Harvard; Founder Member, Credit Union, Northern Ireland, President, 1964-68; Non-Violent Civil Rights Leader, 1968-69; Representative, Londonderry, Northern Ireland Parliament, 1969-72, in Northern Ireland Assembly, 1972-73; Minister of Commerce, Powersharing Executive, 1974; Representative, Londonderry in Northern Ireland Convention, 1975-76; Elected to European Parliament, 1979-; Leader, Social Democratic and Labour Party (SDLP), 1979-2001; Member, Northern Ireland Assembly, 1982-86; MP for Foyle, 1983-; Member for Foyle Northern Ireland Assembly, 1998- (Assembly suspended 2002). Publications: Politics, Peace and Reconciliation in Ireland. Honours include: Nobel Peace Prize (shared), 1998; Martin Luther King Award, 1999; Gandhi Peace Prize, 2002; Freedom of the City of Cork, 2004. Numerous honorary doctorates. Address: 5 Bayview Terrace, Derry BT48 7EE, Northern Ireland.

HUME Robert, b. 6 January 1928, Glasgow, Scotland. Consultant Physician. m. Kathleen Anne Ogilvie Hume, 2 sons, 1 daughter. Education: Ayr Academy; Bellahouston Academy; University of Glasgow; MB ChB, 1948-53; MD (Commend), 1967; DSc, 1985. Appointments: National Service, Intelligence Corps; Commissioned, Gordon Highlanders, India and Germany, 1946-48; Hutcheson Research Scholar, 1955-56, Hall Fellowship, 1956-59, Honorary Clinical Lecturer, 1965, Honorary Sub-Dean, Faculty of Medicine, 1988, University of Glasgow; Consultant Physician, Southern General Hospital Glasgow, 1965-93; Retired, 1993; Member of the Board of Directors, Healthcare International, 1995-2002. Publications: Author of numerous publications on haematological and vascular disorders. Memberships: BMA, 1954; Scottish Society for Experimental Medicine, 1955; British Society for Haematology, 1960; Member, Research Support Group, Greater Glasgow Health Board, 1978-90; Member, Intercollegiate Standing Committee on Nuclear Medicine, UK, 1980-83; Scottish Council, BMA, 1980-83; Chairman, Sub-Committee on Medicine, Greater Glasgow Health Board, 1955-90; RCPS (Glas), Honorary Registrar for Examinations 1971-83, Chairman, Board of Examiners, 1983-88, Visitor and President Elect, 1988, President, 1990-92; Chairman, Conference of Scottish Royal Colleges and Faculties, 1991-92; Chairman, Joint Committee on Higher Medical Training of Royal Colleges of UK, 1990-93; Member, Scottish Society of Physicians, 1965; FRCPS, 1968; FRCPE, 1969; Honorary Member, Association of Physicians of Great Britain and Ireland, 1971; Honorary FACP, 1991; Honorary RACP, 1991; Member, Academy of Medicine of Malaysia, 1991; Honorary FCM(SA); Honorary FRCPS (Canada); FRCPath, 1992; FRCSEd, 1992; FRCPI, 1993; Member, Buchanan Castle Golf Club; The Royal Philosophical Society of Glasgow;

Glasgow Antiques and Fine Arts Society; National Trust of Scotland. Address: 6 Rubislaw Drive, Bearsden, Glasgow G61 1PR, Scotland.

HUMPRHEYS David A, b. 7 November 1956, Epsom, England. Research Scientist. m. 1 daughter. Education: Sutton Valence School, 1974; BSc (Hons), Electronics, Southampton University, 1978; PhD, Electronic Engineering, London University UCL, 1990. Appointments: Scientific Officer, 1978-83, Higher Scientific Officer, 1983-86, Senior Scientific Officer, 1986-91, Grade 7, Civil Service, 1991-95, Principal Research Scientist, 1995-, National Physical Laboratory, Teddington; Guest Editor, IEE Proc Opto OFMC Special Edition Vol 153, No 5. Publications: More than 16 journal and 50 conference papers. Honours: IEE Ambrose Fleming Premium, 1987. Memberships: Chartered Engineer, Engineering Council, 1987; Corporate Member, Institution of Engineering and Technology (UK), 1987; Senior Member, Institute of Electrical and Electronic Engineers, USA, 1990; Royal Institution of Great Britain. Address: National Physical Laboratory, Communication Technologies, F3-A7, Hampton Road, Teddington, Middlesex TW11 0LW, England. E-mail: david.a.humphreys@iee.org

HUMPHREYS Emyr Owen, b. 15 April 1919, Clwyd, Wales. Author. m. Elinor Myfanwy, 1946, 3 sons, 1 daughter. Education: University College, Aberystwyth; University College, Bangor. Publications: The Little Kingdom, 1946; The Voice of a Stranger, 1949; A Change of Heart, 1951; Hear and Forgive, 1952; A Man's Estate, 1955; The Italian Wife, 1957; A Toy Epic, 1958; The Gift, 1963; Outside the House of Baal, 1965; Natives, 1968; Ancestor Worship, 1970; National Winner, 1971; Flesh and Blood, 1974; Landscapes, 1976; The Best of Friends, 1978; The Kingdom of Bran, 1979; The Anchor Tree, 1980; Pwyll a Riannon, 1980; Miscellany Two, 1981; The Taliesin Tradition, 1983; Salt of the Earth, 1985; An Absolute Hero, 1986; Open Secrets, 1988; The Triple Net, 1988; Bonds of Attachment, 1990; Outside Time, 1991; Unconditional Surrender, 1996; The Gift of a Daughter, 1998; Collected Poems, 1999; Dal Pen Rheswm, 1999; Ghosts and Strangers, 2000; Conversations and Reflections, 2002; Old People are a Problem, 2003; The Shop, 2005. Honours: Somerset Maugham Award, 1953; Hawthornden Prize, 1959; Society of Authors Travel Award, 1978; Welsh Arts Council Prize, 1983; Honorary DLitt, University of Wales, 1990; Welsh Book of the Year, 1992, 1999; Honorary Professor of English, University College of North Wales, Bangor. Membership: Fellow, The Royal Society of Literature, 1991; Cymmrodorion Medal, 2003. Address: Llinon, Penyberth, Llanfairpwll, Ynys Môn, Gwynedd LL61 5YT, Wales.

HUMPHRIES (John) Barry, b. 17 February 1934, Australia. Actor; Writer. m. (1) Rosalind Tong, 1959, 2 daughters, (2) Diane Millstead, 2 sons, (3) Lizzie Spender, 1990. Education: University of Melbourne. Appointments: Various one-man shows; film appearances. Publications: Bizarre I, 1965; Innocent Australian Verse, 1968; Wonderful World of Barry McKenzie, 1968; Bazza Pulls It Off, 1972; Adventures of Barry McKenzie, 1973; Bazza Holds His Own, 1974; Dame Edna's Coffee Table Book, 1976; Bazza Comes Into His Own, 1978; Les Patterson's Australia, 1979; Barry Humphries' Treasury of Australian Kitsch, 1980; Dame Edna's Bedside Companion, 1982; Les Patterson: The Traveller's Tool, 1985; Dame Edna: My Gorgeous Life, 1989; More Please, 1992; Women in the Background, 1996; Barry Humphries' Flashbacks, 1999; My Life As Me, 2002. Honours: Society of West End Managements Award, 1979; OBE, 2007. Memberships: President, Frans de Boewer Society, Belgium; Vice President, Betjeman Society, 2001-.

HUMPHRY Derek John, b. 29 April 1930, Bath, England. Journalist; Author; Broadcaster. Appointments: Messenger Boy, Yorkshire Post, London, 1945-46; Cub Reporter, Evening World, Bristol, 1946-51; Junior Reporter, Evening News, Manchester, 1951-55; Reporter, Daily Mail, 1955-61; Deputy Editor, The Luton News, 1961-63; Editor, Havering Recorder, 1963-67, Hemlock Quarterly, 1983-92, Euthanasia Review, 1986-88, World Right to Die Newsletter, 1992-04; Home Affairs Correspondent, The Sunday Times, 1966-78; Special Writer, Los Angeles Times, 1978-79. Publications: Because They're Black, 1971; Police Power and Black People, 1972; Passports and Politics, 1974; The Cricket Conspiracy, 1976; False Messiah, 1977; Jean's Way, 1978; Let Me Die Before I Wake, 1982; The Right to Die!: Understanding Euthanasia, 1986; Final Exit, 1991; Dying with Dignity, 1992; Lawful Exit, 1993; Freedom to Die, 1998; The Good Euthanasia Guide, 2004. Contributions to: New Statesman; Independent, London; USA Today. Honours: Martin Luther King Memorial Prize, UK, 1972; The Saba Medal for contribution to the World Right-to-Die Movement, 2000. Memberships: Founder and Chief executive Officer, The Hemlock Society, 1980-92; President, World Federation of Right to Die Societies, 1988-90; Founder and President, The Euthanasia Research and Guidance Organization (ERGO), 1993-. Address: 24829 Norris Lane, Junction City, OR 97448-9559, USA.

HUMPHRYS John, b. 17 August 1943. Broadcaster. Divorced, 2 sons, 1 daughter. Appointments: Washington Correspondent, BBC TV, 1971-77, Southern Africa Correspondent, 1977-80, Diplomatic Correspondent, 1981; Presenter, BBC Nine o'Clock News, 1981-87; Presenter, BBC Radio 4 Today Programme, 1987-, On the Record, BBC TV, 1993-, John Humphrys Interview Radio 4, 1995-. Publication: Devil's Advocate, 1999; Great Food Gamble; Lost for Words: The Mangling and Manipulation of the English Language, 2004; Beyond Words, 2006; In God We Doubt, 2007. Honours: Fellow, Cardiff University, 1998; Honorary DLitt, Dundee, 1996; Honorary MA, University of Wales, 1998; Honorary LLD, St Andrews, 1999. Address: BBC News Centre, Wood Lane, London W12, England.

HUNT Anthony James, b. 22 June 1932, London, England. Structural Engineer. m. (1) Patricia Daniels, 1957, dissolved, 1972, remarried, 1975, dissolved, 1982, 1 son, 1 daughter, (3) Diana Joyce Collett. Education: CEng, Westminster Technical College, 1961; FIStructE, 1973. Appointments: Articled via Founders' Co to J L Wheeler Consulting Engineer, 1948-51; F J Samuely and Partners, Consulting Engineers, 1951-59; Morton Lupton, Architects, 1960-62; Founded Anthony Hunt Associates, Consulting Engineers, 1962, Stood down as Chairman of Anthony Hunt Associates, became a consultant to them in 2002; Acquired by YRM plc, Building Design Consultants, 1988; Became separate limited company, 1997; Major buildings: Sainsbury Centre for the Visual Arts, Norwich, 1978, 1993; Willis Faber Dumas HQ, Ipswich, 1975; Inmos Micro Electronics Factory, Gwent, 1982; Schlumberger Cambridge Research, 1985; Waterloo International Terminal, 1993; Law Faculty, Cambridge, 1995; National Botanic Garden, Wales, 1998; New Museum of Scotland, Edinburgh, 1998; Lloyd's Register of Shipping, London, 2000; Eden Project, Cornwall, 2001; Willis Visiting Professor of Architecture, Sheffield University, 1994-. Publications: Tony Hunt's Structures Notebook, 1997; Tony Hunt's Sketchbook, 1999. Honours: FRSA, 1989; Honorary FRIBA, 1989; Gold

Medallist, IStructE, 1995; Honorary DLitt, Sheffield, 1999; Graham Professor of Architecture, Graduate School of Fine Arts, University of Pennsylvania, 2002; Honorary DEng, Leeds, 2003; Visiting Professor, Chinese University of Hong Kong; Visiting Professor, IST, Lisbon. Address: Stancombe Farm, Bisley with Lippiatt, Stroud, Gloucestershire, GL6 7NF, England. E-mail: tony@huntprojects.co.uk

HUNT David Roderic Notley, b. 22 June 1947, Brighton, England. Barrister. m. Alison Connell Jelf, 2 sons. Education: MA Honours, Law, Trinity College, Cambridge, 1968; Inns of Court School of Law, 1968-69. Appointments: Called to the Bar, Gray's Inn, 1969; Queen's Counsel, 1987; Recorder, 1991; Master of the Bench of Gray's Inn, 1995. Publications: Article in the Solicitor's Journal. Address: Blackstone Chambers, Blackstone House, Temple, London EC4Y 9BW, England. E-mail: davidhunt@blackstonechambers.com

HUNT Helen, b. 15 June 1963, Los Angeles, USA. Actress. m. Hank Azaria, 1999 (divorced). Creative Works: Stage appearances include: Been Taken; Our Town; The Taming of the Shrew; Methusalem; Films include: Rollercoaster; Girls Just Want to Have Fun; Peggy Sue Got Married; Project X; Miles From Hume; Trancers; Stealing Home; Next of Kin; The Waterdance; Only You; Bob Roberts; Mr Saturday Night; Kiss of Death; Twister; As Good As It Gets; Twelfth Night; Pay It Forward, 2000; Dr T and the Women, 2000; Cast Away, 2000; What Women Want, 2000; The Curse of the Jade Scorpion, 2001; A Good Woman, 2004; Bobby, 2006; Then She Found Me, 2007. TV includes: Swiss Family Robinson; Mad About You; Empire Falls. Honours include: Emmy Award, 1996, 1997; Golden Globe Award, 1997; Academy Award, Best Actress, 1998. Address: c/o Connie Tavel, 9171 Wilshire Boulevard, Beverly Hills, CA 90210, USA.

HUNT Jeffrey H, b. 18 April 1957, Passaic, New Jersey, USA. Optical Scientist. m. Rebecca Johanna Hunt, 1 daughter. Education: BS, Physics, Massachusetts Institute of Technology, 1979; MA, Physics, 1982, PhD, Physics, 1988, University of California, Berkeley. Appointments: Research Assistant, 1977-79, Teaching Assistant, 1978-79, Massachusetts Institute of Technology; Teaching Assistant, 1979-81, Research Associate, 1980-87, University of California, Berkeley; Engineering Specialist, Rockwell Corporation, 1988-96; Technical Fellow, The Boeing Company, 1997-. Publications include: Laser Beam Diagnostics; Optical Parametric Oscillation. Honours: Fellow of the American Physical Society, 2007. Memberships: American Physical Society. Address: The Boeing Company WB54, 8531 Fallbrook Avenue, West Hills, CA 91304, USA.

HUNT Mary Elizabeth, b. 1 June 1951, Syracuse, New York, USA. Theologian. Education: Bachelor of Arts, Marquette University, 1972; Master of Theological Studies, Harvard Divinity School, 1974; Master of Divinity, Jesuit School of Theology at Berkeley, 1978; PhD, Philosophical and Systematic Theology, 1980. Appointments: Frontier Internship in Mission, Buenos Aires, 1980-82; Co-founder, Co-director, Women's Alliance for Theology Ethics and Ritual, Silver Spring, 1983-; Visiting Assistant Professor, Religion, Colgate University, New York, 1986-87; Adjunct Assistant Professor, Women's Studies, Georgetown University, Washington, 1995-99; Research Fellow, Center for the Study of Values in Public Life, Harvard Divinity School, 2000-2001. Publications: Fierce Tenderness: A Feminist Theology of Friendship; From Woman-Pain to Woman-Vision (editor); La sfida del femminismo alla teologia (editor); Good Sex: Feminist Perspectives from the World's Religions (co-editor),

2001; A Guide for Woman in Religion – Finding Your Way From A to Z (editor), 2004; Many chapters, articles, book reviews and booklets. Honours: Isaac Hecker Award; Women's Ordination Conference Prophetic Figure Award; Crossroad Women's Studies Prize; Mary Rhodes Award. Memberships: American Academy of Religion; Society for Christian Ethics; Alpha Sigma Nu. Address: 8121 Georgia Ave #310, Silver Spring, MD 20910, USA.

HUNTER Alexis, b. 4 November 1948, Auckland, New Zealand. Artist. m. Baxter Mitchell. Education: Diploma of Fine Arts in Painting, Auckland University, 1970; Teaching Diploma, Auckland Teachers College, 1971; City & Guilds, London, 1972; London Graphics Academy, 2001. Appointments: Curator, UK and overseas, 1986; Assistant Professor of Painting and Photography, Houston University, Texas, USA; Lecturer, UK and overseas, 1981-98. Publications: Numerous articles and papers. Honours: Major Award, Greater London Arts Association, 1981; Grant, Arts Council of New Zealand, 1981; British Council Travel Award, 1982; Grant, Lake District Residency, Greater London Arts Council, 1983; Travel Grant, British Council, 1986; Grant, Arts Council of New Zealand, 1988; Travel Grant, British Council, 1994. Memberships: Artists Alliance of New Zealand; Foundation of Women's Art; London Institute of Directors; Wellesley Club. Address: 13 Hillier House, 46 Camden Square, London NW1 9XA, England. Website: www.alexishunter.co.uk

HUNTER David John, b. 4 November 1949, Maidstone, Kent, England. Retired Nurse. m. Marilyn Carol, 1 son, 1 daughter. Education: BA; RGN; RMN; RNT; Dip OH&S; DipASE; CertAdEd; CertEd; LIC&G; OHNC (pt1); Cert Mgmt, MIFI, current studies, BA(Hons) Health Studies. Appointments: Student Nurse; Staff Nurse; Charge Nurse; Nursing Officer; Unqualified Tutor; Nurse Tutor; Lecturer/ Practitioner; Occupational Health Advisor; Occupational Health Practitioner. Publications: Paramedic UK; 3 articles on suicide. Honours: Knight, Order of St Andrew of Jerusalem; Serving Brother, Order of St John; Centenary Medal, British Fire Services Association. Membership: British Fire Services Association; Royal College of Nursing. Address: 10 Brecon Avenue, Cheadle Hulme, Cheadle, Cheshire SK8 6DA, England.

HUNTER Holly, b. 20 March 1958, Atlanta, Georgia, USA. Actress. m. J Kaminski, divorced. Education: Career: Theatre includes: on Broadway: Crimes of the Heart; The Wake of Jamey Foster; The Miss Firecracker Contest; Other Stage Appearances include: The Person I Once Was; Battery, New York; A Lie of the Mind, Los Angeles; By the Bog of Cat, London, 2004; Regional work; Films include: Broadcast News, Raising Arizona, 1987; Once Around, 1990; The Piano and The Firm, 1993; Copycat, 1995; Crash, 1996; Living Out Loud, 1998; Time Code, O Brother Where Art Thou? 2000; When Billie Beat Bobby, Festival in Cannes, 2001; Goodbye Hello, 2002; Levity, Thirteen, 2003; Levity, 2003; The Incredibles (voice), Little Black Book, 2004; Nine Lives, The Big White, 2005; Saving Grace (TV), 2007. Honours: 2 for TV appearances: Best Actress Emmy for Roe vs Wade, 1989; Best Actress Award, American TV Awards, 1993; Best Actress Award, Cannes Film Festival Award, 1993; Academy Award, 1994. Memberships: Director, California Abortion Rights Action League. Address: 41 Stutter Street, #1649, San Francisco, CA 94104, USA.

HUPPERT Herbert E, b. 26 November 1943, Sydney, Australia. m Felicia Ferster, 2 sons. Education: BSc, Honours, Sydney University, 1964; MSc, Australian National University, 1966; MS, University of California at San Diego, 1967; PhD, California, 1968; MA, Cambridge, 1971; ScD, Cambridge, 1985. Appointments: ICI Research Fellow, 1968-69; Assistant Director of Research in DAMTP, 1970-81; University Lecturer in DAMTP, 1981-88; Reader in Geophysical Dynamics, University of Cambridge, 1988-89, Professor of Theoretical Geophysics and Foundation Director of the Institute of Theoretical Geophysics, 1989-; Professor of Mathematics, University of New South Wales, 1991-96; Member, NERC Council, 1993-99; Visiting Scientist, Australian National University, University of California at San Diego, Canterbury University, Caltech, MIT, University of New South Wales, University of Western Australia, the Weizmann Institute, Woods Hole Oceanographic Institute; Chairman, Royal Society Working Group on Bioterrorism, which published a report, Making the UK Safer, 2004, 2002-. Publications: Author or co-author of approximately 200 papers discussing applied mathematics, crystal growth, fluid mechanics, geology, geophysics, oceanography, meteorology and science in general. Honours: Sydney University Medal and Baker Prize in Mathematics, 1964; Fellow, King's College Cambridge, 1970-; Maurice Hill Research Fellow of the Royal Society, 1977; Royal Society Anglo-Australian Research Fellow, 1991, 1995; Evnin Lecturer, Princeton University, 1995; Midwest Mechanics Lecturer, USA, 1996-97; Henry Charnock Distinguished Lecturer, Southampton Oceanography Centre, 1999; Smith Industries Lecturer, Oxford University, 1999; Elected to National Academy of America's Arthur L Day Prize and Lectureship, 2005; Distinguished Israel Pollak Lecturer of the Technion, 2005; William Hopkins Prize, Cambridge Philosophical Society, 2005; Royal Society Wolfson Merit Award, 2006; Murchison Medal London Geological Society, 2007. Memberships: Elected Fellow: Royal Society, 1987, American Geophysical Union, 2002, American Physical Society, 2004; Royal Society Dining Club, 1993. Address: Institute of Theoretical Geophysics, DAMTP, University of Cambridge, Centre for Mathematical Sciences, Wilberforce Road, Cambridge CB3 0WA, England. E-mail: heh1@esc.cam.ac.uk Website: www.itg.cam.ac.uk/people/heh/index.html

HUR Seung-Ho, b. 12 October 1965, Daegu, South Korea. Associate Professor. m. Jung-Hyang Park, 1 son. Education: Bachelor degree, School of Medicine, 1990, Master of Science, 1993, PhD, 1997, Graduate School, Keimyung University, Daegu. Appointments: Internship, 1990-91, Resident, Internal Medicine, 1991-95, Fellowship, Cardiovascular Medicine, 1995-97, Keimyung University Dongsan Medical Center; Korean Board of Cardiovascular Medicine, 1997; Military Physician (Army Captain), Nonsan Military Hospital, 1997-2000; Postdoctoral Research Fellow, Cardiovascular Medicine, Stanford University School of Medicine, 2000-01, 2005-06; Clinical Instructor, 2001-02, Assistant Professor, 2003-07, Associate Professor, 2008-, Keimyung University School of Medicine. Publications: Numerous articles in professional journals. Memberships: Korea Medical Association; Korean Society of Internal Medicine; Korean Society of Circulation; American College of Cardiology; Korean Society of Interventional Cardiology/Hypertension/Echo Cardiography. Address: 194 Dongsan-dong, Jung-gu, Keimyung University, Dongsan Medical Center, Daegu, 700-712, South Korea. E-mail: shur@dsmc.or.kr

HURD Douglas (Richard) (Hurd of Westwell), b. 8 March 1930, Marlborough, England. Politician; Diplomat; Writer. m. (1) Tatiana Elizabeth Michelle, 1960, divorced, 3 sons, (2) Judy Smart, 1982, 1 son, 1 daughter. Education: Trinity College, Cambridge. Appointments: HM Diplomatic Service,

1952-66; Joined Conservative Research Department, 1966, Head, Foreign Affairs Section, 1968; Private Secretary to the Leader of the Opposition, 1968-70; Political Secretary to the Prime Minister, 1970-74; Member of Parliament, Conservative Party, Mid-Oxon, 1974-83, Witney, 1983-97; Opposition Spokesman on European Affairs, 1976-79; Visiting Fellow, Nuffield College, 1978-86; Minister of State, Foreign and Commonwealth Office, 1979-83, Home Office, 1983-84; Secretary of State for Northern Ireland, 1984-85, Home Secretary, 1985-89, Foreign Secretary, 1989-95; Candidate for Conservative Leadership, 1990; Deputy Chairman, NatWest Markets, 1995-98; Director Natwest Group, 1995-99; Deputy Chairman, Coutts & Co, 1998-; Chairman, Hawkpoint Advisory Committee, 1999-2003; Chairman British Invisibles, 1998-2000; Chairman, Prison Reform Trust, 1997-2001; President, Prison Reform Trust, 2001-; Chairman, The Booker Prize Committee, 1998; Chairman, Council for Effective Dispute Resolution, 2001-04; High Steward, Westminister Abbey, 2000-; Joint President, Royal Institute for Internal Affairs, 2002-. Publications: The Arrow War, 1967; Send Him Victorious (with Andrew Osmond), 1968; The Smile on the Face of the Tiger (with Andrew Osmond), 1969; Scotch on the Rocks (with Andrew Osmond), 1971; Truth Game, 1972; Vote to Kill, 1975; An End to Promises, 1979; War Without Frontiers (with Andrew Osmond), 1982; Palace of Enchantments (with Stephen Lamport), 1985; The Search for Peace (BBC TV Series), 1997; The Shape of Ice, 1998; Ten Minutes to Turn the Devil, 1999; Image in the Water, 2001; Memoirs, 2003. Honours: Commander of the Order of the British Empire, 1974; Privy Councillor, 1982; Spectator Award for Parliamentarian of the Year, 1990; Companion of Honour, 1995; Baron Hurd of Westwell, 1997. Address: House of Lords, London SW1A OPW, England.

HURLEY Elizabeth, b. 10 June 1965, England. Model; Actress; Producer. m. Arun Nayer, 2007, 1 son previous relationship. Career: Former model and spokeswoman, Estée Lauder; Head of Development for Simian Films, 1996; Films include: Aria, 1987; The Skipper, 1989; The Orchid House, 1990; Passenger '57, 1992; Mad Dogs and Englishmen, 1994; Dangerous Ground, 1995; Samson and Delilah, Produced Extreme Measures, Austin Powers: International Man of Mystery, 1996; Permanent Midnight, 1997; My Favorite Martian, EdTV, Austin Powers: The Spy Who Shagged Me, 1999; The Weight of Water, Bedazzled, 2000; Serving Sara, The Weight of Water, Double Whammy, 2002; Method, 2004. Address: c/o Simian Films, 3 Cromwell Place, London SW7 2SE, England.

HURSH Ray, b. 2 March 1935, Superior, Wisconsin, USA. Retired. m. Helen M Hughes, 3 sons, 1 daughter. Education: Theatre Arts, Speech and Drama, California College of Theater Arts, Pasadena, California, 1953-55; Communications, University of Minnesota, Duluth, Minnesota, 1957-60; Degree in Marketing and Business Management, Wisconsin Indianhead Technical College, 1972-74; Diploma, Fitness and Nutrition, International Correspondence School, Pennsylvania, 1987; Stress Management, International Business Systems, Las Vegas, Nevada, 1987; Stress Management, University of Wisconsin, 1988. Appointments: Musician and Performer; Psychiatric Technician and E R CNA, Dallas Texas Hospital, 1961-72; CNA, nursing homes and home health care, Minnesota and Wisconsin, 1972-85; Personal Trainer and Fitness Instructor, teaching aerobics, body building and individual sports training, specialised in stress management and psychological training, 1983-94; Fine Dining Waiter, 1994-99; Retired, concentrating on writing, 2000-; Lay Minister, Hospice Volunteer. Publications include: A Prism

of Thought, 1997; Best Poets of 1998; Outstanding Poets of 1998; Rustling Leaves, 1998; In the Shadow of Midnight, 2000; America in the Millennium, 2000; Nature's Echoes, 2001; Silk Clouds and Velvet Dreams, 2002; Letters From the Soul, 2003; Theatre of the Mind, 2003; Colours of the Heart, 2004; Desert of Despair, 2004; Seven Shades of Pale, 2005; Labours of Love, 2005; Music: Composed full mass for Catholic Church, 2004. Honours include: Outstanding Speaker of the Year, Wisconsin Rotary Club, 1952; Outstanding Achievement in Journalism, University of Minnesota, 1959; Winner Love Poem Contest, Le Courte Orielles Community College, Hayward, Wisconsin, 1997; Editors Choice Award, 1997, 2002; International Poet of Merit, International Society of Poets; International Peace Prize, United Cultural Convention, USA, 2006; Listed in Who's Who publications and biographical dictionaries. Address: 10654 Reinke Street, Apartment #8, Hayward, WI 54843, USA.

HURSTHOUSE Miles Wilson, b. 27 October 1919, Hastings, New Zealand. Medical Practitioner. m. Jillian, 2 sons, 1 daughter. Education: MB, ChB, Auckland University College, Otago University, Sydney University, Australian College of Dermatologists, Sydney, Australia. Appointments: Civil Servant; Army Service WW2, 5 years New Zealand Artillery reaching rank of Captain; Hospital Service as House Surgeon, 2 years; Private Medical Practice, 48 years, including 3 years postgraduate study in Australia; Anaesthetist, Nelson Hospital, 16 years; Lecturer, Obstetrics Nelson Hospital, 10 years; Specialist Dermatologist, Nelson Hospital, 10 years; Retired, still registered medical practitioner for emergencies; Managing Director, Private Property Company. Publications: Autobiography, Vintage Doctor: 50 Years of Tears and Laughter, 2001; 10 scientific papers on subjects including: Melanoma incidence in the Nelson-Marlborough region of New Zealand, use of topical Retinoic acid in bullous ichthyosiform erythroderma, confusing rashes and exanthemata, basal cell carcinoma in burn scars. Honours: International Silver C Gliding Award; Member of winning car team, Southland Centennial Car Trial (International); New Zealand University Blue, Shooting, 1950; Otago University Blues, Shooting, 1949, 1950; Navigation Cup, Nelson Aero Club, 1964; Numerous cups and trophies for local motor sport; Honorary Life Member, Nelson Car Club and Nelson Gliding Club. Memberships include: President: Nelson Car Club, Nelson Gliding Club, Nelson Division, New Zealand Medical Association, Nelson Branch New Zealand Cancer Society, Nelson Branch, New Zealand Heart Foundation, New Zealand Dermatological Association, New Zealand Faculty Australasian College of Dermatologists, Stoke Tahunanui Probus Club; Member, Nelson Area Health Board. Address: 306 Princes Drive, Nelson, New Zealand.

HURT David, b. 7 September 1961, San Francisco, California, USA. Storeworker; Business Owner. 1 foster son. Education: BS, Business Management, Liberty University. Appointments: Business Owner, 1981-2007; Storeworker, 1985-2007; Consumer Panels Worker, 2005-2006. Publication: Better Home and Garden. Honours: Diploma of Expertise in Computers and Business; Man of the Year; 500 Greatest Geniuses of the 21st Century; American Ambassadors Medal; American Medal of Honor. Membership: Costco Business; ABI Advisory Directorate International. Address: 218 Calle de La Palmoa, Fallbrook, CA 92028, USA. E-mail: dchurt@earthlink.net

HURT John, b. 22 January 1940, Chesterfield, England. m. (1) Annette Robertson, (2) Donna Peacock, 1984, divorced 1990, (3) Jo Dalton, 1990, divorced 1995, 2 sons, (4) Ann

Rees Meyers, 2005. Education: Lincoln Academy of Dramatic Art; Royal Academy of Dramatic Art. Appointments: Painter; Actor. Creative Works: Stage appearances include: Chips With Everything, 1962; The Dwarfs, 1963; Hamp, 1964; Inadmissible Evidence, 1965; Little Malcolm and His Struggle Against the Eunuchs, Belcher's Luck, 1966; The Only Street, 1973; Travesties, 1974; The Shadow of a Gunman, 1978; The London Vertigo, 1991; A Month in the Country, 1994; Krapp's Last Tape, 2000, Gate Theatre, 2001; Afterplay, 2002; Films include: The Elephant Man, 1980; King Ralph, Lapse of Memory, 1991; Dark at Noon, 1992; Monolith, Even Cowgirls Get the Blues, Rob Roy, 1994; Wild Bill, 1995; Dead Man, 1996; Contact, 1997; Love and Death on Long Island, 1998; All the Little Animals, You're Dead, The Love Letter, 1999; Lost Souls, Night Train, 2000; Captain Corelli's Mandolin, Harry Potter and the Philosopher's Stone, Tabloid, Bait, Miranda, Owning Mahony, 2001; Crime and Punishment, 2002; Miranda, Dogville (voice), 2003; Hellboy, 2004; Short Order, Valiant (voice), The Proposition, Shooting Dogs, Manderlay (voice), The Skeleton Key, V for Vendetta, 2005, Boxes, Outlander, 2007; Lezione 21, The Oxford Murders, 2008. TV: The Waste Places, 1968; Nijinsky: God of the Dance, The Naked Civil Servant, 1975; I, Claudius, 1976; Treats, 1977; Crime and Punishment, 1979; Poison Candy, Deadline, 1988; Who Bombed Birmingham? 1990; Journey to Knock, Red Fox, 1991; Six Characters in Search of an Author, 1992; Prisoner in Time, Saigon Baby, 1995; Alan Clark Diaries, 2004. Honours: Best Television Actor, 1975; British Academy Award, 1975; Emmy Award, 1978; British Academy Award, Best Supporting Actor, 1978; Golden Globe, Best Supporting Actor Award, 1978; Variety Club, Best Actor Award, 1978; British Academy Award, Best Actor, 1980; Variety Club, Best Film Actor Award, 1980; Evening Standard, Best Actor Award, 1984; Cable Ace Award, 1995; Richard Harris Award for Outstanding Contribution to British Film, British Film Industry Awards, 2003. Address: c/o Julian Belfrage & Associates, 46 Albemarle Street, London W1X 4PP, England.

HURT William, b. 20 March 1950, Washington, USA. Actor. m. (1) Mary Beth Hurt, (2) Heidi Henderson, 1989 (divorced), 2 sons. Education: Tufts University; Juilliard School. Creative Works: Stage appearances include: Henry V, 1976; Mary Stuart; My Life; Ulysses in Traction; Lulu; Fifth of July; Childe Byron; The Runner Stumbles; Hamlet; Hurlyburly; Beside Herself, 1989; Ivanov, 1991; Films include: Altered States; Eyewitness; Body Heat; The Big Chill; Corky Park; Kiss of the Spider Woman; Children of a Lesser God; Broadcast News, 1987; A Time of Destiny, 1988; The Accidental Tourist, 1989; The Plastic Nightmare; I Love You to Death, The House of Spirits, 1990; The Doctor, Until the End of the World, 1991; Mr Wonderful, The Plague, 1993; Trial By Jury, Second Best, 1994; Jane Eyre, Secrets Shared With a Stranger; Smoke, 1995; Michael; Loved; Lost in Space, One True Thing, Dark City, 1998; The Miracle Marker, 2000; AI: Artificial Intelligence, The Flamingo Rising, Rare Birds, 2001; Changing Lanes, Nearest to Heaven, Tuck Everlasting, 2002; The Blue Butterfly, The Village, 2004; The King, A History of Violence, Neverwas, Syriana, 2005; The Legend of Sasquatch (voice), Beautiful Ohio, The Good Shepherd, 2006; Mr Brooks, Noise, Into The Wild, 2007; Vantage Point, Yellow Handkerchief, 2008. Honours include: Theatre World Award, 1978; Best Actor Award, Cannes Film Festival, 1985; Academy Award, Best Actor, 1985; 1st Spencer Tracy Award, 1988. Address: c/o Hilda Quille, William Morris Agency,151 El Camino Drive, Beverly Hills, CA 90212, USA.

HUSBANDS Sir Clifford (Straughn), b. 5 August 1926, Barbados. Governor-General. m. Ruby C D Parris, 1 son, 2 daughters. Education: Parry School; Harrison College, Barbados; Middle Temple, Inns of Court, London, England. Appointments: Called to Bar, Middle Temple, 1952; Private Practice, Barbados, 1952-54; Deputy Registrar (Ag) Barbados, 1954; Legal Assistant to Attorney General, Grenada, 1954-56; Magistrate, Grenada, 1956-57; Magistrate, Antigua, 1957-58; Crown Attorney, Magistrate and Registrar, Montserrat, 1958-60; Crown Attorney (Ag), St Kitts-Nevis-Anguilla, 1959; Attorney General (Ag), St Kitts-Nevis-Anguilla, 1960; Assistant to Attorney-General and Legal Draughtsman, Barbados, 1960-63; Assistant to Attorney General, Barbados, 1960-67; Director of Public Prosecutions, Barbados, 1967-76; Queen's Counsel, 1968; Judge, Supreme Court, Barbados, 1976-91; Justice of Appeal, Barbados, 1991-96; Chairman, Community Legal Services, 1985-96; Member, Judicial and Legal Service Commission, Barbados, 1987-96; Chairman, Penal Reform Committee, Barbados, 1995-96; Governor-General of Barbados, 1996; President of the Privy Council for Barbados, 1996. Honours: Queen's Silver Jubilee Medal, 1977; Gold Crown of Merit, 1989; Companion of Honour of Barbados, 1989; Knight of St Andrew, 1995; Knight of Grand Cross of the Most Distinguished Order of Saint Michael and Saint George, 1996; Paul Harris Fellowship Award, 2001; Knight of Grace in the Most Venerable Order of the Hospital of St John of Jerusalem, 2004. Memberships: Vice President, Barbados Lawn Tennis Association, 1970's; President, Old Harrisonian Society, 1983-87; Council Member, Barbados Family Planning Association, 1960-96. Address: Government House, Government Hill, St Michael, Barbados.

HUSSAIN AJMAL Ibrahim, b. 15 May 1935, Palayamkottai, Tamil Nadu, India (British citizen). Engineering Manager. 2 sons. Education: BE, Civil Engineering, UNI, Madras, 1955; Diploma, Imperial College, London, 1964; MBA, Cranfield, 1973; Chartered Engineer, 1962. Appointments: Assistant Engineer, Kymore Cement Works Associate Cement Companies Ltd, Bombay, 1956-57; Training with Sir William Halcrow & Partners, London, 1957-60; Civil Engineer, Designer, Nuclear Power Division, Simon Carves Ltd, London, 1960-61; Design Engineer, L G Mouchel & Partners, London, 1962-63; Engineer, Senior Engineer, Bertlin & Partners, London, Bombay, 1963-69; Senior Assistant Engineer, London Borough, Hillingdon, 1969-71; Senior Engineer, Project Manager, Peter Fraenkel & Partners, London, 1973-75; Senior Resident Engineer, Halcrow Group, London, Al Jubail, 1976-80; Site Engineer, Dar Al Handasah, Noble Associates, London Underground, Luanda, London, 1980-82; Senior Engineer, Construction projects and Maintenance Directorate, Ministry Works, Power and Water, Bahrain, 1983-85; Support to Associate Consultant on Planning Applications, Roughton & Partners for the Maidstone Borough Council, 1985-86; Noro Project Manager/Co-ordinator, SIG Ministry of Transport Works and Utilities, Honiara Solomon Islands (seconded as technical co-operation officer by ODA, Glasgow) 1987-89; Freelance Engineer, Scott Wilson Associates, Fluor Daniel and others, 1990-95; Structural Engineer/Design Group Advisor, Devonport Management Ltd, Plymouth, 1996-2000; Project Manager, Hyder Consulting, London, 2000; Associate Consultant, Advisory Service to Peter Fraenkel Maritime Ltd, Dorking, London Borough of Hounslow and others, 2001-; Advisor, London Borough of Richmond Building Control on Structural Safety and Construction Design Management, 2007-. Memberships: English Bridge Union.

Address: 3 Chase Court, Wimbledon Chase, London SW20 9ER, England. E-mail: ajmalih@hotmail.com Website: www.professionalassociates.com

HUSSAIN Syed Muzammil, Freelance Columnist; Multilingual Translator; Social Worker; Media Consultant. Education: BA, University of the Punjab, Lahore, 1986; BA (Hon), Media, Higher Institute of Islamic Da'wah and Journalism, Muhammad Bin Saud University, Riyadh, Saudi Arabia, 1988; Master, Arabic, Punjab University, Lahore, 1988; Master, Mass Communication, Allama Iqbal Open University, Islamabad, 2000. Appointments: Programme Producer, 1989, In-charge Public Relations to Rector, 1997-, Da'wah Academy, International Islamic University; Urdu-Arabic translator, Kashmir-ul-Muslima magazine, 1990-95; Social Worker, Chapman Kot, district Bagh (Poonch), Azad Kashmir, 15 years; General Secretary, Literary Society, Government Degree Muzaffarabad and Azad Kashmir; Member, editorial board of Higher Institute of Islamic Da'wah, Madina Munawwara's Magazine; Scout, Saudi Arabia, 3 years. Honours: 3rd position, All Pakistan Syed Abul A'la Maududi memorial essay competition, Karachi, 1980; Participated in numerous cultural and popular programmes. Memberships: Historical and Archaeological Association of Pakistan; Daira; AAA Translators Inc, Canada; Shah-e-Hamdan International Islamic Association; Honorary Member, Board of Governors, ABI. Address: PO Box No 1485, Islamabad, Pakistan. E-mail: muzamil58@yahoo.com

HUSSAIN Syed Sarfraz, b. 4 April 1957, Gujrat, Punjab, Pakistan. Doctor. m. Seema, 2 sons. Education: MBBS; MD; PhD; PhD Diplomate, Board Certified American Academy of Traumatic Stress; Diplomate, Board Certified in Pain Management. Appointments: Intern, Fellow/Registrar, Psychiatry and Neurology, Jinnah Postgraduate Medical Centre, Karachi, 1981-85; Chief Resident, Psychiatrist & Neurologist, Aga Khan University Hospital; Consultant Psychiatrist, MidEast Hospital; Consultant Psychiatrist & Neurologist, The Retreat Lahore-Pakistan, 2000-. Publications include: Environment & Mental Health study; Dhatt Syndromes; Dubai Syndrome; History of Neuro-Psychopharmacology. Honours: High School Scholarship; ICIC (WHO) Scholar; Ship Institute of Psychiatry, London; ECFMG Certification. Memberships include: Pakistan Psychiatric Society, Karachi; Pakistan Research Council, Islamabad; American Association of Psychology; American Academy of Neurology. Address: 318-H, Block H, Johar Town, Lahore 53781, Pakistan. E-mail: sarfraz71@hotmail.com

HUSSEIN Queen Noor (HM), b. 23 August 1951. m. King Hussein I of Jordan, deceased 2 February 1999, 4 children. Education: BA, Architecture, Urban Planning, Princeton University, USA 1974. Appointments: Architectural and Urban Planning Projects in Australia, Iran and Jordan; Founded in Jordan, Royal Endowment for Culture and Education, 1979; Annual Arab Children's Congress, 1980; Annual International Jerash Festival for Culture and Arts, 1981; Jubilee School, 1984; Noor Al Hussein Foundation, 1985; National Music Conservatory, 1986; National Task Force for Children; Advisory, Committee for the UN University International Leadership Academy, Amman; Patron of the General Federation of Jordanian Women and the National Federation of Business and Professional Women's Clubs; Patron, Royal Society for the Conservation of Nature; Honorary President, Jordan Red Crescent; The Jordan Society, Washington DC, 1980; Patron, International Union for the Conservation of Nature and Nature Rescue, 1988; Founding Member, International Commission on Peace and Food, 1992;

President, United World Colleges, 1995; Honorary President, Birdlife International, 1996; Director, Hunger Project. Honours: Numerous Honorary Doctorates, International Relations, Law, Humane Letters; International Awards and Decorations. Memberships: International Eye Foundation Honorary Board; Trustee, Mentor Foundation; General Assembly of the SOSKinderdorf International; International Council of the Near East Foundation. Address: Bab Al Salam Palace, Amman, Jordan.

HUSTON Anjelica, b. 8 July 1951, Los Angeles, California, USA. Actress. m. Robert Graham, 1992. Creative Works: Stage appearances include: Tamara, Los Angeles, 1985; TV appearances include: The Cowboy and the Ballerina, NBC-TV Film, 1984, Faerie Tale Theatre, A Rose for Miss Emily, PBS Film, Lonesome Dove, CBS Mini-Series; The Mists of Avalon, 2001; Iron Jawed Angels, 2004; Films include: Sinful Davey; A Walk with Love and Death, 1969; The Last Tycoon, 1976; The Postman Always Rings Twice, 1981; Swashbuckler; This is Spinal Tap, The Ice Pirates, 1984; Prizzi's Honor, 1985; Gardens of Stone; Captain Eo; The Dead; Mr North; A Handful of Dust; The Witches; Enemies; A Love Story; The Grifters; The Addams Family; Addams Family Values; The Player; Manhattan Murder Mystery; The Crossing Guard, The Perez Family, 1995; Buffalo '66, Phoenix, 1997; Director, Bastard Out of Carolina, 1995, Phoenix, 1997; Agnes Browne, 1999; The Golden Bowl, 2001; The Royal Tenenbaums, Blood Work, The Man from Elysian Fields, 2002; Daddy Day Care, 2003; The Life Aquatic with Steve Zissou, 2004; These Foolish Things, Art School Confidential, Material Girls, Seraphim Falls, 2006; The Darjeeling Limited, 2007. Honours include: Academy Award, Best Supporting Actress, 1985; NY & Los Angeles Film Critics Awards, 1985; Best Supporting Actress in a Series, Miniseries or TV Movie, Golden Globe Awards, 2005. Address: c/o International Creative Management, 8942 Wilshire Boulevard, Beverly Hills, CA 90211, USA.

HUTCHISON John Bower, b. 9 July 1938, London, England. Neuroscientist. m. Rosemary, 4 daughters. Education: Belmont School, Hassocks, Sussex; Newcastle High School, Newcastle, Natal, South Africa; Department of Zoology, University of Natal, South Africa; Department of Zoology, University of Cambridge; St John's College, Cambridge. Appointments: Temporary Junior Lecturer, Zoology, University of Natal, Republic of South Africa, 1962-64; Research Student, 1964-67, Research Fellow, 1967-1970, Department of Zoology, University of Cambridge; CSIR Research Fellow, Republic of South Africa, 1964-67; Senior Research Scientist, 1967-1970, College Lecturer, Physiology, 1976-1996, St John's College, Cambridge; Fullbright Scholar, MRC Travel Award, Fellow in Research, Department of Biology, Princeton University, 1971-72; Visiting Professor, MRC Overseas Travel Award, 1981-82; Tenured Scientist, Medical Research Council, MRC Unit, Madingley, Cambridge, 1987-99; Head of MRC, Neuroendocrine Development and Behaviour Group, Head, Behavioural Development Laboratory, Brabraham Institute, Cambridge, 1987-99; Life Fellow, St John's College, Cambridge, 1996-. Publications: Book, Biological Determinants of Sexual Behaviour, 1977; Over 100 scientific papers and articles for professional journals. Honours: Fellow, Institute of Biology, Princeton, America; CSIR Overseas Bursary for Research; Fulbright Scholarship; Fellowship, St John's College, Cambridge; Emeritus Member, Society for Neuroscience, America; Senior Member, Society for Endocrinology. Memberships: Society for Neuroscience, America; Society for Endocrinology; Association for the

Study of Animal Behaviour. Address: St John's College, Cambridge, Cambridgeshire, CB2 1TD, England. E-mail: jghi@uni.cam.uk

HUTSON Jeremy Mark, b. 7 May 1957, West Kirby, Cheshire, England. Professor of Chemistry. Education: BA, 1st Class, Chemistry, Wadham College, Oxford University, 1975-79; DPhil, Physical Chemistry, Hertford College, Oxford University, 1979-81. Appointments: NATO/SERC Postdoctoral Research Fellow, University of Waterloo, Canada, 1981-83; Drapers Company Research Fellow, 1983-84, Stokes Research Fellow, 1984-86, Pembroke College, Cambridge and Theoretical Chemistry Department, University of Cambridge; Lecturer, 1987-93, Reader, 1993-96, Professor, 1996-, Head of the Department of Chemistry, 1998-2001, University of Durham; Vice-Chair, Gordon Conference on Molecular and Ionic Clusters, Ventura, 2006. Numerous invited lectures at international conferences include most recently: American Physical Society DAMOP Meeting, Knoxville, 2006, Gordon Conference on Atomic and Molcular Interactions, New London, New Hampshire, 2006, Heraeus Seminar on Cold Molecules, Bad Honnef, Germany, 2006. Publications: 145 scientific publications with over 5,300 citations up to August 2005; Editor, International Reviews in Physical Chemistry; Specialist Editor, Computer Physics Communications. Honours: Corday-Morgan Medal, Royal Society of Chemistry, 1991; Visiting Fellowship, Joint Institute for Laboratory Astrophysics, Boulder, Colorado, USA, 1991; Nuffield Foundation Science Research Fellowship, 1993-94; Visiting Professorship, University of Colorado, 2001-2002; Kołos Medal, University of Warsaw and Polish Chemical Society, 2007; Award in Computational Chemistry, Royal Society of Chemistry, 2006. Memberships: Fellow, Royal Society of Chemistry, UK; Fellow, Institute of Physics, UK. Address: Department of Chemistry, University of Durham, Durham DH1 3LE, England.

HUTTON Gabriel Bruce, b. 27 August 1932, Minchinhampton, Gloucestershire, England. Circuit Judge (Retired). m. Deborah Leigh Windus, 1 son, 2 daughters. Education: Trinity College, Cambridge, 1951-54. Appointments: Called to Bar, Inner Temple, 1956; Deputy Chairman, Gloucester Quarter Sessions, 1971; Recorder, Crown Court, 1972-78; Circuit Judge, Western Circuit, 1978-2003; Resident Judge, Gloucester Crown Court, 1987-2003. Address: Chestal House, Dursley, Gloucestershire GL11 5AA, England.

HUTTON, Baron of Bresagh in the County of Down, (James) Brian Edward Hutton, b. 29 June 1931, United Kingdom. Retired Law Lord. m. (1) Mary Gillian Murland, deceased, 2000, 2 daughters, (2) Rosalind Anne Nickols, 2 stepsons, 1 stepdaughter. Education: BA, Balliol College, Oxford; Queen's University, Belfast. Appointments: Called to the Bar, Northern Ireland, 1954; Junior Counsel to Attorney General of Northern Ireland, 1969; Queen's Counsel, Northern Ireland, 1970; Senior Crown Counsel, Northern Ireland, 1973-79; Judge of the High Court of Justice, Northern Ireland, 1979-88, Lord Chief Justice of Northern Ireland, 1988-97; a Lord of Appeal in Ordinary, 1997-2004; Chairman, Hutton Inquiry, 2003-2004; Member, Joint Law Enforcement Commission, 1974; Deputy Chairman, Boundary Commission for Northern Ireland, 1985-88. Honours: Kt, 1988; Privy Councillor, 1988; Life Peer, 1997. Memberships: President, Northern Ireland Association for Mental Health, 1983-90; Visitor, University of Ulster, 1999-2004. Address: House of Lords, London SW1A 0PW, England.

HUTTON Rt Hon John, b. 6 May 1955, London, England. Secretary of State for Business, Enterprise and Regulatory Reform; Member of Parliament for Barrow and Furness. m. Rosemary Caroline Little, 1978, divorced 1993, 3 sons, 1 daughter. Education: Westcliffe High School for Boys, Essex; BA, 1976, BCL, 1978, Magdalen College, Oxford. Appointments: Research Associate, Templeton College, Oxford, 1980-81; Senior Law Lecturer, Newcastle Polytechnic, 1981-82; Member of Parliament for Barrow and Furness, 1992-; Minister, Department of Health, 1998-2005; Chancellor of the Duchy of Lancaster, 2005; Secretary of State for the Department of Work and Pensions, 2005-07; Secretary of State for Business, Enterprise and Regulatory Reform, 2007-.

HUTTON Ronald Edmund, b. 19 December 1953, Ootacamund, India. Historian. m. Lisa Radulovic, 5 August 1988. Education: BA, Cantab, 1976; MA, 1980; DPhil, 1980. Appointments: Professor of History, Bristol University, 1996-. Publications: The Royalist War Effort, 1981; The Restoration, 1985; Charles II, 1989; The British Republic, 1990; The Pagan Religions of the Ancient British Isles, 1991; The Rise and Fall of Merry England, 1994; The Stations of the Sun, 1996; The Triumph of the Moon: A History of Modern Pagan Witchcraft, 1999; Shamans, 2001; Witches, Druids and King Arthur, 2003; Debates in Stuart History, 2004; The Druids, 2007. Contributions to: Journals. Honour: Benjamin Franklin Prize, 1993. Memberships: Royal Historical Society; Folklore Society; Fellow, Society of Antiquaries. Address: 13 Woodland Road, Bristol BS8 1TB, England.

HUTTON Timothy, b. 16 August 1960, Malibu, California, USA. Actor. m. (1) Debra Winger, 1986, divorced, 1 son. (2) Aurore Giscard d'Estaing, 2000, 1 child. Career: Plays: Prelude to a Kiss, 1990; Babylon Gardens, 1991; TV: Zuma Beach, 1978; Best Place to Be; Baby Makes Six; Sultan and the Rock Star; Young Love; First Love; Friendly Fire, 1979; Nero Wolfe Mystery, 2001; WW3, 2001; 5ive Days to Midnight, 2004; Films: Ordinary People, 1980; Taps, 1981; Daniel, 1983; Iceman, 1984; Turk, The Falcon and the Snowman, 1985; Made in Heaven, 1987; A Time of Destiny, Everybody's All-American, Betrayed, 1988; Torrents of Spring, Q&A, 1990; The Temp, The Dark Half, 1993; French Kiss, City of Industry, Scenes From Everyday Life, 1995; The Substance of Fire, Mr and Mrs Loving, Beautiful Girls, 1996; City of Industry, Playing God, 1997; The General's Daughter, 1999; Just One Night, Deliberate Intent, Deterrence, Lucky Strike, 2000; Sunshine State, 2002; Secret Window, Kinsey, 2004; Turning Green, 2005; Last Holiday, Stephanie Daley, The Kovak Box, Heavens Fall, Falling Objects, Off the Black, The Good Shepherd, 2006; The Last Mimzy, When a Man Falls in the Forest, Lymelife, The Alphabet Killer, Brief Interviews with Hideous Men, Multiple Sarcasms, 2007. Honours: Oscar, Best Supporting Actor, 1980. Address: CAA, 9830 Wilshire Boulevard, Beverly Hills, CA 90212, USA.

HUXLEY George Leonard, b. 23 September 1932, Leicester, England. Scholar. m. Davina Best, 3 daughters. Education: BA, Magdalen College, Oxford, 1955. Appointments: Fellow, All Souls College, Oxford, 1955-61; Professor of Greek, The Queen's University of Belfast. 1962-83; Director, Gennadius Library, American School of Classical Studies, Athens, Greece, 1986-89; Research Associate, later Honorary Professor, Trinity College, Dublin, 1983-. Publications: Books and articles on Greek and Byzantine subjects. Honours: Hon DLitt, Belfast; Hon Litt D, Dublin. Memberships: Athenaeum; Fellow of the

Society of Antiquaries; Member of the Royal Irish Academy; Member, Academia Europaea. Address: School of Classics, Trinity College, Dublin 2, Ireland.

HUXLEY Hugh Esmor, b. 25 February 1924, Birkenhead, England. Physiologist. m. Frances Frigg, 1966, 2 stepsons, 1 daughter, 1 stepdaughter. Education: Graduated, Christ's College, Cambridge, 1943; PhD, 1952. Appointments: Radar Officer, RAF Bomber Command and Telecommunications Research Establishment, Malvern, 1943-47; Research Student, Medical Research Council Unit for Molecular Biology, Cavendish Laboratory, Cambridge, 1948-52; Commonwealth Fund Fellow, Biology Department, MIT, 1952-54; Research Fellow, Christ's College, Cambridge, 1952-56; Member, External Staff, 1962-87, Joint Head, Structural Studies Division, 1976-87, Deputy Director, 1977-87, Medical Research Council Laboratory of Molecular Biology, Cambridge; Professor of Biology, 1987-97, Director, 1988-94, Professor Emeritus, 1997-, Rosenstiel Basic Medical Sciences Research Center, Brandeis University, Boston, Massachusetts; Fellow, King's College, Cambridge, 1961-67; Fellow, Churchill College, Cambridge, 1967-87; Harvey Society Lecturer, New York, 1964-65; Senior Visiting Lecturer, Physiology Course, Woods Hole, Massachusetts, 1966-71; Wilson Lecturer, University of Texas, 1968; Dunham Lecturer, Harvard Medical School, 1969; Croonian Lecturer, Royal Society of London, 1970; Ziskind Visiting Professor of Biology, Brandeis University, 1971; Penn Lecturer, University of Pennsylvania, 1971; Mayer Lecturer, MIT, 1971; Miller Lecturer, State University of New York, 1973; Carter-Wallace Lecturer, Princeton University, 1973; Pauling Lecturer, Stanford University, 1980; Jesse Beams Lecturer, University of Virginia, 1980; Ida Beam Lecturer, University of Iowa, 1981. Publications: Articles in scientific journals. Honours: Feldberg Award for Experimental Medical Research, 1963; William Bate Hardy Prize of the Cambridge Philosophical Society, 1965; Honorary DSc, 1969, 1974, 1976, 1988; Louis Gross Horwitz Prize, 1971; International Feltrinelli Prize for Medicine, 1974; International Award, Gairdner Foundation, 1975; Baly Medal, Royal College of Physicians, 1975; Royal Medal, Royal Society of London, 1977; E B Wilson Medal, American Society for Cell Biology, 1983; Albert Einstein World Award of Science, 1987; Franklin Medal, 1990; Distinguished Scientist Award, Electron Microscopy Society of America, 1991; Copley Medal, Royal Society of London, 1997. Memberships: Member, Advisory Board, Rosensteil Basic Medical Sciences Center, Brandeis University, 1971-77; Member, Council of Royal Society of London, 1973-75, 1984-86; Member, Scientific Advisory Committee, European Molecular Biology Laboratory, 1975-81; Member, Board of Trustees, Associated Universities Inc, 1987-90; Member, Germany Academy of Science, Leopoldina, 1964; Foreign Associate, NAS, 1978; American Association of Anatomists, 1981; American Physiological Society, 1981; American Society of Zoologists, 1986; Foreign Honorary Member, American Academy of Arts and Sciences, 1965; Danish Academy of Sciences, 1971; American Society of Biological Chemists, 1976; Honorary Fellow, Christ's College, Cambridge, 1981. Address: Rosensteil Basic Medical Sciences Research Center, Brandeis University, Waltham, MA 02254, USA.

HUXTABLE Ada Louise, b. New York, New York, USA. Architecture Critic; Writer. m. L Garth Huxtable. Education: AB, magna cum laude, Hunter College, New York City; Postgraduate Studies, Institute of Fine Arts, New York University. Appointments: Assistant Curator of Architecture and Design, Museum of Modern Art, New York, 1946-50;

Contributing Editor, Progressive Architecture and Art in America, 1950-63; Architecture Critic, The New York Times, 1963-82, The Wall Street Journal, 1996-; Cook Lecturer in American Institutions, University of Michigan, 1977; Hitchcock Lecturer, University of California at Berkeley, 1982. Publications: Pier Luigi Nervi, 1960; Classic New York, 1964; Will They Ever Finish Bruckner Boulevard?, 1970; Kicked a Building Lately?, 1976; The Tall Building Artistically Reconsidered: The Search for a Skyscraper Style, 1985; Goodbye History, Hello Hamburger, 1986; Architecture Anyone?, 1986; The Unreal America: Architecture and Illusion, 1997. Contributions to: Various publications. Honours: Many honorary doctorates; Fulbright Fellowship, 1950-52; Guggenheim Fellowship, 1958; Architectural Medal for Criticism, American Institute of Architects, 1969; 1st Pulitzer Prize for Distinguished Criticism, 1970; Medal for Literature, National Arts Club, 1971; Diamond Jubilee Medallion, City of New York, 1973; Secretary's Award for Conservation, US Department of the Interior, 1976; Thomas Jefferson Medal, University of Virginia, 1977; John D and Catharine T MacArthur Foundation Fellowship, 1981-86; Henry Allen Moe Prize in the Humanities, American Philosophical Society, 1992. Memberships: American Academy of Arts and Letters; American Philosophical Society; American Academy of Arts and Sciences, fellow; New York Public Library, director's fellow; Society of Architectural Historians. Address: 969 Park Avenue, New York, NY 10028, USA.

HUYNH My Hang V, b. 30 May 1962, Saigon, Vietnam (Naturalized US citizen). Chemist. Education: BS, Chemistry, BA, Mathematics, State University College of New York at Geneseo, 1987-91; PhD, Co-ordination Chemistry, State University of New York at Buffalo, 1998; Post-Doctoral Research Associate, University of North Carolina, Chapel Hill, North Carolina, 1998-2000; Post-Doctoral Research Associate, 2000, Director-Funded Postdoctoral Fellow, 2001-02, Los Alamos National Laboratory, New Mexico; PhD, Chemistry (Co-ordination Chemistry). Appointments: Tutor, Chemistry and Mathematics, State University College of New York at Geneseo, 1988-90; Lecturer, Chemistry, State University of New York at Buffalo, 1992-1997; Synthetic Organic and Inorganic Chemist in High-Nitrogen Energetic Materials, Dynamic Materials Property and Energetic Materials Science Division, Los Alamos National Laboratory, Los Alamos, 2002-. Publications: Numerous appearances in national and international media resulting from Green Primary Explosives; 58 articles in scientific journals; 12 patents. Honours include: Director-Funded Postdoctoral Fellow, Los Alamos National Laboratory, 2001-02; Postdoctoral Distinguished Performance Award, Los Alamos National Laboratory, 2002; Living Science Award for Services to Research, Application, Healthcare and Education in all Scientific Fields, 2004; Distinguished Licensing Award, Los Alamos National Laboratory, 2005; Individual Distinguished Performance Award, Los Alamos National Laboratory, 2005; 21st Century Award for Achievement, 2005; R&D 100 Award Winner: Combustion Synthesis of Nano-structured Metal Foams, 2005; R&D 100 Award Winner: Green Primaries – Enviro-Friendly Energetic Materials, 2006; National Registry of Environmental Professional (NREP) Awards in Health and Safety, 2006; Ernest Orlando Lawrence Award for Chemistry, 2006; Best-in-class Pollution Prevention, DOE/NNSA Award, Green Primaries – Enviro-Friendly Energetic Materials, 2007; International Medal of Honor, 2007; Geneseo Alumni Association Professional Achievement Award, 2008; Best-in-Class Pollution Prevention DOE/NNSA Award, Ultrapure Carbon and Carbon Nitrides nano-materials; MacArthur Fellowship Genius Award, 2008-12; Pollution

Prevention P2 Star Award Honorable Mention, Green Primary-Enviro-Friendly Energetic Materials; Listed in several Who's Who and biographical publications. Address: Los Alamos National Laboratory, High Explosive Science and Technology Group, MS C920 Los Alamos National University, New Mexico 87545, USA. E-mail: mhuynh@los-alamos.net

HWANG Ki-Young, b. 7 September 1957, Republic of Korea. Researcher. m. Soo-San Lee, 2 sons. Education: BSME, Ulsan Institute of Technology, 1980; Certificate, First Class Heat Control Engineering, 1980; MSME, 1986, PhD, Mechanical Engineering, 1994, Yonsei University. Appointments: Researcher, 1979-, Senior Researcher, 1988-2002, Principal Researcher, 2003-, Agency for Defense Development; Researcher, Graduate School, Yonsei University, 1990-94. Publications: 17 papers published in professional scientific journals including: A Hybrid Numerical Analysis of Heat Transfer and Thermal Stress in a Solidifying Body using FVM and FEM, 1996; Thermal Analysis of a Thermal Liner under a Severely Convective Boundary Load using PATRAN and ABAQUS, 1996; Effects of a Density Change and Natural Convection on the Solidification Process of a Pure Metal, 1997; Numerical Analysis for the Optimum Design of a Triple-glazed Airflow Window, 1997; Two-dimensional Thermal Analysis for Carbonacious Thermal Liner of Rocket Nozzle with Ablation and In-depth Pyrolysis, 1999. Honours: Korean Defense Science Prize, 1986, 1989, 1999, 2000. Memberships: Korean Society of Mechanical Engineers; Korean Society of Aeronautical and Space Sciences; Korean Society of Propulsion Engineers; Korean Society of Air-conditioning and Refrigerating Engineers. Address: Agency for Defense Development, PO Box 35-5, Yuseong, Taejon 305-600, Taejon, Republic of Korea. E-mail: kyhwang@sunam.kreonet.re.kr

HWANG Min Cheol, b. 27 March 1980, Gwang-Ju, Korea. Graduate Student. m. 2007. Education: BS, 2003, PhD in progress, Electronic Engineering, Korea University, Seoul. Publications: Numerous articles in professional journals. Honours: 2nd Prize, 7th TI DSP Design Contest, 2006; Listed in international biographical dictionaries. Memberships: Student Member, Institute of Electrical and Electronic Engineering. E-mail: charles99@dali.korea.ac.kr

HWANG So-Min, b. 19 January 1965, Korea. Medical Doctor. m. Eun-Ju Park, 1 daughter. Education: MB, 1989, MM, 1997, MD, 2000, Inje University, Korea. Appointments: Resident course, Board Qualified Plastic Surgeon, Plastic & Reconstructive Surgery, Paik Hospital, 1993-97; Instructor, 1997-99, Assistant Professor, 1999-2004, Pusan National University Hospital; Fellowship, Australian Craniofacial Unit, Adelaide, Australia, 2003-04; Chief, Aesthetic, Plastic & Reconstructive Surgery Center, 2004-. Memberships: Korean Society of Plastic & Reconstructive Surgery; Korean Society for Surgery of the Hand; IPRAS; IFSSH. E-mail: sominhwang@hanmail.net

HWANG Sun Wook, b. 9 November 1971, Seoul, Korea. Professor. m. Young Shin Park, 1 son. Education: BS, Pharmacy, 1994, MS, Pharmacology, 1996, PhD, Pharmacology, 2001, Seoul National University, College of Pharmacy, Seoul. Appointments: Research Associate, Sensory Research Center, National Creative Research Initiatives sponsored by Ministry of Science and Technology, College of Pharmacy, Seoul National University, 1998-2001; Lecturer, Graduate School of Health Science and Social Welfare, Sahmyook University, Seoul, 2001; Lecturer, College of Pharmacy, Duksung Women's University, Seoul, Korea, 2001; Postdoctoral

Research Associate, The Institute for Childhood and Neglected Diseases, Department of Cell Biology, The Scripps Research Institute, La Jolla, California, USA, 2002-05. Publications: 19 articles in professional scientific journals. Honours: Fellowship of National Creative Research Initiatives, Ministry of Science and Technology, 1998-2001; Leading Health Professional, IBC, 2006. Memberships: Society for Neuroscience, USA; The Korean Physiological Society; The Korean Society for Brain and Neuroscience; The Pharmaceutical Society of Korea. Address: Korea University, Ansan Hospital #3513, Gojan-1-Dong, Danwon-Gu, Ansan-Shi, Gyeonggi-Do, 425-707, Korea. E-mail: sunhwang@korea.ac.kr

HWANG Sung Kyoo, b. 13 July 1953, Yeongju, Korea. Professor. m. Hyun Sook Woo, 2 sons, 1 daughter. Education: MD, 1977, Master of Medicine, 1981, Kyungpook National University; PhD, Chunbuk National University, 1991. Appointments: Internship, 1977-78, Residency, Neurosurgery, 1978-82, Kyungpook University Hospital; Chairman, St Luke's Hospital, 1985-86; Full-time Instructor, Kyungpook University Hospital, 1986-89; Visiting Researcher, New York University Medical Center, 1989-90; Assistant Professor, 1989-93, Associate Professor, 1993-98, Professor, 1998-, Director, Office of Education and Research, 2001-2003, Chairman, Department of Neurosurgery, 2004-, Kyungpook University Medical School and Hospital; Director, Clinical Trial Center (funded by Korean Ministry of Health and Welfare), Kyungpook University Hospital, 2005-; President, Korean Society for Paediatric Neurosurgery, 2002; President, Korean Society of Spina Bifida, 2005-2006. Publications: Articles in scientific journals as co-author include most recently: Surgical treatment of ossified cephalhematoma, 2004; Traumatic vertebral artery dissection in a child with brachial plexus injury, 2005; Outcome of surgical management for tethered spinal cord, 2006. Memberships: Korean Medical Society; Korean Neurosurgical Society; Korean Society for Paediatric Neurosurgery; International Society for Paediatric Neurosurgery; American Association of Neurological Surgeons. Address: Department of Neurosurgery, Kyungpook University Hospital, 50 Samdukdong, Chungku, Daegu, 700-721 Korea. E-mail: shwang@knu.ac.kr Website: http://bh.knu.ac.kr/~shwang

HWANG Tzu-Yang, b. 21 September 1953, Taiwan, Republic of China (nationalised US citizen, 1994). Professor; President; Senior Pastor; Honorary Chair. m. Wei-Chih, 1 adopted son. Education: Humanity Sciences, Tung-Hai University, Taiwan, 1977-78; The Workshop of Pastoral Church Growth and Field Education, 1983-84; International Workshop on Theology and Asian Studies, 1984; Missiology, Fuller Theological Seminary, 1987; Master of Divinity, Systematics and Church History, Tainan Theological Seminary; Masters of Theology, Systematic Theology, The History of Christian Doctrine, Princeton University Theological Seminary; PhD, Religious Philosophy, Theology and Culture, Chinese for Christ Theological Seminary, USA, 1990; Researching Religions, Culture, Philosophy, Theology at Harvard University Divinity School, and Duke University Divinity School, 1991-92; Master Diploma, Religion, Philosophy and Cultural Theology; Missio-History; Education; Culture; History and Missions; Religious Philosophy; Theology. Appointments: President, Sunday School of King-Men Church; Preacher, Ta-Tseng Church, Taiwan; Chair, Erhin District Changhua Union Church; The Bible Study in University Center for University Students for Presbyterians of Chenghua and Taichung; Teaching Assistant, Tainan Theological Seminary; Founder, Youth Fellowship, Kingston Taiwanese American Fellowship Presbyterian Church, USA;

Head Pastor, Good Shepherd Presbyterian Church, USA; Chair for Philosophy and Theology, Chinese for Christian Theological Seminary; Adjunct Professor, Holy Light Theological Seminary; President, Supreme Master, Grand Master, Distinguished Professor, CEO, Founder, Honorary Chair, Chair of the Faculty Committee, Chair of the Research Department; Honorary Doctor of Philosophy, American Chichou Theo-Philosophical Institute, El Monte, California, USA; Senior Pastor, Founder, President, Honorary Chair, Light Christ Church, USA; President, Incorporator, CEO, Founder, Chair, Charter Governor, Light Christ Foundation. Publications: Numerous publications; Over 700 items for numerous awards, prizes, orders, laureates, medals, ranks, citations, certificates and diplomas; Over 36 books; Over 600 professional and academic articles and papers; Over 50 international biographical dictionaries and books. Honours: Numerous awards and prizes including: International Order of Ambassador; Minister of Culture; Secretary General, UCC, American Registry of Outstanding Professionals; Ambassador-General of the USA, UCC; International Top 100 Scientists; Leading Scientists of the World; International Governor; International Order of Fellowships; International Top 100 Educator; Leading Educators of the World; Diploma of Experts, Leading International Leaders of Achievement; The Certificate of Leading Scientists of the World; Leading Professionals of the World; Senator, World Nations Congress Global Fellowship; World Academy of Letters; Gold Medal, United States; International Medal of Honour (3 times); Sovereign Ambassador of the Order of American Ambassador; Meritorious Decoration (4 times), IBC; International Cultural Diploma of Honor (5 times), ABI; Presidential Seal of Honor; International Sash of Academia; International Directory of Experts and Expertise; The Ambassador of Grand Eminence; Mutual Loyalty Award, IBC; International Expert; Registry of the World's Most Respected Expert; Noble Laureate; Genius Laureate of the United States; World Laureate; International Registry of Profiles; International Ambassador of Goodwill; Greatest Intellectuals; Greatest Living Legends; Grand Master, Supreme Master; Adviser of Arts and Humanities to the Director General; International Medal of Honor; Life Member, Research Council of Biography; International Order of Distinction; Adviser on Arts and Humanities to the Director General, IBC; Greatest Minds; Greatest Lives; Leading Intellectuals of the World (Founding Member, Charter Member, Noble Member, Hall of Fame); Leading Educators of the World; Leading Scientists of the World; The Tzu-Yang Hwang Award Foundation; Vice President, Recognition Board of the World (United) Congress for Arts, Science and Communications to UNO; Socratic Chair; Humanities and Philosophy; World Academy of Letters; Board Member, International Order of Merit; Founding Cabinet Member, Presidential Dedication, World Peace and Diplomacy Forum to the United Nations Organisation; Founder, Life Academician, Diplomatic Counsellor, London and International Diplomatic Academy; The Royal Book of Diplomacy and Science; Albert Schweitzer International University to UNO; Prominent Member, Cavalier/Commander, International and The World Order of Sciences, Culture and Education, European and International Academy of Informatization, Belgium and World Distributed Information University to UNO; World Distributed University; International Information Center; Deputy Governor, Continental Governor for the USA, American Biographical Institute; Deputy Director General, Continental Governor for the USA, Honorary Director General, International Biographical Centre; Founder of the Order; Founder, American Order of Excellence (medal); many others. Memberships: Harvard Co-operative Society; American Chi-Chou Theo-Philosophical Institute; Light

Christ Church; Light Christ Foundation; American Academy of Religion; The Society of Biblical Literature; The Scientific Study of Religion, Purdue University; Decree Number 4 of Only One Hundred for Decree of Excellence in Education; Pinnacle Achievement Award for Education; Cogressional Medal of Excellence; Gold Laureates; International Medal of Vision; Man of Achievement; Outstanding Achievement Award, 3 times; Light Christ Church Foundation; National Republican Congressional Committee's Member (Sustaining Member & Gold Member); Register of Congressional Order of Merit (US House); Honorary Chairman, Prestigious House Republican Trust, premier group of Advisors to Republican Leadership, US House of Representatives; Member, National Geography; Member, USA Olympic Team Committee; Member, Harvard Co-operative Society; American Chi Chou Theo-Philosophical Institute recognised and accredited to California Government (CPSVE), Association of Theological Schools (ATS), USA, Canada, Taiwan, and mainland China; World Nations and United Nations Organisations (UNO); Muriel Van Orden Jennings Society, Princeton Theological Seminary; Diamond Leader, Gold Leader, Disabled American Veteran, Commander's Club; Gallery of Excellence; President Award; World Medal of Freedom; World Citizen; World Cup; Noble Prize; Legion of Honor; President's Citation; Gold Laurel; International Expert Elite; World Record Holder; 500 Greatest Genius of 21st Century; Ambassador (Consular) of the International Order of Merit; The Top 200 of the IBC; The Rev Dr Professor Tzu-Yang Hwang, HonDG Foundation; Vice-Chancellor, World Academy of Letters; (Senator; Supreme Master, Vice President, Recognition Board, World Nations Congress); International Profile of the Accomplished Leader; Greatest Intellectuals; Outstanding 2000 Intellectuals of 21st Century Triptych Award & Medal of Inclusion; Dictionary of Greatest Intellectuals Dedication; World Record Holder; International Peace Prize; others. Address: 11768 Roseglen Street, El Monte, CA 91732, USA.

HWANG Won-Joo, b. 27 September 1971, Busan, Republic of Korea. Professor. m. Su-Yeon Kim. Education: Bachelor's degree, 1998, Master's degree, 2000, Computer Engineering, Pusan National University, Busan; PhD, Information Systems Engineering, Osaka University, Japan, 2002. Appointments: Visiting Scholar, University of Missouri at Kansas City, USA, 2002; Professor, 2002-, Vice Director, Office of Admission, 2007, Inje University, Gimhae, Gyeongnam; Director, Korea Multimedia Society, 2007. Publications: Over 70 papers and patents related on u-Home (Ubiquitous Home Networks); Wireless Sensor Networks; Internet QoS and Network Optimization. Honours: Korean Government Overseas Scholarship, 2000-03; Best Paper Award, MITA, 2006. Memberships: Life Member, Korea Multimedia Society; Life Member, Korean Institute of Communication and Sciences; Licentiate, IEEE. Address: Inje University, 607 Obangdong, Gimhae, Gyeongnam 621-749, Republic of Korea. E-mail: ichwang@inje.ac.kr

HWANG Yunhan, b. 25 July 1957, Korea. Professor. m. Youngim Cho, 2 sons. Education: BA, Elementary Education, College of Education, 1987, M Ed, Graduate School, 1987, University of Illinois at Chicago, USA; PhD, Education, Graduate School, University of Alabama, Tuscaloosa, USA, 1994. Appointments: Elementary School Teacher, Eastern Kumsan Elementary School, 1980-82; Teaching and Research Assistant, University of Alabama, USA, 1990-94; Director, Hangchon Special Education Institute, 1994-95; Associate Director, Center for the Study of Elementary Education, 1995-97; Director, Center for the Study of Elementary Education, 1997-99; Lecturer, 1994-95, Full time Lecturer,

1995-97, Assistant Professor, 1997-2002, Chair, Curriculum & Instruction Major, 1999-, Chair, Department of Elementary Education, 2000-01, Associate Professor, 2001-06, Chair, Curriculum & Instruction Major, 2005-07, Professor, 2006-, Dean of Academic Affairs, 2007-, Gwangju National University of Education; Visiting Scholar, University of Iowa, USA, 2002; Committee Member, Special Economic Zone for Regional Development, Ministry of Knowledge Economy, 2006-08; Evaluation Committee Member, Department of Education in Colleges, Deputy Prime Minister and Minister of Education & Human Resources Development, 2007. Publications: 10 books; 88 articles, papers, presentations in professional journals. Honours: Two Chancellor's Student Service Awards, 1987, 1988, Scholarship Association Award, 1987-88, University of Illinois at Chicago; Faculty Recognition Award, University of Alabama, 1992; Academic Honor, Kappa Delta Pi, 1992; Most Outstanding Graduate Research Assistant Award, 1993; Korean Student Association of the University of Alabama Award, University of Alabama, 1993; Appreciation Plaque, Korean Multiple Intelligences Eduation Association, 2005; 10th Year Award of Teaching, 2005, Professor of the Year (Research Area), 2007, Gwangju National University of Education; Listed in international biographical dictionaries. Memberships: Korean Society for the Elementary Education; Korean Society for the Studies of Teacher Education; Korean Society for the Studies of Educational Administration; Korean Association for Multiple Intelligences Education; Association of Supervision and Curriculum Development. Address: Gwangju National University of Education, 1-1 Poonghyang-dong, Buk-gu, Gwangju, 500-703, Korea. E-mail: yhhwang@gnue.ac.kr Website: http://www.edu4ts.net

HYAM Ronald, b. 16 May 1936, Isleworth, England. Historian. Education: Isleworth Grammar School, 1947-1954; Royal Air Force, 1954-56; St John's College Cambridge, 1956-60; First Class in both parts of the Historical Tripos, 1958-59, BA, 1959, MA, 1963, PhD, 1963. Appointments: Fellow, Magdalene College Cambridge, 1962-; Reader, British Imperial History, University of Cambridge, 1996; Emeritus, 1999-; Sometime Librarian, Archivist, Admissions Tutor and President of Magdalene College, Cambridge. Publications: Books on imperial history including: Empire and Sexuality, 1990, 1991, 1992; Britain's Imperial Century 1915-1914, 3rd edition, 2002; The Lion and the Springbok: Britain and South Africa Since the Boer War (with Peter Henshaw), 2003; Britain's Declining Empire: The Road to Decolonisation 1918-1968, 2006. Honour: LittD, University of Cambridge, 1993. Membership: Project Committee, British Documents on the End of Empire Project 1991-2005. Address: Magdalene College, Cambridge CB3 0AG, England.

HYATT Derek James, b. 21 February 1931, Ilkley, Yorkshire, England. Artist; Teacher; Writer. m. Rosamond Joy Rockey, 1 daughter. Education: NDD Illustration, 1st class honours, Leeds College of Art, 1948-52; Part-time studies, Norwich School of Art, 1953; 1st class honours, Royal College of Art, 1954-58; Part-time courses, Film Studies, 1960, Philosophy, 1962, London University. Career: Solo exhibitions annually, throughout UK, 1958-; Visiting Lecturer, Art History and Foundation Course, Kingston School of Art, Surrey, 1959-64; Senior Lecturer, Visual Studies and Illustration Studies, Leeds Polytechnic, 1964-84; Visiting Professor, Cincinnati University, USA, 1980; Full-time artist and writer, 1984-. Publications: Numerous articles in professional art journals and magazines; Author and Illustrator, The Alphabet Stone, 1992; Co-author, Stone Fires-Liquid Clouds, The Shamanic Art of Derek Hyatt, monograph, 2001. Honours: Phil May

Drawing Prize, 1954; Royal Scholar Prize, RCA, 1956; Landscape Painting Prize, RCA, 1958; Companion of the Guild of St George, Ruskin Society, 1990; Yorkshire Arts Award, Bradford Art Gallery, Retrospective, 2001. Memberships: Artists for Nature Foundation International, Extremadura, Spain, 1998. Address: Rectory Farmhouse, Collingham, Wetherby, Yorkshire LS22 5AS, England.

HYDON Kenneth John, b. 3 November 1944, England. Accountant. m. Sylvia, 1 son, 1 daughter. Education: FCMA; FCCA; FCT. Appointments: Financial Director: Racal SES Ltd, 1979-81; Racal Defence Radar and Avionics Group Ltd, 1981-85; Vodafone Group plc, 1985-2005; Non-Executive Director: Verizon Wireless (USA), 2000-05; Reckitt Benckiser plc, 2003-; Tesco plc, 2004-; Royal Berkshire Hospital NHS Trust, 2005-; Pearson plc, 2006-. Membership: Leander.

HYLLSETH Bjorn, b. 30 May 1927, Skoger, Norway. Professor Emeritus. m. Randi, 2 sons, 2 daughters. Education: BVetSci, Sydney, Australia, 1958; PhD, Virology, Royal Veterinary College, Stockholm, Sweden, 1973. Appointments: Veterinarian, Franklin Veterinary Club, New Zealand, 1958-64; Laboratory Veterinarian, National Veterinary Institute, Stockholm, 1965-73; Professor, Virology, The Norwegian School of Veterinary Science, 1973-95. Publications: Several articles in professional journals. Membership: Norwegian Veterinary Association. Address: Alfheim 23, N-1384 Asker, Norway.

HYMAN Timothy James, b. 17 April 1946, Hove, Sussex, England. Painter; Writer. m. Judith Ravenscroft. Education: Slade School of Fine Art, 1963-67. Career includes: 8 London solo exhibitions including, Austin/Desmond Fine Art, 1990, 2000, 2003, 2006; Has shown widely in mixed exhibitions including: Royal Academy Summer Exhibition; Hayward Annual; Whitechapel Open; National Portrait Gallery; Works in public collections including: Arts Council Collection; British Museum; Government Art Collection; Los Angeles County Museum; Contemporary Art Society; Museum of London; Swindon Art Gallery; Deutsche Bank; Artist-in-Residence, Lincoln Cathedral, 1983-84; Artist-in Residence, Sandown Racecourse, 1992; Curated, Narrative Paintings, ICA, London and tour, 1979-80; Curated, Stanley Spencer, Tate Britain, 2001; Curated, British Vision, Ghent, 2007. Publications include: Bonnard, 1998; Bhupen Khakhar, 1998; Carnivalesque, 2000; Sienese Painting, 2003; Frequent contributions to The Times Literary Supplement, 1990-. Honours: Leverhulme Award, 1992; Wingate Award, 1998; Honorary Research Fellow, University College, London; Beato Angelico Medal, Florence, 2004. Address: 62 Myddelton Square, London EC1R 1XX, England.

HYND Ronald, b. 22 April 1931, London, England. Choreographer. m. Annette Page, 1 daughter. Education: Ballet Rambert School, Mercury Theatre, Notting Hill Gate. Appointments: Principal Dancer, Ballet Rambert, 1949-51, Royal Ballet, 1951-70; Roles as principal dancer noble: Siegfried in Swan Lake; Florimund in Sleeping Beauty; Albrecht in Giselle; Les Sylphides; Prince of the Pagodas; Lady and the Fool; The Firebird; and a diverse repertoire of classical and dramatic leads; Ballet Director, Bavarian State Ballet, Munich, 1970-73, 1984-86; Freelance Choreographer, Full length ballets include: The Merry Widow, 1975; Rosalinda, 1978; Papillon, 1979; The Nutcracker, 1976; Coppelia, 1985; The Sleeping Beauty, 1993; Le Diable a Quatre, 1984; Ludwig II, 1986; One act ballets include: Le baiser de la Fee; Dvorak Variations; Mozartiana; La Chatte; Valses Nobles et Sentimentales; La Valse; Wendekreise; The Seasons; In a

Summer Garden; Charlotte Bronte; Scherzo Capricciosso; Performed by international companies including: La Scala, Milan; Deutsche Oper Berlin; Vienna State Opera; Bavarian State Ballet, Munich; Royal Danish Ballet; Australian Ballet; National Ballet of Canada; London Festival Ballet/ English National Ballet; Royal Sadler's Wells; American Ballet Theatre; Houston Ballet; Pacific Northwest Ballet; Tokyo Ballet; Grands Ballets Canadiens; Maggio Musicale, Florence; Ballet de Santiago, Chile; Slovenian Ballet; Hong Kong Ballet; TV productions include: The Nutcracker; The Sanguine Fan; Merry Widow; Rosalinda. Honours: Listed in international biographical directories.

HYNDE Chrissie, b. 7 September 1951, Akron, Ohio, USA. Singer; Songwriter; Musician. 1 daughter with Ray Davies, m. (1) Jim Kerr, divorced, 1 daughter, (2) Lucho Brieva, 1999, separated. Appointments: Contributor to New Musical Express; Co-Founder, Chrissie Hynde and the Pretenders, 1978, Singer, Songwriter, Guitarist, New Band Formed, 1983; Tours in Britain, Europe & USA. Creative Works: Singles include: Stop Your Sobbing, 1978; Kid; Brass in Pocket; I Go to Sleep, 1982; Back on the Chain Gang, 1982; Middle of the Road, 1984; Thin Line Between Love and Hate; Don't Get Me Wrong; Hymn to Her; Albums include: Pretenders, 1980; Pretenders II, 1981; Extended Play, 1981; Learn to Crawl, 1985; Get Close, 1986; The Singles, 1987. Honours: Platinum and gold discs.

HYNDMAN Robin John, b. 2 May 1967, Melbourne, Victoria, Australia. Professor of Statistics. m. Leanne, 1989, 2 sons, 2 daughters. Education: BSc (Hons), 1988, PhD, 1992; University of Melbourne; A Stat, Statistical Society of Australia, 2000. Appointments: Statistical Consultant, Statistical Consulting Centre, University of Melbourne, 1985-92; Lecturer, Department of Statistics, 1993-94; Lecturer, Department of Mathematics, Monash University, 1995-96; Senior Lecturer, Department of Mathematics and Statistics, 1997-98; Senior Lecturer, Department of Econometrics and Business Statistics, 1998-; Visiting Professor, Department of Statistics, CO State University, 1998; Director of Consulting, 1999-2006, Director, Business & Economic Forecasting Unit, 2001-, Professor of Statistics, 2003-, Department of Econometrics & Business Statistics, Monash University; Editor-in-Chief, International Journal of Forecasting, 2005-; Director, International Institute of Forecasters, 2005-. Publications: 4 books; 52 refereed papers; 5 conference proceedings; 13 unrefereed research papers; 14 other statistical publications; 152 statistical consulting reports; 9 non-statistical books. Honours: Second Maurice H Belz Prize in Statistics, 1986, Norma McArthur Prize in Statistics, 1987, Dwights Prize in Statistics, 1988, University of Melbourne; Finalist, Channel Ten Young Achiever Awards, 1990; Award for Excellence in Teaching, Monash Science Society, 1998; Belz Lecturer, Statistical Society of Australia, 2006; Moran Medal for Statistical Science, Australian Academy of Science, 2007; Listed in international biographical dictionaries. Memberships: International Statistical Institute; International Institute of Forecasters; International Association for Statistical Computing; American Statistical Association; Statistical Society of Australia; Australian Population Association. Address: Department of Econometrics & Business Statistics, Monash University, VIC 3800, Australia. E-mail: rob.hyndman@buseco.monash.edu.au Website: www.robhyndman.info

HYNES H B Noel, b. 20 December 1917, Devizes, Wiltshire, England. Biologist. m. Mary Hinks, deceased, 1999, 3 sons, 1 daughter. Education: ARCS, BSc Special, Imperial College,

University of London, 1938; External Research Student (London), Freshwater Biological Association Laboratory, Ambleside, Westmorland, PhD, 1941, DSc, London, 1958. Appointments: Wireworm Survey, Ministry of Agriculture, Shropshire, England, 1941; Entomologist, Agriculture Branch of the Colonial Office, 1941-46; Training in Tropical Crops, Imperial College of Tropical Agriculture, Trinidad, 1941; Inducted into Locust Control Programme, Colonial Office, served in Ethiopia, Kenya and Somalia; Lecturer then Senior Lecturer, Liverpool University, 1947-64; Invited to make a Department of Biology, University of Waterloo, Canada, 1964; Retired as Distinguished Professor Emeritus, 1983; After retirement taught at new University of Addis Ababa, Ethiopia and University of Louisville, Kentucky, USA; Served on various committees for Canadian Government and World Health Organisation. Publications: Books: The Biology of Polluted Waters, 1960; The Ecology of Running Waters, 1970; Nunc Dimittis – A Life in the River of Time (autobiography), 2001; More than 200 papers in scientific journals. Honours: Canada Centennial Medal; Elected Fellow, Royal Society of Canada; Hilary Jolly Award, Australian Society of Limnology; Honorary DSc, Universities of Waterloo and New Brunswick; Naumann/Thieneman Medal, International Association of Limnology, 1998; Man of the Year 2005, American Biographical Institute; Listed in Who's Who publications and biographical dictionaries. Memberships: International Society for Limnology; Freshwater Biological Association; North American Benthological Society. Address: 127 Iroquois Place, Waterloo, Ontario, N2L 2S6, Canada. E-mail: nhynes@sciborg.uwaterloo.ca

HYODO Haruo, b. 3 March 1928, Japan. Radiologist. m. Keiko Tomita, 1 son, 2 daughters. Education: Dokkyo University School of Medicine, Japan; Tokushima University, Japan. Appointment: Radiologist. Publications: 2 Japanese patents. Honours: Gold Medal, Honorary Member, Japanese Society of Interventional Radiology; Japan Billiary Association; Listed in international biographical publications. Memberships: Several Japanese associations. Address: 1-9-3 Saiwai-cyo, Mibu-machi, Shimotsuga tochigi, 321-0203 Japan. E-mail: hyodo283@green.ocn.ne.jp

HYPPÖNEN Elina Tuulikki, b. 1 May 1970, Tampere, Finland. Scientist. m. Alexander Hedger, 1 son. Education: MSc, Nutrition, 1996, Master of Public Health, 1997, University of Kuopio, Finland; Authorised Nutritionist, National Board of Medicolegal Affairs, 1996; MSc, Medical Statistics, LSHTM, England, 2000; PhD, Epidemiology, University of Tampere, Finland, 2001. Appointments: Research Trainee, Centre de Nutrition Humaine, University of Nancy, France, 1993-94; Researcher, 1996-97, Graduate School Researcher, 1997-2001, Tampere School of Public Health, Adjunct Professor in Epidemiology, 2005-, University of Tampere; Research Fellow, 2001-04, Senior Research Fellow, 2004-05, Lecturer, 2005-, Centre for Paediatric Epidemiology and Biostatistics, Institute of Child Health, London, England. Publications: 27 articles in professional medical journals. Honours: Public Health Career Scientist, Department of Health, England, 2004. Memberships: International Epidemiological Association; Nutrition Society (UK); Association for the Study of Obesity (UK); Society of Social Medicine (UK); Finnish Society of Nutrition Research. Address: Centre for Paediatric Epidemiology and Biostatistics, Institute of Child Health, 30 Guilford Street, London WC1N 1EH, England. E-mail: e.hypponen@ich.ucl.ac.uk

I

IBITOLA Gilbert Akin, b. 18 January 1962, Ayere, Nigeria. Senior Lecturer. m. Ruth Anyango Odallo, 2 sons, 1 daughter. Education: BSc, University of Sokoto, 1984; MSc, University of Ilorin, 1988; PhD, Devi Ahilya University, Indore, India, 1998; Diploma, CIM, Ambala City, India, 1995. Appointments: NYSC Lecturer, Physics, Electronics, The Polytechnic, Ibadan, Nigeria, 1984-85; Part-time Graduate Assistant, Assistant Lecturer, Physics, University of Ilorin, Ilorin, Nigeria, 1985-88; Lecturer, Physics/Electronics, Kwara State Polytechnic, Ilorin, Nigeria, 1987-89; Assistant Lecturer, Lecturer I and II, Physics/Electronics, Federal University of Technology, Minna, Nigeria, 1989-96; Part-time Lecturer, Electronics, Devi Ahilya University, Indore, India, 1993-96; Part-time Lecturer, Electronics, University of Nairobi, Nairobi, Kenya, 1996-2006; Lecturer, Senior Lecturer, Physics with Electronics, Kenyatta University, Nairobi, Kenya, 1997-. Publications: Over 30 papers presented at conferences, workshops and seminars include most recently: Adaptive IIR Filtering of Delta-Sigma Modulated Signals, 2003; Web Caching Policies – A Comparison, 2003; A Multi-Destination Routing Approach to Improve Web Server Response, 2004; Web Server: Browsing of the Web Through E-Mail, 2004; Current Trends in Computational Electromagnetic Techniques, 2005. Honours include: Vice-Chancellor's Prize to best all-round BSc Student, University of Sokoto, Nigeria, 1984; Commonwealth Scholarship and Fellowship Scheme Award, 1992-96; Great Minds of the 21st Century, ABI, USA, 2004. Memberships: Indian Academy for Instructional Planning; Life Member, Indian National Institute-Industry Forum for Energy; Professional Member, Central Institute of Management of India; Life Member, Kenya Meteorological Society; Life Member, Solar Energy Society of India; New York Academy of Sciences; American Association for the Advancement of Science; Institute of Electrical and Electronics Engineers, USA; Association for Computing Machinery of USA. Address: Department of Physics, Kenyatta University, PO Box 43844, Nairobi, Kenya. E-mail: ibitolaieee1@yahoo.com

IBRAHIM Shams El Din, b. 27 May 1948, Cairo, Egypt. Assistant Professor. Education: PhD, Agriculture (Soil Science). Appointments: Assistant Professor, Soil, Water & Environmental Research Institute, Agricultural Research Centre. Publications: Some desertification aspects as related to soil fertility status, 2002; Utilization of some organic farm residues for improving the productivity of the newly reclaimed soils at El Fayoum governorate, 2002; The role of proline and organic manure in plant salt tolerance, 2003; Response of maize yield grown on calcereous soil to some organic and inorganic amendments under irrigation with saline drainage water, 2003; Response of corn plants grown on calcereous soil organic fertilization and sulphur, 2003; Effect of Gypsum and mineral fertilizers on yields and nutrients concentration of peanut and wheat grown on sandy soil, 2005; Response of wheat plant to macro and micronutrients fertilization, 2005. E-mail: shamseldin81@hotmail.com

ICE-T (Tracy Marrow), b. Newark, New Jersey, USA. Rap Singer; Actor. m. (1) Darlene Ortiz, 1 child, (2) Nicole Austin, 2005-. Creative Works: Albums: Rhyme Pays, 1987; The Iceberg/Freedom of Speech; Just Watch What You Say, 1989; O G Original Gangster, Havin' a "T" Party (with King Tee), 1991; Body Count, 1992; Home Invasion, The Classic Collection, 1993; Born Dead (with Body Count), 1994; 7th Deadly Sin, 1999; Ice-T Presents the Westside, 2004; Films: Breakin', 1984; New Jack City, Ricochet, 1991;

Trespass, 1992; Surviving the Game, 1994; Tank Girl, Johnny Mnemonic, 1995; Below Utopia; Final Voyage, Corrupt, 1999; Leprechaun 5, Sonic Impact, The Alternate, 2000; Hip Hop Crime Partners, 2000; Out Kold, Ablaze, Tara, Stranded, Kept, Air Rage, 2001; Tracks, Pimpin' 101, On the Edge, 2002; Lexie, 2004; Tracks II, 2005; Copy That, 2006; Thira, 2007. Publication: The Ice Opinion, 1994. Address: Priority Records, 6430 West Sunset Boulevard, Los Angeles, CA 90028, USA. Website: www.mcicet.com

IDOWU Samuel Olusegun, Senior Lecturer. 3 daughters. Education: Diploma, Public Administration, Glasgow College of Technology, 1979; DMS, CNAA, Dundee College of Technology, 1980; Institute of Chartered Secretaries & Administrators, Sheffield City Polytechnic, 1982; MSc, Accounting & Finance, University of Stirling, 1983; City & Guilds Teachers Certificate, North East Surrey College of Technology, 1990. Appointments: Assistant Accountant, K B Films International Ltd, 1983-85; Accountant/Office Manager, Swaybest Ltd, 1985-88; Part time Lecturer, Merton College, Morden, Surrey, 1987-92; Lecturer, Senior Lecturer, North East Surrey College of Technology, 1988-2001; Part time Lecturer, Management Accounting, Croydon College, 1999-2001; Part time Lecturer, Management Accounting, Kingston University, 2000-01; Senior Lecturer, London Guildhall University, 2002; Senior Lecturer, London Metropolitan University, 2002-. Publications: Numerous papers and articles in professional journals including most recently: Corporate social responsibility: An analysis of ideology and practical implementation in enterprises, 2006; Are the CSR matters based on good intentions of false pretences? 2007 Honours: Freeman, City of London, 2004. Memberships: Fellow, Royal Society of Arts; Fellow, Institute of Chartered Secretaries & Administrators; British Accounting Association. Address: London Metropolitan University, 84 Moorgate, London, EC2 6SQ. E-mail: s.idowu@londonmet..co.uk

IGBOJI Paul Ola, b. 24 September 1963, Igbeagu, Nigeria. Environmental Scientist; Consultant. m. Maria, 2 sons. Education: HND/OND, General Agriculture, 1989; PGD, Soil Science and Crop Production, 1991; MSc, Soil Science, 1995; PhD, Environmental Sciences, 2006. Appointments: Chief Agricultural Extension Officer, National Agricultural Land Development Authority, Enugu State Directorate, Nigeria, 1994-96; Senior Agricultural/Horticultural Officer, Ministry of Agriculture and Natural Resources, Ebonyi State, Nigeria, 1996-97; Lecturer, Ebonyi State University, Nigeria, 1998-. Publications: Numerous articles in professional journals; 3 books/monographs; 8 workshop/conference papers. Honours: Listed in international biographical dictionaries; Secretary, Think Tank on Agriculture, Enugu State, Nigeria. Memberships: American Society of Agronomy; Soil Science Society of America; Crop Science Society of America; Society for General Microbiology. Address: Department of Soil Science and Environmental Management, Ebonyi State University, PO Box 699, Abakaliki, Nigeria. E-mail: paul.igboji@ntlworld.com

IGLESIAS Enrique, b. 8 May 1975, Madrid, Spain. Singer; Songwriter. m. Anna Kournikova, 2004. Career: Sings in English and Spanish; Albums: Enrique Iglesias, 1995; Master Pistas, Vivir, 1997; Cosas Del Amor, 1998; Enrique, 1999; Escape, 2001; Quizas, 2002; 7, 2003; Insomniac, 2007. Singles: Experienca Religiosa, No Llores Por Mi, Bailamos, Rhythm Divine, 1999; Be With You, Solo Me Importas Tu, Sad Eyes, 2000; Hero, 2001; Escape, Don't Turn Off the Lights, Love To See You Cry, Maybe, 2002; Addicted, 2003; Not In Love …, 2004. Honours: Grammy Award, 1997; 8

Premios Los Nuestro; Billboard Awards for Artist of the Year; Album of the Year, 1997; ASCAP Award for Songwriter of the Year, 1998; American Music Award for Favorite Latin Artist, 2002. Address: c/o Interscope Records, 2220 Colorado Avenue, Santa Monica, CA 90404, USA. Website: www.enriqueiglesias.com

IGLESIAS Julio (Julio Jose Iglesias de la Cueva), b. 23 September 1943, Madrid, Spain. Singer; Songwriter. m. Isabel Preisler, 20 January 1971, divorced, 3 sons, Partner: Mirander Rijnsburger, 3 children. Education: Law student, Cambridge University. Musical Education: Learnt to sing in hospital (recovering from car crash). Career: Goalkeeper, Real Madrid junior team; Winner, Spanish Song Festival, Benidorm, 1968; Professional singer, songwriter, 1968-; Winner, Eurovision Song Contest, Netherlands, 1970; Major success in Latin America, 1970s; English Language releases, 1981-; Concerts and television appearances worldwide; In excess of 100 million records sold to date. Compositions include: La Vida Sigue Igual; Mi Amor; Yo Canto; Alguien El Alamo Al Camino; No Ilores. Recordings: Over 70 albums include: Soy, 1973; El Amor, 1975; A Mis 33 Anos, 1977; De Nina A Mujer, 1981; 1100 Bel Air Lace, 1984; Un Hombre Solo, 1987; Starry Night, 1990; La Carretera, 1995; Tango, 1996; Corazon Latino, 1998; Noche de Cuatro Lunas, 2000; Una Donna Puo Cambiar la Vita, 2000; Ao Meu Brasil, 2000; Divorcio, 2003; Love Songs; 2004; l'homme que Je suis, 2005; Romantic Classics, 2006; Quelque chose de France, 2007. Also on: Duets (with Frank Sinatra), 1993; Hit singles include: Manuela, 1975; Hey, 1979; Begin The Beguine, 1981; To All The Girls I've Loved Before, duet with Willie Nelson, 1983; My Love, duet with Stevie Wonder, 1988. Publications: Autobiography: Entre El Cielo y El Infernierno, 1981. Honours: Grammy, Best Latin Pop Performance, 1987; Diamond Disc Award, Guinness Book Of Records (most records in most languages), 1983; Medaille de Vermeil de la Ville de Paris, 1983; Eurovision Song Contest Winner, 1970. Membership: Hon member, Spanish Foreign Legion. Address: c/o Anchor Marketing, 1885 NE 149th Street, Suite G, North Miami, FL 33181, USA. Website: www.julioiglesias.com

IIDA Yôichi, b. 21 August 1940, Kobe, Japan. Chemist; Molecular Biologist. m. Hiroko Yokoyama, 1 son, 1 daughter. Education: BS, University of Tokyo, 1963; MS, University of Tokyo, 1965; DSc, University of Tokyo, 1969. Appointments: Research Associate, 1965-77, Lecturer, 1977-95, Associate Professor, 1995-, Hokkaido University, Japan. Publications: Author, Seminar Book of Basic Physical Chemistry, 1992; Human Genome Project and Bioinformatics, 1995; Handbook of Multivariate Statistical Analysis and Examples, 2002; Contributor of articles to professional journals. Memberships: Physical Society of Japan; Chemical Society of Japan; Biophysical Society of Japan; Molecular Biological Society of Japan. Address: Division of Chemistry, Graduate School of Science, Hokkaido University, 060-0810 Sapporo, Hokkaido, Japan. E-mail: chemjimu@sci.hokudai.ac.jp

IIDA Yukisato, b. 24 August 1918, Tokyo, Japan. Lawyer. m. Turuko Aoki, 3 sons. Publications: Drafting of English Patent Specifications; English-Japanese Dictionary of Patent Terms; Japanese-English Dictionary of Patent Terms; Text of EU Trademarks; English-Japanese Encyclopaedia of the Language of the Industrial Property; and others. Honours: Yellow Ribbon Medal, Japanese Government; 5th Order of Merit of the Rising Sun, Japanese Emperor. Memberships: Japanese Patent Attorney's Association; AIPPI; and others. Address: 5-18-13 Koenji-Minami, Suginami-Ku, Tokyo 166-0003, Japan.

IKE Adebimpe Olurinsola, b. 29 June 1933, Ijebu Igbo, Ogun State, Nigeria. Librarian; Administrator; Teacher. m. Chukwuemeka Ike OFR, 1 son. Education: BA (Hons), London, 1960; MA, Ghana, 1974; PG Dip Lib, Ibadan, 1965. Appointments: Sub-Librarian, University of Nigeria, Nsukka, 1962-71; Readers Adviser, Ghana Library Board, Accra, Ghana, 1972-74; Assistant Documentalist, Association of African Universities, Accra, Ghana, 1974-75; Senior Librarian, Principal Librarian, University of Lagos, 1976-81; Pioneer University Librarian, Abubakar Tafawa Balewa University, Bauchi, 1981-93; National Co-Ordinator NADICEST Project, 1988-; Visiting Lecturer, Department of Library Science and Archives, University of Ghana, Legon, Ghana, 1975-76; Professor of Library Science, Nnamdi Azikiwe University, Awka, 1995-. Publications: 60 contributions in monographs, scholarly journals, conferences, seminars, workshops and technical reports. Honours and awards include: Lions Club Merit Award for Professional Excellence; Fellow, Nigerian Library Association; Mothers in Unity, Nigeria; Federal Government Scholarships, Secondary School and University. Memberships include: Life Member, Chartered Institute of Library and Information Professionals, UK; Founding Member, Nigerian Library Association; Member, Nigerian Institute of Management; Member, Nigeria National Committee; ICSU; IGBP. Address: National Documentation and Information Centre for Science and Technology, Nnamdi Azikiwe University, PO Box 1132, Awka, Anambra State, Nigeria.

IKEMOTO Keiko, Psychiatrist; Neuroscientist; Educator. Education: MD, 1985, PhD, 1996, Shiga University of Medical Science, Otsu, Japan. Appointments: Resident, 1985-86, Assistant Professor, 1986-88, Department of Psychiatry, Visiting Assistant Professor, Department of Legal Medicine, 2001-, Shiga University of Medical Sciences, Otsu; Bousière du Government France, Department of Experimental Medicine, Claude Bernard University, Lyon, France, 1995-96; Assistant Professor, Department of Anatomy, Fujita Health University School of Medicine, Toyoake, 1997-2000; Head, Laboratory of Biochemistry, Clinical Research Institute, 2002-04; Chief, Sect Clinical Examination, National Minami Hanamaki Hospital, Japan, 2002-04; Chief, Department of Psychiatry, Taiyonokuni Hospital, Japan, 2004-; Associate Professor, Department of Neuropsychiatry, Fukushima Medical University School of Medicine, 2006-. Publications: Author, Points of Psychiatry, 1986; Research in Monoamine Neuronal Systems and Brain Research of Psychoses. Honours: Grant, Japan Society for Promotion of Science, 1998-. Memberships: Society for Neuroscience. Address: Department of Neuropsychiatry, Fuskushima Medical University School of Medicine, Fukushima 960-1295, Japan. E-mail: ikemoto@fmu.ac.jp

IKEUCHI Hiroshi, b. 5 July 1924, Japan. Orthopaedic Surgeon. m. Setsuko. Education: Graduate, Tohoku University, 1949; PhD, 1960. Appointments: Vice Chairman, 1966, Chairman, 1984, Emeritus Chairman, 1990-94, Department of Orthopaedic Surgery, Tokyo Teishin Hospital, 1949-; Resident Doctor and Fellowship Professor (under instruction of Dr David M Bosworth), Department of Orthopaedic Surgery, St Giles Hospital, Sea View Hospital, St Luke's Hospital and Policlinic Hospital, New York, USA, 1959-62; Visiting Lecturer, Tokyo University, 1974-78; Instructor, UCLA, 1978-85; Visiting Lecturer, Shinshu University, 1982-91; Visiting Professor, Kansas University, 1982. Publications include: Total Meniscectomy of Complete Discoid Lateral Meniscus under Arthroscopic Control; Arthroscopic Peripheral Repair of the Menisci. Honours: Purple Ribbon

Medal, Ministry of Science and Technology, 1972; Maejima Hisoka Prize, Tele-Communication Association, 1991; Award, Japanese Orthopaedic Association, 1991; Third Order of Merit with the Sacred Treasure, 1994. Memberships: Japanese Orthopaedic Association; Japanese Rheumatism Association; Arthroscopy Association of North America; German Speaking Association of Arthroscopy; French Arthroscopy Association; Argentina Arthroscopy Association; Ikeuchi Intern Society for Arthroscopy and Musculoskeletal Endoscopy. Address: Ozenji-nishi, 6-chome, 24-14, Asao-ku, Kawasaki-shi, Kanagawa-ken, 215-0017, Japan.

IKUTA Shigeru, b. 21 February 1949, Yamagata prefecture, Japan. Professor. m. Atsuko, 1 son, 1 daughter. Education: Bachelor's degree, Shizuoka University, Japan, 1971; Master's degree, 1973, Doctor of Science, 1976, Tohoku University, Sendai, Japan. Appointments: Postdoctoral Staff, Institute of Chemical and Physical Research, Wako, Japan, 1976-77; Researcher, 1977-83, Associate Professor, 1984-90, Professor, 1990-2005, Tokyo Metropolitan University; Postdoctoral Staff, University of Alberta, Edmonton, Canada, 1980-82; Visiting Professor, University of Sydney, Australia, 1988; Visiting Professor, City University of New York, USA, 1994; Vice President, Council for Improvement of Education through Computers, 1998-2002, 2004-; Principal, Senior High School Affiliated to Tokyo Metropolitan University, 2001-03; Professor, University of Tsukuba, 2005-08; Professor, Otsuma Women's University, 2008-; Member, Special Committee of National Institution for Academic Degrees and University Evaluation, 2006-08; Editor, High School Chemistry Textbook, Daiichi Gakushusha, 2006-. Publications: Basic Principle of Electric Computer, 1988; Introduction of Information Science, 1993; Molecular Orbital Method, 1994; Internet Activities in Chemistry, 2000; How to Learn an Information Science in Primary and Secondary Schools, 2001; 168 articles in professional journals. Memberships: Society for Information Technology & Teacher Education; Association for Computing Machinery; Japan Society for Education Technology; Council for Improvement of Education through Computers; The Chemical Society of Japan. Address: 2-38-80 Bessho, Hachioji-Shi, Tokyo 192-0363, Japan.

ILLSLEY Eric, b. 9 April 1955, Barnsley, South Yorkshire, England. Member of Parliament. m. Dawn Illsley, 2 daughters. Education: LLB, Law, University of Leeds. Appointments: Head of Administration, Yorkshire National Union of Mineworkers; Member of Parliament, Barnsley Central, 1987-; Member, Select Committee, on Energy, 1987, 1991, on Televising Proceedings of the House of Commons, 1988-91, on Procedure, 1991-; on Foreign Affairs, 1997-; Opposition Whip, 1991-94; Opposition spokesperson, on health, 1994-95, on local government, 1995, on Northern Ireland, 1995-97. Memberships: Member, Co-operative Party and MSF; Joint Chair, All Party Parliamentary Glass Committee; Treasurer, Yorkshire Labour Group of Members of Parliament; Member, Chairman's Panel; Vice Chair, Parliamentary and Scientific Committee; Vice Chair, Commonwealth Parliamentary Association UK Branch; Executive Committee Member, Inter Parliamentary Union. Address: House of Commons, London SW1A 0AA, England. E-mail: illsleye@parliament.uk

ILYUMZHINOV Kirsan Nikolayevich, b. 5 April 1962, Elista, Kalmykia. President of the Republic of Kalmykia. m. 1 son. Education: Graduate, Moscow State University for International Relations, 1989. Appointments: Elected President of the Republic of Kalmykia, 1993, re-elected, 1995, 2002-. Publications: President's Crown of Thorns (a documentary novel), 1995; Kalmykia at the turn of centuries

(research work), 1997; Kalmykia. Heading toward democracy (research work), 1998. Honour: Order of Friendship by the Decree of the Russian President, 1997. Address: House of Government, 35800 Elista, Republic of Kalmykia, Russian Federation. E-mail: 1p@kalm.ru

ILYUSHIN Michael, b. 8 June 1945, Chapaevsk Kuibyshev Region, USSR. Professor; Chemistry. m. Shugalei Irina V, 1 daughter. Education: Engineer Chemist-Technologist Diploma, Leningrad Liensovet Institute of Technology (LTI), 1969; Candidate of Chemical Sciences (PhD), LTI, 1975; Doctor of Chemical Sciences, State Institute of Technology, St Petersburg, 1995. Appointments: Engineer, 1969-72; Aspirant (post-postgraduate), 1972-75; Researcher, 1975-78; Assistant Professor, 1978-93, Associate Professor, 1993-95, Professor, 1995-. Publications: 11 papers, many on explosives, in journals or other professional publications. Honours: Medal, Inventor of the USSR, 1981; Soros Associate Professor, Russia, 1997; Award for Achievement, 1998; 20th Century Award for Achievement, 1999; International Man of the Year, 1997-98, 1999-2000; International Man of the Millennium, 1999. Membership: All-Russian Chemical Society, 1972. Address: St Petersburg State Institute of Technology (Technical University), Moskovsky pr 26, 190013, St Petersburg, Russia.

IM Hana, b. 25 August 1963, Seoul, Korea. Professor. m. Hyeong Jin Kim, 2 sons. Education: BS, Microbiology, Seoul National University, 1986; PhD, Microbiology, University of Texas at Austin, USA, 1993. Appointments: Research Associate, University of Wisconsin at Madison, USA, 1993-95; Senior Research Scientist, Korea Research Institute of Bioscience & Biotechnology, 1996-2000; Professor, 2000-, Chairman, 2005-, Department of Molecular Biology, Sejong University. Publications: Numerous articles in professional scientific journals; 3 patents. Honours: Silla Cultural Foundation Fellowship, Korea, 1984-86; Texas State Fellowship, USA, 1991; Outstanding Scholar of the Year, Daeyang Foundation, Korea, 2001; Who's Who in the World, 2005; Outstanding Publication Award, Journal of Microbiology, 2005. Memberships: Member, Protein Society, USA, 1995; Member, Korean Society of Biochemistry and Molecular Biology; Editor, Journal of Microbiology, 2002. Address: Department of Molecular Biology, Sejong University, 98 Gunja-dong, Kwangjin-gu, Seoul 143-747, Republic of Korea. E-mail: hanaim@sejong.ac.kr

IMAMURA Hiromi, b. 29 April 1959, Gifu, Japan. Professor. m. Takakazu Imamura. Education: Master of Arts, Nanzan University, Nagoya, Japan, 1984. Appointments: Professor, 2004-, Director, Department of Foreign Languages, 2007-, Chubu University, Aichi, Japan. Publications: An Invitation to Sociolinguistics, 1996; TOEIC TEST General Course, 2007; New Grade 2 STEP Test Success Course, 2007. Honours: Excellence in Teaching Award, Japan Association of College English Teachers, 1999. Memberships: TESOL; Japan Association of College English Teachers; Language Education and Technology; JALT; and others. Address: Department of Foreign Languages, Chubu University, 1200 Matsumoto-cho, Kasugai, Aichi 487-8501 Japan.

IMAN (Iman Abdul Majid), b. 25 July 1956, Model. m. (1) Spencer Haywood, divorced 1987, 1 child, (2) David Bowie, 1992, 1 daughter. Education: Nairobi University. Appointments: Fashion Model, 1976-90; Has modelled for Claude Montana and Thierry Mugler; Signed Revlon Polish Ambers Contract (1st black model to be signed by an international cosmetics co), 1979; Numerous TV appearances;

Appeared in Michael Jackson video. Creative Works: Films include: Star Trek VI: The Undiscovered Country; Houseparty II; Exit to Eden; The Deli, 1997; Omikron: The Nomad Soul, 1999. Publications: Naomi, 1996; I Am Iman, 2001; Beauty of Color: The Ultimate Beauty Guide for Skin of Color, 2006. Address: c/o Elite Model Management, 40-42 Parker Street, London WC2B 5PQ, England.

IMMELMAN Niel, b. 13 August 1944, Bloemfontein, South Africa. Pianist. Education: Royal College of Music, 1964-69; Private studies with Ilona Kabos, 1969-70, Maria Curcio, 1970-76; LRAM; ARCM; LGSM; LTCL. Career: Debut with London Philharmonic Orchestra, 1969; Concert appearances, London's Royal Festival Hall, Royal Albert Hall and Amsterdam Concertgebouw; Concert tours of every continent; Compact disc recordings for Etcetera and Meridian labels; Professor of Piano, Royal College of Music, London, 1980-; Masterclasses at Berlin Hochschule, The Chopin Academy, Warsaw and Moscow Conservatoire. Publications: Commercial recordings of Beethoven, Schubert, Schumann, Dale, Suk and Bloch; First pianist in history to record complete piano works of Josef Suk; Articles on pianists Lamar Crowson and Annie Fischer. Honours: Chappell Gold Medal, 1969; Fellow, Royal College of Music, 2000. Memberships: Royal Society of Musicians of Great Britain; EPTA. Address: 41 Ashen Grove, London, SW19 8BL, England. E-mail: immelman@lineone.net

IMYANITOV Naum Solomonovich, b. 31 December 1935, Novocherkassk, Russia. Scientist. m. Kira Rozinova, 1 son. Education: MS, 1958; PhD, 1964; DSc, 1980; Diplomas: Fine Chemical Engineering, 1958; Research Chemist, 1962; Senior Research Chemist, 1967. Appointments: Research Scientist, 1958-65; Senior Scientist, 1965-76; Department Leader, 1976-86; Chief Scientist, 1986-, VNII Neftekhim, Leningrad, St Petersburg; Project Leader, SciVision, St Petersburg, Academic Press, 1998-2000; Project Leader, MDL Information Systems, Inc, St Petersburg, 2000-; Chief Scientist, Eurochim-SPb-Trading, St Petersburg, 2003-. Publications: Author, 230 articles and patents; Editor, 2 monographs. Honours: Badge, Inventor of Czechoslovakia, 1979; Badge, Inventor of USSR, 1986; Medal, Veteran of Labour, 1988. Memberships: Mendeleev Chemical Society, 1959; World Wide Club Chemical Community, 1999. Address: ul Bryantseva 18, kv 155, 195269 St Petersburg, Russia. E-mail: naum@itcwin.com

IN Man-Jin, b. 11 October 1963, Dangjin, Chungnam, Korea. Professor. m. Ok-Joo Kim, 1 son, 1 daughter. Education: BS, 1985, MS, 1987, PhD, 1997, Seoul National University, Seoul. Appointments: Senior Researcher, Daesang Corp, Seoul, 1986-98; Research Professor, Korea Nutritional Research Institute, Korea University, 1998-99; Associate Professor, Chungwoon University, Hongseong, Korea, 1999-. Publications: Papers and articles in professional scientific journals. Honours: Young Scientist Award, Korean Society for Applied Biological Chemistry, 2006; Universal Award of Accomplishment, ABI, 2007; International Scientist of the Year, IBC, 2007. Memberships: Korean Academic Industrial Society; Korean Society of Food Science and Nutrition; Korean Food Professional Engineers; Korean Society of Microbiology and Biotechnology; Korean Society of Food Science and Technology; Korean Society of Applied Biological Chemistry. Address: Department of Human Nutrition and Food Science; Chungwoon University, San 29, Namjang-ri, Hongseong-eup, Hongseong-kun, Chungnam 350-701, Korea. E-mail: manjin@chungwoon.ac.kr

ING Bruce, b. 1 September 1937, London, England. Mycologist. m. Eleanor Scouller, 1 son, 1 daughter. Education: BA, 1960, MA, 1964, Cambridge University; MSc, St Andrews University, 1967; PhD, Liverpool University, 1979. Appointments: Assistant Organiser, Conservation Corps, 1960-64; Director, Kindrogan Field Study Centre, 1964-67; Conservation Officer, Hertfordshire and Middlesex Trust, 1967-71; Lecturer, Senior Lecturer in Biology, Chester College, 1971-94; Professor of Environmental Biology, University of Chester, 1999-. Publications: Over 200 papers on myxomycetes, fungi, ecology and conservation, 1959-; Publications in over 10 countries; The Phytosociology of Myxomycetes, 1994; The Myxomycetes of Britain and Ireland, 1999. Honours: Benefactors Medal, British Mycological Society, 1995. Memberships: Institute of Biology; Linnean Society; British Mycological Society; many other botanical, mycological and natural history societies worldwide. Address: 24 Avon Court, Mold, Flintshire, CH7 1JP, England. E-mail: bruce.ing@which.net

INGALALLI Rachappa I, b. 12 March 1948, Jodalli-Dharwad, India. Teacher; Researcher; Administrator. m. Basavanti, 2 sons. Education: BSC, 1969, MA, 1972, PhD, 1982, Karnatak University, Dharwad; DSc, Open International University, Calcutta, 2005. Appointments: Lecturer, Logic, ASM College, Bellary, Karnatak, 1972-85; Lecturer, 1985, Reader, 1985, Professor, 1994-, Department of Philosophy, Karnatak University; Chairman of Department, 1994-96, 1999-; Chairman, Board of Studies, Philosophy, 1997-99; Chairman, Board of Examinations, Philosophy, 1997-99, 2001-2002; President of Philosophy Alumni Association, 2006. Publications: Books: Testimony (s'abda-pramāna): an Epistemological Analysis, 1988; Meaning and Knowledge, 1989; Jnana Yoga, 1989; A Study in Relation of Identity, 1990; Knowledge of Action, 1992; Modern Symbolic Logic, 2000; Validity of Knowledge, 2001; God in World Religions, 2005; 80 articles in national and international journals. Honours: Karnatak University Scholar, 1970-72; University Grants Commission's Teacher Fellowship, 1977-81. Memberships: Academic Council, Faculty of Society Sciences, Board of Studies; Member of Faculty of Social Sciences, Member of University Students Welfare Board, Member of Board of University Teaching; Editorial boards of several journals; Listed in Who's Who publications. Address: Department of Philosophy, Karnatak University, Dharwad 580003, India.

INGEL Lev, b. 15 May 1946, Nizhny Tagil, USSR. Geophysicist. m. Irina Sklobovskaya, 1 daughter. Education: Graduate, Gorky State University, 1968; PhD, Institute of Experimental Meteorology, Obninsk, 1979; Dr in Physics and Mathematics, Hydrometeo Centre, Moscow, 1998. Appointments: Engineer, Institute 'Salute', Gorky, 1969-73; Engineer, Institute of Experimental Meteorology, Obninsk, 1973-75; Scientist, Senior Scientist, Institute of Experimental Meteorology, Obninsk, 1975-. Publications: More than 140 articles in scientific journals in meteorology, geophysics, hydrodynamics, astrophysics, quantum electronics. Honours: Grantee, International Science Foundation; Russian Foundation of Basic Research, 1997, 1998, 2001, 2004. Membership: Academic Board, Institute of Experimental Meteorology; Izvestia Newspaper Club, Moscow Address: Mira St 4, Flat 45, 249038 Obninsk, Kaluga Reg, Russia. E-mail: lingel@obninsk.com

INGHAM John, b. 16 February 1958, Halifax, England. Journalist. m. Christine, 1 son, 1 daughter. Education: BA (Hons), 1980, PhD, 1990, History, Durham University; MA, American Studies, Bowling Green State University,

Ohio, USA, 1981; Visiting Researcher, Georgetown University, Washington, 1982-83. Appointments: Freelance Sports Reporter, Sunday Express, 1986-89; Deputy Editor, BNFL News and Editor, Sellascene, 1984-87; Northern Correspondent, Building & Chartered Surveyor Weekly Magazines, 1987-89; News Reporter, Defence & Diplomatic Correspondent, Foreign Desk, Political Correspondent, Environment Correspondent, 1989-99, Environment, Transport & Defence Editor, 1999-2006, Daily Express. Address: Daily Express, 10 Lower Thames Street, London EC3, England. E-mail: john.ingham@express.co.uk

INGLE Stephen James, b. 6 November 1940, Ripon, Yorkshire, England. Professor Emeritus. m. Margaret Anne Farmer, 1964, 2 sons, 1 daughter. Education: BA, 1962, DipEd, 1963, MA, 1965, University of Sheffield; PhD, Victoria University, New Zealand, 1967. Appointment: Professor, University of Stirling. Publications: Socialist Thought in Imaginative Literature, 1979; Parliament and Health Policy, 1981; British Party System, 1987, 1989, 2000; George Orwell: A Political Life, 1993; British Party System (3), 2000; Narratives of British Socialism, 2002; Social and Political Thought of George Orwell: A Reassessment, 2006. Many contributions to fields of Politics and Literature. Honours: Commonwealth Scholar, 1964-67; Erasmus Scholar, 1989; Visiting Research Fellow, Victoria University, New Zealand, 1993; Opm Society Overseas Fellow, 2006-. Memberships: Political Studies Association; Society of Authors. Address: Department of Politics, University of Stirling, Stirling FK9 4LA, Scotland.

INGLIS-JONES Nigel John, b. 7 May 1935, London, England. Queen's Counsel. m. (1) Lenette Bromley-Davenport, deceased 1986, 2 sons, 2 daughters, (2) Ursula Jane Drury Culverwell, 1 son. Education: Trinity College, Oxford, 1955-58. Appointments: Subaltern, Grenadier Guards, National Service, 1953-55; Called to the Bar, 1959; Recorder of the Crown Court, 1978-93; Took Silk, 1982; Deputy Social Security Commissioner, 1993-2002; Bencher of the Inner Temple, 1981-. Publication: The Law of Occupational Pension Schemes, 1989. Honour: Queen's Counsel. Membership: MCC. Address: Outer Temple Chambers, 222 The Strand, London WC2R 1BA, England.

INGRAM David Stanley, b. 10 October 1941, Birmingham, England. Botanist; Horticulturalist; Conservationist. m. Alison, 2 sons. Education: Yardley Grammar School, Birmingham; BSc, PhD, University of Hull; MA, ScD Cantab. Appointments: Research Fellow, University of Glasgow; Senior Scientific Officer, Agricultural Research Council Unit of Developmental Botany; Lecturer, then Reader in Plant Pathology, University of Cambridge; Regius Keeper, Royal Botanic Garden, Edinburgh; Master, St Catharine's College, Cambridge. Publications: 9 books; Newspaper and magazine articles; Research papers, reviews and articles in peer-reviewed scientific and specialist journals. Honours: OBE; FIBiol, 1986; FRSE, 1993; FIHort, 1995; FRCPEd, 1998; Hon FRSGS, 1998; Hon D University, Open University, 2000; Victoria Medal of Honour, Royal Horticultural Society, 2004. Memberships: Senior Visiting Fellow, Department of Plant Sciences, University of Cambridge; Honorary Professor and Special Adviser to University of Edinburgh on the Public Understanding of Science, Engineering and Technology; Honorary Professor, Glasgow University; Honorary Fellow and Visiting Professor, Myerscough College, Lancashire; Honorary Fellow, Royal Botanic Garden, Edinburgh; Downing College and St Catharine's College, Cambridge; Worcester College, Oxford; Independent Member and Deputy

Chair, Joint Nature Conservation Committee; Senior Visiting Fellow, ESRC Genomics Forum, Edinburgh; Programme Convenor and Chairman, Steering Group on Science and Society, Royal Society of Edinburgh; Formerly Chairman, Darwin Initiative for the Survival of Species; Visiting Professor, Napier University. Address: Town End House, 56 High Street, Burton-in-Lonsdale, LA6 3JF, England.

INMAN Edward Oliver, b. 12 August 1948, Oslo, Norway. Chief Executive. 1 son, 2 daughters, 2 stepdaughters. Education: MA, Gonville and Caius College, 1969; School of Slavonic Studies, London, 1970. Appointments: Research Assistant, then Directing Staff, Imperial War Museum, London, 1972-78; Keeper, 1978-82, Director, 1982-2004, Imperial War Museum, Duxford, Cambridge; Chief Executive, South Bank Employers' Group, 2004-. Honours: Order of the British Empire, 1998; Fellow, Royal Aeronautical Society, 1999. Address: South Bank Employers' Group, 103 Waterloo Road, London SE1 8UL, England. E-mail: einman@iwm.org.uk

INNES Brian, b. 4 May 1928, Croydon, Surrey, England. Writer; Publisher. m. (1) Felicity McNair Wilson, 5 October 1956, (2) Eunice Lynch, 2 April 1971, 3 sons. Education: BSc, King's College, London, 1946-49. Appointments: Assistant Editor, Chemical Age, 1953-55; Associate Editor, The British Printer, 1955-60; Art Director, Hamlyn Group, 1960-62; Director, Temperance Seven Ltd, 1961-; Proprietor, Brian Innes Agency, 1964-66; Immediate Books, 1966-70, FOT Library, 1970-; Creative Director, Deputy Chairman, Orbis Publishing Ltd, 1970-86; Editorial Director, Mirror Publishing, 1986-88. Publications: Book of Pirates, 1966; Book of Spies, 1967; Book of Revolutions, 1967; Book of Outlaws, 1968; Flight, 1970; Saga of the Railways, 1972; Horoscopes, 1976; The Tarot, 1977; Book of Change, 1979; The Red Baron Lives, 1981; Red Red Baron, 1983; The Havana Cigar, 1983; Crooks and Conmen, 1993; Catalogue of Ghost Sightings, 1996; The History of Torture, 1998; Death and The Afterlife, 1999; Dreams, 1999; Bodies of Evidence, 2000; Profile of a Criminal Mind, 2003; The Body in Question, 2005; Fakes and Forgeries, 2005; Serial Killers, 2006. Contributions to: Encyclopaedia Britannica; Grove Dictionary of Jazz; Man, Myth & Magic; Take Off; Real Life Crimes; Fire Power; The Story of Scotland; Discover Scotland; Marshall Cavendish Encyclopaedia of Science; Numerous recordings, films, radio and television broadcasts; Many photographs published. Honour: Royal Variety Command Performance, 1961. Memberships: Chartered Society of Designers; Royal Society of Literature; Royal Society of Chemistry; Royal Society of Arts; Institute of Paper, Printing and Publishing (IP3); Crime Writers Association; British Actors' Equity; Chelsea Arts Club. Address: Les Forges de Montgaillard, 11330 Mouthoumet, France.

INOMATA Nobumichi, b. 14 November 1936, Ashio Tochigi, Japan. m. Nobuko Kuraoka, 13 June 1971, 1 son, 1 daughter. Education: BAgri, 1961; MAgri, 1963; DAgri, 1973. Appointments: Assistant, Osaka Prefectural University, 1970; Associate Professor, Okayama University 1977, Professor, Okayama University, 1982, Emeritus Professor, 1999, Okayama University; Professor, Konan Women's University, 2007. Publications: Experimental Manipulation of Ovule Tissues, 1985; Biotechnology in Agriculture and Forestry, 1990; Breeding Oilseed Brasica, 1993; Recent Advances in Oilseed Brassicas, 1997; Genetic Resources, Chromosome Engineering and Crop Improvements, Vegetable Crops, 2007. Address: 180-3 Shinogoze, Okayama City, Okayama, 703-8201, Japan.

INOUE Hiroshi, b. 14 July 1954, Kobe-shi, Japan. Mechanical Engineer; Researcher. m. Fumiyo Yoshida. Education: Bachelor's degree, 1977, Master's degree, 1979, Mechanical Engineering, Tokyo Institute of Technology. Appointments: Researcher, 1979-93, Senior Researcher, 1993-95, Mechanical Engineering Research Laboratory, Hitachi Ltd, Tsuchiura-shi, Japan; Senior Researcher, Power and Industrial Systems R&D Laboratory of Hitachi Ltd, Hitachinaka-shi, Japan, 1995-. Publications: Development of Multi Cluster burner for fuel grade dimethyl ether; Methane/Oxygen combustor for carbon dioxide recover closed-cycle gas turbine; and others. Honours: Listed in international biographical dictionaries. Memberships: Gas Turbine Society of Japan; Japan Society of Mechanical Engineers. Address: 2-2-11 Motoyama-cho, Mito-shi, Ibaraki 310-0032, Japan.

INSALL Donald William, b. 7 February 1926, Clifton, Bristol, England. Architect. m. Amy Elizabeth (Libby) Moss, 2 sons, 1 daughter. Education: RWA School of Architecture, Bristol University, Bristol; Royal Academy School of Architecture, London; School of Planning and Research for Regional Development; Lethaby Scholar, The SPAB. Appointments: Founder Director, Donald Insall Associates, Architects and Historic Building Consultants, London, Bath, Canterbury, Cambridge, Chester, Conwy, Shrewsbury, 1957-; Member, Historic Buildings Council for England, 1971-84; Founder-Commissioner, English Heritage, 1984-89. Publications: The Care of Old Buildings Today; Historic Buildings: Action to Maintain the Expertise for their Care and Repair, Council of Europe; Chester: A Study in Conservation; Contributor: Encyclopaedia Britannica and numerous technical journals; Arts Council Film: Buildings: Who Cares? Honours: Queen's Silver Jubilee Medal, 1977; OBE, 1981; CBE, 1995; Honorary LLD, 2004; Honorary Freeman of the City of Chester; Europa Nostra Medal of Honour; Harley J McKee Award, Association for Preservation Technology, International; Plowden Medal, Royal Warrant Holders' Association. Memberships include: Fellow, RIBA; Fellow (Rtd), RTPI; Fellow, Society of Antiquaries of London; Academician, Royal West of England Academy; Liveryman, Worshipful Company of Goldsmiths; Member, Europa Nostra; Member of Committees, European Union; Council Member, ICOMOS, UK; UK Committee, World Monuments Fund; Past and present Member of Fabric Committees, Westminster Abbey, Canterbury and Southwark Cathedrals; Vice-president, City of Winchester Trust; Honorary Life Member, Bath Preservation Trust; Patron; Kew Society, Environmental Trust for Richmond upon Thames, Bedford Park Society; Fellow, Royal Society of Arts; Rolls Royce Enthusiasts' Club; The Athenaeum. Address: Donald Insall Associates, 19 West Eaton Place, London SW1X 8LT, England. E-mail: donald.insall@insall-lon.co.uk

INSAROV Gregory E, b. 14 November 1948, Moscow, USSR. Ecologist. m. Irina D, 1 daughter. Education: MS, Mathematics, Moscow State University, USSR, 1970; PhD, Biology, Moscow State Forestry University, Moscow, USSR, 1975; Junior Research Scientist, 1976-77, Senior Research Scientist, 1978-79, Institute of Applied Geophysics, Moscow, USSR; Senior Research Scientist, Natural Environment and Climate Monitoring Laboratory, Moscow, USSR/Russia, 1979-91; Leading Research Scientist, Institute of Global Climate and Ecology, Moscow, Russia, 1991-. Publications: Over 100 publications as author or co-author; Books: Mathematical methods in forest protection, 1980; Effects of SO_2 on plants, 1984; Quantitative characteristics of the state of epiphytic lichenflora of biosphere reserves. The Zakatal reserve, 1987; Numerous book chapters, articles in scientific journals and conference proceedings include most recently: Assessment of lichen sensitivity to climate change, 1996; Computer-aided multi-access key IDENT for identification of the Negev lichens, 1997; A system to monitor climate change with epilithic lichens, 1999; Long term monitoring of lichen communities response to climate change and diversity of lichens in the Central Negev Highlands, Israel, 2001; Lichen Monitoring and Global Change, 2002; Towards an Early Warning System for Global Change, 2004. Honours: Expedition leader, former USSR and Sweden, co-ordinated and guided expeditions to remote protected areas with emphasis on lichen monitoring, 1978-92; Editorial Board, Series Problems of Ecological Monitoring and Ecosystem Modelling, 1987-; Visiting Professor, University of Arkansas at Monticello, USA, 1990; Research Associate, Swedish Environmental Protection Agency, Sweden, 1991-92; Research Associate, Ben-Gurion University of the Negev, Israel 1993-97; Marie Curie Experienced Fellow, University of Evora, Portugal, 1997; Leading Research Scientist, Institute of Geography of the Russian Academy of Sciences, Moscow, Russia, 1998-; Director, NATO Advanced Research Workshop on Lichen Monitoring, Wales UK, 2000; Expert, Intergovernmental Panel on Climate Change, 2001-; Research Fellow, Acid Deposition and Oxidant Research Center, Japan, 2004; Network of Soil and Vegetation Monitoring Specialists of the Acid Deposition Monitoring Network in East Asia, 2004-; Project Leader, Air Quality Management in Moscow and London, 2006-07; Listed in national and international biographical directories. Memberships: Moscow Society of Naturalists, 1972-; British Lichen Society, 1993-; American Association for the Advancement of Science, 1997-98; American Bryological and Lichenological Society, 1998-; European Association for the Science of Air Pollution, 2001-; Russian National Committee on Human Dimensions on Global Environmental Change, 2004; Nordic Lichen Society, 2005-. Address: Institute of Global Climate and Ecology, Glebovskaya 20B, Moscow 107258, Russia. E-mail: insarov@lichenfield.com

IOSEBASHVILI Alexander, b. 26 January 1965, City of Tbilisi, Georgia, USSR. Scientist. Education: Doctor of Science, 1991; Scientific Diploma, 1993; Professor, 1993. Appointments: Scientist; Researcher; Philosopher; Psychologist; Applied Mathematician; Lawyer; Medical Reformer; Medical Student; Fraud and Corruption Investigator. Publications include: Physico-cosmological works on Psychology, Politics and Ethics; An Alternative of the Criticism of the Science admitting Psychoanalisis; Albert Einstein and Mendelev and his Periodical Table of Chemical Element for Myth? Honours include: Noble Prize, 2002; American Medal of Honor, 2002, 2003, 2004, 2006, 2007; International Peace Prize, 2004, 2006; The World Order of Science-Education-Culture, 2002, 2005. Memberships: Smithsonian; American Association for the Advancement of Science; New York Academy of Sciences; Academy of Political Science; American Psychological Society; National Geographic Society; American Institute of Chemical Engineers; American Museum of Natural History; The Mathematical Association of America; American Chemical Society; American Bar Association; London Diplomatic Academy. Address: 99-05, 63rd Dr Apt 9-V, Rego-Park, NY 11374, USA.

IP David, b. 21 August 1960, Hong Kong. Orthopaedic Surgeon. m. Fu Nga Yue. Education: Graduate, Hong Kong University Medical School, 1985; Fellow Royal College of Surgeons of Edinburgh, 1999; Fellow, Hong Kong College of Orthopaedic Surgeons. Publications: Numerous articles in scientific journals as chief author include: Comparison of

DICTIONARY OF INTERNATIONAL BIOGRAPHY

two total knee prostheses on the incidence of patella clunk syndrome; Management of forearm deformities in multiple exostoses; Early results of nexgen total knee anthroplasty; Sequential Hip Fragility Fractures in the Elderly; Premature fixation failure of distal fixation screws of IC nail; Rare complications of segmental medullary tube breakage of intramedullary nailing; Orthopaedic Principles – A Resident's Guide, 2005; Orthopaedic Traumatology – A Resident's Guide, 2006; Orthopaedic Rehabilitation, Assessment and Enablement, 2007. Honours: Lifetime Achievement Award, IBC; Deputy Director General, IBC; Scientific Advisor, IBC; Member, Order of International Fellowship; International Healthcare Professional of the Year Award, 2004; IBC Award of Biographical Recognition; Order of Distinction, IBC; Member, Order of Ambassadors, ABI; Winner of the Universal Award for Achievement for the Year 2004, ABI; Universal Award of Accomplishment, ABI; Outstanding Professional Award, ABI; IBC Award of Biographical Recognition; Key Award, Leader in Science, ABI; International Peace Prize, United Cultural Convention, USA; Scientific Advisor, ABI; Deputy Governor, ABI Research Association; American Medal of Honor, IBA; Elected Fellow of American Biographical Institute Listed in Who's Who publications and biographical dictionaries including: Who's Who in the World; Great Minds of the 21st Century; 2000 Intellectuals of the 21st Century; Leading Intellectuals of the 21st Century; The Cambridge Blue Book; Who's Who in Science and Engineering. Memberships: Royal College of Surgeons of Edinburgh; Life Fellow, IBC; World Peace and Diplomacy Forum; Hong Kong College of Orthopaedic Surgeons; Overseas Member, American Association of Orthopaedic Surgeons; Fellow, American Biographical Institute. Address: 3B Highland Mansion, Cleveland Street, Causeway Bay, Hong Kong. E-mail: ipd8686@pacific.net.hk

IPATOV Sergei Ivanovich, b. 10 November 1952, Moscow, Russia. Applied Mathematician in Astronomy. m. Valentina Ipatova (Artioukhova), 1 son. Education: Moscow State University, Department of Mechanics and Mathematics, 1970-75; PhD (Kandidat of Physical and Mathematical Sciences), 1982; Doctor of Physical and Mathematical Sciences, 1997. Appointments: From Probationer Investigator to Leading Scientist, Keldysh Institute of Applied Mathematics of Russian Academy of Sciences, Moscow, 1975-2003; Lecturer, Moscow State University, 1998; Visiting USA via NASA grant, July 2001- April 2002; NRC Senior Research Associate in NASA Goddard Space Flight Centre, May 2002-April 2003; Visiting Senior Research Associate, George Mason University, May 2003-April 2004; Research Associate, Catholic University of America, 2004; Research Associate, University of Maryland, 2005-06; Visiting Scientist, Department of Terrestrial Magnetism of Carnegie Institution of Washington, 2006-. Publications: Published over 240 scientific works including papers in international, Soviet and Russian journals, and the book: Migration of Celestial Bodies in the Solar System, (in Russian), 2000. Honours: Asteroid 14360 Ipatov; Medals: Outstanding People of the 20th Century, 2000 Outstanding Scientists of the 20th Century, 2000 Outstanding Intellectuals of the 21st Century, 2000 Outstanding Scientists of the 21st Century, One Thousand Great Intellectuals, International Scientist of the Year, International Biographical Centre, Cambridge, England, 1998, 2002 and 2003; Medal of Honor, 1999, Leading Intellectuals of the World, 2002, American Medal of Honor, 2003, American Biographical Institute; Various grants. Memberships: European Astronomical Society, 1995-; Euro-Asian Astronomical Society, 1995-; New York Academy of Sciences, 1995-96, 2004-; Associate, Committee

on Space Research, 1996-; Russian Academy of Natural Sciences, 2000-; Russian Academy of Sciences and Arts, 2000-; American Astronomical Society, 2002-; International Astronomical Union, 2003-; American Geophysical Union, 2006-; Member, Editorial Board of the Journal, Solar System Research, 2003-. E-mail: siipatov@hotmail.com Website: http://www.dtm.ciw.edu/ipatov

IQBAL Bahar, b. 1 September 1960, Jessore, Bangladesh. Writer. m. Shobnom, 2 daughters. Education: Graduate. Appointments: Author, 1987-. Publications: Takhon Ami Shazade; Laile Moznu; Alor Vobona Andokar. Honours: Local and national awards. Memberships: Jhikorgacha Press Club; many other organisations. Address: Jhikorgacha 7420, Parbazar, Jessore, Bangladesh.

IRONS Jeremy, b. 19 September 1948, Isle of Wight, England. Actor. m. (2) Sinead Cusack, 1978, 2 sons. Creative Works: TV appearances include: Notorious Woman; Love for Lydia; Langrishe Go Down; Voysey Inheritance; Brideshead Revisited; The Captain's Doll; Tales From Hollywood, 1991; Longtitude 2000; Films: Nijinsky, The French Lieutenant's Woman, 1980; Moonlighting, 1981; Betrayal, 1982; The Wild Duck, Swann in Love, 1983; The Mission, 1986; A Chorus of Disapproval, Dead Ringers, 1988; Australia, Danny, The Champion of the World, 1989; Reversal of Fortune, 1990; Kafka, Damage, 1991; Waterland, 1992; M. Butterfly, House of the Spirits, 1994; Die Hard with a Vengeance, 1995; Stealing Beauty, Lolita, 1996; The Man in the Iron Mask, 1997; Chinese Box, 1998; Dungeons and Dragons, 2000; The Time Machine, 2001; Callas Forever, 2002; The Merchant of Venice, Being Julia, 2004; Kingdom of Heaven, Casanova, 2005; Inland Empire, Eragon, 2006. Stage appearances: The Real Thing, Broadway, 1984; Rover, The Winter's Tale, Richard II, Stratford, 1986. Honours include: NY Critics Best Actor Award, 1988; Academy Award, 1991; Tony Award; European Film Academy Special Achievement Award, 1998. Address: c/o Hutton Management, 4 Old Manor Close, Askett, Buckinghamshire HP27 9NA, England.

IRONSIDE 2nd Baron, Edmund Oslac Ironside, b. 21 September 1924, Camberley, Surrey, England. Businessman. m. Audrey Marigold Morgan-Grenville, 1 son, 1 daughter. Education: Tonbridge School. Appointments: Lieutenant Royal Navy, 1943-52; Marconi Co, 1952-59; English Electric Leo Computers, 1959-64; International research and Development Co Ltd, 1968-84; NEI plc, 1984-89; Defence Consultant, Rolls Royce IPG, 1989-95. Publication: Book: Highroad to Command, 1972. Honours: Honorary FCGI, 1986; Member of Court of Assistants, Worshipful Company of Skinners, Master, 1981-82; Honorary Fellow, City and Guilds Institute (Hon FCGI). Memberships: Organising Committee, British Library, 1972-74, Select Committee European Communities, 1974-90; Chairman, Science Reference Library Advisory Committee, 1975-85; President: Electric Vehicle Association of Great Britain, 1975-83, European Electric Road Vehicle Association, 1980-82, Sea Cadet Corps, Chelmsford, 1959-88; Vice-President: Institute of Patentees and Inventors, 1976-90, Parliamentary and Scientific Committee, 1977-80, 1983-86; Treasurer, All Party Energy Studies Group, 1979-92; Honorary Secretary, 1992-94, Chairman 1994-2000, All-Party Defence Study Group; Privy Council Member of Court, City University, 1971-96 and Council, 1987-89; Court, University of Essex, 1982; Club: Royal Ocean Racing. Address: Priory House, Old House Lane, Boxted, Colchester, Essex CO4 5RB, England.

IRVIN Albert, b. 21 August 1922, London, England. Artist. m. Beatrice Nicolson, 2 daughters. Education: Northampton School of Art, 1940-41; Navigator, Royal Air Force, 1944-46; Goldsmiths College, University of London, 1946-50. Career: Teacher, Goldsmiths College, 1962-83; Solo exhibitions include: New Art Centre, London, regularly during 1960's and 70's; Gimpel Fils Gallery, London, regularly since 1982; Aberdeen Art Gallery, 1976, 1983; Third Eye Centre, Glasgow, 1983; Ikon Gallery, Birmingham, 1983; Talbot Rice Gallery, Edinburgh, 1989; Spacex Gallery, Exeter, 1990; Serpentine Gallery, London, 1990; Welsh Arts Council, Cardiff, 1990; Royal Hibernian Academy, Dublin, 1995; Centre d'Art Contemporain, Meymac, France, 1998; Royal West of England Academy, 1999; Storey Gallery, Lancaster and Scott Gallery, Lancaster University, 2003; Peppercanister Gallery, Dublin 2003, 2006; Gimpel Fils Gallery, London, 2004, 2007; Advanced Graphics Gallery, London, 2002, 2005; Galleries and museums in USA, Australia, Austria, Germany, France, Belgium, Spain, Dubai, Finland, Ireland, Italy, Saudi Arabia, Sweden, Switzerland; Works in public collections including Tate Gallery, Royal Academy, Victoria and Albert Museum, Arts Council, British Council and in public collections internationally; Commissions include: Painting for Homerton Hospital, Hackney, 1987; Design for Diversions Dance Company, 1994; Painting for Chelsea and Westminster Hospital, 1996. Publications: Albert Irvin: Life to Painting by Paul Moorhouse, 1998; Television: A Feeling for Paint, BBC2, 1983; Off the Wall: The Byker Show, BBC2 1994; Albert Irvin: Artist At Work, Artsworld, 2000; Albert Irvin: Portrait, Injam, Paris, 2001; Radio: Interview with Joan Bakewell, BBC Radio 3, 1990; Private Passions interview with Humphrey Berkeley, BBC Radio 3, 2001. Honours: Arts Council Awards, 1968, 1975, 1980; Prize Winner, John Moores Liverpool Exhibition, 1982; Gulbenkian Award for Printmaking, 1983; Giles Bequest Award, Victoria and Albert and British Museum, 1986; Korn/Ferry Award, Royal Academy, 1989; Honorary Fellow, Goldsmiths College, 2002; Listed in Who's Who publications and biographical dictionaries. Memberships: London Group, 1985-2006; Royal Academician, 1998, Honorary Member, Royal West of England Academy, 2000. Address: 19 Gorst Road, London SW11 6JB, England.

IRVINE Robin Francis, b. 10 February 1950, Wales. Professor of Molecular Pharmacology. m. Sandra Jane, 2 sons. Education: MA, BA (Hons), Biochemistry, St Catherine's College, Oxford, 1972; PhD, Agricultural Research Council Unit of Developmental Botany, Cambridge, 1976. Appointments: Beit Memorial Fellow, 1975-78, Higher Scientific Officer, 1978, Senior Scientific Officer, 1980, Principal Scientific Officer, 1983, Senior Principal Scientific Officer (UG6), 1987, Deputy Chief Scientific Officer (UG5) and Head of Development and Signalling, 1993-95, AFRC Institute of Animal Physiology, Babraham, Cambridge; Royal Society Research Professor of Molecular Pharmacology, Department of Pharmacology, University of Cambridge. Publications: Over 150 papers as author, co-author and first author published in refereed journals include: Back in the water: the return of the insitol phosphates, 2001; Inositol lipids are regulated during cell cycle progression in the nuclei of murine erythroleukaemia cells, 2001; Inositol 1,4,5-triphosphate 3-kinase A associates with F-actin and dendritic spines via its N terminus, 2001; Type IIα phosphatidylinositol phosphate kinase associates with the plasma membrane via interaction with type I isoforms, 2002. Honours: Pfizer Academic Award, 1988; Transoceanic Lecturer, The Endocrine Society, USA, 1989; FEBS Lecturer, 1993; FRS, 1993; Morton Lecturer, Biochemical Society, 1993; FIBiol, 1998; FMedSci (Founding Fellow), 1998.

Memberships: Editorial Boards: Cellular Signalling, 1989-, Current Biology, 1994, Cell, 1996, Molecular Pharmacology, 2000-; Chairman, Molecular and Cellular Pharmacology Group 1999-, Council Member, 1999-, Biochemical Society; Royal Society Council, 1999-2001; Royal Society Research Fellowships Committee, 2000-. Address: Department of Pharmacology, University of Cambridge, Tennis Court Road, Cambridge CB2 1PD, England. E-mail: rfi20@cam.ac.uk

IRVING Amy, b. 10 September 1953, Palo Alto, California, USA. Actress. m. Steven Spielberg, 1985, divorced, 1 son, 1 son by Bruno Barreto. Education: American Conservatory Theater and London Academy of Dramatic Art. Career: Plays: Romeo and Juliet, 1982-83; Amadeus, 1981-82; Heartbreak House, 1983-84; The Road to Mecca, 1988; Films: Carrie; The Fury; Voices; Honeysuckle Road; The Competition; Yentl; Mickey and Maude; Rumpelstiltskin; Crossing Delancey; A Show of Force; Benefit of the Doubt; Kleptomania; Acts of Love; I'm Not Rappaport; Carried Away; Deconstructing Harry; One Tough Cop, 1998; Blue Ridge Fall, 1999; The Confession; The Rage: Carrie 2, 1999; Traffic, 2000; Bossa Nova, 2000; Thirteen; Conversations About One Thing, 2002; Tuck Everlasting, 2002; Hide and Seek, 2005.

ISAAC Luc Jean-Marie Michel Ghislain, b. 15 August 1954, Jemappes, Belgium. Professor. Divorced, 4 sons. Education: Doctor in Philosophy and Letters, Romance Philology, Catholic University of Louvain, Belgium, 1981; Equivalent State's Doctorate, France, 1990. Appointments: Assistant, Catholic University of Louvain, Belgium, 1976-83; Associated Master Assistant, University of Nancy II, France, 1983-84; Substitute Professor, University of Antwerp, Belgium, 1987-89; Associated Master of Conferences, University of Limoges, France, 1989-90; Professor of Linguistics, University of Bretagne Occidentale, Brest, France, 1990-. Publications: Calcul de la flexion verbale en français contemporain, 1985; Règles d'orthographe dialectale du Borinage, de Mons et des environs, mises au point par la Commission dialectale de Jemappes, 1985; Linguistica Perennis, in Apples of Gold. Mélanges en mémoire de Daniel Le Gall, 2000. Honours: Lauréat du concours universitaire, 1976, Lauréat du concours pour l'attribution des bourses de voyage, 1982, Ministère de l'Education Nationale et de la Culture Française, Belgium; Lifetime Achievement Award (World Congress of Arts, Science and Communications), 2006; Universal Award of Accomplishment (ABI), 2006; International Educator of the Year 2006 (IBC); Listed in Who's Who publications and biographical dictionaries. Memberships: Member of the Order of International Fellowship; International Order of Merit; Order of International Ambassadors. Address: Université de Bretagne Occidentale, 20 rue Duquesne, CS 93837, F-29238 Brest, Cedex 3, France. E-mail: luc.isaac@univ-brest.fr

ISAACS Jeremy Israel, Sir, b. 28 September 1932. Arts Administrator. m. (1) Tamara Weinreich, 1958, 1 son, 1 daughter, (2) Gillian Widdicombe, 1988. Education: Glasgow Academy; Merton College, Oxford. Appointments: TV Producer, Granada TV, 1958, Associated Rediffusion, 1963, BBC TV, 1965; Controller of Features, Associated Rediffusion, 1967; Thames TV, 1968-78; Producer, The World at War, 1974, Cold War, 1998; Director of Programmes, 1974-78; Special Independent Consultant, TV Series, Hollywood ITV, A Sense of Freedom, ITV Ireland, TV Documentary, BBC, Battle for Crete, NZ TV, Cold War, Turner Broadcasting; CEO, Channel 4 TV Co, 1981-88; General Director, Royal Opera House, 1988-96 (director 1985-97); Chief Executive, Jeremy Isaacs Productions, 1998-. Publications: Storm Over Four: A Personal Account, 1989; Cold War, 1999; Never

Mind the Moon, 1999. Honours include: Desmond Davis Award, Outstanding Creative Contribution to TV, 1972; George Polk Memorial Award, 1973; Cyril Bennett Award, 1982; Lord Willis Award, Distinguished Service to TV, 1985. Memberships include: British Film Institute; Fellow, Royal TV Society, 1978.

ISAYEV Avraam, b. 17 October 1942, Privolnoe, Azerbaijan. Engineer; Educator. m. Lubov M Dadasheva, 1 daughter. Education: MSChemE Azerbaijan Institute of Oil and Chemistry, Baku, 1964; PhD, Polymer Engineering, Russian Academy of Sciences, Moscow, 1970; MS, Applied Mathematics, Institute of Electronic Machine Building, Moscow, 1975. Appointments: Research Associate, State Research Institute of Nitrogen Industries, Severodonetsk, Russia, 1965-66; Predoctoral, Institute of Petrochemical Synthesis, Russian Academy of Sciences, Moscow, 1967-69; Research Associate, 1970-76; Senior Research Fellow, Israel Institute of Technology, Haifa, 1977-78; Senior Research Associate, Cornell University, Ithaca, New York, 1979-83; Associate Professor, Institute of Polymer Engineering, 1983-87, Professor, 1987-2000, Director, Moulding Technology, 1987-, Distinguished Professor, 2001-, University of Akron, Ohio; Visiting Professor, several universities and institutions. Publications: Numerous articles in professional journals; Books and encyclopaedias; 1 monograph; Edited 4 books. Honours include: Distinguished Corporation Inventor, American Society of Patent Holders, 1995; Silver Medal, Institute of Materials, London, 1997; Melvin Mooney Distinguished Technology Award, Rubber Division, American Chemical Society, 1999; OMNOVA Solutions University Signature Award, 2000 and 2002; Vinogradov Prize, GV Vinogradov Society of Rheology, Moscow, 2000; Fellow, Society of Plastic Engineers, 2008. Memberships: American Chemical Society; New York Academy of Sciences; Society of Plastic Engineers; Polymer Processing Society; Society of Rheology. Address: University of Akron, Institute of Polymer Engineering, 250 South Forge Street, Akron, OH 44325-0301, USA.

ISHIHARA Shintaro, b. 30 September 1932, Kobe, Japan. Politician; Author. m. Noriko, 4 sons. Education: Law Graduate, Hitotsubashi University, Tokyo, Japan. Appointments: Member, House of Councilors, 1968-72; Member, House of Representatives, 1972-95; Director-General, Environment Agency, 1976-77; Minister of Transport, 1987-88; Candidate, Liberal Democratic Party, Presidential Election, 1988; Governor of Tokyo, (currently serving third term), 1999-. Publications: The Season of the Sun, (Akutagawa Prize for Literature, 1956); The Forest of Fossils; The Japan that Can Say "No"; The State Becomes An Illusion; Undercurrents – Episodes from a Life on the Edge; Victorious Japan. Honours: Akutagawa prize, 1956. Memberships: Member, Selection Committee for Akutagawa Prize, 1995. Address: Tokyo Metropolitan Government, 2-8-1, Nishi-Shinjuku, Shinjuku-ku, Tokyo 163-8001, Japan. E-mail: S0000573@section.metro.tokyo.jp

ISHIKAWA Seiichi, b. 25 April 1950, Kitakyushu-city, Fukuoka, Japan. Environmentalist; Educator. Education: BS, Engineering, Kyushu Institute of Technology, Japan, 1973. Appointments: Economical Bureau of Kitakyushu-city, 1973-77; Institute of Environmental and Health Sciences, Kitakyushu-city, 1977-93; Sewage Bureau, Kitakyushu-city, 1993-99; Institute of Environmental Sciences, Kitakyushu-city, 1999-2006; University of Kitakyushu, 2006-. Honours: Paper Prize, Japanese Society of Water Environment, 1985; Eng D, Kyushu University, 1992; Iki-Iki Sewage Prize, Ministry of

Construction in Japan, 1997; Prize, Association of Prefectoral and Municipal Environmental Institute, 2002. Memberships: Japan Society of Waste Management Experts; Japanese Society of Water Environment; Society of Environmental Science, Japan. Address: Makiyama, 2-12-405, Tobata-ku, Kitakyushu-city, Fukuoka, 804-0053, Japan. E-mail: ishikawa@env.kitakyu-u.ac.jp

ISLAM Rafiqul, b. 31 March 1956, Bangladesh. University Professor. Education: MSc, Petro-Chemical Engineering & Technology, Azerbaijan Institute of Petroleum & Chemistry, 1980; PhD, Chemical Engineering, Azerbaijan Institute of Petro-Chemical Processes Academy of Sciences, 1985. Appointments: Process Engineer, Eastern Refinery Ltd, 1981; Scientist, Central Research Laboratory, Baku Petroleum Refinery, 1982-86; Engineer, Process Design, Bangladesh Chemical Industries Corporation (Chittagong Urea Fertilizer Ltd), 1986-87; Assistant Professor, 1987, Associate Professor, 1992, and Professor, 1997, Chairman, 2004-07, Department of Applied Chemistry & Chemical Technology, University of Dhaka. Publications: Around 50 articles in national and international journals. Honours: Winner, Moscow Olympiad of Young Scientists; Marie Curie Bursary, Commission of the European Communities; Great Wall Award, State Education Commission of China and UNESCO; Alexander von Humboldt Post-Doctoral Fellowship; Europe Research Fellowship; Commonwealth Academic Staff Fellowship; Listed in international biographical dictionaries. Memberships: Environment Study Centre, Bangladesh; Bangladesh Chemical Society; Bangladesh Association for the Advancement of Science; Asiatic Society of Bangladesh; Institution of Engineers, Bangladesh; Association of Humboldt Fellows Bangladesh; Bangladesh Society of Pharmaceutical Chemists. Address: Department of Applied Chemistry & Chemical Technology, University of Dhaka, Dhaka 1000, Bangladesh.

ISMAIL Michael, b. 26 February 1964, Hong Kong. Corporate Management. m. Catherine. Education: BEng (Hons); MBA. Appointments: Senior Administrative Officer; Senior Branch Manager, 2002; Head of Management Services, 2006-; Publications: Study of Ports: Planning, Design, Operation. Honours: Awarded CFPcm; FChFP; CIAM; FLMI; ACS; AIAA; Various company awards. Membership: MIET; MIEEE; LUA, Full Member; GAMA, Full Member; IFPAS, Associate; HKSI. Address: PO Box 10821, General Post Office, Hong Kong. E-mail: mmismai@attglobal.net

ISMAILOV Tagir Abdurashidovich, 5 December 1953, Ikhrek, Rutulsky District, Republic of Daghestan. Physicist. m. Gulnara Magomedovna, 1 son, 2 daughters. Education: Honours Degree, Daghestan State University, 1975; Candidate of Technology, 1982, Doctor of Technology, 1992, Leningrad Technological Institute of Refrigeration Industry. Appointments: Junior Researcher, 1975-76, Senior Scientist, 1976-79, Assistant Lecturer, 1983-85, Senior Lecturer, 1985-88, Associate Professor, 1988-89, Head, Department of Theoretical and General Electrotechnology, 1989-90, Dean, Faculty of Informatics and Management and Professor, 1993-97, Pro-rector of Informatization, Dean of Faculty of Informatics and Management, Professor, 1997-2000, Pro-rector of Studies, Professor, 2000-01, 1st Pro-rector, Professor, 2001-02, Rector, Daghestan State Technical University (Daghestan State Polytechnic Institute before 1995), 2002-08; Chairman, Rectors Council of Higher Education Institutions, Republic of Daghestan, 2007-08. Publications: 679 publications; 92 inventions with patents. Honours: 2 Letters of Commendation, Presidium of the Supreme Soviet of the Republic of Daghestan; Prize winner,

Komsomol Committee, Republic of Daghestan; Honoured Inventor, Republic of Daghestan; Honoured Science Worker, Russian Federation; Honorary Worker of Higher Professional Education, Russian Federation; State Prize, Republic of Daghestan, 2003; Rector of the Year, Russian Federation, 2004 and 2005; Order of Saint Sofia, Oxford, England; Order of Zvezda Otechestva; Order of Honour, Russian Federation. Memberships: International Academy of Refrigeration; International New York Academy of Sciences; International Academy of Informatization; International Academy of Open Education; Deputy of People's Assembly of the Republic of Daghestan. Address: 70 Imam Shamil Avenue, Makhachkala, 367015, Republic of Daghestan. E-mail: dstu@dstu.ru Website: www.dstu.ru

ISOKRARI Ebenezer, b. 7 May 1955, Buguma, Rivers State, Nigeria. Business. m. Rossanah Fanty, 3 sons, 6 daughters. Education: BSc, Political Science, 1977. Appointments: Member, Rivers State Advisory Council; National Chairman, Rivers State. Publications: Numerous articles in professional journals. Honours: Several awards for outstanding service to humanity; 24 chieftancy titles including Ochiariri of Isiokpo and Odozi Obodo of Ozalla. Memberships: Several clubs. Address: No 1 Elelenwon St, Port Harcourt, Nigeria. E-mail: ebednezarisokrari@yahoo.com

ITO Atsuko, b. 7 July 1933, Tokyo, Japan. Professor Emeritus. Education: BSc, Ochanomizu University, 1956; MSc, 1959, DSc, 1962, University of Tokyo, Japan. Appointments: Assistant, University of Tokyo, 1963-68; Assistant Professor, 1968-77, Professor, 1977-99, Retired, 1999, Ochanomizu University; Research Adviser, RIKEN. Publications: 170 papers published in scientific journals. Memberships: Physical Society of Japan, 1958-; Council for University Chartering and School Juridical Person, 1993-2000; University Council Subcommittee on organisation and management, 1993-99; Educational Personnel Training Council, 1993-95; Geodesy Council, 1994-2000; Research Advisor, RIKEN, 1999-; University Administrative Council, Yamanashi University, 2000-04; Textbook Authorisation Council, 2001-02;IIAS Fellow, International Institute for Advanced Studies, 2003-; Committee Member, Administrative Council, Akita University, 2006-08. Address: Iwasaki Advanced Meson Science Laboratory, Nishina Center, RIKEN, Hirosawa 2-1, Wako-Shi, Saitama 351-0198, Japan.

ITOH Chiaki, b. 4 February 1939, Akita, Japan. Professor. m. Katsuko, 1 son, 1 daughter. Education: PhD, Tokyo University of Education, 1966. Appointments: Lecturer, Meiji Gakuin University, Tokyo, 1968-71; Assistant Professor, 1971-78; Professor, 1978-2007; Professor Emeritus, 2007-. Publications: Unified Gauge Theory of Weak Electromagnetic and Strong Interactions, 1973. Honours: International Man of the Year, IBC, 1994-95; Most Admired Man of the Decade, ABI, 1995; The International Order of Merit, IBC, 1996. Memberships: The American Physical Society. Address: Department of Physics, Meiji Gakuin University, 1518 Kamikuratacho, Totsuka, Yokohama 244-8539, Japan. Website: http://www.meijigakuin.ac.jp/~citoh/eng.htm

ITOH Katsu, b. 20 March 1938, Nishikata-Mura, Fukushima, Japan. Artist; Painter. m. Jacqueline Ito. Education: Studied Painting under Master Kakuichi Ichikawa, Osaka, 1956-61; Studied at the School of Drawing, Osaka, 1958-60; Studies at the Alliance Française, Paris, 1970-71; Studied at the Ateliers des Beaux Arts, Montparnasse, Paris, 1972-73; Studied Printmaking under Stanley W Hayter, Atelier-17, Paris 1974-76. Career: Currently living and painting in Paris.

Publications: Works included in various publications which include: Arts Critic, by R Bouillot, 1982; Profils Arts, by C Dorval, 1987; Portraits d'Artists, 1998; Dictionary Editions Alba, Italy, 1999; Les Artistes de l'An 2000, 1999; La Vigne et le Vin, 2001. Honours: Prize of Karl Beule, Institute in France, Academy of Fine Arts in France, 1971; Salon Figuration Critique, Guest of Honour, Paris La Défense, France, 1989. Address: 695-0017, 603-29 Waki-Cho, Gotsu-Shi, Shimane-ken, Japan. E-mail: contact@drouot-cotation.org

IVANISEVIC Goran, b. 13 September 1971, Split, Croatia. Former Professional Tennis Player. Appointments: Winner, US Open Junior Doubles with Nargiso, 1987; Turned Professional, 1988; Joined Yugoslav Davis Cup Squad, 1988; Runner-up, Wimbledon Championship, 1992, 1994, 1998; Semi-Finalist, ATP World Championship, 1992; Winner, numerous ATP tournaments, include Kremlin Cup, Moscow, 1996; Winner, Wimbledon Championship, 2001; Winner, 22 tours singles and 9 doubles titles to date; Retired, 2004. Honours include: Bronze Medal, Men's Doubles, Barcelona Olympic Games, 1992; BBC Overseas Sports Personality of the Year Award, 2001. Membership: President, Children in Need Foundation, 1995. Website: www.goranivanisevic.com

IVANOV Victor Petrovich, b. 12 May 1950, Novgorod, Russia. Deputy Head of Administration of the President of the Russian Federation. m. 1 son, 1 daughter. Education: Graduate, Leningrad Professor M. Bonch-Bruyevich Electrical Engineering Institute of Communications, 1974; Served in Soviet Army, 1974-75; Engineer, Leningrad Scientific-Production Association "Vector", 1975-77; Served in State Security Bodies, Specialisation - fight against organised crime, 1977-; Head, Directorate of Administrative Bodies, St Petersburg Mayor's Office, 1994-96; Director General, Teleplus Television Company, 1996-98; Head of Directorate, Federal Security Service of the Russian Federation, 1998-99; Deputy Director, Head of Department of Economic Security, Federal Security Service of the Russian Federation, 1999-2000; Deputy Head of Administration of the President of the Russian Federation, 2000-04; Adviser to the President, 2004-. Honours: Order "For Merits to the Motherland" 4th class; Order of Honour; Medal "For Merits in Combat". Address: Administration of President of Russian Federation, Staraya pl 4, 103132 Moscow, Russia.

IVES Kenneth James, b. 29 November 1926, St Pancras, London, England. Civil Engineer. m. Brenda Grace Tilley, 1 son, 1 daughter. Education: BSc, Engineering, 1948, PhD, 1955, DSc, Engineering, 1967, University College London. Appointments: Junior Engineer, Metropolitan Water Board, London, 1948-55; Lecturer, Reader, Professor of Civil Engineering, 1955-92, Emeritus Professor, 1992-, University College London; Postdoctoral Fellow, Harvard University, USA, 1958-59; Visiting Professor, University of North Carolina, USA, 1964; Adviser on Environmental Health, World Health Organisation, 1967-86; Visiting Professor, Delft University, Netherlands, 1977. Publications: About 120 scientific papers and articles; 3 books: The Scientific Basis of Filtration, 1975; The Scientific Basis of Flocculation, 1978; The Scientific Basis of Flotation, 1984. Honours: Gans Medal of the Society for Water Treatment and Examination, 1966; Gold Medal, Filtration Society, 1983; Jenkins Memorial Medal, International Association for Water Pollution Research and Control, 1990; Freeze Award and Lecture, American Society of Civil Engineers, 1994; Commander of the Order of the British Empire, CBE, 1996. Memberships: Fellow, Royal Academy of Engineering; Life Fellow, Institution of Civil Engineers; Foreign Associate, National Academy of

Engineering, USA; Life Member, American Society of Civil Engineers; Life Member, American Water Works Association; Life Member, Water Environment Federation, USA. Address: Department of Civil and Environmental Engineering, University College London, Gower St, London WC1E 6BT, England.

IVES William George Herbert, b. 30 September 1922, Woodlea Municipality, Manitoba, Canada. Forest Entomology. m. Marion Florence Taylor, deceased, 3 daughters. Education: BSc, Agriculture, The University of Manitoba, 1951; MSc, The Iowa State College, 1953. Appointments: Lead Aircraftsman, Royal Canadian Air Force, 1942-46; Student Assistant, 1949-50, Technical Officer and Research Officer, Grades 1 through 4, 1951-67, Forest Insect Laboratory, Winnipeg, Manitoba; Research Scientist 2, Forest Biology Laboratory, Winnipeg, 1967-70; Research Scientist 3, 1970-89, Research Scientist 4 (part time), 1989-92, Canadian Forestry Service, Edmonton, Alberta. Publications: Numerous books, articles and papers in professional scientific journals include: Environmental factors affecting 21 forest insect defoliators in Manitoba and Saskatchewan, 1945-69, 1981; Dispersal of Olesicampe benefactor and Mesochorus dimidiatus in western Canada, 1984; Tree and Shrub Insects of the Prairie Provinces (co-author), 1988; Factors affecting the survival of immature lodgepole pine in foothills of west-central Alberta (co-author), 1993; Forest Insect Pests in Canada (co-editor), 1995. Honours: Founders Award, Executive of the Western Forest Insect Work Conference, 1999; Great Minds of the 21st Century, ABI, 2004; Top 100 Scientists, IBC, 2005. Memberships: New York Academy of Sciences; American Association for the Advancement of Science. Address: 11459 – 42 Avenue, Edmonton, Alberta T6J 0W2, Canada.

IVUT Roman, b. 17 July 1949, Grodno, Republic of Belarus. Scientist. m. Aldona, 1 daughter. Education: Engineer Mechanic, Belarussian Polytechnic Institute, 1972; Department of English Language, Minsk State Pedagogical Institute, 1985. Appointments: Teacher, Technical School, 1972-74; Assistant Professor, Professor, Manager, Belarussian National Technical University, 1974-; Probationer, Californian University, 1986-87; Probationer, FRG, 1994; Chairman, State Expertial Council of the Committee of Science & Technologies, 1995-96; Chairman, Expertial Committee of Higher Attestation Commission, 2001-03. Publications: 5 books. Honours: Honorable Transport Worker; Excellent Pupil in Education of the Republic of Belarus. Memberships: International Academy of the Information Technologies; Belarussian Engineer Academy. Address: 39-74 Vostochnaja Street, Minsk 220040, Belarus.

IWAHASHI Hidehiko, b. 9 June 1967, Miyazaki, Japan. Cardiovascular Surgeon. m. Mitsue, 2 sons. Education: MD, 1994; PhD, 2001. Appointments: Assistant Professor, Cardiovascular Surgery, 2001, Assistant Professor, Cardiovascular Surgery, 2004, Lecturer, Associate Professor, Cardiovascular Surgery, 2005, Fukuoka University School of Medicine; Adjunct Instructor, Department of Surgery, Baylor College of Medicine, USA, 2003. Publications: Determination of plasma prothrombin level by Ca2+-dependent prothrombin Activator (CA-1) during warfarin anti-coagulation, 2001; Development of the oxygenator: past, present and future, 2004; New method of thermal coronary angiography for intraoperative patency control in off-pump and on-pump coronary artery bypass grafting, 2007. Honours: Listed in international biographical dictionaries. Memberships: Asian Cardiovascular Surgery. Address: 7-45-1 Nanakuma Jonan-ku, Fukuoka, 814-0180, Japan. E-mail: hiwahasi@siren.ocn.ne.jp

IWUGO Kenneth Ogugua, b. 30 December 1944, Lagos, Nigeria. Professor; Programme Director. m. Etmonia Joyce Florence, 1 son, 4 daughters. Education: BSc (Hons, Chemical Technology, Huddersfield Polytechnic, 1969; MSc, Advanced Analytical Chemistry, University of Bristol, 1970; PhD, Public Health Engineering, University of Birmingham, 1977. Appointments: Applied Science Student Assistant, Atomic Energy Research Establishment, Harwell, England, 1967-68; Senior Assistant Chemist, Mersey & Weaver River Authority, England, 1970-72; Chemist/Industrial Effluent Inspector, Altrincham Corporation, England, 1972; Principal Professional Officer, National Council for Scientific Research, Zambia, 1972-75; Researcher, University of Birmingham, England, 1975-77; Consultant Sanitary Engineer, World Bank, Washington, UK/USA, 1977-78; Professor and Head of Department of Civil Engineering, University of Lagos, Nigeria, 1984-94; Regional Adviser, World Health Organisation, Congo, 1988-90; Principal Lecturer & Consultant, University of the West of England, England, 1994-2000; Senior Academic & Professional Practice Advisor and Co-ordinator, 1998-2007, Programe Director, PGCPD/WEM, 2007-, PGCPD/CIWEM, University of Bristol, England. Publications: Over 85 papers and articles in professional journals, books and booklets. Memberships: Chartered Chemist & Member, Royal Society of Chemistry, UK; Fellow, Institution of Public Health Engineers; Fellow, Council and Accreditation Panel Memberships Chartered Institution of Water and Environmental Management, UK; Member, Strategic Council of the International Water Association; Member, American Association of Environmental and Engineering Professors; Life Member, Asian Society for Environmental Protection; Fellow, Nigeria Environmental Society; Member, International Water Association; Registered Member, UK Higher Education Academy; Editorial Board, Waterlines International Journal; Advisory Board, International Rainwater Harvesting Association; Regional Environment Protection Advisory Committee, UK Environment Agency; Chairman, British Broadcasting Corporation; West Regional Advisory Council and Member, English National Forum; Standards Board of England. Address: 17, Sixth Avenue, Filton, Bristol BS7 0LT, England. E-mail: kenneth.iwugo@bristol.ac.uk

IYER Vijayan Gurumurthy, b. 10 June 1964, Mayuram, India. University Professor. m. Shanthi. Education: Diploma, Mechanical Engineering, 1982; Diploma, Production Management, Annamalai University, 1988; Post Diploma, Automobile Engineering, Victoria Jubilee Technical Institute, Mumbai, 1992; AMIE, Mechanical Engineering, Institution of Engineers, India, 1990; Master's, 1997, PhD, 2003, Environmental Science and Engineering, Indian School of Mines University, Dhanbad; Post-doctoral Researcher, World Scientific and Engineering Academy and Society, Greece, 2006. Appointments: Technical Officer, Indian Council of Agricultural Research Service, Central Institute of Agricultural Engineering, Bhopal, 1985-; Central Institute for Research on Cotton Technology, -1998; Professor, Hindustan College of Engineering, Rajalakshmi Engineering College, MNM Jain Engineering College; Professor, Environmental Engineering, Dr M G R University, Chennai. Publications: Over 120 research publications in the field of environmental science and mechanical engineering and education; Reviewer: WSEAS, ASABE, Environmental Monitor Journals. Honours: Kendriya Sachivalaya Hindi Parishad, 1988; Bharat Jyothi, 2000; Prominent citizens of India and Best Citizen of India, 2001; Rashtriya Ratna, 2001; NCERT Special Education Award, 2003; Rashtriya Gaurav, 2004; Tamil Nadu Government Best Environmental Research Essay Award, 2005; Postdoctoral Fellowship Award, 2006. Memberships:

Indian Society for Technical Education; Loss Prevention Association of India; World Scientific and Engineering Academy and Society, Greece; Institution of Engineers, Bangladesh; Aeronautical Society of India; Bioinformatics Institute of India; Consultancy Development Center; Mining Engineers Association of India; Indian Society for Training and Development; American Society of Mechanical Engineers; Fellow: Institution of Engineers, India; Institution of Valuers, India; Textile Association, India; All India Management Association. Address: 36, (New No 5) Venkatesh Nagar Main Road, Chennai 600 092, Tamilnadu, India. E-mail: gvijayan33@hotmail.com Website: www.gviyer.net

J

JACK Kenneth Henderson, b. 12 October 1918, North Shields, Northumberland, England. University Professor. m. Alfreda Hughes, deceased 1974, 2 sons. Education: BSc, 1939, DThPT, 1940, MSc, 1944, King's College, University of Durham, Newcastle upon Tyne, England; PhD, 1950, ScD, 1978, Fitzwilliam College, University of Cambridge, England. Appointments: Experimental Officer, Ministry of Supply, London, England, 1940-41; Lecturer in Chemistry, King's College, University of Durham, 1941-45, 1949-52, 1953-57; Senior Scientific Officer, British Iron and Steel Research Association, 1945-49; Research, Crystallographic Laboratory, Cavendish Laboratory, Cambridge, 1947-49; Research Engineer, Westinghouse Electric Corporation, Pittsburgh, Pennsylvania, USA, 1952-53; Research Director, Thermal Syndicate Ltd, Wallsend, Tyne and Wear, 1957-64; Professor of Applied Crystal Chemistry, University of Newcastle Upon Tyne, 1964-84; Director, Wolfson Research Group for High-Strength Materials, England, 1970-84; Leverhulme Emeritus Fellow, 1985-87; Emeritus Professor, University of Newcastle Upon Tyne, 1984-; Consultant, Cookson Group plc, England, 1986-94; Honorary Professor of Materials Engineering, University of Wales, Swansea, 1996-2011. Publications: 200 papers in scientific journals and conference proceedings covering solid state chemistry, crystallography, metallurgy, ceramic science and glass technology. Honours: 18 major awards including: Elected Fellow of The Royal Society (FRS), 1980; Prince of Wales Awrd for industrial Innovation and Production, 1984; Appointed Officer of the Most Excellent Order of the British Empire (OBE), 1997. Memberships: Fellow, The Royal Society (Elected); Fellow, The Royal Society of Chemistry; Distinguished Life Member, The American Ceramic Society, 2007; Honorary Member, Société Française de Métallurgie et de Matériaux; Honorary Member, the Ceramic Society of Japan; Honorary Member, The Materials Research Society of India. Address: 147 Broadway, Cullercoats, Tyne and Wear, NE30 3TA, England.

JACK Ronald Dyce Sadler, b. 3 April 1941, Ayr, Scotland. University Professor. m. Kirsty Nicolson, 8 July 1967, 2 daughters. Education: MA, Glasgow, 1964; PhD, Edinburgh, 1968; DLitt, Glasgow. Appointments: Lecturer, Department of English Literature, Edinburgh University, 1965; Reader, 1978; Professor, 1987; Visiting Professor, University of Virginia, 1973-74; Director, Universities Central Council on Admissions, 1988-94; Visiting Professor, University of Strathclyde, 1993; Distinguished Visiting Professor, University of Connecticut, 1998-2004; Professor Emeritus, 2004-. Publications: Scottish Prose 1550-1700, 1972; The Italian Influence on Scottish Literature, 1972; A Choice of Scottish Verse 1560-1660, 1978; The Art of Robert Burns (co-author), 1982; Sir Thomas Urquhart (co-author), 1984; Alexander Montgomerie, 1985; Scottish Literature's Debt to Italy, 1986; The History of Scottish Literature, Vol I, 1988; Patterns of Divine Comedy, 1989; The Road to the Never Land, 1991; Of Lion and Unicorn, 1993; The Poems of William Dunbar, 1997; Mercat Anthology of Early Scottish Literature, 1997, 2nd revised edition, 2000; New Oxford Dictionary of National Biography (associate editor), 2004; Scotland in Europe (co-editor), 2006. Contributions to: Review of English Studies; Modern Language Review; Comparative Literature; Studies in Scottish Literature. Memberships: Medieval Academy of America; Scottish Text Society; Fellow, Royal Society of Edinburgh, 2001; Fellow, English Association, 2001. Address: David Hume Tower, George Square, Edinburgh EH8 9JX, Scotland.

JACK Simon Michael, b. 29 October 1951, Indore, India. Judge. m. Christine, separated, 1 son, 2 daughters. Education: Winchester College, 1965-69; Degree in French, German and Law, Trinity College, Cambridge, 1970-73; Bar Exams, Inns of Court School of Law, 1973-74. Appointments: Called to the Bar of England and Wales, 1974; Barrister on North Eastern Circuit, 1975-2003; Assistant Recorder, 1992-96; Recorder, 1996-2004; Circuit Judge, based at Hull, 2004-. Honours: Scholarship to Winchester College; Head Boy of Winchester College; Middle Temple Harmsworth Exhibition; Exhibition to Trinity College, Cambridge. E-mail: simonjack@hotmail.com

JACKEVICIUS Algirdas, b. 3 August 1926, Panevezis reg, Lithuania. Surgeon. m. Marija Jackeviciene, 1 daughter. Education: MD, Vilnius University, 1948; Presentation of thesis of doctor of medicine, 1953; Surgeon, Vilnius First Hospital, 1951-1957; Habil Doctor of Medicine, Vilnius, 1969. Appointments: Senior Research Worker, Lithuanian Institute of Oncology, 1957-79; Chief of the Department of Thoracic Surgery, Lithuanian Institute of Oncology, 1979-90; Professor, 1994; Professor of the Clinic of Surgery, Lithuanian Oncology Center, 1990-2002; Professor of Surgery, Institute of Oncology, Vilnius University, 2004- Publications: 278, 1952-2006; 6 books include: Lung Cancer, 1975; Textbook: Oncology (editor), 1992; Lung and Mediastinum Tumors, 2002. Honours: Medal: Veteran of Works, 1986; Sign of Advanced Worker of Health Service. Memberships: International Association for the Study of Lung Cancer; European Association for Cardio-Thoracic Surgery; Lithuanian Society of Thoracic and Cardio Surgeons; Lithuanian Society Against Cancer; Lithuanian Society of Surgeons, Lithuanian Senological Society, Vilnius. Address: Department of Thoracic Surgery, Institute of Oncology, Vilnius University, Santariskiu 1, Vilnius 08660, Lithuania. E-mail: algirdasj@is.lt

JACKLIN Tony, b. 7 July 1944, Scunthorpe, England. Golfer. m. Vivien Jacklin, 1966, deceased 1988, 2 sons, 1 daughter, (2) Astrid May Waagen, 1988, 1 son, 1 stepson, 1 stepdaughter. Appointments: Lincolnshire Open Champion, 1961; Professional, 1962-85, 1988-; Won, British Assistant Professional's Title, 1965; Won, Dunlop Masters, 1967, 1973; First British player to win British Open since 1951, 1969; US Open Champion, 1970; First British player to win US Open since 1920 and first since 1900 to hold US and British Open titles simultaneously; Greater Greensboro Open Champion, USA, 1968, 1972; Won, Italian Open, 1973, German Open, 1979, Venezuelan Open, 1979, Jersey Open, 1981, British PGA Champion, 1982 and 15 major tournaments in various parts of the world; Played in 8 Ryder Cup matches and 4 times for England in World Cup; Captain of 1983 GB and European Ryder Cup Team; Captain of European Ryder Cup Team, 1985 (1st win for Europe since 1957), 1987; BBC TV Golf Commentator; Director of Golf, San Roque Club, 1988-; Golf course designer. Publications: Golf With Tony Jacklin, 1969; The Price of Success, 1979; Jacklin's Golfing Secrets, with Peter Dobereiner; The First Forty Years, with Renton Laidlaw, 1985; Your Game and Mine, with Bill Robertson, 1999. Honours include: Honorary Fellow, Birmingham Polytechnic, 1989. Memberships include: British Professional Golfers Association. Address: Tony Jacklin Golf Academy, Plaza del Rio Office Centre, 101 Riverfront Boulevard, Suite 610, Bradenton, FL 34205, USA.

JACKMAN Brian, b. 25 April 1935, Epsom, Surrey, England. Freelance Journalist; Writer. m. (1) 14 February 1964, divorced December 1992, 1 daughter, (2) January 1993. Education: Grammar School. Appointment: Staff,

Sunday Times, 1970-90. Publications: We Learned to Ski, 1974; Dorset Coast Path, 1977; The Marsh Lions, 1982; The Countryside in Winter, 1986; My Serengeti Years, editor, 1987; Roaring at the Dawn, 1996; The Big Cat Diary, 1996; Touching the Wild, 2003. Contributions to: Sunday Times; The Times; Daily Telegraph; Daily Mail; Country Living; Condé Nast Traveller; BBC Wildlife. Honours: TTG Travel Writer of Year, 1982; Wildscreen Award, 1982. Memberships: Royal Geographical Society; Fauna and Flora Preservation Society. Address: Spick Hatch, West Milton, Nr Bridport, Dorset DT6 3SH, England.

JACKSON Betty, b. 24 June 1949, Lancashire, England. Couturier. m. David Cohen, 1985, 1 son, 1 daughter. Education: Birmingham College of Art and Design. Appointments: Chief Designer, Quorum, 1975-81; Founder, Betty Jackson Ltd, 1981, Director, 1981-; Opened, Betty Jackson Retail Shop, 1991; Part-time Tutor, RCA, 1982-; Visiting Professor, 1999; Established Award for Arts by Preston City Council, 2004. Memberships: Fellow, Birmingham Polytechnic, 1989; University of Central Lancashire, 1993. Honours: Designer of the Year, 1985; Royal Designer for Industry, Royal Society of Arts, 1988, 1989; Fil d'Or, International Linen, 1989; Honorary Fellow, 1989, part time tutor, 1982-, visiting professor, 1999, RCA; Contemporary Designer of the Year, 1999. Address: Betty Jackson Ltd, 1 Netherwood Place, Netherwood Road, London W14 0BW, England. Website: www.bettyjackson.com

JACKSON Christopher Murray, b. 24 May 1935, Norwich, Norfolk, England. Politician; Businessman. m. Carlie Elizabeth Keeling, 1 son, 1 daughter. Education: BA Hons (Physics), MA, Magdalen College, Oxford; Studies in German and Economics, Frankfurt University; Postgraduate studies in Economics and Accounting, London School of Economics. Appointments: Commissioned Pilot, Royal Air Force, 1954-56; Member, Unilever Management Development Scheme, (Marketing Manager, Lever Bros, 1966, Senior Manager, 1967), Unilever plc, 1959-69; General Marketing Manager, Director of S&P Services, Save & Prosper Group, 1969-71; Contested UK General Election, East Ham South, 1970; Head of Corporate Planning, Donald Macpherson Group plc, 1971-74; Contested UK General Election, Northampton North, 1974; Director of Corporate Development, Spillers Group, 1974-80; Member, European Parliament for Kent East, 1974-94; Non-executive Director, Westminster Communications Ltd, 1988-95; Non-executive Director, Politics International Ltd, 1995-98; National Chairman, Agriculture & Countryside Forum, 1995-98; Member, National Executive, Conservative Party, 1995-98; Chairman, Natural Resources International Ltd, 1997-2003; Director and Former Chairman, CJA Consultants Ltd, 1995-; Chairman, Wekmeade Ltd, 1997-; Chairman, Board of Governors, Bethany School, 1999-. Publications: Numerous articles in popular press and professional journals; People Centred Development, 1985; Industrial Property Rights, 1998. Honours: Honorary Member of European Parliament. Memberships: Member, Conservative Party, 1959-99, 2007-; Royal Institute of International Affairs; Executive Committee, Society for Long Range Planning, 1969-79; Royal Parish Church of St Martin-in-the-Fields: Voluntary Social Worker, 1963-67, PCC, 1965-69, Treasurer, 1968-69; The Athenaeum, 2005-. Address: Flackley Ash Farmhouse, Peasmarsh, Rye, TN31 6TB, England. E-mail: c.jackson@btconnect.com

JACKSON Colin Ray, b. 18 February 1967. Athlete. Career: Honours for 110m hurdles include: Silver Medal, European Junior Championships, 1985; Gold Medal, World Junior Championships, 1986; Silver Medal, Commonwealth Games, 1986; Silver Medal, European Cup, 1987; Bronze Medal, World Championships, 1987; Silver Medal, Olympic Games, 1988; Silver Medal, World Cup, 1989; Gold Medal, European Cup, 1989, 1993; Gold Medal, Commonwealth Games, 1990; Gold Medal, World Cup, 1992; Gold Medal (new world record), Silver Medal (relay), World Championships, 1993; Honours for 60 hurdles include: Silver Medal World Indoor Championships, 1989, 1993; Silver Medal, 1987, Gold Medal 1989, 1994, European Indoor Championships; Gold Medal, European and Commonwealth Championships, 1994; Gold Medal, European Championships, 1998, 2002; Gold Medal, World Championships, 1999; Numerous Welsh, UK, European and Commonwealth records; Most capped British athlete ever (70 vests), 2003; Total of 25 medals; Announced retirement in 2003. Honours: MBE, 1990; CBE, 1992; Hon BA, Aberystwyth, 1994; Hon BSc, University of Wales, 1999; Athlete of the Decade, French Sporting Council; Hurdler of the Century, German Athletic Association; Athlete of the Year, 1993-94; British Athletics Writers Sportsman of the Year, 1994; Sports Writers Association. Memberships: Brecon Athletics Club UK International, 1985-. Address: 4 Jackson Close, Rhoose, Vale of Glamorgan, CF62 3DQ, Wales. Website: www.mtc-uk.com

JACKSON Frank Cameron, b. 31 August 1943, Australia. Professor. m. Morag Fraser, 2 daughters. Education: BA, 1968, BSc, 1964, University of Melbourne; PhD, La Trobe University, 1975. Appointments: William Evans Visiting Fellow, Otago University, 1986; Visiting Professor of Philosophy, Harvard University, 1988; Senior Humanities Council Fellow, Department of Philosophy, Princeton University, 1990; Inaugural Daniel Taylor Visiting Fellow, Otago University, 1990; John Locke Lecturer, Oxford University, 1995; James B and Grace J Nelson Philosopher in Residence, University of Michigan; 1998; Erskine Visitor, University of Canterbury NZ, May 1998; Overseas Visiting Scholar, St John's College, Cambridge, 2002; Distinguished Professor of Philosophy, 2003-; Director, Research School of Social Sciences, Australian National University, 2004-07; Tang Chun-I Visiting Professor, the Chinese University of Hong Kong 2006. Publications: Perception: a Representative Theory, 1977; Conditionals, 1987; Philosophy of Mind and Cognition (with David Braddon-Mitchell) 1996, 2nd edition 2006; From Metaphysics to Ethics –a Defence of Conceptual Analysis, 1998. Memberships: Elected to the Fellowship of the Australian Academy of the Humanities, 1981; Elected to the Fellowship of the Academy of the Social Sciences in Australia, 1998; Elected Corresponding Fellow of the British Academy, 2000; ISI Citation Laureate, 2004; Order of Australia (AO), 2006. Address: 75 Napier Crescent, Montmorency, VIC 3094, Australia

JACKSON Glenda, b. 9 May 1936, Birkenhead, Cheshire, England. Member of Parliament; Actress. m. Roy Hodges, 1958, divorced 1976, 1 son. Education: Royal Academy of Dramatic Art. Appointments: Actress, Royal Shakespeare Company; Other Theatre includes: The Investigation, Hamlet, US, 1965; Three Sisters, 1967; The Maids, 1974; Hedda Gabler, 1975; The White Devil, 1976; Antony and Cleopatra, 1978; The House of Bernada Alba, 1986; Scenes from an Execution, 1990; Mermaid, 1990; Mother Courage, 1990; Mourning Becomes Electra, 1991; Films include: Women in Love, 1969; Sunday, Bloody Sunday, Mary, Queen of Scots and The Boyfriend, 1971; A Touch of Class, 1973; The Abbess of Crewe, 1976; House Calls, 1978; Salome's Last Dance, 1988; The Rainbow, 1989; The Secret Life of Sir Arnold Bax, 1992; TV includes: Elizabeth R, 1971; The Morecambe and

Wise Show; Elected Labour MP Hampstead and Highgate, 1992-; Parliamentary Under Secretary of State, Department for the Environment and Transport, 1997-99; Adviser on Homelessness, GLA, 2000-. Honours: CBE, Honorary DLitt, Liverpool, 1978; Honorary LLM, Nottingham, 1992; Honorary Fellow, Liverpool Polytechnic, 1987; 2 Academy Awards, 1971, 1974. Memberships: President, Play Matters, 1976-; Director, United British Artists, 1986-. Address: c/o House of Commons, London SW1A 0AA, England.

JACKSON Janet, b. 16 May 1966, Los Angeles, USA. Singer; Actress. m. El DeBarge, 1984, annulled 1986. Rene Elizondo, 1991, divorced. Career: First appearance with family singing group The Jacksons, aged 7; Television actress, 1977-81; Appeared in US television series: Good Times, CBS-TV; Diff'rent Strokes; Fame; A New Kind Of Family; Solo recording artiste, 1982-; Concerts and tours include: Rhythm Nation World Tour (US, Europe, Far East), 1990; Film debut, Poetic Justice, 1993. Recordings: Albums: Janet Jackson, 1982; Dream Street, 1984; Control, 1986; Janet Jackson's Rhythm Nation, 1989; Janet, 1993; Design Of A Decade 1986-1996, 1995; The Velvet Rope, 1997; All For You, 2001; Damita Jo, 2004. Hit singles include: What Have You Done For Me Lately, Nasty, When I Think Of You, 1986; Control, Let's Wait Awhile, The Pleasure Principle, 1987; Miss You So Much, 1989; Rhythm Nation, Escapade, Alright, Come Back To Me, Black Cat, 1990; Love Will Never Do (Without You), 1991; The Best Things In Life Are Free, duet with Luther Vandross, from film Mo' Money, 1992; That's The Way Love Goes, If, Again, 1993; Whoops Now, Scream, Runaway, 1995; Twenty Foreplay, When I Think of You, 1996; Got Til It's Gone, Together Again, 1997; Go Deep, Every Time, I Get Lonely, 1998; Girlfriend, What's It Gonna Be, 1999; Doesn't Really Matter, 2000; All For You, Someone To Call My Lover, Got Til It's Gone, Son of a Gun, 2001; Just a Little While, All Nite Don't Stop, 2004; So Excited, 2006. Films: Poetic Justice, 1992; Nutty Professor II: The Klumps, 2000; Why Did I Get Married?, 2007. Numerous honours include: Billboard Awards, 1986-; American Music Awards, 1987-; Soul Train Awards, 1987-; MTV Video Music Awards, 1987-; Grammy, Best Music Video, Rhythm Nation 1814, 1990; Star on Hollywood Walk Of Fame, 1990; Janet Jackson Week, Los Angeles, 1990; Humanitarian Of The Year Award, Starlight Foundation of Southern California, 1990; Chairman's Award, NAACP Image Awards, 1992; First artist to have seven US Top 5 hits from one album, 1990-91; International Dance Award, Achievement In Dance, 1995. Address: RDWM Services (UK) Ltd, 37 Limerston Street, London, SW10 0BQ, England. Website: www.janet-jackson.com

JACKSON Jesse Louis, b. 8 October 1941, Greenville, North Carolina, USA. Clergyman; Civic Leader. m. Jacqueline Lavinia Brown, 1964, 3 sons, 2 daughters. Education: University of Illinois; Illinois Agricultural and Technical College; Chicago Theological Seminary. Appointments: Ordained to Ministry Baptist Church, 1968; Active, Black Coalition for United Community Action, 1969; Co-Founder, Operation Breadbasket, Southern Christian Leadership Conference; Coordinating Council, Conmunity Organsations, Chicago, 1966, National Director, 1966-77; Founder, Executive Director, Operation PUSH (People United to Save Humanity), Chicago, 1971-; TV Host, Voices of America, 1990-. Honours include: President's Award, National Medical Association, 1969; Humanitarian Father of the Year Award, National Father's Day Committee, 1971. Address: c/o Rainbow PUSH Coalition, 930 East 50th Street, Chicago, IL 60615, USA.

JACKSON Michael David, (Gen Sir Mike) b. 21 March 1944, Sheffield, England. Soldier. m. Sarah Coombe, 4 May 1985, 2 sons, 1 daughter. Education: BSoc Sc, Birmingham University, 1967. Appointments: Chief of Staff Berlin Infantry Brigade, 1977-78; Co-Commander, 2nd Battalion, The Parachute Regiment, 1979-80; Directing Staff, Staff College, 1981-83; Commanding Officer, 1st Battalion, The Parachute Regiment, 1984-86; Directing Staff, Joint Services Defence College, 1987-88; Service Fellow, Wolfson College Cambridge 89; Commander, 39 Infantry Brigade, 1990-91; Director Personal Services, 1992-93; Commander 3 (UK) Division, 1994-96; Commander Multinational Division South West, Bosnia, 1996; Director, Development and Doctrine, MOD, 1996-97; Commander, Allied Command Europe Rapid Reaction Corps, 1997-1999; Commander, Kosovo Force, 1999; Commander in Chief, UK Land Force, 2000-03; Chief of the General Staff, 2003-. Honours: MBE, 1979; Freeman, City of London, 1988; CBE, 1992; CB, 1996; KCB, 1998; DSO, 1999; Kt Grand Cross, Order of the Bath, 2005. Membership: RUSI. Address: Office of the Chief of the General Staff, Ministry of Defence, Main Building, Whitehall, London, SW1A 2HB, England. E-mail: webmaster@dgics.mod.uk Website: www.mod.uki

JACKSON Michael Joseph, b. 29 August 1958, Gary, Indiana, USA. m. (1) Lisa Marie Presley, divorced, (2) Debbie Rowe, divorced, 2 sons, 1 daughter. Career: Lead singer, family singing group Jackson Five (later the Jacksons), 1969-75; Solo artist, 1971-; Lengthy world tours, including Bad Tour 1987; Dangerous World Tour, 1992; Film appearances: The Wiz, 1978; Captain Eo, 1986; Moonwalker, 1988; Founder, Heal The World Foundation (children's charity); Owner, ATV Music Company (including rights for John Lennon and Paul McCartney songs); Owner, MJJ record label. Compositions include: Co-writer with Lionel Richie, We Are The World, USA For Africa famine relief single, 1985. Recordings: Albums: with Jackson Five/Jacksons include: Diana Ross Presents The Jackson Five, 1969; ABC, Third Album, 1970; Goin' Back To Indiana, Maybe Tomorrow, 1971; Looking Through The Windows, 1972; Farewell My Summer, Get It Together, Skywriter, 1973; Dancing Machine, 1974; Moving Violation, 1975; Joyfull Jukebox, Music, The Jacksons, 1976; Goin' Places, 1977; Destiny, 1978; Triumph, Boogie, 1980; Live, 1981; Victory, 1984; Solo albums: Got To Be There, 1971; Ben, 1972; Music And Me, 1973; Forever Michael, The Best Of, 1975; The Wiz (film soundtrack), 1978; Off The Wall, 1979; ET - The Extra Terrestrial (film soundtrack), Thriller (Number 1 in every Western country), 1982; Bad (Number 1, UK and US), 1987; Dangerous (Number 1, US and UK), 1991; HIStory - Past, Present And Future Book I, Scream, Childhood, 1995; Invincible, 2001; Numerous solo hit singles include: Got To Be There, 1971; Rockin' Robin, Ain't No Sunshine, Ben (Number 1, US), 1972; Don't Stop Till You Get Enough (Number 1, US), Off The Wall, 1979; Rock With You (Number 1, US), She's Out Of My Life, 1980; One Day In Your Life (Number 1, UK), 1981; The Girl Is Mine, duet with Paul McCartney (Number 1, UK), 1982; Billie Jean (Number 1, US and UK), Beat It (Number 1, US), Wanna Be Startin' Somethin', Human Nature, Say Say Say, duet with Paul McCartney, Thriller, 1983; I Can't Stop Loving You (Number 1, UK and US), Bad (Number 1, US), 1987; The Way You Make Me Feel (Number 1, US), 1988; Dirty Diana (Number 1, US), 1988; Leave Me Alone, 1989; Black And White (Number 1, UK and US), 1991; Remember The Time, Heal The World, Give In To Me, 1992; Scream (with Janet Jackson), You Are Not Alone, Earth Song, 1995; They Don't Care About Us, 1996; Ghosts, Stranger in Moscow, Blood on the Dance Floor, 1997; You Rock My World, Cry,

2001; Contributor, recordings by Minnie Ripperton; Carol Bayer Sager; Donna Summer; Paul McCartney. Publications: Moonwalk (autobiography), 1988; Dancing The Dream (poems and reflections), 1992. Honours include: Numerous Grammy Awards, 1980- (including 7 awards, 1984; Song Of The Year, 1986; Legend Award, 1993) Numerous American Music Awards, 1980- (including 11 awards, 1984; Special Award of Achievement, 1989); BRIT Awards: Best International Artist, 1984, 1988, 1989; Artist Of A Generation, 1996; Soul Train Awards, 1988-; MTV Video Vanguard Award, 1988; 2 NAACP Image Awards, 1988; Entertainer of the Decade, American Cinema Awards Foundation, 1990; First recipient, BMI Michael Jackson Award, 1990; 3 World Music Awards, 1993; Most successful album ever, Thriller (50 million copies sold worldwide); Star on Hollywood Walk Of Fame, 1984; Numerous magazine poll wins and awards; Gold and Platinum records; Honorary Director, Exeter City Football Club, 2002-.

JACKSON Peter, b. 31 October 1961, Pukerua Bay, North Island, New Zealand. Film Director. m. Frances Walsh, 1 son, 1 daughter. Films: Bad Taste, 1987; Meet the Feebles, 1989; Valley of the Stereos, 1992; Ship to Shore, 1993; Heavenly Creatures, 1994; Jack Brown Genius, 1994; Forgotten Silver, 1995; The Frighteners, 1996; The Lord of the Rings: The Fellowship of the Ring, 2001; The Lord of the Rings: The Two Towers, 2002; The Long and Short of It, 2003; The Lord of the Rings: The Return of the King, 2003; The Long and Short of it, 2003; King Kong, 2005. Honours: Honorary Graduation, Massey University, 2001; BAFTA Award for Best Director, 2001; New Zealand Order of Merit, 2002; Voted Man of the Year 2002, Australian Empire Magazine, 2003; Golden Globe Award, Best Director, 2004; Critics' Choice Award, Best Director, 2004; Academy Award, Best Director, Best Picture, 2004; Oscar, Best Director, 2004. Address: c/o ICM, 8942 Wilshire Boulevard, Beverly Hills, CA 90211, USA.

JACKSON Samuel L, b. 21 December 1948, Washington, USA. Actor. m. LaTanya Richardson, 1 daughter. Education: Morehouse College. Appointments: Co-Founder, Member, Just Us Theatre Company, Atlanta. Creative Works: Stage appearances: Home; A Soldier's Story; Sally/Prince; Colored People's Time; Mother Courage; Spell No 7; The Mighty Gents; The Piano Lesson; Two Trains Running; Fences; TV appearances: Movin' On, 1972; Ghostwriter, 1992; The Trial of the Moke, 1978; Uncle Tom's Cabin, 1987; Common Ground, 1990; Dead and Alive: The Race for Gus Farace, 1991; Simple Justice, 1993; Assault at West Point, Against the Wall, 1994; Films include: Together for Days, 1972; Ragtime, 1981; Eddie Murphy Raw, 1987; Coming to America, School Daze, 1988; Do The Right Thing, Sea of Love, 1989; A Shock to the System, Def by Temptation, Betsy's Wedding, Mo' Better Blues, The Exorcist III, GoodFellas, Return of the Superfly, 1990; Jungle Fever, Strictly Business, 1991; Jumpin' at the Boneyard, Patriot Games, Johnny Suede, 1992; Jurassic Park, True Romance, 1993; Hail Caesar, Fresh, The New Age, Pulp Fiction, 1994; Losing Isaiah, Kiss of Death, Die Hard With a Vengeance, 1995; The Great White Hype, A Time to Kill, 1996; The Long Kiss Goodnight; Jackie Brown; Trees Lounge; Hard Eight; Out of Sight; The Negotiator; Deep Blue Sea; Sphere; Eve's Bayou; Star Wars Episode I: The Phantom Menace, Rules of Engagement, 1999; Shaft, Unbreakable, 2000; The Caveman's Valentine, The 51st State, 2001; Changing Lanes, Star Wars Episode II: Attack of the Clones, The House on Turk Street, XXX, 2002; Basic, S.W.A.T, 2003; Country of My Skull, Twisted, Kill Bill: Vol 2, The Incredibles (voice), 2004; Coach Carter, Mr Incredible and Pals, xXx: State of the Union, Star Wars: Episode III-Revenge of the Sith, The Man,

2005; Farce of the Penguins, Freedomland, Snakes on a Plane, Home of the Brave, 2006; Resurrecting the Champ, 1408, Cleaner, 2007; Jumper, Iron Man, 2008. Honours include: Best Actor Award, Cannes International Film Festival; New York Film Critics Award. Address: c/o ICM, 8942 Wilshire Boulevard, Beverly Hills, CA 90211, USA.

JACKSON Siti Mariah Mansor, b. 29 May 1953, Kedah, Malaysia. Artist. m. (1) Billy Morrow Jackson, deceased, (2) Brian John Sullivan, 2008. Education: Diploma in Art and Design (Textile Design) and Art Teacher's Diploma, Mara Institute of Technology, Malaysia, 1978-79; MA, Art Education, University of Illinois, 1988. Appointments: Art Teacher, Lecturer, Malaysian Schools and Teachers Colleges, 1979-85; Ceramic Sculptor, 1988-; Vice President, Jackson Studios, Illinois; Invitational and Juried Local and National Group Art Exhibitions and Show Cases. Publication: Book, On This Island: An Artistic View of Martha's Vineyard, 2005. Honours: First Award, Fabric Design on Paper for Stewardess Uniform, Malaysian Airline System, 1978; Federal Teaching Art Scholarship, Ministry of Education, Malaysia, 1985; Elected Member, Kappa Delta Pi, 1987; Award of Excellence, Manhattan Arts International Cover Art Competition, New York, 1995; 2nd Place, Watercolour, 10th International Juried Exhibition, Laredo Center for the Arts, 2002. Memberships: Smithsonian Institution, Washington, DC; National Museum of Women in the Arts, Washington, DC; International Women Artists Council, USA-Malaysia; Krannert Art Museum, University of Illinois, Champaign; Art Exhibition Advisory Committee, Springer Cultural Center, Champaign. Address: 706 West White Street, Champaign, IL 61820, USA. E-mail: mrartist2@cs.com Web site: http://www.soltec.net/jacksonstudios/

JACKSON Victoria (Vicky), b. 6 August 1934, London, England. m. Antoine Jackson, 1 son, 1 daughter. Education: Colchester College of Further Education; Dartington College of Arts. Appointments: Professional Singer, 1969-78; Singing Teacher, 1980-83; BBC Recording Artist; Accounts Controller, Executive Director, Chief Executive Officer, 1987-. Honour: Life Fellow, International Biographical Association. Memberships: Membership Secretary, World Foundation of Successful Women; Royal Horticultural Society. Address: Withycot, Ely Road, Prickwillow, Cambridgeshire CB7 4UJ, England.

JACKSON William David, b. 15 July 1947, Liverpool, England. Freelance Journalist; Translator; Poet. m. Christine Range, 3 June 1972, 1 son, 1 daughter. Education: BA, Honours, English Language and Literature, St Catherine's College, Oxford, 1968. Publications: Then and Now (book), 2002; From Now to Then (book), 2005. Contributions to: Acumen; Agenda; The Amsterdam Review; Babel; Blithe Spirit; The Dark Horse; Haiku Quarterly; Iron; Leviathan Quarterly; The London Magazine; Metre; Modern Poetry in Translation; Oasis; Orbis; Outposts; Oxford Poetry; Pennine Platform; Poetry Nottingham; Poetry Review; Poetry Wales; The Rialto; The Shop; Stand; Staple. Address: Clemensstrasse 66, 80796 Munich, Germany.

JACKSON (William) Keith, b. 5 September 1928, Colchester, Essex, England. Emeritus Professor. m. (1) 3 children, (2) Jennifer Mary Louch, 21 December 1990. Education: London University Teaching Certificate, 1947; BA, Honours, University of Nottingham, 1953; PhD, University of Otago, New Zealand, 1967. Publications: New Zealand Politics in Action (with A V Mitchell and R M Chapman), 1962; New Zealand (with J Harré), 1969; Editor, Fight for Life, New

Zealand, Britain and the EEC, 1971; New Zealand Legislative Council, 1972; Politics of Change, 1972; The Dilemma of Parliament, 1987; Historical Dictionary of New Zealand (with A D McRobie), 1996, 2nd edition, 2005; New Zealand Adopts Proportional Representation: Accident? Design? Evolution? (with Alan McRobie), 1998. Contributions to: Numerous professional journals. Honours: Mobil Award for Best Spoken Current Affairs Programme, Radio New Zealand, 1979; Henry Chapman Fellow, Institute of Commonwealth Studies, London, 1963; Canterbury Fellowship, 1987; Asia 2000 Fellowship, 1996. Address: 92A, Hinau Street, Christchurch 4, New Zealand.

JACOBI Derek George, Sir, b. 22 October 1938, London, England. Actor. Education: St Johns College, Cambridge. Appointments: Birmingham Repertory Theatre, 1960-63; National Theatre, 1963-71; Prospect Theatre Company, 1972, 1974, 1976-78; Artistic Association, 1976-; Old Vic Company, 1978-79; Joined Royal Shakespeare Company, 1982; Vice-President, National Youth Theatre, 1982-; Artistic Director, Chichester Festival, 1995-. Creative Works: TV appearances include: She Stoops to Conquer; Man of Straw; The Pallisers; I Claudius; Philby; Burgess and Maclean; Tales of the Unexpected; A Stranger in Town; Mr Pye; Brother Cadfael, 1994-; Inquisition, 2002; Mr Ambassador, 2003; The Long Firm, 2004; Films: Odessa File; Day of the Jackal; The Medusa Touch; Othello; Three Sisters; Interlude; The Human Factor; Charlotte, The Man Who Went up in Smoke, The Hunchback of Notre Dame, 1981; Inside the Third Reich, 1982; Little Dorrit, 1986; The Tenth Man, 1988; Henry V, The Fool, 1990; Dead Again, Hamlet, 1996; Love is the Devil, 1997; Gladiator, 2000; Gosford Park, The Revengers Tragedy, Night's Noontime, Two Men Went to War, 2002; Cloud Cuckoo Land, Strings, 2004; Bye Bye Blackbird, Project Huxley, Nanny McPhee, 2005; Underworld: Evolution, 2006; Guantanamero, The Riddle, Anastezsi, 2007; Morris: A Life with Bells On, Adam Resurrected, 2008. Plays: The Lunatic; Lover and the Poet, The Suicide, 1980; Much Ado About Nothing; Peer Gynt; The Tempest, 1982; Cyrano de Bergerac, 1983; Breaking the Code, 1986; Richard II, 1988; Richard III, 1989; Kean, 1990; Becket, 1991; Mad, Bad and Dangerous to Know; Ambassadors, 1992; Macbeth, 1993; Hadrian VII, Playing the Wife, 1995; Uncle Vanya, 1996; God Only Knows, 2000; Director: Hamlet, 1988, 2000. Honours: Honorary Fellow, St Johns College, Cambridge; Variety Club Award, 1976; British Academy Award, 1976; Press Guild Award, 1976; Royal TV Society Award, 1976; CBE, 1985; KBE, 1994; Evening Standard Award Best Actor, 1998. Address: Chichester Festival Theatre, Oaklands Park, Chichester, West Sussex PO19 4AP, England.

JACOBS Cecilia, b. 8 January 1961, Cape Town, South Africa. Academic. m. Keith Ivor Jacobs, 1 son, 1 daughter. Education: Bachelor of Arts, 1981; Higher Diploma in Education, 1982; Master's degree, Education, 1998; Doctoral Degree, Education, 2006. Appointments: Secondary School Teacher, 1983-90; Lecturer, University of Western Cape, 1990-91; Lecturer, Researcher & Faculty of Engineering Teaching & Learning Co-ordinator, Cape Peninsula University of Technology, 1991-2007. Publications: 10 articles in peer-reviewed journals & conference proceedings; 1 book chapter; 18 national conference papers; 6 international conference papers; Reviewer and Guest Editor for South African Scholarly Journal. Honours: 2 research grants; 2 doctoral scholarships; 1 international symposium keynote address; 1 plenary address at conference; 12 invited seminars; Listed in international biographical dictionaries. Memberships: South African Applied Linguistics Association; South African

Academic Development Association. Address: 14 Aaron Figaji Street, Beroma, Bellville, 7530, Western Cape, South Africa. E-mail: jacobsc@cput.ac.za

JACOBS David Lewis, b. 19 May 1926, London, England. Broadcaster. m. (1) Patricia Bradlaw, 16 September 1949, divorced 1972, 1 son deceased, 3 daughters; (2) Caroline Munro, 1975, deceased 1975; (3) Lindsay Stuart Hutcheson, 1 August 1979, 1 stepson. Education: Belmont College, London. Career: Royal Navy; Impressionist, Navy Mixture, 1944; Chief Announcer, Radio SEAC, Ceylon; BBC announcer and newsreader; Freelance broadcaster; Radio includes: Housewives Choice; BBC Jazz Club; Pick Of The Pops; Saturday Show Band Show; Any Questions?; Any Answers?; Melodies For You; Founder member, Capital Radio; Own programme, BBC Radio 2, 6 years; Television includes: Juke Box Jury; Top Of The Pops; David Jacobs' Words And Music; Sunday Night With David Jacobs; Where Are They Now?; What's My Line?; Eurovision Song Contest; A Song For Europe; Miss World; Little Women; Come Dancing; Presents musical concerts and one-man show, An Evening with David Jacobs. Publications: Jacobs Ladder; Caroline; Any Questions? (with Michael Bowen). Honours: 6 Royal Command Performances; Top British DJ, BBC and Radio Luxembourg, 6 years; TV Personality of Year, Variety Club of Great Britain, 1960; BBC Radio Personality of Year, 1975; Sony Gold Award, 1984; Sony Hall of Fame; Richard Martin Award (animal welfare); Honorary Doctorate, Kingston University, 1994; CBE, 1996; Deputy Lieutenant of and for Greater London, 1983; Representative Deputy Lieutenant for the Royal Borough of Kingston-upon-Thames; Honorary Freeman of the Royal Borough of Kingston-upon-Thames, 1997; Chairman, Thames Radio. Memberships include: Vice-President, Society of Stars; Vice-President, Royal Star & Garter Home, Richmond; Vice-President, Kingston Arts Festival; Director, Chairman, Kingston Theatre Trust. Hobbies: Travel; Hotels; Talking; Listening. Current Management: Billy Marsh Associates. Address: 174 North Gower Street, London, NW1 2NB, England.

JACOBS Peter, b. 21 March 1934, Pretoria, South Africa. m. Margaret Ann (Diane) Botbyl, 21 January 1961, 2 sons. Education: Matriculated, Prince Edward School, 1948; MB, BCh, 1959, MD, 1966, PhD, 1974, University of Witwatersrand. Appointments: Chief Medical Technologist, Pasteur Institute and Public Health Laboratory, Salisbury; Chief Technologist, Dr George V Blaine Laboratory, Central Africa, 1951-54; Director, Division of Haematology, Department of Laboratory Medicine, University Hospital and King County Medical Centre, Seattle, USA; Therapeutic Trials Physician, Department of Medicine, University of the Witwatersrand and Johannesburg General Hospital; Foundation Professor of Haematology, University Cape Town, Chief Specialist, Groote Schuur Hospital, 1971; Director, University Cape Town Leukaemia Centre; Emeritus Professor of Haematology, University of Cape Town, 1995; Honorary Consultant Physician, Groote Schuur Hospital Teaching Group, 1995; Honorary Professor of Haematology, Stellenbosch University –Tygerberg Academic Hospital, 1996; Professor of Internal Medicine, College of Medicine – University of Nebraska Medical Centre; Foundation Professor and Head, Division of Clinical Haematology, Department of Internal Medicine, University of Stellenbosch and Tygerberg Academic Hospital, 2003. Publications: Author of books, chapters and numerous professional articles in scientific journals. Honours include: Eli Lilly International Fellowship; Andries Blignault Memorial Medal; Ernest Oppenheimer Memorial Scholarship; Chalarick Solomon Memorial Scholarship; David Lurie Memorial Prize;

Medical Graduate Prize in Medicine; University Washington Research Fellowship; S L Sive Memorial Travelling Fellowship; Ernest Oppenheimer Memorial Travelling Fellowship; Fellowships: The Royal Society of Medicine; The Royal College of Physicians of Edinburgh; The Royal College of Pathologists in the UK; The American College of Physicians; American Society of Internal Medicine The Royal Society of South Africa; The Colleges of Medicine of South Africa. Memberships: Association of Cancer Research; The American Society of Clinical Haematology; The College of American Pathologists; Consultancies: Drug Monitoring for World Health Organization – Uppsala. Address: Department of Haematology and Bone Marrow Transplant Unit Incorporating The Searll Research Laboratory for Cellular and Molecular Biology, Constantiaberg Medi-Clinic, PO Box 294, Plumstead, 7801, Cape Town, South Africa.

JACOBSON Dan, b. 7 March 1929, Johannesburg, South Africa. Professor Emeritus; Writer. m. Margaret Pye, 3 sons, 1 daughter. Education: BA, University of the Witwatersrand; Honorary Ph.D., University of Witwatersrand. Appointments: Visiting Fellow, Stanford University, California, 1956-57; Professor, Syracuse University, New York, 1965-66; Fellow, 1981, Australian National University; Lecturer, 1975-80, Reader, 1980-87, Professor, 1988-94, Professor Emeritus, 1994-, University College, London. Publications: The Trap, 1955; A Dance in the Sun, 1956; The Price of Diamonds, 1957; The Evidence of Love, 1960; The Beginners, 1965; The Rape of Tamar, 1970; The Confessions of Josef Baisz, 1979; The Story of the Stories, 1982; Time and Time Again, 1985; Adult Pleasures, 1988; Hidden in the Heart, 1991; The God Fearer, 1992; The Electronic Elephant, 1994; Heshel's Kingdom, 1998; A Mouthful of Glass, translation, 2000; Ian Hamilton in Conversation with Dan Jacobson, interview, 2002; All for Love, 2005. Contributions to: Periodicals and newspapers. Honours: John Llewelyn Rhys Memorial Award, 1958; W Somerset Maugham Award, 1964; H H Wingate Award, 1979; J R Ackerley Award, 1986; Honorary DLitt, University of the Witwatersrand, 1987; Mary Elinore Smith Prize, 1992; Honorary Fellow, University College, London, 2005. Address: c/o A M Heath & Co Ltd, 79 St Martins Lane, London WC2, England.

JACOBSON Howard, b. 25 August 1942, Manchester, England. Novelist. m. (1) Rosalin Sadler, 1978, divorced 2004, 1 son, (2) Jenny De Yong, 2005. Education: BA, Downing College, Cambridge. Appointments: Lecturer, University of Sydney, 1965-68; Supervisor, Selwyn College, Cambridge, 1969-72; Senior Lecturer, Wolverhampton Polytechnic, 1974-80; Television Critic, The Sunday Correspondent, 1989-90; Into the Land of Oz, (Channel 4), 1991; Writer/Presenter, Yo, Mrs Askew! (BBC2), 1991, Roots Schmoots (Channel 4 TV), 1993, Sorry, Judas (Channel 4 TV), 1993, Seriously Funny: An Argument for Comedy (Channel 4 TV), 1997; Columnist, The Independent, 1998-; Howard Jacobson Takes on the Turner (Channel 4 TV), 2000; Why The Novel Matters: A South Bank Show Special (ITV), 2002. Publications: Shakespeare's Magnanimity: Four Tragic Heroes, Their Friends and Families, 1978; Coming From Behind, 1983; Peeping Tom, 1984; Redback, 1986; In the Land of Oz, 1987; The Very Model of a Man, 1992; Roots Schmoots, 1993; Seeing With the Eye: The Peter Fuller Memorial Lecture, 1993; Seriously Funny, 1997; No More Mister Nice Guy, 1998; The Mighty Walzer, 1999; Who's Sorry Now?, 2002; The Making of Henry, 2004; Kalooki Nights, 2006. Honours: Winner Jewish Quarterly and Wingate Prize, 2000; Winner of the first Bollinger Everyman Wodehouse

Prize, 2000. Membership: Modern Painters, editorial board. Address: Curtis Brown, Haymarket House, 28-29 Haymarket, London SWIY 4SP, England.

JACOBSON Jerry I, b. 25 January 1946, New York, USA. Medical Researcher, Biophysicist; Theoretical Physicist. 1 son; 4 daughters. Education: BA, City University of New York, 1966; DMD, DDS, Temple University, Philadelphia, USA, 1970; PhD, Bundel Khand University, India, 2002. Appointments: President, Institute of Theoretical Physics and Advanced Studies for Biophysical Research; Chairman, President, The Perspectivism Foundation, Florida, USA; Chairman of the Board, President, CEO, Jacobson Resonance Enterprises Inc, Public Biotechnology Corporation; Chief Magnetic Therapist, Magnetic Resonance Therapy Inc, Nassau, Bahamas; Chief Science Officer, Applied Magnetics LLC, Denver, Colorado and Pico Tesla Magnetic Therapies LLC. Publications: 12 US patents; 15 foreign patents; 3 books; 4 book chapters; 80 full length science articles; 10 full length philosophy articles. Honours: International Order of Merit, IBC; Champion of Freedom Award; Invited Lecturer, Karolinska Institute; Special Achievement in Medical Research, Bundel Khand University. Memberships: Cardiology in Review; American Physical Society Medical Hypotheses; American Association for Advancement of Sciences; Bioelectromagnetics Society; Bundel Khand University; Advisory Board, Center for Frontier Sciences, Temple University, Philadelphia, USA; New York Academy of Sciences, USA. Address: Institute of Theoretical Physics, 2006 Mainsail Circle, Jupiter, FL 33477-1418, USA. E-mail: drjijacobson@yahoo.com

JAFFE Edward E, b. 22 September 1928, Vilna, Poland. Chemist. m. Ann Swirski, 1 son, 2 daughters. Education: BS, City College, City of New York, 1952; MS, 1954, PhD, 1957, New York University. Appointments: Research Chemist, 1957-63, Senior Research Chemist, 1963-65, Research Associate, 1965-73, Research Supervisor, 1973-75, Technical Superintendent, 1975-78, Research Manager, 1978-80, Research Fellow, 1980-84, DuPont Company; Distinguished Research Fellow, 1984-87, Director of Research, 1987-88, Vice President of R&D, 1988-95, CIBA-GEIGY Corporation; Retired, 1995-; Exclusive Consultant to CIBA Speciality Chemical Corp, 1995-2003; Independent consultant, 2003-. Publications: 67 US patents; Over 300 international patents; Many articles in professional journals and chapters in scientific books. Honours: Founders Day Award, New York University; Armin J Bruning Award, Outstanding Contribution to the Science of Colour; Recipient of the American Chemical Society Delaware Section Award, for Conspicuous Scientific Achievement in the Area of Chemistry, 2000. Memberships: American Chemical Society; Delaware Chemical Society Chapter; Organic Section of ACS; Sigma Xi Society. Address: 6 Penny Lane Court, Wilmington, Delaware 19803, USA. E-mail: eejaffe@comcast.net

JAGGER Bianca, b. 2 May 1950, Nicaragua. Actress; Film Maker; Human Rights Advocate. divorced, 1 daughter. Education: Political Science, Institute of Science Politics, Paris, France; Film School, New York University. Appointments: Lecturer, Colleges and Universities. Civic Activities: Executive Director, Leadership Council, Amnesty International, USA; Advisory Committee of Human Rights, Watch America; Coalition, International Justice; Board Director, People for The American Way; Special Advisor, Indigenous Development International, University of Cambridge, England. Publications: Several articles in professional journals, newspapers and magazines. Honours include: United Nations Earth Day International Award, 1994; Green Globe Award, Rainforest Alliance, 1997; Right Livelihood Award, 2004. Commissions and Creative Works: Produced and directed a documentary "Nicaragua in Transition"; Appeared in many feature films and television productions. Address: 530 Park Avenue, 18D New York, NY 10021, USA.

JAGGER Sir Michael (Mick) Philip, b. 26 July 1943, Dartford, Kent, England. Singer; Songwriter. m. (1) Bianca Pérez Morena de Macias, 1971, divorced, 1979, 1 daughter, (2) Jerry Hall, 2 sons, 2 daughters; 1 daughter by Marsha Hunt; 1 son Luciana Gimenez. Education: London School of Economics. Career: Member, Rolling Stones, 1962-; Numerous tours, concerts include: National Jazz & Blues Festival, Richmond, 1963; Debut UK tour, 1963; Debut US tour, 1964; Free concert, Hyde Park, 1969; Free concert, Altamont Speedway, 1969; Knebworth Festival, 1976; Live Aid, Philadelphia, 1985; Solo tour including Japan, 1988; Steel Wheels North American tour, 1989; National Music Day Celebration Of The Blues, with Gary Moore, 1992; Voodoo Lounge World Tour, 1994-95; Bridges to Babylon Tour, 1997-98; Films include: Ned Kelly, 1970; Performance, 1970; Freejack, 1992; Bent, 1996. Compositions: Co-writer for the Rolling Stones, with Keith Richards (under the pseudonym The Glimmer Twins). Recordings: Albums include: The Rolling Stones, 1964; The Rolling Stones No 2, 1965; Out Of Our Heads, 1965; Aftermath, 1966; Between The Buttons, 1967; Their Satanic Majesties Request, 1967; Beggar's Banquet, 1968; Let It Bleed, 1969; Get Yer Ya-Ya's Out, 1969; Sticky Fingers, 1971; Exile On Main Street, 1972; Goat's Head Soup, 1973; It's Only Rock And Roll, 1974; Black And Blue, 1976; Some Girls, 1978; Emotional Rescue, 1980; Still Life, 1982; Steel Wheels, 1989; Flashpoint, 1991; Stripped, 1995; Bridges to Babylon, 1997; Forty Licks, 2002; Live Licks, 2004; The Very Best of Mick Jagger, 2007. Solo albums: She's The Boss, 1985; Primitive Cool, 1987; Wandering Spirit, 1993; Goddess in the Doorway, 2001; Singles include: It's All Over Now; Little Red Rooster; (I Can't Get No) Satisfaction; Get Off Of My Cloud; Jumping Jack Flash; Let's Spend The Night Together; Brown Sugar; 19th Nervous Breakdown; Harlem Shuffle; Ruby Tuesday; Paint It Black; It's Only Rock'n'Roll; Start Me Up; Undercover Of The Night; Dancing In The Street (with David Bowie); Ruthless People, 1986; Let's Work, 1987; Sweet Thing, 1993; Don't Tear Me Up, 1993; God Gave Me Everything, 2001; Visions of Paradise, 2002; Old Habits Die Hard (with Dave Stewart), 2004. Honours: with Rolling Stones include: Grammy Lifetime Achievement Award, 1986; Inducted into Rock And Roll Hall Of Fame, 1989; Q Award, Best Live Act, 1990; Ivor Novello Award, Outstanding Contribution To British Music, 1991; Golden Globe Award for Best Original Song, 2005. Address: c/o Rupert Loewenstein, 2 King Street, London SW1Y 6QL, England.

JAHN Ilse Margarete (Trommer), b. 2 February 1922, Chemnitz (Sachsen). Biologist. m. Wilhelm Jahn, deceased, 1 daughter. Education: Studied Biology, 1941-42, 1952-56, Diploma in Biology, 1956, Dr rer nat, 1963; University of Jena; DrScNat (habil), Humboldt University, 1979; Docent, Berlin, 1980. Appointments: Assistant Ernst-Haeckel-Haus Jena, 1956-62; Research Fellow (Editor), A-Von-Humboldt Commission, Academy of Science, Berlin, 1962-67; Curator of Exposition in Museum für Naturkunde, Humboldt University, 1967-80; Docent of Museology, Humboldt University, Berlin, 1980-82. Publications: Dem Leben auf der Spur, 1969; Die Jugendbriefe Alexander von Humboldts (co-editor), 1973; Charles Darwin, 1982; Geschichte der Biologie (co-editor), 1982, 1985, 1998, 2002; Grundzüge der Biologieschichte,

1990; Darwin and Co (co-editor), 2001; 220 scientific articles and biographies. Honours: Vice-Director, Museum für Naturkunde, 1971-74; President, section/biological museums, (council of museums GDR) 1971-82; Title, Obermuseumsrat (Ministry of Culture), 1984; German Society of History and Theory of Biology; President, 1991-93. Memberships: Deutsche Akademie der Naturforscher Leopoldina, 1986-; Corresponding Member, Senckenberg Naturf Ges (SNG), 1992-; New York Academy of Sciences, 1995-; Dr h c, University of Jena, 2002. Address: Eyke-von-Repkow-Pl.2, 10555 Berlin, Germany.

JAHRREISS Heribert, b. 15 January 1924, Leipzig, Germany. University Professor of Physics. m. Ingeborg Kunkel, 1 son, 1 daughter. Education: Diploma, Physics, 1951; DPhil, 1952; Habilitation, 1959. Appointments: Scientific Assistant, 1952, Assistant, Lecturer, 1959, Assistant Professor, 1966, Associate Professor, 1970, Professor, 1980. Publications include: Introduction to Physics, 1977, 5th edition, 1993. Honours: Cross of Honour, President of the Federal Republic of Germany; Medal of Honour, University of Köln. Memberships include: Secretary General, 1974-83, Vice President, 1983-86, 1989-92, President, 1986-89, International Union for Vacuum Science, Technique and Application. Address: Nassestr 36, D-50939 Cologne, Germany.

JAIN B M, b. 2 September 1946. Researcher; Teacher. m. Manju, 1 son, 1 daughter. Education: MA, PhD, Political Science. Appointments: Research Scientist, Political Science, South Asia Studies Centre, University of Rajasthan, India, 1988-2006; Visiting Professor, Asian and Asian American Studies, State University of New York, USA, 2006-07. Publications: More than 12 books; Over 72 articles in refereed journals and chapters in edited volumes. Honours: Member, Editorial Board, Project South Asia, Missouri Southern State College, USA; UGC Teacher Fellow, 1977-81; ICCSR Fellow, New Delhi, 1987; Visiting Scholar, Institute for Far Eastern Studies, Korea, 1997; Charles Wallace Trust Grantee, 1998; Visiting Scholar, Henry L Stimson Center, Washington, USA, 1998; Gerald Ford Foundation Grantee, 2001; Member, International Advisory Council, Toda Institute for Global Peace and Policy Research, Hawaii, USA; Honorary Academician and Research Professor, International Noble Academy, Toronto, Canada; Visiting Fellow, University of Pennsylvania, USA, 2001; Visiting Fellow, University of Hong Kong, 2002; Visiting Professor, University of Jaume I Castellon, Spain, 2008; Listed in international biographical dictionaries; Numerous invited lectures abroad. Memberships: International Political Science Association; Association of Asia-Pacific Research Association; Association of Third World Studies; International Peace Research Association; International Congress of Psychology; International Association of Historians in Asia; Indian Political Science Association; Indian Congress of Defence Studies. Address: 4/87 Jawahar Nagar, Near Power House, Jaipur – 302004, India. E-mail: jainbm2001@yahoo.com

JAKOBSSON Thor Edward, b. 5 October 1936, Wynyard, Sask, Canada. Retired Research Scientist. m. Johanna Johannesdottir, 1 son, 1 daughter. Education: Cand Mag, University of Oslo and Bergen, Norway, 1964; Cand Real, Meteorology, University of Bergen, Norway, 1966; PhD, Meteorology, McGill University, Montreal, Canada, 1973. Appointments: Research Assistant, University of Bergen, Norway, 1966-68; Research Scientist, Atmospheric Environment Service, Toronto, Canada, 1973-79; Research Scientist and Project Manager, Icelandic Meteorological Office, Reykjavik, Iceland, 1979-2006; Adjunct Professor,

University of Iceland, 1980-2002; Retired, 2006. Publications: Popular and scientific articles, reports and book chapters; numerous articles on various subjects in newspapers and journals. Memberships: American Meteorological Society; Canadian Meteorological and Oceanographic Society; International Biometeorological Society. Address: Espigerdi 2 (2E), IS-108 Reykjavik, Iceland, Europe.

JAMES Alan Morien, b. 20 January 1933, Newport, Monmouthshire, Wales. Retired University Teacher. m. (1) Valerie Hancox, 4 sons, 2 daughters, (2) Lorna Lloyd. Education: BSc Economics, first class honours, London School of Economics and Political Science, 1954. Appointments: Civil service, 1955-57; Assistant Lecturer, Lecturer, Senior Lecturer, Reader in International Relations, London School of Economics, 1957-73; Professor of International Relations, Keele University, 1974-98. Publications: 8 books. Honours: Rockefeller Research Fellow, Columbia University, 1968; Visiting Professor, University of Ife, 1981; Visiting Professor, Jawaharlal Nehru University, 1983; Guest Professor, National Institute for Defense Studies, Japan, 1993. Memberships: Committees of Social Science Research Council; Council for National Academic Awards; University Grants Committee. Address: 23 Park Lane, Congleton, Cheshire CW12 3DG, England.

JAMES Anthony, (A R James), b. 17 March 1931, London, England. Literary Researcher; Author. m. (1) Jacqueline, 19 April 1952, deceased, (2) Anne, 27 September 1997, 1 son, 2 daughters. Appointments: General Manager, Wimbledon Stadium, 1956-91; Secretary, NGRC Racecourse Promoters, 1989-2005. Publications: W W Jacobs Companion, 1990; Wimbledon Stadium - The First Sixty Years, 1993, new enlarged edition, 2000; Informing the People, 1996; W W Jacobs (biography), 1999; WW Jacobs Book - Hunter's Field Guide, 2001. Contributions to: Book and Magazine Collector; Antiquarian Book Monthly; W W Jacobs Appreciation Society Newsletter; WWII HMSO Paperbacks Society Newsletter. Memberships: Secretary and Editor, W W Jacobs Appreciation Society, WWII HMSO Paperbacks Society. Address: 3 Roman Road, Southwick, W Sussex BN42 4TP, England.

JAMES Clive Vivian Leopold, b. 7 October 1939. m. Prue Shaw, 2 daughters. Writer; Broadcaster; Journalist. Education: Sydney University; Pembroke College, Cambridge. Appointments: President, Footlights, Cambridge; TV Critic, 1972-82, Feature Writer, 1972-, The Observer; Director, Watchmaker Productions, 1994-; Lyricist for Pete Atkin; TV series including: Cinema; Up Sunday; So It Goes; A Question of Sex; Saturday Night People; Clive James on Television; The Late Clive James; The Late Show with Clive James; Saturday Night Clive; Fame in the 20th Century; Sunday Night Clive; The Clive James Show; Numerous TV documentaries including: Clive James meets Katherine Hepburn, 1986; Clive James meets Jane Fonda; Clive James meets Mel Gibson, 1998; Clive James meets the Supermodels, 1998; Postcard series, 1989-; Publications: Non-Fiction: The Metropolitan Critic, 1974; The Fate of Felicity Fark in the Land of the Media, 1975; Peregrine Prykke's Pilgrimage Through the London Literary World, 1976; Britannia Bright's Bewilderment in the Wilderness of Westminster, 1976; Visions Before Midnight, 1977; At the Pillars of Hercules, 1979; First Reactions, 1980; The Crystal Bucket, 1981; Charles Charming's Challenges on the Pathway to the Throne, 1981; From the Land of Shadows, 1982; Glued to the Box, 1982; Flying Visits, 1984; Snakecharmers in Texas, 1988; The Dreaming Swimmer, 1992; Fame, 1993; The Speaker in Ground Zero, 1999; Novels: Brilliant Creatures, 1983; The Remake, 1987; Unreliable

Memoirs (autobiography), 1980; Falling Towards England: Unreliable Memoirs Vol II, 1985; Unreliable Memoirs Vol III, 1990; May Week Was in June, 1990; Brrm! Brrm! or The Man From Japan or Perfume at Anchorage, 1991; Fame in the 20th Century, 1993; The Metropolitan Critic, 1993; Criticism: Clive James on Television, 1993; The Silver Castle, 1996; Evan as We Speak, 2005; North Face of Soho, 2006. 4 volumes of poetry. Address: c/o Watchmaker Productions, The Chrysalis Building, Bramley Road, London W10 6SP, England.

JAMES David Geraint, b. 2 January 1922, Treherbert, Wales. Doctor of Medicine. m. Sheila Sherlock, deceased, 2 daughters. Education: MA, MD, Jesus College, Cambridge; MRCS, LRCP, MRCP, Middlesex Hospital, University of London. Appointments: Surgeon-Lieutenant RNVR, 1946-48; Consultant Physician, Royal Navy, 1972-85; Dean of Studies, 1968-88, Consultant Physician, 1959-, Royal Northern Hospital, London; Professor of Medicine, University of London and Miami; Consultant Ophthalmic Physician, St Thomas' Hospital, London. Publications: Textbook of Infections, 1957; Colour Atlas of Respiratory Diseases, 1981; Sarcoidosis, 1985. Honours: Worshipful Society of Apothecaries, 1960-; Freeman, City of London; Honorary LLD University of Wales, 1982; FRCP, 1964; Honorary FACP, 1990. Memberships: President: Harvey Society, London; Osler Club, London; Medical Society, London; Member: London Medical Ophthalmology Society; World Congress History of Medicine; RCP; Hunterian Society; World Association of Sarcoidosis; International Journal of Sarcoidosis; Postgraduate Medical Federation; Thoracic Society of France, Italy and Portugal; French National Academy of Medicine; London Glamorganshire Society; White Robed Member, Bardic Circle of Wales. Address: 41 York Terrace East, London NW1 4PT, England.

JAMES Geraldine, b. 6 July 1950, Maidenhead, Berkshire, England. Actress. m. Joseph Blatchley, 1 daughter. Education: The Drama Centre, London. Career: Theatre includes: UN Inspector; The Cherry Orchard; Home; Faith Healer; Give Me your Answer Do; Death and the Maiden; Hedda Gabler; Lysistrata; The Merchant of Venice; Cymbeline; The White Devil; 4 years repertory including 18 months with the Northcott Theatre, Exeter; TV includes: Poirot; Jane Hall's Big Bad Bus Ride; Little Britain; White Teeth; The Sins; Kavanagh QC; Band of Gold; Blott on the Landscape; The Jewel in the Crown; The History Man; Dummy, Hearts of Gold; He Knew He Was Right; Hex; The Sins; White Teeth; Hearts of Gold; Little Britain; Jane Hall; The Battle of Rome; A Harlot's Progress, 2006; The Amazing Mrs Pritchard, 2006; The Time of Your Life, 2007; Medieval Heist, 2007; The Last Enemy, 2007. Films: Gandhi; The Tall Guy; Wolves of Willoughby Chase; She's Been Away; The Luzhin Defense; An Angel for May; Calendar Girls; Radio includes most recently: The Raj Quartet; Brought to Book; Turtle Diaries; King Lear; The Master and Marguerita; Alexander the Great; The Deptford Wives; The Hours; Whale Music; Richard III. Honours: TV Critics Award, Best Actress, 1978; Venice Film Festival Best Actress, 1989; Drama Desk Award, New York, 1990; OBE, 2003. Address: c/o Julian Belfrage Associates, Adam House, 14 New Burlington Street, London W15 3BQ, England.

JAMES Glen William, b. 22 August 1952, London, England. Solicitor. m. Amanda Claire Dorrell, 3 daughters. Education: New College, Oxford. Appointments: Articled Clerk, 1974-76, Assistant Solicitor, 1976-83, Partner, 1983-, Slaughter and May. Publications: Various professional articles contributed to books and other publications associated with corporate and commercial law. Memberships: Law Society; City of London Solicitors' Company; Securities Institute; Royal Automobile Club. Address: c/o 1 Bunhill Row, London EC1Y 8YY, England.

JAMES Michael Leonard, b. 7 February 1941, Cornwall, England. Government Official; Writer and Broadcaster. m. Jill Tarján, 2 daughters. Education: MA, Christ's College, Cambridge; FRSA. Appointments: Entered Government Service, GCHQ, 1963; Private Secretary to Rt Hon Jennie Lee, Minister for the Arts, 1966-68; DES, 1968-71; Planning Unit of Rt Hon Margaret Thatcher, Secretary of State for Education and Science, 1971-73; Assistant Secretary, 1973; Deputy Chief Scientific Officer, 1974; Adviser, OECD, Paris and UK Governor, International Institute for Management of Technology, Milan, 1973-75; International Negotiations on Non-Proliferation of Nuclear Weapons, 1975-78; Director, IAEA Vienna, 1978-83; Adviser, International Relations, 1983-85, Consultant, 1985-2001, Commission of the European Union, Brussels; Chair, Civil Service Selection Boards, 1983-93; Chair, The Hartland Press Ltd, 1985-2001, Wade Hartland Films Ltd, 1991-2000; Feature Writer and Book Reviewer for The Times, (Resident Thriller Critic, 1990-91); Sunday Times, Guardian and Daily Telegraph, (Resident Thriller Critic, 1993-). Publications: Co-author, Internationalization to Prevent the Spread of Nuclear Weapons, 1980; Novels, as Michael Hartland: Down Among the Dead Men, 1983; Seven Steps to Treason, 1985 (South West Arts Literary Award, dramatised for BBC Radio 4, 1990); The Third Betrayal, 1986; Frontier of Fear, 1989; The Year of the Scorpion, 1991; As Ruth Carrington: Dead Fish, 1998; TV and radio include: Sonja's Report, ITV, 1990; Masterspy (interviews with KGB defector Oleg Gordievsky), BBC Radio 4, 1991. Honours: Honorary Fellow, University of Exeter, 1985-. Memberships: Governor, East Devon College of Further Education, Tiverton, 1985-91, Colyton Grammar School, 1985-90, Sidmouth Community College, 1988-; (Chair, Board of Governors, 1998-2002); Chair, Board of Governors, Axe Vale Further Education College, Seaton, 1987-91; Member, Immigration Appeal Tribunal, 1987-; Devon and Cornwall Rent Assessment Panel, 1990-; Chairman, General Medical Council, Professional Conduct Committee, 2000-. Address: Cotte Barton, Branscombe, Devon, EX12 3BH, England.

JAMES P(hyllis) D(orothy) (Baroness James of Holland Park), b. 3 August 1920, Oxford, England. Author. m. Ernest Connor Bantry White, 9 August 1941, deceased 1964, 2 daughters. Appointments: Member, BBC General Advisory Council, 1987-88, Arts Council, 1988-92, British Council, 1988-93; Chairman, Booker Prize Panel of Judges, 1987; Governor, BBC, 1988-93; President, Society of Authors, 1997-. Publications: Cover Her Face, 1962; A Mind to Murder, 1963; Unnatural Causes, 1967; Shroud for a Nightingale, 1971; The Maul and the Pear Tree (with T A Critchley), 1971; An Unsuitable Job for a Woman, 1972; Innocent Blood, 1980; The Skull Beneath the Skin, 1982; A Taste for Death, 1986; Devices and Desires, 1989; The Children of Men, 1992; Original Sin, 1994; A Certain Justice, 1997; Time to be in Earnest, 1999; Death in Holy Orders, 2001; The Murder Room, 2003; The Lighthouse, 2005. Honours: Order of the British Empire; Honorary Fellow, St Hilda's College, Oxford, 1996, Downing College, Cambridge, 2000, Girton College, Cambridge, 2000; Honorary DLitt, University of Buckingham, 1992, University of Hertfordshire, 1994, University of Glasgow, 1995, University of Durham, 1988, University of Portsmouth, 1999; Honorary LittD, University of London, 1993; Dr hc, University of Essex, 1996; Grand Master Award,

Mystery Writers of America, 1999. Memberships: Fellow, Royal Society of Literature; Fellow, Royal Society of Arts. Address: c/o Greene & Heaton Ltd, 37 Goldhawk Road, London W12 8QQ, England.

JAMIL Tariq, b. 9 November 1965, Pakistan. Lecturer; Engineer. m. Saiqa, 1 son, 1 daughter. Education: BSc, Electrical Engineering, NWFP University of Engineering and Technology, Pakistan, 1989; MS, Computer Engineering, 1992; PhD, Computer Engineering, Florida Institute of Technology, USA, 1996. Appointments: Graduate Teaching Assistant, Florida Institute of Technology, USA, 1994-96; Assistant Professor, Faculty of Computer Science and Engineering, GIK Institute of Engineering Sciences and Technology, Pakistan, 1997; Lecturer, School of Computer Science and Engineering, University New South Wales, Sydney, Australia, 1997-98; Lecturer, School of Computing, University of Tasmania, Launceston, Australia, 1999-2000; Assistant Professor, Department of Electrical & Computer Engineering, Sultan Qaboos University, Muscat, Oman, 2000-. Publications include: An Investigation into the Application of Linear Feedback Shift Registers for Steganography, 2002; Hardware Implementation and Performance Evaluation of Complex Binary Adder Designs, 2003; Implementation of a CAM-based Dataflow Processor for Parallel Computations, 2004; A case study approach to investigate the usefulness of AHP in developing SSADM customization model, 2005; Design and implementation of a nibble-size multiplier for $(-1+j)$-base complex binary numbers, 2005; Design and Implementation of an Automatic Emergency Management System, 2006; Impact of Shift Operations on $(-1+j)$-base Complex Binary Numbers, 2008. Honours include: National Talent Scholarship, 1981-89; President's Cash Award and Gold Medal, 1983, Best Graduate and Gold Medal, 1989; Quaid-e-Azam Scholarship, 1990-94; Award for Academic Excellence, IEEE Computer Society, 1996; Distinguished Speaker, IEEE Computer Society, 2005-07. Memberships: IEEE, USA; Institution of Engineering and Technology, UK; Institution of Electrical and Electronic Engineers, Pakistan; Chartered Engineer, UK; Professional Engineer, Pakistan. Address: Electrical and Computer Engineering Department, Sultan Qaboos University, PO Box 33, Muscat 123, Sultanate of Oman.

JAMMEH Alhaji Yahya A J J, b. 25 May 1965, Kanilai, Foni Kansala District, The Gambia. Colonel (retired); Doctor; President of the Republic of The Gambia. m. Zineb Souma. Education: Passed Common Entrance Examination and awarded a Government Scholarship, 1978; General Certificate of Education 'O' Level, Gambia High School, 1983; Diploma in Military Science, four-month Military Police Officers basic course, Fort McClellon, Alabama, USA, 1993. Appointments: Joined Gambia National Gendarmerie then assigned to Special Intervention Unit of The Gambia National Army, 1984; Private (later Sergeant), Special Guards Unit of the Mobile Gendarmerie, 1986; Escort Training Instructor (later Cadet Officer), Gendarmerie Training School, 1987; In charge of Presidential Escort (later Second Lieutenant), Presidential Guards, 1989-90; Security Officer for Visiting Heads of State at the ECOWAS Summit and as Officer-in-charge of the ECOWAS Peace Conference for Liberia, Kairaba Beach Hotel, 1990; Officer Commanding, Mobile Gendarmerie, 1991; Officer Commanding, The Gambia National Gendarmerie's Military Police Unit, 1991; Officer Commanding (later First Lieutenant), The Gambia National Army Military Police, Yundum Barracks 1991-92; Officer-in-charge both of His Holiness and entourage, and of VIP security at State functions including visiting Heads of

State on the visit of Pope John Paul II, 1992; Special Officer in charge of the close protection of the visiting ECOMOG Field Commander, 1993; Chairman, Armed Forces Provisional Ruling Council and Head of State, 1994; Promoted to Captain, 1994, Colonel, 1996, retired, 1996; Elected President of the Republic of The Gambia, 1996-; Elected Chairman of CILSS during its 12th Conference of Heads of State and Government, The Gambia, 1997. Honours: Honorary Citizen of the State of Georgia, USA, 1993; Honorary Lieutenant-Colonel ADC of Alabama State Militia, USA, 1994; Highest Libyan Insignia, Grand Commander of the Order of Al-Fatah, 1995; Highest Chinese Insignia, the Order of Brilliant Jade with Grand Cordon of the Republic of China, 1996; Pan-African Humanitarian Award, Pan-African Foundation and the World Council of Culture, 1997; Man of the Year, ABI, 1997; Gold Record of Achievement, ABI, 1998; Honorary Admiral in the Alabama State Navy, Governor of Alabama, 1998; Grand Order of Bravery by Colonel Gadaffi of Libya, 1998; Islamic Worldwide Grand Prix, Cheikhna Cheikh Saad Bouh Foundation of Dakar, Senegal, 1998; Honorary Doctorate of Civil Law from St Mary's University, Halifax, Canada, 1999; Deputy Governor of the ABI Research Association, 1999; Millennium Medal of Honour, ABI, 2000. Address: Office of the President, State House, Banjul, The Gambia.

JANES J(oseph) Robert, b. 23 May 1935, Toronto, Ontario, Canada. Writer. m. Gracia Joyce Lind, 16 May 1958, 2 sons, 2 daughters. Education: BSc, Mining Engineering, 1958, MEng, Geology, 1967, University of Toronto. Publications: Children's books: The Tree-Fort War, 1977; Theft of Gold, 1980; Danger on the River, 1982; Spies for Dinner, 1984; Murder in the Market, 1985. Adult books: The Toy Shop, 1981; The Watcher, 1982; The Third Story, 1983; The Hiding Place, 1984; The Alice Factor, 1991; St Cyr/Kohler series: Mayhem, 1992; Carousel, 1992; Kaleidoscope, 1993; Salamander, 1994; Mannequin, 1994; Dollmaker, 1995; Stonekiller, 1995; Sandman, 1996; Gypsy, 1997; Madrigal, 1999; Beekeeper, 2001; Flykiller, 2002. Non-Fiction: The Great Canadian Outback, 1978. Textbooks: Holt Geophoto Resource Kits, 1972; Rocks, Minerals and Fossils, 1973; Earth Science, 1974; Geology and the New Global Tectonics, 1976; Searching for Structure (co-author), 1977. Teacher's Guide: Searching for Structure (co-author), 1977; Airphoto Interpretation and the Canadian Landscape (with J D Mollard), 1984. Contributions to: Toronto Star; Toronto Globe and Mail; The Canadian; Winnipeg Free Press; Canadian Children's Annual. Honours: Grants: Canada Council; Ontario Arts Council; J P Bickell Foundation; Thesis Award, Canadian Institute of Mining and Metallurgy; Works-in-progress Grant, Ontario Arts Council, 1991; Hammett Award Nominee, International Association of Crime Writers (North American Branch). Memberships: Crime Writers Association (UK); Historical Novel Society (UK); International Association of Crime Writers (North American Branch). Address: PO Box 1590, Niagara-on-the-Lake, Ontario L0S 1J0, Canada. Website: www.jrobertjanes.com

JANG Se Bok, b. 27 May 1962, Jinju, South Korea. Professor. m. Mi Suk Jeong, 1 son, 1 daughter. Education: PhD, Pusan National University, 1995. Appointments: Postdoctoral studies, University of California at Berkeley, USA; Associate Professor, Pusan National University. Publications: Numerous articles in professional journals. Honours: Best Graduate Student's Award. Memberships: American Chemical Society; Biophysical Society. Address: Department of Molecular & Biology, College of Natural Sciences, Pusa National University, Busan 609-735, Korea. E-mail: sbjang@pusan.ac.kr

JANI Mayank, b. 15 February 1968, Kheralu District, Mahesana, India. Doctor. m. 2 sons. Education: Bachelor of Homoeopathic Medicine & Surgery, Sardar Patel University, Viddanagar, Anand, 1991; Postgraudate Diploma of Medical Laboratory Technology, Gujarat Institute of Technical Education, Baroda, 1992; Postgraduate Diploma in Information Technology, Manipal Academy of Higher Education, Manipal, 2000; MD, Sardar Patel University, V V Nagar, 2007. Appointments: General Practitioner, 1991-. Address: 6-b Shivam Swaminarayan Society, Behind Sardar Ganj, Anand 388001, Gujarat, India. E-mail: drmayank123@yahoo.com

JANNER Greville Ewan, Baron Janner of Braunstone, b. 11 July 1928, Cardiff, South Wales. Working Peer; Barrister; Queen's Counsel; Author; Jewish Leader. m. Myra Louise Sheink, deceased, 1 son, 2 daughters. Education: MA, Trinity Hall, Cambridge, 1946-49; Harvard Law School, 1950-51; Hon PhD, Haifa, 1984; Hon LLD, De Montfort University, Leicester, 1998. Appointments: Member of Parliament, Leicester North West, 1970-74; Member of Parliament, Leicester West, 1974-97; Chairman, Select Committee on Employment, 1992-96; Vice Chairman, British Israel and British India Parliamentary Groups; Vice President, World Jewish Congress; Founder President, Commonwealth Jewish Council; Chairman, Holocaust Educational Trust; President, Maimonides Foundation; Former President, Board of Deputies of British Jews, 1978-84; Founder, President, JSB Ltd; Former Director, Labroke plc. Publications: Author, 65 books mainly on employment and industrial relations law, presentational skills and public speaking; One Hand Alone Cannot Clap. Memberships: Magic Circle; International Brotherhood of Magicians. Address: House of Lords, London SW1A 0PW, England.

JANSEN N Elly, b. 5 October 1929, Wisch, Holland. Retired Charity Director. m. Alan Brian Stewart (George Whitehouse), 3 daughters. Education: Paedologisch Institute, Free University, Amsterdam, Boerhave Kliniek (SRN), University of London. Appointments: Founder and CEO, Richmond Fellowship for Community Mental Health, 1959-91; Founder, Richmond Fellowship College, 1967; Founder and CEO, Richmond Fellowship International, 1981-2000; Founder and Executive Trustee, Fellowship Charitable Foundation (now Community Housing and Therapy), 1983-93; Founder, Richmond Fellowship Workshops, 1986; Founded: Richmond Fellowship of America (1968), Australia (1973), New Zealand (1977), Austria (1978), and subsequently of Barbados, Bangladesh, Bolivia, Canada, Costa Rica, France, Ghana, Grenada, Hong Kong, India, Israel, Jamaica, Malta, Mexico, Nigeria, Peru, Philippines, Trinidad & Tobago, Uruguay and Zimbabwe; Organised international conferences on therapeutic communities and courses on mental illness and drug rehabilitation; Acted as adviser to many governments on issues of community care. Publications: Editor, The Therapeutic Community Outside the Hospital, 1980; Contributor: Mental Health and the Community, 1983; Towards a Whole Society, 1985; R D Laing, Creative Destroyer, 1997; Contributions to American Journal of Psychiatry, L'Information Psychiatrique and other journals. Honours: Fellowship, German Marshall Memorial Fund, 1977-78; OBE, 1980; Templeton Award, 1985. Address: Clyde House, 109 Strawberry Vale, Twickenham, TW1 4SJ, England.

JANTUAH Kwame Sanaa-Poku (formerly John Ernest Jantuah), b. 21 December 1922, Kumasi, Ashanti, Ghana. Educationist; Lawyer; Diplomat; Politician. m. (1) 2 sons, 5 daughters, (2) Agnes Owusua, 1 son, 1 daughter. Education: Cambridge (UK) Senior Secondary School Certificate, 1941;

Teacher's Certificate A Grade 1, St Augustine's Teacher Training College, 1943-44; Politics & Economics Diploma course, Catholic Workers College (now Plater College), Oxford, 1946-48; BL and LLB (Hons Lond), Gibson & Weldon School of Law, London, England, 1964-66; Called to the English Bar, Lincoln's Inn, 1966 and to the Ghana Bar, 1967. Appointments: Teacher, Roman Catholic Senior School, Ejisu, 1945-46; Headmaster, Asante Youth Association Day Secondary School, Kumasi, 1953; Deputy General Secretary, Asante-man Council, Kumasi, 1948-50; Elected CPP Member, Kumasi Town Council, 1950; Editor, The Asante Sentinel, Kumasi, 1950-51; Elected Member, Gold Coast Legislative Assembly, 1951 and appointed Ministerial Secretary to Minister of Justice & Attorney General; Minister of Agriculture & Fisheries, 1954-56; Deputy High Commissioner of Ghana to London, 1957-59 (Acting High Commissioner for latter part of 1958); Ambassador of Ghana to France, 1959-62, to Brazil, 1962-64, to Berlin (GDR), 1985-90; Legal Practice, City Chambers, Accra, 1967-79; Minister of Local Government, Rural Development & Co-operatives, 1979-81; Minister of Interior, October to December, 1981 (interrupted by coup d'etat of December 1981). Publications: Ne Nos Inducas in Tentationem (dissenting comment on the Lord's Prayer), 1989; Christianity, Culture and Change, 1997. Honours: Grand Officier de l'Ordre du Mèrite (Republic of Senegal), 1981; Certificate of Honour, The Pan-Africanists Forum, 1999. Memberships: Royal Oyoko Abohyen Clan of Ashanti; President, Asante Youth Association (AYA), 1952-53; Platernian Association, Oxford; Guild of Catholic Lawyers, Ghana; Ghana Bar Association; Oxford and Cambridge Association of Ghana, Accra; United Gold Coast Convention; Convention People's Party; People's National Party. Address: PO Box AN6467, Accra-North, Accra, Ghana.

JAROENRAT Kairat, b. 5 April 1976, Nakhon Pathom, Thailand. Lecturer. m. Natchamol Srichumroenrattana. Education: BSc, Petrochemicals and Polymeric Materials, 1997; MSc, Information Technology, 2000; PhD, Information Technology, 2008. Appointments: Lecturer. Nakhon Pathom Rajabhat University, Thailand. Publications: On routing performance of MENTOR algorithm, 2006; On routing performance of a network algorithm, 2006. Honours: Listed in international biographical dictionaries. Address: 47 Nasang-Nakhum Road, T Nakhon Pathom, A Muang, Nakhon Pathom, 73000, Thailand. E-mail: kairat@kairat.com Website: www.kairat.com

JARRATT Sir Alexander Anthony, b. 19 January 1924, London, England. Retired Civil Servant; Company Executive. m. Mary Philomena Keogh, 1 son, 2 daughters. Education: BCom, 1st Class Honours, Birmingham University, 1946-49. Appointments: Petty Officer Fleet Air Arm; Civil Servant Ministry of Power, 1949-64; Seconded to the Treasury, 1953-54; Cabinet Office, 1964-65; Secretary, Prices and Incomes Board, 1964-68; Deputy Under Secretary, Department of Employment and Productivity, 1968-70; Deputy Secretary Ministry of Agriculture, 1970; Chief Executive IPC and IPC Newspapers, 1970-74; Chairman and Chief Executive, Reed International, 1974-85, Director, 1970-85; Chairman, Smiths Industries plc, 1985-91, Director, 1984-96; Director, Thyssen-Bornemisza Supervisory Board, 1972-89; Deputy Chairman: Midland Bank plc, 1980-91, Prudential Corporation, 1987-91 and 1992-94; Non-Executive Director, ICI plc, 1975-91; President Advertising Association, 1979-83; Former Member, NEDC; Former Chairman, CBI Economic Policy Committee; CBI Employment Policy Committee; Former Member, Presidents Committee, CBI; Chairman, Industrial Society, 1975-79; Henley Administrative Staff College, 1976-89; Centre for Dispute Resolution, 1990-2000, president, 2001-; Chancellor, University of Birmingham, 1983-2002. Honours: Companion of the Bath, 1968; Knight Bachelor, 1979; Honorary LLD, University of Birmingham; Honorary DSc, Cranfield; Honorary D Univ, Brunel and Essex; Honorary, CGIA; FRSA; Honorary FCGI. Address: Barn Mead, Fryerning, Essex CM4 0NP, England.

JARRE Jean-Michel, b. 24 August 1948, Lyons, France. Musician (synthesizers, keyboards); Composer; Record Producer. m.(1) Flore Guillard, 1975, divorced, 1 child (2) Charlotte Rampling, 1977' divorced, 1 son (3) Anne Parillaud, 2005-. Musical Education: Piano and guitar from age 5; Conservatoire de Paris, with Jeanine Reuff. Career: Solo debut, Paris Opera, 1971; Youngest composer to appear, Palais Garnier, 1971; Major concerts, often including lasers and fireworks, filmed for video releases include: Beijing, China, 1981; Bastille Day, Place De La Concorde, 1979; Houston, Texas (1.3 million audience), 1986; London Docklands, 1988; La Defense, Paris (2.5 million audience), 1990; Sun City, Johannesburg, South Africa, 1993; Member of jury, First International Visual Music Awards, Midem, France, 1992. Compositions include: Oxygène Part IV, used for several television themes; Ballet and film scores include: Des Garçons Et Des Filles, 1968; Deserted Palace, 1972; Les Granges Brûlées, 1973; La Maladie De Hambourg, 1978; Gallipoli, 1979. Recordings: Albums (all self-composed and produced): Deserted Palace, 1971; Oxygène, 1977; Magnetic Fields, 1981; The Concerts In China, 1982; The Essential Jean-Michel Jarre, 1983; Zoolook, 1984; Rendez-Vous, 1986; In Concert Lyons/Houston, 1987; Revelations (Number 2, UK), 1988; Jarre Live, 1989; Waiting For Cousteau, 1990; Images - The Best Of Jean-Michel Jarre, 1991; Chronologie, 1993; Jarre Hong Kong, 1994; Cities in Concert, 1997; Oxygène 7-13, 1997; China Concert, 1999; Odyssey Through 2, 1998; Metamorphoses, 2000; Aero, 2004; Teo & Tea, 2007. Honours: First Western artist to play in China, 1981; Grand Prix, Academie Du Disque, Zoolook, 1985; Best Instrumental Album, Victoire de la Musique, 1986; Numerous Platinum and Gold discs worldwide. Address: c/o Dreyfus Records, 26 Avenue Kléber, 75116 Paris, France.

JARRE Maurice Alexis, b. 13 September 1924, Lyons, France. Composer. m. (1) France Pejot, 1946, 1 son, (2) Dany Saval, 1965, 1 daughter, (3) Laura Devon, 1967 (divorced). Musical Education: Conservatoire National Supéreur de Musique. Career: Musician, Radiodiffusion Française, 1946-50; Director of Music, Théâtre National Populaire (TNP), 1950-63. Compositions: Symphonic music; Music for theatre and ballet include: Roland Petit's Notre-Dame de Paris (Paris Opera), 1966; Numerous film scores include: Lawrence Of Arabia, 1963; Dr Zhivago, 1965; Ryan's Daughter, 1970; Shogun, 1980; Doctors In Love, 1982; A Passage To India, 1985; The Mosquito Coast, 1987; Tai-Pan, 1987; Gaby, 1988; Gorillas In The Mist, 1989; Ghost; Dead Poets Society, 1990; Fatal Attraction; Les Vendanges de feu, 1994; Sunchaser, 1996; Jour et la nuit, Le, 1997; Sunshine, 1999; I Dreamed of Africa, 2000. Honours: Officer, Légion d'Honneur, Commander des Arts et Lettres; Prix Italia, 1955, 1962; Grand Prix du Disque, Academy Charles Cross, 1962; Hollywood Golden Globe, 1965, 1984; People's Choice Award, 1988. Address: c/o Paul Kohner Inc, 9169 Sunset Boulevard, Los Angeles, CA 90069, USA.

JARSKÝ Čeněk, b. 11 June 1953, Prague, Czech Republic. Civil Engineer; Professor of Technology of Structures. m. Václava Jarská, 1 son. Education: MSc, Civil Engineering, 1976, PhD, Technology of Structures, 1982, DSc, Technology of Structures, 2001, all at the Czech Technical University, Prague; Postgraduate Course in Theoretical Cybernetics, Charles University, Prague, 1983; Diploma of Chartered Engineer, Czech Chamber of Civil Engineers, Prague, 1991. Appointments: Lecturer, Czech Technical University, Prague, 1976-82; Scientific Officer, Building Research Establishment, Garston, UK, 1980-81; Scientific Officer, 1982-84, Division Head, 1984-90, Research Institute of Civil Engineering, Prague; General Manager, Owner, CONTEC Construction Technology Consulting, Kralupy n. Vlt, 1990-; Associate Professor, 1997-2005, Professor of Technology of Structures, 2005-, Czech Technical University, Prague. Publications: Automated Preparation and Management Realization of Structures (book, author), 2000; Planning and Realization of Structures (book, main author), 2003; Mathematical Modeling in Preparation and Management of Projects (monograph, author), 2005. Honours: Bronze Medal, Ministry of Civil Engineering, Prague, 1989; Award Certificate, Grand Prix For Arch (exhibition), 2000; Silver Plaque, Slovak Technical University, 2004. Memberships: Czech Society of Project Management, Prague; Czech Chamber of Chartered Civil Engineers, Prague; International Association for Bridge and Structure Engineering, Zurich. Address: Mánesova 819, 27801 Kralupy n. Vlt, Czech Republic. E-mail: jarsky@contec.cz Website: www.contec.cz

JASON Sir David, b. 2 February 1940, England. Actor. m. Gill Hinchcliffe, 2005, 1 daughter. Creative Works: Theatre includes: Under Milk Wood, 1971; The Rivals, No Sex Please...We're British!, 1972; Darling Mr London (tour), Charley's Aunt (tour), 1975; The Norman Conquests, 1976; The Relapse, 1978; Cinderella, 1979; The Unvarnished Truth (Middle/Far East tour), 1983; Look No Hands! (tour and West End), 1985; Films: Under Milk Wood, 1970; Royal Flash, 1974; The Odd Job, 1978; Only Fools and Horses, Wind in the Willows, 1983; TV includes: Do Not Adjust Your Set, 1967; The Top Secret Life of Edgar Briggs, 1973-74; Mr Stabbs, 1974; Ronnie Barker Shows, Open All Hours, Porridge, Lucky Feller, 1975; A Sharp Intake of Breath, 1978; Del Trotter in Only Fools and Horses, 1981-91; Porterhouse Blue, 1986; Jackanory, 1988; A Bit of A Do, 1988-89; Single Voices: The Chemist, Amongst Barbarians, 1989; Pa Larkin in The Darling Buds of May, 1990-92; A Touch of Frost, 1992-2006; The Bullion Boys, 1993; Micawber, 2001; The Second Quest, 2005; Diamond Geezer, 2005-2007; Ghostboat, Hogfather, 2006. Voice work: Dangermouse; Count Duckula; The Wind in the Willows. Honours include: Best Actor Award, BAFTA, 1988; BAFTA Fellowship, 2003; OBE, 2005. Address: c/o Richard Stone Partnership, 2 Henrietta Street, London WC2E 8PS, England.

JASON Gillian Brett, b. 30 June 1941, England. Art Gallery Director. m. Neville Jason, 21 March 1961, 1 son, 1 daughter. Education: Dominican Convent School, Brewood, Staffordshire; Royal Ballet School, London, 1958-60; London Opera Centre, London, 1965-67. Appointments: Director, Gillian Jason Gallery, London, 1981-94; Director, Jason and Rhodes, London, 1994-99; Gillian Jason, Modern and Contemporary Art, 1999-. Honours: BBO Award, Royal Ballet School, 1958; Countess of Munster Award, London Opera Centre, 1965. Membership: Society of London Art Dealers, 1994-. Address: 114 New Cavendish Street, London, W1W 6XT, England. Email: art@gillianjason.com Website: www.gillianjason.com

JASPER David, b. 1 August 1951, Stockton on Tees, England. University Teacher; Clergyman. m. Alison Elizabeth Collins, 29 October 1976, 3 daughters. Education: Dulwich College,

1959-69; Jesus College, Cambridge, 1969-72; BA, MA, 1976, BD, 1980, Keble College, Oxford; PhD, Hatfield College, Durham, 1983; DD, Keble College, Oxford, 2002; Theol Dr hc, Uppsala University, 2007. Appointments: Director, Centre for the Study of Literature and Theology, Durham University, 1986-91, Glasgow University, 1991-; Editor, Literature and Theology; Professor of Literature and Theology, University of Glasgow, 1998-. Publications: Coleridge as Poet and Religious Thinker, 1985; The New Testament and the Literary Imagination, 1987; The Study of Literature and Religion, 1989; Rhetoric Power and Community, 1992; Reading in the Canon of Scripture, 1995; The Sacred and Secular Canon in Romanticism, 1999; The Sacred Desert, 2004; General Editor, Macmillan Series, Studies in Religion and Culture. Honours: Dana Fellow, Emory University, Atlanta, 1991; Honorary Fellow, Research Foundation, Durham University, 1991; Ida Cordelia Beam Distinguished Visiting Professor, University of Iowa, 2003; Doctorate of Theology – Honoris Causa, University of Uppsala, Sweden, 2007. Memberships: International Society for Religion, Literature and Culture secretary; American Academy of Religion; Fellow, Society for Arts, Religion and Culture, 2000; Fellow, Royal Society of Edinburgh, 2006. Address: Netherwood, 124 Old Manse Road, Wishaw, Lanarkshire ML2 0EP, Scotland.

JAY Peter, b. 7 February 1937. Writer; Broadcaster. m. (1) Margaret Ann Callaghan, 1961, dissolved 1986, 1 son, 2 daughters, (2) Emma Thornton, 1986, 3 sons. Education: MA, 1st class honours, Politics, Philosophy and Economics, Christ Church Oxford, 1960. Appointments: Midshipman and Sub-Lieutenant, RNVR, 1956-57; Assistant Principal, 1961-64, Private Secretary to Joint Permanent Secretary, 1964, Principal, 1964-67, HM Treasury; Economics Editor, The Time, 1967-77; Associate Editor, Times Business News, 1969-77; Presenter, Weekend World, ITV series, 1972-77; The Jay Interview, ITV series, 1975-76; Ambassador to USA, 1977-79; Director, Economist Intelligence University, 1979-83; Consultant, Economist Group, 1979-81; Chairman and Chief Executive, TV-AM Ltd, 1980-83, and TV-AM News, 1982-83; President, TV-AM, 1983-; Presenter, A Week in Politics, Channel 4, 1983-86; COS to Robert Maxwell, Chairman of Mirror Group Newspapers Ltd, 1986-89; Visiting Scholar, Brookings Institution, Washington, 1979-80; Wincott Memorial Lecturer, 1975; Copland Memorial Lecturer, Australia, 1980; Shell Lecturer, Glasgow, 1985; Governor, Ditchley Foundation, 1982-; Author and Presenter, Road to Riches, BBC TV series, 2000. Publications: The Budget, 1972; Contributor, America and the World, 1979, 1980; The Crisis for Western Political Economy and other Essays, 1984; Apocalypse 2000, with Michael Stewart, 1987; Contributor, Foreign Affairs journal, Road to Riches, or The Wealth of Man, 2000. Honours: Political Broadcaster of the Year, 1973; Harold Wincott Financial and Economic Journalist of the Year, 1973; RTS Male Personality of the Year, Pye Award, 1974; SFTA Shell International TV Award, 1974; RTS Home News Award, 1992; Honorary DH, Ohio State University, 1978; Honorary DLitt, Wake Forest University, 1979; Berkeley Citation, University of California, 1979. Address: Hensington Farmhouse, Woodstock, Oxfordshire OX20 1LH, England.

JAYACHANDRAN Divakaran, b. 10 November 1957, Kokkottukonam, Trivandrum, India. Senior Medical Social Worker. m. S Lissa, 1 son, 1 daughter. Education: BSc, 1979, MA, Sociology, 1981, MA, Psychology, 1995; PhD in Behavioural Sciences, 2007. Appointments: Research Scientist, Loyola College of Social Sciences, 1981-82; Psychiatric Social Worker, Medical College, Kozhikode, 1982-85; Senior Medical Social Worker, Comprehensive Epilepsy Program,

SCT Institute of Medical Sciences, Trivandrum, 1985-. Publications: Clinical trial of yoga meditation in Medically Refractory Epilepsy; Numerous articles in medical journals. Honours: Best Scientific Paper Award (non medical), IEA/ IES, 1995, 2005. Memberships: Governing Council IEA, Governing Body, State Resource Centre, Kerala; Patron, Epilepsy Self Help Group, Advisory Committee Newsletters; Senior Faculty and Course Co-ordinator, CACEE, University of Kerala; Faculty in Social Sciences, INNOU; Member, CAOA; Editor, Epilepsy newsletter 'Pratheekesha'; ISHA; ARDSI; ISSA; IAGP; Member, International Conclave on Epilepsy and Disability. Address: Department of Neurology, SCT Institute of Medical Science and Technology, Trivandrum 695011, India. E-mail: sijass@hotmail.com

JAYAWARDENE Kirikankanange Albert Thistlethwayte Wilhelm Perera, b. 9 November 1928, Moratuwa, Sri Lanka. Consultant Anaesthetist. m. Amara, 1 son, 2 daughters. Education: MBBS, Ceylon, 1956; DA, London, 1962; FRCA, England, 1963; FACC, USA, 1985. Appointments: Retired Consultant Anaesthetist, Cardiothoracic Unit and Surgical Intensive Care Unit, National Hospital, Sri Lanka. Publications: Several articles in professional medical journals. Honours: Most Outstanding Citizen Award for Medicine, 1995; 20th Century Achievement Award; Vishva Prasadhini Award for Distinguished Service to the Nation, 1996; Listed in national and international biographical dictionaries. Memberships: President, College of Anaesthesiologists of Sri Lanka, 1984, 1985, 1986; President, Sri Lanka Medical Association, 1991; Vice President, Sri Lanka Heart Association, 1994-; Vice President, Organisation of Professional Associations of Sri Lanka, 2001, 2006-07; Patron, Sri Lankan Critical Care and Emergency Medicine Society, 2002-; Director and Vice President, Critical Care, Ceylon Hospitals Ltd; Director, Durdans Heart Surgical Centre. Address: 14 Albert Place, Dehiwela, Sri Lanka.

JAYSTON Michael, b. 29 October 1935, Nottingham, England. Actor. m. (1) Lynn Farleigh, 1965, divorced 1970, (2) Heather Mary Sneddon, divorced 1977, (3) Elizabeth Ann Smithson, 1978, 3 sons, 1 daughter. Career: Actor, RSC, 1965-69, National Theatre, 1976-79; Films: Cromwell, 1970; Nicholas and Alexandra, 1971; Follow Me, 1972; Bequest to the Nation, 1972; Tales That Witness Madness, 1973; Craze, 1973; The Internecine Project, 1974; Dominique, 1978; Zulu Dawn, 1979; Element of Doubt, 1996. TV: Power Game; Charles Dickens; Beethoven; Solo-Wilfred Owen; Quiller, 1975; Tinker, Tailor, Soldier, Spy, 1979; Dr Who, 1986; A Bit of A Do, 1988; Kipling's Sussex, 1989; About Face, 1989; Darling Buds of May, 1992; Outside Edge, 1995-96; Only Fools and Horses, 1996; Flesh and Blood, 1980; Dust to Dust, 1985; Doctor Who. 1986; Highlander III: The Sorcerer, 1994; The Bill, 2006. Theatre: Private Lives, 1980; Sound of Music, 1981; Way of the World, 1984-85; Woman in Mind; Beethoven Readings with Medici String Quartet, 1989; Dancing at Lughnasa, 1992; Wind in the Willows, 1994; Racing Demon, 1998; Easy Virtue, 1999. Address: Michael Whitehall Ltd, 125 Gloucester Road, London SW7 4TE, England.

JEAL Tim, b. 27 January 1945, London, England. Author. m. Joyce Timewell, 11 October 1969, 3 daughters. Education: MA, Christ Church, Oxford. Publications: For Love of Money, 1967; Somewhere Beyond Reproach, 1969; Livingstone, 1973; Cushing's Crusade, 1974; Until the Colours Fade, 1976; A Marriage of Convenience, 1979; Baden-Powell, 1989; The Missionary's Wife, 1997; Deep Water, 2000; Swimming with my Father, 2004; Stanley: The Impossible Life of Africa's Greatest Explorer, 2007. Honours: Joint Winner,

Llewelyn Rhys Memorial Prize, 1974; Writers Guild Laurel Award; Sunday Times Biography of the Year, 2007; Winner, American National Book Critics Circle Award for Biography, 2007. Membership: Society of Authors. Address: 29 Willow Road, London NW3 1TL, England.

JEAN Ming-Der, b. 4 December 1957, Taiwan, Republic of China. Science Educator; Researcher. m. Yuh-Ing Hwang, 1986, 2 daughters. Education: BS, Aerospace and Systems Engineering, Feng-Chia University, 1981; MS, Materials Science, National Sun Yat Sen University, Taiwan, 1986. Appointments: Lecturer, Yung-Ta Institute and Commerce Taiwan, 1986-2003; Lecturer, Ping-Tung University of Technology, Taiwan, 1990-92; Associate Professor, 2004-. Publications: 24 articles in professional scientific journals. Honours: Listed in national and international biographical directories. Memberships: American Chemical Society. Address: 316 Chung-Shan Road, Lin-Lo, Ping-Tung, 900 Taiwan, Republic of China.

JEBASHVILI Manana, b. 21 January 1961, Tbilisi, Georgia. Doctor. m. Shalva Gabeskiria, 1 daughter. Education: Medical Institute of Tbilisi, 1984; Postgradaute, Georgian State Institute of Hospital Therapy, 1986; Doctor Medical Science (PhD), 2001. Appointments: Member, Committee of Health and Social Affairs, Georgian Parliament. Publications: 52 scientific works. Honours: Diploma of Expertise, Gastroenterology and Hepatology, 2006; Woman of the Year, ABI. Memberships: General Secretary, Georgian National Association of Gastroenterology. Address: Paliashvili 6, Tbilisi, Georgia. E-mail: mananajeb@yahoo.com

JEE Jung-Hoon, b. 21 June 1972, Masan, Republic of Korea. Fisheries Biologist; Director. m. Yoo-Hwa Keum. Education: BSc, Fisheries Science, Fish Pathology, 1997, MSc, Aquatic Toxicology, 1999, PhD, Environment Toxicology, 2003, Pukyong National University. Appointments: Senior Researcher, Institute of Fisheries Science, 2003-05; Research Instructor, Pukyong National University, 2004-05; Deputy Director, Ministry of Maritime Affairs & Fisheries, 2006-. Publications: 42 articles in professional scientific journals. Honours: Korea Science and Engineering Foundation Award, 2003-04; Korea Research Foundation Award, 2005; Listed in international biographical dictionaries. Memberships: Korean Fisheries Society; Korean Society of Fish Pathology. Address: International Co-operation Bureau, MOMAF, #140-2, Gye-dong, Jongno-Gu, Seoul, 110-703, Republic of Korea. E-mail: aquajee@momaf.go.kr

JEFFCOTT Leo B, b. England. Professor of Veterinary Science. m. Tisza Jacqueline Hubbard, 14 June 1969, 2 daughters. Education: Bachelor of Veterinary Medicine, Royal Veterinary College, University of London, 1961-66; PhD, 1972; FRCVS, 1978; DVr Pt 1, 1973; DVSc, 1989; Specialist in Equine Medicine, 1990; MA, 1994; VetMedDr hc (Uppsala), 2000. Appointments: Assistant Pathologist, 1967-71, Radiologist, 1972-77, Head of Clinical Department, 1977-82, Equine Research Station, Animal Health Trust, Newmarket, England; Accredited Event Veterinarian, FEI, 1977-; Professor of Clinical Radiology, 1981-82, Visiting Professor, 1990-91, Swedish University of Agricultural Sciences, Uppsala, Sweden; Professor of Veterinary Clinical Sciences, 1982-91, Deputy Dean, Faculty of Veterinary Science, 1985, Head of Department, Veterinary Clinical Sciences, 1985-89, Director, Department of Veterinary Clinic & Hospital, 1986-91, University of Melbourne, Australia; Official Veterinarian at Olympic Games, 1988, 1992, 1996, 2000, 2004, 2008; Professor of Veterinary Clinical Studies,

Department of Clinical Veterinary Medicine, 1991-2004, Dean, Veterinary School, 1991-2004, Professorial Fellow, Pembroke College, 1993-2004, University of Cambridge, England; Dean, Faculty of Veterinary Science, University of Sydney, 2004-. Publications: Over 300 scientific publications related to equine science; Co-author of 10 textbooks. Honours include: Share Jones Lectureship in Veterinary Anatomy, 1993; Animal Health Trust Outstanding Scientific Achievement Award, 1994; Sefton Award 1997 for services to Equestrian Safety, 1997; Dalrymple Champneys Prize and Cup, 2001; J D Stewart Address, 2004; R R Pascoe Peroration, 2005; Honorary Member, Bureau of the Federation Equestre Internationale, 2006. Memberships: British Veterinary Association; British Equine Veterinary Association; Member, Bureau of Federation Equestre Internationale and Chairman, Veterinary Committee, 1998-2006; Royal College of Veterinary Surgeons; World Society for the Protection of Animals; International Committee on Equine Exercise Physiology. Address: Faculty of Veterinary Science, University of Sydney, J D Stewart Building B01, NSW 2006, Australia. E-mail: leoj@vetsci.usyd.edu.au

JEFFS Julian, b. 5 April 1931, Wolverhampton, England. Author; Editor. m. Deborah Bevan, 3 sons. Education: Downing College, Cambridge. Appointments: Sherry Shipper's Assistant, Spain, 1956; Barrister, Gray's Inn, 1958; QC, 1975; Recorder, 1975-96; Bencher of Hon Society of Gray's Inn, 1981; Deputy High Court Judge (Chancery Division), 1981-96; Retired from practice, 1991. Publications: Sherry, 1961, 5th edition, 2004; Clerk & Lindsell on Torts, 13th edition, 1969 to 16th edition, 1989 (an editor); The Wines of Europe, 1971; Little Dictionary of Drink, 1973; Encyclopaedia of UK and European Patent Law, 1977, co-editor; The Wines of Spain, 1999. Honours: Office International de la Vigne et du Vin, 1962, 2001; Gran Orden de Caballeros del Vino; Glenfiddich Wine Writers Award, 1974 and 1978. Memberships: Member of Committee, Wine and Food Society, 1965-67, 1971-82; Chairman, Patent Bar Association, 1980-89; President, Circle of Wine Writers, 1992-96. Address: Church Farm House, East Ilsley, Newbury, Berkshire RG20 7LP, England.

JENKINS David, 1 March 1926, Birmingham, England. Ecologist. m. Margaret Wellwood Johnston, 1 son, 1 daughter. Education: MRCVS, Royal Veterinary College, 1948; Degree in Zoology, MA,1952, Emmanuel College, Cambridge; D Phil, 1956, Bureau of Animal Population, Zoology Department, Oxford University; DSc (Oxon); FRSE, 1986. Appointments: Team Leader, Nature Conservancy/Aberdeen University Unit of Grouse and Moorland Ecology, 1956-66; Assistant Director, Research (Scotland), Nature Conservancy, 1966-72; Head of Banchory Research Station, Institute of Terrestrial Ecology, 1972-86; Honorary Research Fellow, 1956-86, Honorary Professor of Zoology, 1986-, Aberdeen University; Chairman, Scientific Advisory Committee, World Pheasant Association, 1975-94; Member, North-east Regional Board, Nature Conservancy Council for Scotland/Scottish Natural Heritage, 1992-98. Publications: Population studies in partridges, 1961 et seq; Population studies on red grouse in north-east Scotland (with A Watson and G R Miller), 1963 et seq.; Structure and regulation of a shelduck population (with M G Murray and P Hall), 1975 et seq.; Ecology of otters in north-east Scotland (alone and with others), 1976 et seq.; Of Partridges and Peacocks – And Of Other Things About Which I Knew Nothing, 2003. Address: Whitewalls, 1 Barclay Park, Aboyne, Aberdeenshire AB34 5JF, Scotland.

JENKINS Ivor, b. 25 July 1913, Gorseinon, South Wales. Metallurgist. m. Caroline Wijnanda James. 2 sons. Education: Folland Scholar in Metallurgy, BSc, MSc, DSc, University College of Wales, 1931-34; Industrial Bursar, GEC Research Laboratories, Wembley, England, 1934-36. Appointments: Scientific Staff, GEC Research Laboratories, Wembley, 1936-44; Deputy Chief Metallurgist, Whitehead Iron and Steel Co, Newport, Monmouthshire, Wales, 1944-46; Head of Metallurgy Department, 1946-52, Chief Metallurgist, 1952-61, GEC, Wembley; Director and Director of Research, Manganese Bronze Holdings, Ltd, 1961-69; Director of Research, Delta Metal Co and Director, Delta Metal (BW) Ltd, 1969-73; Deputy Chairman, Delta Materials Research Ltd, 1977-78; Group Director of Research, Delta Metal Co Ltd and Managing Director, Delta Materials Research Ltd, 1973-78; Consultant, 1978-95; Retired, 1995. Publications: Controlled Atmospheres for the Heat Treatment of Metals, 1946; Joint Editor, Powder Metallurgy Series, Institute of Metals, 1993-; More than 100 contributions to learned societies at home and abroad on metallurgical and related topics. Honours: Williams Prize, Iron and Steel Institute, 1946; CBE, 1970; Fellow, American Society of Metals, 1974; Platinum Medallist, Institute of Metals, 1978; Fellow, University College, Swansea, 1985. Memberships: Fellow, Royal Academy of Engineering; Institute of Metals 1932-, President, 1969-70; Iron and Steel Institute, 1937-; Fellow, Institution of Metallurgists, 1948, President, 1965-66; Fellow, Royal Society of the Arts; Honorary Member, European Powder Metallurgy Association, 1992; American Society of Metals. Address: 31 Trotyn Croft, Aldwick Fields, Bognor Regis, West Sussex PO21 3TX, England.

JENKINS Margaret Anne, b. 20 April 1944. Biochemist. m. Ian McPherson Jenkins, 28 January 1966, 1 son, 1 daughter. Education: BS, Monash University, 1964; MAACB (Member, Australian Association of Clinical Biochemists), 1982; Diploma, Financial Planning, Deakin University, 1992. Appointments: Biochemist, Queen Victoria Hospital, Melbourne, Australia, 1965; Sole Technology, 1965-68; Relieving Technology, 1968-72, Sole Biochemist, West Gippsland Hospital, Warragul, Australia, 1972-76; Biochemist, Preston and Northcote Community Hospital, Preston, 1976-83; Biochemist, Repatriation Campus, 1983-95, Biochemist, Austin Campus, Austin Health, Heidelberg, Australia, 1995-. Publications: 20 papers, 4 reviews and 4 chapters in professional journals including: Laboratory Investigation of Paraproteins by Capillary Electrophoresis, 1996; Automated Capillary Electrophoresis, 1998; Introduction Chapter: Clinical Applications of Capillary Electrophoresis, 1999. Honours: Travelling Scholarship, Australian Association of Clinical Biochemists Annual Science Meeting, 1991; Nancy Dale Scholarship, Australian Association of Clinical Biochemists, 1993; Roche Poster Prize, Australian Association of Clinical Biochemists, 1999; Listed in Who's Who publications and biographical dictionaries. Memberships: Australasian Association of Clinical Biochemists, 1981-, Committee Member, Victorian Branch; Branch Education Representative, Victorian Branch, 1987-91; Australian Electrophoresis Society, 1994-, Committee Member, 1996-98. Address: Austin Campus, Austin Health, Studley Road, Heidelberg, Vic 3084, Australia.

JENKINS Michael Nicholas Howard (Sir), b. 13 October 1932, Sevenoaks, Kent, England. Company Chairman. m. Jacqueline Frances, 3 sons. Education: Merton College, Oxford, 1953-56. Appointments: IBM, 1962-67; Management Consultant, Robson Morrow & Co, 1967-71; Technical Director, London Stock Exchange, 1971-77; Managing

Director, European Options Exchange, 1977-80; Chief Executive, London International Futures and Options Exchange, 1981-92; Chairman, Futures and Options Association, 1992-2000; Chairman, London Commodity Exchange, 1992-96; London Clearing House, 1991- Chairman, 1996-; Deputy Chairman, Easyscreen plc, 1999-; Chairman, E. Crossnet Ltd, 1999-. Honours: OBE, 1991; Knighthood, 1997. Address: London Clearing House, Aldgate House, 33 Aldgate High Street, London EC3N 1EA, England.

JENKINS Michael R H (Sir), b. 9 January 1936. Former President, Boeing UK; Consultant. m. Maxine Louise Hodson, 1 son, 1 daughter. Education: BA Honours, King's College, Cambridge. Appointments: Entered HM Diplomatic Service, 1959; Foreign and Commonwealth Office and British Embassies, Paris and Moscow, 1959-68; Seconded, General Electric Company, London, 1968-70; British Embassy, Bonn, 1970-73; European Commission, Brussels, 1973-83; Assistant Under-Secretary of State, Foreign and Commonwealth Office, 1983-85; Minister and Deputy Head of Mission, British Embassy, Washington DC, 1985-87; British Ambassador, The Netherlands, 1988-93; Executive Director and Member of Group Board, Kleinwort Benson Group, 1993-96; Vice-Chairman, Dresdner Kleinwort Wasserstein, 1996-2003; President, 2003-2005, Part-time Consultant, 2005-, Boeing UK; President's Advisory Council, Atlantic Council, 1994; Non-Executive Director, Aegon NV, 1995; Chairman of Directors, Action Centre for Europe, 1995; Chairman, British Group, Member of the European Executive Committee, Trilateral Commission, 1996-98; Adviser, Sage International, 1997; Chairman, Dataroam Ltd, 1999-2002; Non-Executive Director, EO, 2000; Chairman, MCC, 2000-02, Trustee, 2002-; Council of Britain in Europe, 2000-; The Pilgrims, 2001-; Advisory Council Prince's Trust, 2002-; Companion, Royal Aeronautical Society, 2004. Publications: Arakcheev, Grand Vizier of the Russian Empire, 1969; A House in Flanders, 1992. Honour: KCMG, 1989. Address: The Boeing Company, 16 St James's Street, St James's, London SW1A 1ER, England.

JENKINS Simon David, b. 10 June 1943, Birmingham, England. Journalist; Editor. m. Gayle Hunnicutt, 1978. Education: BA, St John's College, Oxford. Appointments: Staff, Country Life Magazine, 1965; News Editor, Times Educational Supplement, 1966-68; Leader Writer, Columnist, Features Editor, 1968-74, Editor, 1977-78, Evening Standard; Insight Editor, Sunday Times, 1974-76; Political Editor, The Economist, 1979-86; Editor, 1990-92, Columnist, 1992-2005, The Times; Columnist, Evening Standard, 1993-2005; Columnist, Guardian, Sunday Times, 2005-; Director, Faber and Faber (Publishers) Ltd, 1981-90. Publications: A City at Risk, 1971; Landlords to London, 1974; Newspapers: The Power and the Money, 1979; The Companion Guide to Outer London, 1981; Images of Hampstead, 1982; The Battle for the Falklands, 1983; With Respect, Ambassador, 1985; Market for Glory, 1986; The Selling of Mary Davies, 1993; England's Thousand Best Churches, 1999; England's 1000 Best Houses, 2002; Thatcher & Sons, 2006. Address: 174 Regents Park Road, London NW1, England.

JENKYNS Richard Henry Austen, b. 18 March 1949, Steyning, Sussex, England. University Professor. Education: Balliol College, Oxford, 1966-71; Corpus Christi College, Oxford, 1971-72, BA, 1971, M Litt, 1975. Appointments: Fellow of All Souls College, Oxford, 1972-81; Lecturer in Classics, University of Bristol, 1978-81; Fellow in Classics, Lady Margaret Hall, Oxford, 1981-; Reader in Classical Languages and Literature, University of Oxford, 1996-99;

Professor of the Classical Tradition, University of Oxford, 1999-. Publications: The Victorians and Ancient Greece, 1980; Three Classical Poets, 1982; Dignity and Decadence, 1991; Classical Epic, 1992; The Legacy of Rome (editor), 1992; Virgil's Experience, 1998; Westminster Abbey, 2004; A Fine Brush on Ivory, 2004. Honours: Arts Council Book Award for creative Non-Fiction, 1980; Yorkshire Post "Best First Work 1980" Prize. Address: Lady Margaret Hall, Oxford OX2 6QA, England. E-mail: richard.jenkyns@lmh.ox.ac.uk

JENNINGS Alex Michael, b. 10 May 1957, Upminster, Essex. Actor. Partner: Lesley Moors, 1 son, 1 daughter. Education: BA honours, Warwick University, 1978; Bristol Old Vic Theatre School, 1978-80. Career: Theatre includes: Richard II, 1990-91; The Importance of Being Ernest, 1993; Hamlet, 1997-98; Speer, 2000; The Winter's Tale, 2001; The Relapse, 2001; My Fair Lady, 2002 Films include: War Requiem, 1988; A Midsummer Night's Dream, 1996; The Wings of the Dove, 1997; The Hunley, 1998; Four Feathers, 2002; Five Children and It, 2004; Bridget Jones: The Edge of Reason, 2004; Riot at the Rite, 2005; Babel, 2006; The Queen, 2006; TV includes: Smiley's People; Inspector Morse; Ashenden; Inspector Alleyn Mysteries; Hard Times; Bad Blood; London; A Very Social Secretary; The State Within; Cranford Chronicles; Waking the Dead.. Honours: Best Actor for Too Clever By Half, London Theatre Critics Awards; Olivier Award, Best Comedy Performance for Too Clever By Half; Oliver Award, Best Actor for Peer Gynt; Helen Hayes Award, Best Actor for Hamlet, 1998; Hon D Litt, Warwick University, 2000; Best Actor, Evening Standard Drama Award, 2001. Address: c/o ICM, Oxford House, 76 Oxford Street, London W1N 0AX, England.

JENNINGS John Michael, b. 27 August 1944, Christchurch, New Zealand. Academic Evaluator. m. Cynthia Margaret Bensemann, 1 son, 1 daughter. Education: BMus with honours, University of Canterbury, New Zealand, 1966; MMus, University of Sydney, Australia, 1969; Licentiate of the Royal Schools of Music, London, 1963; Licentiate of the Trinity College of Music, London, 1965. Appointments: Assistant Lecturer, 1967-69, Lecturer, 1969-77, Senior Lecturer, 1978-2003, Dean of Arts, 1986-92, Deputy Chair, Chair, Academic Administration Committee, 1995-98, Quality Assurance Facilitator, 1998-2001, University of Canterbury; Director, New Zealand Universities Academic Audit Unit, 2002-. Publications: Books on music education and articles in musicological journals. Honours: University Prize Award, Commonwealth Scholarship and Fellowship Plan, 1966-67; Fellow, Institute of Registered Music Teachers in New Zealand, 1989. Memberships: Institute of Registered Music Teachers in New Zealand, 1972-; New Zealand Organisation for Quality, 1999-. Address: New Zealand Universities Academic Audit Unit, 178 Willis Street, Wellington, New Zealand. E-mail: director@nzuaau.ac.nz Website: www.nzuaau.ac.nz

JENNINGS Marie Patricia, b. 25 December 1930, Quetta, India. Author; Consumer Affairs Consultant. m. Walter Hayman, 1 son. Education: Presentation Convent College, Strinagar, Kashmir. Appointments: Managing Director, The Roy Bernand Co Ltd, 1960-65; Special Adviser, Stanley Tools, 1961-89, The Unit Trust Association, 1976-90, The Midland Bank, now HSBC, 1978-2004; Director, Lexington Ltd, 1971-75, The PR Consultants Association, 1979-84, Cadogan Management Ltd, 1984-90; Patron and Former President, National Association of Womens Clubs, 1998-; Member, Council and Deputy Chairman, Insurance Ombudsman Bureau, 1986-2001; Member, Council of Financial International Managers and Brokers Regulatory

Association, 1986-98; Executive Committee Member, Wider Share Ownership Council, 1987-91; Consumer Panel, Personal Investment Authority, PIA, Chairman, National Federation of Consumer Groups, 1998-2000; Chairman, President and Founder, Consumer Policy Institute, 2000-04; Consultant Editor, Finance, Good Housekeeping Magazine, 1992-2000; Founder and President, The Money Management Council, 1984-2004; Member, FSA Consumer Education Forum, 1998-2004. Publications: Many books including: Women and Money; Ten Steps to the Top; Guide to Good Corporate Citizenship; Perfect Insurance; National TV series: Moneyspinner, C4; Money Go Round, LWT; Translations; Articles for newspapers. Honours: MBE. Memberships: Institute of Directors; RAC Honorary Member, Public Relations Consultants Association; Institute of Public Relations; National Union of Journalists. Address: Cadogan Grange, Calfway Lane, Bisley, Stroud, Gloucestershire, GL6 7AT, England. Email: MLocke1162@aol.com

JENSEN Arthur S, b. 24 December 1917, Trenton, New Jersey, USA. Engineering Physicist. m. Lillian Elizabeth Reed, 2 sons, 1 daughter. Education: BS, Physics, 1938, MS, Physics, 1939, PhD, Physics, 1941, University of Pennsylvania; Diploma of Advanced Engineering, 1972, Computer Science, 1977, Westinghouse School of Applied Science, Baltimore. Appointments: Teacher of Physics and Physics of Aviation, Department of Electrical Engineering, US Naval Academy, 1941-46; Research Physicist, RCA Laboratories, Princeton, NJ, 1946-57; Consulting Physicist, Westinghouse Defence and Space Centre, 1957-94. Publications: Novel, Persian Gulf Jeopardy, 2007; 25 patents; 60 articles in physics and engineering journals and conferences. Honours: Captain, US Navy, retired; Westinghouse Special Corporate Patent Award; American Defence Service Medal; American Campaign Medal; World War II Victory Medal; Naval Reserve Medal; Armed Forces Reserve Medal; Biographical listing in several Who's Who books; Maryland Governor's Citation; Engineers' Council of Maryland's Outstanding Service Award. Memberships: American Association for Advancement of Science; Fellow, Institute of Electrical and Electronic Engineers; American Physical Society; SPIE; Fellow, Washington Academy of Science; Maryland Academy of Science; New York Academy of Science; Life Member, Retired Officers' Association; National Eagle Scout Association; Vigil Honor, Order of the Arrow; Sigma Xi; American Association of Physics Teachers. Address: Chapel Gate 1104, Oak Crest Village, 8820 Walther Boulevard, Parkville, MD 21234-9022, USA.

JENSH Ronald P, b. 14 June 1938. Emeritus Professor of Pathology, Anatomy and Cellular Biology. m. Ruth-Eleanor Dobson, 1962, 2 daughters. Education: BA, 1960, MA, 1962, Bucknell University; PhD, Jefferson Medical College, 1966. Appointments include: Faculty Member, Jefferson Medical College, 1966-; Faculty Member, Graduate School, Thomas Jefferson University, 1970-; Assistant Professor, Radiology and Anatomy, 1974-82, Associate Professor, Anatomy, 1974-82, Associate Professor, Radiology, 1974-91, Professor of Anatomy, 1982-94, Vice Chairman, Department of Anatomy, 1984-94, Section Chief, Microscopic Anatomy, 1988-, Associate Professor, Pediatrics, 1991-, Professor, Department of Pathology, Anatomy and Cellular Biology, 1994-2005, Retired (emeritus), 2005-, Jefferson Medical College. Publications: (author or co-author) 68 papers and books; 69 abstracts; 32 computer programs; 2 Sound and Light Programs - produced; 2 8mm movies produced, 1975; 11 photographic art exhibits including One-Man Shows, Haddonfield, New Jersey, 1987, 1988, Thomas Jefferson University, 1996; 10 photographs published, 1979-. Honours

include: Phi Sigma, 1961; Psi Chi, 1961; Sigma Xi, 1967-; Phi Beta Kappa, Mu Chapter, 1986; Hon Life Member, Jefferson Medical College Alumni Association, 1994; Alumni Award, Bucknell University, Lewisburg, Pennsylvania, 1997; Borough of Haddonfield (New Jersey) "Dr Ronald Jensh Recognition Day", 31 May 1997. Memberships include: Neurobehavioral Teratology Society, President, 1985-86; American Association of Anatomists; American Association of University Professors; Teratology Society; International Association of Human Biologists; Radiation Research Society; Society for Experimental Biology and Medicine. Address: 230 East Park Ave, Haddonfield, NJ 08033-1835, USA.

JEON Byong-Hun, b. 20 July 1970, Hongsung, South Korea. Professor. m. Duk-Ja Lee, 2 daughters. Education: BS, Hanyang University, Seoul, Korea, 1996; MS, 1998, PhD, 2001, Pennsylvania State University, USA. Appointments: Research Associate, Pennsylvania State University, 2002; Research Scientist, University of Alabama, USA, 2002-04; Post doctoral Researcher, PNNL, USA, 2004-05; Assistant Professor, Yonsei University, South Korea, 2005-. Publications: 23 publications in professional scientific journals. Honours: Best Abstract Award, CECG Symposium, Pennsylvania State University, 1999; Honorable Mention Award, CECG Symposium, Pennsylvania State University, 2001; Listed in international biographical dictionaries. Memberships: ACS; KOSSGE. Address: Choeng-gu Apt 202-1201, Myeongnyun-dong, Wonju City, Gangwon-do, South Korea. E-mail: bhjeon@yonsei.ac.kr/

JEON Jae-Ho, b. 22 March 1961, Busan, Korea. Research Scientist. m. Sun-Mi Jin, 4 daughters. Education: BS, Busan National University, Korea, 1984; PhD, Korea Advanced Institute of Science and Technology (KAIST), 1994. Appointments: Research Assistant, 1988-93, Researcher, 1994-95, Korea Advanced Institute of Science and Technology; Research Fellow, IRC, Birmingham University, England, 1996-98; Principal Research Scientist, Korea Institute of Materials Science (KIMS), 1995-. Publications: Over 20 articles in international journals as co-author include most recently: Effect of $SrTiO_3$ concentration and sintering temperature on microstructure and dielectric property of $Ba_{1-x}Sr_xTiO_3$, 2004; Effect of Initial Porosity on mechanical properties of C/SiC Composites Fabricated by Silicon Melt Infiltration Process, 2004; Development of Functionally Graded Anti-oxidation Coatings for Carbon/Carbon Composites, 2004; Densification and Dielectric Property of B_2O_3-doped $Ba_{1-x}Sr_xTiO_3$ Graded Ceramics, 2004; Constitutional Design and Dielectric Properties of BST Graded Ceramics, 2004; Microstructural and Compositional Study of a Bulk PMN-PT Single Crystal Grown from ABT Seed, 2007; 5 articles in domestic journals; 28 papers in conference proceedings; 6 patents. Memberships: Korean Ceramic Society; Korean Institute of Metals and Materials; Korea Powder Metallurgy Institute; Materials Research Society of Korea; International Association of Layered and Graded Materials; Korean Go Association. Address: 105-403, Union Village, Seongju-Dong, Changwon 641-939, Korea. E-mail: jjh@kims.re.kr

JEONG Dong-Soo, b. 11 May 1952, Korea. Principal Researcher. m. Young-Ock Choi, 1 son, 2 daughters. Education: BSc, Mechanical Engineering, Seoul National University, 1977; MSc, Mechanical Engineering, Korea Advanced Institute of Science & Technology, 1988; PhD, Mechanical Engineering, Pusan National University, 1995. Appointments: Compulsory Military Service, 1973-75; Technical trainnig at OPEL, Ruesselsheim, Germany, 1978-79; Technical training at SCHENCK, Germany, 1980; On the job training, Engine Division of Southwest Research Institute, San Antonio, Texas, USA, 1982; Collaboration for T/C diesel engine design, Ricardo, UK, 1984; Director, KIMM, Europe Office, London, 1995-98; Principal Researcher, Engine R&D Lab, Korea Institute of Machinery & Materials (KIMM), Korea, 1977-; Part-time Lecturer, Internal Combustion Engine, ME Department, Changwon National University, Korea, 1988-91; Part-time Lecturer, Engine, Pusan National University, Korea, 1995; Professor, University of Science & Technology, Korea, 2005-. Publications: 12 papers and articles in professional journals. Honours: Technical Prize, KSAE, 1989; R&D Reward, Minister of Science & Technology Development, 1989; Sliver Prize, Annual Academic Achievement, KIMM; Listed in international biographical dictionaries, 2004/2005. Memberships: Society of Automotive Engineers; IANGV; Korea Auto Forum; KT Mark Award Committee; Korean Society of Automotive Engineers; Korean Society of Mechanical Engineers. Address: Engine Laboratory, Korea Institute of Machinery & Materials, 171 Jangdong, Yusung, Daejeon, Korea. E-mail: dsjeong@kimm.re.kr

JEONG Dongwon, b. 20 April 1972, Gunsan, Jeollabuk-do, Korea. Professor. m. Hyunjung Kim. Education: BS, Computer Science, Kunsan National University, 1997; MS, Computer Science, Chungbuk National University, 1999; PhD, Computer Science, Korea University, 2004. Appointments: Full time Instructor, Advanced Institute of Information Technology, Korea, 1999-2000; Senior Researcher, Jigunet Corporation, Korea, 2000-01; Committee Member, TTA PG406, Korea, 2002-; Researcher, Lime Media Technologies Co Ltd, Korea, 2002-05; Research Assistant Professor, Research Institute of Information and Communication Technology, Korea University, 2004-05; Visiting Research Scholar (Post doctorate), School of Information Sciences & Technology, Pennsylvania State University, 2005; Professor, Kunsan National University, 2005-; Korean National Committee Member, ISO/IEC JTC1/SC32, Korea, 2006-. Publications: Numerous papers and articles in professional scientific journals. Honours: Listed in international biographical dictionaries. Memberships: Korean Information Processing Society; Korea Information Sic Society; IEICE, Japan. Address: Department of Informatics & Statistics, Kunsan National University, San 68, Miryong-dong, Gunsan, Jeollabuk-do, 573-701, Republic of Korea. E-mail: djeong@kunsan.ac.kr Website: http://ist.kunsan.ac.kr/

JEONG Gang-Hoan, b. 17 October 1964, Iksan, Korea. Professor. m. Hye-Young Chun, 1 daughter. Education: BA, English, Hankuk University of Foreign Studies, 1986; MS, Hospitality and Tourism, University of Wisconsin, 1987; PhD, Recreation, Park & Leisure Studies, University of Minnesota, 1992. Appointments: Director, Tourism Event Center, 1996-2007, Dean of Tourism College, 2002-05, Paichai University, Daejeon, Korea; National Review Committee of Cultural Tourism Festival, 1996-2006; Developed Buryong Mud Festival (Best Festival ranked in Korea), 1997; Vice Chairman, Korean Academic Society of Tourism, 2003; Vice President, Korean Academic Society of Leisure & Tourism, 2004; National Advisor to Primister Department, Ministry of Culture & Tourism, Ministry of Administration, 2006. Publications: 21st Century Local Development Festivals, 2004; The Benchmarking of the Canadian Winter Festivals, 2006; 3 other books; 35 articles in professional journals. Honours: President's Award, Ministry of Culture & Tourism, Korea, 2001; The Best Tourism Person of the Year 2006.

Memberships: Korea Academic Society of Tourism; National Board of Cultural Tourism Festival Committee, Ministry of Culture & Tourism, Korea. E-mail: jghon@pcu.ac.kr

JEONG Hyeong-Tae, b. 26 January 1973, Seoul, Korea. Engineer. m. Hyun-Jeong Yoo, 1 son, 1 daughter. Education: Bachelor's degree, Electrical Engineering, 1995, Master's degree, Electronic Engineering, 1997, PhD, Electrical Engineering, 2006, Sogang University, Seoul. Appointments: Senior Engineer, Samsung Electronics Co Ltd, Korea, 1997-2002; Higher Senior Engineer, Powerwave UK, 2006-. Publications: 4 articles in professional journals. Honours: Best Paper Award, Asia-Pacific Microwave Conference, 2003. Address: 7 Buckstone Green, Alwoodley, Leeds LS17 5HA, England. E-mail: B612@sogang.ac.kr

JEONG KeeSam, b. 1 November 1965, Daegu, Korea. Professor. m. Yunkyeng Cho, 2 sons. Education: Bachelor's degree, 1988, Master's degree, 1990, PhD, 1997, Electrical Engineering, Yonsei University, Seoul. Appointments: Programmer, Military Service, Seoul District Hospital, Seoul, 1990-92; R&D Manager, EOS Technologies Korea, Seoul, 1992-93; H/W Engineer, EOS Technologies, San Jose, California, USA, 1993-94; Lecturer, Yonsei University, Seoul, 1995-97; Project Manager/Consultant, LG-EDS System, Seoul, 1997-99; Department Head, Leader of Wearable Computer Research Group, Professor, Department of Medical Information System, Yong-In Songdam College, Yong-In, Korea, 1999-. Publications: 6 articles in professional journals; 5 papers presented at conference. Memberships: IEEE; Korean Society of Medical Informatics; Korean Society of Medical & Biological Engineering; Korean Society for Emotion & Sensibility; Ubiquitous IT Korea Forum; Hospital Information System Forum. Address: Yongin Songdam College, Department of Medical Information Systems, 571-1 Mapyung, Gyeonggi Yongin, 449-710, Korea. E-mail: ksjeong@ysc.ac.kr

JERVIS Simon Swynfen, b. 9 January 1943, Yoxford, Suffolk, England. Art Historian. m. Fionnuala MacMahon, 1 son, 1 daughter. Education: Corpus Christi College, Cambridge, 1961-64. Appointments: Student Assistant, Assistant Keeper of Art, Leicester Museum and Art Gallery, 1964-66; Assistant Keeper, 1966-75, Deputy Keeper, 1975-89, Acting Keeper, 1989, Curator, 1989-90, Department of Furniture, Victoria and Albert Museum; Director and Marlay Curator, Fitzwilliam Museum, Cambridge, 1990-95; Director of Historic Buildings, The National Trust, 1995-2002. Publications: 7 books on furniture and design; Many articles in learned journals. Memberships: Member, 1964-, Arts Panel, 1982-95, Chairman, 1987-95, Properties Committee, 1987-95, National Trust; Member, 1966-, Council, 1977-79, 1981-83, 1986-87, Editor, 1988-92, Chairman, 1999-, Furniture History Society; Member, 1968-, Stafford Terrace Committee, 1980-90, Victorian Society; Member, Southwark Diocesan Advisory Committee, 1978-87; Member, 1982-, Council, 1987-1991, Royal Archaeological Institute; Elected Fellow, 1983, Council, 1986-88, Executive Committee, 1987-92, House Working Party, 1988-, President, 1995-2001, Kelmscott Committee, 2001-, Society of Antiquaries of London; Director, 1993-, Trustee, 1996-, The Burlington Magazine; Member, 1988-, Council, 1990-95, Chair, 2004-, Walpole Society; Guest Scholar, The J Paul Getty Museum, 1988-89, 2003; Member, Museums and Galleries Commission, Acceptance in Lieu Panel, 1992-2000; Trustee, The Royal Collection Trust, 1993-2001; Trustee, 1998-2002, Life Trustee, 2002-, Sir John Soane's Museum; Member, Advisory Council,

National Art Collections Fund, 2002-; Iris Foundation Award for Outstanding Contributions to the Decorative Arts, 2002. Address: 45 Bedford Gardens, London W8 7EF, England.

JESS Digby Charles, b. 14 November 1953, Plymouth, England. Barrister; Chartered Arbitrator. m. Bridie, 1 son, 1 daughter. Education: BSc Honours, Aston University, 1976; Called to the Bar, 1978; LLM, 1986, PhD, 1999, University of Manchester; FCIArb, 1992; Chartered Arbitrator, 1999. Appointments: Barrister, Private Practice specialising in insurance claims and building disputes, 1978-; Treasury Counsel (Northern Region), 1992-2003; Legal Assessor, General Medical Council, Council Fitness to Practice Panels, 2002-; Member, Association of Chartered Certified Accountants' Disciplinary and Licensing Committees, 2002-; Chairman CIArb North West Branch, 1992-93; Chairman, BIIBA Liability Society (NW), 1995-99; President, Manchester Liability Society, 2006-; Sometime Part-time Lecturer in Law, University of Manchester. Publications: The Insurance of Commercial Risks: Law and Practice, 1986, 3rd edition 2001; The Insurance of Professional Negligence Risks: Law and Practice, 1982, 2nd edition, 1989; Professional Indemnity Insurance Law (co-author with Enright), 2nd Edition, 2007. Memberships: Northern Circuit Commercial Bar Association; Technology and Construction Court Bar Association. Address: Exchange Chambers, 7 Ralli Courts, West Riverside, Manchester M3 5FT, England. E-mail: jess@exchangechambers.co.uk

JESTY Ronald Cyril Benjamin, b. 7 May 1926, Weymouth, Dorset, England. Graphic Designer; Artist. m. Margaret Ellen Johnson. Appointments: Apprentice Draughtsman, Vickers Armstrong, 1941-45; Freelance Graphic Designer, 1947-78; Artist (watercolours), 1978-; Part-time Art Teacher, 1978-2002. Publications: Learn To Paint Seascapes, 1996; Various articles in Leisure Painter Magazine and International Artist Magazine; Contributor to several books on art and painting. Membership: Royal Society of British Artists, 1982-92. Address: 11 Pegasus Court, South Street, Yeovil, Somerset, BA20 1ND, England.

JHA Rudra Narayan, b. 3 February 1953. Consultant Gynaecologist. m. Ranjana, 1 son, 2 daughters. Education: MBBS, MD (Gynae), Miraj Medical College, India. Appointments: Tutor, Department of Obstetrics and Gynaecology, Miraj Medical College, India, 1983; Medical Officer, Ministry of Health, HMG, 1984; Consultant Gynaecologist, Janakpur Medical Center & Nursing Home, 1985; Consultant Gynaecologist, Sanjivani Medical & Safe Motherhood Centre, Janakpur, 2005-. Honours: International Achiever's Award (Gold Medal), New Delhi, 2004; Man of the Year Medal, ABI, USA, 2005; Order of International Ambassador, ABI, USA, 2006; Marie Curie Award, IBC, Cambridge, 2006; Lifetime Achievement Award, IBC, Cambridge, 2006; American Medal of Honour, ABI, USA, 2007; Gold Medal for Nepal, ABI, USA, 2007; Order of American Ambassador, ABI, USA, 2007; Deputy Governor, ABI, USA, 2007. Memberships: Lions Club, Janakpur; Red Cross Society, Janakpur; ISCKON. Address: Care Medical Centre, Mills Area, Janakpur-1, Nepal. E-mail: caremedical2005@yahoo.com

JI Dong-Sun, b. 10 July 1951, Pyeong Chang, Republic of Korea. Professor. m. 1980, 2 sons. Education: BA, 1979, MA, 1982, PhD, 1990, Dankook University. Appointments: Lecturer, 1982-88, Assistant professor, 1988-90, Daejeon Medical Junior College, Republic of Korea. Assistant Professor, 1990-94, Associate Professor, 1994-2000,

Professor, 2000-, Dankook University, Republic of Korea. Publications: Synthesis and Hydrophilicities of Poly(ethylene 2,6-naphthalate)/Poly(ethylene glycol) Copolymers, 2003; Effects of In Vitro Degradation on the Weight Loss and Tensile Properties of PLA/LPCL/HPCL Blend Fibers, 2005; Preparation of PLA/PEG Block Copolymer via Melt Blend, 2006; Synthesis and Hydrophilicity of Poly(butylene 2,6-naphthalate)/Poly(ethylene glycol) Copolymers, 2006. Honours: Excellent Prize for Young Scientists, 1999; Chairman, 5th Asian Textile Conference. Memberships: The Korean Fiber Society; The Polymer Society of Korea. Address: 117-102 Samsung Raemian 1st Apt 629 Mabuk-dong, Kiheung-gu, Yongin-si, Gyeonggi-do 446-557, Republic of Korea. E-mail: dsunji@dku.edu

JI Wonsoo, b. 28 April 1971, Yeongdeok-gun, Kyungsangbuk-do, Korea. Engineer. m. Ji-hyun Lim, 2 sons. Education: BS, Physics, Hallym University, 1999; Master of Engineering, Electronic Material Engineering, 2001, PhD, Information and Communication Engineering, 2005, Inha University. Appointments: Researcher, Optics & Photonics Elite Research Academy, 2002-04; Adjunct Professor, Inha Technical College, Korea, 2004-05; Senior Engineer, Samsung Electro-Mechanics Co Ltd, Korea, 2005-. Publications: NSOM based characterization method applicable to optical channel waveguide with a solid-state cladding, 2005; Characterization of a Focusing Waveguide Grating Coupler Using Bloch Wave Analysis-Based Local Linear Grating Model and Near-Field Scanning Optical Microscope, 2005; Hybrid control method of Near-field Scanning Optical Microscope for characterization of optical waveguide devices, 2005. Honours: 1st prize winner, Samsung Electro-Mechanics Technical Forum, 2005. Memberships: Optical Society of America; The Korean Physical Society. E-mail: ws.ji@samsung.com

JIMBOW Kowichi, b. 4 June 1941, Nagoya, Japan. Physician; Dermatologist; Professor. m. Mihoko Jimbow, 1 son, 4 daughters. Education: MD, Sapporo Medical College, Sapporo, Japan, 1966; PhD, Sapporo Medical College Graduate School, Sapporo, Japan, 1974. Appointments: Professor and Chair, Department of Dermatology, Sapporo Medical University, School of Medicine, 1995-; Chief, Division of Dermatology, Division of Plastic Surgery (Adjunct), Sapporo Medical University Hospital, 1995-; Adjunct Professor, Department of Medicine, Dermatology and Cutaneous Sciences, University of Alberta, Edmonton, Canada, 1996-; Dean, Sapporo Medical University, Graduate School of Medicine, 2000-; Dean, Sapporo Medical University School of Medicine, 2000-. Honours include: Alfred Marchionini Prize, International Association of Dermatology, 1982; Seiji Memorial Award, Japanese Society of Dermatology, 1984; Alberta Heritage Medical Scientist Award, Canada, 1988, 1993; Henry Stanley Raper Award, European Society of Pigment Cell; Hokkaido Physician Award, Japan, 2001; Hokkaido Science and Technology Award, Japan, 2002. Memberships: Alberta Medical Association; American Academy of Dermatology; American Association for Cancer Research; American Society for Cell Biology; American Society of Photobiology; Canadian Dermatological Association; Canadian Society for Clinical Investigation; Canadian Society for Investigative Dermatology; International Society of Pigment Cell Research; Society for Investigative Dermatology; Japanese Dermatological Association; Japanese Burn Association; WHO Councillor for Evaluation and Methods of Diagnosis and Treatment of Melanoma. Address: Institute of Dermatology & Cutaneous Sciences, Odori 17, Chuo-ku, Sapporo, Hokkaido, 060-0042, Japan. E-mail: jimbow@sapmed.ac.jp

JIN Jong-Youl, b. 15 September 1958, Korea. Professor. m. Ki-Sook Kim, 1 son, 1 daughter. Education: MD, 1983, PhD, 1994, Catholic University of Korea. Appointments: Professor, Internal Medicine, Holy Family Hospital, Catholic University of Korea. Publications: Immunology – Janeway. Honours: Listed in international biographical directories; International Health Professional of the Year, IBC, 2007. Memberships: Korean Society of Haematology, Oncology and Internal Medicine. Address: 512-501 Mok-Dong Apt, Mok-Dong, Seoul 158-755, Korea. E-mail: drjin@catholic.ac.kr

JO Deokjun, b. 22 April 1963, Seoul, Korea. Professor. m. Eunsook Kim, 1 daughter. Education: Bachelor, Civil Engineering, Civil Engineering Department, 1989, Master, 1991, PhD, 2007, Water Engineering, Civil & Environmental Engineering Department, Korean University. Appointments: Daewoo Engineering Company, 1991-2002; Disaster Protection Research Center, 2002-05; Professor, Dongseo University, 2005-. Memberships: KWRA; Professional Engineer. Address: Department of Civil Engineering, Dongseo University, San 69-1, Jurye-Dong, Sasang-Gu, Pusan 617-716, Republic of Korea. E-mail: water21c@gdus.dongseo.ac.kr

JO Jong Chull, b. 9 September 1955, Kyungnam-do, Republic of Korea. Research Scientist. m. Yeong-Kyeong Kim, 1 son, 1 daughter. Education: BS, 1979, MS, 1981, PhD, 1985, Mechanical Engineering, Hanyang University, Seoul. Appointments: Teaching and Research Assistant, 1979-81, Lecturer, 1985-86, Department of Mechanical Engineering, Hanyang University, Seoul; Assistant Professor of Mechanical Engineering, Induk Institute of Technology, Seoul, 1981-86; Senior Researcher, 1986-92, Principal Researcher, 1993-, Nuclear Safety Review and Inspection Department, Project Manager, Development of Integral-Type Reactor Regulatory Technology, 2002-, Chair, Safety Issue Research Department, 2005-, Korea Institute of Nuclear Safety; Visiting Scientist, Division of Nuclear Technology, TUEV Hannover eV, Germany, 1987-88; Visiting Scientist, Office of Nuclear Reactor Regulation, US Nuclear Regulatory Commission, 1995-96; Lecturer, Mechanical Engineering, Graduate School of Jeonju University, Jeonju, 2003-05; Member, National R&D Projects Evaluation Committee, 2007. Publications: Over 130 papers in professional scientific journals. Honours: Korean Prime Ministerial Citation, 1994; Korean Presidential Citation, 2004; Certificate of Recognition, 2005; Tenure Evaluation of an Associate Professor of Engineering Science and Mechanics, Penn State University, 2006; Outstanding Technical Paper Award, Korean Nuclear Society, 2006; Invited contributor, 3rd Edition of Companion Guide for ASME B&PV Codes, American Society of Mechanical Engineers, 2007; Invited author, Topic 'Fluid-Structure Interaction' for Pressure Vessels and Piping Systems, The Encyclopaedia of Life Support Systems, UNESCO, 2007-08. Listed in international biographical directories. Memberships: Korea Foundation of Science and Technology; American Society of Mechanical Engineers; Korean Society of Pressure Vessels and Piping; Korean Nuclear Society; Korean Society of Mechanical Engineers; and others. Address: Korea Institute of Nuclear Safety, 19 Kusung-dong, Yusung-gu, Taejeon (Daejeon) 305-338, Korea. E-mail: jcjo@kins.re.kr

JOEL Billy (William Martin Joel), b. 9 May 1949, Bronx, New York, USA. Musician; Singer; Songwriter. m. (1) Elizabeth Weber, 1971, (2) Christie Brinkley, 23 March 1989, 1 daughter, (3) Katie Lee, 2004. Education: LHD (honorary), Fairfield University, 1991; HMD (honorary), Berklee College of Music, 1993. Appointment: Solo Recording Artist, 1972-. Creative Works: Turnstiles; Streetlife Serenade; The Stranger, 1978; 52nd Street, 1978; Glass Houses, 1980; Songs In the Attic, 1981; Nylon Curtain, 1982; An Innocent Man, 1983; Cold Spring Harbour, 1984; Piano Man, 1984; Greatest Hits, Vols I & II, 1985; The Bridge, 1986; KOHUEPT-Live in Leningrad, 1987; Storm Front, 1989; River of Dreams, 1994; 2000 Years: Millennium Concert, 2000; Fantasies & Delusions, 2001; My Lives, 2005. Publications: Goodnight My Angel: A Lullabye, 2004. Honours: 6 Grammy Awards; 10 Grammy Nominations; Grammy Legend Award, 1990; Songwriters Hall of Fame, 1992.

JOFFE Joel Goodman (Lord Joffe), b. 12 May 1932. Human Rights Lawyer; Businessman; Chairman and Trustee of Charities; National Health Services Chairman. m. Vanetta Joffe, 3 daughters. Education: B Com LLB, Witwatersrand University, Johannesburg. Appointments: Solicitor, then Barrister, Johannesburg, 1952-65; Secretary and Administrative Director, Abbey Life Assurance, London, 1965-70; Founder Director, Joint Managing Director, Deputy Chairman, Allied Dunbar Assurance, 1971-91; Founding Trustee, Chairman, Allied Dunbar Charitable Trust, 1974-93; Chairman, Thamesdown Voluntary Services Council, 1974-1980; Trustee, Honorary Secretary, Chairman of the Executive Committee, Chair, Oxfam, 1979-2001; Chairman, Swindon Private Hospital plc, 1982-87; Council Member, IMPACT, 1984-; Chairman, Swindon Health Authority, 1988-93; Campaigner to protect consumers from the excesses of the Financial Services Industry, 1992-97; Chairman, Swindon and Marlborough National Health Trust, 1993-95; Special Adviser to South African Minister of Transport, 1997-98; Chair of The Giving Campaign, 2000-04; Trustee, J G and V L Joffe Charitable Trust. Memberships: Member, Royal Commission for the Care of the Elderly, 1997-99; Member, Home Officer Working Group on the Active Community, 1998-99. Address: Liddington Manor, Liddington, Swindon, Wiltshire SN4 0HD, England.

JOHANSEN Stein Erik, b. 16 June 1954, Trondheim, Norway. Professor. 1 daughter. Education: PhD, Philosophy, 1985, DSc, Philosophy of Economics, 1991, University of Bergen, Norway; University degrees in other disciplines: Economics, Anthropology; Sociology; and Mathematical Logic. Appointments: Associate Professor, Sociology, University of Oslo, Norway, 1991-92; Associate Professor, Social Anthropology, Norwegian University of Science and Technology, Trondheim, 1992-; Full Professor, Division of Physics, Institute for Basic Research, USA, 2002-. Publications: Books include: Quo Vadis, Sapiens .. . Prelude to a subject-oriented theory of culture, 1987; 24 Hour People, 1988; The Concept of Labour Time Content: A Theoretical Construction. A revisionist contribution to the foundation of form reflected capital theory, 1991; Outline of Differential Epistemology, 2007; Articles include: Initiation of Hadronic Philosophy. The philosophy underlying hadronic mechanics and chemistry, 2006. Address: Jacob Rolls Gt 22, N-7016 Trondheim, Norway. E-mail: stein.johansen@svt.ntnu.no

JOHANNSON Scarlett, b. 22 November 1984, New York, USA. Film Actress. Career: Films: North, 1994; Just Cause, 1995; If Lucy Fell, Manny & Lo, 1996; Fall, 1997; Home Alone 3, 1997; The Horse Whisperer, 1998; My Brother the Pig, 1999; Ghost World, 2000; An American Rhapsody, The Man Who Wasn't There, 2001; Eight Legged Freaks, 2002; The Girl with a Pearl Earring, Lost in Translation, 2003; The Perfect Score, A Love Song for Bobby Long, A Good Woman, The SpongeBob SquarePants Movie (voice), 2004; In Good Company, Match Point, The Island, 2005; Scoop, The Black Dahlia, The Prestige, 2006; The Nanny Diaries, The Other

Boleyn Girl, 2007. Honours: Hollywood Reporter Young Star Award, 1998; Best Supporting Actress, Toronto Film Critics Association, 2000; Countercurrent Prize for Best Actress, Venice Film Festival, 2003; Best Actress, Boston Society of Film Critics, 2003; BAFTA Award for Best Actress, 2004. Address: c/o United Talent Agency, 9560 Wilshire Boulevard, Floor 5, Beverly Hills, CA 90212-2400, USA.

JOHN Biju, b. Kerala, India. Priest; Scientist; Researcher; Inspirational Speaker & Writer. Education: Degree, Philosophy, Kerala University, India, 1991; Diploma, Visual Basics, India, 2000; Master's degree, Information Technology, Charles Sturt University, Australia, 2003; Diploma, Business, London, England, 2005; PhD Researcher, Kingston University, Faculty of CISM, 2005-07; Research, Semantic e-Marketing, Kingston University, London, 2005-07. Appointments: Director and Administrator, Metrotech Institute of Computer Technology, 2000; St Mary's Metropolitan Cathedral, Kerala, 1998-2000; Priestly Ministry, Kerala and London, 1998-2007; First Syro-Malabar Co-ordinator, London, 2005-07; Director, Magnificata Charitable Society, 2006-; Conference Chair Semantic e-Marketing and Enterprise Computing, 2007-08. Publications: Numerous articles in professional journals. Honours: Honours in Information Technology, 2005; Founder, International Kerala Computer Society. Memberships: Syro-Malabar Catholic Church; Archdiocese of Southwark; Magnificata Productions, Technology and Oriental Studies charity; British Computer Society; Semantic e-Marketing and Enterprise Computing; International Kerala Computer Society; Kingston University. E-mail: john@seec.eu

JOHN Elton (Sir) (Reginald Kenneth Dwight), b. 25 March 1947, Pinner, Middlesex, England. Singer; Songwriter; Musician (piano). m. Renate Blauer, 1984, divorced 1988; partner, David Furnish, 2005. Musical Education: Piano lessons aged 4; Royal Academy of Music, 1958. Career: Member, Bluesology, 1961-67; Worked at Mills Music Publishers; Solo artiste, 1968-; Long-term writing partnership with Bernie Taupin, 1967-; Partnership wrote for Dick James Music; Founder, Rocket Records, 1973; Own publishing company, Big Pig Music, 1974; Performances include: Wembley Stadium, 1975; First Western star to perform in Israel and USSR, 1979; Live Aid, Wembley, 1985; Wham's farewell concert, Wembley, 1985; Prince's Trust concerts, London, 1986, 1988; Farm Aid IV, 1990; AIDS Project Los Angeles - Commitment To Life VI, 1992; Chair, The Old Vic Theatre Trust, 2002-; Concert for Diana, 2007. Film appearance, Tommy, 1975. Recordings: Hit singles include: Your Song, 1971; Rocket Man, 1972; Crocodile Rock (Number 1, US), Daniel, Saturday Night's Alright For Fighting, Goodbye Yellow Brick Road, 1973; Candle In The Wind, Don't Let The Sun Go Down On Me, 1974 (live version with George Michael, Number 1, UK and US, 1991); Philadelphia Freedom, Lucy In The Sky With Diamonds (Number 1, US), Island Girl (Number 1, US), 1975; Pinball Wizard, from film Tommy, Don't Go Breaking My Heart, duet with Kiki Dee (Number 1, UK and US), Sorry Seems To Be The Hardest Word, 1976; Song For Guy, 1979; Blue Eyes, 1982; I Guess That's Why They Call It The Blues, I'm Still Standing, Kiss The Bride, 1983; Sad Songs (Say So Much), 1984; Nikita, 1986; Sacrifice (Number 1, UK), 1989; True Love (with Kiki Dee), 1993; Made In England, Blessed, Believe, 1995; You Can Make History, 1996; If The River Can Bend, 1998; Written in the Stars, 1999; I Want Love, This Train Don't Stop There Anymore, 2001; Are You Ready for Love, 2003; All That I'm Allowed (I'm Thankful), 2004; Contributor, That's What Friends Are For, Dionne Warwick And Friends (charity record), 1986; Albums include: Elton John, 1970; Tumbleweed

Connection, Friends, 17-11-70, 1971; Madman Across The Water, Honky Chateau, 1972; Don't Shoot Me, I'm Only The Piano Player, Goodbye Yellow Brick Road, 1973; Caribou, 1974; Captain Fantastic And The Brown Dirt Cowboy, Rock Of The Westies, 1975; Here And There, Blue Moves, 1976; A Single Man, 1978; Lady Samantha, 21 At 33, 1980; Jump Up!, 1982; Too Low For Zero, 1983; Breaking Hearts, 1984; Ice On Fire, 1985; Leather Jackets, 1986; Live In Australia, 1987; Reg Strikes Back, 1988; Sleeping With The Past, 1989; The One, 1992; Made In England, Love Songs, 1995; Big Picture, 1997; Aida, 1999; El Dorado, 2000; Songs From the West Coast, 2001; Elton John – Greatest Hits, 1970-2002, 2002; Peachtree Road, 2004; Wrote music for stage musicals, The Lion King, 1994 and Billy Elliot, 2004. Honours include: First album to go straight to Number 1 in US charts, Captain Fantastic..., 1975; Numerous Ivor Novello Awards for: Daniel, 1974; Don't Go Breaking My Heart, 1977; Song For Guy, 1979; Nikita, 1986; Sacrifice, 1991; Outstanding Contribution To British Music, 1986; Star on Hollywood Walk Of Fame, 1975; Madison Square Gardens Honours: Hall Of Fame, 1977; Walk Of Fame (first non-athlete), 1992; American Music Awards: Favourite Male Artist, Favourite Single, 1977; Silver Clef Award, Nordoff-Robbins Music Therapy, 1979; BRIT Awards: Outstanding Contribution To British Music, 1986; Best British Male Artist, 1991; Grammy, Best Vocal Performance By A Group, 1987; MTV Special Recognition Trophy, 1987; Hitmaker Award, National Academy of Popular Music, 1989; Honorary Life President, Watford Football Club, 1989; Inducted into Songwriters Hall Of Fame (with Bernie Taupin), 1992; Q Magazine Merit Award, 1993; Officer of Arts And Letters, Paris, 1993; KBE, 1998; Dr hc Royal Academy of Music, 2002; Grammy Lifetime, Achievement Award, 2000; Kennedy Center Honors, 2004. Address: c/o Simon Prytherch, Elton Management, 7 King Street Cloisters, Clifton Walk, London, W6 0GY, England.

JOHN Ricky, b. 2 May 1957, Trinidad, West Indies. Education: BSc, Electrical Engineering, New Jersey Institute of Technology (NJIT), 1981; MSc, Management, NJIT, 1992; PhD, Engineering Management, Kennedy-Western University, 2000. Appointments: Flight Test Engineer for experimental test flights of US Space Shuttle Columbia, member, NASA Space Shuttle Launch Team, Kennedy Space Center, 1981-82; Systems Engineer, Airway Facilities Modernization Program, US Federal Aviation Administration (FAA), 1983-85, Selected to test one of world's first Weather Radar Display Systems, 1983; Program Administrator, New Jersey Department of Energy, 1985; Conceptual designer and installer: first multi-campus integrated computerized energy management system, New Jersey University of Medicine and Dentistry; Largest geothermal energy system of its kind, Stockton State College, New Jersey; Visiting Lecturer, John Donaldson Technical Institute in Port-of-Spain, Trinidad, 1982; Member, New Jersey Martin Luther King Commission Education Committee, 1987-90; Technical Advisor, New Jersey Board of Public Utilities, 1996-; Judge and presenter, NASA Awards for annual North New Jersey Regional Science Fair for secondary students, 1993-. Memberships: New Jersey Institute of Technology Alumni Association, Board of Trustees, 1991-, Vice President for Public Relations, 1996-98; Institute of Electrical and Electronic Engineers; New Jersey Aviation Hall of Fame; Notary Public, State of New Jersey, 1988-; Board of Directors, New Jersey Inventors Hall of Fame, 2003-. Address: 350 Davis Avenue, Kearny, NJ 07032, USA.

JOHNS David John, b. 29 April 1931, Bristol, England. Chartered Engineer. Education: BSc (Eng), Aero Engineering, 1950-53, MSc (Eng), 1959, University of Bristol; PhD, 1967, DSc, 1985, Loughborough University. Appointments: Apprentice up to Section Leader, Bristol Aeroplane Co Ltd, 1949-57; Technical Officer, Sir W G Armstrong Whitworth Aircraft Ltd, 1957-58; Lecturer, Cranfield College of Aeronautics, 1958-64; Reader, Professor, 1964-83, Head of Department of Transport Technology, 1972-82; Senior Pro-Vice-Chancellor, 1982-83, Loughborough University; Foundation Director, City Polytechnic of Hong Kong, 1983-89; Vice-Chancellor and Principal, University of Bradford, 1989-98; Chairman, Prescription Pricing Authority, 1998-2001; Chairman, North and East Yorkshire and Northern Lincolnshire Strategic Health Authority; Chairman, Genetics and Insurance Committee. Publications: Monograph, Thermal Stress Analyses; 126 Technical articles; 40 papers on education, training et al. Honours: British Association for the Advancement of Science Brunel Lecturership in Engineering; Commander of the Order of the British Empire (CBE). Memberships: Chartered Engineer, Engineering Council, 1964; Fellow, Royal Aeronautical Society, 1969; Fellow, Institute of Acoustics, 1977-85; Fellow, Chartered Institute of Transport, 1977-85; Fellow, Hong Kong Institution of Engineers, 1984; Life Fellow, Aeronautical Society of India, 1986; Fellow, Royal Academy of Engineering, 1990. Address: 8 Swan Court, York Road, Harrogate, N. Yorks HG1 2QH, England. E-mail: david@johnshg1.fsnet.co.uk

JOHNSON Alan Arthur, b. 17 May 1950, London, England. Secretary of State for Health; Member of Parliament for Hull West and Hessle. Education: Sloane Grammar School, Chelsea. Appointments: Postman, 1968; Member, National Executive Council, 1981-, Union Official, 1987-, Union of Communication Workers; General Secretary, Communication Workers Union, 1992; Member, Labour's National Executive Committee; Member of Parliament for Hull West and Hessle, 1997-; Parliamentary Private Secretary to Dawn Primarolo, 1997; Minister, Department of Trade & Industry, 1999; Minister for Higher Education, Department of Education and Skills, 2003; Secretary of State for Work and Pensions, 2004; Secretary of State for Productivity, Energy and Industry, 2005; Secretary of State for Education and Skills, 2006; Secretary of State for Health, 2007.

JOHNSON Alan Michael Borthwick, b. 7 June 1944, Liverpool, England. Barrister. Education: Liverpool College, 1951-63; Corpus Christi College, Oxford, 1963-67. Appointments: Barrister at 1, Gray's Inn Square; Called to the Bar 1971; Member of the Middle Temple and Gray's Inn. Honours: MA; Harmsworth Scholarship, Middle Temple. Memberships: Oxford Society; South Eastern Circuit; Criminal Bar Association. Address: 1, Gray's Inn Square, Gray's Inn, London WC1R 5AA, England.

JOHNSON (Alexander) Boris, b. 19 June 1964, New York, USA. Member of Parliament. m. Marina Wheeler, 2 sons, 2 daughters. Education: Brakenbury Scholar, BA, Balliol College, Oxford. Appointments: Trainee Reporter, The Times, 1987; Reporter, Wolverhampton Express and Star, 1988; Leader Writer, 1988, European Community Correspondent, Brussels, 1989-94, Assistant Editor, 1994, The Daily Telegraph; Editor, The Spectator, 1999-2005; Member of Parliament, Conservative, Henley-on-Thames, 2001-; Shadow Minister for the Arts, April-November 2004; Appearances on Radio and TV. Publications: Books: Friends, Voters and Countrymen, 2001; Lend Me your Ears, 2003; Seventy Two Virgins, 2004; The New British Revolution, 2005; Dream of

Rome; Weekly column for the Daily Telegraph. Honours: Political Commentator of the Year, What the Papers Say, 1997; National Journalist of the Year, Pagan Federation of Great Britain, 1998; Editors' Editor of the Year, 2003; Columnist of the Year, British Press Awards, 2004; Channel 4 News Award for the person who made the biggest impression on the politics of 2004, 2005; Columnist of the Year, What the Papers Say, 2005. Address: House of Commons, London SW1A 0AA, England.

JOHNSON Benjamin Sinclair Jr, b. 30 December 1961, Falmouth, Jamaica. Professional Athlete; Coach. Honours: Phil Edwards Memorial Outstanding Track Athlete, 1984, 1985, 1986, 1987; Inducted into the Canadian Amateur Hall of Fame, 1985; Olympic Champion Award, 1985; Morton Crowe Award for Male Athlete of the Year, 1985, 1986, 1987; CTFA Track Jack W Davies Outstanding Athlete of the Year, 1985, 1986, 1987; Athlete of the Month, October 1985, January 1986, August 1987, January 1988, Sports Federation of Canada; Sports Excellence Award, 1986; IAAF/Mobil Grand Prix Standings (Indoor), 1986; Lionel Connacher Award for Male Athlete of the Year, 1986, 1987; Jesse Owens International Trophy for Athletic Excellence, 1987; World Champion Award, 1987; The Tribute to Champions; Outstanding Athlete of the Year, 1986, 1987; Order of Canada, 1987; Disqualified for doping lost 1987-88 records. E-mail: benjohnson979@mail.com

JOHNSON Betsey Lee, b. 10 August 1942, Hartford, Connecticut, USA. Fashion Designer. m. (1) John Cale, 1966, 1 daughter, (2) Jeffrey Olivier, 1981. Education: Pratt Institute, New York; Syracuse University. Appointments: Editorial Assistant, Mademoiselle Magazine, 1964-65; Partner, Co-Owner, Betsey, Bunky & Nini, New York, 1969-; Shops in New York, Los Angeles, San Francisco, Coconut Grove, Florida, Venice, California, Boston, Chicago, Seattle; Principal Designer for Paraphernalia, 1965-69; Designer, Alvin Duskin Co, San Francisco, 1970; Head Designer, Alley Cat by Betsey Johnson (division of LeDamor Inc), 1970-74; Freelance Designer for Junior Women's Division, Butterick Pattern Co, 1971, Betsey Johnson for Jeanette Maternities Inc, 1974-75; Designer for Gant Shirtmakers Inc (women's clothing), 1974-75, Tric-Trac by Betsey Johnson (women's knitwear), 1974-76, Butterick's Home Sewing Catalog (children's wear), 1975-; Head Designer, Junior Sportswear Co; Designed for Star Ferry by Betsey Johnson & Michael Miles (children's wear), 1975-77; Owner, Head Designer, B J Inc, Designer, Wholesale Co, New York, 1978; President, Treasurer, B J Vines, New York; Opened Betsey Johnson Store, New York, 1979. Honours include: Merit Award, Mademoiselle Magazine, 1970; Coty Award, 1971; 2 Tommy Print Awards; Fashion Walk of Fame, 2002. Memberships: Council of Fashion Designers; American Women's Forum. Address: 110 East 9th Street, Suite A889, Los Angeles, CA 90079, USA.

JOHNSON Charles (Richard), b. 23 April 1948, Evanston, Illinois, USA. Professor of English; Writer. m. Joan New, June 1970, 1 son, 1 daughter. Education: BA, 1971, MA, 1973, Southern Illinois University; Postgraduate Studies, State University of New York at Stony Brook, 1973-76. Appointments: Assistant Professor, 1976-79, Associate Professor, 1979-82, Professor of English, 1982-, University of Washington, Seattle. Publications: Faith and the Good Thing, 1974; Oxherding Tale, 1982; The Sorcerer's Apprentice: Tales and Conjurations, 1986; Being and Race: Black Writing Since 1970, 1988; Middle Passage, 1990; All This and Moonlight, 1990; In Search of a Voice (with Ron Chernow),

1991; Dreamer, 1998; Turning the Wheel, 2003. Honours: Governor's Award for Literature, State of Washington, 1983; National Book Award, 1990. Address: c/o Department of English, University of Washington, Seattle, WA 98105, USA.

JOHNSON Christopher Louis McIntosh, b. 12 June 1931, Thornton Heath, England. Economic Adviser. m. Anne Robbins, 1958, 1 son, 3 daughters. Education: MA 1st class honours, Philosophy, Politics and Economics, Magdalen College, Oxford. Appointments: Journalist, 1954-76, Paris Correspondent, 1959-63, The Times and Financial Times; Diplomatic Correspondent, Foreign Editor, Managing Editor, Director, Financial Times, 1963-76; Chief Economic Adviser, 1977-91, General Manager, 1985-91, Lloyds Bank; Visiting Professor of Economics, Surrey University, 1986-90; Visiting Scholar, IMF, 1993; Specialist Adviser to the Treasury Select Committee, House of Commons, 1981-97; Chairman, British Section of the Franco-British Council, 1993-97; UK Adviser, Association for the Monetary Union of Europe, 1991-2002. Publications: Editor, Lloyds Bank Review and Lloyds Bank Economic Bulletin, 1985-91; 4 books; Newspaper articles; Lectures on the euro and other economic and financial topics. Honours: Chevalier de la Legion d'Honneur, 1996. Memberships: Member, National Commission on Education, 1991-92; Member, Council of the Britain in Europe Campaign for the Euro; Member, Council of the Institute for Fiscal Studies; Chairman, New London Orchestra, 2001-04. Address: 39 Wood Lane, London N6 5UD, England. E-mail: johnson.c@blueyonder.co.uk

JOHNSON Daniel Benedict, b. 26 August 1957, London, England. Journalist; Writer. m. Sarah Johnson, 2 sons, 2 daughters. Education: BA 1st class, Modern History, Magdalen College, Oxford, 1978; Research Student, Cambridge, 1978-81; Shakespeare Scholar, Berlin, 1979-80. Appointments: Teaching Assistant, German History, Queen Mary College, London, 1982-84; Director of Publications, Centre for Policy Studies, 1983-84; The Daily Telegraph: Leader Writer, 1986-87; Bonn Correspondent, 1987-89; Eastern Europe Correspondent, 1989-90; The Times: Leader Writer, 1990-91; Literary Editor, 1992-96; Assistant Editor, Comment, 1996-98; The Daily Telegraph, Associate Editor, Culture, 1998-; Reported, New York Sun. Publications: Contributions to: The New Yorker; New York Times; Wall Street Journal; Washington Post; Commentary; The National Interest; Civilisation; The Spectator; Times Literary Supplement; Literary Review; Prospect; Encounter; many other journals; Books: Co-editor, German Neo-Liberals and the Social Market Economy, 1989; Introduction, Thomas Mann: Death in Venice and Other Stories; Introduction, Collected Stories, 2001. Address: c/o The Daily Telegraph, 1 Canada Square, Canary Wharf, London, E14 5DT, England. E-mail: daniel.johnson@telegraph.co.uk

JOHNSON David, b. 26 August 1927, Meir, Staffordshire, England. Historian. Education: Repton; Sandhurst. Publications: Sabre General, 1959; Promenade in Champagne, 1960; Lanterns in Gascony, 1965; A Candle in Aragon, 1970; Regency Revolution, 1974; Napoleon's Cavalry and its Leaders, 1978; The French Cavalry 1792-1815, 1989; Bonaparte's Sabres, 2003. Contributions to: The Armourer (1914: The Riddle of the Marne); Skirmish Magazine (The Quest for Arthur). Address: 64B John Street, Porthcawl, Mid-Glam CF36 3BD, Wales.

JOHNSON Earvin (Magic Johnson), b. 14 August 1959, Lansing, Michigan, USA. Basketball Player. m. Cookie Kelly, 1 son. Education: Michigan University. Appointments:

Professional Basketball Player, Los Angeles Lakers National Basketball Association (NBA), 1979-91, (retired), Returned to professional sport, 1992, later announced abandonment of plans to resume sporting career; Chairman, Johnson Development Corporation, 1993-, Magic Johnson Entertainment, 1997-; Vice-President, Co-Owner, Los Angeles Lakers, 1994-, Head Coach, 1994; Presenter, TV Show, The Magic Hour, 1998-. Publications: Magic, 1983; What You Can Do to Avoid AIDS, 1992; My Life (autobiography), 1992. Honours include: Named, Most Valuable Player, NBA Playoffs, 1980, 1982, 1987, NBA, 1987, 1989, 1990. Memberships include: NCAA Championship Team, 1979; National Basketball All-Star Team, 1980, 1982-89; National Basketball Association Championship Team, 1980, 1982, 1985, 1987, 1988; National AIDS Association. Address: Magic Johnson Foundation, Suite 1080, 1600 Corporate Pointe, Culver City, CA 90230, USA.

JOHNSON Gabriel Ampah, b. 13 October 1930, Aneho, Togo. Professor of Biology. m. Louise Chipan, 3 sons, 3 daughters. Education: Licence-es-Sciences, 1950-54, Doctorat-es- Sciences d'État, 1954-59, Universite de Poitiers, France. Appointments: Research Fellow, CNRS, France, 1958-60; Professor and Chair of Biology, 1966; Founding Rector, Universite du Benin, Lome, Togo, 1970-86; Chancellor of Togolese Universities, 1998-. Publications: Articles and papers in professional scientific journals. Honours: Chevalier de l'Ordre National de la Côte-d'Ivoire, 1966; Officier de la Légion d'Honneur, France, 1971; Commandeur de l'Ordre National du Gabon, 1977; Grand Officier de la Croix du Sud, Ordre du Cruzeiro do Sul, Brazil, 1977; Commandeur de l'Ordre du Mérite, France, 1983; Certificate of Merit, IBC, 1983; Commandeur de l'Ordre des Palmes Académiques, France, 1986; Commandeur de l'Ordre National de Mérite de la Tunisie, 1986; Commandeur de l'Ordre du Mono, Togo, 2000; Commandeur de l'Ordre des Palmes Académiques, Togo, 2006; Universal Award of Accomplishment, ABI, 2006; International Medal of Honor, IBC, 2006; American Medal of Honor, ABI, 2006. Memberships: The Africa Club; World Association of Social Prospective; UNESCO. Address: Boîte Postale 7098, Lome, Togo, West Africa. E-mail: apa.g.johnson@ids.tg

JOHNSON Jenny, (Jennifer Hilary Harrower), b. 2 November 1945, Bristol, England. m. Noel David Harrower, 28 April 1990, 1 son. Education: The Red Maids' School, Bristol. Career: Choreographer; Illustrator; Reiki Practitioner; Writer. Publications: Poetry: The Wisdom Tree, 1993; Neptune's Daughters, 1999; Recent contributions to: Grapevine, GreenSpirit Journal and Poetry Salzburg Review. Honours: 4 Literature Awards, Southwest Arts (now Arts Council England, South West); BETW, 1978-1982. Memberships: The Reiki Association; GreenSpirit. Address: Ground Floor Flat, 6 Lyndhurst Road, Exmouth, Devon EX8 3DT, England. E-mail: jennyharrower@btinternet.com

JOHNSON Michael, b. 13 September 1967, Dallas, USA. Athlete. Education: Baylor University. Appointments: World Champion 200m, 1991, 400m & 4 x 400m, 1993, 200m, 400m & 4 x 400m (world record), 1995, 400m, 1997; Olympic Champion 4 x 400m (world record), 1992, 200m, 400m, 1996, World Record Holder 400m (indoors) 44.63 seconds, 1995, 4 x 400m (outdoors) 2.55.74, 1992, 2.54.29, 1993; Undefeated at 400m, 1989-97; First man to be ranked World No 1 at 200m and 400m simultaneously, 1990, 1991, 1994, 1995; Olympic Champion, 200m (world record), 400m, Atlanta, 1996; Olympic Champion, 400m, Sydney 2000. Awards:

Jesse Owens Award, 1994; Track and Field US Athlete of the Year (four times). Address: USA Track & Field, PO Box 120, Indianapolis, IN 46206, USA.

JOHNSON Peter Alec Barwell, b. 26 July 1936, England. m. Gay Marilyn Lindsay, 2 daughters. Education: Uppingham. Appointments: Founder, The British Sporting Art Trust; East Anglian Committee and Member, Executive Council, Historic Houses Association; Chairman and Managing Director, Arthur Ackermann & Peter Johnson Ltd; Council Member, British Antique Dealers' Association, 1970-80; Chairman, Hans Town Ward Conservatives, 1969-72; Chairman, Cleaner Royal Borough, 1989-91; British Delegate, Conseil Internationale de la Chasse; Governor, Kimbolton School, 1993-2000; Member, Cromwell Museum Management Committee; Founder Trustee, Colvin Fire Prevention Trust, 2000-; Guide, Chelsea Physic Garden; Inventor (with John Barwell) of a weed-gathering hoe (Jo-Hoe), 1994. Publication: Book, The Nasmyth Family (with E Money, 1977). Memberships: Buck's; Hurlingham. Address: 16 Church Street, Great Gransden, Sandy, Bedfordshire, England.

JOHNSON Rex Sutherland, b. 24 August 1928, Essex, England. Chartered Architect; Arbitrator; Expert Witness. m. Betty E Johnson, deceased, 2 sons. Education: Diploma of Architecture, London University. Appointments: Assistant Architect, Senior Architect, T P Bennett and Son; Junior Partner, Oliver Law and Partners, 1961-63; T P Bennett and Son, 1963-65; Associate Partner, 1965-69, Senior Partner, 1969-90, Ronald Ward and Partners; Retired, 1990; Consultant, Design 5, London. Memberships: Fellow, Royal Institute of British Architects; Fellow, Chartered Institute of Arbitrators; Founder Member, Society of Expert Witnesses; Trustee, Royal Wanstead Childrens Foundation. Address: Whitepines, Longmill Lane, Crouch, Nr Sevenoaks, Kent TN15 8QB, England. Email: beejons@aol.com

JOHNSON Robin Stanley, b. 23 January 1944, High Wycombe, Buckinghamshire, England. University Lecturer; Academic Mathematician. m. Rosalind Ann, 2 sons. Education: Sir William Borlase's School, Marlow; BSc (Eng), Aeronautics, MSc, Theoretical Aerodynamics, 1962-66, PhD, 1967-69, Imperial College, London. Appointments: Lecturer, Applied Mathematics, 1969-81, Senior Lecturer, Applied Mathematics, 1981-94, Reader in Applied Mathematics, 1994-2005, Professor of Applied Mathematics, 2005-, University of Newcastle upon Tyne. Publications: Books: Solitons: an Introduction (with P G Drazin), 1989, reprinted with corrections, 1993; An introduction to the mathematical theory of water waves, 1997; Singular perturbation theory, 2004; Articles in scientific journals include most recently: The classical problem of water waves: a reservoir of integrable and nearly integrable equations, 2003; The Camassa-Holm equation for water waves moving over a shear flow, 2003; On solutions of the Camassa-Holm equation, 2003; Some contributions to the theory of edge waves, 2005. Memberships: Fellow, Institute of Mathematics and its Applications; Chartered Mathematician; Chartered Scientist. Address: School of Mathematics and Statistics, University of Newcastle upon Tyne, Newcastle upon Tyne NE1 7RU. E-mail: r.s.johnson@ncl.ac.uk

JOHNSON Stanley P, b. 18 August 1940. Writer. m. (1) Charlotte Fawcett, 1963, dissolved 1979, 3 sons, 1 daughter, (2) Jennifer Arnell, 1981, 1 son, 1 daughter. Education: BA, MA, Exeter College, Oxford, 1959-63; Harkness or Commonwealth Fund Fellowship, State University of Iowa and Columbia University, New York, 1964; Diploma,

Agricultural Economics, Oxford, 1964-65. Appointments: United Kingdom Foreign Office, 1964-65; World Bank, Washington DC, 1966-69; United Nations Association of the United States, UNA-USA, 1968-69; Ford Foundation Fellow, London School of Economics, 1969-70; Conservative Research Department, 1969-70; International Planned Parenthood Federation, 1970-73; Head of EC's Prevention of Pollution and Nuisances Division, Adviser to EC Director-General for Environment, European Commission, Brussels, 1973-79; MEP for East Hampshire and the Isle of Wight, Vice Chairman of Committee on the Environment, Public Health and Consumer Protection, European Parliament, 1979-84; Adviser to Director-General Environment, Director of Energy Policy (DG XVII), European Commission, Brussels, 1984-90; Food and Agriculture Organisation of the United Nations, 1990-92; Director, International and Policy Services, Environmental Resources Management, 1992-94; Special Adviser on the Environment to Coopers and Lybrand, 1994-96; Senior Adviser, International Fund for Animal Welfare, 1996-2003. Publications: Author, 20 books (11 non-fiction and 9 fiction); Articles in professor and popular journals; Speeches at national and international conferences. Honours: Newdigate Prize for English Verse, Oxford University, 1962; Greenpeace Prize for Outstanding Services to the Environment, 1984; Royal Society for the Prevention of Cruelty to Animals, Richard Martin Award for Outstanding Services to Animal Welfare, 1984; Cited by London Times as "environmentalist of the year" for work on EU habitats directive, 1989; Consultant, UNDP/UNFPA, 1969-97; Consultant, World Bank Operations Evaluation Unit, 1970; Member, UK Countryside Commission, 1971-73; General Editor, Kluwer Law International series of books on Environmental Law and Policy, 1987-97; Consultant (at Coopers and Lybrand) to UNEP, 1992-92; Consultant FAO for follow-up to Rio Forest Principles, 1994; Trustee, Earthwatch Institute Europe, 1995-2001; Trustee, Plantlife International, 2002-05; Trustee, Gorilla Organisation, 2004-. Address: 34 Park Village East, London NW1 7PZ, England.

JOHNSON William, b. 20 April 1922, Manchester, England. University Professor. m. Heather M Thornber, 1946, 3 sons, 2 daughters. Education: BSc.Tech., UMIST, 1943; REME Commd. 1943-47; BSc Mathematics, London, 1948; DSc, Manchester University, 1960; FRS, 1982 FREng, 1983. Appointments: Professor of Mechanical Engineering, UMIST, 1960-75; Professor of Mechanics, Engineering Department, University of Cambridge, 1975-82; Visiting Professor, Industrial Engineering Department, 1984-85, United Technologies Distinguished Professor of Engineering, 1987-89, Purdue University, Indiana, USA; Visiting Professor of Mechanical Engineering and History of Science, UMIST, 1992-94. Publications (with co-authors): Plasticity for Mechanical Engineers, 1962; Mechanics of Metal Extrusion, 1962; Bibliography of Slip Line Fields, 1968; Impact Strength of Materials, 1972; Engineering Plasticity, 1973; Engineering Plasticity: Metal Forming Processes, 1978; Crashworthiness of Vehicles, 1978; Bibliography of Slip Line Fields, 1982; Collected papers on Benjamin Robins, 2001-03; Record and Services Satisfactory, 2003. Honours include: Safety in Mechanical Engineering Prize (jt), 1980, 1990; James Clayton Prize (jt), Institution of Mechanical Engineers, 1987 and Bernard Hall Prize, 1965, 1967. Silver Medal, Institute of Sheet Metal, 1987; AMPT Gold Medal, Dublin, 1995; ASME Engineer-Historian Award, 2001; Honorary DSc, Bradford University, 1976, Sheffield University, 1986, UMIST, 1995. Memberships: Institution of Mechanical Engineers, 1942-; Foreign Fellow, Academy of Athens, 1982; Foreign Member, Russian Academy of Science, Ural Branch, 1993;

Indian National Academy of Engineering, 1999; Fellow of University College, London, 1981. Address: 5 Epworth Court, King Street, Cambridge, CB11LR, England.

JOHNSON-LAIRD Philip Nicholas, b. 12 October 1936, Rothwell, Yorkshire, England. Psychologist. m. Maureen M Sullivan, 1 son, 1 daughter. Education: BA (Hons), PhD, University College, London. Appointments: Quantity Surveyor, Librarian, miscellaneous jobs, 1952; Assistant Lecturer, 1966, Lecturer, 1967, Psychology, University College, London; Visiting member, Institute for Advanced Study, Princeton, USA, 1971-72; Reader, 1973, Professor, 1978, Experimental Psychology, University of Sussex; Visiting Professor, Stanford University, 1980, 1985; Assistant Director, Medical Research Council's Applied Psychology Unit, Cambridge, 1982; Visiting Professor of Psychology, 1986, 1987, 1988, Professor of Psychology, 1989, Stuart Professor of Psychology, 1994, Princeton; Visiting Professor, New York University, 1992. Publications: Numerous articles and papers published in professional scientific journals. Honours: Rosa Morison Memorial Medal, 1964; James Sully Scholarship, 1964; Spearman Medal, 1974; Honorary Doctorate, University of Gothenburg, 1983; Presidents' Award, British Psychological Society, 1985; Fellow, Darwin College, Cambridge, 1985-89; Medaglia d'Onore, University of Florence, 1989; Honorary Laurea, University of Padua, Italy, 1997; Honorary DSc, Trinity College, University of Dublin, Ireland, 2000; Honorary Doctorate in Psychology, Universidad Nacional de Educacion a Distancia, Madrid, Spain, 2000; Honorary Doctorate, University of Ghent, Belgium, 2002; Honorary Laurea, University of Palermo, Sicily, 2005; Fyssen International Prize, 2002; Mind and Brain Prize, Turin University, 2004; Honorary Laurea, University of Palermo, Sicily, Italy, 2005. Memberships: Fellow, British Academy; Fellow, Royal Society of London; Fellow, University College, London; Member, American Philosophical Society; Member, National Academy of Sciences; Member of numerous other psychological societies. Address: Department of Psychology, Princeton University, Princeton, NJ 08540, USA. E-mail: phil@princeton.edu Website: www.princeton.edu/~psych/psychsite/~phil.html

JOHNSTON Barrie Colin, b. 7 August 1925, London, England. Retired Merchant Banker. m. Cynthia Anne, 1 son, 1 daughter. Appointments: Junior Clerk, Helbert Wagg & Co Ltd, 1941-43; War Service, Royal Marines, Commissioned, 1945, Qualified as Intelligence Officer, Served in 34th Amphibious Regiment RM in SEAC, 1943-46; Rejoined Helbert Wagg, 1946, amalgamated in 1960 to J Henry Schroder Wagg & Co Ltd; Promoted later to Assistant Director of the Bank; Created Schroder Life Assurance, on the Board for 2 years; Member of team that formed first Property Unit Trust for Pension Funds in 1966, began lecturing on Pension and Property matters, 1946-72; Director, Charterhouse Japhet, 1972-84; Chairman, Charterhouse Bank, Jersey for 5 years; Retired, 1984; Non-executive Director, Charterhouse Investment Management, 1984-86; Additional Business Interests: The Pension Fund Property Unit Trust, 1966-89; The Charities Property Unit Trust, 1967-88; The Pension Fund Agricultural Property Trust, 1976-89; Non-executive Director, T H White Ltd, 1980-87; Director, Mornington Building Society, 1988-91; Director, ML-MIM European Equity Revival Fund NV, 1990-98; Chairman, Honorary Treasurer, or Trustee of 20 charities, 1984-2003. Publications: Articles in professional magazines and newspapers; lectures to professional bodies; Book, Life's a Lottery – or is it?, 2001. Honour OBE, 1994. Memberships: Fellow, Pensions Management Institute; Associate UK Society of Investment Professionals; Honorary

Fellow, Royal College of Radiologists; Honorary Member, Royal Electrical and Mechanical Engineers Institution; Fellow, Royal Society of the Arts. Address: Yew Cottage, 8 The Green, Ewell, Surrey KT17 3JN, England.

JOHNSTONE Alexander Henry, b. 17 October 1930, Edinburgh, Scotland. Retired University Professor. m. Martha Y Cuthbertson, 2 sons. Education: Leith Academy, 1942-49; BSc (1st Class), Chemistry, 1953, PGCE, 1954, University of Edinburgh; PhD, Chemical Education, University of Glasgow, 1972. Appointments: Chemistry Master, George Watson's College, Edinburgh; Principal Chemistry Master, Stirling High School; Senior Lecturer in Chemistry, Reader in Chemistry, Professor in Chemistry, Director of Teaching & Learning Service, Director of Centre for Science Education, Professor of Science Education, University of Glasgow. Publications: 8 chemistry textbooks; 200 academic research papers; Supervision of 80 higher degree students. Honours: Nyholm Medal, Royal Society of Chemistry; Illuminati Medal, Italian Chemical Society; Mellor Medal, Royal Australian Chemical Society; Brasted Medal, American Chemical Society; Verhagen Titular Chair, Limburg University; FECS Lecture, Federation of European Chemical Societies; Galen Lectureship, University of Dublin. Memberships: Fellow, Royal Society of Chemistry. E-mail: alexjo@btinternet.com

JOLEVSKI Ivan, b. 3 July 1963, Bitola, Republic of Macedonia. Historian; Manager. 1 daughter. Education: Master of History, St Cyril and Methodius University, Skopje. Appointments: Manager, History Archive, The Institute, Museum and Gallery, Bitola, 1987-99; Restoration of Macedonia's Sirok Sokak; Manager, PC for management with housing and business shortage in Bitola; Part time Journalist in culture and politics. Publications: Author and co-author of several scientific articles for professional journals. Honours: Person of the Year, City of Bitola. Memberships: OMPEM. Address: Strcin 79, Bitola 7000, Republic of Macedonia. E-mail: ivanc063@freemail.com.mk

JOLIE Angelina, b. 1975, USA. Actress. m. (1) Jonny Lee Miller, 1996, divorced 1999, (2) Billy Bob Thornton, 2000, divorced 2003, 1 adopted son, 1 adopted daughter, 1 daughter with Brad Pitt. Education: Lee Strasberg Institute, New York. Career: Goodwill Ambassador, UNHCR, 2001; Films: Lookin' To Get Out, 1982; Cyborg II: Glass Shadow, Hackers, 1995; Foxfire, Mojave Moon, Love Is All There Is, 1996; True Women, George Wallace, Playing God, 1997; Hell's Kitchen, Gia, 1998; Playing by Heart, Girl, Interrupted, 1999; Tomb Raider, Original Sin, 2001; Life or Something Like It, 2002; Lara Croft Tomb Raider: Cradle of Life, Beyond Borders, 2003; Taking Lives, Shark Tale (voice), Sky Captain and the World of Tomorrow, Alexander, 2004; Mr & Mrs Smith, 2005; The Good Shepherd, 2006; A Mighty Heart, Beowulf, 2007; Kung Fu Panda, 2008. Honours: Golden Globe, 1998, 1999; Screen Actors Guild Award, 1999; Academy Award for Best Supporting Actress, 1999. Address: c/o Richard Bauman & Associates, Suite 473, 5757# Wilshire Boulevard, Los Angeles, CA 90036, USA.

JONAS Peter (Sir), b. 14 October 1946, London, England. General and Artistic Director, Bavarian State Opera. m. Lucy Hull, 1989, divorced 2001. Education: BA honours, University of Sussex; LRAM, FRNCM, 2000, Royal Northern College of Music; CAMS, Fellow, FRCM 1989, Royal College of Music; Eastman School of Music, University of Rochester, USA. Appointments: Assistant to Music Director, 1974-76, Artistic Administrator, 1976-85, Chicago Symphony Orchestra; Director of Artistic Administration, Orchestral

Association of Chicago, Chicago Symphony Orchestra, Chicago Civic Orchestra, Chicago Symphony Chorus, Allied Arts Association, Orchestra Hall, 1977-85; General Director, ENO, 1985-93; General and Artistic Director, Bavarian State Opera, 1993-; Chairman, Deutsche Opernkonferenz (Congress of German and European Opera House Directors), 1999-2005. Publications: with Mark Elder and David Pountney, Power House, 1992; Co-author, Eliten und Demokratie, 1999-2005; Lecturer, University of St Gallen (CH), 2001-; Lecturer, University of Zürich, 2003-. Honours: FRSA, 1989; CBE, 1993; Honorary DrMus, Sussex, 1994; Knighted 2000; Bayerische Verdienstorden (Distinguished Service Cross), 2001; Bavarian Constitutional Medal, 2001; Queen's Lecture, Berlin, 2001; Visiting Lecturer, St Gallen University, 2003-, University of Zurich, 2004-; Member, Bavarian Academy of Fine Arts, 2005-. Memberships: Advisory Board, Hypo-Vereinsbank, 1994-2004; Board of Governors, Bayerische Rundfunk, 1999-2006; Board of Management, National Opera Studio, 1985-93; Council, RCM, 1988-95; Council, London Lighthouse, 1990-94. Address: Bayerische Staätsoper, Nationaltheater, Max-Joseph-Platz 2, 80539 München, Germany.

JONCKHEERE Inge, b. 26 May 1977, Ghent, Belgium. Education: MSc, Bio-Engineering, Land and Forestry Management, 2000; PhD, BioScience Engineering, 2005. Appointments: Research Associate, Kuleuven, 2001-05; Postdoctoral Research Fellow, Kuleuven, 2005-06; European Collaborative Research Co-ordinator, European Science Foundation, 2006-. Publications: 15 peer-reviewed articles; 4 book chapters; More than 20 national and international conference proceedings. Honours: Postdoctoral Grant, Flemish Science Foundation, 2006-09; Laureate, Belgian Stichting Roeping, 2006; Listed in international biographical dictionaries. Memberships: IEEE; EGU; AGU; EPWS; EuroScience. Address: Andre Devaerelaan 102, 8500 Kortrijk, Belgium. E-mail: ijonckheere@esf.org

JONES Catherine Zeta, b. 25 September 1969, Swansea, Wales. Actress. m. Michael Douglas, 1 son, 1 daughter. Creative Works: Stage appearances include: The Pyjama Game; Annie; Bugsy Malone; 42nd Street; Street Scene; TV appearances include: Darling Buds of May; Out of the Blue; Cinder Path, 1994; Return of the Native, 1995; Titanic, 1996; Film appearances include: Scheherazade; Coup de Foudre; Splitting Heirs, 1993; Blue Juice, 1995; The Phantom, 1996; The Mask of Zorro, 1997; Entrapment, 1998; The Haunting, 1999; Traffic, 2000; America's Sweethearts, 2001; Chicago, 2002; Monkeyface, 2003; Intolerable Cruelty, 2003; The Terminal, 2004; Ocean's Twelve, 2004; Legend of Zorro, 2005; No Reservations, 2007; Death Defying Acts,2007. Honours: Best Supporting Actress, BAFTA Awards, 2003; Screen Actors Guild Awards, 2003; Academy Awards, 2003. Address: c/o ICM Ltd, Oxford House, 76 Oxford Street, London W1N 0AX, England.

JONES Douglas Gordon, b. 1 January 1929, Bancroft, Ontario, Canada. Retired Professor; Poet. Education: MA, Queen's University, Kingston, Ontario, 1954. Appointment: Professor, University of Sherbrooke, Quebec, 1963-94. Publications: Poetry: Frost on the Sun, 1957; The Sun Is Axeman, 1961; Phrases from Orpheus, 1967; Under the Thunder the Flowers Light Up the Earth, 1977; A Throw of Particles: Selected and New Poems, 1983; Balthazar and Other Poems, 1988; The Floating Garden, 1995; Wild Asterisks in Cloud, 1997; Grounding Sight (poetry), 1999. Other: Butterfly on Rock: A Study of Themes and Images in Canadian Literature, 1970. Honours: President's Medal,

University of Western Ontario, 1976; Governor General's Award for Poetry, 1977, and for Translation, 1993; Honorary DLitt, Guelph University, 1982. Address: 120 Hougton Street, North Hatley, Quebec JOB 2CO, Canada.

JONES George Glenn, b. 12 September 1931, Saratoga, Texas, USA. Country Singer; Musician (guitar). m. (1) Tammy Wynette, 1969-75; (2) Nancy Sepulveda, 1983. Career: Recording artist, 1953-; Worked under names of Johnny Williams, Hank Davis, Glen Patterson; Worked with The Big Bopper; Johnny Preston; Johnny Paycheck; Recorded duets with Gene Pitney; Melba Montgomery; Tammy Wynette; Elvis Costello; James Taylor; Willie Nelson. Compositions include: The Window Up Above, Mickey Gilley; Seasons Of My Heart, Johnny Cash, Jerry Lee Lewis. Recordings: 150 Country hits include: Why Baby Why; White Lightning; Tender Years; She Still Thinks I Care; You Comb Her Hair; Who Shot Sam?; The Grand Tour; He Stopped Loving Her Today; Recorded over 450 albums; Recent albums include: First Time Live, Who's Gonna Fill Their Shoes, 1985; Wine Coloured Roses, 1986; Super Hits, Too Wild Too Long, 1987; One Woman Man, 1989; Hallelujah Weekend, You Oughta Be Here With Me, 1990; And Along Came Jones, Friends In High Places, 1991; Salutes Bob Wills and Hank Williams, Live At Dancetown USA, Walls Can Fall, 1992; One, 1995; I Lived to Tell It All, 1996; In a Gospel Way, 1997; It Don't Get Any Better Than This, 1998; The Cold Hard Truth, Live with the Possum, 1999; with Tammy Wynette: We Can Go Together, 1971; Me And The First Lady, 1972; Golden Ring, 1976; Together Again, 1980. Address: Razor & Tie, 214 Sullivan Street, Suite 4A, New York, NY 10012, USA.

JONES George William, b. 4 February 1938, Wolverhampton, England. Retired University Professor. m. Diana Mary, 1 son, 1 daughter. Education: Jesus College, Oxford, 1957-60; Nuffield College, Oxford, 1960-63. Appointments: Assistant Lecturer in Government, 1963-65, Lecturer in Government, 1965-66, Leeds University; Lecturer in Political Science, 1966-71, Senior Lecturer in Political Science, 1971-74, Reader in Political Science, 1974-76, Professor of Government, 1976-2003, Professor Emeritus, 2003-, London School of Economics; Honorary Professor, University of Birmingham, 2003-; Visiting Professor, Queen Mary College, London, 2004-. Publications: Borough Politics, 1969; Herbert Morrison, 1973, 2nd edition 2001; Case for Local Government, 2nd edition 1985; West European Prime Ministers, 1991; At the Centre of Whitehall, 1998; Regulation Inside Government, 1999. Honours: BA, 1960; MA, 1965; D Phil, 1965; FRHisS, 1980; OBE, 1999. Memberships: Honorary Fellow, University of Wolverhampton, 1986; Layfield Committee on Local Government Finance, 1974-76; Joint Working Party on Internal Management of Local Authorities, 1992-93; Beacon Council's Advisory Panel, 1999-2002; National Consumer Council, 1991-99; Honorary Member, Chartered Institute of Public Finance and Accountancy, 2003-; Honorary Member, Society of Local Authority Chief Executives, 2003-. Address: Department of Government, LSE, Houghton Street, London WC2A 2AE, England. E-mail: g.w.jones@lse.ac.uk

JONES Grace, b. 19 May 1952, Spanishtown, Jamaica. Singer; Model; Actress. m. Atila Altaunbay, 1996. Education: Syracuse University. Appointments: Fashion Model, New York, Paris; Made 1st Album, Portfolio, for Island Records, 1977; Debut as Disco Singer, New York, 1977; Founder, La Vie en Rose Restaurant, New York, 1987. Creative Works: Films include: Conan the Destroyer; A View to a Kill, 1985; Vamp; Straight to Hell; Siesta; Boomerang, 1991; Cyber

Bandits, 1995; McCinsey's Island, 1998; Palmer's Pick Up, 1999; No Place Like Home, 2006. Albums include: Fame; Muse; Island Life; Slave to the Rhythm.

JONES Huw, b. 5 May 1948, Manchester, England. Broadcasting Executive. m. Siân Marylka Miarczynska, 1979, 1 son, 1 daughter. Education: BA, Modern Languages (French), MA, Oxon. Appointments: Pop Singer, Recording Artist, Television Presenter, 1968-76; Director, General Manager, Sain Recording Company, 1969-81; Chairman, Barcud Cyf (TV Facilities), 1981-93; Managing Director, Producer, Teledu'r Tir Glas Cyf (independent production company), 1982-93; First Chairman, Teledwyr Annibynnol Cymru (Welsh Independent Producers), 1984-86; Chief Executive, S4C (Welsh Fourth Channel), 1994-2005. Honours: Honorary Fellow, University of Wales, Aberystwyth; Member, Gorsedd of Bards National Eisteddfod of Wales; Fellow, Royal Television Society. Memberships: Chairman, Celtic Film and Television Co Ltd, 2001-2004; Director, Sgrin Cyf; Director, Skillset Ltd; Chairman, Skillset Cymru; Member, British Screen Advisory Council. Address: S4C, Parc Ty Glas, Llanishen, Cardiff, C14 5DU, Wales. E-mail: huw.jones@s4c.co.uk

JONES James Earl, b. 17 January 1931, Mississippi, USA. Actor. m. Cecilia Hurt, 1982, 1 child. Education: University of Michigan. Creative Works: Numerous stage appearances on Broadway and elsewhere including, Master Harold...And the Boys, Othello, King Lear, Hamlet, Paul Robeson, A Lesson From Aloes, Of Mice & Men, The Iceman Cometh, A Hand is on the Gate, The Cherry Orchard, Danton's Death, Fences; Frequent TV appearances; Voice of Darth Vader in films Star Wars, The Empire Strikes Back, The Return of the Jedi; Films include: Matewan; Gardens of Stone; Soul Man; My Little Girl; The Man; The End of the Road; Dr Strangelove; Conan the Barbarian; The Red Tide; A Piece of the Action; The Last Remake of Beau Geste; The Greatest; The Heretic; The River Niger; Deadly Hero; Claudine; The Great White Hope; The Comedians; Coming to America; Three Fugitives; Field of Dreams; Patriot Games; Sommersby; The Lion King (voice); Clear and Present Danger; Cry the Beloved Country; Lone Star; A Family Thing; Gang Related; Rebound; Summer's End; Undercover Angel, 1999; Quest for Atlantis, 1999; On the Q.T., 1999; Finder's Fee, 2001; Recess Christmas: A Miracle on Third Street (voice), 2001; Robots (voice), 2005; Star Wars: Episode III – Revenge of the Sith, 2005; The Benchwarmers (voice), 2006; The Better Man, 2008. Honours include: Tony Award; Golden Globe Award; Honorary DFA, Princeton, Yale, Michigan.

JONES John Henry, b. 29 April 1942, Lingfield, Surrey, England. Chemist; Historian. m. Patricia, 3 sons. Education: Balliol College, Oxford, 1961-67. Appointments: Fellow, 1966-, Dean, 1972-2002, Vicegerent, 2000-01, 2006, Vice-Master, 2002-2007, Balliol College, Oxford. Publications: Numerous papers and articles in professional scientific journals. Honours: MA; D Phil; C Chem; FRSC; FRHistS. Address: Balliol College, Oxford, OX1 3BJ, England. E-mail: john.jones@balliol.ox.ac.uk

JONES Keith John, b. 20 October 1951, Portsmouth, England. Mathematician. m. Deborah Jane, 1 stepson, 3 daughters. Education: BSc (Hons), Mathematics, London University; MSc, Applicable Mathematics, Cranfield Institute of Technology; PhD, Computer Science, Birkbeck College, London University. Appointments: Mathematician/Algorithmist/Programmer, Standard Telecommunications Laboratories Ltd, 1978-83; Mathematician/Algorithmist/

Programmer, Thorn-EMI Electronics Ltd, Somerset, 1983-85; Mathematician/Algorithmist/Programmer, Bae Underwater Research & Eng Unit, Dorset, 1985-87; Mathematician/Algorithmist/Programmer, Dowty Maritime Systems Ltd, Dorset, 1987-89; Mathematician/Algorithmist/Programmer, GEC Marconi Naval Systems Ltd, Somerset, 1989-96; Mathematician/Algorithmist/Programmer, DERA/QinetiQ, Dorset, 1996-2001; Company Director, Algosoft Solutions Ltd, 2001-; Consultant Mathematician, TRL Technology Ltd, Gloucestershire, 2002-. Publications: Numerous articles in professional journals; 4 patents. Address: 8 Westhill Road, Wyke Regis, Weymouth, Dorset, DT4 9NA, England. E-mail: keith.jones-algosoft@homecall.co.uk

JONES Lawrence William, b. 16 November 1925, Evanston, Illinois, USA. Professor Emeritus. 1 son, 2 daughters. Education: BSc, 1948, MSc, 1949, Northwestern University, Evanston, Illinois; PhD, University of California at Berkeley, 1952. Appointments: Professor of Physics, 1952-98, Chair, Department of Physics, 1982-87, Professor Emeritus, 1998, University of Michigan; Scientist, Midwestern Universities Research Association, 1956-57; Ford Foundation Fellow, CERN, Geneva, Switzerland, 1961-62; Guggenheim Foundation Fellow, CERN, 1965; Visiting Professor and Science Research Council Fellow, Westfield College, London, England, 1977; Visiting Professor, Tata Institute for Fundamental Research, Bombay, India, 1979; Distinguished Visiting Scholar, University of Adelaide, Australia, 1991; Visiting Professor, University of Sydney, Australia, 1991; Visiting Scientist, University of Auckland, New Zealand, 1991. Publications: Over 300 journal publications; Over 200 publications in conference proceedings; Over 30 book chapters or sections. Honours: Phi Beta Kappa and Sigma Xi; Fellow, American Physical Society; Award, Quest for Technology, University of Michigan; Honoree, Symposium in Honor of LW Jones, CERN, Geneva. Memberships: American Physical Society; American Association for the Advancement of Science; Phi Beta Kappa. Address: Department of Physics, University of Michigan, 450 Church Street, Ann Arbor, MI 48109-1040, USA. E-mail: lwjones@umich.edu

JONES Martyn David, b. 1 March 1947, Crewe, Cheshire, England. Member of Parliament. Divorced, 1 son, 1 daughter. Education: Liverpool College of Commerce; CIBiol, Liverpool Polytechnic; MIBiol, Trent Polytechnic. Appointments: Microbiologist, Wrexham Lager Beer Company, 1969-87; Councillor, Clwyd County Council, 1981-89; MP for Clwyd South (formerly Clwyd South West), 1987-; Opposition Spokesperson on Food, Agriculture and Rural Affairs, 1994-95; Labour Whip; 1988-92; Speaker's Panel of Chairmen, 1993-94; Chairman, Welsh Affairs Select Committee, 1997. Memberships: Council Member, Royal College of Veterinary Surgeons; SERA, Fabian Society; Christian Socialist Movement; Federation of Economic Development Authorities; Institute of Biology. Address: House of Commons, London, SW1A 0AA, England. E-mail: jonesst@parliament.uk

JONES Norah, b. 30 March 1979, New York, USA. Singer; Pianist. Education: Booker T Washington High School for the Performing and Visual Arts, Dallas; North Texas University. Career: Member, Wax Poetic; Formed band with Jesse Harris, Lee Alexander and Dan Rieser; Solo artist, 2001-; Albums: Come Away With Me, 2002; Feels Like Home, 2004; Not Too Late, 2007. Singles: First Sessions, 2001; Don't Know Why, 2002; Feelin' The Same Way, 2002; Come Away With Me, 2002; Turn Me On, 2003; Sunrise, 2004; What Am I To You? 2004; Here We Go Again, 2004. Honours: MOBO Award,

Best Jazz Act, 2002; VH1 Best Young Female Singer Award, 2002; Grammy Awards: Best New Artist, 2003; Album of the Year, 2003, Best Pop Vocal Album, 2003, Record of the Year, 2003, Best Pop Vocal Performance, 2003, Best Female Pop Vocal Performance, 2005, Record of the Year, 2005; BRIT Award for International Breakthrough Artist, 2003; World Music Awards for Best Female Artist, 2004. Address: Macklam Feldman Management, Suite 200, 1505 W Second Avenue, Vancouver, BC V6H 3Y4, Canada. Website: www.norahjones.com

JONES Peter Ivan, b. 14 December 1942, Cosham, Hampshire, England. Chairman of the Tote. m. Elizabeth Gent, 2 sons, 2 daughters. Education: BSc Economics, London School of Economics, 1964; MIPA, 1967. Appointments: Chief Executive, Boase Massimi Pollitt, 1988-89; Chief Executive, 1989-93, Director, 1989-97, Omnicom UK plc; President, Racehorse Owners Association, 1990-93; Member, Horserace Betting Levy Board, 1993-95; Director, British Horseracing Board, 1993-97; President, Diversified Agency Services, 1993-97; Chairman, Dorset Police Authority, 1997-2003; Director, 1995-97, Chairman, 1997-, Horserace Totalisator Board. Publications: Trainers Record, annually, 1973-87; Editor, Ed Byrne's Racing Year, annually, 1980-83. Memberships: Bridport and West Dorset Golf Club. Address: Melplash Farmhouse, Melplash, Bridport, Dorset DT6 3UH, England. E-mail: pjones@tote.co.uk

JONES Quincy, b. 14 March 1933, Chicago, Illinois, USA. Record Producer; Composer; Arranger; Musician; Conductor. m. (1) 3 children, (2) Peggy Lipton, 2 daughters. Education: Seattle University; Berklee College of Music; Boston Conservatory. Appointments: Trumpeter, Arranger, Lionel Hampton Orchestra, 1950-53; Arranger, various singers; Leader, own orchestra, concerts, TV appearances, 1960-; Music Director, Mercury Records, 1961, Vice-President, 1964. Creative Works: Solo Albums: You've Got It Bad Girl, 1973; Walking In Space, 1974; Body Heat, 1974; Mellow Madness, 1975; I Heard That!, 1976; Quintessence, 1977; Sounds And Stuff Like That, 1978; The Dude, 1981; Bossa Nova, 1983; The Q, 1984; Back On The Block, 1989. Honours: Golden Note, ASCAP, 1982; Honorary Degree, Berklee College, 1983; Over 20 Grammy Awards; Lifetime Achievement, National Academy of Songwriters, 1989; Jean Hersholt Humanitarian Award, 1995; Scopus Award; Producers' Guild of America Award, 1995; Crystal Award, World Economic Forum, 2000; Marian Anderson Award, 2001; Ted Arison Prize, National Foundation for Advancement in the Arts, 2001; Kennedy Center Honor, 2001. Address: Rogers and Cowan, 3800 Barham Boulevard, Suite 503, Los Angeles, CA 90068, USA.

JONES Russell Alan, b. 26 May 1960. Director. Education: BA Honours, British Government and Politics and History (also studied with conductor and musicologist, Harry Newstone), University of Kent at Canterbury, 1978-81. Appointments: Orchestra Manager, Royal Liverpool Philharmonic, 1981-86; Concerts Manager, Scottish Chamber Orchestra, 1986; Chief Executive, National Federation of Music Societies, 1987-97; Chairman, National Music Council, 1995-2000; Numerous appointments (Director of Operations and Director of Policy & Public Affairs), ABSA/Arts and Business, 1997-2002; Co-creator, Arts & Business New Partners programme; Director, Association of British Orchestras, 2002-; Former Chairman, Young Musicians Symphony Orchestra; Former Vice Chairman, Academy of Live & Recorded Arts, -2005. Memberships: President, International Alliance of Orchestral Associations; Freeman, City of London; Liveryman,

Worshipful Company of Musicians; Past Master, Billingsgate Ward Club; Fellow, Royal Society of Arts; Lords Taverner; Chevalier, Order of Champagne. Address: 12 Eastern Road, Bounds Green, London N22 4DD, England.

JONES Tom Sir (Thomas Jones Woodward), b. 7 June 1940, Pontypridd, Wales. Entertainer. m. Melinda Trenchard, 1956, 1 son. Career: Former bricklayer, factory worker, construction worker; Singing debut, aged 3, later sang in clubs, dance halls, with self-formed group The Playboys; Became Tom Jones, 1963; First hit record It's Not Unusual, 1964; Appeared on radio, television; Toured US, 1965; Television show, This Is Tom Jones, 1969-71; Many international hits, albums in Top 10 charts, Europe, USA; Over 30 million discs sold by 1970; Toured continuously, television appearances, 1970s-; Score, musical play Matador; Hit single: A Boy From Nowhere, 1987; Frequent Amnesty International; Simple Truth, 1991; Rainforest Foundation, 1993; Shelter, 1993; Television series: The Right Time, 1992; Glastonbury Festival of Contemporary Performing Arts, 1992; Live stage appearance, Under Milk Wood, Prince's Trust, 1992; Performed in Amnesty International 40th Anniversary Special, 2001. Recordings: Hits include: It's Not Unusual, 1964; What's New Pussycat, 1965; Thunderball, 1966; Green Green Grass Of Home, 1966; Delilah, 1968; Love Me Tonight, 1969; Can't Stop Loving You; She's A Lady; Letter To Lucille, 1973; Say You Stay Until Tomorrow, 1976; A Boy From Nowhere, 1987; It's Not Unusual (reissue), 1987; If I Only Knew, 1994; Burning Down the House, 1999; Baby It's Cold Outside, 1999; Mama Told Me Not To Come, 2000; Sex Bomb, 2000; You Need Love Like I Do, 2000; Tom Jones International, 2002. Albums include: Green Green Grass Of Home, 1967; Delilah, 1968; This Is Tom Jones, 1969; Tom, 1970; I Who Have Nothing, 1970; Close Up, 1972; The Body and Soul Of TJ, 1973; I'm Coming Home, 1978; At This Moment, 1989; After Dark, 1989; The Lead And How To Swing It, 1994; Reload, 1999; Mr Jones, 2002; Reload 2, 2002. Honours: OBE, 1999; BRIT Award for Best British Male Solo Artist, 2000; Nodnoff Robbins Music Therapy Silver Clef Award, 2001; Q Magazine Merit Prize, 2002; BRIT Award for Outstanding Contribution to Music, 2003; Knight Bachelor, 2006. Memberships: SAG; AFTRA: AGVA. Address: Tom Jones Enterprises, 10100 Santa Monica Blvd, Ste 205, Los Angeles, CA 90067, USA.

JONES Tommy Lee, b. 15 September 1946, San Saba, Texas, USA. Actor. m. (1) Kimberlea Cloughley, 1981, (2) Dawn Laurel, 2001. Education: Harvard University. Creative Works: Broadway appearances include: A Patriot for Me; Four in a Garden; Ulysses in Night Town; Fortune and Men's Eyes; TV appearances include: The Amazing Howard Hughes; Lonesome Dove; The Rainmaker; Cat on a Hot Tin Roof; Yuri Nosenko; KGB; April Morning; Films include: Love Story, 1970; Eliza's Horoscope; Jackson County Jail; Rolling Thunder; The Betsy; Eyes of Laura Mars; Coal Miner's Daughter; Back Roads; Nate and Hayes; River Rat; Black Moon Rising; The Big Town; Stormy Monday; The Package; Firebirds; JFK; Under Siege; House of Cards; The Fugitive; Blue Sky; Heaven and Earth; Natural Born Killers; The Client; Blue Sky; Cobb; Batman Forever; Men in Black, 1997; Volcano, 1997; Marshals, 1997; Small Soldiers (voice), 1998; Rules of Engagement, 1999; Double Jeopardy, 1999; Space Cowboys, 2000; Men in Black II, 2002; The Hunted, 2003; The Missing, 2003; Man of the House, 2005; The Three Burials of Melquiades Estrada, 2005; A Prairie Home Companion, 2006; No Country for Old Men, 2007; In the Valley of Elah, 2007. Honours include: Emmy Award.

JONES Trevor Mervyn, b. 19 August 1942, Wolverhampton, England. Director. m. Verity Ann Bates, 1 son, 1 daughter. Education: BPharm, Honours, PhD, Kings College, London. Appointments: Lecturer, University of Nottingham; Head of Development, The Boots Co Ltd; Director, Research and Development, Wellcome Foundation; Chairman, Reneuron Holdings plc; Director of Merlin Fund, Merlin Biosciences; Director General, Association of the British Pharmaceutical Industry; Director, Allergan Inc; Director, NextPharm Ltd. Publications: Numerous scientific papers in learned journals; Books: Drug Delivery to the Respiratory Tract; Advances in Pharmaceutical Science. Honours: Honorary degrees: PhD, University of Athens; DSc, University of Nottingham; DSc, University of Strathclyde; DSc, University of Bath; Honorary Fellowships: Royal College of Physicians, Faculty of Pharmaceutical Medicine; British Pharmacological Society; The School of Pharmacy; Charter Gold Medal, Pharmaceutical Society; Gold Medal, Comenius University. Memberships: Fellow, Kings College London; Fellow, Royal Society of Chemists; Fellow, Royal Pharmaceutical Society; Member, College of Pharmacy Practice; Member, WHO Commission on Intellectual Property Rights Innovation and Public Health; Liveryman, Worshipful Society of Apothecaries; Atheneum Club; Surrey County Cricket Club. Address: 18 Friths Drive, Reigate, Surrey, RH2 0DS, England. E-mail: trevor.m.jones@btinternet.com

JONG Erica Mann, b. 26 Mar 1942, New York, USA. Author; Poet. m. Kenneth David Burrows, 1 daughter. Education: BA, Barnard College, 1963; MA, Columbia University, 1965. Appointments: Faculty, English Department, CUNY, 1964-65; Overseas Division of Maryland, 1969-70; Member, Literary Panel, NY State Council on Arts, 1972-74; Faculty Bread Loaf Writers Conference, Middlesex, VT, USA, 1982; Mbr, Faculty Salzburg Seminar, Salzburg, Austria, 1993. Publications: Author: (poems) Fruits and Vegetables, 1971, reissued, 1997; Half Lives, 1973; Loveroot, 1975; At the Edge of the Body, 1979; Ordinary Miracles, 1983; Becoming Light: Poems New and Selected, 1992; (Novels) Fear of Flying, 1973; How to Save Your Own Life, 1977; Fanny: Being the True History of Fanny Hackabout-Jones, 1980; Parachutes and Kisses, 1984; Serenissima, 1987, reissued as Shylock's Daughter: a Novel of Love in Venice; Any Woman's Blues, 1990; The Devil at Large: Erica Jong on Henry Miller, 1993; Fear of Fifty: A Midlife Memoir, 1994; Inventing Memory: A Novel of Mothers and Daughters, 1997; What Do Women Want? Bread. Roses. Sex. Power, 1998.; Sappho's Leap, 2003; Seducing the Demon: Writing for My Life, 2006; Bad Girls: My Dirty Secret, 2007. Honours: Woodrow Wilson Fellow; Recipient Bess Hokin Prize Poetry Magazine, 1971; Named Mother of the Year, 1982; National Endowment Arts Grantee, 1973. Literary Agent: Ed Victor Ltd. Address: 6 Bayley St, Bedford Square, London WC1B 3HB, England.

JONSON Guy, b. 5 November 1913, London, England. Concert Pianist. m. Patricia Burrell, deceased, 2 daughters. Education: Royal Academy of Music, London, 1930-35; MacFarren Gold Medal, 1934. Appointments: WWII Army: RA seconded Personal Selection, 1940-46; Professor of Pianoforte, Tobias Matthay Pianoforte School, London, 1936-39; Professor, Tutor, Royal Academy of Music, 1939-85; Examiner, Royal Schools of Music, 1947-89; Adjudicator, Competitive Festivals throughout UK and Canada, 1949-85; Solo Recitalist, Soloist with major orchestras world-wide; CD Recordings on the Manuscript label. Honours: FRAM; Hon FTCL; FRSA. Memberships: Incorporated Society of Musicians; Royal Philharmonic Society; RAM Club; Royal Society of Arts. Address: 18 Bracknell Gardens, Hampstead, NW3 7EB, London, England. E-mail: guyjonson@blueyonder.co.uk

JONUŠIENĖ Laimutė, b. 30 January 1939, Lithuania. Journalist. m. Antanas Jonušas, 1 son. Education: Philology, Vilnius University, 1961; Private studies of art, music and history in Lithuania and abroad. Appointments: Editor, Culture Life Department at the Lithuania National Radio, 1964-2002; Culture Life Observer for the press, 2002-; Broadcasts for International Radio University (URTI), 1994-98. Publications: Reports on the most prestigious summer festivals for Lithuanian National Radio and the Magazine "Muzikos Barai" (traditions, innovations and personalities); Reports on world-wide places of culture for "Muzikos Barai" and "Kelionių magija". Honours: Grants for cultural initiatives: URTI, Paris, 1994-98, Kultur Kontakt, Vienna, 1996, 1998, Open Society Fund, 1996, Lucerne Summer Festival, 2002, Salzburger Festspiele, 1998-2001, Bayreuther Festspiele, 2000-2001. Memberships: Lithuanian Journalists Union; International Federation of Journalists; Lithuanian Association of Artists; Art Creators; European Council of Artist; ECA. Address: Basanavičiaus 17-21, LT-03108 Vilnius, Lithuania. E-mail: laima.jonusiene@gmail.com

JOO Sang-Yeol, b. 30 August 1951, Uljin, Gyeongsangbuk-do, Korea. m. Jeong-Hee Kwon, 2 sons. Education: BSc, Kangwon National University, 1978; MSc, 1981, DSc, 1991, Korea University. Appointments: Full Instructor, 1982-84, Assistant Professor, 1984-88, Associate Professor, 1988-93, Full Professor, 1993-, Dean, College of Natural Sciences, 2005-07, Kangwon National University. Publications: Numerous articles in professional journals. Memberships: Korean Mathematical Society; Korean Statistical Society; Korean Data Analysis Society; Korean Reliability Society. Address: Department of Statistics, Kangwon National University, Hyoja 2-dong, Chunchon 200700, Republic of Korea. E-mail: syjoo@kangwon.ac.kr

JORDAN Bill (Lord), b. 1936, Birmingham, England. m. Jean, 3 daughters. Appointments: Machine Tool Fitter, 1951; Joined engineering union, served as Shop Steward, Convenor at GKN and District President; Elected Divisional Organiser, West Midlands Division, 1977; Elected National President, Amalgamated Engineering Union, 1986; General Secretary, International Confederation of Free Trade Unions, 1994-2002. Honours: CBE; Honorary Doctorate, University of Central England, 1993; Honorary Doctorate, University of Cranfield, 1995. Memberships: General Council of the British TUC; National Economic Development Council; European Metalworkers' Federation; International Metalworkers' Federation; European Trade Union Confederation; Victim Support Advisory Committee; English Partnership; Winston Churchill Trust; Governor, London School of Economics; Governor, Ashridge Management College; RSA; Member, UN High Level Panel on Youth Employment; Member, UN Global Compact Advisory Council; Chairman, English Partnerships Pension Scheme, 2003-.

JORDAN Michael Jeffrey, b. 17 February 1963, Brooklyn, New York, USA. Basketball and Baseball Player. m. Juanita Vanoy, 1989, 2 sons, 1 daughter. Education: University of North Carolina. Appointments: Player, Chicago Bulls National Basketball Association (NBA), 1984-93, 1995-98, (NBA Champions, 1991, 1992, 1993, 1996, 1997, 1998); Birmingham Barons Baseball Team, 1993; Member, NCAA Championship Team, 1982, US Olympic Team, 1984, NBA All-Star Team, 1985-91; with Nashville Sounds, 1994-95;

Holds record for most points in NBA Playoff Game with 63; Retired, 1998-; Came out of retirement to play for Washington Wizards, 2001-; Founder, Jordan Motorsports/Suzuki, 2004. Publications: Rare Air: Michael on Michael (autobiography), 1993; I Can't Accept Not Trying: Michael Jordan on the Pursuit of Excellence. Honours include: Seagram's NBA Player of the Year, 1987; Most Valuable Player, NBA All-Star Game, 1988; NBA Most Valuable Player, 1988, 1991, 1992, 1996, 1998; Named, World's Highest Paid Athlete, Forbes Magazine, 1992. Memberships: President, Basketball Operations, Washington Wizards, 1999-. Address: Washington Wizards, 718 7th Street NW, Washington, DC 20004, USA.

JORDAN Neil Patrick, b. 25 February 1950, Sligo, Ireland. Author; Director. 3 sons, 2 daughters. Education: BA, 1st Class Honours, History/English Literature, University College, Dublin, 1972. Appointment: Co-Founder, Irish Writers Cooperative, Dublin, 1974. Publications: Night in Tunisia, 1976; The Past, 1979; The Dream of a Beast, 1983; Sunrise with Sea Monster, 1994; Nightlines, 1995. Films as a Director: Angel, 1982; The Company of Wolves, 1984; Mona Lisa, 1986; High Spirits, 1988; We're No Angels, 1989; The Miracle, 1990; The Crying Game, 1992; Interview With the Vampire, 1994; Michael Collins, 1996; The Butcher Boy, 1997; In Dreams, 1999; The End of the Affair, 1999; In Dreams, 1999; Double Dawn, 2001; The Good Thief, 2002; Shade, 2005; Breakfast on Pluto, 2005; The Brave One, 2007; Heart Shaped Box, 2007. Honours: Guardian Fiction Prize, 1979; The London Evening Standard's Most Promising Newcomer Award, 1982; London Film Critics Circle Awards, 1984; Oscar, 1992; Los Angeles Film Critics Award, 1992; New York Film Critics Circle Award, 1992; Writers Guild of America Award, 1992; BAFTA Award, 1992; Golden Lion, Venice Film Festival, 1996; Silver Bear, Berlin Film Festival, 1997; BAFTA Award, 2000. Address: c/o Jenne Casarotto Co Ltd, National House, 60-66 Wardour Street, London W1V 3HP, England.

JOSÉ Alan Spencer MacIntosh, b. 19 October 1953. Registrar. m. Gwendoline Elizabeth Emmerson, 1 daughter. Education: Harrow High School, Harrow College of Education. Appointments: A carer spanning some 30 years, mostly with local government, specialising in crematoria and cemetery management. Publications: Articles in Journal of ICCM and Motoring Club magazines. Honours: Freeman of the City of London, 1991. Memberships: Institute of Cemetery and Crematorium Management (FICCM), 1996-; Secretary, ICCM Northern Branch Forum, 2004-; Chair, Community Service Committee, Rotary Club of Durham, 2007-08; President, Durham Circle; Catenian Association; Jaguar Enthusiasts Club; National Trust Life Member. Address: Links View, South Road, Durham, DH1 3TQ, England and Le Pont, 53600 Voutré, France.

JOSEPH Jane Elizabeth, b. 7 June 1942, Dorking, Surrey. Painter; Printmaker. Education: Camberwell School of Arts & Crafts, 1961-65. Career: Solo shows include: Morley Gallery, London, 1973; The Minories, Colchester, 1982; Angela Flowers Gallery, London, 1987; Flowers East, London, 1989; Flowers East, London, 1992; Edinburgh Printmakers, 1994; Chelsea and Westminster Hospital, London, 1995; Morley Gallery, London, 1997; Scarborough Art Gallery, 1999; "Twenty Etchings for Primo Levi", Morley Gallery, London, Hebrew Union College, New York, Italian Cultural Institute, London, 2000; The Stanley Picker Gallery, Kingston University, 2000; Worcester City Art Gallery, 2001; "Etchings 1985-2001", Victoria Art Gallery, Bath, 2002; "Commonplaces", School of Art Gallery, Aberystwyth, 2004; Group shows include:

Royal Academy Summer Exhibition, London, 1971-97/01/05; Flowers East, 1990, 1994, 1999; Rocket Gallery, London, 1996; Inaugural exhibition, Artsway, Lymington, 1997; The Hunting Art Prizes, London, 1997, 2003; Cheltenham Open Drawing Exhibition and tour, 1998, (prizewinner), 2000; Portrait of the Artist, touring exhibition, UK, 1999; "Printworks", Eagle Gallery, London, 2002; The Art of Aging, Hebrew Union College, New York, 2003; International Biennieale of Graphic Arts, Ljubljana, 2005; Drawing Breath, Wimbledon College of Art and Touring; "Flora", Eagle Gallery, London; Work in collections: School of Art Gallery, Aberystwyth; Ben Uri Art Gallery, London; Birmingham City Museum and Art Gallery; Brecknock Museum, Brecon; The British Museum; Chelsea and Westminster Hospital, London; Fitzwilliam Museum, Cambridge; New Hall College, Cambridge; Government Art Collection, London; Hebrew Union College, New York; Imperial College, London; Lindley Library, London; The National Art Library, Victoria and Albert Museum; Castle Museum, Norwich; Ashmolean Museum, Oxford; Unilever House, London; Worcester City Art Gallery; Yale Center for British Art, New Haven, Connecticut, USA; The British Library, London. Commission: Chelsea and Westminster Hospital, 1994; Folio Society, etchings for "If This is a Man" by Primo Levi, 1999, and "The Truce" by Primo Levi, 2002. Publications: "A Little Flora of Common Plants" with text by Mel Gooding, 2002. Honours: Leverhulme Travelling Award, 1965-66; Invited Artist, Pécs Workshop for Graphic Art, Hungary, 1989, Abbey Award in Painting, British School at Rome, 1991, 1995; Elephant Trust Award, 1997; Wimbledon School of Art Research and Development Grant, 2000. Address: 6A Eynham Road, London W12 0HA, England. E-mail: jane_joseph2003@yahoo.co.uk

JOSEPHSON Brian David, b. 4 January 1940, Cardiff, Wales. Physicist. Education: Cambridge University. Appointments: Fellow, Trinity College, Cambridge, 1962-; Research Assistant Professor, University of Illinois, 1965-66; Professor of Physics, Cambridge University, 1974-; Faculty Member, Maharishi European Research University, 1975; Helped discover the tunnelling effect in superconductivity, called the Josephson effect. Publications: Co-editor, Consciousness and the Physical World, 1980; The Paranormal and the Platonic Worlds, in Japanese, 1997; Research papers on superconductivity, critical phenomena, theory of intelligence, science and mysticism. Honours: Honorary Member, Institute of Electrical and Electronic Engineers; Foreign Honorary Member, American Academy of Arts and Sciences; New Scientist Award, 1969; Research Corporation Award, 1969; Fritz London Award, 1970; Hughes Medal, Royal Society, 1972; Joint Winner, Nobel Prize for Physics, 1973. Address: Cavendish Laboratory, Madingley Road, Cambridge, CB3 0HE, England. E-mail: bdj10@cam.ac.uk

JOSHI Rangnath Nathrao, b. 29 July 1940, Aite Tq Bhoom district Osmanabad, Maharashtra, India. Retired Superintendent in Law and Judiciary Department; Poet; Writer; Actor; Sweet Poetry Singer; Music Director. Education: HMDs; BTMD; DLit, Colombo; DLit, Nanded; PhD, Calcutta; 25 other literary degrees. Appointments: Composer of poems and lyrics in Marathi, Hindi, English and Sanskrit, Proze and Poetry; Singer of own compositions, 3051 performances in various states and cities in India; Singer, Actor, Director, Literary researcher, artist of radio and television; Many Performances; Approved Poet of AIR; Prominent personality in various posts in several sansthas and state institutions. Publications: 7,050 poems (gits); Publications include: Sangram Tutari; Dhaktya Tuljapurchi Tuljabhavani; Bhavdhara; Shri Tuljabhavani Mahima;

Gitbhavani; Dundubhi; Sachitra Gitashree; Lokmata Ahilya deviholkar; Shri Manik Prabhu Gitayan; Bhaktikaustubha; Ahilyadevi Holkar Gitayan; Shrikashi Jagadguru Charitra Gitganga; Dharmatma; Shri Mahadev Maharaj Lilamrut; Shri Sadguru Ramrang Darshan Kavya; Chan Chan bad bad gite; Tuljaiche Abhang, Bhavani Darshan. Honours: Eight First prizes, 1953, 1974, 1976, 1980, 1999, 2001, 2006, 2007; Special Merit Certificate Pune, 1976; Numerous medals, awards, cups, certificates, Sanman Patra for literary, musical, dramatic, poetic work, yoga; International Man of the Year 2001 & 2006; Presided at several literary, cultural, yoga conferences; Life member, Maharashtra Shahir Parishad Pune; Invited Chief Poet for Kavi Sammelen, arranged by Station Director of All India Radio Aurangabad, 1981, etc; Chief guest, invitee, president, inaguarator, examiner, many literary, musical, dramatic and social institutions; Chief and Judge in numerous competitions. Memberships include: All India Rajendra Samajik Kalyan Parishad Patna 1974-; Gita Ramayan Prachar Sangha Swargashram, 1975, etc; Chief Consultant, Editor, Dharma Prbha magazine, 1984-, and others; Master in Palmistry; ShakatiPat [Kundlini] diksha Sadguru; Jyotish Maharshi; Pandit Samrat; Main Actor in 25 dramas; Composed samargits, war songs, national songs, performed programmes in national institutions and in public programmes; Has done social service, cultural service and national service; Posted on the greatest post of His Holiness as Kundlini Shakti Pat Dikshant Jagadguru Mahaswami. Address: 335 Kaviraj, Near Papnash Tirtha, At PO Tq, Tuljapur District, Osmanabad 413601, Maharashtra State, India.

JOSIPOVICI Gabriel David, b. 8 October 1940, Nice, France. Professor of English; Writer; Dramatist. Education: BA, Honours, 1st Class, St Edmund Hall, Oxford, 1961. Appointments: Lecturer in English, 1963-76, Reader in English, 1976-84, Professor of English, 1984-99, Research Professor, Graduate School of Humanities, 1999-, University of Sussex. Publications: Novels: The Inventory, 1968; Words, 1971; Mobius the Stripper: Stories and Short Plays, 1974; The Present, 1975; Migrations, 1977; The Echo Chamber, 1979; The Air We Breathe, 1981; Conversations in Another Room, 1984; Contre-Jour, 1986; In the Fertile Land, Shorter Fiction, 1987; The Big Glass, 1990; In a Hotel Garden, 1993; Moo Pak, 1994; Now, 1998; Goldberg: Variations, 2002; Everything Passes, 2006. Non-Fiction: The World and the Book, 1971; The Lessons of Modernism, 1977; Writing and the Body, 1982 The Book of God: A Response to the Bible, 1988; Text and Voice, 1992; Touch, 1996; On Trust, 1999; A Life, 2001; The Singer on the Shore, 2006. Contributions to: Encounter; New York Review of Books; London Review of Books; Times Literary Supplement. Honours: Sunday Times Playwriting Award, 1969; BBC nominations for Italia Prize, 1977, 1989; South East Arts Literature Prize, 1978; Lord Northcliffe Lecturer, University of London, 1981; Lord Weidenfeld Visiting Professor of Comparative Literature, University of Oxford, 1996-97; Fellow of the Royal Society of Literature, 1997; Fellow of the British Academy, 2001. Address: c/o John Johnson, Clerkenwell House, 45-47 Clerkenwell Green, London EC1R 0HT, England.

JOSS Timothy Hans, b. 27 June 1955, London, England. Artistic Director. m. Elizabeth Morag Wallace, 1 daughter. Education: The Queen's College, Oxford, England, 1973-76; University of Grenoble, 1976; Royal Academy of Music, England, 1976-79. Appointments: Mathematics lecturer, Davies's College, London WC1; Community worker, Pitt Street Settlement, London SE15; Commissioned composer and record producer for 1980 World Energy Conference; Researcher for Richard Baker, 1979-81; Assistant Administrator, Live

Music Now!, 1981-82; Music and Dance Officer, North West Arts, 1982-89; Concerts Director, Bournemouth Sinfonietta rising to Senior Manager, Bournemouth Orchestras, 1989-93; Director (Artistic Director and Chief Executive), Bath Festivals Trust, 1993-2004; Director, The Rayne Foundation, 2005-. Publications: Editor: UK Directory of Black, Asian and Chinese Musics, 1989; UK Directory of Community Music, 1992. Honours: Fellow, Royal Society of Arts; Honorary Associate, Royal Academy of Music; Chevalier Dans L'Ordre Des Arts Et Lettres. Memberships: Council Member, London Sinfonietta, Trustee, The Richard Feilden Foundation. Address: The Old Barn, West Yatton, Chippenham, Wiltshire SN14 7EW, England. E-mail: timjoss@timjoss.com

JOYNER-KERSEE Jaqueline, b. 3 March 1962, East St Louis, Illinois, USA. Athlete. m. Bobby Kersee, 1986. Education: University of California, Los Angeles; Training: Husband as coach. Career: Athlete in the Heptathlon; Assistant Basketball Coach, UCLA; World Record Heptathlon Scores: 7,158 points, Houston, 1986; 7,215 points, US Olympic Trial, Indianapolis, 1988; 7,291 points, Seoul, 1988; 7,044 points, Olympic Games, Barcelona 1992; Honours: 3 Olympic Gold Medals; 4 World Championships; Record erased by IAAF, 1999; With Richmond Rage in American Basketball League; Winner, IAAF Mobil Grand Prix, 1994; Chair, St Louis Sports Commission, 1996-; Jim Thorpe Award, 1993; Jackie Robinson Robie Award, 1994; Jesse Owens Humanitarian Award, 1999; Hon DHL, Spellman College, 1998, Howard University, 1999, George Washington University, 1999. Publications: A Kind of Grace, autobiography, 1997. Address: Elite International Sports Marketing Inc, 1034 South Brentwood Boulevard, Suite 1530, St Louis, MO 63117, USA.

JOZWIAK Ireneusz Jozef, b. 10 March 1951, Poddebice, Poland. Professor Dr Hab; Engineer. m. Elzbieta, 2 sons, 2 daughters. Education: School of Electronics Technology, Zdunska Wola, 1970; MSc, Department of Electronics, 1975, Dr, Institute of Engineering Cybernetics, 1979, Wroclaw University of Technology; Habilitation, Polish Academy of Sciences, 1994. Appointments: Secretary General, International Conference on Relcomex, Ksiaz Castle, 1979-89; Director, Catholic Secondary School, Wroclaw, 1996-; Councillor, City Council of Wroclaw, 1994-2002; Professor, Wroclaw University of Technology, Wroclaw, Poland, 1998-; Chancellor, High School of Teleinformatics Technologies, Swidnica, Poland, 2001-. Publications: Co-editor, Performance Evaluation, Reliability and Exploitation of Computer Systems, 1989; Author, Application of the Weibull Proportional Hazards Model to the Engineering Systems Reliability Assessment, 1991; Co-author, O/S2 3.0 Warp Operating System Architecture and Function, 1998; Contributor of 150 articles to professional journals. Honours: Gold Polish Medal for Work, 2008. Memberships: Society of Education, President, 2005-; Society of Polish Informatics, President, 1995-; Association of Miraculous Medal, Member of Board, 1996-. Address: Wroclaw University of Technology, Institute of Applied Informatics, Department of Computer Science and Management, Wybrzeze Wyspianskiego str 27, 50-370 Wroclaw, Poland. E-mail: ireneusz.jozwiak@pwr.wroc.pl

JUAN CARLOS I (King of Spain), b. 5 January 1938, Rome. Education: Private, Fribourg, Switzerland, Madrid, San Sebastian; Institute of San Isidro, Madrid; Colegio del Carmen; General Military Academy, Zaragoza; University Madrid. Appointments: Inaugurated as King of Spain, 1975; Named as Captain-General of the Armed Forces, 1975. Honours include: Charlemagne Prize, 1982; Bolivar Prize, UNESCO, 1983; Gold Medal Order, 1985; Candenhove

Kalergi Prize, Switzerland, 1986; Nansen Medal, 1987; Humanitarian Award, Elie Wiesel, USA, 1991; Houphouet Boigny Peace Prize, UNESCO, 1995; Franklin D Roosevelt Four Freedoms Award, 1995. Memberships include: Foreign Member, Académie des sciences morales et politiques. Address: Palacio de la Zarzuela, 28071 Madrid, Spain.

JUDD Frank Ashcroft, Baron Judd, b. 28 March 1935, Sutton, Surrey, England. Specialist in International Affairs. m. Christine Willington, 2 daughters. Education: City of London School, BScEcon, London School of Economics and Political Science, 1953-56. Appointments: F/O RAF, 1957-59; Secretary General, International Voluntary Service, 1960-66; Member of Parliament, Labour, Portsmouth West, 1966-74, Portsmouth North, 1974-79; Parliamentary Private Secretary to Leader of the Opposition, 1970-72; Member of the Parliamentary Delegation to the Council of Europe and Western European Union, 1970-73; Shadow Navy Minister, 1972-74; Parliamentary Under Secretary of State for Defence (Navy), 1974-76; Minister of State for Overseas Development, 1976-77; Minister of State, Foreign and Commonwealth Office, 1977-79; Associate Director, International Defence and Aid Fund for Southern Africa, 1979-80; Director, Voluntary Service Overseas, 1980-85; Director, Oxfam, 1985-91; Created Life Peer, 1991; Member, Sub-committee, (Environment, Agriculture, Public Health and Consumer Protection) of the European Community Committee in the House of Lords, 1997-2001; Member, Procedure Committee, 2001-04, and Ecclesiastical Committee in the House of Lords, 2001-; Joint Committee (Commons & Lords) on Human Rights, 2003-; Member, Parliamentary Assembly of the Council of Europe & Western European Union, 1997-2005; Joint Chair, Joint Working Group on Chechnya, Council of Europe, 2000-03; A Non-Executive Director, Portsmouth Harbour Renaissance Ltd; Trustee of Saferworld and of the Ruskin Foundation; Consultant Advisor to De Montfort University. Publications: Radical Future (jointly), 1967; Fabian International Essays (jointly), 1970; Purpose in Socialism (jointly), 1973; Imagining Tomorrow (jointly), 2000. Honours: Honorary DLitt, University of Bradford, University of Portsmouth; Honorary LLD, University of Greenwich; Honorary Fellow, University of Portsmouth and Selly Oak Colleges; Freeman of the City of Portsmouth; Member of Court, London School of Economics; Member of Court, University of Lancaster and University of Newcastle. Memberships include: Royal Institute of International Affairs; The Royal Society of Arts; The British Council; The Oxfam Association; The Labour Party; The Fabian Society; President, YMCA (England), 1996-2005; Vice-President Council for National Parks and United Nations Association; Convenor, Social Responsibility Forum of Churches Together in Cumbria, 1999-2005. Address: House of Lords, London SW1A 0PW, England.

JUERGENS Uwe, b. 29 January 1942, Frankfurt am Main, Germany. Zoologist. m. Christl, 1 daughter. Education: Abitur, Luitpold Gymnasium, Munich, 1961; Doctor Degree, 1969, Habilitation, 1976, University of Munich, Germany. Appointments: Research Associate, Max Planck Institute of Psychiatry, Munich, 1969-91; Professor, Zoological Institute, Head, Neurobiology Department, German Primate Centre, Goettingen, 1991-2007. Publications: Over 160 articles in international journals; Co-Editor, Nonverbal Vocal Communication, 1992; Co-Editor, Current Topics in Primate Vocal Communication, 1995; Associate Editor, Journal of Medical Primatology, 1996-2004. Retired in 2007. Address: 37075 Goettingen, Germany. E-mail: ujuerge@t-online.de

JUGNAUTH Anerood, b. 29 March 1930, Quatre-Bornes, Mauritius. President of the Republic. m. Sarojni, 1 son, 1 daughter. Education: Palma Church of England Aided School; Regent College, Quatre Bornes; Lincoln's Inn, United Kingdom, 1951; Called to the Bar, 1954. Appointments: Leader, Mouvement Socialist Militant, 1983-2003; President, Mouvement Militant Mauricien, 1973-82; Member, Legislative Assembly, 1963; Minister of State for Development, 1965-67; Minister of Labour, 1967; District Magistrate, 1967-69; Crown Counsel, 1969; Senior Crown Counsel, 1971; Leader of the Opposition, 1976-82; Prime Minister, Mauritius, 1982-95, 2000-03; President of the Republic of Mauritius, 2003-. Honours: Named Queen's Counsel, 1980; Doctor of Civil Law (Honoris Causa), University of Mauritius, 1985; Doctor (Honoris Causa), Université Aix-en-Provence, 1985; Member, Her Majesty's Most Honourable Privy Council, 1987; The First Class Order of the Rising Sun, Japan, 1988; Knighted Commander of the Most Distinguished Order of St Michael and St George, UK, 1988; Grand Officier de l'Ordre de la Legion d'Honneur, France, 1990; Doctor (Honoris Causa), Chennai University, 2001; Grand Commander of the Order of the Star and Key of the Indian Ocean, 2003. Address: La Caverne, Vacoas, Mauritius. E-mail: president@mail.gov.mu

JUHAS Pavol, b. 4 July 1941, Teplicany, District Kosice, Slovak Republic. Civil Engineer; Professor. m. Emilia. 2 sons. Education: Ing, Civil Engineering Faculty, Technical University, 1965; PhD, Scientific Study, 1973; Doctor of Sciences, 1988; Associate Professor, 1992; University Professor, 1993. Appointments: Designer, Eastern Slovak Steel Works, 1965-68; Scientific Worker, Institute of Construction and Architecture, 1968-93; Scientific Secretary, 1980-85; Vice Director, 1985-90; Professor, Civil Engineering Faculty, 1993-; Dean, 1994-2000; Head of the Department, 2000-. Publications: Theory and design of civil engineering steel structures; Elasto plastic analyses; Global and local stability; Postcritical behaviour and load carrying capacity; Fatigue strength and lifetime of structures; Economical utilisation of higher strength steels; Geometrical and material optimalisation of steel structures. Honours: Award, Slovak Academy of Sciences; Medals, Technical University; Member, Scientific Committee and Boards; 1 medals, Technical University; 2 medals, Faculty of Civil Engineering; Medal, Faculty of Mechanical Engineering. Memberships: Slovak Association for Steel Structures; International Association for Bridge and Structural Engineering; Structural Stability Research Council; Slovak Chamber of Civil Engineers; American Society of Civil Engineers. Address: Civil Engineering Faculty, Technical University Kosice, Vysokoskolska 4, 042 00 Kosice, Slovak Republic.

JULIUSON Adetominiyi D Akinsanya, Diplomacy Practitioner; Writer; Businessman; Political Strategist. Appointments: Director, Academy of Commercial Diplomacy; Executive President, Association of Certified Commercial Diplomats; Director, Graduate School of Advanced Diplomatic Studies; President Emeritus & Chairman, Congress of Diplomats & Parliamentarians; Sponsor and Campaigner, National Society for the Prevention of Cruelty to Children; Chairman, Europa Academy Books; Founder/Chairman, Royal Society of St George of England (Docklands Branch); Founder, Juliuson Books (formerly Delberg Professional Books). Publications: Over 25 published articles on democracy & politics, leadership and diplomacy. Honours include: Honorary Doctorate, Business Administration; Certified Master of Business Administration (CMBA); Certified Doctor of Business Administration (CDBA); Certified Business Finance Consultant (BFC);

Chartered Diplomat (C Dipl); The Honorable, Datuk of the Royal Order of Kiram (by HM Sultan Moh'd Faud Kiram I); The Honorable, Datuk (Baronet) of the Royal Order of Sulu & Sabah (by HM Sultan Kiram I); Freedom of the City of London; Noble Order Global Award of Excellence for Charity and Community Service (Philippines); First African Liveryman of the City of London; Honorary Fellow, Australian-Asian Institute of Civil Leadership, Queensland (HonFAAICL); Listed in 2005 Edition of Royal Book of Diplomacy of London Diplomatic Academy; Honoured by the National Society for the Prevention of Cruelty to Children; Stevie Award for Best Executive, USA; International Order of Merit; Companion of the Order of St Andrew of Scotland; Certificate of Distinction; Medal of Honour (IIU Cambridge); Great Minds of the 21st Century; Man of the Year, ABI; International Peace Prize, UCC; Distinguished Fellow, Academy of Commercial Diplomacy; Fellow, Association of the Certified Commercial Diplomats; Listed in Who's Who publications and biographical dictionaries. Memberships: Fellow, Atlantic Council of the United Kingdom; Assembly Member, International Diplomatic Academy; Pan-European Federation of Heritage (Europa Nostra); Diplomatic Member, London Diplomatic Academy; Member, Royal Society of St George of England and Wales; Honourable Member, Congress of Diplomats; Member, Commonwealth Magistrates and Judges Association; Member, Guild of Freemen of the City of London; Member, King Richard III Society; Member, Guild of Freemen of the City of York; Member, City of London Branch, Agency for Bank of England's Business Panel; Member, European-Atlantic Group; Member, 1912 Club (Palace of Westminster); Companion, Nautical Institute (CNI); Fellow, Royal Institution of Great Britain; Doctoral, Institute of Professional Financial Managers; Affiliate Professional, Chartered Institute of Marketing, London; Member, Defence and Security Forum of GB; Member, Cities of London and Westminster Conservatives, UK; Member, Political Studies Association; Member, 5 of the Ward Clubs and United Wards Club of the City of London; Member, City Livery Yacht Club; Member, Dubai Society; Full Member, Institute of Directors, City of London (MIoD); European Institute of Public Administration. Address: PO Box 50561, Docklands, London E16 3WY, England. E-mail djuliuson@hotmail.co.uk

JUN Tae-Youn, b. 9 January 1954, Jinhae, Gyeongsangnam-do, Korea. Professor. m. Hyejung Jun Lee, 1 son, 1 daughter. Education: MD, College of Medicine, 1978, Master of Medical Science, 1981-83, Doctor of Medical Science, 1987-90, The Catholic University of Korea. Appointments: Research Fellow, Laboratory of Immunogenetics, Memorial Sloan-Kettering Cancer Center, New York, New York, USA, 1992-93; Director, Department of Psychiatry, St Mary's Hospital, 2001-; Professor, Department of Psychiatry, College of Medicine, The Catholic University of Korea, 2001-; Director of Scientific Committee, KNPA, 2003-05; Principal Investigator, Government sponsored Clinical Research Centre for Depression, 2005-; Director, Yeongdeungpo-gu Community Mental Health Centre, 2006-; Regular Member, National Academy of Medicine of Korea, 2006-. Publications: Articles in medical journals include: Possible association between G308A tumor necrosis factor-alpha gene polymorphism and major depressive disorder in the Korean population, 2003; TNFB polymorphism may be associated with schizophrenia in the Korean population; No association of TAP2 polymorphism in Korean patients with schizophrenia, 2004; Monocyte chemoattractant protein-1 (MCP1) promoter-2518 polymorphism may confer a susceptibility to major depressive disorder in the Korean population, 2004; Quinone oxidoreductase (NQO1) gene polymorphism (609/T) may be associated with tardive dyskinesia, but not with the development of schizophrenia, 2004; The merlin tumor suppressor interacts with Ral guanine nucleotide dissociation stimulator and inhibits its activity, 2005; Fine mapping of schizophrenia locus at chromosome 6q23: increased evidence for linkage and reduced linkage interval, 2005. Honours: Paul Janssen Schizophrenia Research Award, 2004; WFSBP Research Prize, 2007. Memberships: American Psychiatric Association; Korean Neuropsychiatric Association; Korean Neurological Association; World Federation of Societies of Biological Psychiatry. Address: #62 Yeouido-dong, Yeongdeungpo-gu, Seoul 150-713, Korea. E-mail: tyjun@catholic.ac.kr

JUNG Dieter, b. 9 October 1941, Bad Wildungen, Germany. Multimedia Artist; Professor. m. Annette, 1 daughter. Education: MA, Fine Arts, Hochschule für bildende Künste, Berlin, and École Nationale des Beaux Arts, Paris, 1962-68; Diploma, Experimental Film, German Film and Television Academy, Berlin, 1971-74. Appointments: Guest Professor, Universidade Federal da Bahia, Salvadore, Brazil, 1975; Studies in Holography, New York School of Holography, New York, 1977; Collaboration with Dr Donald White, Bell Laboratories, 1977-82; Collaboration with Jody Burns, Holoplate, New York, 1982-86; Guest lecturer, Harvard University, MIT and Sorbonne University, Paris, 1989; Professor hc, Interamerican University of Humanistic Studies, Florida, 1990-2007; Professor, Creative Holography and LightArt, Academy of Media Arts Cologne; Development of Holokinetic Mobiles, HoloMobiles XYZ and Transoptical Mobiles, 1998; Development of Floor Holograms, 2001; Research into interactive Laser installations ORACULUM, 2001; Light installations, Strings, Light in Flight, and Loops; Numerous lectures, workshops, solo and group exhibitions in Europe, USA, South America and Asia. Publications: Book, Holographic Network, 2003; Articles in professional journals. Honours: Fellowship, Institut Francais, École des Beaux Arts, Paris, 1965-66; The German National Merit Foundation, 1967; USA Fellowship, German Academic Exchange Service, 1968-69; Artist-in-Residence, The MacDowell Colony, 1977; Artist-in-Resident, Yaddo, 1978; Grant, Cabin Greek Center for Work and Environmental Studies; Artist-in-Resident Grant, Museum of Holography, New York, 1983; Rockefeller Fellow, Center for Advanced Visual Studies, MIT, 1985-86; Grant, Council for the Arts, MIT; Award, Shearwater Foundation, USA, 1988, 2003; Listed in international biographical dictionaries. Memberships: Member, Founding Council, Academy of Media Arts, 1990, 1991; Member, Board of Trustees, Center for Art and Media/ZKM, Karlsruhe, 1992-96; Director, international conference and exhibition, Holographic Network: Art – Science – Technology, Akademie der Künste, Berlin, 1996; Member, MIT Advisory Council on Art-Science-Technology, 1979-97. Address: Vionvillestr 11, 12167 Berlin, Germany.

JUNG Gyung-woo (Simon), b. 17 September 1958, Busan, Korea. Urologist; Medical Doctor. m. In-Ja Lee (Veronica), 2 sons. Education: Master's degree, 1988, PhD, 1995, Department of Medicine, Graduate School, Pusan National University; Postdoctoral studies, University of California at San Francisco, 1995-97. Appointments: Intern, 1984-85, Resident in Urology, 1985-88, Chief Resident, Department of Urology, 1986-87, Pusan National University; Chairman, Urology, Pusan Daedong Hospital, Busan, 1988-91; Instructor, 1991-94, Assistant Professor, 1994-98, Associate Professor, 1998-2001, Head of Sexual Dysfunction and Andrology, 1991-2001, Chief Professor and Chairman, 2001, Department of Urology, College of Medicine, Dong-A University, Pusan;

Member, Editorial Committee, Dong-A Medical Journal, 1992-95; Research Fellow, Sexual Dysfunction Center University of California at San Francisco, 1995-97; Member, Editorial Committee, The Korean Journal of Andrology, 1997-99, 2001-02. Publications: 6 articles in professional journals; ASPIR book on erectile dysfunction, 1999. Honours: Winner of paper contest in clinical research, 4th Asia Pacific Society for Sexual and Impotence Research, 1993; First Prize, 8th International Society for Sexual and Impotence Research, 1998. Memberships: American Urological Association; European Urological Association; International Urological Association; International Society for Sexual Medicine; Asia Pacific Society for Sexual Medicine; Asia Urologic Association; Korean Urological Association; Korean Medical Association; Korean Andrological Society; Korean Prostate Society; Korean Urological Cancer Society; Korean Continence Society; Korean Pediatric Urological Society. Address: Smile Jung's Urology, Wongwang Medical Center, 485-6 Bujeon-Dong, Jin-Gu, Busan 614-849, Korea. E-mail: topandro@unitel.co.kr

JUNG Kwang Am, b. 27 February 1970, Chang Won city, Korea. Orthopaedic Surgeon. m. Su Jeong Song, 2 sons. Education: B Med, 1992, Master's degree, 1996, Postgraduate studies, 1998-2000, Yeungnam University, Taegu, Korea. Appointments: Intern, 1996-97, Resident, 1997-2001, Yeungnam University Hospital; Chief, Orthopaedic Surgery, 16th Air Force Base Hospital, Yecheon, 2001-03; Chief, Orthopaedic Surgery, Armed Forces Daegu Hospital, Taegu, 2003-04; 13th, 15th, 17th, 19th, 21st ISAKOS approved Severance Arthroscopy Knee Cadaver Workshop Table Instructor, 14th, 16th, 18th, 20th, 22nd, 24th ISAKOS approved Severance Arthroscopy Shoulder Cadaver Workshop Table Instructor, 2004-05, 13th-15th ISAKOS approved Severance Arthroscopy Live Surgery Faculty, 2004-05, Severance Hospital, Seoul; Orthopaedic Doctor, Arthroscopy & Reconstructive Surgery of Shoulder, Knee and Sports Medicine, Himchan Hospital, Incheon, 2005-. Publications: 11 international and domestic articles in professional scientific journals; 2 presentations at international conference; Co-translator, Manual of Arthroscopic Surgery. Honours: Award for Great Service to the Air Force Base; Award for Establishment of Arthroscopy & Joint Research Institute; Listed in biographical directories; Great Minds of the 21st Century, 2007; Outstanding Professional Award, 2007; Men of the Year, 2007. Memberships: American Academy of Orthopaedic Surgeons; Arthroscopy Association of North America; International Society of Arthroscopy, Knee Surgery and Orthopaedic Sports Medicine; Yonsei University of Arthroscopy & Joint Research Institute; Korean Medical Association; Korean Orthopaedic Association; Korean Shoulder & Elbow Society; Korean Fracture Society; Korean Knee Society Member; Korean Arthroscopy Society. Address: Mokdong Himchan Hospital, 404-3, Mok-dong, Yangcheon-gu, Seoul 158-806, Republic of Korea.

JUSTICE James Walcott, b. 16 December 1932, New York City, New York, USA. Physician. m. A Harras, 3 sons, 1 daughter. Education: BA, Chemistry, Bucknell University, 1954; MD, Medicine, New York Medical College, 1958; Master of Public Health, Johns Hopkins School of Hygiene and Public Health, 1962. Appointments: Commissioned, United States Public Health Service, 1959-85 (retired 1985); Served in Indian Health Service, Alaska, Oklahoma and Arizona and Peace Corps, Korea; Community Medicine, Health Science Centre, University of Arizona, 1987-97. Publications: Telemedicine in a Rural Health System, 1979; Twenty Years of Diabetes on the Warm Springs Indian

Reservation, 1989; Cancer Profiles of Two American Indian Tribes, 1992; Diabetes in the Desert People, 1993. Honours: Public Health Service Meritorious Service Award; Foreign Service Award; Hazardous Duty Award. Memberships: American Public Health Association; Physicians for Social Responsibility; Clinical Society of US Public Health Service. Address: 3663 E Kingler Spring Pl, Tucson, AZ 85718, USA.

JUUL Kristian, b. 14 April 1968, Copenhagen, Denmark. Director, Santaris Pharma. m. Signe, 2 sons, 1 daughter. Education: DVM, Royal Veterinary and Agricultural University, Copenhagen, 1994; Philosophy, Danish, Copenhagen University, 1988. Appointments: Scientific Project Manager, Danish Medicines Agency, 1995-97; Clinical Co-ordinator, GEA Pharmaceuticals, 1997-2001; Clinical Research Manager, Ferring Pharmaceuticals, 2001-04; Clinical Trial Manager, Coloplast, 2004-06; Head, Director, Coloplast A/S, Clinical Operations, 2006-07; Director, Santaris Pharma, 2007-. Publications: Numerous articles in professional journals. Listed in international biographical dictionaries. Memberships: Board Member, Chairman, Political Committee, Conservative Party, Elsinore. Address: Mariehoj 70, 3000 Elsinore, Denmark. E-mail: juul.familien@gmail.com

K

KABANOV Modest, b. 19 March 1926, St Petersburg, Russia. Psychiatrist. m. Lydia Kabanova. Education: St Petersburg Medical University, 1948. Appointments: Head Physician, District Psychoneurological Dispensary, St Petersburg, 1958-60; Head Physician, IVth City Mental Hospital, 1960-64; Director, V M Bekhterev Psychoneurological Research Institute, 1964-2002; International Programmes Director, V M Bekhterev Psychoneurological Research Institute, 2002-. Publications: Over 260 in Russian and foreign languages including 9 Monographs. Honours: Honoured Scientist of the Russian Federation. Memberships: President, World Association for Dynamic Psychiatry, 1995-2005; World Association for Psychosocial Rehabilitation; World Association for Social Psychiatry. Address: V M Bekhterev Psychoneurological Research Institute 3, Bekhterev Street, St Petersburg 192019, Russia.

KABASAKAL Osman Sermet, b. 16 June 1956, Ankara, Turkey. Chemical Engineer. m. Kadriye Aslan Kabasakal. Education: BS, Chemical Engineering Department, Faculty of Engineering, Hacettepe University, 1984; MS, 1989, PhD, 1995, Chemical Engineering Department, Institute of Science and Technology, Istanbul Technical University. Appointments: Assistant, Chemical Technologies Division, 1985-95, Doktor Associate, 1995-98, Associate Professor, 1998-99, Chemical Engineering Department, ITU Faculty of Chemistry-Metallurgy; Associate Professor, 1999-2005, Professor, 2005-, Chemical Engineering Department, Faculty of Engineering-Architecture, Eskisehir Osmangazi University. Publications: 15 articles authored or co-authored published in journals included in the Source Publications List of Science Citation Index (SCI) by Institute of Scientific Information (ISI). Memberships: Turkish Chamber of Chemical Engineers; Turkish Chemical Association; IUPAC Affiliate Member. Address: Eskisehir Osmangazi University, Faculty of Engineering & Architecture, Chemical Engineering Department, Bati Meselik, Eskisehir, 26480, Turkey. E-mail: osk@ogu.edu.tr

KABASAWA Uki, b. 21 January 1965, Namerikawa, Japan. Physicist. Education: Bachelor Degree, 1988, Master Degree, 1990, Osaka University. Appointments: Researcher, Central Research Laboratory, 1990-96, Engineer, Electronic Device Manufacturing Equipment and Engineering Division, 1996-99, Engineer, Instruments, Beam Technology Centre, 1999-2001, Hitachi Ltd; Engineer, Hitachi High-Technologies Corporation, Research and Development Division, 2001-. Publications include: Studies of High Temperature Superconductors, volume 1, 1989, volume 6, 1990; Advances in Superconductivity VI, vol 2, 1994; Quantum Theory of Many-Body Systems, 1999; Elements of Advanced Quantum Theory, 2000; Introduction to Mesoscopic Physics (translator), 2000; The Physics of Quantum Fields (translator), 2002; The Case of the Missing Neutrinos (translator), 2002; The Physics of Low-Dimensional Semiconductor, translator, 2004; An Introduction to the Standard Model of Particle Physics (translator), 2005. Memberships: American Association for the Advancement of Science; New York Academy of Sciences; Physical Society of Japan; Japan Society of Applied Physics. Address: Hitachi High-Technologies Corporation, Beam Technology Centre, 882 Ichige, Hitachinaka-shi, Ibaraki-ken 312-8504, Japan. E-mail: kabasawa-uki@naka.hitachi-hitec.com

KABBAH Alhaji Ahmad Tejan, b. 6 February 1932, Pendembu, Kailahun District, Sierra Leone. President of Sierra Leone. m. Patricia Tucker (deceased), 4 children. Education:

Bachelor's degree in Economics, University College, Aberystwyth, Wales, 1959; Law studies. Appointments: Barrister-at-Law, Honourable Society of Gray's Inn, London, 1969; National and international civil servant in Western Area and in all Provinces of Sierra Leone; District Commissioner, Bombali and Kambia (Northern Province), Kono (Eastern Province), and Moyamba and Bo (Southern Province); Permanent Secretary in various ministries (Trade and Industry, Social Welfare and Education); Deputy Chief, West Africa Division, UN Development Programme (UNDP), New York; Head and Resident Representative, UNDP's operation in Lesotho, 1973; Head of operations in Tanzania, Uganda and Zimbabwe, Head, Eastern and Southern Africa Division, Deputy Director and Director of Personnel, Director of Division of Administration and Management, UNDP; Leader, Sierra Leone Peoples Party; Elected President of Sierra Leone, 1996-2002, 2002-. Honours: Chancellor, University of Sierra Leone; Honorary Doctor of Laws degree, University of Sierra Leone; Honorary Doctor of Laws degree, Southern Connecticut State University, USA; Honorary Doctor of Laws, University of Bradford, England; Grand Commander, Order of the Republic of Sierra Leone; Grand Commander of the Republic of the Gambia, 2001. Address: Presidential Lodge, Hill Station, Freetown, Sierra Leone. E-mail: info@statehouse-sl.org Website: www.statehouse.sl

KAČERGIENĖ Nella (Vernickaitė), b. 19 October 1935, Minsk, Belarus. Physician; Paediatrician; Scientific Researcher. Education: Doctor's Assistant, Obstetrician, Kaunas Paramedical and Obstetrical School, 1954; Physician, Kaunas Medical Institute, 1962; Clinical Physician diploma, 1970, Postgraduate, 1973, Diploma, Candidate of Medical Science, Institute of Paediatrics, USSR, Academy of Medical Sciences, Moscow, 1973; Senior Research Diploma, USSR, 1984; Diploma, Med Sci Doctor's degree, USSR Academy of Medical Sciences, 1987; Senior scientific researcher, Vilnius, 1984; Paediatrician of highest category, Vilnius, 1991; Diploma, Dr Sci habilitas, 1993. Appointments: Nurse, Surgery Department, Kaunas Town Hospital No 2, 1952-54; Doctor's Assistant-Obstetrician, Jieznas Hospital, 1954-56; Paediatrician, Prienai District Hospital, 1962-67; Republican Vilnius Children's Hospital, 1967-68; Clinical Physician of the Institute of Paediatrics, USSR, Academy of Medical Sciences, Moscow, 1968-70; Postgraduate of the Institute of Paediatrics, USSR Academy of Medical Sciences, Moscow, 1970-73; Junior Research Worker, 1973-79, Senior Research Worker, 1979-85, Department of Paediatrics of the Lithuanian Scientific Research Institute of Experimental and Clinical Medicine; Senior Research Worker, Lithuanian Scientific Research Institute of Mother and Child Care, 1985-91; Chief Scientific Researcher, Centre of Paediatrics of Vilnius University Children's Hospital, 1991-97, Centre of Paediatrics of Vilnius University, 1998-2001. Publications: (monograph) SOS to the Life on Earth: The Effect of Environmental Factors and Atmospheric Chemical Pollutants on the Human Organism at Certain Periods of Its Ontogenesis, 1999; Book, The Road to Happiness, 2006; 210 scientific works and 2 inventions. Honours include: Gold Record of Achievement in Honour of Career Excellence and Outstanding Contributions to International Society, ABI, USA; 20th Century Award for Achievement, IBC, MCM, 1900-2000, England, Silver Medal, 1998; Gold Medal, Leading Intellectuals of the World, ABI, 1998; Gold and Silver Medal, 2000 Outstanding Scientists of the 20th Century, IBC, England, 1999; Gold Medal, International Scientist of the Year, IBC, England, 2001; The IBC Millennium Time Capsule, IBC, England, 1999; Torch of Global Inspiration, ABI, USA, 2000; Presidential Seal of Honour, for Exemplary Achievements in the Fields of Pediatry and Ecology, USA, 2000; Scientific Excellence – Gold Medal, USA, 2001; Secretary General of the United Cultural Convention, USA, 2001; Ambassador General, UCC, USA, 2006; 21st Century Genius Gold Medal, ABI, USA, 2006; Great Minds of the 21st Century Gold Medal, USA, 2002; International Peace Prize, United Cultural Convention, USA, 2003; The World Order of Science-Education-Culture, European Academy of Informatisation, Brussels, 2002; Dame (rank), Belgium, 2002; Albert Schweitzer Gold Medal for Science and Peace, Albert Schweitzer International University, Spain, 2004; American Medal of Honor, ABI, USA, 2004; World Medal of Freedom, ABI, USA, 2004; Da Vinci Diamond, IBC, 2004; Living Legends, Gold Medal, IBC, 2004; Edict as a Sovereign Ambassador , Order of American Ambassadors, ABI, USA, 2006; Proclamation: The Genius Elite (Documented in Leading Intellectuals of the World, ABI, 2004); 21st Century Genius of Distinction, ABI, USA, 2005; Numerous diplomas including: Greatest and Great Minds of the 21st Century Diploma, USA, 2002; Ambassador of Grand Eminence, Diploma, USA, 2002; Researcher of the Year, 2001, Diploma, USA, 2002; The World Order of Science – Education – Culture, European Academy of Informatisation, Brussels, 2002; Da Vinci Diamond, IBC, 2004; Scroll of Legend, IBC, 2005; 21st Century Genius, ABI, 2005; Genius Laureate of Lithuania, ABI, 2006; 500 Greatest Geniuses of the 21st Century, ABI, 2006; Global Year of Medicine and Healthcare, Marie Curie Award, IBC, 2006; Cambridge Blue Book Laureate, IBC, 2006; Order of American Ambassadors, ABI, 2006. Memberships include: Lithuanian Paediatric Academic Council, 1973-; Russian Academy of Medical Science Committee of Chronobiology and Chronomedicine, 1985; National Geographic Society, USA, 1991; International Society of Biometeorology, USA, 1991; International Committee for Research and Study of Environmental Factors, Brussels, Belgium, 1992; Scientific Excellence European Academy of Informatization, Belgium, 2002; Founder Diplomatic Counsellor, London Diplomatic Academy, 2000; International Diplomatic Academy, London, 2002; Member of the Assembly of the International Diplomatic Academy, Geneva, 2002; Order of American Ambassadors, 2006; DDG, FIBA, MOIF, IBC, England, 1995-97. Address: Viršuliškių 89-22, LT-05117 Vilnius, Lithuania.

KADRI S Manzoor, b. India. Physician. Education: MBBS, Government Medical College, Srinagar, Kashmir, India, University of Kashmir, Srinagar, Kashmir, India; Postgraduate Training: Certified Course in HIV/AIDS & STD Management, 2002, Certified Course in Geriatric Medicine, 2004, Indian Medical Association. Appointments: Currently, Faculty Member, Regional Institute of Health and Family Welfare, Directorate of Health Services, Kashmir, India; Associated with undergraduate theoretical and practical teaching programme for MBBS, BDS students and laboratory technologists; Associated with laboratory work, serology, bacteriology, screening of tuberculosis and voluntary counselling and testing centre for HIV/AIDS at the SMHS Hospital, Srinagar; Involved in training of medical doctors and para-medics in newer concepts of disease like revised national tuberculosis control programme, awareness regarding HIV/AIDS, reproductive and child health, disease surveillance and working as a Nodal Officer for disease surveillance for the districts of Kupwara and Leh under the Integrated Disease Surveillance Programme (IDSP); FETP, WHO, 2006. Publications: Book chapters in: Psychology, 2004; Agricultural Development and Vector Borne Disease, 2004; A Guide to Common Diseases, 2004; Epidemiology for Health Professionals, 2004; Health Care Waste Management (An Introduction) for the Health Care Worker, 2004; Food, Waste

and Family Health – A Manual for Health Educators, 2004; More than 60 articles in medical journals: Scientific Reviewer for Chest, Journal of the American College of Chest Physicians; Scientific Reviewer for Thorax (BMJ Group of Publications); Editorial Board, Indian Journal for the Practising Doctor. Memberships: Medical Advisor, Gerson Lehrman Group's Council of Healthcare Advisors, New York, USA. New York Academy of Sciences; All India Advisory Board, Journal of the Indian Medical Association; Indian Medical Association; Indian Society of Health Administrators; Indian Association of Medical Informatics; Computer Society of India; Brand Ambassador, Bioinformatics Institute of India. Address: Post Pox 1143, GPO, Srinagar 190001, Kashmir, India. E-mail: kadrism@gmail.com Website: http://rihfwk.indmedica.com

KAFELNIKOV Yevgeny Aleksandrovich, b. 18 February 1974, Sochi, Russia. Tennis Player. m. 2 daughters. Education: Krasnodar Pedagogical Institute. Appointments: Started playing tennis in Sochi Children Sports School, 1982; Later with coach Anatoly Lepeshin; ATP Professional, 1992-; Won 17 ATP tournaments including Milan, St Petersburg, Gstaad, Long Island; Won French Open (singles and doubles), 1996; Won, Moscow Kremlin Cup, 1997; Won, Australian Open, 1999; Member, Russian Federation Davis Cup Championship Team, 1993; Runner-up, World Championship, Hanover, 1997; Highest ATP Rating 1st, 1999; Olympic singles champion, Sydney, 2000; Winner of 51 pro titles by 2002. Address: All-Russian Tennis Association, Luzhnetskaya nab 8, 119871 Moscow, Russia.

KAGAYA Hiroshi Kan, b. 8 August 1930, Tokyo, Japan. Professor Emeritus. m. Kazuko, 2 sons, 1 daughter. Education: MA, Humanities, Tokyo University, 1956. Appointments: Professor, Osaka University of Foreign Studies, 1960-95. Publications: History of Modern Iran, 1975; Urdu-Japanese Dictionary, 2005. Honours: Professor Emeritus, Osaka University of Foreign Studies; Sitara-i Quaid-i Aazam, Government of Pakistan, 2007. Memberships: Academic associations for Islamic, Iranian and South-Asian studies, Japan. Address: Nishiyamacho 4-59, Koyoen, Nishinomiya, Japan 662. E-mail: qnkdr381@yahoo.co.jp

KAHL Lesley Patricia, Research Scientist; Specialist in Clinical Drug Development. Divorced, 1 daughter. Education: BSc (Hons I), University of Newcastle, New South Wales, Australia, 1979; PhD, Medical Biology, University of Melbourne, Victoria, Australia, 1983. Appointments: Postdoctoral Research Fellow, Department of Medicine, Harvard Medical School, Boston, USA, 1983-86; Postdoctoral Research Fellow, Wellcome Laboratories, London, England, 1986-92; Principal/Senior Clinical Research Scientist, Wellcome/Glaxo Wellcome, London, 1992-2004; Senior Manager and Manager, Clinical Development, GlaxoSmithKline, London, 2005-. Publications: Numerous articles to professional journals including bench and clinical research mainly in the area of infectious disease. Honours: University Gold Medal for Excellence in the Science Faculty, University of Newcastle, New South Wales, 1979; NIH Fogarty International Post Doctoral Fellow, Harvard Medical School, Boston, 1983-86; Listed in international biographical directories. Memberships: Institute of Clinical Research. Address: Inflammation and Rheumatology Medicines Development Centre, GlaxoSmithKline, Greenford Road, Greenford, Middlesex UB6 0HE, England. E-mail: lesley.p.kahl@gsk.com

KAHNG Sungtek, b. 17 August 1971, Seoul, Korea. Radio Engineering Professor. m. Nahmjoo Hah, 2 sons. Education: BE, Electronic Engineering, KNU, 1994; PhD, Electronic Telecommunication Engineering, Hanyang University, Seoul, 2000. Appointments: Senior Research Staff, Division of Radio and Broadcasting Research, Electronic Telecommunication Research Institute, Daegon, Korea, 2000-04; Professor, University of Incheon, 2004-. Publications: Design of Dual-Mode Channel Filters and Group-Delay Equalizers for a Ka-bond Satellite Transponder, 2003; Genetic-Algorithm-Based Complex Images of the HMD in Parallel Plate Waveguides, 2003; GA-Optimized Differential Signalling to Damp EM Noise, 2006. Honours: Invited speaker: IEEE EMC Symposium, 2006; EMC Zurich, Singapore, 2006; Session Chair, Asian Pacific Microwave Conference, 2006; Technical Consultant, Korea's Defence Quality Control Program, 2007-. Memberships: IEEE; ACES; ISAP 2005 Steering Committee. E-mail: s-kahng@incheon.ac.kr

KAIBYSHEV Oscar, b. 28 March 1939, Moscow, USSR. Engineer. m. Calina Alexandrovna Grushko, 1 son. Education: Engineer, Physics of Metals, 1962, Graduate studies, 1964-67, PhD, 1976, Full Professor, 1977, Moscow Institute of Steels and Alloys, Moscow. Appointments: Engineer in the Physics of Metals. Memberships: Academician, Russian Academy of Natural Sciences; Academician, Sciences of Bashkortostan Republic. Address: Sivoshkay 7, x 2, ap 8, Moscow, 1175638, Russia.

KAIMENYI Jacob Thuranira, b. 10 July 1952, Meru, Kenya. Periodontologist. m. Stella Gatirithu, 2 sons, 3 daughters. Education: Bachelor, Dental Surgery, 1978, PhD, 1998, University of Nairobi, Kenya; Master, Dental Surgery, University of Mangalore, India, 1982. Appointments: Dental Officer (Intern), 1979-82, Head, Department of Periodontology, KNH, 1982-85, Senior Dental Officer, 1982-85, Deputy Officer in chage of the National Dental Unit, 1983-85, Ministry of Health; Chairman, Dental School, 1989-92; Head, Division of Periodontology, 1992-95; Chairmam, Department of Periodontology/Community/Preventive Dentistry, 1995-2000; Dean, Faculty of Dental Sciences, 2000-04; DVC (AA), UoN, 2005-. Publications: Chapters in 2 dental text books; 51 articles in refereed journals; 10 articles in unrefereed medical and dental publications. Honours: Commonwealth Scholarship, 1979; President, Commonwealth Dental Association; Ambassador of Peace, 2006; Listed in international biographical dictionaries. Memberships: Commonwealth Dental Association; Kenya National Academy of Sciences; Kenya Dental Association. Address: University of Nairobi, Harry Thuku Road, PO Box 30197, 00100 Nairobi, Kenya. E-mail: jkaimenyi@uonbi.ac.ke

KAKATI Dinesh Chandra, b. 1 February 1941, Soalkuchi, Assam, India. Doctor of Medicine. m. Bhabhni, 1 son, 1 daughter. Education: MBBS, Guwahati University, India, 1967; Diploma in Tropical Medicine, University of Liverpool, England, 1970; Diploma in Thoracic Medicine, Diploma in Cardiac Medicine, University of London, 1984; Diploma in Geriatric Medicine, Royal College of Physicians of London, 1985; Vocational Training Certificate, Royal College of General Practitioners, 1987; Intra-Uterine Device, Family Planning Certificate, Joint Committee on Contraception, 1987. Appointments: House Officer, Senior House Officer, Gauhati Medical College Hospital, Assam, India, 1967-68; General Medicine, Ingham Infirmary, South Shields, England, 1969; Senior House Officer, Registrar, Sunderland General Hospital, Sunderland, 1969-72; Registrar, Addenbrookes Hospital and

Chesterton Hospital, Cambridge, 1972-74; Internal Medicine, University of Edinburgh, Scotland, 1973; Registrar, London Hospital and Bethnal Green Hospital, London, 1974-77; Specialist and Consultant, Oldchurch Hospital, Romford, 1977-83; Postgraduate Student, National Heart Hospital, Brompton Hospital, London Chest Hospital, London, 1983-84; Clinical Assistant, Romford Group of Hospitals based at St George's Hospital, Hornchurch, 1984-2002; General Practice Principal, Berwick Surgery, Rainham, 1997-. Publications: Numerous articles in professional journals. Honours: Class examination medals; 4th place, Guwahati University Order of Merit; Distinction, MBBS, Guwahati University. Memberships: Cultural Association of Assam in the UK; Chairman, Sankar Jayanty Celebration Committee, UK; Assamese Bihu Committee, UK; British Medical Association; Royal College of General Practitioners of London; Royal Society of Health. Address: Assam Manor, 99 Ardleigh Green Road, Hornchurch, Essex RM11 2LE, England. E-mail: kakati.dinesh@ntlworld.com

KALABUKHOVA Tatyana Nikolaevna, b. 19 April 1939, Moscow, USSR. Biophysicist; Lecturer; Poet; Writer; Illustrator. Education: Diploma with distinction, Moscow State University, Moscow, 1962; Postgraduate, Institute of Biophysics, USSR Academy of Sciences, Moscow, 1965-68; Diploma of Candidate of Science, Moscow, 1971. Appointments: Stager, Researcher, 1962-64, Junior Scientist, Collaborator, 1964-65, Institute of Biophysics, USSR Academy of Sciences, Moscow; Junior Scientist, Collaborator, Institute of Biophysics, USSR Academy of Sciences, Pushchino, 1968-90; Scientist, Collaborator, Institute of Cell Biophysics, USSR Academy of Sciences, Pushchino, 1991; Senior Scientist, Collaborator, Institute of Cell Biophysics, Russian Academy of Sciences, Pushchino, 1992-; Lecturer, Pushchino Ecology Museum, 2003-; Book Illustrator, 2007-; Volunteer Scientist and Biophysicist; Retired. Publications: Numerous articles published in professional scientific journals. Honours: Medal of Veteran of Labour of Presidium of Supreme Soviet of USSR, 1988; Medal of President of Russian Federation, 1997; Grantee, Russian Fund for Basic Researches, 1996-98. Memberships: Chairman, Pushchino Branch of Ultraviolet Radiation Section of Science Council on Biophysics Problems, USSR Academy of Sciences, 1976-1980. Address: Microregion (G)-25-116, Pushchino-on-Oka, Moscow Region, 142290, Russia.

KALMBACH Gudrun, b. 27 May 1937, Grosserlach, Germany. Professor. Education: Dr rer. nat. University of Göttingen, Germany. Appointments: Assistant, University of Göttingen, Germany, 1963-66; Lecturer, University of Illinois, Urbana, USA, 1967-69; Assistant Professor, University of Massachusetts, Amherst, USA, 1970-71; Assistant Professor, Pennsylvania State University, University Park, USA, 1969-75; Professor, University of Ulm, Germany, 1975-2002; Director, MINT, 2003-. Publications: 12 books; Articles in professional journals on algebra, topology, quantum structures, education; Chief Editor, Journal MINT. Honours: 4 medals; 2 titles; 2 books in honour of 60th Birthday. Memberships: AMS; AWM; ECHA; Emmy-Noether-Verein (Chair); FDP; LDA; OIA. Address: PF 1533, D-86818 Bad Woerishofen, Germany. E-mail: mint-01@web.de

KALTENBACH Anneliese Elisabeth, b. Karlsruhe-Durlach, Germany. Retired Senior Civil Servant. Education: Diplomas, Commercial French and English Studies, Russian Language and Literature, Karlsruhe, Germanic, General Linguistics, and History Studies; Paris Lic-ès-Lettres, 1957; PhD, Paris, 1962; Appointments: Employee, German Embassy Paris and

Ministry for Foreign Affairs, Bonn, 1951-60; Deputy Chief for West European Affairs, Press and Information Office, Federal Government of Bonn, 1961-82. Publications include: Ludwig Haeusser, Historien et patriote (1818-1867), 1965. Honours include: Gold Medal, Robert Schuman, Silver Gilt Medal, Municipality of Paris, Bronze Medal Académie Française, 1966; Commander Order of Oranje-Nassau, 1972; Order of Leopold II, 1972; Commandeur de l'Ordre du Mérite du Grand-Duché de Luxembourg, 1973; Silver Medal, French-German Youth Office, 1982; Commandeur de l'Ordre National du Mérite de la République Française, 1980; Merit Cross First Class, Federal Republic of Germany, 1982; Officer dans l'ordre des Palmes Académiques, 1995. Address: Duerenstrasse 29, D 53173 Bonn, Germany.

KALRA G L, b. 1 July 1941, Londkhor, Pakistan. Teacher; Researcher. m. Raj Kalra, 2 daughters. Education: MSc, 1962, PhD, 1967, University of Delhi. Appointments: Senior Research Fellow, University of Delhi, 1966-69; Fellow, Flinders University of South Australia, 1969-70; RA, University of Delhi, 1970-74; Lecturer, 1974-84; Reader, 1984-86; Associate Professor, Al Fateh University, Tripoli, 1986-87; Reader, University of Delhi, 1984-94; Professor in Physics, University of Delhi, 1994-2006. Publications: 50 research papers mostly in international scientific journals. Honours: Hari Om Ashram Prerit Dr Vikram Sarabhai Research Award in Planetary and Space Sciences, 1985; Australia VC's Committee Visiting Fellowship, 1990; Offered New York Academy of Sciences Membership. Memberships: Founder Member, Astronomical Society of India; Founder Member of Plasma Science Society of India; Listed in Who's Who and biographical publications. Address: G-89 Ashok Vihar, Delhi 110052, India.

KALVITIS Aigars, b. 27 June 1966, Riga, Latvia. Politician. m. Kristine, 3 sons. Education: Bachelor's degree, 1992, Master's degree, 1995, Agricultural Economics, Latvian University of Agriculture; Master's course, Food Industry Business Administration, University College, Cork, Ireland, 1993; In-service Training, Holstein Association, University of Wisconsin, USA, 1995. Appointments: Milkman and Tractor Driver, Alamnas Bruk AB, Sweden, 1990-91; Director, Agro Biznesa Centrs, 1992-94; Chairman of the Board, Zemgales piens, 1994; Chairman, Commission of the Central Union of Latvian Dairying, 1994-98; Member, 7th Saeima, Member of the Budget and Finance (Taxation) Committee and Public Expenditure and Audit Committee, 1998-99; Minister for Agriculture, 1999-2000; Minister for Economics, 2000-02; Member, 8th Saeima, 2002-04; Chairman, Parliamentary Group of the People's Party, 2002-04; Prime Minister of the Republic of Latvia, 2004-07. Memberships: The People's Party. Address: 36 Brivibas Blvd, Riga, LV-1520, Latvia.

KAMANDA Kama Sywor, b. 11 November 1952, Luebo, Congo-Kinshasa. Writer; Poet; Novelist; Playwright; Essayist; Lecturer; Storyteller. Education: State Diploma in Literary Humanities, 1968; Degree in Journalism, Journalism School, Kinshasa, Congo, 1969; Degree in Political Sciences, University of Kinshasa, 1973; Licence in Philosophy, University of Kinshasa, 1975; HD, University of Liège, 1981. Appointments: Lecturer, various universities, schools and cultural centres; Literary Critic, various newspapers. Publications: Les Contes du griot, Volume 3 (Les Contes des veillées africaines), 1967, 1985, 1998; Les Résignations, 1986, 1997; Éclipse d'étoiles, 1987, 1997; Les Contes du griot, Volume 1, 1988, 1997; La Somme du néant, 1989, 1999; Les Contes du griot, Volume 2 (La Nuit des griots), 1991, 1996; L'Exil des songes, 1992; Les Myriades des temps vécus, 1992, 1999; Les Vents de l'épreuve, 1993, 1997; Quand dans l'âme les mers s'agitent, 1994, 1998; Lointaines sont les rives du destin, 1994, 2000; L'Étreinte des mots, 1995; Chants de brumes, 1997, 2002; Œuvre poétique, 1999; Les Contes du crépuscule, 2000; Le Sang des solitudes, 2002; Contes, 2003, 2004; La Joueuse de Kora, 2006; La Traversée des Mirages, 2006. Honours: Paul Verlaine Award, French Academy, 1987; Louise Labé Award Jury, 1990; Literature Award, Black African Association of French-Speaking Writers, 1991; Special Poetry Award, Academy Institute in Paris, 1992; Silver Jasmin for Poetical Originality, 1992; Special Prize, French-Speaking Countries General Council Agency, 1992; Théophile Gautier Award, French Academy, 1993; Melina Mercouri Award, Greek Poets and Writers Association, 1999; Poet of the Millennium, 2000 Award; International Poets Academy, India, 2000; Honorary Citation, Joal Fadiouth, Senegal, 2000; Poetry Award, International Society of Greek Writers, 2002; Top 100 Writers, IBC, 2005; Professional of the Year, IBC, 2005; Man of the Year, ABI, 2005; Exceptional Contribution Honor Certificate, Maurice-Cagnon, International Council for French Studies, 2005; Master Diploma for Speciality Honors in Writing, World Academy of Letters, USA, 2006; International Peace Prize, United Cultural Convention, 2006; Subject of Kamanda au Pays de Conte (MC de Conninck), 1993; Kama Kamanda, Poète de l'exil (Pierette Sartin), 1994; Kama Sywor Kamanda, chantre de la mémoire égyptienne (Isabelle Cata and Frank Nyalendo), 2003. Memberships: Society of French Poets; French Society of Men of Letters; Association of African Writers; PEN Club; Association of French-Speaking Writers; International Council of French-Speaking Studies; SABAM (Belgian Society of Authors, Composers and Editors). Address: 18 Am Moul, L-7418 Buschdorf, Luxembourg. E-mail: kamanda@pt.lu Website: www.kamanda.net

KAMEDA Hisao, b. 15 April 1942, Gifu-City, Gifu, Japan. University Professor. m. Mieko Kameda, 3 sons. Education: Bachelor of Science, 1965, Master of Science, 1967, Doctor of Science, 1970, University of Tokyo, Tokyo, Japan. Appointments: Research Associate, University of Tokyo, 1970-71; Assistant Professor, University of Electro-Communications, 1971-73; Visiting Scientist, IBM T J Watson Research Center, 1973-74; Visiting Researcher, University of Toronto, 1974-75; Associate Professor, 1973-85, Professor, 1985-92, University of Electro-Communications; Professor, 1992-96, Professor Emeritus, 2006-, University of Tsukuba. Publications: Articles in professional journals including: JACM, ACM Transactions on Computer Systems, IEEE Transactions on Computer, IEEE Transactions Software Engineering, IEEE Transactions on Automatic Control, IEEE Transactions on Parallel and Distributed Systems. Honours: Fellow, IEICE; Fellow, IPSJ; Fellow, ORSJ; Best Paper Award, IEEE NACON '97; Listed in numerous Who's Who and biographical publications. Address: Department CS, Graduate School of SIE, University of Tsukuba, 1-1-1 Tennodai, Tsukuba Science City, Ibaraki 305-8573, Japan. Website: www.osdp.cs.tsukuba.ac.jp/~kameda

KAMENAR Boris, b. 20 February 1929, Susak-Rijeka. University Professor. m. Maja Perusko, Vedrana. Education: Diploma in Chemical Technology, University of Zagreb, 1953; PhD, Chemistry, University of Zagreb, 1960; Postdoctoral Fellowship, University of Oxford, England, 1964. Appointments: Head, Testing Laboratory, Metal Factory, Rijeka, 1953-56; Research Scientist, Rudjer Boskovic Institute, Zagreb, 1956-62; Assistant and Associate Professor, University of Zagreb, 1962-72; Professor of Chemistry, University of Zagreb, 1972-99; Professor Emeritus, 1999-;

Visiting Fellow, All Souls College, Oxford, 1971-72; Visiting Professor, University of Auckland, New Zealand, 1980; Visiting Professor, Massey University, Palmerston North, New Zealand, 1989-90, 1995. Publications: About 160 articles in scientific journals. Honours: Scientific Award, Republic of Croatia, 1970; Scientific Award, City of Zagreb, 1980; Scientific Award for Life Achievement, Republic of Croatia, 1999; Božo Težak Medal, Croatian Chemical Society, 2002. Memberships: President, Croatian Chemical Society, 1976-80; President, European Crystallographic Committee, 1978-81; Croatian Academy of Sciences and Arts, 1988-, Foreign Secretary, 2000-2004; Fellow of the World Academy of Art and Science, 2005-; President, Croatian Crystallographic Association, 1992-2006. Address: Laboratory of General and Inorganic Chemistry, Faculty of Science, University of Zagreb, Horvatovac 102A, 10000 Zagreb, Croatia.

KAMERER Jocelyne Maria, b. 6 September 1950, Pont-a-Moussons, France. Poet. Education: Kaiserlautern American High School, Kaiserlautern, West Germany. Career: Secretary; Poet; Cocktail Waitress. Publications: Reflections, 1990; Contributions to many poetry journals including Poets of Now, Glory Be To God, The Oak/Shepherd, and others. Honours: Association for Advancement of Poetry, 10 awards, including: Gold Quill Award, 1990, Silver Quill Award, 1991; Plowman, 1st Place, Southern Poetry Association, 4 awards, 1991; Khepera, 2 awards, 1994; More than 15 1st Place, Robert Bennett's Viewpoint; Certificate for Teaching Christian Doctrine, Thomas Aquinas Cathedral, Reno, Nevada, 1984-85; Listed in international biographical dictionaries. Memberships: Sponsor of veterans' groups such as Disabled American Veterans; Sponsor of numerous charities such as foundations for the blind and animal charities. Address: 6256 Village Lane, Colorado Springs, CO 80918, USA.

KAMEYAMA Michitaka, b. 12 May 1950, Utsunomiya, Japan. Professor. m. Kimiko Owashi, 1 son, 2 daughters. Education: Bachelor Degree, Electronic Engineering, 1973, Master Degree, Electronic Engineering, 1975, Doctor Degree, Electronic Engineering, 1978, Tohoku University. Appointments: Research Associate, 1978-81, Associate Professor, 1981-91, Professor, 1991-, Tohoku University. Publications include: A Multiplier Chip with Multiple-Valved Bidirectional Current-Mode Logic Circuits, IEEE Computer, 1988. Membership: Fellow, IEEE. Address: 6-10-8 Minami-Yoshinari, Aoba-ku, Sendai, Japan.

KAMINSKI Wlodzimierz, b. 16 April 1924, Skierniewice, Poland. Scientist; Economist. m. Krystyna Tyszkowska, 1 son. Education: MS, 1947, LLD, 1948, University of Cracow; DAgricEcon, 1961, Professor, Economic Sciences, 1973-92, doctor honoris causa, 2000, Agricultural University, Warsaw. Appointments: Researcher, Economist, 1959-92, Extraordinary Professor, 1973-80, Ordinary Professor, 1980-92, Faculty of Food Technology, Agricultural University, Warsaw; Editorial Board, International Journal of Refrigeration, 1975-99; Ordinary Professor, 1997-, Prorector, 1998-2004, Warsaw College of Economics, Warsaw; Visiting Professor, various universities and institutions; Head, Division for Spatial Research, 1983-92, Director, 1990, Institute of Agricultural and Food Economics. Publications: 25 books, over 300 publications in 8 languages; Author, Regional Aspects of Food Economy, 1989; Booklet, Refrigeration and the Worldwide Food Industry on the Threshold of the 21st Century, 1995. Honours: Knight, Officer and Commander Cross of Polonia Restituta, 1964, 1979, 1987; 5 awards, Ministry of Education, 1975-85; 1st scientific award, Ministry of Agriculture, 1991; Cross of National Army, Polish Government, 1994;

Croix d'Officier du Merite Agricole, French Government, 1995; Award, International Institute of Refrigeration, 1999; Man of the Year, 2004; Professor Pijanowski Award, Polish Scientific Society of Food Industry, 2006. Memberships: Polish Scientific Society of Food Industry; Polish Academy of Sciences; 2 committees, Association of Agricultural Economists; Hungarian Scientific Society of Food Industry; French Academy of Agriculture; International Institute of Refrigeration, Paris; New York Academy of Sciences. Address: Smolna 15, Room 11, 00375 Warsaw, Poland.

KAMIYA Kanichi, b. 10 December 1941, Inabe, Mie, Japan. Chemist; Educator. m. Machiko Shoji, 1 son, 1 daughter. Education: Bachelor's Degree, 1964, Master's Degree, 1966, Faculty of Engineering, PhD, 1969, Nagoya University, Japan. Appointments: Postdoctoral Fellow, University of New York at Buffalo, 1969-70; Researcher, Toyota Institute of Science and Chemistry, 1969-71; Associate Professor, 1971-83, Professor, 1983-2005, Professor Emeritus, 2005-, Mie University, Japan. Publications: Book chapters: Fine Ceramics, 1988; Sol-Gel Optics, 1994; Handbook of Sol-Gel Science and Technology, 2005; 250 papers on sol-gel and structure of glasses in scientific journals including: Physics and Chemistry of Glasses, 1998, Journal of Non-Crystalline Solids, 1998; Journal of Sol-Gel Science and Technology, 1999, Materials Research Bulletin, 2005. Honours: Academic Award for Young Scientist, Tokai Association of Chemical Engineering, Japan, 1981; Academic Award, Ceramic Society of Japan, 1987. Memberships: American Ceramic Society; Chemical Society of Japan; Director, 1998-99, Ceramic Society of Japan; Vice-Chair, 2003-, Japan Society of Sol-Gel Science and Technology. Address: 1044-2 Uga, Daian, Inabe, Mie 511-0286, Japan. E-mail: kanichi-kamiya@apost.plala.or.jp

KAMU Okko, b. 7 March 1946, Helsinki, Finland. Conductor. Education: Violin studies with Väinö Arjava from 1949 and with Professor Onni Suhonen at the Sibelius Academy, Helsinki, 1952-67. Career: Leader of the Suhonen Quartet, 1964; Leader of the Finnish National Opera Orchestra, 1966-69; Conducted Britten's The Turn of the Screw in Helsinki, 1968; Guest Conductor, Swedish Royal Opera, 1969; Chief Conductor, Finnish Radio Symphony Orchestra, 1971-77; Music Director, Oslo Philharmonic, 1975-79; Music Director, Helsinki Philharmonic,1981-88; Principal Conductor, Dutch Radio Symphony, 1983-86; Principal Guest Conductor, City of Birmingham Symphony Orchestra, 1985-88; Principal Conductor, Sjaelland Symphony Orchestra (Copenhagen Philharmonic), 1988-89; Guest engagements with the Berlin Philharmonic, Suisse Romande Orchestra, Vienna Symphony Orchestra and orchestras in the USA, Far East, Australia, South America and Europe; Conducted the premieres of Sallinen's operas The Red Line and The King Goes Forth to France; Metropolitan Opera, 1983, US premiere of The Red Line; Covent Garden, 1987, in the British premiere of The King Goes Forth to France; Principal Conductor of the Helsingborg Symphony Orchestra, 1991-2000; Music Director of the Finnish National Opera, 1996-2000; Principal Guest Conductor, Singapore Symphony Orchestra, 1995-2001, 2006 and principal Guest Conductor of Lausanne Chamber Orchestra, 1999-2002. Recordings: About 70 recordings for various labels; Sallinen's Shadows, Cello Concerto and 5th Symphony. Honours: Winner, 1st Herbert von Karajan Conductors' Competition, Berlin, 1969; Member of the Royal Swedish Academy of Music. Address: Villa Arcadia, C/Mozart 7, Rancho Domingo, 29639 Benalmadena Pueblo, Spain.

KAN Chi-Wai, b. 13 October 1970, Hong Kong. Textile Chemist. m. Oi-Yee Agnes Lai. Education: BSc, 1994, PhD, 1998, Textile Chemistry, The Hong Kong Polytechnic University; MSc, Total Quality Management and Business Excellence, Sheffield Hallam University, England, 2002; Master of Education, Christian Education, Research Institute of Christian Education, Hong Kong, 2005. Appointments: Research Assistant, 1994-95, 1995, Tutor, 1995-97, Research Student, 1995-98, Research Associate, 2003-05, Lecturer, 2006-, Institute of Textiles and Clothing, The Hong Kong Polytechnic University; Assistant Laboratory Manager, Specialised Technology Resources (HK) Ltd, Hong Kong, 1998; Instructor, Li Ka Shing Institute of Professional and Continuing Education, Open University of Hong Kong, 2005; Occupational Safety Officer II, Labour Department, Government of the Hong Kong Special Administrative Region, Hong Kong, 1998-2005. Publications: 2 monographs; Over 60 referred journals; 19 professional journals; Over 40 international conference and symposium proceedings. Memberships: American Chemical Society; Royal Society of Chemistry; Institution of Occupational Safety and Health; Hong Kong Quality Management Association; Associateship, Society of Dyers and Colourists; Associateship, Textile Institute; Member, Hong Kong Institution of Textile and Apparel. Address: Institute of Textiles and Clothing, Hung Hom, Kowloon, Hong Kong. E-mail: tccwk@inet.polyu.edu.hk

KANEMATSU Hideyuki, b. 21 November 1957, Sakai, Osaka, Japan. Researcher. m. Reiko Komori, 1 son, 1 daughter. Education: B Eng, 1981, M Eng, 1983, PhD, 1989, Materials Science and Engineering, Nagoya University. Appointments: Research Associate, Department of Materials Science and Engineering, Faculty of Engineering, Nagoya University, 1986; Research Associate, Department of Materials Science and Engineering, Faculty of Engineering, Osaka University, 1990; Research Associate, 1992, Assistant Professor, 1994, Associate Professor, 1997, Full Professor, 2007, Department of Materials Science and Engineering, Suzuka National College of Technology. Publications: 8 books; 185 scientific papers; 19 patent applications. Honours: Listed in international biographical dictionaries; Professional Member, 2001, Fellow, 2007, Institute of Metal Finishing in UK; Wood Badge, Scout Association of Japan, 2002; Outstanding Achievement Award, American Chemical Society, 2002; President Award, Association of National Colleges of Technology, Japan, 2003; Educational Incentive Award, Suzuka National College of Technology, 2003; Chem Luminary Award, American Chemical Society, 2004; Long Service Award for 20 Years, Institute of National Colleges of Technology, 2006. Memberships: Institute of Metal Finishing in UK; National Association for Surface Finishing, USA The Minerals, Metals & Materials Society, USA; ASM International; American Society for Engineering Education, USA; Japan Institute of Metals; Iron and Steel Institute of Japan; Japanese Society for Engineering Education; Surface Finishing Society of Japan; Japan Society of Heat Treatment; Japan Industrial Archaeology Society. Address: 2-4-31 Shinonome Nishi-machi, Sakai-ku, Sakai, Osaka 590-0013, Japan. E-mail: kanemats@mse.suzuka-ct.ac.jp

KANG Bubjoo, b. 20 August 1961, Yesan, Chungnam, Korea. Professor. m. Bokhee Byun, 1 daughter. Education: BSc, Electronic Engineering, Kyunghee University, 1983; MSc, 1985, PhD, 1996, Electronic Engineering, Yonsei University. Appointments: Team Manager, ETRI, Daejeon, Korea, 1988-2001; Chairman, TTA IMT-2000 Evaluation Group, 1995-97; Professor, Dongguk University, Kyongju, Korea, 2001-. Publications: 2 papers: Performance evaluation of

DS/CDMA Hybrid Acquisition in Multipath Rayleigh Fading Channel; A performance comparison of Code Acquisition Techniques in DS-CDMA System; 2 patents: Channel Encoding Apparatus Using Single Concatenated encoder; Code Acquisition Device using Two-step Search processes in DS-CDMA UWB Modem and Thereof. Memberships: Life Member, KICS; Life Member, KIMICS; Member, IEEE; Member, IEICE. Address: Hanmaru Apt 103-1001, Dunsan-Dong, Seo-gu, Daejeon 302-773, Republic of Korea. E-mail: bjkang@dongguk.ac.kr

KANG Do-Young, b. 20 September 1966, Busan, Korea. Physician; Professor. m. Soo-Jeong Yi, 2 daughters. Education: Bachelor of Medicine, Dong-A University College of Medicine, 1991; Master of Medicine, 1995, Doctor of Medicine, 1998, Done-A University Postgraduate School. Appointments: Intern, 1991-92, Resident, 1992-96, Fellowship, 1996-97, Dong-A University Hospital; Fellowship, Seoul Asan Medical Centre, 1997-98; Instructor, Kyungpook National University College of Medicine, 1998-2000; Instructor, 1998-2000, Kyungpook National University College of Medicine; Instructor, 2000-2002, Assistant Professor, 2002-2006; Associate Professor, director, 2006-, Dong-A University College of Medicine. Publication: Identification of vasopressin-induced genes in AQP2-transfected MDCK cells by suppression subtractive hybridization, 2004. Honour: Scientific Award of Daiichi, Korean Society of Nuclear Medicine, 1999. Memberships: Korean Association of Nuclear Medicine; Society of Nuclear Medicine; European Society of Nuclear medicine; American Society of Nuclear Cardiology. Address: 3-ga 1 Dongdaesin-Dong, Seo-Gu, Busan 602-715, Korea. E-mail: dykang@dau.ac.kr

KANG Dong-Wha, b. 6 April 1967, Daegu, South Korea. Neurologist; Professor. m. In-Kyong Jeong, 1 daughter. Education: MD, 1991, PhD, Neuroscience, 2001, Seoul National University College of Medicine; Diplomate, Ministry of Health & Welfare, Republic of Korea, 1991. Appointments: Resident, 1995-99, Fellow, 1999-2001, Department of Neurology, Seoul National University Hospital; Postdoctoral Fellow, Stroke Branch, National Institutes of Health, Bethesda, Maryland, USA, 2001-03; Assistant Professor, Asan Medical Centre, Seoul, Korea, 2003-. Publications: 90 articles in professional journals. Honours: Medical College Graduate Student Excellence Award, 1991; Young Investigator Award, Korean Neurological Association, 2006. Memberships: American Heart Association Stroke Council; Korean Stroke Society; Korean Neurological Association; Korean Society for Human Brain Mapping. Address: Department of Neurology, Asan Medical Centre, 388-1 pungnap-2 dong, Songpa-gu, Seoul, 138-736, South Korea. E-mail: dwkang@amc.seoul.kr

KANG Hang-Bong, b. 20 November 1957, Jinhae, Korea. Professor. m. Jae Yeon Park, 2 sons. Education: BS, Electronic Engineering, Hanyang University, Seoul, 1980; MS, Computer Engineering, Ohio State University, USA, 1989; PhD, Computer Engineering, Rensselaer Polytechnic Institute, 1993. Appointments: Principal Researcher, Samsung Advanced Institute of Technology, 1994-97; Professor, Catholic University of Korea, 1997-. Publications: A Dynamic Bayesian Network-based Framework for Visual Tracking, 2006. Memberships: IEEE; ACM. Address: Department of Computer Engineering, Catholic University of Korea, #43-1 Yokkok 2-dong, Wonmi-Gu, Bucheon, Gyonggi-Do, Korea.

KANG Intae, b. 13 January 1970, Busan, Korea. Electronics Engineer. m. Kihee Kim, 2 sons. Education: BS, Seoul National University, Korea, 1994; MS, Johns Hopkins

University, Baltimore, USA, 1996; PhD, University of Washington, Seattle, USA, 2004. Appointments: Teaching Assistant, 1998-2001, Research Assistant, 2001-04, University of Washington; Software Engineer, Optometrix Inc, Kent, Washington, 2001-02; Senior Engineer, Telecomm R&D Center, Samsung Electronics, Suwon, Kyunnni-Do, 2006-. Publications: Numerous articles in professional journals. Honours: Listed in international biographical dictionaries. Memberships: IEEE; Eta Kappa Nu (Honor Society). Address: Michellan-Chereville D-1304, Bundang, JeongJa, SeongNam, Kyunggi 463-834, Korea. E-mail: kangit@gmail.com

KANG Jian, b. 2 August 1964, Shanxi, China. University Professor. m. Mei Zhang, 2 sons. Education: BEng, 1984, MSc, 1986, School of Architecture, Tsinghua University, Beijing; PhD, The Martin Centre, University of Cambridge, England, 1996. Appointments: Assistant Lecturer, 1987-89, Lecturer, 1989-92, Building Science Department, School of Architecture, Tsinghua University, Beijing; BFT Scholar, 1992-93, Humboldt Postdoctoral Fellow, 1997-98, Fraunhofer Institute of Building Physics, Stuttgart, Germany; Research Fellow, Wolfson College, University of Cambridge, England, 1996-99; Senior Research Associate, The Martin Centre, University of Cambridge, England, 1998-99; Lecturer, 1999-2001, Reader, 2001-03, Full Professor, 2003-, School of Architecture, University of Sheffield. Publications: 3 books; More than 90 refereed journals and book chapters; Over 150 refereed conferences. Honours: Newman Medal, Acoustical Society of America, 1996; Lloyd's of London Fellowship, 1998; A V Humboldt Fellowship, Germany, 1997-98; Fellow, Cambridge University Wolfson College, UK, 1996-99; Visiting Professor, Harbin Institute of Technology, and South China University of Technology, 2005-; Distinguished Overseas Experts, Chinese Academy of Sciences, 2005-; Chang-Jiang Visiting Chair Professorship, China Ministry of Education, 2007-; Tyndall Medal, Institute of Acoustics, 2008. Memberships: Fellow, Institute of Acoustics, UK; Fellow, Acoustical Society of America; German Society of Acoustics; Acoustical Society of China; European Acoustics Association; International Institute of Acoustics and Vibration; Chairman, UK Chinese Association of Resources and Environment. Address: School of Architecture, University of Sheffield, Western Bank, Sheffield S10 2TN, England. E-mail: j.kang@sheffield.ac.uk Website: www.shef.ac.uk/acoustics

KANG Joon-Wun, b. 17 January 1954, Seoul, Korea. Professor. m. Ran A Park, 2 sons. Education: BS, Yonsei University, Korea, 1979; MS, Chemical Engineering, University of Oklahoma, 1984; PhD, Environmental Engineering, UCLA, 1989. Appointments: Research Consultant, James M Montgomery, 1987; Postdoctoral, University of North Carolina, 1989; Professor, Department of Environmental Engineering, Yonsei University, 1990-; Visiting Professor, California Institute of Technology, 1997; Dean of General Affairs, Yonsei University Wonju Campus, 2002-04; Visiting Professor, University of Illinois at Urbana-Champaign, 2004; Dean, College of Health Science. Publications: The chemistry of water treatment processes involving ozone, hydrogen peroxide and ultraviolet radiation, 1987. Honours: Harvey M Rosen Memorial Award, 1989; Yonsei Academic Award, 1999; Best Paper Award, Korean Society of Environmental Engineering, 2005. Memberships: International Ozone Association; International Water Association; American Chemical Society. Address: Chong-gu Apt 101-1103, Wonju City, South Korea. E-mail: jwk@yonsei.ac.kr

KANG Seong-Seung, b. 10 October 1967, Muan, Republic of Korea. Research Professor. m. Si-Sun Yu. Education: BS, Resource Engineering, Chosun University, Gwangju, 1993; MS, Geophysics and Engineering Geology, Kwangwoon National University, Chuncheon, 1996; PhD, Rock Mechanics and Rock Engineering, Kumamoto University, Japan, 2000. Appointments: Brain Korea 21, Researcher, Earth Science, Seoul National University, 2001-04; Visiting Research Fellow, Kumamoto University, 2004-06; Research Professor, Sunchon National University, 2006-. Publications: Evaluation of core disking rock stress and tensile strength via the compact conical-ended borehole overcoring (CCBO) technique. Honours: Yomeyama Scholarship, International Rotary Club, 1999-2000; Best Paper Award, Society of Mining and Materials Processing, Institute of Japan, 2006. Memberships: International Society of Rock Mechanics; Korean Society of Civil Engineering; Korean Society of Geosystem Engineering. Address: Research Institute of Basic Sciences, Sunchon National University, 315 Maegok, Suncheon, Jeonnam 540-742, Republic of Korea. E-mail: kangss67@yahoo.co.kr

KANG Seong-Woong, b. 11 October 1959, Jinzu, Republic of Korea. Physiatrist; Professor. m. Hyun-Sook Kim, 2 sons. Education: Bachelor, 1985, Master, 1991, PhD, 1996, Yonsei University College of Medicine; Internship, 1985-86, Residency, 1989-92, Yongdong Severance Hospital. Appointments: Instructor, 1994-96, Assistant Professor, 1996-2002, Associate Professor, 2000-06, Professor, 2006-, Yonsei University College of Medicine; Chairman, Department of Rehabilitation Medicine, Yongdong Severance Hospital, 2004-; Board of Directors: Korean Association of Amyotrophy Lateral Sclerosis; Korean Organisation of Rare Disease; Korean Academy of Rehabilitation Medicine. Publications: 74 articles; Book chapter, Major key topics concerning pulmonary rehabilitation in patients with neuromuscula disease. Honours: Best Paper Award, 2002; Korean Academy of Rehabiliation Medicine. Memberships: International Society of Physical and Rehabilitation Medicine; Korean Academy of Rehabiliation Medicine; Korea Academy of Clinical Geriatrics. E-mail: kswoong@yumc.yonsei.ac.kr Website: www.breatheasyclub.com

KANTARIS Sylvia, b. 9 January 1936, Grindleford, Derbyshire, England. Poet; Writer; Teacher. m. Emmanuel Kantaris, 11 January 1958, 1 son, 1 daughter. Education: Diplôme d'Études Civilisation Française, Sorbonne, University of Paris, 1955; BA, Honours, 1957, Cert.Ed, 1958, Bristol University; MA, 1967, PhD, 1972, University of Queensland, Australia. Appointments: Tutor, University of Queensland, Australia, 1963-66, Open University, England, 1974-84; Extra-Mural Lecturer, Exeter University, 1974-; Cornwall's First Writer in the Community, 1986. Publications: Time and Motion, 1975; Stocking Up, 1981; The Tenth Muse, 1983; News From the Front (with D M Thomas), 1983; The Sea at the Door, 1985; The Air Mines of Mistila (with Philip Gross), 1988; Dirty Washing: New and Selected Poems, 1989; Lad's Love, 1993. Contributions to: Many anthologies, newspapers, and magazines. Honours: National Poetry Competition Award, 1982; Honorary Doctor of Letters, Exeter University, 1989; Major Arts Council Literature Award, 1991; Society of Authors Award, 1992. Memberships: Poetry Society of Great Britain; South West Arts, literature panel, 1983-87; literary consultant, 1990-. Address: 14 Osborne Parc, Helston, Cornwall TR13 8PB, England.

KAPETANAKIS Basil, b. 19 July 1974, Chicago, USA. Medical Doctor; Obstetrics and Gynaecology. Education: Medical diploma, University of Athens School of Medicine,

1999; Affiliated Residency Program, Northwestern University, St Joseph Hospital, Chicago, 2001-05; Galloway Fellowship, Gynaecologic Oncology, Memorial Sloan-Kettering Cancer Center, New York, 2004; Reproductive Endocrinology, Lubeck Medical University, Germany, 2005. Appointments: 1st Assistant, Surgical Obstetrics and Gynaecology, Iaso Maternity Hospital, Athens, 1999-2000; Clerk rotation, Obstetrics and Gynaecology, Rush Presbyterian-St Lukes Hospital, Chicago, 2000; Assistant, Division of Reproductive Endocrinology and Infertility, Center of Reproductive Medicine and Genetics, Athens, Greece, 2005-07; 1st Assistant, Laparoscopic Surgery, Ygeia Hospital, Athens, 2005-07; Director, Division of Reproductive Medicine and Genetics, Athens, Greece, 2005-08. Publications: Numerous articles in professional journals and at conference. Honours: Cum Laude Medical Diploma, University of Athens, School of Medicine; Outstanding Lapaoendoscopic Resident, 2005; Resident Achievement Award, Society of Laparoendoscopic Surgeons; Chief Senior Resident, S Joseph Hospital, Northwestern University, 2004-05; Resident Research Award for Outstanding Research, Organon USA Inc, 2004. Memberships: Junior Fellow, American College of Obstetricians & Gynecologists; American Medical Association; Hellenic Laparoscopic Association. Address: Kalliga 78, Filothei, Athens 15237, Greece. E-mail: vkapertas@yahoo.com

KAPLAN Ben-Zion, b. 13 February 1936, Tel-Aviv, Israel. Professor of Electrical Engineering. Education: BSc, Cum Laude, Electrical Engineering, 1954-58, MSc, Electrical Engineering, 1962-64, Technion, Israel Institute of Technology, Haifa, Israel; Doctor of Philosophy, Applied Science (Electrical Engineering), The University of Sussex, England, 1968-71. Appointments: Electronics Engineering Officer, Israel Defence Forces, 1958-61; Engineer, Electronics Department, The Weizmann Institute of Science, Rehovot, Israel, 1961-68; Tutorial and Research Fellow, Inter-University Institute of Engineering Control, University of Sussex, England, 1968-71; Senior Lecturer, 1973-79, Associate Professor, 1979-85, Professor, 1985-2006, Professor Emeritus, 2006-, Incumbent of the Chinita and Konrad Abrahams-Curiel Chair in Electronic Instrumentation, 1988-2006, Department of Electrical and Computer Engineering, Ben-Gurion University of the Negev, Israel; Sabbatical Year, Department of Physics, University of Otago, New Zealand, 1991-92. Publications: More than 135 publications in refereed journals as author and co-author on various subjects such as: Sensing magnetic fields, sensing electric DC fields, nonlinear and chaotic oscillations, chaos control, magnetic levitation; More than 80 conference publications including some proceedings publications. Honours: Fellow, Electromagnetic Academy; Prize in the Field of Applied Electronics, Polish-Jewish Ex-Servicemen's Association, London, 1993. Memberships: Association of Engineers and Architects in Israel; Senior Member, IEEE; Israeli Committee of URSI and its Metrology Subcommittee. Address: Department of Electrical and Computer Engineering, Ben-Gurion University of the Negev, Beer-Sheva 84105, Israel. E-mail: kaplan@ee.bgu.ac.il

KARAN Donna, b. 2 October 1948, Forest Hills, New York, USA. Fashion Designer. m. (1) Mark Karan, 1 daughter, (2) Stephen Weiss, 1983, deceased 2001. Education: Parsons School of Design, New York. Appointments: Designer, Anne Klein & Co, Addenda Co, 1968; Returned to Anne Klein, 1968, Associate Designer, 1971, Director of Design, 1974-84; Owner, Designer, Donna Karan Co, New York, DKNY, 1984-96; Designer, Donna Karan International, 1996-2001; Chief Designer, LVMH, 2001-. Honours: Coty Awards, 1977, 1981; Fashion Designers of America Women's

Wear Award, 1996; FEMMY Designer of the Year Award, 1999; FIFI Best National Advertising Campaign of the Year Award, 2001; Fashion Group International Superstar Award, 2003. Membership: Fashion Designers of American. Address: Donna Karan International, 15th Floor, 5550 Seventh Avenue, New York, NY 10018, USA.

KARANDE Sunil, b. 29 July 1961, Bombay, India. Paediatrician; Researcher. Education: MBBS, 1984; DCH, 1988; MD, 1989; Diploma in Information Technology, Advanced Computing Training School, Pune, 2000. Appointments: Medical Officer, Government of India, 1990-91; Surgeon Lieutenant, Indian Navy, 1991-92; Lecturer, Paediatrics, Seth GS Medical College and KEM Hospital, Bombay, 1992-98; Associate Professor, Paediatrics, Lokmanya Tilak Municipal Medical College and Lokmanya Tilak Municipal General Hospital, Bombay, 1998-; Committee Member and Resource Person for AIDS Awareness in Junior Colleges in Mumbai, UNICEF and Mumbai Districts AIDS Control Society, 2000-. Publications: 72 indexed articles in peer reviewed journals; Written chapters in 2 books. Honours: Expert, Essential Drug List, Indian Pharmacological Society of Clinicians and Pharmacologists, 1994; First Prize, Free Paper, VII Maharashtra State Indian Academy of Paediatrics Conference, 1996; Reviewer for Indian Paediatrics, Indian Journal of Paediatrics, Journal of Postgraduate Medicine and Neurology India, British Journal of Clinical Pharmacology, Paediatric Rehabilitation, Emerging Infectious Diseases, Indian Journal of Medical Sciences; Expert Review of Pharmacoeconomics and Outcomes Research; American Journal of Medical Genetics Part B, Neuropsychiatric Genetics, Journal of Pediatric Neurology indexed journals. Memberships: Member of Technical Committee: WHO/ Adverse Drug Reaction Monitoring Programme, 1997-99; Life Member, Indian Academy of Paediatrics; Life Member, Indian Medical Association; Member, New York Academy of Sciences, 1996. Address: Flat 24, Joothica, 5th Floor, 22A Naushir Bharucha Road, Mumbai 400007, India. E-mail: karandesunil@yahoo.com

KARASIN Grigory B, b. 1949, Moscow, Russia. Diplomat; Ambassador Extraordinary and Plenipotentiary. m. Olga V Karasina, 2 daughters. Education: Graduate, College of Oriental Languages, Moscow State University, 1971. Appointments: Embassy in Senegal, 1972-76; Embassy in Australia, 1979-85; Embassy in the United Kingdom, 1988-92; Director, Department of Africa, MFA, 1992-93; Director, Department of Information and Press, MFA, 1993-96; Deputy Minister of Foreign Affairs of the Russian Federation, 1996-2000; Ambassador to the Court of St James's, 2000-. Address: The Russian Embassy, 13 Kensington Palace Gardens, London W8 4QX, England.

KARAVANIĆ Ivor, b. 27 June 1965, Zagreb, Croatia. Archaeologist. m. Snježana. Education: BA, Archaeology, 1990, MA, Archaeology, 1993, University of Zagreb; PhD, Archaeology, 1999, University of Zagreb. Appointments: Research Assistant, 1991-2001; Assistant, 1993-99, Senior Assistant, 1999-2001, Assistant Professor, 2001-05, Associate Professor, 2005-, Head of Department, 2005-, Department of Archaeology, Faculty of Humanities and Social Sciences, University of Zagreb, 1991-. Publications include: Néandertaliens et Paléolithique supérieur dans la grotte de Vindija, co-author, 1998; Gornjopaleolitičke kamene i koštane rukotvorine iz špilje Vindije, 1994; Upper Paleolithic occupation levels and late-occurring Neanderthal at Vindija Cave (Croatia) in the Context of Central Europe and the Balkans, 1995; The Middle/Upper Paleolithic Interface and the Relationship of Neanderthals and Early Modern Humans in the Hrvatsko Zagorje, co-author, 1998; The Early Upper Paleolithic of Croatia, 1998; Neanderthal Diet at Vindija and Neanderthal Predation: The Evidence from Stable Isotopes, co-author, 2000; Stones that Speak, Šandalja in the Light of Lithic Technology, co-author, 2000; Olschewian and Appearance of Bone Technology in Croatia and Slovenia, 2000; ESR and AMS-based ^{14}C dating of Mousterian Levels at Mujina Pećina, Dalmatia, Croatia, co-author, 2002; Osvit tehnologije, co-author, 2003; Život neandertalaca, 2004; Odiseja čovječanstra, co-author, 2005. Honours: Fellowship, French Government, 1995, 2001; Constantin-Jireček Fellowship, 1995; Fulbright Fellowship, 1996-97; International Scientist of the Year, IBC, 2001; Plaquette of Zagreb City, 2006; Faculty of Humanities and Social Sciences Medal, 2006; Listed in several Who's Who and biographical publications. Memberships: Croatian Archaeological Society; Society for American Archaeology; European Association of Archaeologists; INQUA National Committee, Croatia; Serra International, Zagreb; Croatian Fulbright Alumni Association; L'Association croate des boursiers du governement Français. Address: Department of Archaeology, Faculty of Humanities and Social Sciences, University of Zagreb, Ivana Lučića 3, 10000 Zagreb, Croatia. E-mail: ikaravan@ffzg.hr

KARDORFF Bernd, b. Mönchengladbach, Germany. Dermatologist; Laser Specialist; Author; Inventor; Allergologist. m. Maria, 1 son, 1daughter. Education: Doctor of Medicine, Heinrich-Heine University, Dusseldorf; Specialist in Dermatology (Medical), Specialist in Allergology (Medical), Specialist in Environmental Medicine (Medical), Aerztekammer Nordrhein, 2000; Specialist in Acupuncture, 2006. Appointments: Head Physician, Laser Medicine, 1996-99, Registrar, 1998-99, St Barbara Hospital, Duisburg, Northrhine-Westphalia; Vice Head Physician, Rhein-Klinik St Joseph, Duisburg-Beeckerwerth, Northrhine-Westphalia, 1996-99; Chief Dermatologist and Allergologist, Kardorff & Dorittke Out Patients Clinic, Mönchengladbach, 1999; President, Dachverband für Wohnortnahe Dermatologische Rehabilitation und Therapie chronischer Hautkrankheiten, 2000; Advisory Board Member, DERM Specialist periodical, Omnimed-Verlag, Hamburg, 2001; Head Physician, Skin, Allergy and Venous Clinic, Korschenbroich, 2007. Publications: Papers and articles in professional scientific and medical journals; Author, several scientific books. Honours: Award for Paediatric Dermatology, 1999; Literary Awards, Georg Thieme Publishing Company, 1995, 1998, 2002. Memberships: Deutsche Akademie für Akupunktur und Auriculomedizin; NVV Lions Mönchengladbach; Westgerman Basketball Mastership, 2000; Deutsche Dermatologische Gesellschaft; Arbeitsgemeinschaft Dermatologische Kosmetologie; Vereinigung für operative Dermatologie; Dachverband für Wohnortnahe Dermatologische Rehabilitation und Therapie chronischer Hautkrankheiten. Address: Dermatology & Laser Out Patients Clinic, Marktstrasse 31, Mönchengladbach, Northrhine-Westphalia 41236, Germany. E-mail: info@dorittke-kardorff.de Website: www.dorittke-kardorff.de

KARIM Fawzi, b. 1 July 1945, Baghdad, Iraq. Poet; Writer; Editor; Publisher. m. 31 December 1980, 2 sons. Education: BA, Arabic Literature, College of Arts, Baghdad, 1967. Appointment: Editor-in-Chief and Publisher, Al-Lahda Al-Shiriya, quarterly, London. Publications: Where Things Begin, 1968; I Raise My Hand in Protest, 1973; Madness of Stone, 1977; Stumbling of a Bird, 1985; We Do Not Inherit the Earth, 1988; Schemes of Adam, 1991; Pestilential Continents, 1992; Collected Poems, 1968-1992, 1993. Other: Essays

and short stories. Contributions to: Reviews and periodicals. Memberships: Poetry Society, England; Union of Iraqi Writers. Address: PO Box 2137, London W13 0TY, England.

KARLIS Athanasios, b. 17 April 1967, Athens, Greece. Lecturer. m. Kiriaki Felekidou, 2 daughters. Education: Bachelor, Electrical Engineering, 1991, PhD, 1996, Electrical and Computer Engineering, Aristotle University of Thessaloniki, Greece. Appointments: Electrical Engineer, private sector, 1991-2000; Lecturer, Department of Electrical and Computer Engineering, Democritus University of Thrace, Greece, 2000-. Publications: Approximately 30 articles in scientific journals and international conferences. Honours: Listed in international biographical dictionaries. Memberships: IEEE; Technical Chamber of Greece; Hellenic Institute of Electric Vehicles; Rotary Club of Xanth. E-mail: akarlis@ee.duth.gr

KARPOV Anatoliy Yevgenievich, b. 23 May 1951, Zlatoust, Russia. Chess Player. m. (1) Irina, 1 son, (2) Ntalia Bulanova, 1 daughter. Education: Leningrad University. Career: Member, CPSU, 1980-91; USSR Candidate Master, 1962, Master, 1966; European Junior Champion, 1967, 1968; World Junior Champion, 1969; International Master, 1969; International Grandmaster, 1970; USSR Champion, 1976, 1983, 1988; World Champion, 1975-85; Became world champion when holder, Bobby Fischer, refused to defend title; Retained title against Viktor Korchnoi, 1978 and 1981; Defended title against Garry Kasparov, Moscow, 1984 (match later adjourned due to illness of both players); Lost to Kasparov, 1985; Unsuccessfully challenged Kasparov, 1986, 1987, 1990; Won World Championship title under FIDE after split in chess organisations, 1993, 1996, 1998; Has won more tournaments than any other player (over 160); People's Deputy of USSR, 1989-91; President, Soviet Peace Fund (now International Association of Peace Funds), 1982-; President, Chernobyl-Aid organisation, 1989-; UNICEF Ambassador for Russia and Eastern Europe, 1998-; Chair, Council of Directors Federal Industrial Bank, Moscow. Publications: Chess is My Life, 1980; Karpov Teaches Chess, 1987; Karpov on Karpov, 1991; How to Play Chess; 47 other books. Honours: Winner, Oscar Chess Prize, 1973-77, 1979-81, 1984, 1994; Fontany di Roma Prize for Humanitarian Achievements, 1996; Honorary Texan; Honorary Citizen of Tula, Zlatoust, Orsk and other cities in Russia, Belarus and Ukraine. Memberships: Soviet (now Russian) UNESCO Affairs Commission; Board, International Chess Federation; Editor in Chief, Chess Review 64 magazine, 1980-91. Address: International Peace Fund, Prechistenka 10, Moscow, Russia.

KARRAZ Mazen, b. 7 July 1964, Sednaya, Syria. Physician; Anaesthesiologist. Education: MD, University of Damascus, Syria, 1987; Certificate, Anaesthesia Specialist: Damascus University, Syria, 1993; University of Paris V, 1995; Acupuncture Specialist diploma, University of Paris XIII, 1999; Pain Management Diploma, University of Paris, XII, France, 2000. Appointments: Anaesthesiologist: Bicetre University Hospital, Paris, 1994-95; Beauvais Hospital, 1996-2001; Evry Hospital, 2001-02; Verdun Hospital, 2003-; Expert: Columnist Sociedad Iberoamnericana de Information Cientifica, 2003-; Consultant, Council of Healthcare Advisors, 2003-. Publications: Numerous articles in professional medical journals. Honours: Nominated finalist, loco-regional Anaesthesia Prize, French Association of Anaesthesiologists, 2002, 2003. Memberships: French Pain Management Association; French Anaesthesia Association;

Euroanaesthesia Association; World Anaesthesia Association. Address: 57 Planchat St, 75020 Paris, France. E-mail: mazenkarraz@hotmail.com

KARUNARATNE Vidanage Pemananda, b. 10 October 1942, Colombo, Sri Lanka, Management, Marketing and Training Consultant. m. Nanda Vijitha Karunaratne, 2 daughters. Education: BA, Economics (Ceylon), 1961-65; Expert's Certificate in Insurance Management (Japan), 1988; Postgraduate Diploma, Marketing Management (Sri Lanka), 1990-92; MBA (Sri Lanka), 1993-96; Associate of Ceylon Insurance College (Sri Lanka), 1993; Chartered Marketer, Chartered Institute of Marketing (UK), 1998. Appointments: Assistant Manager, Life Department, 1968-69, Assistant Manager and Manager, Housing Loans Department, 1970-79, Manager and Head, Publicity Advertising, Training and Public Relations Department, 1980-91, Insurance Corporation of Sri Lanka; Manager, Training Department, Ceylinco Insurance Company, 1991-95; Academic and Administative Head, Ceylinco Insurance College, 1995-97; Visiting Senior Lecturer, University of Sri Jayewardenepura, Sri Lanka, 1991-; Management, Marketing and Training Consultant, 1997-. Publications: The Neglected But Essential Element of the Marketing Mix for Insurance - Personalised Service - The Case of Insurance in Sri Lanka; Transformation Through the People for the People – The Indian Experience: The Lessons Sri Lankans Can Learn From It. Honours: Consulting Editor, ABI, USA, 2002; Man of the Year 2005, ABI, USA, Listed in Who's Who publications and biographical dictionaries. Memberships: Chartered Institute of Marketing, UK, 1993; Chartered Management Institute, UK, 1994; Chartered Institute of Public Relations, 1995; Institute of Management of Sri Lanka, 1996; Research Board of Advisors, ABI, 2003. Address: 3A Wimalawatta Road, Nugegoda, Sri Lanka.

KARWOWSKI Jacek Andrzej, b. 23 March 1940, Vilna, Lithuania. Physicist. m. Anna Maria Karwowska, 2 sons, 1 daughter. Education: MSc, 1962; Doctorate, 1968; Dr hab, 1974; Professor, 1988. Appointments: Assistant, 1962-69, Adjunct, 1969-75, Docent, 1975-88, Professor, 1988-2005, Professor Emeritus, 2005-, N Copernicus University, Torun, Poland; Postdoctoral Fellow, Department of Chemistry, University of Alberta, Edmonton, Canada, 1972-73; Visiting Scientist, Max Planck Institute für Astrophysik, Garching bei München, Germany, 1-3 months yearly, 1984-2000; Visiting Professor, Consejo Superior de Investigaciones Científicas, Madrid, Spain, 1987-88. Publications: 182 scientific papers in international journals; Co-author, 2 books. Honour: Cavalier Cross, Order of Polonia Restituta, 1994. Memberships: Polish Physical Society; European Physical Society; International Society for Theoretical Chemical Physics; Polish Chemical Society; Polish Alpine Society. Address: Cegielnik 18, 87-134 Zławieś Wielka, Poland. E-mail: jka@fizyka.umk.pl

KASER Michael Charles, b. 2 May 1926, London, England. Economist. m. Elizabeth Piggford, 4 sons, 1 daughter. Education: BA, 1946, MA, 1950, Economics, King's College, Cambridge; MA, 1960, DLitt, 1993, Oxford University. Career: Chief Scientific Advisor's Department, Ministry of Works, 1946-47; HM Foreign Service, including HM Embassy, Moscow as Second Secretary, Commercial Secretariat, 1947-51; United Nations Economic Commission for Europe, Geneva, 1951-63; Fellow, 1960-93, Emeritus Fellow, 1993-, St Antony's College; Lecturer, 1963-72, Reader, 1972-93, Reader Emeritus, 1993-, University of Oxford; Honorary Chair, Institute for German Studies, University of Birmingham, 1993-. Publications: Author, Editor, 23 books and 390 articles in journals on the East European, Russian and

Central Asian economies; Books include: Soviet Economics, 1970; Health Care in the Soviet Union and Eastern Europe, 1976; Privatisation in the CIS, 1995; The Economies of Kazakstan and Uzbekistan, 1997. Memberships: General Editor, International Economic Association, 1986-2007; Councillor, 1979-92, Chairman, 1980-92, Central Asia and Caucasus Advisory Board, 1993-2003, Royal Institute of International Affairs; Trustee, Council of the Keston Institute, 1994-2002 and Cumberland Lodge, Windsor, 1987-2006; Former President, British Association of Former UN Civil Servants; Former President, Albania Society of Britain; Member, Advisory Group on Former Soviet and East European Studies of the Higher Education Funding Council for England; Reform Club. Honours: Papal Knighthood, Order of St Gregory; Knight's Cross of the Order of Merit, Poland; Order of Naim Frasheri, Albania; Hon DSocSc, Birmingham; Honorary Member, European Association of Comparative Economics. Address: 31 Capel Close, Oxford, OX2 7LA, England.

KASIPATHI Chinta, b. 17 October 1955, Rajahmundry, India. Professor of Geology. m. Hemalatha, 2 sons. Education: BSc, 1973, M Sc (Tech), 1976, PhD, 1981, Andhra University. Appointments: Research Assistant, 1976-80; Research Associate, 1980-84, Officer Pool, 1984; Lecturer, Assistant Professor, 1984-86; Reader, Associate Professor, 1986-94; Professor, 1998-; Supervised doctoral and masters theses; Supervised 28 PhD students; organised two national seminars and two national workshops; Consultant, several mining organisations; Adviser, national and international bodies. Publications: 168 research papers in field of Indian ore mineral studies; Editorial Board, 5 journals. Honour: Young Scientist Award, 1984; Recognised Qualified Person, Government of India; Man of the Year 2005; Vijay Rattan Award, IIFS, New Delhi; Glory of India Gold Medal, IISA; Bharata Jyothi Award, IISA; Gold Medal and Citation from Environmental Research Academy International, India. Memberships: New York Academy of Sciences; AGID; IGC; GSI; GMMSI; IMSA; IEA; IGC, India; IMA; IGI; IAGS; SGAT; MMR; JDW; FGW; INS; AEG; ISAG; Secretary, Andhra University Geology Alumni Association; FISCA; FAPA Sc; F GARC; FEnRA. Address: Department of Geology, Andhra University, Visakhapatnam 530 003, Andhra Pradesh, India.

KASPAROV Garri Kimovich, b. 13 April 1963, Baku. Chess Player. m. (1) Masha Kasparova, 1 daughter, (2) Yulia Kasparova, 1 son. Education: Azerbaijan Pedagogical Institute of Foreign Languages. Appointments: Azerbaijan Champion, 1975; USSR Junior Champion, 1975; International Master, 1979, International Grandmaster, 1980; World Junior Champion, 1980; Won USSR Championship, 1981, subsequently replacing Anatoliy Karpov at top of world ranking list; Won match against Viktor Korchnoi, challenged Karpov for World Title in Moscow, 1985, the match being adjourned due to the illness of both players; Won rescheduled match to become the youngest ever World Champion; Successfully defended his title against Karpov, 1986, 1987, 1990; Series of promotional matches in London, 1987; Won Times World Championship against Nigel Short, 1993; Stripped of title by World Chess Federation, 1993. Publication: Child of Change (with Donald Trelford), 1987; London-Leningrad Championship Games, 1987; Unlimited Challenge, 1990. Honours include: Oscar Chess Prize, 1982-83, 1985-89; World Chess Cup, 1989. Membership: Professional Chess Association. Address: Mezhdunarodnaya-2, Suite 1108, Krasnopresnenskaya nab 12, 123610 Moscow, Russia. E-mail: maiavia@dol.ru Website: www.kasparovchess.com

KASUYA Koichi, b. 1 February 1943, Osaka, Japan. University Professor. m. Keiko Nakamura, 2 sons. Education: BSME, 1965, MSME, 1967, PhD, Engineering, 1970, Osaka University, Japan. Appointments: Research Associate, Osaka University, 1970-78; Humbolt Fellow, University of Karsruhe, Germany, 1976-77; Associate Professor, Tokyo Institute of Technology, 1978-; Member, Advisory Committee, International Symposium on Gas Flow and Chemical Lasers and High Power Laser Conference, 1982-; Research Collaborator, Nagoya University, 1978-91, Osaka University, 1992-. Publications: Several books and many research reports on plasma engineering, laser developments, plasma and laser applications, nuclear fusion (science and technology). Honours: Prize of Kudo Foundation in Japan; Travels Grants, 1967-; Grants-in-Aid for Research Work, Ministry of Education and Hattori Foundation. Memberships: Institute of Electrical Engineering of Japan; Institute of Electric and Electronic Engineers, USA; American Physical Society; Japan Society of Plasma Science and Nuclear Fusion; Laser Society of Japan. Address: Department of Energy Sciences, Interdisciplinary Graduate School of Science and Engineering, Tokyo Institute of Technology, G3-35, 4259 Nagatuta, Midori-ku, Yokohama, Kanagawa 226-8502, Japan.

KATAI Satoshi, b. 1 November 1965, Ota-ku, Tokyo, Japan. Medical Doctor; Neurologist. m. Hiroko Masatsuka Katai, 1 daughter. Education: MD, 1991, PhD (Doctor of Medical Science), 2000, Shinshu University School of Medicine, Matsumoto, Nagano, Japan. Appointments: Resident in Internal Medicine, 3rd Department of Medicine, Shinshu University School of Medicine, Matsumoto, Nagano, Japan; Resident in Internal Medicine, Kenwakai Hospital, Ida, Nagano, Japan, 1992; Medical Staff, Internal Medicine, Komoro Kousei General Hospital, Komoro, Nagano, Japan, 1993; Medical Staff, Internal Medicine, Fukuyama Cardiovascular Hospital, Fukuyama, Hiroshima, Japan, 1994; Medical Staff, Internal Medicine (Neurology), Kakeyu Rehabilitation Centre and Clinic, Ueda, Nagano, Japan, 1995-; Visiting Scientist in Neurophysiology, Section of Brain Research, Primate Research Institute, Kyoto University, Inuyama, Aichi, Japan. Publications: Articles in medical journals as co-author include: A case of corticobasal degeneration presenting with primary progressive aphasia, 1997; Everyday memory Impairment in Parkinson's Disease, 1999; Event based and time based prospective memory in Parkinson's disease, 2003. Who's Who in Medicine and Healthcare, 2005; Great Minds of the 21st Century, 2006; Lifetime Achievement Award, 2006. Memberships: Japanese Society of Neurology; Japanese Neuroscience Society; Neuropsychology Association of Japan; Japan Society for Higher Brain Dysfunction. Address: Department of Neurology, Kakeyu Rehabilitation Centre and Clinic, 1308 Kakeyu Onsen, Ueda, Nagano 386-0396 Japan. E-mail: skatai@kakeyu-hp.com

KATILIUS Ramunas, b. 15 October 1935, Kaunas, Lithuania. Physicist; Scientific Researcher. m. Elmira Sabirova, 2 sons. Education: Diploma (cum laude), Faculty of Physics and Mathematics, Vilnius University, 1959; Postgraduate Studies, Institute of Physics and Mathematics, Lithuanian Academy of Sciences, Vilnius, 1959-62; Candidate of Physics and Mathematics (PhD), Institute for Semiconductors of the Academy of Sciences of the USSR, Leningrad, 1969; Doctor of Science (Physics and Mathematics), Ioffe Physical-Technical Institute of the Academy of Sciences of the USSR, Leningrad, 1986; Senior Research Fellow, Academy of Sciences of the USSR, 1989; Doctor Habilitatus (Nat Sci), Republic of Lithuania, 1993; Professor (Nat Sci), Vytautas Magnus University, 1993. Appointments: Junior Research Fellow,

Institute of Physics and Mathematics of the Lithuanian Academy of Sciences, Vilnius, 1962-66; Junior Research Fellow, Institute for Semiconductors of the Academy of Sciences of the USSR, Leningrad, 1966-72; Junior Research Fellow, Senior Research Fellow, Ioffe Physical-Technical Institute of the Academy of Sciences of the USSR, Leningrad, 1972-88; Extraordinary Professor, Faculty of Physics and Mathematics, 1992-93, Professor of Physics, Environment Research Faculty, 1993-2000, Vytautas Magnus University, Kaunas; Principal Research Fellow, Semiconductor Physics Institute, Vilnius, 1988-. Publications: Over 130 papers in professional journals; 7 review articles and book chapters; 3 books. Honours: Lithuanian National Science Award, 1995; ISI Citation Index: 500+. Memberships: Lithuanian Physical Society; Associate Member, Institute of Physics, UK; Board Member, Lithuanian Association of Non-Linear Analysis; Editorial Board Member, Nonlinear Analysis – Modelling and Control; Board Member, Open Society Fund, Lithuania, 1990-2000. Address: Semiconductor Physics Institute, Gostauto 11, Vilnius, LT-01108, Lithuania. E-mail: ramunas@osf.lt

KATSANOS Nicholas, b. 14 January 1930, New Agathoupolis, Greece. University Professor. m. Hara Sideri, 3 sons. Education: Doctorate Degree, Chemistry, 1963; Post-graduate Diploma in Radiochemistry, 1961; Degree in Chemistry, 1954. Appointments: Teaching Assistant, University of Thessaloniki, Greece; Research Associate, Head of Research Group, Professor of Physical Chemistry, Director of Physical, Inorganic and Nuclear Chemistry Department, University of Patras, Greece. Publications: Articles in international journals and/or presented in scientific symposia; 180 original research papers; 10 books in Greek; 2 books in English. Honours: Empirikion Scientific Prize, 1972; Academy of Athens Prize, 1983; Desty Memorial Prize, Waters Ltd. Memberships: Fellow and Chartered Chemist of Royal Society of Chemistry, England; Greek Chemist Association; Chromatographic Society; New Academy of Sciences. Address: 5 Chilonos Patreos, 26224 Patras, Greece.

KATSOURIS Andreas G, b. 1940, Meniko, Cyprus. Professor. m. Despoina, 2 daughters. Education: BA, MA, University of Athens, Greece, 1963; PhD, Greek Drama, University of Leeds, England, 1972. Appointments: Lecturer in Classics, 1973, Associate Professor, 1982, Full Professor, 1997-, University of Ioannina. Publications: 10 books; Many articles. Honours: Stipendiat, Alexander von Humboldt-Stiftung; Fellow, Center for Hellenic Studies. Address: Department of Classics, University of Ioannina, 45332 Ioannina, Greece.

KATSURA Fumiko, b. 21 February 1944, Kyoto, Japan. Professor. Education: BA, 1966, MA, 1968, Kyoto University; Visiting Scholar, UCLA, 1977-78; Visiting Scholar, St Edmunds College, 1989-90; Visiting Scholar, Cambridge, 1997; Research Fellow, Kyoto University, 2001-02. Appointments: Assistant, Kyoto University, 1970-72; Instructor, 1972-76, Associate Professor, 1976-91, Professor, 1991-, Ryukoku University; Owner and manager, Kameoka Katsura Hall (a private hall for classical music and cultural activities). Publications: A History of English Poetry; Men and Literature; For Those Who Read English Poetry; George Meredith's The Ordeal of Richard Feveral; B T Gates' Victorian Suicide; E B Browning's Aurora Leigh; English Sonnets from Southey to Swinburne. Memberships: The Browning Institute; The Renaissance Institute; The English Literary Society of Japan; The Victorian Studies Society of Japan. Address: 51 Hatago-Cho, Kameoka, Kyoto, Japan 621-0866.

KATZENBERG Jeffrey, b. 1950, USA. Film Executive. m. Marilyn Siegal, 1 son, 1 daughter. Appointments: Assistant to Chair, CEO, Paramount Pictures, NY, 1975-77; Executive Director, Marketing, Paramount TV, California, 1977, Vice President, Programming, 1977-78; Vice President, Feature Production, Paramount Pictures, 1978-80, Senior Vice President, Production, Motion Picture Division, 1980-82, President, Production, Motion Pictures & TV, 1982-94; Chairman, Walt Disney Studios, Burbank, California, 1994-; Co-Founder, Dreamworks SKG, 1995-. Address: Dreamworks SKG, 100 Flower Street, Glendale, CA 91201, USA.

KAUFFMAN Teresa Jo, b. 24 August 1951, San Francisco, California, USA. Professor; Creative Artist; Therapist; TV Writer; Producer; Director; Journalist. Education: BA, Journalism, University of California, Berkeley, 1974; Master's degree, Communication, University of Texas, Austin, 1980; PhD, Psychology, Communication and Creative Expression Therapy, The Union Institute, 1996, with distinction. Appointments: Writer, film and TV producer and director, artist, poet, composer of lyrics and melody, vocalist, expressive arts and communication therapist; Worked in television, radio and video for over 25 years; TV news anchor and reporter, ABC affiliate, 1974, Texas; Researcher, Writer, Alberta Educational Television, Canada, 1976; Senior writer-producer-director, Ampex Corporation, California, 1981; Lecturer, Department of Communication, North Carolina State University, 1985-2000; Early frame by frame computer art animation in the world; Adjunct faculty in Arts and Studies at NCSU, Adjunct Professor, Meredith College in Raleigh, former Adjunct Faculty, Department of Radio, Television and Motion Pictures, University of North Carolina in Chapel Hill; Teacher of a variety of arts and communication courses; Founder and Director of Creative Spaces. Publications include: Poetry; Textbook: The Script as Blueprint: Content and Form Working Together - Writing for Radio, television, Video and Film, 1997. Honours: 1 Emmy nomination; More than 15 first-place national television and video awards; National Broadcasting Society Outstanding Professional member of the Year, 1994; Outstanding Lecturer of the Year, College of Humanities and Social Sciences at North Carolina State University, 1996; Finalist Outstanding Teacher, North Carolina State University; Phi Kappa Phi. Memberships include: American Psychological Association; Berkeley Honor Society; California Scholastic Federation; National Association of Television Arts and Sciences; Also Community Service work in professional field. Address: 407 Furches St, Raleigh, NC 27607, USA.

KAULBARS Alexey Alexandrovich, b. 15 March 1964, Moscow, USSR. Economist. m. Nathalie Kovalyov. Education: Plekhanov Institute of National Economy, Moscow, 1981-86. Appointments: Economist, State Customs Committee, USSR, 1988-91; Accountant, 1991-94; General Director, JSC Business Trading, 1994-97; Deputy Director, 1997-98, Deputy Chairman, 1998-2004, Department of State Customs Committee, Russian Federation; First Deputy to Minister of Economic Development and Trade, 2003-04, Director, Foreign Trade Regulation Department, 2004-, Ministry of Economic Development and Trade, Russian Federation. Address: 4 General Antonov str, Moscow, 117279, Russia. E-mail: kaulbars@mail.ru

KAVATKAR Anita, b. 9 August 1969, Wai, Satara, India. Medical Doctor; Pathologist. m. Neelkanth C Kavatkar. Education: MBBS, 1990; MD, 1994. Appointments: Lecturer, 1995-2004, Associate Professor, 2004-, Department of Pathology, B J (Byramjee Jeejeebhoy) Medical College, Pune, Maharashtra, India. Publications: Articles in medical journals as co-author: Cytological study of neck masses with special emphasis on tuberculosis, 1996; Sclerosing mediastinitis with oesophageal involvement in miliary tuberculosis – A case report, 2000; Granulocytic sarcoma presenting as a mediastinal mass – a case report, 2002; Infantile Hepatic Hemangioendothelioma – A Case Report, 2003; Fatal Outcome of Colloid Cyst of Third Ventricle – A report of three cases, 2003; Fine needle aspiration cytology in lymphadenopathy of HIV positive patients, 2003; Autopsy study of maternal deaths, 2003; Benign linitis plastica – a case report, 2004. Honours: Smt Kuntidevi Mehrotra Award for research publication; International Fellowship, Indian Council of Medical Research, 2005; Listed in Who's Who publications and biographical dictionaries. Memberships: Life Member: Indian Association of Pathologists and Microbiologists, Research Society, BJ Medical College, Indian Academy of Cytologists. Address: BJ Medical College, Department of Pathology, Sassoon Road, Pune 411001, Maharashtra, India. E-mail: kavatkaranita@rediffmail.com

KAWAHATA Masahiro, b. 8 September 1936, Tokyo, Japan. Professor; Executive. m. Keiko Kohra, 1 son. Education: BE, Mechanical Engineering, 1960; ME, Control Engineering, 1963; PhD, Systems Engineering, 1966, University of Tokyo. Appointments: Consulting Professor, Electrical Engineering, Stanford University; Provost's Distinguished Visiting Professor, University of Southern California; Full Professor, Management Engineering, Tokai University; Visiting Professor, Industrial Engineering, University of Washington; Chairman/CEO of eCharge Co Ltd; Member of the Board of Directors, Terabeam Corporation; Senior Vice President, eCharge² Corp, Board Member, Visualant Inc, CEO Nextelligent Inc; Partner, The Branded Asset Management Group, LLC; Chairman & CEO, Branded Asset Management Group Co Ltd; Chairman & CEO, Visualant Co Ltd. Publications: 130 books and articles for professional journals. Honours: Awarded by Minister of International Trade and Industry for outstanding contribution to the development of Information Society of Japan, 1986; University of Washington Pioneer Award, 1995; Honoured by MITI for outstanding contribution for Public Understanding of High Technologies, 1996; University of Southern California Provost's Distinguished Visiting Professor, 1997. Memberships: Numerous memberships including: Board of Trustees, Japan Systems Engineering Society; Board of Trustees, Japan CAI Society; Board of Trustees, Seijo University and Affiliated Schools; Secretary IEEE Tokyo Branch. Address: 3-18-2 Denenchofu Ota-ku, Tokyo 145-0071, Japan.

KAWANO Ietoshi, b. 6 July 1941, Shimane, Japan. Electronics Engineer. m. Machiko, 2 sons. Education: BSEE, 1964, MS in Electronics, 1966, University of Kyoto. Appointments: Telecommunication Division, Hitachi Ltd, 1966-95; Executive Officer, Hitachi Shonan Denshi Co, 1995-2001; Assistant Professor, Shibaura Institute of Technology, 2003-. Publications: 14 papers in scientific journals. Honours: Hitachi President Award in Software Engineering; Listed in international biographical dictionaries. Memberships: IEEE; Information Processing Society of Japan; The Institute of Electronics, Information and Communication Engineers. Address: 1-5-9-36 Osone, Kohoku-ku, Yokohama 222-0003, Japan. E-mail: ikawano@dream.com

KAY Steven Walton, b. 4 August 1954, Amman, Jordan. Lawyer; Barrister. m. Valerie, 1 son, 1 daughter. Education: Epsom College; LLB (Hons), Leeds University; Inns of Court School of Law, 1976-77. Appointments: Called to the Bar, Inner Temple, 1977; Bar Rights of Audience in the Crown Court, 1995; Bar Council Committee, Efficiency in the Criminal Justice System, 1994; Prime Minister's Special Committee on Victims in the Criminal Justice System, 1995; Secretary Criminal Bar Association, 1993-96; Queens Counsel, 1997; Recorder, 1997; Treasurer, European Criminal Bar Association, 1998-2000; Defence Counsel, Dusko Tadic, UN International Criminal Tribunal for the Former Yugoslavia , 1996; Defence Counsel, Alfred Musema, UN Criminal Tribunal for Rwanda, 1997-; Amicus Curiae, Trial of Slobodan Milosevic, UN International Tribunal for the Former Yugoslavia, 2001-04; Assigned Counsel, Slobodan Milosevic, 2004-2006; Advising Syria re: UN Resolutions 1595, 1636, 1644, 2005; Other notable trials include: R-v-Winzar (an allegation of murder by insulin injection); R-v-Lomas (a European agricultural regulations fraud); R-v-Hannon (an international time share fraud); R-v-Clemente (an international money laundering case). Publication: Role of Defence in International Criminal Court, Commentary on ICC (editors: Casese, Jones, Gaeta), 2003. Honour: QC, 1997. Memberships: Criminal Bar Association; Forensic Science Society; Association of Defence Council. Listed in national biographical dictionaries. Address: 9 Bedford Row, London WC1R 4HD, England. E-mail: goodnightvienna@gmail.com

KAY Vernon, b. 28 April 1974, Bolton, England. TV Presenter; DJ; Former Model. m. Tess Daly, 2003, 1 daughter. Career: Model; DJ, BBC Radio 1, 2004-; TV appearances: T4, Channel 4 TV; Boys and Girls, 2003; A Wife for William, 2004; HeadJam, 2004; Hit Me Baby One More Time, 2005; The Prince's Trust 30th Birthday: Live, 2006; All Star Family Fortunes, 2006-; Co-presenter, with Tess Daly, Just the Two of Us, 2006; Gameshow Marathan, 2006, 2007; Extras, 2007; Thank God You're Here, 2008; Happy Birthday Brucie! 2008.

KAYO Olga S, b. 27 June 1979, Letnerechenskij, Karelia, USSR. Senior Algorithm Designer. m. Sila Kayo, 1 daughter. Education: MSc, University of Joensuu, Finland, 2001; Diploma, St Petersburg State University, Russia, 2002; PhD (Dr Tech), University of Oulu, Finland, 2006. Appointments: Researcher, 2001-02, Senior Researcher, 2002-06, University of Oulu, Finland; Senior Algorithm Designer, Nokia, 2007-. Publications: 13 conference and journal papers including: Incremental locally linear embedding, 2005. Honours: Best Finnish Master's Thesis in Pattern Recognition, Pattern Recognition Society of Finland, 2001. Memberships: Pattern Recognition Society of Finland.

KAZANTZIS Judith, b. 14 August 1940, Oxford, England. Poet; Fiction Writer. 1 son, 1 daughter. Education: Honours Degree, Modern History, Oxford, 1961. Appointments: General Council, Poetry Society, member, 1991-94; Royal Literary Fund fellow, University of Sussex, 2005-2006. Publications: Non Fiction: The Gordon Riots, 1966; Women in Revolt, 1968; Poetry Collections: Minefield, 1977; The Wicked Queen, 1980; Touch Papers (co-author), 1982; Let's Pretend, 1984; Flame Tree, 1988; A Poem for Guatemala, pamphlet, 1988; The Rabbit Magician Plate, 1992; Selected Poems 1977-92, 1995; Swimming Through the Grand Hotel, 1997; The Odysseus Papers: Fictions on the Odyssey of Homer, 1999; In Cyclops' Cave, Homeric translation, 2002; Just After Midnight, 2004; Fiction: Of Love And Terror, 2002; Short Fiction: London Magazine; Comparative Criticism; Critical Quarterly; Serpents Tail Anthologies; Contributions to: Stand; Agenda; London Magazine; Poetry London; Poetry Wales; New Statesman; Red Pepper; Poetry Review; Ambit; Verse; Honest Ulsterman; Anthologies: Poems on the Underground;

Key West Reader; Faber Book of Blue Verse; Virago Book of Love Poetry; Second Light Anthologies; The Light Unlocked; Red Sky at Night; Criticism: Poetry in Poetry Review, London Magazine; Fiction, in Banipal, 2007-08. Honours: Judge, Sheffield Hallam Poetry Competition, 1995-96; Judge, Stand International Poetry Competition, 1998; Royal Literary Fund Fellow, University of Sussex, 2005-06; Cholmondeley Award, 2007. Memberships: CND; Palestine Solidarity Campaign. Address: 32 St Annes Crescent, Lewes, East Sussex, BN7 1SB, England. Website: www.judithkazantzis.com

KAZI Rehan, b. 24 August 1972, Bombay, India. Head & Neck Cancer Surgeon. m. Irfana, 1 son. Education: MBBS, 1995; MS, 1998; DNB, 2002; DOHNS (Eng), 2004; DLORCS (Eng), 2002; PhD (London), 2007. Appointments: Consultant Head and Neck Cancer Surgeon, Jaslok, Saifee, and Holy Family Hospitals, Mumbai. Publications: Over 20 scientific articles in national and international peer-reviewed journals; Presented papers and posters at more than 25 international and national meetings/workshops; Written and contributed to chapters in 3 medical books and numerous patient education leaflets. Honours: ICRETT Scholarship for MSC Institute, Poland, UICC; International Scholarship, Sun Yat Sen Cancer Centre, Taipei, Taiwan; ICRETT Scholarship, to Royal Marsden Hospital, London, UICC; Cancer Aid Foundation Merit Award, Cancer Aid Foundation, Bombay, 2004; Byers Award, American Head and Neck Society, Chicago, USA, 2006; British Journal of Surgery Prize, British Association of Surgical Oncology, 2006. Memberships: Numerous head-neck professional bodies and societies; Secretary General, CARF (cancer NGO). Address: Bridge View, 10th Floor, 16 Hansraj Lane, Byculla, Bombay 400027, India. E-mail: rehan_kazi@yahoo.com Website: headandneckcancersurgeon.com

KAZIM Ahmed, b. 1 January 1932, Dubai, United Arab Emirates. Orthopaedic Surgeon. m. Sultana, 1 son, 2 daughters. Education: Fellow, Royal College of Surgeons, Edinburgh, 1958; Fellow, Royal College of Surgeons, London, 1960. Appointments: Senior Orthopaedic Surgeon, Trinidad, West Indies, 1966-74; Head of Orthopaedic Department, Dubai Hospital, Dubai, United Arab Emirates, 1976-2003. Publications: For Whom the Bell Tolls, 1996. Honours: Lisboa Gold Medal, University of Bombay; Honorary Consul General for Pakistan in Trinidad, West Indies. Memberships: British Orthopaedic Association; American Academy of Orthopaedic Surgeons. Address: PO Box 11889, Dubai, United Arab Emirates. E-mail: aakazim@emirates.nat.ae

KE Bin, b. 10 December 1953, Guangxi, China. Physician; Researcher. m. Yunfei Liang, 1 daughter. Education: Bachelor, Medical diploma, Guangxi Medical University, Guangxi, 1978; Doctor of Medicine, School of Medicine, Ryukyu University, Okinawa, Japan, 1992. Appointments: Physician, Guangxi Province General Hospital, Guangxi, China, 1978-88; Researcher, Okinawa Health Center, Okinawa, Japan, 1993-96; Guest Professor, Guangxi University of Chinese Medicine, Guangxi, 1998-; Senior Researcher, Medical Consultant, EM Research Organization, Okinawa, 1997-; Vice Director, EM Wellness Center, Okinawa, 2005-. Publications: 3 books: EM Medical Revolution, 2000; Get Rid of Sub-Health, 2005; Clinical and Basic Medical Research on EM-X, 2000-04; Articles: Evaluation of the toxicity and safety of the antioxidant beverage effective micro-organisms-X (EM-X) in animal models. Honours: Listed in international biographical dictionaries. Memberships: Vice Chairperson of Chinese Society of Sub-Health; Fellow, Okinawa Society of Alternative Medicine; Member, Japanese Society of Diabetes.

Address: Effective Micro-Organisms Wellness Center, 1478 Kishaba, Kitanagausuku, Okinawa 901-2311, Japan. E-mail: kebin@emro.co.jp

KEACH Stacy, b. 2 June 1941, Savannah, Georgia, USA. Actor; Director. m. Malgossia Tomassi, 1986, 2 daughters. Career: Plays: Hamlet, 1964; A Long Day's Journey into Night; Macbird; Indians; Deathtrap; Hughie; Barnum; Cyrano de Bergerac; Peer Gynt; Henry IV (Parts I & II); Idiot's Delight; The King and I, 1989; Love Letters, 1990-93; Richard III, 1991; Stieglitz Loves O'Keefe, 1995; Director: Incident at Vichy; Six Characters in Search of an Author; Films: The Heart is a Lonely Hunter; End of the Road; The Travelling Executioner; Brewster McCloud; Doc; Judge Roy Bean; The New Centurions; Fat City; The Killer Inside Me; Conduct Unbecoming; Luther; Street People; The Squeeze; Gray Lady Down; The Ninth Configuration; The Long Riders; Road Games; Butterfly; Up in Smoke; Nice Dreams; That Championship Season; The Lover; False Identity; The Forgotten Milena; John Carpenter's Escape from LA, Prey of the Jaguar, 1996; The Truth Configuration, American History X, 1998; Icebreaker, 1999; Unshackled, Militia, Mercy Streets, 2000; Sunstorm, 2001; When Eagles Strike, Jesus, Mary and Joey, 2003; Caught in the Headlights, Galaxy Hunter, El Padrino, The Hollow, 2004; Man with the Screaming Brain, Keep Your Distance, 2005; Come Early Morning, Jesus, Mary and Joey, Death Row, 2006; Honeydipper, 2007; The Portal, 2008; TV: Mike Hammer, Private Eye, 1997; The Courage to Love, Titus, 2000; Lightning: Fire From The Sky, 2001; Rods! The Santa Trap, 2002; Miracle Dogs, Frozen Impact, 2003; Prison Break, 2005-07; ER, 2007. Publications: Keach, Go Home! 1996. Memberships: Artists Committee, Kennedy Center Honors, 1986-; Hon Chair, American Cleft Palate Foundation, 1995-. Honours: Vernon Rice Drama Desk Award; 3 Obie Awards; Pasadena Playhouse Alumni Man of the Year, 1995; Pacific Pioneers Broadcasters' Association Diamond Circle Award, 1996. Address: c/o Palmer & Associates, #950, 23852 Pacific Coast Highway, Malibu, CA 90265, USA.

KEANE Fergal Patrick, b. 6 January 1961, Ireland. Journalist; Broadcaster. m. Anne Frances Flaherty, 1986, 1 son. Education: Terenure College, Dublin; Presentation College, Cork. Appointments: Trainee Reporter, Limerick Leader, 1979-82; Reporter, Irish Press Group, Dublin, 1982-84, Radio Telefis, Eireann, Belfast, 1986-89 (Dublin 1984-86); Northern Ireland Correspondent, BBC Radio, 1989-91, South Africa Correspondent, 1991-94, Asia Correspondent, 1994-97, Special Correspondent, 1997-; Presenter, Fergal Keane's Forgotten Britain, BBC, 2000. Publications: Irish Politics Now, 1987; The Bondage of Fear, 1994; Season of Blood: A Rwandan Journey, 1995; Letter to Daniel, 1996; Letters Home, 1999; A Stranger's Eye, 2000; There Will be Sunlight Later: A Memoir of War, 2004; All of These People, 2006. Honours: Reporter of the Year Sony Silver Award, 1992, Sony Gold Award, 1993; International Reporter of the Year, 1993; Amnesty International Press Awards; RTS Journalist of the Year, 1994; OBE, 1996; BAFTA Award, 1997; Hon DLitt, Strathclyde, 2001, Staffordshire, 2002. Address: c/o BBC Television, Wood Lane, London W12 7RJ, England.

KEANE Marie-Henry, b. 26 May 1937, Limerick, Ireland. Theologian; Academic. Education: University of South Africa; Visiting Scholar, Catholic University of America; Harvard Divinity School and Weston School of Theology, Cambridge, Massachusetts, USA; BA (Hons); BTh, BTh (Hons); MTh; DTh; South Africa Teacher's Diploma, Natal; Dip Rel Educ, London. Appointments: Associate Professor, Department of Systematic Theology and Theological Ethics,

University of South Africa; Visiting Professor, Pastoral Institute, Johannesburg, South Africa; External Examiner, Natal University, South Africa; External Examiner, Rhodes University, South Africa; President, Dominican Association of England and Ireland; Tutor, Systematic Theology, 1994-2000; Administrator, Niland Conference Centre, Bushey Heath. Publications: Word and Life, 1981; The Meaning in of History, 1990; Towards an Authentic and Transforming Spirituality for Women in South Africa, 1991; Women in the Theological Anthropology of the Early Fathers, 1988; Harvard and Women's Contributions to the University, 1992; Freedom, Theology and Deliverance, 1995; A Theology and Spirituality of Divine and Human Compassion with Special Reference to the Stewardship of Earth, 1998; The Church as Servant in Today's World, 2000; Doctoral thesis, The Pathos of God as the Theological Basis for a Servant Model of Church. Address: Rosary Priory, 93 Elstree Road, Bushey, Bushey Heath, Herts WD23 4EE, England. E-mail: mhkeaneop@nilandcentre.co.uk

KEANELY Terri Lilya, b. 21 March 1938, Fort Stockton, Texas, USA. Consultant; Educator; Artist. m. Roger C Keanely, 2 daughters. Education: Licensed Massage Therapist. Career: Consultant (Personal Growth and Development Director, Motivator, Teacher, Adviser, Author, Counsellor); Artist/Photographer, 11 pictures displayed at The George Bush Library and Museum, College Station, Texas; Founder, Krashada Acupressure Body Work Therapy; Creator, Multi-Body Release (Method of Releasing, Cleansing and Healing Traumas on Physical, Emotional, Mental and Spiritual Levels); Dress Designer/Dressmaker, 15 years; Jeweller, over 30 years. Publications: The Heaven and Earth Photo Collection; A Balanced Path to Mastery and Enlightenment, 1971. Honours: Speaker, Leader, Business and Professional Women's Convention, Dallas, Texas, 1972; Speaker, 7th International Human Unity Conference, Chicago, Illinois, 1980; Name placed on Wall of Tolerance, 2004; Best Jeweller in the Southwest Award, Art and Craft Shows. Memberships: National Association for Female Executives; National Campaign for Tolerance. Address: Dallas, TX 75220, USA.

KEATING Henry Reymond Fitzwalter, b. 31 October 1926, St Leonards-on-Sea, Sussex, England. Author. m. Sheila Mary Mitchell, 1953, 3 sons, 1 daughter. Education: BA, Trinity College, Dublin. Publications: The Perfect Murder, 1964; Inspector Ghote Trusts the Heart, 1972; The Lucky Alphonse, 1982; Under a Monsoon Cloud, 1986; Dead on Time, 1989; The Iciest Sin, 1990; The Man Who (editor), 1992; The Rich Detective, 1993; Doing Wrong, 1994; The Good Detective, 1995; The Bad Detective, 1996; Asking Questions, 1996; The Soft Detective, 1997; Bribery, Corruption Also, 1999; Jack the Lady Killer, 1999; The Hard Detective, 2000; Breaking and Entering, 2000; The Dreaming Detective, 2002; A Detective at Death's Door, 2003; One Man and His Bomb, 2006; Rules, Regs and Rotton Eggs, 2007; Inspector Ghote's First Case, 2008; Contributions to: Crime books reviews, The Times, 1967-83. Honours: Gold Dagger Awards, 1964, 1980, Diamond Dagger Award, 1996, Crime Writers Association. Memberships: Crime Writers Association, chairman, 1970-71; Detection Club, president, 1986-2001; Royal Society of Literature, fellow; Society of Authors, chairman, 1982-83. Address: 35 Northumberland Place, London W2 5AS, England.

KEATING Paul John, b. 18 January 1944. Australian Politician. m. Anna Johanna Maria Van Iersel, 1975, 1 son, 3 daughters. Education: De La Salle College, Bankstown, New South Wales. Appointments: Research Officer, Federal

Municipal & Shire Council Employees Union of Australia, 1967; MP for Blaxland, 1969-96; Minister for Northern Australia, 1975; Shadow Minister for Agriculture, 1976, for Minerals & Energy, 1976-80, for Resources & Energy, 1980-83; Shadow Treasurer, 1983; Federal Treasurer of Australia, 1983-91; Deputy Prime Minister, 1990-91; Prime Minister of Australia, 1991-96. Publication: Engagement: Australia Faces the Asia Pacific, 2000. Memberships: Chairman, Australian Institute of Music, 1999-; Board of Architects of New South Wales, 2000-.

KEATING Ronan, b. 3 March 1977, Dublin, Ireland. Vocalist. m. Yvonne, 1 son, 1 daughter. Career: Lead Singer, Boyzone; Co-Host, Eurovision Song Contest, Ireland. Recordings: Singles: Working My Way Back To You, 1994; Key To My Life, Love Me For A Reason, So Good, Father and Son, Coming Home Now, 1995; Words, 1996; Isn't It A Wonder, Baby Can I Hold You Tonight, Mystical Experience, 1997; I Love The Way You Love Me, You Needed Me, Solo: When You Say Nothing At All, Everyday I Love You, 1999; Life Is a Rollercoaster, The Way You Make Me Feel, 2000; Lovin' Each Day, 2001; If Tomorrow Never Comes, I Love The Way We Do, We've Got Tonight, 2002; Iris, 2006. Albums: Different Beat, 1996; Where We Belong, 1998; By Request – the Greatest Hits, 1999; Ronan, 2000; Destination, Turn It On, 2002; 10 Years of Hits, 2004; Bring You Home, 2006. Publications: No Matter What, 2000; Life is a Rollercoaster, 2000.. Honours: BMI European song-writing Award, 2003; Fair Trade Ambassador for Christian Aid. Address: The Outside Organisation, 180-182 Tottenham Court Road, London, W1P 9LE, England.

KEATON Diane, b. 5 January 1946, California, USA. Adopted 2 children. Education: Student at Neighbourhood Playhouse, New York. Career: Theatre in New York includes: Hair, 1968; The Primary English Class, 1976; Films include: Lovers and Other Strangers, 1970; The Godfather, 1972; Sleeper, 1973; Annie Hall, 1977; Manhattan, 1979; Shoot the Moon, 1982; Crimes of the Heart, 1986; Baby Boom, 1988; The Godfather III, 1991; Manhattan Murder Mystery, 1993; Father of Bride II, 1995; Marvins's Room, The First Wives Club, 1996; The Only Thrill, 1997; Hanging Up (also director), The Other Sister, Town and Country, 1999; Sister Mary Explains It All, 2001; Wildflower, 2002; Something's Gotta Give, 2003; Terminal Impact, The Family Stone, 2005; Because I Said So, Smother, 2007; Mama's Boy, Mad Money, 2008. Publications: Reservations, Still Life, editor. Honours: Academy Award, Best Actress, 1977; Golden Globe Award, Best Actress in a Musical or Comedy, 2004. Address: c/o John Burnham, William Morris Agency, 151 El Camino, Beverly Hills, CA 90212, USA.

KEATON Michael, b. 9 September 1951, Pittsburgh, USA. Actor. m. Caroline MacWilliams, divorced, 1 son. Education: Kent State University. Appointments: With Comedy Group, Second City, Los Angeles; TV appearances include: All in the Family; Maude; Mary Tyler Moore Show; Working Stiffs; Report to Murphy; Roosevelt and Truman (TV film); Body Shots (producer), 1999. Creative Works: Films: Night Shift, 1982; Mr Mom, 1983; Johnny Dangerously, 1984; Touch and Go, Gung Ho, 1987; Beetlejuice, Clean and Sober, 1988; The Dream Team, Batman, 1989; Much Ado About Nothing, 1992; My Life, The Paper, Speechless, 1994; Multiplicity, Jackie Brown, 1997; Desperate Measures, Jack Frost, 1998; A Shot at Glory, 2000; Quicksand, 2001; First Daughter, 2004; White Noise, Game 6, Herbie Fully Loaded, 2005; Cars (voice), The Last Time, 2006. Address: c/o ICM Management, 8942 Wilshire Boulevard, Beverly Hills, CA 90211, USA.

KEATS Reynold Gilbert, b. 15 February 1918, Pt Pirie, South Australia, Australia. Emeritus Professor of Mathematics. m. Verna Joy, 2 daughters. Education: Diploma in Accountancy, 1939; BSc, 1948, PhD, 1966, University of Adelaide. Appointments: Clerk, Savings Bank of South Australia, 1934-40; Private to Lieutenant, 2/48th Battalion, Australian Imperial Forces, 1940-45; Visiting Research Scientist, Royal Aircraft Establishment, Farnborough, England, 1948-51; Scientific Officer, Australian Government Department of Supply, Melbourne, Victoria, 1951, 1952; Senior Scientific Officer, 1952-57, Principal Scientific Officer, 1957-61, Australian Government Department of Supply, Weapons Research Establishment, Salisbury, South Australia; Senior Lecturer, University of Adelaide, South Australia, 1961-67; Professor of Mathematics, 1968-83, Dean, Faculty of Mathematics, 1971-76, 1980-83, Member of Council, 1977, 1978, Deputy Chairman of Senate, 1977, 1978, Emeritus Professor, 1983-, Honorary Professor, 1984-88, University of Newcastle, New South Wales. Honours: Fellow, Australian Society of Certified Practising Accountants, 1952; Fellow, Institute of Mathematics and its Applications, 1973; Honorary DMath, University of Waterloo, Ontario, Canada, 1979; Chartered Mathematician, Institute of Mathematics and its Applications, 1993; Fellow, Australian Mathematical Society, 1995; Fellow, Australian Computer Society, 1997. Membership: The Legacy Club of Newcastle. Address: 39 Woodward St, Merewether, NSW 2291, Australia.

KEATS-ROHAN Katharine S B, b. 3 June 1957. Historian. m. John Lyttleton Lloyd, deceased 2004, 1 son. Education: BA, History, 1984, MA, Medieval Studies, 1985, PhD, Classics, 1987, London. Appointments: Junior Research Fellow, Linacre College, Oxford, 1987-89; Research Assistant, Department of History, University of Sheffield, 1988-89; Adjunct (Research) Fellow, Linacre College, Oxford, 1992-97; Founder and Director, Unit for Prosopographical Research, 1993-; Fellow, European Humanities Research Centre, Oxford, 1997-. Publications include: Ioannis Saresberiensis Metalogicon (co-editor), 1991; Ioannis Saresberiensis Policraticus Libri I-IV (V-VII to follow), 1993; Domesday Names: An Index of personal and Place Names in Domesday Book, 1997; Domesday People: A Prosopography of Persons Occurring in English Documents 1066-1166, Volume I, Domesday Book, 1999; Continental Origins of English Landholders 1966-1166 Database, 2002; Domesday Descendants: A Prosopography of Persons Occurring in English Documents 1066-1166 Volume II Pipe Rolls to Cartae Baronum, 2002; The Cartulary of the Abbey of Mont-Saint-Michel, 2006; Editor, Prosopography Approaches and Applications A Handbook, 2007; Numerous articles in academic journals and conference proceedings; General editor and publisher, Prosopographica et Genealogica (www.coelweb.co.uk). Honours: W F Masom Scholarship in Classics, University of London, 1986-88; Clay Scholarship, Bedford College, London, 1985-86; British Council Research Visitor to the University of Prague, 1985; Leverhulme Trust Grant, 1992-96; Prix Brant IV de Koskull 1998 for Domesday People, Confédération Internationale de Généalogie et d'Héraldique. Memberships: Société d'Histoire et d'Archéologie de Bretagne, 1991-; Haskins Society, 1991-; Fellow, Royal Historical Society, 2002. Address: European Humanities Research Centre, 41 Wellington Square, Oxford OX1 2JF, England. E-mail: katharine.keats-rohan@history.ox.ac.uk

KEAY John (Stanley Melville), b. 18 September 1941, Devon, England. Author. Education: BA, Magdalen College, Oxford, 1963. Publications: Into India, 1973; When Men and Mountains Meet, 1977; The Gilgit Game, 1979; India

Discovered, 1981; Eccentric Travellers, 1982; Highland Drove, 1984; Explorers Extraordinary, 1985; The Royal Geographical Society's History of World Exploration, 1991; The Honourable Company, 1991; Collins Encyclopaedia of Scotland, 1994; Indonesia: From Sabang to Meranke, 1995; The Explorers of the Western Himalayas, 1996; Last Post, 1997; India: A History, 2000; The Great Arc, 2000; Sowing the Wind, 2003; Mad About the Mekong, 2005; The Spice Route, 2005. Address: Succoth, Dalmally, Argyll, Scotland.

KEEFFE Barrie (Colin), b. 31 October 1945, London, England. Playwright. m. (1) Dee Truman, 1969, divorced 1979, (2) Verity Bargate, 1981, deceased 1981, 2 stepsons, (3) Julia Lindsay, 1983, divorced 1993. Appointments: Writer; Actor; Director; Journalist; Tutor; Dramatist-in-Residence, Shaw Theatre, London, 1977, Royal Shakespeare Company, 1978; Associate Writer, Theatre Royal Stratford East, London, 1986-91; Board of Directors, Soho Poly Theatre, 1976-81; Associate Director, Soho Poly Theatre, 1989-96; Board of Directors, Theatre Royal, Stratford East, 1981-89; Ambassador, United Nations, 50th anniversary year, 1995; Tutor, City University, London, 2002-05; Judith E Wilson Fellow, Christ's College Cambridge, 2003-4. Plays: A Mad World, My Masters, 1977, Gimme Shelter, 1977; Barbarians, 1977; Frozen Assets, 1978, revised version, 1987; Sus, 1979; Heaven Scent, 1979; Bastard Angel, 1980; Black Lear, 1980; She's So Modern, 1980; Chorus Girls, 1981; A Gentle Spirit (with Jules Croiset), 1981; The Long Good Friday (screenplay), 1984; Better Times, 1985; King of England, 1986; My Girl, 1989; Not Fade Away, 1990; Wild Justice, 1990; I Only Want to Be With You, 1997; Shadows on the Sun, 2001; Still Killing Time, 2006; Novels: Gadabout, 1969; No Excuses, 1983; Journalism: Numerous articles contributed to national newspapers, including Sunday Times; The Independent; The Guardian; Evening Standard. As Director: A Certain Vincent, 1974; A Gentle Spirit, 1980; The Gary Oldman Fan Club, 1998. Radio Plays: Good Old Uncle Jack, 1975; Pigeon Skyline, 1975; Self-Portrait, 1977; Paradise, 1990; On the Eve of the Millennium, 1999; Tales, 2000; Feng Shui and Me, 2000; The Five of Us, 2002. Television Plays: Gotcha, 1977; Champions, 1978; Hanging Around, 1978; Nipper, 1978; Waterloo Sunset, 1979; No Excuses Series, 1983; King, 1984; Honours: French Critics Prix Revelation, 1978; Giles Cooper Award, Best Radio Plays, 1978; Edgar Allan Poe Award, Mystery Writers of America, 1982. Membership: Société des Auteurs et Compositeurs Dramatiques. Address: 110 Annandale Road, London SE10 0JZ, England.

KEEFFE Emmet Britton, b. 12 April 1942, San Francisco, California, USA. Physician. m. Melenie Marie Laskey, 2 sons, 1 daughter. Education: BS, 1964, Teaching Credential, 1965, University of San Francisco, California, USA; MD, Creighton University, 1969; Intern and Resident, Gastrointestinal Fellow, Oregon Health and Science University, 1974; Liver Fellow, University of California, San Francisco, 1979. Appointments: Professor of Medicine, Oregon Health and Science University, 1979-92; Clinical Professor of Medicine, UCSF, 1992-95; Medical Director, Liver Transplant Program and Chief, Division of Gastroenterology, California Pacific Medical Center, 1992-95; Professor of Medicine, Chief of Hepatology, Medical Director of Liver Transplant Program, Stanford University Medical Center, 1995-2008; Vice President and Chief Medical Officer, Romark Laboratories, LC. Publication: Flexible Sigmoidoscopy, 1985; Handbook of Liver Disease, 1998, 2004; Atlas of Gastrointestinal Endoscopy, 1998. Honours: Best Doctors in America, Cited, 1992, 1994; America's Top Doctors, 2000-08. Memberships: President, 1995, American Society for Gastrointestinal Endosocopy;

Board of Directors, 1991-95, American Liver Foundation; President, 1991, Western Gut Club; President, 2004, American Gastroenterological Association; American Association for the Study of Liver Diseases; Master, American College of Physicians; American Gastroenterological Association; American Society for Gastrointestinal Endoscopy; Royal College of Physicians of Ireland; Fellow, American College of Gastroenterology; American Medical Association. Address: Stanford University Medical Center, 750 Welch Road, Suite 210, Palo Alto CA 94304-1509, USA.

KEEGAN John (Desmond Patrick) (Sir), b. 15 May 1934, London, England. Editor; Writer; Defence Correspondent. m. Susanne Everett, 1960, 2 sons, 2 daughters. Education: BA, 1957, MA, 1962, Balliol College, Oxford. Appointments: Senior Lecturer in Military History, Royal Military Academy, Sandhurst, 1960-86; Fellow, Princeton University, 1984; Defence Editor, Daily Telegraph, 1986-; Delmas Distinguished Professor of History, Vassar College, 1997. Publications: The Face of Battle, 1976; Who's Who in Miltary History (co-author), 1976; World Armies (editor), 1979, new edition, 1982; Six Armies in Normandy, 1982; Zones of Conflict (co-author), 1986; The Mask of Command, 1987; The Price of Admiralty, 1988, reissued as Battle at Sea, 1993; The Times Atlas of the Second World War, 1989; Churchill's Generals (editor), 1991; A History of Warfare, 1993; Warpaths: Travels of a Military Historian in North America, 1995; War and Our World: The Reith Lectures, 1998; The Penguin Book of the War: great miltary writings (editor), 1999; Winston Chruchill, 2002; Intelligence in War, 2003; The Iraq War, 2004. Honours: Officer of the Order of the British Empire, 1991; Duff Cooper Prize, 1994; Honorary Doctor of Law, University of New Brunswick, 1997; Honorary Doctor of Literature, Queen's University, Belfast, 2000; Knighted, 2000; Honorary Doctor of Letters, University of Bath, 2001. Address: The Manor House, Kilmington, near Warminster, Wilts BA12 6RD, England.

KEEGAN Kevin Joseph, b. 14 February 1951, Armthorpe, England. Professional football manager; Former professional football player. m. (1) Jean Woodhouse, 1974, 2 daughters. Career: Player: Scunthorpe United, Liverpool, 1971-77 (won League Championships three times, FA Cup 1974, European Cup, 1977, UEFA Cup, 1973, 1976), SV Hamburg, 1977-80, Southampton, 1980-82, Newcastle United, 1982-84; Retired, 1984; Scored 274 goals in approximately 800 appearances; Capped for England 63 times (31 as captain), scoring 21 goals; Manager: Newcastle United, 1992-97; Fulham, 1998-99, England national team, 1999-2000, Manchester City, 2001-05. Publications: Kevin Keegan, 1978; Against the World: Playing for England, 1979; Kevin Keegan: My Autobiography, 1997. Honours: Footballer of the Year, 1976; European Footballer of the Year, 1978, 1979. Address: c/o Manchester City Football Club, City of Manchester Stadium, Manchester, England.

KEEN Richard, b. 29 March 1954, Rustington, Sussex, England. Queen's Counsel. m. Jane Carolyn Anderson, 1 son, 1 daughter. Education: Beckman Scholar, University of Edinburgh. Appointments: Admitted to Faculty of Advocates (Scottish Bar), 1980; Counsel to DTI in Scotland, 1986-93; Queen's Counsel, 1993-; Chairman, Appeal Committee, Institute of Chartered Accountants Scotland (ICAS), 1996-. Treasure, Faculty of Advocates. Address: The Castle, Elie, Fife KY9 1DN, Scotland. E-mail: rskeenqc@compuserve.com

KEENE Raymond Dennis, b. 29 January 1948, London, England. Author; Publisher. m. Annette Sara Goodman Keene, 1 son. Education: MA, Trinity College, Cambridge, 1967-72.

Career: Chess Correspondent, The Spectator, 1977-; Co-owner, GM Racing (winner of 1984/85 UK historic Formula 3 Championship); The Times, 1985-; The Sunday Times, 1996-; International Herald Tribune, 2001-08; Organiser, World Chess Championships, London, 1986, 1993, 2000; Director, Hardinge Simpole Publishing; Organiser, World Memory Championship; Founding President, Commonwealth Chess Association; International Arbiter of Mental World Records & Director of The International Academy of Mental World Records. Publications: 130 books written and published on chess; Daily chess article in The Times; Weekly chess column in The Spectator and the Sunday Times; Weekly IQ column in The Times. Honours: International Chess Grandmaster, 1976; OBE, 1985. Memberships: The Garrick; Director, The Brain Trust Charity. Address: 86 Clapham Common, North Side, London SW4 9SE, UK. E-mail: rdkobe@aol.com

KEESOM Pierre Henri Marie, b. 21 August 1943, Heerleu, The Netherlands. Trademark Attorney; Translator. m. Xiaodu Liu, 3 sons. Education: Sworn Translator (English), Sworn Translator (French), 1981; JDrs, Catholic University, Nymegen, 1988; idem Interpreter (French), 2002; Diploma, Justice Department, Translator and Interpreter (English), 2004. Appointments: Trademark Attorney, Member of Management Team, Markgraaf, 1965-75; Principal, Keesom & Hendriks, 1975-. Publications: The New Benelux Trade Marks Act, 1986; Contributor of many articles to professional publications. Honours: Knight 6th Grade; Order of Orange – Nassau; Officer, Most Venerable Order of the Hospital of St John of Jerusalem. Memberships: Fellow, Chartered Institute of Linguists; Fellow, Royal Society for the Encouragement of the Arts, Manufacturers & Commerce; Member, Netherlands Association of Interpreters and Translators; Member, Royal Netherlands Society for Genealogy and Heraldry. E-mail: phmkeesom@keesom.hl Website: www.keesom.nl

KEEY Roger Brian, b. 11 March 1934, Birmingham, England. Chemical Engineer. m. Daphne Pearl Griffiths, 18 March 1959, 1 son, 3 daughters. Education: BSc, 1954; PhD, University of Birmingham, 1957; DSc (Hon), Technical University of Lódź, 2002. Appointments: Chemical Engineer, DCL Ltd, Saltend, 1957-62; Lecturer, Senior Lecturer, Reader, University of Canterbury, New Zealand, 1962-78; Professor, 1978-97, Professor Emeritus, 1997-, Chemical Engineering; Director, Wood Technology Research Centre, 1997-2001; Forest Guardian, Hurunui District Council, 1999-; Hanmer Springs Community Board, 2001-. Publications: Drying Principles and Practice; Introduction to Industrial Drying Operations; Reliability in the Process Industries; Drying of Loose and Particulate Materials; Wainui Incident; Kiln-Drying of Lumber; Management of Engineering Risk; Lambent Flames. Honours: Cadman Medal; NZIE Angus Award; NZIE Skellerup Award; IPENZ Rabone Award; IPENZ Skellerup Award; Proctor and Gamble Award, Excellence in Drying Research; Award for outstanding achievement and excellence in Drying R and D, 1st Nordic Drying Conference; Chemeca Medal, 2005; Distinguished Fellow IPENZ, 2006; Listed in several Who's Who publications. Memberships: former Council Member IPENZ; former Council Member, Christchurch Polytechnic; former Council Member, New Zealand Dairy Research Institute; FRSNZ; FIChemE; Dist FIPENZ; FNZIC; CEng. Address: PO Box 31080, Ilam, Christchurch, New Zealand 8444.

KEIGHTLEY Richard Charles, b. 2 July 1933, Aldershot, England. Army Major General. m. Caroline Rosemary Butler, 3 daughters. Education: Royal Military Academy Sandhurst, 1951-53; Army Staff College, 1963; National

Defence College, 1971-72; Royal College of Defence Studies, 1980. Appointments: Various Regimental and Staff appointments, 1953-70; Commander, 5th Royal Inniskilling Dragoon Guards, 1972-75; Colonel GS, 1st Division, 1977; Commander 33 Armoured Brigade, 1978-79; Brigadier General Staff, UK Land Forces, 1981; GOC Western District, 1982-83; Commandant, Royal Military Academy Sandhurst, 1983-87; Chairman, Dorset Healthcare NHS Trust, 1995-97; Chairman, Dorset Health Authority, 1988-95, 1998-2001; Chairman, Southampton University Hospitals NHS Trust, 2002-. Honour: CB, 1987. Memberships: President, Dorset County Royal British Legion; President, Dorset Relate; Member, St John Council for Dorset. Address: Kennels Farmhouse, Tarrant Gunville, Dorset DT 11 8JQ, England.

KEILLOR Garrison, (born Gary Edward Keillor), b. 7 August 1942, Anoka, Minnesota, USA. Writer; Radio Host. Education: BA, University of Minnesota, 1966. Appointments: Creator-Host, national public radio programmes, A Prairie Home Companion and American Radio Company. Publications: Happy to Be Here, 1982; Lake Wobegon Days, 1985; Leaving Home, 1987; We Are Still Married: Stories and Letters, 1989; WLT: A Radio Romance, 1991; The Book of Guys, 1993; Wobegon Boy, 1997; Lake Wobegon Summer 1956, 2001; Love Me, 2004; Homegrown Democrat, 2004; Good Poems for Hard Times, 2005; Pontoon, 2007. Children's Books: Cat, You Better Come Home, 1995; The Old Man Who Loved Cheese, 1996; Sandy Bottom Orchestra, 1997; ME by Jimmy (Big Boy) Valente as Told to Garrison Keillor, 1999. Contributions to: Newspapers and magazines. Honours: George Foster Peabody Award, 1980; Grammy Award, 1987; Ace Award, 1988; Best Music and Entertainment Host Awards, 1988, 1989; American Academy and Institute of Arts and Letters Medal, 1990; Music Broadcast Communications Radio Hall of Fame, 1994; National Humanities Medal, 1999. Address: c/o Minnesota Public Radio, 45 East 7th Street, St Paul, MN 55101, USA.

KEINÄNEN Matti Tapio, b. 1 January 1953, Kuopio, Finland. Docent. m. Kristina, 2 sons, 1 daughter. Education: Licentiate of Medicine, 1977; Doctor of Medicine and Surgery, 1981; Specialist in Psychiatry, 1985; Psychoanalytic Psychotherapy Training, 1986; Specialist-level Psychotherapy Training, 1992; Advanced Specialist-level Individual Psychotherapy Training, 1997; Docent in Psychiatry, Turku University, 2002; Family Therapy Training, Finnish Mental Health Society, 1987; Licentiate Psychotherapist, 1995; Licentiate Advanced Specialist-level Individual Psychotherapist, 1998, National Authority for Medicolegal Affairs; Supervising Member, Finnish Balint-Group Organisation, 1999; Docent in Clinical Psychology, Jyväskylä University, 2000. Appointments: Psychiatrist, Finnish Student Health Service, Turku; Docent in Psychiatry, Turku University; Docent in Clinical Psychology, Jyväskylä University. Publications: Articles on biological basic study of psychiatry, family research and symbolic function research in individual psychoanalytic psychotherapy; Book: Psychosemiosis as a Key to Body-Mind Continuum. The Reinforcement of Symbolization – Reflectiveness in Psychotherapy, 2006. Honours: International Peace Prize, 2005. Memberships: Finnish Medical Association; Finnish Psychiatric Association; International Semiotic Association; Finnish Psychodynamic Psychotherapy Association; Finnish Adolescent Psychiatry Association; Finnish Balint-Group Association; International Association of Relational Psychoanalysis and Psychotherapy, 2005. Address: Finnish Student Health Service, Kirkkotie 13, FIN-20540 Turku, Finland.

KEITEL Harvey, b. 13 May 1939, USA. Actor. m.(1) Lorraine Bracco, divorced, 1 daughter, (2) Daphna Kastner, 2001, 1 child. Education: Actors Studio. Appointments: US Marines. Creative Works: Stage appearances: Death of a Salesman, Hurlyburly; Films: Mean Streets; Alice Doesn't Live Here Anymore; That's the Way of the World; Taxi Driver; Mother Jugs and Speed Buffalo Bill and the Indians; Welcome to LA; The Duelists; Fingers; Blue Collar; Eagle's Wing; Deathwatch; Saturn 3; Bad Timing; The Border; Exposed; La Nuit de Varennes; Corrupt; Falling in Love; Knight of the Dragon Camorra; Off Beat; Wise Guys; The Men's Club; The Investigation; The Pick-up Artist; The January Man; The Last Temptation of Christ; The Two Jakes; Two Evil Eyes (The Black Cat); Thelma & Louise; Tipperary; Bugsy; Reservoir Dogs; Bad Lieutenant; Mean Streets; The Assassin; The Young Americans; The Piano; Snake Eyes; Rising Sun; Monkey Trouble; Clockers; Dangerous Game; Pulp Fiction; Smoke; Imaginary Crimes; Ulyssees' Gaze, Blue in the Face, 1995; City of Industry; Cop Land, Head Above Water; Somebody to Love, 1996; Simpatico, 1999; Little Nicky, U-571, Holy Smoke, 2000; Nailed, Taking Sides, Grey Zone, 2001; Nowhere, Ginostra, Red Dragon, Beeper, 2002; Crime Spree, Galindez File, Dreaming of Julia, Puerto Vallarta Squeeze, 2003; National Treasure, The Bridge of San Luis Rey, 2004; Shadows in the Sun, Be Cool, The Shadow Dancer, 2005; A Crime, The Stone Merchant, Arthur and the Invisibles (voice), 2006; My Sexiest Year, The Ministers, National Treasure: Book of Secrets, 2007. Address: c/o William Morris Agency, 151 South El Camino Drive, Beverly Hills, CA 90212, USA.

KEITH Penelope Anne Constance, b. 2 April 1940, Sutton, Surrey, England. Actress. m. Rodney Timson, 1978. Education: Webber Douglas School, London. Creative Works: Stage appearances include: Suddenly at Home, 1971; The Norman Conquests, 1974; Donkey's Years, 1976; The Apple Cart, 1977; The Millionairess, 1978; Moving, 1980; Hobson's Choice, 1982; Captain Brassbound's Conversation, 1982; Hay Fever, 1983; The Dragon's Tail, 1985; Miranda, 1987; The Deep Blue Sea, 1988; Dear Charles, 1990; The Merry Wives of Windsor, 1990; The Importance of Being Ernest, 1991; On Approval, 1992; Relatively Speaking, 1992; Glyn and It, 1994; Monsieur Amilcar, 1995; Mrs Warren's Profession, 1997; Good Grief, 1998; Star Quality, 2001; Film appearances include: Rentadick; Take a Girl Like You; Every Home Should Have One; Sherlock Holmes; The Priest of Love; TV appearances include: The Good Life (Good Neighbors in USA), 1974-77; Private Lives, 1976; The Norman Conquests, 1977; To the Manor Born, 1979-81; On Approval, 1980; Spider's Web; Sweet Sixteen; Waters of the Moon; Hay Fever; Moving; Executive Stress; What's My Line?, 1988; Growing Places; No Job for a Lady, 1990; Law and Disorder, 1994; Teletubbies (voice) 1997; Next of Kin; Coming Home, 1999; Margery and Gladys, 2003. Honours include: Best Light Entertainment Performance, British Academy of Film & TV Arts, 1976; Best Actress, 1977; Show Business Personality, Variety Club of Great Britain, 1976; BBC TV Personality, 1979; Comedy Performance of the Year, Society of West End Theatre, 1976; Female TV Personality; TV Times Awards, 1976-78; BBC TV Personality of the Year, 1978-79; TV Female Personality, Daily Express, 1979-82. Address: London Management, 2-4 Noel Street, London W1V 3RB, England.

KELLEHER Graeme George, b. 2 May 1933, Sydney, Australia. Civil Engineer; National Resource Manager. m. Fleur Meachen, 1 son, 2 daughters. Education: BE (Civil), 1955. Appointments: Engineer Project Manager, 1955-75; Commissioner, Ranger Uranium Inquiry, 1976-77; Deputy Chair, Non-proliferation Task Force, 1977-78; Chair, CEO, Great Barrier Reef Marine Park Authority, 1979-94; Professor, Systems Engineering, James Cook University, 1991-94; Vice Chair, World Commission on Protected Areas, 1986-98; Senior Advisor and Leader on High Seas Marine Protected Areas Task Force, World Commission on Protected Areas, 1999-; Chair, CSIRO Marine Advisory Committee, 1995-99; Co Chair, Life Sciences, Co-operative Research Centres Program, 1995-2002; Director, Graeme Kelleher and Associates, 1995-; Member, Religious and Scientific Committee, Religion, Science and the Environment, 1996-; Member, Independent Community Engagement Panel, Murray-Darling Ministerial Council, 2002-2004. Publications: Ranger Uranium Environmental Inquiry; Guidelines for Marine Protected Areas; A Global Representative System of Marine Protected Areas; Many papers and articles. Honours: Churchill Fellowship, 1972; Monash Medal, 1986; Member, Order of Australia, 1988; Officer of the Order of Australia, 1996; Packard International Parks Merit Award, 1998; Centenary Medal, 2003; Institution of Engineers, Canberra Hall of Fame, 2005 Memberships: Institution of Engineers (Fellow); Australian Academy of Technological Sciences and Engineering (Fellow); Environmental Institute of Australia and New Zealand (Fellow). Address: 12 Marulda Street, Aranda, Canberra ACT 2614, Australia.

KELLER Evelyn Fox, b. 20 March 1936, New York, New York, USA. Professor of History and Philosophy of Science; Writer. 1 son, 1 daughter. Education: BA, Brandeis University, 1957; MA, Radcliffe College, 1959; PhD, Harvard University, 1963. Appointments: Visiting Fellow, later Scholar, 1979-84, Visiting Professor, 1985-86, MIT; Professor of Mathematics and Humanities, Northeastern University, 1982-88; Senior Fellow, Cornell University, 1987; Member, Institute for Advanced Study, Princeton, New Jersey, 1987-88; Professor, University of California at Berkeley, 1988-92; President, West Coast History of Science Society, 1990-91; Professor of History and Philosophy of Science, Massachusetts Institute of Technology, 1992-; MacArthur Fellow, 1992-97; Guggenheim Fellowship, 2000-01; Moore Scholar, California Institute of Technology, 2002; Winton Chair, University of Minnesota, 2002-05; Dibner Fellow, 2003; Radcliffe Institute Fellow, 2005; Rothschild Lecturer, Harvard University, 2005; Plenary Speaker, International History of Science Congress, Beijing, 2005. Publications: A Feeling for the Organism: The Life and Work of Barbara McClintock, 1983, 2nd edition, 1993; Reflections on Gender and Science, 1985, new edition, 1995; Women, Science and the Body (editor with Mary Jacobus and Sally Shuttleworth), 1989; Conflicts in Feminism (editor with Marianne Hirsch), 1990; Keywords in Evolutionary Biology (editor with Elisabeth Lloyd), 1992; Secrets of Life, Secrets of Death: Essays on Language, Gender, and Science, 1992; Refiguring Life: Metaphors of Twentieth Century Biology, 1995; Feminism and Science (editor with Helen Longino), 1996; The Century of the Gene, 2000; Making Sense of Life, 2002. Contributions to: Scholarly journals. Honours: Distinguished Publication Award, Association for Women in Psychology, 1986; Alumni Achievement Award, Brandeis University, 1991; Honorary Doctorates, Holyoke College, 1991, University of Amsterdam, 1995, Simmons College, 1995, Rensselaer Polytechnic Institute, 1995, Technical University of Lulea, Sweden, 1996; John D and Catharine T MacArthur Foundation Fellowship, 1992-97; Medal of the Italian Senate, 2001; Numerous honorary degrees. Address: c/o Program in Science, Technology and Society, Massachusetts Institute of Technology, 77 Massachusetts Avenue, Cambridge, MA 02139, USA.

DICTIONARY OF INTERNATIONAL BIOGRAPHY

KELLEY Patricia Marie Hagelin, b. 8 December 1953, Cleveland, Ohio, USA. Geology Educator. m. Jonathan Robert Kelley, 1 son, 1 daughter. Education: BA, Geology, College of Wooster, 1975; AM, Geology, 1977; PhD, Geology, Harvard University, 1979. Appointments: Instructor, New England College, 1979; Assistant Professor, 1979-85, Associate Professor, 1985-89, Acting Associate Vice-Chancellor for Academic Affairs, 1988, Professor of Geology and Geological Engineering, 1989-90, University of Mississippi; Programme Director for Geology and Paleontology and Geological Record of Global Change Programmes, National Science Foundation, 1990-92; Professor and Chair of the Department of Geology and Geological Engineering, University of North Dakota, 1992-97; Professor and Chair, Department of Earth Sciences, 1997-2003, Professor of Geology, 2003-, University of North Carolina at Wilmington. Publications: Over 60 books, articles in scientific journals and book chapters as author and co-author include most recently: The fossil record of drilling predation on bivalves and gastropods, in Predator-Prey Interactions in the Fossil Record, 2003; Moonsnail Project: a scientific collaboration with middle school teachers and students, 2003; Predators, Prey and Their Fossil record: The PS Short Course, 2002; Paleoecological patterns in molluscan extinctions and recoveries: Comparison of Cretaceous-Tertiary and Eocene-Oligocene extinctions in North America, 2004; The influence of anti-predatory morphology on survivorship of the Owl Creek Formation molluscan fauna through the end-Cretaceous extinction, 2005; Comparisons of class and lower taxon level patterns in naticid gastropod predation, 2006; A case for cannibalism: Confamilial and conspecific predation by naticid gastropods, 2007. Honours include: Sigma Xi, 1975; National Science Foundation Graduate Fellowship, 1976-79; An Outstanding Young Woman of America, 1983; Outstanding Faculty Member, School of Engineering, University of Mississippi, 1989-90; Award Paper, 13th Annual Conference on College Teaching and Learning, 2002; Association for Women Geoscientists Outstanding Educator Award, 2003; Faculty Scholarship Award, University of North Carolina, Wilmington, 2005; Centennial fellow of the Palentological Society, 2006. Memberships include: Fellow, Geological Society of America; Fellow, American Association for the Advancement of Science; President, Paleontological Society, 2000-2002; President, Board of Trustees, Paleontological Research Institution, 2004-2006; National Center for Science Education; Society for Sedimentary Geology; Association for Women Geoscientists. Address: Department of Geography and Geology, University of North Carolina Wilmington, 601 South College Road, Wilmington, NC 28403-5944, USA. E-mail: kelleyp@uncw.edu

KELLY Anthony, b. 25 January 1929, Hillingdon, Middlesex, England. Consultant. Education: BSc, 1st class, Physics, University of Reading, 1949; PhD, Trinity College, Cambridge, 1953; ScD, University of Cambridge, 1968. Appointments: Research Associate, University of Illinois, 1953-55; ICI Fellow, University of Birmingham, 1955; Assistant Professor, Associate Professor, The Technological Institute, Northwestern University, Chicago, 1956-59; University Lecturer, University of Cambridge, 1959-67; Superintendent, 1967-69, Deputy Director, 1969-75, National Physical Laboratory, Middlesex; Seconded to ICI plc, 1973-75; Consultant to many international companies, 1973-; Vice Chancellor and Chief Executive, University of Surrey, 1975-94; Founder, Surrey Research Park, 1979; Director, Johnson Wax UK Ltd, 1981-96; Director, QUO-TEC Ltd, 1984-2000; Director, NPL Management Ltd, 1994-2001; Distinguished Research Fellow, Department of Materials Science and Metallurgy, University of Cambridge, 1994-.

Publications: 200 papers in scientific and technical journals; Numerous books; Many lectures. Honours include: CBE, 1988; Gold Medal, American Society of Materials, 1991; Platinum Medal, Institute of Materials, 1992; Knight of St Gregory, 1992; Deputy Lieutenant for the County of Surrey, 1993; DUniv, University of Surrey, 1994; Honorary Fellow, Institution of Structural Engineers, 1996; Hon DSc, University of Birmingham, 1997; Honorary Fellow, Institution of Civil Engineers, 1997; Acta Metallurgica Gold Medal, 2000; Honorary DEng, Hanyang University, Korea, 2001; Honorary Doctor of Science, University of Reading, 2002. Memberships: Institute of Metals; British Non-Ferrous Metals Research Association; Engineering Materials Requirements Board, Department of Trade and Industry; European Association of Composite Materials; Royal National Institute for the Deaf; Institute of Materials. Address: Churchill College, Cambridge, CB3 0DS, England. E-mail: ak209@cam.ac.uk

KELLY Donald Francis, b. 20 July 1933, Manchester, England. Veterinary Pathologist. m. Patricia Ann Holt, 3 sons. Education: BVSc, Bristol, 1957; MRCVS, 1957; MA, PhD, Cantab, 1963; FRCPath, Dipl ECVP. Appointments: Demonstrator in Pathology, University of Cambridge, 1962-66; Assistant/Associate Professor, University of Pennsylvania, 1966-70; Senior Lecturer, University of Bristol, 1970-79; Professor of Veterinary Pathology, University of Liverpool, 1979-2000; Honorary Senior Fellow, Emeritus Professor, University of Liverpool, 2000-. Publications: 200 contributions to textbooks, scientific veterinary literature in medicine, surgery and pathology. Honours: Founding President, European College of Veterinary Pathologists, 1995-97. Memberships: MRCVS; FRCPath; Diplomate, European College of Veterinary Pathologists. Address: Department of Veterinary Pathology, University of Liverpool, Faculty of Veterinary Science, Elmhurst, Neston, Wirral CH64 7TE, England. E-mail: donpatkel@aol.com

KELLY J Vincent, b. 18 October 1950, Cork, Ireland. Chartered Engineer; Ergonomist; Chartered Safety & Health Practitioner. m. Claire Collins, 2 sons. Education: Bachelor of Engineering, National University of Ireland, 1972; Diploma in Safety, Health & Welfare at Work, University College, Cork, 1995; Master of Science, Health Ergonomics, 1998, Doctor of Philosophy, 2004, University of Surrey. Appointments: Design Engineer, Site Engineer, and Resident Engineer with local authorities, consultants and contractors, 1972-79; Self-employed Consulting Engineer, 1979-; Self-employed Consulting Ergonomist, 1998-; Member of Research Team, Robens Centre for Health Ergonomics, European Institute of Health and Medicine Science, University of Surrey. Publications: The principle of ergonomics within European Union Directives, 2003; The role of work stress and psychological factors in the development of musculoskeletal disorders – The Stress and MSD Study, 2004; Legal Issues in Work Related Musculoskeletal Disorders: a European Perspective from the UK, 2005. Honours: ICE, 1976; IEI, 1979; FEANI, 1988; CREE, 2001; ACEI, 2003; IOSH, 2005. Memberships: Institution of Civil Engineers; Fellow, Institution of Engineers of Ireland; Fellow, Chartered Institute of Arbitrators; Institution of Occupational Safety & Health; Ergonomic Society. Address: Ballydehob, Co Cork, Ireland.

KELLY Rt Hon Ruth Maria, b. 9 May 1968, Limavady, Northern Ireland. Member of Parliament for Bolton West; Secretary of State for Transport. m. Derek John Gadd, 1996, 1 son, 3 daughters. Education: Edgarley Hall; Sutton High School; Westminster School; Philosophy, Politics and Economics, Queen's College, Oxford, 1989;

MSc, Economics, London School of Economics, 1992. Appointments: Economics Writer, The Guardian newspaper, 1990-94; Deputy Head, Inflation Report Division, Bank of England, 1994; Member of Parliament for Bolton West, 1997-; Parliamentary Private Secretary to Nick Brown at the Ministry for Agriculture, Fisheries and Food; Economic Secretary and Financial Secretary, HM Treasury; Minister for the Cabinet Office; Secretary of State for Education and Skills, 2004; Minister for Women and Equality, 2006; Secretary of State at the Department for Communities and Local Government, 2006; Secretary of State for Transport, 2007-.

KELNER Simon, b. 9 December 1957, Manchester, England. Newspaper Editor. m. Sally Ann Lasson, 1 daughter. Education: Pre-entry Journalism course, Preston Polytechnic, 1975-76. Appointments: Trainee Reporter, Neath Guardian, 1976-79; Sports Reporter, Extel, 1979-80; Sports Editor, Kent Evening Post, 1980-83; Assistant Sports Editor, Observer, 1983-86; Deputy Sports Editor, The Independent, 1986-89; Sports Editor, Sunday Correspondent, 1989-90; Sports Editor, Observer, 1990-91; Editor, Observer magazine, 1991-93; Sports Editor, The Independent on Sunday (launched first national stand-alone sports section), 1993-95; Night Editor, The Independent, 1995; Features Editor, The Independent, 1995-96; Editor of Night & Day magazine (review section of Mail on Sunday), 1996-98; Editor-in-Chief, The Independent, 1998-. Honours: Winner, Magazine of the Year (Observer magazine), 1992; Honorary Fellowship, University of Central Lancashire; The Edgar Wallace Award, 2000; Editor of the Year, What the Papers Say Awards, 1999, 2003; Newspaper of the Year, What the Papers Say Awards, 2004; Newspaper of the Year, British Press Awards, 2004; Newspaper of the Year, London Press Club, 2004; GQ Editor of the Year, GQ Awards, 2004; Media Achiever of the Year, Campaign Media Awards, 2004; Marketeer of the Year, Marketing Week Effectiveness Awards, 2004. Publications: To Jerusalem and Back, 1996. Memberships: The Groucho Club; Kirtlington Golf Club. Address: The Independent, 191 Marsh Wall, London E14 9RS, England.

KELSALL Malcolm Miles, b. 27 February 1938, London, England. Professor Emeritus of English. m. Mary Emily Ives, 5 August 1961. Education: BA, Oxon, 1961; BLitt, Oxon, 1964; MA, Oxon, 1965. Appointments: Staff Reporter, The Guardian Newspaper, 1961; Assistant Lecturer, Exeter University, 1963-64; Lecturer, Reading University, 1964-75; Professor, 1975-2003, Professor Emeritus, 2005-, University of Wales, Cardiff; Visiting Professor: University of Paris VII, 1978, University of Hiroshima, 1979, Charles University, Prague, 1994, University of Madison, Wisconsin, 1996; Visiting Scholar in residence, International Centre for Jefferson Studies, 1997. Publications: Editor, Sarah Fielding, David Simple, 1969; Editor, Thomas Otway, Venice Preserved, 1969; Christopher Marlowe, 1981; Congreve: The Way of the World, 1981; Studying Drama, 1985; Byron's Politics, 1987; Editor, Encyclopaedia of Literature and Criticism, 1990; The Great Good Place: The Country House and English Literature, 1992; Editor, J M Synge, The Playboy of the Western World, 1997; Editor, William Congreve, Love For Love, 1999; Jefferson and the Iconography of Romanticism, 1999; Literary Representations of the Irish Country House, 2003. Contributions to: Byron Journal; Cambridge Companions to Byron and Pope; DNB; Encyclopaedia of the Essay; Encyclopaedia of the Romantic Era; Essays in Criticism; Irish University Review; Theatre Research International; Review of English Studies; Studies in Romanticism. Honours: Elma Dangerfield Prize, 1991; British Academy Warton Lecturer, 1992; Marchand Lecturer, 2005; Honorary Fellow, Graduate School of European Romanticism, Glasgow University. Membership: Advisory Editorial Board, The Byron Journal, Litteraria Pragensia. E-mail: malcolm.kelsall@btinternet.com

KEMP Terence James, b. 26 June 1938, Watford, Hertfordshire, England. Professor. m. Sheila Therese, 1 son, 2 daughters. Education: BA, 1961, MA, DPhil, 1963, Jesus College, Oxford. Appointments: DSIR Research Fellow, Cookridge Laboratory, University of Leeds, 1962; Assistant Lecturer, 1966-66, Lecturer, 1966-70, Senior Lecturer in Chemistry, 1970-74, Reader in Chemistry, 1974-80, Professor of Chemistry, 1980-, Pro-Vice Chancellor, 1983-89, University of Warwick. Publications: Introductory Photochemistry, 1971; Dictionary of Physical Chemistry, 1992; 240 original scientific articles. Honours: Meldola Medal, Royal Institute of Chemistry, 1967; Order of Merit, Polish People's Republic, 1978; Nagroda, 2nd prize, Marie Curie-Slodowska Society for Radiation Research, 1992. Address: Department of Chemistry, University of Warwick, Coventry CV4 7AL, England. E-mail: t.j.kemp@warwick.ac.uk

KENDAL Felicity, b. 25 September 1946. Actress. m. (1) 1 son, (2) Michael Rudman, 1983, divorced 1991, 1 son. Career: Plays: Minor Murder; Henry V; The Promise; Back to Methuselah; A Midsummer Night's Dream; Much Ado About Nothing; Kean; Romeo and Juliet; 'Tis Pity She's a Whore; The Three Arrows; The Norman Conquests; Once Upon a Time; Arms and The Man; Clouds; Amadeus; Othello; On the Razzle; The Second Mrs Tanqueray; The Real Thing; Jumpers; Made in Bangkok; Hapgood; Ivanov; Hidden Laughter; Tartuffe; Heartbreak House; Arcadia; An Absolute Turkey; Indian Ink; Mind Millie for Me; The Seagul; Waste; Alarms and Excursions; Fallen Angels; Humble Boy; Happy Days; TV includes: The Good Life; Solo; The Mistress; The Woodlanders; Edward VII; Rosemary and Thyme, 2003-06. numerous other plays and serials; Films: Shakespeare Wallah, 1965; Valentino, 1976; Parting Shots. Publications: White Cargo, 1998. Honours: Variety Club Most Promising Newcomer, 1974; Best Actress, 1979; Clarence Derwent Award, 1980; Evening Standard Best Actress Award, 1989; Variety Club Best Actress Award, 2000. Address: c/o Chatto and Linnit, 123A Kings Road, London SW3 4PL, England.

KENDALL Bridget, b. 27 April 1956, Oxford, England. Journalist. Education: Lady Margaret Hall, Oxford, 1974-78; Harvard, USA, 1978-80; St Antony's College, Oxford, 1980-83; Voronegh State University, 1976-77; Moscow State University, 1981-82. Appointments: Trainee, BBC World Service, 1983; Presenter and Producer, Newsnight, BBC2, 1983-84; Producer, Reporter, BBC World Service Radio, 1984-89; BBC Moscow Correspondent, 1989-93; BBC Washington Correspondent, 1994-98; BBC Diplomatic Correspondent, 1998-. Publications: Co-author, David the Invincible, annotated translation (classical Armenian philosophy), 1980; Kosovo and After: The future of spin in the digital age (Jubilee Lecture for St Antony's College, Oxford), 2000; Co-author, The Day that Shook the World (BBC correspondents on September 11th 2001), 2001. Honours: British Council Scholar to USSR, 1976-77, 1981-82; Harkness Fellow, USA, 1978-80; Sony Award, Reporter of the Year (Bronze Award), 1992; James Cameron Award for distinguished journalism, 1992; Voice of the Listener and Viewer Award, 1993; MBE, 1994; Honorary Doctorate, University of Central England, Birmingham, 1999; Honorary Doctorate in Law, St Andrew's University, 2001; Honorary Doctorate in Law, Exeter University, 2002; Honorary Fellow, St Anthony's College, Oxford. Memberships: Advisory Board, Russian and Eurasian Programme at Chatham House,

DICTIONARY OF INTERNATIONAL BIOGRAPHY

Royal Institute of International Affairs, 2000-; Member of Council, Royal United Services Institute, 2001-05; Member of Advisory Council, European Research Institute, University of Birmingham. Address: BBC Television Centre, Wood Lane, London W12, England.

KENNEDY Alexander, b. 20 April 1933, Manchester, England. Retired Consultant Histopathologist. Education: MB ChB, Liverpool, 1956; MD, Liverpool, 1964; MRCPath, 1967; FRCPath, 1985. Appointments: House Office, Stanley and Royal Liverpool Children's Hospitals, 1956-58; Short Service Commission, Royal Air Force Medical Branch, 1958-61; Pathologist, RAF Hospital, Wroughton, 1958-61; Lecturer, University of Liverpool, 1961-67; Visiting Assistant Professor, University of Chicago, 1968; Senior Lecturer, University of Sheffield, 1969-77; Consultant Histopatholgist, 1977-97, Retired, 1997-, Northern General Hospital, Sheffield. Publications: 4 books; Over 50 articles in professional journals; Abstracts, letters and other publications. Memberships: Pathological Society of Great Britain and Ireland; British Thoracic Society; British Division of the International Academy of Pathology; Trent Regional Thoracic Society; Sheffield Medico-Chirurgical Society. Address: 16 Brincliffe Gardens, Sheffield, S11 9BG, England. E-mail: sandy.kennedy@care4free.net

KENNEDY (George) Michael (Sinclair), b. 19 February 1926, Manchester, England. Music Critic; Author. m. (1) Eslyn Durdle, 16 May 1947, deceased 2 January 1999, (2) Joyce Bourne, 10 October 1999. Education: Berkhamsted School. Appointments: Staff, 1941-, Northern Music Critic, 1950-, Northern Editor, 1960-86, Joint Chief Music Critic, 1986-89, The Daily Telegraph; Music Critic, The Sunday Telegraph, 1989-2005. Publications: The Hallé Tradition: A Century of Music, 1960; The Works of Ralph Vaughan Williams, 1964, revised edition, 1980; Portrait of Elgar, 1968, 3rd edition, 1987; Elgar: Orchestral Music, 1969; Portrait of Manchester, 1970; A History of the Royal Manchester College of Music, 1971; Barbirolli: Conductor Laureate, 1971, revised edition, 2003; Mahler, 1974, revised edition, 1990; The Autobiography of Charles Hallé, with Correspondence and Diaries (editor), 1976; Richard Strauss, 1976, revised edition, 1995; The Concise Oxford Dictionary of Music (editor), 1980, revised edition, 1995 and 2007; Britten, 1981, revised edition, 1993; The Hallé 1858-1983, 1983; Strauss: Tone Poems, 1984; The Oxford Dictionary of Music (editor), 1985, 2nd edition, revised, 1994 and 2006; Adrian Boult, 1987; Portrait of Walton, 1989; Music Enriches All: The First 21 Years of the Royal Northern College of Music, Manchester, 1994; Richard Strauss, Man, Musician, Enigma, 1999; The Life of Elgar, 2004. Contributions to: Newspapers and magazines. Honours: Fellow, Institute of Journalists, 1967; Honorary MA, Manchester, 1975; Officer of the Order of the British Empire, 1981; Fellow, Royal Northern College of Music, 1981; Commander of the Order of the British Empire, 1997; Companion, Royal Northern College of Music, 1999; Hon DMus, Manchester, 2003; Honorary Member, Royal Philharmonic Society, 2005. Address: The Bungalow, 62 Edilom Road, Manchester M8 4HZ, England.

KENNEDY Iain Manning, b. 15 September 1942, Northampton, England. Company Director. m. Ingrid Annette, 2 daughters. Education: Pembroke College, Cambridge, 1961-64. Appointments: Joined staff, 1969, Production Director, 1976, Chief Executive, 1998, Chairman, 2001, Church and Co plc; Chairman, SATRA, 1989; Governor, University College, Northampton, 1998; Retired, 2001.

Honours: OBE, 2002. Address: 3 Townsend Close, Hanging Houghton, Northampton, NN6 9HP, England. E-mail: iain@hanghoughton.fsnet.co.uk

KENNEDY Jane Hope, b. 28 February 1953, Loughborough, England. Architect. m. John Maddison, 2 sons. Education: Dip Arch, Manchester Polytechnic; Registered Architect, RIBA. Appointments: British Waterways Board, 1978-80; Assistant, David Jeffcoate Architect, 1980-81; Self-employed, 1981-86; Norwich City Council Planning Department, 1986-88; Architect, 1988-, Partner, 1992-, Purcell Miller Tritton; Surveyor to the fabric of Ely Cathedral, 1994-. Memberships: Institute of Historic Building Conservation; Fellow, Royal Society of Arts; Architect Accredited in Building Conservation. Address: Purcell Miller Tritton, 46 St Mary's Street, Ely, Cambridgeshire CB7 4EY, England. E-mail: janekennedy@pmt.co.uk

KENNEDY John Maxwell, b. 9 July 1934, Cardiff, Wales. Solicitor. m. Margaret, 4 sons. Education: LLB, University College, London University, 1954. Appointments: Allen & Overy: Joined, 1954, qualified as a Solicitor, 1957, Partner, 1962, Senior Partner, 1986; Involved in advising major international corporations, banks, governments on a wide variety of commercial, financial and oil-related work; International capital markets, involving debt and equity financings by governments and international corporations; Acted for the national oil company in Saudi Arabia and the central bank and the Ministry of Defence; Retired, 1994; Chairman, Law Debenture Corporation plc (Investment Trust), 1994-2000; Board Member, Financial Services Authority, 1994-1999; Chairman, 1996-98, Director and Chairman, Remuneration Committee and Member of the Audit Committee, 1993-2004, Amlin plc (formerly Angerstein Underwriting Trust plc); Chairman, Lloyd's Corporate Capital Association, 1995-98; Trustee, Director (appointed by the Secretary of State)of the Nuclear Trust (fund set up to provide for the decommissioning costs of British Energy's nuclear power stations), 1996-; Carried out Senior Management Review on behalf of the Cabinet Office on the Treasury Solicitor's Department, 1996. Memberships: City of London Club; City Law Club; Hurlingham Club; Royal Wimbledon Golf Club. Address: 16 Kensington Park Road, London W11 3BU, England.

KENNEDY Sir Ludovic (Henry Coverley), b. 3 November 1919, Edinburgh, Scotland. Writer; Broadcaster. m. Moira Shearer King, 1950, 1 son, 3 daughters. Education: MA, Christ Church, Oxford. Appointments: Broadcaster, numerous radio and television programmes, 1955-90; Columnist, Newsweek International, 1974-75, Sunday Standard, 1981-82; Director, The Spectator, 1988-90. Publications: Sub-Lieutenant, 1942; Nelson's Band of Brothers, 1951; One Man's Meat, 1953; Murder Story, 1956; Ten Rillington Place, 1961; The Trial of Stephen Ward, 1964; Very Lovely People, 1969; The British War (general editor), 1973-77; Pursuit: The Chase and Sinking of the Bismarck, 1974; A Presumption of Innocence: The Amazing Case of Patrick Meehan, 1979; Menace: The Life and Death of the Tirpitz, 1979; The Portland Spy Case, 1979; Wicked Beyond Belief, 1980; A Book of Railway Journeys (editor), 1980; A Book of Sea Journeys (editor), 1981; A Book of Air Journeys (editor), 1982; The Airman and the Carpenter, 1985; On My Way to the Club (autobiography), 1989; Euthanasia: The Good Death, 1990; Truth to Tell (collected writings), 1991; In Bed with an Elephant: A Journey Through Scotland's Past and Present, 1995; All in the Mind: A Farewell to God, 1999; 36 Murders and Two Immoral Earnings, 2002. Honours: Rockefeller Foundation Atlantic Award in Literature,

1950; Winner, Open Finals Contest, English Festival of Spoken Poetry, 1953; Cross, 1st Class, Order of Merit, Germany, 1979; Richard Dimbleby Award, British Association of Film and Television Arts, 1988; Knighted, 1994; F.R.S.L., 1998; Several honorary doctorates. Memberships: Russian Convoy Club, patron, 1989-; Voluntary Euthanasia Society, president, 1995-. Address: c/o Rogers, Coleridge and White, 20 Powis Mews, London W11 1JN, England.

KENNEDY Nigel, b. 28 December 1956, England. Violinist. Partner, Eve Westmore, 1 son. Education: Yehudi Menuhin School; Juilliard School of Performing Arts. Creative Works: Chosen by the BBC as the subject of a 5 year documentary on the development of a soloist following his debut with the Philharmonic Orchestra, 1977; Appeared with all the major British orchestras; Appearances at all the leading UK Festivals and in Europe at Stresa, Lucerne, Gstaad, Berlin & Lockenhaus; Debut at the Tanglewood Festival with the Boston Symphony under André Previn, 1985, at MN with Sir Neville Marriner, at Montreal with Charles Dutoit; Given concerts in the field of jazz with Stephane Grappelli at Carnegie Hall and Edinburgh, runs his own jazz group; Recordings include: Elgar Sonata with Peter Pettinger; Tchaikovsky; Sibelius; Vivaldi; Mendelssohn; Bruch; Walton Viola & Violin Concertos; Elgar Concerto with London Philharmonic Orchestra; Bach's Concerto with Berlin Philharmonic. Publication: Always Playing, 1991. Honours include: Best Classical Disc of the Year Award, London, 1985; Golden Rose of Montreux, 1990; Variety Club Showbusiness Personality of the Year, 1991; Hon DLitt, Bath, 1991; BRIT Award for Outstanding Contribution to British Music, 2000; Male Artist of the Year, 2001. Memberships include: Senior Vice President, Aston Villa FC, 1990-. Address: Askonas Holt Ltd, Lonsdale Chambers, 27 Chancery Lane, London WC2A 1PF, England. Website: www.askonasholt.co.uk

KENNEDY, Rt Hon Lord Justice, Rt Hon Sir Paul Joseph Morrow Kennedy, b.12 June 1935, Sheffield, England. m. Virginia Devlin, 2 sons, 2 daughters. Education: MA, LLM, Gonville and Caius College, Cambridge, 1955-59; Called to Bar at Gray's Inn, 1960, Bencher, 1982, Vice-Treasurer, 2001, Treasurer, 2002. Appointments: Recorder, 1972-83; Queen's Counsel, 1973; Presiding Judge, North East Circuit, 1985-89; High Court Judge, Queen's Bench Division, 1983-92; Lord Justice of Appeal, 1992-; Member Judicial Studies Board and Chairman of Criminal Committee, 1993-96; Vice-President, Queen's Bench Division, 1997-2002; Member Sentencing Guidelines Council, 2004-. Honours: Kt, 1983; PC, 1992; Honorary Fellow, Gonville and Caius College, Cambridge, 1998; Honorary LLD, University of Sheffield, 2000. Address: Royal Courts of Justice, Strand, London WC2A 2LL, England.

KENNEDY Peter Graham Edward, b. 28 March 1951, London, England. Professor of Neurology. m. Catherine Ann Kennedy, 1 son, 1 daughter. Education: University College London and University College Hospital Medical School, 1969-74; MB BS, 1974; PhD, 1980; MD, 1983; FRCP (London), 1988; FRCP (Glasgow), 1989; DSc, 1991; FRSE, 1992; MPhil, 1993; MLitt, 1995; FRCPath, 1996; FMedSci, 1998. Appointments: Honorary Research Assistant, MRC Neuroimmunology Project, University College, London, 1978-80; Registrar, then Senior Registrar, National Hospital for Nervous Diseases, London, 1982-84; Visiting Assistant Professor of Neurology, Johns Hopkins University Hospital, USA, 1985; Senior Lecturer, Neurology and Virology, University of Glasgow, 1986-87; Burton Professor of Neurology, University of Glasgow and Consultant Neurologist, Institute of Neurological Sciences, Southern

General Hospital, Glasgow, Scotland, 1987-. Publications: Numerous articles in learned journals on Neurology and Neurovirology; Books: Infections of the Nervous System (with R T Johnson), 1987; Infectious Diseases of the Nervous System (with L E Davis), 2000. Honours: BUPA Medical Foundation Doctor of the Year Research Award, 1990; Linacre Medal and Lectureship, Royal College of Physicians, London, 1991; TS Srinivasan Gold Medal and Endowment Lecturer, Madras, 1993; Fogarty International Scholar-in-Residence, National Institutes of Health, Bethesda, USA, 1993-94; James W Stephens Honored Visiting Professor, Department of Neurology, University of Colorado Health Sciences Center, Denver, USA, 1994; Livingstone Lecture, Royal College of Physicians and Surgeons of Glasgow, 2004. Memberships: Association of Physicians of Great Britain and Ireland; Corresponding Member, American Neurological Association; Association of British Neurologists; Fellow of the Royal Society of Edinburgh; Founder Fellow, Academy of Medical Sciences; Secretary, 2000-03, President, 2004-, International Society for Neurovirology; Chairman, EFNS Scientist Panel on Infections including AIDS; Member Editorial Boards several medical journals. Address: Glasgow University Department of Neurology, Institute of Neurological Sciences, Southern General Hospital, Glasgow G51 4TF, Scotland. E-mail: p.g.kennedy@clinmed.gla.ac.uk

KENNEFICK Christine Marie, b. 4 July 1962, Washington DC, USA. Materials Scientist. Education: BSc, 1984, MSc, 1986, Stanford University; PhD, Cornell University, 1991. Appointments: National Research Council Associate, NASA Lewis Research Center, Cleveland, Ohio, 1991-93; Guest Scientist, Max-Planck Institute, Stuttgart, Germany, 1994-96; ASEE Postdoctoral Fellow, US Army Research Laboratory, Aberdeen, Maryland, 1997-98; Senior Research Associate, Air Force Research Laboratory, Dayton, Ohio, 1998-2000; Visiting Assistant Professor, Shippensburg University, Pennsylvania, 2001-02; Lecturer, Howard University, Washington, DC, 2005-07. Honours: BSc with Distinction and in Departmental Honors Program; International Woman of Year, IBC, 1998-2001; Outstanding Woman of the Twentieth Century, ABI, 1999; Listed in biographical publications. Memberships: Life Fellow, International Biographical Association; Fellow, Deputy Governor, American Biographical Institute; International Order of Merit; Order of International Ambassadors. Address: 2029 Turtle Pond Drive, Reston, VA 20191, USA.

KENNET 2nd Baron, (Wayland Hilton Young), b. 2 August 1923, England. Politician; Writer; Journalist. m. Elizabeth Ann Adams, 24 January 1948, 1 son, 5 daughters. Education: Trinity College, Cambridge. Appointments: Royal Navy, 1942-45; Staff, Foreign Office, 1946-47, 1949-51; Delegate, Parliamentary Assemblies, Western European Union and Council of Europe, 1962-65; Editor, Disarmament and Arms Control, 1962-65; Parliamentary Secretary, Ministry of Housing and Local Government, 1966-70; Opposition Spokesman on Foreign Affairs and Science Policy, 1971-74; Member, European Parliament, 1978-79; Chief Whip, 1981-83, Spokesman on Foreign Affairs and Defence, 1981-90, Social Democratic Party, House of Lords; Vice President, Parliamentary and Scientific Committee, 1989-. Publications: As Wayland Young: The Italian Left, 1949; The Deadweight, 1952; Now or Never, 1953; Old London Churches (with Elizabeth Young), 1956; The Montesi Scandal, 1957; Still Alive Tomorrow, 1958; Strategy for Survival, 1959; The Profumo Affair, 1963; Eros Denied, 1965; Thirty-Four Articles (editor), 1965; Existing Mechanisms of Arms Control, 1965. As Wayland Kennet: Preservation, 1972;

The Futures of Europe, 1976; The Rebirth of Britain, 1982; London's Churches (with Elizabeth Young), 1986; Northern Lazio; An Unknown Italy (with Elizabeth Young), 1990; Parliaments and Screening, 1995. Address: 100 Bayswater Road, London, W2 3HJ, England.

KENSIT Patsy (Jude), b. 4 March 1968, London, England. Film Actress. m. (1) Dan Donovan, (2) Jim Kerr, divorced, 1 son, (3) Liam Gallagher, divorced, 1 son. Creative Works: Films include: The Great Gatsby; The Bluebird; Absolute Beginners; Chorus of Disapproval; The Skipper; Chicago Joe and The Showgirl; Lethal Weapon II; Twenty-One; Prince of Shadows; Does This Mean We're Married; Blame It On the Bellboy; The Turn of the Screw; Beltenebros; Bitter Harvest; Angels and Insects; Grace of My Heart; Human Bomb; Janice Beard; Pavillions, 1999; Best; Things Behind the Sun, 2000; Bad Karma; Who's Your Daddy, 2001; The One and Only, 2001; Darkness Falling, 2002; Quest for the Kingdom: A fairy tale; shelter Island, 2003; Played, 2006; TV appearances: Great Expectations; Silas Marner; Tycoon: The Story of a Woman; Adam Bede; The Corsican Brothers (US TV); Aladdin; Emmerdale; Holby City; Play: See You Next Tuesday, 2003; Played, 2006. Address: c/o Steve Dagger, 14 Lambton Place, London W11 2SH, England.

KENT Alexander James, b. 24 August 1977, Dover, Kent, England. Cartographer. Education: BSc (Hons), Geography and Cartography, Oxford Brookes University, 1998; M Phil, GIS and Remote Sensing, Queens' College, Cambridge University, 1999; PhD, Geography, University of Kent, Canterbury, 2007. Appointments: Independent Geo-Information Consultant, 1999-2007; Cartographic Editor, Atlas Project, Oxford Centre for Islamic Studies, 1999-2007; Lecturer, GIS and Remote Sensing, Oxford Brookes University, 2000-05; Sessional Lecturer, Cartography, Canterbury Christ Church University, 2004-07; Technical Consultant, Williams Performance Tenders, 2007; Researcher, Oxford Dictionary of National Biography, 2007; Head, Cartography Unit, School of Geography, University of Southampton, 2008-. Publications: Numerous articles in professional journals. Honours: Robert White Prize, Harvey Grammar School, 1995; PCI Geomatics Prize, Oxford Brookes University, 1998; 1st Prize, Queens' College Graduate Photography Competition, 1999; International Cartographic Association Travel Award, 2007; National Geographic Award, 2007. Memberships: Fellow, British Cartographic Society; Fellow, Royal Geographical Society; Committee Member, Charles Close Society for the Study of Ordnance Survey Maps. Address: School of Geography, University of Southampton, Highfield, Southampton SO17 1BJ, England. E-mail: a.j.kent@soton.ac.uk

KENT Paul Welberry, b. 19 April 1923, Doncaster, England. Biochemist. m. Rosemary Shepherd, 3 sons, 1 daughter. Education: BSc, PhD, Birmingham University; MA, DPhil, Jesus College, DSc, Christchurch, Oxford University. Appointments: Assistant Lecturer then ICI Fellow, Birmingham University; Visiting Fellow, Princeton University, New Jersey, 1948-49; Demonstrator in Biochemistry, Oxford University, 1950-72; Tutor and Dr Lees Reader, 1955-72, Emeritus Fellow (Student), 1973- Christ Church, Oxford; Master, Van Mildert College, Durham University, 1972-82. Publications: Biochemistry of Amino Sugars, 1955; Membrane-Mediated Information, 1973; Some Scientists in the Life of Christ Church, Oxford, 2001; Robert Hooke and the English Renaissance, 2005. Honours: JP; Honorary DSc, CNAA; Honorary LHD, Drury University, USA; Order of Merit, Germany. Memberships: Royal Society of Chemistry; Biochemical Society; Athenaeum. Address: 18 Arnolds Way, Cumnor Hill, Oxford OX2 9JB, England.

KENTFIELD Graham Edward Alfred, b. 3 September 1940, Buckhurst Hill, Essex, England. Retired Bank of England Official. m. Ann Hewetson, 2 daughters. Education: BA (Lit Hum, 1st Class), St Edmund Hall, Oxford, 1963. Appointments: Head of Monetary Policy Forecasting, 1974-76, Governor's Speechwriter, 1976-77, Editor, Quarterly Bulletin, 1977-80, Senior Manager, Banking and Money Supply Statistics, 1980-84, Adviser, Banking Department, 1984-85; Deputy Chief Cashier, 1985-91, Chief Cashier and Chief of Banking Department, 1991-94, Chief Cashier and Deputy Director, 1994-98, Bank of England. Honour: Fellow of Chartered Institute of Bankers, 1991; Memberships: Bank of England Director BACS Ltd, 1988-95; Bank of England Director, Financial Law Panel, 1994-98; Bank of England Representative, Council of Chartered Institute of Bankers, 1991-98; Bank of England Representative, APACS Council, 1991-98; Member, Building Societies Investor Protection Board, 1991-2001; Member, Deposit Protection Board (Banks), 1991-98; Chairman, Insolvency Practices Council, 2000-04; Honorary Treasurer, Society for the Promotion of Roman Studies, 1991-; Trustee, 1994- Chairman, 2000-, Chartered Institute for Bankers Pension Fund; Trustee, 1999-, Chairman, 2005-, Overseas Bishoprics Fund; Member, Council of London University, 2000-. Address: 27 Elgood Avenue, Northwood, Middlesex, HA6 3QL, England.

KENWRIGHT Bill, b. 4 September 1945, England. Theatre Producer. Education: Liverpool Institute. Appointments: Actor, 1964-70; Theatre Producer, 1970-; Chairman, Everton Football Club, 2004; Launched, Everton Tigers basketball team, 2007. Creative Works: Plays directed include: Joseph and The Amazing Technicolor Dreamcoat, 1979; The Business of Murder, 1981; A Streetcare Named Desire, 1984; Stepping Out, 1984; Blood Brothers, 1988; Shirley Valentine, 1989; Travels With My Aunt, 1993; Piaf, 1994; Lysistrata, 1993; Medea, 1993; Pygmalion, 1997; A Doll's House; An Ideal Husband; The Chairs, 2000; Blood Brothers; Ghosts; The Female Odd Couple. Honours: CBE, 2000. Address: Bill Kenwright Ltd, 106 Harrow Road, London, W2 1RR, England.

KENYON Ronald James, b. 24 May 1951, Penrith, England. Chartered Accountant. m. Ann Christine Kenyon, 1 son, 1 daughter. Education: Trent Polytechnic, Nottingham; Foundation Course, Institute of Chartered Accountants. Appointments: Pricewaterhouse, Leeds, 1968-69; Chartered Accountant, 1974-, Partner, 1980-, F T Kenyon and Son, Kyle and Kenyon, Kyle Saint and Co, Saint and Co; Chairman, Cumberland Society of Chartered Accountants, 1991. Publications: Rock Climbing in the North of England, 1978; Rock Climbing Guide to Borrowdale, 1986, 1990. Honours: Fellow, Institute of Chartered Accountants; Vice President, Fell and Rock Climbing Club. Memberships: Fell and Rock Climbing Club; Eden Valley Mountaineering Club; Penrith Agriculture Society; Eden Sports Council; Penrith Partnership; Penrith Mountain Rescue Team, 1967-92; Penrith Lions Club, 1979-2004.

KENZO Takada, b. 1940, Kyoto, Japan. Fashion Designer. Education: Bunka Fashion College, Japan. Appointments: Designer of patterns, Tokyo magazine; Freelance Designer to Louis Feraud, Paris, 1964-70; Owner of own shop, Jungle

Jap, 1970; Director and Writer of film, Yume, Yume no Ato, 1981; Head, Kenzo fashion house; Retired, 1999; Created Yume label, 2002.

KERAMIDAS Dimitrios Constantine, b. 28 May 1935, Athens, Attica, Greece. Paediatric Surgeon. m. Dimitra Anagnostou, 1 daughter. Education: Medical Diploma, University of Athens School of Medicine, 1960; Training in General Surgery and Qualification, Athens, 1967; Training in Paediatric Surgery and Qualification, Athens, 1970; Doctorate Thesis, 1967, Associate Professorship Thesis, 1978 Athens University; European Board of Paediatric Surgery, 1999. Appointments: Associate in Paediatric Surgery, Children's Hospital Aglaia Kyriakou of Athens, 1971-73, 1974-85; Research Fellow, University of Southern California, USA, 1973-74; Chief of Paediatric Surgery, Children's Hospital, Aghia Sophia, Athens, 1985-2002; Professor of Paediatric Surgery, University of Patras, Greece, 1998-2000; Consultant Paediatric Surgeon, Mitera Maternity and Children's Hospital, Athens, 2003-. Publications: Experimental research: Presse Med, 1968; British Journal of Surgery, 1969; Journal of Paediatric Surgery, 1974, 1980, 1994 (letter); Z Kinderchirurgie, (Clinical), 1984; Paediatric Surgery International, 1991; Surgical Techniques: Surgery, 1979; British Journal of Urology, 1995; European Journal of Paediatric Surgery, 1995, 1997; Contributions to books: Hypospadias Surgery, 2004; Liver and Biliary Tract Surgery, 2006; Chapters in 14 textbooks in Greek; 241 contributed articles to professional journals (in Greek and English). Honours: President, Greek Association of Paediatric Surgeons, 1991-92; President, Mediterranean Association of Paediatric Surgeons, 2000-2002; President, Greek Surgical Society, 2003. Memberships: British Association of Paediatric Surgeons; European Paediatric Surgeons Association; Mediterranean Association of Paediatric Surgeons. Address: Mitera Maternity and Paediatric Hospital, 6 Erythrou Stavrou Str, 16123 Athens, Greece. E-mail: dimit940@otenet.gr

KERC Janez, b. 22 May 1962, Podrecje. Pharmacist. Education: BSc, 1987, MSc, 1990, PhD, 1995. Appointments: Researcher, 1988-94, Senior Researcher, 1994-2002, Head of NDS Department, 2002-, Lek Pharmaceuticals d.d. Ljubljana; Assistant Professor, 1997-2007, Associated Professor, 2007-, Faculty of Pharmacy, University of Ljubljana. Publications: Patents in pharmaceutical field; Articles in professional journals. Honours: KRKA Award, 1985; Minarik Award, 1999. Memberships: Slovenian Pharmaceutical Society; Controlled Release Society. Address: Podrecje 6, 1230 Domzale, Slovenia.

KERNAN Roderick Patrick, b. 20 May 1928, Dublin, Ireland. Physiologist. m. Mary Kavanagh, 1 son, 1 daughter. Education: BSc Special (1st Honours), 1951, MSc, 1952, PhD, 1956, DSc, 1964, University College, Dublin, National University of Ireland; Medical Research Fellowships, 1951-65; Scholarships: Foreign Students Summer Project, MIT, Cambridge, Massachusetts, USA, 1956, and Deutscher Akademischer Austauschdienst, 1974. Appointments: Department of Physiology of Reproduction, Rockefeller Institute, New York, 1957-58; Visiting Professor of Physiology, George Washington University, Washington, DC, 1969-70; Rae Professor of Biochemistry, Royal College of Surgeons, Dublin, 1964-66; Associate Professor of Physiology, University College, Dublin, 1966-93; Vice President, 1979-80, 1988-89, Science, Secretary, 1993-2000, Royal Irish Academy. Publications: Books: Cell K, 1965; Butterworth Inc, Washington DC; Cell Potassium, 1980; John Wiley & Sons, New York; Chapters in: Transport and

Accumulation in Biological Systems, 1972; Membranes and Ion Transport Vol 1, 1970; 61 papers in international journals. Honours: Conway Medal, Royal Academy of Medicine in Ireland, 1979. Memberships: Royal Irish Academy, 1964; Physiological Society, 1963; British Biophysical Society, 1966; Royal Academy of Medicine in Ireland, 1963; Biomedical Engineering Society of Ireland, 1971. Address: 37 Templeville Drive, Templeogue, Dublin 6W, Ireland. E-mail: roddy_kernan@yahoo.com

KERNICK Robert Charles, b. 11 May 1927, Istanbul, Turkey. Wine Merchant. m. (1) Gillian Burne, 1 son, 1 daughter, (2) Adelaide Anne Elizabeth White. Education: Blundells and Sidney Sussex, Cambridge. Appointments: Director, Grandmetropolitan Ltd, 1972-75; Managing Director, International Distillers and Vintners, 1972-75; Clerk of the Royal Cellars, 1979-92; Chairman, Corney and Barrow Ltd, 1981-88; Clerk of the Prince of Wales's Cellar, 1992-99. Honours: Commander of the Royal Victorian Order; Chevalier de l'Ordre du Merite Agricole. Memberships: Merchant Taylors' Company; Leathersellers' Company; Cavalry and Guards Club; MCC; Swinley Forest Golf Club. Address: 79 Canfield Gardens, London NW6 3EA, England.

KERRICH Robert, b. 15 December 1948, Dorking, England. Professor. m. Beverly, 1 stepson, 1 stepdaughter. Education: BSc, Birmingham University, England, 1970; MSc, 1972, PhD, 1995, Imperial College, London, England; DSc, Saskatchewan of University, Canada, 1991. Appointments: Postdoctoral Fellow, ALTECH, 1975; Postdoctoral Fellow, 1975-76, Professor, 1976-86, University of Western Ontario; George McLeod Research Chair, University of Saskatchewan, 1987-. Publications: 23 chapter reviews; 215 refereed papers; 2 edited volumes; 8 short course chapters; 34 invited papers in conference proceedings; 201 abstracts; 23 technical reports; 1 book. Honours: NATO Postdoctoral Fellowship, 1975-77; Florence Bucke Science Prize, Faculty of Sciences, University of Western Ontario, 1986; EWR Steacie Fellowship, Natural Science and Engineering Research Council of Canada, 1987-89; W H Gross Medal, Young Mineral Deposits Geologist, GAC, 1988; Distinguished Lecturer, Canadian Institute of Mining and Metallurgy, 1989; Undergraduate Teaching Award, 1989; Past President's Medal, Mineralogical Association of Canada, 1989; Fellow, Royal Society of Canada, 1992; DSc, University of Saskatchewan, 1996; Elected Foreign Fellow, Geological Society of America, 1997; Willett G Miller Medal of Royal Society, 1999; Distinguished Researcher Award, University of Saskatchewan, 2000; Elected Member, European Academy of Sciences, 2001; USSC Teaching Award, 2003; Duncan Derry Medal, Geological Association of Canada, 2003; Killan Research Fellowship, Canada Council, 2003-05; Saskatchewan Centenary Medal, 2006; Career Achievement Award, Volcanology and Igneous Petrology Division, GAC, 2006. Memberships: Geological Association of Canada; Geological Society of America. Address: Geological Sciences, University of Saskatchewan, Saskatoon, S7N 5E2, Canada. E-mail: robert.kerrich@usask.ca

KESBY John Douglas, b. 14 April 1938, London, England. Anthropologist; Educator. m. Sheila Anne Gregory. Education: BA, 1960, Diploma in Anthropology, 1961, BLitt, 1963, MA, 1967, DPhil, 1971, Oxford University, England. Appointments: Lecturer, Pitt Rivers Museum, Oxford, 1967-68; College Lecturer, King's and Newnham Colleges, Cambridge, 1968-71; Lecturer, University of Kent, Canterbury, 1971-98. Publications include: The Cultural Regions of East Africa, 1977; The Rangi of Tanzania, 1981; Progress and the Past among the Rangi of Tanzania, 1982; Rangi Natural History,

1986; Entry in Encyclopaedia Britannica: Eastern Africa: the Peoples: East Africa. Memberships include: Association of Social Anthropologists; University and College Union; Royal Society for the Protection of Birds; Kent Trust. Address: 32 St Michael's Place, Canterbury, Kent CT2 7HQ, England.

KESSELYÁK Péter, b. 7 February 1936, Budapest, Hungary. Research Engineer. m. Judit Bontó, 2 sons, 4 daughters. Education: MSc, Mathematics & Physics, University of Szeged, Hungary, 1958; Postgraduate, Environmental Testing, 1960, Reliability Engineering, 1962, Computer Engineering, 1977, Technical University of Budapest. Appointments: Research Engineer, BHG Telecommunication Works, Budapest, 1959-91; Senior Counsellor, Communications Authority, Hungary, 1991-2006; Board Member, European Telecom Standards Institute, 1996-2005; Issue Manager, CEEC/EU Enlargement Affairs, 1996-2004; Expert, Hungarian National Accreditation Body, 1997-2006. Publications: Over 50 articles in periodicals; Quality; Hiradastechnika; many others. Honours: Annual Award of European Organisation for Quality, 1983; 2nd Prize, National Competition for Microelectronics, 1983; Baross Gábor Ministerial Award, 1994. Memberships: International Electrotechnical Commission (IECTC56, Dependability); Hungarian National Committee for EOQ; EOQ Software Group. Address: National Communications Authority, Ostrom u 23-25, H-1525 Budapest, Hungary. E-mail: p.kesselyak@chello.hu

KETOLA Tarja Niina Elina, b. 6 January 1959, Poytya, Finland. Academic. Education: MSc, Turku School of Economics, Finland, 1983; Higher Education Teacher Training, Finland, 1988; Lic Sc, Turku School of Economics, Finland, 1992; MA, University of Sussex, United Kingdom, 1993; Diploma of the Imperial College, PhD, Imperial College, University of London, United Kingdom, 1995. Appointments: Active Partner, Kyron Viikkolehti Ky newspaper, Finland, 1977-88; Departmental Assistant, Turku School of Economics, 1982-83; Lecturer, Turku Commercial College, 1983-93; Academy of Finland Researcher, University of Sussex, UK, 1991-92, and Imperial College, UK, 1992-94; Lecturer B, Department of Management Studies, Brunel University, UK, 1995-99; Post-doctoral Researcher, mostly Foundation for Economic Education Scholar, Finland, 1999-2003; Research Scholar, Department of Social Psychology, London School of Economics, UK, 2003; Head of Research, Senior Researcher and Lecturer, Turku School of Economics, Finland, 2004-06; Lecturer, Helsinki School of Economics & University of Helsinki, Finland, 2006; Adjunct Professor, Environmental Management, Turku School of Economics, Finland, 2004-; Associate Professor, Sustainable Development, University of Vaasa, Finland, 2006-. Publications: Author, 4 books; Editor, 4 scientific books; Numerous articles in professional journals. Honours: Prize, Pioneering Environmental Management Research, Nordic Business Environmental Management Network, Finland, 1997; Listed in international biographical dictionaries. Memberships: Nordic Academy of Management; European Academy of Management; European Business Ethics Network; Greening of Industry Network Society; International Sustainable Development Research Society; International Association for Business and Society; Sustainable Development Teaching Advancement Forum; Eco-Campus Working Group. Address: University of Vaasa, Wolffintie 34, 65100, Vaasa, Finland. E-mail: tarja.ketola@uwasa.fi

KETTLEY John Graham, b. 11 July 1952, Halifax, West Yorkshire, England. Presenter; Weather Consultant. m. Lynn, 2 sons. Education: BSc honours, Applied Physics, Coventry University. Appointments: Meteorological Office, 1970-2000; National BBC TV broadcast meteorologist, Domestic TV manager and lead presenter, 1985-2000; Founded, British Weather Services, 2000; Appearances on numerous TV series; Ambassador for Cricket World Cup, 1999; Presenter and host, Triangular NatWest One-day International cricket, 2001; Freelance presenter and weather consultant, John Kettley Enterprises; Contract weather presenter and sporting features for BBC Radio 5Live, 2001-. Publications: Several articles for cricket journals, travel and leisure brochures; Foreword, Rain Stops Play, book by Andrew Hignell, 2002. Memberships: Lord's Taverner, 1990-; Institute of Broadcast Meteorology, 1995-; Fellow, Royal Meteorological Society, 2001-. Address: c/o PVA Management, Hallow Park, Hallow, Worcester WR2 6PG, England. E-mail: johnkettley@bbc.co.uk

KEVELAITIS Egidijus, b. 27 July 1961, Kaunas, Lithuania. Medical Doctor. m. Sigita, 2 sons. Education: MD, 1985; PhD, 1988; DSc, 1993; Docent diploma, 1994. Appointments: Assistant Professor, Department of Physiology and Pathophysiology, Kaunas Medical Institute, 1985-88; Senior Lecturer, Department of Physiology and Pathophysiology, Kaunas Medical Academy, 1988-92; Associate Professor, Department of Physiology, 1992-2001, Professor, Department of Physiology, 2001-, Chairman, Department of Physiology, 2002-, Kaunas Medical University. Publications: Articles to medical journals; Editor, textbook: Human Physiology, 1999, 2002; Journal, Medicina, 2001-. Honours: Award, Lithuanian Academy of Sciences, 1984; Research Fellowship, European Society of Cardiology, 1997. Memberships: Lithuanian Physiological Society, Vice-President, 1992-2005; President, 2005-; European Society of Cardiology; New York Academy of Sciences; Danish Society of Pharmacology. Address: Department of Physiology, 9 Mickeviciaus, Kaunas Medical University, 3000 Kaunas, Lithuania.

KEYS Alicia, b. 25 January 1981, New York, USA. Singer; Pianist; Songwriter. Education: Professional Performing Arts School, Manhattan; Classically trained pianist. Career: Signed to Clive Davis' new J Records label, 1999; Appeared in charity telethon in aid of World Trade Center victims, 2001; Prince's Trust Urban Music Festival, London, 2004; Collaborations with Angie Stone and Jimmy Cozier. Recordings: Albums: Songs In a Minor, 2001; The Diary of Alicia Keys, 2003; Unplugged, 2005; As I Am, 2007. Singles: Girlfriend, 2001; Fallin', 2001; A Woman's Worth, 2001; How Come You Don't Call Me Any More, 2002; You Don't Know My Name, 2003; If I Ain't Got You, 2004. Honours: Grammy Award, Best New Artist, 2001; Grammy Award, Best R&B Album, 2001; Grammy Award, Song of the Year, Best Female R&B Vocal Performance, Best R&B Song, 2001; American Music Award Favorite New Artist, Pop/Rock, Favourite New Artist, Soul/R&B, 2002; MTV Award, Best R&B Act, 2002; MOBO Award for Best Album, 2002; American Music Award for Best Female Soul/R&B Artist, 2004; Source Hip Hop Music Award for Female Artist of the Year, 2004; Grammy Award, Best R&B Album, 2005; Grammy Award, Best R&B Song, 2005. Address: William Morris Agency, 1325 Avenue of the Americas, New York, NY 10019, USA. Website: www.aliciakeys.net

KHAJA Naseeruddin, b. 1 April 1954, Gulbarga, India. Medical Teacher. m. Syeda Mahmooda Banu, 2 sons. Education: MBBS, Karnatak University, Dharwad, 1975; DLO, Mysore University, 1978; MS (ENT), Bangalore University, 1981. Appointments: Lecturer in ENT, GMC Bellary, 1982-88; Assistant Professor in ENT, MMC, Mysore, 1988-93; Professor of ENT, KMC, Hubli, 1993-95; Professor & HOD of ENT, KIMS, Hubli, 1995-; Director, Vijayanagar

Institute of Medical Sciences Bellary, Karnataka, India, 2006-. Publications: Papers and articles in professional journals. Honours: First PhD Guide at Department of ENT, KIMS, Hubli; Fellowship of Indian Academy of Otolaryngology; President, AOI Karnatak Branch, 2004-05. Memberships: IMA & IMA-AMS; AOI; ISO; APOI; NES; FHNO; Academy of Allergy; Life Associate, MAAS; Life Member, Telemedicine Society of India. Address: Vijayanagar Institute of Medical Sciences, Bellary-583104, Karnataka State, India. E-mail: drknaseeruddin@rediffmail.com

KHAN Gulfaraz, b. 7 February 1965, Pakistan. Academic Pathologist. m. Rosina Murtaza, 1 daughter. Education: BSc, 1988; MSc, 1989; PhD, 1993. Appointments: Senior Scientist, St Batholomew's Hospital Medical College, London, 1993-94; Research Fellow, Tufts University School of Medicine, Boston, USA, 1995-96; Postdoctoral Scientist, University of Glasgow, 1996-99; Lecturer, Pathology, ARU, Cambridge, 2002-04; Senior Lecturer, Cellular Pathology, Kingston University, 2004-. Publications: Over 24 articles in professional journals; 1 book; 2 book chapters. Honours: Honorary Senior Lecturer, St George's Hospital, University of London, 2005-; Visiting Scientist, Spanish National Cancer Institute, 2005-; Editor, Pakistan Journal of Pathology online, 2005-; Editor, Pakistan Journal of Medical Sciences, 2005-; Editor, Scientific Journals International, 2006-; Visiting Lecturer, Middlesex University, 2007-; Listed in international biographical dictionaries. Memberships: Fellow, Royal Institute of Public Health; Fellow, Royal Society of Medicine; Pathological Society of Great Britain & Ireland. Address: Kingston University, School of Life Sciences, Penrhyn Road, Kingston Upon Thames, Surrey KT1 2EE, England. E-mail: g.khan@kingston.ac.uk

KHAN Imran Niaza, b. 25 October 1952, Lahore, Pakistan. Politician; Former Professional Cricketer. m. Jemima Goldsmith, 1995, divorced 2004, 2 sons. Education: Keble College, Oxford. Career: Right-arm fast bowler, middle-order right-hand batsman; Played for Lahore, 1969-71, Worcester, 1971-76, Oxford University, 1973-75 (Captain, 1974), Dawood, 1975-76, PIA, 1975-81, Sussex, 1974-88, NSW, 1984-85; 88 test matches for Pakistan, 1971-92, 48 as captain, scoring 3,807 runs and taking 362 wickets; Toured England 1971, 1974, 1975 (World Cup), 1979 (World Cup), 1982, 1983 (World Cup), 1987; Scored 17,771 first-class runs and took 1,287 first-class wickets; 175 limited-overs ints, 139 as captain (including 1992 World Cup victory); Special Representative for Sports, UNICEF, 1989; Editor in Chief, Cricket Life, 1989-90; Founder, Imran Khan Cancer Hospital Appeal, 1991-; Founder, 1996, Leader, 1996-, Tehrik-e-Insaf (Movement for Justice). Publications: Imran, 1983; All-Round View (autobiography), 1988; Indus Journey, 1990; Warrior Race, 1993; Syndicated newspaper column. Honours: Honorary Fellow, Keble College, Oxford, 1988; Wisden Cricketer of the Year, 1983; Hilal-e-Imtiaz, 1993. Address: c/o Shaukat Khanum Memorial Trust, 29 Shah Jamal, Lahore 54600, Pakistan.

KHAN Jemima, b. 30 January 1974, London, England. Charity fund-raiser. m. Imran Khan, 1995, divorced 2004, 2 sons. Education: Bristol University. Career: Developed own brand of tomato ketchup; Established Jemima Khan Designs fashion label; Campaigned to improve literacy levels in Pakistan; UK Special Representative, UNICEF, 2001-; Founded Jemima Khan Appeal; Reporter and presenter, Channel 5, Bangladesh, 2002-; Fund-raiser, Shaukat Khanum Memorial Cancer Hospital. Honours: Rover People's Award

for Best Dressed Female Celebrity, British Fashion Awards, 2001. Address: c/o UNICEF, 3 United Nations Plaza, New York, NY 10017, USA.

KHAN Md Mahbub Ul Karim, b. 15 October 1955, Bangladesh. Associate Professor. m. Halima, 1 daughter. Education: MBBS, Mymensingh Medical College, Dhaka University, Bangladesh, 1980; D Ped, University of Vienna, Austria, 1987; MCPS, 1995; DCH, 1999; DTM&H, 2000. Appointments: Medical Officer, Rural Health Complex, Dewanganj & Madarganj, Jamalpur, Bangladesh, 1982-83; Assistant Registrar, Rangpur Medical College Hospital, Bangladesh, 1983; Medical Officer, Department of Paediatrics, Shahid Rezae Hospital, Kazerun, Fars, Iran, 1983-86; Private Practice as Paediatrician, Mymensingh town, Bangladesh, 1987-97; Associate Professor, Department of Paediatrics, Community Based Medical College, Bangladesh, 1997-. Publications: Case study profile of congenital heart diseases, 1999; Disease profile of the admitted neonates in CBMCB hospital paediatric unit, 2002; Audit of the blood transfusion in CBMCB paediatric unit, 2003; Laboratory diagnosis of malaria, 2003; Experiences of cranial ultrasonography in admitted symptomatic neonates, 2003; Case report – Brittle bones disease, 2004; Is severe malnutrition declining in Bangladesh, 2006; Case report: Hyper Reactive Malarial splenomegaly, 2006. Memberships: Bangladesh Medical Association; International Lions Club; American Medical Society; National Heart Foundation, Bangladesh. Address: Department of Paediatrics, Community Based Medical College, Mymensingh, Bangladesh. E-mail: mkarim_ khan@yahoo.com

KHAN Mohammad, b. 19 August 1942, Kanpur, India. Educator. m. Zubaida Hamid, 2 sons, 5 daughters. Education: BS (Mech), 1963; ME (Prod), 1966; PhD (Prod), 1979. Appointments: Lecturer, University of Roorkee, India, 1966-70; Assistant Professor, MNNIT, Allahabad, India, 1970-80; Assistant Professor, Basrah University, Iraq, 1980-84; Professor (Mech), Garyousis University, Benghazi, Libya, 1984-2001; HOD (Mech), Dean, Engineering, Integral University, India, 2002-. Publications: 2 books: Industrial Engineering, Welding Science and Technology; 29 research papers. Honours: Institution of Engineers; Prize, 1976-77, Certificate of Merit, 1978; Bharat Jyoti Award, 1999. Memberships: Fellow, Institution of Engineers; Senior Member, SME, USA. Address: 94/6 Nai Sarak, Kanpur, Uttar Pradesh, 208001, India. E-mail: mikyh_20@yahoo.com

KHAN Sujoy, b. 16 June 1976 (arrived in UK 2002). Immunologist. m. Sanchita Saha, 2004, 1 daughter. Education: MBBS, Christian Medical College, Vellore, India, 1999. Appointments: Resident, Christian Medical College & Hospital, Vellore, 2000-02; Senior House Officer, NHS Trust, Wales, 2002-05; Specialist Registrar, Immunopathology, Barts and the London NHS Trust, London, 2005; Specialist Registrar, Immunology, Path Links Immunology, Scunthorpe, England, 2005-. Publications: Numerous articles in professional journals. Honours: Research Award, Christian Medical College & Hospital, 1999. Memberships: RCP; Association of Clinical Pathologists; European Academy of Allergy and Clinical Immunology; American Academy of Allergy, Asthma and Immunology. Address: Path Links Immunology, Scunthorpe General Hospital, Scunthorpe, DN15 7BH, England. E-mail: sujoykhan@gmail.com

KHARE Mukesh, b. 1 January 1956, Varanasi, India. Civil Engineer. Education: BEng in Civil Engineering, 1977; MEng in Civil Engineering, Environmental Engineering,

1979, University of Roorkee; PhD, Faculty of Engineering, University of Newcastle upon Tyne, 1989. Appointments: Assistant Design Engineer, Uttar Pradesh State Irrigation Department, 1979-81; Assistant Environmental Engineer, Pollution Control Board, Agra, 1981-84; Research Scholar, Demonstrator, University of Newcastle upon Tyne, England, 1984-89; Fellow to Council of Scientific and Industrial Research, National Environmental Engineering Research Institute, India, 1989-90; Lecturer, Assistant Professor, 1990-96, Assistant Professor, 1997-2000, Associate Professor, February 2000-2005, Professor, 2005- Department of Civil Engineering, Indian Institute of Technology, Delhi; Lecturer II, University of Technology, Lae, Papua New Guinea, 1996-97; Atlantic LMG Chair Professor, University of West Indies, St Augustine, Trinidad & Tobago, 2006-07; Invited Lecturer, Urban Vehicular Pollution, Department of Environmental and Applied Sciences, Harvard University, USA, 2002 and EMN, Nantes, France, 2002; Founder, Co-Ordinator, Indo-French unit on Water and Waste Technologies, joint venture between, Institute of Technology, Delhi and Ministry of Education, France; Co-ordinator, IITD-ENPC, France MOU on Transport and Environment, and Remote Sensing; Reviewer: Research Management Group, Philip Morris Inc, USA, National Research Foundation, Pretoria, S Africa, Foundation for Research Development, Pretoria, S Africa; Member, Technical Advisory Board, Blacksmith Institute, USA. Publications: More than 50 in international and national refereed journals, proceedings, symposia, 1990-, in field of industrial and water pollution, indoor and outdoor air pollution; Author, Institute Water Quality Monitoring Programme; Founder, Editorial Board Member, International Journal on Environment and Waste Management, 2006-; Founder, Editorial Board Member, International Journal on Environmental Science & Engineering, 2008-; Editor, Special issue on Urban Air Pollution, in print; Book: Modelling Urban Vehicle Emissions, 2002; WIT Press UK; Artificial Neural Network in Vehicular Pollution Modelling, 2007; Aluminium Smelting & Engineering, Environmental and Health Perspectives, 2008; Contributed chapter, Fuel Options, to Handbook of Transport and Environment Vol 4, 2003; Sectoral Analysis of Air Pollution Control in Delhi, 2004; Principal Investigator, International Sustainable Technology Alliance (ISTA): Sustainable Development programme, Arizona State University, USA; Member, Expert, Examination Committee, All India Council for Technical Education, India; University Grant Commission, India; Union Public Service Commission, India, Consultant to Associate in Rural Development (ARD), USA and Delhi Pollution Central Committee, India. Honours: National Merit Scholar, 1969-77; Best Outgoing Student, Civil Engineering Department, University of Roorkee, 1977; Best Solo Singer, University of Roorkee Cultural Society, 1977; Fellowship, University Grant Commission, 1977-79; National Scholarship for Study Abroad, 1984-89; Overseas Research Student Award, Committee of Vice-Chancellors and Principals, UK, 1987-89. Memberships include: Fellow, Wessex Institute of Great Britain; Fellow, Indian Water Works Association; Life Member: Indian Society for Wind Engineers; Indian Association for Environmental Management; Indian Society for Environmental Management; Indian Association for Air Pollution Control; Newcastle University and Roorkee University Alumni Associations. Address: Indian Institute of Technology, Hauz Khas, New Delhi 110016, India. E-mail: mukeshk@civil.iitd.ernet.in

KHINTIBIDZE Elguja, b. 7 June 1937, Georgia. Philologist. m. Mzia Menabde, 2 sons. Education: Student of Tbilisi State University, 1955-60; Postgrad Student, 1960-63; Cand Philol, 1963; DrPhilol, 1971; Professor, 1973; Corresponding Member, Georgian Academy Sciences, 1997. Appointments: Assistant Professor, 1966, Professor, 1973, Deputy Dean Philology Department, 1965-66, The Dean of Philology Department, 1976-85, Vice Rector, Tbilisi State University, 1985-93; Director, Centre of Georgian Studies, 1992-; Head, Laboratory of Georgian-Foreign Literature Contacts, 1993-; Head, Chair of Old Georgian Literature, 2000-. Publications: 180 scholarly works including 14 monographs; Georgian-Byzantine Literary Contacts, 1996; The Designation of Georgians and Their Etymology, 1998; Georgian Literature in European Scholarship, 2001. Honours: Ivane Javakhishvili Prize, 1983; International Order of Merit, 1994; Georgia's Order of Merit, 2003. Memberships: Membre Titulaire de Société Internationale pour l'Etude de la Philosophie Médiévale (Belgique Louvan La Neuve). Address: Side Street Ateni 18A Apt 13, Tbilisi 0179, Georgia.

KHORANA Har Gobind, b. 9 January 1922, Raipur, Punjab Region, India (US Citizen). Chemist. m Esther Elizabeth Sibler, 1952, 1 son, 2 daughters. Education: Bachelor's Degree, 1943, Master's Degree, 1945, Chemistry, Punjab University; Doctorate, Liverpool University; Postdoctoral work in Zurich, Switzerland. Appointments: Organic Chemist, working with Sir Alexander Todd, Cambridge, 1950-52; Organic Chemist, National Research Institute, Canada, 1952-60; Professor and Co-Director, Institute of Enzyme Chemistry, University of Wisconsin, 1960-64; Conrad A Elvehjem Professor in Life Sciences, 1964-70; Andrew D White Professor at Large, Cornell University, Ithaca, 1974-80; Alfred P Sloan Professor, 1970-97, Professor Emeritus and Senior Lecturer, 1997-, Massachusetts Institute of Technology. Publications: Some Recent Developments in the Chemistry of Phosphate Esters of Biological Interest, 1961; Articles on Biochemistry in various journals. Honours: Joint Winner, Nobel Prize for Physiology or Medicine, 1968; Louisa Gross Horwitz for Biochemistry, 1968; American Chemical Society Award for creative work in Synthetic Chemistry, 1968; Lasker Foundation Award, 1968; American Academy of Achievement Award, 1971; Willard Gibbs Medal, 1974; Gairdner Foundation Annual Award, 1980; National Medal of Science, 1987; Paul Kayser International Award of Merit, 1987; Numerous honorary degrees and international awards. Memberships: NAS; Foreign Academician, USSR Academy of Sciences; Foreign Member, Royal Society, London; Pontifical Academy of Sciences. Address: Departments of Biology and Chemistry, Massachusetts Institute of Technology, 77 Massachusetts Avenue, Room 68-680, Cambridge, MA 02139, USA.

KIDALOV Vladimir N, b. 7 April 1948, Redkino, Tverskaya obl, Russia. Doctor; Radiobiologist. m. Liudmila Belenova, 1 son. Education: Military Doctor's diploma; Candidate of Medical Sciences; Certificate, Senior Scientific Employee, Radiobiology; Diploma, Doctor of Medical Sciences, Internal Illnesses and Radiobiology. Appointments: Chief, Medical Aid Station; Scientific Employee, Senior Scientific Employee, Deputy Chief of Laboratory, Chief of Research Group, Army-Medical Group; Senior Scientific Employee, Laboratory of Biophysics; Head, Organisational-Methodical Department, Professor, Faculty of Internal Illnesses. Publications: 120 papers; 5 monographs; 40 articles. Honours: Diploma, International Academy for Information, Communication and Management in Technics, Nature and Society. Memberships: International Academy for Information, Communication and Management in Technics, Nature and Society; Associate Editor, Bulletin of New Medical Technologies. Address: Ave Aviakoustruktorov 11-1-122, St Petersburg 197372, Russia. E-mail: vkidalov@mail.ru

KIDD Jodie, b. 1979, Surrey, England. Fashion Model. Education: St Michael's School, W Sussex. Appointments: Modelled for numerous fashion magazines, also top international catwalk model for designers include: Gucci, Prada, Karl Lagerfeld, Yves Saint Laurent, Chanel, John Galliano, Calvin Klein, Yohji Yamamoto; Make-up Model for Chanel, 1999 season. Honours: Former National Junior Athletics Champion; Holder, Under 15s High Jump Record for Sussex; Many awards as junior show jumper. Address: c/o IMG Models, Bentinck House, 3-8 Bolsover Street, London, W1P 7HG, England.

KIDMAN Fiona (Judith) (Dame), b. 26 March 1940, Hawera, New Zealand. Writer; Poet. m. Ernest Ian Kidman, 20 August 1960, 1 son, 1 daughter. Appointments: Founding Secretary/ Organiser, New Zealand Book Council, 1972-75; Secretary, 1972-76, President, 1981-83, New Zealand Centre, PEN; President, 1992-95, President of Honour, 1997-, New Zealand Book Council. Publications: Novels: A Breed of Women, 1979; Mandarin Summer, 1981; Paddy's Puzzle, 1983, US edition as In the Clear Light, 1985; The Book of Secrets, 1987; True Stars, 1990; Ricochet Baby, 1996; The House Within, 1997; Songs from the Violet Café, 2003; The Captive Wife, 2005. Short stories: Unsuitable Friends, 1988; The Foreign Woman, 1994; The Best of Fiona Kidman's Short Stories, 1998; A Needle in the Heart, 2002; Songs from the Violet Café, 2003; The Best New Zealand Fiction, 2004, 2005. Poetry: Honey and Bitters, 1975; On the Tightrope, 1978; Going to the Chathams, Poems: 1977-1984, 1985; Wakeful Nights: Poems Selected and New, 1991; Other: Search for Sister Blue (radio play), 1975; Gone North (with Jane Ussher), 1984; Wellington (with Grant Sheehan), 1989; Palm Prints (autobiographical essays), 1995; New Zealand Love Stories: An Oxford Anthology (editor), Best New Zealand Fiction, 1999. Contributions to: Periodicals. Honours: Scholarships in Letters, 1981, 1985, 1991, 1995; Mobil Short Story Award, 1987; Queen Elizabeth II Arts Council Award for Achievement, 1988; Officer of the Order of the British Empire, 1988; Victoria University Writing Fellowship, 1988; President of Honour, New Zealand Book Council, 1997; Dame Companion of the New Zealand Order of Merit, for services to literature, 1998. Memberships: International PEN; Media Women; New Zealand Book Council, president, 1992-95; Patron, Cambodia Trust Aotearoa. Address: 28 Rakau Road, Hataitai, Wellington 3, New Zealand.

KIDMAN Nicole, b. 20 June 1967, Hawaii, USA, Australian nationality. Actress. m. (1) Tom Cruise, 1990, divorced 2001, 1 adopted son, 1 adopted daughter, (2) Keith Urban, 2006, 1 daughter. Education: St Martin's Youth Theatre, Melbourne; Australian Theatre for Young People, Sydney. Appointments: Goodwill Ambassador, UNICEF. Acting début in Australian film aged 14; Actress, TV mini-series, Vietnam, 1987; Bangkok Hilton, 1989. Creative Works: Films: The Emerald City; The Year My Voice Broke; Flirting; Dead Calm, Days of Thunder, 1990; Billy Bathgate, 1991; Far and Away, 1992; Malice, My Life, 1993; Batman Forever, To Die For, 1995; Portrait of a Lady, 1996; The Peacemaker, Eyes Wide Shut, 1998; Practical Magic, Moulin Rouge, 1999; The Others, 2000; Moulin Rouge, Birthday Girl, The Hours, 2001; Dogville, Cold Mountain, The Human Stain, Birth, 2003; The Interpreter, Alexander the Great, 2004; Bewitched, 2005; Fur: An Imaginary Portrait of Diane Arbus, Happy Feet, 2006; The Invasion, His Dark Materials: The Golden Compass, Margot at the Wedding, 2007. Play: The Blue Room, 1998-99. Honours: Best Actress Award, Australian Film Institute; Actress of the Year, Australia; Seattle International Film Festival Award, 1995; London Film Critics Award, 1996; Best Actress, Golden

Globe Award, 1996; BAFTA Nominee, 1996; Best Actress in a Musical, Golden Globe Award, 2001; Best Dramatic Actress, Golden Globe Award, 2003; BAFTA Award for Best Actress in a Leading Role, 2003; Academy Award for Best Actress, 2003. Address: c/o Ann Churchill-Brown, Shanahan Management, PO Box 478, Kings Cross, NSW 2011, Australia.

KIEHL Reinhold, b. 8 October 1947, Worms, Germany. Chemist; Biochemist; Human Biologist. m. Ilse Gertraud Schoyerer, divorced, 2 daughters. Education: BEng, Engineering School, Mannheim, 1971; MS, Chemistry, University of Heidelberg, 1974; DSc, 1977; MEng, Fachhochschule, Mannheim, 1982. Appointments: Registered Eco-Audit Specialist, Research Fellow Max Planck Institute, Heidelburg, 1977; Postdoctoral Fellow Scripps Clinic, La Jolla, 1977-79; Assistant Professor, Ruhr University, Bochum, 1979-85; Associate Professor, Bielefeld University, 1985-87; Head of Laboratory And Research, Clinic Neukirchen, 1987-94; Professor, Director; Freelance Workshop And Course Instructor, 1995-. Publications: Over 50 articles to professional journals. Memberships: American Heart Association; Max Planck Society; Royal Society of Chemistry; AAAS; British Society of Allergy and Clinical Immunology; International Union of Pure and Applied Chemistry; New York Academy of Science. Address: RKI Institut(e) (Lab Research Molecular Med/Biol), Saliterweg 1, 93437 Furth Im Wald, Germany. E-mail: kiehl@rki-i.com Website: www.rki-i.com

KIKAWADA Masayuki, b. 29 November 1963, Tokyo, Japan. Medical Doctor. m. Naoko, 1 son, 2 daughters. Education: MD, 1993, PhD, Immunology, 1999, Tokyo Medical University. Appointments: Resident, Internal Medicine, 1993-95, Fellow, Pulmonary Medicine, 1995-98, Fellow, 1998-2000, Attending Physician, 2000-04, Instructor, 2004-, Physician in Chief, 2006-07, Geriatric Medicine, Tokyo Medical University; Assistant Professor, Clinical Welfare College, Tokyo, 2003-; Assistant Professor, Ryogoku Rehabilitation College, Tokyo, 2003-. Publications: Papers and articles published in professional scientific journals worldwide. Honours: Listed in national and international biographical dictionaries. Memberships: ACP; The Japanese Society of Internal Medicine; The Japan Geriatrics Society; The Japanese Respiratory Society; Japan Society for Respiratory Endoscopy; The Japan Lung Cancer Society; The Japanese Association of Infectious Disease. Address: Department of Geriatric Medicine, Tokyo Medical University, 6-7-1 Nishishinjuku, Shinjuku-ku, Tokyo 160-0023, Japan.

KILBERGER Harry (Jindřich), b. 10 July 1921, Plzeň, Czech Republic. m. Margaret Robinson. Education: Technical Architectural studies, Czechoslovakia, 4 years; Technician in Civil Engineering, International Refugee Organisation Area 3, Würzberg, US Zone, Germany, 1949; Architectural College, Australia, last 2 years from 6 years. Honours: Hobart Technical College Prize, 1958; Credits for structural design and for research (thesis) of parking problems and solutions in big cities; Special Clarence Municipality Prize for Civic Centre Design; Building alteration for accommodation of the Royal Visit of Queen Elizabeth II and Prince Philip to Alice Springs, Northern Territory, Australia, 1963; American Public Ambassadors Delegation, Chinese Republic, 1991; Professional of the Year, 2007; International Order of Merit, 2007. Memberships: Member, 1960-, Fellow, 1970-, Royal Australian Institute of Architects; Member, 1961-, Chartered Member, Royal Institute of British Architects; Registered Architect, Tasmania, Australia, 1960-. Address: 9/17 Chapman St, Bellerive, Tasmania 7018, Australia.

KILMER Val, b. 31 December 1959, Los Angeles, USA. Actor. m. Joanne Whalley, divorced, 1 son, 1 daughter. Education: Hollywood's Professional's School; Juilliard. Creative Works: Stage appearances include: Electra and Orestes, Henry IV Part One, 1981; As You Like It, 1982; Slab Boys, 1983; Hamlet, 1988; Tis Pity She's A Whore, 1992; TV Films: Top Secret, 1984; Real Genius, 1985; Top Gun, 1986; Willow, 1988; Kill Me Again, 1989; The Doors, Thunderheart, 1991; True Romance, The Real McCoy, Tombstone, 1993; Wings of Courage, Batman Forever, Heat, 1995; The Saint, The Island of Dr Moreau, The Ghost and the Darkness, Dead Girl, 1996; Joe the King, 1999; Pollock, Red Planet, 2000; The Salton Sea, Run for the Money, 2002; Masked and Anonymous, Wonderland, The Missing, 2003; Spartan, Mind Hunters, Alexander, 2004; Kiss, Kiss, Bang, Bang, 2005; Moscow Zero, 10th & Wolf, Played, Summer Love, Déjà vu, The Ten Commandments: The Musical, 2006; Delgo, Have Dreams, Will Travel, 2007; Conspiracy, Columbus Day, Alpha Numeric, 2008. Address: c/o CAA, 9830 Wilshire Boulevard, Beverly Hills, CA 90212, USA.

KIM Byung-Nam, b. 6 April 1962, Seoul, South Korea. Researcher. m. Eun-Kyung Lee, 1 son, 1 daughter. Education: Bachelor's degree, Yonsei University, Korea, 1986; Master's degree, 1989, Doctor's degree, 1992, University of Tokyo, Japan. Appointments: Researcher, 1992-93, Research Associate, 1995-98, University of Tokyo; Research Associate, Tokyo Metropolitan University, 1993-95; Senior Researcher, National Institute for Materials Science, 1998-; Visiting Scholar, University of Pennsylvania, USA, 2003-04. Publications: Articles and papers in professional scientific journals. Honours: Paper Award, 1994, Meritorious Honor Award, 2003, Japan Institute of Metals. Memberships: Japan Institute of Metals; Commendation for Science and Technology, Minister of Education, Culture, Sports, Science and Technology, Prizes for Science and Technology, 2007. Address: National Institute for Materials Science, 1-2-1 Sengen, Tsukuba, Ibaraki 305-0047, Japan. E-mail: kim.byung-nam@nims.go.jp

KIM Chongsoon, b. 23 February 1953, South Korea. Medical Doctor. m. Eunhee Han, 1981, 1 son, 1 daughter. Education: MD, 1977, MS, 1980, PhD, 1987, Seoul National University, Korea. Appointments: Rotating Internship, 1977-78; Residency, 1978-82; Visiting Scholar, MD Anderson Cancer Center, 1988-89; Visiting Scholar, Kyoto University Hospital, Research Center Julich, 1994; Chief, Department of Nuclear Medicine, 1985-89, Chief, Department of Internal & Nuclear Medicine, 1989-, Hanil Hospital; Director, Radiation Health Research Institute, KHNP, 1999-. Publications: Clinical Cancer Research, 2005; Oncology Reports, 2005; Environmental Toxicology and Chemistry, 2005; Oncology Reports, 2005; Radiation Protection Dosimetry, 2006. Honours: Distinguished Service Awards: Korea Society of Nuclear Medicine, 1997; Ministry of Science and Technology, 2001; Korean Hydro & Nuclear Power, 2002. Memberships: EANM; SNM; IAR. Address: Radiation Health Research Institute, 388-1, Ssang Moon Dong, Do Bong Gu, Seoul 132-703, Korea. E-mail: kjsoon@khnp.co.kr

KIM Dohyeon, Assistant Professor. Education: BSc, 1993, MSc, 1995, Aerospace Engineering, PhD, Mechanical and Aerospace Engineering, 1998, Seoul National University; ABD, University of Warwick. Appointments: Private, Korean Army, 1990-91; Senior Associate, 1998-99, Consultant, 2000, The Boston Consulting Group, Seoul; Lecturer, Woosuk University, Wanju, Korea, 1999-2002; Team Leader (Deputy Director), Strategic Planning Team, SBSI, Seoul, 2000-02; Director (Partner), NAC Corporate Finance Group, Seoul, 2002-03; Director (Partner), I&S Business Consulting Group, Seoul, 2003-05; Invigilator, Seminar Lecturer, Warwick Business School, Coventry, England, 2005-06; Assistant Professor, College of Business Administration, Kookmin University, Seoul, 2006-; Advisor, Lian Accounting Corporation, 2006-; Member of Advisory Committee, Korean Consulting Association, 2006-; Member of Advisory Committee, Korean Technology Transfer Corporation, 2006-. Address: College of Business Administration, Kookmin University, Songbuk-gu, Seoul, Korea. E-mail: drkiim@kookmin.ac.kr

KIM Dosik, b. 8 March 1964, Seoul, Republic of Korea. Principal Researcher. m. Wonyoung Kim, 2 sons. Education: Bachelor's degree, 1987, Master's degree, 1990, PhD, 1994, Hanyang University, Seoul. Appointments: Lecturer, Seoul National University of Technology, 1994-95; Visiting Scholar, Stanford University, USA, 1995-97; Lecturer, Inha University, Inchon, Korea, 1997-98; Postdoctoral Fellow, 1998-2000, Principal Researcher, 2000-, Korea Atomic Energy Research Institute, Korea. Publications: Notched Strength and Fracture Criterion in Fabric Composite Plate Containing a Circular Hole; Low Temperature Effects on the Fracture Behavior of STS 304 Stainless Steel for Membrane of LNG Storage Tank; Tensile Test Techniques for Nuclear Fuel Cladding in a Hot Cell. Honours: Paper Award, Korean Nuclear Society, 2005; Paper Award, Materials Research Society of Korea, 2006. Memberships: Korean Society of Mechanical Engineers; Korean Institute of Metals and Materials; Korean Nuclear Society; Materials Research Society of Korea. Address: Korea Atomic Energy Research Institute, Irradiated Materials Examination Facility, 150 Dukjin-Dong, Yusong-Gu, Daejeon 305-353, Republic of Korea. E-mail: kimds@kaeri.re.kr

KIM Hakyong, b. 4 July 1972, Daejon, South Korea. Research Engineer. Education: BE, Electronics Engineering, Chungnam National University, 1995; MS, 1997, PhD, 2001, Information and Communications, Gwangju Institute of Science and Technology. Appointments: Research Professor, Ultrafast Fiber-Optic Networks Research Center of GIST, 2001; Senior Researcher, Corecess Inc, 2001-03; Senior Researcher, Samsung Networks Inc, Seoul, Korea, 2003-. Publications: Over 40 papers in professional journals; 3 patents pending. Honours: Best Paper Award, Korea Telecom, 1994, 1995; Listed in international biographical directories. Memberships: Associate Member: IEEE; IEEK; IEICE. Website: http://hykim.net

KIM In-Ju, b. 17 October 1961, Seoul, Korea. Researcher; Lecturer. m. Eun-Sun Oh, 1 daughter. Education: MSc, Applied Biomechanics, 1996, PhD, 2001, University of Sydney. Appointments: Research Assistant, 1997-2001, Teaching Staff and Honorary Research Fellow, 2002, School of Exercise and Sport Science, Faculty of Health Sciences, University of Sydney; Research Fellow and Lecturer, School of Sport and Health Sciences, University of Exeter, England, 2003-; Invited Industry Consultant, Medical Engineering Section, Pera, UK, 2005-; Invited Industry Consultant, Healthcare Council, The Gerson Lehrman Group, USA, 2005-. Publications: Numerous articles in professional journals. Honours: Research Award for Generating Innovative Research Ideas to Prevent Fatalities and Injuries in the Workplace, American Society of Safety Engineers Foundation, 2002; Best Paper Award, Journal of Korean Association of Science and Technology, Australia, 2003; Research Grant (Category 1), ACT Health and Medical Research Council's Research Support Program, Australia, 2004; Man of the Year, ABI, 2006; Listed in Who's Who publications and national and international biographical dictionaries. Memberships: British Association of Sport and Exercise Sciences; The Ergonomics Society; International Society of Biomechanics; International Researcher, Contact Group for Slips, Trips and Falls; International Ergonomics Association; Ergonomics Society of Australia; and many others. Address: 9 Derry Street, Monash, ACT 2904, Australia. E-mail: i.kim@exeter.ac.uk

KIM Jong Il, b. 16 February 1942, Mount Paekdu, Korea. Leader of the Democratic People's Republic of Korea; General Secretary of the Workers' Party of Korea; Chairman of the National Defence Commission of the Democratic People's Republic of Korea. Education: Graduated, Kim Il Sung University, Pyongyang. Career: Officer, Section Chief, Deputy Director, Director, Department of the Central Committee of the Worker's Party of Korea, 1964-73; Member, Central Committee of the Workers' Party of Korea, 1972; Secretary, Central Committee of the Workers' Party of Korea, 1973; Member, Political Committee Central Committee of the Workers' Party of Korea, 1974; Member, Presidium of Political Bureau, Central Committee of the Workers' Party of Korea and Member, Military Commission of the Central Committee of the Workers' Party of Korea, 1980; Deputy, Supreme People's Assembly of the Democratic People's Republic of Korea, 1982-; First Vice-Chairman, National Defence Commission, Democratic People's Republic of Korea, 1990-93; Chairman, National Defence Commission, Democratic People's Republic of Korea, 1993-; Supreme Commander, Korean People's Army, 1991-; Marshal, Democratic People's Republic of Korea, 1992-; General Secretary, Worker's Party of Korea, 1997. Publications: Kim Jong Il Selected Works, 14 volumes; For the Completion of the Juche Revolutionary Cause, 10 volumes; Many other works. Honours: 3 times, The Hero of the Democratic People's Republic of Korea; 3 times, The Kim Il Sung Order; The Kim Il Sung Prize; Many other domestic and foreign orders and medals, honorary titles and titles of doctorate. Address: The Central Committee of the Workers' Party of Korea, Pyongyang, Democratic People's Republic of Korea.

KIM Jong-Bo, b. 18 January 1971, Seoul, Korea. Researcher. m. Eun-Hee Park, 1 son, 1 daughter. Education: BA, Horticulture, 1989-96, MSc, Floriculture, 1996-98, Kon-kuk University, Korea; PhD, Plant Biotechnology, Wageningen University, The Netherlands, 1999-2005. Appointments: Teaching Assistant, 1996-98, Research Assistant, 1997-98; Senior Researcher, Central Research Centre, Neobio Co Ltd, 2006-; Associate Researcher, Turfgrass and Environment Research Institute, Samsung Everland Inc, 2003-06; Associate Researcher, Central Research Institute, Neobio Co Ltd, 2006; Principal Researcher, Genomine Inc, 2006-2007; Assistant Professor, Kon-kuk University, 2007-. Publications: Articles as co-author in scientific journals including: Korean Journal of Turfgrass Society, 1997 (2), 2004; Acta Horticulturae, 2001, 2002; In Vitro Cellular & Developmental Biology-Plant, 2005; Euphytica, 2005; Plant Cell Tissue and Organ Culture, 2006; Research in Plant Disease, 2006 (submitted); Genetics, 2007. Honour: National Scholarship in the field of Agrimony and Horticulture, 1999-2001. Listed in Who's Who publications and biographical dictionaries. Memberships: Director, Korean Society for Plant Biotechnology; Director, Turfgrass Society of Korea, 2004-; International Society of Horticultural Science, 1999-; Society for In Vitro Biology, 2000-; International Plant Molecular Biology, 2001; Botanical Society of Korea, 2003-; Korean Breeding Society, 2003-. Address: Department of Horticulture, School of Natural Sciences, Kon-kuk University, Chung-Ju si, 380-701, Korea. E-mail: jbhee1011@kku.ac.kr

KIM Jun-Gyu, b. 20 February 1967, Masan, Kyongnam, Korea. Patent Examiner. m. Yeon-Suk Jeong, 27 February 2000, 1 son. Education: PhD, University of Tokyo, Japan, 1999. Appointments: Senior Researcher, Inha University, Korea; Research Professor, Inha University, Korea; Patent Examiner, Korean Intellectual Property Office. Publications: 48 articles. Honours: Listed in various Who's Who Publications. Address: Korean Intellectual Property Office, Inorganic Chemistry Examination Team, Gov. Complex Daejeon Bldg 4 Dunsan, 302-701, South Korea. E-mail: iamjgkim@hanmail.net

KIM Jung Whee, b. 4 May 1940, Gimcheon, Republic of Korea. Medical Doctor. m. Myung-Ja Son, 2 sons. Education: Premedical course, Liberal Arts & Sciences College, 1958-60, Medical Doctor, School of Medicine, 1960-64, Kyungpook National University. Appointments: Intern, First Army Hospital, Daegu, 1964-65; Medical Officer, Korea Army, 1964-69; Resident, Department of Neuro-Psychiatry, 1970-74, Lecturer, Department of Neuro-Psychiatry, 1985-90, Kyungpook National University; Director, Korea Neuro-Psychiatric Clinic, Daegu, 1974-; Neuropsychiatrist, Daegu Juvenile Detention & Classification Home, Ministry of Justice, 1979-2000; Lecturer, Legal Research and Training Institute, Ministry of Justice, 1980-2000; President, Daegu & Kyungbook Sections, Korean Neuro-Psychiatric Association, 1984-85; Director, Board of Directors, Daegu Section, The Life Line, 1985-2002; President, Nam-gu Medical Association, Daegu City, 1991-92; Member, Advisory Committee for medical affairs, Daegu District Public Prosecutor's Office, 1991-94; Lecturer, Daegu Education & Training Institute, Daegu Metropolitan Office of Education, 1993-96; Committee Member for Special Education, Daegu Metropolitan Office of Education, 1995-; Committee Member for Mental Hygiene, Daegu Metropolitan City Hall, 1997-2000. Publications: Over 40 research papers in professional journals; Book, The effects of meditation on a measure of Ego-Identity in Delinquent Adolescents, Daegu Juvenile Detention & Classification Home, 1997. Honours: Prime Minister's Citation Award, 2000. Memberships: Korean Medical Association; Korean Society of Neuropsychiatry. Address: 556-2, Daemyung Dong, Nam Gu, Daegu, 705-306, Korea. E-mail: koreakim@ppp.kornet21.net

KIM Ki Hang, b. 5 August 1936, Pyong-Nam, Korea. Distinguished Professor of Mathematics. m. Myong-Ja Hwang, 1 son, 1 daughter. Education: BSc, 1960, MSc, 1961, Mathematics, University of Southern Mississippi; MPhil, 1970, PhD (Dissertation guided by Gian-Carlo Rota of MIT), 1971, Mathematics, George Washington University. Appointments: Instructor of Mathematics, University of Hartford, 1961-66; Lecturer of Mathematics, George Washington University, 1966-68; Associate Professor of Maths and Chairman, St Mary's College of Maryland, 1968-70; Associate Professor of Mathematics, University of North Carolina at Pembroke, 1970-74; Distinguished Professor of Mathematics, Alabama State University, 1974-. Publications: 7 books and over 150 articles in Mathematics; Mathematical Social Sciences, Editor-in-Chief, 1981-94. Honours: 6 National Science Foundation research grant awards. Memberships: Korean Academy of Science and Technology. Address: 416 Arrowhead Drive, Montgomery, AL 36117, USA.

KIM Ki-Won, b. 26 March 1962, Wonju, Kangwondo, Korea. Orthopaedic Surgeon. m. Heasook Kim, 3 daughters. Education: BS, 1987, MS, 1997, PhD, 2005, Catholic University School of Medicine, Korea. Appointments: Instructor, 1995-99, Assistant Professor, 2000-2004, Associate Professor, 2005-, Department of Orthopaedics, St Mary's Hospital, Catholic University, Korea. Publications: Articles in medical journals including: Spine; Journal of Bone and Joint Surgery, CORR; Journal of Spine Disorders. Honours: Paper of the Year, Korean Orthopaedic Association; Paper of the Year, Korean Society of Spinal Surgery, 2004; Listed in Who's Who publications and biographical dictionaries. Address: Department of Orthopaedic Surgery, St Mary's Hospital, The Catholic University, 62 Yoido-dong, Youngdeungpo-ku, Seoul 150-713, Korea.

KIM Kwang Seog, b. 5 April 1963, Gwangju, Korea. Plastic and Reconstructive Surgeon; Professor. m. Ji Young Park, 1 son, 1 daughter. Education: Bachelor of Medical Science, 1988, Master of Medical Science, 1994, Doctor of Philosophy, 1997, Graduate School, Chonnam National University, Gwangju, Korea. Appointments: Public Health Doctor, National Public Health Care Centre, 1988-91; Internship, 1991-92, Residency, 1993-97, Chonnam National University Hospital, Gwangju, Korea; Lectureship, Graduate School, Chonnam National University, Gwangju, Korea, 1997-99; Fellowship, 1999-2000, Clinical Professor, 2000-2004, Chonnam National University Hospital, Gwangju, Korea; Assistant Professor, 2004-2008, Associate Professor, 2008-, Graduate School, Chonnam National University; Assoc Director, Hand Surgery Centre, 2000-2002, Director, Microsurgery Centre, 2003-2007, Chonnam National University Hospital. Publications: Numerous articles in medical journals include most recently: Resurfacing of a totally degloved hand using thin perforator-based cutaneous free flaps, 2003; Distally based dorsal forearm fasciocutaneous flap, 2004; Radial midpalmar island flap, 2005; Combined transcutaneous transethmoidal/ transorbital approach for the treatment of medial orbital blowout fractures, 2006. Honours: Korean Certification for Medical Practice, 1988; Korean Certification for Speciality Board of Plastic and Reconstructive Surgery, 1997; Korean Certification for Subspecialty Board in surgery of the hand, 2005; Research Grants, Chonnam National University, 1999-2008. Memberships: International Confederation of Plastic, Reconstructive and Aesthetic Surgery; Korean Society of Plastic and Reconstructive Surgeons; Korean Society of Aesthetic Plastic Surgery; Korean Society of Surgery of the Hand; Korean Cleft Palate-Craniofacial Association. Address: Department of Plastic and Reconstructive Surgery, Chonnam National University Medical School, 8 Hak-dong, Dong-gu, Gwangju, 501-757, Korea. E-mail: pskim@chonnam.ac.kr

KIM Kyoung Soo, b. 15 March 1964, Seoul, Korea. Chief Executive Officer. m. Chun Kyun Park, 2 daughters. Education: BS, Chemistry, Kyung Hee University, Korea, 1986; MS, Chemistry, 1988, PhD, Chemistry, 1990, Korea Advanced Institute of Science and Technology (KAIST). Appointments: Senior Researcher, Korea Research Institute of Chemical Technology, 1990-95; Research Manager, Hanmi Pharmaceutical Co Ltd, 1995-98; Research Director, ChemTech Research Incorporation, 1998-2002; Chief Executive Officer, Chirogenix Co Ltd, 2002-; Advisor, HS Holdings Inc, 2005-. Publications: Chemistry Letters, 1988; Tetrahedron Letters, 1989 (2), 1991; Journal of Physical Organic Chemistry, 1990; Chemical Industry (London), 1992; Synthetic Communications, 1992; Pure and Applied Chemistry, 1993; Reviews on Heteroatomic Chemistry, 1990; 42 patents. Honours: Award for Excellence, Kyung Hee University, Korea, 1986; Distinguished Service Award, Korea Research Institute of Chemical Technology, Korea, 1993; Distinguished Service Award, ChemTech Research Incorporation, Korea, 2001; International Order of Merit, IBC, England, 2005; The Order of International Fellowship, IBC, 2005; Lifetime Achievement Award, The World Congress of Arts, Sciences and Communications, England, 2005; The IBC

Medal of Honour, IBC, 2005; Year 2005 Universal Award of Accomplishment, ABI, 2005; Top 100 Scientists Pinnacle of Achievement Award, IBC, 2005; 21st Century Award for Achievement, IBC, 2005; IBC Hall of Fame, 2005; IBC's Salute to Greatness Award, 2005; The IBC Meritorious Decoration, IBC, 2005; The Da Vinci Diamond, IBC, 2005; The Order of International Ambassadors, ABI, 2005; IBC Lifetime of Achievement Award, 2005; International Commendation of Success, ABI, 2005; The Key Award, ABI, 2005; American Medal of Honor, ABI, 2005; Decree of Excellence, IBC, 2005; Man of the Year, ABI, 2005; Award for Excellent Venture Entrepreneurs, Gyonggi Regional Service, Small and Medium Business Administration, 2005; International Medal of Vision, ABI, 2006; The Statesmen's Award of Ambassador of Grand Eminence, ABI, 2006; International Cultural Diploma of Honor, ABI, 2006; The Archimedes Award, IBC, 2006; World Lifetime Achievement Award, ABI, 2006; The World Medal of Freedom, ABI, 2006; International Peace Prize, UCC, 2006; Legion of Honor, UCC, 2006; Presidential Citation, The Korea Government, 2006; The Master Diploma, The World Academy of Letters, 2006; Scientist of the Year, IBC, 2006; Leading Scientists of the World, IBC, 2006; American Hall of Fame, ABI, 2006; Order of American Ambassadors, ABI, 2006; Presidential Award, The Korea Government, 2006; New Intelligent Korean of the Year, 2006; Small and Medium Business Administration, 2006; Letter of Commendation, Small and Medium Business Administration, 2006; Listed in numerous national and international biographical directories. Memberships: Life Fellow, Korean Chemical Society, Korea, 1990; Editorial Member, Korea Specialty Chemical Industry Association, 2001; Member, main committee of Clinical Trial Center for Functional Foods, 2004; Member, Venture Enterprises Special Committee, 2005; Regular Member, American Chemical Society, USA, 2005; Life Fellow, International Biographical Association, IBC, 2005; Life Patron, International Biographical Association, IBC, 2005; Member, International Order of Merit, IBC, 2005; Member, Order of International Fellowship, 2005; Member, The Research Board of Advisors, ABI, 2005; Lifetime Deputy Governor, ABI Research Association, USA, 2005; Founding Member, The American Order of Excellence, ABI, 2005; Honorary Director General, IBC, 2006; Deputy Director General, IBC, 2006; Governor, IBA, 2006; Adviser to Director General, IBC, 2006; Senator, World Nations Congress, 2006; Ambassador-General, United Cultural Convention, 2006; Vice-President, The World Congress of Arts, Sciences and Communications, 2006. Address: Chirogenix Ltd, 801, Kowoon Institute of Technology Innovation, Suwon University, Whasung-City, Kyunggi-do, Korea 445-743. E-mail: kskimpc@chirogenix.com

KIM Man Deuk, b. 18 February 1967, Daegu, Korea. Professor. m. Joo Sun Yune, 1 son, 1 daughter. Education: Bachelor's degree, Yonsei University, 1992; Master's degree, Chungnam University, 2002. Appointments: Resident, Severance Hospital, Yonsei University, 1993-96; Assistant Professor, Bundang CHA Hospital, Pochon CHA University, 2001-; Research Fellowship, Oregon Health & Science University, 2005-06. Publications: Uterine artery embolization for adenomyosis without fibroids, 2004; Pregnancy following uterine artery embolization with polyvinyl alcohol particles for patients with uterine fibroid or adenomyosis, 2005; Uterine restoration after repeated sloughing of fibroids or vaginal expulsion following uterine artery embolization, 2005; Longterm results of uterine artery embolization for symptomatic adenomyosis, 2007. Honours: Pregnancy following uterine artery embolization with PVA particles, SIR meeting, 2003. Memberships: Society of Interventional Radiology. E-mail: mdkim@cha.ac.kr

KIM Nam-Il, b. 28 December 1972, Seoul, South Korea. Research Professor. Education: BS, 1996, MS, 1998, PhD, 2004, Sungkyunkwan University, South Korea. Appointments: Post Doctoral Fellow, 2004-05, Research Professor, 2006-, Sungkyunkwan; Faculty Research Associate, University of Maryland, USA, 2005-06. Publications: About 42 papers in leading journals. Honours: Post Doctoral Fellowship, Korean Science and Engineering Foundation, 2005; Post Doctoral Fellowship, Sungkyunkwan University, 2004; Listed in international biographical directories. Memberships: KSCE. Address: Civil and Environmental Engineering, Sungkyunkwan University, Cheoncheon-Dong, Jangan-ku, Suwon 440-746, South Korea. E-mail: kni8501@gmail.com

KIM Sang-Wook, b. 8 August 1966, Seoul, Korea. Professor. m. Suk-Yeon Hwang, 1 son, 1 daughter. Education: BS, Seoul National University, 1989; MS, 1991, PhD,1993, Korea Advanced Institute of Science and Technology, Seoul. Appointments: Visiting Researcher, Stanford University, California, USA, 1991; Senior Researcher, Information & Electronic Research Center, Daejeon, Korea, 1994-95; Postdoctorate, IBM TJ Watson Research Center, New York, USA, 1999-2000; Associate Professor, Kangwon National University, Chooncheon, Korea, 1995-2003; Professor, Hanyang University, Seoul, 2003-. Publications: Concurrency Control in a Main Memory DBMS; Shape-Based Retrieval in Time-Series Databases; A Subsequence Matching Algorithm that Supports Normalization Transform; Efficient Processing of Similiarty Search Under Time Warping in Sequence Databases; A High Performance Index Manager in a Main Memory DBMS; On Batch-Constructing B+-trees. Honours: Best Paper Award, SIGDB, 2005; Best Research Award, Kangwon National University, 2003; Postdoctorate Fellowship, KOSEF, 1999-2000; SANHAK Foundation Scholarship, 1987-89. Memberships: ACM; IEEE; SIGMOD; SIGKDD; SIGDB; KISS; KIPS; KICS. Address: School of Information & Communication, Hanyang University, 17 Haengdang, Seongdong, Seoul, Korea. E-mail: wook@hanyang.ac.kr

KIM Sangkyun, b. 23 August 1973, Seoul, Korea. Computer Company Executive. m. Hyunjoo Yang, 2 daughters. Education: PhD, Computer Science & Industrial Engineering, 2005. Appointments: CTO, SecureSoft, 1996-99; Manager, KCC I&C, 2000-02; Professor, Yonsei University, 2001-; Director, Somansa, 2002-. Publications: More than 100 papers in domestic and international journals including: Journal of Systems & Software; International Journal of Technology Management; Internet Research; Industrial Management & Data System. Honours: New Software Grand Award; Ministry of Information & Communication; NT Award, Small & Medium Business Administration; IR52 & KT Award, Ministry of Science. Memberships: SERG; KSII; KSCI; Emerald Literati Club. Address: Department of Industrial Enginnering, Kangwon National University, 192-1 Hyojadong, Chuncheonsi, Kangwondo 200-701, Korea. E-mail: saviour@yonsei.ac.kr

KIM Soon Keol, b. 12 July 1967, Seoul, South Korea. Plastic & Aesthetic Surgery. m. Jung-Keum Park, 1994, 2 sons. Education: MD, Inje University School of Medicine, Pusan, Korea, 1985-91; Medical Master's degree, 2000-02, Medical Doctor's degree, 2003-05, Inje University. Appointments: Chief Doctor of Plastic Surgery, Seoul Hospital, 1997-98; Chief Professor of Plastic and Reconstructive Surgery, Ilsan

Paik Hospital, Inje Medical Center, 2000-; Associate Professor, China Medical University, 2004-; Chief of Soonjeong Plastic Surgery Clinic, 2004-. Publications: 15 articles in professional medical journals including most recently: The Clinical Usefulness of the Endoscopy assisted Reduction Mandibular Angleplasty, 2002; The Technique for Correction of Male Nipple hypertrophy: The Sinusoidal Wave Form Excision and Purse-String Suture Method, 2003; Reconstruction of wide soft tissue defect of frontal area with Terudermis ® and Hydrogel ®, 2003; The Use of Porous Polyethylene Implants (Medpor®) in cross pattern and case of Extensive Blow out fracture, 2003; The Utility of Thin Section CT in Pediatric Nasal Bone Fracture, 2003; Double eyelid operation in middle-aged women by buried suture method, 2004. Memberships: Korean Society of Plastic & Reconstructive Surgeons; Korean Society of Aesthetic Plastic Surgery; Korean Cleft Palate-Craniofacial Association; Oriental Society of Aesthetic Plastic Surgery; International Society of Aesthetic Plastic Surgery; International Confederation for Plastic & Reconstructive Surgery; The American Society for Aesthetic Plastic Surgery; European Society of Plastic Reconstructive & Aesthetic Surgery. Address: SoonJeong Plastic Surgery, 2239, Daehwa-Dong, Ilsan-Gu, Koyang-Si, Kyungki=Do, 411-806, South Korea. E-mail: soonjeongps@naver.com

KIM Su Gwan, b. 23 August 1964, Haenam, Korea. Professor; Oral and Maxillofacial Surgeon; Educator. Education: DDS, 1989, MSD, 1992, PhD, 1998, Chosun University, Gwangju, Korea. Appointments: Professor, Vice-Dean, Chosun University, Gwangju, Korea; Chairman, Department of Oral and Maxillofacial Surgery, Chosun University Dental Hospital, Gwangju, Korea, 1999; Director, Korean Academy of Laser Dentistry, 2001; Director, Korean Association of Maxillofacial Plastic and Reconstructive Surgeons, 1990; Director, Korean Association of Oral and Maxillofacial Surgeons, 1990. Publications: Over 490 publications in scientific journals and books include: Grafting of large defects of the jaws with a particulate dentin-plaster of Paris combination, 1999; Combined implantation of particulate dentin, plaster of Paris and a bone xenograft (Bio-Oss) for bone regeneration in rats, 2001; The use of particulate dentin-plaster of Paris combination with/without platelet-rich plasma in the treatment of bone defects around implants, 2002; The Effect of High Local Concentrations of Antibiotics on Demineralized Bone Induction in Rats, 2004. Honours include: Presidential Award, 5 times, 1999-2003; Scientific Research Award, 62 times. Memberships: Affiliate Member, American Association of Oral and Maxillofacial Surgeons; Fellow, International Association of Oral and Maxillofacial Surgeons, 1998; Academy of Laser Dentistry, 2001; Academy of Osseointegration, 2002; International Association of Dental Research; American College of Oral and Maxillofacial Surgeons, 2003; Official Journal of the Asian Association of Oral and Maxillofacial Surgeons; International Congress of Oral Implantologists; European Association of Osseointegration, 2005. Address: 421, Seosuk-dong, Dong-gu, Gwangju-City, Korea, 501-825. E-mail: sgckim@mail.chosun.ac.kr

KIM Sung Soo, b. 12 April 1945, Sungsong, Korea. Vocational Education Educator. m. Young Hee Kim, 1 son, 2 daughters. Education: BS, Seoul National University, 1967; MEd summa cum laude, 1971; PhD, University of Minnesota, 1979. Appointments: 1st Lieutenant, Korean Artillery, 1967-69; Assistant, Seoul National University, 1971-75; Consultant, Ministry of Education, Seoul, 1972-75; Assistant University of Minnesota, St Paul, USA, 1976-80; Senior Researcher, Korea Educational Development Institute, 1980-81; Assistant Professor to Professor, Seoul National University,

1981-; Consultant, Ministry of Education, Seoul, 1983-84; Extension Specialist, Rural Development Administration, Suwon, 1990-; Head Professor, Agricultural Management Course, 1993-. Publications: Rural Community Development, 1984; Methodology for Adult Education, 1988; Integrated Rural Development, 1989; Agricultural Extension, 1992; Understanding Agriculture & Rural Community, 2002; Rural Youth, 2004; Editor, Journal Korean Agricultural Education, 1982-. Honours: Ever Green Cultural Award, College of Agriculture, Seoul National University, 1966; Chief of Staff Award, Korean Army, 1967; Student Leadership Award, President, University of Minnesota, 1978; Honorary State FFA Degree, Minnesota FFA, 1980; Honorary American FFA Degree, 1999. Memberships: Life Member, Society of Korean Agricultural Education; Life Member, Korean Society of Study Education; Life Member, Korean Association for Adult Education; Executive Secretary and Vice-President, 1982-, President, 1995-, Korean Vocational Association; Secretary, 1994-96, President, 1997-, Korean Association for Agricultural Extension; Phi Delta Kappa; Secretary general 1982-, Korean Association for Rural Youth Education. Address: College of Agriculture & Life Sciences, Seoul National University, Seoul 151-921 Korea. E-mail: agkss@snu.ac.kr

KIM Sungwon, b. 15 March 1968, Gimcheon, Republic of Korea. Professor; Educator; Civil Engineer. m. Ji-Young Yun, 1995, 1 daughter. Education: BA, 1992, MS, 1994, PhD, 1998, Civil Engineering, Yeungnam University, Republic of Korea. Appointments: Adjunct Professor, Department of Civil Engineering, Pohang 1st College, 1997-98; Postdoctoral Fellow, Department of Civil Engineering, Colorado State University, USA, 1999-2000; Senior Lecturer, Department of Civil and Environmental Engineering, 2001-05, Assistant Professor, Department of Railroad and Civil Engineering, 2005-, Dongyang University. Publications: Over 100 research papers including: Uncertainty Reduction of Flood Stage Forecasting using Neural Networks Model. Honours: Listed in international biographical directories; Vice President, Recognition Board, World Congress of Arts, Sciences and Communications; Order of International Fellowship; Hall of Fame; International Order of Merit; IBC Lifetime Achievement; The Da Vinci Diamond; Life Fellowship, IBA; Order of International Ambassadors; Research Board of Advisors; The American Order of Excellence; International Peace Prize; American Hall of Fame. Memberships: International Association of Hydraulic Engineering & Research; American Society of Civil Engineers; International Water Resources Association; Korean Water Resources Association; Korean Society of Civil Engineers; Korean Society of Water and Wastewater; Korean Society of Hazard Mitigation; Korean Wetlands Society. Address: 1356-3, MetroPalace APT 109-107, Suseong, Daegu, 706-746, Republic of Korea. E-mail: swkim68@phenix.dyu.ac.kr

KIM Ung-Yong, b. 7 March 1963, Seoul, South Korea. Civil & Environmental Engineering. m. Kyong-Ja Cho, 2 sons. Education: Bachelor, Konkuk University, South Korea, 1970; Master, 1989, Doctor in Engineering, 1998, Chungbuk National University, South Korea. Appointments: Visiting Professor, Hanbat National University, South Korea, 1993-; Lecturer, Chungbuk National University, South Korea, 1996-; Principal Researcher, Korea Advanced Institute of Science & Technology (KAIST), Korea, 1999-2004; Technical Adviser, Ministry of Government Administration and Home Affairs, Korea, 2001-; Principal Researcher, Korea Research Institute for Environmental & Development, South Korea, 2005-. Publications: Books: Ask To Stars, 1968; Hydrology Practice, 2005; Principal papers: Scour Countermeasure

using Additional Facility in front of Bridge Pier, 2005; New Estimation Technique for Special Pattern of Delivery Rate using GIS/RS, 2005; 80 other papers. Honours: IQ recorded at over 210, Guinness Book of Records, 1972-80; Best Paper Awards, Korea Water Resources Association, Korea, 2004; Listed in international biographical dictionaries. Memberships: Associate Member, Korea Water Resources Association, 1994-; Professional Association, Korea Society of Civil Engineering, 1996-. Address: 104-1401 Hyoseong Apt, Kakyong-dong, Heungduk-gu, Cheongju, Chungbuk, 361-736, Republic of Korea. E-mail: uykim@kaist.ac.kr

KIM Yong Jig, b. 26 January 1957, Choongju, Choongbuk, Korea. Professor of Naval Architecture. m. Sung Hee Yoon, 1 son, 1 daughter. Education: Bachelors, 1979; Masters, 1981; PhD, 1985, Seoul National University, Seoul, Korea. Appointments: Chairman of Department of Naval Architecture and Marine Systems Engineering, Pukyong National University, Busan, Korea, 1989-91, 1999-2001; Editorial Director, the Society of Naval Architects of Korea, Seoul, Korea, 2002-05; Full time Lecturer/Professor, Pukyong National University, Busan, Korea, 1984-. Publications: Over 70 technical papers including Numerical Calculation and Experiment of Green Water on the Bow-Deck in Regular Waves, Transactions of the Society of Naval Architects of Korea, 2005. Honours: Excellent Paper Award, the Society of Naval Architects of Korea, 1997; Excellent Paper Award, the Korean Federation of Science and Technology Societies, 2004. Memberships: The Society of Naval Architects and Marine Engineers; Life Member, the Society of Naval Architects of Korea; Life Member, the Korean Society of Ocean Engineers. Address: Department of Naval Architecture and Marine Systems Engineering, Pukyong National University, 599-1 Daeyeon 3-dong, Nam-gu, Busan, 608-737, Republic of Korea. E-mail: yjkim@pknu.ac.kr

KIM Yong Kuk, b. 15 February 1952, Jeonbuk, Korea. Safety Director. m. Soon Young Cho, 1 son. Education: Bachelor of Mechanical Engineering, Inha University, 1977; Master of Mechanical Engineering, Yeon-Se University, 1996. Appointments: Manager of Mechanical Department, Daewoo Engineering Co, 1977-89; Safety Director, Korea Occupational Safety & Health Agency, 1990-. Publications: Book: Safety Engineering for Transporation, 1981; Articles: Safety diagnosis technics of Tower crane after typhoon, 1996; Study for stability at assembling & disassembling of Tower crane, 2004. Honours: Minister Awards, Labor Minister of Korea, 1993; President Awards, President of Korea, 2000. Memberships: Korea Safety Society; Korean Professional Engineers Association. Address: 706 Ho, 103 Dong, Keukdong-Apt, Hyeonjeo Dong, Sendaemun Gu, Seoul 120-796, Korea. E-mail: ykkim@kosha.net

KIM Yong-Nam, b. 10 April 1973, Seoul, Korea. Materials Engineer; Researcher. m. Jung-Mi Kwon, 1 son. Education: BS, 1996, MS, 1998, PhD, 2004, Ceramic Engineering, Yonsei University. Appointments: Senior Researcher, ICT Ltd, 2004-05; Senior Researcher, Korea Testing Laboratory, 2005-. Publications: Papers and articles in professional scientific journals. Honours: Listed in international biographical dictionaries. Memberships: The Korean Ceramic Society. Address: Korea Testing Laboratory, 222-13, Guro3-Dong, Guro-Gu, Seoul 152-718, Korea. E-mail: ynkim@ktl.re.kr Website: www.ktl.re.kr

KIM Young-Han, b. 16 July 1961, Daegu, South Korea. Professor of Economics. m. Hyebok Lee, 1 daughter. Education: PhD, Economics, Indiana University, Bloomington,

DICTIONARY OF INTERNATIONAL BIOGRAPHY

USA, 1997. Appointments: Professor, Department of Economics, Sungkyunkwan University, Seoul, 2001-. Publications: Optimal Foreign Market Penetration under Informational Barriers, 1999. Memberships: AEA. E-mail: kimyh@skku.edu

KIMANI Leonard Njunge, b. 25 May 1949, Kiambu, Kenya. Economist; Statistician. m. Roxanah M, 2 sons, 2 daughters. Education: MSc, Computer Science; MSc, Project Planning & National Development; B (Hons) Statistics. Appointments: Senior Economist, Statistician, 1990-94; Principal Economist, Statistician, 1994-97; Deputy Chief Economist, Statistician, 1994-2005; Chief Economist, Statistician & Ag Secretary, 2004-06; Ag Secretary, National Economic & Social Council & Director, Economic Sector, 2006-08. Publications: Public Census Report, 1984 (Statistics Chapter); Joint Report on Recovery Programme for Kenya, 1992, 2003; Taskforce Member; e-Government Strategy; Co-ordinator, 24hr Economy Strategy; Research Co-ordinator, Research Fellows program; Joint Report, National Environment Action Plan, 1993-94; Chapter Author, Ministerial Rationalisation & Staff Rightsizing; Revised Blue Book on District Focus for Rural Development; Chairman, Ambassadors Development Agency; Chairman, Mwanadu Road Safety Association (MROSA). Honours: Listed in Marquis Who's Who 2007; Cited in 2000 Intellectuals of the 21st Century. Memberships: Institute of Statisticians; IEEE. Address: PO Box 55407-00200, Nairobi, Kenya. E-mail: lnkimani@hotmail.com

KIMŌTŌ Kyoji, b. 20 June 1942, Osaka, Japan. Professor of Mechanical Engineering. m. Kyoko Komatsu, 1 son, 3 daughters. Education: BSc, Kobe University, 1965; Dr of Engineering, Kyoto University, 1978. Appointments: Emeritus Professor, Osaka Prefectural College of Technology. Publications: Article: Education for Engineers to the Students in Colleges of Technology, 1998. Editor: Textbook Series of Mechanical Engineering; Author: Engineering Heat Transfer, 1992; Engineering Thermodynamics, 2001; Engineering of Thermal Energy and Environment Conservation, 2002; Introduction to Mechanical Engineering, 2002. Memberships: Japan Society of Mechanical Engineers. Address: 19-2 Seifu-Cho, Otsu, Shiga Prefecture, 520-0225 Japan.

KIMURA Masashi, b. 26 January 1966, Japan. Research Scientist. Education: Biological Sciences, 1986-93, PhD, Department of Biological Sciences, 1999, University of Tsukuba; Appointment: Research Scientist, Department of Molecular Pathobiochemistry, Division of Disease Control, Gifu University School of Medicine, 1993-. Publications: Articles in scientific journals including: Journal of Biological Chemistry, 1997, 1999; Cancer Research, 1999; Molecular Cell Biology, 2002; Book: Function of Aurora Kinases in Mitosis and Cancer, 2005. Honours: International Scientist of the Year, IBC, 2004; Greatest Living Legends, IBC, 2004; Outstanding Professional Award, ABI, 2004; Universal Award of Accomplishment, ABI, 2004; Lifetime Achievement Award, IBC, 2005; Top 100 Scientist, IBC, 2005; Leading Scientists of the World, IBC, 2005; Hall of Fame, IBC; Universal Award of Accomplishment, ABI, 2004; Outstanding Professional Award, ABI, 2004; Man of the Year 2005; World Lifetime Achievement Award, ABI, 2005; Listed in Who's Who publications and biographical dictionaries. Memberships: Molecular Biology Society of Japan; Japanese Biochemical Society; Japan Society for Cell Biology; American Society for Cell Biology. Address: Department of Molecular Pathobiochemistry, Division of Disease Control, Gifu University Graduate School of Medicine, Yanagido 1-1, Gifu 501-1194, Japan. E-mail: yo@cc.gifu-u.ac.jp

KINDERSLEY Tania, b. 30 January 1967, London, England. Writer. Education: MA, Christ Church, Oxford. Publications: Goodbye, Johnny Thunders, 1997; Don't Ask Me Why, 1998; Elvis Has Left the Building, 2001; Nothing to Lose, 2002. Address: Home Farm, Aboyne, Aberdeenshire AB34 5JP, Scotland. E-mail: pulch66@totalscne.co.uk

KING B B (Riley), b. 16 September 1925, Itta Bena, Mississippi, USA. Singer; Musician (guitar). Musical Education: Self-taught guitar. Career: Performed with the Elkhorn Singers; Played with Sonny Boy Williamson, 1946; Regular broadcast slot, The Sepia Swing Show, Radio WDIA; Averaged 300 performances a year, 1950s-70s; Numerous worldwide tours with wide variety of R&B and pop artistes; Appearances include: Newport Jazz Festival, 1969, 1989; Atlantic City Pop Festival, 1969; Atlanta Pop Festival, 1970; Mar Y Sol Festival, Puerto Rico, 1972; Kool Jazz Festival, New York, 1983; Live Aid concert, Philadelphia, 1985; Benson & Hedges Blues Festival, Dallas, 1989; JVC Jazz Festival, Newport, 1990; Memphis In May Festival, 1991; Montreux Jazz Festival, 1991; San Francisco Blues Festival, 1991; Guitar Legends, Expo '92, Seville, Spain, 1991; Westbury Music Fair, New York, 1993; Pori Jazz, Finland, 1995; Opened B B King's Memphis Blues Club, Memphis, Tennessee, 1991. Recordings: Albums: Completely Well, 1970; The Incredible Soul Of B B King, 1970; Indianola Mississippi Seeds, 1970; Live In Cook County Jail, 1971; Live At The Regal, 1971; B B King In London, 1971; LA Midnight, 1972; Guess Who, 1972; The Best Of.., 1973; To Know You Is To Love You, 1973; Friends, 1974; Lucille Talks Back, 1975; King Size, 1977; Midnight Believer, 1978; Take It Home, 1979; Now Appearing At Ole Miss, 1980; There Must Be A Better World Somewhere, 1982; Love Me Tender, 1982; Blues'n'Jazz, 1984; Six Silver Strings, 1986; Live At San Quentin, 1991; Blues Summit, 1993; Lucille and Friends, 1995; Live in Japan, 1999; with Bobby Bland: Together For The First Time - Live, 1974; Together Again - Live, 1976; Hit singles include: Three O'Clock Blues; You Didn't Want Me; Please Love Me; You Upset Me Baby; Sweet Sixteen; Rock Me Baby; The B.B.Jones (used in film soundtrack For The Love Of Ivy); The Thrill Is Gone; Blues Come Over Me; Also featured on: Happy Anniversary, Charlie Brown!, 1989; When Love Comes To Town, U2, 1989; Heroes And Friends, Randy Travis, 1990; The Simpsons Sing The Blues, 1990. Honours include: Grammy Awards: Best Male R&B Vocal Performance, 1971; Best Ethnic or Traditional Recording, 1982; Best Traditional Blues Recording, 1984, 1986, 1991, 1992; Inducted into Rock And Roll Hall Of Fame, 1987; Lifetime Achievement Awards include: NARAS, 1988; Songwriters Hall Of Fame, 1990; Gibson Guitars, 1991; Star in Hollywood Walk Of Fame, 1990; MTV Video Award, with U2, 1989; Q Inspiration Award, 1992. Memberhsip: Co-chairman, Foundation For The Advancement Of Inmate Rehabilitation And Recreation. Current Management: Sidney A. Seidenberg Inc., 1414 6th Avenue, New York, NY 10019, USA.

KING Billie Jean, b. 22 November 1943, California, USA. Tennis Player. m. Larry King, 1965, divorced. Education: Los Angeles State University. Career: Amateur status, 1958-67; Professional, 1967-; Championship Titles: Australia, 1968; South Africa, 1966, 1967, 1969; Wimbledon 20 Titles, 10 doubles, 4 mixed and 6 singles, 1966, 1967, 1968, 1972, 1973, 1975, Italy, 1970; Federal Republic of Germany, 1971; France, 1972; Winner, 1/046 singles tournaments, 1984; Other: Sports Commentator ABC-TV, 1975-78; Founded Women's Tennis Association, 1973; Publisher of Women's Sports, 1974-; US Tennis Team Commissioner, 1981-; CEO World Team

Tennis, 1985-; US Federation Cup Team Captain, 1995-2004; Women's Olympic Tennis Coach, 1996, 2000; Virginia Simms Championship Series Consultant; Chair, US Tennis Association, Tennis High Performance Committee, 2005-. Publications: Tennis to Win, 1970; Billie Jean, w K Chapin, 1974; We Have Come a Long Way: The Story of Women's Tennis, 1988. Honour: Top Woman Athlete of the Year, 1973. Address: c/o World Team Tennis, 445 North Wells, Suite 404, Chicago, IL 60610, USA.

KING Don, b. 20 August 1931, Clevelend, USA. Boxing Promoter. m. Henrietta, 2 sons, 1 daughter. Career: Boxing promoter, 1972-; Owner, Don King Productions Inc, 1974-; Fighters promoted include: Mohammad Ali, Sugar Ray Leonard, Mike Tyson, Ken Norton, Joe Frazier, Larry Holmes, Roberto Duran, Tim Witherspoon, George Foreman, Evander Holyfield; Founder, The Don King Foundation; Actively supports other charities including: The Martin Luther King Jr Foundation. Honours: International Boxing Hall of Fame, 1997. Address: Don King Productions Inc, 501 Fairway Drive, Deerfield Beach, FL 33441, USA.

KING Francis Henry, (Frank Cauldwell), b. 4 March 1923, Adelboden, Switzerland. Author; Drama and Literary Critic. Education: BA, 1949, MA, 1951, Balliol College, Oxford. Appointment: Drama Critic, Sunday Telegraph, 1978-88. Publications: Novels: To the Dark Tower, 1946; Never Again, 1947; An Air That Kills, 1948; The Dividing Stream, 1951; The Dark Glasses, 1954; The Firewalkers, 1956; The Widow, 1957; The Man on the Rock, 1957; The Custom House, 1961; The Last of the Pleasure Gardens, 1965; The Waves Behind the Boat, 1967; A Domestic Animal, 1970; Flights, 1973; A Game of Patience, 1974; The Needle, 1975; Danny Hill, 1977; The Action, 1978; Act of Darkness, 1983; Voices in an Empty Room, 1984; Frozen Music, 1987; The Woman Who Was God, 1988; Punishments, 1989; Visiting Cards, 1990; The Ant Colony, 1991; Secret Lives (with Tom Wakefield and Patrick Gale), 1991; The One and Only, 1994; Ash on an Old Man's Sleeve, 1996; Dead Letters, 1997; Prodigies, 2001; The Nick of Time, 2003; With My Little Eye, 2007. Short Stories: So Hurt and Humiliated, 1959; The Japanese Umbrella, 1964; The Brighton Belle, 1968; Hard Feelings, 1976; Indirect Method, 1980; One is a Wanderer, 1985; A Hand at the Shutter, 1996; The Sunlight on the Garden, 2006. Other: E M Forster and His World, 1978; A Literary Companion to Florence, 1991; Autobiography: Yesterday Came Suddenly, 1993. Honours: Somerset Maugham Award, 1952; Katherine Mansfield Short Story Prize, 1965; Officer, 1979, Commander, 1985, of the Order of the British Empire. Memberships: English PEN, president, 1976-86; International PEN, president, 1986-89, vice-president, 1989-; Royal Society of Literature, fellow. Address: 19 Gordon Place, London W8 4JE, England. E-mail: fhk@dircon.co.uk

KING Larry, b. 19 November 1933, Brooklyn, USA. Broadcaster. m. (1) Alene Akins, 1 daughter, (2) Sharon Lepore, 1976, (3) Julia Alexander, 1989, 1 son, (4) Shawn Southwick, 1997. Appointments: Disc Jockey, various radio stations, Miami, Florida, 1957-71; Freelance Writer, Broadcaster, 1972-75; Radio Personality, Station WIOD, Miami, 1975-78; Writer, Entertainment Sections, Miami Herald, 7 years; Host, The Larry King Show, 1978-, 1990 Goodwill Games, WLA-TV Let's Talk, Washington DC; Columnist, USA Today, Sporting News; Currently hosts Larry King Live,nightly on CNN. Appeared in films, Ghostbusters, 1984, Lost in America, 1985. Publications: Mr King, You're Having a Heart Attack (with B D Colen), 1989; Larry King: Tell Me More, When You're From Brooklyn, Everything

Else is Tokyo, 1992; On the Line (jointly), 1993; Daddy Day, Daughter Day (jointly), 1997. Honours: Several broadcasting and journalism awards. Address: c/o CNN Larry King Live, 820 1st Street NE, Washington, DC 20002, USA.

KING Mervyn Allister, b. 30 March 1948, Chesham Bois, England. Economist; Central Banker. Education: BA honours, King's College, Cambridge. Appointments: Junior Research Officer, 1969-73; Kennedy Scholarship, Harvard University, 1971-72; Research Officer, 1972-76; Lecturer, Faculty of Economics, Cambridge, 1976-77; Fellow, St John's College, Cambridge, 1972-77; Esmee Fairbairn Professor of Investment, University of Birmingham, 1977-84; Visiting Professor of Economics, Harvard University, 1982-83, Visiting Professor of Economics, Massachusetts Institute of Technology, 1983-84; Visiting Professor of Economics, Harvard University, and Senior Olin Fellow, National Bureau of Economic Research, 1990; Professor of Economics, London School of Economics, 1984-95; Chief Economist and Executive Director, Bank of England, 1991-98; Visiting Professor of Economics, London School of Economics, 1996-; Deputy Governor, Bank of England, 1998-2003; Governor, Bank of England, 2003-. Publications: Indexing for Inflation, 1975; Public Policy and the Corporation, 1977; The British Tax System, 1978, 5th edition, 1990; The Taxation of Income from Capital, a comparative study of the US, UK, Sweden & West Germany, 1984; Numerous articles in various journals. Honours include: Stevenson Prize, Cambridge University, 1970; Medal of the University of Helsinki, 1982; Honorary Fellow, St John's College, Cambridge, 1997; Honorary degrees from Birmingham and London Guildhall and City (London) and Wolverhampton Universities and London School of Economics; Honorary Fellow, King's College, Cambridge, 2004; Honorary Doctorate, University of Helsinki, 2006; Honorary Life Member of IFS, 2006; Honorary Degree, Doctor of Laws, University of Cambridge, 2006; Other activities: Advisory Council, London Symphony Orchestra, 2001-; Chairman of OEDC's Working Party 3 Committee, 2001-03; Member, Group of Thirty, 1997-; President of Institute for Fiscal Studies, 1999-2003; Visiting Fellow, Nuffield College, Oxford, 2002-; Patron, Worcestershire County Cricket Club; Trustee, National Gallery; Committee Member, All England Lawn Tennis and Croquet Club. Address: Bank of England, Threadneedle Street, London EC2R 8AH, England.

KING Stephen Edwin, (Richard Bachman), b. 21 September 1947, Portland, Maine, USA. Author. m. Tabitha J Spruce, 1971, 2 sons, 1 daughter. Education: University Maine. Appointments: Teacher, English, Hampden Academy, Maine, 1971-73; Writer-in-Residence, University of Maine, Orono, 1978-79. Publications: Carrie, 1974; Salem's Lot, 1975; The Shining, 1977; The Stand, 1978; The Dead Zone, 1979; Firestarter, 1980; Danse Macabre, 1981; Cujo, 1981; Christine, 1983; Pet Sematary, 1983; The Talisman (w Peter Straub), 1984; Cycle of the Werewolf, 1985; It, 1986; The Eyes of the Dragon, 1987; Misery, 1987; The Tommyknockers, 1987; The Dark Half, 1989; Four Past Midnight, 1990; Needful Things, 1991; Gerald's Game, 1992; The Girl Who Loved Tom Jordan, 1999; Hearts in Atlantis, 1999; Storm of the Century (adapted to mini-series), 1999; Riding the Bullet, 2000; On Writing, 2000; Dreamcatcher, 2001; Everything's Eventual, 2002; From a Buick 8, 2002; The Dark Tower Stories: Vol I: The Gunslinger, 1982, Vol II: The Drawing of the Three, 1984, Vol III: The Waste Lands, 1991, Vol IV: Wizard and Glass, 1997, Vol: V: Wolves of the Cala, 2003, Vol VI: Song of Susannah, 2004, VII: The Dark Tower, 2004. Short Story Collections: Night Shift, 1978; Different Seasons, 1982; Skeleton Crew, 1985; Gerald's Game, 1992;

Dolores Claiborne, 1993; Nightmares & Dreamscapes, 1993; Insomnia, 1994; As Richard Bachman: Thinner, 1984; The Bachman Books: Rage, The Long Walk, Roadwork, The Running Man, 1985; Over 200 stories including 50 best selling horror and fantasy novels. Honours: Medal for Distinguished Contribution to American Letters, National Book Foundation, 2003. Memberships: Authors Guild of America; Screen Artists Guild; Screen Writers of America; Writers Guild. Address: 49 Florida Avenue, Bangor, ME 04401, USA. Website: www.stephenking.com

KING OF BRIDGWATER, Baron of Bridgwater in the County of Somerset, Thomas Jeremy (Tom) King, b. 13 June 1933, Glasgow, Scotland. Politician. m. Elizabeth Jane Tilney, 1 son, 1 daughter. Education: Emmanuel College, Cambridge. Appointments: National Service, Somerset Light Infantry and Kings African Rifles, Tanganyika and Kenya; With E S & A Robinson Ltd Bristol, rising to Division General Manager; Director, 1965-79, Chairman, 1971-79, Sale Tilney & Co; Member of Parliament, Conservative, Bridgwater, 1970-2001; Parliamentary Private Secretary to Minister of Posts and Telecommunications, 1970-72, to Minister for Industrial Development, 1972-74; Vice-Chairman, Conservative Parliamentary Industry Committee, 1974; Shadow Secretary of State for Energy, 1976-79; Minister of State for Local Government, 1979-83; Secretary of State for Environment, 1983; Secretary of State for Transport, 1983; Secretary of State for Employment, 1983-85; Secretary of State for Northern Ireland, 1985-89, Secretary of State for Defence, 1989-92; Member of Nolan Committee on Standards in Public Life, 1994-97; Chairman of Intelligence and Security Committee which oversees MI5, MI6 and GCHQ, 1994-2001; Entered House of Lords as Lord King of Bridgwater, 2001; Chairman, London International Exhibition Centre Ltd; Director, Electra Investment Trust; Part Time Vice Chairman, Conservative National and International Security Policy Group, 2006-. Honours: PC, 1979; CH, 1992. Address: c/o The House of Lords, London SW1A 0PW, England.

KING-HELE Desmond George, b. 3 November 1927, Seaford, Sussex, England. Scientist; Author; Poet. m. Marie Therese Newman, 1954, separated 1992, 2 daughters. Education: BA, 1st Class Honours, Mathematics, 1948, MA, 1952, Trinity College, Cambridge. Appointments: Staff, 1948-68, Deputy Chief Scientific Officer, Space Department, 1968-88, Royal Aircraft Establishment; Editor, Notes and Records of the Royal Society, 1989-96; Various lectureships. Publications: Shelley: His Thought and Work, 1960, 3rd edition, 1984; Satellites and Scientific Research, 1960; Erasmus Darwin, 1963; Theory of Satellite Orbits in an Atmosphere, 1964; Space Research V (editor), 1965; Observing Earth Satellites, 1966, 2nd edition, 1983; Essential Writings of Erasmus Darwin (editor), 1968; The End of the Twentieth Century?, 1970; Poems and Trixies, 1972; Doctor of Revolution, 1977; Letters of Erasmus Darwin (editor), 1981; The RAE Table of Earth Satellites (editor), 1981, 4th edition, 1990; Animal Spirits, 1983; Erasmus Darwin and the Romantic Poets, 1986; Satellite Orbits in an Atmosphere: Theory and Applications, 1987; A Tapestry of Orbits, 1992; John Herschel (editor), 1992; A Concordance to the Botanic Garden (editor), 1994; Erasmus Darwin: A Life of Unequalled Achievement, 1999; Antic and Romantic (poems), 2000; Charles Darwin's Life of Erasmus Darwin (editor), 2002; The Collected Letters of Erasmus Darwin (editor), 2006. Contributions to: Numerous scientific and literary journals. Honours: Eddington Medal, Royal Astronomical Society, 1971; Charles Chree Medal, Institute of Physics, 1971; Lagrange Prize, Académie Royale de Belgique, 1972;

Honorary Doctorates, Universities of Aston, 1979, and Surrey, 1986; Nordberg Medal, International Committee on Space Research, 1990; Society of Authors Medical History Prize, 1999. Listed in national and international biographical dictionaries. Memberships: British National Committee for the History of Science, Medicine and Technology, chairman, 1985-89; Fellow, Institute of Mathematics and Its Applications; Fellow, Royal Astronomical Society; Fellow, Royal Society; Bakerian Lecturer, Royal Society, 1974; Wilkins Lecturer, Royal Society, 1997. Address: 7 Hilltops Court, 65 North Lane, Buriton, Hampshire GU31 5RS, England.

KINGSHOTT Brian Frederick, b. 18 November 1944, London, England (Permanent resident, USA). Terrorism and Counter Terrorism. Education: Technical Qualification Electronics (BSc Associate Degree Equivalent): Higher National Certificate PMG 1 & 2; Radar Installation & Maintenance Certification (Board of Trade Certification, British Merchant Navy) City & Guilds of London: Radio Am Operation Certification; Radio, Television & Electronics Maintenance Certification; British Merchant Navy Polytechnic, University of Plymouth, Plymouth, England, 1962-64; BA, Art History, Open/Keele University, Milton Keynes, England, 1990; MA, Criminal Justice/Police Studies, 1994, PhD, Police Studies, 2003, University of Exeter, England. Appointments: Radio/Electronics Officer, British Merchant Navy, 1962-68; Radio & Television Industry, 1968-69; Government Communications Officer, GCHQ, 1969-70; Police Officer, Devon & Cornwall Constabulary, England, 1970-2001; Visiting Professor, Terrorism, 2002, Assistant Professor, Terrorism, 2003-, Grand Valley State University School of Criminal Justice. Publications: Numerous articles in professional journals including most recently: The Role of Management and Leadership within the Context of Police Service Delivery, 2006; An Assessment of the Terrorist Threat to Use a Nuclear (IND) or Radiological (RDD) Device in an Attack, 2006; Book reviews; Conference presentations. Honours: Queen's Silver Jubilee Medal (Police), 1977; Chief Constablees Commendation with Star for Bravery & Leadership, 1986; Police Long Service & Good Conduct Medal, 1993; Honorable Discharge (Exemplary Conduct), Devon & Cornwall Constabulary, 2001. Memberships: Elected Fellow, Royal Society of Arts, London; Academy of Criminal Justice Sciences; North Eastern Academy of Criminal Justice Sciences; American Society of Law Enforcement Trainers; Center for American and International Law; Honorary Fellow, Hypatia Trust; South Africa's National Research Foundation. Address: Grand Valley State University, School of Criminal Justice, 275C De Vos Center, 401 West Fulton Street, Grand Rapids, Michigan 49504, USA. E-mail: kingshob@gvsu.edu

KINGSLEY Ben, b. 31 December 1943, England. Actor. m. 3 sons, 1 daughter. Appointments: RSC, 1970-80, National Theatre, 1977-78; Associate Artist, RSC. Creative Works: Stage appearances include: A Midsummer Night's Dream; Occupations; The Tempest; Hamlet (title role); The Merry Wives of Windsor; Baal; Nicholas Nickleby; Volpone; The Cherry Orchard; The Country Wife; Judgement; Statements After An Arrest; Othello (title role); Caracol in Melons; Waiting for God; TV appearances include: The Love School, 1974; Kean; Silas Marner; The Train, 1987; Murderous Amongst Us, 1988; Anne Frank; Several plays; Films: Gandhi, Betrayal, 1982; Harem, Turtle Diary, 1985; Without A Clue, Testimony, Pascali's Island, 1988; Bugsy, 1991; Sneakers, Innocent Moves, Dave, 1992; Schindler's List, 1993; Death and the Maiden, 1994; Species, 1995; Twelfth Night, 1996; Photographing Fairies, 1997; The Assignment, Weapons of Mass Destruction, Sweeney Todd, 1998; The Confession,

Sexy Beast, Rules of Engagement, What planet Are You From? Spooky House, 1999; A.I., Triumph of Love, Anne Frank, 2000; Tuck Everlasting, 2001; Sound of Thunder, Suspect Zero, House of Sand and Fog, 2002; Thunderbirds, Suspect Zero, 2004; A Sound of Thunder, Olive Twist, BloodRayne, 2005; Lucky Number Slevin, 2006; You Kill Me, The Last Legion, The Ten Commandments, Transsiberian, War, Inc, Elegy, 2007. Honours include: 2 Hollywood Golden Globe Awards, 1982; NY Film Critics Award; 2 BAFTA Awards; Los Angeles Film Critics Award, 1983; Best Actor, British Industry Film Awards, 2001; Screen Actors' Guild Award for Best Actor, 2002. Address: c/o ICM, 76 Oxford Street, London W1N 0AX, England.

KINGSOLVER Barbara, b. 8 April 1955, Annapolis, Maryland, USA. Author; Poet. m. (1) Joseph Hoffmann, 1985, divorced 1993, 1 daughter, (2) Steven Hopp, 1995, 1 daughter. Education: BA, DePauw University, 1977; MS, University of Arizona, 1981. Appointments: Research Assistant, Department of Physiology, 1977-79, Technical Writer, Office of Arid Land Studies, 1981-85, University of Arizona, Tucson; Journalist, 1985-87; Author, 1987-; Founder, Bellwether Prize to recognize a first novel of social significance, 1997. Publications: The Bean Trees (novel), 1988; Homeland and Other Stories, 1989; Holding the Line: Women in the Great Arizona Mine Strike of 1983 (non-fiction), 1989; Animal Dreams (novel), 1990; Pigs in Heaven (novel), 1993; Another America (poems), 1994, new edition, 1998; High Tide in Tucson: Essays from Now or Never, 1995; The Poisonwood Bible (novel), 1998; Prodigal Summer (stories), 2000; Small Wonder, 2002; Last Stand, 2002; Animal, Vegetable, Miracle, 2007; Notes to a Future Historian, 2007. Contributions to: Many anthologies and periodicals. Honours: Feature-Writing Award, Arizona Press Club, 1986; American Library Association Awards, 1988, 1990; PEN Fiction Prize, 1991; Edward Abbey Ecofiction Award, 1991; Los Angeles Times Book Award for Fiction, 1993; PEN Faulkner, 1999; American Booksellers Book of the Year, 2000; National Humanities Medal, 2000; Governor's National Award in the Arts, Kentucky, 2002; John P McGovern Award for the Family, 2002; Physicians for Social Responsibility National Award, 2002; Academy of Achievement Golden Plate Award, 2003. Address: PO Box 31870, Tucson, AZ 85751, USA.

KINNEY Arthur F(rederick), b. 5 September 1933, Cortland, New York, USA. Author; Editor; Teacher; Director, Massachusetts Center for Renaissance Studies. Education: AB, magna cum laude, Syracuse University, 1955; MS, Columbia University, 1956; PhD, University of Michigan, Ann Arbor, 1963. Appointments: Instructor, Yale University, 1963-66; Assistant Professor, University of Massachusetts, Amherst, 1966-69; Associate Professor, 1969-75, Professor, 1975-84, Thomas W Copeland Professor of Literary History, University of Massachusetts, 1984-; Adjunct Professor of English, Clark University, 1971-; Adjunct Professor of English, New York University, 1991-. Publications: Over 30 books including: Humanist Poetics; Continental Humanist Poetics; John Skelton: Priest as Poet; Lies Like The Truth: Shakespeare Macbeth and the Cultural Moment; Dorothy Parker Revisited; Faulkner's Narrative Poetics; Go Down, Moses: The Miscegenation of Time; Shakespeare by Stages; Shakespeare's Webs: Networks of Meaning; Shakespeare and Cognition; Editor: Renaissance Historicism; Cambridge Companion to English Literature 1500-1600; Tudor England: An Encyclopedia; Elizabethan Backgrounds; Titled Elizabethans; Rogues, Vagabonds and Sturdy Beggars; Nicholas Hilliard's Art of Lymning; Women in the Renaissance; Renaissance Drama; New Critical Essays on Hamlet; A Companion to Renaissance Drama; Challenging

Humanism Founding Editor, English Literary Renaissance, journal; Massachusetts Studies in Early Modern Culture, book series; Twayne English Authors – Renaissance, book series. Honours: Phi Beta Kappa; Breadloaf Scholar in Fiction; Morse Fellow, Yale; Fulbright Scholar and Teacher, Oxford University, 1977-78; Senior NEH Fellow, 1973-74, 1981-82, 2003-2004; Senior Folger Fellow, 1974, 1982, 1991, 1995; Senior Huntington Library Fellow, 1973, 1977, 1990; Paul Oskar Kristeller Lifetime Achievement Award, Renaissance Society of America, 2006; Listed in several biographical publications. Memberships include: President, Renaissance English Text Society; President, MLA Council of Editors of Learned Journals; Trustee, Shakespeare Association of America; Executive Council, Renaissance Society of America; Executive Council, Folger Library Institute; MLA. Address: 25 Hunter Hill, Amherst, MA 01002, USA.

KINNOCK Glenys, b. 7 July 1944, Roade, Northamptonshire, England. Member of European Parliament, Wales. m. Neil Kinnock, 1 son, 1 daughter. Education: BA, Dip Ed, University College, Cardiff, 1962-66. Appointments: Primary and Secondary School Teacher, 1966-93; European Parliamentary Labour Party Spokesperson on Development, Co-President of the African, Caribbean and Pacific States ACP-EU Joint Parliamentary Assembly; Member of European Parliament, South Wales East, 1994-99; Member of European Parliament, Wales, 1999-. Publications: Books: Voices for One World, 1987; Eritrea – Images of War and Peace, 1989; Nambia - Birth of a Nation, 1991; Could Do Better – Where is British Education in the European League Tables?; By Faith and Daring, 1993; Zimbabwe: On the brink, 2003; The rape of Darfur, 2006. Honours: Honorary Fellow, University of Wales College, Newport and University of Wales, Bangor; Honorary Doctorates from: Thames Valley, Brunel and Kingston Universities; Fellow, Royal Society of Arts. Memberships: NUT; GMB; President, One World Action; Patron, Saferworld; Council Member, Voluntary Service Overseas; Patron, Drop the Debt Campaign; Vice President, Parliamentarians for Global Action; Board Member, World Parliamentarian Magazine; President, Coleg Harlech; Patron, Welsh Woman of the Year; Vice President, Wales Council for Voluntary Action, South East Wales Racial Equality Council; Vice President, St David's Foundation; Special Needs Advisory Project, Cymru; UK National Breast Cancer Coalition Wales; Community Enterprise Wales and Charter Housing; Patron, Burma Campaign UK; Crusaid; Elizabeth Hardie Ferguson Trust; Medical Foundation for Victims of Torture; National Deaf Children's Society; Council Member, Britain in Europe.

KINNOCK Neil Gordon (Lord Kinnock of Bedwellty), b. 28 March 1942, Wales, United Kingdom. Politician. m. Glenys Elizabeth Parry, 1967, 1 son, 1 daughter. Education: Lewis School, Pengam; University College, Cardiff. Appointments: Elected President, University College Cardiff Students Union, 1965-66; Tutor, Organizer, Industrial & Trade Union Studies, Workers' Educational Association, 1966-70; Labour MP for Bedwellty, 1970-83, for Islwyn, 1983-95; Member, Welsh Hospital Board, 1969-71; Parliamentary Private Secretary to Secretary of State for Employment, 1974-75; Member, National Executive Committee, Labour Party, 1978-94; Leader of Labour Pty, 1983-92; Leader of the Opposition, 1983-92; EC Commissioner with Responsibility for Transport, 1995-99; President, Cardiff University, 1998-; Vice-President, European Commission, 1999-2004; Chairman, British Council, 2004-; Life Peer, 2005. Publications: Wales and the Common Market, 1971; Making Our Way, 1986; Thorns and Roses, 1992; Numerous contributions in periodicals, newspapers and books including The Future of Social Democracy, 1999. Honours: Several honorary doctorates; Alex de Tocqueville Prize, 2003. Address: British Council, 10 Spring Gardens, London SW1A 2BN, England.

KINSKI Natassja, b. 24 January 1961, West Berlin, Germany. Actress. m. I Moussa, 1984, divorced, 1 son, 1 daughter; 1 daughter with Quincy Jones. Career: Debut in Falsche Bewegung, 1975; Films include: Stay as You Are, 1978; Cat People, 1982; Moon in the Gutter, 1983; Unfaithfully Yours; Paris; Texas and the Hotel New Hampshire, 1984; Magdalene, 1989; Terminal Velocity, 1994; One Night Stand, 1997; Sunshine, 1998; Town and Country, 1999; The Claim, 2000; The Day the World Ended, 2001; An American Rhapsody, 2001; Say Nothing, 2001; Beyond the City Limits, 2001; .com for Murder, 2002; Paradise Found, 2003; Á ton image, 2004; Inland Empire, 2006. Address: c/o Peter Levine, William Morris Agency, 151 South El Camino Drive, Beverly Hills, CA 90212, USA.

KINTSURASHVILI Ketevan, b. 16 May 1956, Tbilisi, Georgia. Art Historian. m. Dimitri Janiashvili, 2 sons. Education: BA (Hons), 1978; PhD, 1987. Appointments: Laboratory Researcher, Researcher, Senior Researcher, G Chubinashvili Georgian Art History Institute, 1978-2006; Visiting Professor, Mount Holyoke College, Massachusetts, USA, 1995, 2004, 2007; Researcher, Yale University, Connecticut, USA, 1996-98; Lecturer, Tbilisi State Academy of Art, 1998-2003; Researcher, Balliol College, Oxford University, England, 2001-; Professor, Sh Rustaveli University of Theatre & Film, 2005-. Publications: David Kakabadze – A 20th Century Classic, 2002 (in Russian), 2006 (in English); 20th Century Art, 2005. Honours: Salzburg Seminar Fellow, 1999, 2006; Fulbright Scholar, 2003-04; RSEP/IREX, 1998; Soroj Foundation, 1995-96. Address: 51/15 Chavcharvadze Ave, Tbilisi 0162, Georgia. E-mail: ketskin@hotmail.com Website: www.z-kkal.iatp.ge

KIRBY Michael Donald, b. 18 March 1939, Sydney, Australia. Judge. Partner: Johan A van Vloten. Education: BA, 1959, LLB, 1962, LLM, first class honours, 1967, BEc, 1966, Sydney University. Career: Solicitor and Barrister; Deputy President, Australian Conciliation and Arbitration Commission, 1975-83; Foundation Chairman, Australian Law Reform Commission, 1975-84; Judge, Federal Court of Australia, 1983- 84; President, New South Wales Court of Appeal, 1984-96; President, Court of Appeal of the Solomon Islands, 1995-96; One of seven Justices of the High Court of Australia, Australia's Federal Supreme Court, 1996-; Acting Chief Justice of Australia, 2007, 2008. Honours: Companion of the Order of St Michael and St George, 1983; Honorary Fellow, New Zealand Research Foundation, 1984; Honorary DLitt, University of Newcastle, New South Wales, 1987; Companion of the Order of Australia, 1991; Australian Human Rights Medal, 1991; Hon LLD, Macquarie University, 1994; Hon LLD, Sydney University, 1996; Hon LLD, National Law School, India, 1997; UNESCO Prize for Human Rights Education, 1998; Hon DLitt, University of Ulster, 1998; Hon LLD, Buckingham, 1999; Hon DUniv, Univerity of South Australia, 2002; Hon D Litt, James Cook University, 2003; Hon LLD, Australian National University, 2004; Lifetime Achievement Award, Australian Law Awards, 2005; Included in 100 Most Influential Australians, 2006; Honorary Bencher, Inner Temple, London, 2006; Hon D University, Southern Cross University, 2007; Hon LLD, University of South Wales, 2008. Memberships include: Member, UNAIDS Global Reference Group on HIV/AIDS and Human Rights; Member, Judicial Integrity Group of UN Office on Drugs and Crime; Honorary Member, Australian National Commission for UNESCO, 1996-2007; Member, American Law Institute. Address: Judges' Chambers, High Court of Australia, Box 6309, Kingston, Canberra, ACT 2604, Australia. E-mail: kirbyj@hcourt.gov.au

KIRK Nicholas Kenneth, b. 27 December 1945, Bradford, West Yorkshire, England. Musician (New Orleans Jazz Banjo); Electronics Engineer. Education: BSc, Honours, University of Wales; Postgraduate Diploma in Communications, Southampton University; Postgraduate Diploma in R F and Microwave, Bradford University. Career: Appearances on radio and television Wales with Clive Evans' River City Stompers, 1966-67; Appeared at the Keswick Jazz Festival, Bude Jazz Festival, Marsden Jazz Festival, and at jazz clubs and pubs in Yorkshire, Wales and South of England, with the Dennis Browne Creole Band; Appeared at the 100 Club in London with the New Era Jazzband; Currently proprietor, P&P Electronics and P&P Electrical. Publications: Author of British Patent for apparatus for Recording and Replaying Music (The Musical Arranger and Sequencer), subsequent sale of patent rights to Waddingtons House of Games. Composition: Clouds. Recording: Float Me Down The River, with the Dennis Browne Creole Band, cassette; City Of A Million Dreams, cassette; Live at the Ritz, CD, by the Dennis Armstrong Jazz Band; Alternative Theory of the Red Shift in the Universe. Memberships: Fellow, Royal Microscopical Society. Address: 36 Kilpin Hill Lane, Staincliffe, Near Dewsbury, West Yorkshire WF13 4BH, England.

KIRK Raymond Maurice, b. 31 October 1923, Beeston, Nottinghamshire, England. Surgeon, retired. m. Margaret Schafran, 1 son, 2 daughters. Education: King's College, London; Charing Cross Hospital, London; University of London. Appointments: Ordinary Seaman to Lieutenant RNVR, 1942-46; House Surgeon and Casualty Officer, Charing Cross Hospital, 1952; Lecturer in Anatomy, King's College, London, 1952-53; House Surgeon and Resident Surgical Officer, Royal Postgraduate Medical School, Hammersmith Hospital, London, 1953-56; Registrar and Senior Registrar, Charing Cross Hospital, 1956-60; Senior Surgical Registrar, Royal Free Hospital, 1961; Consultant Surgeon, Willesden General Hospital, 1962-72; Consultant Surgeon and Honorary Senior Lecturer, Royal Free Hospital, 1964; Part-time Lecturer in Anatomy and Developmental Biology, University College, London; Honorary Professor of Surgery, Honorary Consulting Surgeon, Royal Free Hospital and Royal Free and University College, London School of Medicine, 1989-. Publications: Author and co-author, 8 books; Numerous articles and chapters in professional medical journals. Memberships: Royal College of Surgeons of England; Court of Examiners; Royal Society of Medicine; Hunterian Society; Medical Society of London; Association of Surgeons of Poland; Association of Surgeons of Sri Lanka. Address: 10 Southwood Lane, Highgate Village, London N6 5EE, England. E-mail: r.kirk@medsch.ucl.ac.uk

KIRK-GREENE Anthony (Hamilton Millard), b. 16 May 1925, Tunbridge Wells, England. m. Helen Sellar, 1967. University Lecturer; Fellow; Writer; Editor. Education: BA, 1949, MA, 1954, Clare College, Cambridge; MA, Oxford University, 1967. Appointments: Senior Lecturer in Government, Institute of Administration, Zaria, Nigeria, 1957-62; Professor of Government, Ahmadu Bello University, Nigeria, 1962-65; University Lecturer and Fellow, St Antony's College, Oxford, 1967-92, Emeritus Fellow, 1992-; Director, Oxford University Colonial Records Project, 1979-84; Director, Foreign Service Programme, Oxford University,

1986-90; Associate Professor, Stanford University (Oxford Campus), 1992-99; Co-editor/Academic Consultant: Methuen Studies in African History, 1969-75, Hoover Colonial Studies, 1975-85, Holmes and Meier, Africana, 1978-83, Gregg Press Modern Revivals in African Studies, 1990-95, Radcliffe Press Overseas Memoirs, 1992-; Reviews Editor: Corona Club Bulletin, 1984-2000, Britain-Nigeria Association Newsletter, 2001-07; Associate Editor, Oxford Dictionary of National Biography, 1996-2005. Publications: Barth's Travels in Nigeria, 1962; The Emirates of Northern Nigeria (co-author), 1966; Crisis and Conflict in Nigeria, 1971; A Biographical Dictionary of the British Colonial Service, 1939-66, 1991; On Crown Service, 1999; Britain's Imperial Administrators, 2000; The British Intellectual Engagement with Africa in the 20th Century (co-editor), 2000; Glimpses of Empire, 2001; Symbol of Authority, 2006. Contributions to numerous reference books and scholarly journals. Honours: Member of the Order of the British Empire, 1963; Hans Wolff Memorial Lecturer, 1973; Fellow, Royal Historical Society, 1985; Festschrift, 1993; Leverhulme Emeritus Fellowship, 1993; Companion of the Order of St Michael and St George, 2001; African Studies Association (UK) Distinguished Africanist Award, 2005. Memberships: Royal African Society; International African Institute; Britain – Nigeria Association, Council Member, 1985-2007; African Studies Association of UK, President, 1988-90; Vice President, Royal African Society, 1992-2006. Address: c/o St Antony's College, Oxford OX2 6JF, England.

KIRKHOPE Timothy John Robert, b. 29 April 1945, Newcastle upon Tyne, England. Solicitor. m. Caroline Maling, 4 sons. Education: Law Society College of Law, Guildford, Surrey. Appointments: Qualified as Solicitor, 1973; Partner, Wilkinson Maughan, now Eversheds, Newcastle upon Tyne, 1977-87; Conservative, Member of Parliament, Leeds North East, 1987-97; Government Whip, 1990-95; Vice Chamberlain to HM the Queen, 1995; Under Secretary of State, Home Office, 1995-97; Business Consultant, 1997-; Member of European Parliament, Yorkshire and the Humber, 1999-; Spokesman on Citizens Rights, Justice and Home Affairs, 1999-; Chief Whip, Conservative Delegation, 1999-2001; Member, Future of Europe Convention, 2002-. Memberships: Fountain Society; Northern Counties Club; Dunstanburgh Castle Golf Club; Newcastle Aero Club, private pilot. Address: c/o ASP 14E, 246 European Parliament, Rue Wiertz, B-1047 Brussels, Belgium. E-mail: tkirkhope@europarl.eu.int

KIRSCH Philippe, b. 1 April 1947, Namur, Belgium. President of the International Criminal Court. Education: Bachelor's degree, Stanislas College, Montreal, 1966; LL L, 1969, LL M, 1972, University of Montreal; Called and admitted to Quebec Bar, 1970; Academy of International Law, The Hague, 1979. Appointments: Chairman, Sixth (Legal) Committee UN General Assembly, 1982-83; President, International Conference on Air Law, 1988; Ambassador and Deputy Permanent Representative of Canada, United Nations, New York, 1988-92; Director General, Bureau of Legal Affairs, 1992-94, Assistant Deputy Minister of Legal and Consular Affairs, 1994-96, Legal Advisor, 1994-99, Department of Foreign Affairs and International Trade, Ottawa; Chairman, United Nations Ad Hoc Committee for the Elaboration of an International Convention on the Safety of United Nations and Associated Personnel, 1993-94; Chairman, United Nations Ad Hoc Committee for the Suppression of Acts of Terrorism, 1997-99; Chairman, Committee of the Whole, United Nations Diplomatic Conference of Plenipotentiaries on the Establishment of an International Criminal Court, 1998; Chairman, Preparatory Commission for the International Criminal Court, 1999-2002; Ambassador of Canada to the Kingdom of Sweden, 1999-2003; Member of the Group of international advisors, International Committee of the Red Cross, 2000-03; President, International Criminal Court and judge on its Appeals Chamber, 2003-. Publications: Articles: The Expanding Peacemaking Role of the United Nations, 1992; The Rome Conference on an International Criminal Court: The Negotiating Process, 1999; Reaching Agreement at the Rome Conference, 2002; The International Criminal Court: a New and Necessary Institution Meriting Continued International Support, 2005; Book chapter, La Cour pénale internationale face à la souveraineté des Etats, 2002. Honours: Queen's Counsel, 1988; Robert S Litvack Human Rights Memorial Award, 1999; Minister of Foreign Affairs' Award for Foreign Policy Excellence, 1999; William J Butler Human Rights Medal Award, 2001; Parliamentarians for Global Action Defender of Democracy Award, 2002; Canada Sweden Human Rights Awards, 2003; Medal of the Law Faculty, University of Montreal, 2003; Honorary Doctorate of Laws, University of Quebec in Montreal, 2003; Distinguished Achievement Award for Advancement of the Rule of Law and Civil Society, University of British Columbia, 2003; Honorary Doctorate of Laws, University of Montreal, 2003; World Peace Award, World Federalist Movement, Canada, 2004; Honorary Doctorate of Laws, University of Ottawa, 2004; Honorary Doctorate of Laws, National University of Ireland, 2004; International Humanitarian Award for Advancing Global Justice, Case Western Reserve University, 2005; Honorary Doctorate of Laws, Odessa National Academy of Law, 2007. Memberships: Associate Member, Institute of International Law; Member of the Board of Advisors, Parliamentarians for Global Action; Member of the Board of Advisors, Journal of International Criminal Justice; Bar of the Province of Quebec. Address: Office of the President, International Criminal Court, Maanweg 174, 2516 AB The Hague, The Netherlands.

KIRSZENSTEIN-SZEWINSKA Irena, b. 24 May 1946, Leningrad, Russia. Athlete. m. 2 sons. Education: Warsaw University. Appointments: Athlete, 1961-80 (100m, 200m, long jump, 4 x 100m relay, 4 x 400m relay); Took part in Olympic Games, Tokyo, 1964, Munich, 1972; 10 times world record holder for 100m, 200m, 400m; President, Polish Women's Sport Association, 1994-, Polish Athletic Association, 1997-; Vice President, Polish Olympic Committee, 1988, Polish Olympians Association, 1993, World Olympians Association, 1995-; Member, Council European Athletic Association, 1995-, Women's Committee, International Association of Athletics' Federation, International Olympic Committee, 1998-, President, Irena Szewinska Foundation-Vita-Aktiva, 1998, IOC Coordination Committee, Athens, 2004-; Head, Polish Federation of Athletics, 2004; Member, International Olympic Committee, 2004. Honours include: Gold Cross of Merit, 1964; Officer Cross, Order of Polonia Restituta, 1968; Commander's Cross, Order of Polonia Restituta, 1972, with Star, 1999; Order of Banner of Labour, 2nd class, 1976. Address: Polish Athletic Association, ul Ceglowska 68/70, 01-809 Warsaw, Poland.

KISER Nagiko Sato, b. 7 August 1923. Retired Librarian. Education: Secondary Teaching Credential, Tsuda College, Tsuda Juku University, Tokyo, Japan, 1945; BA, Journalism, Trinity University, San Antonio, Texas, 1953; BFA, 1956, MA, Art History, 1959, Ohio State University; MLS, Library Media Specialist Certificate, State University of New York, Albany, 1974. Appointments include: Reporter, Personal Relations Department, The Mainichi Newspapers, Osaka, Japan, 1945-50; Contract Interpreter, United States Department of State, Washington DC, 1956-58, 1966-67; Resource Specialist, Richmond (CA) Unified School District,

1968-69; Editing Supervisor, CTB/McGraw-Hill, Monterey, California, 1969-71; Multi-Media Specialist, Monterey Peninsular Unified School District, 1975-77; Librarian, Sacramento City Unified School District, 1977-79, 1981-85; Librarian, Nishimachi International School, Tokyo, 1979-80; Senior Librarian, Professional Library, Camarillo State Hospital and Development Center, 1985-93. Listed in: Who's Who in the World; The World Who's Who of Women; Who's Who of American Women; Who's Who in the West. Address: 1101 Mission Verde Drive, Camarillo, CA 93010, USA.

KITANO Hirohisa, b. 28 January 1931, Toyama, Japan. Tax Law Educator. m. Hachie Aoyama, 3 sons. Education: LLB, Ritsumeikan University, Kyoto, Japan, 1955; LLM, Waseda University, Tokyo, 1962; LLD, Ritsumeikan University, 1974. Appointments: Staff, Bureau of Tax, Ministry of Finance, Tokyo, 1955-60; Lecturer, University of Toyama, 1962-89; Lecturer University of Tokyo, 1963-64, 1977-79; Assistant Professor, 1964-66, Associate Professor, 1966-71, Professor, 1971-2001, Professor Emeritus, 2001-, Nihon University, Tokyo; Chief, Nihon University Comparative Law Institute, 1996-98, President, Nihon University Law Library, 1998-99; Visiting Scholar, University of California, Berkeley, 1975-76. Publications: Structures of Modern Tax Law, 1972; Rights of Taxpayers, 1981; Japanese Constitution and Public Finance 1983; Taxpayers Fundamental Rights, 1991; Theory of Business Tax Law, 1994; Japanese General Consumption Tax, 1996; Study of Tax Professional, 1997; Fundamental Theory of Science of Tax Law, 2003. Honours: Onoazusa Prize, Waseda University, 1962; Nihon University Award, 1977, 1995; Prize, Japan Association of Tax Consultants, 1973, 1977; Honorary Professor, Southwest University of Political Science and Law, China, 2000; Visiting Professor, Peking University, China, 2005. Memberships: President, Japan Taxpayers Association, 1977-; Director, Japan Civil Liberties Union, 1978-2002; Tokyo Bar Association, 1981-; President, Japan Association of Public Financial Law, 1991-2000; President, Japan Democratic Lawyers Association, 1993-; President, Japan Association of Science of Taxation, 1995-2007; Science Council of Japan, 1994-2003; Vice-president, Japan Lawyers International Solidarity Association, 1995-2007. Address: 5-9-25 Kitamachi, Kokubunji, Tokyo 1850001, Japan.

KITE Thomas O Jr, b. 9 December 1949, Austin, Texas, USA. Golfer. m. Christy Kite, 2 sons, 1 daughter. Appointments: Won Walker Cup, 1971; Turned Professional, 1972; Won Ryder Cup, 1979, 1981, 1983, 1985, 1987, 1989, 1993, European Open, 1980, US Open, Pebble Beach, CA, 1992; LA Open, 1993; 10 US PGA Wins; Appointed Captain, US Team for 1997 Ryder Cup, Valderrama, Spain; Joined Sr PGA Tour 2000; Numerous wins including The Countryside Tradition, 2000; MasterCard Championship, 2002; Spokesman for Chrysler Jr Golf Scholarship Programme. Address: c/o PGA Tour, 112 Tpc Boulevard, Ponte Vedra Beach, FL 32082, USA.

KITIS Eliza, b. 27 February 1946, Thessaloniki. Professor; Linguistics. m. George Kitis, 2 sons. Education: MA, Theoretical Linguistics, University of Essex, England, 1975; PhD, Philosophy of Language, University of Warwick, England, 1982. Appointments: Lecturing at Department of English, Aristotle University, Thessaloniki, Greece, 1981-. Publications: Names of periodicals, Journal of Pragmatics, 1987, 1997, 1999; Word and Image, 1997; Pragmatics and Cognition, 2000, many others. Honours: Various studentships, Department of Education and Science, England; Major 3 year studentship, 1976. Memberships: LAGB, IASS, AIMAV,

ESSE, HASE, ICLA; IPrA. Address: Department of English, Aristotle University, Thessaloniki 54124, Greece. E-mail: ekitis@enl.auth.gr

KITT Eartha Mae, b. 26 January 1928, South Carolina, USA. Actress; Singer. m. William MacDonald, 1960, divorced, 1 daughter. Career: Soloist, Katherine Graham Dance Group, 1948; Night Club Singer, 1949-; Theatre Work includes: Dr Faustus, Paris, 1951; New Faces, 1952; Timbuktu, 1978; Blues in the Night, 1985; The Wizard of Oz, 1998; The Wild Party, 2000; Films include: New Faces, 1953; Accused, 1957; Anna Lucasta, 1958; Synanon, 1965; Up the Chastity Belt, 1971; Boomerang, 1991; Fatal Instinct, 1993; Harriet the Spy, 1996; The Emperor's New Groove (voice), 2001; On the One, 2005; And Then Came Love, 2007; Numerous TV appearances. Publications: Thursday's Child, 1956; A Tart is Not a Sweet, Alone with Me, 1976; I'm Still Here, 1990; Confessions of a Sex Kitten, 1991. Publications: Thursday's Child, 1956; A Tart is Not a Sweet, Alone with Me, 1976; I'm Still Here, 1990; Confessions of a Sex Kitten, 1991; Down to Earth (jointly), 2000; How to Rejuvenate: It's Not Too Late (jointly), 2000. Honour: National Association of Negro Musicians Woman of the Year, 1968. Address: c/o Eartha Kitt Productions, Flat 37, 888 7th Avenue, New York, NY 10106, USA.

KITTLEMAN Martha Adrienne, b. 31 December 1936, Houston, Texas, USA. Caterer; Decorator; Florist. m. Edmund Taylor Kittleman, 3 sons, 2 daughters. Education: BA, University of Mississippi; 2 years, University of Tulsa; UNC; Silver Jubilee, Oxford University, England, 1977; Correspondence degrees, Floristry, Interior Decorating, Antiques; Administrative Medical Assistant, Stratford Career Institute, 2005; Plainchant course in Latin, Liturgical Institute of Tulsa, 2007-09. Appointments: Owner, Chef, Adrienne's Tea Room, Bartlesville, Oklahoma, 1979; Head Cook, Bluestem Girl Scout Council, Bartlesville, 1993; Head Cook, Washington/Nowata Counties Community Action Fund Inc (WNCCAF), Dewey, Oklahoma, 1993; Supervisor, Aftercare Program, St John School, Bartlesville, 1994-95; Gourmet Cook, International Mozart Festival, Bartlesville, 1998; Sampler, Auntie Anne's Pretzels, Bartlesville, 1998; Director Associate of RBC; Abundant Health Associates, Independent Member of RBC. Honours: Advisory Council, IBC; Nominee, Woman of the Year, IBC; Member, Society of Descendants of Knights of the Most Noble Order of the Garter; Listed in biographical dictionaries. Memberships: Bartlesville Choral Society; Eucharistic Minister; Magna Carta Dames; Plantagenet Society; Delta Delta Delta Sorority. Address: 110 Fleetwood Place, Bartlesville, OK 74006, USA. E-mail: kittlemana@aol.com

KITTNAROVA Olga, b. 15 August 1937, Prague, Czechoslovakia (Czech Republic). Pedagogue; Journalist. Divorced, 1 daughter. Education: Musicology, Faculty of Philosophy and History, Charles University, Prague, 1955-60; PhD, 1971. Career: Editor, Supraphone, 1960-65; Teacher of Music, Music History and Theory, Prague Conservatoire, 1973-91; Pedagogue, Department of Musical Education, Pedagogical Faculty, Charles University, Prague; Permanent Reviewer for newspapers and magazines including the musical journal Harmonie; Co-operation with 400 programmes for Prague Radio; Interested in musical ecology; Delivered the Women of Europe Award Lecture, The Excess of Sound in Contemporary Music, at Barcelona, 1994. Compositions include: Songs about Music with own texts, piano and Orff's instruments, published, 1995. Publications: Prague Quartet, 1974; Prague Quartet, Memorial Volume, UNESCO Symposium, 1978. Contributions to: Critical Miscellany,

Musical Inventor A Hába, 1991; Jarmil Burghauser, 1992; Memorial Volume from Ecological Congress-Warning Memento of Sound Excess, 1995; Analysis of Musical Interpretation, University textbook, 1999; The Resounding Scores as a Guide of Performing Art, 2002; A History of Music in Outlines (in English), 2007. Memberships: Association of Musical Artists and Musicologists, Society for Music Ecology. Address: Benesovska 4, 10100 Prague 10, Czech Republic.

KIVELÄ Sirkka-Liisa, b. 14 January 1947, Temmes, Finland. Professor. m. Mauri Akkanen. Education: Medical Doctor, 1971; Doctor of Philosophy, 1983; Associate Professor in Family Medicine, 1984; Specialist in Family Medicine, 1976; Specialist in Geriatrics, 1985. Appointments: Chief Physician, Posio Health Centre, 1971-80; Senior Lecturer in Geriatrics, Tampere University, 1980-88; Professor in Public Health, Oulu University, 1988-90; Professor in Family Medicine, Oulu University, 1990-2000; Professor in Family Medicine, Turku University, 2000-. Publications: Over 300 scientific articles in national and international journals on depression, falls, abuse, coronary heart disease, chronic pulmonary diseases in old age; 40 publications for medical education; 2 books. Honours: Eeva Jalavisto Prize, 1996; Sv Aa og Magda Friederichens Prize, 1999. Membership: International Association of Psychogeriatrics. Address: University of Turku, Department of Family Medicine, Lemminkaisenkatu 1, 20014 University of Turku, Finland. Website: www.med.utu.fi/yleislaak/kivela.html

KIWERSKI Jerzy Edward, b. 24 June 1937, Warsaw, Poland. Physician. m. Szymczak Dorota, 1 son, 3 daughters. Education: Physician, 1963; Doctor of Medical Sciences, 1971; Habilitation, 1975; Professor of Medicine, 1984. Appointments: Head and Chairman, Rehabilitation Clinic, Warsaw Medical University, 1982-; Regional Consultant in Rehabilitation, 1981-2002; National Consultant in Rehabilitation, 2002-; Vice President, 1990, President, 1999-, Committee of Rehabilitation, Polish Academy of Sciences; Director, Metropolitan Rehabilitation Center, 1991-98; President, Polish Society of Rehabilitation, 1992-99; Honorary Member, Polish Society of Rehabilitation, 2002-; New York Academy of Sciences, 1993; Vice-President, Polish Society of Biomechanics, 1994-2000. Publications: 17 handbooks; Over 530 articles in national and international periodicals; Over 340 lecture and congress papers. Honours: Ministry of Health Awards; President of Warsaw Award, National Orders; Outstanding Man of 21st Century, ABI; 2000 Outstanding Intellectuals of the 20th Century, IBC; Man of the Year 2001, 2004 ABI; One of the Genius Elite, ABI, 2004; Listed in several biographical publications. Memberships: International Medical Society of Paraplegia; European Spine Society; International Rehabilitation Medical Association; European Board of Physical Medicine and Rehabilitation; The World Federation for Neurorehabilitation. Address: Chyliczki, Orchidei 4, 05-500 Piaseczno, Poland.

KIZAWA Makoto, b. 18 April 1925, Kiryu, Japan. Former University Professor. m. Yukiko Nishi, 21 January 1951, 2 sons, Education: BA, Dept of EE, University of Tokyo, 1948; DEng, University of Tokyo, 1969. Appointments: Electrotechnical Laboratory, 1948-70; Professor, Osaka University, 1970-80; Professor, 1980-83, Vice-President, 1983-87, University of Library and Information Science. Publications: Digital Magnetic Recording, 1979; A Treatize of Data in Science and Technology, in Japanese, 1983; Co-Editor, Dictionary of Terms in Computer Technology, in Japanese, 1973. Honours: Niwa Prize, Japan Information Centre of Science and Technology, 1969; Standardisation Award,

Ministry of International Trade and Industry, Japan, 1989; Decorated with the Third Order of the Sacred Treasure, 2002. Memberships: ICSU/CODATA Task Group on Computer Use, 1967-76; Secretary, ICSU/CODATA Task Group on Accessibility and Dissemination of Data, 1972-80; Member, CODATA Nomination Committee, 1986-98. Address: 3-13-6 Hachimanyama, Setagaya-ku, Tokyo, 156-0056, Japan.

KLEES Pierre, b. 20 June 1933, Brussels, Belgium. Company Director. m. Marianne Delange, 2 sons, 1 daughter. Education: Degree of Mechanical and Electrical Civil Engineer, Brussels University, 1956; Advanced Management, Westinghouse Learning Corporation, USA, 1960. Appointments: General Manager, 1986-87, Director General Manager, 1987-89, ACEC; Director General Manager and Vice-Chairman of the Management Committee, Union Minière, 1989-92; Managing Director, 1993-2003, Executive Chairman, 2003-2004, BIAC; Currently: Director of Concours Musical International Reine Elisabeth; Chairman, European Confederation of Directors Associations; Chairman, Belgian Association of Directors; Director, Airport Council International Fund; Director of Proviron; Director of MCM (Metaal Constructies/Constructions Métalliques; Director of Alstrom ACEC ENERGIE; Director of Trasys S.A.; Vice-Chairman, Commission Energie 2003; Honorary Chairman of the Belgian Post; Chairman of the Vinçotte Group; Academic appointments: Chairman: Comité de l'Académie pour les Applications de la Science, Royal Belgian Academy Council for Applied Sciences, Impact Cooremans; Visiting Professor, Université de Mons-Hainaut; Member: Conseil Stratégique de l'Université Libre de Bruxelles (ULB), Schumpeter Group (Group gathering of entrepreneurs), ULB, Conseil Scientifique de la Chaire de l'Ethique des Affaires, ULB. Publications: Author of over 120 reports on subjects including: Technical and economic aspects of nuclear power stations and gas turbine power stations, on the potential development of alternative energy sources, on the sustainable development of transports, on the management, security and environmental protection of airports. Honours: Honorary Chairman and Managing Director, Brussels International Airport Company; Honorary Chairman, Alcatel-Etca; Honorary Professor, Université Libre de Brussels; Honorary Chairman, Société Royale Belge des Ingénieurs et des Industriels; Expert for the European Commission DG-IV Airport Competition, 1995; Man of the Year 1995, Aviation Press Club; Nominated Manager of the Year 1998, Trends Tendences; Commandeur de l'Ordre de Leopold; Commandeur de l'Ordre de Leopold II. Memberships: ASME; New York Academy of Science, Fondation Tolson D'Or; American Nuclear Society. Address: 120 rue Dodonée, 1180 Brussels, Belgium. E-mail: general.management@aib-vincotte.be

KLEIN Calvin Richard, b. 19 November 1942, New York, USA. Fashion Designer. m. (1) Jayne Centre, 1964, 1 daughter, (2) Kelly Rector, 1986, divorced 2006. Education: Fashion Institute of Technology, New York. Appointments: Own Fashion Business, 1968; President, Designer, Calvin Klein Ltd, 1969-; Consultant, Fashion Institute of Technology, 1975-. Honours: Coty Award, 1973, 1974, 1975; Coty Hall of Fame; FIT President's Award, Outstanding Design Council of Fashion Designers of America. Memberships: Council of Fashion Designers. Address: Calvin Klein Industries Inc, 205 West 39th Street, NY 10018, USA.

KLEIN George, b. 28 July 1925, Budapest, Hungary. Professor; Head of Department. Education: MD, Karolinska Institute, 1951; PhD (hc), Hebrew University, Jerusalem, 1989; DSc (hc), University of Nebraska, 1991; PhD (hc), Tel

Aviv University, 1994. Appointments: Instructor in Histology, 1945, Instructor in Pathology, 1946, Budapest University; Research Fellow, 1947-49, Assistant Professor of Cell Research, 1951-57, Professor of Tumour Biology and Head of Department of Tumour Biology, 1957-93, Research Group Leader, Microbiology and Tumour Biology Centre, 1993-, Karolinska Institute; Guest Investigator, Institute for Cancer Research, Philadelphia, USA, 1950; Visiting Professor, Stanford University, USA, 1961; Forgarty Scholar, NIH, USA, 1972; Visiting Professor, Hebrew University, Hadassah Medical School, 1973-93. Publications: Over 1,280 papers in professional scientific journals. Honours include: DSc (hon), University of Chicago, 1966; MD (hon), University of Debrecen, Hungary, 1988; Institute of Human Virology Lifetime Achievement Award, 1998; Honorary Doctor of Medical Science, Osaka University, 2001; Paracelsus Medal, 2001; The Wick R Williams Memorial Lecture Award, 2001; Ingemar Hedenius Prize, 2002. Memberships: Royal Swedish Academy of Sciences; Foreign Member, Finnish Scientific Society; Foreign Associate, National Academy of Sciences of the United States; Honorary Member, Hungarian Academy of Sciences; Honorary Member, American Association of Immunologists; Foreign Member, American Philosophical Society; Honorary Member, French Society of Immunology; Honorary Foreign Member, American Academy of Arts and Sciences; Honorary Member, American Association for Cancer Research; Member, Scientific Advisory Board, Ludwig Institute; Editor, Advances in Cancer Research; Member, Nobel Assembly of Karolinska Institutet; Titular Member, European Academy of Sciences, Arts and Humanities; Academy of Cancer Immunology; Honorary Fellow, Euorpean Association for Cancer Research. Address: Karolinska Institutet, Box 280, 171 77 Stockholm, Sweden. E-mail: georg.klein@mtc.ki.se

KLEMP Harold, b. USA. Ministry Writer; Lecturer. Education: Colleges in Milwaukee, Fort Wayne, Indiana. Appointments: US Air Force; Radio Intercept Operator, Goodfellow AFB, Texas. Publications: The Wind of Change; Soul Travelers of the Far Country; Child in the Wilderness; The Living Word, Books 1 and 2; The Book of ECK Parables, vols 1-4; The Spiritual Exercises of ECK; Ask the Master, Books 1 and 2; The Dream Master; We Come as Eagles; The Drumbeat of Time; The Slow Burning Love of God; The Secret of Love; Our Spiritual Wake-Up Calls; A Modern Prophet Answers Your Questions About Life; The Art of Spiritual Dreaming, 1999; Autobiography of a Modern Prophet, 2000; How to Survive Spiritually in Our Times, 2001; The Spiritual Laws of Life, 2002; Past Lives, Dreams and Soul Travel, 2003; The Language of Soul, 2003; Your Road Map to the ECK Teachings: ECKANKAR Study Guide, 2 vols, 2003; Youth Ask a Modern Prophet about Life, Love and God, 2004; Love – the Keystone of Life, 2004; Animals Have Souls Too! 2005; Those Wonderful ECK Masters, 2005; Truth Has No Secrets, 2005; ECK Masters and You: An Illustrated Guide, 2006; Touching the Face of God, 2006. Address: c/o Eckankar, PO Box 2000, Chanhassen, MN 55317-2000, USA.

KLETZ Trevor Asher, b. 23 October 1922, Darlington, England. Chemical Engineer. m. Denise, deceased, 2 sons. Education: BSc, Chemistry, Liverpool University, 1941-44; DSc, Chemical Engineering, 1986, Hon D Tech, 2006, Loughborough University. Appointments: Various Research, Production and Safety appointments, ICI Ltd, 1944-82; Professor, Department of Chemical Engineering, 1978-86, Senior Visiting Research Fellow, 1986-2000, Visiting Professor, 2000-, Loughborough University; Adjunct Professor, Texas A&M University, 2003-. Publications: 11 books; Over 100 peer-reviewed papers. Honours: OBE, 1997. Memberships:

Fellow, Royal Academy of Engineering; Institution of Chemical Engineers; Royal Society of Chemistry; American Institute of Chemical Engineers. Address: 64 Twining Brook Road, Cheadle Hulme, Cheadle, Cheshire SK8 5RJ, England. E-mail: t.kletz@lboro.ac.uk

KLEVER Paul, b. Germany. Entrepreneur; Scientist; Educator. Education: Master of Science in Mechanical Engineering (MEng), University of Applied Sciences, Cologne, Germany; Master of Science in Chemical Engineering (MSc), Technical University of Berlin, Germany; Doctor of Science in Chemistry (DSc), University of North London, England; Doctor of Science in Chemistry (Dr), Vasile Goldis Western University, Arad, Romania; Master of Business Administration in Economics (MBA), Trinity College & University, Texas, USA; Doctor of Business Administration (DBA), Universidad Empresarial de Costa Rica, San Jose, Costa Rica; Doctor in Economics (Dr), Moscow State University, Moscow, Russia; Numerous training and business courses. Appointments: Managing Director, K + K Publishing Group, Bonn, Germany; Sales Manager Computer Systems, Control Data GmbH, Frankfurt and Hamburg, Germany; Sales Manager Computer Systems, Computervision GmbH, Hamburg and Munich, Germany; Director Marketing and Key Account Sales Manager, McDonnel Douglas Information Systems Group, Frankfurt and London; Managing Director, Data Business Partner GmbH, Dusseldorf and Frankfurt, Germany; Researcher and Lecturer, University of Essen, and Technical University of Dortmund, Germany; Director & CEO, Lexington Asset Holdings Corp, Palm Beach and New York, USA and London, UK; Visiting Professor, Vasile Goldis Western University, Arad, Romania; Vice-Rector and Honorary Professor, Albert Schweitzer International University, Geneva, Madrid and New York; Official Representative and Counsellor to the United Nations Geneva, International Commission on Distance Education (CODE), Geneva, Switzerland and Madrid, Spain; Senior Professor and Dean, Universidad Empresarial de San Jose, Costa Rica; Counsellor and Advisory in Trans American European Businesses over 15 years. Publications: Numerous articles, research papers and technical journals; Presented numerous papers in his areas of expertise. Honours: Netaji Subhash Chandra Bose National Award for Excellence, UNESCO, Nagpur, India; Kentucky Colonel, awarded by the Governor of the State of Kentucky, Frankfort, Kentucky, USA; Meritorious Service Medal awarded by the United States Army (USAVR), Los Angeles, California, USA. Memberships include: Chamber of Commerce, Boca Raton, Florida, USA; Knight Grand Cross, Sovereign Order of the Knights of Justice, Malta and UK; Knight Commander, Order of Saint Constantine the Great, USA; Knight of Grace; Knights of Malta, Italy; Researcher and Lecturer, University of Essen, and Technical University of Dortmund, Germany; Counsellor, London Diplomatic Academy, London, England; Honorary Life Member, Albert Schweitzer International Society, Geneva, Madrid, New York; Honorary Life Member, Jagruthi Kiran Foundation, Nagpur, India; Fellow, The Augustan Society, California, USA; Membre, Chambre Européenne Experts (CEE) Commission Parlement Européenne, Brussels - Paris - Rome. Address: London, England. E-mail: euroclass@gmx.net

KLINE Kevin Delaney, b. 24 October 1947, St Louis, USA. Actor. m. Phoebe Cates, 1989, 1 son, 1 daughter. Education: Indiana University; Julliard School of Drama. Appointments: Founding Member, The Acting Co, NY, 1972-76. Creative Works: Films include: Sophie's Choice; Pirates of Penzance; The Big Chill, 1983; Silverado, Violets Are Blue, 1985; Cry Freedom, 1987; A Fish Called Wanda,

1988; January Man, I Love You to Death, 1989; Soapdish, Grand Canyon, 1991; Consenting Adults, Chaplin, 1992; Dave, 1993; Princess Caraboo, 1994; Paris Match, French Kiss, 1995; Fierce Creatures, 1996; The Ice Storm, In and Out, 1997; A Midsummer Night's Dream, Wild Wild West, 1999; The Anniversary Party, Life as a House, 2001; Orange County, The Emperor's Club, The Hunchback of Notre Dame II (voice), 2002; De-Lovely, 2004; The Pink Panther, A Prairie Home Companion, As You Like It, 2006; Trade, 2007; Definitely, Maybe, 2008. Theatre includes: Numerous Broadway appearances in On the Twentieth Century, 1978; Pirates of Penzance, 1980; Arms and the Man, 1985; Several off-Broadway appearances including Richard III, 1983; Henry V, 1984; Hamlet (also director), 1986, 1990; Much Ado About Nothing, 1988; Measure for Measure, 1995; The Seagull, 2001. Honours include: Tony Award, 1978, 1980; Academy Award, Best Supporting Actor, 1989. Address: c/o William Morris Agency, 1325 Avenue of the Americas, New York, NY 10019, USA.

KLINGER Thomas Scott, b. 4 May 1955, Kalamazoo, Michigan, USA. Professor. 1 son, 1 daughter. Education: AA, Bradford College, 1974; BA, Macalester College, 1975; MA, 1979, PhD, 1984, University of South Florida. Appointments: Adjunct Assistant Professor, Saint Leo College, 1984-85; Assistant Professor, 1985-90, Associate Professor, 1990-96, Professor, 1996-, Bloomsburg University. Publications include: Numerous articles in scientific journals. Honours: Fellowship, University of South Florida, 1978-80; Honorable mention, Florida Academy of Sciences, 1980; Science Departmental Award, Bradford College; Midwest Newspapers Scholarship Prize; Mary C Barret Scholarship Prize; Mary C Barret Community Service Award; Antarctic Service Medal, 1999; Listed in numerous Who's Who and biographical publications. Memberships: Society for Integrative and Comparative Biology; American Microscopial Society; Sigma Xi; American Association for the Advancement of Science. Address: Department of Biology, Bloomsburg University, 400 East Second Street, Bloomsburg, PA 17815, USA. E-mail: tklinger@bloomu.edu

KLINSMANN Jurgen, b. 30 June 1964, Germany. Football Coach; Former Professional Football Player. m. Debbie, 1995, 1 son, 1 daughter. Appointments: Started career with Stuttgarter Kickers, before moving to Stuttgart, 1984-89; Member, Winning Team, World Cup, 1990, UEFA Cup with Inter Milan, 1991 and Bayern Munich, 1996; With Inter Milan, 1989-92; AS Monaco, 1992-94; Tottenham Hotspur, 1994-95, 1997-98, played for Bayern Munich, 1995-97, Sampdoria, 1997; International Ambassador for SOS Children's Villages in partnership with FIFA; Founder, children's care charity AGAPEDIA; Vice President, Soccer Solutions; International Ambassador, FIFA World Cup Germany 2006; Head Coach, German National Football Team, 2004-. Honour: Footballer of the Year, 1988, 1994; English Footballer of the Year, 1995. Address: Soccer Solutions LLC, 744 SW Regency Place, Portland, OR 97225, USA. Website: www.soccersolutions.com

KNAPMAN Roger Maurice, b. 20 February 1944, Crediton, Devon, England. Chartered Surveyor. m. Carolyn Eastman, 1 son, 1 daughter. Education: Royal Agricultural College, Cirencester, England. Appointments: Conservative Member of Parliament for Stroud, 1987-97; Parliamentary Private Secretary to the Minister of State for the Armed Forces, 1991-93; Junior Government Whip, 1995-96; Senior Government Whip and Lord Commissioner of the Treasury, 1996-97; UKIP Political Advisor, 2000-01, Leader,

2001-2006, UK Independence Party; UKIP MEP for South West of England, 2004-. Address: Coryton House, Coryton, Okehampton, Devon, EX20 4PA, England.

KNECHT Robert Jean, b. 20 September 1926, London, England. Professor of French History Emeritus. m. (1) Sonia Hodge, deceased 1984 (2) Maureen White, 28 August 1986. Education: BA, 1948, MA, 1953, King's College, London; DLitt, Birmingham, 1984. Appointments: Assistant Lecturer, Modern History, 1956-59, Lecturer, Modern History, 1959-68, Senior Lecturer, Modern History, 1968-78, Reader in French History, 1978-85, Professor of French History, 1985-94, Emeritus Professor of French History and Honorary fellow of Institute for Advanced Research in the Humanities, 1998-, University of Birmingham. Publications: The Voyage of Sir Nicholas Carewe, 1959; Francis I and Absolute Monarchy, 1969; The Fronde, 1975; Francis I, 1982; French Renaissance Monarchy, 1984; The French Wars of Religion, 1989; Richelieu, 1991; Renaissance Warrior and Patron, 1994; The Rise and Fall of Renaissance France, 1996; Catherine de'Medici, 1998; Un Prince de la Renaissance: François Ier et son royaume, 1998; The French Civil Wars, 2000; The Valois, 2004. Honour: Chevalier dans l'Ordre des Palmes académiques, 2001. Memberships: Fellow, Royal Historical Society; Society of Renaissance Studies, chairman, 1989-92; Chairman, Society for the Study of French History, 1994-97; Society of Authors. Address: 79 Reddings Road, Moseley, Birmingham B13 8LP, England.

KNEESE Carolyn C, b. 16 September 1941, Austin, Texas, USA. Retired Associate Professor. Education: BA, University of Texas, 1962; MA, Houston Baptist University, 1990; Ed D, University of Houston, 1994. Appointments: Teacher, Austin Independent School District, Texas, 1963-64; Teacher, Highland Park Independent School District, Texas, 1964-67; Research Assistant, University of Houston, 1993; Research Associate, Texas A&M University, 1994; Program Evaluator, Alameda Unified School District, California, 1995; Adjunct Professor, Center for Professional Teacher Education, University of Texas, 1998; Assistant Professor, 1998-2002, Associate Professor, 2003, Education Administration, Texas A&M Commerce. Publications: Co-author of book, School Calendar Reform: Learning in all Seasons, 2006; Numerous journal articles, monographs, books and book chapters. Honours: Research Award, American Education Research Association, 2000; Listed in international biographical dictionaries. Memberships: American Educational Research Association; Southwest Educational Research Association; Phi Delta Kappa; American Association of University Women; National Association of Year Round Education; Texas Chapter, National Association of Year Round Education; Texas Professors of Educational Administration; National Association of Secondary School Principals; Association for Supervision and Curriculum Development; Texas Council of Women School Executives. Address: 1100 Uptown Park Blvd #33, Houston TX 77056, USA. E-mail: cckneese@aol.com

KNEŽEVIĆ Radovan, b. 17 May 1943, Doboj, Serbia. Professor. m. Slobodanka, 1 son, 1 daughter. Education: Bachelor's degree, University of Novi Sad, 1966; Master's degree, Postgraduate School, Institute of Economic Science, Belgrade, 1970; Professional Management Specialisation, PA International Management Consultants Ltd, London, UNIDO Fellowship, 1972; PhD, Marketing, Belgrade University, 1993. Appointments: Researcher, Federal Institute for Statistics, Belgrade, 1967-70; Researcher and Management Consultant, Institute of Economic Science, Belgrade, 1971-80; Professor, 1981-2007, Dean, 2001-04, of

Marketing, Belgrade Business School; Lecturer, Marketing, Brother's Karic University, Belgrade (First Private University in form Yugoslavia); Recognised Yugos-Lavian and Serbian Marketing Academic. Publications: Author, 12 books; Over 90 scientific articles in all Yugoslavian business journals and numerous proceedings; Author or co-author, 60 practical management studies and projects; Management Consultant to leading Yugoslavian and Serbian companies; Author, Marketing, 10th edition, prestigious marketing publication in former Yugoslavia. Honours: May Awards, Belgrade Town, 1988. Memberships: Serbian Association of Marketing; Editorial Board, Journal of Marketing, Belgrade. Address: Belgrade Business School, Kraljice Marije 149, Belgrade, Serbia. E-mail: radovan.knezevic@bbs.edu.yu

KNIGHT Edith Joan, b. 18 May 1932, Great Houghton, Barnsley, England. Retired Teacher; Singer; Poet. m. John Wyndham Knight, deceased. Education: Certificate in Education, Leeds University; RSA Diplomas in Shorthand, Typewriting Teaching, 1969; Qualifications in Music and Singing. Appointments: Secretarial Posts including Confidential Secretary, Barnsley British Co-operative Society, 1949-56; Head of Commercial Studies, 1969-87, Deputy Head of Middle School, 1973-76, Assistant to Head of Upper School, 1976-87, Wombwell High School; Solo singer for 63 years; Formerly, Oratorio Contralto Soloist, Joan Parkin. Publications: Anthologies: Voices on the Wind, 1996; A Lasting Calm, 1997; The Secret of Twilight, 1998; Millennium Memories, 2000; Books including: Way Back Then, 1999; A Word of Peace, 2000; The Triplet Times, 2001; The Prime of Life, 2002; Sweet Memories, 2002; Rondeau Challenge, 2003; A Story to Share, 2004; Love Hurts, 2004; Looking On, 2004; Labours of Love, 2005; The Way of God, 2005; Songs of Honour, 2006; Dodger & Friends, 2006; Animal Antics, 2007; Sights to Behold, 2007; Poetry in magazines including: Poems of the World; Retford Writers; Triumph Herald (hymn); Poetry Now (The Great War Unvisited). Honour: Bronze Medallions, International Society of Poets' Washington Conventions, 1997, 2005, 2006. Membership: Friend of Poetry-Next-The-Sea, Wells, Norfolk; International Society of Poetry. Address: Great Houghton, Barnsley, South Yorkshire, England.

KNIGHT Gladys, b. 28 May 1944, Atlanta, Georgia, USA. Singer. Career: Singer, Gladys Knight and the Pips, 1957-89; Signed to Motown Records, 1966; Appearances include: Grand Gala Du Disque, Amsterdam, 1969; European tour, 1974; Kool Jazz Festival, San Diego, 1977; London Palladium, 1978; World Music Festival, 1982; Solo artiste, 1989-; Concerts include: Westbury Music Fair, New York, 1992; Recordings: Albums: Everybody Needs Love, 1967; Feelin' Bluesy, 1968; Silk'n'Soul, 1969; Gladys Knight And The Pips' Greatest Hits, 1970; If I Were Your Woman, 1971; Standing Ovation, 1972; Neither One Of Us, 1973; All I Need Is Time, 1973; Imagination, 1974; Anthology, 1974; Knight Time, 1974; Claudine, 1974; A Little Knight Music, 1975; I Feel A Song, 1975; 2nd Anniversary, 1975; The Best Of Gladys Knight And The Pips, 1976; Pipe Dreams, 1976; Still Together, 1977; 30 Greatest, 1977; The One And Only, 1978; About Love, 1980; A Touch Of Love, 1980; Visions, 1983; The Collection - 20 Greatest Hits, 1984; Solo: Good Woman, 1991; Just for You, 1994; Many Different Roads, 1998; At Last, 2000; Christmas Celebrations, 2002; Best Thing That Ever Happened To Me, 2003; One Voice, 2005; Before Me, 2006; A Christmas Celebration, 2006. Numerous honours include: Top Female Vocalist, Blues and Soul magazine, 1972; American Music Awards, 1975, 1976, 1984, 1989; Grammy Awards: Best Group Vocal Performance, Best R&B

Vocal Performance, 1974; Heritage Award, Soul Train Music Awards, 1988; Honoured, Essence Awards, 1992; NAACP Image Award; Magazine awards from Cashbox, Billboard, Record World, Rolling Stone; Star on Hollywood Walk of Fame, 1995; Gladys Knight and the Pips inducted into Rock 'n' Roll Hall of Fame, 1996; Pinnacle Award, 1998. Current Management: Newman Management Inc, 2110 E Flamingo Road, Ste 300, Las Vegas, NV 89119, USA.

KNIGHT Gregory, b. 4 April 1949, Blaby, Leicestershire, England. Member of Parliament; Solicitor. Education: College of Law, London. Appointments: Member of Parliament for Derby North, 1983-97; Assistant Government Whip, 1989-90; Lord Commissioner of the Treasury, 1990-93; Government Deputy Chief Whip, 1993-96; Minister of State for Industry, Department of Trade and Industry, 1996-97; MP for East Yorkshire, 2001-; Shadow Deputy Leader, House of Commons, 2001-03; Shadow Minister for Culture, 2003; Shadow Minister for Railways and Aviation, 2003-05; Shadow Minister for Roads, 2005-. Publications: Westminster Words, 1988; Honourable Insults, 1990; Parliamentary Sauce, 1993; Right Honourable Insults, 1998; Naughty Graffiti, 2005. Honour: Privy Councillor, 1995. Memberships: Member of Conservative Party, 1966-; Member of Law Society, 1973; Member, Bridlington Conservative Club, 2001-. Address: House of Commons, Westminster, London SW1A 0AA, England. E-mail: secretary@gregknight.com

KNIGHT Michael James, b. 29 August 1939, London, England. Surgeon. m. Phyllis Mary, 1 son, 1 daughter. Education: MB BS (London), 1963; LRCP MRCS (Conjoint Board), 1963; FRCS (Royal College of Surgeons), 1967; MS, London, 1975. Appointments: Consultant Surgeon, St George's Hospital, London, St James Hospital, London, Royal Masonic Hospital, London; Honorary Senior Lecturer, St George's Hospital Medical School; Research Registrar, St George's Hospital; Research Registrar, Washington University, St Louis, USA. Publications: Chapters and articles on pancreatic and biliary diseases, and pancreatic islet transplantation. Honours: Hunterian Professor, Royal College of Surgeons, 1975; Member, Court of Examiners of the Royal College of Surgeons; Maingot Prize; External Examiner, Glasgow, Edinburgh, Sri Lanka and Abu Dhabi; Independent Adviser, Health Service Commissioner for England. Membership: Founder, Honorary Secretary and President, Pancreatic Society of Great Britain and Ireland. Address: 33 Sherwood Court, Chatfield Road, London SW11 3UY, England. E-mail: michaelknightms@aol.com

KNIGHT (Sir) Peter, b. 12 August 1947, Bedford, England. Professor. m. Christine Knight, 2 sons, 1 daughter. Education: BSc, 1968, DPhil, 1972, University of Sussex. Appointments: Research Associate, University of Rochester, USA, 1972-74; SRC Research Fellow, Sussex University, 1974-76; Jubilee Research Fellow, Royal Holloway College, 1976-78; SERC Advanced Fellow, 1978-83, Lecturer, 1983-87, Reader, 1987-88, Professor, 1988-, Head of Quantum Optics and Laser Science Group, 1992-2001, Head of Physics Department, 2001-, Acting Principal of the Faculty of Physical Sciences, 2004-05, Imperial College, London. Publications: Over 400 scientific papers in international journals; 2 textbooks, Concepts of Quantum Optics, 1983; Introductory Quantum Optics, 2005. Honours: Fellow, Royal Society; Fellow, Institute of Physics; Fellow, Optical Society of America; Thomas Young Medal, Institute of Physics; Einstein Medal and Prize, Eastman Kodak Co; Parsons Medal, Royal Society and Institute of Physics; Elected Vice President, 2002, President Elect, 2003, President, 2004, Optical Society of

America; Knight Bachelor, 2005. Memberships: Royal Society; Optical Society of America; Institute of Physics. E-mail: p.knight@imperial.ac.uk

KNIGHT Peter Leonard, b. 12 August 1947, Bedford, England. Educator. m. Christine, 2 sons, 1 daughter. Education: BSc, 1968, DPhil, 1972, University of Sussex. Appointments: Research Associate, University of Rochester, New York, USA, 1972-74; SRC Research Fellow, Sussex University, 1974-76; Jubilee Research Fellow, 1976-78, SERC Advanced Fellow, 1978, Royal Holloway College London; SERC Advanced Fellow, 1978-83, Lecturer, 1983-87, Reader, 1987-88, Professor, 1988-, Head of Physics Department, 2002-05; Principal, Faculty of Natural Sciences, 2005-, Imperial College London; Chief Scientific Advisor, National Physical Laboratory, 2002-05. Publications: Principles of Quantum Optics, 1983; Introductory Quantum Optics, 2004; Author of over 400 articles in scientific literature. Honours: Honorary Doctorates: INAOE Mexico, Slovak Academy of Sciences; Alexander von Humboldt Research Award, 1993; Einstein Medal and Prize for Laser Science, Society of Optical and Quantum Electronics, 1996; Parsons Medal Institute of Physics and Royal Society, 1997; European Physical Society Lecturer, 1998-99; Thomas Young Medal and Prize, Institute of Physics, 1999; Knighthood, 2005; President, Optical Society of America, 2004. Memberships: Fellow, Institute of Physics; Fellow, Optical Society of America; European Physical Society; The Royal Society; Mexican Academy of Sciences; Academia Europaea. Address: Faculty Building, Imperial College, London SW7 2AZ, England.

KNOBLER Robert, b. 6 December 1945, Bolivia. Professor of Dermatology. Education: BA, 1967, BS, 1969, Columbia University; MD, University of Vienna, 1977. Appointments: Lecturer, Department of Dermatology, Columbia University, 1983-; Professor, Dermatology, University of Vienna Medical School, 1996-; Head, Photoimmunotherapy Center, Dermatology, Vienna; Chairman, 2000-06, Past Chairman, 2006-, EORTC Cutaneous Lymphoma Task Force. Publications: Over 100 in professional medical journals. Honours: Unilever Award, 1981; Gold Medal, American Academy of Dermatology, 1992; Research Award, AESCA & Company, 1993. Memberships: New York Academy of Sciences; AAD; ILDS; SID; ESDR; EORTC; SIDLA; European Academy of Dermatology and Venerology (EADV). Address: Medical University of Vienna General Hospital, Department of Dermatology, Wahringerguertel 18-20, A-1090 Vienna, Austria.

KNOPFLER Mark, b. 12 August 1949, England. Guitarist; Songwriter. m. Lourdes Salomone, 1983, 2 sons. Education: Leeds University. Career: Former music journalist, Yorkshire Evening Post; Former member of bands: Brewer's Droop, Café Racers; Former member, Dire Straits, 1977-88, 1991-95; Toured world-wide; Own band, Notting Hillbillies, 1989; Solo artist, 1984-; Guest on numerous albums by other artists. Film music composition: Local Hero, 1983; Cal, 1984; Comfort and Joy, 1984; Alchemy Live, 1984; The Princess Bride, 1987; Last Exit to Brooklyn, 1989; Tishina, 1991; Wag the Dog, 1998; Hooves of Fire, 1999; Metroland, 1999; A Shot at Glory, 2001; numerous other films; Recordings: Albums: with Dire Straits: Dire Straits, 1978; Communique, 1979; Making Movies, 1980; Love Over Gold, 1982; Extendedanceplay, 1983; Alchemy: Dire Straits Live, 1984; Brothers In Arms, 1985; Money For Nothing, 1988; On Every Street, 1991; On The Night, 1993; Live at the BBC, 1995; Sultans of Swing, 1998; Solo: Comfort and Joy, 1984; Neck and Neck, 1990; Golden Heart, 1996; Sailing to Philadelphia,

2000; The Ragpicker's Dream, 2002; Shangri-La, 2004; with Notting Hillbillies: Missing... Presumed Having a Good Time, 1990; Singles: with Dire Straits: Sultans of Swing, 1978; Lady Writer, 1979; Romeo and Juliet, 1980; Making Movies, 1980; Tunnel of Love, 1981; Private Investigations, 1982; Twisting By the Pool, 1983; So Far Away; Money for Nothing, 1985; Brother In Arms, 1985; Walk of Live, 1986; Your Latest Trick, 1986; Calling Elvis, 1991; Heavy Fuel, 1991; On Every Street, 1992; Encores, 1993; Solo: Going Home, 1983; Darling Pretty, 1996; Sailing to Philadelphia, 2000; Why Aye Man, 2002; Boom Like That, 2004; Kill to Get Crimson, 2007. Honours: Hon DMus (Leeds), 1995; Ivor Novello Awards for Outstanding British Lyric, 1983, Best Film Theme, 1984, Outstanding Contribution to British Music, 1989; Nordorff-Robbins Silver Clef Award for Outstanding Services to British Music, 1985; Grammy Award for Best Rock Performance, 1986; Grammy Awards for Best Country Performance (with Chet Atkins), 1986, 1991; OBE, 1999; Hon D Mus (University Sunderland), 2007. Address: William Morris Agency, 1325 Avenue of the Americas, New York, NY 10019, USA. Website: www.markknopfler.com

KNOWLES Colin George, Lord Knowles of Houghton and Burnett, b. 11 April 1939, Southport, England. Retired. m. Rosalie Marion Lander, 3 daughters. Education: CEDEP, Fontainebleau France; MA, PhD, Trinity College, Delaware, USA. Appointments: Company Secretary and Head of Public Affairs, Imperial Tobacco Ltd, 1960-80; Chairman, Griffin Associates, Ltd, UK, 1980-83; Director, TWS Public Relations (Pty) Ltd, Johannesburg, 1984; Chairman, Concept Communications (Pty) Ltd, Johannesburg, 1983-84; Director of Development and Public Affairs, University of Bophuthatswana, 1985-95; Chairman, Bophuthatswana Region Public Relations Institute of South Africa, 1988-91; Chairman, St John Ambulance Foundation, Bophuthatswana, 1989-94; Member Chapter (Governing Body) Priory of St John for South Africa, 1992-99; Director, The Consumer Council of Bobhuthatswana, 1991-94; Director, Association for Business Sponsorship of the Arts, 1975-84, Chairman, 1975-80; Director, The Bristol Hippodrome Trust Ltd, 1977-81; Director, The Bath Archaeological Trust Ltd, 1978-81; Director, The Palladian Trust Ltd, 1978-81. Honours: Freeman City of London, 1974; Liveryman, Worshipful Company of Tobacco Pipe Makers and Tobacco Blenders, London, 1973; OStJ, 1977, CStJ, 1991; KStJ, 1995; Lord Knowles of Houghton and Burnett, 2006; Listed in national and international biographical dictionaries. Memberships: Chancellor of the Duchy of Lancaster's Committee of Honour on Business and the Arts, 1980-81; MInstM; MIPR; FIMgt; FRSA; FPRI (SA); APR; Associate Member, Association of Arbitrators of South Africa (AAArb); Carlton Club; MCC. Address: 15 Standen Park House, Lancaster LA1 3FF, England. E-mail: lkhb@talktalk.net

KNOWLES Evelyn, b. 14 April 1931, London, England. Retired City Councillor. 1 son, 2 daughters. Education: BA Honours, Psychology, Ealing College of Higher Education. Appointments: President, Cambridge MS Society; Chair, Cambridge Citizens Advice Bureau; Cambridge City Councillor, 1986-2002; Director, St Lukes Community Centre, 1989-98; Mayor of Cambridge, 2000-01; Non-executive Director, Cambridge Primary Care Trust, 1998-2005; Member, Liberal Democrat Executive Committee, Isle of Wight, 2005-. Memberships: Fellow, Royal Society of Arts; Life Member, National Trust; Friend of University Botanic Garden; Friend of British Library; Member, Fawcett Society; Friends of the Earth. Address: Carisbrooke, 1b Madeira Road, Ventnor, PO38 1QP, England.

DICTIONARY OF INTERNATIONAL BIOGRAPHY

KNOX (Alexander John) Keith, b. 27 November 1933, Belper, Derbyshire, England. Electronic Engineer (retired); Record Producer. m. Ingrid Zakrisson Knox, 1 son, 2 stepchildren. Education: BSc, Physics and Maths, Southampton University, London; Brighton College of Advanced Technology; Course with Richard Goodman, Decision Mathematics for Management. Appointments: Electronic Engineer, with EMI, 1957-59, Brush Clevite Company, Hythe, Hampshire, UK, 1959-62; Redifon Ltd, Crawley, Sussex, UK, 1962-64; Amplivox Ltd, Wembley, Middlesex, UK, 1964-65, Transitron Electronic SA, Switzerland, 1965-67; Transitron Electronic Sweden AB, 1967-72; Freelance sound record producer, Caprice Records/Sonet Records/WEA-Metronome Records (Stockholm), Storyville Records (Copenhagen), 1971-85; Manager for music group, "Sevda", 1971-74; Manager for music group "Music for Xaba", 1972-73; Marketing and liaison engineer, Sonab AB, Solna, Sweden, 1972-74; English language copywriter for advertising agency, Andersson and Lembke AB, Sundbyberg, Sweden, 1974-75; Support Engineer, Royal Institute of Technology (KTH), Stockholm, Sweden, 1975-98; Executive Producer, Silkheart Records, Stockholm, Sweden, 1986-. Publications: (biography, Lars Gullin) Jazz Amour Affair, 1986; Numerous articles for jazz publications and underground press. Address: PO Box 64, 04638 Mojácar, Almeria, Spain.

KNOX David Laidlaw (Sir), b. 30 May 1933, Lockerbie, Dumfriesshire, Scotland. Member of Parliament, retired. m. Margaret Eva Mackenzie, 2 stepsons, 1 deceased. Education: BSc Honours, Economics, London University. Appointments: Production Manager, printing industry, 1956-62; Internal Company Management Consultant, 1962-70; Parliamentary Adviser, Chartered Institute of Management Accountants, 1980-97; Member of European Legislation Select Committee, 1976-97; Member of Speakers Panel of Chairmen, 1983-97; Member of Parliament for Leek, 1970-83; Vice Chairman, Conservative Party, 1974-75; Member of Parliament for Staffordshire Moorlands, 1983-97; Chairman, London Union of Youth Clubs, 1998-99; Deputy Chairman, London Youth, 1999-. Publications: 4 pamphlets. Honours: Knighted, 1993. Memberships: Past member, Federation of Economic Development Authorities; Past member, Industry and Parliament Trust; Past Honorary Fellowship, Staffordshire University; Member, Conservative Party; Member, Conservative Group for Europe; Member, Tory Reform Group; Member, One World Trust. Address: The Mount, Alstonefield, Ashbourne, Derbyshire, DE6 2FS, England.

KNOX-JOHNSTON Robin (Sir), b. 17 March 1939, London, England. Master Mariner m. Suzanne Singer, 1962, deceased 2003, 1 daughter. Education: Berkhamstead School; DOT Masters Certificate, 1965 Appointments: Merchant Navy, 1957-67; First Person to sail single-handed non-stop around the World, 1968-69; Managing Director, St Katharine's Yacht Haven Ltd, 1975-76; Director, Mercury Yacht Harbours Ltd, 1970-73; Rank Mariner International, 1973-75; Troon Marina Ltd, 1976-83; National Yacht Racing Centre Ltd, 1979-86; Knox-Johnston Insurance Brokers Ltd, 1983-; Managing Director, St Katherine's Dock, 1991-93; Chairman, Clipper Ventures plc; Set record for sailing circumnavigation, 1994; Completed 2nd solo circumnavigation of the World in Yacht, SAGA Insurance, finishing 4th in Velux 5 Oceans Race, 2007. Publications: A World of My Own, 1969; Sailing, 1975; Twilight of Sail, 1978; Last But Not Least, 1978; Bunkside Companion, 1982; Seamanship, 1986; The BOC Challenge 1986-1987, 1988; The Cape of Good Hope, 1989; History of Yachting, 1990; The Columbus Venture, 1991; Sea, Ice and Rock, 1992; Beyond Jules Verne, 1995. Honours: CBE,

1969; Sunday Times Golden Globe, 1969; Royal Institute of Navigation Gold Medal and fellowship, 1992; Jules Verne Trophy, 1994; Book of the Sea Award; Knighthood, 1995; Honorary DSc, Maine Maritime Academy; Honorary DSc, Nottingham Trent University. Memberships: Member, RNLI Council, 1972-; Younger Brother, Trinity House, 1972; Trustee, National Maritime Museum, Greenwich, 1993-2003; Trustee, National Maritime Museum, Cornwall, England; Sports Council Lottery Panel, 1995-99; Fellow, Royal Institute of Navigation; Member, English Sports Council, 1999-2003; President, Sail Training Association, 1992-2001; Honorary Member, Royal Yacht Squadron. Address: St Francis Cottage, Torbryan, Newton Abbot, Devon TQ12 5UR, England. Website: www.robinknox-johnston.co.uk

KNUDSEN Dagfinn Andreas, b. 11 April 1942, Drevja, Norway. Metallurgist. m. Karin Nilssen, 1 daughter. Education: Engineering Degree, Metallurgical Techniques, Trondheim Tekniske Skole, 1967. Appointments: Assistant Engineer, Årdal Verk, ÅSV, 1967-72; Project Engineer, Sunndal Verk, ÅSV, 1972-86; Process Engineer, Franzefoss Bruk, 1986; Service Engineer, Østlandsmeieriet, 1989; Service Engineer, Autodisplay AS, 1991. Publications: Microstructure of Commercial Silicon Material, 1983; Essay on Sensational Journalism, 1989; About Modern Industrial Culture; About Norwegian International Fish Industry; About Employees, Managers, Company & Loyalty. Honours: Vice President, World Congress of Arts, Sciences and Communications. Memberships: Order of International Fellowship, IBC. Address: Rådhusgata 29, N 8657 Mosjøen, Norway.

KNUTSSON Henry Hoffding, b. 4 August 1930, Copenhagen, Denmark. Structural Engineer. 1 son, 1 daughter. Education: Structural Engineer, 1954. Appointments: Chairman or Secretary, Code of Practise for Lightweight Concrete, 1965-84; Masonry, 1978-97; Safety of Structures and Load for Design, 1974-99. Secretary for CEN/TC 124, Timber Structures, 1989-96. Publications: Wall ties for cramping veneer walls, 1976; Constructions for low rise houses until 2 floors, 1977, 1981; General control for building products, 1979, 1986; Foundation for low rise buildings, 1980 (editing only), 1985; Mortar, brickwork, plastering, 1981; Reinforced concrete floors, 1985; Constructions for low rise buildings, 1985; Veneer walls for external insulation, 1988; Wall ties for cramping veneer walls and cavity walls, 1989; Windloads on structures (editing only), 1989; Masonry: materials and properties, 1992; Low rise buildings: insulation, moisture, sound, fire, ventilation, carrying capacity (one of 8 editors), 1998; Author, chapter on brickwork, Handbook for Structures. Memberships: Board Member, 1947-57, Chairman, 1955-57, UNF (The Scientific Society for Youth). Address: Askevaenget 39, 2830 Virum, Denmark.

KOBAYASHI Keiji, b. 15 May 1938, Yokkaichi-city, Mie, Japan. Researcher. m. Kazuko, 2 daughters. Education: Bachelor's degree, Nagoya Institute of Technology; Doctor's course, Tokyo Institute of Technology. Appointments: Central Research Laboratory, 1960, Chief Researcher, Research and Development Centre, 1977, Toshiba; Assembly man, Kuramae Association of Tokyo Institute of Technology. Publications: About 75 papers published; 200 patents held; Numerous articles in professional journals. Honours: Japan Ceramic Society Award, 1962; 47 patent registration awards, Toshiba, 1960-2006; . Memberships: Japan Ceramic Society; Chemical Society of Japan; Applied Physics Society of Japan. Address: 241-0814, 3-11-12, Nakazawa, Asahi, Yokohama, Japan.

KOBAYASHI Nagao, b. 21 January 1950, Nagano, Japan. Professor of Chemistry. m. Yayoi Enomoto, 2 daughters. Education: MTech, 1975; DSc, 1978; DPharm, 1986. Appointments: Technician, Pharmacy Institute, Tohoku University, 1978-83; Assistant Professor, Chemical Research Institute, Tohoku University, 1983-85; Assistant Professor, Pharmacy Institute, Tohoku University, 1986-95; Professor, Department of Chemistry, Graduate School of Science, Tohoku University, 1995-. Publications: Several articles in professional journals. Memberships: Chemical Society of Japan; Polymer Society of Japan; Japan Society of Co-ordination Chemistry, Society of Porphyrins and Phthalocyanines. Address: Department of Chemistry, Graduate School of Science, Tohoku University, Sendai 980-8578, Japan.

KOCSIS Richard N, b. New Zealand (Australian citizen). Forensic Psychologist; Criminologist. Education: Certificate of Business Management, VET; Bachelor of Arts, Psychology, Macquarie University; Honours, Psychology, University of New England; Master of Criminology, Bond University; PhD, Psychology, University of New England. Appointments: University of New England, 1997-98; Charles Sturt University, 1999-2000. Honours: Dean's List Scholar, 1995; D R Grey Research Scholarship, 1996; Australian Postgraduate Award (Industry), 1997; Keith & Dorothy McKay Academic Award, 1998; Australian Museum Eureka Award, 2000; Listed in international biographical dictionaries. Memberships: Registered Psychologist, NSW Psychologists Registration Board. Address: PO Box 662, Dee Why, NSW 2099, Australia. E-mail: richard_kocsis@hotmail.com

KOENIGSBERGER Helmut Georg, b. 24 October 1918, Berlin, Germany. Historian. m. Dorothy Romano, 2 daughters. Education: BA, 1940, MA, 1944, PhD, 1949, Gonville and Caius College, Cambridge. Appointments: Royal Navy, 1944-45; Lecturer, Economic History, Queen's University, Belfast, 1948-51; Senior Lecturer, Economic History, Manchester University, 1951-60; Professor of Modern History, Nottingham University, 1960-66; Professor of History, Cornell University, USA, 1966-73; Professor of History, King's College, London, 1973-84. Publications: The Practice of Empire, 1951, 1969; Europe in the 16th Century (with G L Mosse), 1968, 1989; Estates and Revolutions, 1971; The Habsburgs and Europe, 1971; Politicians and Virtuosi, 1986; Medieval Europe 400-1500, 1987; Early Modern Europe 1500-1789, 1987; Republiken und Republikanismus (editor), 1988; Monarchies, States Generals and Parliaments, 2001. Honours: Guggenheim Fellow, 1970-71; Fellow, Historical College, Munich, 1984-85; Encomienda Order of Isobel the Catholic, 1997; Fellow of King's College London, 1999. Membership: President, International Commission for the History of Parliaments, 1980-85; Royal Historical Society, Vice-President, 1982-85; Fellow, British Academy, 1989-. Address: 116 Waterfall Road, Southgate, London N14 7JN, England.

KOGAN Norman, b. 15 June 1919, Chicago, Illinois, USA. Professor Emeritus of Political Science. m. Meryl Reich, 18 May 1946, 2 sons. Education: BA, 1940, PhD, 1949, University of Chicago. Appointments: Faculty, University of Connecticut, 1949-88; Visiting Professor, University of Rome, 1973, 1979, 1987. Publications: Italy and the Allies, 1956; The Government of Italy, 1962; The Politics of Italian Foreign Policy, 1963; A Political History of Postwar Italy, 1966; Storia Politica dell' Italia Repubblicana, 1982, 2nd edition, revised and expanded, 1990; A Political History of Italy: The Postwar Years, 1983. Contributions to: Yale Law Journal; Il Ponte; Western Political Quarterly; Journal of Politics; Comparative Politics; Indiana Law Journal. Honour: Knight in the Order of Merit of the Italian Republic, 1971; Lifetime of Achievement Award, 2003. Address: 13 Westwood Road, Storrs, CT 06268, USA.

KOH Choon-Myung, b. 14 August 1938, Seoul, Korea. Professor Emeritus. m. Sun Ja Kim, 1 son, 2 daughters. Education: BSc, Biology, 1964, MPH, Infectious Disease, 1970, Yonsei University, Seoul, Korea; PhD, Food Engineering, Dongkuk University, Seoul, 1979; PhD, Microbiology, Dankuk University, Seoul, 1989. Appointments: Chairman, Student Affairs, 1978-86, Chairman, Department of Microbiology, 1978-92, Yonsei University, Wonju College of Medicine, Wonju; Campus Dean, Wonju Campus, Yonsei University, 1990-92; Director, Institute of Basic Medical Science, Yonsei University, 1994-98; Vice President of Faculty Senator, Yonsei University, 1996-98; Vice President of Korean Society for Medical Mycology, Korea, 1996-98; President, Korean Society for Microbiology, Korea, 1999-2000; Advisor NIH, Korea, 2003-; President Emeritus, Korea, 2003-; Chair Professor, Kyungdong University, Korea, 2006-; President, Board of Foundation, KyungBok College, 2007-. Publications: Articles in professional scientific journals. Honours: Appreciation Plaque, Ministry of Government Administration and Home Affairs, Republic of Korea, 1980; The Hwangjo-Keunjung Medal, President, Republic of Korea, 2003. Memberships: Korean Society for Microbiology; Korean Society for Medical Mycology; Korean Society for Immunology; International Society for Human and Animal Mycology; Asia Pacific Society for Medical Mycology; Research Board of Advisors, ABI. Address: 14-19, Yeoui-Sibum Apt, Yeouido-dong, Youngdungpo-ku, Seoul 150-761, Republic of Korea. E-mail: yuwmckoh@chol.com

KOH John Seng Siew, b. 29 June 1946, Malacca, Malaysia. Architect. m. Judith Loh Foong Lin, 2 sons, 1 daughter. Education: RIBA, Part I, University of Singapore, 1970; Bachelor of Architecture (1st class honours), University of Liverpool, 1973. Appointments: Principal, Arkitek Majubina Chartered Architects, 1981-97; Partner, Arkitek Majubina TSP Architects & Planners, 1987-2001; Managing Director, Arkitek Maju Bina Sdn Bhd, 1997-; Managing Director, Majubina Horizons Sdn Bhd, 1997-. Publications: Over 20 articles in professional and popular journals, 1972-. Honours: Special Mention Award, Malaysia Institute of Architects Competition, 1988; Honorary Mention Award, Awards for Excellence, Malaysian Institute of Interior Designers, 1995; Winner, Leisure and Entertainment, Awards for Design Excellence, Malaysian Institute of Interior Designers, 2005; Bronze Award (Colour on Buildings), Malaysia Institute of Architects, 2006; Mention Award in Interior Design, Malaysia Institute of Architects, 2006. Memberships: FRAIA; RIBA; SIA; APAM; IPDM; WACA; Member, RAIA International Area Committee, 2006-08; Secretary-General of Eastern Regional Organisation for Planning & Housing (Earoph), 1994-2002; Honorary Secretary, Malaysian Institute of Architects, 1988-90; Honorary Council Member, Heritage of Malaysia Trust, 1995-97; Member, Board of Trustees, Malaysian Nature Society, 1998-. Address: Arkitek Maju Bina Sdn Bhd, 3A10, Block C, Phileo Damansara 1, 9 Jalan 16/11, Petaling Jaya, Selangor, Malaysia. E-mail: ssjohnkoh@gmail.com

KOIDE Samuel S, b. 6 October 1923, Honolulu, Hawaii, USA. Physician. m. Sumi M Mitsudo, 2 sons. Education: BS, University of Hawaii, 1945; MD, 1953, MS, 1954, PhD, 1960, Northwestern University. Appointments: Associate, Sloan Kettering Institute for Cancer Research, New York,

USA, 1960-65; Senior Scientist, Population Council, New York, USA, 1965-2004. Publications: Over 300 paper in Biomedical Journals. Honours: Career Development Award, NIH, PHS, USA, 1963-65. Memberships: American Society of Molecular Biology and Biochemistry; The Biochemical Society; American Society of Cell Biology; Marine Biological Laboratory; USA Society for Experimental Biology and Medicine. Address: Koide Desk, 134 Lefurgy Ave, Dobbs Ferry, NY 10522, USA. E-mail: koide@optonline.net

KOLEROVA Nadezda, b. 4 January 1970, Moscow, USSR. Doctor. m. Uriy Kolerov, 2 daughters. Education: Medical Degree, Samara Medical University, 1993. Appointments: Senior Psychiatrist, Medical Institution, RF Interior Troops, RF Interior Office, Moscow, 1993-2002; Psychiatrist-Narcologist, Narcological Hospital #17, Moscow, 2002-04; Psychologist, Health and Beauty Salon, Moscow, 2004-05; Psychologist, Specialist Language School #1218, Moscow, 2005-. Publications: Food as integrated living processes element; Express diagnostics for living systems. Honours: Silver Medal, The New Time International Workshop for Innovations and New Technologies, 2006; Certificate of Recognition, Russian Society of Inventors and Efficiency Experts of St Petersburg and Leningrad Oblast, 2007; Forumul Inventatorilor Romani Cup, 2007; Silver Medal, EXPO TRANSILVANIA, 2007; Silver Medal, INFO INVENT, 2007. Memberships: Scientific School for Studies in Causality. E-mail: n_bir@zmail.ru

KOLOMVOS Nikolaos, b. 5 June 1969, Athens, Greece. Oral and Maxillofacial Surgeon. m. Aikaterini Lachlali. Education: Dentistry, 1994; Post-graduate diploma (MSc), Oral Patho-Biology, 1999; Advanced Trauma Life Support Course, ACS Committee on Trauma, 2002, and 2007; Course Certificate, Microsurgery of Vessels and Nerves, 2002; Oral and Maxillofacial Surgery, 2002; Doctora, 2006; Medicine, 2007. Appointments: Scientific Collaborator, Oral and Maxillofacial Surgery Clinic, Dental School of University of Athens, 1994-96, 2002-; Scientific Collaborator, Aglaia Kiriakou Children's Hospital, 1994-96, 2002-; General Surgery, St Olga's General Hospital, Athens, 1996-97; Oral and Maxillofacial Surgery, Evangelismos General Hospital, Athens, 1999-2002; Private clinic, 2003-; Doctor, University of Athens, 2006-; Speaker at many conferences, congresses and sessions. Publications: Reasons for inferior alveolar nerve's block anaesthesia failure and suggestive alternative technique; Histopathological check of the carotid sheath for possible metastatic disease in patients with cancer of the oral cavity; Many articles in Greek in professional international magazines. Honours: Dimitriou Arapoglou Scholarship; Greek State Scholarship; Highest grade during introductory exams in Oral and Maxillofacial Surgery. Memberships: Hellenic Association for Oral and Maxillofacial Surgery; Dental Association of Athens; Stomatological Society of Greece; International Association of Aesthetic Medicine. Address: 18 Sivitanidou Str, Kallithea 176 76, Athens, Greece.

KOLTOVER Vitaliy Kiva, b. 15 May 1944, Orekhovo-Zuyevo, Russia. Biophysicist. 1 son. Education: MS, Physics, Kiev State University, 1966; PhD, Physics and Mathematics, Institute of Chemical Physics, Moscow, 1971; DSc, Biophysics, Moscow, 1988. Appointments: Plant Physiology Institute, Kiev, Ukraine, 1966-68; Predoctoral Fellow, Junior Scientist, Senior Scientist, Head Bioreliability Group Institute of Problems of Chemical Physics, 1968-. Publications: Books and articles in professional journals on reliability, aging, radiation ecology, metallofullerenes. Honours: Outstanding Achievement Diploma of President of Russian Academy of Sciences. Memberships: International

Union of Radioecology; Expert Board, Russian Foundation for Basic Research. Address: Institute of Problems of Chemical Physics, Russian Academy of Sciences, Chernogolovka 142432, Moscow, Russia.

KOMAKI Hisatoki, b. 29 August 1926, Kyoto, Japan. Honorary President of International Earth Environment University. m. Yoriko. Education: Graduated from PhD Course of Kyoto University; PhD in Agricultural Chemistry. Appointments: Professor, Mukogawa University; Founder of International Earth Environment University (IEEU); Honorary President, IEEU. Publications: Selected Works of Professor Dr Hisatoki Komaki – Four Steps to Absolute Peace, Vols I to IX, in English, French, German, Italian, Spanish and Russian, 1998. Honours: Medal of Honour with Dark Blue Ribbon, Japanese Government; Nobel Prize for Physiology and Medicine (Nomination); Highest Gold Medal (Red Cross). Memberships: Japan Society of Bioscience; Japan Academy of Science; Society of Nutrition and Food Science; Paul Harris Fellow of Rotary International. Address: 12 Donokamicho, Matsugasaki, Sakyo, Kyoto, Japan.

KOMATSU Toshiki, b. 16 November 1968, Japan. Chemical Scientist. Education: BS, 1991, MS, 1993, PhD, 2000, University of Tsukuba. Appointments: NEC Corp, Japan, 1998; AIST, MITI, Japan, 2000; IMS, University of Tsukuba, 2002; NIMS, Japan, 2004; Chisso Petrochemical Corp, 2005. Publications: Articles in professional scientific journals. Memberships: American Chemical Society; Chemical Society of Japan; Photochemical Society of Japan. Address: 75 Goi Research Center, Chisso Petrochemical Corp, Ichihara 290-8551, Japan. E-mail: komatsu@big.or.jp

KONDO Yasuto, b.17 October 1962, Nagoya, Japan. Pediatrician. m. Kayo. Education: MD, School of Medicine, 1987, PhD, Post Graduate Course of Medical Science, 1993, Fujita Health University, Aichi-Ken, Japan. Appointments: Resident, Department of Pediatrics, Fujita Health University, 1987-89; Pediatrician, Kamo Hospital, Toyota, 1993-94; Guest Researcher, ALK Laboratory, Denmark, 1994-95; Fogarty Fellow, FDA/DAPP/CBER, MD., USA, 1995-97; Researcher, 1997, Assistant Professor, 1997-2005, Department of Pediatrics, School of Medicine, Fujita Health University; Post-Doctoral Fellow, University of Texas Medical Branch, Galveston, Texas, 2002-03; Associate Professor, Department of Pediatrics, School of Medicine, Fujita Health University, 2005-. Publications: Co-author of articles in medical journals including most recently: Transient pancytopenia associated with parvovirus infection in a healthy child, 2002; Assessment of cross-reactivity between Japanese cedar (Cryptomeria japonica) pollen and tomato fruit extracts by RAST inhibition and immunoblot inhibition, 2002; IgE cross-reactivity between fish roes (salmon, herring and pollock) and chicken egg in the patients who have anaphyalaxis to salmon roe, 2002; Grades of 43 Fish Species in Japan Based on IgE-binding Activity, 2006; Structural basis for epitope sharing between group 1 allergens of cedar pollen, 2006; Parvalbumin is not responsible for cross-reactivity between Tuna and Marlin: A case report. Honours: Listed in Leading Health Professionals of the World 2006. Memberships: American Academy of Allergy, Asthma and Immunology; Japanese Society of Pediatric Allergy and Clinical Immunology; Japanese Society of Allergology; Japan Pedatric Society.

KOO Hyun-Jin, b. 27 February 1967, Seoul, Korea. Textile Engineer; Principal Researcher. m. Karpjoo Jeong, 1 son. Education: BSc, Textile Engineering, Inha University, Incheon, Korea, 1989; MSc, Textile Technology & Management,

1993, PhD, Fiber & Polymer Science, 1996, North Carolina State University, USA. Appointments: Postdoctoral Fellow, College of Textiles, North Carolina State University, 1996-99; Postdoctoral Fellow, Department of Textile Engineering, Hanyang University, 1999-2001; Senior Researcher, Division of International Co-operation, Korean Institute of Industrial Technology, 2001-; Principal Researcher, Reliability Assessment Center, FITI Testing & Research Institute, 2002-; Expert, ISO TC 38 (Textiles) SC2/ISOTC221 (Geosynthetics), Korean Agency for Technology & Standards, 2003-; Editor, Fiber Technology & Industry, Korean Fiber Society, 2004-. Publications: Variance Tolerancing & Decomposition in Short-Staple Spinning Processes: Part I – Modeling of Spun Yarn Strength through Intrinsic Components, 2001; Lifetime Prediction of Geogrids for Reinforcement of Embankments and Slopes, 2005; Reliability Assessment of Seatbelt Webbings through Accelerated Life Testing, 2005. Honours: Materials & Components Technology Prize, Minister of Korea Ministry of Commerce, Industry & Energy, 2006. Memberships: Korean Reliability Society; Korean Fiber Society; International Geosynthetic Society; Korean Geosynthetic Society; ASTM International. Address: Reliability Assessment Center, FITI Testing and Research Institute, 892-64 Jegi2-dong, Dongdaemun-gu, Seoul 130-864, Korea. E-mail: koohh@fiti.re.kr

KOOK Yoon-Ah, b. 16 May 1960, Iksam, Korea. Professor. m. Seon-Hwa Jin, 1 son, 1 daughter. Education: DDS, Wonkwang University, 1985; PhD, Chon-buk University, 1995; MSD, University of Southern California, USA, 2000. Publications: Orthotads: The Clinical Guide and Atlas, 2007. Address: The Catholic University of Korea, Kangnam St Mary's Hospital, #505 Banpo-Dong, Seocho-Gu, Seoul 137-701, Korea.

KOONTZ Dean R(ay), (David Axton, Brian Coffey, Deanna Dwyer, K R Dwyer, John Hill, Leigh Nichols, Anthony North, Richard Paige, Owen West), b. 9 July 1945, Everett, Pennsylvania, USA. Writer. m. Gerda Ann Cerra, 15 October 1966. Education: BS, Shippensburg University, 1966. Publications: Star Quest, 1968; The Fall of the Dream Machine, Fear That Man, 1969; Anti-Man, Beastchild, Dark of the Woods, The Dark Symphony, Hell's Gate, 1970; The Crimson Witch, 1971; A Darkness in My Soul, The Flesh in the Furnace, Starblood, Time Thieves, Warlock, 1972; A Werewolf Among Us, Hanging On, The Haunted Earth, Demon Seed, 1973; Strike Deep, After the Last Race, 1974; Nightmare Journey, The Long Sleep, 1975; Night Chills, Prison of Ice, 1976, revised edition as Icebound, 1995; The Vision, 1977; Whispers, 1980; Phantoms, 1983; Darkfall, 1984; Twilight Eyes, The Door to December, 1985; Strangers, 1986; Watchers, 1987; Lightning, 1988; Midnight, 1989; The Bad Place, 1990; Cold Fire, 1991; Hideaway, Dragon Tears, 1992; Mr Murder, Winter Moon, 1993; Dark Rivers of the Heart, 1994; Strange Hideways, Intensity, 1995; Tick-Tock, 1996; Fear Nothing, 1998; False Memory, 1999; From the Corner of the Eye, 2000; One Door Away from Heaven, 2001; By the Light of the Moon, 2002; The Face, Odd Thomas, 2003; Life Expectancy, 2004.; Forever Odd, 2005; The Husband, Brother Odd, 2006; The Good Guy, The Darkest Evening of the Year, 2007; Dead and Alive, 2008. Contributions to: Books, journals, and magazines. Honours: Daedalus Award, 1988; Honorary DLitt, Shippensburg University, 1989. Address: William Morris Agency, 1325 Avenue of the Americas, New York, NY 10019, USA.

KORDA Petr, b. 23 January 1968, Prague, Czech Republic. Tennis Player. m. Regina Rajchrtova, 1992, 1 son, 2 daughters. Appointments: Coached by his father until 18 years old; Coached by Tomas Petera, 1991-; Winner, Wimbledon Junior Doubles, 1986; Turned Professional, 1987; Winner, Stuttgart Open, 1997, Australian Open, 1998, Qatar Open, 1998; Member, Czechoslovak Davis Cup Team, 1988, 1996; Retired, 1999, after winning 20 professional titles including 10 singles titles; Currently plays in Seniors Tour; Winner, Honda Challenge, 2002; Chairman, Board of Supervisors, Karlštejn golf resort.

KORNBERG Arthur, b. 3 March 1918, Brooklyn, New York, USA. Biochemist. m. (1) Sylvy R Levy, deceased 1986, 3 sons, (2) Charlene W Levering, 1988, deceased 1995. Education: Pre-Medical Course, College of the City of New York, BS, 1937; Medical Degree, University of Rochester School of Medicine, 1941. Appointments: Commissioned Officer, US PUBLIC Health Service, 1941-42; National Institutes of Health, Bethesda, Maryland, 1942-52; Professor and Chairman, Department of Microbiology, Washington University School of Medicine, 1953-59; Executive Head, 1959-69, Professor, 1959-88, Professor Emeritus, 1988-, Department of Biochemistry, Stanford University School of Medicine, Palo Alto; Made the first synthetic molecules of DNA; Synthesized a biologically active artificial viral DNA. Publications: For the love of Enzymes: the odyssey and a biochemist (autobiography), 1989; Numerous original research papers and reviews on subjects in biochemistry, particularly enzymatic mechanisms of biosynthetic reactions. Honour: Joint Winner, Nobel Prize in Medicine and Physiology, 1959; Several honorary degrees; numerous other awards. Memberships: NAS; American Philosophical Society; American Academy of Arts and Sciences, Foreign member, Royal Society, 1970. Address: Department of Biochemistry, Stanford, University Medical Center, Stanford, CA 94305, USA.

KORNBERG Hans Leo, b. 14 January 1928, Herford, Germany (British Citizen). Professor of Biochemistry. Education: BSc, 1949, PhD, 1953, Sheffield University. Appointments: John Stokes Research Fellow, University of Sheffield, 1952-53; Member, Medical Research Council Cell Metabolism Research Unit, University of Oxford, 1955-61; Lecturer in Biochemistry, Worcester College, Oxford, 1958-61; Professor of Biochemistry, University of Leicester, 1961-75; Sir William Dunn Professor of Biochemistry, University of Cambridge, 1975-95; University Professor and Professor of Biology, Boston University, Massachusetts, USA, 1995-; Fellow, 1975-, Master, 1982-95, Christ's College, Cambridge. Publications: Numerous articles in scientific journals. Honours: Commonwealth Fund Fellow, Yale University and Public Health Research Institute, New York, 1953-55; Colworth Medal, Biochemical Society, 1963; Warburg Medal, Gesellschaft für biologische Chemie der Bundersrepublik, 1973; Honorary member of: Society of Biological Chemistry (USA), 1972; Japanese Biochemical Society, 1981; American Academy of Arts and Sciences, 1987; Honorary FRCP, 1989; Numerous honorary fellowships and degrees. Memberships: German Academy of Sciences, Leopoldina, 1982; Foreign associate, NAS, 1986; Academie Europaea, 1988; Fellow, American Academy of Microbiology, 1992; Foreign member, American Philosophical Society, 1993; Foreign member, Accademie Nazionale dei Lincei, Italy, 1997. Address: The University Professors, Boston University, 745 Commonwealth Avenue, Boston, MA 02215, USA.

KORNFELD Robert Jonathan, b. 3 March 1919, Newtonville, Massachusetts, USA. Dramatist; Writer; Poet. m. Celia Seiferth, 23 August 1945, 1 son. Education: AB, Harvard University, 1941; Attended, Columbia University, Tulane University, New York University, New School for Social Research, Circle-in-the-Square School of Theatre, and Playwrights Horizons Theatre School and Laboratory. Appointment: Playwright-in-Residence, University of Wisconsin, 1998. Publications: Plays: Great Southern Mansions, 1977; A Dream Within a Dream, 1987; Landmarks of the Bronx, 1990; Music For Saint Nicholas, 1992; Hot Wind From the South, 1995; The Hanged Man, 1996. Plays produced: Father New Orleans, 1997; The Queen of Carnival, 1997; The Celestials, 1998; Passage in Purgatory, Shanghai, China, 2000; The Gates of Hell, New York, 2002; Starry Night, New York, 2003; The Celestials, New York, 2005; The Art of Love, New York, 2006; Music for St Nicholas, New York, 2006. Other: Fiction and poetry. Contributions to: Various publications; Six play readings (theatres, universities and clubs), 2005. Honours: Numerous awards and prizes; Visiting Artist, Fellow, American Academy, Rome, 1996. Memberships: Authors League; Dramatists Guild; National Arts Club; New York Drama League; PEN Freedom to Write Committee; Times Square Playwrights. Address: The Withers Cottage, 5286 Sycamore Avenue, Riverdale, NY 10471, USA.

KORPINEN Leena Helena, b. 15 May 1963, Turku, Finland. Professor. Education: MSc, Technology, Tampere University of Technology, 1986; Licenced Physician, 1989, Doctor of Medicine, 1993, Tampere University; Doctor of Technology, 1996, Lappeenranta University of Technology. Appointments: Research Engineering, 1988-93, Acting Associate Professor, 1995, Head of Institute of Power Engineering, 1997-2001, Associate Professor, 1995, Professor, 1998, Head of the Laboratory of Electrical Engineering and Health, 2001-, Tampere University of Technology. Honours: Docent, Medical Technology, Tampere University, 1996.

KORZENIK Diana, b. 15 March 1941, New York, New York, USA. Professor Emerita; Painter; Writer. Education: Oberlin College; BA, Vassar College; Master's Programme, Columbia University; EdD, Graduate School of Education, Harvard University. Appointments: Professor Emerita, Massachusetts College of Art, Boston. Publications: Chapter in Art and Cognition (editors, Leondar and Perkins), 1977; Drawn to Art, 1986; Art Making and Education (with Maurice Brown), 1993; The Cultivation of American Artists (co-editor with Sloat and Barnhill), 1997; The Objects of Art Education, 2004. Contributions to: Professional journals and to magazines. Honours: Boston Globe L L Winship Literary Award, 1986; National Art Education Association Lowenfeld Award, 1998; American Library Association LEAB Award for excellence in museum publications, 2005. Memberships: Friends of Longfellow House, founder, board member; American Antiquarian Society; Massachusetts Historical Society. Address: 7 Norman Road, Newton Highlands, MA 02461, USA.

KOSHY Thomas, b. 21 August 1942, Kozhancheri, Kerala, India. Professor. m. Gracy, 1 son, 1 daughter. Education: BSc (1st class) Mathematics and Physics, 1962, MSc (1st class) Mathematics, 1964, University of Kerala; PhD, Error-Correcting Codes and Applied Algebra, Boston University, USA, 1971. Appointments: Lecturer, Mar Thomas College, University of Kerala, 1964-67; Teaching Fellow, Boston University, 1967-70; Assistant Professor, 1970-73, Associate Professor, 1973-78, Professor, 1978-, Framingham

State College. Publications: 90 articles in professional journals. Honours: First Prize for Proficiency in Mathematics, University of Kerala, 1962, 1964; Honour, Kappa Chi Chapter of Kappa Delta Pi, 1979; Distinguished Service Award, 1984; College Citation for Meritorious Service Award, 1987; Commonwealth Citation for Outstanding Performance, 1988; Excellence Award for Outstanding Contributions to Education, 2004; Distinguished Faculty of the Year Award, 2007; Listed in international biographical dictionaries. Address: Department of Mathematics, Framingham State College, 100 State Street, Framingham, MA 01701-9101, USA.

KOSSYI Igor Antonovich, b. 6 April 1935, Tbilisi, USSR. Physicist; Researcher. m. Natalya Dmirievna Buchinskaya, 1 son, 1 daughter. Education: Diploma, Experimental Nuclear Physics, Moscow Physical-Engineering Institute, 1959; PhD Diploma, Lebedev Physical Institute, Moscow, 1974; Professor of Physics Diploma, Prokhorov General Physics Institute, 1980. Appointments: Junior Research Associate, Physical –Technical Institute of Georgian Academy of Sciences, Sukhumi, USSR, 1959-62; Senior Research Associate, Head of Laboratory, Lebedev Physical Institute of RAS, Moscow, 1966-74; Head of Laboratory, Prokhorov General Physics Institute of RAS, 1974-. Publications: Plasma Physics and Plasma Electronics; Nonlinear and Turbulent Processes in Plasma Physics; Physics and Chemistry of Gas Discharges in Microwave Beams; 250 publications in plasma physics, gas discharges physics, and microwave discharges applications. Address: General Physics Institute of RAS, Vavilov Street 38, Moscow 119 991, Russia.

KOUBA Vaclav, b. 16 January 1929, Vrabi, Czech Republic. Epizootiologist. m. Anna Holcapkova, 1 son, 1 daughter. Education: Diploma, Veterinary Medicine, 1953, PhD, 1961, Habil Docent 1966, DrSc, 1978, Professor, Epizootiology, 1988, University of Veterinary Medicine, Brno, Czech Republic. Appointments: Lecturer, 1952-56, University of Veterinary Medicine, Brno, Czech Republic; National Chief Epizootiologist, Prague, 1956-78; Visiting Professor, University of Havana, 1967-71; Animal Health Officer (Research/Education), Animal Health Officer (Veterinary Intelligence), Senior Animal Health Officer, FAO-UN, Rome, Italy, 1978-85; Initiator and Founder, Veterinary Faculty, Lusaka University, Zambia, 1981; Professor, Founder of Faculty and Institute of Tropical Veterinary Medicine, Brno, 1985-88; Chief, Animal Health Service (responsible for United Nations animal health policy), Food and Agriculture Organisation of the United Nations, Rome, 1988-91; Visiting Professor, Mexico City University, 1993; Visiting Professor, University of Kosice, 1993-98; Visiting Professor, University of Prague, 1999-; Founder of modern epizootiology; Achievements as leading specialist: Eradication of bovine brucellosis, 1964, bovine tuberculosis, 1968, Teschen disease, 1973 and foot and mouth disease, 1975 in Czechoslovakia; Foot and mouth disease in Mongolia, 1964; African swine fever in Cuba, 1971; Myiasis Cochliomyia hominivorax in Northern Africa, 1991 regaining free status of the whole Eastern hemisphere; First isolation of Aujeszky disease virus in Czechoslovakia, 1954. Publications include: General Epizootiology textbooks; FAO-WHO-OIE World Animal Health Yearbook, editor-in-chief; Over 700 articles on epizootiology; Software: Epizoo, Epizmeth, Epiztext, electronic textbook. Honours: Polar Star Order, Mongolian Government; Outstanding Work Order, Czechoslovak Government; Veterinary Public Health Expert, World Health Organization, Geneva; Informatics Expert, International Office of Epizootics, Paris; Honourable President, Cuban Veterinary Scientific Society. Memberships: World Veterinary

Association, Education Committee; International Society of Veterinary Epidemiology and Economics; World Association for the History of Veterinary Medicine. Address: PB 516, 17000 Praha 7, Czech Republic. Website: www.cbox.cz/vaclavkouba

KOUH Taejoon, b. 6 October 1970, Seoul, Korea. Professor. m. Imsoon Kim, 1 daughter. Education: BA, Boston University, USA, 1994; ScM, 1996, PhD, 2002, Physics, Brown University, USA. Appointments: Postdoctoral Research Associate, Boston University, 2002-05; Tenured Lecturer, 2005-07, Assistant Professor, 2007-, Kookmin University, Korea. Publications: Numerous articles in professional journals. Honours: Phi Beta Kappa; Sigma Xi. Memberships: American Physical Society; Korean Physical Society; Korean Magnetics Society. Address: Department of Physics, Kookmin University, 861-1 Jeongneung-dong, Seongbuk-gu, Seoul, 136-702, Korea. E-mail: tkouh@kookmin.ac.kr

KOVE Miriam, b. 17 February 1941, Chotin, Bassarabia. Psychoanalytic Psychotherapist. Divorced, 2 daughters. Education: BA, Sir George University, Montreal, Canada, 1962; MS, Education, Hunter College, 1976; Certificate in Psychoanalytic Psychotherapy, New Hope Guild Centres, New York, 1979; M of SW, Adelphi University, 1983; Diplomat, American Board of Examiners, NYC, 1991-. Appointments: Private practice, 25 years; Faculty Supervisor, New Hope Guild Centres Training Programme; Adjunct Lecturer, Early Childhood, Kingsborough: Intake Director, Marble Collegiate Church, Institute for Religion and Health. Publications: Articles to professional journals; Presentations; 2 books: Myths and Madness; Mid-Life Murders. Honours: Presenter, National Conference of the Society of Clinical Social Work, Chicago; Who's Who Among Human Service Professionals; Who's Who in American Women. Memberships: National Association of Social Work; American Board of Examiners in Clinical Social Work. Address: 320 E 25th St, #8EE, New York, NY 10010, USA.

KOWALSKA Maria T, b. 8 June 1932, Wielun, Poland. Research Scientist. m. W Kowalski, 1 son, 1 daughter. Education: BA, Lyceum of General Education, Lodz, Poland, 1950; MS in Pharmacy, 1954, PhD in Pharmacy, 1964, Dr Hab in Phytochemistry, 1978, Medical Academy, Poznan. Appointments: Assistant Professor, Pharmacy, Medical Academy, Poznan, 1955-67; Postdoctoral Fellowship, Department of Pharmacy, University of Paris, France, 1969-70; Associate Professor of Agriculture, Department of Technology of Wood, Poznan, 1970-80; Professor of Pharmacognosy, National University of Kinshasa, Zaire, 1980-82; Research Associate, Research Center, Fairchild Tropical Garden, Miami, Florida, USA, 1985-90; Adjunct Assistant Professor, Department of Biochemistry and Molecular Biology, University of Miami, School of Medicine, 1990-2001. Publications: 53 scientific publications in the field of phytochemistry and pharmacognosy in international scientific periodicals. Honours: Dean's Award, Medical Academy in Poznan, 1962-64; PI grants, International Palm Society, 1986-87; PI grants, World Wildlife Fund, 1988. Memberships: Polish Pharmaceutical Society, 1960-72; American Society of Phytochemistry, 1990-92. Address: 6421 SW 106 Street, Miami, FL 33156, USA. E-mail: kellin242@aol.com

KOZÁK János, b. 20 December 1945, Kenderes, Hungary. Professor. m. Erzsébet Barna, 3 sons, 2 daughters. Education: Agricultural Engineer, 1968, Professional Agricultural Engineer, 1975, Agricultural Doctor of the University, 1979,

University of Agricultural Sciences, Gödöllő, Hungary; Candidate of Economy (PhD), The Hungarian Committee of Scientific Qualifications, Budapest, Hungary, 1988; Habilitation, Szent István University, Gödöllő, Hungary 1998. Appointments: Assistant, Co-operative Farm, Aranykalász, Törökszentmiklós; Manager, Farm Machinery Institute, Gödöllő, 1970; Chief Animal Breeder, Co-operative Farm, Lenin, Kunság Népe, Kunhegyes, 1970-78; Director, Goose Breeding Research Station, 1978-99, 2001-05; Assistant Professor, Professor, University of Agricultural Sciences, Gödöllő, 1990-99; Professor, Szent István University, Gödöllő, 2000-. Publications: Books: Vertical relations and possibilities for the improvement of interest in goose production; Miscellaneous poultry breeding; Examination of environmental conditions in the light of European Union requirements; Poultry Industry in Hungary; Works on technologies, market regulation and animal welfare. Honour: Outstanding Worker of Agriculture Award, Ministry of Agriculture and Food Industry. Memberships: World's Poultry Science Association Working Group No 8 Waterfowl, Hungarian Branch; Technical Commission of International Down and Feather Bureau; Chairman, Hungarian Standard National Technical Committee MSZT/MB 626, Feather and Down; Poultry Breeding Department, Association of Hungarian Foodstuffs Industry Science; World Rabbit Science Association, Hungarian Branch; Hungarian Association of Agricultural Economists; World Council of Hungarian University Professors; Association of Hungarian Specialists; Public Body of the Hungarian Academy of Sciences. Address: Szent István University; Department of Pig and Poultry Breeding. Address: Páter Károly u 1, H-2103 Gödöllő, Hungary. E-mail: kozak.janos@mkk.szie.hu

KOZHAMTHADAM Job, b. 30 November 1945, Kaduthuruthy, Kerala, India. Jesuit Priest; Professor. Education: MS, Physics, Patna University, India, 1971; MA, History and Philosophy of Science, University of Notre Dame, USA, 1980; PhD, History and Philosophy of Science, University of Maryland, College Park, USA, 1986. Appointments: Professor, Philosophy of Science, 1986-; Member, International Society for Science & Religion, Cambridge, England; Member, Academic Senate, Jnana-Deepa, 1990-93; Dean, Faculty of Philosophy, 1995-2001, President, , 2006-, Jnana-Deepa Vidyapeeth (Pontifical Athenaeum), Pune, India; Founder-President, Indian Institute of Science & Religion, 2001-; Member, Indian National Commission for History of Science, Indian National Science Academy, 2000-03. Publications: The Discovery of Kepler's Laws, 1994; Contemporary Science & Religion in Dialogue, 2002; Science, Technology & Values, 2003; East-West Interface of Reality, 2003; Religious Phenomena in a World of Science, 2004; Modern Science, Religion & the Quest for Unity, 2005; Chief Editor, Omega, Indian Journal of Science & Reglion, 2002-. Honours: Gold Medal, Best Graduate of the Year, University of Ranchi, 1969; National Merit Scholarship, Government of India; Author, Outstanding Academic Book of the Year, 1994; Templeton Awards. Memberships: New York Academy of Sciences; British Society for Philosophy of Science; Philosophy of Science Association; History of Science Society; Association of Christian Philosophers; IFCU Board. Address: Jnana-Deepa Vidyapeeth (Pontifical Institute of Philosophy & Religion), Ramwadi, Pune 411014, India. E-mail: jobksj@gmail.com

KOZLOVSKIY Vladimir, b. 16 February 1928, Saint Petersburg, Russia. Physicist-Engineer. m. Irina Foox, 1 son. Education: Diploma, Polytechnic Institute of Saint Petersburg, 1944-50; Post Graduate Student, Institute of

Silicate Chemistry, Saint Petersburg, 1952-56; Bachelor of Physical Mathematical Science, 1964; Doctor of Physical Mathematical Science, 1996. Appointments: Engineer, Works 211, Saint Petersburg, 1950-53; Scientific Collaborator, Institute of Semiconductors, Saint Petersburg, 1956-59; Scientific Collaborator, Raw Materials Synthesis Institute, Moscow, 1960-68; Lecturer and Scientific Collaborator, Technical University of Electronics and Mathematics, Moscow, 1968-91. Publications: 100 publications in Russian magazines and transactions of conferences and the Jewish Scientific Society, Berlin on the subject of solid corps physics, phase transitions, segnettelectricity. Honours: Medal for Defence of Leningrad; Man of the Year 2005; ABI Ambassador; Medal of Cambridge; Key of Success; Presidential Seal of Honor; Distinguished Service to Humankind Award. Memberships: Jewish Scientific Society in Berlin; Moscow Mathematical Society. Address: Saarmunderstr 85, 14478 Potsdam, Germany. E-mail: v.kozlovskiy@gmx.de

KOZLOWSKI Wlodzimierz, b. 12 August 1955, Warsaw, Poland. Physicist. Education: MSc, 1979, PhD, 1983, Moscow Power Engineering Institute – Technical University. Appointments: Expert, Institute of Nuclear Research, Poland, 1980-84; Assistant Professor, Institute of Fundamental Technological Research, Polish Academy of Sciences, Warsaw, 1984-91; Assistant Professor, Institute of Nuclear Chemistry and Technology, Warsaw, 1992-94; Assistant Professor, Institute of Biocybernetics and Biomedical Engineering, Polish Academy of Sciences, Warsaw, 1994-2002. Publications include most recently: Method of Discrete Displacements..., 1996; A Note on Varying Lattice Isotropy, 2002; Opportunity for Regulating the Collective Effect of Random Expansion with Manifestations of Finite Size Effects in a Moderate Number of Finite Systems, 2003 (http://arxiv.org/cond-mat/0307215 and http://arxiv.org/cond-mat/0505674). Honours: Listed in Who's Who in science and biographical dictionaries. Address: Bialostocka 9, Apt 25, Warsaw 03-741, Poland. E-mail: wlodekak@ibb.waw.pl

KRA Pauline, b. 30 July 1934, Lodz, Poland. Professor. m. Leo D. Children: 2 sons. Education: Physics, Radcliffe College, Boston, Massachusetts, USA, 1951-53; BA, Mathematics, Barnard College, New York, USA, 1955; MA, French, 1963, PhD, French, 1968, Columbia University, New York, USA; MA, Computer Science, Queens College, City University of New York, USA, 1990. Appointments: Lecturer in French, 1964-65, Research Assistant, Computer Science, 1992, Queens College; Visiting Lecturer, Rutgers University, 1968; Assistant Professor, 1968-76, Associate, 1976-82, Professor, 1982-99, Professor Emerita, 1999-, French, Yeshiva University; Senior Programmer Analyst, Columbia University, 1998-2007; Senior Programmer, University of Chicago, 2007-. Publications including: The Invisible Chain of the Lettres persanes, 1963; Religion in Montesquieu's Lettres persanes, 1970; A knowledge model for analysis and simulation of regulatory networks, 2000; Rousseau et la politique du caractère national, 2001; GENIES: a natural-language processing system for the extraction of molecular pathways from journal articles, 2001; The concept of national character in 18th century France, 2002; Two biomedical sublanguages: a description based on the theories of Zellig Harris, 2002; Of truth and pathways: chasing bits of information through myriads of articles, 2002; Automating terminological networks to link heterogeneous biomedical databases, 2004; GeneWays: a system for extracting, analyzing, visualizing, and integrating molecular parthway data, 2004; Annotation of Montesquieu, Lettres persanes, 2004; La Religion dans les Pensees de Montesquieu, 2005; La

Defense des Lettres persanes, 2005. Honours: Phi Beta Kappa; Dissertation awarded Distinction. Memberships: MLA; AATF; American Society for 18th Century Studies; Société Montesquieu; Société Française d'etude du dix-huitième siècle; Association for Literary and Linguistic Computing; Association for Computers and the Humanities; Phi Beta Kappa. E-mail: pauline.kra@dbmi.columbia.edu

KRAJICEK Richard, b. 6 December 1972, Rotterdam, Netherlands. Tennis Player. m. Daphne Dekkers, 1999, 1 son, 1 daughter. Appointments: Started playing tennis, 3 years; Reached semi-finals, Australian Open, 1992; Wimbledon Men's Singles Champion, 1996; Won 20 titles to date; Director, ABN AMRO World Tennis Tournament, 2004. Publications: Fast Balls, 2005. Address: ATP Tour, 201 ATP Tour Boulevard, Ponte Vedra Beach, FL 32082, USA.

KRALJEVIĆ Miro, b. 16 February 1949, Ljubljana, Slovenia. Ichthyologist; Scientific Researcher. m. Živana Crvelin, 1 son. Education: BSc, Faculty of Natural Science and Mathematics, 1974, MSc, 1977, PhD, 1995, University of Zagreb, Croatia; Qualified as Assistant Professor, Faculty of Marine Fishery, University of Split, 1998. Appointments: Research Assistant, 1977-95, Senior Research, 1995-98, Assistant Professor, 1998-2002, Professor, 2002-, Institute of Oceanography and Fisheries, University of Split, Croatia. Publications: Numerous articles as co-author in scientific journals including most recently: Age and growth of sharpsnout seabream (Diplodus puntazzo) in the eastern Adriatic Sea, 2007; On the record of read seabream (Pagrus major) in the Adriatic Sea, 2007; Growth of juvenile sharpsnout seabream (Diplodus puntazzo) in the Kornati Archipelago, eastern Adriatic Sea, 2007; Age, growth, maturity, mortality and yield-per-recruit for annual sea bream (Diplodus annularis L) from the middle eastern Adriatic Sea, 2007; Age, growth and mortality of brown comber (Serranus hepatus) in the eastern Adriatic (Croatian coast), 2007; Growth of juvenile striped seabream (Lithognathus mormyrus) in the Adriatic Sea, 2007. Honours: Listed in numerous biographical publications. Memberships: Croatian Biology Association; Croatian Ecological Association; CIESM Association. Address: Institute of Oceanography and Fisheries, Šetalište Ivana Meštrovića 63, 21000 Split, Dalmatia, Croatia. E-mail: kraljevic@izor.hr

KRAMER Herbert J, b. 24 December 1939, Bad Kreuznach, Germany. Professor of Medicine. m. Hella, 2 sons. Education: Medical School, Munich, 1958-60; Medical School, Sorbonne University, Paris, France, 1960-61; MD, 1963, PhD, 1967, Medical School, University of Saarland. Appointments: Resident, Research Fellow, UCLA, California, USA, 1968-70; Resident, 1964-68, Chief Resident, 1970-72, Medical Faculty, Assistant Professor of Medicine, 1972, University of Saarland; Associate Professor of Medicine, 1976, Professor of Medicine/ Nephrology, 1980-, University of Bonn. Publications: Over 300 publications in professional journals. Honours: Claude-Bernard Prize, University of Saarland, 1972; Theodor Frerichs Prize, German Society of Internal Medicine, 1973. Memberships: International Society of Nephrology; American Society of Nephrology; German Society of Nephrology; International Society of Hypertension; American Society of Hypertension; German Society of Hypertension; New York Academy of Sciences; American Society of Physiology; and others. Address: Augustastrasse 67, 53173, Bonn-Bad Godesberg, Germany. E-mail: hkramer@uni-bonn.de

KRAMER Stephen Ernest, b. 12 September 1947, Hampton Court, England. Circuit Judge. m. Miriam Leopold, 1 son, 1 daughter. Education: BA, 1969, MA, 1987, Keble College,

Oxford; Université de Nancy, France. Appointments: Called to the Bar (Gray's Inn), 1970; Assistant Recorder, 1987-91, Recorder of the Crown Court, 1991-; Standing Counsel (Crime) to HM Customs and Excise South Eastern Circuit, 1989-95; Member, Bar Council, 1993-95, Committee, South Eastern Circuit, 1997-2000; Chairman Liaison Committee, Bar Council/Institute of Barristers' Clerks, 1996-99; Committee Member, 1993-98, Acting Vice Chairman, 1998-99, Vice Chairman, 1999-2000, Chairman, 2000-2001, Criminal Bar Association; Queen's Counsel, 1995; Bencher Gray's Inn, 2001-; Head of Chambers, 2 Hare Court Temple, London, 1996-2003; Circuit Judge, 2003-05, Senior Circuit Judge sitting at Central Criminal Court, Old Bailey, 2005-.

KRASILNIKOV Nikolay, b. 22 January 1927, Irkutsk, USSR. Communications Educator; Researcher. m. Olga Krasilnikova, 1 son. Education: Graduate, Leningrad Politechnical Institute, 1950; PhD, Leningrad Institute of Aviation Instrument Making, 1952; DSc, Academy of Communication, Leningrad, 1964; Diploma of Professor, 1965. Appointments: Engineer, Institute of Television, Leningrad, 1950-54; Assistant Professor, 1954-57, Head of Department of Transmitting and TV Devices, Leningrad Institute of Aviation Instrument Making, 1957-1994; Professor, State University of Aerospace Instrumentation, Saint Petersburg, 1994-. Publications: 230 including 8 monographs, 1961, 1976, 1986, 1999, 2001; Articles in professional journals. Honours: Medal for Leningrad Defence, 1944; Honoured Scientific and Technical Worker of Russia, 1992; Honoured Professor of State University of Aerospace Instrumentation, St Petersburg, 1997. Memberships: Fellow, Science and Technology Society of Radio Engineering, Electronics and Communications, 1951; New York Academy of Sciences, 1995. Address: State University of Aerospace Instrumentation, 67 Bolshaia Morskaia, 190000 Saint Petersburg, Russia.

KRASNOYAROVA Nadezhda, b. 14 November 1950, Almaty City, Kazakhstan. Doctor. m. Alexey Kraznoyarov, 1 son. Education: Medical Diploma (Distinction), 1975; Doctor of Medical Sciences, Russian Federation, 1997; Doctor of Medical Sciences, Kazakhstan, 2003; Professor of Medicine, 2005. Appointments: Medical Student, 1969-75; Neuropathologist, 1975-89; Junior Researcher, Neurology Department, 1989-93; Assistant, 1993-97, Associate Professor, 1997-2005, Professor, 2005-, Department of Traditional Medicine. Publications: 4 medical books; 135 articles. Honours: Woman of the Year, 2007. Memberships: FIMM. Address: Gaydara Str, h87, f85, Almaty City, 050009, Kazakhstan.

KRAU Edgar, b. 9 April 1929, Stanislau, Poland. University Professor; Scientist; Educator. m. Mary Epure, 1 daughter. Education: MA, Psychology, Education, 1951, PhD, Psychology, 1964, University of Cluj, Romania. Appointments include: High School Teacher, Gherla, Romania, 1952-61; Chief Research Fellow, Institute of Pedagogical Sciences, Cluj, 1961-63; Consecutive positions, University of Cluj, 1963-77; Head, Psychological Department, Academy of the Romanian Republic, Cluj Branch, 1968-77; Member International Test Commission, 1971-73; Professor, University of Haifa, Israel, 1977-81; Professor, Tel-Aviv University, 1981-97; Chairman International Colloquium on Human Resources Development, Jerusalem, 1984; Member, Scientific Committee, XXI International Congress of Applied Psychology, 1986. Publications: Books: Co-author, Treatise of Industrial Psychology, 1967; Author, editor, Self-realization, Success and Adjustment, 1989; Author, The Contradictory Immigrant Problem, 1991; Co-author: Projet professionnel - projet de vie,

1992; Organizations and Management: Towards the Future, 1993; Author: The Realization of Life Aspirations through Vocational Careers, 1997; Social and Economic Management in the Competitive Society, 1998; A Meta-Psychological Perspective on the Individual Course of Life, 2003; Over 70 papers in leading scientific journals; Editor-in-Chief, Man and Work (journal of labour studies), 1987-. Honours include: Vasile Conta Prize, Romanian Academy, 1972; Award, High Centre for Logic and Comparative Sciences, Bologna, Italy, 1972; Honorary Mention, Journal of Vocational Behavior, 1986; Homagial Biography, Bibliography, Revue Européenne de Psychologie Appliquée, 1993; Dedication, Outstanding People of the 20th Century, IBC; 20th Century Achievement Award, ABI, 1999; Honours List, International Biographical Centre, 2000; Cavalier, World Order of Science, Education and Culture, 2002; American Order of Excellence, 2003; Legion of Honor, United Cultural Convention, 2005; Order of American Ambassadors, 2006; Listed in numerous international biographical publications. Memberships: International Association of Applied Psychology, 1970-, Executive Committee, Division of Psychology and National Development, 1982-86; Member-Instructor, Israeli Psychological Association, 1978-; Affiliate, American Psychological Association, 1993-; Active Member, New York Academy of Sciences, 1998-; Member of Academic Council, London Diplomatic Academy, 2002; Einsteinian Chair of Sciences, World Academy of Letters, 2004-. Address: 2 Hess Str, 33398 Haifa, Israel.

KRAVCHENKO Peter, b. 21 June 1921, Kyiv, Ukraine. Designer of Special Effects. m. Valentyna Ponomarenko, 1 son, 1 daughter. Education: Diploma, Kyiv State Taras Shevchenko Art School; Diploma, Institute of Commercial Art, Australia; Diploma, School of Television Skill, Australia. Appointments: Visual Artist, Designer of Special Effects, Wardrobe Department, TV Studio, ABN 2, 20 years; Director, Board of Directors and Ukrainian Studies Foundation, Australia, 1991-98; Participated in art exhibitions in Australia and Ukraine. Publications: Many articles published as Approbated Correspondent, Ukrainian Weekly, The Free Thought; Book: Costumes of Ukraine, 1999. Honours: Honourable Diplomas from: President of Ukraine; Mayor of Kyiv, Ukraine; Minister of Culture and Art in Ukraine; Council Ukrainian Organisation in Australia; International Charity Funds: Spiritual Legacy, Ukrainian Khata, Cambridge University; International Peace Award, Cultural Assembly of USA; World Congress of Arts, Sciences and Communications Lifetime Achievement Award. Memberships: Honorary Member, National Society of Artists in Ukraine; International Charity Fund, Spiritual Heritage, Kyiv; Co-founder, Member and Secretary, Ukrainian Artists Society in Australia. Address: 57 Georges Avenue, Lidcombe, New South Wales, Australia 2141.

KRAYBILL Herman F, b. 27 June 1914, Marietta, Pennsylvania, USA. Biomedical Research Scientist. m. Dorothy, deceased, 1 son, 2 daughters. Education: BS, Franklin & Marshall College, 1936; MS, 1938, PhD, 1941, Biochemistry, University of Maryland. Appointments: Chief of Biochemistry Division, US Army Medical Research & Nutrition Laboratory, Denver, Colorado, 1953-60; Associate Director, Bureau of Foods and Science, Food & Drug Administration, Washington DC, 1960-66; Director and Co-ordinator, Environmental Cancer Program, National Cancer Institute, Bethesda, Maryland, 1966-84. Publications: 150 science journal papers; Editor and co-editor, 4 books in biomedical research area. Honours: Distinguished Alumnus Award, Franklin & Marshall College, 1976; Merit Award, National Cancer Institute in Bethesda, 1981; Outstanding

Alumnus Award, 1996, Established Dr Kraybill Fellowships in Biochemistry, 2006, University of Mryland College Park. Memberships: American Chemical Society; Society of Toxicology; New York Academy of Science; Pan-American Medical Association; American Institute of Nutrition; Sigma Xi; American Council on Science and Health; Alpha Chi Sigma.

KREBS John Richard (Lord Krebs of Wytham), b. 11 April 1945, Sheffield, England. Chairman; Professor; Principal. m. Katharine Anne Fullerton, 1968, 2 daughters. Education: BA, 1966, MA, 1970, D Phil, 1970, Pembroke College, Oxford. Appointments: Assistant Professor, Institute of Animal Resource Ecology, UBC, Canada, 1970-73; Lecturer in Zoology, University College of North Wales, Bangor, 1973-75; University Lecturer in Zoology, Edward Grey Institute of Field Ornithology, Oxford, 1976-88; Fellow, Wolfson College, Lecturer in Zoology, Oriel, St Anne's and Pembroke Colleges, 1976-81; E P Abraham Fellow in Zoology, Pembroke College, 1981-88; Storer Lecturer, University of California, 1985; Official Fellow, 1988-2005, Honorary Fellow, 2005-, Pembroke College; Royal Society Research Professor, Oxford University, 1988-2005; Director, AFRC Unit of Ecology and Behaviour, 1989-94; Director, NERC Unit of Behavioural Ecology, 1989-94; Chief Executive, Natural Environment Research Council, UK, 1994-99; Chairman, UK Food Standards Agency, 2000-05; Principal, Jesus College, Oxford University, 2005-. Publications: 2 books; 144 refereed publications; 45 book chapters; 27 other articles; 11 abstracts; 25 book reviews. Honours include: Association of the Study of Animal Behaviour Medal, 2000; Benjamin Ward Richardson Gold Medal, Royal Society for Promotion of Health, 2002; ISI Highly Cited Researcher, 2002; Wooldridge Medal, British Veterinary Association, 2003; Croonian Lecture, Royal Society, London, 2004; Lord Rayner Memorial Medal, 2005; Award for Outstanding Achievement, Society for Food Hygiene Technology, 2005; Harben Gold Medal, Royal Institute of Public Health, 2006; Life Peerage (cross bencher), 2007; Numerous DSc honoris causa. Memberships: Honorary Fellow, German Ornithologists' Society, 2003; Foreign Honorary Member, US National Academy of Sciences, 2004; Fellow, Academy of Medical Sciences, 2004. Address: Jesus College, Oxford OX1 3DW, England. E-mail: principal@jesus.ox.ac.uk

KREBS Rolf, b. 1940, Mainz, Germany. Professor. m. Ingeborg, 2 daughters. Education: MD, Mainz University, 1967; Specialist (lic Physician) in Pharmacology and Clinical Pharmacology; Professor of Pharmacology and Toxicology, University of Mainz, 1971. Appointments: Head, Clinical Research, Bayer AG, 1976-83; Head, R&D Pharmaceuticals worldwide, Bayer, 1984-86; Vice Director, General Bayer Italia, Milan, 1986-89; Vice Chairman and Head, Pharmaceuticals, 1989-2000, Chairman, Board of Managing Directors, 2001-04, Boehringer Ingelheim. Publications: The effect of barbiturates on the myocardium, 1979; Klinische Pharmakologie der Herzglykoside, 1980; Coronary Disease, text book, 1975-85. Honours: Boehringer Ingelheim award, 1971; Ernst v Bergmann medal, 1974; Honorary Doctor, University of Athens, Greece, 1994; Honorary Member, Bulgarian Academy of Medicine, 1995; Grand Decoration of Honour, Republic of Austria, 1999; Officer's Cross of the Order of Merit of the Federal Republic of Germany, 2003; Member, European Academy of Science & Art, 2003; BTG Lifetime Achievement Award, 2006. Memberships: President, European Federation of Pharmaceutical Industries and Associations, 1996-98; President, International Federation

of Pharmaceutical Manufacturers Association, 2000-02. Address: Grosse Gallusstrasse 18, 60311 Frankfurt/Main, Germany. E-mail: krebs.rolf@web.de

KREMENYUK Victor, b. 13 December 1940, Odessa, Ukraine. Professor; Research Scholar. m. Liudmila. Education: Moscow Institute for International Relations of the Foreign Ministry (MGIMO), USSR, 1957-63; Courses at the Soviet Military Academy, 1963-64; PhD, MGIMO, 1965-67; Candidate, EconSci (World Economy), 1968; Doctor of History, Institute for USA and Canada Studies, 1980. Appointments: Military Service, 1963-68; Journalist, International Affairs, 1968-70; Research Scholar, Institute for USA and Canada Studies, 1970-; Lecturer and Professor: Salzburg seminar, Austria; NATO (SHAPE) School, Oberammergau, Germany; NATO Defense College, Rome, Italy; Marshall Center for European Security Studies, Garmisch-Partenkirschen, Germany; University of Paris, France; University La Sagesse, Beirut, Lebanon; Consultant and Advisor: USSR Supreme Soviet and Russian State Duma; Soviet and Russian Foreign Ministry; International Institute for Applied Systems Analysis, Laxenburg, Austria. Publications: Over 350 books, monographs, collective publications, articles in the press and academic journals worldwide. Honours: 2 medals for military service; Soviet National Prize for Science and Technology, 1980; CPR Institute for Dispute Resolution, New York, Book Award, 2002; Russian Ministry for Emergencies Prize for Strategic Risk Analysis, 2005. Memberships: US National Geographical Society, 1982-. Address: Institute for USA and Canada Studies, Russian Academy of Sciences, Khlebny per 2/3, Moscow 123995, Russian Federation. E-mail: vkremenyuk@yahoo.com

KREMER Erhard K, b. 19 January 1953, Löhnberg, Germany. Professor. Education: Diploma, Mathematics, University of Giessen, Germany, 1977; PhD, Mathematics, University of Hamburg, Germany, 1979; Habilitation, Mathematics, University of Hamburg, Germany, 1983. Appointments: Scientific Assistant, 1977-80, University Assistant, 1981-83, Professor of Applied Mathematical Statistics, 1983-, Mathematics Department, University of Hamburg, Germany; Mathematical Referent, Bavarian Re in Munich, Germany, 1980-81; President, Non-profit Association on Applied Mathematical Statistics and Risk Theory, Hamburg, 1986-98; Deputy Governor, American Biographical Institute Research Association, Raleigh, USA, 1996-; Consular Representative of the United Cultural Convention, 2001-. Publications: Over 150 mathematical articles, notes, books and further. Honours: Man of the Year, ABI, 1995, 1996, 2006; Most Admired Man of the Year, ABI, 1995; Most Admired Man of the Decade, ABI, 1995; 20th Century Award for Achievement, IBC, 1995; Gold Record of Achievement, 1995; Who's Who of the Year, 1995; World Lifetime Achievement Award, 1996; Personality of Year, ABI, 1996; 2000 Millennium Medal of Honour, ABI, 1998; Platinum Record for Exceptional Performance, ABI, 1998; Outstanding Man of the 20th Century, ABI, 1999; Outstanding Man of the 21st Century, ABI, 2000; Presidential Seal of Honor, ABI, 2000; International Intellectual of the Year, IBC, 2001; World Citizen of the Year 2002, ABI, 2002; International Scientist of the Year, IBC, 2002; Outstanding Professional Award, ABI, 2006; Genius Laureate of Germany, ABI, 2005; American Hall of Fame, ABI; Lecturer, world-wide, including: Hamburg, 1981, Prague, 1982, Tel Aviv, 1986, Berlin, 1988, Rio de Janeiro, 1988, New York, 1989, Quebec, 1989, Cairo, 1991, Munich, 1992, Tokyo, 1994, Athens, 1996, Cairns, 1997; Peking, 1998; Washington, 2001; Listed in international biographical dictionaries. Memberships: International Actuarial Association; German Mathematicians

Association; German Actuarial Association; German University Union; Order of International Ambassadors; Legion of Honor, United Cultural Convention. Address: Hagenbeckstrasse 154A, D-22527 Hamburg, Germany.

KRENEK Mary, b. 8 December 1951, Wharton, Texas, USA. Researcher; Educator; Army Reserve Officer. Education: AA, Wharton County Junior College, 1972; BA, Texas A & I University, Corpus Christi, 1974; MA, St Mary's University, San Antonio, 1992; Czech Language Certificate, Charles University, Prague, Czech Republic, 1994. Appointments: Certificate, Secondary and Elementary Teacher, Texas; Polygraph Examiner, San Antonio, Texas 1979-81; Industry Contractor Market, Political and Social Researcher, San Antonio and Houston, 1982-; Substitute Teacher, Teacher, San Antonio School District, 1981-82, Houston School District, 1991-98, 2002-; Delegate, Texas Democrat Convention, 1971-72; 1st Lieutenant, US Army, 1975-78; Lieutenant Colonel, USAR, 1978-, Retired USAR, 2003; Associate, J C Penney Co Inc, 1994-2000; Instructor, Government, Wharton County Junior College, Wharton, Texas, 1997-99; Actor, Southwest Casting, 2006-. Memberships: National Association of Self-Employed; Reserve Officers Association, Secretary-Treasurer, Alamo Chapter, (Junior Vice-President Department Texas), St Mary's University Alumni Association; Alumni Association Presidential Classroom for Young Americans; Pi Sigma Alpha; Political Science Honor Society; American Legion; Czech Ex Students Association of Texas; Wharton County Historical Museum Association; Women in Military Service for America Memorial Foundation (Charter); Houston Czech Cultural Center; American Political Science Association; Point/Counterpoint (Local Houston Chapter); Elected, Secretary of the Board of Directors, Egypt Plantation Museum. Address: PO Box 310, Egypt, TX 77436-0310, USA. E-mail: marykrenek01@aol.com

KRET Yana, b. 21 November 1974, Ukraine. Lector; Psychologist. m. Igor Kret, 1 daughter. Education: Specialist in Practical Psychology, 1997, Candidate of Science in Psychology (PhD), 2000, Certificate on Doctorate Completion, 2006, Zaporozhye State University, Ukraine. Appointments: Practical Psychologist, Secondary School for Deaf Children, Zaporozhye, Ukraine, 1997-2000; Lector, Zaporozhye State University, 2000-03; Bi-lingual Teacher, Dungannon Primary School, Dungannon, Northern Ireland, 2003-. Publications: Correction of the Psychophysical Development of the Deaf Children of the Elder Pre-School Age, Kiev, Ukraine; Early Diagnostic and Correction of the Psychomotion of Children with Psychophysical Disability, Zaporozhye, Ukraine, 2007; Early Diagnostic and Correction of Psychomotion of Children with Autism, Zaporozhye, 2007. Honours: Certificate of Secondary Education, 1992; Diploma of Candidate of Science in Special Psychology, 2000; Award for Teaching Assistant of the Year, Northern Ireland, 2005; Certificate on Doctorate Completion, 2006. Memberships: General Teaching Council for Northern Ireland. Address: 40 Killymerron Park, Dungannon, Northern Ireland, BT71 6DN, United Kingdom.

KRETSIS Nicholaos, b. 11 September 1959, Krikello, Evrytania, Greece. Researcher; Businessman. Education: JMB, English, 1979, GCE, Mathematics and Economics, 1981, Tutorial College of Chichester, West Sussex, England. Appointments: Research on The Theory of Relativity; Research into cancer genetics; Research into cosmology; Philosophical Research; Amateur photographer; Discovery of the Pandavrehi waterfalls in the Krikellopotamos river, and caves with stalactites and stalagmites in Krikello at the place of Panayia, on the mountain Anilia; Discovery and exposure

of an international drug and smuggling net; Businessman. Publications: Numerous articles in Greek press and other magazines and newspapers. Honours: Vice President, Greek Cancer Society; Active Member, NYAS, USA; Regural Member, AAAS, USA; Member, American Chemical Society. Memberships: National Geographic Society, USA; National Geographic Society, Greece; The Folio Society, London, England. Address: Krikello, PS 360 76, Evrytania, Greece.

KRIEGER César Amorim, Director of the Directorate of Information and Intelligence. Education: LLB, 1986, SJD/PhD, 2002, Laws, State and Society, Federal University of Santa Catarina School of Law, Brazil; LLM (Honours), Exeter University, England, 1996. Appointments: Associate, Banco de Desenvolvimento do Estado de Santa Catarina S/A, 1982-87; Partner, Krieger, Brasil & Silveira Advogados Associados, 1987-89; Chief Police Officer, Policia Civil do Estado de Santa Catarina, 1988-; Special Legal Adviser, Secretaria do Desenvolvimento Economico e Mercosul do Estado de Santa Catarina, 1997-98; Adjunct Professor of International Relations, Universidade do Vale do Itajai, 1997-; Adjunct Professor, International Relations, Universidade do Sul de Santa Catarina, 1997-; Lecturer, Civil Police Academy of Santa Catarina, 1998-. Publications: Papers and articles in professional legal journals. Memberships: Alumni Association of Exeter University; American Society of International Law; Brazilian Society of Airspace Law; Brazilian Criminal Law Society; Nereu de Oliveira Ramos Lodge; Brazilian Chief Police Officers Association; Brazilian Red Cross; Commander, The Military and Hospitaller Order of Saint Lazarus of Jerusalem, Malta Obedience; Friend of the Brazilian Army; Friend of the Brazilian Navy. Address: Rua Paulino Pedro Hermes, 2231, 88.108-370 – São José, SC, Brazil. E-mail: camorim@ssp.sc.gov.br

KRIPALANI Lakshmi, b. 24 August 1920, Hyderabad, Sindh, Pakistan. Educator. 1 adopted son. Education: BS (Hons), Experimental Psychology, University of Bombay, India; MA, Education, with certificates in Pre-education, Elementary Education, Supervision and Administration, Seton Hall University; Protegee of Dr Maria Montessori, trained by her in 1946. Appointments: Volunteered to teach after high school graduation, Karachi, India, 1936-42; Ran one room middle school in Karachi, India, 1942-43; Pioneered New India School in protest to the method of teaching in Karachi and classes for women who were widows or single and lived a life of deprived individuals, 1943-47; Pioneered Pawani Refugee Camp School without walls in the camp for refugee children, Bombay, India, 1947-48; Pioneered Garrison School for Services after British left India, 1948-62; Pioneered first Montessori school, Iowa City Iowa, 1962-64; Pioneered Hilary School in Ironbound section, Newark, New Jersey, 1964-65; Pioneered Montessori Center of New Jersey with Montessori teacher training classes and children's classes, 1966-84; Columnist, national newspaper "Public School Montessorian", 1987-; Continuing as Montessori Consultant, Lecturer, Writer and Poet. Honours include: Resolution passed by Senate of New Jersey for her work in Early Childhood Education and Training of Montessori Teachers, 1970; Maha Rishi Award, 1973; Community Leaders and Noteworthy Americans Award, 1978; Golden Award World of Poetry, 1986, 1987; Certificate of Appreciation, Montclair Lion's Club, 1993; Iliad Literary Awards Program, 1998; Honourable Mention, 1998 Literary Awards Program, 1998; Woman of the Year Award, 2005, ABI; International Peace Prize, UCC, 2007; Listed in Who's Who publications and biographical dictionaries. Memberships: Life Member, Association Montessori Internationale; Life Member American Montessori Society; Life Member, North American

Montessori Teachers Association; Life Member, Association of the Displaced People of Sindh, Pakistan (after the partition of India); Board Member, UNA, USA, 1964-, Past President of the Montclaire Chapter, New Jersey, 1968-70; League of Women Voters; Friends of Barnet; Mensa; College Women's Association; Gardening Club; Cosmopolitan Club. Address: 340 North Fullerton Avenue, Upper Montclair, NJ 07043, USA. E-mail: lkriplani@concst.net

KRISTINSSON Magnús, b. 13 June 1943, Eyjafjörður, Iceland. Freelance Teacher; Teacher's Trainer; Translator; Interpreter; Tourist Guide; Editor; Lecturer. m. Brigitte Kristinsson, 1 son. Education: BA (Hons), English Language and Literature, German, Icelandic and Philosophy, University of Leeds, 1967; Study of German, University of Kiel, Germany, 1967-68; Study of Foreign Language Didactics, Computer Science and Data Processing, Giessen, Germany, 1987-88; Authorised Tourist Guide, Iceland (German, English, Icelandic), 1970-; Publicly appointed Translator and Interpreter for German, English and Icelandic in Iceland, Icelandic Ministry of Justice, 1975; Accredited Translator and Interpreter for German and Icelandic in Germany, Stuttgart Regional Court, 1998. Career: Junior Teacher, Secondary Boarding School Eiðar, Iceland, 1963-64; Director, Adult Education Department, Akureyri Junior College, 1975-81; Executive and Publicity Manager, Icelandic Social-Political Movement "Samtök um jafnrétti milli landshluta", 1985-86; Teacher of German and English, Junior College, Akureyri, Iceland, 1968-85, 1986-87, 1988-90; Part-time, 1970-90, Full-time, 1990-94, Tourist Guide and Translator, Iceland; Freelance Teacher (English, Icelandic, PC-Computing), Translator, Interpreter, Editor, Tourist Guide and Lecturer, Germany, 1994-. Publications: Several articles, books and book chapters in Icelandic include: Book: Úr torfbæjum inn í tækniöld (chief editor, translator, co-author), 2003; Fjallabálkurinn umhverfis Glerárdal (book chapter), 1991; Article: Glerárdalur, lýsing og örnefnatal, 1978; Translations of books from German and English into Icelandic. Honour: Best Non-Fiction Book of the Year in Iceland for "Úr torfbæjum inn í tækniöld", 2003. Memberships: BDÜ (Federal Association of Interpreters and Translators), Germany; FLDS (Association of Certified Court Interpreters and Document Translators), Iceland; VVU (Association of Accredited and Sworn Court Interpreters and Appointed and Sworn Document Translators) Baden-Württemberg, Germany; HAGÞENKIR (Union of Icelandic Non-Fiction Writers). Address: Schmidener Strasse 241, D-70374 Stuttgart, Germany. E-mail: kristinsson@gmx.net

KROCKOVER Gerald Howard, b. 12 November 1942, Sioux City, Iowa, USA. Professor. m. Sharon Diane Shulkin, 2 sons. Education: BA, Chemistry, Secondary Education, 1964; MA, Science Education, Geology, 1966, PhD, Science Education, Geology, 1970, University of Iowa. Appointments: Science Teacher, Bettendorf and Iowa City, 1964-70; Assistant Professor, Associate Professor, Purdue University, West Lafayette, Indiana, 1970-80; Professor of Earth and Atmospheric Science Education, Purdue University, 1980-. Publications: 13 textbooks; 5 elementary science series; 121 journal publications. Honours include: Outstanding Science Educator, Association for the Education of Teachers of Science, 1973; Distinguished Teacher Educator Award, National Association of Teacher Educators, 1990. Memberships include: American Association for the Advancement of Science; International Organisation for Science and Technology Education. Address: Purdue University, 550 Stadium Mall Drive, West Lafayette, IN 47907-2051, USA.

KROGH Geo Von, b. 25 January 1943, Bergen, Norway. Medical Doctor. Education: Graduate, University of Bergen, Norway, 1967; Training in Sweden, 1970-; Specialist in Dermatovenereology, 1978. Appointments: Associate Professor, Karolinska University Hospital Solna, Stockholm, Sweden, retired 2006. Publications: 119 publications of which 51 are original research contributions; 80 articles and 2 textbooks relating to the management of condylomas; Articles in medical journals as co-author include: Adolescent girls investigated for sexual abuse: history, physical findings and legal outcome, 1999; European course on HPV associated pathology: guidelines for primary care physicians for the diagnosis and management of anogenital warts, 2000; European guideline for the management of anogenital warts, 2001; Condyloma eradication: self-therapy with 0.15%-0.5% podophyllotoxin versus 20-25% podophyllin – an integrated safety assessment, 2001; Potential human papillomavirus reactivation following topical corticosteroid therapy of genital lichen sclerosus and erosive lichen planus, 2002; Screening and genotyping of genital Chlamydia trachomatis in urine specimens from male and female clients of youth-health centres in Stockholm County, 2002; The cost-effectiveness of patient-applied treatments for anogenital warts, 2003; Numerous surveys. Memberships include: Swedish Academy of Dermatology; Scandinavian Society of Genito-urinary Medicine; International Society for the Study of Vulvar Disease; Swedish Physicians Against AIDS; European Academy of Dermatology and Venereology; International AIDS Society; European Academy of Dermatology and Venereology; International Society for STD Research; Medical Society for the Study of Venereal Diseases; American Venereal Disease Association; Swedish Society for Dermatologic Surgery; American Academy of Dermatology; International Union against Sexually Transmitted Infections, European Branch, Honorary Treasurer, 2002-2003. Address: Korphoppsgatan 29, 12064 Stockholm, Sweden. E-mail: geo.von-krogh@bredband.net

KRONDAHL Hans, Professor Emeritus; Fibre Artist; Fabric Designer. Education: Graduate, University College of Arts Crafts and Design, Stockholm, Sweden; Further studies in Europe and the Far East. Appointments: Teacher, Fibre Art and Textile Design in art schools, 1960-; Working in own studio for Tapestry Weaving and Fabric Design, 1963-; Senior Lecturer, Head of Textile Department, University College of Arts Crafts and Design, Stockholm, Sweden, 1977-78; Head of Textile Design Department, National College of Art and Design, Oslo, Norway, 1978-79; Head of Textile Design Department, HDK College, 1981-88, Professor of Textile Art, Gothenburg University, Sweden, 1988-94; Worked as UNIDO Expert in Textile Design, Indonesia, 1979-80; Exhibits in Sweden and abroad most recently works included in "Katja of Sweden", Kulturen Museum, Lund, 2002-2003; "Heliga Kläder", Klostret Museum, Ystad, 2004-2005; Permanent representation in museum collections in Europe and USA; Tapestries, front curtains, rugs, carpets, ecclesiastical textiles and vestments commissioned for the public environment. Publications: Works included in: The Lunning Prize Exhibition Catalogue, 1986; Svenska Textilier 1890-1990, by Jan Brunius, etc, 1994; Contemporary Textile Art by Charles S Talley, 1982; Fiberarts Magazine, 1996; The Design Encyclopedia; Museum of Modern Art, New York, 2004. Honour: Prince Eugen Medal, 2002. Address: Smedjegatan 8, S 21421 Malmö, Sweden.

KROPACHEV Nikolay, b. 8 February 1959, Leningrad, Russia. Lawyer; Judge. m. Natalia Alexandrovna Sidorova, 1 son. Education: Graduate, Law Faculty, 1981, PhD Student,

1981-84, PhD (Candidate of Law), Law Faculty, 1985, Doctor of Law Degree, 2000, St Petersburg State University. Appointments: Assistant (Junior) Lecturer, 1985-92, Senior Lecturer, 1992-2000, Professor, 2000-, Dean of the Special Law Faculty, 1992-98, Dean of the Law Faculty, St Petersburg State University, 1998-; Chairman, St Petersburg Charter Court, 2000-05; First Vice-Rector of Saint Petersburg State University, 2006. Publications: Mechanism of Criminal Law Regulation, 1989; Penal Law (textbook), 1989; Criminology (textbook), 1992, 2003, 2005; Criminal Law on a Contemporary Stage, 1992; Russian Criminal Legislation (Comparative Analysis), 1996; Criminal Law Regulation: Mechanism and System, 1999; Criminal Law Regulation: the criminal liability, 2000; Criminal Law of Russia (co-author), (textbook), 2006. Honours: A F Koni Medal, Ministry of Justice, 1999; Russian President's Prize, 2002; Order of Honour, 2004. Memberships: Vice-President, Interregional Association of Law Schools, 1996-; President, St Petersburg and Lenningrad Region Association of Lawyers; Member, Association of Lawyers of Russia; Member of Presidium of Association of Russian Lawyers. Address: Faculty of Law, St Petersburg State University, 22 aya liniya 7, R-199026 VO St Petersburg, Russia. E-mail: office@jurfak.spb.ru

KROSNICK Mary Lou Wesley, b. 11 June 1934, Bayonne, New Jersey, USA. Musician; Pianist; Teacher. m. Aaron B Krosnick, 1 son. Education: BS, Juilliard School of Music, 1957; MA, University of Wisconsin, 1958; MM, Yale University School of Music, 1961. Appointments: Head of Piano Department, Sewanee Summer Music Center, 1976-85; Assistant Professor of Music, 1978, Associate Professor of Music, 1985, Professor of Music, 1992, Distinguished Performer-in-Residence, 2000-, Jacksonville University, Florida; Performances: Soloist with The Boston Pops Orchestra under Arthur Fiedler, 1961; Soloist with The Jacksonville Symphony Orchestra, Kennedy Center and Carnegie Hall under Willis Page, 1972; Soloist with The Jacksonville Symphony Orchestra under Morton Gould, 1981; Performances as a soloist and composer on Radio Stations: WaXR, WNYC, WOR-TV, Radio Free Europe, 1950-51; Composition: The Rain Comes (performed under Leopold Stokowsky in a version orchestrated by him by the New York Philharmonic-Symphony Orchestra, 1949). Publication: Book chapter in Isabella Vengerova: Beloved Tyranna by Joseph Rezits, 1995. Honours: 1st Place, New York Philharmonic Symphony's Young Composers' Contest, 1949; 1st Place, National Guild of Piano Teachers' International Recording Competition, Collegiate Division, 1957, Teachers' Division, 1972; 1st Place, University of Redlands, California, National American Music Competition, 1961; Listed in national and international biographical dictionaries. Memberships include: Florida State Music Teachers; Music Teachers National Association; National Federation of Music Clubs; Address: 13734 Bermuda Cay Court, Jacksonville, FL 32225, USA. E-mail: abkmlk@hotmail.com

KRUG Arno, b. 16 February 1935, Schneidemuhl, Germany. Surgeon. m. Christine, 3 sons, 1 daughter. Education: MD, Berlin-Marburg, 1959; PhD, Surgery, 1972, Professor, 1978, Kiel. Appointments: Chief Surgeon, City Hospital, Hof/Saale, Germany, 1978-98; Retired, 1998-. Publications: Blood supply of the myocardium after temporary coronary occlusion; Alteration in myocardial hydrogen concentration: a sign of irreversible cell damage; The extent of ischemic damage in the myocardium of the cat after permanent and temporary coronary occlusion. Memberships: German Society of Surgery. Address: Theodor-Fontane-Str 20, D-95032 Hof/Saale, Germany. E-mail: arnokrug@yahoo.de

KRUGLOV Victor Victorovich, b. 31 July 1951, Krasnoslobodsk, Russia. Lawyer. m. Lyudmila Evgenievna, 2 sons, 1 daughter. Education: LLB, 1970, LLD, 1999, Urals State Law Academy, Ekaterinburgh, Russia; LLM, Moscow State University, Moscow, 1972. Appointments: Teacher, 1974-82, Assistant Professor, 1982-2000, Head, Environmental Department, 1994-, Professor, 2000-, Councillor of Rector, 2001-, Urals State Law Academy, Ekaterinburgh; Expert, Land Environmental Law, Consultant, Oblast Duma Government, Sverdlovsk Region, Ekaterinburgh, 1993-; Corresponding Member, 1995-98, Academician, 1998, Russian Ecological Academy, Moscow. Address: Box 759, 620 100 Yekaterinburgh, Russia.

KRUKOWSKI Zygmunt Henderson, b. 11 December 1948, Crimond, Aberdeenshire, Scotland. Surgeon. m. Margaret Anne, 1 son, 2 daughters. Education: MB ChB, 1966-72, PhD, 1978, University of Aberdeen; FRCS (Edinburgh), 1976; FRCP (Edinburgh), 2001. Appointments: Basic and higher surgical training in Aberdeen, Inverness and London, Ontario; Lecturer in Surgery, 1977-86, Senior Lecturer, 1988-96, Reader, 1996-99, Professor of Clinical Surgery, 1999-, University of Aberdeen; Consultant Surgeon, 1986-; Surgeon to the Queen, 2004-. Publications: Publications on surgical audit, surgical infections, surgical technique, laparoscopic surgery, endocrine surgery and health services research. Honour: Honorary FRCS (Glasgow), 2000. Memberships: National Committees on Audit and Quality; President, British Association of Endocrine Surgeons, 2005-. Address: Aberdeen Royal Infirmary, Foresterhill, Aberdeen AB25 2ZN, Scotland.

KRUPATKIN Alexander Ilych, b. 17 February 1961, Moscow, Russia. Medical Doctor. Education: MD, Medical Institute, Tver, Russia, 1983; Dr Neurology, 1984; Consultant in Psychotherapy, 1987; PhD, 1989; DMSci, 1999; Professor of Pathophysiology, 2006. Appointments: Physician, Regional Hospital, Tver, Russia, 1983-84; Junior Researcher, Senior Researcher, Leading Researcher, Central Institute of Traumatology and Orthopaedics, Moscow, 1984-. Publications include: Polarographic Method in Traumatology and Orthopaedics, 1986; Laser Doppler Flowmetry in Traumatology and Orthopaedics, 1998; Clinical Neuroangiophysiology of the Limbs (perivascular innervation and nervous trophics), 2003. Honours: Man of the Year, 2000, IBC, England. Memberships: New York Academy of Sciences; Russian Association of Functional Diagnostics. Address: ul Priorova 10, CITO, 127299 Moscow, Russia.

KRUSZEWSKI Eugeniusz Stanislaw, b. 13 November 1929, Zbaszyn, Poland. University Professor; Historian. m. Marta Bialecka, 2 daughters. Education: MAEc, Poland, 1962; Post-graduate studies, Denmark, 1971-74; PhD, 1975, Dr. hab. 1980, Polish University, London. Appointments: Drafted into Polish Army, 1950-57, 1962-64, Financial Officer, Warsaw, Gdynia; Teacher, Secondary School, Gdańsk, 1965-69; Civil Servant, Governmental Centre of Documentation and Information, Copenhagen, Denmark, 1976-97; Reader, 1980-85, Professor of the History of International Relations, 1985-, Polish University, London; Polish-Scandinavian Research Institute, Copenhagen, Denmark, 1985-. Publications: 8 books on Polish-Scandinavian history, immigration and emigrations history; Over 260 scientific articles, reviews, biographical articles. Honours: Army Medal, 1948; Home Army Cross, London, 1973; Knight Cross of the White Cross International, Sydney, Australia, 1990; Gold Medal of the Polish Cultural Congress, 1985, 1995; The Writers Award, Polish Combatants Association, London,

1992; Award of the Union of Polish Writers Abroad, London, UK, 2000. Memberships: Danish Catholic Historians Society; Polish Historical Society in Great Britain; Polish Society of Arts and Sciences Abroad, London, UK; Union of Polish Writers Abroad, London; Albert Schweitzer Society, Cracow, Poland; President, Polish-Scandinavian Research Institute; Member, Polish PEN Club, Warsaw. Address: POB 2584, DK-2100 Copenhagen Ø – Denmark.

KUAN Hon, b. 17 March 1956, Taiwan. Researcher. m. Gui-Yu Chen, 2 sons. Education: Bachelor, 1984, Master, 1991, Doctor, 1996, National Cheng-Kung University. Appointments: Associate Professor, Department of Electrical Engineering, Southern Taiwan University of Techology, 1996-2000; Manager, Department of Epitaxy, South Epitaxy Corporation, 2000-02; Manager, Department of Technology, LandMark Optoelectronics Corporation, 2002-03; Director, Center of Optoelectronics, Far East University, 2003-06. Publications: A Gate-Recessed InGaN-Channel HFET with Improved Carrier Performance, 2006; Determination of Microwave Dielectric constant by Two Microstrip Line Method Combined with EM Simulation, 2006. Address: Optoelectronic Center, Far East University, No 49 Chung Hua Road, Hsia-Shi Country, Tainan 744, Taiwan, ROC. E-mail: hkuan@cc.feu.edu.tw

KUBIK Gerhard, b. 10 December 1934, Vienna, Austria. Cultural Anthropologist; Ethnomusicologist; Psychoanalyst. m. Lidiya Malamusi. Education: PhD, University Vienna, 1971; Habilitation with the work Theory of African Music, 1980. Appointments: Field work since 1959 in 18 countries of sub-Saharan Africa, since 1974 also in Venezuela and Brazil, leading to the world's most comprehensive collection of documented recordings of African music and oral literature; Present status, University Professor. Publications: 290 works, including several books. Honours: Twice a recipient of a Körner Foundation Prize in Vienna; Life affiliateship to the Centre for Social Research, University of Malawi; Elected to Honorary Fellowship of the Royal Anthropological Institute of Great Britain and Ireland, London, 1995. Memberships: Sigmund Freud Museum, Vienna; Centre for Black Music Research, Chicago; Royal Anthropological Institute of Great Britain and Ireland, London; Oral Literature Research Programme, Blantyre, Malawi. Address: Burghardtgasse 6/9, A 1200 Vienna, Austria.

KUBILIUS Jonas, b. 27 July 1921, District Jurbarkas, Lithuania. Mathematician. m. Valerija Pilypaité, 1 son, 1 daughter. Education: Diploma with Honours, Vilnius University, 1945; Candidate of Science, Leningrad University, 1951; DSc, Steklov Institute, Moscow, 1957. Appointments: Laboratory Assistant, Assistant Professor, 1945-48, Associate Professor, Professor, 1951-, Rector, 1958-92, Vilnius University; Member, Praesidium, Academy of Sciences of Lithuania, 1962-92; People's Deputy of USSR, 1989-91; Member of Parliament of Lithuania, 1992-96. Publications: Probability methods in the Number Theory (7 editions), 1959; Real Analysis, 1970; Probability and Statistics (2 editions), 1980; Limit Theorems, 1988; Book of Essays, 1996; Antanas Baranauskas and Mathematics, 2001; Several hundred papers. Honours: State Prize in Sciences, 1958, 1980; Dr hc, Greifswald, Prague, Latvian, Salzburg universities, several orders. Memberships: Founder and President, Lithuanian Mathematical Society, 1962-; President, Lithuanian-USA Association, 1991-; President, Club, Experience, 1995-. Address: Faculty of Mathematics and Informatics, Vilnius University, Naugarduko 24, Vilnius LT-03225, Lithuania.

KUČEROVÁ Helena, b. 18 April 1949, Olomouc, Czech Republic. Psychiatrist. Education: College of Medicine, Olomouc, Czech Republic, 1974; Diploma, Psychiatry Level I, Prague, 1979; Diploma, Psychiatry Level II, Prague, 1983. Appointments: Assistant Lecturer, College of Medicine, Hradec Králové, Czech Republic, 1974-76; Medical Registrar, Mental Teaching Hospital, Hradec Králové, 1976-83; Junior Consultant, Mental Hospital, Brno, 1983-86; Junior Consultant, Mental Hospital, Šternberk, 1986-90; Outpatient Psychiatrist Consultant, Private Practice, Hranice, Czech Republic, 1991-. Publications: 49 articles in professional scientific journals. Honours: Listed in national and international biographical dictionaries. Memberships: New York Academy of Sciences; American Association for the Advancement of Science; Czech Medical Chamber; Czech Psychiatric Society. Address: Svatoplukova 10, 753 01 Hranice na Moravě, Czech Republic.

KÜHLER Martin Franz, b. 4 August 1970, South Africa. Reliability Engineer. m. Magdalena, 3 sons, 1 daughter. Education: BSc, Electrical Engineering, Almeda University, 2003. Appointments: Project Supervisor, Reliability Engineer, Tranfield Services, New Zealand; Plant Performance Engineer, Meridian Energy, New Zealand; Reliability Strategist, Tranfield Services, Worley, 2007-. Publications: Article: Electrical engineer shows why he's Mr Reliable, 2006. Honours: Generation Award Winner, ESITO Excellence Awards, 2006. Memberships: IEEE. Address: 4 Oakhill Drive, Ranford, Canning Vale, Perth, WA 6155, Australia. E-mail: mfkuhler@bigpond.com

KUHRT Gordon Wilfred, b. 15 February 1941, Madras, South India. Clergyman. m. Olive, 3 sons. Education: BD, Honours, London University, 1960-63; Oakhill Theological College, 1965-67; Doctor in Professional Studies, Middlesex University, 2001. Appointments: Religious Education Teacher, 1963-65; Curate, St Illogan, Truro, England, 1967-70; Curate, Holy Trinity, Wallington, England, 1970-73; Vicar of Shenstone, Lichfield, England, 1973-79; Vicar of Emmanuel, South Croydon, England, 1979-89; Rural Dean, Croydon Central, 1981-86; Honorary Canon of Southwark Cathedral, 1987-89; Archdeacon of Lewisham, 1989-96; Chief Secretary of the Advisory Board for Ministry, 1996-98; Director of Ministry, Ministry Division, Archbishop's Council, 1999-. Publications: Handbook for Council and Committee Members, 1985; Believing in Baptism, 1987; Doctrine Matters (editor), 1993; To Proclaim Afresh (editor), 1995; Issues in Theological Education and Training, 1998; Clergy Security, 1999; An Introduction to Christian Ministry, 2000; Ministry Issues for the Church of England – Mapping the Trends, 2001; Bridging the Gap: Reader Ministry Today, 2002. Membership: Fellow of the College of Preachers. Address: Ministry Division, Archbishops' Council, Church House, Great Smith Street, London SW1P 3NZ, England. E-mail: gordon.kuhrt@mindiv.c-of-e.org.uk

KUIJKEN Barthold, b. 1949, Belgium. Musician. Education: Modern Flute, Bruges Conservatory and the Royal Conservatories of Brussels and The Hague. Career: Researcher on authentic instruments in museums and private collections; Specialist on the performance of early music from the 17th and 18th centuries on original instruments; Member of Brussels-based ensemble Musiques Nouvelles focusing on avant garde music; Performances with his brothers Wieland (viola da gamba, baroque cello) and Sigiswald (baroque violin, viola da gamba); Performances with Rene Jacobs (counter tenor), Paul Dombrecht (baroque oboe), Lucy van Dael (baroque violin) and with harpsichordists, Robert Kohnen,

Gustav Leonhardt, Ewald Demeyere and Bob van Asperen; Baroque Flutist in the Orchestra, Collegium Aureum and in La petite Bande; Chamber music concerts world-wide; Professor of Baroque Flute, Royal Conservatories of Brussels and The Hague; Guest Professor and Member of International Juries. Publications: Numerous scholarly works include: Annotated Urtext edition of J S Bach's Flute Music. Recordings: Numerous recordings on various record labels. Honours: Le Choc de l'Année 2001, France; Diapason d'Or de l'Année 2002, France. Address: Zwartschaapstraat 38, B-1755 Gooik, Belgium.

KUKLA Cynthia Mary, b. 23 June 1952, Chicago, Illinois, USA. Artist; Professor of Art. 2 sons. Education: BFA, School of the Art Institute of Chicago, Chicago, Illinois, 1973; MFA, University of Wisconsin-Madison, Madison, Wisconsin, 1983. Appointments: Assistant Professor of Art, 1983-1989, Associate Professor of Art, 1989-93, Northern Kentucky University, Highland Heights, Kentucky; Associate Professor of Art, 1993-2003, Professor of Art, 2004-, Illinois State University, Normal, Illinois; Visiting Professor, Aristotle Thessaloniki University, Thessaloniki, Greece, 2006. Exhibitions: Over 50 solo exhibitions include: Headley Whitney Museum, Lexington, Kentucky, 1985; Armory Art Gallery, Blacksburg, Virginia, 1985; Chautauqua Art Center, New York, 1995; University of Illinois, 2000; Contemporary Art Center, Peoria, Illinois, 2005; Over 200 group exhibitions include: Springfield Art Museum, Springfield, Missouri, 1980, 1983, 2006; Laguna Beach Art Museum, Laguna Beach, California, 1983; American Embassy, Quito, Ecuador, 1989; Grand European National Centre, Arts e Lettres, Nice, France, 1990; Canton Art Institute, Canton, Ohio, 1992; Kharkov Art Museum, Ukraine, 1992; Arrowmount Center, Gatlinburg, Tennessee, 1993, 1995, 2004, 2006; Rockford Art Museum, Rockford, Illinois, 1995 and 2006; Ft. Sztuki Association, Krakow, Poland, 1998; Palace of Art, Budapest, Hungary, 1999; Lakeview Art Museum, Peoria, Illinois, 2002 and 2005; Vivarosi Gallery, Budapest, Hungary, 2004. Honours: University grants for sculpture, 1994, 1997, 2003; University technology grants to develop "Lost Art" website: www.cfa.ilstu.edu/cmkukla, 1997, 1998, 1999; Fellowships, Hungarian Multicultural Council, Balatonfured, Hungary and Vermont Studio Center, Johnson, Vermont, 2003; Keynote Speaker, Cincinnati Art Museum, 2004; Fellowship, Virginia Center for Creative Arts, Amhurst, 2005; Travel grant for panel participation in Impact.Kontakt Art Conference, Berlin and Poznan, 2005; Commission: 5 paintings for inauguration of Spurlock Museum of World Culture, University of Illinois, Champaign-Urbana, 2001. Memberships: American Association of University Women; Art Institute of Chicago; College Art Association; Contemporary Art Center, Cincinnati; McLean County Art Center, Bloomington; National Watercolor Honor Society; National Museum of Women Artist, Washington, DC; Rotary International. Address: 1001 Broadmoor Drive, Bloomington, IL 61704-6109. E-mail: cmkukla@ilstu.edu

KULICHENKO Anatoly, b. 18 March 1948, St Petersburg, Russia. Textile and Clothing Scientist. Divorced, 2 daughters. Education: Engineer, Leningrad Institute of Textile and Light Industry (LITLI), 1972; Candidate of Technical Sciences (PhD), LITLI, 1978; Docent, LITLI, 1985; Professor, St Petersburg University of Technology and Design, SUTD (former LITLI), 1995; Visiting Professor, De Montfort University, Leicester, UK, 1998; Doctor of Technical Sciences, 2005. Appointments: Engineer, Technologist, Designer, Clothing Manufacturing Companies, Leningrad, 1972-75; Research Course, Department of Textile Science, LITLI,

1975-78; Lecturer, Senior Lecturer (Docent), Professor, Department of Textile Science, LITLI-SUTD, 1978-; Dean of Faculty, Clothing Design and Technology, SUTD, 1994-2002; Head, Department of Textile Science, 2000-, Pro-Rector, 2002-, First Vice Rector, 2005-, for University Development, SUTD; Doctor of Technical Sciences Degree, Moscow, 2005-, Pro-Rector for International Lincs 2007-. Publications: About 100 publications in the area of textile and clothing science and higher education in Russia, UK, USA, Canada, Hong Kong, Ukraine, France, Finland and others. Honours: Distinguished Leadership Diploma; Man of the Year, 2000, ABI; Meritus Worker of Higher Professional Education Medal, Russian Federation, 2000; Honorary Degree of Doctor of Technology, De Montfort University, UK, 2003. Memberships: European Textile Network; The Textile Institute, UK; The Fibre Society, USA. Address: State University of Technology and Design, 18 Bolshaja Morskaja Str, St Petersburg, Russia 191186.

KULKARNI Chandrashekhar Vishwanath, b. 27 February 1979, Satara, India. Research; Science. Education: BSc (1st class), Chemistry, 1999, MSc (1st class), Industrial Chemistry, 2001, Shivaji University, Kolhapur. Appointments: Research Student (Project Assistant), Complex Fluids and Polymer Engineering Group, National Chemical Lab, Pune, India, 2002-04; PhD, Membrane Biophysics Group, Department of Chemistry, Imperial College, London, England, 2005-. Publications: 3 articles in professional journals; 9 proceedings and posters. Honours: Shivaji University Merit Scholarship for MSc; Marie Curie Fellowship for PhD; Marie-Curie Grant to attend 56th Lindau Meeting of Nobel Laureates, Germany, 2006. Address: A/P: Tadavale, Tal: Koregaon, Dist: Satara, Maharashtra, PIN 415010, India. E-mail: c.kulkarni@imperial.ac.uk

KULMAGAMBETOV Ilyas, b. 21 June 1954, Republic of Kazakhstan. Medical Doctor. m. Farida Nurmanbetova, 1 son. Education: Medical Doctor, Almaty State Medical Institute, Republic of Kazakhstan, 1977; Candidate of Medical Sciences Degree, 1983, Doctor of Medical Sciences Degree, 1991, Moscow; Professor of Medicine Degree, Republic of Kazakhstan, 1994; Academician of National Academy of Sciences of the Republic of Kazakhstan, 2004. Appointments: Assistant Professor, Department of Internal Diseases, Almaty State Medical Institute, Almaty, Republic of Kazakhstan, 1982-85; Head, Department of Clinical Pharmacology, Kazakh State Medial University, Almaty, 1988-2001; Rector of Karaganda State Medial Academy, Karaganda, 2001-. Publications: 280 articles; 1 textbook; 12 monographs; 33 inventions; 20 rational proposals. Honours: Best Young Innovator of Moscow, 1981; Laureate of Lenin Komsomol Prize of Kazakhstan, 1982; Diploma of Honor and Bronze Medal of Exhibition of National Economy Progress of USSR, 1986; Medal, 10 Years of Independence of the Republic of Kazakhstan, 2001; Brestplate, Honorary Distinction in Health Care of the Republic of Kazakhstan, 2003; Brestplate, For Merit in Development of Sciences of the Republic of Kazakhstan, 2004; Medal, 10 Years of Constitution of the Republic of Kazakhstan, 2005; Yuriy Gagarin Medal, Federation of Cosmonauts of Russia, 2006; Honorary Worker of Education of the Republic of Kazakhstan, 2006; Laureate of Socrates International Award, UK, 2006. Memberships: Academician, National Academy of Sciences of the Republic of Kazakhstan. Address: Karaganda State Medical Academy, 40, Gogolya Street, Karaganda, 100008, Republic of Kazakhstan. E-mail: kgma@nursat.kz

KUMAGAI Takashi, b. Tokyo, Japan. Physician; Researcher. m. Hiroko Anzai, 1 son. Education: BS, Tokyo University, 1984; MD, 1990, PhD, 1999, Tokyo Medical and Dental University, Tokyo. Appointments: Resident, Internal Medicine, Tokyo Medical and Dental University, 1990-91; Resident, Internal Medicine, Ohme Municipal General Hospital, 1991-93; Resident, Hematology, Tokyo Medical and Dental University, 1993-94; Resident, Hematology, Tokyo Metropolitan Komagome Hospital, 1994-95; Staff Physician, Hematology, Tokyo Teishin Hospital, 1999-2001; Research Fellow, Department of Hematology/Oncology, Cedars-Sinai Medical Center, UCLA School of Medicine, 2001-04; Deputy Director, 2004-07, Director, 2007-, Department of Hematology, Ohme Municipal General Hospital; Clinical Associate Professor, Tokyo Medical and Dental University, 2008-. Publications: Papers and articles in professional medical journals. Honours: Tanaka Michiko Award, Tokyo Medical and Dental University, 1999; Listed in international biographical dictionaries. Memberships: Fellow and Board-Certified Instructor, Japanese Society of Hematology; Fellow and Board-Certified Instructor, Japanese Society of Internal Medicine; Member, American Society of Hematology; Member, American Association for Cancer Research. Address: 3-13-7, Room 201, Morooka-cho, Ohme, Tokyo, 198-0031, Japan. E-mail: kumamed1_2001@yahoo.co.jp

KUMM Dietmar Alfred, b. 20 January 1959, Munich, Germany. Orthopaedic Surgeon. m. Patricia Anne Schneider, 1 son, 2 daughters. Education: Medical Student, Friedrich-Wilhelms University, Bonn Germany, 1978-84; MD, University of Bonn, 1984; PhD, 1985. Appointments: Intern, Basle University, Switzerland, 1984; Assistant Surgeon, EV Hospital, Badgodesberg, 1984-89; Assistant, University of Cologne, Cologne, Germany, 1989-94; Assistant Professor, University of Cologne, Cologne, Germany, 1984-86; Senior Doctor, University of Witten-Herdecke, Witten, 1996-2003; Chief Doctor, Department Director, Head of Department, Bethesda, Hospital, Duisburg, Germany, 2003. Publications: Consultant in field; Contributor of articles to professional journals; Numerous patents: Achievements include: Invention of Periprothet Halterungs Systeme; Gewindestift fuer Femurepiphyse. Memberships: New York Academy of Sciences; German Association for Orthopaedics and Traumatology; BVO; American Association for the Advancement of Science; German Association for Sports Medicine; American Academy of Orthopedic Surgery. Address: Orthopädische Klinik, Bethesda KRHS, Heerstr 219, D-47053 Duisburg, Germany.

KUMPINSKY Enio, b. Porto Alegre, Brazil. Chemical Engineer. m. Marsha Gail Brum, 4 children. Education: BSChemE, Federal University of Rio Grande do Sul, 1976; MSChemE, Federal University of Rio de Janeiro, 1978; PhD, Chemical Engineering, University of Houston, 1983. Appointments: Research Engineer, DuPont, Wilmington, Delaware, 1984-89; Division Engineer, DuPont, Louisville, 1989-91; Senior Staff Research Engineer, 1991-98, Principal Engineer, 1998-2004, Research Fellow, 2004-, Ashland Inc, Columbus; Calorimetry and Heat Transfer Consultant, Ashland Inc, Worldwide, 1995-2002; Lean Six Sigma and Design for Six Sigma Initiatives, 2003-; Six Sigma Master Black Belt. Publications: Several articles in professional journals. Listed in biographical dictionaries. Address: Ashland Inc, PO Box 2219, Columbus, OH 43216, USA.

KUNDT Wolfgang Helmut, b. 3 June 1931, Hamburg, Germany. Astrophysics Professor. m. Ulrike Schümann, 1 son, 1 daughter. Education: Dipl Phys, 1956, Promotion,

1959, Habilitation, 1965, Hamburg University, under Pascual Jordan. Career: Professor, Hamburg, Bielefeld, Bonn; Visiting Scientist: Pittsburgh, Pennsylvania; Edmonton; Cern; Kyoto; Boston; Bangalore; Linz; Maribor. Publications: Over 260 articles on fundamental physics, astrophysics, geophysics and biophysics; 6 books including: Astrophysics: a New Approach, 2004. Honours: NASA Group Achievement Award, 1975. Memberships: AG; EPS. Address: Institut für Astrophysik der Universität, Auf Dem Hügel 71, D-53121, Bonn, Germany. E-mail: wkundt@astro.uni-bonn.de

KUNERT Günter, b. 6 March 1929, Berlin, Germany. Poet; Author; Dramatist. m. Marianne Todten. Education: Hochschule für angewandte Kunst, Berlin-Weissensee. Publications: Poetry: Wegschilder und Mauerinschriften, 1950; Erinnerung an einen Planeten: Gedichte aus Fünfzehn Jahren, 1963; Der ungebetene Gast, 1965; Verkündigung des Wetters, 1966; Warnung vor Spiegeln, 1970; Im weiteren Fortgang, 1974; Unterwegs nach Utopia, 1977; Abtötungsverfahren, 1980; Stilleben, 1983; Berlin beizeiten, 1987; Fremd daheim, 1990; Mein Golem, 1996; Erwachsenenspiele, autobiography, 1997; Nachtvorstellung, poems, 1999. Novel: Im Namen der Hüte, 1967. Other: Der ewige Detektiv und andere Geschichten, 1954; Kramen in Fächen: Geschichten, Parabeln, Merkmale, 1968; Die Beerdigung findet in aller Stille statt, 1968; Tagträume in Berlin und andernorts, 1972; Gast aus England, 1973; Der andere Planet: Ansichten von Amerika, 1974; Warum schreiben?: Notizen ins Paradies, 1978; Ziellose Umtriebe: Nachrichten von Reisen und Daheimsein, 1979; Verspätete Monologe, 1981; Leben und Schreiben, 1983; Vor der Sintflut: Das Gedicht als Arche Noah, 1985; Die letzten Indianer Europas, 1991. Honours: Heinrich Mann Prize, 1962; Heinrich Heine Prize, Düsseldorf, 1985; Hölderlin Prize, 1991; Georg-Trakl Prize, Austria, 1997. Memberships: Deutsche Akademie für Sprache und Dichtung e.v., Darmstadt. Address: Schulstrasse 7, D-25560 Kaisborstel, Germany.

KÜNG Hans, b. 19 March 1928, Lucerne, Switzerland. Professor of Ecumenical Theology Emeritus; Author. Education: Gregorian University, Rome; Institut Catholique, Paris; Sorbonne, University of Paris. Appointments: Ordained Roman Catholic Priest, 1954; Practical Ministry, Lucerne Cathedral, 1957-59; Scientific Assistant for Dogmatic Catholic Theology, University of Münster/Westfalen, 1959-60; Professor of Fundamental Theology, 1960-63; Professor of Dogmatic and Ecumenical Theology, 1963-80; Director, Institute of Ecumenical Research, 1963-96; Professor of Ecumenical Theology, 1980-96, Professor Emeritus, 1996-, University of Tübingen; President, Foundation Global Ethic, Germany, 1995, Switzerland, 1997; Various guest professorships and lectureships throughout the world. Publications: The Council: Reform and Reunion, 1961; That the World May Believe, 1963; The Council in Action, 1963; Justification: The Doctrine of Karl Barth and a Catholic Reflection, 1964, new edition, 1981; Structures of the Church, 1964, new edition, 1982; Freedom Today, 1966; The Church, 1967; Truthfulness, 1968; Infallible?: An Inquiry, 1971; Why Priests?, 1972; On Being a Christian, 1976; Signposts for the Future, 1978; The Christian Challenge, 1979; Freud and the Problem of God, 1979; Does God Exist?, 1980; The Church: Maintained in Truth, 1980; Eternal Life?, 1984; Christianity and the World Religions: Paths to Dialogue with Islam, Hinduism and Buddhism (with others), 1986; The Incarnation of God, 1986; Church and Change: The Irish Experience, 1986; Why I Am Still A Christian, 1987; Theology for a Third Millennium: An Ecumenical View, 1988; Christianity and Chinese Religions (with Julia Ching), 1989; Paradigm Change in Theology: A Symposium for the Future, 1989; Reforming the Church Today, 1990; Global Responsibility: In Search of a New World Ethic, 1991; Judaism, 1992; Mozart: Traces of Transcendence, 1992; Credo: The Apostles' Creed Explained for Today, 1993; Great Christian Thinkers, 1994; Christianity, Its Essence and History, 1995; Islam, in preparation; A Dignified Dying; A plea for personal responsibility (with Walter Jens) 1995; A Global Ethic for Global Politics and Economics, 1997; The Catholic Church, A Short History, 2001; Tracing the Way, Spiritual Dimensions of the World Religions, 2002; My Struggle for Freedom, Memoirs I, 2003; The Beginning of All Things, Science and Religion, 2007; Islam: Past, Present and Future, 2007. Honours: Oskar Pfister Award, American Psychiatric Association, 1986; Göttingen Peace Award, 2002; 22nd Niwano Peace Prize, Tokyo, 2005; Many honorary doctorates. Address: Waldhäuserstrasse 23, 72076 Tübingen, Germany.

KUNINAKA Akira, b. 16 January 1928, Tokyo, Japan. Professor. m. Sumiko Tanaka, 1 son, 2 daughters. Education: Bachelor of Agriculture, 1951, Doctor of Agriculture, 1959, University of Tokyo. Appointments: Researcher, 1953-2004, Director, 1978-86, Managing Director, 1986-95, Yamasa Corporation; Research Associate, Department of Biochemistry, MIT, 1963-66; President, Japan Immuno-Monitoring Centre, 1982-86; Chairman, Japan Sect Institute of Food Technologists, 1991-92; Guest Professor: Tokyo University of Agriculture, 1994-98, Chiba University, 1995-96, Chiba Institute of Science, 2005-. Publications: Papers and articles in professional scientific journals. Honours: Agricultural Chemistry prize, 1960; Imperial Invention prize, 1964; Purple Ribbon medal, Prime Minister, Tokyo, 1983. Memberships: Japan Society for Bioscience, Biotechnology, and Agrochemistry; Japan Bioindustry Association; American Chemical Society; Brewing Society of Japan. Address: 2-15-21 Araoi-cho, Choshi-shi, Chiba-ken 288-0056, Japan. E-mail: kunisan@isis.ocn.ne.jp

KUNITSYN Valery Georgievich, b. 23 November 1941, Chita, Russia. Biophysic. m. Marina F Nekrasova, 1 son, 2 daughters. Education: Higher, Tomsk University, 1965; Postgraduate, Institute of Physiology, SB RAN, Novosibirsk, Russia, 1972. Appointments: Assistant, 1973-84, Lecturer, 1984-87, Researcher, 1987-2007, Medical State University, Institute of Biochemistry RAMS. Publications: 4 articles in professional journals. Address: Polzunova 3, Flat 4, Novosibirsk 630057, Russia. E-mail: kunitsyn@ngs.ru

KURIYAMA Shinichi, b. 5 October 1962, Osaka, Japan. Physician; Epidemiologist. m. Yuka Goto, 3 sons. Education: BS, Department of Physics, Tohoku University, 1987; MD, Osaka City University Medical School, 1993; PhD, Department of Public Health and Forensic Medicine, Tohoku University Graduate School of Medicine, 2004. Appointments: Medical Director, The Daido Mutual Life Insurance Company, 1993-2003; Assistant Professor, 2003-05, Associate Professor, 2005-, Department of Public Health and Forensic Medicine, Tohoku University Graduate School of Medicine. Publications: 63 articles in professional journals. Honours: Young Investigator Award, Japan Epidemiological Association, 2005; Gold Prize, Tohoku University School of Medicine, 2008. Memberships: Japan Epidemiological Association; Japanese Society of Public Health; Japan Society for the Study of Obesity; Japanese Society of Child Neurology. Address: Department of Public Health and Forensic Medicine, Tohoku University Graduate School of Medicine, 2-1 Seiryo-machi, Aoba-ku, Sendai, 980-8575, Japan.

KURODA Haruhiko, b. 25 October 1944, Japan. Banker. Education: BA, Law, University of Tokyo, Japan, 1967; M Phil, Economics, University of Oxford, England, 1971. Appointments: Joined Japan's Ministry of Finance, 1967. Secondment to International Monetary Fund, Washington DC, USA, 1975-78; Director, International Organisations Division, International Finance Bureau, 1987-88; Secretary to the Minister of Finance, 1988-89; Director of several divisions including International Tax Affairs Division, Tax Bureau, 1989-92; Deputy Vice Minister of Finance for International Affairs, 1992-93; Commissioner, Osaka Regional Taxation Bureau, 1993-94; Deputy Director-General, International Finance Bureau, 1994-96; President, Institute of Fiscal and Monetary Policy, 1996-97; Director-General International Finance Bureau, 1997-99; Vice Minister of Finance for International Affairs, 1999-2003; Special Adviser to the Cabinet, 2003-2005; Professor, Hitotsubashi University, Graduate School of Economics, 2003-2005; President, Asian Development Bank, 2005-. Publications: Several books on monetary policy, exchange rate, international finance policy co-ordination, international taxation and international negotiations. Address: Asian Development Bank, 6 ADB Avenue, Mandaluyong City, 1550 Metro Manila, Philippines. E-mail: information@adb.org

KURODA Kagayaki, b. 10 February 1962, Tokyo. Associate Professor. m. Mihari, 1 daughter. Education: BS, Instrumentation Engineering, Faculty of Engineering, 1984, Instrumentation Engineering, School of Engineering, Kobe University, Japan, 1986; PhD, School of Engineering, Osaka City University, Japan, 1992. Appointments: Satellite Systems Engineer, Nippon Electric Company, Yokohama, Kanagawa, Japan, 1986-88; Research Associate, Faculty of Engineering, Osaka City University, Osaka, Japan, 1989-98; Visiting Researcher, 1995-96, Visiting Assistant Professor, 2000, Department of Radiology, Harvard Medical School, Boston, Massachusetts, USA; Assistant Professor, Institute of Science and Technology, 1999-2000, Associate Professor, School of Information Science and Technology, 2001-, Tokai University, Hiratsuka, Kanagawa, Japan; Deputy Director, Department of Image-Based Medicine, 2001-04, Senior Research Scientist, Group of Molecular Imaging, 2006-, Institute of Biomedical Research and Innovation, Kobe, Hyogo, Japan. Publications: 2 book chapters; Numerous articles in professional journals. Honours: Grants: Nakatani Electronic Measuring Technology Association of Japan, 1993, 1998; Shimadzu Science and Technology Promotion Foundation, 1998; Toyoda Rikagaku Kenkyusho, 2005; Ministry of Science and Education, Japan, 1991-94, 1996-; Special Award, Japanese Society for Magnetic Resonance in Medicine, 1998; Educational Exhibit Award, 2003; Research-Promotive Award, Japanese Society for Hyperthermic Oncology, 2006. Memberships: International Society for Magnetic Resonance in Medicine; The Institute of Electrical and Electronics Engineering; The Optical Society of Japan; Japanese Society of Hyperthermic Oncology; Japan Society of Medical Electronics and Biological Engineering; The Institute of Electronics, Information and Communication Engineers; Japanese Society of Magnetic Resonance in Medicine; Japan Radiology Society. Address: School of Information Science and Technology, Tokai University, 1117 Kitakaname, Hiratsuka, Kanagwa 259-1292, Japan. E-mail: kagayaki@keyaki.cc.u-tokai.ac.jp

KURODA Tatsuaki, b. 11 March 1955, Shirakawa, Japan. Professor of Economics. m. Junko Otani, 18 October 1980, 2 daughters. Education: BS, 1978, MS, 1980, Kyoto University; PhD, University of Pennsylvania, 1989. Appointments: Research Associate, Kyoto University, 1985;

Assistant Professor, Toyahashi University of Technology, 1989; Associate Professor, 1991, Professor, 1998, Nagoya University; Visiting Scholar, LSE and University of Reading, England, 2003; Dean, Graduate School of Environmental Studies, 2004. Publications: City Planning for Promoting Amenity, 1984; Location of Public Facilities with Spillover Effects, 1989; A Power Index of Multistage and Multiagent Decision Systems, 1993; Advertising and City Formation with Local Public Goods, 1995. Honour: Graduate Prize, University of Pennsylvania, 1987. Membership: American Economic Association; Regional Science Association International; Applied Regional Science Conference; Japan Economics Association. Address: 4-4-18 Takamoridai, Kasugai 487-0032, Japan.

KURTE-JARDIN Michael, b. 28 June 1973, Paderborn, Germany. Doctor of Polymer Engineering. m. Melanie Jardin, 1 son. Education: Dipl Ing, Mechanical Engineering, University of Paderborn, 2001; Dr Ing, Institute of Polymer Engineering KTP, University of Paderborn, 2005. Appointments: Scientific Assistant, Institute of Polymer Engineering KTP, University of Paderborn, 2001-05; R&D Manager, XPS Technology, URSA Deutschland GmbH, Leipzig, 2005-06; Manager, Extrusion Technology, R&D XPS, URSA Insulation, SA, Madrid, 2006-. Publications: 27 articles in professional scientific journals in field of polymer extrusion and injection moulding. Address: Grundsteinheimer Weg 6, 33165 Lichtenau, Germany. E-mail: m.kurte-jardin@gmx.de

KURTOVIC Sefko, b. 26 August 1937, Gacko, Bosnia and Herzegovina. Lawyer; University Professor. m. Nives, 1 son. Education: LB, 1962, LLM, 1968, University of Zagreb, Croatia; Postgraduate Diploma, Law, University of Strasbourg, France, 1965; Postgraduate Diploma, Law, King's College, London, 1970; LLD, University of Ljubljana, Slovenia, 1972. Appointments: Assistant, General History of State and Law, 1963-73, Associate Professor, General History of State and Law, Professor, History of Political Theories, 1973-84, Read Professor, General History of State and Law, Professor, History of Political Theories, 1984-2008, Law Faculty, University of Zagreb, Croatia. Publications: General History of the State and Law (from Antiquity to the Second World War) vols I-II, 1987-2007; Chrestomathy of General History of State and Law (from Hammurabian Law to the Second World War) vols I-II, 1999-; Studies and Articles in General History of State and Law, vols I-III, 2002; Articles include: Supreme executive power of French Third Republic, 1871-87; Historical premises of Paris Commune; Dissolution of parliament in French Third Republic; French Socialist Party, 1905-1914; Magna Carta 1215 and its constitutional analysis; Historical genesis of political representation; etc. Address: II Cvjetno naselje 26, 10000 Zagreb, Croatia.

KURUPPUARACHCHI Lalith Asoka, b. 31 March 1959, Badulla, Sri Lanka. Professor; Consultant Psychiatrist. m. K G Indralatha, 1 son. Education: MBBS, Peradeniya, Sri Lanka, 1982; MD, Psychiatry, Postgraduate Institute of Medicine, Colombo, Sri Lanka, 1988; MRCPsych (UK), Royal College of Psychiatrists, UK, 1992; Fellowship, Royal College of Psychiatrists, UK, 2006. Appointments: Acting Consultant Psychiatrist, General Hospital, Kandy, Sri Lanka, 1992; Consultant Psychiatrist, G H Badulla, Sri Lanka, 1992-94; Head, Department of Psychiatry, University of Kelaniya, Sri Lanka, 1994-2002; Senior Lecturer, Psychiatry, Faculty of Medicine, Ragama University of Kelaniya, Sri Lanka, 1994-2004; Professor, Psychiatry, University of Kelaniya, Sri Lanka, 2004-. Publications: Book, Identification of Psychiatric Illnesses, 2004; Book chapters, Psychiatry

in Sri Lanka; Contributed articles to several professional journals. Honours: President's Research Award, Sri Lanka, 2000, 2001; Fellowship, WHO, 1997; Kenneth Rawnsley Travelling Fellowship, Royal College of Psychiatrists, 2000. Memberships: Sri Lanka Medical Association; Kandy Society of Medicine; Sri Lanka College of Psychiatrists; Peradeniya Medical School Alumni Association. Address: 284 Thalapathpitiya Road, Madiwela, Kotte, Sri Lanka. E-mail: lalithkuruppu@lycos.com

KURUVILLA Bill (Kollanparampil), b. 20 July 1943, Kodukulanji, Kerala, India. Engineer. m. Santha, 1 son, 3 daughters. Education: BSc, Electrical Engineering, Kerala, India, 1965; MBA, Business Administration, USA; Student in Theology, USA (PhD on hold); PhD programme in Philosophy and Apologetics; PhD, Business Administration, USA, 1997; Diploma in Children's Writing, CT, USA, 2000. Appointments: Lecturer, MA College of Engineering, Kerala, India, 1965-66; Executive Engineer, Kerala State Electricity Board, India, 1966-88; Electrical Engineer, Zesco, Lusaka, Zambia, 1972-75; Chief of Power Station, Sher, Ministry of Power, Mozambique, 1979-81; Design Engineer, Septa, Philadelphia, PA, USA, 1989-. Publications: Numerous articles; Author, 5 books (4 unpublished); 1 US patent. Honours: Lifetime Royal Patronage and Citizen of the Year, 1994, 1996; Listed in national and international biographical directories; Honored Member, America's Registry of Outstanding Professionals for the Year, 2000-01, 2001-02, 2002-03, 2003-04, 2004-05, 2005-06; International Peace Prize, UCC, USA: Excellence Award and Gold Medal, 2006; Glory of India Award, Friendship Forum of India, 2006. Memberships: World Affairs Council of Philadelphia; Institute of Engineers (India); Associate, Library of Congress, USA; Handiham Club of USA. Address: 2407 Sentry Court, E Norriton, PA 19401, USA.

KUSHNER Jack, b. 5 December 1939, Montgomery, Alabama, USA. Physician Executive. m. Annetta, 2 children. Education: University of Sheffield, England, 1959; BA (History), Tulane University, 1960; MD, University of Alabama, 1964; Surgical Intern, George Washington, 1965; Surgical Resident, Michigan, 1966; Neurosurgical Resident, Wake Forest, 1968-72; Master's (Finance) MGA, University of Maryland, 1990. Appointments: Chairman, American Opportunity Portal; Chief Executive Officer, Futuristic Instruments; Neurosurgeon, Annapolis. Publications: Author, When Physicians Change Careers, 1995. Honours: Bronze Star, Combat Surgeon, Viet-Nam, 1967; Board Certification, Neurological Surgery, 1975; Guest Speaker, British Neurological Surgeons, Cork, 1982; Man of the Year, ABI, 2004; Most Distinguished Alumnus, University of Maryland, 2004; Top 100 Health Care Professionals; America's Top Surgeons; Marie Curie Award, IBC, 2006; Lifetime Achievement Award, IBC; IBC Hall of Fame; Military Leadership Circle University of Maryland; Tulane University Alumni Board of Directors; Senior Tournament Director, United States Naval Academy Golf Association; Listed in international biographical dictionaries; First Place, World Dance-o-Rama, Ball Room Dancing, Las Vegas, 2007. Memberships: American Association of Neurological Surgeons; Congress of Neurosurgeons; Southern Neurological Surgery; Pacific Neurosurgeons; Board of Managers, Anne Arundel Medical Center; Committee of Emerging Technology and Education, American College of Surgeons; National Security Forum @Air War College-Maxwell AFB; New York Academy of Sciences; Alpha Epsilon Delta Honor Society; Eta Sigma Phi Honor Society; Fellow, Tropical Medicine in Panama with Louisiana State University; White House

Conference on Camp David Middle East Accords; Fellow, American College of Surgeons; Fellow, International College of Surgeons; 1902 Society for Anne Arundel Medical Center; Co-founder, Transcriptions International, 1989; Community Leaders of America, ABI; Men of Achievement, IBC, 1980; 2000 Outstanding People of the 20th Century, IBC, 1998. Address: 2030 Homewood Road, Ferry Farms, Annapolis, MD 21409, USA. E-mail: jkaoportal@comast.net

KUSIN Vladimír Victor, b. 2 December 1929, Frydek-Mistek, Czech Republic. Historian. m. Daniela Cihacek, 1 son, 1 daughter. Education: Commercial Academy Frydek-Mistek, 1949; Economic University, 1953; PhDr, Charles University, 1968. Appointments: Lecturer, Manual Worker, Translator, Journalist, Czechoslovakia, 1953-68; Research Fellow, University of Lancaster, England, 1968-69; Research Fellow, University of Glasgow, Scotland, 1970-78; Executive Committee, International Committee for Soviet and East European Studies, Glasgow, 1974-78; Director, information centre, 1975-78; Editor, ICSEES Newsletter, 1976-78; Chief Analyst, Radio Free Europe-Radio Liberty, Munich, Germany, 1980-91; Lecturer in field; Retired, 1991-. Publications: The Intellectual Origins of the Prague Spring, 1971; Political Grouping in the Czechoslovak Reform Movement, 1972; From Dubcek to Charter 77, 1978; Co-author, Czechoslovakia 1969-69, 1975; Editor, The Czechoslovak Reform Movement, 1968, 1973; Translator: Geoffrey Bocca, The Life and Death of Harry Oakes, 1965; Translator: Tom Stoppard, Rosencrantz and Guildenstern Are Dead, 1968; Contributor of numerous articles to professional publications. Honours: Research Grant, Social Science Research Council, 1970-71; Margery and Huntly Sinclair Trust, 1974; International Scholarly Co-operative Grant, Volkswagen Foundation, 1976-78. Address: Jiriho Felixe 1688, CZ-74401 Frenštát p R, Czech Republic.

KUTCHER Ashton (Christopher), b. 7 February 1978, Ceder Rapids, Iowa, USA. Actor. m. Demi Moore, 2005-. Education: Biochemical Engineering Student, University of Iowa. Career: Sweeper, General Mills plant; Modeling. Film Appearances include: Coming Soon, 1999; Down To You, 2000; Reindeer Games, 2000; Dude Where's My Car?, 2000; Texas Ranger, 2001; Just Married, 2003; My Boss's Daughter, 2003; Cheaper by the Dozen, 2003; The Butterfly Effect, 2004; Guess Who, 2005; A Lot Like Love, 2005; Bobby, 2006; The Guardian, 2006; Open Season (voice), 2006. TV Appearances include: Just Shoot Me, 1997; That 70's Show, 1998; Grounded for Life, 2002; The Tonight Show with Jay Leno, 2003; RI:SE, 2003; Entertainment Tonight, 1981; Celebrities Uncensored, 2003; The Bernie Mac Show, 2004; T4, 2004. Honours: Young Artist Award, 1999; Sierra Award, 2000; MTV Movie Award, 2001; Razzie Award, 2004.

KUTILEK Miroslav, b. 8 October 1927, Trutnov, Czech Republic. Professor of Soil Science and Soil Physics. m. Xena Radova, 1 son, 1 daughter. Education: Ing, CTU, Prague, 1946-51; CSc, 1952-55; DrSc, 1966. Appointments: Associate Professor, CTU Prague, 1968-73; Reader, University of Khartoum, Sudan, 1965-68; Professor, CTU, Prague, 1973-90, 1992-93; Deputy Dean, 1974-85; Visiting Professor, Institute de Mechanique, Grenoble, France, 1979-80, 1985, 1991; Visiting Professor, University of California, 1981-82; Visiting Professor, Technische Universitat, Braunschweig, 1989; Professor, Bayreuth University, Fachbereich Geookologie, Germany, 1990-92. Publications: Research papers in journals; Scientific Books in Czech; Four books on Soil Science, Soil Hydrology, Porous Materials; Scientific books and monograph chapters in English; Others; Seven fiction books in Czech.

Honours: Felber's Award, Technical Sciences; Mendel's Award, Biological Sciences; Honorary Member, IUSS. Memberships: International Soil Science Society; New York Academy of Sciences; International Commission on Irrigation and Drainage; International Council of Scientific Unions; European Cultural Club; Others. Address: Nad Patankou 34, 160 00 Prague 6, Czech Republic.

KUTTNER Paul, b. 20 September 1922, Berlin, Germany. Publicity Director; Author. m. (1) Myrtil Romegialli, 1956, divorced 1961, (2) Ursula Timmermann, 1963, divorced, 1970, 1 son. Education: Bismarck Gymnasium, Berlin, 1932-38; Bryanston College, Blandford, Dorset, 1939-40. Appointments: Child Actor, aged nine, in films including: Kameradschaft (directed by G W Pabst); Emil und die Detektive (based on Erich Kästner's international juvenile best-seller, opposite Fritz Rasp); M (directed by Fritz Lang, starring Peter Lorre), Germany, 1931; US Publicity Director for the Guinness Book of World Records, 1964-89; Publicity Director, Sterling Publishing Co Inc, 1989-98. Publications: Translator of nine American books from German into English, 1963-76; The Man Who Lost Everything, 1976 (Best Seller in Spanish Language Edition, 1982); Condemned, 1983; Absolute Proof, 1984; The Iron Virgin, 1985; History's Trickiest Questions, 1990; Arts & Entertainment's Trickiest Questions, 1993; Science's Trickiest Questions, 1994; The Holocaust: Hoax or History? - The Book of Answers to Those Who Would Deny the Holocaust, 1997; Autobiography, An Endless Struggle – Reminiscences and Reflections, 2007. Contributions to: Der Weg; London Week. Address: Apt 5C, 37-26 87th Street, Jackson Heights, NY 11372, USA.

KVARATSKHELIA Ramaz, b. 15 November 1935, Tbilisi, Georgia. Chemist. m. Lyudmila Mladznovskaya, 1 son, 1 daughter. Education: Chemist-Engineer diploma, 1954-59, Candidate of Sciences, 1965, Georgian Polytechnical Institute; Institute of Inorganic Chemistry, 1959-; Doctor of Sciences, Kiev, Ukraine, 1987. Appointments: Junior, Senior and Chief Scientist, Institute of Inorganic Chemistry and Electrochemistry, 1959-; Professor, Georgian Technical University, 1989-95. Publications: 2 monographs; 1 invention; 150 articles in the fields of electrochemistry, physical chemistry and organic chemistry. Memberships: New York Academy of Sciences. Address: I Javakhishvili str 73, 0112 Tbilisi, Georgia. E-mail: ekvarats@hotmail.com

KWAK Chan, b. 1 June 1969, Seoul, Korea. Researcher. m. Minhee Park, 2 sons. Education: BS, 1993, MS, 1995, PhD, 2000, Chemical Engineering, Seoul National University. Appointments: Postdoctoral Researcher, Korea Institute of Science and Technology, 2000-02; Postdoctoral Scholar, Caltech, 2002-04; Senior Researcher, Samsung SDI, 2004-08; R&D Staff Member, Samsung Advanced Institute of Technology, 2008-. Publications: 15 peer reviewed articles in energy and material science; 48 registered patents; 119 filed patents in Korea, Japan, US, China and Europe. Address: Sungwon Sante Ville 3cha 222-1402, Sanghyun-dong, Yongim-si, Kyungki-do, 448-519, South Korea. E-mail: kcpmhkj@yahoo.com

KWAK Keun-Chang, b. 1 May 1971, Cheongju, Korea. Researcher. m. Young-Mi Jo, 2 daughters. BS, 1996, MS, 1998, PhD, 2002, Department of Electrical Engineering, Chungbuk National University, Korea. Appointments: Postdoctoral studies, Chungbuk National University, 2002-03; Postdoctoral studies, University of Alberta, Canada, 2003-05; Adjunct Professor, Korea University of Science and Technology, 2006-; Senior Researcher, ETRI, Intelligent

Robot Division, 2005-. Publications: 19 international journal papers; 24 international conference papers; 19 domestic journal papers; 50 domestic conference papers; 9 paten applications regarding Human-Robot Interaction. Honours: Best Poster Award, Korea Robot Society, 2006; Best Paper Award, Korean Nuclear Society, 1999; Listed in international biographical dictionaries. Memberships: IEEE; IEICE; IEEE Trans on Systems, Mom and Cybernetics; Cybernetics Society. Address: 161 Gajeong-dong, Yuseong-gu, Daejeon 305-700, Korea. E-mail: kwak@etri.re.kr

KWAUK Mooson, b. 9 May 1920, Hangyang, Hubei Province, China. Research Professor. m. Huichun Kwei, 2 sons, 1 daughter. Education: BS, Chemistry, University of Shanghai, 1943; MSc, Chemical Engineering, Princeton University, 1946. Appointments: Chemical Engineer, Hydrocarbon Research Inc, New York, 1947, 1952-56; Chemical Engineer, The Coca-Cola Export Corp, New York, 1948-52; Professor, 1956-, Director, 1978-86, Director Emeritus, 1986-, Institute of Chemical Metallurgy, Academia Sinica, 1956-; Distinguished Exchange Scholar, National Academy of Sciences, USA, 1984; Visiting Professor, Virginia Polytechnic Institute and State University, 1986-87; Visiting Professor, Ohio State University, 1989. Publications include: Fluid-Bed Technology for Extractive Metallurgy, 1958; Fluidized Leaching and Washing, 1979; Idealized and Bubbleless Fluidization, 1992; Fast Fluidization, 1994; Geometric Mobiles, 1998. Honours: Sigma Xi, 1947; Chesterman Award, New York, USA, 1951; Member, Chinese Academy of Sciences; Corresponding Member, Swiss Academy of Engineering Science; International Fluidization Award, Banff, Canada, 1989; Lectureship Award in Fluidization, Los Angeles, USA, 1997. Memberships: American Chemical Society; American Institute of Chemical Engineers; Chemical Industry and Engineering Society of China, Vice president; CIESC Institute of Chemical Engineering, President; Chinese Society of Particuology, President; Chinese Society of Metals; Chinese Society of Chemistry. Address: Apartment 402, Building 810, Dormitory of Academia Sinica, Zhongguan Village, Beijing 100080, China. E-mail: mooson@lcc.icm.ac.cn

KWOK Hong Kin, Assistant Professor; Researcher. Education: BSSc, Sociology, 1978, MPhil, Sociology, 1980, PhD, Sociology, 2000, The Chinese University of Hong Kong, Hong Kong. Appointments: Lecturer, Department of Social Sciences, Lingnan College, Hong Kong, 1980-96; Assistant Professor, Department of Sociology and Social Policy, Lingnan University, Hong Kong, 1996-; Researcher, Global Development Network (GDN), World Bank Institute of the World Bank; External Examiner, Springboard Programme, Lingnan Institute of Further Education, Lingnan University, 2001-; Assessor, Research grant proposal of research Grants Council of Hong Kong, University Grants Committee, 2002. Publications: Analysing Hong Kong Society, 1989; Chinese Family in Transition, 1997; Theory and Practice of Mother-tongue Education, 1998; Quality Education in the 21st Century: The Development of Mainland China, Hong Kong, Macau and Taiwan, 2000; 70 Years of Education in Hong Kong, 2004; Numerous journal articles. Honours: 1st Class Award, Best Chinese Thesis, Committee for the Scientific Studies in Chinese Management, 2002; Listed in numerous Who's Who and biographical publications: Memberships: Hong Kong Professional Teachers' Union, 1988-; Canadian Sociology and Anthropology Association, 1994-; Hong Kong Sociological Association, 1998-; Hong Kong Teachers' Association, 1998-; Board Member, International Sociological Association, Research Committee on Sociology of Ageing, 2002-06,

2006-10. Address: Department of Sociology and Social Policy, Lingnan University, 8 Castle Peak Road, Tuen Mun, New Territories, Hong Kong. E-mail: kwokhk@ln.edu.hk

KWON Bong Cheol, b. 15 November 1969, Seoul, Korea. Orthopaedic Surgeon; Hand Surgeon. m. Jung Kyong Lee, 1 daughter. Education: MD, 1994, PhD, 2008, Seoul National University. Appointments: Resident, Orthopaedic Surgery, 1998-2002, Fellow, Hand Surgery, 2002-03, Seoul National University; Assistant Professor, College of Medicine, Hallym University, 2003-. Publications: The effect COX-2 inhibitors on periprosthetic osteolysis, 2004; Comparative study between minimal medial and epidondylectomy and anterior subcutaneous transposition of the ulnar nerve for cubital tunnel syndrome, 2006; Fluoroscopic diagnosis of scapholunate interosseous ligament injuries in distal radius fractures, 2008; Comparison of sonography and electrodiagnostic testing in the diagnosis of carpal tunnel syndrome, 2008. Memberships: Korean Society for Surgery of the Hand; The Korean Orthopaedic Association; The International Federation of Societies for Surgery of the Hand. Address: Department of Orthpaedic Surgery, Hallym University Sacred Heart Hospital, PyeongChon-dong, DongAn-gu, Anyang-si, Kyeonggi-do, 431-070, South Korea.

KWON Oh-Heon, b. 30 May 1958, Daegu, South Korea. Professor. m. Myung-Hwa Son, 2 daughters. Education: BA, 1981, MD, 1983, Engineering, Kyungpook National University; PhD, University of Tokyo, 1991. Appointments: Researcher, LG Electronics, 1984-86; Professor, Pukyong National University, 1993-. Publications: Mechanical Safety Engineering; The stress analysis and the crack behaviour according to the characteristic of the interfacial region in fibre reinforced MMC; The effect of load orientation for crack propagation and acoustic emission evaluation on plainwoven CFRP; and others. Memberships: Korean Society of Mechanical Engineers; Korean Society of Safety. Addrss: Prugio 110-2705, Millak-Dong, Busan 613-771, Republic of Korea. E-mail: kwon@pknu.ac.kr

KWON Sook-Hyung (Sam), b. 2 May 1959, Andong, South Korea. Process Engineer; Vice President. m. Young Suk Song, 2 daughters. Education: BS, Chemical Engineering, University of Seoul, 1983, MS, Chemical Engineering, Yonsei University, 1987. Appointments: Engineer, Chon Engineering Company, 1982-84; Engineer, Lucky Engineering Company, 1984-87; Vice President, SK Energy, 1987-. Publications include: VHVI Base Oils from Fuels Hydrocracker Bottoms, 1999; Hydrogen Production Alternatives in an IGCC Plant, 1999; VHVI Base Oils and White Oils from Fuels Hydrocracker Bottoms, 2000; Best Practices in Operation, 2000; Raising the Bar-Premium Base Oils Produced by the All-Hydroprocessing Route, 2004; SK's Lube Base Oil Production – Successful Completion of 2nd LBO Project, 2005. Honours: Dasan Technology Award, Korea Economic Daily, 2000; KPEA Technology Award, Korea Professional Engineers Association, 2001. Memberships: Korea Professional Engineers Association; API Standard Committee; ISO-Technology Committee 185; Korean Institute of Chemical Engineers. Address: 110 Kosa-Dong, Nam-Gu, Ulsan, 680-130, South Korea. E-mail: shkwon@skenergy.com

KWON Soon Yong, b. 8 February 1963, Kyungi province, Korea. Orthodontist. m. Eun Joo Kim, 1 son, 1 daughter. Education: DMD, 1988; MSD, Certified in Orthodontics, 1994; PhD, Oral Biology, 1998. Appointments: Teaching Assistant, 1992-93, Scholarship Teaching Assistant, 1993-94, Department of Orthodontics, Kyung Hee University, School of

Dental Medicine; Full time Associate Professor, Department of Orthodontics, Hallym Medical University School of Dental Medicine, 1996-2000; Representative President, Network of Central Orthodontic Office, 2000-. Publications: The effects of high pull headgear in mixed dentition with class II malocclusion, 1994; An experimental study of distraction osteogenesis upon canine mandible, 1998; Orthodontic treatment using skeletal anchorage I, II and III, 2002; Clinical application of the tongue elevator, 2002. Memberships: Korean Association of Orthodontics; American Association of Orthodontics; World Federation of Orthodontics. Address: Central Dental Office 202, 1305-2 Youhwa B/D, Seocho-Dong, Seocho-Gu, Seoul 137-070, Korea. E-mail: braceman@naver.com Website: www.central28.com

KWON Soon-Kyoung, b. 14 October 1940, Anjoo, Korea. Professor. m. Sin-Kang Park, 1 son, 1 daughter. Education: BS, Seoul, 1962; MS, Seoul, 1964; PhD, Munster, Germany, 1975. Appointments: Assistant Professor, 1978-82, Associate Professor, 1982-87, Professor, 1987-2006, Professor Emeritus, 2006-, Vice President, 1992-93, Dean, College Pharmacy, 1998-2000; President, 2001, Duk-Sung Women's University. Publications: Medicinal Chemistry, 1985, 1996, 1999, 2005; The World of Drugs, 1988; The Advices of Drugs and Health, 2000. Honours: Prize for Distinguished Scientist, 1980; Golden Tower Prize for Distinguished Pharmacist, 1992; Prize for Commentator on Pharmaceutical Affairs, 1997; Dong-Am prize in pharmacy, Korean Pharmaceutical Industry News, 2001; Prize for Distinguished Pharmaceutical Educator, 2006. Memberships: American Chemical Society; Pharmaceutical Society of Korea; Korean Chemical Society; Korean Society of Applied Pharmacology. Address: Sooyoo-dong 572-25, Kangbook-Ku, Seoul 142-880, Korea.

KWONG Daniel W, b. 1 August 1958, Hong Kong. Business Owner; Investor; Global Strategist. Divorced, 1 daughter. Education: BA, Political Science, California State University at Los Angeles, USA, 1982; JD, Law, Thomas Jefferson College of Law, Florida, USA, 1993. Appointments: Chairman/CEO, Global Investment and Management Institute Inc; Chairman/CEO, Golden Harvest Holdings Ltd; Honorary Chairman and Non-Executive Director, KingHarvests.Com, Shanghai, China; Visiting Professor, World Eminent Chinese Business College, Beijing, China; Contributing Editor, Politics on Line; Independent Non-Executive Director, MingNetwork.Com. Publications: A Hidden Tool (an investment book), 1990; Cass' Story (song), 1991. Honours: Founding Sponsor, Flight 93 National Memorial Monument (invited by Governor Tom Ridge); Co-Founder, Ronald Reagan Republican Center, DC; Founder, National History Center, DC; Conference Chair/Key Note Speaker, Real Estate Investments in China, San Francisco, 2007. Memberships: Life Member, Republican National Committee; Life Member, Republican Presidential Task Force; Fellow, Hong Kong Institute of Directors; Vice Chairman, Board of Trustees, World Eminent Chinese Business Association, Beijing, China. Address: 601 South Cecil Street, Monterey Park, CA 91755, USA. E-mail: ghh_dwk@sbcglobal.net

KYPRAIOS Ioannis, b. 22 December 1979, Thessalonika, Greece. Greek Orthodox Christian; Engineering Research Fellow; Associate Tutor. Education: B Eng (First Class with Honours), Computer Systems Engineering, MSc (distinction), Modern Digital Communication Systems, D Phil, Engineering (Object Recognition/Image Processing), 2005, University of Sussex, Brighton, England. Appointments: Associate Tutor in Engineering, 2000-, Visiting Research Fellow in Engineering, Laser and Photonics Systems Research Group, 2005-, University of Sussex, Brighton; Hellenic Armed Forces Service, 2006-07. Publications: An investigation of the non-linear properties of correlation filter synthesis and neural network design, 2002; A non-linear training set superposition filter derived by neural network training methods for implementation in a shift invariant optical correlator, 2003; Object recognition within cluttered scenes employing a hybrid optical neural network (HONN) filter, 2004; Performance assessment of unconstrained Hybrid Optical Neural Network (U-HONN) filter for object recognition tasks in clutter, 2004; Fully invariant object recognition in cluttered scenes, 2005; Review of agent-based recommendation systems, 2006; Object recognition within cluttered scenes employing the Modified-Hybrid Optical Neural Network filter, 2006/2007; Performance assessment of the Modified-Hybrid Optical Neural Network filter, 2006/2007; Design and implementation of the Hybrid Optical Neural Network (HONN) family of object recognition filters, mathematical modelling and implementation of a deterministic design method for a convolutional-type Artificial Neural Network Architecture; Design and implementation of 4th type non-iterative Artificial Neural Network (SINA NNET). Honours: Top 10 Best Performance, Local (Crete) Students' Mathematics Competition (part of the National Qualifiers for the Maths' Olympics), 1996-97; 3 year Research Fund, EU Bursary, 2000-03; 1st Joint Prize, Best Poster Exhibition, 2001-02, School of Science and Technology, Department of Engineering and Design, University of Sussex; Listed in international biographical directories. Memberships: IEEE, USA; IET (IEE), England; BMVA, England.

KYRIAKOPOULOS Grigorios, b. 11 September 1972, Athens, Greece. Research Scientist. Education: Degree, Chemical Engineering, National Technical University of Athens, 1996; MS, Hellenic Open University, Patra, Greece, 2004; PhD, School of Chemical Engineering, National Technical University of Athens, Greece, 2005; MS, entitled Techno-economical Systems, National Technical University, Athens, Greece, 2007. Appointments: Research Fellow, Organic Chemical Technology, Laboratory of National Technical University of Athens, 1996-2006; Participant in the postgraduate programme "Protection of Monuments" organised by the Schools of Architectural Engineering, Chemical Engineering, Civil Engineering and Agronomist-Topographer Engineering, National Technical University of Athens with the experimental study: Removal of pesticides from aqueous solution by adsorption on polymeric resins, 1998-99 and 1999-2000; Academic Studies Auditor, Hellenic National Academic and Information Centre, Hellenic Ministry of Education, 2005-2006; Lecturer, Technical University of Pedagogical and Technical Education, Athens, Greece, 2004-2008; Lecturer, Hellenic Naval Academy of Greece, 2006-2008; Public Servant, Engineer, National Technical University of Athens, 2007-. Publications: Articles in scientific journals and papers in conference proceedings as co-author include: Adsorption of pesticides on resins, 2003; Removal of pesticides from aqueous solutions by adsorption, 2004; Effect of ionic strength and pH on the adsorption of selected herbicides on amberlite, 2006; Adsorption of pesticides on carbonaceous and polymeric materials from aqueous solutions. A review, 2006; Treatment of contaminated water with pesticides via adsorption, 2006. Honours: Scholarships: National Technical University of Athens, 1998-2001; Hellenic Open University, 2001-2002, 2002-2003, 2003-2004; Postdoctoral Research, State Scholarship Foundation of Greece; Prix Afas, 2000, Société d'Encouragement au Progrès (French Institution) in the Municipality of Athens, 2000; Thomaidio Award, National Technical University of Athens, 2003, 2004 and 2005;

Reviewer in the following journals: Chemical Engineering Science, Journal of Hazardous Materials, Chemosphere, Carbon, WSEAS International Conferences, Journal of Environmental Management and Chemical Engineering Journal. Memberships: Technical Chamber of Greece; Panhellenic Society of Chemical Engineers. Address: National Technical University of Athens, 9 Heroon Polytechniou Street, School of Electrical and Computer Engineering, Electric Power Division, Zografou Campus, GR 15780, Athens, Greece. E-mail: gregkyr@chemeng.ntua.gr

KYTE Peter Eric, b. 8 May 1945, Rawalpindi, Pakistan. Barrister. m. Virginia Cameron, 1 son, 1 daughter. Education: MA, Trinity Hall, Cambridge, 1968. Appointments: Teacher of Classics and French, 1964-65; Manager, Charter Consolidated Ltd, London, Mauritania and Congo, 1968-73; Account Executive, Merrill Lynch, London and New York, 1973-74; Joined Chambers of Daniel Hollis QC, now Hollis Whiteman Chambers, 1974-; Recorder, 1988; Queen's Counsel, 1996; Legal Assessor for the General Medical Council and General Dental Council. Honours: Recommended as Leading Silk in the field of Criminal Fraud in Chambers Guide to the Legal Profession, 2000-. Memberships: New York Stock Exchange; Chicago Board of Trade; Gray's Inn; Criminal Bar Association; Aula Club. Address: Forge House, Lower Heyford, Oxfordshire, OX25 5NS, England. E-mail: peter@kyte.u-net.com

L

LA PLANTE Lynda, b. 15 March 1946, Formby, England. Television Dramatist; Novelist. m. Richard La Plante, divorced. Education: Royal College of Dramatic Art. Appointments: Former Actress. Creative Works: Actress in The Gentle Touch, Out, Minder; Founder and Chair, La Plante Productions, 1994-; TV dramas include: Prime Suspect, 1991, 1993, 1995; Civvies; Framed; Seekers; Widows (series); Comics, 2 part drama, 1993; Cold Shoulder 2, 1996; Cold Blood; Bella Mafia, Trial and Retribution, 1997-; Killer Net, 1998; Mind Games, 2000; The Warden, 2001; Framed, Widows (mini-series), 2002; The Commander, 2003-. Publications include: The Widows, 1983; The Widows II, 1985; The Talisman, 1987; Bella Mafia, 1991; Framed, Civvies, Prime Suspect, 1992; Seekers, Entwined, Prime Suspect 2, 1993; Lifeboat, Cold Shoulder, Prime Suspect 3, 1994; She's Out, 1995; The Governor, Cold Blood, 1996; Trial and Retribution, 1997; Cold Heart, Trial and Retribution 2, 1998; Trial and Retribution 3, 1999; Trial and Retribution 4, Sleeping Cruelty, 2000; Trial and Retribution 5, Trial and Retribution 6, Royal Flush, 2002; Like a Charm (short stories), Above Suspicion (novel), 2004; The Red Dahlia, 2006; Clean Cut, 2007. Honours: CBE, 2008. Address: La Plante Productions Ltd, Paramount House, 162-170 Wardour Street, London, W1F 8ZX, England. Website: www.laplanteproductions.com

LAAR Mart, b. 22 April 1960, Tallinn, Estonia. Prime Minister. m. Katrin Laar, 1981, 1 son, 1 daughter. Education: MA, Philosophy, BA, History, Tartu University. Appointments: Member, Supreme Council, 1990-92; Member, Constitutional Assembly, 1992; Prime Minister of Estonia, 1992-94, 1999-2002; National Coalition Fatherland Party Chairman, 1992-95; Member of Parliament, Riikogu, VII Session, 1992-95; Member of Parliament, Riigikogu, VIII Session, 1995-98; Chairman, Pro Patria, 1998-; Prime Minister, Republic of Estonia, 1999. Publications: Variety of Estonian and English language books and publications on history. Honours: The Year's Best Young Politician in the World Award, 1993; European Tax Payer Association Year Prize, 2001; European Bull, Davastoeconomic Forum, Global Link Award, 2001; Adam Smith Award, 2002; Cato Institute's Milton Friedman Prize for Advancing Liberty, 2006. Memberships: Chairman, Jaan Tonisson Institute; Estonian Christian Democratic Union; Pen Club; Estonian University Students Society; Mont Pelerin Society, 2007. Address: State Chancellery, Lossi Plats 1a, Tallinn 15161, Estonia.

LACEY Nicholas Stephen, b. 20 December 1943, London, England. Architect. m. (1) Nicola, (2) Juliet, 2 sons, 3 daughters. Education: MA, Emmanuel College Cambridge; AADipl, Architectural Association, London. Appointments: Partner, Nicholas Lacey and Associates, 1971-83; Partner, Nicholas Lacey and Partners, 1983-. Honours: Winner, Wallingford Competition; Winner, Crown Reach (Millbank) Competition; Joint Winner, Arunbridge Competition; Prize Winner, Paris Opera House Competition; RIBA Regional Awards; Civic Trust Awards. Memberships: Royal Institute of British Architects (RIBA); Architecture Club; Athenaeum; Royal Dorset Yacht Club. Address: Reeds Wharf, 33 Mill Street, London SE1 2AX, England. E-mail: nicholaslacey@lineone.net

LACHELIN Gillian Claire Liborel, b. 5 February 1940, Reigate, Surrey, England. Emeritus Consultant in Obstetrics and Gynaecology. Education: MA, MB, BChir, 1964, MRCOG, 1969, MD (London), 1981, FRCOG, 1982, Cambridge University and St Thomas' Hospital Medical School. Appointments: Reader and Consultant in Obstetrics and Gynaecology, 1977-2000, Emeritus Reader and Consultant in Obstetrics and Gynaecology, 2000-, University College London and University College Hospitals Trust. Publications: Numerous articles on reproductive endocrinology; Books: Miscarriage: The Facts; Introduction to Clinical Reproductive Endocrinology. Memberships: Committee on Safety of Medicines, 1993-96; Society for Gynecologic Investigation (USA), 1982-. Address: Department of Obstetrics and Gynaecology, Royal Free and University College Medical School, 88-96 Chenies Mews, London WC1E 6HX, England.

LACHINOV Mikhail, b. 31 March 1957, Gorkovskaya Region, Russia. Engineer; Economist. 1 son, 1 daughter. Education: M Eng, Moscow Civil Engineering University, 1979; PhD, 1987; Master of Economics, State Financial Academy of the Russian Federation Government, 1991; Postgraduate Courses, London School of Business, Holborn College, London, England, 1994. Appointments: Professor of Economics, Moscow State Civil Engineering University, 1995-2002; Head, Director, Institution of Civil Engineers representation in Russia, 1996-2003; Deputy Director, Economics, "Mospromstroi" Construction Corporation, 2002-2006; International Construction and Industrial Association (Mossib), 2006; Department of Management Directors. Publications: Textbook: Foreign Economic Relations in Construction, 2001; More than 30 scientific articles. Honours: Medal, Krasnoyarsk Region Development Award; Medal, For International Links Development. Memberships: Fellow, Institution of Civil Engineers (UK); Fellow, Russian Society of Civil Engineering; Chartered Engineer. Address: Bolshoy Patriarshi Perevlok, H3 build 1 "pik-group" Moscow 123001, Russia. E-mail: lachinov@rambler.ru

LACHOWICZ Tadeusz Zygmunt, b. 11 December 1919, Drohobycz. Physician; Microbiologist; Chemist. m. Wanda Jadwiga Schmager, deceased. Education: MD, 1948, Master's degree in Chemistry, 1951, Jagellonian University; Candidate of Medical Sciences, 1958; Lecturer, 1960; Extraordinary Professor, 1968; Ordinary Professor, 1974. Appointments: Assistant, Adjunct, State Institute of Hygiene, 1946-50; Lecturer in Epidemiology in Military Service, 1951-52, Chief of Laboratory; Chief of the Microbiological Department in District Laboratory, 1954-63; Chief of Microbiology Department, 1963-65; Chief of Research, 1965-1980, Retired, 1980, Military Institute of Hygiene and Epidemiology. Publications: 135 experimental works, 2 manuals, 2 patents, over 100 interviews to radio, press and television; Investigations on Staphylococcins, 1962; Purification and properties of Staphylococcin A, 1968; The use of Immunofluorescence Adsorption Test for Titrating Tetanus Anatoxins, 1968. Honours: Awards of Ministry of Military Affairs, I, II, II, Grade, 1971, 1977, 1980; Awards of City of Krakow, 1973, 1978; Knight Cross, 1963; Man of the Year, ABI, 1991, 1992, 1993, 1995, 1999, 2000 with Commemorative Medal, 2004; Man of the Year, IBC, 1991-92, 1995-96, IBC; International Order of Merit, 1994; ABI Laureate of Poland, 1999; Key of Success Medical Excellence from ABI, 2000; 2000 Outstanding Scientists of the 20th Century, IBC, 2000; 2000 Outstanding Scholars of the 20th Century, IBC, 2000; Companion of Honour, IBC, 2002; Adviser to the Director General, IBC, 2003; Scroll of Legend, Medal, Living Legends, IBC, 2003; Honorary Member, IBC, 2003; International Register of Profiles, 12th Edition, 2003; International Peace Prize, United Cultural Convention United States of America; The First Five Hundred, IBC, 2003; International Medal of Honour, IBC, 2003; Ambassador of Grand Eminence, ABI, 2003; Greatest Lives, IBC, 2004; Personality of the Year, 2004; Great Minds of the 21st Century, 2004; Noble Laureate, 2004; American Hall of Fame and Medal, ABI, 2004; The Genius Elite, ABI, 2004; Certificate of Authenticity in the Book of Knowledge, ABI, 2005; IBC Hall of Fame, 2005; Top 100 Scientists, IBC, 2005. Memberships: International Society of Pathology of Infectious Diseases; Polish Physician Society; International Biographical Association; American Biographical Institute's Research Association. Address: Krowoderskich Zuchow 23m44, 31-271 Krakow, Poland.

LACROIX Christian Marie Marc, b. 16 May 1951, Arles, France. Fashion Designer. m. Francoise Roesenstiehl, 1989. Education: Université Paul Valéry, Montpellier; Université Paris, Sorbonne; Ecole du Louvre. Appointments: Assistant, Hermès, 1978-79, Guy Paulin, 1980-81; Artistic Director, Jean Patou, 1981-87, Christian Lacroix, 1987-, Emilio Pucci, 2002-; Design for Carmen, Nîmes, France, 1988, for L'as-tu revue?, 1991, for Les Caprices de Marianne, 1994, for Phèdre a la Comèdie Francaise, 1995; Created costumes for Joyaux, Opera Garnier, 2000; Decorated the TGV Mediterranee, 2001; Creative Director, Emilio Gucci, 2002. Publications: Pieces of a Pattern, 1992; Illustrations for albums, Styles d'aujourd'hui, 1995; Journal d'une collection, 1996. Honours include: Dés d'or, 1986, 1988; Council of Fashion Designers of America, 1987; Prix Balzac, 1989; Goldene Spinnrad Award, Germany, 1990; Commander, Ordre des Arts es Lettres, 1991; Prix Molière, for costumes in Phèdre, 1996; Chevalier, Legion d'honneur, 2002. Address: 73 rue de Faubourg Saint Honoré, 75008 Paris, France.

LADYMAN Stephen John, b. 6 November 1952, Ormskirk, Lancashire, England. Member of Parliament. m. Janet Baker, 2 stepsons, 1 daughter, 1 stepdaughter. Education: BSc, Applied Biology, Liverpool Polytechnic; PhD, Strathclyde University. Appointments: Research Scientist, MRC Radiobiology Unit, 1979-85; Head of Computing, Kennedy Institute, 1985-91; Head, Computer Support, Pfizer Central Research, 1991-97; Member of Parliament, South Thanet, 1997-; Treasurer, All Party British Fruit Industry Group, 2000-; Chair, All Party Parliamentary Group on Autism, 2000-; Liaison MP for The Netherlands, 2001-; Chair, All Party British-Dutch Group, 2001-; Parliamentary Private Secretary to the Minister for the Armed Forces, 2001-. Address: House of Commons, London SW1A 0AA, England. E-mail: ladymans@parliament.uk

LAFON Jacqueline Lucienne, b. 4 October 1941, Paris, France. Law Educator. Education: Baccalaureat, Paris, France, 1960; Doctorate in Law, Paris University, 1972. Appointments: Associate Professor, Paris XI Law Faculty, 1973-2007; Associate Professor, Sorbonne University (Paris IV), 1973-80; Associate Dean, Paris XI Law Faculty, 1980-87; Lecturer, Florida State University Study Centre, Florence, Italy, 1983; Lecturer, Florida International University, Miami, USA, 1984; Lecturer, Harvard University, Massachusetts, USA, 1984; Lecturer, Boston University Overseas Programs, Paris, 1985; Lecturer, Missouri University, Kansas, USA, 1987; Associate Professor, University Pantheon-Sorbonne (Paris I), 1990-. Publications: 5 books; 8 articles in professional journals. Honours: Laureate in Private Roman Law, University of Paris, 1962; Award for thesis, University of Paris II, 1972; Award for thesis, Association of the Historians of Law Faculties, 1973; Grant, Centre National de la Recheche Scientifique, 1979. Memberships: Le cercle France-Amériques, Paris; L'association France-Canada, Paris; Association Vieilles maisons Françaises, Paris.

LAGERFELD Karl-Otto, b. 1938, Hamburg, Germany. Fashion Designer. Education: Art School, Hamburg. Appointments: Fashion Apprentice, Balmain and Patou, 1959; Freelance Designer, associated with Fendi, Rome, 1963-, Chloe, Paris, 1964-83, Chanel, Paris, 1982-, Isetan, Japan; Designer, Karl Lagerfeld's Women's Wear, Karl Lagerfeld France Inc, 1983-; First collection under own name, 1984; Honorary Teacher, Vienna, 1983; Costume Designer for film, Comédie d'Amour, 1989; Designed tour outfits for Maddona; Kylie Minogue, Mariah Carey, 2004; New collection K Karl Lagerfeld, 2006. Publications: Lagerfeld's Sketchbook, 1990; Karl Lagerfeld Off the Record, 1995. Honours include: Golden Thimble, 1986. Address: Karl Lagerfeld France Inc, 75008 Paris, France.

LAGOS Ricardo, b. 2 March 1938, Santiago, Chile. Politician. m. Luisa Durán, 5 children. Education: University of Chile; Duke University, North Carolina, USA; PhD. Appointments: Professor, 1963-72, former Head, School of Political and Administrative Sciences, former Director, Institute of Economics, General Secretary, 1971, University of Chile; Chairman, Alianza Democrática, 1983-84; Chairman, Partido por la Democracia, 1987-90; Minister of Education, 1990-92; Minister of Public Works, 1994; President of Chile, 2000-06. Publications: Numerous books and articles on economics and politics. Address: Office of the President, Palacio de la Moneda, Santiago, Chile.

LAGRAVENESE Richard, b. 30 October 1959, Brooklyn, New York, USA. Film Screenplay Writer, Director and Producer. m. Ann Weiss, 1986, 1 daughter. Education: Emerson College; BFA, New York University. Appointments: Producer, The Ref, film, 1994; Director, Living Out Loud, film, 1998. Creative Works: Screenplays: Rude Awakening, 1991; The Fisher King, 1991; The Ref, 1994; A Little Princess, 1995; The Bridges of Madison County, 1995; The Horse Whisperer, 1998; Living Out Loud (also Director), 1998; Unstrung Heroes; Defective Detective, 2002; Paris, je t'aime, 2006; The Secret Life of Walter Mitty, 2006; Freedom Writers, 2007; P.S. I Love You, 2008. Honours: Independent Film Project Writer of the Year. Address: c/o Kirsten Bonelli, 8383 Wilshire Boulevard, Suite 340, Beverly Hills, CA 90211, USA.

LAHOUD Emile (General), b. 1936, Baabdate, Lebanon. Politician; Naval Officer. m. Andrée Amadouni, 2 sons, 1 daughter. Education: Brumana High School; Cadet Officer, Military Academy, 1956; Naval Academy courses, UK, USA, 1958-80. Appointments: Ensign, 1959, Sub-Lieutenant, 1962, Lieutenant, 1968, Lieutenant-Commander, 1974, Commander, 1976, Captain, 1980, Rear-Admiral, 1985, General, 1989; Commander of Second Fleet, 1966-68, First Fleet, 1968-70; Staff of Army Fourth Bureau, 1970-72; Chief of Personal Staff of General and Commander of Armed Forces, 1973-79; Director of Personnel, Army Headquarters, 1980-83; President of Military Office, Ministry of Defence, 1983-89; General and Commander of Armed Forces, 1989-; President of Lebanon, 1998-. Publications: Procedure and Modus Operandi, 1998. Honours: Medal of Merit and Honour, Haiti, 1974; Lebanese Medal of Merit, General Officer, 1989; War Medals, 1991, 1992; Dawn of the South Medal, 1993; National Unity Medal, 1993; Medal of Esteem, 1994; Grand Cordon, Order of the Cedar, Lebanon, 1993; Commandeur, Légion d' Honneur, France, 1993; Order of Merit, Senior Officer Level, Italy, 1997; Grand Cross of Argentina, 1998; Order of Hussein ibn Ali, Jordan, 1999; Necklace of Independence, Qatar, 1999. Address: Presidential Palace, Baabda, Lebanon. E-mail: opendoor@presidency.gov.lb

LAI Shih-Kung, b. 15 November 1957, Taiwan. Professor. m. Chiung-Ku Lee, 15 October 1993. Education: BSE, Urban Planning, National Cheng Kung University, 1979; MCRP, City and Regional Planning, Ohio State University, 1985; PhD, Regional Planning, University of Illinois at Urbana-Champaign, 1990. Appointment: Director, Centre for Land and Environmental Planning, Associate Professor, Professor, Department of Real Estate and Built Environment, National Taipei University and Department of Urban Planning, National Cheng Kung University. Publication: Meanings and Measurements of Multiattribute Preferences, 1996; Omega, Environment and Planning B, Decision Sciences, The Annals of Regional Science. Honour: Research awards of National Science Council, Republic of China, 1993-. Memberships: American Planning Association; INFORMS; Taiwan Planning Association. Address: 67, Section 3, Min Sheng East Road, Taipei, Taiwan, Republic of China. E-mail: sklai@mail.ncku.edu.tw

LAIDLAW Christopher Charles Fraser (Sir), b. 9 August 1922. Business Executive. m. Nina Mary Prichard, 1952, 1 son, 3 daughters. Education: St John's College, Cambridge. Appointments: War Service, Europe, Far East, Major on General Staff, 1939-45; With British Petroleum Co Ltd, 1948-83: Representative, Hamburg, 1959-61, General Manager, Marketing Department, 1963-67, Director, BP Trading, 1967, President, BP Belgium, 1967-71, Director of Operations, 1971-72, Chairman, BP Germany, 1972-83, Managing Director, BP Co Ltd, 1972-81, Deputy Chairman, BP Co Ltd, 1980-81, Chairman, BP Oil Ltd, 1977-81, Chairman, BP Oil International 1981; Director, Commercial Union Assurance Co, 1978-83, Barclays Bank International Ltd, 1980-87, Barclays Bank, 1981-88; Chairman, ICL, 1981-84; President, ICL France, 1983; Director, Amerada Hess Corporation, 1983-94; Director, Barclays Merchant Bank, 1984-87; Chairman, Boving and Co, 1984-85; Chairman, UK Advisory Board, 1984-91, Director, 1987-94, INSEAD; Director, Amerada Ltd, 1985-98; Chairman, Bridon PLC, 1985-90; Director, Daimler-Benz UK Ltd, 1994-99. Honours: Honorary Fellow, St John's College, Cambridge. Memberships: President, German Chamber of Industry and Commerce, 1983-86; Master, Tallow Chandlers Company, 1988-89; Vice-President, British-German Society, 1996-. Address: 49 Chelsea Square, London SW3 6LH, England.

LAIDLAW (Henry) Renton, b. 6 July 1939, Edinburgh, Scotland. Journalist. Education: James Gillespie's School, Edinburgh, Scotland; Daniel Stewart's College, Edinburgh, Scotland. Appointments: Sports Reporter, Edinburgh Evening News, 1957-68; Newsreader, Interviewer, Grampian Television, 1968-70; BBC Reporting Scotland Anchorman, 1970-73; Golf Reporter, Evening Standard, London, 1973-98; BBC radio, ITV, TWI, Eurosport, Screensport, Sport on 2, BBC Radio Scotland, PGA European Tour Productions, 1985-2002; Golf Channel, USA, 1995-. Publications: Golfers Handbook (editor); Tony Jacklin – the First 40 Years; Play Better Golf; Play Golf (with Peter Alliss); Golfing Heroes; Ryder Cup 1985; Ryder Cup, 1987; Ryder Cup, 1989; Captain at Kiawah (with Bernard Gallacher); Wentworth – 70 Years; Sunningdale Centenary. Honours: Lifetime Achievement Award in Journalism, PGA of America, 2003; Memorial Journalism Award, USA, 2001. Memberships: R and A; Sunningdale; Royal Burgess; Ballybunion; Caledonian Club. Address: c/o Kay Clarkson, 10 Buckingham Place, London SW1E 6HX, England. E-mail: renton@rentonlaidlaw.com

LAINE Cleo (Clementina Dinah Dankworth), b. 28 October 1927, Southall, Middlesex, England. Singer. m. (1) George Langridge, 1947, 1 son, (2) John Philip William Dankworth, 1958, 1 son, 1 daughter. Appointments: Joined, Dankworth Orchestra, 1953; Lead, Seven Deadly Sins, Edinburgh Festival and Sadler's Wells, 1961; Acting roles in Edinburgh Festival, 1966, 1967; Founder, Wavendon Stables Performing Arts Centre, 1970; Many appearances with symphony orchestras; Frequent tours and TV appearances and productions including Last of the Blonde Bombshells, 2000. Publications: Cleo: An Autobiography, 1994; You Can Sing If You Want To, 1997. Honours include: Woman of the Year, 9th Annual Golden Feather Awards, 1973; Edison Award, 1974; Variety Club of GB Show Business Personality Award, 1977; TV Times Viewers' Award for Most Exciting Female Singer on TV, 1978; Grammy Award, Best Jazz Vocalist, Female, 1985; Best Actress in a Musical, 1986; Theatre World Award, 1986; Lifetime Achievement Award, 1990; Vocalist of the Year, British Jazz Awards, 1990; Lifetime Achievement Award, USA, 1991; ISPA Distinguished Artists Award, 1999. Memberships include: National Association of Recording Merchandisers. Address: The Old Rectory, Wavendon, Milton Keynes MK17 8LT, England.

LAING (John) Stuart, b. 22 July 1948, Limpsfield, England. Diplomat.1 son, 2 daughters. Education: Rugby School; Corpus Christi College, Cambridge. Appointments: Served with the UK Diplomatic Service in Saudi Arabia, Brussels, Cairo, Prague and the Foreign and Commonwealth Office, London. British High Commissioner, Brunei, 1998–2002; British Ambassador to Oman, 2002-2005; British Ambassador to Kuwait, November 2005-. Membership: Athenaenum Club. Address: British Embassy, PO Box 2 Safat, 13001 Kuwait. E-mail: stuart.laing@fco.gov.uk

LAINSON Ralph, b. 21 February 1927, Upper Beeding, Sussex, England. Parasitologist. m. Zéa Constante Lins-Lainson, 1 son, 2 daughters. Education: BSc, 1947-51, London University; PhD, 1952-55, DSc, 1964, University of London, London School of Hygiene and Tropical Medicine. Appointments: Lecturer, Department of Medical Protozoology, London School of Hygiene and Tropical Medicine, 1955-59; Director, Leishmaniasis Unit, Baking Pot, Cayo, Belize, Central America, 1959-62; Research Worker, London School of Hygiene and Tropical Medicine, 1962-65; Director, Wellcome Parasitology Unit, Instituto Evandro Chagas, Belém, Pará, Brazil, 1965-92. Publications: 350 articles in scientific journals and textbooks of parasitic diseases, particularly Leishmaniasis, Malaria and Toxoplasmosis. Honours: Chalmer's Medal, Royal Society of Tropical Medicine and Hygiene, 1971; Manson Medal, Royal Society of Tropical Medicine and Hygiene, 1984; Fellow, Royal Society of London, 1982; Associate Fellow, Third World Academy of Sciences, 1989; OBE, 1996; American Medal of Honour, 2004; Listed in National and international biographical dictionaries. Memberships: Honorary Member, London School of Tropical Medicine and Hygiene; Honorary Member, British Society of Parasitology; Honorary Member, Royal Society of Tropical Medicine and Hygiene; Honorary Member, Society of Protozoologists. Address: Avenida Visconde de Souza Franco 1237, Apto 902, 66053-000, Belém, Pará, Brazil. E-mail: ralphlainson@iec.pa.gov.br

LAIRD Gavin Harry (Sir), b. 14 March 1933, Clydebank, Scotland. Trade Union Official. m. Catherine Gillies Campbell, 1956. Appointments: Shop Stewards Convener, Singer, Clydebank, 7 years; Regional Officer, 1972-75, Executive Councillor for Scotland and North-West England, 1975-82,

General Secretary, Union Section, 1992-95, Amalgamated Engineering Union, formerly Amalgamated Union of Engineering Workers; Scottish Trades Union Congress General Council, 1973-75; Part-time Director, Highlands and Islands Development Board, 1974-75; Part-time Director, British National Oil Corporation, 1976-86; Trades Union Congress General Council, 1979-82; Industrial Development Advisory Board, 1979-86; Chairman, The Foundries Economic Development Committee, 1982-85; Arts Council, 1983-86; Director, Bank of England, 1986-94; Non-Executive Director, Scottish TV Media Group PLC, 1986-99; Non-Executive Director, Britannia Life, 1988-; Non-Executive Director, GEC Scotland, 1991-99; Non-Executive Director, Edinburgh Investment Trust, 1994-; Chairman, Greater Manchester Buses North, 1994-96; Armed Forces Pay Review Body, 1995-98; Employment Appeal Tribunal, 1996-; Non-Executive Director, Britannia Investment Managers Ltd and Britannia Fund Managers Ltd, now Britannia Asset Managers Ltd, 1996-; Chairman, Murray Johnstone Venture Capital Trust 4, 1999-; Murray Johnstone Private Acquisition Partnership Advisory Committee, 1999-. Honours: Commander, Order of the British Empire. Memberships: Trustee, John Smith Memorial Trust; Advisory Board, Know-How Fund for Poland, 1990-95; Trustee, Anglo-German Foundation, 1994-; President, Kent Active Retirement Association, 1999-; Vice-President, Pre-Retirement Association of Great Britain and Northern Ireland, 1999-; Editorial Board, European Business Journal. Address: 9 Cleavedon House, Holmbury Park, Bromley BR1 2WG, England.

LAKATANI Sani, Politician. Appointments: Leader, Niue People's Party; Prime Minister of Niue, 1999-2001; Minister for External Affairs, Finance, Customs and Revenue, Economic and Planning Development and Statistics, Business and Private Sector Development, Civil Aviation, Tourism, International Business Company and Offshore Banking, Niue Development Bank, 1999-2001; Chancellor, University of the South Pacific, Fiji, 2000-03; Deputy Premier and Minister for Planning, Economic Development and Statistics, the Niue Development Bank, Post, Telecommunication and Information Computer Technology Development, Philatelic Bureau and Numismatics, Shipping, Investment and Trade, Civil Aviation and Police, Immigration and Disaster Management, 2002-. Address: c/o Office of the Prime Minister, Alofi, Niue, South Pacific.

LALLAAICHA (HRH Princess), Diplomatist. Appointments: Moroccan Ambassador to UK, 1965-69; Moroccan Ambassador to Italy and accredited to Greece, 1969-73. Honours: Grand Cordon, Order of the Throne of Morocco. Membership: President, Moroccan Red Crescent. Address: c/o Ministry of Foreign Affairs, ave Franklin Roosevelt, Rabat, Morocco.

LAMB Allan Joseph, b. 20 June 1954, Langebaanweg, Cape Province, South Africa. Cricketer. m. Lindsay Lamb, 1979, 1 son, 1 daughter. Education: Abbotts College. Appointments: Mid-Order Right-Hand Batsman; Teams: Western Province, 1972-82, 1992-93, OFS, 1987-88, Northamptonshire, 1978-95, Captain 1989-95; Qualified for England 1982 and played in 79 Tests, 1982-92, 3 as Captain, scoring 4,656 runs, average 36.0, including 14 hundreds; Toured Australia, 1982-83, 1986-87, 1990-91; Scored 32,502 1st Class Runs, 89 hundreds; 1,000 15 times; 122 limited-overs internationals; Director, Lamb Associates Event Management Company, Grenada Sports Ltd; Contributor, Sky Sports Cricket. Publication: Silence of the Lamb, autobiography, 1995. Address: Lamb Associates, First Floor, 4 St Giles Street, Northampton NN1 1JB, England.

LAMB Andrew (Martin), b. 23 September 1942, Oldham, Lancashire, England. Writer on Music. m. Wendy Ann Davies, 1 April 1970, 1 son, 2 daughters. Education: Corpus Christi College, Oxford, 1960-63; MA, Honours, D Litt, 2006, Oxford University. Publications: Jerome Kern in Edwardian London, 1985; Ganzl's Book of the Musical Theatre (with Kurt Ganzl), 1988; Skaters' Waltz: The Story of the Waldteufels, 1995; An Offenbach Family Album, 1997; Shirley House to Trinity School, 1999; 150 Years of Popular Musical Theatre, 2000; Leslie Stuart: Composer of Florodora, 2002; Fragson: The Triumphs and the Tragedy (with Julian Myerscough), 2004; The Merry Widow at 100, 2005. Editor: The Moulin Rouge, 1990; Light Music from Austria, 1992; Leslie Stuart: My Bohemian Life, 2003. Contributions to: Oxford Dictionary of National Biography; The New Grove Dictionary of Music and Musicians; The New Grove Dictionary of American Music; The New Grove Dictionary of Opera; Gramophone; Musical Times; Classic CD; BBC Music Magazine; American Music; Music and Letters; Wisden Cricket Monthly; Cricketer; Listener; Notes. Memberships: Fellow, Institute of Actuaries; Lancashire County Cricket Club. Address: 12 Fullers Wood, Croydon CR0 8HZ, England.

LAMB Willis Eugene Jr, b. 12 July 1913, Los Angeles, California, USA. Physicist. m. (1) Ursula Schaefer, 1939, deceased 1996, (2) Bruria Kaufman, 1996. Education: University of California; PhD. Appointments: Instructor, 1938, Professor of Physics, 1948-52, Columbia University, New York City; Loeb Lecturer, Harvard University, 1953-54; Professor of Physics, Stanford University, Stanford, California, 1951-56; Wykeham Professor of Physics and Fellow, New College, University of Oxford, England, 1956-62; Henry Ford II Professor of Physics, 1962-72, J Willard Gibbs Professor of Physics, 1972-74, Yale University, USA; Professor of Physics and Optical Sciences, 1974-, Regents Professor, 1990-, University of Arizona, Tucson; Senior Alexander von Humboldt Fellow, 1992-94. Honours: Rumford Premium, American Academy of Arts and Sciences, 1953; Honorary ScD, University of Pennsylvania, 1953; Co-recipient, Nobel Prize in Physics, 1955; Research Corporation Award, 1955; Guggenheim Fellow, 1960; Honorary LHD, Yeshiva University, 1964; Honorary ScD, Gustavus Adolphus College, 1975; Honorary ScD, Columbia University, 1990; Humboldt Fellowship, 1992; Honorary Fellow, Royal Society of Edinburgh. Memberships: National Academy of Sciences. Address: Optical Sciences Center, University of Arizona, Tucson, AZ 85721, USA.

LAMBERT Nigel Robert Woolf, b. 5 August 1949, London, England. Barrister; Queens Counsel. m. Roamie Elisabeth Sado, 1 son, 1 daughter. Education: College of Law, London. Appointments: Called to the Bar, Gray's Inn, 1974; Ad eundem Member of Inner Temple, 1986; Chairman, South Eastern Circuit, Institute of Barristers Clerks Committee; Assistant Recorder, 1992-96; Recorder, 1996-; Queens Counsel, 1999; Chairman, North London Bar Mess, 2001-; Bencher, Gray's Inn, 2003. Memberships: Life Vice President, Cokethorpe Old Boys Association; North London Bar Mess Committee, 1991-; Criminal Bar Association, Committee, 1993-2000; Member, Bar Council, 1993-2000; Member, South Eastern Circuit, Executive Committee, 2001-; Inner Temple Bar Liaison Committee, 2002-04. Address: 2-4 Tudor Street, London EC4Y 0AA, England. E-mail: nigellambertqc@hotmail.com

LAMBERT Richard Peter, b. 23 September 1944. Journalist. m. Harriet Murray-Browne, 1973, 1 son, 1 daughter. Education: Balliol College, Oxford; BA Oxon. Appointments: Staff, 1966-2001, Lex Column, 1972, Financial Editor, 1978,

New York Correspondent, 1982, Deputy Editor, 1983, Editor, 1991-2001, Financial Times; Lecturer and Contributor to The Times, 2001-; External Member, Bank of England Monetary Policy Committee, 2003-; Director, Confederation of British Industry, 2006-. Honours: Hon DLitt, City University, London, 2000; Princess of Wales Ambassador Award, 2001; World Leadership Forum Business Journalist Decade of Excellence Award, 2001. Memberships: Director, London International Financial Futures Exchange; AXA Investment Mans, International Rescue Committee, UK; Chair, Visiting Arts; Governor, Royal Shakespeare Co; UK Chair, Franco-British Colloque; Member, UK-India Round Table; Member, International Advisory Board, British-American Business Inc. Address: Bank of England, Threadneedle Street, London EC2R 8AH, England.

LAMINE LOUM Mamadou, b. Senegal. Politician. Appointments: Formerly Minister of Economics, Finance and Planning, Senegal; Prime Minister of Senegal, 1998-99. Memberships: Parti Socialiste. Address: Office of the Prime Minister, ave Leopold Sedar Senghor, Dakar, Senegal.

LAMONT Norman Stewart Hughson (Baron Lamont of Lerwick in the Shetland Islands), b. 8 May 1942, Lerwick, Shetland, Scotland. Politician; Writer; Businessman. m. Alice Rosemary White, 1971. Education: BA Economics, Fitzwilliam College, Cambridge. Appointments: Personal Assistant to Duncan Sandys MP, 1965; Staff, Conservative Research Department, 1966-68; Merchant Banker, N M Rothschild and Sons, 1968-79; Director, Rothschild Asset Management; Conservative Member of Parliament for Kingston-upon-Thames, 1972-97: Parliamentary Private Secretary to Norman St John Stevas, 1974, Opposition Spokesman on Prices and Consumer Affairs, 1975-76, Opposition Spokesman on Industry, 1976-79, Parliamentary Under-Secretary of State, Department of Energy, 1979-81, Minister of State, Department of Trade and Industry, 1981-85, Minister of State, Department of Defence Procurement, 1985-86, Financial Secretary to Treasury, 1986-89, Chief Secretary to Treasury, 1989-90, Chancellor of the Exchequer, 1990-93; Non-Executive Director, N M Rothschild and Sons Ltd, 1993-95; Chairman, Archipelago Fund, Food Fund and Indonesia Investment Trust, 1995-; Chairman, Conservatives Against a Federal Europe, 1998; Vice-Chairman, International Nuclear Safety Commission; Chair, Bruges Group, 2003-; House of Lords Select Committee on European Union, 2001-03; Director, Balli Group PLC. Publications: Sovereign Britain, 1995; In Office, 1999. Honour: Life Peeerage, 1998; Privy Councillor. Memberships: Chairman, Cambridge University Conservative Association, 1963; President, Cambridge Union, 1966. Address: c/o Balli Group plc, 5 Stanhope Gate, London, W1Y 5LA, England.

LAMPI Rauno Andrew, b. 12 August 1929, Gardner, Massachusetts, USA. Food Scientist; Engineer. m. Betty, 3 sons, 1 daughter. Education: BS, 1951, MS, 1955, PhD, 1957, Food Technology, University of Massachusetts. Appointments: Technical Director, New England Apple Products; Manager, Food Technology Section, Central Engineering, FMC Corporation; Research Physical Scientist, US Army Natick R and D Centre; Physical Science Administrator, N Labs; Independent Food Scientist/Engineer. Publications: Over 80, including 5 book chapters: 3 patents. Honours: US Army Exceptional Civilian Service Medal; Institute of Food Technology's Industrial Achievement Award; Institute of Food Technology Riester-Davis Award. Memberships: Fellow, Institute of Food Technology. Address: 20 Wheeler Road, Westborough, MA 01581, USA.

LANDAU David, CBE, b. 22 April 1950, Tel Aviv, Israel. Company Chairman. m. Marie-Rose Kahane, 1 son, 1 daughter. Education: MD, University of Pavia, Italy, 1978; MA, Wolfson College, Oxford, 1979. Appointments: Supernumerary Fellow, Worcester College, Oxford, 1980-; Print Curator, The Genius of Venice, Royal Academy, 1983; Founder and Editor, Print Quarterly, 1984-; Founder and Joint Managing Director, Loot, 1985-95; Founder, 1986, Chairman, 1990-91, Free-Ad Papers International Association; Chairman, Steering Committee, Andrea Mantegna Exhibition, Royal Academy and Metropolitan Museum of Art, New York, 1992; Chairman, Loot Group of Companies, 1994-2000; Director, 1995-2003, Chairman, 1998-2003, National Gallery Company (formerly National Gallery Publications); Director, Getty Images, 2003-06; Chairman, Saffron Hill Ventures, 2000-. Publications: Georg Pencz, 1978; Federica Galli, 1982; The Renaissance Print (with Prof P Parshall), 1994; Articles in Print Quarterly; Master Drawings, The Burlington Magazine, etc. Honours: CBE; Commendatore dell'OMRI. Memberships: Trustee: British Friends of Art Museums of Israel, 1995-; National Gallery Trust, 1996-; The Art Fund 1996-; National Gallery, 1996-2003; Venice in Peril Fund, 1996-, Treasurer, 1997-; Courtauld Institute, 2002-. Address: 51 Kelso Place, London W8 5QQ, England. E-mail: dlandau@saffronhill.com

LANDSBERGIENE Grazina, b. 28 January 1930, Anyksciai, Lithuania. m. Vytautas Landsbergis, 1 son, 1 daughter. Education: Panevezys Gymnasium for Girls, 1948; Lithuanian Academy of Music, 1959. Appointments: Accompanist, National Theatre of Opera and Ballet, 1958-85; Associate Professor, Professor, Lithuanian Academy of Music, 1990-; Numerous concerts and records with various singers. Honours: Vilnius Glory Award, 1998; Order of Grand Duke Gediminas, 1999; Barbora Radvilaite Award, Vilnius, 2005. Memberships: Lithuanian Society of Political Prisoners and Deportees; Chairperson, Vytautas Landsbergis Foundation. Address: Traidenio 34-15, LT 2004 Vilnius, Lithuania.

LANDSBERGIS Vytautas, b. 18 October 1932, Kaunas, Lithuania. Musicologist; Politician. m. Grazina Rucyte, 1 son, 2 daughters. Education: J Gruodis Music School, 1949, Ausra gymnasium, Kaunas, 1950; Lithuanian Music Academy, Vilnius, 1955. Appointments include: Chairman, 1988-90, Honorary Chairman, 1991-, Lithuanian Reform Movement, Sajudis; President of the Supreme Council of the Republic of Lithuania (Head of State), 1990-92; Member of Seimas (Parliament), Republic of Lithuania and Leader of Opposition, 1992-96, member, Lithuanian Delegation to Parliamentary Assembly of Council of Europe, 1992-96, 2000-02, and to the Baltic Assembly, 1992-96, 2000-04; Chairman, Lithuanian Conservative Party, 1993-2003; President, Seimas (Parliament) Republic of Lithuania, 1996-2000; Candidate, Presidential elections, 1997; Member of the Seimas (Parliament) of the Republic of Lithuania, 2000-04; Observer to the European Parliament, 2003-04, and MEP, 2004-. Publications include: Books: (in Lithuanian) The Hope Regained, 1990, 1991; The Case of Freedom, 1992; The Cross-roads, 1995; Autobiography, Years of Decision (in German and Lithuanian), 1997, Lithuania Independent Again (in English), 2000; Numerous others include: Monographs on the artist and composer M K Ciurlionis, 1965, 1971 and 1975 (in Russian), 1976, 1986, 1992 (in English); Intermezzo (poems), 1991, 2004; Who are We? (poems), 2004; Waves Give Me the Road (memories of the kid), 2004; Glimmers of History (poems), 2006; It's Serious, Children (poems), 2006; Editions of Documents: Together. The Council of the Baltic States 1990-92 (in English), 1996; The Act of 11 March. Facsimiles, 2000; The Heavy Freedom (in Lithuanian) volumes I-III, 2000; The Cousin Mathew. The Book on Stasys Lozoraitis from His Letters and Messages (in Lithuanian), 2002, 2003; Koenigsberg and Lithuania (in Lithuanian), 2003; Unknown Documents on January 13 (in Lithuanian), 2003, 2004; In the European Parliament I,II and III (in Lithuanian), 2004, 2005, 2006; Lithuania's Road to NATO (in Lithuanian), 2005; Forgotten Soviet war Crime (in English), 2005, (in Lithuanian), 2006, 2007; Soldier Seeks Justice (in Lithuanian), 2006. Honours include: Norwegian People's Peace Prize, 1991; Fondation de Future (France), 1991; Hermann-Ehlers-Preis, Germany, 1992; 9th International Ramon Llull Prize of the Catalonian Culture Congress Foundation (Spain), 1994; Legion of Honour Order 2nd Class, France, 1997; Order of Grand Duke Vytautas, 1st Class, Lithuania, 1998; Vibo Valentia Testimony Prize, Italy, 1998; Royal Norwegian Order of Merit (Grand Cross), 1998; Grand Cross Order of the Republic of Poland, 1999; UNESCO Medal, 1999; Order of Merit (Grand Cross) of the Order of Malta, 1999; Grand Croix de l'Ordre de l'Honneur of Greece, 1999; Truman-Reagan Freedom Award (USA), 1999; Pleiade Ordre de la Frankophonie (France), 2000; Three Stars Order, 2nd Class, Latvia, 2001; Order of the Cross of St Mary's Land, 1st Class, Estonia, 2002; Order of Grand Duke Vytautas with Golden Collar, 2003; Sixteen Honorary doctorates, including University of Sorbonne. Memberships include: Lithuanian Composers Union; European St Sebastian's Order of Knights; Honorary Doctor of St Lucas Academy, The Netherlands, 2004; Chairman: M K Ciurlionis Society; M K Ciurlionis International Competition; Member of International Advisory Council of the Victims of Communism Memorial Foundation (USA), 1995-2007; Knight of the Grand Order de Coeurs, 2004-. Address: Traidenio 34-15, LT 2004 Vilnius, Lithuania.

LANG Helmut, b. 10 March 1956, Vienna, Austria. Fashion Designer. Career: Established own studio, Vienna, 1977; Opened made-to-measure shop, Vienna, 1979; Developed ready-to-wear collections, 1984-86; Presented Helmut Lang's Women's Wear, 1986, Helmut Lang's Menswear, 1987-, Paris Fashion Week; Started licensed business, 1988; Professor, Masterclass of Fashion, University of Applied Arts, Vienna, 1993-; Helmut Lang Underwear, 1994; Helmut Lang Protective Eyewear, 1995; Helmut Land Jeans, 1996; Helmut Lang, Footwear and Accessories, 1990; Helmut Lang Fragrances, 1999. Honours: Council of American Fashion Designers of the Year Award, 1996; CFDA Designer of the Year, 2004; Fashion Group International "The Imagineers of Our Time" Award, 2004; LEAD Award, 2005. Address: c/o Michele Montagne, 184 rue St Maur, 75010 Paris, France.

LANG k d (Kathryn Dawn Lang), b. 2 November 1961, Consort, Alberta, Canada. Singer; Composer; Actress. Career: Played North American clubs with own band, 1982-87; Performed at closing ceremony, Winter Olympics, Calgary, 1988; Headlining US tour, 1992; Royal Albert Hall, 1992; Earth Day benefit concert, Hollywood Bowl, 1993; Sang with Andy Bell, BRIT Awards, 1993; Television includes: Late Night with David Letterman; Wogan; The Arsenio Hall Show; The Tonight Show; Top of the Pops; Subject, South Bank Show documentary, ITV, 1995; Film appearance, Salmonberries, 1991. Recordings: Albums: A Truly Western Experience, 1984; Angel with a Lariat, 1986; Shadowland, 1988; Absolute Torch and Twang, 1990; Ingénue, 1992; Even Cowgirls Get the Blues (soundtrack), 1993; All You Can Eat, 1995; Drag, 1997; Australian Tour, 1997; Invincible Summer, 2000; Live By Request, 2001; A Wonderful World (with Tony Bennett), 2003; Hymns of the 49th Parallel, 2004; Reintarnation, 2006; Features on soundtrack to Dick Tracy; Hit singles include:

Crying (duet with Roy Orbison); Constant Craving; Mind of Love; Miss Chatelaine; Just Keep Me Moving; If I Were You. Honours: Canadian CMA Awards: Entertainer of Year, 1989; Album of Year, 1990; Grammy Awards: Best Female Country Vocal Performance, 1990; Best Pop Vocal, 1993; Album of the Year, Ingénue, 1993; Best Traditional Pop Vocal Album, 2004; American Music Award: Favourite New Artist, 1993; Songwriter of The Year, with Ben Mink, 1993; BRIT Award, Best International Female, 1995.

LANGE Jessica, b. 20 April 1949, Cloquet, Minnesota, USA. Actress. m. Paco Grande, 1970, divorced, 1 daughter with Mikhail Baryshnikov; 1 son, 1 daughter with Sam Shepard. Education: University of Minnesota; Mime, Etienne DeCroux, Paris. Appointments: Dancer, Opera Comique, Paris; Model, Wilhelmina Agency, New York. Creative Works: Films include: King Kong, 1976; All That Jazz, 1979; How to Beat the High Cost of Living, 1980; The Postman Always Rings Twice, 1981; Frances, Tootsie, 1982; Country, 1984; Sweet Dreams, 1985; Crimes of the Heart, 1986; Everybody's All American, 1989; Far North, 1991; Night and the City, 1993; Losing Isaiah, Rob Roy, Blue Sky, 1994; A Thousand Acres, 1997; Hush, Cousin Bette, 1998; Titus, 1999; Prozac Nation, Normal, Masked and Anonymous, Great Performances, Big Fish, 2003; Don't Come Knockin', Neverwas, 2005; Bonneville, 2006; Play: Long Day's Journey Into Night, 2000; Star Showtime TV Production, Cat On A Hot Tin Roof, 1984. Honours include: Theatre World Award, Golden Globe, 1996. Address: c/o CAA, Ron Meyer, 9830 Wilshire Boulevard, Beverly Hills, CA 90212, USA.

LANGE Roderyk, b. 5 October 1930, Bydgoszcz, Poland. Choreologist; Anthropologist. Widower. 1 son. Education: Dance Studies prior to university; Movement and Notation studies, Folkwang Hochschule, Essen, Germany, 1959; MA, Cultural Anthropology, Universities of Toruń and Wrocław, Poland, 1965; PhD, Polish University, London, 1975; Habilitation, 1977; Professor nomination, 1979. Appointments: Lecturer, Laban Art of Movement Studio, Addlestone, Surrey, 1967-1972; Lecturer, Queen's University, Belfast, Northern Ireland, 1975-82; Director, Centre for Dance Studies, Jersey, Channel Islands, UK, 1971-2003; Lecturer, Laban Centre, Goldsmiths' College, London University, 1976-93; Professor, Polish University, London, 1979-92; Professor, A Mickiewicz University, Poznań, Poland, 1989-2003; Director, Institute of Choreology, Poznań, Poland, 1993-; Lecturer, Academy of Music, Warsaw, Poland, 1999-; Leader of the European Seminar for Kinetography, 1980-96. Publications: Numerous publications on the anthropology of dance, movement analysis and notation; Monographs include: The Nature of Dance: An Anthropological Perspective, 1975; Handbook of Kinetography according to the Laban-Knust method, 1975; Folklore of Cuiavia (co-author), 1979; Guidelines for Fieldwork on Traditional Dance: Methods and Checklist, 1984. Honours: Honorary Citizen of Poznań, Poland, 1988; Oskar Kolberg Medal, Warsaw, 1990; Chevalier de L'Ordre des Arts et des Lettres, Paris, 2005. Memberships: Fellow, Royal Anthropological Institute, London; Co-chairperson, ICTM Study Group of Ethnochoreology, 1986-92; Fellow, International Council of Kinetography Laban; Member, Conseil International de la Danse, UNESCO, Paris and of other scholarly associations. Address: The Lodge – Hamptonne, La Rue de la Hague, St Peter, Jersey, JE3 7DB, Channel Islands.

LANGHAM John Michael, b. 12 January 1924, Stroxton, UK. Chartered Engineer. m. Irene Elizabeth Morley, 2 sons, 1 daughter. Education: MA (Cantab), Mechanical Sciences Tripos, Queen's College, Cambridge, England; Administrative

Staff College. Appointments: Engineer Officer, Royal Navy, 1944-46; Various Appointments, 1947-67, Executive Director, 1967-80, Stone-Platt Industries, plc; Director, BPB Industries plc, 1976-92; Chairman: Vacu-Lug Traction Tyres Ltd, 1973-95; Chairman, Langham Industries, Ltd, 1980-; External Appointments: Member, CBI Council, 1967-79; Chairman, CBI Production Committee, 1970-79; Member, Executive Board, British Standards Institute, 1969-76; Deputy Chairman, Quality Assurance Council, 1971-79; Member, General Council, 1974-82, Member, Management Board, 1979-82, Vice-President, Executive Committee, 1978-82, E.E.F. Publications: Presented British Exchange Paper to 21st International Foundry Congress, Italy; Article: The Manufacture of Marine Propellers with Particular Reference to the Foundry. Honours: Commander of the Order of the British Empire (CBE); Diploma, Institute of British Foundrymen, 1954, 1963; British Foundry Medal and Prize, 1955; Award of American Foundrymen's Society, Detroit Congress, 1962, Dorset Business Man of the Year, 1996. Memberships: Fellow, Institution of Mechanical Engineers; Fellow, Institute of Marine Engineers; Fellow, Institute of British Foundrymen, Companion of the Institute of Management. Address: Bingham's Melcombe, Dorchester, Dorset DT2 7PZ, England.

LANKA Vaclav, b. 25 October 1941, Hredle, near Rakovník, Czech Republic. Teacher. 1 son. Education: Diploma, Faculty of Natural Science, Charles University, Prague, 1974; Diploma Biologist. Appointments: Teacher, to 1994; Vice-Mayor, Town of Rakovník, 1994-98; Currently Teacher. Publications: Co-author, books: Amphibians and Reptiles, 11 editions, 6 languages, 1985; Wolfgang Böhme, 1999; Handbuch der Reptilien und Amphibien Europas, Vol 3/IIA; Monographs: Dice Snake, Natrix tessellata, 1975; Variabilität und Biologie der Würfelnatter, Natrix tessellata LAURENTI, 1976; Several hundred popular articles on nature and ecology; Several hundred specialist and popular lectures. Membership: Entomological Society of the Czech Republic, 1956-; Species Survival Commission, International Union for the Conservation of Nature and Natural Resources. Address: Jilská ul. 1061, 269 01 Rakovník, Czech Republic.

LANSBURY Angela Brigid, b. 16 October 1925, United Kingdom. Actress. m. (2) P Shaw, 1949, 1 son, 1 step-son, 1 daughter. Education: School of Singing and Dramatic Art, London; School of Drama and Radio, New York. Career: with MGM, 1943-50; Freelance, 1951-; Films include: Gas Light, National Velvet, 1944; The Picture of Dorian Gray, 1945; If Winter Comes, The Three Musketeers, 1948; Kind Lady, 1951; Please Murder Me, 1956; The Reluctant Debutante, 1958; Blue Hawaii, 1961; The Greatest Story Ever Told, The Amorous Adventures of Moll Flanders, 1965; Bedknobs and Broomsticks, 1971; Death on the Nile, 1978; The Mirror Crack'd, The Lady Vanishes, 1980; The Pirates of Penzance, 1982; The Company of Wolves, 1983; Voice of Mrs Potts in Beauty and the Beast, 1991; Nanny McPhee, 2005; Theatre includes: Broadway debut in Hotel Paradiso, 1957; Mame, New York Winter Garden, 1966-68; Gypsy, 1974; Anna, The King and I, 1978; Sweeny Todd, 1979; Mame, 1983; Deuce, 2007; TV includes: Madeira! Madeira!, The Ming Llama, Lace, Murder She Wrote, 1984-96; The Shell Seekers, 1989; Miss Arris Goes to Paris, 1992; Mrs Santa Claus, 1996; South by Southwest, 1997; A Story to Die For, 2000; The Blackwater Lightship, 2004; Law & Order: Special Victims Unit, 2005; Law & Order: Trial by Jury, 2005.; Kingdom Hearts II (voice), 2005. Publication: Positive Moves, co-author and video. Honours include: Academy Award Nomination, Best Supporting Actress, 1944; Nomination, Academy Award, The

Manchurian Candidate; Pudding Theatre Woman of the Year, 1968; Antoinette Perry Awards for Mame, 1968; Dear World, 1969; Gypsy, 1975; Sweeney Todd, 1982; Sarah Siddons Awards, 1974, 1980; BAFTA Lifetime Achievement Award, 1992; CBE; National Medal of Arts, 1997; Nomination, 16 Emmy Awards; Winner, 6 Golden Globe Awards, nominated 8 Golden Globe Awards. Address: c/o MCA Universal, 100 Universal City Plaza, Universal City, CA 91608, USA.

LANSING Sherry, b. 31 July 1944, Chicago, Illinois, USA. Business Executive. m. (2) William Friedkin, 1991. Education: BS, Northwestern University, Evanston, Illinois. Appointments: Mathematics Teacher, Public High Schools, Los Angeles, California, 1966-69; Model, TV commercials, Max Factor Co and Alberto-Culver, 1969-70; Appeared in films Loving and Rio Lobo, 1970; Executive Story Editor, Wagner International, 1970-93; Vice-President for Production, Heyday Productions, 1973-75; Executive Story Editor, then Vice-President for Creative Affairs, MGM Studios, 1975-77; Vice-President, then Senior Vice-President for Production, Columbia Pictures, 1977-80; President, 20th Century Fox Productions, 1980-83; Founder, Jaffe-Lansing Productions, Los Angeles, 1982-; Produced films including Racing with the Moon, 1984, Firstborn, 1984; Fatal Attraction, 1987; The Accused, 1989; Black Rain, 1990; School Ties, 1992; Indecent Proposal, 1993; The Untouchables: Capone Rising, 2006; Chairperson, Paramount Pictures, 1992-. Honour: Jean Hersholt Humanitarian Award, 2007. Address: Paramount Pictures Corporation, 555 Melrose Avenue, Los Angeles, CA 90038, USA.

LANZINGER Klaus, b. 16 February 1928, Wörgl, Tyrol, Austria. University Professor. m. Aida Schüssl, 1 son, 1 daughter. Education: BA, Bowdoin College, Brunswick, Maine, USA, 1951; PhD, University of Innsbruck, Austria, 1952. Appointments: Research Assistant, University of Innsbruck, 1957-67; Associate Professor, 1967-77, Professor of Modern Languages, 1977-97, Professor Emeritus, 1997-, University of Notre Dame, Indiana; Chairman, Department of German and Russian, 1989-96. Publications: Epik im amerikanischen Roman, 1965; Editor, Americana-Austriaca, 5 vols, 1966-83; Jason's Voyage: The Search for the Old World in American Literature, 1989; America – Europe: A Transatlantic Diary 1961-1989, online 2006; Articles include: The Foreign Response to the Declaration of Independence, 1978; Thomas Wolfe's Modern Hero: Goethe's Faust, 1983; Jason's Voyage: The International Theme of Thomas Wolfe, 1992. Honours: Fulbright Research Grant, 1961; Zelda Gitlin Literary Prize, Thomas Wolfe Society, 1993; Lifetime Achievement Award, IBC. Memberships: Modern Language Association of America (MLA); Deutsche Gesellschaft für Amerkastudien; European Association for American Studies; Thomas Wolfe Society. Address: 52703 Helvie Drive, South Bend, IN 46635, USA.

LAPTEV Vladimir, b. 28 April 1924, Moscow, Russia. Professor of Law. m. Maya Lapteva, 2 sons. Education: Graduate, Law Department, Moscow Institute for Foreign Trade, 1949. Appointments: Chief of Section of Economic Law, Institute of State and Law of Russian Academy of Sciences, Moscow, 1959; Chief, Centre of Entrepreneurial and Economic Law, 1992; Chief scientific researcher of the Institute, 1997; Head of Chair of Entrepreneurial Law of Academic Law University, Moscow, 1997. Publications: More than 350 scientific books and articles in fields of economic and entrepreneurial law. Honour: Professor, Doctor of Law,

Honoured Scientist of Russian Federation. Membership: Russian Academy of Sciences. Address: Institute of State and Law, Znamenka 10, Moscow, Russia.

LARA Brian Charles, b. 2 May 1969, Santa Cruz. Cricketer. Appointments: Started playing cricket aged 6; Played football for Trinidad Under 14; Played cricket for West Indies Under-19; Captain, West Indies Youth XI against India, scoring 186; Left-Hand Batsman; Teams: Trinidad and Tobago, 1987-, Captain 1993-; Warwickshire, 1994, Captain 1988; Making world record 1st class score of 501 not out, including most runs in a day, 390, and most boundaries in an innings, 72, v Durham, Edgbaston, 1994; 112 Tests for West Indies 1990-, 18 as Captain, scoring 10,094 runs, average 52.84, including 26 hundreds, highest score 400, world record v England, St John's, Antigua, 2004; Has scored 19,835 1st class runs, 55 hundreds, to 2002, including 2,066 off 2,262 balls for Warwickshire, 1994, with 6 hundreds in his first 7 innings; Toured England, 1991, 1995; 246 One Day Internationals, scoring 9,031 runs (average 42.39); Retired, 2007. Honours: Wisden Cricketer of the Year, 1995; Federation of International Cricketers' Associations International Cricketer of the Year, 1999. Publication: Beating the Field, autobiography, 1995. Address: c/o West Indies Cricket Board, PO Box 616, St John's, Antigua.

LARGE Andrew McLeod Brooks (Sir), b. 7 August 1942, Goudhurst, Kent, England. Banker and Regulatory Official. m. Susan Melville, 1967, 2 sons, 1 daughter. Education: University of Cambridge; Euorpean Institute of Business Administration, Fontainebleau; MA, Economics; MBA. Appointments: British Petroleum, 1964-71; Orion Bank Ltd, 1971-79; With Swiss Bank Corporation, 1980-89, as Managing Director, 1980-83, Chief Executive, Deputy Chairman, 1983-87, Group Chief Executive, 1987-88, SBCI London; Board, Swiss Bank Corporation, 1988-90; Non-Executive Director, English China Clays, 1991-96; Chairman, Large, Smith and Walter, 1990-92; Chairman, Securities and Investments Board, 1992-97; Member, Board on Banking Supervision, 1996-97, Deputy Governor, 2002-, Bank of England; Deputy Chairman, 1997-2002, Director, 1998-2002, Barclays Bank; Chairman, Euroclear, 1998-2000. Address: Bank of England, Threadneedle Street, London EC2R 8AH, England. Website: www.bankofengland.co.uk

LARSON Gary, b. 14 August 1950, Tacoma, Washington, USA. Cartoonist. m. Toni Carmichael, 1988. Education: Washington State University. Career: Performed in jazz duo, 1972-75; Worked in a music store; Sold first cartoons to Pacific Search magazine; Subsequently sold cartoons to Seattle Times, San Francisco Chronicle, Chronicle Features Syndicate; Founder, FarWorks Inc; Announded retirement, 1994. Exhibitions include: The Far Side of Science, California Academy of Sciences, 1985; Smithsonian National Museum of Natural History; American Museum of Natural History, New York; Los Angeles County Museum of Natural History; Films: Gary Larson's Tales from The Far Side, 1994; Gary Larson's Tales from The Far Side II, 1997. Publications: The Far Side; Beyond The Far Side; In Search of The Far Side; Bride of The Far Side; Valley of The Far Side; It Came From The Far Side; Hound of The Far Side; The Far Side Observer; Night of the Crash-test Dummies; Wildlife Preserve; Wiener Dog Art; Unnatural Selections; Cows of Our Planet; The Chickens Are Restless; The Curse of Madame "C"; Last Chapter and Verse, 1996; Anthologies: The Far Side Gallery 1, 2, 3, 4 and 5; The PreHistory of The Far Side; There's A Hair in My Dirt! A Worm's Story, 1998. Honours: National Cartoonists Society Award for best syndicated panel of 1985;

Outstanding Cartoonist of the Year Award, 1991, 1994; Max and Moritz Prize for Best International Cartoon, 1993; Insect named in his honour, Strigiphilus garylarsoni (biting louse), also butterfly, Serratoterga larsoni; Grand Prix, Annecy Film Festival, 1995. Address: c/o Andrews McMell Publishing, 4520 Main Street, Suite 700, Kansas City, MO 64111, USA. Website: www.thefarside.com

LASKIER Michael M, b. 5 May 1949, Givataim, Israel. Historian. m. Anat, 1 son, 1 daughter. Education: BA (magna cum laude), 1971, MA, 1973, PhD, 1979, University of California at Los Angeles. Appointments: Associate Director, New York Office, Alliance Israelite Universelle, 1979-80; Lecturer, Jewish and Middle East History Departments, Tel-Aviv University, 1980-89; Louis Susman Associate Professor of History, Spertus College of Judaica, Chicago, USA, 1990-91; Executive Director, The Sephardic Educational Center, Los Angeles, USA, 1992-94; Adjunct Associate Professor of History, 1993-94; Associate Professor of History and Political Science, Chair, Political Science Department, Ashqelon Academic College, 1995-2003; Associate Professor, 2002-2005, Professor, 2005-, Department of Middle East History; Director, Menachem Begin Center for the study of Resistance and Underground Movements, 2006, Bar-Ilan University. Publications: Author/editor, numerous books; Over 40 refereed chapters in books; 86 refereed articles in journals; 27 book reviews. Honours: US National Jewish Book Award, 1994. Memberships: Association for Jewish Studies, USA; Israel Oriental Society. Address: Shimon Ben-Tzvi 40, Apt #63, Givataim 53633, Israel. E-mail: michael1949@barak-online.net

LATHAM Anthony John Heaton, b. 30 October 1940, Wigan, England. Retired University Lecturer; Musician; Writer. m. Dawn Catherine Farleigh, 10 November 1990, 1 son. Education: Merton College, Oxford, 1959-60; BA (Hons) Medieval and Modern History, Birmingham, 1964; PhD, African Studies, Birmingham, 1970. Appointments: Lecturer and Senior Lecturer, University of Wales, Swansea, 1967-2003; Visiting Professor, University of Illinois, 1979, 1988. Publications: CD, John Latham's Jazz Timers, Sandy & Co, 1998; CD, Oxford Jazz Through the Years 1926-1963, 2002; CD, John Latham's Jazz Timers, with Bill Nicholes, 2004; Discographies: Sandy Brown, 1995; Al Fairweather, 1994; Stan Greig, 1995; Articles in Jazz Journal, Journal of International Association of Jazz Record Collectors, Jazz Rag, Just Jazz; British Jazz Times; New Orleans Music; Oxford Today; New Oxford Dictionary of National Biography, 2004. Honours: Postmastership, Merton College, Oxford, 1959; Baxter Prize for Local History, University of Birmingham, 1964. Membership: Musicians' Union; Secretary, Sandy Brown Society. Address: 2 Church Meadow, Reynoldston, Swansea SA3 1AF, Wales.

LATYSHEV Pyotr Mikhailovich, b. 30 August 1948, Khmelnitsky, Ukraine. Politician; Security Officer. m. 2 sons. Education: Omsk Higher School of Ministry of Internal Affairs, Academy of Ministry of Internal Affairs. Appointments: Inspector, the Head, Perm Division for the Fight against Economic Crime, 1970-86; Head, Department of Internal Affairs, Perm oblast, 1986-91; People's Deputy of the Russian Federation, 1990-93; Member of the Committee of Supreme Soviet on Law and the Fight against Crime, 1993; Head, Department of Internal Affairs Krasnador Territory, 1991-94; Deputy Minister of Internal Affairs Russian Federation, 1994-2000; Plenipotentiary Representative of the President of the Russian Federation in the Urals Federal District, 2000-. Honours: State Orders. Address: Office of the

Plenipotentiary Representative of the President of the Russian Federation in the Urals Federal District, Oktyabrskaya pl 3, 620031 Yekaterinburg, Russia. Website: www.uralfo.ru

LAU Mo Kiu, b. 28 December 1955, Toishan, Guangdoug, China. Radiologist. m. Mei Chen Li, 1 son. Education: MD, China Medical College, Taiwan, 1986; Resident, Cathay General Hospital, Taipei, 1986-90; Resident, National Taiwan University Hospital, 1990; Diplomate, Diagnostic Radiology. Appointments: Attendant Radiologist, Cathay General Hospital, Taipei, 1990-98; Director of Medical Imaging, Yee Zen General Hospital, Taiwan, 1998-2004; Radiologist, Saint Paul Hospital, 2004-06; Radiologist, Hwa Young Hospital, 2006-08. Publications: Eosinophilic gastroenteritis involving esophagus and CBD, a case report; The value of CT in the evaluation and intervention of pregnancy related complications; Delayed CT for retrocaval ureter, a case report; The value of modified Rosenberg method of knee; A custom-made remote injection device for HSG and others; Production of High Quality Black and White Slides with Colour Film and Standard Viewboxes; Is it infallible to identify opaque stone on a single KUB before an IVP study; The value of after contrast opaque stone in IVU; Alagille syndrome a case report; MRI of normal aortomesenteric angle related data; MRI of Ebstein's anomaly; MRI in Asplenia with congenital cardiovascular disease; MRI of acoustic schwannoma; The policy of reduced CT dose in children in Taiwan; What volume of contrast medium is applicable for an IVU study?; The Incidence of failure to detect fracture on one view radiograph; The value of KUB in the primary screening of mature ovarian cyst teratoma. Honours: Listed in Who's Who publications and biographical dictionaries. Memberships: American Roentgen Ray Society; European Society of Paediatric Radiology. Address: No 2 Chang Ping Street, Lane 82, 4th Floor, Hsin Chuang 242, Taipei, Taiwan, Republic of China.

LAUDA Andreas-Nikolaus, b. 22 February 1949, Vienna, Austria. Racing Driver. m. Marlene Knaus, 1976, 2 sons. Appointments: Competed in hill climbs, 1968, later in Formula 3, Formula 2, Sports Car Racing; Winner, 1972 John Player Brit Formula 2 Championship; Started Formula 1 racing in 1971; World Champion, 1975, 1977, 1984, runner-up, 1976; Founder, Owner, Own Airline, Austria. Creative Works: Grand Prix Wins: 1974 Spanish, Ferrari, 1974 Dutch, Ferrari, 1975 Monaco, Ferrari, 1975 Belgian, Ferrari, 1975 Swedish, Ferrari, 1975 French, Ferrari, 1975 US, Ferrari, 1976 Brazilian, Ferrari, 1976 South African, Ferrari, 1976 Belgian, Ferrari, 1976 British, Ferrari, 1977 South African, Ferrari, 1977 German, Ferrari, 1977 Dutch, Ferrari, 1978 Swedish, Brabham-Alfa Romeo, 1978 Italian, Brabham-Alfa Romeo; Retired, 1979; Returned to racing, 1981; Won US Formula 1 Grand Prix, British Grand Prix, 1982, Dutch Grand Prix, 1985; Retired, 1985; Chair, Lauda Air, -2000; CEO Ford's Premier Performance Division, 2001-02; Head, Jaguar Racing Team, 2001-02. Honours include: Victoria Sporting Club International Award for Valour, 1977. Address: Sta Eulalia, Ibiza, Spain.

LAUDER Leonard Alan, b. 19 March 1933, New York City, New York, USA. Business Executive. m. Evelyn Hausner, 1959, 2 sons. Education: Wharton School, University of Pennsylvania. Appointments: Joined, 1958, Executive Vice-President, 1962-72, President, 1972-, Chief Executive Officer, 1982-, now also Chairman, Estee Lauder Inc, cosmetics and fragrance company, New York; Trustee, University of Pennsylvania, 1977-; President, Whitney Museum of American Art, 1977-; Trustee, Aspen Institute

for Humanistic Studies, 1978-; Governor, Joseph H Lauder Institute of Management and International Studies, 1983-. Address: Estee Lauder Inc, 767 Fifth Avenue, New York, NY 10153, USA.

LAUGHTON Anthony Seymour (Sir), b. 29 April 1927. Oceanographic Scientist. m. (1) Juliet A Chapman, 1957, dissolved 1962, 1 son, (2) Barbara C Bosanquet, 1973, 2 daughters. Education: King's College, Cambridge; John Murray Student, Columbia University, New York, 1954-55; PhD. Appointments: Served Royal Naval Volunteer Reserve, 1945-48; Oceanographer, 1955-88, later Director, National Institute of Oceanography, later Institute of Oceanographic Sciences; Member, 1974-, Chairman, 1986-, Joint IOC-IHO Guiding Committee, GEBCO, ocean charts; Member, 1981-, Chairman, 1995-, Governing Body, Charterhouse School; Council, University College, London, 1983-93; Co-ordinating Committee for Marine Science and Technology, 1987-91; Trustee, Natural History Museum, 1990-95. Publications: Papers on marine geophysics. Honours: Silver Medal, Royal Society of Arts, 1958; Prince Albert the 1st of Monaco Gold Medal, 1980; Founders Medal, Royal Geographical Society, 1987; Murchison, Geological Society, 1989. Memberships: Fellow, Royal Society; President, Challenger Society for Marine Science, 1988-80; President, Society for Underwater Technology, 1995-97; President, Hydrographic Society, 1997-99. Address: Okelands, Pickhurst Road, Chiddingfold, Surrey GU8 4TS, England.

LAUNDER Brian Edward, b. 20 July 1939, United Kingdom. Professor. m. Dagny Simonsen, 1 son, 1 daughter. Education: BScEng, Imperial College London; SM, ScD, Massachusetts Institute of Technology; DScEng, University of London; DSc, University of Manchester; DEng, UMIST. Appointments: Research Assistant, Massachusetts Institute of Technology, 1961-64; Lecturer in Mechanical Engineering, 1964-72, Reader in Fluid Mechanics, 1972-76, Imperial College London; Professor of Mechanical Engineering, University of California Davis, 1976-80; Professor of Mechanical Engineering, 1980-98, Head of Thermodynamics and Fluid Mechanics Division, 1980-90, Head of Mechanical Engineering Department, 1983-85, 1993-95, Research Professor, 1998-, Chairman Environmental Strategy Group, 1998-2004, UMIST (now University of Manchester since October 2004); Adjunct Professor, Pennsylvania State University, 1984-88; Associate Editor ASME Fluids Engineering Journal, 1978-81; Editor-in-Chief, International Journal of Heat and Fluid Flow, 1987-; Regional Director, Tyndall Centre for Climate Change Research, 2000-05. Publications: Mathematical Models of Turbulence (with D B Spalding), 1972; Turbulence Models and Their Application (with W C Reynolds and W Rodi), 1985; Closure Strategies for Turbulent and Transitional Flows (with N Sandham), 2002; Author of over 250 scientific articles. Honours: Honorary Professor, Nanjing University of Aeronautics and Astronautics, People's Republic of China, 1993; Hon DUniv, INP, Toulouse and Aristotle University of Thessaloniki, Greece; FRS; FREng, 1994; James Clayton Lifetime Research Achievement Prize, 2004 Memberships: FIMechE, 1981; FASME, 1983; FRAeS, 1996. Address: Department of Mechanical, Aerospace and Civil Engineering, The University of Manchester, PO Box 88, Manchester M60 1QD, England. E-mail: brian.launder@manchester.ac.uk

LAUREN Ralph, b. 14 October 1939, Bronx, New York, USA. Couturier. m. Ricky L Beer, 1964, 3 sons. Appointments: Salesman, Bloomingdale's, New York, Brooks Brothers, New York; Assistant Buyer, Allied Stores, New York; Representative, Rivetz Necktie Manufacturers, New York; Neckwear Designer,

Polo Division, Beau Brummel, New York, 1967-69; Founder, Polo Menswear Company, New York, 1968-, Ralph Lauren's Women's Wear, New York, 1971-, Polo Leathergoods, 1978-, Polo Ralph Lauren Luggage, 1982-, Ralph Lauren Home Collection, 1983-; Chair, Polo Ralph Lauren Corporation, 66 stores in USA, over 140 worldwide. Honours: Several fashion awards, including: American Fashion Award, 1975; Council of Fashion Designers of America Award, 1981. Address: Polo Ralph Lauren Corporation, 650 Madison Avenue, New York, NY 10022, USA.

LAURENTS Arthur, b. 14 July 1917, New York, New York, USA. Dramatist; Writer; Director. Education: BA, Cornell University, 1937. Publications: Plays: Home of the Brave, 1946; The Bird Cage, 1950; The Time of the Cuckoo, 1952; A Clearing in the Woods, 1956; Invitation to a March, 1960; The Enclave, 1973; Scream, Houston, 1978; The Hunting Season, The Radical Mystique, Jolson Sings Again, 1995; My Good Name, 1997; Big Potato, 2000; Venecia, Claude Lazlo, 2001; The Vibrator, Closing Bell, 2002; Attacks on the Heart, Two Lives, 2003; Collected Plays, 2004. Musical Plays: West Side Story, 1957; Gypsy, 1959; Anyone Can Whistle, Do I Hear a Waltz?, 1964; Hallelujah Baby, 1967; Nick and Nora, 1991. Screenplays: The Snake Pit, Rope, Caught, 1948; Anna Lucasta, 1949; Anastasia, 1956; Bonjour Tristesse, 1958; The Way We Were, 1973; The Turning Point, 1977. Novels: The Way We Were, 1972; The Turning Point, 1977; Original Story By (memoir), 2000. Honours: Tony Awards, 1967, 1984; Drama Desk Awards, 1974, 1978; Golden Glove Award, 1977; Writers Guild of America, 1977; Best Director Award, 1985; William Inge Festival Award, 2004. Memberships: Academy of Motion Picture Arts and Sciences; Authors League; Dramatists Guild; PEN; Screenwriters Guild; Theatre Hall of Fame. Address: c/o William Morris Agency, 1325 Avenue of the Americas, New York, NY 10019, USA.

LAURIE Hugh, b. 11 June 1959, Oxford, England. Actor; Comedian. m. Jo, 2 sons, 1 daughter. Education: Cambridge University. Appointments: President, Footlights, Cambridge University; TV Appearances include: Santa's Last Christmas; Alfresco, The Crystal Cube, 1983; Mrs Capper's Birthday, 1985; Saturday Live (writer), 1986; A Bit of Fry and Laurie, 1989-91; The Laughing Prisoner, Blackadder the Third, Up Line, 1987; Blackadder: The Cavalier Years, Les Girls, Blackadder's Christmas Carol, 1988; Blackadder Goes Forth, Hysteria 2! 1989; Jeeves and Wooster, 1990-92; Treasure Island, All or Nothing at All, 1993; Look at the State We're In! (also director), The Adventures of Mole, 1995; The Best of Tracey Takes On..., 1996; The Place of Lions, 1997; Blackadder Back & Forth, 1999; Little Grey Rabbit, Preston Pig, 2000; Life with Judy Garland: Me and My Shadows, Second Star to the Left, 2001; Spooks, 2002; Stuart Little, Fortysomething (also director), The Young Visiters, 2003; House, 2004-; Film Appearances include: Plenty, 1985; Strapless, 1989; Peter's Friends, 1992; A Pin for the Butterfly, 1994; Sense and Sensibility, 1995; 101 Dalmatians, The Snow Queen's Revenge, 1996; The Borrowers, Spice World, The Ugly Duckling, 1997; The Man in the Iron Mask, Cousin Bette, 1998; Stuart Little, 1999; Carnivale, Maybe Baby, Lounge Act, 2000; The Piano Tuner, Chica de Rio, 2001; Stuart Little 2, 2002; Flight of the Phoenix, 2004; Valiant (voice), Stuart Little 3: Call of the Wild, The Big Empty, 2005. Publications: Fry and Laurie 4, (with Stephen Fry), 1994; The Gun Seller, 1996. Honours: Golden Globe Award, Best Actor in a TV Series, 2006. Address: Hamilton Asper Ltd, Ground Floor, 24 Hanway Street, London W1P 9DD, England.

LAURIE Richard Thomas, b. 4 October 1935, Bagshot, Surrey, England. Writer; Musician; Gardener. m. Susan Dring, divorced, 2 sons; 1 daughter. Education: Bradfield College 1949-1954. Appointments: National Service, 2 Lieutenant, RASC; Creative Director, Brockie Haslam, 1970-81; Group Head, Ted Bates, 1982-84; Band Leader, Dick Laurie's Elastic Band, 1983-; Creative Director, Breen Bryan Laurie and Dempsey, 1985-89; Creative Director, The Medicine Men 1993-; Producer, Zephyr Records, 1995-2000; Director, The Jobbing Gardener, 2002-. Publications: Editor: Soho Clarion, 1977-99, Docklands Business News, 1994-96, Journal for European Private Hospitals, 1995-96; Founder/ Publisher/Editor, Allegedly Hot News International, 1987-; Numerous articles, reviews and interviews. Memberships: Soho Society Executive Committee, 1976-2000, Advertising Creative Circle Council Member 1980-90; Director, Creative Circle Radio Workshop, 1988-90; Listed in Who's Who publications and biographical dictionaries. Address: 27 Clarendon Drive, Putney, London SW15 1AW, England. E-mail: alasdick@waitrose.com

LAURSEN (Kirsten Marie) Benedicte, b. 6 September 1933, Trustrup, Denmark. Doctor of Medical Science. Education: MD, Copenhagen University, Denmark, 1961; Authorised Specialist of Internal Medicine, 1969, Authorised Specialist of Haematology, 1983, National Health Service, Denmark. Appointments: Specialist Training, different departments in University Hospitals, Copenhagen, 1963-80; Extensive teaching and lecturing activity, 1963-2004; Consultant, Associate Head, Department of Haematology and Internal Medicine B, 1980-2004, Aalborg Hospital; Retired, 2004-. Publications: Over 50 papers and articles in professional medical journals. Honours: Research Fellowship, Department of Internal Medicine, Enzymology, Washington University School of Medicine, St Louis, Missouri, USA, 1970-71; Member, Regional Scientific Ethical Committee, 1990-98. Memberships: Danish Medical Association; Danish Society of Haematology; International Society of Haematology; Danish Central Scientific Ethical Committee, 1994-98. Address: Skolemestervej 10, 9000 Aalborg, Denmark.

LAVENDER Justin, b. 4 June 1951, Bedford, England. Opera Singer. m. Louise Crane, 1 son, 1 daughter. Education: Queen Mary College, University of London; Guildhall School of Music and Drama. Career: Operatic Tenor; Leading roles with most of the world's major opera houses, 1980-; Title role, Faust (Gounod) Royal Opera, Covent Garden, 2004; Concert engagements with major orchestras and conductors worldwide; Numerous recordings, most recently Schnittka's Faust Cantata. Publications: Regular contributions to The Irish Examiner, original articles and book reviews, 1996-; Contributions to various professional journals. Membership: Newlands Rowing Club. Address: c/o Athole Still International Management Ltd, 25-27 Westow Street, London SE19 3RY, England.

LAVER Rod(ney) George, b. 9 August 1938, Rockhampton, Queensland, Australia. Tennis Player. m. Mary Benson, 1966, 1 son. Education: Rockhampton High School. Career: Played Davis Cup for Australia, 1958, 1959, 1960, 1961, 1962, and first open Davis Cup, 1973; Australian Champion, 1960, 1962, 1969; Wimbledon Champion, 1961, 1962, 1968, 1969; USA Champion, 1962, 1969; French Champion, 1962, 1969; First player to win double Grand Slam, 1962, 1969; Professional from 1963; First Player to win over 1,000,000 US $ in prize money. Publications: How to Play Winning Tennis, 1964; Education of a Tennis Player, 1971. Honours: Member, Order of the British Empire; Melbourne Park centre court renamed

Rod Laver Arena in his honour, 2000. Address: c/o Tennis Australia, Private Bag 6060, Richmond South, VIC 3121, Australia.

LAVERDANT Alain Michel, b. 2 February 1954, Thionville, France. Researcher. m. Patricia Simone Vandon, 1 son. Education: Aeronautics Engineer, ETACA, 1976; DEA Meca flu, Energ, 1978, Doctorat 3rd cycle, 1981, Orléans University; Doctor of Sciences, Rouen University, 1991. Appointments: Doctoral Candidate, 1978-81; Research Engineer, 1981-93; Master of Research, 1994. Publications: Papers and articles in professional scientific journals. Honours: Prix Estrade-Delcros; Houllevigue Saintour Jules Mahyer de l'Académie des Sciences, 1991. Address: 9 résidence de la Boële, 91700 Sainte-Geneviève-des-Bois, France. E-mail: laverdan@onera.fr

LAVIELLE Lisette, b. 14 April 1941, Mulhouse, France. Retired Researcher. m. Jean-Pierre Lavielle, 2 daughters. Education: Graduate, Chemical Engineering, École Nationale Supérieure de Chimie, Mulhouse, 1964; Doctor of Engineering, University of Strasbourg, France, 1968; DSc, University of Haute-Alsace, Mulhouse, 1971. Appointments: Research Associate, Thin Films Laboratory, CNRS, École Nationale Supérieure de Chimie, Mulhouse, 1964-70; Research Associate, Mineral Chemistry Laboratory, CNRS, Mulhouse, 1971-76; Engineer, European Society of Propulsion, Vernon, 1978-79; Research Associate, Macromolecular Chemistry Laboratory, CNRS, Rouen, 1980-81; Research Associate, Centre for Physical Chemistry Solid Surfaces, CNRS, Mulhouse, 1981-94; Research Associate, General Photochemistry Department, CNRS, 1995-2001. Publications: Polymer Surface Dynamics, chapter, 1987; Polymer Characterisation by Inverse Gas Chromotography, chapter, 1989; UV Phototreatment of Polymer Film Surface: Self-Organization and Thermodynamics of Irreversible Processes, chapter, 1999. Honour: Recipient, Emilio Noelting Prize, École Nationale Supérieure de Chimie de Mulhouse, 1964. Address: 6 rue la Fayette, 68100 Mulhouse, France.

LAW Jude, b. 29 December 1972, London, England. Actor. m. Sadie Frost, 1997, divorced 2003, 2 sons, 1 daughter. Appointments: National Youth Music Theatre; Co-founder, Natural Nylon (production company), Director, 2000-03; Stage appearances include: Joseph and the Amazing Technicolour Dreamcoat; Les Parents Terribles, 1994; Ior, 1995; Tis Pity She's A Whore, 1999; Doctor Faustus, 2002; Film appearances include: Shopping, 1994; I Love You I Love You Not, 1996; Wilde, 1997; Gattaca, Midnight in the Garden of Good and Evil, 1997; Bent; Music From Another Room, Final Cut, The Wisdom of Crocodiles, 1998; eXistenZ, The Talented Mr Ripley, 1999; Final Cut; Enemy at the Gates, Love Honour and Obey, 2000; Artificial Intelligence: AI, 2001; Road to Perdition, 2002; Cold Mountain, 2003; Sky Captain and the World of Tomorrow, Alfie, I Heart Huckabees, The Aviator, Lemony Snicket's A Series of Unfortunate Events (voice), 2004; All the King's Men, Breaking and Entering, The Holiday, 2006; My Blueberry Nights, Sleuth, 2007. Honours: BAFTA Award, Best Supporting Actor, 1999. Address: c/o Julian Belfrage Associates, 46 Albemarle Street, London, W1S 4DF, England. Website: www.jude-law.net

LAWRENCE Roderick John, b. 30 August 1949, Adelaide, Australia. m. Clarisse Christine Gonet, 3 sons. Education: BArch, University of Adelaide, 1972; MLitt, University of Cambridge, England, 1978; DSc, Ecole Polytechnique Fédérale de Lausanne, Switzerland, 1983. Appointments: Design-Research Architect, South Australian Housing Trust,

Adelaide, 1974; Architect, Percy Thomas Partnership, Cardiff, Wales, 1978; Tutor, Department of Architecture, Ecole Polytechnique Fédérale de Lausanne, 1978-84; Consultant, Committee on Housing Building and Planning, Economic Commission for Europe, 1984-85; Visiting Lecturer, Faculty of Architecture and Town Planning, University of Adelaide, Visiting Research Fellow, School of Social Sciences, Flinders University, 1985; Master of Teaching and Research, Centre for Human Ecology and Environmental Sciences, University of Geneva, 1986; Professor, Faculty of Social and Economic Sciences, 1999-; Member of 4 Scientific Editorial Boards. Publications include: An Ecological Blueprint for Healthy Housing, 1993; Mythical and Ritual Constituents of the City, 1994; Type as Analytical Tool: Reinterpretation and Application, 1994; Sustaining Human Settlement: A Challenge for the New Millennium, 2000. Over 120 articles in scientific journals and 50 book reviews. Honours: Wormald Prize in Architecture, University of Adelaide, 1971; Milne Travelling Scholarship, 1974; Lawson Postgraduate Research Fellowship, 1974; Travel and Study Scholarship, National Science Foundation of Switzerland, 1984; Eurasmus Mundus Professor's Scholarship, 2007-08; Listed in national and international biographical dictionaries. Memberships: Associate Member, Royal British Institute of Architects, 1973-98; People and Physical Environment Research, Sydney; International Association for People – Environment Studies, Guildford, England; Co-ordinator, European Network for Housing Research, Working Group on Housing and Health; Member, Scientific Advisory Board of the World Health Organisation's European Centre for Environment and Health, 1994-98; Member, The New York Academy of Sciences, 1997-; Chairperson, Evaluation Advisory Committee of World Health Organisation's Healthy Cities Project, 1998-; Member, World Health Organization's European Taskforce on Housing and Health, 2001-. Address: Faculty of Social and Economic Sciences, Pole Environment, University of Geneva, Site Battelle, CH-12227 Carouge (CE), Switzerland. E-mail: roderick.lawrence@unige.ch

LAWSON Charles Nicholas, b. 4 May 1940, Crawley, Sussex, England. Publisher. m. Marion Victoria Lawrence, 1 son, 1 daughter. Education: Wellington College, Berkshire, England, 1967-71; Surrey County Technical College, 1971-73; Cambridge College of Arts and Technology, 1973-74. Appointments: Production Director, Hawthorne Press Ltd, 1982-88; Chief Executive, Snipe Publishing, 1988-; Director, Eddison Press Ltd, 1986-; Director, Academy of Children's Writers Ltd, 1986-. Memberships: International Platform Association; Cambridge Business and Professional Club; University of Cambridge Club; National Trust. Address: The Poplars, 90 Aldreth Road, Haddenham, Ely, Cambridgeshire CB6 3PN, England.

LAWSON Dominic Ralph Campbell (Hon), b. 17 December 1956, London, England. Journalist; Editor. m. (1) Jane Fiona Wastell Whytenead, 1982, divorced 1991, (2) Hon Rosamond Monckton, 1991, 2 daughters. Education: Christchurch, Oxford; BA Oxon. Appointments: World Tonight and The Financial World Tonight, BBC, 1979-81; Staff, Energy Correspondent, Lex Columnist, 1987-90, Columnist, 1991-94 The Financial Times; Deputy Editor, 1987-90, Editor, 1990-95, The Spectator; Editor, The Spectator Cartoon Book; Columnist, Sunday Correspondent, 1990; Columnist, Daily Telegraph, 1994-95; Editor, The Sunday Telegraph, 1995-2005; Columnist, The Independent, 2006-. Publications: Korchnoi, Kasparov, 1983; Britain in the Eighties, co-author, 1989; The Spectator Annual, editor, 1992, 1993, 1994; The Inner Game, editor, 1993. Honours: Editor of the Year, Society of Magazine Editors, 1990. Memberships: Fellow, Royal Society of Arts. Address: The Sunday Telegraph, 1 Canada Square, Canary Wharf, London E14 5AR, England.

LAWSON Lesley (Twiggy), b. 19 September 1949, London. England. Model; Singer; Actress. m. (1) Michael Whitney Armstrong, 1977, deceased, 1983, 1 daughter, (2) Leigh Lawson, 1988. Career: Model, 1966-70; Manager, Director, Twiggy Enterprises Ltd, 1966-; Own musical series, British TV, 1975-76; Founder, Twiggy and Co, 1998-; Made several LP records; Appearances in numerous TV dramas, UK and USA; Appeared in films including The Boy Friend, 1971, There Goes the Bride, 1979, Blues Brothers, 1981, The Doctor and the Devils, 1986, Club Paradise, 1986, Harem Hotel, Istanbul, 1988, Young Charlie Chaplin, TV film, 1989, Madame Sousatzka, 1989, Woundings, 1998; Appeared in plays: Cinderella, 1976; Captain Beaky, 1982; My One and Only, 1983-84; Blithe Spirit, Chichester, 1997; Noel and Gertie, USA, 1998; If Love Were All, New York, 1999; Blithe Spirit, New York, 2002; Play What I Wrote, 2002; Mrs Warren's Profession, 2003. Publications: Twiggy: An Autobiography, 1975; An Open Look,1985; Twiggy in Black and White, co-author, 1997. Honours: 2 Golden Globe Awards, 1970. Address: c/o Peters Fraser and Dunlop, Drury House, 34-43 Russell Street, London WC2B 5HA, England. E-mail: postmaster@pfd.co.uk

LAWSON of BLABY, Baron of Newnham in the County of Northamptonshire, Nigel Lawson, b. 11 March 1932, London, England. Politician. m. (1) Vanessa Salmon, divorced. 1980, deceased. 1985, (2) Thérèse Mary Maclear, 1980, 2 sons, 4 daughters, 1 deceased. Education: Christ Church, Oxford; MA Oxon. Appointments: Sub-Lieutenant, Royal Naval Volunteer Reserve, 1954-56; Editorial Staff, Financial Times, 2956-60; City Editor, Sunday Telegraph, 1961-63; Special Assistant to Prime Minister, 1963-64; Columnist, Financial Times and Broadcaster, BBC, 1965; Editor, The Spectator, 1966-70; Regular Contributor to Sunday Times and Evening Standard, 1970-71, The Times, 1971-72; Fellow, Nuffield College, Oxford, 1972-73; Special Political Adviser, Conservative Party Headquarters, 1973-74; Member of Parliament for Blaby, Leicestershire, 1974-92; Opposition Whip, 1976-77; Opposition Spokesman on Treasury and Economic Affairs, 1977-79; Financial Secretary to the Treasury, 1979-81; Secretary of State for Energy, 1981-83; Chancellor of the Exchequer, 1983-89; Non-Executive Director, Barclays Bank, 1990-98; Chairman, Central European Trust, 1990-; Adviser, BZW, 1990-91; Non-Executive Director, Consultant, Guinness Peat Aviation, 1990-93; Director, Institute for International Economics, Washington DC, 1991-; International Advisory Board, Creditanstalt Bankverein, 1991-; International Advisory Board, Total SA, 1994-; Advisory Council, Prince's Youth Business Trust, 1994-; President, British Institute of Energy Economics, 1995-; Chairman, CAIB Emerging Russia Fund, 1997-; Privy Councillor. Publications: The Power Game, co-author, 1976; The View from No 11: Memoirs from a Tory Radical, 1992; The Nigel Lawson Diet Book, co-author, 1996; Various pamphlets. Memberships: President, British Institute of Energy Economics, 1995-; Governing Body, Westminster School, 1999-2005; President, British Institute of Energy Economics, 1995-2004. Honours: Finance Minister of the Year, Euromoney Magazine, 1988; Honorary Student, Christ Church, Oxford, 1996. Address: House of Lords, London SW1A 0PW, England.

LAYARD, Baron of Highgate in the London Borough of Haringey, Peter Richard Grenville, b. 15 March 1934, Welwyn Garden City, England. Economist. m. Molly Meacher, 1991. Education: BA, Cambridge University; MSc, London School of Economics. Appointments: Schoolteacher, London County Council, 1959-61; Senior Research Officer, Robbins Committee on Higher Education, 1961-64; Deputy Director, Higher Education Research Unit, 1964-74, Lecturer, 1968-75, Head, Centre for Labour Economics, 1974-90, Reader, 1975-80, Professor of Economics, 1980-99, Director, Centre for Economic Performance, 1990-, London School of Economics; Consultant, Centre for European Policy Studies, Brussels, 1982-86; University Grants Committee, 1985-89; Chairman, Employment Institute, 1987-92; Ch-Chairman, World Economy Group, World Institute for Development Economics Research, 1989-; Economic Adviser to Russian Government, 1991-97. Publications: Cost Benefit Analysis, 1973; Causes of Poverty, co-author, 1978; Microeconomic Theory, co-author, 1978; More Jobs, Less Inflation, 1982; The Causes of Unemployment, co-editor, 1984; The Rise in Unemployment, co-editor, 1986; How to Beat Unemployment, 1986; Handbook of Labour Economics, co-editor, 1987; The Performance of the British Economy, co-author, 1988; Unemployment: Macroeconomic Performance and the Labour Market, co-author, 1991; East-West Migration: the alternatives, co-author, 1992; Post-Communist Reform: pain and progress, co-author, 1993; Macroeconomics: a text for Russia, 1994; The Coming Russian Boom, co-author, 1996; What Labour Can Do, 1997; Tackling Unemployment, 1999; Tackling Inequality, 1999; What the Future Holds; Happiness: Lessons from a New Science, 2005. Honours: Created Life Peer, 2000. Memberships: Fellow, Econometric Society. Address: 45 Cholmeley Park, London N6 5EL, England.

LE BLANC Matt, b. 25 July 1967, Newton, Massachusetts, USA. Actor. m. Melissa McKnight, 2003, 1 daughter. Education: Newton High School; Trained as carpenter. Career: Actor: Television includes: TV 101, 1988; Top of the Heap, 1991; Vinnie and Bobby, 1992; Red Shoes Diaries, 1993; Friends, 1994-2004; Reform School Girl, 1994; Red Shoes Diaries 7, 1997; Joey, 2004-2006; Commercials: Levi's 501 jeans, Coca Cola, Doritos, Heinz Ketchup; Producer, The Prince, 2006; Films include: Lookin' Italian, 1994; Ed, 1996; Lost in Space, 1998; Charlie's Angels, 2000; All the Queens Men, 2001; Charlie's Angels: Full Throttle, 2003; TV guest appearances include: Just the Ten of Us, 1989; Monsters, 1990; Married... with Children, 1991; The Rosie O'Donald Show, 1996; The Tonight Show with Jay Leno, 1996; Entertainment Tonight, 2003; Opera Winfrey Show, 2003; Celebrities Uncensored, 2003; Tonight with Jay Leno, 2004. Honours: TV Guide Award, 2000; Teen Choice Award, 2002. Address: c/o United Talent Agency, 9560 Wilshire Boulevard, Suite 500, Beverly Hills, CA 90212, USA.

LE BRUN Christopher Mark, b. 20 December 1951, Portsmouth, England. Artist. m. Charlotte Verity, 2 sons, 1 daughter. Education: DFA, Slade School of Fine Art, 1970-74; MA, Chelsea School of Art, 1974-75. Career: Visiting Lecturer: Brighton Polytechnic, 1975-82, Slade School of Fine Art, 1978-83, Wimbledon School of Art, 1981-83; Professor of Drawing, RA, 2000-02, Chair, Education Committee RA, 2000-, Royal Academy; Trustee, Prince of Wales's Drawing School, 2004-; Trustee: Tate Gallery, 1990-95, National Gallery, 1996-2003, Dulwich Picture Gallery, 2000-05; Chair, Academic Advisory Board, Prince of Wales Drawing School, 2004-; Trustee, Princes' Drawing School, 2004-; Numerous one-man and group exhibitions internationally since 1979; Public Collections include: Tate Gallery, British Museum,

Victoria and Albert, MOMA, New York; British Council; National Portrait Gallery; Scottish National Gallery of Modern Art; Walker Art Gallery. Publications: Works feature in: 50 Etchings, 1991; Christopher Le Brun, 2001. Honours: John Moores Liverpool Prizewinner, 1978, 1980; Gulbenkian Printmakers Commission, 1983; DAAD Fellowship, Berlin, 1987-88; Turner Watercolour Medal, 2005. Membership: Royal Academician (RA), 1996. Address: Royal Academy of Arts, Piccadilly, London W1J 0BD, England.

LE MARCHANT Francis Arthur (Sir), b. 6 October 1939, Hungerton, UK. Artist; Farmer. Education: Byam Shaw School of Drawing and Painting; Certificate, RAS, Royal Academy Schools. Career: One man exhibitions include: Museum of Art and Science, Evansville, USA; Agnews; Roy Miles Fine Art; Group exhibitions include: Royal Academy Summer Exhibitions; Leicester Galleries, Spink; Bilan de l'Art Contemporain, Paris; Spink; Collections include: Government Art Collections, 2 paintings; Financial Times; The Museum of Evansville, USA; University of Evansville, USA; Collection of the late Mrs Anne Kessler. Honour: Silver Medal, Bilan de l'Art Contemporain, Paris. Memberships: Savile Club; Reynolds Club (Alumni Association of Royal Academy Schools). Address: c/o HSBC, 88 Westgate, Grantham, Lincolnshire NG31 6LF, England.

LE ROUX Deborah Anne, b. 17 March 1967, Bolton, Lancashire, England. Chiropractor. m. Brian Underwood, 2 sons. Education: BSc, Chiropractic; MSc, Chiropractic. Appointments: Chiropractor, private practitioner, Nailsea. Bristol, England; Regional tutor, postgraduate chiropractic students, North Somerset, England. Publications: Papers and articles for professional national and international journals. Honours: DC, Doctor of Chiropractic; FCC, Ortho, Fellowship of the Faculty of Rehabilitation and Chiropractic Orthopaedics, College of Chiropractors. Memberships: BCA, British Chiropractic Association; GCC, General Council of Chiropractic; CoC, College of Chiropractors; FRCO, Faculty of Rehabilitation and Chiropractic Orthopaedics. Address: Nailsea Chiropractic Clinic, 22 Colliers Walk, Nailsea, Bristol, North East Somerset, BS48 1RG, England.

LEACH Henry (Conyers) (Admiral of the Fleet Sir), b. 18 November 1923. Naval Officer. m. Mary Jean McCall, 1958, deceased 1991, 2 daughters. Education: Royal Naval College, Dartmouth. Appointments: Served cruiser Mauritius, South Atlantic and Indian Ocean, 1941-42, battleship Duke of York, 1943-45, destroyers, Mediterranean, 1945-46; gunnery, 1947; Gunnery appointments, 1948-51; Gunnery Officer, cruiser Newcastle, Far East, 1953-55; Staff appointments, 1955-59; Commanded destroyer Dunkirk, 1959-61; Captain, 27th Squadron and Mediterranean, frigate Galatea, 1965-67; Director of Naval Plans, 1968-70; Commanded Commando Ship Albion, 1970; Assistant Chief of Naval Staff, Policy, 1971-73; Flag Officer, First Flotilla, 1974-75; Vice-Chief of Defence Staff, 1976-77; Commander-in-Chief and Allied Commander-in-Chief, Channel and Eastern Atlantic, 1977-79; Chief of Naval Staff, First Sea Lord, 1979-82; First and Principal ADC to the Queen, 1979-82; Deputy Lieutenant; Chairman, 1987-98, Honorary Vice-President, 1991-, Council, King Edward VII Hospital; Governor, Cranleigh School, 1983-93; Chairman, 1983-98, Honorary Vice-President, 1999-, St Dunstan's; Governor, St Catherine's, 1987-93. Publications: Endure No Makeshifts, autobiography. Honours: Knight Grand Cross, Order of the Bath; Honorary Freeman, Merchant Taylors, Shipwrights, City of London. Memberships: Royal Bath and West of England Society, President, 1993, Vice-President, 1994-; Royal Naval Benevolent Society,

President, 1984-93; Sea Cadet Association, President, 1984-93; Patron, Meridian Trust Association, 1994-; Patron, Hampshire Royal British Legion, 1994-. Address: Wonston Lea, Wonston, Winchester, Hants SO21 3LS, England.

LEAH Philip, b. 23 October 1948, Dulwich, London, England. Music Educator. Divorced, 2 sons. Education: Northern School of Music, Manchester, 1968-71; Awarded GNSM, 1971; Studies in flute, piano and composition; Padgate College of Education, Warrington, 1971-72; Postgraduate Certificate in Education. Appointments: Peripatetic Music Teacher, Glamorgan, 1972-73; Peripatetic Music Teacher, City of Birmingham, 1973-90; Lecturer, North Worcestershire College of Education, 1977-80; University of Wolverhampton, 1982-90; Founder and Musical Director, West Birmingham Schools Wind Band, 1985-90; Founder and Musical Director, Halesowen Symphony Orchestra, 1986-89; Examiner, Guildhall School of Music and Drama, 1988-; Flute Tutor, University of Wales, Aberystwyth, 2000-05. Compositions: Concertino for bass tuba and orchestra; Sinfonia for flute and strings; Acme, a suite for chamber orchestra; Sinfonia for chamber orchestra; Elegy for string sextet; Prelude and Scherzo for string quartet; Three Penny Bit for wind; Wind quintet; Fanfare, 1969; Fanfare for a Golden Jubilee; Conversations for flute and piano; Chorale Prelude on 'Austria' for organ; Wedding Suite for organ; In Annum for tenor solo, SATB choir and string quartet; Winter for SATB choir and string quartet; Song: Meditation for soprano and piano; Psychological Songs for bass voice and piano; Various arrangements for woodwind instruments. Honours: First prize, Horatio Albert Lumb Composition Competition, 1992. Memberships: Royal Society of Musicians of Great Britain; Incorporated Society of Musicians; SPNM (Society for Promotion of New Music); Musicians' Union. Address: 15 Oak Tree Crescent, Lapal, Halesowen, West Midlands, B62 9DA, England. E-mail: philleah@aol.com

LEAPER David John, b. 23 July 1947, York, England. Professor of Surgery. m. Francesca Ann, 1 son, 1 daughter. Education: Leeds Modern Grammar School, 1957-65; MBChB with honours, University of Leeds Medical School, 1970; MD, 1979, ChM, 1982. Appointments: House Officer, Leeds General Infirmary, 1970-71; MRC Fellow, 1971-73; Registrar, Leeds General Infirmary and Scarborough, 1973-76; Senior Registrar in Surgery, CRC Fellow, Westminster and Kings College Hospitals, London, 1976-87; Professor of Surgery, University of Hong Kong, 1988-90; Senior Lecturer in Surgery, University of Bristol, 1981-95; Professor of Surgery, 1995-2004, Emeritus Professor, 2004-, University of Newcastle; Visiting Professor, Cardiff University, 2004-; Visiting Professor, University of Southampton, 2006-; Visiting Professor, Imperial College, London, 2006-; Director, Salisbury Wound Research Centre, 2006-. Publications: Books: International Surgical Practice; Oxford Handbook of Clinical Surgery; Oxford Handbook of Operative Surgery; Handbook of Postoperative Complications: Series: Your Operation, Preparation for the MRCS, 2006; Member, Editorial Board of Medical, Educational and Surgical Journals; Papers on wound healing, surgical infections, colorectal and breast cancer. Honours: Fellow, Royal College of Surgeons of England, 1975, of Edinburgh, 1974, of Glasgow, 1998; Hunterian Professor, 1981-82; Zachary Cope Lecturer, 1998; Fellow, American College of Surgeons, 1998; Past Member, Court of Examiners, Royal College of Surgeons of England; Intercollegiate Fellowship Examiner, 2000-04. Memberships: Founder Member, Past Recorder and Past President, European Wound Management Association; Surgical Infection Society of Europe; Past Vice President, Section of Surgery, Royal

Society of Medicine; Past Committee Member, Surgical Research Society; Programme Director, Higher Surgical Training, Northern Deanery, 2000-04; Member, Specialist Advisory Committee, Higher Surgical Training, UK, 2000-05; Chair, Subcommittee Surgical Site Infection, Steering Group on Healthcare Associated Infection; Day Case Champion, Modernisation Agency, 2002-04; Member, 2015 Forum; Chair, NICE guideline development group, Surgical Site Infection; Expert Member Antimicrobial Resistance and Healthcare Associated Infection Advisory Group. Address: 33 Peverell Avenue East, Poundbury, Dorchester, Dorset DT1 3RH, England. E-mail: profdavidleaper@doctors.org.uk

LEAPMAN Michael Henry, b. 24 April 1938, London, England. Writer; Journalist. m. Olga Mason, 15 July 1965, 1 son. Appointment: Journalist, The Times, 1969-81. Publications: One Man and His Plot, 1976; Yankee Doodles, 1982; Companion Guide to New York, 1983; Barefaced Cheek, 1983; Treachery, 1984; The Last Days of the Beeb, 1986; Kinnock, 1987; The Book of London (editor), 1989; London's River, 1991; Treacherous Estate, 1992; Eyewitness Guide to London, 1993; Master Race (with Catrine Clay), 1995; Witnesses to War, 1998; The Ingenious Mr Fairchild, 2000; The World for a Shilling 2001; Inigo, 2003. Contributions to: Numerous magazines and journals. Honours: Campaigning Journalist of the Year, British Press Award, 1968; Thomas Cook Travel Book Award, Best Guide Book of 1983; Garden Writers Guild Award, 1995; Times Education Supplement Senior Book Award, 1999. Memberships: Society of Authors; Royal Society of Arts, National Union of Journalists. Address: 13 Aldebert Terrace, London SW8 1BH, England.

LEAVER Christopher (Sir), b. 3 November 1937, London, England. Business Executive. m. Helen Mireille Molyneux Benton, 1975, 1 son, 2 daughters. Appointments: Commissioned, Royal Army Ordnance Corps, 1956-58; Member, Retail Food Trades Wages Council, 1963-64; Justice of the Peace, Inner London, 1970-83; Council, Royal Borough of Kensington and Chelsea, 1970-73; Court of Common Council, Ward of Dowgate, 1973, Sheriff, 1979-80, Lord Mayor, 1981-82, City of London; Justice of the Peace, City, 1974-93; Board, Brixton Prison, 1975-78; Governor, Christ's Hospital School, 1975; Governor, City of London Girls School, 1975-78; Board of Governors, 1978-, Chancellor, 1981-82, City University; Chairman, Young Musicians Symphony Orchestra Trust, 1979-81; Trustee, Chichester Festival Theatre, 1982-97; Church Commissioner, 1982-83, 1996-; Chairman, London Tourist Board Ltd, 1983-89, Trustee, London Symphony Orchestra, 1983-91; Deputy Chairman, 1989-93, Chairman, 1993-94, Vice-Chairman, 1994-2000, Thames Water PLC; Adviser to Secretary of State on Royal Parks, 1993-96; Non-Executive Director, Unionamerica Holdings, 1994-97; Chairman, Eastbourne College. Honours: Knight Grand Cross, Order of the British Empire; Knight, Order of St John of Jerusalem; Honorary Colonel, 151 Regiment, Royal Corps of Transport (Volunteers), 1983-89; Honorary Colonel, Royal Corps of Transport, 1988-91; Honorary Liveryman, Farmers Company; Fellow, Chartered Institute of Transport; Honorary Freeman, Company of Water Conservators; Freeman, Company of Watermen and Lightermen; Order of Oman. Memberships: Vice-President, Playing Fields Association. Address: c/o Thames Water PLC, 14 Cavendish Place, London W1M 0NU, England.

LEAVER Peter Lawrence Oppenheim, b. 28 November 1944. Lawyer; Football Executive. m. Jane Rachel Pearl, 1969, 3 sons, 1 daughter. Education: Trinity College, Dublin; Called to Bar, Lincoln's Inn, 1967. Appointments: Member,

Committee on Future of the Legal Profession, 1986-88, Council of Legal Education, 1986-91, General Council of the Bar, 1987-90; Chairman, Bar Committee, 1989, International Practice Committee, 1990; Director, Investment Management Regulatory Organisation, 1994-2000; Recorder, 1994-; Bencher, 1995; Queen's Counsel; Chief Executive, Football Association Premier League, 1997-99; Deputy High Court Judge. Memberships: Chartered Institute of Arbitrators; Member, Dispute Resolution Panel for Winter Olympics, Salt Lake City, 2002. Address: 5 Hamilton Terrace, London NW8 9RE, England.

LEBED Aleksander Ivanovich (Lieutenant General), b. 20 April 1950, Novocherkassk, Russia. Army Officer. m. 2 sons, 1 daughter. Education: Ryazan Higher School of Airborne Troops; M Frunze Military Academy. Appointments: Platoon then Company Commander, Ryazan Higher Airborne Troops Commanding School, 1973-81; Battalion Commander, Afghanistan, 1981-82; Regimental Commander, 1985-86; Deputy Commander, Airborne Troops Formation, 1986-88; Commander, Tula Airborne Troops Division, 1989-92; Stood guard with paratrooper battalion at Supreme Soviet building during attempted coup, August, 1991; Deputy Commander, Airborne Troops and Military Education Institute, 1991; Commander, 14th Russian Army, Pridniestr Republic, 1992-94; Deputy Chairman, National Council, Congress of Russian Communities, 1995-96; Member, State Duma, 1995-96; Candidate, Presidential Election, 1996; Secretary, Security Council of Russia, 1996; Started negotiations with Chechen separatists; Founder, Russian People's Republican Party; Governor, Krasnoyarsk Territory; Member, Council of Russian Federation, 1998-. Publications: It is a Pity for the Power, 1995; My Life and My Country, 1997; Ideology of Common Sense, 1997. Honours: Several military orders. Address: House of Administration, Mira prospect 110, 660009 Mrasnoyarsk, Russia.

LEBED Aleksey Ivanovich, b. 14 April 1955, Novocherkassk, Rostov Region, Russia. m. Yelizaveta Vladimirovna, 1 son, 1 daughter. Education: Ryazan Higher School of Airborne Troops; Military Academy; Saint Petersburg State University. Appointments: Served in the Soviet Army, 1979-88; Served in Afghanistan, 1982, Pskov, 1991; Military operations, various parts of USSR, 1980-92; Regimental Commander, 300th Paratroop Regiment, 1995-96; State Duma Deputy, 1996-; Head of Government, Republic of Khakassia, 1996-2001; Member, Council of Russian Federation, 1996-; Member, Congress of Russian Communities. Honours: Order of the Red Star; Medal for Courage; Honoris Causa Degree, Khakassia Kalanov State University; Peter the Great Prize, 2001. Address: House of Government, Prospect Lenina 67, R-665019 Abakan, Russia. E-mail: pressa@khakasnet.ru

LEBEDEV Alexander A, b. 3 June 1938, Voronezh, USSR. Diplomat. m. Nina Lordkipanidze, 1963. Education: Honours Graduate, Moscow Institute of International Relations, 1961; Doctorate, European Community Enlargement, Institute of World Economy and International Relations, USSR Academy of Sciences, 1976. Appointments: Various positions in national and international NGO's during the 1960's and 70's include: Vice-President, USSR Students Union; Vice-President, International Union of Students; Secretary World Peace Council; Head of International Service; Member of Board of USSR Copyright Agency; Twice on Staff of Central Committee of Soviet Communist Party, International Department, 1970-73; Head, International Information Division, Central Committee of Soviet Communist Party, 1987-90; Deputy Head Soviet Delegation, OSCE Information

Forum, London, 1989: Spokesman on Soviet Foreign Policy, Council on Foreign Relations, New York, 1990; Minister-Councilor, USSR Embassy, Czechoslovakia, Prague, 1990-91; Ambassador of USSR then Russian Federation, to Czechoslovakia then the Czech Republic, 1990-96; Head, United Nations Liaison Office, Zagreb, 1996-98; Ambassador at Large, Foreign Ministry of the Russian Federation, 1998; Ambassador of the Russian Federation, Republic of Turkey, Ankara, 1998-. Publications: Books: Essays of British Foreign Policy, 1988; The New Soviet Foreign Policy, 1989; Numerous publications in Soviet and international magazines and newspapers on problems of Soviet and Russian Foreign Policy, relations between USSR and the West, European security, world diplomacy; Numerous interviews for television and radio at home and abroad. Address: Embassy of the Russian Federation, Ankara, Turkey.

LEBEDEV Vladimir Alekseyevich, b. 8 May 1940, Novosibirsk, Russia. Physicist-Researcher; Teacher-Psychologist. m. Valentine Aleksandrovna Rechling, 1965, 2 sons. Education: State Institute of Railway, Novosibirsk, 1957-59; MSc, State University of Novosibirsk, 1965; Patent Lawyer Diploma, Central Institute of Study of Patents, 1971; History/Philosophy Educator Diploma, Regional University of History & Philosophy, 1979. Appointments: Probationer, State Institute of Railway, Novosibirsk, 1957-59; Probationer, Russian Academy of Sciences, Siberian Branch, Institute of Thermophysics, Novosibirsk, 1963-65; Probationer Researcher, 1965-67, Engineer, 1967-78, Research Assistant, 1978-2003, Senior Research Assistant, 2003-, one of the Organisers and First Ideologist, Teacher-Psychologist, The School for the Sick Child, The Centre for the Social Habilitation by Out-of-Medicine Methods, Novosibirsk, 1991-2004; Physics, Music, Art and History Lecturer, Home of Scientists, TV, Child Organisation, etc, Novosibirsk, 1970-; Teacher-Psychologist, Lecturer, State University, Novosibirsk, 2004-; Consultant, Seminars on methods of child psychology correction, TV, various medical and educational organisations, Russia, 1992-2006; Lecturer, Clinic of Research Institute of Physiology, Medical Academy of Russia, 2005-; Special Educator, Pedagogue, 2005-. Publications: More than 120 books, papers and reports on gravitation, thermophysics and psychology. Honours: Medal, The Science in Siberia authors' competition, 1979; Honorary title and Medal, Honoured Veteran of Russian Academy of Science, 1997; Soros Foundation Grant, 1997; Grand Gold Medal of Siberian Market, Education XXI age, 1998; Honorary Insignia, Silver Sigma, 2007. Memberships: Emperor Peter I Academy of Sciences and Arts. Address: Institute of Thermophysics, Russian Academy of Sciences, Siberian Branch, Lavrent'ev Ave, 1, Novosibirsk, 630090, Russia. E-mail: leb_vlad@mail.ru

LECHEVALIER Hubert Arthur, b. 12 May 1926, Tours, France. Microbiologist. m. Mary Jean Pfeil, 2 sons. Education: Licence ès Sciences, 1947, MS, 1948, Laval University, Quebec, Canada; PhD, Rutgers University, New Brunswick, New Jersey, 1951. Appointments: Assistant Professor, Microbiology, College of Agriculture then Waksman Institute, Rutgers University, 1951-56; Associate Professor, Microbiology, 1956-66, Professor, Microbiology, 1966-91, Associate Director, 1980-88, Waksman Institute of Microbiology, Rutgers University; Professor Emeritus, Rutgers, The State University of New Jersey, 1991-. Publications: Author or co-author of over 140 scientific papers, co-author or co-editor of 10 books including: A Guide to the Actinomycetes and Their Antibiotics, 1953; Antibiotics of Actinomycetes, 1962; Three Centuries of Microbiology,

1965, reprint 1974; The Microbes, 1971; 4 US patents. Honours include: Honorary Member, the Société Française de Microbiologie 1972-; Charles Thom Award (jointly with Mary P Lechevalier), 1982; DSc, Laval University, 1983; Bergey Trust Award for contributions to bacterial taxonomy, 1989; New Jersey Inventors Hall of Fame, 1990; Honorary member of the Society for Actinomycetes, Japan, 1997. Address: 131 Goddard-Nisbet Rd, Morrisville, VT 05661-8041, USA. E-mail: mheques@together.net

LEDERER Helen, b. 24 September 1954, United Kingdom. Comedienne; Actress. m. Chris Browne, 1 daughter. Education: Hatfield Polytechnic (now Hatfield University); Central School of Speech and Drama. Career: Early work at the Comedy Store and similar venues; Theatre includes: Bunny in House of Blue Leaves, Lilian Bayliss Theatre; Rita in Educating Rita; Doreen in Having a Ball, Comedy Theatre; Vagina Monologues, West End, 2002; Full House and The Hairless Diva, Palace Theatre, Watford; Television appearances include: The Young Ones; Girls on Top; The French and Sauders Show; Flossie in Happy Families, BBC2; 4 series of Naked Video, writing and performing own material between sketches, BBC2; Wogan; Hysteria; The New Statesman; Bottom; 5 series of Absolutely Fabulous, BBC; One Foot in the Grave, BBC; Heartbeat; Occasional presenter, The Heaven and Earth Show, BBC; Radio includes: In One Ear; Life With Lederer (writer and performer, 2 series), Radio 4; Short story readings, Radio3 and Radio 4; Comic Cuts, Radio 5; Regular writer and performer of comic monologues for Woman's Hour, Radio 4; Presenter of Home Truths (as stand in for the late John Peel), BBC Radio 4; Films: Solitaire for Two; Dance to Your Daddy; Speak Like a Child; Clark. Publications: Coping with Lederer; Single Minding; Contributing author: Girl's Night In/Big Night Out; Author of numerous articles for newspapers and magazines. Memberships: Groucho; Soho House; Princes Trust Ambassador; Fawcett Society. Address: Jessica Carney Associates, 4th Floor, 23 Golden Square, London, W1F 9JP, England. E-mail: info@jcarneyassociates.co.uk

LEE Ang, b. 1954, Pingtung, Taiwan. Film maker. m. Jane Lin, 1983, 2 sons. Education: National Taiwan College of Arts, 1975; BFA Degree in Theatre/Theater Direction, University of Illinois Urbana-Champaign; Masters Degree in Film Production, New York University. Career: Films include: Joe's Bed-Stuy Barbershop: We Cut Heads, 1983; Pushing Hands, 1992; The Wedding Banquet, 1993; Eat Drink Man Woman, 1994; Sense and Sensibility, 1995; The Ice Storm, 1997; The Civil War drama Ride With The Devil, 1999; Crouching Tiger, Hidden Dragon, 2000; Hire, The Chosen (short film), 2001; Hulk, 2003; Brokeback Mountain, 2005; Se, jie, 2007. Honours: Golden Bear, Berlin Film Festival; Best Director, National Board of Review and the New York Film Critics Circle, 1995; Best Screenplay at Cannes, 1997; Best Foreign Language Film, 2000; Best Director at the Golden Globes, 2000; Oscar, Best Director, 2006.

LEE Chan-Yun, b. 19 July 1952, Hwa-Liang, Taiwan. Technical Staff Member Associate Professor of Physics. m. Chia-Li Grace Yang, 1 son, 2 daughters. Education: BS, Physics, Soochow University, 1974; MS, Physics, University of Southern California, 1980; PhD, Physics, University of Notre Dame, 1994. Appointments: Assistant Professor, Physics, TIT, 1982-86; Associate Professor, Physics, TIT, 1986-88; Chairman, Physics Section, TIT, 1986-88; Consultant, TSD, 1983-88; Director, TNSM, 1986-88; Senior Engineer, LRC, 1994-99; Professor, Physics, SJCC, 1998-2000; Key Account for South Asia Area, LRC, 1997-99; Technical Staff, 1999-, West Coast Process Co-ordinator, 2000, TEA. Publications:

DICTIONARY OF INTERNATIONAL BIOGRAPHY

Over 20 articles published in professional journals. Honours: 27th Science and Technology Personnel Research Award, 1988; Excellent Researchers Prize, 1986, 1987; Outstanding Academic Publication Prize, 1987, 1988. Memberships: Chinese Physics Association; American Vacuum Association. Address: 471 Via Vera Cruz, Fremont, CA 94539-5325, USA.

LEE Christopher Frank Carandini, b. 27 May 1922, London, England. Actor; Author; Singer. m. Birgit Kroenke, 1961, 1 daughter. Education: Wellington College. Appointments: Served RAF, 1941-46; Mentioned in Despatches, 1944; Film industry, 1947-; Appeared in over 200 motion pictures; Films include: Moulin Rouge, 1953; The Curse of Frankenstein, 1956; Tale of Two Cities, 1957; Dracula, 1958; The Hound of the Baskervilles, The Mummy, 1959; Rasputin the Mad Monk, 1965; The Wicker Man, The Three Musketeers, The Private Life of Sherlock Holmes, 1973; The Four Musketeers, The Man with the Golden Gun, 1975; To the Devil a Daughter, 1976; Airport 77, Return from Witch Mountain, How the West Was Won, Caravans, The Silent Flute, 1977; The Passage, 1941, Bear Island, 1978; The Serial, 1979; The Salamander, 1980; An Eye for an Eye; Goliath Awaits; Charles and Diana; The Return of Captain Invincible; The Howling Z; Behind the Mask; Roadstrip; Shaka Zulu; Mio my Mio; The Girl. Un Metier du Seigneur; Casanova; The Disputation (TV); Murder Story; Round the World in 80 Days (TV); Return of the Musketeers; Outlaws; Gremlins II, 1989; Sherlock Holmes; Rainbow Thief; L'Avaro; Wahre Wunder, 1990; Young Indy, Cybereden, 1991; Death Train, 1992; The Funny Man, Police Academy, Mission in Moscow, 1993; A Feast at Midnight, 1994; The Stupids, Moses, 1995; Jinnah, 1997; Sleepy Hollow, 1999; The Lord of the Rings, 2000, 2001, 2003; Star Wars Episode II, 2002 and Episode III, Charlie and the Chocolate Factory, The Corpse Bride, Greyfriars Bobby, 2005; The Heavy, 2008. Publications: Christopher Lee's Treasury of Terror, Christopher Lee's Archive of Evil, 1975; Christopher Lee's The Great Villains, 1977; Tall Dark and Gruesome, 1977, 2002; Christopher Lee: Lord of Misrule, 2004. Honours: Officier, Ordre des Arts et des Lettres, 1973; Commander, St John of Jerusalem, 1997; Commander of the Order of the British Empire, 2001. Address: c/o Diamond Management, 31 Percy Street, London, W1T 2DD, England.

LEE David Jiunn Chieh, b. 20 December 1972, Kuala Lumpur, Malaysia. Company Director; Consultant. Education: Bachelor of Commerce; Bachelor of Science; Master of Commerce (First Class Honours), Management; PhD, Information Systems. Appointments: Lecturer, 2001-02, Lecturer, 2004-06, The University of Auckland; Director, J C Lee Limited, 2004-. Publications: Articles in professional journals. Honours: Senior Prize, Management Science and Information Systems, The University of Auckland; The University of Auckland Doctoral Scholarship; Top 40 Doctoral Students in the World, International Conference on Information Systems Doctoral Consortium, 2000. Memberships: MENSA. E-mail: david.lee@jclee.co.nz

LEE Don Yoon, b. 7 April 1936, Seoul, Korea. Academic Researcher; Writer; Publisher. Education: BA, University of Washington, 1963; MA, St Johns University, 1967; MS, Georgetown University, 1971; MA, Indiana University, 1975, 1990; PhD, World Information Distributed University, 2003. Appointments: Publisher, Academic Researcher, Writer, Founder, Eastern Press Inc, Bloomington, 1981-. Publications: History of Early Relations Between China and Tibet, 1981; An Introduction to East Asian and Tibetan Linguistics and Culture, 1981; Learning Standard Arabic, 1988; An Annotated

Bibliography of Selected Works on China, 1981; Light Literature and Philosophy of East Asia, 1982; An Annotated Biography on Inner Asia, 1983; An Annotated Archaeological Bibliography of Selected Works in Northern and Central Asia, 1983; Traditional Chinese Thoughts, 1990; Arabic Verb Frequency, 1991. Address: PO Box 881, Bloomington, IN 47402-0881, USA.

LEE Doyung, b. 28 December 1930, South Korea. Businessman; Community Leader. m. Grace Lee, 2 sons, 1 daughter. Education: BA, Korea University; Georgetown University, USA, 3 years. Appointment: President, Hansan Lee Trading Corp, 32 years; Retired 2000. Honours: Americans by Choice, 1987; Medal of Dong Baek, South Korea, 1988; Medal of Freedom, 1994, 1999, 2002. Memberships: President, 1974, 1977-78, 1991-92, Korean-American Association of Washington Metropolitan Area; Founding President, 1977-78, Federation of Korean-American Associations; President, 1990, Korean-American Republican of Virginia. Address: 5815 Governors View Lane, Alexandria, VA 22310-2356, USA. E-mail: doyung@msn.com

LEE Hong-Koo, b. 9 May 1934, Seoul, Korea. Politician; Political Scientist. m. 1 son, 2 daughters. Education: Seoul National University; Emory University; Yale University; PhD. Appointments: Assistant Professor, Emory University, USA, 1963-64; Assistant Professor, Case Western Reserve University, 1964-67; Assistant Professor, Associate Professor, Professor of Political Science,1968-88, Director, Institute of Social Sciences, 1979-82, Seoul National University, Korea; Fellow, Woodrow Wilson International Center for Scholars, Smithsonian Institution, Washington DC, 1973-74; Fellow, Harvard Law School, 1974-75; Minister of National Unification, Korea, 1988-90; Special Assistant to President, 1990-91; Ambassador to UK, 1991-93; Commission on Global Governance, 1991-95; Senior Vice-Chairman, Advisory Council for Unification, Chairman, Seoul 21st Century Committee, The World Cup 2002 Bidding Committee, 1993-94; Deputy Prime Minister, Minister of National Unification, 1994; Prime Minister, 1994-95; Chairman, New Korea Party, 1996; Ambassador to USA, 1998-. Publications: An Introduction to Political Science; One Hundred Years of Marxism; Modernization. Address: Embassy of the Republic of South Korea, 2450 Massachusetts Avenue NW, Washington, DC 20008, USA. E-mail:korinfo@koreaemb.org

LEE Hung, b. 21 November 1954, Taiwan. Professor. m. Colleen McCann, 1 son, 1 daughter. Education: BSc, honours, Biochemistry, University of British Columbia, 1977; PhD, Biochemistry, McGill University, 1982. Appointments: Research Associate, Division of Biological Sciences, National Research Council, Canada, 1983-86; Assistant Professor, Department of Environmental Biology, 1986-91, Adjunct Professor, School of Engineering, 1992-, Associate Professor, Department of Environmental Biology, 1991-99, University of Guelph; Visiting Professor, Biotechnology Laboratory, University of British Columbia, 1992-93; Affiliated Network Investigator, Protein Engineering Network Center of Excellence, 1998-; Professor, Department of Environmental Biology, University of Guelph, 1999-; Regional Associate Editor for the journal, Environmental Toxicology, 2000-; Network Investigator, Canadian Water Network Centre of Excellence, 2001-; Visiting Professor, Department of Wood Science, University of British Columbia, 2005-2006; Editorial Board Member, Antonie van Leeuwenhoek International Journal of General and Molecular Microbiology, 2007-. Publications: 151 original research papers, 28 original review papers, 16 refereed book chapters, 1 patent, 178 conference abstracts, 12 non-refereed technical reports, 4 disclosures. Honours include: Canadian MRC Studentship, McGill University, 1978-82; Research Excellence Citation, Imperial Oil Limited, 1990; Presidential Distinguished Professor Award, University of Guelph, 2002-04; Listed in national and international biographical dictionaries. Membership: American Society for Microbiology. Address: Department of Environmental Biology, University of Guelph, Guelph, Ontario N1G 2W1, Canada.

LEE Jae-Man, b. 6 August 1930, Korea. Professor Emeritus. m. Eun-Hong Kim, 1 son, 1 daughter. Education: BS, 1956, MA, 1957, Jeon-Buk University; PhD, Tsukuba University, Japan, 1995. Appointments: Shin-Heung High School, Jeon-Ju, 1952-66; Korean Armed Forces, 1953-55; Professor, Kun-San National Junior Teachers College, 1966-78; Professor, Kun-San National Woman's College, 1978-79; Professor, 1979-95, Emeritus Professor, 1996, Kun-San National University; Professor, Ewha Woman's University, Seoul, 1979-80; Professor, Nagoya University, Japan, 1982; Professor, Tsukuba University, 1988-89. Publications: Author: Junior Science Education, 1968; Natural Science, 1970; University Physical Experiments, 1989. Honours: Eduation Merit Prize, Ministry of Education, Seoul, 1991; Kuhkmin-Huhnjang Dong-BaekJang, Merit Prize, Seoul, 1995. Memberships: Society of Korean Physics. Address: 185 Kosa-Dong, Jeon-Ju, Jeon-Buk, 560-802, Republic of Korea.

LEE Jeong-Kyu, b. 15 July 1950, Choongmoo, South Korea. Educational Scholar; Researcher; Professor; Academic Administrator; Columnist. m. Ok-Hee Yang, 1980, 1 daughter. Education: BA, Theology, Korean Union College, Sahmyook University, Seoul, 1981; M Ed, Education Administration, University of Montana, USA, 1994; PhD, Higher Education Administration, University of Texas at Austin, USA, 1997. Appointments: Teacher and Counsellor, Unbong and Sunhwa Vocational Senior High Schools, Incheon, South Korea, 1981-85; Viniculturalist, Seowoon-myon, Kyungki-do, South Korea, 1985-88; Instructor, 1995-96, Research Internship, Institutional Research, 1996, Office of Institutional Studies and Planning, University of Texas at Austin; Director, National Statistics of Korean Higher Education, 1998-99; Research Fellow, Division of Educational Policy Research, Korean Educational Development Institute, Seoul, 1998-2004; Instructor, 2000-01, Joint Professor, 2001-03, Graduate School of Educational Administration and Management, Hongik University, Seoul; Instructor, Graduate School of Education, Yonsei University, Seoul, 2001-02; Instructor, Graduate School of Education, Dongkuk University, Seoul, 2002; President, Central College, Burnaby, Canada, 2003-04; Visiting Scholar/Faculty, Department of Educational Studies, University of British Columbia, Canada, 2003-04; Expert Adviser, Future Unification Institution, 1999-; Expert Adviser and Professional Columnist, Hankook Daehak Shinmoon (Korean University newspaper), 2003-. Publications: Numerous articles in professional journals, government and grant research works and 5 books. Honours: Henderson Scholarship, 1996, Academic Competitive Scholarship, 1996-97, University of Texas at Austin. Memberships: Association of Asian Studies; Korean Social Study of Educational Administration; Phi Kappa Phi. Address: 6846-190 St, Surrey, BC V4N 5P2, Canada. E-mail: jeongkyuk@hotmail.com

LEE Jong-Wook, b. 29 May 1964, Seoul, Korea. Medical Educator. m. Eun-Jung Jo, 2 daughters. Education: Bachelor's degree, 1989; Master's degree, 1995; PhD, 2003; Diplomate, Ministry of Health and Welfare, Korea, 1989; Board Certified in Hand Surgery, Korean Society for Surgery of Hand,

Korea, 2003. Appointments: Professor, Hallym University, Department of Plastic & Reconstructive Surgery, 1995-; Director, Insurance Committee, Korean Burn Society; Director, Korean Society for Surgery of Hand; Director, Korean Society for Head & Neck Oncology, 2003-06; Medical Consultant, Korean Human Tissue Bank; Committee Member, Korean Society of Plastic & Reconstructive Surgery. Publications: Pediatric Electrical Burn: Outlet Injury Caused by Steel Chopstick Misuse, 2004; Use of the Artificial Dermis for Free Radical Flap Donor Site, 2005; Pediatric Hand Injury Induced by Treadmill, 2005; Esthetic and Functional Reconstruction for Burn Deformities of the Lower Lip and Chin with Free Radial Forearm Flap, 2006; Burns in Epilepsy: Seven Years of Experience from the Hallym Burn Center in Korea, 2006; Face Burns Caused by Flambe Drinks, 2006. Honours: Listed in international biographical dictionaries; International Health Professional of the Year, 2006. Address: 94-200 Youngdungpo-Dong, Youngpungpo-Gu, Department of Plastic & Reconstructive Surgery, Hangang Sacred Heart Hospital, Seoul 150-719, Korea.

LEE Jung Eun, b. 4 January 1972, Seoul, Korea. Postdoctor (KIST). Education: BS, Chemistry, 1994, MS, Physical Chemistry, 1997, Sookmyung Women's University; Diploma, Computer Aided Molecular Design Centre Soong Sil University; Invited Researcher, University of California Davis, 2003; PhD Environmental Chemistry, Pohang University of Science and Technology, 2006. Appointments: Postdoctoral, Center for Environmental Technology Research, Korea Institute of Science and Technology. Publications: Articles as co-author in scientific journals including: Bulletin of the Korean Chemical Society, 1999, 2003; Journal of Molecular Spectroscopy, 2000; Journal of the American Chemical Society, 2002; Journal of Physical Chemistry A, 2003, 2004. Honours: Listed in many international biographical directories. Memberships: American Chemical Society; Korean Chemical Society; Global Association of Culture and Peace; Christian Gospel Missionary. Address: Center for Environmental Technology Research, Korea Institute of Science and Technology, Seoul 136-791, Korea. E-mail: lje4523@postech.ac.kr Website: www.postech.ac.kr/lab/see/art

LEE Keun-Young, b. 27 July 1953, Seoul, Korea. Medical Doctor; Obstetrician and Gynaecologist. m. Sung-Ji Nam, 2 sons. Education: MD, Chun-Ang University Medical College, Seoul, Korea, 1978; Board (Obstetrics and Gynaecology), Hallym University Medical College, Seoul, Korea, 1983; PhD, Biochemistry, Chun-Ang University Medical College, Seoul, Korea, 1984. Appointments: Fellowship, Maternal-Foetal Medicine, 1983-85, Assistant Professor, Department of Obstetrics and Gynaecology, 1985-87, Hallym University; Visiting Assistant Professor, Department of Obstetrics and Gynaecology, University of Maryland, USA, 1988-89; Associate Professor, 1989-95, Professor, 1997-, Department of Obstetrics and Gynaecology, Hallym University, Seoul, Korea; President, Kangnam Sacred Heart Hospital, Hallym University, 2006-. Publication: Article in medical journal: Interleukin-6, but not relaxin, predicts outcome of rescue cerclage in women with cervical incompetence, 2004. Honours: Award, Korean Health Association Minister, 2004; Best Paper of the Year, Korean Society of Obstetrics and Gynaecology, 2005. Memberships: Vice-President, Korean Society for Maternal-Foetal Medicine; Society for Maternal Foetal Medicine. Address: Department of Obstetrics and Gynaecology, Hallym University, Kang Nam Sacred Heart Hospital, #948-1 Daelim 1-Dong, Youngdeungpo-Gu, Seoul 150-950 Korea. E-mail: mfmlee@korea.com

LEE Kok Loong, b. 23 June 1976, Kuala Lumpur, Malaysia. Materials Technologist. Education: BEng, Mechanical Engineering, 1998, PhD, Materials Science, 2004, Leicester University, England. Appointments: Researcher, Chungnam National University, Korea, 2003; Materials Technologist, Corus UK, 2003-06; Technology Transfer Specialist, Bodycote, 2006-. Publications: Structure Property Relations in Non Ferrous Metals (materials science textbook); Articles in scientific journals: Metallurgical and Materials Transaction A; Scripta Materialia; Materials Science and Engineering A; Journal of Materials Science; Composites Part A: Applied Science and Manufacturing. Honours: PhD Scholarship; Winner of the Lincolnshire Iron and Steel Institute Ironmaster's Young Members Paper; Listed in Who's Who publications and biographical dictionaries. Membership: Institute of Materials. Address: 20 Berkely Drive, Chelmsford, Essex, CM2 6XR, England. E-mail: kokLoong1@hotmail.com

LEE Lung-Sheng, b. 15 May 1954, Nantou, Taiwan. Professor. m. Chun-Chin Lai, 1 son, 1 daughter. Education: Bachelor in Industrial Education, National Taiwan Normal University, 1978; Master in Industrial Education, National Taiwan Normal University, 1980; PhD, Technology Education, Ohio State University, 1991. Appointments: Instructor, National Taipei Institute of Technology, 1982-84; Instructor, National Taiwan Normal University, 1984-86; Associate Professor, National Taiwan Normal University, 1986-93; Professor, National Taiwan Normal University, 1993-; Dept Chair, National Taiwan Normal University, 1995-2001; College Dean, National Taiwan Normal University, 2001-2004; Adviser, Ministry of Education, Taiwan, Republic of China, 1997-2000; President, National United University, 2005-; President, Association for Curriculum and Instruction, Tawian, 2006-; President, Ohio State University Alumni Club of Taiwan, 2007-. Publications: Over 100 articles; Issues in Technology Education and Vocational Education. Honours: Leader to Watch, International Technology Education Association, 1996; Alumni Award of Excellence, Technology Education, Ohio State University, 1999; Prakken Professional Co-operation Award, ITEA, 2002. Memberships: ITEA; Industrial Technology Education Association, Taiwan. Address: National United University, 1 Lien Da, Kung Ching Li, Miaoli 360, Taiwan. E-mail: lslee@nuu.edu.tw Website: www.nuu.edu.tw/~president/

LEE Martin Chu Ming, b. 8 June 1938, Hong Kong. Politician; Barrister. m. Amelia Lee, 1969, 1 son. Education: BA, University of Hong Kong. Appointments: Queen's Counsel; Justice of the Peace; Hong Kong Legislative Council, 1985-; Basic Law Drafting Committee, 1985-90; Hong Kong Law Reform Commission, 1985-91; Chairman, Hong Kong Consumer Council, 1988-91; Founder, 1989, Leader, 1990-, United Democrats of Hong Kong; Chairman, Democratic Party, 1994-2002; Goodman Fellow, University of Toronto, 2000. Publications: The Basic Law: some basic flaws, co-author, 1988. Honours: International Human Rights Award, American Bar Association, 1995; Prize for Freedom, Liberal International, 1996; Democracy Award, National Endowment for Democracy, USA, 1997; Honorary LLD, Holy Cross College, 1997; Honorary LLD, Amherst College, USA, 1997; Statesmanship Award, Claremont Institute, USA, 1998; Schuman Medal, European Parliament, 2000. Memberships: Chairman, Hong Kong Bar Association, 1980-83. Address: Democratic Party of Hong Kong, 4th Floor, Hanley House, 776-778 Nathan Road, Kowloon, Hong Kong Special Administrative Region, China. E-mail: oml@martinlee.org.hk Website: www.martinlee.org.hk

LEE Ook, b. 3 January 1965, Seoul, South Korea. Professor. m. Mikyung Kim, 2 sons. Education: BS, Computer Science and Statistics, Sould National University, 1987; MS, Computer Science, Northwestern University, Evanston, USA, 1989; PhD, Management Information System, The Claremont Graduate University, USA, 1997. Appointments: Professor, Hansung University, South Korea, 1997-99; Professor, North Carolina A&T State University, USA, 1999-2000; Professor, University of Nevada at Las Vegas, USA, 2000-01; Senior Lecturer, University of Queensland, Australia, 2001-02; Professor, Information Systems, Chair, Department of Information Technology Management, College of Information and Communications, Hanyang University, South Korea, 2002-. Publications: Over 100 journal articles, conference papers and book chapters; Book, Internet Marketing Research: Theory and Practice. Honours: First to utilise critical social theory in understanding cyberspace behaviour such as Internet addiction, Cyber democracy and Travel anxiety. Memberships: Advisory Board, InfoSci Corporation, USA; Editorial Review Board, International Journal of Information Technology Cases; Korean Government Advisor to APEC Small to Medium Business Forum. Address: Department of Information Technology Management, College of Information and Communications, Hanyang University, Seoul, South Korea. E-mail: ooklee@hanyang.ac.kr

LEE Seong Jin, b. 13 January 1970, Seoul, Republic of Korea. Medical Doctor; Professor. Education: MD, 1995, PhD, 2004, Hanyang University, Seoul; MSc, University of Ulsan, Seoul, 2001. Appointments: Intern, 1995-96, Resident, Internal Medicine, 1996-2000, Clinical and Research Fellowship, Endocrinology, 2000-01, Asan Medical Centre, Seoul; Research Fellowship, Endocrinology, Harvard Medical School, 2001-02; Assistant Professor, Department of Internal Medicine, 2002-, Member, Clinical Trial and Research Committee, 2002-, ChunCheon Sacred Heart Hospital. Publications: 40 articles and papers in professional journals. Honours: Best Article Award, 1999, 2002, 2006, Best Academic Award, 2004, Young Investigator's Award, 2005, Korean Society of Endocrinology; Research Grant Award, Hallym Medical Center, 2005. Memberships: Korean Medical Association; Korean Association of Internal Medicine; Korean Society of Endocrinology; Korean Diabetes Association; American Diabetes Association. Address: Division of Endocrinology and Metabolism, Department of Internal Medicine, College of Medicine, Hallym University, ChunCheon Sacred Heart Hospital, Gyo-Dong 153, ChunCheon-Si, Kangwon-Do 200-704, Republic of Korea. E-mail: leesj@hallym.ac.kr

LEE Spike (Shelton Jackson Lee), b. 20 March 1957, Atlanta, Georgia, USA. Film Maker; Actor. m. Tonya Lewis, 1993, 1 daughter. Education: Morehouse College; Atlanta University; New York University; Institute of Film and TV. Appointments: Wrote Scripts for Black College; The Talented Tenth; Last Hustle in Brooklyn; Produced, Wrote, Directed, Joe's Bed-Stuy Barbershop; We Cut Heads; Has directed music videos; TV Commercials; Films include: She's Gotta Have It, 1985; School Daze, 1988; Do the Right Thing, 1989; Love Supreme, Mo' Better Blues, 1990; Jungle Fever, 1991; Malcolm X, 1992; Crooklyn; Girl 6; Clockers, Tales from the Hood, 1995; Girl 6; Get on the Bus; 4 Little Girls; He Got Game, 1998; Summer of Sam, 1999; Bamboozled, The Original Kings of Comedy, 2000; Lisa Picard is Famous, A Huey P Newton Story, 2001; The 25th Hour, 2003; CSA: Confederate States of America, She Hate Me, 2004; Jesus Children of America, 2005; Inside Man, 2006; Lovers & Haters, 2007; TV includes: Sucker Free City, 2004; Miracle's Boys, 2005; When the Levees Broke: A Requiem in Four Acts,

Shark, 2006; M.O.N.Y, 2007. Publications: Spike Lee's Gotta Have It: Inside Guerilla Filmmaking, 1987; Uplift the Race, 1988; The Trials and Tribulations of the Making of Malcolm X, 1992; Girl 6; Get on the Bus, 1996. Honours: Cannes Film Festival Prize for Best New Film, 1985; Cannes Film Festival, Best New Director, 1986; LA Film Critics' Association Awards, 1986, 1989; Chicago Film Festival Critics' Awards, 1990, 1992; Golden Satellite, Best Documentary, 1997; Dr h c, New York University, 1998; Inducted into National Association for the Advancement of Colored People Hall of Fame, 2003; Commander des Arts et des Lettres, 2003. Address: Forty Acres and a Mule Filmworks, 124 De Kalb Avenue, Brooklyn, New York, NY 11217, USA.

LEE William Johnson, b. 13 January 1924, Oneida, Tennessee, USA. Attorney. m. Marjorie Young, 20 August 1949, 2 sons. Education: Akron University; Denison University; Harvard University Graduate School; Ohio State University Law School; Admitted, Ohio Bar, Florida Bar, Federal US District Court Northern and Southern Districts, Ohio and the Southern District of Florida. Appointments: Research Assistant, Ohio State University Law School, 1948-49; Served in the USAF; Attorney Examiner, Assistant State Permit Chief, State Permit Chief, Assistant State Liquor Control Director, Liquor Purchases Chief, Ohio Department of Liquor Control, 1951-57; Assistant Counsel, Hupp Corporation,1957-58; Lawyer in general practice, Acting Municipal Judge, Ohio, 1959-62; Part-time Instructor, College Business Administration, Kent State University, 1961-62; Papy & Carruthers law firm, Florida, 1962-63; Special Counsel, City Attorney's Office, Fort Lauderdale, Florida, 1963-65; Private practice in law, Fort Lauderdale, 1965-66; Assistant Attorney General, Office of the Attorney General, State of Ohio, 1966-70; Administrator, State Medical Board, Ohio, 1970-85; Member, Editorial Board, Ohio State Law Journal; Member, Federated State Board's National Commission for Evaluation of Foreign Medical Schools, 1981-83; Member, Flex 1/Flex 2 Transitional Taskforce, 1983-84. Publications: Several articles. Honours: Outstanding People of the 20th Century; Outstanding People of the 21st Century; Wall of Tolerance, Montgomery, Alabama. Memberships: Ohio State Bar Association; Broward County Bar Association; Akron Bar Association; Columbus Bar Association; Franklin County Trial Lawyers Association; Association of Trial Lawyers of America; American Legion; Phi Kappa Tau; Pi Kappa Delta; Delta Theta Phi; Experimental Aviation Association of South West Florida; Honorary Ambassador and Speaker, World Forum, St Catherine's University, Oxford, England, 2006. Address: 704 Country Club Drive, Apple Valley, Howard, OH 43028, USA.

LEE Yang Hun, b. 17 April 1954, Millyang, Republic of Korea. Professor. m. Hi Ryun Lee, 2 sons. Education: Bachelor degree, 1980, Master degree, 1982, Doctor degree, 1987, Engineering, Busan National University, Republic of Korea. Appointments: Instructor, 1983-86, Assistant Professor, 1986-90, Associate Professor, 1990-95, Professor, 1995-, Dong-A University, Republic of Korea; Visiting Scholar, University of Massachusetts, USA, 1992-93. Publications: Book, Textile Measurements, 1992; Papers: Studies in the steps for the Polar Polymers – Iodine Complex Formation and Their Applications, 30 papers; The variations of the structure and properties of the synthetic fibers by solvent treatment, 7 papers; The applications of the solvent-bonding of the cellulose fibers by using N-methylmorpoline N-oxide, 7 papers. Memberships: The Korean Fiber Society; The Polymer Society of Korea; The Korea Society of Dyers and Finishers. Address: Division of Fashion and Textiles, Dong-A University, 840 Hadan-dong, Saha-gu, Busan 604-714, Republic of Korea. E-mail: leeyh@daunet.donga.ac.kr

LEE Young Woo, b. 9 March 1937, Ulsan City, Korea. Neuroscientist; Neurosurgeon; Biomedical Engineer. m. Kyung Ja Kim, 1 son, 1 daughter. Education: MD, School of Medicine, 1962, MSc, Medicine, 1965, PhD, 1973, Graduate School, Pusan National University, Pusan, Korea; Rotating Internship, 1962-63, Residency, General Surgery, 1963-65, Residency, Neurosurgery, 1965-67, Pusan National University Hospital, Pusan, Korea; Fellowship, Neurosurgery, Long Island College Hospital, Brooklyn, New York, USA, 1980-81. Appointments: Army Service, 1967-70; Instructor, Assistant Professor, Associate Professor, Professor, 1971-2002, Chairman, Department of Neurosurgery, 1975-2002, Pusan National University School of Medicine and Pusan National University Hospital, Pusan, Korea; Honorary Professor, Pusan National University, 2002-; Honorary Superintendent, Dong-Rae Bong Seng Hospital and Chairman of Department of Neurosurgery in Bong Seng Hospital, 2002-; Research Fellow, Department of Neurology, University of Alabama in Birmingham School of Medicine and Medical Center, USA, 1974-75; Fellowship, Department of Neurosurgery, Montreal Neurological Institute, McGill University, Montreal, Canada, 1998-99. Publications: Over 150 articles in scientific journals as author and co-author include most recently: Clinical Analysis Spondylolisthesis Treated with Pediatric Screw Instrumentation, 1998; Clinical Analysis of Thoracolumbar and Lumbar Spine Fracture Treated with Instrumentation; 1999; Prognosis of Surgically Treated Acute Subdural Hematoma, 2003; Chemical Hypoxia-Induced Cell Death in Human Glioma Cells: Role of Reactive Oxygen Species and Lipid Peroxidation; Role of Oxidative Stress in Amyloid-β Peptide-induced Death of Human Glioma Cells; H_2O_2-Induced Cell Death in Human Glioma Cells: Role of Lipid Peroxidation and PARP Activiation, 2001; Underlying Mechanism of Cisplatin-induced Apoptosis in PC-12 Cells, 1998; Modulation of Immune Responses by Capsaicin in Mice, 2000; Books in collaboration: Neurosurgery, 1989, 1996, 2001; The Great Medical Encyclopedia, 1991. Honours include: Military Medal in Vietnam War, President of the Republic of Korea, 1968; 2 Medals, Vietnam Government, 1969; Pfizer's Medical Company Prize, 1997; Madison Biomedical Prize, Korean Society of Biomedical Engineering, 1999; Educational Prizes, 2001, Korean Teacher Association; Pusan Teacher Association; Research Prize, Korean Neurosurgical Society, 2001. Numerous Memberships include: Korean Medical Association; Korean Neurosurgical Society; International College of Surgeons; Korean Society of Medical and Biological Engineering; New York Academy of Sciences; Korean Brain Tumour Study Group; Korean Society for Brain and Neural Science (Neuroscience); Korean Veterans Society.

LEE Yuan Tseh, b. 29 November 1936, Hsinchu, Taiwan. Professor of Chemistry. m. Bernice W Lee, 1963, 2 sons, 1 daughter. Education: National Taiwan University; National Tsinghua University, Taiwan; University of California, Berkeley; PhD. Appointments: Assistant Professor, 1968-71, Associate Professor, 1971-72, Professor of Chemistry, 1973-74, James Franck Institute and Department of Chemistry, University of Chicago, Illinois, USA; Professor of Chemistry, 1974-94, Professor Emeritus, 1994-, University of California, Berkeley; Head, Academia Sinica, 1994. Publications: Articles in professional journals. Honours: Sloan Fellow, 1969; Guggenheim Fellow, 1976; Miller Professorship, 1981; E O Lawrence Award, US Department of Environment, 1981;

Co-recipient, Nobel Prize for Chemistry, 1986; Many other awards and prizes. Memberships: American Academy of Arts and Sciences. Address: Department of Chemistry, University of California, Berkeley, CA 94720, USA.

LEECH Geoffrey Neil, b. 16 January 1936, Gloucester, England. Emeritus Professor of English Linguistics; Writer. m. Frances Anne Berman, 29 July 1961, 1 son, 1 daughter. Education: BA, English Language and Literature, 1959, MA, 1963, PhD, 1968, University College London; DLitt, Lancaster University, 2002. Appointments: Assistant Lecturer, 1962-64, Lecturer, 1965-69, University College London; Reader, 1969-74, Professor of Linguistics and Modern English, 1974-2001, Emeritus professor of English Linguistics, 2002-, University of Lancaster; Visiting Professor, Brown University, 1972, Kobe University, 1984, Kyoto University, 1991, Meikai University, Japan, 1999. Publications: English in Advertising, 1966; A Linguistic Guide to English Poetry, 1969; Towards a Semantic Description of English, 1969; Meaning and the English Verb, 1971, 2nd edition, 1987, 3rd edition 2004; A Grammar of Contemporary English (with R Quirk, S Greenbaum, and J Svartvik), 1972; Semantics, 1974, 2nd edition, 1981; A Communicative Grammar of English (with J Svartvik), 1975, 2nd edition, 1994, 3rd edition, 2002; Explorations in Semantics and Pragmatics, 1980; Style in Fiction (with M Short), 1981, 2nd edition, 2007; English Grammar for Today (with R Hoogenraad and M Deuchar), 1982, 2nd edition, 2005; Principles of Pragmatics, 1983; A Comprehensive Grammar of the English Language (with R Quirk, S Greenbaum, and J Svartvik), 1985; Computers in English Language Teaching and Research (editor with C N Candlin), 1986; The Computational Analysis of English (editor with R Garside and G Sampson), 1987; An A-Z of English Grammar and Usage, 1989, 2nd edition (with B Cruickshank and R Ivanič), 2001; Introducing English Grammar, 1992; Statistically-driven Computer Grammars in English (editor with E Black and R Garside), 1993; Spoken English on Computer (editor with G Myers and J Thomas), 1995; Corpus Annotation (editor with R Garside and T McEnery), 1997; Longman Grammar of Spoken and Written English (with D Biber, S Johansson, S Conrad and E Finegan), 1999; Longman Student Grammar of Spoken and Written English (with D Biber and S Conrad), 2002; Longman Student Grammar of Spoken and Written English Workbook (with S Conrad and D Biber), 2002; A Glossary of English Grammar, 2006; English – One Tongue, Many Voices (with J Svartvik), 2006. Contributions to: A Review of English Literature; Lingua; New Society; Linguistics; Dutch Quarterly Review of Anglo-American Letters; Times Literary Supplement; Prose Studies; The Rising Generation; Transactions of the Philological Society; Language Learning; International Journal of Corpus Linguistics; English Language and Linguistics. Honours: FilDr, University of Lund, 1987; British Academy, fellow, 1987; Hon DLitt, University of Wolverhampton, 2002; Listed in numerous Who's Who and biographical publications. Membership: Academia Europea; Member, Det Norske Videnskaps-Akademi, 1993. Address: Department of Linguistics and English Language, Lancaster University, Lancaster, LA1 4YT, England.

LEEM Kanghyun, b. 21 May 1970, Seoul, South Korea. Associate Professor. Education: BS, 1995, MA, 1997, PhD, 2001, Oriental Medicine, Kyung Hee University, Seoul, South Korea. Appointments: Assistant Professor, 2003-06, Associate Professor, 2007-, Chairman, 2007-, Department of Oriental Medicine, College of Oriental Medicine, Semyung University, Chungbuk. Publications: Effects of egg yolk proteins on the longitudinal bone growth of adolescent male rats, 2004;

Traditional Korean Medicine: Now and the Future, 2007. Honours: Letter of Commendation, Commissioner of Korea Food & Drug Administration, 2004. Address: Department of Herbology, College of Oriental Medicine, Semyung University, 579, Shinwol-Dong, Jechon-City, Chungbuk 390-711, South Korea.

LEES Andrew John, b. 27 September 1947, Liverpool, England. Professor of Neurology. m. Juana Luisa Pulin Perez Lopez, 1 son, 1 daughter. Education: Royal London Hospital Medical College, University of London; Post Graduate Training, L'Hopital Salpetriere, Paris, University College London Hospitals, National Hospital for Neurology and Neurosurgery. Appointments: Consultant Neurologist, National Hospital for Neurology and Neurosurgery; Professor of Neurology, Institute of Neurology; Director, Reta Lila Weston Institute of Neurological Science; Appeal Steward to the British Boxing Board of Control. Publications: Ray of Hope, authorised biography of Ray Kennedy; Tic and Related Disorders; 820 articles in peer reviewed medical journals. Honours: Charles Smith Lecturer, Jerusalem, 1999; Cotzias Lecturer 2000, Spanish Neurological Association. Memberships: Member, Royal Society of Medicine; Fellow, Royal College of Physicians; President, of the Movement Disorders Society; Former Editor-in-Chief, Movement Disorders. Address: The Reta Lila Weston Institute for Neurological Studies, The Windeyer Building, 46 Cleveland Street, London, W1T 3AA, England. E-mail: a.lees@ion.ucl.ac.uk

LEES David (Bryan) (Sir), b. 23 November 1936, Aberdeen, Scotland. Business Executive. m. Edith Bernard, 1961, 2 sons, 1 daughter. Education: Chartered Accountant. Appointments: Articled Clerk, 1957-62, Senior Audit Clerk, 1962-63, Binder Hamlyn and Co, Chartered Accountants; Chief Accountant, Handley Page Ltd, 1964 0-68; Financial Director, Handley Page Aircraft Ltd, 1969; Chief Accountant, 1970-72, Deputy Controller, 1972-73, Director, Secretary, Controller, 1973-76, GKN Sankey Ltd; Group Finance Executive, 1976-77, General Manager Finance, 1977-82, GKN Ltd; Finance Director, 1982-87, Group Managing Director, 1987-88, Chairman, 1988-, Chief Executive Officer, 1988-97, GKN PLC; Commissioner, Audit Commission, 1983-90; Council Member, 1988-, Chairman, Economic Affairs Committee, 1988-94, Member, President's Committee, currently, Confederation of British Industry; Governor, 1986-, Chair, 2004-, Shrewsbury School; Listed Companies Advisory Committee, 1990-97; Director, 1991-, Chairman, Courtaulds, 1996-98; Director, Bank of England, 1991-99; National Defence Council, 1995-2004; European Round Table, 1995-2002; Panel on Takeovers and Mergers, 2001-; Governor, Sutton's Hospital in Charterhouse, 1995-; Director, Royal Opera House, 1998-; Currently Chairman, Tate and Lyle PLC. Honours: Officer's Cross, Order of Merit, Germany, 1996; Founding Societies Centenary Award for Chartered Accountants, 1999. Memberships: Companion, British Institute of Management; Fellow, Institute of Chartered Accountants; Fellow, Royal Society of Arts; President, Engineering Employers Federation, 1990-92; President, Society of Business Economists, 1994-99. Address: Tate and Lyle PLC, Sugar Quay, Lower Thames Street, London EC3R 6DQ, England.

LEES David James, b. 9 February 1960, Tottenham, England. Geotechnical Engineer. m. Jacqueline Lawson, 1 son, 1 daughter. Education: Diploma, 1980, BSc, Mining, 1983, Associate, 1983, Camborne School of Mines; MSc, Engineering, University of Witwatersrand, 1989. Appointments: Mining Engineer, Johannesburg Consolidated Investment Co, South Africa, 1983-88; Senior Geotechnical

Engineer, Ove Arup & Partners, London, England, 1988-91; Principal Tunnelling Engineer, Babtie Group, UK, 1991-94; Resident Engineer, Geo Engineering, Jersey, UK, 1994-95; Tunnelling Engineer, Snowy Mountains Engineering Corporation, Australia, 1995-99; Editor, Australasian Tunnelling Society Journal, 1997-; Director, David Lees & Associates, Sydney, Australia, 1999-; Manager, Tunnelling, NSW Civil Manager KBR, 2002-04; Editorial Board, Tunnelling and Underground Space Technology, 2003-07; Director, Grouting and Foundation Works, Australia, 2004-; Director, EA Media, 2002-. Publications: Numerous articles in professional journals. Honours: Chartered Professional Engineer (CPEng); Listed in international biographical dictionaries. Memberships: Institution of Engineers, Australia; Australian Underground Construction and Tunnelling Association; Institution of Mining and Metallurgy, UK; British Tunnelling Society. Address: 1 Endeavour Avenue, La Perouse, NSW 2036, Australia. E-mail: d.lees@gfwaust.com Website: www.gfwaust.au

LEEWER William G Jr, b. 17 November 1950, Camden, New Jersey, USA. Educator. Education: BA, Literature, Richard Stockton State College, New Jersey, 1975; MEd, 1987, PhD, 2000, University of South Missouri. Appointments: School Bus Driver, 1975-77; High School English Teacher, 1977-92; District Director, Gifted & Talented, 1987-92; Adjunct Communications Professor, Rowan University of New Jersey, 1984-95; Visiting Assistant, Professor of Education, USM, 2002-03; Assistant Professor of Education & Graduate Co-ordinator, MSU, 2003-. Publications: Involvment: Building Partnerships; Lowering the Failure Rate in Secondary Schools; The Teachers School Security & Safety; Torts for Teachers: A Primer for Educators. Honours: Eagle Scout, 1967; Who's Who Among American Teachers, 1992, 2004; Great Minds of the 21st Century, 2006; Outstanding Professional Award in Education, 2006. Memberships: NCTE; NCTM; KDP; PDK; SPLC Leadership Council; Research Board of Advisors, ABI; ACLU; Founding/Charter Member: WWII National Museum, Washington DC; Wall of Tolerance; MLK, Junior National Memorial Project; National D-Day Museum, Louisiana; National Law Enforcement Memorial & Museum; Disabled Veteran Life Member Foundation; The Wall Society, Vietnam Veterans Memorial. E-mail: wleewer@meridion.msstate.edu

LEGGE-BOURKE Victoria Lindsay, b. 12 February 1950, Witchford, Cambridgeshire, England. Business Executive. Education: Benenden and St Hilda's College, Oxford. Appointments: Social Attaché, British Embassy, Washington, USA, 1971-73; Director, Junior Tourism LTD, 1974-81; Lady-in-Waiting, HRH The Princess Royal, 1974-86; Extra Lady-in-Waiting, HRH The Princess Royal, 1986-; Special Assistant, 1983-89, Head of Protocol, 1991-94, American Embassy, London; Council of the American Museum in Britain, 1995-; Executive Director, 1995-98, Executive Director of Cultural and Social Affairs, 1999-, Goldman Sachs International; Governor of the English Speaking Union, 1996-99; Director, Lehman Brothers, 1998-99. Honours: LVO, 1986; Meritorious Honor Award, US State Department, 1994. Membership: The Pilgrims. Address: 72 Albany Mansions, Albert Bridge Road, London SW11 4PQ, England. E-mail: victoria.legge-bourke@gs.com

LEGH Davis Piers Carlis (The Hon), b. 21 November 1951, Compton, England. Chartered Surveyor. m. Jane Wynter Bee, 2 sons, 2 daughters. Education: Eton, Royal Agricultural College, Cirencester. Appointments: Senior Partner, John German, 1994-99; Senior Partner, Germans,

1999-2000; Chairman, Fisher, German Chartered Surveyors, 2000-. Honour: FRICS. Memberships: Chairman, Taxation Committee, CLA. 1993-97; Chairman, East Midlands Region Country Land and Business Association (CLA), 2002-. Address: Cubley Lodge, Ashbourne, Derbyshire DE6 2FB, England.

LEGRIS Manuel Christopher, b. 19 October 1964, Paris, France. Ballet Dancer. Education: Paris Opera School of Dancing. Career: Member, Corps de Ballet, 1980, Danseur Etoile, 1986-, Paris Opéra; Major roles, Paris Opéra, include Arepo, Béjart, 1986, In the Middle Somewhat Elevated, Forsythe, 1987, Magnificat, Neumeier, 1987, Rules of the Game, Twyla Tharp, 1989, La Belle au Bois Dormant, Nureyev, 1989, Manon, MacMillan, 1990, Dances at the Gathering, Robbins, 1992; In Hamburg created Cinderella Story and Spring and Fall, Neumeier; Appearances, Bolshoi Ballet, Moscow, La Scala, Milan, Royal Ballet, London, New York City Ballet, Tokyo Ballet, Stuttgart Ballet, elsewhere. Honours: Gold Medal, Osaka Competition, 1984; Prix du Cercle Corpeaux, 1986; Nijinsky Prize, 1988; Benois de la Danse Prize, 1998; Chevalier des Arts et des Lettres, 1998; Nijinsky Award, 2000. Address: Théâtre National de l'Opéra de Paris, 8 rue Scribe, 75009 Paris, France.

LEHMANN Christian, b. 3 August 1957, Morat, Switzerland. Scientist. Education: Chemistry Studies, 1977-81, Doctoral Thesis, Laboratory of Organic Chemistry, 1981-86, Swiss Federal Institute of Technology, Zurich, Switzerland. Appointments: Postdoctoral Researcher on RNA synthesis, MRC Laboratory of Molecular Biology, Cambridge, England, 1987-88; G. S. Rosenkranz Fellow, Laboratory of Organic Chemistry, Swiss Federal Institute of Technology, Zurich, 1989-90; Researcher, Pharma Research New Technologies, F Hoffmann-La Roche AG, Basel, 1991-95; Responsible for molecular modelling, Institute of Organic Chemistry, 1995-2001, Scientific Host to the Faculty of Sciences, independent studies on various topics in molecular biostructural design, 2001-2003, University of Lausanne; Scientific Host to the Faculty of Environmental Sciences, project design in various areas, Ecole Polytechnique Fédérale de Lausanne, 2003-; Development of a Center of Excellence for Chemistry Concepts in 3 Dimensions (C3D-Center). Publications: Numerous articles in scientific journals and papers presented at conferences as author and co-author include most recently: Molecular Modelling Methods: Molecular Modelling: Indispensable Tool at the Interface between Structural Analysis and Molecular Design, 2000; Crystal Structure of a Synthetic Cyclodecapeptide Template for TASP Design, 2001; Bicyclo[3.2.1]amide-DNA: a chiral, non-chiroselective base-pairing system, 2002; One Good Turn Deserves Another: Regular Turns in Peptide and Nucleic Acid Templates, 2003; Polarization Alternation Driven Electron Transfer (PADET) in Nucleic Acid and Porpho-Helicene Structures, 2006; Lifetime forwarding E-mail addresses of both Swiss Polytechnics: lehmannc.3d@a3.epfl.ch and lehmannc3d@alumni.ethz.ch. Honours: G. S. Rosenkranz Fellowship, 1989; Silver Medal, American Peptide Society, 2001; Elected Fellow of the World Innovation Foundation, 2002; Nominated Member of the Steering Committee of the Science Advisory Board, 2003-2004; Archimedes Award, Da Vinci Diamond, IBC, 2006; IBA Scientist of the Year 2006; Founding Member, American Order of Excellence (FAOE); International Order of Merit (IOM); American Medal of Honor, Presidential Seal of Honor, ABI, 2006; Universal Award of Accomplishment, ABI, 2006; International Peace Prize and Legion of Honor Laureate, United Cultural Convention, USA, 2006; Vice-President of the World Congress of Arts, Sciences and Communications,

2007; Listed in Who's Who publications and biographical dictionaries. Memberships: Swiss Chemical Society; European Peptide Society; American Peptide Society; Fellow, World Innovation Foundation. Address: Ecole Polytechnique Fédérale and University of Lausanne, CH-1015 Lausanne, Switzerland. E-mail: christian.lehmann@epfl.ch

LEHOTKA Gabor, b. 20 July 1938, Vác, Hungary. Organist; Composer; Educator. Education: Degree of Organist-Educator, 1963, Degree of Composer-Music Theory Teacher, 1965, Ferenc Liszt Academy of Music. Career: Soloist, National Philharmonic Society, 1963-80; Organ Teacher, Béla Bartók Conservatoire, 1969-85; Organ Teacher, Ferenc Liszt Academy of Music, 1975-; Organ Construction: Vác (organ built by Jehmlich Company of Dresden), 1976; Training organ for in-practice organists, Vigadó, Budapest (Aqunincum Organ Factory), 1978; Franciscan Church, Vác (Aquincum Organ Factory), 1979; Bartók Hall, Szombathely (Jehmlich Co), 1980; Kodály Grammar School, Kecskemét (Jehmlich Co), 1983; The House of Arts, Szekszárd (Jehmlich Co), 1989; Music Academy of Budapest (Jehmlich Co), 1995; Dohány Street Synagogue, Budapest (Jehmlich Co), 1996; Jury Member of several organ competitions, 1978-99. Compositions: Numerous compositions from 1959 onwards include: Works published in print: Published in USA: Noël pour Orgue, 1981; Suite Française pour Orgue, 1984; Organ Symphony No 4 for Organ Solo, 1983; Veni, Creator Spiritus for SATB Chorus and Organ, 1993; Sabbato ad vesperas Hymn for SATB Soli, SATB Chorus and Organ, 1994; Published in Germany: Präludium, Choral und Fuge für eine Silbermannorgel, 1988; Barock-Sonate für Trompete und Orgel, 1988; Vier Koreanischen Volkslieder fur Trompete und Orgel, 2006; Trompetenkonzert fur Trompete und Orchester, 2006; Published in France: Quintette pour instruments à vent, 1991; Major works: Sermon on the Mount – Oratorio for mixed choir, soloists and full orchestra, 2002; Eszter (Esther) – Opera in three acts, 2005; The Jáki Mass for mixed choir and full orchestra (re-orchestrated in 1999); Hommage à Händel – Organ Concerto (re-orchestrated in 1999; 2nd Organ Concerto for organ and full orchestra, 2003; Violin Concerto for full orchestra, 1984; Amor Sanctus, fifteen choral works with organ accompaniment on Medieval poems, 1990-92; Latin Mass for mixed choir, 1993. Recordings: Almost 50 recordings including solo albums, collaborations, accompaniments and continuo, 1965-. Publications: Books: My Instrument, the Organ, 1993; The 20th Anniversary of the Vác Organ, 1996; The Methodology of Teaching to Play the Organ, 2000; Articles in music journals. Honours include: Ferenc Liszt Prize, 1974; Artist of Merit of the People's Republic of Hungary, 1978; Chevalier de l'Ordre des Arts et des Lettres, 1986; Deputy Director General, IBC, 2005. Memberships: Founding Member, Ferenc Liszt Society; Founding Member, Zoltán Kodály Society. Address: Vam Utca 6, 2600 Vác, Hungary

LEHTONEN Hannu Jalmari, b. 28 December 1942, Vihti, Finland. Civil Engineer (Technician). Education: Civil Engineer, Soil and Hydraulic Engineering, 1967; First Class Foreman of Concrete Construction, Capacitate qualifications for bearing constructions, 1988. Appointments: Assistant Controller, 1967, Planner, 1968-72, Assistant Controller, 1973, Foreman, 1974-75, Responsible Foreman, 1976-84, Building Engineer, Technician, 1984-86, Managing Director, 1987-90, Responsible Foreman, 1990-91, Unemployed, 1992-2002, Pensioner, 2003-. Publications: Coherent Theory®, 2000; General Coherent Theory®, 2001; Coherent Jurisdiction Theory®, 2002; Specific Coherent Theory®, 2003; The Basic Axioms of Specific Coherent Theory®,

2003; The Basic Axioms of Coherent Gravitational Theory®, 2003; The Basic Axioms of Coherent Vacuum Ball Magnet Theory®, 2003; The Basic Axioms of Coherent Vacuum Ball Theory®, 2003; The Final Summarise of Coherent Science®, 2003; The Applications Model of Coherent Science®, 2004; Coherent Neutrino Vacuum Ball Physics®, 2004; The Theory Verifications of Coherent Science®, 2004; Neutrino Vacuum Ball Chemistry of Coherent Science®, 2005; Supra-Synthesis of the Coherent Science®, 2005; General Theory of Coherent Science, 2006; General Theory of the Crosswise Attraction Power Actions, 2006. Memberships: Finnish Artificial Intelligence Society; Rakennusmestarien Keskuliitto r y. Address: Maijanojantie 314, 03400 Vihti, Finland.

LEIBOVITZ Annie, b. 2 October 1949, Connecticut, USA. Photographer. Education: San Francisco Art Institute. Career: Photographed rock'n'roll stars and other celebrities for Rolling Stone magazine, 1970s; Chief Photographer, Vanity Fair, 1983-; Proprietor, Annie Leibovitz Studio, New York; Celebrity portraits include studies of John Lennon, Mick Jagger, Bette Midler, Louis Armstrong, Ella Fitzgerald, Jessye Norman, Mikhail Baryshnikov, Arnold Schwarzenegger, Tom Wolfe; Retrospective exhibition, Smithsonian National Portrait Gallery, Washington DC, 1991. Publications: Photographs 1970-90, 1992; Women, with Susan Sontag, 2000. Honours: Innovation in Photography Award, American Society of Magazine Photographers, 1987. Address: Annie Leibowitz Studio, 55 Vandam Street, New York, NY 10013, USA.

LEIGH Elisabeth Sarah, b. 14 July 1939, London, England. Writer; Lecturer. Education: BA, French and Italian, Somerville College, Oxford; Piccolo Teatro School of Mime, Milan; Central School of Speech and Drama, London. Appointments: Researcher, Producer, Director, BBC Television, 1963-68; Producer, Director, Yorkshire Television, 1969; Independent documentary film producer/director, films for BBCTV, Thames TV and Yorkshire TV, 1969-82; Contributor, food and magazine features, Sunday Times, 1984-91; Novelist, 1989-; Lecturer in Creative Writing, City of Westminister College, London, 1999-. Publications: 5 novels; Sunday Times Guide to Enlightened Eating; Articles for Sunday Times, Elle and Evening Standard. Honours: British Association for the Advancement of Science: Experiment in Time, 1969; BISFA Award, Call for Help, 1971; Argos Award for Consumer Journalism, 1987. Memberships: Society of Authors. Address: c/o David Higham Associates, 5-8 Lower John Street, London W1R 4HA, England.

LEIGH Jennifer Jason, b. 5 February 1962, Los Angeles, California, USA. Actress. Career: Appeared in Walt Disney TV movie The Young Runaways, age 15; Other TV films include The Killing of Randy Webster, 1981, The Best Little Girl in the World, 1981; Film appearances including Eyes of a Stranger, 1981, Fast Times at Ridgemont High, 1982, Grandview, USA, 1984, Flesh and Blood, 1985, The Hitcher, The Men's Club, 1986, Heart of Midnight, The Big Picture, 1989, Miami Blues, Last Exit to Brooklyn, 1990, Crooked Hearts, Backdraft, 1991, Rush, Single White Female, 1992, Short Cuts, 1993, The Hudsucker Proxy, Mrs Parker and the Vicious Circle, 1994, Georgia, 1995, Kansas City, 1996, Washington Square, 1997, eXistenZ, 1999; The King is Alive, 2000; The Anniversary Party, 2001; Crossed Over, Road to Perdition, 2002; In The Cut, 2003; The Machinist, Childstar, 2004; The Jacket, Palindromes, Easter Sunday, Rag Tale, 2005; Margot at the Wedding, Lymelife, 2007; Stage appearances including Sunshine, Off-Broadway, 1989. Address: c/o Elaine Rich, 2400 Whitman Place, Los Angeles, CA 90211, USA.

LEIGH Mike, b. 20 February 1943, Salford, Lancashire, England. Dramatist; Film and Theatre Director. m. Alison Steadman, 1973, divorced 2001, 2 sons. Education: Royal Academy of Dramatic Arts; Camberwell School of Arts and Crafts; Central School of Art and Design; London Film School. Publications: Plays: The Box Play, 1965; My Parents Have Gone to Carlisle, The Last Crusade of the Five Little Nuns, 1966; Nenaa, 1967; Individual Fruit Pies, Down Here and Up There, Big Basil, 1968; Epilogue, Glum Victoria and the Lad with Specs, 1969; Bleak Moments, 1970; A Rancid Pong, 1971; Wholesome Glory, The Jaws of Death, Dick Whittington and His Cat, 1973; Babies Grow Old, The Silent Majority, 1974; Abigail's Party, 1977, also TV play; Ecstasy, 1979; Goose-Pimples, 1981; Smelling a Rat, 1988; Greek Tragedy, 1989; It's a Great Big Shame!, 1993; Two Thousand Years, 2005. TV films: A Mug's Game, Hard Labour, 1973; The Permissive Society, The Bath of the 2001 F A Cup, Final Goalie, Old Chums, Probation, A Light Snack, Afternoon, 1975; Nuts in May, Knock for Knock, 1976; The Kiss of Death, 1977; Who's Who, 1978; Grown Ups, 1980; Home Sweet Home, 1981; Meantime, 1983; Four Days in July, 1984; Feature films: Bleak Moments, 1971; The Short and Curlies, 1987; High Hopes, 1988; Life is Sweet, 1990; Naked, 1993; Secrets and Lies, 1996; Career Girls, 1997; Topsy Turvy, 1999; All or Nothing, 2002; Vera Drake, 2004. Radio Play: Too Much of a Good Thing, 1979. Honours: Golden Leopard, Locarno Film Festival, 1972; Golden Hugo, Chicago Film Festival, 1972; George Devine Award, 1973; Evening Standard Award, 1981; Drama Critics Choice, London, 1981; Critics Prize, Venice Film Festival, 1988; Honorary MA, Salford University, 1991, Northampton, 2000; OBE, 1993; Best Director Award, Cannes Film Festival, 1993; Palme D'Or, Cannes Film Festival, 1996; Honorary DLitt, Stafford, 2000, Essex, 2002; Best British Independent Film, 2005; Best Director, British Independent Film Awards, 2005; Best Film, Evening Standard British Film Awards, 2005; David Lean Award for Achievement in Direction; BAFTA Awards, 2005. Address: The Peters, Fraser and Dunlop Group Ltd, 503/4 The Chambers, Chelsea Harbour, London SW10 0XF, England.

LEITH Jake Quintin, b. 18 November 1958, Bushey, Hertfordshire, England. Chartered Designer. Education: BA, Honours, Textiles (Printed and Woven), Loughborough College of Art and Design, 1981; MA, Textiles and Fashion, Birmingham Institute of Art and Design, 1982. Appointments: Export Designer, Everest Fabrics, Ghaziabad, India, 1983-84; Design Consultant, Europa Shop Equipment Ltd, 1984-85; Interior Designer, Fantasy Finishes, London, 1985-86; Senior Partner, The Jake Leith Partnership (an interior design consultancy), 1986-. Publications: Article: Realising Entrepreneurial Ambition, CSD Magazine, 2001; The Designer Magazine, 2002. Memberships: Fellow, Chartered Society of Designers, 1995-, Vice President, 2004-07, Honorary Secretary, 2008-; FRSA, 1996. Address: Holly Cottage, 16 Chapel Cottages, Hemel Hempstead, Hertfordshire HP2 5DJ, England. E-mail: jake@jlp.uk.com Website: jlp.uk.com

LEITH Prudence Margaret, b. 18 February 1940, Cape Town, South Africa. Caterer; Author. m. Rayne Kruger, 1 son, 1 daughter. Education: Haywards Heath, Sussex; St Mary's, Johannesburg; Cape Town University; Sorbonne, Paris; Cordon Bleu School, London. Appointments: Founder and Managing Director: Leith's Ltd (formerly Leith's Good Food Ltd), 1960-65; Leith's Restaurant, 1969-95; Leith's School of Food and Wine, 1975-95; Board Member: Whitbread plc, 1995-2005; Triven VCT, 1999-2003; Halifax plc, 1995-99; Safeway plc (formerly Argyll Group plc), 1989-96; Leeds Permanent Building Society, 1992-95; British Railways Board, 1980-85; British Transport Hotels, 1977-83; Cookery Correspondent: Daily Mail, 1969-73; Sunday Express, 1976-80; The Guardian, 1980-85; The Mirror, 1995-98; Non-Executive Director: Woolworths, 2001-; Omega International plc, 2004-; Consultant, Compass Group plc, 2001-. Publications include: 12 cookbooks including Leith's Cookery Bible with Caroline Waldegrave; 3 novels in print; TV series include: Best of British, BBC2; Take 6 Cooks, Channel 4; Tricks of the Trade, BBC1. Honours: Corning Award Food Journalist of the Year, 1979; Glenfiddich Trade Journalist of the Year, 1983; Honorary Fellow, Hotel, Catering and Institutional Management Association, 1986; Order of the British Empire, 1989; Veuve Clicquot Business Woman of the Year, 1990; Honorary Fellow, Salford University, 1992; Honorary Fellow, The City and Guilds of London Institute, 1992-97; Visiting Professor, University of North London, 1993; Freedom of the City of London, 1994; Honorary DSc, The University of Manchester, 1996; Honorary Doctor of Business Administration, Greenwich University, 1996; Honorary Doctor of Letters, Queen Margaret College, Edinburgh, 1997; Honorary Doctorate, The Open University, 1997; Master of the University of North London, 1997; Deputy Lieutenant of Greater London, 1998-; Doctor of the University, Oxford Brookes, 2000; Honorary Doctorate, City University, 2005. Memberships: Trustee/Director, Training for Life, 1999; Commissioner, Lord Griffiths Debt Commission, 2004-05; Chairman: The British Food Trust, 1997-; 3E's Enterprises Ltd, 1998; Kings College for Technology and the Arts, 2000-; Ashridge Management College, 2002-; 3C's Limited, 2002-. Address: Castleton Glebe, Moreton in Marsh, Gloucester, GL56 0SZ, England.

LELAS Snjezana, b. 29 April 1971, Zagreb, Croatia. Pharmacologist. Education: BA, 1992, D Phil, 1996, University of Oxford, England. Appointments: Postdoctoral Fellow, Louisiana State University, Medical Center, New Orleans, Louisiana, USA, 1997-99; Postdoctoral Fellow, Harvard Medical School, Southborough, Massachusetts, USA, 1999-2001; Senior Research Investigator, Bristol-Myers Squibb, Wallingford, Connecticut, USA, 2002-. Publications: Articles in professional journals. Honours: Nuffield Scholar, 1991, Overseas Research Student Award, 1995, University of Oxford. Memberships: Society for Neuroscience; American Society for Pharmacology and Experimental Therapeutics; Behavioural Pharmacology Society. Address: 3B Oak Hill Drive, Clinton, CT 06413, USA. E-mail: snjezana.lelas@bms.com

LEMPER Ute, b. 4 July 1963, Munster, Germany. Singer; Dancer; Actress. Education: Max Reinhardt-Seminar, Vienna. Appointments: Leading Role, Viennese Production of Cats, 1983; Appeared in Peter Pan, Berlin, Cabaret, Düsseldorf and Paris; Chicago, 1997-99; Life's A Swindle tour, 1999; Punishing Kiss tour, 2000; Albums include: Ute Lemper Sings Kurt Weill, 1988; Vol 2, 1993; Threepenny Opera, 1988; Mahoganny Songspiel, 1989; Illusions, 1992; Espace Indécent, 1993; City of Strangers, 1995; Berlin Cabaret Songs, 1996; All that Jazz/The Best of Ute Lemper, 1998; Punishing Kiss, 2000; Film appearances include: L'Autrichienne, 1989; Moscou Parade, 1992; Coupable d'Innocence, 1993; Prêt à Porter, 1995; Bogus, 1996; Combat de Fauves, 1997; A River Made to Drown In, 1997; Appetite, 1998; Ute Lemper: Blood & Feathers, 2005. Honours: Moliere Award, 1987; Laurence Oliver Award; French Culture Prize, 1993. Address: c/o Oliver Gluzman, 40 rue de la Folie Regnault, 75011 Paris, France.

LENDL Ivan, b. 7 March 1960, Czechoslovakia (US citizen, 1992). Retired Professional Tennis Player. m. Samantha Frankel, 1989, 5 daughters. Appointments: Winner, Italian Junior Singles, 1978; French Junior Singles, 1978; Wimbledon Junior Singles, 1978; Spanish Open Singles, 1980, 1981; South American Open Singles, 1981; Canadian Open Singles, 1980, 1981; WCT Tournament of Champion Singles, 1982; WCT Masters Singles, 1982; WCT Finals Singles, 1982; Masters Champion, 1985. 1986; French Open Champion, 1984, 1986, 1987; US Open Champion, 1985, 1986, 1987; US Clay Court Champion, 1985; Italian Open Champion, 1986; Australian Open Champion, 1989, 1990; Finalist Wimbledon, 1986; Held, World No 1 Ranking for a Record 270 weeks; Named World Champion, 1985, 1986, 1990; Retired, 1994. Publication: Ivan Lendl's Power Tennis. Honours: Granted American Citizenship, 1992; ATP Player of the Year, 1985, 1986, 1987; Inducted, International Tennis Hall of Fame, 2001. Memberships: Laureus World Sports Academy. Address: c/o Laureus World Sports Academy, 15 Hill Street, London W1 5QT, England.

LENNARTSSON Olof Walter, b. 27 October 1943, Sweden. Physicist. m. Nancy Karllee, 1 son. Education: MEng, 1969, PhD, Plasma Physics, 1974, Royal Institute of Technology, Stockholm, Sweden. Appointments: NAS/NRC Research Associate, 1974-76; Docent, Royal Institute of Technology, Sweden, 1976-78; Staff Scientist, Lockheed Martin Missiles and Space, 1979-. Publications: Numerous articles in scientific journals and books. Memberships: American Geophysical Union; American Institute of Physics. Address: Lockheed Martin Space Systems Co, Advanced Technology Center, ADCS, B255, 3251 Hanover Street, Palo Alto, CA 94304, USA.

LENO Jay (James Douglas Muir Leno), b. 28 April 1950, New Rochelle, New York, USA. Comedian; TV host. m. Mavis Nicholson. Education: Emerson College, Boston, USA. Career: Standup comedian and comedy writer, 1970s; One of several guest hosts, 1986, Executive guest host, 1987-92, Host, 1992-, Tonight Show (NBC); Films include: American Hot Wax, 1978; Silver Bears, 1978; Americathon, 1979; What's Up; Hideous Sun Demon (voice), 1983; Collision Course, 1989; We're Back! A Dinosaur's Story (voice), 1993; The Flintstones, 1994; Providence (voice), 1999; The Fairly OddParents (voice), 2001-05; Robots (voice), 2005; Ice Age 2: The Meltdown (voice), 2006; The Jimmy Timmy Power Hour 3: The Jerkinators (voice), 2006; Payback, 2006; Christmas Is Here Again (narrator), 2007. Honours: Emmy Award, 1995. Address: The Tonight Show with Jay Leno, 3000 West Alameda Avenue, Burbank, CA 91523, USA. Website: www.nbc.com/The_Tonight_Show_with_Jay_Leno/index.shtml

LENTNER Csaba, b. 30 August 1962, Papa, Hungary. Economist; Educator. Education: BS, Economics, College of Finance and Accountancy, Zalaegerszeg, 1984; MSc, 1989, Doctorate, 1991, Economics, University of Economics, Budapest; Dr fin habil, West Hungarian University, Sopron, 2003; CPA, Hungarian Judicial Chamber, 1994; PhD, CSc, Economics, Hungarian Academy of Sciences, Budapest, 1995. Appointments: Analyst Economist, Hungarian National Bank, Budapest, 1990-91; Financing Section Head, Hungarian Foreign Trading Bank, Budapest, 1991-93; Director, Danube Bank Joint-Stock Co, Budapest, 1993-96; Board of Directors, Agricultural and Food Industrial Joint Stock Co, Fertod, 1994-98; President, Control Sub Commission, Budapest General Assembly, 1996-98; President, Control Commission, Funeral Joint-Stock Co, 1997-98; Associate Professor, Head of

Department, West Hungarian University, Sopron, 1996-2007; Member, Hungarian Parliament, Budapest, 1998-2002; President, Hungarian-Slovanian Section, Interparliamentary Union, Brussels, 1998-2002; Vice-Dean, WHU for Faculty of Economics, 2003-05; Study of British monetary and fiscal policy, England, 2007-; Chairman, Advisory Board for Public Foundation of Gyor, 2007-; Professor, Head Advisor, Private Business College of Wekerle Alexander, 2008-. Publications: Books: Change-over and Financial Policy, 2005; Regulation of Money Markets in Hungary, 2006; Financial Policies Strategies at the Beginning of the XXI Century, The Health Care System as a New Competitive Factor in the Light of the Convergence Programme, 2007; Articles: The Competitiveness of Hungarian University-Based Knowledge Centres in European Economic and Higher Education Area, 2007. Memberships: Hungarian Academy of Sciences Committee for Future Research; Hungarian Accreditation Committee for Economics. Address: 51 Dozsa Gyorgy rkp, Gyor 9026, Hungary. E-mail: dr.lentnercsaba@gmail.com Website: www.lentnercsaba.hu

LEONARD Elmore (John, Jr), b. 11 October 1925, New Orleans, Louisiana, USA. Novelist. m. (1) Beverly Cline, 30 August 1949, 3 sons, 2 daughters, divorced 7 October 1977, (2) Joan Shepard, 15 September 1979, deceased, 13 January 1993, (3) Christine Kent, 15 August 1993. Education: BA, University of Detroit, 1950. Publications: 33 novels including: Hombre, 1961; City Primeval, 1980; Split Images, 1981; Cat Chaser, 1982; Stick, 1983; Labrava, 1983; Glitz, 1985; Bandits, 1986; Touch, 1987; Freaky Deaky, 1988; Killshot, 1989; Get Shorty, 1990; Maximum Bob, 1991; Rum Punch, 1992; Pronto, 1993; Riding the Rap, 1995; Out of Sight, 1996; Pagan Babies, 2000; Fire in the Ole, 2001; When the Women Come Out to Dance, 2002; Tishomingo Blues, 2002; A Coyote's in the House, 2003; Mr Paradise, 2004; The Hot Kid, 2005; Up in Honey's Room, 2007. Other: The Tonto Woman and Other Western Stories, 1998; Screenplays: Cuba Libre, 1998; Be Cool, 1999. Honours: Edgar Allan Poe Award, 1984, and Grand Master Award, 1992, Mystery Writers of America; Michigan Foundation for the Arts Award for Literature, 1985; Honorary degrees in Letters from Florida Atlantic University, 1995, University of Detroit Mercy, 1997. Memberships: Writers Guild of America; PEN; Authors Guild; Western Writers of America; Mystery Writers of America. Address: c/o Michael Siegel, Brillstein-Grey Entertainment, 9150 Wilshire Boulevard, Beverly Hills, CA 90212, USA.

LEONARD Hugh, (John Keyes Byrne), b. 9 November 1926, Dublin, Ireland. Playwright. m. Paule Jacquet, 1955, 1 daughter. Publications: Plays: The Big Birthday, 1957; A Leap in the Dark, 1957; Madigan's Lock, 1958; A Walk on the Water, 1960; The Passion of Peter Ginty, 1961; Stephen D, 1962; The Poker Session, 1963; Dublin 1, 1963; The Saints Go Cycling In, 1965; Mick and Mick, 1966; The Quick and the Dead, 1967; The Au Pair Man, 1968; The Barracks, 1969; The Patrick Pearse Motel, 1971; Da, 1973; Thieves, 1973; Summer, 1974; Times of Wolves and Tigers, 1974; Irishmen, 1975; Time Was, 1976; A Life, 1977; Moving Days, 1981; The Mask of Moriarty, 1984. Television: Silent Song, 1967; Nicholas Nickleby, 1977; London Belongs to Me, 1977; The Last Campaign, 1978; The Ring and the Rose, 1978; Strumpet City, 1979; The Little World of Don Camillo, 1980; Kill, 1982; Good Behaviour, 1982; O'Neill, 1983; Beyond the Pale, 1984; The Irish RM, 1985; A Life, 1986; Troubles, 1987; Parnell and the Englishwoman, 1988; A Wild People, 2001. Films: Herself Surprised, 1977; Da, 1984; Widows' Peak, 1984; Troubles, 1984; Books: Home Before Night, autobiography, 1979; Out After Dark, autobiography, 1988; Parnell and the Englishwoman, 1989; I, Orla! 1990; Rover and other Cats, a memoir, 1992; The Off-Shore Island, novel, 1993; The Mogs, for children, 1995; Magic, 1997; Fillums, 2003. Honours: Honorary DHL (RI); Writers Guild Award, 1966; Tony Award; Critics Circle Award; Drama Desk Award; Outer Critics Award, 1978; Doctor of Literature, Trinity College, Dublin, 1988. Address: 6 Rossaun Pilot View, Dalkey, County Dublin, Ireland.

LEONARD Ray Charles (Sugar Ray), b. 17 May 1956, Wilmington, North Carolina, USA. Boxer. m. Juanita Wilkinson, 1980, divorced 1990, 2 sons. Appointments: Amateur Boxer, 1970-77; won 140 of 145 amateur fights; World amateur champion, 1974; US amateur athletic union champion, 1974; Pan-American Games Gold Medallist, 1975; Olympic Gold Medallist, 1976; Guaranteed Record Purse of $25,000 for first professional fight, 1977; Won, North American Welterweight title from Pete Ranzany, 1979; Won World Boxing Council Version of World Welterweight title from Wilfred Benitez, 1979; Retained title against Dave Green, 1980; Lost it to Roberto Duran, Montreal, 1980; Regained title from Duran, New Orleans, 1980; World Junior Middleweight title, World Boxing Association, 1981; Won, WBA World Welterweight title from Tommy Hearns to become undisputed World Champion, 1981; Drew rematch, 1989; 36 professional fights, 33 wins, lost 2, 1 draw; Retired from boxing, 1982; returned to ring, 1987; Won World Middleweight title; Lost to Terry Norris, 1991; retired, 1991, 1997; returned to ring, 1997; Lost International Boxing Council Middleweight title fight to Hector Camacho, 1992; Commentator, Home Box Office TV Co; Motivational speaker; Co-host, The Contender. Address: Suite 303, 4401 East West Highway, Bethesda, MD 20814, USA.

LEONARD Todd Jay, b. 16 November 1961, Shelbyville, Indiana, USA. University Professor. Education: BA with Honors and Distinction, Humanities, 1985, MA, History, 1987, Purdue University, Indiana, USA; Diploma, Teaching English as a Foreign Language, English Language Centre, London, England, 1993; PhD, Social Science, Empresarial University of Costa Rica, 2004. Appointments include: Visiting Professor, La Universidad de las Americas, Costa Rica, 1987; Visiting Lecturer, 1988, Course Coordinator, 1988-89, Department of Foreign Languages and Literatures, Purdue University, Indiana, USA; Assistant English Teacher, Japan Exchange and Teaching Programme, 1989-92; Associate Professor of English, Hirosaki Gakuin University, Japan, 1992-; Part-time Lecturer, Faculty of Education, 1993-, Part-time Lecturer, Faculty of Liberal Arts, 1993-, Hirosaki University, Japan; English Language Committee Member, National Entrance Examination, Daigaku Nyushi Center, Tokyo, 1998-2002; Ordained Minister, Universal Spiritualist Association, Muncie, Indiana, 2003. Publications: Academic books include: East Meets West: Understanding Misunderstandings between ALTs and JTEs, 1999; Orbit English Reading, 2004; ESL related textbooks include: Team-Teaching Together: A Bilingual Resource Handbook for JTES and AETS; East Meets West: An American in Japan, 1998; Trendy Traditions! A Cross-Cultural Skills-Based Reader of Essays on the United States, 2001; Business as Usual: An Integrated Approach to Learning English, 2004; Talking to the Other Side: A History of Modern Mediumship and Spiritualism-a study of the Religion, Science, Philosophy and Mediums that encompass this American-made Religion, 2005; Numerous academic articles and book reviews. Honours include: Dean's List, Purdue University; Outstanding and Distinguished Graduate Instructor, Purdue University, 1987; Rotary Scholar, La Universidad de Costa Rica, 1987; Governor Appointed

Trustee for the Committee on Foreigners Living in Aomori, Aomori Foundation for International Relations, 1991-92; Pi Sigma Alpha; Sigma Delta Pi; Phi Alpha Theta; Phi Kappa Phi; Best of JALT 2002 Award. Memberships include: Japan Association for Language Teachers; Modern Language Journal Association; Japan Association of Comparative Culture; Life Member Purdue Alumni Association; Association for the Scientific Study of Religion (ASSR); Indiana Association of Historians; Indiana Association of Spiritulists (IAOS); Universal Spiritulist Association (USA). Address: Jyonan 4-3-19, Hirosaki-shi, Aomori-ken 036-8232 Japan. E-mail: tleonard@infoaomori.ne.jp Website: www.toddjayleonard.com

LEONHARDT Joyce LaVon, b. 17 December 1927, Aurora, Nebraska, USA. Poet. Education: BS, Union College, Lincoln, 1952. Appointments: High School Teacher, 1952-76; Junior College Instructor, 1981-90. Contributions to: Several books of poems. Honours: Honourable Mention Certificates; Golden Poet; Silver Poet. Membership: World of Poetry. Address: 1824 Atwood Street, Longmont, CO 80501, USA.

LEONI Tea, b. 25 February 1966, New York, USA. Actress. m. David Duchovny, 1997, 1 son, 1 daughter. Career: Film appearances in Switch, 1991, A League of Their Own, 1992, Wyatt Earp, 1994, Bad Boys, 1995, Flirting with Disaster, 1996, Deep Impact, 1998, There's No Fish Food in Heaven, 1999; The Family Man, 2000; Jurassic Park III, 2001; Hollywood Ending, 2002; People I Know, 2002; House of D, 2004; Spanglish, 2004; Fun with Dick and Jane, 2005; You Kill Me, 2007; Appeared in TV sitcoms Naked Truth, 1995, Flying Blind, 1995. Address: c/o ICM, 8942 Wilshire Boulevard, Beverly Hills, CA 90211, USA.

LEONIDOPOULOS Georgios, b. 19 April 1958, Kalamata, Messinia, Greece. Electrical, Computer and Electronics Engineer; Researcher; Educator. Education: Diploma, Electrical and Computer Engineering, Patra University, Greece, 1981; Postgraduate, Iowa State University, USA, 1982, Wayne State University, USA, 1983; MSc, 1984; PhD, Electronic and Electrical Engineering, Strathclyde University, Glasgow, Scotland, 1988. Appointments: Trainee Electrical Engineer, Public Electricity Co, Kalamata, Greece, 1979; Teaching Assistant, Strathclyde University, Scotland, 1984-87; Engineering Educator, Secondary School, Kalamata, Greece, 1991-94; Professor, Engineering, Institute of Technology, Kalamata, Greece, 1994-97; Professor, Engineering, Electrical Engineering Department, Institute of Technology, Lamia, Greece, 1997-. Publications include: A method for locating polymeric insulation failure of underground cables, 1998; On the convergence of three series, 1998; Root investigation of third degree algebraic equation, 1998; A mathematical method for solving a particular type of linear differential equations using complex symbolism, 2000; Trigonometric form of the quadratic algebraic equation solution, 2000; Greenhouse dimensions estimation and short time forecast of greenhouse temperature based on net heat losses through the polymeric cover, 2000; Greenhouse daily sun-radiation intensity variation, daily temperature variation and heat profits through the polymeric cover, 2000; Test methods of the four basic mathematical operations, 2001. Honours: Referee of research articles; Patentee in field; Examiner for Greek postgraduate scholarships; Selectee, Euratom research position, Joint European Torus, Culham, Oxford, England, 1990; Head of Electrical Engineering Department, 2000-03; Listee, expert evaluator of European Commission's scientific research and development programmes; European programme Socrates, Greece, 2000-; Grant, Schilizzi Foundation, 1987; Grant,

Empeirikeion Foundation, 1994. Memberships: New York Academy of Sciences; IEEE; National Geographic Society; AMSE. Address: Kilkis 11, Kalamata 24100, Messinia, Greece. E-mail: georgiosleonidopoulos@yahoo.gr

LEONOV Aleksey Arkhipovich (Major-General), b. 30 May 1934, Listianka, Kamerovo Region, Russia. Cosmonaut. m. Svetlana Leonova, 2 daughters. Education: Chuguevsky Air Force School for Pilots; Zhukovsky Air Force Engineering Academy; Cosmonaut Training, 1960. Appointments: Pilot, 1956-59; Member, CPSU, 1957-91; Participant, space-ship Voskhod 2 flight, becoming first man to walk in space, 1965; Pilot Cosmonaut of USSR; Chairman, Council of Founders, Novosti Press Agency, 1969-90; Deputy Commander, Gagarin Cosmonauts Training Centre, 1971; Participant, Soyuz 19-Apollo joint flight, 1975; Major-General, 1975; Deputy Head, Centre of Cosmonaut Training, 1975-92; Director, Cheteck-Cosmos Co, 1992-; Vice-President, Investment Fund Alfa-Capital, 1997-; Vice President, Alpha Bank, 2000. Publications: Numerous books, papers and articles; Two Sides of the Moon (with David Scott), 2004. Honours: Honorary DrScEng; Hero of the Soviet Union, 1965, 1975; Hero of Bulgaria; Hero of Vietnam; Order of Lenin, twice; USSR State Prize, 1981. Memberships: Co-Chairman, Board, International Association of Cosmonauts. Address: Alfa-Capital, Academician Sakharov Prospect 12, 107078 Moscow, Russia.

LÉOTARD François Gérard Marie, b. 26 March 1942, Cannes, France. Politician. m. (1) France Reynier, 1976, (2) Isabelle Duret, 1992, 1 son, 1 daughter. Education: Faculté de Droit, Paris; Institut d'Etudes Politiques, Paris; Ecole Nationale d'Administration. Appointments: Secretary of Chancellery, Ministry of Foreign Affairs, 1968-71; Administration, Town Planning, 1973-76; Sous-Préfet, 1974-77; Mayor of Fréjus, 1977-92, 1993-97; Deputy to National Assembly, for Var, 1978-86, 1988-92, 1995-97; 1997-2002; Conseiller-Général, Var, 1980-88; Secretary, 1982-88, President, 1988-90, 1995-97, Honorary President, 1990-95, Général Parti Républican; Vice-President, 1983-84, President, 1996-, Union pour la Démocratie Française; Minister of Culture and Communications, 1986-88; Member, Municipal Council, Fréjus, 1992; Minister of National Defence, 1993-95; With EU Special Envoy to Macedonia, 2001-; Inspector General de Finances pour l'extérieur, 2001-; Convicted of money-laundering and illegal party funding, received 10 month suspended sentence, 2004. Publications: A Mots Découverts, 1987; Culture: Les Chemins de Printemps, 1988; La Ville aimée: mes chemins de Fréjus, 1989; Pendant la Crise, le spectacle continue, 1989; Adresse au Président des Républiques françaises, 1991; Place de la République, 1992; Ma Liberté, 1995; Pour l'honneur, 1997; Je vous hais tous avec douceur, 2000; Paroles d'immortels, 2001. Honours: Chevalier, Order Nationale du Mérite. Address: Nouvelle UDF, 133 bis rue de l'Université, 75007 Paris, France.

LEPOSA Ronald, b. 5 March 1947, Cleveland, Ohio, USA. Military; Engineering. m. Catherine, 1 daughter. Education: German Language School, 1960-62; Company Mascot, 508th AAA Missile Battalion (NIKE), Warrensville Station, Cleveland, 1958; Communications Specialist, Southeastern Signal School, Fort Gordon, Georgia, 1966; USARPAC, Korea, 1967-68; Communications Electronics, Cryptographic Operators Course, S/G 31 E#47, Lenggreis, Germany, 1968; Attack of the USS Pueblo, 1968; USAREUR, Germany, 1968-69; Exercise Reforger I, Communications Zone, Europe, 1968-69. Appointments: Engineer, East Ohio Gas

Co, 1969-2001. Publications: Article on Pueblo Attack, Benedictine Newspaper, 1968. Address: 18964 Windward Way, Strongsville, Ohio 44136, USA.

LEROY Miss Joy, b. 8 September 1927, Riverdale, Illinois, USA. Miss LeRoy - Model; Narrator; Designer; Author. Education: Texas Technological College, Lubbock, 1946; BS (Honours), Purdue University, West Lafayette, Indiana, 1949. Further studies include sewing, theatre, computer programming, fine arts, music, photography. Appointments: Model, sales representative for Jacques and sales representative for the book department at Loebs, Lafayette, 1950-52; window trimmer, Marshall Field and Co, 1952-53, and sales and display representative, Emerald House, 1954-55, Evanston, Illinois; Turned professional in Detroit in the field of design, modelling and narrating; Model and narrator for companies including: American Motors Corp (Auto and Kelvinator); Speedway Petroleum Co; Ford Motor Company (Auto and Tractor); The Sykes Co; Coca Cola Co; Hoover Vacuum Co; General Motors Co (Chevrolet and Oldsmobile); J L Hudson Co; Jam Handy Organization; Boston, 1962-70 model for "Copley 7" and tour guide, model, free lance writer for The Christian Science Monitor and The Christian Science Publishing Society; later, Special Events Co-ordinator for Opening of the Sheraton Hotel and Prudential Insurance Co; From 1976 to 2008 she has travelled around the seven continents and has earned awards from Maupintours, INTRAV, Royal Viking, and the Crystal Society; She has completed 137 cruises, 5½ years, 2,013 days at sea, 1977-2008. Publications: Articles in field of fashion writing, creative ideas for Youth, and educational Puzz-its, copyrights from 1986-. Honours: Numerous include: Congressional Certificate of Appreciation, 1991; Republican National Hall of Honour, 1992; Republican Presidential Legion of Honour, Republican Presidential Task Force, Wall of Honour, 1993; Republican Senatorial Medal of Freedom, Order of Liberty National Republican Committee, Republican Presidential Legion of Merit and National Republican Senatorial Order of Merit, 1993; Republican Campaign Council, 1994; Ronald Wilson Reagan Eternal Flame of Freedom, 1995; Grand Club, Republican Party of Florida, 1996; International Women of the Year, 1996-99; Woman of the Year, 1998-99, 2000, 2001, 2002, 2003, 2005, 2006, 2007, 2008; Presidential Task Force, Medal of Merit, Republican Party and Life Member Republican Senatorial Inner Circle, 1997; Distinguished 20th Century Republican Leader, 1998; Republican Senatorial Millennium Medal of Freedom, World Laureate of England, Deputy Director General in 1999; Presidential Roundtable Representative from Florida, 2000 to 2008, Ronald Wilson Reagan Founder's Wall, 2002; ABI: 2000 Notable American Women; Deputy Governor and Continental Governor; Millennium Medal of Honour and Presidential Medal of Honour; a Noble Member of the Order of International Ambassadors; International Order of Merit, 2000; Presidential Seal of Honor, 2000; American Order of Excellence, 2000; Secretary-General, Ambassador General, 500 Leaders of Influence - Hall of Fame, 2001; Charter Member of International Honour Society, 2001; Congressional Medal of Excellence, ABI, 2001; Leading Intellectuals of the World; IBC: 2000 Outstanding Intellectuals of the 20th and 21st Century; 500 Founders of the 21st Century; Honours List and American Medal of Honor; American Hall of Fame, 2003; International Medal of Honour, IBC, 2003; World Lifetime Achievement Award, ABI, 2003; Outstanding People of the 21st Century and Who's Who in the 21st Century Medals, 2003; Intellectual of the Year; One Thousand Great Americans, 2003; Noble Prize, and International Peace Prize and Lifetime Achievement Award, United Cultural Convention, 2002; International Register of Profiles,

2003-2005; Vice Consul, 2001; Lifetime Achievement Award, IBC, 2002; Republican Senatorial Medal of Freedom, Star, 2003-2005, and the Republican Senatorial American Spirit Medal, 2006, "The highest honor the Republican members of the US Senate can bestow"; International Visual Artist of the Year, International Hall of Fame, World Academy of Letters, with honours, Living Legends, Da Vinci Diamond and Statesman's Award as Ambassador of Grand Eminence, 2004; World Peace and Diplomacy Presidential Dedication, International Register of Profiles and Living Legends, 13th edition, World Medal of Freedom, Top 100 Artists, 2005; Noble and Genius Laureate for the Leading Intellectuals of the World, ABI, 2005; IBC Meritorious Decoration; Salute to Greatness; Honorary Director General, IBC, 2006; Order of American Ambassadors, 2006; Global Year of Excellence, Life Patron, IBC, 2006; Secretary-General, Lifetime Achievement Statuette, United Cultural Convention, 2006; Vice-President, The President's Cup, World Forum Federation Arts, Science and Communications, Ambassador of International Order of Merit, Gold Laurels for Triumphant Deeds, President's Citation for Recognition of Excellence (Gold Medal for the United States of America – Passion, Courage, Commitment, Success, Excellence, Virtue, Spirit); Director General's Leadership Award, 2007; 2000 Outstanding Intellectuals of the 21st Century & Distinguished Service Order & Cross, ABI, 2008; 500 Great Leaders, Honors Edition for Genius Laureates, ABI, 2008; Lifetime of Greatness Award and member of the Legion of Honour, IBC, 2008; Legion of Honor Medal, ABI, United Cultural Convention, 2008. Address: Apt 2104, 2100 S Ocean Lane, Fort Lauderdale, FL 33316-3827, USA.

LESLIE John, b. 11 July 1923, Philadelphia, USA. Artist; Designer; Sculptor; Fine Art; Photographer. m. (1) Kathryn Elizabeth Frame, (2) Mary Frances Huggins, 3 children. Education: Graduate, Commercial Art with Harry Brodsky, Murrell Dobbins Tech, Philadelphia, 1941; Postgraduate, Fleisher Art Memorial, Philadelphia, 1939-42, Philadelphia Museum School of Industrial Art, 1944, Philadelphia Musical Academy, 1965-67, Pennsylvania State University, 1982-. Appointments include: Staff Artist, Philadelphia Daily News, 1942; Founder, Creative Director, Graphic-Ad Displays Inc, Philadelphia, 1944; Collaborative Designer, Thanksgiving Day Parade and Fashion Show Stage Set Designer, Gimbel Brothers, Philadelphia, 1945; Artist, Muralist, Bonwit Teller, Philadelphia Eagles Football Team, PSFS Bank; Stage Set Designer, Bessie V Hicks School of Dramatic Arts, Philadelphia, 1944-46; Art Director, Dupiex Display and Manufacturing Company Inc, Philadelphia, 1947-54; Designer, Leslie Creations Inc, Lafayette Hill, 1954-65; Founder, Mail Order Methods Inc, Lafayette Hill, Pennsylvania, 1954-57; Artist-Designer, World Treasures, Seven Seas House Inc, Lafayette Hill, Pennsylvania, 1960-65; President, Lions, Lafayette Hill, 1960-71; Founder, Creative Director & Designer of 150 Kopy Kat Inc, franchised Instant Printing Centers in 31 States, Ft Washington, PA, 1968-77; Art Director, Designer, Jesse Jones Industries Inc, Philadelphia, 1978-79; Co-Founder, Art Director, Galerie Marjole Inc, Sanatoga, PA, 1987-89; Lecturer, Limited Edition Fine Arts Prints, 1987-; Fine Art Spokesman, Radio and Television, 1989-; Author, Lasting Impressions, a weekly column on fine art photography, Englewood Herald, Florida, 2000-. Honours: Walter Emerson Baum Award for American Impressionist Painting; Sellers Museum Award for Impressionism in Fine Art Photography; King of Prussia Pastel Painting Award; AMVETS Award for Outstanding Artistic Designs; Playboy Magazine Award for Artistic Merit; Japanese Graphic Arts Industry Award; Works in 23 US museums, US Embassy, Paris, France, and numerous private collections. Memberships:

Woodmere Art Museum, Philadelphia; Arts and Humanities Council, Port Charlotte, Florida; Boca Grande, Florida, Art Alliance; New York Oil Pastel Association; US Army's 8th Armored Division Association; National AMVETS; Military Heritage & Aviation Museum, Punta Gorda, Florida; Les Amis de Veterans Français. Commissions and Creative Works: Designer, Mannequettes, 3-D miniature human figures with cylindrical wooden heads and paper sculptured clothing; Plasti-Coil: An expandable-retractable coil of multicoloured plastic tubing wound over a soft wire core; 3-D's (3 dimensional collages of paper sculpture, painted artwork & layered composition board), all used in major specialty shop and department store windows and interiors across the USA; The Crystal Mall: a climate controlled glass atrium enclosing entire existing downtown shopping districts; Proposed US Veterans of WWII Memorial Hall of Honor; Proposed museum building & interior design for Military Heritage & Aviation Museum, Punta Gorda, Florida; Designer, First avant-garde A-Frame Home on US Atlantic Coast; Collaborative designer of 11 Coarctare Homes, Englewood, Florida, 1997-99; Creator, Inventor: Functional Metal Sculpture – a collection of welded-chromed steel occasional furniture pieces; The Slab Chair: of interlocking leather-covered foam rubber panels; Numerous exhibitions and works in public and private collections. Address: Blueberry Hill Studios, 6318 Zeno Circle, Port Charlotte, FL 33981, USA.

LESSING Doris May, b. 22 October 1919, Kermanshah, Persia. Writer. m. (1) Frank Charles Wisdom, 1939, divorced 1943, 1 son, 1 daughter, (2) Gottfried Anton Nicholas Lessing, 1945, divorced 1949, 1 son. Publications: The Grass Is Singing 1950; Children of Violence, 1952; A Proper Marriage, 1954; Retreat to Innocence, 1956; The Golden Notebook, 1962; A Ripple from the Storm, 1965; The Four-Gated City, 1969; Briefing for a Descent into Hell, 1971; The Summer Before the Dark, 1973; The Memoirs of a Survivor, 1974; Canopus in Argos: Archives, 1979-1983; The Diary of a Good Neighbour, 1983; If the Old Could, 1984; The Diaries of Jane Somers, 1984; The Good Terrorist, 1985; The Fifth Child, 1988; Love, Again, 1996; Mara and Dann, 1999; Ben, in the World, 2000; The Old Age of El Magnifico, 2000; The Sweetest Dream, 2001; The Story of General Dann and Mara's Daughter, Griot and the Snow Dog, 2005; Short stories: Collected African Stories, 2 volumes, 1951, 1973; Five, 1953; The Habit of Loving, 1957; A Man and Two Women, 1963; African Stories, 1964; Winter in July, 1966; The Black Madonna, 1966; The Story of a Non-Marrying Man and Other Stories, 1972; A Sunrise on the Veld, 1975; A Mild Attack of Locusts, 1977; Collected Stories, 2 volumes, 1978; London Observed: Stories and Sketches, 1992; The Grandmothers, 2004; Non-fiction includes: Going Home, 1957, 1968; Particularly Cats, 1967; Particularly Cats and More Cats, 1989; African Laughter: Four Visits to Zimbabwe, 1992; Under My Skin, 1994; Walking in the Shade, 1997. Plays: Each to His Own Wilderness, 1958; Play with a Tiger, 1962; The Singing Door, 1973; Other publications include: Fourteen Poems, 1959; A Small Personal Voice, 1974; Doris Lessing Reader, 1990; Timebites, 2005. Honours: 5 Somerset Maugham Awards, Society of Authors, 1954-; Prix Médicis for French translation, Carnet d'or, 1976; Austrian State Prize for European Literature, 1981; Shakespeare Prize, Hamburg, 1982; W H Smith Literary Award, 1986; Palermo Prize and Premio Internazionale Mondello, 1987; Grinzane Cavour Award, Italy, 1989; Woman of the Year, Norway, 1995; Los Angeles Times Book Prize, 1995; James Tait Memorial Prize, 1995; Premi Internacional Catalunya, Spain, 1999; David Cohen Literary Prize, 2001; Principe de Asturias, Spain, 2001; PEN Award, 2002. Memberships: Associate Member,

American Academy of Arts and Letters, 1974; National Institute of Arts and Letters, USA, 1974; Member, Institute for Cultural Research, 1974; President, Book Trust, 1996-. Address: c/o Jonathon Clowes Ltd, Iron Bridge House, Bridge Approach, London NW1 8BD, England.

LESTER Alexander Norman Charles Phillips, b. 11 May 1956, Walsall, England. Broadcaster. Education: Diploma, Communication Studies, Birmingham Polytechnic, 1978. Appointments: BBC Local and Independent Radio, 1977-86; BBC Radio 2, 1987-; Alex Lester Show, Radio 2, 1991-; Presenter, The Boat Show, BBC2 TV, Appearances on: Call My Bluff, BBC TV; Waterworld, Carlton TV; Lunchtime Live, Meridian TV; Announcer/Voice Over on numerous satellite and terrestrial TV and radio channels. Honours: Patron St Michael's Hospice, St Leonards-on-Sea; Ambassador, Hospital Radio Association. Memberships: Hastings Winkle Club; Equity. Address: c/o MPC Management, MPC House, 15-16 Maple Mews, Maida Vale, London NW6 6UZ, England. E-mail: alex.lester@bbc.co.uk

LESTER Richard, b. 19 January 1932, Philadelphia, USA. American Film Director. m. Deirdre V Smith, 1956, 1 son, 1 daughter. Education: William Penn Carter School; University of Pennsylvania. Appointments: TV Director, CBS, 1952-54; ITV, 1955-59; Composer, 1954-57; Film Director, 1959-; Films directed: The Running, Jumping and Standing Still Film, 1959; It's Trad ad, 1962; The Mouse on the Moon, 1963; A Hard Day's Night, 1963; The Knack, 1965; Help!, 1965; A Funny Thing Happened on the Way to the Forum, 1966; How I Won the War, 1967; Petulia, 1969; The Bed Sitting Room, 1969; The Three Musketeers, 1973; Juggernaut, 1974; The Four Musketeers, 1974; Royal Flash, 1975; Robin and Marian, 1976; The Ritz, 1976; Butch and Sundance: The Early Days, 1979; Cuba, 1979; Superman II, 1980; Superman III, 1983; Finders Keepers, 1984; The Return of the Musketeers, 1989; Get Back, 1990. Honours: Academy Award Nomination, 1960; Grand Prix, Cannes Film Festival, 1965; Best Director, Rio de Janeiro Festival, 1966; Gandhi Peace Prize, Berlin Festival, 1969; Best Director, Tehran Festival, 1974. Address: c/o Creative Artists Agency, 9830 Wilshire Boulevard, Beverley Hills, CA 90212, USA.

LESTER OF HERNE HILL, Baron of Herne Hill in the London Borough of Southwark, Anthony Paul Lester, b. 3 July 1936, London, England. Lawyer. m. Catherine Elizabeth Debora Wassey, 1971, 1 son, 1 daughter. Education: Trinity College, Cambridge; BA, Cantab; LLM, Harvard Law School; Called to Bar, Lincoln's Inn, 1963, Bencher, 1985. Appointments: Special Adviser to Home Secretary, 1974-76, to Northern Ireland Standing Advisory Commission on Human Rights, 1975-77; Appointed Queen's Counsel, 1975; Member, Board of Overseers, University of Pennsylvania Law School, Council of Justice, 1977-90; Member, Court of Governors, London School of Economics, 1980-94; Honorary Visiting Professor, University College London, 1983-; Board of Directors, Salzburg Seminar; President, Interights, 1996-2000; Recorder, South-Eastern Circuit, 1987-93; Co-Chair, Board, European Roma Rights Center; Governor, British Institute of Human Rights; Chair, Board of Governors, James Allen's Girls' School, 1987-93; Chair, Runnymede Trust, 1990-93; Governor, Westminster School, 1998-; Member, Advisory Committee, Centre for Public Law, University of Cambridge, 1999-; International Advisory Board, Open Society Institute, 2000-; Member, House of Lords Select Committee on European Communites Sub Committee E (Law and Insts), 2000-04, 2004-; Parliamentary Joint Human Rights Commission, 2001-04; Foreign Honorary Member, American Academy of Arts and Sciences, 2002; Foreign Member, American Philosophical Society, 2003; Adjunct Professor, Faculty of Law, University College, Cork, Ireland, 2005; Special Advisor on Constitutional Reform to the Secretary of State for Justice, 2007. Publications: Justice in the American South, 1964; Race and Law, co-author, 1972; Butterworth's Human Rights Cases, editor-in-chief; Halsbury's Laws of England Title Constitutional Law and Human Rights, 4th edition, consultant editor, contributor, 1996; Human Rights Law and Practice, co-editor, 1999; Articles on race relations, public affairs and international law. Honours: Honorary degrees and fellowships, Open University, University College, London University, Ulster University, South Bank University; Liberty Human Rights Lawyer of the Year, 1997. Address: Blackstone Chambers, Blackstone House, Temple, London EC4Y 9BW, England.

LETSIE III, King of Lesotho, b. 17 July 1963, Morija, Lesotho. Monarch. Education: National University of Lesotho; Universities of Bristol, Cambridge and London. Appointments: Principal Chief of Matsieng, 1989; Installed as King of Lesotho, 1990, abdicated, 1995, reinstated after father's death, 1996-; Patron, Prince Mohato Award. Address: Royal Palace, Masero, Lesotho.

LETTE Kathy, b. 11 November 1958, Sydney, Australia. Author. m. Geoffrey Robertson, 1990, 1 son, 1 daughter. Education: Sylvania High School, Sydney. Publications: Puberty Blues, 1980; HIT and MS, 1984; Girl's Night Out, 1988; The Llama Parlour, 1991; Foetal Attraction, 1993; Mad Cows, 1996; Altar Ego, 1998; Nip 'n Tuck, 2001; Dead Sexy, 2003; How to Kill Your Husband: And Other Handy Household Hints, 2006; Plays: Wet Dreams, 1985; Perfect Mismatch, 1985; Grommitts, 1988; I'm So Sorry For You, I Really Am, 1994; Radio: I'm So Happy For You, I Really Am; Essays: She Done Him Wrong, 1995; The Constant Sinner in Introduction to Mae West, 1995. Address: c/o Ed Victor, 6 Bayley Street, London, WC1B 3HB, England.

LETTERMAN David, b. 12 April 1947, Indianapolis, USA. Broadcaster. m. Michelle Cook, 1969, divorced 1977. Education: Ball State University. Appointments: Radio and TV Announcer, Indianapolis; Performer, The Comedy Store, Los Angeles, 1975-; TV Appearances include: Rock Concert, Gong Show; Frequent guest host, The Twilight Show; Host, David Letterman Show, 1980; Late Night with David Letterman, 1982; The Late Show with David Letterman, CBS, 1993-; TV Scriptwriting includes, Bob Hope Special; Good Times; Paul Lynde Comedy Hour; John Denver Special. Publications: David Letterman's Book of Top Ten Lists, 1996. Honours: Recipient, Six Emmy Awards. Address: Late Show with David Letterman, Ed Sullivan Theater, 1697 Broadway, New York, NY 10019, USA.

LETTS Quentin Richard Stephen, b. 6 February 1963, Cirencester, Gloucestershire, England. Journalist. m. Lois Rathbone, 1 son, 1 daughter. Education: Trinity College, Dublin; Jesus College, Cambridge. Appointments: Daily Telegraph, 1988-95, 1997-2000; New York Bureau Chief, The Times, 1995-97; Parliamentary Sketchwriter, Daily Mail, 2000-. Membership: The Savile Club. Address: Scrubs' Bottom, Bisley, Gloucestershire GL6 7BU, England.

LETTS-CIARRAPICO Rosa Maria, b. 30 May 1937, Rome, Italy. Art Historian. m. Anthony A Letts, 1 son, 1 daughter. Education: Maturitá Classica, 1955; Degree in Law, University of Rome, 1955-59; MA Course, Brandeis University, Massachusetts, USA (Fulbright Scholarship),

1959-60; BA (Hons), European History of Art, Courtauld Institute, University of London, 1966-69; MPhil (Hons), Combined Historical Studies on the Renaissance, Warburg Institute, University of London. Appointments: Lecturer, History of Art and Architecture, University of London Extra Mural Department, 1966-80; Lecturer on Italian European Art (Renaissance and Baroque), Exhibitions Consultant, Victoria and Albert Museum, 1975-82; Lecturer in Renaissance and Baroque Art, Italian Modern Art, Design and Architecture, Sotheby's Art Courses, 1978-85; Phillips Courses on Contemporary Design, Architecture and Fashion, 1985-86; Founding Director, Accademia Italiana delle Arti delle Arti Applicate, London, 1988-2002; Cultural Counsellor, Italian Embassy, London, 1992-96; Juror, European Design Award, Royal Society of Arts, 1992-93; Artistic Director, Accademia Club, London, 2002-08; Artstur Italian Art and Culture, 2008-; Curator of numerous exhibitions, 1981-2002. Publications: Books: La Pittura Fiorentina, 1970; Art Treasures of London (in the series English Art Guides), 1981; Renaissance, Cambridge Introduction to the History of Art, 1981, 3rd edition, 1991; Catalogues include: Italia Ao Luar, 1989; Italy by Moonlight 1550-1850, 1990, 2nd edition, 1991; Catalogues essays and articles. Honours: Cavaliere Ufficiale della Repubblica Italiana; Fiorino D'Oro della Città di Milano offerta dal Sindaco di Milano. Address: Artstur Italian Art & Culture, 59 Knightsbridge, London SW1X 7RA, England. E-mail: artstur@googlemail.com

LEU Paul, b. 26 June 1927, Carja-Murgeni, Romania. Educator and Researcher. m. Magdalena, 2 sons, 1 daughter. Education: Philology Graduate (Head of Promotion), Al I Cuza University, Iasi, Romania, 1954; Diploma in Teaching Language, Literature and Literature Theory. Appointments: Teacher, 1949-96; Associate Professor, 1965; Lecturer, 1968; Extensive researches into subjects including: literary history, ethnography, history of music, teaching and history of teaching, history of Bucovina during Austria's domination, also researches into the unpublished works of S Fl Marian, Ciprian Porumbescu, Iraclie Porumbescu, Bishop Grigore Leu, Archbishop Victor Leu and others. Publications: 39 books include: Ciprian Porumbescu – documente si marturii, 1971; Ciprian Porumbescu, monograph, 1972, 1978; Basme din Tara de Sus, 1975; Legende istorice din Bucovina, 1981; Marthir of the Heart, monograph, 1995; Nuvele si amintiri, 1996; Simion Florea Marian, monograph, 1996; Romanian Folk Stories II, III and IV, 1997-98; The S Fl Marian Academician - Monograph, 1998; S Fl Marian, Facerea lumii, 1998; S Fl Marian, Legende botanice, 1999; Founder of the Romanian Ethnography – Monograph I and II, 1998-99; S Fl Marian, Plantele noastre, 2000; Colegiul National Stefan cel Mare Suceava – Monograph I, Etapia austriacă, 2000; Iraclie Prumbescu - Monograph, 2000; Quo vadis romane!, 2001; Gr-or KK Obergymnasium din Suceava, in intampinarea unirii Bucovinei cu Romania, 2003; S Fl Marian, Cosmogeneza, 2004; Basme populare romanesti, I and II, 1986-2004; Martiri ai credintei in Hristos, 2005; Episcopi romani rapiti si asasinati de KGB, 2005; Grigorie Leu, arhiereu-vicar al mitropoliei Moldovei şi Bucovinei, 2006; Victor Leu, arhepiscop de la Gibraltar la Marea Roşie, 2006; Martyrs of Christian Faith: Killed and Kidnapped by the KGB, 2006; Martiri ai Bisericii Neamului, 2006; Kidnapped by KGB and Sentenced to Death, 2007; 600 articles, documents and book reviews; Script for the short TV Movie, Remember Ciprian Porumbescu, 1996. Honours: Front Ranking Teacher Award, Romanian Ministry of Education, 1964; Second Degree Teacher Diploma, 1965; First Degree teaching Diploma, 1976; A Pen on Two Continents, summary of Paul Leu's works by Octavian Nestor; Listed in: The Romanian Ethnology Dictionary, I

and II, 1998; Bibliographie zur Kultur und Landeskunde der Bukowina, 1965-1990; Muzica in Bucovina, 1981; Scriitori bucovineni Mic dictionar, 1992; Dictionar de literature – Bucovina, 1993; The International Directory of Distinguished Leadership, 11th edition, 2003; The Contemporary Who's Who, 2nd edition, 2005; 2000 Outstanding Intellectuals of the 21st Century, 2004; Enciclopedia Bucovinei, I and II, 2005; Dictionary of International Biography 32nd Edition, 2005, 33rd edition, 2007, 34th edition, 2008; Great Minds of the 21st Century, 2005; Dictionarul etnologilor romani, 2006; Bibliografie si referinte critice despre Paul Leu, octogenar, 2007; Books stored in the most important national, academical and university libraries in the world. Membership: Member and President, Society of Romanian Language and Literature; Founder Member, The Victims of the Communism Representative Committee, Romania. Address: 7217 175th Street, Unit #113, NE, Kenmore, WA 98028, USA. E-mail: paulleu@hotmail.com

LEUNG Kam Tim, b. 21 June 1931, China. Educator. Education: Sun Yat-sen University, 1953. Appointments: Teacher, secondary schools, college and universities, mainland China, 1953-95; Tutor, Open University of Hong Kong, 1997-99; Part-time Tutor, Hong Kong University, 2001. Publications: 30 articles in top journals. Honours: Senior Lecturer Certificate, Educational Department of Guangdong Province, China, 1987; Listed in national and international biographical publications. Memberships: Regular Member, International Association of Chinese Linguistics, 1994-. Address: PO Box 91360, Tsim Sha Tsui Post Office, Kowloon, Hong Kong.

LEUNG Nigel Chun Ming, b. 19 July 1977, Hong Kong. Airline Pilot. Education: MEng (First Class Honours), Aeronautical Engineering, Imperial College, London, 2001. Appointments: Principal Engineer, BMT Reliability Consultants Ltd, Hampshire, 2001-02; Cadet Pilot Programme, HK Dragon Airlines Ltd, Adelaide, Australia, 2002-03; Australian Private Pilot Licence (Multi Engine), HK Commercial Pilot Licence and Command Instrument Rating, First Officer, Airbus A330-300, HK Dragon Airlines Ltd, 2004-. Honours: Numerous academic and sports awards and titles during academic life. Memberships: Associate Member, Royal Aeronautical Society. E-mail: aerofoil2415@hotmail.com

LEUNG Thomas Kim-Ping, b. 28 July 1955, Hong Kong. Associate Professor. m. May Mei-Lin Leung, 1 son. Education: BA, University of Saskatchewan, Canada; MComm, University of New South Wales, Australia; PhD, University of Western Sydney, Australia. Appointments: Various executive positions in multi-national companies, 1980-91; Lecturer, Assistant Professor, Associate Professor, Hong Kong Polytechnic University, 1991-. Publications: Over 80 articles in international referred journals, book chapters and referred conferences; Book: Guanxi: Relationship in a Chinese Context (co-author), The Haworth Press. Address: Department of Management and Marketing, The Hong Kong Polytechnic University, Hung Hom, Kowloon, The Hong Kong SAR. E-mail: msthomas@polyu.edu.hk

LEVENE OF PORTSOKEN, Baron of Portsoken in the City of London, Peter Keith Levene, b. 8 December 1941, Pinner, Middlesex, England. Business Executive; Justice of the Peace. m. Wendy Ann Levene, 1966, 2 sons, 1 daughter. Education: BA, University of Manchester. Appointments: Joined, 1963, Managing Director, 1968, Chair, 1982, United Scientific Holdings; Member, South-East Asia Trade

Advisory Group, 1979-83; Personal Adviser to Secretary of State for Defence, 1984; Alderman, 1984, Sheriff, 1995-96, Lord Mayor, 1998-99, City of London; Chair, European NATO National Armaments Directors, 1990-91; Special Adviser to Secretary of State for the Environment, 1991-92; Chair, Docklands Light Railway Ltd, 1991-94; Chair, Public Competition and Purchasing Unit, H M Treasury, 1991-92; Deputy Chair, Wasserstein Perella and Co Ltd, 1991-94; Adviser to Prime Minister on Efficiency, 1992-97; Special Adviser to President of Board of Trade, 1992-95; Chair, Chief Executive Officer, Canary Wharf Ltd, 1993-96; Senior Adviser, Morgan Stanley and Co Ltd, 1996-98; Director, Haymarket Group Ltd, 1997-; Chair, Bankers Trust International, 1998-99; Chair, Investment Banking Europe, Deutsche Bank AG, 1999-2001; Director, 2001-04, Head, Chairman, nominations committee, 2004-, J Sainsbury plc; Vice Chair, Deutsche Bank, UK, 2001-02; Chair, Lloyds of London, 2002-; Member, Supervisory Bd Deutsche Boerse AG, 2004-. Honours: Honorary Colonel Commandant, Royal Corps of Transport, 1991-93; Master, Worshipful Company of Carmen, 1992-93; Honorary Colonel Commandant, Royal Logistics Corps, 1993-; Fellow, Queen Mary and Westfield College, London University, 1995; Knight Commander, Order of St John of Jerusalem; Commander, Ordre National du Mérite, 1996; Honorary DSc, City University, 1998; Knight Commandants Order of Merit, Germany, 1998; Middle Cross Order of Merit, Hungary, 1999; Knight Commander, Order of the British Empire. Memberships: Fellow, Chartered Institute of Transport; Companion, Institute of Management; Defence Manufacturers Association, Council, 1982-85, Vice-Chair, 1983-84, Chair, 1984-85. Address: 1 Great Winchester Street, London EC2N 2DB, England. E-mail: peter.k.levene@db.com

LEVENSON David, b. 8 October 1965, Bronx, New York, USA. Physician. m. Marissa, 4 sons. Education: BA cum laude, 1985, BS cum laude, 1985, University of Miami; MD, Honours in Physiology and Biophysics, New York University School of Medicine, 1989. Appointments: Residency Training Programme, Long Island Jewish Medical Centre, 1989-92; Endocrinology Fellowship, Cornell University Programme, 1992-94; Geriatric Fellowship, University of Miami, Florida, 1994-95; Private Practice, 1995-. Publications: Electrophysiologic Changes Accompanying Wallerian Degeneration in Frog Sciatic Nerve Brain Research; Candida Zeylenoides: Another opportunistic yeast; Peripheral facial nerve palsy after high dose radio iodine therapy in patients with papillery thyroid cancer; A review of calcium preparations; A multi-centre trail of Gallium Nitrate in patients with advanced Pagets disease of bone. Honour: AMA Physicians' Recognition Award. Memberships: Fellow, American College of Endocrinology; Fellow, American College of Physicians; American Association of Clinical Endocrinology; Endocrine Society. Address: 7301 West Palmetto Park Road, Suite 108B, Boca Raton, FL 33433, USA.

LEVER, His Honour Judge Bernard Lewis, b. 1 February 1951, Manchester, UK. Judge. m. Anne Helen Ballingall, 2 daughters. Education: MA, The Queen's College, Oxford. Appointments: Called to the Bar, Middle Temple, 1975; Barrister, Northern Circuit, 1975-2001; Recorder, 1995-2001; Standing Counsel to the Inland Revenue, 1997-2001; Circuit Judge, 2001. Honour: Neale Exhibitioner, Oxford University. Membership: Vincent's Club. Address: Manchester Crown Court, Minshull Street, Manchester M1 3FS, England.

LEVER Tresham Christopher Arthur Lindsay (Sir) (3rd Baronet), b. 9 January 1932, London, England. Naturalist; Writer. m. Linda Weightman McDowell Goulden, 6 November 1975. Education: Eton College, 1945-49; BA, 1954, MA, 1957, Trinity College, Cambridge. Appointments: Commissioned 17th/21st Lancers, 1950; Peat Marwick Mitchell & Co, 1954-55; Kitkat & Aitken 1955-56; Director John Barran & Sons Ltd, 1956-64. Publications: Goldsmiths and Silversmiths of England, 1975; The Naturalized Animals of the British Isles, 1977; Naturalized Mammals of the World, 1985; Naturalized Birds of the World, 1987; The Mandarin Duck, 1990; They Dined on Eland: The Story of the Acclimatisation Societies, 1992; Naturalized Animals: The Ecology of Successfully Introduced Species, 1994; Naturalized Fishes of the World, 1996; The Cane Toad: The History and Ecology of a Successful Colonist, 2001; Naturalized Reptiles and Amphibians of the World, 2003; Naturalised Birds of World, 2005; The Naturalised Animals of Britain and Ireland, 2009. Contributions to: Books, Art, Scientific and general publications. Honours: Honorary Life President, Tusk Trust, 2004; Fellow, WWF-UK, 2005; Editorial Board, Journal of Applied Herpetology, 2005-; Vice-Patron, Conservation Foundation, 2005-2006. Memberships: Fellow, Linnean Society of London; Fellow, Royal Geographical Society; World Conservation Union Species' Survival Commission, 1988-; Council of Ambassadors, WWF (UK), 1999-2005; Honorary Life Member, Brontë Society, 1988. Address: Newell House, Winkfield, Berkshire SL4 4SE, England.

LEVEY Michael (Vincent) (Sir), b. 8 June 1927, London, England. Writer. m. Brigid Brophy, deceased 1995, 1 daughter. Education: Exeter College, Oxford. Appointments: Assistant Keeper, 1951-66, Deputy Keeper, 1966-68, Keeper, 1968-73, Deputy Director, 1970-73, Director, 1973-87, National Gallery, London; Slade Professor of Fine Art, Cambridge, 1963-64, Oxford, 1994-95. Publications: Six Great Painters, 1956; National Gallery Catalogues: 18th Century Italian Schools, 1956; The German School, 1959; Painting in 18th Century Venice, 1959, 3rd edition, 1994; From Giotto to Cézanne, 1962; Dürer, 1964; The Later Italian Paintings in the Collection of HM The Queen, 1964, revised edition, 1991; Canaletto Paintings in the Royal Collection, 1964; Tiepolo's Banquet of Cleopatra, 1966; Rococo to Revolution, 1966; Bronzino, 1967; Early Renaissance, 1967; Fifty Works of English Literature We Could Do Without (co-author), 1967; Holbein's Christina of Denmark, Duchess of Milan, 1968; A History of Western Art, 1968; Painting at Court, 1971; The Life and Death of Mozart, 1971, 2nd edition, 1988; The Nude: Themes and Painters in the National Gallery, 1972; Art and Architecture in 18th Century France (co-author), 1972; The Venetian Scene, 1973; Botticelli, 1974; High Renaissance, 1975; The World of the Ottoman Art, 1976; Jacob van Ruisdael, 1977; The Case of Walter Pater, 1978; The Painter Depicted, 1981; Tempting Fate, 1982; An Affair on the Appian Way, 1984; Pater's Marius the Epicurean (editor), 1985; Giambattista Tiepolo, 1986; The National Gallery Collection: A Selection, 1987; Men at Work, 1989; The Soul of the Eye: Anthology of Painters and Painting (editor), 1990; Painting and Sculpture in France 1700-1789, 1992; Florence: A Portrait, 1996; The Chapel is on Fire (memoir), 2000; The Burlington Magazine, anthology, 2003; Sir Thomas Lawrence, 2005. Contributions to: Periodicals. Honours: Hawthornden Prize, 1968; Knighted, 1981; Honorary Fellow, Royal Academy, 1986; Banister Fletcher Prize, 1987; Lieutenant, Royal Victoria Order, 1965. Memberships: Ateneo Veneto, foreign member; British Academy, fellow; Royal Society of Literature, fellow. Address: 36 Little Lane, Louth, Lincolnshire LN11 9DU, England.

LEVI-MONTALCINI Rita, b. 22 April 1909, Turin, Italy. Neuroscientist. Education: Graduated, Medicine, University of Turin, 1936. Appointments: Neurological research in Turin and Brussels, 1936-41, in Piemonte, 1941-43; In hiding in Florence during German occupation, 1943-44; Medical Doctor working among war refugees, Florence, 1944-45; Resumed academic positions at University of Turin, 1945; Worked with Professor Viktor Hamburger, 1947, Associate Professor, 1956, Professor, 1958-77, St Louis, USA; Director, 1969-78, Guest Professor, 1979-89, Guest Professor, Institute of Neurobiology, 1989-, Institute of Cell Biology of Italian National Council of Research, Rome. Publications: In Praise of Imperfection: My Life and Work, 1988. Honour: Joint Winner, Nobel Prize for Medicine, 1986. Address: Institute of Neurobiology, CNR Viale Marx 15, 00137, Rome, Italy.

LÉVI-STRAUSS Claude, b. 28 November 1908, Brussels, Belgium. Anthropologist; University Professor; Writer. m. (1) Dina Dreyfus, 1932, (2) Rose Marie Ullmo, 1946, 1 son, (3) Monique Roman, 1954, 1 son. Education: University of Paris-Sorbonne. Appointments: Professor, University of São Paulo, Brazil, 1935-39; Visiting Professor, New School of Social Research, New York, USA, 1942-45; Cultural Counsellor, French Embassy, USA, 1946-47; Associate Director, Musée de l'Homme, Paris, France, 1949-50; Director of Studies, Ecole Pratique des Hautes Etudes, Paris, 1950-74; Professor, 1959-82, Honorary Professor, 1983-, Collège de France. Publications: La vie familiale et sociale des indiens Nambikwara, 1948; Les structures élémentaires de la parenté, 1949; Tristes tropiques,, 1955; Anthropologie structurale, 1958; Le totémisme aujourd'hui, 1962; La pensée sauvage, 1962; Le cru et le cuit, 1964; Du miel aux centres, 1967; L'origine des manières de table, 1968; L'homme nu, 1971; Anthropologie structurale deux, 1973; La voie des masques, 1975, 1979; Le regard éloigné, 1983; Paroles données, 1984; La potière jalouse, 1985; De près et de loin, co-author, 1988; Histoire de Lynx, 1991; Regarder, écouter, lire, 1983; Saudades do Brasil, 1994. Honours: Dr hc, Brussels, Harvard, Yale, Chicago, Columbia, Oxford, Stirling, Zaire, Mexico, Uppsala, Johns Hopkins, Montreal, Québec and Visva-Bharati University, India; Prix Paul Pelliot, 1949; Huxley Memorial Medal, 1965; Viking Fund Gold Medal, 1966; Gold Medal, Centre National de la Recherche Scientifique, 1967; Erasmus Prize, 1973; Aby M Warburg Prize, 1996; Grand Croix, Légion d'Honneur; Commandeur, Ordre National du Mérite, des Palmes Académiques, des Arts et des Lettres. Memberships: Académie Française; Foreign Member, Royal Academy of the Netherlands, Norwegian Academy of Sciences and Letters, American Academy of Arts and Sciences, American Academy and Institute of Arts and Letters, British Academy; Foreign Associate, National Academy of Sciences, USA; Honorary Member, Royal Anthropological Institute, American Philosophical Society, London School of Oriental and African Studies. Address: 2 rue des Marronniers, 75016 Paris, France.

LEVICK William Russell, b. 5 December 1931, Sydney, Australia. Neuroscience Researcher. m. Patricia Lathwell, 1 son, 1 son deceased, 1 daughter. Education: BSc, honours, 1953, MSc, 1954, MBBS, honours, 1957, University of Sydney. Appointments: C J Martin Travelling Fellow, Cambridge University, University of California, Berkeley, 1963-64; Professorial Fellow, 1967-83, Professor, 1983-96, Australian National University, Canberra. Honours: Fellowship, Australian Academy of Sciences, 1973, Optical Society of America, 1977, Royal Society of London,

1982. Memberships: Society for Neuroscience; Australian Neuroscience Society; Australian Physiological Society. Address: 33 Quiros Street, Red Hill, ACT 2603, Australia.

LEVIN Ira, b. 27 August 1929, New York, New York, USA. Novelist; Dramatist. m. (1) Gabrielle Aronsohn, 20 August 1960, divorced January 1968, 3 sons, (2) Phyllis Finkel, 1979, divorced 1981. Education: Drake University, 1946-48; AB, New York University, 1950. Appointments: US Army, 1953-55. Publications: Novels: A Kiss Before Dying, 1953; Rosemary's Baby, 1967; This Perfect Day, 1970; The Stepford Wives, 1972; The Boys From Brazil, 1976; Silver, 1991; Son of Rosemary, 1997. Plays: No Time for Sergeants, 1956; Interlock, 1958; Critic's Choice, 1961; General Seeger, 1962; Drat! The Cat! 1965; Dr Cook's Garden, 1968; Veronica's Room, 1974; Deathtrap, 1979; Break a Leg, 1981; Cantorial, 1990. Contributions to: Television and films. Honours: Edgar Allan Poe Awards, Mystery Writers of America, 1953, 1980. Memberships: American Society of Composers, Authors and Publishers; Authors Guild; Authors League of America; Dramatists Guild. Address: c/o Harold Ober Associates, 425 Madison Avenue, New York, NY 10017, USA.

LEVITAS Valery, b. 3 April 1956, Kiev, Ukraine. Researcher; Educator. m. Natasha Levitas, 20 January 1993, 2 sons. Education: MS honours, Mechanical Engineering, Kiev Polytechnic Institute, 1978; PhD, Materials Science, Institute of Superhard Materials, Kiev, 1981; DSc, Continuum Mechanics, Institute of Electronic Machine Building, Moscow, 1988; DEng habil, Continuum Mechanics, University of Hannover, Germany, 1995; Registered Professional Engineer, Texas, 2001. Appointments: Leader, Research Group, 1982-95, Associate Research Professor, 1984-88, Research Professor, 1989-95, Consultant, 1995-, Institute for Superhard Materials, Ukrainian Academy of Sciences, Kiev; Humboldt Research Fellow, 1993-95, Visiting and Research Professor, 1995-99, University of Hannover, Germany; Associate Professor, 1999-2002, Professor, 2002-, Director, Center for Mechanochemistry and Synthesis of New Materials, 2002-2007, Texas Tech University, Lubbock; President, Firm "Material Modeling", Lubbock, 2002-; Consultant, Los Alamos National Laboratory, 2001-; Schaefer 2050 Challenge Professor, Department of Mechanical Engineering and Department of Aerospace Engineering; Courtesy Appointment, Department of Material Science & Engineering, Iowa State University, Ames, Iowa, 2008-; Adjunct Professor, Department of Mechanical Engineering, Texas Tech University, Lubbock, 2008-. Publications include: Large Elastoplastic Deformations of Materials at High Pressure, 1987; Thermomechanics of Phase Transformations and Inelastic Deformations in Microinhomogeneous Materials, 1992; Large Deformation of Materials with Complex Rheological Properties at Normal and High Pressure, 1996; Continuum Mechanical Fundamentals of Mechanochemistry, 2004. Honours: Medal, Ukrainian Academy of Sciences, 1984; Alexander von Humboldt Foundation Fellowship, Germany, 1993-95; International Journal of Engineering Sciences Distinguished Paper Award, 1995; Richard von Mises Award, Society of Applied Mathematics and Mechanics, 1998; Best Professor Award, Pi Tau Sigma, Mechanical Engineering Department, Texas Tech University, 2001; American Medal of Honor, ABI, 2004; Barnie E Rushing Jr Faculty Distinguished Research Award, Texas Tech University, 2005. Memberships: International Association for the Advancement of High Pressure Science and Technology; American Society of Mechanical Engineers; American Physical Society; Society of Engineering Science; Society of Applied Mathematics and Mechanics; Minerals,

Metals and Materials Society. Address: Texas Tech University, Department of Mechanical Engineering, Lubbock, TX 79409-1021, USA.

LEVITT Arthur, Jr, b. 3 February 1931, Brooklyn, New York, USA. Business Executive. m. Marylin Blauner, 1955, 1 son, 1 daughter. Education: Williams College. Appointments: Assistant Promotion Director, Time Inc, New York, 1954-59; Executive Vice-President, Director, Oppenheimer Industries Inc, Kansas City, 1959-62; Joined, 1962, President, 1969-78, Shearson Hayden Stone Inc, now Shearson Lehmann Bros Inc, New York; Chair, Chief Executive Officer, Director, American Stock Exchange, New York, 1978-89; Chair, Levitt Media Co, New York, 1989-93; Chair, New York City Economic Development Corporation, 1990-93; Chair, Securities and Exchange Commission, 1993-2001; Various directorships and other business and public appointments. Honours: Honorary LLD, Williams College, 1980, Pace, 1980, Hamilton College, 1981, Long Island, 1984, Hofstra, 1985. Address: Securities and Exchange Commission, 450 Fifth Street NW, Washington, DC 20001, USA.

LEVITT Stephan Hillyer, b. 9 February 1943, Brooklyn, New York, USA. Indologist. Education: Diploma, High School of Music and Art, New York City, 1956-60; BA, Columbia College, Anthropology, 1960-64; PhD, University of Pennsylvania, Department of Oriental Studies, 1964-73. Appointments: Cataloguer, Indic MSS, University of Pennsylvania Library for Institute for Advanced Studies of World Religions, Stony Brook, New York, 1971-72; Research Assistant, to Emeritus Professor, Dr W Norman Brown, University of Pennsylvania, 1972-74; Visiting Assistant Professor, Anthropology Department and Humanities Program, University of Denver, 1974-76; Tutor, English Department and Student/Faculty Co-ordinator, Humanities Program, Queensborough Community College, New York City, 1977-78; Private tutor, consulting work for University of Pennsylvania Library, Center for Judaic Studies, University of Pennsylvania (formerly Annenberg Research Institute), Burke Library, Union Theological Seminary, 1978-. Publications: Articles in professional journals. Honours: National Defense Foreign Language Fellowship (Tamil), 1964-67; American Council of Learned Societies Fellowship for Summer Study in Linguistics, 1967; American Institute of Indian Studies Travel-Study Award, 1974; University of Denver Faculty Research Grant, 1975. Memberships: American Oriental Society; Friends of the Library of the University of Pennsylvania; Societas Linguistica Europaea; Bhandarkar Oriental Research Institute; Dravidian Linguistics Association. Address: 144-30 78th Road, Apt 1H, Flushing, New York 11367-3572, USA.

LEVY Alain M, b. 19 December 1946, France. Record Company Executive. Education: Ecole des Mines, France; MBA, University of Pennsylvania. Appointments: With CBS, Assistant to the President, CBS International, New York, 1972, Vice-President, Marketing for Europe, Paris, 1973, Vice-President, Creative Operations for Europe and Manager, CBS Italy, 1978; Managing Director, CBS Disques, France, 1979; Chief Executive Officer, PolyGram, 1984; Executive Vice-President, PolyGram Group, France and Federal Republic of Germany, 1988; Manager, US Operations PolyGram Group, 1990-; President, Chief Executive Officer, Member, Board of Management, PolyGram USA, 1991-; Member, Group Management Committee, Philips Electronics, 1991-; Majority Shareholder, PolyGram USA, 1991-98; Chair, Board EMI Group plc, 2001-, Chair and Chief Executive Officer, EMI Recorded Music, 2001-. Address: EMI Group plc, 4 Tenterden Street, Hanover Square, London W1A 2AY, England.

LEVY, His Honour Dennis Martyn, b. 20 February 1936, Liverpool, England. Queen's Counsel. m. Rachel Jonah, 1 son, 1 daughter. Education: BA, 1960, MA, 1963, Gonville and Caius College, Cambridge. Appointments: Called to the Bar, Gray's Inn, 1960, Hong Kong, 1985, Turks and Caicos Islands, 1987; Granada Group, 1960-63; Time Products Ltd, 1963-67; In practice at the Bar, 1967-91; Queen's Counsel, 1982; Recorder, 1989-91; Circuit Judge, 1991-2007; Accredited Mediator, 2007; Member: Employment Appeals Tribunal, 1994-2004, Lands Tribunal, 1998; Trustee of Fair Trials International; Chairman, The United Kingdom Association of Jewish Lawyers and Jurists. Address: 25 Harley House, Marylebone Road, London, NW1 5HE, England.

LEVY John Court (Jack), b. 16 February 1926, London, England. Engineer; Consultant; Managing Director. m. Sheila F Krisman, 2 sons, 1 daughter. Education: BSc, Engineering, Imperial College of Science and Technology, London, England, 1943-46; MS, University of Illinois, USA, 1953-54; PhD, University of London, 1961. Appointments: Stress Analyst, Boulton Paul Aircraft, 1946-48; Assistant to Chief Engineer, Fullers Ltd, 1948-52; Lecturer, Senior Lecturer, Reader, 1952-66, Head (Professor) of Mechanical and Manufacturing Engineering, 1966-83, City University, London; Director, Engineering Profession at Engineering Council, 1983-90; Consulting Engineer, 1990-97; Consultant to Engineering Council, 1997-; Managing Director, Levytator Ltd, 2000-. Publications: Most recent publications include: UK Manufacturing – Facing International Challenge, 1994; Co-author, Sustaining Recovery, 1995; The University Education and Industrial Training of Manufacturing Engineers for the Global Market, 1996; UK Developments in Engineering Education, Including the Matching Section, 1998; Keynote address at international conference, The Impact of Globalization on Engineering Education and Practice, Balaton, Hungary, 1999. Honours: OBE, 1984; Member, Board of Governors, Middlesex University, 1990-2003; Freeman of City of London, 1991; Honorary Doctorates, City University, London, University of Portsmouth, Leeds Metropolitan University. Memberships: Fellow, Royal Academy of Engineering; Fellow, Institution of Mechanical Engineers; Fellow, Royal Aeronautical Society; Fellow, City and Guilds of London Institute; Fellow, Royal Society of Arts; Fellow, Institution of Engineers of Ireland. Address: 18 Woodberry Way, Finchley, London N12 0HG, England. E-mail: jack.levy1@btopenworld.com

LEVY, Baron of Mill Hill, Michael Abraham Levy, b. 11 July 1944, London, England. Consultant. m. Gilda Altbach, 1 son, 1 daughter. Education: Hackney Downs Grammar School (formerly the Grocers Company School); Qualified as Chartered Accountant. Appointments: Accountancy practice, 1967-73; Built up MAGNET, worldwide record and music publishing group of companies (sold to Warner Brothers) (now part of Time Warner), 1973-88; Built up and sold a second successful company in the music and entertainment business, 1992-97; Consultant to various international companies, 1998-. Honours: B'nai B'rith First Lodge Award, 1994; Elevated to the Peerage as Baron Levy of Mill Hill, 1997; Friends of the Hebrew University of Jerusalem Scopus Award, 1998; Honorary Doctorate, Middlesex University, 1999; Israel Policy Forum (USA) Special Recognition Award, 2003. Memberships: Vice Chairman, Central Council for Jewish Social Services, 1994-; Chairman, Chief Rabbinate

Awards for Excellence, 1992-; Chairman, Foundation for Education, 1993-; Patron, British Music Industry Trust, 1995-; Member, World Commission on Israel-Diaspora Relations, 1995-; Chairman, Jewish Care Community Foundation, 1995-; Member, Advisory Council to the Foreign Policy Centre, 1997-; Patron, Prostate Cancer Charitable Trust, 1997-; Member, International Board of Governors, Peres Center for Peace, 1997-; Member, NCVO Advisory Committee, 1998-; Patron, Friends of Israel Educational Trust, 1998-; President, Community Service Volunteers, 1998-; Trustee, Holocaust Educational Trust, 1998-; President, Jewish Care, 1998-; Member, Community Legal Service Champions Panel, 1999-; Patron, Save A Child's Heart Foundation, 2000-; Member, Honorary Committee of the Israel Britain and the Commonwealth Association, 2000-; Honorary President, UJIA, 2000-; President, JFS School, 2001-; Patron, Simon Marks Jewish Primary School Trust, 2002-; Honorary Patron, Cambridge University Jewish Society, 2002-; President, Specialist Schools and Academies Trust, 2005-; Trustee and member of the Executive Committee of the Jewish Leadership Council JLC; President, Jewish Lads and Girls Brigade JLGB, 2006-. Former positions: Founder, Former Chairman, British Music Industry Awards Committee (now Music Industry Trust); Vice-Chairman, British Phonographic Industry Ltd, 1984-87; Vice-Chairman, Phonographic Performance Ltd, 1979-84; Honorary Vice-president, UJIA, 1994-2000; Chairman, Jewish Care, 1992-97; National Campaign Chairman, JIA, 1982-85; Member, Keren Hayesod World Board of Governors, 1991-95; Member, World Board of Governors of the Jewish Agency, representing Great Britain, 1990-95; World Chairman, Youth Aliyah Committee, Jewish Agency Board of Governors, 1991-95; Governor, JFS School, 1990-95; Executive Committee Member, Chai-Lifeline, 2001-2002; Chairman, Academy Sponsors Trust; Chairman, Board of Trustees of New Policy Network Foundation, 2000-2006. Address: House of Lords, Westminster, London SW1, England.

LEVY Suzy Hug, b. 2 June 1944, Istanbul, Turkey. Plastic Arts; Sculptor; Installation, Performance, Video Artist. m. Henry Levy, 1 son, 1 daughter. Education: BA, Robert College, American College for Girls. Career: Artist and Sculptor; Numerous national and international exhibitions include most recently: Solo exhibitions: Newspapers, APEL Gallery, Istanbul and Emlak Bank Gallery, Ankara, Turkey, 1999; A Celebration, installation, video, performance, Milli Reasurans Art Gallery, Istanbul, Turkey, 2000; Fragile Images, installation, photography, performance, video, Iş Sanat Gallery, Istanbul, 2001; Arcadia, installation, performance, video, Milli Reasurans Art Gallery, Istanbul, 2001; INAX Gallery, Tokyo, Japan, 2001; To be a woman, G-art Gallery, Istanbul, 2005; Selected international group exhibitions: Designed Landscape Forum, San Francisco Museum of Modern Art, USA, 1996; Global Fine Arts Gallery, JCCNV, Pilgrims Gallery, DFI Gallery, Washington DC, USA; Documenta, Detroit Museum of Modern Art, USA, 2001; As You See Me But I Am Not, Frauen Museum, Bonn and Communale Gallerie, Berlin, Germany, 2001; Tunis Biennial, Tunis, 2002; Between Two Quays, MAAS Gallery, Rotterdam, Holland, 2002; Nazim Hikmet Commemoration Day, Nakano, Japan, 2002; Comparisons, Tokyo and Kyoto University, Japan, 2003; Gunther Verheugen's Choice, Contemporary Painting and Sculpture from Turkey, European Union Building, Brussels, Belgium, 2003; Dialogues Plastiques, Hotel de Ville Gallery, Brussels, Belgium, 2004; Contemporary Painting and Sculpture from Turkey, Lyngby Cultural Centre, Denmark and Melina Mercouri Cultural Centre, Athens, Greece, 2004; Finalists Show, London Jewish Museum of Art, Ben Uri

Gallery and Tram Studios, London, England, 2004; Installed the Flying Carpets exhibit at Dolmabahçe Cultural Centre, Istanbul, 2000; Curator, Auschwitz exhibit, 2001, Anne Frank: A History for Today exhibit, 2002, Terezin Children's drawings exhibit, 2004, Schneidertempel Cultural Centre, Istanbul; Designed the Holocaust Menorah, 2002; Installed the Kuzgun Acar Retrospective exhibit, Kibele Art Gallery, Istanbul, 2004. Honours: Contemporary Artist of the Year Award, Painting and Sculpture Museum Association, Istanbul, 1991; Il Sharjah Biennial Award, United Arab Emirates, 1997; Artist of the Year on Sculpture, Ankara Arts Council, 1998, 1999, 2000; Tunis Biennial Award, 2002; International Jewish Artist of the Year Award in Sculpture, London Jewish Museum of Art, Ben Uri Gallery, 2004; Beijing Biennial, 2005; Listed in international biographical dictionaries. Memberships: Founder, Istanbul Modern Art Museum Foundation; Founder, Schneidertempel Cultural Centre; Istanbul Philharmonic Orchestra Association; PCD-UNESCO Plastic Arts Association; SANART Art and Cultural Organisation. Address: Karakütük Cad. 52, Sariyer, Istanbul, Turkey. E-mail: suzy@levi.com.tr

LEW Julian D M, b. 3 February 1948, South Africa. Lawyer; Queen's Counsel. m. Margot Gillian Perk, 2 daughters. Education: LLB honours, University of London, 1969; Doctorat special en droit international, Catholic University of Louvain, Belgium, 1977; Fellow, Chartered Institute of Arbitrators. Appointments: Called to Bar in England, 1970; Admitted Solicitor, 1981; New York State Bar, 1985; Barrister, Arbitrator, 20 Essex Street, London; Visiting Professor, Head of School of International Arbitration, Centre for Commercial Law Studies, Queen Mary, University of London; Partner, Herbert Smith, 1995-2005. Publications: Numerous books and articles on international commercial arbitration and international trade including: Applicable Law in International Commercial Arbitration, Oceana, 1978; Comparative International Commercial Arbitration, co-author, Kluwer, 2003. Memberships: General Council of the Bar of England and Wales; International Bar Association; American Bar Association; Swiss Arbitration Association; American Arbitration Association; French Committee for Arbitration; British Institute of International and Comparative Law; Chairman, Committee on arbitration practice guidelines of Chartered Institute of Arbitrators, 1996-2001; Chairman, Committee on Intellectual Property Disputes and Arbitration, International Chamber of Commerce, 1995-99; Member, Council of the ICC Institute of World Business Law; Director and Member of Court, London Court of International Arbitration. Address: 20 Essex Street, London WC2R 3AL, England. E-mail: jlew@20essexst.com

LEWIN Christopher George, b. 15 December 1940, Poole, Dorset. Actuary. m. Robin Lynn, 2 sons. Education: Cooper's Company School, London, 1951-55; Actuaries Tuition Course, Institute of Actuaries 1956-62. Appointments: Actuarial Assistant, Equity & Law Life, 1956-63; Actuarial Assistant, London Transport, 1963-67; Actuarial Assistant, 1967-70, Controller, Corporate Pensions, 1970-80, Co-ordinator, Private Capital, 1980-89, British Rail; Pensions Director, Associated Newspapers, 1989-92; Head of Group Pensions, Guinness PLC, 1992-98; Head of UK Pensions, Unilever PLC, 1998-2003; Pensions Manager, EDF Energy plc, 2005; Part-time appointments: Member of Investment Committee, The Pensions Trust, 2004-; Chairman of Training Standards Initiative, National Association of Pension Funds, 2004-2006; Chairman of Trustees, Marconi Pension Fund, 2004-05; Reviewer, Department of Work and Pensions Deregulatory Review of Private Pensions, 2007. Publications: Book: Pensions and Insurance Before 1800 - A Social History,

2003; Article: The Philosophers' Game (Games and Puzzles Magazine), 1973; Enterprise Risk Management and Civil Engineering, Civil Engineering, vol 159, Special Issue 2, 2006; Various papers in technical journals on investment appraisal, manpower planning, funding of pension schemes and capital projects. Honours: Sir Joseph Burn Prize, Institute of Actuaries, 1962; Finlaison Medal, Institute of Actuaries, 1999; Pensions Manager of the Year, Professional Pensions Magazine, 2003. Memberships: Fellow Institute of Actuaries, 1962; Fellow, Pensions Management Institute, 1976; Governor, Pensions Policy Institute; Governor, National Institute for Economic and Social Research; Chairman of joint working party with the Actuarial Profession and the Institution of Civil Engineers to develop a successful risk methodology for projects known as RAMP, 1992-; Member of Steering Group for the Stratrisk Initiative, 2002-. E-mail: thirlestane1903@aol.com

LEWIN Michael Zinn, b. 21 July 1942, Cambridge, Massachusetts, USA. Writer; Dramatist. 1 son, 1 daughter. Education: AB, Harvard University, 1964; Churchill College, Cambridge, England. Appointment: Co-Editor, Crime Writers Association Annual Anthology, 1992-94. Publications: Author of 18 novels including: Called by a Panther, 1991; Underdog, 1993; Family Business, 1995; Rover's Tales, 1998; Cutting Loose, 1999; Family Planning, 1999; Eye opener, 2004. Other: Various radio plays, stage plays and short stories Contributions to: Indianapolis for New York Times Sophisticated Traveller. Honours: Maltese Falcon Society of Japan Best Novel, 1987; Raymond Chandler Society of Germany Best Novel, 1992; Mystery Masters Award, 1994. Memberships: Detection Club; Crime Writers Association; Authors Guild. Address: Garden Flat, 15 Bladud Buildings, Bath BA1 5LS, England.

LEWIN Russell Mark Ellerker, b. 21 March 1958, Woolwich, England. Solicitor. 2 sons. Education: BA, Jurisprudence, 1980, MA, Jurisprudence, 1990, St John's College, Oxford. Appointments: Articled Clerk, 1981-83, Solicitor, 1983-, Partner, 1990, Recruitment Partner, 1994-98, European Regional Council, 1997-, Policy Committee, 1998-, Managing Partner, 1998, Baker & McKenzie, London. Publications: Various articles on topics of Intellectual Property and EU Competition Law. Memberships: City of London Solicitors' Guild; Academy for Chief Executives; Liberal Democrats. Address: c/o Baker & McKenzie, 100 New Bridge Street, London EC4V 6JA, England. E-mail: russell.lewin@bakernet.com

LEWIS Adrian Mark, b. 25 June 1951, Swansea, Wales. University Lecturer. m. Valerie Josephine Barber. Publication: BA, Modern History, Oxford University, 1973; MA, History of Art, University of London, 1975; PhD, History of Art, University of Manchester, 1996. Appointments: Lecturer, Bristol Polytechnic, 1975-76; Education Officer, Walker Art Gallery, Liverpool, 1970-79; Lecturer, 1979, MA Course Leader, 2000-2003, History of Art, De Montfort University Leicester; Visiting Associate Professor, Creighton University, Omaha, USA, 1999; External Assessor, Bristol Polytechnic, 1988-92. Publications: Books: The Last Days of Hilton, 1996; Roger Hilton, 2003; Exhibition catalogue: Roger Hilton: The Early Years, 1984; 76 reviews and articles in Art History; Art Monthly; Art Book; Artscribe; Burlington Magazine; Connoisseur; Sculpture Journal. Address: History of Art and Material Culture, De Montfort University, The Gateway, Leicester LE1 9BH, England. E-mail: alewis@dmu.ac.uk

LEWIS Bernard Walter, b. 24 July 1917, Lincoln, England. Flour Miller. m. Joyce Ilston Storey, 1943, 1 son, 1 daughter. Education: University of Manchester. Appointments: Joined King's Own Regiment, served in Middle East, 1940-46; RASC, 1941; Captain, 1942; Major, 1943; Chairman and Managing Director, Green's Flour Mills Ltd, 1955-90; General Tax Commissioner, 1957-93; Chairman, Dengie and Maldon Essex Bench, 1970-88; Chairman, Maldon Harbour Commissioners, 1978-2001; Chairman, Flour Advisory Bureau, 1979-88; President, National Association of British and Irish Millers, 1985-86; Chairman, Edward Baker Holdings Ltd, 1983-89; Retired, 1989. Honour: CBE, 1973. Memberships: Financial Board, Conservative Party, 1966-75; Chairman, Board of Governors, Plume School, 1968-83; Liveryman, Worshipful Company of Bakers, 1973. Address: Roughlees, 68 Highlands Drive, Maldon, Essex CM9 6HY, England.

LEWIS Carl, b. 1 July 1961, Birmingham, Alabama, USA. Athlete. Education: University of Houston. Appointments: Bronze Medal, Long Jump, Pan-American Games, 1979; Won World Cup Competition, 1981; First World Championships (with 8.55 metres); Achieved World Record 8.79 metre jump, 1983; Gold Medals, Olympic Games, 100 metres, 200 metres, Long Jump, 4x100m, 1984; 65 Consecutive wins in Long Jump, 1985; Silver Medal, 200 metres; Gold Medal, 100 metres, Olympic Games, 1988; Jumped 8.64 metres, New York, 1991; World Record, 100 metres 9.86 seconds, 1991; Gold Medal, Long Jump, Olympic Games, 1992; Gold Medal for long jump (27ft. 10.75 in), Olympic Games, 1996; Retired, 1997; Attached to Trialtir, 1997. Honours: Track and Field News Athlete of the Decade, 1980-89; Athlete of the Century, IAAF, 1999. Address: c/o Carl Lewis International Fan Club, P O Box 57-1990, Houston, TX 77257-1990, USA.

LEWIS Denise, b. 27 August 1972, West Bromwich, England. Athlete. Career: Specialises in heptathlon; Commonwealth Heptathlon Record Holder (6,736 points), 1977; Fifth European Junior Championships, 1991; Gold Medal, Commonwealth Games, 1994; Gold Medal, European Cup, 1995; Bronze Medal, Olympic Games, 1996; Silver Medal, World Championships, 1997; Gold Medal, European Championships, 1998; Gold Medal, Commonwealth Championships, 1998; Silver Medal World Championship, 1999; New Commonwealth Record (6,831 points), 2000; Gold Medal, Olympic Games, 2000. Publications: Denise Lewis: Faster, Higher, Stronger, autobiography, 2001. Honours: British Athletics Writers Female Athlete of the Year, 1998, 2000; Sports Writers Association Sportswoman of the Year, 2000. Address: c/o MTC (UK) Ltd, 20 York Street, London, W1U 6PU, England. E-mail: info.mtc-uk.com

LEWIS Ernest Sidney, b. 27 April 1924, London, England. Company Secretary. m. Constance Sylvia, 1 son. Education: John Ruskin School, Croydon. Appointments: Company Secretary in investment companies; Retired. Publications: Occasional contributions to entomological periodicals. Honours: Presentational clock in appreciation of 35 years service with Continental Union Trust Company Ltd, 1976. Memberships: Royal Entomological Society; Linnean Society; Croydon Natural History & Scientific Society; Friends of the Natural History Museum; Devon Invertebrate Forum. Address: 24 New Street, Chagford, Devon TQ13 8BB, England.

LEWIS Esyr ap Gwilym, b. 11 January 1926, Clydach Vale, Glamorgan, Wales. Retired Judge. m. Elizabeth Hoffmann, 4 daughters. Education: Exhibitioner and Foundation Scholar, Trinity Hall, Cambridge, 1947-50. Appointments: Army Intelligence Corps, 1944-47; Called to Bar at Gray's Inn, 1951; Law Supervisor, Trinity Hall, Cambridge, 1951-57; Queens Counsel, 1971; Recorder, Crown Court, 1972-84; Deputy

High Court Judge, 1978-84; Official Referee, London Official Referees Courts, 1984-98, Senior Official Referee, 1994-98; Leader, Welsh Circuit, 1978-82; Member, Criminal Injuries Compensation Board, 1977-84. Publications: Articles in legal publications. Honour: Queen's Counsel. Memberships: Fellow, Chartered Institute of Arbitrators; Vice-President, Academy of Experts; Honorary Fellow, Society of Advanced Legal Studies; Bencher of Gray's Inn, 1978-, Treasurer, 1997. Address: 2 South Square, Gray's Inn, London WC1R 5HT, England.

LEWIS Geoffrey David, b. 13 April 1933, Brighton, East Sussex, England. Museum Consultant. m. Frances May Wilderspin, 3 daughters. Education: MA, University of Liverpool; Diploma of the Museums Association. Appointments include: Museum Assistant, 1950-58, Assistant Curator, 1958-60, Worthing Museum and Art Gallery; Deputy Director and Keeper of Antiquities, Sheffield City Museum, 1960-65; Honorary Lecturer in British Prehistory, University of Sheffield, 1965-72; Director, Sheffield City Museums, 1966-72; Director, Liverpool City Museums, 1972-74; Director, Merseyside County Museums, 1974-77; Director of Museum Studies, University of Leicester, 1977-89; Museum Consultant, 1989-; President, 1983-89, Chair, Ethics Committee, International Council of Museums, 1996-2004; Chair of Governors, Wolvey School, 1998-2003; President, Museums Association, 1980-81. Publications: The South Yorkshire Glass Industry, 1964; Prehistoric and Roman Times in the Sheffield Area (co-author), 1968; For instruction and recreation: a centenary history of the Museums Association, 1989; Manual of Curatorship: A guide to museum practice (co-editor), 1984, 2nd edition, 1992; Contributor to Encyclopaedia Britannica, 1984, 1998, 2006, Britannica On-line, 2007; Contributor to many books and articles relating to archaeology, ethics and museums. Honours: Honorary Fellow, Museums Association, 1989; Honorary Member, International Council of Museums, 2004; Listed in biographical dictionaries. Memberships: Diploma and Associate, 1958, Fellow, 1966, Museums Association; Fellow, Society of Antiquaries of London, 1969. Address: 4 Orchard Close, Wolvey, Hinckley LE10 3LR, England. E-mail: dib@geoffreylewis.co.uk

LEWIS, Baron of Newnham in the County of Cambridgeshire, Jack Lewis b. 13 February 1928, Barrow, England. Professor of Chemistry. m. Elfreida M Lamb, 1951, 1 son, 1 daughter. Education: Universities of London and Nottingham; PhD. Appointments: Lecturer, University of Sheffield, 1954-56; Lecturer, Imperial College, London, 1956-57; Lecturer-Reader, 1957-61, Professor of Chemistry, 1967-70, University College, London; Professor of Chemistry, University of Manchester, 1961-67; Professor of Chemistry, University of Cambridge, 1970-95; Fellow, Sidney Sussex College, Cambridge, 1970-77; Warden, Robinson College, Cambridge, 1975-. Publications: Papers in scientific journals. Honours include: Honorary Fellow, Sidney Sussex College, Cambridge; Honorary Fellow, Royal Society of Chemistry; 21 honorary degrees; Davy Medal, Royal Society, 1985; Chevalier, Ordre des Palmes Académiques; Commander Cross of the Order of Merit, Poland; Royal Medal, Royal Society, 2004. Memberships: Fellow, Royal Society; Foreign Associate, National Academy of Sciences, USA; Foreign Member, American Philosophical Society, 1994; Foreign Member, Accademia Nazionale dei Lincei, 1995; Numerous committees. Address: Robinson College, Grange Road, Cambridge CB3 9AN, England.

LEWIS Jerry (Joseph Levitch), b. 16 March 1926, Newark, New Jersey, USA. Comedian; Writer; Director; Producer; Actor. m. (1) Patti Palmer, 1944, divorced, 5 sons, (2) SanDee Pitnick, 1983, 1 daughter. Career: Comedian, night-clubs, then with Dean Martin, 500 Club, Atlantic City, New Jersey, 1946; Professor of Cinema, University of Southern California; Film debut with Dean Martin in My Friend Irma, 1949; Other films, many also as producer and director, include My Friend Irma Goes West, 1950, That's My Boy, 1951, The Caddy, Sailor Beware, 1952, Jumping Jacks, The Stooge, Scared Stiff, 1953, Living It Up, Three Ring Circus, 1954, You're Never Too Young, 1955, Partners, Hollywood or Bust, 1956, The Delicate Delinquent, 1957, The Sad Sack, Rock a Bye Baby, The Geisha Boy, 1958, Visit to a Small Planet, 1959, The Bellboy, Cinderfella, 1960, It's Only Money, 1961, The Errand Boy, 1962, The Patsy, The Disorderly Orderly, 1964, The Family Jewels, Boeing-Boeing, Three On a Couch, 1965, Way Way Out, 1966, The Big Mouth, 1967, Don't Raise the Bridge, Lower the River, 1968, One More Time, Hook, Line and Sinker, 1969, Which way to the Front?, 1970, The Day the Clown Cried, 1972, Hardly Working, 1979, King of Comedy, 1981, Slapstick of Another Kind, 1982, Smörgåsbord, 1983, How Did You Get In?, 1985, Mr Saturday Night, 1992, Funny Bones, Appeared in play, Damn Yankees, 1995, on tour, 1995-97; Television appearances including Startime, The Ed Sullivan Show and the Jazz Singer. Publications: The Total Film-Maker, 1971; Jerry Lewis in Person, 1982. Address: Jerry Lewis Films Inc, 3160 W Sahara Avenue, C-16, Las Vegas, NV 89102, USA. Website: www.jerrylewiscomedy.com

LEWIS Jerry Lee, b. 29 September 1935, Ferriday, Louisiana, USA. Singer; Musician (piano); Entertainer. m. 6 times. Career: Appeared on Louisiana Hayride, 1954; Film appearances: Jamboree, 1957; High School Confidential, 1958; Be My Guest, 1965; Concerts include: National Jazz & Blues Festival, 1968; Rock'n'Revival Concert, Toronto, 1969; First appearance, Grand Ole Opry, 1973; Rock'n'Roll Festival, Wembley, 1974; Numerous appearances with own Greatest Show On Earth; Subject of biographical film, Great Balls Of Fire, 1989. Recordings: Hit singles include: Whole Lotta Shakin' Goin' On', 1957; Great Balls Of Fire, Breathless, High School Confidential, 1958; What I'd Say, 1961; Good Golly Miss Molly, 1963; To Make Love Sweeter For You, 1969; There Must Be More To Love Than This, 1970; Would You Take Another Chance On Me?, 1971; Me And Bobby Gee, Chantilly Lace, 1972. Albums include: Jerry Lee Lewis, 1957; Jerry Lee's Greatest, 1961; Live At The Star Club, The Greatest Live Show On Earth, The Return Of Rock, Whole Lotta Shakin' Goin' On, Country Songs For City Folks, 1965; By Request - More Greatest Live Show On Earth, Breathless, 1967; Together, with Linda Gail Lewis, 1970; Rockin' Rhythm And Blues, 1971; Sunday Down South, with Johnny Cash, 1972; The Session, with Peter Frampton, Rory Gallagher, 1973; Jerry Lee Lewis, 1979; When Two Worlds Collide, 1980; My Fingers Do The Talking, 1983; I Am What I Am, 1984; Keep Your Hands Off It, 1987; Don't Drop It, 1988; Great Balls Of Fire! (film soundtrack), 1989; Rocket, 1990; Young Blood, 1995; Many compilations; Contributor, film soundtracks: Roadie, 1980; Dick Tracy, 1990. Honours include: Inducted into Rock'n'Roll Hall Of Fame, 1986; Star on Hollywood Walk Of Fame, 1989. Address: Warner Bros Records, 75 Rockefeller Plaza, New York, NY 10019, USA.

LEWIS Peter Tyndale, b. 1929, London, England. Retail Businessman. m. Deborah Anne Collins, 1 son, 1 daughter. Education: Christ Church, Oxford, 1949-52. Appointments: 2nd Lieutenant, Coldstream Guards, 1948-49; Pilot Officer, RAFVR, 1951-52; Barrister, Middle Temple, 1955-59; Joined

John Lewis Partnership, 1959; Director, John Lewis Department Stores, 1967-71; Chairman, John Lewis Partnership plc and John Lewis plc, 1972-93. Honours: Companion, Institute of Management; Fellow, Royal Society of Arts. Memberships: Executive Committee, Industrial Society, 1968-79; Executive Committee, Design Council, 1971-74; Chairman, Retail Distributors Association, 1971-72; Governor, Windlesham House School, 1979-95; Governor, NIESR, 1983-2000; Trustee, Bell Educational Trust, 1987-97; Governor, Queen's College, Harley Street, 1994-2000; Trustee, Southampton University Development Trust, 1994-2004. Address: 34 Victoria Road, London W8 5RG, England.

LEWIS-SMITH Anne Elizabeth, b. 14 April 1925, London, England. Poet; Writer; Editor; Publisher. m. Peter Lewis-Smith, 17 May 1944, 1 son, 2 daughters. Appointments: Assistant Editor, 1967-83, Editor, Envoi Poetry Magazine, 1984-90; Editor, Aerostat, 1972-77; Editor, WWNT Bulletin, 1981-83; British Association of Friends of Museums Yearbook, 1984-91; Publisher, Traeth Publications, 1990-; Publisher, Envoi Poets Publications, 1990-; Balloonist, 1969-. Publications: The Beginning, 1964; Seventh Bridge, 1965; Flesh and Flowers (three impressions), 1967; Dandelion Flavour, 1971; Dinas Head, 1980; Places and Passions, 1986; In the Dawn, 1986; Circling Sound, 1996; Feathers Fancies and Feelings, 1999; Off Duty!, 2006; Every Seventh Wave, 2006. Poetry in over 40 different poetry magazines world-wide and 16 anthologies translated into various languages, including Hebrew and Spanish; Regular Contributor to Newspapers and magazines. Honours: Swedish Ballooniana-Prizet for Services to Aviation; Tissandier Award for Services to Aviation, 1983; Debby Warley Award for Services to International Aviation; Dorothy Tutin Award for Services to Poetry. Memberships: PEN; Society of Women Writers and Journalists; Honorary member, Balloon Federation of America; Balloon Club of South Africa. Address: Pen Ffordd, Newport, Pembrokeshire, SA42 0QT, Wales.

LEYCEGUI GARDOQUI Beatriz, b. 10 November 1964, Veracruz, Mexico. Lawyer. 2 sons, 1 daughter. Education: Master of International Affairs, Columbia University, New York City, USA, 1988-90; JD, Escuela Libre de Derecho, Mexico City, 1982-87. Appointments: Legal Assistant, Ministry of the Interior, Mexico City, 1984-88; Research Assistant, Columbia University, New York City; Legal Counsel, Ministry of Foreign Affairs, Mexico City, 1990; Director, Legal Analysis, Office in Charge of NAFTA negotiations, Ministry of Trade and Industrial Development, Mexico City, 1990-92; Professor and Researcher, ITAM, Mexico City, 1993-99; Partner, SAI Consultores, SC, 1999-2006; Under-secretary for International Trade Negotiations, Ministry of the Economy, Mexico City, 2006-. Publications: Books: Some Thoughts Regarding the Prevention, Administration and Resolution of Disputes under NAFTA Chapters 18 & 20, 1993; Trading Punches: Trade Remedy Law Disputes under NAFTA, US, 1995, Mexico, 1997; Natural Partners?: Five Years of the North American Free Trade Agreement (NAFTA), 2000; Articles: Prevention of Disputes under the Free Trade Agreement: Chapter XVII Analysis, 1994; A Legal Analysis of Mexico's Antidumping and Countervailing Regulatory Framework, 1995; Eliminating Unfairness within North America Region: A Look at Antidumping, 1997; Agreement to disagree: Disputes Resolution under NAFTA, 2000; Trading Remedies to Remedy Trade: the NAFTA Experience, 2003-04; The Ten Major Problems with the Anti-dumping Instrument in Mexico, 2005. Honours: 1st Class Award, Escuela Libre de Derecho; Honorary Mention, Professional Exam, Ford Foundation, Columbia University and Bank of Mexico Scholarships.

Memberships: Mexican Bar Law College, Mexican Council for Foreign Affairs; Institute of Latin American Studies; Advisory Board, Columbia University; Legal Studies Department, CIDE; Member, Advisory Board, International Business Law Masters Degree, Iberoamerican University. Address: Alfonso Reyes 30-90 Floor, Hipodromo Condesa, Mexico DF 06140, Mexico City, Mexico. E-mail: bleycegui@economia.gob.mx and bleyceguiga@yahoo.com.mx

LEYDEN Michael J II (Lei Jie Ming), b. 26 February 1950, Wenatchee, Washington, USA. Entrepreneur; Educator; Writer. m. Xu Zhong Yu, 1 son, 2 daughters. Education: AA, Wenatchee Valley College, Washington, 1970; University of the Virgin Islands, 1971; BA, Central Washington University, 1972; MA, Washington State University, 1974; Certificate, Small Business Management Program, University of Hawaii-Hilo, 1975; DBA, Newport University, Utah, 1997. Appointments: Lecturer, Philosophy, Washington State University, and University of New Brunswick, 1972-75; Founder/Corporate Owner, international business, Real Estate, trader, 1975-86; Visiting Scholar & Invited Guest Lecturer, International Business, University of Guam, 1988; Lecturer, Economics, University of Hawaii, 1989; Professor, International Economics, Nankai University, 1994; Professor, International Politics, Peking (Beijing) University, 1995; Professor, International Management Economics (MBA), Tsinghua University, 1996; Professor, Economics, Shanghai University, 1997; Professor, College of Business Management, Tianjin Polytechnic University & Graduate School, 2002-03; Deputy (Vice) General Manager, Beijing & Tianjin Prosperty Advertising Co Ltd, Tianjin & Peking, 2003-04; International Business Affairs Manager & Director, Michael Trading & Consulting Co Ltd, Beijing, 2003-04; Professor, Economics & English Literature, Beijing Wuzi University, 2006; Professor, International Finance, International & Global Banking, Shandong University of Science & Technology, and Technology International Education Centre, 2006-07; Professor, School of Business, Zhanjiang Normal University, School of Business, Guangzhou, 2007-; Professor, Emirates Aviation College, Dubai, United Arab Emirates, 2007-; Managing Partner, Strategic Project Management LLC, Honolulu, Hawaii. Publications: 3 books; Numerous articles in professional journals. Honours include: No 1 Australian Government USA Importer of the Year, 1986; Outstanding Teaching Excellence Award, Peking University, 1996; Departmental No 1 Professor, Shanghai University, 1997; Large Silver Medal, ACPF China National Philatelic Exhibition, 2003; Large Silver Medal for Literature, International Philatelic Exhibition, 2003; Distinguished Foreign Faculty, Tianjin Polytechnic University, 2003. Memberships: Independent Scholars of Asia; American Association of University Professors. Address: PO Box 22124, Honolulu, HI 96823-2124, USA. E-mail: michelleyden@yahoo.com

LEYGRAF Hans, b. 7 September, 1920, Stockholm, Sweden. Concert Pianist; Music Educator. m. Margarethe Stehle, 1 son, 1 daughter. Education: Piano with Gottfrid Boon, Stockholm, Sweden, 1928-38; Piano with Anna Hirzel-Langenhan, Schloss Berg, Thurgau, Switzerland, 1938-41; Composition, Conducting, Music Academy, Stockholm, Sweden, 1936-40; Composition, Conducting, Music Academy, Munich, Germany, 1941-42. Career: Concert Pianist in more than 30 countries, 1938-; Piano Teacher, Music Academy, Darmstadt, Germany, 1954-62; Visiting Piano Teacher, Edsberg Music School, Stockholm, Sweden, 1958-70; Piano Teacher, Music University, Hannover, Germany, 1962-85; Piano Professor, University Mozarteum, Salzburg, Austria, 1972-; Visiting Piano Professor, Music University of Berlin, 1988-97.

Recordings: 5 CDs: Mozart, all piano sonatas, 1982-85; 3 CDs, Schubert, 3 recitals, 1994. Honours: Litteris et Artibus, Stockholm, Sweden, 1977; Das österreichische Ehrenkreuz, Vienna, Austria, 1984; Das grosse silberne Ehrenzeichen, Vienna, Austria, 1994. Memberships: Swedish Academy of Music, Stockholm, 1961; Honorary Member, University of Mozarteum, Salzburg, 1988-; Honorary Doctor, University of Luleå, Sweden, 2003. Address: Am Irrsee 15, A-4893 Zell am Moos, Austria.

LI Ching-Chung, b. 30 March 1932, Changshu, China. Professor of Electrical Engineering and Computer Science. m. Hanna Wu Li, 2 sons. Education: BSEE, National Taiwan University, 1954; MSEE, 1956, PhD, 1961, Northwestern University. Appointments: Professor, Electrical Engineering, University of Pittsburgh, 1967-; Professor, Computer Science, University of Pittsburgh, 1977-. Publications: Over 200 papers. Memberships: Fellow, IEEE; Fellow, IAPR; Fellow, AAAS; Biomedical Engineering Society; Pattern Recognition Society. Address: 2130 Garrick Drive, Pittsburgh, PA 15235-5033, USA.

LI Hua, b. 25 August 1960, Wuhan, People's Republic of China. Assistant Professor. m. Dong-Ping Yuan, 1 daughter. Education: BSc, 1982, MSc, 1987, Wuhan University of Technology; PhD, National University of Singapore, 1999. Appointments: Managing Director, Wuhan University of Technology Press, 1990-94; Research Scholar, Senior Research Engineer, Principal Research Engineer, National University of Singapore, Institute of High performance Computing, 1994-2000; Postdoctoral Associate, University of Illinois Urbana-Champaign, USA, 2000-2001; Research Scientist, Division Manager, Institute of High Performance Computing, Singapore, 2001-2006; Assistant Professor, School of Mechanical and Aerospace Engineering, Nanyang Technological University, 2006-2007. Publication: Hermite-cloud: a novel true meshless method, 2003; Rotating Shell Dynamics, 2005. Honour: Silver Award of HPC Quest – The Blue Challenge – presented by IMB & IHPC. Memberships: Singapore Society of Theoretical and Applied Mechanics; Association for Computational Mechanics, Singapore. Address: Blk 612 #09-302, Clementi West St 1, Singapore 120612. E-mail: lihua@ntu.edu.sg

LI Lingwei, b. 1964. Badminton Player. Career: Participant in international championships; Won Women's Singles Title, 3rd World Badminton Championships, Copenhagen, 1982; Won Women's Singles and Women's Doubles, 5th ALBA World Cup, Jakarta, 1985; Won Women's Singles, World Badminton Grand Prix finals, Tokyo, 1985; Won Women's Singles at Dunhill China Open Badminton Championship, Nanjing, and Malaysian Badminton Open, Kuala Lumpur, 1987; Won Women's Singles at World Grand Prix, Hong Kong, China Badminton Open, and Danish Badminton Open, Odense, 1988; Won Women's Singles, All-England Badminton Championships, 1989; Winner, Women's Singles, 6th World Badminton Championships, Jakarta. Honours: Elected 7th in list of 10 Best Chinese Athletes. Address: China Sports Federation, Beijing, People's Republic of China.

LI Shuliang, b. 15 February 1963, P R China. Senior Lecturer. m. W Wang, 2 sons. Education: Bachelor's degree, Computer Science (Electronic Computing), 1984, Master's degree (M Phil equivalent), Management Science (Industrial Management Engineering), 1993, Southwest Jiaotong University, China; PhD, Hybrid Intelligent Decision Support systems, University of Luton, Bedfordshire, England, 2001. Appointments: Associate Professor, School of Economics and Business Administration, Southwest Jiaotong University, 1994-99; Senior Lecturer, Business Information and Intelligent Systems, Westminster Business School, University of Westminster, 2001-. Publications: The Development of a Hybrid Intelligent System for Developing Marketing Strategy, 2000; A Web-Enabled Hybrid Approach to Strategic Marketing Planning: Group Delphi + a Web-Based Expert System, 2005; AgentStra: An Internet-Based Multi-Agent Intelligent System for Strategic Decision Making, 2007. E-mail: lish@wmin.ac.uk

LI Tzu-yin, b. 3 March 1931, Gulangyu District, Xiamen Municipality, Fujian Province, China. Professor; Research Scientist. m. Qing-Liang Huang, 3 daughters. Education: BS, Department of Biology, Beijing Normal University, China, 1954; MS, 1987; PhD, 1990; Postdoctor, 1990-93, Department of Entomology, Texas A and M University, USA. Appointments: Biology Teacher, Beijing 15th Middle School, 1954-56; Lecturer, Professor, Department of Biology, Beijing Normal University, 1956-85; Visiting Scientist, Department of Zoology, J W Gothe University, Frankfurt, Germany, 1981-82; Research Assistant, Postdoctoral, Research Scientist, Department of Entomology, Texas A and M University, USA, 1983-2001. Publications: 6 books (4 co-author); Numerous articles for scientific journals. Honours: Certified Outstanding Teacher in Beijing, 1956; Certificate of Honour for lifelong scientist, Department of Zoology, J W Gothe University, 1982; Board Certified Entomologist, 1993, Emeritus Membership, 1996, Entomology Society of America; Certified as one of 2000 Outstanding Scientists of the 20th Century by IBC, Cambridge England, 2000; Award for Scientific Achievement as one of 500 World Leaders of Influence, ABI, USA, 2001; Honourable Professor, Beijing Normal University, China, 2002; Lifetime of Achievement Award, IBC, 2007; Excellent Overseas Chinese Entrepreneur, Chinese Enterprises Association; Included in several most reputed international biographical dictionaries. Memberships: Entomological Society of America; Sigma Xi, Scientific Research Society; Honour Society of Agriculture, Gamma Sigma Delta. Address: 35-30 73rd Street, Apt 3H, Jackson Heights, NY 11372, USA. E-mail: litzuyin@yahoo.com

LI-LAN, b. 28 January 1943, New York, New York, USA. Artist. Appointments: Regional Council, Parrish Art Museum, Southampton, New York, 1984-87; Artists Advisory Board, East Hampton Center for Contemporary Art, East Hampton, New York, 1989-90. Publications: Canvas With an Unpainted Part: An Autobiography, Tokyo, Japan, 1976; Texts in exhibition catalogues and books, numerous articles. Commissions and Creative Works: Collections in numerous museums including: Virginia Museum of Fine Arts, Richmond, Virginia; The Parrish Art Museum, Southampton, New York; William Benton Museum of Art, Storrs, Connecticut; Arkansas Arts Center, Little Rock; The Baltimore Museum of Art, Baltimore, Maryland; San Diego Museum of Art, San Diego, California; The Sezon Museum of Modern Art, Karuizawa, Japan; Ohara Museum of Art, Kurashiki, Japan; Other collections include: Estee Lauder Inc, Mobil Oil Corporation, Lifetime TV, Chermayeff and Geismer Associates, New York; Gap Inc, Flagship Store, Oahu, Hawaii; Art For Peace Collection, Fischer Pharmaceuticals Ltd, Tel Aviv, Israel; Seattle First National Bank, Washington; Security Pacific National Bank, Los Angeles, California; Weatherspoon Art Gallery, Greensboro, North Carolina; Werner Kramarsky Collection, New York; Solo exhibitions in USA, Japan, Taiwan include: Robert Miller Gallery, New York, 1978; OK Harris Gallery, New York, 1983, 1985, 1987; The William Benton Museum of Art, Storrs, Connecticut,

1990; Lin & Keng Gallery, Taipei, Taiwan, 1995, 1997, 2001, 2006; Art Projects International, New York, New York, 1994, 1996; DoubleVision Gallery, Los Angeles, California, 2003; Nabi Gallery, New York, 2004; Jason McCoy Inc, New York, 2006; Numerous group exhibitions in USA, Japan and Taiwan. Honours: Artists Grant, Artists Space, New York, 1988, 1990; Certificate of Merit: Chinese American Cultural Pioneer, New York City Council, 1993.

LIANG Xue-Zhang, b. 1 December 1939, Pingdu, Shandong, China. University Professor. m. Feng-Jie, 2 sons, 1 daughter. Education: Diploma, 1962; Postgraduate thesis and diploma, 1965. Appointments: Assistant, 1965; Lecturer, 1978; Associate Professor, 1983; Professor, 1990; PhD Supervisor, 1993. Publications: Articles in journals: Lagrange representation of multivariate interpolation, 1989; On the convergence of Hakopian interpolation and cubature, 1997; On the integral convergence of Kergin interpolation on the disk, 1998; Solving second kind integral equation by Galerkin methods with continuous orthogonal wavelets, 2001; The application of Cayley-Bacharach theorem to bivariate Lagrange interpolation, 2004. Honours: Natural Science Award, China, 1982; Scientific and Technical Progress Award, Education Committee of China, 1988. Membership: Jilin Province Expert Association of China. Address: Institute of Mathematics, Jilin University, Changchun, Jilin 130012, China.

LIAO Shutsung, b. 1 January 1931, Taiwan. m. Shuching, 4 daughters. Education: BS, Agricultural Chemistry, 1953, MS, Biochem, 1956, National Taiwan University; PhD, Biochemistry, University of Chicago, 1961. Appointments: Research Associate, 1960-63; Assistant Professor, 1964-69, Associate Professor, 1969-71, Professor, 1972, Department of Biochemistry and Molecular Biology Ben May Institute for Cancer Research, University of Chicago, 1972; Chairman of the Board of Trustees and CEO, Anagen Therapeutics Inc, 1999-; Director, Tang Center for Herbal Medicine Research, 2000-2002; Consultant to various national and international conferences, agencies, foundations and workshops. Publications: Member, Editorial Board: Journal Steroid Biochemistry and Molecular Biology, The Prostate and Receptors and Signal Transduction; Associate Editor, Cancer Research, 1982-89; Over 250 articles to professional journals. Honours: NIH Grantee, 1962-; Pfizer Lecture Fellow Award, Clinical Research Institute, Montreal, 1972; Science-Technology Achievement Prize, Taiwanese-American Foundation, 1983; Gregory Pincus Medal and Award, Worcester Federation for Experimental Biology, 1992; Tzongming Tu Award, Formosan Medical Association, 1993; C H Li Memorial Lecture Award, 1994; Achievements include: Discovery of androgen activation mechanism and androgen receptors; Cloning and structural determination of androgen receptors, and other nuclear receptors, receptor gene mutation, molecular basis of cancer growth and progression, molecular approaches to chemoprevention and therapeutic treatment of hormone sensitive and insensitive cancers as well as cardiovascular and Alzheimer diseases; Memberships: American Society of Biochemistry and Molecular Biology; American Association of Cancer Research; Endocrine Society; North American Taiwanese Professors Association, President, 1980-81, Executive Director, 1981-; Member, National Academy, Taiwan, 1994; Fellow, American Academy of Arts and Sciences, 1997. Address: University of Chicago, Ben May Institute for Cancer Research, 929 E 57th Street, Chicago, IL 60637-1463, USA.

LIDDLE Peter (Hammond), b. 26 December 1934, Sunderland, England. Historian; Author; Archive Director. Education: BA, University of Sheffield, 1956; Teacher's Certificate, University of Nottingham, 1957; Diploma in Physical Education, Loughborough University of Technology, 1957. Appointments: History Teacher, Havelock School, Sunderland, 1957; Head, History Department, Gateacre Comprehensive School, Liverpool, 1958-67; Lecturer, Notre Dame College of Education, 1967; Lecturer, 1967-70, Senior Lecturer in History, 1970-87, Sunderland Polytechnic; Keeper of the Liddle Collection, University of Leeds, 1988-99; Director, The Second World War Experience Centre, Leeds, 1999-2007; Founder and Editor, The Poppy and the Owl, 1990; Founder and Editor, Everyone's War, 1999. Publications: Men of Gallipoli, 1976; World War One: Personal Experience Material for Use in Schools, 1977; Testimony of War 1914-18, 1979; The Sailor's War 1914-18, 1985; Gallipoli: Pens, Pencils and Cameras at War, 1985; 1916: Aspects of Conflict, 1985; Home Fires and Foreign Fields (editor and contributor), 1985; The Airman's War 1914-18, 1987; The Soldier's War 1914-18, 1988; Voices of War, 1988; The Battle of the Somme, 1992; The Worst Ordeal: Britons at Home and Abroad 1914-18, 1994; Facing Armageddon: The First World War Experienced (co-editor and contributor), 1996; Passchendaele in Perspective: The Third Battle of Ypres (editor and contributor), 1997; At the Eleventh Hour (co-editor and contributor), 1998; For Five Shillings a Day (co-author), 2000; The Great World War, 1914-45, volume I, 2000, volume II, 2001, (co-editor and contributor); D-Day: By Those Who Were There, 2004. Contributions to: Journals and other books; Oral History Consultant. Honours: MLitt, University of Newcastle, 1975; PhD, University of Leeds, 1997; Life President, Second World War Experience Centre. Memberships: British Audio Visual Trust; Fellow, Royal Historical Society. Address: Prospect House, 39 Leeds Road, Rawdon, Leeds LS19 6NW, England.

LIEBERMAN Louis Stuart, b. 23 May 1938, Swan Hill, Victoria, Australia. Barrister; Solicitor; Director. m. Marjorie Cox, 2 sons, 1 daughter. Education: New South Wales Barristers and Solicitors Admission Board; Studied and worked as Articled Law Clerk; Qualified as a Solicitor, New South Wales and High Court and Barrister and Solicitor, Victoria; Diploma in Law (SAB). Appointments include: Senior Partner, Harris Lieberman & Co Barristers and Solicitors, 1974-76; Chair, House of Representatives Standing Committee on Aboriginal and Torres Strait Islander Affairs; Parliamentary Secretary to Leader of Opposition, Commonwealth Parliament; Shadow Minister for Health, Further Education, Water Resources, Property and Services; Minister for Planning, Assistant Health, Minerals and Energy, Mines; Member for Benambra, Legislative Assembly, Parliament of Victoria, 1976-92, retired; Member for Indi, House of Representatives, Commonwealth of Australia, 1993-2001, retired; Director, Hume Building Society Ltd, 1999. Memberships: Fellow, Australian Institute of Company Directors; Law Society of New South Wales; Law Institute, Victoria; Australian War Memorial Foundation; Patron Bandiana Military Museum; La Trobe University Council; Wodonga Technical College Council; Rotary. Address: PO Box 151, Wodonga, Victoria, Australia 3689.

LIEBERSON Stanley, b. 20 April 1933, Montreal, Canada. Professor of Sociology. Education: MA, Sociology, 1958, PhD, Sociology, 1960, University of Chicago, USA. Appointments: Instructor to Assistant Professor of Sociology, 1959-61, University of Iowa, USA; Assistant Professor to Professor of Sociology, University of Wisconsin, 1961-67; Professor of Sociology, University of Washington, 1967-71;

Professor of Sociology, University of Chicago, 1971-74; Professor of Sociology, University of Arizona, 1974-83; Professor of Sociology, University of California, Berkeley, 1983-88, Professor of Sociology, 1988-, Abbott Lawrence Lowell Professor, 1991-2006, Abbott Lawrence Lowel Research Professor, 2007-, Harvard University. Publications include most recently: Book: A Matter of Taste: How Names, Fashions, and Culture Change, 2000; Articles in academic journals: The Instability of Androgynous Names: The Symbolic Maintenance of Gender Boundaries, 2000; Barking Up the Wrong Branch: Scientific Alternatives to the Current Model of Sociological Science (co-author), 2002; Popularity as a Taste (co-author), 2003; The Frequency Distribution Mechanism (co-author), 2006; Book chapters: Index of Isolation in the Encyclopedia of Housing, 1998; Examples, Submerged Statements and the Neglected Application of Philosophy to Social Theory in What is Social Theory?: The Philosophical Debates, 1998; Jewish Names and the Names of Jews in These are the Names: Studies in Jewish Onomastics, 2003; Popularity as a Taste: An Application to the Naming Process, The Frequency Distribution Mechanism. Honours include: Guggenheim Fellowship, 1972-73; Distinguished Contribution to Scholarship Award, American Sociological Association, 1982; Honorary MA, Harvard University, 1988; Honorary Degree of Doctor of Humane Letters, University of Arizona, 1993; Christensen Visiting Fellow, St Catherine's College, University of Oxford, 2001; Co-recipient, Best Book in the Sociology of Culture, Culture Section, American Sociological Association, 2001; Mirra Komarovsky Book Award, Eastern Sociological Association, 2002. Memberships include: Population Association of America; American Sociological Association; Sociological Research Association; American Academy of Arts and Sciences; National Academy of Sciences; American Philosophical Society. Address: Department of Sociology, Harvard University, William James Hall, Room 436, 33 Kirkland Street, Cambridge, MA 02138, USA.

LIEBESCHUETZ John Hugo Wolfgang Gideon, b. 22 June 1927, Hamburg, Germany. Retired Professor of Classical and Archaeological Studies; Writer. m. Margaret Rosa Taylor, 9 April 1955, 1 son, 3 daughters. Education: BA, 1951, PhD, 1957, University of London. Appointments: Professor and Head of Department of Classical and Archaeological Studies, University of Nottingham, 1979-92. Publications: Antioch, 1972; Continuity and Change in Roman Religion, 1979; Barbarians and Bishops, 1992; From Diocletian to the Arab Conquest, 1992; The Decline and Fall of the Roman City, 2000; Ambrose of Milan, Political Letters and Speeches, 2005; Decline and Change in Late Antiquity, 2006. Honours: Fellow, British Academy, 1992; Corresponding Fellow, German Archaeological Institute, 1994; Fellow, University College, London, 1997; Fellow, Society of Antiquaries. Address: 1 Clare Valley, The Park, Nottingham NG7 1BU, England.

LIEBOWITZ Daniel S F, b. 26 November 1921, New York City, USA. Physician; Author; Clinical Professor Emeritus. Widower, 2 sons, 1 daughter. Education: BA, Columbia College, Columbia University, 1943; MD, New York University, 1946; Postgraduate Training, Bellevue Hospital, New York City, Goldwater Memorial Hospital, New York City, and Western Reserve's Crile VA Hospital, Cleveland, Ohio. Appointments: Gastroenterologist, Redwood City, California, 42 years; Director of Medical Education, Sequoia Hospital, Redwood City, 30 years; Teacher, University of California School of Medicine, San Francisco, 3 years; Part time Teacher, Stanford University School of Medicine, 1963-95; Clinical Professor of Medicine Emeritus; Volunteer Physician, hospital ship USS Hope; Research trips to Africa; Several lectures on various topics. Publications: Numerous books including The Last Expedition, 2005. Honours: Listed in international biographical dictionaries. Memberships: American Medical Association; Royal Geographic Society; Explorers' Club. E-mail: eminpasha@aol.com

LIGAA Urtnasangiin, b. 10 March 1932, Galt sum, Khovsgol aimag, Mongolia. Botanist; Economic Botanist. m. Norjingiina Ninjil, 1 son, 4 daughters. Education: VS, Veterinary Sciences, Mongolian State University, Ulaanbaatar, Mongolia. 1951-56; Chemistry and Pharmacology of Medicinal Plants, Veterinary Institute and Institute of Medicinal Plants, Budapest, Hungary, 1965-66; Postgraduate Botany, Economic Botany, (PhD), V L Komarov Botanical Institute, Academy of Sciences of Leningrad (St Petersburg), Russia, 1969-72. Appointments: Veterinary, State Farm "Erentsav", 1956-63; Scientific Researcher, Agricultural Institute of Mongolian Academy of Sciences, 1964-68; Scientific Researcher, Chief Scientist, Leading Scientist, Chief Advisor for Economic Botany Sector, Member, Academic Council, Institute of Botany, Mongolian Academy of Science, 1973-92; Teacher, Traditional Medicine Institute "Mamba Datsan", 1993-94; Leading Scientist, National Institute of Mongolian Traditional Medicine, 1995-97; Teacher of Medicinal and Useful Plants, 1998-2000, Senior Leading Scientist, Project Executor, 2001-, Mongolian State University of Agriculture. Publications: 21 books and numerous papers to specialist journals, conferences and seminars. Address: Ulaanbaatar 46, POB 743, Mongolia.

LIKHACHEV Vasily, b. 5 January 1952, Gorki, Russia. Lawyer. m. Nailya Likhacheva, 2 daughters. Education: Diploma in International Law, Kazan State University, 1970-75; Doctor of Legal Science, 1990. Appointments: Professor, Kazan State University, 1978-90; Vice-President of Tatarstan, 1990-95; Chief of the Parliament, Republic of Tatarstan, 1995-96; Permanent Representative of the Russian Federation to the European Community, 1998-2003; Senator of the Council of the Federation, 2004-. Publications: More than 300 scientific papers including: A Legal Status of Tatarstan, 1996; On the Way to Law and Justice, 1997; Russia and the EU in the international system, 2004. Honours: A number of national and international honours and awards; Rank of Ambassador Extraordinary and Plenipotentiary. Address: 26 B. Dmitrovka, Moscow 103426, Russia. E-mail: vnlikhachev@council.gov.ru

LILA Lila, b. 12 April 1950, Chhaprohal, India. Medicine. m. Baltej Singh, 1 daughter. Education: BSc; MBBS; MS (Ortho); FRACGP. Appointments: Medical Officer, Agriculture University, Solan, 1976; Medical Officer, Rural Hospital, Karsog, 1977-78; Orthopaedic Surgeon, District Hospital, Solan & Nahan, 1982-92; Medical Officer in Charge, ESI Hospital, Parwanoo, 1992-94; RMO, Nepean Hospital, Australia, 2000-02; General Practitioner, NSW, Australia, 2002-. Honours: First girl child in community and family to go to school; Scholarship from Class 5 onwards; Merit Scholarship holder from Class 10 onwards; First lady doctor from State to do Master's in Orthopaedics and Practical Orthopaedics. Memberships: Indian Medical Association; NSW Medical Association; Australian Medical Association. Address: 216 Glenwood Pk Dr, Glenwood, NSW, 2768, Australia. E-mail: lila_ortho@hotmail.com

LILLEY Right Honourable Peter Bruce, b. 23 August 1943, Kent, England. Politician. m. Gail Ansell, 1979. Education: Clare College, Cambridge; MA, Cantab. Appointments: Chairman, Bow Group, 1973; Member of Parliament for

St Albans, 1983-97, for Hitchin and Harpenden, 1997-; Economic Secretary, 1987-89, Financial Secretary, 1989-90, to Treasury; Secretary of State for Trade and Industry, 1990-92, for Social Security, 1992-97; Opposition Front Bench Spokesman for Treasury, 1997-98; Deputy Leader of the Opposition, 1998-99; Former Director, Greenwell Montague, Oil Analyst; Chairman, Globalisation and Global Poverty policy group, 2007. Publications: The Delusion of Incomes Policy, co-author, 1977; The End of the Keynesian Era, 1980; Thatcherism: The Next Generation, 1990; Winning the Welfare Debate, 1996; Patient Power, 2000; Common Sense on Cannabis, 2001; Taking Liberties, 2002; Save on Pensions, 2003. Honour: Privy Councillor. Address: House of Commons, London SW1A 0AA, England.

LILLIE Betty Jane, b. 11 April 1926, Cincinnati, Ohio, USA. Professor of Biblical Studies. Education: BSEd, 1955, BA, 1961, College of Mt St Joseph; MA, 1967, MA, 1975, Providence College, Rhode Island; PhD, Hebrew Union College, Cincinnati, Ohio, 1982. Appointments: Teaching at graduate and undergraduate levels, Faculty, Athenaeum of Ohio, Cincinnati, Ohio, 1982-2007; Athenaeum Summer Program: Progoff Intensive Journal I, 1986, Progoff Intensive Journal II, 1987, Women in the Biblical Tradition, 1988; Athenaeum Israel Study Program in Israel, Summer 1989; Athenaeum Summer Lecture Series: Women in the Biblical Tradition, 1990; Participant in faculty development workshops, 1992, 1993, 1996, 1997, 1999, 2002, 2003, 2004, 2005, 2006 and 2007; Faculty, Evening College of the University of Cincinnati, 1984-2003; Academic committees; Involvement in Church ministry and life. Publications: Book: A History of the Scholarship on the Wisdom of Solomon from the Nineteenth Century to our Time; Biblical Exegesis for Weekday Homily Helps; Weekly column on Sunday Scripture readings every third month, 1988-; Numerous articles and papers on religious topics. Honours include: International Peace Prize, 2003; World Medal of Freedom, 2006; Named Woman of the Year, 1993, 1994, 1995, 1996, 1997, 1999, 2000; International Woman of the Year, 1992-93, 1996-97, 1998-99, 1999-2000, 2001-02, 2007; Named for: Decree of International Letters for Cultural Achievement, 1996, 1997; Lifetime Achievement Award, ABI, 1997; International Cultural Diploma of Honour, 1997, 1999; Presidential Seal of Honor, 1997; Order of International Fellowship, 1997; Millennium Hall of Fame, 1998; Named Educator of the Year, IBC, 2006; Great Minds of the 21st Century, ABI, 2002, 2007-08; Listed in Cambridge Blue Book, IBC, 2007; International Peace Prize, United Cultural Convention, USA, 2003. Memberships: Catholic Biblical Association; Society for Biblical Literature; Biblical Archaeology Society; Eastern Great Lakes Biblical Society, Vice President, 1992; President, 1993; Council of Societies for the Study of Religion; Women's Center for Theological Studies; Ohio Humanities Council; Listed in Who's Who publications and biographical dictionaries. Address: 2704 Cypress Way Appt 3, Cincinnati, OH 45212-1773, USA.

LIM Chee Wah, b. 27 January 1965, Batu Pahat, Johor, Malaysia. Associate Professor. m. Moi Peng Choo, 1 son, 1 daughter. Education: BEng (honours), Mechanical Engineering (Aeronautics), University of Technology, Malaysia, 1989; MEng, Mechanical Engineering, National University of Singapore, 1992; PhD, Mechanical Engineering, Nanyang Technological University, Singapore, 1995. Appointments: Research Assistant, National University of Singapore, 1989-91; Research Assistant, Teaching Assistant, Nanyang Technological University, Singapore, 1992-94; Research Assistant, 1994-95, Postdoctoral Research Fellow, 1995-97, University of Queensland, Australia; Research Fellow,

University of Hong Kong, 1998-2000; Assistant Professor, 2000-03, Associate Professor, 2003-, City University of Hong Kong; Professional Consultant, Green Technology Consultants Limited, Hong Kong, 2000-; Associate Editor (Asia-Pacific Region), Advances in Vibration Engineering, 2002-; Technical Reviewer for John Wiley & Sons, Kluwer Academic Publishers and more than 30 international journals. Publications: Contributed more than 140 technical papers to professional journals; 1 book; 1 book chapter; More than 60 international conference papers; miscellaneous research reports. Honours: Public Service Commission Scholarship, Malaysia, 1985-89; Best Academic Performance, Mechanical Engineering, (Aeronautics), 1989; University of Queensland Postdoctoral Research Fellowship, 1995-97; University of Hong Kong Research Fellowship, 1998-2000; Listed in several biographical dictionaries; Fellowship, International Biographical Association. Memberships: American Society of Mechanical Engineers; American Society of Civil Engineers; Acoustical Society of America; Structural Engineering Institute of ASCE. Address: Department of Building and Construction, City University of Hong Kong, Tat Chee Avenue, Kowloon, Hong Kong. E-mail: bccwlim@cityu.edu.hk

LIM Chwen Jeng, b. 1964, Malaysia. Architect. Education: AA Dipl, Architectural Association, School of Architecture, London, England, 1982-87. Appointments: Director, Studio 8 Architects, 1994-; Director, Bartlett Architecture Research Laboratory, University College, London, 1999-; Visiting Professor, Glasgow School of Art, 2001-; Exhibitions include: RMIT, Melbourne, Australia, 1996; Stadelschule, Frankfurt, 1997; ARCHILAB Fonds Regional d'Art Contemporain du Centre, France, 1999; Mackintosh Museum, Glasgow, 2004; Venice Architecture Biennale 04, British Pavilion, 2004; Other group exhibitions include: Dulwich Picture Gallery, 1990; National Gallery Alexandros Soutzos Museum, Athens, 1990; Museo Nazionale Di Castel St Angelo, Rome, 1994; Nara World Architecture Triennale, Japan, 1996; Defence Corp Building, Jyvaskyla, Finland, 1997; CUBE Gallery, Manchester, 2000; Academie de France, Rome, 2000; RIBA, London, 2000; Architecture Foundation, London, 2001; Gallery 312, Chicago, USA, 2001; Rubelle + Norman Schafler Gallery, New York, 2001; Storefront Gallery, New York, 2001; Thread Waxing Gallery, New York, 2001; Chicago Architecture Foundation, USA, 2001; Mediatheque d'Orleans, France, 2002; Drawings in permanent collections include: The Victoria and Albert Museum, London; Fonds Regional d'Art Contemporain du Centre, France; RIBA British Architectural Library, London. Publications: Articles in international periodicals and newspapers; Monographs include: Sins and Other Spatial Relatives, 2001; How Green is Your Garden, 2003; Neo Architecture, 2005; 5 edited books. Honours: Award winning research-based architectural competitions include: Housing: A Demonstration Project, UK, 1987; Bridge of the Future, Japan, 1987; UCL Museum, UK, 1996; Ideal Home Concept House, UK, 1999; GlassHouse, Japan, 2001. RIBA Award for Academic Contribution in Architectural Education, 1997, 1998, 1999; Selected to represent the UK in the Venice Architecture Biennale 04, 2004; Chosen as one of the New British Talent in Architecture by the Guardian and Independent Newspapers, 2004. Address: Studio 8 Architects, 95 Greencroft Gardens, London NW6 3PG, England. E-mail: mail@cjlim-studio8.com Website: www.cjlim-studio8.com

LIM Hanjo, b. 2 September 1947, Kyungbuk, South Korea. Professor. m. Yeun Hong, 1 son, 2 daughters. Education: BS, Physics, 1971, MS, Solid State Physics, 1974, Seoul National University, Korea; PhD, Solid State Physics, Universite de Montpellier II, France. Appointments: Professor, Department of Electrical & Computer Engineering, 1975-, Vice President for Research Affairs, 1993-95, 2002-03, Ajou University, Korea; Director, Brain Korea 21 Program, Ajou University, 1999-2001; Editor in Chief, Korean Journal of Applied Physics, Korean Physical Society, 1995-97; Member & Chairman, Planning Committee for Creative Research Initiative, 2001-06; President, Korea Nanotechnology Research Society, 2003-06; Director General, Korea Science & Engineering Foundation (KOSEF), 2006-07. Publications: About 160 papers in international scientific or technical journals; Around 50 research papers in domestic scientific journals; 6 books on solid-state physics or semiconductor physics. Honours: President's Award, Korean Government, 1990. Memberships: Korean Physical Society, Institute of Electronics Engineers of Korea. Address: Department of Electrical & Computer Engineering, Ajou University, Youngtong-ku, Suwon 443-749, South Korea. E-mail: hanjolim@ajou.ac.kr

LIM Hyun-Sul, b. 15 July 1952, Iksan-si, Jeonbuk-do, Korea. Professor. m. Hae-Gyeong Kim, 1 son, 1 daughter. Education: MD, College of Medicine, 1978, MPH, School of Public Health, 1981, PhD, College of Medicine, 1986, Seoul National University. Appointments: Korean Medical License for Practice, Ministry of Health and Social Welfare, 1978; Korean Board of Preventive Medicine, 1983; Korean Board of Family Medicine, 1989; Korean Board of Occupational Medicine, 1997; Assistant Professor, 1990-94, Associate Professor, 1994-99, Full Professor & Chair, 1999-, Preventive Medicine, College of Medicine, Dongguk University; Visiting Scientist, Environmental Epidemiology Services, Department of Veterans Affairs, Washington DC, USA, 1999-2000; Head, Medical Institute of Dongguk University, 2001-03; President, Korean Society of Epidemiology, 2004-06; Committee Member, National Academy of Medicine of Korea, 2004-08; Reform Mass Screening, Korea Ministry of Health and Welfare, 2005-; Vice President, Korean Society for Zoonoses, 2006-08; President, Korean Association of Agricultural Medicine & Community Health, 2007-09. Publications: Books: Preventive Medicine, 2004; Environmental Epidemiology, 2005; From Glass Fiber Wastes to Avian Influenza, 2005; 5 articles in professional scientific journals. Honours: The Testimonial of the President in the Republic of Korea, 2003; Award of Academy for Veterans, 2006. Memberships: Korean Medical Association; Korean Society for Preventive Medicine; Korean Society of Epidemiology; Korean Academy of Independent Medical Examiners; Korean Academy of Family Medicine; Korean Society of Toxicology; Korean Association of Agricultural Medicine & Community Health; Korean Society of Occupational and Environmental Medicine; American Public Health Association; Korean Society for Indoor Environment; Korean Society for Zoonoses. Address: Department of Preventive Medicine, Dongguk University, College of Medicine, 707 Seokjang-dong, Gyeongju-si, Gyeongsongbuk-do 780-714, Korea. E-mail: wisewine@dongguk.ac.kr

LIM Tae-Gyoon, b. 24 January 1962, Gwangju, Republic of Korea. Mechatronics Engineer; Consultant; Researcher. m. Hong-Soun Kim 1997, 1 son. Education: BSME, Hanyang University, Seoul, 1985; MSME, Korea Advanced Institute of Science and Technology, Daejeon, 1987; Doctorate, 1993. Appointments: Postdoctoral Fellow, Korea Institute of Science and Technology, Seoul, 1993-94; Senior Researcher, Research Institute of Industrial Science and Technology, Pohang, 1994-; Guest Professor, Yeungnam University, Gyeongsan, 1996-97; Evaluator, University Industrial Technology Force, Yongin, 2003-; Korea Institute of Industrial Technology Evaluation and Planning, Seoul, 2004-; Certified Valuation Analyst,

Korea Valuation Association, 2005-. Publications: 22 patents; 10 patents pending; 71 articles and reports in professional journals. Honours: Excellent Paper Award, Metal Industry Committee, IEEE Industry Application Society, 2003; Listed in international biographical dictionaries. Memberships: IEEE; Institute of Control, Robotics and System Engineers, Korea; Korean Society of Mechanical Engineers; Korea Valuation Association. Address: Facility & Automation Research Center, Research Institute of Industrial Science and Technology, PO Box 135, Pohang, Kyungbuk 790-600, Republic of Korea. E-mail: tglim@rist.re.kr Website: www.rist.re.kr/team/mert/

LIM Timothy H, b. 24 April 1960 (Dual British and Canadian nationality). Professor. m. Laura Perler, 1 son, 1 daughter. Education: BA (first class), University of British Columbia, 1982; MCS (first class), New Testament, Regent College, 1985; Grad Dipl (first class), Ancient History, Macquarie University, 1986; M Phil, 1988, D Phil, 1991, Faculty of Oriental Studies, University of Oxford. Appointments: Kennicott Hebrew Fellow, Faculty of Oriental Studies, University of Oxford, and Junior Research Fellow, Oxford Centre for Hebrew and Jewish Studies and St Hugh's College, Oxford, 1991-93; Lecturer, Dead Sea Scrolls and Christian Origins, 1994-98, Reader, Hebrew and Old Testament Studies, 1998-2004, Professor of Hebrew Bible and Second Temple Judaism, 2005-, University of Edinburgh. Publications: 9 authored and edited books; Over 30 articles in professional journals. Honours include: Lady Davis Doctoral Fellowship, Hebrew University of Jerusalem, Department of Bible, 1989-90; Junior Research Fellowship, Wolfson College, University of Oxford, 1990-91; Kennicott Junior Research Fellow, Oriental Institute, Oxford Centre for Hebrew and Jewish Studies and St Hugh's College, Oxford, 1991-93; Post-Doctoral Fellowship, Social Sciences and Humanities Research Council of Canada, 1993-94; BP Prize Lectureship in the Humanities, Royal Society of Edinburgh, 1998. Address: New College, Mound Place, Edinburgh EH1 2LX, Scotland.

LIM Won Kyun, b. 4 July 1953, Incheon, South Korea. Professor. m. Chung-Hyo Lee, 2 sons. Education: BS, Mechanical Engineering, 1972-76, MS, Mechanical Engineering, 1979-81, PhD, Mechanical Engineering, 1981-88, Inha University, Incheon, South Korea. Appointments: Professor, 1981-, Mechanical Department Chairman, MyongJi University, Kyonggido, South Korea, 1986-88; Visiting Professor, Cornell University, Ithaca, New York, 1990-1991; Visiting Professor, University of Florida, Gainesville, Florida, USA, 1999-2000; Visiting Professor, Vienna University of Technology, Vienna, Austria, 2006-2007; Standard Development Committee Member, Korea Automotive Technology Institute, Cheonan, South Korea, 2001-2004; Director, Korean Society of Mechanical Engineers, Seoul, 2005-06; Central Construction Technical Committee Member, Ministry of Construction and Transportation, Seoul, South Korea, 2006-. Publications: Articles in scientific journals including: Engineering Fracture Mechanics, 1998, 2001; Journal of Composite Materials, 2002; International Journal of Fatigue, 2003; Transactions of the Korean Society of Mechanical Engineers, 2006. Honours: Full Scholarship, Inha University, 1972-76; Grants, Korea Research Foundation, 1995-97. Memberships: Korean Society of Mechanical Engineers; Editor, Journal of Korean Society of Precision Engineering. Address: Department of Mechanical Engineering, MyongJi University, 38-2 Namdong, Yongin, Kyonggido 449-728, South Korea. E-mail: limwk@mju.ac.kr

LIMERICK, Sylvia Countess of; Sylvia Rosalind Pery, b. 7 December 1935, Cairo, Egypt. m. 6th Earl of Limerick, deceased 2003, 2 sons, 1 daughter. Education: MA, Lady Margaret Hall, Oxford. Appointments include: Research Assistant, Foreign and Commonwealth Office, 1959-62; Volunteer, British Red Cross, 1962-66; President and Chairman, Kensington and Chelsea Division, British Red Cross, 1966-72; Member of Board of Governors, St Bartholomew's Hospital, 1970-74; Vice Chairman, Foundation for the Study of Infant Deaths, 1971-; President, 1972-79, Vice President, 1979-99, UK Committee for UNICEF; Vice-Chairman, Community Health Council, 1974-77; Member, Committee of Management, Institute of Child Health, London, 1976-96; Member Area Health Authority, Kensington, Chelsea and Westminster, 1977-82; Council Member, King Edward's Hospital Fund for London, 1977-; Vice President, 1978-84, President, 1984-2002, Community Practitioners and Health Visitors' Association; Trustee, Child Accident Prevention Trust, 1979-87; President, 1973-84, Vice President, 1985-90, National Association for Maternal and Child Welfare; Reviewed National Association of Citizens' Advice Bureau for H M Government, 1983; Vice-Chairman, 1984-85, Chairman of Council, 1985-95, Chairman Emeritus, 1995-97, British Red Cross Society; Advisory Board, Civil Service Occupational Health Service, 1989-92; Board Member, Eastman Dental Hospital Special Health Authority, 1990-96; Trustee, Voluntary Hospital of St Bartholomew, 1991-2004; Vice President, International Federation of Red Cross and Red Crescent Societies, 1993-97; Vice Chairman, Institute of Neurology/Hospital for Neurology and Neurosurgery Joint Research Ethics Committee, 1993-2004; Non-Executive Director, University College London Hospitals NHS Trust, 1996-97; Chairman, CMO's Expert Group to Investigate Cot Death Theories, 1994-98; Trustee, Child Health Research Appeal Trust, 1995-2006; Chairman, Committee of Management, Eastman Dental Institute, 1996-99; Chairman, Eastman Dental Research Foundation, 1996-2002; Chairman, CPHVA Charitable Trust, 1997-2002; Patron, Child Advocacy International, 1998-; Honorary Vice President, British Red Cross Society, 1999-; Patron, CRUSE. Publications: Co-author, Sudden Infant Death: patterns, puzzles and problems, 1985; Over 65 articles in medical and other journals on cot death and on International Red Cross and Red Crescent Movement. Honours: CBE, 1991; Hugh Greenwood Lecturer, Exeter University, 1987; Hon D Litt, Council for National Academic Awards, 1990; Samuel Gee Lecturer, RCP, 1994; European Women of Achievement Humanitarian Award, 1995; Hon LLD, University of Bristol, 1998. Memberships: Fellow, Royal Society of Medicine, 1977-; Hon MRCP, 1990, Hon FRCP, 1994, Royal College of Physicians; Freeman Honoris Causa, Worshipful Company of Salters, 1992; Honorary Fellow, Institute of Child Health, London, 1996; Honorary Member, 1986-, Honorary Fellow, 1996, Royal College of Paediatrics and Child Health; Freeman, Worshipful Company of World Traders, 2003; Order of the Croatian Star, 2003. Address: Chiddingly, West Hoathly, West Sussex, RH19 4QT. E-mail: srlimerick@aol.com

LIN Chia-Hsiang, b. 7 September 1977, Taipei City, Taiwan. Electrical and Electronics Technologist. Education: College degree, Electronic Engineering, National Taipei Institute of Technology (now National Taipei University of Technology), Taipei City, 1997; Master's degree, Electrical Engineering, National Taiwan University, Taipei City, 2002; Project Management Professional, Project Management Institute, USA, 2005. Appointments: Military Legal and Discipline Affairs Officer, military service, Military Police, Taipei City Headquarters, 1997-99; Researcher, High Performance Computing Lab, Taipei City, 2000-02; Research and Development Engineer, R&D Engineer, LITE-ON IT Corporation (LITE-ON Group), Taipei City, 2002-05; Research & Development Solution Consultant, Projects, 2005-06; Assistant Manager, Project Management & Product Management, Yoko Technology Corporation, Taipei City, 2007-. Publications: Numerous articles in professional journals on embedded system and project risk management. Honours: 6 approved patents; Listed in international biographical dictionaries; Invited Lecturer, Yen Tjing Ling Industrial Research Institute, and Graduate Institute of Electrical Engineering, National Taiwan University. Memberships: Institute of Electrical and Electronics Engineers Computer Society. Address: 5F, No 61, Lane 81, Sec 2, Jhonghua Road, Jhongjheng District, Taipei City 100, Taiwan, ROC. E-mail: xiangn.chlin@msa.hinet.net

LIN In-Tsang, b. 5 May 1981, Tainan, Taiwan. Electrical Engineer; Researcher. Education: BSEE, National Taiwan University, 2003, MSEE, Department of Electrical Engineering, Interdisciplinary MRI/MRS Laboratory, 2005, PhD Student, Department of Electrical Engineering and Graduate Institute of Communication Engineering, 2007-, National Taiwan University, Taiwan. Appointments: Researcher, Department of Electrical Engineering, Interdisciplinary MRI/MRS Laboratory, 2003-05. Publications: 3 journal papers; 8 conference papers. Honours: Student Stipend Award, International Society for Magnetic Resonance in Medicine, 2004; Communication Stipend Award, Okwap Company, Taiwan, 2005; 3rd place, 27th IEEE EMBS Annual International Conference, Design Paper Competition, 2005; 3rd prize, 4th National Innovation Award in the Student Section, Institute for Biotechnology and Medicine Industry, 2007; Listed in international biographical dictionaries. Memberships: IEEE Student Member; ISMRM Member. E-mail: r92921112@ntu.edu.tw

LIN Jia-Chuan, b. 31 January 1967, Taipei, Taiwan. Professor. m. Zhen-Di, 1 son. Education: PhD, Electrical Engineering, National Cheng Kung University, 1996. Appointments: Dean, Academic Affairs, 2004-07, Vice President, 2007-, St John's University, Taiwan. Publications: The Improved Electrical Contact Between a Metal and Porous Silicon by Deposition Using a Supercritical Fluid, 2006; Photoluminescence from N-type Porous Silicon Layer Enhanced by a Forward-Biased NP-Junction, 2006; Manufacturing Method for N-type Porous Silicon Based on Hall Effect without Illumination, 2006; The Enhancement of Photoluminescence of N-Type Porous Silicon by Hall-Effect Assistance During Electrochemical Anodization, 2007; Light-Emission and Negative-Differential-Conductance of N-Type Nanoporous Silicon with Buried P-Layer Assistance, 2007. Honours: Best Paper Award, Electronics Devices and Materials Association, 2006. Address: St John's University, No 499, Sec 4, Tam King Road, Tamsui, 25135, Taiwan. E-mail: jclin@mail.sju.edu.tw

LIN Mei-Mei (Rose), b. 7 December 1958, Taipei, Taiwan. Historian. Education: BA, General History, 1981, MA, Modern China, 1984, National Cheng Chi University, Taiwan; MA, US History, 1987, PhD, US History, 1994, University of Texas at Austin, USA. Appointments: Associate Professor, Department of History, National Chung Cheng University, Chia-Yi, Taiwan, 1994-2000; Associate Professor, 2000-05, Full Professor, 2005-, Department of History, National Dong Hwa University, Hualien, Taiwan. Publications: Over 30 papers and articles in professional journals. Honours: Modern Chinese History Scholarship, Ministry of Education, Taiwan, 1982-84; US History Scholarship, National Society of the Colonial Dames of America in the State of Texas, 1990; Teaching Assistantship, 1986-91, Dora Boham

Research Fund, 1991, History Department, UT-Austin; New Faculty Research Fund, National Chung Cheng University, 1994-95; National Science Council Research Grant, National Science Council Research Award, 1997-98, National Science Council, Taiwan; Scholarship, the USIA of State Department, USA, 1999; Special Book Grant, USIS Taipei and USIA of State Department, USA, 2002; Project Grant, National Science Council, Taiwan, 2000-02, 2002-03; First, Second and Third Year Project Grant, National Science Council, Taiwan, 2003-2006; Women in Missology: Taking the Four Churches of Taiwan Episcopal Church in Northern Taiwan as Case-in-point, Project Grant, 2006-2007; National Science Council, Executive Yuan, Taiwan, ROC. Listed in national and international biographical dictionaries. Memberships: The Taiwan Association for Religious Studies; American Studies Association of the ROC; American Historical Association; Association for Asian Studies; Historical Society of American Episcopal Church; Organisation of American Historians; Chinese Society of the Modern History. Address: 2F, No1, Alley 11, Lane 208, Ray-An Street, Taipei (10661), Taiwan, ROC. E-mail: mmlin@mail.ndhu.edu.tw

LIN Ping-Wha, b. 11 July 1925, China. Company President; Consultant. Education: BS, Jiaotong University, Shanghai, China, 1947; PhD, Purdue University, USA. Appointments: Consulting Engineer; Consultant, 1962-66, 1984, Project Manager, 1979-81, World Health Organisation; Lawrence L Dresser Chair Professor and Professor Emeritus, Tri-State University, Angola, Indiana; President, Lin Tech Incorporated. Publications: Author of over 60 papers in professional journals including articles on Lin's Theory of Flux and Its Applications. Honours: DOE Grant, 1984; Honoured Member of American Inventors, 1990 and 1992-97; Man of the Year, American Biographical Institute, 1991; International Man of the Year, International Biographical Centre, 1991-92; Honorary Award, Chinese Electrical Engineering Society, 1999; Listed in national and international biographical dictionaries. Memberships: Fellow, American Society of Civil Engineers; American Chemical Society, American Association for the Advancement of Science; New York Academy of Sciences; Sigma Xi; Life Member AWWA. Address: 506 S Darling Street, Angola, IN 46703, USA.

LIN Wei-Song, b. 25 January 1951, Taiwan. Electrical Engineering Educator. m. Shieh-Ying, 1 son, 1 daughter. Education: Bachelor, 1973, Master, 1975, National Cheng Kung University; PhD, National Taiwan University, 1982. Appointments: Researcher, Telecom Research Institute, Taiwan, 1977-78; Researcher, Telecom Training Institute, Taiwan, 1978-80; Lecturer, 1981-83, Associate Professor, 1983-87, Professor, 1987-, National Taiwan University. Publications: Synthesized affine invarian function for 2D shape recognition; Tracking the radiometric performance of the Rocsat-1 ocean color imager; Self-organizing fuzzy control of multivariable systems using LVQ network. Honours: Excellent Research Awards, National Science Council, 1991, 1994; Success of Satellite Mission Award, National Satellite Program Office, 2002; Best Paper Award, Chinese Institute of Image Processing & Pattern Recognition. Memberships: IEEE; International Union Radio Science. Address: Department EE, No 1, Sec 4, Roosevelt Rd, Taipei 106, Taiwan. E-mail: weisong@cc.ee.ntu.edu.tw

LIN Yuzheng, b. 28 September 1937, Guang-Dong Province, People's Republic of China. Professor. m. Bao Zhen Qi, 2 daughters. Education: BS, Tsinghua University, People's Republic of China, 1962. Appointments: Lecturer, 1979, Associate Professor, 1985, Professor, 1990, Tsinghua

University, People's Republic of China. Publications: Applications of low energy accelerators in China; Applications of low energy linacs in China, 2002; Medical Accelerators (in Chinese), 2004. Honours: Science and Technology Advancement First Class Award, Education Ministry, China, 2001; National Science and Technology Advancement First Class Award, China, 2004. Membership: Vice-President, Chinese Accelerator Society. Address: Accelerator Laboratory, Department of Engineering Physics, Tsinghua University, Beijing 100084, People's Republic of China. E-mail: linyz@mail.tsinghua.edu.cn

LIN Zhisheng, b. 10 December 1944, Puning, Guangdong, People's Republic of China. Professor. m. Xiaodong Lian, 1 son, 1 daughter. Education: University Diploma in Physics, Department of Physics, Sun Yat-Sen (Zhongshan) University, Guangzhou, Guangdong, People's Republic of China, 1964-69. Appointments: Assistant Lecturer, Department of Physics, 1969-79, Assistant Lecturer, 1979-83, Lecturer, 1983-92, Associate Professor, 1992-98, Department of Radio Electronics, Associate Professor, 1998-2001, Professor, 2001-, Department of Electronics and Communication Engineering, Sun Yat-Sen (Zhongshan) University, Guangzhou, Guangdong, People's Republic of China. Publications: Books: Principal and Service of Black and White Television Sets, 1994; Electronic Circuits and AM Radio Sets, 1995; Signals and Systems (Chinese Translation of the book Signals and Systems by Simon Haykin et al), 2004; Signals and Linear Systems, 2007; Over 30 journal papers. Honours: Prizes for 3 research projects and 6 science and technology articles. Listed in Who's Who publications and biographical dictionaries. Membership: Senior Member, Chinese Institute of Electronics. Address: Department of Electronics and Communication Engineering, Zhongshan University, Guangzhou, People's Republic of China. E-mail: isslzs@mail.sysu.edu.cn

LINDSAY (John) Maurice, b. 21 July 1918, Glasgow, Scotland. Poet; Writer; Editor. m. Aileen Joyce Gordon, 3 August 1946, 1 son, 3 daughters. Education: Glasgow Academy, 1928-36; Scottish National Academy of Music, 1936-39. Appointments: Programme Controller, 1961-63, Production Controller, 1963-66, Chief Interviewer, 1966-67, Border Television; Director, The Scottish Civic Trust, 1967-83; Consultant, 1983-2002, Honorary Trustee, 2000-, The Scottish Civic Trust; Editor, Scottish Review, 1975-85; Honorary Secretary General, Europa Nostra, 1983-90; President, Association for Scottish Literary Studies, 1982-83. Publications: The Advancing Day, 1940; Predicament, 1942; No Crown for Laughter, 1943; The Enemies of Love: Poems, 1941-45, 1946; Selected Poems, 1947; At the Wood's Edge, 1950; Ode for St Andrew's Night and Other Poems, 1951; The Exiled Heart: Poems, 1941-56, 1957; Snow Warning and Other Poems, 1962; One Later Day and Other Poems, 1964; This Business of Living, 1971; Comings and Goings, 1971; Selected Poems, 1942-72, 1973; The Run from Life: More Poems, 1942-72, 1975; Walking Without an Overcoat: Poems, 1972-76, 1977; Collected Poems, 2 volumes, 1979, 1993; A Net to Catch the Wind and Other Poems, 1981; The French Mosquito's Woman and Other Diversions, 1985; Requiem for a Sexual Athlete and Other Poems and Diversions, 1988; The Scottish Dog, with Joyce Lindsay, 1989; The Theatre and Opera Lover's Quotation Book, with Joyce Lindsay, 1993; News of the World: Last Poems, 1995; Speaking Likenesses, 1997; Worlds Apart, poems, 2000; Glasgow: Fabric of a City, 2000; The Edinburgh Book of 20th Century Scottish Poetry, with Lesley Duncan, 2005. Other: Editions of poetry, plays, etc. Honours: Territorial Decoration; Commander of the Order of the British Empire, 1979; DLitt, University of Glasgow,

1982. Memberships: Association of Scottish Literary Studies; Honorary Fellow, Royal Incorporation of Architects in Scotland. Address: Park House, 104 Dumbarton Road, Bowling, G60 5BB, Scotland.

LINDSAY Michael Samuel Benjamin, b. 28 September 1959, Colombo, Sri Lanka. Director. m. Sonali Sandhya Suriyagoda, 4 sons. Education: B Bus, Business, Banking and Finance; MAPKE (Migration Agents Professional Knowledge Exam); PS 146, Financial Planners Authority; Diploma in Occupational Health and Safety; Certificate in Uniform Consumer Credit Code (Banking); Certificate in Management, Human Resources; Certificate IV, Mortgage Broking. Appointments: Business Development Manager, Public Transport Corporation, Australia, 1990-98; Business Manager, Macquarie Bank, Australia, 1998-99; Director, Lincom Trading Pty Ltd, 1998-; Director, MBL Services Pty Ltd, 1999-; Director, Digitcom Pty Ltd, 2005-; Director, Comprehensive Wealth Solutions Pty Ltd, 2005-; Director, Infinity Migration Services Pty Ltd, 2006-. Publications: Public Transport in Victoria; Skilled Migration to Australia; Residential Property Investment in Australia; Business Migration to Australia; Credit Process in Australia. Honours: Highest Achiever, Smartline Finance Broking Awards, 2004, 2005, 2006; District Champion, Table Tennis, 1997, 1998. Memberships: Associate Member, Mortgage Industry Association of Australia; Migration Institute of Australia; Australian Professionals, Engineers, Scientists and Managers Association; Migration Agents Registration Association, Australia.

LINDSAY Oliver John Martin, b. 30 August 1938, Lincolnshire, England. Author; Editor; Historian. m. Lady Clare Giffard, 1 son, 2 daughters. Education: Eton; Royal Military Academy, Sandhurst, UK; Staff College, Camberley, UK; National Defence College, Latimer, UK. Appointments: Commissioned in the Grenadier Guards and on the Staff serving in many parts of the world including: Cameroons, Germany, Cyprus, Rhodesia, Hong Kong and Canada, 1957-93; Retired in rank of Colonel; Trust Director and Fund Raiser, Treloar Trust for 300 disabled children, 1993-99; Editor, Guards Magazine, 1993-; International Lecturer. Publications: Books: The Lasting Honour: the Fall of Hong Kong 1941, 1978; At the Going Down of the Sun: Hong Kong and South East Asia 1941-45, 1981; A Guards General: the Memoirs of Sir Allan Adair (editor), 1986; Once a Grenadier: the History of the Grenadier Guards 1945-1995, 1996; The Battle for Hong Kong: Hostage to Fortune, 2005; Articles published in three continents. Honours: CBE; FRHist S; Member of the Queen's Body Guard for Scotland, Royal Company of Archers. Membership: Boodles Club. Address: Church Farm, Beer Hackett, Sherborne, Dorset DT9 6QT, England.

LINDSAY Robert, b. 13 December, 1949, Ilkeston, Derbyshire, England. Actor. m. Cheryl Hall, divorced; 1 daughter with Diana Weston; 2 sons with Rosemarie Ford. Education: Royal Academy of Dramatic Art. Career: Stage career commenced at Manchester Royal Exchange; Appeared in Me and My Girl, London, Broadway and Los Angeles, 1985-87; Appeared as Henry II in Anouilh's Beckett, London, 1991, Cyrano de Bergerac, London, 1992; Film appearances in Bert Rigby, You're a Fool, Loser Takes All, Strike It Rich, Fierce Creatures, 1996; Television appearances including Edmund in King Lear, Granada, Wolfie in comedy series Citizen Smith, Michael Murray in serial GBH, Channel 4, 1991; Admiral Sir Edward Pellew, Hornblower, 1998-. My Family, BBC, 2000-; Space Race (narrator), BBC2,

2005; Tony Blair in A Very Social Secretary, More4, 2005; Jericho, ITV1, 2005; Friends and Crocodiles, 2006; Gideon's Daughter, 2006. Other performances in Genghis Cohn, Jake's Progress, Goodbye My Love, 1996, Oliver, 1998, Richard III, 1998, Fagin in Oliver Twist, 1999. Honours: Olivier, Tony and Fred Astaire Awards for performance in Me and My Girl; Olivier Award for Best Actor in a Musical, 1998. Address: Hamilton Asper Management, Ground Floor, 24 Hanway Street, London W1P 9DD, England.

LINEKER Gary Winston, b. 30 November 1960, Leicester, England. Former Footballer; Television Host. m. Michelle Denise Cockayne, 1986-2006 (divorced) 4 sons. Career: Debut as professional footballer, Leicester City, 1978; Everton, 1985; Represented England, 1986 World Cup, Mexico, 1990 World Cup, Italy; Captain, England, 1991-92; FC Barcelona, Spain, 1986-89; Transferred to Tottenham Hotspur, 1989-92; 80 international caps; Scored 48 goals, June 1992; Grampus Eight Team, Japan, 1994; Presenter, Match of the Day, BBC TV, 1995-. Honour: MA, Leicester, 1992, Loughborough, 1992; OBE, 1992. Address: c/o SFX Sports Group, 35/36 Grosvenor Street, London W1K 4QX, England.

LING Sergey Stepanovich, b. 7 May 1937. Politician and Agronomist. m. 3 children. Education: Belarus Agricultural Academy; Higher CPSU School, CPSU Central Committee. Appointments: Agronomist Sovkhoz, Lesnoye Kopylsk District; Chief Agronomist Sovkhoz, Chief Agronomist, Krynitsa Kopylsk District; Deputy Director, Lyuban Production Co; Chief, Soligorsk Production Agricultural Administration; Deputy Chairman, then Chairman, Slutsk District Executive Committee, Secretary, Smolevichi District CPSU Committee, 1960-72; Chief, Agricultural Division, Secretary, Minsk Regional Belarus Communist Party Committee, 1972-82; First Deputy Chairman, then Chairman, Executive Committee, Minsk Regional Soviet, 1982-86; Chairman, Belarus State Committee on Prices, Deputy Chairman, State Planning Committee, 1986-90; Head, Agricultural Division, Secretary, Central Committee, Belarus Communist Party, 1990-91; Deputy Chairman, Belarus Council of Ministers; Chairman, State Committee on Economics and Planning, 1991-; Deputy Prime Minister, 1994-96, Acting Prime Minister, 1996-97, Prime Minister, 1997-2000, Belarus. Address: c/o Council of Ministers, pl Nezavisimosti, 220010 Minsk, Belarus.

LINGARD Brian Hallwood, b. 2 November 1926, Melbourne, Australia. Architect. m. Dorothy, 2 sons, 1 daughter. Education: DA, Manchester College of Art, School of Architecture. Appointments: Royal Navy, 1944-46; Associate, Royal Institute of British Architects (ARIBA), 1949; Commenced private architectural practice, 1950; Fellow, Royal Institute of British Architects (FRIBA), 1957; Formed architectural partnership, Brian Lingard and Partners, 1972; Formed landscape architecture partnership, Ecoscape (now Lingard Styles Landscape), 1975; Formed architectural historians partnership, Gallery Lingard, 1982; Chairman, Architects Benevolent Society, 1988-92. Publications: The Opportunities for the Conservation and Enhancement of Our Historic Resorts; Special Houses for Special People. Honours: RIBA Regional Award (Wales); DOE/RIBA Housing Medals/Commendations (7 awards); Civic Trust Awards/ Commendations (21 awards); TIMES/RICS Conservation Awards (2 awards); Prince of Wales Conservation Awards (3 awards); Life Vice-President, Architects Benevolent Society, 2002. Memberships: Carlton Club; Royal Automobile Club; Sloane Club. Address: Le Bouillon House, St George's Esplanade, St Peter Port, Guernsey.

LINGEN-STALLARD Andrew Phillip, b. 10 August 1962, Worcester, England. Honorary Senior Midwife; Midwife Advisor. m. (1) Avril Clare Dove, 1985, divorced, 1996, 3 sons; Civil Partner, Lee Winter, 2005. Education: Registered General Nurse, 1985; Registered Midwife, 1988; BSc (Hons), Midwifery, 1996, MSc, Advancing Midwifery, 2006, Kings College, University of London. Appointments include: Midwife, Grade E, Princess Margaret Hospital, Swindon, 1988-92; Midwife Grade F, Roehampton Hospital, Roehampton, 1992-93; Midwife Grade G, Kings College Hospital, NHS Trust, 1993-96; Supervisor of Midwives, Lambeth, Southwark and Lewisham SHA, 1997-; Clinical Midwifery Manager, Clerical and Administration Manager, Supervisor of Midwives, Grade H, 1996-99, Senior Nurse for Surgery Grade I, 2000-2001, Clinical Midwifery Manager (Acting Assistant and Head of Midwifery), Supervisor of Midwives, 2001, Lewisham University Hospital, Lewisham; Modern Matron, Senior Midwife Manager Grade I, Kings College Hospital, 2001-2005; Appointed by Secretary of State for Health to Midwifery Support Team, Department of Health, 2005; Honorary Senior Midwife, Kings College Hospital, 2005-; Midwife Advisor, London Ambulance Service, 2005-; Managing Director and Trustee, Royal College of Midwives, 2003-07; Managing Director, Lingen-Stallard & Winter Estates Ltd (Property portfolio), 2005-; Managing Director, Lingen-Stallard & MacDonald Entertainment Ltd, 2006-; Midwife Advisor, Nursing & Midwifery Council in UN, 2006-. Publications: Contributor of articles, letters and comment to professional journals. Honours: Grantee, Her Majesty's College of Arms, 2003; Fellow, Royal Society of Arts, 2005; Elected UK Council Member, Royal College of Midwives, 2003-07, Professional Policy Committee, 2003-07, Employment Relations Committee, 2003-2005. Memberships: Royal College of Midwives; Labour Party; Amnesty International; Genealogical Society; White Lion Society; Heraldic Society; National Trust; Royal Society for the Protection of Birds; Royal Horticultural Society. Address: 36 Romola Road, Tulse Hill, London SE24 9AZ, England. E-mail: aplingenstallard@aol.com

LINKLATER Richard, b. 30 July 1960, Houston, Texas, USA. Film Director. Appointments: Founder, Director, own film company, Detour Films, Austin, Texas; Founder, Artistic Director, Austin Film Society; Director, films, Slacker, 1991, Dazed and Confused, 1993, Before Sunrise, 1995, Suburbia, 1997, The Newton Boys, 1998; Waking Life, 2001; Tape, 2001; Live From Shiva's Dance Floor, 2003; The School of Rock, 2003; Before Sunset, 2004; $5.15/Hr, 2004; Bad News Bears, 2005; Fast Food Nation, 2006; A Scanner Darkly, 2006; Inning by Inning: A Coach's Progress, 2008. Honours: Silver Bear, Berlin Film Festival, 1995.

LINSCOTT Gillian, b. 27 September 1944, Windsor, England. Journalist; Writer. m. Tony Geraghty, 18 June 1988. Education: Honours Degree, English Language and Literature, Somerville College, Oxford University, 1966. Appointments: Journalist, Liverpool Post, 1967-70; Northern Ireland Correspondent, Birmingham Post, 1970-72; Reporter, The Guardian,1972-79; Sub Editor, BBC Radio News, Local Radio Parliamentary Reporter, 1979-90; Freelance Writer, 1990-. Publications: A Healthy Body, 1984; Murder Makes Tracks, 1985; Knightfall, 1986; A Whiff of Sulphur, 1987; Unknown Hand, 1988; Murder, I Presume, 1990; Sister Beneath the Sheet, 1991; Hanging on the Wire, 1992; Stage Fright, 1993; Widow's Peak, 1994; Crown Witness, 1995; Dead Man's Music, 1996; Dance on Blood, 1998; Absent Friends, 1999; The Perfect Daughter, 2000; Dead Man Riding, 2002; The Garden, 2002; Blood on the Wood, 2003. Honours:

Herodotus Award, The Historical Mystery Appreciation Society, 1999; Ellis Peters Historical Dagger, Crime Writers Association, 2000. Memberships: Society of Authors; Crime Writers Association. Address: Wood View, Hope Under Dinmore, Leominster, Herefordshire HR6 0PP, England.

LIOTTA Ray, b. 18 December 1954, Newark, New Jersey, USA. Actor. m. Michelle Grace, 1997-2004 (divorced), 1 daughter. Education: BFA, University of Miami. Career: Various television appearances: Another World, NBC, 1978-80; Hardhat & Legs, CBS movie, 1980; Crazy Times, ABC pilot, 1981; Casablanca, NBC, 1983; Our Family Honour, NBC, 1985-86; Women Men – In Love there Are No Rules, 1991; The Rat Pack, 1998; Point of Origin, 2002; Film appearances: The Lonely Lady, 1983; Something Wild, 1986; Arena Brains, 1987; Dominick and Eugene, 1988; Field of Dreams, 1989; Goodfellas, 1990; Article 99, Unlawful Entry, 1992; No Escape, Corrina, Corrina, 1994; Operation Dumbo Drop, 1995; Unforgettable, 1996; Turbulence, Phoenix, Copland, 1997; The Rat Pack, 1998; Forever Mine, Muppets From Space, 1999; Blow, Heartbreakers, Hannibal, 2001; John Q, A Rumor of Angels, Narc, 2002; Identity, 2003; Last Shot, Slow Burn, Control, 2004; Revolver, 2005; Even Money, Local Color, Comeback Season, Smokin' Aces, 2006; In the Name of the King: A Dungeon Siege Tale, Wild Hogs, Battle in Seattle, Crossing Over, Hero Wanted, 2007; Powder Blue, 2008.. Address: c/o Endeavor Talent Agency, 9701 Wilshire Boulevard, 10th Floor, Beverly Hills, CA 90212, USA.

LIPAEV Vladimir Vasilievitch, b. 14 June 1928, Moscow, Russia. Physicist. m. Elena Sopatch, 1 daughter. Education: Graduate, Physical Faculty, 1950, PhD, 1957, DSc, 1965, Professor, 1970, Moscow State University. Appointments: Employee, Moscow Research Institute for Instrument Automation; Chief Designer and Chair, Co-ordinating Council for Software Design Automation; Director, Prometeus integrated project, 1954-88; Chief Scientist, Institute for System Programming, Russian Academy of Science; Professor, MSTU Stankin. Publications: More than 41 monographs and textbooks; Over 300 periodical publications; Author, Software Engineering, Methodological Foundations textbook, 2006. Honours: Honoured Worker for Science and Technology, Russian Federation, 1983; Laureate Prize, Council of Minister of the USSR, 1985; Laureate Prize, Russian Government in the field of education, 2001. Address: Gamalei 23-2-10, Moscow, 123098, Russia. E-mail: www.lip@ispras.ru Website: www.ispras.ru/lipaev/index.htm

LIPMAN Maureen, b. 10 May 1946, Hull, England. Actor. m. Jack Rosenthal, deceased, 1 son, 1 daughter. Education: Newland High School for Girls, Hull; London Academy of Music and Dramatic Art. Appointments: TV: Cold Enough for Snow, 1997; Hampstead on the Couch, Coronation Street, George Eliot: A Scandalous Life, Jonathan Creek, 2002; Winter Solstice, 2003; Art Deco Designs, 2004; The Fugitives, 2005. Stage: The Rivals, 1996; Okahoma! 1998, 1999, 2002; Peggy For You, 1999; Sitting Pretty, The Vagina Monologues, The Play What I Wrote, 2001; Thoroughly Modern Milly, 2004; Film: Captain Jack, 1997; Solomon & Gaenor, 1998; The Discovery of Heaven, The Pianist, 2001; Lighthouse Hill, Supertex, 2002; Standing Room Only, 2004; Stories of Lost Souls, 2006; Bridge of Lies, 2007. Radio: The Lipman Test, 1996-97; Choice Grenfell, 1998; Home Truths, 2002. Publications: How Was It For You? 1985; Something to Fall Back On, 1987; You Got an 'Ology?, with Richard Phillips, 1989; Thank You For Having Me, 1990; When's It Coming Out? 1992; You Can Read Me Like a Book, 1995; Lip Reading, 1999. Honours: CBE; Hon D Litt, Hull and

Sheffield; Hon MA, Salford. Memberships: BAFTA; Equity. Address: c/o Conway van Gelder Ltd, 18-21 Jerryn Street, London SW1Y 6HP, England.

LIPWORTH Maurice Sydney (Sir), b. 13 May 1931, Johannesburg, South Africa. Barrister; Businessman. m. Rosa Liwarek, 1957, 2 sons. Education: BCom, LLB, University of Witwatersrand. Appointments: Practising Barrister, Johannesburg, 1956-64; Non-Executive Director, Liberty Life Association of Africa Ltd, 1956-64; Executive, Private Trading Companies, 1964-67; Executive Director, Abbey Life Assurance PLC, 1968-70; Vice-President, Director, Abbey International Corporation Inc, 1968-70; Co-Founder, Director, 1970-88, Deputy Managing Director, 1977-79, Joint Managing Director, 1979-84, Deputy Chairman, 1984-88, Allied Dunbar Assurance PLC; Director, J Rothschild Holdings PLC, 1984-87; Director, BAT Industries PLC, 1985-88; Deputy Chairman of Trustees, 1986-93, Chairman, 1993-, Philharmonia Orchestra; Chairman, Monopolies and Mergers Commission, 1988-92; Non-Executive Director, Carlton Communications PLC, 1993-; Deputy Chairman, Non-Executive Director, National Westminster Bank, 1993-2000; Chairman, Financial Reporting Council, 1993-2001; Non-Executive Director, 1994-99, Chairman, 1995-99, Zeneca Group PLC; Member, Senior Salaries Review Body, 1994-; Trustee, South Bank Ltd, 1996-. Honours: Honorary Queen's Council, 1993. Memberships: Chairman, Bar Association for Commerce, Finance and Industry, 1991-91; European Policy Forum. Address: 41 Lothbury, London EC2P 2BP, England.

LISBERG Harvey Brian, b. 2 March 1940, Manchester, England. Impressario; Artist Manager. m. Carole Gottlieb, 5 November 1969, 2 sons. Education: Manchester University. Musical Education: Self-taught piano, guitar. Career: First in discovering: Graham Gouldman; Andrew Lloyd Webber; Tim Rice; Herman's Hermits; Tony Christie; Sad Café; Godley and Creme; 10cc; Currently representing: 10cc; Graham Gouldman; Eric Stewart; George Stiles; Anthony Drewe; Cleopatra. Address: Kennedy House, 31 Stamford Street, Altrincham, Cheshire WA14 1ES, England.

LISHMAN Arthur Gordon, b. 29 November 1947, Bolton, England. Director General of National Charity. m. Margaret Ann, 1 son, 2 daughters. Education: BA (Econ), University of Manchester, 1968; Honorary Fellow, University of Central Lancashire, 2002. Appointments: Field Officer, 1974-77, Head of Fieldwork, 1977-87, Operations Director, 1987-2000, Director General, 2000-, Age Concern, England. Honours: OBE, 1993; CBE, 2006. Memberships: MCMI; FRSA. E-mail: directorgeneral@ace.org.uk

LISOWSKI Józef Andrzej, b. 10 September 1943, Łuków, Poland. Professor; Rector. m. Regina, 2 daughters. Education: MSc, 1967; PhD, 1973; DSc, 1979; Professor, 1989. Appointments: Assistant and Associate Professor, Technical University of Gdansk, 1967-80; Full Professor, 1980-2008, Rector, 1989-96, 2002-08, Gdynia Maritime University. Publications: 17 books and monographs; 57 scientific papers in journals; 110 conference papers; 4 patents; 63 research projects; 9 PhD in control theory application in marine technology. Honours: Gold Badge of Honour, UNESCO International Centre for Engineering Education, 2005; Officer Cross of Poland Renaissance Order, 2002. Memberships: Polish Science Academy, KAIR; International Association of Maritime Universities. Address: Gdynia Maritime University, ul Morska 83, 81-225 Gdynia, Poland. E-mail: jlis@am.gdynia.pl Website: www.am.gdynia.pl

LISTER David George, b. 19 September 1943, Tadcaster, Yorkshire, England. Physical Chemist. Education: BSc, University of Leeds, 1968; PhD, 1984, DSc, University of Glasgow. Appointments: Research Assistant, University College, London, 1968-70; Royal Society Fellowship, Istituto di Spettroscopia Molecolare, Bologna, Italy, 1970-71; Research Fellow, University of Wales, Bangor, Wales, 1971-73; Senior Lecturer, University of Dar Es Salaam, Tanzania, 1975-76; Professor of Physical Chemistry, University of Messina, Italy, 1987-. Publication: Book: Internal Rotation and Inversion, 1978 (co-author). Memberships: European Academy of Sciences; Royal Society of Chemistry; American Chemical Society. Address: Dipartimento di Chimica Industriale e Ingegneria dei Materiali, Salita Sperone 31, 29, I98166 Sant'Agata di Messina, Italy. E-mail: listerd@unime.it

LITHERLAND Sheila Jacqueline, b. 18 September 1936, Birmingham, England. Poet; Creative Writing/Literature Tutor. Divorced, 1 son, 1 daughter. Education: Regent Street Polytechnic, 1955; Ruskin College, Oxford, 1986; BA, University College, London, 1989. Publications: The Long Interval; Fourpack; Half Light; Modern Poets of Northern England; New Women Poets; The Poetry of Perestroika; Flowers of Fever; The Apple Exchange;The Forward Book of Poetry, 2001; The Work of the Wind; The Homage. Contributions to: Iron Magazine; Writing Women Magazine; Oxford Magazine; Green Book. Honour: Annaghmakerrig Residence, 1994; Nothern Writers Award, 2000. Memberships: Colpitts Poetry; Poetry Society; Vane Women Writers' Collective. Address: 6 Waddington Street, Durham City DH1 4BG, England.

LITTEN Julian William Sebastian, b. 6 November 1947, Wolverhampton, England. Architectural Historian. Education: South West Essex Technical College and School of Art, Walthamstow, 1964-66; PhD, Department of History and Archaeology, Cardiff University, 1993-2002. Appointments: Museum Assistant, Department of Sculpture, 1966-74, Senior Museum Assistant, 1974-82, Research Assistant, 1982-84, Department of Prints and Drawings, Accommodation Officer, 1984-90, Front-of House Manager, 1990-99, Victoria and Albert Museum, London; Visiting Lecturer in Built Heritage Conservation, Canterbury Christ Church University College, Canterbury, 1999-2005. Publications: Books: St Mary's Church, Woodford, Essex, 1978; The English Way of Death: The Common Funeral Since 1450, 1991, 2nd edition, 1992, 3rd edition, 2002; Folklore Traditions of Our Lady, 1994; The Eucharistic Year, 2001; St Barnabas and St James the Greater, Walthamstow, 2003; Co-author: St Mary the Virgin, Radwinter, 1994; Guide to the Management of safety in Burial Grounds, 2001; Numerous chapters and articles in academic journals. Honours: PhD; FSA; FSA (Scot). Memberships: Fellow, Society of Antiquaries of London; Fellow Society of Antiquaries of Scotland; International Institute of Risk and Safety Management. Address: Friarscot, Church Street, King's Lynn, Norfolk PE30 5EB, England. E-mail: julian.litten@btopenworld.com

LITTEN Nancy Magaret, b. 30 September 1951, Dartford, Kent, England. Musician. m. Clinton Davis, 2 sons, 1 daughter. Education: LRAM Violin (Teacher's), 1970, LRAM Piano (Teacher's), 1971, Royal Academy of Music; Cert Ed, Exeter, 1972; ATCL Voice (Performer's), 2001. Appointments: Teacher of Piano, Singing, Violin and Keyboard, Kent Music School, 1997-; ABRSM Examiner, 1998-; Founder, Director, Kent Keyboard Orchestra, 1999-, and Kent Music's Singing Days for Instrumentalists; Freelance Accompanist and Adjudicator. Publications: Contributor to the Federation of Music Services,

A Common Approach, 2002, keyboard section; Consultant to ABRSM for Electronic Keyboard Music Medals, 2004-. Honours: Elizabeth Stokes Open Piano Scholarship, 1968; Janet Duff Greet Prize for most deserving British scholar, 1970, 1971. Membership: Incorporated Society of Musicians. Address: Springfield, 39 Ashford Road, Maidstone, Kent ME14 5DP, England.

LITTLE Tasmin, b. 13 May 1965, London, England. Violinist. m. Michael Hatch, 1 daughter. Education: Yehudi Menuhin School; Guildhall School of Music; Private studies with Lorand Fenyves, Canada. Career: Performed with New York Philharmonic, Leipzig Gewandhaus, Berlin Symphony, London Symphony, Philharmonia, Royal Philharmonic, Royal Liverpool Philharmonic, European Community Chamber, Royal Danish and Stavanger Symphony orchestras; Has played in orchestras conducted by Kurt Masur, Vladimir Ashkenazy, Leonard Slatkin, Tadaaki Otaka, Sir Charles Groves, Andrew Davis, Jerzy Maksymiuk, Vernon Handley, Yan Pascal Tortelier, Sir Edward Downes, Yehudi Menuhin and Sir Simon Rattle; Played at Proms since 1990; Concerto and recital performances in UK, Europe, Scandinavia, South America, Hong Kong, Oman, Zimbabwe, Australia, New Zealand, USA and Japan; Numerous TV appearances including BBC Last Night of the Proms, 1995, 1998. Recordings include: Concertos of Bruch, Dvořák, Brahms, Sibelius, Delius, Rubbra, Saxton, George Lloyd, Ravel, Debussy, Poulenc, Elgar, Bax, Finzi; Dohnanyi violin sonatas, Bruch Scottish Fantasy, Lalo Symphonie Espagnole, Part Spiegel im Spiegel and Fratres. Publication: paper on Delius' violin concerto. Honours: Hon DLitt (Bradford), 1996; Hon DMus (Leicester), 2002. Address: c/o Askonas Holt Ltd, 27 Chancery Lane, London WC2A 1PF, England.

LITTLE RICHARD (Richard Penniman), b. 5 December 1935, Macon, Georgia, USA. Singer; Musician (piano). Education: Theological college, 1957. Career: R&B singer, various bands; Tours and film work with own band, The Upsetters; Gospel singer, 1960-62; World-wide tours and concerts include: Star Club, Hamburg, Germany, with Beatles, 1962; European tour, with Beatles, Rolling Stones, 1963; UK tour with Everly Brothers, 1963; Rock'n'Revival Concert, Toronto, with Chuck Berry, Fats Domino, Jerry Lee Lewis, Gene Vincent, Bo Diddley, 1969; Toronto Pop Festival, 1970; Randall Island Rock Festival, with Jimi Hendrix, Jethro Tull, 1970; Rock'n'Roll Spectaculars, Madison Square Garden, 1972-; Muhammad Ali's 50th Birthday; Benefit For Lupus Foundation, Universal City, 1992; Westbury Music Fair, 1992; Giants Of Rock'n'Roll, Wembley Arena, 1992; Film appearances: Don't Knock The Rock, 1956; Mr Rock'n'Roll, 1957; The Girl Can't Help It, 1957; Keep On Rockin', 1970; Down And Out In Beverly Hills, 1986; Mother Goose Rock'n'Rhyme, Disney Channel, 1989. Recordings: Albums: Here's Little Richard, 1957; Little Richard Is Back, 1965; Greatest Hits, 1965; Freedom Blues, 1970; The King Of Rock'n'Roll, 1971; God's Beautiful City, 1979; Lifetime Friend, 1987; Featured on: Folkways - A Vision Shared (Woody Guthrie tribute), 1988; For Our Children, 1991; Shake It All About, 1992; Little Richard and Jimi Hendrix, 1993; Shag on Down by the Union Hall,1996; Hit singles include: Tutti Frutti, 1956; Long Tall Sally, 1956; The Girl Can't Help It, 1957; Lucille, 1957; She's Got It, 1957; Jenny Jenny, 1957; Keep A Knockin', 1957; Good Golly Miss Molly, 1958, Baby Face, 1959; Bama Lama Bama Loo, 1964. Honours include: Inducted, Rock'n'Roll Hall of Fame, 1986; Star, Hollywood Walk Of Fame, 1990; Little Richard Day, Los Angeles, 1990;

Penniman Boulevard, Macon, named in his honour; Platinum Star, Lupus Foundation Of America, 1992; Grammy Lifetime Achievement Award, 1993.

LITTLEJOHN Joan Anne, b. 20 April 1937, London, England. Creative Artist. Education: Royal College of Music, 1955-59; Postgraduate Study, Howells and Others; LRAM, 1957; GRSM, 1958. Appointments: Freelance Composer, Musicologist, Photographer, 1959-; Administrative Staff, Royal College of Music, 1960-83; Piano Teacher, Harrow School, 1972-73. Publications: Poems and Music. Honours: RVW Trust and Patrons Fund Awards in the 1970's; Recipient Howells' Composing Piano, 1984; Award of Merit, Golden Poet Award, 1985 and Silver Poet Award, 1986; Millennium Medal of Honour, 1998; Archives destined for The Nation, to be housed at The Devon Record Office. Memberships: PRS; ABIRA. Address: Shepherds Delight, 49 Hamilton Lane, Exmouth, Devon EX8 2LW, England.

LITTLEMORE Christopher Paul, b. 8 March 1959, Warwickshire, England. Architect. m. Jane Evelyn Chalk, 1 son, 1 daughter. Education: BA (Hons), B.Arch, Manchester University, 1977-83; MSc, Conservation of Historic Buildings, Bath University, 1998-99. Appointments: Associate, 1986, Director, 1989, Managing Director, 2002, The Charter Partnership, Architects. Membership: Royal Institute of British Architects. Address: Meadow House, Broad Chalke, Nr Salisbury, Wilts, England. E-mail: cplittlemore@charter.eu.com

LITTON Andrew, b. 16 May 1959, New York City, New York, USA. Orchestral Conductor; Pianist. Education: Mozarteum, Salzburg; Juilliard School of Music; MM. Appointments: Assistant Conductor, La Scala, Milan, 1980-81; Exxon-Arts Endowment Assistant Conductor, then Associate Conductor, National Symphony Orchestra, Washington DC, 1982-86; Principal Guest Conductor, 1986-88, Principal Conductor, Artistic Adviser, 1988-94, Conductor Laureate, 1994-, Bournemouth Symphony Orchestra; Music Director, Dallas Symphony Orchestra, 1994-2006; Guest Conductor, many leading orchestras world-wide including Chicago Symphony, Philadelphia, Los Angeles Philharmonic, Pittsburgh Symphony, Toronto Symphony, Montreal Symphony, Vancouver Symphony, London Philharmonic, Royal Philharmonic, London Symphony, English Chamber, Leipzig Gewandhaus, Moscow State Symphony, Stockholm Philharmonic, RSO Berlin, RAI Milan, Orchestre National de France, Suisse Romande, Tokyo Philharmonic, Melbourne Symphony and Sydney Symphony orchestras; Opera debut with Eugene Onegin, Metropolitan Opera, New York, 1989; Conducted Leoncavallo, La Bohème and Falstaff, St Louis Opera, Hansel and Gretel, Los Angeles Opera, 1992, Porgy and Bess, Royal Opera House, Covent Garden, 1992, Salome, English National Opera, 1996; Music Consultant to film The Chosen. Publications: Recordings including Mahler Symphony No 1 and Songs of a Wayfarer, Elgar Enigma Variations, complete Tchaikovsky symphony cycle, complete Rachmaninov symphony cycle, Shostakovich Symphony No 10, Gershwin Rhapsody in Blue, Concerto in F, Bernstein Symphony No 2, Brahms Symphony No 1; As piano soloist and conductor, Ravel Concerto in G. Honours: Winner, William Kapell Memorial US National Piano Competition, 1978; Winner, Bruno Walter Conducting Fellowship, 1981; Winner, BBC-Rupert Foundation International Conductors Competition, 1982; Honorary DMus, Bournemouth, 1992. Address: c/o IMG Artists Europe, Media House, 3 Burlington Lane, London W4 2TH, England.

LIU Angela Leitmannová, b. 14 January 1952, Slovakia (former Czechoslovakia). Professor in Biophysics. m. George Shih-jan Liu, 1 son, 1 daughter. Education: MSc, Humboldt University, Berlin, Germany, 1974; PhD, Biophysics, 1977; Associate Professor, 1989; DrSc, 1995, Professor, 2001. Appointments: Humboldt University, 1972-77; Slovak Academy of Sciences, 1977-81; Slovak Technical University, 1981-; Visiting Associate Professor, 1991-2001, Visiting Professor, Biophysics, Michigan State University, East Lansing, 2001-. Publications: Over 180 in professional journals. Honours: Several. Memberships: Union of Slovak Mathematicians and Physicists; Slovak Medical Society; Slovak Cybernetic Society at Slovak Academy of Sciences. Address: Department of Physiology, Biomedical and Physical Sciences Building, Michigan State University, East Lansing MI 48824, USA.

LIU Qiang, b. 12 October 1979, XuZhou, China. Postdoctoral. Education: MD, Nanjing Medical University, China. Appointments: Postdoctoral Fellow, 2003-06. Publications: Iptakalim inhibits nicotine-induced enhancement of extracellular dopamine and glutamate levels in the nucleus accumbens of rats, 2006. Honours: Postdoctoral Fellow; Excellent Student Scholarship. Address: Barrow Neurological Institute, St Joseph's Hospital – CHW, 350 W Thomas Rd, Phoenix, AZ 85013, USA. E-mail: qiang.liu@chw.edu

LIU Yuliang, b. 24 August 1963, Hengyang City, Hunan province, P R China. Professor. m. Wei Su, 1 son, 2 daughters. Education: BA, Applied Linguistics, Hengyang Teachers University, 1984; MA, Educational Psychology, Northwest Normal University, 1990; PhD, Educational Psychology, Texas A&M University, Commerce, Texas, USA, 2000. Appointments: Classroom Teacher, Middle School, Hengyang City, P R China, 1984-87; Instructor, Department of Education and Psychology, Northwest Normal University, 1990; Research Associate and Director, Changsha Educational and Scientific Research Institute, 1990-95; Teaching/Research Fellow, Department of Psychology and Special Education, 1995-99, Assistant Multimedia Specialist, 1997-98, Texas A&M University, Commerce; Visiting Assistant Professor, Department of Psychology and Counseling, Southeastern Oklahoma State University, USA, 1999-2000; Faculty Mentor for Visiting International Scholar, University of Ibadan, Nigeria, 2006-07; Consultant, Capella University, Minneapolis, USA, 2006-; Assistant Professor, Department of Educational Leadership, 2000-06, Graduate Program Director, Instructional Technology, 2003-, Associate Professor, 2006-, Southern Illinois University, Edwardsville. Publications: Numerous articles in professional journals. Honours: Scholarships, travel and research grants; Competitive Student Travel Award, American Psychological Association, 1999; The Graduate Research Competition Award, Southwestern Psychological Association Annual Conference, Dallas, 2000; The Jerry and Marilyn Morris Distinguished Doctoral Student Award of the Year, 1999-2000, Alumni Ambassador Award, 2003, Outstanding Alumni, 2005, College of Education and Human Services, Texas A&M University; Listed in international biographical dictionaries. Memberships: Society of International Chinese in Educational Technology; American Education Research Association; Association for the Advancement of Computing in Education; Association for Educational Communications and Technology; International Society for Technology in Education. Address: 7060 Stallion Drive, Edwardsville, IL 62025, USA. E-mail: yliu63@gmail.com

LIU Zhaorong, b. 1 June 1937, Zuoquan County, Shanxi Province, China. Educator. m. Shaohua Zhao, 1 son, 3 daughters. Education: Mathematical Department, Harbin Teachers' College. Appointment: Teacher, Yuci Railway Middle School, 1962-95. Publications: The Proof of Goldbach's Conjecture; Numerous other mathematical research papers. Honours: The Golden Medal of the First Special Contribution Experts awarded by the World ESCH Organisation; Listed in Who's Who publications and biographical dictionaries. Membership: Mathematical Association of America; World ESCH Group; American Mathematical Society. Address: #168 Anning Street, Yuci District, Jinzhong City, Shanxi Province 030600, People's Republic of China. E-mail: lzronga@163.com

LIVELY Penelope Margaret, b. 17 March 1933, Cairo, Egypt. Writer. m. Jack Lively, 27 June 1957, 1 son, 1 daughter. Education: Honours Degree, Modern History, Oxford University, England. Publications: Fiction: The Road to Lichfield, 1977; Nothing Missing But the Samovar, and Other Stories, 1978; Treasures of Time, 1979; Judgement Day, 1980; Next to Nature, Art, 1982; Perfect Happiness, 1983; Corruption and Other Stories, 1984; According to Mark, 1984; Moon Tiger, 1986; Pack of Cards: Stories 1978-86, 1987; Passing On, 1989; City of the Mind, 1991; Cleopatra's Sister, 1993; Heat Wave, 1996; Beyond the Blue Mountains: Stories, 1997; Spider Web, 1998; The Photograph, 2003; Making It Up, 2005. Non-Fiction: The Presence of the Past: An Introduction to Landscape History, 1976; Oleander, Jacaranda, 1992; A House Unlocked, 2001. Children's Books: Astercote, 1970; The Whispering Knights, 1971; The Driftway, 1972; Going Back, 1973; The Ghost of Thomas Kempe, 1974; Boy Without a Name, 1975; Fanny's Sister, 1976; The Stained Glass Window, 1976; A Stitch in Time, 1976; Fanny and the Monsters, 1978; The Voyage of QV66, 1978; Fanny and the Battle of Potter's Piece, 1980; The Revenge of Samuel Stokes, 1981; Uninvited Ghosts and Other Stories, 1984; Dragon Trouble, Debbie and the Little Devil, 1984; A House Inside Out, 1987; In Search of A Homeland: The Story of the Aeneid, 2001; The House in Norham Gardens, 2004. Contributions to: Numerous journals and magazines. Honours: Officer of the Order of the British Empire, 1989; Hon DLitt (Tufts University), 1993, (Warwick), 1998; Hon Fellow, Swansea University, 2002; Commander of the British Empire, 2002; Several honorary degrees and literary awards. Memberships: Society of Authors; PEN. Address: c/o David Higham Associates, 5-8 Lower John Street, Golden Square, London W1R 4HA, England.

LIVERPOOL, Bishop of, Rt Rev James Stuart Jones, b. 1948, Glasgow, Scotland. Anglican Bishop. m. Sarah Jones, 3 daughters. Education: BA honours, Theology, Exeter University, 1970; PGCE, Drama and Religious Education, 1971; Theological Training, Wycliffe Hall, Oxford. Appointments: Teacher of Religious Education and Latin; Producer at Scripture Union; Reader, 1976; Deacon, 1982; Priest, 1983; Bishop, 1994; Curate and then Associate Vicar, Christ Church with Emmanuel, Clifton, Bristol; Visiting Lecturer, Media Studies, Trinity College, Bristol; Vicar of Emmanuel Church, South Croydon, 1990; Bishop of Southwark's Examining Chaplain; Bishop's Selector; Bishop of Hull, 1994; Bishop of Liverpool, 1998-. Publications: Author of books on Christian spirituality; Various articles for newspapers. Honours: Honorary Doctor of Divinity, University of Hull, 1999; Honorary Doctor of Letters, University of Lincolnshire and Humberside, 2001. Memberships: Chair, Governing Body, St Francis of Assisi City Academy; Chair, Wycliffe Hall, Oxford; President Church Pastoral Aid Society; Co-president, Liverpool Hope College; Member, Governing Council of

Liverpool University; Fellow, University of Gloucestershire; Foundation Governor, Blue Coat School, Liverpool; Visitor, Liverpool College, Liverpool; Member, Urban Bishops Panel of the Church of England; Vice President, Tear Fund. Address: Bishop's Lodge, Woolton Park, Liverpool L25 6DT, England.

LIVESLEY Brian, b. 31 August 1936, Southport, Lancashire, England. Medical Practitioner. m. Valerie Anne Nuttall, 1 son, 2 daughters. Education: MB, ChB, Leeds University Medical School, 1960. Appointments: Clinical Training and Teaching posts, University and District Hospitals, Leeds, Manchester and Liverpool, 1961-69; Harvey Research Fellow, King's College Hospital Medical School, London, 1969-72; Consultant Physician, Geriatric Medicine, Southwark, London, 1973-88; University of London's Foundation Professor in the Care of the Elderly, Honorary Consultant Physician in General and Geriatric Medicine, Chelsea and Westminster Hospital NHS Trust, London, 1988-2001; North West Thames Regional Adviser, Postgraduate Education, British Postgraduate Medical Federation, 1990-96; Invited Expert on the care of adults for several Police Constabularies and HM Coroner's offices, 1999-; The University of London's Emeritus Professor in the Care of the Elderly, 2003-. Publications: Over 150 professional publications. Honours: Officer Brother, 1992, Knight, 1994, Most Venerable Order of St John of Jerusalem. Memberships: Osler Lecturer, 1975, Gideon de Laune Lecturer, 2001, Master, 2005-2006, Past Master & Court of Assistants, Worshipful Society of Apothecaries of London; Royal Society of Medicine; Royal College of Physicians of London; British Academy of Forensic Sciences. Address: PO Box 295, Oxford OX2 9GD, England. E-mail: brian.livesley@doctors.org.uk

LIVINGSTON Dorothy Kirby, b. 6 January 1948, Gosforth, Northumberland. Solicitor. 2 daughters. Education: MA, Jurisprudence, Hugh's College, Oxford, 1966-69. Appointments: Trainee, 1970, Assistant Solicitor, 1972, Partner, 1980, Herbert Smith; Member, Advisory Board, Centre for European Law, King's College, London, 1996; Member, City of London Law Society Competition Law Committee, 1998; Chairman, City of London Law Society Financial Law Committee, 1999; Solicitor Advocate (Civil), 2005. Publications: Competition Law and Practice, 1995; The Competition Act 1998: A Practitioner's Guide, 2001; Competition Law chapters in Leasing and Asset Finance, 3rd edition 1997, 4th edition 2003. Address: Herbert Smith, Exchange House, Primrose Street, London EC2A 2HS, England. E-mail: dorothy.livingston@herbertsmith.com

LIYANAGE Sunil, b. 27 September 1941, Colombo, Sri Lanka. Consultant Rheumatologist. m. Isabela Nallamanickam, 2 sons. Education: MBBS (Ceylon), 1965; FRCP (UK); DCH (Eng); DipMedAc. Appointments: Consultant Rheumatologist in East Berkshire, 1975-2005; Medical Director, Heatherwood and Wexham Park NHS Trust, 1991-95. Publications: Chapters in: Recent Advances in Rheumatology; Textbook of Rheumatology; Handbook of Drug Interactions. Memberships: British Society for Rheumatology; American Society for Bone and Mineral Research; British Medical Acupuncture Society, former Chairman. Address: The Princess Margaret Hospital, Windsor, SL4 3SJ, England. E-mail: rheumatology@lineone.net Website: www.medicalacupuncture.co.uk

LLEWELLIN (John) Richard (Allan), b. 30 September 1938, Haverfordwest, South Wales. Bishop. m. Jennifer Sally House, 1 son, 2 daughters. Education: Clifton College, Bristol; Theological studies, Westcott House and Fitzwilliam College, Cambridge, 1961-64. Appointments: Articled to Messrs Farrer

and Co of Lincoln's Inn Fields; Solicitor, Messrs Field Roscoe and Co, London; Assistant Curate, Radlett, Hertfordshire, 1964-68; Assistant Priest, Johannesburg Cathedral, South Africa, 1968-71; Vicar of Waltham Cross, 1971-79; Rector of Harpenden, 1979; Bishop of St Germans, 1985; Bishop of Dover and Bishop in Canterbury, 1992; Bishop at Lambeth and Head of Staff to the Archbishop of Canterbury, 1999-. Address: Lambeth Palace, London, SE1 7JU, England. Email: richard.llewellin@lampal.c-of-e.org.uk

LLEWELLYN SMITH Sir Christopher Hubert, b. 19 November 1942, Giggleswick, England. Physicist. m. Virginia Grey, 1 son, 1 daughter. Education: BA, Physics with First Class Honours, 1964, DPhil, Theoretical Physics, 1967, Oxford University. Appointments: Royal Society Exchange Fellow, Physical Institute, Academy of Sciences, Moscow, USSR, 1967-68; Fellow in the Theoretical Studies Division, European Laboratory for Particle Physics (CERN), Geneva, Switzerland, 1968-70; Research Associate, Stanford Linear Accelerator Center, Stanford, California, USA, 1970-72; Staff Member, Theoretical Studies Division, CERN, Geneva, 1972-74; Fellow, St John's College, Oxford, 1974-98; Lecturer, 1974-80, Reader, 1980-87, Professor of Theoretical Physics, 1987-98, Chairman of Physics, 1987-92; Science Research Council Senior Fellow, 1978-81; Director General of CERN (on secondment from Oxford), 1994-98; Provost and President, University College London, 1999-2002; Senior Research Fellow, Department of Physics, University of Oxford, 2002-2003; Director, UKAEA Culham Division and Head of the Euratom/UKAEA Fusion Association, 2003-; Chairman, Consultative Committee for Euratom on Fusion, 2004-. Publications: Numerous articles on high energy physics, fusion energy, science policy and international collaboration in science. Honours: Maxwell Prize and Medal, Institute of Physics, Fellow of the Royal Society, 1984; Academia Europaea, 1989; Fellow, American Physical Society, 1994; Honorary DSc, Bristol, UK, 1997; Honorary D.Cien., Granada, Spain, 1997; Honorary DSc, Shandong China, 1997; Medal, Japanese Association of Medical Sciences, 1997; Gold Medal, Slovak Academy of Science, 1997; Foreign Fellow, Indian National Science Academy; Honorary Fellow, University of Wales, Cardiff, 1998; Distinguished Associate Award, US Department of Energy, 1998; Distinguished Service Award, US National Science Foundation, 1998; Glazebrook Medal, Institute of Physics, 1999; Honorary Fellow, St John's College, Oxford, 2000; Knight Bachelor, 2001; Honorary Fellow, New College, Oxford, 2002; Honorary Fellow, Institute of Mathematics and its Applications, 2003; Fellow, Energy Institute, 2005. Address: Culham Science Centre, Abingdon, Oxon OX14 3DB, England. E-mail: chris.llewellyn-smith@ukaea.org.uk

LLOYD Christopher, b. 22 October 1938, Stamford, Connecticut, USA. Actor. m. Catherine Boyd 1959-1971 (divorced), Carol Vanek 1988-1991 (divorced). Education: Neighbourhood Playhouse, New York. Appointments: Film Debut, One Flew Over the Cuckoo's Nest, 1975; Films include: Butch and Sundance: The Early Days; The Onion Field; The Black Marble; The Legend of the Lone Ranger; Mr Mom; To Be or Not to Be; Star Trek III: The Search for Spock; Adventures of Buckaroo Banzai; Back to the Future; Clue; Who Framed Roger Rabbit?; Track 29; Walk Like a Man; Eight Men Out; The Dream Team; Why Me?; Back to the Future, Part II; Back to the Future, Part III; The Addams Family; Twenty Bucks; Dennis the Menace; Addams Family Values; The Pagemaster; Camp Nowhere; The Radioland Murders; Things To Do in Denver When You're Dead; Cadillac Ranch; Changing Habits; Dinner at Fred's; Baby Geniuses; My Favorite Martian; Man on the Moon; Chasing Destiny, 2000; When Good Ghouls Go Bad, 2001; Wit, 2001; Wish You Were Dead, 2003; Interstate 60, 2003; Haunted Lighthouse, 2003; Merry Christmas Space Case (voice), 2003; Admissions, 2004; Wallflowering, 2005; Enfants Terribles, 2005; Flakes, 2007; Fly Me to the Moon, 2007; Jack and the Beanstalk, 2008; Foodfight, 2008; The Tale of Despereaux, 2008. TV includes: Taxi; Best of the West; The Dictator; Tales from Hollywood Hills; Pat Hobby - Teamed with Genius; September Gun; Avonlea; Alice in Wonderland; Right to Remain Silent; The Edge; Quicksilver Highway; Spin City; Cyberchase; Tremors; Malcolm in the Middle; The Big Time; I Dream (series), 2004; Clubhouse (series), 2004; Stacked, 2005-2006; A Perfect Day, 2006. Honours: Winner, Drama Desk and Obie Awards, Kaspar, 1973. Address: The Gersh Agency, 252 North Canon Drive, Beverly Hills, CA 90210, USA.

LLOYD Clive Hubert, b. 31 August 1944, British Guiana, now Guyana. Cricketer. m. Waveney Benjamin, 1 son, 2 daughters. Career: Left-Hard Batsman, Right-Arm Medium-Paced Bowler; Played for British Guiana and Guyana, 1963-83; Played, 1968-86, Captain, 1981-83, 1986, for Lancashire; 110 Tests for West Indies, 1966-85, with record 74 as Captain, scoring 7,515 runs, averaging 46.6, including 19 centuries; Toured England, 1969, 1973, 1975 in World Cup, 1976, 1979 in World Cup, 1980, 1983 in World Cup, 1984; Scored 31,232 first-class runs including 79 centuries; Director, Red Rose Radio PLC, 1981; Executive Promotions Officer, Project Fullemploy, 1987-; West Indies Team Man, 1988-89, 1996-; International Cricket Council Referee, 1992-95. Publications: Living for Cricket, co-author, 1980; Winning Captaincy, co-author, 1995. Honours: Commander, Order of the British Empire. Address: c/o Harefield, Harefield Drive, Wilmslow, Cheshire SK9 1NJ, England.

LLOYD (David) Huw (Owen), b. 14 April 1950, London, England. Family Doctor. m. Mary Eileen, 1 son, 3 daughters. Education: Gonville and Caius College, Cambridge, 1968-71; Guy's Hospital, London, 1971-74; Somerset Vocational Training Scheme, 1976-79. Appointments: Principal, Cadwgan Surgery, Old Colwyn; Clinical Governance Lead, Conwy Local Health Group. Memberships: Fellow, Royal College of General Practitioners; Chairman, Mental Health Task Group, RCGP; Deputy Chairman, North Wales Local Medical Committee; Member, Welsh Council, RCGP; General Practitioners Committee, Wales. Address: Maes yr Onnen, Abergele Road, Llanddulas; Abergele LL22 8EN, Wales. E-mail: huwlloyd@welshnet.co.uk

LLOYD Elisabeth Anne, b. 3 September 1956, Morristown, New Jersey, USA. Professor. Education: BA Science and Political Theory, University of Colorado, Boulder, 1980; PhD, Princeton University, 1984. Appointments: Assistant Professor, Department of Philosophy, University of California, San Diego, 1985-88; Assistant Professor, Department of Philosophy, 1988-90, Associate Professor, 1990-97, University of California, Berkeley; Affiliated Faculty, History and Philosophy of Science Programme, University of California, Davis, 1990-98; Professor, Department of Philosophy, University of California, Berkeley, 1997-99; Professor, Department History and Philosophy of Science, Professor, Department of Biology, 1998-; Chair, Department of History and Philosophy of Science, 2000-04; Tanis Chair of History and Philosophy of Science, 2001-, Professor, Department of Biology, Indiana University, Bloomington, 1998-. Publications: 3 books; 40 articles in professional journals; 4 book reviews; numerous presentations and invited lectures; Articles and books in progress. Honours: University

of California: Resident Fellow and Fellow, UC Humanities Research Institute; National Science Foundation Scholar's Award; Humanities Graduate Research Assistance Fellowship; Several grants; Regents Summer Faculty Fellowship; Princeton University: National Science Foundation Graduate Fellow; Garden State Graduate Award; University of Colorado: Phi Beta Kappa; Van Ek Award; Bonnie and Vern L Bullough Award, Foundation for the Scientific Study of Sexuality. Memberships include: American Philosophical Association; Philosophy of Science Association; International Society for the History, Philosophy and Social Studies of Biology. Address: History and Philosophy of Science Department, Goodbody Hall 130, Indiana University, Bloomington, IN 47405-2401, USA. E-mail: ealloyd@indiana.edu

LLOYD Sir Geoffrey (Ernest Richard), b. 25 January 1933, London, England. Emeritus Professor of Ancient Philosophy and Science; Writer. m. Janet Elizabeth Lloyd, 1956, 3 sons. Education: BA, 1954, MA, 1958, PhD, 1958, King's College, Cambridge. Appointments: Fellow, 1957, Senior Tutor, 1969-73, King's College, Cambridge; Assistant Lecturer in Classics, 1965-67, Lecturer in Classics, 1967-74, Reader in Ancient Philosophy and Science, 1974-83, Professor of Ancient Philosophy and Science, 1983-2000, Cambridge University; Bonsall Professor, Stanford University, 1981; Sather Professor, University of California at Berkeley, 1984; Visiting Professor, Beijing University and Academy of Sciences, 1987; Master, Darwin College, 1989-2000; Professor at Large, Cornell University, 1990-96; Zhu Kezhen Visiting Professor, Institute for the History of Natural Science, Beijing, 2002. Publications: Polarity and Analogy, 1966; Early Greek Science: Thales to Aristotle, 1970; Greek Science After Aristotle, 1973; Magic, Reason and Experience, 1979; Science, Folklore and Ideology, 1983; Science and Morality in Greco-Roman Antiquity, 1985; The Revolution of Wisdom, 1987; Demystifying Mentalities, 1990; Methods and Problems in Greek Science, 1991; Adversaries and Authorities, 1996; Aristotelian Explorations, 1996; The Way and the Word (with N Jivin), 2002; In the Grip of Disease, Studies in the Greek Imagination, 2003; Ancient Worlds, Modern Reflections, 2004; The Delusions of Invulnerability, 2005; Principles and Practices in Ancient Greek and Chinese Science, 2006. Editor: Hippocratic Writings, 1978; Aristotle on Mind and Senses (with G E L Owen), 1978; Le Savoir Grec (with Jacques Brunschwig), 1996, English edition, 2000. Contributions to: Books and journals. Honours: Sarton Medal, 1987; Honorary Fellow, King's College, Cambridge, 1990; Honorary Foreign Member, American Academy of Arts and Sciences, 1995; Knighted, 1997; Hon LittD (Athens), 2003. Memberships: British Academy, fellow; East Asian History of Science Trust, chairman, 1992-; International Academy of the History of Science, 1997. Address: 2 Prospect Row, Cambridge CB1 1DU, England.

LLOYD John Nicol Fortune, b. 15 April 1946. Journalist. m. (1) Judith Ferguson, 1974, divorced 1979, (2) Marcia Levy, 1983, divorced 1997, 1 son. Education: MA, University of Edinburgh. Appointments: Editor, Time Out, 1972-73; Reporter, London Programme, 1974-76; Producer, Weekend World, 1976-77; Industrial Reporter, Labour Correspondent, Industrial and Labour Editor, Financial Times; 1977-86; Editor, 1986-87, Associate Editor, 1996-, New Statesman; Other Financial Times assignments, 1987-, including Moscow Correspondent, 1991-95; Freelance journalist, 1996-. Publications: The Politics of Industrial Change, co-author, 1982; The Miners' Strike: Loss Without Limit, co-author, 1986; In Search of Work, co-author, 1987; Counterblasts, contributor, 1989; Rebirth of a Nation: an Anatomy of Russia,

1998; Re-engaging Russia, 2000; The Protest Ethic, 2001; What the Media are Doing to Our Politics, 2004. Honours: Journalist of the Year, Granada Awards, 1984; Specialist Writer of the Year, IPC Awards, 1985; Rio Tinto David Watt Memorial Prize, 1997. Address: New Statesman, Victoria Station House, 7th Floor, 191 Victoria Street, London SW1E 5NE, England. E-mail: info@newstatesman.co.uk

LLOYD Kathleen Annie, (Kathleen Conlon, Kate North), b. 4 January 1943, Southport, England. Writer. m. Frank Lloyd, 3 August 1962, divorced, 1 son. Education: BA, Honours, King's College, Durham University. Publications: Apollo's Summer Look, 1968; Tomorrow's Fortune, 1971; My Father's House, 1972; A Twisted Skein, 1975; A Move in the Game, 1979; A Forgotten Season, 1980; Consequences, 1981; The Best of Friends, 1984; Face Values, 1985; Distant Relations, 1989; Unfinished Business, 1990; As Kate North: Land of My Dreams, 1997; Gollancz, 1997. Contributions to: Atlantic Review; Cosmopolitan; Woman's Journal; Woman; Woman's Own. Membership: Society of Authors. Address: 26A Brighton Road, Birkdale, Southport PR8 4DD, England.

LLOYD Robert Andrew, b. 2 March 1940, Southend-on-Sea, England. Broadcaster; Opera Singer; Teacher; Writer. m. Lynda Anne Powell, 1 son, 3 daughters. Education: MA, Modern History, Keble College, Oxford, 1962; London Opera Centre Certificate, 1969. Appointments: Teacher, various secondary schools, 1962; Lieutenant, Royal Navy, 1962-65; Civilian Tutor, Bramshill Police College, 1966-68; Student, London Opera Centre, 1968-69; Principal Bass, Sadlers Wells Opera, 1969-72; Principal Resident Bass, Royal Opera, Covent Garden, 1972-83; Freelance Broadcaster, Opera Singer, Teacher and Writer, 1983-; Senior Artist, Royal Opera Covent Garden, 2004; Master Teacher, San Francisco Merola Program, 2004. Publications: Over 80 recordings; Radio and TV performances. Honours: Charles Santley Award; Chaliapin Commemoration Medal, St Petersburg; Best Foreign Singer Award, Buenos Aires; Commander of the British Empire, 1990; Honorary Fellow, Keble College; Honorary Member, Royal Academy of Music, Fellow of Royal Welsh College of Music and Drama. Memberships: President, British Youth Opera; Member, Executive Committee, Musicians Benevolent Fund; President, Abertillery Orpheus Male Voice Choir; President, Southend Choral Society; President 2005-6, Incorporated Society of Musicians; Sponsor, Brecon Cathedral Endowment Appeal; Tooley Committee, HEFCE, Advisory Committee of Friends of Covent Garden. Address: 57 Cholmeley Crescent, London N6 5EX, England. E-mail: robtlloyd@blueyonder.co.uk

LLOYD Ursula E, b. 10 July 1943, London, England. Consultant Obstetrician and Gynaecologist. m. William Lloyd, 2 daughters. Education: MB BS, MRCS, LRCP, 1967; FRCOG, 1987. Appointments: Training posts in Obstetrics and Gynaecology, 1967-81; Consultant, St George's Hospital, 1981-92; Private Medical Practice, Portland Hospital, London, 1992-. Memberships: Royal Society of Medicine; British Medical Association; Apothecaries Livery Co. Address: Basement Flat, 75 Harley Street, London, W1G 8QL, England.

LLOYD WEBBER Andrew, (Baron Lloyd Webber of Sydmonton) b. 22 March 1948, London, England. Composer. m. (1) Sarah Jane Hugill, 1971, divorced 1983, 1 son, 1 daughter, (2) Sarah Brightman, 1984, divorced 1990, (3) Madeleine Gurdon, 1991, 2 sons, 1 daughter. Education: Magdalen College, Oxford; Royal College of Music, FRCM, 1988. Career: Composer and producer, musicals; Composer,

film scores; Deviser, board game, And They're Off; Owner, Really Useful Group. Compositions: Musicals: Joseph And The Amazing Technicolour Dreamcoat (lyrics by Tim Rice), 1968; Jesus Christ Superstar (lyrics by Tim Rice), 1970; Jeeves (lyrics by Alan Ayckbourn), 1975; Evita (lyrics by Tim Rice), 1976; Tell Me On A Sunday (lyrics by Don Black), 1980; Cats (based on poems by T S Eliot), 1981; Song And Dance, 1982; Starlight Express (lyrics by Richard Stilgoe), 1984; The Phantom Of The Opera (lyrics by Richard Stilgoe and Charles Hart), 1986; Aspects Of Love (lyrics by Don Black and Charles Hart), 1989; Sunset Boulevard (lyrics by Don Black and Christopher Hampton), 1993; By Jeeves (lyrics by Alan Ayckbourn), 1996; Whistle Down The Wind (lyrics by Jim Steinman), 1996; The Beautiful Game (book and lyrics by Ben Elton), 2000; The Woman in White (book by Charlotte Jones, lyrics by David Zippel), 2004; The Sound of Music, 2006 (lyrics by Oscar Hammerstein II); The Phantom of Manhattan, 2009 (lyrics by David Zippel). Film Scores: Gumshoe, 1971; The Odessa File, 1974; Jesus Christ Superstar, 1974; Others: Requiem, 1985; Variations On A Theme Of Paganini For Orchestra, 1986; Amigos Para Siempre (official theme for 1992 Olympic Games), 1992; When Children Rule The World (official theme for the opening ceremony 1998 Winter Olympics). Publications: Evita (with Tim Rice), 1978; Cats: The Book of the Musical, 1981; Joseph And The Amazing Technicolour Dreamcoat (with Tim Rice), 1982; The Complete Phantom of the Opera, 1987; The Complete Aspects of Love, 1989; Sunset Boulevard: From Movie to Musical, 1993; Restaurant Columnist, the Daily Telegraph, 1996-99; Film: The Phantom of the Opera, 2004-05. Honours include: 5 Laurence Olivier Awards; 6 Tony Awards; 4 Drama Desk Awards; 3 Grammy Awards; Triple Play Award, ASCAP, 1988; Knighthood, 1992; Praemium Imperiale Award, 1995; Richard Rogers Award, 1996; Oscar, Best Song, (with Tim Rice), 1997; Honorary Life Peer, 1997; Critics Circle Award Best Musical, 2000. Address: 22 Tower Street, London WC2H 9NS, England.

LLOYD WEBBER Julian, b. 14 April 1951, London, England. Cellist. m. (1) Celia M Ballantyne, 1974, divorced 1989, (2) Zohra Mahmoud Ghazi, 1989, divorced, 1999, son, (3) Kheira Bourahla, 2001. Education: Royal College of Music. Appointments: Debut, Queen Elizabeth Hall, 1972; Debut, Berlin Philharmonic Orchestra, 1984; Appears in major international concert halls; Undertaken concert tours throughout Europe, North and South America, Australasia, Singapore, Japan, Hong Kong and Korea; Numerous TV appearances and broadcasts in UK, Netherlands, Africa, Germany, Scandinavia, France, Belgium, Spain, Australasia, USA; Recordings include: World Premieres of Britten's 3rd Suite for Solo Cello; Bridge's Oration; Rodrigo's Cello Concerto; Holst's Invocation; Gavin Bryar's Cello Concerto; Philip Glass Cello Concerto; Tchaikovsky Rococo Variations; Sullivan's Cello Concerto; Vaughan Williams' Fantasia on Sussex Folk Tunes; Andrew Lloyd Webber's Variations; Elgar's Cello Concerto; Dvorak Concerto; Saint Saens Concerto; Lalo Concerto; Walton Concerto; Britten Cello Symphony; Philip Glass Cello Concerto, Phantasia. Publications: Frank Bridge, Six Pieces, 1982; Young Cellist's Repertoire, 1984; Travels with my Cello, 1984; Song of the Birds, 1985; Recital Repertoire for Cellists, 1986; Short Sharp Shocks, 1990; The Great Cello Solos, 1992; The Essential Cello, 1997; Cello Moods, 1999; Classical Journeys, 2004; Elgar Cello Concerto, 2005. Honours: British Phonographic Industry Award for Best Classical Recording, 1986; Crystal Award World Economic Forum, 1998; FRCM; Honorary Doctorate, (University of Hull) 2003, (Thames Valley

University) 2004. Address: c/o IMG Artists Europe, Lovell House, 616 Chiswick High Road, London, W4 5RX, England. Website: www.julianlloydwebber.com

LLOYD-JONES Sir (Peter) Hugh (Jefferd), b. 21 September 1922, St Peter Port, Jersey, Channel Islands. Classical Scholar. m. (1) Frances Hedley, 1953, divorced 1981, 2 sons, 1 daughter, (2) Mary R Lefkowitz, 1982. Education: Christ Church, Oxford; MA (Oxon), 1947. Appointments: Fellow, Jesus College, Cambridge, 1948-54; Fellow, Corpus Christi College, Oxford, 1954-60; Regius Professor of Greek and Student of Christ Church, Oxford, 1960-89. Publications: The Justice of Zeus, 1971, 2nd edition, 1983; Blood for the Ghosts, 1982; Supplementum Hellenisticum (with P J Parsons), 1983; Sophoclis Fabulae (with N G Wilson), 1990; Sophoclea (with N G Wilson), 1990; Academic Papers, 2 volumes, 1990; Greek in a Cold Climate, 1991; Sophocles (editor and translator), 3 volumes, 1994-96; Sophocles: Second Thoughts (with N G Wilson), 1997. Contributions to: Numerous periodicals. Honours: Honorary DHL, University of Chicago, 1970; Honorary PhD, University of Tel Aviv, 1984; Knighted, 1989; Honorary DPhil, University of Thessalonica, 1999, Göttingen, 2002. Memberships: British Academy, fellow; Academy of Athens, fellow; Corresponding Member; American Academy of Arts and Sciences; American Philosophical Society; Rheinisch-Westfälische Akademie; Bayerische Akademie der Wissenschaften; Accademia di Lettere, Archeologia e Belle Arti, Naples. Address: 15 West Riding, Wellesley, MA 02482, USA.

LO Shou-Chih, b. 5 March 1970, Taiwan. Assistant Professor. m. Hsing-Min Ko, 2 daughters. Education: BS, Chiao Tung University, 1993; MS, 1994, PhD, 2000, Tsing Hua University. Appointments: Postdoctoral Researcher, Computer and Communication Research Center, National Tsing Hua University, Taiwan, 2000-04; Assistant Professor, Department of Computer Science & Information Engineering, National Dong Hwa University, Taiwan, 2004-. Publications: Architecture for QoS and Mobility Support in IP-Based Wireless Networks, An Efficient Multipolling Mechanism for IEEE; Efficient Index and Data Allocation for Wireless Broadcast Services. Honours: Listed in international biographical dictionaries. Memberships: IEEE; IEICE. Address: No 1, Sec 2, Da Hsueh Road, Shoufeng, Hualien, 974 Taiwan. E-mail: sclo@mail.ndhu.edu.tw Website: www.csie.ndhu.edu.tw/~robert

LO Wen-Lin, b. 1 January 1958, Kaohsiung, Taiwan. Dermatologist. m. Yung-Jung Ho, 1 son, 1 daughter. Education: MD, National Yang-Ming Medical College, Taipei, 1982. Appointments: Resident, Dermatology, 1984-89, Attending Physician, 1989-91, Veterans General Hospital, Taipei; Lecturer, National Yang-Ming Medical College, 1989-91; Attending Physician, 1991-93, Section Chief, 1993-94, Chutong (Taiwan) Veterans Hospital; Private Practice, 1994-. Publications: Contributor of articles in professional journals. Memberships: Fellow, American Academy of Dermatology; Asian Dermatological Association; International Society of Dermatology; Chinese Dermatological Society; Laser Medicine Society. Address: 2/F #2 Lane 14, Chung Shan North Sec 7, Taipei 111, Taiwan.

LOACH Kenneth, b. 17 June 1936, Nuneaton, England. Film Director. m. Lesley Ashton, 1962, 3 sons (one deceased), 2 daughters. Education: St Peter's Hall, Oxford. Appointments: BBC Trainee, Drama Department, 1963; Freelance Film Director, 1963-; Films include: Poor Cow, 1967; Kes, 1969; In Black and White, 1970; Family Life, 1971; Black Jack,

1979; Looks and Smiles, 1981; Fatherland, 1986; Hidden Agenda, 1990; Riff Raff, 1991; Raining Stones, 1993; Ladybird Ladybird, 1994; Land and Freedom, 1995; Carla's Song, 1996; My Name is Joe, 1998; Bread and Roses, 2001; The Navigators, 2001; Sweet Sixteen, 2002; 11.09.01 UK Segment, 2002; Ae Fond Kiss, 2004; Tickets, 2007; McLibel, 2005; The Wind That Shakes the Barley, 2006; To Each His Cinema, 2007; It's a Free World, 2007. TV includes: Diary of a Young Man, 1964; Three Clear Sundays, 1965; The End of Arthur's Marriage, 1965; Up the Junction, 1965; Coming Out Party, 1965; Cathy Come Home, 1966; In Two Minds, 1966; The Golden Vision, 1969; The Big Flame, 1970; After a Lifetime, 1971; The Rank of File, 1972; Auditions, 1980; A Question of Leadership, 1980; The Red and the Blue, 1983; Questions of Leadership, 1983; Which Side are You On?, 1984; The View from the Woodpile, 1988; Time to Go, 1989; Dispatches: Arthur Scargill, 1991; The Flickering Flame, 1996; Another City, 1998. Honours: Hon DLitt, St Andrews; Staffordshire University, Bristol; Dr hc, Royal College of Art, 1988; Honorary Fellow, St Peter's College, Oxford; Léopard d'honneur for Lifetime Achievement, Locarno Film Festival, 2003; Praemium Imperiale, 2003; London Film Critics' Circle Award for Outstanding Contribution to Cinema, 2005. Address: c/o Parallax Pictures, 7 Denmark Street, London, WC2H 8LS, England.

LOADER Clive Robert (Sir), Air Chief Marshal. Education: Judd School, Tonbridge; University of Southampton. Appointments: University Cadet, RAF, 1972; Officer Training, 1973-74; Flying Training (Jet Provost, Gnat, Hunter), 1974-76, Joined Harrier Force, 1976; Served tours on all front-line Harrier squadrons including: Cmd 3 (Fighter) Squadron, 1993-95, OC RAF Laarbruch, Germany, 1996-99; Flown on ops in Belize, Falkland Islands, Iraq, Bosnia; Personal Staff Officer to Commander-in-Chief Strike Command, 1991-93, head major review of administration support in RAF, 1999-2000, Air Commodore Harrier RAF High Wycombe, 2000-01, ACOS J3 UK Permanent Joint HQ, 2001-02, ACDS (Ops) MOD, UK, 2002-04, Deputy Commander-in-Chief, Strike Command, 2004-2007; Commander-in-Chief Air Command, 2007. Honour: OBE, 1996; Knighted, 2006. Memberships: FRAeS; President, RAF Cricket and Combined Services Cricket; President, RAF Rugby; President, RAF Sailing. Address: Commander-in-Chief Air Command, Headquarters Air Command, RAF High Wycombe, Buckinghamshire HP14 4UE, England.

LOADES David Michael, b. 19 January 1934, Cambridge, England. Retired Professor of History; Writer. m. Judith Anne Atkins, 18 April 1987. Education: Emmanuel College, Cambridge, 1955-61, BA, 1958, MA, PhD, 1961, LittD, 1981. Appointments: Lecturer in Political Science, University of St Andrews, 1961-63; Lecturer in History, University of Durham, 1963-70; Senior Lecturer, 1970-77, Reader, 1977-80, Professor of History, 1980-96, University College of North Wales, Bangor; Director, British Academy John Foxe Project, 1993-2004; Honorary Research Professor, University of Sheffield, 1996-. Publications: 22 books and collections include: Two Tudor Conspiracies, 1965; The Oxford Martyrs, 1970; The Reign of Mary Tudor, 1979; The Tudor Court, 1986; Mary Tudor: A Life, 1989; The Tudor Navy, 1992; John Dudley: Duke of Northumberland, 1996; Tudor Government, 1997; England's Maritime Empire, 2000; The Chronicles of the Tudor Queens, 2002; Elizabeth I, 2003; Intrigue and Treason: the Tudor Court 1547-1558, 2004. Editor: The Papers of George Wyatt, 1968; The End of Strife, 1984; Faith and Identity, 1990; John Foxe and the English Reformation, 1997; John Foxe: an historical perspective, 1999; with C S Knighton,

The Anthony Roll of Henry VIII, 2000; Letters from the Mary Rose, 2002; John Foxe: At Home and Abroad, 2004; Word and Worship, 2005; The Church of Mary Tudor (co-editor with E Duffy), 2006; Mary Tudor: The Tragical History of the First Queen of England, 2006; Henry VIII: Court, Church and Conflict; Contributions to academic journals. Memberships: Royal Historical Society, Fellow; Society of Antiquaries of London, Member; Ecclesiastical History Society; Navy Records Society. Address: The Cottage, Priory Lane, Burford, Oxon OX18 4SG, England.

LOBODA-CACKOVIC Jasna, b. Homec, Slovenia, resident in Berlin, Germany, 1970-. Scientist; Research Physicist; Artist; Sculptor; Painter; Photoartist. m. Hinko Cackovic. Education: Art education: Sculpturing and painting in the artist's studio of father, Peter Loboda, Artist, Sculptor, Professor at the Academy Ljubljana, Slovenia and continued by self-education; Education in Music, Literature, Theatre from mother, Jelena Loboda Zrinski, Artist, Writer; Science Education: Diploma in Science, Physics, 1960, MSc, Solid State Physics, 1964, University of Zagreb, Croatia; PhD, 1970, Fritz-Haber-Institut der Max-Planck-Gesellschaft, Berlin-Dahlem, Germany and University of Zagreb. Appointments: Scientist, Atom Institute Ruder Boskovic, Zagreb, 1960-71; Hon Assistant, University of Zagreb, 1961-65; Postdoctoral, 1970-71, Scientist, 1965-67, 1970-97, Fritz-Haber-Institut der Max-Planck-Gesellschaft, Berlin-Dahlem; Freelance in multidisciplinary fields, concerning universal art and new fields in science and technology, different aspects of human living and activity, 1997-; Always searching for new ways; Scientific achievements include: Physics of Polymers, synthetic and biological molecules; Reactions at the surface of single crystals and alloys; Memory in Nature, 1971; Self-ordering of the matter; Memory of Solid and Fluid Matter; Order/disorder phenomena in the atomic, molecular and colloidal dimensions; Mutual dependence of order between atomic and colloidal entities; Self preparing of the structure in atomic dimensions to make processes in future possible; Theoretical and Experimental development of small and wide angle X-rays scattering analysis, magnetic susceptibility and of broad line nuclear magnetic resonance analysis; Development of physical instruments. Creative Art Works include new principals of creation in art, "Fracture as a Principle of Forming", developed in the 80th, as complex scopes of expression: Rebuilding a new volume and aesthetic relations from fragments of an already finished sculpture or painting; In spite of fracturing this is a live affirming process; The presence of time is the fourth dimension in the sculptures; Arrangement of several identical or different sculptures, or paintings, to multiple-artworks; Composition of sculptures and paintings into volume-collages; Drawings and paintings act as sculpture, stay free in volume; Sculptures/Drawings act as players on a stage; Creative activity in sculpturing/painting/photoart and science (physics, mathematics, chemistry) influenced by literature, music, theatre, astrophysics and cosmology; Developing of Universal Art including mentioned multidisciplinary fields; Intention to contribute: to synthesis of science, art and harmony, to the ethic and aesthetic part of human living and activity, to freedom in all it's facet's through culture in the widest sense; Many of 1490 sculptures, reliefs and paintings presented at exhibitions in Germany, Austria, France, Monaco, Switzerland, Croatia, Luxembourg, 1968-, and Internet galleries, 1998-; Innovative Works, Two-Artist Cooperation JasHin, with Hinko Cackovic from 1997; Permanent art representations in Gallery for Sculpture (Bildhauergalerie Plinthe), Berlin, 1987-95, Paintings in Gallery Kleiner Prinz, Baden-Baden, Germany, 1987-; In Internet, 1999-;

Cyber Museum wwwARTchannel (www.art-channel.net), Gallery "artgala" of Jean-Gebser-Akademie eV, Germany (www.artgala.de). Publications: About 70 articles to professional scientific journals and in books; Featured in art journals, books and numerous catalogues. Honours: Grants: Atom Institute Ruder Boskovic, Zagreb, Croatia, 1965-66; Deutsche Forschungsgemeinschaft Germany, 1966; Deutscher Akademischer Austauschdient, Germany, 1966-67; Alexander von Humboldt Stiftung, Bad Godesberg, Germany, 1970-71; Career achievements, accomplishments and contributions to society: New Century Award, Europe 500, Leaders for the New Century, 2000; Presidential Award, 500 Great Minds, 2001; Presidential Award, 500 Distinguished Professors & Scholars of the BWW Society, 2004; 20th and 21st Century Achievement Award, 1999, 2003; Certificate for merit in nature protection and preservation of species, 2004; Science award for contributions to the field of Physics, 2007; Gold Medal for Germany for Success, Passion, Courage, Spirit, Commitment, Excellence, Virtue, 2006; Awards for Outstanding Contribution to Art, Science and their Creative Interaction: The Da Vinci Diamond, 2004; Dedication, Dictionary of International Biography, 33rd Edition, 2006; Salute to Greatness Award, 2007; IBC Lifetime Achievement Award, 2006; Roll of Honour, 2007-; Art awards include: Euro gold medal, Art and Culture, Exhibition Zürich, Switzerland, 1989; Euro Art Plaquette, Exhibition Paris, France, 1989; 3 Euro honorary prizes, Exhibitions, Berlin, Dresden and Baden-Baden, Germany, 1993, 1994, 1995; Sculpture Prize, 5th Open Art Prize, Bad Nauheim, Germany, 1995; International Virtual Internet Art Competitions of the Forschungs-Instituts Bildender Kunste, Germany, 1998, 2000, 2001; magna cum laude for the oeuvre at the Virtual Internet Art Competitions of the Jean-Gebser-Akademie, Germany, 2002/2003, 2004/2005; Grants: Atom Institute Ruder Boskovic, Zagreb, Croatia, 1965-66; Deutsche Forschungsgemeinschaft, Germany, 1966; Deutscher Akademischer Austauschdienst, Germany, 1966-67; Alexander von Humboldt Stiftung, Bad Godesberg, Germany, 1970-71. Memberships: Deutsche Physikalishe Gesellschaft, 1972-95; New York Academy of Science, 1996; Member, Cyber Museum Euro art channel, 1998-; Fellow, International Biographical Association, 1998-2001; Member of the Virtual Gallery "artgala.de" by Forschungs-Institut Bildende Künste (FIBK) and Jean-Gebser-Akademie eV, Germany, 1999-; Member, The Europe 500, 2000; Founding Member of the BWW (Bibliotheque World Wide) Society, 2001; Europäischer Kulturkreis Baden-Baden, 2002-; Member, 500 Great Minds, 2002; Archaeology, Astronautics and SETI Research Association, 2002-; The International Order of Merit, 2007-; Active member, various organisations working against child poverty, sponsoring their education, 2006-; Sovereign Ambassador, Order of American Ambassadors, 2006; Vice President, Recognition Board, The World Congress of Arts, Sciences and Communication, 2007-; Secretary-General, United Cultural Convention, 2007-09. Address: Im Dol 60, 14195 Berlin, Germany.

ŁOCH Eugenia, b. 10 November 1926, Dębica, Poland. University Professor. m. Władysław Łoch. Education: MA, Polish Philology, Jagiellonian University, Kraków, 1958; PhD, Pedagogical University, Kraków, 1968; Post-doctoral (Habilitationsschrift), Jagiellonian University, Kraków, 1978; Full Professor, Maria Curie-Skłodowska University, 1996. Appointments: Member of Polish Parliament, 1972-76; Vice-Dean, Faculty of Humanities, WSP Rzeszòw, 1972-74; Vice-Dean, Faculty of Humanities, UMCS, Lublin, 1982-84; Director, Institute of Polish Philology, 1989-92; Head, Department of Literature of Positivism and Young Poland, UMCS, 1977-96. Publications: 31 scientific books as author,

DICTIONARY OF INTERNATIONAL BIOGRAPHY

editor and co-editor including: Short Stories of Iqnacy Maciejowski-Sewer, Kraków, 1971; Elements of Mysticism in Jarosław Iwaszkiewicz's Short Stories, Rzeszów, 1978; Focus on Modernism, Lublin, 1996; Jerzy Żuławski: Life and Work, Rzeszów, 1976; The Romantic Legacy in Polish Positivist Literature and the Literature of Young Poland, Lublin, 1988; Expressionism in Young Poland Literature and its Background of Polish and Overseas Literatures of 20th Century, Lublin, 1988; Modernism and the National Literatures, Lublin, 1999; Between Literature and Medicine, Lublin, 2005; Numerous articles in popular and professional journals. Honours: Award, Ministry of Education, 1969, 1979; Golden Cross of Merit, 1975; Kawalerski Cross, 1984. Memberships: Association Internationale des Literatures Comparees; Committee for Literary Sciences PAN, Warszawa, 1985-87; Philology Commission PAN, Kraków, 1971-; Chairman, Philological Commission, Lublin, 1991-. Address: ul Paryska 6m5, 20-854 Lublin, Poland. E-mail: eloch@klio.umcs.lublin.pl

LOCKHART James, Conductor. Education: Edinburgh University, Scotland, 1947-1951; Royal College of Music, London, 1951-1954. Appointments: Assistant Conductor, Yorkshire Symphony Orchestra, Leeds, 1954-55; Repetiteur and Assistant Conductor, Städtische Bühnen, Münster, 1955-56; Repetiteur and Assistant Conductor, Bayerische Staatsoper, München 1956-57; Director of the Opera Workshop, University of Texas, Austin, Texas, 1957-59; Repetiteur and Assistant Conductor, Glyndebourne Festival Opera, 1957-59; Repetiteur and Assistant Conductor, The Royal Opera House, Covent Garden, 1959-60; Assistant Conductor, BBC Scottish Symphony Orchestra, Glasgow, 1960-61; Conductor, Sadlers Wells Opera, London, 1960-62; Repetiteur and Conductor, The Royal Opera House, Covent Garden, London, 1962-68; Music Director, Welsh National Opera, Cardiff, 1968-73; Generalmusikdirektor, Staatstheater, Kassel, 1972-80; Generalmusikdirektor, Koblenz Opera, 1981-88; Generalmusikdirektor, Rheinische Philharmonie, Koblenz, 1981-91; Principal Guest Conductor, BBC Concert Orchestra, 1982-87; Director of Opera, Royal College of Music, 1986-1992; Director of Opera, Royal College of Music and Royal Academy of Music, 1992-96; Opera Consultant, Royal College of Music and Royal Academy of Music, London, 1996-98; Guest Professor of Conducting, Tokyo National University of Fine Arts and Music, (Tokyo Geidai), 1998-2001; Professor of Conducting, Sydney Conservatorium of Music, 2005; Professor Emeritus, Tokyo National University of Fine Arts and Music, (Tokyo Geidai); Ehrendirigent, Rheinische Philharmonie, Koblenz; Freelance Conductor. Address 105 Woodcock Hill, Harrow, Middlesex, HA3 0JJ, England. E-mail lockgrog@aol.com

LODER Robert Reginald (Robin), b. 12 November 1943, Titchfield, Hampshire, England. Landowner. m. Jane Royden, 2 sons, 2 daughters. Education: MA, Trinity College, Cambridge. Appointments: Owner, Leonardslee Gardens; High Sheriff of West Sussex, 2000-01. Address: Leonardslee Gardens, Lower Beeding, Horsham, West Sussex RH13 6PP, England. E-mail: gardens@leonardslee.com

LODGE David John, b. 28 January 1935. Honorary Professor of Modern English Literature. m. Mary Frances Jacob, 1959, 2 sons, 1 daughter. Education: BA, honours, MA (London); PhD, Birmingham; National Service, RAC, 1955-57. Appointments: British Council, London, 1959-60; Assistant Lecturer, 1960-62, Lecturer, 1963-71, Senior Lecturer, 1971-73, Reader of English, 1973-76, Professor of Modern English Literature, 1976-87, Honorary Professor, 1987-2000, Emeritus Professor, 2001-, University of Birmingham;

Harkness Commonwealth Fellow, 1964-65; Visiting Associate Professor, University of California, Berkeley, 1969; Henfield Writing Fellow, University of East Anglia, 1977. Publications: Novels: The Picturegoers, 1960; Ginger, You're Barmy, 1962; The British Museum is Falling Down, 1965; Out of the Shelter, 1970, revised edition, 1985; Changing Places, 1975; How Far Can You Go?, 1980; Small World, 1984; Nice Work, 1988; Paradise News, 1991; Therapy, 1995; Home Truths, 1999; Thinks...., 2001; Author, Author, 2004. Criticism: Language of Fiction, 1966; The Novelist at the Crossroads, 1971; The Modes of Modern Writing, 1977; Working with Structuralism, 1981; Write On, 1986; After Bakhtin (essays), 1990; The Art of Fiction, 1992; The Practice of Writing, 1996; Consciousness and the Novel, 2002; The Year of Henry James: The Story of a Novel, 2006. Honours: Yorkshire Post Fiction Prize, 1975; Hawthornden Prize, 1976; Whitbread Book of the Year Award, 1980; Sunday Express Book of the Year Award, 1988; Chevalier de L'Ordre des Arts et des Lettres, 1997; CBE, 1998. Address: Department of English, University of Birmingham, Birmingham B15 2TT, England.

LODGE Oliver Raymond William Wynlayne, b. 2 September 1922, Painswick, Gloucestershire, England. Retired Barrister. m. Charlotte Young, deceased, 1990, 1 son, 2 daughters. Education: Officer Cadet, Royal Fusiliers, 1942; BA, 1943, MA, 1947, King's College, Cambridge. Appointments: Called to the Bar by Inner Temple, 1945; Practiced at Chancery Bar, 1945-74; Admitted ad eundam to Lincoln's Inn, 1949; Member of Bar Council, 1952-56, 1967-71; Member of Supreme Court Rules Committee, 1968-71; Bencher of Lincoln's Inn, 1973; Permanent Chairman of Industrial Tribunals, 1975-92, Part-time Chairman, 1992-94; Regional Chairman of London South Region of Industrial Tribunals, 1980-92; General Commissioner of Income Tax for Lincoln's Inn District, 1983-91; Treasurer of Lincoln's Inn, 1995. Publications: Editor, 3rd edition, Rivington's Epitome of Snedl's Equity, 1948; Editor, article on Fraudulent and Voidable Conveyances in 3rd edition of Halsbury's Laws of England, 1956. Memberships: Garrick Club; Bar Yacht Club. Address: Southridge House, Hindon, Salisbury, Wiltshire SP3 6ER, England.

LÖFFLER di CASAGIOVE Harti Hanns, b. 21 March 1936, Munich, Bavaria. University Professor. m. Edyta, 1 son. Education: BA, Munich Interpreters' School, 1963; MA, Munich University, 1968; Teacher Training Exam, State of Bavaria, 1970; PhD, Harvard University, USA, 1978; Postgraduate Ethics Studies (Philosophy), Munich, State Exam, 1988. Appointments: Assistant Lecturer, German (English), Bocconi University, Milan, Italy, 1963-66; Assistant Researcher, Linguistics, Munich University, 1966-68; Faculty Member, Maryland University, European Division, 1968-71; Language Co-ordinator, German-English-Italian, Munich Olympics, 1971-72; Lecturer, Munich and Landshut Fachhochschulen, 1972-77; Civil Service High School Teacher, Languages, Munich, 1978-88; Co-ordinator, Munich Municipality Education Authority, 1988-91; Freelance Language and Ethics Teacher, Orbetello, Tuscany, Italy, 1991-95; Freelance Language Teacher and Interpreter, Munich, 1995-2001; Freelance Language Teacher and Interpreter, Pietrasanta, Tuscany, 2001-02, 2005-07; Faculty Member, European School of Economics, Italy, 2002-04; Associate Professor, German, Camerino University, Italy, 2004-05; Managing Member, CONI (National Olympic Committee of Italy), Lucca County, 2007; Probo viro, Member of the Disciplinary Court of Panathlon International, Lucca County, 2007. Publications: Grüß Gott, lieber Kinder, 1964; Corso di lingua tedesca, 1966; Dizionario base tedesco-italiano/

- 665 -

italiano-tedesco, 1965; Ski Dictionary Italian-German, Italian-English, 1968. Honours: Viscount Casagiove; Fellow, Academy of Political Science; Judge of both German and Italian Sailing Federations; Grand Master Legal Scholar, 2006; DDG, IBC, 2007. Address: cp 192, Marina di Pietrasanta, I-55044, Italy. E-mail: languages@harti-it.eu

LOFTHOUSE Geoffrey (Lord Lofthouse of Pontefract), b. 18 December 1925, Featherstone, England. Deputy Speaker, House of Lords. m. Sarah, deceased, 1 daughter. Education: Leeds University, 1954-57. Appointments: Member, Pontefract Borough Council, 1962; Mayor of Pontefract, 1967-68; Leader, Pontefract Borough Council, 1969-73; First Chairman, Wakefield MDC, 1973; Chairman, Housing Committee, 1973-79; Elected Member of Parliament for Pontefract and Castleford, 1978; Elected Deputy Speaker of the House of Commons, 1992-97; Elected Deputy Speaker of the House of Lords, 1997-; Chairman of Wakefield Health Authority, 1998. Publications: A Very Miner MP (autobiography), 1985; Coal Sack to Woolsack (autobiography), 1999. Honours: Knighthood, 1995; Peerage, 1997. Memberships: Member of the Imperial Society of Knights Bachelor; Appointed Magistrate, 1970; President, British Amateur Rugby League Association. Address: 67 Carleton Crest, Pontefract, West Yorkshire WF8 2QR, England.

LOGUE Christopher (John), b. 23 November 1926, Portsmouth, Hampshire, England. Poet; Writer; Dramatist. m. Rosemary Hill, 1985. Education: Prior College, Bath. Publications: Poetry: Wand and Quadrant, 1953; Devil, Maggot and Son, 1954; The Weakdream Sonnets, 1955; The Man Who Told His Love: 20 Poems Based on P Neruda's "Los Cantos d'amores", 1958, 2nd edition, 1959; Songs, 1960; Songs from "The Lily-White Boys", 1960; The Establishment Songs, 1966; The Girls, 1969; New Numbers, 1970; Abecedary, 1977; Ode to the Dodo, 1981; War Music: An Account of Books 16 to 19 of Homer's Iliad, 1981; Fluff, 1984; Kings: An Account of Books 1 and 2 of Homer's Iliad, 1991, revised edition, 1992; The Husbands: An Account of Books 3 and 4 of Homer's Iliad, 1994; Selected Poems (edited by Christopher Reid), 1996; All Day Permanent Red, 2003. Plays: The Lily-White Boys (with Harry Cookson), 1959; The Trial of Cob and Leach, 1959; Antigone, 1961; War Music, 1978; Kings, 1993. Screenplays: Savage Messiah, 1972; The End of Arthur's Marriage, 1965; Crusoe (with Walter Green), 1986. Other: Lust, by Count Plamiro Vicarion, 1955; The Arrival of the Poet in the City: A Treatment for a Film, 1964; True Stories, 1966; The Bumper Book of True Stories, 1980. Editor: Count Palmiro Vicarion's Book of Limericks, 1959; The Children's Book of Comic Verse, 1979; London in Verse, 1982; Sweet & Sour: An Anthology of Comic Verse, 1983; The Children's Book of Children's Rhymes, 1986. Honours: 1st Wilfred Owen Award, 1998; Whitbread Poetry Award, 2005. Address: 41 Camberwell Grove, London SE5 8JA, England.

LOHSE Andrea, b. 28 April 1964, Kellinghusen, Schleswig-Holstein, Germany. University Lecturer. Education: First State Examination, Christian-Albrechts University, Kiel, 1988; Dr iur, LLD, Christian-Albrechts University, Kiel, 1991; Second State Examination, after 3 years practical training in judicial or other legal work, Schleswig-Holstein, 1993. Appointments: Research Assistant, Christian-Albrechts University, 1984-89; Stagaire, trainee, Commission, European Community, Direction General Competition, Brussels, 1989-90; Administrative Assistant, ERASMUS, student exchange, program, 1990-93, Academic Assistant, civil law, 1993-94, Christian-Albrechts University; Lecturer, Academy

of the Savings Banks, Kiel, 1991-94; Academic Assistant, civil, business and competition law, Free University Berlin, 1994-2001; Lawyer, Hengeler Mueller, 2003-04; University Lecturer, Johann Wolfgang Goethe University, 2004-05; University Lecturer, Ruhr-University Bochum, 2005-2006. Publications: Indonesian law concerning prohibition of monopolistic practices and unfair business competition, 2000, 2001; Law in Cases: Antitrust Law and Unfair Business Competition Law, 2001; The Prohibition of Cartels and the EEC Umbrella Regulation, 2001; Corporate Governance – the duties of the members of the management and supervisory board, 2005. Honours: Scholarships: Schleswig-Holstein, 1989-90, University Association Schleswig-Holstein, 1992; Faculty Award, Law, Christian-Albrechts University, 1992; Kieler Doctores Juris Association, 1993; Furtherance Honor, Hermann-Ehlers-Foundation, 1992; Scholarship, German Research Foundation, 2002-03. Membership: Protestant Church, 1964-. Address: Uhlenweg 30A, 25548 Kellinghusen, Germany. E-mail: lohse.andrea@web.de

LÖKER Altan, b. 6 November 1927, Kütahya, Turkey. Electrical Engineer, retired. Education: MS in Electrical Engineering, Technical University of Istanbul, 1951; MS in Physics, Stevens Institute of Technology, USA, 1957. Appointments: Electrical Engineer in Turkey, USA, Canada, and Saudi Arabia; Project Manager, Subcontractor, Contractor in Turkey; Graduate Assistant at the Technical University of Istanbul and Physics Department of Stevens Institute of Technology. Publications: Film and Suspense, 1976, 2nd edition, 2005; Dreams and Psychosynthesis, 1987; Cognitive-Cybernetic Theory and Therapy, 1993; Dreams, Migraine, Neuralgia, 1993; Theory in Psychology: The Journal of Mind and Behaviour, 1999; Cognitive Behavioural Cybernetics of Symptoms, Dreams, Lateralization, 2001, 2nd edition, 2002; Migraines and Dreams, 2003. Memberships: Turkish Chamber of Electrical Engineers, retired. Address: Lalasahin 23/5, Ferikoy, Istanbul 80260, Turkey. E-mail: alloker@superonline.com

LOLLOBRIGIDA Gina, b. 4 July 1927, Sibiaco. Italian Actress. m. Milko Skofic, 1949, 1 son. Education: Liceo Artistico, Rome. Appointments: First Screen Role, Pagliacci, 1947; Appeared in numerous films including: Campane a Martello, 1948; Cuori Senza Frontiere, 1949; Achtung, bandit!, 1951; Enrico Caruso, 1951; Fanfan la Tulipe, 1951; Altri Tempi, 1952; The Wayward Wife, 1952; Les belles de la nuit, 1952; Pane, amour e fantasia, 1953; La Provinciale, 1953; Pane, amour e gelosia, La Romana, 1954; Il Grande Gioco, 1954; La Donna piu Bella del Mondo, 1955; Trapeze, 1956; Notre Dame de Paris, 1956; Solomon and Sheba, 1959; Never So Few, 1960; Go Naked in the World, 1961; She Got What She Asked For, 1963; Woman of Straw, 1964; Le Bambole, 1965; Hotel Paradiso, 1966; Buona Sera Mrs Campbell, 1968; King, Queen, Knave, 1972; The Bocce Showdown, 1990; Plucked, Bad Man's River; The Lonely Woman; Bambole; Donna in fuga, Una, 1996; XXL, 1997. Publications: Italia Mia, 1974; The Philippines. Address: Via Appia Antica 223, 00178 Rome, Italy.

LOMAS Herbert, b. 7 February 1924, Yorkshire, England. Poet; Critic; Translator. m. Mary Marshall Phelps, 29 June 1968, 1 son, 1 daughter. Education: BA, 1949, MA, 1952, University of Liverpool. Appointments: Teacher, Spetsai, Greece, 1950-51; Lecturer, Senior Lecturer, University of Helsinki, 1952-65; Senior Lecturer, 1966-72, Principal Lecturer, 1972-82, Borough Road College. Publications: Chimpanzees are Blameless Creatures, 1969; Who Needs Money?, 1972; Private and Confidential, 1974; Public

Footpath, 1981; Fire in the Garden, 1984; Letters in the Dark, 1986; Trouble, 1992; Selected Poems, 1995; A Useless Passion, 1998; The Vale of Todmorden, 2003. Translations: Territorial Song, 1991; Contemporary Finnish Poetry, 1991; Fugue, 1992; Wings of Hope and Daring, 1992; The Eyes of the Fingertips are Opening, 1993; Black and Red, 1993; Narcissus in Winter, 1994; The Year of the Hare, 1994; Two Sequences for Kuhmo, 1994; In Wandering Hall, 1995; Selected Poems, Eeva-Lisa Manner, 1997; Three Finnish Poets, 1999; A Tenant Here, 1999; Not Before Sundown, 2003. Contributions to: London Magazine and other reviews, journals, and magazines. Honours: Prize, Guinness Poetry Competition; Runner Up, Arvon Foundation Poetry Competition; Cholmondeley Award; Poetry Book Society Biennial Translation Award; Knight First Class, Order of the White Rose of Finland, 1991: Finnish State Prize for Translation, 1991. Memberships: Society of Authors; Finnish Academy; Finnish Literary Society; President, Suffolk Poetry Society, 1999-. Address: North Gable, 30 Crag Path, Aldeburgh, Suffolk IP15 5BS, England.

LOMU Jonah, b. 12 May 1975, Auckland, New Zealand. Rugby Football Player; Athlete. m. (1) Tanya Rutter, divorced, (2) Fiona Taylor, 2003. Appointments: Bank Officer, ASB Bank of New Zealand; Youngest Ever Capped All Black; Wing; International Debut, New Zealand versus France, 1994; Semi Finalist at World Cup, South Africa, 1995; Affilliated to Rugby Union; Ran 100m in 10.7 Seconds; With All Blacks, 1999; Signed for Cardiff Blues, 2005. Website: www.jonahlomu.com

LONE Khalid Parvez, b. 26 August 1949, Lahore, Pakistan. University Professor. m. Asifa, 1 son, 1 daughter. Education: BSc, Chemistry and Zoology, Gordon College, 1969; MSc, First Class First, Punjab University, Lahore, Pakistan, 1971; PhD, School of Health and Life Sciences, Department of Biological Sciences, University of Aston in Birmingham, England, 1980. Appointments: Research Trainee, Pakistan Medical Research Centre and International Center for Medical Research and Training, University of Maryland, USA, 1972-73; Lecturer, Department of Zoology, Punjab University, Lahore, 1973-76; Demonstrator, 1976-80, Postdoctoral Fellow, 1980-81, University of Aston in Birmingham; Director of Research and National Co-ordinator, Directorate of Fisheries, Pakistan Agricultural Research Council, 1981-82; Assistant Professor, 1982-90, Associate Professor, 1990-95, Professor, 1995-2000, Department of Zoology, Punjab University, Lahore, Pakistan; Research Scientist, Mariculture and Fisheries Department, Food Resources Division, Kuwait Institute for Scientific Research, 1987-90, 1992-95, 1997-2003; Professor and Chairman, Department of Biological Sciences, Dean, Faculty of Science and Technology, University of Education, Lahore, Pakistan, 2004-05; Professor, Zoology Department, G C University, Lahore. Publications: More than 80 articles in numerous scientific journals include most recently: Effect of Diethylstilbestrol on the development of Drosophilia melanogaster: studies on nucleic acids and proteins, 2004; Changes in chemical composition of defatted rice polishing after treatment with HCl and hydrogen peroxide and extrusion cooking, 2004; Metabolizable energy of physically and chemically treated defatted rice polishing, 2004; 53 published abstracts. Honours: Sir William Robert Gold Medal, Punjab University; Gold Medal, Professor Abdus-Salam (Nobel Laureate) Award, 1984; Young Scientist of the Year Gold Medal, Pakistan Academy of Sciences, 1986. Memberships: 4 editorial boards; Eco-Ethics International Union, Germany; International Union for the Conservation of Nature; Treasurer, Life Fellow Zoological Society of Pakistan; Founder Member, Asian Fisheries Society; Institute of Biology, UK; Network

of Tropical Aquaculture Scientists. Address: Department of Zoology, GC University, Katchery Road, Lahore-54000, Pakistan. E-mail: kplone@yahoo.com

LONERAGAN Owen William, b. 26 March 1924, Maylands, Western Australia. Forestry; Esperanto. m. Joan Edith Shaw, deceased 2005, 2 sons, 1 daughter. Education: Sport: South Perth Soccer Club, 1933-41, Captain, 1946-48, WA State Team Reserve, 1948, Canberra ACT, 1949; School Swimming Classes, 1934-39; Cricket, 1934-36; Life Saving Certificate, 1936; Perth Boys School Soccer Team, 1937-39; Tennis, Country Golf Clubs, 1959; Golf in retirement, 2007; Music: Junior Brass Band, 1937-39; French Horn, RSL Band, 1940-41; Arts I, 1946, Science I and II, 1947-48, University of Western Australia; Australian Forestry School, Canberra, 1949-50, Diploma, 1951; BSc, 1954, MSc, 1963, University of Western Australia. Appointments: Junior, Health Department, Western Australia, 1940-41; Australian Military Forces, 1942; RAAF attached RAF aircrew Wireless Operator, 1943-45; Clerk, Commonwealth Repatriation Commission, Perth, 1945-46; University Trainee, Commonwealth Reconstruction Training Scheme, 1946-51; Professional Forester, Forests Department, Western Australia, Forest Assessor, Jarrahdale, 1951-52; Assistant Divisional Forest Officer, Dwellingup-Pemberton, 1952-60; Research Silviculturist, Manjimup-Como, 1961-79; Senior RS, 1980-84; Regeneration and treatments, Growth and Ecology of Jarrah, Karri, Sandalwood, Forest Parks and Reserves; Dedication to code of principles for harmony in sustainable living; Promotion of unique phonetic language Esperanto across cultures; Saving Australia's forests with annual yield rotation. Publications include: Review of Sandalwood Research, 1990; Karri Phenological Studies, 1979; Co-author, Vegetation Complexes, 1980; Ecology of Jarrah, 1986; Triple A Title – Harmony Week to Harmony World, working plan for local/state/regional/world harmony purpose: How to Stop Being Violent & Dehumanising People, 2007; Carbon Pollution Reduction Working Plan Model, 2007; Federal Pulpmill Tasmania, Assessment Process Debate. Honours: War Medals, 1939-45; University of Western Australia Hackett Bursary, 1947; Forests Department of Western Australia Bursary, 1949-50; United Nations Association of Australia Peace Award, 1996; Deputy Director General, IBC. Memberships include: Life Member, Institute of Foresters of Australia; Life Member, United Nations Association of Australia (WA), President, 1982-85; UN Year of the Tree and inaugural member of Greening Australia (WA), 1982; Tree Society (WA); RAAF Association (WA); Returned and Services League, (WA); Australian Conservation Foundation (WA); Life Member, Esperanto League (WA), Honorary Treasurer, 1976-85, 1997-2002; Multicultural Education Council (WA), 1978-80; Life Member, Australian Esperanto Association, Honorary Treasurer, 1986-95, Esperanto Examination Certificates Elementa, 1985, Meza, 2002; Vice President, Australia-Bangladesh Aid Inc, 1987; Inaugural member, World Peace and Diplomacy Forum, International Biographical Centre, 2003; Deputy Director General for Oceania, 2004, HonDG, 2005, IBC. Address: 26 Second Avenue, Claremont, WA 6010, Australia.

LONG Derek Albert, b. 11 August 1925, Gloucester, England. Scientist; Author; Antiquarian. m. Moira Hastings (Gilmore), 3 sons. Education: MA, D Phil, Jesus College, Oxford. Appointments: Fellow, University of Minnesota, USA, 1949-50; Research Fellow, Spectroscopy, University of Oxford, 1950-55; Lecturer, Senior Lecturer, Reader in Chemistry, University College, Swansea, 1956-66; Professor of Structural Chemistry, 1966-92, Professor Emeritus, 1992-, Chairman of the Board of Physical Sciences, 1976-79, Director, Molecular

Spectroscopy Unit, 1982-88, University of Bradford; OECD Travelling Fellow, Canada and USA, 1964; Leverhulme Research Fellow, 1970-71; Visiting Professor: Reims, Lille, Bordeaux, Paris, Bologna, Florence, Keele; Chairman, Second International Conference on Raman Spectroscopy, Oxford, 1970; Co-Director, NATO Advanced Studies Institute, Bad Winsheim, 1982; Member, Italian-UK Mixed Commission for Implementation of Cultural Convention, 1985; Vice Chairman, Euro Laboratory for Non-Linear Spectroscopy, Florence, 1986-92. Publications: Founder, Journal of Raman Spectroscopy, Editor, Editor-in-Chief, 1973-99, Emeritus Editor, 2000-; Books (sole author): Raman Spectroscopy, 1977; The Raman Effect, 2002; Books (joint editor): Essays in Structural Chemistry, 1971; Specialist Periodical Reports in Molecular Spectroscopy (vols 1-6), 1973-79; Non-Linear Raman Spectroscopy and Its Chemical Applications, 1988; Proceedings Eleventh International Conference on Raman Spectroscopy, 1988; About 200 papers in scientific journals relating to Raman Spectroscopy; Other papers: Sevres Service des Arts Industriels, 1997; The Goodmanham Plane, 2002; More Early Planes, 2006. Honours: Fellow, Royal Society of Chemistry, Chartered Chemist; Foreign Member, Lincei Academy, Rome, Italy; Honorary, Docteur es Sciences, Reims, France. Membership: Oxford and Cambridge Club. Address: 19 Hollingwood Rise, Ilkley, W Yorks, LS29 9PW, England. E-mail: dal@profdalong.demon.co.uk

LONGACRE Glenn V, b. 26 June 1961, Charleston, West Virginia, USA. Archivist. m. Mary Kathleen, 1 daughter. Education: BA, History, 1987, MA, Public History, 1988, West Virginia University. Appointments: Project Archivist, West Virginia and Regional History Collection, West Virginia University, Morgantown, West Virginia, 1987-88; Reference Archivist, Ohio Historical Society, Archives-Library Division, Columbus, Ohio, 1989-93; Archivist, National Archives and Records Administration - Great Lakes Region, Chicago, Illinois, 1993-. Publications: Co-author, 2 books; Author, 2 articles for professional journals; 3 Book reviews. Memberships: Army Historical Foundation; Association for Documentary Editing; Chicago Area Archivists; Midwest Archives Conference; World War Two Studies Association; 82nd Airborne Association; 504th Parachute Infantry Regiment Association. Address: National Archives and Records Administration - Great Lakes Region, 7358 South Pulaski Road, Chicago, Il 60629, USA. E-mail: glenn.longacre@nara.gov

LONGMORE, Rt Hon Lord Justice, Rt Hon Sir Andrew Centlivres, b. 25 August 1944, Liverpool, England. Judge. m. Margaret McNair, 1 son. Education: Lincoln College, Oxford. Appointments: Called to Bar, 1966; Queen's Counsel, 1983; Recorder of Crown Court, 1992; High Court Judge, 1993; Lord Justice of Appeal, 2001. Publications: Co-editor, 6th, 7th, 8th and 9th edition of MacGillirray's Law of Insurance. Honours: Knight, 1993; Privy Councillor, 2001. Memberships: Middle Temple, 1962-. Address: Royal Courts of Justice, London WC2A 2LL, England.

LONIGAN Paul R, b. 27 May 1935, New York City, USA. Professor of Romance Languages. m. Cynthia Hartley, 2 daughters. Education: BA, Romance Languages and Classics, Queens College, New York, 1960; PhD, Romance Languages, Johns Hopkins University, 1967. Appointments: Instructor, Russell Sage College, Troy, New York, 1963-65; Associate Professor, State University College, Oswego, New York, 1965-67; Queens College, CUNY, 1967-, Professor, 1983; Professor, CUNY Graduate Center, 1968-. Publications on subjects: Medieval epic, romance, hagiography, Early Irish

church, the Druids, Chrétien de Troyes, Villon, Rabelais, Montaigne, Ruben Darío, Women in the Middle Ages, Shamanism in the Old Irish Tradition, The Romance Languages and the Celtic Monks, The Three Kings of the Nativity, Napoleon's Irish Legion; Editor, poetry of María Victoria Carreño Montás, Respuestas Del Corazón, 1999; 'Protest Through Fasting'; 'Seamus Heaney's translation of Beowulf'; The Song of Roland; General Richard Montgomery (of The American Revolution). Editor, Provincial prize winning poetry of María Victoria Carreño Montás, 'Fragmentos de una tarde', Dominican Republic, Cocolo Editorial, 2004. Honours: National Defence Fellow; Phi Beta Kappa; Delta Phi Alpha; Magna cum laude; Chevalier dans l'Ordre des Palmes Académiques; International Order of Merit, 1999; Commemorative Medal of Honour, 2001; Plaque of Distinction as Sponsor of Le Cercle Francais, Queens College; World Medal of Freedom, 2006; Listed in national and international biographical dictionaries. Memberships: Círculo de Cultura Panamericano; Irish Texts Society; Contributing Editor of Oidhreacht, Newsletter of Celtic Heritage Books; Association of Literary Scholars and Critics; Archaeological Institute of America; American Society of the French Academic Palms; Hugenot Heritage, New York City, New York; The Biblical Archaeology Society. Address: PO Box 243, Montgomery, NY 12549, USA.

LOOS Katja, b. 11 February 1971, Frankfurt am Main, Germany. Chemist. Education: Vordiplom, Chemistry, 1990-92, Diploma, Organic Chemistry, 1993-96, Johannes Gutenberg Universität, Mainz, Germany; Dr rer nat, Polymer Science, Universität Bayreuth, Germany. Publications: Several articles in scientific journals. Honours: DAAD Fellowship, University of Massachusetts, Amherst, USA, 1997; DAAD Fellowship, Universidade Rio Grande do Sul, Brazil, 1999; Feodor-Lynen Research Fellowship Polytechnic University, Brooklyn, USA, 2001-03; State University, Groningen, The Netherlands, 2003-; Poster Award Makromolekulares Kolloquium, Freiburg, Germany, 1999, and others. Address: Hattersheimer Str 14, 65779 Kelkheim, Germany. E-mail: katjaloos@web.de

LOPATIN Pavel Konstantinovich, b. 29 May 1968, Kemerovo, Russia. Robotics Professor; Researcher. Education: Mechanical Engineering degree, Technical University of Budapest, Hungary, 1991; Candidate, Technical Sciences, Siberian State Aerospace University, Krashoyarsk, Russia, 1998. Appointments: Programmer, Krasnoyarsk Polytechnical Institute, 1991-92; Krasnoyarsk Metallurgical Plant, 1992-93; Assistant, Siberian State Aerospace University, Krasnoyarsk, 1994-97; Senior Teacher, Siberian State Aerospace University, Krasnoyarsk, 1997-99; Docent, Siberian State Aerospace University, Krasnoyarsk, 1999-. Publications: Algorithm of a manipulator movement amidst unknown obstacles, 2001; Manipulating Robots: Kinematics Dynamics Control, 2005; Using the Forward Search and the Polynomial Approximation Algorithms for Manipulator's Control in an Unknown Enviornment, 2006; Using the Polynomial Approximation Algorithm in the Algorithm2 for Manipulator's Control in an Unknown Environment, 2007; Algorithm for Dynamic Systems' Control in an Unknown Static Environment, 2007. Honours: Grantee, Russian Foundation for Basic Research, 2005; Scholar, President of Russia, 1996-97; Scholar, German Academic Exchange Service, 2003; Listed in international biographical dictionaries. Memberships: Krasnoyarsk Historical and Educational Society Memorial; IEEE; Krasnoyarsk Esperanto Club; Political Party Union of Right Forces. E-mail: pavel-lopatin@yandex.ru

LOPES Eliezer Pereira, b. 31 January 1961, Rio de Janeiro, Brazil. Communications Educator and Researcher. Education: Proficiency in English, University of Cambridge, England, 1981; Degree, Electrical Engineering, Systems Engineering, Rio de Janeiro State University, 1984; Telecommunications Engineering Postgraduate Studies, Rio de Janeiro Federal University, 1985; MS, Electrical Engineering, Rio de Janeiro Federal University, 1989; BEd, Rio de Janeiro State University, 1992; Doctor of Science, Electrical Engineering, Federal University of Santa Catarina, 1998. Appointments: Consultant, Unisul/Epagri, 1999-2007; Telecommunications Researcher and Professor, Southern Santa Catarina University, 2001-07; Dean and Professor of Telecommunications and Network Systems, Bandierantes University, 2007-; Implementor of meteorological, oceanic and subsurface radar systems; Research, development and design of atmospheric discharge detection networks, nowcasting systems and radar. Publications: 17 articles in professional scientific journals. Honours: Listed in international biographical directories; Marquis Who's Who in the World, 2006, 2007, 2008, 2009; 2000 Outstanding Intellectuals of the 21st Century (and Dedication Section), 2006, 2007, 2008; Great Minds of the 21st Century (and Dedication Section), 2007, 2008; Deputy Governor, ABIRA, 2007; Cambridge Blue Book (Front Section), 2007; Man of the Year, USA, 2006, 2007; Vice President, Recognition Board, World Congress of Arts, Sciences and Communications, 2007; International Directory of Experts and Expertise, 2006; Honorary Director General, IBC, 2006; Deputy Director General, IBC, 2006; Scientific Advisor to Director General, IBC, 2006; Lifetime Fellowship, International Biographical Association, 2006; Great Lives of the 21st Century, 2007; Dictionary of International Biography, 2006, 2007; Hall of Fame, 2006; 500 Greatest Geniuses of the XXI Century, 2008. Memberships: Brazilian Geophysics Society, 1994; Engineering and Architecture Regional Council, Rio de Janeiro, 1985; Marquis Who's Who, 2006, 2007, 2008, 2009; International Biographical Centre, Honorary Director General, 2006; American Biographical Institute, Deputy Governor, 2006; ABI Order of International Ambassadors, 2007; United Cultural Convention, Ambassador General, 2006; Ambassador, International Order of Merit, 2007. Address: Bandeirantes University - Uniban, PO Box 951, Santa Catarina, Florianópolis, 88010-970, Brazil. E-mail: elihzeu@terra.com.br

LOPES Elizeu Pereira, b. 22 September 1963, Rio de Janeiro, Brazil. Communications Educator and Researcher. Education: Proficiency in English, University of Cambridge, England/Brazilian Society of English Culture, Rio de Janeiro, 1981; Degree, Electrical Engineering (cum laude), 1985, MS, 1989, Rio de Janeiro Federal University; Bachelor of Education Degree, Rio de Janeiro State University, 1992; DS, Santa Catarina Federal University, Florianópolis, 1998. Appointments: Consultant, Unisul/Epagri – Santa Catarina State Research Company, Florianópolis, 1999-2007; Telecommunications Researcher, Southern Santa Catarina University, 2000-07; Head, National Graduation Examination Board, 2003; Dean and Professor of Telecommunications and Network Systems, Bandeirantes University, 2007-; Implementor of meteorological, oceanic and subsurface radar systems; Research, development and design of atmospheric discharge detection networks, nowcasting systems and radar. Publications: 17 articles and papers in professional scientific journals. Honours: Marquis Who's Who in the World, 2006, 2007, 2008, 2009; 2000 Outstanding Intellectuals of the 21st Century (and Dedication Section), 2006, 2007, 2008; Great Minds of the 21st Century (and Dedication Section), 2007, 2008; Deputy Governor, ABIRA, 2007; Cambridge Blue Book (Front Section), 2007; Man of the Year, USA, 2006, 2007; Vice President, Recognition Board, World Congress of Arts, Sciences and Communications, 2007; International Directory of Experts and Expertise, 2006; Honorary Director General, IBC, 2006; Deputy Director General, IBC, 2006; Scientific Advisor to Director General, IBC, 2006; Lifetime Fellowship, International Biographical Association, 2006; Great Lives of the 21st Century, 2007; Dictionary of International Biography, 2006, 2007; Hall of Fame, 2006; 500 Greatest Geniuses of the XXI Century, 2008. Memberships: Brazilian Geophysics Society, 1994; Engineering and Architecture Regional Council, Rio de Janeiro, 1985; Marquis Who's Who, 2006, 2007, 2008, 2009; International Biographical Centre, Honorary Director General, 2006; Deputy Governor, American Biographical Institute, 2006; ABI Order of International Ambassadors, 2007; United Cultural Convention, Ambassador General, 2006; Ambassador, International Order of Merit, 2007. Address: Bandeirantes University - Uniban, PO Box 951, Santa Catarina, Florianópolis, 88010-970, Brazil. E-mail: elihezer@terra.com.br

LOPEZ Jennifer, b. 24 July 1970, Bronx, New York, USA. Actress; Dancer; Singer. m. (1) Ojani Noa, 1997, (2) Cris Judd, 2001, (3) Marc Anthony, 2004, Twins. Appointments: Album: On the 6; J Lo, 2001; J To Tha L-O! This Is Me... Then, 2002; Rebirth, 2005; Como Ama una Mujer, Brave, 2007; Singles: If You Had My Love, Waiting for Tonight, 1999; Feelin' So Good, Let's Get Loud, 2000; Love Don't Cost a Thing, Amor se paga con amor, Play, Ain't It Funny, I'm Real, 2001; I'm Gonna Be Alright, Jenny From the Block, 2002; All I Have, I'm Glad, Reel Me, 2003; Baby I Love You, Shall We Dance? 2004. Film appearances include: My Little Girl, 1996; My Family – Mia Familia, Money Train, 1995; Jack, Blood and Wine, 1996; Anaconda, Selena, U-Turn, 1997; Out of Sight, 1998; Thieves, Pluto Nash, 1999; The Cell, The Wedding Planner, 2000; Angel Eyes, 2001; Enough, Maid in Manhattan, 2002; Gigli, 2003; Jersey Girl, Shall We Dance? 2004; Monster-in-Law, An Unfinished Life, 2005; Border Town, El Cantante, 2006; TV appearances include: Second Chances; Hotel Malibu; Nurses on the Line; The Crash of Flight 7. Honours: Golden Globe, 1998; MTV Movie Award, 1999; Billboard Latin Award for Hot Latin Track of the Year, 2000; MTV Video Music Award for Best Dance Video, 2000; VH1/Vogue Fashion Versace Award, 2000; MTV Europe Music Award for Best Female Act, 2001; MTV Award for Best Female, 2002. Address: International Creative Management, 8942 Wilshire Boulevard, Beverly Hills, CA 90211, USA. Website: www.jenniferlopez.com

LOPEZ GARCIA Angel, b. Madrid, Spain. Telecommunication Engineer. m. Maria Del Mar, 2 daughters. Education: Telecommunication Engineer, ETSIT, Madrid, Spain, 1980-1986. Appointments: Systems Analyst, Siemens S A, 1986-1989; Project Leader, Sener S A, 1989-1991; Project Leader, Indra Sistemas S A, 1991-2005; Senior Consultant, IT Deusto SA, 2005-. Honours: Graduate with honours, Telecommunication Engineering. Address: Caleruega, 73, 28033, Madrid, Spain. E-mail: augellopezgarcia@wanadoo.es

LÓPEZ-COBOS Jesús, b. 25 February 1940, Toro, Spain. Orchestral Conductor. Education: DPhil, Madrid University; Composition, Madrid Conservatory; Conducting, Vienna Academy. Appointments: Worked with major orchestras including London Symphony, Royal Philharmonic, Philharmonia, Concertgebouw, Vienna Philharmonic, Vienna Symphony, Berlin Philharmonic, Hamburg NDR, Munich Philharmonic, Cleveland, Chicago Symphony, New York

Philharmonic, Philadelphia, Pittsburgh; Conducted new opera productions at La Scala, Milan, Covent Garden, London, Metropolitan Opera, New York; General Musikdirektor, Deutsche Oper, Berlin, 1981-90; Principal Guest Conductor, London Philharmonic Orchestra, 1981-86; Principal Guest Conductor, Artistic Director, Spanish National Orchestra, 1984-89; Music Director, Cincinnati Symphony Orchestra, 1986-2000; Music Director, Lausanne Chamber Orchestra, 1990-2000; Orchestre Français des Jeunes, 1998-2001; Music Director, Tetro Real, Madrid, 2003-. Publications: Recordings including: Bruckner symphonies; Haydn symphonies; Donizetti's Lucia di Lammermoor; Rossini's Otello; Recital discs with José Carreras. Honours: 1st Prize, Besançon International Conductors Competition, 1969; Prince of Asturias Award, Spanish Government, 1981; Founders Award, American Society of Composers, Authors and Publishers, 1988; Cross of Merit, 1st Class, Federal Republic of Germany, 1989. Address: c/o Terry Harrison Artists, The Orchard, Market Street, Charlbury, Oxon OX7 3PJ, England.

LOPUSZANSKI Jan (Tadeusz), b. 21 October 1923, Lwów (Leopol), Poland. Theoretical Physicist. m. (1) Halina Pidek, (2) Barbara Zaslonka, 1 son. Education: MA, University Wroclaw, Poland, 1950; PhD, Jagellonian University, Cracow, Poland, 1955. Appointments: Assistant to Associate Professor, University of Wroclaw, 1947-68, Full Professor, 1968-95, Retired, 1995; Vice Dean, Mathematics, Physics and Chemistry Faculty, University of Wroclaw, 1957-58, Dean, 1962-64; Visiting Professor, University of Utrecht, 1958, NYU, 1960-61; Institute for Advanced Study, Princeton, 1964-65, SUNY, Stony Brook, 1970-71, University of Göttingen, 1984, 1991-92; Director, Institute of Theoretical Physics, University of Wroclaw, 1970-84. Publications: Books: Fizyka Statystyczna, 1969 (Coll A Pawlikowski) An Introduction to the Conventional Quantum Field Theory, 1976; Rachunek Spinorow, 1985; An Introduction to Symmetry and Supersymmetry in Quantum Field Theory, 1991; The Inverse Variational Problem in Classical Mechanics, 1999; Over 100 articles in professional journals. Honours: Member, Editorial Board, Reports on Mathematical Physics and Fortschritte der Physik; Recipient: Chevalry Cross Order Polonia Restituta, 1965; Officer Cross OPR, 1991; Member, Polish Academy of Sciences, correspondent, 1976-86, permanent, 1986-; Polish Academy of Arts and Sciences, Cracow, correspondent, 1996-; Celebration of the 50th anniversary of the PhD, Jagellonian University, 2005. Memberships: Polish Physics Society; Association of Members of the Institute for Advanced Study in Princeton; International Association of Mathematical Physics; International Union of Pure and Applied Physics. Address: Institute of Theoretical Physics, University of Wroclaw Pl Max Born 9, 50204 Wroclaw, Poland. E-mail: lopus@ift.uni.wroc.pl

LOREN Sophia, b. 20 September 1934, Rome, Italy. Actress. m. Carlo Ponti, 1957 (marriage annulled 1962) m. Carlo Ponti 1966-2007 (deceased), 2 sons. Education: Scuole Magistrali Superiori. Appointments: First Screen Appearance, as an extra in Quo Vadis; Appeared in many Italian and other Films including: E Arrivato l'Accordatore, 1951; Africa sotto i Mari (first leading role); La Tratta delle Bianche, La Favorita, 1952; Aida, Il Paesedei Campanelli, Miseria e Nobilta, Il Segno di Venere, Tempi Nostri, Carosello Napoletano, 1953; L'Oro di Napoli, Attila, 1954; Peccatoche sia una canaglia, la Bella Mugnaia, La Donna del Fiume, 1955; Boccaccio, 1970; Matromonio All; Italiana; American Films include: The Pride and the Passion, 1955; Boy on a Dolphin, Legend of the Lost, 1956; Desire Under the Elms, 1957; That Kind of Woman, Houseboat, The Key, 1958; The Black Orchid, 1959;

The Millionairess, Two Women, El Cid, 1961; Yesterday, Today and Tomorrow, 1963; The Fall of the Roman Empire, 1964; Lady L, Judith, A Countess from Hong Kong, 1965; Arabesque, 1966; More than a Miracle, 1967; The Priest's Wife, Sunflower, 1970; Man of La Mancha, 1972; Brief Encounter, (TV), The Verdict, 1974; The Cassandra Crossing, A Special Day, 1977; Firepower, 1978; Brass Target, 1979; Blood Feud, 1981; Mother Courage, 1986; Two Women, 1989; Pret a Porter, Grumpier Old Men, 1995; Soliel, 1997; Francesca e Nunziata (TV), 2001; Between Strangers, 2002; Lives of the Saints (TV), Peperoni ripienie pesci in faccia, 2004. Memberships: Chair, National Alliance for Prevention and Treatment of Child Abuse and Maltreatment. Publications: Eat with Me, 1972; Sophia Loren on Women and Beauty, 1984. Honours: Venice Festival Award for the Black Orchid, 1958; Cannes Film Festival Award for Best Actress, 1961; Honorary Academy Award, 1991; Chevalier Legion d'Honneur; Goodwill Ambassador for Refugees, 1992. Address: Chalet Daniel, Burgenstock, Luzern, Switzerland.

LOTFY Michael Wasef, b. 12 August 1960, Cairo, Egypt. President, Better Egypt for Educational Services. m. Hala Aziz Rizkalla, 1 son. Education: BS, Commerce, 1981, Certificate of Completion, Computer Science, Faculty of Science, 1981, Ain Shams University; Certificate of Participation, European Community's Private Sector Development Program, 1998. Appointments: Director, London Business Institute, El Sahafieen and Heliopolis, 1981-90; Vice President, Nozha, Misr El Ghedida Culture Association, 1991-2000; Vice President, Better Egypt for Information Technology, Training and Consultancy, 2000-03; President, Setup Systems, President, Better Egypt for Educational Services, 2003-. Publications: Numerous articles in professional journals. Honours: Certificate of Honor, Egyptian Union of Tourist Chambers and the Chamber of Tourist Premises, 1993; Two Certificates of Honor, Egyptian Union of Tourist Chambers and the Chamber of Tourist Items and Antiques, 1994; Certificate of Honor, Egyptian Union of Tourist Chambers and the Chamber of Tourist Hotels, 2000; Certificate of Honor, Ministry of Tourism, 2003. Memberships: Suez Canal Company for Educational Services; Board of Trustees, October 6 University; Board of Egypt's Company for Consultancy; Board Member, Suez Canal Company for Touristic Transportation. Address: 37, Shahin St, Agouza, Giza 12411, Egypt. E-mail: betteregypt@laycos.com

LOTOREV Alexander Nikolaevich, b. 10 September 1948, Alexandrovka Village, Zolotukhinsky District, Kursk Region, USSR. Public Servant. m. Liubov Lotoreva, 2 sons, 1 daughter. Education: Postgraduate Diplomas, Kursk State Pedagogical Institute and Russian Academy of Public Service; Valid State Adviser of the Russian Federation 1st class. Appointments: Served in the Red Army, 1967-69; Toolmaker and Secretary of the Comsomol Committee, State Steel Bearing Factory, Kursk, 1970-76; Assistant to the Commander of a Company and Commander of a Company, Armed Forces, 1976-78; Director, Technical Training College No 22, Kursk, 1978-82; Deputy Director, Technical Training College, Surgut, Director of the Technical Training College, Nefteyugansk, Autonomous Region of Khanty, 1982-90; Elected Chairman, Executive Committee of the City of Nefteyugansk, 1990-92, Vice-Head, Administration of Nefteyugansk, 1992-; Elected Deputy of the State Duma of Khanty-Mansyisk. 1995, re-elected. 1999; Vice-President of the Deputy Group "Regions of Russia"; State Duma Committee on Power Transport and Communication; State Duma Mandate Committee; Co-ordinator of the deputy group on relations with Turkmenia; Active participant in the Co-ordinations Council of the Centrist Deputy Association

DICTIONARY OF INTERNATIONAL BIOGRAPHY

"Unity", "Fatherland-All Russia" "People's Deputy", "Regions of Russia"; Secretary General (Head of Staff), State Duma of the Federal Assembly, Russian Federation, 2002-. Honours: Honorary PhD, Economics; Medals: 60 Years of the USSR Armed Forces, 1978, In Memory of 850 Years of Moscow, 1997, 300 Years of Saint Petersburg, 2003; Honoured Certificate of the State Duma of the Federal Assembly of the Russian Federation, 2002; Order of Honour, 2003. Address: State Duma of the Federal Assembly of the Russian Federation, Okhotny ryad 1, 103265 Moscow, Russian Federation. E-mail: lotorev@duma.gov.ru

LOUISY Calliopa Pearlette, b. 8 June 1946, St Lucia, West Indies. Governor General. Education: BA, University of the West Indies, 1969; MA, Laval University, 1975; PhD, University of Bristol, 1994. Appointments: Principal, St Lucia A Level College, 1981-86; Dean, 1986-94, Vice Principal, 1994-95, Principal, 1996-97, Sir Arthur Lewis Community College; Governor General, 1997. Publications: The Changing Role of the Small State in Higher Education; Globalisation and Comparative Education: A Caribbean Perspective; Whose Context for What Quality? Informing Eduation Strategies for the Caribbean; Nation Languages and National Development in the Caribbean: Reclaiming Our Own Voices. Honours: Student of the Year, 1968; Grand Cross of the Order of St Lucia, 1997; International Woman of the Year, 1998, 2001; Grand Cross of the Order of St Michael and St George, 1999; Honorary Degree of Doctor of Law (LLD) University of Bristol, 1999 and University of Sheffield, 2003; Dame of Grace of the Most Venerable Order of the Hospital of St John of Jerusalem, 2001; Listed in International Biographical Dictionaries. Membership: Fellow, Royal Society of Arts, 2000. Address: Government House, Morne Fortune, Castries, St Lucia, West Indies. E-mail: govgenslu@candw.lc

LOUKANTCHEVSKY Milen, b. 14 July 1959, Troyan, Bulgaria. Telecom Executive. Education: MS, Computer Engineering, Rousse University, Bulgaria, 1984; PhD, Computer Systems, Kiev Polytechnic Institute, USSR, 1991. Appointments: Lecturer, 1985-93, Senior Lecturer, 1993-, Rousse University; Telecom Executive, Teletronic Ltd, 1998-. Publications: Author, System Programming for Single-Chip Microcontrollers, 1993; Translator, Windows Wisdom for C and C++ Programmers, 1996; Telecommunications - Principles, Technology, 1999. Honours: Listed in international biographical dictionaries. Memberships: IEEE Communications Society; IEEE Computer Society; Association of Computing Machinery. Address: 3 Rodopi Str, PO Box 38, Rousse 7005, Bulgaria. E-mail: mil@ieee.org

LOUSADA Peter Allen, b. 30 March 1937, Amesbury, Wiltshire, England. Businessman. m. Jane Gillmor, 2 sons, 1 daughter. Appointments: Pilot Officer, RAF, National Service, Canada, 1956-58; Advertising and Marketing, Unilever group companies Lintas, Gibbs, 1958-64; Director, Middle East, Bristol-Myers International Inc, Teheran, 1965-69; Vice President, Canada Dry Corporation, including operations in Africa and Europe, 1970-86; Director, Schweppes International, 1986-90; Chairman, Cadbury Schweppes, Portugal, 1988; Supervisory Board Apollinaris and Schweppes, 1988-90; Vice President, Cadbury Beverages Europe, 1986-90, Board of Management, BSDA, 1988-96; Founder Member, International Soft Drinks Council, Washington DC, 1994-95; Director, UNESDA-CISDA, 1988-95, Elected President, Berlin, 1990; Senior Vice President, Cadbury Beverages, 1990-96; Chairman, Faraday Consulting, 1997-2003; Non-Executive Chairman, Canadean Ltd, 1997-2003; Commander, St John Ambulance, 1999-2005, Deputy Lieutenant, 2003-,

Bedfordshire. Memberships: Honorary Member, BSDA; Honorary Member, UNESDA-CISDA; Woburn Golf Club; RAF Club. Address: Well Cottage, Bow Brickhill, Milton Keynes, MK17 9JU, Buckinghamshire, England.

LOVE Courtney, b. 9 July 1964, San Francisco, USA. Singer; Musician (guitar); Actress. m. Kurt Cobain, 24 February 1992-1994, deceased, 1 daughter. Career: Member, Faith No More, 1 year; Founder, singer/guitarist, Hole, 1991-2002; Solo artist, 2003-; Tours include: Support tour to Nine Inch Nails; Reading Festival, 1994, 1995; Film appearances: Straight To Hell; Sid And Nancy; Feeling Minnesota; The People vs Larry Flynt; Man on the Moon; Beat, 2000; Julie Johnson, 2001; Trapped, 2002; Trailer for a Remake of Gore Vidal's Caligula, 2005. Recordings: Albums: Pretty On The Inside, 1991; Live Through This, 1994; Celebrity Skin, 1998; Solo album: America's Sweetheart. Singles: Doll Parts, 1994; Ask for It, 1995; Celebrity Skin, 1998; Malibu, 1998; Awful, 1999; Solo single: Mono, 2004. Address: Q-Prime Inc, 729 Seventh Avenue, 14th Floor, New York, NY 10019, USA. Website: www.courtneylove.com

LOVELL (Alfred Charles) Bernard (Sir), b. 31 August 1913, Oldland Common, Gloucestershire, England. Professor of Radio Astronomy Emeritus; Writer. m. Mary Joyce Chesterman, 1937, deceased 1993, 2 sons, 3 daughters. Education: University of Bristol. Appointments: Professor of Radio Astronomy, 1951-80, Professor Emeritus, 1980-, University of Manchester; Director, Jodrell Bank Experimental Station, later Nuffield Radio Astronomy Laboratories, 1951-81; Various visiting lectureships. Publications: Science and Civilisation, 1939; World Power Resources and Social Development, 1945; Radio Astronomy, 1951; Meteor Astronomy, 1954; The Exploration of Space by Radio, 1957; The Individual and the Universe, 1958; The Exploration of Outer Space, 1961; Discovering the Universe, 1963; Our Present Knowledge of the Universe, 1967; The Explosion of Science: The Physical Universe (editor with T Margerison), 1967; The Story of Jodrell Bank, 1968; The Origins and International Economics of Space Exploration, 1973; Out of the Zenith, 1973; Man's Relation to the Universe, 1975; P M S Blackett: A Biographical Memoir, 1976; In the Centre of Immensities, 1978; Emerging Cosmology, 1981; The Jodrell Bank Telescopes, 1985; Voice of the Universe, 1987; Pathways to the Universe (with Sir Francis Graham Smith), 1988; Astronomer By Chance (autobiography), 1990; Echoes of War, 1991; The Effect of Science on the Second World War, 2000. Contributions to: Professional journals. Honours: Officer of the Order of the British Empire, 1946; Duddell Medal, 1954; Royal Medal, 1960; Knighted, 1961; Ordre du Mérite pour la Recherche et l'Invention, 1962; Churchill Gold Medal, 1964; Gold Medal, Royal Astronomical Society, 1981; Many honorary doctorates. Memberships: American Academy of Arts and Sciences, honorary foreign member; American Philosophical Society; International Astronomical Union, vice-president, 1970-76; New York Academy; Royal Astronomical Society, president, 1969-71; Royal Society, fellow; Royal Swedish Academy, honorary member. Address: The Quinta, Swettenham, Cheshire CW12 2LD, England.

LOVELL Mary Sybilla, b. 1941, Prestatyn, North Wales. Writer. m. (2) Geoffrey A H Watts, 1991, 1 son, 2 stepsons, 2 stepdaughters. Publications: Hunting Pageant, 1980; Cats as Pets, 1982; Boys Book of Boats, 1983; Straight on till Morning, 1987; The Splendid Outcast, 1988; The Sound of Wings, 1989; Cast No Shadow, 1991; A Scandalous Life, 1995; The Rebel Heart, 1996; A Rage to Live, 1998; The Mitford Sisters, 2001; Bess of Hardwick, 2005. Contributions to: Many technical articles on the subjects of accounting and software. Memberships: Society of Authors; R S Surtees Society, vice president, 1980-; Fellow, Royal Geographical Society. Address: c/o Louise Ducas (Literary Agent), The Barn House, 244 Westside Road, Norfolk CT 06058, USA.

LOVESEY Peter, (Peter Lear), b. 10 September 1936, Whitton, Middlesex, England. Writer. m. Jacqueline Ruth Lewis, 30 May 1959, 1 son, 1 daughter. Education: BA, Honours, English, University of Reading, 1958. Publications: The Kings of Distance, 1968; Wobble to Death, 1970; The Detective Wore Silk Drawers, 1971; Abracadaver, 1972; Mad Hatters Holiday, 1973; Invitation to a Dynamite Party, 1974; A Case of Spirits, 1975; Swing, Swing Together, 1976; Goldengirl, 1977; Waxwork, 1978; Official Centenary History of the Amateur Athletic Association, 1979; Spider Girl, 1980; The False Inspector Dew, 1982; Keystone, 1983; Butchers (short stories), 1985; The Secret of Spandau, 1986; Rough Cider, 1986; Bertie and the Tinman, 1987; On the Edge, 1989; Bertie and the Seven Bodies, 1990; The Last Detective, 1991; Diamond Solitaire, 1992; Bertie and the Crime of Passion, 1993; The Crime of Miss Oyster Brown (short stories), 1994; The Summons, 1995; Bloodhounds, 1996; Upon a Dark Night, 1997; Do Not Exceed the Stated Dose (short stories), 1998; The Vault, 1999; The Reaper, 2000; Diamond Dust, 2002; The Sedgemoor Strangler (short stories), 2002; The House Sitter, 2003; The Circle, 2005; The Secret Hangman, 2007. Honours: Macmillan/Panther 1st Crime Novel Award, 1970; Crime Writers Association Silver Dagger, 1978, 1995, 1996 and Gold Dagger, 1982 and Cartier Diamond Dagger, 2000; Grand Prix de Littérature Policière, 1985; Prix du Roman D'Aventures, 1987; Anthony Award, 1992; Macavity Award 1997, 2004. Memberships: Crime Writers Association, chairman, 1991-92; Detection Club; Society of Authors. Address: 59 Crescent Road, Leigh-on-Sea, Essex SS9 2PF, England.

LOWE Gordon, b. 31 May 1933, Halifax, England. University Professor. m. Gwynneth Hunter, 2 sons. Education: BSc, ARCS, 1954, PhD, DIC, 1957, Royal College of Science, Imperial College, London University; MA, Oxford University, 1960. Appointments: University Demonstrator, 1959-65, Weir Junior Research Fellow, University College, 1959-61, Official Fellow, Tutor in Organic Chemistry, Lincoln College, 1962-99, University Lecturer, 1965-88, Sub-Rector, Lincoln College, 1986-89, Aldrichian Praelector in Chemistry, 1988-89, Professor of Biological Chemistry, 1989-2000, Emeritus Professor of Biological Chemistry, Supernumerary Fellow, 2000-, Oxford University; Director, Founder, Scientific Consultant, Pharminox Ltd, 2002-. Publications: Around 240 articles in learned journals. Honours: CChem, FRSC, 1981; Charmian Medal for Enzyme Chemistry, Royal Society of Chemistry, 1983; FRS, 1984; DSc, Oxon, 1985; Royal Society of Chemistry Award for Stereochemistry, 1992. Memberships: Fellow, Royal Society, London; Fellow, Royal Society of Chemistry, London. Address: 17 Norman Avenue, Abingdon, Oxfordshire, OX14 2HQ, England. E-mail: gordon.lowe@chem.ox.ac.uk

LOWE Robert Helper, b. 17 March 1964, Virginia, USA. Actor. m. Sheryl Berkoff, 1991, 2 sons. TV: A New Kind of Family, 1979; The West Wing, 1999-2006; Jane Doe, 2001; Framed, 2002; The Christmas Shoes, 2002; The Lyon's Den, 2003; Salem's Lot, 2004; Perfect Strangers, 2004; Beach Girls, 2005; The Christmas Blessing, 2005; Brothers and Sisters, 2006-08; Dr Vegas, 2004-06; A Perfect Day, 2006; Family Guy, 2007; Stir of Echoes: The Homecoming, 2007; Film: The Outsiders, 1983; St. Elmo's Fire, 1985; About Last

Night, 1986; Wayne's World, 1992; Austin Powers: The Spy Who Shagged Me, 1999; Under Presure, 2000; The Specials, 2000; Proximity, 2001; Austin Powers in Goldmember, 2002; View from the Top, 2003; Thank You for Smoking, 2005.

LOWNIE Andrew (James Hamilton), b. 11 November 1961, Kenya. Literary Agent; Writer; Editor. m. Angela Doyle, 2 May 1998, 1 son, 1 daughter. Education: Magdalene College, Cambridge, 1981-84; BA, Cantab; MA, Cantab; MSc, University of Edinburgh, 1989. Appointments: Agent, 1985-86, Director, 1986-88, John Farquharson Literary Agents; Director, Andrew Lownie Associates, 1988-; Partner, Denniston and Lownie, 1991-93; Director, Thistle Publishing, 1996-. Publications: North American Spies, 1992; Edinburgh Literary Guide, 1992; John Buchan: The Presbyterian Cavalier, 1995; John Buchan's Collected Poems (editor), 1996; The Complete Short Stories of John Buchan, Vols 1 - 3 (editor), 1997-98; The Literary Companion to Edinburgh, 2000; The Edinburgh Literary Companion, 2005; Contributions to: Books and periodicals. Honour: English Speaking Union Scholarship, 1979-80. Memberships: Association of Authors' Agents; Society of Authors; Secretary, The Biographer's Club, 1998-; Executive Committee, PEN, 2000. Address: 36 Great Smith Street, London, SW18 3BU, England.

LOWRY John Christopher, b. 6 June 1942, Timperley, Cheshire, England. Consultant Surgeon. m. Valerie Joyce Smethurst, 1 son, 1 daughter. Education: BDS, 1963; MB ChB, 1970, University of Manchester; FDSRCS (Eng), 1968; FRCS (Ed), 1984; MHSM (OU), 1994; FDSRCS (Ed), Ad Ho, 1999; FRCS (Eng) by election, 2002; FFGDP (UK) Ad Eund, 2005. Appointments: House Officer, Senior House Officer, University of Manchester, Manchester Royal Infirmary, 1963-65; Registrar, Plastic and Maxillofacial Unit, Bradford, 1965-67; House Officer, Professorial Surgical and Medical Units, University Hospital South Manchester, Senior House Officer in Surgery, University Hospital South Manchester, 1970-72; Senior Registrar, North West Region, 1972-76; Consultant Maxillofacial and Oral Surgeon, Royal Bolton Hospital, 1976-; Part-time Lecturer in Biological Sciences, University of Manchester, 1976-2000; Visiting Professor of Surgery, University of Central Lancashire, 2004-; Chairman, Cosmetic Surgery Interspeciality Committee, Senate of Surgery of Great Britain & Ireland, 2005-. Publications: Maxillofacial Trauma; Economics of Healthcare Delivery; Salivary Disease; Telemedicine. Honours: Honorary Member, Hungarian Association for Maxillofacial Surgery; Honorary Fellow, American Association for Oral and Maxillofacial Surgery; Honorary Member, Croatian Society for Maxillofacial, Plastic and Reconstructive Head and Neck Surgery; Down Surgical Prize, British Association for Oral and Maxillofacial Surgery; Tomes Medal, British Dental Association; CBE, 2003; Golyer Gold Medal, Royal College of Surgeons of England, 2006; Doctor Honoris Causa, University of Iasi, Romania, 2006; Honorary Assistant Professor, University of Bucharest, Romania, 2007; FRCA by Election, 2007. Memberships: European Association for Cranio-Maxillo-Facial Surgery, Secretary General, 1998-; British Association of Oral and Maxillofacial Surgeons, Honorary Secretary, 1989-92, President, 2001; Manchester Medical Society, President, 2004-2005; Royal College of Surgeons (Eng), Dean of Faculty, 2001-2004, Member of Council, 2001-, Examiner Surgical Royal Colleges of UK and Ireland, 1996-2001. Address: The Valley House, 50 Ravens Wood, Heaton, Bolton BL1 5TL, England. E-mail: johnlowry1@btinternet.com

LOYD Francis Alfred (Sir), b. 5 September 1916, Berkhamsted, England. Colonial Service Officer. m. (1) Katharine Layzell, deceased 1981, 2 daughters, (2) Monica Murray Brown. Education: Trinity College, Oxford, England. Appointments: Appointed to Colonial Service, 1938; District Officer, Kenya, 1939; Military Service, East Africa, 1940-42; Private Secretary to Governor of Kenya, 1942-45; District and Provincial Commissioner, 1945-62; Commonwealth Fund Fellowship to USA, 1953-54; Permanent Secretary, Governor's Office, 1962-63; H.M. Commissioner for Swaziland, 1964-68; Director, London House for Overseas Graduates, 1969-79; Chairman, Oxfam Africa Committee, 1979-85. Honours: MBE, 1951; OBE, 1954; CMG, 1961; KCMG, 1965. Memberships: Vincent's Club (Oxford). Address: 53 Park Road, Aldeburgh, Suffolk IP15 5EN, England.

LU Jiqiang, b. 23 September 1977, China. Computer Scientist. m. Xiao Yan Yan. Education: BSc, Applied Mathematics, Yantai University, China, 2000; M Eng, Information and Communication Engineering, Xidian University, 2003; PhD, Information Security Group, Royal Holloway, University of London, 2008. Appointments: Government Officer, Intellectual Property Office, Department of Science and Technology, Government of Shandong Province, China, 2003; Research Assistant, Information Security, Information and Communication University, South Korea, 2003-04; Visual C++ Software Engineer, Network Security Products, ONETS Wireless & Internet Security Tech Co Ltd, China, 2004-05; Visual C++ Software Engineer, Network Security Products, The Beijing R&D Institute, Huawei Technologies Co Ltd, China, 2005. Publications: Numerous articles in professional journals. Honours: Prize, Associated Mathematical Contest of National High School Students, Chinese Mathematical Society, 1995; Prize, Mathematical Contest in Modeling of National College Students, Chinese Mathematical Society, 1999; Distinguished Graduate, Yantai University, 2000; Distinguished Postgraduate Student, Xidian University, 2002; Best Master Thesis Prize, Xidian University, 2003; British Chevening/Royal Holloway Scholarship, 2005-08. Address: Information Security Group, Royal Holloway, University of London, Egham, Surrey, TW20 0EX, England. E-mail: lvjiqiang@hotmail.com

LU Li Ying, b. 18 March 1951, Taipei City, Taiwan. Chinese Medicine. Education: BCh MD, Chinese Medical College, Hong Kong, 2004. Appointments: Associated Professor, Physician Course, American Naturopathic Association, Taiwan Branch. Publications: Homeopathic Clinical Trial for the Myopia of the Elementary Schoolchildren; Acupuncture Treatment for the Sciatic Patients. Honours: Kaz-Mo Medical Medal, Health for Society, Taiwan. Memberships: Life Member, Hong Kong Chinese Medical Association; Life Fellowship, British Institute of Homeopathy, 2007.

LUBAG Leandro Sapinoso, b. 14 May 1957, Malolos, Bulacan, Philippines. Electrical Engineer. m. Cristina P Yuvienco, 2 daughters. Education: BS, Electrical Engineering, Mapua Institute of Technology, Manila, 1979. Appointments: Senior Electrical Engineer, KEO International Consultants, Qatar; Senior Building Services Engineer, Taiwan High Speed Rail Corporation, Taiwan; Systems Co-ordination Engineer, Kowloon-Canton Railway Corporation, Hong Kong; Construction Engineer, Airport Authority, Hong Kong; Senior Building Services Engineer, Slipform Engineering Ltd, Hong Kong. Honours: Listed in international biographical dictionaries. Memberships: Institution of Electrical Engineers, London; Institution of Engineering and Technology, London; United Service Lodge No 1341, EC.

LUCAS George, b. 14 May 1944, Modesto, California, USA. Film Director. M. Marcia 1969-1983 (divorced). Education: University of South California. Appointments: Warner Brothers Studio; Assistant to Francis Ford Cappola, The Rain People; Director, Documentary on making The Rain People; Formed, Lucasfilm Ltd; Director, Co-Author, Screenplay Films THX-1138, 1970; American Graffiti, 1973; Director, Author, Star Wars, 1977; Director, Author, To Prequel The Phantom Menace, 1999; Executive Producer, More American Graffiti, 1979; The Empire Strikes Back, 1980; Raiders of the Lost Ark, 1981; Return of the Jedi, 1982; Indiana Jones and the Temple of Doom, 1984; Howard the Duck, 1986; Labyrinth, 1988; Willow, 1988; Tucker: The Man and His Dream, 1988; Co-Executive Producer, Mishima, 1985; Indiana Jones and the Last Crusade, 1989; Star Wars Episode I: The Phantom Menace, 1999; Star Wars Episode II: Attack of the Clones, 2002; Star Wars Episode III: Revenge of the Sith, 2005; The Adventures of Young Indiana Jones Documentaries, 2007. Executive Producer, The Young Indiana Jones Chronicles (TV series), 1992-93; Radioland Murders, 1994. Honours: Dr hc, University of South California, 1994; Irving Thalberg Award, 1992. Address: Lucasfilm Ltd, P O Box 2009, San Rafael, CA 94912, USA.

LUCAS John (Randolph), b. 18 June 1929, England. Philosopher; Writer. m. Morar Portal, 1961, 2 sons, 2 daughters. Education: St Mary's College, Winchester; MA, Balliol College, Oxford, 1952. Appointments: Junior Research Fellow, 1953-56, Fellow and Tutor, 1960-96, Merton College, Oxford; Fellow and Assistant Tutor, Corpus Christi College, Cambridge, 1956-59; Jane Eliza Procter Visiting Fellow, Princeton University, 1957-58; Leverhulme Research Fellow, Leeds University, 1959-60; Gifford Lecturer, University of Edinburgh, 1971-73; Margaret Harris Lecturer, University of Dundee, 1981; Harry Jelema Lecturer, Calvin College, Grand Rapids, 1987; Reader in Philosophy, Oxford University, 1990-96. Publications: Principles of Politics, 1966, 2nd edition, 1985; The Concept of Probability, 1970; The Freedom of the Will, 1970; The Nature of Mind, 1972; The Development of Mind, 1973; A Treatise on Time and Space, 1973; Essays on Freedom and Grace, 1976; Democracy and Participation, 1976; On Justice, 1980; Space, Time and Causality, 1985; The Future, 1989; Spacetime and Electromagnetism, 1990; Responsibility, 1993; Ethical Economics, 1996; The Conceptual Roots of Mathematics, 1999; An Engagement with Plato's Republic, 2003; Reason and Reality, 2006; Contributions to scholarly journals. Memberships: British Academy, Fellow; British Society for the Philosophy of Science, president, 1991-93. Address: Lambrook House, East Lambrook, Somerset TA13 5HW, England. Website: http://users.ox.ac.uk/~jrlucas

LUCKMAN Steven Paul, b. 3 July 1973, Walsall, England. Research Scientist. Education: BSc, Biochemistry, University of York, 1995; PhD, University of Sheffield Medical School and University of Aberdeen, 1999. Appointments: Postdoctoral studies, Connective Tissue Biology Labs, University of Cardiff School of Biosciences, Cardiff, 1999-2002; Postdoctoral studies, Institute of Clinical Medicine, Section for Neurology, Haukeland University Hospital, Bergen, Norway, 2002-. Publications: Numerous highly cited papers and articles in professional scientific journals. Honours: JBMR Anniversary Classic Paper, 2005; Listed in international biographical dictionaries. E-mail: stevel_37@hotmail.com

LUGTON Charles Michael Arber, b. 5 April 1951, Johannesburg, South Africa. Government Civil Servant. m. Elizabeth Joyce Graham, 2 sons. Education: St John's College, Johannesburg; The Edinburgh Academy; University of Edinburgh. Appointments: Private Secretary to Permanent Under Secretary of State, Scottish Office, 1976-78; Head of Branch, Police Division, 1978-83; Head of Town and Country Planning Policy Branch, 1983-87; Head of Public Health Division, 1988-90; Head of Criminal Justice and Licensing Division, Scottish Home and Health Department, 1990-95; Principal Private Secretary to the Secretary of State for Scotland, 1995-97; Director of Corporate Development, 1998-99; Head of Constitution and Parliamentary Secretariat, Scottish Executive, 1999-2004; Head of Constitution and Legal Services Group, 2004-. Memberships: Governor, Merchiston Castle School, Edinburgh; Board Member, Civil Service Healthcare Society Limited. Address: Scottish Executive, Victoria Quay, Edinburgh EH6 6QQ, Scotland. E-mail: michael.lugton@scotland.gsi.gov.uk

LUKE William Ross, b. 8 October 1943, Glasgow, Scotland. Chartered Accountant. m. Deborah Jacqueline Gordon Luke, 3 daughters, 1 deceased. Appointment: Senior Partner, Luke, Gordon & Co, Chartered Accountants, 1983-. Honours: Metropolitan Police Commendation, 1983; Life Vice-President, London Scottish Rugby Football Club, 1995-. Memberships: Fellow, Institute of Chartered Accountants in England and Wales; Member, London Scottish Rugby Football Club; Member, Caledonian Society of London; Qualified Sub-Aqua Advanced Open Water Diver (PADI). Address: 105 Palewell Park, London SW14 8JJ, England.

LUKOSEVICIUS Viktoras, b. 9 August 1939, Kaunas, Lithuania. University Teacher. m. Emilija Lukoseviciene, 2 sons. Education: Diploma Engineer of Geodesy, Kaunas Polytechnical Institute, Lithuania, 1962; PhD, Engineering, Institute of Surveying, Aerial Photography and Cartography, Moscow, 1966; Associate Professor, Kaunas Polytechnical Institute, 1970. Appointments: Head of Basic Science Department, 1967-70, Head of Civil Engineering Department, 1970-81, KPI; Vice Dean and Associate Professor, Panevezys Faculty, Kaunas University of Technology, 1981-87, Head of Civil Engineering Department, Associate Professor and Faculty Council Chair of Panevezys Campus, Kaunas University of Technology, 1988-2001; Head of Civil Engineering Department, Associate Professor of Panevezys Institute, KTU, 2002-. Publications include: Books: Over 60 scientific articles; Participant in conferences in USA, Brazil, Sweden, Norway, Russia. Honours: Certificate, Governor of State of Ohio, USA for outstanding contribution of the continued success of the Columbus National Program, 1995; Fellowship Winner, NATO and Italy National Science Competition, 1996. Memberships: Senate Member, Kaunas University of Technology, 1992-2001; Council Member, KTU, Panevezys Institute, Faculty of Technology; International Association for Continuing Engineering Education; Association for the Advancement of Baltic Studies; Council Member, Lithuanian Liberal Society, 1992-2004; Candidate, Lithuanian Republic Parliament, 1992,1996; Board Member, Panevezys Department, Lithuanian Scientists Union; President, Panevezys Lithuanian and Swedes Society. Address: Statybininku 56-66, Lt 37348 Panevezys, Lithuania.

LUMB William V, b. 26 November 1921, Sioux City, Iowa, USA. University Professor. m. Lilly I Carlson, 25 June 1949, 1 son. Education: DVM, Kansas State University, 1943; MSc, Texas A&M University, 1953 Graduate Studies, 1952-54, PhD, 1957, University of Minnesota; Doctor of Science

(Honorary), The Ohio State University, 1999. Appointments: Us Army Veterinary Corps, 1943-46; Intern, Resident, Angell Memorial Animal Hospital, Boston, 1946-48; Assistant and Associate Professor, Texas A&M University, 1949-52; Associate Professor, Department of Clinics and Surgery, 1954-58, Colorado State University; Associate Professor, Department of Surgery and Medicine, Michigan State University, 1958-60; Associate Professor, Department of Medicine, 1960-63, Professor and Director of Surgical Laboratory, Department of Clinical Sciences, College of Veterinary Medicine and Biomedical Sciences, 1963-82, Colorado State University; Professor Emeritus, Colorado State University, 1982; Professor, Ross University, St Kitts, West Indies, 1986; President and Chief Executive Officer, The Lubra Company, 1972-99. Publications: Numerous articles in professional journals; Books: Small Animal Anesthesia, 1963; Veterinary Anesthesia (co-author), 1979, 2nd edition, 1984; Book chapters, papers, films; 2 patents. Honours include: The Gaines Medal, 1965; Ralston Purina Award, 1980; Colorado Veterinarian of the Year, 1981; Distinguished Service Award, Veterinary Medicine, Kansas State University, 1982; American College of Veterinary Anesthesiologists, Service Award, 1982; Jacob Markowitz Award, Academy of Surgical Research, 1987; Phi Zeta; Gamma Sigma Delta; Sigma Xi; Glover Distinguished Faculty Award, 2004, Colorado State University. Memberships include: President and Chairman of the Board, American College of Veterinary Surgeons, 1974-75; Founding Diplomate, American College of Veterinary Anesthesiologists; American Veterinary Medical Association; American Animal Hospital Association; Fellow, American Association for the Advancement of Science. Address: 1905 Mohawk Street, Fort Collins, CO 80525-1501, USA.

LUMLEY Joanna, b. 1 May 1946, Kashmir, India. Actress. m. (1) Jeremy Lloyd, divorced, (2) Stephen Barlow, 1 son. Career: TV includes: Release; Comedy Playhouse; Satanic Rites of Dracula, 1973; Coronation Street; General Hospital, 1974-75; The New Avengers, 1976-77; Steptoe & Son; Are You Being Served?; Sapphire & Steel, 1978; Absolutely Fabulous, 1992-94, 1996, 2001; Class Act, 1994; Joanna Lumley in the Kingdom of the Thunder Dragon, 1997; Coming Home, 1998; A Rather English Marriage, 1998; Nancherrow; Dr Willoughby MD; Mirrorball, 1999; Giraffes on the Move, 2001; Up In Town, 2002; Absolutely Fabulous Special, 2002; Marple, 2004; Sensitive Skin, 2005, 2nd series, 2007; Jam and Jerusalem, 2006; The Friday Night Project, 2007; Films include: Some Girls Do; Tam Lin; The Breaking of Bumbo; Games That Lovers Play; Don't Just Lie There, Say Something; On Her Majesty's Secret Service; Trail of the Pink Panther; Curse of the Pink Panther; That Was Tory; Mistral's Daughter; A Ghost in Monte Carlo; Shirley Valentine; Forces Sweetheart; Innocent Lies; James and the Giant Peach; Cold Comfort Farm; Prince Valiant; Parting Shots; Mad Cows; Maybe Baby; The Cat's Meow; Ella Enchanted; Eurotrip, 2004; The Magic Roundabout (voice), 2005; The Corpse Bride (voice), 2005; Dolls, 2006; The Audition, 2006; Theatre includes: Blithe Spirit, 1986; Vanilla, 1990; The Letter, 1995; all in London. Publications: Stare Back and Smile, memoirs, 1989; Girl Friday, 1994; Joanna Lumley in the Kingdom of the Thunder Dragon, 1997; No Room for Secrets (autobiography), 2004. Honours: OBE; Hon DLitt, Kent, 1994; D University, Oxford Brookes, 2000; BAFTA Award, 1992, 1994; Special BAFTA, 2000. Address: c/o Caroline Renton, 23 Crescent Lane, London SW4, England.

LUMSDEN David (James) (Sir), b. 19 March 1928, Newcastle upon Tyne, England. Musician. m. Sheila Gladys Daniels, 28 July 1951, 2 sons, 2 daughters. Education: Selwyn

College, Cambridge; MA, 1955; DPhil, 1957. Career: Fellow, Organist at New College Oxford; Rector, chori, Southwell Minster; Founder and Conductor of Nottingham Bach Society; Director of Music, Keele University; Visiting Professor at Yale University; Principal: Royal Scottish Academy of Music and Drama and Royal Academy of Music, London; Hugh Porter Lecturer at Union Theological Seminary, New York, 1967; Director, European Union Baroque Orchestra, 1985-. Publications: An Anthology of English Lute Music, 1954; Thomas Robinson's Schoole Musike 1603, 1971. Contributions to: The Listener; The Score; Music and Letters; Galpin Society Journal; La Luth et sa Musique; La musique de la Renaissance. Honours: Knight, 1985; Honorary Fellow, Selwyn College, Cambridge, 1986; Honorary DLitt, Reading, 1990; Honorary Fellow of Kings College, London, 1991; Honorary Fellow, New College, Oxford, 1996. Memberships: Incorporated Society of Musicians, President, 1984-85; Royal College of Organists, President, 1986-88; Incorporated Association of Organists, President, 1966-68; Honorary Editor, Church Music Society, 1970-73; Chairman, National Youth Orchestra of Great Britain, 1985-94; Chairman, Early Music Society, 1985-89; Board, Scottish Opera, 1977-83; Board, ENO, 1983-88. Address: Melton House, Soham, Cambridgeshire CB7 5DB, England.

LUNAN (Charles) Burnett, b. 28 September 1941, London, England. Medical Practitioner. m. Helen Russell Ferrie, 2 sons, 1 daughter. Education: MB ChB, 1965, MD, 1977, University of Glasgow. Appointments: Research Fellow, MRC Unit, Strathclyde University, UK, 1971-72; Lecturer, University of Aberdeen, UK, 1973-75; Senior Lecturer, University of Nairobi, Kenya, 1975-77; Consultant Obstetrician, Gynaecologist, North Glasgow University NHS Trust, 1977-; Consultant to WHO, Bangladesh, 1984-85; Short term Consultant to WHO, ODA, Bangladesh, 1988-94. Publications: Various chapters and articles on female sterilisation, infection in pregnancy, diabetes in pregnancy, Caesarean section, health care in the developing world. Honours: MRCOG, 1970, FRCOG, 1983, Royal College of Obstetricians and Gynaecologists, London; FRCS, 1985, Royal College of Physicians and Surgeons of Glasgow. Memberships: Secretary, 1978-82, Vice President, 1998-2002, President, 2002-, Glasgow Obstetrical and Gynaecological Society; Treasurer, 1982-90, Vice President, 1990-91, President, 1991-92, Royal Medico-Chirurgical Society of Glasgow. Address: Princess Royal Maternity, 16 Alexandra Parade, Glasgow G31 2ER, Scotland.

LUNDGREN Dolph, b. 3 November 1959, Stockholm, Sweden. Actor. Education: Washington State University; Massachusetts Institute of Technology; Royal Institute of Technology, Sweden. Career: Doorman, Limelight disco, New York; Films include: A View to a Kill; Rocky IV; Masters of the Universe; Red Scorpion; The Punisher; I Come in Peace; The Eleventh Station; Dark Angel; Showdown in Little Tokyo; Universal Soldier; The Joshua Tree; Meltdown; Army of One; Johnny Mnemonic; The Shooter; The Algonquin Goodbye; The Peacekeeper, 1997; The Minion; Sweepers, 1999; Storm Catcher, 1999; Bridge of Dragons, 1999; The Last Patrol, 2000; The Last Warrior, 2000; Agent Red, 2001; Hidden Agenda, 2001; Detention, 2003; Direct Action, 2004; Fat Slags, 2004; Retrograde, 2004; The Defender, 2004; The Mechanik, 2005; Diamond Dogs, 2007; Missionary Man, 2007.

LUO Zhi-Shan, b. 20 August 1936, Da-pu, Guangdong, China. Teacher; Researcher of Mechanics. m. Wang Xiu-Yin, 2 sons. Education: Graduate, Tianjin University, China, 1958. Appointments: Assistant, 1958-79, Lecturer, 1979-85,

Associate Professor, 1986-93, Director, Laboratory of Mechanics, 1984-85; Director, Teaching and Research Section, 1985-86, Professor of Mechanics, 1993-, Tianjin University; Visiting Professor, Mechanical Engineering, University of Hong Kong, 1992; Technical Consultant, Shanton Jingyi Machinery Co, Shanton, China, 1992-94, Hong Kong Press Publications, 1996-97; Chief Engineer, Director of Research, Tianjin Xingu Intelligent Optical Measuring Technique Company, 2000-02; Civil Engineering Inspect and Determine Institute Board of Tianjin University, 2002-; Member, ABI Research Board of Advisors, 2004-; Chief Expert, Enterprise Development Research Center Expert Committee, Chine Management Science Institute, 2006-. Publications: The Principle and Application of Sticking Film Moire Interferometry; Ultra-high Sensitivity Moiré Interferometry for Subdynamic Tests in Normal Light Environment; Research of Instrumentation and Intellectualization for Moiré Interferometry; Ultra-High Sensitivity Moiré Interferometry by the Aid of Electronic-liquid Phase Shifter and Computer; Moiré Interferometer of Intelligent Mode and Its Application; New Computer Adjusted-and-Processing Moiré Interferometer's Applied Research to Mechanical Property Measure of Concrete; Application of Moiré Interferometry in study for Destructive Mechanism of Concrete; The Advance Instrumentation and its Prospects of Engineering Application for Moiré Interferometry. Honours: Medal of Gold, 2nd Invention Exhibition of China, 1986; Advanced Award of Science and Technology, China Education, 1986, 1997; Medal of Gilding, 15th International Exhibition of Invention and New Technique, Geneva, 1987; National Award of Invention, China, 1987; Award of Invention, Tianjin, China, 1998; Gold Medal, WCC for Promotion of Patent, 2005; Award of Special Grade, 2006; Gold Medal of the Divine Land Personages, 2006; The Golden Title of Nobility Medal of 100 Excellent Personage, 2007; Honor Figure of Harmonius China, Gold Award, 2008; Highest Award of Gold, 2008. Memberships: China Mechanics Society; China Invention Society; Society for Experimental Mechanics, Inc. Address: Department of Mechanics, Tianjin University, Tianjin 300072, China. E-mail: lzstju@sina com.cn

LUPESCU Grigore, b. 30 August 1931, Târgu-Jiu, România. Doctor of Medicine; Specialist in Cardiology. m. Iuliana Popescu, 1 son, 1 daughter. Education: PhD, Medical Sciences, Faculty of General Medicine, Bucharest, 1983. Appointments: Doctor in Medicine, Specialist in Cardiology, Head of Cardiology Department, Târgu-Jiu Hospital; Head of Romanian Medical Association, Gorj County Department, Romania. Publications include: Over 70 papers and abstracts in diverse journals. Honours: Citizen of Honour, Târgu-Jiu Town; Honorary Member, IBC Advisory Council; Member, ABI Research Board of Advisors. Memberships: New York Academy of Sciences; Academy of Medical Sciences of Romania; Mediterranean Society of Cardiology; Balkan Medical Union; Founding Member, Society of Writers and Journalist Doctors of Romania. Address: Str Traian No 3, 210120, Târgu-Jiu, Romania.

LUPU Radu, b. 30 November 1945, Galati, Romania (British citizen). Concert Pianist. Education: Piano lessons at age 6 with Lia Busuioceanu; Subsequent teachers: Florica Muzicescu and Cella Delavrancea; High School, Brasov; Scholarship, Moscow Conservatoire, Russia, 1961-69; Studied with Heinrich Neuhaus and Stanislav Neuhaus. Appointments: Debut at age 12; Plays regularly with leading orchestras and conductors in all major capitals and centres throughout the world; London debut, 1969; Berlin debut, 1971; American debut, in New York with Cleveland

Orchestra and Barenboim, and in Chicago with Chicago Symphony and Giulini, 1972; World Premiere of Andre Tchaikowsky Piano Concerto, London, 1975. Publications: Recording include: Beethoven Piano Concertos; Brahms 1; Schumann; Grieg; Mozart K467; Mozart Double with Murray Perahia; Solo repertoire by Brahms, Beethoven, Schubert and Schumann; Leider with Barbara Hendricks; Piano duets with Daniel Barenboim and Murray Perahia; Chamber Music with Kyung Wha Chung, and Szymon Goldberg. Honours: 1st Prize, Van Cliburn Competition, 1966; Enescu Competition, 1967; Leeds Competition, 1969; Abbiati Prize, 1989, 2006; Edison Award, 1995; Grammy Award, 1995; The Premio Internazionale Arturo Benedetti Michelangeli, 2006. Address: Terry Harrison Artists Management, The Orchard, Market Street, Charlbury, Oxfordshire OX7 3PJ, England. E-mail: artists@harrisonturner.co.uk Website: www.harrisonturner.co.uk

LURIE Alison, b. 3 Sept 1926, Chicago, Illinois, USA. Professor of English; Author. 3 sons. Education: AB, magna cum laude, Radcliffe College, 1947. Appointments: Lecturer, 1969-73, Adjunct Associate Professor, 1973-76, Associate Professor, 1976-79, Professor of English, 1979-, Cornell University. Publications: Love and Friendship, 1962; The Nowhere City, 1965; Imaginary Friends, 1967; Real People, 1969; The War Between the Tates, 1974; V R Lang: Poems and Plays, With a memoir by Alison Lurie, 1975; Only Children, 1979; Clever Gretchen and Other Forgotten Folktales (juvenile), 1980; The Heavenly Zoo (juvenile), 1980; The Language of Clothes (non-fiction), 1981; Fabulous Beasts (juvenile), 1981; Foreign Affairs, 1984; The Truth About Lorin Jones, 1988; Don't Tell the Grownups: Subversive Children's Literature, 1990; Women and Ghosts, 1994; The Last Resort, 1998. Contributions to: Many publications. Honours: Guggenheim Fellowship, 1966-67; Rockefeller Foundation Grant, 1968-69; New York State Cultural Council Foundation Grant, 1972-73; American Academy of Arts and Letters Award, 1984; Pulitzer Prize in Fiction, 1985; Radcliffe College Alumnae Recognition Award, 1987; Prix Femina Etranger, 1989; Parents' Choice Foundation Award, 1996. Literary Agent: Melanie Jackson Inc, 250 W 57th Street, New York 10107. Address: c/o Department of English, Cornell University, Ithaca, NY 14853, USA.

LUSCOMBE Lawrence Edward, b. 10 November 1924, Torquay, England. Anglican Bishop. m. Doris Luscombe, deceased, 1 daughter. Education: Kings College, London, 1963-64; LLD, 1987, MPhil, 1991, PhD, 1993, University of Dundee. Appointments: Indian Army, 1942-47; Chartered Accountant, Partner, Galbraith, Dunlop and Co, later Watson and Galbraith, 1952-63; Rector, St Barnabas, Paisley, 1966-71; Provost of St Paul's Cathedral, Dundee, 1971-75; Bishop of Brechin, 1975-90; Primus of the Scottish Episcopal Church, 1985-90. Publications: The Scottish Episcopal Church in the Twentieth Century; A Seminary of Learning; Matthew Luscombe, Missionary Bishop; The Representative Man. Honours: Chaplain, Order of St John; Honorary Research Fellow, University of Dundee; Honorary Canon, Trinity Cathedral, Davenport, Iowa, USA. Memberships: Institute of Chartered Accountants of Scotland; Society of Antiquaries of Scotland; Royal Society of Arts. Address: Woodville, Kirkton of Tealing, By Dundee, DD4 0RD, Scotland.

LUTTWAK Edward N(icholae), b. 4 November 1942, Arad, Romania (US citizen, 1981). Political Scientist; Author. m. Dalya Iaari, 14 December 1970, 1 son, 1 daughter. Education: Carmel College, England; BSc, London School of Economics and Political Science, 1964; PhD, Johns Hopkins University,

1975. Appointments: Associate Director, Washington Center of Foreign Policy Research, District of Columbia, 1972-75; Visiting Professor of Political Science, Johns Hopkins University, 1973-78; Senior Fellow, 1976-87, Research Professor in International Security Affairs, 1978-82, Arleigh Burke Chair in Strategy, 1987-, Director, Geo-Economics, 1991-, Senior Fellow, 2004, Center for Strategic and International Studies, Washington, DC; Nimitz Lecturer, University of California, Berkeley, 1987; Tanner Lecturer, Yale University, 1989. Publications: A Dictionary of Modern War, 1971, new edition with Stuart Koehl, 1991; The Grand Strategy of the Roman Empire: From the First Century A.D. to the Third, 1976; The Economic and Military Balance Between East and West 1951-1978 (editor with Herbert Block), 1978; Sea Power in the Mediterranean (with R G Weinland), 1979; Strategy and Politics: Collected Essays, 1980; The Grand Strategy of the Soviet Union, 1983; The Pentagon and the Art of War: The Question of Military Reform, 1985; Strategy and History, 1985; On the Meaning of Victory: Essays on Strategy, 1986; Global Security: A Review of Strategic and Economic Issues (editor with Barry M Blechman), 1987; Strategy: The Logic of War and Peace, 1987; The Endangered American Dream: How to Stop the United States from Becoming a Third World Country and How to Win the Geo-Economic Struggle for Industrial Supremacy, 1993; Turbo-Capitalism: Winners and Losers in the Global Economy, 1999; La renaissance de la puissance aerienne stategique, 1999; Che cos'é davvero la democrazia (with Susanna Creperio Verratti); Il Libro delle Liberta, 2000; Strategy Now (editor), 2000; Strategy: The Logic of War and Peace, 2002. Contributions to: Numerous books and periodicals. Address: c/o Center for Strategic and International Studies, Georgetown University, 1800 K Street North West, Washington, DC 20006, USA.

LUX Jonathan Sidney, b. 30 October 1951, London, England. Solicitor. m. Simone, 1 son, 2 daughters. LLB Honours, Nottingham University, 1973; Diplom d'Etudes Superieures, University of Aix-Marseilles, 1974; Solicitor: England and Wales, 1977, Hong Kong, 1986. Appointments: Trainee Solicitor, 1975-77, Solicitor, 1977-83, Partner, London Office, 1983-2001 and 2004-, Managing Partner, Hamburg, Germany, 2001-2003, Ince & Co (international law firm). Publications: Co-author: The Law of Tug, Tow and Pilotage, 1994; The Law and Practice of Marine Insurance and Average, 1996; Alternative Dispute Resolution, 2002; Bunkers, 2004; Corporate Social Responsibility, 2005; Classification Societies, in preparation; Editor: Classification Societies, 1993; Maritime Law Handbook, ongoing. Contributor of articles to professional journals. Honours: University Exhibition, 1972; French Government Scholarship, 1973; Freeman of City of London; Fellow, Chartered Institute of Arbitrators. Memberships: Law Society; Fellow, Chartered Institute of Arbitrators; Accredited Mediator (CEDR, The Academy of Experts, ADR Net); London Maritime Arbitrators Association; German Maritime Arbitrators Association; China Maritime Arbitration Commission; Association of Average Adjusters; Steering Committee, London Shipping Law Centre; Former Chair and current Chair of various Committees, International Bar Association; Athenaeum Club; Arbitrator: CIETAC (China); Hong Kong Arbitration Commission (HKIAC); Sports Disputes Resolution Board (SDRP); International Bunker Industry Association (IBIA). Address: c/o Ince & Co, International House, 1 St Katharine's Way, London E1W 1UN, England. E-mail: jonathan.lux@incelaw.com

LYALL John Adrian, b. 12 December 1949, Thundersley, Essex, England. Architect. m. Sallie Davies, 1 son, 1 daughter. Education: Architectural Association, School of Architecture,

London, 1968-74. Appointments: Partner, Alsop & Lyall, 1979-91; Managing Director, John Lyall Architects, 1991-; Chair and Deputy Chair, 2004-07, RIBA Vice President, RIBA Trust; Council Member, Architectural Association, 2005-; CABE National Design Review Panel, 2007-. Publications: Books: A Guide to Recent Architecture: London, 1993; A Guide to Recent Architecture: England, 1995; Context: New Buildings in Historic Settings, 1998; Architecture 99: The RIBA Awards, 1999; John Lyall: Contexts and Catalysts, 1999; Numerous articles and contributions to professional journals. Honours: RIBA National Awards, 1991, 1999; RIBA White Rose Award, 1991; Leeds Award for Architecture, 1990, 1992; Ironbridge Award, British Archaeological Society, 1990, 1992, 1998; Civic Trust Commendation, 1991; Europa Nostra Award, 1991; British Council of Shopping Centres Award, 1991; Design Week Award, 1991; Aluminium Imagination Award, 1993; RICS Urban Renewal Award, 1995; The Ironbridge Award of Awards, 1998; RIBA Regional Award, 1999; RIBA National Category Award, 1999; Civic Trust Commendation, 2000; Architectural Review/MIPIM Future Projects Award, 2005. Memberships: Architectural Association; Royal Institute of British Architects; Fellow, Royal Society of Arts; Chelsea Arts Club; Committee Member, Stour Valley Arts and Music Society. Address: Newlands, Gandish Road, East Bergholt, Suffolk CO7 6TP, England. E-mail: john.lyall@johnlyallarchitects.com

LYKLEMA Johannes, b. 23 November 1930, Apeldoorn, The Netherlands. Professor. m. 2 children. Education: Studies in Chemistry and Physics, State University of Utrecht, 1948-55; PhD, Utrecht, 1956; Honorary Doctorate, Universite Catholic, Louvain-la-Neuve, Belgium, 1988, Royal Institute of Technology, Stockholm, Sweden, 1997; Universidad de Granada, Spain, 2007. Appointments: Military Service, 1956-58; Science Co-Worker, University of Utrecht, 1958-61; Visiting Associate Professor, University of South California, Los Angeles, USA, 1961-62; Professor, Physical and Colloid Chemistry, Wageningen Agricultural University, 1962-; Visiting Professor, University of Bristol, England, 1971, Australian National University, Canberra, 1976, University of Tokyo, Japan, 1988; Visiting Professor, University of Florida, Gainesville, USA, 1997-. Publications: Over 335 articles in professional journals. Honours: Nightingale Award for Medical Electronics, 1963; Gold Medal, Centre for Marine Research, Ruder Boskovic, Zagreb, 1986; Knight in the Order of the Dutch Lion, 1991; Koninklijke Shell Prize, 1995; Thomas Graham Prize, 1995. Memberships: 90 national and local committees; 105 international. Address: Wageningen University, Department of Physical Chemistry and Colloid Science, De Dreijen 6, 6703 HB Wageningen, The Netherlands.

LYNCH David, b. 20 January 1946, Missoula, Montana, USA. Film Director. m. (1) Peggy Reavey, 1967, divorced, 1 daughter, (2) Mary Fisk, 1977, divorced, 1 son, (3) Mary Sweeney, 2006, 1 child. Education: Hammond High School, Alexandria; Corcoran School of Art, Washington, DC; School of Museum of Fine Arts, Boston; Pennsylvania Academy of Fine Arts, Philadelphia. Appointments: Films include: The Grandmother, 1970; Eraserhead, 1977; The Elephant Man, 1980; Dune, 1984; Blue Velvet, 1986; Wild at Heart, 1990; Storyville, 1991; Twin Peaks; Fire Walk With Me, 1992; Lost Highway, 1997; Crumb, 1999; The Straight Story, 1999; Mullholland Drive, 2001; Darkened Room, 2002; Rabbits, 2002; Dumbland, 2002; Inland Empire, 2006; Boat, 2007. TV includes: Twin Peaks, 1990; Mulholland Drive, 2000. Honours: Fellow, Centre for Advanced Film Study, American Film Institute, Los Angeles, 1970; Dr hc, Royal College of

Art; Golden Palm, Cannes; Stockholm Institute Film Festival Lifetime Achievement Award, 2003; Best Director, Cannes Film Festival, 2001. Address: c/o CAA, 9830 Wilshire Boulevard, Beverly Hills, CA 90212, USA.

LYNCH John, b. 11 January 1927, Boldon, England. Professor Emeritus; Historian. Education: MA, University of Edinburgh, 1952; PhD, University of London, 1955. Appointments: Lecturer in History, University of Liverpool, 1954-61; Lecturer, Reader and Professor of Latin American History, University College, London, 1961-74; Professor of Latin American History and Director of Institute of Latin American Studies, University of London, 1974-87. Publications: Spanish Colonial Administration 1782-1810: The Intendant System in the Viceroyalty of the Río de la Plata, 1958; Spain Under the Habsburgs, 2 volumes, 1964, 1967, 2nd edition, revised, 1981; The Origins of the Latin American Revolutions 1808-1826 (with R A Humphreys), 1965; The Spanish American Revolutions 1808-1826, 1973, 2nd edition, revised, 1986; Argentine Dictator: Juan Manuel de Rosas 1829-1852, 1981; The Cambridge History of Latin America (with others), Vol 3, 1985, Vol 4, 1986; Bourbon Spain 1700-1808, 1989; Caudillos in Spanish America 1800-1850, 1992; Latin American Revolutions 1808-1826: Old and New World Origins, 1994; Massacre in the Pampas, 1872: Britain and Argentina in the Age of Migration, 1998; Latin America between Colony and Nation, 2001; Simón Bolívar: A Life, 2006. Honours: Encomienda Isabel La Católica, Spain, 1988; Doctor, Honoris Causa, University of Seville, 1990; Order of Andres Bello, 1st Class, Venezuela, 1995. Membership: Fellow, Royal Historical Society. Address: 8 Templars Crescent, London N3 3QS, England.

LYNCH John Edward Jr, b. 3 May 1952, Lansing, Michigan, USA. Lawyer. m. Brenda Jayne Clark, 4 sons, 1 daughter. Education: AB, Hamilton College, 1974; JD, Case Western Reserve University, 1977; Appointments: Bar: Connecticut, 1978, Ohio, 1980; US District Court (no. dist), Ohio, 1980, US Court of Appeals (6th Circuit), 1980, Texas, 2000; Associate, Thompson, Weir & Barclay, 1977-78; Law Clerk, US District Judge, Cleveland, 1978-80; Associate, 1980-86, Partner, 1986-96, Squire, Sanders and Dempsey, Cleveland; Vice President, General Counsel, Secretary, Caliber System Inc, Akron, Ohio, 1996-98; Senior Vice-President, General Counsel, BP America Inc, 1998-99; Associate General Counsel, Upstream Western Hemisphere BP, 1999-2002; Associate General Counsel, E&P, GP&R; Global BP plc, London, 2003-06; Group Compliance & Ethics Officer, BP plc, London, 2006-. Address: BP Plc, 1 St James's Square, London SW1Y 4PD, England. E-mail: lynchj@bp.com

LYNCH Timothy Jeremy Mahoney, b. 10 June 1952, San Francisco, California, USA. Lawyer; Classical Scholar; Author; Business Executive. Education: MS, JD, Civil Law, Taxation Law, Golden Gate University; MA, PhD, University of San Francisco, 1983; PhD, Classics, Divinity, Harvard University, 1988; JSD, Constitutional Law, Hastings Law Center, San Francisco; Postdoctoral research, Writing in Classics. Appointments: Chairman, Patristic, Biblical, Latin and Greek Literary Publications Group, Institute of Classical Studies; Chairman, Postdoctoral Research and Writing in Humanities Group, National Association of Scholars; Fellow, Harvard University Center for Hellenic Studies, 1991, 1993; Senior Research and Writing Fellow, Medieval Theological Philosophy manuscripts of St Gallen Monks, Medieval Academy of America; Research Professor, University of California at Berkeley, 1996-99; Graduate Theological Union, 1998-; Senior Fellow, History of Religion Project,

Harvard University, 1998. Publications: History of Europe, 5 volumes, 1987; Essays and Papers on US-Soviet Relations, Iran-British Relations, 1988; Legal Essays, 1990-94; Musical Papers, 1994; History of Classical Tradition, 20 volumes, 1995; Poems for children; Textbooks; Co-editor, co-author: Commentary on Classical Philology; Greek Hellenic Philosophy, Literary Translations and Commentary on Philodemus Project, 1995; 50 volumes on classical philology, literary styles and analysis of Old Testament Exegesis, history of mediaeval and modern moral and ecumenical theological institutes; Love Duchess; Odyssey of Clotilda; Composer of Operas, Symphonies; Plays; Books; Cello Percussion Pieces. Contributions to: Journals. Honour: Member, International Platform Association; Eminent Scholar of the Year, National Association of Scholars, 1993; Academy Award, American Academy of Achievement, 1998; Royal Society Special Citation for Exceptional Performance in Literary Performing Arts; Elected, American Academy of Poets; Presidential Seal of Honor. Memberships: American Philological Association, president, 1996-97; American Historical Association; Law Society of America; Society of Biblical Literature; American Institute of Archaeology. Address: 501 Forest Avenue, Suite 108, Palo Alto, CA 94301, USA.

LYNDEN-BELL Donald, b. 5 April 1935. Astronomer. m. Ruth Marion Truscott, 1 son, 1 daughter. Education: Marlborough College, Wiltshire, 1948-53; PhD, Theoretical Astrophysics, Clare College, University of Cambridge, 1960. Appointments: Harkness Fellow of the Commonwealth Fund New York, California Institute of Technology & Mt Wilson & Palomar Observatories, 1960-62; Research Fellow, Clare College, 1960-62; Assistant Lecturer in Mathematics, University of Cambridge, 1962-65; Director of Studies in Mathematics, Clare College, 1962-65; Official Fellow of Clare College, 1962-65; Principal Scientific Officer, later Senior Principal Scientific Officer, Royal Greenwich Observatory, Herstmonceux Castle, Sussex, 1965-72; Professor of Astrophysics, University of Cambridge, 1972-2001; Visiting Appointments: Oort Professor, Leiden University; Visiting Professor, University of Sussex, 1969-72; South African Astronomical Observatory, 1973-90; Fairchild Scholar, CALTECH, 1979; Mt Stromlo Observatory, Australia, 1987; Einstein Fellow, Israeli Academy, Jerusalem, 1990; Carnegie Observatories, Pasadena, California, 2002; Queen's University, Belfast, 1996-2003, David Bates Lecturer, 2003. Publications: Numerous papers in scientific journals; Monthly Notices of Royal Astronomical Society. Honours: Murgoci Prize for Physics, Clare College, 1956; Honorary Scholar of Clare College, 1957; Schwarzschild Lecturer and Medallist of the Astronomische Gesellschaft, 1983; Eddington Medal, 1984, Gold Medal, 1993, Royal Astronomical Society; Medal, Science Faculty, Charles University, Prague; Honorary DSc, Sussex, 1987; Brouwer Award in Dynamical Astronomy of the AAS, 1990; Bruce Medal of the Astronomical Society of the Pacific, 1998; J J Carty Award, NAS, 1999; Russell Lecturer, American Astronomical Society, 2000; CBE, 2000. Membership: Fellow, Clare College; Fellow, Royal Society; Fellow, Royal Astronomical Society; Fellow, Cambridge Philosophical Society; Honorary Fellow, Inter-University Centre for Astronomy and Astrophysics, Pune, India; Foreign Associate, US National Academy of Sciences; Honorary Foreign Member, American Academy of Arts and Sciences; Foreign Associate, Royal Society of South Africa; Honorary Member, American Astronomical Society. Address: 9 Storey's Way, Cambridge CB3 0DP, England. E-mail: dlb@ast.cam.ac.uk

LYNDON SKEGGS Barbara Noel, b. 29 December 1924, London, England. Retired. m. Michael Lyndon Skeggs, 2 sons, 2 daughters. Appointments include: Served 6 months in Aircraft Factory and 2½ years in the WRNS during World War II; Joined Conservative Party, holding various constituency positions over the years, 1945-; Manager of Ford Primary School, 1963-88; Appointed Justice of the Peace, 1966-94; Conservative County Councillor for Crookham, 1968-81; Appointed Tax Commissioner, 1984-94; Appointed Deputy Lieutenant for Northumberland, 1988-; Appointed High Sheriff of Northumberland, 1994-95. Honours: Freeman of the City of London, 1973; Badge of Honour for Distinguished Service, BRCS, 1987; MBE, 1990. Memberships: Berwick Infirmary Management Committee, 1966-74; Area Health Authority, 1974-90; Northumberland Family Practitioner Committee, 1980-90; Northumberland Magistrates Committee, 1980-94; Ford and Etal PCC, 1961-96; Board of Northern Opera, 1971-81. Address: Dalgheal, Evanton, Ross-shire IV16 9XH, Scotland.

LYNN Vera (Margaret Lewis) (Dame), b. 20 March 1917. Singer. m. Harry Lewis, 1941, 1 daughter. Career: Debut performance, 1924; Appeared with Joe Loss, Charlie Kunz, 1935; Ambrose, 1937-40; Applesauce, Palladium, London, 1941; Became known as the Forces Sweetheart, 1939-45; Radio show Sincerely Yours, 1941-47; Tour of Burma, entertaining troops, 1944; 7 Command performances; Appearances, Europe; Australia; Canada; New Zealand; Performed at 50th Anniversary of VE Day Celebrations, London, 1995; Own television shows: ITV, 1955; BBC1, 1956; BBC2, 1970; First British artist to top Hit Parade. Numerous recordings include: Auf Wiederseh'n (over 12 million copies sold). Publication: Vocal Refrain (autobiography), 1975. Honours: Order of St John; LLD; MMus. Address: c/o Anglo-American Enterprises, 806 Keyes House, Dolphin Square, London SW1V 3NB, England.

LYON Martin, b. 10 February 1954, Romford, Essex, England. Librarian; Poet. Education: BA, 1976. Appointments: Principal Library Assistant, University of London. Contributions to: Acumen; Agenda; Orbis; Outposts Poetry Quarterly; Pen International; Spokes. Honour: Lake Aske Memorial Award. Address: 63 Malford Court, The Drive, South Woodford, London E18 2HS, England.

LYONS Roger Alan, b. 14 September 1942, London, England. Consultant. m. Kitty Horvath, 2 sons, 2 daughters. Education: BSc (Econ) Hons, University College London, 1966. Appointments: General Secretary, MSF Union, 1992-2002; Member, Merger and Monopolies Commission, 1996-2002; Member, Design Council, 1998-2004; Member, Central Arbitration Committee, 1998-; Judge, Employment Appeals Tribunal, 1999-; Joint General Secretary, Amicus Union, 2002-04; President, TUC, 2003-04; Adviser to Business Services Association, 2005-. Publications: Contributions to: Handbook on Industrial Relations; Handbook on Management Development; Free and Fair, 2004. Memberships: Fellow, University College London; Fellow, Royal Society of Arts. Address: 22 Park Crescent, London N3 2NJ, England. E-mail: rogerlyons22@hotmail.com

LYSENKO Mikhail, b. 12 May 1955, Moscow, Russia. Diplomat. m. Luidmila, 1 son, 1 daughter. Education: Graduate, Moscow State Institute of International Relations, 1977. Appointments: Joined Ministry of Foreign Affairs, 1977; Served at the Embassies of USSR/Russia in USA, 1980-85, and Canada, 1996-2000; Director, International Security and Disarmament Department, Ministry of Foreign

Affairs of the Russian Federation, 2001-04; Ambassador Extraordinary and Plenipotentiary of the Russian Federation to New Zealand, 2004-. Publications include: Curbing the Star Wars Threat: a Russian View, 2006. Honours: Diplomatic Rank, Minister Extraordinary and Plenipotentiary First Class; PhD, International Law. Address: Embassy of the Russian Federation, 57 Messines Road, Karori, Wellington, New Zealand.

M

MAAFI Mounir, b. 1 January 1966, Sétif, Algeria. Senior Lecturer. m. Wassila Damerdji, 1 son. Education: Engineer's degree, Industrial Chemistry, Institut National de Chimie Industrielle, Algeria, 1989; DEA, Spectrochemistry, Paris 6 – Paris 7 Universities, France, 1991; PhD, Chemistry, Paris 7 University, 1996. Appointments: Teaching Assistant, Marne La Vallee University, 1992-95; Invited Researcher, Department of Analytical Chemistry, University of Extremadura, Badajoz, Spain, 1995, 1997; Associate Professor, Teaching and Research, Paris 7 University, 1995-97; Associate Professor, CPCM, Paris, 1997-98; Research Fellow, Institute of Topology and System Dynamics, Paris, 1997-98; Research Fellow, Karolinska Institute, Karolinska Pharmacy, Stockholm, 1998-99; Research Fellow, Teaching Associate, University of Glamorgan, Cardiff, Wales, 2001-04; Senior Lecturer, Leicester School of Pharmacy, De Montfort University, 2005-. Publications: 30 scientific papers; 21 scientific communications; 2 books. Honours: Listed in international biographical dictionaries. Memberships: European Photochemistry Association. Address: Leicester School of Pharmacy, De Montfort University, The Gateway, Leicester, LE1 9BH, England. E-mail: mmaafi@dmu.ac.uk

MAC KEY James Fredrik, b. 20 November 1919, Varberg, Sweden. Professor; Doctor. m. Kerstin Anne-Marie Madsen, 2 daughters. Education: MSc, Agronomy, 1945, DPh, Genetics, 1953, DSc, Genetics, 1954, Royal Agriculture College of Sweden, Uppsala. Appointments: Assistant Teacher, Chemistry, Royal Agriculture College of Sweden, 1942-44; Assistant Plant Breeder, (Uppsala substation) 1944-45, (Svalöf main station) 1945-57, Head Plant Breeder, 1958-62, Swedish Seed Association ; Professor of Plant Breeding, 1962-84, Active Professor Emeritus, 1985-, Royal Agricultural College and Swedish University of Agricultural Sciences, Uppsala. Publications: Over 200 scientific publications pertaining to applied and theoretical genetics with special reference to self-fertilising crops, spontaneous and induced mutations, race-specific disease resistance and yield structure including root patterns of cereals, evolution and revision of taxonomy of cultivated plants, evolution and genetics of polyploidy and origin of agriculture. Honours: Knight of the Royal Order of the Polar Star, Sweden 1967; The Nilsson-Ehle Gold Medal, Swedish Academy of Forest and Agriculture, 1994; Rockefeller Research Fellowship, USA, 1954-55; Foreign Senior Scientist Award, National Science Foundation, USA, 1970-71; Weseman Foreign Scientist Award, Iowa State University, Ames, USA, 1980. Memberships: Swedish Seed Association; Hungarian Academy of Sciences; Yugoslavian Society of Genetics; Mendelian Society; Royal Academy of Forest and Agriculture; Royal Society of Arts and Sciences, Uppsala; Royal Physiographic Society, Lund. Address: Department of Plant Biology and Forest Genetics, Swedish University of Agricultural Sciences, POB 7080, SE-750 07, Uppsala, Sweden.

MacCARTHY Fiona, b. 23 January 1940, London, England. Biographer; Cultural Historian. m. David Mellor, 1966, 1 son, 1 daughter. Education: MA, English Language and Literature, Oxford University, 1961. Appointments: Staff Writer, The Guardian, 1963-69; Women's Editor, Evening Standard, 1969-71; Reviewer, The Times, 1981-91, The Observer, 1991-98. Publications: The Simple Life: C R Ashbee in the Cotswolds, 1981; The Omega Workshops: Decorative Arts of Bloomsbury, 1984; Eric Gill, 1989; William Morris: A Life for our Time, 1994; Stanley Spencer, 1997; Byron Life and Legend, 2002; Last Curtsey: The End of the Debutantes,

2006. Contributions to: Times Literary Supplement; New York Review of Books. Honours: Royal Society of Arts Bicentenary Medal, 1987; Honorary Fellowship, Royal College of Art, 1989; Wolfson History Prize, 1995; Honorary D Litt, University of Sheffield, 1996; Senior Fellowship, Royal College of Art, 1997; Fellow, Royal Society of Literature, 1997; Honorary Doctorate, Sheffield Hallam University, 2001; Honorary Fellowship, Lady Margaret Hall, Oxford, 2007. Memberships: PEN Club; Royal Society of Literature. Address: The Round Building, Hathersage, Sheffield S32 1BA, England.

MacCORMACK Geoffrey Dennis, b. 15 April 1937, Canterbury, Kent, England. Retired Professor of Law. 1 daughter. Education: University of Sydney, Australia, 1954-60; University of Oxford, England, 1960-65. Appointment: Professor of Jurisprudence, University of Aberdeen, 1971-96. Publications: Traditional Chinese Law, 1990; The Spirit of Traditional Chinese Law, 1996. Address: School of Law, King's College, University of Aberdeen, Old Aberdeen AB24 3UB, Scotland. E-mail: g.maccormack@abdn.ac.uk

MacCRACKEN Michael, b. 20 May 1942, USA. Atmospheric Scientist. m. Sandra Svets, 2 sons. Education: BS, Engineering, Princeton University, 1964; PhD, University of California, Davis, 1968. Appointments: Physicist, Atmospheric Scientist, University of California, Lawrence Livermore National Laboratory, 1968-2002; Executive Director, National Assessment Co-ordination Office, 1997-2001; Senior Scientist, Office US Global Change Research Program, 2001-2002; Chief Scientist for Climate Change Programs, Climate Institute, Washington, DC, 2003-. Publications: Co-editor 5 books; Several dozen articles in professional journals. Memberships: Fellow, American Association for the Advancement of Science; American Geophysical Union; American Meteorological Society; International Association of Meteorology and Atmospheric Sciences, President 2003-2007; The Oceanography Society. Address: 6308 Berkshire Drive, Bethesda, MD 20814, USA.

MacDONALD Angus D, b. 9 October 1950, Edinburgh, Scotland. Headmaster. m. Isabelle M Ross, 2 daughters. Education: MA (Hons), Cambridge University, 1969-71; Dip Ed, Edinburgh University, 1971-72. Appointments: Assistant Teacher, Alloa Academy, 1972-73; Assistant Teacher, King's School, Paramatta, 1978-79; Assistant Teacher, Edinburgh Academy, 1973-82; Head of Geography, 1982, Deputy Principal, 1982-86, George Watson's College; Headmaster, Lomond School, 1986-. Honour: Exhibition to Cambridge University. Membership: Chairman, Clan Donald Lands Trust. Address: 8 Millig Street, Helensburgh, Argyll & Bute, Scotland.

MacDONALD Betty Ann Kipniss, b. 1936, Brooklyn, New York, USA. 4 children. Education: Art School, Museum of Modern Art, Manhattan; Art Students League; Sumie Drawing, Chinese Institute night school; MA, Teachers College, Columbia University. Appointments: Teacher of Art, elementary school and junior high school, 5 years; Editorial Assistant of children's books; Teacher of Art, Montshire Museum; Board Member, New Hampshire Art Association; Teacher, Lebanon College; Printmaking; Teacher, Smithsonian Institution, 10 years; Artist, Central Intelligence Agency. Publications: Poetry published in the Potomac Quarterly; Commissions for music book covers; Washington Women's Investment Club funded murals for a shelter for the homeless. Honours: Purchase Award Prize, Delta National Small Prints Exhibition; Museum Award for Graphics, Washington

County Museum of Fine Arts; Best in Show in "Small Prints, Big Impressions", Maryland Federation of Arts; 1st Place Award, 72nd Annual International Exhibition of Fine Art in Miniature; Artwork held in a dozen galleries across the USA and in many museums and permanent collections around the world. Address: PO Box 1202, McLean, VA 22101, USA.

MacDONALD Douglas Andrew, b. 2 June 1967, Barrie, Ontario, Canada. Psychologist; Associate Professor of Psychology. m. Clementina Iampietro, 2 daughters. Education: BA (Hons), Psychology, 1990, MA, Psychology, 1992, PhD, Clinical Psychology, 1998, University of Windsor, Windsor, Ontario. Appointments: Academic: Teaching/Graduate Assistant, 1989-92, Sessional Instructor, Department of Psychology, 1993-94, University of Windsor, Windsor, Ontario; Part-time Faculty, Saybrook Graduate School and Research Center, San Francisco, California, USA, 2001-; Associate Professor of Psychology, University of Detroit Mercy, Detroit, Michigan, USA, 2000-; Clinical/Applied: Practicum Student, Guelph Assessment and Treatment Unit, Guelph Correctional Centre, Guelph, Ontario, 1991; Intern (half-time), University of Windsor Psychological Services Centre, 1992-93, Intern (half-time), Windsor Regional Hospital, Western Campus, 1994-95; Behavioural Consultant (half-time), Essex County Board of Education, Essex, Ontario, 1995-97; Psychologist, Windsor Board of Education, 1997-98; Psychologist, Greater Essex County District School Board, 1998-2004. Publications: Book: Approaches to transpersonal measurement and assessment (co-editor), 2002; Peer-reviewed journal articles as co-author include most recently: Using transpersonal tests in humanistic psychological assessment, 2002; Transpersonal psychology, physical health and mental health: Theory, research and practice, 2003; Validation of Self-Expansiveness Level Form with an Indian Sample, 2004; Confirmatory factor analysis of the Allport and Ross Religious Orientation Scale with a Polish Sample, 2006; Numerous papers presented a conferences and symposia. Honours: University of Windsor Tuition Scholarships, 1992-93, 1993-94; Ontario Graduate Scholarship, 1992-93; Research Development Grant, Floraglades Foundation; Recipient, 2006 Carmi Harari Early Career Contributions Award, American Psychological Association; Invited Reviewer for several psychological journals; Member of several editorial boards; Listed in Who's Who publications and biographical dictionaries. Memberships: American Psychological Association, 1998-; Division 32, Humanistic Psychology, 2005-; Canadian Psychological Association, 2000-. Address: University of Detroit Mercy, Department of Psychology, 4001 W McNichols Road, Detroit, MI 48221, USA. E-mail: macdonda@udmercy.edu

MacDONALD Ian, b. 22 December 1921, London, England. Emeritus Professor of Applied Physiology. m. (1), 2 sons, 1 daughter, (2) Rose Philomena. Education: MB BS, PhD, MD, DSc, University of London and Guy's Hospital. Appointments: RAMC, 1946-48; Professor of Applied Physiology, 1967-89, Head, Department of Physiology, 1977-89, Professor Emeritus, 1989-, Guy's Hospital, London; Member, UK Food Additives and Contaminants Committee, 1977-83; President, UK Nutrition Society, 1980-83; Chairman, Joint WHO/FAO Expert Committee of Dietary Carbohydrates, 1980; Chairman, 1983-85, Vice-President, 1990-2005, British Nutrition Foundation; Member, UK Food Advisory Committee, 1983-86; Chairman, Nutrition Consultative Panel, UK Dairy Industry, 1984-88. Publications: Books: Effects of Carbohydrates on Lipid Metabolism (editor), 1973; Metabolic Effects of Dietary Carbohydrates (editor), 1986; Sucrose (editor), 1988; Published research on gastric physiology and on foetal growth, main research interest:

dietary carbohydrate in man. Honours: Freeman of the City of London, 1967; Freeman, Worshipful Society of Apothecaries, 1967; International Award for Modern Nutrition, 1973. Memberships: FIBiol. E-mail: rosian@onetel.com

MacDONALD Simon Gavin George, b. 5 September 1923, Beauly, Inverness-shire, Scotland. University Professor of Physics, retired. m. Eva Leonie Austerlitz, 1 son, 1 daughter. Education: First Class Honours, Mathematics and Natural Philosophy, Edinburgh University, 1941-43, 1946-48; PhD, St Andrews University, 1953. Appointments: Junior Scientific Officer, Royal Aircraft Establishment, Farnborough, 1943-46; Lecturer in Physics, 1948-57, Senior Lecturer in Physics, 1962-67, University of St Andrews; Senior Lecturer in Physics, University College of the West Indies, Jamaica, 1957-62; Senior Lecturer in Physics, 1967-72, Dean, Faculty of Science, 1970-73, Professor of Physics, 1973-88, Vice-principal, 1974-79, University of Dundee. Publications: 3 books; Numerous articles in scientific journals on x-ray crystallography. Honours: Fellow, Institute of Physics, 1958; Fellow, Royal Society of Edinburgh, 1972; Chairman, Dundee Repertory Theatre; Chairman, Federation of Scottish Theatres. Address: 7a Windmill Road, St Andrews, Fife KY16 9JJ, Scotland.

MacDOWELL Andie, b. 21 April 1958, South Carolina, USA. Film Actress. m. (1) Paul Qualley, divorced, 1 son, 2 daughters, (2) Rhett DeCamp Hartzog, 2001-2004 (divorced). Appointments: TV appearances include: Women and Men 2, In Love There are no Rules, 1991; Sahara's Secret; Films include: Greystoke, 1984; St Elmo's Fire, 1985; Sex, Lies and Videotape, 1989; Green Card, 1990; Hudson Hawk, 1991; The Object of Beauty, 1991; The Player, 1992; Ruby, 1992; Groundhog Day, 1993; Short Cuts, 1993; Bad Girls, 1994; Four Weddings and a Funeral, 1994; Unstrung Heros, 1995; My Life and Me, 1996; Multiplicity, 1996; The End of Violence, 1997; Town and Country, 1998; Shadrack, 1998; The Scalper, 1998; Just the Ticket, 1998; Muppets From Space, 1999; The Music, 2000; Harrison's Flowers, 2000; Town and Country, 2001; Crush, 2001; Ginostra, 2002; The Last Sign, 2004; Beauty Shop, 2005; Tara Road, 2005; Barnyard (voice), 2006; Intervention, 2007. Address: c/o ICM 8942 Wilshire Boulevard, Beverly Hills, CA 90211, USA.

MacDOWELL Douglas Maurice, b. 8 March 1931, London, England. Professor of Greek; Writer. Education: BA, 1954, MA, 1958, DLitt, 1992, Balliol College, Oxford. Appointments: Assistant Lecturer, Lecturer, Senior Lecturer, Reader in Greek and Latin, University of Manchester, 1958-71; Professor of Greek, 1971-2001, Professor Emeritus, Honorary Research Fellow, 2001-, University of Glasgow. Publications: Andokides: On the Mysteries (editor), 1962; Athenian Homicide Law, 1963; Aristophanes: Wasps (editor), 1971; The Law in Classical Athens, 1978; Spartan Law, 1986; Demosthenes: Against Meidias (editor), 1990; Aristophanes and Athens, 1995; Antiphon and Andocides (with M Gagarin), 1998; Demosthenes: On the False Embassy (editor), 2000; Demosthenes: Speeches 27-38 (translator), 2004. Honours: Fellow, Royal Society of Edinburgh, 1991; Fellow, British Academy, 1993. Address: Department of Classics, University of Glasgow, Glasgow G12 8QQ, Scotland.

MacFARLANE Sheila Margaret, b. 2 May 1943, Aberdeen, Scotland. Artist. 1 daughter. Education: DA, Edinburgh College of Art, 1960-64, Dip Ed, Morray House College of Education, 1964-65; Atelier 17, Paris, 1967-68. Appointments: Lecturer in Charge of Printmaking, Duncan of Jordanstone College, Dundee, 1970-76; Founder, Director, Kirktower

House Print Studio, Montrose, 1976-88; Art-Drama Specialist to children with special needs in Angus, Occasional Visiting Lecturer to Ruskin School, Oxford University, 1984-2004; Selector, Researcher for SAC Exhibition "Relief Printing", 1984-85. Publications: The Finella Prints, Printmaking Today, 1997; The Finella Prints, The Leopard Magazine, 2002. Membership: Dundee Contemporary Arts Print Studio. Address: 1 Tangleha, St Cyrus, Montrose, Angus, DD10 0DQ, Scotland.

MacGINNIS John, b. 17 November 1962, England. Archaeologist. Education: BA, Near Eastern Archaeology and Assyriology, Trinity College, Cambridge, 1982-86; PhD, Near Eastern Archaeology and Assyriology, Darwin College, Cambridge, 1987-91. Appointments: British Academy Research Scholarship, 1987-91; Fellow, Wolfson College, Oxford, 1992-97, Freelance Archaeologist, 1997-2000; Research Fellow, McDonald Institute for Archaeological Research, Cambridge, 2001-; Excavation experience: Coppergate, York, 1980; Walton-le-dale, Lancashire, 1981; Danebury, Hampshire, 1981; Landesamt für Vor- und Frügeschichte Schleswig-Holstein, Germany, 1982, 1984; Kissonerga, Cyprus, 1983; Nineveh, Iraq, 1986, 1989; Tell Brak, Syria, 1987, 1990, 1991, 1992, Rojdi, Gujarat, 1993; Charsada, NWFP, Pakistan, 1993, 1996; Meröe, Sudan, 1994; Merv, Turkmenistan, 1994; Jamestown, Virginia, 1995; Car Dyke, Cambridgeshire, 1997; Armana, Egypt, 1998, 1999, 2000, 2003, 2004; Ziyaret, Turkey, 2000, 2001, 2002, 2003, 2004; Souakin, Sudan, 2002; Qasr Ibrim, Egypt, 2004, 2005. Publications: Monographs: Letter Orders from Sippar and the Administration of the Ebabbara in the Late Babylonian Period, 1995; Road Archaeology in the Middle Nile (co-author), in press; Numerous articles in archaeological journals. Membership: British School of Archaeology in Iraq. Address: McDonald Institute for Archaeological Research, Downing Street, Cambridge CB2 3ER, England. E-mail: johnmacginnis@aol.com

MacGREGOR John Roddick Russell (Lord MacGregor of Pulham Market), b. 14 February 1937, Glasgow, Scotland. Politician; Businessman. m. Jean Mary Elizabeth Dungey, 1 son, 2 daughters. Education: MA, First Class Honours, St Andrew's University; LLB, King's College, London. Appointments: University Administrator, 1961-62; Editorial Staff, New Society, 1962-63; Hill Samuel & Co, 1968-79; Director, Hill Samuel and Co, 1973-79; Deputy Chairman, Hill Samuel Bank Ltd, 1994-96; Non-Executive Director: Slough Estates plc, 1995-, Associated British Foods plc, 1994, Unigate plc (now Uniq), 1996-, Friends Provident plc, 1998-; European Supervisory Board, DAFS Netherlands NV; Political Career: Special Assistant to Prime Minister, 1963-64; Head, Leader of Opposition's Office, 1965-68; Member of Parliament for South Norfolk, 1974-2001; Lord Commissioner of the Treasury, 1979-81; Parliamentary Under Secretary of State for Industry with particular responsibility for small businesses, 1981-83; Minister of State for Agriculture, Fisheries and Food, 1983-85; Chief Secretary to the Treasury, 1985-87; Minister for Agriculture, Fisheries and Food, 1987-89; Secretary of State for Education, 1989-90; Lord President of the Council and Leader of the Commons, 1990-92; Secretary of State for Transport, 1992-94; Member of the House of Lords, 1991-. Honours: OBE, 1971; PC, 1985; Honorary Fellow, King's College, London, 1990; Honorary LLD, University of Westminster, 1995. Address: House of Lords, London SW1A 0PW, England.

MACHADO Maria Augusta Soares, b. 5 January 1950, Brazil. Mathematics. 2 sons. Education: Graduate, Mathematics; Master, Mathematics; Doctor, Engineering. Appointments: CASNAV, Naval Analysis Center, 1980-95; IPQM, Naval Institute of Research, 1994-2000; IBMEC, Business School, 2000-. Publications: 5 mathematics books; 2 soft computing books; Several articles of operations research, statistics and soft computing. Honours: Best Patent Award, 2006.

MACHIDA Curtis A, b. 1 April 1954, San Francisco, USA. Molecular Neurobiologist. Education: AB, University of California, Berkeley, 1976; PhD, Oregon Health Sciences University, 1982. Appointments: Postdoctoral Fellow, Biochemistry, Oregon Health Sciences University, 1982-85; Postdoctoral Fellow, Vollum Institute, 1985-88; Assistant Scientist, 1988-95, Assistant Professor, 1989-95; Associate Scientist, Associate Professor, 1995-2002 Neuroscience, Oregon National Primate Research Center, Oregon Health Sciences University; Research Associate Professor, Integrative Biosciences, Oregon Health Sciences University, 2002-05; Research Professor, Integrative Biosciences, 2005-; Adjunct Faculty, Biochemistry and Biophysics, Oregon State University, 1997-2001. Publications: Over 100 articles and abstracts in professional journals; Patent holder; Editor, Adrenergic Receptor Protocols; Editor, Viral Vectors for Gene Therapy: Methods and Protocols; Member, Editorial Boards, Molecular Biotechnology, Frontiers in Bioscience and World Medicine/International Journal of Biomedical Sciences. Honours include: NIH First Award; AHA Established Investigator Award; NIH Grant Recipient. Memberships: AAAS; ASM; ASBMB; ASGT; AHA Scientific Council. Address: Department of Integrative Biosciences, School of Dentistry, Oregon Health Sciences University, 611 SW Campus Drive, Portland, OR 97239, USA.

MACKAY William Morton, b. 26 March 1934, Dundee, Scotland. Educator. m. Catherine, 30 July 1959, 2 sons, 1 daughter. Education: MA (honours), St Andrews University; Dip Ed, St Andrews University, 1957; Diploma of Theological Studies, Free Church of Scotland College, Edinburgh, 1959. Appointments: Teacher, Buckhaven High School, 1959-61; Ordained, 1961; Teacher, Supervisor of Secondary Studies and Headmaster (1966-78), St Andrew's College, Lima, Peru, 1961-78; Teacher, Lothian Region, 1978-85; Principal, Presbyterian Ladies' College, Melbourne, Australia, 1986-97; Lecturer, Church History, Free Church of Scotland College, Edinburgh, 1998-2005; Clerk of Public Questions, Religion and Morals Committee, Free Church of Scotland, 1999-2002; Chairman, International Missions Board, 2002-. Publications: Thomas Chalmers: A Short Appreciation, 1980; Articles: Formative Aims in the Teaching of History, in "The Teaching of History", Catholic University of Peru, 1979; Church and School and the Care of Youth, in "Crown Him Lord of All", 1993; Andrew Melville and the Scottish Universities, and The Getting of Wisdom, in "A Witness for Christ", 1996. Honours: Diploma of Honour for services to Education in Peru, Peruvian Government, 1981; Moderator of Synod, Presbyterian Church of East Australia, 1993; Moderator of General Assembly, Free Church of Scotland, 2001. Memberships: Australian College of Educators; Association of Heads of Independent Schools of Australia; Associate Fellow, Australian Principals Centre; Fellow, Institute of Contemporary Scotland; Professional Associate, Council Member, 2003-06, Royal Scottish Geographical Society. Address: 53 Lauderdale Street, Edinburgh EH9 1DE, Scotland.

MacKENZIE Kenneth John, b. 1 May 1943, Glasgow, Scotland. Civil Servant. m. Irene Mary Hogarth, 1 son, 1 daughter. Education: Open Exhibitioner, BA, Modern History, 1964, MA, 1970, Pembroke College, University of Oxford; Dorothy Chandos Smyllie Scholarship in Department of History, Stanford University, California, 1964-65; Fulbright Travel Scholarship, 1964; Graduate AM in History, Stanford, 1965. Appointments: Principal Private Secretary to Secretaries of State for Scotland, 1977-79; 2 Assistant Secretary Posts in Scottish Office, 1979-85; 3 Under Secretary Posts in Scottish Office including Principal Finance Officer, 1985-92; Member, Biotechnology and Biological Sciences Research Council, 1992-95; Head of Scottish Office Agriculture and Fisheries Department, 1992-95; Head of Economic and Domestic Secretariat, 1995-97, Head of Constitution Secretariat, 1997-98, Cabinet Office; Head of Scottish Executive Development Department, 1998-2001; Quinquennial Reviewer, Lord Chancellor's Department, 2001-2002; Chairman, Historic Scotland Foundation, 2001-; Member, British Waterways Scotland Group, 2002-; Honorary Professor, Department of Politics, University of Aberdeen, 2001-04; Lead Consultant with Public Administration International advising the Government of Kosovo on structure and organisation of a Prime Minister's Office, 2004-; Board Member, Christian Aid, 2005-. Publications: Articles: Planner Shortage in Strathclyde, 1976; Tears Before Bedtime: A Look Back at the Constitutional Reform Programme since 1997, 2005. Honour: Companion of the Bath (CB), 1996. Address: 30 Regent Terrace, Edinburgh EH7 5BS, Scotland. E-mail: kjmackenzie@freeuk.com

MACKERRAS Sir (Alan) Charles, b. 17 November 1925, Schenectady, New York, USA. Orchestral Conductor. m. Helena Judith Wilkins, 22 August 1947, 2 daughters. Education: Sydney Grammar School, Sydney Conservatorium of Music, Studies with Vaclav Talich, Prague Academy of Music, 1947-48. Appointments: Principal Oboist, Sydney Symphony Orchestra, 1943-46; Oboist, Sadler's Wells Opera Orchestra, 1947; Staff Conductor, Sadler's Wells Opera, 1948-54; Freelance Conductor, orchestras in Britain, European Continent, USA, Australia, 1957-66; First Conductor, Hamburg State Opera, 1966-69; Musical Director, Sadler's Wells Opera, later English National Opera, 1970-77; Chief Guest, Conductor, BBC Symphony Orchestra, 1976-79; Chief Conductor, Sydney Symphony Orchestra, Australian Broadcasting Company, 1982-85; Principal Guest Conductor, Royal Liverpool Philharmonic, 1986-88; Scottish Chamber Orchestra, 1992-95; Conductor Laureate, 1995-; Musical Director, Welsh National Opera, 1987-92; Conductor Emeritus, 1992-; Principal Guest Conductor, San Francisco Opera, 1993-96; Conductor Emeritus, 1996-; Royal Philharmonic Orchestra, 1993-96; Czech Philharmonic Orchestra, 1997-2003; Music Director, Orchestra of St Luke's, 1998-2001, Music Director Emeritus, 2001-; Principal Guest Conductor, Philharmonia Orchestra, 2002-; President, Trinity College of Music, 2000-. Publications: Ballet arrangement of Pineapple Poll, 1951 (Sullivan) and The Lady and the Fool, 1954 (Verdi); Reconstruction of Arthur Sullivan's lost cello concerto, 1986; Contributed 4 appendices to Charles Mackerras: a musicians' musician, by Nancy Phelan, 1987; Numerous articles in musical journals and magazines. Honours: CBE, 1974; Knighthood, 1979; AC (Companion of Order of Australia), 1997; Medal of Merit, Czech Republic, 1996; CH, 2003; Hon RAM, 1969; Hon FRCM, 1987; Honorary Fellow, Royal Northern College of Music, Manchester, 1999; Honorary Fellow, Trinity College of Music, London, 1999; Honorary Fellow, Saint Peter's College, Oxford, 1999; Cardiff University, 2003; Honorary DMus: University of Hull, 1990,

Nottingham, 1991, Brno (Czech Republic), York and Griffith (Brisbane), 1994, Oxford, 1997; Prague Academy of Music, 1999; Napier University, 2000; Melbourne and Sydney, 2003; Janacek Academy of Music, Brno, 2004; University of London, 2005; First Recipient, Queen's Medal for Music, 2005; Royal Philharmonic Society Gold Medal, 2005; BBC Radio 3 Listeners' Award for Artist of the Year, 2005. Address: c/o Askonas Hold Limited, Lonsdale Chambers, 28 Chancery Lane, London WC2A 1PF, England.

MACKESY Piers Gerald, b. 15 September 1924, Cults, Aberdeenshire, Scotland. Historian; Writer. Education: BA, Christ Church, Oxford, 1950; DPhil, Oriel College, Oxford, 1953; DLitt, Oxford, 1978. Appointments: War Service: Lieutenant, The Royal Scots Greys, N.W. Europe, 1943-7; Harkness Fellow, Harvard University, 1953-54; Fellow, 1954-87, Emeritus, 1988-, Pembroke College, Oxford; Visiting Fellow, Institute for Advanced Study, Princeton, New Jersey, 1961-62; Visiting Professor, California Institute of Technology, 1966. Publications: The War in the Mediterranean 1803-1810, 1957; The War for America 1775-1783, 1964, 1993; Statesmen at War: The Strategy of Overthrow 1798-1799, 1974; The Coward of Minden: The Affair of Lord George Sackville, 1979; War without Victory: The Downfall of Pitt 1799-1802, 1984; British Victory in Egypt, 1801: The End of Napoleon's Conquest (Templer Medal), 1995. Memberships: National Army Museum, council member, 1983-92; Society for Army Historical Research, council member, 1985-94, currently Vice President; British Academy, fellow, 1988. Address: Westerton Farmhouse, Dess, by Aboyne, Aberdeenshire AB34 5AY, Scotland.

MACKEY Barbara Wood Jensen, b. 30 April 1927, Salt Lake City, Utah, USA. Interior Designer. m. (1) Lowell Jensen, deceased, 2 sons, 1 daughter, (2) Tom A Mackey. Education: Fellow, Institute of Professional Designers, London, England; Fellow, AID, USA. Appointments: Barbara Jensen Interiors Corp, Salt Lake City, 1960-80; Barbara Jensen Associates, Salt Lake City, 1980-86; Barbara Jensen Designs, Las Vegas, Nevada, Hawaii, St George, Utah, Salt Lake City, Utah, 1986-2000; Retired, 2004-. Publications: Author of books on interior design and geneology; Autobiography; Numerous articles in professional journals, local newspapers and magazines; TV appearances. Honours: Listed in international biographical dictionaries; Fellow, IPD, London; Fellow, AID, USA. Memberships: Saturday Night Dance Club; Hi Stepper Dance Club; Bloomington Golf Club, St George; Fort Douglas Club, Salt Lake City; Daughters of Pioneers Museum; Morman Church – Buildings & Restoration; Started 1st Women's Bank, Salt Lake City, Utah, 1980 (sold bank in 1985).

MacKIERNAN Francis Joseph, b. 3 February 1926, Co Leitrim, Ireland. Catholic Bishop. Education: BA (Honours), 1947, BD, (Honours), 1950, Higher Diploma in Education, 1953, St Patrick's College, Maynooth and University College, Dublin. Appointments: Teacher of Classics, St Malachy's College, Belfast, 1951-52; Teacher of Classics and Irish, St Patrick's College, Cavan, 1952-62; President, St Felim's College, Ballinamore, Co Leitrim, 1962-72; Bishop of Kilmore, 1972-88; Retired, 1988. Publications: Bishops and Priests of the Diocese of Kilmore 1136-1988, 1988; St Mary's Abbey, Cavan, 2000; Many historical articles in Breifne, Journal of the Breifne Historical Society, 1958-. Membership: Editor of Breifne Journal, Secretary, Breifne Historical Society. Address: 5 Brookside, Cavan, Ireland.

MACKINTOSH Cameron Anthony (Sir), b. 17 October 1946, Enfield, England. Theatre Producer. Education: Prior Park College, Bath. Appointments: Stage Hand, Theatre Royal, Drury Lane; Assistant Stage Manager; Worked with Emile Littler, 1966; Robin Alexander, 1967; Producer, 1969-; Chair, Cameron Mackintosh, 1981-; Director, Delfont Mackintosh, 1991-; Productions: Little Women, 1967; Anything Goes, 1969; Trelawney, 1972; The Card, 1973; Winnie the Pooh, 1974; Owl and the Pussycat Went to Sea, 1975; Godspell, 1975; Side by Side by Sondheim, 1976; Oliver!, 1977; Diary of a Madam, 1977; After Shave, 1977; Gingerbread Man, 1978; Out on a Limb, 1978; My Fair Lady, 1979; Oklahoma!, 1990; Tomfoolery, 1980; Jeeves Takes Charge, 1981; Cats, 1981; Song and Dance, 1982; Blondel, 1983; Little Shop of Horrors, 1983; Abbacadabra, 1983; The Boyfriend, 1984; Les Miserables, 1985; Cafe Puccini, 1985; Phantom of the Opera, 1986; Follies, 1987; Miss Saigon, 1989; Just So, 1990; Five Guys Named Moe, 1990; Moby Dick, 1992; Putting it Together, 1992; The Card, 1992; Carousel, 1993; Oliver!, 1994; Martin Guerre, 1996; The Fix, 1997; Oklahoma!, 1999; The Witches of Eastwick, 2000; My Fair Lady, 2001. Honours: Observer Award for Outstanding Achievement; Laurence Oliver Award, 1991; Knighted. Address: Cameron Mackintosh Ltd, 1 Bedford Square, London, WC1B 3RA, England.

MACKLIN Elizabeth, b. 28 October 1952, Poughkeepsie, New York, USA. Poet. Education: BA in Spanish, State University of New York at Potsdam, 1973; Graduate School of Arts and Sciences, New York University, 1975-78. Appointment: Editorial Staff, 1974-99, Query Editor, 1981-99, The New Yorker Magazine; Poetry Editor, Wigwag Magazine, 1989-91; Freelance Editor and Writer, 2000-. Publications: A Woman Kneeling in the Big City, 1992; You've Just Been Told, Poems, 2000; Meanwhile Take My Hand, Poems by Kirmen Uribe (translation), 2007. Contributions to: Nation; New Republic; New York Times; New Yorker; Paris Review; Threepenny Review. Honours: Ingram Merrill Foundation Award in Poetry, 1990; Guggenheim Fellowship, 1994; Amy Lowell Poetry Travelling Scholarship, 1998-99; PEN Translation Fund grant, 2005; Listed in Who's Who publications. Memberships: Authors Guild; PEN American Center, executive board, 1995-96. Address: 207 West 14th Street, 5F, New York, NY 10011, USA. E-mail: elizabethmacklin@writersartists.net

MACKMIN Michael, b. 20 April 1941, London, England. Psychotherapist; Poet; Editor. Divorced, 2 daughters. Education: BA, 1963; MA, 1965. Appointment: Editor, The Rialto. Publications: The Play of Rainbow; Connemara Shore; 23 poems. Address: PO Box 309, Aylsham, Norwich NR11 6LN, England.

MacLACHLAN Kyle, b. 22 February 1959, Yakima, Washington, USA. Actor. m. Desiree Gruber, 2002-. Education: University of Washington, Seattle. Career: Stage: Regional Shakespeare productions and off-Broadway in Palace of Amateurs; Films: Dune, 1984; Blue Velvet, 1986; The Hidden, 1988; Don't Tell Her It's Me, 1990; The Doors, 1991; Where the Day Takes You, Twin Peaks: Fire Walk With Me, 1992; The Trial, Rich in Love, 1993; Against the Wall, The Flintstones, Roswell, 1994; Showgirls, 1995; Trigger Effect, Mad Dog Time, 1996; One Night Stand, 1997; X-Change, Hamlet, Timecode, 2000; Perfume, Me Without You, 2001; Miranda, 2002; Northfork, 2003; Touch of Pink, 2004; Free Jimmy (voice), 2006. Plays: Palace of Amateurs, Minetta Lane Theatre (off Broadway), New York; On An Average Day, Comedy Theatre, London, 2002; TV: Northwest

Passage; The O'Conners; Twin Peaks, 1990-91; Sex and the City, 2000-02; Mysterious Island, 2005; In Justice, 2006; Desperate Housewives, 2006-2007. Address: UTA, 9560 Wilshire Boulevard, 5th Floor, Beverly Hills, CA 90212, USA.

MacLAINE Shirley, b. 24 April 1934, Richmond, Virginia, USA. Film Actress; Writer; Film Director. m. Steve Parker, 1954-1982 (divorced) 1 daughter. Education: Grammar School; Lee High School, Washington. Appointments: Chorus Girl and Dancer; Films include: The Trouble with Harry; Artists and Models; Around the World in 80 Days; Hot Spell; The Matchmaker; Can-Can; Career; The Apartment; Two for the Seesaw; The Children's Hour; Irma La Douce; What a Way to go; The Yellow Rolls-Royce; Gambit; Woman Times Seven; The Bliss of Mrs Blossom; Sweet Charity; Two Mules for Sister Sara; Desperate Characters; The Possessions of Joel Delaney; The Turning Point, 1977; Being There, 1979; Loving Couples, 1980; The Change of Seasons, Slapstick, 1981; Terms of Endearment, 1984; Out on a Limb, 1987; Madame Sousatzka, Steel Magnolias, 1989; Waiting for the Light, Postcards from the Edge, 1990; Used People, 1993; Wrestling Ernest Hemingway, Guarding Tess, 1994; Mrs Westbourne, The Evening Star, 1995; Mrs Winterbourne, The Celluloid Closet; The Evening Star, 1996; Looking for Lulu; Bet Bruce; Joan of Arc, 1999; The Dress Code, 2000; In Her Shoes, 2004; Bewitched, Rumor Has It, 2005; Closing the Ring, 2007. Revues: If My Friends Could See Me Now, 1974; To London with Love, 1976; London, 1982; Out There Tonight, 1990; TV Film: The West Side Waltz, 1994; Joan of Arc; These Old Broads, 2001; Video: Shirley MacLaines's Inner Workout, 1989; Producer and Co-director, The Other Half of the Sky - A China Memoir, 1973. Publications: Don't Fall From Here, 1975; Out on a Limb, 1983; Dancing in the Light, 1985; It's all in the playing, 1987; Going Within, 1989; Dance While You Can, 1991; My Lucky Stars, 1995; The Camino, 2000. Honours: Star of the Year Award, Theatre Owners of America, 1967; Best Actress Award, Desperate Characters, Berlin Film Festival, 1971; Academy Award, Best Actress, 1984; Golden Globe Award, Best Actress, 1989; Lifetime Achievement Award, Berlin Film Festival, 1999. Address: MacLaine Enterprises Inc, 25200 Malibu Road, Suit 101, Santa Monica, CA 90265, USA.

MACLAVERTY Bernard, b. 14 September 1942, Belfast, Northern Ireland. Novelist; Dramatist. m. Madeline McGuckin, 1967, 1 son, 3 daughters. Education: BA, Honours, Queen's University, Belfast, 1974. Publications: Bibliography: Secrets and Other Stories, 1977; Lamb (novel), 1980; A Time to Dance and Other Stories, 1982; Cal (novel), 1983; The Great Profundo and Other Stories, 1987; Walking the Dog and Other Stories, 1994; Grace Notes (novel), 1997; The Anatomy School (novel), 2001; Matters of Life & Death, 2006. For Young Children: A Man in Search of a Pet, 1978; Andrew McAndrew, 1988, US edition, 1993. Radio Plays: My Dear Palestrina, 1980; Secrets, 1981; No Joke, 1983; The Break, 1988; Some Surrender, 1988; Lamb, 1992; Grace Notes, 2003. Television Plays: My Dear Palestrina, 1980; Phonefun Limited, 1982; The Daily Woman, 1986; Sometime in August, 1989. Screenplays: Cal, 1984; Lamb, 1985; Bye-Child, 2003. Drama Documentary: Hostages, 1992, US edition, 1993; Television Adaptation: The Real Charlotte by Somerville and Ross, 1989. Honours: Northern Ireland and Scottish Arts Councils Awards; Irish Sunday Independent Award, 1983; London Evening Standard Award for Screenplay, 1984; Joint Winner, Scottish Writer of the Year, 1988; Society of Authors Travelling Scholarship, 1994; Shortlisted, Saltire Society Scottish Book of the Year, 1994, 2001; Grace Notes awarded

The Saltire Scottish Book of the Year Award, 1997; A Scottish Arts Council Book Award; Shortlisted for: The Booker Prize; the Writers Guild Best Fiction Book; The Stakis Scottish Writer of the Year; The Whitbread Novel of the Year; Creative Scotland Award, the Scottish Arts Council, 2003; Nominated, BAFTA Best Short Film for Bye-Child, 2004; BAFTA Scotland, Best First Director for Bye-Child, 2004; The Lord Provost of Glasgow's Award for Literature, 2005.

MACLEAY John (Iain) Henry James, b. 7 December 1931, Inverness Scotland. Retired Clergyman. m. Jane Speirs Cuthbert, 1 son, 1 daughter. Education: BA, 1954, MA, 1960, St Edmund Hall, Oxford; College of the Resurrection, Mirfield, Yorkshire. Appointments: Deacon, 1957; Priest, 1958; Curate, St John's, East Dulwich, England, 1957-60; Curate, 1960-62, Rector, 1962-70, St Michael's, Inverness, Scotland; Priest-in-Charge, St Columba's, Grantown-on-Spey with St John the Baptist, Rothiemurchus, Scotland, 1970-78; Canon, St Andrew's Cathedral, Inverness, 1977-78; Rector of St Andrew's, Fort William, 1978-99; Synod Clerk of Argyll and the Isles, Canon of St John's Cathedral, Oban, 1980-87; Dean of Argyll and the Isles, 1987-99; Honorary Canon of Oban, 2001. Address: 47 Riverside Park, Lochyside, Fort William PH33 7RB, Scotland.

MacMAHON James Ardle, b. 25 November 1924, Curragh, Co Kildare, Ireland. Catholic Priest. Education: St Macartan's College, Monaghan; Holy Cross College, Clonliffe, Dublin; University College, Dublin; Gregorian University, Rome. Appointments: Ordained Priest, 1949; Doctorate in Canon Law, 1954; Secretary to the Archbishop of Dublin, 1954-72; Parish Priest, 1975-2000; Commission for Charitable Donations and Bequests for Ireland, 1975-2000; Director of Religious Education in Vocational Schools, 1976-79; Vicar Forane, 1977-80; Episcopal Vicar for Religious, 1980-86; Prelate of Honour of His Holiness, 1985; Chancellor, Dublin Metropolitan Chapter of Canons, 2003. Honour: Silver Medal in Licentiate in Canon Law, 1954. Membership, Foxrock Golf Club, Dublin. Address: Queen of Peace Centre, 6 Garville Avenue, Rathgar, Dublin 6, Ireland.

MacPHERSON Elle, b. 29 March 1963, Killara, Australia. Model; Actress; Business Executive. m. G Bensimon, divorced 1990, 2 sons with Arpad Busson. Career: Founder, Elle Macpherson Intimates, and Macpherson Men lingerie and underwear companies; Released fitness video, Stretch and Strengthen, The Body Workout, 1995; Chief Executive, Elle Macpherson Inc; Co-owner, Fashion Café, New York; Films: Sirens; Jane Eyre; If Lucy Fell; The Mirror Has Two Faces; Batman and Robin; The Edge; Beautopia; With Friends Like These; South Kensington. Address: c/o Artistmanagement Associates Inc, 414 East 52nd Street, Penthouse B, New York, NY 10022, USA.

MacQUEEN Hector Lewis, b. 13 June 1956, Ely, Cambridgeshire, England. Professor of Law. m. Frances Mary, 2 sons, 1 daughter. Education: LLB Honours, 1974-78, PhD, 1985, University of Edinburgh. Appointments: Lecturer, Senior Lecturer, Reader, 1979-94, Professor of Private Law, 1994-, Faculty of Law, Dean of the Faculty of Law, 1999-, University of Edinburgh; Visiting Professor, Cornell University, USA, 1991, Utrecht University, Netherlands, 1997; Director, The David Hume Institute, 1991-99. Publications: Copyright, Competition and Industrial Design, 1989, 2nd edition, 1995; Common Law and Feudal Society in Medieval Scotland, 1993; Studying Scots Law, 1993, 2nd edition, 1999; Contract Law in Scotland (with J M Thomson), 2000; Numerous articles in learned and professional journals and collections. Honour:

Fellow of the Royal Society of Edinburgh. Memberships: Chair, Scottish Records Advisory Council, 2001-; Literary Director, Stair Society, 1999-; Heriots FP Cricket Club. Address: Faculty of Law, University of Edinburgh, Edinburgh EH8 9YL, Scotland. E-mail: hector.macqueen@ed.ac.uk

MacRAE (Alastair) Christopher (Donald) (Summerhayes) (Sir), b. 3 May 1937, Burleigh, Gloucestershire, England. Retired Diplomat. m. Mette Willert, 2 daughters. Education: BA Hons, Lincoln College, Oxford; Henry Fellow, Harvard University, USA. Appointments: Royal Navy, 1956-58; Second Secretary, Dar es Salaam, Tanzania, 1963-65; Middle East Centre for Arab Studies, 1965-67; Second Secretary, Beirut, Lebanon, 1967-68; Principal, Near East Department, Foreign and Commonwealth Office, 1968-70; 1st Secretary and Head of Chancery, Baghdad, Iraq, 1970-71; 1st Secretary and Head of Chancery, Brussels, Belgium, 1972-76; On loan to European Commission, 1976-78; Ambassador to Gabon, 1978-80, concurrently to Sao Tome and Principe; Head of West Africa Department, Foreign and Commonwealth Office, and Non-resident Ambassador to Chad, 1980-83; Political Counsellor, Paris, France, 1983-87; Head of Mission, Tehran, Iran, 1987; Assistant Under Secretary, Cabinet Office, 1988-91; British High Commissioner to Nigeria, 1991-94 and concurrently Ambassador to Benin; British High Commissioner to Pakistan, 1994-97; Secretary General Order of St John, 1997-2000. Honours: CMG, 1987; KCMG, 1993; KStJ, 1997. Memberships: Royal Commonwealth Society; Board Member, Aga Khan Foundation (UK); Chairman, Pakistan Society; President St John Ambulance, Ashford District. Address: 4 Church Street, Wye, Kent TN25 5BJ, England. E-mail: christophermacrae@btinternet.com

MACY William H, b. 13 March 1950, Miami, Florida, USA. Actor. m. Felicity Huffman, 2 daughters. Education: Goddard College, Vermont. Appointments: Co-founder, St Nicholas Theatre Company; Atlantic Theatre Company; Stage appearances include: The Man in 605, 1980; Twelfth Night; Beaurecrat; A Call from the East; The Dining Room; Speakeasy; Wild Life; Flirtations; Baby With the Bathwater; The Nice and the Nasty; Bodies Rest and Motion; Oh Hell!; Prairie du Chien; The Shawl; An Evening With Dorothy Parker; The Dining Room; A Call From the Sea; The Beaver Coat; Life During Wartime; Mr Gogol and Mr Preen; Oleanna; Our Town; Play director: Boy's Life; Film appearances include: Without a Trace; The Last Dragon; Radio Days; Somewhere in Time; Hello Again; House of Games; Things Change; Homicide; Shadows and Fog; Benny and Joon; Searching for Bobby Fischer; The Client; Oleanna; The Silence of the Lambs; Murder in the First; Mr Holland's Opus; Down Periscope; Fargo; Ghosts of Mississippi; Air Force One; Wag the Dog; Pleasantville; A Civil Action; Psycho; Magnolia; State and Main; Panic; Focus; Jurassic Park III; Welcome to Collinwood; The Cooler; Stealing Sinatra; Out of Order; Seabiscuit; Spartan; Cellular; Sahara; Bobby, 2006; Inland Empire, 2006; Wild Hogs, 2007; He Was a Quiet Man, 2007; The Deal, 2008; The Tale of Despereaux (voice), 2008; Film director: Lip Service; TV appearances include: Chicago Hope; The Murder of Mary Phagan; Texan; A Murderous Affair; The Water Engine; Heart of Justice; A Private Matter; The Con; A Slight Case of Murder. Address: 8383 Wilshire Blvd, #550, Beverly Hills, CA 90211, USA.

MADACKI Sasa, b. 17 January 1972, Sarajevo, Bosnia & Herzegovina. Librarian. m. Alma Voloder-Madacki, 1 son. Education: BA, Comparative Literature, BSc, Library Science, 1993-98, University of Sarajevo. Appointments: Librarian, State Archives of Bosnia & Herzegovina, Sarajevo,

1994-97; Referral Archivist, Federal Archives of Bosnia & Herzegovina, INDOC Service, 1997-98; Research Librarian, Library, Soros Media Centre, 1998-99; Head of Information Research and Library Department, 1999-2003, Head, Research and Development Department, 2004-, Human Rights Centre, University of Sarajevo; Advisor for Judical Training Database, Serbia and Montenegro, 2006; Information Management Advisor, United Nations Development Programme, Serbia, 2007. Publications: Articles and papers in professional journals. Honours: President of Conference, Association of Librarians of Bosnia & Herzegovina, 2003. Memberships: Association of Archivists of Bosnia & Herzegovina; Association of Librarians of Bosnia & Herzegovina; Association for the Advancement of Information Science. Address: Human Rights Centre, University of Sarajevo, Zmaja od Bosne 8, 71000 Sarajevo, Bosnia & Herzegovina. E-mail: sm@hrc.unsa.ba

MADDEN John, b. 8 April 1949, Portsmouth, England. Film Director. Appointments: TV includes: Inspector Morse; Prime Suspect IV; Ethan Frome; Films: Mrs Brown, 1997; Shakespeare in Love, 1998; Captain Corelli's Mandolin, 2001; Proof, 2005; Killshot, 2008. Honours: Academy Award for Best Film; BAFTA Award for Best Film, 1998.

MADDOCKS Morris Henry St John, b. 28 April 1928, Elland, West Yorkshire, England. Bishop. m. Anne. Education: MA (Cantab), Trinity College, Cambridge, 1956; Chichester Theological College. Appointments: Curate, St Peter's Ealing, London, 1954-55; Curate, St Andrew's, Uxbridge, 1955-58; Vicar, Weaverthorpe, Helperthorpe and Luttons Ambo, 1958-61; Vicar, St Martin's-on-the-Hill, Scarborough, 1961-71; Bishop of Selby, 1972-83; Co-founder, with Anne Maddocks, The Acorn Christian Healing Trust, 1983; Adviser to the Archbishops of Canterbury and York for the ministry of health and healing, 1983-95; Assistant Bishop, Diocese of Chichester, 1987-; Canon of Chichester Cathedral, 1992. Publications: Books: The Christian Healing Ministry, 1981; The Christian Adventure, 1983; Journey to Wholeness, 1986; A Healing House of Prayer, 1987; Twenty Questions About Healing, 1988; The Vision of Dorothy Kerin, 1991. Honour: Cross of St Augustine, 1995. Membership: Founding Life President (with Anne Maddocks), The Acorn Christian Foundation. Address: 3 The Chantry, Cathedral Close, Chichester, West Sussex PO 19 1PZ, England.

MADDOX Jerry Aven, b. 27 September 1935, Atlanta, Georgia, USA. Retired Catalogue Executive. m. Roberta Eddy, 2 sons, 1 daughter. Education: BBA, Emory University Business School, 1957; JD, Emory University Law School, 1964. Appointments: Catalogue Management Executive, Sears Roebuck & Co, 1957-88; School System Substitute Teacher, DeKalb County, Georgia, 1992-2000; Author (writer), 2000-07. Publications: Books on genealogy, historical fiction and non-fiction. Honours: DeKalb County Jaycees; US Marine Corps Active & Reserves, 1957-63; Outstanding Atlantans, Heritage Pub Co, 1977-78; Life Member, National Eagle Scout Association; Jackson Medal, 2000. Memberships: Life Member, Dunwoody Preservation Trust; Dunwoody United Methodist Church; Clan Hay; Clan Grant; St Andrew's Society; Sons of Confederate Veterans; Military Order of Stars & Bars; Life Member, Ft Delaware Society. Address: 4917 Cambridge Drive, Dunwoody, GA 30338, USA.

MADDY Penelope Jo, b. 4 July 1950, Tulsa, Oklahoma, USA. Professor. Education: BA, Mathematics, University of California, Berkeley, 1972; PhD, Philosophy, Princeton University, 1979. Appointments: Assistant Professor, University of Notre Dame, 1978-83; Associate Professor,

University of Illinois, Chicago, 1983-87; Associate Professor, 1987-89, Full Professor, 1989-, University of California, Irvine. Publications: Believing the Axioms, 1988; Realism in Mathematics, 1990; Nationalism in Mathematics, 1997; Second Philosophy, 2007. Honours: Westinghouse Scholarship, 1968; Marshall Scholarship, 1972; American Academy of Arts & Science, 1998; Lakatos Prize, 2002. Memberships: Association for Symbolic Logic; American Philosophical Association; Philosophical Science Association. Address: Department of Logic & Philosophy of Science, University of California Irvine, Irvine, CA 92697-5100, USA.

MADONNA (Madonna Louise Veronica Ciccone), b. 16 August 1958, Bay City, Michigan, USA. Singer; Songwriter; Actress. m. (1) Sean Penn, 1985, divorced 1989; 1 daughter with Carlos Leon, (2) Guy Ritchie, 2000, 1 son, 1 adopted son. Education: University Of Michigan, 1976-78. Career: Dancer, New York, 1979; Actress, 1980-; Solo singer, 1983-; Film appearances include: Vision Quest, Desperately Seeking Susan, 1985; Shanghai Surprise, 1986; Who's That Girl, 1987; Bloodhounds On Broadway, Dick Tracy, 1990; A League Of Their Own, 1992; Evita, 1996; The Next Best Thing, 2000; Swept Away, Die Another Day, 2002; Numerous worldwide concerts, 1983-; Major appearances include: Live Aid, Philadelphia, 1985; Don't Bungle The Jungle, ecological awareness benefit, 1989; Television includes: In Bed With Madonna, documentary, 1991; Stage performance, Speed The Plow, Broadway, 1988; Up For Grabs, Wyndhams Theatre, 2002; Owner, Maverick record label. Compositions include: Co-writer, own hits: Live To Tell; Open Your Heart; Justify My Love; Co-writer, Each Time You Break My Heart, Nick Kamen, 1986. Recordings: Hit singles include: Holiday, 1983; Lucky Star, Borderline, Like A Virgin, 1984; Material Girl, Crazy For You, Angel, Into The Groove, Dress You Up, Gambler, 1985; Live To Tell, Papa Don't Preach, True Blue, Open Your Heart, 1986; La Isla Bonita, Who's That Girl, Causin' A Commotion, The Look Of Love, 1987; Like A Prayer, Express Yourself, Cherish, Dear Jessie, 1989; Oh Father, 1990; Keep It Together, Vogue, I'm Breathless, Hanky Panky, Justify My Love, Rescue Me, 1991; This Used To Be My Playground, Erotica, Deeper And Deeper, 1992; Bad Girl, Fever, Rain, 1993; Frozen, Ray of Light, Power of Goodbye, 1998; Nothing Really Matters, Beautiful Stranger: theme song from Austin Powers: The Spy Who Shagged Me, 1999; American Pie, Music, Don't Tell Me, 2000; What It Feels Like For A Girl, 2001; Die Another Day, 2002; American Life, Hollywood, 2003; Hung Up, 2005; Albums: Madonna, 1983; Like A Virgin, 1985; True Blue, 1986; Who's That Girl?, film soundtrack, 1987; You Can Dance, 1988; Like A Prayer, 1989; I'm Breathless, The Immaculate Collection, Dick Tracy film soundtrack, 1990; Erotica, 1992; Bedtime Stories, 1994; Something To Remember, 1995; Evita, film soundtrack, 1996; Ray of Light, 1997; Music, 2000; American Life, 2003; Remixed and Revisted, 2004; Confessions on a Dance Floor, 2005. Publications: Sex, 1992; The English Roses, 2003; Mr Peabody's Apples, 2003; Yaokov and the Seven Thieves, 2004; The Adventures of Abdi, 2004. Honours include: Numerous MTV Video Awards, including Vanguard Award, 1986; American Music Awards: Favourite Female Video Artist, 1987; Favourite Dance Single, 1991; Oscar, Best Song, 1991; Juno Award, International Song Of The Year, 1991; Grammy Award, Best Longform Music Video, 1992; Grammy Award, Best Electronic/Dance Album, 2007; Numerous awards from Billboard, Vogue and Rolling Stone magazines. Address: c/o Norman West Management, 9348 Civic Centre Drive, Beverly Hills, CA 90210, USA.

DICTIONARY OF INTERNATIONAL BIOGRAPHY

MADSEN Michael, b. 25 September 1958, Chicago, USA. Actor. m. (1) Jeannine Bisignano, divorced, 1 son, (2) Georganne La Piere (divorced), (3) De Anna Morgan 1996-, 3 children. Appointments: Began acting career, Steppenwolf Theatre, Chicago; Appeared in plays including: Of Mice and Men; A Streetcar Named Desire; Appeared in Broadway Production of A Streetcar Named Desire, 1992; Films: Wargames; The Natural; Racing with the Moon; The Killing Time; Shadows in the Storm; Iguana; Blood Red; Kill Me Again; The Doors; The End of Innocence; Thelma and Louise; Fatal Instinct; Inside Edge; Reservoir Dogs; Straight Talk; Almost Blue; Free Willy; A House in the Hills; Money for Nothing; Trouble Bound; Wyatt Earp; The Getaway; Dead Connection; Species; Free Willy II: The Adventure Home; The Winner; Red Line; Mulholland Falls; Man with a Gun; The Last Days of Frankie the Fly; Rough Draft; The Marker; Donnie Brasco; Catherine's Grove; Papertrail; The Girl Gets Moe; Executive Target; The Thief and the Stripper; Supreme Sanction; The Florentine; Species II; Detour; Code of the Dragon, 2000; The Ghost, 2000; High Noon, 2000; LAPD Conspiracy, 2001; LAPD To Protect and Serve, 2001; Welcome to America, 2002; Die Another Day, 2002; My Boss's Daughter, 2003; Kill Bill 1,2, 2003-04; Smatyvay udochki, 2004; Hoboken Hollow, 2005; Sin City, 2005; The Last Drop, 2005; Last Hour, 2006; Scary Movie 4, 2006; House, 2007; Vice, 2007; Deep Winter, 2007; Hell Ride, 2008; The Portal, 2008. TV: Our Family House, 1985-86; Special Bulletin, 1983; War and Remembrance, 1988; Montana, 1990; Baby Snatcher, 1992; Beyond the Law, 1994. Address: Grant and Tane, 9100 Wilshire Boulevard, Beverley Hills, CA 90212, USA.

MADUAKOR Obiajuru, b. 5 July 1938, Isulo, Anambra State, Nigeria. University Professor of English Language and Literature and of African Literature. m. Chijioke Obiageli, 3 sons. Education: BA, Honours English, University of Ibadan, Nigeria, 1962-65; MA, English Literature, University of Leeds, UK, 1971-72; PhD, English Literature, University of Ottawa, Canada, 1972-77. Appointments: Lecturer, English Literature, University of Ife, Nigeria, 1978-81; Senior Lecturer, 1981-84, Associate Professor, 1984-87, Professor, English Literature, 1987-, University of Nigeria, Nsukka, Nigeria. Publications: Book: Wole Soyinka: An Introduction to His Writing, 1986; 50 articles. Honours: DAAD Scholar, University of Mainz, 1993; Visiting Fellow, University of Hull, 1992; Visiting Fellow, University of Leeds, 1993; Visiting Professor, University of Guelph, 1997-99; Adjunct Professor, Tyndale University College, Toronto, 2004-. Memberships: African Literature Association; Modern Language Association; Literary Society of Nigeria; American Studies Association of Nigeria. Address: 20-540 Dorchester Drive, Oshawa, Ontario L1J 6M5, Canada. E-mail: obimaduakor@hotmail.com

MAEHLER Herwig Gustav Theodor, b. 29 April 1935, Berlin, Germany. Emeritus Professor of Papyrology. m. Margaret, 2 daughters. Education: Classics and Classical Archaeology, Universities of Hamburg, Tübingen and Basel, 1955-61; PhD, University of Hamburg, 1961; Postdoctoral British Council Fellowship, Oxford University, England, 1961-62; Habilitation, Freie Universität, Berlin, 1975. Appointments: Research Assistant, University of Hamburg, 1962-63; Research Assistant, Hamburg University Library, 1963-64; Keeper of Greek Papyri, Egyptian Museum, West Berlin, 1964-79; Reader in Papyrology, 1979-81, Professor of Papyrology, 1981-2000, Professor Emeritus, 2000-, University College, London. Publications: Die Auffassung des Dichterberufs im frühen Griechentum bis zur Zeit Pindars, 1963; Die Handschriften der S Jacobi-Kirche in Hamburg,

1967; Urkunden römischer Zeit, 1968; Papyri aus Hermupolis, 1974; Die Lieder des Bakchylides Part I, 1982, Part II, 1997; Greek Bookhands of the Early Byzantine Period (with G Cavallo), 1987; Urkunden aus Hermupolis, 2005; Editions of Bacchylides, 1970, 2003; Bacchylides: A Selection, 2004; Pindar, 1971, 1975, 1989; About 120 articles in learned journals. Honours: Fellow, British Academy, 1986; Fellow, Accademia Nazionale dei Lincei, Rome 2001; Honorary Fellow, University College London, 2001; Honorary PhDs: University of Helsinki, 2000, University of Budapest, 2001, Rome II Tor Vergata, 2003. Membership: Corresponding Member, German Archaeological Institute, 1979; Academia Europea; Association Internationale des Papyrologues. Address: Zeltgasse 6/12, A-1080 Wien, Austria. E-mail: hgt.maehler@virgin.net

MÄELTSEMEES Sulev, b. 7 August 1947, Lihula, Estonia. Professor. m. Helle Evert, 1 daughter. Education: Diploma (cum laude), 1970, PhD, 1975, Tartu University. Appointments: Researcher, Estonian Branch, USSR Academy of Sciences Central Institute of Economic Mathematics, 1970-78; Head of Chair of Service Economy, Tallinn University of Technology, 1978-86; Director of Research, Institute of Economics of Estonian Academy of Sciences, 1986-92; Chairman, Tallinn City Council, 1992-93; Rector, Estonian Institute of Public Administration, 1993-97; Professor, Regional Policy, 1998-, Dean, Faculty of Humanities, 2004-, Tallinn University of Technology. Publications: Local Government in Estonia, Decentralization: Experiments and Reforms, 2000; The Capital City in the Local Self-Government System in Europe, 2005; Wirtschafts und Verwaltungspolitik-zusammenhänge und Gegensätze, 2005. Honours: Medal, Order of White Star 4th Class, President of Estonia, 2002; Badge of Merit, City of Tallinn, 2007. Memberships: Estonian Union of Scientists; Estonian Geographical Society; Estonian Economic Association. Address: 10125 Fachlmanni 34-9, Tallinn, Estonia.

MAES Michael H J, b. 10 March 1954, Ghent, Belgium. Professor; Psychiatrist. m. Rinlaphat Thanapuntasit, 3 daughters. Education: MD, 1979; Psychiatrist, 1986; PhD, 1991. Appointments: Assistant Professor of Psychiatry, University of Antwerp, Belgium, 1986-91; Assistant Professor of Psychiatry, CWRU, Cleveland, Ohio, USA, 1991-96; Director, Clinical Research, Centre of Mental Health, Antwerp, 1995-; Adjunct Professor, Vanderbilt University, Nashville, Tennessee, USA, 1997-; Professor of Psychiatry, Department of Psychiatry, University of Maastricht, The Netherlands, 1999-2005. Publications: Book: Van Freud tot Omega-3 (Standaard); Over 400 articles in international journals. Honours: ECNP Award, 1991; The Klerman Award for Outstanding Research, NARSAD, 1998; Prize, Rimauz-Bartier, FWO, 1999; Listed in several biographical publications. Memberships: World Psychiatric Association; Society of Biological Psychiatry. Address: Olmenlaan 9, 2610 Wilrijk, Belgium. E-mail: crc.mh@telenet.be

MAGEE Bryan, b. 12 April 1930, London, England. Writer. m. Ingrid Söderlund, 1 daughter. Education: MA, Keble College, Oxford University, 1956; Yale University, 1955-56. Appointments: Theatre Critic, The Listener, 1966-67; Lecturer in Philosophy, Balliol College, Oxford, 1970-71; Visiting Fellow, All Souls College, Oxford, 1973-74; Regular Columnist, The Times, 1974-76; Member of Parliament for Leyton, 1974-83; President, Critics Circle of Great Britain, 1983-84; Honorary Senior Research Fellow, 1984-94, Visiting Professor, 1994-2000, King's College, London; Honorary Fellow, Queen Mary College, London, 1988-; Fellow,

Queen Mary and Westfield College, London, 1989-; Visiting Fellow: Wolfson College, Oxford, 1991-94, New College, Oxford, 1995, Merton College, Oxford, 1998, St Catherine's College, Oxford, 2000, Peterhouse College, Cambridge, 2001. Publications: Go West Young Man, 1958; To Live in Danger, 1960; The New Radicalism, 1962; The Democratic Revolution, 1964; Towards 2000, 1965; One in Twenty, 1966; The Television Interviewer, 1966; Aspects of Wagner, 1968; Modern British Philosophy, 1971; Popper, 1973; Facing Death, 1977; Men of Ideas, 1978, reissued as Talking Philosophy, 2001; The Philosophy of Schopenhauer, 1983; The Great Philosophers, 1987; On Blindness, 1995, reissued as Sight Unseen, 1998; Confessions of a Philosopher, 1997; The Story of Philosophy, 1998; Wagner and Philosophy, 2000; Clouds of Glory, 2003; A Hoxton Childhood, 2003. Contributions to: Numerous journals. Honours: Silver Medal, Royal Television Society, 1978; J R Ackerley Prize for Autobiography, 2004. Memberships: Critics Circle; Society of Authors; Arts Council of Great Britain and Chair, Music Panel, 1993-94; Honorary Fellow, Keble College, Oxford, 1994-; Silver Medal, Royal TV Society; Life Member, Clare Hall, Cambridge, 2004. Address: Wolfson College, Oxford OX 2 6UD, England.

MAGER Peter Paul, b. 18 June 1946, Klostergeringswalde, Saxony, Germany. m. Christine, 2 daughters. Education: Approbation in Medicine, Leipzig, 1973; MD, 1974; Mathematics in Chemistry, 1975, Degree in Pharmacology and Toxicology, 1978, Halle; DSc, 1982; Degree in Educational and Didactic Methodology in University Teaching, 1983; Facultas docendi, 1990; Dr med habil, 1991. Appointments: Assistant, Pharmacology and Toxicology, University of Greifswald, 1973-75; Assistant in Internal Medicine, Doesen/Saxony, 1975-76; Senior Researcher, Institute of Pharmacy, University of Halle, 1976-80; Head of Research Group of Pharmacochemistry, University of Leipzig, 1980-; Co-ordinator, Research Programme, FMC Co, Princeton, New Jersey, USA, 1984-90; Consultant, Clinical Pharmacology, Leipzig, 1985-90; Consultant, Biostructure SA, France, 1991-94; Managing Director, Institute of Pharmacology and Toxicology, University of Leipzig, 1993-95; Professor, 1996. Publications: Co-editor and Referee of scientific periodicals; Around 230 papers in scientific periodicals and handbooks; 3 monographs. Honour: Leibniz Award. Memberships include: New York Academy of Sciences; American Association for the Advancement of Science; Affiliate, International Union of Pure and Applied Chemistry; German Society of Pharmacology and Toxicology; Medicinal Chemistry Division, Computer Chemistry Division, German Chemical Society; Deutsche Hochschulverband. Address: Institute of Pharmacology and Toxicology, Haertelstr 16-18, Leipzig D-04107, Germany. E-mail: magp@server3.medizin.uni-leipzig.de

MAGNUSSON Tomas Herbert, b. 1 April 1949, Linköping, Sweden. Dentist. m. Annica Birgitta Hedmo, 3 daughters. Education: L D S, 1974; Odont Dr, PhD, 1981; Docent, Reader, 1986; Professor, 2006; Certified Specialist in Stomatognathic Physiology, 1993. Appointments: General Practitioner, Jokkmokk, Sweden, 1974-1979; Assistant Professor, University of Göteborg, Sweden, 1979-1980; Head, Senior Consultant, Lulea, Sweden, 1980-1988; Senior Consultant, 1988-2000, Head, Senior Consultant, 2000-, Jonkoping, Sweden. Publications: Published more than 70 scientific papers in peer review national and international journals mainly in the field of temporomandibular disorders; One out of two authors of four textbooks and author of four separate book chapters, all in the field of temporomandibular disorders. Honours: The Forsberg Dental Foundation Award for extraordinary clinical achievements, 1990; The Henry

Beyron Award for unique research, 2000; Corresponding member, Finnish Dental Society, 2002. Memberships: Swedish Dental Association; Swedish Dental Society; Swedish Academy of Temporo Mandibular Disorders; Board member and past president of the Society of Oral Physiology. Address: The Institute for Postgraduate Dental Education, Box 1030, SE-55111 Jonkoping, Sweden. E-mail: tomas.magnusson@lj.se

MAGUIRE Adrian Edward, b. 29 April 1971, Ireland. Jockey. m. Sabrina, 1995, 1 daughter. Education: Kilmessan National School; Trim Vocational School. Appointments: Champion Pony Race Rider, 1986; Champion Point to Point Rider, 1990-91; Champion Conditional Jockey, 1991-92; Winner of the Following Races: Cheltenham Gold Cup; Irish Grand National; Galway Plate; Imperial Cup; Greenalls Gold Cup; Queen Mother Champion Chase; King George VI Chase; Triumph Hurdle and Cathcort Chase; Holds record for most Point to Point winners in a season; Most winners in a season for a conditional jockey (71), 1991-92; Retired due to neck injury having won over 1,000 races, 2002. Address: The Jockey Club (Jockey Section), 42 Portman Square, London, W1H 0EM, England.

MAGUIRE Robert Alfred, b. 6 June 1931, London, England. Retired Architect; Sculptor. m. Alison Margaret, 4 daughters. Education: Leverhulme Scholar, AA Diploma with Honours, Architectural Association School of Architecture, London, 1948-53. Appointments: Buildings Editor, Architect's Journal, 1954-59; Partner, Robert Maguire & Keith Murray, 1959-89; Chairman, Maguire & Co, 1988-2003, Maguire & Co International, 1989-2002; Consultant, Maguire & Co, 2003-2004; Surveyor of the Fabric to The Queen's Free Chapel of St George at Windsor Castle, 1975-87; Head, Oxford School of Architecture, 1976-85; Trustee, Stowe House Preservation Trust, 1998-2007. Publications: Book: Modern Churches of the World (co-author with Keith Murray); Numerous articles on architectural theory, architectural critiques and conservation; Major paper: Continuity and Modernity in the Holy Place (Annual Lecture to the Society of Architectural Historians of Great Britain), 1995. Honours: OBE, 1983; 4 buildings of his own design listed as Buildings of Historic Interest: St Paul's Church, Bow Common, London; St Matthew's Church, Perry Beeches, Birmingham; St Mary's Abbey Church, West Malling; Residences at St Mary's Abbey, West Malling. Memberships: Royal Society of Arts; Oxford University Club. Address: Hopewater House, Ettrickbridge, Selkirk TD7 5JN, Scotland.

MAGUIRE Tobey Vincent, b. 27 June 1975, Santa Monica, California, USA. Actor. m. Jennifer Meyer, 2007, 1 child. Career: Various Commercials as child; Films include: Pleasantville, 1998; Ride with the Devil, 1999; Tales from the Whoop: Hot Rod Brown Class Clown, 1990; Empire Records, 1995; Fear and Loathing in Las Vegas, 1998; The Cider House Rules, 1999; Wonder Boys, 2000; Cats and Dogs, voice, 2001; Dons Plum, 2001; Spider-Man, 2002; Seabiscuit, 2003; Spider-Man 2, 2004; The Good German, 2006; Spider-Man 3, 2007. TV appearances include: Celebrities Uncensored; The Tonight show with Jay Leno; Rove Live; Tracey Takes On...; Roseanne; The Wild and Crazy Kids; Great Scott!. Honours include: Academy of Science Fiction, Fantasy & Horror Films, USA, Best Performance by a Young Actor, Pleasantville, 1999.

MAHBOOB Soltanali, b. 14 April 1944, Meshkinshahr, Iran. Professor. m. Lakestani-Amineh, 1 son, 1 daughter. Education: BS, MSc Degrees, Iran, 1965; CES, DEA, Doctorate Degree,

France, 1969; Sabbatical Leave, USA, 1974-75. Appointments: Dean of Pharmacy School, 1975-76; Head of Biochemistry and Nutrition Department, 1976-80; Associate Visiting Professor, USA, 1984-85; Dean of Health and Nutrition School, Tabriz University of Medical Sciences, Tabriz, Iran, 1990-2002; Director of Food and Nutrition Security Program in Tabriz, 2002-05; Director, Nutritional Research Centre, 2005-; Vice Chancellor, Education and Research Affairs, Unviersity of Rabe-Rashidi, 2008-. Publications: 90 articles in national and international journals; 150 articles presented at international and national congresses. Honours: Outstanding Professor of Tabriz University of Medical Science, 1985, 1996, 1998; Outstanding Professor of Iran, 1997; Outstanding Researcher of Tabriz University of Medical Science, 1998, 1999, 2003; Outstanding Researcher of Iran, 1998; Outstanding Manager of Tabriz University of Medical Science, 2000. Memberships: Iranian Society of Nutrition; Iranian Society of Physiology and Pharmacology; FASEB; Sigma Xi Scientific Research Society; Nutrition Today; Iranian Society of Trace Elements Research. Address: Department of Biochemistry and Clinical Nutrition, Faculty of Public Health and Nutrition; Tabriz University of Medical Science, Tabriz, Iran. Address: University of Rabe-Rashidi, Valiasr, Tavanir Avenue, Tabriz, Iran. E-mail: mahbooba@tbzmed.ac.ir

MAHFOUZ Soheir Mahmoud, b. 12 April 1950, Cairo, Egypt. Professor. m. Khalid Aly Sorour, 1 son, 1 daughter. Education: MBBCh, 1974, MSc, Pathology, 1980; PhD, Pathology, 1984, Faculty of Medicine, Cairo University. Appointments: Pathology Instructor, 1976-78; Assistant Lecturer, 1980-84; Assistant Professor of Pathology, 1989-94; Head of Cytology, 1989-, Professor of Pathology, 1994-, Chair of Pathology, 2007, Pathology Department, Kasr Al Ainy Hospital, Cairo University. Publications: Articles in scientific journals: Distribution of the major connective matrix components of the stromal reaction of breast carcinoma, 1987; Synovial Sarcoma, 1990. Honours: Graduated Excellent with Honours, Faculty of Medicine, Cairo University; Woman of the Year 2004, ABI; World Lifetime Achievement Award, 2004, ABI. Memberships: Egyptian Society of Pathologists; Arab Division of the International Academy of Pathology; Vice President of the Commission of EOLSS, Medical Sciences Theme, UNESCO-EOLSS. Address: Pathology Department, Kasr Al Ainy Hospital, Cairo University, Manial, Cairo, Egypt. E-mail: soheirmahfouz@yahoo.com

MAHJOUB Bechir Mohamed, b. 18 June 1935, Mahdia, Tunisia. Professor. m. Aicha Zouari, 2 sons, 1 daughter. Education: Licence de Mathématiques, Institut des Hautes Études de Tunis, 1960; Diplôme D'Études Supérieures, University of Tunis, 1963; Doctorat d'État es Sciences Mathématiques, Paris Sorbonne, 1970. Appointments: Professor of Mathematics, University of Tunis, 1974-; Director General, Higher Education of Tunisia, 1977-88; Delegate of Tunisia at UNESCO, 1988-92; Professor, University of Qatar, 1992-2000. Publications: Book: Cours D'Analyse, 1983; Numerous articles on mathematics published in the proceedings of the Academy of Sciences of Paris and in the annals of the Institute Henri Poincare. Honours: Officier de l'Ordre de la Republique, Tunisia, 1978; Officier de la Légion d'Honneur, France, 1983; Officier de l'Ordre National du Merite, France, 1984. Memberships: Société Mathématique de Tunisie; Association Tunisienne des Sciences Mathématiques. Address: 9 rue des Narcisses, 1004 Elmenzah 5, Tunisia. E-mail: b.mahjoub@yahoo.fr

MAHMOUD Mervat Mostafa, b. 14 April 1941, Egypt. Professor of Medicine. m. Mohamed El Fayoumy, 1 son, 2 daughters. Education: MD, Neurology, Faculty of Medicine, Cairo University, 1972. Appointments: Professor of Neurology, Chairman of Neurology, Head of Neurology Department, 1998-2001, Faculty of Medicine, Cairo University. Publications: Numerous articles in professional journals. Honours: National Award in Medical Sciences, 1982; Award, Egyptian Syndicate (Medical). Memberships: Fellow, American Academy of Neurology, USA; Fellow, World Federation of Neurology; Fellow, Egyptian League Epilepsy. Address: 5 Giamet El Kahera Street, Giza, Egypt.

MAIA Luis Alberto Coelho Rebelo, b. 3 July 1971, France (Portuguese nationality). Auxiliar Professor of Psychology. 1 daughter. Education: Clinical Psychologist, Minho University, Portugal, 1998; MSc, Neuroscientist, Medical School of Lisbon, Portugal, 2001; Graduation, Investigative Proficiency on Psychobiology, 2005, Graduation, Clinical Neuropsychology, 2005, PhD, Clinical Neuropsychologist, 2006, USAL, Spain; Medico Legal Perit, Medicine Institute Abel Salazar, 2007. Appointments: Clinical Psychologist, mental health hospital, 1999-2002; Auxiliar Professor, Beira Interior University, 2002-; Clinical Director, private clinic department, 2007-. Publications: Numerous books and articles in professional journals. Honours: 4 Scholar Merit Awards, 1995, 1996, 1997, 1998, Eng Antonio de Almeida Award, 1998, Minho University, Portugal; Listed in international biographical dictionaries. Memberships: Portuguese Association for Experimental Psychology; Clinical Neuropsychology Portuguese Society; Multiple Sclerosis Portuguese Society; National Psychologist Syndicate; National Syndicate for Superior Studies. Address: Av da Anil, nº 3-A, Esc 8 e 9, 6200-502 Covilhã, Portugal. E-mail: luismaia.gabinete@gmail.com

MAINWARING Scott Patterson, b. 18 July 1954, Pittsburgh, Pennsylvania, USA. Political Scientist; Educator. m. Susan M Elfin, 1 son, 1 daughter. Education: BA, Political Science, 1972-76, MA, Political Science, 1975-76, Yale University; PhD, Political Science, Stanford University, 1978-83. Appointments: Assistant Professor, Government, 1983-88, Associate Professor, Government, 1988-93, Professor of Government, 1993-96, Chair, Government Department 1996-97, Eugene Conley Professor of Political Science, 1996-, Director, Kellogg Institute for International Studies, 1997-2002, 2003-07, University of Notre Dame, Indiana, USA. Publications: Author, The Catholic Church and Politics in Brazil 1916-1985, 1986; Author, Rethinking Party Systems in the Third Wave of Democratization: The Case of Brazil, 1999; Edited books: The progressive Church in Latin America, 1989; Issues in Democratic Consolidation, 1992; Building Democratic Institutions: Party Systems in Latin America, 1995; Presidentialism and Democracy in Latin America, 1997; Christian Democracy in Latin America, 2003; The Third Wave of Democratization in Latin America, 2005; Democratic Accountability in Latin America, 2003; The Crisis of Democratic Representation in the Andes, 2006. Honours: Phi Beta Kappa, Yale University; Magna Cum Laude, Yale University, 1976; Washburn Clark Prize, Yale University, 1976; Hubert Herring Prize for the best dissertation on a Latin American subject, 1983-84; 7 Research Grants and Fellowships include: Fulbright Hays, 1980-81; Social Science Research Council, 1980-81; Fulbright-Hays, 1987-88; Hoover Institute, Stanford, 1990-91; Woodrow Wilson Centre, 1995-96; Guggenheim Fellow, 2000; Listed in national and international biographical dictionaries. Memberships: Council on Foreign Relations, 1986-91; Research Council, International Forum for Democratic Studies, National Endowment for Democracy,

Washington DC, 1994-.Address: Kellogg Institute for International Studies, 231 Hesburgh Center, Notre Dame, IN 46556, USA. E-mail: mainwaring.1@nd.edu

MAJI Debabrata, b. 6 September 1961, Deulpur, Howrah, West Bengal. m. Tapati, 1 son, 1 daughter. Co-ordinator. Education: NTC, Ramakrishna Mission Ashrama, Narendrapur, 24 Parganas, 1982; BSc (2nd Year), Uluberia College, 1984; ASC, 1984, AVTS, 1992, Advanced Training Institute, Calcutta, Dasnagar, Howrah; SDP, Central Staff Training and Research Institute, Calcutta, 1987; FIMI, Institution of Motor Industries, Chennai, 1992; FIAE, Institution of Automotive Engineers, Chennai, 1993.Appointments: Instructor, Industrial Training Institute, Roing, Arunachal Pradesh, 1984-87; Instructor, 1987-93, Foreman, 1993-2001, Department of Mechanical Engineering, Transport Officer, 2001-07, Central Automobile Workshop, Assistant Project Officer, Community Polytechnic Scheme of MHRD, 2007, Co-ordinator, Centre for Appropriate Technology & Rural Development, 2007-, NERIST, Nirjuli, Arunachal Pradesh. Publications: Numerous book chapters, research papers in professional journals and proceedings of international & national conferences, seminars, workshops; Articles in magazines, souvenirs and newspapers. Honours: Several awards for sports activities; Listed in international biographical dictionaries; Award in State Level Essay Competition, 1994; Promising Social Workmanship Award, 1995, 2001; Best Organisation of the Year for Social Activities, 1995; Best Paper Presenter Award, 2000; 15th Indian Engineering Congress Award, 2000; Certificate of Appreciation, 2006; International Scientist Award, 2008; Chairman in Technical Sessions; Invited Guest in conferences, seminars, workshops, exhibitions and meetings. Memberships: Institution of Motor Industries; Institution of Automotive Engineers; Institution of Mechanical Engineers (India); Karnataka Environment Research Foundation; Indian Society for Technical Education. Address: Centre for Appropriate Technology & Rural Development, North Eastern Regional Institute of Science and Technology (Deemed University), Nirjuli (Itanagar) – 791 109, Arunachal Pradesh, India. E-mail: dmaji2004@gmail.com

MAJOR Clarence, b. 31 December 1936, Atlanta, Georgia, USA. Poet; Writer; Artist; Professor. m. (1) Joyce Sparrow, 1958, divorced 1964, (2) Pamela Ritter. Education: BS, State University of New York at Albany, 1976; PhD, Union Graduate School, 1978. Appointments: Editor, Coercion Review, 1958-66, Writer-in-Residence, Center for Urban Education, New York, 1967-68, Teachers and Writers Collaborative-Teachers College, Columbia University, 1967-71, Aurora College, Illinois, 1974, Albany State College, Georgia, 1984, Clayton College, Denver, 1986, 1987; Associate Editor, Caw, 1967-70, Journal of Black Poetry, 1967-70; Lecturer, Brooklyn College of the City University of New York, 1968-69, 1973, 1974-75, Cazenovia Collge, New York, 1969, Wisconsin State University, 1969, Queens College of the City University of New York, 1972, 1973, 1975, Sarah Lawrence College, 1972-75, School of Continuing Education, New York University, 1975; Columnist, 1973-76, Contributing Editor, 1976-86, American Poetry Review; Assistant Professor, Howard University, 1974-76, University of Washington, 1976-77; Visiting Assistant Professor, University of Maryland at College Park, 1976, State University of New York at Buffalo, 1976; Associate Professor, 1977-81, Professor, 1981-89, University of Colorado at Boulder; Editor, 1977-78, Associate Editor, 1978-, American Book Review; Professor, 1989-, Director, Creative Writing, 1991-, University of California at Davis. Publications: Poetry: The Fires That Burn in Heaven, 1954; Love Poems of a Black

Man, 1965; Human Juices, 1965; Swallow the Lake, 1970; Symptoms and Madness, 1971; Private Line, 1971; The Cotton Club: New Poems, 1972; The Syncopated Cakewalk, 1974; Inside Diameter: The France Poems, 1985; Surfaces and Masks, 1988; Some Observations of a Stranger at Zuni in the Latter Part of the Century, 1989; Parking Lots, 1992; Configurations: New and Selected Poems 1958-1998, 1998; Waiting for Sweet Baby, 2002. Fiction: All-Night Visitors, 1969; new version, 1998; NO, 1973; Reflex and Bone Structure, 1975; Emergency Exit, 1979; My Amputations, 1986; Such Was the Season, 1987; Painted Turtle: Woman with Guitar, 1988; Fun and Games, 1990; Dirty Bird Blues, 1996. Other: Dictionary of Afro-American Slang, 1970; The Dark and Feeling: Black American Writers and Their Work, 1974; Juba to Jive: A Dictionary of African-American Slang, 1994; Necessary Distance: Essays and Criticism, 2001; Come by Here: My Mother's Life, 2002. Editor: Writers Workshop Anthology, 1967; Man is Like a Child: An Anthology of Creative Writing by Students, 1968; The New Black Poetry, 1969; Calling the Wind: Twentieth Century African-American Short Stories, 1993; The Garden Thrives: Twentieth Century African-American Poetry, 1995. Honours: Fulbright-Hays Exchange Award, 1981-83; Western States Book Award, 1986; Pushcart Prize, 1989; National Book Award Bronze Medal Finalist, 1998. Address: c/o Department of English, 1 Shields Avenue, University of California at Davis, Davis, CA 95616, USA.

MAJOR John (Sir), b. 29 March 1943. Politician; Former Member of Parliament. m. Norma Major, 1970, 1 son, 1 daughter. Education: Associate, Institute of Bankers. Appointments: Various executive positions, Stand Chartered Bank, UK and overseas, 1965-80; Served, Lambeth Borough Council, 1968-71, including Housing and Finance Committees, also Chairman, Accounts Committee and Housing Committee, 1969; Contested Camden, St Pancras North, February and October 1974; Member, Board, Warden Housing Association, 1975-93; Member of Parliament for Huntingdonshire, 1979-83, for Huntingdon, 1983-2001; Parliamentary Private Secretary to Ministers of State, Home Office, 1981-83; Assistant Government Whip, 1983-84; Lord Commissioner of Treasury, Senior Government Whip, 1984-85; Parliamentary Under-Secretary of State, Department of Health and Social Security, 1985-86; Minister of State, Social Security and the Disabled, 1986-87; Chief Secretary to the Treasury, 1987-89; Secretary of State for Foreign and Commonwealth Affairs, 1989; Chancellor of the Exchequer, 1989-90; Elected Leader, Conservative Party, 1990; Prime Minister, 1st Lord of the Treasury, Minister for the Civil Service, 1990-97. Publication: The Autobiography, 1999. Honours: Member, Order of the Companions of Honour, 1999; Knight Companion of the Most Noble Order of the Garter, 2005. Memberships: Parliamentary Consultant to Guild of Glass Engravers, 1979-83; President, Eastern Area Young Conservatives, 1983-85; National Asthma Campaign, 1998-; Chair, Carlyle Group, 2001-; Non-Executive Director, Mayflower Corporation, 2000-; Member, Main Committee, MCC, 2001-; Honorary Master of the Bench of the Middle Temple, 1992.. Address: House of Commons, London, SW1A 0AA, England.

MAJOR Malvina (Lorraine) (Dame), b. 28 January 1943, Hamilton, New Zealand. Opera Singer (Soprano). m. Winston William Richard Fleming, 16 January 1965, deceased 1990, 1 son, 2 daughters. Education: Grade VIII, Piano, Singing, Theory, Convent at Ngaruawahia, Waikato; Singing continued under Dame Sister Mary Leo, St Mary's Music School, Auckland, 1960-65 and Ruth Packer, Royal

College of Music, London, London Opera Centre, UK, 1965-67. Debut: Camden Town Festival, 1968 in Rossini's La Donna del Lago. Career includes: Performances as: Belle, Belle of New York, New Zealand, 1963; Pamina, Magic Flute, London Opera Centre, 1967; 1st non Mormon Soloist to sing with Mormon Tabernacle Choir, 1987; Matilda in Elisabetta Regina d'Inghilterra, Camden Town, 1968; Rosina, Barber of Seville, Salzburg (conductor, Claudio Abbado), 1968-69; Gala Concert, King and Queen of Belgium, Centenary Antwerp Zoological Society, 1969; Marguerite, Gounod's Faust, Neath and London, 1969; Bruckner's Te Deum, conductor Daniel Barenboim, 1968; Cio Cio San, Madam Butterfly; Widow, The Merry Widow; Gilda in Rigoletto; Tosca; Constanze in Die Entführung; Arminda in La Finta Giardiniera, Brussels, 1986; Donna Elvira, Don Giovanni, Brighton Festival, 1987; Donna Anna in Don Giovanni at Sydney, Australia, 1987; Operas include recent productions of Rosalinda (Die Fledermaus) and Lucia di Lammermoor, Mimi in La Bohème and Constanze in New York and Australia; Sang Arminda at Lausanne, 1989, Constanze with the Lyric Opera of Queensland; Season 1992-93 with Lucia at Adelaide, Arminda at Salzburg, Violetta and Gilda at Wellington; Sang in Eugene Onegin and Don Giovanni with Wellington City Opera, 1997. Recordings: To The Glory of God, 1964; L'amico Fritz, opera (Caterina), 1969; Songs for All Seasons, Mahler Symphony No 4, 1970; Scottish Soldiers Abroad, 1975; Alleluia, 1974; Operatic Arias, conductor John Matheson, 1987; La Finta Giardiniera, Brussels. Contributions to: London Sunday Times (article by Desmond Shawe-Taylor). Honours: New Zealand Mobil Song Quest, 1963; Melbourne Sun Aria, Australia, 1964; Kathleen Ferrier Scholarship, London, 1966; OBE, 1985; DBE, 1991; Honorary D Litt, 1993; Honorary D Waik, 1993. Address: P O Box 4184, New Plymouth, New Zealand.

MAKARCHIAN Masoud, b. 23 July 1959, Hamadan, Iran. Education: MSc, Engineering, Faculty of Engineering, University of Tehran, Iran, 1987; PhD, Geotechnical Engineering, School of Civil and Mining Engineering, The University of Sydney, Australia, 1995. Appointments: Employed as Lecturer, Bu-Ali Sina University, Iran and transferred to the Ministry of Culture and Higher Education; Design, control and supervision of bridges (over 15 designed), Civil Engineering Committee, Ministry of Jehad-e-Sazandegi, Iran, 1986-88; Manager, Academic Staff Employment Section, Office of Supervision and Evaluation of Education, Ministry of Culture and Higher Education, Iran, 1988-90; Some casual jobs in teaching and civil engineering design, 1995-; Assistant Professor, Bu-Ali Sina University, Hamadan, Iran, 1995-. Publications: 18 papers published in English include most recently: Review of Rock Slop Stability, 1998; An Experimental Study of Foundation Underpinning by Piles, 2002; K_0 Triaxial Tests on C1C Kaolin Clay, 2003; Primary and Secondary Consolidation of Kaolin Clay, 2003 (under review). Memberships: British Geotechnical Association; Iranian Society of Civil Engineers; International Society of Soil Mechanics and Geotechnical Engineering; Indian Geotechnical Society; Iranian Geotechnical Society; Iranian Association of Rail Transport Engineering. Address: Faculty of Engineering, Bu-Ali Sina University, PO Box 65178-4161, Hamadan, Iran. E-mail: makarchian@yahoo.com

MAKAROV Alexander, b. 23 November 1955, Moscow, Russia. Mining Surveyor. m. Alla, 2 sons, 1 daughter. Education: Mining Engineer, 1978, PhD (Mining), 1982, Dr of Sciences (Mining), Professor, 1992, Moscow State Geological Prospekting University. Appointments: Scientific Worker, 1978-92, Professor, 1992-2000, Department Chair, 2000-, Department of Mine Surveying, State Geological Prospekting

University, Moscow, Russia; Chief Geomechanik-Advisor, Kazakhmys Corporation, Kazakhstan, 1996-. Publications: More than 100 publications; Books: Rock Pressure, 1986; Rock Mechanics, 2006; Practical Geomechanics, 2006. Memberships: Russian Association of Surveyors. Address: Apt 23, Building 1, Street of 1905 year, Moscow 123100, Russia. E-mail: abm51@mail.ru

MAKEPEACE John, b. 6 July 1939, Solihull, Warwickshire, England. Designer; Furniture Maker. Education: Denstone College, Staffordshire, 1952-57; Pupil to Keith Cooper, Furniture Maker, 1957-59; City and Guilds Teaching Certificate (Crafts), 1957-59; Study tours in: Scandinavia, 1957; USA, 1961, 1974; Italy, 1968; West Africa, 1972. Career: Established own furniture-making business Director, John Makepeace Furniture Ltd, 1963-; Founder Member, Crafts Council, 1972-77; Furniture commissioned by corporate and private clients in UK, Europe and USA; Consultancy Tours: India, 1974, 1977; Australia, 1980; Japan, 1978, 1994; Korea, 2001; Trustee, Victoria and Albert Museum, 1987-91; Founder and Director, The Parnham Trust, 1976-2001. Publications: Publisher, Conran Octopus, 1995; Makepeace: A Spirit of Adventure in Craft and Design by Professor Jeremy Myerson; Numerous articles in professional and popular journals. Honours: Observer Design Award, 1972; OBE for services to furniture design, 1988; Master's Award, Worshipful Company of Furniture Makers, 1999; Award of Distinction, The Furniture Society, USA, 2002. Memberships: Fellow: Institute of Management; Chartered Society of Designers; Royal Society for the Arts; Member, Contemporary Art Society; Member, Contemporary Applied Arts. Address: Farrs, Whitcombe Road, Beaminster, Dorset DT8 3NB, England.

MAKINDE Moses Akinola, b. 3 March 1942, Ado-Ekiti, Nigeria. Professor of Philosophy. m. Juliana Taiwo, 3 sons. Education: BA, First Class Hons, Philosophy, PhD, University of Toronto; MA, University of Western Ontario. Appointments: Lecturer in Philosophy: Obafemi Awolowo University, 1974-89; Professor of Philosophy, 1989-; Head, Department of Philosophy, 1992-95; Dean, Faculty of Arts, 1997-99. Publications: Books: African Philosophy, Culture and Traditional Medicine, 1988; Awo as a Philosopher, 2002; African Philosophy: The Demise of a Controversy, 2005; Logico-Philosophical Papers, 2008; Several book chapters; Refereed conference proceeding papers; Book reviews; Plenary addresses, guest lectures and numerous articles in scholarly journals. Honours: Fellowship Award, Institute of Administrative Management of Nigeria (IAMN); Certified and Distinguished Administrator (CDA); Qualified and Incorporated Administrative Manager (QIAM); Justice of the Peace; Dean's Honours List, University College, Toronto; Visiting Fulbright Scholar, Ohio University, Athens, Ohio, 1983-84. Memberships: Nigerian Philosophical Association; Canadian Philosophical Association, 1980-83; Ohio Philosophical Association, 1983-85; Institute of Encyclopedia of Human Ideas on Ultimate Reality and Meaning; International Society for Metaphysics; International Federation of Philosophical Societies; Committee Member, Teaching Philosophy of the FISP, 1990-99; Member of the Executive, Nigerian Academy of Letters. Address: Department of Philosophy, Obafemi Awolowo University, Ile-Ife, Nigeria. E-mail: mssmakinde@yahoo.com

MAKKI Mohammad Shawqi I, Administrator. Education: BA, KSU, 1970; MA, 1975, PhD, 1979, University of Durham; Associate Professor, 1985; Professor, 1993. Appointments: Consultant, Centre of Crime Control, 1984-85; Chairman,

Geographical Places Name Unit, 1999-; Deputy Chairman, 1984, Chairman of Geography Department, 1986, KSU; Treasurer, 1985-89, Chairman, 2004, Saudi Geographical Society. Publications: More than 50 published books, articles and reports, etc in the field of Urban Geography and Population Geography. Memberships: Town and Country Planning Association; Editorial Advisory Board, AWG. Honours: Award of Medina Prize, 1997; King Abdul Aziz Award, First Grade, 2000; Award of Medina Cultural Club, 2001; Meritorious Decoration Award, 2006. Address: PO Box 67208, Riyadh 11596, Saudi Arabia. E-mail: makki16@hotmail.com

MAKOWER Peter, b. 12 September 1932, Greenwich, London, England. Architect; Town Planner. m. Katharine Chadburn, 2 sons, 1 daughter. Education: The Royal Engineers, 1951-52; Territorial Army, 1952-56; Master of Arts, Trinity College, University of Cambridge, 1959; Diploma in Architecture, The Polytechnic, London, 1959; Diploma in Town Planning, University of London, 1969. Appointments: Architect, 1959-62, Associate, 1962-82, Frederick Gibberd Partners, London; Executive Architect, Chapman Taylor Partners, 1982-85; Solo Principal, Peter Makower Architects and Planners, 1985-99. Publications: The World is Not Enough – an account of the filming of part of the river chase in the Bond film of that name; The Boater, The Quarterly Magazine of the Thames Vintage Boat Club, 2000. Honours: Conservation and Design Award, London Borough of Richmond upon Thames and the Mortlake with East Sheen Society; Lay Reader, Church of England. Memberships: Associate, 1961-70, Fellow, 1970-, Royal Institute of British Architects; Royal Town Planning Institute, 1972-. Address: 89 Hartington Road, Chiswick, London W4 3TU, England.

MALFITANO Catherine, b. 18 April 1948, New York City, New York, USA. Singer (Soprano). Education: High School of Music and Art; Manhattan School of Music; With violinist father and dancer/actress mother; Voice with Henry Lewis. Debut: Nannetta in Falstaff, Central City Opera, 1972. Career: With Minnesota Opera, 1973, New York City Opera, 1973-79, debut as Mimi/La Bohème; Netherlands Opera: Susanna in Figaro, 1974, Eurydice, 1975, Mimi, 1977; Tosca 1998; Salzburg Festival: Servilia in Tito, 1976, 1977, 1979, 3 Hoffmann roles, 1981, 1982, Salome, 1992, 1993, Elvira in Giovanni, 1994, 1995, 1996; Jenny in Mahagonny, 1998; Met debut as Gretel, 1979, returning for many other roles; Vienna Staatsoper: Violetta, 1982, Manon, 1984, Grete in Schreker's Der Ferne Klang, 1991, Salome and Butterfly, 1993; Wozzeck, 1997; Maggio Musicale Florence: Suor Angelica, 1983, Jenny in Weill's Mahagonny, 1990, Salome, 1994; Teatro Comunale, Florence: Antonia in Hoffmann, 1980-81, Mimi, 1983, Faust, 1985, Butterfly, 1988, Poppea, 1992; Munich: Berg's Lulu, 1985, Mimi, 1986, Daphne, 1988; Covent Garden: Susanna, Zerlina, 1976, Butterfly, 1988, Lina (Stiffelio), Tosca, Tatyana, 1993, Salome, 1995, 1997; Berlin Deutsche Oper: Butterfly, 1987, Amelia in Boccanegra, Mimi, Susanna, 1989, Salome, 1990; Berlin Staatsoper, Marie (Wozzeck), 1994, Leonore (Fidelio), 1995; Geneva: Fiorilla (Turco), 1985, Poppea, Manon, 1989, Leonore, 1994; La Scala: Daphne, 1988, Butterfly, 1990; Wozzeck, 1997; Lyric Opera, Chicago: Susanna, 1975, Violetta, 1985, Lulu, 1987, Barber's Cleopatra, 1991, Butterfly, 1991-92, Liu, 1992; McTeague/Bolcom, 1992; Makropulos Case, 1995-96; 3 Roles/Il Trittico, 1996; Salome, 1996; Butterfly 1997, 1998; Mahagonny, 1998; View from Bridge/Bolcom, 1999; Macbeth, 1999; World premiere roles created: Conrad Susa's Transformations, 1973, Bilby's Doll (Carlisle Floyd), 1976, Thomas Pasatieri's Washington Square, 1976, William Bolcom's McTeague, 1992. Recordings: Rossini Stabat Mater, conductor Muti; Gounod Roméo et Juliette, conductor Plasson; Strauss's Salome, conductor Dohnányi; Music for Voice and Violin with Joseph Malfitano; Tosca - Zubin Mehta; Others; Videos include Tosca with Domingo; Stiffelio with Carreras and Salome. Honours: Emmy, Best Performance in Tosca film; Honorary Doctorate De Paul University, Chicago.

MALICK Terrence, b. 30 November 1943, Ottawa, Illinois, USA. Film Director. Education: Center for Advanced Film Study; American Film Institute. Appointments: Films: Bedlands; Days of Heaven, 1978; The Thin Red Line, 1998; The Moviegoer; The New World, 2005. Honours: NewYork Film Critics Award, National Society of Film Critics Award, 1978; Cannes Film Festival Award, 1978; Golden Berlin Bear Award, 1999; Chicago Film Critics Association Award, 1999; Golden Satellite Award, 1999. Address: c/o DGA, 7920 Sunset Boulevard, Los Angeles, CA 90046, USA.

MALIK Art. b, 13 November, 1952. Actor. m. Gina Rowe, 1980, 2 daughters. Career: TV: The Jewel in the Crown; Chessgame; The Far Pavilions; The Black Tower; Death is Part of the Process; After the War; Shadow of the Cobra; Stolen; Cleopatra; In the Beginning, 2000; The Seventh Scroll, 2001; Holby City, 2003-05; The English Harem, 2005; Mayo, 2006; Dalziel and Pascoe, 2006; The Path to 9/11, 2006; Jackanory Junior, 2007. Films: Richard's Things; A Passage to India; Underworld; Living Daylights; Side Streets; City of Joy, 1992; Wimbledon Poisoner, 1994; True Lies, 1994; A Kid in King Arthur's Court, 1995; Path to Paradise, 1997; Booty Call, 1997; Side Streets, 1998; Tabloid, 2001; Out Done, 2002; Tempo, 2003; Fakers, 2004; Nina's Heavenly Delights, 2007. Theatre: Othello; Cymbeline; Great Expectations.

MALIK Zubeida, Journalist. Appointments: Correspondent, Today programme, Radio 4, Reporter, Newsnight, BBC2; Interviewed key figures including: Kofi Anan, President Musharraf, Tony Blair, Prince Saud Al Faisal, Archbishop Tutu, Hamas Sheikh Yassin. Honours: BT Press Award for Radio News Broadcaster of the Year, 1997; Young Journalist of the Year, Foreign Press Association, 2000; Best Radio News Journalist, EMMA, 2001, 2002; Media Personality of the Year, Asian Women of Achievement Awards, 2002; Winner, Carlton TV Multicultural Achievement Award for Television and Radio, 2003; Voted as one of the Good Housekeeping Role Models, 2004. Publications: Contributions to September 11 2001, Feminist Perceptives. Address: Today Programme, BBC Radio 4, Room G630, Stage 6, Television Centre, Wood Lane, London W12 7RJ, England.

MALIŃSKI Mirosław, b. 17 May 1955, Koszalin, Poland. Physicist. m. Teresa Glócko, 1 son, 1 daughter. Education: Master of Science, 1979, PhD, 1988, N C University, Toruń, Poland; DSc, University of Technology, Wroclaw, Poland, 2005. Appointments: Reliability Specialist, Semiconductor Research and Product Centre, 1979-93; Tutor, 1993-2003, Press Agent 1999-2003, Professor and Vice-Dean for Scientific Research, Faculty of Electronic and Computer Science, 2006-08,Technical University of Koszalin, Publications: 83 pieces in professional scientific journals. Honours: Science Awards of the Rector, Technical University of Koszalin, 1998, 2003, 2005, 2007; Outstanding Paper Award, IEEE, USA, 1998; West-Pomeranian Nobel Prize Winner, 2003. Address: 103 Francuska St, 75-430 Koszalin, Poland. E-mail: miroslaw.malinski@tu.koszalin.pl

MALKOVICH John, b. 9 December 1953, Christopher, Illinois, USA. m. (1) Glenne Headley, 1982, divorced, (2) Nicoletta Peyran, 1989, 2 children. Education: Eastern Illinois and Illinois State University. Appointments: Co-Founder, Steppenwolf Theatre, Chicago, 1976; Theatre appearances include: True West, 1982; Death of a Salesman, 1984; Burn This, 1987; Director, Balm in Gilead, 1984-85; Arms and the Man, Coyote Ugly, 1985; The Caretaker, 1986; Burn This, 1990; A Slip of the Tongue, 1992; Libra, Steppenwolfe, 1994; Film appearances include: Places in the Heart, The Killing Fields, 1984; Eleni, 1985; Making Mr Right, The Glass Menagerie, Empire of the Sun, 1987; Miles from Home, 1988; Dangerous Liaisons, Jane, La Putaine du roi, Queen's Logic, The Sheltering Sky, 1989; The Object of Beauty, 1991; Shadows and Fog, Of Mice and Men, 1992; Jennifer Eight; Alive; In the Line of Fire; Mary Reilly, 1994; The Ogre, 1995; Mulholland Falls, Portrait of a Lady, 1996; Con Air; The Man in the Iron Mask, 1997; Rounders, Tune Regained, 1998; Being John Malkovich, The Libertine, Ladies Room, Joan of Arc, 1999; Shadow of the Vampire, 2000; Je Rentre à la Maison, Hotel, Knockaround Guys, 2001; The Dancer Upstairs, director and producer, 2002; Ripley's Game, Johnny English, Um Filme Falado, 2003; The Libertine, 2004; The Hitchiker's Guide to the Galaxy, Colour Me Kubrick; 2005; Art School Confidential, Klimt, The Call, Eragon, 2006; In Transit, Drunkboat, Gardens of the Night, Beowulf, Disgrace, 2007; The Mutant Chronicles, The Great Buck Howard, Afterwards, 2008. Executive Producer, The Accidental Tourist. Address: c/o Artists Independent Network, 32 Tavistock Street, London, WC2E 7PB, England.

MALLARD John Rowland, b. 14 January 1927, Northampton, England. Professor of Medical Physics and Medical Engineering. m. Fiona Lawrance, 1 son, 1 daughter. Education: BSc honours, Physics, University College, Nottingham, 1947; PhD, Magnetism, 1952, DSc, Medical Physics, 1972, University of Nottingham. Appointments: Assistant Physicist, Radium Institute, Liverpool, 1951-53; Senior then Principal Physicist, 1953-56, Head, Department of Physics, 1956-62, Hammersmith Hospital, London; Reader, Medical Physics, Postgraduate Medical School, University of London, 1962-64; Reader, Biophysics, St Thomas's Hospital Medical School, London, 1964-65; Professor of Medical Physics, Head of Department of Bio-Medical Physics and Bio-Engineering, University of Aberdeen and Grampian Health Board, 1965-92. Publications: Over 240 papers, review articles and lectures in medical and scientific journals. Honours include: OBE, 1992; Royal Society Wellcome Gold Medal, 1984; Royal Society Mullard Gold Medal, 1990; Honorary DSc, University of Hull, 1994; Norman Veall Prize Medal, British Nuclear Medicine Society, 1995; Honorary DSc, University of Nottingham, 1996; Keith of Dunottar Silver Medal, Royal Scottish Society of Arts, 1996; Honorary DSc, University of Aberdeen, 1997; Royal Gold Medal, Royal Society of Edinburgh, 2002; Gold Medal, Royal College of Radiologists, 2004; Medal of European Federation of Organisations of Medical Physics, 2004; Freedom of the City of Aberdeen as a Pioneer of Medical Imaging, 2004. Memberships include: Fellow: Royal Society of Edinburgh; Royal Academy of Engineering; Institution of Electrical Engineers; Institute of Physics; Royal College of Pathologists; Honorary Fellow: Institute of Physics and Engineering in Medicine; British Institute of Radiology; British Nuclear Medicine Society; Founder Fellow, International Society of Magnetic Resonance and Medicine; Founder President, International Union of Physics and Engineering in Medicine. Address: 121 Anderson Drive, Aberdeen, AB15 6BG, Scotland. E-mail: h.parry@biomed.abdn.ac.uk

MALLET Philip Louis Victor, b. 3 February 1926, London, England. Member of HM Diplomatic Service (Retired). m. Mary Moyle Grenfell Borlase, 3 sons. Education: Balliol College, Oxford, England. Appointments: Army, 1944-47; HM Foreign Diplomatic Service, 1949-82; Served in Iraq, Cyprus, Aden, Germany, Tunisia, Sudan and Sweden; British High Commissioner in Guyana and non-resident Ambassador to Suriname, 1978-82. Honour: CMG. Address: Wittersham House, Wittersham, Kent TN30 7ED, England.

MALLON Maurus Edward, b. 10 July 1932, Greenock, Scotland. Teacher. Education: MA, Honours, University of Glasgow, 1956; BEd, University of Manitoba, Winnipeg, 1966. Appointments: Retired after 30 year teaching career. Publications: Basileus, 1971; The Opal, 1973; Pegaso, 1975; Way of the Magus, 1978; Anogia, 1980; Bammer McPhie, 1984; Treasure Mountain, 1986; Postcards to a Certain Michel (essays), 1991; Ex Novo Mundo (short stories), 1992; Poems, Satire, Philosophy Compendulum, 1993; A Matter of Conscience (play), 1994. Honours: Gold Records of Excellence, 1994, 1995, Lifetime Achievement Award, 1996, Platinum Records for Exceptional Performance, 1997, 1998, ABI; Gold Medal of Honor, 2000. Memberships: Living Authors' Society; National Writers' Association, USA; PEN, Canada. Address: Box 331, Deep River, Ontario K0J 1P0, Canada.

MALONE Vincent, b. 11 September 1931, Liverpool, England. Bishop. Education: BSc, Liverpool University, 1959; Cert Ed, 1960, Dip Ed, 1962, Cambridge University. Appointments: Chaplain to Notre Dame Training College, Liverpool, 1955-59; Assistant Priest, St Anne's, Liverpool, 1960-61; Assistant Master, Cardinal Allen Grammar School, Liverpool, 1961-71; Chaplain to Liverpool University, 1971-79; Administrator (Dean), Liverpool Metropolitan Cathedral, 1979-89; Auxiliary Bishop of Liverpool, 1989-2006; Vicar General, 2006-. Membership: Fellow, College of Preceptors. Address: 17 West Oakhill Park, Liverpool L13 4BN, England. E-mail: vmalone@onetel.com

MALOUF (George Joseph) David, b. 20 March 1934, Brisbane, Queensland, Australia. Poet; Novelist. Education: BA, University of Queensland, 1954. Appointments: Assistant Lecturer in English, University of Queensland, 1955-57; Supply Teacher, London, 1959-61; Teacher of Latin and English, Holland Park Comprehensive, 1962; Teacher, St Anselm's Grammar School, 1962-68; Senior Tutor and Lecturer in English, University of Sydney, 1968-77. Publications: Poetry: Bicycle and Other Poems, 1970; Neighbours in a Thicket: Poems, 1974; Poems, 1975-1976, 1976; Wild Lemons, 1980; First Things Last, 1981; Selected Poems, 1981; Selected Poems, 1959-1989, 1994. Fiction: Johnno (novel), 1975; An Imaginary Life (novel), 1978; Child's Play (novella), 1981; The Bread of Time to Come (novella), 1981, republished as Fly Away Peter, 1982; Eustace (short story), 1982; The Prowler (short story), 1982; Harland's Half Acre (novel), 1984; Antipodes (short stories), 1985; The Great World (novel), 1990; Remembering Babylon (novel), 1993; The Conversations at Curlow Creek (novel), 1996; Dream Stuff (stories), 2000; Made in Britain, 2003; Every Move You Make, 2006; Typewriter Music, 2007. Play: Blood Relations, 1988. Opera Libretti: Voss, 1986; Mer de Glace; Baa Baa Black Sheep, 1993. Memoir: Twelve Edmondstone Street, 1985. Editor: We Took Their Orders and Are Dead: An Anti-War Anthology, 1971; Gesture of a Hand (anthology), 1975. Contributions to: Four Poets: David Malouf, Don Maynard, Judith Green, Rodney Hall, 1962; Australian; New York Review of Books; Poetry Australia; Southerly;

Sydney Morning Herald. Honours: Grace Leven Prize for Poetry, 1974; Gold Medals, Australian Literature Society, 1975, 1982; Australian Council Fellowship, 1978; New South Wales Premier's Award for Fiction, 1979; Victorian Premier's Award for Fiction, 1985; New South Wales Premier's Award for Drama, 1987; Commonwealth Writer's Prize, 1991; Miles Franklin Award, 1991; Prix Femina Etranger, 1991; Inaugural International IMPAC Dublin Literary Award, 1996; Neustadt Laureat, 2000. Address: 53 Myrtle Street, Chippendale, New South Wales 2008, Australia.

MALPAS John Peter Ramsden, b. 14 December 1927, Colombo, Ceylon. Stockbroker. m. Rosamond Margaret Burn, 3 sons. Education: MA (Oxon), P.P.E., New College Oxford. Appointments: Imperial Chemical Industries, 1951-56; Chase, Henderson and Tennant, 1956-58; Deputy Chairman, Quilter Goodison, 1959-87; London Stock Exchange, 1961-88; Non Executive Director, Penny & Giles International, 1988-92; Management Board, 1988-2002, Honorary Treasurer, 1988-98, Royal Hospital for Neuro Disability; Non Executive Director, West Wittering Estate, 1998. Honour: MA (Oxon). Memberships: Itchenor Sailing Club; Ski Club Great Britain. Address: 48 Berwyn Road, Richmond, Surrey TW10 5BS, England. E-mail: peter.malpas@ukgateway.net

MAMET David Alan, b. 30 November 1947, Chicago, USA. Playwright; Director. m. (1) Lindsay Crouse, 1977, divorced, 2 children (2) Rebecca Pidgeon, 1991, 2 children. Education: Goddard College, Plainfield, Vermont. Appointments: Artist in Residence, Goddard College, 1971-73; Artistic Director, St Nicholas Theatre Company, Chicago, 1973-75; Guest Lecturer, University of Chicago, 1975, 1979; New York University, 1981; Associate Artistic Director, Goodman Theatre, Chicago, 1978; Associate Professor of Film, Columbia University, 1988; Director, House of Games, 1986; Things Change, 1987; Homicide, 1991; Play, A Life in the Theatre, 1989. Publications: The Duck Variations, 1971; Sexual Perversity in Chicago, 1973; The Reunion, 1973; Squirrels, 1974; American Buffalo, 1976; A Life in the Theatre, 1976; The Water Engine, 1976; The Woods, 1977; Lone Canoe, 1978; Prairie du Chien, 1978; Lakeboat, 1980; Donny March, 1981; Edmond, 1982; The Disappearance of the Jews, 1983; The Shawl, 1985; Glengarry Glen Ross, 1984; Speed-the-Plow, 1987; Bobby, Guild in Hell, 1989; The Old Neighborhood, 1991; Oleanna, 1992; Ricky Jay and his 52 Assistants, 1994; Death Defying Acts, 1996; Boston Marriage, 1999; Screenplays: The Postman Always Rings Twice, 1979; The Verdict, 1980; The Untouchables, 1986; House of Games, 1986; Things Change, 1987; We're No Angels, 1987; Oh Hell!, 1991; Homicide, 1991; Hoffa, 1991; Glengarry Glen Ross, 1992; The Rising Sun, 1992; Oleanna, 1994; The Edge, 1996; The Spanish Prisoner, 1996; Wag the Dog, 1997; Boston Marriage, 2001; Childrens' books: Mr Warm and Cold, 1985; The Owl, 1987; The Winslow Boy, 1999; Lakeboat, 2000; State and Main, 2000; Hannibal, 2001; Heist, 2001; Spartan, 2004; Edmond, 2005; Redbelt, 2008. Essays: Writing in Restaurants, 1986; Some Freaks, 1989; On Directing Film, 1990; The Hero Pony, 1990; The Cabin, 1992; A Whore's Profession, 1993; The Cryptogram, 1994; The Village (novel), 1994; Passover, 1995; Make-Believe Town: Essays and Remembrances, 1996; Plays, 1996; Plays 2, 1996; The Duck and the Goat, 1996; The Old Religion, 1996; True and False, 1996; The Old Neighbourhood, 1998; Jafsie and John Henry, 2000; State and Maine, (writer, director), 2000. Honours: Outer Critics Circle Award, for contributions to American Theatre, 1978; Honorary DLitt (Dartmouth College), 1996; Pulitzer Prize for

Drama, New York Drama Critics Award. Address: c/o Howard Rosenstone, Rosenstone/Wender Agency, 38 East 29th Street, 10th Floor, New York, NY 10016, USA.

MANA Samira Al, b. 25 December 1935, Basra, Iraq. Writer. m. Salah Niazi, July 1959, 2 daughters. Education: BA, Honours, University of Baghdad, 1958; Postgraduate Diploma in Librarianship, Ealing Technical College, 1976; Chartered Librarian, British Library Association, 1980. Appointments: Arabic Language and Literature Teacher, Secondary School, Baghdad, 1958-65; Chief Librarian, Iraqi Cultural Centre, London, 1976-81; Assistant Editor, Alightrab Al-Adabi (Literature of the Exiled), 1985-2002. Publications: The Forerunners and the Newcomers (novel), 1972; The Song (short stories), 1976; A London Sequel (novel), 1979; Only a Half (play in two acts), 1979; The Umbilical Cord (novel), 1990; The Oppressers (novel), 1997; The Soul and Other Stories, 1999; Just Look at Me, Look at Me (novel), 2002. Contributions to: Alightrab Al-Adabi; Many short stories in Arabic magazines; Translations in Dutch and English periodicals; Translation into English, The Umbilical Cord, 2005. Address: 46 Tudor Drive, Kingston-Upon-Thames, Surrey KT2 5PZ, England.

MANDAL Anil Kumar, b. 2 January 1958, West Bengal, India. Doctor. m. Vijaya Kumari Gothwal. Education: MBBS, NRS Medical College, Calcutta, India, 1983; MD, All India Institute of Medical Sciences, New Delhi, 1987; Diplomate, National Board for Practice of Ophthalmology, 1987. Appointments: Junior Ophthalmologist, 1990, Assistant Ophthalmologist, 1991-94, Associate Ophthalmologist, 1994-97, Head, 1997-, Director, 2002-, Children's Eye Care Center, Professor of Ophthalmology, 1998-, L V Prasad Eye Institute, Hyderabad. Publications: In professional journals. Honours: Best Resident, Ophthalmologic Research Association, AIIMS, New Delhi, 1990; Best Thematic Film, All India Ophthalmological Society, India, 1997; Professor P Siva Reddy Gold Medal, All India Ophthalmological Society, 1997; Achievement Award, American Academy of Ophthalmology, 2000; Shanti Swarup Bhatnager Prize, CSIR, 2003; Apollo Award of Medical Excellence, Apollo Hospitals Group, 2004-05. Memberships: Life Member, All India Ophthalmological Society; Elected International Member, American Academy of Ophthalmology; International Member, Association for Research and Vision in Ophthalmology. Address: Flat #202, Palace View Estate, Plot 88/89, Road #2, Banjara Hills, Hyderabad 500 034 AP, India.

MANDEL H(arold) George, b. 6 June 1924, Berlin, Germany. Pharmacologist. m. Marianne Klein, 2 daughters. Education: BS, 1944, Yale University; PhD, 1949. Appointments: Laboratory Instructor in Chemistry, Yale University, 1942-44; 1947-49; Research Associate, 1949-50, Assistant Research Professor, 1950-52, Associate Professor Pharmacology, 1952-58, Professor, 1958-, Chairman, 1960-96, Department of Pharmacology, George Washington University School of Medicine and Health Sciences. Publications: Numerous publications on cancer chemotherapy, mechanism of growth inhibition, antimetabolites, drug disposition, chemical carcinogenesis. Honours: Advanced Commonwealth Fund Fellow, Molteno Institute, Cambridge (England) University, 1956; Commonwealth Fund Fellow, University Auckland, New Zealand, and University Medical Sciences, Bangkok, Thailand, 1964; American Cancer Society Eleanor Roosevelt International Fellow, Chester Beatty Research Institute, London, 1970-71; several other scholarships and research grants; Recipient, John J Abel Award in Pharmacology, Eli Lilly & Co, 1958; Distinguished Achievement Award, Washington Academy of Sciences, 1958; Golden Apple

Teaching Award, AMA, 1969, 1985, 1997; George Washington Award, 1998; Who's Who in America, since 1978; Fellow, American Association for the Advancement of Science (AAAS), 2007; Listed in national and international biographical dictionaries. Memberships: Fellow, Medical Research Council Toxicology Unit, Carshalton, England, 1986; Cancer Chemotherapy Com International Union Against Cancer, 1966-73; Board of Advisors, Roswell Park Cancer Institute, Buffalo, New York, 1972-74; Fellow, Lyon, France, 1989; Honorary Fellow, University College, London, 1993-; Consultant, Bureau of Drugs, FDA, 1975-79, EPA, 1978-82; Member various NRC-NAS committees, 1965-86; AAAS; American Chemical Society; American Society Biochemistry and Molecular Biology; President, 1973-74, American Society Pharmacology and Experimental Therapeutics; Chairman, National Caucus of Basic Biomedical Science Chairs, 1991-; American Association for Cancer Research; President, 1976-78, Association for Medical School Pharmacology Chairs. Address: 4956 Sentinel Drive, Bethesda, MD 20816 3562, USA.

MANDELA Nelson Rolihlahla, b. 1918, Umtata, Transkei. President (retired); Lawyer. m. (1) Evelyn Mandela, divorced 1957, 4 children, 2 deceased, (2) Winnie Mandela, 1958, divorced 1996, 2 daughters, (3) Graca Machel, 1998. Education: University College, Fort Hare; University of Witwatersrand. Appointments: Legal Practice, Johannesburg, 1952; On trial for treason, 1956-61 (acquitted); Sentenced to 5 years imprisonment, 1962; Tried for further charges, 1963-64, sentenced to life imprisonment; Released, 1990; President, African National Congress, 1991-97; President of South Africa, 1994-99; Chancellor, University of the North, 1992-; Joint President, United World Colleges, 1995-. Publications: No Easy Walk to Freedom, 1965; How Far We Slaves Have Come: South Africa and Cuba in Today's World, co-author, 1991; Nelson Mandela Speaks: Forging a non-racial democratic South Africa, 1993; Long Walk to Freedom, 1994. Honours: Jawaharlal Nehru Award, India, 1979; Simon Bolivar Prize, UNESCO, 1983; Sakharov Prize, 1988; Liberty Medal, USA, 1993; Nobel Peace Prize (Joint Winner), 1993; Mandela-Fulbright Prize, 1993; Honorary Bencher, Lincoln's Inn, 1994; Tun Abdul Razak Award, 1994; Anne Frank Medal, 1994; International Freedom Award, 2000; Honorary QC, 2000; Honorary Freeman of London; Johannesburg Freedom of the City Award, 2004; Numerous honorary doctorates. Address: c/o ANC, 51 Plein Street, Johannesburg 2001, South Africa.

MANDELBROT Benoit B, b. 20 November 1924, Warsaw, Poland (French Citizen). Mathematician. Education: Graduated, Ecole Polytechnique, Paris, 1947; MS, California Institute of Technology, 1948; PhD, Sorbonne, Paris, 1952. Appointments: Staff Member, Centre National de la Recherche Scientifique, Paris, 1949-57; Institute of Advance Study, New Jersey, 1953-54; Assistant Professor of Mathematics, University of Geneva, 1955-57; Junior Professor of Applied Mathematics, Lille University; Professor of Mathematical Analysis, Ecole Polytechnique, Paris; Research Staff Member, IBM Thomas J Watson Research Centre, New York, 1958; IBM Fellow, 1974; Abraham Robinson Professor of Mathematical Science, 1987-99, Sterling Professor, 1999-, Professor Emeritus, 2005-, Yale University, New Haven, Connecticut; Visiting Professor, Harvard University, 1962-64, 1979-80, 1984-87; Devised the term Fractal to describe a curve or surface. Publications: Logique, Langage et Théorie de l'Information, co-author, 1957; Fractals: Form, Chance and Dimension, 1977; Fractal Geometry of Nature, 1982; Fractals and Scaling in Finance: Discontinuity, Concentration, Risk,

1997; Fractales, hasard et finance, 1997; Multifractals and Low-Frequency Noise: Wild Self-Affinity in Physics, 1998; Gaussian Self-Similarity and Fractals, 2000; Nel mondo dei frattali, 2001; Globality, The Earth, Low-frequency Noise and R/S, 2002; Fractals, Graphics and Mathematical Education, with M L Frame, 2002; Fractals in Chaos and Statistical Physics, 2003; The (Mis) Behaviour of Markets: A Fractal View of Risk, Ruin and Reward, 2004; Numerous scientific papers; Editorial Boards, several journals. Honours: Several honorary degrees; Numerous awards and medals including Chevalier, L'Ordre de la Légion d'Honneur, 1989; L F Richardson Medal for Geophysics, 2000; Procter Prize of Sigma Xi, 2002; Japan Prize for Science and Tech, 2002. Address: Mathematics Department, Yale University, New Haven, CT 06520, USA.

MANDELL Gordon Keith, S, b. 6 March 1947, New York City, New York, USA. Aerospace Engineer. Education: BS, Aeronautics, Astronautics, 1969, MS, Aeronautics, Astronautics, 1970, Massachusetts Institute of Technology. Appointments: Staff Member, Fluid Dynamics Research Laboratory, Massachusetts Institute of Technology, 1970-72; Consulting Aerospace Engineer, 1973-76; Federal Aviation Administration Designated Engineering Representative, 1976-82; Federal Aviation Administration Aerospace Engineer, determining compliance of aircraft designs with safety standards, 1982-. Publications: Missile Recovery by Extensible Flexwing, 1966; Numerous articles in Model Rocketry magazine, 1968-72; Co-author, Lenticular Re-entry Vehicle, 1970; Co-author, editor, book, Topics in Advanced Model Rocketry, 1973. Honours: Louis de Florez Award; James Means Memorial Prize; Grumman Scholar, Massachusetts Institute of Technology, 1965-69; National Science Foundation Fellow, Massachusetts Institute of Technology, 1969-70; Admitted to: Tau Beta Pi; Sigma Gamma Tau; Sigma Xi. Memberships: National Association of Rocketry; National Space Society; Planetary Society; Team SETI. Address: Post Office Box 671388, Chugiak, AK 99567-1388, USA.

MANDELSON Peter Benjamin, b. 21 October 1953, England. Politician. Education: St Catherine's College, Oxford. Appointments: Joined TUC, with Economic Department, 1977-78; Chair, British Youth Council, 1978-80; Producer, London Weekend TV, 1982-85; Director of Campaigns and Communications, Labour Party, 1985-90; MP for Hartlepool, 1992-2004; Opposition Whip, 1994-97, Shadow Frontbench Spokesman on Civil Service, 1995-96, on Election Planning, 1996-97; Chair, General Election Planning Group, 1995-97; Minister without Portfolio, 1997-98; Secretary of State for Trade and Industry, 1998; for Northern Ireland, 1999-2001 (resigned); EU Commissioner for Trade, 2004-; Vice-Chair, British Council, 1999-. Publications: Youth Unemployment: Causes and Cures, 1977; Broadcasting and Youth, 1980; The Blair Revolution: Can New Labour Deliver? 1996. Memberships include: Council, London Borough of Lambeth, 1979-82; International Advisory Committee, Centre for European Policy Studies, 1993-; Trustee, Whitechapel Art Gallery, 1994-; Panel 2000, 1998-.

MANDL Anita Maria, b. 17 May 1926, Prague, Czechoslovakia. Sculptor. m. Denys Jennings, deceased. Education: BSc honours, Zoology, Birkbeck College, University of London, 1947; Part-time, Birmingham College of Art. Appointments: Research Assistant, London Hospital, 1946-47; Lecturer and Senior Lecturer, Reader in Reproductive Physiology, Department of Anatomy, University of Birmingham, 1948-65; Freelance Sculptor, 1965-.

Publications: Numerous scientific papers in professional journals; Exhibitions of artwork in London, across the UK and Channel Islands. Honours: PhD, 1951, DSc, 1960, University of Birmingham. Memberships (past and present): Society of Endocrinology; Devon Guild of Craftsmen; Royal West of England Academy; Royal Society of Marine Artists; Royal British Society of Sculptors; National Trust; Campaign for the Protection of Rural England; Zoological Society of London.

MANFREDI Roberto, b. 22 June 1964, Bologna, Italy. Professor of Infectious Diseases. Education: MD, 1988; Infectious Disease Specialist, University of Bologna, 1992. Appointments: Researcher, Grantee, 1986-91, Medical Assistant, Infectious Diseases, 1991-93, Associate, 1993-, Contract Professor of Infectious Diseases, Postgraduate School of Infectious Diseases, 1996-2005, Associate Professor of Infectious Diseases, 2005-, University of Bologna; Board of Associate Professors of Infectious Diseases, 2003. Publications: Over 1,900 scientific publications in textbooks, congress proceedings and professional journals; 13 monographs. Honours: L Concato Award, University of Bologna, 1988; F Schiassi Award, 1989; G Salvioli Award, University of Bologna, 1991; FESCI Young Investigator Award, 2000; Heracles Award, 2006. Memberships: International Society of Infectious Diseases; Italian Society for Infectious and Tropical Diseases; European AIDS Clinical Society; Editorial Board and Reviewer of many scientific journals. Address: Via di Corticella 45, I-40128, Bologna, Italy.

MANGLA Pramod B, b. 5 July 1936, Chhachhrauli, India. University Professor. m. Raj Mangla, 1 son, 1 daughter. Education: MA, History (Pb); MLibSC, Delhi; MSLS, Columbia, New York; DLSc, MI Inf Sc, London; FILA. Appointments: Professor and Head, Department of Library & Information Science, 1967-69, 1972-79, 1985-88 and 1994-96; Dean, Faculty of Arts, University of Delhi, 1976-78, 1984-88; Professor and Head/Visiting Professor, Department of Library Science, Tabriz University, Iran, 1970-72, 1974-75; UNESCO Expert, Guyana, West Indies, 1978-79; Associated with numerous organisations including Government of India, State governments, universities and other academic institutions in India and abroad, 1970-; Visited around 45 countries on professional assignments. Publications: Author of numerous research articles, books, and technical reports, etc. Honours: Rockefeller Foundation Grant for Higher Studies, 1961; Travel/exchange fellowship grants from organisations such as: UGC (India) National Lecturer, 1984-86; British Council, IDRC and UNESCO; Honorary Fellowship, ILA, 1983; Shiromani Award for Human Excellence, 1990; IFLA Gold Medal, 1991; 2-volume Festschrift, India, 1997; Certificate of Honour, IASLIC, 2006. Memberships: Indian Library Association; IASLIC; Executive Board, 1985-91, Vice President, 1987-91, IFLA; Board of Management, National Library of india, Kolkata, 2003-; Working Group, National Knowledge Commission, Government of India, 2006-. Address: EB-210 Maya Enclave, New Delhi –110064, India. E-mail: manglapb@yahoo.co.in

MANHOLD John Henry, b. 20 August 1919, Rochester, New York, USA. Dental Educator; Consultant. m. (1) Beverly Schecter, 1953, divorced 1969, 1 child, (2) Enriqueta Andino, 1971. Education: BA, University of Rochester, 1940; MD, Harvard University, 1944; MA, Washington University, 1956. Appointments: Instructor, College of Medicine, Tufts University, Boston, 1948-50; Assistant Professor, Chairman, General and Oral Pathology, College of Dentistry, University of Washington, St Louis, 1954-56; From Assistant Professor to Professor, Chairman, Department of General and Oral Pathology, Seton Hall College of Medicine and Dentistry (now University of Medicine and Dentistry, Newark, New Jersey), 1956-87; Medical Director, Woog International, 1987-89; Retired, 1989; Consultant, Johnson & Johnson, New Brunswick, New Jersey, 1960-70, Richardson-Vicks, Shelton, Connecticut, 1981-87, Los Produits Associates, Geneva, 1965-87, Health Care Development Group, New Jersey, 1990-2005, Health Care Development Group, Pennsylvania, 1990-2005, Consumer Commission Network, New York, 1990-2005, Consumer Commission Network, Connecticut, 1990-; Lecturer in field. Publications: Author, Introductory Psychosomatic Dentistry, 1956; Author, Outline of Pathology, 1960; Editor, Clinical Oral Diagnosis, 1965; Author, Tissue Respiration and Oxigenating Agents, 1977; Author, Practical Dental Management: Patients and Practice, 1984; Author, Illustrated Dental Terminology: A Lexicon for the Dental Profession (in 4 languages), 1985; Co-author, Handbook of Pathology, 1987; Editor, Clinical Preventive Dentistry Journal, 1979-92; Contributor of articles to professional journals. Honours: Distinguished Alumni, Harvard University, 1989; Senior Society, Harvard School of Dental Medicine, 1984; President's Award, Alumni Association, University of Medicine and Dentistry, New Jersey, 1980; Letter of Appreciation, Japan, 1980; Certificate of Achievement, University of Maryland, 1965. Memberships: Fellow, Academy of Psychosomatic Medicine; International College of Dentists; American College of Dentists; APA; International Association of Dental Research; American Society of Clinical Pathologists; Moon Valley Country Club; St Petersburg Yacht Club; Sigma Xi. Address: 26027 N 44th Ave, Phoenix, AZ 85083, USA. E-mail: kupferce@cox.net

MANIDAS Sadanandan, b. 29 December 1953, Njekkad, Kerala, India. Physician. m. P M Beena, 10 April 1989, 1 son. Education: MB BS, India, 1979; MRCS, England, 1983; LRCP, London, 1983; LMSSA, London, 1983; FRSM, London, 1983; FRSH, London, 1988; JCPTGP Cert, RCGP (London), 1988; FP Cert, RCOG (London and RCGP (London), 1988; T, (GP), 1991; FICA (USA), 1991; DFFP RCOG, London, 1993; FICS, USA, 1995; FCCP (USA), 1997; H E 1999; O I A, 1999; Advance Trauma Life Support Certificate (ATLS, London), 2003; Advanced Life Support Certificate (ALS, London), 2003; (FRCS (England), 2005; DSc Medicine (USA), 2006. Appointments: GP Registrar, Fieldway Medical Centre, Croydon, UK, 1987-88; Freelance, Family Physician, 1988-; Staff Physician, Stoke Mandeville Hospital, Aylesbury, England, 1995-96; Staff Physician, Kettering General Hospital, Kettering, England, 1996-97; Staff Physician, Warwick General Hospital, Warwick, England, 1997-98; Senior Staff Physician, Accident and Emergency Medicine, The Whittington University Hospital, University College London Medical School, London, England, 1999-. Honours: Distinguished Leadership Award, American Biographical Institute, USA, 1998; Medical Excellence Key Award, ABI, USA, 1998; International Cultural Diploma of Honor, ABI, USA, 1998; Certificate of Merit, Iinternationa Biographical Centre, 1999; Order of International Ambassador, ABI, USA, 1999; Listed in several Who's Who publications. Memberships: Fellow, Royal Society of Medicine, London, 1983; Faculty of History and Philosophy, Medicine and Pharmacy, Worshipful Society of Apothecaries, London, 1983; Royal Society of Health, London, 1989; Fellow, International College of Angiology, USA, 1991; Fellow, International College of Surgeons, USA, 1995; Member New York Academy of Sciences, 1996; Member, Migraine in Primary Care Advisors, Surrey, England, 1997; Fellow, American College of Chest Physicians, 1997; Member, Society of 500 Intellectuals of the World, ABI, 1999; Member, Primary Care Cardivascular Society (PCCS), London, 2000; Associate Member, The Royal College of Physicians, London; Member, Primary Care Rheumatology Society, UK; Member, Primary Care Diabetes Society, UK; Member, Primary Care Dermatology Society, UK; Member, National Obesity Forum (NOF), UK; Fellow, The Royal College of Surgeons, England; Fellow, The Royal Society of Arts (FRSA), London. Address: 1 Wadhurst Court, Wadhurst Close, Penge, London, SE20 8TA, England. E-mail: smanidas@doctors.org.uk

MANILOW Barry (Pinkus), b. 17 June 1946, Brooklyn, New York, USA. Singer; Musician (piano); Songwriter. Education: Advertising, New York City College; Musical Education: NY College Of Music; Juilliard School Of Music. Career: Film Editor, CBS-TV; Writer, numerous radio and television commercials; Member, cabaret duo Jeanne and Barry, 1970-72; MD, arranger, producer for Bette Midler; Solo entertainer, 1974-; Numerous world-wide tours; Major concerts include: Gala charity concert for Prince and Princess of Wales, Royal Albert Hall, 1983; Arista Records 15th Anniversary concert, Radio City Music Hall, 1990; Royal Variety performance, London, 1992; Television film Copacabana, 1985; Numerous television specials and television appearances; Broadway show, Barry Manilow At The Gershwin, 1989; West End musical, Copacabana, 1994. Recordings: Albums include: Barry Manilow, 1973; Barry Manilow II, 1975; Tryin' To Get The Feelin', 1976; This One's For You, 1977; Barry Manilow Live (Number 1, US), 1977; Even Now, 1978; Manilow Magic, 1979; Greatest Hits, 1979; One Voice, 1979; Barry, 1981; If I Should Love Again, 1981; Barry Live In Britain, 1982; I Wanna Do It With You, 1982; Here Comes The Night, 1983; A Touch More Magic, 1983; Greatest Hits Volume II, 1984; 2.00 AM Paradise Café, 1984; Barry Manilow, Grandes Exitos En Espanol, 1986; Swing Street, 1988; Songs To Make The Whole World Sing, 1989; Live On Broadway, 1990; The Songs 1975-1990, 1990; Because It's Christmas, 1990; Showstoppers, 1991; The Complete Collection And Then Some, 1992; Hidden Treasures, 1993; The Platinum Collection, 1993; Singin' with the Big Bands, 1994; Another Life, 1995; Summer of '78, 1996; Manilow Sings Sinatra, 1998; Here at the Mayflower, 2001; A Christmas Gift of Love, 2002; Two Nights Live, 2004; The Greatest Songs of the Seventies, 2007. Scores: Songs from Copacabana and Harmony, 2004; Hit singles include: Mandy (Number 1, US), 1975; Could It Be Magic, 1975; I Write The Songs (Number 1, US), 1976; Tryin' To Get The Feelin', 1976; Weekend In New England, 1977; Looks Like We Made It (Number 1, US), 1977; Can't Smile Without You, 1978; Copacabana (At The Copa), from film Foul Play, 1978; Somewhere In The Night, 1979; Ships, 1979; I Made It Through The Rain, 1981; Let's Hang On, 1981; Bermuda Triangle, 1981; I Wanna Do It With You, 1982. Honours: Grammy Awards: Song Of The Year, I Write The Songs, 1977; Best Male Pop Vocal Performance, Copacabana (At The Copa), 1979; Emmy Award, The Barry Manilow Special, 1977; American Music Awards, Favourite Male Artist, 1978-80; Star on Hollywood Walk Of Fame, 1980; Tony Award, Barry Manilow On Broadway show, 1976; Academy Award Nomination, Ready To Take A Chance Again, 1978; Hitmaker Award, Songwriters Hall Of Fame, 1991; Named, Humanitarian of the Year, Starlight Foundation, 1991; Society of Singers Ella Award, 2003; Platinum and Gold records. Address: Arista Records, 6 W 57th Street, NY 10019, USA.

MANJORO Apphia Clara, b. 12 August 1948, Gutu, Zimbabwe. m. Bartholomew Manjoro, 2 sons, 1 daughter. Education: Diplomas: Teaching, 1969, Leadership, 1984; Degree: Bachelor of Sacred Theology, 1988, Counselling, 1990. Appointments: Reverend; Prophetess; Pastor; Author; Songwriter and Composer; Counsellor; Teacher; Marriage Therapist; Marriage Officer; Ordained Minister; Christ for the Nations Alumni; Founder and President of Virtuous Women Community International; Founder and President, Apphia C Manjoro Rescue Ministry; Conference Speaker; Host of yearly women's conferences and marriage therapy seminars. Honours: Listed in Who's Who publications and biographical dictionaries; Great Women of the 21st Century; Outstanding Female Executive Award; Woman of the Year, 2004-06; Affectionately known as Mother General. Address: The Herald, PO Box 396, Harare, Zimbabwe. E-mail: theherald@zimpapers.co.zw Website: www.drbmanjoroministries.org

MANN (Colin) Nicholas Jocelyn, b. 24 October 1942, Salisbury, Wiltshire, England. Emeritus Professor. m. (1) Joëlle Bourcart, 1 son, 1 daughter, divorced, (2) Helen Stevenson, 2 daughters. Education: BA 1st class, Modern and Medieval Languages, 1964, MA, PhD, 1968, King's College, Cambridge. Appointments: Research Fellow, Clare College, Cambridge, 1965-67; Lecturer in French, University of Warwick, 1967-72; Visiting Fellow, All Souls College, Oxford, 1972; Fellow and Tutor in Modern Languages, 1973-90, Dean of Graduates, 1976-80, Senior Tutor, 1982-86, Emeritus Fellow, 1991-2007, Honorary Fellow, 2007, Pembroke College, Oxford; Member of Council, Museum of Modern Art, 1984-92; Director of the Warburg Institute and Professor of the History of the Classical Tradition, 1990-2001, Senior Research Fellow of the Warburg Institute, 2002-08, University of London; Member of Council of Contemporary Applied Arts, 1994-2006; Distinguished Visiting Scholar, Center for Reformation and Renaissance Studies, Victoria University, Toronto, Canada, 1996; Professeur au Collège de France, 1998; Visiting Professor, University of Calabria, Cosenza, 1999-2000; Fellow, 1992-; Foreign Secretary and Vice President of the British Academy, 1999-2006; Dean of the School of Advanced Study and Professor of Renaissance Studies, 2002-07, Pro-Vice Chancellor, 2003-07, Emeritus Professor, 2007-, University of London; Vice President, ALLEA (Federation of European Academies), 2007-. Publications: Books and articles on Petrarch and other topics in professional journals. Honours: CBE, 1999; Hon DLitt, University of Warwick, 2006; Member of many advisory and editorial boards. Address: Rue du Tourneur, 46160 Cajarc, France. E-mail: nicholas.mann@free.fr

MANN Jessica, b. England. Writer. Publications: A Charitable End, 1971; Mrs Knox's Profession, 1972; The Only Security, 1973; The Sticking Place, 1974; Captive Audience, 1975; The Eighth Deadly Sin, 1976; The Sting of Death, 1978; Funeral Sites, 1981; Deadlier Than the Male, 1981; No Man's Island, 1983; Grave Goods, 1984; A Kind of Healthy Grave, 1986; Death Beyond the Nile, 1988; Faith, Hope and Homicide, 1991; Telling Only Lies, 1992; A Private Inquiry, 1996; Hanging Fire, 1997; The Survivor's Revenge, 1998; Under a Dark Sun, 2000; The Voice From the Grave, 2002; Out of Harm's Way (non-fiction), 2005; The Mystery Writer, 2006. Contributions to: Daily Telegraph; Sunday Telegraph; Various magazines and journals. Memberships: Detection Club; Society of Authors: PEN; Crime Writers Association. Address: Lambessow, St Clement, Cornwall, England.

MANN Michael K, b. 5 February 1943, Chicago, USA. Producer; Director; Writer. m. Summer Mann, 1974, 4 children. Education: University of Wisconsin; London Film School. Appointments: Executive Producer, (TV) Miami Vice,

Crime Story, Drug Wars: Camarena Story, Drug Wars: Cocaine Cartel, Police Story, Starsky & Hutch. Creative Works: Films directed include: The Jericho Mile, 1981; The Keep, 1981; Manhunter, 1986; Last of the Mohicans, 1992; Heat, 1995; The Insider, 1999; Ali, 2001; Collateral, 2004; The Aviator, 2005; Miami Vice, 2006; The Kingdom, 2007; Empire, 2009. Honours include: 2 Emmy Awards; Best Director, National Board of Review, 2004; BAFTA Awards, Best Film, 2005. Memberships: Writers Guild; Directors Guild. Address: c/o Creative Artists Agency, 9830 Wilshire Boulevard, Beverly Hills, CA 90212, USA.

MANNERS Gerald, b. 7 August 1932, Ferryhill, County Durham, England. Economic Geographer. m. Joy Edith Roberta Turner, 2 sons, 2 daughters. Education: BA, 1954, MA, 1958, Undergraduate and Scholar, First Class Geographical Tripos, St Catharine's College Cambridge. Appointments: Commissioned Officer, Royal Air Force, 1955-57; Lecturer, Geography, University College, Swansea, 1957-67; Visiting Scholar, Resources for the Future Inc., Washington DC, USA, 1964-65; Reader in Geography, University College London, 1968-80; Visiting Associate, Joint Center for Urban Studies, Harvard University and Massachusetts Institute of Technology, 1972-73; Visiting Fellow, Centre for Resource and Environmental Studies, Australian National University, 1991; Professor of Geography, 1980-97, Emeritus Professor, 1997-, University College London. Publications include: The Geography of Energy, 1964; South Wales in the Sixties, 1964; Spatial Policy Problems of the British Economy, 1971; The Changing World Market for Iron Ore 1950-1980, 1971; Regional Development in Britain, 1972; Minerals and Men, 1974; Coal in Britain: an Uncertain Future, 1981; Office Policy in Britain, 1986. Honours include: Governor, 1978-95, Chairman, 1986-95, Vice-President, 1995-99, Sadler's Wells Foundation; Trustee, 1993-, Eaga Partnership Charitable Trust; Specialist Adviser to the House of Lords Select Committee on Sustainable Development, 1994-95; Trustee, 1977-, Chairman, 1996-2004, City Parochial Foundation and the Trust for London; Specialist Adviser, House of Commons Environmental Audit Committee, 1999-2001; Chairman, Association of Charitable Foundations, 2003-; OBE, 2005. Memberships: Fellow, Royal Geographical Society (with the Institute of British Geographers); British Institute of Energy Economics; Regional Studies Association. Address: 338 Liverpool Road, London N7 8PZ, England. E-mail: g.manners@ucl.ac.uk

MANNING Jane Marian, b. 20 September 1938, Norwich, Norfolk, England. Singer (Soprano); Lecturer. m. Anthony Payne. Education: Royal Academy of Music, London; Scuola di Canto, Cureglia, Switzerland. Career: Freelance solo singer specialising in contemporary music; More than 350 world premiers including operas; Regular appearances in London, Europe, USA, Australia, with leading orchestras, conductors, ensembles and at major festivals; Lectures and master classes at major universities in USA including Harvard, Princeton, Cornell, Stanford; UK universities and leading conservatories in Europe and Australia; Visiting Professor, Mills College, Oakland, USA, 1981, 1984, 1986; Artistic Director, Jane's Minstrels, 1988-; Artist-in-Residence, universities in USA, Canada, Australia and New Zealand; Currently AHRC Creative Arts Research Fellow, Kingston University, UK, 2004-07; Visiting Professor, Royal College of Music, London; Honorary Professor, Keele University, 1996-2002; Many CDs, radio broadcasts worldwide. Publications: Books, New Vocal Repertory – An Introduction; New Vocal Repertory 2; Chapter on the vocal cycles in A Messiaen Companion; Numerous articles and reviews in newspapers and professional journals.

Honours: Special Award, Composers Guild of Great Britain; FRAM, 1980; Honorary Doctorate, University of York, 1988, OBE, 1990; FRCM, 1998; Hon Doctorate, University of Keele, 2004. Memberships: Vice-President, Society for the Promotion of New Music; Chairman, Nettlefold Trust (Colourscape Festival); Executive Committee, Musicians Benevolent Fund; Royal Philharmonic Society; Incorporated Society of Musicians. Address: 2 Wilton Square, London N1 3DL, England. E-mail: janetone@gmail.com

MANNING Patrick Augustus, b. 17 August 1946, San Fernando, Trinidad, West Indies. Geologist. m. Hazel, 2 sons. Education: San Fernando Government School, 1953-57; Presentation College, San Fernando, 1958-65; University of the West Indies, Mona, Jamaica, 1966-69. Appointments: Parliamentary Representative for San Fernando East, 1971-; Parliamentary Secretary, Ministry of Petroleum and Mines, 1971-73; Parliamentary Secretary to the Prime Minister, 1973; Parliamentary Secretary to the Prime Minister, Ministry of Planning and Development, 1973-74; Parliamentary Secretary, Ministry of Industry and Commerce, 1974-76; Parliamentary Secretary, Ministry of Works, Transport and Communication, 1978; Minister, Ministry of Finance (Maintenance and Tobago), 1978-79; Minister, Ministry of Finance, Public Service Portfolio and Minister, Ministry of the Prime Minister (Information Division), 1979-81; Minister of Information and Minister of Industry and Commerce, 1981; Minister of Energy and Natural Resources, 1981-86; Political Leader, The People's National Movement, 1987-; Leader of the Opposition, 1988-90; Opposition Member of Parliament, 1990-91; Prime Minister, The Republic of Trinidad and Tobago, 1991-95, 2001-; Leader of the Opposition, 1995-2001. Honours: Democracy Prize, Guyana Institute for Democracy, 2003; Star of the Caribbean Award, Caribbean-Central American Action, 2004. Membership: People's National Movement. Address: Office of the Prime Minister, Whitehall, 29 Maraval Road, Port of Spain, Trinidad & Tobago, West Indies. E-mail: pmsec@opm.gov.tt

MANOCHA Anshu, b. 10 October 1971, India. Pharmacologist. Education: B Pharm, 1993, M Pharm, 1995, Faculty of Pharmacy, Jamia Hamdard (Hamdard University), India; PhD, Pharmacology, University College of Medical Sciences and Guru Teg Bahadur Hospital, Delhi University, India, 2000. Appointments: Junior Research Fellow, Department of Pharmacology, Faculty of Pharmacy, Jamia Hamdard, India, 1993-95; Senior Research Fellow, Department of Pharmacology, University College of Medical Sciences and Guru Teg Bahadur Hospital, Shahdara, India, 1996-2000; Lecturer, 2000-04, Senior Lecturer, 2004-, Department of Pharmacology, Faculty of Pharmacy, Jamia Hamdard, New Delhi, India. Publications: 11 published articles in national and international journals; 7 published abstracts. Honours include: University Gold Medal for B Pharm and M Pharm, Jamia Hamdard; National Merit Scholarship, 1987; Hakim Abdul Majeed Scholarship, 1992-93; Junior Research Fellowship, Indian Institute of Technology, 1993-95; Senior Research Fellowship, Council of Scientific and Industrial Research 1996-2000; Servier Young Investigators' Award, Institutet de Recherches Internationales Servier, France, 1999. Memberships: Life Member, Indian Pharmaceutical Association; Life Member, Indian Pharmacological Society; Listed in national and international biographical dictionaries. Address: Department of Pharmacology, Faculty of Pharmacy, Jamia Hamdard, New Delhi 110062, India. E-mail: anshumanocha@hotmail.com

MANSELL Nigel, b. 8 August 1953, Upton-on-Severn, England. Racing Driver. m. Rosanne Perry, 2 sons, 1 daughter. Appointments: Began in Kart-racing, then Formula Ford, Formula 2, 1978-79, first Grand Prix, Austria, 1980; Winner, South African Grand Prix, 1992; Member, Lotus Grand Prix Team, 1980-84, Williams Team, 1985-88, 1991-92, Ferrari Team, 1989-90, Newman-Haas IndyCar Team, 1992-95, McLaren Team, 1995; Winner of 31 Grand Prix; Surpassed Jackie Stewart's British Record of 27 wins; World Champion, 1992; PPG IndyCar World Series Champion, 1993; Editor-in-Chief, Formula One Magazine, 2001. Publications: Mansell and Williams (with Derick Allsop), 1992; Nigel Mansell's IndyCar Racing (with Jeremy Shaw), 1993; My Autobiography (with James Allen), 1995. Honours include: Honorary DEng, Birmingham, 1993; OBE, 1990; BBC Sports Personality of the Year, 1986, 1992; Special Constable for 12 years; Awarded Honorary Fellowship of Centre for Management of Industrial Reliability, Cost and Effectiveness (MIRCE), 1997; Awarded Grand Fellowship of the MIRCE Akademy, 2000; Appointed President, UK Youth Charity, 2002; President, Institute of Advanced Motorists. Address: c/o Nicki Dance, Woodbury Park Golf & Country Club, Woodbury Castle, Woodbury, Exeter, Devon EX5 1JJ, England.

MANSER Martin Hugh, b. 11 January 1952, Bromley, England. Reference Book Editor; Language Trainer; Consultant. m. Yusandra Tun, 1979, 1 son, 1 daughter. Education: BA, Honours, University of York, 1974; MPhil, C.N.A.A., 1977. Publications: Concise Book of Bible Quotations, 1982; A Dictionary of Everyday Idioms, 1983, 2nd edition, 1997; Listening to God, Pocket Thesaurus of English Words, Children's Dictionary, 1984; Macmillan Student's Dictionary, 1985, 2nd edition, 1996; Penguin Wordmaster Dictionary, 1987; Guinness Book of Words, Dictionary of Eponyms, Visual Dictionary, Bloomsbury Good Word Guide, Printing and Publishing Terms, Marketing Terms, Guinness Book of Words, 1988, 2nd edition, 1991; Bible Promises: Outlines for Christian Living, 1989; Oxford Learner's Pocket Dictionary, 2nd edition, 1991; Get To the Roots: A Dictionary of Words and Phrase Origins, The Lion Book of Bible Quotations, Oxford Learner's Pocket Dictionary with Illustrations, 1992; Guide to Better English, Chambers Compact Thesaurus, Bloomsbury Key to English Usage, 1994; Collins Gem Daily Guidance, 1995; NIV Thematic Study Bible, 1996; Chambers English Thesaurus, Dictionary of Bible Themes, NIV Shorter Concordance, 1997; Guide to English Grammar, Crash Course in Christian Teaching, Dictionary of the Bible, Christian Prayer (large print), 1998; Bible Stories, Editor: Millennium Quiz Book, I Never Knew That Was in the Bible, Pub Quiz Book, Trivia Quiz Book, Children's Dictionary, Compiler, Lion Bible Quotation Collection, Common Worship Lectionary, 1999; The Eagle Handbook of Bible Promises, 2000; The Westminster Collection of Christian Quotation, Wordsworth Crossword Companion, Biblical Quotations: A Reference Guide, NIV Comprehensive Concordance, 365 Inspirational Quotations, Writer's Manual, The Facts On File Dictionary of Proverbs, 2001; Dictionary of Foreign Words and Phrases, 2002; Getting to Grips with Grammar, A Treasury of Psalms, Dictionary of Classical and Biblical Allusions, The Joy of Christmas, 2003; Editor, Synonyms and Antonyms, Editor, The Chambers Thesaurus, Compiler, Best Loved Hymns, Poems and Readings, Editor, The Really Useful Concise English Dictionary, Editor, Dictionary of Saints, 2004; Editor, World's Best Mother, A Treasury of Quotations, 2005; Editor, Wordsworth Thesaurus, Editor, Wordsworth Dictionary of Proverbs, Editor Pocket Writer's Handbook, Editor, Collins Dictionary for Writers and Editors, Editor, Thematic Dictionary 1, Thematic Dictionary 2, 2006; Editor, Facts on File Dictionary of Proverbs 2nd edition, Editor, Good Word Guide, 6th Edition, 2007; Compiler, Wordworth Book of Hymns, 2006; Co-author, Facts on File Guide to Style, 2006. Address: 102 Northern Road, Aylesbury, Bucks HP19 9QY, England.

MANSFIELD Eric Arthur, b. 14 April 1932, Southend, Essex, England. RAF Officer; Consulting Engineer. m. Marion Byrne, 1 son, 1 daughter. Education: RAF Apprenticeship, 1949-52; MA, St John's College, Cambridge, England, 1953-56; RAF Flying and Training to Wings Standard, 1957-58; MSc, Southampton University, 1962-63; RAF Staff College, 1968-69. Appointments: Tours with RAF Chief Scientist, Exchange with USAF, 1963-68; Nimrod Aircraft Engineering Authority and OC Engineering Wing, RAF Cottesmore, 1969-74; Chief Electrical Engineer, HQ RAF Germany, 1974-78; Staff, HQ 18 Group, 1978-82; Staff, Ministry of Defence, 1983-86; Staff, NATO HQ AFSOUTH, 1986-88; Staff, RAF Support Command, 1986-89; Association of Consulting Engineers, 1989-94; Independent Consultant, 1994-95; Retired, 1995. Memberships: Royal Aeronautical Society; Chartered Engineer. Address: 33 Chalgrove End, Stoke Mandeville, Bucks HP22 5UH. E-mail: ericandmarion@eamansfield.freeserve.co.uk

MANSFIELD Michael, b. 12 October 1941, London, England. Barrister. m. (1) Melian Mansfield, 1967, divorced 1992, 3 sons, 2 daughters, (2) Yvette Mansfield, 1992, 1 son. Education: Keele University. Appointments: Began Practising, 1967; Founder, Tooks Court Chambers, 1984; Speciality, Civil Liberties Work; Professor of Law, Westminster University, 1996. Creative Works: Films for BBC TV: Inside Story, 1991; Presumed Guilty. Publication: Presumed Guilty. Honours: Honorary Fellow, Kent University; Several Honorary Degrees. Membership: Patron Acre Lane Neighbourhood Chambers, Brixton, 1997-. Address: Tooks Court Chambers, 14 Tooks Court, Cursitor Street, London EC4Y 1JY, England.

MANTHIRAM Arumugam, b. 15 March 1951, Amarapuram, India. Teacher; Researcher. m. Rajeswari, 1 son, 1 daughter. Education: BS, 1974; MS, 1976; PhD, 1980. Appointments: Lecturer, Madurai Kamaraj University, 1981-85; Postdoctoral Fellow, University of Oxford, 1985-86; Postdoctoral Researcher, University of Texas, Austin, 1986-91; Assistant Professor, 1991-96, Associate Professor, 1996-2000, Professor, 2000-. Publications: 300 research papers. Honours: Faculty Excellence Award, 1994; Faculty Leadership Award, 1996; Charlotte Maer Patton Centennial Fellowship in Engineering, 1998; Ashley H Priddy Centennial Professorship in Engineering, 2002; Fellow, American Ceramic Society, 2004; Fellow, World Academy of Materials and Manufacturing Engineering, 2006; BFGoodrich Endowed Professorship in Engineering, 2006. Memberships: American Ceramic Society; American Chemical Society; Materials Research Society; Electrochemical Society; National Institute of Ceramic Engineers; American Association for the Advancement of Science. Address: Department of Mechanical Engineering, 1 University Station C2200, University of Texas, Austin, TX 78712, USA.

MANTOVANI John F, b. 17 January 1949, St Louis, Missouri, USA. Paediatric Neurologist. m. Janice, 1 son, 1 daughter. Education: BA, cum laude, Chemistry, University of Evansville, Indiana, 1971; MD, with honours, University of Missouri, 1974; Residencies in Paediatrics, Neurology and Child Neurology, Washington University School of Medicine, 1974-79. Appointments include: Assistant Professor, Clinical

Neurology, University of Wisconsin, 1980-84; Instructor, Clinical Paediatrics and Neurology, 1985-94, Assistant Professor, 1994-99, Associate Professor, Clinical Paediatrics and Neurology, 1999-, Washington University School of Medicine; Currently, Director of Child Neurology, Medical Director, Mercy Child Development Center; Medical Director, St John's Mercy Children's Hospital. Publications: 20 articles as first author and co-author in peer-reviewed professional journals; 6 abstracts, letters and book chapters; Over 70 scientific presentations and invited lectures. Honours: Board Certifications: Paediatrics, 1980, Neurology and Child Neurology, 1981; Neurodevelopmental Disabilities, 2001; Outstanding Resident Teacher in Neurology, Washington University School of Medicine, 1977; Professional Leadership Award in the Field of Developmental Disabilities, University of Missouri, 1989; Listed in Who's Who publications and biographical dictionaries. Memberships: American Academy for Cerebral Palsy and Developmental Medicine; American Academy of Pediatrics; American Board of Psychiatry and Neurology. Address: 621 South New Ballas Road, Suite 5009, St Louis, MO 63141, USA.

MANUEL Carlos Mariano, b. 9 March 1957, Piqui, Vige, Angola. Pathologist; University Professor. m. Teresa Candeeiro. 2 sons, 2 daughters. Education: Graduate, University of Angola (Agostinho Neto University), 1978-83; PhD, Pathology, Humboldt University, Berlin, Germany, 1988-93. Appointments: Physician and Young Assistant, Teaching Hospital, Luanda and Huambo, Angola, 1983-88; Deputy Dean,, 1993-94, Professor of Pathology and Dean, 1994-2002, Head, Department of Pathology, 1994-, Medical School, University of Luanda, Angola. Publications: Book: O ensino da Medicina en Angola (in Portuguese, 1997, 1999; Gangarten der Arteriosklerosis, 1993; Flow citometry. Relevant research and clinical applications in Angola, 2000; Several oral presentations at congresses in English, Portuguese, French and German. Honours: Several awards received at national and some international scientific congresses in the field of pathology. Memberships include: International Academy of Pathology; European Association of Hematopathology; European Society of Pathology. Address: Faculty of Medicine, CP 12098, Luanda, Angola.

MANVILLE Stewart Roebling, b. 15 January 1927, White Plains, New York, USA. Archivist; Curator. m. Ella Viola Brandelius-Ström Grainger, 17 January 1972. Education: Hunter College Opera Workshop, 1950-52; Akademie für Musik und Darstellende Kunst, Vienna, 1952-53; BS, Columbia University, 1962. Appointments: Assistant Stage Director, European Opera Houses, 1952-57; Editor, 1959-63; Archivist of Percy Grainger's music, curator of the Percy Grainger House in White Plains New York, 1963-. Publications: Manville-Manvel Genealogy, 1948-; Seeing Opera in Italy, 1955; Seeing Opera in Central Europe, 1956. Memberships include: Soc des Antiquaires de Picardie; National Trust for Historic Preservation; Westchester County Historical Society; St Nicholas Society of New York. Address: 46 Ogden Ave, White Plains, NY 10605-2323, USA.

MAO Zai-Sha, b. 3 July 1943, Chengdu, China. Research Chemical Engineer. m. Junxian Zhou, 2 daughters. Education: BEng, Department of Chemical Engineering, Tsinghua University, Beijing, China, 1966; MS, Institute of Chemical Metallurgy, Chinese Academy of Sciences, Beijing, China, 1981; PhD, Department of Chemical Engineering, University of Houston, Texas, USA, 1988. Appointments: Research Professor, Institute of Process Engineering, Chinese Academy of Sciences; Professor, Graduate School, Chinese

Academy of Sciences; Associate Editor in Chief, Chinese Journal of Chemical Engineering, Beijing; Associate Editor in Chief, Chinese Journal of Process Engineering, Beijing. Publications: 117 papers in peer-reviewed journals; 82 conference presentations; 7 patents on multiphase chemical reactor design. Honours: Best Fundamental Paper, South Texas Section, AIChE, USA, 1992; Excellent Postgraduate Adviser, Graduate School, Chinese Academy of Sciences, Beijing, 2001. Memberships: Chemical Industry and Engineering Society of China. Address: Institute of Process Engineering, CAS, PO Box 353, Beijing 100190, China.

MAOGOTO Jackson Nyamuya, b. 12 October 1975, Nairobi, Kenya. Senior Lecturer in Law. Education: Bachelor of Laws (1st class honours), Moi University, 1999; LLM, University of Cambridge, England, 2001; PhD, University of Melbourne, Australia, 2002. Appointments: Graduate Assistant, Moi University; Research Assistant, Sessional Lecturer, University of Melbourne; Senior Lecturer, University of Newcastle, Australia; Member, International Criminal Law Committee, International Law Association. Publications: Prolific publications in leading international specialist journals: Over 25 refereed journal articles; 3 books: International Criminal Law & State Sovereignty, 2003; War Crimes & Realpolitik, 2004; Battling Terrorism, 2005. Honours: Fellow, Cambridge Commonwealth Society; Melbourne International Scholarship; Shell Centenary Award; Chancellor's Medal. Memberships: Royal Institute of International Affairs; Australian Institute of International Affairs; Australian Lawyers for Human Rights; American Society of International Law; Newcastle Law Society; Australian & New Zealand Society of International Law; Nuclear Age Foundation. E-mail: jackson.maogoto@newcastle.edu.au

MAR AND KELLIE, Earl of, James Thomas Erskine (Jamie), b. 10 March 1949, Edinburgh, Scotland. Peer. m. Mary. Education: Diploma in Social Work, Moray House College of Education, 1968-71; Certificate in Building, Inverness College, 1987-88. Career: Social Work, 20 years; Building Work, 4 years; Hereditary Peer, 1994-99; Life Peer, 2000-; Liberal Democrt Assistant Whip; Liberal Democrat Assistant Transport Spokesman. Honours: Life Peerage: Lord Erskine of Alloa Tower, 2000. Memberships: Chairman, Clackmannanshire Heritage Trust; Non-Executive Director, Clackmannanshire Enterprise; Select Committee on the Constitution, 2001-04. Address: Hilton Farm, Alloa FK10 3PS, Scotland.

MARABLE Darwin William, b. 15 January 1937, Los Angeles, California, USA. Historian; Lecturer; Critic; Curator. m. Joan Ynez Frazell. 1 daughter. Education: BA, University of California at Berkeley, 1960; MA, San Francisco State University, 1972; PhD, History of Photography, University of New Mexico, 1980. Appointments: Lecturer, San Francisco State University, 1977-78, 1982, California College of the Arts, Oakland, 1977-79; San Francisco Art Institute, 1977, 2001; St Mary's College, Moraga, 1990-91, 1992; Academy of Art University, 2001, 2006; Instructor, University of California at Berkeley Extension, 1995-; Mentor, University of California at Berkeley Student-Alumni Mentor Program; Volunteer, University of New Mexico Outreach; Board Member, Diablo Symphony Orchestra, Walnut Creek, 1979-81, Lafayette Arts and Science Foundation, 1980-81, Contra Costa Alliance for the Arts, 1981-82; Docent, Friends of Photography, San Francisco, 1995-2001; Arts Commissioner, Contra Costa County Arts Commission, 2003-. Publications: Numerous articles in popular and professional journals. Memberships: History of Photography Group; Friends of Photography; San

Francisco Museum of Modern Art; Society for Photographic Education; Photo Alliance, San Francisco. Commissions and Creative Works: Guest Curator: Hearst Art Gallery, St Mary's College, Moraga, The Crucifixion in Modern Art, 1992; California College of Arts and Crafts, Oakland, Vilem Kriz Memorial Exhibition, 1996; JJ Brookings Gallery, San Francisco, Visual Dialogue Foundation, Revisited, 2000. Honours: Listed in Who's Who publications and biographical dictionaries. Address: 166 Valley Hill Drive, Moraga, CA 94556, USA.

MARADONA Diego Armando, b. 1960, Lanus, Argentina. Footballer. m. Claudia Villafane, 1989-2004 (divorced) 2 daughters. Appointments: Boca Juniors, Argentina, 1982; Barcelona Football Club; Naples Football Club, 1984-91; Sevilla (Spain), 1992, Boca Juniors, 1997, Badajoz, 1998-; Founder, Maradona Producciones; Former Ambassador for UNICEF; Banned from football for 15 months after drugs test; Convicted by Naples Court on charges of possession of cocaine, 14 month suspended sentence and fine of 4 million lira, 1991; Federal Court in Buenos Aires ruled he had complied with the treatment; Suspended for 15 months for taking performance-enhancing drugs in World Cup Finals, 1994; Indicted for shooting an air rifle at journalists, 1994; Resigned as coach of Deporto Mandiyu, 1994; Captain of Argentina, 1993. Sports Vice President, Boca Juniors, 2005-2006; Television Host, 2005-. Publication: Yo Soy El Diego, 2000. Honour: Footballer of the Century Award, Féderation Internationale de Football Association (France), 2000. Membership: President, International Association of Professional Footballers, 1995-.

MARAKHOUSKI Yury, b. 4 September 1945, Georgia, USSR. Physician. m. Svetlana Rogkova, 1 son. Education: Internal Medicine, 1969; PhD, 1974; Certificate, Patentologia, 1983; Certificate, Public Health Management, Informatics and Statistic, 1985; Docent, Internal Medicine, 1988; Certificate, High Degree of Gastroenterologist, 1996; Doc Med Science, 1991; Certificate (GCP), 2001; Professor, Clinical Medicine, 2005. Appointments: Resident, Soviet Army Hospital, Belarus, 1969-71; Endocrinology Post-graduate Student, Radiation Endocrinology Laboratory, Byelorussian Academy of Sciences, Belarus, 1971-75; Head, Gastroenterology Department, City Clinical Hospital No 1, Minsk, Belarus, 1977-81; Docent in Department of Internal Medicine, Minsk State Medical Institute, 1981-89; Head, Republican Gastroenterology Center, Minsk, Belarus, 1989-99; Professor, Department of Gastroenterology and Nutrition, Byelorussian Medical Academy Postgraduate Education, 1999-2001; Head, Department of Gastroenterology and Nutrition, Byelorussian Medical Academy Postgraduate Education, 2001-. Publications: Advances and disadvances in endoscopical examination at the chronic gastritis, 2001; Clinical importance of hepatic injury in adult patients with celiac disease, 2002; Immunodeficiency and gut pathology, 2002; Gallstone today, 2003; Dose-escalation improves 5-ASA response in active ulcerative colitis. Results from a clinical trial comparing novel mesalazine pellets with mesalazine tablets, 2005. Memberships: President, Byelorussian Gastroenterology Association; International Department of the Physicians Association of the Republic of Belarus; Research Committee of World Organisation of Gastroenterology. E-mail: rscg@open.by/belgastro.com

MARBER Patrick, b. 19 September 1964, London, England. Playwright; Director. 1 son. Education: BA, English Language and Literature, Wadham College, Oxford University, 1983-86. Publications: Plays: Dealer's Choice, 1995; After Miss Julie,

1996; Closer, 1997; Howard Katz, 2001; Old Street, 2004; Closer, 2004; Asylum, 2005; Notes on a Scandal, 2006; The Tourist, 2007; Saturday, 2008. Honours: Writer's Guild Award for Best West End Play, 1995; Evening Standard Award for Best Comedy, 1995; Evening Standard Award for Best Comedy, 1997; Critic's Circle Award for Best Play, 1997; Olivier Award for Best Play, 1997; New York Critics' Award for Best Foreign Play, 1999. Address: c/o Judy Daish Associates, Ltd, 2 St Charles Place, London W10 6EG, England.

MARC'HADOUR Germain, b. 16 April 1921, Langonnet, Brittany. Priest; Professor. Education: Licence ès Lettres, 1945; Doctorat ès Lettres, 1969; Honorary Doctorate of Theology, 1999. Appointments: High School Teacher, 1945-52; Assistant Professor, 1952, Professor, 1969, Catholic University; Founding Secretary, Amici Thomae Mori, 1963. Publications: 6-volume work on Thomas More and the Bible; 200 articles in professional journals; 10 books. Honours: 4 medals; Dedicatee of a Festschrift, 1989; Honorary President, 2005. Memberships: Renaissance Society of America; Modern Language Association; Third Order of St Francis; Editorial Board of Tyndale Project; Charter member of Erasmus of Rotterdam Society. Address: 126, rue Chèvre, 49044 Angers, France.

MARCEAU Sophie (Sophie Danièle, Sylvie Maupu), b. 17 November 1966, Paris, France. Actress. 1 son, 1 daughter. Creative Works: Stage appearances include: Eurydice, 1991; Pygmalion, 1993; Films: La Boum, 1981; La Boum 2, 1982; Fort Saganne, 1984; Joyeuses Pâques, 1985; L'Amour Braque, 1985; Police, 1985; Descente aux Enfers, 1986; Chouans!, 1987; L'Etudiante, 1988; Mes Nuits Sont Plus Belles Que Vos Jours, 1989; Pacific Palisades, 1989; Pour Sacha, 1991; La Note Bleue, 1991; Fanfan, 1993; La Fille de D'Artagnan, 1994; Braveheart, 1995; Beyond the Clouds, 1995; Firelight, 1988; Anna Karenina, 1996; Marquise, 1997; The World is Not Enough, 1998; La Fidelité, 1999; Belphégor, 2001; Alex and Emma, 2003; Je reste! 2003; Les Clefs de bagnole, 2003; Nelly, 2004; Anthony Zimmer, 2005; Disparue de Deauville, La, 2007; Cendrillon, 2008; Femmes de l'ombre, Les, 2008. Publication: Menteuse, 1996. Address: c/o Artmedia, 10 avenue George V, 75008 Paris, France.

MARCINIAK Jan Jozef, b. 10 March 1943, Tarnowskie Gory, Poland. Mechanical Engineer. m. Marianna Joanna Melcer, 3 daughters. Education: MA, Silesian University of Technology, Gliwice, Poland, 1968; PhD, 1972; DSc, 1982; Professor, 1990. Appointments: Master of Metal Physics Team, Institute of Metal Science, Silesian University of Technology, 1975-80; Director of Science, 1982-85; Head, Metal Science Department, 1984-88; Director of Institute, 1985-93; Head, Special Materials and Techniques, 1991; President, Association of Faculty Mechanics, Gliwice, 1983-88; Chairman of Board, Silesian University of Technology, 1985; Director of Centre of Bioengineering since 1999. Publications: Biomaterials in Surgery, 1992; Biomaterials, 2002; Menace of Electromagnetic Environment, 1995, 2000; Co-author: Metal Science and Head Treatment of Tool Materials, 1990; Intramedullary Nailing in Osteosynthesis, 2006; Stents for Minimal Invasive Surgery, 2006; 29 books; 28 patents; 360 publications. Honours: Award in Gold, Chief Technical Organization, Katowice, 1980; Order of Merits for Development, Voivode of Katowice 1986; Order of Merits, Leszno, 1988; Gold Medal, INPEX XIII, Pittsburgh, 1997; Golden Key Award, London International Inventions Fair, 1997. Memberships: Rehabilitations Engineering and Social Adaption Committee, Committee of Materials Engineering, Applied Mechanics Committee, Polish Academy of Science;

Scientific Committee of journals; Acta of Bioengineering and Biomechanics, Engineering of Biomaterials; Member, scientific committees of Internationale Conference on Materials, Mechanical and Manufacturing Engineering; Polish Society of Biomechanics; Polish Society of Biomaterials; Polish Society of Applied Electromagnetics; Polish Club of Ecology. Address: Silesian University of Technology, Institute of Engineering and Biomedical Materials, Konarskiego 18a, 44-100 Gliwice, Poland.

MARCOS Imelda Romualdez, b. 1930, Philippines. Politician; Social Leader. m. Ferdinand E Marcos deceased, 1 son, 2 daughters. Appointments: Governor, Metro Manila, 1975-86; Roving Ambassador; Visited Beijing, 1976; Took part in negotiations in Libya over self-government for southern province, 1977; Leader, Kilusan Bagong Lipunan (New Socialist Movement), 1978-81; Member, Batasang Pambansa (Interim Legislative Assembly), 1978-83; Minister of Human Settlements, 1978-79, 1984-86, of Human Settlements and Ecology, 1979-83; Meber, Cabinet Executive Committee, 1982-84; Chair, Southern Philippines Development Authority, 1980-86; Indicated for embezzlement, 1988, acquitted, 1990; Returned to Philippines, 1991; Sentenced to 18 to 24 years imprisonment for criminal graft, 1993; Convicted of two charges of corruption, sentenced to 9-12 years on each, 1993; Sentenced on appeal to Supreme Court; Facing 4 charges of graft, 1995; Presidential Candidate, 1992; Senate, 1995-; 10 pending graft cases, 2007. Creative Works: Records include: Imelda Papin, featuring songs with Mrs Imelda Romualdez Marcos, 1989.

MARCOU Giorgio S, b. Halandri, Greece. Historian. Education: PhD (Honours), Law School of Rome, 1971, and Panteion University, Athens, 1973; Postgraduate diplomas in History of Law. Appointments: Academic Assistant, Researcher, Italian National Research Foundation, Law School of the University of Rome, 1969-76; Lawyer, Athens, 1971-2005; Professor of Byzantine and Post-Byzantine Law, Law School of the Pontifical Institute of Eastern Studies, 1976-79; Visiting Professor, Common Law, University of Trapani, 1979, Naples, 1980, and Rome, 1976-88; Visiting Professor, Post-Byzantine Law, Panteios University of Eastern Studies, 1979; Member, Board of Directors, Ionian Insurance Company, 1990-93; Visiting Professor, University of Macerata, Italy, 1992-93, 1993-94, 1994-95; Visiting Professor, Diplomatic Academy of the Italian Ministry of Foreign Affairs, 1994; Visiting Professor, Higher School of National Security and Defense, Athens, 1997-2001. Publications: Numerous articles in professional journals. Honours: Fontane di Roma, Colosseum, City of Todi, City of Rome, City of Nemi, City of Florence, Prefecture of Rome (Lazio), Todi, Umbria and Florence (Tuscany) awards; Italian Ministry of Culture award; Euro-African Foundation award; Rome Artists' Association ANDROMEDA award; Community of European Journalists award; UNICEF; UNESCO; Honorary Consul of Italy in Dodecanese; Founder and President of UNESCO Dodecanese; House of Europe in Dodecanese; OMMEPO, 1993, 1995; Award for discovery of the Nobel Collection and foundation of the Museum of the Hellenic Nobel Collection, 2000; City of Holargos award, 2003; Honour, Italian Carabiniery Force, 2005; Cavaliere dell'Ordine al merito della Repubblica Italiana; Ifestos Award; Ifestos Award, 2006; University of Thessaly Award, 2007. Memberships: Hellenic UNESCO Federation. Address: 79 Olimpou Street, Hallandri, 15234, Athens, Greece. Website: www.museum-hellenic-nobel-collection.gr

MARGOLYES Miriam, b. 18 May 1941, Oxford, England. Actor. Education: BA (Hons) English Literature, Cambridge University. Career: Films: Stand Up Virgin Soldiers; The Awakening; The Apple; Reds; Coming Out Of The Ice; Scrubbers; Yentl; Electric Dreams; Handel - Honour, Profit And Pleasure; The Good Father; Little Shop Of Horrors; Little Dorrit; Wiesenthal - The Murderers Among Us; I Love You To Death; Pacific Heights; The Fool; Dead Again; The Butcher's Wife; As You Like It; The Age Of Innocence; Ed And His Dead Mother; The White Horse; Immortal Beloved; Babe (Voice); James And The Giant Peach; Crossing The Border; Romeo and Juliet; Sunshine; End Of Days; Alone; Harry Potter and the Chamber of Secrets; Cold Comfort Farm; Different For Girls; Dreaming Of Josephe Lees; Cats & Dogs; The First Snow Of Winter; The Life And Death Of Peter Sellers; Modigliani; Being Julia; Ladies In Lavender; Sir Billi the Vet (voice); Flushed Away; Happy Feet (voice); The Dukes. Television: Fall Of Eagles; Girls Of Slender Means; Kizzy; The Widowing Of Mrs Holroyd; Glittering Prizes; Stanley Baxter Christmas Show; Tales Of The Unexpected: Fat Chance; The History Man; The Lost Tribe; Take A Letter Mr Jones; A Kick Up The 80s (Various); Scotch And Wry; The First Schlemiel; Freud; Strange But True: Flight Of Fancy; A Rough State: The Mexican Rebels; The Young Ones; Alternative Society; Oliver Twist; Blackadder; Blackadder II; Blackadder III; Life And Loves Of A She Devil; The Little Princess; Poor Little Rich Girl; Body Contact; Mr Majeika; The Finding; Doss; City Lights; Old Flames; Orpheus Decending; Hands Across The Sea; Ways And Means; The Comic Strip - Secret Ingredient; Frannie's Turn; Just William; Phoenix And The Carpet; Fall Of The House Of Windsor; The Lost Tribe; Tuscany To Go; Miss Marple; Wallis And Edward; Theatre: The Cherry Orchard; The Killing Of Sister George; She Stoops To Conquer; Dickens' Women; Orpheus Descending; Man Equals Man; Gertrude Stein And A Companion; 84 Charing Cross Rd; Flaming Bodies; Cloud Nine; The White Devil; Threepenny Opera; Kennedy's Children; Canterbury Tales; Fiddler On The Roof; Romeo And Juliet; The Vagina Monologues; The Way Of The World; Blithe Spirit. Honours: Joint winner (with Genevieve Bujold), Best Supporting Actress, LA Critics Circle, 1989; Talkies Performer of the Year, 1991; BAFTA Best Supporting Actor, 1993; Sony Radio Best Actress on Radio, 1993; Best Children's Entertainment, The Royal Television Society, 1999; Best Animation for Children, BAFTA, 1999; Best Independent Production, The Prix Danube, 1999; 2nd Prize, Children's Jury for Best Animation, Chicago International Children's Film Festival, 1999; Grand Prize, Best Short Film, Kinderfilmfest, Tokyo, 1999; Best Film Audience Award Jury Award, Washington DC International Film Festival, 1999 Prix Jeunesse, Best Children's Programme (0-6 fiction), 2000; OBE, 2001. Memberships: BAFTA: Equity; AFTRA; Academy of Motion Pictures. Address: c/o PFD, Drury House, 34-43 Russell Street, London WC2B 5HA, England. Website: www.miriammargolyes.com

MARGRETHE II H.M. (Queen of Denmark), b. 16 April 1940, Denmark. m. Count Henri de Laborde de Monpezat (now Prince Henrik of Denmark), 1967, 2 sons. Education: University of Copenhagen; University of Aarhus; University of Cambridge; University of Sorbonne, Paris; London School of Economics. Appointments: Illustrator, The Lord of the Rings, 1977, Norse Legends as Told by Jorgen Stegelmann, 1979, Bjarkemaal, 1982; Poul Oerum's Comedy in Florens, 1990; Cantabile poems by HRH the Prince Consort, 2000. Publications: (trans) All Men are Mortal (with Prince Henrik), 1981; The Valley, 1988; The Fields, 1989; The Forest (trans), 1989. Honours include: Honorary LLD, Cambridge, 1975,

London, 1980; Honorary Bencher, Middle Temple, 1992; Honorary Fellow, Girton College, Cambridge, 1992; Medal of the Headmastership, University of Paris, 1987; Hon KG, 1979. Address: Amalienborg Palace, 1257 Copenhagen K, Denmark.

MARINELLI Carlo, b. 13 December 1926, Rome, Italy. Musicologist; Discologist; Discographer. 1 son, 1 daughter. Education: Degree in Letters, La Sapienza University of Rome, 1948. Career: Founder and Editor, Microsolco magazine, 1952-59; Professor, History of Music, 1970-98, Associate, 1985-98, Associate, History of Modern and Contemporary Music, 1992-98, Department of Comparative Cultures, Faculty of Letters, University of L'Aquila; Professor, Discography and Musical Videography, 1998-2002, DAMS, Faculty of Letters, University of Bologna; President, Institute for Research on Musical Theatre, Rome. Publications: Discographies of Mozart, Rossini, Monteverdi, Donizetti, Bellini, Verdi, Puccini; Editor, catalogues of Italian audiovisual and sound sources of Mozart and Rossini; Editor: Notizie Videoarchivio Opera e Balletto, Notizie Archivio Sonoro Musica Contemporanea, IRTEM "Quaderni"; Le cantate profane di J S Bach, 1966; La musica strumentale da camera di Goffredo Petrassi, 1967; Lettura di Messiaen, 1972; Cronache di musica contemporanea, 1974; L'opera ceca, l'opera russa, l'opera in Polonia e Ungheria, 1977; Opere in disco. Da Monteverdi a Berg, 1982; Di Goffredo Petrassi, un'antologia, 1983; Prolegomeni ad una nuova disciplina scientifica: Discografia e videografia musicale, 1998; Prolegomena to a new scientific discipline: musical discography and videography, 2000; I documenti musicali sonori e visivi quali fonti di conoscenza, informazione e transmissione, 2002; Sound and Visual Musical Documents as Sources of Knowledge, Information and Transmission, 2002; Rilettura digitale come alterazione di documenti sonori originali, 2004; Analogue-to-Digital Conversion Viewed as an Alteration of Original Sounds Documents, 2004; Discological Critical Edition: Giovanni Paisiello, Il re Teodoro in Venezia, 1994. Discographies: Faust e Mefistofele nelle opere sinfonico-vocali, 1986; Le opere di Mozart su libretti di Da Ponte, 1988; Mozart Singspiele, 1993; Mozart, Opere serie italiane, 1995; Monteverdi, Balli e Madrigali in genere rappresentativo, 1996; De Falla, Atalantida, 1996; Rossini, Il barbiere di Siviglia, 1998; Verdi, Rigoletto, Il trovatore, La traviata, 1999; Monteverdi, Opere teatrali, 2000; Rossini, Opere teatrali 1820-1829, 2001; Verdi, Don Carlo, Otello, Falstaff, 2002; Verdi, Oberto, Giorno di regno, Nabucco, Lombardi, Ernani, Due Foscari, 2003; Verdi, Don Carlos, La forza del destino, 2003, Verdi, Aida, 2004; Mozart, Opere buffe italiane, Serenate, azioni teatrali, balletti, Drammi sacri e oratori, 2006; Un itinerario donizettiano, 2006; Verdi 1844-1850, Giovanna d'Arco, Alzira, Atilla, Macbeth, 1 masnadieri, Jerusalem Il corsaro, La battaglia di Legnano, Luisa Miller, Stiffelio, 2007; Opera Discography Encyclopaedia, 2004-07 onwards. Honours: Honorary Member, International Association of Sound and Audiovisual Archives; Academician, Accademia Santa Cecilia, Rome: Memberships: President, Associazione Italiana Archivi Sonori Audiovisivi; Board Member, Internationales Musik Zentrum, 1993-95; Chairman, Discography Committee, IASA, 1996-99; International, American, Australian, French, Spanish and Italian Musicological Societies; International Association of Music Libraries; Association of Recorded Sound Collectors; Australasian Sound Recording Association; Association Française Archives Sonores; Associazione Italiana Studi Nord Americani; Associazione Docenti Universitari Italiani Musica. Address: Via Francesco Tamagno 65-67, I-00168 Rome, Italy. E-mail: carlomarinelli@mclink.it Website: www.carlomarinelli.it

MARINO Marialuisa, b. 4 January 1945, Milan, Italy. Artist; Poet; Writer. 3 sons. Education: Ballet Diploma, La Scala Opera House, Italy, 1962; Teachers Diploma, Advanced Diploma, Chechetti, Italy, 1963; Principal Soloist, Performing Arts Council of Transvaal, South Africa; Studies in art, Witwatersrand Technical College of Art, South Africa. Appointments: 6 appointments for voluntary community and honorary officer, 1976-85; First solo art exhibition, 1990; Joined family business founded by father in 1967, became Managing Director, 1978, Marmernova and Building Products Pty Ltd; Only woman member, Master Mason Association and the Building Industries Federation; Trustee and Director of Events, City Ballet of London. Publications: Illustrations, Diana: An English Rose, 1998; Beyond Fantasy, painting and poetry book, 2000; Annuario d'Arte Moderna Artisti Contemporanei, 2000; Merry Mischief – A Childhood Celebration of Queen Elizabeth, The Queen Mother, 2001; Royalty; Savonarola; 3 childrens books: The Fantastical Journey of George Green I, 2007, II, 2007, III, 2008; Portraits: Alexander Thynn, Marquis of Bath; Homage to the Queen, 2006; George Green, Miller Mathematician of Nottingham, 1793-1843; Dame Alicia Marcova; HRH Prince William of Wales; Queen Elizabeth, The Queen Mother; Sir Malcolm Arnold CBE; Paloma Picasso. Honours: La Scala Opera House, 1962; 10 gold medals, South Africa Premiere Exhibition, Witwatersrand Easter Show, 1976-85; Annuario d'Arte Moderna, 1999, 2000; Paul Harris Fellow, Rotary Foundation; Citta di Firenze: Professore HC, for painting "Diana, Princess of Wales", 2000; Cavaliere dell'Etruria: Groseto, Italy, 2000; Coppa Libertas, for Symphony No 9, 2001; New Art Promotion "Sirena del Mare", Cervia, Italy, 2001; Statua della Liberta, Accademia del Fiorano, New York, USA, 2001; Award for "Merry Mischief", Accademia Italiana Etruschi, Cita di Milano, 2001; Cavaliere della Pace, Firenze, Italy, for painting of President Nelson Mandela, 2001; N D Marialuisa Marino, Accademica Gentilizia (Classe) Belle Arti, 2001; N D Professor Marialuisa Marino, Il Marzocco dalla Firenze dei Signori l'Illustrissimo Corpo Accademico, (Classe) Belle Arti, 2001; Arte in Italia l'Elite, 2002, 2003; Associazione Culturale: Amici del Quadro Gold Medal, Milan, 2003; Accademia il Marzocco, Gran Premio Internazionale, Genova la Superba citta della Cultura, 2004; Promotore della Pace, for Celebration: A Portrait of Julian Lloyd Webber, 2004; Accademia Internazionale Città Di Roma Award for Venus Through a Mirror of Time, 2004; Salento Porta d'Oriente, 2006, Premio Rembrandt, 2006, Regione Publica Universita di Studi di Lecce; Grand Prix Mediceo Cosimo I Granduca della Toscana città di Livorno, 2007; International Prize, Unversita del Salento, Dipartimento di Scienza dei Materiali, 2007; Rassegna "Folgore" Dr Livorno (Caserma Vannucci) "Premio Italia 2008" for painting and poetry, 2008. Memberships: Life Member, British/Italian Society; International Society of Poets, 2000; Accademia Il Marzocco ND for Belle Arte, 2001; Rotary International Rotary Club of Kensington; The Fine Art Trade Guild, 2000; Academical Commander Ordine Accademico del Verbano, 2004; Avanguardie Artistisce, 2004, 2005. Address: The Mill House, Belvoir Hill, Sneinton, Nottingham NG2 4LF, Nottinghamshire, England.

MARKESINIS Sir Basil, b. 10 July 1944, Athens, Greece. Barrister; QC, Bencher of Gray's Inn, 1991; Professor of Law. m. Eugenie Trypanis, 1 son, 1 daughter. Education: LLB "starred first", 1965, Doctor Iuris, Summa Cum Laude, 1968, Athens; MA, PhD, 1970, LLD, 1988, Cambridge; DCL, Oxford, 1996. Appointments: Advocate, Supreme Court, Athens, 1976-86; Acting Director, 1987-88, Deputy Director, Centre for Commercial Law Studies, 1986-93, Director International Affairs for the Faculty of Laws, 1989-93,

Professor of Comparative Law, 1986-95, Queen Mary College, London; Founder-Director, Institute of Anglo-American Law, Leiden, The Netherlands, 1987-99; Professor of European Law, 1995-98, Professor of Comparative Law, 1998-2000, University of Oxford; Founder-Director, Oxford Institute of European and Comparative Law, 1997-2001; Founder-Director, Institute of Transnational Law, University of Texas at Austin, USA, 1999; Clifford Chance Special Adviser for European Affairs, 1998-2001; Professor of Common and Civil Law, 2000-, Founder and first Chairman, Institute of Global Law, 2001-, University College London; Conseiller Scientifique du Premier Président de la Cour de Cassation, France, 2002-. Publications: 31 books including most recently: Always on the Same Path: Essays on Foreign Law and Comparative Methodology vol 2, 2001; The German Law of Tort: A Comparative Treatise (co-author), 2002; Comparative Law in the Courtroom and Classroom, 2003; Compensation for Personal Injury in England, Germany and Italy, 2004; Rechtsvergleichung in Theorie und Praxis, 2004; The German Law of Contract. A Comparative Treatise (co-author), 2006; Foreign Law in National Courts: A New Source of Inspiration (co-author), 2006; Good and Evil in Art and Law, 2007; Over 120 articles in national and international legal journals. Honours include: Honorary degrees from: University of Gent, Paris I, University of Munich; Officier des Palmes Academiques, France, 1991; Queens Counsel, honoris causa, 1998; Commander of the Order of Honour, Greece, 2000; Knight Grand Cross of the Order of Merit, Italy, 2002; Knight Commander of the Order of Merit, Germany, 2003; Commander of the Order of the Légion d'Honneur, France, 2004; Knight Bachelor, 2005; Doctor hc, Athens, 2007; Knight Grand Cross of Order of Merit, France, 2007. Memberships: Fellow, British Academy; Foreign Fellow, Royal Belgian Academy; Royal Netherlands Academy; Accademia dei Lincei (Rome); Corresponding Fellow, Institut de France (Académie des Sciences Morales et Politiques); Corresponding Fellow, Academy of Athens; Member, American Law Institute. Address: Middleton Stoney House, Middleton Stoney, Bicester, Oxon OX25 4TE, England.

MARKHAM Jehane, b. 12 February 1949, Sussex, England. Poet; Playwright. 3 sons. Education: Central School of Art, 1969-71. Publications: The Captain's Death, 1974; Ten Poems, 1993; Virago New Poets, 1993; Twenty Poems, 1999; Between Sessions and Beyond the Couch, 2002; In The Company of Poets, 2003; Thirty Poems, 2004. Radio Plays: More Cherry Cake, 1980; Thanksgiving, 1984; The Bell Jar; Frost in May. Television Play: Nina, 1978. Theatre Plays: One White Day, 1976; The Birth of Pleasure, 1997; Hermes, 2006. Contributions to: Women's Press; Longmans Study; Sunday Times; BBC 2 Epilogue; Bananas Literary Magazine; Camden Voices; Independent; Observer; Acorn; Ambit; New Statesman; Cork Literary Review; Images of Women, 2006. Memberships: Poetry Society; Highgate Literary and Scientific Society; NFT; Poetry Book Society. Address: 56 Lady Somerset Road, London, NW5, 1TU, England.

MARKHAM Richard, b. 23 June 1952, Grimsby, England. Concert Pianist. Education: Piano privately with Shirley Kemp and Max Pirani; National Youth Orchestra of Great Britain; Royal Academy of Music, London, 1969-73. Career: Concert Pianist; Tours in over 40 countries as David Nettle/Richard Markham Piano Duo, 1977-; Examiner for Associated Board of the Royal Schools of Music, 1984-. Recordings include: Nettle and Markham in America; Nettle and Markham in England; Nettle and Markham in France; Complete Two-Piano Works of Brahms. Honours: ARCM, 1967; LRAM, 1968; Nora Naismith Scholarship, 1969; Bronze

Medal, Geneva International Competition, 1972; Countess of Munster Musical Trust Awards, 1973, 1974; Frederick Shinn Fellowship, 1975; Gulbenkian Foundation Fellowship, 1976-78; ARAM 1983; MRA Award for Excellence, 1985. Memberships: Incorporated Society of Musicians; RAM Club; Gymnos; Friend of Stonewall. Address: The Old Power House, Atherton Street, London SW11 2JE, England. E-mail: richardpiano@aol.com

MARKS Isaac, b. 16 February 1935, Cape Town, South Africa. Doctor. m. Shula, 1 son, 1 daughter. Education: MB ChB, 1956, MD, 1963, Cape Town University; DPM, London University, 1963; FRCPsych, 1970. Appointments: Professor, Consultant Psychiatrist, Institute of Psychiatry, Bethlem-Maudsley Hospital, Kings College London, 1978-2000; Professor Emeritus, 2000-. Publications: 430 scientific articles; 13 books. Honours: Salmon Medallist, New York Academy of Medicine; Honorary Professor, Vrije Universiteit, Amsterdam, 2005-; Fellow, Centre for Advanced Study in Behavioural Science, Stanford, USA. Membership: Fellow, Royal College of Psychiatrists.

MARLAND Michael, b. 28 December 1934, London, England. Retired Headteacher; Educational Author. m. (1) Eileen, deceased 1968, 4 sons, 1 daughter, (2) Linda, 1 son. Education: BA, Sidney Sussex College, Cambridge, 1954-57. Appointments: English Teacher: Der Halepaghen Oberschule, Buxtehude, Germany; Simon Langton Grammar School, Canterbury; Head of English: Abbey Wood Comprehensive School, London; Crown Woods Comprehensive School, London then Director of Studies at that school; Headteacher: Woodberry Down School, London; Founder Headteacher, North Westminster Community School, London; General Editor: Blackie: Student Drama Series, Longman: Imprint Books, Heinemann: School Management Series. Publications: Numerous books include: School Management Skills, 1986; Multilingual Britain, 1987; The Tutor and Tutor Group, 1989; Headship Matters (with Peter Ribbins), 1994; The Art of the Tutor (with Rick Rogers), 1997; Managing Arts in the Curriculum (with Rick Rogers), 2002; The Craft of the Classroom (revised version), 2002; A Vision for Today (with Gillian Klein), 2003; How to be a Successful Form Tutor (with Rick Rogers), 2004; The Complete Teacher, 2007; Compiled and edited 30 literary anthologies for classroom study, 1969-84; Over 100 articles in journals, booklets, newspapers and symposia on educational matters. Honours: CBE; Fellow, College of Preceptors; Hon. Dr. Education, Kingston; Kidscape Children's Champion; Hon. Dr. University, Surrey Roehampton; Honorary Fellow, Institute of Education, London; Fellow, British Educational Leadership, Management and Administration Society. Memberships: National Council, BELMAS; Vice-President, City of Westminster Arts Council; Education Committee, English Speaking Union; Master of Teaching Steering Committee, Institute of Education; Editorial Board, NAPCE; Patron, Tagore Centre, UK; Chair, Upper Street Association, Islington, London; Board Member, Young Person's Concert Foundation. Address: 22 Compton Terrace, London N1 2UN, England.

MAROVIC Pavao, b. 26 January 1954, Split, Croatia. University Professor; Civil Engineer. m. Vladica Herak, 1 son. Education: Faculty of Civil Engineering, University of Zagreb, 1972-77; Graduate, Civil Engineer, 1977; PhD, Faculty of Civil Engineering, University of Zagreb, 1987. Appointments: Teaching Assistant, 1978-88, Assistant Professor, 1988-92, Head of Department, Testing and Technology of Materials, 1988-91, Vice Dean of the Faculty, 1991-94, President, University Assembly, 1991-93, Associated Professor,

1992-96, Vice Rector, 1994-98, Professor, 1996-, Head of the Chair for Strength of Materials, Testing of Structures, 1998-, Dean of the Faculty, 2000-2006, University of Split; Associated Member, Croatian Academy of Technical Sciences, 2000. Publications: International Conference on Nonlinear Engineering Computations, 1991; Nonlinear Calculations of R/C Structures, 1993; International Congress of Croatian Society of Mechanics, 1997, 2000; Symposium on The Use of Computers in Civil Engineering; Co-editor of 25 Croatian Conference proceedings; Approximately 160 scientific and professional papers in journals and conference proceedings; Many others. Honours: Rector's Student Award; Plaque of the CAD/CAM Congress; Decorated by the President of the Republic of Croatia; County Splitsko-dalmatinska Yearly Award for Science; 2000 Outstanding Scientists of the 20th Century Silver Medal, International Biographical Centre; World Lifetime Achievement Award, American Biographical Institute. Memberships: International Association for Computer Methods in Geomechanics; International Association for Bridge and Structural Engineering; Central European Association for Computational Mechanics; European Scientific Association for Material Forming; National Geographic Society; Croatian Society of Mechanics; Croatian Society of Structural Engineers; Many others. Address: Faculty of Civil Engineering and Architecture, University of Split, Matice hrvatske 15, HR-21000 Split, Croatia.

MARQUES Eduardo Jorge de Sousa Ferreira, b. 2 February 1964, Tondela, Portugal. Medical Doctor; Eye Surgeon. Education: Medical Degree, 1987, Clinical Oncology Fellowship, 1989, University of Coimbra, Portugal; Assistant in Ophthalmology, Ministry of Health, Portugal, 1995; Ophthalmology Specialty, Portuguese Medical Association, 1995. Appointments: Member, National Executive Board, Portuguese Medical Association, 1992-98; Ophthalmology Assistant, Coimbra University Hospital, Portugal, 1995-96; Ophthalmology Assistant, Clipóvoa Hospital, Portugal, 1996-99; President, Permanent Working Group of European Junior Doctors, 1998-2001; Ophthalmology Consultant, Centro Oftalmológico de Lisboa, Lisbon, Portugal, 1999-; Member, European Board of Ophthalmology, 2000-03; Member, Consulting Board, Portuguese Medical Association, 2001-; Member, Continuing Medical Education Committee, European Board of Ophthalmology. Publications: 62 presentations; 33 publications including 25 articles and 8 books. Honours: Portuguese Society of Ophthalmology Award, 1995. Memberships: Portuguese Medical Association; Portuguese Society of Ophthalmology; Portuguese Group of Implant and Refractive Surgeons; European Society of Cataract and Refractive Surgeons; American Society of Cataract and Refractive Surgeons; Portuguese Board of Ophthalmology; American Academy of Ophthalmology; International Society of Refractive Surgeons. E-mail: em.lx@netcabo.pt

MARSDEN Simon Neville Llewelyn (Sir), b. 1 December 1948, Lincoln, Lincolnshire, England. Photographer; Author. m. Caroline Stanton, 1 son, 1 daughter. Education: Ampleforth College, Yorkshire, England; Sorbonne, Paris, France. Career: Professional photographer and author; Photographs in the following collections: J Paul Getty Museum, California, USA; Victoria and Albert Museum, London; Bibliothéque Nationale, Paris, France; The Cleveland Museum of Art, USA; The Maryland Historical Society, Baltimore, USA; The University of Arizona, USA; Flanders Field Museum, Ypres, Belgium. Publications: In Ruins: The Once Great Houses of Ireland, 1980; The Haunted Realm – Ghosts, Witches and Other Strange Tales, 1986; Visions of Poe- A Personal Selection of E A Poe's Stories and Poems, 1988; Phantoms of the Isles – Further Tales from the Haunted Realm, 1990; The Journal of a Ghosthunter – In search of the Undead from Ireland to Transylvania, 1994; Beyond the Wall – The Lost World of East Germany, 1999; Venice - City of Haunting Dreams, 2002; The Twilight Hour – Celtic Visions from the Past, 2003; This Spectred Isle – A Journey Through Haunted England, 2005. Memberships: Chelsea Arts Club; The Arthur Machen Society. Address: The Presbytery, Hainton, Market Rasen, Lincolnshire LN8 6LR, England. E-mail: info@marsdenarchive.com Website: www.simonmarsden.co.uk

MARSDEN-SMEDLEY Christopher, b. 9 February 1931, London, England. Retired Architect. m. Susan Penelope King, 2 sons 1 daughter. Education: BA, (Arch), University College, London, 1956. Appointments: Partner, 1961-96, Senior Partner, 1990-96, Nealon Tanner Partnership; High Sheriff, Avon, 1994-95; Deputy Lieutenant, Somerset, 2000. Publications: Burrington, Church and Village; Articles in various architectural papers. Honours: ARIBA, 1959; FRIBA, 1969. Memberships: Honorary Secretary, Bristol Civic Society, 1966-71; Governor, 1969-75, Chairman, 1972-75, Fairfield School; Committee Member, 1974-97, Chairman, 1988-97, Vice President, 1997-, Bristol Age Care; President, Bristol Commercial Rooms, 1988; Trustee, Wells Cathedral, 1997-; Committee Member, 1997-, President 2000-2001, Canynges Society. Address: Church Farm, Burrington, Near Bristol BS40 7AD, England.

MARSH Eric M, b. 25 July 1943, Preston, England. Hotelier. m. Elizabeth Margaret, 2 sons, 2 daughters. Education: National Diploma in Hotelkeeping and Catering, Courtfield Catering College, Blackpool, Lancashire, England, 1960-63. Appointments: Dorchester Hotel, London, 1963-68; Rank Hotels, London, 1968-73; Director and General Manager, Newling Ward Hotels, St Albans, Hertfordshire, England, 1973-1975; Tenant of Cavendish Hotel from Chatsworth Estate, 1975-; Managing Director, Paludis Ltd (Trading as Cavendish Hotel), 1975-; Managing Director of Eudaemonic Leisure Ltd (Trading as George Hotel), 1996-; Managing Director, Cavendish Aviation Ltd (Operating at Gamston Airfield), 1975-. Publications: Several articles in Caterer and Hotelkeeper magazine and Pilot magazine. Memberships: Institute of Marketing; Institute of Advanced Motorists; Director, Committee Member, British Aerobatic Association. Address: Cavendish Hotel, Baslow, Derbyshire DE45 1SP, England. E-mail: info@cavendish-hotel.net

MARSH Francis Patrick, b. 15 April 1936, Birmingham, England. Consultant Physician. m. Pamela Anne Campbell, 1 son, 2 daughters. Education: BA, Natural Science Tripos, Gonville and Caius College, 1957; London Hospital Medical College, 1957-60; MB BChir, Cambridge, 1960; MA, Cambridge, 1961; MRCP, London, 1963; FRCP, London, 1976. Appointments: House Physician, 1960-61, House Surgeon, 1961, The London Hospital; Senior House Officer in Medicine, Kent and Canterbury Hospital, 1961-62; Registrar in Medicine, Royal Free Hospital, 1962-63; Registrar in Medicine, The London Hospital, 1963-65; Research Fellow, 1965-67, Lecturer, Senior Registrar, 1967-70, The London Hospital and London Hospital Medical College; Honorary Consultant Physician, Bethnal Green Hospital, 1970-71; Senior Lecturer in Medicine, The London Hospital Medical College, now St Bartholomew's and the Royal London School of Medicine and Dentistry, 1970-2001; Consultant Nephrologist, Barts and the London NHS Trust, 1971-2001; Dean of Medical Studies and Governor, The London Hospital Medical College, 1990-95; Board of Directors, American

University of the Caribbean, 2000-; Honorary Senior Lecturer in Medicine, Bartholomew's and the Royal London School of Medicine and Dentistry, 2001-; Emeritus Consultant Nephrologist, Barts and the London NHS Trust, 2001-. Publications: Around 80 original research papers; Author, 26 book chapters; Editor, Postgraduate Nephrology; Refereed many medical journals and for regional and national prizes. Memberships include: Joint Formulary Committee, British National Formulary; Renal Association; Specialist Advisory Committee on Renal Disease; North East Thames Regional Medical Advisory Committee; North East Thames Regional Committee for Hospital Medical Services; Council of the Section of Medicine, Experimental Medicine and Therapeutics (Royal Society of Medicine); Central Committee for Hospital Medical Services. Address: Butchers End, 20 Butchers Lane, East Dean, West Sussex, PO18 0JF, England. E-mail: frank.marsh@virgin.net

MARSH Laurie Peter, Consultant; Property Restoration. Education: National Service RASC and Intelligence Corps, 1950-51, commissioned; Reserve Captain, 1954. Appointments: Chairman, Chief Executive Officer, Raincheque Ltd sold to Blacketts Stores plc, Director of plc, 1956; Chairman, Chief Executive Officer, Wadey Davison and L P Marsh (Properties) Ltd, Director, Greenaways (Builders), London, 1958; Chairman, Booty Jewellery, London, 1962; Director, Tigon Film Group, 1969; Acquired Classic Cinemas, 1971; Chairman, Town and District Properties plc and Laurie Marsh Group plc, 1971; Aquired Essoldo Cinema Group and part Rank cinemas, expanded multiple cinemas; LMG expanded into Europe, name changed to Intereuropean Prop Holdings plc, 1974; Chairman and Director, theatre group with Brian Rix and Ray Cooney, acquired 6 London theatres and 1 on Broadway, New York, 1976; Elected Vice President, 1978, President, 1979, Cinematograph Exhibitors Association; Sold IPH plc to ACC Leisure Group, Lord Grade, 1980; Chairman, Cosgrove Hall Properties Inc, New York, 1980; Chairman, Theatre Royal Bath; Restored theatres in London and New York, 1981; Chairman, F and GP LAMDA, UK National Charity, 1991; Founder, Libertas Charity Group, Chairman, Soundalive Tours Group (now International Heritage Group), 1986-98; Non-Executive Chairman, Cole Kitchen Theatre Group, 1994; Non-Executive Chairman, London Crystal Cleaners and Capital Property Services, 1999; Consultant to major property groups; Property restoration, theatre, financial consultancy. Address: 30 Grove End Road, St John's Wood, London NW8 9LJ, England. E-mail: lauriemarsh@onetel.com

MARSHALL Albert Selwyn, b. 26 September 1934, Tatsfield, Surrey, England. Retired Diplomat. m. Joan Margaret Lashwood, deceased, 1985, 1 son, 1 daughter. Education: Kent Horticultural College, Kent, England. Appointments: Royal Corps of Signals, Korea, Suez Canal, Cyprus, 1952-57; Foreign Office, 1957-61; Communications Officer, UK Mission to UN, New York, 1961-64; Archivist, British Embassy, Prague, 1954-65; ECO, British High Commission, Kingston, Jamaica, 1965-68; Foreign and Commonwealth Office, London, England, 1968-72; Management Officer, British Embassy, Addis Ababa, Ethiopia, 1972-75; British Vice-Consul, Belgrade, Yugoslavia, 1975-77; HM Vice-Consul, Tokyo, Japan, 1977-81; Foreign and Commonwealth Office, London, England, 1981-86; Management Officer, British Embassy, Washington DC, USA, 1986-90; HM Consul, Tel Aviv, Israel, 1990-94; Retired, 1994. Honour: MBE, 1968. Memberships: Treasurer, Merrow

Horticultural Society; Volunteer, National Trust, Polesden Lacey. Address: 4 Tansy Close, Guildford, Surrrey GU4 7XN, England. E-mail: albert@asmarshall.freeserve.co.uk

MARSHALL Enid Ann, b. 10 July 1932, Boyndie, Scotland. University Academic. Education: 1st Class Honours, Classics, 1950-55, LLB, with distinction, 1955-58, PhD (part-time), Scots Company Law, 1960-66, University of St Andrews, Fife, Scotland. Appointments: Apprentice Solicitor, Cupar, Fife, 1956-59; Lecturer in Law, Dundee College of Technology, Dundee, Scotland, 1959-72; Lecturer in Business Law, 1972-74, Senior Lecturer in Business Law, 1974-77, Reader in Business Law, 1977-94, Head of Scots Law Research Unit, 1994-99, University of Stirling, Scotland. Publications: General Principles of Scots Law, 1971, 7th edition, 1999; Scots Mercantile Law, 1983, 3d edition, 1997; Scottish Cases on Contract, 1978, 2nd edition, 1993; Scottish Cases on Agency, 1980; Scottish Cases on Partnerships and Companies, 1980; Oliver and Marshall's Company Law, 10th edition, 1987, 11th edition, 1991, 12th edition, 1994; Gill: The Law of Arbitration, 3rd edition, 1983, 4th edition, 2001; Editor, Arbitration Section, Journal of Business Law, 1976-; Editor, Scottish Law Gazette, 1983-2001. Honours: Honorary Associate, RICS; Solicitor. Memberships: ACI arb; FRSA; Law Society of Scotland. Address: 3 Ballater Drive, Stirling FK9 5JH, Scotland.

MARSHALL Hugh Phillips, b. 13 July 1934, London, England. Anglican Priest (Retired). m. Diana Elizabeth Gosling, 1 son, 3 daughters. Education: BA, MA, Sidney Sussex College, Cambridge; Bishops Hostel, Lincoln. Appointments: Royal Navy, 1952-54; Ordained Deacon, 1959, Priest, 1960, Diocese of London; Curate, St Stephen and St John, Westminster, 1959-65; Vicar of St Paul, Tupsey, Hereford, 1965-74; Vicar and Team Rector of Wimbledon, 1974-87; Rural Dean of Merton, 1979-85; Vicar of Mitcham, Surrey, 1987-90; Chief Secretary, ABM, 1990-96; Vicar of Wendover, 1996-2001. Honours: Honorary Canon, Southwark Cathedral, 1989; Honorary Canon Emeritus, 1990; Canon St John's Cathedral Bulawayo, 1996; Commissary to Bishop of Matabeleland, 1989-. Memberships: Chairman, Betty Rhodes Fund, 1966-2007, Member, 1989-2007; South East Regional Committee, National Lottery Charities Board, 1998-2002; Honorary Secretary, Oxford Diocesan Board of Patronage, 2001-; Foundation Governor, Deddington Voluntary Aided School, 2002. Address: 7 The Daedings, Deddington, Oxon OX15 0RT, England.

MARSHALL Valerie Ann, b. 23 September 1939, Middlesex, England. Senior Supervisor. m. Derek, 29 April 1970, 2 sons, 1 daughter. Appointments: Private Secretary, The War Office; Senior School Supervisor, 31 years. Publication: Starlight Dreams, 1998; A Week of Special Happenings, Childrens Stories and Poems and Fully Illustrated By Myself, 2000. Contributions to: Anthologies, reviews, quarterlies, journals, magazines, periodicals and newspapers. Honours: Editor's Choice Awards, 1997, 1998; Special Commendation, 1997; Showcase Award, 1998. Address: 147 Warwick Road, Scunthorpe, North Lincs DN16 1HH, England.

MARSHALL-ANDREWS Robert, b. 10 April 1944, London, England. Member of Parliament; Queen's Counsel; Writer. m. Gillian Diana, 1 son, 1 daughter. Education: University of Bristol; Gray's Inn. Appointments: Member of Bar, 1967; Recorder, Crown Court, 1982; Queen's Counsel, 1987; Deputy High Court Judge, 1996; Bencher, Gray's Inn, 1996; Member of Parliament, 1997-. Publications: Numerous political articles in national (UK) newspapers and publications: Novels: Palace of Wisdom, 1989; A Man Without Guilt, 2002. Honours: Winner Observer Mace, 1967; Spectator Parliamentary Award, 1997. Address: House of Commons, London SW1A 0AA, England.

MARSHANSKY Vladimir, b. 5 January 1957, Bai-Jaak, Russia. Assistant Professor. 1 son. Education: MSc and MD, Russian State Medical University, 1974-80; PhD, Biochemistry, Moscow State University, 1980-84. Appointments: Professor and Director, Department of Biochemistry, The Javeriana University, Bogota, Colombia, 1989-92; Research Assistant Professor, Department of Medicine, University of Montreal, Canada, 1993-98; Instructor in Medicine, 1998-2002, Assistant Professor of Medicine, 2003, Department of Medicine, Harvard Medical School, Boston, USA. Publications: 36 articles in professional scientific journals; 1 book chapter. Memberships: Canadian Society of Biochemistry and Molecular Biology; American Society for Cell Biology; American Society for Biochemistry and Molecular Biology; The American Physiological Society; The Salt and Water Club; Proteomic Society; American Diabetes Association. E-mail: vladimir_marshansky@hms.harvard.edu

MARSTON Jeffery Adrian Priestley, b. 15 December 1927, London, England. Surgeon. m. Sylvie Colin, 2 sons, 1 daughter. Education: MA (Oxon), 1952, DM MCh, 1963, Magdalen College, Oxford; St Thomas' Hospital Medical School; Harvard University; FRCS (Eng), 1958. Appointments: Training Posts at St Thomas' Hospital, St Mark's Hospital, 1959-65; Consultant Surgeon, The Middlesex Hospital, The Royal Northern Hospital, 1970-85, University College Hospital, 1985-92; Consultant Vascular Surgeon, The Manor House Hospital, 1974-93, The National Heart Hospital, 1985-91, The Royal National Orthopaedic Hospital, 1985-91; Emeritus Consultant Surgeon, University College London Hospitals, 1993-; Dean, Royal Society of Medicine. Publications: Books: Intestinal Ischaemia, 1977, Contemporary Operative Surgery, 1979; Vascular Disease of the Gut, 1980; Visceral Artery Reconstruction, 1984; Splanchnic Ischaemia and Multiple Organ failure, 1989; Hamilton Bailey: A Surgeons Life, 1999; Over 130 papers on vascular surgery and gastro-enterology. Honours: MD (honoris causa), Université de Nice, 1983; Gimbernat Prize, University of Barcelona, 1986; Honorary Fellow, Collegio Brasileiro de Cirugões; Honorary Fellow, College of Physicians and Surgeons of Pakistan; Chevalier d'Honneur, Ordre National du Mérite de la République Française. Memberships include: Vice-President, Royal College of Surgeons of England; President, Association of Surgeons of Great Britain and Ireland; President Vascular Surgery Society; British Medical Association; Royal Society of Medicine; Association of Surgeons; Medical Society of London; Membre d'Honneur, Association Française de Chirurgie; Socio de Honor, Asociación Española de Cirugía. Address: 4 Hereford Square, London SW7 4TT, England. E-mail: adrimar@btinternet.com

MARTIN Bill, b. 9 November 1938, Govan, Glasgow, Scotland. Songwriter; Music Publisher. m. Jan, 1 son, 3 daughters. Education: Govan High School; Royal Scottish Academy of Music Certificate. Career: Songwriter; First song, Kiss Me Now, released 1963; Writing partnership with Tommy Scott, 1964-65; Writing partnership with Phil Coulter, 1965-83; Martin-Coulter publishing company, 1970-; Producer of musical, Jukebox, 1983; Producer, publisher and writer, Angus Publications; Acquisitions and Back Catalogue Consultant, SONY/ATV Music, 2000-. Honours: 20 Gold albums; 4 Platinum albums; 3 Ivor Novello Awards; 3 ASCAP Awards; First British Winner, Eurovision Song Contest with Puppet on a String, 1967; Rio de Janeiro Award of Excellence, 1967, 1969; Antibes Song Festival Award for the Best Song, 1971; Japanese Yamaha Best Song Award, 1978; Variety Club Silver Heart, 1979; Scotland's Songwriter of the Decade, 1980; Four No 1s in the UK and three in USA. Memberships: BASCA; PRS; Society of Distinguished Songwriters; Freeman of the City of London; Freeman of the City of Glasgow; Member, Worshipful Company of Distillers; Member, MCC; Past Golf Captain, Royal Automobile Club; Member, St George's Hill Golf Club. Address: 14 Graham Terrace, Belgravia, London SW1W 8JH, England. E-mail: bill.puppetmartin@virgin.net Website: www.billmartinsngwriter.com

MARTIN David (Alfred), b. 30 June 1929, London, England. Professor of Sociology Emeritus; Priest; International Fellow; Writer. m. (1) Daphne Sylvia Treherne, 1953, 1 son, (2) Bernice Thompson, 30 June 1962, 2 sons, 1 daughter. Education: DipEd, Westminster College, 1952; External BSc, 1st Class Honours, 1959, PhD, 1964, University of London; Postgraduate Scholar, London School of Economics and Political Science, 1959-61. Appointments: Assistant Lecturer, Sheffield University, 1961-62; Lecturer, 1962-67, Reader, 1967-71, Professor of Sociology, 1971-89, Professor Emeritus, 1989-, London School of Economics and Political Science; Ordained Deacon, 1983, Priest, 1984; Scurlock Professor of Human Values, Southern Methodist University, Dallas, 1986-90; International Fellow, Institute for the Study of Economic Culture, Boston University, 1990-; Various visiting lectureships. Publications: Pacifism, 1965; A Sociology of English Religion, 1967; The Religious and the Secular, 1969; Tracts Against the Times, 1973; A General Theory of Secularisation, 1978; Dilemmas of Contemporary Religion, 1978; Crisis for Cranmer and King James (editor), 1978; The Breaking of the Image, 1980; Theology and Sociology (co-editor), 1980; No Alternative (co-editor), 1981; Unholy Warfare (co-editor), 1983; Divinity in a Grain of Bread, 1989; Tongues of Fire, 1990; The Forbidden Revolution, 1996; Reflections on Sociology and Theology, 1997; Does Christianity Cause War?, 1997; Pentecostalism: The World Their Parish, 2000; Christian Language and the Secular City, 2002; Christian Language and its Mutations; On Secularization, 2005. Honours: Honorary Assistant Priest, Guildford Cathedral, 1983-; Honorary Professor, Lancaster University, 1993-2002; Sarum Lecturer, Oxford University, 1994-95; Honorary Doctor of Theology, Helsinki, 2000. Membership: International Conference of the Sociology of Religion, president, 1975-83. Address: Cripplegate Cottage, 174 St John's Road, Woking, Surrey GU21 7PQ, England.

MARTIN David McLeod, b. 30 December 1922, Glasgow, Scotland. Artist; Teacher. m. Isobel A F Smith, deceased, 2000, 4 sons. Education: Glasgow School of Art, 1940-42; RAF War Service, 1942-46; Completed training at Glasgow School of Art, 1948; Diploma in Art, 1948; Jordanhill Teachers' Training College, 1948-49. Career: Commenced a teaching career in Glasgow schools in 1949 ending as a Principal Teacher of Art, Hamilton Grammar School; Retired early in 1983 to paint full-time. Publications: Works appear in books including: Paintings from the Clydesdale Bank Collection by Patrick Bourne; Scottish Watercolour Painting by Jack Firth; Articles in the Artist Magazine. Honours: Elected Professional Member: Society of Scottish Artists, 1949, Royal Society of Painters in Watercolour, 1961, Royal Glasgow Institute of the Fine Arts, 1982; Honorary membership, Society of Scottish Artists, 2007; Listed in biographical dictionaries. Address: The Old Schoolhouse, 53 Gilmour St, Eaglesham, Glasgow G76 0LG, Scotland.

DICTIONARY OF INTERNATIONAL BIOGRAPHY

MARTIN Deborah Louise Morgan, b. 21 October 1917, Goodview, Virginia, USA. Retired Realtor Associate. m. John Dick Martin Jr, deceased 1983, 1 son, deceased, 1963. Education: National Business College, 1935-37; Real Estate Diploma, Newport News Hampton Board of Realtors; Real Estate Law, St Leo College, Fort Eustis, Virginia, 1971; Class A, Realtors Institute, University of Virginia, Charlottesville, Virginia, 1976; 30 credits, University of Virginia, Roanoke, Virginia; Certificate of Merit in Education, Newport News Hampton Board of Realtors; 3 credits, Christopher Newport University, 1997, 2002; Two Get Motivated Business Seminar Certificates, Virginia, 1997, 2006; Humor Course, Adirondack Community College, Queensburg, New York, 2006; Many seminars, workshops, in real estate and business. Appointments: Secretarial positions, 1937-43; Clerk-Stenographer, West Virginia, Virginia, South Carolina, 1943-45; Owner, Marlou Grocery, 1945-46; Project Manager, Federal Public Housing Authority, Morgan City, Louisiana, and Bearden, Arkansas, 1945-46; Assistant to Project Manager, Erection of Low Rent Housing, City of Roanoke, Virginia, Federal Public Housing Authority, 1946-47; Owner, Martin Center Grocery, 1947-52; Office Manager, John D Martin Co, Vinton, Virginia, 1947-49; Owner, Station 4, US Post Office, Roanoke, 1947-49; Temporary Substitute Clerk, Roanoke Main Post Office, 1949-50; Beauty Advisor, Peggy Newton Cosmetics, 1953-62; Branch Sales Manager, House of Hollywood Cosmetics of California, Vinton, 1955-68; Sales Agent, Original Greeting Cards, Vinton, 1961-70; Realtor Associate, Ward Realty and Insurance Co, Newport News, Virginia, 1973; Landon Realty, Hampton, Virginia, 1973; Chuck Klein Realty, Newport News, 1974-77; Eagle Properties, Grafton, Virginia, 1977-79; Powell & Associates, Newport News, 1980-96. Publications: Poetry and non-fiction published in many US states, England, South Korea, India, Philippines, Thailand; Many journal and newspaper articles, many states. Honours: Selected Best-Dressed Woman, Propeller Club of United States Convention aboard the HMS Queen Mary, docked at Long Beach, California, 1982; HRH Prince Kevin, Prince Regent of Hutt River Principality, Queensland, Australia, designated her International Citizen of the Year 1995; Over 300 awards, trophies, medals, plaques, certificates and ribbons for poetry and non-fiction; Numerous certificates and ribbons for Toastmaster International speeches and contests; Cavalier Club 596; 10 certificates and 14 medals for Louise Martin Love and Laughter Poetry Show, at International Congress on Arts and Communications and 30th Anniversary International Congress on Science, Culture and Arts in the 21st Century on 4 continents; Delegate certificates, 25 Congresses on 5 continents; Dr Ernest Kay Foundation Award, Keble College, Oxford University, England, 1997; Only delegate to chair the Poetry Seminar at Congresses both at Cambridge University and Oxford University; Woman of the Year, ABI, 2001, 2003; Noble Prize Certificate, Gold Medal; Gold Pin, The United Cultural Convention, 2003; Laureate Woman of Letters Gold Crown, United Poets Laureate International, Thailand, 2002; Honorary Cultural Doctorate in Humane Letters, World University, 2002; Best Costume, Toastmasters International District 66 Fall Conference, Chesapeake, Virginia, 2002; 100 Most Intriguing People Metal Plaque on Wood, ABI, 2003; General audience with Pope John Paul II, Vatican City, Italy, 1987; Listed in many Who's Who books in US, England, India, Thailand and in 25 books of international congress on Arts and Communications and World Forum on five continents; Listed in Republican Presidential Task Force Life Member Book, held in President Ronald Reagan Library, Simi Valley, California; Listed in United States of America Congressional Record, Vol 130, No 60, Washington, DC, 10 May 1984, as Virginia delegate to Jefferson Meeting on the Constitution,

Williamsburg, Virginia; Honored at World Forum, Washington, DC, 2007, Delegate Certificate, 25 years of Sustained Allegiance; Longtime Ambassador; One of 150 World Poets, Guest of Chinese government, 2005; Life Member, Famous Poets Society, 2005; Honorary Lifetime Secretary General, United Cultural Convention, 2006; Honorary Life Fellow, International Biographical Association, 2007; Member, Carter Center of Past USA President Jimmy Carter, 2007. Memberships: Richmond Friendship Force, 1978-present; American Biographical Institute, 1979-present; International Biographical Centre, 1981-present; International Platform Association, International Academy of Poets, Speaking Ladder, 1981-2001; Life Member, Republican Presidential Task Force, 1981-present; International Biographical Association, 1982-present; United Poets Laureate International World Congress of Poets, 1988-present; Poetry Society of Virginia, 1988-present; Cavalier Club, 1988-present, Vice-President Public Relations, 1990-1999, Toastmasters International; Autumn/Men's Retirement Club; Parrish Chapel United Methodist Church, 1929-; People to People Council of 100+; United Nations Association of the Virginia Peninsula, 1984-; International Society of Poets, 1990-; Hampton Roads Republican Womens Club, 2004-; United Nations Association of the United States of America, 2006-; National Active and Retired Federal Employees Association, Peninsula Chapter 682, 2007-; Vice-president, Recognition Board, World Congress of Arts, Sciences and Communications, 2007-. Address: 106 Booth Road, Hidenwood, Newport News, VA 23606-2259, USA.

MARTIN George (Henry), b. 3 January 1926, England. Music Industry Executive; Producer; Composer. m. (1) Sheena Rose Chisholm, 1948, 1 son, 1 daughter, (2) Judy Lockhart Smith, 1966, 1 son, 1 daughter. Education: Guildhall School of Music and Drama. Appointments: Sub-Lieutenant, RNVR, 1944-47; Worker, BBC, 1950, EMI Records Ltd, 1950-65, Chair, 1965-; Built AIR Studios, 1969; Built AIR Studios, Montserrat, 1979; Completed new AIR Studios, Lyndhurst Hall, Hampstead, 1992; Co-merged with Chrysalis Group, 1974, Director, 1978-; Chair, Heart of London Radio, 1994-; Scored the music of 15 films; Produced by George Martin, 2001; The Family Way, 2003. Publications: All You Need is Ears, 1979; Making Music, 1983; Summer of Love, 1994; Playback (autobiography), 2002. Honours include: Ivor Novello Awards, 1963, 1979; Grammy Awards, 1964, 1967 (two), 1973, 1993, 1996; CBE, 1996. Address: c/o AIR Studios, Lyndhurst Hall, Hampstead, London, NW3 5NG, England.

MARTIN Michael John, b. 3 July 1945. Politician. m. Mary McLay, 1 son, 1 daughter. Education: St Patrick's Boys' School, Glasgow, Scotland. Appointments: Glasgow City Councillor, 1973-79; Member of Parliament, Glasgow, Springburn (now Glasgow North East), 1979-; Deputy Speaker and Deputy Chairman of Ways and Means, 1997-2000; Speaker of the House of Commons, 2000-. Address: Speaker's House, House of Commons, London SW1A 0AA, England.

MARTIN Ricky, (Enrique Martin Morales), b. 24 December 1971, Puerto Rico. Singer; Actor. Career: Joined group Menudo, aged 13; Numerous tours and recordings; Left Menudo, 1989; Acted in Mexican soap opera Alcanzur una Estrella II; Began releasing Spanish language albums; Role as bartender in General Hospital; Won the role of Marius in Broadway production of Les Miserables; Dubbed voice in Spanish version of Disney film Hercules; Released first English Language album including a duet with Madonna; Numerous television appearances and tour dates. Recordings:

Singles: Maria, 1996; 1 2 3 Maria, 1997; Cup of Life, 1998; La Bomba, 1999; Livin' La Vida Loca, 1999; She's All I Have Had, 1999; Shake Your Bon-Bon; Story, with Christine Aguilera; Albums: Ricky Martin, 1991; Me Amarás, 1993; A Medio Vivir, 1995; Vuelve, 1998; Ricky Martin, 1999; Sound Loaded, 2000; La Historia, 2001; Almas del Silencio, 2003; Life, 2005; MTV Unplugged, 2006. Honour: Grammy Award, Best Latin Pop Album, 1999; Hollywood Walk of Fame, 2007. Address: c/o Sony Music Latin, 550 Madison Avenue, New York, NY 10022, USA.

MARTIN Steve, b. 14 August 1945, Waco, Texas, USA. Actor; Comedian. m. Victoria Tennant, 1986-1994 divorced, (2) Anne Stringfield, 2007. Education: Long Beach State College; University of California, Los Angeles. Appointments: TV Writer, several shows; Nightclub Comedian; TV Special, Steve Martin: A Wild and Crazy Guy, 1978. Creative Works: Recordings: Let's Get Small, 1977; A Wild and Crazy Guy, 1978; Comedy is Not Pretty, 1979; The Steve Martin Bros; Film appearances include: The Absent Minded Waiter; Sgt Pepper's Lonely Hearts Club Band, 1978; The Muppet Movie, 1979; The Jerk, 1979; Pennies From Heaven, 1981; Dead Men Don't Wear Plaid, 1982; The Man With Two Brains, 1983; The Lonely Guy, 1984; All of Me, 1984; Three Amigos, 1986; Little Shop of Horrors, 1986; Roxanne, 1987; Planes, Trains and Automobiles, 1987; Parenthood, 1989; My Blue Heaven; L.A. Story; Grand Canyon; Father of the Bride; Housesitter, 1992; Leap of Faith, 1992; Twist of Fate, 1994; Mixed Nuts, 1994; Father of the Bride 2; Sgt Bilko, 1995; The Spanish Prisoner; The Out of Towners; Bowfinger, 1999; Joe Gould's Secret, 2000; Novocaine, 2002; Bringing Down the House, 2003; Cheaper By The Dozen, 2003; Jiminy Glick in La La Wood, 2004; Shopgirl, 2005; Cheaper By The Dozen 2, 2005; The Pink Panther, 2006. Honours: Grammy Award, 1977, 1978; National Society of Film Critics Actor's Award. Address: ICM, 8942 Wilshire Boulevard, Beverly Hills, CA 90211, USA.

MARTIN Todd, b. 8 July 1970, Hinsdale, Illinois, USA. Tennis Player. Education: Northwestern College. Appointments: Winner, New Haven Challenger, 1989; Turned professional, 1990; Semi-Finalist, Stella Artois Grass Court Championships, London, 1993, Champion, 1994, Champion (doubles with Pete Sampras), 1995; Finalist, Australian Open, 1994, Grand Slam Cup, Munich, 1995; Semi-Finalist, US Open, 1994, Wimbledon, 1994, 1996, Paris Open, 1998; Champion, Scania Stockholm Open, 1998; Winner of 13 pro titles by end of 2002; Special Adviser, US Tennis High Performance Program, 2003-; Retired, 2004-. Honours include: Adidas/ATP Tour Sportsmanship Award, 1993, 1994; ATP Tour Most Improved Player, 1993. Memberships: US Davis Cup Team, 1994-99; President, ATP Players' Council, 1996-97. Address: c/o Advantage International, 1751 Pinnacle Drive, Suite 1500, McLean, VA 22102, USA.

MARTIN Victoria Carolyn, b. 22 May 1945, Windsor, Berkshire, England. Writer. m. Tom Storey, 28 July 1969, 4 daughters. Education: Winkfield Place, Berks, 1961-62; Byam Shaw School of Art, 1963-66. Publications: September Song, 1970; Windmill Years, 1975; Seeds of the Sun, 1980; Opposite House, 1984; Tigers of the Night, 1985; Obey the Moon, 1987. Contributions to: Woman; Woman's Own; Woman's Realm; Woman's Journal; Good Housekeeping; Woman's Weekly; Redbook; Honey, 1967-87. Address: Newells Farm House, Lower Beeding, Horsham, Sussex RH13 6LN, England.

MARTIN Vivian, b. Detroit, Michigan, USA. Opera and Concert Singer. m. Education: Graduate, Wayne State University, Detroit; Conservatoire de Fountainebleau, France; Detroit Conservatory of Music; France; New York; Munich; Berlin; Detroit. Debut: Operatic debut, Leonardo, Verdi's La Forza Del Destino, 1971. Career: Major opera roles including Leonora, Verdi's Il Trovatore; Rezia, Weber's Oberon; Selika, Meyerbeer's L'Africane; Bess, Gershwin's Porgy and Bess, more than 500 times; Major opera houses and concert halls in Europe, Asia, USA, South America; TV and radio appearances; Toured and soloist with numerous orchestras; Symphonies in Sweden, Berlin, Munich, Nurenberg; Philharmonic orchestras in Germany, Slovenska Philharmonia, Detroit Symphony Orchestra; Sang in Tivoli Garden, Copenhagen, Denmark; Grosser Konzert Saal, Vienna, Austria; Théâtre des Champs Elysees, Paris, France, Kongress Saal, Munich, Germany; Participated in World of Gershwin; Festival with concerts with St Petersburg National Symphony Orchestra in Shostakovich Philharmonic Hall, St Petersburg; Moscow Symphony Orchestra in Tschaikovsky, Moscow, Russia; Concerts and performances in USA and abroad during 1994-2004. Honours: First prize and Jean Paul award, Conservatoire de Fountainbleau, 1953; Eighteen singing scholarships and awards. Memberships: AFTRA; American Guild of Music Artists; Actors Equity Association; Wayne State University Alumni Association; Alpha Kappa Alpha. Address: c/o Dr Gösta Schwark International APS, Opera-Concert-Theatre, 18 Groennegade, 1 Floor, DK-1107 Copenhagen, Denmark.

MARTIN-QUIRK Howard Richard Newell, b. 8 August 1937, Sanderstead, Surrey, England. Architectural Historian. m. Mitzi Quirk. 1 son. Education: BA (Cantab), 1959, MA, 1961, Christs College, Cambridge University; BSc, Bartlett School of Architecture, London University, 1967; MSc, University College, London, 1985. Appointments: Architectural Assistant, Greater London Council, 1966-67; Senior Research Assistant, Kingston College of Art, 1967-70; Director of Undergraduate Studies, School of Architecture, Kingston Polytechnic, 1970-94; Principal Lecturer and Director of History, School of Architecture, Kingston University, 1994-; Chief Oenologist, Chiddingstone Vineyards, 1971-83; Partner, Martin Quirk Associates Architects, 1980-90; Freelance Writer and Journalist. Publications: Meaning and Metaphor in Architecture, 1983; The Crime of the Century (with Kinglsey Amis), 1989; Fame in Architecture, 2001; Articles and reviews in many architectural publications. Honours: Silver Medal, International Wine and Spirit Society, 1991. Memberships: Society of Architectural Historians; Victorian Society; Wagner Society; Architectural Association; NATFHE; Ecclesiological Society. Address: The Old Coach Road, Chiddingstone, Kent TN8 7BH, England. E-mail: howardmartinquirk@hotmail.com

MARTINAC Vanja, b. 28 January 1959, Split, Croatia. Full Professor. 1 son. Education: BSc, 1982, MSc, Chemical Engineering, 1987, PhD, Chemical Engineering, 1994, Faculty of Technology, University of Split. Appointments: Trainee, Graduate Student, 1984-87, Scientific Assistant, 1987-94, Assistant PhD, 1994-96, Faculty of Technology, Assistant Professor, 1996-2001, Associate Professor, 2001-06, Full Professor, 2006-, Faculty of Chemistry and Technology, University of Split. Publications: 33 scientific articles in field of chemical engineering; Co-author, The Book of Technical Thermodynamics, 2nd edition, 2007. Honours: Dean Award, 1982. Memberships: Croatian Chemical Society; Croatian Society of Chemical Engineering & Technologists;

Association of Chemical Engineering & Technology, Split. Address: Faculty of Chemistry and Technology, Teslina 101V, 2100 Split, Croatia. E-mail: martinac@ktf-split.hr

MARTINEZ Conchita, b. 16 April 1972, Monzon, Spain. Tennis Player. Appointments: Turned Professional, 1988; Reached last 16, French Open, 1988, quarter-finals, French Open, 1989, 1990, 1991, 1992, 1993, semi-finals, Italian Open, 1991, French Open, 1994, Australian, French and US Opens and Wimbledon, 1995, French and US Opens, 1996, quarter-finals, Olympic Games, 1992; With Arantxa Sanchez-Vicario, won Olympic Doubles Silver Medal, 1992; Won, Italian Open, 1993, Hilton Head (SC), Italian Open, Stratton (Vt), 1994; Wimbledon Singles Champion, 1994; by end of 2002 had won 42 WTA tour titles; Retired 2006. Honours: WTA Tour Most Impressive Newcomer, 1989; Most Improved Player, Tennis Magazine, 1994; ITF Award of Excellence, 2001; International Tennis Hall of Fame, 2001.

MARTINEZ Seledon C, b. 19 December 1921, Chimayo, New Mexico, USA. Retired Educational Administrator; Real Estate and Land Developer. m. Josephine V Martinez, 1 son, 3 daughters. Education: Kansas State Teachers College, 1940-42; BA, Inter-American Affairs, Education, University of New Mexico, Albuquerque, 1945; Advanced Graduate Work, University of California at Los Angeles, 1952-53; MA, Public School Administration, Counselling and Guidance, Physical Education, Highlands University, Las Vegas, New Mexico, 1953; Colorado State University, 1965. Appointments: Military Service, US Marine Corps, South Pacific Theatre Operations, 1943-44; Coach, Director, Athletics, Social Science Teacher, Santa Cruz High School, New Mexico, 1945-56; Superintendent, Rio Arriba County Schools, Tierra Amarilla, New Mexico, 1957-58; Principal, Dulce Independent Schools, New Mexico, 1959-62; Assistant to President, Director, Curriculum, Planing, Counselling, Northern New Mexico Technical Vocational School, El Rito, 1962-69; Assistant to President, Campus Director, Northern New Mexico Technical Vocational School, Espanola Campus, 1969-72; Director, Federal Programs, Title I and Migrant Education, Espanola Municipal Schools, 1972-81; Board Regents, Northern New Mexico Community College, El Rito and Espanola, 1989-94; Currently: Real Estate and Land Developer; Owner, Rancho Los Barrancos, Lower Chimayo, New Mexico; Consultant, American Bureau International Education, Caracas, Venezuela. Publications: Policies, Practices and Procedures for Espanola Board of Education, 1973; Career Education Guide (K-12), Espanola Municipal Schools, 1978; Affirmative Action Plan, Espanola Municipal Schools, 1979. Honours include: Full Track Scholarship to Kansas State Teachers College, 1940; Ford Foundation Scholarship, 1952-53; Technical-Vocational Fellowship, 1965; Menaul High School Athletic Hall of Fame, 1990; Northern Rio Grande Conference Hall of Fame, 1993; Living Legends, Tesoro Vivo de Rio Arriba, 1997; ZIA Award, University of New Mexico Alumni Association, 1997; Listed in Who's Who publications and biographical dictionaries. Memberships: Disabled Veterans of America; American Legion, Chimayo, New Mexico; VFW; American Association Vocational Educators; Foreign Policy Issues Association. Address: PO Box 182, Chimayo, NM 87522, USA.

MASADA Hiromitsu, b. 3 February 1938, Nishinomiya, Hyogo, Japan. Chemistry Researcher. m. Yoko Danno, 1 daughter. Education: Bachelor of Engineering, Osaka University, 1962; Master of Engineering, 1964, Doctor of Engineering, 1967, Kyoto University. Appointments: Assistant Professor, 1967-72, Associate Professor, 1972-96,

Professor, 1996-2003, Kanazawa University. Honour: Seikyo Newspaper Culture Award, Tokyo, 1986; Who's Who in the World, 1998; Nominator, Nobel Prize in Chemistry, 2001. Address: 7-6 Hongo 3 Chome, Kashiwara City, Osaka Prefecture 582-0001, Japan.

MASIN Ronald, b. Rotterdam, The Netherlands. Musician. m. Maria Kelemen, 1 son, 1 daughter. Education: Private studies on the violin with Betty Pack, Joseph Spira and others; Further studies at Royal Brussels Music Conservatory with Andre Gertler. Career: Concert Master (Leader), Netherlands Philharmonic Orchestra; Formed chamber music group, Amsterdam Kern Ensemble; Solo and chamber music performances worldwide; Head, String Department, Cape Town University, South Africa; Co-founder with Maria Kelemen, Young European Strings School of Music. Publications: Violin Technique – the Natural Way; Numerous works recorded for EMI, commissioned and performed. Memberships: Founder and Member, Irish Branch, European String Teachers Association; Artistic Director, Music Instrument Fund of Ireland. Address: 21 The Close, Cypress Downs, Dublin 6W, Ireland. Website: www.youngeuropeanstrings.com

MASON Dean Towle, b. 20 September 1932, Berkeley, California, USA. Physician; Cardiologist. m. Maureen O'Brien, 2 daughters. Education: BA, Chemistry, Phi Beta Kappa, 1954, MD (first in class), Alpha Omega Alpha, 1958, Duke University; Osler Medical Residency, Johns Hopkins Hospital, Baltimore, 1958-61; Cardiology Fellow, National Heart Institute, National Institutes of Health, Bethesda, 1961-63. Appointments: United States Forest Service Firefighter, 1950; Professional Baseball Player, 1951; United States Air Force Jet Pilot Training, 1953; Cardiology Associate, 1961-63, Co-Director, 1963-68, Cardiac Catheterization Laboratory, National Institutes of Health; Senior Investigator and Attending Physician, National Heart Institute, 1963-68; Professor of Medicine and Physiology, Founding Chief of Cardiology Division, University of California at Davis, 1968-82; Editor-in-Chief, American Heart Journal, 1980-96; Physician-in-Chief, Western Heart Institute, 1983-2000; Chairman, Department of Cardiovascular Medicine, St Mary's Medical Center, San Francisco, California, 1986-99; Honorary Medical Staff, 2000-. Publications: Over 1,500 medical articles and 3,000 medical abstracts; Author, 50 books. Honours: Over 100 academic honours and awards; American Therapeutic Society Research Award, 1965; Outstanding Professor, 1972; Faculty Research Award, 1978; Distinguished Alumnus Award, Duke University Medical School, 1979; Honorary Professor of Medicine, Peking University, 1987; Wisdom Society Award Honour, 1997; Medal of Honour Winston Churchill Society, 1998; Armand Hammer Creative Genius Award, 1998; Dwight D Eisenhower Admirable American of Achievement Award, 1998; Eminent Physician of Wisdom Award, 1999; Medal of Wisdom Award, 2001; Wisdom Cardiologist of the Century, 2001; Albert Schweitzer Fellow of World Humanitarians, 2002; Jonas Salk Award, 2003; Albert Einstein Scientific Research Award, 2003; John Wayne Pioneer of America Award, 2003; Ernest Hemingway Award, 2003; Will Durant Philosopher-Physician Award, 2004; Paul Dudley White Award, 2004; Newton Kugelmass Children's Cardiology Crusader Award, 2004; Norman Vincent Peale Healing Power of Prayer Award, 2005; Teaching delegation to over 50 developing countries, United States State Department and American College of Cardiology; Editorial boards of 32 medical journals; Visiting professor to over 500 medical institutions; Listing in several who's who publications. Memberships: Alpha Omega Alpha Medical Honour Society, 1958; American Society for Clinical Investigation, 1965;

American Society for Clinical Research, President Western Society, 1974-75; American College of Cardiology, President, 1977-78, Master, 1998. Address: 44725 Country Club Drive, El Macero, CA 95618, USA.

MASON OF BARNSLEY, Baron of Barnsley in the County of South Yorkshire, Roy Mason, b. 18 April 1924, England. Member of the House of Lords. m. Marjorie Sowden, 2 daughters. Education: TUC Scholarship, London School of Economics; D University, Hallam University, Sheffield. Appointments: Coal Miner, 1938-53; Labour Candidate for Bridlington, 1951-53; Member of Parliament for Barnsley, 1953-83, Barnsley Central, 1983-87; Opposition Spokesman on Defence and Post Office Affairs, 1960-64; Minister of State for Shipping, Board of Trade, 1964-67; Minister of Defence Equipment, 1967-68; Postmaster General, 1968; Minister of Power, 1968-69; President, Board of Trade, 1969-70; Principal Spokesman on Board of Trade Affairs, 1970-74; Member, Council of Europe and Western European Union, 1973; Secretary of State for Defence, 1974-76; Secretary of State for Northern Ireland, 1976-79; Principal Opposition Spokesman on Agriculture, Fisheries and Food, 1979-81. Publication: Paying the Price, autobiography. Honours: PC, 1968; Peerage, 1987. Memberships: Yorkshire Miners' Council, 1949-53; Council of Europe, 1970-71; Yorkshire Group of Labour MPs, 1970-74, 1981-84; Miners' Group of MPs, 1973-74, 1980-81; Railway and Steel Union MPs, 1979-80; National Rivers Authority, 1989-92. Address: 12 Victoria Avenue, Barnsley, South Yorkshire, S70 2BH, England.

MASSEY Roy Cyril, b. 9 May 1934, Birmingham, England. Cathedral Organist. m. Ruth Carol Craddock. Education: University of Birmingham, 1953-56; Private tuition under Sir David Willcocks, Worcester Cathedral. Appointments: Accompanist, City of Birmingham Choir, 1953-60; Church and School appointments, 1956-65; Warden, Royal School of Church Music, 1965-68; Organist and Master of the Choristers, Birmingham Cathedral, 1968-74; Organist and Master of the Choristers, Hereford Cathedral, 1974-2001. Publication: The Organs of Hereford Cathedral (in Hereford Cathedral, a history), 2000. Honours: Honorary Fellowship, Royal School of Church Music, 1971; Lambeth Degree, Doctor of Music, 1991; MBE for Services to Music, 1997; Honorary Fellowship, Guild of Church Musicians, 2000; President, Royal College of Organists, 2003-05. Address: 2 King John's Court, Tewkesbury, Gloucestershire GL20 6EG, England. E-mail: drroymassey@ukonline.co.uk

MASTERSON Kleber Sanlin Jr, b. 26 September 1932, San Diego, California, USA. Physicist; Military Operations Researcher. m. Sara Cooper Masterson, 2 sons. Education: BS (Engineering), US Naval Academy, 1954; MS (Physics), US Naval Postgraduate School, 1961; PhD (Physics), University of California at San Diego, 1963; Graduate, Advanced Management Programme, Harvard Business School, 1980. Appointments: Commanding Officer, USS Preble; Antiship Missile Defence Project Manager; Assistant Deputy Commander, Naval Sea Systems Command for Anti-Air and Surface Warfare Systems; Chief, Studies Analysis and Gaming Agency; Office of the Joint Chiefs of Staff; Retired as Rear Admiral, US Navy, 1950-82; Principal, 1982-87, Vice President, Partner, 1987-92 Booz, Allen and Hamilton; Senior Vice President, Science Applications International Corporation, 1992-96; President, The Riverside Group Ltd, 1994-; President, Military Operations Research Society, 1988-89; President, Massachusetts Society of the Cincinnati, 2001-04; Assistant Secretary-General, The Society of the Cincinnati, 2001-04; Treasurer General, The Society of

the Cincinnati, 2004-2007; Vice President General, The Society of the Cincinnati, 2007-. Publications: Numerous articles and invited presentations; Created NELIAC ALGOL compiler, 1958-59. Honours: Defence Superior Service Medal; Legion of Merit with 2 gold stars for subsequent awards; Navy Commendation Medal with Combat 'V' and 2 gold stars. Memberships: American Physical Society; Society of Sigma Xi; Society of the Cincinnati. E-mail: skidmasterson@compuserve.com

MATHESON Michael, b. 8 September 1970, Glasgow, Scotland. Member of the Scottish Parliament. Education: BSc, Occupational Therapy, Queen Margaret College, Edinburgh, 1988-92; BA, Diploma in Applied Social Sciences, Open University, 1992-96. Appointments: Community Occupational Therapist, Stirling Council, Central Regional Council and Highland Regional Council, 1992-99; Member of the Scottish Parliament, 1999-; Shadow Minister for Culture and Sport, 2004-2006; Falkirk West, 2007. Memberships: State Registered Occupational Therapist, Health Professions Council; Member, Ochils Mountain Rescue Team; Former Member, Scottish Parliament Justice Committee; Member, Enterprise and Culture Committee. Address: The Scottish Parliament, Edinburgh, EH99 1SP, Scotland. E-mail: michael.matheson.msp@scottish.parliament.uk

MATHESWARAN Manickam, b. 2 July 1978, Tamil Nadu, India. Student. Education: Bachelor of Chemical Engineering, 1999; Diploma in Industrial Safety, 2000; Master of Chemical Engineering, 2001; Diploma in Enterprise Java Technologies, 2002; Doctor of Philosophy in Chemical Engineering, in progress. Appointments: Lecturer, 2002, NSS Programme Officer, 2003. Publications: Separation Science and Technology, 2006; Water Science & Technology, 2006; Catalysis Communications, 2007; Journal of Industrial and Engineering Chemistry, 2007; Journal of Hazardous Materials, 2007; Bulletin of Korean Chemical Society, 2007; Chemosphere, 2007; The Korean Journal of Chemical Engineering, 2007. Memberships: Korean Chemical Society; Korean Institute of Chemical Engineers; Indian Institute of Chemical Engineering. Address: 53, Thillaiamman Nagar, Chidambaram, Tamil Nadu, 608001, India. E-mail: math_chem95@rediffmail.com Website: www.geocities.com/math_chem

MATHIAS Peter, b. 10 January 1928. Historian. m. Elizabeth Ann Blackmore, 2 sons, 1 daughter. Education: BA, 1951, MA, 1954, Jesus College, Cambridge; LittD (Oxon), 1985; DLitt (Cantab), 1987. Appointments include: Research Fellow, Jesus College, Cambridge, 1952-55; Assistant Lecturer, Lecturer, Faculty of History, University of Cambridge, 1955-68; Director of Studies in History, Fellow, Queens' College, Cambridge, 1955-68; Tutor, 1957-68, Senior Proctor, 1965-66, University of Cambridge; Chichele Professor of Economic History, University of Oxford, Fellow All Souls College, 1969-87; Curator Bodleian Library, 1972-87; Master, Downing College, Cambridge, 1987-95; Visiting Professor: Toronto University, 1961; Delhi University, 1967; California University, Berkeley, 1967; Pennsylvania University, 1972; Virginia Gildersleeve Professor, Columbia University, 1972; Johns Hopkins University, 1979; Natal University, 1980; Australian National University, 1981; Geneva University, 1986; Leuven University, 1990; San Marino University, 1990; Waseda University, 1996; Osaka Gakuin University, 1998; Bolzano Free University, 1999; Kansai University, 2006; Chairman, Business Archives Council, 1967-72, President, 1984-95, Vice-President, 1995-;Chairman, International Advisory Committee, University of Buckingham, 1979-84; National

Advisory Council, British Library, 1994-2000; Chairman, 1997-2005, President, 2005-, Great Britain Sasakawa Foundation; Member Syndicate Fitzwilliam Museum, Cambridge, 1987-98; Chairman, Fitzwilliam Museum Enterprises, 1990-99; Member, Board of Patrons, European Association for Banking History; Honorary Treasurer, British Academy, 1980-89. Publications: The Brewing Industry in England 1700-1830, 1959, reprinted 1993; English Trade Tokens, 1962; Retailing Revolution, 1967; The First Industrial Nation, 1969, revised edition, 1983; The Transformation of England, 1979; Editor and contributor, Science and Society, 1972; Co-editor and contributor, The First Industrial Revolutions, 1989; Co-editor and contributor, Innovation and technology in Europe, 1991; L'Economia Britannica dal 1815-1914, 1994; Cinque lezioni de teoria e storia, Naples, 2003; General editor, Cambridge Economic History of Europe, 1968-93. Honours: Fellow, Royal Historical Society, 1972; Fellow, British Academy, 1977; CBE, 1984; Honorary Fellow, Jesus College, 1987, Queens' College, 1987, Downing College, 1995; Honorary LittD, University of Buckingham, 1985, University of Hull, 1992, University of Warwick, 1995, De Montfort University, 1995; Honorary DLitt, University of Birmingham, 1988, UEA, 1999; Honorary Doctorate, Russian Academy of Sciences, 2002; Grand Cordon, Order of the Rising Sun, 2003; Honorary Doctorate, Kansai University, Japan, 2006. Memberships include: President, 1974-78, Honorary President, 1978- International Economic History Society; Vice President, 1975-80, Honorary Vice-President, 2001-, Royal Historical Society; President, 1989-92, Vice President, 1992-, Economic History Society; Academia Europaea; Foreign Member: Royal Danish Academy, Royal Belgian Academy. Address: 33 Church Street, Chesterton, Cambridge, CB4 1DT, England.

MATHUR Anand Behari Lal, b. 8 November 1939, Jaipur, Rajasthan, India. Retired education educator. m. Kanti, 4 children. Education: M Com, First Division, 1960, PhD in Commerce, 1971, University of Rajasthan, Jaipur. Appointments: Teacher of B Com, M Com, M Phil, BSc Management Studies, MBA and PG Diploma students, University of Rajasthan, University of Calabar (Nigeria) on foreign assignment by the Government of India to the Government of Nigeria for 4 years, and J N Vyas University (Jodhpur, India), 39 years; Guest Faculty, Indira Gandhi National Open University, the Bhartiya Vidya Bhawan, the Indian Institute of Rural Management, the Aravali Institute of Management, and the Pacific Institute of Management; Founder Editor, Editor and Chairman of Editorial Board, The Indian Journal of Business Administration, 1996-97, 1997-98, 1998-99, and Head of Department of Business Administration, J N Vyas University, Jodhpur, India, 1996-99, Retired, 1999. Publications: Author of over 50 research papers published nationally and internationally including World Bank Publication, widely recognised by experts and authorities like the International Trade Centre, UNCTAD/GATT, Geneva, Switzerland and the Indian institute of Management, Ahemadabad; Indo-US Trade Relations, 2001 (doctoral thesis updated); Readings in Marketing, 2002; Readings in Management, 2002. Supervisor of over 30 research projects in India and Nigeria in the fields of Marketing and General Management; Participated in numerous national and international seminars, conferences, workshops and symposia. Honours: Invited by the Irish Export Board, Dublin (Ireland) to co-operate in Trade Development Training Programme, 1989; Served as expert at several prominent organisations in India including the University Grants Commission, Banking Service Recruitment Board, and Public Service Commissions; Founded Research Cell, Department

of Business Administration, J N Vyas University, 1997; Nominee, International Educator of the Year, IBC, 2005; Listed in prestigious biographical directories. Memberships: Life Member, The Indian Commerce Association; The Indian Marketing Association; The Pitman Fellowship, London, 1964; A scout; Participated in National Service Scheme. Address: House No 153, EA-1 Zone, Raghuvanshi Nagar, Bhuj 370 001 Gujarat, India. E-mail: mathur1alok@rediffmail.com

MATIN Abdul, b. 1 March 1932, Sawabi, Mardan, Pakistan. Economist. m. Azra, 3 sons. Education: MA, PhD, Economics, Bonn, Germany. Appointments: Minister, Foreign Service, Pakistan Embassy, Ankara, 1973-76; Secretary, Senior Executive Director, Agricultural Development, Bank of Pakistan, 1977-85; Vice Chancellor, Peshawar University, 1987-89. Publications: Industrialization of NWFP, 1970; 95 articles in professional journals, 1957-; Numerous official reports, 1992-. Honours: Award for Excellence of Services, Hamdard Foundation, Karachi, 1992; Award for outstanding services, Khawaja Farid Sang, Lahore, 2004. Memberships: Quaid-e-Azam Management Board, Karachi; Pakistan Bait-ul-Mal, Board of Management, Islamabad, Government of Pakistan; Ex-Member, Higher Education Commission, Government of Pakistan; Member, Search Committee for selection of Vice Chancellors of the Public Universities; Ex-Chairman, Committee on Higher Secondary Education; Ex-Member, Finance Commission; Member, Health Regulatory Authority; Member, Economic Reform Commission, Government of NWFP. Address: House No 27, Street No 9, D3, Phase – I, Hayatabad Peshawar NWFP, Pakistan.

MATOUŠEK Jiří, b. 4 April 1930, Příbram, Czech Republic. Chemical Engineer. m. Dagmar Matoušková, 1 son, 1 daughter. Education: Dipl Eng (Chem), Czech Technical University, Prague and Military Technical Academy, Brno, 1954; PhD (CSc), Military Technical Academy, Brno, 1958; DSc, Military Academy of Chemical Protection, Moscow, 1967; Associate Professor, Special Technology, Military Academy, Brno, 1966; Professor, Organic Chemistry, Palacký University, Olomouc, 1983. Appointments: Assistant Professor, Military Technical Academy, Brno, 1954-59, Head of Department, 1959-63; Director, NBC Defence R & D Establishment, Brno, 1963-71; Deputy Head, Department of Toxicology, Purkyne Medical Research Institute, Hradec Králové, 1971-81; Director for Research, NBC Defence R & D Establishment, Brno, 1981-89; Senior Research Fellow, Academy of Science, Prague, 1989-90; Professor of Toxicology, Masaryk University, Brno, 1990-; Visiting Professor International Institute for Peace, Vienna, 1990-; Director Institute of Environmental Chemistry and Technology, Brno University of Technology, 1992-2000. Publications: Over 520 articles in professional and scientific journals; About 135 research reports, 90 patents and improvement suggestions, mostly realised in production and use; More than 450 conference papers, mostly international; 24 books and 39 chapters in monographs dealing with chemistry and analysis of toxic agents, chemical and biological disarmament, verification, conversion, ecological, environmental and other global problems, mostly in English but also in German, French, Russian, Czech and Slovak. Honours: 8 state and military orders and medals; Memorial Medal of Masaryk University, 1991; Memorial Medal of Brno University of Technology, 1999; American Medal of Honor, 2002; International Peace Prize, 2005. Memberships: International Network of Engineers and Scientists; World Federation of Scientific Workers; Pugwash Conferences; Accredited Representative of World Federation of Scientific Workers at UNO and conference of NGOs; Chairman,

Scientific Advisory Board, Organisation for the Prohibition of Chemical Weapons; Foreign Member, Bologna Academy of Sciences; Honorary Member, NBC Defence Forum, Vienna; Many other professional organisations. Address: Krásného 26, CZ-636 00 Brno, Czech Republic. E-mail: matousek@recetox.muni.cz

MATSUDA Wakoto, b. 6 April 1968, Onomichi, Hiroshima, Japan. Neurosurgeon; Researcher. m. Kiyoe Nakazawa, 2 sons, 1 daughter. Education: MD, Faculty of Medicine, University of Tsukuba, Ibaraki, Japan, 1990-96; Diplomat in Neurosurgery, Japan Neurosurgical Society, 2002. Appointments: Residency, Department of Neurosurgery, University of Tsukuba Hospital, Tsukuba, Ibaraki Japan, 1996-2002; Clinical Fellow, Department of Neurosurgery, Tsukuba Medical Centre Hospital, Tsukuba, Ibaraki, Japan, 2002-2003; Postgraduate, 2003-2006, Research Assistant, 2004-2006, Department of Morphological Brain Science, Graduate School of Medicine, Kyoto University, Kyoto, Japan; Assistant Professor, Division of Anatomy and Cell Biology, Shiga University of Medical Science, 2006-. Publications: Articles in: Journal of Neurology, Neurosurgery and Psychiatry, 2003, 2004; Neuropsychological Rehabilitation, 2005; Journal of Trauma, 2008. Honours: The Best Resident Award of the Year, Department of Neurosurgery, Institute of Clinical Medicine, University of Tsukuba, 2002; Iwadare Scholarship, Iwadare Scholarship Foundation, 2003; Listed in Who's Who publications and biographical dictionaries. Memberships: Japan Neurosurgical Society, Tokyo, Japan; Japanese Congress of Neurological Surgery, Tokyo, Japan; Japan Neuroscience Society, Tokyo, Japan; Japanese Association of Anatomists, Tokyo, Japan. Address: Division of Anatomy and Cell Biology, Department of Anatomy, Shiga University of Medical Science, Tsukinowa-cho, Seta, Otsu, Shiga 520-2192, Japan. E-mail: wako@mua.biglobe.ne.jp

MATSUHASHI Nobuyuki, b. 7 November 1956, Tokyo. Physician. 3 daughters. Education: BM, 1982, MD, 1991, University of Tokyo. Appointments: Resident, University of Tokyo, 1982-84; Assistant Professor, Tokyo Women's Medical College, 1984-85; Resident, Jichi Medical School, 1985-86; Research Fellow, National Institute of Radiological Sciences, 1988-89; Assistant Professor, University of Tokyo, 1989-2003; Chairman, Department of Endoscopy and Department of Gastroenterology, 2006-, Kanto Medical Center, NTT East. Publications: Articles in professional medical journals including: Journal of Immunology, Gut, Lancet, Gastroenterology, Gastrointestinal Endoscopy, Journal of Experimental Medicine, Cancer Research. Honours: Academic Prize of the Japanese Gastroenterological Endoscopy Society, 1999. Memberships: Japanese Society for Gastroenterology; Japanese Society for Gastroenterological Endoscopy; Japanese Society for Immunology; Japanese Society for Internal Medicine; American Gastroenterological Association; Society for Mucosal Immunology; American Society for Gastrointestinal Endoscopy. Address: Department of Endoscopy, Kanto Medical Center, NTT East, 5-9-22 Higashi-gotanda, Shinagawa-ku, Tokyo 141-8625 Japan. E-mail: nmatuha-tky@umin.ac.jp

MATSUMORI Nobuaki, b. 10 September 1969, Atsugi, Kanagawa, Japan. Chemistry Professor. Education: BS, 1992, MS, 1994, PhD, 1997, Chemistry, University of Tokyo. Appointments: Postdoctoral Fellow, University of Tokyo, Japan, 1997-99; Assistant Professor, Osaka University, Japan 1999-; Visiting Scientist, MIT, Cambridge, Massachusetts, USA, 2000-01. Publications: Sorrell Organic Chemistry; About 50 research papers and 10 review papers. Honours:

Inoue Young Scientist Research Award, 1999; Education and Research Award, Osaka University, 2006. Memberships: American Chemical Society; Chemical Society of Japan. Address: 1-1 Machikaneyama, Toyonaka, Osaka 560-0043, Japan. E-mail: matsmori@chem.sci.osaka-u.ac.jp

MATSUMOTO Seiichi, b. 8 November 1916, Kamakura, Japan. President, Japan Family Planning Association. m. Sadako Ohkochi, 8 November 1948, 1 son, 1 daughter. Education: Graduate, Tokyo University School of Medicine, 1941; Dr Med Sci, Tokyo University, 1947. Appointments: Assistant Professor, Showa Medical College, 1945-50; Chief, Department of Maternal Health, Aiiku Institute, 1950-54; Chief, Department of Obstetrics and Gynaecology, Kanto Teishin Hospital, 1954-58; Professor, Obstetrics and Gynaecology, Gunma University School of Medicine, 1958-72; Professor, Obstetrics and Gynaecology, 1972-92, Director, 1974-85, Professor Emeritus, 1992-; Jichi Medical School Hospital; President, Jichi Medical School, School of Nursing, 1987-91; Professor Emeritus, Gunma University, 1988-; Chairman of the Board of Directors, 1985-2000, President, 2000-, Japan Family Planning Association. Publications: Menstruation and its Disorders, 1956; Maternal Care, 1968; Introduction to Maternal and Child Health, 1973; Recent Contraceptive Methods, 1975; Maternal Health Care, 1977; Adolescent Health, 1982; Studies on Women's Senses and Behaviours about Menstruation, 1990; Adolescent Clinic, 1995; Studies on PMS, 1995; Menstruation of Japanese Women, 1999; Lecture for Easier Menstruation, 2004. Honours: Award, Minister of Health and Welfare, 1977; Public Health Award, 1989; Order of Sacred Treasure, Gold and Silver Star, 1991; Award, FIGO, 1994; Gold Medal, World Association for Sexology, 1995. Memberships: Honorary President, Japan Federation of Sexology; Honorary Chairman, Japan Society of Adolescentology; Japan Society of Maternal Health; Executive Board Member, Japan Association of Sex Education. Address: 1-11-17 Yuigahama, Kamakura 248-0014, Japan.

MATSUSHIRO Nobuhito, b. 27 February 1957, Hyogo Prefecture, Japan. Scientist. Education: PhD, Information Engineering, University of Electronic Communications, Tokyo, Japan, 1996; PhD, Colour Science, 2006, PhD student (part time), School of Medicine, Chiba University, Chiba, Japan. Appointments: Manager, 1995-99, General Manager, Researcher, 2000-04, Executive Senior Researcher, 2004-, Oki Data Corp, Takasaki, Japan; Visiting Scientist, 1999-2004, Guest Scientist, 2005-, Rochester Institute of Technology, New York, USA. Publications: 20 journal papers; 50 patents; 3 books. Memberships: Society for Imaging Science and Technology. Address: 3-24-4, Mirokuji, Fujisawa-shi, Kanagawa-ken, 251-0016, Japan. E-mail: no-matusiro@oki.com

MATSUSHITA Junichi, b. 4 July 1959, Yokosuka, Japan. Professor. Education: B Eng, 1983, PhD, 1991, Tokai University, Japan; M Eng, Toyota Technological Institute, Japan, 1986. Appointments: Assistant Professor, 1996-98, Associate Professor, 1998-2001, Department of Applied Chemistry, Associate Professor, 2001-04, Professor, 2004-, Chairman, 2007-, Department of Materials Science, Tokai University; Visiting Professor, Department of Materials Science, University of Cambridge, England, 2005. Publications: Over 100 papers; 3 books; 20 patents. Honours: Award, Electrical Technology Encouragement Prize, Japan Society of Electric Science Technology; Award, Prize of Powder and Powder Metallurgy, Japan Society of Powder and Powder Metallurgy; The Award of the Prize of the Ceramic Society of Japan; Member, Ceramic Society of Japan;

European Academy of Science. Memberships: The Ceramic Society of Japan; Japan Society of Powder and Powder Metallurgy.

MATSUURA Koichiro, b. 29 September 1937, Tokyo, Japan. Director-General of UNESCO. m. Takako Kirikae, 2 sons. Education: Faculty of Law, University of Tokyo, 1956-69; Faculty of Economics, Haverfod College, USA, 1959-61. Appointments: Third Secretary, Embassy of Japan, Ghana, 1961-63; Second Secretary, then First Secretary, Japanese Delegation to the OECD, Paris, 1968-72; Various posts in central administration, 1963-68, 1972-74, Director, First North American Division (Political Affairs), 1974-75, Director, Development Co-operation Division, 1975-77, Director, Aid Policy Division, 1980-82, Director-General, Economics Co-operation Bureau, 1988-90, Director-General, North American Affairs Bureau, 1990-92, Ministry of Foreign Affairs; Counsellor, Embassy of Japan, USA, 1977-80; Director, General Affairs Division, Deputy Director-General, Foreign Minister's Office, 1982-85; Consul General of Japan in Hong Kong, 1985-88; Deputy Minister for Foreign Affairs (Sherpa for Japan at the G-7 Summit), 1992-94; Ambassador of Japan to France and concurrently to Andorra and Djibouti, 1994-99; Chairperson, World Heritage Committee of UNESCO, 1998-99; UNESCO Director-General (elected for a 6-year term on 15 November 1999), 1999-2005; Re-elected UNESCO Director-General for a 4-year term on 15 November 2005), 2005-. Publications: In the Forefront of Economic Co-operation Diplomacy, 1990; History of Japan-United State Relations, 1992; The G-7 Summit: Its History and Perspectives, 1994; Development & Perspectives of the Relations between Japan and France, 1995; Japanese Diplomacy at the Dawn of the 21st Century, 1998. Address: Office of the Director-General, UNESCO, 7, place de Fontenoy, 75352 Paris 07 SP, France. Website: www.unesco.org

MATTESSICH Richard, b. 9 August 1922, Trieste, Italy. Professor Emeritus. m. Hermine. Education: Mech Engineer Diploma, 1940; Dipl Kaufmann, 1944; Dr rer pol, 1945; Dr honoris causa, Madrid, 1998; Bordeaux, 2006; Malaga, 2006. Appointments: Research Fellow, Austrian Institute of Economic Research, 1945-47; Lecturer, Rosenberg College, Switzerland, 1947-52; Department Head, Mount Allison University, Canada, 1953-58; Associate Professor, University of California, Berkeley, 1959-67; Professor, Ruhr University, Bochum, 1965-66; Professor, University of British Columbia, 1967-88; Professor, University of Technology, Vienna, 1976-78; Professor Emeritus, University of British Columbia, 1988-. Publications: Books: Accounting and Analytic Methods, 1964; Simulation of the Firm, 1964; Instrumental Reasoning and Systems Methods, 1978; Modern Accounting Research, 1984; Accounting Research in the 1980's, 1991; Critique of Accounting, 1995; Foundational Research in Accounting, 1995; The Beginnings of Accounting, 2000; La Representacion Contable y el modelo de Capas-Cebolla de la Realidad, 2003; Two Hundred Years of Accounting Research, 2007. Honours: Ford Founding Fellow, USA, 1961, 62; Erskine Fellow, New Zealand, 1970; Killam Senior Fellow, Canada, 1971; Literary Awards, AICPA, 1972, CAAA, 1991; Drhc, University of Montesquieu, Bordeaux, 2006; Drhc, University of Málaga, 2006; Listed in Who's Who publications. Memberships: Accademia Italiana di Econ Aziendale, 1980-; Austrian Academy of Science, 1984-; Life member, American Accounting Association; Life member, Academy of Accounting Historians; Officially Nominated for the Nobel Prize in Economics, 2002; Drhc. (Univ. of Madrid,

1998). Address: Sauder School of Business, University of British Columbia, Vancouver, British Columbia, Canada V6T 1Z2. E-mail: richard.mattessich@sauder.ubc.ca

MATTHEW Christopher Charles Forrest, b. 8 May 1939, London, England. Writer and Broadcaster. m. Wendy Mary Matthew, 19 October 1979, 2 sons, 1 daughter. Education: King's School, Canterbury; MA (Hons), St Peter's College, Oxford. Appointments: Editor, Times Travel Guide, 1972-73. Publications: A Different World; Stories of Great Hotels, 1976; Diary of a Somebody, 1978; Loosely Engaged, 1980; The Long-Haired Boy, 1980; The Crisp Report, 1981; Three Men in a Boat, annotated edition, with Benny Green, 1982; The Junket Man, 1983; How to Survive Middle Age, 1983; Family Matters, 1987; The Amber Room, 1995; A Nightingale Sang in Fernhurst Road, 1998; Now We Are Sixty, 1999; Knocking On, 2000; Now We Are Sixty (And a Bit), 2003; Summoned by Balls, 2005; When We Were Fifty, 2007; Contributions to: Many leading newspapers; Columnist for Punch, 1983-88; Restaurant Critic for English Vogue, 1983-86; Book reviewer for Daily Mail; Radio: Freedom Pass (R4), 2003-. Membership: Society of Authors; Chelsea Arts Club. Address: 35 Drayton Gardens, London SW10 9RY, England.

MATTHIESEN Patrick David Albert Francis Jonathan, b. 1 March 1943, London, England. Art Dealer. m. Hiromi Kaminishi, 2 daughters. Education: Briscoe Owen Scholar, MA, Oriel College, Oxford; Courtauld Institute of Art, London. Appointments: Supervisor of restoration sculpture project in Florence after floods, 1966-67; Supervisor in founding Conservation Institute in Venice in liaison with the Victoria and Albert Museum, 1968-69; Independent Art Dealer, 1970; Associate, Queensbury Investments Ltd property developers, 1970-71; Associate Independent Consultant, 1972, In Charge of the Research Department, 1973-73, General Manager, 1973-75, Director, Old Master Paintings Department, 1976-77, P & D Colnaghi Ltd; Founder, Chairman and Managing Director, Matthiesen Fine Art Ltd, 1978-; Exhibitions mounted by Matthiesen Fine Art include: Important Italian Painting 1600-1700, 1981; Early Italian Paintings and Works of Art 1300-1400, 1983; From Borso to Cesare d'Este: School of Ferrara 1450-1628, 1984; Around 1610: The Onset of Baroque, 1985, Varlin, 1985, Baroque III, 1986; Paintings from Emila 1500-1700, 1987; The Settecento: Italian Rococo and Early Neoclassical Paintings 1700-1800, 1987; A Selection of French Paintings 1700-1840, 1989; Louis Léopold Boilly's L'Entrée du Jardin Turc, 1991; Fifty Paintings 1535-1925, 1993; Paintings 1600-1912, 1996; Gold Backs 1250-1480, 1996; An Eye on Nature, 1997; Collectanea: 1700-1800, 1998; A Del Sarto Rediscovered, 2002; Il Porto di Ripetta, 2002; Chardin's Têtes d'Études au Pastel, 2003. Publications include most recently: Virtuous Virgins: Classical Heroines, Romantic Passion and the Art of Suicide, 2004; Bertin's Ideal Landscapes, 2004; Polidoro Da Caravaggio: La Lignamine's Lamentation. Articles: The S&S 34, 2002; Bob Derecktor and the S&S Family of Gulfstreams, 2003; NY32 & CAL 32: The Forthcoming Duel, 2004; Pocket Cruisers and Racers, 2005; Argyll's Racing History, 2005; Sprats and Minnows: Some S&S Small Fry, 2006. Honours: Honorary Secretary, The Sparkman & Stephens Association, 2000-07. Memberships: RAC; Chairman and Founder, The Matthiesen Foundation. Address: Matthiesen Gallery, 7-8 Mason's Yard, Duke Street, London SW1, England. E-mail: gallery@matthiesengallery.com Website: www.thematthiesenfoundation.org

MATULIONIS Arvydas, b. 1 April 1940, Kupiskis, Lithuania. Professor of Physics. m. Ilona, 3 sons, 1 daughter. Education: Diploma in Physics, Vilnius University, Lithuania, 1961; Candidate of Science, Physics and Mathematics, 1967, DSc, Physics and Mathematics, 1981, Vilnius University, Lithuania; Doctor Habilitus, Nature Science, Lithuania, 1993. Appointments: Research Associate, Institute of Optics, University of Rochester, USA, 1969-70; Senior Research Associate, 1972-74, Head of Laboratory, 1974-91, Associate Professor (part-time), 1983-85, Professor of Physics and Principal Research Associate, 1991-95, 2007-, Professor of Physics and Head of Fluctuation Research Laboratory, 1995-2007, Semiconductor Physics Institute, Vilnius; Professor of Physics (part-time), Vytautas Magnus University, Kaunas, Lithuania, 1991-95. Publications: Over 180 in professional journals; Monograph: H L Hartnagel, R Katilius, A Matulionis, Microwave Noise in Semiconductor Devices, John Wiley and Sons, New York, 2001. Honours: Lithuanian National Award in Science, 1983, 1995. Memberships: Lithuanian Physical Society; International Advisory Committee, International Conference on Noise and Fluctuations; International Advisory Committee, European Workshop on Compound Semiconductor Devices and Integrated Circuits (WOCSDICE). Address: Fluctuation Research Laboratory, Semiconductor Physics Institute Vilnius, 11 A Gostauto, Vilnius 01108, Lithuania.

MATUSSEK Thomas, b. 18 September 1947, Lauda, Germany. Ambassador. m. Ursula Matussek, 1 son, 2 daughters. Education: Studied Law and History at the Universities of Paris (Sorbonne) and Bonn, 1979-72; First State Examination in Law, 1973. Appointments: Judge's Assistant/Assistant Lecturer, University of Bonn, 1973-76; German Foreign Office, Bonn, 1975-77; German Embassy, London, 1977-80; Federal Chancellery, European Affairs, 1980-83; German Embassy, New Delhi, 1983-86; German Embassy, Lisbon, 1986-88; German Foreign Office, Bonn, 1988-92; Head of the Minister's Office, 1992-93, Chief of the Cabinet of the Minister, 1993-94, Foreign Office, Bonn; Deputy Chief of Mission, German Embassy, Washington, 1994-99; Director-General, Political Department, Foreign Office, Berlin, 1999; Ambassador of the Federal Republic of Germany to the Court of St James's, 2002-; German ambassador to the United Nations, 2006. Memberships: Athenaeum; Royal Automobile; Naval and Military Club; Travellers Club; Beefsteak Club; Capital Club. Address: German Embassy, 23 Belgrave Square, London SW1X 8PZ, England. E-mail: amboffice@german-embassy.org.uk

MATVIENKO Vladimir, b. 5 January 1938, Zhytomyr Region, Ukraine. Economist. m. Yallina Matvienko, 1 son, 1 daughter. Education: Kiev Financial Economic Institute, 1959; Kiev Institute of National Economy; Docent, Faculty of Economics, 1979; Professor of Economics, 1992. Appointments: Specialist, Deputy Manager of Donetsk Regional Office; Manager, Dnepropetrovsk Regional Office of Budbank, USSR, 1959-79; Deputy Manager, Manager, Ukrainian Republic Office of Budbank of USSR, 1979, 1987; Chairman, Board of Ukrainian Republic Bank of Prombudbank, 1987-91; Chairman, Board of National Bank of Ukraine, 1991; Chairman, Board of Prominvestbank, 1992-. Publications: The State and the Bank, monograph; Autograph at gryvnya, monograph; Scientific works on economic development; Collections of poems: I Love My Ukraine; On My Native Land; My Starry Song. Honours: Order of Prince Yaroslav the Wise of V Level, the International Friendship and Slavs Prizes; Hero of the Ukraine, Government Order,

2004. Memberships: Full Member, Engineer-Academy of Ukraine; Ukranian Ecological Academy of Science. Address: Grushevskogo Str 9, Apt 6, Kyiv 01021, Ukraine.

MAUNDER Leonard, b. 10 May 1927, Swansea, Wales. Engineer. m. Moira Anne Hudson (deceased), 1 son, 1 daughter. Education: BSc, University College of Swansea, 1947; PhD, Edinburgh University, 1950; ScD, MIT, 1954. Appointments: Instructor and Assistant Professor, Mechanical Engineering, MIT, 1950-54; Section Leader, Aeronautical Research Lab, Wright Air Development Center, US Air Force, 1954-56; Lecturer, University of Edinburgh, 1956-61; Professor, Applied Mechanics, King's College, Professor, Mechanical Engineering and Dean of Engineering, University of Newcastle upon Tyne, 1961-92. Publications: Numerous articles in professional journals; Books: Gyrodynamics and its Engineering Applications with R N Arnold, 1961; Machines in Motion, 1986. Honours: OBE, 1977; I Mech E Leonardo da Vinci Lecturer, 1978; Royal Institution Christmas Lecturer, 1983. Memberships: Fellow, Royal Academy of Engineering; Fellow, Institution of Mechanical Engineers; Fellow, University of Swansea, Wales; Honorary Foreign Member, Polish Society of Applied Mechanics. Address: 46 Moorside South, Newcastle upon Tyne, NE4 9BB, England. E-mail: leonard.maunder@ncl.ac.uk

MAURICE-WILLIAMS Robert Stephen, b. 14 June 1942, Southampton, England. Consultant Neurosurgeon. m. Elizabeth Anne Meadows, 1 son, 3 daughters. Education: Pembroke College, Cambridge, St Thomas' Hospital Medical School, London; MA, MB, BChir, Cambridge; FRCS (England); FRCP(London). Appointments: Chief Assistant in Neurosurgery, St Bartholomew's Hospital, 1973-77; Consultant Neurosurgeon, Brook Hospital, 1977-80; Consultant Neurosurgeon, 1980-, Senior Neurosurgeon, 1982-, The Royal Free Hospital; Editor, British Journal of Neurosurgery, 1992-99; Member, Court of Examiners, Royal College of Surgeons, 1992-98. Publications: Books: Spinal Degenerative Disease, 1981; Subarachnoid Haemorrhage, 1988; Over 80 papers in peer-reviewed scientific journals and 8 chapters in medical textbooks. Honours: Open Scholarship in Natural Sciences, Pembroke College, Cambridge, 1960; First Class Honours, Natural Sciences Tripos, Cambridge, 1964; Cheselden Medal, St Thomas' Hospital, 1967; Hallett Prize, Royal College of Surgeons, 1971. Memberships: Athenaeum Club, London; Pitt Club, Cambridge; Society of British Neurological Surgeons, Officer, 1996-2006, Member of the Council, 1992-2006. Address: Neurosurgical Unit, Wellington Hospital, London NW8 9LE, England.

MAVOR Elizabeth (Osborne), b. 17 December 1927, Glasgow, Scotland. Author. Education: St Andrews, 1940-45; St Leonard's and St Anne's College, Oxford, England, 1947-50. Publications: Summer in the Greenhouse, 1959; The Temple of Flora, 1961; The Virgin Mistress: A Biography of the Duchess of Kingston (US edition as The Virgin Mistress: A Study in Survival: The Life of the Duchess of Kingston), 1964; The Redoubt, 1967; The Ladies of Llangollen: A Study in Romantic Friendship, 1971; A Green Equinox, 1973; Life with the Ladies of Llangollen, 1984; The Grand Tour of William Beckford, 1986; The White Solitaire, 1988; The American Journals of Fanny Kemble, 1990; The Grand Tours of Katherine Wilmot, France 1801-3 and Russia 1805-7, 1992; The Captain's Wife, The South American Journals of Maria Graham 1821-23, 1993.

MAVROPOULOS Georgios, b. 30 July 1964, Moschato, Attiki, Greece. Mechanical Engineer; Researcher. Education: Dipl Ing, Mechanical Engineering, 1989, Dr Ing, 2001, National Technical University of Athens; Certificate of Proficiency in English, University of Michigan, USA, 2004. Appointments: Research Assistant, National Technical University of Athens, 1993-97; Product Design Engineer, Ceremetal se SA, 1998-2000; Product Development Engineer, 2000-05, Responsible for Cooling Systems Development, 2006-, Bosch-Siemens Oikiakes Syskeves. Publications: Author, more than 20 papers in international journals and conferences; Scientific consultant on university textbook, Internal Combustion Engines – Exercises in Dynamics. Honours: Two-year Scholarship for Postgraduate Studies, National Technical University of Athens, 1993-95; Annual Scholarship, Toyota Hellas, 1995-96; Excellence in Research and Development, Bosch-Siemens Oikiakes Syskeves, 2002, 2003, 2005; Society of Automotive Engineers, Best Presentation Award, 2004. Memberships: Technical Chamber of Greece; Hellenic Association of Mechanical and Electrical Engineers; Society of Automotive Engineers. Address: 7 Pallikaridi Street, 18345 Moschato, Greece. E-mail: mavrop@otenet.gr

MAXWELL DAVIES Peter (Sir), b. 8 September 1934, Manchester, England. Composer. Education: Royal Manchester College of Music; Mus B (Hons), Manchester University, 1956. Musical Education: Studies with Goffredo Petrassi in Rome, 1957; Harkness Fellowship, Graduate School, Princeton University, studied with Roger Sessions, Milton Babbitt, Earl Kim. Career: Director of Music, Cirencester Grammar School, 1959-62; Founder and co-director (with Harrison Birtwistle) of the Pierrot Players, 1967-71; Founder, Artistic Director, Fires of London, 1971-87; Founder, Artistic Director, St. Magnus Festival, Orkney Islands, Scotland, 1977-86; Artistic Director, Dartington Summer School of Music, 1979-84; President, Schools Music Association, 1983-; President, North of England Education Conference, 1985; Visiting Fromm Professor of Composition, Harvard University, 1985; Associate Composer/Conductor, Scottish Chamber Orchestra, 1985-94; President, Composer's Guild of Great Britain, 1986-; President, St Magnus Festival, Orkney Islands, 1986-; President, National Federation of Music Societies, 1989-; Major retrospective festival as South Bank Centre, London, 1990; Conductor/Composer, BBC Philharmonic, 1992-; Associate Conductor/Composer, Royal Philharmonic Orchestra, 1992-; President, Cheltenham Arts Festival, 1994-; Composer Laureate of Scottish Chamber Orchestra, 1994-; President, Society for the Promotion of New Music, 1995-. Compositions: Stage: Operas Taverner 1962-70; The Martydom of St Magnus 1976-77; The Two Fiddlers 1978; The Lighthouse, 1979; Theatre Pieces: Notre Dame des Fleurs 1966; Vesalii Icones 1969; Eight Songs for a Mad King 1969; Nocturnal Dances, ballet 1969; Blind Man's Buff 1972; Miss Donnithorne's Maggot 1974; Salome, ballet 1978; Le Jongleur de Notre Dame 1978; Cinderella 1980; The Medium 1981; The No 11 Bus 1983-84; Caroline Mathilde, ballet, 1990; Operas: Resurrection 1987 and The Doctor of Myddfai 1996. Orchestra and Ensemble: Alma Redemptoris Mater for 6 wind instruments 1957; St Michael, sonata for 17 wind instruments 1957; Prolation 1958; Ricercar and Doubles for 8 instruments 1959; 5 Klee Pictures 1959, rev 1976; Sinfonia 1962; 2 Fantasias on an In Nomine of John Taverner 1962-64; 7 In Nomine 1963-65; Shakespeare Music 1965; Antechrist 1967; Stedman Caters 1968; St Thomas Wake 1969; Worldes Blis 1969; Renaissance Scottish Dances 1973; Ave Maris Stela 1975; 4 Symphonies 1973-76, 1980, 1984, 1988; Runes from a Holy Island 1977; A mirror of Whitening

Light 1977; Dances from Salome, 1979; The Bairns of Brugh 1981; Image Reflection, Shadow 1982; Sinfonia Concertante 1982; Sinfonietta Accademica 1983; Unbroken Circle 1984; An Orkney Wedding, with Sunrise 1985; Jimmack the Postie, overture 1986; 10 Strathclyde Concertos for Violin 1985, Trumpet 1987, Oboe 1988, Clarinet 1990, Violin and Viola, 1991, Flute 1991, Doublebass 1992, Bassoon, 1993, Chamber Ensemble 1994, Orchestra 1995; Vocal: 5 Motets 1959; O Magnum Mysterium 1960; Te Lucis ante Terminum 1961; Frammenti di Leopardi, cantata 1962; Veni Sancte Spiritus 1963; Revelation and Fall; The Shepherds' Calendar 1965; Missa super L'Homme Arme 1968, rev 1971; From Stone to Thorn 1971; Hymn to St Magnus 1972; Tenebrae super Gesualdo 1972; Stone Litany 1973; Fiddlers at the Wedding 1974; Anakreontika 1976; Kirkwall Shopping Songs 1979; Black Pentecost 1979; Solstice of Light 1979; The Yellow Cake Review, 6 cabaret songs 1980; Songs of Hoy 1981; Into The Labyrinth for tenor and orchestra 1983; First Ferry to Hoy 1985; The Peat Cutters 1985; House of Winter 1986; Excuse Me 1986; Sea Runes, vocal sextet 1986; Hymn to the Word of God, for tenor and chorus, 1990; The Turn of the Tide for orchestra and children's choir, 1992; Chamber music includes: String Quartet 1961; The Kestrel Paced Round the Sun 1975; Sonatina 1981; The Pole Star 1982; Sea Eagle 1982; Sonata for violin and cimbalon 1984; Piano Sonata 1981; Organ Sonata, 1982; Latest works: Sails in St Magnus I-III, 1997-98; Job, oratorio for chorus, orchestra and soloists, 1998; A Reel of Seven Fishermen for orchestra, 1998; Sea Elegy, for chorus, orchestra and soloists, 1998; Roma Amor Labyrinths, 1998; Maxwell's Reel with Northern Lights, 1998; Swinton Jig, 1998; Temenos with Mermaids and Angels, for flute and orchestra, 1998; Spinning Jenny, 1999; Sails in Orkney Saga III: An Orkney Wintering, for alto saxophone and orchestra, 1999; Trumpet Quintet, for string quartet and trumpet, 1999; Mr Emmet Takes a Walk, 1999; Horn Concerto, 1999; Orkney Saga IV: Westerly Gale in Biscay, Salt in the Bread Broken, 2000, Symphony No 7, 2000; Antarctic Symphony, Symphony No 8, 2000; Canticum Canticorum, 2001; De Assumtione Beatae Mariae Virginis, 2001; Crossing Kings Reach, 2001; Mass, 2002; Naxos Quartet No 1, 2002; Piano Trip, 2002; Naxos Quartet No 2, 2003. Honours: Many honours including: Fellow, Royal Northern College of Music, 1978; Honorary Member, Royal Academy of Music, 1979; Honorary Member, Guildhall School of Music and Drama, 1981; CBE, 1981; Knight Bachelor, for services to music, 1987; L'officier dans L'Ordre des Arts et des Lettres, France, 1988; First Award, Association of British Orchestras, outstanding contribution and promotion of orchestral life in UK; Gulliver Award for Performing Arts in Scotland, 1991; Fellowship, Royal Scottish Academy of Music and Drama, 1994; Charles Grove Award, outstanding contribution to British Music, 1995; Master of the Queen's Music, 2007. Member of the Bayerische Akademie der Schönen Künste, 1998. Address: c/o 50 Hogarth Road, London SW5 0PU, England.

MAY Derwent James, b. 29 April 1930, Eastbourne, Sussex, England. Author; Journalist. m. Yolanta Izabella Sypniewska, 1 son, 1 daughter. Education: MA, Lincoln College, Oxford, 1952. Appointments: Theatre and Film Critic, Continental Daily Mail, Paris, 1952-53; Lecturer in English, University of Indonesia, 1955-58; Senior Lecturer in English, Universities of Lodz and Warsaw, 1959-63; Chief Leader Writer, Times Literary Supplement, 1963-65; Literary Editor, The Listener, 1965-86; Literary and Arts Editor, Sunday Telegraph, 1986-90, The European, 1990-91; European Arts Editor, The Times, 1992-. Publications: Novels: The Professionals, 1964; Dear Parson, 1969; The Laughter in Djakarta, 1973; A Revenger's Comedy, 1979. Non-Fiction: Proust, 1983; The Times Nature

Diary, 1983; Hannah Arendt, 1986; The New Times Nature Diary, 1993; Feather Reports, 1996; Critical Times: The History of the Times Literary Supplement, 2001; The Times: A Year in Nature Notes, 2004. Contributions to: Encounter; Hudson Review. Honours: Member, Booker Prize Jury, 1978; Hawthornden Prize Committee, 1987-; FRSL. Membership: Beefsteak Club; Garrick Club. Address: 45 Burghley Road, London, NW5 1UH, England.

MAY Geoffrey John, b. 7 May 1948, London, England. Chartered Engineer. m. Sarah, 2 sons. Education: MA, Double First Class Honours, Natural Sciences Tripos, Materials Science, Fitzwilliam College, University of Cambridge; PhD, Department of Metallurgy and Materials Science; Fellow of the Institute of Metals; Chartered Engineer. Appointments: Research Officer, Central Electricity Generating Board, 1973-74; Technical Manager, Chloride Silent Power Ltd, 1974-78; Design and Development Manager, Chloride Technical Ltd, 1978-82; Technical Director, 1982-86, Operations Director, 1986-88, Tungstone Batteries Ltd; General Manager, Brush Fusegear Ltd, 1988-90; Managing Director, Barton Abrasives Ltd, 1990-91; Group Director of Technology, Hawker Batteries, 1991-97; Group Director of Technology, BTR Power Systems, 1997-2000; Chief Technology Officer, Fiamm SpA, 2000-03; Principal, The Focus Partnership, 2003-. Publications: Numerous publications in technical and trade journals and conference proceedings. Address: Troutbeck House, Main Street, Swithland, Loughborough, Leicestershire LE12 8TJ, England. E-mail: geoffrey.may@tiscali.co.uk

MAY John F, b. 10 March 1950, Elisabethville, Belgian Congo. Demographer. m. Anne Legrand, 1 son, 1 daughter. Education: BA, Modern History, 1973; MA, Demography, 1985, University of Louvain, Leuven; PhD, Demography, University of Paris, Sorbonne, 1996. Appointments: Associate Expert in Demography, United Nations, Haiti, 1976-79; Expert in Demography, United Nations South Pacific Commission, 1980-83; Training Co-ordinator, International Union for the Scientific Study of Population, 1985-86; Senior Scientist, The Futures Group International, 1987-97; Senior Population Specialist, Africa Region, World Bank, 1997-. Publications: Numerous papers in peer-reviewed journals. Honours: Andrew W Mellon Foundation Visiting Scholarship at the Population Reference Bureau. Memberships: International Union for the Scientific Study of Population; Population Association of America. Address: The World Bank, 1818 H Street NW, MSN # J9 – 901, Washington, DC 20433, USA. E-mail: jmay@worldbank.org

MAY Naomi Young, b. 27 March 1934, Glasgow, Scotland. Novelist; Journalist; Painter. m. Nigel May, 3 October 1964, 2 sons, 1 daughter. Education: Slade School of Fine Art, London, 1953-56; Diploma, Fine Art, University of London. Publications: At Home, 1969, radio adaptation, 1987; The Adventurer, 1970; Troubles, 1976. Contributions to: Anthologies, newspapers, and magazines. Honour: History of Art Prize, Slade School of Fine Art. Membership: PEN. Address: 6 Lion Gate Gardens, Richmond, Surrey TW9 2DF, England.

MAY OF OXFORD, Baron of Oxford in the County of Oxfordshire, Sir Robert McCredie May, b. 1 August 1936, Professor. Education: BSc, PhD, Theoretical Physics, Sydney University. Appointments: Gordon MacKay Lecturer, Applied Mathematics, Harvard University; Senior Lecturer in Theoretical Physics, Personal Chair in Physics, Sydney University; Class of 1877 Professor of Zoology,

1973, Chairman of the Research Board, 1977-88, Princeton University, USA; Royal Society Research Professor, 1988; Chief Scientific Adviser, UK Government, 1995-2000; Head, UK Officer of Science and Technology, 1995-2000; Joint Professorship, Department of Zoology, Oxford University and Imperial College, London; Fellow, Merton College, Oxford University; President, The Royal Society, 2000-05. Publications: Numerous books; Several hundred papers in major scientific journals; Broader contributions to scientific journalism in newspapers, radio and TV. Honours: Knighthood, 1996; Companion of the Order of Australia, 1998; Crafoord Prize, Royal Swedish Academy; Swiss-Italian Balzan Prize; Japanese Blue Planet Prize; Order of Merit (OM), 2002. Memberships: Foreign Member, US National Academy of Sciences; Overseas Fellow, Australian Academy of Sciences. Address: Department of Zoology, University of Oxford, South Parks Road, Oxford, OX1 3PS, England. E-mail: robert.may@zoo.ox.ac.uk

MAY Simon Philip Walter, b. 9 August 1956, London, England. Writer; Businessman. Education: BA, PhD, Philosophy, Birkbeck College, London University; MA, Physiological Sciences (1st class honours), Oxford University. Appointments: Advisor on European Affairs to the Rt Hon Douglas Hurd, 1977-79; Advisor on Foreign Affairs to Rt Hon Edward Heath, 1979-83; Member of Cabinet of Vice President of the EU, Christopher Tugendhat, 1983-85; Member of Cabinet of the President of the EU, 1985-86; Director, Business Strategy and Development, Nortel Europe, 1986-88; Founder and Chief Executive, Mondiale Information Technology Associates, 1989-93; College Research Fellow, Birkbeck, University of London, 1997-; Visiting Professor, Tokyo University, 2000-01; Member, International Investment Committee, ACTIV Investment Fund, Tokyo, 2001-07; Deputy Chairman, Whatman plc, 2001-08. Publications: 5 books; Articles in professional journals. Address: School of Philosophy, Birkbeck College, Malet Street, London WC1E 7HX, England. E-mail: s.may@philosophy.bbk.ac.uk

MAY Theresa Mary, b. 1 October 1956. Politician. m. Philip John May, 1980. Education: St Hugh's College, Oxford. Career: Bank of England, 1977-83; Inter-Bank Research Org, 1983-85; Association for Payment Clearing Services, 1985-97 (Head of European Affairs Unit, 1989-96); Member, (Conservative Party) Merton, London Borough Council, 1986-94; Contested (Conservative Party), Durham NW, 1992, Barking, 1994; MP (Conservative), Maidenhead, 1997-; Opposition Frontbench Spokeswoman on Education and Employment, 1998-99; Shadow Secretary of State for Education and Employment, 1999-2001; Shadow Secretary of State for Transport, Local Government and the Regions, 2001-02; Chair, Conservative Party, 2002-03; Shadow Secretary of State for Environment and Transport, 2003-04, for Families, 2004-05; Shadow Leader of the House, 2005. Address: House of Commons, Westminster, London SW1A 0AA, England.

MAYALL Richard Michael (Rik), b. 7 March 1958, England. Comedian; Actor; Writer. m. Barbara Robin, 1 son, 2 daughters. Education: University of Manchester. Creative Works: Theatre includes: The Common Pursuit, 1988; Waiting for God, 1991-92; The Government Inspector, 1995; Cell Mates, 1995; The New Statesman, 2006; TV includes: The Young Ones (also creator and co-writer), 1982, 1984; The Comic Strip Presents, 1983-2005; George's Marvellous Medicine, 1985; The New Statesman, 1987-88, 1990, 1994; Bottom, 1990, 1992, 1994; Rik Mayall Presents, 1992-94; Wham Bham Strawberry Jam!, 1995; The Alan B'Stard

Interview with Brian Walden, 1995; In the Red, 1998; The Bill, 1999; Jonathan Creek, 1999; The Knock, 2000; Murder Rooms, 2000; Tales of Uplift and Moral Improvement, 2000; All About George, 2005; Films include: Whoops Apocalypse, 1982; Drop Dead Fred, 1990; Horse Opera, 1992; Remember Me, 1996; Bring Me the Head of Mavis Davis, 1996; Guest House Paradiso, 1999; Merlin – The Return, 1999; Kevin of the North, 2000; Jesus Christ, Super Star, 2000; Blanche-Neige, la suite, 2007. Several voices for animations; Live Stand Up includes: Comic Strip, 1982; Kevin Turvey and Bastard Squad, 1983; Rik Mayall, Ben Elton, Andy De La Tour, UK tour and Edinburgh Fringe 1983; Rik Mayall and Ben Elton, 1984-85, Australian tour 1986, 1992; Rik Mayall and Andy De La Tour, 1989-90; Rik Mayall and Adrian Edmondson, UK tours, 1993, 1995, 1997, 2001. Honours include: BAFTA, Best New Comedy, 1990; British Comedy Awards, Best New Comedy, 1992, Best Comedy Actor, 1993. Address: c/o The Brunskill Management Ltd, Suite 8A, 169 Queen's Gate, London SW7 5HE, England.

MAYBANK Stephen John, b. 23 February 1954, London, England. Professor. m. Mari Carmen. Education: Worthing High School for Boys, 1965-72; King's College, Cambridge, 1973-77; Birkbeck College, 1981-88. Appointments: Research Scientist, Marconi Command and Control Systems, Frimley, 1980-89; Research Scientist, GEC Marconi Hirst Research Centre, 1989-95; Lecturer, 1995-98, Reader, 1998-2003, Department of Computer Science, University of Reading; Professor of Computer Science, Birkbeck College, 2004-. Publications: Book, Theory of Reconstruction from Image Motion; Many scientific articles in professional journals. Honours: Scholarship, King's College, Cambridge, 1973-77; Armitage Smith Memorial Prize, Birkbeck College, 1988; EPSRC/Royal Society Industrial Research Fellow, 1993-95. Memberships: Fellow: Institute of Mathematics and its Applications; Fellow, Royal Statistical Society; Senior Member, IEEE; BMVC; Societe Mathematique de France; Higher Education Academy. E-mail: sjmaybank@dcs.bbk.ac.uk Website: www.dcs.bbk.ac.uk/~sjmaybank

MAYER Sydney L, b. 2 August 1937, Chicago, USA. Publisher. m. Charlotte W M Bouter. Education: BA, MA, University of Michigan; MPhil, Yale University. Appointments: Lecturer, University of Maryland, USA, 1966-77; Visiting Assistant Professor, University of Southern California, 1969-74; UK Director, University of Maryland, 1972-73; Managing Director, Bison Books Ltd, 1973-95; President, CEO, Brompton Books Corporation, 1982-98; President, Twin Books Corporation, 1985-98; Chairman, Twin Films Ltd, 1997-. Publications: 22 books including: The World of Southeast Asia (with Harry J Benda), 1971; The Two World Wars (with William J Koenig), 1976; Signal, 1975; World War Two, 1981; hundreds of articles. Honours: Angell Society, University of Michigan, 1989; Honorary Fellow, Oriel College, Oxford, 1993; Fulbright Advisory Board, London, 1993-. Address: 2 Shrewsbury House, 42 Cheyne Walk, London, SW3 5LN, England.

MAYER-KOENIG Wolfgang, b. 28 March 1946, Vienna, Austria. University Professor; Writer. 1 son. Education: DFA, DLitt; University Professor, Austrian Government, 1987. Appointments: Founder, Literarische Situation, Austrian University Cultural Centre, 1968; Head of Division, Corporation of Public Law, Austrian universities, 1968-70; Member, Cabinet of Chancellor Kreisky, Austria, 1971-78; Coordinator, International Governmental Meeting on Future of Science and Technology, 1972; Chairman, Austrian Meetings of Executives, 1972-77; Lecturer, universities

in France, Italy, Germany, USA, 1973-86; Coordinator, negotiations between Austria and Arab States, 1975; Member, Board of Austrian Research Conflict, 1975-82; Industrial Director, Board member, Porr Cy, 1978-90; Chairman, Munich-Brenner-Verona infrastructure consortium, 1986-90; Permanent Representative UN, 1991-92; Founder of high quality wine production in Vienna, Poetenfass Vineyards, 1994-; President, Mozart Company; Member of Board, Karl Renner Institute; Vice President, Pro Austria Nostra; Executive Director, Transportbeton KG; Member, Advisory Board, Porr International AG; Chairman, Humanitarian Aid and Recovery Programme, Indochina and earthquake victims, Italy; Editor of LOG, international journal and magazine. Publications: Visible Pavilions, 1968; Stichmarken, 1968; Psychology and Language, 1975; Language-Politics-Aggression, 1977; Goethes Journey to Italy, 1978; Possibilities of Robert Musil; Chagrin non dechiffre, 1986; Colloqui nella Stanza, 1986; The Corselet of the Mighty, 1986; Modern Grammar, 1986; Fire and Ice, 1986; Mirror Wading, 1986; A hatalom bonyolult angyala, 1989; Behind Desires Deficits, 1997; Confessions of an angry loving European, 1998; Grammatik der Seele, 2004; Verzögertes Vertrauen, 2004; The Three Dolphins, 2005; The Adoption, 2005. Honours include: Cross of Honour for Science and Arts, Austria, 1976; Ordre des Arts et des Lettres, France, 1987; Officer, Order of Merit, Egypt; Grand Cross of Merit, Austrian Province of Carinthia; Commendatore, Republic of San Marino; Order of the Eagle in Gold of the Province of Tyrol; Cross of Honour, Lower Austria; Papal Lateran Cross; Papal Cross of Leo XIII; American Medal of Honor; Gold Cross in Honour of Greek Orthodox Patriarch of Alexandria; Golden Medal, Chamber of Agriculture and Poetenfass Wines granted as "Best Viennese Wines"; International Peace Prize, 2005; Plato Award; Austrian Cross of Honour for Science and Arts First Class, 2006; Grand Cross of Honour of Styrias Government, 2006; Cross of Honour of Governments of Upper Austria; Honorary Medal of City of Vienna. Memberships include: International PEN Club; Accademia Tiberina Roma; Accademia Cosentina; Grand Master of the Order "Pour le Merite"; Grand Master of the Order Merito Navali. Address: Hernalser Guertal 41, A-1170 Vienna, Austria. E-mail: univ.prof.mayer-koenig@aon.at

MAYNE Alfred Rickard, b. 14 August 1937, Oamaru, New Zealand. Research Scientist. m. Lois, deceased, 1 son, 1 daughter. Education: CH CH, Technical College, 1950; Self-taught engineer. Appointments: Self-employed, development of part-steam, part-gaseoline engine, 30 years; Lecturer, numerous universities worldwide (China, Australia, UK, New Zealand, USA, Hong Kong, France and Slovakia). Publications: Numerous articles in professional and popular journals including: Automotive Engineering International and London Times. Memberships: SAE America; SAE Australia. Address: 191 Nerang St, Southport, Queensland 4215, Australia.

MAYNE Richard (John), b. 2 April 1926, London, England. Writer; Broadcaster. m. Jocelyn Mudie Ferguson, 2 daughters. Education: MA, PhD, Trinity College, Cambridge, 1947-53. Appointments: Rome Correspondent, New Statesman, 1953-54; Assistant, Tutor, Cambridge Institute of Education, 1954-56; Official of the European Community, Luxembourg and Brussels, 1956-63; Personal Assistant to Jean Monnet, Paris, 1963-66; Paris Correspondent, 1963-73, Co-Editor, 1990-94, Encounter; Visiting Professor, University of Chicago, 1970; Director, Federal Trust, London, 1971-73; Head, UK Offices of the European Commission, London, 1973-79; Film Critic, Sunday Telegraph, London, 1987-89, The European, 1990-98. Publications: The Community of Europe, 1962; The

Institutions of the European Community, 1968; The Recovery of Europe, 1970; The Europeans, 1972; Europe Tomorrow (editor), 1972; The New Atlantic Challenge (editor), 1975; The Memoirs of Jean Monnet (translator), 1978; Postwar: The Dawn of Today's Europe, 1983; Western Europe: A Handbook (editor), 1987; Federal Union: The Pioneers (with John Pinder), 1990; Europe: A History of its Peoples (translator), 1990; History of Europe (translator), 1993; A History of Civilizations (translator), 1994; The Language of Sailing, 2000; In Victory, Magnanimity, in Peace, Goodwill: a History of Wilton Park, 2003; Cross Channel Currents: 100 Years of the Entente Cordiale, co-editor, 2004; Nuances, 2006; Contributions to: Newspapers and magazines. Honour: Scott-Moncrieff Prize for Translation from French, 1978; Officier de L'Ordre des Arts et des Lettres, 2003. Memberships: Society of Authors; Royal Institute of International Affairs; Federal Trust for Education and Research. Address: Albany Cottage, 24 Park Village East, Regent's Park, London NW1 7PZ, England.

MAYO Edward John, b. 24 May 1931, Lyme Regis, England. Army Officer. m. (1) Jacqueline Margaret Anne Armstrong, deceased, 1 son, (2) Pamela Joyce Shimwell. Education: King's College, Taunton, 1943-49. Appointments: Commissioned, Royal Artillery, 1951; ADC to Governor of Malta, 1953-54, 2 RHA, 1955-57; ADC to Commander in Chief, BAOR, 1958-60; Adjutant 20 FD Regiment, Malaya, 1961-63; Instructor, RMAS, 1964-66; Instructor, Staff College, 1970-72; Commanded 17 Training Regiment, 1972-75; Colonel General Staff, 1979-93; Director General, Help the Aged, 1983-97; Trustee, Helpage, India, 1984-2001; Trustee, Helpage, Sri Lanka, 1986-; Trustee, Helpage, Kenya, 1984-; Trustee, Ex-Services Mental Welfare, 1996-2005; Trustee, Global Cancer, 1996-2004; Patron, Global Cancer, 2005-; Patron, The Homeless Fund, 1998-2000; Patron, Employers' Retirement Association, 2004-; Chairman of Commissioners, Jurby, Isle of Man, 2002-2004; Director, Executive Communication Consultants, 1999-. Publications: Miscellaneous articles on military matters; Articles on ageing. Honour: OBE, 1976. Memberships: Army and Navy Club; Special Forces Club; MCC; Royal Society of Arts, 1985-97; Woodroffes. Address: Ballamoar Castle, Sandygate, Jurby, Isle of Man, IM7 3AJ, United Kingdom. E-mail: mayo@manx.net

MAYOWE Varaidzo, b. 22 October 1980, Harake, Zimbabwe. Clinical Trials Co-ordinator. m. Tapiwa Marvin Mapunde. Education: BSc (Hons), Technology Management, Bradford University, England, 2003; Diploma in Clinical Research, 2005. Appointments: Operations Assistant, IBM UK, 2000-01, 2002; Clinical Trials Co-ordinator, Sheffield Children's NHS Foundation Trust, England, 2004-. Publications: 3 articles in professional journals. Honours: Bronze Award, The Pharma Clinical Researcher of the Year 2005; Listed in international biographical dictionaries. Memberships: Cochrane Airways Group and Cochrane Back Group; Institute of Clinical Research. E-mail: missmayowe@yahoo.co.uk

MAYS Sally, b. Melbourne, Australia. Pianist; Composer; Teacher. m. John Elsom, 2 sons. Education: AMusA, aged 13 years; LRSM, aged 15 years; ARCM, aged 19 years; Studied at University Conservatorium; Clarke Scholarship, Royal College of Music, London; Further studies with Marcel Ciampi in Paris and Irene Kohler in London. Appointments: Recital pianist in Australia, aged 12 years; First UK recital, Wigmore Hall, 1956; Numerous tours of Australia, New Zealand and South Africa; Appearances in Europe, San Diego, Singapore and Abu Dhabi; Piano tuition and music appreciation, Goldsmiths College, University of London, the

City Literary Institute, Marylebone Institute and Roehampton Institute in London; Examiner for the Associated Board of the Royal Schools of Music, in UK and all over the world, 1984-2005; Played with Alexandra Ensemble and leading orchestras around the world; Featured solo performer with London Ballet Orchestra on Margot Fonteyn's Farewell Tour; Premiered: Ann Carr-Boyd's Piano Concerto in Hobart, 1991; Eric Gross's Piano Concerto in Melbourne and Perth, 1983-84; and Edwin Carr's Second Piano Concerto in Wellington and Perth, 1987 and 1992; Broadcasts for Australian Broadcasting Corporation and other broadcasting stations annually; Currently, member of Trio LaVolta and Sounds Positive. Publications: Compiler and editor, four volume series of contemporary Australian Piano Music; Composed for Sounds Positive and for the stage. Honours: Sounds Australia Award for services to music; Chappell Gold Medal, Royal College of Music. Memberships: Founder Member, The Mouth of Hermes, 1968-72; Member, Sounds Positive, 1988-; Fellow, Trinity College, London. Address: 14 Homersham Road, Norbiton, Kingston-upon-Thames, Surrey KT1 3PN, England.

MAZIÈRE Marie-Noëlle, b. 25 December 1943, Paris, France. Artist; Painter. 1 son, 1 daughter. Education: Beaux-Arts de Paris; Diplômée de l'école Camondo – Arts Décoratifs de Paris; Lauréate de la Chambre d'Agriculture de Charente-Maritime. Appointments: Designer: Maison Française; Journal de la Maison; Cent Idées; Maison de Marie-Claire; Mon Jardin Ma Maison; Saveurs; Traffic; Cultural Service Journalist: Libération; Matin de Paris; Humanité Dimanche; Radio Journalist/Producer: France Culture "les Nuits Magnétiques"; Série sur Marguerite Duras; Série sur l'Histoire de la Television; Author, Producer, Journalist and Presenter: Arte Film sur G Brassens "J'ai rendez-vous avec vous", France 2; Professor, Ecole CREAPOLE, Paris; Artist: Exhibitions in France, China, England, Monaco, Switzerland, USA and Belgium, 2002-08. Address: 27, Bd de l'Ocèan, 17450 Fouras, France. E-mail: mnmaziere@aol.com

MAZZOLAI Giovanni, b. 28 December 1966, Rome, Italy. Materials Scientist. Education: Degree, Electrical Engineering, University of Perugia, Italy, 1997. Appointments: Research Contract, Electronics Department, 1997-98, Research Fellowship, 1999-2002, Research Contract (under Ministry of Education), 2005-06, Research Associate, 2007-, Tutor on General Physics in Engineering Courses, 2001-04, Assistant Professor on Biomechanics of Human Movement, 2003-, University of Perugia, Italy; Research Contract, National Institute of the Physics of Matter, Italy, 2003-05; Professor, General Physics (in Engineering Courses), telematic university (e-campus), 2008-. Publications: Advances in Science and Technology, 2000; Scripta Materialia, 2001; Defect and Diffusion Forum, 2002; Acta Materialia, 2003; Materials Science & Engineering A, 2004; Chemical Engineering Transactions, 2005; Journal of Solid State Phenomena, 2006; Journal of Alloys and Compounds, 2007; Defect and Diffusion Forum, 2008. Memberships: Materials Research Society. Address: via del Campeggio 1, Spello (PG), 06038, Italy. E-mail: giovanni.mazzolai@fisica.unipg.it

McADARAGH Raymon Michael, b. 19 February 1951, Springfield, Ohio, USA. Aerospace Engineering Psychologist; Independent Song Writer; Recording Artist. Education: BS, Christopher Newport University, Virginia, 1980; BS, Applied Science & Technology, Thomas A Edison State College, Trenton, New Jersey, 1990; Master of Aeronautical Science, Embry-Riddle Aeronautical University, Florida,

1994; PhD, University of Florida, 1999. Appointments: Air Traffic Control Tower Specialist, US Army, Grafenwohr, Germany, 1970-73; Flight Simulator Ground Instructor, US Army, Fort Rucker, Alabama, 1973-74; Laboratory Technician, Hampton Roads Sanitation District, Newport News, Virginia, 1980-81; Air Traffic Control Specialist, Williamsport, Pennsylvania, 1982-88, Gainesville, Florida, 1988-99, Engineering Research Psychologist, NASA Langley Research Center, Hampton, Virginia, 1999-, Federal Aviation Administration. Publications: Human Circadian Rhythms and the Shift Work Practices of Air Traffic Controllers, 1995; Chronopsychological Learning Effects of Rapidly-Rotating Shift Work on Day-Shift Adaptation, 1999; Toward a Concept of Operations for Aviation Weather Information Implementation in the Evolving National Airspace System, 2002. Honours: Turning Goals into Reality, NASA Office of Aerospace Technology, 2002; Certificate of Appreciation, NASA Aviation Programs Office, NASA Langley Research Center, 2002; Outstanding R&D Contributions, NASA Aviation Safety & Security Program, 2004. Memberships: Aerospace Medical Association; Aerospace Human Factors Association; Tidewater Human Factors of Ergonomic Society. Address: 40 Lodge Road, Poguoson, VA 23662, USA. E-mail: raymon.mcadaragh@nasa.gov

McALEESE Jonathan James, b. 14 December 1971, Belfast, Northern Ireland. Medical Doctor. m. Veronica, 2 sons, 1 daughter. Education: Trinity College, Cambridge University, 1990-93; Edinburgh University Medical School, 1993-96. Appointments: Registrar, Clinical Oncology, Royal Marsden, London, 2000-02; Registrar, Clinical Oncology, Belvoir Park, Belfast, 2002-05; Consultant, Clinical Oncology, Belfast City Hospital, 2005-. Publications: Hypofractionated radiotherapy for poor prognosis malignant glooma: matched pair survival analysis with MRC controls, 2003; Monotherapy for T1-2 Prostate Cancer, 2005; Randomised phase II study of GM-CSF to reduce mucositis caused by accelerated radiotherapy of laryngeal cancer, 2006; PETCT staging in lung cancer: survival advantage compared to conventional staging, 2006; An audit of re-treatment with EBRT for NSCLC, 2006; Neuroendocrine carcinoma arising in soft tissue: three case reports and literature review, 2007; The role of radiotherapy in the treatment of malignant pleural merothehoma, 2007; Failure to achieve a PSA S1 after neoadjuent UIRHa Therapy predicts for lower biochemical control rate and overall survival in localised prostate cancer treated with radiotherapy, 2007. Honours: First Class Degree, Medical Sciences Tripos, Cambridge. Memberships: Fellow, Royal College of Radiologists; Member, Royal College of Physicians, London. E-mail: jonathan.mcaleese@bch.n-i.nhs.uk

McALEESE Mary Patricia, b. 27 June 1951, Belfast, Northern Ireland. President of Ireland. m. Martin, 1976, 1 son, 2 daughters. Education: LLB, The Queen's University, Belfast, 1969-73; BL, Inn of Court of Northern Ireland, 1973-74; MA, Trinity College, Dublin, 1986; Diploma in Spanish, The Chartered Institute of Linguistics, 1991-94. Appointments: Reid Professor, Criminal Law, Criminology and Penology, Trinity College, Dublin, 1975-79, 1981-87; Current Affairs Journalist, Presenter, Irish National TV, 1979-81; Part-time Presenter, -1975; Director, Institute of Professional Legal Study, Queen's University of Belfast, 1987-97; Pro-Vice Chancellor, 1994-97; President, Ireland, 1997-. Publications: The Irish Martyrs, 1995; Reconciled Beings, 1997. Honours: Several honorary degrees; Silver Jubilee Commemoration Medal, Charles University, Prague. Memberships: European Bar Association; International Bar Association; Inns of Court, North Ireland; King's Inn, Dublin; Former Member: Institute of Advanced Study; Irish Association of Law Teachers; Society of Public Teachers of Law; British and Irish Legal Technology Association. Address: Áras an Uachtaráin, Phoenix Park, Dublin 8, Ireland. E-mail: webmaster@president.ie

McARTHUR Christine Louise, b. 14 March 1953, Lennox Town, Scotland. Artist. m. (1) Alistair Lyon, divorced, 2 daughters, (2) Roger Billcliffe. Education: Glasgow School of Art, 1971-76. Career: Artist full-time, 1980-; Part-time Lecturer, Glasgow School of Art and Glasgow University Extra Mural Department, 1980-96. Exhibitions: Peter Potter Gallery, Haddington, 1984; Sue Rankin Gallery, London, 1986, 1990; Fine Art Society Glasgow, 1990; Portland Gallery, London, 1992; Roger Billcliffe Fine Art, Glasgow, 1992, 1994, 1996, 1998, 2000, 2002 (2); Ancrum Gallery, Roxburgh, 1993; Open Eye Gallery, Edinburgh, 1993, 1996; Thackeray Gallery, London, 1995; John Martin of London, Summer Show, 1996, 1998; Courtyard Gallery, Crail, 1997; John Martin of London, 1999, 2001, 2003; Gertsev Gallery, Moscow, 2004; Gertsev Gallery, Atlanta, USA, 2004; Lemon Street Gallery, Truro, 2005; John Martin, London, 2006; Roger Bukliffe Gallery, 2007; Works in collections: Lord Irvine of Lairg; Scottish Arts Council; Arthur Anderson; Scottish Nuclear PLC; University of Strathclyde; Amerada Hess Corporation; Craig Capital Organisation; Lillie Art Gallery, Milngavie; Argyll Group PLC; Clydesdale Bank PLC; MacFarlane Group (Clansman) PLC; Royal Bank of Scotland; Export and Import Bank of Japan; John Lewis Partnership (Glasgow, Nottingham, Edinburgh and Peter Jones, London); Gertsev Gallery, Moscow. Honours: Arts Council Award, Glasgow Society of Women Artist's Trust Fund Award, Lauder Award; N S McFarlane Award, RGI; Alexander Graham Munro Prize, RSW; Scottish Arts Council Travel Bursary; Commissions: 4 large murals for the John Lewis Glasgow Store, 1999; Murals for extension to John Lewis Peter Jones Store, Sloane Square, London, 2002. Memberships: Honorary Secretary, 2000-02, Royal Glasgow Institute of Fine Arts; Royal Scottish Society of Painters in Watercolour. Address: Glen Rowan, Shore Road, Cove, Argyll & Bute, G84 0NU, Scotland. E-mail: clm@rbfa.demon.co.uk

McCALL Carolyn Julia, b. 13 September 1961, Bangalore, India. Chief Executive. m. Peter Framley, 2 sons, 1 daughter. Education: BA, PGCE (Distinction), MA (Distinction); Advanced Management Programme, Wharton, 2000. Appointments: Analyst, Costain Group plc, 1984-86; Planner/ Sales Executive/Group Head, 1986-92; Advertisement Manager/Deputy Advertisement Director, 1992-95; Commercial Director, 1995-2000, Guardian Newspapers Limited; Non-Executive, New Look plc, 1999-2005; CEO, Guardian News & Media Ltd, 2000-06; Chair, Opportunity Now, 2005-; Non-Executive, Tesco plc, 2005-08; Group CEO, Guardian Media Group, 2006-. Address: Guardian Media Group, 60 Farringdon Road, London EC1R 3GA, England.

McCALL Davina, b. 16 October 1967, London, England. TV Presenter. m. Mathew Robinson, 1 son, 2 daughters. Education: St Catherine's, Bramley; Godolphin & Latymer, London. Appointments: God's Gift, MTV; Don't Try This At Home, 4 series; The Brits, 2000, 2003; Big Brother, 7 series, 2000-06; Sam's Game, 2001; Popstars – The Rivals, 2002; Reborn in the USA, 2003; Love on a Saturday Night, 2004; Comic Relief, 2004, 2007; The BAFTA Television Awards, ITV, 2004, 2006; He's Having a Baby, 2005; Davina, BBC, 2006; Sport Relief, 2006; Let's Talk Sex, 2007. Address: c/ o John Noel Management, 2nd Floor, 10A Belmont Street, London NW1 8HH, England.

McCANNY John Vincent, b. 25 June 1952, Ballymoney, Co. Antrim, Northern Ireland. m. Mary (Maureen) Bernadette Mellon, 1 son, 1 daughter. Education: BSc, Physics, Manchester, 1973, Chartered Engineer and Physicist; PhD, Physics, Ulster, 1978; DSc, Electronic Engineering, Queen's University Belfast, 1998. Appointments: Lecturer in Physics, University of Ulster, Coleraine, 1977-79; Higher Scientific Officer, 1979-81, Senior Scientific Officer, 1981-83, Principal Scientific Officer, 1983-84, RSRE (now Qinetiq), Malvern; EPSRC IT Research Lecturer, 1984-87; Director, Institute of Advanced Microelectronics in Ireland (involving Queen's University Belfast, Trinity College Dublin, National Microelectronics Research Centre at University College Cork), 1989-92; Reader, 1984-87, Professor of Microelectronics Engineering, 1988-, Director, Institute of Electronics, Communications and Information Technology, 2000-, Queen's University Belfast; Head of School of Electronics, Electrical Engineering and Computer Science, Queen's University, Belfast, 2005-. Publications: 320 research papers in learned journals and major international conferences; 5 research books; 25 patents; Associate Editor, Journal of VLSI Signal Processing, 1988-; Associate Editor, IEEE Transactions. Circuits, Systems and Devices; Analog and Digital Signal Processing, 2000-05. Honours: UK Royal Academy of Engineering Silver Medal, 1996; IEEE (USA) Millennium Medal, 2000; CBE, 2002; Royal Dublin Society/Irish Times Boyle Medal, 2003; British Computer Society (Belfast Branch) IT Professional of the Year, 2004; IET Faraday Medal, 2006. Memberships: Fellow: Institution of Electrical Engineers, Institute of Physics, Royal Academy of Engineering, Institute of Electrical and Electronic Engineers, USA, Royal Society of London, Irish Academy of Engineering, Engineers Ireland; Member, Royal Irish Academy; European Academy of Sciences. Address: Institute of Electronics, Communications and Information Technology, Queen's University Belfast, Northern Ireland Science Park, Queen's Road, Queen's Island, Belfast BT3 9DT, Northern Ireland.

McCARTER Keith Ian, b. 15 March 1936, Scotland. Sculptor. m. Brenda, 1 son, 1 daughter. Education: The Royal High School of Edinburgh, 1948-54; Edinburgh College of Art, 1956-60. Appointments: Designer, Steuben Glass, New York, USA, 1961-63; Self-employed Sculptor, 1964-; Over 40 public-sited works worldwide. Publications: Many articles published relative to work. Honours: Otto Beit Medal, Royal Society of British Sculptors; Fellow, Royal Society of Arts; DA (Edin). Memberships: The Farmers Club; Melrose RFC. Address: 10 Coopersknowe Crescent, Galashiels, TD1 2DS, Scotland.

McCARTHY Cormac, (Charles McCarthy Jr), b. 20 July 1933, Providence, Rhode Island, USA. Author; Dramatist. m. Lee Holleman, 1961, divorced 1 child, (2) Anne deLisle, 1967, divorced, (3) Jennifer Winkley, 2006, 1 son. Publications: Novels: The Orchard Keeper, 1965; Outer Dark, 1968; Child of God, 1974; Suttree, 1979; Blood Meridian, or The Evening Redness in the West, 1985; All the Pretty Horses, 1992; The Crossing, 1994; Cities of the Plain, 1998; No Country for Old Men, 2005; The Road, 2006; The Sunset Limited, 2006. Plays: The Gardner's Son, 1977; The Stonemason, 1994. Honours: Ingram Merrill Foundation Grant, 1960; William Faulkner Foundation Award, 1965; American Academy of Arts and Letters Travelling Fellowship, 1965-66; Rockefeller Foundation Grant, 1966; Guggenheim Fellowship, 1976; John D and Catharine T MacArthur Foundation Fellowship, 1981; National Book Award, 1992; National Book Critics

Circle Award, 1993; Pulitzer Prize, 2007; James Tait Black Memorial Prize, 2007. Address: 1011 N Mesa Street, El Paso, TX 79902, USA.

McCARTNEY (James) Paul (Sir), b. 18 June 1942, Liverpool, England. Singer; Songwriter; Musician. m. (1) Linda Eastman, 12 March 1969, deceased 1998, 1 son, 2 daughters, 1 stepdaughter, (2) Heather Mills, 2002-2006, divorced, 1 daughter. Education: Self-taught in music. Appointments: Member, The Quarrymen, 1957-59; The Beatles, 1960-70; Founder, Apple Corporation Ltd; Founder, MPL Group of Companies; Founder, Wings, 1970-81; Solo Artiste, 1970-; International tours, concerts, TV, radio, films; Founder, Liverpool Institute of Performing Arts, 1995. Creative Works: Numerous albums with The Beatles. Solo Albums: McCartney, 1970; Ram, 1971; McCartney II, 1980; Tug of War, 1982; Pipes of Peace, 1983; Give My Regards to Broad Street, 1984; Press to Play, 1986; All the Best, 1987; Flowers in the Dirt, 1989; Tripping the Light Fantastic, 1990; Unplugged, 1991; Choba b CCCP, 1991; Paul McCartney's Liverpool Oratorio, 1991; Off the Ground, 1993; Paul is Live, 1993; Flaming Pie, 1997; Standing Stone, symphonic work, 1997; A Garland for Linda, composition with 8 other composers for a capella choir, 2000; Paul McCartney: The Music and Animation Collection, DVD, 2004; The McCartney Years, DVD, 2007. Publications: Paintings, 2000; The Beatles Anthology (with George Harrison and Ringo Starr), 2000; Sun Prints (with Linda McCartney), 2001; Many Years From Now, autobiography, 2001; Blackbird Singing: Poems and Lyrics 1965-1999, 2001. Honours: MBE, 1965; Numerous Grammy Awards; 3 Ivor Novello Awards; Freeman, City of Liverpool, 1984; Doctorate, University of Sussex, 1988; Guinness Book of Records Award, 1979; Q Merit Award, 1990; Knighted, 1997; Fellowship, British Academy of Composers and Songwriters, 2000. Address: c/o MPL Communications, 1 Soho Square, London W1V 6BQ, England.

McCARTNEY Stella, b. 13 September 1971. Fashion Designer. m. Alasdhair Willis, 1 son, 1 daughter. Education: Central St Martins College of Art and Design. Appointments: Work with Christian Lacroix at age 15 and later with Betty Jackson; Work experience in Fashion Department, Vogue magazine; After graduation, set up own design company in London; Chief Designer for Chloe, Paris; Designed collection for Gucci, 2001; Established own fashion house, in partnership with Gucci Group, 2001-; Launched skincare line CARE, 2007. VH/1 Vogue Fashion and Music Designer of the Year, 2000; Woman of Courage Award, 2003; Designed costumes for film, Sky Captain and the World of Tomorrow, 2004. Address: Stella McCartney London, 30 Bruton Street, London, W1J 6LG, England. Website: www.stellamccartney.com

McCLURE Gillian Mary, b. 29 October 1948, Bradford, England. Author; Illustrator. 3 sons. Education: BA, Combined Honours in French, English and History of Art, Bristol University; Teaching Diploma, Moray House. Publications: 19 children's books, 1974-06. Honours: Shortlisted for Smarties Award and Highly Commended in Kate Greenaway Award, 1985; US Parents Guide to Children's Media Award for Outstanding Achievement in Children's Books. Membership: CWIG Society of Authors, committee member, 1989-; PLR Advisory Committee, 1992; Royal Literary Fund Writing Fellow, 2005-08. Address: 9 Trafalgar Street, Cambridge CB4 1ET, England.

McCOLGAN Elizabeth, b. 24 May 1964, Dundee, Scotland. Athlete. m. Peter McColgan, 3 sons, 1 daughter. Education: Coached by Grete Waitz. Appointments: Gold

Medal Commonwealth Games 10,000 m, 1986, 1990; Silver Medal, Olympic Games 10,000m, 1988; Silver Medal, World Indoor Championships 3,000m, 1989; Bronze Medal, Commonwealth Games, 3,000m, 1990; Gold Medal, World Championships 10,000m, 1991; Gold Medal, World Half Marathon Championships, 1992; First in New York City Marathon, 1991; First in Tokyo Marathon, 1992; Third in London Marathon, 1993; Fifth in 1995; First in 1996; Second in 1997, 1998; Retired, 2001; Returned to competitive athletics with victory in Scottish Cross Country Championships, 2004; Runs own fitness centre and coaches young athletes in Dundee. Honours: MBE. Address: c/o Marquee UK, 6 George Street, Nottingham NG1 3BE, England.

McCONAUGHEY Matthew, b. 4 November 1969, Ulvade, Texas, USA. Actor. Education: University of Texas, Austin. Appointments: Film appearances include: Dazed and Confused; The Return of the Texas Chainsaw Massacre; Boys on the Side; My Boyfriend's Back, 1993; Angels in the Outfield, 1994; Scorpion Spring; Submission, 1995; Glory Daze; Lone Star; A Time to Kill, 1996; Larger Than Life, 1997; Amistad; Contact; Making Sandwiches; Last Flight of the Raven; Newton Boys; South Beach; EdTV, 1999; U-571, 2000; The Wedding Planner, 2001; Reign of Fire, 2001; Frailty, 2001; 13 Conversations About One Thing, 2001; Tiptoes, 2003; How to Lose a Guy in Ten Days, 2003; Sahara, 2005; Two for the Money, 2005; Failure to Launch, 2006; We Are Marshall, 2006; Surfer Dude, 2008; Fool's Gold, 2008. Address: c/o J K Livin, POB 596, Zachary, LA 70791, USA.

McCONNELL Charles Stephen, b. 20 June 1951, Yorkshire, England. Chief Executive. m. Natasha Valentinovna, 1 son, 1 daughter. Education: BA Honours, Politics, MPhil, Community Development. Appointments: European and Public Affairs Director, Community Development Foundation, London, 1989-93; Chief Executive, Scottish Community Education Council, 1993-99; Director, Secretary General, International Association for Community Development, 1998-2002; Chief Executive, Community Learning Scotland, 1999-2002; Chairman, UK National Training Organisation for Community Learning and Development, 1999-2002; Head of Community Education and Community Development, Scottish Executive, 2002-03; Chief Executive, Carnegie UK, 2003-07. Publications: Author, editor, co-editor, over 15 books; Many other articles, research and conference papers. Membership: Fellow, Royal Society of Arts. E-mail: charlie@carnegieuk.org

McCORMICK John Owen, b. 20 September 1918, Thief River Falls, Minnesota, USA. Professor of Comparative Literature Emeritus; Writer. m. Mairi MacInnes, 4 February 1954, 3 sons, 1 daughter. Education: BA, 1941, MA, 1947, University of Minnesota; PhD, Harvard University, 1951. Appointments: Senior Tutor and Teaching Assistant, Harvard University, 1946-51; Lecturer, Salzburg Seminar in American Studies, Austria, 1951-52; Professor of American Studies, Free University of Berlin, 1952-53, 1954-59; Professor of Comparative Literature, 1959-, now Emeritus, Rutgers University, New Brunswick, New Jersey. Publications: Catastrophe and Imagination, 1957, 1998; Versions of Censorship (with Mairi MacInnes), 1962; The Complete Aficionado, 1967, 2nd edition, 1998; The Middle Distance: A Comparative History of American Imaginative Literature, 1919-1932, 1971; Fiction as Knowledge: The Modern Post-Romantic Novel, 1975, 1998; George Santayana: A Biography, 1987, 2001; Sallies of the Mind: Essays of Francis Fergusson (editor with G Core), 1997; Seagoing: Memoir, 2000; Another Music, 2008. Contributions to: Numerous

magazines, journals and reviews. Honours: Longview Award for Non-Fiction, 1960; Guggenheim Fellowships, 1964-65, 1980-81; National Endowments for the Humanities Senior Fellow, 1983-84; American Academy and Institute of Arts and Letters Prize, 1988. Address: 31 Huntington Road, York YO31 8RL, England.

McCOY Anthony Peter, b. 5 May 1974, Ballymena, Northern Ireland. National Hunt Jockey. Education: St Ollans School, Randalstown, Northern Ireland. Career: 12 times record breaking Champion National Hunt Jockey. Publications: Autobiography: McCoy, 2002; DVD Documentary "The Real McCoy", 2002. Honours: Honorary Doctorate for services to sport, Queens University, Belfast, 2002; MBE, 2003; Winner, Variety Club of Great Britain Award, 2004. Address: Lodge Down, Lambourn Woodlands, Hungerford, Berks, RG17 7BJ, England. E-mail: ap.mccoy@talk21.com

McCREA Anna Maria, b. 1 February 1959, Lodz, Poland. Civil Engineer. m. Peter Whitehouse. Education: MEng, Civil Engineering, Lodz Institute of Technology, Poland, 1977-82; MSc, Structures, 1985-87, PhD, Robotics and Automation in Construction, 1993-99, City University, London; Programme of IT Courses, Learning Tree International, London, 1998-99; Diploma in Management Studies, South Bank University, 1998-99. Appointments: Assistant Civil Engineer, Construction and Repair Department of District Administration of Penitentiaries, Lodz, Poland, 1983-84; Assistant Civil and Structural Engineer, Alan Baxter and Associates, London, 1987-89; Structural Engineer, Aukett Europe, 1989-92; Senior Lecturer, South Bank University, 1992-98; Co-ordinator of EU-funded Construction Project Futurehome for Communication, Dissemination and Commercial Exploitation, City University, 1998-2000; Product Development Manager, Minglo.com, 2000; Online Product and Content Developer, Construction Plus – Emap Construction Network, 2000-2002; Contract-based Expert for Assessment of Technical Projects submitted for EU funding, European Commission, 2000-; Visiting Lecturer in IT and Structural Form and Function, University College London, 2000; Research and Management Senior Consultant, Davis Langdon Management Consulting, 2002-07; Life Cycle Costing & Sustainability Senior Consultant, Thinkwell Consulting, 2007-. Publication: 3 publications in refereed journals and 9 at refereed conferences. Honours: MEng; MSc; PhD. Memberships: MASCE; MICE. Address: 340 King's Road, London SW3 5UR, England. E-mail: anna.mccrea@bohemians.biz

McCRYSTAL Cahal, (Cal McCrystal), b. 20 December 1935, Belfast, Northern Ireland. Journalist; Broadcaster; Author. m. Stella Doyle, 15 October 1958, 3 sons. Education: St Mary's College, Dundalk; St Malachy's College, Belfast. Appointments: Reporter, Northern Herald; Labour Correspondent, Belfast Telegraph; Crime Reporter, Chief Reporter, Foreign Correspondent, New York Bureau Chief, News Editor, Foreign Features Editor, Sunday Times, London; Senior Writer, Independent-on-Sunday; Senior Writer, The Observer. Publications: Watergate: The Full Inside Story (co-author), 1973; Reflections on A Quiet Rebel, 1997. Contributions to: Vanity Fair, British Magazines, and British Journalism Review; Independent-on-Sunday and Financial Times (book reviews); Poetry, Ireland Review. Honours: Various journalism awards; Belfast Arts Council Literary Award, 1998; Broadcasts for BBC, Radio Eireann, ABC TV and CBC. Membership: Editorial Board, British Journalism Review. Address: c/o 37 Goldhawk Road, London W12 8QQ, England.

McCULLOCH Nigel Simeon (The Right Reverend Bishop of Manchester), b. 17 January 1942, Anglican Bishop. m. Celia Hume, 2 daughters. Education: Selwyn College, Cambridge; Cuddesdon College, Oxford. Appointments: Assistant Curate, Ellesmere Port, 1966-70; Chaplain and Director of Studies in Theology, Christ's College, Cambridge, 1970-73; Diocesan Missioner, Norwich, 1973-78; Rector of St Thomas's, Salisbury, 1978-86; Archdeacon of Sarum, 1979-86; Bishop of Taunton, 1986-92; Bishop of Wakefield, 1992-2003; Bishop of Manchester, 2003-. Member of the House of Lords, 1997-; Lord High Almoner to H.M. The Queen, 1997-. Publications: A Gospel to Proclaim; Barriers to Belief; Credo Columnist for the Times, 1996-2000. Honour: MA. Memberships: Chairman, Sandford St Martin Religious Broadcasters Awards; National Chaplain, The Royal British Legion; National Chaplain, The Royal School of Church Music. Address: Bishop's Lodge, Wakefield WF2 6JL, England. E-mail: bishop@wakefield.anglican.org

McCULLOUGH Colleen, b. 1 June 1937, Wellington, New South Wales, Australia. Writer. m. Ric Robinson, 1984. Education: Holy Cross College, Woollahra, Sydney University; Institute of Child Health, London University. Appointments: Neurophysiologist, Sydney, London and Yale University Medical School, New Haven, Connecticut, USA, 1967-77; Relocated to Norfolk Island, South Pacific, 1980. Publications: Tim, 1974; The Thorn Birds, 1977; An Indecent Obsession, 1981; Cooking with Colleen McCullough and Jean Easthope, 1982; A Creed for the Third Millennium, 1985; The Ladies of Missalonghi, 1987; The First Man in Rome, 1990; The Grass Crown, 1991; Fortune's Favorites, 1993; Caesar's Women, 1996; Caesar, 1997; The Song of Troy, 1998; Roden Cutler, V.C. (biography), 1998; Morgan's Run, 2000; The October Horse, 2002; The Touch, 2003; Angel Puss, 2004; On, Off, 2006; Anthony and Cleopatra, 2007. Honour: Doctor of Letters (honoris causa), Macquarie University, Sydney, 1993. Address: "Out Yenna", Norfolk Island, Oceania (via Australia).

McDAID Perry, (Phoenix Martin, Pam Louis, Blythe Stitt, Naomi de Plume), b. 10 October 1959, Derry City, Ireland. Writer; Poet. Education: BTEC, Business Studies, 1984; BA (Hons), Social Sciences; Certificate in Creative Writing, 2005. Branch Secretary, NICSA, 1980; Civil Servant; Regional Administrative Officer, Industrial Development Board; Manager, Foyle Chess Club; Accounting Officer, Author Operations Manual for Civil Service Pensions; Quizmaster; Retired due to ill health; Managing Editor, Narwhal Publishing. Publications: Over 600 different poems in 800 listings worldwide; Short Stories: Earlyworks, Banksnotes, Professional Anthologies. Honours: Honorary Appointment, The Research Board of Advisors, ABI, 2006; Numerous editor's choice awards; Distinguished Member, International Society of Poets. Memberships: Lifetime member, Metverse, ISP; PCOF; Salopean Society. Address: 6 Rathmore Road, Rathmore Estate, Derry, BT48 9BS, Northern Ireland.

McDERMOTT Patrick Anthony, b. 8 September 1941, Ripley, Surrey, England. Her Majesty's Diplomatic Service, Retired. m. (1) 2 sons, (2) Christa Herminghaus, 2 sons. Education: Clapham College, London. Appointments: Foreign and Commonwealth Office, London, 1961-63; Mexico City, 1963-66; New York, 1966-71; Belgrade, 1971-73; Foreign and Commonwealth Office, London, 1973; Bonn, 1973-76; Paris, 1976-79; Foreign and Commonwealth Office, London, 1979-83; HM Consul-General and Economic and Financial Adviser to the British Military Government, West Berlin, 1984-88; Foreign and Commonwealth Office, London, 1988-89; Counsellor, Paris, 1990-95; Foreign and Commonwealth Office, London, 1996-97; HM Consul General, Moscow and to the Republic of Moldovia, 1998-2001; Retired, 2001-; Management Consultant, Diplomatic Consulting, 2001-02; Deputy Burser, Ampleforth College, 2002-; Board of Trustees, Helmsley Walled Garden, 2005-. Honours: Member, Royal Victorian Order, 1972; Freeman of the City of London, 1986. Address: Linkfoot House, 10 Acres Close, Helmsley, York YO62 5DS, England.

McDONALD Catherine Donna, b. 20 December 1942, Vancouver, British Columbia, Canada. Writer; Arts Administrator. m. Robert Francis McDonald, 28 August 1965. Education: BA, 1964. Publications: Illustrated News: Juliana Horatia Ewing's Canadian Pictures 1867-1869; The Odyssey of the Philip Jones Brass Ensemble; Lord Strathcona; A Biography of Donald Alexander Smith; Milkmaids and Maharajas: A History of 1 Palace Street. Contributions to: Periodicals and journals. Address: 10 Chelwood Gardens, Richmond, Surrey TW9 4JQ, England.

McDONALD Forrest, b. 7 January 1927, Orange, Texas, USA. Distinguished University Research Professor; Historian; Writer. m. (1) 3 sons, 2 daughters, (2) Ellen Shapiro, 1 August 1963. Education: BA, MA, 1949, PhD, 1955, University of Texas. Appointments: Executive Secretary, American History Research Centre, Madison, Wisconsin, 1953-58; Associate Professor, 1959-63, Professor of History, 1963-67, Brown University; Professor, Wayne State University, 1967-76; Professor, 1976-87, Distinguished University Research Professor, 1987-, University of Alabama, Tuscaloosa; Presidential Appointee, Board of Foreign Scholarships, Washington, DC, 1985-87; Advisor, Centre of Judicial Studies, Cumberland, Virginia, 1985-92; James Pinckney Harrison Professor, College of William and Mary, 1986-87; Jefferson Lecturer, National Endowment for the Humanities, 1987. Publications: We the People: The Economic Origins of the Constitution, 1958; Insull, 1962; E Pluribus Unum: The Formation of the American Republic, 1965; The Presidency of George Washington, 1974; The Phaeton Ride, 1974; The Presidency of Thomas Jefferson, 1976; Alexander Hamilton: A Biography, 1979; Novus Ordo Seclorum, 1985; Requiem, 1988; The American Presidency: An Intellectual History, 1994; States' Rights and the Union 1776-1876, 2000; Recovering the Past: A Historian's Memoir, 2004. Contributions to: Professional journals. Honours: Guggenheim Fellowship, 1962-63; George Washington Medal, Freedom's Foundation, 1980; Frances Tavern Book Award, 1980; Best Book Award, American Revolution Round Table, 1986; Richard M Weaver Award, Ingersoll Foundation, 1990; First Salvatori Award, Intercollegiate Studies Institute, 1992; Salvatori Book Award, Intercollegiate Studies Institute, 1994; Mount Vernon Society Choice, One of the Ten Great Books on George Washington, 1998. Memberships: American Antiquarian Society; Philadelphia Society; The Historical Society. Address: PO Box 155, Coker, AL 35452, USA.

McDONALD Paul Ian, b. 20 December 1946, Stockport, England. Managing Director. Education: BA (Hons), Geography, University College London, 1965-68; PhD, Civil Engineering, University of Leeds, 1968-71; Cert Ed, New College Oxford, 1971-72. Appointments: Research Fellow, University of Aston, 1975-78; Head of Information Services, National Oil Company of Saudi Arabia, 1978-83; Senior Oil Analyst, Shearson Lehman Brothers, 1983-86; Managing Director, Pearl Oil Ltd, Hong Kong, 1986-2003; Managing Director, Pearl Oil, Great Britain. Publications: Various articles in Nature; New Scientist; Times Literary Supplement;

Economist Foreign Report; International Affairs; Japanese Institute of Middle Eastern Economies Review; Zeitschrift für Internationale Politik; Books on Middle East and North Africa; Oil Trading in Asia; Deregulation in Japan; Chinese Oil Industry; Oil and Gas in Iraq; The Oil Industry in the USSR; Agriculture in Thailand. Honour: University research exhibited at the Science Museum, London. Memberships: Institute of Petroleum; Oxford Union; Sri Lanka Club, Hong Kong. Address: Springfields, Hawker's Lane, Hambridge, Langport, Somerset TA10 0AU, England.

McDONALD Sir Trevor, b. 16 August 1939, Trinidad. Broadcasting Journalist. m. 2 sons, 1 daughter. Appointments: Worked on newspapers, radio and TV, Trinidad, 1960-69; Producer, BBC Caribbean Service and World Service, London, 1969-73; Reporter, Independent TV News, 1973-78; Sports Correspondent, 1978-80; Diplomatic Correspondent, 1980-87; Newscaster, 1982-87; Diplomatic Editor, Channel 4 News, 1987-89; Newscaster, News at 5.40, 1989-90; News at Ten, 1990-99; ITV Evening News, 1999-2000; ITV News at Ten, 2001-04, News at 10.30, 2004-2005; Chairman, Better English Campaign, 1995-97; Nuffield Language Inquiry, 1998-2000; Governor, English-Speaking Union of the Commonwealth, 2000; President, European Year of Languages, 2000. Publications: Clive Lloyd: a biography, 1985; Vivian Richard's biography, 1987; Queen and Commonwealth, 1989; Fortunate Circumstances, 1993; Favourite Poems, 1997; World of Poems, 1999. Honours: Hon DLitt, Nottingham, 1997; Dr hc, Open University, 1997; Honorary Fellow, Liverpool John Moores University, 1998; Newscaster of the Year, TV and Radio Industries Club, 1993, 1997, 1999; Gold Medal, Royal Television Society, 1998; Richard Dimbleby Award for Outstanding Contribution to Television, BAFTA, 1999; OBE; Knighted, 1999. Royal Television Society Lifetime Achievement Award, 2005. Address: c/o ITN, 200 Gray's Inn Road, London, WC1 8XZ, England.

McDONALD SMITH Paul, b. 26 November 1956, Melbourne, Australia. Artist. Education: HSC, Scotch College Melbourne, 1975; Fine Art (Painting), RMIT, 1976-78; Private Study, 1973-1979; Numerous European Study Tours; Camberwell Travel Scholarship, 1986; Studies and painted in England, Italy, France, Holland, Belgium, Denmark, Austria and Greece. Appointments: Artist, Painter, Tutor, Judge, Curator; Tutorial Appointments, 1977-; Many guest lecture appointments in Victoria and interstate; Self Employed Artist, 1978-; Various Community Arts Appointments, 1981-; Established and tutored a wide range of painting classes in Eastern, Western and Northern suburbs of Melbourne, oil, water colour, media in plein-air and studio landscape painting, portrait, still-life and life subjects; Numerous Judging Appointments, 1982-; Convenor, Cato Gallery Committee, 1992-97; Editor, VAS Publications, 1997-2003; President, Victorian Artists Society, 1998-2003; Chairman, Camberwell Judging Panel, 2002; Exhibitions include: Major solo exhibitions in Melbourne: Mansourah Galleries, 1980; Ash Tree Galleries, 1980, 1983; Gallery 21, Cato Gallery, 1990, 1993; Numerous commissions: Portrait, Landscape, Flowers; Works in private, corporate, municipal and public collections in Australia and private collections in UK, USA, Japan, the Philippines, New Guinea. Publications: Oils, The Medium of The Masters, 1989; Biographical Catalogues include: Alan Moore, 1994; Ludmilla Meilerts, 1994; Euguene Fromentin, 1996; VAS President's Message, 1998-; Numerous editorial contributions to VAS Newsletter, magazines and professional journals. Honours: Numerous including: VAS Signatory Award, 1991; Norwich Landscape Award, 1992; Heidelberg Prize, 1994; RSPCA National Australia Bank Award, 1995;

Outstanding Achievement Award, 1998; Camberwell Club Award, 1998; Norman Kaye Memorial Medallion, 1998 and 1999; Bright '99; Mt Waverley, 1999; Mildura, 1999; Major Award Royal Overseas League, Australia, 2000; Cardinia Shire Award, 2001, VAS Artist of the Year, 2001; Alexandra Award, 2002; Finalist, Victorian Artist of the Year Exhibition, 1990-94, 1996-2006 (no exhibition, 1995); Order of Australia Medal, 2005; Emerald, 2005; Warragul, 2005; Bright, 2006; Balranald Outback Art Award, 2006; Listed in Who's Who publications and international biographical directories. Memberships: FVAS; FRSA; Bottle Brush Club; Twenty Melbourne Painters' Society; RAS, NSW; MOIF; FIBA; LFABI; DDG; Honorary Member, Boxhill Art Group Inc; Hobson's Bay Art Society Inc; Order of Australia Association; President, Twenty Melbourne Painters Society Inc, 2003-; Chairman, AME Bale Travelling Scholarship Judging/ Advisory Panel, 2003-; Chairman, VAS Distinguished Awards Committee, 2004-; President, Honorary Member, Gleneira Cheltenham Art Group Inc, 2003-04. Address: 3 Perry Court, Kew, Victoria 3101, Australia. E-mail: paulmcdonaldsmith@ozemail.com.au

McDORMAND Frances, b. 23 June 1957, Illinois, USA. Actress. m. Joel Coen 1984, 1 son. Education: Yale University, School of Drama. Appointments: Stage Appearances include: Awake and Sing, 1984; Painting Churches, 1984; The Three Sisters, 1985; All My Sons, 1986; A Streetcar Named Desire, 1988; Moon for the Misbegotten, 1992; Sisters Rosenweig, 1993; The Swan, 1993; Films include: Blood Simple, 1984; Raising Arizona, 1987; Mississippi Burning, 1988; Chattaboochee, 1990; Darkman, 1990; Miller's Crossing, 1990; Hidden Agenda, 1990; The Butcher's Wife, 1991; Passed Away, 1992; Short Cuts, 1993; Beyond Rangoon, 1995; Fargo, 1996; Paradise Road, 1997; Johnny Skidmarks, 1997; Madeline, 1998; Talk of Angels, 1998; Wonder Boys, 1999; Almost Famous, 2000; The Man Who Wasn't There, 2001; Upheaval, 2001; Laurel Canyon, 2002; City By the Sea, 2003; Something's Gotta Give, 2003; Last Night, 2004; North Country, 2005; Æon Flux, 2005; Friends with Money, 2006; Miss Pettigrew Lives for a Day, 2008. Has appeared in several TV series. Honours: Screen Actors' Guild Award, 1996; London Film Critics' Circle Award, 1996; Independent Spirit Award, 1996; American Comedy Award, 1997; LA Film Critics Award, 2000. Address: c/o William Morris Agency, 1325 Avenue of the Americas, New York, NY 10019, USA.

McDOUGALL Bonnie Suzanne, b. 12 March 1941, Sydney, Australia. Professor of Chinese. m. H Anders Hansson, 1 son. Education: BA honours, 1965, MA honours, University Medal, 1967, PhD, 1970, University of Sydney. Appointments: Lecturer in Oriental Studies, University of Sydney, 1972-76; Research Fellow, East Asian Research Center, Harvard University, 1976-79; Associate in East Asian Studies, John King Fairbank Center, Harvard University, 1979-80; Visiting Lecturer on Chinese, Harvard University, 1977-78; Editor and Translator, Foreign Languages Press, Peking, 1980-83; Teacher of English, College of Foreign Affairs, Peking, 1984-86; Senior Lecturer in Chinese, University of Oslo, 1986-87; Professor of Modern Chinese, University of Oslo, 1987-90; Professor of Chinese, University of Edinburgh, 1990-. Publications: Numerous books and articles on Chinese Literature. Memberships: Association for Asian Studies; European Association of Chinese Studies; British Association of Chinese Studies; Universities' China Committee in London; Scots Australian Council. Address: Scottish Centre for Chinese Studies, School of Asian Studies, University of Edinburgh, 8 Buccleuch Place, Edinburgh EH8 9LW, Scotland.

McDOWALL David Buchanan, b. 14 April 1945, London, England. Writer. m. Elizabeth Mary Risk Laird, 19 April 1975, 2 sons. Education: MA, 1966-69, M.Litt, 1970-72, St John's College, Oxford. Appointments: Subaltern, Royal Artillery, UK and Hong Kong, 1963-70; British Council, Bombay, Baghdad and London Headquarters, 1972-77; Contributions Officer, United Nations Relief and Works Agency for Palestine Refugees in the Near East, 1977-79; Consultant to voluntary agencies re development in Middle East, 1979-84; Full-time Writer, 1984-. Publications: Lebanon: A Conflict of Minorities, 1984 Palestine and Israel: The Uprising and Beyond, 1989; An Illustrated History of Britain, 1989; Europe and the Arabs: Discord or Symbiosis?, 1992; Britain in Close Up, 1993, 1998; The Palestinians: The Road to Nationhood, 1994; A Modern History of the Kurds, 1996; Richmond Park: The Walker's Historical Guide, 1996; Hampstead Heath: The Walker's Guide (co-author Deborah Wolton), 1998; The Kurds of Syria, 1998; The Thames from Hampton to Richmond Bridge: The Walkers Guide, 2002; The Thames From Richmond to Putney Bridge: The Walker's Guide, 2005. Contributions to: World Directory of Minorities, Middle East section, 1997. Honour: The Other Award. Address: 31 Cambrian Road, Richmond, Surrey TW10 6JQ, England.

McDOWELL Malcolm, b. 13 June 1943, Leeds, England. Actor. m. (1) Mary Steenburgen, 1980, 1 son, 1 daughter, (2) Kelley Kuhr, 1991, 1 child. Appointments: Began career with Royal Shakespeare Company, Stratford, 1965-66; Early TV appearances in such series as Dixon of Dock Green; Z Cars; Stage Appearances: RSC, Stratford, 1965-66; Entertaining Mr Sloane, Royal Court, 1975; Look Back in Anger, New York, 1980; In Celebration, New York, 1984; Holiday Old Vic, 1987; Another Time, Old Vic, 1993; Films Include: If..., 1969; Figures in a Landscape, 1970; The Raging Moon, A Clockwork Orange, 1971; O Lucky Man, 1973; Royal Flash, 1975; Aces High, 1976; Voyage of the Damned, Caligula, 1977; The Passage, 1978; Time After Time, 1979; Cat People, 1981; Blue Thunder, Get Crazy, 1983; Britannia Hospital, 1984; Gulag, 1985; The Caller, Sunset, 1987; Sunrise, 1988; Class of 1999, Il Maestro, 1989; Moon 44; Double Game; Class of 1999; Snake Eyes, Schweitzer; Assassin of the Tsar, 1991; The Player; Chain of Desire; East Wind; Night Train to Venice; Star Trek: Generations, Tank Girl, 1995; Kids of the Round Table; Where Truth Lies; Mr Magoo, 1998; Gangster No 1, Island of the Dead, 2000; Just Visiting, The Void, Dorian, 2001; The Barber, Between Strangers, Superman: Shadow of Apokolips, I Spy, 2002; I'll Sleep When I'm Dead, Tempo, Inhabited, Red Roses and Petrol, The Company, 2003; Hidalgo, Evilenko, Bobby Jones, Stroke of Genius, Tempesta, Pinocchio 3000, 2004 (voice); Rag Tale, 2005; Cut Off, Bye Bye Benjamin, 2006; The List, Exitz, Halloween, Doomsday, 2007; Delgo, 2008. Numerous TV appearances including: Our Friends in the North; War and Peace; Phineas and Ferb. Address: c/o Markham and Froggatt, 4 Windmill Street, London, W1P 1HF, England.

McELLISTREM Marcus T, b. 19 April 1926, St Paul, Minnesota, USA. Emeritus Professor of Physics. m. Eleanor, 1 son, 5 daughters. Education: BA, St Thomas College, St Paul; MS, 1952, PhD, 1956, University of Wisconsin, Madison. Appointments: Research Associate, Indiana University, 1955-57; Assistant Professor, 1957-60, Associate Professor, 1960-65, Professor, 1965-, University of Kentucky; Director, Accelerator Laboratory, University of Kentucky, 1974-. Publications: 95 articles in professional journals. Honours: Distinguished Professor, Arts and Sciences, 1981-82; Kentucky Distinguished Scientist Award, 1992; President, Kentucky Academy of Sciences, 1997. Memberships: Fellow, American Physical Society; Kentucky Academy of Sciences. Address: Department of Physics and Astronomy, University of Kentucky, Lexington, KY 40506-0055, USA.

McENROE John Patrick, b. 16 February 1959, Wiesbaden, Federal Republic of Germany. Lawn Tennis Player. m. (1) Tatum O'Neil, 1986, 2 sons, 1 daughter, (2) Patty Smyth, 2 daughters, 1 step-daughter. Education: Trinity High School, New Jersey; Stanford University, California. Appointments: Amateur Player, 1976-78; Professional, 1978-93; USA Singles Champion, 1979, 1980, 1981, 1984; USA Doubles Champion, 1979, 1981, 1989; Wimbledon Champion (doubles), 1979, 1981, 1983, 1984, 1992 (singles) 1981, 1983, 1984; WCT Champion, 1979, 1981, 1983, 1984, 1989; Grand Prix Champion, 1979, 1983, 1984; Played Davis Cup for USA, 1978, 1979, 1980, 1982, 1983, 1984, 1985; Only Player to have reached Wimbledon semi-finals (1977) as pre-tournament qualifier; Semi Finalist, 1989; Tennis Sportscaster, USA Network, 1993; Member, Men's Senior's Tours Circuits, 1994; Winner, Quality Challenge, Worldwide Senior Tennis Circuit, 1999; ATP Tour, 2006 (doubles); Owner, John McEnroe Gallery; Coach, British Lawn Tennis Association, 2003-; TV: Presenter, The Chair (game show), 2002; McEnroe (talk show), CNBC, 2004. Publication: You Cannot Be Serious, autobiography, 2002. Honour: National Father of the Year Award, 1996; International Tennis Hall of Fame, 1999. Address: The John McEnroe Gallery, 41 Greene Street, New York, NY 10013, USA.

McEWAN Geraldine, b. 9 May 1932, Old Windsor, Berkshire, England. Actress. Education: Windsor County Girls' School. Career: TV: The Prime of Miss Jean Brodie, 1978; L'Elégance, The Barchester Chronicles, Come Into the Garden, Maude, 1982; Mapp and Lucia, 1985-86; Oranges are Not the Only Fruit, 1990; Mulberry, 1992-93; Red Dwarf, 1999; Thin Ice, Victoria Wood's Christmas Special, 2000; Carrie's War, 2003; Marple, 2004-2007; Films: The Adventures of Tom Jones, 1975; Escape from the Dark, 1978; Foreign Body, 1986; Henry V, 1989; Robin Hood: Prince of Thieves, 1991; Moses, 1995; The Love Letter, 1999; Titus, Love's Labours Lost, The Contaminated Man, 2000; The Magdalene Sisters, Food for Love, Pure, 2002; The Lazarus Child, Vanity Fair, 2004; Stage: Debut, Theatre Royal, Windsor, 1949; London stage: Who Goes There? 1951; Sweet Madness; For Better, For Worse; Summertime; Shakespeare Memorial Theatre, Straford on Avon, 1956, 1958, 1961; USA stage: School for Scandal, 1962; The Private Eat and The Public Eye, 1963; Member, National Theatre, 1965-71; Numerous other theatre appearances; Radio: Arrived, 2002; Director: As You Like It, 1988; Treats, 1989; Waiting for Sir Larry, 1990; Four Door Saloon, 1991; Keyboard Skills, 1993. Honours: TV Critics Best Actress Award, 1978; BAFTA Best Actress Award, 1990; Evening Standard Drama Award for Best Actress, 1983 and 1995. Address: c/o ICM Oxford House, 76 Oxford Street, London W1D 1BS, England.

McEWAN Ian, b. 21 June 1948, Aldershot, Hampshire, England. Author. m. (1) Penny Allen, 1982, divorced, 1995, 2 sons, 2 step daughters, (2) Annalena McAfee, 1997. Education: Woolverstone Hall; University of Sussex; University of East Anglia; Hon D Phil, Sussex, 1989; East Anglia, 1993. Publications: First Love, Last Rites, 1975; In Between the Sheets, 1978; The Cement Gardens, 1978; The Imitation Game, 1980; The Comfort of Strangers, 1981; Or Shall we Die?, 1983; The Ploughman's Lunch, 1983; The Child in Time, 1987; Soursweet (screenplay), 1987; A Move Abroad, 1989; The Innocent, 1990; Black Dogs, 1992; The Daydreamer, 1994; The Short Stories, 1995; Enduring Love,

DICTIONARY OF INTERNATIONAL BIOGRAPHY

1997; Amsterdam (novel), 1998; Atonement, 2001; Saturday, 2005; On Chesil Beach, 2007; For You (Opera), 2008. Honours: Somerset Maugham Prize, 1975; Primo Letterario, Prato, 1982; Whitbread Fiction Prize, 1987; Prix Femina, 1993; Booker Prize, 1998; Shakespeare Prize, 1999; CBE, 2000; National Book Critics Circle Award, 2003; James Tait Black Memorial Prize, 2005. Address: c/o Jonathan Cape, Random Century House, 20 Vauxhall Bridge Road, London SW1V 2SA, England. Website: www.ianmcewan.com

McFALL John, b. 4 October, 1944, Member of Parliament. m. Joan McFall, 3 sons, 1 daughter. Education: BSc honours, Chemistry; BA honours, Education; MBA. Appointments: School Teacher, Assistant Head Teacher, -1987; Member of Parliament for Dumbarton, 1987-; Opposition Whip with responsibility for Foreign Affairs, Defence and Trade and Industry, 1990; Deputy Shadow Secretary of State for Scotland with responsibility for Industry and Economic Affairs; Employment and Training; Home Affairs, Transport and Roads; Highland and Islands, 1992-97; Lord Commissioner, 1997-98; Parliamentary Under Secretary of State, Northern Ireland Office, 1998-99; Chairman of the Treasury Select Committee, 2001-05. Memberships: British/Hong Kong Group; British/Italian Group; British/Peru Group; Retail Industry Group; Roads Study Group; Scotch Whisky Group; Parliamentary and Scientific Committee; Select Committee on Defence; Select Committee on Sittings of the House; Executive Committee Parliamentary Group for Energy Studies; Information Committee; Executive Committee Parliamentary Group for Energy Studies. Address: House of Commons, London SW1A 0AA, England. E-mail: mcfallj@parliament.uk

McFAYDEN Jock, b. 18 September 1950, Paisley, Scotland. Artist. m. (1) Carol Hambleton, divorced, 1 son, (2) Susie Honeyman, 1 daughter, 1 son. Education: BA, MA, Chelsea School of Art, London, 1973-77. Career: Over 40 solo exhibitions including: Artist-in-Residence, National Gallery, 1982; Camden Arts Centre, 1988; Imperial War Museum, 1991; Talbot Rice Gallery, Edinburgh, 1998; Pier Arts Centre, Orkney, 1999; Agnew's Gallery, London, 2001; Works in over 30 public collections, including the Tate Gallery, the National Gallery, the Victoria and Albert Museum, the British Museum; Works in many private and corporate collections in Britain, Europe and America. Publication: Jock McFayden – A Book About a Painter, by David Cohen, 2001. Honours: Arts Council Major Award, 1979; Prizewinner John Moores Liverpool, 1991; Designed sets and costumes for Sir Kenneth MacMillan's ballet, The Judas Tree, Royal Opera House, 1992. Membership: Vintage Japanese Motorcycle Club. Address: 15 Victoria Park Square, Bethnal Green, London E2 9PB, England.

McGAVIN David Douglas Murray, b. 9 August 1938, Shanghai, China. Doctor of Medicine. m. Ruth, 2 sons, 1 deceased, 1 daughter. Education: Kelvinside Academy, Glasgow, 1945-46; Shanghai British School, 1947-48; Kelvinside Academy, Glasgow, 1949-56; University of Glasgow, 1956-62. Appointments: Project & Medical Director, Noor Eye Institute, Kabul, Afghanistan, 1976-81; Founder Editor, Journal of Community Eye Health, London, 1988-2003; Medical Director, International Resource Centre for the Prevention of Blindness, 1990-2003; Executive Director, International Community Trust for Health & Educational Services, 1999-. Publications: Editorial Consultant (Founder): Journal of Developing Mental Health, Journal of Community Ear & Hearing Health and Journal of Community Dermatology; Chapters in international medical journals. Honours: Listed in international biographical dictionaries; Honorary Fellowship, Royal College of Physicians of Edinburgh. Memberships: British Medical Association; Royal College of Surgeons, Edinburgh; Royal College of Ophthalmologists; Royal College of Physicians, Edinburgh; Royal Society of Medicine; Royal Geographical Society; Afghan Ophthalmological Society. Address: West Hurlet House, Glasgow Road, Hurlet, Glasgow G53 7TH, Scotland.

McGEACHIE Daniel, b. 10 June 1935, Barrhead, Glasgow, Scotland. Journalist; Company Director. m. Sylvia Andrew, 1 daughter. Appointments: Journalist, Scotland and Fleet Street, 1955-60; Foreign Correspondent, Daily Express, 1960-65; Parliamentary Correspondent, Diplomatic and Political Correspondent, Daily Express, 1965-75; Political Advisor, Conoco UK Ltd, 1975-77; Director, General Manager, Government and Public Affairs, Conoco UK Ltd, 1977-2000. Honours: OBE for services to Industry and Government relations, 1992. Memberships: Member, Royal Institute of International Affairs; Member, Reform Club. Address: 27 Hitherwood Drive, London SE19 1XA, England. E-mail: danmcgeachie@ukgateway.net

McGEOUGH Joseph Anthony, b. 29 May 1940, Kilwinning, Ayrshire, Scotland. University Professor. m. Brenda Nicholson, 2 sons, 1 daughter. Education: BSc, 1963, PhD, 1967, Glasgow University; DSc, Aberdeen University, 1982. Appointments: Senior Research Fellow, Queensland University, 1967; Research Metallurgist, International Research and Development Co Ltd, Newcastle, 1968-69; Senior Research Fellow, Strathclyde University, 1969-72; Lecturer, 1972-77, Senior Lecturer, 1977-80, Reader, 1980-83, University of Aberdeen; Regius Professor of Engineering, 1983-2005, Emeritus Professor, 2005-, University of Edinburgh; Vice-President, Institution of Mechanical Engineers, 2006-07. Publications: Books include: Principles of Electrochemical Machining, 1974; Advanced Methods of Machining, 1988; Micromachining of Engineering Materials (editor), 2001. Honour: FRSE, 1990. Memberships: FIMechE; FIET; FCIRP. Listed in national and international biographical dictionaries. Address: 39 Dreghorn Loan, Edinburgh EH13 0DF, Scotland. E-mail: j.a.mcgeough@ed.ac.uk

McGINNIS Callie B, Dean of Libraries; Associate Professor. Education: BA, English, Rhodes College, Memphis, Tennessee, 1966; MS, Library Science, Louisiana State University, Baton Rouge, Louisiana, 1969. Appointments: Public Services Librarian (Assistant Professor), Macon State College, 1969; Reference Librarian (Assistant Professor), 1974-75, Head of Circulation (Assistant Professor), 1975-76, Co-ordinator of Technical Services (Assistant Professor), 1977-85, Acting Director (Associate Professor), 1982-84, Co-ordinator of Public Services (Associate Professor), 1985-91, Co-ordinator of Technical Services (Associate Professor), 1991-98, Acting Library Director (Associate Professor), 1997-98, Library Director (Associate Professor), 1998-2003, Dean of Libraries (Associate Professor), 2004-, Columbus State University, Georgia. Publications: Numerous papers and articles in professional and popular journals. Honours: Historic Preservation Award, Historic Columbus Foundation, 1985; Faculty Development Awards, 1986, 1989, 1993; Soroptomist Woman of the Year, Columbus Chapter, 2003; Gracious Lady of Georgia, 2004. Memberships: Regents' Academic Libraries Committee; GALILEO Steering Committee; American Library Association; Georgia Library Association; Columbus Area Library Association. Address: 2238 15th Street, Columbus, GA 31906, USA.

McGOUGH Roger, b. 9 November 1937, Liverpool, England. Poet. m. Hilary Clough, 1986, 3 sons, 1 daughter. Education: St Mary's College, Crosby; BA and Graduate Certificate of Education, Hull University. Appointments: Fellow of Poetry, University of Loughborough, 1973-75; Writer-in-Residence, West Australian College of Advanced Education, Perth, 1986. Publications: The Mersey Sound (with Brian Patten and Adrian Henri), 1967; Strictly Private (editor), 1982; An Imaginary Menagerie, 1989; Blazing Fruit (selected poems 1967-87), Pillow Talk, 1990; The Lighthouse That Ran Away, You at the Back (selected poems 1967-87, Vol 2), 1991; My Dad's a Fire Eater, Defying Gravity, 1992; The Elements, Lucky, 1993; Stinkers Ahoy!, 1994; The Magic Fountain, 1995; The Kite and Caitlin, Sporting Relations, 1996; Bad, Bad Cats, Until I Met Dudley, 1997; The Spotted Unicorn, The Ring of Words (editor), 1998; The Way Things Are, 1999; Everyday Eclipses, Good Enough to Eat, Moonthief, Wicked Poems (editor), 2002; Collected Poems of Roger McGough, What on Earth Can It Be? 2003. Honours: Honorary Professor, Thames Valley University, 1993; Officer of the Order of the British Empire, 1997; Honorary MA, 1998; Cholmondeley Award, 1998; Fellow, John Moores University, Liverpool, 1999; CBE, June 2004; Honorary degree, Roehampton University, 2006; Honorary doctorate, University of Liverpool, 2006. Address: c/o The Peters, Fraser and Dunlop Group Ltd, Drury House, 34 – 43 Russell Street, London WC2B 5HA, England.

McGREGOR Ewan, b. 31 March 1971, Perth, Scotland. Actor. m. Eve Mavrakis, 1995, 3 daughters. Education: Guildhall School of Music and Drama. Appointments: Formerly with Perth Repertory Theatre; Theatre includes: What the Butler Saw; Little Malcolm and his Struggle against the Eunuchs, Hampstead Theatre Club, 1989; TV includes: Lipstick on Your Collar; Scarlet and Black; Kavanagh QC; Doggin Around; Tales from the Crypt; ER; Films include: Being Human; Family Style; Shallow Grave; Blue Juice; The Pillow Book; Trainspotting; Emma; Brassed Off; Nightwatch; The Serpent's Kiss; A Life Less Ordinary; Velvet Goldmine; Star Wars Episode I: The Phantom Menace; Little Voice; Rogue Trader; Eye of the Beholder; Nora; Moulin Rouge, 2001; Black Hawk Down, Stars Wars Episode II: Attack of the Clones, 2002; Down with Love, Young Adam, Faster, Big Fish, 2003; Robots (voice), Stay, Valiant (voice), Star Wars Episode III: Revenge of the Sith, The Island, 2005; Stormbreaker, Scenes of a Sexual Nature, Miss Potter, 2006; Cassandra's Dream, The Tourist, 2007; Incendiary, Jackboots on Whitehall, 2008. Documentary and book: The Long Way Round, motorcycle trip around the world for UNICEF with Charley Boorman, 2004; Long Way Down, 2007. Honours: Best Actor Dinard Film Festival, 1994; Best Actor, Berlin Film Festival; Empire Award; Variety Club Awards; Film Critics' Awards.

McGREGOR Harvey, b. 25 February 1926, Aberdeen, Scotland. Barrister. Education: The Queen's College, Oxford University; Harvard University. Appointments: Flying Officer, Royal Air Force, 1946-48; Barrister in Private Practice, 1955-58, 1965-; Executive, J Walter Thompson, 1959-62; Visiting Professor, New York University, USA, 1963-64; Visiting Professor, Rutgers University, USA, 1964-65; Consultant to Law Commission, 1965-73; Fellow, 1972-85, Warden, 1985-96, New College, Oxford; Visiting Professor, University of Edinburgh, 1998-. Publications: International Encyclopaedia of Comparative Law (contributor), 1972; Contract Code, 1993; McGregor on Damages, 17th edition, 2003; European Contract Code (translation from French), 2004. Honours: MA (Oxon); Doctor of Civil Law (DCL), Oxford; Doctor of Juridical Science (SJD), Harvard; Queen's Counsel;

Bencher, Inner Temple; Honorary Fellow, New College, Oxford. Memberships: Past President, Harvard Law School Association of UK, 1981-2001; Member of Editorial Board, Modern Law Review, 1986-; Chairman, London Theatre Council and Theatre Council, 1992-; President, Oxford Stage Co, 1992-; Member, Academy of European Private Lawyers, 1994-; Past Chairman, Trustees of Oxford Union, 1994-2004; Trustee, Migraine Trust, 1999-; Privilegiate, St Hilda's College, Oxford, 2001; Associate Member of Writers to the Signet, 2002-. Address: 29 Howard Place, Edinburgh EH3 5JY, Scotland. E-mail: harvey.mcgregor@hailshamchambers.com

McGREGOR Richard Ewan, b. 22 March 1953, Glasgow, Scotland. Professor of Music. m. Helen Frances Card, 1 son, 1 daughter. Education: B Mus (Hons), University of Glasgow, 1971-75; PhD, University of Liverpool; PGCE, Westminster College, Oxford. Appointments: Director of Music, Luton Sixth Form College, 1981-92; Head of Performing Arts, 1992-99, Principal Lecturer in Music, 1999-2006, Professor of Music, 2006-, St Martin's College, Lancaster. Publications: The Early Music of Peter Maxwell Davies, 1986; The Maxwell Davies Manuscripts in the British Library, 1996; Perspectives on Peter Maxwell Davies, 2000; Reading the Runes, 2000; Laus Deo: Composers' Views of Their Spirituality, 2006; The Persistence of Parody in Peter Maxwell Davies's Music, 2006; Stepping Out: Salome as Transitional Work, 2006; Transubstantiated into the Musical: a critical study of Veni Veni Emmanuel by James Macmillan, 2007; Hunting and Forms: an interview with Wolfgang Rihm, 2007; Numerous compositions. Honours: Glasgow University Class Prize, 1973; Goudie Prize for Harmony, 1974; Martha Vidor Scholarship, University of Liverpool, 1976-79; Italian Government Scholarship, 1982; Paul Sacher Stiftung Stipendium, 2002. Memberships: Higher Education Academy; Scottish Music Centre (Composer); Newsletter Editor, NAMHE, 2001-; Fellow, Society of Antiquaries (Scotland). Address: University of Cumbria, Lancaster Campus, Bowerham Road, Lancaster LA1 3JD, England. E-mail: REMcGregor@ucsm.ac.uk

McGUINNESS Martin, b. Derry, Northern Ireland. Politican. m. 4 children. Appointments: Took part in secret London Talks between Secretary of State for Northern Ireland and Irish Republicans Army (IRA), 1972; Imprisoned for six months during 1973, Irish Republic, after conviction for IRA membership; Elected to North Ireland Association, Refused Seat; Stood against John Hume in General Elections of 1982, 1987, 1992; MP for Mid-Ulster, House of Commons, 1997-; Member, Ulster-Mid, Northern Ireland Association, 1998-2000, Association suspended 11 February 2000; Minister of Education, 1999-2000; Spokesperson for Sinn Féin; Member of National Executive; Involved in Peace Negotiations with British Government.

McGURN Barrett, b. 6 August 1914, New York, New York, USA. Author. m. Janice Ann McLaughlin, 5 sons, 1 daughter. Education: AB, Fordham University, 1935. Honorary Doctor of letters 1958. Appointments: Reporter, New York Herald Tribune, 1935-66, Bureau Chief, Rome, Paris, Moscow, 1946-62; US Foreign Service, Rome, Saigon; Foreign Service Officer, State Department, Washington, 1966-72; Communications Director, US Supreme Court, 1973-82; Communications Director, Archdiocese of Washington, 1983-89. Publications: Decade in Europe, 1958; A Reporter Looks at the Vatican, 1962; A Reporter Looks at American Catholicism, 1967; America's Court, The Supreme Court and the People, 1997; The Pilgrim's Guide to Rome for the Millennium, 1999; Yank, Reporting the Greatest Generation, 2004. Honours: Best US Foreign Correspondent, Long

Island University Award, New York, 1956; Best US Foreign Correspondent, Overseas Press Club, 1957; Honorary Doctorate of Letters, Fordham University, New York, 1958; Grand Knight, Italian National Order of Merit, 1962; Pulitzer Prize Nomination, 1966; US State Department Meritorious Honour Award, 1972. Listed in national and international dictionaries. Memberships: Overseas Press Club of America, President, 1963-65; Association of Foreign Correspondents in Italy, President, 1961, 1962; National Press Club, Washington DC; Cosmos Club, Washington DC. Kenwood Club, Bethesda, Maryland 20816. Address: 5229 Duvall Drive, Bethesda, MD 20816, USA. E-mail: jmcgurn@erols.com

McHARD James L, b. 23 June 1942, Bay City, Michigan, USA. Retired Financial Analyst; Author; Lecturer; Composer. m. Alice Brallie Dekle, 1 son, 1 daughter. Education: BS, Mathematics, University of Michigan, Ann Arbor, 1964; Post Graduate, Finance, Wayne State University. Appointments: Financial Analysis, Ford Motor Co, Michigan, 1966-96; Lecturer, Author, Composer, 1997-. Publications: The Future of Modern Music, 2001; Gerard Pape (article), 2002; Murmulles del Paramo: Rapture in Whispers & Secrets, 2004; Julio Estrada (biography), 2007. Memberships: Southeast Michigan Horn Club; Voice of Reason; Electric Music Foundation. E-mail: release10@sbcglobal.net Website: www.futureofmodernmusic.com

McINTYRE Ian (James), b. 9 December 1931, Banchory, Kincardineshire, Scotland. Writer; Broadcaster. m. Leik Sommerfelt Vogt, 1954, 2 sons, 2 daughters. Education: BA, 1953, MA, 1960, St John's College, Cambridge; College of Europe, Bruges, Belgium, 1953-54. Appointments include: National Service, Commissioned in the Intelligence Corps, 1955-57; BBC Current Affairs Talks Producer, 1957; Editor, At Home and Abroad, 1959; Programme Services Officer, Independent Television Authority, 1961-62; Director of Information and Research, Scottish Conservative Central Office, 1962-70; Writer, Broadcaster, 1970-76, Controller, Radio 4, 1976-78, Controller, Radio 3, 1978-87, British Broadcasting Corporation; Associate Editor, The Times, London, 1989-90. Publications: The Proud Doers: Israel After Twenty Years, 1968; Words: Reflections on the Uses of Language, editor, contributor, 1975; Dogfight: The Transatlantic Battle over Airbus, 1992; The Expense of Glory: A Life of John Reith, 1993; Dirt and Deity: A Life of Robert Burns, 1996; Garrick, 1999; Joshua Reynolds: The Life and Times of the First President of the Royal Academy, 2003. Honour: Winner, Theatre Book Prize, 1999. Memberships; Union Society, Cambridge; Beefsteak Club. Address: Spylaw House, Newlands Avenue, Radlett, Hertfordshire WD7 8EL, England.

McINTYRE James Archibald, b. 2 September 1926, Stranraer, Scotland. Retired Farmer. m. Hilma Wilson Brown, 1 son, 2 daughters. Education: Oxford University, 1944, 6 months short army course. Commissioned 12 H Royal Lancers, 1945-47; West of Scotland Horticultural College, 1948-49. Appointments: Council Member, 1962-72, President, 1969, National Farmers Union, Scotland; Member, 1973-, Chairman, 1985-95, Dumfries and Galloway Health Board; Board Member, NFU Mutual Insurance, 1983-93. Honours: JP, 1989; OBE, 1989; CBE, 1995; O St J, 1979; C St J, 2000. Memberships: National Farmers Union, Scotland, 1950-; Member, Order of St John, 1972-. Address: Glenorchy, Broadstone Road, Stranraer, Scotland.

McINTYRE Richard Harold, b. 20 August 1947, Sydney, Australia. Musician. m. (1) Gillian Rae de Beyer Bailey, (2) Megan Anne Taylor, 4 sons, 1 daughter. Education: Bachelor of Music, Sydney University, 1968. Appointments: Associate Principal Bassoon, Sydney Symphony Orchestra, 1968-78; Lecturer then Senior Lecturer in Bassoon, Canberra School of Music, Australian National University, 1978-; Founding Member, The Canberra Wind Soloists, 1980-; Principal Bassoon, Canberra Symphony Orchestra, 1978-; Chief Conductor and Music Director, Canberra Youth Orchestra, 1980-90; Conductor and Music Director, The Llewellyn Choir, 1992-2005, Oriana Chorale, 2000-2002; Freelance Conductor; Guest Principal Bassoon, most leading Australian orchestras, 1973-. Recordings: 1 Vinyl recording and 3 compact discs as member of the Canberra Wind Soloists; Wind quintet arrangements of Ravel "Mother Goose", Mussorgsky "Pictures at an Exhibition", Stravinsky "Petrushka"(with piano), "Pulcinella". Honours: Canberran of the Year 1986; Advance Australia Award, 1991; Sounds Australian Award, 1991; Medal of the Order of Australia, 1992. Memberships: International Double Reed Society; Australian Double Reed Society; Media, Entertainment and Arts Alliance; National Tertiary Education Union. Address: 48 Green Street, Narrabundah, ACT 2604, Australia. E-mail: rmac@apex.net.au

McISAAC Ian, b. 13 July 1945. Chartered Accountant. m. (1) Joanna Copland, dissolved, 1 son, 1 daughter, (2) Debrah Ball, 1 son, 1 daughter. Education: Charterhouse scholar. Appointments: Partner, Touche Ross (UK), 1979-88; Touche Ross (Canada), 1983-85; Chief Executive, Richard Ellis Finanacial Services, 1988-91; Partner, Deloitte and Touche (formerly Touche Ross), 1991-2005; Global Head, Reorganisation Service, 1999-, UK Chairman, Emerging Markets, 2000-; Chairman, Society of Turaround Professionals, Director, Care International (UK). Honours: Freeman of the City of London; Member of the Worshipful Company of Chartered Accountants; ACA, 1969; FCA, 1979. Memberships: City of London Club; Hurlingham Club; Royal Mid-Surrey Golf Club; High Post Golf Club; OCYC. Address: 28 Hereford Square, London SW7, England. E-mail: imcisaac@deloitte.co.uk

McKAY Brenda Doris, b. 26 January 1947, Johannesburg, South Africa. Writer; Academic Researcher. Education: BA, Classical Culture, History of Art, English and Biblical Studies, 1979, Honours in Ancient History and Latin, 1981, 3rd year course in English III (equivalent to BA major in English), 1981, University of Witwatersrand, Johannesburg; Diploma, Abnormal Psychology, London University, 1986; MA (cum laude) Victorian Studies, 1990, PhD, English Research, 1996, Birkbeck College, London University. Appointments: Antiques dealer, -1988, South Africa and London; Lecturer, English, Birkbeck College, -1996; Teacher, Gender Studies, English and American Literature, University of Hertfordshire, 1997; Independent Scholar and Writer, 1997-. Publications: General articles and reviews on Victorian Culture, Elizabeth Gaskell and Charles Darwin; Extensive writings on George Eliot. Honours: Monograph, George Eliot & Victorian Attitudes to Racial Diversity, Darwinism, Colonialism, Class, Gender and Jewish Culture & Prophecy, honoured by CHOICE as one of 2003's outstanding academic books. Memberships: George Eliot Society; Gaskell Society; Bronte Society. Address: 11 Pinehurst Court, London W11 2BH, England.

McKEEVER Paul Edward, b. 3 December 1946, Pasadena, California, USA. Professor. m. Mary Olivia, 1 son, 2 daughters. Education: BS Biology, Brown University, Providence Rhode

Island, 1964-68; MD, University of California, 1972; PhD, Medical University of South Carolina, 1976. Appointments: Anatomic Pathology Intern and Cardiopulmonary Trainee, University of California, 1972-73; Neuropathology Fellow and Anatomic Pathology Resident, Medical University of South Carolina, 1973-6; Research Associate, 1976-79, Consultant in Neuropathology, 1976-83, Clinical Associate Professor, 1978-83, Neuropathologist, 1979-83, Pathology Consultant, 1980-83, Bethesda, Maryland; Chief, Department of Pathology, 1983-, Staff Physician, 1983-, Associate Professor, 1983-99, Director, Nerve and Muscle Biopsy Service, 1985-89, Director, Neurohistology Laboratory, 1996, Professor, University of Michigan, 1999-. Publications: Numerous books and articles. Honours include: Mosby Book Award, 1972; Who's Who in the East, 1978; American Men and Women of Science, 1980. Memberships: Society for Neuroscience; American Association of Pathologists; Children's Oncology Group; Histochemical Society; Editorial Board, Constitution Committee, American Association of Neuropathologists. Address: Pathology Department, University of Michigan, Box 0602, 1301 Catherine Rd, Rm M4207, Ann Arbor, MI 48109-0602, USA.

McKELLEN Ian Murray (Sir), b. 25 May 1939, Burnley, Lancashire, England. Actor. Education: Bolton School; St Catherines College, Cambridge. Appointments: First stage appearance, Roper (A Man for All Seasons), Belgrade Theatre, Coventry, 1961; Numerous other parts including: Royal National Theatre: Bent, Max; King Lear, Kent; Richard III, world tour then US tour, 1990-92; Napoli Milionaria, 1991; Uncle Vanya, 1992; An Enemy of the People, Peter Pan, 1997; The Seagull, Present Laughter, The Tempest, West Yorkshire Playhouse, 1998-99; Dance of Death, Broadhurst Theatre, New York, 2001, London, 2003, Australia, 2004; Aladdin, Old Vic, London, 2004-05; Films include: Alfred the Great, The Promise, A Touch of Love, 1969; Priest of Love, 1981; The Keep, 1982; Plenty, Zina, 1985; Scandal, 1988; The Ballad of Little Jo, I'll do Anything, 1992; Last Action Hero, Six Degrees of Seperation, 1993; The Shadow, Jack and Sarah, Restoration, 1994; Richard III, 1995; Bent, Swept From Sea, 1996; Apt Pupil, 1997; Gods and Monsters, 1998; X-Men, 1999; Lord of the Rings: The Fellowship of the Ring, 2001; Lord of the Rings: The Two Towers, 2002; X-Men 2, Emile, Lord of the Rings: The Return of the King, 2003; Neverwas, 2005; The Da Vinci Code, X-Men: The Last Stand, Flushed Away (voice), 2006; For the Love of God, Stardust (voice), The Golden Compass (voice), 2007; TV appearances include: David Copperfield, 1965; Ross, 1969; Richard II; Edward II; Hamlet, 1970; Hedda Gabler, 1974; Macbeth; Every Good Boy Deserves Favour, Dying Day, 1979; Acting Shakespeare, 1981; Walter; The Scarlet Pimpernel, 1982; Walter and June, 1983; Countdown to War, 1989; Othello, 1990; Tales of the City, 1993; Cold Comfort Farm, 1995; Rasputin, 1996; Coronation Street, 2005. Publications: William Shakespeare's Richard III, 1996. Honours: Clarence Derwent Award, 1964; Hon D Litt, 1989; Variety and Plays and Players Awards, 1966; Actor of the Year, Plays and Players, 1976; Society of West End Theatres Award for Best Actor in a Revival, 1977, for Best Comedy Performance, 1978, for Best Actor in a New Play, 1979; Tony Award, 1981; Drama Desk, 1981; Outer Critics Circle Award, 1981; Royal TV Society Performer of the Year, 1983; Laurence Olivier Award, 1984, 1991; Evening Standard Best Actor Award, 1984, 1989; Cameron Mackintosh Professor of Contemporary Theatre Oxford University, 1991; Screen Actor's Guild Award for besting supporting Actor, 2000; British Industry Film Awards, Variety UK Personality Award, 2003. Address: c/o ICM 76 Oxford Street, London, W1N 0AX, England.

McKENDRICK Melveena Christine, b. 23 March 1941, Crynant, Neath, Wales. Hispanist. m. Neil McKendrick, 2 daughters. Education: BA 1st class honours, Spanish, King's College, London; PhD, Girton College, Cambridge, 1967. Appointments: Jex-Blake Research Fellow, 1967-70, Tutor, 1970-83, Senior Tutor, 1974-81, Director of Studies in Modern Languages, 1984-95, Girton College, Cambridge; Lecturer in Spanish, 1980-92, Reader in Spanish Literature and Society, 1992-99, Professor of Spanish, Golden-Age Literature, Culture and Society, 1999-, University of Cambridge; British Academy Reader, 1992-94, Visiting Professor, University of Victoria, 1997; Fellow of the British Academy, 1999-; Pro-Vice-Chancellor (Education), University of Cambridge, 2004-. Publications: Author and co-author, numerous books; Articles on Early Modern Spanish theatre in many journals. Memberships: General Board, Cambridge University, 1993-97; Humanities Research Board, British Academy, 1996-98; Arts and Humanities Research Board, 1998-99; Consultant Hispanic Editor, Everyman, 1993-99; Editorial board, Donaire, 1994-; Revista Canadiense de Estudios Hispanicos, 1995-; Bulletin of Hispanic Studies, Glasgow, 1998-. Address: Department of Spanish & Portuguese, Faculty of Modern and Medieval Languages, University of Cambridge, Sidgwick Avenue, Cambridge, CB3 9DA, England.

McKENDRICK Neil, b. 28 July 1935, Formby, Lancashire, England. Historian. m. Melveena Jones, 2 daughters. Education: BA 1st class honours with Distinction, History, 1956, MA, 1960, Christ's College, Cambridge; FRHistS, 1971. Appointments: Research Fellow, 1958, Christ's College Cambridge; Assistant Lecturer in History, 1961-64, Lecturer, 1964-95, Secretary to Faculty Board of History, 1975-77, Chairman, History Faculty, 1985-87, Cambridge University; Fellow, 1958-96, Lecturer in History, 1958-96, Reader in Social and Economic History, 1995-2002, Director of Studies in History, 1959-96, Tutor, 1961-69, Master, 1996-2005, Gonville and Caius College; Lectures: Earl, University of Keele, 1963; Inaugural, Wallace Gallery, Colonial Williamsburg, 1985; Chettyar Memorial, University of Madras, 1990; Master, Gonville and Caius College, 2006-. Publications: Author and Editor of numerous publications; Author of articles in learned journals. Memberships: Tancred's Charities, 1996; Sir John Plumb Charitable Trust, 1999-; Properties Committee, National Trust, 1999-; Vice President, Caius Foundation in America, 1998-; Glenfield Trust, 2001-. Address: The Master's Lodge, Gonville and Caius College, Cambridge, CB2 1TA, England.

McKENNA Virginia Anne, b. 7 June 1931, London, England. Actress; Conservationist. m. Bill Travers, deceased 1994, 3 sons, 1 daughter. Education: Central School of Speech and Drama, London. Career: TV includes: The Whistle Blower; Pucini; The Camomile Lawn; The Deep Blue Sea; A Passage to India; Waters of the Moon; September; Films include: Born Free; Ring of Bright Water; Carve Her Name with Pride; The Cruel Sea; The Smallest Show on Earth; Waterloo; The Barretts of Wimpole Street; Staggered; An Elephant Called Slowly; Sliding Doors. Theatre includes: Season, Old Vic; The Devils; A Winters Tale; Penny for a Song; The River Line; A Little Night Music; The Beggars Opera; Winnie; I Capture the Castle; Hamlet; The King and I. TV includes: The Whistle-Blower; The Scold's Bridle; Marple: A Murder Is Announced,. Publications: Books: On Playing with Lions (with Bill Travers); Some of My Friends Have Tails; Into the Blue; Back to the Blue; Journey to Freedom; Co-editor and contributor to: Beyond the Bars; Contributor to: Women at Work. Honours: Best Actress Award for Born Free, Variety Club; Belgian Prix Femina for Carve Her Name with Pride;

SWET Award for The King and I (theatre); Best Actress Award, Romeo and Juliet (TV); Best Actress Award for A Town Like Alice, BAFTA; OBE, 2004. Memberships: Special Forces Club; Patron of: Plan International UK, Children of the Andes, Elizabeth Fitzroy Support; Wildlife Aid, Swallows and Amazons; Founder, Trustee, The Born Free Foundation. Address: The Born Free Foundation, 3 Grove House, Foundry Lane, Horsham, West Sussex RH13 5PL, England. E-mail: wildlife@bornfree.org.uk

McKENZIE Dan Peter, b. 21 February 1942, Cheltenham, England. Earth Scientist. m. Indira Margaret, 1 son. Education: BA, MA, PhD, King's College, University of Cambridge. Appointments: Senior Assistant in Research, 1969-75, Assistant Director of Research, 1975-79, Reader in Tectonics, 1979-84, Royal Society Professor of Earth Sciences, Department of Earth Sciences, University of Cambridge. Publications: Author of various papers in learned journals. Honours: Honorary MA, University of Cambridge, 1966; Fellow, Royal Society, 1976; Foreign Associate, US National Academy of Sciences, 1989; Balzan Prize (with F J Vine and D H Matthews), International Balzan Foundation, 1981; Japan Prize (with W J Morgan and X Le Pichon), Technological Foundation of Japan, 1990; Royal Medal of the Royal Society, 1991; Crafoord Prize, 2002; Companion of Honour, 2003. Address: Bullard Laboratories, Madingley Road, Cambridge CB3 0EZ, England.

McLACHLIN Beverley, b. 7 September 1943, Pincher Creek, Canada. Chief Justice. m. (1) Roderick McLachlin (deceased), (2) Frank E McArdle, 1992. Education: BA, 1964, MA (Philos), 1968, University of Alberta. Appointments: Called to Bar of Alta, 1969, Bar of British Columbia, 1971; Practised law, Wood, Moir, Hyde & Ross, Edmonton, 1969-71; Thomas, Herdy, Mitchell & Co, Fort St John, British Columbia, 1971-72; Bull, Housser & Tupper, Vancouver, 1972-75; Lecturer, Associate Professor and Professor with tenure, University of British Columbia, 1974-81; Appointed to County Court of Vancouver, 1981; Appointed to Supreme Court of British Columbia, 1981, Court of Appeal of British Columbia, 1985; Appointed Chief Justice of the Supreme Court of British Columbia, 1988; Appointed to Supreme Court of Canada, 1989; Sworn to Privy Council, 2000; Chief Justice of Canada, Supreme Court of Canada, 2000-. Publications: Author of numerous articles and papers in professional journals. Honours: 1st female Chief Justice in history of Canada's highest court; Honorary LLD from: University of British Columbia, 1990; University of Alta, 1991; University of Toronto, 1995; York University, 1999; Law Society of Upper Canada, 2000; University of Ottawa, 2000; University of Calgary, 2000; Brock University, 2000; Simon Fraser University, 2000; University of Victoria, 2000; University of Alta, 2000; University of Lethbridge, 2001; Bridgewater State College, 2001; Mount Saint Vincent University, 2002; University of Prince Edward Island, 2002; University of Montreal, 2003; University of Manitoba, 2004; Queen's University, Belfast, 2004; Dalhousie University, 2004; Carleton University, 2004; University of Fort Kent (Maine), 2005; Aleneo de Manila University, 2006; One of Canada's Most Powerful Top 100 Women; Women's Executive Network, 2003, 2004. Address: Supreme Court Bldg, 301 Wellington St, Ottawa, Ontario K1A 0J1, Canada.

McLAIN John Anthony (Lain), b. 5 June 1933, Chingford, London, England. Composer; Songwriter; Retired Statistician. Education: BSc Mathematics, London University, 1955. Appointments: National Service (REME), 1955-57; CAV Ltd, 1957-59; Statistical Officer, Royal Society for the Prevention of Accidents, 1959-70; Manpower Planner, ICI Plastics, 1970-85; British Aerospace, 1985-87; Television performances: Our Father, Who Art in Heaven, performed by the Gibside Singers, Tyne Tees TV. Recordings: Now You Have Gone, by Tony Jacobs with Jim Barry (piano); Why Don't They Write the Songs?, by Tony Jacobs with Jim Barry Sextet; Adlestrop (poem by Edward Thomas); I Came to Oxford (Gerald Gould); The Old Railway Line (Anne Allinson); The Demise of Harpenden Junction Box (Sue Woodward), by Gordon Pullin (tenor) with John Gough (piano); Winter's Spring, Clock-a-Clay, November, The Cuckoo (settings of John Clare poems), by Grodon Pullin with Andrew Plant (piano). Other compositions (published): Psalm (The Lord is my Shepherd); Mamble (John Drinkwater); Faintheart in a Railway Train (Thomas Hardy); Dream Awhile; The Poop Scoop Song. Listed in national and international biographical dictionaries. Memberships: Performing Right Society Ltd; British Academy of Composers and Songwriters; Light Music Society; Robert Farnon Society; Mensa. Address: 42 Osidge Lane, Southgate, London N14 5JG, England.

McLEAN Don, b. 2 October 1945, New Rochelle, New York, USA. Singer; Instrumentalist; Composer. m. Patrisha Shnier, 1987, 1 son, 1 daughter. Education: Villanova University; Iona College. Appointments: President, Benny Bird Corporation Inc; Member, Hudson River Slope Singers, 1969; Solo concert tours throughout USA, Canada, Australia, Europe, Far East; Numerous TV appearances; Composer of film scores for Fraternity Row; Flight of Dragons; Composer of over 200 songs including Prime Time; American Pie; Tapestry; Vincent; And I Love You So; Castles in the Air; Recordings include: Tapestry, 1970; American Pie, 1971; Don McLean, 1972; Playin' Favourites, 1973; Homeless Brother, 1974; Solo, 1976; PrimeTime, 1977; Chain Lightning, 1979; Believers, 1982; For the Memories, Vol I, Vol II, 1986; Love Tracks, 1988; Headroom, 1991; Don McLean Christmas, 1992; Favourites and Rarities, 1993; The River of Love, 1995; Christmas Dreams, 1997; Sings Marty Robbins, 2001; Starry Starry Night (Live), 2001; You've Got to Share: Songs for Children, 2003; The Western Album, 2003; Christmas Time, 2004; Rearview Mirror: An American Musical Journey, 2005. Numerous compilation packages. Publications: Songs of Don McLean, 1972; The Songs of Don McLean, Vol II, 1974. Honours: Recipient of many gold discs in USA, Australia, UK and Ireland; Israel Cultural Award, 1981. Address: Benny Bird Co, 1838 Black Rock Turnpike, Fairfield, Connecticut 06432, USA.

McLEAN Donald Millis, b. 26 July 1926, Melbourne, Australia. Professor Emeritus of Pathology. m. Joyce. Education: MBBS, 1950; MD, University of Melbourne, 1954; MRCPath, 1963; FRCPC, 1967; FRCPath, 1970. Appointments: Harrison Watson Research Fellow, Clare College, Cambridge, 1955-56; Virologist, The Hospital for Sick Children, Toronto, 1958-67; Professor, Medical Microbiology, University of British Columbia, 1967-91; Professor Emeritus, Pathology, 1991-. Publications: 6 books, 120 original scientific papers. Memberships include: British Medical Association; American Society of Virology. Address: 2720 Yukon Street, Vancouver, British Columbia V5Y 3R1, Canada.

McLELLAN David Thorburn, b. 10 February 1940, Hertford, England. Professor of Political Theory; Writer. m. Annie Brassart, 1 July 1967, 2 daughters. Education: MA, 1962, DPhil, 1968, St John's College, Oxford. Appointment: Professor of Political Theory, Goldsmiths College, University of London. Publications: The Young Hegelians and Karl

Marx, 1969; Karl Marx: His Life and Thought, 1974; Engels, 1977; Marxism After Marx, 1980; Ideology, 1986; Marxism and Religion, 1987; Simone Weil: Utopian Pessimist, 1989; Unto Caesar: The Political Importance of Christianity, 1993; Political Christianity, 1997; Karl Marx: A Biography, 2006; Marxism after Marx, 2007. Contributions to: Professional journals. Address: 13 Ivy Lane, Canterbury, Kent, CT1 1TU, England. E-mail: david@mclellankent.com

McLEOD James Graham, b. 18 January 1932, Sydney, Australia. Neurologist. m. Robyn Edith Rule, 13 January 1962, 2 sons, 2 daughters. Education: BSc, 1953, MB BS, 1959, DSc, 1997, University of Sydney; DPhil, Oxon, 1956; Institute of Neurology, London University, 1963-65; Harvard University, Department of Neurology, 1965-66. Appointments: Pro-Dean, Faculty of Medicine, University of Sydney, 1974-94; Chairman, Department of Neurology, Royal Prince Alfred Hospital, 1978-95; Bosch Professor of Medicine, 1972-97, Bushell Professor of Neurology, 1978-97, Professor Emeritus, 1997-, University of Sydney; Consultant Neurologist, Royal Prince Alfred Hospital, Sydney, 1997-. Publications: A Physiological Approach to Clinical Neurology (co-author), 1981; Introductory Neurology (co-author), 1995; Peripheral Neuropathy in Childhood (co-author), 1991, 1999; More than 200 principal scientific publications. Honours: Rhodes Scholarship, 1953; Nuffield Travelling Fellowship, 1964-65; Sir Arthur Sims Commonwealth Travelling Professorship, 1983; AO, 1986; Commonwealth Medical Senior Fellowship; Honorary Doctorate, University of Aix-Marseille. Memberships: Fellow, Royal Australian College of Physicians, 1971; Fellow, Royal College of Physicians, 1977; Fellow, Australian Academy of Science, 1981; Fellow, Australian Academy of Technological Sciences and Engineering, 1987; Australian Science and Technology Council, 1987-93. Address: 2 James Street, Woollahra, NSW 2025, Australia. E-mail: jmcl7953@mail.usyd.edu.au

McMAHAN Michael Lee, b. 17 May 1946, Memphis, Tennessee, USA. Professor of Biology. m. Brenda Perry McMahan, 2 sons. Education: BS, 1968, MS, 1971, University of Mississippi; PhD, Louisiana State University, 1976. Appointments: Assistant Professor, Associate Professor, Department of Biology, Campbellsville University, 1975-80; Assistant Professor, Associate Professor, Professor, University Professor, Department of Biology, Union University, Jackson, Tennessee, USA, 1980-. Publications: Articles in scientific journals as co-author: A Re-evaluation of Pristina longiseta (Oligochaeta:Naididae) in North America, 1975; Solenopsis invicta Buren: Influence on Louisiana pasture soil chemistry, 1976; As author: Protozoan parasites of some terrestrial oligochaetes, 1975; Preliminary notes on a new megadrile species, genus and family from the southeastern United States, 1976; Anatomical notes on Lutodrilus multivesiculatus (Annelida: Oligochaeta), 1979; Ecology of the limicolous megadrile Lutodrilus multivesiculatus, 1998. Memberships: American Microscopical Society; Biological Society of Washington; Association of Southeastern Biologists. Address: Department of Biology, Union University, 1050 Union University Drive, Jackson, TN38305, USA.

McMANUS Jonathan Richard, b. 15 September 1958, Heywood, England. Barrister. Education: First Class Honours in Law, Downing College, Cambridge, 1978-81; Called to the Bar, 1982; Appointments: Commenced practice at the bar, 1983; Government A panel of Counsel, 1992-1999; QC, 1999. Publication: Education and the Courts, 1998. Honour: Maxwell Law Prize, Cambridge, 1981. Memberships: Administrative Law, Bar Association; National Trust; English Heritage; Friend of the Royal Opera House. Address: 4 and 5, Gray's Inn Square, Gray's Inn. London WC1R 5AH, England.

McMICKLE Robert Hawley, b. 30 July 1924, Paterson, New Jersey, USA. Physicist. m. Gwendolyn Gill, 3 sons, 2 daughters. Education: BA, Physics, Oberlin College, 1947; MS, Physics, University of Illinois, 1948; PhD, Physics, Pennsylvania State University, 1952. Appointments: Research Physicist, BF Goodrich Company, Brecksville, Ohio, 1952-59; Professor, Physics, Robert College, Istanbul, Turkey, 1959-71, University of the Bosphorus, Istanbul, Turkey, 1971-79, Schreiner College, Kerrville, Texas, 1979-80, Luther College, Decorah, Iowa, 1980-81; Adjunct Professor, Physics, Memphis State University, Tennessee, 1981-83; Accreditation Co-ordinator, Northeast Utilities, Seabrook, New Hampshire, 1983-94, Retired, 1994. Publications include: Diffusion Controlled Stress Relaxation, 1955; The Compressions of Several High Molecular Weight Hydrocarbons, 1958; Introduction to Modern Physics, 1979. Honours include: Fellowship, American Petroleum Institute, 1950-52; Research grant, Optics, Innovative Systems Research Inc, Pennsauken, New Jersey, 1976; Distinguished Service Award, University of the Bosphorus, Istanbul, Turkey, 1989. Memberships: American Association of Physics Teachers; Physical Society of Turkey; Sigma Xi. Address: 3032 Fernor Street, Allentown, PA 18103, USA.

McNEAL Jane Erskine, b. 29 October 1958, Somers Point, New Jersey, USA. Musician; Music Teacher. Education: Music Studies, Wheaton College, Illinois; BA, Psychology, Stockton State College, Pomona, New Jersey; Crescendo Music Certification, Academy of Community Music, Philadelphia area, Pennsylvania; Kindermusik Certification, Westminster Choir College, Princeton, New Jersey. Appointments: Piano and Vocal Instructor, 1975-; Recitalist and Professional Accompanist, 1980-; Church and Synagogue Organist and Music Director, Organist, 1982-; Advocate for the mentally ill. Honours: Music Scholarship, Wheaton College; National Merit Corporate Scholarship; Psi Chi Honor Society; Graduated College cum laude; Marquis Who's Who; American Biographical Institute; Biltmore Who's Who. Memberships: Life Member, Republican National Committee; American Federation of Musicians; American Guild of Organists. Address: 2112 Newcombtown Road, Millville, NJ 08332, USA.

McQUEEN Alexander, b. 17 March 1969, London. Education: St Martin's School of Art, London; m. George Forsyth, 2000. Appointments: London Tailors, Anderson and Shepherd, Gieves and Hawkes; Theatrical Costumiers, Berman and Nathans; Des Koji Tatsuno; Romeo Gigli, Rome; Final Collection, St Martin's, 1992 established his reputation; Subsequent shows include: The Birds; Highland Rape; The Hunger; Dante; La Poupee; It's a Jungle Out There; Untitled; Aquired Italian manufacturing company Onward Kashiyama; Chief Designer, Givenchy, Paris, 1996-2000; of Gucci, 2000-. Honours: Designer of the Year, London Fashion Awards, 1996, 2000; 2003; Joint Winner, with John Galliano, 1997; Special Achievement Award, London Fashion Awards, 1998; CBE. Address: c/o Gucci Group NV Rembrandt Tower, 1 Amstelplein, 1096 MA Amsterdam, The Netherlands. Website: www.gucci.com

McVIE J Gordon, b. 13 January 1945, Glasgow, Scotland. Director Cancer Intelligence; Professor. Education: BSc (Hons), Pathology, 1967, MB, ChB, 1969, University of Edinburgh, Scotland; ECFMG, USA, 1971; Accreditation in

Internal Medicine and Medical oncology, Joint Committee on Higher Medical Training, 1977; MD, Edinburgh, 1978; FRCPE, Edinburgh, 1981; FRCPS, Glasgow, 1987; DSc (Hon), University of Abertay, Dundee, Scotland, 1996; DSc (Hon), University of Nottingham, England, 1997; FRCP, 1997; FMedSci, 1998; DSc (Hon), University of Portsmouth, England; FRCSE, Edinburgh, 2001. Appointments: House Officer, Royal Infirmary, Edinburgh and Royal Hospital for Sick Children, Edinburgh, 1969-1970; Medical Research Council Research Fellow, Department of Pathology and Therapeutics, Edinburgh University; 1970-1971; Temporary Lecturer in Therapeutics, 1971-73, Lecturer in Therapeutics, 1973-76, Edinburgh University; Honorary Registrar, 1971-73, Honorary Senior Registrar, 1973-76, Lothian Health Board, Scotland; Senior Lecturer, The Cancer Research Campaign Department of Clinical Oncology, University of Glasgow, 1976-1980; Honorary Consultant in Medical Oncology, Greater Glasgow Health Board, 1976-1980; Head, Clinical Research Unit, Consultant Physician, and Chairman, Division of Experimental Therapy, The National Cancer Institute, Amsterdam, The Netherlands, 1980-84; Clinical Research Director, The National Cancer Institute of the Netherlands, 1984-1989; Scientific Director, 1989-1996, Director General, 1996-2002, The Cancer Research Campaign; Director General, Cancer Research UK, 2002-; Director, Cancer Intelligence, 2003-. Publications: Extensive within this field; Membership of numerous medical editorial boards. Honours: Gunning Victoria Jubilee Prize in Pathology, 1967; Honeyman Gillespie Lecturer in Oncology 1977; Visiting Fellow, Department of Medical Oncology, University of Paris, 1978; Visiting Fellow, Netherlands Cancer Institute, Amsterdam; Consultant, Carcinogenesis of Cytostatic Drugs, International Agency, Research in Cancer, WHO, Lyon, 1980; Visiting Professor, University of Sydney, NSW, Australia; Visiting Professor, British Postgraduate Medical Federation, London University; 1990-96; Chairman, UICC Fellowships Program, 1990-98; President, European Organisation for Research and Treatment of Cancer, 1994-97; First European Editor of Journal of the National Cancer Institute, 1994-; Visiting Professor, University of Glasgow, 1996-; Semmelweis Medal for Excellence in Science. Memberships: European Organisation for Research on Treatment of Cancer (EORTC), 1979-; Numerous advisory committees and examination boards including: Member, Steering Committee, Alliance of World Cancer Research Organisations, 1999; Cancer Research Funders Forum, 1999-2001; Member, AACR Membership Committee, 2000-01; Member, AACR Clinical Cancer Research Committee, 2001-. Address: Cancer Intelligence, 4 Stanley Rd, Cotham, Bristol BS6 6NW, England. E-mail: gordonmcvie@doctors.org.uk

MEACHER Michael Hugh (Rt Hon), b. 4 November 1939, Hemel Hempstead, Hertfordshire, England. Member of Parliament. m. Lucianne Sawyer, 2 sons, 2 daughters. Education: Greats, Class 1, New College, Oxford; Diploma in Social Administration, London School of Economics. Appointments: Lecturer, Social Administration, York and London School of Economics, 1966-70; Member of Parliament for Oldham West, 1970-; Minister for Industry, 1974-75; Minister for the Department of Health and Social Security, 1975-76; Minister for Trade, 1976-79; Member of the Shadow Cabinet, 1983-97; Minister for the Environment, 1997-2003. Publications: Taken for a Ride (about the care of the elderly), 1972; Socialism with a Human Face, 1982; Diffusing Power, 1992. Memberships: Labour Party; Fabian Society; Child Poverty Action Group. Address: House of Commons, Westminster, London, SW1A 0AA, England.

MEAD Sidney Moko, b. 8 January 1927, Wairoa, Hawkes Bay, New Zealand. Lecturer. m. June Terina Walker, 3 daughters. Education: Auckland Teachers' College, 1944-45; Third Year Art Training, 1946; Diploma in Teaching, Education Department, 1962; BA, 1964, MA, 1965, University of Auckland; PhD, University of Southern Illinois, 1968. Appointments: Manutahi Maori District High School, Ruatorea, 1947-48; Itinerant Art Advisor, East Coast Schools, 1949; Itinerant Art Teacher, Urewera, Whakatane, Tauranga, 1950; Headmaster, Minginui Maori School, Urewera, 1951-57; Headmaster, Waimarama Maori School, Hawkes Bay, 1957-60; Headmaster, Whatawhata School, Waikato, 1960-62; Assistant Lecturer, 1963-65, Lecturer, 1968-70, Senior Lecturer, 1970-71, University of Auckland; Associate Professor, McMaster University, 1971-72, 1973-76; Canadian Commonwealth Fellow, University of British Columbia, 1972-73; Professor of Maori, Victoria University of Wellington, 1977-91; Part time Lecturer, Te Whare Wanaga o Awanuiarangi, 1992-. Publications: Numerous articles in professional journals; Research reports; Books and monographs; Lectures and keynote addresses. Honours: Peter Buck Bursary, 1964; Anthropology Prize, University of Auckland, 1965; Carnegie Commonwealth Scholar, 1965-67; Wenner-Gren Pre-doctoral Museum Fellowship, 1967-68; Canadian Commonwealth Research Fellowship, 1972-73; Elsdon Best Memorial Medal, 1983; Pacific Arts Association Manu Daula (Frigate Bird) Award, 1984; Fellow, Royal Society of New Zealand, 1990; Goodman Fielder Wattie Book Award, 1991; Distinguished Service Medal, Order of Ruatara, 1991; Distinguished Alumni Award, Auckland University, 1999; Distinguished Professor, Te Whare Wanaga o Awainuiarangi, 2002; Montana NZ Book Awards Winner, 2002; Distinguished Author Award, Reed Publishing Ltd, 2002; Distinguished Companion of The New Zealand Order of Merit, DCNZM, Queen's Birthday Honours, 2006. Memberships: New Zealand Geographic Board; Maori University Teachers' Association; The Skinner Fund; Bioethics Council; Waitangi Tribunal. Address: 10 Spiers St, Karori, Wellington 6012, New Zealand.

MEDVEDEV Dmitry Anatolyevich, b. 14 September 1965, Leningrad, Russia SFSR, Soviet Union. President of Russia. m. Svetlana Linnik, 1 son. Education: Graduate, Law Department, 1987, PhD, Private Law, 1990, Leningrad State University. Appointments: Docent, Saint Petersburg State University (previously Leningrad State University), 1991-99; Legal Expert, International Relations Committee, St Petersburg Mayor's Office, 1991-96; Legal Affairs Director, Ilim Pulp Enterprise, St Petersburg, 1993; Elected Member, Board of Directors, Bratskiy LPK Paper Mill, 1998-99; Deputy Head, Presidential Staff, Russian Government, 1999-; Chair, 2000-01, 2002, Deputy Chair, 2001-02, Gazprom's Board of Directors; Presidential Chief of Staff, 2003; First Deputy Prime Minister, Russian Government, 2005-; President of Russia, 2008-. Publications: Numerous articles in professional journals. Honours: Person of the Year, Expert magazine, 2005. Address: The Kremlin, Moscow, Russia.

MEDVEDKIN Gennady, b. 30 October 1954, St Petersburg, Russia. Physicist; Researcher. m. Liza Shvets, 2 sons, 1 daughter. Education: MS, Electrical Engineering University, St Petersburg, 1977; PhD, 1981, DSc, 1993, Ioffe Physical Technical Institute, St Petersburg; Vocational Certificate in X-Ray Diffraction, Stanford University, 2006. Appointments: Laboratory Assistant, 1972-77, Probationer-Researcher, 1977-79, Junior Researcher, 1979-86, Researcher, 1986-99, Senior Scientist, 1999-2005, Ioffe Physical Techn Institute, St Petersburg; Director General, Joint-St Co Standard, St

Petersburg, 1997-98; Vice Director, Profit Ltd, St Petersburg, 1999-2000; Visiting Professor, Tokyo University of Agriculture and Technology, 1999-2001; Director General, FERROBIT Ltd, St Petersburg, 2004-2006; Visiting Scholar, Stanford University, 2005-2006. Publications: Monograph, Semiconductor Crystals for Optical Sensors of Linearly Polarized Radiation, 1992; Patentee in field; Over 90 publications in professional refereed journals; More than 70 presentations at international conferences including 5 invited talks. Honours: Honour Plaque for Outstanding Inventors of Russian Federation, 1984; Outstanding Poster Award, Boston, 2000; Best Publication Award, Japan, 2001. Listed in Who's Who publications and biographical dictionaries. Memberships: OSA; MRS; MSJ; JSAP; Institute of Physics, UK; American Association for the Advancement of Science, USA. Address: 4111 West 239th Street, Torrance CA 90505, USA. E-mail: g.a.medvedkin@hotmail.com

MEFED Anatoly Egorovich, b. 7 December 1938, Gorodische, Bryansk, Russia. Physicist; Researcher of NMR in solids; Consultant. m. Lyudmila Ivanovna Putilova, 1 daughter. Education: Graduate, Moscow University, 1962; PhD, Russian Academy of Sciences, 1972. Appointments: Professor, Physics and Maths, Institute Radioengineering and Electronics Russian Academy of Sciences, Fryazino, 1989; Professor, Kazan State University, 1989. Publications: Author and co-author: Discovery, A New Physical Law in Spin Thermodynamics in Solids, 1968; Contribution to more than 80 research papers to professional journals. Honours: Recipient USSR diploma for discovery of a new physics law in spin thermodynamics in solids, 1987; USSR inventor medal Russian Academy of Sciences; Listed in biographical publications. Membership: New York Academy of Sciences, Russian Academy of Natural Sciences. Address: Russian Academy of Sciences Institute of Radioengineering & Electronics, Vvedenskogo Sq, 141190 Fryazino, Moscow, Russia. E-mail: aem228@ire216.msk.su

MEIGHAN Roland, b. 29 May 1937, Sutton Coldfield, England. Writer; Publisher; Consultant. m. (1) Shirley, deceased, (2) Janet, 1 son, 2 stepsons. Education: DSocSc; PhD; BSc; LCP. Appointments: Various school teacher positions; Lecturer, Senior Lecturer in Education, University of Birmingham; Special Professor of Education, University of Nottingham; Independent Writer and Consultant; Director and owner, Educational Heretics Press, Nottingham; Director and Trustee, Centre for Personalised Education Trust. Publications: A Sociology of Educating, 1981, 2nd edition, 1986, 3rd edition, 1999, 4th edition, 2003, 5th edition, 2006; Flexischooling, 1988; Theory and Practice of Regressive Education, 1993; The Freethinkers' Guide to the Educational Universe, 1994; John Holt: Personalised Education and the Reconstruction of Schooling, 1995; The Next Learning System, 1997; The Next Learning System: Pieces of the Jigsaw, 2000; Natural Learning and the Natural Curriculum, 2001; Learning Unlimited; John Holt: personalised learning instead of 'uninvited teaching', 2002; Comparing Learning Systems, 2005. Contributions to: Natural Parent Magazine; Observer; Yorkshire Post; Times Educational Supplement. Membership: Fellow of the Royal Society of Arts. Address: 113 Arundel Drive, Bramcote Hills, Nottingham NG9 3FQ, England. Website: www.edheretics.gn.apc.org

MELEZINEK Adolf, b. 3 October 1932, Vienna, Austria. Emeritus University Professor. m. Vera Melezinek, 1 son, 1 daughter. Education: Dipl Ing, Electronics, 1957; Dr phil, Pedagogy, 1969. Appointments: Chief Engineer; Assistant Professor; University Professor, Chair of Engineering Pedagogy. Publications: More than 200 publications including 20 specialist books such as: Ingenieurpädagogik, in German, Czech, Hungarian, Slovenian, Ukrainian, Polish and Russian editions. Honours: Gold Ring, International Society for Engineering Education; Golden Felber Medal, Czech Technical University, Prague; Honorary Senator, Technical University, Budapest; Grand Gold Medal, Carinthia; Austrian Honorary Cross 1st Class for Science and Art; Dr honoris causa, 1997, 2000, 2001, 2005; Listed in several Who's Who and biographical publications. Membership: Founder and Honorary Life President, International Society for Engineering Education (IGIP). Address: Akazienhofstrasse 79, A-9020 Klagenfurt, Austria. E-mail: adolf.melezinek@uni-klu.ac.at

MELICA Claudia, b. 19 September 1961, Rome, Italy. Lecturer. Education: MA (1st class honours), 1987, PhD, Philosophy, 1994, Postdoctorate Philosophy, 1996-98, University Rome I La Sapienza. Appointments: Temporary research/teaching position, Erasmus University, Rotterdam, Netherlands, 1995-98; Seminars, Istituto Italiano per gli Studi Filosofici, Naples, 1997, 2003, 2004; Lecturer, Philosophy, University Trento, Italy, 2003-. Publications: Hegel on Shadows and the Blue of the Sky, 1993; Hemsterhuis's Optics and his Relationship with Italian Scientists, 1995. Honours: Annual Grant for Study and Research, Istituto Italiano Studi Storici, Naples, 1987-88; DAAD, Heidelberg; DDR Grant, 1989. Memberships: Hegel Society of Great Britain; Hegel-Vereinigung; Centrum Voor Duitse Idealisme; Società Fisosofica Italiana. Address: Department of Philosophy, University of Trento, via S Croce, 65 38100, Trento, Italy. E-mail: claudia.melica@lett.unitn.it

MELLERS Wilfrid (Howard), b. 26 April 1914, Leamington, Warwickshire, England. Professor of Music (retired); Composer; Author. m. (1) Vera M Hobbs, (2) Pauline P Lewis, 3 daughters, (3) Robin S Hildyard. Education: Leamington College, 1933; BA, 1936, MA, 1938, Cambridge University; DMus, University of Birmingham, 1960. Appointments: Staff Tutor in Music, University of Birmingham, 1948-60; Andrew Mellon Professor of Music, University of Pittsburgh, 1960-63; Professor of Music, University of York, 1964-81; Visiting Professor, City University, 1984-. Publications: Music and Society: England and the European Tradition, 1946; Studies in Contemporary Music, 1947; François Couperin and the French Classical Tradition, 1950, 2nd edition, revised, 1987; Music in the Making, 1952; Romanticism and the 20th Century, 1957, 2nd edition, revised, 1988; The Sonata Principle, 1957, 2nd edition, revised, 1988; Music in a New Found Land: Themes and Developments in the History of American Music, 1964, 2nd edition, revised, 1987; Harmonious Meeting: A Study of the Relationship between English Music, Poetry, and Theatre, c.1600-1900, 1965; Caliban Reborn: Renewal in Twentieth-Century Music, 1967; Twilight of the Gods: The Music of the Beatles, 1973; Bach and the Dance of God, 1980; Beethoven and the Voice of God, 1983; A Darker Shade of Pale: A Backdrop to Bob Dylan, 1984; Angels of the Night: Popular Female Singers of Our Time, 1986; The Masks of Orpheus: Seven Stages in the Story of European Music, 1987; Le Jardin Retrouvé: Homage to Federico Mompou, 1989; Vaughan Williams and the Vision of Albion, 1989, new enlarged edition, 1997; The Music of Percy Grainger, 1992; Francis Poulenc, 1994; Between Old Worlds and New: Occasional Writings on Music by Wilfrid Mellers, 1998; Singing in the Wilderness, 2001; Celestial Music, 2002. Contributions to: Reference works and journals. Honours: Honorary DPhil, City University, 1981; Officer of the Order of the British Empire, 1982. Membership: Sonneck Society, honorary member. Address: Oliver Sheldon House, 17 Aldwark, York, YO1 7BX, England.

MELLING John Kennedy, b. 11 January 1927, Westcliff-on-Sea, Essex, England. Drama Critic; Editor; Writer; Lecturer; Broadcaster; Chartered Accountant. Appointments: Drama Critic, The Stage, 1957-90; Drama Critic, Fur Weekly News, 1968-73; Editor, The Liveryman Magazine, 1970-75, Chivers Black Dagger Series of Crime Classics, 1986-91; Radio Crime Book Critic, BBC London, 1984-85, BBC Essex, 1987. Publications: Discovering Lost Theatres, 1969; Southend Playhouses from 1793, 1969; Discovering London's Guilds and Liveries, 6 editions, 1973-03; Discovering Theatre Ephemera, 1974; The Poulters of London Booklet, 1977; She Shall Have Murder, 1987; Murder in the Library, 1987; Fantasy Games' Influence on the Young, 1987; Social Development of Theatres, 1987; Crime Writers' Handbook of Practical Information (editor), 1989; Gwendoline Butler: Inventor of the Women's Police Procedural, 1993; Alchemy of Murder, 1993; Murder Done to Death, 1996; Scaling the High C's (with John L Brecknock), 1996; A Little Manual of Etiquette for Gentlemen, 2004; The Constructors: Genesis and Growth, 2004; A Little Manual of Etiquette for Ladies, 2005; Plays include: George....From Caroline, 1971; Old Christmas, 1979; The Toast is ... (series), 1979-84; Diarists' Pleasures, 1982; Murder at St Dunstan's, 1983; Regular columnist, Crime Time magazine, 1996-2002. Honours: Knight Grand Cross; Order of St Michael; Master of the Worshipful Company of Poulters, 1980-81; Police Medal of Honour, USA, 1984; Knight, Order of St Basil, 1984; Crime Writers Association Award for Outstanding Services, 1989; Listed in national and international biographical dictionaries. Memberships: British Academy of Film and Television Arts; Institute of Taxation, fellow; Faculty of Building, Royal Society of Arts, fellow; Crime Writers' Association, committee member, 1985-88; Governor of the Corporation of the Sons of the Clergy, 1981-; Member, Drugs Task Force, National Association of Chiefs of Police as Honorary Chief of Police, USA; Honorary International Life Vice-President, American Federation of Police; Founder-President, First Honorary Life Member, Westcliff Film and Video Club; Member, Cookery and Food Association; Member, City Livery Club; Liveryman, Worshipful Companies of Bakers, Farriers, and Constructors; Marylebone Rifle and Pistol Club. Addresses: 44 A Tranquil Vale, Blackheath, London SE3 0BD, England; 85 Chalkwell Avenue, Westcliff-on-Sea, Essex, SS0 8NL, England.

MELLOR D(avid) H(ugh), b. 10 July 1938, England. Professor of Philosophy; Writer. Education: BA, Natural Sciences and Chemical Engineering, 1960, PhD, 1968, ScD, 1990, M in English, 1992, Pembroke College, Cambridge; MSc, Chemical Engineering, University of Minnesota, 1962. Appointments: Research Student in Philosophy, Pembroke College, 1963-68, Fellow, Pembroke College, 1965-70, University Assistant Lecturer in Philosophy, 1965-70, University Lecturer in Philosophy, 1970-83, Fellow, 1971-, and Vice-Master, 1983-87, Darwin College, University Reader in Metaphysics, 1983-85, Professor of Philosophy, 1986-99, Professor Emeritus, 1999-, Pro-Vice-Chancellor, 2000-01, Cambridge University; Visiting Fellow in Philosophy, Australian National University, Canberra, 1975; Honorary Professor of Philosophy, University of Keele, 1989-92. Publications: The Matter of Chance, 1971; Real Time, 1981; Cambridge Studies in Philosophy, (editor), 1978-82; Matters of Metaphysics, 1991; The Facts of Causation, 1995; Real Time II, 1998; numerous articles on philosophy of science, metaphysics and philosophy of mind. Contributions to

Scholarly journals. Memberships: Aristotelian Society, president, 1992-93; British Academy, fellow; British Society for the Philosophy of Science, president, 1985-87; British Humanist Association. Address: 25 Orchard Street, Cambridge CB1 1JS, England.

MELVILLE David Murray, b. 2 October 1953, Epsom, Surrey, England. Surgeon. m. Sarah Taylor, 3 sons, 1 daughter. Education: Epsom College; Merton College, Oxford; St Thomas'. Appointments: Consultant Surgeon, St George's Hospital, London. Publications: Intestinal Disorders; Medical Education. Memberships: Royal Society of Medicine; Royal Automobile Club; Association of Surgeons. Address: 18 Caroline Place, London W2 4AN, England. E-mail: david@melville.clara.co.uk

MEMOS Constantine Demetrius, b. 26 November 1946, Patras, Greece. Civil Engineer. m. Maria Antonopoulou, 2 sons. Education: MEng, Civil Engineering, National Technical University of Athens, Greece, 1969; Diploma, Mathematics, University of Patras, Greece, 1972; DIC, PhD, University of London, Imperial College, 1977. Appointments: Educator, Civil Engineering Department, National Technical University of Athens, 1978-; Professor, Maritime Hydraulics and Port Engineering, 2004-; Engineer, Consultant, Port Planning and Design, 1978-. Publications: Over 120 articles in journals and conference proceedings, including Journal of Fluid Mechanics, Coastal Engineering, ASCE Journal of Ports and Waterways, Coastal Engineering Conference, Journal of Hydraulic Research. Honours: Unwin Prize, Imperial College, 1977; Embeirikeio Prize of Technological Science, with Award, Greece, 1988; David Hislop Award, Institution of Civil Engineers, London, 2004; President, ASCE Hellenic Group; Engineers of the Earth. Memberships: Technical Chamber of Greece; Fellow, ASCE; Member, PIANC; IAHR; New York Academy of Sciences. Address: National Technical University of Athens, 5 Heroon Polytechneiou, 15780 Zografos, Greece. E-mail: memos@hydro.ntua.gr

MENDELSON Paul Anthony, b. 6 April 1951, Newcastle upon Tyne. Scriptwriter. m. Michal Mendelson, 2 daughters. Education: MA Law, Emmanuel College, Cambridge. Appointments: Group Head, Ogilvy & Mather, 1973-80; Deputy Creative Director, Wasey Campbell-Ewald, 1980-82; Creative Group Head Dorland Advertising, 1982-88; Creative Director, Capper Granger, 1988-90; Scriptwiter, 1990-; Creator and writer: Losing It, ITV; My Hero, BBC1; So Haunt Me, BBC1; May to December, BBC1; The Dover Series, Radio 4; Snap, Radio 4; A Meeting in Seville, Radio 4; Neighbours from Hell (US in development). Honours: TV and Best Radio Commercial and Best Radio Campaign for Don't Drink and Drive, 1980; Best Media Commercial Clio, 1982; Best Radio Commercial (food) Clio, 1986 BAFTA Nomination for From May to December, 1990. Memberships: Writers Guild of Great Britain; Groucho Club. Address: c/o Alan Brodie Representation, 6th Floor, Fairgate House, 78 New Oxford Street, London WC1A 1HB, England.

MENDES Sam, b. 1 August 1965, England. Theatre Director. m. Kate Winslet, 1 son. Education: Magdalen College School; Oxford University; Peterhouse, Cambridge University. Appointments: Artistic Director, Minerva Studio Theatre, Chichester; Artistic Director, Donmar Warehouse, 1992-2002. Creative Works: Plays directed include: London Assurance, Chichester; The Cherry Orchard, London; Kean, Old Vic, London; The Plough and the Stars, Young Vic, London, Troilus and Cressida, RSC, The Alchemist, RSC, 1991; Richard III, RSC, 1992; The Tempest, RSC, 1993; National Theatre debut with The Sea, 1991; The Rise and Fall of Little Voice, National and Aldwych, 1992; The Birthday Party, 1994; Othello (also world tour); Assassins, Translations, Cabaret, Glengarry Glen Ross, The Glass Menagerie, Company, Habeas Corpus, The Front Page, The Blue Room, To the Green Fields Beyond, (all at Donmar Warehouse) 1992-2000; Uncle Vanya and Twelfth Night, Donmar Warehouse, 2002; Oliver!, London Palladium; Cabaret, The Blue Room, Broadway, New York; Gypsy with Bernadette Peters, Broadway. Films: American Beauty, 1999; The Road to Perdition, 2002; Jarhead, 2005; Starter for Ten, 2006; The Kite Runner, 2007; Things We Lost in the Fire, 2007; Revolutionary Road, 2008. Honours include: Commander of the British Empire, 2000; Critics' Circle Award, 1989, 1993, 1996; Olivier Award for Best Director, 1996; Tony Award, 1998; LA Critics' Award, Broadcast Critics' Award, Toronto People's Choice Award, Golden Globe Award, 1999; Shakespeare Prize, Academy Award for Best Director (also Best Film) for American Beauty, 2000; The Hamburg Shakespeare Prize; Oliver Award for Best Director (also Special Award), 2003. Address: 26-28 Neal Street, London, WC2H 9QQ, England. E-mail: mleigh@scampltd.com

MÉNDEZ RODRÍGUEZ José Manuel, b. 19 March 1955, Reinosa, Spain. Professor of Logic. 2 sons. Education: BA, History, 1978; BA, Philosophy, 1979; PhD, 1983. Appointments: Assistant Lecturer, 1980, Associate Professor, 1981, Professor, 1988-. Publications: Several articles in professional journals. Honours: 1st Class Distinction 1979; Special Distinction, 1983. Member of the Association for Symbolic Logic. Address: Departamento de Filosofia, Universidad de Salamanca, Edificio FES, Campus Unamuno, 37007 Salamanca, Spain. E-mail: sefus@usal.es Website: http//web.usal.es/n.sefus

MENEM Carlos Saul, b. 2 July 1935, Anillaco, La Rioja, Argentina. Politician. m. (1) Zulema Fatima Yoma, 1966, divorced, 1 son, deceased, 1 daughter, (2) Cecilia Bolocco, 2001, 1 child. Education: Cordoba University. Appointments: Founder, Juventud Peronista, Peron Youth Group, La Rioja Province, 1955; Defended political prisoners following 1955 Coup; Legal Advisor, Confederacion General del Trabajo, La Rioja Province, 1955-70; Candidate, Provincial Deputy, 1958; President, Partido Justicialista, La Rioja Province, 1963-; Elected Govenor, La Rioja, 1973, re-elected, 1983, 1987; Imprisoned following military coup, 1976-81; Candidate for President, Argentine Republic for Partido Justicialista, 1989; President of Argentina, 1989-2001; Vice President, Conference of Latin-American Popular Parties, 1990-; Arrested for alleged involvement in illegal arms sales during his presidency, June 2001, charged, July 2001, placed under house arrest for five months; Presidential Candidate, 2003. Publications: Argentine, Now or Never; Argentina Year 2000; The Productive Revolution, with Eduardo Duhalde. Address: Casa de Gobierno, Balcarce 50, 1064 Buenos Aires, Argentina.

MENKEN Alan, b. 22 July 1949, New York, USA. m. Janis, 1972, 2 children. Composer. Education: New York University. Creative Works: Theatre music including: God Bless You Mr Rosewater, 1979; Little Shop of Horrors, with Howard Ashman; Kicks; The Apprenticeship of Duddy Kravitz; Diamonds; Personals; Let Freedom Sing; Weird Romance; Beauty and the Beast; A Christmas Carol; Film music includes: Little Shop of Horrors, 1986; The Little Mermaid, 1988; Beauty and the Beast, 1990; Lincoln, 1992; Newsies, 1992; Aladdin, 1992; Life with Mikey, 1993; Pocahontas, with Stephen Schwartz, 1995; The Hunchback of Notre Dame, 1996; Hercules, 1997; Home on the Range, 2004; Noel, 2004;

The Shaggy Dog, 2006; Enchanted, 2007. Honours include: Several Academy Awards, 1989, 1993, 1996; Golden Globe Award, 1996. Address: The Shukat Company, 340 West 55th Street, Apt 1A, New York, NY 10019, USA.

MENNEN Ulrich, b. 1 July 1947, Barberton, Mpumalanga, South Africa. m. Johanna Margaretha Louw, 2 sons, 1 daughter. Education: MBChB, University of Pretoria, 1970; FRCS, Glasgow, 1978, Edinburgh, 1978; FCS (SA) Ortho, 1979; MMed, Orthopaedics, University of Pretoria, 1979; FHMVS (DUMC) 1983; MD, Orthopaedics, 1983; DSc (Med), 2007. Appointments include: Senior Surgeon, 1980, Principal Surgeon, 1981; Associate Professor and Principal Surgeon, 1983, Orthopaedics, Pretoria Academic Hospital; Microsurgery Fellow, Duke University Medical Centre, Durham, North Carolina, USA, 1983; Professor and Head, Department of Hand- and Microsurgery, Medical University of Southern Africa, 1985-; Honorary Head, Hand Surgery Unit, Pretoria Academic Hospital; Head, Department of Orthopaedic Surgery, Medical University of Southern Africa, 1990-91; Visiting Professor, Hong Kong, Australia, USA, Vietnam, Iran, South Korea, Botswana, Ethiopia, Uganda, Tanzania; Private Hand Surgery Practice, 1992-; Founder and Member, Pretoria Hand Institute, Jakaranda Hospital, 1997-; Originates and develops: MIRA (Mennen Interposition Replacement Arthoplasty) prosthesis for digital joint replacement; DSc (Med), 2007. Publications: Chirurgiese Sinopsis, 1978; Co-author, Surgical Synopsis, 1983; Editor, The Hand Book, 1988, second edition, 1994, third edition, 2007; Co-editor, Principles of Surgical Patient Care, vols 1 and 2, 1990, second edition, 2003; The History of South African Society for Surgery of the Hand 1969-1994, 1994; 195 articles in professional journals and book chapters. Honours include: Registrar's Prize for Best Paper, 1978, 1979; G F Dommisse Orthopaedic Registrar Prize, 1979; Mer-National Literary Prize, for article, 1982; Smith and Nephew Literary Award, South African Orthopaedic Association, 1985; Chamber of Mines Research Grant, 1987; Glaxo Literary Award, 1990; Finalist, Wellcome Medal for Medical Research, 1990; Research Excellence Award, Faculty of Medicine, MEDUNSA, 1997; Masimanyane Award, Engineering Association, 1997; South African Bureau of Standards Design Institute Award, Overall Chairman's Award for Excellence, 1997; 14 times winner, SASSH Annual Isidore Kaplan Literary Prize; Numerous other literary prizes; Originator and developer of the Mennen Clamp-on Bone Fixation System, the Mennen Interposition Replacement Arthroplasty (MIRA prostheses) and the Mennen Tendon Suture (MTST); Pioneer in End-to-side Nerve Suture Technique; South African Orthopaedic Association Presidents Essay Medal, 2005. Memberships include: South African Medical Association; SA Orthopaedic Association; SA Association for Arthritis and Rheumatic Diseases; Cripples Research Association of South Africa; International Member, American Society for Surgery of the Hand; Executive Member and Past President, South African Society for Surgery of the Hand; Founding Member, South African Society for Hand Therapy; Executive Member, Past-Secretary-General and President-Elect, International Federation of Societies for Surgery of the Hand. Address: 374 Lawley Street, Waterkloof, 0181, Pretoria, South Africa.

MEOLA Carosena, b. 11 June 1955, Greci, Avellino, Italy. Senior Researcher Staff Member. Education: Doctor in Aeronautical Engineering, University of Naples Federico II, 1981; Preliminary English Test PET, 1990, First Certificate in English, 1991, University of Cambridge; Thermographer Level II. Appointments: Research Fellowship, Laboratorio Ricerche ed Esperienze dell'Aeritalia di Pomigliano d'Arco, Naples,

1982-83; Research Fellowship, Institute of Gasdynamic, University of Naples, 1984-85; Research Staff Member, 1985-, Consultant Health, Safety and Risk Management, 2000-, Department of Energetics Thermofluidynamics and Environmental Control, University of Naples Federico II; Senior Researcher Staff Member, Department of Aerospace Engineering; Main interests: application of infrared thermography in Fluid Dynamics, Technological Field and Cultural Heritage. Publications: Over 80 scientific papers including 35 published in international journals; 2 review articles in international journals; Invited entry, Encyclopedia of Chemical Processing (ECHP); Many papers presented at international conferences; Enclosed in Database: Aerospace & High Technology Database, Frost & Sullivan Database, CSA/ ASCE Civil Engineering Abstracts; Referee for more than 10 international journals. Honours: Degree Award, Fondazione Politecnica per il Mezzogiorno d'Italia, 1981. Memberships: Ergonomic Society. Address: DIAS Università di Napoli Federico II, Piazzale Tecchio, 80, 80125 Naples, Italy. E-mail: carmeola@unina.it

MERK P Evelyn, b. 8 December 1943, Macon, Georgia, USA. Librarian. Education: AB, Mercer University, 1966; M Ed, University of Georgia, 1973; MLS, Emory University, 1987. Appointments: English Teacher, East Laurens School, East Dublin, Georgia, 1966-68; English Teacher, Westside School, McDonough, Georgia, 1968-70; English Teacher, Brantley County High School, Nahunta, Georgia, 1970-72; School Media Specialist, Mary Persons High School, Forsyth, Georgia, 1973-75; Technical Services Librarian, 1975-76, Reference Librarian, 1976-77, Head Librarian, 1977-96, Assistant Director, 1996-2002, Library Consultant/Trainer, 2002-06, Retired, 2007-, Houston County Public Library, Warner Robins, Georgia. Publications: Editor: AAUW Warner Robins Newsletter, 1977-80; Houston County Friends of the Library Newsletter, 2007-; AAUW Warner Robins Yearbook, 1989-; AAUW Georgia Directory, 2005-. Honours: BPW Woman of Achievement, 1997. Memberships: American Association of University Women; Business and Professional Women; International Federation of University Women; American Library Association; Public Library Association; Southeastern Library Association; Georgia Library Association; Warner Robins Pioneers; University of Georgia Alumni Association; Theatre Macon; Macon Little Theatre; Warner Robins Little Theatre; Warner Robins Community Concert Association; American Association of Retired Persons; Friends of Georgia's Libraries; Houston County Friends of the Library; Emory University Friends of the Library; Houston Arts Alliance. Address: 293 Peachtree Cir, Warner Robins, GA 31088-4448, USA. E-mail: pemerk@yahoo.com

MERKEL Angela, b. 17 July 1954, Hamburg, Germany. Chancellor of Germany. Education: Physics doctorate, 1978. Appointments: Chemist, scientific academy, East Berlin; Joined the Christian Democratic Union (CDU), 1990; Minister for Women and Youth, 1991-94; Minister for Environment, Nature Protection and Reactor Safety, 1994-98; General Secretary, 1993-2000, Chairman, 1998-2000, CDU Deutschlands; Chairman, CDU/CSU-Bundestagsfraktion, 2002-; Chancellor of Germany, 2005-. Publications: The Price of Survival: Ideas and Conversations about Future Tasks for Environmental Policy, 1997. Member: Council of Women World Leaders, 2007. Address: Office of the Federal Chancellor, Willy-Brandt-Strasse 1, D-10557, Berlin, Germany. Website: www.cdu.de

MERKURYEV Yuri, b. 30 April 1954, Riga, Latvia. Educator. m. Galina Merkuryeva, 1 daughter. Education: Electrical Engineer, Automation and Remote Control, 1976, Candidate of Technical Sciences, 1982, Doctor of Engineering, 1992, Habilitated Doctor of Engineering, 1997, Riga Technical University; Sabbatical year in Finland: Abo Akademi, Turku and Helsinki University of Technology, Helsinki, 1987-88. Appointments: Research Assistant, Department of Automatic Control Systems, 1976-78, Doctoral Student, 1978-81, Teaching Assistant, Senior Lecturer, Associate Professor, Acting Head of the Department of Automatic Control Systems, 1982-93; Associate Professor, Head of the Department of Modelling and Simulation, 1993-97, Full Professor, Head of the Department of Modelling and Simulation, 1997-, Riga Technical University; Part-time Professor, University of Rezekne, 1998-2002. Publications: 233 publications including 4 books and a textbook: Logistics Information Systems; 180 scientific papers including chapters in the books: Bounding Approaches to System Identification, 1996, Supply Chain Optimisation: Product/process design, facility location and flow control, 2005; Papers in scientific journals and conference proceedings; 17 teaching publications and 18 edited books. Honours: Best Paper Award, European Simulation Symposium, Dresden, Germany, 1992; Annual Award of the Latvian National Organisation on Automation, 1997; Corresponding Member, Latvian Academy of Sciences, 2004. Memberships include: Senior Member, Board Member, European Council; Director, Latvian MISS Centre; Society for Modelling and Simulation International; Chartered Fellow, British Computer Society; President, Latvian Simulation Society; Baltic Operations Research Society; National Geographic Society; Latvian Scientists Union; Latvian Association of University Professors; Board Member, Latvian Transport Development and Education Association; Editorial Boards: Simulation & Gaming: An Interdisciplinary Journal of Theory, Practice and Research; International Journal of Simulation and Process Modelling; SCS Publishing House. Address: Riga Technical University, Kalku Street 1, LV-1658 Riga, Latvia. E-mail: merkur@itl.rtu.lv

MEYER Conrad John Eustace, b. 2 July 1922, Bristol, England. Retired Roman Catholic Priest. m. Mary Wiltshire. Education: Pembroke College, Cambridge; Westcott House, Cambridge; Ordained Priest in the Roman Catholic Church, 1995. Appointments: War Service, 1942-46; Lieutenant (S), Chaplain, RNVR, retired 1954; As Anglican: Diocesan Secretary for Education, 1960-69; Archdeacon of Bodmin, Truro Diocese, 1969-79 Honorary Canon, Truro Cathedral, 1960-79; Provost, Western Division of Woodard Schools, 1970-92; Examining Chaplain to the Bishop of Truro, 1973-79; Area Bishop of Dorchester, Oxford Diocese, 1979-87; Honorary Assistant Bishop, Truro Diocese, 1990-94; As Roman Catholic: Honorary Canon, Plymouth Roman Catholic Cathedral, 2001. Memberships: Formerly Chairman of Appeal Committee, Vice-Chairman of Society, 1989-90, Vice-President, 1990-, Society for Promoting Christian Knowledge (SPCK); Chairman, Cornwall Civil Aid and County Commissioner, 1993-96; Honorary Fellow, Institute for Civil Defence and Disaster Studies. Address: Hawk's Cliff, 38 Praze Road, Newquay, Cornwall TR7 3AF, England.

MIANO Eliphelet, b. 18 November 1932, Meru, Kenya. Civil Engineer. m. Zipporah Murugi, 2 sons, 3 daughters. Education: Makerere University, Kampala, Uganda, 1950-52; University of Alberta, Canada, 1961-65. Appointments: Engineering Assistant, 1953-61, Civil Engineer, 1965-67, Mowlem Construction Company; East African Engineering Consultants, 1967-; Appointed Director, 1969, Chairman,

1978. Honours: Elder of the Order of Burning Spear (EBS), Republic of Kenya, 1985. Memberships: Fellow, Institution of Engineers of Kenya; Association, Consulting Engineers of Kenya. Address: PO Box 21045, 00505 Ngong Road, Nairobi, Kenya.

MICHAEL George (Georgios Kyriacos Panayiotou), b. 25 June 1963, Finchley, London, England. Singer; Songwriter; Producer. Career: Singer, The Executive, 1979; Singer, pop duo Wham! with Andrew Ridgeley, 1982-86; Solo artiste, 1986-; Worldwide appearances include: Live Aid, with Elton John, Wembley, 1985; Prince's Trust Rock Gala, Wham's 'The Final' concert, Wembley, 1986; Nelson Mandela's 70th Birthday Tribute, 1988; Rock In Rio II Festival, Brazil, 1991; A Concert For Life, tribute to Freddie Mercury, Wembley Stadium, Elizabeth Taylor AIDS Foundation Benefit, Madison Square Garden, New York, 1992; Dispute with Epic record label, and parent company Sony Entertainment, 1992-95; Television special, Aretha Franklin: Duets, 1993. Recordings: Albums: with Wham!: Fantastic, 1983; Make It Big, 1984; The Final, 1986; Solo albums: Faith, 1987; Listen Without Prejudice, Vol 1, 1990; Older, 1996; Older and Upper, Ladies and Gentlemen: The Best of George Michael, 1998; Songs from the Last Century, 1999; Patience, 2004; Contributor, Duets, Elton John, 1991; Two Rooms, 1992; Hit singles include: with Wham!: Wham Rap, Young Guns (Go For It), 1982; Bad Boys, Club Tropicana, 1983; Wake Me Up Before You Go Go, Last Christmas, 1984; Careless Whisper, Everything She Wants, 1984; Freedom, I'm Your Man, 1985; The Edge Of Heaven, Solo: A Different Corner, 1986; I Knew You Were Waiting For Me, duet with Aretha Franklin, I Want Your Sex, Faith, 1987; Father Figure, One More Try, Monkey, Kissing A Fool, 1988; Praying For Time, Freedom 90, 1990; Don't Let The Sun Go Down On Me, duet with Elton John; Too Funky, 1992; Five Live EP, Somebody To Love, with Queen, 1993; Jesus To A Child, 1995; Fast Love, 1996; Star People, You Have Been Loved, 1997; Outside, 1998; As, with Mary J Blige, 1999; If I Told You That, with Whitney Houston, 2000; Freeek!, Shoot the Dog, 2002; Amazing, 2004; Contributor, Do They Know It's Christmas?, Band Aid, 1985; Nikita, Elton John, 1985. Publication: Bare, with Tony Parsons (autobiography). Honours include: BRIT Awards: Best British Group, 1985; Outstanding Contribution to British Music, 1986; Best British Male Artist, 1988; Best British Album, 1991; Ivor Novello Awards: Songwriter Of The Year, 1985, 1989; Most Performed Work (Careless Whisper), 1985; Hit Of The Year (Faith), 1989; Grammy, with Aretha Franklin, 1988; Nordoff-Robbins Silver Clef Award, 1989; American Music Awards: Favourite Pop/Rock Male Artist, Soul R&B Male Artist, Favourite Album, 1989; ASCAP Golden Note Award, 1992. Address: c/o Connie Filipello Publicity, 17 Gosfield Street, London W1P 7HE, England.

MICHAEL (H M King), b. 25 October 1921, Romania. King of Romania. m. Princess Anne of Bourbon-Parma, 1948, 5 daughters. Appointments: Declared heir apparent, ratified by Parliament 1926; Proclaimed King, 1927, deposed by his father, 1930; Succeeded to the throne of Romania following his father's abdication, 1940; Led coup d'etat against pro Nazi dictator Ion Antonescu, 1944; Forced to abdicate following communist takeover of Romania, 1947; Subsequently ran chicken farm in Hertfordshire, England; Went to Switzerland as a Test Pilot, 1956; Worked for Lear Incorporated; Founder, Electronics Company; Stockbroker; Deported from Romania on first visit since exile, 1990; Returned to Romania, 1992; Romanian citizenship and passport restored, 1997; Undertook official mission for Romania's integration into NATO and EU 1997. Honours: Order of Victoria, USSR, 1945; Chief

Commander, Legion of Merit, USA, 1946; Honorary KCVO. Address: 17 La Croix-de-Luisant, 1170 Aubonne, Vaud, Switzerland.

MICHALEK Pavel, b. 27 April 1968, Pardubice, Czech Republic. Consultant Anaesthetist. m. Michaela Vesela, 2 sons, 1 daughter. Education: MD, Medical Faculty, Charles University, Prague, Czech Republic, 1992; Board Certification of 2nd Degree, Anaesthesia and Intensive Care, Prague, 2000; PhD, Medical Faculty, Masaryk University, Brno, 2002. Appointments: Registrar, SHO, District Hospital, Louny, Czech Republic, 1992-98; Consultant, Specialist Registrar, IKEM, Prague, 1998-2001; Chief, Department of Cardiovascular Anaesthesiology and Intensive Care, Nahomolce Hospital, Prague, 2001-05; Senior Lecturer, Medical Faculty, Charles University, Prague, 2001-; Consultant Anaesthetist, Antrim General Hospital, 2005-. Publications: Articles in professional medical journals including: Interventional pain management, 2002; Techniques of regional anaesthesia and analgesia, 2002; Sedation in dental office, 2007. Honours: Reviewer, Journal of Clincal Anaesthesia, USA; Reviewer, BMJ Learning, UK. Memberships: European Society of Regional Anaesthesia; Difficult Airway Society; International Association for Study of Pain; Czech Pain Society; Board Member, Czech Society of Anaesthesia and Intensive Care. Address: 4 Alexandra Park, Muckamore, BT41 4RD, Northern Ireland, United Kingdom. E-mail: pafkamich@yahoo.co.uk

MIDDLEBURGH Charles Hadley, b. 2 October 1956, Hove, East Sussex, England. Rabbi. m. Gilly Blyth. Education: BA (Hons) Ancient and Medieval Hebrew and Aramaic, 1979, PhD, Aramaic, 1982, University College, London. Rabbinic Ordination, Leo Baeck College, 1986. Appointments: Reader, Brighton and Hove, Progressive Synagogue, 1975-77; Minister, Kingston Liberal Synagogue, 1977-83; Rabbi, Harrow and Wembley Progressive Synagogue, 1983-97; Executive Director, Union of Liberal and Progressive Synagogues, 1997-2002; Rabbi, Dublin Jewish Progressive Congregation, 2002-; Rabbi, Progressive Judaism in Denmark, 2002-; Rabbi, Cardiff Reform Synagogue, 2005-; Lecturer in Aramaic, Bible and Practical Rabbinics, 1984-2002, Senior Lecturer in Rabbinics, 2003-, Leo Baeck College; Lecturer, Irish School of Ecumenics, Trinity College, Dublin, 2003-. Publications: Siddur Lev Chadash, Daily, Sabbath and Festival Liturgy, Union of Liberal and Progressive Synagogues (associate editor), 1995; Machzor Ruach Chadashah, High Holyday Liturgy, Union of Liberal and Progressive Synagogues (joint editor), 2003; Book reviews in the Jewish Chronicle, Church Times, Expository Times. Memberships: Fellow, Royal Society of Arts; Fellow, Zoological Society of London. Address: c/o Leo Baeck College, Centre for Jewish Education, The Sternberg Centre, 80 East End Road, Finchley N3 2SY, England. E-mail: charles@middleburgh.co.uk Website: www.middleburgh.co.uk

MIDDLETON Roger, b. 19 May 1955. Professor; Writer. Education: BA, First Class Honours, Victoria University of Manchester, 1976; PhD, Cambridge University, 1981. Appointments: Lecturer in Economic History, University of Durham, 1979-87; Lecturer in Economic History, 1987-90; Senior Lecturer in Economic History, 1990-97, University of Bristol; Reader in the History of Political Economy, 1997-2006. Publications: Towards the Managed Economy, 1985; Government Versus the Market, 1996; Charlatans or Saviours?, 1998; The British Economy Since 1945, 2000; Exemplary Economists (editor with R E Backhouse), 2000; Economic Policy under the Conservatives (with A Ringe & N Rollings), 2004. Contributions to: Economic, history and computing journals. Honours: T S Ashton Prize, Economic History Society, 1980; Choice Outstanding Academic Book, 1996, 1998; Royal Historical Society, fellow; Academician of the Social Sciences. Memberships: Royal Economic Society; Economic History Society; Political Studies Association; Institute of Fiscal Studies. Address: Department of Historical Studies, University of Bristol, Bristol BS1 1TB, England.

MIDDLETON Stanley, b. 1 August 1919, Bulwell, Nottingham, England. Novelist. m. Margaret Shirley Charnley, 22 December 1951, 2 daughters. Education: University College, Nottingham; BA, London University; Cert Ed, Cambridge University; MEd, Nottingham University. Appointments: H M Forces, 1940-46; Head of English, High Pavement College, Nottingham; Judith E Wilson Visiting Fellow, Emmanuel College, Cambridge. Publications: A Short Answer, 1958; Harris's Requiem, 1960; A Serious Woman, 1961; The Just Exchange, 1962; Two's Company, 1963; Him They Compelled, 1964; The Golden Evening, 1968; Wages of Virtue, 1969; Brazen Prison, 1971; Holiday, 1974; Still Waters, 1976; Two Brothers, 1978; In a Strange Land, 1979; The Other Side, 1980; Blind Understanding, 1982; Entry into Jerusalem, 1983; Daysman, 1984; Valley of Decision, 1985; An After Dinner's Sleep, 1986; After a Fashion, 1987; Recovery, 1988; Vacant Places, 1989; Changes & Chances, 1990; Beginning to End, 1991; A Place to Stand, 1992; Married Past Redemption, 1993; Catalysts, 1994; Toward the Sea, 1995; Live and Learn, 1996; Brief Hours, 1997; Against the Dark, 1997; Necessary Ends, 1999; Small Change, 2000; Love in the Provinces, 2004; Brief Garlands, 2004; Sterner Stuff, 2005. Honours: Co-Recipient, Booker Prize, 1974; Honorary MA, Nottingham University; Honorary MUniv, Open University; Honorary DLitt, De Montfort University; FRSL; Honorary DLitt, Nottingham Trent University, 2000. Membership: PEN. Address: 42 Caledon Road, Sherwood, Nottingham NG5 2NG, England.

MIDLER Bette, b. 1 December 1945, Paterson, New Jersey, USA. Singer; Actress; Comedienne. m. Martin von Haselberg, 1984, 1 daughter. Education: Theatre studies, University of Hawaii. Career: As actress: Cast member, Fiddler On The Roof, Broadway, 1966-69; Salvation, New York, 1970; Rock opera Tommy, Seattle Opera Company, 1971; Nightclub concert performer and solo artiste, 1972-; Numerous television appearances include: Ol' Red Hair Is Back, NBC, 1978; Bette Midler's Mondo Beyondo, HBO, 1988; Earth Day Special, ABC, 1990; The Tonight Show, NBC, 1991; Now, NBC, 1993; Films include: Hawaii, 1965; The Rose, 1979; Jinxed!, 1982; Down And Out In Beverly Hills, 1985; Ruthless People, 1986; Outrageous Fortune, 1987; Big Business, 1988; Beaches, 1988; Stella, 1990; Scenes From A Mall, 1990; For The Boys (also co-producer), 1991; Hocus Pocus, 1993; Gypsy, 1993; The First Wives Club, 1996; That Old Feeling, 1997; Drowning Mona, 2000; Isn't She Great, 2000; The Stepford Wives, 2004; Then She Found Me, 2007. Own company, All Girls Productions, 1989-. Recordings: Albums include: The Divine Miss M, 1972; Bette Midler, 1973; Songs For The New Depression, 1976; Broken Blossom, 1977; Live At Last, 1977; Thighs And Whispers, 1979; The Rose, film soundtrack, 1979; Divine Madness, film soundtrack, 1980; No Frills, 1984; Beaches, film soundtrack, 1989; Some People's Lives, 1991; Best Of, 1993; Bette Of Roses, 1995; Experience the Divine, 1997; Bathhouse Betty, 1998; From a Distance, 1998. Singles include: The Rose; Wind Beneath My Wings (Number 1, US), from Beaches soundtrack, 1989; From A Distance, 1991. Publications: A View From A Broad; The Saga Of Baby Divine. Honours: After Dark Award, Performer Of The Year, 1973; Grammy Awards: Best New Artist, 1973;

Best Female Pop Vocal Performance, The Rose, 1981; Record Of The Year, Song Of The Year, Wind Beneath My Wings, 1990; Special Tony Award, 1973; Emmy, Ol' Red Hair Is Back, 1978; Golden Globe Awards: The Rose, 1979; For The Boys, 1991; Oscar Nomination, Best Actress, The Rose, 1980; Contributor, We Are The World, USA For Africa, 1985; Oliver And Company, 1988. Address: c/o All Girls Productions, Animation Bldg #3B-10, 500 South Buena Vista, Burbank, CA 91521, USA.

MIKHAILUSENKO Igor Georgievich, b. 20 April 1932, Moscow, Russia. Translator; Poet; Journalist. Education: Graduate, Maurice Thorez Foreign Languages Institute, Moscow, 1958; Higher Education Diploma, Translator from Russian into English. Appointments: Various posts as translator and English-language speaker; USSR Travel Agency, Intourist; Various assignments as a free-lance journalist; Poetry writer. Publications: Contributor to numerous publications including Dostoinstvo newspaper, 1995-2004; Many poems set to music, which became popular songs; Articles include: Tribute to Third Millennium (book), 2001; Memoirs of Moscow's Man (book); Poet's Dreams (book), 2001; A Peaceful Travel – USA Through Foreign Eyes, (book), 2001; What I Wish (Oh I Wish) I Had Said (book), 2002; Poems That Mirror My Soul (book), 2003; Poems about Flowers (book), 2004; The Will of Baron De Couberten – International Olympic Museum through the eyes of Moscow's poet (book), 2004. Honours: Many awards and citations for international peace efforts, including Badge of Honour, Moscow Peace Committee, 1982; Recognised by the United Poets Laureate International, 1987; Award, Editors of Fine Arts Press, Knoxville, USA, for noteworthy contribution to book: Rainbows and Rhapsodies and his excellence in poetry, 1988; Laureate Man of Letters, awarded the Laurel Wreath, 1997; Listed in several prestigious international biographical directories. Memberships: Laurel Leaves, Official Organ of the United Poets Laureate International; Board of Directors, International Writers and Artists Association. Address: Bolshaya Gruzinskaya Street, House 63, Apartment 87, Moscow 123056, Russia. E-mail: vitaigor@list.ru Website: http:remdate.narod.ru/mikhailusenko.htm

MIKOLAJEWSKA Barbara, b. 3 December 1947, Poland. Sociologist; Author; Publisher. m. FEJ Linton. Education: Master's degree, Sociology. 1970, PhD, Sociology, 1979, Warsaw University, Poland. Appointments: Assistant, Warsaw Polytechnic University, 1970-72; Senior Assistant, 1972-79, Adjunct Professor, 1979-2002, Warsaw University; Co-proprietor, The Lintons' Video Press, New Haven, Connecticut, 1997-. Publications: Sociology of Small Groups, 1985; Ethnic Names as a Factor in Ethnic Distance, 1987; Community, 1989, second edition, revised, 1999; Who are Jews, 1989; Polish Translation of René Giraud's A Theater of Envy: William Shakespeare, 1996; Desire Came Upon That One in the Beginning, 1997, 1999; This Is Us – Doing Math, 1999, Symposium, 1999, Facing Off, 1999; Child's Play, 2000;The Adventures of Marysia, 14 volumes, 2000-04; Good Violence Versus Bad, 2004; The Mahabharata Retold (in Polish): Books I & II, 2007, Book III, 2007; Numerous web publications in English and Polish. Honours: Rector's Achievement Awards, Warsaw University, 1980, 1987, 1988, 1989, 1990. Memberships: Colloquium on Violence and Religion; Society for Indian Philosophy and Religion; Inner Circle, GCT. Address: 36 Everit Street, New Haven, CT, 06511-2208, USA. E-mail: bmikolajewska@gmail.com

MIKRIN Evgeny Anatolievich, b. 15 October 1955, Lebedyan, Russia. Engineer; Mathematician. m. Nataliya Vladimirovna, 1 son, 1 daughter. Education: Engineer-Mechanic, N Bauman Technical University, 1979; Engineer-Mathematician, Avionics Institute, Moscow, 1984; Doctor of Engineering Science, Control Sciences Institute, Moscow, 2001. Appointments: Engineer, 1981-85, Chief of Department, 1985-95, Deputy Chief of Division, 1995-2001, Chief of Division, 2001-07, First Deputy General Designer, 2007-, Rocket Space Corporation Energia; Assistant Professor, 1991-2000, Professor, 2000-, N Bauman Technical University. Publications: On-board Control Complexes for Space Vehicles and Designing of their SW, 2003; Theoretical Basis of Designing of Informational Control Systems for Space Vehicles, 2006. Honours: Medal for Services to Motherland, 2001; Russian Federation President's Grant, 2004, 2005; The Petrov Prize of Russian Academy of Sciences, 2007. Memberships: Russian Academy of Sciences; IEEE; International Academy of Guidance Navigation and Control Systems. Address: Rocket Space Corporation Energia, 4a Lenin Street, Korolev, Moscow Region, 141070, Russia. E-mail: eugeny.mikrin@rsce.ru

MILES Sarah, b. 31 December 1941, England. Actress. m. Robert Bolt, 1967, divorced 1976, re-married 1988, deceased 1995. Education: Royal Academy of Dramatic Art, London. Creative Works: Films include: Those Magnificent Men in Their Flying Machines, 1964; I Was Happy Here, 1966; The Blow-Up, 1966; Ryan's Daughter, 1970; Lady Caroline Lamb, 1972; The Hireling, 1973; The Man Who Loved Cat Dancing, 1973; Great Expectations, 1975; Pepita Jiminez, 1975; The Sailor Who Fell From Grace With the Sea, 1976; The Big Sleep, 1978; Venom, 1981; Hope and Glory, 1987; White Mischief, 1988; The Silent Touch, 1992; Jurij, 2001; Days of Rage, 2001; The Accidental Detective, 2003. Theatre appearances include: Vivat! Regina!; Asylum, 1988; TV appearances include: James Michener's Dynasty; Great Expectations; Harem; Queenie; A Ghost in Monte Carlo; Dandelion Dead; Ring Around the Moon; The Rehearsal. Publications: Charlemagne, play, 1992; A Right Royal Bastard, memoirs, 1993; Serves Me Right, memoirs, 1994; Bolt From the Blue, memoirs, 1996.

MILIBAND Rt Hon David, b. 15 July 1965, London, England. Secretary of State for Foreign and Commonwealth Affairs. m. Louise, 1 child. Education: Degree in Politics, Philosophy and Economics, Corpus Christi College, Oxford; SM degree, Political Science, Massachusetts Institute of Technology, USA, 1990. Appointments: National Council for Voluntary Organisations; Research Fellow and Political Analyst, Institute for Public Policy Research, 1989-94; Secretary, Commission on Social Justice, 1992-94; Head of Policy and Head of the Prime Minister's Policy Unit, 1994-2001; MP for South Shields, 2001-; Schools Minister, Department for Education and Skills, 2002-04; Cabinet Office Minister, 2004-05; Minister of State for Communities and Local Government, 2005-06; Secretary of State for Environment, Food and Rural Affairs, 2006-07; Foreign Secretary, 2007-. Publications: Editor: Paying for Inequality: Economic Cost of Social Justice; Reinventing the Left. Memberships: President of South Shields football club, the Mariners.

MILIBAND Rt Hon Edward Samuel, b. 24 December 1969, St Pancras, England. Member of Parliament for Doncaster North; Minister for the Cabinet Office; Chancellor of the Duchy of Lancaster. Education: Philosophy, Politics and Economics, Corpus Christi College, Oxford; Economics, London School of Economics. Appointments: Television Journalist; Speechwriter and Researcher for Harriet Harman, and later, Shadow Chancellor Gordon Brown; Special Adviser to Gordon Brown in the Treasury; Chair of the Council of Economic Advisers; Visiting Lecturer, Department of Government, Harvard University, 2003-04; Visiting Scholar, Centre for European Studies, 2003; Member of Parliament for Doncaster North, 2005-; Parliamentary Secretary to the Cabinet Office, 2006-07; Chair, All Party Group on Young People; Minister for the Cabinet Office, 2007-; Chancellor of the Duchy of Lancaster, 2007.

MILICHOVSKY Miloslav, b. 13 February 1945, Babice, near Havlickuv Brod, Czech Republic. Senior Lecturer. m. Svatava Dostalova, 2 sons. Education: MS, Physical Chemistry, Institute of Chemical Technology, Pardubice, 1968; Organic Chemistry, ICT, Prague, 1975; CSc, Macromolecular Chemistry, ICT Pardubice, 1977; DrSc, Wood Chemistry and Technology, 1989. Appointments: Graduate Technologist, South Bohemian Papermill Vetrni, 1968; Assistant Professor, ICT Pardubice, 1976; Full Professor, Chemistry and Technology of Wood, Pulp and Paper, ICT Pardubice, 2003; Head of Department, Wood, Pulp, Paper, University of Pardubice. Publications: More than 100 scientific articles in more than 8 scientific and professional journals. Memberships: Technical Association of Pulp and Paper Industry TAPPI; Association of Pulp and Paper Industry SPPaC; Czech and Slovak Papermaking Association SPPC. Address: University of Pardubice, Department of Wood, Pulp and Paper, Studentska 95, CZ 53210 Pardubice, Czech Republic.

MILLER (James) David Frederick, b. 5 January 1935, Wolverhampton, England. Retired Company Director. m. Saffrey Blackett, 3 sons, 1 deceased, 1 daughter. Education: MA, Emmanuel College, Cambridge, Diploma, IPM, London School of Economics. Appointments: Director, J & P Coats Ltd, 1972-79, Coats Patons plc, 1977-92, Royal Scottish National Orchestra, 1985-93, Outward Bound Trust, Ltd, 1985-95, Coats Viyella plc, 1986-92, The Wolverhampton & Dudley Breweries plc, 1984-2001, (chairman 1992-2001), Scottish Life Assurance Co, 1995-2001, J&J Denholm Ltd, 1997-2005, Scottish Enterprise Forth Valley, 1994-2003 (vice-chairman, 1996-2003). Honours: Freeman City of London, 1983; Freeman, Worshipful Company of Needlemakers, 1983; Honorary DUniv: University of Stirling, 1984, University of Paisley, 1997; CBE, 1997. Memberships: Chairman: Scottish Vocational Education Council, 1992-97, Court, University of Stirling, 1992-99, Scottish Examination Board, 1995-97, Scottish Qualifications Authority, 1996-2000, Fairbridge in Scotland, 1998-2006, Clackmannon College of Further Education, 1992-99, 2004-05; Director, Edinburgh Military Tattoo, 1990-2000., 2003-05. Address: Blairuskin Lodge, Kinlochard, Aberfoyle, by Stirling FK8 3TP, Scotland.

MILLER Jeanne-Marie, b. 18 February 1937, Washington DC, USA. Graduate Professor Emerita of English. m. Nathan J Miller. Education: BA, 1959, MA, 1963, PhD, 1976, English, Howard University. Appointments: Instructor, 1963-76, Graduate Assistant Professor, 1976-79, Graduate Associate Professor, 1979-92; Assistant Director, Institute for the Arts and the Humanities, 1973-75, Assistant for Academic Planning, Office of the Vice President for Academic Affairs, 1976-90; Director, Graduate Studies Program in English, 1991-97; Graduate Professor of English, 1992-97; Professor Emerita of English, 1997-, Howard University. Publications: 80 articles in variety of academic books and journals. Honours: Fellow, Ford Foundation, 1970-72; Fellow, Southern Fellowships Fund, 1972-74; Grantee, Howard University Faculty Research Grant, 1975, 1976-77, 1994-95, 1996-97; Grantee, American

Council of Learned Societies, 1978-79; National Endowment for the Humanities, 1981-84; Pi Lambda Delta. Memberships: American Association of Higher Education; American Studies Association; College Language Association; National Council of Teachers of English; Modern Language Association; American Association of University Women; Corcoran Gallery of Art Association; Founder Member, John F Kennedy Memorial Centre for the Performing Arts; Washington National Opera Society; Associate, Metropolitan Museum of Art; Metropolitan Opera Guild; Ibsen Society of America; Drama League of New York; Folger Shakespeare Library; Shakespeare Theatre Guild. Address: 504 24th Street, NE, Washington DC 20002-4818, USA.

MILLER Sir Jonathan (Wolfe), b. 21 July 1934, London, England. Theatre, Film, and Television Director; Writer. m. Helen Rachel Collet, 1956, 2 sons, 1 daughter. Education: MB, BCh, St John's College, Cambridge, 1959. Appointments: Theatre, film, and television director; Resident Fellow in the History of Medicine, 1970-73, Fellow, 1981-, University College, London; Associate Director, National Theatre, 1973-75; Visiting Professor in Drama, Westfield College, London, 1977-; Artistic Director, Old Vic, 1988-90; Research Fellow in Neuropsychology, University of Sussex. Publications: McLuhan, 1971; Freud: The Man, His World, His Influence (editor), 1972; The Body in Question, 1978; Subsequent Performances, 1986; The Don Giovanni Book: Myths of Seduction and Betrayal (editor), 1990; The Afterlife of Plays, 1992; Dimensional Man, 1998; On Reflection, 1998; Nowhere in Particular, 1999. Honours: Silver Medal, Royal Television Society, 1981; Commander of the Order of the British Empire, 1983; Albert Medal, Royal Society of Arts, 1990; Honorary Doctor of Letters, University of Cambridge. Memberships: Royal Academy, fellow; American Academy of Arts and Sciences. Address: c/o IMG Artists, Media House, 3 Burlington Lane, London W4 2TH, England.

MILLER Michael Dawson, b. 12 March 1928, London, England. Solicitor; Author; Insurance Manager. m. Gillian Margaret Gordon Fleming, 3 daughters. Education: Rugby School, 1941-45; Course for training solicitors, Law Society. Appointments: Parachute Regiment Regulars, 1946-48; Territorial Army, 1949-55; Articled Clerk, 1949-53; Qualified Solicitor, 1953; Solicitor in practise, 1954-55; Executive, 1955-61, Partner, 1962-90, Thos R Miller & Son (London); Honourable Artillery Co, 1957-63; Partner, Thos R Miller & Son (Bermuda), 1969-90; Technical Advisor, NATO Planning Board for Ocean Shipping, 1970-92; Director, Shipowners Insurance Management, Montreal, 1973-84; A/B Indemnities, Stockholm, 1983-90; Thos R Miller War Risks Ltd, London, 1985-90. Publications: Marine War Risks, 1st edition 1990, 2nd edition, 1994, 3rd edition 2005; Wars of the Roses, 2000; Uncommon Lawyer, 2001. Honours: Silver Medal, Hellenic Merchant Marine. Memberships: Hurlingham; City Club; Royal Bermuda Yacht Club; Royal Thames Yacht Club; Royal Ocean Racing Club; Law Society; London Maritime Arbitrators Association; Liveryman Shipwrights Co and Solicitors Company. Address: 52 Scarsdale Villas, London W8 6PP, England. E-mail: somerisle@btinternet.com

MILLER Patrick Figgis, b. 22 March 1933, Calcutta, India. College Principal; Priest. m. (1) Margaret Bruzelius, 1 son, 1 daughter, (2) Susanne Oberholzer. Education: St John's School, Leatherhead, Surrey, 1945-51; Christ's College, Cambridge, 1953-56; Cuddesdon College, Oxford, 1956-58; PhD, Surrey University, 1995. Appointments: National Service, 1951-53; Parish Priest, St Cuthbert's Church, Portsmouth, 1958-61; Parish Priest, SCM Chaplain, Great

St Mary's, Cambridge, 1961-63; Head of Religious Studies, Manchester Grammar School, 1963-69; Canon Residentiary, Southwark Cathedral, 1969-72; Director of Social Studies, Queen Mary's College, Basingstoke, 1972-79; Principal, CEO, Esher College, Surrey, 1980-98; Project Director, Learning for Living, a Templeton Foundation Project, 2000-04. Publications: Creeds and Controversies, 1969; New Movements in RE, 1975; Book reviews. Honours: Korean and UN medals. Memberships: London Flotilla; HMS, President, Retired Officers' Association; British Legion. Address: 9 Fairfax Ave, Epsom, Surrey KT17 2QN, England. E-mail: patrickmiller@ntlworld.com

MILLETT Peter James, b. 31 December 1967, Pennsylvania, USA. Orthopaedic Surgeon. m. Sarah, 3 daughters. Education: BS, University of Scranton, 1990; MD, Dartmouth Medical School, 1995; MSc, University of Cambridge, 1995; Orthopaedic Residency, Cornell University and Hospital for Special Surgery, 2000. Appointments: Assistant Professor, Harvard Medical School, 2001-; Co-director, Harvard Shoulder Service, 2001-05; Director, Harvard Musculoskeletal Proteomics Research Group, 2003-05; Director, Shoulder Surgery, Steadman Hawkins Clinic, 2005-. Publications: Numerous articles in professional medical and scientific journals. Memberships: American Academy of Orthopaedic Surgeons; AOSSM; AANA; Orthpaedic Research Society; American Shoulder & Elbow Surgery. Address: Steadman Hawkins Clinic, 181 West Meadow Drive, Vail, Colorado 81657, USA. Website: www.drmillett.com

MILLETT, Baron of St Marylebone in the City of Westminster, Peter Julian Millett, b. 23 June 1932, London, England. Judge. m. Ann Mireille Harris, 2 sons. Education: Double First in Classics and Law, Trinity Hall, Cambridge. Appointments: Junior Counsel, Chancery Bar, 1958-73; Standing Counsel to Department of Trade and Industry, 1967-73; Queen's Counsel, 1973-86; Member Insolvency Law Review Committee, 1976-82; High Court Judge, Chancery Division, 1986-94; Lord Justice of Appeal, 1994-98; Lord of Appeal in Ordinary, 1998-2004; Non-Permanent Judge, Court of Final Appeal, 2000-; Editor-in-Chief, Encyclopaedia of Forms and Precedents, 1990-. Publications: Various in legal journals. Honours: Knighted, 1986; Privy Counsellor, 1992; Honorary Fellow, Trinity Hall, Cambridge, 1992; Baron Millett of St Marylebone, 1998; Honorary LLD, London University, 2000. Memberships: Bencher Lincoln's Inn, 1980 (Treasurer, 2004); Home House. Address: 18 Portman Close, London W1H 9BR, England. E-mail: lord.millett@btinternet.com

MILLIKEN Peter, b. 12 November 1946, Kingston, Ontario, Canada. Lawyer. Member of Parliament. Education: Queen's University; Oxford University; Dalhousie University. Appointments: Lawyer and Partner, Cunningham, Swan, Carty, Little and Bonham, 1973-89; President, Kingston and the Islands Liberal Association, 1985-87; Elected to House of Commons, 1988; Re-elected, 1993; Parliamentary Secretary to the Government House Leader, 1993-96; Councillor, Canadian NATO Parliamentary Association, 1996; Elected Deputy Chairman of Committees of the Whole House, 1996-97; Re-elected, 1997; Deputy Speaker and Chairman of the Committees of the Whole House, 1997; Member, Board of Internal Economy; Re-elected, 2000; Speaker, 2001, Chair of the Board of Internal Economy; Re-elected, 2004; Speaker of the House of Commons, 2004; Re-elected, 2006; Speaker of the House of Commons, 2006. Address: Room 316-N, House of Commons, Ottawa, Ontario K1A 0A6, Canada.

MILLINGTON Barry (John), b. 1 November 1951, Essex, England. Music Journalist; Writer. Education: BA, Cambridge University, 1974. Appointments: Music Critic, Times, 1977-2001; Reviews Editor, BBC Music Magazine; Artistic Director, Hampstead and Highgate Festival. Publications: Wagner, 1984, revised edition, 1998; Selected Letters of Richard Wagner (translator and editor with S Spencer), 1987; The Wagner Compendium: A Guide to Wagner's Life and Music (editor), 1992; Wagner in Performance (editor with S Spencer), 1992; Wagner's Ring of the Nibelung: A Companion (editor with S Spencer), 1993. Contributions to: Articles on Wagner to New Grove Dictionary of Opera, 1992, New Grove Dictionary of Music and Musicians, 2nd edition, 2001; Newspapers and magazines. Membership: Critics' Circle. Address: 50 Denman Drive South, London NW11 6RH, England.

MILLOT Jean-Louis, b. 21 August 1947, Noisy-le-Sec, France. Medical Advisor. Widower. Education: MD, Faculty of Medicine, Lyon, 1975; Maitrise Biomathematics and Statistics, Faculty of Medicine, Kremlin-Bicêtre, France, 1985-. Appointments: Private Practitioner, France, 1976-80; Medical Advisor, EDF Gaz de France, Annecy, France, 1980-. Publications: La place du lithium dans le traitement de l'hyperthyroïdie, 1977; Les accidents de sport chez les salariés d'EDF Gaz de France des régions Rhône-Alpes et Bourgogne-Fréquence et Gravité, 2000; Reduced efficiency of influenza vaccine in prevention of influenza-like illness in working adults: a 7-month prospective survey in EDF Gaz de France employees in Rhône-Alpes 1996-97, 2002. Address: EDF Gaz de France Distribution, 5 bd Decouz, BP 2334, 74011 Annecy Cedex, France. E-mail: jean-louis.millot@edfgdf.fr

MILLS Hayley Catherine Rose Vivien, b. 18 April 1946, London, England. Actress. m. Roy Boulting, 1971, divorced 1977, 2 sons. Education: Elmhurst Ballet School; Ist Alpine Vidamanette. Creative Works: Films include: Tiger Bay, 1959; Pollyanna, 1960; The Parent Trap, 1961; Whistle Down the Wind, 1961; Summer Magic, 1962; In Search of the Castaways, 1963; The Chalk Garden, 1964; The Moonspinners, 1965; The Truth About Spring, 1965; Sky West & Crooked, 1966; The Trouble with Angels, 1966; The Family Way, 1966; Pretty Polly, 1967; Twisted Nerve, 1968; Take a Girl Like You, 1970; Forbush and the Penguins, 1971; Endless Night, 1972; Deadly Strangers, 1975; The Diamond Hunters, 1975; What Changed Charley Farthing?, 1975; The Kingfisher Caper, 1975; Appointment with Death, 1987; After Midnight, 1990; A Troll in Central Park (voice), 1994; 2BPerfectlyHonest, 2004; Stricken, 2005. TV appearances include: The Flame Trees of Thika, 1981; Parent Trap II, 1986; Good Morning Miss Bliss; Murder She Wrote; Back Home; Tales of the Unexpected; Walk of Life, 1990; Parent Trap III, IV, Amazing Stories; Back Home; Wild At Heart; Numerous stage appearances. Publication: My God, 1988. Honours include: Silver Bear Award, Berlin Film Festival, 1958; British Academy Award; Special Oscar, USA; Golden Globe Award. Address: c/o Chatto & Linnit, Prince of Wales Theatre, Coventry Street, London W1V 7FE, England.

MILLS Ian (Sir), b. 19 November 1935, Hampshire, England. Chartered Accountant. m. Elizabeth Dunstan, 1 son, 1 daughter. Education: Taunton's Grammar School, Southampton, 1946-54; Beal, Young & Booth, Chartered Accountants, Southampton, 1954-60. Appointments: Financial Consultant, World Bank team, Pakistan, 1962; Chief Accountant, University of Ibadan, Nigeria, 1965-68; Manager, Price Waterhouse, London, 1960-65, 1968-70; Partner, then Senior Partner, Price Waterhouse, London,

1973-92, (i/c Management Consultancy Services (MCS), Newcastle-upon-Tyne & Scotland, 1970-73; MCS, Africa, 1973-83; Central Government Services, 1983-85; Business Development, Europe, 1988-92); Director of Finance, NHS Executive, 1985-88; Chair, Lambeth, Southwark & Lewisham Health Authority, 1991-96; Chair, North Thames Region of NHS, 1996-98; Chair, London Region of NHS, 1998-2001; Appointments Commissioner, London Region of NHS, 2001-03. Publications: Articles on management, information systems and financial planning and control in professional journals, 1965-88; Pamphlets and brochures on heritage issues, 1984-; Rebirth of a Building: the story in pictures of a 16-year programme of renovation, 2000; Craftsmen of St Margaret: illustrations of the work of 12 Victorian architects and craftsmen, 2007. Honours: Knighted, 2001; Fellow, Royal Society of Arts, 1994-; Fellow, Institute of Health Service Management, 1985-; Fellow, Chartered Institute of Management Consultants, 1963-; Fellow, Institute of Chartered Accountants, 1960-. Memberships: Chair, Independent Remuneration Panel, London Borough of Lewisham, 2001; Chair, Blackheath Historic Buildings Trust, 2003-. Address: 60 Belmont Hill, London SE13 5DN, England. E-mail: ianmills@mysector.co.uk

MILNER Arthur David, b. 16 July 1943, Leeds, England. Professor of Cognitive Neuroscience. Education: BA, 1965, MA, 1970, University of Oxford, England; Dip Psych, London, 1966; PhD, Experimental Psychology, University of London, 1971. Appointments: Research Worker, Institute of Psychology, London, 1966-70; Lecturer and Senior Lecturer in Psychology, 1970-85, Reader in Neuropsychology, 1985-90, Head Department of Psychology, 1983-88, 1994-97, Professor of Neuropsychology, 1990-2000, Dean, Faculty of Science, 1992-94, Honorary Professor of Neuropsychology, 2000-, University of St Andrews, Scotland; Professor of Cognitive Neuroscience, University of Durham, 2000-. Publications: Co-author and/or editor or co-editor of 6 books; Author and co-author of over 140 chapters in books and articles in refereed journals; Numerous invited lectures and workshops. Honours: Fellow, Royal Society of Edinburgh, 1992; Leverhulme Trust Research Fellow, 1998-2000; FC Donders Lecturer, Max-Planck-Institut, Nijmegen, 1999; Member, Scientific Council, Helmholtz Instituut, Netherlands, 2002-; Chichele Lecturer and Visiting Fellow, All Souls College, Oxford, Trinity Term, 2006. Memberships: Experimental Psychology Society; International Neuropsychological Symposium; International Association of Attention and Performance; Royal Society of Edinburgh; European Brain and Behaviour Society. Address: Wolfson Research Institute, University of Durham, Queen's Campus, Stockton-on-Tees TS17 6BH, England. E-mail: a.d.milner@durham.ac.uk

MILNER Peter Marshall, b. 13 June 1919, Nr Barnsley, Yorkshire, England (Canadian citizen). Professor Emeritus. m. Susan Walker, 1 son. Education: BSc, Electrical Engineering (Hons 1st Class), Leeds University, 1941; MSc, 1950, PhD, 1954, Psychology, McGill University, Canada. Appointments: Scientific Officer, Air Defence R&D, 1941-44, Senior Scientific Officer, Atomic Energy Canada, 1944-48, UK Ministry of Supply; Research Associate, Radiation Laboratory, 1948-50, Research, Teaching Assistant, 1950-54, Research Associate, 1954-56, Assistant Professor, 1956-59, Associate Professor, 1959-67, Professor, 1967-91, Chairman, 1980-83, Professor Emeritus, 1991-, Psychology Department, McGill University; Consultant, IBM Research Lab, Poughkeepsie, New York, 1955-58; Research Associate, Carnegie Institute, Washington, 1960-64; Consultant, Rand Corp, Santa Monica, California, 1963-67; Visiting

Professor, Psychology Department, Cambridge University, England, 1971-72; Honorary Visiting Professor, Institute of Neurology, Queen Street, London, 1979-80. Publications: Numerous articles in professional journals. Honours: Gold Medal for Distinguished Lifetime Contributions to Canadian Psychology, Canadian Psychology Association. Memberships: Canadian Psychological Association; American Psychological Association; Psychonomics Society; Animal Behaviour Society; Sigma Xi; International Brain Research Organisation. Address: Department of Psychology, McGill University, 1205 Docteur Penfield Ave, Montréal, Qué, Canada, H3A 1B1. E-mail: peter.milner@mcgill.ca

MIN Pok-Kee, b. 5 September 1968, Daegu, Korea. Dermatologist. m. Younghee Kim, 1 son, 2 daughters. Education: Premedical Course, College of Natural Science, 1987-89, BS, MD, College of Medicine, 1989-93, Internship & Dermatology Residency, 1993-98, Kyung-pook National University Hospital; MSc, Kyung-pook National University, 1996; National Boards on Dermatology, 1998; PhD, Kyung-pook National University College of Medicine, 2004. Appointments: Military Service, 1998-2001; Scientific Director, Botulinum Institute, 2000-; Dermatologist, Chief of AllforSkin Severance Dermatologic Clinic & Hair Center, Daegu, Korea, 2001-; Scientific Director, Daegyeong KAPD Academic Affairs, 2002-; Director, Association of Korean Dermatologists, 2003-05; Member, New Clinical Method Committee, Association of Korean Dermatologists, 2003-05; Professor, Taekyeung College, 2004-; Treasurer, Daegyeong Korean Dermatological Association, 2004-05; Education Director, Korean Hair Research Society, 2004-; Director, Korean Society of Dermatologic Surgery, 2005-; Clinical Professor, Department of Dermatology, Kyung-pook National University School of Medicine, 2005-; Education Director, Association of Korean Dermatologists, 2005-; Clinical Professor, Department of Dermatology, College of Medicine, Kyung-pook National University, 2005-. Publications: 13 books; 2 articles in professional journals. Honours: First Prize, Korean Dermatological Association, 1997; Scientific Award, Korean Military Medical Association, 1999; Distinguished Service Medal, 1999, First Scientific Award, 2000, Korean Military Medical Association; Distinguished Service Medal, 50th Infantry Division ROK Army, 2000; Distinguished Service Medal, 2nd ROK Army Command, 2001; Appreciation Plaque, 2nd ROK Army Command, 2002; Appreciation Plaque, Taekyeung College, 2005; Appreciation Plaque, Daegyeong KAPD Academic Affairs, 2005; Appreciation Plaque, Kyung-pook National University, 2006. Memberships: Korean Medical Association; Korean Dermatological Association; Association of Korean Dermatologists; Korean Hair Research Society; Daegyeong KAPD Academic Affairs; Korean Society of Dermatologic Surgery; Korean Society of Aesthetic Surgery; International Society of Hair Restoration Surgery. Address: Allforskin Clinic & Hair Center, 4th Floor, DNP Building, 59 sa il-dong, jung-gu, Daegu, Korea. E-mail: pkmin68@hanmail.net Website: www.allforskin.com

MINA Fayez Mourad, b. 29 July 1940, Sohag, Egypt. University Professor. m. Theresa Nabih Abdo, 1 son, 1 daughter. Education: BSc, Mathematics and Education, 1964, Special Diploma in Education, 1969, MA, Education, 1973, Faculty of Education, Ain Shams University, Egypt; PhD, University of London, Institute of Education, 1978. Appointments: Mathematics Teacher, 1964-72, Demonstrator and Assistant Lecturer, 1972-78, Lecturer, 1978-83, Associate Professor, 1988-89, Professor, 1989-2000, Emeritus Professor, 2000-, Faculty of Education, Ain Shams University, Egypt; Assistant Professor, 1983-84, Associate Professor,

1984-88, University of Bahrain. Publications: More than 100 publications including books, articles, studies, conference papers and researches (individually and jointly) in the areas of curriculum, mathematics education, comparative education, teacher education, sociology of education, adult education, research methodology and futurology. Honours: The State Prize in Education, Egypt, 1983; Medal of Science and Arts of the First Degree, Egypt, 1985; The Recognition Award Fellowship, Project Milestones, Columbia University, 1992. Memberships: Fellow Institute of Mathematics and its Applications; Elected Member, International Statistical Institute; Board Member, WCCI, 1984-98; Vice-President, ECCI. Address: Faculty of Education, Ain Shams University, Roxy, Heliopolis, Cairo, Egypt. E-mail: fmmina@link.com.eg

MINCHEW Kaye Lanning, Archivist. Education: BA, History (magna cum laude), University of North Carolina at Asheville, 1978; MA, American History, 1980, MSLS, 1981, University of North Carolina at Chapel Hill. Appointments: Archivist, 1983-85, Director, 1985-, Troup County Archives, LaGrange; Numerous education projects, community activities and consulting work. Memberships: Troup County Historical Preservation Commission; Georgia Historical Society; Society of American Archivists; Society of Georgia Archivists; Academy of Certified Archivists. Address: Troup County Archives, 136 Main Street, PO Box 1051, LaGrange, GA 30241, USA. E-mail: kaye@trouparchives.org

MINNELLI Liza, b. 12 March 1946, USA. Singer; Actress. m. (1) Peter Allen, 1967, (2) Jack Haley Jr, 1974, (3) Mark Gero, 1979, divorced 1992, (4) David Gest, 2002, divorced. Creative Works: Films: Charlie Bubbles, 1968; The Sterile Cuckoo, 1969; Tell Me That You Love Me; Junie Moon, 1971; Cabaret, played Sally Bowles, 1972; Lucky Lady, 1976; A Matter of Time, 1976; New York, New York, 1977; Arthur, 1981; Rent-a-Cop, 1988; Arthur 2: On the Rocks, 1988; Sam Found Out, 1988; Stepping Out, 1991; Parallel Lives, 1994; TV specials: Liza; Liza With a Z, 1972; Goldie and Liza Together, 1980; Baryshnikov on Broadway, 1980; A Time to Live, 1985; My Favourite Broadway: The Leading Ladies, 1999; plus numerous TV appearances. Theatre: The Best Foot Forward, 1963; Flora, the Red Menace, 1965; Chicago, 1975; The Act, 1977-78; Liza at the Winter Garden, 1973; The Rink, 1984; Victor-Victoria, 1997; Recordings: Liza with a Z; Liza Minnelli: The Singer; Liza Minnelli: Live at the Winter Garden; Tropical Nights; The Act; Liza Minnelli: Live at Carnegie Hall; The Rink; Liza Minnelli at Carnegie Hall; Results, 1989; Maybe This Time, 1996; Minelli on Minelli, 2000; Liza's Back, 2002; The Very Best of Liza Minnelli: Life is a Cabaret! 2002. Honours include: Academy Award, Best Actress; Hollywood Foreign Press Golden Globe Award; British Academy Award; David di Donatello Award. Address: Angel Records, 810 7th Avenue, Floor 4, New York, NY 10019, USA.

MINOGUE Kylie (Ann), b. 28 May 1968, Melbourne, Victoria, Australia. Singer; Actress. Appointments: Actress, Australian TV dramas: Skyways, 1980; The Sullivans, 1981; The Henderson Kids, 1984-85; Neighbours, 1986-88; Film Appearances: The Delinquents, 1989; Streetfighter, 1994; Biodome, 1995; Sample People, 1998; Cut, 1999; Moulin Rouge, 2001; As Singer, biggest selling single of decade in Australia, Locomotion, 1987; Highest UK chart entry for female artist, Locomotion, Highest debut album chart entry, Australia, UK, Kylie, 1988; First ever artist with 4 Top 3 singles from an album; First female artist with first 5 singles to receive Silver discs; Performances worldwide. Creative Works: Albums: Kylie, 1988; Enjoy Yourself, 1989; Rhythm of Love, 1990; Let's Get To It, 1991; Kylie - Greatest Hits, 1992; Kylie Minogue, 1994; Kylie Minogue, 1997-98; Light Years, 2000; Fever, 2001; Body Language, 2003; X, 2007. Singles: Locomotion, 1987; I Should Be So Lucky, Je Ne Sais Pas Pourquoi, 1988; Especially For You, Never Too Late, 1989; Confide In Me, 1994; Put Yourself in My Place, Where Is The Feeling, Where The Wild Roses Grow, 1995; Some Kind of Bliss, 1997; Did it Again; Breathe, GBI (German Bold Italic), 1998; Spinning Around, On A Night Like This, Please Stay, 2000; Can't Get You Out of My Head, 2001; In Your Eyes, Love at First Sight, 2002; Red Blooded Woman, 2004. Honours: Numerous Platinum, Gold and Silver Discs; 6 Logies (Australia); 6 Music Week Awards (UK); 3 Smash Hits Awards (UK); 3 Australian Record Industry Association Awards; 3 Japanese Music Awards; Irish Record Industry Award; Canadian Record Industry Award; World Music Award; Australian Variety Club Award; MO Award (Australian Showbusiness); Amplex Golden Reel Award; Diamond Award, (Belgium); Woman of the Decade (UK); MTV, Australian Female Artist of the Year, 1998; Pop Release of the Year, Light Years, ARIA; Best International Solo Female Artist and Best International Album, 2002; Grammy Award, Best Dance Recording, 2004; New waxwork model Madame Tussaud's, 2007; Order of the British Empire, 2008. Address: c/o Terry Blamey Management, P O Box 13196, London SW6 4WF, England.

MINOGUE Valerie Pearson, b. 26 April 1931, Llanelli, South Wales. Professor Emeritus. m. Kenneth Robert Minogue, 16 June 1954, separated 1978, divorced 2001, 1 son, 1 daughter. Education: BA, 1952, MLitt, 1956, Girton College, Cambridge. Appointments: Assistant Lecturer, University College, Cardiff, Wales, 1952-53; Contributor, Cambridge Italian Dictionary, 1956-61; Lecturer, 1963-74, Senior Lecturer, 1975-81, French Department, Queen Mary, London University, England; Professor, 1981-88, Research Professor, 1988-96, Professor Emeritus, 1996-, University of Wales Swansea. Publications: Proust: Du Côté de chez Swann, 1973; Nathalie Sarraute: The War of the Words, 1981; Zola: L'Assommoir, 1991; Eight texts, Pléiade Oeuvres complètes of Nathalie Sarraute (editor, with notes and critical essays), 1996. Contributions to: Romance Studies, Editor, 1982-98, General Editor, 1998-2004; Quadrant; Literary Review; Modern Language Review; French Studies; Romance Studies; Forum for Modern Language Studies; New Novel Review; Revue des Sciences Humaines; The Times; Times Literary Supplement; Esprit Créateur; Theatre Research International; Numerous chapters in books. Honours: Listed in international biographical dictionaries. Memberships: Modern Humanities Research Association; Society for French Studies; Institute of Germanic and Romance Studies; Emile Zola Society (President, 2005-); Société Marguerite Duras du Royaume Uni; Société des Dix-Neuviémistes; The Art Fund; Friends of the Royal Academy; Friends of Wigmore Hall; Friends of the Victoria and Albert Museum. Address: 23 Richford Street, London, W6 7HJ, England.

MIR Mohammad Afzal, b. 6 May 1936, Kashmir. Physician. m. Lynda, 1 son, 2 daughters. Education: MBBS, 1962; DCH, 1965; MRCP, 1972; FRCP, 1985. Appointments: Senior House Officer, Alder Hey Children's Hospital, Liverpool; Medical Registrar, North Ormesby Hospital, Middlesborough; Resident Medical Officer, Queen Mary's Hospital, Sidcup; Medical Registrar, Manchester Royal Infirmary; Senior Medical Registrar, Manchester Royal Infirmary; Senior Lecturer and Consultant Physician, University of Wales, College of Medicine. Publications: Numerous papers in acute leukaemia, metabolic disorders, sodium transport and obesity;

10 books on basic clinical skills, PLAB and MRCP; 38 video tapes on basic clinical skills. Honours: Young Research Investigator's Award, British Cardiac Society, 1976; British Heart Foundation, European Travelling Fellowship, 1977. Memberships: British Cardiac Society; British Diabetic Association; British Hypertension Society; Medical Research Society; British Hyperlipidaemia Association. E-mail: afzal.mir@virgin.net

MIRREN Dame Helen, b. 26 July 1945, London, England. Actress. m. Taylor Hackford, 1997. Creative Works: Roles include: The Faith Healer, Royal Court, 1981; Antony & Cleopatra, 1983, 1998; The Roaring Girl, RSC, Barbican, 1983; Extremities, 1984; Madame Bovary, 1987; Two Way Mirror, 1989; Sex Please, We're Italian, Young Vic, 1991; The Writing Game, New Haven, Connecticut, 1993; The Gift of the Gorgon, NY, 1994; A Month in the Country, 1994; Orpheus Descending, 2001; Dance of Death, New York, 2001; Films include: Age of Consent, 1969; Savage Messiah, O Lucky Man!, 1973; Caligula, 1977; The Long Good Friday, Excalibur, 1981; Cal, 1984; 2010, 1985; Heavenly Pursuits, 1986; The Mosquito Coast, 1987; Pascali's Island, 1988; When the Whales Came, 1988; Bethune: The Making of a Hero, 1989; The Cook, the Thief, his Wife and her Lover, 1989; The Comfort of Strangers, 1989; Where Angels Fear to Tread, 1990; The Hawk, The Prince of Jutland, 1991; The Madness of King George, 1995; Some Mother's Son, 1996; Killing Mrs Tingle, 1998; The Pledge, 2000; No Such Thing, 2001; Greenfingers, 2001; Gosford Park, 2001; Calendar Girls, 2003; The Clearing, 2004; Raising Helen, 2004; The Hitchiker's Guide to the Galaxy (voice), 2005; Shadowboxer, 2005; The Queen, 2006; National Treasure: Book of Secrets, 2007; Inkheart, 2008. TV include: Miss Julie; The Apple Cart; The Little Minister; As You Like It; Mrs Reinhardt; Soft Targets, 1982; Blue Remembered Hills; Coming Through; Cause Celebre; Red King, White Knight; Prime Suspect, 1991; Prime Suspect II, 1992; Prime Suspect III, 1993; Prime Suspect IV: Scent of Darkness, 1996; Prime Suspect V: Errors of Judgement, 1996; Painted Lady, 1997; The Passion of Ayn Rand, 1998; Prime Suspect VI: The Last Witness, 2003; Elizabeth I, 2005; Prime Suspect: The Final Act, 2006. Honours include: BAFTA Award, 1991; Emmy Award, 1996; Screen Actor's Guild Award for Best Supporting Actress, 2001; Screen Actor's Guild Award for Best Supporting Actress, 2002; BAFTA, The Queen, 2007; Broadcast Film Critics Association Awards, Best Actress, The Queen, 2007; Oscar, Best Performance by an Actress in a Leading Role for The Queen, 2007. Address: c/o Ken McReddie Ltd, 91 Regent Street, London W1R 7TB, England.

MIRZA Qamar, b. 19 March 1927, Ferozepur, India. Librarian. Education: BA, 1947; Certificate in LSc, 1951; Registration Exam Library Association, London, 1953-54; Masters degree in LSc, 1968-69. Appointments: Assistant Librarian, Northumberland County Library, 1954-62; Deputy Librarian, University of Peshawar, Pakistan, Teacher at Department of LSc, 1962-68, 1971-74; Graduate Librarian, Western Institute of Technology, Australia, 1975-76; Librarian, Umm Al-Qura University, Makkah, Saudi Arabia, 1977-98. Publications: Perspective of Past, Present and Future of L-Services in the University of Peshawar, in Pakistan Librarianship, 1963-64; Islamic Subject Headings in LC Subject Headings, 1992. Honours: Beta Phi Mu. Memberships: Life Member, Pakistan Library Association. Address: 17/46 Wahdat Colony, Disposal Road, Gujranwala, Pakistan.

MIRZOEFF Edward, b. 11 April 1936, London, England. Television Producer. m. Judith Topper, 3 sons. Education: MA (Oxon), Open Scholarship in Modern History, The Queen's College, Oxford. Appointments: Market Researcher, Social Surveys (Gallup Poll) Ltd, 1959-58; Public Relations Executive, Duncan McLeish and Associates, 1960-61; Assistant Editor, Shoppers' Guide, 1961-63; BBC Television, 1963-2000; Executive Producer, Documentaries, 1983-2000; Freelance TV Producer, Director, 2000-; Director and Producer of many film documentaries including: Metro-land, 1973; A Passion for Churches, 1974; The Queen's Realm: A Prospect of England, 1977; The Front Garden, 1977; The Ritz, 1981; The Englishwoman and the Horse, 1981; Elizabeth R, 1992; Torvill and Dean: Facing the Music, 1994; Treasures in Trust, 1995; John Betjeman - The Last Laugh, 2001; Series Editor: Bird's-Eye View, 1969-71; Year of the French, 1982-83; In at the Deep End, 1983-84; Just Another Day, 1983-85; Editor, 40 Minutes, 1985-89; Executive Producer of many documentary series including: The House, 1992, Full Circle with Michael Palin, 1997; The 50 Years War: Israel and the Arabs, 1998; Children's Hospital, 1998-99; Queen Elizabeth The Queen Mother, 2002; The Lords'Tale, 2003; A Very English Village, 2005. Honours: CVO, 1993; CBE, 1997; BAFTA Award for Best Documentary, 1981; BAFTA Awards for Best Factual Series, 1985, 1989; BFI TV Award, 1988; Samuelson Award, Birmingham Festival, 1988; British Video Award, 1993; BAFTA Alan Clarke Award for Outstanding Creative Contribution to Television, 1995; International EMMY, 1996; Royal Philharmonic Society Music Award, 1996; British Press Guild Award for Best Documentary Series, 1996. Memberships: Vice-Chairman TV, 1991-95, Chairman, 1995-97, Trustee, 1999-, British Academy of Film and Television Arts (BAFTA); Trustee, 1999-, Vice Chair, 2000-02, Chair, 2002-06, Grierson Trust; Board Member, Director's and Producer's Rights Society, 1999-; Salisbury Cathedral Council, 2002-. Address: 9 Westmoreland Road, London, SW13 9RZ, England.

MISEVICIUS Alfonsas, b. 10 December 1962, Marijampole, Lithuania. Engineer-Mathematician. m. Laimute Ona Peleckaite, 1 son, 1 daughter. Education: Graduation from secondary school, Gold Medal, 1981; Diploma with Honour, Engineer in Applied Mathematics, 1986, PhD, 1996, Kaunas University of Technology. Appointments: Engineer, 1986-88, Junior Research Fellow, 1988-91, Doctoral Student, 1991-96, Assistant Professor, 1996-98, Associate Professor, 1998-2006, Kaunas University of Technology. Publications: Author of over 70 papers and academic texts on different topics of computer science; Articles in scientific journals. Honour: Best Refereed Technical Paper Award, British Computer Society, Specialist Group on Artificial Intelligence, 2003; J Kazickas Prize, 2004, 3rd Award, Young Scientists' Competition, Kaunas University of Technology. Memberships: Technical Committee of Specialist Group on Artificial Intelligence, British Computer Society; Lithuanian Scientific Society, LSS; Lithuanian Computer Society, LIKS; Lithuanian Operational Research Society, LITORS. Address: Kaunas University of Technology, Department of Multi-Media Engineering, Studentu St. 50-400a/416a, LT-51368, Kaunas, Lithuania. E-mail: alfonsas.misevicius@ktu.lt

MISHIMA Hiroyuki, b. 8 January 1952, Koriyama, Fukushima, Japan. Professor. m. Amiko Tanaka, 1 son, 2 daughters. Education: BSc, Tokai University, Tokyo, 1974; PhD, Nihon University, Tokyo, 1986. Appointments: Teacher, High School, Shimizu, Japan, 1974-75; Prefectural High School, Gyoda, Japan, 1975-77; Assistant, 1977-78, Instructor, 1978-95; Assistant Professor, 1995-2003, Nihon University School of Dentistry at Matsudo; Visiting Assistant Professor, University of South Carolina, 1991-92; Professor, Kochi Gakuen College, 2003-. Publications: (in journals and proceedings) Tooth Enamel IV, 1984; Tooth Enamel V, 1989; Mechanisms and Phylogeny of Mineralization in Biological Systems, 1992; Biomineralization 93, 1994; Dental Morphology 98, 1999; Neanderthal Burials Excavations of the Dederiyeh Caves, Afrin, Syria, 2002; Biomineralization (B1OM 2001), 2004. Memberships: International Association for Dental Research; Japanese Association of Anatomists; Japanese Association of Oral Biology; Microscopy Society of America; New York Academy of Sciences; Society of Vertebrate Palaeontology. Address: Kochi Gakuen College, 292-26 Asahitenjincho, Kochi, 780-0955 Japan.

MISHRA Raghu Nath (HEH Mt Hon Lord Sir), b. 7 April 1947, Amwa Digar, UP, India. Philosopher. m. Miss Abha, 30 January 1973, 2 sons. Education: BSc Electrical Engineering, 1st Class Honours I, 1969; MTech, 1971; PhD, 1975; MA, Engineering Education, 1985; DCTech, 1988; DSc, DCS Business Management, DD, LLD, DIL magna cum laude, 1992; DSc, Telematics and Communication, DSc Cybernetics, DCE, 1993; MUniv, 1994. Appointments: Senior Research Assistant, Electrical Engineering, Indian Institute of Technology (IIT), Kanpur, 1973-75; Assistant Professor, Electrical Engineering, 1975-87, University Professor, 1977-, Associate Professor, Electrical Engineering (Computer Science), 1987-97, Professor, Computer Engineering, 1997-, Head, Computer and Information Technology, 2002-2004; Head Computer Engineering Department, 2005-2007, College of Technology, GBUAT, PantNagar. Publications include: Application of Memory Gradient Methods to Economic Load Dispatching Problem, 1972; Univariate or One-Dimensional Search Techniques for Power Flow Optimisation Problems, 1973; Estimation, Detection and Identification Methods in Power System Studies, 1975; International System of Units, 1978; Memory Gradient Method via Bridge Balance Convergence, 1979; Assumptions in Theory of Ballistic Galvanometer, Hybrid Algorithm for Constrained Minimisation, Convergence of Nonlinear Algorithms, 1980. Honours: National Scholarship, Board of High School and Intermediate Education, Uttar Pradesh, 1963-69; Trainee as Student Engineer, Hindustan Steel Limited (now, Steel Authority of India Limited), summer vacations, 1967, 1968; Lala Balak Ramji Kohinoor Memorial Gold Medal; The RBG Modi Medal; NVR Nageswar Iyer Prize, BH University, 1969; Institute Scholarship, IIT Kanpur, 1969-73; International Register of Profiles Certificate, 1982, Medal, 1991; International Biographical Roll of Honour, 1983, 1984, 1985; CSIR registration as Instrumentation/Technologist, 1983; Men of Achievement, certificate of merit, 1984, Medal, 1991; First Five Hundred medal, plaque, 1985; Commemorative Medal of Honour, Pewter, 1986, Gold, 1993, Research Fellow Gilt Silver Coins, 1994, 1995; IBC Paperweight and Letter Opener, 1987; IBC Certificate of Appreciation, Member of Merit for Life, Confederation of Chivalry, 1988; International Leaders in Achievement, medal, International Who's Who of Intellectuals, Dictionary of International Biography, medals, 1990; Who's Who in Australasia and Far East, medals, Count of San Ciriaco, 1991; KLUO, KtT, 1992; Baron of Bohemian Crown (Royal Order), General Knighthood (NOBLE, JUST and CHILVALROUS) Medal for merit for life, CSC, CU, MIDI pins, Coptic Cross, CaptAM, 1993; KHG, 1994; Bharat Gaurav, 1998; Eminent Personalities of India, proclamation, 1999; Expert, Union Public Service Commission in Electrical Engineering for Civil Services (preliminary) and Engineering Services Examinations, 1994-2001; Dictionary of International Biography 30th Anniversary Edition Certificate, 2002;

Uttaranchal Public Service Commission Specialist in Computer Science for Civil Services (preliminary) examinations, 2002, 2005, syllabus Revision, 2004; Invitation for Best Citizens of India Award, 2002; Expert, Union Public Service Commission in Electronics and Telecommunication Engineering for Engineering Services Examinations, 2003-04; Nominations for World Medal of Honor for Strong Character and personal dignity, International Peace Prize for Positive Peace and Justice, 2003; The World Book of Knowledge; Member of the Board of Studies of Vikram University, Ujjain, 2004; Top 100 Scientist, 2005; The World Medal of Freedom; Man of the Year, 2006; Top 100 Engineers, 2006; Leading Engineers of the World; International Directory of Experts and Expertise. Listed in numerous international biographical publications including 1000 Great Scientists, 2000 Outstanding Scientists of the 20th Century, 2000 Outstanding Scientists of the 21st Century; The Cambridge Blue Book, 2007; Great Minds of the 21st Century; International Who's Who in Engineering. Memberships: Deputy, International States Parliament for Safety and Peace, 1992-2002; Lifelong Member, World Academy Association of the Masters of the Universe; Lifelong Fellow, Australian Institute for Co-ordinated Research; ABI; ABI Research Association; International Advisor, Life Member, Indian Society for Technical Education; IIT Kanpur Alumni Association; Indian Alumni of the World University; Academy of Ethical Science; Indian Citizens Association; International Cultural Correspondence Institute; MIDI. Address: College of Technology Computer Department, GBP University of Agriculture and Technology, PantNagar, 263 145, India.

MISHRICKY Edward, b. 21 September 1956, Egypt. Doctor. m. Hanaa, 2 sons. Education: Bachelor of Medicine, 1979; Bachelor of Surgery, 1979; Fellow, Royal College of General Practitioners, 2000; Fellow, Australian College of Rural and Remote Medicine; Diploma in Aesthetic Surgery; Diploma in Anti-aging Medicine. Appointments: General Practitioner; Orthopaedic Surgeon; Aesthetic and Anti-aging Physician. Publications: Treatment of postoperative infections in orthopaedic surgery; Total knee replacement and postoperative positioning outcome; Compression garments in surgery and medicine. Honours: MBBS; FRACGP; FACRRM; Diploma of Aesthetic & Anti-aging Medicine. Memberships: Australian Medical Association; Rural Faculty of RACGP; American Academy of Aesthetic Medicine; Australian Society of Cosmetic Medicine; American Academy of Anti-aging Medicine; Australian Academy of Anti-aging. Address: 26 Mallee Road, Wagga Wagga, NSW 2650, Australia.

MITCHELL Adrian, (Volcano Jones, Apeman Mudgeon, Gerald Stimpson), b. 24 October 1932, London, England. Poet; Writer; Dramatist; Lyricist. 2 sons, 3 daughters. Education: Christ Church, Oxford, 1953-55. Appointments: Granada Fellow, University of Lancaster, 1968-70; Fellow, Wesleyan University, 1972; Resident Writer, Sherman Theatre, 1974-75, Unicorn Theatre for Children, 1982-83; Judith Wilson Fellow, University of Cambridge, 1980-81; Fellow in Drama, Nanyang University, Singapore, 1995; Dylan Thomas Fellow, UK Festival of Literature, Swansea, 1995. Publications: Novels: If You See Me Coming; The Bodyguard; Plays: Plays with Songs, 1995; Out Loud; Heart on the Left; Blue Coffee; All Shook Up; For children: Robin Hood and Maid Marian; Nobody Rides the Unicorn; Maudie and the Green Children; also adaptions of numerous foreign plays; Television: Man Friday, 1972; Daft as a Brush, 1975; Glad Day, 1978; Pieces of Piece, 1992; Poetry: Paradise Lost and Paradise Regained; 5 programmes of Brecht's poetry, 1998; Radio plays: Animals Can't Laugh; White Suit Blues;

Anna on Anna; Plays: Tyger Tyger Two; Man Friday; Mind Your Head; A Seventh Man, White Suit Blues; Uppendown Money; Hoagy; In the Unlikely Event, Satie Day/Night; The Pied Piper; The Snow Queen; Jemima Puddleduck; The Siege; The Heroes; The Lion, The Witch and the Wardrobe; The Mammoth Sails Tonight; Who Killed Dylan Thomas; Films: Man Friday, 1975; The Tragedy of King Real, 1982; Music: The Ledge, opera libretto, 1961; Houdini, opera libretto, 1977; Start Again, Oratorio, 1998. Contributions to: Newspapers, magazines, and television. Honours: Eric Gregory Award; PEN Translation Prize; Tokyo Festival Television Film Award; Honorary Doctorate, North London University, 1997; CLPE Poetry Award, 2005. Memberships: Royal Society of Literature; Society of Authors; Writers Guild. Address: c/o Peters, Fraser and Dunlop Group Ltd, Drury House, 34-43 Russell Street, London WC2B 5HA, England.

MITCHELL David John, b. 24 January 1924, London, England. Writer. m. 1955, 1 son. Education: Bradfield College, Berkshire; MA, Honours, Modern History, Trinity College, Oxford, 1947. Appointment: Staff Writer, Picture Post, 1947-52. Publications: Women on the Warpath, 1966; The Fighting Pankhursts, 1967; 1919 Red Mirage, 1970; Pirates, 1976; Queen Christabel, 1977; The Jesuits: A History, 1980; The Spanish Civil War, 1982; Travellers in Spain, 1990; The Spanish Attraction, editor, 2001. Contributions to: Newspapers and magazines. Honours: Civil List Pension for services to Literature. Membership: Society of Authors. Address: 20 Mountacre Close, Sydenham Hill, London SE26 6SX, England.

MITCHELL Enid G D, b. London, England. Sculptor; Ceramist. 1 son, 2 daughters. Education: The Lady Eleanor Holles School; Intermediate Arts and Crafts, Ealing School of Art, 1947-50; Study of Sculpture with Robert Thomas, Ealing School of Art, 1964-68; Visual Arts Diploma, London University (Extra Mural), 1967-71; Diploma in Art and Design with Merit, Ceramics, Chelsea School of Art, 1976-79. Career: Independent Sculptor and Ceramist; Exhibitions: Regular exhibitor, Society of Portrait Sculptors, 1967-78; Exhibitor, Royal Society of British Sculptors, 1974-; RBS Exhibitions include: Scone Palace, Scotland; Taliesin Centre, Swansea University; Work in permanent collection, Leamington Spa Museum and various schools; Work in private collections in England, Eire, Israel, Holland, Australia, Brunei (ceramics), USA and Wales. Honour: Gilchrist Prize, London University, 1971. Memberships: Society of Portrait Sculptors, 1967-78; Associate, 1974, Fellow, 1983, Royal Society of British Sculptors. Address: Medmenham 2, 32 Stanier Street, Swindon, Wiltshire SN1 5QX, England.

MITCHELL George John, b. 20 August 1933, Waterville, USA. Politician; Lawyer. 1 daughter. Appointments: Called to Bar, 1960; Trial Attorney, US Department of Justice, Washington, 1960-62; Executive Assistant to Senator Edmund Muskie, 1962-65; Partner, Jensen & Baird, Portland, 1965-77; US Attorney for Maine, 1977-79; US District Judge, 1979-80; US Senator from Maine, 1980-85; Majority Leader, US Senate, 1988-95; Special Advisor to President Clinton for Economic Initiatives in Ireland, 1995; Chancellor designate, Queen's University, Belfast, 1999-; Adviser, Thames Water, 1999-; Chairman, The Walt Disney Company, 2004-2007. Publications; Great American Lighthouses, 1989; World on Fire, 1991; Not For America Alone, 1997; Making Peace, 2000. Memberships: Chair, Maine Democratic Committee, 1966-68; Member, National Committee, Maine, 1968-77; Chair, Committee on Northern Ireland, 1995. Honours: Hon LLD, Queens University, Belfast, 1997; Honorary

KBE, 1999; Shared, Honphouet-Boigny Peace Prize, 1999; Presidential Medal of Freedom, 1999; Tipperary International Peace Award, 2000. Address: c/o Verner, Liipfert, Bernhard, 901 15th Street, NW, #700, Washington, DC 20005, USA.

MITCHELL Julian, b. 1 May 1935, Epping, Essex, England. Author; Dramatist. Education: BA, Wadham College, Oxford, 1958. Appointment: Midshipman, Royal Naval Volunteer Reserve, 1953-55. Publications: Imaginary Toys, 1961; A Disturbing Influence, 1962; As Far as You Can Go, 1963; The White Father, 1964; A Heritage and Its History (play), 1965; A Family and a Fortune (play), 1966; A Circle of Friends, 1966; The Undiscovered Country, 1968; Jennie Lady Randolph Churchill: A Portrait with Letters (with Peregrine Churchill), 1974; Half-Life (play), 1977; Another Country (play), 1982, (film), 1984; Francis (play), 1983; After Aida (play), 1985; Falling Over England (play), 1994; August (adaptation of Uncle Vanya) (play), 1994, (film), 1995; Wilde (film script), 1997; Consenting Adults (TV play), 2007; Contributions to: Welsh History Review; Monmouthshire Antiquary. Honours: Scottish BAFTA Award, 2007. Address: 47 Draycott Place, London SW3 3DB, England.

MITCHELL Lucille Anne, b. 19 October 1928, Dayton Corners, Illinois, USA. Retired Elementary School Educator. m. Donald L Mitchell, 1 son, 3 daughters. Education: BS, Education, Augustana College, 1966; MS, Education, Western Illinois University, 1972; Education Specialist, 1974. Appointments: Teacher, Carbon Cliff, Elementary School, Illinois, 1962-65; Moline Board of Education, Illinois, 1967-92; Board Representative and Member, Illinois Network for School Development, Springfield, Illinois, 1973; Member, Textbook Selection Committee, Moline Board of Education, 1967-84; Teacher of Gifted, Moline Board of Education, 1985-87; Counsellor to Pastor, Community of Christ, 2001-02, 2006-07; Elder in priesthood. Publications: Contributor of poetry: Footprints Through the Forest, 2000; Best Poems and Poets of 2001; Best Poems and Poets of 2004; International Who's Who in Poetry, 2004; Published in International Who's Who in Poetry, 2005 and 2006; Labours of Love, Noble House, 2005. Honours: Master Teacher, State of Illinois, 1984; International Peace Prize, United Cultural Convention, 2005; American Medal of Honor, 2006; Listed in Who's Who in the World, 2005-06 and biographical dictionaries. Memberships: Various committees, Illinois Education Association; Various committees, Moline Education Association; Programme Chairman, 1978-79, Recording Secretary, 1980-81, Delta Kappa Gamma. Address: 3214 55th Street Ct, Moline, IL 61265-5740, USA.

MITCHELL (Raymond) Bruce, b. 8 January 1920, Lismore, New South Wales, Australia. Academic. m. Mollie Miller. Education: MA (Melb), 1952; MA (Oxon), 1955; DPhil (Oxon), 1959; DLitt (Oxon), 1986. Appointments: Teacher, Education Department of Victoria, 1936-40; Commissioned Service, Australian Imperial Force, 1941-46; Manager, Firm of Typesetters, Stereotypers and Lithographers, Melbourne, 1946-47; Student, Tutor, Lecturer, University of Melbourne, 1947-52; Australian National University Scholarship, Oxford University, 1952-54; Fellow and Tutor, St Edmund Hall, 1955-87; University Lecturer, Oxford University, 1955-87; Visiting Professor or Lecturer in 17 countries including Brown University, 1966-67. Publications include: A Guide to Old English, 1965, 2nd edition, 1968, reprinted 1971, 1975, 1978, 1981; A Guide to Old English Revised with Texts and Glossary 3rd edition (with Fred C Robinson), 1982, reprinted 1983, 1984; Old English Syntax, 2 volumes, 1985, reprinted 1985, 1985, 1997-98; A Guide to Old English Revised with

Prose and Verse Texts and Glossary, 4th edition (with Fred C Robinson), 1986, reprinted 1987, 1988; On Old English: Selected papers, 1988; A Critical Bibliography of Old English Syntax to the End of 1984, 1990; A Guide to Old English, 5th edition (with Fred C Robinson), 1992, reprinted 1992 (twice), 1995, 1995, 1996 (twice) 1997 (twice), 1998, 1999, 2000; An Invitation to Old English and Anglo Saxon England, 1995, reprinted 1996 (twice), 1997 (twice), 1998, 2000; Beowulf : An Edition (with Fred C Robinson), 1998, reprinted 2000; Graham St Edmund Hall Oxford 1941-1999 (with Reggie Alton), 2000; Beowulf Repunctuated (with Susan Irvine), 2000; A Guide to Old English, 6th edition 2001, 7th edition, 2006 (with Fred C Robinson); Into Old English: Essays in Honour of Bruce Mitchell, 2006; over 80 articles in academic journals. Honour: Phil Dr honoris causa, Turku, 1986. Memberships: Finnish Academy of Arts and Sciences, 1989; Honorary Member, International Society of Anglo Saxonists, 1989; Honorary Fellow, Australian Academy of Humanities, 2002. Address: 39 Blenheim Drive, Oxford OX2 8DJ, England.

MITCHELL William Joseph, b. 4 January 1936, Bristol, England. Catholic Priest. Education: MA, Jurisprudence, Corpus Christi College, Oxford, 1956; Seminaire S. Sulpice, Paris France, 1956-61; Ordained Priest, 1961; License in Canon Law, Pontifical Gregorian University, Rome, 1963. Appointments: Curate, Pro-Cathedral, Bristol, 1963-64; Secretary to the Bishop of Clifton, 1964-75; Parish Priest, St Bernadette, Bristol, 1975-78; Rector, Pontifical Beda College, Rome, 1978-87; Parish Priest, St John's, Bath, 1988-90; Parish Priest St Anthony's, Bristol, 1990-96; Parish Priest, St Mary-on-the-Quay, Bristol, 1996-97; Dean of Clifton Cathedral, 1997-2001; Parish Priest, St Michael's Tetbury, Gloucestershire, 2001-; Judicial Vicar and Episcopal Vicar for Matrimonial Matters, 2002-. Honours: Prelate of Honour (Monsignor), Pope John Paul I, 1978-; Canon of Cathedral Chapter, 1987-, Vicar General, 1987-2001, Diocese of Clifton. Membership: Chaplain to the Knights of the Holy Sepulchre, 2003. Address: St Michael's Presbytery, 31 Silver Street, Tetbury, Gloucestershire, GL8 8DH, England. E-mail: billmitchell@tetbury31.freeserve.co.uk

MITCHINER Michael Bernard, b. 8 February 1938, Croydon, England. Medical Practitioner. m. Rosaleen Mary, 2 sons, 2 daughters. Education: St George's College, Weybridge, Surrey; Guy's Hospital Medical School, London, 1957-64; BSc, Physiology, 1961, MBBS, 1964, PhD, Pathology, 1969, London University; LRCP, MRCS, 1964. Appointments: House Physician and House Surgeon, Royal Surrey County Hospital, Guildford, 1964-65; University Lecturer in Pathology, Guy's Hospital Medical School, London University, 1965-71; General Medical Practitioner, Sanderstead, 1971-92; Medical and numismatic work, India, 1992, 1993; General Practice, England and abroad, 1993-2007. Publications: A car journey across Asia, 1964; Articles in professional medical journals; Numerous books and articles on coinage and history. Honours: Harris Prize for Anatomy, 1960; Wooldridge Prize for Physiology, 1960; First Prize for Proficiency, 1960; Lubbock Prize Certificate of Honour for Clinical Pathology, 1962; Nuffield Foundation Travelling Scholarship to Hong Kong University, 1963. Memberships: British Medical Association; Royal Society of Medicine; Royal Numismatic Society; Royal Asiatic Society; British Numismatic Society.

MITENKOV Feodor Mikhailovitch, b. 25 November 1924, Klyuchi, Saratovskiy, Russia. Nuclear Scientist; Engineer. m. Ludmila Ivanova, 1 son, 1 daughter. Education: School No

3, Saratov, 1931-1941; Law, All-Union Extra-Mural Institute of Law, Saratov, 1941-1948; Engineering-Physics, Faculty of Physics, Saratov State University, Saratov, 1948-1950. Appointments: Design Engineer, GMZ Works, Russia, 1950-57; Head of Analytical Department, OKBM, 1957-67; Deputy Director and Deputy Chief Designer, OKBM, 1967-69; Director and Chief Designer, OKBM, 1969-97; Scientific Leader, OKBM, 1997-. Publications: Drive mechanisms of control and safety rods for fast sodium-cooled reactors, 1980, co-author; Slightly boiling reactors' stability, Mechanisms of instable processes in thermal and nuclear power engineering, 1981, co-author; Main circulating pumps for Nuclear Power Plants, 1984, co-author; Editor, Encyclopaedia of Mechanical Engineering, 2000-04. Honours: Cand of Techn Sci, NIKIET, Moscow, 1959; PhD, FEI, Obninsk, 1967; Professor, GPI, Gorky, 1968; Honoured science and engineering worker, 1997; President, Russian Nuclear Society, 1992-93; Global Energy International Award 2004. Memberships; Full member, Russian Academy of Sciences, 1990-; Honorary member, European Nuclear Society. Address: OKB Mechanical Engineering, Burnakovsky proezd, 15, Nizhny Novgorod, 603074, Russia. E-mail: okbm@okbm.nnov.ru

MITROVIĆ R Ljubiša, b. 16 February 1943, Mokra, Bela Palanka, Serbia. Sociologist; Professor. m. Svetlana, 2 daughters. Education: Graduate, Sociology, Faculty of Philosophy, University of Belgrade, 1970; Master's Degree, Political Sciences, University of Belgrade, 1975; PhD, Sociological Sciences (General Sociology), University of Niš, 1977. Appointments include: Assistant Teacher, Faculty of Philosophy, 1971, Dean of the Faculty of Philosophy, 1983-87, Full-time Professor, Faculty of Philosophy, 1987, Vice-Rector, 1987-89, University of Niš; Director, Macroproject dealing with regional and cultural co-operation in the Balkans, identity of the Balkan nations, interethnic relationships and the culture of peace, 1996-; Professor, by invitation, World University Association "Plato", Greece, 2001; Director, Centre for Balkan Studies, 2002-; Writer of poetry. Publications: 30 books; Over 350 papers and articles; Most important books: Sociology and Contemporary Times, 1984; Sociology of Development, 1992; Contemporary Society – Strategies of Development and Their Actors, 1996; Globalization and the Balkans, 2002; Contemporary Balkans within the Context of the Sociology of Social Change, 2003; General Sociology, Theory and Modern Society, 2003; The Road to Dependent Society, 2004; Towards the Culture of Peace in the Balkans, 2005; The Crossroads and Alternatives on the Balkans, 2006; 11 collections of poetry including: The New Barbarians, 2000; Orpheus of the Suva Mountain, 2001; Dreading the Big Beast, 2005; The Cosmic Nomads, 2005. Some of his scientific and literary works have been translated into English, French, Bulgarian and Macedonian. Honours: October Prize of the City of Niš, 1987; University Rewards, 1985, 1987; Medal for Deserving Citizens of the Socialist Federative Republic of Yugoslavia, 1988. Memberships: Sociological Association of Serbia; Association for Political Sciences of Serbia; Centre for Balkan Studies. Writers Association of Serbia. Address: Oblačića Rada 24/4, 18000 Niš, Serbia.

MIYACHI Iwao, b. 27 September 1916, Kochi, Japan. Professor of Engineering. m. Kazuko Nagano, 2 daughters. Education: Bachelor in Engineering, 1940, Doctor in Engineering, 1953, University of Tokyo. Appointments: Lecturer, 1940, Professor, 1957, Nagoya University; Professor, 1980, Guest Professor, 1989, Aichi Institute of Technology. Publications: Articles for Institute of Electrical Engineers, Japan, on Power Transmission and Distribution, Electrical Power Engineering, Electrical Power Generation. Honours:

Meritorious Contribution Award and four others, Institute of Electrical Engineers, Japan, 1968-90; Officier des Palmes Académiques, France, 1975; Second Order of National Merits, Japan, 1990. Memberships: SEE, France, 1960-; Honorary Member, Institute of Electrical Engineers of Japan, 1986; Distinguished Member, Conférence Internationale des Grands Réseaux Electriques, 1996. Address: 3-6-5 Nishizaki-cho, Chikusa, Nagoya 464-0825, Japan.

MIYAKE Issey, b. 22 April 1939, Tokyo, Japan. Fashion Designer. Education: Tama Art University; Tokyo and La Chambre Syndicale de la Couture Parisienne, Paris. Appointments: Assistant Designer to Guy Laroche, Paris, 1966-68, to Hubert de Givenchy, Paris, 1968-69; Designer, Geoffrey Beene (ready-to-wear firm), New York, 1969-70; Founder, Miyake Design Studio, Tokyo, 1970; Director, Issey Miyake International, Issey Miyake and Associates, Issey Miyake Europe, Issey Miyake USA, Issey Miyake On Limits, Tokyo; Executive Advisor, Planner, First Japan Culture Conference, Yokohama, 1980. Creative Works: Works exhibited in Paris, Tokyo and MIT, appears in collections of Metro Museum of Art, New York and Victoria and Albert Museum, London. Honours: Japan Fashion Editors Club Awards, 1974, 1976; Mainichi Design Prize, 1977; Pratt Institute Award, New York, 1979; Dr.h.c. Royal College of Art, 1993.

MIYOSHI Isao, b. 15 July 1932, Tokushima, Japan. Physician; Educator. m. Shigeko Kagawa, 3 sons. Education: MD, 1957, PhD, 1965, Okayama University, Japan. Appointments: Intern US Army Hospital, Tokyo, 1957-58; Resident Ohio State University, Columbus, 1958-59; Fellow, University of Texas, Houston, 1959-60; Member, Okayama University Hospital, Japan, 1966-81; Associate Professor, Kochi Medical School, Japan, 1981-82; Professor of Medicine, 1982-98; Professor Emeritus, 1998-. Publications: Numerous articles published in Medical Journals, 1961-2006. Honours: Recipient Hideyo Noguchi Prize, 1983; Princess Takamatsu Cancer Prize, 1984; Hammer Prize, 1985; Asahi Prize, 1987; Medal with Purple Ribbon, 1996. Memberships: Japanese Cancer Association; American Association of Cancer Research. Address: Kochi Medical School, Kochi 783-8505, Japan.

MIZRAHI Isaac, b. 14 October 1961, Brooklyn, New York, USA. Fashion Designer. Education: Parsons School of Design. Appointments: Apprenticed to Perry Ellis, 1982, full-time post, 1982-84; Worked with Jeffrey Banks, 1984-85, Calvin Klein, 1985-87; Founder, own design firm in partnership with Sarah Hadad Cheney, 1987; First formal show, 1988, First spring collection, 1988; First menswear line launched, 1990, Announced closure of firm, 1998.

MIZUNO Koichi, b. 23 December 1965, Tokyo, Japan. Surgeon; Researcher. m. Mihoko, 1 son, 2 daughters. Education: MD, 1990, PhD, Graduate School, 2004, Tokyo Medical and Dental University. Appointments: Department of Orthopaedic Surgery, Saiseikai Kawaguchi Hospital, Saitama, Japan, 1994-95; Yokosuka National Hospital, Kanagawa, Japan, 1995-96; Kudanzaka Hospital, Tokyo, Japan, 1996-2005; Suwa Central Hospital, Nagano, Japan, 2005-07; Kudanzaka Hospital, 2007-. Honours: Japan Orthopaedic Surgery Specialist, 1997; Japan Spinal Surgery Specialist, 2002. Memberships: Japanese Orthopaedic Association; Japanese Society of Spinal Surgery and Related Disease.

MIZUNO Masahiro, b. 28 October 1965, Shiga, Japan. Process Chemist; Researcher. m. Minako Komiyama, 1 son, 1 daughter. Education: BS, 1988, MS, 1990, PhD,

2007, Gifu Pharmaceutical University, Japan; Pharmacist's Certificate, Japan, 1988. Appointments: Researcher, 1990-97, Assistant Research Head, 1997-, Takeda Pharmaceutical Company Ltd, Osaka, Japan. Publications: Articles and papers in professional scientific journals. Honours: Listed in international biographical dictionaries. Memberships: Society of Synthetic Organic Chemistry, Japan; Japanese Society for Process Chemistry. Address: 17-85, Jusohonmachi 2-chome, Yodogawa-ku, Osaka 532-8686, Japan. E-mail: mizuno-masahiro@takeda.co.jp

MO Timothy (Peter), b. 30 December 1950, Hong Kong. Writer. Education: Convent of the Precious Blood, Hong Kong; Mill Hill School, London; BA, St John's College, Oxford. Publications: The Monkey King, 1978; Sour Sweet, 1982; An Insular Possession, 1986; The Redundancy of Courage, 1991; Brownout on Breadfruit Boulevard, 1995; Renegade or Halo², 1999. Contributions to: Periodicals. Honours: Gibbs Prize, 1971; Geoffrey Faber Memorial Prize, 1979; Hawthornden Prize, 1983; E M Forster Award, American Academy of Arts and Letters, 1992; James Tait Black Memorial Prize, 1999. Address: c/o Chatto & Windus, 20 Vauxhall Bridge Road, London SW1V 2SA, England.

MOAT John, b. 11 September 1936, India. Author; Poet. m. 1962, 1 son, 1 daughter. Education: MA, Oxford University, 1960. Publications: 6d per Annum, 1966; Heorot (novel), 1968; A Standard of Verse, 1969; Thunder of Grass, 1970; The Tugen and the Toot (novel), 1973; The Ballad of the Leat, 1974; Bartonwood (juvenile), 1978; Fiesta and the Fox Reviews and His Prophecy, 1979; The Way to Write (with John Fairfax), 1981; Skeleton Key, 1982, complete edition, 1997; Mai's Wedding (novel), 1983; Welcombe Overtunes, 1987; The Missing Moon, 1988; Firewater and the Miraculous Mandarin, 1990; Practice, 1994; The Valley (poems and drawings), 1998; 100 Poems, 1998; Rain (short stories), 2000; Hermes & Magdalen (poems and etchings), 2004; The Founding of Arvon (belles lettres), 2006. Address: Crenham Mill, Hartland, North Devon EX39 6HN, England.

MOBBERLEY David Winstone, b. 12 July 1948, Birmingham, England. Poet; Didgeridoo Player. Divorced, 1 son. Appointments: Pharmaceutical Process Technician, 1964-71; Postman, 1971-2005. Publications: Equilibrium of Forces, 1992; Beneath the Darkness A Light is Shining, 1993; Sacred Journey, 1995; Revelations, 2007; First and Last, 2007; Contributions to Iota; San Fernando Poetry Journal, USA; Envoi; The Plowman Journal; Poetry Now. Honours: 1st Prize, The Plowman Poetry Contest, 1997, 1999, 2001; World Record, Greatest Draw of a Flatbow, Commandery Civil War, Centre, Worcester, 1999. Memberships: Reivers Archery Club, Gordon, Scotland; A Friend of the Classic Malts, Glasgow, Scotland. Address: 87 Woodthorpe Road, Kings Heath, Birmingham B14 6EG, England.

MOBERLEY Gary Mark, b. Sydney, New South Wales, Australia. Musician (keyboards); Composer; Writer; Programmer. Musical Education: Grade 6, Australian Conservatory of Music, New South Wales. Career: Left Australia for London, 1971; Musical Director for soul acts with American Promotions Bureau, 1973; Recorded and toured with Tina Charles, 1974-76; Joined John Miles touring GB, Europe, USA and Canada, supporting Elton John, 1976; Joined The Sweet, 1978; Session work in Florida, USA recording with many Spanish artists, 1981; Returned to London and become involved with major recording studios and recording labels as a session musician, 1982; Live work/ recorded with: The Sweet; John Miles Band; Terence Trent

D'Arby; Prefab Sprout; Wet Wet Wet; The Damned; The Alarm; Hipsway; The The (Infected Album); Jodie Watley; Girlschool; Drum Theatre; Sigue Sigue Sputnik; Little Richard; Haywoode; Nicole; Big Country (remix); Loose Ends; The Associates; Talk Talk; Kiki Dee; Band Of Holy Joy; Dangerous Grounds; Funkadelia; Steel Pulse; Trevor Horn; The JBs; Red Beans and Rice; ABC; Fine Young Cannibals; The Foundations; Jean Jacques Perrey; Live work with: Bee Gees; Paul Rodgers; Bonnie Tyler; Wilson Pickett; Eddie Floyd; Rufus Thomas; Ben E King; Arthur Conley; Andrew 'Junior Boy' Jones; Cookie McGhee; Texas Blues Summit; Memphis Blues Summit; 34 European tours; 9 American tours; 3 world tours; 5 albums of radio and TV themes used world-wide, including Eastenders theme. Address: 43 High Street, Haddenham, Bucks, HP17 8ET, England. E-mail: gm@musicworld.fsbusiness.co.uk

MOBY, b. 11 September 1965, New York, New York, USA. Musician (Guitar, Drums, Keyboards); Producer; Composer; Remixer. Education: University Philosophy Student, University of Connecticut; Private Classical Education, 1976-83. Career: Production & remixes for: Metallica; Smashing Pumpkins; Michael Jackson; Depeche Mode; Soundgarden; Blur; David Bowie; Orbital; Prodigy; Freddie Mercury; Brian Eno; B-52's; Ozzy Osbourne; John Lydon; Butthole Surfers; Erasure; Aerosmith; OMD; Pet Shop Boys; Jon Spencer Blues Explosion; Tours: Lollapalooza, 1995; Red Hot Chili Peppers, 1995; Soundgarden, 1996; Big Top, 1997; Prodigy, 1993, 1995; many solo tours. Recordings: Albums: Moby, 1992; Underground, 1993; Move, 1994; Ambient, 1994; Everything is Wrong, 1995; Underwater, 1995; Animal Rights, 1996; Collected B-Sides, 1996; I Like to Score, 1997; The End of Everything, 1997; Play, 1999; Mobysongs, 2000; 18, 2002; Play: The B Sides, 2004; Hotel, 2005; Singles: That's When I Reach for My Revolver; Come on Baby; Dog Heaven; Why Can't It Stop?; Fucked Up; Higher/Desperate; Into the Blue; Everytime You Touch Me; Feeling So Real; Hymn; Move; UHF; Rock the House; James Bond Theme; Go; Drug Fits the Face; Honey; Run On; Bodyrock; Next Is The E; Why Does My Heart Feel So Bad?; Natural Blues; Full movie score: Double Tap, 1997; Movie soundtrack contributions: Cool World, 1993; Heat, Scream, Joe's Apartment, 1996; Tomorrow Never Dies, the Saint, The Jackal, Spawn, 1997; Gattaca, Senseless, Rounders, Species II, Ever After, Blade, The Bumblebee Flies Anyway, Dangerous Beauty, Permanent Midnight, Playing By Heart, 1998; Any Given Sunday, The Next Best Thing, The Beach, Big Daddy. Honours: Eveything Is Wrong, Album of the Year, Spin Magazine, 1995; Top 5 Albums of the Year, Village Voice, Entertainment Weekly & Go; Live Performer in Germany, 1995, Frontpage Magazine; Nominated Grammy 2000; Nominated Brit 2000. Memberships: BMI; PMRS; AF of M; SAG; AFTRA. Address: c/o Mr Eric Härle, Deutsch-Englische Freundschaft Ltd, PO Box 2477, London NW6 6NQ, England.

MOCUMBI Pascoal Manuel, b. 10 April 1941, Maputo, Mozambique. Medical Doctor. m. Adelina Isabel Bernadino Paindane, 3 January 1966, 2 sons, 2 daughters. Education: MD, University of Lausanne, 1973; Diploma, Health Planning, Institut Planification Sanitaire, University of Dakar, 1975. Appointments: Chief Medical Officer, Sofala Province, 1976-80; Minister of Health, 1980-87; Foreign Minister, 1987-94; Prime Minister, 1994-2004; High Commissioner, European-Developing Countries Clinical Trials Programme, 2004-. Publications: Co-author, Manual de Obstetricia Pratica, Intervencoes Obstétricas; Health for All by the Year 2000?, 1996. Honours: National decorations; International decorations, Brazil, Chile. Memberships: Mozambique

Medical Association; Mozambique Public Health Association; Mozambique Family Development Association. Address: Praça da Marinha, Maputo, Mozambique. E-mail: dgpm.gov@teledata.mz

MOELLER Christoph, b. 27 December 1969, Muensingen, Germany. Child and Adolescent Psychiatrist; Psychotherapist. m. Kirsten, 2 daughters. Education: Medical Doctor, University of Witten/Herdecke, 1997. Appointments: Paediatric Physician, Herdecke, 1997-98; Child and Adolescent Psychiatrist, Osnabrueck, Hannover, 1998-2001; Consultant, Child and Adolescent Psychiatrist/Psychotherapist and Family Therapist, Group Therapist, Hannover, 2002-; Teaching: Balintgroups and Group Therapy. Publications: Author, Seeking Adolescence, 2003; Author and editor, Drug Abuse in Adolescence, 2005; Author and Editor, The Positive Sight of Addiction in Adolescent, 2007; Several articles in journals, newspapers and on TV. Honours: Listed in Who's Who in the World, 2006-08; Who's Who in Science and Engineering. Leading Health Professionals of the World, 2006, 2000 Outstanding Intellectuals of the World 2006-2007. Address: Kinderkrankenhaus auf der Bult, Janusz-Korczak-Allee 12, 30173 Hannover, Germany. E-mail: moeller@hka.de

MOFFATT Henry Keith, b. 12 April 1935, Edinburgh, Scotland. Emeritus Professor. m. Katharine (Linty) Stiven, 2 sons, 1 deceased, 2 daughters. Education: George Watson's College, Edinburgh, 1943-53; Lycee Henri IV, Paris, France, 1953; BSc (1st class honours), Mathematical Science, Edinburgh University, 1953-57; Wrangler, 1958, BA (1st class), 1959, Smith's Prize, 1960, PhD, Magnetohydrodynamic Turbulence, 1962, ScD, 1987, Cambridge University. Appointments: Assistant Editor, 1962-65, Editor, 1966-83, Journal of Fluid Mechanics; Professor of Applied Mathematics, Bristol University, 1977-80; Fellow, 1962-76, 1980-, Tutor, 1970-74, Senior Tutor, 1975-76, Trinity College, Cambridge; Assistant Lecturer, 1962-64, Lecturer, 1964-76, Head of Department of Applied Mathematics and Theoretical Physics, 1983-91, Professor of Mathematical Physics, 1980-2002, Cambridge University; Director, Isaac Newton Institute for Mathematical Sciences, Cambridge, 1996-2001; Blaise Pascal Professorship, ENS, Paris, 2001-03; Leverhulme Emeritus Fellowship, 2003-05. Publications: Numerous papers and articles in professional scientific journals; Books: Magnetic Field Generation in Electrically Conducting Fluids, 1978; Topological Aspects of the Dynamics of Fluids and Plasmas (editor), 1992; Tubes, Sheets and Singularities in Fluid Dynamics (editor), 2002. Honours: FRS, 1986; FRS (Edin), 1988; Doctor hc: Institut National Polytechnique de Grenoble, 1987; State University of New York (Utica), 1990; Edinburgh University, 2001; Technical University of Eindhoven, 2006; Foreign Member: Royal Netherlands Academy of Arts and Sciences, 1991; Academia Europaea, 1994; Académie des Sciences, Paris, 1998; Accademia Nazionale dei Lincei, Rome, 2001; Officier des Palmes Académiques, 1998; Panetti-Ferrari International Prize and Gold Medal, 2001; Euromech Prize in Fluid Mechanics, 2003; Caribbean Award for Fluid Dynamics, 2004; London Mathematical Society Senior Whitehead Prize, 2005; Royal Society Hughes Medal, 2005. Memberships: Member of Bureau, 1992-, President, 2000-04, Vice President, 2004-, International Union of Theoretical and Applied Mechanics; Trustee and Member of Council, African Institute for Mathematical Sciences, 2003-; Fellow, American Physical Society, 2003-. Website: www.damtp.cam.ac.uk/user/hkm2

MOH Za Lee, b. 10 July 1928, Shanghai, China. Engineer. m. Jeannette C S Yin, 1 daughter. Education: BSCE, National Taiwan University, Taipei, Taiwan; MSCE, PhD, Purdue University, Indiana, USA. Appointments: Highway Engineer (Structure), Indiana State Highway Department, Indiana, USA, 1958-61; Assistant Professor, Associated Professor, West Virginia University, USA, 1961-66; Associated Professor, University of Hawaii, USA, 1966-69; Chairman, MAA Group Consulting Engineers, Hong Kong; Chairman, Moh and Associates Inc, Taiwan. Honours: Tau Beta Pi; Sigma Xi; Distinguished Engineering Alumna, Purdue University, 1995. Memberships: Fellow, American Society of Civil Engineers; Fellow, Institute of Structural Engineers; Fellow, Chinese Institute of Civil & Hydraulic Engineers; Fellow, Hong Kong Institute of Engineers; Member, American Association of Engineering Education; Member, Earthquake Engineering Research Institute; Member, ASTM, ACI. Address: 11F, #3 Tunhwa S Rd, Sec 1, Taipei, Taiwan. E-mail: zalee.moh@maaconsultants.com

MOHAN Chander, b. 8 October 1939, Jehlum, Pakistan. Professor. m. Tripta Kumari, 1 son, 1 daughter. Education: BA Honours, Mathematics, 1957, MA, Mathematics, 1960, Panjab University, Chandigarh, India; PhD, Mathematics, Roorkee University, Roorkee, India, 1967. Lecturer, Mathematics, Multaninal Modi College, Modinagar, India, 1961-64; Lecturer, 1964-70, Reader, 1970-85, Professor, 1985-2000, Head, Mathematics Department, 1994-1999, Roorkee University, Roorkee, India; Professor and Dean, Amity School of Computer Science, Noida (UP), India, 2000-02; Professor and Head, Mathematics Department, IILM College of Engineering and Technology, Greater NOIDA, (UP) India 2002-04; Professor, Department of Computer Science, Ambala College of Engineering & Applied Research, Ambala (Haryana) 2004-. Publications: Over 90 research publications in national and international research journals; 3 books on technical subjects. Honours: Khosla Research Award, 1990; Millennium Award of Honour American Biographical Institute; Listed in several Who's Who publications. Memberships: International Astronomical Union; Operations Research Society of India; Founder Member Indian Astronomical Society; Founder Member, Executive Committee Member, Indian Society for Industrial and Applied Mathematics. Address: 2821, Durgacharam Road, Ambala Cantt, (Haryana), India. E-mail: chander_mohan2@rediff.mail.com

MOIR (Alexander) (Thomas) Boyd, b. 1 August 1939, Bolton, Lancashire, England. Medical Practitioner; Scientist. m. Isobel May Shechan, deceased, 1 son, 2 daughters. Education: MBChB, BSc, PhD, Edinburgh University. Appointments: Rotating Intern, New York City, USA, 1964-65; Scientific Staff, 1965-67, Clinical Scientific Staff, 1968-73, Medical Research Council; Senior Medical Officer, 1972-77, Principal Medical Officer, 1977-85, Director of Chief Scientist Organisation, 1986-96, Scottish Health Department; Currently, Honorary Appointments, Edinburgh and Glasgow Universities; Consultancy and Clinical Services. Publications: Publications on Neuroscience, Pharmacology, Biochemistry, Toxicology, Research Management, Public Health. Honours: FRCP (Edin); FRCP (Glasgow); FRCPath; FFPHM; FIBiol; FIFST; MFOM; MFPM; FRSS. Memberships: UK Royal Colleges of Physicians and their Faculties; Royal College of Pathologists; Institute of Biology; Association of Chemists and Biochemists; Pharmacology Society. Address: 23 Murrayfield Gardens, Edinburgh EG 12 6DG, Scotland. E-mail: boyd_moir@msn.com

MOK Ho Ming Joseph, b. 16 September 1967, Hong Kong. Physicist. Education: BSc (Hons), Physics, University of Hong Kong, 1989. Appointments: Teaching Assistant, City University of Hong Kong, 1989-91; Physicist, Department of Health, Hong Kong SAR Govt, 1991-. Publications: Numerous articles in professional journals; Monograph, Cosmic rays: Weather, Climate and Applications. Honours: Vice President, Recognition Board, World Congress of Arts, Sciences and Communications; Foremost Scientists in the World, IBC, 2008; Deputy Director General, IBC; Life Fellowship, International Biographical Association; The Order of International Fellowship, IBC, Cambridge, 2008; IBC Foremost Scientists of the World, 2008; Outstanding Professional Award, 2008; The Order of International Ambassadors, ABI; Listed in international biographical dictionaries; Research Board of Advisors, ABI. Memberships: New York Academy of Science; American Chemical Society; The New Millennium Committee of the Planetary Society; Hong Kong Association of Medical Physics; Hong Kong Radiation Protection Society; Union of Physicists of Hong Kong. Address: Radiation Health Unit, 3/F, Saiwanho Health Centre, 28 Tai Hong St, Sai Wan Ho, Hong Kong. E-mail: jhmmok@netvigator.com

MOKEME Nnaemeka Igwebueze, b. 20 July 1956, Aba, Nigeria. Naturopathic Physician. m. Linda, 1 son, 2 daughters. Education: Minneapolis Technical Institute, Minnesota, USA, 1987; Nigeria College of Natural Medicine, Federal Ministry of Science and Technology, Lagos, Nigeria. Appointments: CEO/Consultant, Naturopath, Emmy Forever Healthcare & Research Centre; Medical Consultant, Naturopath, Model Clinic, Nigeria Natural Medicine Development Agency, Federal Ministry of Science & Technology, Lagos; Lecturer, Nigeria College of Natural Medicine, Federal Ministry of Science & Technology; Consultant, Naturopath, Nigeria Natural Medicine Development Agency; Lecturer, Federal College of Alternative & Traditional Medicine, Lagos; Technical Consultant, The Museum of African Culture; Nursing/Ward Orientation Technician, Willows South (now Walter on Lyndale); Patient-Doctor Liaison Officer, St Mary's Hospital, Health Care Management, University Health Care Hospital. Publications: Cleanse Yourself Internally and Reclaim your Health Naturally, 2000; Ways to Detoxify Your System, 2001; Nature's Green Pharmacy, 2001; Good Nutrition Best Therapy, 2001; Natural Body Builders, 2001; Herbal Treatment of Peptic Ulcer, 2001; Halitosis, 2001; The Truth About Stroke, 2005. Honours: Award of Excellence and Employee of the Month, 1988; Honourable Mention, World of Poetry, USA, 1990; Award of Excellence for Research & Development of Curative Drugs, and Natural Medicine Award for Innovative Concepts, Nigerian Alternative Medicine, 2004; Listed in international biographical dictionaries. Memberships: President, Nigeria Naturopathic Medical Association; Sec, Lagos State Government Board of Traditional Medicine, Hospital & Clinic Standard Committee; National Expert Committee on Research Development in Natural Medicine, Health Science Department of Federal Ministry of Science & Technology; Association of Therapeutics of African Medicine; Nigeria Society of Holistic Medicine; Nigeria Academy of Natural Medicine; Contact Teleministries, USA. E-mail: emmyforever2001@yahoo.com

MOLDEN Nigel Charles, b. 17 August 1948, Oxford, England. Company Director. m. Julia, 3 sons. Education: BSc (Hons), London University, 1970; MSc, Brunel University, 1986; PhD, Fairfax University Institute, 1996. Appointments: General Manager, Warner Bros. Records, 1976-78; International General Manager, WEA Records, 1978-80; Head of International Marketing, Thorn EMI Screen Entertainment, 1980-84; Chairman, Magnum Music Group, 1984-97; Chairman, Magnum America Inc, 1995-97; Chief Executive, Synergie Logistics, 1997-; Thames Valley

Magistrates Courts Service, 2002-2005; HM Courts Service for the Thames Valley, 2005-. Publications: Enemies Within, 1993; Research Provides No Scapegoat, 1993; Thinking Positive, 1994; Adrift On The Waves, 1995. Honours: Fellow, Chartered Institute of Marketing, 1988; Freeman of the City of London, 1990; Fellow, Institute of Directors, 1994; Fellow, Royal Society of Arts, 1995; Fellow, British Management Institute, 1995. Address: Ashcombe House, Deanwood Road, Jordans, Buckinghamshire HP9 2UU, England. E-mail: synergielogistics@btconnect.com

MÖLDER Leevi, b. 4 July 1933, Tudulinna, Estonia. Professor of Chemical Engineering. m. Maila Vägi, 1961, 2 sons, 1 daughter. Education: MSc, Chemical Engineering, 1957, PhD, 1963, Tallinn Technical University. Appointments: Researcher, 1957-62, Associate Professor, 1962-73, Professor 1973-85, 1992-2000, Emeritus Professor, 2001-, Tallinn Technical University; Head of Department, Institute of Chemistry, Estonian Academy of Sciences, 1983-97; Vice Chairman, Council Oil Shale, Estonian Academy of Sciences, 1989-99; Chairman, Commission on Liquid Fuels Quality Specification, Ministry of Economics, Tallinn, 1994-97; Consultant, RAS Kiviter Chemical Co, Kohtla-Jarve, Estonia, 1995-98. Publications: Technology of Heavy Chemicals, co-author, 1970; English-Estonian-Russian Dictionary of Chemistry, co-author, 1998; 203 articles in professional journals; 11 inventions. Honours: Mente et manu Medal, Tallinn Technical University, 1983, 1993; Paul Kogerman Medal, Estonian Academy of Sciences, 1987; White Star Order of Merit, 2004; Listed in numerous biographical publications. Memberships: American Society for Testing and Materials; Estonian Chemical Society; Union of Estonian Scientists; Estonian Society for Nature Conservation. Address: Tallinn Technical University, 5 Ehitajate tee, Tallinn 19086, Estonia. E-mail: leevi.molder@ttu.ee

MOLIN Yury, b. 3 February 1934, Romodanovo Village, USSR. Chemist. m. Galina Jakovleva, 2 daughters. Education: MA, Moscow Institute of Physics and Technology, 1957; Candidate (PhD), 1962, Doctor, 1971, Institute of Chemical Kinetics and Combustion, Novosibirsk. Appointments: Researcher Institute of Chemical Physics, Moscow, 1957-59; Researcher, 1959, Head of Laboratory, 1967, Director, 1971, Head of Laboratory, 1993, Advisor of Russian Academy of Sciences, 2004-, Institute of Chemical Kinetics and Combustion, Novosibirsk; Lecturer, 1966, Professor, 1974-, Novosibirsk State University. Publications: Spin Exchange, 1980; Spin Polarization and Magnetic Effects in Radical Reactions, 1984; Infrared Photochemistry, 1985; 300 articles in scientific journals. Honours: National (Lenin) Prize, 1986; Mendeleev Lecturer, 1992; Fellow of EPR/ESR Society, 1998; N N Semenov Golden Medal, Russian Academy of Sciences, 2006. Memberships: Corresponding Member, 1974, Full Member, 1981, USSR (Now Russian) Academy of Sciences; Editorial boards of journals. Address: Institute of Chemical Kinetics and Combustion, 3 Institutskaya Str, Novosibirsk 630090, Russia. E-mail: molin@ns.kinetics.nsc.ru

MOLINA Alfred, b. 24 May 1953, London, England. Actor. m. Jill Gascoigne. Education: Guildhall School of Music and Drama. Career: Theatre: RSC and National Theatre, Royal Court Theatre, Donmar Warehouse, Minskoff Theater and Broadway; Films: Indiana Jones and the Raiders of the Lost Ark, 1981; Anyone for Denis, 1982; Number One, 1984; Eleni, Ladyhawke, A Letter to Brezhnev, 1985; Prick Up Your Ears, 1987; Manifesto, 1988; Not Without My Daughter, American Friends, Enchanted April, 1991; When Pigs Fly, The Trial, American Friends, 1993; White Fang 2: Myth of the White

Wolf, Maverick, 1994; Hideaway, The Perez Family, A Night of Love, The Steal; Species, 1995; Before and After, Dead Man, Scorpion Spring, Mojave Moon, 1996; Anna Karenina, The Odd Couple II, Boogie Nights, The Man Who Knew Too Little, 1997; The Imposters, 1998; Magnolia, Dudley Do-Right, 1999; The Trial, Chocolat, 2000; Texas Rangers, Agatha Christie's Murder on the Orient Express, 2001; Pete's Meteor, Road to Perdition, 2002; Frida, My Life Without Me, Coffee and Cigarettes, 2003; Spider-Man 2, Steamboy (voice), 2004; Sian Ka'an, 2005; The Da Vinci Code, As You Like It, The Hoax; Orchids, 2006; The Moon and the Stars, Silk, The Little Traitor, The Ten Commandments (voice), 2007. TV: El Cid; Year in Provence; Nervous Energy; Ladies Man; Murder on the Orient Express; Bram and Alice; Justice League; Joan of Arc; The Company. Website: www.alfred-molina.com

MONTAGU OF BEAULIEU Edward John Barrington Douglas-Scott-Montagu, 3rd Baron, b. 20 October 1926, London, England. Museum Administrator; Author; Elected Peer. m. (1) Elizabeth Belinda, 1959, divorced, 1974, 1 son, 1 daughter, (2) Fiona Herbert, 1974, 1 son. Education: St Peter's Court, Broadstairs; Ridley College, St Catharines, Ontario; New College, Oxford. Appointments: Founder, Montagu Motor Car Museum, 1952, world's first Motor Cycle Museum, 1956, National Motor Museum, Beaulieu, 1972; Founder-Editor, Veteran and Vintage magazine, 1956-79; Chairman, Historic Buildings and Monuments Commission, 1983-92; Free-lance motoring journalist; Hereditary Peer, 1947-99, Elected Peer, 1999-, House of Lords. Publications: The Motoring Montagus, 1959; Lost Causes of Motoring, 1960; Jaguar: A Biography, 1961, revised edition, 1986; The Gordon Bennett Races, 1963; Rolls of Rolls-Royce, 1966; The Gilt and the Gingerbread, 1967; Lost Causes of Motoring: Europe, 2 volumes, 1969, 1971; More Equal Than Others, 1970; History of the Steam Car, 1971; The Horseless Carriage, 1975; Early Days on the Road, 1976; Behind the Wheel, 1977; Royalty on the Road, 1980; Home James, 1982; The British Motorist, 1987; English Heritage, 1987; The Daimler Century, 1995; Wheels within Wheels, 2000. Memberships: Federation of British Historic Vehicle Clubs, president, 1989-; Federation Internationale des Voitures Anciennces, president, 1980-83; Historic Houses Association, president, 1973-78; Museums Association, president, 1982-84; Union of European Historic Houses, president, 1978-81; Guild of Motoring Writers. Address: Palace House, Beaulieu, Brockenhurst, Hants SO42 7ZN, England.

MONTAGU-POLLOCK Sir Giles Hampden (5th Baronet of the Khyber Pass), b. 19 October 1928, Oslo, Norway. Management Consultant. m. Caroline Veronica Russell, 1 son, 1 daughter. Education: Eton College; de Havilland Aeronautical Technical School. Appointments: Airspeed Ltd, 1949-51; G P Eliot at Lloyd's, 1951-52; de Havilland Engine Co Ltd, 1952-56; Advertising Manager, Bristol Aeroplane Co Ltd, 1956-59; Advertising Manager, Bristol Siddley Engines Ltd, 1959-61; Associate Director, J Walter Thompson Co Ltd, 1961-69; Director: C Vernon & Sons Ltd, 1969-71, Acumen Marketing Group, 1971-74; 119 Pall Mall Ltd, 1972-78; Management Consultant in Marketing, 1974-; Associate: John Stork & Partners, Ltd, 1980-88, Korn/Ferry International, 1988-2002. Address: The White House, 7 Washington Road, London SW13 9BG, England.

MONTEALEGRE Alberto, b. 21 June 1923, Florida (Valle), Colombia. Educator; Priest. Education: Graduate in Philosophy, Pontificia Universidad Javeriana, Bogota, 1952; PhD, Pedagogical Sciences, University of Louvaine, Belgium, 1957. Appointments: Rector, Franciscan Seminary, Cali, 1957-58; Professor, Rector, International Pedagogical Institute, Grottaferrata, Rome, 1958-64; Dean, Philosophy Faculty, San Buenaventura University, Bogata, 1965; General Counselor, Franciscan Order, Rome, 1965-67; Counselor, Franciscan Province of Santa Fe de Colombia, 1969-75, 1984-90, 1996-99; Rector General, Universidad de San Buenaventura, 1975-84, 1987-93; Provincial Vicar, 1984-90; Rector, Universidad de San Buenaventura, Bogata, 1984-90; Member, International Commission for the Athenaeum Pontifical, Rome, 1999-2000; Rector, Universidad de San Buenaventura, Cartagena, 2000-. Publications: Numerous articles and papers in professional scientific journals. Honours: Parchment, City of Santiago de Cali, 1984; Medal of Civic Merit, Cali City Hall, 1984; Order of the Confederated Cities in Valle del Cauca, Colombia, 1984; Member of Honour, Medical Sofrology International School, Barcelona, 1989; Order of San Buenaventura, Great Academic Distinctions Category, 1985; Recognition Award, Santiago de Cali University, 2001; Civic Medal of Cartagena, 2002; University Recognition Diploma for Personal Merits, Universidad de San Buenaventura, 2006. Memberships: Board of Directors, World Education Science Association, Gante, Belgium; Corresponding Member, History Academy of Cartagena, 2003; Franciscan Community. Address: Universidad de San Buenaventura de Cartagena, Calle Real de ternera, Cartagena, Colombia. E-mail: amontea@usbctg.edu.co Website: www.usbctg.edu.co

MONTENEGRO ALVARADO Jose Miguel, b. 20 February 1974, Ponce, Puerto Rico. Chemical Engineer. Education: BS, 1998, MS, 2001, Chemical Engineering, Mayaguez Campus, University of Puerto Rico. Appointments: Senior Technical Services Specialist, Pfizer Pharmaceuticals LLC, Global Manufacturing Division, Caguas Plant, Puerto Rico, 2001-; Process Analytical Technology (PAT) Champion, 2004; Leader, Latin America/Puerto Rico Region Drug Product Chapter, Pfizer's Global Process Analytical Technology Community of Practice, 2006. Publications: Modeling and Automation of a Fluid Bed Dryer for Deterimination of Optimum Drying End Points of Pharmaceutical Granulations. Honours: Engineering Board of Honor Students, University of Puerto Rico, Mayaguez; Professional of the Year in Engineering, 2006; Man of the Year, 2007; Listed in international biographical dictionaries. Memberships: College of Engineers and Surveryors of Puerto Rico; Institute of Chemical Engineers of Puerto Rico; National Society of Professional Engineers; American Institute of Chemical Engineers. Address: Urb Vista Bahla, 211 Paseo del Puerto, Penuelas, PR 00624, Puerto Rico. E-mail: jose.m.montenegro.alvarado@pfizer.com

MONTEREE-ZALESKI Elizabeth, b. 9 April 1942, Warsaw, Poland. Artist in Figurative Expressionism; Painter; Gallery Curator. m. Anthony, 1 son. Education: Diploma, Portraiture and Design, Warsaw Academy of Fine Arts, 1964. Appointments: Valuer and Gallery Advisor, National and Mutual Gallery, 1967-72; Gallery Curator, Studio Art Gallery, 1972-84; Freelance Journalist, Art Criticism, for Polish Newspapers, 1972; Gallery Curator, Studio Art Gallery, Olinda, Victoria, Australia, 1984-2004; Gallery Curator, Walter Jona Gallery, Olinda, Victoria, Australia, 2004-. Honour: Awarded Diploma of Merit by Committee for 500th Anniversary of Nicholas Copernicus for promoting and exhibiting Polish artists in Australia, 1973; Presidential Seal of Approval, ABI, USA, 2005; Decree of Excellence in Art, IBC, 2005; Gold Medal for Australia, ABI, 2006. Memberships: AICA International; NVAA, Australia. Address: 1486 Mt Dandenong Tourist Road, Olinda, Vic 3788, Australia.

MONTGOMERIE Colin, b. 23 June 1963, Glasgow, Scotland. Golfer. m. Eimear Wilson, 1990-2006 divorced) 1 son, 2 daughters. Education: Baptist University, Texas, USA. Career: Professional Golfer, 1987-; Member, Walker Cup team, 1985, 1987, Ryder Cup team, 1991, 1993, 1995, 1997, 1999, 2002, 2004, Dunhill Cup Team, 1988, 1991-2000, World Cup Team, 1988, 1991, 1992, 1993, 1997, 1998, 1999; Leader, European Tour Order of Merit, 1993-99; 28 European Tour wins as at end December 2002; Signed contract to play Yonex Clubs from 2004. Honours: Winner: Scottish Stroke Play, 1985; Scottish Amateur Championship, 1987; European Tour Rookie of the Year, 1988; Portuguese Open, 1989; Scandinavian Masters, 1991, 1999, 2001; Heineken Dutch Open, 1993; Volvo Masters, 1993; Spanish Open, 1994; English Open, 1994; German Open, 1994; Volvo German Open, 1995; Trophee Lancome, 1995; Alfred Dunhill Cup, 1995; Dubai Desert Classic, 1996; Murphy's Irish Open, 1996, 1997, 2001; Canon European Masters, Million Dollar Challenge, 1996; World Cup Individual, 1997; Andersen Consulting World Champion, 1997; Compaq European Grand Prix, 1997; King Hassan II Trophy, 1997; PGA Championship, 1998, 1999, 2000; German Masters, 1998; British Masters, 1998; Benson and Hedges International Open, 1999; BMW International Open, 1999; Standard Life Loch Lomond Invitational, 1999; Cisco World Matchplay, 1999; Skins Game, US, 2000; Novotel Perrier Open de France, 2000; Ericsson Australian Masters, 2001; Volvo Masters Andalucia, 2002; TCL Classic, 2002; Macan Open, 2003; Caltex Masters Singapore, 2004; Dunhill Links Championships, 2005; Hong Kong Open, 2006; Smurfit Kappa European Open, 2007. Member: winning European Ryder Cup team, 1995, 1997, 2002, 2004. Address: c/o IMG, McCormack House, Burlington Lane, London W4 2TH, England.

MONTGOMERY John Warwick, Baron of Kiltartan, Lord of Morris, Comte de St Germain de Montgommery, b. 18 October 1931, Warsaw, New York, USA. m. Lanalee de Kant, 26 August 1988, 1 adopted son. Education: AB, Philosophy with distinction, Cornell University, 1952; BLS, 1954, MA, 1958, University of California at Berkeley; BD, 1958, MST, 1960, Wittenberg University, USA; PhD, University of Chicago, USA, 1962; Docteur de l'Universite, mention Theologie Protestante, University of Strasbourg, France, 1964; LLB, La Salle Extension University, 1977; Diplome cum laude, International Institute of Human Rights, Strasbourg, 1978; MPhil in Law, University of Essex, England, 1983; Dr (hon), Institute of Religion and Law, Moscow, 1999; LLM, 2000, LLD, 2003, Cardiff University, Wales; Bar: Virginia, 1978; California, 1979; DC, 1985; Washington State, 1990; US Supreme Court, 1981; England & Wales, 1984; Paris, 2003; Licenced Real Estate Broker, California; Certificate, Law Librarian; Diplomate, Medical Library Association; Ordained to ministry, Lutheran Church, 1958; Librarian, general reference service, University of California Library, Berkeley, 1954-55; Instructor, Biblical Hebrew, Hellenistic Greek, Medieval Latin, Wittenberg University, Springfield, Ohio, 1956-59; Head Librarian, Swift Library of Divinity and Philosophy, member Federated Theological Faculty, University of Chicago, 1959-60; Associate Professor, Chairman, Department of History, Wilfred Laurier University, Ontario, Canada, 1960-64; Professor, Chairman, Division of Church History, History of Christian Thought, Director, European Seminar Programme, Trinity Evangelical Divinity School, Deerfield, Illinois, 1964-74; Professor, Law and Theology, International School of Law, Washington DC, 1974-75; Theology consultant, Christian Legal Society, 1975-76; Director of Studies, International Institute of Human Rights, Strasbourg, France, 1979-81; Founding Dean, Professor Jurisprudence, Director of European Programme, Simon Greenleaf University School of Law, Anaheim, California, 1980-88; Distinguished Professor of Theology and Law, Faith Evangelical Lutheran Seminary, Tacoma, Washington, 1989-91; Principal Lecturer, Reader in Law, 1991-93, Professor of Law and Humanities, Director, Centre of Human Rights, 1993-97, Emeritus Professor, 1997-, Bedfordshire University, England; Distinguished Professor of Apologetics, Law, and History of Christian Thought, Vice President, Academic Affairs, UK and Europe, 1997-2007, Trinity College and Theological Seminary, Newburgh, Indiana; Director, International Academy of Apologetics, Evangelism and Human Rights, Strasbourg, France, 1997-; Distinguished Research Professor of Philosophy and Christian Thought, Patrick Henry College, Purcellville, Virginia, 2007-; Distinguished Professor of Law, Regent University, Virginia, 1997-99; Senior Counsel, European Centre for Law and Justice, 1997-2001; Visiting Professor, Concordia Theological Seminary, Springfield, Illinois, 1964-67, DePaul University, Chicago, 1967-70, Concordia University, Irvine, California, 2006; Honorary Fellow, Revelle College, University of California, San Diego, 1970; Lecturer, Research Scientists Christian Fellowship Conference, St Catherine's College, Oxford University, 1985; International Anti-Corruption Conference, Beijing, China, 1995; Pascal Lecturer on Christianity and the University, University of Waterloo, Ontario, Canada, 1987; A Kurt Weiss Lecturer, Biomedical Ethics, University of Oklahoma, 1997; Adjunct Professor, Puget Sound University School of Law, Tacoma, Washington, 1990-91; Worldwide Advocacy Conference lecturer, Inns of Court School of Law London, 1998; Law and Religion Colloquium lecturer, University College, London, 2000; numerous other functions. Publications: Author, 60 books, most recently: The Transcendental Holmes, 2000; The Repression of Evangelism in Greece, 2000; Christ Our Advocate, 2002; Tractatus Logico-Theologicus, 2002; Editor, Contributing Editor, Film and TV series; Contributor of articles to academic, theological, legal encyclopaedias and journals, and chapters to books. Honours: Ordre des chevaliers du Saint-Sepulcre Byzantin; Patriarch's Medal, Romanian Orthodox Church; Phi Beta Kappa; Phi Kappa Phi; Beta Phi Mu; Awards: National Lutheran Educational Conference Fellow, 1959-60; Canada Council Postdoctoral Senior Research Fellow, 1963-64; American Association of Theological Schools Faculty Fellow, 1967-68; Recipient Angel Award, National Religious Broadcasters, 1989, 1990, 1992; Fellow: Trinity College, Newburgh, Indiana; Royal Society of Arts, England; Victoria Institute, London (Honorary Vice-President); Academie Internationale des Gourmets et des Traditions Gastronomiques, Paris; American Scientific Affiliation; Society for Advanced Legal Studies, UK. Memberships: European Academy of Arts, Sciences and Humanities; Heraldry Society, UK (Advanced Certificate); Lawyers' Christian Fellowship (Honorary Vice-President); National Conference of University Professors; International Bar Association; World Association of Law Professors; Middle Temple and Lincoln's Inn; American Society for International Law; Union Internationale de Avocats; National Association of Realtors; ALA; Tolkien Society of America; New York C S Lewis Society; American Historical Society; Society for Reformation Research; Creation Research Society; Tyndale Fellowship, England; Stair Society, Scotland; Presbyterian Historical Society, Northern Ireland; American Theological Library Association; Bibliographical Society, University of Virginia; Evangelical Theological Society; International Wine and Food Society; Societe des Amis des Arts; Chaine des Rotisseurs; Athenaeum Club; Freeman of the City of London and Liveryman of the Scriveners' Company; Players'

Theatre Club; Sherlock Holmes Society of London; Honorary Member, Societe Sherlock Holmes de France; Club de Casseroles Lasserre, Paris. Address: 2, rue de Rome, 67000 Strasbourg, France.E-mail: 106612.1066@CompuServe.com

MOODY A David, b. 21 January 1932, New Zealand. University Teacher; Writer. m. Joanna S Moody. Education: BA, 1951, MA, 1952, Canterbury College, University of New Zealand; BA, 1st Class Honours, Oxford University, 1955. Appointments: Assistant Information Officer, UNHCR, Geneva; Lecturer, Senior Lecturer in English, University of Melbourne, 1958-65; Member, Department of English and Related Literature, 1966-99, Emeritus Professor of English and American Literature, 1999-, University of York. Publications: Virginia Woolf, 1963; Shakespeare: The Merchant of Venice, 1964; The Waste Land in Different Voices (editor), 1974; Thomas Stearns Eliot: Poet, 1979, 1994; At the Antipodes: Homage to Paul Valéry, 1982; News Odes: The El Salvador Sequence, 1984; Cambridge Companion to T S Eliot (editor), 1994; Tracing T S Eliot's Spirit: essays on his poetry and thought, 1996; Ezra Pound: Poet, A Portrait of the Man and His Work, vol 1, The Young Genius 1885-1920, 2007. Honours: Shirtcliffe Fellow, University of New Zealand, 1953-55; Nuffield Foundation Travelling Fellow, 1965; British Academy/Leverhulme Visiting Professor, 1988; Honorary Member, T S Eliot Society, USA; Fellow, English Association. Memberships: International Association of University Professors of English; Association of University Teachers; National Poetry Foundation; Member of the Editorial Board: Paideuma: A Journal of Scholarship on British and American Modernist Poetry, 2002-; Society of Authors. Address: Church Green House, Old Church Lane, Pateley Bridge, North Yorkshire HG3 5LZ, England.

MOOK Sarah, b. 29 October 1929, Brooklyn, New York, USA. Chemist. Education: BA, Hunter College, 1952; Graduate Coursework, Columbia University, 1954-57; Coursework, University of Hartford, 1958-59; Language Course, Columbia University, 1962-65; New York City Citizens Police Academy, 2001. Appointments: Cartographic Aide, US Geological Survey, 1952-54; Research Assistant, Columbia University, 1954-57; Analytical Chemist, Combustion Engineering, 1957-59; Research Scientist, Radiation Applications Inc, 1959-62; Chemist, Marks Polarised Corp, 1962-64; Senior Chemist, NRA Inc, 1964-74; Clinical Technologist, Coney Island Hospital, 1974-84; Supervisor, 1984-89, Principal Chemist, 1989-95, Bellevue Hospital; Retired, 1995-. Publications: Several professional articles. Honours: Woman of the Year, New York City Council, 2004; Margaret M McCord Woman of Year Memorial Award, Sheepshead Bay Historical Society, 2004; Woman of the Year Humanitarian Award, New York State Senate, 2004; Distinguished Leadership in Community Award, New York City Office of Comptroller, 2004. Memberships: American Chemical Society; American Association for the Advancement of Science; American Association for Clinical Chemistry; New York Academy of Science; Van Slyke Society; Citizens Police Academy Alumni Association. Address: 2042 East 14th Street, Brooklyn, NY 11229, USA.

MOOLLAN Cassam Ismael (Sir), b. 26 February 1927, Port Louis, Mauritius. Legal Consultant; Arbitrator. m. Rassoolbibie Adam Moollan, 1 son, 2 daughters. Education: LLB, London School of Economics and Political Science, University of London, 1947-50; Barrister at Law, Lincoln's Inn, London, 1951. Appointments: Private Practice at Mauritian Bar, 1951-55; District Magistrate, 1955-58; Crown Counsel, 1958-64; Senior Crown Counsel, 1964-66; Solicitor

General, 1966-70; Puisne Judge Supreme Court, 1970; Senior Puisne Judge, Supreme Court, 1978; Chief Justice of Mauritius, 1982-88; Acting Governor General on several occasions every year, 1984-88; Retired, 1989. Publications: Editor, Mauritius Law Reports, 1982-88. Honours: Queen's Counsel, 1969; Knight Bachelor, 1982; Chevalier dans l'Ordre National de la Legion d'Honneur, France, 1986. Address: 22 Hitchcock Avenue, Quatre Bornes, Mauritius. E-mail: sircassam@chambers.sirhamid.intnet.mu

MOON Cheol-Hyun, b. 14 March 1960, Seoul, South Korea. Professor. m. Je Kim, 2 sons. Education: Bachelor, DDS, 1984, PhD, 1996, Kyung Hee University; MSc, Chon Nam National University, 1987. Appointments: Military Service, 1987-90; Chair, Department of Orthodontics, Gil Medical Center, 1990-; Professor, Gachon Medical University, 1999-. Publications: Clinical use and Failure of Skeletal Anchorage System, 2002; Orthodontic Treatment with Various Mini-Implant, 2007; Intrusion of Overerupted Molars by Corticotomy and Orthodontic Skeletal Anchorage, 2007. Honours: Man of the Year, ABI, 2007. Memberships: American Association of Orthodontists; Korean Association of Orthodontists. Address: Gachon Medical School, Gil Medical Center, Department of Orthodontics, 1198, Guwol-Dong, Namdong-Gu, Inchon 405-760, South Korea. Website: www.gilhospital.com

MOON Dong Ju, b. 1 May 1962 Hae Nam, South Korea. Principal Research Scientist. m. Eun Kyung Han, 1990, 1 son, 1 daughter. Education: BA, 1985, MS, 1987, Chonnam National University, Kwang Ju, Korea; PhD, Korea University, Seoul, 1998; Postdoctoral studies, Michigan University, USA, 1998-99. Appointments: Researcher, 1989-98, Senior Researcher, 1999-2004, Principal Researcher, 2005-, Korea Institute of Science and Technology, Seoul; Research Fellow, Michigan University, Ann Arbor, USA, 1998-99; Advisor, TC Science Co, Sung Nam, 2000-; Advisor, Nam Young Oil Chemical Industry Co, Ahn San, 2005-; Visiting Professor, Korea University, 2001-; Professor, UST, 2005-. Publications: 50 articles and 194 presentations in professional journals; 35 patents filed; 48 patent applications. Honours: Excellent Research Team, Korea Institute of Science and Technology, 1992-93; Outstanding R&D Team, 1998; Fellow, Exemplary Researcher, 1997; Postdoctoral Fellowship, KOSEF, 1998; Research Fellowship, Michigan University; KIST Person Award, 2005. Memberships: Korea Society for Energy Engineering; Korean Hydrogen & New Energy Society; Korean Society for Industry & Engineering Chemistry; Korean Institute of Chemical Engineering; American Chemical Society. Address: Korean Institute of Science and Technology, 39-1 Hawolgok-dong, Sungbuk-ku, Seoul 130-650, Republic of Korea. E-mail: djmoon@kist.re.kr

MOON Du Geon, b. 29 December 1961, Pusan, Korea. Professor; Urologist. m. Young Kyung Shin, 1 son, 1 daughter. Education: Bachelor degree, MD, Korea University College of Medicine, Seoul, 1990; Master degree, 1995, PhD, 1997, Korea University Graduate School, Seoul. Appointments: Served in Korean Army, 1981-84; Intern, 1990-91, Resident, Urology, 1993-97, Korean University Medical Center; General Practice, Gupo-Jeil Private Clinic, Pusan, 1991-92; Korean Board of Urology, 1997; Clinical Instructor, Department of Urology, Korean University Guro Hospital, 1997-98; Clinical Instructor, Department of Urology, Korean University Anam Hospital, 1998-99; Assistant, Associate Professor, Korean University College of Medicine, 2000; Chief, Department of Urology, Korea University Ansan Hospital, 2002; Research Fellow, Institute of Regenerative Medicine, Wake Forest University, North Carolina, USA, 2004-05; Chief,

Department of Urology, Korea University Guro Hospital, 2006. Publications: Over 20 manuscripts, papers and articles in professional journals. Honours: Pharmacia & Upjohn Award, 1999; 3rd AOCA Award, 2000; Executive Committee Board, Korean Andrological Society, 2001; Editorial Board, Korean Journal of Andrology, 2002; Pfizer Research Award, 2004; Secretary General, Korean Andrological Society, 2004-06; Secretary General, Korean Society for Aging Male Research, 2006; Secretary Medicare, Korean Andrological Society, 2006. Memberships: Korean Medical Association; Korean Urological Association; Korean Andrological Society; American Urological Association; International Society for Sexual and Impotence Research; Asia-Pacific Society for Sexual and Impotence Research; Korean Society of Sexology; International Children's Continence Society; Korean Pediatric Urologic Association; American Society for Regenerative Medicine; Korean Society for Aging Male Research; International Society for the Aging Male. Address: Department of Urology, Korean University Guro Hospital, #80 Guro-Dong, Guro-ku, Seoul 152-703, Korea. E-mail: dgmoon@korea.ac.kr

MOON Yong-Jae, b. 21 February 1967, Boseong, Republic of Korea. Astronomer. m. Young Ma, 2 sons. Education: BS, 1989, PhD, 1999, Astronomy, Seoul National University, Korea. Appointments: Researcher, 1996-98, Senior Researcher, 1998-, Korea Astronomy and Space Science Institute; Post doctoral Research Associate, New Jersey Institute of Technology, Big Bear Solar Observatory, 2001-03. Publications: About 80 referred publications in the field of solar activity and Sun-Earth connection studies. Honours: 2 Academic Accomplishment Awards, 2002, 2003; Excellent Academic Accomplishment Award, 2004. Memberships: Korea Astronomical Society; Korea Space Science Society; American Astronomical Society; American Geophysical Union. Address: Korea Astronomy and Space Science Institute, 61-1 Whaamdong, Yooseong, Daejeon 305-348, Republic of Korea.

MOORE Adrian William, b. 29 December 1956, Kettering, England. University Professor and Lecturer. Education: The Manchester Grammar School, 1968-75; BA, MA, King's College, Cambridge, 1975-78; BPhil, DPhil, Balliol College, Oxford, 1978-82. Appointments: Lecturer in Philosophy, University College, Oxford, 1982-85; Junior Research Fellow in Philosophy, King's College, Cambridge, 1985-88; Tutorial Fellow and University Lecturer in Philosophy, St Hugh's College, Oxford, 1988-; University Professor in Philosophy, St Hugh's College, Oxford, 2004-. Publications: Points of View, 1997; The Infinite, 2nd edition, 2001; Noble in Reason, Infinite in Faculty: Themes and Variations in Kant's Moral and Religious Philosophy, 2003; Making Sense of Things: The Evolution of Modern Metaphysics, forthcoming; Editor, Meaning and Reference, 1993; Infinity, 1993; Bernard Williams, Philosophy as a Humanistic Discipline, 2006. Honours: Leverhulme Major Research Fellowship, 2006-09. Memberships: Council of the Royal Institute of Philosophy; Executive Committee of the British Philosophical Association; Executive Committee of the Mind Association; Editorial Committee of the European Journal of Philosophy; Visiting Fellow at the Australian National University. Address: St Hugh's College, Oxford, OX2 6LE, England. E-mail: Adrian.moore@philosophy.ox.ac.uk.

MOORE Brian C J, b. 10 February 1946. Professor of Auditory Perception. Education: BA, 1968, MA, 1971, Natural Sciences, PhD, Experimental Psychology, 1971, University of Cambridge, England. Appointments: Lecturer, Psychology,

University of Reading, England, 1971-73; Fulbright-Hayes Senior Scholar and Visiting Professor, Department of Psychology, Brooklyn College of CUNY, 1973-74; Lecturer, Psychology, University of Reading, 1974-77; Lecturer, Experimental Psychology, University of Cambridge, 1977-89; Fellow, Wolfson College, Cambridge, 1983-; Visiting Researcher, University of California at Berkeley, USA, 1985; Reader in Auditory Perception, 1989-95, Professor of Auditory Perception, 1995-, University of Cambridge. Publications: Books include most recently: An Introduction to the Psychology of Hearing, 4th edition, 1997, 5th edition, 2003; Cochlear Hearing Loss, 1998; New Developments in Hearing and Balance (co-editor), 2002; Over 84 book chapters and papers in conference proceedings; Over 332 publications in refereed journals. Honours include: T S Littler Prize, British Society of Audiology, 1983; Honorary Fellow, British Society of Hearing Aid Audiologists, 1999; Invitation Fellowship, Japanese Society for the Promotion of Science, 2000; Carhart Memorial Lecturer, American Auditory Society, 2003; Silver Medal, Acoustical Society of America, 2003. Memberships: Experimental Psychology Society; Fellow, Acoustical Society of America; Cambridge Philosophical Society; British Society of Audiology; American Speech-Language-Hearing Association; Audio Engineering Society; Acoustical Society of Japan; American Auditory Society; Association for Research in Otolaryngology; American Academy of Audiology; Fellow, Academy of Medical Sciences; Fellow, Royal Society. Address: Department of Experimental Psychology, University of Cambridge, Downing Street, Cambridge CB2 3EB, England. Website: http://hearing.psychol.cam.ac.uk

MOORE David Moresby, b. 26 July 1933, Barnard Castle, County Durham, England. Professor Emeritus of Botany. m. Ida Elizabeth Shaw, 2 sons. Education: BSc, Honours, Botany, 1954, PhD, 1957, DSc, 1984, University College and Botany Department, University of Durham. Appointments: Research Officer, Genetics Section, Division of Plant Industry, CSIRO, Canberra, ACT, Australia, 1957-59; Research Fellow, Department of Botany, University of California at Los Angeles, 1959-61; Lecturer, Genetics, Department of Botany, University of Leicester, England, 1961-68; Reader, Plant Taxonomy, 1968-76, Professor of Botany, 1976-94, Reading University, England. Publications: About 100 articles on taxonomy, geography, cytogenetics of plants; 19 books include: Vascular Flora of the Falkland Islands, 1968; Plant Cytogenetics, 1976; Flora Europaea Check-List and Chromosome-Number Index, 1982; Green Planet, 1982; Flora of Tierra del Fuego, 1983; Garden Earth, 1991. Honours: Botany Field Prize, University of Durham, 1954; British Association Studentship, University of Durham; Plaque for services to Magellanic Botany, Instituto de la Patagonia, Punta Arenas, Chile, 1976; Premio Perito Francisco P Moreno, Sociedad Argentina de Estudios Geográficos, 1985; Enrique Molina Gold Medal, University of Concepción, Chile. Memberships: Botanical Society of the British Isles; Editorial Committees: Webbia, Italy, Polish Botanical Journal, Anales del Instituto de la Patagonia, Flora de Chile. Address: 26 Eric Avenue, Emmer Green, Reading, Berks, RG4 8QX, England.

MOORE Demi, b. 11 November 1962, Roswell, New Mexico, USA. Actress. m. (1) Bruce Willis, divorced 2000, 3 daughters; (2) Ashton Kutcher, 2005-. Career: Started in TV, also Model; Films include: Blame it on Rio; St Elmo's Fire; One Crazy Summer; About Last Night...; Wisdom; The Seventh Sign; Ghost; Mortal Thoughts, also co-producer; The Butcher's Wife; A Few Good Men; Indecent Proposal; Disclosure; The Scarlet Letter; Striptease, 1995; The Juror, 1996; GI Jane, 1996; The Hunchback of Notre Dame, 1996;

Now and Then, produced & acted, 1996; Deconstructing Harry, 1997; Passion of Mind, 2000; Airframe; Charlie's Angels: Full Throttle, 2003; Half Light, 2006; Bobby, 2006; Flawless, 2007; Mr Brooks, 2007; The Magic 7, 2008. Producer, Austin Powers: International Man of Mystery, 1997; Austin Powers: The Spy Who Shagged Me, 1999; Austin Powers in Goldmember, 2002; Theatre: The Early Girl; TV: General Hospital, Bedroom. Honour: Theatre World Award for The Early Girl. Address: c/o Creative Artists Agency, 9830 Wilshire Boulevard, Beverly Hills, CA 90212, USA.

MOORE Julianne, b. 3 December 1960, USA. Actress. Education: Boston University School for Arts. m. (1) Sundar Chakravarthy 1983-85 (divorced); (2) John Gould Rubin 1986-1995 (divorced); (3) Bart Freundlich 2003-, 2 children. Creative Works: Stage appearances include: Serious Money, 1987; Ice Cream with Hot Fudge, 1990; Uncle Vanya; The Road to Nirvana; Hamlet; The Father; Film appearances include: Tales From the Darkside, 1990; The Hand That Rocks the Cradle, The Gun in Betty Lou's Handbag, 1992; Body of Evidence, Benny & Joon, The Fugitive, Short Cuts, 1993; Vanya on 42nd Street, 1994; Roommates, Safe, Nine Months, Assassins, 1995; Surviving Picasso, 1996; Jurassic Park: The Lost World, The Myth of Fingerprints, Hellcab, Boogie Nights, 1997; The Big Lebowski, 1998; Eyes Wide Shut, The End of The Affair, Map of the World, Magnolia, Cookie's Fortune, An Ideal Husband, 1999; Hannibal, The Shipping News, 2000; Far From Heaven, The Hours, 2002; Marie and Bruce, Laws of Attraction, The Forgotten, 2004; Trust the Man, The Prize Winner of Defiance, Ohio, 2005; Freedomland, Children of Men, 2006; Next, Savage Grace, I'm Not There, 2007; Blindness, 2008. TV appearances include: As the World Turns, series; The Edge of Night, series; Money, Power Murder, 1989; Lovecraft, 1991; I'll Take Manhattan; The Last to Go; Cast a Deadly Spell. Honours: Best Actress, Venice Film Festival, 2002. Address: c/o Creative Artists Agency, 9830 Wilshire Boulevard, Beverly Hills, CA 90212, USA.

MOORE Patrick Alfred Caldwell (Sir), b. 4 March 1923, England. Astronomer; Broadcaster; Writer. Appointments: Served with RAF during World War II; Officer, Bomber Command, 1940-45; Presenter, TV Series, The Sky at Night, 1957-; Special programme to commemorate 50th anniversary of The Sky at Night, 2007. Radio Broadcasts; Director, Armagh Planetarium, Northern Ireland, 1965-68; Freelance, 1968-; Composer, Perseus and Andromeda (opera), 1975; Play, Quintet, Chichester, 2002. Publications: Over 170 books and numerous articles include: Moon Flight Atlas, 1969; Space, 1970; The Amateur Astronomer, 1970; Atlas of the Universe, 1970; Guide to the Planets, 1976; Guide to the Moon, 1976; Can You Speak Venusian?, 1977; Guide to the Stars, 1977; Guide to Mars, 1977; Atlas of the Universe, 1980; History of Astronomy, 1983; The Story of the Earth, 1985; Halley's Comet, 1985; Patrick Moore's Armchair Astronomy, 1985; Stargazing, 1985; Exploring the Night Sky with Binoculars, 1986; The A-Z of Astronomy, 1986; Astronomy for the Under Tens, 1987; Astronomers' Stars, 1987; The Planet Uranus, 1988; Space Travel for the Under Tens, 1988; The Planet Neptune, 1989; Mission to the Planets, 1990; The Universe for the Under Tens, 1990; A Passion for Astronomy, 1991; Fireside Astronomy, 1992; Guinness Book of Astronomy, 1995; Passion for Astronomy, 1995; Stars of the Southern Skies, 1995; Teach Yourself Astronomy, 1996; Eyes on the Universe, 1997; Brilliant Stars, 1998; Patrick Moore on Mars, 1999; Yearbook of Astronomy AD 1000, 1999; Data Book of Astronomy, 2001; Stars of Destiny, 2004. Honours include: Officer of the Order of the British Empire, 1968; Numerous Honorary Degrees; Honorary Member, Astronomic-Geodetic Society of the Soviet Union, 1971; Royal Astronomical Society's Jackson-Gwilt Medal, 1977; CBE, 1987; Fellow, Royal Society, 2001; Knight Bachelor, 2001; Minor Planet No 2602 is named in his honour; BAFTA Special Award, 2002. Memberships: Royal Astronomical Society; Member, British Astronomical Association, President, 1982-84; Athenaeum; Life Member, Sussex Cricket Club; Lord's Taverners. Address: Farthings, 39 West Street, Selsey, Sussex PO20 9AD, England.

MOORE Sir Roger, b. 14 October 1927, London, England. Actor. m. (1) Doorn van Steyn, divorced, (2) Dorothy Squires, 1953, divorced, (3) Luisa Mattioli, 2 sons, 1 daughter, divorced; (4) Christina 'Kiki' Tholstrup, 2002. Education: Royal Academy of Dramatic Arts. Appointment: Special Ambassador for UNICEF, 1991-. Creative Works: Films include: Crossplot, 1969; The Man With the Golden Gun, 1974; That Lucky Touch, Save Us From Our Friends, Shout At The Devil, 1975; Sherlock Holmes in New York, The Spy Who Loved Me, 1976; The Wild Geese, 1977; Escape to Athens, Moonraker, 1978; Esther, Ruth and Jennifer, 1979; The Sea Wolves, Sunday Lovers, For Your Eyes Only, 1980; Octopussy, The Naked Face, 1983; A View to a Kill, 1985; Key to Freedom, Bed and Breakfast, Bullseye!, 1989; Fire, Ice and Dynamite, 1990; The Quest, 1997; Boat Trip, 2002; The Fly Who Loved Me (voice), 2004; Here Comes Peter Cottontail: The Movie (voice), Foley & McColl: This Way Up, 2005; Agent Crush (voice), 2008. TV appearances include: The Alaskans; The Saint, 1962-69; The Persuaders, 1972-73; The Man Who Wouldn't Die, 1992; The Quest, 1995. Publication: James Bond Diary, 1973.

MOORE Terence, b. 24 December, 1931, London, England. Retired Businessman. m. Tessa Catherine, 2 sons, 1 daughter. Education: BSc, Economics, London; AMP, Harvard, USA. Appointments: Various positions, Shell International, 1948-64; Economics Analyst, Investment Banking, 1964-65; Various positions, 1965-87, Managing Director, Supply and Trading, 1979-87, Chief Executive Officer, Conoco Ltd, 1987-95; Currently, Trustee Energy Institute Pension Fund. Publications: Various technical and business articles. Honour: CBE. Memberships: Fellow, Energy Institute; Associate, Chartered Insurance Institute; Associate, Institute of Chartered Shipbrokers; Friend: Royal Academy of Art, Tate Gallery, Imperial War Museum, National Trust. Address: 67 Merchant Court, 61 Wapping Wall, London EW1 3SJ, England. E-mail: terrymoore@terrymoore.demon.co.uk

MOORHOUSE (Cecil) James (Olaf), b. 1 January 1924, Copenhagen, Denmark. European Politician. m. (1) 1 son, 1 daughter, (2) Catherine Hamilton Peterson. Education: King's College, 1942-44 and Imperial College, 1945-46, University of London: BSc (Eng); DIC Advanced Aeronautics; C Eng. Appointments: Designer with De Havilland Aircraft Co, 1946-48; Project Engineer, BOAC, 1949-53; Technical Adviser, 1953-68, Environmental Conservation Adviser, 1968-72, Shell International Petroleum; Environmental Adviser, Shell Group of Companies in UK, 1972-73; Group Environmental Affairs Adviser, Rio-Tinto Zinc Corporation, 1973-80; Consultant, 1980-84; MEP for London South, 1979-84; MEP, London South and Surrey East, 1984-99. Publications: Righting the Balance: A New Agenda for Euro-Japanese Trade (with Anthony Teasdale), 1987; Numerous articles and papers on aviation. Memberships: Club: Sloane; University (Washington, DC); The English Speaking Union; President, Help Tibet Trust (UK). Address: 211 Piccadilly, London W1J 9HF, England. E-mail: jamesmoorhouse@aol.com

MOORHOUSE Geoffrey, b. 29 November 1931, Bolton, Lancashire, England. Author. m. (1) Janet Marion Murray, 1956, 2 sons, 2 daughters, 1 deceased, (2) Barbara Jane Woodward, 1974, divorced, 1978, (3) Marilyn Isobel Edwards, 1983, divorced, 1996. Appointments: Editorial Staff, Bolton Evening News, 1952-54, Grey River Argus, New Zealand, Auckland Star, and Christchurch Star-Sun, 1954-56, News Chronicle, 1957, Guardian, Manchester, 1958-70. Publications: The Other England, 1964; The Press, 1964; Against All Reason, 1969; Calcutta, 1971; The Missionaries, 1973; The Fearful Void, 1974; The Diplomats, 1977; The Boat and the Town, 1979; The Best-Loved Game, 1979; India Britannica, 1983; Lord's, 1983; To the Frontier, 1984; Imperial City: Rise and Rise of New York, 1988; At the George, 1989; Apples in the Snow, 1990; Hell's Foundations: Town, Its Myths and Gallipoli, 1992; Om: Indian Pilgrimage, 1993; A People's Game: Centenary History of Rugby League Football 1895-1995, 1995; Sun Dancing: Medieval Vision, 1997; Sydney, 1999; The Pilgrimage of Grace: the rebellion that shook Henry VIII's throne, 2002; Great Harry's Navy: How Henry VIII Gave England Seapower, 2005. Contributions to: Newspapers and magazines. Honours: Cricket Society Award, 1979; Fellow, Royal Society of Literature, 1982; Thomas Cook Award, 1984; Nominated Booker Prize, 1997. Address: Park House, Gayle, near Hawes, North Yorkshire DL8 3RT, England.

MORAWIEC Henryk Zygmunt, b. 14 September 1933, Katowice, Poland. Academic Lecturer. m. Jadwiga Grabowska. Education: MSc, Technical University, Gliwice, 1958; PhD, 1967, DSc, 1978, Technical University Silesia, Katowice. Appointments: Head of Workshop, Institute of Non-ferrous Metals, Gliwice, 1961-72; Head of Department, 1972-78, Dean of Faculty, Director of Institute, 1990, University of Silesia, Katowice. Publications: Several articles in professional journals; Editor of Proceedings, Conference on Applied Crystallography, 1992, 1994, 1997, 2000, 2003; Editor in Chief, Archives of Materials Science, 2003-06. Honours: Award, Polish Academy of Sciences, 1961; Diploma, Technical University, Brno, 1985; Award, Foundation for Electron Microscopy, Polish Science Foundation, 1994; Listed in numerous Who's Who and biographical publications. Memberships: Committee, Materials Science and Committee, Crystallography, Polish Academy of Sciences; Gerson Lehrman Group's Healthcare Council, 2004; Chairman, Scientific Council, Institute of Non-ferrous Metals, 1995-2002 . Address: University of Silesia, Bankowa 12, 40-007 Katowice, Poland.

MOREL Pierre Jean Louis, b. 27 June 1944, Romans, France. Diplomat. m. Olga Bazanoff, 2 sons, 1 daughter. Education: Ecole Nationale d'Administration; Licence en Droit; Institut d'Etudes Politiques de Paris. Appointments: Political Director, Ministry of Foreign Affairs, 1985-86; Ambassador to the Conference on Disarmament, 1986-90; Diplomatic Adviser to the President, 1991-92; Ambassador in Russia, 1992-96; Ambassador in China, 1996-2002; Ambassador in the Holy See, 2002-05; European Union Special Representative for Central Asia, 2006. Honours: Officier de la Legion d'Honneur; Officier de l'Ordre National de Merite. Memberships: International Institute for Strategic Studies, London, England. Address: 42 rue du Bac, 75007 Paris, France. E-mail: pierre.morel@consilium.europa.eu

MORENO JUAREZ Delia, b. 28 May 1950, Morelia, Michoacan, Mexico. Chemical Engineer. m. Miguel Angel Mora Hernandez, 2 sons, 1 daughter. Education: Degree, Chemical Engineering, Mexico, 1979, Mastery in Administration, 1997, DSc, Regional Development, 2008, UMSNH. Appointments: Postgraduate Maintenance Engineer, IMSS, Morelia, 1975-76; Quality Control, Quimic SA De CV, 1976-81; Teacher, UMSNH, 1977; Dean, Faculty Chemical Engineer, 2004; Trading Manager, Quimic-Quimagra, Lerma, 1981-82; Quality Control Manager, Santa Lucia SA De CV, Morelia, 1982-88; Mexican Institute of Chemical Engineering. Publications: Design and preparation of a condensing-separator, 2005; Tallow pre-cure of low quality for elaboration, 2005; Obtaining untables product with low content of isomers cacao butters trans substitute, 2006; Utilization of solid organic urban residues to produce Biogas, 2008. Honours: Better Students of Mexico, Diary of Mexico Atenalcyt, 1990. Memberships: Associate, Mexican Institute of Chemical Engineers. Address: Av Madero Pte, No 2921, Zip Code 58140, Morelia, Michoacan, Mexico. E-mail: dmjuarez@zeus.umich.mx

MORGAN David Gwyn, b. 24 July 1944, Llandeilo, South Wales. Veterinary Pathologist. m. Patricia, 1 son, 2 daughters. Education: BVSc (Hons), University of Liverpool, 1967; PhD, Viral Oncology, University of Bristol, 1975; Member of the Royal College of Veterinary Surgeons. Appointments: Adjunct Associate Professor, Department of Pathology, School of Veterinary Medicine, University of Pennsylvania, 1982-2001; Assistant Lecturer, Lecturer, Veterinary Comparative Pathology, University of Bristol, 1968-78; Assistant Director, Associate Director and Group Director of Pathology, Group Director, Pathology and Toxicology, Vice-President of Safety Assessment, SmithKline and French laboratories, Philadelphia, USA, 1978-90; Vice-President and Director, Worldwide Safety Assessment, SmithKline Beecham Pharmaceuticals, 1990-2001; Member, Board of Trustees, Health and Environmental Sciences Institute (International Life Sciences Institute, Washington, DC), 1997-2001; Chair, Drug Safety Sub-Section Steering Committee, Pharmaceutical Research and Manufacturers Association, USA, 1994-97; Chair, International Safety Evaluation Advisory Board, Centre for Medicines Research, London, England, 1998-2001; Scientific Advisor to the Academy of Medical Sciences Forum, London, 2002-05. Publications: More than 70 publications: Articles in peer reviewed journals, book chapters, and abstracts on topics related to veterinary pathology, immunotoxicology, arterial toxicity, nephrotoxicity, molecular toxicology and drug safety assessment; 52 invited presentations to international scientific societies and academic departments. Honours: World Health Organisation (IARC) Post-doctoral Research Training Fellowship, Yale University School of Medicine, New Haven Connecticut, USA, 1976; SmithKline Beecham Vice-President's Award for significant scientific contribution, 1993; SmithKline Beecham President's Award for significant scientific contribution, 1994; Safety Pharmacology Society Award for Meritorious Service to the Discipline of Safety Pharmacology, 2004. Memberships: Pathological Society of Great Britain and Ireland; Society of Toxicologic Pathologists, USA; Elected Regional Fellow, Royal Society of Medicine, 2004. Address: Trefri Hall, Aberdovey, Gwynedd LL35 0RD, Wales. E-mail: drgwynmorgan@aol.com

MORGAN David Vernon, b. 13 July 1941, Llanelli, Wales. Distinguished Research Professor. m. Jean, 1 son, 1 daughter. Education: BSc (Wales), 1963; MSc (Wales), 1964; PhD (Cambridge), 1967; DSc (Leeds). Appointments: University of Wales Fellow, Cavendish Laboratory Cambridge, 1966-68; Fellow, Harwell, 1968-70; Lecturer, 1970-77, Senior Lecturer, 1977-80, Reader, 1980-85, University of Leeds; Professor, 1985-, Head of School, 1992-2002, Distinguished Research Professor, Microelectronics, 2002-, Cardiff

University. Publications: 230 papers published in scientific journals and international conferences; Authored and Edited 14 books including: An Introduction to Semiconductor Microtechnology, 1983, 2nd edition, 1990. Honours: FREng, 1996; FCGI for Services to Higher Education, 1998; Papal Cross (Pro Ecclesia et Pontifice) Services to Academe, 2004; Hon Fellowship, University of Wales, 2005. Memberships: FInstP; FIEE; Welsh Livery Guild. Address: School of Engineering, Cardiff University, Cardiff CF24 0YF, Wales. E-mail: morgandv@cf.ac.uk

MORGAN Edward Patrick William, b. 17 September 1927, Shorncliff, Kent, England. Retired; Lay Theologian. m. Nora Jane, 1 son, 1 daughter. Education: English, Honours, University of Birmingham, Teaching Diplomas, St Mary's College, University of London, 1950-53; B Theol, Honours, University of South Africa, 1982-87; Diploma, Credit Management Institute of South Africa; Diploma, Public Relations Institute of South Africa and of Market Research Institute, South Africa. Appointments: Secondary School Teacher, Hertfordshire County Council, Barnet then at St Dominic's, Haverstock Hill, (LCC), 1953-57; Rhodesia Government High School Teacher, Chaplin High School, Gwelo, Southern Rhodesia, 1957-63; St George's Jesuit College, Salisbury, Rhodesia, 1963-67; National Fund Raising Manager, Marist, South Africa, 1967-70; South African Government High School Teacher, Johannesburg, 1970-72; National Marketing Manager, then National Credit Manager in Johannesburg and Director of companies in Harare and Johannesburg, 1965-93; Retired 1993. Publications: Life of St Paul (series for Jesuit Magazine, Salisbury, Rhodesia), 1961; Regional Correspondent for weekly "Southern Cross", South Africa. Memberships: Executive Member for Wexford, Irish Senior Citizens' Parliament, 2005-; Public Relations Institute and Marketing Management Institute, South Africa; Founder-Treasurer, Catenian Association of South Africa; Catholic Theological Society of South Africa and Theology Associations of Great Britain and Ireland; European Society of Theologians. Address: 21 St Brendan's, Rosslare Harbour, County Wexford, Ireland. E-mail: patemorgan@eircom.net

MORGAN Kenneth, b. 9 June 1945, Llanelli, Wales. Professor. m. Elizabeth Margaret Harrison, 2 sons. Education: BSc, 1966, PhD, 1970, DSc (Eng), 1987, University of Bristol; CMath; CEng; FIMA, 1978; FICE, 1993; FREng, 1997. Appointments: Scientific Officer, Mathematical Physics Division, UKAEA, AWRE Aldermaston, 1969-72; Lecturer, Department of Mathematics, University of Exeter, 1972-75; Lecturer, 1975-84, Senior Lecturer, 1984-86, Reader, 1986-88, Professor, 1988-89, Department of Civil Engineering, University of Wales, Swansea; Zaharoff Professor of Aviation, Department of Aeronautics, Imperial College, London 1989-91; Professor, Department of Civil Engineering, 1991-2002, Head of Department, 1991-96, Dean of Engineering, 1997-2000, Professor, School of Engineering, 2002-, Head Civil and Computational Engineering Centre, University of Wales, Swansea, 2003-; Visiting Scientist, Joint Research Centre of the EC, Ispra, Italy, 1980; Visiting Research Scientist, Institute for Computer Applications in Science and Engineering, NASA, Langley Research Center, Virginia, USA, 1985; Visiting Research Professor, Old Dominion University, Norfolk, Virginia, 1986-87; Visiting Research Professor, University of Virginia, 1988-92; Council, International Association for Computational Mechanics, 1993-; Management Board, European Committee for Computational Methods in the Applied Sciences, 1993-; Inter Research Council High Performance Computing Management Committee, 1995-98; Governor, Ysgol Gynradd

Gymraeg, Bryn-y-Môr, Swansea, 2000-. Publications: Finite Elements and Approximations (co-author), 1983; The Finite Element Method in Heat Transfer Analysis (co-author), 1996. Honours: Special Achievement Award, NASA, Langley Research Center, 1989; Computational Mechanics Award, International Association for Computational Mechanics, 1998; Honorary Fellow, International Association for Computational Fluid Dynamics, 2003; Fellow, International Association for Computational Mechanics, 2004. Address: 137 Pennard Drive, Southgate, Swansea SA3 2DW, Wales. E-mail: k.morgan@swansea.ac.uk

MORGAN Piers Stefan, b. 30 March 1965, Guildford, England. Journalist. m. Marion E Shalloe, 1991, separated, 3 sons. Education: Harlow Journalism College. Career: Reporter, Surrey and South London newspapers, 1987-89; Showbusiness Editor, The Sun, 1989-94; Editor, The News of the World, 1994-95; Daily Mirror (later The Mirror) 1995-2004; First News, 2006.TV: Presenter, The Importance of Being Famous, Channel 4, 2004; Morgan & Platell, Channel 4, 2005-; America's Got Talent, 2006; Comic Relief Does The Apprentice, 2007; Britains Got Talent, 2007; You Can't Fire Me, I'm Famous, 2007; Piers Morgan on Sandbanks, 2008. Publications: Private Lives of the Stars, 1990; Secret Lives of the Stars, 1991; Phillip Schofield, To Dream A Dream, 1992; Take That, Our Story, 1993; Take That: On the Road, 1994; Va Va Voom!: A Year with Arsenal, 2003-04; The Insider (memoir), 2005; Don't You Know Who I Am?, 2007. Honours: Atex Award for National Newspaper Editor of the Year, 1994; What the Papers Say Newspaper of the Year Award, 2001; GQ Editor of the Year, 2002; British Press Awards Newspaper of the Year, 2002; Magazine Design & Journalism Awards, Columnist of the Year Live, 2007.

MORGAN Trefor Owen, b. 11 March 1936, New South Wales, Australia. Medical Researcher; Vigneron. m. Olive Lawson, 1 son, 1 daughter. Education: University of Sydney, 1953-59; BScMed, 1958; MBBS, 1960; MD, 1972; Fellow, Royal Australian College of Physicians, 1972; Charles Stuart University, 1987-91; BApplSci, Wine, 1992. Appointments: Intern, Resident, Registrar, Clinical Supervisor, Royal Prince Alfred Hospital, 1960-66; Visiting Scientist, National Institutes of Health, USA, 1966-69; Renal Physician, Princess Alexandra Hospital, Australia, 1969-71; Assistant in Medicine, 1971-77, Professor of Physiology, 1984-2004, University of Melbourne, Victoria; Distinguished Professor of Medicine, Universiti Tecknologica Mara, Shah Alam, Malaysia, 2004-; Visiting Professor, University of Munich, Germany, 1975; Foundation Professor of Medicine, University of Newcastle, Australia, 1977-81; Specialist in Charge of Medicine, Repatriation Hospital, 1981-84; Visiting Professor, University Lausanne, 1996. Publications: 350 scientific papers; 3 books. Honour: Honorary Professor, Shandong Academy of Medical Sciences, China. Memberships: International Society of Hypertension; High Blood Pressure Research Council of Australia; Secretary, Asian Pacific Society of Hypertension. Address: Department of Physiology, University of Melbourne, Parkville 3052, Victoria, Australia.

MORGAN William Richard, b. 27 March 1922, Cambridge, Ohio, USA. Mechanical Engineer. m. Marjorie Eleanor Stevens, 17 February 1946, 1 son, 1 daughter. Education: BSME, Ohio State University, 1944; MSME, Purdue University, 1950; PhD, Mechanical Engineering, 1951. Appointments: Licensed Professional Engineer, Ohio; Power Plant Design Engineer, Curtiss Wright Corp, Columbus, Ohio, 1946-47; Instructor and Westinghouse Research Fellow, Purdue University; West Lafayette Indiana, 1947-51; Supervisor,

Experimental Mechanical Engineering, GE, Cincinnati, 1951-55; Manager, Controls Analysis Development, Aircraft Gas Turbine Division, GE, 1955-59; Manager, XV5A vertical take-off and landing aircraft programme, GE, 1959-65; Manager, Acoustic Engineering, Flight Propulsion Division, GE, 1965-69; Manager, quiet engine programme 1969-71; President, Cincinnati Research Corporation, 1971-73; Vice President, SDRC International, Cincinnati, 1973-79; Engineering and Management Consultant, Cincinnati, 1979-. Publications: Geometric Configuration Factors in Radiant Heat Transmission (PhD Dissertation), 1951; Numerous papers presented in seminars and symposia and articles in professional journals. Memberships: ASME; Sigma Xi; Pi Tau Sigma; Pi Mu Epsilon. Address: 312 Ardon Ln, Cincinnati, OH 45215, USA.

MORIARTY Kieran John, b. 31 May 1951, Cheshire, England. Consultant Gastroenterologist. m. Theresa Butler, 2 sons, 2 daughters. Education: Trinity College, Cambridge, 1969-72; The London Hospital Medical College, 1972-75. Appointments: Senior House Officer to Dr Mike Lancaster-Smith, General Medicine and Gastroenterology, Queen Mary's Hospital, Sidcup, Kent, 1976-77; Clinical Research Fellow in Gastroenterology to Sir Anthony Dawson, Dr Mike Clark and Dr Chris Williams, St Bartholomew's Hospital, London, 1979-83; Tutor in Medicine to Professor Lord Leslie Turnberg, University Department of Medicine, Hope Hospital, Salford, 1983-90; Consultant Gastroenterologist, Royal Bolton Hospital, 1990-. Publications: Holy Communion Wafers and Celiac Disease (prompted the Vatican to change Canon Law and allow use of low gluten communion wafers), 1989; Understanding Irritable Bowel Syndrome (written for patients), 2001; Recorded: CD: Dr Kieran Moriarty - Irish Songs and Ballads (to fund nurses going to Lourdes to help the sick and disabled), 2002. Honours: British Hospital Doctor of the Year for multidisciplinary care for alcoholic patients, 1999; Team Leader of Winning British Hospital Doctor Gastroenterology Team of the Year, 1999; CBE for services to medicine, 2002; Mayo Association of Manchester Award for caring for the sick and disabled, 2003. Memberships: English Member of International Medical Committee of Lourdes; Chief Medical Officer, Salford Diocesan Pilgrimage to Lourdes; Adviser on alcohol to Chief Medical Officer; Director of Strategy and Health Intelligence Officer at the Department of Health; Parliamentary Office of Science and Technology on Binge Drinking; Fellow, Royal College of Physicians of London; Honorary Fellow, Royal College of Physicians of Ireland, 2005; Member, British Society of Gastroenterology, American Gastroenterological Association; Helped formulate Italian Government's nutritional policy. Address: 20 Bramhall Park Road, Bramhall, Stockport SK7 3DQ, England. E-mail: kieran.moriarty@rbh.nhs.uk

MORINAGA Masahiko, b. 20 August 1946, Osaka, Japan. Professor. m. Kazue, 1 son, 1 daughter. Education: BS, 1969, MS, 1971, Kyoto University, Japan; PhD, Northwestern University, USA 1978. Appointments: Lecturer, 1979-83, Associate Professor, 1983-91, Professor 1991-94, Toyohashi University of Technology; Professor, Nagoya University, 1994-; Chair, 176th Committee on the Process-Created Materials Function in the Japan Society for the Promotion of Science, 2004-. Honours: The Meritorious Award of the Japan Institute of Metals, 1989; The Nagai Science Award, 1991; Memorial Lecture for the Korean Institute of Metals, 1997; The Science Award of the DV-Xα Society of Japan, 2001. Memberships: The Minerals, Metals and Materials Society; The Japan Institute of Metals, Vice-President, 2005-06; Iron and Steel Institute of Japan; Physical Society of Japan; DV-Xα Society

of Japan, President, 2004-. Address: Department of Materials Science and Engineering, Graduate School of Engineering, Nagoya University, Furo-cho, Chikusa-ku, Nagoya 464-8603, Japan. E-mail: morinaga@numse.nagoya-u.ac.jp

MORISSETTE Alanis, b. 1 June 1974, Ottawa, Canada. Singer. Career: Solo recording artiste; Appeared on Canadian cable TV, aged 10; Signed contract as songwriter with MCA Publishing aged 14; Concerts include: Twix Mix Jamboree, with David Bowie, Birmingham NEC, 1995; 16 million albums sold. Recordings: Albums: Alanis, 1991; Now Is The Time, 1992; Jagged Little Pill, 1995; Space Cakes (live), Supposed Former Infatuation Junkie, 1998; Alanis Unplugged (live), 1999; Under Rug Swept, 2002; So-called Chaos, 2004; Jagged Little Pill Acoustic, Alanis Morissette: The Collection, 2005; Flavors of Entanglement, 2008. Singles: Fate Stay With Me; You Oughta Know, One Hand In My Pocket, 1995; Ironic, You Learn, Head Over Feet, 1996; All I Really Want, Thank U, You Oughta Know, 1998; Joining You, Unsent, So Pure, So Real, That I Would Be Good, 1999; Hands Clean, Precious Illusions, 2002; So-called Chaos, 2004. Film: Dogma, 1999; Jay and Silent Bob Strike Back, 2001; De-Lovely, American Dreams, 2004; Degrassi: The Next Generation, Fuck, Just Friends, 2005; Lovespring International, Nip/Tuck, 2006; Head-case, 2007; Radio Free Albemuth 2007/08. Honour: BRIT Award, Best International Newcomer, 1996; Four Grammy Awards, including Album of the Year and Best Rock Album; Best Female Award, MTV European Music Awards, 1996. Address: Maverick Recording Company, 9348 Civic Center Drive, Suite 100, Beverley Hills, CA 90210, USA. Website: www.alanismorissette.com

MORITA Masami, b. 1 December 1927, Nagasaki, Japan. Retired Professor of English. m. Masue Okuhara, 1 son, 2 daughters. Education: BA, 1951, MA, 1961, Waseda University; Visiting Scholar, Clare Hall, University of Cambridge, England, 1973-74; Visiting Fellow, Yale University, 1983-84; M Phil, University of Sussex, 2006. Appointments: Lecturer, 1967-68, Associate Professor, 1968-74, Professor, 1974-87, Takasaki City University of Economics; Professor, Kanda University of International Studies, 1987-98. Publications: Shelley's Self-Identification with Nature and His Ideas of Reform; Articles on British and American Romantic Literature, especially Wordsworth, Coleridge, Byron, Keats, Shelley, Emerson, Whitman and Poe. Honours: Grant for studies and researches abroad, Japanese Ministry of Education; Fulbright Fellowship, Japan-US Educational Commission. Memberships: Modern Language Association of America; Keats-Shelley Association of America; Japan Shelley Studies Centre; Caledonia Society; Cambridge Society. Address: 662-3 Shokanji, Takasaki, Gunma 370-0008, Japan.

MORRELL David William James, b. 26 July 1933, Glasgow, Scotland. University Administrator; Ombudsman. m. Margaret Rosemary, 2 sons, 1 daughter. Education: MA (Hons), 1954, LLB, 1957, University of Edinburgh. Appointments: Apprentice Solicitor, Shepherd & Wedderburn WS, 1954-57; Administrative Assistant, King's College, University of Durham, 1957-60; Assistant Registrar, University of Exeter, 1960-64; Senior Assistant Registrar, University of Essex, 1964-66; Academic Registrar, 1966-73, Registrar and Secretary, 1973-89, University of Strathclyde; Consultant to Institutional Management in Higher Education Programme of OECD, Paris, 1989-90; Lay Observer for Scotland, 1989-91; Scottish Legal Services Ombudsman, 1991-94; Chairman, 1995-96, Vice-Chairman, 1996-99, Lomond Healthcare NHS Trust; Member, Argyll and Clyde Health Board, 1999-2001;

Chairman of University of Paisley, 1997-2002. Publications: Various on management in higher education and on lawyer/client relationships. Honours: Honorary Degree, Doctor of the University, University of Paisley, 2005. Memberships: National Trust for Scotland; Historic Scotland; Church of Scotland; Fellow, Institute of Contemporary Scotland.

MORRIS Desmond John, b. 24 January 1928, Purton, Wiltshire, England. Zoologist; Author; Broadcaster; Artist. m. Ramona Baulch, 30 July 1952, 1 son. Education: BSc, Birmingham University, 1951; DPhil, Oxford University, 1954. Appointments: Zoological Research Worker, University of Oxford, 1954-56; Head of Granada TV and Film Unit, Zoological Society of London, 1956-59; Curator of Mammals, Zoological Society of London, 1959-67; Director, Institute of Contemporary Arts, London, 1967-68; Privately engaged writing books, 1968-73; Research Fellow, Wolfson College, Oxford, 1973-81; Privately engaged writing books and making television programmes, 1981-2005. TV series: Zootime, 1956-67; Life, 1965-67; The Human Race, 1982; The Animals Roadshow, 1987-89; The Animal Contract, 1989; Animal Country, 1991-96; The Human Animal, 1994; The Human Sexes, 1997; Solo exhibitions (paintings): Art galleries across England and in Holland, Belgium, France, USA and Ireland. Publications include: The Biology of Art, 1962; The Big Cats, 1965; Zootime, 1966; The Naked Ape, 1967; The Human Zoo, 1969; Patterns of Reproductive Behaviour, 1970; Intimate Behaviour, 1971; Manwatching, 1977; Animal Days, 1979; The Soccer Tribe, 1981; Bodywatching: A Field Guide to the Human Species, 1985; Catwatching, 1986; Dogwatching, 1986; Catlore, 1987; The Human Nestbuilders, 1988; The Animal Contract, 1990; Animal-Watching, 1990; Babywatching, 1991; Christmas Watching, 1992; The World of Animals, 1993; The Naked Ape Trilogy, 1994; The Human Animal, 1994; Bodytalk: A World Guide to Gestures, 1994; Catworld: A Feline Encyclopaedia, 1996; The Human Sexes: A Natural History of Man and Woman, 1997; Illustrated Horsewatching, 1998; Cool Cats: The 100 Cat Breeds of the World, 1999; Body Guards: Protective Amulets and Charms, 1999; The Naked Ape and Cosmetic Behaviour (with Kaori Ishida), 1999; The Naked Eye, Travels in Search of the Human Species, 2000; Dogs: a Dictionary of Dog Breeds, 2001; Peoplewatching, 2002; The Silent Language (in Italian), 2004; The Nature of Happiness, 2004; The Naked Woman, 2004; Linguaggio muto, 2004. Contributions to: Many journals and magazines. Honour: Honorary DSc, Reading University, 1998. Membership: Scientific Fellow, Zoological Society of London. Address: c/o Jonathan Cape, Random Century House, 20 Vauxhall Bridge Road, London SW1V 2SA, England.

MORRIS Frederick, b. 1 December 1929. Law. m. Valerie Rose Farrell, 2 daughters. Education: Glenstal Abbey, Murroe, Co Limerick; UCD, National University of Ireland. Appointments: Kings Inns, Dublin; Call to the Irish Bar, 1952; Barrister at Law; Called to the Inner Bar in Ireland, 1982, Senior Counsel; Called to the Bar in England, 1969; Judge, 1990, President, 1999, High Court of Ireland; Member, Counsel of State of Ireland, 1999; Trustee, Council of European Law, Trier, 1993; Sole Member, Tribunal of Inquiry into Garda Misconduct, 2001. Publications: Interim Report on Tribunal of Inquiry, 2003; Second Interim Report, 2005; Third, Fourth and Fifth Interim Report, 2006. Honours: Granted Freedom of the City of Waterford, 1976. Memberships: Blainroe Golf Club; Milltown Golf Club; Royal Irish Yacht Club; University College Dublin Rugby Club. Address: Belfield Office Park, Beaver Row, Clonskeagh, Dublin 4, Ireland.

MORRIS Richard Francis Maxwell, b. 11 September 1944, Sussex, England. Chief Executive. m. Marian Sperling, 9 April 1983, 2 daughters. Education: New College, Oxford, 1963-66; College of Law, London, 1967. Appointments: Solicitor, Farrer & Co, 1967-71; Banker, Grindlay Brandts, 1971-75; Director, Invicta Radio plc, 1984-92; General Manager, Corporate Finance, SG Warburg & Co, 1975-79; Managing Director, Edward Arnold Ltd. 1987-91; Finance Director, Joint Managing Director, Hodder & Stoughton, 1979-91; Founder, Almaviva Opera, 1989-; Trustee, Governor, Kent Opera, 1985-90; Director, Southern Radio plc, 1990-92; Chief Executive, Associated Board of the Royal Schools of Music, 1993-; Trustee, Director, Kent Music School, 2001-; Member, Executive Committee, Chairman, Music Education Council, 1995-; Trustee, Council for Dance Education and Training, 1999-2005; Governor, The Yehudi Menuhin School, 2004-. Honours: Honorary RCM; Honorary RNCM; MA (Oxon). Memberships: Incorporated Society of Musicians. Address: 24 Portland Place, London W1B 1LU, England. E-mail: rmorris@abrsm.ac.uk

MORRIS Richard Graham Michael, b. 27 June 1948, Worthing, Sussex, England. Neuroscientist. m. Hilary Ann Lewis, 2 daughters. Education: MA, Trinity Hall, University of Cambridge, 1966-69; DPhil, Sussex University, 1969-73. Appointments: Senior Scientific Officer, British Museum, Natural History, Researcher, BBC Television, Science and Features Department, 1973-75; Lecturer, Psychology, 1977-86, MRC Research Fellow, 1983-86, University of St Andrews; Reader in Neuroscience, 1986-93, Professor of Neuroscience, 1993-, Director, Centre for Neuroscience, 1993-97, Chairman, Department of Neuroscience, University of Edinburgh, 1998-2002; Co-Director, Edinburgh Neuroscience, 2005-; Editorial roles in various scientific journals, 1990-. Publications: Over 150 papers in academic journals; Neuroscience: The Science of the Brain (booklet for secondary school children); Parallel Distributed Processing: Implications for Psychology and Neurobiology (editor), 1989; Neuroscience: Science of the Brain, 1994, 2003; Long Term Potentiation, 2004. Honours: Fellow, Academy of Medical Sciences, 1998-; Decade of the Brain Lecturer, 1998; Zotterman Lecturer, 1999; Forum Fellow, World Economics Forum, 2000; Life Sciences Co-ordinate OST Foresight Project on Cognitive Systems, 2002-04; Yngve Zotterman Prize, Karolinska Institute, 1999; Henry Dryerre Prize, Royal Society of Edinburgh, 2000. Memberships: Experimental Psychology Society, Honorary Secretary, 1984-88; British Neuroscience Association, Chairman, 1991-95; Society for Neuroscience, USA; European Brain and Behaviour Society; American Academy of Arts and Sciences, 2004-. Address: Neuroscience, University of Edinburgh, 1 George Square, Edinburgh EH8 9JZ, Scotland.

MORRIS William (Bill), Baron Morris of Handsworth, b. 1938, Jamaica. Trade Union General Secretary. m. Minetta, deceased 1990, 2 sons. Appointments include: Joined engineering company, Hardy Spicers, Birmingham; Joined T&G, 1958; Elected Shop Steward, Hardy Spicers, 1962; Involved in first industrial dispute, 1964; Elected Member, T&G's General Executive Council, 1972; District Officer, T&G, Nottingham/Derby District, 1973; Northampton District Secretary, T&G, 1976; National Secretary of the Passenger Service Trade Group, T&G, 1979; Deputy General Secretary, T&G, 1986-92; Elected General Secretary, 1991, re-elected, 1995-2003; Member, TUC General Council, 1988-2003; Member, TUC Executive Committee, 1988-; Member, Commission for Racial Equality, 1980-87; Member, Executive Board of the International Transport Worker's

Federation, 1986; Member, New Deal Task Force, 1997-2000; Member, Court of the Bank of England, 1998-; Member of Committee for Integrated Transport, 1999-; Member, Governing Councils, Luton University and Northampton University; Chancellor, University of Technology, Jamaica, 1999-, Staffordshire University, 2004-; Chair, Morris Enquiry, 2003-04; Non-executive Director, England and Wales Cricket Board, 2007-. Honours: Numerous Honorary Degrees; Honorary Professorship, Thames Valley University, 1997; Honorary Fellowship, Royal Society of Arts, 1992; Honorary Fellowship City & Guilds London Institute, 1992; Order of Jamaica, 2002; Public Figure of the Year, Ethnic Multicultural Media Awards, 2002; Knighted, 2003. Memberships: Board of Fullemploy, 1985-88; Trustee, 1987-90, Advisory Committee, 1997- Prince's Youth Business Trust. Address: 156 St Agnells Lane, Grove Hill, Hemel Hempstead, Hertfordshire, HP2 6EG, England.

MORRISON Madison, b. 28 June 1940, USA. Writer. Education: BA, Yale University, 1961; AM, 1962, PhD, 1969, Harvard University. Appointments: Assistant, Humanities courses, 1963-1965, Tutor, 1967-1969, Harvard University; Instructor, University of Maryland on military bases in Germany, France and Greece, 1965-1967; Professor, University of Oklahoma, 1969-92. Publications: 19 of the 26 volumes in Sentence of the Gods; 7 other books; Academic monograph: Frank W Stevenson, Chaos and Cosmos in Morrison's Sentence of the Gods, Collection of essays about: MM: The Sentence Commuted. Honours: National Endowment for the Arts; National Endowment for the Humanities; Ingram Merrill Foundation; Fulbright Lecturer, India; Visiting Professor, University of Rome, Italy; Visiting Professor, Thammasat University, Thailand, etc. Address: PO Box 22-106, Taipei, Taiwan. E-mail: madison_morrison@attglobal.net

MORRISON Marion, b. 18 August 1939, Melton, Suffolk, England. m. Tony, 30 July 1965, 1 son, 1 daughter. Education: BA Hons, History, University of Wales, 1958-61. Publications: Let's Visit Uruguay, Indians of the Amazon, Indians of the Andes, 1985; An Inca Farmer, Atahualpa and the Incas, 1986; Let's Visit Venezuela, Let's Visit Paraguay, 1987; Bolivia, People and Places Brazil, 1988; Venezuela, People and Places Argentina, People and Places Central America, 1989; Colombia, 1990; World in View Ecuador, Peru, Bolivia, 1991; Uruguay, World in View Central America, 1992; Paraguay, Fact File Brazil, Amazon Rainforest and Its People, 1993; French Guiana, Highlights Brazil, Focus on Mexico, Real World Mexico and Central America, 1995; Belize, Highlights Peru, Highlights Argentina, Discovering Mexico, Discovering Brazil, Country Insights Brazil, 1996; Country Insights Cuba, 1997; Costa Rica, Peoples of the Americas (major contributor), 1998; Cuba, Colombia, Highlights Costa Rica, 1999; Peru, Ecuador, 2000; El Salvador, 2001; Children's Press: EOW Nicaragua, 2001; EOW Guyana, 2004; EPW Uruguay, 2005; EOW Guatemala, 2005; EOW Costa Rice, 2007; EOW Colombia, 2007, World Almanac Library Great Cities of the World, Mexico City, 2003; Rio de Janeiro, 2004; Buenos Aires, 2005; Evans Countries of the World: Chile, 2006. Contributions: Various magazines and journals. Address: 48 Station Road, Woodbridge, Suffolk IP12 4AT, England. E-mail: morrison@southamericanpictures.com

MORRISON Samuel James, b. 18 February 1917, Glasgow, Scotland. Engineer. m. Mary, 2 daughters. Education: Shawlands Academy, Glasgow, 1922-29; Allan Glen's School, Glasgow, 1929-34; BSc, Electrical Engineering, University of Glasgow, 1935-40. Appointments: Apprentice, 1940-42, Research Engineer, 1945-56, British Thomson

Houston; Shrinkage Engineer, Cosmos Manufacturing, 1942-45; Statistician, Standard Telephones & Cables, 1956-60; Statistician, British Ropes, 1960-63; Lecturer, 1963-78, Head of Department of OR, 1978-82, Honorary Research Associate, 1982-86, Retired, Senior Fellow, 1986, University of Hull. Publications: Over 30 articles in various professional journals; Numerous conference presentations; Author, Introduction to Statistical Engineering. Honours: National Academic Prize, Undiscovered Authors Competition, 2006; Greenfield Industrial Medal, Royal Statistical Society, 2007; IET Achievement Medal, Institution of Engineering and Technology, 2007. Memberships: Fellow, Institution of Engineering and Technology; Fellow, Institution of Mechanical Engineers; Fellow, Chartered Management Institute; Fellow, Royal Statistical Society; Senior Member, American Society for Quality. Address: 4 The Vale, Kirkella, East Yorkshire, HU10 7PS, England.

MORRISON Toni (Chloe Anthony), b. 18 February 1931, Lorain, Ohio, USA. Novelist. m. Harold Morrison, 1958, divorced 1964, 2 children. Education: Howard University; Cornell University. Appointments: Teacher, English and Humanities, Texas Southern University, 1955-57, Howard University, 1957-64; Editor, Random House, New York, 1965-; Associate Professor of English, State University of New York, 1971-72; Schweitzer Professor of the Humanities, 1984-89; Robert F Goheen Professor of the Humanities, Princeton University, 1989-. Publications: The Bluest Eye, 1970; Sula, 1974; Song of Solomon, 1977; Tar Baby, 1983; Beloved, 1987; Jazz, 1992; Playing in the Dark: Whiteness and the Literary Imagination, 1992; Nobel Prize Speech, 1994; Birth of a Nation'hood: Gaze, Script and Spectacle in the O J Simpson Trial, 1997; The Big Box (poems), 1999; The Book of Mean People, 2002; Love, 2003; Remember: The Journey to School Integration, 2004. Who's Got Game?: The Ant or the Grasshopper, The Lion or the Mouse, 2003; Poppy or the Snake, 2004; The Mirror or the Glass, 2007. Honours include: Pulitzer Prize and Robert F Kennedy Book Award, for Beloved, 1988; Nobel Prize for Literature, 1993; Commander, Ordre des Arts et des Lettres; National Medal of Arts, 2000. Membership: Council, Authors' Guild. Address: c/o Suzanne Gluck, International Creative Management, 40 57th Street West, NY 10019, USA.

MORRISON Van (George Ivan Morrison), b. 31 August 1945, Belfast, Northern Ireland. Singer; Songwriter; Composer; Musician. 1 daughter; Partner, Michelle Rocca, 1 son, 1 daughter. Career: Founder, lead singer, Them, 1964-67; Solo artiste, 1967-; Appearances include: Knebworth Festival, 1974; The Last Waltz, The Band's farewell concert, 1976; Played with Bob Dylan, Wembley Stadium, 1984; Self Aid, with U2, Dublin, 1986; Glastonbury Festival, 1987; Prince's Rock Trust Gala, 1989; Performance, The Wall, by Roger Waters, Berlin, 1990; Concert in Dublin, with Bono, Bob Dylan, 1993; Phoenix Festival, 1995. Recordings: Singles include: Gloria; Brown-Eyed Girl; Moondance; Domino; Wild Night; Albums include: Blowin' Your Mind, 1967; Astral Weeks, 1968; Moondance, 1970; His Band And Street Choir, 1973; Tupelo Honey, 1971; St Dominic's Preview, 1972; Hard Nose The Highway, 1973; It's Too Late To Stop Now, 1974; TB Sheets, 1974; Veedon Fleece, 1974; This Is Where I Came In, 1977; A Period Of Transition, 1977; Wavelength, 1978; Into The Music, 1983; Bang Masters, 1990; Common One, 1980; Beautiful Vision, 1982; Inarticulate Speech Of The Heart, 1983; Live At The Opera House Belfast, 1984; A Sense Of Wonder, 1984; No Guru, No Method, No Teacher, 1986; Poetic Champions Compose, 1987; Irish Heartbeat, 1988; Best Of..., 1990; Avalon Sunset, 1989; Enlightenment, 1990; Hymns To

The Silence, 1991; Too Long In Exile, 1993; Best Of..., Vol 2, 1993; A Night in San Francisco, 1994; Days Like This, 1995; Songs of the Mose Allison: Tell Me Something, 1996; The Healing Game, 1997; The Skiffle Sessions: Live in Belfast, 1998, 2000; Brown Eyed Girl, 1998; The Masters, 1999; Super Hits, 1999; Back on Top, 1999; You Win Again, 2000; Down The Road, 2002; What's Wrong With This Picture? 2003; Also recorded on albums: with The Band: Cahoots, 1971; The Last Waltz, 1978; with John Lee Hooker: Folk Blues, 1963; Mr Lucky, 1991; with Bill Wyman: Stone Alone, 1976; with Jim Capaldi: Fierce Heart, 1983; with Georgie Fame: How Long Has This Been Going On, 1996; Pay the Devil, 2006. Honours include: Inducted into Rock And Roll Hall Of Fame, 1993; BRIT Award, Outstanding Contribution to British Music, 1994; Q Award, Best Songwriter, 1995; OBE, 1996; BMI Icon Award, 2004. Website: www.vanmorrison.co.uk

MORRISS Peter, b. 7 January 1940, Chesterfield, England. Retired. m. Joan Margaret, 7 September 1963, 1 son, 1 daughter. Publications: Published in over 100 anthologies of poetry by: Poets England; Forward Press; Poetry Now; Arrival Press; Anchor Books; Poetic Hours; Dogma Publications; United Press; Aural Images; Poetry Today; United Reformed Church Sounds of Fury Anthology; Through My Eyes (poetry collection), 1999; Painting the Town Red (epic Poem), 2002; Tape, Just Poetry (for the Leicestershire Royal Society for the Blind), 1994; Poetry also published in various magazines. Honours: Commendation Poetry Club, 1996, Triumph House, 1997; Editors Choice Award, International Society of Poets, 1996; Editors Choice Award International Library of Poetry, 1998. Membership: Society of Authors; Lapidus (Literary Arts In Personal Development); Poetry Society; British Haiku Society. Address: Pitnamoon Farmhouse, Laurencekirk AB30 1ES, Scotland. E-mail: petermorriss@btinternet.com Website: www.scribesnook.co.uk

MORT Graham Robert, b. 11 August 1955, Middleton, England. Poet. m. Maggie Mort, 12 February 1979, 3 sons. Education: BA, University of Liverpool, 1977; PGCE, St Martin's College, Lancaster, 1980; PhD, University of Glamorgan, 2000. Appointment: Creative Writing Course Leader, Open College of the Arts, 1989-2000. Publications: A Country on Fire; Into the Ashes; A Halifax Cider Jar; Sky Burial; Snow from the North; Starting to Write; The Experience of Poetry, Storylines; Circular Breathing; A Night on the Lash; Visibility: New and Selected Poems. Contributions to: Numerous literary magazines and journals. Honours: 1st Prizes, Cheltenham Poetry Competition, 1979, 1982; Duncan Lawrie Prizes, Arvon Poetry Competition, 1982, 1992, 1994; Major Eric Gregory Award, 1985; Authors Foundation Award, 1994. Memberships: Society of Authors; National Association of Writers in Education. Address: 2 Chapel Lane, Burton-in-Lonsdale, Carnforth, Lancs LA6 3JY, England.

MORTENSEN Finn Hauberg, b. 26 July 1946, Copenhagen, Denmark. Professor. m. Ella Bredsdorff, 3 sons, 2 daughters. Education: Cand. Phil. 1972, Mag. Art. 1975, Lic. Phil. 1979, Copenhagen University, Denmark. Appointments: Research Fellow, 1972-74, Assistant Professor, 1974-76, Associate Professor, 1976-89, Docent, 1989-91, Professor, 1991-, University of Southern Denmark; Research Professor, Copenhagen University, 1994-91; Guest Professor, Kwansei Gakuin University, 1997, 2002; Research Fellow, University of California, Berkeley, 2003, 2004, 2005, 2006, 2007; Chair, Institute of Philosophy, Education and the Study of Religions; University of Southern Denmark, 2005-06; Chair, Institute of Scandinavian Studies and

Linguistics, University of Copenhagen, 2007-. Publications: Litteraturfunktion og symbolnorm 1-2, 1973; Danskfagets didaktik 1-2, 1979; Kierkegaards Either/Or, 1989; A Tale of Tales – H C Andersen, 1989; Funderinger over faget dansk, 1993; Kierkegaard Made in Japan, 1996; Villy Sørensen: Talt, 2002; Abe and Søko, Uddannelsesdebat 1969-2001, 2002; Bibliografi over Villy Sørensens Forfatterskab, 2003; Laeselist, Litteraturpaedagogiske essays 1-2, 2003. Honours: Gold Medal, Copenhagen University, 1969; Knighted by the Queen of Denmark. Memberships: Royal Danish Academy of Sciences and Letters; Council of Arts, Ministry of Culture; Chairman, Society for Danish Language and Literature; Chairman, Council of Literature, Ministry of Culture. Address: Thorsvej 33, 3140 Ålsgårde, Denmark.

MORTIMER Sir John (Clifford), b. 21 April 1923, Hampstead, London, England. Author; Barrister; Playwright. m. (1) Penelope Fletcher, 1949, 1 son, 1 daughter, (2) Penelope Gollop, 2 daughters. Education: Brasenose College, Oxford. Appointments: Called to the Bar, 1948; Master of the Bench, Inner Temple, 1975; Member, Board of National Theatre, 1968-; Chairman, Council Royal Society of Literature, 1989; Chairman, Council Royal Court Theatre, 1990-; President, Howard League for Penal Reform, 1991-. Publications: Novels: Charade, 1947; Rumming Park, 1948; Answer Yes or No, 1950; Like Men Betrayed, 1953; Three Winters, 1956; Will Shakespeare, 1977; Rumpole of the Bailey, 1978; The Trials of Rumpole, 1979; Rumpole's Return, 1981; Rumpole and the Golden Thread, 1983; Paradise Postponed, 1985; Rumpole's Last Case, 1987; Rumpole and the Age of Miracles, 1988; Rumpole a la Carte, 1990; Clinging to the Wreckage (autobiography), 1982; In Character, 1983; Character Parts (interviews), 1986; Summer's Lease, 1988; The Narrowing Stream; Titmuss Regained, 1990; Dunster, 1992; Rumpole on Trial, 1992; The Best of Rumpole, 1993; Murderers and Other Friends (autobiography), 1993; Rumpole and the Angel of Death, 1995; Rumpole and the Younger Generation, 1996; Felix in the Underworld, 1997; Rumpole's Return, 1997; The Third Rumpole Omnibus, 1997; The Sound of Trumpets, 1998; The Summer of a Dormouse (autobiography), 2000; Rumpole Rests His Case, 2001; Rumpole and the Primrose Path, 2002; Rumpole and the Penge Bungalow Murders, 2002; Where There's A Will, 2003; Quite Honestly, 2005; The Scales of Justice, 2005; Rumpole and the Reign of Terror, 2006. Numerous plays and translations. Honours include: British Academy of Writers' Award, 1979, 1980; British Book Award for Lifetime Achievement, 2005.

MOSES Daniel, b. 4 December 1954, Hartsville, South Carolina, USA. Human Resources Consultant; Author. m. Burlean Smith, 1 son. Education: BS, Business Management, Coker College; Masters Degree, Human Resources, Kennedy Western; PhD, Business Administration. Appointments: Manager, Jewel Companies, Jacksonville, Florida, 1981-85; Manager, Pharmor Drug Store, Columbia, South Carolina, 1985-88; Agent, Lincoln Benefit Life, Columbia and Lincoln, Nebraska, 1989-97; Consultant, Bridge Counseling Centre, Benedict College, Columbia, 1989-92; Recruiter, Edward Waters College, Jacksonville, Florida, 1995-96; Publisher, Researcher, Genealogist, Daniel Moses Inc, Delaware, South Carolina, 1994-; Co-founder, Project Heritage Quest Inc; Former Professor, Jones College, Jacksonville; Professor, Phoenix University, Jacksonville; Board of Directors, Theatre Works. Honours: Recipient, Towney Award, Town Theater, Columbia, South Carolina, 1987; Merit Award, International Music Festival, 1993; Junior Achievement, Carolina Music Academy, 1992-94; Ramses Hilton Award. Memberships: SHRM; American Parliamentary Association; International

Platform Association; American Institute of Parliamentarians; South Carolina Philharmonic Orchestra; WWII Tank Destroyer Society; Southside Businessmen's Club; Fort Mose Historical Society; African-American Community of Freedom Inc; Congress World Poets; World Academy of Arts and Sciences; Honorable Order of Kentucky Colonels; Columbia C of C; Jacksonville C of C; Southside Business Mens Club. Address: PO Box 2403, Jacksonville, FL 32203, USA.

MOSIMANN Anton, b. 23 February 1947, Switzerland. Chef; Restaurateur. m. Kathrin Roth, 1973, 2 sons. Appointments: Apprentice, Hotel Baeren, Twann; Worked in Canada, France, Italy, Sweden, Japan, Belgium, Switzerland, 1962-; Cuisinier, Villa Lorraine, Brussels, Les Prés d'Eugénie, Eugénie-les-Bains, Les Frères Troisgros, Roanne, Paul Bocuse, Collonges au Mont d'Or, Moulin de Mougins; Joined Dorchester Hotel, London, 1975, Maitre Chef des Cuisines, 1975-88; Owner, Mosimann's, 1988-, Mosimann's Party Service, 1990-, The Mosimann Academy, 1995-, Creative Chefs, 1996-; Numerous TV appearances. Publications: Cuisine a la Carte, 1981; A New Style of Cooking: The Art of Anton Mosimann, 1983; Cuisine Naturelle, 1985; Anton Mosimann's Fish Cuisine, 1988; The Art of Mosimann, 1989; Cooking with Mosimann, 1989; Anton Mosimann – Naturally, 1991; The Essential Mosimann, 1993; Mosimann's World, 1996. Honours: Freedom of the City of London, 1999; Royal Warrant from HRH the Prince of Wales for Caterers, 2000; OBE, 2004; Lifetime Achievement Award (Hotel & Caterer), 2004; Numerous others. Address: c/o Mosimann's, 11B West Halkin Street, London SW1X 8JL, England.

MOSS Kate, b. 16 January 1974, Addiscombe, England. Model. 1 daughter. Career: Modelled for Harpers and Queen; Vogue; The Face; Dolce & Gabana; Katherine Hamnett; Versace, Yves St Laurent; Exclusive world-wide with Calvin Klein, 1992-99. Publication: Kate, 1994. Film: Unzipped, 1996. TV: Inferno, 1992; Blackadder Back & Forth, 1999. Honour: Female Model of the Year, VH-1 Awards, 1996. Address: Storm Model Management, 1st Floor, 5 Jubilee Place, London SW3 3TD, England.

MOSS Linda Elaine Tribble, b. 29 March 1950, Lebanon, Missouri, USA. Education. m. Leonard Joe Moss, 2 daughters. Education: BSc in Agriculture, University of Missouri, Columbia, 1972; BSc, Chemistry Education, 1991, MSc, Chemistry Education, 1991, Specialist Community College Teaching, Biology Education, 1993, Doctor of Education, Educational Leadership, 2000, Arkansas State University; Project Wet, Wild and Learning Tree Facilitator Certification, 2004. Appointments: Science and Foreign Language Teacher, Poughkeepsie High School, 1987-89; Science and Foreign Language Teacher, Evening Shade High School, 1987-95; Adjunct Physical Science and Biology Instructor, Ozarka College, 1993-95; Science Professor, Black River Technical College, 1995-; Project Wet, Wild and Learning Tree Facilitator, 2004-. Publications: Tested Overhead Projector Demonstrations for High School Chemistry, Master degree thesis, 1991; Tested Overhead Projector Demonstrations for High School Chemistry, 1992; Effects of Domestic Wastewater Effluent on the Water Quality and Aquatic Macroinvertebrates in a Sharp County, Arkansas Street, 1993; Recruitment, Retention and Mentoring of Female and Minority Faculty in Higher Education, Doctoral degree thesis, 2000. Honours: Arkansas Academy of Science, Best Graduate Student Presentation, Kappa Delta Phi Honor Society, 1995; Student Body Choice Teacher, Black River Technical College Student Council, 1997; Faculty Scholar, Phi Theta Kappa International Honor Society, 2002; Appreciation of Outstanding Service,

and Most Distinguished Faculty Advisor, Oklahoma/ Arkansas Region, Phi Theta Kappa, 2006; ABI Fellow, 2007; ABI Professional Women's Advisory Board, 2007; Listed in national and international biographical dictionaries. Memberships: Phi Theta Kappa International Honor Society; Kappa Delta Pi Honor Society; Arkansas Academy of Science; National Education Association; National Science Teachers Association; Arkansas Science Teachers Association; American Chemical Society. Address: Black River Technical College, Highway 304 East, PO Box 468, Pocahontas, AR 72455, USA. E-mail: lindam@blackrivertech.org

MOSS Malcolm, b. 6 March 1943, Audenshaw, Manchester, England. Member of Parliament; Member, Foreign Affairs Select Committee. m. Sonya Alexandra McFarlin, May 2000, 2 daughters. Education: Audenshaw Grammar School, 1954-62; St John's College, Cambridge University, 1962-66. Career: Assistant Master, Blundell's School, Tiverton, Devon, 1966-68; Head of Department of Geography and Economics, Blundell's School, 1968-70; Insurance Broking Consultant, Barwick Associates Ltd, Worcestershire, 1971; General Manager Barwick Associates Ltd, Wisbech, 1972; Co-Founder, Mandrake Ltd, 1974; Wisbech Town Councillor, 1979; Deputy Mayor of Wisbech, 1981; Mayor of Wisbech, 1982; Fenland District Councillor, 1983; Cambridgeshire County Councillor, 1985; Member of Parliament, 1987-. Address: 111 High Street, March, Cambridgeshire, PE15 9LH, England.

MOSS Sir Stirling, OBE, b. 17 September 1929, London, England. Racing Driver. m. (1) Katherine Stuart Moson, 1957, dissolved 1960, (2) Elaine Barbarino, 1964, 1 daughter, dissolved 1968, (3) Susie Paine, 1980, 1 son. Education: Haileybury and Imperial Service College. Appointments: British Champion, 1951; Built Own Car, The Cooper-Alta, 1953; Drove in HWM Formula II Grand Prix Team, 1950, 1951, Jaguar Team, 1955; Leader, Maserati Sports & Grand Prix Teams, 1956, Aston Martin Team, 1956; Member, Vanwall, Aston Martin, Maserati Teams, 1958; Events include New Zealand, Monaco Grand Prix, Nurburgring 1,000km, Argentine 1,000km. UK, Pescara, Italy, Moroccan Grand Prix; Managing Director, Stirling Moss Ltd; Director, 28 companies; Journalist; Lecturer; President, Patron, 28 Car Clubs. Publications: Stirling Moss, 1953; In the Track of Speed, 1957; Le Mans 59, 1959; Design and Behaviour of the Racing Car, 1963; All But My Life, 1963; How to Watch Motor Racing, 1975; Motor Racing and All That, 1980; My Cars, My Career, 1987; Stirling Moss: Great Drives in the Lakes and Dales, 1993; Motor Racing Masterpieces, 1995; Stirling Moss, autobiography, 2001. Honours include: Honorary FIE, 1959; Gold Star, British Racing Drivers Club, 10 times, 1950-61; Driver of the Year, Guild of Motoring Writers, 1954; Sir Malcolm Campbell Memorial Award, 1957; International Motorsports Hall of Fame, 1990; Segrave Trophy, 2005; FIA gold medal, 2006. Address: c/o Stirling Moss Ltd, 46 Shepherd Street, Mayfair, London W1Y 8JN, England. E-mail: stirlingmossltd@aol.com

MÖSSBAUER Rudolf Ludwig, b. 31 January 1929, Munich, Germany. Physicist. Education: Graduated, Munich Institute of Technology, 1952; PhD, 1958; Postgraduate Research, Max Planck Institute for Medical Research, Heidelberg, 1958. Appointments: Professor of Physics, California Institute of Technology, Pasadena; Concurrent Professorship, Munich Institute of Technology; Discovered the Mössbauer Effect. Publications: Papers on Recoilless Nuclear Resonance Absorption and on Neutrino Physics. Honour: Nobel Prize for Physics, 1961. Address: Fachbereich Physik, Physik Department E 15, Technische Universität Mënchen, D-85747 Garching, Germany. E-mail: beatrice.vbellen@ph.tum.de

MOSSELMANS Carel Maurits, b. 9 March 1929, East Knoyle, Wiltshire, England. Investment Banker. m. Prudence Fiona McCorquodale, 2 sons. Education: Stowe; MA, Trinity College, Cambridge. Appointments: Joined Sedgwick Collins & Co, 1952, Director, 1963; Director, Sedgwick Forbes Holdings, 1978; Sedgwick Forbes Bland Payne, 1979; Chairman, Sedgwick Ltd, 1981-84; Deputy Chairman, 1982-84, Chairman, 1984-89, Sedgwick Group plc; Chairman, Sedgwick Lloyd's Underwriting Agents (formerly Sedgwick Forbes (Lloyds Underwriting Agents), 1974-89; Chairman, The Sumitomo Marine & Fire Insurance Co (Europe), 1981-90 (Director, 1975-81); Chairman, Rothschild Asset Management, 1990-93 (Director, 1989-99); Director, Coutts & Co, 1981-95; Director, Rothschild Continuation Ltd, 1990-97; Director, Tweedhill Fisheries, 1990-; Chairman, Committee of Management, Lionbrook Property Fund 'B' (formerly Five Arrows Property Unit Trust Manager Ltd), 1993-2003; Member, Investors' Committee Lionbrook Property Partnership, 1997-2003; Chairman, Indoor Golf Clubs plc, 1998-2004; Vice President, BIIBA, 1987-89. Memberships: Clubs: White's; Cavalry and Guards; Royal St George's Golf; Sunningdale Golf; Swinley Forest Golf; Royal & Ancient Golf, St Andrews. Address: 15 Chelsea Square, London SW3 6LF, England.

MOSZCZYNSKI Paulin, b. 3 January 1936, Janów, Lubelski, Poland. Haematologist. m. Maria Otto, 1 son, 1 daughter. Education: University Medical School, Cracow, Poland, 1960; MD, 1968; Full Professor of Medicine, 1991. Appointments: Head, Department of Medicine, L Rydygier Hospital, Brzesko, Poland, 1975-; Head, Provincial Immunology Laboratory, Brzesko, 1978-; Consultant Haematologist, 1975-; President, International Institute of University Medicine, Tarnow, Poland, 1996-. Publications: Over 420 publications to professional journals; Epidemiology, The Analyst, Arch, Medicine, Research; Industrial Hematology. Honours: Individual Prize Ministry of Health and Social Welfare, 1989; Gloria Med Medal, 1994; Health, 1995; A Schweitzer Golden Medal, 1996, 1999. Memberships: Polish Academy of Medicine; New York Academy of Sciences; Albert Schweitzer World Academy of Medicine. Address: Wyzwolenia 7, 32-800 Brzesko, Poland.

MOTION Andrew, b. 26 October 1952, England. Biographer; Poet; Poet Laureate of the United Kingdom, 1999-. m. (1) Joanna J Powell, 1973, dissolved 1983, (2) Janet Elisabeth Dalley, 1985, 2 sons, 1 daughter. Education: Radley College and University College, Oxford. Appointments: Lecturer in English, University of Hull, 1977-81; Editor, Poetry Review, 1981-83; Poetry Editor, Chatto & Windus, 1983-89, Editorial Director, 1985-87; Professor of Creative Writing, University of East Anglia, Norwich, 1995-2004; Professor of Creative Writing, Royal Holloway, University of London, 2004-; Chair, Literary Advisory Panel Arts Council of England, 1996-98; Poet Laureate of the United Kingdom, 1999-. Publications: Poetry: The Pleasure Steamers, 1978; Independence, 1981; The Penguin Book of Contemporary British Poetry (anthology), 1982; Secret Narratives, 1983; Dangerous Play, 1984; Natural Causes, 1987; Love in a Life, 1991; The Price of Everything, 1994; Selected Poems, 1996-97, 1998; Salt Water, 1997; Here to Eternity, anthology, 2000; Public Property, 2001; Here to Eternity: An Anthology of Poetry, 2001; As Poet Laureate: Remember This: An Elegy on the Death of HM Queen Elizabeth The Queen Mother, 2002; A Hymn for

the Golden Jubilee, 2002; On the Record (for Prince William's 21st birthday), 2003; Spring Wedding (for the wedding of Prince Charles and Camilla Parker Bowles), 2005; Criticism: The Poetry of Edward Thomas, 1981; Philip Larkin, 1982; William Barnes Selected Poems (ed), 1994; Biography: The Lamberts, 1986; Philip Larkin: A Writer's Life, 1993; Keats, 1997; Wainewright the Poisoner, novel, 2000; The Invention of Dr Cake, novel, 2003. Honours include: Rhys Memorial Prize, 1984; Somerset Maugham Award, 1987; Whitbread Biography Award, 1993; Honorary DLitt, Hull, 1996, Exeter, 1999, Brunel, 2000, APU, 2001, Open University, 2002; Sheffield Hallam, 2003; Sheffield, 2005. Address: c/o Faber & Faber, 3 Queen Square, London WC1, England.

MOUILLET Alain Charles Maurice Yves, b. 11 September 1944, Saint Germain Sur Meuse, France. Retired Professor. m. Viviane Albert, 1 son, 2 daughters. Education: Agregation de Sciences Physiques, Paris, 1968; PhD, University of Technology, Compiegne, 1975. Appointments: Assistant Professor, University of Paris XI, Cachan, Val de Marne, 1968-73; Assistant Professor, University of Technology, Compeigue-OISE, 1973-88; Professor, University of Burgundy, IVT Le Creusot, 1988-93; Professor, University Paul Cezanne, 1993-2006. Publications: 35 papers on electrical engineering and electromagnetism. Memberships: Societe des Electriciens et Electroniciens. Address: 140 Avenue Anselme Mathieu, F-84810 Aubignan, France. E-mail: amouil@club-internet.fr

MOULDS Phillip Andrew, b. 4 October 1967, Narrabri, Australia. Education. m. Deborah Cai, 1 son, 1 daughter. Education: Bachelor of Science, 1989, Bachelor of Music, 1991, Bachelor of Educational Studies, 1993, Bachelor of Educational Studies (Honours) Class I, 1996, Doctor of Philosophy, 2002, University of Queensland. Appointments: Boarding Housemaster, 1991-98, Secondary Teacher, 1991-95, Head of Chemistry, 1996-98, Deputy Head of Boarding, 1999-2001, Head of Science, 1989-2003, Deputy Headmaster, Brisbane Grammar School, 2004-; QSA State Review Panel, 2002-06; On-line Coach, 2003-, On-line Instructor, 2005-, Harvard Graduate School of Education; Ministerial Task Force Science Education, 2004-06. Publications: Numerous articles in professional journals. Honours: Golden Key National Honors Society; Westfield Premier's Scholarship for Teaching Excellence, 2003; Australian College of Education Teacher Excellence Award, 2004; Ambassador of Learning Award, Harvard Graduate School of Education, 2005; Listed in international biographical dictionaries. Memberships: Australian College of Education Leadership; Australian College of Educators; ASCD; RACI; STAQ. Address: 20 Fletcher Pde, Bardon, Queensland 4065, Australia. E-mail: moulds@staff.bgs.qld.edu.au

MOUNT William Robert Ferdinand, b. 2 July 1939, London, England. Novelist; Journalist; Editor. m. Julia Lucas, 20 July 1968, 2 sons, 1 daughter. Education: BA, Christ Church, Oxford, 1961. Appointments: Political Editor, 1977-82, 1985, Literary Editor, 1984-85, Spectator; Head of Prime Minister's Policy Unit, 1982-84; Political Columnist, The Times, 1984-85, Daily Telegraph, 1985-90; Editor, Times Literary Supplement, 1991-2002; Fellow, 1991, Council, 2002-05, RSL; Senior Columnist, The Sunday Times, 2002-04. Publications: Very Like a Whale, 1967; The Theatre of Politics, 1972; The Man Who Rode Ampersand, 1975; The Clique, 1978; The Subversive Family, 1982; The Selkirk Strip, 1987; Of Love and Asthma, 1991; The British Constitution Now, 1992; Umbrella, 1994; The Liquidator, 1995; Jem (and Sam), 1998; Fairness, 2001; Mind the Gap, 2004; Heads You

Win, 2004; The Condor's Head, 2007; Cold Cream, 2008. Contributions to: Spectator; Encounter; National Interest; London Review of Books. Honour: Hawthornden Prize, 1992; Honorary Fellow, University of Wales, Lampeter, 2002. Address: 17 Ripplevale Grove, London N1 1HS, England.

MOURA Marcelo Francisco de Sousa Ferreira de, b. 12 February 1962, Lourenço Marques, Mozambique. Auxiliary Professor. m. Ana Cristina Moura, 1 daughter. Education: Graduate, Mechanical Engineering, 1985; Doctor's Diploma, 1996, Faculty of Engineering, University of Porto, Portugal. Appointments: Assistant, 1986-96, Auxiliary Professor, 1996-, Faculty of Engineering, University of Porto, Portugal. Publications: More than 130 publications including papers in international scientific journals, international and national conferences, technical reports, dissertations and lecture notes. Memberships: Mecanica Experimental e Novos Materias, Research Group; Instituto de Engenharia Mechanica e Gestao Industrial; International Association of Computational Mechanics. Address: Faculdade de Engenharia da Universidade do Porto, R Dr Roberto Frias s/n, 4200-465 Porto, Portugal. E-mail: mfmoura@fe.up.pt

MOWAT David, b. 16 March 1943, Cairo, Egypt (British citizen). Playwright. Education: BA, New College, Oxford, 1964. Publications: Jens, 1965; Pearl, 1966; Anna Luse, 1968; Dracula, Purity, 1969; The Normal Woman, and Tyypi, Adrift, The Others, Most Recent Least Recent, Inuit, 1970; The Diabolist, John, 1971; Amalfi (after Webster), Phoenix-and-Turtle, Morituri, 1972; My Relationship with Jayne, Come, 1973; Main Sequence, The Collected Works, The Memory Man, The Love Maker, 1974; X to C, 1975; Kim, 1977; Winter, 1978; The Guise, 1979; Hiroshima Nights, 1981; The Midnight Sun, 1983; Carmen, 1984; The Almas, 1989; Jane, or The End of the World, 1992. Radio Plays. Honour: Arts Council Bursaries. Address: 7 Mount Street, Oxford OX2 6DH, England.

MOWLE Arthur Frank, b. 21 November 1946, Perth, Western Australia. Psychotherapist; Educationalist; Biomedical Scientist. Education: LTh, Melbourne College of Divinity, 1971; Diploma in Nursing, Royal Perth Hospital, 1972; BA, Immanuel College, 1974; WA Teachers Certificate & Diploma, College of Preceptors, England, 1978; PG Dip in Clinical Nutrition, Sydney & DSc (Health Science), CPU, 1982; EdD, California Coast University, 1988; B Hum, Pastoral Care, CSR, 1992; Dip Specific Learning Difficulties, Royal Society of Arts, 1995; MA, CSR, 1997; Dip Psynth Cnslg, South Australia, 2000; ThSoc, CSR, 2004; Cert Clin Hypnotherapy, NSW School of Hypnotic Sciences, 2005; Cert Clin Hypnotherapy, American Institute of Hypnotherapy, 2006. Appointments: Commissioned Officer RAAMC (Reserve), 1972-78; Registered Nurse, Royal Perth Hospital, 1972-73; Teacher and Registered Nurse, Salvado College, New Norcia, 1973-74; Teacher and Registered Nurse, St Mark's Christian Brothers College, Bedford, 1975-80; Teacher and Registered Nurse, Christian Brothers Agricultural School, Tardun, 1981-82; Senior Nurse Educator, Gippsland Base Hospital, Victoria, and in Western Australia, 1983-85; Senior Teacher, Health Officer & Counsellor, Servite College, Tuart Hill, 1986-99; Senior Teacher & Counselling Therapist, Kolbe Catholic College, Rockingham, 2000-; Ordained Priest, Liberal Catholic Church, and later appointed Director of Liberal Catholic Institute of Studies (Australia), 2002; Vicar, Cathedral Church of St John the Divine, Perth, 2005-. Publications: Numerous articles in professional medical journals; Research into role of Vitamin C in health and disease conditions as well as in HIV/AIDS. Honours: The Plato

Award, 2006. Memberships: Fellow, College of Nursing, 1980; Fellow, Australasian College of Biomedical Scientists, 1980; Fellow, Central School of Religion, 1995; Full Member, Psychotherapists & Counsellors Association of Western Australia, 1993; Psychotherapists & Counsellors Federation of Australia, 2004; Western Australian College of Teaching, 2005; Australian Society of Clinical Hypnotherapists, 2006. Address: 53A East St, Guildford, WA 6055, Australia. E-mail: psychehealth@westnet.com.au

MOXLEY Raymond James (Ray), b. 28 June 1923, Sheffield, England. Chartered Architect. m. Ann March, 1 son, 2 daughters. Education: Oxford School of Architecture, 1939-42; War service, 1942-46; Demobilised as Captain Royal Engineers; Dipl Arch, Oxford School of Architecture, 1946-49. Appointments: Assistant Architect, Bristol City Architects Department, 1949-51; Own Practice, 1953; Senior Partner, Moxley, Jenner and Partners, 1970-95; Commissions: Chelsea Harbour & Excel Exhibition Centre, London, et al; Founder, Chairman of the Society of Alternative Methods of Management; Co-Founder, Association of Consultant Architects; Commodore, Cargreen Yacht Club, Cornwall, 2002-2004. Publications: Architects Eye; Building Management by Professionals; An Architects Guide to Fee Negotiation. Honours: Honorary Fellow, University of the West of England; First Honorary Librarian of the Royal Institute of British Architects. Memberships: Fellow, Past Vice President, Royal Institute of British Architects; Past President, Association of Consultant Architects; Fellow, Royal Society of Arts; The Worshipful Company of Chartered Architects; Academician, Royal West of England Academy; The Royal West of England Yacht Club; Cargreen Yacht Club, Cornwall. Address: March House, Cargreen, Cornwall PL12 6PA, England.

MOYLES Chris (Christopher David), b. 22 February 1974, Leeds, England. Radio DJ; Presenter. Career: Presenter, Radio Aire; The Pulse of West Yorkshire; Chiltern Radio; Horizon Radio; Capital FM; Radio Luxembourg; Presenter Radio 1, 1997; Afternoon Show Radio 1, 1998; The Breakfast Show, 2004. TV Appearances: Live With Chris Moyles, The Chris Moyles Show, Look North, 1999; Later With Jools Holland, 2001; Fame Academy, 2002; Liquid News, 2003; Top Of The Pops, 2004; The Great Big Bid, Destination Three, Chris Moyles' Red Nose Rally, Comic Relief In Da Bungalow, Dick And Dom In The Bungalow, Mercury Music Prize, Newsround – Newsround Showbiz, Live 8, Comic Relief Does Fame Academy, 2005; Midlands Today, 2004; Powerhouse, 2004; Jools' 11th Annual Hootenanny, 2003; Ou – Steel/03; Sigmund Freud, 2003; Celebdaq, 2003; Dale's Wedding, 2003; This Is Your Life – David Dickinson, 2003; Patrick Kielty Almost Live, 2002; The Saturday Show, 2002; Radio 1 TV, 2001; Urban Icons – Instant Food, 2001; East Midlands Today, 2001; A Question Of Pop, 2000; Children In Need, 1999; Radio 1 Live From Heaton Park, Manchester, 1999; Real Lives – Radio 1 Goes Mad In Ibiza, 1999; Clubbing Night, 1999; Never Mind The Buzzcocks, 1998; The O Zone, 1998; Fully Booked, 1998; News, 1998; Stupid Punts, 2001; I Love The Nineties, 1992; Look East, 1998; BBC Breakfast News, 1999; Monster Wars, 1998; Viz, 2006; The X Factor: Battle Of The Stars, 2006. Singles Released: Dogz Don't Kill People (Wabbitz Do), 2004. Publications: The Gospel According to Chris Moyles, 2006; The Difficult Second Book, 2007. Honours: Faces For '97, Sky Magazine, 1997; DJ Of The Year, Sony Silver Awards, 1998; DJ Of The Year, The Sun Readers, Best Entertainment Show, Sony Gold Radio Award, 2006; Fastest-Ever Selling Download, Guinness Book Of Records.

MUELLER Rudhard Klaus, b. 20 August 1936, Glauchau, Saxony. Forensic Toxicologist; University Professor. m. Ursula Hanni, 3 daughters. Education: Study of Chemistry, College of Chemistry, Merseburg, 1954-55 and Leipzig University, Diploma (MSc equivalent), 1955-60; Study of Medicine, Leipzig University, 1956-61. Appointments: Member, Institute of Forensic Medicine, Leipzig University, 1960-2003; Dr rer nat in Chemistry, Leipzig University, 1965; Expert in Toxicology, Academy of Advanced Medical Studies, Berlin, 1981; Head, Postgraduate Study Programme Toxicology, Leipzig University, 1987-2003; Professor of Forensic Toxicology, Leipzig University, 1989; Expert in Forensic Toxicology, Society for Toxicological and Forensic Chemistry, 1991; Director, Institute of Doping Analysis and Sports Biochemistry, Dresden, 1992-2006; Member, Thuringian Academy of Sciences, 1993; Federal Commissioner for Doping Analysis, Federal Institute of Sports Sciences, Cologne, 1996-2006; EUROTOX Registered Toxicologist, 1998, 2003. Publications: Over 400 publications including numerous books; Over 600 presentations at scientific meetings. Honours: Virchow Award, Ministry of Health, Berlin, 1977; Leibniz Award, University of Leipzig, 1979; Kockel Medal, Society of Forensic Medicine, Leipzig, 1982; Honorary Member, Society of Medical Sciences, Czech Federal Republic, Prague, 1983; Order of Merit, Federal Republic of Germany, 2003; Alan Curry Award, International Association of Forensic Toxicologists, 2004. Memberships: International Association of Forensic Toxicologists; National Antidoping Agency, Germany; Working Group on Science, Antidoping Convention of the European Council; World Antidoping Agency, 2000-06. Address: Dresdner Str 12, D-01731, Kreischa, near Dresden, Germany. E-mail: rkmueller.leipzig@t-online.de

MUIR WOOD David, b. 17 March 1949, Folkestone, Kent, England. Civil Engineer. m. Helen Rosamond Piddington, 2 sons. Education: Royal Grammar School, High Wycombe, 1959-66; BA, 1970, MA, 1974, Peterhouse, Cambridge; PhD, Cambridge University, 1974. Appointments: William Stone Research Fellow, Peterhouse, Cambridge, 1973-75; Royal Society Research Fellow, Norwegian Geotechnical Institute, Oslo, 1975; Fellow, Emmanuel College, Cambridge, 1975-87; University Demonstrator in Soil Mechanics, Cambridge University Engineering Department, 1975-78; Geotechnical Engineer, Scott, Wilson, Kirkpatrick and Partners, Hong Kong, 1978; University Lecturer in Soil Mechanics, Cambridge University Engineering Department, 1978-87; Associate, Geotechnical Consulting Group, 1983-; Visiting Research Associate, University of Colorado, Boulder, USA, 1986; Cormack Professor of Civil Engineering, University of Glasgow, Scotland, 1987-95; Elder, Cairns Church of Scotland, Milngavie, 1993-98; Royal Society Industry Fellow, Babtie Group, 1995-96; Professor of Civil Engineering, University of Bristol, 1995-; Consultant, Babtie Group, Glasgow, 1997-2006; Head, Department of Civil Engineering, University of Bristol, 1997-2002; MTS Visiting Professor of Geomechanics, University of Minnesota, 2000; Foundation for Industrial Science Visiting Professor, Institute for Industrial Science, University of Tokyo, 2003; Dean, Faculty of Engineering, University of Bristol, 2003-07. Publications: 52 papers in journals; 102 papers in academic conferences. Honours: Rex Moir Prize, 1969; Archibald Denny Prize, 1970; British Geotechnical Society Prize, 1978; Fellow, Royal Academy of Engineering, 1998; 20th Bjerrum Lecture, 2005. Memberships: American Society of Civil Engineers; British Geotechnical Society; Remote Sensing and Photogrammetry Society; Society for Earthquake and Civil Engineering

Dynamics; Fellow, Institution of Civil Engineers. Address: Leigh Lodge, Church Road, Abbots Leigh, Bristol BS8 3QP, England. E-mail: d.muir-wood@bristol.ac.uk

MUKHERJEE Tara Kumar, b. 20 December 1923, Calcutta, India. Retired. Education: Scottish Church College; Calcutta University, India. Appointments: Shop Manager, Bata Shoe Company, India, 1941-44; Buyer, Brevitt Schoes, 1951-56; Sundries Buyer, British Shoe Corporation, 1956-66; Production Administrator, Priestly Footwear Ltd, 1966-68; Head Store Manager, British Shoe Corporation, 1968-70; District Manager, 1970-78; Branch Manager, 1978-84; Save and Prosper Group; Area Manager, Guardian Royal Exchange, 1985-88; Managing Director, OWL Financial Services, 1988. Honours: Honorary Doctor of Philosophy, Middlesex University; FLIA; FRSA. Memberships: First Class Cricketer, Ranjy Trophy, Bihar, India; Leicestershire County Cricket Club; Indian National Club; Chairman, European Multicultural Foundation; President, Confederation of Indian Organisations (UK); President, European Union Migrants Forum; Royal Commonwealth Society; European Movement; President, India Film Society. Address: 51 Viking Way, Brentwood, Essex CM15 9HY, England. E-mail: emf@mbebrentwood.co.uk

MULDOON Paul, b. 20 June 1951, Portadown, County Armagh, Northern Ireland. Poet; Writer; Dramatist; Professor in the Humanities. m. Jean Hanff Korelitz, 1987. Education: BA, English Language and Literature, Queen's University, Belfast, 1973. Appointments: Producer, 1973-78, Senior Producer, 1978-85, Radio Arts Programmes, Television Producer, 1985-86, BBC Northern Ireland; Judith E Wilson Visiting Fellow, University of Cambridge, 1986-87; Creative Writing Fellow, University of East Anglia, 1987; Lecturer, Columbia University, 1987-88; Lecturer, 1987-88, 1990-95, Director, Creative Writing Programme, 1993-, Howard G B Clark Professor in the Humanities, 1998-, Princeton University; Professor of Poetry, University of Oxford, 1999-04; Writer-in-Residence, 92nd Street Y, New York City, 1988; Roberta Holloway Lecturer, University of California at Berkeley, 1989; Visiting Professor, University of Massachusetts, Amberst, 1989-90; Bread Loaf School of English, 1997-. Publications: Poetry: Knowing My Place, 1971; New Weather, 1973; Spirit of Dawn, 1975; Mules, 1977; Names and Addresses, 1978; Immram, 1980; Why Brownlee Left, 1980; Out of Siberia, 1982; Quoof, 1983; The Wishbone, 1984; Meeting the British, 1987; Madoc: A Mystery, 1990; Incantata, 1994; The Prince of the Quotidian, 1994; The Annals of Chile, 1994; Kerry Slides, 1996; New Selected Poems, 1968-94, 1996; Hopewell Haiku, 1997; The Bangle (Slight Return), 1998; Hay, 1998; Poems 1968-98, 2001; Moy Sand and Gravel, 2002; Medley for Morin Khur, 2005; Sixty Instant Messages to Tom Moore, 2005; Horse Latitudes, 2006; General Admission, 2006. Theatre: Monkeys (television play), 1989; Shining Brow (opera libretto), 1993; Six Honest Serving Men (play), 1995; Bandanna (opera libretto), 1999. Essays: To Ireland, I, 2000. Translator: The Astrakhan Cloak, by Nuala Ni Dhomhnaill, 1993; The Birds, by Aristophanes (with Richard Martin), 1999. Editor: The Scrake of Dawn, 1979; The Faber Book of Contemporary Irish Poetry, 1986; The Essential Byron, 1989; The Faber Book of Beasts, 1997; All Souls Night, 2000; To Ireland, I, 2000; Oxford Lectures in Poetry, 2006. Children's Books: The O-O's Party, 1981; The Last Thesaurus, 1995; The Noctuary of Narcissus Batt, 1997. Contributions to: Anthologies and other publications. Honours: Eric Gregory Award, 1972; Sir Geoffrey Faber Memorial Awards, 1980, 1991; Guggenheim Fellowship, 1990; T S Eliot Prize for Poetry, 1994; American

Academy of Arts and Letters Award, 1996; Irish Times Poetry Prize, 1997; Pulitzer Prize for Poetry, 2002; Shakespeare Prize, 2004. Memberships: Aosdana; Poetry Society of Great Britain, president, 1996-; Royal Society of Literature, fellow; American Academy of Arts and Sciences, 2000. Address: Creative Writing Programme, Princeton University, Princeton, NJ 08544, USA.

MULINDI-KING Luzili Ruth, b. 21 July 1947, Lusengeli village, Maragoli, Kenya. Music Educator; Choral Director; Ethnomusicologist. m. Roger P King, 2 daughters. Education: Lusengeli, Kaimosi GBS and Alliance Girls High School; GNSM, Northern School of Music, 1972; Cert Ed, Music, Drama, Bretton Hall College, 1973; MA, Social Anthropology, Ethnomusicology, Queen's University, Belfast, 1984; Singing with Mama Rosalina Ellen Ajando Apungu and Delcie Tetsill; Piano with Julia Moss and Margaret Gifford; Choral Training with Graham Hyslop and Maggie Burton-Page; Ethnomusicology with Professors John Blacking and John Baily. Appointments: Head of Music, AGHS, Kenya, 1973-77; Lecturer, Music Department, Kenyatta University, Nairobi, 1977-91; Head of Music, Lucton School, 1993-2004; School Music, Singing, Piano, St Richard's School, Bredenbury, England, 1999-; Visiting Lecturer, Goshen College, Indiana, USA, also Manchester University, UK; One of two directors of Norwegian Girls' Choir at Sophie Prize Ceremony honouring environmentalist Professor Wangari Mathai, 2004. Publications: Editor, Music Time, 1991; Music in Logoli Culture, 1998; After the Bomb (in The Friend), 1999; Song: Chunga Maji Yasipungue, 1986; Report: Towards an Inclusive Singing Culture, 2004; British Council Scholarship for Postgraduate study at QUB; CD: Music Safari, 2004. Honour: First African Kenyan to win the KMF Leonard Machin Cup for the Bach Class (Prelude and Fugue), Best KMF Choral Director, 1976; Herefordshire Choir of the Year, 1999; Winston Churchill Fellow, 2002. Memberships: Incorporated Society of Musicians; Association of British Choral Directors; National Association of Music Educators; Kenya Music Trust. Address: Brick Cottage, Yarpole, Leominster, Herefordshire, HR6 0BA, England.

MÜLLER Kurt Bernd, b. 3 September 1943, Blens/Eifel, Germany. Professor of American Literature. m. Rosa Gomez Cagigal, 1 son, 1 daughter. Education: State Exam, English and German Philology, University of Cologne, Germany, 1970; PhD, 1976, Habilitation, 1988, University of Freiburg, Germany. Appointments: Academic Councillor, University of Freiburg, Germany, 1979-90; Deputy Professor, University of Trier, Germany, 1990-92; Professor and Chair of American Studies, University of Jena, Germany, 1992-. Publications: Books: Konventionen und Tendenzen der Gesellschaftskritik im expressionistischen amerikanischen Drama der zwanziger Jahre, 1977; Identität und Rolle bei Theodore Dreiser: Eine Untersuchung des Romanwerks unter rollentheoretischem Aspekt, 1991; Inszenierte Wirklichkeiten: Die Erfahrung der Moderne im Leben und Werk Eugene O'Neills, 1993; Ernest Hemingway: Der Mensch, der Schriftsteller, das Werk, 1999; Das amerikanische Drama, 2006. Managing Editor, Literaturwissenschaftliches Jahrbuch; Numerous articles as author and co-author in professional journals. Memberships: Deutscher Anglistenverband; Deutsche Gesellschaft für Amerikastudien; Gesellschaft für Kanadastudien; Görres-Gesellschaft zur Pflege der Wissenschaften. Address: Ernst-Abbe-Platz 8, D-07743 Jena, Germany. E-mail: kurt.mueller@uni-jena.de

MUN Cheol, b. 7 January 1970, Mokpo, Cheonranam-do, Republic of Korea. Assistant Professor. m. Min-Gyeong Kang, 1 son, 1 daughter. Education: BS, Electronic Engineering, Yonsei University, Seoul, Republic of Korea; MS, Electronic Engineering, PhD, Electrical & Electronic Engineering, Yonsei Graduate School, Seoul. Appointments: Engineer, Telecommunication and System Division, Samsung Electronics, Suwon, Republic of Korea, 2001-02; Assistant Professor, Department of Electronic Communication Engineering, Chungju National University, 2002-; Committeeman, Korea ITU-R Study Group 9, 2003; Technical Reviewer, IEEE Communication Society and IEEE Vehicular Technology, 2003-. Publications: 45 technical papers including: Transmit antenna selection for spatial multiplexing with ordered successive interference cancellation, 2006. Honours: Award for Excellence in academic research, Yonsei Graduate School, 2000; listed in numerous Who's Who editions. Memberships: IEEE Communication Society. Address: Department of Electronic Communication Engineering, Chungju National University, Chungju, Republic of Korea 380-702. E-mail: chmun@cju.ac.kr

MUNDA Ivka Maria, b. 7 July 1927, Ljubljana, Slovenia. Scientific Official. Education: Diploma, Biology, Chemistry; PhD, Marine Biology, University of Ljubljana, 1963; PhD, Marine Botany, University of Gothenbourg, Sweden, 1963. Appointments: Assistant, Biological Institute, Medical Faculty, University of Ljubljana; National Research Association, Technical University of Trondheim; Water Research Institute, Oslo; Yearly Grants, Icelandic Research Foundation, Reykjavík, Iceland, for Algological Research, 1963-80; Scientific Official, Hydrobiologish Instituute, Yerseke, Holland, 1964-65; Scientific Official, Biological Institute, Centre for Scientific Research of the Slovene Academy of Science and Arts, 1966-2006; Grants from the Alexander von Humboldt Foundation, Bonn, Germany, 1975-76, for work at the Biologische Anstalt Helgoland, Germany. Scientific Official collaborating on international projects (eg INTERREG), Germany and Italy; Participated at 35 international congresses on phycology and marine biology. Publications: 125 scientific papers, marine algal ecology, geographic distribution and biochemistry, international journals. Honours: Slovene Award, Boris Kidrič; 20th Century Achievement Award, International Biographical Centre; New Century Award, The Europe 500; 1000 Leaders of World Influence; Leading Intellectuals of the World, 2000-2001; Presidential Award, 500 Great Minds; Order of International Ambassadors; American Medal of Honour, Profiles of Excellence. Memberships: British Phycological Society; Phycological Society of America; International Phycological Society; COST; CIESM; Deutsche Botanische Geselschaft; The New York Academy of Sciences; Board of Governors, American Biographical Institute; Research Board of Advisors, ABI; The Planetary Society; Deputy Director General, Biographical Centre, Cambridge; Secretary General, United Cultural Convention, USA; Scientific Advisor to the Director General, IBC; The BWW Society, USA. Address: Centre for Scientific Research, Slovene Academy of Science and Arts, Novi trg 2, 1000 Ljubljana, Slovenia.

MUNKHAMMAR Johnny Mattias, b. 24 September 1974, Hultsfred, Småland, Sweden. Policy Director. Education: Master of Social Science, Uppsala University, 1998. Appointments: Sergeant, Royal Swedish Navy (Military Service), 1993-95; Expert in Economic Policy, Federation of Swedish Industry, Brussels, Belgium, 1998-99; Senior Advisor and Partner, Guller Group Consultancy, Stockholm, Sweden, 1999-2001; Senior Policy Advisor, Confederation of Swedish Enterprise, Stockholm, Sweden, 2002-05; Policy Director, Timbro, 2005-. Publications: European Dawn, Beyond the European Social Model; Index of Economic Freedom (chapter), 2007; Columnist in daily journals and magazines; Author of several papers, books and other studies. Memberships: Member, Society of Economists and the Center for Business and Policy Studies. Address: Timbro, Grev Turegatan 19, Box 5234, SE-102 45, Stockholm, Sweden. E-mail: johnny@munkhammar.org Website: www.munkhammar.org

MUNN Bob (Robert William), b. 16 January 1945, Bath, Somerset, England. Academic. m. Patricia Lorna Moyle, 1 son, 1 daughter. Education: BSc, Chemistry, 1965, PhD, Theoretical Chemistry, 1968, Bristol University; DSc, Manchester University, 1982. Appointments: Postdoctorate Fellow, National Research Council of Canada, 1968-70; ICI Postdoctoral Fellow, Edinburgh University, 1970-71; Lecturer in Chemistry, 1971-80, Reader in Chemistry, 1980-84, Professor of Chemical Physics, 1984-2004, Vice Principal for Finance, 1987-90, Dean, 1994-99, UMIST; Visiting Fellow, Australian National University, 1982; Vice President for Teaching and Learning, The University of Manchester, 2004-07. Publications: Over 200 research-based publications; 2 co-authored books; 2 co-edited books. Memberships: Fellow, Royal Society of Chemistry; Chartered Chemist; Fellow, Institute of Physics; Chartered Physicist; Fellow, Higher Education Academy; Chartered Scientist. Address: The University of Manchester, Manchester M13 9PL, England. E-mail: bob.munn@manchester.ac.uk

MUNRO Alice, b. 10 July 1931, Wingham, Ontario, Canada. Author. m. (1) James Armstrong Munro, 29 December 1951, divorced 1976, 3 daughters, (2) Gerald Fremlin, 1976. Education: BA, University of Western Ontario, 1952. Publications: Dance of the Happy Shades, 1968; A Place for Everything, 1970; Lives of Girls and Women, 1971; Something I've Been Meaning to Tell You, 1974; Who Do You Think You Are?, 1978, US and British editions as The Beggar Maid: Stories of Flo and Rose, 1984; The Moons of Jupiter, 1982; The Progress of Love, 1986; Friend of My Youth, 1990; Open Secrets, 1994; Selected Stories, 1996; The Love of a Good Woman, 1998; Hateship, Friendship, Courtship, Loveship, Marriage, 2001; Runaway (short stories), 2004; The View from Castle Rock, 2006. Honours: Governor-General's Awards for Fiction, 1968, 1978, 1986; Guardian Booksellers Award, 1971; Honorary DLitt, University of Western Ontario, 1976; Marian Engel Award, 1986; Canada-Australia Literary Prize, 1994; Lannan Literary Award, 1995; W H Smith Literary Award, 1996; National Book Critics Circle Award, 1998; Giller Prize, 1999; O Henry Award, 2001. Address: The Writers Shop, 101 5th Avenue, New York, NY 10003, USA.

MURAKAMI Jun, b. 9 March 1975, Hyogo Prefecture, Japan. Assistant Professor. Education: DDS, Okayama University Dental School, 1999; PhD, Graduate School of Medicine & Dentistry, Okayama University, 2002. Appointments: Assistant Professor, Department of Oral & Maxillofacial Radiology, Graduate School of Medicine & Dentistry, Okayama University, Japan, 2003-. Publications: 16 articles in professional journals. Honours: Japan Scholarship Foundation Scholarship for Post Graduate School Student, 1999-2002; Grant in Aid for Research Assistant, 2001-02; Listed in international biographical dictionaries. Memberships: Founding Fellow, International Academy of Oral Oncology, 2005. Address: Department of Oral &

Maxillofacial Radiology, Graduate School of Medicine & Dentistry, Okayama University, 2-5-1 Shikata-cho, Okayama, Japan. E-mail: jun-m@md.okayama-u.ac.jp

MURCHISON Duncan George, Consultant. Education: BSc Honours, Geology, University of Durham, 1952; PhD, University of Durham, 1957. Appointments: Geologist, Royal Dutch Shell, 1957-58; Research Associate, 1958-60, Lecturer, 1960-64, University of Durham; Lecturer, 1964-68, Senior Lecturer, 1968-71, Reader in Geochemistry, 1971-76, Professor of Organic Petrology, 1976-93, Dean of the Faculty of Science, 1980-83, Head of the Department of Geology, 1982-86, Pro-Vice-Chancellor, 1986-90, Acting Vice-Chancellor, 1991, Pro-Vice-Chancellor, 1992-93, Chairman of numerous university committees, University of Newcastle. Publications: Author and Co-author, books and articles (geology, organic petrology, organic geochemistry) in professional scientific journals. Honours: Fellowship, Royal Society of Edinburgh, 1973; Honorary Fellow, Royal Microscopical Society, 1979; Thiessen Medal of the International Committee for Coal Petrology, 1987; Honorary Fellow, International Committee for Coal Petrology, 1994; Honorary Lifetime Member, Society for Organic Petrology, 2002. Memberships: Royal Society of Edinburgh; Geological Society of London, Vice-President, 1995-97, Treasurer, 2000-06; Royal Microscopical Society, President, 1976-78; International Committee for Coal Petrology, President, 1979-83; Edinburgh Geological Society; Yorkshire Geological Society. Address: School of Civil Engineering and Geosciences, Drummond Building, University of Newcastle, NE1 7RU, England. E-mail: duncan@dmurchison.freeserve.co.uk

MURDOCH Keith Rupert, b. 11 March 1931, Melbourne, Australia (American citizen, 1985-). Publishing and Broadcasting Executive. m. (1) Patricia Booker, divorced, 1 daughter, (2) Anna Maria Torv, 28 April 1967, divorced, 2 sons, 1 daughter, (3) Wendy Deng, 1999, 2 daughters. Education: MA, Oxon, Worcester College, Oxford, England, 1953. Appointments: Chief Executive Officer, 1979-, Chairman, 1991-, News Corporation; Owner, numerous newspapers, magazines and TV operations in UK, US, Italy, Asia and Australia. Honours: AC, 1984; Commander of the White Rose, First Class, 1986; Knight of St Gregory the Great, 1998. Address: News Corporation, 1211 Avenue of the Americas, New York, NY 10036, USA.

MURDOCH Lachlan Keith, b. 8 September 1971, Australia (American citizen). Business Executive. m. Sarah O'Hare, 1999. Education: Princeton University. Appointments: Reporter, San Antonio Express News, The Times (UK); Sub-Editor, The Sun (UK); General Manager, Queensland Newspapers Pty Ltd, 1994-95; Executive Director, News Ltd, 1995; Director, Beijing PDN Xinren Information Technology Co Ltd, 1995-; Deputy Chair, Star Television, 1995-; Deputy Chief Executive, News Ltd, 1995-96; Director, The Herald & Weekly Times Ltd, 1996-, News Corporation, 1996-, Deputy COO, 2000-, Independent Newspapers Ltd (NZ), 1997-; Executive Chair, Chief Executive Officer, News Ltd, 1997; Senior Executive Vice-President, US Print Operations News Corporation, 1999-2005; Publisher, NY Post newspaper, 2002-. Address: New York Post, 1211 Avenue of the Americas, New York, NY 10036-8790, USA. Website: www.nypost.com

MURÍN Gustáv, b. 9 April 1959, Bratislava, Slovakia. Author. m. Jana, 2 daughters. Education: BSc, 1983, MSc, 1984, PhD, 1991, Comenius University, Bratislava. Publications: Author: 17 books (including 5 in Czech, 1 in Hindi and 1 French translation): Novel, novella, 2 collections of stories, collection of sci-fi stories, 7 collections of essays, extensive essay study, 2 encyclopaedias of sex, 2 collections of travel stories; Collection of stories in electronic form, Net-Book-Club, Denmark, 1997; Selection of translated texts, Gustáv Murín in Translation, PEEM, Bratislava, 2004; Co-author, 12 different story or essay collections in Slovakia and 8 abroad (4 in Czech Republic, Ukraine, Romania, Cyprus and USA); Author, 12 radio-dramas, TV documents, TV play and script for art movie; Author of more than 1,000 articles in 39 major Slovak, Czech and international newspapers and magazines; Numerous translations. Honours: Best Slovak story, 1979; Best Czech and Slovak story, 1981; Best Czech and Slovak novella, 1986; Special prize in Slovak radio drama, 1988; Honorary Fellow in Writing, University of Iowa, 1995; E E Kisch Award, 2003; Active participation in international literary conferences. Memberships: Member, 1993-, Secretary, 1995-97, President, 2000-04, Slovak Centre of the PEN International; Member, Slovak Centre of Roma Club, 1994-; Member, Slovak Syndicate of Journalists, 1995-. Address: J Hagaru 17, 831 51 Bratislava, Slovak Republic. E-mail: gmurin@fns.uniba.sk

MURPHY Eddie (Edward Regan), b. 3 April 1951, Brooklyn, New York, USA. Film Actor. m. (2) Nicole Mitchell, divorced, 5 children. Creative Works: Films include: 48 Hours, 1982; Trading Places, Delirious, 1983; Best Defence, Beverly Hills Cop, 1984; The Golden Child, 1986; Beverly Hills Cop II, Eddie Murphy Raw, 1987; Coming to America, 1988; Harlem Nights, 1989; 48 Hours 2, 1990; Boomerang, Distinguished Gentleman, 1992; Beverly Hills Cop III, 1994; The Nutty Professor, 1996; Dr Dolittle, Holy Man, Life, 1998; Bowfinger, Toddlers, Pluto Nash, 1999; Nutty Professor II: The Klumps; Dr Dolittle 2, 2001; Showtime, 2002; I-Spy, Daddy Day Care, The Haunted Mansion, Shrek 4-D (voice), 2003; Shrek 2 (voice), Far Far Away Idol (voice), 2004; Dreamgirls, 2006; Norbit, Shrek 3 (voice), 2007; Starship Dave, 2008. Tours with own comedy show; Comedy Albums: Eddie Murphy, 1982; Eddie Murphy: Comedian, 1983; How Could It Be, 1984; So Happy, 1989; Recorded 7 albums of comedy and songs. Honours include: Numerous awards and nominations. Address: c/o Jim Wiatt, ICM, 8942 Wilshire Boulevard, Beverly Hills, CA 90211, USA.

MURPHY Michael, b. 2 May 1951. Consultant Haematologist. m. (Elizabeth) Sarah Green, 1 son, 1 daughter. Education: Medical School, St Bartholomew's Hospital Medical College, London, 1968-73. Appointments: Research Registrar, Haematology, 1978; Registrar, Haematology, Senior Registrar, Haematology, 1980-84, Senior Lecturer, Honorary Consultant, Haematology, 1985-96, St Bartholomew's Hospital London; Consultant Haematologist, National Blood Service and Department of Haematology, Oxford Radcliffe Hospitals NHS Trust, Oxford, 1996-; Senior Clinical Lecturer in Blood Transfusion, 1998-2004, Professor of Blood Transfusion Medicine, 2004-, University of Oxford; Secretary, Chief Medical Officer's National Blood Transfusion Committee, Department of Health, 2001-; Member, Scientific Committee, 1999-, Co-Chair, Transfusion Safety Group, 2001-, Biomedical Excellence for Safer Transfusion Collaborative; Chair, Royal College of Pathologists Transfusion Medicine Subcommittee, 2006-; Member, Royal College of Pathologists Council, 2006-. Publications: Over 70 articles as first author and co-author in medical journals; Over 30 book chapters and reviews; Book: Practical Transfusion Medicine (co-editor), 2001, 2nd edition, 2005. Honours: Kenneth Goldsmith Award, British Blood Transfusion Society, 1994; Thames Valley Health Care Awards, 2004; Winner, Working Smarter category for Barcode technology for safer transfusion; Numerous research grants.

Memberships include: British Society for Haematology; Royal College of Physicians; American Association of Blood Banks; International Society of Blood Transfusion; Royal College of Pathologists. Address: National Blood Service, John Radcliffe Hospital, Oxford OX3 9BQ, England. E-mail: mike.murphy@nbs.nhs.uk

MURPHY Rt Hon Paul, b. 25 November 1948, Usk, Gwent, Wales. Secretary of State for Wales. Member of Parliament for Torfaen. Education: St Francis RC School, Abersychan; West Monmouth School, Pontypool; Oriel College, Oxford. Appointments: Management Trainee, CWS ; Lecturer in Government and History, Ebbw Vale College of Further Education (now Coleg Gwent); Member, Torfaen Borough Council, 1973-87; Member of Parliament for Torfaen, 1987-; Shadow Spokesman on Welsh Affairs, 1988-94, Northern Ireland, 1994-95, Foreign Affairs, 1995, and Defence, 1995-97; Minister of State for Northern Ireland, 1997-99; Appointed to Privy Council, 1999; Secretary of State for Northern Ireland, 2002-05; Chair of the Intelligence and Security Committee, 2005; British Chair of the British-Irish Inter-Parliamentary Body; Executive Committee member, British-American Parliamentary Group; Secretary of State for Wales, 1999-2002, 2008-. Honours: Knight Commander of Merit with Star of the Sacred Military Constantinian Order of St George; Honorary Fellow, Oriel College, 2000; Visiting Parliamentary Fellow, St Anthony's College, Oxford.

MURRAY Andrew (Andy), b. 15 May 1987, Dunblane, Scotland. Tennis Player. Career: Started playing tennis aged 3 years; Won Orange Bowl, Florida aged 12 years; Won U S Open Tennis Boys' Title, 2004; Turned professional aged 18 years; Won doubles with David Sherwood for Great Britain's Davis Cup team against Israel, 2005; Reached semi-finals of the Boys' tournament at the French Open, 2005; Reached the third round of the Stella Artois tournament, 2005; Reached the third round of Wimbledon, 2005; Beat Tim Henman at the Swiss Indoors in Basel, 2005; Won the SAP Open tournament, 2006; Took over from Tim Henman as British number one, 2006; World Ranking 11, 2007. Honours: BBC Young Sports Personality of the Year, 2005. Website: www.murraysworld.com

MURRAY Bill, b. 21 September 1950, Evanston, Illinois, USA. Actor; Writer. m. (1) Margaret Kelly, 1980, divorced, 2 son; (2) Jennifer Butler, 1997, 4 children. Education: Loyola Academy; Regis College, Denver; Second City Workshop, Chicago. Appointments: Performer, Off-Broadway National Lampoon Radio Hour; Regular Appearances TV Series Saturday Night Live; Appeared in Radio Series Marvel Comics' Fantastic Four; Co-Producer, Director, Actor, Quick Change, 1990; Writer, NBC-TV Series Saturday Night Live, 1977-80; Films: Meatballs, 1977; Mr Mike's Mondo Video, 1979; Where the Buffalo Roam, Caddyshack, 1980; Stripes, 1981; Tootsie, 1982; Ghostbusters, The Razor's Edge, Nothing Lasts Forever, 1984; Little Shop of Horrors, 1986; Scrooged, 1988; Ghostbusters II, 1989; Quick Change, 1990; What About Bob?, 1991; Mad Dog and Glory, Groundhog Day, 1993; Ed Wood, 1994; Kingpin, Larger Than Life, Space Jam, 1996; The Man Who Knew Too Little, 1997; With Friends Like These, Veeck as in Wreck, Rushmore, 1998; Wild Things, 1998; The Cradle Will Rock, Hamlet, Company Man, 1999; Charlie's Angels, 2000; The Royal Tenenbaums, Osmosis Jones, 2001; Lost in Translation, Coffee and Cigarettes, 2003; Garfield: The Movie (voice), The Life Aquatic with Steve Zissou, 2004; Broken Flowers, The Lost City, 2005; Garfield: A Tail of Two Kitties, (voice), 2006; The Darjeeling Limited, 2007. Honours include: Emmy Award, Best Writing for

Comedy Series, 1977; BAFTA Award for Best Actor, 2004. Address: c/o William Carroll Agency, 139 N San Fernando Road, Suite A, Burbank, CA 91502, USA.

MURRAY Noreen Elizabeth, b. 26 February 1935, Read, Nr Burnley, Lancashire, England. Scientist; University Teacher. m. Kenneth Murray. Education: BSc, Botany, King's College, London, 1953-56; PhD, Microbial Genetics, University of Birmingham, 1956-59. Appointments: Research Associate, Department of Biological Sciences, Stanford University, 1960-64; Research Fellow, Botany School, Cambridge, 1964-67; Member, MRC Molecular Genetics Unit, 1968-74, Lecturer, 1974-80, Department of Molecular Biology, University of Edinburgh; Group Leader, European Molecular Biology Laboratory, Heidelberg, Germany, 1980-82; Reader, Department of Molecular Biology, 1982-88, Professor of Molecular Genetics (Personal Chair), 1988-2001, Professor Emeritus 2002-, University of Edinburgh. Publications: Numerous publications in scientific journals, including early papers in the field of genetic engineering. Honours: Member, European Molecular Biology Organisation, 1980; Fellow Royal Society, 1982; Fellow Royal Society of Edinburgh, 1989; Member, Academica Europaea, 1989; Royal Society Gabor Medal, 1989; Society of General Microbiology Fred Griffiths Lecturer, 2001; CBE for services to science, 2002; AstraZeneca Award, The Biochemical Society, 2005; Honorary DSc, UMIST, Birmingham and Warwick; Fellow, King's College London. Memberships: Genetics Societies of UK and USA; UK Societies of Biochemistry and General Microbiology; President, Genetics Society of UK, 1987-90; Trustee, The Darwin Trust of Edinburgh, 1990-; Member of Board, International Genetics Federation, 1998-2002; Council Member of BBSRC, 1994-98; Council Member, The Royal Society, 1992-93, 2002-2004; Royal Commission of the Exhibition of 1851, Science Scholarship Committee, 2002-; Honours Committee for Science and Technology, 2005-; Member of the Athenaeum Club, 2001. Address: Institute of Cell Biology, University of Edinburgh, Darwin Building, King's Buildings, Mayfield Road, Edinburgh, EH9 3RJ, Scotland. E-mail: noreen.murray@ed.ac.uk

MURRAY Thomas Kenneth, b. 25 June 1958, Edinburgh, Scotland. m. Sophie Mackenzie, 3 daughters. Education: Sedbergh School; LLB, Dundee University. Appointments: Partner, Gillespie Macandrew WS, Solicitors, 1983-; Law Clerk, Incorporation of Goldsmiths of the City of Edinburgh, 1988-; Chairman, Trefoil House, 2001-; Purse Bearer to Lord High Commissioner of The Church of Scotland, 2003-; Member, 1994-, Chairman, 2004-, British Hallmarking Council; Director, Ludus Baroque orchestra; Director, Silver of the Stars charity. Memberships: Law Society Practicing Certificate Committee; Law Society Investor Protection Committee; Member of The Queens Bodyguard for Scotland; The Royal Company of Archers. Address: 26 Gayfield Square, Edinburgh, EH1 3PA, Scotland.

MURRAY-LYON Iain Malcolm, b. 28 August 1940, Edinburgh, Scotland. Consultant Physician. m. Teresa, 1 son, 1 daughter. Education: University of Edinburgh, 1958-64. Appointments: Consultant Physician and Gastroenterologist, Charing Cross Hospital and Chelsea and Westminster Hospital, London, 1974-2002; Honorary Consultant Physician and Gastoenterologist, Chelsea and Westminster Hospital, 2002-; Honorary Senior Lecturer in Medicine, Imperial College School of Medicine, 1993-. Publications: More than 200 articles on topics in gastroenterology and liver disease and the medical effects of chewing Khat (Qat) leaves. Honours: BSc (Hons), 1962; MB ChB, 1964; MD, 1973; FRCP, 1980;

FRCPE, 1980; International Fellowship, National Institute of Health (NIH), USA, 1971-72. Memberships: British Society of Gastroenterology; British Association for the Study of the Liver; European Association for the Study of the Liver; International Association for the Study of the Liver; Brooks's; Hurlingham Club. Address: 149 Harley Street, London W1G 6DE, England.

MURSELL (Alfred) Gordon, b. 4 May 1949, Guildford, England. Priest in Church of England. m. Anne. Education: Pontifical Institute of Sacred Music, Rome, 1966-67; Brasenose College, Oxford, 1967-71; Cuddesdon College, Oxford, 1971-73; BA, History; BA, Theology; ARCM, Organ Performance; BD, Theology. Appointments: Curate, Walton, Liverpool, 1973-77; Vicar, St John's East Dulwich, London, 1977-86; Tutor, Salisbury-Wells Theological College, Salisbury, 1986-91; Team Rector, Stafford, 1991-99; Provost, 1999-2002, Dean, 2002-2005, Birmingham Cathedral. Publications: The Theology of Carthusian Life, 1989; Out of the Deep: Prayer as Protest, 1989; The Wisdom of the Anglo-Saxons, 1997; The Story of Christian Spirituality (editor), 2001; English Spirituality (2 volumes), 2001. Address: 103a Selly Park Road, Birmingham, B29 7LH, England. E-mail: gordonmursell@beeb.net

MURTON John Evan, b.18 March 1972, UK. Diplomat. m. Sarah, 2 sons, 1 daughter. Education: BA, MA, Geography, Cambridge University, 1991-1994; PhD, Cambridge University, 1997. Appointments: British Embassy, Tokyo, 2000-04; Deputy Director, Secretary General's Private Office, NATO, 2004-07; British High Commissioner, Mauritius, and British Ambassador, Madagascar & Comoros, 2007-. Publications: PhD Thesis, Coping With More People, 1994.

MURZA Vitalij Petrovich, b. 1 January, 1929, Serdegivka, Shpolyanskij, Cherkaskay, Ukraine. Professor, Doctor. 1 daughter. Education: The Chercaskij State Medical Institute, 1953. Appointments: Chief, Kyiv Scientific Research Institute of Medical Problems in Physical Culture; Chair, Medical Culture and Sport Medicine, Kyiv Medical University, AA Bogomoletz Institute of Physiology, Kiev; Chair, Rehabilitation, Open International University for Human Development, Ukraine. Publications: Psychically-physical rehabilitation, 2005; The Sport Medicine, 2006; Articles include 350 research works. Honours: The Order of the Red Flag; High Quality of Health Protection; High Quality of Peoples Education; other medals. Memberships: Member of the Ukrainian Academy of Science; Member of the Academy of Untraditional Methods of Treatment. Address: 1-2 (9) Horiva St. 04071 Kiev, Ukraine

MUSETEANU Crisan, b. 17 December 1947, Bucharest, Romania. Archaeologist. m. Liliana, 1 daughter. Education: Archaeology Department, Faculty of History, Bucharest University, 1970; PhD, History, Archaeological Institute, Vasile Parvan, Bucharest, 1993. Appointments: Member, Organisation Committee, Rei Cretarie Congress, Timisoara, 1994; General Manager, Romanian National History Museum, 1997-; Member, National Commission for Museums and Collections, 1999-2000; Vice President, Archaeological National Commission, 1999-. Publications: Lampes Romanes de Durostorum, 1983; Roman Pottery Workshops, 2003; The Antique Bronzes Typology, Chronology, Authenticity the Acta, 2004. Honours: The Radu Florescu Award and The Emil Condurachi Award, Ministry of Culture. Memberships: National Commission for Museums and Collections.

MUSHA Takaaki, b. 17 September 1951, Toumi-shi, Nagano-ken, Japan. Government Official. m. Yumiko Suzuki, 1 son, 1 daughter. Education: BE, 1974, ME, 1977, Shinshu University; PhD, Mechanical Engineering, 1994. Appointments: Technical Officer, Japan Maritime Self Defense Force, 1977-89; Researcher, Acoustics Laboratory, ONO SOKKI Co Ltd, 1989-94; Research Engineer, 5th Research Center, Technical Research & Development Institute, Defense Agency of Japan, 1995-2006; Deputy Director, Department of Naval Systems Development, TRDI, Ministry of Defense, Japan, 2006-. Publications: Speculations in Science and Technology, 1998; Journal of Theoretics, 2000, 2001, 2002, 2004; Infinite Energy, 2004, 2006; International Journal of Simulation and Process Modeling, 2006; Physics Essays, 1994, 2005; Applied Acoustics, 1993, 1999, 2004, 2005. Honours: Best Paper Award, Marine Acoustics Society of Japan, 2000 and 2003. Memberships: IEEE Ocean Engineering Society; Japan Society of Mechanical Engineers; Marine Acoustics Society of Japan. Address: 3-11-7-601, Namiki, Kanazawa-ku, Yokohama 236-0005, Japan. E-mail: takaaki.musha@gmail.com

MUSIL Robert Kirkland, b. 27 October 1943, New York, USA. Professor. m. Caryn McTighe, 2 daughters. Education: BA, Yale University, 1964; MA, 1966, PhD, 1970, Northwestern University; MPH, Johns Hopkins University, 2001. Appointments: Executive Director, The Professionals' Coalition for Nuclear Arms Control, 1988-92; Executive Director and CEO, Physician for Social Responsibility, 1992-2006; Scholar in Residence, American University, School of International Service, Program in Global Environmental Politics, 2006-; Visiting Scholar, Churches' Center for Theology and Public Policy, Wesley Theological Seminary, 2007-. Publications: Hope for a Heated Planet: How Americans are Fighting Global Warming and for the Future, 2008. Memberships: Board of Directors, Population Connection; Board of Directors, The Council for a Livable World; President, The Scoville Peace Fellowships; Chairman of the Board, 20/20 Vision. Honours: The Armstrong Award for Excellence in Radio Broadcasting, 1985, 1986; Visiting Fellow, The London School of Hygiene & Tropical Medicine, 2001; Visiting Fellow, Pembroke College, Cambridge University, 2001. Address: 8600 Irvington Avenue, Bethesda, MD 20817, USA. E-mail: bmusil1@yahoo.com

MUSIL Rudolf, b. 5 May 1926, Brno, Czech Republic. Emeritus University Professor. m. Ing Liba Kochová, 26 July 1952, 2 sons. Education: RNDr, 1952, CSc, 1960, Habil, 1966, DSc, 1968, Full Professor, 1980, Education, Masaryk University, Charles University. Appointments: Full Professor, Institute of Geological Sciences, Faculty of Science, Masaryk University, Brno. Publications: Personalities of the Faculty of Science, 1997; Climatic Comparison of Terrestrial and Marine Sediments, 1997; Ende des Pliozäns und Unteres bis Mittleres Pleistozän, 1997; Hunting game analysis, 2000; Domestication of wolves in Central European Magdalenien sites, 2000; The environment in Moravia during the stage OIS 3, 2000; Hunting in Central Europe at the End of the Last Glacial, 2003; The Middle and Upper Palaeolithic Game Suite in Central and Southeastern Europe, 2000; Domestication of wolves in Central European Magdalenien sites, 2005; Animal prey in Pavlov I Southeast. A window into the Gravettian Lifestyles; Die Barenpopulation von Bilzingsleben – eine neue mittelpleistozane, 2005-2006; Environmental changes spanning the Early-Middle Pleistocene transition, 2005. Honours: Silver Medal, National Museum, 1968; Silver Medal, Humboldt Universität, Berlin; Medal, Moravian Museum, 1968; Medal, Slaskie University, Poland, 1983; Medal,

Velkopolskie Towarzystwo, 1983; Silver Medal, Academy, 1986; Gold Medal, Masaryk University, 1997; Medal, Faculty of Science, Komensky University, Slovakia, 2006. Memberships: Czech Society of Geology and Mineralogy; Czech Society of Speleology; National Committee INQUA; International Commission on History of Geological Sciences. Address: Kotlárska Str 2, 61137 Brno, Czech Republic. E-mail: rudolf@sci.muni.cz

MUSKER Alison Awdry Chalmers, b. 9 September 1938, Southampton, England. Watercolour Painter. m. Roger, 1 son, 2 daughters. Education: Sherborne School for Girls; SRN, The Middlesex Hospital, London; Studied under Jacqueline Groag and Edward Wesson, Ecole des Arts, Paris, 1956, and under Leslie Orriss, Reading College of Art, 1968. Career: Solo exhibitions: Brotherton Gallery, Walton Street, London, 1981; King Street Gallery, St James's, London, 1983, 1985; The Royal Geographical Society, London, 1986, Richmond Gallery, Cork Street, London, Italy and Albania, 1990; Watercolour auctioned for Red Cross Appeal for the Gulf War, Pennant Melangell Church, Wales for CADW, 1991; Richmond Gallery, Cork St WI, Save Britain's Heritage, 1992; Numerous group exhibitions include: Royal Institute of Painters in Watercolours, 1958, 1977-91; Singer and Friedlander Exhibition, Mall Galleries, 1998, 1999, 2000; Royal Academy, 1999, 2002, 2003, 2005, 2006; New English Art Club, Mall Galleries, 1993-98, 2003, 2004, 2005; The Small Paintings Group, Century Gallery, 2003; W H Patterson and Select Seven Exhibition, 1995-2007; Work in collections including: John Julius Norwich, Lady Dashwood, Barry Munn, Martin Vandersteen, HRH The Prince of Wales; Peter Boizot Collection, The late Queen Mother, The late Shah of Persia, The Landmark Trust, 1994: Charity work includes: Guest Lecturer for National Trust, 1993; Wardour Chapel Appeal, Christies, London, 1994; British Red Cross Society, 1994, 1995; Friends of the City Churches, London, 1995; APA, Mall Galleries, London, 1995; Music in Country Churches, 1996-2007; Painswick House, Rococco Garden Exhibition, 1998; Watercolour donated to North Hampshire Hospital, 2002; Paintings given to Koestler Award Trust, 2002. Publications: Works mentioned in numerous articles and reference works; The Artist's Manual, 1995; Light and Colour Techniques in Watercolour, 1998; Travellers' Survival Kit – Indian drawings, 1997; Creative Watercolour Techniques, 1998; The Enchanted River, 200 Years of the RWS by Simon Fenwick, 2004; The Watercolour Expert by Royal Watercolour Society, Cassell, 2004; Watercolour Masters – Then and Now, by Royal Watercolour Society, 2006; The Dictionary of Artists in Britain since 1945 – David Buckman, 2005; Who's Who in Art, 30th edition, 2002, 32nd edition, 2006; Watercolour Masters: Then & Now, 2006; Cassell. Honours: Agnes Reeve Memorial Prize, 1989, 1991; Award, International Watercolour Biennale, Mexico, 2000; The William-Powlett Prize, 2001; Listed in international biographical dictionaries. Memberships: Chelsea Art Society, 1980; The Small Paintings Group, 2000; Associate Member of RWS, 2000, Full member, Royal Watercolour Society, 2003. Address: Rose Cottage, Beech Hill, Reading, Berkshire RG7 2AZ, England.

MUSSON Cecile Norma, b. 13 August 1914, Bermuda. Educator. m. James A C Smith, 1955. Education: Graduate, Ontario Business College, Canada, 1946; Certificates: American International College, University of Maryland and Queens University, 1955, Cambridge University, 1932, 1956, Bermuda College, 1972. Appointments: Brownie Leader, 1935; News Editor, Recorder, 1941; RCAF, 1946-47; Freelance, Staff, Parliamentary Reporter, 1947; Founder, Head, Commercial School, 1947; Social Welfare Board,

1965; Arts Council, Juveniles Court, 1969; Now serving Family Court, Updating. Publications: Zephyrs, A Collection of Poetic Thoughts, 1937, reprint in 1942 with donation to RAF War Fund, High Critical Praise from Mid-Ocean News. Contributions to: World's Fair Anthology of Verse, 1940; South and West International, 1942; Poem on BBC, 1961; Rome, Date With The Past, Enjoyment of Poetry, 1965; Poetic Voices of America, 1994. Honours: Honorary Representative, CSSI Leonardo da Vinci, 1963; Honorary Medal, Merit Diploma, 1965; International Great Glory Prize, Rome, 1982; FAME Arts Award, 1983; Government Appreciation, 1989; International Order of Merit, IBC, 1990; Woman of the Year, IBC, 1992-93. Memberships: Founder, 1957, President for 16 years, Bermuda Writers Club; Founding Member, Arts Council, 1969, Board of Governors, ABI; WL Fellow, Academy of Poets; Life Member, IBC Associate Poets Laureate International. Address: Cavendish Apt 2, Block 7, Hibiscus, Devonshire DV 03, Bermuda.

MUSTAFA Walid Said, b. 10 October 1942, Al-Bireh, Palestine. Geographer; Educator. m. Valentina Korenda, 2 sons, 1 daughter. Education: BA, Geography, Damascus University, 1965; PhD, Kiev State University, Ukraine, 1972. Appointments: Lecturer, Department of Geography, Jordan University, Amman, Jordan, 1973-78; Acting Head, Department of Geography, Al-Najah University, Nablus, Palestine, 1979-80; Head, Research Centre, Department of Occupied Territory, Palestinian Liberation Organisation, Amman, Jordan, 1980-94; Senior Researcher and Lecturer, Department of History, Geography and Political Science, Bir Zeit University, Palestine, 1994-95; Dean of Students, 1996-2001, Lecturer, Department of Humanities, 2001-03, Dean, Faculty of Arts, Bethlehem University, Palestine, 2004-. Publications: Author: Bethlehem, The Story of the City, 1990; Jerusalem, Population and Urbanization, 1850-2000, English edition, 2000; Co-author: Collective Destruction of Palestinian Villages and Zionist Colonization, 1881-1982, 1987; Collective Books: Palestinian Encyclopaedia – General Edition, 1984; Toward Palestinian Strategy for Jerusalem, 1998; Palestinian Perspectives, 1999; Editor: Abu-Shusheh Village, 1995; Biet Jibreen Village, 1995; Biet-Nabala Village, 1998; Translator: The Death of a Little Girl and Other Stories, 1980; Gorbachev, MC, Perestroika – For Us and The World, 1990. Honours: Assistant Professor, 1973; Associate Professor, 1999. Memberships: Palestinian National Council, 1987-; Central Committee, Palestinian People's Party, 1982-98; Vice-President, Board of Trustees, Arab Thought Form, Jerusalem, 1998-; Board of Trustees, Applied Research Institute, Jerusalem, 1999-; Board of Trustees, Palestinian Human Rights Monitoring Group, 2000. Address: Bethlehem University, Frier Street, PO Box No 9, Bethlehem, Palestine. E-mail: wshmustafa@yahoo.com

MUTH Richard Ferris, b. 14 May 1927, Chicago Illinois, USA. Economist. m. Helene Louise Martin, 2 daughters. Education: US Coast Guard Academy, 1945-47; AB, 1949, MA, 1950, Washington University, St Louis; PhD, University of Chicago, 1958; Master of Theology Studies, Emory University, 1995. Appointments: Associate Professor, University of Chicago, 1959-64; Professor of Economics, Washington University St Louis, 1966-70; Professor, Stanford University, 1970-83; Professor, 1983-2001, Chair, 1983-90, Professor Emeritus, 2001-, Emory University. Publications: With others: Regions, Resources & Economic Growth, 1960; Cities & Housing, 1969; Public Housing, 1974; Urban Economic Problems, 1975; The Economics of Housing Markets (with Allen C Goodman), 1989. Honour: Phi Beta Kappa. Address: Department of Economics, Emory University, Atlanta, GA 30322-2240, USA. E-mail: rmuth@emory.edu

MWENDA Kenneth Kaoma, b. 5 January 1969, Livingstone City, Zambia. Lawyer; Diplomat. Education: LLB, Zambia, 1990; BCL/MPhil, Oxford, 1994, Gr Dip, LCCI, 1991; Adv Dip, IoC; AHCZ; MBA, Hull, 1995; DBA, Pacific Western, 1996; PhD, Pacific Western, 1999; DCL, Trinity; Gr Cert, Warwick, 1998; PhD, Warwick, 2000; FCI; FRSA; Rhodes Scholar; Professor of Corporate Law. Appointments: Staff Development Fellow, Lecturer in Law, University of Zambia, 1991-95; Lecturer in Law, University of Warwick, UK, 1995-98; Visiting Professor of Law, University of Miskolc, Hungary, 1997; Young Professional, Counsel, Legal Department, 1998-99; Projects Officer, 2000-2003, Senior Projects Officer, 2003-04, Senior Counsel, 2004-, The World Bank; Visiting Professor, University of Zambia School of Law, Lusaka, 2001-02. Publications: Books: Legal Aspects of Corporate Capital and Finance, 1999; Banking Supervision and Systemic Bank Restructuring: An International and Comparative Legal Perspective, 2000; The Dynamics of Market Integration: African Stock Exchanges in the New Millennium, 2000; Contemporary Issues in Corporate Finance and Investment Law, 2000; Zambia's Stock Exchange and Privatisation Programme: Corporate Finance Law in Emerging Markets, 2001; Banking and Micro-Finance Regulation and Supervision: Lessons from Zambia, 2002; Principles of Arbitration Law, 2003; Frontiers of Legal Knowledge: Business and Economic Law in Context, 2003; Legal Aspects of Financial Services Regulation and the Concept of a Unified Regulator, 2006; Combating Financial Crime: Legal, Regulatory and Institutional Frameworks, 2006; The Legal Administration of Financial Services in Common Law Jurisdictions, 2006; More than 60 published journal and law review articles. Honours: Law Association of Zambia Best Student in Jurisprudence Prize, 1990; Selected to World Bank's Young Professionals Programme, 1998; University of Yale Law Faculty Fellowship, 1998; International Cultural Diploma of Honour, American Biographical Institute, 2001; Outstanding Professional Award in Corporate Law, ABI, 2001; International Commendation of Achievement and Success in Corporate Law, ABI, 2001; Listed in numerous biographical dictionaries and Who's Who publications. Memberships: Fellow, Royal Society of Arts of England; Fellow, Institute of Commerce of England; International Bar Association; Law Association of Zambia; British Association of Lawyers for the Defence of the Unborn. Address: The World Bank, 1818 H Street NW, Washington DC 20433, USA. E-mail: kmwenda@worldbank.org

MYERS Mike, b. 25 May 1963, Toronto, Ontario, Canada. Actor; Writer. m. Robin Ruzan, 1993. Creative Works: Stage appearances: The Second City, Toronto, 1986-88, Chicago, 1988-89; Actor and Writer, Mullarkey & Myers, 1984-86; TV show, Saturday Night Live, 1989-94; Films: Wayne's World, 1992; So I Married an Axe Murderer, 1992; Wayne's World II, 1993; Austin Powers: International Man of Mystery, 1997; Meteor, 1998; McClintock's Peach, 1998; Just Like Me, 1998; It's A Dog's Life, 1998; 54, 1998; Austin Powers: The Spy Who Shagged Me, 1998; Pete's Meteor, 1999; Austin Powers: Goldmember, 2002; Shrek (Voice), 2003; Cat in the Hat, 2003; Shrek 2 (Voice), 2004; Far Far Away Idol, (voice), 2004; Shrek 3, (voice), 2007. Honours: Emmy Award for outstanding writing in a comedy or variety series, 1989; MTV Music Award, 1998; Canadian Comedy Award, 2000; American Comedy Award, 2000; Blockbuster Entertainment Award, 2000; Teen Choice Award, 2000; MTV Music Award, 2003; AFI Star Award, 2003. Address: c/o Creative Artists Agency, 9830 Wilshire Boulevard, Beverly Hills, CA 90212, USA.

N

N'DOUR Youssou, b. 1959, Dakar, Senegal. Musician; Singer; Songwriter. Career: Member, Sine Dramatic, 1972; Orchestre Diamono, 1975; The Star Band (houseband, Dakar nightclub, the Miami Club), 1976-79; Founder, Etoile De Dakar, 1979; Re-formed as Super Etoile De Dakar, 1982-; International tours include support to Peter Gabriel, US tour, 1987. Recordings: Albums: A Abijan, 1980; Xalis, 1980; Tabaski, 1981; Thiapathioly, 1983; Absa Gueye, 1983; Immigres, 1984; Nelson Mandela, 1985; The Lion, 1989; African Editions Volumes 5-14, 1990; Africa Deebeub, 1990; Jamm La Prix, 1990; Kocc Barma, 1990; Set, 1990; Eyes Open, 1992; The Best Of Youssou N'Dour, 1994; The Guide, 1995; Gainde - Voices From The Heart Of Africa (with Yande Codou Sene), 1996; Immigrés/Bitim Rew, 1997; Inedits 84-85, 1997; Hey You : The Essential Collection, 1988-1990; Best of the 80's, 1998; Special Fin D'annee Plus Djamil, 1999; Joko: From Village to Town, 2000; Batay, 2001; Le Grand Bal, Bercy, 2000; Le Grand Bal 1 & 2, 2001; Birth of a Star, 2001; Nothing's in Vain, 2002; Et Ses Amis, 2002; Sant Allah (Homage to God), 2003; Egypt, 2004; The Best of Youssou N'Dour, 2004; Rokku Mi Rokka, 2007; Instant Karma, 2007. Hit Single: Seven Seconds, duet with Neneh Cherry, 1995; How Come Shakin' the Tree, 1998; Recorded with: Paul Simon, Graceland, 1986; Lou Reed, Between Thought and Expression, 1992; Otis Reading, Otis! The Definitive Otis Reading, 1993; Manu Dibango, Wafrika, 1994; Cheikh Lo, Ne La Thiass, 1996; Alan Stivell, I Dour, 1998. Honours: Best African Artist, 1996; African Artist of the Century, 1999; BBC Radio 3 World Music Award for Album of the Year, 2005. Address: Youssou N'Dour Head Office, 8 Route des Almadies Parcelle, BP 1310, Dakar, Senegal. E-mail: yncontact@yahoo.fr Website: www.youssou.com

NAESS Orvar Almar, b. 25 October 1922, Horten, Norway. Lector (Lecturer). m. Margit, deceased 2006, 1 son, 2 daughters. Education: Examen Artium, 1942; Teachers' College, 1942-44; Cand phil, Oslo University, 1945-51; Master's degree, American Literature, Fulbright stipend, University of Illinois, USA, 1951-52. Appointments: Teacher, elementary school, Oslo, 1944-51; Teacher, state school, Tingvoll, 1952-53; Lector (Lecturer), Molde secondary school, 1953-59; Lector (Lecturer), Sofienberg secondary school, 1959-70; Secretary, Ministry of Education, 1962-65; Vice Principal, Hovin secondary school (gymnasium for adult education), Oslo, 1973-75; Lecturer, Main Teacher, Persbraaten secondary school, 1975-92; Lecturer, Teacher, People's University (Oslo gymnasium), Oslo, 1992-2007. Publications: John Ruskin – The Personality of a Great Artist, 1951; Series of articles on literary themes in Norwegian newspapers. Honours: Stipend from Norway-America Association, 1966; 7th Degree Order of Druids, Norway; Vice President, IGLD, 1970-80. Memberships: Norway-America Association; Norway Conservative Party. Address: Vestliveien 20A, 0750 Oslo, Norway. E-mail: orvnae@frisurf.no

NAGAI Masaru, b. 22 July 1965, Tokyo, Japan. Researcher. Education: Diploma, Faculty of Engineering, 1991, Diploma, Graduate School of Engineering, 1994, Kyoto University; Master's degree, Polymer Science, 1994. Appointments: Staff Engineer, MEMC Co Ltd, 1995-2000; Staff Researcher, TDK Co Ltd, 2000-04; Senior Researcher, Research Institute of Organics Electronics, 2004-06; Assistant Manager, Fuji Electric Advanced Technology Co Ltd, 2007-. Publications include: Dark spot formation and growth in Color-Filter based OLED devices, 2007; Macromolecular contamination on haze generation in an a-Si film by CVD, 2007; Crystallization and Aggregation Processes of vacuum evaporated TPD films, 2008. Honours: Listed in international biographical dictionaries. Memberships: Active Member, Electrochemical Society. Address: 4-13-13-1207 Tsukama, Matsumoto City, Nagano 390-0821, Japan. E-mail: m_nagai@f4.dion.ne.jp

NAGAMINE Toshinobu, b. 19 September 1973, Hyuga, Miyazaki, Japan. Applied Linguist; Educator. m. Tomoko Kariya, 2007. Education: BA, Miyazaki Municipal University, Japan, 1997; MA, Murray State University, Kentucky, USA, 2000; PhD, Indiana University of Pennsylvania, USA, 2007. Appointments: Certified English Teacher, Prefectural Board of Education, Miyazaki, 1997; Teaching Assistant, Department of Education, Murray State University, 1998-2000; CALL Assistant, ESL program, 1999-2000; Research Assistant, Department of Education, 1999-2000; Teaching Associate, English Department, Indiana University of Pennsylvania, 2002-03; Lecturer, Higashi-Omiya Junior High School, Miyazaki, Japan, 2003-04; Senior Lecturer, Yastsushiro National College of Technology, Kumamoto, Japan, 2004-06; Senior Lecturer, 2006-08, Associate Professor, 2008-, Prefectural University of Kumamoto, Japan; Member, Editorial Board, Asian EFL Journal, Institute of National Colleges Technology, Japan; Council Member, Academic Consultant, Kumamoto Prefectural Council for Promotion of Scholastic Studies, 2006-; English Textbook Editor and Developer, Tokyo Shoseki, 2006-; Presenter in field. Publications: Contributed articles to professional journals. Honours: Deputy Superintendent, Buddhist organisation, Soka Gakkai International, Kumamoto; Grantee, Ministry of Education, Science, Sports and Culture, Japan, 2007-08. Memberships: TESOL; Japan Association for Language, Education and Technology; Language and Culture Association of Japan; Japan Association for Language Teaching; The Japan Association for the Study of Teaching English; Phonetic Society of Japan; Life Member, Phi Kappa Phi. Address: Prefectural University of Kumamoto, 3-1-100 Tsukide, Kumamoto 862-8502, Japan.

NAGANO Shinichiro, b. 24 January 1961, Toyonako, Osaka, Japan. Electronics Engineer. m. Hikari, 1 daughter. Education: BS, 1984, MS, 1986, Physics, University of Tokyo; PhD, University of Electro-Communications, 2006. Appointments: Member, Plasma Display Technical Meeting Committee, 2000-04; Head Engineer, Development of Plasma Display Panel Technologies, Mitsubishi Electric Corp, 2000-04; Section Manager, Development of Plasma Display Panel Technologies, Mitsubishi Electric Corp, 2002-04; Manager, Development Promotion Center for Development of Thermal Printing Head Technologies, Shandong Hualing Electronics Co Ltd, 2005-. Publications: 6 articles in professional scientific journals. Honours: Listed in international biographical directories. Memberships: Institute of Electronics, Information and Communication Engineers; Institute of Image Information and Television Engineers. Address: 2-12-3-120 Kitakutsukake Ooe, Nishikyo, Kyoto 610-1101, Japan. E-mail: saaya@gaia.eonet.ne.jp

NAGASAWA Shin'ya, b. 21 September 1955, Niigata City, Japan. Professor. m. Sachiko Kato, 2 daughters. Education: B Eng, 1978, M Eng, 1980, Dr Eng, 1986, Waseda University, Tokyo. Appointments: Research Associate, Meiji University, Tokyo, 1981-88; Assistant Professor, Sanno College, Tokyo, 1988-90; Associate Professor, Asia University, Tokyo, 1990-95; Professor, Ritsuneikan University, Kyoto, 1995-2003; Professor, Waseda Business School, Tokyo, 2003-. Publications: Creating Customer Experience on Long-Standing Companies, 2006; Marketability of Environment-Conscious

Products, 2007; The Principles of Louis Vuitton: The Strongest Brand Strategy, 2007. Honours: Nikkei Publishing Award in Quality Control, 2001; Best Paper Award, EcoDesign, 2003; Publishing Award in Waste Technology, 2006; Publishing Awards, Japan Society of Kansei Engineering, 2002, 2005, 2006, 2007. Memberships: Japan Society of Kansei Engineering; Association of Product Development and Management. Address: 7F Nishiwaseda Bldg, 1-21-1 Nish-Waseda, Shinjuku-ku, Tokyo 1690051, Japan. E-mail: nagasawa@waseda.jp Website: www.waseda.jp/wbs

NAGASHIMA Kazunori, b. 20 May 1965, Japan. Physician. Education: MD, Akita University, 1992; PhD, Tokyo Medical University, 2003. Appointments: Research fellow, Tokyo Medical University, Tokyo, Japan; Research Scholar, Postdoctoral fellow, Columbia University, New York, USA; Health Care Physician, Isesaki-Sawa Medical Association Hospital, Gunma, Japan. Publications: Articles in medical journals: Clarification of changes of serum lipids according to age in males and females who requested a medical health check up, 2000; Changes regarding age and correlations between serum lipids and body mass index in humankind, 2002; Effects of the PPARγ agonist pioglitazone on lipoprotein metabolism in patients with type 2 diabetes mellitus, 2005. Honours: Symposiast, 40th Annual Congress of Japanese College of Angiology, Hiroshima, Japan, 1999; Man of the Year 2005, ABI, 2005; Great Minds of the 21st Century, ABI, 2005; Noble Order of International Ambassadors, ABI, 2005; 2000 Outstanding Intellectuals of the 21st Century, IBC, 2005, 2006; Deputy Director General, IBC, 2006; 500 Greatest Geniuses of the 21st Century, ABI, 2006; Deputy Governor, ABI, 2006; Great Lives of the 21st Century, IBC, 2006; American Medal of Honor, ABI, 2006; International Order of Merit, IBC, 2006; Gold Medal for Japan, ABI, 2006; Top 100 Health Professionals, IBC, 2006; Director Generals Roll of Honour, IBC, 2007; Greatest Minds of the 21st Century, ABI, 2007. Memberships: International Health Evaluation and Promotion Association; Japanese Society of Internal Medicine; Japanese Circulation Society; Japan Atherosclerosis Society; Japanese College of Angiology; Japan Society of Health Evaluation and Promotion; Japan Society of Ningen Dock; American Heart Association; Council on Arteriosclerosis, Thrombosis and Vascular Biology; International Atherosclerotic Society; Council on Epidemiology and Prevention; Interdisciplinary Working Group of Atherosclerotic Peripheral Vascular Disease; American Diabetes Association; New York Academy of Sciences. Address: 23-13 Chuo-cho, Prime Square ISESAKI Rm 901, Isesaki-shi, Gunma-ken, 372-0042, Japan. E-mail: kanagashima-circ@umin.ac.jp

NAGY Endre László, b. 25 December 1942, Terehegy, Baranya, Hungary. Electrical Engineer; Researcher; Educator. m. Ritsuko Mine. Education: Budapest Technical University, 1961-66; PhD, Computing and Automation Research Institute of Hungarian Academy of Sciences, and Budapest Technical University, 1970-73. Appointments: Scientific Associate, Research Institute for Electric Energy Industry, Budapest, 1966-70, 1973-74; Associate Professor, Kandó Kálmán College for Electrical Engineering, Budapest, 1974-84; Chief Researcher, Birds Information Research Institute, Tokyo, 1987-89; Head of Department, Sanrura Inc, Tokyo/Yokohama, 1990-93; Basic research on control systems, 1994-. Publications: Several articles, studies and presentations at conferences: International Federation of Automatic Control; World Multi-Conference on Systematics, Cybernetics and Informatics; International Conference on Nonlinear Problems in Aviation & Aerospace; American Control Conference, etc. Honours: Diploma Prize, Electrotechnical Society, Budapest,

1966; Proclamation Plaque Certificate, ABI, 2008; Universal Award of Accomplishment, 2008; Listed in international biographical dictionaries. Memberships: International Federation of Automatic Control; International Institute of Informatics & Systematics; Society of Instrument and Control Engineers of Japan. E-mail: nagy@mtd.biglobe.ne.jp

NAIPAUL V(idiadhar) S(urajprasad) (Sir), b. 17 August 1932, Chaguanas, Trinidad. Author. m. (1) Patricia Ann Hale, 1955, deceased 1996, (2) Nadira Khannum Alvi, 1996. Education: Queen's Royal College, Trinidad; BA, Honours, English, University College, Oxford, 1953. Publications: Novels: The Mystic Masseur, 1957; The Suffrage of Elvira, 1958; Miguel Street, 1959; A House for Mr Biswas, 1961; Mr Stone and the Knights Companion, 1963; The Mimic Men, 1967; A Flag on the Island, 1967; In a Free State, 1971; Guerrillas, 1975; A Bend in the River, 1979; The Enigma of Arrival, 1987; A Way in the World, 1994; Beyond Belief, 1998; Letters Between a Father and Son, 1999; Reading and Writing: a Personal Account, 2000; Half a Life, 2001. Other: The Middle Passage, 1962; An Area of Darkness, 1964; The Loss of El Dorado, 1969; The Overcrowded Barracoon, and Other Articles, 1972; India: A Wounded Civilization, 1977; The Return of Eva Perón, 1980; Among the Believers, 1981; Finding the Centre, 1984; A Turn in the South, 1989; India: A Million Mutinies Now, 1990; Beyond Belief: Islamic Excursions Among the Converted Peoples, 1998; Literary Occasions, 2004; Magic Seeds, 2004. Contributions to: Journals and magazines. Honours: John Llewelyn Rhys Memorial Prize, 1958; Somerset Maugham Award, 1961; Hawthornden Prize, 1964; W H Smith Award, 1968; Booker Prize, 1971; Honorary Doctor of Letters, Columbia University, New York City, 1981; Honorary Fellow, University College, Oxford, 1983; Honorary DLitt, University of Cambridge, 1983, University of Oxford, 1992; Knighted, 1990; British Literature Prize, 1993; Nobel Prize for Literature, 2001. Memberships: Royal Society of Literature, fellow; Society of Authors. Address: c/o Gillon Aitken Associates, 29 Fernshaw Road, London SW10 0TG, England.

NAIR Govindapillai Achuthan, b. 17 February 1946, Trivandrum, India. Teacher; Researcher; University Professor. m. P Lakshmi Nair, 1 son, 2 daughters. Education: MSc, Zoology, Birla Institute of Technology and Science, Pilani, India, 1969; PhD, Aquatic Biology, 1981; DSc, Ecology, Kerala University, India, 2001. Appointments: CSIR, Government of India, Junior, Senior and Postdoctoral Fellow; Research Associate, Department of Ocean Development and US PL (480) Smithsonian Project; Deputy Director and Project Co-ordinator, ERRC, India; Assistant Professor, Associate Professor, Professor, Department of Zoology, University of Garyounis, Benghazi, Libya; Director and Professor of Bio-Sciences in SAFI Institute of Advanced Study, Calicut, India, 2005; Visiting Professor, Department of Environmental Sciences, Kerala University, India, 2006-. Publications: 110 papers published on the subjects of general biology/ecology, breeding and population biology, feeding and nutritional biology, haematobiology, parasitology, biometrics, toxicology, pollution biology. Honours: Sri Chitra Prize, Kerala University for best research publications; Best Academician 2001-2002, University of Garyounis, Benghazi, Libya; Listed in Who's Who publications and biographical dictionaries. Memberships: Fellow, Linnean Society of London; New York Academy of Sciences; Asian Fisheries Society, Philippines. Address: Sankara Bhavan-4, Sasthamangalam, Thiruvananthapuram-695010, Kerala State, India. E-mail: gachuth@yahoo.com

DICTIONARY OF INTERNATIONAL BIOGRAPHY

NAKAGAWA Akio, b. 25 September 1949, Japan. Chief Fellow. m. Masami Morie, 2 daughters. Education: BSc, 1972, MSc, 1974, PhD, Electrical Engineering, 1984, University of Tokyo. Appointments: Joined company, 1974-, Senior Fellow, Advanced Device Laboratory, 2005-, Toshiba R&D Centre; Visiting Scholar, Department of Electrical & Computer Engineering, University of Massachusetts, USA, 1981-83; Chief Fellow, Toshiba Corporation, Semiconductor Company. Publications: More than135 technical papers including: A time- and temperature-dependent simulation of the GTO turn-off process, 1982; Non-latch-up 1200V 75A bipolar-mode MOSFET with large ASO, 1984; New 500V output device structure on silicon oxide film, 1990; Over 105 Japanese patents; Over 110 US patents. Address: 580-1 Horikawa-Cho, Saiwai-Ku, Kawasaki 212-8520, Japan. E-mail: akio.nakagawa@toshiba.co.jp

NAKAGAWA Hachiro, b. 27 August 1931, Osaka, Japan. Director. m. Fumiko, deceased, 1 son, 1 daughter. Education: MD, Osaka University School of Medicine, 1956; PhD, Graduate School of Medicine, Osaka University, 1961. Appointments: Professor, Director, Institute of Protein Research, Osaka University; Director, R&D Center, BML Co; Visiting Professor, Akita University; Director, International Institute of Alternative Medicine. Publications: Central Regulation of Energy Metabolism with Special Reference to Circadian Rhythm; Biological Rhythms and Their Central Mechanism; Brain Nutrition; and others. Honours: Emeritus Professor of Osaka University. Memberships: Honorary Member, Japanese Biochemical Society; New York Academy of Sciences. Address: 21-10 Harima-cho 1 Chome, Abeno-Ku, Osaka City, Osaka 545-0022, Japan. E-mail: nakagawah@oct.zaq.ne.jp

NAKAGAWA Masahiko, b. 4 September 1968, Tokyo, Japan. Forestry Researcher. Education: Bachelor of Science, Humboldt State University, 1992; Master of Agriculture, University of Tokyo, 1995.; Doctor of Agriculture, University of Tokyo, 2006. Appointments: Bureaucrat, Forestry Agency, Ministry of Agriculture, Forestry and Fisheries, 1995-96; Forester, Shibiutan Forester Office, Japan National Forest, 1996-98; Forester, Tokyo Metropolitan Government, Tokyo Metropolitan Forest, 1998-99; Forester, Abasiri-seibu Forest Centre, Hokkaido Prefectural Forest, 1999-2003; Forestry Researcher, Hokkaido Forestry Research Institute, 2003-. Publications: Numerous articles in professional journals. Honours: Phi Kappa Phi; magna cum laude, 1992; Listed in national and international biographical dictionaries. Memberships: Japan Forest Engineering Society; Forest Management and Research Network; Iwamizawa Aikido Association. Address: Kyosai Dai-ich Apt #102, 1376-1 Aza-Bibai, Bibai-shi, Hokkaido, 072-0042, Japan.

NAKAYAMA Akiyoshi, b. 13 July 1930, Kyoto, Japan. History Educator. m. Yoko Sugimura, 1960, 2 children. Education: MA, Literature, 1956, D Litt, 1992, Kyoto University. Appointments: Research Fellow, Warsaw University, Poland, 1962-65, University of Vienna, Austria, 1965-2001; Lecturer to Professor of History, Sangyo University, Kyoto, Japan, 1968-; Guest Professor, University of London, England, 1981. Publications: Author, Poland – It's Climate and Course of History, 1971; Modern Europe and Historical Eastern Europe, 1991; Contributor of articles to professional journals. Honours: Cultural Merit Medal, Ministry of Culture and Art of Poland, 1974. Memberships: Japanese Society for Slavic and East European Studies; Japanese Society of Western History. Address: 2-6 Hirabayashi, Misasagi, Kyoto 607-8406, Japan.

NAM Charles Benjamin, b. 25 March 1926, Lynbrook, New York, USA. Demographer; Sociologist. m. Marjorie Tallant, deceased, 1 son, 1 daughter. Education: BA, Applied Statistics, New York University, 1950; MA, Sociology, 1957, PhD, Sociology, 1959, University of North Carolina. Appointments: Staff, 1950-53, Branch Chief, 1957-63, US Bureau of the Census; Professor, Florida State University, 1964-95; Professor Emeritus and Author, Research Associate, Centre for Demography and Population Health, Florida State University, 1995-. Publications: 13 books, including The Golden Door, 2006; Over 100 articles and chapters. Honours: Fellow, American Association for the Advancement of Science; Fellow, American Statistical Association. Memberships: American Association for the Advancement of Science; Population Association of America, Past President; American Statistical Association; Society for the Study of Social Biology; American Sociological Association; International Union for the Scientific Study of Population. Address: 820 Live Oak Plantation Road, Tallahassee, FL 32312-2413, USA. E-mail: charlesnam2@embarqmail.com

NAM Eunsoo, b. 28 October 1960, Daegu, Korea. Principal Research Scientist. m. Sungwol Kwon, 1 son, 1 daughter. Education: BS, Physics, Kyungpook National University, 1983; MA, 1993, PhD, 1995, Physics, State University of New York (Buffalo), USA. Appointments: Head, Wideband Transceiver Module Team and Ultra High Speed Communication IC Team, Electronics and Telecommunications Research Institute, 1985-; Member, Board of National Technology Evaluation in Korean National Science Foundation, Korean Ministry of Science & Technology, and Korean Ministry of Communication, 2000-; Visiting Scholar, Harvard University, USA, 2005-06. Publications: Several articles in professional journals including: Stable two-wavelength lasers by use of a double alpha-type fiber cavity with fiber grating mirrors, 2005; Photoreceiver of selectively detecting light of specific wavelength and method. Memberships: IEEE; Korean Physical Society. Address: IT Convergence Lab, ETRI, 161 Gajung-dong, Yusung-gu, Daejeon, 305-350, South Korea. E-mail: esnam@etri.re.kr Website: www.etri.re.kr

NAM Ki-Chan, b. 28 September 1959, Andong, South Korea. Professor. m. Hyang Sug Yi, 2 sons. Education: B Eng, Korea Maritime University, 1984; MSc, 1989, PhD, 1992, University of Wales, United Kingdom. Appointments: Lecturer, Associate Professor, Professor, 1993-; Committee Member, Council of Port Development, Ministry of Maritime Affairs & Fisheries, 1997-; Dean of Student Affairs, Korea Maritime University, 2003-04; Director, Port & Logistics Education Project, 2004-; Committee Member, Busan Port Authority, 2006-. Publications: Book, Logistics Planning; Articles: Evaluation of Handling Systems for Container Terminal; Simulation Study of Container Terminal Performance; Determinants for the Development of a Logistics Hub. Memberships: Korea Institute of Navigation & Port Research; Korea Logistics Association; Korean Society of Transportation. Address: Korea Maritime University, 1 Dongsam-Dong, Pusan 606-791, South Korea. E-mail: namchan@hhu.ac.kr

NANDARGI Shobha, b. 2 May 1960, Pune, India. Research in Hydrometeorology. Education: MSc, Pune University, Pune; PhD, Environmental Sciences, Pune University, Pune. Appointments: Junior Research Assistant, 1984-, Research Senior Scientist C, Indian Institute of Tropical Meteorology, Pashan, Pune. Publications: Mostly research in the field of Hydrometeorology, especially the occurrence of severe rainstorms and floods in the Indian Region; Over 100 publications. Membership: Indian Meteorological Society. E-mail: nshobha@tropmet.res.in

NANDEDKAR Deepak Prabhakar, b. 26 January 1944, Indore, Madhya Pradesh, India. Educator. m. Tarala, 1 son. Education: BSc, 1st Class with V Rank/Merit, Vikram University, 1963; MSc, Physics with Electronics and Radio Physics, 1st Class with II Rank/Merit, Indore University, 1965; MTech, Electrical Engineering with specialisation in Electron-Devices Technology, 1967, PhD, 1970, IIT Mumbai. Appointments: Lecturer, 1969-76, Assistant Professor, 1976-2001, Associate Professor, 2001-2006, Retired 2006, Department of Electrical Engineering, IIT, Powai, Mumbai, India. Publications: Numerous and various articles as co-author/author in engineering and scientific journals, and at symposiums. Honours: American Biographical Institute Awards: Distinguished Leader Brass Medal, 2002; Certification and American Bronze Medal of Honor, 2002; World Laureate of India, 2002-03; Teaching Excellence Award, 2003; Outstanding Professional Award, 2004; Man of the Year, 2005; World Gold Medal, 2005; United Cultural Convention Awards: International Peace Prize, 2003, 2005; Lifetime Achievement Award, 2005; International Biographical Centre Awards: Awards Roster, International Educator of the Year, 2004; Silver Medallion & Certification, Leading Educators of the World, 2005; Silver Medallion & Certification, Top 100 Scientists, 2005; India International Friendship Society Awards: Bharat Jyoti Award, 2006; Rajiv Gandhi Excellence Award, 2006; Indira Gandhi Shiromani Award, 2006; Glory of India Award, International Institute of Success Awareness, 2006; Best Citizens of India Award, International Publishing House, India, 2006; Friendship Forum of India Awards: Bharat Excellence Award, 2006; Rashtrya Jewel Award, 2006; Glory of India International Award, 2006; Lifetime Achievement Award, 2006; Listed in Who's Who publications and biographical dictionaries. Memberships: Research Board of Advisors, 2002-; Life Fellow, 2002-; Consulting Editor, Contemporary Who's Who, ABI, 2002-2003; Life Member, Fellow, Institution of Electronics and Telecommunication Engineers, New Delhi, 2004-; Life Member, Indian Society for Technical Education, New Delhi, India, 2004-; Life Member, Indian Institute of Technology Alumni Association, Mumbai, India, 2005-. Address: Building Number G-01, Flat Number 301, Brahmand Phase VIII, New Brahmand Annex Co-operative Housing Society Ltd, Dharmacha Pada, Azad Nagar, Kolshet, Sandoz Baug Post Office, Thane – 400607, Maharashtra State, India.

NAPIER William McDonald, (Bill Napier), b. 29 June 1940, Perth, Scotland. Astronomer. m. Nancy Miller Baillie, 7 July 1965, 1 son, 1 daughter. Education: BSc, 1963; PhD, 1966. Publications: The Cosmic Serpent, 1982; The Cosmic Winter, 1990; The Origin of Comets, 1990; Nemesis (novel), 1998; Revelation (novel), 2000; The Lure (novel), 2002; Shattered Icon (novel), 2003. Contributions to: New Scientist; Astronomy Today. Honour: Honorary Professor, Cardiff University; Joint recipient, Arthur Beer Memorial Prize, 1986-87. Membership: Royal Astronomical Society, fellow; International Astronomical Union; Spaceguard UK; Committee on Space Research. Address: County Cork, Ireland.

NARAGHI Akhtar, Writer. m. Javad Ebadi, deceased, 1 son, 1 daughter. Education: PhD, English Literature, McGill University, Canada, 1991. Appointments: Teacher at Teachers Training College, Tehran; Teacher, McGill University. Publications: Legacy: Selected Poems, 1992; The Big

Green House: A Novel in Twelve Short Stories (translated into German, French and Persian), 1994, 5th edition, 2001; Solitude: Selected Poems, 1996; Blue Curtains: A Novel in Six Stories, 1999; With Mara That Summer: A Novel in Four Stories, 2004; Ghazal: The Poems of Safai Naraghi (editor), 1972; Contributor of forewords, articles, short stories and poems to numerous journals. Honours: The Big Green House shortlisted for the 1995 QSPELL Hugh MacLennan Prize for Fiction; Several interviews for newspapers, radio and television Listed in Who's Who publications and biographical dictionaries. Memberships: Founding President, International Organisation of the Helen Prize for Women, 1987; Member, Quebec Writers' Association. Address: PO Box 781, Place du Parc, Montreal, QC H2X 4A6, Canada. E-mail: persica@sypatico.ca

NARASIMHA RAO Sabnavis, b. 21 December 1949, Bangalore, India. Teacher. m. M Vimala, 1 daughter. Education: BSc (Hons), 1969; MSc, 1971; DBA, 1972; BASM, 2002; MD (AM), 2003. Appointments: Research Assistant, Department of Physiology, St John's Medical College, Bangalore, 1971-72; Lecturer in Zoology, 1972-, Professor, 1988-, Head of the Department, 2003-, MES College of Arts, Commerce and Science, Bangalore, India. Publications: Presented papers at various national conferences. Honours: Certificate of Appreciation, Government of Karnataka for Russian Festival in India; Dasara State Sports Award; Man of the Year, IBC, 2006; 2000 Outstanding Individuals of the 21st Century; Top 100 Educators; Order of International Ambassadors; Listed in international biographical dictionaries. Memberships: Fellow, Zoological Society of India; Ethological Society of India; Institute of Holistic Therapy, Mexico; Fellow, World Society of Alternative Medicine, USA. Address: #42, Kanakapura Road, Basavanagudi, Bangalore, Karnataka, India. E-mail: narasirao@gmail.com

NAROTZKY Norman D, b. 14 March 1928, Brooklyn, New York, USA. Artist; Painter; Printmaker. m. Mercedes Molleda, 2 daughters. Education: High School of Music and Art, 1945; BA, Brooklyn College, 1949; Art Students League, New York City, 1945-49; Cooper Union Art School, 1952; Atelier 17, Paris, 1954-56; Kunstakademie, Munich, 1956-57; New York Institute of Fine Arts, 1957-58; BFA, Cooper Union Art School, 1979. Appointments: 56 solo exhibitions in Europe and USA; Group shows: Brooklyn Museum of Art; National Gallery, Oslo; Salon de Mai and Salon des Réalités Nouvelles, Paris; Vi Bienal Sao Paulo, Brazil; Museum of Modern Art, New York; Baltimore Museum of Art; San Francisco Museum of Art; Whitney Museum of Art, New York; Palazzo Strozzi, Florence; Haus der Kunst, Munich; Fundació Miro, Barcelona; Work in collections of museums in USA and Europe. Publications: The Raven Edgar Allan Poe: limited edition Artists Book with 9 original colour etchings, 1993; Various articles in professional journals and magazines. Honours: Wooley Foundation Fellowship, 1954; French Government Fellowship, 1955; Fulbright Fellowship, 1956; First Prize, Hebrew Educational Society, Brooklyn, New York, 1959; Painting Grant, Generalitat de Catalunya, 1983; Grand Prize, II Bienal D'Art FC, Barcelona, 1987; Listed in national and international biographical dictionaries. Memberships: Life Member, Art Students League of New York; Catalan Association of Visual Artists, Barcelona; Cercle d'Art Sant Lluc, Barcelona. Address: Putxet 84, 08023 Barcelona, Spain. E-mail: narotzky@compuserve.com Website: http://ourworld.compuserve.com/homepages/narotzky

NASIR Babar Murad, b. 25 October 1955, Karachi, Pakistan. Consultant. Education: BSc, 1st Class Honours, Electronics, 1975, D Phil, 1979, University of Sussex, England. Appointments: Lecturer, University of Ibadan, Nigeria, 1979-80; Principal System Analyst, NWDB, Nigeria, 1981; Researcher A, University of Greenwich, England, 1984-86; Postdoctoral Research Fellow, King's College, University of London, England, 1986-88; Research Fellow, Birkbeck College, University of London, 1989-90. Publications: Sole author 1994-98 of: 14 Colloquium Digest Articles, IEE; 1 UK Patent; 4 International conference proceedings articles. Honours: Nominated by ABI: Man of the Year; Man of Achievement; International Peace Prize; American Medal of Honor; Master Diploma with Honors, 2004; World Medal of Freedom, 2005; Listed in Who's Who publications and biographical dictionaries. Membership: IEE. Address: 14 Cool Oak Lane, London NW9 7BJ, England. E-mail: nsrbbr@yahoo.com

NASR Seyyed Hossein, b. 7 April 1933, Tehran, Iran. University Professor. m. Soussan Daneshvary, November 1958, 1 son, 1 daughter. Education: BS, MIT, 1954; MSc, 1956, PhD, History of Science and Philosophy, 1958, Harvard University. Appointments: Professor of Philosophy and History of Science, 1958-79, Dean of Faculty of Letters, 1968-72, Vice Chancellor, 1970-71, Tehran University; Visiting Professor, Harvard University, 1962, 1965; Aga Khan Professor of Islamic Studies, American University of Beirut, 1964-65; President, Aryamehr University, 1972-75; Founder, 1st President, Iranian Academy of Philosophy, 1974-79; Distinguished Visiting Professor, University of Utah, 1979; Professor of Religion, Temple University, 1979-84; University Professor, The George Washington University, 1984-; A D White Professor-at-Large, Cornell University, 1991-97. Publications: Over 50 books and 500 articles in magazines and journals throughout the world. Honours: Royal Book Award of Iran, 1963; Honorary Doctorate, University of Uppsala, 1977; Gifford Lecturer, 1981; Honorary Doctorate, Lehigh University, 1996. 2001 volume of the Library of Living Philosophers. Address: The George Washington University, Gelman Library, 709-R, 2130 H Street, NW Washington, DC 20052, USA.

NASTASE Ilie, b. 19 July 1946, Bucharest, Romania. Tennis Player. m. (1) 1 daughter, (2) Alexandra King, 1984. Appointments: National Champion (13-14 age group), 1959, (15-16 age group) 1961, (17-18 age group) 1963, 1964; Won, Masters Singles Event, Paris, 1971, Barcelona, 1972; Boston, 1973, Stockholm, 1975; Winner, Singles, Cannes, 1967, Travemunde, 1967, 1969, Gauhati, Madras, 1968, 1969, New Delhi, 1968, 1969, Viareggio, 1968, Barranquilla, Coruna, Budapest, Denver, 1969, Salisbury, Rome, 1970, Omaha, Nice, Monte Carlo, 1971, 1972, Baastad, Wembley, Stockholm, Richmond, Hampton, Istanbul, 1971, Forest Hills, Baltimore, Madrid, Toronto, S Orange, Seattle, 1972, Roland Garros, US Open, 1973; Winner, Doubles, Roland Garros (with Ion Tiriac), 1970; Played 130 matches for the Romanian team in the Davis Cup; Retired, 1985. Publication: Breakpoint, 1986. Honours: ILTF Grand Prix, 1972, 1973; Best Romanian Sportsman of the Year, 1969, 1970, 1971, 1973. Address: Clubul Sportiv Steaua, Calea Plevnei 114, Bucharest, Romania.

NATH Ashish, b. 16 August 1971, Allahabad, India. Engineer. m. Jaya, 1 son. Education: BE (Hons), Electrical, MMM Engineering College, Gorakpur, 1993; PGDIE, NITIE, Mumbai, 1997. Appointments: Director (EI), CEA, Ministry of Power, Government of India, 1997-99; SO II E/

M, CEAF, Military Engineers Services, 1999-2000; AGEC E/M, Gecgarhi, MES, 2000-02; AGECI, Research and Development, Kanpur MES, 2002-05; Deputy Director, CEAF Allahabad, 2005; GE (W), Allahabad MES, 2005-. Honours: Raza DM Merit Scholarship; College of Merit Scholarship, MMM Engineering College; Listed in international biographical dictionaries. Memberships: IEEE: Comp Society; Industrial Appliance Society; Power Engineering Society; Engineering Management Society; Communication Society; Power Engineering Society; Society on Social Implication of Technology, IIIE. Address: 1/37 Stanley Road, Justice Mulla Campus, Allahabad 211002, India. E-mail: nath_ashish@rediffmail.com

NATH Indranil, b. 11 September 1969, Kolkata, India. Managing Director. m. Sumitra, 2 sons. Education: BA (Hons), Japanese and Linguistics, 1991; MBA, 1995; Graduate Diploma in Training & Development, 1995; PhD, Engineering Management, 2006; Certified IT Project Manager, 2002; Chartered IT Professional, 2007. Publications: Several articles in professional journals. Honours: Fellow, Chartered Management Institute, England. Memberships: IEEE; Project Management Institute; Indian Society of Training & Development; Institute of Corporate Directors; British Computer Society. Address: 3-15-16 Shin Yamashita, Naka-ku, Yokohama 231-0801, Japan. E-mail: indranil@nationaline.com

NATHAN Peter Geoffrey, b. 27 July 1929, London, England. Solicitor. m. Caroline Mullen, 2 sons, 2 daughters. Education: MA, Oriel College, Oxford; Diplôme Etudes de Civilisation Française, University of Paris. Appointments: Writer RN, 1948-49; Admitted Solicitor, 1958 Herbert Oppenheimer Nathan & Vandyk, 1954-88, Partner, 1959-88; Consultant: Boodle Hatfield, 1988-92, Wood & Awdry (formerly Wood Awdry Wansbroughs), 1992-2000; Governor, Sports Aid Foundation, 1999-2002; Chairman, 1999-2002 Honorary President, 2003-, Sports Aid London; Chairman, 1984-97, Vice-President, 1997-, Deputy Chairman Peter May Memorial Appeal, 1995-97; London Playing Fields Society; Vice-President, Croydon Playing Fields Society, 1996-; National Heritage Secretary's Ministerial Nominee, London Council for Sport and Recreation, 1992-95; Trustee until 1996, Patron, 1996-, Oriel College Development Trust; Chairman, Oriel Law Society until 1996; Chairman, Oriel Law Fellowship Appeal until 1996; Chairman, Chiddingfold Branch of the Farnham Conservative Association, 1965-70. Honours: Freeman City of London, 1961; Master Worshipful Company of Gold and Silver Wyre Drawers. 1989; DL, Greater London, 1991; National Playing Fields Association President's Certificate, 1992; OBE, 1999. Memberships include: Community Health Council for Kensington, Chelsea and Westminster representing Royal Borough of Kensington and Chelsea, 1974-78; Council, British Heart Foundation, 1976-93; Council, Anglo-Swiss Society, 1988-2005; Court, City University, 1989-93; Livery Consultative Committee, Corporation of London, 1994-97; Law Society; Honorary Member, Geographical Association; Clubs: MCC; Vincent's (Oxford); Oriental; City University. Address: Kites Nest House, Bourton, Dorset SP8 5AZ, England.

NAUGHTIE (Alexander) James, b. 9 August 1951, Aberdeen, Scotland. Journalist. m. Eleanor Updale, 1986, 1 son, 2 daughters. Education: University of Aberdeen; Syracuse University. Appointments: Journalist, The Scotsman (newspaper), 1977-84, The Guardian, 1984-88, Chief Political Correspondent; Presenter, The World at One, BBC Radio, 1988-94, The Proms, BBC Radio and TV, 1991-, Today, BBC

Radio 4, 1994-, Book Club, BBC Radio 4, 1998-. Publication: The Rivals, 2001; The Accidental American, 2004. Honour: LLD, Aberdeen. Membership: Council, Gresham College, 1997-. Radio Personality of the Year, 1991; Voice of the Listener and Viewer Award, 2001. Address: BBC News Centre, London W12 7RJ, England.

NAUMOVA Irina, b. 10 October, 1951, Samtredia, Georgia. Educator; Researcher. m. Boris Nikolaevich Naumov, 1 son. Education: BSc (Hons) Piano, Kutaisi College of Music "M Balanchivadze", 1970; MSc (Hons), Philology, Kutaisi State Pedagogical Institute " A Culukidze", 1973; PhD, Philology, 1982, Postdoctoral Fellowship, Philology, 1993, Academy of Pedagogical Sciences of the USSR, Moscow. Appointments: Lecturer, English and Russian, Kutaisi State Polytechnical Institute "N Muskhelshvili", Kutaisi, 1974-79; Postgraduate Student, Academy of Pedagogical Sciences of the USSR, Moscow, 1979-82; PhD Senior Lecturer, English, Kharkiv State Municipal Academy, 1983; Retraining Courses, 1989-90, Postdoctoral Research Fellow, 1991-93, Academy of Pedagogical Sciences of the USSR, Moscow; Head of Foreign Languages Department, Associate Professor, Kharkiv National Municipal Academy, 1985-. Publications: Articles in professional journals, conference proceedings and chapters in books include most recently: Phraseological units of English origin in present-day Russian, 2000; Phraseological units of German origin in Russian and English, 2001; Phraseological commonalities of the Russian and English Languages, 2001; Phraseological commonalties of Biblical origin in Russian and English, 2001; Phraseology in a mirror of national mentality, 2002; English Origin of Phraseological Neologisms of the Russian Language, 2002; Culturological Codes of Language Nomination, 2003; Semantic Evolution of Biblical Interfrazemes in Russian and English, 2003; Current Phraseology of Russian and English Languages, 2003; English Sources of Political Linguistics of the Russian Language, 2004; Contemporary Phraseology and Art, 2004; On the Origin of Popular Words and Phrases Borrowed from English, 2004. Honours: certificates for Research Programmes, Dundee Business School and School of Science and Engineering, Abertay Dundee University, 1999, 2000, 2001; Acmeology Course Certificate, Russian Academy of Education, Institute of Adult Education, Saint Petersburg, 2001; Award for Outstanding Support to the International YMCA, New York, 2003; Certificates for Participation and Assistance to III Jornadas Andaluzas de Eslavistica, 2004; Listed in Who's Who publications and biographical dictionaries. Memberships: European Association of Lexicography; European Association of Researchers of Phraseology; British Association of Slavonic and Eastern European Studies; The Slavists Cognitive Linguistics Association; Dictionary Society of North America; International Association of Teachers of English as Foreign Language; Research Board of Advisors, ABI; IATEFL, Kiev; TESOL-Ukraine, Kiev; UAPRYAL, Kiev. Address: Ap 116, 195 Klochkovskaya St, Kharkiv 61 145, Ukraine. E-mail: irina@bi.com.ua

NAURYZBAI Zhumagali, b. 21 October 1949, Zhezkazgan, Karaganda region, Kazakhstan. Rector of the university; Doctor of Pedagogic Science; Professor. m. Abdigulova Zhannat, 3 sons, 1 daughter. Education: Chemistry and Biology Teacher, Karaganda State University, 1972; Graduate (1st class honours), Science of Law, Abai University of Almaty, 1998; PhD, Pedagogics, 1988, 1998. Appointments: Adviser of the President's Council on Education and International Relations, 1990-91; Executive, Head of the advisers in the President's office and Cabinet of Ministers, 1991-93; Secretary of the National Council on State Policy in the President's office;

Akim Deputy, Zhezkazgan Region, 1994-95; Majilis Deputy of Parliament of the Republic of Kazakhstan, 1995-99; Rector of Baikonurov University, Zhezkazgan, 2000-. Publications: 44 books; 3 monographs; 3 textbooks; 2 electronic manuals; More than 500 articles in the field of education; Author, 4 poetic collections; CD of own songs. Honours: 4 State Awards, Baitursynov, 2003, Altynsarin medal, 2006; Kazakhstan Journalist League prizewinner; Ana Tili's winner for Person of the year; Parasat's winner for Person of the Year; Gold Medal, French Association SPI, 2002; International Award Gold Bullion, Switzerland, 2006; Honorary Citizen of Zhezkazgan; Honour Scholar of Education, Republic of Kazakhstan. Memberships: Academician, International Academy of Sciences; Academician, Academy of Pedagogical Sciences of the RK; Union of Journalists of the RK; Thesis Commission of Doctors in Buketov University of Karaganda; Editorial Board of Higher Education of Kazakhstan, Kazakhstan Mektebi, Tarbie Kuraly and Ulagat. Address: Alashakhan Street, 1b, Zhezkazgan, Karaganda oblast, RK, 100602, Kazakhstan. E-mail: univer@zhez.kz Website: www.zhez.kz

NAVARRO David Michael, b. 7 June 1967, Santa Monica, California, USA. Songwriter, Writer, Musician (piano, guitar, drums and bass guitar). m. (3) Carmen Electra, 2003, Separated. Musical Education: Piano lessons aged 6; Guitar lessons. Career: Various TV and radio show appearances; Co-hosting Tv show Rock Star:INXS; Bands: South Dakota Railroad, Dizastre, 1983; Jane's Addiction, 1986; Red Hot Chilli Peppers, 1993; Nancy Raygun (Swallow), 1999; Spread, 1997; Camp Freddy, 2002; The Panic Channel, 2004. Recordings: Singles released include: Rexall; Hungry; Sunny Day; Mourning Son; Everything; Not for Nothing; Avoiding the Angel; Very Little Daylight; Venus in Furs; Slow Motion Sickness; The Bed; Somebody Else; Easy Girl; Why Cry; Teahouse of the Spirits. Albums include: Nothing's Shocking, 1988; Trust No One, 2001; One, 2006. Publications: Don't Try This at Home, 2004. Website: www.6767.com.

NAVRATILOVA Martina, b. 18 October 1956, Prague, Czech Republic (now American Citizen). Tennis Player. Career: Defected to the US in 1975, professional Player since; Titles: Wimbledon Singles, 1978, 1979, 1982, 1983, 1984, 1985, 1986, 1987, 1990; Doubles: 1976, 1979, 1982, 1983, 1984, 1985; Avon, 1978, 1979, 1981; Aust, 1981, 1983, 1985; France, 1982, 1984; US Open, 1983, 1984, 1986, 1987; Finalist at Wimbledon, 1988, 1989; Federation Cup for Czechoslovakia, 1973, 1974, 1975; 54 Grand Slam Titles (18 Singles, 37 Doubles); World Champion, 1980; Ranked No 1, 1982-85; 8 Wimbledon Titles, 1993; Women's Record for Consecutive wins, 1984; 100th Tournament win, 1985; only player to win 100 Matches at Wimbledon, 1991; Record 158 singles victories, 1992; 1,400 Victories, 1994; 167 Singles Titles, 1994; Made comeback in 2000 (in doubles only); Winner, Mixed Doubles, Australian Open, 2003 (oldest winner of a grandslam title); 177 doubles titles; Retired doubles, 2006. Appointments: President, Women's Tennis Association, 1979-80; Designs own fashionwear; Representative of USA in Federation Cup, 2003. Publications: Being Myself, 1985; The Total Zone (with Liz Nickles, novel, 1994); The Breaking Point (with Liz Nickles), 1996; Killer Instinct, (with Liz Nickles), 1998. Address: IMG, 1360 E 9th Street, Cleveland, OH 44114, USA.

NAYDENOV Nayden Milev, b. 1 June 1959, Plovdiv, Bulgaria. Engineer. m. Anusha, 1 daughter. Education: MS, Diploma Engineer in Automation, 1986, Social Psychology, 1985, Technical University, Rousse; Business Organisation and Management, Academy of Economics,

2001. Appointments: Maintenance Team Head; Engineer; Instrumentation and Control Department Head, KNPP Branch, 1987-98; Executive Director, Digtech Isc, Sofia,1998-2001; Units 5 & 6, Modernisation Programme Project Manager, Kozloduy Nuclear Power Plant, 2001-. Publications: Study and analysis of degradation processes in the electronic equipment operating at Kozloduy, 2005; Pre-and post-service microhardness measurements of electrical contacts operating at Kozloduy NPP, 2006; Articles in professional scientific journals. Honours: Power Engineer of the Year, Bulgarian Power Engineering Branch Chamber, 2003. Memberships: Union of Bulgarian Scientists; Rotary Club. Address: Block 13, Entr B, Floor 6, Ap 36, Kozloduy 3320, Vratza District, Bulgaria.

NEASOM Norman, b. 7 November 1915, Tardebigge, Worcestershire, England. Artist; Art Teacher. m. Jessie Mary Davis, 2 daughters. Education: Drawing, Painting, Composition and Illustration, Birmingham College of Arts and Crafts, 1931-35. Career: Teacher, Painting School Birmingham College of Art, 1946-54; Teacher, Redditch School of Art, 1954-80; Retired, 1980; Artist since childhood; Exhibitions: Royal Academy, 1970, 1974, 1976; Royal Watercolour Society; Royal Birmingham Society of Artists; Stratford Art Society; Mall Galleries; Work in collections: West Midlands Arts Council, Birmingham City Arts Collection and various private collections. Publications: Works reproduced by firms including Medici prints; Articles for Leisure Painter; Covers for Readers Digest; Illustrations for local history books. Honours: Twice winner James Priddy Award, Royal Birmingham Society of Arts. Memberships: Patron and Honorary Member, Stratford-on-Avon Art Society; Royal Watercolour Society; Royal Birmingham Society of Artists. Address: 95 Bromfield Road, Redditch, Worcestershire, B97 4PN, England.

NEBE Michael, b. 28 July 1947, Nordenbeck, Waldeck, Germany. Cellist; Conductor. Education: Educational Diploma and Teaching Qualifications, Dortmund Conservatorium; MMus, King's College, University of London, England, studied under Thurston Dart, Brian Trowell, Antony Milner, Geoffrey Bush; Licentiate, Royal Academy of Music, studying with Florence Hooton and Colin Hampton; Conducting, private studies in Germany and at Morley College, London under Lawrence Leonard; International Conductors' Seminar, Zlin, Czech Republic, 1991 and 1993 under Kirk Trevor, Jiri Belohlavek, Georg Tintner and Zdenek Bilek. Debut: Wigmore Hall, London, 1977. Career: Member, London Piace Consort, London Piace Duo, both until 1987, Plaegan Piano Quartet; Numerous performances as soloist and chamber music player throughout UK; Tours in Germany, Netherlands, USA, Canada, Australia; Conductor and Musical Director of Whitehall Orchestra (The Orchestra of the British Civil Service), 1990-; Associated Conductor, Surrey Sinfonietta until 1994; Founder and Musical Director, Fine Arts Sinfonia of London, 1994-; Appearances as conductor in the UK, Germany Spain, Turkey; Teacher, conductor, freelance musician, soloist, translator, writer, lecturer and adjudicator; Made numerous live and recorded radio and television appearances, CD recordings; Conducted over 150 British and world Premieres. Publications: Translation into German, Eta Cohen's Violin Tutor, 1979; Cello Tutor, 1984; Articles for British newspapers and magazines. Membership: Dvorak Society; Incorporated Society of Musicians; Musicians' Union. Address: c/o Thornton Management, 24 Thornton Avenue, London SW2 4HG, England.

NECHAEV Yury Ivanovich, b. 25 January 1933, Vereja, Moscow, Russia. Shipbuilder. m. Victoria Anatolievna, 2 daughters. Education: Cand Sc, 1966, Dr Sc, 1976, Professor, 1977, Shipbuilding Department, Moscow Technical Institute. Appointments: Head of Laboratory, Moscow Technical Institute, 1958-59; Assistant Professor, Kaliningrad State Technical Institute, 1959-69; Assistant Professor, 1959-71, Head of Department, 1971-81, Vice Rector, 1979-85, Sebastopol Device Institute; Director-Chief Constructor, Construction Bureau of Information and Control Systems, 1985-95; Head of Department, Professor of Computer Science Department, State Marine Technical University, 1995-. Publications: Artificial neural network and genetic algorithms in identification problems and ship's behaviour forecast in real time intelligence systems, Gamburg, Germany, 2003; Principles of neural network use in on-board intelligence systems. Neurocomputers: development and application, Moscow, Russia, 2004; Ships safety navigation in conditions of the Arctic shelf, Osaka-Sakai, Japan, 2004; Data mining at designing and operation of marine dynamic object, Naples, Italy, 2005; Neuroapproximation and neuroforecast in on-board intelligence systems, Moscow, Russia, 2005; On-board intelligence systems, Moscow, Russia, 2006. Honours: Honorary Member, Russian Academy of Natural Science, 2003; Knight of Science and Arts, 2004; Honorary Figure of Science, Russian Federation, 2006. Memberships: Honorary Member, Academician, Russian Academy of Natural Science; Head, St Petersburg Department, Russian Association of Neuroinformatics; Member, Editorial Board, Morskoy Vestnik magazine; Vice Chairman, Dissertation Soviet; Prepared 11 doctors of science and 17 candidates of technical, physical and mathematical science. Address: Kusnetsovskaya str, 22-93, Box 13, St Petersburg 196128, Russia. E-mail: int@csa.ru

NEELEY G Steven, b. Cincinnati, Ohio, USA. Professor of Philosophy; Attorney at Law; Philosophical Psychotherapist. Education: BS BA, Magna Cum Laude, Xavier University, 1980; JD, University of Cincinnati School of Law, 1985; MA, 1987, PhD, 1989, University of Cincinnati. Appointments: Law Clerk, Law Offices of T D Shackleford, 1982-84; Attorney-At-Law, Private Practice, 1985-; Adjunct Professor, Union Institute (Union for Experimenting Colleges and Universities), 1989-; Visiting Assistant Professor of Philosophy, Xavier University, 1989-92; Adjunct Professor of Philosophy, College of Mount St Joseph, 1992-93; Assistant Professor of Philosophy, 1993-97, Associate Professor of Philosophy, 1997-2003, Saint Francis College; Professor of Philosophy, Saint Francis University, 2003-; Philosophical Psychotherapist, Private Practice, 1997-. Publications: Books: The Constitutional Right to Suicide: A Legal and Philosophical Examination, 1994, 2nd edition, 1996; Schopenhauer: A Consistent Reading, 2003; Numerous articles in professional journals. Honours include: Swatsworth Faculty Award, Saint Francis, 1997; American Philosophical Association, Excellence in Teaching Award, 1998; Finalist, Saint Francis College Honour Society Distinguished Faculty Award, 1998, 1999, 2000, 2001, 2002, 2003; 2004; Student Government Association Teacher of the Year Award, 2004, 2005; Who's Who Among American Teachers, 2005. Address: Saint Francis University, PO Box 6000, Loretto, PA 15940, USA.

NEELY William Robert Nicholas (Bill), b. 21 May 1959, Belfast, Northern Ireland. TV Journalist. m. Marion Kerr, 2 daughters. Education: BA Honours, Queens University, Belfast. Appointments: Reporter, BBC, Northern Ireland, 1981-87; Reporter, BBC Network, 1987-88; Reporter, Presenter, Sky TV, 1989 (January to June); ITN Reporter, 1989-90, ITN

Washington Correspondent and US Bureau Chief, 1990-97, Europe Correspondent, 1997-2002, International Editor and Newscaster, 2002-, ITN. Honours: Royal Television Society News Award, 1999, 2001, 2006; Golden Nymph Trophy, Monte Carlo TV Festival, 2000. Listed in biographical dictionaries. Address: 200 Gray's Inn Road, London WC1X 8XZ, England. E-mail: bill.neely@itn.co.uk

NEESON Liam, b. 5 June 1952, Ballymena, Northern Ireland. Actor. m. Natasha Richardson, 1994, 2 children. Education: St Mary's Teachers College, London. Appointments: Forklift Operator; Architect's Assistant. Creative Works: Theatre includes: Of Mice and Men, Abbey Theatre Co, Dublin; The Informer, Dublin Theatre Festival; Translations, National Theatre, London; The Plough and the Stars, Royal Exchange, Manchester; The Judas Kiss; Films include: Excalibur; Krull; The Bounty; The Innocent; Lamb; The Mission; Duet for One; A Prayer for the Dying; Suspect Satisfaction; High Spirits; The Dead Pool; The Good Mother; Darkman; The Big Man; Under Suspicion; Husbands and Wives; Leap of Faith; Ethan Frome; Ruby Cairo; Schindler's List; Rob Roy; Nell; Before and After; Michael Collins; Les Misérables, 1998; The Haunting; Star Wars: Episode 1 – The Phantom Menace; Gun Shy, 1999; Gangs of New York, 2000; K19: The Widowmaker, 2002; Love Actually, 2003; Kinsey, 2004; Kingdom of Heaven, 2005; Batman Begins, 2005; The Proposition, 2005; Breakfast on Pluto, 2005; The Chronicles of Narnia: The Lion, the Witch and the Wardrobe, 2005; Seraphim Falls, 2006; Taken, 2008. TV includes: Arthur the King; Ellis Island; If Tomorrow Comes; A Woman of Substance; Hold the Dream; Kiss Me Goodnight; Next of Kin; Sweet As You Are; The Great War and the Shaping of the 20th Century; Comic Relief VIII; Empires: The Greeks – Crucible of Civilization; The Endurance: Shackleton's Legendary Antarctic Expedition; Inside the Space Station; The Man Who Came to Dinner; The Greeks; Revenge of the Whale; Nobel Peace Prize Concert; Uncovering the Real Gangs of New York; The Maze; Inside the Playboy Mansion; Martin Luther; Evolution; Liberty's Kids: Est 1776; Happy Birthday Oscar Wilde. Honours include: Best Actor, Evening Standard Award, 1997; Best Actor, Los Angeles Film Critics' Association, 2004. Address: c/o ICM, 8942 Wilshire Boulevard, Beverly Hills, CA 90211, USA.

NEGRI SEMBILAN Yang di-Pertuan Besar, Tuanku Jaafar ibni Al-Marhum Tuanku Abdul Rahman, b. 19 July 1922, Malaysia. Malaysian Ruler. m. Tuanku Najihar binti Tuanku Besar Burhanuddin, 1943, 3 sons, 3 daughters. Education: Malay College; Nottingham University. Appointments: Entered Malay Administrative Service, 1944; Assistant District Officer, Rembau, 1946-47; Parti, 1953-55; Chargé d'Affaires, Washington DC, 1947; 1st Permanent Secretary, Malayan Permanent Mission to UN, 1957-58; 1st Secretary, Trade Counsellor, Deputy High Commissioner, London, 1962-63; Ambassador to United Arab Republic, 1962; High Commissioner, concurrently in Nigeria and Ghana, 1965-66; Timbalan Yang di-Pertuan Agong (Deputy Supreme Head of State), 1979-84, 1989-94; Yang di-Pertuan Agong (Supreme Head of State), 1994-99.

NÉHER-NEUMANN Erzsébet, b. 20 February 1935, Rábatamási, Hungary. Retired Chemical Engineer; Researcher in Solution Chemistry. Education: Diploma of Chemical Technician, Chemical Technical School, 1953; Diploma of Honour in Chemical Engineering, 1958, Technical Dr, 1964, University of Chemical Industries, Veszprèm, Hungary; Technical Dr, equivalent to PhD, Royal Institute of Technology, Stockholm, Sweden, 1987. Appointments: Assistant, 1958-64,

1st Assistant to Professor, 1965-67, University of Chemical Industries, Veszprèm, Hungary; Assistant, 1967-77, Research Engineer, 1977-2000, Department of Inorganic Chemistry, Royal Institute of Technology, Stockholm, Sweden; Retired, 2000. Publications: Articles in scientific journals including Acta Chemica Scandinavica, 1979, 1984, 1985, 1992, 1994, 1997, 1998, 1999; Journal of Solution Chemistry, 2003, 2006. Honour: 21st Century Award for Achievement with Illuminated Diploma of Honour, International Biographical Centre, Cambridge, England. Address: Smedsbacksgatan 7, 3tr, 115 39 Stockholm, Sweden.

NEHORAI Arye, b. 10 September 1951, Haifa, Israel. Professor. m. Shlomit, 1 son, 1 daughter. Education: BSc, Technion, Israel, 1976; MSc, Technion, Israel, 1979; PhD, Stanford University, 1983. Appointments: Research Engineer, Systems Control Technology Inc, 1983-85; Assistant Professor, Yale University, 1985-89; Associate Professor, Yale University, 1989-95; Professor, University of Illinois, Chicago, 1995-2005; Professor and Chair, Electrical and Systems Engineering, Washington University in St Louis, St Louis, 2006-. Publications: More than 120 journal papers; 200 conference papers. Honours: University Scholar, University of Illinois; IEEE Signal Processing Society Senior Award for Best Paper, 1989; Magazine Paper Award, 2003; Fellow, IEEE; Fellow, Royal Statistical Society; Editor in Chief, IEEE Transactions on Signal Processing, 2000-2002; Vice President, Publications, IEEE Signal Processing Society, 2003-05; Technical Achievement Award, IEEE Signal Processing Society, 2006. Memberships: IEEE; Royal Statistical Society; IEEE Signal Processing Society Distinguished Lecturer, 2003-05. Address: ESE Department, Washington University in St Louis, One Brookings Drive, St Louis, MO 63130, USA. E-mail: nehorai@ese.wustl.edu

NEIL Andrew, b. 21 May 1949, Paisley, Scotland. Publisher; Broadcaster; Editor; Columnist; Media Consultant. Education: MA, University of Glasgow. Appointments: Conservative Party Research Department, 1971-73; Correspondent, The Economist, 1973-83; UK Editor, 1982-83, Editor, Sunday Times, 1983-94; Executive Chairman, Sky Television, 1988-90; Executive Editor and Chief Correspondent, Fox News Network, 1994; Contributing Editor, Vanity Fair, New York, 1994-; Freelance Writer and Broadcaster, 1994-97; Publisher, (Chief Executive and Editor-in-Chief), The Scotsman, Edinburgh, The Business, London, 1996-; Chief Executive, The Spectator and Apollo magazines, handbag.com, London, 2004-; Anchorman, BBC TV's Despatch Box, ITV's Thursday Night Live; BBC Radio's Sunday Breakfast, 1998-2000; BBC TV's This Week with Andrew Neil; BBC TV's Daily Politics, 2003-; Lord Rector, University of St Andrews, 1999-2002; Fellow, Royal Society for Arts, Manufacture and Commerce. Publications: The Cable Revolution, 1982; Britain's Free Press: Does It Have One?, 1988; Full Disclosure (autobiography), 1996: British Excellence, 1999, 2000, 2001. Address: Glenburn Enterprises Ltd, PO Box 584, London SW7 3QY, England.

NEILL John Robert Winder, b. 17 December 1945, Dublin, Ireland. Archbishop. m. Betty Anne Cox, 3 sons. Education: Foundation Scholar, 1965, First Class Moderatorship, 1966, Trinity College, Dublin, 1962-66; Theological Tripos, 1968, Jesus College, Cambridge, 1966-69; General Ordination Examination, 1969, Ridley Hall, Cambridge, 1968-69. Appointments: Ordained Deacon, 1969, Priest, 1970, Bishop, 1986; Curate of Glenageary, Dublin, 1969-71; Bishop's Vicar, St Canice's Cathedral, Ossory, 1971-74; Rector of Abbeystrewry, Cork, 1974-78; Vicar of Saint Bartholomew's,

Dublin, 1978-84; Dean of Waterford, 1984-86; Bishop of Tuam, 1986-97; Bishop of Cashel and Ossory, 1997-2002; Archbishop of Dublin and Primate of Ireland, 2002-. Honours: BA, University of Dublin, 1966; BA, University of Cambridge, 1968; MA, University of Dublin, 1969; MA, University of Cambridge, 1972; LLD (Honoris Causa), National University of Ireland, 2003. Address: The See House, 17 Temple Road, Dublin 6, Ireland. E-mail: archbishop@dublin.anglican.org

NEILL Sam, b. 14 September 1947, Northern Ireland. Actor. m. Noriko Watanabe, 1 daughter. 1 son by Lisa Harrow. Education: University of Canterbury. Creative Works: Toured for 1 year with Players Drama Quintet; Appeared with Amamus Theatre in roles including Macbeth and Pentheus in The Bacchae; Joined New Zealand National Film Unit, playing leading part in 3 films, 1974-78; Moved to Australia, 1978, England, 1980; TV appearances include: From a Far Country; Ivanhoe; The Country Girls; Reilly: Ace of Spies; Kane and Abel (mini-series); Submerged (film), 2001; Framed (film), 2002; Dr Zhivago (mini-series), 2002; Stiff, 2004; Jessica, 2004; To The Ends of the Earth, 2005; Mary Bryant, 2005; The Triangle, 2005; Merlin's Apprentice, 2006; The Tudors, 2007; Iron Road, 2008. Films: Sleeping Dogs, 1977; The Journalist; My Brilliant Career; Just Out of Reach; Attack Force Z; The Final Conflict (Omen III); Possession; Enigma; Le Sand des Autres; Robbery Under Arms; Plenty; For Love Alone; The Good Wife; A Cry in the Dark; Dead Calm; The French Revolution; The Hunt for Red October; Until the End of the World; Hostage; Memoirs of an Invisible Man; Death in Brunswick; Jurassic Park; The Piano; Sirens; Country Life; Restoration; Victory; In the Month of Madness; Event Horizon; The Horse Whisperer; My Mother Frank; Molokai; The Story of Father Damien; Bicentennial Man; The Dish, 2000; Monticello; The Zookeeper, 2001; Jurassic Park III, 2001; Dirty Deeds, 2002; Perfect Strangers, 2002; Yes, 2004; Wimbledon, 2004; Little Fish, 2005; Irresistible, 2006; Angel, 2007; How to Change in 9 Weeks, 2008. Address: c/o ICM, 8942 Wilshire Boulevard, Beverly Hills, CA 90211, USA.

NERMUT Milan Vladimir, b. 19 March 1924, Kyjov, Czech Republic. Divorced, 4 daughters. Education: Medical Bacteriology, 1956, CSc degree, 1958, Medical Faculty, Readership in Cytology, 1965, Faculty of Science, Purkyne University, Brno. Appointments: Department of Biology, Medical Faculty, Brno, 1947-62; Institute of Microbiology, Czechoslovak Academy of Sciences, Prague, 1962-65; Head of Electron Microscopy Laboratory, Institute of Virology, Czechoslovak Academy of Sciences, Bratislava, 1965-70; Max-Planck Institute for Virus Research, Tubingen, Germany, 1970-71; National Institute for Medical Research, MRC, London, 1971-89; National Institute for Biological Standards and Control, South Mimms, UK, 1991-2005; Visiting Scientist, National Institute for Medical Research, MRC, London, 2006-; Visiting Scientist in France, Canada, USA, Australia, Switzerland, Spain and University College, London. Honours: Hlavka Memorial Medal, Czechoslovak Academy of Sciences, 1992; J E Purkyne Gold Medal, Medical Faculty, Masaryk University, Brno, 1992; Honorary Degree (DSc), Slovak Academy of Sciences, Bratislava, 1995; Memorial Medal, Masaryk University, Brno, 2003; Babak Medal, Biological Society, Brno, Czech Republic; Listed in national and international biographical dictionaries. Memberships: Society of General Microbiology; Research Board of Advisors, ABI, 2007; Editorial Board Member: Micron; Veterinary Medicine; Microscopy and Analysis; Scripta Medica. Address: 12 Milton Road, London NW7 4AX, England. E-mail: mvnermut@nimr.mrc.ac.uk

NETANYAHU Benjamin, b. 21 October 1949. Politician; Businessman. m. 3 children. Education: BSc, 1974, MSc, 1976, MIT. Appointments: Managing Consultant, Boston Consulting Group, 1976-78; Executive Director, Jonathan Institute, Jerusalem, 1978-80; Senior Manager, Rim Inds, Jerusalem, 1980-82; Deputy Chief of Mission, Israeli Embassy, Washington DC, 1982-84; Permanent Representative to UN, 1984-88, Deputy Minister of Foreign Affairs, 1988-91, Deputy Minister, PM's Office, 1991-92; Leader, Likud, 1993-99; 2006-; Minister of Foreign Affairs, 2002-03, of Finance, 2003-. Publication: A Place Among the Nations: Israel and the World, 1993; Fighting Terrorism, 1995; A Durable Peace, 2000. Address: Ministry of Finance, POB 13191, 1 Rehov Kaplan, Kiryat Ben-Gurion, Jerusalem 91008, Israel.

NETTLETON Michael Arthur, b. 30 August 1932, Leeds, Yorkshire, England. Retired Academic. Widower, 2 daughters. Education: BSc, Applied Chemistry, Glasgow University & ARTC, Royal Technical College, 1953; PhD, Applied Physical Chemistry, Imperial College, London University, 1960; DSc, Strathclyde University, 1979. Appointments: REME, Malaysia, 1953-55; Electrochemical Engineering, 1955-58; Imperial College, 1958-60; Vickers Research, 1960-62; Central Electricity Research Laboratories, 1962-85; Mechanical Engineering and later Chemical Engineering, University of Queensland, 1985-97. Publications: Over 80 articles in reputable scientific journals. Honours: Research Fellow, Physics Department, University College of Wales; Research Fellow, Mechanical Engineering Department, Leeds University; Hunterhill Bursary, Glasgow, General Service Medal; Honorary Professor, University of Queensland. Memberships: Returned Servicemen Club, Australia. Address: Acorns, 11 Grendon Close, Horley, Surrey RH6 8JW, England. E-mail: MNettl5993@aol.com

NEUFELD Karl H, b. 16 February 1939, Warendorf, Germany. Professor of Theology. Education: Lic phil, 1965, Lic Theol, 1970, Lyon-Fouvière; Dr theol, Catholic Institute of Paris, 1975; Dr theol habil, Innsbruck University, 1980; Dr phil, München-Hochschule für Philosophie, 1983. Appointments: Assistant of K Rahner, 1971-73; Professor of Theology, Rome Pont University Gregoriana, 1978-1989; Professor of Theology, Innsbruck, 1990-2007. Publications: Books and articles about French Theology; Studies about the work of Ad Von Harnack, Philosophy and Theology, History of Thought and History of Theology, Theology of Religions. Honours: Honorary member, Direct Committee of Istituto di Scienze Religiose, Trento, Italy. Memberships: ASS Internationale Card Henri de Lubac, Paris; German Cercle of Theologians, Dt Hochschulverband. Address: Sillgasse 6, P'fach 569 A- 6021, Innsbruck, Austria.

NEWBY Richard Mark (Baron of Rothwell in the County of West Yorkshire), b. 14 February 1953, UK. Member of the House of Lords. m. Ailsa Ballantyne Thomson, 2 sons. Education: BA, Philosophy, Politics and Economics, 1971, MA, St Catherine's College, Oxford. Appointments: Private Secretary to Permanent Secretary, 1977-79, Principal Planning Unit, 1979-81, HM Customs and Excise; Secretary, SDP Parliamentary Committee, 1981; National Secretary, SDP, 1983-88; Executive, 1988-90, Director, 1991, Corporate Affairs, Rosehaugh plc; Director, Matrix Communications Consultancy Ltd, 1992-99; Chairman, Reform Publications, 1993-; Liberal Democrat, Treasury Spokesman, House of Lords, 1997-; Member, Centre Forum Advisory Board; Director, Flagship Group, 1999-2001; Chief of Staff to Charles Kennedy MP, 1999-2006; Chairman Live Consulting, 2001-. Honour: OBE, 1990. Memberships: Trustee, Allachy Trust;

Trustee, Coltstaple Trust; MCC; Trustee: Fatimid Foundation UK; IDS UK; David Lloyd George Statue Appeal Trust; NW University UK; Playing Alive Foundation; FRSA. Address: House of Lords, London SW1A 0PW, England. E-mail: newbyr@parliament.uk

NEWELL Mike, b. 28 March 1942, St Albans, England. Film Director. m. Bernice Stegers, 1979, 3 children. Education: University of Cambridge. Appointments: Trainee Director, Granada TV, 1963. Creative Works: TV work includes: Big Breadwinner Hog (series), 1968; Budgie (series); Thirty Minute Theatre and other TV plays; Director, European Premiere of Tennessee Williams' The Kingdom of the Earth, Bristol Old Vic; Films: The Man in the Iron Mask, 1976; The Awakening, 1979; Bad Blood, 1980; Dance with a Stranger, 1984; The Good Father, 1985; Amazing Grace and Chuck, 1986; Soursweet, 1987; Common Ground, 1990; Enchanted April, 1991; Into the West; Four Weddings and a Funeral, 1994; An Awfully Big Adventure, 1994; Donnie Brasco, 1997; Pushing Tin, 1998; Photographing Fairies (executive producer), 1997; 200 Cigarettes, 1999; Best Laid Plans, 1999; High Fidelity, 2000; Traffic, 2000; I Capture the Castle, 2003; Mona Lisa Smile, 2003; Harry Potter and the Goblet of Fire, 2005; Love in the Time of Cholera, 2007. Honours include: BAFTA Award, Best Director, 1995. Address: c/o ICM, Oxford House, 76 Oxford Street, London W1N 0AX, England.

NEWEY Jon Wilton, b. 12 January 1951, London, England. Editor; Publisher. m. Jill Newey, 1 son, 1 daughter. Education: Bec Grammar School; Graphic Art Diploma Course, Kennington College. Appointments: Professional Musician, 1970-74; Department Head, Dalton's Weekly, 1974-77; Advertisement Manager, Sounds Magazine, 1977-91; Publisher, Top Magazine, 1991-99; Editor and Publisher, Jazzwise Magazine, 2000-. Publications: Books: The Tower Jazz Guide (editor); Tapestry of Delights (consultant editor); Music Mart Drum Guide (author); Jazz-Rock – A History (discographer); Articles in magazines including: Sounds, Music Mart, Mojo, Record Collector, Jazzwise, Jazz on CD, Jazz at Ronnie Scotts, Music Business, MI PRO. Honour: Journalist of the Year, Parlimentary Jazz Awards, 2006. E-mail: jonnewey@jnal.com

NEWING Peter, b. 10 May 1933, Littlebourne, Canterbury, England. Clerk in Holy Orders. m. Angela Newing. Education: Cert Ed, Birmingham, Worcester College of Education, 1953-55; BA and Long Prize (Proxime Accesit), St John's College, Durham, 1960-65; B Ed, Bristol University, 1976; BSc, State University of New York, USA, 1985; Ed D, Pacific Western University, USA, 1988; Diploma, Religious Studies, Cambridge University, 1991. Appointments: National Service, RAF, London, 1951-53; Science Teacher, Bedfordshire County Council, 1955-60; Curate of Blockley with Aston Magna, 1965-69; Deacon, 1965, Priest, 1966, Gloucester; Priest in Charge of Taynton and Tibberton, 1969-75; Lecturer, Gloucestershire College of Arts and Technology, now University of Gloucestershire, 1972-82; Tutor, Open University, 1975-76; Rector of Brimpsfield, Elkstone and Syde, 1975-95; Rector of Brimpsfield, Daglingworth, The Duntisbournes, etc., 1995-2001; Curate of Redmarley, Bromesberrow, Dymock etc., 2001-03, Honorary Curate, 2003-. Publications: Pamphlet, The Literate's Hood and Hoods of the Theological Colleges of the Church of England, 1959; Various articles on church bells. Honours: Fellow Society of Antiquaries, Scotland, 1959; Fellow Royal Society of Arts, London, 1960; Fellow The College of Preceptors, London (F.Coll.P), 1995; Honorary Fellow, Victoria College

of Music, London; B Th, Trinity College, 2007. Memberships: Bishop of Gloucester's Visitor to Church Schools, 1976-94; Member of Court, University of Bristol, 1977-2004; Member, Gloucester Diocesan Synod, 1982-2001, re-elected 2003-2009; Member, Gloucester Diocesan Board of Finance, 1982-2004; Member, Gloucester Diocesan Board of Patronage, 1985-93, 2001-; Member, Panel of Advisers Incumbents (Vacation of Benefices) Measure 1977, 1985-; Member, Central Council of Church Bellringers, 1985-2004. Address: The Rectory, Albright Lane, Bromesberrow, Ledbury, Herefordshire HR8 1RU, England.

NEWKIRK Herbert William, b. 23 November 1928, Jersey City, New Jersey, USA. Materials Scientist. m. Madeleine Dorothy, 2 sons, 1 daughter. Education: AA, Pre-Engineering, Jersey City Junior College, 1948; BSc, Polytechnic Institute of Brooklyn, 1951; PhD, Ohio State University, 1956. Appointments: Chemist, General Electric, Hanford Research Laboratories, 1956-59; Chemist, RCA, David Sarnoff Research Center, 1959-60; Group Leader, Materials Scientist, Lawrence Livermore National Laboratory, 1960-92; Consultant and Participating Guest, Environmental Restoration Division, Lawrence Livermore National Laboratory; Visiting Research Professor, Aachen Technical Institute and Philips Laboratories, Aachen, Germany, Philips Laboratories, Eindhoven, Netherlands, 1969-71. Publications: Over 50 publications and articles on various topics of materials science; 2 inventions. Honours: First Prize and Best of Show – Ceramographic Exhibit, American Ceramic Society, 1965; Research and Development 100 Magazine Award for Technologically Most Significant Invention, 1991; William L Dickinson High School Scholastic Hall of Fame, 2001. Memberships: American Association of Crystal Growth, Treasurer, Northern California Section; Phi Lambda Upsilon; Sigma Xi Fraternity. Address: 1141 Madison Avenue, Livermore, CA 94550, USA. E-mail: newkirk01@sbcglobal.net

NEWMAN Nanette, b. Northampton, England. Actress. m. Bryan Forbes, 2 daughters. Education: Italia Conti School; Royal Academy of Dramatic Art. Appointments: Varied Career in Films, Stage and TV. Creative Works: Appearances in Films including: The Wrong Box; The Stepford Wives; The Raging Moon; International Velvet; The Endless Game; The Mystery of Edwin Drood; Talk Show, The Fun Food Factory; TV Series, Stay With Me Till Morning; Comedy Series, Let There Be Love, Late Expectations. Publications: God Bless Love, That Dog, The Pig Who Never Was, Amy Rainbow, The Root Children; The Fun Food Factory; Fun Food Feasts; My Granny Was a Frightful Bore; The Cat Lovers Coffee-Table Book; The Dog Lovers Coffee-Table Book; The Cat and Mouse Love Story; The Christmas Cookbook; Pigalev; The Best of Love; Archie; The Summer Cookbook; Small Beginnings; Bad Baby; Entertaining with Nanette Newman and Her Two Daughters Sarah and Emma; Charlie The Noisy Caterpillar; Sharing; Cooking for Friends; Spider the Horrible Cat; There's A Bear in the Bath; A Bear in the Classroom; Take 3 Cooks; To You With Love, 1999; Up to the Skies and Down Again, 1999; Bad Baby Good Baby, 2002; Small Talk, 2004; Ben's Book, 2005; Eating In, 2005. Honours include: Best Actress Award, Variety Club; Best Actress, Evening News. Address: Chatto & Linnit Ltd, 123 King's Road, London SW3 4PL, England.

NEWSTEAD Charles George, b. 8 April 1956, London, England. Clinical Director. m. Catherine Lucy McEwen, 3 sons, 1 daughter. Education: Davenant Foundation Grammar School, 1967-74; Guy's Hospital Medical School, 1974-81; BSc, 1st class honours, Basic Medical Sciences and Physiology,

University of London, 1978; MB BS, University of London, 1981; MRCP (UK), 1986; MD, University of London, 1991; FRCP (London), 1997; Diploma in Health Services Management, University of York, 1998. Appointments: House Physician, Lewisham Hospital, 1981-82; House Surgeon, Guy's Hospital, 1982; Senior House Officer/Registrar Training Scheme, The Royal London Hospital, 1982-86; Lecturer in Renal Medicine, The Royal London Hospital Medical College (University of London), Honorary Registrar, The London Hospital, 1986-89; Honorary Lecturer Medical Unit, The Royal London Hospital Medical College, supported by The Medical Research Council, 1989-90; Clinical Lecturer in Medicine, University of Manchester, Honorary Senior Registrar (Renal and General Medicine), Manchester Royal Infirmary, 1990-93; Lead Clinician, Renal Services Leeds Teaching Hospitals NHS Trust, Consultant Renal Physician, St James's University Hospital, Leeds, Honorary Senior Lecturer, University of Leeds, 1990-93; Lead Clinician, Renal Services Leeds Teaching Hospitals NHS Trust, Consultant Renal Physician, St James's University Hospital, Leeds; Honorary Senior Lecturer, University of Leeds, 1993-2001; Clinical Director and Chair of Clinical Management Team, Renal Services Leeds Teaching Hospitals NHS Trust, 2003-. Publications: Co-author or author of over 30 peer-reviewed papers; More than 15 editorials, reviews and book chapters; Over 100 short reports or conference abstracts; Principal editor of 6 sets of clinical guidelines. Honours: Ian Howat Memorial prize; British Nutrition Foundation/Nestle Bursary Award; MRC Project Grant; National Kidney Research Fund Grant. Memberships: The Physiological Society; The Renal Association; European Dialysis and Transplant Association; European Renal Association; International Society of Nephrology; British Transplantation Society; The Royal College of Physicians of London; The Transplantation Society. Address: Renal Unit, St James's Hospital, Leeds LS9 7TF, England. E-mail: chas.newstead@leedsth.nhs.uk

NEWTON Thandie, b. 6 November 1972, Zambia. Actress. m. Oliver Parker, 1998, 2 daughters. Education: Downing College, Cambridge. Career: Films: Flirting, 1991; The Young Americans, 1993; Interview with a Vampire, 1994; Loaded, 1994; Jefferson in Paris, 1995; The Journey of August King, 1995; The Leading Man, 1996; Gridlock'd, 1997; Besieged, 1998; Beloved, 1998; Mission Impossible II, 2000; It Was An Accident, 2000; The Truth About Charlie, 2002; Shade, 2003; The Chronicles of Riddick, 2004; Crash, 2004; The Pursuit of Happyness, 2006; Norbit, 2007; Run, Fat Boy, Run, 2007. TV: Pirate Prince, 1991; In Your Dreams, 1997; ER, 2003-05.

NEWTON-JOHN Olivia, b. 26 September 1948, Cambridge, England. Singer; Actress. m. Matt Lattanzi, 1984-1995 (divorced) 1 daughter. Career: Moved to Australia, aged 5; Singer in folk group as teenager; Local television performer with Pat Carroll; Winner, National Talent Contest, 1964; Singer, actress, 1965-; Represented UK in Eurovision Song Contest, 1974; Music For UNICEF Concert, New York, 1979; Film appearances include: Grease, 1978; Xanadu, 1980; Two Of A Kind, 1983; It's My Party, 1995; Sordid Lives, 2001; Own clothing business, Koala Blue, 1984-. Recordings: Albums: If Not For You, 1971; Let Me Be There, 1974; Music Makes My Day, 1974; Long Live Love, 1974; If You Love Me Let Me Know (Number 1, US), 1974; Have You Ever Never Been Mellow, 1975; Clearly Love, 1975; Come On Over, 1976; Don't Stop Believin', 1976; Making A Good Thing Better, 1977; Greatest Hits, 1978; Grease (film soundtrack), 1978; Totally Hot, 1979; Xanadu (film soundtrack), 1980; Physical, 1981; 20 Greatest Hits, 1982; Olivia's Greatest Hits Vol 2, 1983; Two Of A Kind, 1984; Soul Kiss, 1986; The Rumour,

1988; Warm And Tender, 1990; Back To Basics: The Essential Collection 1971-92, 1992; Gaia - One Woman's Journey, 1995; More than Physical, 1995; Greatest Hits, 1996; Olivia, 1998; Back with a Heart, 1998; Highlights from the Main Event, 1999; Greatest Hits: First Impressions, 1999; Country Girl, 1999; Best of Olivia Newton John, 1999; Love Songs: A Collection: Hit singles include: If Not For You, 1971; What Is Life, 1972; Take Me Home Country Roads, 1973; Let Me Be There, 1974; Long Live Love, 1974; If You Love Me (Let Me Know), 1974; I Honestly Love You (Number 1, UK), 1974; Have You Never Been Mellow (Number 1, US), 1975; Please Mr Please, 1975; Something Better To Do, 1975; Fly Away, duet with John Denver, 1976; Sam, 1977; You're The One That I Want, duet with John Travolta (Number 1, US and UK, third-best selling single in UK), 1978; Summer Nights, duet with John Travolta (UK Number 1, 9 weeks), 1978; Hopelessly Devoted To You (Number 2, UK), 1978; A Little More Love, 1979; Deeper Than The Night, 1979; I Cant Help It, duet with Andy Gibb, 1980; Xanadu, with ELO (Number 1, UK), 1980; Magic (Number 1, US), 1980; Physical (US Number 1, 10 weeks), 1981; Make A Move On Me, 1982; Heart Attack, 1982; Twist Of Fate, from film soundtrack Two Of A Kind, 1983; Back with a Heart, 1998; Grease (Remix), 1998; I Honestly Love You, 1998; Physical Remix 1999, 1999. Honours include: OBE; Grammy Awards: Record of the Year, 1974; Best Country Vocal Performance, 1974; Best Pop Vocal Performance, 1975; Numerous American Music Awards, 1975-77, 1983; CMA Award, Female Vocalist Of Year (first UK recipient), 1975; Star on Hollywood Walk Of Fame, 1981; Numerous other awards from Record World; Billboard; People's Choice; AGVA; NARM; Goodwill Ambassador, UN Environment Programme, 1989. Address: MCA, 70 Universal City Plaza, North Hollywood, CA 91608, USA.

NG Leong Loke, b. 10 October 1954, Ipoh, Malaysia. Professor of Medicine and Therapeutics. Education: Anglo Chinese School, Ipoh, Perak, Malaysia; The Leys School, Cambridge, England; University of Cambridge School of Medicine; The London Hospital Medical College, Whitechapel, London, England. Appointments: Registrar in Medicine, Addenbrooke's Hospital, Cambridge, 1982-84; MRC Fellow, Radcliffe Infirmary, Oxford, 1984-87; Lecturer in Clinical Pharmacology, University of Oxford, 1988-90; Senior Lecturer, Clinical Pharmacology, 1990-96, Reader, 1996-2001, Professor, 2001-, Medicine & Therapeutics, University of Leicester. Publications: Articles in medical journals. Memberships: Member, British Pharmacological Society, 1990; Fellow, Royal College of Physicians, London, 1996; Member, Association of Physicians of Great Britain and Ireland, 2003. Address: Pharmacology and Therapeutics Group, Department of Cardiovascular Sciences, University of Leicester, Robert Kilpatrick Clinical Sciences Building, Leicester Royal Infirmary, Leicester, LE2 7LX, England. E-mail: lln1@le.ac.uk

NG Yuen-Yee Jenny, b. 21 July 1957, Hong Kong. Physiotherapist. m. Tam Sing Fai, 2 daughters. Education: Professional Diploma, Physiotherapy, 1981; Postexperience Certificate, Peripheral Manipulation, 1991; Master of Science in Training, 1995; Exercise Specialist, American College of Sport Medicine, 2003. Appointments: Student Physiotherapist, 1978-81, Physiotherapist II, 1981-83, Physiotherapist I, 1983-, Grantham Hospital, Hong Kong; Training Officer, Allied Health, Hospital Authority, Hong Kong, 2006-. Publications: Preliminary evidence on the measurement properties of the Chinese version of the Child Health Questionnaire, 2005; Papers and articles in professional journals. Honours: Honorary Lecturer, Hong Kong Polytechnic University, 1996-2003;

Honorary Clinical Tutor, 1993-99; Invited Paper Reviewer, 2001-; Best Hospital Program Award, 1998, 2000; Listed in international biographical dictionaries. Memberships: Hong Kong Physiotherapy Association: American College of Sport Medicine. E-mail: yuenyeejenny.ng@gmail.com

NGAI Sik Chong David, b. 26 March 1955, Hong Kong. Chartered Surveyor. m. A Tsui, 1 son, 2 daughters. Education: Bachelor in Law (with Honours), University of Wolverhampton, England. Appointments: Director, UK based international construction consultancy firm, 1982-95; Self-employed construction, costing and project management consultant, 1995-97; Estimator/Project Manager of a general contractor, 1997-98; Senior Estimator/Risk Manager, PCL Construction Management Inc, 1998-99; Partner, professional quantity surveyor/project management consultant firm, Canada, 1999-2000; Instructor, British Columbia Institute of Technology, Canada, 1999-; Consultant/Senior Estimator, PCL Constructors Canada Inc, 2000-01; Instructor, Mechanical Contractors Association of British Columbia, 2001-; Director, professional quantity surveying company, Canada, 2001-. Honours: Arbitrator, Better Business Bureau of Mainland BC, Canada. Memberships: Professional Member, Royal Institution of Chartered Surveyors; Bachelor of Law (with Honours); Professional Member, Quantity Surveyors Society of British Columbia; Professional Member, Canadian Institute of Quantity Surveyor; Full Member, American Association of Cost Engineers; Gold Seal Certified, Canadian Construction Association; Chartered Member, British Columbia Arbitration & Mediation Institute; Chartered Member, ADR Institute of Canada. Address: 9391 Patterson Road, Richmond, British Columbia V6X 1P8, Canada. E-mail: dscngai@hotmail.com

NGUYEN Khue Vu, b. 24 September 1952, Hanoi, Vietnam. Research Scientist. m. Martine Françoise Juilleret, 2 sons, 1 daughter. Education: Bachelor of Science, Biochemistry, 1979, Master of Science, Molecular Biology, 1980, PhD, Macromolecular Physical Chemistry, 1983, PhD, Physical Sciences, 1986, Université Louis Pasteur, Strasbourg, France. Appointments: Research Scientist, Ecole Européenne des Hautes Etudes des Industries Chimiques, Strasbourg, France, 1983-86; Research Scientist, Institut de Bacteriologie de la Faculté de Médecine, Strasbourg, France, 1986-87; Research Scientist, Anda Biologicals Company, Strasbourg, France, 1987-97; Research Scientist, Neurofit Company, Strasbourg, France, 1997-99; Research Scientist, Department of Biochemical Genetics and Metabolism and Mitochondrial Disease Center, University of California, San Diego, USA, 1999-. Publications: Numerous research articles in the areas of biopolymer chemistry, physical and analytical chemistry, enzymology, immunology and molecular biology in scientific journals including: Journal of Polymer Science, 1986; Journal of Medical Microbiology, 1990; Biochemical Biophysical Research Communications, 2002; Annals of Neurology, 2004; Many patents. Honours: Listed in numerous Who's Who publications and biographical dictionaries. Memberships: American Chemical Society; American Society for Microbiology; American Association for the Advancement of Science; New York Academy of Sciences. Address: Biochemical Genetics and Metabolism, The Mitochondrial and Metabolic Disease Center, UCSD School of Medicine, 214 Dickinson Street, Building CTF, Room C-103, San Diego, CA 92103-8467, USA. E-mail: k25nguyen@ucsd.edu

NGUYEN Phuong, b. 30 June 1950, Saigon, Vietnam. Mechanical Engineer. Divorced, 1 son, 1 daughter. Education: BS, Mechanical Engineering, Dalat University, Vietnam, 1974; MS, Mechanical Engineering, Bristol University,

England, 1983; PhD, Applied Mechanics, Cranfield University (the then Cranfield Institute of Technology), Bedford, 1987. Appointments: Lecturer, Department of Mechanical Engineering, Cantho University, Vietnam, 1978-80; Pipe Stress Engineer, Santa Fe Brown (UK) Ltd, Milton Keynes, England, 1988; Structural Assessment Group, BNFL Magnox Generation and predecessor organisations, Gloucestershire, England, 1989-. Publications: The Historical Battles of the Vietnam War 1963-75, 1993; The Vietnam War Collection: From the First Battle Until the Last, 2001. E-mail: phuong.d.nguyen@magnox.co.uk

NICHOLS Mike (Michael Igor Peschowsky), b. 6 November 1931, Berlin, Germany. Stage and Film Director. m. (1) Patricia Scot 1957, (2) Margot Callas, 1974, 1 daughter, (3) Annabel Nichols, (4) Diane Sawyer, 1988. Education: University of Chicago. Creative Works: Shows directed: Barefoot in the Park, New York, 1963; The Knack, 1964; Luv, 1964; The Odd Couple, 1965; The Apple Tree, 1966; The Little Foxes, 1967; Plaza Suite, 1968; Films (director/producer): Who's Afraid of Virginia Woolf?, 1966; The Graduate, 1967; Catch-22, 1969; Carnal Knowledge, 1971; Day of the Dolphin, 1973; The Fortune, 1975; Annie, 1977; Gilda Live, 1980; Silkwood, 1983; Heartburn, 1985; Biloxi Blues, 1987; Working Girl, 1988; Postcards From the Edge, 1990; Regarding Henry, Wolf, 1994; Mike Nicholas, 1995; The Birdcage, 1998; Primary Colors, 1998; What Planet Are You From?, 2000; All the Pretty Horses, 2000; Closer, 2004; Charlie Wilson's War, 2007. Plays directed: Streamers, 1976; Comedians, 1976; The Gin Game, 1978; Lunch Hour, 1980; The Real Thing, 1984; Hurlyburly, 1984; Waiting for Godot, 1988; Death and the Maiden, 1992; Blue Murder, 1995; The Seagull, 2001; Spamalot, 2005. Honours include: Tony Awards; National Association of Theatre Owners' Achievement Award. Address: c/o Mike Ovitz, CAA, 9830 Wilshire Boulevard, Beverly Hills, CA 90212, USA.

NICHOLSON Bryan Hubert (Sir), b. 6 June 1932, Rainham, Essex, England. Chairman. m. Mary, 1 son, 1 daughter. Education: Politics, Philosophy and Economics, Honours, Oriel College, Oxford, 1952-55. Appointments include: Unilever Management Trainee then District Manager, 1955-60; Sales Manager, Jeyes Group, 1960-64; Sales Director, UK, General Manager, Australia, Managing Director, UK and France, Remington, 1964-72; Director, Operations, 1972-76, Executive Main Board Director, 1976-79, Chairman, UK, Chairman, Germany, Supervising Director, France and Italy, Executive Main Board Director, 1979-84, Rank Xerox Ltd; Chairman, Manpower Services Commission, 1984-87; Chairman, The Post Office, 1987-92; Chairman, Council for National Academic Awards, 1988-91; Chairman, National Council for Vocational Qualifications, 1990-93; Chancellor, Sheffield Hallam University, 1992-2001; Chairman, Varity Europe Ltd, 1993-96; President, Confederation of British Industry, 1994-96; Chairman, Cookson Group plc, 1998-2003; Pro-Chancellor and Chair of the Council of the Open University, 1996-2004; Chairman, 2001-2003, Deputy Chairman, 2003-2004, Chairman, 2004-2005, Goal plc (renamed Educational Development International plc); Chairman, 1992-2001, Vice-president, 2001-05, President, 2005-, BUPA; Chairman, Financial Reporting Council, 2001-05; Current Non-Executive Directorships: Equitas Holdings plc, 1996-2005, Education Development International plc, 2005-; President, Wakefield Trinity Wildcats, 2000-; President, National Centre For Young People with Epilepsy (NCYPE), 2005-; Trustee, International Accounting Standards Committee Foundation (IASCF); EU Observer, Public Interest Oversight Board (PIOB) of the International

Federation of Accountants (IFAC); Senior Advisor, Penfida; Member, Proudfoot European Advisory Board. Honours: KB, 1987; GBE, 2005; Companion of the Institute of Management, 1985-; FRSA, 1986-; Honorary FGCI, 1989; Honorary Fellow: Oriel College, Oxford, Manchester Metropolitan University, 1990, Scottish National Vocational Council, 1994-, Scottish Qualifications Authority, 1997; Elected Fellow, Chartered Institute of Marketing, 1991; Hon D Ed, Council for National Academic Awards, 1992; Honorary Doctor, Open University, 1994; Honorary Companion, Chartered Institute for Personnel and Development, 1994; Honorary Doctor of Letters, Glasgow Caledonian University, 2000; Honorary Doctor, Sheffield Hallam University; Honorary Fellow, Open University, 2006; Listed in national and international biographical dictionaries. Membership: Oxford and Cambridge Club. Address: Flat 21, 192 Emery Hill Street, London SW1P 1PN, England. E-mail: bryanhnicholson@aol.com

NICHOLSON Geoffrey Joseph, b. 4 March 1953, Sheffield, England. Writer. Education: MA, English, Gonville and Caius College, Cambridge, 1975; MA, Drama, University of Essex, Colchester, 1978. Publications: Street Sleeper, 1987; The Knot Garden, 1989; What We Did On Our Holidays, 1990; Hunters and Gatherers, 1991; Big Noises, 1991; The Food Chain, 1992; Day Trips to the Desert, 1992; The Errol Flynn Novel, 1993; Still Life with Volkswagens, 1994; Everything and More, 1994; Footsucker, 1995; Bleeding London, 1997; Flesh Guitar, 1998; Female Ruins, 1999; Bedlam Burning, 2000; The Hollywood Dodo, 2004; Sex Collectors, 2006; Contributions to: Ambit magazine; Grand Street; Tiger Dreams; Night; Twenty Under 35; A Book of Two Halves; The Guardian, Independent; Village Voice; New York Times Book Review; L.A. Weekly, Bookforum, Daily Telegraph; Salon.Com; Modern Painters, Art Review. Honour: Shortlisted, Yorkshire Post 1st Work Award, 1987; Shortlisted, The Whitbread Prize, 1998. Address: c/o A P Watt, 20 John Street, London EC1N 2DR, England.

NICHOLSON Jack, b. 22 April 1937, Neptune, New Jersey, USA. Actor; Film Maker. m. Sandra Knight, 1961, divorced 1966, 1 daughter. Career: Films include: Cry-Baby Killer, 1958; Studs Lonigan, 1960; The Shooting; Ride the Whirlwind; Hell's Angels of Wheels, 1967; The Trip, 1967; Head, 1968; Psych-Out, 1968; Easy Rider, 1969; On a Clear Day You Can See Forever, 1970; Five Easy Pieces, 1971; Drive, He Said, 1971; Carnal Knowledge, 1971; The King of Marvin Gardens, 1972; The Last Detail, 1973; Chinatown, 1974; The Passenger, 1974; Tommy, 1974; The Fortune, 1975; The Missouri Breaks, 1975; One Flew Over the Cuckoo's Nest, 1975; The Last Tycoon, 1976; Goin' South, 1978; The Shining, 1980; The Postman Always Rings Twice, 1981; Reds, 1981; The Border, 1982; Terms of Endearment, 1984; Prizzi's Honor, 1984; Heartburn, 1985; The Witches of Eastwick, 1986; Ironweed, 1987; Batman, 1989; The Two Jakes, 1989; Man Trouble, 1992; A Few Good Men, 1992; Hoffa, 1993; Wolf, 1994; The Crossing Guard, 1995; Mars Attacks! The Evening Star, Blood and Wine, 1996; As Good As It Gets, 1997; The Pledge, 2000; About Schmidt, 2002; Anger Management, 2003; Something's Gotta Give, 2003; The Departed, 2006; The Bucket List, 2007. Honours: Academy Award, Best Supporting Actor, 1970, 1984; Academy Award, Best Actor, 1976; Cecil B De Mille Award, 1999; Kennedy Center Honor, 2001; Commander des Arts et des Lettres; Golden Globe for Best Dramatic Actor, 2003. Address: 12850 Mulholland Drive, Beverly Hills, CA 90210, USA.

NICHOLSON John William, b. 9 February 1955, Hampton Court, Middlesex, England. University Lecturer. m. Suzette, 2 sons, 2 daughters. Education: BSc, Kingston University, 1977; PhD, South Bank University, 1981. Appointments: Research Fellow, South Bank University, 1981-83; Higher Scientific Officer, Senior Scientific Officer, Principal Scientific Officer, Laboratory of the Government Chemist, 1983-94; Senior Lecturer in Biomaterials Science, King's College, London, 1995-97; Reader in Biomaterials Science, King's College, London, 1997-2002; Professor of Biomaterials Chemistry, University of Greenwich, 2002-. Publications: Approximately 150 scientific articles; 4 books: The Chemistry of Polymers, 1991, 2nd edition, 1996, 3rd edition, 2006; Acid Base Cements (with A D Wilson), 1993; Polymers in Dentistry (with M Braden, R Clarke and S Parker), 1996; The Chemistry of Medical and Dental Materials, 2002. Honours: EurChem; CChem; FRSC; Jordan Award, Oil and Colour Chemists Association, 1987; President, 2001, Treasurer, 2003-, UK Society for Biomaterials. Memberships: Fellow, Royal Society of Chemistry; UK Society for Biomaterials; European Society for Biomaterials; International Association for Dental Research. Address: School of Science, University of Greenwich, Chatham, Kent ME4 4TB, England. E-mail: j.w.nicholson@gre.ac.uk

NICKLAUS Jack William, b. 21 January 1940, Columbus, Ohio, USA. Professional Golfer. m. Barbara Jean Bash, 1960, 4 sons, 1 daughter. Education: Ohio State University. Career: Professional, 1961-; Winner: US Amateur Golf Championship, 1959, 1961; US Open Championship, 1962, 1967, 1972, 1980; US Masters, 1963, 1965, 1966, 1972, 1986; US Professional Golfers' Association, 1963, 1971, 1973, 1975, 1980; British Open Championship, 1966, 1970, 1978; 6 times, Australian Open Champion; 5 times, World Series winner; 3 times individual winner, 6 times on winning team, World Cup; 6 times, US representative in Ryder Cup matches; 97 tournament victories; 76 official tour victories; 58 times second, 36 times third; Won US Senior Open, USA; 136 tournament appearances, 1996; Played in 154 consecutive majors, 1999; Designer of golf courses in USA, Europe, Far East; Chairman, Golden Bear International Inc; Captain, US team which won 25th Ryder Cup, 1983 Co-chair, The First Tee's Capital Campaign, More Than A Game, 2000; Retired at the Open Championship at St. Andrews, 2005. Publications: My 55 Ways to Lower Your Golf Score, 1962; Take a Tip From Me, 1964; The Greatest Game of All, autobiography, 1969; Lesson Tee, 1972; Golf My Way, 1974; The Best Way to Better Your Golf, vols 1-3, 1974; Jack Nicklaus' Playing Lessons, 1976; Total Golf Techniques, 1977; On and Off the Fairway, autobiography, 1979; The Full Swing, 1982; My Most Memorable Shots in the Majors; My Story, 1997. Honours: Athlete of the Decade Award, 1970s; Hon LLD, St Andrew's, 1984; 5 times US PGA Player of the Year; Golfer of the Century, 1988. Address: 11780 US Highway #1, North Palm Beach, FL 33408, USA.

NICKS Stevie (Stephanie Nicks), b. 26 May 1948, California, USA. Singer; Songwriter. Appointments: Songwriter with Lindsey Buckingham; Recorded album, Buckingham Nicks, 1973; Joined Group, Fleetwood Mac, 1973. Creative Works: Albums with Fleetwood Mac: Fleetwood Mac, 1975; Rumours, 1977; Tusk, 1979; Fleetwood Mac Live, 1980; Mirage, 1982; Tango in the Night, 1987; Behind the Mask, 1990; 25 Years - The Chain, 1992; Solo albums include: Bella Donna, 1981; The Wild Heart, 1983; Rock a Little, 1985; Time Space, 1991; Street Angel, 1994; Composer of Songs Rhiannon, Landslide, Leather and Lace, Dreams, Sara, Edge of Seventeen, If Anyone Falls (with Sandy Stewart), Stand Back (with Prince

Rogers Nelson), I Can't Wait (with others), The Other Side of the Mirror, Time Space, Street Angel, Seven Wonders (with Sandy Stewart). Address: WEA Corporation, 79 Madison Avenue, Floor 7, New York, NY 10016, USA.

NICOL Donald MacGillivray, b. 4 February 1923, Portsmouth, England. Historian; Professor Emeritus. m. Joan Mary Campbell, 1950, 3 sons. Education: MA, 1948, PhD, 1952, Pembroke College, Cambridge. Appointments: Scholar, British School of Archaeology, Athens, 1949-50; Lecturer in Classics, University College, Dublin, 1952-64; Visiting Fellow, Dumbarton Oaks, Washington, DC, 1964-65; Visiting Professor of Byzantine History, Indiana University, 1965-66; Senior Lecturer and Reader in Byzantine History, University of Edinburgh, 1969-70; Koraës Professor of Modern Greek and Byzantine History, Language and Literature, 1970-88, Assistant Principal, 1977-80, Vice Principal, 1980-81, Professor Emeritus, 1988-, King's College, University of London; Editor, Byzantine and Modern Greek Studies, 1973-83; Birbeck Lecturer, University of Cambridge, 1976-77; Director, Gennadius Library, Athens, 1989-92. Publications: The Despotate of Epiros, 1957; Meteora: The Rock Monasteries of Thessaly, 1963, revised edition, 1975; The Byzantine Family of Kantakouzenos (Cantacuzenus) ca 1100-1460: A Genealogical and Prosopographical Study, 1968; Byzantium: Its Ecclesiastical History and Relations with the Western World, 1972; The Last Centuries of Byzantium 1261-1453, 1972, 2nd edition, 1993; Church and Society in the Last Centuries of Byzantium, 1979; The End of the Byzantine Empire, 1979; The Despotate of Epiros 1267-1479: A Contribution to the History of Greece in the Middle Ages, 1984; Studies in Late Byzantine History and Prosopography, 1986; Byzantium and Venice: A Study in Diplomatic and Cultural Relations, 1988; Joannes Gennadios - The Man: A Biographical Sketch, 1990; A Biographical Dictionary of the Byzantine Empire, 1991; The Immortal Emperor: The Life and Legend of Constantine Palaiologos, Last Emperor of the Romans, 1992; The Byzantine Lady: Ten Portraits 1250-1500, 1994; The Reluctant Emperor: A Biography of John Cantacuzene, Byzantine Emperor and Monk c. 1295-1383, 1996; Theodore Spandounes: On the Origin of the Ottoman Emperors (translator and editor), 1997. Contributions to: Professional journals. Membership: British Academy, fellow. Address: 4 Westberry Court, Pinehurst, Grange Road, Cambridge, CB3 9BG, England.

NICOLLE Frederick Villeneuve, b. 11 March 1931, Lausanne, Switzerland. Plastic Surgeon. m. Helia Stuart Walker, 1 son, 2 daughters. Education: Eton College; Trinity College, Cambridge; Middlesex Hospital, London. Appointments: Consultant Plastic Surgeon, Royal Postgraduate Medical School and Hammersmith Hospital. Publications: Books: Rheumatoid Arthritis of the Hand; Rhinoplasty; Breast Reduction; Numerous articles in professional medical journals. Honours: Honorary Professor of Plastic Surgery, International Society of Plastic Surgeons; Visiting Professor of Plastic Surgery, North and South America, and numerous other countries; Fellow, Royal College of Surgeons; M Chir, Cambridge; Gillies Memorial Lecturer, Royal College. Memberships: British Association of Aesthetic Plastic Surgery; British Association of Plastic Surgery; International Society of Plastic Surgery; Chelsea Clinical Society; Alpine Surgical Society. Address: Stud Farmhouse, Chilton Foliat, Hungerford, Berkshire RG17 0TE, England.

NIDDRIE Robert Charles, b. 29 January 1935, Southampton, England. Chartered Accountant. m. Maureen Joy, 1 son, 2 daughters. Education: Brockenhurst Grammar

School. Appointments: National Service 1959-61; Whittaker, Bailey & Co, 1952-59, 1962-75, Partner, 1963-75; Senior Partner in Charge, Southampton Office, Price Waterhouse, 1975-92; Trustee, Duphar Pension Scheme, 1992-2003; Local Director, Coutts & Co, 1992-2002; Non-Executive Director: Bournemouth Orchestras, 1986-96, Meridian Broadcasting Charitable Trust, 1993-2000, Sovereign Employee Benefits Ltd, 1993-95, Chairman, Southampton Cargo Handling plc, 1993-98, Hotel du Vin Ltd, 1994-2004; Founder Chairman, Hampshire Branch of Institute of Directors, 1980-86, Member, Institute of Directors Council, 1980-86; Trustee, Mayflower Theatre Trust, 1988-99; Governor King Edward VI School, Southampton, 1989-2003; Winchester Cathedral Guild of Voluntary Guides, 1995-; Trustee, Deputy Chairman, Royal Marines Museum, 1996-2006. Memberships: Fellow, Institute of Chartered Accountants; Associate, Chartered Institute of Taxation; Associate, Institute of Directors. Address: Morestead House, Morestead, Winchester, Hampshire SO21 1LZ, England.

NIEUW AMERONGEN Arie van, Professor of Oral Biochemistry. Education: MSc, Biochemistry, 1970; PhD, Biochemistry, 1974, Vrije Universiteit, Amsterdam. Appointments: Assistant Professor, Dental Faculty, Department of Oral Biochemistry, 1974-78, Associate Professor, 1974-90, Chairman of Department, 1984, Professor of Oral Biochemistry, 1990-, Vrije Universiteit, Amsterdam; Head of the Subdepartment of Oral Biochemistry, 1984-; Chairman, Department of Basic Dental Sciences, 1999-; Chairman, Dutch Dental Research School, 2000-; Supervisor of 22 PhD Students; Organised 3 international congresses: 5th, 6th, 7th, European Symposium on the Application of Saliva in Clinical Practice and Research, Egmond aan Zee, 1999, 2002, 2005. Publications: First author, 100 papers; Co-author 200 papers; Books: Saliva and Salivary Glands, 1988; Saliva and Oral Health, 1994; Saliva and Dental Elements, 1999; Faith and Science, 2001; Saliva, Salivary Glands and Oral Health, 2004. Memberships: Member of the Editorial Boards: Journal of Dental Research, 1998-2001; Journal of Odontology, 2000-2002; Oral Biosciences and Medicine, 2003-07; 8 Patents. Address: Vrije Universiteit, Department of Oral Biochemistry, ACTA, Van Der Boechorststraat 7, 1081 BT Amsterdam, The Netherlands.

NIGAM Prakash Kumar, b. 10 October 1923, Bhainsdahi, M.P. India. Electrical Engineer/Writer. m. Kanta Nigan, 2 sons, 1 daughter. Education: Bachelor of Science, Nagpur University, India, 1944; BS in Electrical Engineering, University of Wisconsin, USA, 1948. Appointments: Testing Engineer, G.E., USA, 1948-49; Electrical Engineer, Assistant Superintendent, Tata Electric Co. Bombay, India, 1950-60; Chief Power Engineer, HEC, Ranchi, India, 1968; Electrical Engineer with United Engineers, Crawford and Russel, Ebasco, New York, Commonwealth Associates, Bechtel Giffels in USA, 1968-81; Consulting Engineer, Accro and ADSC in US, 1983. Conference: Thermo Electric Plants as complement to Hydro-Electric Development in Bombay-Poona Region for World Power Conference, 1952. Publications include: Book, Reflections on History of the World in 20th Century, to be published 2007; 43 articles in newspapers, 1994-2007. Honours: Scholarship for Advance Studies in USA from J N Tata Endowment, Bombay, India. Memberships: Rotary International Club; Lions Club; A.I.E.E. Address: 43/44 Vijay Nagar Colony, Lalghati, Bhopal 462630, India.

NIGHY William (Bill) Francis, b. 12 December 1949, Caterham, Surrey, England. Actor. m. Diana Quick, 1 daughter. Education: St John Fischer School, Purley, Surrey,

England. Career: National Theatre: A Map of the World and Skylight by David Hare; Pravda by David Hare and Howard Brenton; The Seagull by Chekov; Arcadia by Tom Stoppard; Mean Tears by Peter Gill; Blue Orange by Joe Benhall; A Kind of Alaska and Betrayal by Harold Pinter; Films: Still Crazy; Lawless Heart; Lucky Break; Underworld, I Capture the Castle, Love Actually, 2003; Shaun of the Dead, Enduring Love, 2004; The Magic Roundabout, The Hitchhiker's Guide to the Galaxy, The Constant Gardener, 2005; Underworld Evolution, Pirates of the Caribbean: Dead Man's Chest, Stormbreaker, Flushed Away, Notes on a Scandal, 2006; Hot Fuzz, Pirates of the Caribbean: At World's End, 2007; Valkyrie, 2008. TV: Absolute Hell; The Maitlands; The Men's Room; A Masculine Ending; Eye of the Storm; Unnatural Causes; Don't Leave Me This Way; The Maitlands; Kiss Me Kate; Longitude, 2000; The Inspector Lynley Mysteries: Well Schooled in Murder, 2002; Ready When You Are Mr McGill, The Lost Prince, State of Play, The Canterbury Tales (The Wife of Bath's Tale), The Young Visiters, Life Beyond the Box: Norman Stanley Fletcher, 2003; He Knew He Was Right, Poliakoff Films 2004 – 2, The Girl in the Café, Gideons Daughter, 2005. Numerous radio performances. Honours: Theatre Managers Best Actor, 1996; Best Actor, Barclays Theatre Award, 1996; Best Comedy Performance, Evening Standard Peter Sellars Award, 1998; Best Actor, Broadcasting Press Guild Award, 2003; Barclays Best Actor Award, 2004; BAFTA Award for Best Actor in a TV Drama, 2004; Best Supporting Actor, LA Critics' Circle Award, 2004; London Film Critic's Award, 2004; Best Supporting Actor, LA Critics' Circle Award, 2004; BAFTA Award for Best Supporting Actor, 2004. Address: c/o Markham & Froggatt Ltd, Julian House, 4 Windmill Street, London W1P 1HF, England. Website: www.markhamfroggatt.com

NIHEI Mari Mayang Bernabe, b. 18 December 1964, Balite Cabanatuan City. Manager. Education: Graduate, Philippine Statesman Colleges, 1980; International Relation Co-ordinator, Blood Council Programme; International Foreign Correspondent; Interpreter, re Integration; Graduate, French Course, Waseda University, 2006, Graduate Spanish Course, French Course, Waseda University, 2006. Appointments: Cultural Dancer and Singer; Owner, Sushi Bar and Restaurant; Teacher, Elementary School, Tokyo, Japan; Founder, Japan Association of Novo Ecijanos; Executive Adviser, Sweet Memories Friendship Club of DWNE; International Relations Officer, Nueva Ecija Blood Council; Broadcaster Association of the Philippines; Deputy Governor, ABIRA; Ambassador of Goodwill, ABI; Adviser, Nagkahaisang Haranista; Founder of Teatro Kanto Organisation, Tokyo; Founder/President of Japan Association of Novo Ecijanos; Chairperson of Japan Nueva Ecija Foundation. Honours: Certificate of Recognition, Office of the Governor Tomas N Joson III, 1999; Highest Recognition Award, DWNE Radio Station, Nueva Ecija, Philippines, 2000; Award of Distinction, Association of Commentators & Announcers of the Philippines, 2000; Year 2000 Presidential Awards for Filipino Individuals Overseas, President Joseph E Estrada, 2000; Honorary Member, Rotary Midtown Cabanatuan, 2000; Lifetime Deputy Governor, 2000; Award of Accomplishment, 2000; Woman of the Year, 2000; Officers of Japan Association of Novo Ecijano, Rhiga Royal Hotel, Tokyo, Japan, 2001; World Laureate, 2001; Certificate of Attendance, Philippine Educational Theatre Association, Tokyo, 2001; Medal for Outstanding Participation, 28th International Congress on Arts & Communication, Cambridge, England, 2001; Speaker's Certificate and Medallion, 29th International Congress on Arts & Communication, Vancouver, Canada, 2002; Recognition, Philippine President Gloria Macapagal Arroyo, Tokyo,

Japan, 2003; Order of International Ambassadors, ABI; Certificate of Appreciation, Republic of Philippines; Plaques of Appreciation and Recognition: National Voluntary Blood Services Program, Dr Paulino J Garcia Memorial Research and Medical Center, 1999; Department of Health, Center for Health Development, San Fernando, Philippines, 2000; Nagkakaisang Haranistang DWNE, 2000; Silangan Shimbun, Tokyo, 2001; President of Japan Association of Novo Ecijanos; Presidential Award, 2004; Plaque of Appreciation, Philippine Army Fort Magsaysay, 2006; Plaque of Appreciation, Philippine Embassy, Tokyo, 2006; Plaque of Appreciation, Kamakata Group, 2006; Listed in international biographical dictionaries. Memberships: Board of Consultants, Nueva Ecija Blood Council; President of Teatro Kanjo Organisation; President of Japan Association of Novo Ecijanos; Chairperson of Japan Nueva Ecija Foundation. Address: 1-22-2-1102 Higashi Wing, Shinjuku-ku Nishiwaseda, Tokyo 169-0051, Japan. E-mail: mari-nihei1218@xge.biglobe.ne.jp Website: www.ofw-tv.com

NII Shiro, b.12 January 1932, Naruto, Tokushima Prefecture, Japan. College President. m. Etsuko Tada, 1 son, 2 daughters. Education: MD, Osaka University Medical School, 1956; Intern, Hirohata Hospital, Himeji City, 1956-57; License to Practice Medicine, 1957; Doctor of Medical Science, Osaka University Medical School, 1961. Appointments: Research Associate, 1961-66, Associate Professor, 1966-78, Research Institute for Microbial Diseases, Osaka University; Professor, 1978-97, Dean, 1993-95, Okayama University Medical School; Professor, Kawasaki College, 1997-98; President Niimi College, 1998-2002; President, 2003-06, Honorary President, 2006-, CAC Rehabilitation College. Publications: Articles in scientific journals include: Experimental pathology of measles in monkeys, 1963; Electron microscopy of herpes simplex virus, 1968; Electron microscopic study on the development of herpes viruses, 1992. Honours: Seto Award, Japanese Society of Microscopy; Honorary Professor, Jiangxi Medical College, China, 1993; Emeritus Professor, Okayama University, 1997-; Scientific Award, Sanyo Newspaper, 1997; Meritorious Member, Japanese Society of Infectious Diseases, 2003-; Honorary Member, Japanese Society for Virology, 2003-. Memberships: Japanese Society for Virology; Japanese Society of Microscopy; Japanese Association for Infectious Diseases; Japanese Society for Sexually Transmitted Diseases. Address: Famir Okayama 206, Hama 372-1, Okayama 703-8256, Japan. E-mail: cac-iryo@nifty.com

NII Yuko, b. 22 October 1942, Tokyo, Japan. Artist; Philanthropist. Education: BFA, Macalester College, St Paul, Minnesota, 1965; MFA, Pratt Institute, Brooklyn, 1969. Appointments: Artist, Painter; One woman shows include: Elaine Benson Gallery, Long Island, 1977, 1986, 1994, Fairleigh Dickenson University, New Jersey, 1978, Berkshire Museum, Massachusetts, 1979, Monique Knowlton Gallery, New York City, 1979, Vered International Gallery, Long Island, 1979, Haber Theodore Gallery, New York City, 1980, International Monetary Fund, Washington, 1980; Costume and Stage Set Designer: Chiang Ching Dance Company, New York City, 1977-78, Zignal I at La-Mama, 1978-79; Residency, Yaddo, Saratoga Springs, New York, 1980, 1982; Founder, Director, Williamsburg Art and History Centre, Brooklyn, 1996-. Publications: Contributor: New York Journal, Japan, 1982-83; New York Arts Magazine, 2002; 11211 magazine, 2004; Friends and Mentors Art Show catalogue, 2001. Honours: Woman of Year, Office of Brooklyn Borough President Howard Golden, 1998; Woman of Year, Office of Governor of New York State George Pataki, 2001; Woman of Year, Office of Brooklyn Borough President,

Marty Markowitz, 2003; Outstanding Citizen Award, New York City Council, 2003; Fellowship, Pratt Institute, Brooklyn , 1966-69; Scholarship, Macalester College, St Paul, Minnesota, 1963-65. Address: 385 Clinton Avenue, Brooklyn, NY 11238, USA. E-mail: wahcenter@earthlink.net

NIJNIK Maria, b. 7 April 1956, Lviv, Ukraine. Research Scientist. m. Albert Nijnik, 1 daughter. Education: Dipl Engineer/MSc with Distinction, Ukrainian University of Forestry and Wood Technology, 1978; PhD, Economics, National Academy of Sciences of the USSR, 1984; MSc, Environmental Policy and Management, Netherlands, 1995; Diploma, General and Quantitative Economics, Netherlands Network of Economics, 1999; Diploma, Mansholt Graduate School of Social Sciences, Netherlands, 2002; PhD, Social Sciences, Wageningen University, 2002. Appointments: Researcher, Senior Scientific Fellow, National Academy of Sciences of the USSR, Institute of Economics, 1980-91; Associate Professor, Ukrainian National University, 1991-94; Researcher, Institute for Environmental Studies, Vrije Universiteit, Amsterdam, 1995-2000; Post-Doc Research Fellow, Agricultural Economics and Rural Policy, Wageningen University, 2002; Research Scientist, Socio-Economic Research Programme, Macaulay Institute and Fellow of the University of Aberdeen, UK, 2002-. Publications: Over 100 articles and papers in professional scientific journals, books and proceedings of societies. Honours: Honorary Fellow, University of Aberdeen. Memberships: Scottish Economic Society; UK Women Experts in Science, Engineering and Technology; Advisory Group, Agriculture and Rural Development, USA; Royal Netherlands Society for Agricultural Sciences; Academician, Ukrainian Ecological Academy; Ukrainian Scientific Society; European and International Societies for Ecological Economics; International Union of Forest Research Organisations; International Association of Agricultural Economists; International Association for Society and Natural Resources. Address: The Macaulay Institute, Craigiebuckler, Aberdeen, AB15 8QH, Scotland. E-mail: m.nijnik@macaulay.ac.uk Website: www.macaulay.ac.uk/science

NIKS Inessa, b. 6 November 1938, St Petersburg, Russia. Piano Teacher; Musicology Teacher. m. Mikhail Niks, deceased, 1 son, 1 daughter. Education: Studied Piano, Special Music School for Gifted Children, St Petersburg, 1948-56; Master in Musicology, Diploma with Distinction, St Petersburg Conservatory, 1956-61. Career: Teacher of Musicology and Piano, Music College, Novgorod, Russia, 1961-64; Teacher of Musicology and Piano, Music School, St Petersburg, 1966-76; Head of Musicology Department, Pskov Music College, 1976-79; Owner, piano and musicology studio, Redlands, California, 1983-; Co-Founder, Niks Hand Retraining Center, 1991-; Special course for composers based on new research of sound. Publications: Numerous articles in specialist music journals concerning newly developed piano technique; Co-Inventor of Hand Guide, piano training device, 1991; Manual, Play Without Tension, supplement to piano training device, 1998; Manual, Type Without Tension, 2000; Cassette, Mystery of Singing Tone – acoustical breakthrough in piano sound, 1998. Honours: Silver Medal, 1983, Bronze Medal, 1984, International Piano Recording Competition; Finalist, Audio-Visual Piano, 1995. Memberships: Music Teachers' Association of California, 1983-; European Piano Teachers' Association, 1985-; The National League of American Pen Women, 2002-. Address: Niks Hand Retraining Centre, 1434 Fulbright Ave, Redlands, CA 92373, USA. Website: www.nikstechnique.com

NIMMO Ian Alister, b. 14 October 1934, Lahore, Pakistan. Journalist. m. Grace, 1959, 2 sons, 1 daughter. Education: Royal School of Dunkeld; Breadalbane Academy. Appointments: Lieutenant, Royal Scots Fusiliers, 1956; Editor, Weekly Scotsman, 1962; Editor, Evening Gazette, Teesside, 1970; Editor, Evening News, Edinburgh, 1976-89; Publishing Consultant, 1989-. Publications: Robert Burns, 1968; Portrait of Edinburgh, 1969; The Bold Adventure, 1969; Scotland at War, 1989; The Commonwealth Games, 1989; Edinburgh The New Town, 1991; Edinburgh's Green Heritage, 1996; Walking With Murder, 2005; Rhythms of the Celts, stage musical, 1997; Numerous articles and radio programmes. Membership: Scottish Arts Club; Robert Louis Stevenson Club; Edinburgh Sir Walter Scott Club; Vice-President, Newspaper Press Fund. Address: The Yett, Whim Farm, Lamancha, By West Linton, Peeblesshire EH46 7BD, Scotland. E-mail: iannimmoscotland@aol.com

NIMOY Leonard, b. 26 March 1931, Boston, Massachusetts, USA. Actor; Director. m. (1) Sandi Zober, 1954, divorced, 1 son, 1 daughter. (2) Susan Bay, 1988, 1 Child. Education: Boston College; Antioch University. Appointments: US Army, 1954-56; TV appearances include: Star Trek, 1966-69; Eleventh Hour; The Virginian; Rawhide; Dr Kildare; Film appearances include: Old Overland Trail, 1953; Satan's Satellites, 1958; Valley of Mystery, co-producer, 1967; Catlow, co-producer, 1971; Invasion of the Bodysnatchers, co-producer, 1978; Star Trek - The Motion Picture, co-producer, 1979; Star Trek: The Wrath of Khan, co-producer, 1982; Star Trek III: The Search for Spock, Director, 1984; Star Trek IV: The Voyage Home, Director, 1986; Star Trek V: The Final Frontier, 1989; Star Trek VI: The Undiscovered Country; Director, Three Men and a Baby, 1987, The Good Mother, 1988, Funny About Love, 1990, Holy Matrimony, 1994; The Pagemaster (voice), 1994; Carpati: 50 Miles, 50 Years, 1996; A Life Apart: Hasidism in America (voice), 1997; David, 1997; Brave New World, 1998; Sinbad, 2000; Atlantis: The Lost Empire, 2001. Publications: I Am Not Spock, autobiography, 1975; We Are All Children, 1977; Come Be With Me, 1979; I am Spock, 1995. Address: c/o Gersh Agency Inc, 222 North Cannon Drive, Beverly Hills, CA 90210, USA.

NINEHAM Dennis Eric, b. 27 September 1921, Southampton, England. Retired University Professor. m. Ruth Corfield Miller, 2 sons, 2 daughters (1 deceased). Education: King Edward VI School, Southampton; Queen's College, Oxford. Appointments: Warden of Keble College, Oxford; Regius Professor of Divinity, Cambridge; Professor of Divinity, University of London; Fellow and Tutor, Queen's College, Oxford. Publications: The Gospel of St Mark; Explorations in Theology; The Use and Abuse of the Bible; Christianity Medieval and Modern; many others. Honours: DD (Oxon); Hon DD, Birmingham; Hon DD, Yale. Memberships: Honorary Fellow, Keble College, Oxford; Honorary Fellow, Queen's College, Oxford; Fellow, King's College, London. Address: 9 Fitzherbert Close, Oxford, OX4 4EN, England.

NIRENBERG Marshall Warren, b. 10 April 1927, New York, New York, USA. Biochemist. Education: Graduated, Biology, 1948, Master's Degree, 1952, University of Florida; PhD, Biological Chemistry, University of Michigan, 1957. Appointments: National Institute of Health (Arthritic and Metabolic Diseases), 1957-62, Head, Laboratory of Biochemical Genetics, 1962-; Laboratory of Biochemical Genetics, National Heart, Lung and Blood Institute, Bethesda, Washington, DC; Work in deciphering the chemistry of the genetic code. Honour: Honorary Member, Harvey Society; Molecular Biology Award, National Academy of Sciences,

1962; Medal, Department of Health, Education and Welfare, 1963; Modern Medicine Award, 1964; National Medal for Science, President Johnson, 1965; Joint Winner, Nobel Prize for Physiology or Medicine, 1968; Louisa Gross Horwitz Prize for Biochemistry, 1968. Memberships: New York Academy of Sciences; AAAS; NAS; Pontifical Academy of Sciences, 1974; Deutsche Leopoldina Akademie der Naturforscher; Foreign Associate, Academy des Sciences, France, 1989. Address: Laboratory of Biochemical Genetics, National Heart, Lung and Blood Institute, Building 36, Room IC06, Bethesda, MD 20892, USA.

NISH Ian Hill, b. 3 June 1926, Edinburgh, Scotland. Retired Professor. m. Rona Margaret Speirs, 29 December 1965, 2 daughters. Education: University of Edinburgh, 1943-51; University of London, 1951-56. Appointments: University of Sydney, New South Wales, Australia, 1957-62; London School of Economics and Political Science, England, 1962-91. Publications: Anglo-Japanese Alliance, 1966; The Story of Japan, 1968; Alliance in Decline, 1972; Japanese Foreign Policy, 1978; Anglo-Japanese Alienation 1919-52, 1982; Origins of the Russo-Japanese War, 1986; Contemporary European Writing on Japan, 1988; Japan's Struggle with Internationalism, 1931-33, 1993; The Iwakura Mission in America and Europe, 1998; Japanese Foreign Policy in the Inter-War Period, 2002. Honours: Commander of the Order of the British Empire, 1990; Order of the Rising Sun, Japan, 1991; Japan Foundation Award, 1991; Honorary Member, Japan Academy, 2007. Memberships: European Association of Japanese Studies, president, 1985-88; British Association of Japanese Studies, president, 1978. Address: Oakdene, 33 Charlwood Drive, Oxshott, Surrey KT22 0HB, England.

NISHIMATSU Yuichi, b. 16 January 1932, Japan. Consultant Engineer; Professor Emeritus, University of Tokyo. m. Teiko Kawaguchi, 2 daughters. Education: Graduate, Department of Mining, University of Tokyo, 1954; DEng, University of Tokyo, 1969. Appointments: Research Engineer, Coal Research Institute, Tokyo, 1957; Professor, Department of Mining, University of Tokyo, 1976; Professor Emeritus, 1992-. Publications: Several articles in professional journals. Honours: 4 Prizes, Excellent Research Papers. Membership: Engineering Academy of Japan. Address: 31-9-1003 Honcho, Wako City, Saitama 351-0114, Japan.

NISHIURA Hiroyuki, b. 15 February 1953, Itami, Hyogo Prefecture, Japan. Scientist; Professor. Education: BS, 1976, MS, 1978, DS, 1981, Osaka University, Japan. Appointments: Postdoctoral Fellow, Soryushi Shogakukai Foundation, 1981-82; Postdoctoral Fellow, Japan Society for the Promotion of Science, Kyoto University, 1982-83; Postdoctoral Fellow, Johns Hopkins University, 1983-85; Associate Professor, 1991-2000, Professor, 2000-2005, Osaka Institute of Technology, Junior College; Professor, Faculty of Information Science and Technology, Osaka Institute of Technology, 2005-. Memberships: Physical Society of Japan; American Physical Society. Address: Faculty of Information Science and Technology, Osaka Institute of Technology, 1-79-1 Kitayama, Hirakata-city, Osaka 573-0196, Japan. E-mail: nishiura@is.oit.ac.jp

NISHIYAMA Misuzu, b. 15 December 1951, Sapporo, Japan. Anaesthesiologist. m. Hiroaki Nishiyama, 1 daughter. Education: Graduated, 1976, Hokkaido University, Sapporo, Japan. Appointments: Resident, Hokkaido University, 1975-76; Staff Anaesthesiologist, St Luke's International Hospital, Tokyo, 1986-96; Staff Anaesthesiologist, Jikei University School of Medicine, 1996-2000; Staff Anaesthesiologist,

Asahi Central Hospital, 2001-04; Staff Anaesthesiologist, Ito Municipal Hospital, 2007-. Publication: Anaesthesiology Resident Manual, 1994, 2nd edition, 2000, 3rd edition, 2007. Address: 4982-1317 Futo Ito, Shizuoka-ken, Japan.

NISHTAR Sania, b. 16 February 1963, Pakistan. Doctor. m. G Nishtar, 1 son, 1 daughter. Education: MBBS, Khyber Medical College, Peshawar, 1986; PhD, Medicine, Kings College London, 2002. Appointments: Founder, President and Executive Director, Heartfile, Pakistan. Publications: Numerous papers and articles published in professional and popular journals; 2 books: The National Action Plan for NCD Prevention Control and Health Promotion in Pakistan, 2004; The Gateway Paper: Reforming Health Systems in Pakistan – a Strategic View, 2005. Honours: Many awards including: University of Peshawar gold medal and merit scholarship, 1986; President, Pakistan Student Award and gold medal, 1986; Best Graduate, Khyber Medical College and gold medal, 1986; All Pakistan Quaid-e-Azam Merit Scholarship, 1989; Member, 1996, Fellow, 2005, Royal College of Physicians of London; European Union Population Science Award, 2005; Sitara-i-Imtiaz, 2005. Memberships: World Heart Foundation; Asia Pacific Society of Cardiology; Heartfile; Pakistan's Health Policy Forum; Pakistan Health Policy Council; National Commission on Government Reforms; Trust for Voluntary Organisations in Pakistan; Infrastructure Project Development Facility, Pakistan. Address: Zargul Farms, 1 Park Road, Chak Shahzad, Islamabad, Pakistan. E-mail: sania@heartfile.org Website: heartfile.org/founder.htm

NISSAN Ephraim, b. 9 May 1955. Academic Scholar. Education: Dottore, Ingegneria Elettronica, 1982; Engineering Certification Exam, 1983; PhD, Computer Science, 1989. Appointments: Visiting Professor, University of Urbino, Italy, 1993; Researcher, University of Greenwich, London, 1994-2003; Researcher, Computing Department, Goldsmiths College, University of London, 2004. Publications: About 230 publications of which over 70 articles in professional journals; Guest Editor for scholarly journals over 15 times. Honours: Listed in international biographical dictionaries; Honorary posts at University of Manchester, University of Urbino, and Universidad del Salvador in Buenos Aires; Award for PhD project, 1988; Award for second Laurea thesis, nationwide contest, Italy, 1982; Guest Editor, Applied Artificial Intelligence; Artificial Intelligence and Law; Artificial Intelligence for Engineering Design, Analysis and Manufacturing; Computers and Artificial Intelligence; Computing and Informatics; Cybernetics and Systems; Information and Communications Technology Law; International Journal on Artificial Intelligence Tools; Journal of Educational Computing Research; Journal of Intelligent and Fuzzy Systems; New Review of Applied Expert Systems; Joint Editor, Melilah, Manchester. E-mail: ephraimnissan@hotmail.com

NISSEL Siegmund (Walter), b. 3 January 1922, Munich, Germany. Violinist. m. Muriel, 5 April 1957, 1 son, 1 daughter. Education: External Matriculation, Honours Degree, London University; Private violin study with Professor Max Weissgarber until 1938, then with Professor Max Rostal in London. Debut: With Amadeus Quartet at Wigmore Hall in London, 1948. Career: Founder Member of the Amadeus Quartet; innumerable BBC Radio and TV and ITV appearances; International concert career; Quartet disbanded in 1987 after the death of the violist Peter Schidlof. Recordings: Mozart, Beethoven, Schubert and Brahms Quartets; Benjamin Britten; Brahms Sextets; etc. Honours: Honorary DMus, London and York Universities; OBE; Verdienstkreuz für Musik in

Germany and Austria; Honorary LRAM. Memberships: ISM; ESTA. Address: 11 Highgrove Point, Mount Vernon, Frognal Rise, London NW3 6PZ, England.

NISSEN George Maitland, b. 29 March 1930, London, England. Stockbroker. m. Jane Bird, 2 sons, 2 daughters. Education: Eton College; Trinity College, Cambridge. Appointments: Member of London Stock Exchange, 1956-91; Governor, RI Academy of Music, 1990-98; Deputy Chairman, The Stock Exchange, 1988-91; Chairman: Inv Management Regulatory Organisation, 1989-92; The Book Guild, 1993-2007; Girls Day School Trust Enterprises, 1995-; Liberty Syndicate Management, 1997-2002; The Ffestiniog Railway, 2002-03; Friends of Chiswick House, 2002-. Honours: CBE, 1987. Memberships: Brooks's; Beefsteak. Address: Swan House, Chiswick Mall, London W4 2PS, England. E-mail: g.nissen@talk21.com

NIXDORFF Uwe, b. 12 June 1958, Hofheim/Ts, Germany. Cardiologist. m. Sigrid Nixdorff, 1 son, 1 daughter. Education: MD degree, Johann Wolfgang Goethe University, Frankfurt, 1985; Approbation, Licence for practising medicine, 1985; Doctoral Thesis, Johann Wolfgang Goethe University, 1986; Specialisation as Internist, 1993; Subspecialisation as Cardiologist, 1995; Subspecialisation in Sports Medicine, 2003; Habilitation, Johannes Gutenberg University, Mainz, Germany, 1998; Security in Radiation Exposure qualification, 1998. Appointments: Study of Medicine, Johann Wolfgang Goethe University, 1978-85; Internal Department, Military Hospital, Giessen, Germany, 1985-86; Clinic for Heart and Circulatory Diseases, German Heart Centre, Munich, 1986-87; Resident, Johannes Gutenberg University Clinic, Mainz, Germany, 1987-98; Research Fellow, Michael Reese Hospital, Chicago, USA, 1988; Research Fellow, University of Virginia School of Medicine, Charlottesville, USA, 1989; Research Fellow, Harvard Medical School, Boston, USA, 1989; Consultant, Friedrich-Alexander University Clinic, Erlangen, Germany, 1998-. Publications: 52 original papers; 14 casuistic reports; 14 reviews; 144 abstracts; 28 articles in books; 294 lectures and posters. Honours: Young Investigator's Award, International Council on Electrocardiology, 1988; Best Abstract Award, Honourable Mention, International Society of Cardiovascular Ultrasound, 1996; Award for Increasing the Stature and Contributing to the Success of the 2nd World Congress of Echocardiography and Vascular Ultrasound, Beijing, 1996; Best Poster Award, 8th Essen-Mayo-Mainz Symposium, 1996; Fellow, European Society of Cardiology, 2000; Honourable Knight of the Order of St John, 2000; Listed in national and international biographical dictionaries. Memberships: American Heart Association; European Society of Cardiology; German Society of Cardiology; Chairman of Cluster of Working Groups of Cardiovascular Ultrasound, Nuclear Medicine, MRT and Cardio CT; Chairman of Working Group of Cardiovascular Ultrasound; American Society of Echocardiography; New York Academy of Science; German Society of Internal Medicine; Confederation of German Internists; German Society of Ultrasound Medicine; German Heart Foundation, Member of the Editorial Board; German Society of Sport's Medicine. Address: Turmhügelweg 22, D-91058 Erlangen, Germany. E-mail: uwe.nixdorff@t-online.de

NIXON John, b. 25 September 1952, Hemsworth, Yorkshire, England. Health Economist. m. Yumi Nixon, 2 sons, 2 daughters. Education: Certificate in Education (Cert Ed), 1983; BA (Hons), Social Policy, 1995; MSc Health Economics, 1996; PhD, Economics, 2002. Appointments: Lieutenant, Royal Navy, 1968-92; Tutor, Economics, 1996-98, Fellow,

Centre for Reviews and Dissemination, 1998-2007, University of York. Publications: Numerous articles in peer-reviewed journals including most recently: The European Network of Health Economic Evaluation Databases, 2004; The usefulness of the NHS Economic Evaluation Database to researchers undertaking Health Technology Assessment Reviews, 2004; The relationship between health care expenditure and health outcomes: Evidence and caveats for a causal link, 2006. Memberships: International Health Economics Association; UK Health Economics Study Group; Society for Social Medicine. E-mail: jn105@york.ac.uk

NOAKES Vivien, b. 16 February 1937, Twickenham, England. Writer. m. Michael Noakes, 9 July 1960, 2 sons, 1 daughter. Education: MA, D Phil, English, Senior Scholar, Somerville College, Oxford. Appointments: Guest Curator, Exhibition: Edward Lear 1812-1888, Royal Academy of Arts, London and The National Academy of Design, New York, 1985; Consultant of Lear's paintings and manuscripts to all major auction houses; Honorary Governor, Harris Manchester College, Oxford, 1994-; Member, Governing Committees, Quintin Kynaston School, 2001-2003; LEA, Governor, 2004-07; Judge, The Royal Society of Literature W H Heinemann Award, 1999-2004; Judge, The Winifred Holtby Prize for Regional Writing, 1999-2003. Publications: Edward Lear: The Life of a Wanderer, 1968, 4th edition, 2004; For Lovers of Edward Lear, 1978; Scenes from Victorian Life, 1979; Edward Lear 1812-1888, The Catalogue of the Royal Academy Exhibition, 1985; The Selected Letters of Edward Lear, 1988; The Painter Edward Lear, 1991; The Imperial War Museum Catalogue of Isaac Rosenberg, 1998; The Daily Life of the Queen: An Artists Diary, 2000. The Poems and Plays of Isaac Rosenberg, 2004; Voices of Silence: The Alternative Book of First World War Poetry, 2006; Editor, 21st Century Oxford Authors, Isaac Rosenberg, 2008. Contributions to: Times; Times Literary Supplement; Financial Times; Daily Telegraph; New Scientist; Punch; Harvard Magazine; Tennyson Research Bulletin. Honours: Philip and Francis Hofer Lecturer, Harvard University, 1988; The Tennyson Society Memorial Address, Lincoln, 1988; Guest Lecturer, Yale Center for British Art, 2000; Lecturer, Somerville College, Oxford, 1995-96. Memberships: Fellow, Royal Society of Literature; Member, Society of Authors; PEN. Address: Eaton Heights, Eaton Road, Malvern, Worcesterhire WR14 4PE England. E-mail: mail@vivien-noakes.co.uk

NOBLE Tim, b. 19 February 1966, Stroud, England. Artist. Education: Foundation Course, Cheltenham Art College, 1985-86; BA (Hons), Fine Art, Nottingham Trent University, 1986-89; Artist in Residence, Dean Clough, Halifax, West Yorkshire, 1989-92; MA, Sculpture, Royal College of Art, 1992-94. Career: Solo Exhibitions: British Rubbish, IAS, London, 1996; Home Chance, 20 Rivington Street, London, 1997; WOW, Modern Art, London, 1998; The New Barbarians, Chisenhale Gallery, London, 1999; I ♥ YOU, Deitch Projects, New York, 2000; British Wildlife, Modern Art, London, 2000; Masters of the Universe, Deste Foundation, Athens, 2000; Instant Gratification, Gagosian Gallery, Beverly Hills, 2001; Ghastly Arrangements, Milton Keynes Gallery, 2002; Tim Noble & Sue Webster, P S 1 MoMA, New York, 2003; Modern Art is Dead, Modern Art, London, 2004; Tim Noble & Sue Webster, Museum of Fine Arts, Boston, 2004; The Joy of Sex, Kukje Gallery, Seoul, 2005; The Glory Hole, Bortolami Dayan, New York, 2005; Polymorphous Perverse, The Freud Museum, London, 2006; Group Exhibitions: Lift, Atlantis Basement, Brick Lane, London, 1993; Hijack, New York, London, Berlin, 1994; The Fete Worse Than Death, Hoxton Square, London, 1994; Absolut Art, RCA, London, 1994;

The Hanging Picnic, Hoxton Square, London, 1995; Sex and the British, Galerie Thaddaeus Ropac, Salzburg, Paris, 2000; Apocalypse – Beauty and Horror in Contemporary Art, RAA, London, 2000; Form Follows Fiction, Castello di Rivoli Museo – d'Arte Contemporanea, Turin, 2002; 2001 A Space Oddity, The Colony Room Club Artists' Show, London, 2001; State of Play, The Serpentine Gallery, London, 2004; New Blood, Saatchi Gallery, London, 2004; Monument To Now, Dakis Joannou Collection, Athens, 2004. Honours: MA (Sculpture); BA (Hons) Degree in Fine Art. Memberships: The Colony Room Club. E-mail: info@scumbags.org.uk

NOLTE Nick, b. 8 February 1941, Omaha, USA. Film Actor. m. Rebecca Linger, 1984, divorced 1995, 1 son. Education: Pasadena City College; Phoenix City College. Creative Works: Films: Return to Macon County, 1975; The Deep, 1977; Who'll Stop the Rain, 1978; North Dallas Forty, 1979; Heartbeat, 1980; Cannery Row, 48 Hours, 1982; Under Fire, 1983; The Ultimate Solution of Grace Quigley, Teachers, 1984; Down and Out in Beverly Hills, 1986; Weeds, Extreme Prejudice, 1987; Farewell to the King, New York Stories, 1989; Three Fugitives; Everybody Wins; Q & A, Prince of Tides, 1990; Cape Fear, 1991; Lorenzo's Oil, 1992; Blue Chips, I'll Do Anything, Love Trouble, Jefferson in Paris, 1994; Mulholland Falls, Mother Night, 1996; Afterglow, 1997; Affliction, U-Turn; Breakfast of Champions, The Thin Red Line, 1998; The Golden Bowl, 2000; Investigating Sex, Double Down, 2001; The Good Thief, Northfork, Hulk, 2003; Hotel Rwanda, 2004; Neverwas, 2005; Over the Hedge (voice), Paris, I Love You, Peaceful Warrior, A Few Days in September, Off the Black, 2006; The Mysteries of Pittsburgh, 2007; The Spiderwick Chronicles, 2008. Numerous TV and theatre appearances. Address: 6153 Bonsall Drive, Malibu, CA 90265, USA.

NOOR AL-HUSSEIN, H.M. Queen of Jordan, b. Lisa Najeeb Halaby, 23 August 1951. m. King Hussein I of Jordan, 1978, deceased 1999, 4 children. Education: Princeton University. Appointments: Architechtural and Urban Planning Projects, Australia, Iran, Jordan, 1974-78; Founder, Royal Endowment for Culture and Education, Jordan, 1979, Annual Arab Childrens Congress, Jordan, 1980, Annual International Jerash Festival for Culture and Arts, Jordan, 1981, Jubilee School, Jordan, 1984, Noor Al-Hussein Foundation, Jordan, 1985, National Music Conservatory, Jordan, 1986; Chair, National Task Force for Children; Advisory Committee, UN University International Leadership Academy, Amman; Patron, General Federation of Jordanian Women, National Federation of Business and Professional Womens Clubs, Royal Society for Conservation of Nature and various cultural, sporting and national development organisations; WWF International, Aspen International, 2004-; International Alert's Women and Peace-building Campaign, Council of Women World Leaders' Advisory Group, 2004-; Honorary President, Jordan Red Crescent, Birdlife Int, 1996-2004 (Honorary President Emeritus, 2004-). Publication: Leap of Faith: Memoirs of an Unexpected Life, 2002. Honours: Numerous honorary doctorates, international awards and decorations. Memberships include: Honorary President, Jordan Red Crescent; Founding Member, International Commission on Peace and Food, 1992; President, United World Colleges, 1995. Address: Royal Palace, Amman, Jordan.

NORDGREN Mats Olav, b. 9 May 1959, Malmö, Sweden. Head & Neck Surgeon; Consultant. m. Margareta Petersson, 2 sons. Education: Medical Licenciate, 1989; Specialist in Otorhino-laryngology, Head & Neck Surgery, 1997; Specialist, Phoniatrics, 2005; PhD, Lund University, 2005.

Appointments: Resident, Thoracic Surgery, 1990-91; Resident, Urologic Surgery, 1993-94; Resident, Head and Neck Surgery, 1994-97; Consultant, Head and Neck Surgery and Phoniatrics, 1997. Publications: Thesis, Health-Related Quality of Life in Head and Neck Cancer – a Five Year Prospective Multicenter Study. Honours: Listed in international biographical dictionaries. Memberships: International Member, American Academy of Otorhinolaryngology – Head and Neck Surgery; Corresponding member, American Head and Neck Society; Fellow, Swedish Association of Otorhinolaryngology. Address: Ehrensvardsgatan 15A, 21213 Malmö, Sweden. E-mail: mats.nordgren@med.lu.se

NORDMARK Annica Maria Elisabeth, b. 25 August 1944, Sweden. Executive Manager. m. Jan Nordmark, 1 son, 1 daughter. Education: Diploma, Bar-Lock Secretary and Commercial Institute, 1965; Proficiency in English Certificate, Cambridge University Intern Course, 1991. Appointments: Secretarial work, Department of Trade & Industry, Canadian Embassy, Stockholm, 1966-73; Assistant Secretary General for Rockstore 77 and 80 Symposia, Hagconsult AB, 1976-81; Executive Secretary, International Marketing, AB Jacobson & Widmark/Hagconsult AB, 1977-81; Information Officer, Swedish Rock Engineering Research Foundation BeFo, 1981-96; Executive Manager, Secretariat, Swedish National Group, International Tunnelling Association, 1982-2007; Office Manager, BK Swedish Rock Construction Committee, 1996-2007; Executive Council Member, International Tunnelling Association, 2001-04. Publications: Many articles and papers in professional journals. Honours: Paperweight of the US Engineering Foundation, 1990; Medal, International Tunnelling Association, 1998. Memberships: International Tunnelling Association; Swedish Association of Engineering Geology BGS. Address: Swedish Rock Construction Committee, Box 1721, SE-111 87 Stockholm, Sweden. Website: www.bergsprangningskommitten.se

NORDSTRØM Hans-Henrik, b. 26 June 1947, Nakskov, Denmark. Composer. m. Anne Kristine Smith, 1 son. Education: Royal Danish Academy of Music, Copenhagen, 1965-70. Debut: Copenhagen, 1990. Compositions include most recently: Lost Traces (saxophone and percussion), 2001; In the Woods (violin and sinfonietta), 2001; The Twelve Bens (string trio, 2001); Imaginations (harpsichord), 2002; ...if a Tone in the Night (recorder and accordion, 2002; Growth (brass quintet), 2002; Fair Isle (violoncello, 12 woodwinds, 4 French horns), 2002; Riverrun (Septet), 2002; Quarks (string trio), 2002; Tingsominggenting (guitar), 2003; ALP (flute, clarinet, guitar, percussion and violin), 2003; Following the Wake (piano trio), 2003; Sketches from Iceland (piano quartet), 2003; Mourning Knight (mezzo, recorder, saxophone & percussion), 2003; ALP Too (viola and guitar), 2003; Nuages d'Automne (trombone and sinfonietta), 2003-2004; Nuvole Italiane (piano), 2004; Nuages Élégiaques (trombone), 2004; Triskele (wind quintet), 2004; Ante Discum Solis (saxophone and harp), 2004; Røst (clarinet, bassoon and piano), 2004; Diecieis Fragmentos (mezzo, guitar and percussion), 2004; Sjúrður (soprano and saxophone), 2004; Infinite Water (clarinet and tape), 2005; Finnegan's (sinfonietta), 2005; "Stalingrad" (4 saxophones and 2 percussion), 2005; The Place That Is Not (saxophone and organ, 2005; Endro Karnag (flute & cello), 2005; Tres retratos con sombra (mezzo, flute, violincello and accordion), 2006; Rain (flute, percussion and electronics), 2006; Another Kind of Stillness (bassoon and piano), 2006; Dias (accordian and harpiscord), 2006; Tyst November (septet), 2007; Cantos al amor (mezzo, violin, violincello and piano), 2007. Recordings: Hans-Henrik Nordstrøm 1 (Portrait CD), 1997; Hans-Henrik Nordstrøm 2

(Portrait CD), 1999; Hans-Henrik Nordstrøm 3 (Portrait CD), 2001; No 4: In the Woods (Portrait CD), 2003; No 5: North West (Portrait CD), 2005; Starting Points (Portrait CD), 2007; Finnegans, 2007. Honours: Grant, Danish Art Foundation, 1990-; Danish Composer's Society's Grant, 2001; Artistic Co-Director, Contemporary Music in Susaa Festivals, held in August every year since 1993-; Composer of the Year, 2003, Bornholm Music Festival; Composer of the Year, Birkeroed, 2004. Membership: Danish Composers Society. Address: Skovmarksvej 52, Vetterslev, DK-4100 Ringsted, Denmark. E-mail: hans-henrik@nordstroem.dk Website: www.nordstroem.dk

NORMAN Barry Leslie, b. 21 August 1933, London, England. Writer; Broadcaster. m. Diana Narracott, 1957, 2 daughters. Appointments: Entertainments Editor, Daily Mail, London, 1969-71; Weekly Columnist, The Guardian, 1971-80; Writer and Presenter, BBC 1 Film, 1973-81, 1983-88, The Hollywood Greats, 1977-79, 1984, The British Greats 1980, Omnibus, 1982, Film Greats, 1985, Talking Pictures, 1988; Barry Norman's Film Night, BSkyB, 1998-2001; Radio 4 Today, 1974-76, Going Places, 1977-81, Breakaway, 1979-80. Publications: Novels: The Matter of Mandrake, 1967; The Hounds of Sparta, 1968; End Product, 1975; A Series of Defeats, 1977; To Nick a Good Body, 1978; Have a Nice Day, 1981; Sticky Wicket, 1984. Non-Fiction: Tales of the Redundance Kid, 1975; The Hollywood Greats, 1979; The Movie Greats, 1981; Talking Pictures, 1987; 100 Best Films of the Century, 1992, 1998; And Why Not? 2002. Thriller: The Birddog Tape, 1992; The Mickey Mouse Affair, 1995; Death on Sunset, 1998. Honours: British Association of Film and Television Arts Richard Dimbleby Award, 1981; Magazine Columnist of the Year, 1991; Honorary DLitt, University of East Anglia, 1991, University of Hertfordshire, 1996; Magazine Columnist of the Year, 1991; Commander of the Order of the British Empire, 1998.

NORMAN Geraldine (Lucia), (Geraldine Keen, Florence Place), b. 13 May 1940, Wales. U.K. Representative of the State Hermitage Museum. m. Frank Norman, July 1971. Education: MA, Honours, Mathematics, St Anne's College, Oxford, 1961; University of California at Los Angeles, USA, 1961-62. Publications: The Sale of Works of Art (as Geraldine Keen), 1971; 19th Century Painters and Paintings: A Dictionary, 1977; The Fake's Progress (co-author), 1977; The Tom Keating Catalogue (editor), 1977; Mrs Harper's Niece (as Florence Place), 1982; Biedermeier Painting, 1987; Top Collectors of the World (co-author), 1993; The Hermitage: The Biography of a Great Museum, 1997. Contributions to: The Times, The Independent, The Daily Telegraph and other Newspapers. Honour: News Reporter of the Year, 1976; Russian Federation Medal in memory of 300 years of St Petersburg, 2005. Address: 5 Seaford Court, 220 Great Portland Street, London W1, England.

NORMAN Gregory John, b. 10 February 1955, Queensland, Australia. Professional Golfer. m. (1) Laura, 1 July 1981, divorced, 1 son, 1 daughter, (2) Chris Evert. Career: Professional, 1976-; Numerous major victories including: Doral Ryder Open, 1990, 1993, 1996; South African Open, 1996; Players Championship, 1994; PGA Grand Slam of Golf, 1993, 1994; British Open, 1986, 1993; Canadian Open, 1984, 1992; Australian Masters, 1981, 1983, 1984, 1989, 1990; New South Wales Open, 1978, 1983, 1986, 1988; Australian Open, 1980, 1985, 1987; European Open, 1986; World Match-Play, 1980, 1983, 1986; Australian Team, Dunhill Cup, 1985, 1986. Publications: My Story, 1982-83; Shark Attack, 1987-88; Greg Norman's Instant Lessons, 1993; Greg Norman's Better

Golf, 1994. Honours: Inducted into World Golf Hall of Fame, 2001. Address: Great White Shark Enterprises Inc, PO Box 1189, Hobe Sound, FL 33475-1189, USA.

NORODOM RANARIDDH Prince, b. 2 January 1944, Cambodia. m. 1968, 2 sons, 1 daughter. Appointments: President, United National Front for an Independent, Neutral, Peaceful & Co-operative Cambodia; Co-Chair, Provisional National Government of Cambodia; Minister of National Defence, Interior and National Security, 1993; Member, National Assembly, 1993-; Co-Prime Minister, Member, Throne Council, 1993; 1st Prime Minister of Royal Government of Cambodia, 1993-97; Chair, National Development Council, 1993-97; Found guilty of conspiracy with Khmer Rouges to overthrow the government, sentenced to 30 years imprisonment; In Exile; Returned from exile 1998; Professor of Public Law.

NORODOM SIHANOUK Samdech Preah, b. 31 October 1922, Cambodia. King of Cambodia. m. Princess Monique, 14 children (6 deceased). Education: Saigon; Vietnam; Paris; Military Training, Saumur, France. Appointments: Elected King, 1941, Abdicated, 1955; Prime Minister, Minister of Foreign Affairs, 1955, 1956, 1957; Permanent Representative to UN, 1956; Elected Head of State, 1960; Took Oath of Fidelity to Vacant Throne, 1960; Deposed by Forces of Lon Nol, 1970; Resided, Peking; Established, Royal Government of National Union of Cambodia, (GRUNC) 1970; Restored as Head of State when GRUNC forces overthrew Khmer Republic, 1975, Resigned, 1976; Special Envoy of Khmer Rouge to UN, 1979; Founder, National United Front for an Independent Neutral, Peaceful and Co-operative Kampuchea, 1981-89; President, Tripartite National Cambodian Resistance, in exile 13 years, returned to Cambodia, 1991-93; Crowned King of Cambodia, 1993-2004; Colonel in Chief, Armed Forces, 1993-; Abdicated, 2004. Publications: L'Indochine vue de Pékin (with Jean Lacouture), 1972; My War With the CIA (with Wilfred Burchett), 1973; War and Hope: The Case for Cambodia, 1980; Souvenirs doux et amers, 1981; Prisonnier des Khmers Rouges, 1986; Charisme et Leadership, 1989. Address: Khemarindra Palace, Phnom Penh, Cambodia.

NORRIS David, b. 31 July 1944, Leopoldville, Belgian Congo. Retired Academic; Broadcaster; Public Representative (Senator). Education: St Andrew's College, Dublin; The High School, Dublin; Reade Pianoforte School; University of Dublin; Trinity College, Dublin. Appointments: Founding Chairman, North Great George Street Preservation Society; Founding Chairman, James Joyce Centre, Dublin; Founding Chairman, National Gay Federation; Founding Chairman, Campaign for Homosexual Law Reform; Regular Weekly Radio Presenter, Sunday with Norris, Newstalk Radio; Member, Joint Committee on Foreign Affairs; Re-elected Member of Seanad Eireann, 2007. Publications: James Joyce's Dublin; A Beginners Guide to James Joyce; In the Midst of the Hibernian Metropolis, proceedings of the International James Joyce Symposium; Numerous articles on literary, political and sociological topics; TV, radio and film presenter; Writer and performer of one man James Joyce Show (theatre). Honours: Gold Medal, Brazilian Academy of Letters; Gold Medal, University Philosophical Society; Silver Medal, University Philosophical Society; Human Rights Award, University College, Galway, 2007; Diplôme d'Honneur, Centre for the Study of Sexual Minorities, Paris. Memberships: Royal Dublin Society; Royal Zoological Society of Ireland; Amnesty International; North Great George Street Preservation Society; James Joyce Centre, Dublin; Kildare Si; University Club. Address: 18 North Great George St, Dublin I, Ireland.

NORTH Anthony Charles Thomas, b. 7 February 1931, Derby, England. University Professor. m. Margaret, 3 daughters. Education: BSc (Hons), Physics, 1951, PhD, Biophysics, 1955, University of London King's College. Appointments: Professor, Molecular Biophysics, 1972, Professor of Biophysics, Head, 1973, Astbury Department of Biophysics; Astbury Professor of Biophysics, Department of Biochemistry and Molecular Biology, 1990; Professor Emeritus, University of Leeds; Secretary-General, International Union for Pure & Applied Biophysics, 1993-2002. Publications: Numerous articles in professional journals. Honours: Honorary Member, British Biophysical Society; Honorary Member, Hungarian Biophysical Society. Memberships: Fellow, Institute of Physics; Chartered Physicist; Member, British Biophysical Society; Member, Biochemical Society; Member, British Crystallographic Association; Member, Molecular Graphics and Modelling Society. Address: 27 Breary Lane, Bramhope, Leeds LS16 9AD, England. E-mail: actnorth@talktalk.net

NORTON Hugh Edward, b. 23 June 1936, London, England. Business Executive. m. (1) Janet M Johnson, 1965, deceased, 1 son, (2) Joy Harcup, 1998. Education: Winchester College; Trinity College, Oxford. Appointments: Joined British Petroleum Company, 1959, Exploration Department, 1960, in Abu Dhabi, Lebanon & Libya, 1962-70, subsequently held appointments in Supply, Central Planning; Policy Planning, Regional Directorate Mid E & International & Government Affairs departments; Managing Director, BP's Associate Companies, Singapore, Malaysia, Hong Kong, 1978-81, Director of Planning, 1981-83, Regional Director for Near East, Middle East & Indian Sub-Continent, 1981-86, Director of Administration, 1983-86, Managing Director, CEO, BP Exploration Co, 1986-89, Chair, 1989-95, Managing Director, British Petroleum Co PLC, 1989-95; Chair, BP Asia Pacific Private Co Ltd, 1991-95; Director, Inchcape PLC, 1995-, Standard Chart PLC, 1995-, Lasmo PLC, 1997-. Memberships: Council, Royal Institute of Economic Affairs, 1991-. Address: c/o BP Asia Pacific Pte Ltd, BP Tower, 25th Storey, 396 Alexandra Road, 0511 Singapore.

NORWICH John Julius (The Viscount Norwich), b. 15 September 1929, London, England. Writer; Broadcaster. m. (1) Anne Clifford, 5 August 1952, 1 son, 1 daughter, (2) Mollie Philipps, 14 June 1989. Education: University of Strasbourg, 1947; New College, Oxford, 1949-52. Appointments: Writer, Royal Navy, 1947-49; Foreign Office, 1952-64; Third Secretary, British Embassy, Belgrade, 1955-57; Second Secretary, British Embassy, Beirut, 1957-60; First Secretary, Foreign Office, London, 1961; British delegation to Disarmament Conference, Geneva, 1960-64; Writer, Broadcaster, 1964-; Chairman: British Theatre Museum, 1966-71; Venice in Peril Fund, 1970-; Executive Committee, National Trust, 1969-95; Franco-British Council, 1972-79; Board, English National Opera, 1977-81. Publications: Mount Athos, 1966; Sahara, 1968; The Normans in the South, 1967; The Kingdom in the Sun, 1970; A History of Venice, 1977; Christmas Crackers 1970-79, 1980; Glyndebourne, 1985; The Architecture of Southern England, 1985; A Taste for Travel, 1985; Byzantium: The Early Centuries, 1988; More Christmas Crackers 1980-89, 1990; Venice: A Traveller's Companion (editor), 1990; The Oxford Illustrated Encyclopaedia of the Arts (editor), 1990; Byzantium, the Apogee, 1991; Byzantium: The Decline and Fall, 1995; A Short History of Byzantium, 1997; Shakespeare's Kings, 1999; Still More Christmas Crackers 1990-99, 2000; Paradise of Cities, 2003; The Middle Sea: A History of the Mediterranean, 2006. Honours: Commander, Royal Victorian Order; Commendatore, Ordine al Merito della Repubblica Italiana; Award, American Institute of Architects.

Memberships: Fellow, Royal Society of Literature; Fellow, Royal Geographical Society; Fellow, Royal Society of Arts. Address: 24 Blomfield Road, London W9 1AD, England.

NOSOV Valery R, b. 28 June 1939, Moscow, Russia. Mathematician; Engineer; Educator. m. Irina, 1996, 1 son, 1 daughter. Education: MS (Hons), Physics, Moscow State Lomonosov University, 1962; Stage at Institute Henry Poincare, Paris, France, 1965-66; PhD, Physics and Mathematics, Moscow University of Peoples Friendship, 1967; DSc, Engineering, Moscow State Institute of Electronics and Mathematics, 1981. Appointments: Assistant Professor and Professor, Moscow State Institute of Electronics and Mathematics, 1969-2000; Bourse de Haut Nivel, University de Pau, France, 1996-97; Professor, Applied Mathematics, Mechanics, Institute Politecnico Nacional de Mexico, 2001-. Publications: Mathematical Theory of Control Systems Design, 1996; Stability of Functional Differential Equations, 1986; Mathematical Theory of Control Systems Design, 1989, 1998, 2003; Stability and Periodic Modes of Control Systems with Aftereffect, 1981; 6 patents; More than 50 articles; Silver medal of All Union Exhibition of People Economy Achievements, Moscow, 1988; Diploma a la Investigación, Instituto Politecnico Nacional de Mexico, 2006. Memberships: STLE; Academy of Nonlinear Science; Moscow Mathematical Society. Address: SEPI-ESIME, Instituto Politecnico Nacionale, Calle Wilfredo Massieu Col, Lindavista CP 07730, Mexico DF, Mexico. E-mail: vnossov@ipn.mx

NOURSE Christopher Stuart, b. 13 August 1946, Salisbury, Wiltshire, England. Arts Administrator. Education: LLB, University of Edinburgh, 1965-68; Middle Temple/Inns of Court School of Law, 1968-69. Appointments: Royal Opera House, English Opera Group, Royal Ballet New Group, 1972-76; General Manager, Sadler's Wells Royal Ballet, 1976-89; Administrative Director, Birmingham Royal Ballet, 1989-91; Assistant to the General Director, Royal Opera House, 1991-96; Administrative Director, Royal Opera House Trust, 1996-97; Executive Director, Rambert Dance Company, 1997-2001; Vice Chairman, London Dance Network, 1998-2000; Managing Director English National Ballet, 2001-2003; Arts and Dance Consultant, 2005-; Administrator, National Dance Awards, 2005-; Trustee, National Youth Dance Trust, 2002-2006; Trustee, Youth Dance, England, 2004-; Director, Dancers Pension Scheme 2006-. Honours: Listed in Who's Who publications and biographical dictionaries. Membership: Fellow, Royal Society of Arts, 1998. Address: 55 Queen's Gate, South Kensington, London SW7 5JW, England.

NOVAK Pavel, b. 7 September 1918, Stribro, Czech Republic. Civil Engineer; University Teacher. m. R Elizabeth Maurer, 1 son, 1 daughter. Education: BSc (Hon), University of London (external), 1941; Ing Dr, 1949, CSc (PhD), 1958, Czech Technical University, Prague; Dr Sc, Technical University, Brno, 1965. Appointments: Assistant Engineer, Trent Navigation Co, Nottingham, 1941-42; Assistant Lecturer, University College, Nottingham, 1942-45; Scientific Officer to Principal Scientific Officer, Hydraulic Research Institute, Prague, 1945-67; Director, Institute of Hydrodynamics, Academy of Sciences, Prague, 1967-68; Senior Lecturer, Department of Civil Engineering, 1968-70; Professor of Civil and Hydraulic Engineering, 1970-83, Head of Department of Civil Engineering, 1981-83, Head of School of Civil & Mining Engineering, 1982-83, University of Newcastle. Publications: Over 100 papers in refereed journals and at international conferences; Author, Co-author and editor of 22 books. Honours: Corresponding Member,

Academy of Science, Toulouse, 1967; James Hardie Speaker, Institution of Engineers, Australia, 1987; Honorary Member, International Association for Hydraulic Engineering and Research, 1989; Hlavka Medal, 1992, Bechyne Gold Medal, 1994, Czechoslovak Academy of Sciences; Hydraulic Structures Medal, American Society of Civil Engineers, 2003. Memberships: Fellow, Institution of Civil Engineers, UK; Fellow, Chartered Institution of Water and Environmental Management; Honorary Member, International Association for Hydraulic Engineering and Research. Address: 5 Glendale Avenue, Whickham, Newcastle upon Tyne, NE16 5JA, England. E-mail: pavel.novak@ncl.ac.uk

NOVAKOVIC Mileva, (Lela Novak), b. 7 September 1938, Zagreb, Yugoslavia. Retired; Poet. m. Svetozar Novakovic, 21 February 1959, 1 son, 1 daughter. Education: Grammar School; Pitman's College, Wimbledon; Short Story Writers Course, Premier School of Journalism, Fleet Street. Appointments: Before retirement worked as: Personal Assistant to Chairmen and Managing Directors, and Business Manager for several large companies. Publications: Contributions to various anthologies, newspapers, and magazines. Honours: Special mentions for distinguished achievements; Fellow, International Biographical Association, Poetry Society of Great Britain; Distinguished Member, International Society of Poets. Address: 39 The Ridgeway, Gunnersbury Park, London W3 8LW, England.

NOVOTNA Jana, b. 2 October 1968, Brno, Czech Republic. Tennis Player. Appointments: Won US Open Junior Doubles, 1986; Turned Professional, 1987; Won 1st Title, Adelaide, 1988; Olympic Silver Medal, Doubles wih Helena Sukova, 1988; Won Australian and US Open Mixed Doubles with Pugh, 1988; Won 6 Women's Doubles Titles, 1989;With Sukova, won Australian Open, French Open, Wimbledon Doubles, 1990; Reached Quarter Finals, French Open, 1991; Won 7 Doubles Titles with Savchenko Neiland, 1992; Won Singles Titles, Osaka and Brighton, 1993; Singles Titles, Leipzig, Brighton, Essen, 1994; Won Wimbledon Singles and Doubles, 1998; Announced retirement, 1999. Honours: Olympic Bronze Medal in Singles, Silver Medal in Doubles, Atlanta, 1996.

NUGEE Edward George, 9 August 1928, Godalming, Surrey, England. Barrister-at-Law. m. Rachel Elizabeth Makower, 4 sons. Education: Law Moderations (Distinction), 1950, BA, Jurisprudence (1st Class), 1952, Eldon Law Scholarship, 1955, MA, 1956, Worcester College, Oxford; Barrister-at-Law, 1955. Appointments: Royal Artillery (Office of Chief of Staff FARELF), 1947-49; Captain, Intelligence Corps (100APIU(TA)), 1950-64; Barrister-at-Law, 1955; Inner Temple: Bencher, 1976, Treasurer, 1996 (read as a pupil with Lord Templeman and Lord Brightman, 1954-55); Queen's Counsel, 1977; Deputy High Court Judge (Chancery Division), 1982-97; Chairman, Committee of Inquiry into the Management of Privately Owned Blocks of Flats, 1984-85. Publications: Joint editor, Halsbury's Laws of England: Landlord and Tenant (3rd edition 1958); Real Property (3rd edition 1960, 4th edition, 1982, re-issue, 1998); Nathan on the Charities Act, 1962; Various articles in legal journals. Honour: TD, 1964. Memberships: The Institute of Conveyancers, 1971-, President, 1986-87; Church Commissioner, 1990-2002, Board of Governors, 1993-2002; Council of Radley College, 1975-95; Governors of Brambletye School, 1972-82, Chairman, 1972-77; Council of Legal Education, 1967-90, Vice-Chairman and Chairman of Board of Studies, 1976-82; Legal Advisory Commission of General Synod,

2001-. Address: Wilberforce Chambers, 8 New Square, Lincoln's Inn, London WC2A 3QP, England. Website: www.wilberforce.co.uk

NUMBERE Geoffrey Dabibi, b. 3 March 1944, Buguma, Nigeria. Clergyman. m. Nonyem Eziamaka, 4 sons, 1 daughter. Education: Government College, Umuahia, 1959-62; Government Secondary School, Owerri, 1963-64; University of Ife, Ife-Ife, 1967-70. Appointments: Work experience, pioneered Pentecostalism in Muslim North of Nigeria; Founder of Evangelical Church of West Africa in Gumel, Jigawa State, 1970-72; International Director, Greater Evangelism World Crusade, 1972; Pioneered Missionary Work and Pentecostal Evangelism in rural areas of Niger Delta, 1972-89; Trustee, Board of Directors, Nigerian Institute of Christian Studies, 1991; Member, Eminent Persons Commission, 1993; Missionary outreaches and church planting, Sierra Leone, 1994; Missionary work and church planting, Kampala and mountainous villages of Uganda, 1995; Missionary work in Rwanda, 1995-98; Missionary work and church planting in Goma, Democratic Republic of Congo, 1999; Missionary work and church planting in Burundi, 2001; Chairman, South-Stouh Zone, Christian Association of Nigeria, 2006; Chairman, Rivers State Christian Association of Nigeria, 2007. Publications: The Eagle Christian; Unity of the Brethren in the Local Church; Symbolism in the Bible; Word Killeth, Word Maketh Alive; Wake Up; Several newspaper articles. Honours: One of Five Thousand Personalities, 1988; Dedication of Rivers State to God, 1992; Man of the Year 2003, Rivers State Television, 2003. Memberships: Christian Association of Nigeria. Address: 47 Isiokpo Street, D/Line, PO Box 946, Port Harcourt, Rivers State, Nigeria. E-mail: greaterworldhqtrs@yahoo.com

NUNN John Francis, b. 7 November 1925, Colwyn Bay, North Wales, United Kingdom. Medical Specialist in Anaesthesia. m. Sheila Doubleday, 1 son, 2 daughters. Education: Wrekin College, Wellington, Shropshire, 1939-43; MB ChB, Birmingham University Medical School, 1948; PhD, 1959, MD (Hons), 1970, DSc, 1992, Birmingham University. Appointments: Professor of Anaesthesia, University of Leeds, 1964-68; Dean of Faculty of Anaesthetists, Royal College of Surgeons, 1979-82; Head of Anaesthesia Division, Medical Research Council, 1968-91. Publications: Nunn's Applied Respiratory Physiology, 4 editions; Ancient Egyptian Medicine, 1996; Approximately 230 publications in professional journals. Honours: Hunterian Professor, Royal College of Surgeons, 1961; First Dudley Buxton Medallist, Royal College of Surgeons, 1968; Vicary Lecturer, Royal College of Surgeons, 1982; Faculty Medal, Royal College of Surgeons, 1988; First Magill Medallist, Association of Anaesthetists, 1988; Hon FRCA, 1991; Sir James Young Simpson Memorial Medal, Royal College of Surgeons of Edinburgh, 1991; Honorary Fellow, Royal Society of Medicine, 1992; MD (Hon), Uppsala, 1993; Laurea (Honoris causa), Turin, 1993. Memberships: Honorary Member, 9 overseas anasthetic societies (USA, Japan, Australia, New Zealand, Germany); 30 overseas visiting professorships; 40 invited lectureships at major conferences; 22 eponymous lectureships; Elected to Fellowship of Geological Society of London, 1991. Address: 3A Dene Road, Northwood, Middlesex HA6 2AE, England.

NUNN Trevor Robert, Sir, b. 14 January 1940, Ipswich, England. Theatre Director. m. (1) Janet Suzman, 1969, 1 son, (2) Sharon Lee Hill, 1986, 2 daughters, (3) Imogen Stubbs, 1994, 1 son, 1 daughter. Education: Downing College, Cambridge. Appointments: Trainee Director, Belgrade Theatre,

Coventry; Associate Director, Royal Shakespeare Company, 1964-86, Director Emeritus, 1986-; Founder, Homevale Ltd, Awayvale Ltd; Artistic Director, Royal National Theatre, 1996-2001. Creative Works: Productions include: The Merry Wives of Windsor, 1979; Once in a Lifetime, 1979; Juno and the Paycock, 1980; The Life and Adventures of Nicholas Nickleby, 1980; Cats, 1981; All's Well That Ends Well, 1981; Henry IV (pts I and II), 1981, 1982; Peter Pan, 1982; Starlight Express, 1984; Les Misérables, 1985; Chess, 1986; The Fair Maid of the West, 1986; Aspects of Love, 1989; Othello, 1989; The Baker's Wife, 1989; Timon of Athens, 1991; The Blue Angel, 1991; Measure for Measure, 1991; Heartbreak House, 1992; Arcadia, 1993; Sunset Boulevard, 1993; Enemy of the People, 1997; Mutabilitie, 1997; Not About Nightingales, 1998; Oklahoma, 1998; Betrayal, 1998; Troilus and Cressida, 1999; The Merchant of Venice, 1999; Summerfolk, 1999; Love's Labour's Lost, 2002; We Happy Few, 2004; The Woman in White, 2004; Acorn Antiques, 2005; Hamlet, 2004; King Lear, 2007; The Seagull, 2007; Gone With the Wind, 2008. TV: Antony and Cleopatra, 1975; Comedy of Errors, 1976; Every Good Boy Deserves Favour, 1978; Macbeth, 1978; Shakespeare Workshops Word of Mouth, 1979; The Three Sisters, Othello, 1989; Porgy and Bess, 1992; Oklahoma!, 1999; Films: Hedda, Lady Jane, 1985; Twelfth Night, 1996; Operas: Idomeneo, 1982; Porgy and Bess, 1986; Cosi Fan Tutte, 1991; Peter Grimes, 1992; Katya Kabanova, 1994; Sophie's Choice, 2002. Publications: British Theatre Design, 1989. Honours: CBE; Knighted, 2002. Address: Royal National Theatre, Upper Ground, South Bank, London SE1 9PX, England.

NUORTEVA Pekka Olavi, b. 24 November 1926, Helsinki, Finland. Professor of Environmental Science. m. Sirkka-Liisa Welling-Vuontela, 1 son, 2 daughters. Education: MSc, Biology, 1951, DrSc, Zoology, 1955, Docent, Entomology, 1955, Competence for Chief of Zoological Museum, 1972, Professor, 1975, Helsinki University. Appointments: Research Worker, Finnish Agricultural Research Institute, Tikkurila, Finland, 1952; Demonstrator, Anatomy, Medical Faculty, Assistant, Department of Ecology and Morphology, Institute of Zoology, 1954, Docent (Lecturer), Institute of Zoology, 1955; Lecturer in Parasitology, Veterinary High School, Helsinki, 1967; Intendent of the Zoological Museum of Helsinki University, 1958; Chief of the Department of Entomology, Zoological Museum, Helsinki University, 1972; Professor of Environmental Science, Helsinki University, 1975-. Publications: More than 300 scientific publications from a field including ecophysiology of insects, agricultural and forest phytopathology, medical entomology and parasitology, subarctic biology, methylmercury pollution of fish, cadmium bioaccumulation and cadmium resistance in ants, circulation of toxic metals and their antagonists in forest biota, blowflies as transmitters of disease germs, population decrease in honeybees and bumblebees, tick transmission by migratory birds; More than 700 popularisations about the above themes including 10 books; The Atlas of Finnish Animals. Honours: Chairman in numerous international congresses on environmental science, entomology and forensic science; National Prize for polularisation of science in Finland, 1974, 1977; Portrait in the Galleria Academica, Helsinki University, 1986; 2 First Class Medals, Finnish White Rose Order; 3 Golden Medals, Finnish League for Environmental Protection; 6 Medals from Scientific Societies. Memberships: Finnish Water Protection Committee, 1969-71; Committee for Environmental Protection in Finland, 1970-73; Finnish Energy Committee, 1987-89; Numerous scientific and environmental societies; Former Co-ordinator of scientific collaboration with some socialist countries on behalf of Helsinki University. Address: Department of Environmental Science, Helsinki University, Caloniuksenk 6 C 64, FIN-00100 Helsinki, Finland.

NUSS Joanne Ruth, b. 2 May 1951, Great Bend, Kansas, USA. Sculptor. Education: Valparaiso University, Indiana, 1969-71; University of Kansas, Kansas, 1972-73; University of Copenhagen, Denmark, 1974; BA, Fort Hays State University, Kansas, 1975; Master's program with Beverly Pepper, 1st Prize in Class Presentation, New Mexico Institute of Fine Arts, Santa Fe, New Mexico, 1991. Career: Bronze casting producing sculptures, 1975-; Exhibited worldwide for over 30 years; Work held in private collections of: King Hassan II of Morocco, Prince of Brunei and Bandarseri Begawan, Brunei; First foreign female artist commissioned for architectural project in Tangiers, Morocco, 1988-90; Exhibits in juried shows throughout USA. Honours: Award of Excellence, Period Gallery, Omaha; First Place Award, University of Northern Iowa Gallery, Cedar Falls, Iowa; Artist in Residence Grants, Taos, New Mexico, 1984, 1990; Best 3-D Award, Kansas Artist Craftsman Award, Wichita, Kansas; Dictionary of American Sculptors 18th Century to the Present, New York, 1984; First Kansas Artist Purchase Award, Kansas Professional Artists Collection, Fort Hays State University, Kansas, 1985; Artist featured working in Morocco, BBC Radio Network, London, 1986; Award of Excellence, Upstream People Gallery, Omaha, Nebraska, 2001-02; Woman of Achievement Award, 2005; America's Registry of Outstanding Professionals, 2005-06. Memberships: National Association of Women Artists; New York National Museum of Women in the Arts; National Sculpture Society, New York; International Sculpture Center, Hamilton, New York. Address: Unique Bronze Sculptures, 152 E Lupita Road, Sante Fe, NM 87505, USA.

NWAFOR Onwuzurigbo Martin Iheonu, b. 15 June 1956, Ihube-Okigwe, Imo State, Nigeria. Mechanical Engineer; Educator. m. Ngozi B, 1 son, 1 daughter. Education: Automobile Engineering, North Worcestershire College, Bromsgrove, England, 1978; BSc (Hons) Mechanical Engineering, Wolverhampton Polytechnic, England, 1982; MSc, Thermodynamics, Birmingham University, England, 1984; PhD, Energy and Power (Automotive Engineering), Reading University, England, 1994. Appointments: JB & S Lees Ltd, Trident Steel Works, West Bromwich, England, 1976-77; Charles Clark Motors Ltd, Wolverhampton, England, 1977; All Saints Motors Ltd, Bromsgrove, England, 1977-78; Design Office, Barton Conducts Ltd, Walsall, England, 1978-79; Lecturer, Anambra State University, 1985-86; Lecturer, Federal University of Owerrri, 1991; Researcher and Lecturer, University of Reading, England, 1991-94; Maintenance and Production Engineer, Linpac Metal Packaging, Woodley, England, 1995-97; Lecturer then Reader, Department of Mechanical Engineering, Federal University of Owerri, Nigeria; Head, Mechanical Engineering Department, Federal University of Technology, Owerri. Publications: More than 35 articles in scientific journals and presented at conferences as author and co-author include most recently: Effect of choice of pilot fuel on emission characteristics of Diesel Engine running on natural gas, 2002; Effect of Advanced Injection Timing on Emission Characteristics of Diesel Engine Running on Biofuel, 2004; Soyabean Oil as a Fuel for Compression Ignition Engine, 2004; Factors affecting the transesterification of Palm Olein, 2004. Memberships: Nigerian Society of Engineers; Associate Member, Institute of Mechanical Engineers, UK; Registered Engineering Council, UK; Registered Engineer, Council for the Regulation of Engineers in Nigeria; Institute of Motor Industry, UK. Address:

Department of Mechanical Engineering, Federal University of Technology, PMB 1526, Owerri, Imo State, Nigeria. E-mail: ominwafor@futo.edu.ng

NWAOZUZU Chijioke, b. 9 January 1963, Port Harcourt, Nigeria. Petroleum Management and Policy. m. Daisy Chioma, 2 sons. Education: BSc (Hons), University of Nigeria, 1983; MBA, Edinburgh Business School, Heriot-Watt University, Edinburgh, 2003; MBA (Oil & Gas Specialization), CEPMLP, Dundee, 2003; PhD, Downstream Petroleum Law & Policy, 2007. Appointments: District Medical Representative, 1985-87, Area Medical Representative, 1987-89, Ranbaxy Pharmaceuticals International (Nig) Ltd; Sales Manager, Glitters Amanda Petroleum Marketing Company (Nig) Ltd, 1989-95; Executive Director, Earth Natural Resources Ltd (Nig), 1996-2001; Part time Graduate Research Assistant, Centre for Energy, Petroleum, Mineral Law and Policy, University of Dundee, 2003-04, 2004-06. Publications: Papers and articles in professional scientific journals. Honours: Federal Merit Award, Federal Government of Nigeria, 1980-82; Best Student, Faculty of Biological Sciences, University of Nigeria, 1980-82; Foundation Scholarship Award, University of Nigeria, 1981-83; Best Graduating Student, Microbiology Department, UNN, 1983; British Chevening Scholarship Award, Foreign & Commonwealth Office, UK, 2001-03; PhD Scholarship Award, University of Dundee, 2003-; PhD Scholarship Award, Ministry of Petroleum Resources, Nigeria, 2003-; International Peace Prize, UCC, 2005; Board of Governors, Research Association, ABI, 2005; Honorary Member, Order of International Ambassadors, ABI, 2005; American Medal of Honor, ABI, 2006; Honorary Member, Research Board of Advisors, ABI, 2005; Man of the Year Award, ABI, 2005; Man of Achievement Award, ABI, 2005; Listed in international biographical dictionaries. Memberships: Graduate Member, Energy Institute; Charter Member, Global Petroleum Club; Life Member, Heriot-Watt University Student's Association, Edinburgh; Founder, Nigerian CEPMLP Association-Dundee University, Scotland; Founder, Nigerian CEPMLP Alumni Association, Nigeria; Member: Information for Energy Group; Scottish Networks International; The Watt Club, Heriot-Watt University; London Alumni Chevening; Nigerian Institute of Management; Nigerian Environmental Society; Nigerian Institute of Marketing. Address: Post-Graduate School of Management & Policy, The Centre for Energy, Petroleum, Mineral Law & Policy, Carnegie Building, University of Dundee, Dundee, DD1 4HN, Scotland. E-mail: c.nwaozuzu@dundee.ac.uk Website: www.cepmlp.org

NWOJI Benson Iroabuchi, b. 18 June 1951, Amaokpu Nilpa, Nigeria. Banking; Finance. 3 sons, 1 daughter. Education: BSc, Management, University of Nigeria, Nsukka, 1979; MBA, Finance, University of Stirling, United Kingdom, 1990; Fellow, Institute of Chartered Secretaries & Administrators, United Kingdom, 2000. Appointments: Head, Corporate Banking Department, Nigeria Merchant Bank, 1992-94; Senior Assistant General Manager, Afribank Nigeria plc, 1994-2000; Management Director/CEO, Afribank Trustees & Investments Ltd, 2000-. Publications: Author, Corporate Finance – Guide to Application in Banking & Financial Services in Nigeria. Honours: Illustrious Award; Specialised Certification of Expertise in Corporate Finances, ABI. Memberships: Institute of Directors, UK/Nigeria. Address: c/o Afribank Trustees & Investments Ltd, 94 Broad Street, Lagos, PMB 12021, Lagos Nigeria. E-mail: ben_nwoji@yahoo.com

NYAM-OSOR Namsrain, b. 3 January 1955, Khentii province, Mongolia. Historian. m. Jambal Tsetsegmaa, 1 son, 1 daughter. Education: BA, History, 1987; MA, Law, 1997;

PhD, History, 1998; ScD, History, 2003. Appointments: Director, Khunnu Company, 1992-94; President, Ikhzasag University, 1994-. Publications: Over 25 books; About 100 articles in professional journals. Honours: ScD; Professor; Meritorious Teacher of Mongolia; Meritorious Scientist of Buryat Republic, Russia. Memberships: Council for Scientists and Experts of President of Mongolia; Academy of Nomadic Culture and Civilization. Address: Ikh Zasag University, Bayanzurkh district, 4 Khoroo, B Dorjiin Street, Ulaanbaatar, Mongolia. E-mail: nyamosor@ikhzasag.edu.mn Website: www.ikhzasag.edu.mn

NYE Robert, b. 15 March 1939, London, England. Author; Poet; Dramatist; Editor. m. (1) Judith Pratt, 1959, divorced 1967, 3 sons, (2) Aileen Campbell, 1968, 1 daughter. Publications: Fiction: Doubtfire, 1967; Tales I Told My Mother, 1969; Falstaff, 1976; Merlin, 1978; Faust, 1980; The Voyage of the Destiny, 1982; The Facts of Life and Other Fictions, 1983; The Memoirs of Lord Byron, 1989; The Life and Death of My Lord Gilles de Rais, 1990; Mrs Shakespeare: The Complete Works, 1993; The Late Mr Shakespeare, 1998. Children's Fiction: Taliesin, 1966; March Has Horse's Ears, 1966; Wishing Gold, 1970; Poor Pumpkin, 1971; Out of the World and Back Again, 1977; Once Upon Three Times, 1978; The Bird of the Golden Land, 1980; Harry Pay the Pirate, 1981; Three Tales, 1983; Lord Fox and Other Spine-Chilling Tales, 1997. Poetry: Juvenilia 1, 1961; Juvenilia 2, 1963; Darker Ends, 1969; Agnus Dei, 1973; Two Prayers, 1974; Five Dreams, 1974; Divisions on a Ground, 1976; A Collection of Poems, 1955-1988, 1989; 14 Poems, 1994; Henry James and Other Poems, 1995; Collected Poems, 1995, 1998; The Rain and the Glass: 99 Poems: 99 Poems, New and Selected, 2004; Plays: Sawney Bean (with Bill Watson), 1970; The Seven Deadly Sins: A Mask, 1974; Penthesilea, Fugue and Sisters, 1976. Translator: Beowulf, 1968. Editor: A Choice of Sir Walter Raleigh's Verse, 1973; The English Sermon, 1750-1850, 1976; The Faber Book of Sonnets, 1976; PEN New Poetry 1, 1986; First Awakenings: The Early Poems of Laura Riding (co-editor), 1992; A Selection of the Poems of Laura Riding, 1994. Contributions to: Magazines and journals. Honours: Eric Gregory Award, 1963; Guardian Fiction Prize, 1976; Hawthornden Prize, 1977. Membership: Royal Society of Literature, fellow.

NYIRI Ferenc (Baron), b. 25 August 1964, Hódmezővásárhely, Hungary. Basstrombone Player. Education: Academy of Music, Franz Liszt, Szeged, 1985. Appointment: Symphony Orchestra of Pécs, 1985-89; Nationaltheater of Szeged, 1989-93; Symphony Orchestra of Szeged, 1993-. Publications: Journal of Hungarian Trombone-Tuba Association. Honours: Competition of Trombone, III Prize, 1984, II Prize, 1985; Prize of Artisjus, 2001; Listed in biographical dictionaries. Memberships: Hungarian Trombone-Tuba Association. Address: Ipoly sor 11/B, H-6724 Szeged, Hungary.

NYUNT U Soe (Alias Htilar Sitthu), b. 18 April 1932, Meiktila, Myanmar. Retired Deputy Minister for Culture. m. Daw Hla Yin Yin Soe, 3 sons, 5 daughters. Education: Arts, University of Adult Education, Yangon, 1952-54; PhD, Poetry, 2004, D Litt, Dublin Metropolitan University, Ireland. Appointments: Enrolled, No 1 Field Artillery Regiment, 1950; 2nd in Command, Ordnance Depot North Burma, Mandalay, 1961-62; Officer on Special Duty, posted to Office of Revolutionary Council Chairman, Ministry of Culture, 1962-63; Company Commander, No 26 Burma Regiment, 1963-65; Chairman, Township Security Council, Kyaikhto, posted to Ministry of Home Affairs, 1965-67; Major, 2nd in Command, No 47 Burma Regiment, 1967; 2nd in Command

and Additional Commander, No 23 Burma Regiment, 1968; Officer on Special Duty, State Timber Board, Yangon, posted in Ministry of Agriculture and Forest, 1968-70; Lieutenant Colonel Commanding Officer, No 50 Burma Regiment, 1970-74; General Staff Grade 1, Defence Service, Psychological Warfare and Public Relations, 1974-76; General Staff Officer Grade 1 and Acting Deputy Commander in part time in Central Command, 1976-78; Chief Editor, Mirror Daily (NPE), posted to Ministry of Information, 1978-84; Director General, Fine Arts Department, promoted and posted to Ministry of Culture, 1984-88; Elected member, Pyithu Hluttaw (People's Parliament), by Myothit Township, 1984-88; Managing Director, News and Periodical Enterprise, transferred to Ministry of Information, 1988-92; Deputy, Ministry of Culture, 1993-2003; Retired, 2003. Publications: Over 2,000 poems; 1500 articles; 88 books including: 24 books of poetry, 11 novels, 11 works of literary criticism and appreciation; 34 books of collected articles; 8 books on political affairs; 24 books translated into English, French, Chinese, German, Japanese and Russian; Most recent works include: Myanmar Classical Poetry, 1998; The Epic Poems of Conquering of Haing Gyi Island and Panwa, 1999; I Shall Never Forget Him, novelettes and short stories, 1999; My Precious Pearl, 2002; Appreciation of Myanmar Patriotic poems, 2004; A review of Myanmar History 1920-1962, 2004; O Sound of Bell from Nagasaki, epic poem, 2004; Odes to Sino-Myanmar Friendship, 2007; Contribution to Anthologies of Myanmar Literature 1916-1993. Honours include: State Military Service Medal, 1952; Diploma and Military Merits (3rd degree), Marshall Tito, President of Yugoslavia, 1954; The People Militia Combating Medal; Medal of the Victory of Foreign Enemy Divisions Agression Battle (KMT); Medal for Excellent Administrative Field (1st class); Medal for Public Service; Medal for State Peace and Tranquility, 1990; Medal for State Law and Order Restoration, 1990; Sarpay Beikman Poem Award, 1962; National Literary Award, 1992; The Great Poet Laureate, Japan, 1996; Honourable Member, Min On Concert Association, Japan, 2000; The Literary Messenger of Friendship Award, China, 2001; Award for Excellent Performance in Literature, Myanmar, 2003; Decree of Prime Minister for Friendship Medal Decoration and Government Medal of LAO Democratic Republic, 2003; IBC Meritorious Achievement, 2004; IBC Decree of Merit, 2004; DPhil, Poetry, 2004, D Litt, 2006, Fellow, 2006, Dublin Metropolitan University, Ireland; ABI Research Board of Advisors, 2007; Lifetime Achievement Award, 2007. Memberships: Founder, Chairman, Myanmar Writers and Journalists Association; Patron, Myanmar Music Association; Patron of Arts and Crafts Association. Address: #152, 45th Street , Botahtaung Township, Yangon, Myanmar. E-mail: minhlaphone@gmail.com

O

O'BRIEN Conor Cruise, (Donat O'Donnell), b. 3 November 1917, Dublin, Ireland. Writer; Editor. m. (1) Christine Foster, 1939, divorced 1962, 1 son, 1 daughter, (2) Máire MacEntee, 1962, 1 adopted son, 1 adopted daughter. Education: BA, 1940, PhD, 1953, Trinity College, Dublin. Appointments: Member, Irish diplomatic service, 1944-61; Vice-Chancellor, University of Ghana, 1962-65; Albert Schweitzer Professor of Humanities, New York University, 1965-69; Member, Labour Party, Dublin North-east, Dail, 1969-77, Senate, Republic of Ireland, 1977-79; Visiting Fellow, Nuffield College, Oxford, 1973-75; Minister for Posts and Telegraphs, 1973-77; Pro-Chancellor, University of Dublin, 1973-; Fellow, St Catherine's College, Oxford, 1978-81; Editor-in-Chief, The Observer, 1979-81; Visiting Professor and Montgomery Fellow, Dartmouth College, New Hampshire, 1984-85; Senior Resident Fellow, National Humanities Center, North Carolina, 1993-94. Publications: Maria Cross, 1952; Parnell and His Party, 1957; The Shaping of Modern Ireland (editor), 1959; To Katanga and Back, 1962; Conflicting Concepts of the UN, 1964; Writers and Politics, 1965; The United Nations: Sacred Drama, 1967; Murderous Angels (play), 1968; Power and Consciousness, 1969; Conor Cruise O'Brien Introduces Ireland, 1969; Albert Camus, 1969; The Suspecting Glance (with Máire Cruise O'Brien), 1970; A Concise History of Ireland, 1971; States of Ireland, 1972; King Herod Advises (play), 1973; Neighbours: The Ewart-Biggs Memorial Lectures 1978-79, 1980; The Siege: The Saga of Israel and Zionism, 1986; Passion and Cunning, 1988; God Land: Reflections on Religion and Nationalism, 1988; The Great Melody: A Thematic Biography and Commented Anthology of Edmund Burke, 1992; Ancestral Voices, 1994; On the Eve of the Millennium, 1996; The Long Affair: Thomas Jefferson and the French Revolution, 1996; Memoir: My Life and Themes, 1998. Honours: Valiant for Truth Media Award, 1979; Honorary doctorates. Memberships: Royal Irish Academy; Royal Society of Literature. Address: Whitewater, Howth Summit, Dublin, Ireland.

O'BRIEN Denis Patrick, b. 24 May 1939, Knebworth, Hertfordshire, England. Economist. m. (1) Eileen Patricia O'Brien, deceased, 1985, 1 son, 2 daughters (2) Julia Stapleton, 1 daughter. Education: BSc, Economics, 1960, University College, London; PhD, Queen's University, Belfast, 1969. Appointments: Assistant Lecturer, 1963-65, Lecturer, 1965-70, Reader, 1970-72, Queen's University, Belfast; Professor of Economics, 1972-97, Emeritus Professor, 1998-, Durham University. Publications: J R McCulloch, 1970; The Correspondence of Lord Overstone (3 volumes), 1971; Competition in British Industry (jointly), 1974; The Classical Economists, 1975; Competition Policy, Profitability and Growth (jointly), 1979; Pioneers of Modern Economics in Britain (jointly), 1981; Authorship Puzzles in the History of Economics (jointly), 1982; Lionel Robbins, 1988; Thomas Joplin and Classical Macroeconomics, 1993; Methodology, Money and the Firm (2 volumes), 1994; The Classical Economists Revisited, 2003; History of Economic Thought as an Intellectual Discipline, 2007, The Development of Monetary Economics, 2007.Honours: FBA, 1988; Distinguished Fellow, History of Economics Society, 2003. Address: c/o Dr Julia Stapleton, Department of Politics, South End House, South Road, Durham DH1 3TG, England.

O'BRIEN Edna, b. 15 December 1936, Tuamgraney, County Clare, Ireland. Author; Dramatist. m. 1954, divorced 1964, 2 sons. Education: Convents; Pharmaceutical College of Ireland. Publications: The Country Girls, 1960; The Lonely Girl, 1962; Girls in Their Married Bliss, 1963; August is a Wicked Month, 1964; Casualties of Peace, 1966; The Love Object, 1968; A Pagan Place, 1970; Night, 1972; A Scandalous Woman, 1974; Mother Ireland, 1976; Johnnie I Hardly Knew You, 1977; Mrs Reinhardt and Other Stories, 1978; Virginia (play), 1979; The Dazzle, 1981; Returning, 1982; A Christmas Treat, 1982; A Fanatic Heart, 1985; Tales for Telling, 1986; Flesh and Blood (play), 1987; Madame Bovary (play), 1987; The High Road, 1988; Lantern Slides, 1990; Time and Tide, 1992; House of Splendid Isolation, 1994; Down by the River, 1997; James Joyce: A Biography, 1999; Wild Decembers, 1999; In the Forest, 2002; Iphigenia (play), 2003; Triptych, 2004; The Light of Evening, 2006. Honours: Yorkshire Post Novel Award, 1971; Los Angeles Times Award, 1990; Writers' Guild Award, 1993; European Prize for Literature, 1995; American National Arts Gold Medal. Address: David Godwin Associates, 14 Goodwin Court, Covent Garden, London WC2N 4LL, England.

O'BRIEN Keith Patrick, b. 17 March 1938, Ballycastle, County Antrim, Northern Ireland. Cardinal in Catholic Church. Education: BSc, University of Edinburgh, 1955-59; St Andrew's College, Drygrange, Melrose, 1959-65; Dip Ed, Moray House College of Education, 1965-66. Appointments: Teacher and Chaplain, St Columba's Secondary School, Fife, 1966-71; Priest, St Patrick's Kilsyth, 1972-75; Priest, St Mary's, Bathgate, 1975-78; Spiritual Director, St Andrew's College, Drygrange, Melrose, 1978-80; Rector, Blairs College, Aberdeen, 1980-85; Archbishop of St Andrew's and Edinburgh, 1985-; Cardinal, 2003. Honours: Equestrian Order of the Holy Sepulchre of Jerusalem, Grand Prior of the Scottish Liertenancy of the Order, 2001; Cardinal in Catholic Church, 2003; Knight Grand Cross, 2003; Honorary LLD, University of St Francis Xavier, Antigonish, Nova Scotia, 2004; Honorary DD, University of St Andrew's, 2004; Honorary DD, University of Edinburgh, 2004; Sovereign Military Order of Malta; Bailiff Grand Cross of Honour and Devotion, 2005. Address: The Archbishop's House, 42 Greenhill Gardens, Edinburgh EH10 4BJ, Scotland. E-mail: cardinal@staned.org.uk

O'BRIEN Stephen, b. 1 April 1957, East Africa. Member of Parliament. m. Gemma, 2 sons, 1 daughter. Education: MA (Hons) Law, Emmanuel College, Cambridge, 1976-79; Final Professional Examination, College of Law, Chester, 1979-80. Appointments: Solicitor, Senior Managing Solicitor, Freshfields Solicitors, City of London, 1981-88; Executive Assistant to the Board, 1988-89, Director of Corporate Planning, 1989-94, Director, International Operating Group, 1994-98, Deputy Chairman, Director, Redland Tile & Brick Ltd (Northern Ireland), 1995-98, Group Committee Member, 1990-98, Group Secretary and Director, Corporate Affairs, 1991-98, Redland PLC; International Business Consultant, 1998-; Member of Parliament for Eddisbury, South West Cheshire, 1999-; Parliamentary Private Secretary to the Chairman of the Conservative Party, 2000-2001; Opposition Whip (Front Bench), 2001-2002; Shadow Paymaster General, 2002-03; Shadow Secretary of State for Industry, 2003-05; Shadow Minister for Skills and Higher Education, 2005; Shadow Minister for Health, 2006. Memberships: CBI, Elected Member, South East Regional Council, 1995-98; Scottish Business in the Community, Council of Members, 1995-98; BMP Construction Products Association, 1995-99. Address: House of Commons, London SW1A 0AA, England. E-mail: obriens@parliament.uk

O'CONNOR Sinead, b. 8 December 1966, Dublin, Ireland. Singer. m. John Reynolds, divorced, 1 son, 1 daughter. Education: Dublin College of Music. Appointments: Band Member, Ton Ton Macoute, 1985-87. Creative Works: Singles include: Heroin, 1986; Mandinka, 1987; Jump in the River, 1988; Nothing Compares 2 U, 1990; Three Babies, 1990; You Do Something to Me, 1990; Silent Night, 1991; My Special Child, 1991; Visions of You (with Jan Wobble's Invaders of the Heart), 1992; Emperor's New Clothes, 1992; Secret Love, 1992; Success Has Made a Failure of Our Home, 1992; No Man's Woman, 2000; Jealous, 2000; Guide Me God, 2003; I Don't Know How To Love Him, 2007.Albums include: The Lion and the Cobra, 1987; I Do Not Want What I Haven't Got, 1990; Am I Not Your Girl?, 1992; Universal Mother, 1994; Gospeloak, 1997; Sean-Nós Nua, 2002; She Who Dwells in the Secret Place of the Most High Shall Abide Under the Shadow of the Almighty, 2003; Collaborations, 2005; Throw Down Your Arms, 2005; Theology, 2007. Video films: Value of Ignorance, 1989; The Year of the Horse, 1991; TV film: Hush-a-Bye-Baby. Honours include: MTV Best Video, Best Single Awards, 1990; Grammy Award, Best Alternative Album, 1991. Address: c/o Principle Management, 30-32 Sir John Rogerson Quay, Dublin 2, Ireland.

O'DONNELL Augustine Thomas (Gus), b. 1 October 1952, London, England. Economist. m. Melanie, 1 daughter. Education: BA, First Class, Economics, University of Warwick, 1973; M Phil, Nuffield College Oxford, 1975. Appointments: Lecturer, Department of Political Economy, University of Glasgow, 1975-79; Economist, H M Treasury, 1979-85; First Secretary, British Embassy, Washington DC, USA, 1985-88; Senior Economic Advisor, H M Treasury, 1988-89; Press Secretary to the Chancellor of the Exchequer (Nigel Lawson then John Major), 1989-90; Press Secretary to the Prime Minister, 1990-94; Deputy Director, H M Treasury, UK Representative to the EU Monetary Committee, 1994-97; UK Executive Director to the International Monetary Fund and the World Bank, Minister (Economic), British Embassy, Washington DC, 1997-98; Head of the Government Economic Service with professional responsibility for 730 economists, 1998-2003; Director, 1998-99, Managing Director, 1999-2002, H M Treasury, Macroeconomic Policy and Prospects; Permanent Secretary to H M Treasury, 2002-. Publications: Adding It Up (PIU report), 2000; Reforming Britain's Economic and Financial Policy (co-editor), 2002; UK Policy Coordination: The Importance of Institutional Design, 2002; Microeconomic Reform in Britain (co-editor), 2004. Honours: Honorary Fellow, Nuffield College, Oxford; Honorary Degrees: Warwick University, Glasgow University. Memberships: Chairman, Treasury Gym Club; Member of World Economics International Advisory Board. Address: H M Treasury, 1 Horse Guards Road, London SW1A 2HQ, England.

O'DONNELL Chris, b. 26 June 1970, Winnetka, Illinois, USA. Actor. m. Caroline Fentress, 1997, 4 children. Creative Works: Films include: Men Don't Leave, 1990; Fried Green Tomatoes, 1991; Scent of a Woman, 1992; School Ties, 1992; The Three Musketeers, 1993; Blue Sky, 1994; Circle of Friends, 1995; Mad Love, 1995; Batman Forever, 1995; The Chamber, In Love and War, Batman and Robin, Cookie's Fortune, 1998; The Bachelor, 1998; Vertical Limit, 2000; 29 Palms, 2002; Kinsey, 2004; The Sisters, 2005; Kit Kittredge: An American Girl, 2008. TV includes: Head Cases, 2005; Grey's Anatomy, 2006; The Company, 2007. Address: c/o Kevin Huvane, CAA, 9830 Wilshire Boulevard, Beverly Hills, CA 90212, USA.

O'DONOGHUE (James) Bernard, b. 14 December 1945, Cullen, County Cork, Ireland. University Teacher of English; Poet. m. Heather MacKinnon, 23 July 1977, 1 son, 2 daughters. Education: MA in English, 1968, BPhil in Medieval English, 1971, Lincoln College, Oxford. Appointments: Lecturer and Tutor in English, Magdalen College, Oxford, 1971-95; Fellow and University Lecturer in English Wadham College, Oxford, 1995-. Publications: The Courtly Love Tradition, 1982; Razorblades and Pencils, 1984; Poaching Rights, 1987; The Weakness, 1991; Seamus Heaney & the Language of Poetry, 1994; Gunpowder, 1995; Here Nor There, 1999; Outliving, 2003. Contributions to: Norton Anthology of Poetry; Poetry Ireland Review; Poetry Review; Times Literary Supplement. Honours: Southern Arts Literature Prize, 1991; Whitbread Poetry Award, 1995. Memberships: Poetry Society, London, 1984-; Fellow, Royal Society of Literature, 1999; Fellow, English Society, 1999; Association of University Teachers. Address: Wadham College, Oxford OX1 3PN, England.

O'DONOGHUE Rodney (Rod) Charles, b. 10 June 1938, Woodford, Essex, England. Retired Director; Historian; Writer. m. Kay Patricia Lewis, 2 sons, 1 daughter. Education: Merchant Taylor's School, 1951-56; Fellow of the Institute of Chartered Accountants. Appointments: Accounting Profession, 1956-63; To Finance and Administration Director, Kimberly-Clark Ltd, 1963-72; To Group Controller, Rank Xerox Group, 1963-72; Group Finance Director (Finance and IT), Pritchard Services Group plc, 1983-86; Main Board and Group Finance Director (Finance and IT), 1986-97, Main Board Director, 1997-1998, Inchcape plc; Retired 1998; Historian, Genealogist and Writer, Founder of The O'Donoghue Society, 1998-. Publications: The O'Donoghue Trail, 1990-95; O'Donoghue People and Places, 1999; Quarterly Journal for the O'Donoghue Society, 2000-; 2 books in progress. Memberships: Society of Genealogists; Irish Genealogical Research Society; Guild of One Name Studies; Highgate Golf Club; The National Trust; English Heritage; RSPB; The Arts Club. Address: 30 Canonbury Park South, London N1 2FN, England. E-mail: rod@odonoghue.co.uk Website: www.odonoghue.co.uk

O'FERRALL Patrick Charles Kenneth, b. 27 May 1934, Wrecclesham, Surrey, England. Clerk in Holy Orders (Non-Stipendiary). m. (1) Mary Dorothea Lugard, deceased, 1 son, 2 daughters, (2) Wendy Elizabeth Barnett. Education: MA, New College, Oxford, 1954-58; Advanced Management Program, Harvard Business School, USA, 1983. Appointments: Various positions, Iraq Petroleum Group, 1958-70; BP Area Co-ordinator for Abu Dhabi Marine Areas Ltd and BP Eastern Agencies, 1971-73; Total CFP, Paris, 1974-77; Commercial Manager, 1977-82, Alwyn North Co-ordination Manager, 1983-85, Projects Co-ordination Manager, 1985-90, Total Oil Marine, London; Director, Total Oil Marine (Engineering Construction) Ltd, 1983-89; Deputy Chairman, 1991-93, Chairman, 1993-99, Lloyd's Register of Shipping; Member, Offshore Industry Advisory Board, 1991-94; Lay Reader, Church of England, 1961-2000; Ordained, Deacon, 2000, Priest, 2001; Curate, Saints Peter and Paul, Godalming, 2000-01. Honours: Longstaff Exhibition, New College, Oxford; Fellow, Royal Society of Arts; Honorary Fellow, Royal Academy of Engineering; Companion, Chartered Management Institute. memberships: Past master, Worshipful Company of Coachmakers and Coach Harness Makers, 1993-94; Liveryman, Worshipful Company of Shipwrights; Member of Court of Common Council, City of London, 1996-2001; Chairman, City Branch Outward Bound Association, 1993-97; President Aldgate Ward Club, 1998, currently Honorary Chaplain; Retired Member of Baltic

Exchange, currently Honorary Chaplain. Address: Catteshall Grange, Catteshall Road, Godalming, Surrey GU7 1LZ, England. E-mail: patrick@oferrall.co.uk

O'GRADY Barbara Ann Vinson, b. 6 July 1928, Alhambra, California, USA. Public Health Nurse. m. Joseph Putnam O'Grady, 3 sons, 2 daughters. Education: Diploma in Nursing, Los Angeles County General Hospital, 1945-48; Baccalaureate in Science (major in Public Health Nursing), UCLA, 1948-51; Masters in Science (major in Public Health Nursing), University of Minnesota, 1970-72. Appointments: Staff Nurse, Los Angeles County General Hospital; Private Duty Nurse, Scripps Hospital; Staff Nurse, University of Minnesota Hospital, periodically between 1951-70; Assistant Professor in Nursing, Gustavus Adolphus College, St Peter, Minnesota, 1972-77; Appointed Director of Ramsey County Public Health Nursing Service, St Paul, Minnesota, 1977-88. Publications: The Collection of Baseline Data for Evaluating Patient Care, 1982. Honours: Innovative State and Local Government Initiatives, Ford Foundation, 1981; Outstanding Achievement Award, Board of Ramsey County Commissioners, 1987; Community Service Award, Minnesota Public Health Association, 1988. Memberships: American Academy of Nursing; American Nurses Association; Women's Environmental Watch; Valley Community Mentoring. Address: 3955 Edgehill Lane, PO Box 624, Santa Ynez, CA 93460, USA. E-mail: jb@syv.com

O'HORA Nathy Patrick Joseph, b. 21 February 1926, Kiltimagh, Co Mayo, Ireland. Astronomer. m. Elizabeth Wilson, 1 son, 2 daughters. Education: Galway University; BSc, London University. Appointments: Joined Time Department, 1949, Night Observer, Transit Circle, Meridian Department, 1957-62, Head of Astronomy Section, Time Department, 1965, Public Information Officer, 1975, Royal Greenwich Observatory. Publications: The Dunsink Observatory, 1964; An Investigation of PZT Observations for Evidence of the Existence of Polar Disturbances Due to Large Earthquakes, 1970; The Longitude of Herstmonceux, 1971; The Free Polar Motion in 1916-1933, 1971; The Herstmonceux PZT, 1972; Semi-Diurnal Tidal Effects in PZT Observations, 1973; Tidal Perturbations in Astronomical Observations, 1973; Fortnightly Terms in PZT Observations, 1973; Rotation of the Earth during the 1972 Solar Event, 1973; The Detection of Recent Changes in the Earth's Rotation, 1975; International Time Transfer between USNO and RGO via NTS-1 Satellite, 1978; L'Observatoire Royal de Greenwich, a Greenwich, et a Herstmonceux, 1980; L'Observatoire de la Roque de los Muchachos, 1980; Sur l'Année d'une Lettre de Halley datée d'un Huitième de Juin, 1985; Astrographic Catalogues of British Observatories, 1987. Memberships: Fellow, Royal Astronomical Society; Member, Institute of Physics; Member, International Astronomical Union; Member, Societe Astronomique de France. Address: Nephin, Hailsham Road, Herstmonceux, East Sussex BN27 4LJ, England.

O'KANE Stephen Granville, b. 26 April 1951, Harrow, Middlesex, England. Writer; Researcher. Education: BA, Politics, History (subsidiary), University of Nottingham, England, 1970-73; MA, Political Thought, University of Keele, England, 1973-75; PhD, Christianity and Socialism in British thought, University of London, London School of Economics, 1975-79; Reading ability in French, 1989-93; Numerous computer courses, 1978-98; Business Enterprise Programme and Extended Business Training, 1989-91. Career: Owing to ill health (asthma and ME/CFS) became researcher and writer rather than pursue an institutional career; Writings and research on the confluence between ethical and political

issues and the implications of that for ethics itself, 1979-; Research into political affairs in individual members of the European Union, 1988-; Part-time Adult Education Teacher, Clerical and Market Research work, 1980-81, 1984-86, 1993; Set up own website (http://www.stgok.mistral.co.uk) adjusted to RNIB guidelines for people with sight difficulties; Member of Assert, charity working for people with Aspergers Syndrome, 2003-. Publications: Books: Politics and Morality under Conflict, 1994; Ethics and Radical Freedom, 2006; Essays on website: Freedom and Thematic Decentralisation; The Spider and the Fly; Moral Judgement: True or False?; Several articles for The Radical Quarterly, 1987-90; 2 articles in FSI News/Business News (Sussex), 1989, 1990; Article, What Right to Private Property? In Economy and Society, 1997; Paper, Ethical Systems and Expansion in Information Circulation, 2003. Memberships: British Society for Ethical Theory; Brighton and Hove Friends of the Earth, 1995-. Address: Flat 25, Homedrive House, 95-97 The Drive, Hove, East Sussex, BN3 6GE, England. E-mail: gs@o-kane.f2s.com Website: www.o-kane.f2s.com

O'MEARA Mark, b. 13 January 1957, Goldsboro, North Carolina, USA. Golfer. Education: Long Beach State University. Career: Professional Golfer, 1980-; Ryder Cup Team, 1985, 1989, 1991, 1997; Won US Amateur Championship, 1979, Greater Milwaukee Open, 1984, Bing Crosby Pro-American, 1985, Hawaii Open, 1985, Fuji Sankei Classic, 1985, Australian Masters, 1986, Lawrence Batley International, 1987, AT&T Pebble Beach National Pro-American, 1989, 1990, 1992, 1997, H-E-B TX Open, 1990, Walt Disney World/Oldsmobile Classic, 1991, Tokia Classic, 1992, Argentine Open, 1994, Honda Classic, 1995, Bell Canada Open, 1995, Mercedes Championships, 1996, Greater Greensboro Open, 1996, Brick Invitational, 1997, US Masters, 1998, British Open, 1998, World Matchplay 1998; Best Finish 2002, 2nd in Buick Invitational and 2nd in Buick Open; Champions Tour, 2007. Honour: All-American Rookie of the Year, Long Beach State University, 1981; PGA Tour Player of the Year, 1998. Address: c/o PGA, Box 109601, Avenue of Champions, Palm Beach Gardens, FL 33410, USA.

O'NEAL Ryan, b. 20 April 1941, Los Angeles, USA. Actor. m. (1) Joanna Moore, divorced, 1 son, 1 daughter, (2) Leigh Taylor-Young, divorced, 1 son, 1 son with Farrah Fawcett. Career: Numerous TV appearances; Films include: The Big Bounce, 1969; Love Story, 1970; The Wild Rovers, 1971; What's Up, Doc? 1972; The Thief Who Came To Dinner, 1973; Paper Moon, 1973; Oliver's Story, 1978; The Main Event, 1979; So Fine, 1981; Partners, 1982; Irreconcilable Differences, 1983; Fever Pitch, 1985; Tough Guys Don't Dance, 1986; Chances Are, 1989; Faithful, 1996; Hacks, 1997; Burn Hollywood Burn, 1997; Zero Effect, 1998; Coming Soon, 1999; Epoch, 2000; People I Know, 2002; Malibu's Most Wanted, 2003; Waste Land, 2007.

O'SULLEVAN Peter John (Sir), b. 3 March 1918. Racing Correspondent; Commentator. m. Patricia Duckworth, 1951. Education: Hawtreys, Charterhouse, College Alpin, Switzerland. Appointments: Chelsea Rescue Service, 1939-45; Editorial work and manuscript reading with Bodley Head Publisher; Racing Correspondent, Press Association, 1945-50, Daily Express, 1950-86, Today, 1986-87; Race Broadcaster, 1946-98; Chair, Osborne Studio Gallery, 1999-. Publication: Calling the Horses: A Racing Autobiography, 1989. Honours include: CBE; Derby Award, Racing Journalist of the Year, 1971, 1986; Racehorse Owner of the Year Award, Horserace Writers Association, 1974; Sport on TV Award,

Daily Telegraph, 1994; Services to Racing Award, Daily Star, 1995; Media Awards Variety Club of Great Britain, 1995; Lester's Award, Jockeys' Association, 1996; Special Award, TV and Radio Industries Club, 1998. Address: 37 Cranmer Court, London SW3 3HW, England.

O'SULLIVAN Sonia, b. 28 November 1969, Cobh, Ireland. Athlete. Education: Accounting Studies, Villanova, USA. Career: Gold Medal 1500m, Silver Medal 3000m, World Student Games, 1991; Holds 7 national (Irish) records; Set new world record (her first) in 2000m, TSB Challenge, Edinburgh, 1994, new European record in 3000m, TSB Games London, 1994; Gold Medal in 3000m European Athletic Championships, Helsinki, 1994; Winner, Grand Prix 3000m, 2nd overall, 1993; Silver Medal, 1500m World Championships, Stuttgart, 1993; Gold Medal, 5000m World Championships, Gothenburg, 1995; Gold Medal, World Cross Country Championships 4km, 8km, 1998; Gold Medal, European Championships 5000m, 10,000m, 1998; Silver Medal, 5,000m 2000 Olympic Games; Silver Medal, 5,000m, 10,000m European Championships, 2002; Retired, 2007. Publications: Running to Stand Still. Honours: Female Athlete of the Year, 1995; Texaco Sports Star of the Year (Athletics), 2002. Address: c/o Kim McDonald, 201 High Street, Hampton Hill, Middlesex TW12 1NL, England.

O'TOOLE Peter Seamus, b. 2 August 1932, Eire, Ireland. Actor. 1 son, 2 daughters. Education: RADA (Diploma), Associate, RADA. Career: Joined Bristol's Old Vic Theatre, played 73 parts, 1955-58; West End debut in Oh My Papa, 1957; Stratford Season, 1960; Stage appearances in, Pictures in the Hallway, 1962; Baal, 1963; Ride a Cock Horse, Waiting for Godot, 1971; Dead Eye Dicks, 1976; Present Laughter, 1978; Bristol Old Vic Theatre Season, 1973; Macbeth Old Vic, 1980; Man and Superman, 1982-83; Pygmalion, 1984, 1987; The Applecart, 1986; Jeffrey Barnard is Unwell, 1989, 1991, 1999; Films include: Kidnapped, The Day They Robbed the Bank of England, 1959; Lawrence of Arabia, 1960; Becket, 1963; Lord Jim, 1964; What's New Pussycat?, 1965; The Bible, 1966; Night of the Generals, Great Catherine, 1967; The Lion in Winter, 1968; Goodbye Mr Chips, 1969; Brotherly Love, Country Dance, 1970; Murphy's War, 1971; Under Milk Wood, The Ruling Class, Man of La Mancha, 1972; Rosebud, 1974; Man Friday, Foxtrot, 1975; Caligula, 1977; Power Play, Stuntman, Zulu Dawn, 1978; The Antagonists, My Favourite Year, 1981; Supergirl, 1984; Club Paradise, The Last Emperor, 1986; High Spirits, 1988; On a Moonlit Night, 1989; Creator, King Ralph, 1990; Wings of Fame, 1991; Rebecca's Daughters, Our Song, Civies, 1992; Fairytale: the True Story, 1997; Coming Home, The Manor, 1998; Molokai: The Story of Father Damien, 1999; Global Heresy, The Final Curtain, 2002; Bright Young Things, 2003; Troy, 2004; Lassie, 2005; Venus, One Night with the King, 2006; Ratatouille (voice), Stardust, Thomas Kinkade's Home for Christmas, 2007. Publications: The Child, 1992; The Apprentice, 1996. Honours: Commander of the Order of Arts and Letters, France; Outstanding Achievement Award, 1999. Address: c/o William Morris Agency, Stratton House, Stratton Street, London, W1X 5FE, England.

OAKLEY Ann (Rosamund), b. 17 January 1944, London, England. Professor of Sociology and Social Policy; Writer. 1 son, 2 daughters. Education: MA, Somerville College, Oxford, 1965; PhD, Bedford College, London, 1974. Appointments: Research Officer, Social Research Unit, Bedford College, London, 1974-79; Wellcome Research Fellow, Radcliffe Infirmary, National Perinatal Epidemiology Unit, Oxford, 1980-83; Deputy Director, Thomas Coram Research Unit, 1985-90, Director, Social Science Research Unit, 1990-, Professor of Sociology and Social Policy, 1991-, University of London. Publications: Sex, Gender and Society, 1972; The Sociology of Housework, 1974; Housewife, 1974, US edition as Women's Work: A History of the Housewife, 1975; The Rights and Wrongs of Women, 1976; Becoming a Mother, 1980; Women Confined, 1980; Subject Women, 1981; Miscarriage, 1984; Taking It Like a Woman, 1984; The Captured Womb: A History of the Medical Care of Pregnant Women, 1984; Telling the Truth about Jerusalem, 1986; What Is Feminism, 1986; The Men's Room, 1988; Only Angels Forget, 1990; Matilda's Mistake, 1990; Helpers in Childbirth: Midwifery Today, 1990; The Secret Lives of Eleanor Jenkinson, 1992; Social Support and Motherhood: The Natural History of a Research Project, 1992; Essays on Women, Medicine and Health, 1993; Scenes Originating in the Garden of Eden, 1993; Young People, Health and Family Life, 1994; The Politics of the Welfare State, 1994; Man and Wife, 1996; The Gift Relationship by Richard Titmuss, 1997; Who's Afraid of Feminism? 1997; Welfare Research: A critical review, 1998; Experiments in Knowing: Gender and Method in the Social Sciences, 2000; Welfare and Wellbeing: Richard Titmuss's contribution to social policy, 2001; Overheads, 2000; Gender on Planet Earth, 2002; Private Complaints and Public Health: Richard Titmus on the National Health Service, 2004; The Ann Oakly Reader: Gender, women and social science, 2005; Fracture: Adventures of a broken body, 2007. Contributions to: Professional journals; Many chapters in academic books. Honours: Hon DLitt, Salford, 1995; Honorary Professor, University College, London, 1996-; Honorary Fellow, Somerville College, Oxford, 2001-. Address: c/o The Sayle Agency, 8B Kings Parade, Cambridge, CB2 1SJ, England.

OAKLEY Robin Francis Leigh, b. 20 August 1941, Kidderminster, Worcestershire, England. Journalist. m. Carolyn, 1 son, 1 daughter. Education: MA, Brasenose College, Oxford. Appointments: Liverpool Daily Post, 1964-70; Crossbencher Columnist and then Assistant Editor, Sunday Express, 1970-79; Assistant Editor, Now! Magazine, 1979-81; Assistant Editor, Daily Mail, 1981-86; Political Editor, The Times, 1986-92; Political Editor, BBC, 1992-2000; European Political Editor, CNN, 2000-; Turf Columnist, The Spectator, 1996-; Racing Correspondent, Financial Times, 2003-; Trustee, Thompson Foundation, 2001-. Publications: Valley of the Racehorse – a portrait of the racing community of Lambourn, 2000; Inside Track – thirty years of political reporting, 2001. Honour: OBE, 2001. Membership: RAC. Address: 17 West Square, London SE11 4SN, England. E-mail: robin.oakley@cnn.com

OBEMBE Lawrence Kayode, b. 7 June 1949, Ekiti, Nigeria. Senior Lecturer; Consultant. m. Ibitola Olufunmike Dada, 2 sons, 3 daughters. Education: Bachelor of Medical Science, Physiology, 1974, Bachelor of Medicine, Bachelor of Surgery, 1977, University of Ibadan. Appointments: House Officer, Adeoyo State Hospital, Ibadan, 1977-78; National Youth Service Corps, National Orthopaedic Hospital, Igbobi, Lagos, 1978-79; Senior House Officer, 1979-80, Senior Registrar, 1984-85, University College Hospital, Ibadan; Rotating Registrar, University College Hospital Obstetrics & Gynaecology, Anaesthesia, General Surgery and Neonatology, 1980-83; Research Registrar, Department of Obstetrics & Gynaecology, Aberdeen Royal Infirmary, University of Aberdeen, Scotland, 1983-84; Lecturer, Consultant, Acting Head, Department of Obstetrics & Gynaecology, University of Maiduguri, Bornu State, 1986; Consultant Obstetrician & Gynaecologist, Chief Medical

Director, Christus Specialists' Hospital (Nig) Ltd, at various locations; Senior Lecturer, Consultant, Ladoke Akintola University of Technology, College of Medicine, Osogbo, 2001-. Publications: Many articles and papers in professional medical journals; Books include: Fundamental Principles of Diagnostic Ultrasonography, 2004. Honours: Numerous awards including: Merit Award, National Association of Resident Doctors, 2003; Merit and Donors Award, Nigerian Medical Association, Oyo State Chapter, 2003; Chairman, Welfare Sub Committee of the Board, National Orthopaedic Hospital, Igbobi, 2003; NMA delegate to First African Health Summit, 2003; Meritorious Service Award, Nigerian Medical Association, Oyo State, 2004. Memberships: Association of General & Private Medical Practitioners of Nigeria; Nigerian National Post Graduate Medical College; Society of Gynaecology and Obstetrics of Nigeria; Sickle Cell Association of Nigeria; West African College of Surgeons; Nigerian Medical Association; International Society of Ultrasound in Obstetrics and Gynaecology; International Society of Laparoendoscopic Surgeons; American Institute of Ultrasound in Medicine; International College of Surgeons; President, Christ's School Alumni Association, Ibadan Chapter; Member, Board of Management University College Hospital, Ibadan; Member, Court of Governors, College of Medicine, University of Ibadan; Chief Executive Officer, Premier Medicaid International HMO, Health Insurance Scheme. Address: Zion Building, PO Box 29259 Sec PO, Ibadan, Oyo State, Nigeria. E-mail: k-obembe@yahoo.co.uk

ODELL Robin Ian, b. 19 December 1935, Totton, Hampshire, England. Writer. m. Joan Bartholomew, 19 September 1959. Publications: Jack the Ripper in Fact and Fiction, 1965; Exhumation of a Murder, 1975; Jack the Ripper: Summing-up and Verdict (with Colin Wilson), 1977; The Murderers' Who's Who (with J H H Gaute), 1979; Lady Killers, 1980; Murder Whatdunit, 1982; Murder Whereabouts, 1986; Dad Help Me Please (with Christopher Berry-Dee), 1990; A Question of Evidence, 1992; Lady Killer, 1992; The Long Drop, 1993; Landmarks in Twentieth Century Murder, 1995; The International Murderer's Who's Who, 1996; Ripperology, 2006; Murderers' Row (with Wilfred Gregg), 2006. Contributions to: Crimes and Punishment; The Criminologist. Honours: FCC Watts Memorial Prize, 1957; International Humanist and Ethical Union, 1960; Edgar Award, Mystery Writers of America, 1980. Memberships: Our Society; Police History Society. Address: 11 Red House Drive, Sonning Common, Reading RG4 9NT, England.

OESER Hans-Christian, b. 12 June 1950, Wiesbaden, Germany. Literary Translator; Travel Book Author; Editor. m. Barbara Proctor, 1 son, 1 daughter. Education: German, Politics, Philosophy and Pedagogy, Marburg and Berlin (West), Germany, 1971-77; First State Examination, 1978; Second State Examination, 1980; MA, 1980; ITI Diploma in Translation, 1989. Appointments: Lecturer in German, University College, Dublin, 1980-83; Lecturer in German, National Institute for Higher Education (now Dublin City University), 1983-84; Teacher, Goethe Institute, Dublin, 1984-2000. Publications: Irland (with M Schmidt), 1989; Dublin. Stadt und Kultur (with J Schneider and R Sotscheck), 1992; Treffpunkt Irland. Ein literarischer Reiseführer, 1996; Irland (with E Wrba and R Sotscheck), 1998; Oscar-Wilde-ABC, 2004; Dublin. Ein Reisebegleiter, 2005; James Joyce (with J Schneider), 2007. Editor of anthologies, almanacs and foreign language editions; Translator of non-fiction, fiction and poetry titles by numerous authors; Author of many essays, articles, reviews and translations in newspapers, journals, anthologies, encyclopaedias and websites. Honours: European Translation Prize Aristeion, 1997; Honorary Membership for Life of the Irish Translators' and Interpreters' Association, 2003. Memberships: Society for Exile Studies; Founder Member, Treasurer, 1986-89, Honorary Secretary, 1989-98, Editor of Translation Ireland, 1995-99, Irish Translators' and Interpreters' Association; PEN Centre of German Speaking Writers Abroad; PEN Centre Germany; PEN Centre Ireland; Irish Writers' Union; Member, Board of Directors, Ireland Literature Exchange, 1995-99. Address: 114 Ballinclea Heights, Killiney, Co Dublin, Ireland. E-mail: hcoeser@eircom.net Website: www.sign-bso.de/hcoeser/html/

OFFER Clifford Jocelyn, b. 10 August 1943, Ightham, Kent, England. Clerk in Holy Orders. m. Catherine, 2 daughters. Education: St Peter's College, Oxford (sent down); BA, Exeter University; Westcott House, Cambridge. Appointments: Curate, Bromley Parish Church, 1969-74; Team Vicar, Southampton (City Centre), 1974-83; Team Rector of Hitchin, 1983-94; Archdeacon of Norwich and Canon, Librarian, Norwich Cathedral, 1994-. Publications: King Offa in Hitchin, 1992; In Search of Clofesho, 2002. Membership: FRSA. Address: 26 The Close, Norwich NR1 4DZ, England. E-mail: archdeacon.norwich@4frontmedia.co.uk

OGAWA Ikuo, b. 30 September 1967, Tokyo, Japan. Research Engineer. m. Sayoko, 2 sons, 1 daughter. Education: BS, MS, Applied Physics, Waseda University, Tokyo, Japan, 1992. Appointments: Research Engineer, NTT Opto-Electronics Laboratories, 1992-; Research Engineer, NTT Wireless Systems Laboratories, 1994-; Senior Research Engineer, NTT Photonics Laboratories, 1996-. Honours: Best Paper Award, Inose Award, IEICE, 2006. Memberships: IEEE/LEOS; Institute of Electronics, Information and Communication Engineers of Japan; Japan Society of Applied Physics; Optical Society of Japan. E-mail: iogawa@aecl.ntt.co.jp

OGG Wilson Reid, b. 26 February 1928, Alhambra, California, USA. Social Scientist; Academician; Philosopher; Lawyer; Poet; Lyricist; Educator. Education: AA, 1947; AB, 1949; JD, University of California, 1952; Hon DD, University of Life Church, 1969; Doctorate, Religious Humanities, 1970. Appointments: Psychology Instructor, US Armed Forces Institute, Taegu, Korea, 1953-54; English Instructor, Taegu English Language Institute, 1954; Trustee Secretary, 1st Unitarian Church of Berkeley, 1957-58; Research Attorney, Continuing Education of the Bar, University of California, 1958-63; Vice President, International House Association, 1961-62; President, Board Chairman, California Society for Psychical Study, 1963-65; Private Law Practitioner, 1955-; Director, Admissions, International Society for Philosophical Enquiry, 1981-84. Publications: Poetry publications in numerous journals and anthologies; Author: The Enfolding Universe, 1995; Constitutional Law: Crisis Facing American Democracy, 2005; Collection of Essays of Wilson Ogg, 2006. Honours: Commendation Ribbon W Medal Pendant; Cultural Doctorate, World University; The International Peace Prize, United Cultural Convention, USA; Commemorative Medal, Medal of Science and Peace, 50th Anniversary of the Nobel Prize of Peace, 1953-2003; Member, International Hall of Fame, 2005; The World Medal of Freedom, 2006; Leading Educators of the World, 2006. Memberships: American Mensa; Emeritus Member, Faculty Club, University at Berkeley; The Triple Nine Society; International House Association; New York Academy of Sciences; London Diplomatic Academy; Scientific Faculty, Cambridge, England; Laureate, Top 100 Scientists for the Year, 2005; International Platform Association; The World's Most Respected Experts, 2006; San

Francisco Bar Association; American Society of Composers, Authors and Publishers; American Bar Association; State Bar of California. Address: Pinebrook at Bret Harte Way, 1104 Keith Avenue, Berkeley, CA 94708, USA. E-mail: wilsonogg@alum.calberkeley.org; www.wilsonogg.com

OGILVIE-GRAHAM Thomas Syme, b. 23 June 1960, Dundee, Scotland. Army Officer, Biologist, Barrister. m. Tinamay Ullens de Schooten, 2 sons, 1 daughter. Education: BVM&S, 1982, DVM&S, 1994, The Edinburgh Academy; Edinburgh University; MSc, CBiol, FIBiol, 1995, Reading University; called to the Bar by Gray's Inn, 1998; Fulbright Fellowship, Cornell University, 2001. Appointments: Active Service, including Intelligence and Airborne Forces appointments in Northern Ireland, Balkans, Africa, Middle East; Served in the King's Troop and Household Cavalry; Army Officer, Brigadier, Director Army Veterinary and Remount Service as well as Honorary Veterinary Surgeon to the Queen, 2007; External interests in Bio fuel Technology, Politics and International Trade. Publications: Numerous articles relating primarily to animal behaviour and wildlife conservation. Honours: Robert Louis Stevenson Silver Medal, 1977; MBE, 1992; Knight of Merit of Constantinian Order, 2004; Officer of Order of St. John, 2005; Knight of Order of St Francis, 2006. Memberships: Royal College of Veterinary Surgeons; British Veterinary Association; Special Professor at Nottingham University; Royal Society of Medicine (Section President); Chairman of Wildlife Vets International; Society for the Protection of Animals Abroad; Welfare Fund for Companion Animals; British Fulbright Scholars Association; Constantinian Order; Zoological Society of London; Steering Group member for Government Veterinary Surgeons. Address: 8 The Terrace, Camberley, Surrey, GU15 4NS. E-mail: tom.ogilvie-graham@virgin.net

OGRAM Geoffrey Reginald, b. 14 October 1937, Ealing, England. Retired College Principal Lecturer. m. Margaret Mary, 3 daughters. Education: BSc (Hons) Industrial Metallurgy, 1958, PhD, 1961, University of Birmingham. Appointments: Research Fellow, University of Birmingham, 1960-62; Research Metallurgist, GKN Group Research Centre, Wolverhampton, 1962-65; Lecturer, Senior Lecturer, Principal Lecturer in Metallurgy, Sandwell College, West Midlands, 1965-95. Publications: Articles in scientific journals: Effect of Alloying Additions in Steel, 1965; Directionality of Yield Point in Strain-aged Steel, 1967; Magical Images – A Handbook of Stereo Photography (author's publication); The Music of Gordon Jacob (in preparation). Honours: MIMMM; C Eng. Memberships: British Magical Society, 1975, President, 1989-90; Magic Circle, 1978-; Catenian Association (Stafford Circle), President, 1980-85, 2001-2002; Provincial Councillor, 1985-91; Birmingham Japan Society, 1991-, Chairman, 1999-2001; Stereoscopic Society, 1997-; Governor St Anne's Roman Catholic Primary School, Stafford, 1997-; Organist, St Anne's Roman Catholic Church, Stafford, 1970-; Stafford Recorded Music Society, Secretary, 2004-. Address: 6 Silverthorn Way, Wildwood, Stafford ST17 4PZ, England. E-mail: geoff.ogram@talktalk.net

OGUCHI Chiaki, b. 11 January 1969, Yokohama, Japan. Researcher; Associate Professor. m. Takashi Oguchi, 1 son, 1 daughter. Education: Master of Science, 1993, Doctor of Science, 1998, University of Tsukuba, Japan. Appointments: Assistant Professor, University of Tsukuba, 1998-2002; JSPS Domestic Research Fellow, Japan International Research Center for Agricultural Sciences, Tsukuba; 2002-2004; Associate Professor, Saitama University, 2004-. Publications: Articles in scientific journals: Weathering rates

over 40,000 years based on the changes in rock properties of porous rhyolite, 1999; Formation of weathering rinds on andesite, 2001; A porosity-related diffusion model of weathering-rind development, 2004. Honours: Special Award for Education and Research, Meikei-Tsukuba University, 2000; Great Women of the 21st Century in the field of Geomorphology, 2005. Memberships: British Geomorphological Research Group; European Geosciences Union; Japan Geomorphological Union; Association of Japanese Geographers; The Clay Science Society of Japan. Address: 255 Shimo-Okubo, Sakura-ku, Saitama, 338-8570 Japan. E-mail: ogchiaki@mail.saitama-u.ac.jp

OGUCHI Takashi, b. 13 March 1963, Matsumoto, Japan. Associate Professor. m. Chiaki, 1 son, 1 daughter. Education: BA, 1985, DSc, 1996, University of Tokyo, Japan. Appointments: Assistant Professor, Department of Geography, Faculty of Science, University of Tokyo, 1991-97; Visiting Scholar, University of Arizona, USA, 1997; Visiting Scholar, Institute of Hydrology, UK, 1997-98; Associate Professor, Center for Spatial Information Science, University of Tokyo, 1998-; Member, Editorial Board, Catena, 1997-; Geomorphology, 1999-2002; Geography Compass, 2006-08; The Open Geology Journal, 2007-; Co-Editor-in-Chief, Geomorphology, 2003-; Member, International Advisory Board, Geographical Research, 2004-; Adjunct Graduate Faculty, University of Memphis, USA, 2007-. Publications: Articles in scientific journals as author and first author include: River water quality in the Humber Catchment: An introduction using GIS-based mapping and analysis, 2000; Fluvial geomorphology and paleohydrology in Japan, 2001; Geomorphology and GIS in Japan: background and characteristics, 2001; An online database of Polish towns and historical landscapes using an Internet map server, 2002; Identification of an active fault in the Japanese Alps from DEM-based hill shading, 2003; Late Quaternary rapid talus dissection and debris-flow deposition on an alluvial fan in Syria, 2004. Honours: Excellent Paper Award for Young Geographers, Association of Japanese Geographers, 1995; International Order of Merit, Order of Distinction, Order of International Fellowship, Lifetime Achievement Award, IBC, 2005-2006; Order of International Ambassadors, American Order of Excellence, ABI, 2005-2006; COMLAND Award, Commission on Land Degradation and Desertification, International Geographical Union, 2008. Memberships: Commission Member: International Geographical Union, International Association of Geomorphologists; Steering Committee Member: Association of Japanese Geographers, Japanese Geomorphological Union, GIS Association of Japan; Honorary Director General, IBC; Deputy Governor, ABI. Address: Centre for Spatial Information Science, University of Tokyo, 5-1-5 Kashiwanoha, Kashiwa 277-8568, Japan. E-mail: oguchi@csis.u-tokyo.ac.jp

OGUN Oluremi, b. 10 October 1957, Owo, Nigeria. Economics Educator. Education: BSc (Honours), Economics, 1981, MSc, Economics, 1983, PhD, Economics, 1990, University of Ibadan, Nigeria; ACIB, London, 1991. Appointments: Visiting Senior Lecturer, University of Lagos, Nigeria, 2006-07. Publications: Several journal articles, 1 book. Honours: African Economic Research Consortium (AERC) Research Grant, 1992, 1994, 1996; Research Fellowship, 1994; Special Service Award, Institute for New Technology, UN University, Maastricht, 1992; Visiting Senior Economist, Financial Institutions Training Centre, Lagos, 1994; Visiting Research Scholar, University of California at Santa Barbara, 1994-96; African Technology Policy Studies (ATPS) Research Grant, 1995; Listed in numerous biographical dictionaries.

Memberships: Nigerian Economics Society, Life Member and Secretary Oyo State Chapter, 1993; AERC; ATPS; West African Economics Association; Chartered Institute of Bankers, London; Economic Development Association; Association of Third World Studies. Address: Department of Economics, University of Ibadan, Nigeria.

OGUNSHAKIN Alex Abimola, b. 2 February 1956, Ondo, Nigeria. Chartered Marketer. m. Joy Ogechi, 1 son, 2 daughters. Education: Diploma in Mass Communication, School of Journalism and TV, Frilsham Hermitage, Berkshire, England, 1976; Diploma in Commerce, Institute of Commerce, London, 1979; HND, Business Studies, Management Services Division, West Bromwich College of Commerce and Technology, England, 1977-80; Diploma in Marketing, Chartered Institute of Marketing, London, 1980; Diploma in Private Detective & Investigation, 2007. Appointments: Assistant Lecturer and Lecturer III, Marketing, Federal Polytechnic, Bida, Niger State, Nigeria, 1981-85; Merchandiser, Domino Stores Ltd, Yaba, Nigeria, 1985-87; Group Manager, Merchandising, UTC Stores, Lagos, Nigeria, 1987-90; Sales and Marketing Manger, John Holt PLC, Shipping Services Division, Nigeria, 1990-92; Cargo Sales Manager then National Cargo Sales Manager, United Parcel Services, Cargo Logistics Division, 1993-98; Commercial Consultant, Folabim Commercial Services, Ikeja, Lagos, Nigeria, 1999-; Marketing Consultant, Bakafaj International (Freight) Ltd, 1998-2001; General Manager, Logistics, TNT Logistics Division, 2001-2002; National Sales and Marketing Manger, Bemil Nig Ltd, Lagos, 2003; General Manager, Alarm Centre Ltd, 2003; Executive Director, Grand Security Nigeria Ltd, 2003-06; Executive Director, Grandsec/Metro-Beam Services (a division of Lexy-Gradsec Services Ltd, Lagos), 2006-. Publications: Concorde Plane: Effect of British Aviation Industry, 1979; Sales Promotion - An Effective Marketing Tool, 1980. Honour: Presidential Merit Award, National Institute of Marketing, Nigeria, 2004. Memberships: Member, Chartered Institute of Marketing, UK; Fellow, British Society of Commerce; Member Institute of Commercial Management, UK; Fellow and Council Member, National Institute of Marketing of Nigeria; Fellow, Institute of Private Detective & Investigation; Fellow, Institute of Chartered Management Accountants of Nigeria; Member, Institute of Management Consultants; Member, Institute of Industrial Security & Safety of Nigeria. Address: PO Box 15056, Ikeja, Lagos, Nigeria.

OGUTI Takasi, b. 31 March 1930, Nagano-ken Japan. Professor. m. Yoko, 1 son, 1 daughter. Education: BS, Graduate, University of Tokyo, 1953; Doctor of Science, 1962. Appointments: Professor, Geophysics, University of Tokyo, 1970; Director, Geophysics Research Laboratory, University of Tokyo, 1985; Director, Solar Terrestrial Environment Laboratory, Nagoya University, 1989-. Publication: Metamorphoses of Aurora. Honours: Tanakadate Prize, 1962; Hasegawa Prize, 1993. Memberships: Society of Geomagnetism and Earth Planetary and Space Sciences. Address: Shakujiicho 7-33-9, Nerimaku, Tokyo 177-0041, Japan.

OH Kwang-Jun, b. 26 September 1968, Seoul, South Korea. Orthopaedic Surgeon; Professor. Education: Premedical course, 1987-89, Medical Doctor, 1993, Korea University College of Medicine; Master of Science, 2001, Doctor of Philosophy, 2003, Korea University Postgraduate School. Appointments: Clinical Fellowship, Department of Trauma & Reconstructive Surgery, Lukaskrankenhaus, Dusseldorf, Germany, 2002; Clinical Fellowship, 2001-03, 2003, Department of Orthopaedic Surgery, Konkuk University

Hospital; Orthopaedic Clinical Research Fellowship, Department of Orthopaedic Surgery, Stanford University Medical Center, USA, 2003-05. Publications: 12 international articles; 30 national articles. Honours: Best Paper Award, 11th Congress IHLAS, Seoul, Korea; President's Initiative Award, 51st AAEM, Savannah, Georgia, USA; Poster Prize, 23rd Triennial SICOT, Istanbul, Turkey; FIMS-EFSMA Travelling Fellowship, 2005. Memberships: Korean Hip & Knee Society; AO (Switzerland) Alumni Association Member; International Member, American Academic Orthopaedic Society. 4-12 Hwayang-dong, Gwangjin-gu, Seoul 143-729, South Korea. E-mail: damioh@gmail.com

OH Sang Ho, b. 10 December 1973, Daejeon, Republic of Korea. Researcher. Education: BS, Materials Science and Engineering, Han Yang University, Seoul, 1996; MS, 1998, PhD, 2002, Materials Science and Engineering, Pohang University of Science and Technology, Pohang. Appointments: Postdoctorate, 2002-03, Visiting Scientist, 2005, Max-Planck-Institute for Metal Research; Senior Researcher, Korea Research Institute of Standards and Science, 2003-05; Scientist, Erich Schmid Institute for Materials Science, 2005-06; Research Associate, North Carolina A&T State University, 2006-07; Visiting Scientist, Oak Ridge National Laboratory, 2006-07; Senior Researcher, Korea Basic Science Institute, 2007-. Publications: More than 30 international scientific peer-reviewed journal papers, including Ordered Liquid Aluminum at the Interface with Sapphire, 2005. Address: Division of Electron Microscopic Research, Korea Basic Science Institute, 52 Eoeun-dong, Yuseong-gu, Daejeon 305-333, Republic of Korea. E-mail: shoh@kbsi.re.kr

OH Yong Seog, b. 17 July 1962, Seoul, Korea. Associate Professor. m. Young Joo Kwak, 1 son, 1 daughter. Education: MD, Catholic University of Korea Medical College, Seoul, 1987; PhD, Catholic University of Korea Postgraduate School, 1999. Appointments: Internship, St Mary's Hospital, 1987-88, Resident, Internal Medicine, 1991-95, Assistant Professor, 2000-04, Associate Professor, 2004-, Catholic University; Instructor of Cardiology, St Vincent Hospital, 1996-99; Research Fellow, Cedars-Sinai Medical Center, Los Angeles, California, 2002-04. Publications: Scar formation after ischemic myocardial injury in MRL mice, 2004; Spatial distribution of nerve sprouting after M2 in mice, 2006; Radiofrequency catheter ablation and nerve growth factor concentration in human heart rhythm, 2006. Address: #62 Yoido-dong Youngdeungpo-Gu, St Mary's Hospital, Seoul 150-713, Korea.

OHASHI Tetsuya, b. 21 August 1951, Sapporo, Japan. Materials Scientist. m. Yoshie Yokouchi, 26 March 1977. Education: BS, 1974, MS, 1976, PhD, 1981, Hokkaido University. Appointments: Researcher, 1982, Senior Researcher, 1991, Hitachi Research Laboratory, Hitachi Ltd; Research Fellow, National Research Institute of Metals, 1997; Professor, Kitami Institute of Technology, 1999-. Publications: Numerical Modelling of Plastic Multislip in Metal Crystals of FCC Type, 1994; Finite Element Analysis of Plastic Slip and Evolution of the Geometrically Necessary Dislocations, 1997. Crystal plasticity analysis of dislocation emission from microvoids, 2005; A multiscale approach for modelling scale-dependent yield stress in polycrysalline metals, 2007. Memberships: Fellow, Japan Society of Mechanical Engineers; Japan Institute of Metals; Materials Research Society; American Association for the Advancement of Science. Address: 3-367-1 Tanno, Kitami, Hokkaido 099-2103, Japan.

OHHIRA Iichiroh, b. 6 February 1936, Osaka, Japan. Researcher. m. Masumi Ohhira. Education: Bachelor's Degree, Agriculture, 1960, Master's Degree, Agriculture, 1973, Doctorate, Natural Science, 1990, Okayama University, Japan; Doctorate of Science in Health Science, Adam Smith University, USA, 2000; Doctorate in Veterinary Medical Science, Azabu University, Japan, 2000. Appointments: Securities Dealer, Ohi Securities Corporation, Okayama, 1960-71; Representative Director, Ohhira Gardens and Parks Design Office, Okayama, 1973-85; Representative Director, Ohhira Plant Pathology Research Centre, Okayama, 1973-85; Representative Director, Bio Activity Research and Development Centre, Okayama, 1974-2000; Founder, BIOBANK CO LTD, Okayama, 2000-; Researcher, Graduate School of Natural Science and Technology, Okayama University; Technical Adviser, Agriculture and Environmental Issues, Chengdu, Suchuan, China; Lecturer Chugoku Junior College, Okayama; Professor, Kangnung National University, Korea; Professor, Pusan Fisheries College, Korea. Publications: Articles in scientific journals include most recently: The Influences of Lactic Acid Bacteria (OM-X) on Bone Structure, 1999; Purification of Anti-Escherichia coli O-157 Components Produced by Enterococcus faecalis TH10, an Isolate from Malaysian Fermented Food, Tempeh, 2000; Antifungal Activity of the Fermentation Product of Herbs by Lactic Acid Bacteria against Tinea, 2002. Honours include: Okayama Nichinichi Newspaper Prize, 1981; Japanese Dairy Science Association Prize, 1991; Presidential Citation, Philippine Medical Association, 2002; Presidential Citation, International College of Surgeons, Philippine Section, 2004; Gusi Peace Prize, Philippines, 2004; Discovery of Enterococcus faecalis TH10, highly active and useful lactic acid bacterium, isolated and identified from Tempeh, a fermented food in Southeast Asia. Memberships include: New York Academy of Sciences; Japanese Society of Food Microbiology; Brewing Society of Japan; The Japanese Society for Virology; The Society for Antibacterial and Antifungal Agents, Japan; Japanese Society for Lactic Acid Bacteria; Japanese Society of Veterinary Science; Japanese Society of Soil Science and Plant Nutrition; Japanese Dairy Science Association; Japanese Society for Bacteriology; The Society for Bioscience, Biotechnology and Agrochemistry; Japanese Society for Food Science and Technology; Japanese Health Food & Nutrition Food Association. Address: BIOBANK CO LTD, 601 Park Square SHOWA 1-7-15, Omote-cho, Okayama, 700-0822 Japan. E-mail: biobank@omx.co.jp

OHLSSON Bertil Gullith, b. 24 July 1954, Malmö, Sweden. Scientist. Education: BS, Biology and Chemistry, 1979, PhD 1987, University of Lund, Sweden; Postdoctoral Fellow, Rockefeller University, New York, New York, 1987-90. Appointments: Assistant Professor, Department of Molecular Biology, Göteborg University, Sweden, 1991-92; Associate Professor, 1993-96, Research Associate, 1997-2004, Associate Professor, 2004-, Wallenberg Laboratory, Sahlgren's University Hospital, Göteborg, Sweden; Research Co-ordinator, Göteborg University, Göteborg, Sweden, 2005-. Publication: Article in Journal of Clinical Investigation, 1996. Address: Research and Innovation Services, External Relations, Göteborg University, Box 100, SE 405 30 Göteborg, Sweden. E-mail: bertil.ohlsson@gu.se

OHSHIO Mitsuo, b. 26 February 1932, Tokyo, Japan. Researcher. m. Yuuko, 3 daughters. Education: BSc, 1956, MSc, 1958, DSc, 1963, University of Tokyo. Appointments: Research Section Chiefs and Planning Section Chief, Radio Research Laboratories, 1963-87; Professor, Electronics & Information Engineering Research Course, Postgraduate Course in Engineering, Graduate School and Department of Electrical & Electronic Engineering, Faculty of Engineering, University of the Ryukyus, 1987-97. Memberships: Society of Geomagnetism and Earth, Planetary and Space Sciences (Japan); American Geophysical Union. Address: 3-1-1-306 Takiyama, Higashi-Kurume, Tokyo 203-0033, Japan.

OHSHIRO Yuzuru, b. 4 December 1966, Okinawa, Japan. Medical Researcher; Educator. m. Rieko, 1 son, 1 daughter. Education: MD, 1997, PhD, 2000, University of the Ryukyus Okinawa, Japan. Appointments: Medical Staff, 1997-2001, Assistant Professor, 2001-03, Assistant Professor, 2005-, Ryukyu University Hospital; Fellow, Joslin Diabes Center, Harvard Medical School, USA, 2003-05. Publications: Research in diabetes and obesity. Honours: Investigator Award, Kange Medical Foundation, 2003; Listed in international biographical dictionaries. Memberships: Japanese Society of Internal Medicine; Japan Diabes Society.

OJEI Andrew Chukwudi, b. 18 December 1958, Agbor, Nigeria. Banker. m. Julie, 3 sons, 1 daughter. Education: HSC, Government College, Ughelli, Delta State; BSc (Hons), University of Lagos. Appointments: Chartered Accountant, Egunjobi Sulaiman & Co, 1984-86; Chartered Accountant, Ibraheem Jimoh & Co, 1989-91; General Manager, Zenith Bank plc, 2000-05; Managing Director, Chief Executive Officer, Zenith Bank (Ghana) Ltd, 2005-. Honours: CEO's Awards as an Outstanding Role Model, 2002-03. Memberships: Achimota Golf Club, Accra, Ghana. Address: 3 Rangoon Close, Cantonments, Accra, Ghana.

OJHA Ek Raj, b. 23 September 1957, Mauwa, Dotee, Nepal. Education: BSc, Agriculture, University of Agricultural Sciences, 1984; BA, English, Tribhuvan University, Kathmandu, 1985; MSc, 1990, PhD, 1995, Rural and Regional Development Planning, Asian Institute of Technology. Appointments: Assistant Agriculture Officer, Department of Agriculture, Kathmandu, 1985-86; Agriculture Officer, Central Bank of Nepal, Kathmandu, 1986-90; Research Associate, 1991-95, Resource Person (Socio-economic Research), 1993, Asian Institute of Technology (AIT), Bangkok; United Nations Researcher, United Nations Centre for Regional Development (UNCRD), Japan, 1995-97; Senior Instructor, Banker's Training Centre, 1998-2000, Research Officer, Research Department, 2000, Central Bank of Nepal; Development Economist, United States Agency for International Development (USAID), Kathmandu, 2000; Visiting Scholar, Indiana University, USA, 2001; Associate Professor (and Associate Director, Human and Natural Resources Studies Centre), Environmental Economics and Entrepreneurship courses, Kathmandu University, 2000-02; Faculty Member, Sustainable Rural Development, 2003-, Agriculture and Rural Development, 2007-, Tribhuvan University; Contract Faculty, Human Dimensions of Development course, Kathmandu University, 2004; Resource Person, Economic Development, 2004, 2004-05; Nepalese Economy, Kathmandu College of Management (KCM), 2007; Rural Development, and Rural Development and Conservation courses, 2006, Rural Development, 2007, Institute of Forestry, Pokhara; Sustainable Rural Development, Padma Kanya Campus, 2005-06; Natural and Human Resources Management, and Rural Resources, Environment and Management courses, Classic College International (CCI), 2006-07; Sustainable Rural Development, K and K College, 2007; Founder Chairman, Centre for Rural Research and Development (CERRED), 2006-. Publications: Co-author: 1 monograph; 1 working paper; 3 institutional reports; Author: 4 books; Numerous articles in professional journals. Memberships: World Futures Studies Federation; Aaroyga Aashram; Kirateshwar Sangeetashram. Address: GPO Box 13313, Kathmandu, Nepal. E-mail: ero@wlink.com.np

OK Min Hwan, b. 29 December 1969, Daegue, South Korea. Researcher. m. MinKyung Jang, 1 son, 1 daughter. Education: MSc, Computer Science, Pusan National University, 1998; PhD Candidate, Computer Science, Korea University, 2000. Appointments: Instructor, Department of IT, Changshin College, 2001-03; Senior Researcher, Informatics Centre, Korea Railroad Research Institute, 2004-. Publications: IEICE Transactions on Information and Systems, 2006; Springer Lecture Notes in Computer Science, 2003-07; A Non-synchronous Update Mechanism of Load-Information for Load-Balancing. Honours: Listed in international biographical dictionaries. Memberships: IEEE. Address: 213-403 Lotte Apt, Changwon, Gyeongnam 641-784, Republic of Korea.

OKA Yoshinari, b. 15 April 1962, Okayama City, Japan. Surgeon. m. Mayumi Sadamori, 2 daughters. Education: Graduate, Medical Division, 1987, Medical Doctor, 1997, Okayama University. Appointments: Surgeon, Okayama University Hospital, 1987; Surgeon, Kagawa Rousai Hospital, 1987-89; Surgeon, Matsuyama Saiseikai Hospital, 1989-92; Surgeon, Saiwaicho Memorial Hospital, 1992-. Publications: Lowering of Oxidative Stress in Hemodialysis Patients by Dialysate Cleaning: in Relation to Arteriosclerosis, 2004; Sevelamer Hydrochloride Exacerbates Metabolic Acidosis in Hemodialysis Patients, Depending on Dosage, 2007. Honours: Listed in international biographical dictionaries. Memberships: Japanese Society for Dialysis Therapy; Soka Gakkai International. E-mail: saiwai@io.ocn.ne.jp

OKADA Ellie, b. 25 March 1958, Kobe, Japan. Intellectual Property Management. Education: BA, Kwansei Gakuin University, 1984; MBA, 1986, DBA, 1999, Kobe University. Appointments: Assistant, 1988, Assistant Professor, 1989, Associate Professor, 1990-98, Department of Business Administration, Associate Professor, 1999-2002, Professor, 2003-, International Graduate School of Social Sciences, Yokohama National University; Visiting Scholar, 1993, Visiting Scholar, 2008-, Center on Japanese Economy and Business, Columbia Business School, Columbia University. Publications: International Harmonization and Adaptation of Japanese Accounting in the Context of Change of Japanese Corporate Governance System, 1997; Firm Valuation in the Context of Intellectual Asset Management, 2001, 2002; Strategic Management on Innovation Competencies and Intellectual Properties, 2003; Strategic Management on Innovation Competencies in the Context of Complex and Compound Project Management, Japanese Project Management, 2008. Honours: Meritorious Service Award, Japan Patent Office, 2005. Memberships: Member, Academy of International Business; Fellow, Intellectual Property Association of Japan; Fellow, Workshop for the Study of Multinational Enterprises, -2006; Fellow, Knowledge Management Society of Japan. Address: 1-10-1-3314, Higashi-Shinbashi, Minato-ku, Tokyo 105-0021, Japan. E-mail: admin@ellie-okada.com Website: www.ellie-okada.com

OKOKO Enobon Etim, b. 11 May 1962, Ikot Eyo, Akwa Ibom State, Nigeria. Town Planner. m. Peace Okoko, 3 sons, 1 daughter. Education: Bachelor of Science, First Class Honours, University of Maiduguri, Nigeria, 1984; Master of Urban and Regional Planning, University of Ibadan, Nigeria, 1987; PhD, Federal University of Technology, Akure, Nigeria, 2002. Appointments: Lecturer, Town and Regional Planning Department, Federal Polytechnic, Nasarawa, Nigeria,

1988-91; Senior Lecturer, Urban and Regional Planning Department, Federal University of Technology, Akure, Nigeria, 1991-, Associate Professor, 2006-. Publications: Book: Quantitative Techniques in Urban Analysis, 2001; Urban Transportation Planning and Modelling, 2006; 3 book chapters; Over 30 articles in learned journals. Honours: Principal's Prize for Best Student of the Year in WASCE Examination, 1978; Dean's Prize for Best Student of the Year, Faculty of Social and Management Sciences, University of Maiduguri, 1984; Listed in Who's Who publications and biographical dictionaries. Memberships: Associate Member, Royal Geographical Society, London; Member, Society for Environment Management and Planning; Corporate Member, Nigerian Institute of Town Planners; Member, International Geographical Union, Commission on Modelling Geographical Systems (United Kingdom); Registered Town Planner, 2000. Address: Department of Urban and Regional Planning, School of Environmental Technology, Federal University of Technology, PMB 704, Akure, Ondo State, Nigeria. E-mail: enookoko@yahoo.com

OKRI Ben, b. 15 March 1959, Minna, Nigeria. British Author; Poet. Education: Urhobo College, Warri, Nigeria; University of Essex, Colchester. Appointments: Broadcaster and Presenter, BBC, 1983-85; Poetry Editor, West Africa, 1983-86; Fellow Commoner in Creative Arts, Trinity College, Cambridge, 1991-93. Publications: Flowers and Shadows, 1980; The Landscapes Within, 1982; Incidents at the Shrine, 1986; Stars of the New Curfew, 1988; The Famished Road, 1991; An African Elegy, 1992; Songs of Enchantment, 1993; Astonishing the Gods, 1995; Birds of Heaven, 1995; Dangerous Love, 1996; A Way of Being Free, 1997; Infinite Riches, 1998; Mental Fight, 1999; In Exilus (play), 2001; In Arcadia, 2002; Starbook Rider, 2007. Contributions to: Many newspapers and journals. Honours: Commonwealth Prize for Africa, 1987; Paris Review/Aga Khan Prize for Fiction, 1987; Booker Prize, 1991; Premio Letterario Internazionale Chianti-Ruffino-Antico-Fattore, 1993; Premio Grinzane Cavour, 1994; Crystal Award, 1995; FRSL, 1997; Honorary DLitt: Westminster, 1997, Essex, 2002, Exeter, 2004; OBE, 2000; Premio Palmi, 2000; FRSA, 2004. Memberships: Society of Authors; Council, Royal Society of Literature, 1999-2004; Vice-president, English Centre, International PEN, 1997-; Board, Royal National Theatre of Great Britain, 1999-. Address: c/o Vintage, Random House, 20 Vauxhall Bridge Road, London SW1 2SA, England.

OLAZABAL Jose Maria, b. 5 February 1966, Spain. Professional Golfer. Career: Member, European Ryder Cup team, 1987, 1989, 1991, 1993, 1997, Kirin Cup Team, 1987, Four Tours World Championship Team, 1989, 1990, World Cup Team, 1989, Dunhill Cup Team, 1986, 1987, 1988, 1989, 1992; Winner, Italian Amateur Award, 1983, Spanish Amateur Award, 1983, European Masters-Swiss Open, 1986, Belgian Open, 1988, German Masters, 1988, Tenerife Open, 1989, Dutch Open, 1989, Benson & Hedges International, 1990, Irish Open, 1990, Lancome Trophy, 1990, Visa Talhoyo Club Masters, 1990, California Open, 1991, Turespana Open de Tenerife, 1992, Open Mediterrania, 1992, US Masters, 1994, 1999, Dubai Desert Classic, 1998; Benson & Hedges International Open 2000, French Open, 2001, Buick Invitational, 2002; Omega Hong Kong Open, 2002; Mallorca Classic, 2005. Tour victories include: NEC World Series of Golf, 1990; The International, 1991; US Masters, 1994, 1999; Dubai Desert Classic, 1998; Golf course designer. Address: PGA Avenue of Champions, Palm Beach Gdns, FL 33418, USA. Website: www.aboutgolf.com/jmo

OLDFIELD Bruce, b. 14 July 1950, England. Fashion Designer. Education: Sheffield City Polytechnic; Ravensbourne College of Art; St Martin's College of Art. Appointments: Founder, Fashion House, Producing Designer Collections, 1975; Couture Clothes for Individual Clients, 1981; Opened Retail Shop, Couture & Ready-to-Wear, 1984; Managing Board, British Knitting & Clothing Export Council, 1989; Designed for films, Jackpot, 1974; The Sentinel, 1976; Vice-President, Barnardo's, 1998; Govenor, London Institute, 1999-; Trustee, Royal Academy, 2000-. Publication: Seasons, 1987. Exhibition: Retrospective, Laing Galleries, Newcastle-upon-Tyne, 2000. Honours: Fellow, Sheffield Polytechnic, 1987; Royal College of Art, 1990; OBE, 1990; Durham University, 1991; Hon DCL (Northumbria), 2001; Hon DUniv (University of Central England), 2005. Publications: Seasons, 1987; Rootless (autobiography), 2004. Address: 27 Beauchamp Place, London SW3, England.

OLDMAN Gary, b. 21 March 1958, New Cross, South London, England. Actor. m. (1) Lesley Manville, 1 son, (2) Uma Thurman, 1991, divorced 1992, (3) Donya Fiorentino, divorced, 2 children. Education: Rose Bruford Drama College; Greenwich Young People's Theatre. Career: Theatre: Massacre in Paris; Chincilla; Desparado Corner; A Waste of Time; Minnesota Moon; Summit Conference; Real Dreams; The Desert Air; War Play I, II, III; Serious Money; Women Beware Women; The Pope's Wedding; The Country Wife; Films: Sid and Nancy; Prick Up Your Ears; Track 29; Criminal Law; We Think The World of You; Chattachoochee; State of Grace; Exile; Before and After Death; Rosencrantz and Guildenstern are Dead; JFK; Dracula; True Romance; Romeo is Bleeding; Immortal Beloved; Murder in the First; Dead Presidents; The Scarlet Letter; Basquiat; Nil by Mouth, The Fifth Element, Air Force One, 1997; Lost in Space, 1998; Anasazie Moon, 1999; Hannibal, The Contender, 2000; Nobody's Baby, Hannibal, 2001; Interstate 60, The Hire: Beat the Devil, 2002; Medal of Honor: Allied Assault – Spearhead (voice), Tiptoes, True Crime: Streets of LA (voice), Sin, 2003; Harry Potter and the Prisoner of Azkaban, Dead Fish, 2004; Batman Begins, Harry Potter and the Goblet of Fire, 2005; Bosque de sombras, 2006; Harry Potter and the Order of the Phoenix, 2007; The Dark Knight, 2008. TV: Remembrance; Meantime; Honest, Decent and True; Rat in the Skull; The Firm; Heading Home; Fallen Angels. Honours: BAFTA Award, 1997. Address: c/o Douglas Urbanski, Douglas Management Inc, 515 N Robertson Boulevard, Los Angeles, CA 90048, USA.

OLIVEIRA Carlos A, b. 1 December 1942, Barras-Piauí, Brazil. Medical Doctor. Widowed, 3 daughters. Education: MD, Faculdade Nacional de Medicina, Rio de Janeiro, 1966; Specialist in Otolanyngology, American Board of Otolaryngology, Chicago Illinois, 1979; Doctor of Philosophy, Otolaryngology, University of Minnesota Graduate School, Minneapolis, Minnesota, USA, 1977; Postdoctoral Fellowship, Harvard Medical School, Boston, Massachusetts, USA, 1989. Appointments: Associate Professor, 1977-97, Professor and Chairman, Department of Otolanryngology, 1997-, Brasilia University Medical School, Brasilia, Brazil. Publications: 82 scientific articles published in Brazil, 18 scientific articles in international journals including, Annals of Otology, Rhinology & Laryngology; Archives of Otolaryngology; Laryngoscope; International Tinnitus Journals. Honours: Physician Recognition Award, American Medical Association, 1977; International Scientist of the Year, IBC. Memberships: Prosper Menière Society; Schuknecht Society, Boston, Massachusetts, USA; Neuroquilibriumetric Society, Bad Kinssingen, Germany; Brazilian Otolaryngology Society; American Otological Society. Address: Avda W-3 Sul Quadra 716, Bloco E, Sala 202, Brasilia DF, Brazil. E-mail: oliv@abordo.com.br

OLIVER (James) Michael (Yorrick), b. 13 July 1940, Worthing, England. Director; Chairman. m. Sally, 2 daughters. Education: Brunswick School; Wellington College. Appointments: Partner, Director, Kitcat & Aitken & Co, 1970-90; Managing Director, Carr Kitcat & Aitken, 1990-93; Director, 1994, 1996, Director of Investment Funds, Scottish Widows Investment Partnership Ltd, 1996-2001; Lord Mayor of the City of London, 2001-2002; Numerous directorships and trusteeships. Honours: LLD (Hon), University of East London, 1999; DLitt (Hon), City University, 2001; Knight of St John, 2001; Knight Bachelor, 2003. Memberships: Alderman of Bishopsgate, The City of London, 1987-; Justice of the Peace, City of London Bench, 1987-2006; Deputy Lieutenant of Cambridgeshire, 2004-; Chairman, St John Ambulance, City of London Centre, 1994-; Trustee, Museum of London, 2003-; Joint Chairman, Museum in Docklands, 2003-; Governor, The Hon The Irish Society, 2007-. Address: Paradise Barns, Buck's Lane, Little Eversden, Cambridge CB23 1HL, England.

OLIVER Jamie Trevor, b. 27 May 1975, Essex, England. Chef. m. Juliette Norton, 2 daughters. Education: Westminster Catering College. Career: Head Pastry Chef, The Neal Street Restaurant; Chef, River Café, 3 years; Established Fifteen, chain of charity restaurants; TV: The Naked Chef, 1999; Comic Relief: Red Nose Ground Force in Practice, 2001; Pukka Tukka, 2001; Jamie's Kitchen, 2002; The Rise of the Celebrity Class, 2004; Jimmy's Farm, 2004; Jamie's School Dinners, 2005; Comic Relief: Red Nose Night Live 05, 2005. Publications: The Naked Chef; Something for the Weekend; The Return of the Naked Chef; Happy Days with the Naked Chef; The Naked Chef Takes Off; Jamie's Kitchen; Jamie's Dinners; Jamie's Italy; Cook With Jamie; Jamie at Home. Honours: MBE, 2003; Beacon Fellowship Prize, 2005.

OLIVER John, b. 14 April 1935, London, England. Retired Bishop. m. Meriel, 2 sons, 1 daughter (deceased). Education: Gonville and Caius College, Cambridge, 1956-59; Westcott House, Cambridge, 1959-60, 1964. Appointments: Curate in the Hilborough Group of parishes, 1964-68; Chaplain of Eton College, 1968-72; Team Rector of South Molton, 1973-82; Team Rector of Central Exeter, 1982-85; Archdeacon of Sherborne, 1985-90; Bishop of Hereford, 1990-2003; Member of the House of Lords, 1997-2003. Publications: The Church and Social Order, 1968; Contributor to: Changing Rural Life (editor Leslie Francis), 2004; Contributions to: Theology; Crucible and occasional journalism. Address: The Old Vicarage, Glascwm, Powys LD1 5SE, Wales.

OLLERENSHAW Kathleen Mary (Dame), b. 1 October 1912, Manchester, England. Mathematician. m. Robert G W Ollerenshaw, deceased, 1 son, 1 daughter both deceased. Education: Open Scholarship, Mathematics, Somerville College, Oxford, 1931-34; Oxford D Phil, Mathematics, 1945. Appointments: Chairman: Association of Governing Bodies of Girls' Public Schools, 1963-69, Manchester Education Committee, 1967-70, Manchester Polytechnic, 1968-72; Elected to Manchester City Council, 1956-81: Alderman, 1970-74, Lord Mayor, 1975-76, Deputy Lord Mayer, 1976-77, Leader of the Conservative Opposition, 1977-79, Honorary Alderman, 1981; Honorary Freeman of the City of Manchester, 1984-; Vice-President, British Association for Commercial and Industrial Education; Member: Central Advisory on Education in England, 1960-63, CNAA,

1964-74, SSCR, 1971-75, Layfield Committee of Enquiry into Local Government Finance, 1974-76; President, St Leonards School, St Andrews, 1976-2003; Deputy Pro Chancellor, University of Lancaster, 1978-91; Pro Chancellor, University of Salford, 1983-89; Director, Manchester Independent Radio Ltd, 1972-83; Deputy Lieutenant, Greater Manchester, 1987-; Honorary Colonel, Manchester and Salford Universities' Officer Training Corps, 1977-81. Publications: Books: Education of Girls, 1958; The Girls Schools, 1967; Returning to Teaching, 1974; The Lord Mayor's Party, 1976; First Citizen, 1977; Most-Perfect Pandiagonal Magic Squares, their Construction and Enumeration (with David Brée), 1998; To Talk of Many Things (autobiography), 2004; Constructing pandiagonal magic squares of arbitrarily large size, 2006; Numerous research papers in mathematical journals, 1940-2004. Honours: Mancunian of the Year, Junior Chamber of Commerce, 1977; DStJ, 1983; Honorary Fellow: Somerville College, Oxford, 1978; Honorary Fellow, City and Guilds, London, 1980; Honorary Fellow, Institute of Mathematics and Its Applications, 1990, Fellow, 1964, Member, Council, 1972-, President, 1979-80; Honorary Fellow, UMIST, 1987; Freeman City of Manchester, 1984-; Honorary DSc Salford, 1975; Honorary LLD, Manchester, 1976; Honorary Colonel, Manchester and Salford Universities Officer Training Corps, 1977-81; Honorary DSc, CNAA; Honorary DSc, Lancaster, 1992; Honorary LLD, Liverpool, 1994; Honorary FIMA, 1988; Catherine Richards Prize, International of Mathematics, 2007. Memberships: President: Manchester Technological Association, 1981, Manchester Statistical Society, 1983-85; Patron, Museum of Science and Technology, Manchester, 2003-; Vice President, Manchester Astronomy Society, 1998-; Chairman, Council Order of St John, Greater Manchester, 1974-89; Member, Chapter General Order of St John, 1978-96; Chartered Mathematician. Address: 2 Pine Road, Manchester M20 6UY, England. E-mail: kmo@mighty-micro.co.uk

OLSZEWSKI Stanislaw Marian, b. 8 December 1932, Warsaw, Poland. Physicist. m. Anna Kalinowska, deceased 1996, 1 son (from a previous marriage). Education: MSc, Theoretical Physics, Warsaw, 1954; Chemical Engineer, Warsaw, 1954; Doctor degree, Solid State Physics, Paris-Orsay, 1962; Habilitation, Chemical Physics, Warsaw, 1964; Professor, 1971. Appointments: Research Worker, Institute of Physical Chemistry, Polish Academy of Sciences, 1955-; Visiting Professor, University of Grenoble, 1982, 1989; Visiting Professor, University of Paris-Sud, 1988; Head of Division, Institute of Physical Chemistry, Polish Academy of Sciences, 1985-2002. Publications: Over 100 research papers. Honours: Golden Cross of Merit, 1980. Memberships: European Academy of Sciences and Arts, Austria; Polish Physical Society; Polish Chemical Society. Address: Institute of Physical Chemistry, Polish Academy of Sciences, Kasprzaka 44/52, 01-224 Warsaw, Poland. E-mail: olsz@ichf.edu.pl

OMAE Iwao, b. 7 August, 1939, Takao, Japan. Chemist; Researcher. m. Junko Hasegawa, 1 son, 2 daughters. Education: BA, Japan National College, 1962; MA, 1965, PhD, Organotin Chemistry, 1968, Osaka University. Appointments: Assistant Professor, Osaka University, 1968-70; Researcher, Teijin Central Research Institute, 1970-77; Adviser, Teijin Technical Information Ltd, 1977-97; Lecturer, Osaka City University, 1997; Professor, Tsuzuki Integrated Education Institute, 1997-2006; Founder and Head, Omae Research Laboratories, 1998-; Lecturer, Nihon Pharmaceutical University, 2006-. Publications: Books as author: Organometallic Intramolecular-coordination Compounds, 1986; Organotin Chemistry, 1989; Applications of Organometallic Compounds, 1998; Global Warming and Carbon Dioxide, 1999; Plastic Recycles, 2000; Associate Editors, Research Journal of Chemistry and Environment, Indore, India, 2003-. Honour: Prize for Outstanding Paper on Organotin Antifouling Paints, 6th International Conference for Maritime Safety and the Environment, NEVA 2001, Russia; Prize for Outstanding Paper on Tin-free Antifouling Paints, 8th International Conference for Maritime Industries and Shipping, NEVA, Russia, 2005. Memberships: Chemical Society of Japan; Society of Synthetic Organic Chemistry, Japan; American Chemical Society. Address: 335-23, Mizuno, Sayama, Saitama 350-1317, Japan. E-mail: um5i-oome@asahi-net.or.jp

OMELCHENKO Nikolay Victorovich, b. 26 June 1951, Kazakhstan, USSR. Professor of Philosophy. m. Svetlana, 2 daughters. Education: Diploma, Philosophy, 1978, Candidate, Philosophy, 1984, Moscow State University by the name of MV Lomonosov, Russia; Doctor, Philosophy, St Petersburg State University, Russia, 1997. Appointments: Assistant Professor, 1982-87, Senior Lecturer, 1987-92, Associate Professor, 1992-99, Philosophy Department, Dean, History and Philosophy Faculty, 1996-2000, Full Professor, Department of Social Philosophy, 1999-, Dean, Faculty of Philosophy and Social Technologies, 2000-, Volgograd State University, Russia; Co-Chairman, 4th International Conference, Human Being in Contemporary Philosophical Conceptions, UNESCO, 2007. Publications: 94 including: Human Creativity and the Teaching of Philosophy, The Mansfield-Volgograd Anthology, 2000; The Pragmatic Effect of Secular Theology (internet), 2004; An Essay in Philosophical Anthropology, Volgograd, 2005; Philosophy as a Productive Orientation, Tuebingen, 2006; The Human Soul and Final Definitions, Ankara, 2006. Honours: Exchange Professor, Mansfield University, Pennsylvania, USA, 1997; Academician of Academy for Humanities, St Petersburg, Russia, 1998-; Fulbright Scholar-in-Residence, Mansfield University, Pennsylvania, USA, 2001-02; Honorary Workman of the Higher Professional Education of the Russian Federation, 2006-; Listed in national and international biographical directories. Memberships: Russian Philosophical Society, 1978-; International Erich Fromm Society, Germany, 1993-; Society for Philosophy of Creativity, USA, 1998-; American Philosophical Association, USA, 2005-. Address: Volgograd State University, 100 Universitetsky Prospect, Volgograd 400062, Russia. E-mail: nomelchenko@mail.ru

OMIDVAR Hedayat, b. 3 January 1966, Abadan, Iran. Senior Expert. Education: BSc, 1995, MSc, 2001, Industrial Engineering. Appointments: Project Management, 1995-2001, Senior Expert, 2001-, Responsible for Strategic Studies, Research and Technology Department, National Iranian Gas Company. Publications: Articles in international journals and international conferences. Memberships: Institute of Industrial Engineers, 1992; American Industrial Hygiene Association, 1994; Iran Institute of Industrial Engineering, 2001; International Gas Union, 2003. Address: No 6 Arghavan Alley, Sabory St, Kashanak, Tehran 1978975981, Iran. E-mail: hedayatomidvar@yahoo.com

OMOROGBE Oluyinka Osayame, b. 21 September 1957, Ibadan, Nigeria. Professor of Law. m. Allan Omorogbe, 1 son, 2 daughters. Education: LLB (Hons), University of Ife, 1978; LLM, London School of Economics, 1982; BL, Nigerian Law School, 1979; Member, Chartered Institute of Arbitration, 2004. Appointments: Private Practice, 1980-81; Lecturer, University of Benin, 1983-90; Senior Lecturer, University of Lagos, 1990-2002; Professor, 2002-, Dean, 2005-, Faculty of

Law, University of Ibadan. Publications: Numerous articles in professional journals. Honours: Listed in international biographical dictionaries. Memberships: Academic Advisory Group of the Section on Energy, Environment & Infrastructure Law, International Bar Association; Deputy President II, Nigerian Society of International Law. Address: Faculty of Law, University of Ibadan, Ibadan, Oyo State, Nigeria. E-mail: yinta.omorogbe@gmail.com

ONDAATJE Michael, b. 12 September 1943, Colombo, Sri Lanka. Author. 2 sons. Education: Dulwich College, London; Queen's University; University of Toronto. Publications include: Poetry: The Dainty Monsters, 1967; The Man With Seven Toes, 1968; There's a Trick with a Knife I'm Learning to Do, 1979; Secular Love, 1984; Handwriting, 1998; Fiction: The Collected Works of Billy the Kid; Coming Through Slaughter; Running in the Family; In the Skin of a Lion; The English Patient; Handwriting; Anil's Ghost, 2000; The Conversations: Walter Murch and the Art of Editing Film, 2002; The Story, 2005; Divisadero, 2007. Honour: Booker Prize for Fiction, 1992; Prix Medicis, 2000; American Cinema Editors Awards, 2003; Kraszna-Krausz Book Award, 2003. Address: 2275 Bayview Road, Toronto, Ontario N4N 3MG, Canada.

ONEGA JAÉN Susana, b. 17 November 1948, Madrid, Spain. Professor of English Literature. m. Francisco Curiel Lorente, 2 sons. Education: Degree, 1975, PhD, 1979, English Philology, University of Zaragoza; Numerous certificates for aptitude in English, French, Italian and German, Madrid, Cambridge, Heidelberg, 1967-77. Appointments: Teacher of English, Official School of Languages, Madrid, 1968-69; Untenured Lecturer, 1975-77, Untenured Associate Professor, 1977-83; Tenured Associate Professor, 1983-86, Full Professor, 1986, Vice-Head of Department, 1989-90, 1995-97, 2000-03; Head of Department, 1987-89, 1991-93, 1993-95, 1997-99, Department of English, University of Zaragoza; Head of Competitive Research Team (projects financed by the Ministry of Education) 1991-95, 1995-98, 1998-2001, 2004-07, (financed by the Ministry of Science and Technology), Government of Aragon, 2003-05 2005-07, 2007-; Research Manager for The Philologies and Philosophy, Ministry of Science and Technology, 2001-03; Member of Committee for recognition of foreign degrees in the Philologies, Ministry of Education and Science, 2005-; Member of Committee for Quality Assessment of Staff in the Humanities, National Agency for Quality Assessment and Validation, 2005-. Publications: Books include: Análisis estructural, método narrativo y "sentido" de The Sound and the Fury de William Faulkner, 1980; Estudios literarios ingleses II: Renacimiento y barroco (editor and author of introduction), 1986; Form and Meaning in the Novels of John Fowles, 1989; Telling Histories: Narrativizing History/Historicizing Literature (editor and author of introduction), 1995; Narratology: An Introduction (co-editor and co-author of introduction), 1996; Peter Ackroyd. The Writer and his Work, 1998; Metafiction and Myth in the Novels of Peter Ackroyd, 1999; London in Literature: Visionary Mappings of the Metroplis (co-editor and co-author of introduction), 2002; Refracting the Canon in Contemporary British Literature and Film (co-editor and co-author of introduction), 2004; George Orwell: A Centenary Celebration, 2005; (Co-editor and co-authorof introduction), Jeanette Winterson, 2006. Numerous articles in professional journals, book chapters, conference papers and translations. Honours: Extraordinary Prize for Degree in Philosophy and Letters, University of Zaragoza, 1976; Extraordinary Prize for Doctorate in Philosophy and Letters, University of Zaragoza, 1980; Enrique García Díez Award,

1990; Honorary Research Fellowship, Birkbeck College, University of London, 1995-96. Memberships: Spanish Association for Anglo-American Studies, 1977-; European Association for American Studies, 1977-; European Society for the Study of English, 1990-; International Association of University Professors of English, 1995-; National Federation of Associations of Spanish University Professors, 1997-2002; Corresponding Fellow, The English Association, 2003-; Association of Women Researchers and Technologists, 2003-. Address: Dpto de Filología Inglesa y Alemana, Facultad de Filosofía y Letras, 50009 Universidad de Zaragoza, Spain. E-mail: sonega@unizar.es

ONG Hean-Choon, b. 10 November 1945, Malaysia. Doctor. Education: MBBS, University of Malaya, 1970; MRCOG, 1975; M MEd O&G, University of Singapore, 1982; FICS, USA, International College of Surgeons, 1983; FRCOG, UK, 1989; FAMM, Academy of Medicine of Malaysia, 1997; FRCP I, 1999. Appointments: Consultant, Obstetrician and Gynaecologist, Pantai Medical Centre; Past Chairman, Malaysian Representative Committee, RCOG, UK; Member, National Estrogen Deficiency Awareness Faculty of Malaysia; Chairman, Preliminary Investigation Committee V, Malaysian Medical Council. Publications: Over 82 scientific papers in local, regional and international journals. Honours: Many honours. Memberships: Royal College of Obstetricians and Gynaecologists, UK; International College of Surgeons; Malaysian Medical Association. Address: Klinik Wanita H C Ong, 148 Jalan Ipoh, 51200 Kuala Lumpar, Malaysia.

ONG HIXSON Patricia, b. 2 August 1969, Singapore. Research Associate. m. Richard Hixson. Education: BSc, National University of Singapore, 1991; MSc, Medical Science, 1993, PhD, Medical Genetics, 1996, University of Glasgow. Appointments: Postdoctoral Research Fellow, Montreal Children's Hospital Research Institute, Montreal, Quebec, Canada, 1996-98; Scientific Officer, Department of Pathology, Singapore General Hospital, Singapore, 1998-2000; Postdoctoral Associate, 2000-03, Postdoctoral Fellow, 2003-2005, Department of Paediatrics, Section of Leukocyte Biology, Research Associate, Department of Molecular and Human Genetics, 2005-06, Research Associate, Center for Cell and Gene Therapy, 2006-, Baylor College of Medicine, Houston, Texas, USA. Publications: Articles in scientific journals including: Molecular and Cellular Probes, 1996, 1997, 1998; Human Heredity, 1998; Kidney International, 1998; Cancer Genetics, Cytogenetics, 2000; Blood, 2004; Veterinary Immunology and Immunopathology, 2005. Honours: Recipient, Glasgow University Postgraduate Research Scholarship, 1994-96; Recipient, Travel Award, Federation of Clinical Immunology Societies, 2004. Memberships: American Society of Human Genetics; British Society of Human Genetics; Human Genome Organisation. Address: Baylor College of Medicine, Center for Cell and Gene Therapy, Room N1010, Houston, TX 77030, USA. E-mail: phixson@bcm.tmc.edu

ONGAN Nilgün Erdal, b. 5 July 1935, Istanbul, Turkey. Architecture; Design. m. Onay. Education: Graduate, Istanbul Austria Lycee; Graduate, Istanbul State's Fine Arts Academy Department of Interior Architecture; Postgraduate education, Italy-Rome State's Fine Arts Academy Department of Artistic Services. Appointments: Painter-Decorator, Schloss Gehrden Historical Castle, Germany, 1963; Stage designer, Franco Zeffirelli's Hamlet, Italy; Manager and Stage Designer, Eliseo Theatre, Rome; Stage Designer, Fallstaff opera, State Opera Hall, Rome, 1964; Designer (action sketches for John Houston's Bible and Roger Vadim's Barbarella), Dino de Laurentiis

Film Studios, 1965-68; TV Set Designer, Ankara Television, Turkey, 1968; Décor-Graphics Chief, Istanbul Television, 1974; Assistant Director of Artistic Services, Istanbul Television; Décor and Artistic Services, Interstar television, 1992; Artistic Services Director, Kanal D, and later HBB TV; Lecturer, Istanbul University Faculty of Communication Radio Television Department, 1994-98. Publications: Pictures printed in Silhouettes of Turkey, 1974-2005. Honours: 2000 Outstanding Intellectuals of the 21st Century, 2000; Honorary Member, Chamber of Interior Architects, 2002; Antalya Golden Orange Film Festival award, 2002; White Pearl TV Awards, 2005; International Professional of the Year, 2005; IBC Top 100 Communicators, 2006; Performance and Visual Arts Award, World Brotherhood Union, Mevlana Supreme Foundation, 2007; ABI Gold Medal for Turkey. Memberships: Fine Arts Society; Fine Arts Academy; Interior Architects Society. Address: Kucuk Bebek Cad Nurhan Apt 51/7 Bebek, 80810 Istanbul, Turkey.

ONIFADE Ademola, b. 26 May 1956, Osogbo, Nigeria. University Teacher. m. Toyin Oluyede, 1 son, 3 daughters. Education: B Ed (Hons), University of Ibadan, 1978; MPE, University of New Brunswick, Frediction, Canada, 1980; PhD, University of Maryland, College Park, USA, 1983. Appointments: Head, Department of Physical and Health Education, Adeyemi College, Ondo State, Nigeria, 1985-86; Head, Department of Physical and Health Education, 1988-90, 1999-2000, Professor, 2000-, Dean, Faculty of Education, 2000-2004, Lagos State University. Publications: Psycho-Social Perspective of Sports, 1993; History of Physical Education in Nigeria, 2001; Emergent Issues in Sociology of Sports, 2001; Britain, Sport and Nation Building in Nigeria, 2004. Honours: Listed in Who's Who publications and biographical dictionaries. Memberships: Nigeria Academy of Education; Nigerian Association for Physical and Health Education and Recreation. Address: Department of Physical and Health Education, Lagos State University, PMB 1087, Apapa, Lagos, Nigeria. E-mail: ademolaonifade@yahoo.com

ONODA Masashige, b. 1 February 1959, Hitachi, Ibaraki, Japan. Physicist. m. Keiko Ogawa, 1 son, 2 daughters. Education: BSc, 1981, MSc, 1983, DSc, 1985, University of Tsukuba, Japan. Appointments: Research Associate, Okazaki National Research Institutes, Okazaki, Aichi, Japan, 1985-90; Associate Professor, University of Tsukuba, Tsukuba, Japan, 1990-; Visiting Fellow, National Institute for Research in Inorganic Materials, Tsukuba, Ibaraki, Japan, 1996-2001; Part time Lecturer, Ibaraki Prefectural University of Health Sciences, Ami, Ibaraki, Japan, 2000-05; Visiting Fellow, National Institute for Materials Science, Tsukuba, Ibaraki, Japan, 2001-06. Publications: Recent articles in Institute of Physics and in American Physical Society. Honours: Award, Thermal & Electric Energy Technology Foundation; IBC International Scientist of the Year, 2007; Listed in international biographical dictionaries. Memberships: Physical Society of Japan. Address: Institute of Physics, University of Tsukuba, 1-1-1 Tennodai, Tsukuba 305-8571, Japan. E-mail: onoda@sakura.cc.tsukuba.ac.jp

OPIE Iona, b. 13 October 1923, Colchester, England. Writer. m. Peter Opie, 2 September 1943, deceased, 2 sons, 1 daughter. Publications: A Dictionary of Superstitions (with Moira Tatem), 1989; The People in the Playground, 1993; With Peter Opie: The Oxford Dictionary of Nursery Rhymes, 1951, new edition, 1997; The Oxford Nursery Rhyme Book, 1955; The Lore and Language of Schoolchildren, 1959; Puffin Book of Nursery Rhymes, 1963; A Family Book of Nursery Rhymes, 1964; Children's Games in Street and Playground, 1969; The Oxford Book of Children's Verse, 1973; Three Centuries of Nursery Rhymes and Poetry for Children, 1973; The Classic Fairy Tales, 1974; A Nursery Companion, 1980; The Oxford Book of Narrative Verse, 1983; The Singing Game, 1985; Babies: an unsentimental anthology, 1990; Children's Games with Things, 1997. Honours: Honorary MA, Oxon, 1962, Open University, 1987, DLitt, University of Southampton, 1987, University of Nottingham, 1991, Doctorate, University of Surrey, 1997; CBE, 1998; FBA, 1998. Address: Mells House, Liss, Hampshire GU33 6JQ, England.

OPIK Lembit, b. 2 March 1965, Bangor, County Down, Northern Ireland. Member of Parliament. Education: BA, Philosophy, Bristol University. Appointments: President, Bristol Students Union, 1985-86; Member, National Union of Students National Executive, 1987-88; Brand Assistant, 1988-91, Corporate Training and Organisation Development Manager, 1991-96, Global Human Resources Training Manager, 1997, Proctor and Gamble; Elected to Newcastle City Council, 1992; Elected as MP for Montgomeryshire, 1997-; Party Spokesperson on Northern Ireland and Young People, 1997; Spokesperson for Wales, Leader of the Welsh Liberal Democrats, Member of Shadow Cabinet, 2001-2007; Liberal Democrat spokesman for Business, Enterprise and Regulatory Reform, 2007-. Publications: Articles on politics in newspapers and magazines; Weekly column in Shropshire Star, The Week in Politics. Honours: Nominated for Channel 4 House Magazine New MP of the Year, 1998; Nominated for Country Life Rural MP of the Year, 1999. Memberships: Agriculture Select Committee, 1998-2001; Co-Chair, All Parliamentary Middle Way Group; Member, Spinal Injuries Association; Speaks on behalf of British Gliding Association; Chair, All Party Parliamentary Motorcycle Group; President, Shropshire, Astronomical Society. Address: House of Commons, London, SW1A 0AA, England. E-mail: opikl@parliament.uk

ORING Stuart August, b. 28 August 1932, Bronx, New York, USA. Publisher; Writer; Photographer; Researcher. m. Mary Carolyn Barth Oring, 2 daughters. Education: Associate Degree, Applied Sciences, 1957, BFA, 1959, Rochester Institute of Technology; MA, American University, 1970. Appointments: Visual Info Specialist, ARS of US Department of Agriculture, 1964-67; AV Specialist, National AV Center, 1967-69; Photojournalist, Office of Economic Opportunity, 1971-74; Visual Information Specialist (Photography), ASCS of US Department of Agriculture, 1974-94; Founded ISIS Visual Communications (researcher, writer, photographer), 1992-. Publications: Books: Understanding Pictures; Theories, Exercises and Procedures; A Beginners Guide to Pictures; Understanding Pictures: A Teacher's Planning Guide; Numerous articles and photographs published. Honour: Certificate of Appreciation, Eastman Kodak Co; Research and development of new approaches for analysing and interpreting art and photographs. Memberships: National Art Education Association; American Society for Psychopathology of Expression. Listed in national and international biographical dictionaries. Address: 2570 Redbud Lane, Owings, MD 20736, USA.

ORLOFF Harold David, b. 24 November 1915, Winnipeg, Manitoba, Canada. Chemist. m. Leah Orloff, 1 son, 2 daughters. Education: BSc, Honours, 1937, MSc, 1939, University of Manitoba; PhD, McGill University, 1941. Appointments: Research Chemist, Canadian Board of Grain Commissioners, 1938; Research Scientist, H Smith Paper Mills, 1941-48; Associate Director of Research, Ethyl Corporation, 1948-82; Adjunct Professor of Chemistry, University of Detroit,

Michigan, USA, 1957. Publications include: Articles and papers in Pulp and Paper Magazine, Canada, 1946; Journal of the American Chemical Society, 1951, 1953, 1954; Chemical Reviews, 1954; Industrial Engineering and Chemistry, 1961; Botyu Kagaku, 1956; Proceedings of the 7th World Petroleum Congress, 1967; Zeolites, 1984; Poultry Science, 1985; Over 50 patents; Co-inventor, Arborite Plastics, also Secondary Chemical Recovery System for use in kraft pulp production. Honours: Isbister Scholar, University of Manitoba, 1934-37; Research Fellow, McGill University, 1940-41; Weldon Memorial Gold Medal, Senior Award of Canadian Pulp and Paper Association, 1948. Memberships: American Chemical Society; Sigma Xi; Pulp and Paper Associations, USA, Canada. Address: 2903 Victoria Circle, Apt D3, Coconut Creek, FL 33066, USA.

ORLOVA Vera, b. 17 May 1951, Blagoveschensk, Russia. Psychiatrist; Psychotherapist. m. Vladimir Kulkov, 2 daughters. Education: Diploma of Physician with excellent honours, 2nd Moscow Medical Institute, 1974; Candidate of Medical Sciences, 1984; Doctor of Medical Sciences, 2000. Appointments: Junior Researcher, Mental Health Research Centre, Russian Academy of Medical Sciences, 1977-97; Head of Psychiatric Expert Commission, Moscow, 1987-88; Senior Researcher, 1988-91, Leading Researcher, 1991-2005, Head of Genetic Unit (equivalent to Professor), 2001-, Chief Researcher, 2007-, Mental Health Research Centre, Russian Academy of Medical Sciences; Head of Integrative Psychiatry, Chair, International University of Fundamental Studies (IUFS), Professor, 2007-. Publications: More than 130 articles as author and co-author in medical journals in the fields of clinical and biological psychiatry, genetics of schizophrenia and theoretical biology. Honours: Gold Medal for Secondary education Diploma, 1968; Grant of British Council, 2000; Grant of Russian Foundation for Basic Research, 2002; Grant of Royal Society, 2004; Travel Grants for: 8th World Congress of Psychiatric Genetics, 1998; XI World Congress of Psychiatry, 1999; 7th and 8th World Congresses of Biological Psychiatry, 2001, 2005; Great Women of the 21st Century, 2006; International Peace Prize of the United Cultural Convention, USA, 2006. Listed in Who's Who publications and biographical dictionaries. Memberships: Society of Neuropathologists and Psychiatrists, Russia; Society of Medical Genetics, Russia; World Federation of Societies of Biological Psychiatry; corresponding member, Russian Academy of Natural Sciences; corresponding member, International Academy of Ecology, Man and Nature Protection. Address: Mental Health Research Centre, RAMS, Zagorodnoe Shosse 2, 113152, Moscow, Russia. E-mail: vorlova@yandex.ru

ORMAN Stanley, b. 6 February 1935, London, England. Consultant. m. Helen Hourman, 1 son, 2 daughters. Education: BSc, 1st Class Honours, Chemistry and Physics, 1957, PhD, Chemistry, 1960, Kings College, London; Fulbright Fellow, Brandeis University Massachusetts, USA, 1960-91. Appointments: Scientist Ministry of Defence, 1961-82, positions held include: Chief Weapons Systems Engineer Chevaline, 1980-82, Minister, British Embassy, Washington, USA, 1982-84, Deputy Director Atomic Weapons research Establishment, 1984-86, Founding Director General, SDI Participation Office, 1986-90; Under Secretary of State, UK Ministry of Defence, 1982-90; Chief Executive Officer, General Technology Systems, USA, 1990-96; Chief Executive Officer, Orman Associates, 1996-. Publications: Author book: Faith in G.O.D.S – Stability in Nuclear Age, 1991; 150 published papers and articles on chemistry, corrosion science, adhesion and defence issues including over 90 articles on

missile defence; Participation in workshops and presentations at over 70 international conferences on defence issues. Honours: Captained London University Track Team, 1956-57; Represented Britain in World Student Games, 3rd in 100m and 7th in Long Jump, 1956; Jelf Medalist, King's College, London, 1957. Address: 17825 Stoneridge Drive, North Potomac, MD 20878, USA. E-mail: or2withdog@comcast.net

ORME Michael Christopher L'Estrange, b. 13 June 1940, Derby, England. University Professor; Medical Practitioner. m. (Joan) Patricia Orme, 1 son. Education: MA, MB, BChir (Cantab), 1964-65; MD, 1975; MRCP, 1967; FRCP, 1980. Appointments: Senior Lecturer, Clinical Pharmacology, 1975, Professor, 1984, Dean, Faculty of Medicine, 1991-96, University of Liverpool; Director of Education and Training, North West Regional Office, NHS Executive, 1996-2001; Retired 2001; Currently Professor Emeritus, University of Liverpool; Consultant Physician Emeritus, Royal Liverpool Hospital. Publications: 275 peer reviewed publications in journals; Books and book chapters on drug interactions, clinical pharmacology of oral contraceptives, drugs in tropical disease, anticoagulants and anti-rheumatic drugs. Honours: FRCGP (Hon), 1996; F Med Sci, 1998; DSc (Hon), Salford, 2000; FFPHM, 2000; Honorary Fellow, University of Central Lancashire, 2001; Honorary MD, International Medical University, Kuala Lumpur, Malaysia, 2004. Memberships: Association of Physicians; British Pharmacological Society. Address: Lark House, Clapton-on-the-Hill, Cheltenham, Gloucestershire GL54 2LG, England. E-mail: morme@eandthome.demon.co.uk

ORMOND Julia, b.4 January 1965, England. Actress. m.(1) Rory Edwards, divorced; (2) Jon Rubin, 1999, 1 child. Education: Farnham Art School; Webber Douglas Academy. Appointments: Worked in Repertory, Crucible Theatre, Sheffield, Everyman Theatre, Cheltenham; On tour with Royal Exchange Theatre, Manchester; Appeared in Faith, Hope and Charity, Lyric, Hammersmith; Treats, Hampstead Theatre; West End Debut in Anouilh's The Rehearsal; My Zinc Bed, 2000. Creative Works: TV appearances: Traffik (Channel 4 series); Ruth Rendell Mysteries; Young Catherine, 1990; Stalin, 1992; Animal Farm (voice), 1999; Varian's War, 2001; Iron Jawed Angels, 2004; The Way, 2006. Films: The Baby of Macon; Legends of the Fall; First Knight; Sabrina; Smilla's Sense of Snow, 1997; The Barber of Siberia, 1998; The Prime Gig, 2000; Resistance, 2003; The Nazi Officer's Wife, 2003; Inland Empire, 2006; I Know Who Killed Me, 2007; Surveillance, 2008; Kit Kittredge; An American Girl, 2008; The Curious Case of Benjamin Button, 2008. Address: c/o CAA, 9830 Wilshire Boulevard, Beverly Hills, CA 90212, USA.

ORMSBY Frank, b. 30 October 1947, Enniskillen, County Fermanagh, Northern Ireland. Poet; Writer; Editor. Education: BA, English, 1970, MA, 1971, Queen's University, Belfast. Appointment: Editor, The Honest Ulsterman, 1969-89. Publications: A Store of Candles, 1977; Poets from the North of Ireland (editor), 1979, new edition, 1990; A Northern Spring, 1986; Northern Windows: An Anthology of Ulster Autobiography (editor), 1987; The Long Embrace: Twentieth Century Irish Love Poems (editor), 1987; Thine in Storm and Calm: An Amanda McKittrick Ros Reader (editor), 1988; The Collected Poems of John Hewitt (editor), 1991; A Rage for Order: Poetry of the Northern Ireland Troubles (editor), 1992; The Ghost Train, 1995; The Hip Flask: Short Poems from Ireland (editor), 2000; The Blackbird's Nest: Anthology of Poetry from Queen's University Belfast (editor),2006;

Selected Poems of John Hewitt (editor with Michael Longley), 2007. Address: 33 North Circular Road, Belfast BT15 5HD, Northern Ireland

ÖRVELL Claes Gunnar, b. 22 April 1945, Stockholm, Sweden. Physician; Virologist. m. Eva Reimert, 2 sons, 3 daughters. Education: MD, 1973, PhD, 1977, Karolinska Institutet. Appointments: Researcher, Department of Virology, Karolinska Institutet, 1978-79; Researcher, Virology, National Bacteriological Laboratory, 1980-92; Associate Professor, Karolinska Institutet, 1988-; Senior Physician, Stockholm City Council, 1992-. Publications: Numerous scientific articles on the subjects structural, clinical and epidemiological studies on viruses. Honours: International Order of Merit, IBC, 2000; Order of International Fellowship, IBC, 2001; Fellow, International Biographical Association, 2001; Founding Member American Order of Excellence, 2001; Presidential Seal of Honor, 2001; Lifetime Achievement Award, IBC, 2001; World Biographee Day, ABI, 2001; Deputy Governor, ABI, 2001; Noble Prize for Outstanding Achievements and Contribution to Humanity, UCC, 2001; Continental Governor, ABI, 2001; Deputy Director General, IBC, 2001; Adviser to the Director General, IBC, 2001; Ambassador of Grand Eminence, ABI, 2002; ABI Hall of Fame, 2002; Minister of Culture, ABI, 2003; International Peace Prize, UCC, 2004; Order of Distinction, IBC, 2004; Life Fellow, ABI, 2005; Order of American Ambassadors, ABI, 2006; Hall of Fame, IBC, 2006. Memberships: FABI. Address: Department of Clinical Virology, Huddinge University Hospital, F68, S-14186 Huddinge, Sweden. E-mail: claes.orvell@karolinska.se

OSBORN John Holbrook (Sir), b. 14 December 1922, Sheffield, England. Semi-retired: Politician; Industrialist; Scientist; Soldier. m. (1) Molly Suzanne Marten, divorced 2 daughters, (2) Joan Mary Wilkinson, deceased, (3) Patricia Felicity Read. Education: MA Cantab, Part II Tripos Metallurgy, Trinity Hall, Cambridge University, England, 1943; Diploma in Foundry Technology, National Foundry College, Wolverhampton Technical College, 1949. Appointments: Royal Corps Signals, 1943-47; Battery Commander, Royal Artillery TA, 1948-55; Assistant Works Manager, Production Controller, Cost Controller, 1947-51, Company Director, 1951-79, Samuel Osborn and Company Limited, Sheffield, England; Conservative Candidate and Member of Parliament, Sheffield Hallam, 1959-87; Parliamentary Private Secretary to Minister for Commonwealth Relations, 1962-64; Joint Honorary Secretary, Conservative 1922 Committee, 1968-87; Former Chairman, Conservative Transport Committee, All-Party Road Study Group, Parliamentary Group Energy Studies; All-Party Channel Tunnel Group; Member of the European Parliament, 1975-79; Former Member of the Interim Licensing Authority; Friends of Progress. Publications: Co-author: Conservative publications: Export of Capital; Trade not Aid; Change or Decay; A Value Added Tax; European Parliamentary publications: Help for the Regions; Energy for Europe; Also Chairman of a Parliamentary and Scientific Committee report on Information Storage and Retrieval. Honours: Knight Bachelor, Birthday Honours 1983, for Public and Political Services; Chairman, Business in Development Committee, UK Chapter of Society of International Development, 1990-1995, attached to Worldaware; Member Executive, 1968-75, 1979-82, Life Member, 1987, IPU, UK branch; Life Member, CPA, UK branch, 1987-; Officer, 1960-87, Life Member, 1987, Parliamentary and Scientific Committee; European Atlantic Group Committee, 1990-; Member, Royal Institute of International Affairs, 1985-; Member, Conservative Group for Europe, European Movement, 1975-;

Council Member, 1963-79, Life Member, Industrial Society; Junior Warden-Searcher, Assistant Searcher, Freeman, 1987-, Company of Cutlers in Hallamshire. Memberships: Fellow, Royal Society for Encouragement of the Arts, Manufacture and Commerce, 1966-; Trustee of many Sheffield Charitable Trusts; President, 1960-96, Honorary Patron, Sheffield Institute of Advanced Motorists; Fellow, Institute of Directors, 1955-; Fellow, Institute of Materials (now IM3), 1947-. Address: Newlands, 147 Hawton Road, Newark, Nottinghamshire, NG24 4QG, England. E-mail: j.p.osborn147@ntlworld.com

OSBORNE Margaret Elizabeth Brenda, b. 21 December 1931, Clifton, Bristol, England. Artist; Painter; Poet. m. Stuart John Osborne, 1 daughter. Education: Intermediate Certificate in Arts and Crafts, West of England College of Art, 1950; National Diploma in Design, 1952; Art Teacher's Diploma, Painting, 1953; Ministry of Education Certificate in Education, 1953. Career: Art Teacher in Schools and Art College for 26 years; Currently, Professional Freelance Painter in oils, gouache painting figurative portraits to commission and domestic pets; Worked for Galleries, Tarmac, Cadbury's and Glynweb for retiring directors and for private collectors; Over 100 commissions; Exhibitions: The Young Contemporaries Exhibition, London, 1952; Works sent to the Pastel Society in the Mall Gallery in London, selected to tour in the provinces in the 1960's; Showed work via one-woman exhibition, Lichfield Art Centre, mid 1970s; Still available for commissions. Honours: Intermediate Art Scholarship, 1948; City Senior Scholarship, Bristol Education Committee, 1950; Senior Drawing Prize, West of England College of Art, 1952; Listed in Who's Who publications and biographical dictionaries. Membership: The Fawcett Society, 2003-. Address: 64 Burton Manor Road, Stafford ST17 9PR, England.

OSBORNE Stuart John, b. 20 May 1925, Weston-Super-Mare, Somerset, England. Modeller; Carver. m. Margaret Elizabeth B Cole, 1 daughter. Education: West of England College of Art, Bristol, 1948-52; ARCA, ATD, Royal College of Art, London; Ed Dip, Bristol University. Appointments: College Lecturer in Clay Modelling, Figure Drawing and Stone and Wood Carving; Ran own 3 year course for 18 years; After retirement work on own projects, mainly figurative modelling, female and male figures and animals in wood and stone; Works known in France, USA, Canada, Japan and Italy. Publications: Numerous mentions in press and magazines. Honours: Prize-winner in Unknown Political Prisoner Competition; Scholarship to study in Florence. Memberships: Society of Portrait Sculptors, 1971-84; Fellow, Royal Society of British Sculptors, 1980-84; Society of Free Painters and Sculptors, -2003. Address: 64 Burton Manor Road, Stafford ST17 9PR, England.

OSBOURNE Ozzy (John), b. 3 December 1948, Aston, Warwickshire, England. Vocalist. m. Sharon Arden, 4 July 1982, 3 children. Career: Vocalist, Black Sabbath (formerly Earth), 1967-79; Numerous concerts worldwide include: Madison Square Garden, New York, 1975; Reunion concerts include: Live Aid, Philadelphia, 1985; Solo artiste, with own backing band Blizzard Of Ozz, 1979-; US Festival, 1983; Rock In Rio festival, 1984; Monsters of Rock Festival, Castle Donington, 1986; Moscow Music Peace Festival, 1989; No More Tears world tour, 1992; Created highly successful yearly touring festival, Ozz Fest, 1996; Has recorded with artists including: Alice Cooper, Motorhead, Ringo Starr, Rick Wakeman. Recordings: Hit singles: with Black Sabbath include: Paranoid; Iron Man; War Pigs; Never Say Die; Solo/with Blizzard Of Ozz: Mr Crowley, 1980; Crazy

Train, 1980; Bark At The Moon, 1983; So Tired, 1984; Shot In The Dark, 1986; The Ultimate Sin, 1986; Close My Eyes Forever, duet with Lita Ford, 1989; No More Tears, 1991; Perry Mason, 1995; I Just Want You, 1996; Get Me Through, 2001; Dreamer, 2002; Changes (with Kelly Osbourne), 2003; Listen and Learn, 2003; Albums: with Black Sabbath: Black Sabbath, 1969; Paranoid, 1970; Sabbath Bloody Sabbath, 1973; Sabotage, 1975; Technical Ecstasy, 1976; Never Say Die, 1978; Reunion, 1998; Numerous compilations; with Blizzard of Ozz/solo: Blizzards Of Ozz, 1980; Diary Of A Madman, 1981; Talk Of The Devil, 1982; Bark At The Moon, 1983; The Ultimate Sin, 1986; Tribute, 1987; No Rest For The Wicked, 1988; Just Say Ozzy, 1990; No More Tears, 1991; Live & Loud, 1993; Ozzmosis, 1995; The Ozzman Cometh, 1997; OzzFest Vol 1: Live, 1997; Diary of a Madman/Bark at the Moon/Ultimate, 1998; Down to Earth, 2001; Live at Budokan, 2002; X-Posed, 2002. Honour: Grammy Award, 1994; NME, 2004. Address: Sharon Osbourne Management, PO Box 15397, Beverly Hills, CA 90209, USA. Website: www.ozzy.com

OSEMWOWA Usiosefe Iyengunmwena, b. 2 February 1950, Utekon, Benin City, Nigeria. Law; Tax Administration. m. Helen Oghogho, 2 sons, 2 daughters. Education: Diploma, BS, Falkirk College of Technology, Scotland, 1979; LLB, University of Benin, Nigeria, 1984; BL Nigeria Law School, Lagos; Executive Development Course, Obafemi Awolowo University, Ile-Ife, 1991; ACTI (Nig) 2004. Appointments: Statistical Assistant, Economic Planning, Ministry of Finance; Executive Officer, Administrator General & Public Trustees Office & the Directorate of Public Prosecution (DPP), Ministry of Justice, Edo State; Principal Executive Officer, Department of Finance & Supply, Department of Administration, Board of Internal Revenue; Secretary, Department of Planning and Research and Statistics, Departmental Tenders Board; Assistant Director of Taxes, Secretary/Member, Pool Betting Arbitration Panel; Member, Tax Assessment Review Committee; Commissioner of Stamp Duty; Head, Capital Gains Tax; Head, Legal Department; Member, Committee to draft Edo State Position; Paper on the review of Nigerian Tax System. Publications: Books: Customary Law of the Binis; Essentials of the Law and Practice of Stamp Duties in Nigeria; the Kingdom of Benin Legacies of Ancient Civilization; Articles: ODUDUWA, Projecture of Yoruba race originated from Benin (Nig); Ijaw, Itsekiri and Urhobo War in Delta State; Papers: Law Review Commission: Law; Review in the 21st Century: Customary Law of Inheritance in the 21st Century; NBA Law Week, Critique of the Customary Law of the Binis; Workers in Nigeria poorly paid; Stamp Duties and Registration of Instruments; Civil Servants Participation in Partisan Politics; Essay: Fundamentals of the Law and Practice of Taxation in Nigeria. Memberships: Associate, Chartered Institute of Taxation (Nig); Member, National Association of Students of Great Britain; Vice Chair, Association of Senior Civil Servants of Nigeria, Edo State; Cash Award, Oba of Benin Kingdom for contribution to knowledge; Member, Research Board of Advisors, American Biographical Institute, Raleigh, USA. Address: PO Box 5274, Benin City, Nigeria. E-mail: usiosemwowa@yahoo.com

OSWALD Angela Mary Rose (Lady), b. 21 May 1938, London, England. Lady-in-Waiting. m. Sir Michael Oswald, 1 son, 1 daughter. Appointments: Extra Woman of the Bedchamber to H M Queen Elizabeth the Queen Mother, 1981-83; Woman of the Bedchamber to H M Queen Elizabeth the Queen Mother, 1983-2002. Honours: LVO, 1993; Freeman

of the City of London, 1995; CVO, 2000. Address: The Old Rectory, Weasenham St Peter, King's Lynn, Norfolk, PE32 2TB, England.

OSWALD (William Richard) Michael (Sir), b. 21 April 1934, Walton-on-Thames, Surrey. Racehorse Stud Manager. m. Lady Angela Oswald, 1 son, 1 daughter. Education: MA, King's College Cambridge. Appointments: 2nd Lieutenant, King's Own Regiment, BAOR, Korea, 1953-54; Captain, Royal Fusiliers (TA), 1955-60; Manager, Lordship and Egerton Studs, Newmarket, 1962-69; Director, Royal Studs, 1970-98; Racing Manager for H M Queen Elizabeth, The Queen Mother, 1970-2002; National Hunt Advisor to H M The Queen, 2002-; Member, Council of Thoroughbred Breeder's Association, 1964-2001, President, 1997-2001; Chairman, Bloodstock Industry Committee, Animal Health Trust, 1986-2002; Liveryman, Worshipful Company of Shipwrights. Honours: LVO, 1979; CVO, 1988; KCVO, 1998; Honorary DSc, De Montfort University, 1997; Honorary Air Commodore, 2620 Sqdn Royal Auxiliary Air Force, 2001-. Memberships: Jockey Club; Army and Navy Club. Address: The Old Rectory, Weasenham St Peter, King's Lynn, Norfolk PE32 2TB, England.

OTTO Brinna Dorothea, b. 21 July 1938, Mannheim, Germany. Archeologist. Education: Certificate, Graphic Arts, Academy Otto-Stössinger, Karlsruhe, 1961; Certificate, Archaeological Volunteer, Landesmuseum, Karlsruhe, 1970; PhD, Classical Archaeology, University of Heidelberg, 1972; Habilitation, 1983, University Professor, 1994, Classical Archaeology, University of Innsbruck. Appointments: Collaborator, Annual Archaeological Excavation in ancient Herakleia (modern Policoro), South Italy, 1965-69; Archaeological Volunteer, Landesmuseum, Karlsruhe, 1969-70; Assistant Teacher, University of Heidelberg, University of Wurzburg, University of Innsbruck, Landesmuseum, Karlsruhe, 1972-83; Lectureship, 1983-94, Professor, Classical Archaeology, 1994-, University of Innsbruck; Field Director, Excavations in the Sanctuary of Demeter at Herakleia/Policoro, South Italy, 1995-2003; Head of Archaeological Scientific Projects, 2003-. Publications include: Geometrische Ornamente auf anatolischer Keramik, 1976; Herakleia in Lukanien und das Quellheiligtum der Demeter, 1996; König Minos und sein Volk, 1997; The Sacrificed God, 1996; Zeus Kretagenes, 2001; Il racconto in immagini della "Tomba del Tuffatore", 2003. Honours: Research Board of Advisors, ABI, 2002; Vice President, Archaeological Society of Innsbruck, 2004-; Research Fellow, American Biographical Institute, 2006. Memberships: Istituto per la storia e l'archeologia della Magna Graecia, Taranto, 2006-. Address: Institute of Archaeologies, University of Innsbruck, A-6020 Innsbruck, Austria. E-mail: brinna.otto@uibk.ac.at

OU Chien-Min, b. 1 February 1956, Taiwan. Electronics Engineering. m. Ying-Tee Tai, 1 son, 1 daughter. Education: Diploma, Chien-Shin Institute of Technology; Master Degree, 2000, PhD, 2003, ChungYuan Christian University. Appointments: Lecturer, Chien Shin Institute of Technology, 1978; Assistant Professor, Ching Yun University, 2003. Publications: About 40 journal papers. Honours: Phi Tau Phi Honour. E-mail: cmou@cyu.edu.tw

OUZTS Eugene Thomas, b. 7 June 1930, Thomasville, Georgia, USA. Minister; Secondary educator. m. Mary Olive Vineyard. Education: MA, Harding University, 1957; Postgraduate: Murray State University, University of Arkansas, Arizona State University, University of Arizona; Northern Arizona University. Appointments: Certificated

Secondary Teacher, Arkansas, Missouri, Arizona; Ordained Minister Church of Christ, 1956; Minister in various Churches in Arkansas, Missouri, Texas, -1965; Teacher, various public schools, Arkansas, Missouri, 1959-65; Teacher, Arizona, 1965-92; Minister in Arizona Church of Christ, Clifton, Morenci, Safford and Duncan, 1965-. Honours: Civil Air Patrol, Arizona Wing Chaplain of Year, 1984; Thomas C Casaday Unit Chaplain, 1985; Arizona, Wing Safety Officer, 1989; Arizona Wing Senior Member, 1994; Meritorious Service Award, 1994; Southwestern Region Senior Member, 1995; Exceptional Service Award, 1997; Life Fellowship, IBA, Cambridge, England. Memberships: Military Chaplains Association; Disabled American Veterans; Air Force Association; American Legion; Elks; Board, Arizona Church of Christ Bible Camp; Airport Advisory Board, Greenlee County, Arizona; Civil Air Patrol/Air Force Auxiliary (Chaplain, 1982, 1st Lieutenant advanced through grades to Lieutenant Colonel, 1989); Assistant Wing Chaplain. Address: 739E, Cottonwood, Duncan, Arizona 85534-8108, USA.

OVENDEN John Anthony, b. 26 May 1945, Epping, Essex, England. Clergyman. m. Christine, 2 sons, 1 daughter. Education: BA, Open University; MA, Kings College, London. Appointments: Precentor and Sacrist, Ely Cathedral; Vicar of St Mary's, Primrose Hill, London; Canon of St George's Chapel, Windsor; Chaplain in the Royal Chapel, Windsor Great Park; Chaplain to H M The Queen; Canon Chaplain, 1998-; Precentor, 2007-. Address: Chaplain's Lodge, The Great Park, Windsor, Berkshire SL4 2HP, England.

OVERILL Richard Edward, b. 29 January 1950, Halstead, Essex, England. Computer Scientist. m. Geraldine, 2 sons. Education: St Christopher School, Letchworth, England, 1960-68; BSc, 1971. PhD, 1975, University of Leicester, England. Appointments: Senior Analyst/Advisor, 1975-1986; Lecturer in Computer Science, 1987-1994; Senior Lecturer in Computer Science, 1994-, King's College London. Publications: 75 papers and articles in academic journals, professional journals and conference proceedings, covering computational science, parallel computing and information security. Memberships: Fellow, British Computer Society; Fellow, Institute of Mathematics; Fellow, Higher Education Academy; Member, Institute of Engineering and Technology; Member, Royal Society of Chemistry. Address: Department of Computer Science, King's College London, Strand, London WC2R 2LS, England. E-mail: richard.overill@kcl.ac.uk

OVODOV Yury S, b. 28 August 1937, Kharkov, Ukraine, USSR. Chemist; Immunochemist. m. Raisa G Ovodova, 1 son. Education: Lomonosov State University, Moscow, 1959; Candidate of Chemical Sciences, 1963; Doctor of Chemical Sciences, 1972; Professor in Bioorganic Chemistry, 1973. Appointments: Senior Laboratory Worker, Novosibirsk Institute of Organic Chemistry, Siberian Branch of the USSR Academy of Sciences, 1959-62; Intern, Institute of Chemistry of Natural Compounds, the USSR Academy of Sciences, Moscow, 1960-62; Junior Scientist, Laboratory of Chemistry of Natural Substances, Vladivostok, 1962-64; Deputy Director, 1967-87, and concurrently Head of Department, 1975-94, Head of Laboratory, 1964-75 and 1979-94, Pacific Institute of Bioorganic Chemistry, Far Eastern Branch, Academy of Sciences, Vladivostok; Elected Corresponding Member of the USSR Academy of Sciences, 1990; Full Member, Russian Academy of Sciences, 1992; Head, Department of Molecular Immunology, 1994-2004, Director, 2004-, Institute of Physiology, Komi Science Centre, the Urals Branch of the Russian Academy of Sciences, Syktyvkar; Concurrently, Director, Educational Scientific Centre, Syktyvkar State University, 2000-; Chief Scientist, Institute of Chemistry, Komi Science Centre, The Urals Branch of the Russian Academy of Sciences, Syktyvkar, 2002-06. Publications: Triterpenic Glycosides of Gypsophila spp; Bioglycans-immunomnodulators; Bacterial Lipopolysaccharides; Oncofetal Antigens and Oncoprecipitins; The Chemical Foundations of Immunity; Selected Chapters of Bioorganic Chemistry; Structural Features and Physiological Activities of Plant Polysaccharides. Honours: Lenin Komsomol Prize, 1972; I I Mechnikov Award, 1993; Y A Ovchinnikov Award, 2003; Laureate Medal, Russian Academy of Sciences and Arts, 2007; Listed in Who's Who publications and international biographical dictionaries. Memberships: The Slav Academy of Science; New York Academy of Sciences; International Endotoxin Society; American Chemical Society; American Association for the Advancement of Science; Russian Biochemical Society; The Urals Immunology Society; Russian Physiological Society; Society of Biotechnologists of Russia. Address: Institute of Physiology, Komi Science Centre, The Urals Branch of the Russian Academy of Sciences, 50 Pervomaiskaya str, 167982 Syktyvkar, Russia.

OW Rosaleen Kong Soon Oi, b. 20 December 1948, Malaysia. Academic Lecturer. m. Danny W K Ow, 1 son, 1 daughter. Education: B Social Science (Hons, Upper), 1971, PhD, Social Work, 1991, National University of Singapore; MSc (Econs), University of Wales, 1976. Appointments: Senior Lecturer, Deputy Head, Department of Social Work, National University of Singapore. Publications: Families in Society; Social Work in Healthcare; Social Work and Health; International Journal of Social Welfare; Asia Pacific Journal of Social Work & Social Development. Honours: Teaching Excellence Award, National University of Singapore, 1994; Listed in international biographical dictionaries. Memberships: Life Member, Singapore Association of Social Workers. Address: Department of Social Work, AS3, National University of Singapore, S 117570, Singapore. E-mail: swkowso@nus.edu.sg

OWEN, Baron of the City of Plymouth, David Anthony Llewellyn Owen, b. 2 July 1938, Plymouth, Devon, England. Physician; Politician; Businessman. m. Deborah Schabert, 2 sons, 1 daughter. Education: MA, MB BChir, Cantab, 1962. Appointments: Neurological Registrar, St Thomas' Hospital, London, 1964-65; Research Fellow, Medical Unit, St Thomas, 1966-68; Member of Parliament for Plymouth, 1966-92; Minister for Navy, 1968-70; Minister of Health, 1974-76; Minister of State for Foreign and Commonwealth Affairs, 1976-77; Foreign Secretary, 1977-79; Leader of the SDP Parliamentary Party, 1981-82; Deputy Leader of SDP, 1982-83; Leader of SDP, 1983-87 and 1988-92; EU Negotiator in Former Yugoslavia, 1992-95. Publications: Papers and articles in medical journals; The Politics of Defense; In Sickness and in Health; Face the Future; The United Kingdom; Our NHS; Autobiography, Time to Declare, 1991; Anthology of poetry, Seven Ages, 1992 and Balkan Odyssey, 1995. Honours: Companion of Honour, 1994; Baron Owen of the City of Plymouth, 1992; Chancellor of Liverpool University, 1996; FRCP, 2005. Address: House of Lords, Westminster, London SW1A 0PW, England.

OWEN Michael James, b. 7 November 1980, Church Village, Pontypridd, Wales. Rugby Union Player. m. Lucy, 2 daughters. Education: Bryn Celynnog Comprehensive School, 1992-99; Diploma of Higher Education, Business Studies, University of Glamorgan, 2000. Career: Wales, 41 caps, 2 tries; Debut, versus South Africa in Bloemfontein, 2002; 5 tests as captain;

7 appearances (2 as captain), British Lions tour, New Zealand, 2005; World XV and Barbarians; 105 games, Pontypridd RFC, 1999-2003; 91 games, Newport Gwent Dragons, 2003-; Joining Saracens, 2008 season.

OWEN Nicholas David Arundel, b. 10 February 1947, United Kingdom. Journalist; Television Presenter. m. Brenda, 2 sons, 2 daughters. Appointments: Journalist: Surrey Mirror, 1964, London Evening Standard, 1968-70, Daily Telegraph, 1970-71, Financial Times, 1972-79, Now! Magazine, 1979-81; Reporter and Presenter, BBC Television News, 1981-84; Presenter, ITN, 1984-; Royal Correspondent, ITV News, 1994-2000; Channel 4 News Business and Economics Correspondent; Presented ITV1's live hour and a half Budget Programme, 2004; Anchor, Parliament Programme, Channel 4's first daytime political series; Presenter of ITV Lunchtime News, 2002-2007; Presenter, BBC New 24, 2007-. Publications: History of the British Trolleybus, 1972; Diana – The People's Princess. Address: c/o Independent Television News, 200 Gray's Inn Road, London WC1X 8XZ, England. E-mail: nicholas.owen@itn.co.uk

OXLEY William, b. 29 April 1939, Manchester, England. Poet; Writer; Translator. m. Patricia Holmes, 13 April 1963, 2 daughters. Education: Manchester College of Commerce, 1953-55. Publications: The Dark Structures, 1967; New Workings, 1969; Passages from Time: Poems from a Life, 1971; The Icon Poems, 1972; Sixteen Days in Autumn (travel), 1972; Opera Vetera, 1973; Mirrors of the Sea, 1973; Eve Free, 1974; Mundane Shell, 1975; Superficies, 1976; The Exile, 1979; The Notebook of Hephaestus and Other Poems, 1981; Poems of a Black Orpheus, 1981; The Synopthegms of a Prophet, 1981; The Idea and Its Imminence, 1982; Of Human Consciousness, 1982; The Vitalist Reader, 1982; The Cauldron of Inspiration, 1983; A Map of Time, 1984; The Triviad and Other Satires, 1984; The Inner Tapestry, 1985; The Mansands Trilogy, 1988; Mad Tom on Tower Hill, 1988; The Patient Reconstruction of Paradise, 1991; Forest Sequence, 1991; In the Drift of Words, 1992; The Playboy, 1992; Cardboard Troy, 1993; The Hallsands Tragedy, 1993; Collected Longer Poems, 1994; Completing the Picture (editor), 1995; The Green Crayon Man, 1997; No Accounting for Paradise (autobiography), 1999; Firework Planet (for children), 2000; Reclaiming the Lyre: New and Selected Poems, 2001; Namaste: Nepal Poems, 2004; London Visions, 2005; Poems Antibes, 2006; Contributions to: Anthologies and periodicals. Address: 6 The Mount, Furzeham, Brixham, South Devon TQ5 8QY, England. E-mail: pwoxley@aol.com

OYAMA Munetaka, b. 5 September 1963, Fukuoka, Japan. Associate Professor. m. Mieko Oyama, 2 sons. Education: Master of Science, 1988, Doctor of Science, 1991, Kyoto University, Japan. Appointments: Research Associate, Nagoya University, Japan, 1991-94; Research Associate, 1994-99, Associate Professor, 1999-, Kyoto University, Japan. Publications: Over 110 articles in scientific journals including: Journal of Physical Chemistry A, 2002; Chemistry Communications, 2002; Perkin 2, 2001, 2002. Honour: Sano Award, Japan Electrochemical Society, 1998. Memberships: Electrochemical Society; International Electrochemical Society. Address: International Innovation Center, Kyoto University, Nishikyo-ku, Kyoto 615-8520, Japan. E-mail: oyama@iic.kyoto-u.ac.jp

OYEYEMI Boboye Olayemi, b. 26 November 1960, Ibadan, Nigeria. Engineer. m. Bolanle Oluyemisi, 2 sons. Education: Diploma in Transportation Management, 1993, Master's degree in Public Administration, 1995, University of Lagos;

Doctoral Candidate (Doctor of Public Administration), University of Nigeria, in progress. Appointments: Ibadan Zone, 1980-82, Educational Service, 1983-85, Federal Radio Corporation of Nigeria, Lagos; Nigerian Television Authority, Sokoto, 1985-87; Officer in Charge, Communications, 1988-92, Area Commander, Plan and Production, 1992-93, Principal Commander in Charge, National Uniform Licensing Scheme, 1993-95, Zonal Commanding Officer, Zone RS9, Sokoto, 1995-96, Deputy Director, Operations, 1996-99, Director, Operations, 1999-2002, Director, Motor Vehicle Administration, RSHQ, Abuja, 2002-03, Zonal Commanding Officer, Zone RS3, Yola, 2003-05, Federal Road Safety Commission, National Headquarters, Abuja. Publications: Productivity in Road Traffic Administration: Issues, Strategies and Impediments, 2003; Strands in Road Traffic Administration in Nigeria, 2003. Honours: Certificate of Commendation/Recognition, FRSC, 1992; Architect of the Club Award, Lagos Welfare Club, 1993; Capital Oil Special Marshal Unit Award, 1993; Road Safety Merit Award, FRSC, 1993; Certificate of Merit, Africa Youth Sports Federation, 1997; Friend of the Muse Award, University of Nigeria, 2001; Public Safety Gold Award, African Safety Agenda, 2002; Certified Distinguished Administrator Award, Institute of Corporate Administration, 2003; American Medal of Honor, ABI, 2004; Man of the Year Award, ABI, 2004; Achiever's Award, FRSC, 2004; Nigerian Youth Organisation Excellence Award, 2005; African Youth Organisation Medal, 2005; Achiever's Award, FRSC, 2005; Member, Order of the Federal Republic. Memberships: Institution of Engineering and Technology, London; Chartered Institute of Personnel Management of Nigeria; Chartered Institute of Administration, Lagos; National Association of Technological Engineers, Lagos; Nigerian Institute of Management, Lagos; Nigerian Institute of Safety Professionals, Lagos; Institute of Management Consultants, Lagos; Chartered Institute of Logistics and Transport, London; International Institute of Risk & Safety Management, London; Institute of Corporate Administration, Abuja; American Society of Safety Engineers, USA; Institute of Road Safety Officers, London; Institute of Transportation Engineers, USA; International Association of Chiefs of Police, USA; Institute of Electrical and Electronics Engineers, USA. Address: Plot 18A, Tunis Street, Wuse Zone 6, PO Box 9084, Wuse Post Office, Abuja, FCT, Nigeria.

OYLER Edmund John Wilfrid, b. 8 February 1934, London, England. Chartered Accountant. m. Elizabeth Kathleen Larkins, 1961, 2 sons, 1 daughter. Education: Trinity College, Cambridge, 1953-56; BA, 1956; MA 1960; University College, London, 1970-72; LLM, 1972; Heythrop College, London, 1997-2000; MTh, 2000. Appointments: National Service, 2nd Lieutenant, Royal Signals, 1951-53; Chartered accountant in public practice, ACA, 1961, FCA, 1972; Articled – Pannell Crewdson and Hardy, 1956-60; Whinney Smith and Whinney, 1961; Partner, Whinney Murray and Co, 1967-79; Partner, Ernst and Whinney, 1979-89; Partner, Ernst and Young, 1989-97; Partner specialising in taxation of insurance companies, 1967-92; National tax partner, 1978-81; Partner with national responsibility for trusts, 1985-89; National compliance partner, 1988-97; Sole Practitioner, 1997-99. Memberships: Athenaeum; Madrigal Society; Georgian Group; Royal Geographical Society; Activities for ICAEW include: Co-opted Member of Council, 1996-99, Chairman, Financial Services Authorisation Committee, 1995-2001, Chairman, Joint Investment Business Committee, 1995-2001, Chairman, London Society of Chartered Accountants, 1996-97, Chairman, Joint Monitoring Unit Limited, 1997-2001. Address: 20 Bedford Gardens, London, W8 7EH, England.

OZ Amos, b. 4 May 1939, Jerusalem, Israel. Author; Professor of Hebrew Literature. m. Nily Zuckerman, 5 April 1960, 1 son, 2 daughters. Education: BA cum laude, Hebrew Literature, Philosophy, Hebrew University, Jerusalem, 1965; MA, St Cross College, Oxford, 1970. Appointments: Teacher, Literature, Philosophy, Huldah High School and Givat Brenner Regional High School, 1963-86; Visiting Fellow, St Cross College, Oxford, England, 1969-70; Writer-in-Residence, Hebrew University, Jerusalem, 1975-76, 1990; Writer-in-Residence, University of California, Berkeley, USA, 1980; Writer-in-Residence, Professor of Literature, The Colorado College, Colorado Springs, 1984-85; Writer-in-Residence, Visiting Professor of Literature, Boston University, Massachusetts, 1987; Full Professor of Hebrew Literature, 1987-2005, Professor Emeritus, 2005, Ben Gurion University, Beer Sheva, Israel; Writer-in-Residence, Tel Aviv University, 1996; Writer-in-Residence, Visiting Professor of Literature, Princeton University, (Old Dominion Fellowship), 1997; Weidenfeld Visiting Professor of European Comparative Literature, St Anne's College, Oxford, 1998. Publications include: Where the Jackals Howl (stories), 1965, My Michael (novel), 1968; Under This Blazing Light (essays), 1978; Black Box (novel), 1987; Don't Call It Night (novel), 1994; All Our Hopes (essays) 1998; The Same Sea, 1999; A Tale of Love and Darkness (novel), 2002; How to Cure a Fanatic, 2006; Rhyming Life and Death, 2007. Honours include: Holon Prize, 1965; Wingate Prize, London, 1988; Honorary Doctorate, Tel Aviv University, 1992; Frankfurt Peace Prize, 1992; Knight's Cross of the National Legion D'Honneur, France, 1997; Honorary Doctorate, Brandeis University, USA, 1998; Israel's Prize for Literature, 1998; My Michael selected by Bertelsmann international publishers' panel as one of the greatest 100 novels of the 20th Century, 1999; Freedom of Expression Prize, Writers' Union of Norway, 2002; Goethe Cultural Award for his life's Work, 2005; Prince of Asturias Award, 2007. Address: c/o Deborah Owen Ltd, 78 Narrow Street Limehouse, London E14 8BP, England.

ÖZSOYLU N Şinasi, b. 29 August 1927, Erzurum, Turkey. Physician. m. F Selma, 2 sons, 1 daughter. Education: Istanbul University, 1951; Ankara University, 1959; Washington University, 1960, 1961; Harvard University, 1963. Appointments: Associate Professor, Paediatrics, Hacettepe University; Professor of Paediatrics and Haematology, 1969; Head, Paediatrics Department, 1976; Head, Haematology and Hepatology Departments, 1973-94; Professor of Paediatrics and Haematology, Fatih University, 1994-2005. Publications: 880 in professional journals. Honours include: İhsan Dogramaci Award, 1979; Mustafa N Parlar Award, 1989; Hacettepe University Excellence in Science Achievement Award, 1991; TUSAV Honorary Award, 2002; Help to Health Honorary Award, 2003; Fatih University Award, 2004; SAMEDER Award, 2005; Physician of the Year, 2007; Listed in Who's Who publications and international biographical dictionaries. Memberships: American Academy of Paediatrics, Honorary Fellow; American Paediatrics Society, Honorary Member; Islamic Academy of Sciences; Turkish Paediatric Society. Address: Fatih University Medical Faculty, Alparslan Türkeş Cad No 57 Emek, Ankara 06510, Turkey.

P

PÄÄSUKE Mati, b. 2 April 1954 Viljandi, Estonia. Professor. m. Maive Pääsuke, 1 son. Education: Diploma Physical Education, 1976, PhD, Physiology, University of Tartu, Estonia. Appointments: Researcher, 1981-88, Associate Professor, 1989-2001, Dean of Faculty of Exercise and Sports Sciences, 1989-98, Head, Institute of Exercise Biology and Physiotherapy, 1998-2004, Professor of Kinesiology and Biomechanics, 2002-, University of Tartu, Estonia. Publications: Over 50 articles in international refereed journals including: Acta Orthopaedica Scandinavica; Acta Physiologica Scandinavica; Annals of Anatomy, Ageing: Clinical and Experimental Research; European Journal of Applied Physiology; Electromyography and Clinical Neurophysiology; Pediatric Exercise Science. Honours: Listed in Who's Who publications and biographical dictionaries. Memberships: Estonian Physiological Society; Estonian Federation of Sports Medicine; International Society of Biomechanics in Sports. Address: Institute of Exercise Biology and Physiotherapy, University of Tartu, 5 Jakobi Street, 51014 Tartu, Estonia. E-mail: mati.paasuke@ut.ee Website: www.ut.ee/KKKB

PACHECO PACIFICO Andrea Maria C, b. 8 October 1971, Maceió, Brazil. University Professor; Lawyer. Education: Bachelor of Law, University of Alagoas, Brazil, 1993; Postgraduate, Lato Sensu, International Law, 1997; Postgraduate, Lato Sensu, Public Law, University of Pernambuco, Brazil, 2000; LLM/MA, International Law, International Relations, University of Lancaster, England; PhD Course, Social Sciences, Catholic University of Sao Paulo, 2005-08. Appointments: General Co-ordinator for Legislative Subjects, Legislative Assembly of Alagoas, Brazil, 1995-97; University Professor, International Law and International Relations and International Human Rights Law, 1997-; Head of Department of Law Course, 1997, 1998; Co-ordinator of Activities of Extension of Law Course, 2002-08. Publications: Book: Drugs, Violence and Criminality in Alagoas, 1995; International Treaties and the Brazilian Constitutional Law, 2002; Articles: Refugees as Subjects of International Law, 2005; Human Rights in the Constitutions of Mercosur, 2005; Migrants within Labour Relations in Brazil, 2006; Integration for Development: The Social Capital Produced by Argentinians and Italians in Maceio/Brazil, 2007. Honours: Scholarship for XXIV Course on International Law, OAS, 1997; Scholarship to take LLM/MA, University of Lancaster, 1998-99; Scholarship, York University, Canada, 2007. Memberships: American Society of International Law; Inter-American Bar Association; Rotary International; Brazilian Bar Association; Brazilian Institute of Human Rights; Brazilian Red Cross. Address: R. Con Antonio F Vasconcelos, 138/202, Jatiúca, Maceió, Alagoas, 57036-470, Brazil. E-mail: apacifico@hotmail.com

PACINO Al (Alfredo James), b. 25 April 1940, New York, USA. Actor. Education: The Actors Studio. Appointments: Messenger, Cinema Usher; Co-Artistic Director, The Actors Studio Inc, New York, 1982-83; Member, Artistic Directorate Globe Theatre, 1997-. Creative Works: Films include: Me, Natalie, 1969; Panic in Needle Park, 1971; The Godfather, 1972; Scarecrow, 1973; Serpico, 1974; The Godfather Part II, 1974; Dog Day Afternoon, 1975; Bobby Deerfield, 1977; And Justice For All, 1979; Cruising, 1980; Author! Author!, 1982; Scarface, 1983; Revolution, 1985; Sea of Love, 1990; Dick Tracy, 1991; The Godfather Part III, 1990; Frankie and Johnny, 1991; Glengarry Glen Ross, 1992; Scent of A Woman, 1992; Carlito's Way, 1994; City Hall, 1995; Heat, 1995;

Donny Brasco, 1996; Looking For Richard, 1996; Devil's Advocate, 1997; The Insider, 1999; Chinese Coffee, 1999; Man of the People, 1999; Any Given Sunday, 1999; Insomnia, 2002; Simone, 2002; People I Know, 2002; The Recruit, 2003; Gigli, 2003; The Merchant of Venice, 2004; Two for the Money, 2005; 88 Minutes, 2007; Ocean's Thirteen, 2007; Righteous Kill, 2008. Honours include: Tony Award, 1996; British Film Award; National Society of Film Critics Award. Address: c/o Rick Nicita, CAA, 9830 Wilshire Boulevard, Beverly Hills, CA 90212, USA.

PACKER William John, b. 19 August 1940, Birmingham, England. Artist; Critic. m. Clare Winn. Education: Wimbledon School of Art, 1959-63; Brighton College of Art, 1963-64. Career: First exhibited Royal Academy 1963, many group exhibitions since then; Teacher in art schools, 1967-77; External Examiner, Visitor and Advisor at various art schools, 1979-; Art Critic, Art and Artists, 1969-74; Art Critic, Financial Times, 1974-; Recent Solo Exhibitions: Piers Feetham Gallery, 1996, 2001, 2004; Exhibitions curated include: British Art Show I, 1979-80; Elizabeth Blackadder Retrospective, 1984; Martin Fuller Retrospective, 2002; Critic's Choice, Lemon Street Gallery, Truro, 2007. Publications: Books include: The Art of Vogue Covers, 1980; Fashion Drawing in Vogue, 1983; Henry Moore, 1986; John Houston, 2003; Numerous freelance reviews, articles and catalogue essays. Honours: Honorary Fellow, Royal College of Art; Honorary RBA; Honorary FRBS; Honorary PS; Inaugural Henry Moore Lecturer, British Institute Florence, 1986; Artist Fellow, Ballinglen Foundation, Co Mayo, Ireland, 1995. Memberships: Crafts Council, 1980-87; Government Art Collection Advisory Committee, 1977-84; Fine Art Board, National Council for Academic Awards, 1976-83; Member, International Association of Arts Critics; New English Art Club; Chelsea Arts Club; Academy Club, Soho; The Garrick Club. Address: 60 Trinity Gardens, London SW9 8DR, England.

PADFIELD Peter Lawrence Notton, b. 3 April 1932, Calcutta, India. Author. m. Dorothy Jean Yarwood, 23 April 1960, 1 son, 2 daughters. Publications: The Sea is a Magic Carpet, 1960; The Titanic and the Californian, 1965; An Agony of Collisions, 1966; Aim Straight: A Biography of Admiral Sir Percy Scott, 1966; Broke and the Shannon: A Biography of Admiral Sir Philip Broke, 1968; The Battleship Era, 1972; Guns at Sea: A History of Naval Gunnery, 1973; The Great Naval Race: Anglo-German Naval Rivalry 1900-1914, 1974; Nelson's War, 1978; Tide of Empires: Decisive Naval Campaigns in the Rise of the West, Vol I 1481-1654, 1979, Vol II 1654-1763, 1982; Rule Britannia: The Victorian and Edwardian Navy, 1981; Beneath the Houseflag of the P & O, 1982; Dönitz, The Last Führer, 1984; Armada, 1988; Himmler, Reichsführer - SS, 1990; Hess: Flight for the Führer, 1991, revised, updated edition; Hess: The Führer's Disciple, 1993; War Beneath the Sea: Submarine Conflict 1939-1945, 1995; Maritime Supremacy and the Opening of the Western Mind: Naval Campaigns that Shaped the Modern World 1588-1782, 1999; Maritime Power and the Struggle for Freedom: Naval Campaigns that Shaped the Modern World 1788-1851, 2003. Novels: The Lion's Claw, 1978; The Unquiet Gods, 1980; Gold Chains of Empire, 1982; Salt and Steel, 1986. Honour: Winner Mountbatten Maritime Prize, 2003. Membership: Society for Nautical Research. Address: Westmoreland Cottage, Woodbridge, Suffolk, England.

PADMANABHAN Krishnan, b. 11 May 1964, Trivandrum City, India. Research and Development Officer. Education: MSc, Eng, Materials Engineering, Indian Institute of Science, Bangalore, 1991; PhD, Materials Engineering, Indian Institute of Science, Bangalore, 1995. Appointments: Postdoctoral Fellow, Nanyang Technological University, Singapore, 1996-98; Guest Researcher, University of Delaware and National Institute of Standards and Technology, USA, 1998-99; Guest Faculty, IIT, Madras, 1999; Research Fellow, Singapore MIT Alliance, 2000-02; Professor, SVCE, Sri Perumbudur. Publications: Over 50 articles in international refereed journals; Proceedings at international conferences and workshops; Many oral and poster presentations, short articles, lectures and seminars. Listed in Who's Who publications and biographical dictionaries. Memberships: Fellow, IIPE; Fellow IE (India). Address: New No 40, 14th Cross Street, New Colony, Chromepet, Chennai 600044, India.

PAEK Mun Cheol, b. 11 September 1957, Seoul, Korea. Research Engineer. m. Sun Young Doe, 1 son, 1 daughter. Education: Bachelor's degree, Department of Petroleum and Minerals, Seoul National University; Master's degree, PhD, Materials Science, Korea Advanced Institute of Science and Technologies, Daejeon. Appointments: Engineering Staff, Electronics Telecommunications Research Institute, Daejeon, 1982-; Paper Referee, Argonne National Laboratories, Argonne, Illinois, USA, 1993-; Visiting Scholar, Lucent Bell Labs, Murray Hill, New Jersey, USA, 1996-97. Publications: 7 US patents. Memberships: Society of Photo-Optical Instrumentation Engineers; Korean Magnetic Society; Korea Institute of Electrical and Electronic Materials Engineers; Korean Vacuum Society; Society of Information Storage System; Korea Institute of Electronics Engineers. Address: 130-106 Hanbit Apt, Oeun-dong, Yuseong-gu, Daejeon, 305-755, Korea. E-mail: backme@etri.re.kr

PAGANO Rosario, b. 10 August 1976, Catania, Italy. VLSI Designer. Education: Laurea Degree, Electronic Engineering, 2001, PhD, Power Electronics, 2005, University of Catania, Italy. Appointments: Application Engineer, Philips Semiconductors, Nijmegen, Netherlands, 2005-06; IC Designer, NXP Semiconductors, Nijmegen, 2006-. Publications: 1 US patent; Over 30 publications in professional journals and conferences. Honours: Fellowship, National Council of Research, Italy, 2003; Listed in international biographical dictionaries. Memberships: IEEE. Address: NXP Semiconductors, 2 Gerstweg, Nijmegen, 6534 AE, The Netherlands. E-mail: rosario.pagano@nxp.com

PAGE Annette (Annette Hynd), b. 18 December 1932, Manchester, England. Retired Ballerina. m. Ronald Hynd, 1957, 1 daughter. Education: Royal Ballet School, 1944. Appointments: Ballerina, Sadler's Wells Theatre Ballet (Royal Ballet touring company), 1950-55; Ballerina, Sadler's Wells Ballet, (major Royal Ballet company), 1955-67; Ballet Mistress, Bayerischestaatsoper, Munich, 1984-86; Roles include: The Firebird; Princess Aurora in Sleeping Beauty; Odette-Odile in Swan Lake; Giselle; Lise in La Fille Mal Gardée; Juliet in Romeo and Juliet; Cinderella; Swanhilda in Coppelia; Nikiya in La Bayadère; Les Sylphides; Miller's Wife in Three Cornered Hat; Terpsichore in Apollo; Blue Girl in Les Biches; Mamzelle Angot; Ballerina in Petrouchka; Symphonic Variations; Les Rendezvous; Beauty and the Beast; La Capricciosa in Lady and the Fool; Queen of Hearts in Card Game; Agon; Polka in Solitaire; Ballerina in Scènes de Ballet; Queens of Fire and Air in Homage to the Queen; Blue Girl in Les Pâtineurs; Tango and Polka in Façade; Julia and Pèpe in A Wedding Bouquet; Moon and Pas de Six in Prince of the Pagodas; Danses Concertantes; Faded Beauty and Young Lover in Noctambules; Flower Festival Pas de Deux; Ballerina in Ballet Imperial. Memberships: Arts Council of Great Britain, 1976-79.

PAGET Julian Tolver (Lt. Col. Sir), b. 11 July 1921, London, England. Army Officer. m. Diana Farmer, 1 son, 1 daughter. Education: MA, Modern Languages, Christ Church Oxford, 1939-40. Appointments: Commission in Coldstream Guards, 1940-68; Served Northwest Europe, 1944-45; Retired as Lieutenant Colonel, 1968; Author, 1967-; Gentleman Usher to H M The Queen, 1971-91. Publications: Counter Insurgency Campaigning, 1967; Last Post, Aden 1964-67, 1969; The Story of the Guards, 1976; The Pageantry of Britain, 1979; The Yeoman of the Guard, 1984; Wellington's Peninsular War, 1990; Hougoumont, 1992; The Coldstream Guards 1650-2000, 2000. Honours: Succeeded as 4th Baronet, 1972; CVO, 1984. Memberships: Cavalry and Guards Club; Flyfishers Club.

PAGLIA Camille (Anna), b. 2 April 1947, Endicott, New York, USA. Professor of Humanities; Writer. Education: BA, State University of New York at Binghamton, 1968; MPhil, 1971, PhD, 1974, Yale University. Appointments: Faculty, Bennington College, Vermont, 1972-80; Visiting Lecturer, Wesleyan University, 1980; Visiting Lecturer, Yale University, 1980-84; Assistant Professor, 1984-87, Associate Professor, 1987-91, Professor of Humanities, 1991-2000, Philadelphia College of the Performing Arts, later the University of the Arts, Philadelphia; Columnist, Salon.com, 1995-2001; University Professor and Professor of Humanities and Media Studies, University of the Arts, 2000-; Contributing Editor, Interview magazine, 2001-. Publications: Sexual Personae: Art and Decadence from Nefertiti to Emily Dickinson, 1990; Sex, Art, and American Culture: Essays, 1992; Vamps and Tramps: New Essays, 1994; Alfred Hitchcock's "The Birds", 1998; Break, Blow, Burn: Camille Paglia Reads Forty-Three of the World's Best Poems, 2005. Contributions to: Journals and periodicals and Internet communications. Address: University of the Arts, 320 South Broad Street, Philadelphia, PA 19102, USA.

PAHANG H.R.H. Sultan of, b. 24 October 1930, Istana Mangga Tunggal, Pekan, Malaysia. m. (1) Tengku Hajjah Afzan binti Tengku Muhammad, 1954, deceased 1988, 2 sons, 5 daughters, (2) Sultanah Hajah Kalsom, 1991, 1 son. Education: Malay College, Kuala Kangsar; Worcester College, Oxford; University College, Exeter. Appointments: Tengku Mahkota (Crown Prince), 1944; Captain, 4th Battalion, Royal Malay Regiment, 1954; Commander, 12th Infantry Battalion of Territorial Army, 1963-65, Lieutenant-Colonel; Member, State Council, 1955; Regent, 1956, 1959, 1965; Succeeded as Sultan, 1974; Timbalan Yang di Pertuan Agong (Deputy Supreme Head of State), Malaysia, 1975-79, Yang di Pertuan Agong (Supreme Head of State), 1979-84, 1985; Constitutional Head, International Islamic University, 1988. Honours include: DLitt, Malaya, 1988, LLD, Northrop, USA, 1993. Address: Istana Abu Bakar, Pekan, Pahang, Malaysia.

PAICHADZE Sergei A, b. 7 June 1936, Batumi, Georgia. Bibliologist. m. Larisa A Kozhevnikova, 1 son, 1 daughter. Education: Leningrad State Institute of Culture, 1956-61; Postgraduate, 1967-70; Candidate of Philological Sciences, 1971; Doctor of Historical Sciences, 1992; Professor, 1994. Appointments: Deputy Director, Krasnoyarsk Regional Book Trading Company, 1962-67; Head, Department of Bibliography, Dean, Pro-Rector on scientific work, Institute of Culture, Khabarovsk, 1971-86; Researcher, 1986-93, Head of Bibliology Group, 1995-2007; Chief Research Officer, Laboratory of Bibliology, State Public Scientific-Technical Library of the Siberian Branch of the Russian Academy of Sciences, 2002-; Member, Editorial Board of 3 scientific journals; Deputy Head, Council on defence of dissertations.

Member: Commission on Book Culture History, Russian Academy of Sciences; Research Board of Advisors, ABI; Individual Member, Russian Book Union. Publications: More than 250 publications, monographs and articles in professional journals; 18 successful postgraduates-candidates of Historical Sciences. Honour: Laureate, All-Russian Competitions of Scientific Works. Address: ul Voschod 15, 630200 Novosibirsk, Russia.

PAIGE Elaine, b. 5 March 1948, Barnet, England. Singer; Actress. Education: Aida Foster Stage School. Creative Works: West End theatre appearances in Hair, 1968, Jesus Christ Superstar, 1973, Grease (played Sandy), 1973, Billy (played Rita), 1974, Created roles of Eva Peron in Evita, 1978 and Grizabella in Cats, 1981, Abbacadabra (played Carabosse), 1983, Chess (played Florence), 1986, Anything Goes (played Reno Sweeney), 1989, Piaf, 1993-94, Sunset Boulevard (played Norma Desmond), 1995-96, The Misanthrope (played Célimène), 1998; The King and I, 2000; Where There's a Will, 2003; Sweeney Todd – The Demon Barber of Fleet Street, 2004; The Drowsy Chaperone, 2007; Numerous solo albums, 4 multi-platinum albums, 8 consecutive gold albums. Honours include: Society of West End Theatres Award, 1978; Variety Club Award, 1986; British Association of Songwriters, Composers & Authors Award, 1993; OBE, 1995; Lifetime Achievement Award, National Operatic and Dramatic Association, 1999. Address: c/o EP Records, M M & M Pinewood Studios, Pinewood Road, Iver, Bucks SL10 0NH, England.

PAISLEY Ian Richard Kyle, b. 6 April 1926, Ireland. Politician; Minister of Religion. m. Eileen E Cassells, 1956, 2 sons, 3 daughters. Education: South Wales Bible College; Reformed Presbyterian Theological College, Belfast. Appointments: Ordained, 1946; Minister, Martyrs Memorial Free Presbyterian Church, 1946-; Moderator, Free Presbyterian Church of Ulster, 1951; Founder, The Protestant Telegraph, 1966; Leader (co-founder), Democratic Unionist Party, 1972; MP (Democratic Unionist), 1974-, (Protestant Unionist 1970-74), resigned seat, 1985 in protest against the Anglo-Irish Agreement; Re-elected, 1986; MP (Protestant Unionist) for Bannside, Co Antrim, Parliament of Northern Ireland (Stormont), 1970-72, Leader of the Opposition, 1972, Chair, Public Accounts Committee, 1972; Member, Northern Ireland Assembly, 1973-74, elected to Second Northern Ireland Assembly, 1982; Member, European Parliament, 1979-; MP for Antrim North, Northern.Ireland Assembly, 1998-2000; Member, Political Committee European Parliament Northern Ireland Assembly, 1998-; First Minister of Northern Ireland, 2007- Publications include: Jonathan Edwards, The Theologian of Revival, 1987; Union with Rome, 1989; The Soul of the Question, 1990; The Revised English Bible: An Exposure, 1990; What a Friend We Have in Jesus, 1994; Understanding Events in Northern Ireland: An Introduction for Americans, 1995; My Plea for the Old Sword, 1997; The Rent Veils at Calvary, 1997; A Text a Day Keeps the Devil Away, 1997. Address: The Parsonage, 17 Cyprus Avenue, Belfast BT5 5NT, Northern Ireland.

PAL Satyabrata, b. 5 April 1945, Calcutta, West Bengal, India. University Professor. m. Sm Swastika Pal, 1 son, 1 daughter. Education: BSc, Honours, 1964, MSc, 1966, PhD, Statistics, 1979, Calcutta University. Appointments: Lecturer, Ashutosh College, Calcutta, 1967-69; Assistant Professor, Kalyani University, 1969-74, Bidhan Chandra Krishi Viswavidyalaya (BCKV), 1974-75; Associate Professor, 1975-82, Professor, 1983-2007, Head, 1979-82, 1985-88, 1995-98, Dean, Post-Graduate Studies, 2003-05,

BCKV; Principal, NSHM College of Management and Technology, Durgapur, West Bengal, 2007-08; Principal, Swami Vivekananda Institute of Management and Computer Science, 2008-. Publications: 105 papers in international and national journals; 2 books on statistics. Honours: Elected Member, International Statistical Institute, Permanent Officer: Netherlands; Fellow: Academy of Science and Technology, West Bengal, Calcutta, India; Inland Fisheries Society of India, Barrackpore, West Bengal, India; Indian Association of Hydrologists, Roorkee, India; Senior Post Doctoral Fellow, International Rice Research Institute, Manila, Philippines; Chairman, Finance Committee, International Biometric Society, USA; Bharat Excellence Award and Gold Medal, Friendship Forum of India, New Delhi, India; Rajib Gandhi Shrimoni Award, India International Friendship Society, New Delhi, India; Shiksha Rattan Puroskar and Certificate of Excellence, 2007 by India International Friendship Society, New Delhi, India. Memberships: Governing Body Member, Life Member of 10 societies and associations; Indian Region. Address: 101/B, Bakul Bagan Road, Kolkata 700025, West Bengal, India. E-mail: satbrpal@vsnl.net

PAL Trivan, b. 21 December 1954, New Delhi, India. Physicist. Divorced, 1 son. Education: BSc (Hon), ARCS, Physics, Imperial College, University of London, England, 1975; MSc, 1977, PhD, 1983, Physics, University of Geneva & CERN, Switzerland. Appointments: Research Fellow, California Institute of Technology, Pasadena, USA, 1983-86; Staff (with tenure), Superconducting, SuperCollider Laboratory, Dallas, Texas, USA, 1992-94; Senior Research Associate, University of Bern and CERN, Switzerland, 1986-98; Staff (with tenure), Computing and Controls, Swiss Light Source, Paul Scherrer Institute, Switzerland, 1998-. Publications: 80 refereed publications in international journals; Numerous citations and acknowledgements in books. Honours: High Honours citations, Master thesis; High Honours citation, Doctoral thesis; Performance Award, PSI/GFA, Villigen, Switzerland, 2002; Listed in international biographical dictionaries. Memberships: Associate, Royal College of Science, London; International Review Committee, Journal of Systems, Cybernetics and Informatics. Address: Paul Scherrer Institute, 5232 Villigen, Switzerland. E-mail: trivan.pal@psi.ch

PALIN Michael Edward, b. 5 May 1943, Sheffield, Yorkshire, England. Freelance Writer and Actor. m. Helen M Gibbins, 1966, 2 sons, 1 daughter. Education: BA, Brasenose College, Oxford, 1965. Appointments: Actor, Writer: Monty Python's Flying Circus, BBC TV, 1969-74; Ripping Yarns, BBC TV 1976-80; Writer, East of Ipswich, BBC TV, 1986; Films: Actor and Joint Author: And Now for Something Completely Different, 1970; Monty Python and the Holy Grail, 1974; Monty Python's Life of Brian, 1978; Time Bandits, 1980; Monty Python's The Meaning of Life, 1982; Actor, Writer, Co-Producer, The Missionary, 1982; Around the World in 80 Days, BBC, 1989; Actor: Jabberwocky, 1976; A Private Function, 1984; Brazil, 1984; A Fish Called Wanda, 1988; Contributor, Great Railway Journeys of the World, BBC TV, 1980; Actor, Co-Writer, American Friends, film, 1991; Actor, GBH, TV Channel 4, 1991; Actor, Fierce Creatures, 1997; Michael Palin's Hemingway Adventure, BBC TV, 1999; Sahara, 2002; Himalaya with Michael Palin, 2004; Michael Palin's New Europe, 2007. Publications: Monty Python's Big Red Book, 1970; Monty Python's Brand New Book, 1973; Dr Fegg's Encyclopaedia of All World Knowledge, 1984; Limericks, 1985; Around the World in 80 Days, 1989; Pole to Pole, 1992; Pole to Pole - The Photographs, 1994; Hemingway's Chair, 1995; Full Circle, 1997; Full Circle - The Photographs, 1997; Michael Palin's Hemingway Adventure,

1999; Sahara, 2002; Himalaya, 2004; For Children: Small Harry and the Toothache Pills, 1981; The Mirrorstone, 1986; The Cyril Stories, 1986. Honours: Writers Guild, Best Screenplay Award, 1991; Dr hc (Sheffield), 1992, (Queen's, Belfast), 2000; Lifetime Achievement Award, British Comedy Awards, 2002; BCA Illustrated Book of the Year Award, 2002; British Book Award, TV & Film Book of the Year, 2005; BAFTA Special Award for Outstanding Contribution to TV, 2005. Address: 34 Tavistock Street, London WC2E 7PB, England.

PALMER Arnold Daniel, b. 10 September 1929, Latrobe, USA. Golfer; Business Executive. m. Winifred Walzer, 1954, 2 daughters. Education: Wake Forest University, North Carolina. Appointments: US Coast Guard, 1950-53; US Amateur Golf Champion, 1954; Professioanl Golfer, 1954-;Winner, 92 professional titles, including British Open 1961, 1962, US Open 1960, US Masters 1958, 1960, 1962, 1964, Canadian PGA 1980, US Seniors Championship 1981; Member, US Ryder Cup Team, 1961, 1963, 1965, 1967, 1971, 1973, Captain 1963, 1975; President, Arnold Palmer Enterprises; Board of Directors, Latrobe Area Hospital. Publications: My Game and Yours, 1965; Situation Golf, 1970; Go for Broke, 1973; Arnold Palmer's Best 54 Golf Holes, 1977; Arnold Palmer's Complete Book of Putting, 1986; Playing Great Golf, 1987; A Golfer's Life (with James Dodson), 1999; Playing by the Rules, 2002; Memories, Stories and Memorabilia, 2004. Honours: LLD, Wake Forest National College of Education; DHL, Florida Southern College; Athlete of the Decade, Associated Press, 1970; Sportsman of the Year, Sports Illustrated, 1960; Hickok Belt, Athlete of the Year, 1960. Address: PO Box 52, Youngstown, PA 15696, USA.

PALMER Frank Robert, b. 9 April 1922, Westerleigh, Gloucestershire, England. Retired Professor; Linguist; Writer. m. Jean Elisabeth Moore, 1948, 3 sons, 2 daughters. Education: MA, New College, Oxford, 1948; Graduate Studies, Merton College, Oxford, 1948-49. Appointments: Lecturer in Linguistics, School of Oriental and African Studies, University of London, 1950-52, 1953-60; Professor of Linguistics, University College of North Wales, Bangor, 1960-65; Professor and Head, Department of Linguistic Science, 1965-87, Dean, Faculty of Letters and Social Sciences, 1969-72, University of Reading. Publications: The Morphology of the Tigre Noun, 1962; A Linguistic Study of the English Verb, 1965; Selected Papers of J R Firth, 1951-1958 (editor), 1968; Prosodic Analysis (editor), 1970; Grammar, 1971, 2nd edition, 1984; The English Verb, 1974, 2nd edition, 1987; Studies in the History of Western Linguistics (joint editor) 1986; Semantics, 1976, 2nd edition, 1981; Modality and the English Modals, 1979, 2nd edition, 1990; Mood and Modality, 1986, 2001; Grammatical Roles and Relations, 1994; Grammar and Meaning, 1995 (editor) 1995; Modality in Contemporary English (joint editor), 2003; English Modality in Perspective (co-editor), 2004. Contributions to: Professional journals. Memberships: Academia Europaea; British Academy, fellow; Linguistic Society of America; Philological Society. Address: Whitethorns, Roundabout Lane, Winnersh, Wokingham, Berkshire RG41 5AD, England.

PALTROW Gwyneth, b. 27 September 1973, Los Angeles, USA. Actress. m. Chris Martin, 2003, 1 daughter. Education: University of California, Santa Barbara. Creative Works: Films include: Flesh and Bone, 1993; Hook; Moonlight and Valentino; The Pallbearer; Seven; Emma, 1996; Sydney; Kilronan; Great Expectations, 1998; Sliding Doors, 1998; A Perfect Murder, 1998; Shakespeare in Love, 1998; The Talented Mr Ripley, 1999; Duets, 1999; Bounce, 2000;

The Intern, 2000; The Anniversary Party, 2001; The Royal Tenenbaums, 2001; Shallow Hal, 2001; Possession, 2002; View From the Top, 2003; Sylvia, 2003; Sky Captain and the World of Tomorrow, 2004; Proof, 2004; Infamous, 2006; Love and Other Disasters, 2006; Running with Scissors, 2006; The Good Night, 2007; Iron Man, 2008. Honours include: Academy Award, Best Actress, 1998. Address: c/o Rick Kurtzman, CAA, 9830 Wilshire Boulevard, Beverly Hills, CA 90212, USA.

PALUMBO Peter Garth, Baron Palumbo of Walbrook in the City of London, b. 20 July 1935. m. (1) Denia, 1959, deceased 1986, 1 son, 2 daughters; (2) Hayat, 1986, 1 son, 2 daughters. Education: Eton College; MA (Hons), Law, Worcester College, Oxford. Appointments: Governor, London School of Economics and Political Science, 1976-94; Chairman: Tate Gallery Foundation, 1986-87; Painshill Park Trust Appeal, 1986-96; Serpentine Gallery, 1994-; Board Member and Director, Andy Warhol Foundation for the Visual Arts, 1994-97; Trustee: Mies van der Rohe Archive, 1977-; Tate Gallery, 1978-85; Whitechapel Art Gallery Foundation, 1981-87; Natural History Museum, 1994-2004; Design Museum, 1995-2005; Trustee and Honorary Treasurer, Writers and Scholars Educational Trust, 1984-99; Chairman, Arts Council of Great Britain, 1989-94; Member of Council, Royal Albert Hall, 1995-99; Chairman of Jury, Pritzker Architecture Prize, 2004-; Chancellor, Portsmouth University, 1992-2007; Governor, Whitgift School, 2002-. Honours: Liveryman, Salters' Co, 1965-; Honorary FRIBA, 1986; Created Life Peer, 1991; Honorary FFB, 1994; Honorary FIStructE, 1994; Honorary DLitt Portsmouth, 1993; National Order of Southern Cross, Brazil, 1993; Patronage of the Arts Award, Cranbrook Academy of Arts, Detroit, 2002.

PALVA Ilmari Pellervo, b. 5 May 1932, South Pirkkala, Finland. Physician; Haematologist. m. Seija Kaivola, 9 June 1956, 1 son, 3 daughters. Education: MD, 1956, PhD, 1962, University of Helsinki. Appointments: Registrar, 1959-63, Consultant, 1964-65, Department of Medicine, University Hospital, Helsinki; Instructor, University of Helsinki, 1963-64; Associate Professor, Internal Medicine, University of Oulu, 1965-74; Professor, Internal Medicine, University of Kuopio, 1974; Acting Professor, Medical Education, University of Tampere, 1975-76; Consultant, City Hospitals, Tampere, 1977-92, Retired, 1992. Publications: Over 250 scientific papers in professional journals. Honours: Knight of 1st Rank Order of Finnish White Rose, 1986; Honorary Member, Finnish Society of Haematology, 1992. Memberships: Finnish Medical Association; Finnish Society of Internal Medicine; Finnish Society of Haematology; International Society of Haematology; American Society of Hematology. Address: Oikotie 8, FIN 33950 Pirkkala, Finland.

PAN Chai-fu, b, 8 September 1936, Loshon, Szechwan, China. Emeritus Professor. m. Maria C Shih, 1 son, 1 daughter. Education: BS, Chemical Engineering, National Taiwan University, 1956; PhD, Physical Chemistry, University of Kansas, USA, 1966. Appointments: Associate Professor, 1966-71, Professor, 1971-91, Emeritus Professor of Chemistry, 1991-, Alabama State University, USA. Publications: Contributions to Journal of Physical Chemistry, Journal of Chemical and Engineering Data, Canadian Journal of Chemistry, Journal of Chemical Society, Faraday Transaction 1, other professional journals. Honours: Phi Lambda Upsilon, 1963; Fellowship, American Institute of Chemists, 1971; Alabama State University Research Award, 1985; More than 30 listings. Memberships: American

Chemical Society; Fellow, American Institute of Chemists. Address: 2420 Wentworth Drive, Montgomery, AL 36106, USA. E-mail: ppan@charter.net

PANCHENKO Yurii Nikolayevich, b. 6 April 1934, Kharkov, Ukraine. Chemist. m. Larisa Grigoriyevna Tashkinova, 1 son. Education: Department of Chemistry, MV Lomonosov Moscow State University, 1959; PhD, Chemistry (Molecular Spectroscopy), 1970. Appointments: Junior Researcher, Karpov Physico-Chemical Institute, 1959-61; Junior Researcher, 1961-77, Senior Researcher, 1977-, Department of Chemistry, Moscow State University. Publications: More than 200 scientific works in numerous scientific journals. Honours: Silver Medal (secondary school), Medal of Eötvös Lorand Budapest University. Membership: Fellow, World Association of Theoretically Oriented Chemists. Address: Laboratory of Molecular Spectroscopy, Division of Physical Chemistry, Department of Chemistry, MV Lomonosov Moscow State University, Vorobiovy gory, Moscow 119899, Russia. E-mail: panchenk@physch.chem.msu.su

PANDEY Jagdish, b. 9 February 1928, Bararhi, PS Dehri-on-Sone, Dist Rohtas, Bihar, India. Retired Chief Engineer, Irrigation Department, Government of Bihar. m. Smt Manorma, 4 sons, 3 daughters. Education: PhD, USA; Fellow, Institution of Engineers, India, FIE, 1987; Chartered Engineer, India, 1988. Appointments: Assistant Engineer, Executive Engineer, Superintending Engineer, Chief Engineer, Irrigation Department, Government of Bihar, India. Publications: Rural Development and Small Scale Industries; Bihar and Small Scale Industries; Problem of Pollution and Science of the Modern Age; Sanskrit Language and Indian Civilisation; Saint Tulsidas and His Devotion; Problem of Unemployment and its Solution in India; Condition of Women and their Problem in India. Honours: Best Citizen of India Award; Man of Achievement Award, International Publishing House, New Delhi; Man of the Year 1998, ABI, USA; Distinguished Leadership Award, Research Board of Advisors, ABI, 1999; Rising Personalities of India Award, International Penguin Publishing House; 20th Century Bharat Excellence Award, Glory of India Award, Friendship Forum of India, New Delhi; National Udyog Excellence Award, International Institute of Education and Management; National Gold Star Award, International Business Council; Jewel of India Award, International Institute of Education and Management; Outstanding Intellectuals of the 20th Century, IBC, Cambridge, England; The Millennium Achiever 2000, All India Achievers' Conference, New Delhi; Mahamana Madan Mohan Malvia Samman; Honour by Sanatan Brahman Samaj North Bihar Muzaffarpur (India); Eminent Personalities of India Award, Board of Trustees of International Biographical Research Foundation India in Recognition of Superb Achievements within the Community of Mankind during 20th Century; Vijay Rattan Award and Certificate of Excellence, India International Friendship Society; Bibhuti Bhushan Award, Jagatguru-Shankaracharya of Gobardhan Pith Puri; Sajio Maha Manav Award, National President Sanatan Brahman Samaj; Bharat Jyoti Award, International Institute of Success Awareness, Delhi; Rashtriya Nirman Award, International Business Council; Honorary Member, Research Board of Advisors, ABI, USA, 1999; Life Time Achievement Award, National and International Compendium Delhi; Gold Medals, Friendship Forum of India; Rashitriya Ratan Shiromani Award, Modern India International Society; Gold Medal and Man of the Year, Mumbai, 2003; Great Achiever of India Award, FNP; Pride of India Award, International Institute of Education and Management; 21st Century Excellence Award, International Business Council; Rashtra

Shresth Nidhi Award, Delhi; Eminent Citizen of India Award, NIC; International Gold Star Award, Taranath Ranabhat M P, Rt Hon Speaker, Pratinidhi Sabha (House of Representatives of Nepal), Kathmandu, 2004; Vijay Shree Award, International Business Council; Goswami Tulsidal Award, Industrial Technology Foundation; Prominent Citizens of India Award, 2004; Vikas Shree Award, IIEM; Rashtra Prabha Award; Rashtra Nirman Ratna Award; Indira Gandhi Excellence Award, Indian Solidarity Council, New Delhi; Golden Heart Award, Delhi; Noble Son of India Award, Delhi; Rajdhani Rattan Gold Medal Award, International Business Council, New Delhi; Golden Lifetime Achievement Award, National Services, Industrial Technology Foundation, Delhi; Man of the Millennium Award and Certificate of Merit, New Delhi; UWA Outstanding Intellectuals of the 21st Century Award, Chennai; Glory of India International Award and Certificate of Excellence, 2006, Bharat Nirman Award & Gold Medal, Certificate of Excellence, Certificate of Feliciation, 2006, Certificate of Participation, Economic Growth & National University, Best Citizens of India Award, 2006, Friendship Forum of India; UWA Outstanding Intellectuals of the 21st Century Award, Chennai, 2007; Rashtriya Vidya Saraswati Puraskar & Certificate, Indian Solidarity Council, New Delhi. Memberships: Fellowship of Institution of Engineers, India; Chartered Engineer, India; Fellow Membership, United Writers' Association; Fellow IBRF, International Biographical Research Foundation, India; President, Sanskrit Sanjivan Samaj; President, Jagjiwan Sanatorium Shankerpuri; President, Sur Mandir; President, Durga Puja Samiti Patna; President, Sanatan Brahman Samaj Bihar; President, Bihar Hindi Sahitya Sammelan Patna; President, Ganga Sewa Sangh, Bihar, Patna; Vice President, Sanatan Brahman Samaj, India; Chief Patron, Subordinate Engineers Association, Bihar, Patna, India; Patron, Sangrakshak Mandal Pragya Samiti, Bihar, Patna; Patron, Bihar-Nepal Sanskritik Munch; Patron, Bihar-Kerala Sanskritik Munch; Member, International Bhojpuri Sammelan, Bihar, Patna. Address: Rajendra Nagar, Road No 6-C, Patna 800016, Bihar, India.

PANG Shiu Fun, b. 22 February 1945, Hong Kong. Biologist; Biotechnologist. m. Celia Sook Fun Ho, 2 sons. Education: BSc, Biology, The Chinese University of Hong Kong, 1969; MA, Biology, California State University, USA, 1971; PhD, Biology, University of Pittsburgh, USA, 1974. Appointment: Vice-President, Chief Technology Officer, CK Life Sciences Limited, Hong Kong, 2000-2006; Principal Scientific Adviser, CK Life Sciences International Inc, 2006-. Publications: More than 230 papers; Books include: Receptor and Non-receptor Mediated Actions of Melatonin; Recent Progress of Pineal Research – 40 Years After Discovery of Melatonin; Melatonin – Universal Photoperiodic Signal with Diverse Actions. Honours: Editor-in-Chief and Managing Editor, Biological Signals, Switzerland, 1990-97; Editor-in-Chief and Managing Editor, Biological Signals & Receptors, Switzerland, 1998-2001. Memberships: European Pineal Society, 1981-; International Brain Research Organisation, 1985-; Chinese Association of Physiological Sciences, China, 1988-. Address: CK Life Sciences Limited, 2 Dai Fu St, Tai Po Industrial Estate, Tai Po N.T., Hong Kong. E-mail: sf.pang@ck-lifesciences.com

PANIN Ivan, b. 1 June 1959. Company Owner and Director. Education: Doctor of Economics. Appointments: Professor; Academician, International Informatization Academy. Publications: Business Management Technologies. Honours: Holder, International Order of Science, Education and Culture. Address: 24 Suvorovskaya str, Moscow, 107061, Russia.

PANKOV Yuri, b. 10 February 1930, Leningrad, USSR. Biochemist; Molecular Biologist. m. Svetlana Chumachenko, 1 son, 1 daughter. Education: Biochemist, Leningrad State University, 1953; PhD, 1963; DSc, 1968; Biophysicist, Moscow State University, 1972; Academician of the USSR Academy of Medical Sciences, 1986; Professor, 1984, MOIF, 2000. Appointments: Senior Scientist, Institute of Experimental Endocrinology and Hormone Chemistry (IEEHC), 1965-70; Deputy Director, IEEHC, 1970-83; Director of IEEHC, 1983-90; Director of Moscow WHO Collaborating Center on Human Reproduction, 1984-97; Director, Moscow WHO Collaborating Center on Diabetes, 1984-90; Head of Laboratory Molecular Endocrinology Endocrine Research Centre, 1990-. Publications: Biochemistry of hormones and hormonal regulation, 1976; Several articles in Nature; Biochemistry; Molecular Biology; Bioorganic chemistry, Vestnick of Russian Academy of Medical Sciences; Problem Endocrinology. Honours: Honorary member, Cuban Society of Endocrinology Metabolism, 1984; Honorary Citizen of Lexington, Kentucky, USA, 1987; Listed in numerous international biographical publications. Memberships: Endocrine Society; Planetary Society; European Association for the Study of Diabetes; American Diabetes Association; Adjunct Professor, Special Educational Programme on Biochemistry, Immunology, Molecular and Cellular Biology, A N Belozersky Institute, Moscow State University, 1999. Address: Endocrine Research Centre, Moscvorechye Str 1, 115478, Moscow, Russia. E-mail: yuri-pankov@mtu-net.ru

PAPADEMOS Lucas, b. 11 October 1947, Athens, Greece. Bank Executive. Education: BSc, Physics, 1970, MSc, Electrical Engineering, 1972, PhD, Economics, 1977, Massachusetts Institute of Technology. Appointments: Research Assistant, Teaching Fellow, Massachusetts Institute of Technology, 1973-75; Lecturer, Economics, 1975-77, Assistant and Associate Professor of Economics, 1977-84, Columbia University, New York; Senior Economist, Federal Reserve Bank of Boston, 1980; Visiting Professor of Economics, Athens School of Economics and Business, 1984-85; Professor of Economics, University of Athens, 1988-; Economic Counsellor (Chief Economist), 1985-93, Head, Economic Research Department, 1988-93, Deputy Governor, 1993-94, Governor, 1994-2002, Bank of Greece; Vice-President, European Central Bank, 2002-; Member, Greece's Council of Economic Experts. Publications: Numerous articles in professional journals and books chapters as author and co-author. Honour: Grand Commander of the Order of Honour, Greece, 1999-. Memberships include: Governor, International Monetary Fund for Greece, 1994-; General Council, 1999-, Governing Council, 2001-, European Central Bank; Chairman, Governor's Club, 2001-. Address: European Central Bank, Kaiserstr 29, D-60211 Frankfurt am Main, Germany.

PAPINEAU David Calder, b. 30 September 1947, Como, Italy. Philosopher. m. Rose Wild, 6 July 1986, 1 son, 1 daughter. Education: BSc, Honours, University of Natal, 1967; BA, Honours, 1970, PhD, 1974, University of Cambridge. Appointment: Professor, King's College, London, 1990-. Publications: For Science in the Social Sciences, 1978; Theory and Meaning, 1979; Reality and Representation, 1987; Philosophical Naturalism, 1993; Introducing Consciousness, 2000; Thinking about Consciousness, 2002; The Roots of Reason, 2003. Membership: British Society for the Philosophy of Science, President, 1993-95. Address: Department of Philosophy, King's College, London WC2R 2LS, England.

PARAVICINI Nicolas Vincent Somerset, b. 19 October 1937, London, England. Private Banker. m. Susan Rose Phipps. 2 sons, 1 daughter. Education: Royal Military College Sandhurst. Appointments: British Army, The Life Guards, 1957-69, retired as Major; Director, Joseph Sebag & Co, 1972-79; Chairman and Chief Executive, Sarasin Investment Management Ltd, 1980-89; Consultant, Bank Sarasin & Co, 1990-; Chief Executive, Ely Place Investments Ltd, 1992-98. Honours: Freeman City of London, 1984, Deputy Lieutenant for Powys, 2006, Listed in biographical dictionary. Memberships: London Stock Exchange, 1972-80; President, Becknockshire Agricultural Society, 1998-99; SSAFA Powys, 2002-; Clubs: White's; Pratt's; Corviglia Ski; Cardiff & County. Address: Glyn Celyn House, Brecon, Powys LD3 0TY, Wales.

PARIS Richard Bruce, b. 23 January 1946, Bradford, England. University Academic. m. Jocelyne Marie-Louise Neidinger, 1 son, 1 daughter. Education: BSc, 1967, PhD, 1971, DSc, Mathematics, 1999, University of Manchester. Appointments: Postdoctoral Fellow, Royal Society of London, 1972-73, Foreign Collaborator, 1973-74, Research Scientist, Euratom, Theory Division, Controlled Thermonuclear Fusion, 1974-87, Commissariat à l'Energie Atomique, France; Senior Lecturer, University of Abertay Dundee, 1987-99; Honorary Readership, University of St Andrews, 1998-; Reader in Mathematics, University of Abertay Dundee, 1999-. Publications: Books: Asymptotics of High Order Differential Equations (with A D Wood), 1986; Asymptotics and Mellin-Barnes Integrals (with D Kaminski), 2001; Author of over 100 papers and technical reports; Publications in Proceedings A Royal Society, Journal of Computational and Applied Mathematics, Physics of Fluids; Author of 2 chapters in Handbook of Mathematical Functions, forthcoming revised edition. Honours: Fellow of the Institute of Mathematics and Applications, 1986; CMath, 1992, DSc, 1999. Memberships: Institute of Mathematics and its Applications; Edinburgh Mathematical Society; Mathematical Association. Address: University of Abertay Dundee, Dundee DD1 1HG, Scotland. E-mail: r.paris@abertay.ac.uk

PARISESCU Vasile, (Parizescu), b. 25 October 1925, Braila, Romania. Fine Artist; Officer Engineer. m. Victoria, 1 daughter. Education: Bachelor of Art, Faculty of Philology and Philosophy, University of Bucharest, 1949; The Military School of Artillery, 1947; The Military technical Academy, 1953, The Fine Art School, Bucharest, 1973; Independent study of paintings with Dumitru Ghiata, Rudolph Schweitzer Cumpana and Gheorghe Vanatoru. Career: Painter; Scientist; General of the Brigade, Romanian Army; Command appointments in the Romanian Army in the field of armours and auto-drivers technology; 17 personal exhibitions in Romania and abroad; Several national and group exhibitions; Many participations at international exhibitions including: Moscow, 1987, Rome, 1990, 1999, Tokyo, Osaka, Yokohama, 1994-95, Paris 2000, Wiene, 2003; Paintings in collections and museums in Romania, Austria, England, Canada, Switzerland, France, Germany, Netherlands, USA, Greece, Cyprus, Sweden, Turkey, Japan, Yugoslavia, Italy. President of the Society of Art Collectors of Romania; Director of the magazine, Pro Arte. Publications: 30 books in the field of science and technology; Over 1000 articles on science, technology and art; Monography Albums, Vasile Parizescu, 1995, 2001; The Encyclopaedia of Romanian Contemporary Artists, 1999, 2003; The Encyclopaedia of Great Personalities from Romanian History, Science and Culture, 5th volume, 2004; Several TV and Radio appearances. Honours: Laureate of the National First Prize for Science, 1979; The First

National Prize, Republican Art Exhibitions, 1981, 1983, 1985, 1987; Laureate with diploma and medal, International Art Festival, Moscow, 1987; First Prize, National Salon of Art, Botosani, Romania, 1988; Cultural Diploma and Plaquette, City of Bucharest, 1988; Honoured Citizen of the city of Brăila, 1994; Albo D'Oro Prize and selected as Effective Senator of the International Academy of Modern Art, Rome, 1999. Memberships: President of Honour, Fine Arts Society, Bucharest; Member of the National Commission of Museums and Collections; National expert for modern and contemporary art. Address: Bd Nicole Balcescu nr 3, Bloc Dunarea 3, scara 1, ap 12, cod 70111, sector 1 Bucharest, Romania. Website: www.stdb.ro/arta/EVPARIZ.HTM

PARK Hee-Sae, b. 6 March 1970, South Korea. Professor. m. Jin-Hee Kwak, 1 son. Education: Bs, Biochemistry, Yeungnam University, 1996; MS, Biochemistry, Kyungpook National University, 1998; PhD, Graduate School of Biotechnology, Korea University, 2000. Appointments: Research Associate, Korea University, 2000-01; Research Associate, Washington University, St Louis, USA, 2001-03; Assistant Professor, 2003-07, Associate Professor, 2007-, Chonnam National University. Publications: Over 30 papers and articles in professional journals including: Integrin-Linked Kinase Controls Notch1 Signalling by Down-Regulation of Protein Stability through FbW7 Ubiquitin Ligase, 2007. Honours: Best Thesis Award, Korea University, 2001; Best Researcher of the Year, Intron Inc, 2001. Memberships: American Society for Cell Biology; Society for Neuroscience. Address: 300, Buk-ku, Yongbong-Dong, Gwangju, Chonnam National University, School of Biological Sciences & Technology, 500-757, South Korea. E-mail: proteome@jnu.ac.kr

PARK Hoanjae, b. 10 July 1960, Taegu, Republic of Korea. Professor. m. Youngran Jeon, 1 son, 1 daughter. Education: BS, 1986, MS, 1989, Economics, KyungBook National University, Seoul; Master of Economics, Ohio State University, USA, 1991; PhD, Economics, North Carolina State University, USA, 1996. Appointments: Department Director, National Statistical Office, Seoul, 1997-98; Professor, Catholic University of Daegu, Taegu, Republic of Korea, 1998-; Director, Catholic University of Daegu, Taegu, 2003-05; Vice President of School Affairs, Catholic University of Daegu, Taegu, 2006-. Publications: Randall and Stoll's bound in an inverse demand system, 1997; On interpreting inverse demand systems: A primal comparison of scale flexibilities and income elasticities, 1999; On inferring individual behaviour from market behaviour in a predetermined quantities model, 2004; Modelling inverse demands for fish: Empirical welfare measurement in Gulf and South Atlantic Fisheries, 2004; The Use of Conditional Cost Functions to Generate Estimable Mixed Demand Systems, 2007. Honours: Grantee, NMFS Sea Grants, National Marine Fisheries Service, USA, 1994-95; 21st Century Award for Achievement, England, 2006. Memberships: Korea Finance and Public Economics Association; Econometrics Association; Environmental Economics Association. Address: Catholic University of Daegu, Department of Economics and Trade, 330 GeumRak-Ri, Hayang-Up, KyungBook, KyungSan 712-702, Republic of Korea. E-mail: parkletters@yahoo.co.kr

PARK Hung Suck, b. 7 November 1956, Kangreung City, Korea. Environmental Engineer; Educator. m. Young Soon Kim, 1 son, 1 daughter. Education: BS, Environmental Engineering, University of Seoul, 1984; MS, 1986, PhD, 1990, Civil Engineering, Korea Advanced Institute of Science and Technology. Appointments: Researcher, Environmental Research Center, KIST, Korea, 1990-92; Manager of

Laboratory, Metropolitan Landfill of Environmental Management Corporation, Korea, 1992-93; Registered Professional Engineering in Water Quality Management, Korea, 1992-; Faculty Position, Department of Civil and Environmental Engineering, University of Ulsan, Korea, 1993-. Publications: Books: Environmental Science and Engineering, 1995; Environmental Engineering, 1998; Management of Water Quality and Water Resources, 1999; 4 patents; Numerous papers in international journals. Honours: Best Scholar Award, University of Seoul, 1984; Award, Ministry of Environment, 2004; Distinguished Service Award, Ulsan Civic Forum, 2006; Column writer for Kyeong Sang daily newspaper; Distinguished invited speaker to China and Japan. Memberships: Korea Organic Waste Recycling Council; Korea Society of Water Quality; Water Environment Federation; America Water Works Association; International Association on Water Quality; Korean Society of Water and Wastewater; Korea Technological Society of Water and Wastewater Treatment; Korean Professional Engineers Association; Korean Society of Waste Management; Korean Environment Preservation Association; Korean Environment Management Federation; Korean Water Works Association; Korean Society of Civil Engineers; Korean Society of Soil and Groundwater Environment; Korean Society of Urban Environment; Ulsan Local Agenda 21; Korean National Council for Conservation of Natural Resources; Presidential Commission for Sustainable Development. Address: Department of Civil and Environmental Engineering, University of Ulsan, Mugeo-Dong, Nam-Gu, Ulsan Metropolitan City, 680-749, Republic of Korea. E-mail: parkhs@ulsan.ac.kr Website: http://cms.ulsan.ac.kr/epcl

PARK Hyuntae, b. 16 December 1970, Seoul, Korea. Research Fellow. Education: PhD, 2007. Appointments: Research Fellow, Laboratory for Physical Education and Medicine, Physical Education and Medicine Research Center, 2003-05; Research & Academic Assistant, Department of Physical and Health Education, The University of Tokyo, 2005-06; Research Fellow, Core Research Team of Genomics for Longevity and Health, Tokyo Metropolitan Institute for Gerontology, 2006-. Publications include: Meteorology and the physical activity of the elderly: the Nakanojo Study, 2005; Yearlong Physical Activity and Depressive Symptoms in Older Japanese Adults: Cross-Sectional Data from the Nakanojo study, 2006; Clinical factors as predictors of the risk of falls and subsequent bone fractures due to osteoporosis in postmenopausal women, 2006; Relationship of bone health to yearlong physical activity in older Japanese adults: cross-sectional data from the Nakanojo Study, 2007; Yearlong Physical Activity and Health-Related Quality of Life in Older Japanese Adults: The Nakanojo Study, 2007; Development and Evaluation of the Physical Activity Questionnaire for Elderly Japanese: The Nakanojo Study, 2007; Genetic risk for metabolic syndrome: examination of candidate gene polymorphisms related to lipid metabolism in Japanese individuals, 2007; Effect of combined exercise training on bone, body balance and gait ability: a randomized controlled study in community dwelling elderly women, 2008. Memberships: American College of Sports Medicine; International Bone and Mineral Society; American Society of Bone and Mineral Metabolism; National Osteoporosis Foundation; The Gerontological Society of America; Japanese Society of Physical and Fitness and Sports Medicine; Japanese Society of Physiology Anthropology; Korean Alliance for Health, Physical Education, Recreation and Dance; MOO. Address: Genomics for Longevity and Health, Tokyo Metropolitan Institute of Gerontology, 35-2 Sakaetso, Itabashi-ku, Tokyo 173-0015, Japan.

PARK Il-Kwon, b. 25 June 1956, Milyang, Kyungnam. Principal Researcher. m. Young-Hee Choi, 2 daughters. Education: BA, 1979, MA, 1981, PhD, 2004, Naval Architecture, Pusan National University, Republic of Korea. Appointments: Design and Construction of Naval Weapon Systems Test Range, 1988-2001; ROKN Technical Officer, 1981-84; Principal Researcher, Agency for Defense Development, 1984-; Battleship Combat System Co-Development with USA, 2005-07. Publications: UDT, 2002; Shock and Vibration, 2003; Patent, Cablewinding Device for Underwater Explosion Shock Test. Honours: Minister's Award, MND, 2002; President's Award, ADD, 2004; Medals of National Defense Science, ADD; Awarded and listed in international biographical dictionaries. Memberships: Life Member, Society of Naval Architects of Korea, 1979-; Editorial Board Member, Ships and Offshore Structures, UK, 2006-07; Life Fellowship, IBA, UK, 2007-; Deputy Director General, IBC, UK, 2007-. Address: Greenbeach Apt 1210, Jewhangsan 25-52, Chinhae, Kyungnam, 645-240, Republic of Korea. E-mail: pik625@hanmail.net

PARK Jung Yul, b. 27 December 1958, Seoul, Korea. Professor; Medical Doctor. m. Hye Soon, 1 son, 1 daughter. Education: MD, BA, Korea University Medical College, 1985; MS, 1987, PhD, 1995, Korea University Medical School; Neurosurgery Board, 1990; Canadian Medical Licence, 1998; Research & Clinical Fellowship, University of Toronto, Canada. Appointments: Head, Department of Neurosurgery, Director, Education & Training, Korea University Medical Centre, Ansah Hospital; Director of SICU & Medical Informatics, Korea University; President, Centre for Minimally Invasive Surgery, Korea University; Delegate & Deputy Editor, Korean Association of Neurosurgical Society; Editor in Chief, Journal of Korean Paediatric & Geriatric Neurosurgical Society. Publications: 13 books; 182 major peer-reviewed articles; 540 abstracts & proceedings. Honours: 10 awards, including 4 times election as Best Doctor in Korea. Memberships: World Federation of Neurological Surgery; IASP; AANS; CNS; KNS; AHA; IAMI; AASFS; KASFS; INS; KNS; KAPN; ISPN; KASS. Address: #215-101 Family Apt, Moonjung-Dong, Songpa-Gu, Seoul 138-200, Korea. E-mail: jypark@kumc.or.kr

PARK Kap Joo, b. 19 November 1956, Seoul, Republic of Korea. Professor. m. Myung Soon Lee, 2 sons. Education: BS, 1986, MS, 1988, PhD, 1994, Konkuk University. Appointments: Biologist, Senior Researcher, Korea Institute of Oriental Medicine, Seoul, 1995-99; Chief Researcher, 1999-2001, Research Professor, 2001-, Konkuk University. Publications: Numerous articles in professional journals; Patents for anti-viral drug for Influenza virus; Anti-viral funcational material for Influenza; Neu Tofu congelator using Korean herb. Honours: Listed in international biographical dictionaries. Memberships: Board Member, Korea Society of Virology, 1996-; Board Member, Editor, Korea Society of Environmental Biology, 2001-; Board Member, Korea Association for Creation Research, 2002-. Address: Department of Biological Sciences, Konkuk University, Kwangjin-gu, Hwayang-dong 1, Seoul 143-701, South Korea.

PARK Kyeongsoon, b. 25 December 1958, Incheon, Korea. Associate Professor. m. Mijin Han Park, 1 son, 1 daughter. Education: BS, Inha University, Korea, 1980; PhD, University of Maryland, USA, 1992. Appointments: Researcher, Agency for Defense Development, Daejeon, Korea; Research Associate, University of Massachusetts, Lowell, USA; Professor, Dean of Engineering College,

Chairman, Department of Advanced Materials Engineering, Sejong University, Seoul, Korea; Director, Centre for Advanced Materials, Seoul, Korea. Publications: Chemical Ordering in Semiconductor Thin Films; Electrical Properties of Ni-Mn-Co-(Fe) Oxide Thick-Film NTC Thermistors Prepared by Screen Printing; Microstructure and Mechanical Properties of Silicon Carbide Fiber-reinforced Aluminum Nitride Composites. Honours: President's Awards, Inha University; President's Awards, Agency for Defense Development, Korea. Memberships: Korea Institute of Metals and Materials; Korea Ceramic Society. Address: Department of Advanced Materials Engineering, Sejong University, 98 Kunja-Dong, Kwangjin-Ku, Seoul 143-747, Korea. E-mail: kspark@sejong.ac.kr

PARK Kyung-Won, b. 7 August 1972, Seoul, Korea. Professor. m. Ji-Hyun Cha, 2 daughters. Education: BA, 1996, MS, 1998, Materials Science & Engineering, Sungkyunkwan University; PhD, Materials Science & Engineering, Gwangju Institute of Science & Technology, 2003. Appointments: Postdoctoral Researcher, Seoul National University, 2003-04; Postdoctoral Researcher, Pennsylvania State University, 2004-05; Full time Lecturer, Soongsil University, 2005-. Publications: Papers and articles in professional scientific journals. Honours: Oronzio de Nora Foundation Prize, International Society of Electrochemistry, 2006; Listed in international biographical dictionaries. Memberships: International Society of Electrochemistry; Electrochemical Society; Korean Society of Industrial and Engineering Chemistry; Korean Chemical Society. Address: Soongsil University, Department of Chemical and Environmental Engineering, 511 Sango-Dong, Dongjak-Gu, Seoul 156-743, Korea. E-mail: kwpark@ssu.ac.kr

PARK Myungkark, b. 24 July 1950, Kangwon-do, Korea. Publisher; Physicist. m. Hyunmi Suh, 1 son. Education: BS, Physics, Seoul National University, 1972; MS, Physics, Wayne State University, 1979; PhD candidate, Physics, Washington State University, 1979-83; PhD Student, Physics, Kent State University, 1983-85; PhD Student, Physics, University of Cincinnati, 1985-87; Computing, SOC, 1987-88. Appointments: Publisher; President and Owner, Prompter Publications; A US Publisher, 1989 (1988)-. Publications: Numerous books, journals, articles, notebooks, etc; ...Electron Emission...1981. Honours: Who's Who Medal, 2000; Great Minds of the 21st Century, 2005 (and its dedication (2005-06)); Man of the Year, 2005; many others. Memberships: AAAS; Inactive Member: APS, AMS, AVS, KPS. Address: PO Box 167, Chongnyangni, Tongdaemoon-gu, Seoul 130-650, Korea.

PARK Namje, Information Scientist. Education: BS, Dongguk University, Republic of Korea, 2000; MS, 2003, PhD, Computer Engineering, 2007, Sungkyunkwan University, Republic of Korea. Appointments: Researcher, Newreka Co Ltd, Daejeon, 2000-03; Officer, Korean Association of Local Informatization, Seoul, 2003; Senior Researcher, Electronics and Telecom Research Institute, Daejeon, 2003; On-line Customs Officer, Korea Customs Service, 2004; Committee Member, Korea Institute of Industrial Technology Evaluation and Planning, Seoul, 2004; Independent Consultant, IT Consulting, Korea IT Information Center, 2004; Session Chairman, Personal Wireless Commission Conference, Spain, 2006; Researcher, Dongguk University, Republic of Korea, 2006; Lecturer, 2007. Publications: Author and Translator, Applications Technology, Security and Privacy, 2007; Author, Techniques, Protocols and System-On-Chip Design; Numerous articles in professional journals. Honours: Early Graduation,

Dongguk University, 2000; Recipient, Research Excellence Award, Electronics and Telecom Research Institute, 2005; Best Paper Award, Guest Journal, 2006; Recognition Award, Mobile RFID Forum, 2007. Memberships: Open Mobile Alliance; IEEE; Organisation for Advancement of Structured Information Standards; Korean Information Processing Society; Korea Institute of Information Security & Cryptology; Mobile RFID Forum. Address: ETRI Info Security Research Division, 161 Gajeong-dong Yuseong-gu, Daejeon, 305-350, Republic of Korea. E-mail: namjepark@etri.re.kr

PARK Nick (Nicholas W), b. 6 December 1958, Preston, Lancashire, England. Film Animator. Education: Sheffield Art School; National Film & TV School, Beaconsfield. Appointments: Aardman Animations, 1985, partner, 1995-. Creative Works: Films include: A Grand Day Out, 1989; Creature Comforts, 1990; The Wrong Trousers, 1993; A Close Shave, 1995; Chicken Run (co-director), 2000; Wallace & Gromit: Curse of the Were-Rabbit, 2005.; Shaun the Sheep, (TV), 2007; Creature Comforts, (TV), 2007. Honours: BAFTA Award, Best Short Animated Film, 1990; Academy Award, 1991, 1994; Oscar, Best Animated Feature Film, 2006. Address: Aardman Animations Ltd, Gas Ferry Road, Bristol BS1 6UN, England.

PARK Sang Chul, b. 28 January 1971, Taegu, Korea. Professor. m. Noh Euna, 2 sons. Education: BS, 1994, MS, 1996, PhD, 2000, Industrial Engineering, Department of Industrial Engineering, KAIST. Appointments: Senior Researcher, Cubictek, 2000-02; Research Engineer, DaimlerChrysler, ITM Department, 2002-04; Associate Professor, Department of Industrial Engineering, Ajou University, 2004-. Publications: Tool-path generation from measured data, 2003; Polygonal extrusion, 2003; Contour-parallel offset machining without tool-retractions, 2003; Knowledge capturing methodology in process planning, 2003; In-Process model generation for the process planning of a prismatic part, 2003; Freeform die-cavity pocketing, 2003; Sculptured surface machining using triangular mesh slicing, 2004; Triangular Mesh Intersection, 2004; Hollowing objects with uniform wall thickness, 2005; A methodology for creating a virtual FMS model, 2005; Pencil curve detection from visibility data, 2005. Honours: Winner, Samsung Software Contest, 1995; Best paper award, CASYS, 2000. Memberships: Editorial Board Member, Computer-Aided Design and Applications, 2005; Editorial Board Member, Entrue Journal of Information Technology, 2006. Address: Department of IE, Ajou University, San 5, Woncheon-dong, Yeongtong-gu, Suwon, 443-749, Korea. E-mail: scpark@ajou.ac.kr

PARK Sehie, b. 28 November 1935, Seoul, Korea. University Professor Emeritus. m. Cha Gyoung Park, 2 sons. Education: BS, 1959, MS, 1961, Seoul National University, Seoul, Korea; PhD, Indiana University, Bloomington, Indiana, USA, 1975. Appointments: Assistant, Instructor, Assistant Professor, 1963-75, Associate Professor, 1975-81, Professor, 1981-2001, Professor Emeritus, 2001-, Seoul National University; President, Korean Mathematical Society, 1982-84. Publications: Fixed point theory of multifunctions in topological vector spaces, 1992; Foundations of the KKM theory, 1996; Ninety years of the Brouwer fixed point theorem, 1999; The KKM principle implies many fixed point theorems, 2004; Fixed points of multimaps in the better admissible class, 2004. Honours: Culture Prize Seoul Metropolitan Government, 1981; Dongbaeg Medal of Civil Merit, 1987; National Academy of Sciences Prize, 1994. Memberships: National Academy of Sciences, Republic of Korea; Korean

Academy of Science and Technology; Korean Mathematical Society; American Mathematical Society. Address: Centreville 103-1104, Dae Chi Dong, Gang Nam Gu, Seoul, Korea.

PARK Seok Beom, b. 2 August 1970, Seoul, South Korea. Dermatologist. m. Han Na Hyun, 1 son, 1 daughter. Education: BS, College of Natural Sciences, 1991, College of Medicine, 1991-95, Intern, 1995-96, MS, School of Medicine, 2000, Resident, 1996-2000, Chief Resident, 1999-2000, Department of Dermatology, Seoul National University; Staff Physician, Korean Hansen Welfare Association, Suwon, Kyunggido, 2000-03; PhD, School of Medicine, Kangwon National University, Kangwondo, 2007-. Appointments: Dermatology Consultant: Korean Hansen Welfare Association, Suwon, 2000-03; Ajou Medical University Hospital, Suwon, 2000-03; Seoul National University Hospital, Seoul, 2003-; Asan Medical Center, 2003-; Samsung Medical Center, Seoul, 2003-; Seoul Medical Center, Seoul, 2007-. Publications: Numerous articles in professional journals. Memberships: American Academy of Dermatology; Korean Medical Association; Korean Dermatological Association; Korean Society for Acne Research; Korean Society for Cutaneous Laser Surgery; Korean Society of Phlebology; Korean Society for the Study of Obesity; Korean Society of Adipose-derived Stem Cell Research. Address: Leaders Clinic, 9th Floor, Seo-Kyeong Building, 184-21, Jamsil-dong, Songpa-gu, 138-861, Seoul, South Korea. E-mail: soyofafa@naver.com Website: www.beautyleader.co.kr

PARK Seong Jin, b. 19 May 1968, Buson, South Korea. Professor. m. Won-Young Kwon, 2 sons, 1 daughter. Education: BS, 1991, MS, 1993, PhD, 1996, Department of Mechanical Engineering, POSTECH, Korea. Appointments: Postdoctoral Program, Department of Mechanical Engineering, POSTECH, 1996; Research Engineer, LG Product Engineering Research Center, LG Electronics Inc, Korea, 1996-2000; Lecturer, LG Learning Center, 1998-2002; Research Manager, R&D Center, Seoul, Korea, 2000-01; Visiting Research Manager, Polymer Research Center, POSTECH, 2000-01; Research Director, R&D Center, FineOptics Inc, Seoul, 2001-; Lecturer, Bestner Inc, 2000-01; Chief Technical Officer, 2001-, Lecturer, 2002-, CetaTech Inc, Sacheon; Visiting Scholar, 2001-03, Research Associate, 2003-05, Center for Innovative Sintered Products, Penn State University, USA; Research Associate II, 2005, Associate Research Professor, 2006-, Center for Advanced Vehicular Systems, Adjunct Associate Professor, Department of Mechanical Engineering, 2006-, Graduate Faculty, Computational Engineering Program, 2006-, College of Engineering, Mississippi State University. Publications: 3 books; 3 patents; Numerous articles in professional journals. Honours: Young Generation Scientist Award, Education Ministry of Korean Government, 1996; Archimedes Award, 2007; Listed in international biographical dictionaries. Memberships: Materials Working Group, Mississippi State University; International Institute for the Science of Sintering. Address: Center for Advanced Vehicular Systems, Mississippi State University, PO Box 5405, Mississippi State, MS 39762-5405, USA. E-mail: sjpark@cavs.msstate.edu

PARK Seung Young, b. 28 September 1974, Kwang-ju, Republic of Korea. Professor. m. Heekyung Cho, 1 son. Education: BS, 1997, MS, 1999, PhD, 2002, Korea University. Appointments: Post Doctoral Research Fellow, Korea University, 2002; Senior Engineer, Samsung Advanced Institute of Technology, Republic of Korea, 2003-05; Post Doctoral Research Fellow, Purdue University, USA, 2006; Assistant Professor, Kangwon National University, Republic of Korea, 2007-. Publications: 18 technical papers on digital communications in international refereed journals. Memberships: IEEE; IEICE. Address: School of Information Technology, Kangwon National University, 192-1 Hyoja-dong, Chuncheon, Kangwon 200-701, Republic of Korea. E-mail: young@ieee.org Website: http://cc.kangwon.ac.kr/~parksy

PARK Sin-Chong, b. 8 October 1945, Seoul, Republic of Korea. Professor. m. Kyung-Hee Kim, 2 sons. Education: BS, Applied Physics, Seoul National University, 1968; MS, Physics, Purdue University, West Lafayette, Indiana, 1973; PhD, Chemical Physics, University of Minnesota, Minneapolis, 1978. Appointments: Laboratory Head, Agency for Defense Development, Daejeon, Republic of Korea, 1978-82; Vice President, Electronics & Telecommunication Research Institute, 1983-97; Expert Member, President, Council of Advisors on Science & Technology, Seoul, 1989-90; Professor, Information and Communication University, Daejeon, 1998-; President System Integration Technology Institute, Daejeon, 2001; Chairman, System on Chip Forum, Seoul, 2003-04. Publications: Over 50 articles in professional journals; More than 20 patents. Honours: President's Award, President of Korea, 1993; New Industry Management Award, New Industry Management Academy, 1994. Memberships: IEEE: IEICE; KICS; IEEK. Address: 103-6, Munji-Dong, Yuseong-Gu, Daejeon, 305-714, Republic of Korea.

PARK Sung Duk, b. 25 October 1951, South Korea. Registered Nurse. m. Wi Hwan Park, 1 son, 1 daughter. Education: Diploma, Kyung Pook National University School of Nursing, South Korea. Appointments: Jesse Brown Veterans Administration Medical Center. Honours: Merit Award, City of Chicago; Leadership Award, Korean Nurses Association of Midwest; Distinguished Service Award, Korean American Association of Chicago; Outstanding Award, Asian American Coalition; Commendation, Republic of Korea. Memberships: Korean Nurses Association of Midwest, USA; American Oncology Nursing Society.

PARK Tae Won, b. 27 February 1961, Goseong Kyungnam, Korea. Researcher. m. Namhee Kim, 1 son, 1 daughter. Education: PhD, Pusan National University, 1995. Appointments: Korean Army, 1985-86; Researcher, Agency for Defense Development (New Materials Development and Evaluation), 1987-; Researcher, High Cycle Fatigue Test for Ti-bAl-4V alloy, Air Force Research Laboratory, Daton, Ohio, USA, 2000-01. Publications: Identification of precipitates appearing in Al-Li-Cu-Zr alloy, 2006; A study on the fatigue properties of Sc added Al alloy, 2007; A study on the aging behavior of Al-Li-Cu-Zr alloy, 2007. Honours: Silver Medal, 1992; Copper Medal, 1999; Silver Medal, 2002. Memberships: Korean Welding Society; Korean Institute of Metals and Materials; Korean Society of Heat Treatment. Address: Chung-gu Narae Apt 109-304, Jeonmin-Dong, Youseong-gu, Daejeon 305-729, Korea. E-mail: parktw9@lycos.co.kr

PARK Yeoung-Geol, b. 29 September 1945, Gwang-Ju, South Korea. Professor; Doctor. m. In-Sook Kim, 1 son, 2 daughters. Education: Bachelor's degree, Chonnam National University Medical School, 1970; Master's degree, Chonnam National University Graduate School, 1980; Doctor's degree, Chonbuk National University Graduate School, 1985. Appointments: Intern, 1970-71, Resident, 1971-75, Chonnam National University Hospital; Full time Instructor, 1978-80, Assistant Professor, 1980-83, 1991-93, Associate Professor, 1993-98, Professor, 1998-, Department of Ophthalmology, Chonnam National University Medical School and Hospital; Director, Korean Strabisms & Pediatric Ophthalmology Society, 1998-2000; Director, Korean Ophthalmological Society,

2007-. Publications: 2 books: Current Concepts in Strabismus, 2004; Ophthalmology, 2006; 139 national and international papers; 160 international and domestic presentations. Honours: Best Poster Award, Asia Pacific Academy of Ophthalmology, 2006. Memberships: Korean Ophthalmological Society; American Academy of Ophthalmology; European Society of Cataract and Refractive Surgery. Address: Department of Ophthalmology, Chonnam National University Medical School and Hospital, 8 Hak-Dong, Dong-Gu, Gwangju, 501-757, South Korea. E-mail: ygpark@chonnam.ac.kr

PARK Yongsoo, b. 14 December 1960, Daegu, Korea. Professor. m. Chang In Suh, 2 sons. Education: MD, 1986, PhD, 1995, College of Medicine, Seoul National University. Appointments: Senior Research Scientist, Biomedical Research Center, Korean Institute of Science & Technology, 1994-95; Assistant Professor, Associate Professor, Professor, Hanyang University, College of Medicine, 1995-; Visiting Professor, Barbara Davis Center for Childhood Diabetes, University of Colorado Health Sciences Center, 1997-99. Publications: Numerous papers and articles in professional medical journals. Honours: Behringer Mannheim Award, American Diabetes Association, 1991; Eli Lilly Award, International Diabetes Federation, 1992; Korean Diabetes Association, Seol-won Award, 1999; Hanyang University Best Teacher's Award, 2002. Memberships: American Diabetes Association; International Diabetes Federation; Korean Diabetes Association. E-mail: parkys@hanyang.ac.kr

PARK Yonmook, b. 1 December 1972, Seoul, Republic of Korea. Senior Engineer. m. Younkyung Moon. Education: BS, 1995, MS, 1999, Control and Instrumentation Engineering, Korea University; PhD, Aerospace Engineering, Korea Advanced Institute of Science and Technology, 2004. Appointments: First Lieutenant, 3-Artillery Brigade, Republic of Korea, 1995-97; Education Assistant, Department of Control and Instrumentation Engineering, Korea University, 1997-99; Invited Speaker, 1st Matlab User Conference, Republic of Korea, 1999; Research Assistant, Division of Aerospace Engineering, Department of Mechanical Engineering, KAIST, 2000-03; Session Chair, 4th Asian Control Conference, Singapore, 2002; Senior Engineer, Satellite Technology Research Center, KAIST, 2003-04; Satellite Attitude Control Team Leader, Satellite Technology Research Center, KAIST, 2004; Invited Speaker, Sensor and Intelligent Control Laboratory, Department of Aerospace Engineering, Sejong University, Republic of Korea, 2004; Senior Engineer, 2004-, Project Leader, 2005, Project Leader, 2006-, Mechatronics & Manufacturing Technology Center, Samsung Electronics Co Ltd; Invited Speaker, Micro Thermal System Research Center, Seoul National University, 2005; Session Chair, 2007 IEEE International Conference on Mechatronics and Automation, China, 2007. Publications: Numerous articles in professional journals including: Optimal stabilization of Takagi-Sugeno fuzzy systems with application to spacecraft control, 2001; Robust and optimal attitude control law design for spacecraft with inertia uncertainties, 2002; Least squares based PID control of an electromagnetic suspension system, 2003; LMI-based design of optimal controllers for Takagi-Sugeno fuzzy systems, 2004; Design and analysis of optimal controller for fuzzy systems with input constraint, 2004; Robust and optimal attitude stabilization of spacecraft with external disturbances, 2005. Honours include: Korea University Staff Scholarship, 1991, 1992, 1993; Work-Study Scholarship, Korea University, 1992, 1993; Special Scholarship, Korea University, 1994; Welfare Scholarship, Korea University, 1994; 3-Artillery Brigade Commander Award, 1997; Education Assistant Scholarship,

Korea University, 1997, 1998, 1999; Silver Prize, 9th Annual Humantech Thesis Prize, Samsung Electronics Co Ltd, 2003; Best Conference Paper Award, 2007 IEEE International Conference on Mechatronics and Automation, China, 2007; Meritorious Service Award, Samsung Electronics Co Ltd, 2008. Memberships: Korean Institute of Electrical Engineers; Institute of Electrical and Electronics Engineers, USA; Institute of Control, Robotics and Systems, Republic of Korea; Korean Society for Aeronautical and Space Sciences. Address: Mechatronics and Manufacturing Technology Center, Samsung Electronics Co Ltd, 416 Maetan-3Dong, Yeongtong-Gu, Suwon-City, Gyeonggi-Do 443-742, Republic of Korea. E-mail: ym-park@kaist.ac.kr

PARK Young W, b. 21 February 1946, Kyung-Nam, South Korea. Professor. m. Eun Y Park, 2 sons. Education: BS, Kon Kuk University, 1973; MS, University of Minnesota, USA, 1976; PhD, Utah State University, 1981; MDiv, Houston Theological Seminary, 1989; DMin, Northern Baptist Theological Seminary, 1998. Appointments: Postdoctoral Research Associate, Utah State University, USA, 1981-82; Research Specialist, 1982-84, Associate Professor, 1984-97, Prairie View A&M University, Texas A&M System; Pastor, Bethany Korean Baptist Church, Houston, Texas, 1990-97; Professor, Fort Valley State University, Georgia, 1997-; Adjunct Professor, The University of Georgia, 2001-; Pastor, Warner Robins Korean Baptist Church, Georgia, 1999-. Publications: More than 58 scientific research papers in American and international refereed scientific journals; Editor, 3 books; More than 20 symposium papers; 25 book chapters; More than 150 abstract papers in proceedings of professional conferences. Honours include: Distinguished Faculty Award, Research Leader Award, Prairie View A&M University, 1985; 1st Place Scientist Paper Award, ARD Symposium, 1989, 1992; Member, Editorial Board, Small Ruminant Research Journal, 1990-; John W Blassingame Outstanding Scholar Award, Fort Valley State University, 2007; President, Sigma Xi, Prairie View A&M Chapter; Listed in numerous Who's Who and biographical publications. Memberships: Sigma Xi; Institute of Food Technologists; American Dairy Science Association; International Goat Association; Federation of American Societies for Experimental Biology; Southern Baptist Convention. Address: Agricultural Research Station, College of Agriculture, Home Economics and Allied Programs, Fort Valley State University, Fort Valley, GA 31030-4313, USA. E-mail: parky@fvsu.edu

PARKER Alan William (Sir), b. 14 February 1944, London, England. Film Director; Writer. m. Annie Inglis, 1966, divorced 1992, 3 sons, 1 daughter. Education: Owen's School, Islington, London. Appointments: Advertising Copywriter, 1965-67; TV Commercial Director, 1968-78; Writer, Screenplay, Melody, 1969; Chair, Director's Guild of Great Britain, 1982-; British Film Institute, 1998-; Member, British Screen Advisory Council, 1985-. Creative Works: Writer, Director: No Hard Feelings, 1972; Our Cissy, 1973; Footsteps, 1973; Bugsy Malone, 1975; Angel Heart, 1987; A Turnip Head's Guide to the British Cinema, 1989; Come See the Paradise, 1989; The Road to Wellville, 1994; Director: The Evacuees, 1974; Midnight Express, 1977; Fame, 1979; Shoot the Moon, 1981; The Wall, 1982; Birdy, 1984; Mississippi Burning, 1988; The Commitments, 1991; Evita, 1996; Angela's Ashes, 1998; The Life of David Gale, 2003. Publications: Bugsy Malone, 1976; Puddles in the Lane, 1977; Hares in the Gate, 1983; Making Movies, 1998. Honours include: BAFTA Michael Balcon Award for Outstanding Contribution to British Film; National Review Board, Best Director Award, 1988; Lifetime Achievement Award, Director's Guild of Great

Britain Lifetime Achievement Award; BAFTA Award, Best Director, 1991; CBE; Officier, Ordre des Arts et des Lettres, 2005. Address: c/o Creative Artists Agency, 9830 Wilshire Boulevard, Beverly Hills, CA 90212, USA.

PARKER Anthony Wayne, b. 3 February 1953, Little Rock, Arkansas, USA. m. Lisa Ann Laird, 3 sons. Education: BA, Magna Cum Laude, History, 1990, MA, American History, 1992, University of Georgia, Athens; PhD, Scottish/ American History, University of St Andrews, Scotland, 1996. Appointments: Teaching Fellow, 1996-98, Course Co-ordinator, Lecturer and Tutor, 1998-2007, Department of History and School of American Studies, Director, School of American Studies, 2000-07, Director, University of Transatlantic Student Exchange & Study Abroad Programmes, 2001-07, Associate Director of Administration and Undergraduate Programmes, Institute for Transatlantic, European and American Studies, 2003-07, University of Dundee; Consultant, Emigration Exhibit Project, New Museum of Scotland, Edinburgh, Scotland, 1998-99; Convenor, Scottish Confederation of University and Research Libraries, North American Studies Group, Scotland, 1999-2007; Editorial Board, Journal of Transatlantic Studies, Scotland; Co-Conference Secretary, Council Member, Economic and Social History Society of Scotland, Scotland; External Academic Reviewer, National Museums of Scotland, Museum of Scotland International, Edinburgh, 2001-02; Consultant, ETL Project, University of Edinburgh collaborating with Universities of Coventry and Durham, 2001-07; Consultant, National Library of Scotland Stakeholder Research and the new Draft Strategy for the National Libraries of Scotland, 2003-04; Consultant, Scottish Executive, USA Strategy 2010 Group, 2006-07. Publications: Book, Scottish Highlanders in Colonial Georgia: the Recruitment, Emigration and Settlement in Darien 1735-1748, 1997, reprinted 2002; Articles in professional journals; Various conference and seminar papers, and book reviews. Honours: Fellow, Higher Education Academy; Fellow, Institute of Contemporary Scotland; Fellow, Charles Warren Center for Studies in American History, Harvard University, International Seminar on the History of the Atlantic World, 1996; elected Phi Kappa Phi and National Honour Society, USA; Honoured by Scottish Government and presented to Queen Elizabeth II at Buckingham Palace, 2007. Memberships: British Association for American Studies; Centre for Enterprise Management, College of Internal Affiliates; Scottish Association for the Study of America; Institute for Learning and Teaching in Higher Education; Organisation of American Historians; Southern Historical Society; Eighteenth Century Scottish Studies Society; Transatlantic Studies Association; Scottish Trans-Atlantic Relations Project; Economic and Social History Society of Scotland. Address: ITEAS, The University of Dundee, Dundee, DD1 4HN, Scotland. E-mail: a.w.parker@dundee.ac.uk

PARKER James Mavin (Jim), b. 18 December 1934, Hartlepool, England. Composer. m. Pauline Ann, 3 daughters. Education: Guildhall School of Music. Career: Composer. Compositions include: A Londoner in New York, 10 brass; Light Fantastic, 10 brass and percussion; Mississippi Five, woodwind quintet; The Golden Section, 5 brass; Clarinet Concerto; Mexican Wildlife, 5 brass and percussion; Boulevard, woodwind quintet; Follow the Star, musical with Wally K Daly; Film and TV music includes: Mapp and Lucia; Wynne and Penkovsky; Good Behaviour; The Making of Modern London; Girl Shy (Harold Lloyd); The Blot; Wish Me Luck; Anything More Would be Greedy; House of Cards; Parnell and the Englishwoman; Soldier Soldier; The House of Elliott; Body and Soul; Goggle Eyes; The Play the King;

The Final Cut; Moll Flanders; Tom Jones; A Rather English Marriage; Lost for Words; Foyle's War; The Midsomer Murders. Honours: BAFTA Awards for Best TV Music for: To Play the King, 1993, Moll Flanders, 1997, Tom Jones, 1997, A Rather English Marriage, 1998; GSM Silver Medal, 1959; LRAM, 1959; Honorary GSM, 1985. Membership: BAFTA. Address: 16 Laurel Road, London SW13 0EE, England. E-mail: jimparker@fairads.co.uk

PARKER John Richard, b. Great Britain. Chartered Architect; Chartered Town Planner; Urban Designer. Education: Polytechnic of Central London and University College London; PhD, DipArch, DipTP; ARIBA; FRTPI; FRSA. Appointments: Job Architect, Department of Architecture and Civic Design, Schools Division, London County Council, 1961-64; Group Leader, Directorate of Development Services, London Borough of Lambeth, 1964-70; Head of Central Area Team, Department of Transportation and Development, Greater London Council, 1970-86; Consultant Planning Inspector, Department of the Environment, 1986-88; Founding Partner and Managing Director, Greater London Consultants Limited (and Partnership), 1986-96; Principal, John Parker Associates, 1996-; Consultant, Greater London Consultants, 1996-; Consultant, Council of Europe and Editor of Revised European Urban Charter, 2004-; Chairman, International Development Forum, 2000-04; Leader, RTPI International Development Network, 2004-; Trustee, Jubilee Walkway Trust, 2002-. Publications: Over 50 publications and public lectures, most recently: Character of Cities, 2002; Built Environment of Towns: Towards a Revised Urban Charter, 2002. Honours: 3 prize-winning entries in architectural competitions; Winston Churchill Fellow, 1967; RIBA Pearce Edwards Research Award, 1969; BALI Landscape Award, 1980; Edwin Williams Memorial Award, 1980; RICS/Times Conservation Award, 1985; British Council Anglo/ Soviet Exchange Award, 1989. Memberships: Associate, Royal Institute of British Architects; Fellow, Royal Town Planning Institute; Fellow, Royal Society of Arts. Address: 4, The Heights, Foxgrove Road, Beckenham, Kent BR3 5BY, England. E-mail: jpa@btinternet.com

PARKER Sarah Jessica, b. 25 March 1965, Nelsonville, Ohio, USA. Actress. m. Matthew Broderick, 1997, 1 son. Creative Works: Stage appearances include: The Innocents, 1976; The Sound of Music, 1977; Annie, 1978; The War Brides, 1981; The Death of a Miner, 1982; To Gillian on Her 37th Birthday, 1983-84; Terry Neal's Future, 1986; The Heidi Chronicles, 1989; How to Succeed in Business Without Really Trying, 1996; Once Upon a Mattress, 1996; Film appearances include: Rich Kids, 1979; Somewhere Tomorrow, 1983; Firstborn, 1984; Footloose, 1984; Girls Just Want to Have Fun, 1985; Flight of the Navigator, 1986; LA Story, 1991; Honeymoon in Vegas, 1992; Hocus Pocus, 1993; Striking Distance, 1993; Ed Wood, 1994; Miami Rhapsody, 1995; If Lucy Fell, 1996; Mars Attacks!, 1996; The First Wives Club, 1996; Extreme Measures, 1996; Til There Was You, 1997; A Life Apart: Hasidism in America, 1997; Isn't She Great, 1999; Dudley Do-Right, 1999; State and Main, 2000; Life Without Dick, 2002; Strangers with Candy, 2005; The Family Stone, 2005; Failure to Launch, 2006; Spinning Into Butter, 2007; Smart People, 2008. Numerous TV appearances include: Equal Justice, 1990-91; Sex and the City, 1998-2004. Honours: Golden Globe for Best Actress in a TV Series, 2001; Emmy, 2004. Address: Creative Artists Agency, 9830 Wilshire Boulevard, Beverly Hills, CA 90212, USA.

PARKES Roger Graham, b. 15 October 1933, Chingford, Essex, England. Novelist; Scriptwriter. m. Tessa Isabella McLean, 5 February 1964, 1 son, 1 daughter. Education: National Diploma of Agriculture. Appointments: Staff Writer, Farming Express and Scottish Daily Express, 1959-63; Editor, Farming Express, 1963; Staff Script Editor, Drama, BBC-TV, London, 1964-70. Publications: Death Mask, 1970; Line of Fire, 1971; The Guardians, 1973; The Dark Number, 1973; The Fourth Monkey, 1978; Alice Ray Morton's Cookham, 1981; Them and Us, 1985; Riot, 1986; Y-E-S, 1986; An Abuse of Justice, 1988; Troublemakers, 1990; Gamelord, 1991; The Wages of Sin, 1992. Contributions to: Daily Express; Sunday Express. Honour: Grand Prix de Littérature, Paris, 1974. Memberships: Writers Guild of Great Britain; Magistrates Association. Address: Cartlands Cottage, Kings Lane, Cookham Dean, Berkshire SL6 9AY, England.

PARKINSON, Baron of Carnforth in the County of Lancashire (Cecil Edward Parkinson), b. 1 September 1931. Politician. m. Ann Mary Jarvis, 1957, 3 daughters, 1 daughter by Sarah Keays. Education: Emmanuel College, Cambridge. Career: Manual trainee, Metal Box Co; Articled Clerk, 1956, Partner, 1961-71, West, Wake, Price & Co; Founder, 1967-, Chair, 1967-79, Director, 1967-79, 1984-, Parkinson Hart Securities Ltd; Director of several other companies, 1967-79; Branch Treasurer, Hemel Hempstead Conservative Association, 1961-64, Constituency Chair, 1965-66, Chair and ex-officio member all committees, 1966-69; Chair, Herts 100 Club, 1968-69; President, Hemel Hempstead Young Conservatives, 1968-71, Northampton Young Conservatives, 1969-71; Contested Northampton, General Election, 1970; MP for Enfield West, 1970-74, for Hertfordshire South, 1974-83, for Hertsmere, 1983-92; Secretary, Conservative Backbench Finance Committee, 1971-72; Parliamentary Private Secretary to Minister for Aerospace and Shipping, 1972-74; Assistant Government Whip, 1974; Opposition Whip, 1974-76; Opposition Spokesman on Trade, 1976-79; Minister of State for Trade, 1979-81; Paymaster General, 1981-83; Chair, Conservative Party, 1981-83, 1997-98; Secretary of State for Trade and Industry, 1983, for Energy, 1987-89, for Transport, 1989-90; Chair, Conservative Way Forward Group, 1991-; Chancellor of the Duchy of Lancaster, 1982-83; Leader, Institute of Directors, Parliamentary Panel, 1972-79; Secretary, Anglo-Swiss Parliamentary Group, 1972-79, Chair, 1979-82; Chair, Anglo-Polish Conservative Society, 1986-98; Chemical Dependency Centre Ltd, 1986-, Jarvis (Harpenden) Holdings, Usborne, 1991-, Midland Expressway Ltd, 1993-, Dartford River Crossing Ltd, 1993-; Director, Babcock International, 1984-87, Sports Aid Foundation, Save and Prosper, 1984-87, Tarmac, 1984-87; Sears PLC, 1984-87. Publication: An Autobiography: Right at the Centre, 1992. Address: House of Lords, London SW1A 0PW, England.

PARKINSON Michael, b. 28 March 1935, Yorkshire, England. TV Presenter; Writer. m. Mary Heneghan, 3 sons. Appointments: The Guardian, Daily Express, Sunday Times, Punch, Listener; Joined Granada TV Producer, Reporter, 1965; Executive Producer and Presenter, London Weekend TV, 1968; Presenter, Cinema, 1969-70, Tea Break, Where in the World, 1971; Hosted own chat show "Parkinson", BBC, 1972-82, 1998-2004, ITV, 2004-2007, "Parkinson One to One", Yorkshire TV, 1987-90; Presenter, Give Us a Clue, 1984-, All Star Secrets, 1985, Desert Island Discs, 1986-88, Parky, 1989, LBC Radio, 1990; Help Squad, 1991, Parkinson's Sunday Supplement, Radio 2, 1994, Daily Telegraph, 1991-; Going for a Song, 1997-; Parkinson's Choice, Radio 2, 1999-2004. Publications: Football Daft, 1968; Cricket Mad, 1969; Sporting Fever, 1974; George Best: An Intimate Biography, 1975; A-Z of Soccer, co-author, 1975; Bats in the Pavilion, 1977; The Woofits, 1980; Parkinson's Lore, 1981; The Best of Parkinson, 1982; Sporting Lives, 1992; Sporting Profiles, 1995; Michael Parkinson on Golf, 1999; Michael Parkinson on Football, 2001. Honours: Sports Feature Writer of the Year, British Sports Jounalism Awards, 1995, 1998; Yorkshire Man of the Year, 1998; BAFTA Award for Best Light Entertainment, 1999; Media Society Award for Distinguished Contribution to Media, 2000; CBE, 2000. Address: CSS Stellar Management Ltd, 1st Floor, Drury House, 34-43 Russell Street, London WC2B 5HA, England.

PARLIER Greg H, b. 10 May 1952, San Luis Obispo, California, USA. Retired Colonel, US Army; Senior Systems Analyst; Independent Consultant; Defense Analyst; Educator; Advisor to Foreign Governments. Education: BS, USMA, West Point, 1974; MS, Naval Postgraduate School, 1983; MA, Walsh School of Foreign Service, Georgetown, 1988; US Marine Corps Command and Staff College, 1989; National Defense Fellow, MIT, 1995; US Army War College, 1996; MIT Sloan Executive Series on Management, Innovation and Technology, 1997-2008; PhD, Wesleyan, 2004. Appointments: Battalion Commander, 5th Battalion (Avenger), 2nd Air Defense Artillery Regiment, 69th ADA Brigade, V Corps, USAREUR, 1992-94; Chief, Resource Plans and Analysis Division, Directorate of Program Analysis and Evaluation, Office of the Chief of Staff, Army, 1996-98; Director, Program Analysis and Evaluation, US Army Recruiting Command, 1998-2002; Director for Transformation and Principal Assistant Deputy Commander, US Army Aviation and Missile Command, 2002-03; Senior Research Scientist, University of Alabama, Huntsville, 2003-05; Adjunct Research Staff, Institute for Defense Analyses, 2003-; Senior Systems Analyst, SAIC, 2005-. Publications: One text and numerous articles in professional journals. Honours: Legion of Merit (3); Bronze Star; Meritorious Service Medal (7); Army Commendation Medal (3); Plaque of Appreciation: Korean National Assembly; German Efficiency Badge in Gold (2nd Award); Honorary Commander, Flugabwehrkanonregiment 8, 1st German Mountain Division; Canadian Parachutist Badge; MORS Graduate Research Award, 1983; Finalist, ORSA Koopman Prize, 1985, 1987; DA Operations Research Analyst of the Year, 1987; US Navy League Cates Award for Superior Research, 1989; Finalist, DA Payne Memorial Award for Excellence in Analysis, 1997, 2001; Finalist, MORS Rist Prize, 1998, 2002; Finalist, INFORMS Edelman Award, 2001; Edelman Laureate, INFORMS, 2006. Memberships: California Scholarship Federation; 82nd Airborne Division Association; Air Defense Artillery Association; Association of the US Army; American Legion; Military Operations Research Society; many others. Address: 255 Avian Ln, Madison, AL 35758, USA. E-mail: gparlier@knology.net

PAROLARI Manoel Carlos de Figueiredo Ferraz, b. 19 November 1946, Sao Paulo, SP, Brazil. Consultant. Divorced, 1 son, 1 daughter. Education: Mechanical Engineer, ITA Instituto Tecnológico da Aeronáutica; Physics, self-taught. Appointments: Author; Independent Researcher. Publications: Articles in professional journals and on the Internet. Honours: Marina Cintra, 1961, 1962; São Luís, 1965; Rhodosá Prize for best mechanical engineer designer, 1971. Memberships: New York Academy of Sciences; American Association for the Advancement of Science; American Chemical Society. E-mail: mcparolari@uol.com.br Website: www.parolari.eng.br

PARR John Brian, b. 18 March 1941, Epsom, England. University Researcher. m. Pamela Harkins, 2 daughters. Education: BSc (Econ), University College London, University of London, 1959-62; PhD, University of Washington, Seattle, USA, 1962-67. Appointments: Assistant Professor of Regional Science, 1967-72, Associate Professor of Regional Science, 1972-75, University of Pennsylvania, USA; Lecturer, Senior Lecturer in Urban Economics, 1975-80, Reader in Applied Economics, 1980-89, Professor of Regional and Urban Economics, 1989-, University of Glasgow. Publications include: Regional Policy: Past Experience and New Directions (co-edited book), 1979; Market Centers and Retail Location: Theory and Applications (co-authored book), 1988; Numerous refereed articles in professional journals include: Outmigration and the depressed area problem, 1966; Models of city size in the urban system, 1970; Models of the central place system: a more general approach, 1978; A note on the size distributions of cities over time, 1985; The economic law of market areas: a further discussion, 1995; Regional economic development: an export-stages framework, 1999; Missing elements in the analysis of agglomeration economies, 2002. Honours: Guest, Polish Academy of Sciences, Warsaw, Poland, 1977; Speaker, August Lösch Commemoration, Heidenheim an der Brenz, Germany, 1978; Speaker at the Ehrenpromotion (award of honorary doctorate) of Professor Dr Martin Beckmann, University of Karlsruhe, Germany, 1981; Participant in Distinguished Visitors Program, University of Pennsylvania, Philadelphia, 1983; Academician, Academy of Learned Societies for the Social Sciences, 2000; Moss Madden Memorial Medal, 2003; Elected Fellow, Regional Science Association International, 2006. Memberships: Royal Economic Society; Regional Science Association International and British and Irish Section; Regional Studies Association; Member of various editorial boards of scientific journals. Address: Department of Urban Studies, University of Glasgow, Glasgow G12 8QQ, United Kingdom.

PARR Robert G, b. 22 September 1921, Chicago, Illinois, USA. Professor. m. Jane Bolstad, 1 son, 2 daughters. Education: AB, magna cum laude, Brown University, 1942; PhD, Physical Chemistry, University of Minnesota, 1947; Dhc, University of Leuven, 1986; Jagiellonian University, 1996. Appointments include: Assistant Professor, Chemistry, University of Minnesota, 1947-48; Assistant Professor, Professor, Chemistry, Carnegie Institute of Technology, 1948-62; Visiting Professor, Chemistry, Member, Center of Advanced Study, University of Illinois, 1962; Professor of Chemistry, Johns Hopkins University, 1962-74; Chairman, Department of Chemistry, 1969-72; William R Kenan Junior Professor of Theoretical Chemistry, University of North Carolina; Wassily Hoeffding Professor of Chemical Physics, 1990-. Publications: Over 200 scientific articles, 2 books. Honour: Langmuir Award, American Chemical Society; Award in Chemical Sciences, National Academy of Sciences. Memberships include: International Academy of Quantum Molecular Science; National Academy of Sciences; American Academy of Arts and Sciences; Indian National Science Academy. Address: Chemistry Department, University of North Carolina, Chapel Hill, NC 27599, USA.

PARRINDER (John) Patrick, b. 11 October 1944, Wadebridge, Cornwall, England. Professor of English; Literary Critic. 2 daughters. Education: Christ's College, 1962-65, Darwin College, 1965-67, Cambridge; MA, PhD, Cambridge University. Appointments: Fellow, King's College, Cambridge, 1967-74; Lecturer, 1974-80, Reader, 1980-86, Professor of English, 1986-, University of Reading. Publications: H G Wells, 1970; Authors and Authority, 1977, 2nd edition, enlarged, 1991; Science Fiction: Its Criticism and Teaching, 1980; James Joyce, 1984; The Failure of Theory, 1987; Shadows of the Future, 1995. Editor: H G Wells: The Critical Heritage, 1972; Science Fiction: A Critical Guide, 1979; Learning from Other Worlds, 2000; Nation and

Novel, 2006. Contributions to: London Review of Books; Many academic journals. Honour: President's Award, World Science Fiction, 1987; Fellow, English Association, 2001. Memberships: H G Wells Society; Science Fiction Foundation; Society of Authors. Address: School of English and American Literature, University of Reading, PO Box 218, Reading, Berkshire RG6 6AA, England.

PARRIS Matthew, b. 7 August 1949, Johannesburg, South Africa. Writer; Broadcaster. Education: Clare College, Cambridge; Yale University. Career: FOC, 1974-76; With Conservative Research Department, 1976-79; MP (Conservative) for West Derbyshire, 1979-86; Presenter, Weekend World, 1986-88; Parliamentary Sketch Writer for The Times, 1988-2001; Columnist, for The Times, 1988-, for The Spectator, 1992; Member, Broadcasting Standards Council, 1992-97. Publications: Chance Witness (memoir), 2001; Various books about travel, politics, insult, abuse and scandal. Honours: Various awards for writing and journalism. Address: c/o The Times, Pennington Street, London E1 9XN, England.

PARROTT Andrew Haden, b. 10 March 1947, Walsall, England. Conductor; Scholar. m. Emily Van Evera, 1 daughter. Education: Open Postmastership, BA, Merton College, Oxford, 1966-71. Appointments: Founder and Director, Taverner Choir, Consort and Players, 1973-; Music Director and Principal Conductor, London Mozart Players, 2000-06; Music Director, New York Collegium, 2002-. Publications: Numerous recordings; Articles include those on Monteverdi, Purcell, Bach in scholarly journals; The New Oxford Book of Carols (co-editor); The Essential Bach Choir, 2000, German edition, 2003. Honours: Honorary Research Fellow, Royal Holloway, University of London, 1995-; Honorary Senior Research Fellow, University of Birmingham, 2000-. Address: c/o Allied Artists, 42 Montpelier Square, London SW7 1JZ, England. E-mail: name@alliedartists.co.uk

PARSONS Susie, b. 29 April 1950, Cuckfield, Sussex, England. Managing Director. Partner, Dave Perry, 1 son. Education: BA (Hons) in French Studies, University of Lancaster, 1972; Post-graduate Certificate in Education, King's College, University of London, 1973. Appointments: Teacher, London Borough of Brent, 1973-74; Education Officer, then Director of Community Education, Shelter, 1974-77; Housing Projects Officer, North Kensington Law Centre, 1977-81; Secretary to Paddington and North Kensington Community Health Council, 1981-84; General Manager, London Energy and Employment Network, 1984-87; Head of Press, Publicity and Information, London Borough of Hackney, 1987-94; Executive Director, then Chief Executive, London Lighthouse, 1994-98; Chief Executive, Commission for Racial Equality, 1999-2001; Independent Management Consultant, 2001-02; Chief Executive, Campaign for Learning, 2002-05; Managing Director, Susie Parsons Management Solutions Ltd, 2005-. Publications: School and Community in the Inner City, 1977; Workout, 1979; London Energy Action Plan, 1986; Good Practice Guide to District Heating, 1988; Taking the Lead, 1992; The Right Side of the Law, 1993; 50/50 – Equality for Women Managers by the Year 2000, 1995; Learning to Learn in Schools, 2003; Give Your Child a Better Chance, 2003; Promoting Diversity in the Workplace, 2004; QCA Futures Programme, 2005; Learning to Learn in Schools, 2005; Learning to Learn for Life, 2005; Reinventing Education, 2005; Numerous magazine articles on health, social care, quality, equality and lifelong learning. Memberships: Kensington & Chelsea Tenant Management Organisation; Golborne Forum; Fellow, Royal Society of Arts. Address: 171 Oxford Gardens, London W10 6NE, England. E-mail: susie@spms.org.uk

PARTINGTON Brian Harold, b. 31 December 1936, Manchester, England. Clergyman. m. Valerie, 2 sons, 1 daughter. Education: St Aidan's Theological College, Birkenhead. Appointments: Curate, Emmanuel, Didsbury, 1963-66, Curate, St Mary's, Deane, 1966-68, Diocese of Manchester; Vicar of Kirk Patrick, 1968-96, Bishop's Youth Officer, 1968-77, Vicar of St Paul's, Foxdale, 1976-96, Vicar of St John's, 1977-96, Rural Dean of Peel, 1976-96, Canon of St Patrick St German's Cathedral, 1985-96, Vicar of St George's, Douglas, 1996-2004, Archdeacon of the Isle of Man, 1996-2005, Diocese of Sodor and Man; Post Office Board, 2006. Honour: OBE, 2002; Memberships: Executive Chairman, Isle of Man Sports Council; Chairman, 1988-96, Vice-President, 1996-, Hospice Care; President, Isle of Man Hockey Association, 1997-2007; President, Isle of Man Cricket Association, 1996-2006; Vice-Chairman, 2001-2005, Chairman, 2005-, International Island Games Association, 2005-; Vice-Captain, 2005, Captain, 2006, Peel Golf Club, Douglas Rotary Club; Royal Commonwealth Society; Ecclesiastical Law Society. Address: Brambles, Patrick Village, Isle of Man, IM5 3AN. E-mail: bpartington@mcb.net

PARTON Dolly Rebecca, b. 19 January 1946, Sevier County, Tennessee, USA. Singer; Composer. m. Carl Dean, 1966. Creative Works: Films include: Nine to Five, 1980; The Best Little Whorehouse in Texas, 1982; Rhinestone, 1984; Steel Magnolias, 1989; Straight Talk, 1991; The Beverly Hillbillies; Frank McKlusky, C.I., 2002; Miss Congeniality 2: Armed and Fabulous, 2005; Albums include: Here You Come Again, 1978; Real Love, 1985; Just the Way I Am, 1986; Heartbreaker, 1988; Great Balls of Fire, 1988; Rainbow, 1988; White Limozeen, 1989; Home for Christmas, 1990; Eagle When She Flies, 1991; Slow Dancing with the Moon, 1993; Honky Tonk Angels, 1994; The Essential Dolly Parton, 1995; Just the Way I Am, 1996; Super Hits, 1996; I Will Always Love You and Other Greatest Hits, 1996; Hungary Again, 1998; Grass is Blue, 1999; Best of the Best –Porter 2 Doll, 1999; Halos and Horns, 2002; Just Because I'm a Woman: Songs of Dolly Parton, 2003; For God and Country, 2003; Live and Well, 2004; Those Were The Days, 2005; Backwoods Barbie, 2008. Composed numerous songs including: Nine to Five. Publication: Dolly: My Life and Other Unfinished Business, 1994. Honours include: Vocal Group of the Year Award (with Porter Wagoner), 1968; Vocal Duo of the Year, All Music Association, 1970, 1971; Nashville Metronome Award, 1979; Female Vocalist of the Year, 1975, 1976; Country Star of the Year, 1978; Peoples Choice, 1980; Female Vocalist of the Year, Academy of Country Music, 1980; East Tennessee Hall of Fame, 1988. Address: RCA, 6 West 57th Street, New York, NY 10019, USA.

PARTRIDGE Derek William, b. 15 May 1931. London, England. Retired Diplomat. Appointments: HM Diplomatic Service: Foreign Office, London, England, 1951-54, Oslo, 1954-56, Jedda, 1956, Khartoum, 1957-60, Sofia, 1960-62, Manila, 1962-65, Djakarta, 1965-67, FCO, 1967-72, Brisbane, 1972-74, Colombo, 1974-77; Head, Migration and Visa Department, FCO, 1981-83; Head, Nationality and Treaty Department, FCO, 1983-86; British High Commissioner, Freetown, Sierra Leone, 1986-91; Liberal Democrat Councillor, London Borough of Southwark, 1994-2002. Honours: CMG, 1987. Memberships: National Liberal Club; Royal African Society. Address: 16 Wolfe Crescent, Rotherhithe, London SE16 6SF, England.

PASCOE Jane, b. 9 May 1955, Bristol, England. Artist. 1 son. Education: Foundation Course, Art and Design, 1973-74, BA Hons, Fine Art, 1st Class, 1977, Bristol Polytechnic Faculty of Art and Design; Art Teacher's Certificate, Brighton Polytechnic School of Art Education, 1977-78. Appointments: Art Teacher, Highbury School, Salisbury, 1979-84; Art Teacher, Blandford Upper School, 1984-86; Head of Art, Bournemouth School for Girls, 1986-88; Head of Art, Kingdown School, Warminster, 1988-89; Head of Art, The Atherley School, Southampton, 1989-2006; Head of Art, Hampshire Collegiate School, Romsey, 2006-. Work exhibited in: Royal West of England Academy of Art; The Festival Gallery; The Victoria Gallery; Beaux Arts Gallery, Bath; Wessex Artists Exhibition, Salisbury; The Eye Gallery, Bristol; The Manor House Gallery, Cheltenham; Parkin Fine Art, London; The Mall Gallery, London; Work also included in numerous private collections including The Cheltenham and Gloucester Building Society and the Public Collection of the RWA, Bristol. Honour: Listed in several Who's Who and biographical publications. Memberships: Associate Member, 1983, Full Member, 1987, Royal West of England Academy of Art. Address: Honeysuckle Cottage, Charmus Road, Old Calmore, Southampton, Hampshire SO40 2RG, England.

PASQUINI Massimo, b. 20 July 1973, Rome, Italy. Psychiatrist. Education: School of Medicine, 1992-98, Resident, Psychiatry, 1998-2002, Sapienza University, Rome; Training in Psychopharmacology, 2000-01; Training in Cognitive Psychotherapy, APC School, 2001-02; American-Italian Cancer Foundation Fellowship, 2003-07. Appointments: Delegate, Maudsley Core Forum for European Psychiatrists; Psychiatrist, Inpatient Clinic S'Alessandro, Rome, 2002-05; Consultant Psychiatrist, Oncology Division of San Camillo Forcalini Hospital, Rome, 2003-05; Psychiatrist, Department of Psychiatry, Division of Emergency Psychiatry, 2006-, Head, Outpatients Clinic of Psychopharmacology in Oncology, 2007, Research Associate, OCD Study Program, 2007, Sapienza University, Rome. Publications: Numerous articles in professional journals. Honours: Award, Italian Society of Psychopathology, 2005. Memberships: Association of European Psychiatrists; Societá Italiana di Psicopatologia; Societá Italiana di Psichiatria; Societá Italiana di Psicooncologia. Address: Department of Psychiatry, Sapienza University of Rome, Viale Dellá Universitá 30, 00135 Rome, Italy. E-mail: massimo.pasquini@uniroma1.it

PATEL Mukesh Thakorbhai, b. 19 June 1969, London, England. Group Quality Assurance Manager; EU Qualified Person. m. Jayana, 1 son, 1 daughter. Education: BSc (Hons) Chemistry, University of Leeds, 1989-92; MCIPS, Chartered Institute of Purchasing & Supply, 2006; CChem MRSC Chartered Chemist, Royal Society of Chemistry, 2003; Graduate, Dale Carnegie Management Programme, 2001; QP Training, David Beg Associates, 2002-05; Qualified Person under permanent provisions of Directive 2001/83EC, 2006; Completed BSI Lead Auditor course, 2006. Appointments: R&D Chemist, 1992-94, Chemicals Buyer, 1994-97, A H Marks & Co Ltd, Bradford; Commercial Buyer, 1997-2001, Pharmaceutical Regulatory Affairs Manager, 2001-02, Pharmaceutical Quality Manager & EU Qualified Person, 2002-05, Masterfoods Complementary Petcare (A division of Mars Inc), Birstall; Pharmaceutical Compliance Manager, InTouch PharmaMed, Cleckheaton, 2006-07; Group Quality Assurance Manager, Matthews InTouch, Cleckheaton, 2007-. Publications: Research in the field of organophosphorus chemistry. Memberships: Royal Society of Chemistry;

Chartered Institute of Purchasing & Supply; Pharmaceutical Quality Group. Address: 2 New Bank Street, Morley, Leeds, LS27 8NA, England. E-mail: patelmukesh69@yahoo.co.uk

PATERSON Howard Cecil, b. 16 March 1920, Edinburgh, Scotland. Retired. Widower, 1 son. Education: Daniel Stewart's College, Edinburgh, 1925-36; Edinburgh College of Art, 1937-39. Appointments: Army Service, Royal Artillery, 1939-45; Personnel Section Officer, 1945-49; TA, 1949-70; Retired as Lieutenant Colonel, 1970; Assistant Personnel Manager, Jute Industries Ltd, 1949-51; Deputy Director, Scottish Country Industries Development Trust, 1951-66; Senior Director, Scottish Tourist Board, 1966-81; Independent Tourism Consultant, Tourism Advisory Services, 1981-2000; Chairman, Taste of Scotland Scheme, 1984-86; Chairman, Scottish International Gathering Trust, 1981-91; Vice-Chairman, 1982-89, Chairman, 1989-90, Scottish Aircraft Collection Trust; Vice-Chairman, John Buchan Society, 1990-95; Chairman, 1990-2003, Honorary Life President, 2003-, Trekking and Riding Society of Scotland. Publications: Tourism in Scotland, 1969; The Flavour of Edinburgh, 1986. Honours: Territorial Decoration (TD) with two clasps; Front Line Britain Medal; Polish Medal, Custodian of Places of National Remembrance. Memberships: Royal Scots Club, Edinburgh; Scottish Reserve Forces and Cadets Association; Royal Artillery Association; Royal Artillery Institution; Founder Member, Firepower; Royal Artillery Museum, Woolwich; City of Edinburgh Artillery Officers Association; 52 Lowland Division Officers Club; Reserve Forces Association; Friend of Historic Scotland; Life Fellow, Royal Society for the Protection of Birds; Fellow, Society of Antiquaries in Scotland; Life Member, National Trust for Scotland; Friend, National Botanic Gardens of Scotland; Art Fund; Friend of the National Galleries of Scotland; Member, Scottish Borders Music and Arts Guild; The Scottish Rural Property and Business Association; Countryside Alliance; British Association for Shooting and Conservation; Scottish Association of Country Sports; World Wildlife Fund; Country Club UK; West Linton Historical Association; West Linton Music Society. Address: Dovewood, Carlops Road, West Linton, Peeblesshire EH46 7DS, Scotland.

PATTARATHAMMAS Vibul, b. 24 April 1932, Bangkok, Thailand. Businessman. m. Amara, 1 son, 1 daughter. Education: Honorary PhD, Business Administration, Christian University, Thailand, 2005. Appointments: President, St Joseph Convent's Parents and Teachers Association, 1975-82; Chairman, The Foundation of Sapan Luang Church, 1975-88; Moderator, District 7, Church of Christ in Thailand, 1975-96; President, Bangkok Christian College's Parents and Teachers Association, 1976-81; President, Franco-Thai Chamber of Commerce, 1977; Moderator, Sapan Luang Church, Bangkok, 1977-81; Chairman, Christham Vithaya School, 1977-81; Chairman, Christham Sueksa School, 1977-81; Moderator, Board of Elders, Sapan Luang Church, 1977-84, 1993-94; Moderator, Church of Christ in Thailand, 1979-82; Chairman, The Foundation of Church of Christ in Thailand, 1979-82; Chairman, The Foundation of Lutheran Church in Thailand, 1979-97; Member, Central Committee of World Council of Churches, 1980-82; Vice Chairman, Christian Mission in Asia, 1980-82; Founder & First Chairman, Board of Directors, Christian College, Bangkok, 1983-86; Chairman, Board of Directors, Bangkok Christian Hospital, 1983-86; Chairman, Board of Directors, Bangkok Institute of Theology, 1983-98; Vice President, Thai Korean Chamber of Commerce, 1987-90; Chairman, The Foundation of Seven Lights, 1987-2000; Founding President, Thai Belgian Luxembourg Business Club, 1990-92; Founding President, Belgian-Luxembourg/

Thai Chamber of Commerce, 1993-99; Vice Chairman, Board of Trade of Thailand, 1994-98. Honours: Chevalier L'Ordre du Merite, France, 1979; Companion of the Most Exalted Order of White Elephant, Thailand, 1982; Thai Red Cross Second Level, 1984; Insignia of Officer of Order of Leopold II of Belgium, 1986; Insignia of Officer of the Order of the Crown of Belgium, 1999. Memberships: Chairman, Organising Committee of the First National Skill Contest & Career Exhibition, Thailand, 1970; President, Rotary Club of Bangkok South, 1972-73; Rotary District Governor's Group Representative, 1973-74, 1976-77; Chairman, Rotary Group Studies Exchange Subcommittee Rotary District 330, 1977-78. Address: 83-85 Soi Anumanrajdhon Off Decho Road, Bangkok 10500, Thailand.

PATTEN Brian, b. 7 February 1946, Liverpool, England. Poet; Writer. Appointment: Regents Lecturer, University of California at San Diego. Publications: Poetry: The Mersey Sound: Penguin Modern Poets 10, 1967; Little Johnny's Confession, 1967; The Home Coming, 1969; Notes to the Hurrying Man: Poems, Winter '66-Summer '68, 1969; The Irrelevant Song, 1970; At Four O'Clock in the Morning, 1971; Walking Out: The Early Poems of Brian Patten, 1971; The Eminent Professors and the Nature of Poetry as Enacted Out by Members of the Poetry Seminar One Rainy Evening, 1972; The Unreliable Nightingale, 1973; Vanishing Trick, 1976; Grave Gossip, 1979; Love Poems, 1981; New Volume, 1983; Storm Damage, 1988; Grinning Jack: Selected Poems, 1990; Armada, 1996; The Utterly Brilliant Book of Poetry (editor), 1998. Editor: Clare's Countryside: A Book of John Clare, 1981; The Puffin Book of 20th Century Children's Verse, 1996; The Story Giant, 2001. Children's Books: Prose: The Jumping Mouse, 1972; Mr Moon's Last Case, 1975; Emma's Doll, 1976; Jimmy Tag-along, 1988; Grizzelda Frizzle, 1992; Impossible Parents, 1994; Beowulf, a version, 1999. Poetry: Gargling With Jelly, 1985; Thawing Frozen Frogs, 1990; The Magic Bicycle, 1993; The Utter Nutters, 1994; The Blue and Green Ark, 1999; Juggling with Gerbils, 2000; Little Hotchpotch, 2000; Impossible Parents Go Green; The Monsters Guide to Choosing a Pet (with Roger McGough), 2004. Contributions to: Journals and newspapers. Honour: Special Award, Mystery Writers of America, 1977; Arts Council of England, Writers Award, 1998; Freedom of the City of Liverpool, 2000; The Cholmondeley Award for Poetry, 2001; Honorary Fellow, John Moores University, 2002; Fellow, RSL. Membership: Chelsea Arts Club. Address: c/o Rogers, Coleridge and White, 20 Powis Mews, London W11 1JN, England.

PATTERSON Most Hon Percival Noel James, b. 10 April 1935, Dias Hanover, Jamaica. Politician; Lawyer. 1 son, 1 daughter. Education: BA, English, University of West Indies, 1958; BLL, London School of Economics, 1963. Appointments: Joined People's National Party, 1958; Party Organiser, People's National Party, 1958; Vice President, People's National Party, 1969; Minister of Industry, Trade and Tourism, 1972; Deputy Prime Minister and Minister of Foreign Affairs and Foreign Trade, 1978-80; Chairman, People's National Party, 1983; Deputy Prime Minister and Minister of Development, Planning and Production, 1989-90; Deputy Prime Minister and Minister of Finance and Planning, 1990-99; President and Party Leader, People's National Party, 1992; Prime Minister, 1992-96. Honours: Sir Hughes Parry Prize for excellence in the Law of Contract; Leverhulme Scholarship, London School of Economics; Appointed to Privy Council of the United Kingdom, 1992; Honorary Doctor of Letters, Northeastern University, 1994; Honorary Degree of Doctor of Laws, Brown University, 1998; Numerous foreign awards include: Order of Jose Marti, Cuba, 1997; Order of

the Volta, Ghana, 1999; Food and Agriculture Organisation Agricola Medal, Jamaica, 2001; Juan Mora Fernandez Great Silver Cross, Costa Rica, 2001. Address: Office of the Prime Minister, 1 Devon Road, Kingston 6, Jamaica. E-mail: jamhouse@cwjamaica.com

PAUL Jeremy, b. 29 July 1939, Bexhill, Sussex, England. Writer. m. Patricia Garwood, 26 November 1960, 4 daughters. Education: King's, Canterbury and St Edmund Hall, Oxford. Publications: Numerous TV plays, series and adaptations, 1960-, including: Upstairs, Downstairs, 1971-75; Country Matters, 1972; The Duchess of Duke Street, 1976; Danger, UXB, 1977; A Walk in the Forest, 1980; The Flipside of Dominick Hide (with Alan Gibson), 1980; Sorrell and Son, 1983; The Adventures, Return and Memoirs of Sherlock Holmes, 1984-94; Lovejoy, 1991-94; Hetty Wainthropp Investigates, 1996-98; Midsomer Murders, 2001. Theatre: David Going Out, 1971; Manoeuvres, 1971; Visitors (with Carey Harrison), 1980; The Secret of Sherlock Holmes, 1988; The Watcher, 1989. Film: Countess Dracula, 1970. Theatre: Dead Easy, 2006; Book, Sing Willow , 2003. Membership: Writers Guild of Great Britain. Address: c/o Eben Foggitt Associates. E-mail: eben.foggitt@btinternet.com. Website: www.jeremypaul.org.uk

PAVLICHENKOV Igor Mikhailovitch, b. 4 December 1934, Reutov City, Moscow Region, Russia. Physicist; Theoretician. m. Olga Yavorskaya, 11 November 1972, 1 son. Education: Physics, Moscow University, 1958; Candidate of Physics, JINR, Dubna, 1964; DPhys, Kurchatov Institute, 1982. Appointments: Junior Researcher, 1958-83, Senior Researcher, 1983-87, Leading Researcher, 1987-93, Principal Researcher, 1993-, Kurchatov Institute. Publications: Several research papers in professional journals. Honours: I V Kurchatov Annual Prize, 1988, 1994. Memberships: Russian Nuclear Research Programme Committee, Moscow, 1986-90; Several scientific boards. Address: Russian Research Centre, Kurchatov Institute, 123182 Moscow, Russia.

PAXMAN Jeremy Dickson, b. 11 May 1950, Leeds, England. Journalist; Author. Education: St Catherine's College, Cambridge. Appointments: Journalist, Northern Ireland, 1973-77; Reporter, BBC TV Tonight and Panorama Programmes, 1977-85; Presenter, BBC TV Breakfast Time, 1986-89, Newsnight, 1989-, University Challenge, 1994-, Start the Week, Radio 4, 1998-2002. Publications: A Higher Form of Killing (co-author), 1982; Through the Volcanoes, 1985; Friends in High Places, 1990; Fish, Fishing and the Meaning of Life, 1994; The Compleat Angler, 1996; The English, 1998; The Political Animal, 2002; Numerous articles in newspapers and magazines. Honours include: Royal TV Society Award, International Reporting; Richard Dimbleby Award, BAFTA, 1996, 2000; Interview of the Year, Royal TV Society, 1997, 1998; Voice of the Viewer and Listener Presenter of the Year, 1994, 1997; Dr h c, Leeds, Bradford, 1999; Variety Club Media Personality of the Year, 1999; Fellow, St Edmund Hall, Oxford, St Catharine's College, Cambridge, 2001. Address: c/o BBC TV, London W12 7RJ, England.

PAYMASTER Nalin Jagmohandas, b. 13 April 1933, Bombay, India. Consultant Anaesthetist. m. Marjorie Elaine, 1 son, 1 daughter. Education: MBBS, Seth G S Medical College, University of Bombay; DA, KEM Hospital, University of Bombay; DA, University of London; FRCA, Royal College of Anaesthetists; ECFMG Certification, USA. Appointments: Resident Physician, St Georges Hospital, Bombay, 1955-56; House Physician, 1956-57, Resident Anaesthetist, 1957-59, KEM Hospital, Bombay; Senior House Officer in

Anaesthesia, United Liverpool Hospitals, England, 1959-60; Anaesthetic Registrar, Liverpool Regional Hospital Board, England, 1960-61; Senior Anaesthetic Registrar, Newcastle Regional Hospital Board, England, 1961-62; Fellow in Anaesthesiology, University of Pennsylvania, Philadelphia, USA, 1962-63; Fellow in Anaesthesiology, University of Washington, Seattle, 1963-64; CSIR Scientists Pool Officer, KEM Hospital, Bombay, India, 1964-65; Consultant Anaesthetist, Mersey Regional Health Authority, England, 1965-94; Consultant Anaesthetist, Wirral and West Cheshire Community NHS Trust, 1994-2001. Publications: Author of articles on: anaesthetic equipment, induction of anaesthesia in children, muscle relaxants in anaesthesia, dental anaesthesia, induced hypotension in anaesthesia, local anaesthetic toxicity, pre-medication, intravenous nutrition, post-operative pain, magnesium metabolism, intracellular pH; Numerous papers presented at national and international medical conferences. Honours: Past Chairman Division of Anaesthesia, Past Chairman, Theatre Users Committee, Clatterbridge Hospital, Wirral; Past Member of Scientific and Medical Committees, Clatterbridge Hospital and Arbowe Park Hospital, Wirral; Past Member, Medical School chess, cricket, table tennis and swimming teams; Winner, Sunday Times Chess Competition; Listed in biographical dictionaries. Memberships: The Debrett Society; Birkenhead Medical Society; Gayton Probus Club; Heswall Duplicate Bridge Club; Wirral Duplicate Bridge Club; Pensby Chess Club. Address: The Close, Chantry Walk, Lower Heswall, Wirral, Merseyside, CH60 8PX, England. E-mail: nalin_paymaster@hotmail.com

PAYNE Margaret Allison, b. 14 April 1937, Southampton, England. Artist; Educationalist. Education: NDD, Painting, Etching, Relief Printmaking, Harrow School of Art, 1955-59; ATC, Goldsmith's College, London University, 1959-60; BA (Hons), History of Art, Birkbeck College, London University, 1977-81; MA, Institute of Education, London University, 1981-83. Appointments: Art Teacher: Haggerston School, London, 1960-61; Harrow Art School, 1961-62, St Hilda's School, Bushey, 1965-68, Sarum Hall School, 1995-97; Senior Lecturer, University of Surrey, Roehampton, 1968-94; Exhibitions include: Annually with the Royal Society of Painter-Printmakers, 1962-90; Royal Academy Summer Exhibition: 1958, 1959, 1960, 1961, 1973, 1977; Young Contemporaries, 1960-61; Paris Salon, 1962-63; Norwich Art Gallery, 1964; Harrogate Art Gallery, 1977; Cardiff Art Gallery, 1978, 1979; Arts Club, London, 1987; Dickens Gallery, Bloxham, 1990; Many Educational Displays include: Art and Appreciation in a Multicultural Nursery School, 1989; Eastwood Nursery School at the Tate, 1989; Works in Sheffield City Art Gallery; Nottinghamshire and Sheffield Pictures for Schools. Publications: Articles in journals include: Under Fives at the Tate, 1989; Teaching Art Appreciation, 1990; Games Children Play, 1993; Froebelian Principles and the Art National Curriculum, 1993; What's in a Picture, 1994; Take Another Look, 1995. Membership: Fellow, Royal Society of Painter Etchers. Address: 11A Wallorton Gardens, East Sheen, London SW14 8DX, England.

PEACOCK Sylvia Elizabeth (Korupp), b. 25 September 1968, York, Pennsylvania, USA (US and German citizen). Assistant Professor; Teacher. Education: Diploma in Sociology, Faculty of Sociology, University of Bremen, Germany, 1995; PhD, Faculty of Social Sciences, Utrecht University, The Netherlands, 2000. Appointments: Research Fellow, Graduate School, Interuniversity Centre for Social Science Theory and Methodology, Utrecht University, 1995-2000; Assistant Professor, Erfurt University, Institute for Empirical Social Research, 2000-; Freelance Teacher,

Survey Methods for the Cultural and Social Sciences, Open University, Hagen, 2005-. Publications: Numerous peer reviewed papers, books, chapters and periodicals. Honours: Several grants; Distinguished teacher award, Erfurt University, 2004-05. Memberships: European Sociological Association; Dutch Sociological Association; German Sociological Association; German University Association. Address: Methods of Social Research; Department of Social Sciences, Erfurt University, Nordhaeuserstr 63, 99089 Erfurt, Germany. E-mail: sylvia.korupp@uni-erfurt.de Website: http://www.uni-erfurt.de/esf/korupp.html

PEARCE Leslie Dennis, b. 20 April 1945, Bow, East London, England. Factory Worker; Road Worker; Security Officer; Local Government Officer; Retired. m. Anne Black, 21 December 1990. Appointments: J Compton Sons & Webb, Uniform Clothing, Cap Cutter; R M Turner and Hunter, Timber Merchants, Trainee Sales; Poplar Borough Council, Road Labourer; United Dairies, Milk Roundsman; Securicor, Brinks Mat, Security Express, Cash In Transit Security Guard; London Borough of Hackney, Cashier, 1975-95, early retired. Publications include: Making Matters Verse; Pre-Conception, poem, 1997; Travellers Moon, 1997; Mirrors of the Soul, 1996; Voices in the Heart, 1997; Expressions, 1997; Tibby, 1998; Winter Warmer, 1998; What Love, 1998; Science, 1998; A Moving Sonnet, 1998, 1999; Three Cheers (poem), 1999; The Love Verses, 2004; This Endless Joy, 2006; The Poet's Dream; A Seasonal Sonnet, 2008. Honour: Editors Choice Award, 1996. Membership: International Society of Poets, Distinguished Member. Address: 29 Eastwood Road, Bexhill-on-Sea, East Sussex, TN39 3PR, England.

PEARSALL Derek Albert, b. 28 August 1931, Birmingham, England. Emeritus Professor of English. m. Rosemary Elvidge, 30 August 1952, 2 sons, 3 daughters. Education: BA, 1951, MA, 1952, University of Birmingham. Appointments: Assistant Lecturer, Lecturer, King's College, University of London, 1959-65; Lecturer, Senior Lecturer, Reader, 1965-76, Professor, 1976-87, University of York; Visiting Professor, 1985-87, Gurney Professor of English, 1987-2000, (Emeritus), Harvard University, Cambridge, Massachusetts, USA. Publications: John Lydgate, 1970; Landscapes and Seasons of the Medieval World (with Elizabeth Salter), 1973; Old English and Middle English Poetry, 1977; Langland's Piers Plowman: An Edition of the C-Text, 1978; The Canterbury Tales: A Critical Study, 1985; The Life of Geoffrey Chaucer: A Critical Biography, 1992; John Lydgate (1371-1449): A Bio-bibliography, 1997; Chaucer to Spenser: An Anthology of Writings in English 1375-1575, 1999; Gothic Europe 1200-1450, 2001; Arthurian Romance: A Short Introduction, 2003. Memberships: Early English Text Society, council member; Medieval Academy of America, fellow; New Chaucer Society, president, 1988-90; American Academy of Arts and Sciences, fellow. Address: 4 Clifton Dale, York YO30 6LJ, England.

PECHERSKY Alexander, b. 3 October 1963, St Petersburg, Russia. Physician. Education: Master in Medicine, Military Medical Academy, St Petersburg, 1987; MD, Medical Academy of Post-Graduate Studies, St Petersburg, 1992. Appointments: Intern, Medical Academy of Post-Graduate Studies, St Petersburg, 1989; Urologist, Centre of Anti-Infertility, St Petersburg, 1989-90; Resident in Urology, Medical Academy of Post-Graduate Studies, St Petersburg, 1990-92; Urologist, Hospital of Professional Pathologies, St Petersburg, 1992-95; Urologist, 1995-2005, Senior Lecturer, 2005-, Medical Academy of Post-Graduate Studies, St Petersburg. Publications: Articles in medical journals include as first-author: Androgen administration in middle-aged and ageing men: effects of oral testosterone undecanoate on dihydrotestosterone, estradiol and prostate volume, 2002; Changes in the level of cytokines among patients with prostate cancer after orchiectomy, 2003; The influence of the level of testosterone on the formation of dihydrotestosterone and estradiol in testosterone-sensitive cell lines of fibroblasts of the foreskin, 2005; Changes in the expression of receptors of steroid hormones in the presence of the development of partial age-related androgen deficiency, 2005; The role of testosterone in regulation of the expression of genes of several proliferation factors, 2006; The influence of partial androgen deficiency among aging men (PADAM) on the impulse mode of the incretion of some hormones and mitotic activity, 2006; Role of partial age-related androgen deficiency (PADAM) in the development of metabolic syndrome and an increase in proliferate activity, 2006. Honours: Medal "Author of Scientific Discovery", Russian Academy of Natural Sciences, Moscow, 2001. Memberships: Russian Association of Urology; International Society of Urology; European Association of Urology; Society of Plastic, Reconstructive and Aesthetic Surgeons; St Petersburg Club of Scientists. Address: St Petersburg Medical Academy of Post-Graduate Studies, 41, Kirochnaya St, St Petersburg 193015, Russia.

PECKHAM Sir Michael John, b. 2 August 1935, Panteg, Wales. Medical Practitioner; University Professor. m. Catherine Stevenson King, 1958, 3 sons. Education: St Catherine's College, Cambridge; University College Hospital Medical School. Appointments: Senior Lecturer, Institute of Cancer Research, 1972-74; Professor and Honorary Consultant, Institute of Cancer Research and Royal Marsden Hospital, 1974-86; Dean, Institute of Cancer Research, 1984-86; Director, British Postgraduate Medical Federation, 1986-90; Editor-in-Chief, European Journal of Cancer, 1990-95; Director of Research and Development, Department of Health, 1991-95; Director, School of Public Policy, University College London, 1996-2000; Vice Chair, Imperial Cancer Research Fund, 1987-90; Chair, Office of Science and Technology, Healthcare Development Foresight Programme, 1999-2000; Chair, National Educational Research Forum, 2000; Chair, Development Forum, 2000. Publications: Oxford Textbook of Oncology, 1995; Clinical Futures, 1999; A Model for Health: Innovation and the Future of Health Services, 2000; 10 solo art exhibitions in Edinburgh, London and Oxford. Honours: Honorary Fellow, St Catharine's College, Cambridge, 1998; Dr hc, Besançon, Catholic University of Louvain, 1993; Honorary DSc, Loughborough, Exeter, 1996. Memberships: Founding President, British Oncological Association, 1986-88; President, Federation of European Cancer Societies, 1989-91; European Society for Therapeutic Radiology and Oncology, 1983-85; Foreign Associate Member, NAS Institute of Medicine, 1994-.

PECORINO Lauren Teresa, b. 17 June 1962, New York, USA. Senior Lecturer; Author. Education: BSc, Biology, 1984, PhD, Cell and Developmental Biology, 1990, State University of New York at Stony Brook; Postdoctoral tenure, Ludwig Institute for Cancer Research, 1991-96. Appointments: Director of Quality and Learning, Programme Leader, Senior Lecturer, University of Greenwich, England, 1996-. Publications: The Molecular Biology of Cancer – Mechanisms, Targets and Therapeutics, 2005; Numerous research publications. Honours: NATO Postdoctural Fellowship. Memberships: Sigma Xi; American Association of the Advancement of Science; The Biochemistry Society;

Institute of Biomedical Science. Address: School of Science at Medway, University of Greenwich, Chatham, Kent, ME4 4TB, England. E-mail: l.pecorino@gre.ac.uk

PEÇULI Velesin, b. 26 December 1949, Vlorë, Albania. University Professor. m. Sara, 2 daughters. Education: Undergraduate studies, Tirana Agricultural University, 1967-72; Graduate studies, Perugia University, Perugia, Italy, 1980-83; PhD, 1986; Qualified Assistant Professor, 1990; Qualified Professor Dr, 1995. Appointments: University Lecturer, Agroecology and Ecology, 1984-, Deputy Rector, 1991-92, Deputy Dean, Agricultural Faculty, 1992-94, Rector, 2000-07, Agricultural University of Tirana. Publications: Nearly 60 scientific articles in domestic and overseas journals; Nearly 20 books in field of agriculture and ecology; Co-author, Albanian Dictionary of Agricultural Terminology. Honours: Citizen of Honor, Davis City, California, USA, 2000; Naim Frashri Golden Order, President of the Republic, 2001. Memberships: Consultative Committee of CIHEAM, Paris, France; Steering Committee, Albanian Centre for Studies in Ecology and Environment. Address: Agricultural University of Tirana, Kodër Kamëz, Tirana, Albania. E-mail: vpeculi@yahoo.com

PEDERSEN Hans Therkild, b. 27 February 1940, Stouby, Denmark. Grand Sire of the Odd Fellow Order of Denmark. m. Valborg Lissau, 2 sons, 1 daughter. Education: Teacher's Certificate Exam, Gedved Seminarium (College of Education), 1962; Parish Librarian Training, Denmark's Library School, 1965; School Librarian Training, 1972. Appointments: Infantry Corporal, Danish Army, 1963; School Teacher, Sandved School, 1963; School Teacher, 1967, School Librarian, 1972-84, Vice-Principal, 1997, Principal, 2000-2002, Fuglebjerg School; School Library Advisor Fuglebjerg Municipality, 1984-97; Admitted to the Odd Fellows Order, 1973; Grand Sire (Head of the Danish Branch of the International Odd Fellows Order), 1993-; Chairman, Federation of Independent European Jurisdictions of The Odd Fellows Order; Vice President, International Council, IOOF, 2006-; Liaison between this association and The Sovereign Grand Lodge in America. Publications: Illustrated Work: Dronning Ingrid I Sønderjylland (Queen Ingrid in South Jutland), 1995; The Odd Fellows Order – Aim, History, Developments (co-author), 1996. Honour: Danish Red Cross Emblem of Merit. Memberships: Vice-Chairman, Odd Fellows Children's Foundation under the Danish Red Cross; Chairman, Odd Fellows Hospice Foundation; Management Board, Thomas Wildey Institute "Institute für klinik und praxisgekoppelte Grundlagenforschung", Munich, Germany; Grand Sire of the Grand Lodge for Europe, 2007. Address: Oestengen 13, Bisserup, 4243 Rude, Denmark. E-mail: hp@oddfellow.dk Website: www.oddfellow.dk

PEDERSEN K George, b. 13 June 1931, Alberta, Canada. Educator. m. Penny, 1 son, 1 daughter. Education: Diploma, BC Provincial Normal School, 1952; BA, University of British Columbia, 1959; MA, University of Washington, 1964; PhD, University of Chicago, 1969. Appointments: Teacher, Vice President and Principal, various public schools, 1952-65; Academic appointments at University of Toronto, 1968-70, University of Chicago, 1970-72; Dean and Academic Vice President, University of Victoria, 1972-79; President, Simon Fraser University, 1979-83; President, University of British Columbia, 1983-85; President, University of Western Ontario, 1985-94; Interim President, University of Northern British Columbia, 1995; Founding President, Royal Roads University, 1995-96. Publications: The Itinerant Schoolmaster; Several book chapters; Innumerable articles. Honours: 10

major scholarships; Fellow, Canadian College of Teachers, Commonwealth Medal, 1992; Officer, Order of Canada, 1993; Order of Ontario, 1994; Order of British Columbia, 2002; Queens Jubilee Medal, 2002; LLD, McMaster University, 1996; D.Litt, Emily Carr Institute of Art and Design, 2003; LLD, Simon Fraser University, 2003; LLD, University of Northern British Columbia; Fellow, Royal Society for the Advancement of the Arts; many others. Address: 2232 Spruce St, Vancouver, BC V6H 2P3, Canada.

PEDERSEN Mette Katharina, b. 24 August 1939, Copenhagen, Denmark. Medical Doctor; Ear-Nose-Throat Specialist. 1 son, 1 daughter. Education: MD; PhD. Appointments: Ear-Nose-Throat Specialist and Voice Disorders, The Medical Centre, Copenhagen. Publications: Numerous papers and articles in professional scientific and medical journals latest including: Acid Reflux Treatment for Hoarseness, 2006; Videostroboscopic expert evaluation of the larynx with running objective voice management at the same time gives more secure results than videos alone, 2006; A discussion of the evidence based approach in research of the singing voice, 2006. Honours: The Danish School System; The Finnish Phoniatric Society; many others. Address: The Medical Centre, Voice Unit, Ostergade 18, 3, DK-1100 Kbh, K, Denmark. E-mail: m.f.pedersen@dadlnet.dk Website: www.mpedersen.org

PEKER Elya, b. 15 June 1937, Moscow, Russia. Artist; Painter. m. Katrina Friedman, 1 son. Education: Diploma, Theater Decoration, Moscow Art Institute, 1956. Appointment: Freelance Artist. Publications: Large series of posters and reproductions of Flower and Still Life paintings published and distributed world-wide. Honours: Cross of Order of International Ambassadors, title His Excellency, ABI, 1996; Listed in: Asian/American Who's Who, 1999, and numerous other Biographical Publications. Memberships: LIMA Licensing Industry Merchandisers' Association; International Platform Association. Commissions and Creative Works: Paintings. Address: 1610 East 19, Street No 297-196, Brooklyn, NY 11229, USA.

PELÉ (Edson Arantes do Nascimento), b. 23 October 1940, Tres Coracoes, Minas Gerais State, Brazil. Football Player; Author. m. Rosemeri Cholbi, 1966, divorced 1978, 1 son, 2 daughters. Education: Santos University. Appointments: Football Player at Bauru, Sao Paulo, Bauru Athletic Club; Joined Santos FC, 1955; 1st International Game v Argentina; Played in World Cup, 1958, 1962, 1966, 1970; Retired with New York Cosmos; Chair, Pelé Soccer Camps, 1978-; Director, Santos FC, 1993-; Special Minister for Sports, Government of Brazil, 1994-; Director, Soccer Clinics. Publications: Eu Sou Pelé, 1962; Jogando com Pelé, 1974; My Life and the Beautiful Game, 1977; Pelé Soccer Training Program, 1982; The World Cup Murders (novel), 1988. Honours: 3 World Cup Winner medals; 2 World Club Championship medals; 110 international caps; 97 goals for Brazil; 1,114 appearances for Santos, 1,088 goals; 9 league championship medals; 4 Brazil Cup medals; Goodwill Ambassador for 1992; UN Conference on Environment and Development, Rio De Janeiro; International Peace Award, 1978; WHO Medal, 1989; Honorary KBE, 1997; FIFA World Footballer of the Century, 2000; Hans Christian Andersen Ambassador, 2003-. Address: 75 Rockefeller Plaza, New York, NY 10019, USA.

PELIKAN Anton, b. 2 February 1945, Banska Bystrica, Czechoslovakia. Surgeon; Professor of Surgery. m. Iva, 1 son. Education: Leaving Examination, 1963; MD, Faculty of Medicine, 1969; CCST, 1977; PhD, 1981; DSc, Doctor of Medical Sciences, 1993; Professor of Surgery, 1996. Appointments: Surgeon, 1969-97, Consultant Surgeon, 1977-, Roosevelt Hospital, Banska Bystrica; Head, Department of Central Operating Theatres and Department of Surgical Oncology, 1978-97; Head of Surgery, later Consultant Surgeon, University Hospital Ostrava, Czech Republic, 1997-99; Locum Consultant Surgeon, Isle of Wight, England, 2005-06; Locum Consultant Surgeon, Aberdeen Royal Hospital, Scotland, 2007. Publications: 165 publications; 235 lectures; Book, Carcinoma of the Colon and Rectum, 1985. Honours: Listed in international biographical dictionaries. Memberships: European Society of Surgical Oncology; Society of Surgical Oncology; Czech Surgical Society; Czech Society of Oncology. Address: Budouatelska 22, 74717 Ludgerovice, Czech Republic. E-mail: anton.pelikan@fnspo.cz

PELLI Moshe, b. 1936, Israel (US citizen). Professor. m. 2 children. Education: BS, Journalism and Liberal Studies, New York University, 1957-60; PhD, The Dropsie College for Hebrew and Cognate Learning, Philadelphia, 1961-67. Appointments: Editor, NIV, Hebrew Literary Quarterly, New York, USA, 1957-66; Executive Director, Hebrew Month, 1962-66; Executive Director, Hanoar Haivri (Hebrew Youth Organization), 1962-66; Founding Editor, 1964-66, Editor, 1983-85, Lamishpaha, Hebrew Illustrated Monthly, New York; Assistant Professor Co-ordinator of Hebrew Language Program, University of Texas, 1967-71; Abstractor, Religious and Theological Abstracts, 1968-71; Senior Lecturer, Staff Representative on University Instructors National Board, Ben-Gurion University, Israel, 1971-74; Associate Professor, Modern Hebrew Language and Literature, Cornell University, New York, USA, 1974-78; Associate Professor, Yeshiva University, Erna Michael College, New York, 1978-84; Judaic Studies Program, 1985-, Associate Professor, Department of Foreign Languages, 1985-88, Director, Interdisciplinary Program in Judaic Studies, Office of the Dean of Arts & Sciences, 1988-, Professor and Director, 1989-, The Abe and Tess Wise Endowed Professor in Judaic Studies, 2004-, College of Arts and Humanities, University of Central Florida. Publications: 12 scholarly books; 2 novels; 8 children's books; Numerous papers presented in scholarly conferences and articles published in professional journals. Honours include: Abraham Friedman Prize for Hebrew Culture in America, 1991; College of Arts and Sciences Excellence Award in Research, 1996; University of Central Florida Distinguished Researcher of the Year, 1996; Lucian N Littauer Foundation grant, 2005; Elected Fellow, Moses Mendelssohn Center, University of Potsdam, Germany, 2000; I Edward Kiev Library Foundation Grant, 2005; Member, Editorial Board, Kesher, 2005; Member, Editorial Board, Hebrew Higher Education, 2005; Elected Vice President, National Association of Professors of Hebrew in USA, 2005; Elected President NAPH, 2007; University of Central Florida Research Incentive Award, 2006; Distinguished Researcher of the Year, College of Arts and Humanities, University of Central Florida, 2006. Memberships: Association for Jewish Studies; American Academy of Religion; American Society of 18th Century Studies; National Association of Professors of Hebrew; World Union of Jewish Studies. Address: University of Central Florida, Judaic Studies Program, PO Box 161992, Orlando, FL 32816-1992, USA. E-mail: pelli@pegasus.cc.ucf.edu

PELLOW Andrew Charles Henry (Newman), b. 29 September 1944, Nettlestone, Isle of Wight, England. Musician; Writer. Education: Diploma, History of Church Music, Williams School, 1986. Appointments: Organist, Nettlestone Methodist Chapel, 1956-93; Clerk, Legal Cashier, John Robinson & Jarvis, 1961-66, Robinson, Jarvis

& Rolf, 1967-90; Freelance Piano Teacher, Accompanist, Calligrapher, 1990-; Musician and Calligrapher, Taylorian Fine Arts, 1990-; Organist, Choir Master, St Helen's (IW) Parish Church, 1993; Organist, Choir Master, Sandown Parish Church, Christ Church, Broadway, 1994-97; Director of Music, Organist, Choir Master, Parish and Priory Church of St Mary-the-Virgin, Carisbrooke, 1997-99; Freelance Organist, 1999-; Sub-Deacon with Traditional Anglican Church in Britain, St Barnabas Mission, Isle of Wight, 2004, Licensed to Office 2005. Publications: Robella Ruby (poems), 1985; Numerous poems in anthologies; Many articles in professional & church magazines and newsletters; Periodic letters and concert critiques in local press. Honours: Associate of the Institute of Legal Cashiers and Administrators, 1984; Winner, Piano, Organ, Composition, Speech, Poetry and Prose, Isle of Wight and Portsmouth Musical Competition Festivals, 1989-2003, 2005, 2006, 2007; Twice winner, four times runner-up, Isle of Wight County Press/Tritone Singers Annual Carol Competition, 1996, 1998, 2000, 2001, 2002 and 2004; LGMS, 1996; Admitted Fellow, Guild of Musicians and Singers (FGMS), 2006; 1st Prize, Poetry, Poetry Today, 1998; Elected a Fellow of the Academy of St Cecilia, 2001; Granted Life Membership of the Central Institute, London (MCIL), 2002; Life Fellow (FCIL), 2006; Piano-Oxford Music Festival, 2003, 2004, 2006 & 2007; Ceremonially admitted to CIL, 2003; Honorary Fellowship (Hon NCM), National College of Music, London, 2007. Memberships: Executive Trustee, 1998-2003, Official Accompanist, 1994-2004, Isle of Wight Musical Competition Festivals; Patron, 2004-; The Betjeman Society, 1990, 2006-; Friend of Winchester Cathedral, 1984-; Guild of Musicians and Singers; Isle of Wight Organists' Association; St Thomas's (Ryde) Heritage Centre Friends & Trust (Honorary Secretary), 1985-2005; Zion Chapel Trust, Swanmore, IW (Chairman), 1989-; Isle of Wight Morris Minor Owners' Club, 1998-; Company Secretary/Treasurer, Primary Flats (Carisbrooke) Management Company Ltd, 1999-; Committee, Royal School of Church Music, Isle of Wight, 1999-; Parochial Church Council & Concert Series' Co-ordinator, St Michael and All Angels, Swanmore, 2000-03; The Folio Society, 2001, 2003-2007; Ryde Arts Festival (Planning Group), 2002-05; Amateur Actor, Bembridge (IW) Little Theatre Club, 2005; Centenary Pageant Carisbrooke Castle (Sir George Carey AD1588), 2007; The Guild of Church Musicians, 2004-; Cornwall Family History Society, 2005-; Trinity College, London – Local Teachers' Forum; Ryde (IW) Social Heritage Group, 2006; Friend of St Michael's Church, Brighton, 2006-; Associate, European Piano Teachers Association (UK) Ltd, 2007; Regular Contributor to CFHS Journal. Address: 2 Radley Cottages, Nettlestone Hill, Nettlestone, Isle of Wight, PO34 5DW, England.

PELZER Charles Francis, b. 5 June 1935, Detroit, Michigan, USA. Human Geneticist. m. Veronica A Killeen, 1 daughter. Education: BS, University of Detroit Mercy, Detroit, Michigan, USA, 1957; PhD, University of Michigan, Ann Arbor, Michigan, USA, 1964. Appointments: Research Associate, Michigan State University, East Lansing, Michigan, USA, 1976-77; Research Fellow, Henry Ford Hospital, Detroit, Michigan, USA, 1982-83, 1989-1992; Assistant Professor, Associate Professor, Professor of Biology, Saginaw Valley State University, Michigan, USA, 1969-; Chair of Biology, Saginaw Valley State University, 2002-. Publications: 15 articles in scientific journals in the general area of molecular genetics. Honours: Kettering Foundation Postdoctoral Fellow, Wabash College, Crawfordville, Indiana, 1965-66; Kellogg Foundation, Predoctoral Trainee, University of Michigan, Ann Arbor, Michigan, 1961; Alumni Award, Saginaw Valley

State University, Michigan, USA, 1971. Memberships include: New York Academy of Science; American Society of Human Genetics; National Association of Biology Teachers; Electrophoresis Society; Council on Undergraduate Research, and 10 others. Address: Biology Department, Saginaw Valley State University, Michigan 48710, USA. E-mail: cfp@svsu.edu

PENA Lorenzo, b. 29 August 1944, Alicante, Spain. University Professor. m. Teresa Alonso, 19 February 1969. Education: American Studies Diploma, Liège University, Belgium, 1978; PhD, Philosophy, Liège University, 1979; Master of Law, Spanish Open University, Madrid, Spain, 2004. Appointments: Professor of Philosophy, Pontifical University of Ecuador, 1973-75, 1979-83; Professor, University of Léon, Spain, 1983-87; Senior Science Researcher, CSIC (Spanish Institute of Advanced Study), 1987-; Visiting Position, Australian national University, Research School of Social Sciences, 1992-93. Publications: Rudiments of Mathematical Logic (Madrid), 1991; Philosophical Findings, 1992. Honours: National Prize for Literary Creation in the Humanities, Madrid, 1988. Memberships: Australian Association of Philosophy; Mind Association; Aristotelian Society; European Society of Analytical Philosophy. Address: Spanish Institute for Advanced Study, Department of Philosophy, Pinar 25, E28006 Madrid, Spain.

PENCHEREK-JACKSON Nancy, b. 25 October 1938, Fort Myers, Florida, USA. Real Estate Broker; Investor. m. (1) John Jackson, 2 sons, 1 daughter, (2) Raymond Pencherek. Education: Florida Realtors Institute I, 1982, FRI, II, 1988; Certified Instructor, FMAR, 1988; Graduate, Realtors Institute, 1989. Appointments: National Retail Advertising Representative; Commercial Bank Teller; Real Estate Salesman; Real Estate Broker; Investment Management Marketing Entrepreneur. Publications: Articles in trade and popular journals. Honours: NAR Honor Society; NAR Diamond Pin Club; FAR Honor Society; Sales Excellence Award; Bank Award of Excellence; ESA Sorority Girl of the Year; United Cultural International Peace Prize; Community and Youth Services Award. Memberships: National and Florida Association of Realtors; Lions Club International; Friends of the Opera Society; USA Dance Organisation; SW Florida Chamber of Commerce; German-American Social Club; Naples Barbershop Chorus Belles; National Association of Female Executives; Florida Sheriff's Youth Ranches; SW Florida Christian Women's Club; International Fellowship of Christians and Jews; Christ Community Christian & Missionary Alliance Church.

PENHALE Bridget, b. 29 August 1955, Holsworthy, Devon, England. Reader. m. Dan Smith, 2 sons. Education: BA (Hons) Psychology, University of Nottingham, 1974-77; MSc, Social Work/CQSW, London School of Economics, University of London, 1980-81. Appointments: Student Community Action Co-ordinator, University of Nottingham, 1977-78; Residential Social Worker, Nottinghamshire Social Services, 1978-79; Social Worker, Sandwell Metropolitan Borough Council, 1979-80; Social Worker, Staffordshire Social Services, 1981-85; Social Worker, Norfolk Social Services, 1986-89; Lecturer in Social Work, University of East Anglia, joint appointment with Norfolk County Council, 1990-92; Team Manager, Norfolk Social Services, 1992-95; Lecturer in Social Work, 1996-2003, Senior Lecturer, 2003-2004, University of Hull; Senior Lecturer in Gerontology, University of Sheffield, 2004-2006; Reader in Gerontology 2006-. Publications include: Books as co-author: The Dimensions of Elder Abuse, 1997; Forgotten People: Positive Practice in Dementia Care,

1998; Stroke at your fingertips, 2000, 2nd edition, 2005; Child Protection and Maternal Mental Health, 2003; Adult Protection, forthcoming, 2007; Numerous book chapters and peer reviewed articles in professional journals. Honour: European Regional Representative, International Network for Prevention of Elder Abuse; Board Member, INPEA, 2006-. Memberships: International Network for the Prevention of Elder Abuse; British Society of Gerontology; Action on Elder Abuse; British Association for Service to Elderly; British Association of Social Workers; Registered Social Worker with General Social Care Council; Child Poverty Action Group. Address: School of Nursing and Midwifery, University of Sheffield, Bartolome House, Winter Street, Sheffield S3 7ND, England. E-mail: b.penhale@sheffield.ac.uk

PENN Sean, b. 17 August 1960, Burbank, California, USA. Actor. m. (1) Madonna, 1985, (2) Robin Wright, 1996, 2 children. Creative Works: Theatre appearances include: Heartland; Slab Boys; Hurlyburly, 1988; Film appearances: Taps, 1981; Fast Times at Ridgemont High, 1982; Bad Boys, 1983; Crackers, 1984; Racing with the Moon, 1984; The Falcon and the Snowman, 1985; At Close Range, 1986; Shanghai Surprise, 1986; Colors, 1988; Judgement in Berlin, 1988; Casualties of War, 1989; We're No Angels, 1989; State of Grace, 1990; Carlito's Way, 1993; Dead Man Walking, 1996; U Turn, 1997; She's So Lovely, 1997; Hurlyburly, 1998; As I Lay Dying, 1998; Up at the Villa, 1998; The Thin Red Line, 1998; Sweet and Lowdown; Being John Malkovich; The Weight of Water; The Pledge, 2000; Up at the Villa, 2000; I am Sam, 2001; Mystic River, 2003; 21 Grams, 2003; The Assassination of Richard Nixon, 2005; The Interpreter, 2005; All the King's Men, 2006; Persepolis, 2007; Crossing Over, 2007. Director, Writer: The Indian Runner, 1991, The Crossing Guard, 1995; The Pledge, 2000. Honours include: Best Actor Award, Berlin Film Festival, 1996; Oscar for Best Actor, Mystic River, 2004; Golden Globe, Best Dramatic Actor, 2004; Critics' Choice Award, Best Actor, 2004; Academy Award, Best Actor, 2004. Address: Suite 2500, 2049 Century Park East, Los Angeles, CA 90067, USA.

PENROSE Roger, b. 8 August 1931, Colchester, Essex, England. Mathematician. Education: University College, London; Doctorate, Cambridge University, 1957. Appointments: Worked with father in the devising of seemingly impossible geometric figures; Lecturing and Research posts in Britain and the USA; Professor of Applied Mathematics, Birkbeck College, London, 1966-73; Rouse Ball Professor of Mathematics, Oxford University, 1973-98; Professor Emeritus, 1998- Important contributions to the understanding of astrophysical phenomena, especially Black Holes. Publications: Techniques of Differential Topology in Relativity, 1973; Spinors and Space-time, with W Rindler, volume I, 1984, volume II, 1986; The Emperor's New Mind, 1989; The Nature of Space and Time, with S Hawking, 1996; The Large, the Small and the Human Mind, 1997; White Mars, with B Aldiss, 1999; The Road to Reality: A Complete Guide to the Laws of the Universe, 2004; articles in scientific journals. Honours: Adams Prize, 1966-67; Dannie Heinemann Prize, 1971; Eddington Medal, 1975; Royal Medal, 1985; Wolf Foundation Prize for Physics, 1988; Dirac Medal and Prize, Institute of Physics, 1989; Einstein Medal, 1990; Science Book Prize, 1990; Naylor Prize, London Mathematics Society, 1991; 8 Dr h c; Hon D University, 1998. Memberships: London Mathematical Society; Cambridge Philosophical Society; Institute for Mathematics and its Applications; International Society for General Relativity and Gravitation; Fellow, Birkbeck College, 1998; Institute

of Physics, 1999; Foreign Associate, National Academy of Sciences, USA, 1998. Address: Mathematical Institute, 24-29 St Giles, Oxford, OX1 3LB, England.

PENTELÉNYI Thomas J, b. 25 February 1939, Budapest, Hungary. Professor of Neurosurgery. m. Mary Pálfalvy, 2 daughters. Education: Graduate, Semmelweis Medical University, Budapest, 1963; Specialised in surgery, 1967; Specialised in neurosurgery, 1974; PhD, 1978. Appointments: Worked with: World Federation of Neurosurgical Societies; European Association of Neurosurgical Societies; Euroacademy for Multidisciplinary Neurotraumatology; International Conferences on Recent Advances in Neurotraumatology; International Medical Society of Paraplegia; International Conferences on Lumbar Fusion and Stabilization; European Spine Society; International Society of Minimally Invasive Spine Surgery; American Spinal Injury Association; European Federation of Neurological Societies; Central European Brain Injury Data Base; Leading Professor, Neurotraumatology and Spinal Surgery, Faculty of Traumatology, Haynal Imre University of Health Sciences, Budapest; Chairman, Subcommittee on Education in Neurotrauma, World Federation of Neurosurgical Societies; President, ICLFS World Conference, Budapest, Hungary, 1995; President, Hungarian Spine Society, Budapest, 1994-96; Head and Chairman, Department of Neurosurgery, National Institute of Traumatology, Budapest, 1986-2005; Member, Scientific Consultation Board, EMN, 2001-; International Senior Neuroscience Consultants' Board, Memphis Neurosciences Center, Tennessee; Subcommittee on Disaster Assistance in Neurotraumatology, WFNS; International Global SHIP Program (Spine and Head Injury Prevention), Taipei, Taiwan; International Advisory Board, International Medical Protection Society, London, UK; Traumatology Advisory Board to the Hungarian Minister of Health, Budapest, Hungary; New York Academy of Sciences; Scientist Panel, European Federation of Neurological Societies; Steering Committee of the WHO Neurotrauma Council, WHO; Central European Brain Injury Data Base, Budapest-New York. Publications: 718 scientific papers and lectures; 198 publications. Honours: Highest Hungarian Medical Professional Medal, 1988; Felicitation Medal of the Indian Neurological Society, Rajkot, Gujarat, India, 2000; Diploma of Achievement in Medicine and Healthcare, IBC, 2005; Honorary Member: Jan Evangelist Purkinje Medical University, Brno; University of Padova, Italy; Sutter Health System, California; Fundacion Instituto Neurologico de Colombia, Bogota, Colombia; Honorary Member, Indian Neurological Society, India. Memberships: Hungarian Neurosurgical Society; Hungarian Neuroradiology Society; Hungarian Neurotrauma Society; Hungarian Spine Society; Hungarian Traumatology Society; Hungarian Diabetes Society; International Medical Society of Paraplegia; European Association of Neurosurgical Societies; World Federation of Neurosurgical Societies; Visiting Professor: University of Tennessee, Memphis, Tennessee; Spinal and Arthritis Center, Cleveland, Ohio; University of Chicago Medical Center, Chicago, Illinois; Temple University, Philadelphia, Pennsylvania; Jefferson University, Philadelphia, Pennsylvania; University of California Davis, Sacramento, California; Xaveriana Medical School, Bogota, Colombia; Head, Hungarian-Japanese Intergovernmental Scientific and Technology Research Project in Neurotraumatology, Budapest-Kurume, 2004-07; 1000 Great Minds of the 21st Century, 2005-06; Deputy Director General, IBC. Address: National Institute of Traumatology, Department of Neurosurgery, VIII Fiumei ut 17, 1081 Budapest, Hungary. E-mail: pentelenyi@obsi.hu

PENZAR Ivan, b. 17 December 1928, Gola, Koprivnica, Croatia. Professor. m. Branka, 2 sons, 1 daughter. Education: BSc, 1951, MSc, 1962, PhD, 1970, Physics of Atmosphere, Faculty of Sciences, University of Zagreb. Appointments: Research Assistant, 1951, Assistant Professor, 1972, Associate Professor, 1984, Full Professor, 1986, Physical Meteorology, Physics of Atmosphere, Dynamics of Atmosphere, Measurements in Meteorology, Basics of Geophysics at Faculty of Sciences, Agroclimatology, University of Zagreb and Osijek, Croatia and University of Mostar, Bosnia and Herzegovina. Publications: 81 scientific papers; 99 other papers; 7 books dealing with solar irradiation, climatology, interaction between the physics of the sea and atmosphere and history of Croatian Meteorology. Honours: The Order of Croatian Danica, with figure of Ruger Boschovich. Memberships: International Solar Energy Society; European Association for Atmosphere Pollution; Croatian Committee for Geodessy and Geophysics; Scientific Council on Energetic, Croatian Academy of Science and Arts. Address: Grskoviceva 9, 10000 Zagreb, Croatia.

PEPE Frank A, b. 22 May 1931, Schenectady, New York, USA. Emeritus Professor. Education: BS, Chemistry, Union College, 1953; PhD, Physical Chemistry, Yale University, 1957. Appointments: Instructor, 1957-60, Associate, 1960-63, Assistant Professor, 1963-65, Associate Professor, 1965-70, Professor, 1970-92, Department of Anatomy, School of Medicine, University of Pennsylvania, Chairman, Department of Anatomy, 1977-90, Professor, Department of Cell and Development Biology, 1992-96, Emeritus Professor, 1996-. Publications: Numerous articles in professional journals; Editor, Motility in Cell Function, 1979. Honours: Fellow, AAAS, 1987; Raymond C Truex Distinguished Lecture Award, Hahneman University, 1988. Memberships: American Association of Anatomists; American Chemical Society; AAAS; Sigma Xi; Micro Society of America. Address: 4614 Pine Street, Philadelphia, PA 19143-1808, USA. E-mail: fpepe@mail.med.upenn.edu

PEPPÉ Rodney Darrell, b. 24 June 1934, Eastbourne, East Sussex, England. Author; Artist. m. Tatjana Tekkel, 16 July 1960, 2 sons. Education: Eastbourne School of Art, 1951-53, 1955-57; London County Council Central School of Art, 1957-59; NDD, Illustration (special subject) and Central School Diploma. Appointments: Art Director, S H Benson Ltd, 1960-64; J Walter Thompson & Co Ltd, 1965-65; Consultant Designer to Ross Foods Ltd, 1965-72; Freelance Graphic Designer, Illustrator, 1965-98; Children's Author and Illustrator, 1968; Toymaker and Automatist. Publications: The Alphabet Book, 1968; Circus Numbers, 1969; The House That Jack Built, 1970; Hey Riddle Diddle!, 1971; Simple Simon, 1972; Cat and Mouse, 1973; Odd One Out, 1974; Henry series, 1975-78; Picture Stories, 1976; Rodney Peppe's Puzzle book, 1977; Ten Little Bad Boys, 1978; Three Little Pigs, 1979; Indoors Word Book, Outdoors Word Book, 1980; Rodney Peppé's Moving Toys, 1980; The Mice Who Lived in a Shoe, 1981; Run Rabbit, Run!, 1982; The Kettleship Pirates, 1983; Little Toy Board Book series, 1983; Make Your Own Paper Toys, 1984; Block Books, 1985; The Mice and the Flying Basket, 1985; Press-Out Circus, Press-Out Train, 1986; Tell the Time with Mortimer, 1986; The Mice and the Clockwork Bus, 1986; Open House, 1987; First Nursery Rhymes, 1988; Thumbprint Circus, 1988; Noah's Ark Frieze, 1989; Huxley Pig series, 1989-90; The Animal Directory, 1989; ABC Index. ABC Frieze, 1990; The Shapes Finder, 1991; The Colour Catalogue, 1992; The Mice on the Moon, 1992; The Mice and the Travel Machine, 1993; The Magic Toybox, 1996; Gus and Nipper, 1996; Hippo Plays Hide and Seek, 1997;

Angelmouse Series, 2000; Automata and Mechanical Toys, 2002; Toys and Models, 2003; Making Mechanical Toys, 2005; TV Series: Huxley Pig, ITV, 1990; Angelmouse, BBC, 2000. Contributions to: Periodicals. Membership: Society of Authors. Address: Stoneleigh House, 6 Stoneleigh Drive, Livermead, Torquay, Devon TQ2 6TR, England.

PERA Marcello, b. 28 January 1943, Lucca, Tuscany, Italy. President of the Italian Senate. Education: Accountancy degree, F Carrara High School, Lucca, 1962; Degree (summa cum laude), Philosophy, University of Pisa, 1972. Appointments: Employee, Banca Toscana, Lucca, 1962-63, Agliana, Pistoia, 1963-64; Employee, Lucca Chamber of Commerce, 1964-73; Assistant Professor, 1976-80, Associate Professor, 1980-89, Full Professor, 1992, Philosophy of Science, University of Pisa; Visiting Fellow, Center for Philosophy of Science, University of Pittsgurgh, USA, 1984; Visiting Fellow, The Van Leer Foundation, Jerusalem, Israel, 1987; Full Professor, Theoretic Philosophy, University of Catania, 1989-92; Visiting Fellow, Department of Linguistics and Philosophy, MIT, Cambridge, Massachusetts, USA, 1990; Co-ordinator, Convention for Liberal Reform, 1995; Visiting Fellow, Centre for the Philosophy of Natural and Social Sciences, London School of Economics, England, 1995-96; Senator, Lucca constituency, Freedom Alliance, 13th Parliament, 1996-2001; Deputy Leader, Forza Italia parliamentary group, 1996-2001; Member, Standing Committee on Education and Cultural Properties, 1996-97; Member, Standing Committee on the Judiciary, 1997-; Member, Joint Committee on Constitutional Reform, 1997-; Member, Forza Italia Steering Committee; Head, Forza Italia Judiciary Department; Re-elected to Senate, Lucca constituency, House of Freedoms, 2001; Elected President of the Senate, 2001-. Publications: Contributions to scientific magazines and editorial activity; Member of advisory panels of and contributor to several journals; Contributions to Italian daily and weekly papers; Co-author (with Cardinal Joseph Ratzinger) of book entitled, Senza radici (Without Roots). Address: Gabinetto del Presidente, Senato della Repubblica, Palazzo Madama, 00186 Rome, Italy. E-mail: d.citi@senato.it

PERAK H.H. Sultan of, Sultan Azlan Muhibbuddin Shah ibni Al-Marhum Sultan Yussuf Ghafarullahu-Lahu Shah, b. 19 April 1928, Batu Gajah, Malaysia. Ruler. m. Tuanku Bainun Mohamed Ali, 1954, 2 sons, 3 daughters. Education: Malay College; University of Nottingham. Appointments: Called to Bar, Lincoln's Inn; Magistrate, Kuala Lumpur; Assistant State Secretary, Perak; Deputy Public Prosecutor; President, Sessions Court, Seremban and Taiping; State Legal Advisor, Pahang and Johre; Federal Court Judge, 1973; Chief Justice of Malaysia, 1979; Lord President, 1982-83; Raja Kechil Bongsu (6th in line), 1962, Raja Muda (2nd in line), 1983; Sultan of Perak, 1984-; Yang di-Pertuan Agong (Supreme Head of State), 1989-94; Pro-Chancellor, University of Saina Malaysia, 1971, Chancellor, University of Malaya, 1986; Honorary Colonel-in-Chief, Malaysian Armed Forces Engineers Corps; Manager, Malaysian Hockey Team, 1972; President, Malaysian Hockey Federation, Asian Hockey Federation; Vice-President, International Hockey Federation, Olympic Council of Malaysia.

PEREDELSKIY Gennadiy Ivanovich, b. 16 September 1937, Prokopyevsk, Russia. University Professor. Divorced, 1 son. Education: Graduated, Tomsk Polytechnical Institute, 1960; Postgraduate Candidate of Technical Science, 1969; Docent, 1971; Doctor of Technical Science, 1989; Professor, 1993. Appointments: Assistant Lecturer, Industrial Electronics Chair of Tomsk Polytechnical Institute, 1960-64;

Docent, Industrial Electronics Chair of Tomsk Institute of Radioelectrics and Electronics Engineering, 1964-74; Head, Chair, Industrial Electronics of Tomsk Institute, Automatised Controlling Systems and Radioelectronics, 1974-91; Head, Chair, Industrial Electronics and Automatics of Kursk Polytechnical Institute, 1991-95; Professor, Orel State Technical University, 1995-2004; Professor, Kursk State Technical University, 2004-. Main research interests: use of test-signals in the form of consecutive pulses with voltage change during their duration, according to extent functions law. Publications: Over 300 articles and papers and 2 monographs; Titles include: Capacitor Transducers fed with Pulsed Voltage, 1968; Induction Transduced with Pulsed Feed, 1969; Induction bridge, feeding by trapezium form voltage, 1969; Independent Compensation Principle of Nonlinearity in Generators of Linearity Varying Voltage, 1971; Maxwell Bridge, Fed by Pulsed Trapezium-Formed Voltage, 1971; Generator of Linear Varying Voltage with Nonlinearity Independent Compensation, 1974; Electric Bridges with Pulsed Feed, Balanced with Active Resistances, 1975; Transformer Bridges with Pulsed Feed, 1977; Bridges with separated equilibrium on three parameters, 1980; Separate Equilibrium of Bridge Circuits for Measuring Parameters of Multi-element Double-Poles, 1984; About the theory of bridge circuits constructions for measuring parameters of four-cells two-terminal networks, 1987; About properties of polyelements circuits, 1989; Simplification of measuring circuits analysis with polyelements two-terminal networks, 1995; Bridge Circuits for Parameters Measuring of Multi-Element Double-Poles, 1995; Definition of equivalence two-terminal networks on the bridge circuits basis with pulsed feed, 1996; Synthesis of bridge circuits with pulsed feeding, 1998; Frequency-Independent Double-Poles on Four-celled Bridge Circuits, 1998; About property of quadripoles with recurring cells which have equal circuits and connecting, 1999; A property of potentially frequency independent two-terminal networks, 2000; About the Equivalency of Frequency Independent Two-Pole Networks, 2002; Mating of pulsed power supply bridge circuits with electron assembly, 2002; Use of potentially frequency-independent, two-terminal networks for solutions of problems for measuring equipment, 2003; Improvement of electric bridges with electronic units coupling based on analogue adder, 2004; About the Frequency-Independent Two-Pole Network of Two Structures, 2006; Multiarm bridge circuits to determine the parameters of multielement two-port network with heterogeneous reactive element, 2006. Honours: Academician of the Electroengineering Sciences Academy of the Russian Federation; Academician of the Metrological Academy of the Russian Federation. Memberships: Scientific-Methodological Council in Industrial Electronics, 1975-80. Address: ul Pyatdesyat Lyet Oktyabrya, 96B-54, 305040 Kursk, Russia. E-mail: rector@kstu.kursk.ru

PEREIRA NEVES José Maria, b. 28 March 1960, Santa Catarina, Santiago Island, Cape Verde. Public Administrator. Divorced, 3 sons. Education: BA, Public Administration, São Paulo School of Business and Administration, São Paulo, Brazil. Appointments: Member, Partido Africano da Independência da Guiné e Cabo Verde, 1980; Co-ordinator, Administration Reform and Modernization Projects, Cape Verde, 1987-88; Consultant, Organisational Development, Human Resources Management and Professional Training, Cape Verde, 1987-96; Consultant/Trainer of Trainers, Organisational Theory, Conflict Management and Local Government Management and Leadership, Cape Verde, 1987-; Director, National Public Administration Training Center, Cape Verde, 1988-89; Secretary General, Juventude Africana

Amilcar Cabral youth organisation, Cape Verde, 1989; Assistant Professor in Management, School of Management, Higher Education Institute, Cape Verde; Chairman, Specialised Committee on Public Administration, Local Government and Regional Development, 1996-2000; Member, National Committee, Inter-Parliamentary Union, 1996-2000; Vice President, PAICV Parliamentarian Group, 1996-2000; Member of the Parliament, Santa Catarina constituency, Cape Verde, 1996-2001; 2nd Vice President, National Assembly, 1996-2000; Mayor, Santa Catarina, Santiago Island, Cape Verde, 2000-01; President, Partido Africano da Independência de Cabo Verde, 2000-; Prime Minister of the Republic of Cape Verde, 2001, re-elected 2006-. Honours: Marechal Floriano Peixoto Merit Award, 2005; Ruby Cross. Address: PO Box 16, Palácio do Governo – Várzea, Praia, Ilha de Santiago, República de Cabo Verde.

PERHAM Michael Francis, b. 8 November 1947, Dorchester, Dorset, England. Bishop of Gloucester. m. Alison Jane Grove, 4 daughters. Education: Hardye's School, Dorchester, 1959-65; BA, 1974, MA, 1978, Keble College, Oxford; Cuddesdon Theological College, Oxford, 1974-76; Honorary Doctor of Philosophy, University of Gloucestershire, 2007. Appointments: Ordained Deacon in Canterbury Cathedral, 1976; Assistant Curate, St Mary's Addington, Croydon, 1976-81; Ordained Priest in Canterbury Cathedral, 1977; Domestic Chaplain to Bishop of Winchester (Bishop John Taylor), 1981-84; Rector, Oakdale Team Ministry, Poole, 1984-92; Canon Residentiary and Precentor, Norwich Cathedral, 1992-98; Vice Dean of Norwich, 1995-98; (Last) Provost of Derby, 1998-2000; (First) Dean of Derby, 2000-04; Ordained Bishop in St Paul's Cathedral, 2004; (40th) Bishop of Gloucester, 2004-. Publications include: A New Handbook of Pastoral Liturgy, 2000; Signs of Your Kingdom, 2003; Glory in our Midst, 2005. Honours: Honorary Fellow, Royal School of Church Music, 2003-. Memberships: Member, Governing Body of SPCK, 2002-, Chairman, 2006-; President, Alcuin Club, 2005-; Bishop Protector of the Society of St Francis, 2005-; Council Member, Pro-Chancellor, University of Gloucestershire, 2007-; President, Retired Clergy Association, 2007-; Chair, Hospital Chaplaincies Council, 2007-. Address: Church House, College Green, Gloucester, GL1 2LY, England. E-mail: bshpglos@glosdioc.org.uk

PERINA Jan, b. 11 November 1936, Mestec Kralove, Czech Republic. Professor of Physics. m. Vlasta Perinova, 1 son, 1 daughter. Education: Palacky University, 1964; PhD, Palacky University, 1966; RNDr, Palacky University, 1967; DSc, Charles University, 1984; Professor, 1990. Appointments: Laboratory of Optics and Joint Laboratory of Optics, Palacky University Olomouc, 1964-; Department of Optics, Palacky University Olomouc, Czech Republic, 1990-. Publications: About 300 publications on coherence and statistics of light; Books: Van Nostrand, 1972; Mir, 1974, 1987; Kluwer, 1984, 1985, 1991, 1994; World Scientific, 1998; J. Wiley, 2001. Honours: Awards of: Columbia University, 1983; Ministry of Education, 1991; Slovakia Academy of Sciences, 1996; Town of Olomouc, 2001; State Award of the Czech Republic, 2002; European Academy of Sciences and Arts, 2006. Memberships: Fellow of American Optical Society, 1984; Learned Society Bohemica, 1995. Address: Kmochova 3, 77900 Olomouc, Czech Republic.

PEŘINOVÁ Vlasta Anna, b. 16 October 1943, Ostravice, Czech Republic. Professor. m. Jan Peřina, 1 son, 1 daughter. Education: Graduate, Faculty of Natural Sciences, 1965, Rerum Naturalium Doctor, Mathematical Analysis, 1967, PhD, Mathematical Analysis, 1981, Associate Professor,

1992, Professor, General Physics and Mathematical Physics, 1995; Palacký University Olomouc, Czech Republic; DSc, General Physics and Mathematical Physics, Charles University, Prague, Czech Republic, 1990. Appointments: Research Worker, Computational Centre, 1966-68, Scientific Worker, Laboratory of Optics, 1968-84, Senior Scientific Worker, Joint Laboratory of Optics of Palacký University and Czechoslovak Academy of Sciences, 1984-90; Leading Scientific Worker, Laboratory of Quantum Optics, 1990-95; Professor, Department of Optics, 1995-, Faculty of Natural Sciences, Palacký University, Olomouc, Czech Republic. Publications: Monograph: Phase in Optics, 1998; Book Chapters in Modern Nonlinear Optics, 1993, Progress in Optics volume 33, 1994, volume 40, 2000, volume 43, 2002; Modern Nonlinear Optics part 1, 2001; Numerous articles in professional scientific journals. Honour: Collective Prize, Ministry of Education, Prague, 1991. Memberships: Union of Czech Mathematicians and Physicists, 1967-; International Society of Optical Engineering - SPIE, 1991. Address: Department of Optics, Faculty of Natural Sciences, Palacký University, Třída Svobody 26, 771 46, Olomouc, Czech Republic. E-mail: perinova@prfnw.upol.cz

PEROT (Henry) Ross, b. 27 June 1930, Texarkana, Texas, USA. Industrialist. m. Margot Birmingham, 1956, 4 children. Education: US Naval Academy. Appointments: US Navy, 1953-57; IBM Corporation, 1957-62; Founder, Electron Data Systems Corporation, 1962, Chair of Board, CEO, 1982-86; Director, Perot Group, Dallas, 1986-; Founder, Perot Systems Corporation, WA, 1988-, Chair, 1988-92, 1992-, Board Member, 1988-; Chair, Board of Visitors, US Naval Academy, 1970-; Candidate for President of USA, 1992, 1996; Founder, Reform Party, 1995. Publications: Not For Sale at Any Price, 1993; Intensive Care, 1995. Address: The Perot Group, PO Box 269014, Plano, TX 75026, USA.

PERRETT Bryan, b. 9 July 1934, Liverpool, England. Author; Military Historian. m. Anne Catherine Trench, 13 August 1966. Education: Liverpool College. Appointment: Defence Correspondent to Liverpool Echo, during Falklands War and Gulf War. Publications: The Czar's British Squadron (with A Lord), 1981; A History of Blitzkrieg, 1983; Knights of the Black Cross: Hitler's Panzerwaffe and its Leaders, 1986; Desert Warfare, 1988; Encyclopaedia of the Second World War (with Ian Hogg), 1989; Canopy of War, 1990; Liverpool: A City at War, 1990; Last Stand: Famous Battles Against the Odds, 1991; The Battle Book: Crucial Conflicts in History from 1469 BC to the Present, 1992; At All Costs: Stories of Impossible Victories, 1993; Seize and Hold: Master Strokes of the Battlefield, 1994; Iron Fist: Crucial Armoured Engagements, 1995; Against All Odds! More Dramatic Last Stand Actions, 1995; Impossible Victories: Ten Unlikely Battlefield Successes, 1996; The Real Hornblower: The Life and Times of Admiral Sir James Gordon, GCB, 1998; The Taste of Battle, 2000; The Changing Face of Battle, 2000; Gunboat!, 2000; Last Convoy, 2000; Beach Assault, 2000; Heroes of the Hour, 2001; Trafalgar, 2002; Crimea, 2002; Waterloo, 2003; For Valour – Victoria Cross and Medal of Honor Battles, 2003; D Day, 2005; U-Boat Hunter, 2005; British Military History for Dummies, 2007. Contributions to: War Monthly; Military History; World War Investigator; War in Peace (partwork); The Elite (partwork). Memberships: Rotary Club of Ormskirk. Address: 7 Maple Avenue, Burscough, Nr Ormskirk, Lancashire L40 5SL, England.

PERRIE Walter, b. 5 June 1949, Lanarkshire, Scotland. Poet; Author; Critic. Education: MA, Honours, Mental Philosophy, University of Edinburgh, 1975; MPhil, English Studies, University of Stirling, 1989. Appointments: Editor, Chapman, 1970-75; Scottish-Canadian Exchange Fellow, University of British Columbia, Canada, 1984-85; Managing Editor, Margin: International Arts Quarterly, 1985-90; Stirling Writing Fellow, University of Stirling, 1991; Part-Time Lecturer, Philosophy and Creative Writing, Perth College, 2000-. Publications: Metaphysics and Poetry (with Hugh MacDiarmid), 1974; Poem on a Winter Night, 1976; A Lamentation for the Children, 1977; By Moon and Sun, 1980; Out of Conflict, 1982; Concerning the Dragon, 1984; Roads that Move: A Journey Through Eastern Europe, 1991; Thirteen Lucky Poems, 1991; From Milady's Wood and Other Poems, 1997; The Light in Strathearn (poems), 2000; Decagon – Selected Poems 1995-2005, 2004; Caravanserai (Poems), 2005; Rhapsody of The Red Cliff (Poems), 2006; As Far As Thales – Beginning Philosophy, 2006; The King of France is Bald: Philosophy and Meaning, 2007; Editor (with John Herdman), FRAS magazine, 2004-; Contributions to: Journals and periodicals. Honours: Scottish Arts Council Bursaries, 1976, 1983, 1994, and Book Awards, 1976, 1983; Eric Gregory Award, 1978; Ingram Merrill Foundation Award, 1987 Scottish Arts Council Writers Bursary, 1999; Society of Authors, Travelling Scholarship, 2000. Memberships: PEN, Scotland; Society of Authors. Address: 10 Croft Place, Dunning, Perthshire PH2 0SB, Scotland.

PERRY Helen, b. 4 March 1927, Birmingham, Alabama, USA. Nurse; Teacher. m. George Perry, deceased, 3 sons, 1 daughter, deceased. Education: Birmingham School of Practical Nursing; Student, LaSalle Extension University, Chicago, 1968; Georgetown University, 1979; Doctorate, Mayanuis Mosaic Society, Duke University, San Antonio, 1979; Certified Paramedic. Appointments include: LPN, 1950-; Minister, Greater Emmanuel Holiness Church, Birmingham, 1957-; Member, Advisory Board, American Security Council, Virginia, 1969-91; Member, Coalition for Desert Storm; Volunteer, ARC, Birmingham, 1970; Notary Public, Alabama, 1970-; LPN Teacher, Wenona High School, City Board of Education, Birmingham, 1977-; Member, Hall of Fame, Presidential Task Force, Washington, 1983-91; Home Health Nurse, University of Alabama Birmingham Hospital, 1988-; Trustee, National Crime Watch, 1989; Member, Crime Watch American Police, Washington, 1989; Image Development Advisory Board; Nominee, National Republican Committee, Washington, 1991, 1992; Selected VIP Guest Delegate, Republican National Convention, Houston, 1992; Life Member Presidential Task Force, Washington, 1992; Member, Finance Committee Fundraiser, Middleton for Congress Campaign, 1994; Delegate, Commonwealth of Ky So Republican Leadership Conference, 2000; Member, Jefferson Committee, 2001; Nominated, Jefferson County Board of Education; Member, Advisory Board, National Congressional Committee, Washington; Teacher, Wilson Elementary School, 2005; Substitute Teacher, 2005-; School Teacher, City Board of Education of LPN Nurse; Clergy Member, ICC; Ordained Elder, Greater Emmanuel Temple Holiness Church Inc East. Publications: Composed song, The Hour of Midnight. Honours include: Named Good Samaritan, Law Enforcement Officers; Award, Alabama Sheriff Association, 1989; Award, Navy League, 1989-91; Certificate of Appreciation, Presidential Congressional Task Force, 1990, Republican National Committee, 1994; Diamond Award, USA Serve America, 1992; Republican Presidential Award, Legion of Merit, 1994; Royal Proclamation, Royal Highness Kevin, Prince Regent of Hutt River Province; Service Award, Alabama Board of Nursing; Outstanding Senior Citizens Certificate of Recognition; Sovereign Ambassador, Order of American Ambassadors, ABI Health Partners in Health Certificate of

Completion, Shepherd's Center Southside; Who's Who in America: Highest Achievers, 2006. Memberships: Alabama Nurses Association; Unknown Players; National Republican Women Association; Life Member, LaSalle Extension University Alumni; Alabama Sheriff Association; Nominated Member, Advisors of Professional Women; Service Award for over 40 years of service as a nurse, Alabama Board of Nursing. Address: 2021 10th Avenue South, Apt 513, Birmingham, AL 35205, USA.

PERRY Matthew, b. 19 August 1969, Williamstown, Massachusetts, USA. Actor. Education: Ashbury College, Ottawa, Canada. Career: Films: A Night in the Life of Jimmy Reardon, 1988; She's Out of Control, 1989; Getting In, 1994; Fools Rush In, 1997; Almost Heroes, 1998; Three to Tango, 1999; Imagining Emily, 1999; The Whole Nine Yards, 2000; Serving Sara, 2002; The Whole Ten Yards, 2004; Hoosiers 11: Senior Year, 2005; Numb, 2007; The Laws of Motion. 2008;The Beginning of Wisdom, 2008; TV: Boys Will be Boys; Home Free; Sydney; Who's The Boss?; The Tracey Ullman Show; Empty; The John Laroquette Show; Beverly Hills 90210; Growing Pains; 240 Roberts; Friends, 1994-2004; Studio 60 on the Sunset Strip, 2006-07; TV films: Second Chance, 1987; Dance 'Til Dawn, 1988; Sydney, 1990; Call Me Anna, 1990; Home Free, 1993; Deadly Relations, 1993; Parallel Lives, 1994; Scrubs, 2001; Play: Sexual Perversity in Chicago, London, 2003; Writing includes: Maxwell House; Imagining Emily. Address: William Morris Agency, 151 El Camino Drive, Beverly Hills, CA 90212, USA.

PERVOLARAKI Eleftheria, b. 6 December 1981, Rhodes, Greece. PhD Student. Education: Foundation Courses in Dandis Foundation School, Chania, Crete, Greece; BSc (Hons), Molecular Biology, Portsmouth University; MSc, Molecular Genetics, Leicester University; M Phil, PhD, University of Cardiff. Appointments: Research Assistant, Biosciences, Cardiff University, 2003-06. Memberships: Clock Biology Club, Leicester University; Neuroscience Society, SFN, USA. E-mail: pervolarakie@cf.ac.uk

PESCI Joe, b. 9 February 1943, USA. Film Actor. Creative Works. M. Claudia Haro (divorced), 1 child. Films include: Death Collector, 1976; Raging Bull, 1980; I'm Dancing as Far as I Can, 1982; Easy Money, 1983; Dear Mr Wonderful, 1983; Eureka, 1983; Once Upon a Time in America, 1984; Tutti Dentro, 1984; Man On Fire, 1987; Moonwalker, 1988; Backtrack, 1988; Lethal Weapon II, 1989; Betsy's Wedding, 1990; Goodfellas, 1999; Home Alone, 1990; The Super, 1991; JFK, 1991; Lethal Weapon III, 1992; Home Alone II, 1992; The Public Eye, 1992; My Cousin Vinny, 1992; A Bronx Tale, 1993; With Honours, 1994; Jimmy Hollywood, 1994; Casino, 1995; 8 Heads in a Duffel Bag, 1997; Gone Fishing, 1997; Lethal Weapon 4, 1998; The Good Shepherd, 2006. Honours include: Academy Award, Best Supporting Actor, 1991.

PESEK Jiri R V, b. 19 April 1936, Prague, Czech Republic. Geologist. m. Jarmila Dobiasova, 2 daughters. Education: Graduate, Faculty of Science, Charles University, 1959; Postgraduate Study, 1962-66; PhD, 1967. Appointments: Institute of Geology Exploration, 1959-60; Assistant Professor, 1967-88, Associate Professor, 1988-91, Professor of Economic Geology, 1991-, Faculty of Science, Charles University. Publications: 16 books and textbooks; About 305 papers in professional journals. Honours: Gold Medal, Faculty of Science; Commemorative Medal, Charles University. Memberships include: Czech Geological Society,

Sub-Commission on Carboniferous Stratigraphy. Address: Charles University Prague, Faculty of Science, 12843 Prague 2, Albertov 6, Czech Republic.

PESONEN Lauri Ilja Waltter, b. 5 October 1976, Helsinki, Finland. Senior Engineer. Education: Deutsche Schule, Helsinki, 1985-95; MSc, Computer Science, Helsinki University of Technology, 2001; PhD, Computer Science, Wolfson College, University of Cambridge, England, 2008. Appointments: Military Service, 1996-97; Software Engineer, More Magic Software, Finland, 1997-98; R&D Engineer, 1999-2001, Customer Care Team Leader, 2001-02, Product Development Manager, 2002, First Hop, Finland; Software Developer, Meridea Financial Software, Finland, 2002-03; Software Developer, IBM Research, Switzerland, 2004; Senior Engineer, Cambridge Consultants, England, 2006-. Publications: Conferences and journals. Memberships: Institute of Engineering and Technology.

PETER Gernot, b. 26 April 1942, Linz, Donau, Austria. Chemist. m. Agnes, 1 son, 1 daughter. Education: Diploma in Organic, Inorganic and Physical Chemistry, Dr phil nat in Biochemistry, Physical Chemistry and Clinical Chemistry, Faculty of Biochemistry and Pharmacy, Johann-Wolfgang-von-Goethe-University, Frankfurt, Germany. Appointments: Scientific Assistant, Centre of Biological Chemistry, Johann-Wolfgang-von-Goethe-University, 1973-81; Part-time Scientific Assistant, Institute of Laboratory Diagnostics and Haematological Paternity Testing, Giessen, 1973-78; Head, Laboratory of Pharmacokinetics, ASTA Medica AG, Frankfurt, 1981-90; Head, Group of Nonclinical Pharmacokinetics, ASTA Medica, 1990-2000; Manager, Senior Scientist, Preclinical Sciences, ADME (since 2002: VIATRIS GmbH & Co KG), 2001-03; Retired. Publications: 30 scientific articles and meeting abstracts; Patents in field of cytostatics; Contribution of pharmacokinetic parts to more than 10 expert opinions in connection with the international approval of drugs; International study reports. Memberships: Society of German Chemists; German Cancer Society; Society of Laboratory Animal Science; European Society for Autoradiography; German Society of Natural Scientists and Physicians; ADME panel in IPACT I and II. Address: Dr-Carl-Henss-Str 28, D-61130 Nidderau, Germany.

PETER Roland, b. 13 March 1940, Vienna, Austria. Biologist; Educator. m. Hedwig Kocko, 25 March 1972. Education: Studies in Biology, Chemistry and Biochemistry, University of Vienna, Thesis in Zoology, PhD, 1971. Appointments: Tutor, University of Vienna; Assistant Professor, 1972-81, Associate Professor (Oberrat), 1982-2001, University Professor of Cell Biology and Genetics, 2001-, Department of Cell Biology, University of Salzburg. Publications: Several articles on electrophoresis, stem cells, regeneration and reproduction in flatworms in scientific journals including: Zeitschrift für zoologische Systematik und Evolutionsforschung, Progress in Zoology, Verhandlungen der Deutschen Zoologischen Gesellschaft, Hydrobiologia, Marine Ecology, Belgian Journal of Zoology. Memberships: Freshwater Biological Association of the UK (Life Member); New York Academy of Sciences; Österreichische Gesellschaft für Biochemie und Molekularbiologie; Deutsche Gesellschaft für Zellbiologie; Deutsche Zoologische Gesellschaft. Address: Department of Cell Biology, University of Salzburg, Hellbrunnerstrasse 34, A-5020 Salzburg, Austria. E-mail: roland.peter@sbg.ac.at

PETROBELLI Pierluigi, b. 18 October 1932, Padua, Italy. University Teacher. Education: Laurea in Lettere, University of Rome, 1957; Master of Fine Arts, Princeton University, USA, 1961. Appointments: Librarian-Archivist, Istituto di studi verdiani, Parma, 1964-69; Professor of Music History, Conservatory "G Rossini", Pesaro, 1970-73; Assistant Professor of Music History, University of Parma, 1970-73; Lecturer in Music, 1973-77, Reader in Musicology, 1978-80, Faculty of Music, King's College, University of London; Director, Istituto nazionale di studi verdiani, Parma, 1980-; Professor of Music History, University of Perugia, 1981-83; Professor of Music History, University of Rome "La Sapienza", 1983-2005. Publications: Books: Tartini- Le fonti biografiche, 1968; Tartini, le sue idee e il suo tempo, 1992; Music in the Theatre, 1994; Some 200 articles in scholarly periodicals on music history, main topics: Italian Ars Nova; 17th Century Italian Opera; Mozart; Italian Opera of the 19th Century, mainly Verdi and Bellini. Honours: Chair of Italian Culture, University of California, Berkeley, 1988; Lauro de Bosis Lecturer in the History of Italian Civilisation, Harvard University, 1996; Visitante distinguido, Universidad Nacional de Cordoba, Argentina, 1996; Foreign Honorary Member, Royal Musical Association, 1997; Corresponding Member of the American Musicological Society, 1989. Memberships: Member, Commission Mixte, Répertoire Internationale des sources musicales, 1973-; Member, Akademie für Mozartforschung, Internationale Stiftung Mozarteum, Salzburg, 1991-; Accademia Europaea, 1992; Corresponding Member, Accademia Nazionale dei Lincei, 2000; National Member, 2005; Member of the External Advisory Board, Faculty of Music, Oxford University; Member, Advisory Board, Forschungsinstitut für Musiktheater, University of Bayreuth; Member of the Directorium, International Musicological Society, 1997-2007. Address: via di S. Anselmo 34, I-00153 Rome, Italy.

PETROV Alexander Alexandrovich, b. 3 February 1934, Orekhovo-Zuevo City, USSR. Applied Mathematician. m. Valentina Alexeevna Golovanova, 1 son. Education: Master's Degree, Moscow Institute of Physics and Technology, 1957; PhD, 1964; Professor, 1973. Appointments: Junior Researcher, 1963-68, Chief of Department, 1968-2005, Computing Centre, Academy of Sciences of USSR (since 1992 Russian Academy of Sciences, since 2004 Dorodnicin Computing Centre of Russian Academy of Sciences). Publications: More than 200 publications in scientific issues including more than 10 monographs; From Gosplan to Market Economy: Mathematical Analysis of the Evolution of the Russian Economic Structures (with I G Pospelov and AA Shaninin). Honours: Order of Friendship, State Prize of the USSR; The Peter the Great Medal (National). Membership: Academician, Russian Academy of Sciences. Address: Ul Vavilova 40, Moscow 119991, Russia. E-mail: petrov@ccas.ru

PETROV Vadim, b. 24 May 1932, Prague, Czech Republic. Composer; Professor of Composition. m. Marta Votápková, 26 June 1954, 1 son, 2 daughters. Education: Graduate, Department of Composition, Academy of Fine Arts, Prague, Czech Republic, 1956. Career: The Giant Mountains Fairy Tales; There Are Some Limits; The Romance of Water Spirit; The Good Old Band; Sonets Chi Seled in Stone; Pax Rerum Optima; The Swans' Lament; The Nightingale and Rose; The Twelve; Johan Doctor Faust Nocturno in G; Burlesque; The Valessian Intermezzo; Song of the Night; The Ditty. Compositions: Melancholical Waltz; Tango Habanero; Scherzo Poetico; Riva Dei Pini; Romans; The Silver Serenade; Russian Evangelium; Song for Jane Eyre; The Autumn Memory; Nigh Tango; Song of Hoping and Belief. Recordings: The Maple Violin; Lucy and Miracles; Anna Snegina; Don Quigxot; Don Jean and others. Publications: Czech and Slovak Composer, 1980; Film and Time, 1983; The Little Czechoslovak Encyclopedia, 1986. Honours: Award Of The Association of Czechoslovak Composers; Czech Television, 1997; Svobodné Slovo, Prague, 1997. Address: Hlubocinka 844, 25168 Kamenice, Czech Republic. E-mail: prof.petrov@seznam.cz Website: www.prof-vadim-petrov.cz

PETROV Valery Danilovich, b. 13 February 1946, Moscow, Russia. Consultant; Educator; Researcher; Lecturer. Education: Honoured Diploma in Physics of Semiconductors, Moscow Technical University, Moscow Power Institute, 1970. Appointments: Engineer, Chief Engineer, Scientist, Chief Scientist, Head of Laboratory, Moscow, 1971-89; Consultant, Educator, Researcher, Lecturer, West Europe, 1992-; Made outstanding contributions to several scientific fields: Physics, Photochemistry, Volumic Imaging, Human Vision; Holography; Research in Extra-Terrestrial Environments; Lectures on computer- and laser-based systems of volumic and quasi-volumic imaging; Proposed a novel concept and mechanism of volumic human and animal vision drastically different from traditional one based on stereoscopic approach, 1995; Some elements of his concept can be traced in Leonardo da Vinci's work "A Treatise on Painting" and in the works of prominent early researchers; Postulated the conceptual notion of volumic view as a basis of volumic data acquisition, 1995; Proposed the unified concept of physical volumic spaces, their artificial imitations and hypothetical computer-generated spaces, 1997; Invented momental holography, 1976-78, the technique was used in space flights, resulting in the first ever holograms and interferograms made in microgravity conditions, 1981-83; Obtained first holograms outdoors, 1978; Recorded first holograms in violet part of visible spectrum and in the near ultra-violet range with semiconductor lasers, 1999; Inventor, several devices for volumic imaging and for measurement of deformations and vibrations, including those capable of working outdoors in unpromising natural environments, 1996-2002; Proposed holographic minirobot for investigations of Mars, 2003; Invented novel bathless techniques for ultra-high resolution silver-halide media, 1996-97; Introduced instantaneous spray-jet holography and holographic interferometry, 1990-2002; Invented dynamic – sliding holographic method permitting to process tremendous amounts of data – over 100 GB per second, 2001-03; In photochemistry field, devised monobath chemical solution for ultra-high resolution silver-halide media, 1976-78. Publications: 110 research articles published in refereed journals and conference proceedings; Over 60 communications at international scientific conferences and invited lectures. Honours: Several Diplomas and Medals from IBC and from Marquis Who's Who in the World; Best Paper Award, from Toyota, 1999; Listed in more than 30 biographical books. Membership: FIBA. Address: Postfach 3350, D-89023, Ulm, Germany.

PETTY William Henry, b. 7 September 1921, Bradford, Yorkshire, England. Retired Educator; Poet. m. Margaret Elaine Bastow, 31 May 1948, 1 son, 2 daughters. Education: Peterhouse, Cambridge, 1940-41, 1945; MA, Cantab; 1950; BSc, London, 1953; D Litt, Kent, 1983. Appointments: Administrative, Teaching, and Lecturing posts, London, Doncaster, North and West Ridings of Yorkshire, Kent, 1945-73; Chief Education Officer, Kent, 1973-84; Chairman of Governors, Christ Church University College, Canterbury, 1992-94. Publications: No Bold Comfort, 1957; Conquest, 1967; Springfield: Pieces of the Past, 1994; Genius Loci (with Robert Roberts), 1995; The Louvre Imperial, 1997;

Interpretations of History, 2000; No-One Listening, 2002; Breaking-time, 2005; Hi-jacked Over China With Jane Austen, 2006. Contributions to: Various anthologies, 1954-2007, reviews, quarterlies, and journals. Honours: Cheltenham Festival of Literature Prize, 1968; Camden Festival of Music and the Arts Prize, 1969; Greenwood Prize, Poetry Society, 1978; Lake Aske Memorial Award, 1980; Commander of the Order of the British Empire, 1981; Swanage Festival of Literature Prize, 1995; Ali Competition Prize, 1995; Kent Federation of Writers Prize, 1995; White Cliffs Prize, 2000; Otaker/Faber Competition, 2003 and 2004; Envoi Competition, 2004; Split the Lark Prize, 2004; Coast to Coast Prize, 2005; Essex Festival Prize, 2006; Newark Poetry Prize, 2007; Listed in biographical dictionaries. Membership: Poetry Society. Address: Willow Bank, Moat Road, Headcorn, Kent TN27 9NT, England.

PEYTON Kathleen Wendy, (Kathleen Herald, K M Peyton), b. 2 August 1929, Birmingham, England. Writer. m. Michael Peyton, 1950, 2 daughters. Education: ATD, Manchester School of Art. Publications: As Kathleen Herald: Sabre, the Horse from the Sea, 1947; The Mandrake, 1949; Crab the Roan, 1953. As K M Peyton: North to Adventure, 1959; Stormcock Meets Trouble, 1961; The Hard Way Home, 1962; Windfall, 1963; Brownsea Silver, 1964; The Maplin Bird, 1964; The Plan for Birdsmarsh, 1965; Thunder in the Sky, 1966; Flambards Trilogy, 1969-71; The Beethoven Medal, 1971; The Pattern of Roses, 1972; Pennington's Heir, 1973; The Team, 1975; The Right-Hand Man, 1977; Prove Yourself a Hero, 1977; A Midsummer Night's Death, 1978; Marion's Angels, 1979; Flambards Divided, 1981; Dear Fred, 1981; Going Home, 1983; The Last Ditch, 1984; Froggett's Revenge, 1985; The Sound of Distant Cheering, 1986; Downhill All the Way, 1988; Darkling, 1989; Skylark, 1989; No Roses Round the Door, 1990; Poor Badger, 1991; Late to Smile, 1992; The Boy Who Wasn't There, 1992; The Wild Boy and Queen Moon, 1993; Snowfall, 1994; The Swallow Tale, 1995; Swallow Summer, 1995; Unquiet Spirits, 1997; Firehead, 1998; Swallow the Star, 1998; Blind Beauty, 1999; Small Gains, 2003; Greater Gains, 2005; Blue Skies and Gunfire, 2006. Honours: New York Herald Tribune Award, 1965; Carnegie Medal, 1969; Guardian Award, 1970. Address: Rookery Cottage, North Fambridge, Chelmsford, Essex CM3 6LP, England.

PFEFFER Philip E, b. 8 April 1941, New York, NY, USA. Biophysicist. m. Judith Stadlen, 2 sons, 1 daughter. Education: BS Chemistry, Hunter College of the City University of New York, 1962; MS, Chemistry, 1964, PhD, Chemistry, 1966, Rutgers University, New Brunswick, NJ. Appointments: Teaching Assistant, 1962-64, Research Assistant, 1964-66, Department of Chemistry, Rutgers University, New Brunswick, NJ; NIH Postdoctoral Research Fellow with Gerhardt Closs, University of Chicago, 1966-68; Research Chemist, Lipid Research Lab, Eastern Regional Research Center, 1968-76; Physical Leader, Physical Chemistry Lab, 1976-80; Lead Scientist, Microbial Biophysics and Biochemistry Lab, 1980-; Visiting Scientist, Department of Plant Physiology, Centre d'Etudes Nuclearies de Grenoble, 1986; Oxford Research Fellow, Department of Plant Science, Oxford University, 1989; Visiting Professor, Insititut de Biologie Vegetale Moleculaire, Universite Bordeaux, 1998; Adjunct Full Professor, Department of Bioscience and Biotechnology, Drexel University, Philadelphia, 1996-. Publications: Author and Co-author of 156 publications. Honours include: Bond Award, American Oil Chemists Society, 1976; Philadelphia Federal Service Award for Scientific Achievement, 1979; Philadelphia American Chemical Society Award, 1982;

USDA Science and Education Award, 1982; Agricultural Research Service North Atlantic Area Scientist of the Year, 1986; Competitive ARS Postdoctoral Research Associate Grants, 1986-1989; New Orleans ACS Award, 1987; Oxford University Visiting Scientist Stipend, 1989; OECD Fellowship, 1995, 1996; National Research Initiative Grant, Awardee, 1997-2000, 2002-2004. Memberships: American Society of Plant Biologists; American Chemical Society; International Society for Plant Microbial Interactions; AAAS. Address: USDA/ARS/Eastern Regional Research Center, Microbial Biophysics and Residue Chemistry, 600 E Mermaid Lane, Wyndmoor, PA 19038, USA.

PFEIFFER Michelle, b. 29 April 1957, Santa Ana, California, USA. Actress. m. (1) Peter Horton, divorced 1987, 1 adopted daughter, (2) David E Kelly, 1993, 2 children. Career: Films include: Grease 2; The Witches of Eastwick; Scarface; Married to the Mob; The Fabulous Baker Boys; Tequila Sunrise; Dangerous Liaisons, 1989; Frankie and Johnnie, 1990; Batman Returns, 1992; The Age of Innocence, 1993; Wolf, 1994; Dangerous Minds, 1997; Up Close and Personal, 1997; To Gillian on Her 37th Birthday, 1997; One Fine Day, 1997; A Thousand Acres, 1997; Privacy, 1997; The Story of US, 1999; The Deep End of the Ocean, 1999; A Midsummer Night's Dream, 1999; Being John Malkovitch, 1999; What Lies Beneath, 2000; I am Sam, 2001; White Oleander, 2002; Sinbad: Legend of the Seven Seas (voice), 2003; I Could Never Be Your Woman, 2007; Hairspray, 2007; Stardust, 2007. TV includes: Delta House; Splendour in the Grass. Address: c/o ICM, 8942 Wilshire Boulevard, Beverly Hills, CA 90211, USA.

PHAT Muny, b. 7 January 1951, Kampong Cham, Cambodia. Governmental Staff. m. U Phany, 2 sons, 2 daughters. Education: Bachelor degree (diploma), Agricultural Sciences, 1989; MSc, Agricultural Economic Development, 2004. Appointments: Staff, Provincial Department of Agriculture, 1979-90; Head of Agronomy Department, 1990-93, Dean, Agriculture Faculty, 1993-95, Vice Rector, 1995-2003, Royal University of Agriculture; Director, Prek Leap National School of Agriculture, 2003-07. Publications: Technical notes on native language (Khmere) on fruit tree propagation, vegetable culture, agroforestry (case study), industrial crops, livelihood income generation based on small business. E-mail: pathmuny@presa.edu.kh

PHEMISTER Pauline Jane, b. 24 April 1959, Renfrewshire, Scotland. Lecturer. 1 son. Education: MA (Hons), Mental Philosophy, 1980, PhD, Philosophy, 1985, University of Edinburgh; Dip Lib, College of Librarianship, Wales, 1981. Appointments: Part time Tutor, University of Edinburgh, 1985-88; Course Tutor, Open University, 1986-88; Sub-Faculty Fellow, Sub-faculty of Philosophy, Oxford University, 1988-91; Assistant Professor, Philosophy, University of Nebraska-Lincoln, 1991-93; Lecturer, Department of Philosophy, University of Liverpool, 1993-2005; Lecturer in Philosophy, 2005-, University of Edinburgh. Publications: 4 books and guest editions; 8 articles in professional journals; Numerous contributions to books, book reviews and shorter pieces. Honours: Bruce of Grange Hill Award, 1980, John Macmurray Prize, 1985, University of Edinburgh; Scottish Education Department Major Studentship, 1981-84; British Academy Post-Doctoral Research Fellowship, 1988-91; AHRB Research Leave Award, 1999. Memberships: G W Leibniz Gesellschaft, Hannover; British Society for the History of Philosophy; Leibniz Society of North America. E-mail: p.phemister@ed.ac.uk

PHILLIPS Anthony Charles Julian, b, 2 June 1936, Falmouth, Cornwall, England. Headmaster. m. Victoria Ann Stainton, 2 sons, 1 daughter. Education: Solicitors Articled Clerk, 1953-58; Qualified as a Solicitor, 1958; Law Society's Honours Examination, 1958; BD First Class, AKC First Class, King's College, London, 1963; PhD, Gonville & Caius College, Cambridge, 1967; Pre-ordination, The College of the Resurrection, Mirfield, 1966. Appointments include: Solicitor, London, 1958-60; Curate, The Good Shepherd, Arbury, Cambridge, 1966-69; Dean, Chaplain and Fellow, Trinity Hall, Cambridge, 1969-74; Honorary Chaplain to the Bishop of Norwich, 1970-71; Chaplain and Fellow, St John's College, Oxford, 1975-86; Lecturer, Theology, Jesus College, Oxford, 1975-86; Examining Chaplain to the Bishop of Oxford, 1979-86; Examining Chaplain to the Bishop of Manchester, 1980-86; Domestic Bursar, St John's College, Oxford, 1982-84; Chairman, Faculty of Theology, 1983-85; S A Cook Bye Fellowship, Gonville and Caius College, Cambridge, 1984; Lecturer, Theology, Hertford College, Oxford, 1984-86; Archbishops of Canterbury and York Interfaith Consultant for Judaism, 1984-85; Examining Chaplain to the Bishop of Wakefield, 1984-86; Canon Theologian of the Diocese of Truro, 1985-2002; Headmaster, The King's School, Canterbury, 1986-96; Honorary Canon of Canterbury Cathedral, 1987-96; County Chaplain to St John Ambulance, 1996-2002; Chapter Canon of Truro Cathedral, 2001-2002, Emeritus Canon, 2002-; The Royal Cornwall Polytechnic Society, Board Member, 2003-, Chairman, 2004-; Governor, SPCK, 1998-2006, Chair of Publishing, 2000-05. Publications: Books: Ancient Israel's Criminal Law, 1970; Deuteronomy, 1973; God BC, 1977; Lower than Angels: Questions raised by Genesis 1-11, 1983, 1996; Preaching from the Psalter, 1988; The Passion of God, 1995; Entering into the Mind of God, 2002; Essays on Biblical Law, 2002, paperback, 2004; Standing Up to God, 2005; Numerous articles in academic journals and newspapers. Honours: Archibald Robertson Prize, 1962, Junior McCaul Hebrew Prize, 1963, King's College, London; Serving Brother to the Order of St John, 2003. Memberships: Society of Old Testament Study; Worshipful Company of Broderers. Address: The Old Vicarage, 10 St Peter's Road, Flushing, Nr Falmouth, Cornwall TR11 5TP, England.

PHILLIPS Francis Douglas, b. 19 December 1926, Dundee, Scotland. Artist; Painter. m. Margaret Parkinson, 1 daughter. Education: DA, Dundee College of Art, 1951. Career: Military service with Army; Illustrator, D C Thomson & Co Ltd; Full time painter, 1966-; Illustrator, over 100 books; Taught water colour painting, Dundee Art Centre; Taught illustration, Dundee College of Commerce; Several paintings reproduced as Limited Edition Prints; Over 1145 covers for magazine, Peoples Friend; Cover work for British and French Readers Digest and Scottish Field; Article in Artists and Illustrators Magazine, 2007; TV interviews, 1991, 1992, 1993, 1996; Radio Tay interview, 1995; Exhibited widely in commercial galleries including: Group Exhibitions: The Royal Scottish Academy; The Royal Glasgow Institute of Fine Art; The Royal Scottish Society of Painters in Watercolour; The Royal Institute of Painters in Watercolour, London; One Person Exhibitions: Stables Gallery, Bathgate, 1986; Dundee Art Galleries, 1987; Step Gallery, Edinburgh, 1989; Cornerstone Gallery, Stirling, 1998; Two Person Exhibitions: Victoria Art Galleries-Albert Institute, Dundee, 1955; Cornerstone Gallery, Dunblane, 1992; Cornerstone Gallery, Stirling, 1995, 1998; Queens Gallery, Dundee, 2002; Leith Gallery, Edinburgh, 2002; Numerous Four Person Exhibitions, Collections, Private Collections and Group Exhibitions. Publications: Contributions to several magazines including: The Artist Magazine; The International Artists Magazine; The Scots Magazine. Membership: Life Member, Royal Glasgow Institute of Fine Art. Address: 278 Strathmore Avenue, Dundee, DD3 6SJ, Scotland.

PHILLIPS Sir Fred, b. 14 May 1918, St Vincent. Queen's Counsel. m. Gloria, 3 sons, 2 daughters. Education: Barrister, Middle Temple, 1956; LL.B, London, 1957; MCL (Master of Civil Law), McGill University, 1968; LLD, Hon, University of the West Indies, 1989. Appointments: Cabinet Secretary, Federal Government of the West Indies, 1960-62; Administrator, St Kitts, Nevis, Anguilla, 1966-67; Governor, St Kitts, Nevis, Anguilla, 1967-69; Chief Legal Adviser in the Caribbean for Cable and Wireless, 1969-97. Publications: Freedom in the Caribbean: A Study in Constitutional Change, 1977; The Evolving Legal Profession in the Commonwealth, 1978; West Indian Constitutions: Post Independence Reforms, 1985; Caribbean Life and Culture: A Citizen Reflects, 1991; Commonweath Caribbean Constitutional Law, 2002; Ethics of the Legal Profession, 2004; Numerous papers in journals. Honours: Commander of the Royal Victorian Order, (CVO); Knight Bachelor, 1967. Address: PO Box 3298, St John's, Antigua.

PHILLIPS Leslie Samuel, b. 20 April 1924, London, England. Actor; Producer; Director. m. four children. Career: Child actor; Vice President, Royal Theatrical Fund, Disabled Living Foundation; Films include: A Lassie From Lancashire, 1935; The Citadel; Train of Events; The Galloping Major; Sound Barrier; The Fake; The Limping Man; Value for Money; The Gamma People; As Long As They're Happy; The Big Money; Brothers in Law; The Barretts of Wimpole Street; Just My Luck; Les Girls; The Smallest Show on Earth; I Was Monty's Double; The Man Who Liked Funerals; Carry on Nurse; This Other Eden; Carry on Teacher; Please Turn Over; Doctor in Love; Watch Your Stern; Carry on Constable; In The Doghouse; Crooks Anonymous; The Fast Lady; Father Came Too; Doctor in Clover; The Magnificent 7 Deadly Sins; Not Now Darling; Don't Just Lie There; Out of Africa; Empire of the Sun; Scandal; King Ralph; Carry on Columbus; Caught in the Act; Day of the Jackal; Cinderella; Saving Grace; August; Lara Croft – Tomb Raider; Harry Potter and the Philosopher's Stone; Thunderpants; Collusion; Doctor in Trouble; Pool of London; Maroc 7; Colour Me Kubrick; With Shadows; Venue. Radio: numerous plays including Navy Lark; Les Miserables; Tales from the Backbench; Round the World in 80 Days; Wind in the Willows; TV: Our Man at St Mark's; Time and Motion Man; Reluctant Debutante; A Very Fine Line; Casanova 74; You'll Never See Me Again; Rumpole; Summer's Lease; Chancer; Lovejoy; Boon; House of Windsor; Love on the Branch Line; Canteville Ghost; The Pale Horse; Dalziel & Pascoe; The Sword of Honour; Into the Void; The Oz Trial; Take a Girl Like You; Tales of the Crypt, Who Bombed Birmingham? Holby City; Midsomer Murders; Where the Heart Is; Theatre: The Merry Wives of Windsor; On the Whole Life's Been Jolly Good; Love for Love; Naked Justice; For Better or Worse; Ghosts of Albion; Charley's Aunt; Camino Real; Deadly Game; Diary of a Nobody; Man Most Likely to…; Passion Play; Walking with Shadows; Heartbeat; Marple: By the Pricking of My Thumbs, The Last Detective. Honours: Evening Standard Lifetime Achievement in Films Award, 1997; OBE, 1998; CBE, 2008. Address: c/o Diamond Management, 31 Percy Street, London W1T 2DD, England.

PHILLIPS Sian, b. 14 May 1934, Bettws, Carmarthenshire, Wales. Actress. m. (1) D H Roy, 1954, (2) Peter O'Toole, 1960, divorced 1979, 2 daughters, (3) Robin Sachs, 1979, divorced 1992. Education: University of Wales; RADA.

Career: Child actress, BBC Radio Wales and BBC TV Wales; Newsreader, Announcer, Member of BBC repertory company, 1953-55; Toured for Welsh Arts Council with National Theatre Company, 1953-55; Arts Council Bursary, 1955; Royal TV Society annual televised lecture, 1992; Theatre includes: Lettice and Loveage, 2001; Divas at The Donmar Season, 2001; My Old Lady, Doolittle Theatre, Los Angeles, 2002, Promenade Theatre, New York, 2002-03; National Tour with The Old Ladies, 2003; The Dark, Donmar, London, 2004; Falling in Love Again, Cabaret, London, Europe, Israel, New York, UK tour; Films include: Becket, 1963; Goodbye Mr Chips, 1969; Laughter in the Dark, 1968; Murphy's War, 1970; Under Milk Wood, 1971; The Clash of the Titans, 1979; Dune, 1983; Ewok II; The Two Mrs Grenvilles; Sian, 1988; Dark River, 1990; The Age of Innocence, 1993; House of America, 1997; Coming and Going, 2001; Gigolo, 2004; TV: Shoulder to Shoulder, 1974; How Green Was My Valley, 1975; I, Claudius, 1976; Boudicca; Off to Philadelphia in the Morning, 1977; The Oresteia of Aeschylus, 1978; Crime and Punishment, 1979; Tinker, Tailor, Soldier, Spy, 1979; Sean O'Casey, 1980; Churchill: The Wilderness Years, 1981; How Many Miles to Babylon, 1982; Smiley's People, 1982; George Borrow, 1983; A Painful Case; Beyond All Reason; Murder on the Exchange; The Shadow of the Noose, 1988; Snow Spider, 1988; Freddie & Max; Emlyn's Moon; Perfect Scoundrels, 1990; Heidi, 1992; The Borrowers, 1992; The Chestnut Soldier, 1992; Huw Weldon TV Lecture, 1993; Summer Silence; The Vacillations of Poppy Carew; Mind to Kill; Ivanhoe, 1997; The Scold's Bridle, 1998; The Aristocrats, 1998; Alice Through the Looking Glass, 1998; Aristocrats, 1999; Nikita, 1999; The Magician's House, 1999, 2000; Cinderella, 2000; Attila, 2001; The Last Detective; The Murder Room; Numerous recordings and radio work. Honours: Honorary Fellow: University of Cardiff, 1981, Polytechnic of Wales, 1988, University of Wales, Swansea, 1998, Trinity College, Carmarthen; Honorary DLitt (Wales), 1984; CBE, 2000; Many awards for work in cinema, theatre and on TV including BAFTA Wales Lifetime Achievement Award, 2001. Memberships: Vice President, Welsh College of Music and Drama; Member, Gorsedd of Bards for services to drama in Wales, 1960; Member, Arts Council Drama Committee for 5 years; Governor, St David's Trust; Former Governor, Welsh College of Music and Drama; Fellow, Royal Society of Arts; Vice President, Actors Benevolent Fund. Address: L King, PDF, Drury House, 34-43 Russell Street, London, WC2B 5HA, England.

PHYSICK John Frederick, b. 31 December 1923, London, England. Museum Curator. m. Eileen Mary Walsh, 2 sons, 1 daughter. Education: Battersea Grammar School; Dr of the Royal College of Art; D Litt, Lambeth. Appointments: Home Guard, 1940-42; Royal Navy, 1942-46; Victoria and Albert Museum, 1948-84, retired as Deputy Director; Currently, Vice-Chairman, Rochester Cathedral Advisory Committee. Publications: The Engravings of Eric Gill, 1965; Designs for English Sculpture 1680-1860, 1969; The Wellington Monument, 1976; Marble Halls, 1975; The Victoria and Albert Museum: the history of its building, 1982; Sculpture in Britain (editor 2nd edition), 1988; The Albert Memorial (contributor), 2000; Westminster Abbey, Henry VII's Chapel (contributor), 2003; A Biographical Dictionary of British Sculptors 1660-1851, (contributor) 2007. Honours: CBE; Fellow, Society of Antiquaries. Memberships: Victorian Society; Society of Architectural Historians; Vice-President, Public Monuments and Sculpture Association; Vice-President, Church Monuments Society. Address: 14 Park Street, Deal, Kent CT14 6AG, England.

PIATTI Polo, b. 25 January 1954, Buenos Aires, Argentina. Freelance Composer. Education: Baccalaureate, Biological Sciences, College Revolución de Mayo, Buenos Aires, 1972; Professor, Nacional de Musica, National Music Conservatory, Buenos Aires, 1979; Maître de Musique et Musicologie, URF de Musicologie, Sorbonne University, Paris, France, 1981; Waldorf Musiclehrer, Anthroposophisch Pädagogisches Seminar, West Berlin, 1982. Appointments: Music & Instrument Teacher, France, Germany & UK, 1983-99; Workshop Leader, Improvisation for Music Teachers, Holland, Austria, Spain & UK, 1984-88; Musical Director & Composer, numerous educational institutions, Britain and abroad; Founder & Director, The First Improvisations Choir, Stuttgart, Germany, 1987-89; Head of Music & Co-Founder, Freie Kleintheaterschule, Stuttgart, Germany, 1987-89; Lecturer, Musical Cosmology, Holland, Austria, Italy, Germany & Switzerland, 1987-99; Co-Founder & Composer, Contemporary Performing Arts Project "Imaginism", Germany, 1988-89; Head of Music, Italia Conti Academy of Theatre Arts, London, 1994-95; Director of Music, World Centre for Performing Arts, England, 1995-96; Singing Tutor/Coach, master classes for professional international singers, London, 1996-2007; Founder, Managing Director & Owner, Polo Piatti Management Ltd, 1999-2005; Freelance Composer, Artistic Director for State & Multimedia Productions, 2004-; Piano concerts and performances throughout Europe; Conductor/ Founder: The First Improvisations Choir, Stuttgart, 1987-89; London Latin American Choir, 1997-2000; Rudolf Steiner Choir & Orchestra School, Stuttgart; Waldorf Students Choir & Orchestra. Publications: Compositions for dance; Original soundtracks; Original compositions for plays; Compositions and arrangements for shows. Honours: Listed in international biographical dictionaries; Musical Director 7 Composer in Residence, Theatre Forum Drei, 1987-89; Winner, Yearly Sponsorship for the Arts, Landes-Wurttemberg Bank, 1988; South Germany Klein Theatre Prize, 1990. Memberships: British Music Writers Council & PAMRA, London, UK. Address: c/o Peter Martin, 10 Harborne Close, South Oxhey, Watford, Hertfordshire WD19 6TZ, England. E-mail: polopiatti@mac.com

PICARD Barbara Leonie, b. 4 December 1917, Richmond, Surrey, England. Author. Publications: Ransom for a Knight, 1956; Lost John, 1962; One is One, 1965; The Young Pretenders, 1966; Twice Seven Tales, 1968; Three Ancient Kings, 1972; Tales of Ancient Persia, reprinted, 1993; The Iliad, 1991; The Odyssey, reprinted 2000; French Legends, Tales and Fairy Stories, 1992; German Hero-sagas and Folk-tales, 1993; Tales of the Norse Gods, 1994; Selected Fairy Tales, 1994; The Deceivers, 1996; The Midsummer Bride, 1999; Numerous other publications. Address: Oxford University Press, Great Clarendon Street, Oxford, England.

PICARD Robert Georges, b. 15 July 1951, Pasadena, California, USA. Professor. m. Elizabeth Carpelan, 1 son, 2 daughters. Education: BA, Loma Linda University, 1974; MA, California State University, Fullerton, 1980; PhD, University of Missouri, 1983. Appointments: Associate Professor (tenured), Assistant Professor, Louisiana State University, Louisiana, 1983-87; Associate Professor, Director of Communication Industries Management Program, Emerson College, Massachusetts, 1987-90; Professor (tenured), Graduate Studies Co-ordinator, 1997-98, Department Chair, 1994-97, California State University, Fullerton, 1990-98; Professor and Director, Media eMBA Programme, 1998-2003, Manager, Media Group, 1998-2003, VTTS Endowed Professorship, Media Economics, 2001-03, Turku School of Economics and Business Administration, Turku, Finland;

Professor, Economics, 2003-, Director, Media Management and Transformation Centre, 2003-, Director of Research, 2007-, Jönköping University, Jönköping International Business School, Sweden. Publications: 20 books; Papers and articles in professional journals. Honours: Numerous grants and contracts from around the world; Listed in international biographical dictionaries. Address: Media Management & Transformation Center, Jönköping International Business School, PO Box 1026, 55111 Jönköping, Sweden. E-mail: robert.picard@ihh.hj.se

PICASSO Paloma, b. 19 April 1949, Paris, France. Designer. m. Rafael Lopez-Cambil (Lopez-Sanchez) 1978, divorced 1998, (2) Eric Thevennet, 1999. Education: University of Paris; Sorbonne; Studied jewellery design and manufacture. Career: Designer, fashion jewellery for Yves St Laurent, 1969; Designer, jewellery for Zolotas, 1971; Designer, costumes and sets, Parisian theatre productions: L'Interpretation, 1975, Succès, 1978; Created Paloma Picasso brand and creations designed for: Tiffany & Co, 1980; L'Oreal; Metzler Optik Partner AG; Villeroy & Boch; KBC; Motif; Pieces in permanent collections of Smithsonian Institute, Musée des Arts Décoratifs and Die Neue Zamlang; Council of Fashion Design of America Accessory Award, 1989. Address: Paloma Picasso Parfums, 1 rue Pasquier, 92698 Levallois-Perret Cédex, France.

PICK Stepan, b. 26 December 1949, Prague, Czech Republic. Physicist. Education: Graduate, 1973, RNDr, 1976, Charles University; CSc, Czechoslovak Academy of Sciences, 1981. Appointments: J Heyrovsky Institute of Physical Chemistry, 1974, Researcher, 1986-; Visiting Professor, University of Nancy, France, 1992, 1993; Visiting Professor, University of Louis Pasteur, Strasbourg, France, 2006. Publications: Over 100 articles in professional journals. Memberships: Union of Czech Mathematicians and Physicists; Czech Union of Nature Conservation. Address: J Heyrovsky Institute of Physical Chemistry, Academy of Sciences of the Czech Republic, Dolejskova 3, CZ 182 23 Prague 8, Czech Republic.

PICKERING Alan Michael, b. 4 December 1948, York, England. Pension Consultant. m. Christine. Education: BA (Hons), Politics and Social Administration, University of Newcastle, 1969-72. Appointments: British Rail Clerical Officer, 1967-69; Head of Membership Services, Electrical, Electronics, Telecommunications and Plumbing Union, 1972-92; Partner, Watson Wyatt, 1992-; Member Occupational Pensions Board, 1992-97; Chairman, National Association of Pension Funds, 1999-2001; Chairman, European Federation for Retirement Provision, 2001-04; Chairman, Plumbing Industry Pension Scheme, 2001-; Non-Executive Director, The Pension Regulator, 2005-. Chairman, Life Academy, 2005-. Publication: A Simpler Way to Better Pensions, HMSO, 2002. Honour: CBE; Memberships: Blackheath and Bromley Harriers, President, 1992; Pensions Management Institute. Address: Watson Wyatt, 21 Tothill Street, London SW1H 9LL, England.

PICKTON David Wallace, b. 28 May 1954, Manchester, England. Marketing Educator; Researcher. m. Margaret Joan Irwin, 1981, 1 son, 1 daughter. Education: MA, University of Lancaster, 1978; Marketing Diploma, Chartered Institute of Marketing, 1975; Creative Diploma in Communications, Advertising and Marketing, CAM Foundation, 1975; International Management Teachers Programme, University of Bocconi, Milan, 1988; Certificate of Education, De Montfort University, 1983; Occupational/Psychometric Administrator, Ase NFER-Nelson, 1990. Appointments: Retail Marketing

and Advertising Manager, Dunlop (NTS), Stockport, England, 1975-76; Public Relations Officer, Metropolitan Borough of Stockport, 1978-79; Account Manager and Planner, Chetwynd Street Advertising, Manchester, 1979-81; Lecturer/Management Trainer, Blackwood Hodge Management Centre, Northampton, 1981-83; Principal Lecturer, 1983-2000, Head, Department of Marketing, 2000-, De Montfort University; Director, Isham Management Associates, Northampton, 1984-93; Visiting Academic, various universities, 1995-; Publisher/Reviewer, Oxford University Press, Oxford, 1998-; Macmillan, Basingstoke, 1998-; Research Bid Reviewer, Economic and Social Research Council, London, 2001; Editorial Board Member, Journal of Marketing Communications, 2002-; Marketing Intelligence and Planning Journal, 2003-; Corporate Communications Journal, 2005-; Registered Marketing Consultant, Department of Trade and Industry, 1988-92; Consultant, Strategic Management Development Ltd, Wadenhoe, Cambridgeshire, 1996-99; Regional Chairman, Marketing Education Group, East Midlands, 1987-90; Academic Adviser, Institute of Practitioners in Advertising, Industry/Academia Com, London, 1998; External examiner and adviser, various universities, 1988-; Assistant Editor, Marketing Intelligence and Planning Journal, Bradford, 2003-; International celebrity speaker, Celebrity Speakers Association, Andorra, 2004-. Publications: Author: Integrated Marketing Communications; Marketing: An Introduction; Applied Strategic Marketing; Contributed articles to professional journals and chapters to books. Honours: Best Paper, International Corporate and Marketing Communications Conference, 2001; Grantee: International Educational Bursary Foundation for Management Education, 1988; Marketing Consultancy, Department of Trade and Industry, 1990-92; Knowledge Transfer Partnerships, 2002-07; Research into Competitive Intelligence and Marketing Strategy, Chartered Institute of Marketing, 2003-04. Memberships: Fellow, Chartered Institute of Marketing; Fellow, Royal Society for the Arts; Communication, Advertising and Marketing Foundation; British Institute of Management; Institute of Learning and Teaching; Academy of Higher Education; Academy of Marketing. Address: De Montfort University, The Gateway, Leicester, Leicestershire LE1 9BH, England. E-mail: dpmar@dmu.ac.uk

PICKWOAD Michael Mervyn, b. 11 July 1945, Windsor, Berkshire, England. Film Designer. m. Vanessa Orriss, 3 daughters. Education: BSc, Honours, Civil Engineering, Southampton University. Career: Exhibitor, Director's Eye, MOMA, Oxford, 1992; Exhibition Design of Treasures of the Mind, Trinity College, Dublin Quatercentury (400 years), 1992; Design of Eastern Art Gallery, Ashmolean Museum, Oxford, 1996; Films: Comrades, 1985; Withnail & I, 1986; The Lonely Passion of Judith Hearne, 1987; How to Get Ahead in Advertising, 1988; The Krays, 1989; Let Him Have It, 1990; Century, 1992; Food of Love, 1996; Honest, 1999; High Heels, 2000; Television: Running Late, 1992; The Dying of the Light, 1994; Cruel Train, 1994; Cider With Rosie, 1998; A Rather English Marriage, 1998; David Copperfield, 1999; Last of the Blonde Bombshells, 1999; Hans Christian Andersen, 2001; Death in Holy Orders, 2002; The Deal, 2003; Death on the Nile, 2003; Archangel, 2004; The Queen's Sister, 2005; Sweeney Todd, 2005; Longford, 2006; Miss Marple, 2006-07; Old Curiosity Shop, 2007; Lost in Austen, 2007. Publications: Architectural paper models for the National Trust, 1972; Landmark Trust, 1973; St Georges Chapel, 1974; Architectural drawings for Hugh Evelyn Prints, 1973. Memberships: BAFTA; GBFD. Address: 3 Warnborough Road, Oxford OX2 6HZ, England.

PIERCE Mary, b. 15 January 1975, Montreal, Canada. Tennis Player. Career: Turned Professional, 1989; Moved to France, 1990; Represented France in Federation Cup, 1991; 1st Career Title, Palermo, 1991; Runner-up, French Open, 1994; Winner, Australian Open, 1995, Tokyo Nichirei, 1995; Semi-Finalist, Italian Open, Candian Open, 1996; Finalist, Australian Open singles, 1997, doubles with Martina Hingis, 2000; Winner of singles and doubles, with M Hingis, French Open, 2000; Highest singles ranking No 3; Winner of doubles, with M Hingis, Pan Pacific; French Federation Cup team, 1990-92, 1994-97; French Olympic team, 1992, 1996; 24 WTA Tour singles and doubles titles (by end 2002); France's (rising star) Burgeon Award, 1992; WTA Tour Comeback Player of the Year, 1997. Address: c/o WTA, 133 First Street North East, St Petersburg, FL 33701, USA.

PIERSCIONEK Barbara Krystyna, b. 20 October 1960, London, England. Academic; Professor. 1 son. Education: BSc (optom), 1983, PhD, 1988, University of Melbourne. MBA, University of Bradford, 2000; Postgraduate Diploma (Law), 2001; Postgraduate Diploma, Legal Practice, 2003, LLM, 2004, Leeds Metropolitan University. Appointments: Schultz Research Fellow, 1991-97; Senior Lecturer, 1998-2000, Senior Research Fellow, 2000-2004, University of Bradford; Professor of Optometry and Vision Science, University of Ulster, 2004-. Publications: Over 80 articles and conference abstracts; 1 book chapter; 1 encyclopaedia article; Numerous articles in professional magazines. Memberships: Society of MBAs; Law Society; Australian Optometric Association. Address: Department of Biomedical Sciences, University of Ulster, Cromore Road, Coleraine BT52 1SA, Northern Ireland. E-mail: b.pierscionek@ulster.ac.uk

PIGOTT-SMITH Tim (Timothy Peter), b. 13 May 1946, Rugby, England. Actor; Director. m. Pamela Miles, 1 son. Education: BA (Hons), Bristol University, 1964-67; Bristol Old Vic Theatre School, 1967-69. Career: Extensive theatre work includes most recently: Mourning Becomes Electra at the Royal National Theatre; Hecuba at the Donmar; Broadway: Sherlock Holmes and the Iceman Cometh; Television includes: The Lost Boys; Angelo and Hotspur for BBC Shakespeare series; Francis Crick in Life Story; Ronald Merrick in Jewel in the Crown; The Chief; The Vice; Richard Hale in North and South; The Last Flight to Kuwait, 2007; Holby City, 2007. Films include: Clash of the Titans; Escape to Victory; Remains of the Day; Bloody Sunday; Alexander; V for Vendetta, 2005; Entente Cordiale, 2005; Flyboys, 2005; Director: The Real Thing, National Tour, 2005; Royal Hunt of the Sun for a National Tour, 1989; Hamlet in Regent's Park, 1994; Samuel Beckett's Company, Edinburgh Fringe and the Donmar; Regular broadcaster. Publications: Out of India, 1986, 1990, 1997; Numerous audio-books. Honours: BAFTA, TV Times and Broadcasting Press Guild Best Actor Awards for the Jewel in the Crown, 1984; Fringe First, Edinburgh Festival for Samuel Beckett's Company; Honorary Dlitt, Leicester University, 2002. Memberships: Special Lecturer, Bristol University Drama Department. Address: Actual Management, 7 Gt Russell Street, London WC1B 3NH, England. Website: www.timpigott.smith.co.uk

PIKE David Alan Wingeate, b. 2 October 1930, Kent, England. Distinguished Professor Emeritus. m. Carol Lynn Tjernell, 2 daughters. Education: BA, McGill University, 1960; MA, Universidad Interamericana Mexico, 1961; Docteur de l'Université de Toulouse, 1966; PhD, Stanford University, 1968. Appointments: Allied Intelligence G2/GSI Trieste, 1950-52; Lloyds Broker, London, 1952-55; Assistant Director, Institute of Hispanic American and Luso-Brazilian

Studies, Stanford, 1962-64; Professor of Contemporary History and Politics, 1968-, Distinguished Professor, 1993-, Emeritus, 2001-, The American University of Paris; Vice-Chairman, California Institute of International Studies, Stanford, 1996-; Director of Research, American Graduate School of International Relations and Diplomacy, 2003-; Board, World Association of International Studies, Stanford, 2006. Publications: Les Français et la Guerre d'Espagne, 1975; In the Service of Stalin, 1993; Españoles en el Holocausto, 2003; Betrifft: KZ Mauthausen, 2005; Franco and the Axis Stigma, 2007. Honours: Sociétaire des Gens de Lettres de France; Fellow of the Royal Historical Society; Medalla de la Universidad Autónoma de Madrid. Listed in Who's Who publications and biographical dictionaries. Memberships: Association de la Presse anglo-américaine de Paris. Address: 62 rue Jean-Baptiste Pigalle, 75009 Paris, France. E-mail: david.pike@aup.fr Website: www.ac.aup.fr

PIKE Edward Roy, b. 4 December 1929, Perth, Western Australia. Physicist. Education: BSc, Mathematics, 1953, BSc, Physics, 1954, PhD, Physics, 1957, University College, Cardiff, Wales. Appointments: Fellow, American Society for Testing Materials, University College, Cardiff, 1954-58; Research Assistant, University of Wales, Cardiff, 1957-58; Instructor, Massachusetts Institute of Technology, USA, 1958-60; Senior Scientific Officer to Chief Scientific Officer, Royal Signals and Radar Establishment, Malvern, England, 1960-86; Visiting Professor of Mathematics, Imperial College of Science and Technology, London, 1984-85; Non-Executive Director, Richard Clay plc (Printers), 1984-86; Clerk Maxwell Professor of Theoretical Physics, King's College, London, 1986-; Head of School of Physical Sciences and Engineering, King's College, London, 1991-94; Chairman, Stilo Technology Ltd (Publishing and World Wide Web software), 1995-2002; Chairman, 2000-02, Non-Executive Director, 2002-04, Stilo International plc; Director, Phonologica Ltd, 2004-. Publications: 300 papers and 10 books in the fields of theoretical physics, X-Ray diffraction, statistics, imaging and optics, inverse problems, compact disc technology. Honours: Charles Parsons Prize, Royal Society, 1975; McRobert Award, Confederation of Engineering Institutions, 1977; Annual Achievement Award, Worshipful Company of Scientific Instrument Makers, 1978; Civil Service Award to Inventors, 1980; Guthrie Medal and Prize, Institute of Physics, 1995; Fellow, University College Cardiff; Fellow King's College London; Fellow of the Institute of Mathematics and Applications; Fellow of the Institute of Physics; Fellow of the Optical Society of America; Fellow of the Royal Society. Address: Physics Department, King's College London, Strand, London WC2R 2LS, England.

PIKE Lionel John, b. 7 November 1939, Bristol, England. University Professor; Organist. m. Jennifer Marguerite Parkes, 2 daughters. Education: BA, Class I, Music, B Mus, MA, D Phil, Pembroke College, Oxford; FRCO; ARCM. Appointments: Organist, 1969-, Lecturer in Music, 1965-80, Senior Lecturer in Music and College Organist, 1980-2004, Professor of Music, 2004-05, Royal Holloway College (University of London), UK; Retired, 2005. Publications: Beethoven, Sibelius and "The Profound Logic", 1978; Hexachords in Late Renaissance Music, 1998; Vaughan Williams and the Symphony, 2003; Pills to Purge Melancholy: The Evolution of the English Ballet, 2004. Honours: Book: Beethoven, Sibelius and "The Profound Logic", named by Choice Magazine as one of the three best academic books in any subject for the year 1978-79; Limpus Prize for FRCO; Honorary Fellowship, Royal Holloway College, 2007. Memberships: Royal College of Organists; Havergal Brian

Society; Robert Simpson Society; Herbert Howells Society; Ralph Vaughan Williams Society. Address: 34 Alderside Walk, Englefield Green, Egham, Surrey, TW20 0LY, England. E-mail: lionel.pike@hotmail.co.uk

PILLAY Gerald John, b. 21 December 1953, Natal, South Africa. Vice Chancellor; Rector. m. Nirmala, 2 sons. Education: Bachelor of Arts, 1975, Bachelor of Divinity (with distinction), 1979, Doctor of Theology, University of Durban-Westville, 1985; Doctor of Philosophy, Rhodes University, 1983; BA, BD, D Theol, Philosophical Theology, Durban; PhD, Ecclesiastical History, Rhodes University. Appointments: Lecturer, Senior Lecturer, Church History, University of Durban-Westville, 1979-87; Professor, Modern Church History, University of South Africa, 1988-96; Foundation Professor of Theology, 1997-2003, Dean of Liberal Arts, 1998-2003, Otago University, New Zealand; Vice Chancellor & Rector, Liverpool Hope University, 2003-. Publications: Numerous articles in professional journals. Honours: FRSA. E-mail: pillayg@hope.ac.uk

PILLINGER Colin Trevor, b. 9 May 1943, Bristol, England. Professor of Planetary Sciences. m. Judith Mary, 1 son, 1 daughter. Education: BSc, PhD, University of Wales; DSc, University of Bristol. Appointments: Research Assistant, Research Associate, University of Bristol, 1968-76; Research Associate, Senior Research Associate, University of Cambridge, 1976-84; Open University Senior Research Fellow, 1984-90; PI of NASA Apollo Programme; Personal Chair in Planetary Services, Department of Earth Sciences, Open University, 1990-97; Principal Investigator, ESA Inc, Rosetta Cometary Mission, 1994-2000; Gresham Professor of Astronomy, 1996-2000; Lead Scientist, Beagle 2 Project for ESA Mars Express Mission, 1997-; Head, Planetary & Space Sciences Research Institute, 1997-2005; Professor, Planetary Sciences, 1997-; Emeritus Gresham Professor of Astronomy. Publications: Over 1,000 refereed papers, conference proceedings, abstracts, reports and scientific journalism; 3 books. Honours: Aston Medal, 2003; CBE, 2004; A C Clarke Award, 2004; BIS Space Achievement Medal, 2005; Reginald Mitchell Memorial Medal, 2006; Asteroid 15614 named Pilinger. Memberships: FRAS, 1981; Fellow, Meteoritical Society, 1986; FRS, 1993; FRGS, 1993; Fellow, IAU, 1993; Fellow, University College, Swansea, 2003. Address: Planetary & Space Sciences Research Institute, The Open University, Walton Hall, Milton Keynes, Buckinghamshire MK7 6AA, England. E-mail: psrg@open.ac.uk

PIMPLE Gajendra Haridas, b. 25 April 1964, Washim (MS), India. Architectural Planner, Interior Designer; Vaastushastra Consultant. m. Manisha, 1 son, 1 daughter. Education: Diploma in Architecture, 1987; Vaastushastra Visharad (equivalent to Bachelor of Vaastu-Science), 2000; Vaastushastra Pandit, (equivalent to Master of Vaastu-Science), 2001. Appointments: Architectural Assistant to Mr Vishawas N Dikhole, M Arch, Nagpur, 1987; Visiting Lecturer, Maharashtra Kala Vidhyalaya, Nagpur, 1988-92; Architectural and Interior Designer, own private practice, 1992; Vaastushastra Consultant, own practice, 2000. Publications: Research papers presented at conferences and seminars; Articles published in popular and professional journals. Honours: Special Guest of Honour, Pune, 1999; Vastu-Shiromani, Raipur, 1999; Vastu-Sadhak, Khajuraho, 2000; Scholar Guest of Honour, Nagpur, 2000; Special Guest of Honour, Moka, Mauritius, 2001; Vastu-Aaditya, Haridwar, 2001; Vastu-Manishi, Surat, 2001; Special Honour, Colombo, Sri Lanka, 2002; Vastu-Alankar, Vrundavan, 2002. Memberships: Life Member, PACE International

Astromedical Academy, Delhi; Super Category Life Member, International Federation of Astrology & Spiritual Science, Jodhpur; Conference Member: Shri Shankar Jyotir-Vidhyalay, Poona; Asian Astrologers Congress, Kolkata; International Vastu Association, Jodhpur; Related Member: Art of Living Foundation, Wardha; Lions Club, Gandhi City, Wardha; Life Member, Bhavsar Jyoti, Pune; Sadbhav, Khamgaon; Executive Member, President, Founder Member, Shri Swami Samartha Sewa Trust, Wardha; Executive Member, Vice President, Bhavsar Society, Wardha; Executive Member, Co-ordinator and Founder Member, Designers and Planners Association, Wardha; Faculty, Visiting Lecturer to Dr R G Bhoyar Institute of Technical Education for Department of Interior Designing & Decoration, Wardha. Address: 33, State Bank Colony, Near Gajanan Apartments, Nalwadi, Wardha – 442 001, Maharashatra State, India.

PINCHER (Henry) Chapman, b. 29 March 1914, Ambala, India. Author. m. (1), 1 daughter, 1 son, (2) Constance Wolstenholme, 1965. Education: BSc Honours, Botany, Zoology, 1935. Appointments: Staff, Liverpool Institute, 1936-40; Royal Armoured Corps, 1940; Defence, Science and Medical Editor, Daily Express, 1946-73; Assistant Editor, Daily Express, Chief Defence Correspondent, Beaverbrook Newspapers, 1972-79; Academician, Russian Academy for Defence, Security and Internal Affairs, 2005-. Publications: Breeding of Farm Animals, 1946; A Study of Fishes, 1947; Into the Atomic Age, 1947; Spotlight on Animals, 1950; Evolution, 1950; It's Fun Finding Out (with Bernard Wicksteed), 1950; Sleep and How to Get More of It, 1954; Sex in Our Time, 1973; Inside Story, 1978; Their Trade is Treachery, 1981; Too Secret Too Long, 1984; The Secret Offensive, 1985; Traitors - the Labyrinth of Treason, 1987; A Web of Deception, 1987; The Truth about Dirty Tricks, 1991; One Dog and Her Man, 1991; Pastoral Symphony, 1993; A Box of Chocolates, 1993; Life's a Bitch!, 1996; Tight Lines!, 1997. Novels: Not with a Bang, 1965; The Giantkiller, 1967; The Penthouse Conspirators, 1970; The Skeleton at the Villa Wolkonsky, 1975; The Eye of the Tornado, 1976; The Four Horses, 1978; Dirty Tricks, 1980; The Private World of St John Terrapin, 1982; Contamination, 1989. Honours: Granada Award, Journalist of the Year, 1964; Reporter of the Decade, 1966; Honorary DLitt, University of Newcastle upon Tyne, 1979; King's College, London, fellow, 1979; Elected, Moscow Academy for Defence, Security & Law & Order, 2005; Russian Order of the Great Victory, 2006. Address: The Church House, 16 Church Street, Kintbury, Near Hungerford, Berkshire RG17 9TR, England.

PINCHUK Leonid, b. 14 May 1938, Gomel, Belarus. Engineer. m. L Kasatkina, 28 July 1966, 1 son, 2 daughters. Education: Graduated Engineer-Mechanic, Belarus Institute of Railway Engineers 1960; PhD, Engineering, 1972; DrSci, Engineering, 1983; Full Professor, Materials Science, Moscow,1990. Appointments: Technologist, Engineer-Designer, Locomotive Plant, Yaroslavl, 1960-68; Engineer, Researcher, Laboratory Chief, Department Head, Metal-Polymer Research Institute, Academy of Sciences of Belarus, Gomel, 1968-. Publications: 21 books; More than 360 articles in magazines and journals; 280 inventions. Honour: Honoured Inventor of Belarus, 2004. Memberships: Academician, Belarus Engineering Academy; Active Member, New York Academy of Sciences; National Geographical Society; Correspondent Member, International Eurasian Academy of Science. E-mail: mpri@mail.ru

PINE Courtney, b. 18 March 1964, London, England. Jazz Musician (saxophone). 1 son, 3 daughters. Career: International tours, with own reggae and acoustic jazz bands;

Trio (with Cameron Pierre, Talvin Singh) opened for Elton John and Ray Cooper, The Zenith, Paris and Royal Albert Hall, London, European Tour, 1994; Teacher's Jazz European tour, 1996; Support to Cassandra Wilson, US and Canada, 1996; Tours, Japan, South Africa and UK, 1996; Festivals in Europe, Japan, Thailand, 1996; Television appearances; Regular guest, Later With Jools Holland; Black Christmas, Channel 4; The White Room, 1996; Featured Artist on BBC's Perfect Day recording. Recordings include: Albums: Journey To The Urge Within, 1987; Destiny's Song, 1988; The Vision's Tale, 1989; Closer To Home, 1990; Within The Realms Of Our Dreams; To The Eyes Of Creation; Modern Day Jazz Stories', 1996; Underground, 1997; Another Story, 1998; History is Made at Night (soundtrack), 1999; Back in the Day (soundtrack), 2000; Featured guest on: Wandering Spirit (with Mick Jagger); Jazzmatazz, Guru; Jazzmatazz II - The New Reality, Guru; Summertime, track on The Glory of Gershwin (Larry Adler tribute album); Evita (with Madonna); Devotion, 2003; Radio: Presenter, BBC Radio 2 series, Millennium Jazz, 1999; 5 series of BBC Radio 2 Jazz Crusade, 1999-2004; UK Black 2003, Jazz Makers. Honours: Mercury Music Prize, one of Albums of the Year, 1996; Best Jazz Act, MOBO, 1996, 1997; Best Jazz Act, BBC Jazz Awards, 2001; Gold Badge, Academy Composers and Songwriters, 2002. Address: c/o 33 Montpelier Street, Brighton, BN1 3DI, England. Website: www.courtney-pine.com

PINNEY Lucy Catherine, b. 25 July 1952, London, England. Author; Journalist. m. Charles Pinney, 14 June 1975, divorced, 2000, 2 sons, 1 daughter. Education: BA, Honours, English, Education, York University, 1973. Publications: The Pink Stallion, 1988; Tender Moth, 1994; A Country Wife, 2004. Contributions to: Sunday Times; Observer; Daily Mail; Telegraph; Company; Cosmopolitan; Country Living; Country Homes and Interiors; She; The Times, columnist, 1998-2003. Honour: Runner-up, Betty Trask Prize, 1987. Address: Egremont Farm, Payhembury, Honiton, Devon EX14 0JA, England.

PINSENT Sir Matthew Clive, b. 10 October 1970, Norfolk, England. Former Oarsman. m. Dee, 2 sons. Education: University of Oxford. Career: First represented UK at Junior World Championships, 1987, 1988; Gold Medal, coxless pairs (with Tim Foster), 1988; Competed 3 times in University Boat Race for Oxford, 1990, 1991, 1993, winning twice; Gold Medal, coxless pairs (with Steve Redgrave), World Championships, 1991, 1993, 1994, 1995; Olympic Games, Barcelona, 1992, Atlanta, 1996; Gold Medal, coxless fours (with Steve Redgrave, Tim Foster and James Cracknell), World Championships, 1997, 1998, 1999, Olympic Games, Sydney, 2000; Gold Medal, coxless pairs (with James Cracknell), World Championships, 2001, 2002 (new world record); Gold Medal, coxless fours (with Cracknell, Coode and Williams) Olympic Games, Athens, 2004; Member, International Olympic Committee, 2002-04; Retired, 2004. Publication: A Lifetime in a Race, 2004. Honours: International Rowing Federation Male Rower of the Year; Member, BBC Sports Team of the Year, 2004; Knighted, 2004. Address: c/o Professional Sports Partnerships Ltd, The Town House, 63 The High Street, Chobham, GU24 8AF, England. Website: www.matthewpinsent.com

PINTO Maria Cristina Rosamond, b. 30 August 1950, Goa, India (Portuguese). Professor of Genetics and Medicine. m. Vice Count Aboim Borges, Joao Paulo, deceased. Education: BSc, 1969, MD, 1978, MA, 1983, University of Lisbon; PhD, Molecular Biology/ Genetics, University of Miami; PhD, Medicine, University of Lisbon, 1988; Board Certified

Geneticist, Portuguese Medical Boards, 1992. Appointments: University Assistant and Educator, 1978-; Assistant Professor, University of Lisbon, 1988; Consultant, Portuguese Board of Sciences & Technology, Representative of Gene Therapy Group in European Community, Associate Professor; Researcher, Molecular Genetics, Studies in Human Fertility; Portuguese and European Support Groups for Genetics Deficiencies and Aged People. Publications: 3 scientific books; Over 300 national and international publications. Honours: Literature Poetry Composition, 1974; Award, Best Rated Medical Graduate with Five Portuguese Medical Schools, 1978; Honours Pfizer Prize, 1981. Memberships: American Society of Human Genetics; American College of Medical Genetics; European Society of Human Genetics; Gene Therapy Society; UNESCO. Address: R Amilcar Cabral, n 21, R/C H 1750-018, Lisbon, Portugal.

PIPERAKI Stavroula Ina, b. 14 September 1965, Athens, Greece. Pharmacist. m. George Theodossopoulos, 2 sons. Education: French Literature Course, Sorbonne IV, 1984; Computer Sciences Course, Hellenic Center of Productivity, 1985; PhD, Pharmaceutical Sciences, University of Athens, 1993. Appointments: Special Postgraduate Scholar, Division of Pharmaceutical Chemistry, Laboratory of Pharmaceutical Analysis, 1990-93; Scientific Training Manager, Pancosmetics Hellas, 1991-92; Researcher Program, National Drug Organisation, 1991-93; Regulatory Affairs Manager, Aventis SA, 1993-96; Researcher, Department of Chemistry, University of York, 1993; Teacher, Postgraduate Program, Division of the Pharmaceutical Technology, University of Athens, 1995; Teacher, Postgraduate Program, Division of the Pharmaceutical Chemistry, University of Athens, 1996-97; Manager, Department of Regulatory Affairs, Pharmacovigilance Department, Aventis SA, 1996-98; Manager and Owner, pharmacy, Athens, 1997-. Publications: Co-author, 17 articles in scientific journals; 20 conference papers; Participant in several congresses, meetings, seminars and workshops. Honours: National School Awards for Excellency, 1979-83; Listed in international biographical dictionaries. Memberships: Pharmaceutical Association of Pharmacists of Attica; Panhellenic Association of Pharmacists; American Association for the Advancement of Science; AMICAL; European Society of Regulatory Affairs.

PIPPARD Sir (Alfred) Brian, b. 7 September 1920, London, England. Physicist. m. Charlotte Frances Dyer, 3 daughters. Education: Clare College Cambridge, 1938-41. Appointments: Demonstrator, Lecturer, Reader in Physics, 1946-60, John Humphrey Professor of Physics, 1960-71, Cavendish Professor of Physics, 1971-82, Cambridge University; President, Clare Hall, Cambridge, 1966-73. Publications: Elements of Classical Thermodynamics, 1957; Cavendish Problems in Classical Physics, 1962; Dynamics of Conduction Electrons, 1965; Forces and Particles, 1972; Physics of Vibration, 2 volumes, 1978, 1983; Response and Stability, 1985; Magnetoresistance, 1989; Many papers in Proceedings of the Royal Society and other journals. Honours: Hughes Medal, Royal Society, 1959; Holweck Medal, 1961; Dannie-Heinemann Prize, 1969; Guthrie Prize, Institute of Physics, 1970; Knight Bachelor, 1975. Memberships: Fellow, Clare College, Cambridge, 1947-66; Fellow of the Royal Society, 1956-; Honorary Fellow, Clare College, 1973-; Honorary Fellow, Clare Hall, 1973; President, Institute of Physics, 1974-76; Honorary Fellow, Institute of Physics. Address: 30 Porson Road, Cambridge CB2 2EU, England.

PIQUET Nelson, b. 17 August 1952, Rio de Janeiro, Brazil. Racing Driver. m. (1) Maria Clara, (2) Vivianne Leao, 1 son. Appointments: 1st Grand Prix, Germany, 1978; Member, Ensign Grand Prix Team, 1978, BS McLaren Team, 1978, Brabham Team, 1978-85, Williams Team, 1986-87, Lotus Team, 1988-89, Benetton Team, 1990; Winner of 23 Grand Prix; Formula One World Champion, 1981, 1983, 1987.

PISARCHIK Alexander N, b. 3 June 1954, Minsk, Belarus. Physicist. m. Liudmila Kotashova, 1 son, 4 daughters. Education: MS, Belorussian State University, 1976; PhD, Institute of Physics, Minsk, 1990. Appointments: Visiting Professor, University Libre, Brussels, 1992; Visiting Professor, Universitat Autonoma de Barcelona, 1993-94, 1997-99; Visiting Professor, University of Iceland, Reykjavik, 1995; Senior Researcher, Institute of Physics, Minsk, 1996-99; Research Professor, Centro de Investigaciones en Optica, Leon, Gto, Mexico, 1999-. Publications: Contributor, articles to professional journals including Physics review A and E; Physics review Letters; Physica D; Physics Letters A; Optical Communications. Honours: First Prize, National Academy of Science, Minsk, 1999. Memberships: European Physical Society, 1994-; Academia Mexicana de Optica, 2000-; Society for Industrial and Applied Mathematics, 2001-; Mexican National System of Researchers (SNI, level 3), 2001-; Mexican National System of Evaluators on Science and Technology (SINECYT), 2002-. Address: Centro de Investigaciones en Optica AC, Loma del Bosque # 115, Col Lomas del Campestre, 37150 Leon, Guanajuato, Mexico. E-mail: apisarch@foton.cio.mx

PISPAS Asterios (Stergios), b. 16 October 1967, Athens, Greece. Chemist. m. Tserepa Charikleia, 1 son. Education: BS, Chemistry, 1989, PhD, Polymer Chemistry, 1994, University of Athens, Greece. Appointments: Post Doctoral Fellow, Department of Chemistry, University of Alabama, Birmingham, USA, 1994-95; Research Associate, Department of Chemistry, University of Athens, Greece, 1997-2004; Associate Researcher, Theoretical and Physical Chemistry Institute, National Hellenic Research Foundation, 2004-. Publications: Over 110 research publications in refereed journals; Over 140 announcements in Scientific Conferences; Co-author, 1 book on Block Copolymers. Honours: American Institute of Chemists Foundation Award for Outstanding Postdoctoral Fellow, 1995; ACS-PMSE Doolittle Award for Best Paper, 2003; Associate Editor, European Physical Journal E: Soft Matter, 2003-. Memberships: Greek Chemists Association; Greek Polymer Society; Editorial Board, The Open Macromolecules Journal, 2007-. Address: Theoretical and Physical Chemistry Institute, National Hellenic Research Foundation, 48 Vassileos Constantinou Ave, 11635 Athens, Greece. E-mail: pispas@eie.gr

PITA João Rui, b. 30 October 1961, Coimbra, Portugal. Professor. Education: Lic, Pharmaceutical Sciences, 1986, PhD, Pharmacy, 1995, Ageregation, Pharmacy (Social Pharmacy, History of Pharmacy), 1999, Faculty of Pharmacy, University of Coimbra, Portugal. Appointments: Assistant, 1986-89, 1989-95, Auxiliar Professor, 1995-99, Researcher, Interdisciplinary Studies on the 20th Century Centre, 1997-, Auxiliar Professor with Aggregation, 1999-2002; Associate Professor with Aggregation, 2002-, University of Coimbra. Publications: 9 books; Over 150 articles; 16 book chapters. Honours: Member, International Academy of the History of Pharmacy, 2001. Memberships: History of Science Society, USA; American Institute of the Historyof Pharmacy, USA; Societe d'Histoire de la Pharmacie, France; Centro de Direito Biomedico, Portugal. Address: Faculty of Pharmacy, University of Coimbra, Rua do Norte, 3000 Coimbra, Portugal. E-mail: jrpita@ci.uc.pt Website: www.uc.pt/coimbra

PITCHER Harvey John, b. 26 August 1936, London, England. Writer. Education: BA, 1st Class Honours, Russian, University of Oxford. Publications: Understanding the Russians, 1964; The Chekhov Play: A New Interpretation, 1973; When Miss Emmie was in Russia, 1977; Chekhov's Leading Lady, 1979; Chekhov: The Early Stories, 1883-1888 (with Patrick Miles), 1982; The Smiths of Moscow, 1984; Lily: An Anglo-Russian Romance, 1987; Muir and Mirrielees: The Scottish Partnership that became a Household Name in Russia, 1994; Witnesses of the Russian Revolution, 1994; Chekhov: The Comic Stories, 1998. Contributions to: Times Literary Supplement. Address: 37 Bernard Road, Cromer, Norfolk NR27 9AW, England.

PITCHES Douglas Owen, b. 6 March 1930, Exning, Suffolk, England. Poet & Artist. m. Barbara Joyce Budgen, 7 August 1954. Education: BA, Honours, Open University, 1979. Publications: Poems, 1965; Prayer to the Virgin Mary (Chaucer Translation), 1965; Man in Orbit and Down to Earth, 1981; Art Demands Love Not Homage, 1992. Contributions to: Orbis; Outposts; Envoi; Tribune; Anthologies: Responding; New Voices; Another 5th Poetry Book and others. Address: 14 Linkway, Westham, Pevensey, East Sussex BN24 5JB, England.

PITELIS Christos Nicholas, b. 10 November 1957, Greece. Academic. 1 son, 1 daughter. Education: Ptychion (BA) Public Administration, Pantion University, Greece, 1979; Postgraduate Diploma, Public and Industrial Economics, University of Newcastle, England, 1980; MA, 1982, PhD, 1984, Economics, Warwick University, England. Appointments: Teaching Assistant, University of Warwick, 1982-84; National Service, Greek Army, 1988; Residential Tutor, University of Nottingham, England, 1984-87; Lecturer, University of Nottingham, 1984-89; Lecturer, University of St Andrews, Scotland, 1989-91; Professor of Strategic Management, The China-Europe Management Institute, Beijing, Peoples Republic of China, 1991; Visiting Professor, University of St Petersburg, 2007; Special Advisor, Minister of Industry, Greece, 1994-95; Economic Advisor to Greek Government & Co-ordinator, The Future of Greek Industry project, Ministry of Development, Athens, 1995-97; Senior Research Fellow, Birmingham Business School, England, 1997-; Director, Centre of International Business and Management, 1997-, University Senior Lecturer, International Business Economics, 2000-04, University Reader, International Business and Competitiveness, 2004-, Judge Business School, University of Cambridge; Part time Professor, Department of Economics, University of Athens, 2006-; Director of Studies, Management, Queens' College, University of Cambridge, 2000-. Publications: 3 monographs; 6 edited books; Numerous articles in professional journals; 7 books, 2 in preparation. Honours: Trustee, Harry Hansen Fellowship Trust; New Century Award, 1999; Listed in international biographical dictionaries. Memberships: Academy of Management; European International Business Academy; Academy of International Business; Consultant to many governments and international organisations; Fellow, Economics, Queens' College, University of Cambridge. Address: Queens' College, University of Cambridge, Silver Street, Cambridge CB3 9ET, England. E-mail: c.pitelis@jbs.cam.ac.uk

PITKEATHLEY Jill Elizabeth, b. 4 January 1940, Guernsey, Channel Islands. Peer of the Realm. 1 son, 1 daughter. Education: Ladies College, Guernsey. Appointments President, Volunteering England; Chair of Cafcas (Children and Families Court Advisory Service); Labour Peer. Publications: Only Child, 1994; Cassandra and Jane, 2005. Honours: Honorary Degrees from Bristol and Metropolitan Universities; OBE, 1993; Peerage, 1997. Address: House of Lords, London, SWIA 0PW, England.

PITMAN Jennifer Susan, b. 11 June 1946, England. Racehorse Trainer. m. (1) Richard Pitman, 1965, 2 sons, (2) David Stait, 1997. Career: National Hunt Trainer, 1975-99; Director, Jenny Pitman Racing Ltd, 1975-99; Racing and Media Consultant, 1999-; Winners include: Corbiere, Welsh National, 1982, Grand National, 1983; Burrough Hill Lad, Welsh National, 1984, Cheltenham Gold Cup, 1984, King George VI Gold Cup, 1984, Hennessy Gold Cup, 1984; Smith's Man, Whitbread Trophy, 1985; Gainsay, Ritz Club National Hunt Handicap, 1987, Sporting Life Weekend Chase, 1987; Garrison Savannah, Cheltenham Gold Cup, 1991; Wonderman, Welsh Champion Hurdle, 1991; Don Valentino, Welsh Champion Hurdle, 1992; Royal Athlete, Grand National, 1995; Willsford, Scottish National, 1995; Last Winner, Scarlet Emperor, Huntingdon, 1999. Publications: Glorious Uncertainty (autobiography), 1984; Jenny Pitman: The Autobiography, 1999; On the Edge, 2002; Double Deal, 2002; The Dilemma, 2003; The Vendetta, 2004. Honours include: Racing Personality of the Year, Golden Spurs, 1983; Commonwealth Sports Award, 1983, 1984; Piper Heidsieck Trainer of the Year, 1983-84, 1989-90; Variety Club of Great Britain Sportswoman of the Year, 1984; OBE, 1998. Address: Owls Barn, Kintbury, Hungerford, Berkshire, RG17 9XS, England.

PITT Brad, b. 18 December 1963, Shawnee, Oklahoma, USA. Film Actor. m. Jennifer Anniston, 2000, divorced, 2005, 1 daughter, twins (son and daughter) with Angelina Jolie. Creative Works: TV appearances include: Dallas (series); Glory Days (series); Too Young to Die? (film); The Image (film); Films include: Cutting Glass, Happy Together, 1989; Across the Tracks, 1990; Contact, Thelma and Louise, 1991; The Favor, Johnny Suede, Cool World, A River Runs Through It, 1992; Kalifornia, 1993; Legend of the Fall, 1994; 12 Monkeys, 1995; Sleepers, Mad Monkeys, Tomorrow Never Dies, 1996; Seven Years in Tibet, The Devil's Own, 1997; Meet Joe Black, 1998; Fight Club, Snatch, 2000; The Mexican, Spy Game, Ocean's Eleven, 2001; Confessions of a Dangerous Mind, 2002; Sinbad: Legend of the Seven Seas (voice), 2003; Troy, Ocean's Twelve, 2004; Mr & Mrs Smith, 2005; Babel, 2006; Ocean's Thirteen, The Assassination of Jesse James by the Coward Robert Ford, 2007; Burn after Reading, 2008. Address: Creative Artists Agency, 9830 Wilshire Boulevard, Beverly Hills, CA 90212, USA.

PITTAWAY Neil John, b. 14 August 1973, Wakefield, England. Artist. Education: BA (Hons) Fine Art, University of Gloucestershire, 1992-96; City & Guilds Teacher's Certificate, Dewsbury College, 1997-98; MA, Printmaking, University of Bradford, 1996-98; Postgraduate Diploma in Fine Art, The Royal Academy Schools, London, 1998-2001; PGCE, University of Huddersfield, 2004. Career: Work held in many private and public collections including: The Ashmolean Museum, Oxford; British Museum (RWS Collection), London; St Paul's Cathedral, London; Victoria and Albert Museum, London; Guildhall Art Library, London; Indian Institute of Contemporary Art, Mumbai, India; Dover Street Arts Club, London; D H Lawrence Museum and Birthplace,

Nottingham; Work for: Great Artists, Channel 5 TV, 2001. Publications: Longitude: Printmaking Today, 2001; Drawings for "London in Poetry and Prose", Enitharmon Press, London, 2003; The RWS, The Watercolour Expert, 2004; Illustration Magazine, 2005; RWS Watercolour Masters Then & Now, 2006. Honours: Selected Awards include: Ashmolean Museum Oxford Prize; The Dover Street Arts Club Excellence in Drawing Award; The Gwen May Re Award; John Smith Award; British Institution prize for printmaking and drawing; Elizabeth Scott Moore Award. Memberships: Elected Associate Member, 2000, Full Member, 2005, Royal Society of Painter-Printmakers; Elected Associate Member, 2002, Full Member, 2005, Royal Watercolour Society; Elected Artist Member, Arts Club Dover Street, London, 2001-. Address: 1 Glenfields, Netherton, Wakefield, West Yorkshire WF4 4SH, England. E-mail: njpittaway@hotmail.com Website: www.njpittaway.co.uk

PIUNOVSKIY Alexei, b. 16 March 1954, Moscow, Russia. Mathematician. m. Galina Piunovskaya, 2 daughters. Education: MSc, Electrical Engineering, 1971-76, MSc, Applied Mathematics, 1980, PhD, Applied Mathematics, 1981, Moscow Institute of Electronic Technology. Appointments: Engineer, Researcher, Moscow Institute of Electronic Technology, 1976-84; Head of Group, Moscow Institute of Physics and Technology, 1984-2000; Senior Lecturer, Reader, University of Liverpool, 2000-. Publications: 64 publications in total; Optimal Control of Random Sequences in Problems with Constraints, Kluwer, 1997; Articles in journals including: Mathematics of Operational Research; Journal of Mathematical Analysis and Applications. Honours: Multiple grants from Russian Fund of Basic Research, EPSRC, Royal Society, LMS, British Council. Membership: Moscow Mathematical Society; The OR Society; American Mathematical Society. Address: Department of Mathematical Sciences, Peach Street, The University of Liverpool, Liverpool L69 7ZL, England.

PIZZI Romain, b. 5 November 1974, Port Elizabeth, South Africa. Veterinary Surgeon. Education: BVSc, Pretoria University, South Africa, 1999; MSc, Wild Animal Health, London Royal Veterinary College and Institute of Zoology, London, England, 2000; CertZooMed, 2002, DZooMed, Avian, 2005, Royal College of Veterinary Surgeons, London; MACVSc, Small Animal Surgery, Australian College of Veterinary Scientists, 2005. Appointments: Private practice, Blackpool, Lancashire, England, 2 years; Field Veterinarian, Haryana state, Northern India; Veterinary Surgeon, Inglis Veterinary Centre, Dunfermline, Scotland, 2003-05; Royal Zoological Society of Scotland Senior Clinical Scholar in Exotic Animal/Wildlife Medicine, Royal (Dick) School of Veterinary Studies, Edinburgh University, 2003-05; Zoo and Wildlife Pathologist, Zoological Society of London, 2005-06; Director, Zoological Medicine Ltd, Roslin, Scotland, 2006-; Special Lecturer, Zoo and Wildlife Medicine, The University of Nottingham, 2007-. Publications: Numerous articles in professional journals, national conferences papers, conference posters, books, book chapters and reviews. Memberships: Royal College of Veterinary Surgeons; British Veterinary Zoological Society; World Association of Wildlife Veterinarians; European Association of Zoo and Wildlife Veterinarians. Address: Zoological Medicine Ltd, 37 Easter Bush, Roslin, Midlothian EH25 9RE, Scotland. E-mail: romain@zoologicalmedicine.org

PLANT Colin Wilfrid, b. 16 November 1952, Burslem, Stoke-on-Trent, England. Consultant Entomologist. m. Lesley Carole Brewitt, divorced, 1 son, 1 daughter. Education: Newcastle-under-Lyme High School; BSc in Applied

Biology, University of London, 1970-74. Appointments: Scientific Officer, North-east Thames Regional Public Health Laboratory, 1975-79; Museum Biologist, Newham Museum Service, 1979-94; Freelance consultancy work, 1989-. Publications: Numerous articles in professional scientific journals. Memberships: Fellow, Royal Entomological Society; Past President: London Natural History Society; British Entomological Society; Essex Field Club; Editor: Entomologist's Record; The Natural History of Buckingham Palace Garden, London, 2001. Address: 14 West Road, Bishops Stortford, Hertfordshire CM23 3QP, England. E-mail: cpauk1@ntlworld.com

PLATER Alan Frederick, b. 15 April 1935, Jarrow on Tyne, County Durham, England. Writer; Dramatist. m. (1) Shirley Johnson, 1958, divorced 1985, 2 sons, 1 daughter, (2) Shirley Rubinstein, 1986, 3 stepsons. Education: King's College, Durham, 1953-57; University of Newcastle. Career: Full time writer, for stage, screen, radio, television, anthologies and periodicals, 1960-; Written extensively for radio, TV, films and theatre, also for The Guardian, Listener, New Statesman, etc; Plays include: The Fosdyke Saga; Films include: It Shouldn't Happen to a Vet; Keep the Aspidistra Flying; TV series include: Z Cars; Softly Softly; TV adaptions include: Barchester Chronicles; The Fortunes of War; A Very British Coup; Campion; A Day in Summer; A Few Selected Exits; Oliver's Travels; Dalziel and Pascoe. Publications: The Beiderbecke Affair, 1985; The Beiderbecke Tapes, 1986; Misterioso, 1987; The Beiderbecke Connection, 1992; Oliver's Travels, 1994; Doggin' Around, 2006 and others. Honours: Various stage, radio and television drama awards; Honorary Fellow, Humberside College of Education, 1983; Honorary DLitt (Hull), 1985; Hon DCL (Northumbria), 1997; Royal TV Society Writers' Award, 1988; BAFTA Writers' Award, 1988; BAFTA Dennis Potter Award, 2005. Memberships: Royal Society of Literature, fellow; Royal Society of Arts, fellow; Co-chair, 1986-87, President, 1991-95, Writer's Guild of Great Britain. Address: c/o 200 Fulham Road, London SW10 9PN, England.

PLATT Theodore, b. 8 September 1937, Moscow, Russia. Conductor; Composer; Double Bassist; Harpsichordist. Education: Degree in Double Bass Performance, Composition and Music Education, Ippolitov-Ivanov Conservatory of Music, 1956; Doctorate, Moscow Conservatory of Music, 1962. Career: Founder and Director, 4 chamber ensembles including first baroque and classical ensembles in USSR (Moscow), 1968-81, and New York Concertino Ensemble, 1981; Live concerts on major classical music radio stations in US; 8 years as Double Bass Soloist of Moscow Chamber Orchestra under Rudolf Barshay (performance with Gilels, Menuhin, Oistrakh, Rostropoivch, others); Discovered and premiered lost baroque works; Teacher and Coach of String Instruments and Voice. Compositions: 2 Symphony Concertos; Cycles of Vocal Compositions; Rapsodietta on Two Japanese songs for Symphony Orchestra; Poem for Sympfony Orchestra, Souvenir of Japan; 1 Quartet. Recordings: Baroque, Romantic and modern works as Double Bass Soloist of Moscow Chamber Orchestra under Rudolf Barshay; Baroque-Early Romantic repertoire (Mozart, Boccherini, Bach, Schubert, others) as Music Director and Soloist with New York Concertino Ensemble. Memberships: Conductors Guild; College Music Society. Address: Sun Coast Chamber Concerts Inc, 12315 Durango Avenue, North Port, FL 34287-1109, USA.

PLENDER Richard Owen, b. 9 October 1945, Epsom, Surrey, England. Barrister; Author. m. Patricia Clare Ward, 2 daughters. Education: Open Exhibition, BA, 1967, LLB, 1968, Queens' College, Cambridge; MA, 1970, PhD, 1971, University of Sheffield; LLM summa cum laude, 1971, JSD, 1983, University of Illinois, USA; LLD, University of Cambridge, 1993. Appointments: Assistant Lecturer, University of Sheffield, 1968-70, University of Illinois, 1971-72, University of Exeter, 1972-74; Called to Bar, Inner Temple, 1974; Lecturer, Reader, Director Centre of European Law, King's College London, 1974-88; Visiting Professor, University of Paris II, 1988-89; Legal Advisor to UN High Commissioner for Refugees, 1976-78; Référendaire, European Court of Justice, 1980-83; Queens Counsel, 1988-. Publications: Books include: International Migration Law, 1972, 2nd edition, 1988; Fundamental Rights, 1973; Cases and Materials on the Law of the European Communities, 1980, 3rd edition, 1993; A Practical Introduction to European Community Law, 1980; Introduccion al Derecho Comunnario, 1985; Basic Documents in International Migration Law, 1988, 2nd edition, 1996, 3rd edition, 2006; Legal History and Comparative Law, 1990; The European Contracts Convention – The Rome Convention on the Choice of Law for Contracts, 1991, 2nd edition, 2001. Honours: Rebecca Squires Prize, University of Cambridge, 1967; College of Law Prize, University of Illinois, 1973; Berridale-Keith Prize, 1972; QC, 1988; Honorary Senior Member, Robinson College, Cambridge; Honorary Visiting Professor, City University. Membership: World Trade Organisation List of Panellists. Address: 20 Essex Street, London WC2R 3AL, England.

PLESKO Ivan, b. 13 June 1930, Selpice, Slovakia. Physician. m. Anna, 2 daughters. Education: MD, Comenius University, Bratislava, 1955; PhD, 1964; DSc, Slovak Academy of Sciences, Bratislava, 1987; Associate Professor, 1968. Appointments: Research Assistant, 1955-68; Assistant Professor, Epidemiology, Comenius University, Bratislava, 1968-76; Host Researcher, Institute Pasteur, Paris, 1968-; Assistant Professor, University of Constantine, Algery, 1971-73; Head, Department of Epidemiology, Cancer Research Institute, Slovak Academy of Sciences, 1976-; Head, National Cancer Registry of Slovakia, 1980-2005. Publications: Atlas of Cancer Occurrence in Slovakia; Epidemiology of Lung Cancer; Atlas of Cancer Mortality in Central Europe; More than 190 papers in professional journals. Honours: Jesenius Medal, Research in medical sciences; Golden Medal, Research and Art; Gold medal of Health Promotion Foundation, Warsaw, Poland; Gold medal of the Slovak Medical Society; Award Panacea for lifelong research activities, 2004; Important individuality of Slovak Academy of Sciences, 2005; others; Listed in national and international dictionaries. Memberships: League Against Cancer, Slovakia; International Association of Cancer Registries; Science Council; Czech National Cancer Registry; European Institute of Oncology. Address: Pri Suchom mlyne 62, 811 04 Bratislava, Slovakia.

PLISCHKE Le Moyne W, b. 11 December 1922, Greensburg, Pennsylvania, USA. Research Chemist. m. Joan Harper. Education: BS, Waynesburg University, Pennsylvania, 1948; MS, West Virginia University, 1952. Appointments: Instructor, Waynesburg University, Pennsylvania, 1948-49; Research Chemist, US Naval Ordnance Test Station, California, 1952-53; Assistant Professor of Chemistry, Virginia Commonwealth University, Virginia, 1953-54; Research Chemist, E I Dupont, New Jersey, 1955-57; Research Chemist, Monsanto, Florida, 1957-. Publications: 18 US patents; 51 foreign patents. Honours: Monsanto Achievement Award.

Memberships: American Chemical Society. Address: 2100 Club House Drive, Lillian, AL 36549-5402, USA. E-mail: plis123@gulftel.com

PLOWRIGHT Dame Joan Anne, b. 28 October 1929, Brigg, Lancashire, England. Actress. m. (1) Roger Gage, 1953, (2) Sir Laurence (later Lord) Olivier, 1961-89 (his death)1 son, 2 daughters. Education: Old Vic Theatre School. Appointments: Member, Old Vic Company, toured South Africa, 1952-53. Creative Works: Plays and films include: Britannia Hospital, 1981; Richard Wagner, Cavell, Brimstone and Treacle, 1982; The Cherry Orchard, 1983; The Way of the World, 1984; Mrs Warren's Profession, Revolution, 1985; The House of Bernardo Alba, 1986; Drowning by Numbers, 1987; Uncle Vanya, The Dressmaker, The Importance of Being Earnest, 1988; Conquest of the South Pole, And a Nightingale Sang, I Love You to Death, 1989; Avalon, 1990; Time and the Conways, Enchanted April, Stalin, 1991; Denis the Menace, A Place for Annie, 1992; A Pin for the Buterfly, Last Action Hero, 1993; Widow's Peak, On Promised Land, Return of the Natives, Hotel Sorrento, A Pyromaniac's Love Story, The Scarlet Letter, Jane Eyre, 1994; If We Are Women, Surviving Picasso, Mr Wrong, 1995; 101 Dalmatians, The Assistant, 1996; Shut Up and Dance, Tom's Midnight Garden, It May Be the Last Time, 1997; America Betrayed, Tea with Mussolini, 1998; Return to the Secret Garden, Frankie and Hazel, 1999; Bailey's Mistake, Global Heresy, 2000; George and the Dragon, Bringing Down the House, 2002; The Great Goose Caper, Absolutely Perhaps, I Am David, 2003; George and the Dragon, Mrs Palfrey at the Claremont, 2005; Goose on the Loose, Curious George (voice);2006; The Spiderwick Chronicles, Knife Edge, 2008. Publications: And That's Not All, autobiography, 2001. Honours include: Best Actress, Tony Award, 1960; Best Actress, Evening Standard Award, 1964; Variety Club Award, 1976; Variety Club Film Actress of the Year Award, 1987; Golden Globe Award, 1993; 18th Crystal Award for Women in Film, USA, 1994. Address: c/o The Malthouse, Horsham Road, Ashurst, Steying, West Sussex BN44 3AR, England.

PLUMMER Christopher, b. 13 December 1929, Toronto, Canada. Actor. m. (1) Tammy Lee Grimes, 1956, 1 daughter, (2) Patricia Audrey Lewis, 1962 (divorced 1966), (3) Elaine Regina Taylor, 1970. Career: Theatre includes: Professional debut, Ottawa Repertory Theatre; Broadway debut, 1951-52; Numerous appearances in USA: Julius Caesar; The Tempest; The Lark; L'Histoire du Soldat; JB, 1951-61; The Resistable Rise of Arturo Ui; The Royal Hunt of the Sun, 1965-66; The Good Doctor, 1973; Othello, 1981; Macbeth, 1988; No Man's Lane, 1994; Barrymore, 1996; Many leading Shakespearean roles, Stratford Canadian Festival Co; British debut, Richard III, 1961; Leading actor, National Theatre Co of Great Britain, 1971-72; Many TV roles; Films include: The Fall of the Roman Empire; The Sound of Music; Inside Daisy Clover; Triple Cross; Oedipus the King; Nobody Runs Forever; Lock Up Your Daughters; The Royal Hunt of the Sun; Battle of Britain; Waterloo; The Pyx; The Spiral Staircase; Conduct Unbecoming; The Return of the Pink Panther; The Man Who Would Be King; Aces High, 1976; The Disappearance, 1977; International Velvet, The Silent Partner, 1978; Hanover Street, 1979; Murder by Decree, The Shadow Box, 1980; The Disappearance, The Janitor, 1981; The Amateur, 1982; Dreamscape, 1984; Playing for Keeps, Lily in Love, 1985; Dragnet, 1987; Souvenir, 1988; Shadow Dancing; Mindfield, Where the Heart Is, 1989; Star Trek VI: The Undiscovered Country, 1991; Malcolm X, 1992; Wolf, Dolores Claiborne, 1994; Twelve Monkeys, 1995; Skeletons, 1996; The Arrow, 1997; The Insider, All the Fine, 1999; The Dinosaur Hunter,

Dracula, 2000; Lucky Break, Blackheart, A Beautiful Mind, Full Disclosure, 2001; Ararat, Nicholas Nickleby, 2002; Blizzard, Cold Creek Manor, 2003; National Treasure, Alexander, 2004; Tma, Our Fathers, Must Love Dog, Syriana, The New World, 2005; Inside Man, The Lake House, 2006; Man in the Chair, Closing the Ring, Emotional Arithmetic, Aldready Dead, 2007; My DogTulip, 2008. Honours: Theatre World Award, 1955; Evening Standard Award, 1961; Delia Australian Medal, 1973; Antoinette Perry (Tony) Award, 1974; Emmy Award, 1977; Genie Award, 1980; Australian Golden Badge of Honour, 1982; Maple Leaf Award, 1982; Tony Award for Best Leading Actor in a Play, 1997. Address: c/o Lou Pitt, The Pitt Group, 9465 Wilshire Boulevard, Suite 480, Beverly Hills, CA 90212, USA.

PODSIADLO Elzbieta, b. 9 August 1938, Doly Opacie, Kielce voivodship, Poland. Lecturer. Education: MS, Natural Sciences, University of Wroclaw, 1962; PhD, Agricultural Sciences, 1972, Assistant Professor in Agricultural Sciences, 1987, The Agricultural University of Warsaw. Appointments: Teacher, secondary school, 1962-63; Laboratory Assistant, Senior Research Assistant, Assistant Professor, Professor, Department of Zoology, Agricultural University of Warsaw, 1963-. Publications include: Morpho-biological studies on primary parasites of scale insects from the genus of Asterodiaspis Signoret in Poland, 1986; Concept of the species of Asterodiaspis variolosa, 1990; Morphological adaptations for respiration in Coccidae, 2005. Memberships: The Polish Entomological Society. Address: Department of Zoology, Agricultural University of Warsaw, Ciszewskiego 8, 02-786 Warsaw, Poland. E-mail: podsiadlo@alpha.sggw.waw.pl

POE Terry Lynn, b. 30 March 1952, Asheboro, North Carolina, USA. Public School Educator; Church Organist. Education: BA, Music Education, Wake Forest University, 1974; Mentor Teacher Certification, 1988. Appointments: Boy Scouts of America, 1965-70; Accompanist/Associate Director, Raleigh Boychoir, 1974-94; Teacher, Wake County Public Schools, 1974-; Church Organist, Trinity United Methodist Church, 1976-; Chapel Organist, St Mary's College, Raleigh, 1979-85; Mentor Co-ordinator, Carroll Middle School, 1996-. Honours: Wake County Executive PTA Secondary Teacher of the Year, 1988; Listed in international biographical dictionaries. Memberships: National Education Association; Music Educators National Conference; American Guild of Organists. Address: 704 Hampstead Place, Raleigh, NC 27610-1720, USA. E-mail: terrylpoe@aol.com

POITIER Sidney, b. 20 February 1927, Miami, Floria, USA. Actor. m. (1) Juanita Hardy, 4 daughters, (2) Joanna Shimkus, 2 daughters. Appointments: Army service, 1941-45; Actor with American Negro Theatre, 1946; Member, 1994-2003, President, 1994-2003, Board of Directors, Walt Disney Company; Ambassador to Japan from the Commonwealth of the Bahamas; Actor, films including: Cry the Beloved Country; Red Ball Express; Go, Man, Go; Blackboard Jungle, 1955; Goodbye My Lady, 1956; Edge of the City, Something of Value, 1957; The Mark of the Hawk, The Defiant Ones, 1958; Porgy and Bess, 1959; A Raisin in the Sun, Paris Blues, 1960; Lilies of the Field, 1963; The Long Ships, 1964; The Bedford Incident, 1965; The Slender Thread, A Patch of Blue, Duel at Diablo, 1966; To Sir With Love, In the Heat of the Night, 1967; Guess Who's Coming to Dinner, 1968; For the Love of Ivy, 1968; The Lost Man, 1970; They Call Me Mister Tibbs, 1970; The Organization, 1971; The Wilby Conspiracy, 1975; Shoot to Kill, 1988; Deadly Pursuit, 1988; Separate But Equal, TV, 1992; Sneakers, Children of the Dust, TV, 1995; To Sir With Love II, TV, 1996; Actor, director,

Buck and Preacher, 1972; Warm December, 1973; Uptown Saturday Night, 1974; Let's Do It Again, 1975; A Piece of the Action, 1977; One Man, One Vote, 1996; Mandela and de Klerk, (TV), 1997; Director, Stir Crazy, 1980; Hanky Panky, 1982; Got For It, 1984; Little Nikita, 1987; Ghost Dad, 1990; Sneakers, 1992; The Jackal, 1997; David and Lisa (TV), 1998; Free of Eden (TV), 1999; The Simple Life of Noah Dearborn (TV), 1999; The Last Brickmaker in America (TV), 2001. Publication: This Life, 1980. Honours: Silver Bear Award, Berlin, 1958; NT Film Critics Award, 1958; Academy Award, Oscar, Best Actor of 1963; Cecil B De Mille Award, 1982; Life Achievement Award, American Film Institute, 1992; Kennedy Centre Honours, 1995; Honorary KBE; Honorary Academy Award for Lifetime Achievement, 2002. Address: c/o CAA, 9830 Wilshire Boulevard, Beverly Hills, CA 90210, USA.

POLAŃSKI Roman, b. 18 August 1933, Paris, France. Film Director; Writer; Actor. m. (1) Barbara Kwiatkowska-Lass, divorced, (2) Sharon Tate, 1968, deceased 1969, (3) Emmannuelle Seigner, 1989, 2 children. Education: Polish Film School, Łódź. Career: Actor: A Generation; The End of the Night; See You Tomorrow; The Innocent Sorcerers; Two Men and a Wardrobe; The Vampire Killers; What? 1972; Blood for Dracula, 1974; Chinatown, 1974; The Tenant, 1976; Chassé-croisé, 1982; Back in the USSR, 1992; A Pure Formality, 1994; Dead Tired, 1994; Tribute to Alfred Lepetit, 2000; The Revenge, 2002; Director: Two Men and a Wardrobe, 1958; When Angels Fall; Le Gros et Le Maigre; Knife in the Water; The Mammals; Repulsion; Cul de Sac; The Vampire Killers, 1967; Rosemary's Baby, 1968; Macbeth, 1971; What? 1972; Lulu (opera), Spoleto Festival, 1974; Chinatown, 1974; The Tenant, 1976; Rigoletto (opera), 1976; Tess, 1980; Vampires Ball, 1980; Amadeus (play), 1981; Pirates, 1986; Frantic, 1988; Tales of Hoffman (opera), 1992; Bitter Moon, 1992; Death and the Maiden, 1984; Dance of the Vampire (play), 1997; The Ninth Gate, 1999; Icons; A Pure Formality; In Stuttgart, 2000; The Pianist, 2002; Zemsta, 2002; Oliver Twist, (Director), 2005; Rush Hour 3, 2007. Publications: Roman (autobiography), 1984. Honours: Prize, Venice Film Festival, 1962; Prize, Tours Film Festival, 1963; Prize, Berlin Film Festival, 1965, 1966; Best Director Award, Society of Film and TV Arts, 1974; Le Prix Raoul-Levy, 1975; Golden Globe Award, 1980; Pris René Clair for Lifetime Achievement, Academy Française, 1999; Best Film, Cannes Film Festival, 2002; Academy Award for Best Director, 2003; BAFTA Award for Best Film and Best Director, 2003. Address: c/o ICM, 8942 Wilshire Boulevard, Beverly Hills, CA 90211-1934, USA. Website: www.icmtalent.com

POLIAKOFF Stephen, b. 1952, London, England. Dramatist; Director. m. Sandy Welch, 1983, 1 son, 1 daughter. Education: Westminster School; University of Cambridge. Theatre: Clever Soldiers, 1974; The Carnation Gang, 1974; Hitting Town, 1975; City Sugar, 1976; Strawberry Fields, 1978; Shout Across the River, 1978; The Summer Party, 1980; Favourite Nights, 1981; Breaking the Silence, 1984; Coming into Land, 1987; Playing with Trains, 1989; Sienna Red, 1992; Sweet Panic, 1996; Blinded by the Sun, 1996; Talk of the City, 1998; Remember This, 1999; Films: Hidden City, 1992; Close My Eyes, 1992; Century, 1995; The Tribe, 1998; Food of Love, 1998; TV plays include: Caught on a Train; She's Been Away; Shooting the Past, 1999; Perfect Strangers, 2001; The Lost Prince, 2003; Friends and Crocodiles, 2005; Gideon's Daughter, 2005; Joe's Palace, 2007; A Real Summer, 2007; Capturing Mary, 2007. Publications: Plays One, 1989; Plays Two, 1994; Plays Three; Sweet Panic; Blinded by the Sun; Talk of the City; Shooting the Past; Remember This. Honours include: Best British Film Award, 1992; Critic's Circle Best

Play Award; Prix Italia; BAFTA Award; Venice Film Festival Prize. Address: 33 Donia Devonia Road, London N1 8JQ, England.

POLISYUK Galina B, b. 13 October 1931, Moscow, Russia. Lector; Professor. m. Emil Polisyuk, 3 daughters. Education: Moscow Evening University of Marx and Lenin; Moscow Energy-Economical Institute of S Orgenekidze. Appointments: Professor, Faculty of Economy of Interbranch Complexes, 1990-; Professor, Faculty of Book Keeping in Trade, 1992; Professor, Faculty of Book Keeping and Audit, REA by G V Pleehanov, 2004. Publications: The economic analysis of efficiency and rates of growth of building manufacture, 1977; Audit (manual), 2000; Audit (text book), 2003; The simplified system of the taxation of the account and reporting of the small enterprises, 2004; Audit: technology of check (manual), 2005. Honours: Doctor of Economic Sciences. Memberships: Professional Auditor, Institute of Professional Book Keepers and Auditors of Russia; Management Council, Protection of the Desertations on a speciality, Book Keeping and Statistics. Address: 11 Parkovaya str, Korpus 344, Moscow 105215, Russia.

POLLOCK John (Charles), b. 9 October 1923, London, England. Clergyman; Writer. m. Anne Barrett-Lennard, 4 May 1949. Education: BA 1946, MA 1948, Trinity College, Cambridge; Ridley Hall, Cambridge, 1949-51. Appointments: Captain, Coldstream Guards, 1943-45; Assistant Master (History and Divinity), Wellington College, Berkshire, 1947-49; Ridley Hall, Cambridge, 1949-51; Ordained Anglican Deacon, 1951, Priest, 1952; Curate, St Paul's Church, Portman Square, London, 1951-53; Rector, Horsington, Somerset, 1953-58; Editor, The Churchman (quarterly), 1953-58; Chaplain to the High Sheriff of Devon, 1990-91. Publications: Candidate for Truth, 1950; A Cambridge Movement, 1953; The Cambridge Seven, 1955, new editions 1985 and 2006; Way to Glory: The Life of Havelock of Lucknow, 1957, new edition, 1996; Shadows Fall Apart, 1958; The Good Seed, 1959; Earth's Remotest End, 1960; Hudson Taylor and Maria, 1962, new edition, 1996; Moody Without Sankey, 1963, new edition, 1995; The Keswick Story, 1964, new edition, 2006; The Christians from Siberia, 1964; Billy Graham, 1966, revised edition, 1969; The Apostle: A Life of Paul, 1969, revised edition, 1985, new edition as Paul the Apostle, 1999; Victims of the Long March, 1970; A Foreign Devil in China: The Life of Nelson Bell, 1971, new edition, 1988; George Whitefield and the Great Awakening, 1972, new edition as Whitefield: The Evangelist, 2000; Wilberforce, 1977, new edition as Wilberforce: God's Statesman, 2001; Bicentenary edition as Wilberforce, 2007; Billy Graham: Evangelist to the World, 1979; The Siberian Seven, 1979; Amazing Grace: John Newton's Story, 1981, new edition as Newton: The Liberator, 2000; The Master: A Life of Jesus, 1984, new edition as Jesus: The Master 1999; Billy Graham: Highlights of the Story, 1984; Shaftesbury: The Poor Man's Earl, 1985, new edition as Shaftesbury: The Reformer, 2000; A Fistful of Heroes: Great Reformers and Evangelists, 1988, new combined edition with On Fire for God, 1998; John Wesley 1989, new edition as Wesley: The Preacher, 2000; On Fire for God: Great Missionary Pioneers, 1990; Fear No Foe: A Brother's Story, 1992; Gordon: The Man Behind the Legend, 1993, new edition as Gordon of Khartoum; An Extraordinary Soldier, 2005; Kitchener: The Road to Omdurman, 1998; Kitchener: Saviour of the Nation, 2000; Kitchener (comprising The Road to Omdurman and Saviour of the Nation), 2001; The Billy Graham Story, 2004; Abolition! Newton, the Ex-Slave Trader and Wilberforce, the Little Liberator, 2007. Contributions to: Reference works including Oxford DNB and religious periodicals. Honours: The John Pollock Award for Christian Biography (annual) founded by Samford University, USA, 1999; Clapham Prize, Gordon College, USA, 2002; Honorary Doctor of Letters, Samford University, USA, 2002. Membership: English Speaking Union Club. Address: Rose Ash House, South Molton, Devonshire EX36 4RB, England.

POLYVODA Sergey, b. 1 February 1953, Dnepropetrovsk, Ukraine. Cardiologist. m. Valentina N Bondareva, 1 daughter. Education: MD, 1976, PhD, 1981, Zaporozhye Medical University; DSc, State Scientific Institute of Cardiology, 1991; Postgraduate Study, Medical Academy of Zaporozhye, 2002, 2008; Appointments: Assistant Professor, 1981, Rector, 1992, Zaporozhye Medical Institute of Postgraduate Education; Assistant Professor, 1987-89, Rector, 1992-94, Head of Department of Hospital Therapy 2, 1994-2001, Zaporozhye Advanced Doctor Training Institute; Department of Therapy, Zaporozhye State Medical University, 1995; Academician, Ukrainian Academy of Science, 2006. Publications: Over 500 articles; 18 reviews; 37 patents; 4 books and book chapters. Honours: Order of Medical Merit, 2008; Scientific Board Member; Doctor's Degree Qualification Council; Ukrainian Academician; Editorial Board Member of 3 medical journals; Medal for Achievement in Cardiology. Memberships: Ukrainian Academy of Science; Ukrainian Scientific Cardiological Society. Address: Str 40 Let Sovetskoy, N86A, 9, 69037 Zaporozhye, Ukraine.

PONCE DE LEAO POLICARPO Armando José, b. 30 April 1935, Portugal. Professor. m. Maria Isabel, 2 sons, 1 daughter. Education: Graduated in Science, Physics and Chemistry, University of Coimbra, Portugal, 1957; Diploma of Advanced Studies in Science, 1960, PhD, University of Manchester, 1963; Doctor of Physics, University of Coimbra, Portugal, 1964. Appointments: Assistant, 1957-63, Associate Professor, 1968, Professor, 1979, Head of Department of Nuclear Physics Studies, University of Coimbra, Portugal; Research Fellow, CERN, Geneva; Research Fellow, Institute of Nuclear Studies, Tokyo; Head of the Physics Department; Director of the Physics Museum; Director, LIP, Particles Laboratory. Publications: Over 250 papers contributed to refereed scientific journals; Milestone papers on GPSC, gas proportional scintillation counters. Honours: Grã-Cruz da Ordem Nacional do Merito Cientifico da República Federativa do Brasil; Grande Oficial da Ordem de Santiago de Espada, Portugal. Memberships: Academia de Ciencias de Lisboa, International Radiation Physics Society; European Physics Society; Committee of Science and Technology Policy (OCDE); ECFA. Address: Department of Physics, University of Coimbra, 3004-516, Coimbra, Portugal. E-mail: policarpo@lipc.fis.uc.pt

PONCELET Christian, b. 24 March 1928, Blaise, Ardennes, France. Chairman of the Senate. m. Yvette Miclot, 1 son, 1 daughter. Education: Saint-Sulpice College, Paris; Post and Telecommunication National School. Appointments: Auditor, French Post and Telecommunication, 1950-53; Member, National Confederation Committee of French Christian Workers, 1953-62; MP, Gaullist Party, 1962; Member, Union Democratic Group of the National Assembly, 1962; Elected General Councillor, Remiremont, 1963, re-elected 1964, 1970, 1982, 1988, 1994; Elected Municipal Councillor, Remiremont, 1965; Re-elected MP, Republic Defense Union group, 1967, 1968, 1973; Social Affairs State Secretary, 1972, State Secretary to the Work, Employment and Population Minister, 1973, Civil Service State Secretary to Prime Minister, 1974, Messmer government; Budget State Secretary to the Economy and Finances Minister, Chirac

government, 1974; Chairman, General Council of Vosges Department, 1976, re-elected 1979, 1982, 1985, 1988, 1992, 1994; Budget State Secretary to the Economy and Finance Minister, 1976, Parliamentary Relations State Secretary to the Prime Minister, 1977, Barre government; Elected Senator, Vosges Department, 1982, re-elected 1986, 1995, 2004; Elected Mayor of Remiremont (Vosges), 1983, re-elected 1989, 1995; Elected Chairman, Finance, Budgetary Control and National Economic Audit Standing Committee of the Senate, 1986, re-elected 1989, 1992, 1995; Elected Chairman of the Senate, 1998, re-elected 2001, 2004. Address: 17 rue des Etats-Unis, 88200 Remiremont, France.

PONG David Bertram Pak-Tang, b. 28 September 1939, Hong Kong. Professor. m. Barbara Mar, 3 daughters. Education: St Paul's College, Hong Kong, 1951-60; BA, Hons, School of Oriental and African Studies, University of London, 1963; PhD, School of Oriental and African Studies, 1969. Appointments: Research Fellow, Institute of Historical Research, University of London, 1965-66; Fellow, Far Eastern History, School of Oriental and African Studies, University of London, 1966-69; Assistant Professor, History, University of Delaware, 1969-73; Associate Professor, History, 1973-89; Research Fellow, Research School of Pacific Studies, Institute of Advanced Studies, Australian National University, 1978-82; Professor, 1989-; Chair, Department of History, 1992-98; Director, East Asian Studies Programme, 1989-; Editor in Chief, Encyclopaedia of Modern China. Publications: Shen Pao-chen (Shen Baozhen) and China's Modernization in the Nineteenth Century: A Critical Guide to the Kwangtung (Guangdong) Provincial Archives Deposited at the Public Record Office of London; Ideal and Reality: Social and Political Change in Modern China, 1860-1949; Resisting Japan: Mobilizing for War in China, 1935-1945; Shen Baozhen pingzhuan: Zhongguo jindaihua de changshi; Taiwan haifang bing kaishan riji; Many other articles. Honours: Research Fellowship, Institute of Historical Research, University of London, 1965-66; American Council of Learned Societies Research Fellowship, 1973-74; Research Fellow, Research School of Pacific Studies, Institute of Advanced Studies, Australian National University, 1978-82; Phi Kappa Phi Honor Society, 1999; Honorary Research Fellow, Modern History Research Centre, Hong Kong Baptist University, 2002-. Memberships: Association for Asian Studies; Society for Qing Studies; History Society of 20th-Century China; Asian Studies Association of Hong Kong; Modern Chinese History Society of Hong Kong; Chinese Military History Society; Phi Kappa Phi Honor Society. Address: Department of History, University of Delaware, Newark, DE 19716, USA.

PONNALA Sandeep, b. 15 September 1945, Secunderabad, India. Teacher; Educator. m. Vindhya Rani, 2 sons, 2 daughters. Education: M Ed, 1971; MA, 1973; M Phil, 1975; PhD, 1978. Appointments: Lecturer in Education, 1978-85; Reader in Education, 1985-94; Director, Centre for Adult Education, 1992-2005; Professor in Education, 1994-2005; Director, Vocation Courses, 1996-99; Principal, IASE, 1999-2000; Director, Centre for Distance Education, 2000-02; Dean, Faculty of Education, 2004-05. Publications: 4 books; 30 articles in national and international journals; 20 evaluation studies. Honours: Bharath Jyothi, 2005; Best Citizens of India, 2006; Distinguished Teacher Educator, 2007. Memberships: Association for Supervision & Curriculum Development, USA; Indian Adult Education Association; Indian Institute of Public Administration. Address: 12-13-677-12, Kimtee Colony, Street No 1, Lane No 1, Tarnaka, Secunderabad – 500017, Andhra Pradesh, India. E-mail: sandeepponnala@yahoo.com

POOL Adam de Sola, b. 5 November 1957, Palo Alto, California, USA. Venture Capitalist. m. Kristina Gjerde, 1 son. Education: BA, University of Chicago, 1981; MA, University of California, 1982; MBA, Massachusetts Institute of Technology. Economist, First National Bank of Chicago, 1980; Research Officer, 1982-83, International Officer, 1983-86, Assistant Vice President, 1986, Industrial Bank of Japan, New York; Associate, Corporate Finance, Salomon Brothers Inc, New York, 1987, 1988-92; Principal Banker, 1992-94, Senior Banker, 1994-95, European Bank for Reconstruction and Development; Chief Investment Officer, Yamaichi Regent ABC Polska, 1995-97; Owner, PP Investments, 1998-. Publications: Published photographer. Memberships: Board member: Relpol Centrum SA; Finesco SA; Korte-Organica RT; Honorary Member, Yale Club. Address: ul Piaskowa 12c, 05-510 Konstanin, Poland. E-mail: pool@eip.com.pl

POOLE Charles P, b. 7 June 1927, Panama. Physicist. m. Kathleen, 2 sons, 3 daughters. Education: BA, Fordham University, 1950; MS, Physics, 1952; PhD, Physics, University of Maryland, 1958. Appointments: Physicist, Westinghouse Electronic Corporation, 1952-53; Physicist, Gulf Research Corporation, 1958-64; Associate Professor, Physics, University of South Carolina, 1964-66; Professor, Physics, 1966-94; Professor Emeritus, 1994-. Publications: 20 books; 16 review articles; 150 research publications; Electron Spin Resonance; Relaxation in Magnetic Resonance; Theory of Magnetic Resonance; Superconductivity; The New Superconductors; others. Honours: Russell Award, University of South Carolina; Jesse W Beams Award, American Physical Society; Fellow, EPR/ESR Society; Fellow, American Physical Society. Memberships: International Society of Magnetic Resonance. Address: Department of Physics, University of South Carolina, Columbia, SC 29208, USA.

POP Iggy (James Jewel Osterburg), b. 21 April 1947, Ypsilanti, Michigan, USA. Singer; Musician (guitar); Actor. Education: University of Michigan. Career: Formed Iguanas, High School band, 1962; Prime Movers, 1966; Concerts in Michigan, Detroit and Chicago; Formed The Stooges (originally the Pyschedelic Stooges), 1967; 3 albums, 1969-73; Solo artiste, 1976-; Collaborations with David Bowie, 1972-; Numerous tours and television appearances; Actor, films including: Sid And Nancy; The Color Of Money; Hardware; Cry-Baby; Atolladero; Tank Girl; Dead Man; The Crow – City of Angels; The Brace; The Rugrats Movie (voice); Snow Day; Coffee and Cigarettes; Miami television series: Miami Vice; The Adventures of Pete & Pete; Compositions include: Co-writer, China Girl, David Bowie; Many film songtracks. Recordings: Albums: with The Stooges: The Stooges, 1969; Jesus Loves The Stooges, 1977; I'm Sick Of You, 1977; Solo albums: Fun House, 1970; Raw Power, 1973; Metallic KO, 1976; The Idiot, 1977; Lust For Life, 1977; TV Eye Live, 1978; Kill City, 1978; New Values, 1979; Soldier, 1980; Party, 1981; I'm Sick Of You, 1981; Zombie Birdhouse, 1982; I Got The Right, 1983; Blah Blah Blah, 1986; Rubber Legs, 1987; Live At The Whiskey A Go Go, 1988; Death Trip, 1988; Raw Stooges, 1988; Raw Stooges 2, 1988; The Stooges Box Set, 1988; Instinct, 1988; Brick By Brick, 1990; American Caesar, 1994; Naughty Little Doggie, 1996; Heroin Hates You, 1997; King Biscuit Flower Hour, 1997; Your Pretty Face is Going to Hell, 1998; Sister Midnight, 1999; Avenue B, 1999; Iggy Pop, 1999; Hippodrome Paris '77 (live), 1999; Beat 'Em Up, 2001; Skull Ring, 2003; Singles: Beside You, 1993; Wild America, 1993; Corruption, 1999; Appears on: Rock at the Edge, 1977; Low, David Bowie, 1977; Trainspotting, 1996; Death in Vegas, Contino Sessions, 1999; Contributor, Red Hot And Blue AIDs

charity record. Publications: Autobiographies: I Need More; Iggy Pop's A-Z, 2005. Address: Art Collins Management, PO Box 561, Pine Bush, NY 12566, USA.

POP Nadia-Cella, b. 13 March 1948, Ariuşd, Romania. Professor; Poet. Education: Bachelor of Philosophy, Babeş-Bolyai University, 1973. Appointments: High School Teacher; Newspaper Reporter; Librarian; Poet. Publications: Poems published in popular journals and poetry anthologies around the world; 3 poetry books: Gânduri de veghe, 1997; Din simfonia vieţii, 2001; Avalanche over impossible, 2006; Works translated into 12 languages; Contributor, 5 plays, Braso, Vienna and Bucharest. Honours: 139 international prizes for literary creations including: Medaille d'Or, Halaf; Grand Prix de l'Europe, Guerande; Medaille d'Argent, Paris; Premio internazionale Goccia di luna, La Spezia; 3 Premio Internazional di Poesia e Prosa, Pomezia Roma; Diplome, La plume ardente, Liege; Medaille de bronze, Luxemburg; Die Goldmedaille und Grosen intern Preis Friedrich Holderlin, Gildekamer; The Best Poet of the Year 2004, Chongqing; Professor Honoris causa, St Lucas Academy, Bamberg, Germany; Academical Knight, Greci-Marino Academy, Vinzaglio, Italy; Several honours and nominations from ABI and IBC. Memberships: 16 literary societies and academies in France, Italy, Germany and USA. Address: Apt 9, 6 Soarelui Street, Brasov, Romania.

POPESCU Casin, b. 17 August 1921, Husi, County Fălciu, Romania. Civil and Building Engineer. m. Mioara Popescu, 1 daughter. Education: Diploma in Civil Engineering, College for Building and Construction, Bucharest, Romania, 1942. Appointments: Assistant Professor, 1943-47, Honorary Secretary, 1945-47, Hydraulics Department, Polytechnic College, Bucharest (relieved of post for political reasons); Emigrated to Germany for political reasons, 1980; Research in the history of antiquity, 1980-2004; Freelance Engineer, Project Inspector, Atomic Energy Research Laboratories, Babcock-Braun-Bowery, Mannheim, Germany, 1982; Member, Centre Roumain de Recherches Etablissement libre d'enseignement supérior declare à l'Académie de Paris, 1984; Co-Founder (with wife), quarterly magazine: Paths of Fate in Balance, 1991; Officially recognised as a scientist and mathematical physicist in Romania, 2004. Publications: Numerous publications include, 1946-80: The Effect of Seismic Force on Metal Railroad Bridges - Shock Absorption and Resonance Phenomena, 1958; New Solution for Calculating the Vibration of Circular Concrete Plates, 1964; Fundamental historical works, 1980-2004: The Bridges over the Istru in the 1st Millennium Before Christ, 1984; The Legends of the Argonaut Saga – Historical Events, 1989; Who are the Etruscans, 1989, 2nd edition, 2004; Danubian Neolithic Writing, 1989; Leuce, the Achilles Island – Localisation and Historical References, 2000; The Romanian People and Their Christian Roots, 2004; Doctrina Chistiana – Prolegumene, 2004; Metaphysics of the Existence, 2006; The Universe in the Bible and the Exact Sciences, 2004-06; Numerous papers for international symposiums on energy and the environment, 1987-90: Sonic Impulses – the Available Clean Energy, 1988; About the Recuperation of Wind Energy by means of Aeroturbosomites, 1988; The Mechanics of Hydrofoil Profiles and a New Generation of Turbines, 1989; Numerous patents: Founder, Theory of Hydrosonicity; Founder, Theory of Compressible Bodies or Sonic Geometry (includes Euclidian geometry, particularly in the case of $b_{p,t} = 0$, where $b_{p,t}$ is the coefficient of compressibility); Studies concerning the force of gravity resulting from the rotation of natural bodies around their axis; Studies concerning The Nature of Space and Time (Stephen Hawking/Roger Penrose) in the hypothesis of the

DICTIONARY OF INTERNATIONAL BIOGRAPHY

compressibility of space and time; The Universe in the Bible and the Exact Sciences, 2004-06. Address: Goldgasse 12, D-77652 Offenburg, Germany.

POPOV Dmitriy Ivanovich, b. 24 November 1939, Ryazan, USSR. Educator. m. Lyudmila Petrovna Tsjiganova, 2 daughters. Education: Graduate, Radio Engineer, Radio Engineering Institute, Ryazan, 1961; Postgraduate, Aviation Institute, Moscow, 1966; Doctor of Engineering Science, Energy Institute, Moscow, 1990; Professor, Moscow, 1992. Appointments: Engineer, Design Office, Moscow, 1961-63; Postgraduate, Aviation Institute, Moscow, 1963-66; Educator, Professor, Ryazan State Radio Engineering University, Russia, 1966-. Publications: Contributed over 70 scientific articles in radio engineering and radar to professional journals; Over 60 inventions. Honours: Breastplate Inventor of USSR, 1988. Memberships: Active member, International Informatization Academy. Address: Krupskoy Street 10-129, Ryazan 390044, Russia. E-mail: dip@popovd.ryazan.ru

POPOV Sergey Valentinovich, b. 29 April 1959, Tomsk, Russia. Cardiologist. m. Galina V Volkova. Education: General Practitioner, Tomsk State Institute of Medicine, 1982; Postgraduate Training: Cardiosurgery, Research Institute of Circulation Pathology, Novosibirsk, Russia, 1982-83; Implantable Pacemakers, 1983, Tachyarrhythmia Surgery, 1985, All Union Centre of Pacing, Kaunas, Lithuania; PhD, Research Institute of Cardiology, Tomsk, Russia, 1988; Certification in Guidant-Intermedics Implantable Pacemakers, Moscow Russia, 1993; Certification in GCP International Regulations, Bristol-Myers-Squibb, Smolensk, Russia, 1996; Doctor of Medicine, Research Institute of Cardiology, Tomsk, Russia, 1996; Certification in Intercardial RF Ablation of Tachycardias, 1997, Joint Investigations of the Efficacy of Tachycardia Radiofrequencey, 1999, Johannes Gutenburg, Universität Mainz Kilinkum Mainz, Germany; Certification in Surgical and Interventional Arrythmology, Federal Centre of Arrhythmology, Moscow, Russia, 1998; Certification in Medtronic Implantable Defibrillators, 2001, Certification in Medtronic Cardiac Resynchronisation Therapy, 2004, Lausanne, Switzerland. Appointments: Junior, Senior and Chief Research Assistant, Cardiac Arrhythmias Department, 1982-92, Head, Federal Siberian Centre of Cardiac Arrythmias, 1992-, Professor of Cardiology, Cardiac Arrhythmias Department, 2000-, Vice-Director, 2002-, Research Institute of Cardiology, Tomsk, Russia. Publications: More than 500 original communications. Memberships: Co-ordinating Board of Surgical and Interventional Arrhythmology, Ministry of Health of the Russian Federation, 1999; Deputy Chairman, Russian Society of Clinical Electrophysiology, Arrhythmology and Pacing, 2002; International Editors Group PACE, 2004; European Society of Cardiology, 2005; European Heart Rhythm Association. Address: Research Institute of Cardiology, Cardiac Arrhythmias Department, 111A Kievskaya St, Tomsk, 634012 Russia. Address: E-mail psv@cardio.tsu.ru

POPOVA Venche, b. 11 January 1931, Svishtov, Bulgaria. Professor of History of Contemporary Bulgarian Language and Bulgarian Stylistics. m. Bahni Bahnev, 1 daughter. Education: Bulgarian Philology, Sofia University "St Klimet Ohridski", 1948-52; Postgraduate studies in Contemporary Bulgarian Language, 1953-56; PhD, Sofia University "St Kliment Ohridski", 1965; Specialisation in Serbian, Croatian and Slovenian Languages in the Universities of Belgrade, Zagreb and Ljubljana, 1968. Appointments: Assistant, Department of Bulgarian Language, Faculty of Slavic Philologies, 1958, Associate Professor (Reader), 1974, Professor, 1991-, Sofia

University "St Kliment Ohridski"; Lecture Courses, Plovdiv University, 1974-85; Practical course in Contemporary Bulgarian Language, Jagiellonian University Krakow, Poland, 1963-66; Lectures abroad in: Universities of Upsala and Stockholm, Sweden, 1971-76, University of Regensburg, Germany, 1978; University of Hamburg, Germany, 1981; Macquire University Sydney and The State University in Melbourne, Australia, 1984. Publications: More than 120 books and studies include: Concise Grammar of Bulgarian Language (co-author), 1972. 2004; Issues of Bulgarian Stylistics, 1975; Stylistic Function of Some Categories Words in Fiction, 1979; Language and Style of Hristo Botev, 1980; History of Bulgarian Literary Language (co-author), 1989; Bulgarian Stylists till the 50's of XX Century, 1994; Wonders of Children's Speech, 1995. Honours: Anniversary Medal "100 Years of Sofia University", Rector's Council of Sofia University "St Kliment Ohridski", 1988; Academic Vladimir Georgiev Award for best study in linguistics, 13th Century Bulgaria Foundation. 1991. Memberships: Translators Union in Bulgaria; Bulgarian Journalist Union; Head, International Summer Seminar in Bulgarian Language and Culture for Foreign Bulgarian scholars and Slavists, 1975-86; Member, International Commission to the International Committee of the Slavists, 1976-91; Specialised Scientific Council of Linguists for Scientific Degrees and Titles defence, 1998-2004; Currently: Member, Higher Testimonial Commission for Awarding Scientific Titles and Degrees. Address: Ul. Gogol 21, app 8, 1124 Sofia, Bulgaria. E-mail: sofiakb@abv.bg

POPOVIC Radivoje S, b. 12 April 1945, Kraljevo, Serbia, Yugoslavia. Professor. m. 2 daughters. Education: Dipl El Ing, University of Belgrade, 1969; Magistar of Science, 1973, DSc, 1978, Electronic Engineering, University of Nis, Yugoslavia. Appointments: Head, CMOS Department, Electronics Industry Corp, Nis, Yugoslavia, 1969-81; Adjunct Lecturer (part time), University of Nis, 1978-81; Adjunct Lecturer (part time), University of Belgrade, 1980-81; Vice President, Corporate R&D, Landis & Gyr Corp, Zug, Switzerland, 1982-93; Co-Founder, Managing Director (part time), Sentron AG, Zug, 1993-2004; Professor, Micro-Systems, Swiss Federal Institute of Technology, Lausanne, Switzerland, 1994-; Co-Founder, Board of Directors (part time), Senronisis AD, Nis, Serbia, 2003-; Co-Founder, Board of Directors (part time), Senis GmbH, Zug, 2004-; Co-Founder, Board of Directors (part time), Ametes AG, Zurich, Switzerland, 2005-. Publications: Book, Hall Effect Devices, 1991 and 2004; 250 papers in scientific journals and conference proceedings; 20 invited talks; 4 book chapters; More than 95 original patent applications (inventions). Honours: Regular Member, Swiss Academy of Engineering Sciences; Foreign Member, Serbian Academy of Engineering Sciences. E-mail: radivoje.popovic@epfl.ch

POPPEL Emanuel S, b. 25 December, 1925, Romania. Professor of Chemical Engineering. m. Mica-Claire Poppel, 1950. Education: MSc, Chemical Engineering, 1950, PhD, 1958, Doctor in Science, 1971, Polytechnic Institute, Iaşi, Romania. Appointments: Assistant, Professor, 1949-52, Lecturer, 1952-60, Associate Professor, 1960-70, Professor, 1970-96, Professor Emeritus, 1996-, Technical University of Iaşi, Romania; Visiting Professor, Dresden and Darmstadt, Germany, 1972, 1974, Graz, Austria, 1995; Lecturer in Hungary, Holland, Poland, Russia, USA, England, Israel, Austria; Supervisor of more than 550 graduate students and 19 PhD theses. Publications: 220 scientific works and 10 licences in the field of fibre structures and rheology, electrokinetics in pulp and paper technology, processes and equipment in the pulp and paper industry; 8 books and monographs. Honour:

International Peace Prize, United Cultural Convention, USA, 2005. Memberships: Fellow, International Academy of Wood Science; Honorary member, PITA/PIRA, England; New York Academy of Science; International Association of Scientific Papermakers. Address: Technical University of Iaşi, Department of Paper Science, Mangeron Str. 71, RO-700050 Iaşi, Romania. E-mail: epoppel@omicron.ch.tuiasi.ro

PÖPPING Bert, b. 20 December 1961, Dortmund, Germany. Director. m. Heike. Education: BSc, 1983, BSc, Biology, 1984; MSc, 1989, PhD, 1993, University of Bochum, Germany. Appointments: Teaching Assistant, 1988-89, Research Assistant, 1989-93, University of Bochum; Senior Research Assistant, University of Durham, 1993-95; Higher Scientific Officer, 1995-97, Head of GMO and Molecular Meat Speciation Service, 1997-99, CSL Food Science Laboratory, Norwich; Company Molecular Biologist, Eurofins, 1999-2000; Scientific Head of Department, 2000-, Eurofins' Biological Analysis Laboratory WEJ, Hamburg, Germany; Director, Molecular Biology and Immunology, Eurofins Scientific Group, 2000-. Publications: Over 80 articles in professional journals. Memberships: AOAC International; Past President, AOAC Europe Section; Member, Scientific Advisory Panel, AACC, CEN TC 275, ISO TAG 34 member; IFSTI; DGHM; VDB. Address: 69a Kilnwick Road, Pocklington, Yorkshire YO42 2JY, England. E-mail: bertpopping@eurofins.com Website: www.eurofins.com

PORTMAN Natalie, b. 9 June 1981, Jerusalem, Israel. Actress. Education: Harvard University. Career: Model, aged 11; Films: Léon, 1994; Developing, 1995; Heat, 1995; Beautiful Girls, 1996; Everyone Says I Love You, 1996; Mars Attacks! 1996; The Diary of Anne Frank, 1997; Star Wars: Episode I – The Phantom Menace, 1999; Anywhere But Here; Where the Heart Is, 2000; The Seagull, 2001; Zoolander, 2001; Star Wars: Episode II – Attack of the Clones, 2002; Cold Mountain, 2003; Garden State, 2004; True, 2004; Closer, 2004; Star Wars: Episode III – Revenge of the Sith, 2005; V for Vendetta, 2006; Paris, Je t'aime, 2006; Goya's Ghosts, 2006; My Blueberry Nights, 2007; Hotel Chevalier, 2007; The Darjeeling Limited, 2007; Mr Magorium's Wonder Emporium, 2007; The Other Boleyn Girl, 2008. Theatre: A Midsummer Night's Dream; Cabaret; Anne of Green Gables; Tapestry. Honours: Best Supporting Actress, Golden Globe Awards, 2005. Address: c/o ICM, 8942 Wilshire Boulevard, Beverly Hills, CA 90211, USA.

PORTWAY Christopher (John), b. 30 October 1923, Halstead, Essex, England. Writer. m. Jaroslava Krupickova, deceased, 1 son, 1 daughter. Publications: Journey to Dana, 1955; The Pregnant Unicorn, 1969; All Exits Barred, 1971; Corner Seat, 1972; Lost Vengeance, 1973; Double Circuit, 1974; The Tirana Assignment, 1974; The Anarchy Pedlars, 1976; The Great Railway Adventure, 1983; Journey Along the Spine of the Andes, 1984; The Great Travelling Adventure, 1985; Czechmate, 1987; Indian Odyssey, 1993; A Kenyan Adventure, 1993; Pedal for Your Life, 1996; A Good Pair of Legs, 1999; The World Commuter, 2001; Flat Feet & Full Steam, Dangerous Devotion, forthcoming; Regular contributions to: Motoring and Leisure Magazine; The Lady; Hidden Europe. Honour: Winston Churchill Fellow, 1993. Membership: Fellow, Royal Geographical Society; Founder Member, British Guild of Travel Writers. Address: Middle Gaynes, Mill Lane, Colne Engaine, Nr Colchester, CO6 2HX, England.

POSOKHOV Yevgen, b. 14 August, 1971, Kharkov, Ukraine. Scientist. m. Daria Bevziuk, 1 son. Education: MS, Chemistry, 1993, PhD, Organic Chemistry, 2000, Kharkov State University. Appointments: Research Fellow, 1993-96, Research Associate, 1997-2000; Postdoctoral Fellow, 2000-2004; Senior Research Scientist, 2004-. Publications: More than 20 articles in peer-reviewed scientific journals. Honours: Postdoctoral Fellowship Grants: Fellowship of ICHF Polish Academy of Science, 2000-2002; NATO-PC (Tubitak) Fellowship Programme, 2002-2003. Memberships: European Photochemical Association, 1998-; Biophysical Society, 2005-. Address: Ul Kharkovskay 2, Apartment 5, Merepha, Kharkov Oblast 62472, Ukraine. E-mail: eugen.a.posokhov@univer.kharkov.ua

POSPÍŠIL Jaroslav, b. 19 February 1935, Charváty, Czech Republic. Professor. Education: MSc, 1957; MEng, 1964; RNDr, 1968; PhD, 1968; DSc, 1992; Graduated in Physics and Mathematics, Palacký University, Olomouc, Electrical Engineering, University of Technology, Brno. Appointments: Researcher, Optics, Institute of Industrial Sciences, Tokyo University; Professor, Optics and Quantum Electronics, Head, Department of Applied Physics, Palacký University, Olomouc. Publications: Over 260 research papers in professional journals mainly in the field of transfer, statistical, digital and informational properties of optical, electrooptical, photographical, optoelectrical and human vision systems. Honours: Gold Medal, Palacký University, 1995; Merit Member and Honorary Member, Union of Czech Mathematicians and Physicists, 1996 and 2002. Memberships: International Society for Optical Engineering; Union of Czech Mathematicians and Physicists; Czech Committee, International Commission for Optics; Optics and Electronics Division of European Physical Society; Czech and Slovak Society for Photonics; Czech Society for Metrology. Address: Ovesná 10, 77900 Olomouc, Czech Republic.

POSSAMAI Adam M, b. 7 January 1970, Auvelais, Belgium. Associate Professor. m. Alpha Possamai-Inesedy, 2 sons, 1 daughter. Education: BSS (Hons), GDIP Ed, Leuven, Belgium; PhD, La Trobe University, Australia. Appointments: Lecturer in Sociology, 1999-2004, Senior Lecturer in Sociology, 2004-, Associate Professor, 2007-, University of Western Sydney. Publications: Religion and Popular Culture, 2005; In Search of New Age Spiritualities, 2005; Perles Noines, 2005; Articles in Journal of Consumer Culture and Culture and Religion. Memberships: Past President, Australian Association for the Study of Religions; Secretary, Research Committee 22 for the Sociology of Religion from the International Sociological Association; Co-editor, The Australian Religion Studies Review. Address: School of Social Sciences (Bankstown Campus), University of Western Sydney, Locked Bag 1737, Penrith South Dr, NSW 1737, Australia. E-mail: a.possamai@uws.edu.au

POSTGATE John Raymond, b. 24 June 1922, London, England. Microbiologist. m. Mary Stewart, 3 daughters. Education: First Class Honours, Chemistry, D Phil, Chemical Microbiology, Balliol College, Oxford; DSc, Oxford. Appointments: Senior Research Investigator to Principal Scientific Officer, Microbiology Group, Chemical Research Laboratory, 1948-59; Principal to Senior Principal Scientific Officer, Microbiological Research Establishment, 1959-63; Assistant Director, 1963-80, Director, 1980-87, AFRC Unit of Nitrogen Fixation, Professor now Emeritus of Microbiology, 1965-, University of Sussex; Visiting Professor, University of Illinois, Champaign-Urbana, USA, 1962-63; Visiting Professor, Oregon State University, Corvallis, USA, 1977-78.

Publications include: Scientific books: The Sulphate-Reducing Bacteria, 1979, 1984; The Fundamentals of Nitrogen Fixation, 1982; Nitrogen Fixation, 1978, 1987, 1998; Microbes and Man, 1969, 1986, 1992, 2000; The Outer Reaches of Life, 1994, 1995; Other books: A Plain Man's Guide to Jazz, 1973; Lethal Lozenges and Tainted Tea, 2001; A Stomach for Dissent (with Mary Postgate), 1994; Over 200 research papers; 30 articles on popular science; Numerous record reviews and writings on jazz music. Honours: Williams Exhibition to Balliol College, Oxford; Honorary DSc, University of Bath, 1990; Honorary LLD, University of Dundee, 1997. Memberships: Fellow, Institute of Biology, 1965, President, 1982-84; Elected Fellow, Royal Society, 1977; President, Society for General Microbiology, 1984-87, Honorary Member, 1988; Honorary Member, Society for Applied Microbiology, 1988; Honorary Associate, Rationalist Press Association, 1995. Address: 1 Houndean Rise, Lewes, East Sussex BN7 1EG, England. E-mail: johnp@sussex.ac.uk

POSTLETHWAITE Pete, b. 16 February 1946, Lancashire, England. Actor. Career: Theatre includes: Macbeth, Bristol; Films include: The Last of the Mohicans; In the Name of the Father; Romeo and Juliet; Alien 3; Dragonheart; Distant Voices; Still Lives; Brassed Off; The Lost World; Jurassic Park; Amistad; The Serpent's Kiss; Among Giants; The Divine Ryans; Wayward Son; When the Sky Falls; Rat; Cowboy Up; The Shipping News; Triggermen; Between Strangers; The Limit; Strange Bedfellows; Red Mercury; Dark Water; The Constant Gardener; Æon Flux; Ghost Son; Valley of the Heart's De;ight; The Omen; Closing the Ring. TV includes: Between the Lines; Lost for Words; Alice in Wonderland; Butterfly Collectors; Animal Farm (voice); The Sins; Shattered City: The Halifax Explosion. Address: c/o Markham and Froggart Ltd, 4 Windmill Street, London, W1P 1HF, England.

POUND Keith Salisbury, b, 3 April 1933, London, England. Clergyman. Education: BA, MA, St Catharine's College, Cambridge, 1951-54; Cuddesdon College, Oxford, 1955-57. Appointments: Curate, St Peter, St Helier, Morden, 1957-61; Training Officer, 1961-64, Warden, 1964-67, Hollowford Training Centre, Sheffield; Rector, Holy Trinity, Southwark, 1968-78; Rector, Thamesmead, 1978-86; Chaplain General and Archdeacon to H M Prison Service, 1986-93; Chaplain, Grendon and Springhill Prisons, 1993-98; Chaplain to H M The Queen, 1990-2003. Publication: Creeds and Controversies, 1965. Membership: Civil Service Club. Address: Adeleine, Pett Road, Pett, East Sussex TN35 4HE, England.

POURMOHAMMADI Mohammad Reza, b. 25 February 1959, Tabriz, Iran. Professor. m. N Badadafshord, 2 sons. Education: BSc, Geography, Tabriz University, 1984; MSc, Urban Planning, UWIST, England, 1986; PhD, Urban Planning, UWCC, England, 1990. Appointments: Head, Faculty of Humanities and Social Science, 1991-96, Vice Chancellor for Student Affairs, 1996-97, Vice Chancellor for Academic Affairs, 1997-2000, Chancellor, 2002-05, Tabriz University. Publications: Books: Planning for Housing; Urban Land Use Planning; 25 articles in the field of urban planning; 7 research projects; Supervision of 23 MSc and 2 PhD theses. Memberships: IAU; Oxford Round Table on Higher Education. Address: Department of Geography and Urban Planning, Tabriz University, Iran. E-mail: pourmohammadi@tabrizu.ac.ir

POWELL Michael Peter, b. 24 July 1950, Oxford, England. Consultant Neurosurgeon. m. Jennifer Shields, 3 daughters. Education: BA, MA, 1980, New College, Oxford, 1968-72; MB BS, Middlesex Hospital Medical School, University of London, 1972-75; FRCS, Royal College of Surgeons, England, 1980. Appointments: Registrar, Neurosurgery, 1980-82, Research Registrar, 1982-83, Bristol; Senior Registrar, National Hospital for Nervous Diseases, 1983-85; Consultant Neurosurgeon, National Hospital for Neurology and Neurosurgery, UCLH (Trust), 1985-. Publication: The Management of Pituitary Tumours (first edition 1996 with Professor S Lightman, second edition, 2003 with Professors S Lightman and E R Laws). Memberships: RCS England; BMA. Address: The National Hospital, Queen Square, London WC1N 3BG, England. E-mail: michael.powell@uclh.org

POWELL Robert, b. 1 June 1944, Salford, Lancashire, England. Actor. m. Barbara Lord, 1975, 1 son, 1 daughter. Career: TV roles include: Doomwatch, 1970; Jude the Obscure, 1971; Jesus of Nazareth, 1977; Pygmalion, 1981; Frankenstein, 1984; Hannay (series), 1988; The Sign of Command, 1989; The First Circle, 1990; The Golden Years, 1992; The Detectives, 1992-97; Escape, 1998; Dalziel and Pascoe, 2005; Marple: The Murder at the Vicarage, 2004; Holby City, 2005-. Theatre roles include: Hamlet, 1971; Travesties (RSC), 1975; Terra Nova, 1982; Private Dick, 1982; Tovarich, 1991; Sherlock Holmes, 1992; Kind Hearts and Coronets, 1998; Film include: Mahler, 1974; Beyond Good and Evil, 1976; Thirty Nine Steps, 1978; Imperative, 1981; Jigsaw Man, 1982; Shaka Zulu, 1985; D'Annunzio, 1987; Chunuk Bair, 1992; The Mystery of Edwin Drood, 1993; Colour Me Kubrick: A True…ish Story, 2005; Hey Mr DJ, 2005. Honours: Best Actor, Paris Film Festival, 1980; Venice Film Festival, 1982; Hon MA, 1990, Hon DLitt (Salford), 2000. Address: c/o Jonathan Altans Associates Ltd, 13 Shorts Gardens, London, WC2H 9AT, England.

POWELL Sandy, b. 7 April 1960. Costume and Set Designer. Education: St Martin's College of Art and Design, Central School of Art, London. Career: Costume designer for Mick Jagger on Rolling Stones European Urban Jungle tour, 1990, all shows by The Cholmondoleys and the Featherstonehaughs; Stage sets include: Edward II (RSC); Rigoletto (Netherlands Opera); Dr Ox's Experiment (ENO); Costumes for films include: Cobachan; The Last Of England; Stormy Monday; The Pope Must Die; Edward II; Caraveggio; Venus Peter; The Miracle; The Crying Game; Orlando; Being Human; Interview with a Vampire; Rob Roy; Michael Collins; The Butcher Boy; The Wings of the Dove; Felicia's Journey; Shakespeare in Love; Velvet Goldmine; Hilary and Jackie; The End of the Affair; Miss Julie; Gangs of New York; Far From Heaven; Sylvia; The Aviator. Honours: Best Technical Achievement Award, Evening Standard Awards, 1994; Academy Award, 1998 and 2005; BAFTA Award, 1998. Address: c/o PFD, Drury House, 34-43 Russell Street, London, WC2B 5HA. E-mail: lmamy@pfd.co.uk

PRACIANO-PEREIRA Tarcisio, b. 1 July 1943, Belém, Pará, Brazil. Mathematician; Educator; University Professor. m. Ana Fátima, 3 sons. Education: BSc, Mathematics, University Federal do Ceará, 1969; PhD, Mathematics, University of Uppsala, Sweden, 1980. Appointments: Associate Professor, Unviersidade de Federal de Goiás, Brazil, 1980-88; Member, University Council of Universidade de Aveiro, Portugal, 1988-89; Associate (Visiting) Professor Universidade de Aveiro, Portugal, 1988-89; Associate Professor, Universidade de Maringá, Paraná, Brazil, -1994; Full Professor, Numerical Analysis, Universidade do Rio Grande, Rio Grande do Sul, Brazil; Full Professor, Numerical Analysis, Universidade Estadual Vale do Acarau, Sobral, Ceará, Brazil. Publications: Numerous articles in professional journals. Honours: Listed in international biographical dictionaries. Memberships: American Mathematical Society; Sociedad Brasileira de Matemática Aplicada e Computacional; Society of Industrial and Applied Mathematics; Mathematical Association of America; Sociedade Paranaense de Matemática. Address: Av da Universidade, 850, 62040-370, Sobral, Ceará, Brazil.

PRANDOTA Jozef, b. 4 June 1941, Czersk, near Warsaw, Poland. Physician. m. Lydia Pankow-Prandota, 1 daughter. Education: Physician, 1965, Doctor of Medicine, 1970, PhD, 1980, Professor of Medical Sciences, 1990, Full Professor, 2005, University Medical School, Wroclaw, Poland; Specialisation in Paediatrics, 1969, 1973; Specialist in Clinical Pharmacology, 1981. Appointments: Assistant-Adjunct, Department of Pharmacology, Medical School, Wroclaw; Adjunct, Clinical Paediatric Nephrology, 1975-77, Vice-Chief, Chief, 1978-2002, Department of Paediatrics, Korczak Memorial Hospital, Wroclaw; Member of Staff, Faculty of Public Health, Faculty of Medicine and Dentistry, University Medical School, Wroclaw, 2002-; Visiting Scientist: Department of Paediatrics, Emory University Medical School, Atlanta, USA, 1973-75, Department of Paediatrics and Pharmacology, Louisiana State University, Shreveport, USA, 1986, Department of Clinical Pharmacology, University Medical School, University of Paris XII, 1977-78; Department of Paediatrics/Paediatric Nephrology, Hannover, Germany, 1993; Head, Department of Social Paediatrics, Faculty of Public Health, 2006. Publications: Articles in scientific journals including: Clinical Pharmacology and Therapeutics, 1975; International Urology and Nephrology, 1977, 1991, 1996; Pediatric Research, 1983; The International Journal of Pediatric Nephrology, 1984; Developmental Pharmacology and Therapeutics, 1986; Pediatric Infectious Diseases Journal, 1987; Drugs, 1988; European Journal of Clinical Pharmacology, 1988, 1991; Xenobiotica, 1991; Autoimmunity, 2001; Allergology and Immunopathology (Madrid), 2002; Several articles in The American Journal of Therapeutics, 2000-2005. Honours: Award for the Best Research Work in 1993, Polish Paediatric Society; Individual Award, Minister of Health, 2004; Team Award (for book, Pediatric Nephrology), Minister of Health, 2005; Listed in Who's Who publications and biographical dictionaries. Memberships: European Society of Paediatric Nephrology; European Society for Paediatric and Perinatal Pharmacology; New York Academy of Sciences; Polish Paediatric Association. Address: University Medical School, Faculty of Public Health, 5 Bartla Street, 51-618 Wroclaw, Poland. E-mail: prandota@ak.am.wroc.pl

PRASAD Braj Kishore, b. 24 January 1956, Bekobar, Jharkhand, India. Research and Development. m. Meera, 1 daughter. Education: BSc Engg, Metallurgical Engineering, BIT, Sindri, 1981; MTech, Metallurgical Engineering, IIT, Kanpur, 1983; PhD, Metallurgical Engineering, University of Roorkee, 1994. Appointments: Research Officer, RRL, Bhopal, 1983-84; Lecturer, Metallurgical Engineering Department, REC Durgapur, 1984-85; Scientist B, 1985-90, Scientist C, 1990-95, Scientist EI, 1995-2000, Scientist EII, 2000-, RRL, Bhopal. Publications: 120 papers in international journals; 49 papers in conference proceedings. Honours: Best Paper Award, 1995; Khosla Research Award, 1997; Maximum Publications Impact Award, RRL Bhopal, 2002-03; Bronze Medal, The Mining, Geological and Metallurgical Institute of India, 2004-05; Listed in national and international biographical dictionaries. Memberships: IIM; SAEST; MSI; MRSI; IE(I); ISE; ISNT; IIME. Address: Regional Research Laboratories, Habibganj Naka, Bhopal 462 026, India. E-mail: braj_kprasad@yahoo.com

PRASANNA Govindarajan, b. 1 June 1983, Omalur, India. Compulsory Residential Rotatory Internee. Education: MBBS. Appointments: Compulsory Residential Rotatory Internee, Govt Mohan Kumaramangalam Medical College, Salem. Publications: HSV II IgG, IgM markers in HIV/AIDS patients; Zinc and Magnesium levels in Lean Body Type II Diabetes Mellitus Patients; Urine Culture and Sensitivity in patients attending STD Clinic; Ophthal Manifestations of HIV/AIDS patients. Honours: Gold Medal in Anatomy, Surgery, Paediatrics Prize Examination; Indian Council of Medical Research projects, 2004, 2005. Memberships: CRRI Representative. Address: 8/4 Chinna Mariamman Koil Street, Omalur (PO), Salem (Dt), Tamilnadu 636455, India. E-mail: dr_prasannag@yahoo.co.in

PRASANNA Sivaprakasam, b. 5 November 1978, Chennai, India. Research Assistant. Education: B Pharm, Bachelor of Pharmacy, 1997-2001; M Pharm, Master of Pharmacy, Medicinal and Pharmaceutical Chemistry, 2001-03; PhD, Medicinal Chemistry, 2004-. Appointments: PhD Student and Research Assistant, University of Mississippi, USA. Publications: 12 articles in scientific journals. Address: 417 Faser Hall, Department of Medicinal Chemistry, School of Pharmacy, University of Mississippi, MS 38677, USA. E-mail: psivapra@olemiss.edu

PRASHAR Usha Kumari (Baroness of Runnymede), b. 29 June 1948, Nairobi, Kenya. Member of the House of Lords. m. Vijay Sharma, July 1973. Education: BA, Honours, University of Leeds, 1967-70; Dip Soc, University of Glasgow, 1970-71. Appointments include: Conciliation Officer, Race Relations Board, 1971-76; Director, Runnymede Trust, 1976-84; Fellow, Policy Studies Institute, 1984-86; Director, National Council for Voluntary Organisations, 1986-91; Numerous activities from 1992-96 include: Membership of the Royal Commission on Criminal Justice, Lord Chancellors Advisory Committee on Legal Education and Conduct; The Arts Council; Chairman Parole Board of England and Wales, 1997-2000; First Civil Service Commissioner, 2000-; Chairman, National Literacy Trust, 2001-04; Chancellor, De Montfort University, 2000-; Chairman, Royal Commonwealth Society, 2001-; Board Member, Salzburg Seminar, 2000-04; BBC World Service Trust, 2002; Judicial Appointments Commission, 2005. Publications include: Contributed to: Britain's Black Population, 1980; The System: a study of Lambeth Borough Council's race relations unit, 1981; Scarman and After, 1984; Sickle Cell Anaemia, Who Cares? A survey of screening, counselling, training and educational facilities in England, 1985; Acheson and After: primary health care in the innercity, 1986. Honours: CBE 1994; Peerage, 1999; Honorary LLD: De Montfort, 1994; South Bank University, 1994; Greenwich, 1999; Leeds Metropolitan, 1999; Ulster, 2000; Oxford Brookes, 2000; Asian Women of Achievement Award, 2002. Address: House of Lords, London SW1A 0PW, England. E-mail: prasharu@parliament.uk

PRATA Pedro Reginaldo, b. 15 May 1954, Rio de Janeiro, Brazil. Medical Doctor; University Senior Lecturer. m. 1 daughter. Education: MD, UERJ, 1978, Resident, Internal Medicine, 1979-80, Resident, Psychiatry, 1981-82, Faculty of Medical Science, Rio de Janeiro State University; Diploma, Social Psychiatry, National School of Public Health, 1982; Diploma, Public Health Policy and Management, Getulio Vargas Foundation, 1983; Diploma, Public Health and Human Resources, ENSPMG/FIOCRUZ, 1984; MSc, Public Health, University of Leeds, England, 1988; PhD, Environmental Sciences, University of East Anglia, England, 2001. Appointments: Member, Polyomielitis Eradication

Programme, Amazon Rain Forest, 1976-78; Member of team who launched first mobile rescue emergency service for accidents and disabled in Brazil, Rio de Janeiro City, 1980s; Member, Measles Eradication Programme, Rio de Janeiro, Brazil, 1983-86; Physician, Rio de Janeiro, 1983-87; Advisor, Public Health, Health State Department, Rio de Janeiro, 1983-84; Head, Department of Public Health and Human Resources, Rio de Janeiro, 1984-86; Secretary General of Health State Council, 1985-86, Head of Health Office, 1986-87, State Government, Rio de Janeiro; Tutor Assistant, Master Course in Public Health, Faculty of Medicine, Leeds University, England, 1989-90; Co-ordinator, Research Programme, State Government Research Foundation, Rio de Janeiro, 1991-92; Visiting Lecturer, Public Health, Federal University of Mato Grosso do Sul, Brazil, 1992; Lecturer, Public Health, Federal University of Bahia, Brazil, 1994-; Co-ordinator, Environmental Health Risk Study Group, 2007-. Publications: Articles in professional journals. Memberships: Fellow, Royal Geographical Society, London; Member, Brazilian Association of Public Health. E-mail: pedrorp@ufba.br

PRATCHETT Terry, b. 28 April 1948, Beaconsfield, Buckinghamshire, England. Author. m. Lyn Marian Purves, 1 daughter. Appointments: Journalist; Writer. Publications: The Carpet People, 1971, revised 1992; The Dark Side of the Sun, 1976; Strata, 1981; The Colour of Magic, 1983; The Light Fantastic, 1986; Equal Rites, Mort, 1987; Sourcery, Wyrd Sisters, 1988; Pyramids, Eric, The Unadulterated Cat, Co-author, Good Omens: The Nice and Accurate Predictions of Agnes Nutter, Truckers, Guards! Guards!, 1989; Moving Pictures, Diggers, Wings, 1990; Reaper Man, Witches Abroad, 1991; Small Gods, Only You Can Save Mankind, 1992; Johnny and the Dead, Lords and Ladies, Men at Arms, Co-author, The Streets of Ankh-Morpork, 1993; Soul Music, Co-author, Interesting Times, The Discworld Companion, 1994; Maskerade, Co-author, The Discworld Map, 1995; Johnny and the Bomb, Feet of Clay, Hogfather, The Pratchett Portfolio, 1996; Jingo, 1997; The Last Continent, Co-author, A Tourist Guide to Loncre, Carpe Jugulum, 1998; Co-author, Death's Domain, Co-author, The Science of Discworld, The Fifth Elephant, Co-author, Nanny Ogg's Cookbook, 1999; The Truth, 2000; Thief of Time, 2001; The Amazing Maurice and His Educated Parents, Night Watch, The Science of the Discworld I, II, III, 2002; Monstrous Regiment, The Wee Free Men, 2003; A Hat Full of Sky, Going Postal, 2004; Nation, 2008. Honours: OBE, 1998; Hon DLitt, (Warwick), 1999; Carnegie Medal, 2001. Address: c/o Colin Smythe, PO Box 6, Gerrards Cross, Buckinghamshire SL9 8XA, England.

PREBBLE Richard, b. 7 February 1948, Kent, England. Leader and List Member of Parliament, ACT New Zealand Party. m. (1) Nancy Prebble, 1970, (2) Doreen Prebble, 1991. Education: BA, LLB honours, Legal-economic problems, Auckland University; Lizzie Rathbone Scholar, 1967-70. Appointments: Admitted to Supreme Court as Barrister and Solicitor, 1971; Admitted to the Fiji Supreme Court Bar, 1973; Chair, Cabinet Committee, 1983-84; Headed privatisation programme; Key Minister, Labour Government, 1984-87; Elected Member of Parliament, Auckland Central, 1975-90; Professional Company Director, Works and Development Corporation, 1994-96; Elected Member of Parliament, Wellington Central, 1996-99; Leader and List Member of Parliament for ACT New Zealand Party, 1996-2004; Speaker and Advisor on regulatory, public sector, labour market, communications and transport reform; Speaking engagements in Europe, UK, USA, Indonesia, Australia and South America. Publications: I've Been Thinking, 1996; What Happens Next,

1997; I've Been Writing, 1999; Out of the Red, 2006. Address: Parliament Buildings, Wellington 1, New Zealand. E-mail: richard.prebble@parliament.govt.nz

PRENDERGAST Francis Joseph (Frank), b. 13 July 1933, Ireland. Retired. m. Mary Sydenham, 3 sons, 1 deceased, 3 daughters, 1 deceased. Education: Christian Brothers School, Limerick; Diploma, Social and Economic Science, University College, Cork, Ireland; MA, Industrial Relations, Keele University, England. Appointments: Baker, Keane's Bakery, Limerick, 1950-73; General President, Irish Bakers and Confectioners and Allied Workers Union, 1967-70; Branch Secretary, ITGWU, Shannon, Clare County Branches, 1973-77; Regional Secretary, ITGWU, Limerick, Clare, 1977-82; Head Office Representative, ITGWU, Clare County, Limerick No 2 Branches, 1987-88; District Secretary, SIPTU, Limerick, 1990-93; Member, Board of Management, Crescent College Comprehensive SJ, 1973-91; Member, Governing Body, University of Limerick, 1974-79; President, Christian Brothers School Past Pupils Union, Limerick, 1995-99; Member, Limerick City Council, 1974-99; Mayor of Limerick, 1977-78, 1984-85; Dáil Eireann (Irish Parliament), Labour Party TD (Member of Parliament), Limerick East Constituency, 1982-87; Vice-President, Bureau of Consultative Council for Regional and Local Authorities Europe, 1990-94; Alternate Member, Committee of Regions, European Union, 1994-98; Chairman, Assembly of Regional Authorities, Ireland, 1995-96; Chairman, General Council of County Councils, Ireland, 1996-97; Chairman, Mid-West Regional Authority, Ireland, 1995-96; Member, Irish Language Steering Group, Department of Local Government and Environment, Ireland, 1984-99; Member, Irish Language Television Council, 1994-2000; Member, Governing Body, School of Celtic Studies, Dublin Institute of Advanced Studies, Dublin, 1996-2000; Member, Irish Place Names Commission, 1997-; Member, Executive Trust, Hunt Museum, Limerick, 2000-; Member, Irish Parliament Trust, 1985-; Chairman, Board of Management, Árd Scoil Ris Christian Brothers School, Limerick, 2003-2006; Cathaoirleach, Gaelcholaiste Luimnigh, 2006-. Publications: History of St Michael's Parish, Limerick, 2000; Limerick's Glory: From Viking Settlement to the New Millennium (co-author), 2002; Articles in: Remembering Limerick – Historical Essays, 1997, North Munster Antiquarian Journal, Old Limerick Journal, AMDG Publications, Ireland, Made in Limerick – Historical Essays, 2003; Dála an Scéil, a book of published newspaper articles in Irish, 2003; Moyross: The Story So Far: Celebrating 30 Years of Corpus Christi Parish, Limerick, 2008; Weekly column in Irish for the Anois and Limerick Leader newspapers. Memberships: Garryowen Football Club; Voices of Limerick Choir; Thomond Archaeological Society; Limerick Thomond Probus Club. Address: "Avondonn", Cratloe Road, Mayorstone Park, Limerick, Ireland.

PRENGLER Mara, b. 1963, Buenos Aires, Argentina. Medical Doctor; Paediatrician. Education: MD, School of Medicine, University of Buenos Aires, 1988; Certificate of Specialist in Paediatrics, Ministry of Health and Social Services, 1993; PhD, Child Health, University College, University of London, England, 2005. Appointments: Complete Residence in Clinical Paediatrics, Hospital de Ninos Dr Ricardo Gutierrez Children's Hospital, Buenos Aires, 1989-93; Practitioner, Neurology Unit, Hospital Dr Ramos Mejia, Buenos Aires, 1993-94; Practitioner, Child Neurology Unit, Hospital de Ninos Dr Ricardo Gutierrez Children's Hospital, Buenos Aires, 1994-96; Fellowship, Center for Developmental Medicine and Child Neurology, Beth Israel Medical Center, University Hospital and Manhattan Campus for the Albert Einstein College of Medicine, New York, USA, 2001; Research Fellow, Specialist Clinical Fellowship in Paediatric Neurology, Institute of Child Health and Great Ormond Street Hospital for Sick Children, London, England, 1996-2000; PhD Student and Research Fellow in Paediatric Neurology, Institute of Child Health, University College, London, 2000-04; Honorary Research Fellow in Paediatric Neurology, Registrar to Professor Robert Surtees, Professor of Child Neurology, Neurosciences Unit, Great Ormond Street Hospital for Children NHS Trust, 2004-06; UK Co-ordinator, Silent Infarct Transfusion Trial in Sickle Cell Disease, 2005. Publications: 15 refereed articles in professional medical journals; 2 book chapters. Honours: K Horemis Prize, Greek Pediatric Society Meeting, 2003. Memberships: Fellow, Royal Society of Medicine; Member, British Medical Association; Member, British Paediatric Neurology Association. Address: 3 Kingsley Walk, Tring, Hertfordshire HP23 5DN, England. E-mail: mprengler@hotmail.com

PRESCOTT John Leslie, b. 31 May 1938, Prestatyn, Wales. Politician; Trade Unionist. m. Pauline Tilston, 1961, 2 sons. Education: Ruskin College, Oxford; Hull University. Appointments: Trainee Chef, 1953-55; Steward, Merchant Navy, 1955-63; Recruitment Officer, General and Municipal Workers Union, 1965; Contested Southport for Labour, 1966; Full-time officer, National Union of Seamen, 1968-70; Member of Parliament, Kingston upon Hull East, 1970-83, Hull East, 1983-97, Kingston upon Hull East, 1997-; Member Select Committee, Nationalised Industries, 1973-79, Council of Europe, 1972-75, European Parliament, 1975-79; Personal Private Secretary to Secretary of State for Trade, 1974-76; Opposition Spokesman on Transport, 1979-81, Regional Affairs and Devolution, 1981-83, on Transport, 1988-89, on Employment, 1993-94; Member, Shadow Cabinet, 1983-97; Member, National Executive Deputy Council, 1989-; Deputy Leader, Labour Party, 1994-2007; Deputy Prime Minister and Secretary of State for the Environment, Transport and the Regions, May 1997-2001; Deputy Prime Minister and First Secretary of State, 2001-2007. Publications: Not Wanted on Voyage: report of 1966 seamen's strike, 1966; Alternative Regional Strategy: A framework for discussion, 1982; Planning for Full Employment, 1985; Real Needs - Local Jobs, 1987; Moving Britain into the 1990s, 1989; Moving Britain into Europe, 1991; Full Steam Ahead, 1993; Financing Infrastructure Investment, 1994; Jobs and Social Justice, 1994; Fighting Talk, 1997; Punchlines: A Crash Course in English with John Prescott, 2003. Honours: North of England Zoological Society Gold Medal, 1999; Priyadarshni Award, 2002. Address: House of Commons, London, SW1A 0AA, England.

PRESCOTT Mark (Sir), b. 3 March 1948, London, England. Racehorse Trainer. Education: Harrow. Appointment: Trainer at Newmarket, 1970-; Training over 1,700 winners including: Pivotal, Alborada, Albanova. Publications: The Waterloo Cup – The First 150 Years (co-author); Occasional contributor to publications including: The Racing Post and Horse and Hound. Address: Heath House, Newmarket, Suffolk CB8 8DU, England

PRESCOTT Richard Chambers, b. 1 April 1952, Houston, Texas, USA. Poet; Writer. m. Sarah Elisabeth Grace. Education: Self-taught. Publications: The Sage, 1975; Moonstar, 1975; Neuf Songes (Nine Dreams), 1976, 2nd edition, 1991; The Carouse of Soma, 1977; Lions and Kings, 1977; Allah Wake Up, 1978, 2nd edition, 1994; Night Reaper, 1979; Dragon Tales, 1983; Dragon Dreams, 1986, 2nd edition, 1990; Dragon Prayers, 1988, 2nd edition, 1990; Dragon

Songs, 1988, 2nd edition, 1990; Dragon Maker, 1989, 2nd edition, 1990; Dragon Thoughts, 1990; Tales of Recognition, 1991; Kings and Sages, 1991; Dragon Sight: A Cremation Poem, 1992; Three Waves, 1992; Years of Wonder, 1992; Dream Appearances, 1992; Remembrance Recognition and Return, 1992; Spare Advice, 1992; The Imperishable, 1993; The Dark Deitess, 1993; Disturbing Delights: Waves of the Great Goddess, 1993; The Immortal: Racopa and the Rooms of Light, 1993; Hanging Baskets, 1993; Writer's Block and Other Gray Matters, 1993; The Resurrection of Quantum Joe, 1993; The Horse and The Carriage, 1993; Kalee Bhava: The Goddess and Her Moods, 1995; Because of Atma, 1995; The Skills of Kalee, 1995; Measuring Sky Without Ground, 1996; Kalee: The Allayer of Sorrows, 1996; The Goddess and the God Man, 1996; Living Sakti: Attempting Quick Knowing in Perpetual Perception and Continuous Becoming, 1997; The Mirage and the Mirror, 1998; Inherent Solutions to Spiritual Obscurations, 1999; The Ancient Method, 1999; Quantum Kamakala, 2000. Contributions to: Articles and essays to professional publications. Address: 8617 188th Street South West, Edmonds, WA 98026, USA.

PRESS Vello, b. 13 October 1934, Tallinn, Estonia. Scientific Worker. m. Lubomira Maria Broniarz. Education: Graduate Engineer, Technical University of Tallinn, 1957; PhD, Academy of Sciences of Estonia 1970; Diploma of Senior Researcher, 1974. Appointments: Heat Power Engineer, The Shipyard and the Factory Building Materials, Tallinn, 1957-60; Junior Researcher, Institute of Thermal Physics and Electrophysics, 1960-70; Senior Researcher, 1970-93; Senior Lecturer, Poznan University of Technology, 1994-2004; Retired, 2004. Publications: Over 50 papers and reports, field of combustion of fuels and the mass transport in multicomponent media. Honours: Medal of Honour 2000 Millennium, American Medal of Honour, 2005, World Medal of Freedom, 2006, American Biographical Institute. Address: Brzoskwiniowa Str 4, PL 62-031, Lubon, Poland.

PRESSER Cary, b. 20 June 1952, Brooklyn, New York, USA. Research Engineer. m. Karen Leslie, 2 daughters. Education: BSc, Aerospace Engineering, Polytechnic Institute of Brooklyn, New York, 1974; MSc, Aeronautical Engineering, Polytechnic Institute of Brooklyn, Farmingdale, New York, 1976; DSc, Aeronautical Engineering, Technion, Israel Institute of Technology, Haifa, Israel, 1980. Appointments: Engineering Assistant, Student Internship Program, Hypersonic Vehicles Division, Langley Research Center, Langley, Virginia, 1973; Teaching Fellow, Department of Aeronautical Engineering, Polytechnic Institute of Brooklyn, Farmingdale, 1975-75; Teaching Instructor, Department of Aeronautical Engineering, Technion, Israel Institute of Technology, Haifa, Israel, 1975-80; Research Engineer, 1980-94, Group Leader, High Temperature Processes Group, 1994-99, Group Leader, Thermal and Reactive Processes Group, 1999-2004, Research Engineer, 2004-, Process Measurement Division, Chemical Science and Technology Laboratory, National Institute of Standards and Technology, Gaithersburg, Maryland. Publications: Numerous articles as author and co-author include most recently: Application of a Benchmark Experimental Database for Multiphase Combustion Modeling, 2006; Transport of High Boiling-Point Fire Suppressants in a Droplet-Laden Homogeneous Turbulent Flow Past a Heated Cylinder, 2006; PIV Measurements of Water Mist Transport in a Homogeneous Turbulent Flow Past an Obstacle, 2006. Honours include: Silver Medal Award for Meritorious Federal Service, 1991, SMART Bonus Award, 1992, US Department of Commerce; AIAA Terrestrial Energy Systems Technical Committee Best Paper Award, 1994; Listed in Who's Who publications and biographical dictionaries. Memberships include: Associate Fellow, American Institute of Aeronautics and Astronautics; Senior Member, Instrumentation Society of America; Fellow, American Society of Mechanical Engineers; American Society for Testing and Materials; American Association for Aerosol Research; American Chemical Society; American Association for the Advancement of Science; New York Academy of Science; Sigma Xi; Sigma Gamma Tau. Address: Nanoscale and Optical Metrology Group, Process Measurements Division, Chemical Science and Technology Laboratory, National Institute of Standards and Technology, 100 Bureau Drive, Stop 8360, Gaithersburg, MD 20899-8360, USA. E-mail: cpresser@nist.gov

PRESSINGER Selwyn Philip Hodson, b. 9 December 1954, Guildford, Surrey, England. Writer; Company Director. Education: Graduate, Aix-en-Provence University France; Graduate, Oxford Brookes University; Postgraduate, The College of Law, Chancery Lane, London, 1973-78. Appointments: Management Consultancy (Company Law, Marketing and Trade Finance), 1981-2005:- SCF (UK), SCT Lille (France), Tennant FM International Ltd, Maygrove Consulting Ltd, Wilton & Partners; Legal Training and Practice, 1977-80:- Solicitors Professional Course and Thicknesse Hull Solicitors, Westminster. Publications: Books: Rupert Pressinger OSB 1688-1741, Benedictine Prior, 1998; Major W.S.R. Hodson 1821-1858 – In Memoriam, 2001; Military & Equine Works of Captain Adrian Jones, 2005; The Knights of St John & Torphichen Scotland, 2005; Contributions to national newspapers and literary magazines including: The Times, The Financial Times, The Universe, The Literary Review, 1990-2005; Articles in military and historical journals including: Army Quarterly and Defence Journal, Soldiers of the Queen, Journal of the Victorian Military Society, Journal of the Society for Army Historical Research, 1998-2005. Honours: Fellow, Royal Geographical Society, 1993; Honorary Member, Hodson's Horse Officers' Association, 1997; Fellow, Royal Society of Arts, 1999. Memberships: Associate, Law Society, 1978; British Institute of Management, 1985; Institute for the Management of Information Systems, 1990; Chartered Institute of Marketing, 1994; Catholic Writers' Guild, 1996. Address: c/o 28 Old Brompton Road, South Kensington, London SW7 3SS, England.

PRESTON-GODDARD John, b. 5 May 1928, Liverpool, England. Painter. Partner, Kathleen Preston-Goddard. Education: Croydon School of Art. Career: Own studios since 1948; Freelance painter in oils and watercolour; Works sold in UK, USA, Europe, South Africa, Canada and South America. Publications: Numerous international publications. Address: The Studio House, 46 Selborne Road, Park Hill Village, Croydon, Surrey CR0 5JQ, England.

PREVIN André George, b. 6 April 1929, Berlin, Germany. Conductor; Pianist; Composer. m. (1) Betty Bennett, divorced, 2 daughters, (2) Dory Langan, 1959, divorced 1970, (3) Mia Farrow, 1970, divorced 1979, 3 sons, 3 daughters, (4) Heather Hales, 1982, 1 son; (5) Anne-Sophie Mutter, 2003, divorced 2006. Education: Berlin and Paris Conservatories. Appointments: Music Director, Houston Symphony, USA, 1967-69; Music Director, Principal Conductor, London Symphony Orchestra, 1968-79, Conductor Emeritus, 1979-; Composer, conductor, approximately 50 film scores; Guest Conductor, Guest Conductor most major world orchestras also, Royal Opera House, Covent Garden, Salzburg, Edinburgh, Osaka, Flanders Festival; Music Director, London South Bank Music Festival, 1972-74; Pittsburgh Symphony

Orchestra, 1976-84, Los Angeles Philharmonic Orchestra, 1984-89; Music Director, Royal Philharmonic Orchestra, 1985-86, Principal Conductor, 1987-92; Chief Conductor and Music Director, 2004-06, Conductor Laureate, 2006-, Oslo Philharmonic Orchestra; Series of TV specials for BBC and American Public Broadcasting Service. Publications: Compositions, major works include: Every Good Boy Deserves a Favour (text by Tom Stoppard), 1977; Pages from the Calendar, 1977; Peaches, 1978; Principals, 1980; Outings, 1980; Reflections, 1981; Piano Concerto, 1984; Triolet for Brass, 1987; Variations for Solo Piano, 1991; Six Songs for Soprano and Orchestra, 1991; Sonata for Cello and Piano, 1992; The Magic Number, 1995; Trio for Bassoon, Oboe and Piano, 1994; Sonata for Violin, 1996; Sonata for Bassoon and Piano, 1997; Streetcar Named Desire (opera), 1998; Books: Music Face to Face, 1971; Orchestra (editor), 1977; Guide to Music, 1983; No Minor Chords: My Days in Hollywood, 1991. Honours include: TV Critics Award, 1972; Academy Awards for Best Film Score, 1959, 1960, 1964, 1965; Honorary KBE, 1995; Glenn Gould Prize, 2005. Address: c/o Columbia Artists, 165 W 57th Street, New York, NY 10019, USA.

PRICE Barrie, b. 13 August 1937, Bradford, England. Chartered Accountant. m. Elizabeth, 4 sons, 1 daughter. Education: St Bede's Grammar School, Bradford, 1948-53; ACA, 1959; FCA, 1968; ACCA, 1974; FCCA, 1980; MCMI, 1979; FCMI, 1980. Appointments: Trainee Accountant, 1953-58; Partner, 1962, Senior Partner 1974-, Lishman Sidwell Campbell and Price; Chairman and Managing Director, Lishman Sidwell Campbell & Price Ltd (formerly Slouand Ltd), 1968-; Director, Eura Audit International, 1999-; Senior Partner, LSCP LLP, 2003-; Senior Partner, ABS LLP, 2004-; Senior Partner, Eura Audit UK, 2005-; Director: Lishman Sidwell Campbell & Price Trustees Ltd, Lishman Sidwell Campbell and Price Financial Services Ltd, Tywest Investments Ltd, Slouand Ltd, Yorks Accountants Ltd, Yorks Consultants Ltd, Yorks Accountants and Auditors Ltd, Financial Centres Ltd, A1 Accountants Ltd, Ripon Accountants Ltd, Ripon Improvement Trust Ltd, Lyons St John Ltd, LSCP Ltd, Yorks Image Ltd, LSCP Properties Ltd, LSCP Nominees Ltd, Accountant UK On Line Ltd, A2Z Financial Services Ltd; Director, Eura Audit International, 1999-; Senior Partner, Eura Audit, UK, 2005-; Vice President Euka Audit International 2006- Various appointments: AUKOL Ltd, Development Sharing (High Skellgate) Ltd, Gibsons Hotel (Harrogate) Ltd, Online Administrator Ltd; Board Member, Eura Audit International Paris, 2001-; Councillor, 1968-91, Mayor, 1980-81, Deputy Mayor, 1974-75, 1982-83, 1987-88, Ripon City Council; Councillor, 1974-91, Deputy Leader, 1987-88, 1990-91, Chairman, Economic Development Committee, Harrogate Borough District Council; Chairman: Ripon Life Care and Housing Trust, Ripon City and District Development Association, 1969-90, Harrogate Theatre Appeal, 2001-, Harrogate Theatre Forward Appeal, 2002-; President, Ripon City Conservative Association; Trustee: City of Ripon Festival, Chairman, 1981-, York Film Archive, Chairman, 1981-91, Ripon Cathedral Appeal, 1994-97, Ripon Museum Trust Appeal, Chairman, 1998-2000. Memberships: Ripon Chamber of Trade and Commerce, 1962-83, President, 1975-77, Life Member, 1983-; Roman Catholic Diocese of Leeds Finance Committee and Board, 1989-94; Ripon Tennis Centre; RSC; Ripon Civic Society; Life Member, Yorkshire Agricultural Society; Life Member, National Trust; Skipton and Ripon Conservative Association; ACA, 1959; FCA, 1968; FCCA; FCMI. Address: Prospect House, 54 Palace Road, Ripon, North Yorkshire HG4 1HA, England. E-mail: b.price@euraaudituk.com

PRICE Janet, b. 5 February 1938, Abersychan, Pontypool, Gwent, South Wales. Singer (Soprano). m. Adrian Beaumont. Education: BMus (1st class honours) and MMus, University of Wales, Cardiff, 1956-62; LRAM (Singing Performer); ARCM (Piano Performer); LRAM (Piano Accompanist); Studied singing with Olive Groves, 1962-64; Special Study of French Vocal Music with Nadia Boulanger, France, 1966. Appointments: Singing career encompassing opera, concerts and recitals throughout the UK and Western Europe, parts of Canada and USA; Worked with leading orchestras and conductors including Haitink, Rozhdestvensky, etc; Sang opera with Glyndebourne Festival Opera, Welsh National Opera, Opera Rara, Kent Opera Co, Handel Opera Society, Northern Ireland Opera Trust, San Antonio Grand Opera Texas, BBC TV, etc; Specialty of resurrecting neglected heroines of the Bel Canto period in operas by Mercadante, Donizetti, Bellini, etc; Numerous important premieres including Belgian premiere of Tippett's 3rd Symphony, Festival of Flanders, 1975; Adjudicator at competitions including Arts Council's Young Welsh Singers' Competition, RTE's Musician of the Future Competition, Dublin, Grimsby International Singers' Competition, Llangollen International Eisteddfod; Singing Professor at Royal Welsh College of Music & Drama, 1984-2004, 2006- and at Royal Academy of Music, London, 1997-2007. Publications: Commercial recordings for EMI, Argo, Philips, Decca, Opera Rara, etc; Role of Hecuba in video of Tippett's opera, King Priam, 1985; Article entitled Haydn's Songs from a Singer's Viewpoint, Haydn Yearbook, 1983. Honours: Winner, Arts Council's first Young Welsh Singers' Competition, 1964; Honorary ARAM, 2000; FRWCMD, 2004. Memberships: Royal Society of Musicians of Great Britain. Address: 73 Kings Drive, Bishopston, Bristol BS7 8JQ, England.

PRICE Margaret (Berenice) (Dame), b. 13 April 1941, Tredegar, Wales. Singer (Soprano). Education: Trinity College of Music, London. Debut: Operatic debut with Welsh National Opera in Marriage of Figaro, 1963. Career: Renowned for Mozart Operatic Roles; Has sung in world's leading opera houses and festivals; Many radio broadcasts and television appearances; Major roles include: Countess in Marriage of Figaro, Pamina in The Magic Flute, Fiordiligi in Così fan tutte, Donna Anna in Don Giovanni, Constanze in Die Entführung, Amelia in Simon Boccanegra, Agathe in Freischütz, Desdemona in Otello, Elisabetta in Don Carlo, Aida and Norma; Sang: Norma at Covent Garden, 1987, Adriana Lecouvreur at Bonn, 1989, Elisabeth de Valois at the Orange Festival; Sang Amelia Grimaldi in a concert performance of Simon Boccanegra at the Festival Hall, 1990; Season 1993-94 in Ariadne auf Naxos at Opera de Lyon and Staatsoper Berlin. Recordings: Many recordings of opera, oratorio, concert works and recitals including, Tristan und Isolde, Le nozze di Figaro, Elgar's The Kingdom, Don Giovanni, Così fan tutte, Judas Maccabeus, Berg's Kingdom, Don Giovanni, Così fan tutte, Judas Maccabeus, Berg's Altenberglieder, Mozart's Requiem and Die Zauberflöte; Jury Member, Wigmore Hall International Song Competition, 1997. Honours: CBE; DBE, 1993. Memberships: Fellow of The College of Wales, 1991; Fellow of The College of Music and Drama of Wales, 1993. Address: c/o Stefan Hahn, Artist Management HRA, Sebastianplatz 3, 80331 Munich, Germany.

PRICE Nick, b. 28 January 1957, Durban, South Africa. Professional Golfer. m. Sue, 1 son, 1 daughter. Career: Professional Golfer, 1977-; Winner, PGA Championship, 1992, 1994, British Open, 1994, 3rd PGA Tour Money Leader, 1992; PGA Tour Money Leader, 1993; Zimbabwe Open, 1995; MCI Classic, 1997; Suntory Open, 1999; CVS Charity Classic, 2001; Mastercard Colonial, 2002; Founder, Nick Price golf course design, 2001; 10 US PGA victories, 25 world-wide victories. Honours: Vardon Trophy, 1993; Named Player of the Year, 1993; Bob Jones Award, United States Golf Association, 2005. Address: c/o PGA Tour, 100 Avenue of the Champions, Palm Beach, FL 33410, USA.

PRICE Richard (John), b. 15 August 1966, Reading, England. Librarian. m. Jacqueline Canning, 6 December 1990, divorced, 2006, 2 daughters. Education: BA, Honours, English Studies and Librarianship, 1988, PhD, 1994, University of Strathclyde. Appointments: Curator, Cataloguing, 1988, Information Officer, 1990, Curator, Modern British Collections, 1992-2003, Head Modern British Collections, 2003-, The British Library. Publications: Sense and a Minor Fever, 1993; Tube Shelter Perspective, 1993; Marks & Sparks, 1995; Hand Held, 1997; Perfume & Petrol Fumes, 1999; A Boy in Summer, 2002; Lucky Day, 2005; British Poetry Magazines 1914-2000 (with David Miller), 2006; Earliest Spring Yet, 2006; Greenfields, 2007. Contributions to: Independent; Verse; Europ; Journal of Comparative Criticism; Object Permanence; New Writing Scotland; Forward Anthology; Angel Exhaust; Poetry Scotland. Honour: 1st Prize, STV, Glasgow and Strathclyde Universities, 1988. Memberships: Poetry Society. Address: c/o Modern British Collections, The British Library, 96 Euston Road, London NW1 2DB, England.

PRICE Roger (David), b. 7 January 1944, Port Talbot, Wales. Professor of Modern History; Writer. Education: BA, University of Wales, University College of Swansea, 1965. Appointments: Lecturer, 1968-82, Senior Lecturer, 1982-83, Reader in Social History, 1984-91, Professor, European History, 1991-94, University of East Anglia; Professor of Modern History, University of Wales, Aberystwyth, 1994-. Publications: The French Second Republic: A Social History, 1972; The Economic Modernization of France, 1975; Revolution and Reaction: 1848 and The Second French Republic (editor and contributor), 1975; 1848 in France, 1975; An Economic History of Modern France, 1981; The Modernization of Rural France: Communications Networks and Agricultural Market Structures in 19th Century France, 1983; A Social History of 19th Century France, 1987; The Revolutions of 1848, 1989; A Concise History of France, 1993, second edition, 2005; Documents on the French Revolution of 1848, 1996; Napoleon III and the French Second Empire, 1997; The French Second Empire: an Anatomy of Political Power, 2001; People and Politics in France, 1848-1870, 2004. Contributions to: Numerous Magazines and journals. Honour: DLitt, University of East Anglia, 1985. Membership: Fellow, Royal Historical Society, 1983. Address: Department of History and Welsh History, University of Wales, Aberystwyth, Ceredigion SY23 3DY, Wales.

PRIDEAUX Humphrey Povah Treverbian, b. 13 December 1915, London, England. Soldier; Businessman. m. Cynthia Birch Reynardson, 4 sons. Education: BA, Hons, 1936, MA, 1945, Trinity College Oxford, 1933-36. Appointments: Regimental and Staff appointments, Regular Army, 1936-53; Director, 1956-73, Chairman, 1963-73, NAAFI; Director, 1964-88, Chairman, 1973-88, London Life; Director, 1968-81, Chairman, 1972-81, Brooke Bond Liebig; Director, 1969-81, Vice-Chairman, 1977-81, W H Smith; Director, 1981-93, Chairman, 1983-93, Morland & Co. Honours: Kt, 1971; OBE; DL. Memberships Cavalry and Guards Club. Address: Kings Cottage, Buryfields, Odiham, Hook, Hampshire RG29 1NE, England. E-mail: hptprideaux@aol.com

PRIEST Graham George, b. 14 November 1948, London, England. Philosopher. m. Anne Catherine Priest, divorced 2001, 1 son, 1 daughter. Education: BA, 1970, MA, 1974, St John's College, Cambridge University; MSc with distinction, Mathematical Logic, Bedford College, London University, 1971; PhD, Mathematics, London School of Economics, 1971-74; LittD, University of Melbourne, 2002. Appointments: Lecturer, Department of Logic and Metaphysics, University of St Andrews, Scotland, 1974-76; Lecturer, 1976-79, Senior Lecturer, 1979-87, Associate Professor, 1987-88, Department of Philosophy, University of Western Australia; Professor, Department of Philosophy, University of Queensland, 1988-2000; Visiting Professorial Fellow, University of St Andrews, Scotland, 2000-; Boyce Gibson Professor of Philosophy, University of Melbourne, 2001-. Publications: Over 150 papers; Books include: In Contradiction: a study of the transconsistent, 1987; Beyond the Limits of Thought, 1995; Introduction to Non-Classical Logic, 2001; Towards Non-Being, 2005; Doubt Truth to be a Liar, 2006; Editor, 6 works; 26 reviews; Numerous papers at conferences and learned societies. Honours: President, Australasian Association for Logic, 1988; President, Australasian Association of Philosophy; Elected Life Member, Clare Hall, Cambridge, 1991; Elected Fellow, Australian Academy of Humanities, 1995-; Chair of the Council, Australasian Association of Philosophy; 1st Vice-President, International Union for Logic, Methodology and Philosophy of Science, 1998-2003. Memberships: Australian Association of Philosophy; Australasian Association for Logic. Address: Department of Philosophy, University of Melbourne, Australia 3010.

PRIEST Jean Hirsch, b. 5 April 1928, Chicago, Illinois, USA. Professor Emeritus. m. Robert Eugene, deceased, 1 son, 2 daughters. Education includes: PhB Hons, 1947, BS, 1950, MD Hons, 1953, University of Chicago; MD, Illinois, 1957-1970; MD, Washington, 1959-1965; MD, Georgia, 1971-; MD, Montana, 1991-97. Appointments include: Clinical Instructor, Department of Pediatrics, Epidemiologist, Laboratory Bacteriologist, 1957-58, University of Illinois, Chicago, Illinois; Staff Physician, Respiratory Center, Columbus Hospital, Chicago Illinois, 1957-58; Clinical Instructor, Department of Pediatrics, University of Washington, Seattle, 1960-62; Instructor, Department of Pediatrics, 1963-65, Director, Birth Defects Clinic, 1964-67, Assistant Professor, Department of Pediatrics and Pathology, 1965-71, University of Colorado Medical Center, Denver, Colorado; Visiting Member of staff, Department of Zoology, University of St Andrews, Scotland, 1969-70; Visiting Professor, Department of Community Health, Research Cytogeneticist, University of Auckland, New Zealand, 1980-81; Director, Prenatal Diagnosis Program, 1973-90, Professor Emeritus, 1990-, Emory University, Atlanta, Georgia; Director, Genetics Laboratory, Physician, Shodair Hospital, Helena, MT, 1990-95; Professor Emeritus, Faculdade de Medicina de Marília, SP, Brasil, 2000-; American Cytogenetics Conference, Distinguished Cytogeneticist Award, 2006. Publications: 3 books; 8 book chapters; 7 book reviews; 27 abstracts; 86 refereed. Memberships: American Society for Cell Biology; Chair, Social Issues Committee, 1976-80, American Society of Human Genetics; American Board of Medical Genetics; Tissue Culture Association; Vice-President, 1977-81, American Dermatoglyphics Society; International Dermatoglyphics Society; Association of Cytogenetic Technologists; Sigma Xi; American Medical Association. Address: 843 Barton Woods Road NE, Atlanta, GA 30307, USA. E-mail: jpriest517@aol.com

PRIMDAHL Soren, b. 16 July 1967, Skanderborg, Denmark. Chemical Engineer. 1 son, 1 daughter. Education: MSc, Chemical Engineering, Technical University of Denmark, 1993; PhD, University of Twente, The Netherlands, 1999. Appointments: Research Scientist, 1993-98, Senior Research Scientist, 1998-2001, Risoe National Laboratory, Denmark; Development Engineer, OFS Fitel Denmark, 2001-04; Project Leader, Rockwool International A/S, 2004-06; Manager, Cell & Stack Production, Topsoe Fuel Cell A/S, 2006-. Publications: Patents and several articles in professional scientific journals. Address: Straedet 7, DK-3550 Slangerup, Denmark. E-mail: spri@topsoe.dk

PRIMOST Norman Basil, b. 25 June 1933, London, England. Barrister. m. Debbie Doris Ferster, 3 sons, 1 daughter. Education: LLB (Hons), London School of Economics, University of London, 1950-53; Research on Comparative Law of Agency, Trinity Hall, Cambridge, 1953-54. Appointments: National Service, Censoring Mail RASC, Military Corrective Establishment, Colchester, 1954-56; Called to the Bar, Middle Temple, 1954; Pupillage with Montague Waters QC, 1956-57; General Common Law Practice specialising in property law with particular emphasis on landlord and tenant law, 1957-; Head of Chambers, Temple Gardens Temple, 1986-94. Publications: Legal Correspondent, Stock Exchange Journal, 1967-69; Editor, Restrictive Practices Reports, 1969-71; President, B'nai B'rith First Lodge of England, 2005-07. Memberships: Wig and Pen Club; King's Head Theatre; Hampstead Theatre. Address: Grande Vue, 98 West Heath Road, London NW3 7TU, England. E-mail: sprimost@hotmail.com

PRINCE (Prince Rogers Nelson), b. 7 June 1958, Minneapolis, Minnesota, USA. Singer; Songwriter; Producer. m. (1) Mayté Garcia, 1996, 1 son (deceased), (2) Manuela Testolini, 2001. Appointments: Leader, Prince and The Revolution; Singer, New Power Generation, 1991-; Numerous tours and concerts. Creative Works: Singles: 1999; Alphabet Street; Controversy; I Could Never Take The Place; If I Was Your Girlfriend; Let's Go Crazy; Little Red Corvette; Purple Rain; Raspberry Beret; Sign O' The Times; U Got The Look; When Doves Cry; Cream; Gold. Albums: For You, 1978; Dirty Mind, 1979; Controversy, 1979; Prince, 1979; 1999, 1983; Purple Rain, 1984; Around the World in a Day, 1985; Parade, 1986; Sign of the Times, 1987; Lovesexy, 1988; Batman, 1989; Graffiti Bridge, 1990; Diamond and Pearls, 1991; Come, 1995; The Gold Experience, 1995; The Rainbow Children, 2002; One Nite Alone – Live! 2002; Musicology, 2004; 3121, 2006; Ultimate, 2006. Honours: Academy Award, Best Original Score, 1984; 3 Grammy Awards, 1985; Brit Awards, 1992, 1993, 1995; Q Award, Best Songwriter, 1990; Special Award, World Soundtrack Awards, 2004; Golden Globe, Best Original Song – Motion Picture, Happy Feet, 2007. Address: Paisley Park Enterprises, 7801 Audoban Road, Chanhassen, MN 55317, USA. Website: www.npgmusicclub.com

PRINGLE Charles Norman Seton (Air Marshal Sir), b. 6 June 1919, Dublin, Ireland. Retired Engineer. m. Margaret Sharp, 1 son (deceased). Education: BA, MA, St John's College, Cambridge. Appointments: Royal Air Force, 1941-76, final appointment, Controller of Engineering Supply and Chief Engineer; Senior Executive, Rolls-Royce (1971) Ltd, 1976-78; Non-Executive Director, Hunting Engineering, 1976-78; Chairman, Council of Engineering Institutions, 1977-78; The Director, Chief Executive, Society of British Aerospace Companies Ltd, 1978-84; Non-Executive Director, Cobham plc, 1985-89. Publications: Technical papers, Royal Aircraft Establishment, 1949. Honours: CBE 1967; KBE, 1973;

Honorary Fellow (President, 1975-76), Royal Aeronautical Society; Fellow, Royal Academy of Engineering; Life Fellow, Wildfowl & Wetland Trust; Life Fellow, RSPB. Memberships: President, Smectonian Society of Civil Engineers, 2006. Address: Appleyards, Fordingbridge, Hampshire SP6 3BP, England

PRINGLE Jack Brown, b. 13 March 1952, Cambuslang, Glasgow, Scotland. Architect. 2 daughters. Education: BA Honours, Bristol University, 1970-73; DipArch, 1974-75; RIBA Pt II, 1977. Appointments: Powell and Moya, 1973-81; Jack Pringle Architects, 1981-86; Pringle Brandon, 1986-; Royal Institute of British Architects, Council, 1980-86, 2003-, Vice-President, 2003-2005, President, 2005-07. Honours: RIBA; FRSA; FICPD. Memberships: PPRIBA; Hon AIA; FRSA. Address: 10 Bonhill Street, London EC2A 4QJ, England.

PRITZKER Andreas E M, b. 4 December 1945, Baden, Switzerland. Physicist. m. (1) Marthi Ehrlich, 1970, deceased 1998, (2) Ursula Reist, 2003. Education: PhD, Physics, Swiss Federal Institute of Technology (ETH), Zurich, Switzerland. Appointments: Scientist, Alusuisse, 1975-77; Consulting Engineer, Motor Columbus, 1977-80; Scientist, Swiss Institute for Nuclear Research, 1980-83; Assistant to President Board of Swiss Federal Institutes of Technology, 1983-87; Head Administration, Paul Scherrer Institute, 1988-98; Head, Logistics and Marketing, Paul Scherrer Institute, 1998-2002; Founder and Chairman, Munda Publishing Company, 2003-. Publications: Filberts Verhangnis, 1990; Das Ende der Tauschung, 1993; Eingeholte Zeit, 2001; Several short stories. Memberships: Swiss Writers Association; PEN Swiss-German Centre. Address: Rebmoosweg 55, CH 5200 Brugg, Switzerland. E-mail: apritzker@bluewin.ch

PROCHASKA Charles Roland, b. 8 December 1941, Nampa, Idaho, USA. Aerospace Engineer. m. Judith Diane Armstrong, 3 sons, 1 stepson, 1 stepdaughter, deceased. Education: Graduated in Aerospace Engineering, University of Michigan, 1965. Appointments: Specialist Engineer, BCAC-BMS-BAC, Renton and Kent, Washington, 1965-79; Senior Specialist Engineer, 767 Division, Boeing Co, Everett, Washington, 1979-82, Boeing Marine Systems, Renton, 1982-87; Principal Engineer, Sea Lance, Boeing Aerospace and Electronics, Kent WA, 1987-90; Principal Engineer, 777 Division, Boeing Co Cargo Systems, Renton, 1990-91; Manager, 777 Division Boeing Co Cargo Furnishings, Everett, 1991-95, 777 Division Boeing Co Insulation, Everett, 1994-95, Payloads, Boeing Co Insulation-New Process, Everett, 1995-97; Option Management, Boeing Co, Everett, 1997-98; Manager, Payloads, Boeing Co Emergency Equipment-Narrow Bodies, Everett, 1998-99; Principal Engineer, Emergency Equipment, 767 Airplane Cabin Interiors, 1999; Principal Engineer, Payloads Concept Center, Boeing Co, Everett, 1999-2002; Owner, Whidstar Construction, 2002-; Owner, Polysteel of Island County, 2006-. Publications: Project POSSUM, Polar Orbiting Satellite System-University of Michigan, 1965; National Aerospace Standard 3610, Cargo Unit Load Devices, 1968; Blueprints for Skyriders, 1968; Minuteman Stage III Hardening Review, Silo Equipment, 1972; Sea Lance Production Readiness Review, 1987; 777 Cargo Systems Critical Design Review, 1992; Option Management, the TBS Process Overview, 1997; Certification Plan, 767-400 Emergency Equipment, 1999; 3 Patents. Honours include: National Merit Award, 1960; East Quadrant Award, University of Michigan, 1964; Dean's List, University of Michigan, 1965; Outstanding Performance Award, Boeing, 1979; Employee of the Month, Boeing, 1989;

Vice-President's Award for Working Together, Alan Mulally et al, 1995; District Award of Merit, Green River District Chief, Seattle Council, Boy Scouts of America; Listed in several Who's Who and biographical publications. Memberships: Society of Professional Engineering Employees in Aerospace; Washington State Grange; Quadrants Society; National Merit Society. Address: 3499 Smugglers Cove Road, Greenbank, WA 98253-9764, USA. E-mail: whidstar@whidbey.com

PROCTER (Mary) Norma, b. 15 February 1928, Cleethorpes, Lincolnshire, England. Opera and Concert Singer. Education: Wintringham Secondary School, Grimsby; Vocal and Music studies in London with Roy Henderson, Alec Redshaw, Hans Oppenheim and Paul Hamburger. Career: London debut, Southwark Cathedral, 1948; Operatic debut, Aldeburgh Festival in Britten's Rape of Lucrecia, 1959, 1960; Royal Opera House, Covent Garden in Gluck's Orpheus, 1961; Specialist in concert works, oratorios and recitals; Performed at festivals and with major orchestras in France, Germany, Netherlands, Belgium, Spain, Italy, Portugal, Norway, Denmark, Sweden, Finland, Austria, Luxembourg, Israel, South America; Performances with conductors including: Bruno Walter, Leonard Bernstein, Jascha Horenstein, Bernard Haitink, Raphael Kubelik, Karl Richter, Pablo Casals, Malcolm Sargent, Charles Groves, David Willcocks, Alexander Gibson, Charles Mackerras, Norman del Mar. Recordings include: The Messiah; Elijah; Samson; Second, Third and Eighth Symphonies and Das Klagende Lied by Mahler; First Symphony by Hartmann; Scenes and Arias by Nicholas Maw; Le Laudi by Hermann Suter; Brahms and Mahler Ballads with Paul Hamburger; Songs of England with Jennifer Vyvyan, 1999; The Rarities by Britten including world premier release of 1957 recording of Canticle II – Abraham and Isaac with Peter Pears and Benjamin Britten, 2001. Honour: Honorary RAM, 1974. Membership: President, Grimsby Philharmonic Society. Address: Nor-Dree, 194 Clee Road, Grimsby, Lincolnshire DN32 8NG, England.

PROST Alain Marie Pascal, b. 24 February 1955, Lorette, France. Motor Racing Team Owner; Former Racing Driver. 2 sons. Education: College Sainte-Marie, Saint-Chamond. Career: French and European Champion, Go-Kart racing, 1973; French Champion, 1974-75; French and European Champion, Formula Three Racing, 1979; Joined Marlboro MacLaren Group, 1980; Winner, French, Netherlands and Italian Grand prix, 1981; World Champion, 1985, 1986, 1989, 1993; Winner, Brazilian, French, Mexican, Spanish and British Grand Prix, 1990; South African, San Marino, Spanish, European, Canadian, French, British, German Grand Prix, 1993; Silverstone Grand Prix, 1993; Estoril Grand Prix; 51 Grand Prix wins; Retired from Grand Prix racing in 1993.Technical consultant to McLaren Mercedes, 1995; Founder and President, Prost Grand Prix team, -. Publication: Vive ma vie, 1993. Honours: Officer, Legion d'honneur; Honorary OBE, 1994. Address: Prost Grand Prix, 7 avenue Eugène Freyssinet, 78286 Guyancourt Cedex, France.

PROUDFOOT (Vincent) Bruce, b. 24 September 1930, Belfast, Northern Ireland. Geographer. m. Edwina V W Field, 2 sons. Education: BA, 1951, PhD, 1957, Queen's University, Belfast. Appointments: Research Officer, Nuffield Quaternary Research Unit, 1954-58; Lecturer, 1958-59, Queen's University, Belfast; Lecturer, 1959-67, Tutor, 1960-63, Librarian, 1963-65, Hatfield College, University of Durham; Associate Professor, 1967-70, Professor, 1970-74, University of Alberta, Canada; Professor of Geography, 1974-93, Emeritus Professor of Geography, 1993-, University of St Andrews; Member of Council, 1975-78, 1992-93,

Honorary Editor, 1978-92, Chairman of Council, 1993-99, Vice-President, 1993-, Royal Scottish Geographical Society. Publications: Books: Frontier Settlement Studies (joint editor with R G Ironside et al), 1974; Site, Environment and Economy (editor), 1983; The Downpatrick Gold Find, 1955; Author and co-author of numerous papers in geographical, archaeological and soils journals and book chapters. Honours: Lister Lecturer, British Association for the Advancement of Science, 1964; Estyn Evans Lecture, Queens University Belfast, 1985; Bicentenary Medal, Royal Society of Edinburgh, 1997; FSA, 1963; FRSE, 1979; FRSGS, 1991; OBE, 1997. Memberships: Fellow Royal Society of Arts; Fellow Royal Anthropological Institute; Fellow Royal Geographical Society with Institute of British Geographers; Fellow Society of Antiquaries Scotland. Address: Westgate, 12 Wardlaw Gardens, St Andrews, Fife KY16 9DW, Scotland.

PROULX E(dna) Annie, b. 22 August 1935, Norwich, Connecticut, USA. Writer. m. (1) H Ridgeley Bullock, 1955, divorced, 1 daughter, (2) James Hamilton Lang, 1969, divorced 1990, 3 sons. Education: BA, University of Vermont, 1969; MA, Sir George Williams University, Montreal, 1973. Publications: Heart Songs and Other Stories, 1988; Postcards, 1992; The Shipping News, 1993; Accordion Crimes, 1996; Brokeback Mountain, 1998; Close Range: Wyoming Stories, 1999; That Old Ace in the Hole, 2002; Bad Dirt: Wyoming Stories 2, 2004; Contributions to: Periodicals. Honours: Guggenheim Fellowship, 1992; PEN/Faulkner Award, 1993; National Book Award for Fiction, 1993; Chicago Tribune Heartland Award, 1993; Irish Times International Fiction Award, 1993; Pulitzer Prize in Fiction, 1994; Alumni Achievement Award, University of Vermont, 1994; New York Public Library Literary Lion, 1994; Dos Passos Prize for Literature, 1996; American Academy of Achievement Award, 1998; The New Yorker Book Award for Best Fiction, 2000; English Speaking Union Ambassador Book Award, 2000; Aga Khan Prize for Fiction, 2004. Memberships: Phi Alpha Theta; Phi Beta Kappa; PEN American Centre. Address: c/o Simon and Schuster Inc, 1230 Avenue of the Americas, New York, NY 10020, USA.

PRUSTY Rabin, 6 October 1939, Cuttack, India. Scientist; Engineer; Award Winning Photographer. Education: MSCE, Masters in Science and Masters in Environmental Engineering, West Virginia University, 1979. Appointments: Environmental Engineer, specialising in pollution control projects, such as analysis of effects of toxic chemicals on humans, and the establishment of health-based safe disposal limits for toxic waste, 1979-. Main research interests: 12 years' research into Multiple Chemical Sensitivity (MCS), Electromagnetic Fields (EMF) Sensitivity; Genetic engineering and the alteration of gene and cell structures due to exposure to toxic chemicals. Publications: Numerous articles contributed to specialist scientific and computer journals; MCS website, www.nettally.com/prusty/mcs.htm. Honours: International Scientist of the Year, 2001; Man of the Year 2004; Two 1st place and one 2nd place prizes at a photography exhibit, North Florida Fair, Tallahassee, Florida, 2005; Two 2nd place and one 3rd place in 2006; One 1st place and two 2nd place prizes in 2007. Listed in numerous Who's Who publications and biographical dictionaries. Membership: The Institute of Electrical and Electronics Engineers, 1993-94. Address: PO Box 20517, Tallahassee, FL 32316-0517, USA. E-mail: rprusty@yahoo.com

PRYBYLA Jan S, b. 21 October 1927, Poland. Professor Emeritus. m. Jacqueline Meyer, 1 son, 1 daughter. Education: BComm, 1949; MEconSc, 1950; PhD, 1953. Appointments:

Professor of Economics, Pennsylvania State University, 1958-95; Visiting Professor of Economics, Nankai University, Tianjin, China, 1987-88; Visiting Scholar, Institute of International Relations, National Chengchi University, Taipei, Taiwan. Publications: Co-author, Russia and China on the Eve of a New Millennium, 1997; Contributor, The Chinese Communist State in Comparative Perspective, 2000; Author, The American Way of Peace: An Interpretation, 2005. Honours: Lindback Award for Distinguished Teaching, Pennsylvania State University, 1971; Distinction in the Social Sciences Award, Pennsylvania State University, 1979; Adjunct Faculty, US Department of State, Foreign Service Institute, Washington, DC, USA. Memberships: President, Conference on European Problems; Member, American Association for Chinese Studies; Member, Association for Comparative Economic Studies. Address: 5197 N Spring Pointe Pl, Tucson, AZ 85749, USA. E-mail: prybyla@comcast.net

PRYCE John Derwent, b. 29 January 1941, Bowness on Windermere, England. University Lecturer. m. (1) Christine, 1967, divorced 1988, 2 sons, 1 daughter, (2) Kate, 1990, 1 daughter. Education: Dragon School, Oxford; Eton College; BA, Mathematics, Trinity College, Cambridge, 1962; PhD, Mathematics, University of Newcastle Upon Tyne, 1965; Cert Ed, University of Bristol, 1966. Appointments: Mathematics Teacher, 1966-68; Lecturer, University of Aberdeen, 1968-75; Lecturer, University of Bristol, 1975-88; Sabbatical Professor, University of Toronto, Canada, 1982-83; Lecturer, Senior Lecturer, Royal Military College of Science, Cranfield University, 1988-2006. Publications: Books: Basic Methods of Linear Functional Analysis, 1973; Numerical Solution of Sturm-Liouville Problems, 1993; 55 articles in refereed journals/conference proceedings. Honours: Co-director, Uniben International Conferences on Scientific Computing, Benin City, Nigeria, 1992, 1994; Guest Editor, Volume on Differential Equations, Special Millennium Edition of Journal Computational and Applied Mathematics, 2000; Steering Committee Member, International Interval Subroutine Library project, 2005-. Memberships: Fellow, Institute of Mathematics and Applications; Chartered Mathematician; Chartered Scientist. Address: 142 Kingshill Road, Old Town, Swindon, Wiltshire, SN1 4LW, England.

PRYCE Jonathan, b. 1 June 1947, North Wales. Actor. Partner, Kate Fahy, 2 sons, 1 daughter. Education: Royal Academy of Dramatic Art. Career: Stage appearances include: The Comedians, 1975, 1976; Hamlet, Royal Court, London, 1980; The Caretaker, National Theatre, 1981; Accidental Death of an Anarchist, Broadway, 1984; The Seagull, Queen's Theatre, 1985; Macbeth, RSC, 1986; Uncle Vanya, 1988; Miss Saigon, Drury Lane, 1989; Oliver!, London Palladium, 1994; My Fair Lady, 2001; A Reckoning, 2003; The Goat, 2004; TV appearances include: Roger Doesn't Live Here Anymore (series), Timon of Athens, 1981; Martin Luther, Praying Mantis, 1983; Whose Line is it Anyway?, 1988; The Man from the Pru, 1990; Selling Hitler, 1991; Mr Wroe's Virgins, Thicker Than Water, Great Moments in Aviation, 1993; David, 1997; Hey, Mr Producer! The Musical World of Cameron Mackintosh, 1998; The Union Came: A Rugby History, 1999; Victoria & Albert, 2001; Confessions of an Ugly Stepsister, 2002; HR, Baker Street Irregulars, 2007. Films include: Something Wicked This Way Comes, 1982; The Ploughman's Lunch, 1983; Brazil, 1985; The Doctor and the Devils, Haunted Honeymoon, 1986; Jumpin' Jack Flash, 1987; Consuming Passions, The Adventures of Baron Munchausen, 1988; The Rachel Papers, 1989; Glen Garry Glen Ross, 1992; The Age of Innocence, A Business Affair, 1993; Deadly Advice, 1994; Carrington, 1995; Evita, 1996;

Tomorrow Never Dies, 1997; Regeneration, 1997; Ronin, 1998; Stigmata, 1999; Very Annie Mary, Unconditional Love, The Affair of the Necklace, Bride of the Wind, 2001; Unconditional Love, Mad Dogs, 2002; What a Girl Wants, Pirates of the Caribbean: The Curse of the Black Pearl, 2003; De-Lovely, 2004; The Brothers Grimm, Living Neon Dreams, Brothers of the Head, The New World, 2005; Ranaissance (voice), Pirates of the Caribbean: Dead Man's Chest, 2006; The Moon and the Stars, Pirates of the Caribbean: At World's End, 2007; My Zinc Bed, Leatherheads, 2008. Recordings: Miss Saigon, 1989; Nine-The Concert, Under Milkwood, 1992; Cabaret, 1994; Oliver!, 1995; Hey! Mr Producer, 1998; My Fair Lady, 2001. Honours: Tony Award, 1976; Oliver and Variety Club Awards, 1991; Tony and Drama Desk Awards, 1994; Best Actor, Cannes Film Festival, 1995; Best Actor, Evening Standard Film Awards, 1996. Address: c/o Julian Belfrage Associates, 46 Albemarle Street, London W1X 4PP, England.

PŠENÁK Oskar, b. 30 September 1973, Nové Zámky, Czechoslovakia. Physician; Researcher; Educator. Education: General Medicine, 1998, Postgraduate study, Department of Pathological Physiology, 1998-2003, 1st Medical School, Charles University, Prague, Czech Republic. Appointments: Clinical Residency, 4th and 3rd Clinic for Internal Medicine, General Teaching Hospital, 1999-2003, Educator, Department of Pathological Physiology, 2001-04, 1st Medical School, Charles University, Prague, Czech Republic; Internal Residency, Teaching Hospital, Paracelsus Private Medical University, Salzburg, Austria, 2004-. Publications: 10 publications; 4 participations at conferences. Honours: 3rd Prize, Student Scientific Conference, 1st Medical School, Charles University, Prague, Czech Republic, 2000; Mayor's Prize for Achievements in Clinical Cancer Research, Nové Zámky, Slovakia, 2005; Listed in international biographical dictionaries. Memberships: Austrian Medical Association. Address: Rudolf-Biebl-Str 2/Top39, 5020 Salzburg, Austria. E-mail: psenak@europe.com

PSYCHOGIDIS Georgios, b. 24 March 1976, Heraklion, Crete, Greece. Child Psychologist. Education: Diploma in Marketing, Institution of Vocational Training, Athens, 1999; BA, Psychology, American College of Greece, 2002; MSc, Child and Adolescent Mental Health, Institute of Psychiatry, King's College, University of London, 2004; Certificate in Dyslexia, University of Macedonia, Thessalonica, 2006. Appointments: Student Librarian, 1999, Assistant to Professor, 1999-2000, Biology, American College of Greece; Assistant to Child Psychologist, Heraklion, Greece, 2002-03; Practising Psychologist, St Thomas Hospital, London, 2003; Volunteer Child Psychologist, Child Mental Health Center, Heraklion, 2004-05; Child Psychologist, private practice, Heraklion, 2005-. Publications: Contributions to newspaper and 2 magazines; Numerous articles in professional journals. Honours: Listed in international biographical dictionaries. Memberships: American Psychological Association; International Association for Applied Psychology; American Mental Health Counselors; Mental Health America; National Autistic Society, UK. Address: 111 Aghias Paraskevis Street, Limin Hersonisou, 70014, Crete, Greece. E-mail: psychogidis@yahoo.gr

PUCKETT Richard Edward, b. 9 September 1932, Klamath Falls, Oregon, USA. Artist; Consultant; Retired Recreation Executive. m. Velma Faye Hamrick, 14 April 1957 (deceased 1985), 1 son, 3 daughters. Education: Southern Oregon College of Education, 1951-56; Lake Forest College, Illinois, 1957-58; Hartnell Junior College, Salinas; College Major, Fine Arts and Education; San Jose State University, California, 1973; BA, Public Service, University San Francisco, 1978. Appointments: Acting Arts and Crafts Director, Ft Leonard Wood, Missouri, 1956-57; Arts and Crafts Director; Assistant Special Services Officer (designed and opened 1st Ft Sheridan Army Museum), Ft Sheridan, Illinois, 1957-59; Arts and Crafts Director, Ft Irwin, California, 1959-60; Arts and Crafts Director, Ft Ord, California (directed and opened 1st Presidio of Monterey, California, Army Museum), 1968; Artist, Consultant, Retired Recreation Executive, Ft Ord, California, 1986; Directed and built the largest and most complex arts and craft program in the Department of Defense; Had the model program for the army; Taught painting classes and workshops for 30 years. Creative Works: Exhibitions: One-Man Shows at Seaside City Hall, 1967-86, 2002, Ft Ord Arts and Crafts Centre Gallery, 6 times, 1967-86, Presidio of Monterey Art Gallery, Del Messa Gallery, Carmel, California, 1998; Southern Oregon Art Gallery, Medford, 2000, Country Rose Gallery, Hollister, California, 2001-03, Walter Avery Gallery Seaside City Hall, 2001-06; Sasoontsi Gallery, 2004; Works in private collections in USA, Canada and Europe; Designed and opened first Ft Sheridan Army Museum, Presidio of Monterey Museum, exhibited in group shows at Salinas Valley Art Gallery, Del Messa Gallery, 2001-03, 2001-06; 2nd place, juried show, Sasoontsi Gallery, 2006; Glass on Holiday, Gatlinburg, Tennessee, 1981-82; Donated over 5,000 photos, slides, scrapbooks, paintings, arts and crafts items, etc to University of Monterey Bay, Ft Ord; Donated photo collection, Hartnell Junior College. Honours: 1st Place, Department of Army Programming Award, 6 times, 1975-84; Exhibited in Smithsonian; 5 USA Army Forces Command 1st Place Awards for Programming and Publicity, 1979-84; 1st and 3rd Place, Modern Sculpture, Monterey, California Fair, Fine Arts Exhibition, 1979; 19 Awards for Outstanding Performance; Commanders Award Medal, 1987; ABI Golden Academy Award for Lifetime Achievement, 1991; International Man of the Year Award, 1991-92; Friend of the Arts Special Tribute Bronze Sculpture, Arts Council for Monterey County; 2nd Place Award, Salinas Valley Arts Exhibition, 2006; Champions of the Arts, 2007; Certificate of Special Congressional Recognition, Senator Sam Farr, 2007; Commendation, Salinas City Council, 2007; Listed in international biographical dictionaries. Memberships: Salinas Fine Arts Association; President, Monterey Peninsula Art Museum Association, 2000-08; President, Salinas Valley Art Association; Ford Ord Alumni Association; International Acrylic Artists Association. Address: 210 San Miguel Ave, Salinas, CA 93901-3021, USA.

PULLMAN Bill, b. 17 December, 1953, Hornell, New York, USA. Actor. Education: University of Massachusetts. m. Tamara, 3 children. Appointments: Former drama teacher, building contractor, director of theatre group; Started acting in fringe theatres, New York; Moved to Los Angeles; Films include: Ruthless People; A League of Their Own; Sommersby; Sleepless in Seattle; While You Were Sleeping; Caspar; Independence Day; Lost Highway, 1997; The End of Violence, 1997; The Thin Red Line, 1998; Brokedown Palace, 1998; Zero Effect, 1998; A Man is Mostly Water, 1999; History is Made at Night, 1999; The Guilt, 1999; Lake Placid, 1999; Coming to Light: Edward S Curtis and the North American Indians (voice), 2000; Titan AE, 2000; Numbers, 2000; Ignition, 2001; Igby Goes Down, 2002; 29 Palms, 2002; Rick, 2003; The Grudge, 2004; The Orphan King, 2005; Dear Wendy, 2005; Alien Autopsy, 2006; Scary Movie 4, 2006; You Kill Me, 2007; Nobel Son, 2007; Your Name Here, 2008; Surveillance, 2008; Bottle Shock, 2008; Phoebe in Wonderland, 2009. Address: c/o J J Harris, 9560 Wilshire Boulevard, Suite 50, Beverly Hills, CA 90212, USA.

PULLMAN Philip, b. 19 October 1946, Norwich, England. Author. m. Jude Speller, 15 August 1970, 2 sons. Education: BA, Oxford University, 1968. Appointments: Teacher, Middle School, 1972-86; Lecturer, Westminster College, Oxford, England, 1986-96. Publications: The Ruby in the Smoke, 1986; The Shadow in the North, 1987; The Tiger in the Well, 1990; The Broken Bride, 1992; The White Mercedes, 1992; The Tin Princess, 1994; Northern Lights, 1995; The Golden Compass, 1996; Spring-Heeled Jack, 1997; Puss in Boots, 1997; The Subtle Knife, 1997; Count Karlstein, 1998; Clockwork, 1998; I Was a Rat! 2000; The Amber Spyglass, 2000; Lyra's Oxford, 2003; The Scarecrow and his Servant, 2004. Contributions to: Reviews in Times Educational Supplement; The Guardian. Honours: Carnegie Medal, 1996; Guardian Children's Fiction Award, 1996; British Book Awards Children's' Book of the Year, 1996; British Book Awards WH Smith Children's Book of the Year, 2000; Whitbread Children's Book of the Year Prize, 2001; Whitbread Book of the Year Award, 2001; BA/Book Data Author of the Year Award, 2001; Booksellers' Association Author of the Year, 2001, 2002; British Book Awards Author of the Year Award, 2002; Whitbread Book of the Year Award, 2002; CBE, 2004. Address: c/o Caradoc King, AP Watt Ltd, 20 John Street, London WC1N 2DR, England. Website: www.philip-pullman.com

PUNCOCHAR Pavel, b. 20 March 1944, Pelhrimov, Czech Republic. Biologist; Ecologist. m. Marcela, 1 daughter. Education: MSc, Faculty of Life Sciences, Charles University, Prague, 1966; RNDr, Hydrobiology, 1969; PhD, Hydromicrobiology, 1972, Appointments: Czech Academy of Sciences, Hydrobiological Laboratory, 1967; Institute of Landscape Ecology, Prague, 1985-86; Water Research Institute, Prague, 1986-97; Director, 1990-97; Director, Department of Watermanagement Policy, 1998, General Director, Section of Watermanagement, 2003, Deputy Minister, 2006-07, Ministry of Agriculture. Publications: More than 350 papers, contributions in Czech and or international journals. Memberships: International Commission for Elber River Protection; International Commission for Danube River Protection; International Commission for Oder River Protection; Member, Research Board, Ministry of the Environment; Czech Academy of Sciences, Hydrobiological Institute; Institute of Hydrobiology and Fishery of South Bohemia University; Institute of Soil Protection and Drainage, Prague; Others. Address: Zitkova 225, 15300 Prague 5, Czech Republic.

PUNTER David Godfrey, b. 19 November 1949, London, England. Professor of English; Writer; Poet. m. Caroline Case, 5 December 1988, 1 son, 2 daughters. Education: BA, 1970, MA, 1974, PhD, 1984, University of Cambridge. Appointments: Lecturer in English, University of East Anglia, 1973-86; Professor and Head of Department, Chinese University of Hong Kong, 1986-88; Professor of English, University of Stirling, 1988-2000; Professor of English, University of Bristol, 2000-. Publications: The Literature of Terror, 1980; Blake Hagel and Dialectic, 1981; Romanticism and Ideology, 1982; China and Class, 1985; The Hidden Script, 1985; Introduction to Contemporary Cultural Studies (editor), 1986; Lost in the Supermarket, 1987; Blake: Selected Poetry and Prose (editor), 1988; The Romantic Unconscious, 1989; Selected Poems of Philip Larkin (editor), 1991; Asleep at the Wheel, 1997; Gothic Pathologies, 1998; Spectral Readings (editor), 1999; Selected Short Stories, 1999; Companion to the Gothic (editor), 2000; Writing the Passions, 2000; Postcolonial Imaginings, 2000. Contributions to: Hundreds of articles, essays, and poems in various publications. Honours: Fellow, Royal Society of Arts; Fellow, Society of Antiquaries

(Scotland); Scottish Arts Council Award; Founding Fellow, Institute of Contemporary Scotland; DLitt, University of Stirling. Address: Department of English, University of Bristol, Bristol BS8 1TB, England.

PURI Sanjay, b. 23 November 1961, Rampur, India. Physicist. m. Bindu Puri, 2 sons. Education: MS Physics, IIT Delhi, India, 1982; PhD, Physics, University of Illinois at Urbana-Champaign, USA, 1987. Appointments: Assistant Professor, 1987-93, Associate Professor, 1993-2001, Professor, 2001-, Jawaharlal Nehru University (JNU), New Delhi. Publications: Approximately 125 papers and books on statistical physics and nonlinear dynamics. Honours: Young Scientist Medal, Indian National Science Academy, 1993; Satyamurthy Medal, Indian Physics Association, 1995; Birla Science Award, Birla Science Centre, 2001; Homi Bhabha Fellowship, Bhabha Fellowships Council, 2003; Elected Fellow, Indian Academy of Sciences, Bangalore, 2006; S S Bhatnagar Prize, Council of Scientific and Industrial Research, 2006. Address: School of Physical Sciences, Jawaharlal Nehru University, New Delhi 110067, India. E-mail: puri@mail.jnu.ac.in

PURKIS Andrew James, b. 24 January 1949, London, England. Charity Director. m. Jennifer Harwood Smith, 1 son, 1 daughter. Education: 1st Class Honours Modern History, Corpus Christi College, Oxford, 1967-70; St Antony's College, Oxford, 1971-74; Doctor of Philosophy, 1978. Appointments: Administrative Trainee, 1973-76, Private Secretary, 1976-77, Principal, 1977-80, Northern Ireland Office; Head of Policy Analysis, 1980-84, Head of Policy Planning, 1984-86, Assistant Director, 1986-87, National Council for Voluntary Organisations; Director, Council for the Protection of Rural England, 1987-91; Public Affairs Secretary to the Archbishop of Canterbury, 1992-98; Chief Executive, Diana, Princess of Wales Memorial Fund, 1998-2005; Chief Executive, Tropical Health and Education Trust (THET), 2005-. Publications: Housing and Community Care (with Paul Hodson), 1982; Health in the Round (with Rosemary Allen), 1983. Honours: OBE; DPhil; MA. Membership: FRSA, 1989. Address: 38 Endlesham Road, Balham, London SW12 8JL, England.

PURNELL Rt Hon James Mark Dakin, b. 2 March 1970, London, England. Member of Parliament for Stalybridge and Hyde; Secretary of State for Work and Pensions. Education: PPE, Balliol College, Oxford. Appointments: Research Fellow, Institute for Public Policy Research; Head of Corporate Planning, BBC; Special Advisor to Prime Minister Tony Blair, 1997-2001; Member of Parliament for Stalybridge and Hyde, 2001-; Member, Work and Pensions Select Committee, House of Commons, 2001-03; Chair, All Party Group on Private Equity and Venture Capital, 2002-03; Chair, Labour Friends of Israel, 2002-04; Parliamentary Private Secretary to Ruth Kelly, 2003-05; Government Whip, 2004; Parliamentary Under-Secretary of State for Creative Industries and Tourism, Department for Culture, Media and Sport, 2005-06; Minister of State for Pensions, Department for Work and Pensions, 2006-; Secretary of State for Culture, Media and Sport, 2007-; Work and Pensions Secretary, 2008-. Honours: Consumer Champion Of The Year by Which? Magazine, 2007.

PURSER Philip John, b. 28 August 1925, Letchworth, England. Journalist; Author. m. Ann Elizabeth Goodman, 18 May 1957, 1 son, 2 daughters. Education: MA, St Andrews University, 1950. Appointments: Staff, Daily Mail, 1951-57; Television Critic, Sunday Telegraph, 1961-87. Publications: Peregrination 22, 1962; Four Days to the Fireworks, 1964; The Twentymen, 1967; Night of Glass, 1968; The Holy

Father's Navy, 1971; The Last Great Tram Race, 1974; Where is He Now?, 1978; A Small Explosion, 1979; The One and Only Phyllis Dixey, 1978; Halliwell's Television Companion (with Leslie Halliwell), 1982, 2nd edition, 1986; Shooting the Hero, 1990; Poeted: The Final Quest of Edward James, 1991; Done Viewing, 1992; Lights in the Sky, 2005. Contributions to: Numerous magazines and journals. Memberships: Writers Guild of Great Britain; British Academy of Film and Television Arts. Address: 10 The Green, Blakesley, Towcester, Northamptonshire NN12 8RD, England.

PURVES Libby, (Elizabeth Mary Purves), b. 2 February 1950, London, England. Journalist; Broadcaster; Writer. m. Paul Heiney, 2 February 1980, 1 son (deceased), 1 daughter. Education: BA, 1st Class Honours, University of Oxford, 1971. Appointments: Presenter-Writer, BBC, 1975-; Editor, Tatler, 1983. Publications: Adventures Under Sail (editor), 1982; Britain at Play, 1982; The Sailing Weekend Book, 1984; How Not to Be a Perfect Mother, 1987; One Summer's Grace, 1989; How Not to Raise a Perfect Child, 1991; Casting Off, 1995; A Long Walk in Wintertime, 1996; Home Leave, 1997; More Lives Than One, 1998; Holy Smoke, 1998; Regatta, 1999; Passing Go, 2000; A Free Woman, 2001; Acting Up, 2004; Love Songs and Lies, 2007. Contributions to: Newspapers and magazines. Honours: Best Book of the Sea, 1984; OBE, Services to Journalism, 1999; Columnist of the Year, 1999; Desmond Wettern Award, 1999. Membership: RSA. Address: c/o Rogers Coleridge White, 20 Powis Mews, London W11 1JN, England.

PUSARA Kostadin, b. 2 June 1939, Ulinje, Gacko, Serbia. University Professor. m. Milica Ostojić, 2 sons. Education: Dipl OECC, Economic Faculty, 1963, MS degree (Magistar), 1979, PhD (Doctorate), 1983, Law Faculty, Belgrade University. Appointments: Foreign Trade Secretary, Invest Import, Belgrade; Government of Republic of Serbia; Federal Government of Yugoslavia; University of Belgrade; Braća Karić University, Belgrade. Publications: International Business Finance. Honours: Award for Best Professor chosen by students, University of Novi Sad, Serbia, 1998; Award for Best Professor chosen by students, Braća Karić University, 2004. Memberships: European Expert Group, Belgrade Office. Address: Ilije Garasanina 25, Belgrade 11000, Serbia. E-mail: kosta@ftb.uni-bk.ac.yu Website: www.pusara.com

PUTIN Vladimir Vladimirovich, b. 7 October 1952, Leningrad, USSR. President, Prime Minister of the Russian Federation. m. Ludmila Alexandrovna Putina, 2 daughters. Education: Graduate, Faculty of Law, Leningrad State University, 1975. Appointments: National Security Service, 1975-90; Assistant Rector, International Affairs, Leningrad State University, Adviser to Chairman, Leningrad City Council, 1990; Head, International Committee, St Petersburg Mayor's Office, 1991-96, concurrently, First Deputy Chairman of the Government of St Petersburg, 1994-96; Deputy Property Manager, under President Yeltsin, Moscow, 1996; Deputy Chief of Staff, Main Control Department of the Administration of the Russian Federation, 1997; First Deputy Chief of Staff in Charge of Russian Regions and Territories, 1998; Director, Russian Federal Security Service, 1998; Secretary, Russian Security Council, 1999; Prime Minister of the Russian Federation, 1999; Acting President, 1999, President of the Russian Federation, 2000-04, 2004-08; Prime Minister of the Russian Federation, 2008-. Honours: Master of Sports in sambo wrestling, 1973; Master of Sports in judo, 1975; Won sambo championships in St Petersburg many times; Candidate of Economic Sciences. Address: The Kremlin, Moscow, Russia. E-mail: president@kremlin.ru

PUTTNAM David Terence (Baron), b. 25 February 1941, London, England. Film Producer. m. Patricia Mary Jones, 1 son, 1 daughter. Appointments: Advertising, 1958-66; Photography, 1966-68; Film production, 1968-; Chairman, Enigma Productions Ltd, 1978-, Spectrum Strategy Ltd, 1999-; Director, National Film Finance Corporation, 1980-85, Anglia TV Group, 1982-99, Village Roadshow Corporation, 1989-99, Survival Anglia, 1989-, Chrysalis Group, 1993-96; Chairman, CEO, Columbia Pictures, USA, 1986-88; President, Council for Protection of Rural England, 1985-92; Visiting Lecturer, Bristol University, 1984-86; Visiting Industrial Professor, 1986-96; Governor, Lecturer, LSE, 1997-; Governor, 1974-, Chair, 1988-96, National Film and TV School; Chair, Teaching Council, 2000-02; Productions include: That'll Be the Day; Mahler; Bugsy Malone; The Duellists; Midnight Express; Chariots of Fire; Local Hero; The Killing Fields; Cal; Defence of the Realm; Forever Young, 1984; The Mission, 1985; Mr Love, 1986; Memphis Belle, 1989; Meeting Venus, 1990; Being Human, 1993; War of the Buttons, 1993; Le Confessional, 1995; My Life So Far, 2000. Publications: Rural England: Our Countryside at the Crossroads, 1988; Undeclared War: The Struggle to Control the World's Film Industry, 1997; My Life So Far, 1999. Honours: Honorary FCSD; Honorary degrees (Bristol, Leicester, Manchester, Leeds, Bradford, Westminster, Humberside, Sunderland, Cheltenham and Gloucester, Kent, London Guildhall Universities, Royal Scottish Academy, Imperial College London; Special Jury prize for the Duellist, Cannes, 1977; 2 Academy Awards, 4 BAFTA Awards for Midnight Express, 1978; 4 Academy Awards, 3 BAFTA Awards for Chariots of Fire, 1981; 3 Academy Awards and 9 BAFTA Awards for The Killing Fields, 1985; Michael Balcon Award, BAFTA, 1982; Palme d'Or, Cannes, 1 Academy Award, 3 BAFTA Awards for The Mission, 1987; Officier, Ordre des Arts et des Lettres, 1986. Memberships include: Vice President, BAFTA; Chancellor, University of Sunderland; Chairman, National Endowment for Science, Technology and the Arts, National Museum of Photography, Film and TV; Education Standards Task Force, 1997-2000. Address: Enigma Productions, 29A Tufton Street, London, SW1P 3QL, England.

PYBUS Rodney, b. 5 June 1938, Newcastle upon Tyne, England. Writer; Poet. m. Ellen Johnson, 24 June 1961, 2 sons. Education: BA, Honours, Classics, English, MA, 1965, Gonville and Caius College, Cambridge. Appointments: Lecturer, Macquarie University, Australia, 1976-79; Literature Officer, Cumbria, 1979-81. Publications: In Memoriam Milena, 1973; Bridging Loans, 1976; At the Stone Junction, 1978; The Loveless Letters, 1981; Talitha Cumi, 1985; Cicadas in Their Summers: New and Selected Poems, 1988; Flying Blues, 1994. Contributions to: Numerous publications. Honours: Alice Hunt Bartlett Award, Poetry Society, 1974; Arts Council Writer's Fellowships, 1982-85; National Poetry Competition Awards, 1984, 1985, 1988; 1st Prize, Peterloo Poetry Competition, 1989; Hawthornden Fellowship, 1988. Prize-winner, Arvon International Poetry Competition, 2006. Memberships: Society of Authors. Address: 21 Plough Lane, Suffolk CO10 2AU, England.

PYO Hyeon-Bong, b. 11 January 1963, Seoul, Korea. Physicist; Research Scientist. m. Se-Hyeon Oh, 1 son, 1 daughter. Education: BSc, Department of Physics, Seoul National University, 1986; Diploma, 1990, PhD, 1995, Fachbereich Physik, University of Hamburg, Germany. Appointments: Postdoctoral Fellow, Basic Research Department, 1996-97, Leader, Biomens Team, IT Convergence & Components Laboratory, 1997-, Electronics and Telecommunications Research Institute. Publications: Over 50 scientific and technical publications in journals and conferences; Over 60 international and Korean patents. Honours; Listed in national and international biographical dictionaries. Memberships: Korean Physical Society; Korean Biochip Society; Deutsche Physikalische Gesellschaft. Address: IT Convergence & Components Laboratory, Biomens Team, ETRI, 161 Gajeong-Dong, Yuseong-Gu, Daejeon 305-350, Republic of Korea. E-mail: pyo@etri.re.kr

PYUN Jae-Young, b. 8 February 1972, Jangsung, Jeollanam-do, Korea. Professor. m. Seong-bok Seo, 1 daughter. Education: BS, Department of Electronics Engineering, Chosun University, 1997; MS, Department of Electronics Engineering, Chonnam University 1999; PhD, Department of Electronics Engineering, Korea University, 2003. Appointments: Research Engineer, Palitech Corporation, 2001-03; Research Engineer, Telecommunication & Network Group, Samsung Electronics Corporation, Korea, 2003-04; Full time Lecturer, 2004-06, Assistant Professor, 2006-, Department of Information & Communication Engineering, Chosun University. Publications: 20 international journal papers. Honours: Listed in international biographical dictionaries. Memberships: IEEE; IEICE; IEEK; KICS. Address: Department of Information & Communication Engineering, Chosun University, 375 Susuk-dong, Dong-gu, Gwang-ju, 501-759, Korea. E-mail: jypyun@chosun.ac.kr

Q

QIU Junping, b. 1 November 1947, Lianyuan city, Hunan province, China. Library and Information Scientist; Educator. m. Jin Lian Yan, 1972, 2 daughters. Education: BSc, 1969, Certified Professor, 1996, Wuhan University. Appointments: Professor, 1996-, Teacher of PhD candidates, 1997-, Dean, Scientific Information Training Centre, Wuhan University, China Scientific Commission; Director, Library and Information Research Centre, Wuhan University, Research Centre for China Scientific Evaluation, Wuhan. Publications: 26 books, 7 important books and over 280 articles in professional journals including: New Advances in the Study of Knowledge and Information Management, 1987; Bibliometics, 1988; Market Economy Informatics, 2001; Network Data Analysis, 2004; Bibliometrics and Content Analysis, 2005; Science of Knowledge Management, 2006; A Report on the Competitiveness Evaluation of Universities and Subjects in China, 2006; An Evaluation Report of Postgraduates Education in China, 2006; Informetrics, 2007; An Evaluation Report of World-Class Universities and Subjects Competitiveness, 2007. Honours: 36 academic awards; Excellent Chinese Communist Party Member Award, Wuhan University, 1985; Excellent Teacher Award, 1987; Excellent Doctoral Superior Award, 2003; Key founder of Chinese bibliometrics; Young expert with extraordinary contribution to Hubei Province, 2001; Expert with special government subsidy by China State Council, 2004. Memberships: School of Information Management and College of Education Science, Wuhan University; Director, Research Centre for Chinese Science Evaluation; Evaluation Expert, Higher Education Evaluation Center of the Ministry of Education; China Management Science Research Institute; Zhejiang University; Nanjing University of Science and Technology; Vice President, The China Society of Indexers; Vice Director, Committee of Scientometrics; Chinese Association of Science and Technology and S&T Policy Research; China Society for Scientific and Technical Information; Chinese Social Sciences Information Society; Society of Competitive Intelligence of China; CSSCI Steering Committee, Ministry of Education, Committee for Translation and Publishing, Library Society of China; Editor of 14 scientific journals; Research in library and information science, bibliometrics, scientometrics, webometrics, scientific evaluation and university evaluation, information management, knowledge management, economy information, competitive intelligence. Address: Wuhan University School of Information Management, Luojia Hill, Wuhan 430072, China. E-mail: jpqiu@whu.edu.cn

QUADRIO CURZIO Alberto, b. 25 December 1937, Tirano, Italy. Professor. Education: Degree, Political Science, Catholic University of Milan, 1961. Appointments: Professor, University of Cagliari, 1965; Professor, 1972, Dean of Faculty, Political Sciences, 1974-75, University of Bologna; Founder, Institute of Economic Sciences, University of Bergamo, 1975-76; Director of the Research Centre in Economic Analysis, 1977-; Professor of Political Economy, 1976-, Dean of the Faculty of Political Sciences, 1989-, Catholic University of Milan; Lecturer, various universities world-wide; Speaker, conferences and seminars world-wide; Columnist, Sole 24 Ore Journal. Publications: about 300, concerning economic theory, history of economic thought; stylized facts of economics, applied and institutional economics relating to economic development. Honours: Prizes for Economics include S Vincent, Walter Tobagi, Cortina Ulisse; Gerolamo Cardano, Rotary Club Pavia International Prize; Targa Premio Nuova Spoleto, Associazione Premio Nuova Spoleto; Gold Medal for cultural merit, from President of Italian Republic, Benemeriti della Scienza e della Cultura, 2000. Memberships include: Many review and research institutions, scientific councils; Representative Economists, Council National Research, CNR, 1977-87; President, Italian Economists Society, 1995-98; Co-founder then Director, Economia Politica, Journal of Analytical and Institutional Economics (Il Mulino); Member, Past President, Istituto Lombardo Accademia di Scienze e Lettere; National Member, National Academy Lincei. Address: Universita Cattolica Del Sacro Cuore, Largo Gemelli 1, 20923 Milano, Italy. E-mail: alberto.quadriocurzio@unicatt.it

QUAID Dennis, b. 9 April 1954, Houston, Texas, USA. Actor. m. (2) Meg Ryan, 1991, divorced, 1 son, (3) Kimberley Buffington, 2004, 2 children. Education: University of Houston. Career: Stage appearances in Houston and New York; Performances with rock band The Electrics; Songwriter for films: The Night the Lights Went Out in Georgia; Tough Enough; The Big Easy; TV appearances: Bill: On His Own; Johnny Belinda; Amateur Night at the Dixie Bar and Grill; Everything That Rises; Films: September 30 1955, 1978; Crazy Mama; Our Winning Season; Seniors; Breaking Away; I Never Promised You a Rose Garden; Gorp; The Long Riders; All Night Long; Caveman; The Night the Lights Went Out in Georgia; Tough Enough; Jaws 3-D; The Right Stuff; Dreamscape; Enemy Mine; The Big Easy; Innerspace; Suspect; DOA; Everyone's All-American; Great Balls of Fire; Lie Down With Lions; Postcards from the Edge; Come and See the Paradise; A 22 Cent Romance; Wilder Napalu; Flesh and Bone; Wyatt Earp; Something To Talk About, 1995; Dragonheart, 1996; Criminal Element, 1997; Going West, 1997; Gang Related, 1997; Savior, 1997; Switchback, 1997; The Parent Trap, 1998; On Any Given Sunday, 1999; Frequency, 2000; Traffic, 2000; The Rookie, 2002; Far From Heaven, 2002; Cold Creek Manor, 2003; The Alamo, 2004; The Day After Tomorrow, 2004; Flight of the Phoenix, 2004; Synergy, 2004; In Good Company, 2004; Yours, Mine and Ours, 2005; American Dreamz, 2006; Terra (voice), 2006; Smart People, 2008; Vantage Point, 2008; The Express, 2008; The Horseman, 2008. Address: POB 742625, Houston, TX 77274, USA.

QUANT Mary, b. 11 February 1934, London, England. Fashion, Cosmetic and Textile Designer. m. Alexander Plunket Greene, 1957, deceased 1990, 1 son. Education: Goldsmith's College of Art, London, England. Career: Started in Chelsea, London, 1954; Director, Mary Quant Group of Companies, 1955-; Joint Chair, Mary Quant Ltd; Design Council, 1971-74; UK-USA Bicentennial Liaison Committee, 1973; Retrospective exhibition of 1960s fashion, London Museum, 1974; Victoria and Albert Museum Advisory Council, 1976-78; Senior Fellow, Royal College of Art, 1991; Director (non-executive), House of Fraser, 1997-. Publications: Quant by Quant, 1966; Colour by Quant, 1984; Quant on Make-up, 1986; Mary Quant Classic Make-up and Beauty Book, 1996. Honours: OBE, 1966; Honorary Fellow, Goldsmiths College, University of London, 1993; Honorary FRSA, 1995; Sunday Times International Fashion Award, Rex Award, USA, Annual Design Medal, Society of Industrial Artists and Designers, Piavolo d'Oro, Italy, Royal Designer for Industry, Hall of Fame Award, British Fashion Council (for outstanding contribution to British fashion), 1990; Fellow, Chartered Society of Designers, winner of the Minerva Medal, the Society's highest award; Dr hc, Winchester College of Art, 2000. Address: Mary Quant Ltd, 3 Ives Street, London SW3 2NE, England.

QUEEN LATIFAH, (Dana Owens), b. 18 March 1970, East Orange, New Jersey, USA. Rap Artist; Actress. Career: Worked for Burger King; Worked with female rap act Ladies Fresh; Recorded with producers Dady-O, KRS-1, DJ Mark the 45 King and members of De La Soul; Moved to Motown Records; Established own label and management company, Flavor Unit; Guest appearance on Shabba Ranks's single Watcha Gonna Do; Other recording collaborations with De La Soul and Monie Love; Films include: Living Single; Jungle Fever, 1991; House Party 2, 1991; Juice, 1992; My Life, 1993; Set It Off, 1996; Hoodlum, 1997; Sphere, 1998; Living Out Loud, 1998; The Bone Collector, 1999; Bringing Out the Dead, 1999; The Country Bears, 2002; Brown Sugar, 2002; Chicago, 2002; Bringing Down the House, 2003; Scary Movie 3, 2003; Barbershop 2: Back in Business, 2004; The Cookout, 2004; Beauty Shop, 2005; Last Holiday, 2006; Ice Age: The Meltdown (voice), 2006; Stranger Than Fiction, 2006; Lost Historical Films on the Ice Age Period (voice), 2006; Life Support, 2007; Hairspray, 2007; The Perfect Holiday, 2007; Mad Money, 2008; What Happens in Vegas, 2008. Many TV appearances. Recordings: Singles: Wrath of My Madness, 1990; How Do I Love Thee, 1990; Ladies First, 1990; Mama Gave Birth to the Soul Children, 1990; Come Into My House, 1993; U.N.I.T.Y., EP, 1994; Just Another Day, EP, 1994; Mr Big Stuff, 1997; It's Alright, 1997; Paper, 1998; Albums: All Hail the Queen, 1989; Latifah's Had It Up 2 Here, 1989; Nature of a Sista, 1991; Black Reign, 1993; Queen Latifah and Original Flava Unit, 1996; Order in the Court, 1998. Address: c/o Universal Records, 2220 Colorado Avenue, Santa Monica, CA 90404, USA. Website: www.queenlatifahmusic.com

QUEIROZ Francisco Manuel Monteiro de, b. 7 June 1951, Kuito-Bie, Angola. Lawyer; Professor of Economic Law. 1 son, 2 daughters. Education: Degree in Law, Agostinho Neto University, Luanda, Angola, 1984; Postgraduate in International Economic Law, Agostinho Neto University, Angola and São Paulo University, Brazil, 1986; Master in Law, Economic Law Sciences, Classic University, Lisbon, Portugal, 1996. Appointments: Magistrate of Public Prosecution, 1979-84; Professor of Economic Law, 1985-, Director of Faculty of Law, 1986-2000, Agostinho Neto University; Parliamentary Affairs Consultant/Advisor, Cabinet of the President of Angola, 2005-; Analyst of Macroeconomics and Political Economics, Angola. Publications: Articles, book chapters and conference papers include: The Constitution Angolan Economic, 1992; The Economic Role of the Angolan State, 1996; Informal Sector of Economy in Angola: Contributes for Understanding and Framing Juridical-Economic (Master's Dissertation), 1996; No Official Sector of Economy in Angola: Juridical Perspective – Economic, 1996; The Importance of the Traditional Economy, 1996; The International Juridical Personality of the Organisations that Follow the Armed Road to Conquer the Power – The Case of UNITA, 1998; The Responsibilities of Angola in Peace in the Process of Economic Integration of SADC, 2002; The Penal Economic Right, 2003; The Rights of Foreign Investor Vis a Vis to the Angolan Investment Law, 2003. Honour: Certificate of Best Professor of the Year 2001, Faculty of Law. Memberships: Angolan Strategic Studies Association; Angolan Lawyers Association; Portuguese Lawyers Association; Canadian Association of African Studies until 2003. Address: Rua Marien N'Gouabi, 101 R/C (Lawyers Office) Luanda, Angola. E-mail: f.queiroz@ebnet.net

QUEL Eduardo Jaime, b. 12 January 1940, Mar del Plata, Argentina. Professor. m. Maria Silvia, 2 sons, 1 daughter. Education: Graduate, Physics, University of La Plata, Argentina, 1962; Doctor, Physical Sciences, University of Louvain, Belgium, 1970; Doctor, Physics, University of La Plata, Argentina, 1973. Appointments: Professor, National Technical University, 1964; Head, Laser Group, Citefa, Argentina, 1972-1980; Director, Ceilap Investigation Centre for Lasers and Applications, 1980-; Professor, National University of San Martin, 1995. Publications include: Laser scientific works presented at international and national Congresses; Papers and articles published in important international and national magazines; Co-Author of 2 books; Co-Editor of 1 book. Honour: Recorrido Dorado Award, 1992. Memberships: Sociedad Cientifica Argentina; Asociacion Fisica Argentina; Optical Society of America; American Geophysical Union. Address: Sucre 3774, 1430 Buenos Aires, Argentina. E-mail: quel@citefa.gov.ar

QUIGLEY Stephen Howard, b. 29 May 1951, Boston, Massachusetts, USA. Executive Editor. m Suzanne Elizabeth Daley, 2 sons, 1 daughter. Education: BA, French and International Relations, Dartmouth College, Hanover, New Hampshire, 1973. Appointments: College Sales Representative, Acquisitions Editor, Regional Sales Manager, Addison-Wesley Publishing Co Inc, Boston, Chicago and DC, 1973-84; Acquisitions Editor, Scott, Foresman and Company, Chicago, 1985-88; Senior Mathematics Editor, PWS Publishing Company, Boston, 1988-95; Executive Editor, John Wiley & Sons Inc, Hoboken, New Jersey and Marblehead, 1995-. Honours: Editor of the Year, 1990; Man of Achievement Award, 2002; Listed in Who's Who publications and biographical dictionaries; Dartmouth Club of the Year, 1990; Association of American Publishers Professional/ Scholarly Publications Book of the Year, 2001, 2002, 2006 and 2007. Memberships include: American Mathematical Society; MAA; National Council of Teachers of Mathematics; American Statistical Association; Association for Supervision and Curriculum Development; Geological Society of America; Massachusetts Bar Association; Boston Rotary International; American Red Cross; Boy Scouts of America; Corinthian Yacht Club, Goldthwaite Reservation. Address: John Wiley & Sons Inc, Two Hooper Street, Marblehead, MA 01945, USA. E-mail: squigley@wiley.com

QUIN Louis DuBose, b. 5 March 1928, Charleston, South Carolina, USA. Professor of Chemistry. m. Gyöngyi Szakal Quin, 2 sons, 1 daughter (by previous marriage). Education: BS, The Citadel, 1947; MA, 1949, PhD, 1952, University of North Carolina. Appointments: Chemical Industry and US Army, 1952-56; Department of Chemistry, Duke University, 1956-86, Assistant Professor to J B Duke Professor, Chair, 1970-76; Department Chemistry, University of Massachusetts, 1986-96, Head, 1986-94; Chemistry Department, University of North Carolina at Wilmington, Distinguished Visiting Professor, 1997-.99 Publications: 250 research publications, 8 authored or edited books. Honours: AE and BA Arbusov Award in Phosphorus Chemistry, 1997; North Carolina Distinguished Lecturer, 1999; Fellow, American Association for the Advancement of Science. Membership: American Chemical Society, Sigma Xi. Address: 15 Aldersgate Court, Durham, NC 27705, USA.

QUINN Aiden, b. 8 March 1959, Chicago, USA. Actor. m. Elizabeth Bracco, 1987, 2 daughters. Career: Worked with various theatre groups, Chicago; Off-Broadway appearances in Sam Shepard plays: Fool for Love; A Lie of the Mind; Hamlet, Chicago; TV: An Early Frost; Empire Falls, 2004; Films: Reckless, 1984; The Mission; All My Sons; Stakeout; Desperately Seeking Susan; Crusoe; The Handmaid's Tale; At Play in the Fields of the Lord; Avalon; Legends of the Fall; Mary Shelley's Frankenstein, 1994; The Stars Fell on Henrietta, 1994; Haunted, 1994; Michael Collins, 1996; Looking for Richard, 1996; Commandants, 1996; The Assignment, 1997; Wings Against the Wind, 1998; This is My Father, 1998; Practical Magic, 1998; Blue Vision, 1998; The Imposters, 1998; 50 Violins, 1999; In Dreams, 1999; Two of Us, 2000; See You In My Dreams, 2000; Evelyn, 2002; A Song for a Raggy Boy, 2003; Bobby Jones: Stroke of Genius, 2004; Plainsong, 2004; Return to Sender, 2005; Nine Lives, 2005; The Exonerated, 2005; Empire Falls, 2005; Dark Matter, 2007; 32A, 2007; Wild Child, 2008. Address: CAA, 930 Wilshire Boulevard, Beverly Hills, CA 90212, USA.

QUINN Sheila Margaret (Dame Sheila Quinn), b. 16 September 1920, Blackpool, Lancashire, England. Nurse. Education: SRN, Lancaster Royal Infirmary, Lancaster, 1943-47; SCM, Lordswood Maternity Hospital, Birmingham, 1948-49; Nurse Tutor Diploma, London University and Royal College of Nursing, 1955-57; BSc (Hons) Economics, London University, 1960-63; Henley Management College, 1968. Appointments: Various Hospital Posts, 1949-57; Principal Nurse Tutor, Prince of Wales Hospital, London, 1957-61; Director, Social and Economic Welfare Division, 1961-66, Executive Director, International Council of Nurses, Geneva, 1966-70; Chief Nurse, Southampton University Hospitals, 1970-74; Chief Area Nurse, Hampshire, 1974-78; Chief Regional Nurse, Wessex, 1978-83; Chief Nursing Advisor, British Red Cross, 1983-89; International Nursing Consultant, 1989-; Advisory Committee on Nursing of European Union, 1979-87, President, 1979-82; Standing Committee of Nurses of the European Union, 1975-89, President, 1983-89. Publications: Nursing in the European Community, 1980; Caring for the Carers, 1981; ICN Past and Present, 1993; Nursing, The European Dimension, 1993; A Dame Abroad (Memoir Club), 2004; Numerous articles in national and international nursing journals. Honours: Fellow Royal College of Nursing, 1977; CBE, 1978; Hon DSc (Soc Sc), Southampton University, 1986; DBE, 1987; Christiane Reimann International Award for Nursing, 1993. Memberships: Life Vice President and Fellow Royal College of Nursing; Fellow, Royal Society of Medicine; Committee Member, 1986-2007, Vice Chair, 2000-2007, Brendon Care Foundation for the Total Care of Elderly, Winchester; Trustee and Former Chair, SCA Community Care Services, Southampton; International Nursing Consultant, Dreyfus Health Foundation, New York, USA. Address: 7 Knightwood Crescent, Shannon Way, Chandlers Ford, Hampshire, SO53 4TL, England. E-mail: dsmq@tesco.net

QUINSEY Vernon Lewis, b. 10 October 1944, Flin Flon, Manitoba, Canada. Professor and Head of Psychology. m. Jill L Atkinson, 4 sons, 1 daughter. Education: BSc, University of North Dakota at Grand Forks, 1966; MSc, 1969, PhD 1970, University of Massachusetts at Amherst. Appointments: Director of Research, Penetanguishene Mental Health Centre, 1976-84 and 1986-88; Visiting Scientist, Institut Philippe Pinel, 1984-86; Professor of Psychology, 1988-, Psychiatry, 1994-, Biology, 2003-, Psychology Department Head, 2004-, Queen's University, Kingston, Ontario, Canada. Publications: 8 books; Over 150 articles and chapters. Honours: Senior Research Fellowship, Ontario Mental Health Foundation, 1997-2001; Career Contribution Award, Canadian Psychological Association. Memberships: Human Behavior and Evolution Society; Association for the Treatment of Sexual Abusers; International Academy of Sex Research; Fellow, Canadian Psychological Association. Address: Psychology Department, Queen's University, Kingston, Ontario, Canada, K7L 3N6.

QUINT David Paul, b. 24 July 1950, Iowa, USA. Investment Banker. m. Kathleen Stern, 2 sons, 2 daughters. Education: Bachelor of Arts, 1972, Juris Doctorate, 1975, University of Notre Dame. Appointments: Attorney, Arter & Hadden, 1975-83; Managing Director, Belden & Blake (UK) Inc., 1983-92; Chief Executive, RP&C International, 1992-. Publications: Articles, Notre Dame Law Review. Honours: Member, Notre Dame Law Review; Fellow, Rotary International. Membership: Ohio State Bar Association. Address: 31A St James's Square, London, SW1Y 4JR, England. E-mail: dquint@rpcint.co.uk

QUIRK Sir Randolph (Baron Quirk of Bloomsbury), b. 12 July 1920, Isle of Man, England. Emeritus Professor of English Language and Literature; Writer. m. (1) Jean Williams, 1946, divorced 1979, 2 sons, (2) Gabriele Stein, 1984. Education: BA, 1947, MA, 1949, PhD, 1951, DLitt, 1961, University College, London. Appointments: Lecturer in English, 1947-54, Professor of English Language, 1960-68, Quain Professor of English Language and Literature, 1968-81, University College, London; Commonwealth Fund Fellow, Yale University and University of Michigan, 1951-52; Reader in English Language and Literature, 1954-58, Professor of English Language, 1958-60, University of Durham; Vice Chancellor, 1981-85, University of London. Publications: The Concessive Relation in Old English Poetry, 1954; Studies in Communication (with A J Ayer and others), 1955; An Old English Grammar (with C L Wrenn), 1955, enlarged edition (with S E Deskis), 1994; Charles Dickens and Appropriate Language, 1959; The Teaching of English (with A H Smith), 1959, revised edition, 1964; The Study of the Mother-Tongue, 1961; The Use of English, 1962, enlarged edition, 1968; Prosodic and Paralinguistic Features in English (with D Crystal), 1964; A Common Language (with A H Marckwardt), 1964; Investigating Linguistic Acceptability (with J Svartvik), 1966; Essays on the English Language: Mediaeval and Modern, 1968; Elicitation Experiments in English (with S Greenbaum), 1970; A Grammar of Contemporary English (with S Greenbaum, G Leech, and J Svartvik), 1972; The English Language and Images of Matter, 1972; A University Grammar in English (with S Greenbaum), 1973; The Linguist and the English Language, 1974; Old English Literature: A Practical Introduction (with V Adams and D Davy), 1975; A Corpus of English Conversation (with J Svartvik), 1980; Style and Communication in the English Language, 1982, revised edition, 1984; A Comprehensive Grammar of the English Language (with S Greenbaum, G Leech and J Svartvik), 1985; English in the World (with H Widdowson), 1985; Words at Work: Lectures on Textual Structure, 1986; English in Use (with G Stein), 1990; A Student's Grammar of the English Language (with S Greenbaum), 1990, revised edition 1997; An Introduction to Standard English (with G Stein), 1993; Grammatical and Lexical Variance in English, 1995. Contributions to: Scholarly books and journals. Honours: Commander of the Order of the British Empire, 1976; Knighted, 1985; Life Peerage, 1994; Numerous honorary doctorates; Various fellowships. Memberships: Academia Europaea; British Academy, president, 1985-89. Address: University College London, Gower Street, London WC1E 6BT, England.

R

RAAD Virginia, b. 13 August 1925, Salem, West Virginia, USA. Concert Pianist; Musicologist. Education: BA, Wellesley College; New England Conservatory; Diploma, Ecole Normale de Musique, Paris; Doctorate, highest honours, University of Paris. Career: Numerous concerts, lectures, master classes, including: Alliance Francaise, Pittsburgh and University of Pittsburgh; Walsh College, Ohio; Special Summer Artist; Middlebury College, Vermont; Wellesley College, Massachusetts; University of Michigan-Dearborn; Elmira and Manhattanville Colleges, New York; Rollins College, Florida; College of William and Mary, Virginia; University of Notre Dame, Indiana; Marietta College, Ohio; Huntington Galleries, West Virginia; Music Teachers' National Association Convention, Houston; Musician in Residence, North Carolina Arts Council and Community Colleges; Mount Mary College, Wisconsin; Portland State University, Oregon; Seton Hill College, Pennsylvania; Mount Union College, Ohio; Berea College, Kentucky; Community concerts, music clubs, TV, radio, USA, Europe; Adjudicator, Grant Reviewer. Recordings: The Piano Works of Claude Debussy, 1995. Publications include: L'Influence de Debussy: Amerique (Etats-Unis), in Debussy et l'evolution de la musique au XXe siècle, 1965; Claude Debussy, Gabriel Faure, both in New Catholic Encyclopaedia, 1967. Contributions to: Musical Courier, 1961; The American Music Teacher, 1968, 1971, 1976, 1977, 1981, 1986; Piano Guild Notes, 1973, 1995; Clavier, 1979, 1986; The Piano Sonority of Claude Debussy, 1994. Honours: Travel Grant, American Council of Learned Societies; French Government grants; Outstanding West Virginia Woman Educator, Delta Kappa Gamma; Biography, Study in pioneering music methods, submitted to the Arthur and Elizabeth Schlesinger Library on History of Women in America, Radcliffe College. Memberships: American, International and French Musicological Societies; College Music Society; Music Teachers' National Association, Musicology Programme Chair, 1983-87; American College of Musicians. Address: 60 Terrace Avenue, Salem, WV 26426, USA. E-mail: virginiaraad@aol.com.

RABINOWITZ Harry, b. 26 March 1916, Johannesburg, South Africa. Conductor; Composer; Musical Director. m. (1) Lorna Thurlow Anderson, 1944, 1 son, 2 daughters, divorced 2000, (2) Mary Cooper Scott, 2001. Education: University of the Witwatersrand; Guildhall School of Music, London. Career: Corporal, SA Forces, 1942-43; Conductor, BBC Radio, 1953-60; Head of Music, BBC Television Light Entertainment, 1960-68; LWT, 1968-77; Freelance Conductor, Composer, Hollywood Bowl, 1983-84, Boston Pops, 1985-92, London Symphony Orchestra, Royal Philharmonic Orchestra, 1996; Conductor for Films including: Chariots of Fire, Manhattan Project, Heat and Dust, The Bostonians, Time Bandits, Camille Claudel, Howard's End, The Remains Of The Day, Shirley Valentine, Business Affair, Le Petit Garçon, La Fille de d'Artagnan, Death And The Maiden, Nelly and Mr Arnold, Secret Agent, La Belle Verte, Surviving Picasso, The English Patient, Amour Sorcier, City of Angels, A Soldier's Daughter Never Cries; Message In A Bottle; Cotton Mary; The Talented Mr Ripley; The Golden Bowl; Cold Mountain; Possession; Television, New Faces, 1987-88, Paul Nicholas Special, 1987-88, Julia MacKenzie Special, 1986, Nicholas Nickleby, Drummonds, the Insurance Man, Absent Friends, Simon Wiesenthal Story, Marti Caine Special, Alien Empire, Battle of the Sexes; Theatre Conductor, World Premieres of Cats and Song & Dance. Compositions: Film: Sign Of Four; TV: Reilly Ace of Spies; The Agatha Christie Hour; Thomas and Sarah; Crocodile Bird. Honours: MBE, 1978; Basca Gold Award, 1986; Radio and Television Industries Award, 1984; Freeman City of London, 1996. Memberships: British Academy of Composers And Songwriters. Address: 7 East View Cottages, Purser's Lane, Peaslake, Surrey GU5 9RG, England. E-mail: mitziscott@aol.com

RACZKA Tony Michael, b. 16 January 1957, Pottsville, Pennsylvania, USA. Artist; Educator. m. Patricia G Martinez, 1 daughter, 1 step-daughter. Education: BFA, Northern Arizona University, Flagstaff, USA, 1978; MFA, Northern Illinois University DeKalb, USA, 1980; Postgraduate Studies, University of California, San Diego, USA, 1991-92. Appointments: Gallery Co-ordinator (and Part-time Instructor of Art), Southwestern College, Chula Vista, California, 1981-84; Instructor of Art, Northern Arizona University, Flagstaff, Arizona, 1983; Registrar, Mingei International Museum of Folk Art, San Diego California, 1985-86; Instructor of Art, San Diego State University, 1987; Senior Museum Preparator, University Art Gallery, University of California, San Diego, 1989-95. Publications: To Consociate and Foster the Self, 2000; Words of Wonder, Wit, and Well?....Well Being, 2000; The Blending of Natures and the Perception of the Real, 2000. Honours: Exhibitions at commercial galleries: Quint Gallery, La Jolla, San Diego, 1982, 1983; Printworks, Chicago, 1982, 1984; Queens College Art Center, CUNY, Flushing, New York, 1999-; Recipient, Pollock-Krasner Foundation Award, 2001. Memberships: International Society of Phenomenology and the Sciences of Life; San Diego Museum of Art. Address: 4430 42nd Street #2, San Diego, CA 92116, USA. E-mail: raczkatony@aol.com

RADCLIFFE Paula Jane, b. 17 December 1973, Northwich, England. Athlete. m. Gary Lough, 1 daughter. Education: University of Loughborough. Career: Distance Runner; World Junior Cross Country Champion, 1992; Started senior career, 1993; 5th, 5,000m, Olympic Games, 1996; Winner, Fifth Avenue Mile, New York, 1996, 1997; 3rd, International Association of Athletics Federations World Cross Challenge series, 1997; 4th, 5,000m, World Championships, 1997; European Cross Country Champion, 1998; 2nd, 10,000m European Challenge, 1998; Silver Medal, 10,000m World Championships, 1999; 4th, 10,000m, Olympic Games, 2000; World Half Marathon Champion, 2000, 2001; World Cross Country Champion, 2002; Gold Medal, 5,000m, Commonwealth Games, 2002; Gold Medal, 10,000m, European Championships, 2002; Winner, London Marathon, 2002, 2003, 2005; Chicago Marathon, 2002, New York Marathon, 2004, 2007; Set world best time for 5,000m in Flora Light 5km, 2003; Winner, Great North Run Half Marathon in world best time, 2003; World record holder for 10,000m, 20,000m and marathon; Captain, GB's Women's Athletic Team, 1998-; Helsinki World Championships, Gold Medal, 2005; Winner San Silvestre Vallecana, 10 Km race, New Years Eve, 2005. Athlete Representative, International Association of Athletics Federations. Publication: Paula My Story So Far, 2004. Honours: Hon DLitt (De Montfort, Loughborough); British Female Athlete of the Year, 1999, 2001 and 2002; IAAF World Female Athlete of the Year, 2002; BBC Sports Personality of the Year, 2002; Sunday Times Sportswoman of the Year, 2002; MBE, 2002. Address: c/o Bedford and County Athletics Club, 3 Regent Close, Bedford MK41 7XG, England.

RADONS Jürgen, b. 21 February 1960, Lünen, Germany. Biologist. m. Vera Beatrix Langhammer, 9 September 1999. Education: Diploma, Biology, 1985; PhD, Biochemistry, 1991; Habilitation, Experimental Medicine, 2004. Appointments:

Postgraduate Fellow, Cellular and Molecular Immunology, Biochemistry, 1986-91; Postdoctoral Fellow, Immunology and Biochemistry, 1991-92, Diabetology, 1992-96; Research Fellow, Rheumatology, 1996-98, Molecular Immunology, 1998-2006; Lecturer, Senior Scientist, Experimental Medicine, 2004-06; Group Leader in Tumour Biology and Molecular Oncology, Lecturer in Biochemistry/Pathobiochemistry, University of Greifswald, Germany, 2006-. Publications: Several articles in professional journals. Honours: International Scientist of the Year 2001; Leader of Science, Technology and Engineering, 2001; Great Minds of the 21st Century; One of 500 Leaders of Influence; 2000 Outstanding Scientists of the 20th Century; 2000 Outstanding Scientists of the 21st Century; 2000 Outstanding Intellectuals of the 21st Century; 2000 Eminent Scientists of Today. Membership: The American Biographical Institute, Research Fellow; International Society of Exercise and Immunology. Address: Obere Bachstrasse 6a, D-17509 Hanshagen, Germany.

RAHMAN Muhammad Mujibur, b. 1 July 1936, Malda, Bangladesh. Teacher. m. Bilkis, 6 sons, 2 daughters. Education: PhD, Rajshahi Varsity, Bangladesh; MA, MOL, BA, IA, HSC, Matric, SSC, Molvi Fazil, Punjab Varsity, Lahore, Pakistan; HS Education Board, Pakistan; MM, Fazil, Dhaka Madrasa Education Board, Bangladesh. Appointments: Teacher, BamaBala DB High School, Okara, Pakistan; Lecturer, Shibli College, Lahore; Lecturer, Associate Professor, Professor, Rashahi Varsity, Bangladesh; Assistant Editor, Testimony bi-weekly journal, New Jersey, USA; Director, LIMS Higher Education Centre, East Meadow, New York. Publications: Approximately 45 books and 200 articles in different languages in professional journals over 25 years. Honours: Rajshahi University Merit Award for Academic Excellence for Completion of both Master and PhD degrees; Medals and certificates from Rashahi Varsity & Indo Arab Cultural Centre, Calcutta, India and East Meadow Higher Education Centre, New York, USA; Syndicate members and all the Boards of Examiners in Bangladesh, Pakistan and India; Several other awards and medals from many other organisations; Listed in international biographical dictionaries. Memberships: Asiatic Society, Dhaka; Indo-Arab Cultural Centre, Calcutta; Bangla Academy, Dhaka; Madrasah National Education and Study Committee, Bangladesh; Islamic Foundation Advisory Committee, Dhaka and Rajshahi; History Parisad, Dhaka; Member, Jamiat-e-Ahle Hadith, Dhaka & Rajshahi; Shah Makhdum Parishad Rajshahi; Uttara Sahitya Majlis, Rajshahi; Asiatic Society, Dhaka; Darus Salaam, Riyadh, KSA; Al-Attique Inc, Canada; Assistant Librarian, RUL Rajshahi, Bangladesh; Life Member, Editorial Board, Asaar-e-Jadeed; Life Member, Editorial Board, Tuba & Tuba, Gujranwala, Pakistan; Life Member, Editorial Board, Darpan, Dhaka, Bangladesh, and Nawa-i-Islam Chah Raha, Delhi, India. Address: 1 Riverside Drive, 72nd St, West End, NY 10023, USA.

RAINE Craig (Anthony), b. 3 December 1944, Shildon, County Durham, England. Poet; Writer. m. Ann Pasternak Slater, 27 April 1972, 3 sons, 1 daughter. Education: Honours Degree in English Language and Literature, 1966, BPhil, 1968, Exeter College, Oxford. Appointments: Lecturer, Exeter College, Oxford, 1971-72; Lincoln College, Oxford, 1974-75; Christ Church, Oxford, 1976-79; Books Editor, New Review, London, 1977-78; Editor, Quarto, London, 1979-80; Poetry Editor, New Statesman, London, 1981; Faber & Faber, London, 1981-91; Fellow, New College, Oxford, 1991-; Editor, Arete magazine, 1999-. Publications: Poetry: The Onion, Memory, 1978; A Journey to Greece, 1979; A Martian Sends a Postcard Home, 1979; A Free Translation, 1981; Rich, 1984;

1953: A Version of Racine's Andromaque, 1990; History: The Home Movie, 1994; Clay. Whereabouts Unknown, 1996; A la recherche du temps perdu, 2000; Collected Poems 1978-99, 2000. Other: The Electrification of the Soviet Union (libretto), 1986; A Choice of Kipling's Prose (editor), 1987; Haydn and the Valve Trumpet (essays), 1990; In Defence of T S Eliot (essays), 2000; Collected Poems 1978-1999, 2000; Rudyard Kipling: The Wish House and Other Stories (editor), 2002; T.S. Eliot: Image, Text and Context, 2007. Contributions to: Periodicals. Honours: 1st Prizes, Cheltenham Festival Poetry Competition, 1977, 1978; 2nd Prize, National Poetry Competition, 1978; Prudence Farmer Awards, New Statesman, 1979, 1980; Cholmondeley Poetry Award, 1983; Sunday Times Award for Literary Excellence, 1998. Memberships: PEN; Royal Society of Literature. Address: c/o New College, Oxford OX1 3BN, England.

RAITT Bonnie, b. 8 November 1949, Burbank, California, USA. Musician (guitar, piano). m. Michael O'Keefe, 1991-1999 (divorced). Education: Radcliffe College. Career: Performer, blues clubs, US East Coast; Concerts include: MUSE concert, Madison Square Garden with Bruce Springsteen, Jackson Browne, Carly Simon, The Doobie Brothers, 1979; Roy Orbison Tribute Concert with artists including: Whoopi Goldberg; kd lang; Bob Dylan; B B King, 1990; Performances with artists including: Stevie Wonder, Bruce Springsteen, Aretha Franklin, Willie Nelson, Elton John. Recordings: Albums include: Bonnie Raitt, 1971; Give It Up, 1972; Takin' My Time, 1973; Streetlights, 1974; Home Plate, 1975; Sweet Forgiveness, 1977; The Glow, 1979; Green Light, 1982; Nine Lives, 1986; Nick Of Time, 1989; The Bonnie Raitt Collection, 1990; Luck Of The Draw, 1991; Road Tested, 1995; Fundamental, 1998; Silver Lining, 2002; Souls Alike, 2005; The Best of Bonnie Raitt on Capital, 1989-2003, 2003; Bonnie Raitt and Friends, 2006. Singles include: Something to Talk About, 1991; Not the Only One, 1992; You Got It, 1995; Lover's Will, 1999; I Will Not Be Broken, 2005; I Don't Want Anything to Change, 2006.. Honours include: 4 Grammy Awards: Album of Year; Best Rock Vocal Performance; Best Female Pop Vocal Performance; Best Traditional Blues Performance (with John Lee Hooker), and numerous nominations; Rock and Roll Hall of Fame, 2000. Address: PO Box 626, Los Angeles, CA 90078, USA.

RAJAGOPAL, b. 11 March 1957, Jagdalpur, India. Professor. m. Arati Jha, 1 son, 1 daughter. Education: MA, 1979, PhD, 1984, Economics, Ravishankar University. Appointments: Senior Assistant Director, National Institute of Rural Development, India, 1984-95; Assistant Professor, Institute of Rural Management, Anand, 1995-97; Programs Coordinator/ Director, National Institute of Agricultural Marketing, Jaipur, 1997-99; Senior Faculty, Administrative Staff College of India, 1999-2001; Professor of Marketing, Monterrey Institute of Higher Education and Technology (ITESM), 2001-. Publications: 27 books; 145 articles and research papers; 63 working papers; 5 book chapters; 42 research and consultancy projects; 52 conferences; 46 management cases; Developed Strategic Moves – The Business Chess and Card Game. Honours: Listed in international biographical dictionaries; National Merit Scholarship, 1977-79; Doctoral Fellow, Ministry of Social Welfare, 1980-82; Doctoral Fellow, Indian Council of Social Science Research, 1983; Fellow, British Council, 1994; Best Research Professor Award, 2004; National Researcher (SNI-2) of National Council of Science and Technology, Mexico, 2004-12; Fellow, Royal Society of Arts, Manufacture and Commerce, London, 2006-. Memberships: Indian Society of Agricultural Economics; Academic Member, Marketing Science Institute, USA;

Business and Economics Society International; Association of Consumer Research; Academy of Marketing Science; Chair, Latin America Chapter, Business and Economics Society International Convention, Mexico, 2009; Editor-in-Chief, International Journal of Leisure and Tourism Marketing. Address: ITESM, 222, Calle del Puente, Col Ejidos de Huipulco, Tlalpan, 14380, D F, Mexico.

RAKOWSKI Andrzej, b. 16 June 1931, Warsaw, Poland. Musicologist; Acoustician. m. Magdalena Jakobczyk, 1 son, 2 daughters. General Education: MSc (electronic engineer), 1957, DSc, 1963, Warsaw University of Technology; Upper PhD (habilitation in musicology), 1977, Warsaw University. Musical Education: MA, State College of Music in Warsaw, 1958. Appointments: Music Producer, Polish Disc Recording Company, 1956-58; Acoustic Consultant, Opera National Theatre, 1966-70; Assistant, Associate, Professor of Musical Acoustics, 1955-2001-, Deputy Rector, 1972-75, Rector (President), 1981-87, Head of the Chair of Music Acoustics, 1968-2001, Chopin Academy of Music, Warsaw; Part-time Professor, Institute of Musicology, Warsaw University, 1987-2003, A Mickiewicz University, Poznan, 1997-; Visiting Professor: Central Institute for the Deaf and Washington University St Louis, USA, 1977-78, McGill University, Montreal, 1985, Hebrew University, Jerusalem, 1991, New University of Lisbon, 2004. Publications: Books: Selected Topics on Acoustics, 1959; Categorical Perception of Pitch in Music, 1978; The Access of Youth to Musical Culture, 1984; Studies on Pitch and Timbre of Sound in Music (editor), 1999; Creation and Perception of Sound Sequences in Music (editor), 2002; Over 120 articles to scientific journals including: Acustica; Acta Acoustica; Journal of the Acoustical Society of America; Psychology of Music; Musicae Scientiae; Perception Psychophysics, Muzyka. Honours: Union of Polish Composers, 1956-; -Awards of the Minister of Culture in Poland, 1966, 1968, 1982, 1987; Polish State Awards, Silver Cross of Merit, 1971, Golden Cross of Merit, 1973; Order of the Revival of Poland, Bachelor's Cross, 1982, Officers Cross, 2002. Memberships: Polish Music Council, Vice President, 1984-89, Committee for Music in Schools, President, 2006-; Polish Academy of Sciences, 1994-, Acoustical Committee President, 1996-2007; European Society for Cognitive Sciences of Music, President, 2000-2003; Honorary Member, Polish Acoustical Society; Honorary Member, Polish Phonetic Association; Fellow, Acoustical Society of America. Listed in Who's Who publications and biographical dictionaries. Address: Pogonowskiego 20, Warsaw 01564, Poland. E-mail: rakowski@chopin.edu.pl

RALPH Richard Peter, b. 27 April 1946, London, England. Diplomat. (1) Margaret Elizabeth Coulthurst, 1970, divorced 2001, 1 son, 1 daughter, (2) Jemma Victoria Elizabeth Marlor, 2002. Education: Honours Degree, Politics, Edinburgh University, Scotland. Appointments: Joined, HM Diplomatic Service, 1969; Third Secretary, Foreign and Commonwealth Office (FCO), 1969-70; Third, then Second, Secretary, Laos, 1970-74; Second, then First, Secretary, Portugal, 1974-77; First Secretary, FCO, 1977-81; First Secretary and Head of Chancery, Zimbabwe, 1981-85; First Secretary, then Counsellor, FCO, 1985-89; Counsellor, Washington, USA, 1989-93; Ambassador, Latvia, 1993-95, Governor, Falkland Islands, Commissioner for South Georgia and the South Sandwich Islands, 1996-99; Ambassador, Romania (also accredited to Moldova), 1999-2002; Ambassador to Peru, 2003-. Honours: Companion of the Order of St Michael and St George (CMG); Commander of the Royal Victorian Order(CVO). E-mail: richard.ralph@fco.gov.uk

RAMA-MONTALDO Manuel Domingo, b. 10 May 1941, Montevideo, Uruguay. International Legal Consultant. Education: Doctor of Law and Social Sciences, University of the Republic, Montevideo, 1960-67; Diploma in Law, International Law and Organisation, Oxford University, 1968-70; British Council Fellowship, Oxford University, 1968-70; Artigas Fellowship for post graduate research, University of the Republic, 1968-70; International Law Fellowship, United Nations Institute for Training and Research, The Hague International Law Academy, and New York (UNITAR), 1971; UNESCO International Law Fellowship, Hague Academy, Rome (FAO), and New York (UNITAR), 1972. Appointments: Professor of Introduction to Law, Montevideo Law College, 1967-73; Associate Professor in charge of full course of International Law, University of the Republic, Montevideo, 1971-73; Senior Legal Advisor, United Nations Legal Office, New York, 1973-94; UNITAR Lecturer, UN-UNITAR Hague Special Seminars on International Law, 1987-94; Deputy Director for Research and Studies, 1994-96, Deputy Director, 1996-2001, United Nations Codification Division, New York; International Legal Consultant, International Law Research Center, Montevideo, 2001-; Consultant, International Criminal Court, The Hague, 2005-07. Publications: Numerous articles and papers in professional journals. Honours: Secretary, UN Programme of Assistance in the teaching, study, dissemination and wider appreciation of International Law, 1976-86; Secretary, Drafting Committee, UN Rome Conference on an International Criminal Court, 1998; Deputy Secretary, UN International Law Commission, Geneva, 1994-2001; Deputy Secretary, Sixth (legal) Committee, UN General Assembly, New York, 1994-2001; Secretary or Deputy Secretary of numerous UN bodies or activities, 1980-2001. Memberships: Uruguayan Bar Association; American Society of International Law; Rotary Club, Montevideo, Uruguay. Address: Rio Negro 1337, Ap 407, Montevideo, Uruguay. E-mail: maramont@adinet.com.uy

RAMACHANDRAN Perumpidil Narayanan, b. 23 December 1945, Cherai, India. Engineering Academician. m. K Radha, 1 son. Education: BSc, Engineering, 1967; M Eng, 1976; DSc, 2006. Appointments: Lecturer, Delhi College of Engineering; Research Associate, AIT, Bangkok; Research Associate, BITS, Pilani; Training Officer, Orient Paper Mills, AML AI; Deputy Director, IIPM, Orissa; Academic Registrar, KIIT, Orissa; Professor & Head of Department, SNMIMT, Kerala; Principal, NCERC, Kerala. Publications: 40 research papers; Editor, 3 books. Honours: National Scholar, 1961; Colombo Plan Scholar, 1988, 1991; Listed in international biographical dictionaries. Memberships: FIE; C ENGG (India); MIEEE; MISTD; MISTE; MIMA. Address: NCERC, Pampady (PO), Thiruvilwamala, Trissur Dist, Kerala 680597, India.

RAMANAUSKAS Rimgaudas Juozapas, b. 3 December 1934, Kaunas, Lithuania. Engineer. 1 daughter. Education: Dairy Technical School, Belvederis, 1954; Dairy Institute, Vologda, Russia, 1959; PhD, 1967; DSc, 1993. Appointments: Chief Technologist, Dairy Plant, Klaipeda, Lithuania, 1959-61; Head of Laboratory, Food Institute, Kaunas, Lithuania, 1964-. Publications: 24 patents; Over 700 scientific publications; 14 books. Honours: Man of Achievement, Man of the Year 1996/97, 2004, IBC; Gold Star Award, IBC, Man of the Year, 1997/98, ABI. Memberships: New York Academy of Sciences; International Academy of Refrigeration; International Academy of Engineering. Address: Food Institute, Taikos 92, Kaunas, Lithuania. E-mail: lmai@lmai.lt

RAMASARMA Ayyagari Venkat Sundar, b. 18 October 1963, Kovvur, India. Advocate. m. Sarada, 1 son. Education: B Com (Honours), 1980; LLB, 1983. Appointments: Secretarial Officer, Swil Ltd; Assistant Company Secretary, Tata Timken Ltd; Head of Trademarks, D P Ahuja; Senior Trademark Attorney, Depennigs; Senior Associate, Anand & Anand; Associate, Khaitan & Co; Partner, Kochhar & Co. Publications: Trends in Patent & Trademark Law; It's All in the Mind; On Your Trademarks, Get Set, Go; How to Keep Data from Prying Eyes; It is All in the Technique; Making Your Mark Work; Copycats Beware, It's All in the Right; If You Have to Copy, Do It Right; Patently Yours; It's All in the Design; Author, Commentary on Intellectual Property Laws. Honours: Listed in international biographical dictionaries. Memberships: International Trade Mark Association; Asian Patent Attorney Association; Bar Association of West Bengal. Address: Kochhar & Co, 177 Annasalai, Suite 503, 5th Floor, Raheja Towers, Chennai 600 002, India. E-mail: ramasarma@chennai.kochhar.com

RAMASWAMY Nachipalayam Muthusamy, b. 14 April 1939, Tiruchengode, India. Former Dean; Emeritus Professor. m. Ms Malini, 1 daughter. Education: BSc, Agriculture and Allied Subjects, 1961, MSc, Cytogenics and Plant Breeding, 1969, PhD, Genetics and Plant Breeding, 1973, Madras University, India. Appointments: Associate Professor/Assistant Professor, 1972-81; Professor and Head, Regional Research Stations, India, 1981-84; Professor, Cytogenics, 1984-86; Post-Doctoral Research Scientist, Biotechnology, IDRC, Carleton University, Ottawa, Canada, 1986-88; Professor and Head, Biotechnology, 1988-94; Consultant, FAO of the United Nations, Somalia, 1989-90; Dean (Post Graduate studies), Tamil Nadu Agricultural University, 1994-97; Professor Emeritus, ICAR, 2000-02; Dean (Research and Development), KSR College of Arts and Science, Tiruchengode, India, 2002-. Publications: In the field of research include: 155 on plant biotechnology, 55 on plant breeding and genetics; Over 50 general/popular articles; Contributed to the release of 7 improved crop varieties; Developed tissue culture protocols in many crops. Honours: Scholarship, Center for Advanced Training in Cell and Molecular Biology, Catholic University of America; Senior Research Fellowship, Department of Atomic Energy; Senior Research Fellowship, ICAR, Government of India; Post-Doctoral Research Fellowship, IDRC, Canada. Memberships: American Association for the Advancement of Science, USA; Indian Society of Genetics and Plant Breeding; Indian Society of Plant Breeders; International Association of Plant Tissue Culture and Biotechnology. Address: Prof NMR Foundation for R&D, PPG Institute of Health Sciences Campus, Saravanampatty, Coimbatore – 641035, India. E-mail: muruga14@rediffmail.com

RAMIREZ-MIRELES Fernando, b. 27 November 1962, Monterrey, Nuevo Leon, Mexico. Professor. m. Gina Miroslava, 2 daughters. Education: BSc, Metropolitan Autonomous University, Mexico City, 1987; MSc, CINVESTAV-IPN, Mexico City, 1988; PhD, University of Southern California, Los Angeles, California, 1998; Professor, CINVESTAV-IPN, Mexico City, 1988-92; MTS, Glenayre/Wireless Access, Santa Clara, CA, 1998-2000; Systems Engineer, Aware Inc, Lafayette, California, 2000-2001; Systems Engineer, Ikanos, Fremont, California, 2001-2003; Professor, ITAM, Mexico City, 2003-; Diplomas in ITAM; Business Administration, 2005; Legal Aspects of TIC, 2006; Intellectual Property, 2007. Publications: Journal articles in IEEE Transactions; Letters and contributions to IEC International Reports; Articles in IEEE Conferences; Referee in IEEE Transactions, Letters and Conferences; Patents: US and European Patents on DSL.

Honours: IEEE Senior Member; Member, National Systems of Researchers; Fulbright Scholarship; University Medal of Merit; Listed in Who's Who publications. Memberships: IEEE; Society of Hispanic Professional Engineers; Tau Beta Pi. Address: Pennsylvania 91, Colonia Napoles, Mexico City DF, CP 03810 Mexico. E-mail: fernandomireles@yahoo.com

RAMOS Theodore Sanchez de Piña, b. 30 October 1928, Oporto, Portugal (Spanish) (British citizen). Portrait Painter. m. Julia Nan Rushbury, separated, 4 sons, 1 deceased. Education: Colégio Araújo Lima, Oporto; The Northern Polytechnic, London; Hornsey School of Art; RAS Dip, Royal Academy Schools, 1949-54. Appointments: Portrait painter; Former Visiting Lecturer, Harrow School of Art; Brighton College of Art; Royal Academy Schools; Represented in permanent collections: National Portrait Gallery; Royal Academy of Arts; Guards Museum; Windsor Guildhall; Chatsworth House; Government House, Perth, Western Australia; Louisiana University; Portraits include: Her Majesty The Queen; Her Majesty Queen Elizabeth the Queen Mother; HRH Prince Philip, Duke of Edinburgh; HRH Prince Charles; The Grand Duke of Luxembourg; Andrew, 11th Duke of Devonshire. Publications: Numerous illustrations for Penguin books and other publishers. Honours: RAS Silver Medal, 1953. Memberships: East India Club; Marylebone Cricket Club; Reynolds Club; Liveryman, The Worshipful Company of Painter-Stainers; The Worshipful Company of Founders. Address: Studio 3, Chelsea Farm House, Milmans Street, London SW10 0DA, England.

RAMOS-SOBRADOS Juan I, b. 28 January 1953, Bernardos, Segovia, Spain. Professor of Mechanical Engineering. m. Mercedes Naveiro, 2 sons. Education; B Aeronautical Engineering, 1975, Dr Engineering, 1983, Madrid Polytechnic University, Spain; MA, Mechanical and Aerospace Engineering, 1979, PhD, Mechanical and Aerospace Engineering, 1980, Princeton University, USA. Appointments: Research Engineer, Helicopter Design, Madrid, 1976-77; Research Assistant, 1977-78, Teaching Assistant, 1979, Department of Mechanical and Aerospace Engineering, Princeton, New Jersey, USA; Instructor, 1979-80, Assistant Professor, 1980-85, Faculty Member of Center for Energy and Environmental Studies, 1980-91, 1991-93, Associate Professor, 1985-89, Professor, 1989-93, Department of Mechanical Engineering, Carnegie Mellon University, Pittsburgh, Pennsylvania, USA; Visiting Professor, Universita degli Studi di Roma Tor Vergata, Rome, 1988-89; Visiting Professor, 1990-91, Professor, 1992- E T S Ingenieros Industriales, Universidad de Malaga, Spain. Publications: Book: Internal Combustion Engine Modelling, 1989; Over 300 papers in journals, proceedings of international conferences on fluid mechanics, combustion and applied mathematics. Honours: Prize Francisco Arranz, Association of Aeronautical Engineers, Madrid, 1975; Aeronautical Engineering Medal, Ministry of Education and Science, Madrid, 1977; National Award in Aeronautical Engineering, King Juan Carlos I of Spain, 1977; Daniel and Florence Guggenheim Fellow, Princeton University September 1977 - January 1978, honorary May to August, 1978; George Van Ness Lothrop Fellowship in Engineering, Princeton, 1979-80; Ralph R Teetor Award, Society of Automotive Engineers, 1981. Address: ETS Ingenieros Industriales, Room I-320-D, Universidad de Malaga, Plaza El Ejido s/n, 29013 Malaga, Spain.

RAMPLING Charlotte, b. 5 February 1946, London, England. Actress. m. (2) Jean Michel Jarre, 1978, 2 sons, 1 stepdaughter (1 son from previous marriage). Career: Films include: The Knack, 1963; Rotten to the Core, Georgy Girl, The Long Duel, Kidnapping, Three, The Damned, 1969; Skibum, Corky, 1970; 'Tis Pity She's a Whore, Henry VIII and His Six Wives, 1971; Asylum, 1972; The Night Porter; Giordano Bruno, Zardoz, Caravan to Vaccares, 1973; The Flesh of the Orchid, Yuppi Du, 1974-75; Farewell My Lovely, Foxtrot, 1975; Sherlock Holmes in New York, Orca – The Killer Whale, The Purple Taxi, 1976; Stardust Memories, 1980; The Verdict, 1983; Viva la Vie, 1983; Beauty and Sadness, 1984; He Died with His Eyes Open, 1985, Max mon Amour, Max My Love, 1985; Angel Heart, 1987; Paris by Night, 1988; Dead on Arrival, 1989; Helmut Newton, Frames from the Edge, Hammers Over the Anvil, 1991; Time is Money, 1992; La marche de Radetsky, TV Film, 1994; Asphalt Tango, 1995; Wings of a Dove, 1996; The Cherry Orchard, 1998; Signs and Wonders, 1999; Aberdeen, 1999; Fourth Angel, Under the Sand, Superstition, 2000; See How They Run, 2002; Summer Things, 2003; I'll Sleep When I'm Dead, 2003; Swimming Pool, 2003; The Statement, 2003; Jerusalem, 2003; Vers le sud, 2004; Basic Instinct 2, 2006; Désaccord parfait, 2006; Angel, 2007; Caótica Ana, 2007; Boogie Woogie, 2008; Babylon A.D., 2008; TV: numerous appearances. Honours: Chevalier Ordre des Arts et des Lettres, 1986; OBE, 2000; Cesar d'honneur, 2001; Chevalier, Legion d'honneur, 2002. Address: c/o Artmédia, 20 avenue Rapp, 75007 Paris, France.

RAMSBOTHAM The Honourable Sir Peter Edward, b. 8 October 1919, London, England. Diplomat. m. (1) Frances Blomfield, deceased, 2 sons, 1 daughter, deceased (2) Zaida Hall, 1985. Education: Eton College, 1932-37; Magdalen College, Oxford, 1938-40. Appointments: High Commissioner, Cyprus, 1969-71; Ambassador to Iran, 1971-74; Ambassador to the United States, 1974-77; Retired from Foreign Service and as Governor and Commander-in-Chief of Bermuda, 1980; Director, Lloyds Bank, 1981-90; Chairman, Regional Board, Lloyds Bank; Director, Commercial Union, 1981-90; Chairman, Ryder-Cheshire Foundation for the Relief of Suffering; Trustee, Leonard Cheshire Foundation; Chairman, World Memorial Fund for Disaster Relief, 1992-96. Publications: Europe's Futures, Europe's Choices, 1969; Partners in Peace and Prosperity – A Premier and a Governor in Bermuda, 2000. Honours: Despatches; Croix de Guerre, 1945; GCVO, 1976; GCMG, 1978; DL; Knight of St John; Honorary Fellow., Magdalen College, Oxford, 1991. Memberships: Governor, Ditchley Foundation; Governor, Kings School, Canterbury, 1983; President, British-American-Canadian Associates, 1990; President, City of Winchester Trust; Hon LLD: Akron University; College of William and Mary; Maryland University; Yale University. Address: East Lane, Ovington, Alresford, Hampshire SO24 0RA, England.

RAMSDEN Jeremy Joachim, b. 13 August 1955, Amersham, England. Biophysics and Nanotechnology Scientist. Education: MA, Cambridge University, 1981; Dr ès Sciences, Ecole Polytechnique Fédérale, Lausanne, Switzerland, 1985. Appointments: Research Scientist, Ilford Ltd, Warley, Essex, England, 1977-81; Research Associate, Princeton University, New Jersey, 1986; Visiting Scientist, Hungarian Academy of Sciences, Bioctr, Szeged, 1987; Scientist, 1988-2002, Privat-docent, 1994-, Basel University, Switzerland; Visiting Scientist, USSR Academy of Sciences, Moscow, 1990; President, Institute of Advanced Study, Basel, 1999-; Research Director, Bionanotechnology, Cranfield University, Kitakyushu, 2003-. Publications: The New World Order, 1991; Bioinformatics, 2004; Spiritual Motivation: New Thinking for Business and Management, 2007; Contributor of articles to professional journals. Memberships: Oxford & Cambridge Club; Swiss Biochemical Society; Mathematical

Association of America; Institute of Materials, Minerals and Mining. Address: Department of Materials, Cranfield University, Bedfordshire, MK43 0AL, England. E-mail: j.ramsden@cranfield.ac.uk

RANSFORD Tessa, b. 8 July 1938, Bombay, India. Poet; Writer; Editor. m. (1) Iain Kay Stiven, 29 August 1959, divorced 1986, 1 son, 3 daughters, (2) Callum Macdonald, 7 December 1989, (deceased). Education: MA, University of Edinburgh, 1958; Teacher Training, Craiglockhart College of Education, 1980. Appointments: Founder, School of Poets, Edinburgh, 1981-; Founder, 1982, Director, 1984-99, Scottish Poetry Library; Editor, Lines Review, 1988-98; Retired, 1999; Freelance Poetry Practitioner and Adviser, 1999-; Royal Literary Fund Writing Fellow, 2001-04, 2006-. Publications: Light of the Mind, 1980; Fools and Angels, 1984; Shadows from the Greater Hill, 1987; A Dancing Innocence, 1988; Seven Valleys, 1991; Medusa Dozen and Other Poems, 1994; Scottish Selection, 1998; When it Works it Feels Like Play, 1998; Indian Selection, 2000; Natural Selection, 2001; Noteworthy Selection, 2002; The Nightingale Question: five poets from Saxony, 2004; Shades of Green, 2005; Sonnet Selection, 2007. Contributions to: Anthologies, reviews, and journals. Honours: Scottish Arts Council Book Award, 1980; Howard Sergeant Award for Services to Poetry, 1989; Heritage Society of Scotland Annual Award, 1996; OBE, New Years Honours, 2000; Society of Authors Travelling Scholarship, 2001. Memberships: Saltire Society, honorary member 1993; Scottish Library Association, honorary member, 1999; Scottish Poetry Library, ex-officio honorary member, 1999; Fellow, Centre for Human Ecology, 2002; Honorary Doctorate, Paisley University (DUniv), 2003; Scottish International PEN, President, 2003--6; Institute of Contemporary Scotland, Honorary Fellow, 2005. Address: 31 Royal Park Terrace, Edinburgh EH8 8JA, Scotland. Website: http://www.wisdomfield.com

RANTZEN Esther, b. 22 June 1940. Television Presenter. m. Desmond Wilcox, 1977, deceased 2000, 1 son, 2 daughters. Education: MA, Somerville College, Oxford. Appointments: Studio manager, making dramatic sound effects, BBC Radio, 1963; Presenter, That's Life, BBC TV 1973-94; Scriptwriter, 1976-94; Producer, The Big Time (documentary series), 1976; Presenter: Esther Interviews..., 1988; Hearts of Gold, 1988, 1996; Drugwatch; Childwatch; The Lost Babies (also producer); Esther (talk show), 1994-; The Rantzen Report, 1996-; Excuse my French, 2006; Old Dogs New Tricks, 2006. Publications: Kill the Chocolate Biscuit (with D Wilcox), 1981; Baby Love, 1985; The Story of Ben Hardwick (with S Woodward), 1985; Once Upon a Christmas, 1996; Esther: The Autobiography, 2000; A Secret Life, 2003. Honours include: BBC TV Personality of 1975, Variety Club of Great Britain; Richard Dimbleby Award, BAFTA, 1988; OBE, 1991; Snowdon Award for Services to Disabled People, 1996; Royal TV Society Hall of Fame Award, 1998; Champion, Community Legal Service, 2000; Hon DLitt, South Bank University, 2000. Memberships: National Consumer Council, 1981-90; Health Education Authority, 1989-95; Chairman, Childline. Address: BBC TV, White City, 201 Wood Lane, London, W12 7RJ, England.

RANU Harcharan Singh, b. Lyallpur, India. Biomedical Scientist; Professor; Biomedical Engineer. Education: BSc, Leicester Polytechnic, Leicester, England, 1963; MSc, University of Surrey, Guildford, Surrey, England, 1968; PhD, University of Westminster and Middlesex Hospital Medical School, London, England, 1976. Appointments: Professor and Director, Louisiana Technical University, USA; Consultant,

Columbia University College of Physicians and Surgeons, New York, USA, 1988-; Professor and Chairman, Department of Biomechanics, New York College of Osteopathic Medicine, USA, 1989-93; Professor and Executive Assistant to President and Director, Life University, 1993-; President, American Orthopaedic Biomechanics Research Institute, Atlanta, Georgia, USA, 1997-. Publications: Numerous articles in professional medical journals and conference proceedings include most recently: Laserectomy of the Herniated Spinal Discs: A New Treatment Technique; Relief From Low-Back Pain in Sports By Infusion of Saline into the Human Nucleus Pulposus and Establishing the Pressure-Volume Relationship (Ranu's Principle), 1999; In Vivo Micro-Fracture Simulation In Olympic Field Hockey Players, 1999; Simulation of Micro-Fracture Injury in Female Gymnasts – An in Vivo Study, 2002; Micro-Fracture Injury Simulation in Pole-Vaulting, 2003; Simulation of Drop in Intradiscal Pressure in the Human Spinal Discs due to Laserectomy by 3-D Modelling, 2003; 3-D Foot Pressure Measurements in Normal and Diabetic Persons, 2005. Honours: Edwin Tate Award, University of Surrey, England, 1967; James Clayton Award, Institution of Mechanical Engineers, London, England, 1974-76; Hilliburton Award, Louisiana Technical University, 1983; President's Prize, The Biological Engineering Society of Great Britain, 1984; Third International Olympic Committee World Congress on Sports Sciences Award, Atlanta, USA, 1995. Memberships include: Fellow, American Society of Mechanical Engineers; Fellow, Institution of Mechanical Engineers, London; Fellow, The Biological Engineering Society (Institute of Physics and Engineering in Medicine), London; American Society of Biomechanics; Orthopaedic Research Society of USA; American Association for the Advancement of Science; Charted Scientist; The Science Council, UK; American College of Sports Medicine. Address: PO Box 724441, Atlanta, GA 31139-1441, USA.

RAO M V M Satyanarayana, b. 22 January 1946, Ramachandrapuram, India. Geophysicist. m. Meenakshi, 1 son, 1 daughter. Education: BSc, 1963, MS, Physics, 1965, PhD, Geophysics, 1974, Osmania University. Appointments: Scientific Assistant, DLRL, 1965-66; Scientific Assistant, 1966-71, Scientist, 1971-92, NGRI; Deputy Director, NIRM, 1992-95, NGRI, 1995-2006; Emeritus Scientist, NGRI, 2006-. Publications: more than 100 research publications. Honours include: DAAD Fellowship, 1976; AP Akademi Young Scientist Award, 1981; US Fulbright Fellowship, 1987; Japan STA Fellowship, 1990; AEWG Gold Medal, 1997; ISNT National Award for Best Technical Paper in Research and Development in NDT, 1999; JSPS Invitation Fellowship from Japan, 2004; CSIR Emeritus Scientist Award, 2006; Listed in Who's Who publications and biographical dictionaries. Memberships: AEWG India; International Society of Rock Mechanics; AP Akademi of Sciences; Indian Geophysical Union; Life Fellow, Ultrasonic Society of India, ISNT, India. Address: NGRI, Uppal Road, Hyderabad-500 007, India.

RAO Nagaraja B K, b. 23 March 1934, Bangalore, India. Professor; Editor; Publisher. m. 2 daughters. Education: BSc, University of Mysore, India, 1955; MSc, University of Southampton, England, 1971; DIISc, The Indian Institute of Science, India, 1963; PhD, 1978, University of Birmingham, England; DTech, University of Sunderland, England, 2004. Appointments: Head of Packaging, LRDE, Bangalore, India, 1956-64; Head of Packaging, Hairlok Co, Bedford, England, 1965-67; Research Fellow, University College London, 1969-70; Post Doctoral Research Fellow, University of Birmingham, England, 1971-79; Senior Lecturer, Birmingham Polytechnic, 1980-89; Reader/Professor,

Southampton Institute, 1990-96; Past Visiting Professor, University of Exeter, University of Sunderland and Glasgow Caledonian University; Past External Examiner for numerous universities throughout UK, also universities in India, Republic of South Africa, Sweden and Canada; Organised international congresses and exhibitions in UK, France, India, Canada, Finland, Australia, USA, Sweden, Portugal, Czech Republic; Published and edited COMADEM congress proceedings distributed worldwide. Publications: Over 120 technical papers in well-known journals; Editor and author, Handbook of Condition Monitoring; Contributed chapters in The Handbook of Condition Monitoring, and Infrasound & Low Frequency Vibration; Editor in chief and publisher, International Journal of Condition Monitoring and Diagnostic Engineering Management. Honours: Visiting Professor, University of Glamorgan, Wales; External Examiner, University of Wales Institute of Cardiff, Wales; Visiting Lecturer: Vaxjo University, Sweden; Lulea University of Technology, Sweden; Vellore Institute of Technology, India. Address: 307 Tiverton Road, Selly Oak, Birmingham, B29 6DA, England. E-mail: rajbknrao@btinternet.com

RAOOF Mohammed, b. 19 November 1955, Tehran, Iran. University Professor. m Mojgan Etemad. Education: BSc (Eng), Civil Engineering (1st class honours), 1975-78, MSc, Concrete Structures and Technology. 1978-79, PhD, Structural Analysis, 1979-83, DSc (Eng), Structural Engineering and Mechanics, 2002, Imperial College, London University. Appointments: Research Assistant, Imperial College, 1981-85; Structural Engineer, Wimpey Offshore Engineers and Constructors Ltd, 1985-86; Lecturer II, 1986, Senior Lecturer, 1988, Bridon Reader, 1991, Bridon Professor of Structural Mechanics, 1992, South Bank University, London, 1986-94; Professor of Structural Engineering, Structures and Materials Group Leader, Civil and Building Engineering Department, Loughborough University, 1994-. Publications: Sole author of 21 international journal and 19 refereed international conference papers; Co-author of 56 international and 16 refereed national journal and 50 refereed international conference papers; Papers presented in 55 international conferences with 43 of them having been held outside the UK in 21 different countries across 4 continents; Reviewed papers for 21 different international journals. Honours: T K Hsieh Award, Institution of Civil Engineers in Conjunction with the Society of Earthquake and Civil Engineering Dynamics, 1985; James Watt Gold Medal, Institution of Civil Engineers, 1991; CEGB Prize, Institution of Mechanical Engineers, 1991; Trevithick Premium, Institution of Civil Engineers, 1993; Henry Adams Award (Diploma), Institution of Structural Engineers, 1993; First winner of the 14th Khwarizmi International Award 2000-2001, Endorsed by UNESCO and presented personally by the President of Iran, 2001. Memberships: Diploma of Membership of Imperial College, 1979; Member, 1995-2000, Fellow, 2000-, Institution of Structural Engineers; Fellow, Institution of Civil Engineers, 2002-. Address: Civil and Building Engineering Department, Loughborough University, Loughborough, Leicestershire LE11 3TU, England. E-mail: m.raoof@lboro.ac.uk

RAPEANU Sevastian, b. 24 July 1932, Richitele, Judetul Arges; Romania. Physicist. m. Doina Constantin Rapeanu, 2 sons. Education: MSc, Mathematics and Physics Faculty, Bucharest University, 1957; Specialization in Sweden, "Atomic motion in solids and liquids by thermal neutrons" through stipend from IAEA, Vienna, Royal Institute of Technology, 1962-63; PhD in Physics, Institute of Atomic Physics, Romanian Academy, Bucharest, 1969; PhD degree supervisor, Reactor Physics and Nuclear Data, 1970, and

Condensed Matter Physics, 1990; Doctor Docent in Physics, Senate of Bucharest University, 1976. Appointments include: Head of Laboratory and Deputy Director, Atomic Physics Institute, 1969-70; Specialty Inspector, Nuclear Power Section – Ministry Council, 1970-71; General Inspector, State Committee for Nuclear Energy, 1971-77; Professor, Machinery Engineering Technology Faculty, Pitesti University, 1978-81; Scientific Director, Nuclear Power Reactors Institute, Pitesti, 1977-82; General Director of National Agency for Atomic Energy, 1994-97; President of Interministerial Council of NAAE, Co-ordinator, Realization of Nuclear National Program, 1996-2010; Member of Board of Directors, National Institute for Electrostatics and Electrotechnologies, Bucharest, 1997-2000; Currently Member, Consultative Council, Nuclear Regulatory Body and Member, Technology Committee, Romanian Academy, 2001-; Co-ordinator, The Explanatory Dictionary – Nuclear Energy (Romanian, English, French), 1999, 2004, 2005; Research activities in fields including: Neutron physics, total reflection of neutrons, neutron polarisation, neutron spectrometry, neutron elastic and inelastic scattering, condensed matter and physics, statics and dynamics of simple liquids and molecular, hydrogen in metals, water, heavy water and water solution, nuclear materials and nuclear energetics. Publications: Over 200 papers in national and international speciality journals; Co-author: Tables and Formulae for Mathematics, Physics and Chemistry, 1967; Atomic and Nuclear Physics, 1976; Techniques and Measurements at Nuclear Reactors, 1983; Translator, Reactor Physics by Shulten and Guth (from English), 1975; Translator, Course of Dosimetry by VI Ivanov (from Russian), 1999; Co-author: Elemente Suport pentru Dezafectarea Reactorului Nuclear de Cercetare VVR-S, Vol 1, 2003; Scientific Control-Treatise, Valorificarea resurselor naturale, vols 1, 2, 3, 2004, 2005; Participant in numerous national and international conferences; Numerous scientific articles for professional journals. Honours: IAEA, Vienna, 1995; INP Pitesti, 1996, 1999; RANE-Bucharest, 1996; JINR Dubna, Russia, 1996; Jubilee Medal, 1996; International Man of the Year, IBC, 2000-2001; Man of the Year, ABI, 2001 and 2006; American Diploma of Honor, ABI, 2002 and 2006; International Diploma of Honour, IBC, 2003; Gould Medal for Romania, 2006; Romania - The United States of America Medal, 30 Years of Co-operation in The Peaceful Use of Nuclear Energy, 1974-2004; Merit Diploma, 2006; Top 100 Scientists, IBC, 2005; Noteworthy Personality in Science, Special Commission of the Romanian Academy of Science; Listed in numerous biographical dictionaries. Memberships: Numerous Professional Societies, including: International Committee for Nuclear Data-IAEA, 1976-79; Chairman of Organising Committee of the 10th ICND Session, Bucharest, 1978; Condensed Matter Physics, JINR-Dubna, Russia, 1994-97; Academy of Romanian Scientists; Romanian Physical Society; European Physical Society. Address: Terasei Alley 8, bl R12A, sc2, et 3, ap 54, PO 82, Sector 4, 041774 Bucharest, Romania.

RAPLEY Christopher Graham, b. 8 April 1947, West Bromwich, England. Director, Science Museum, London. m. Norma Kahn, 2 daughters. Education: BA (Hons) Physics, Oxford University, England, 1969, MA, 1974; MSc, Radioastronomy, Manchester University, 1970; PhD, X-Ray Astronomy, University College London, England, 1976; DSc, Bristol University, 2008. Appointments: Head, Remote Sensing Group, Mullard Space Science Laboratory, University College London, 1982-94; Associate Director, Mullard Space Science Laboratory, 1990-94; Professor, Remote Sensing Science, 1991-97; Executive Director, International Geosphere-Biosphere Programme, Stockholm,1994-97;

Director, British Antarctic Survey, Cambridge, England, 1998-2007; Director, Science Museum, London, 2007-. Publications: Over 120 articles in scientific journals and reports. Honours: Honorary Professorships, UCL and UEA, 1999-; Fellow, St. Edmund's College, Cambridge, 1999; Commander British Empire, 2003; Edinburgh Medal, 2008; Fellow, University College, London, 2008. Memberships: American Geophysical Union; International Polar Year Joint Committee; President, Scientific Committee on Antarctic Research. Address: Science Museum, Exhibition Road, London SW7 2DD, England. E-mail: chris.rapley@sciencemuseum.org.uk

RASHBA Emmanuel Iosif, b. 30 October 1927, Kiev, Ukraine. Physicist. m. Erna Kelman, 1 son, deceased, 1 daughter. Education: Diploma with Honour, Kiev, 1949; PhD, Kiev, 1956; Doctor of Sciences, Ioffe Institute for Physics and Technology, St Petersburg, 1963; Professor of Theoretical and Mathematical Physics, Landau Institute for Theoretical Physics, Moscow, 1967. Appointments: Junior and Senior Scientist, Institute of Physics, Kiev, 1954-60; Head of Theoretical Department, Institute for Semiconductors, Kiev, 1960-66; Head of Department and Principal Scientist, Landau Institute for Theoretical Physics, Moscow, 1966-97; Research Professor, University of Utah, Salt Lake City, 1992-2000; Research Professor, SUNY at Buffalo, 2001-2003; Research Associate, Harvard University, Cambridge, 2004-. Publications: Collection of Problems in Physics, in Russian, 1978, 1987, in English 1986, in Japanese, 1989; Spectroscopy of Molecular Excitons, in Russian, 1981, in English, 1985; Over 230 contributed and review papers in professional journals. Honours: National Prize in Science, USSR, 1966; Ioffe Prize of the Academy of Sciences of the USSR, 1987; ICL Prize, Conference on Lumin. and Optical Spectroscopy, 1999; Arkady Aronov Memorial Lecture, Israel, 2005; Sir Nevill Mott Lecture, England, 2005; Rutherford Professorship in Spintronics, England, 2007; Solomon Pekar Prize, National Academy of Sciences, Ukraine, 2007. Membership: Fellow American Physical Society. Address: Department of Physics, Harvard University, Cambridge, MA 02138, USA. E-mail: erashba@physics.harvard.edu

RASHKOVA Tsetska Grigorova, b. 16 May 1952, Rousse, Bulgaria. Mathematician; Researcher. m. Petar Ivanov Rashkov, 2 daughters. Education: MSc, Mathematics, Sofia University, St Kl Ohridski, 1971-76; PhD, Mathematics, Algebra and Number Theory, 1997. Appointments: Assistant Professor, 1976-79, Senior Assistant Professor, 1979-89, Chief Assistant Professor, 1989-2000, Associate Professor, 2000-, University of Rousse, A Kanchev. Publications: Varieties of metabelian Jordan algebras, co-author, 1989; Varieties of algebras having a distributive lattice of subvarieties, 1995; Identities in algebras with involution, 1999; Matrixalgebras with involution and central polynominals, 2002; Identities in matrix superalgebras with superinvolution, 2003; Involutorial matrix algebras – identities and growth, 2004; Description of the superinvolutions for M(2), 2005; Polynomial identities in superalgebras with superinvolutions, 2005; The role of a theorem of Bergman in investigating identities in matrix algebras with symplectic involution, 2006. Honours: Listed in national and international biographical dictionaries. Memberships: Union of Bulgarian Mathematicians; Union of Scientists in Bulgaria. Address: Department of Algebra and Geometry, Centre of Applied Maths and Informatics, Pedagogical Faculty, University of Rousse "Angel Kanchev", Studentska str 8, Rousse 7017, Bulgaria. E-mail: tcetcka@ami.ru.acad.bg

RATAN John, b. 23 September 1960, Arunachal Pradesh, India. Consultant Paediatric Surgeon. m. Simmi K Ratan, 1 son, 1 daughter. Education: MBBS, 1985, MS, 1989, Jimper, Pondicherry; MCh, Paediatric Surgery, All India Institute of Medical Sciences, 1992. Appointments: Senior Resident, Paediatric Surgery, 1989-92; Consultant, Paediatric Surgery, Jain Medical Centre, Sitaram Bhartiya Institute of Science and Research, Delhi; Consultant, Neonatal Surgery, Maternity and Children Hospital, Najran, Kingdom Saudi Arabia, 2005-. Publications: More than 30 articles in reputed medical journals. Honours: Best Student of Science at State Level; First Surgeon in India to report surgically treated survivor of Type 3 Laryngotracheal Cleft using conservative approach. Memberships: Indian Medical Association; Indian Association of Paediatric Surgeons; Indian Society of Paediatric Urology. Address: E-13/13, Khirki Extension, Malviya Nagar, New Delhi, 110017, India. E-mail: drjohnsimmi@yahoo.com

RATCLIFFE Eric Hallam, b. 8 August 1918, Teddington, Middlesex, England. Retired Physicist and Information Scientist; Writer; Poet; Editor. Appointment: Founder-Editor, Ore, 1955-95. Publications: Over 30, including: The Visitation, 1952; The Chronicle of the Green Man, 1960; Gleanings for a Daughter of Aeolus, 1968; Leo Poems, 1972; Commius, 1976; Nightguard of the Quaternary, 1979; Ballet Class, 1986; The Runner of the Seven Valleys, 1990; The Ballad of Polly McPoo, 1991; Advent, 1992; The Golden Heart Man, 1993; Fire in the Bush: Poems, 1955-1992, 1993; William Ernest Henley (1849-1903): An Introduction, 1993; The Caxton of Her Age: The Career and Family Background of Emily Faithfull (1835-1895), 1993; Winstanley's Walton, 1649: Events in the Civil War at Walton-on-Thames, 1994; Ratcliffe's Megathesaurus, 1995; Anthropos, 1995; Odette, 1995; Sholen, 1996; The Millennium of the Magician, 1996; The Brussels Griffon, 1996; Strange Furlongs, 1996; Wellington - A Broad Front, 1998; Capabilities of the Alchemical Mind, 1999; Cosmologia, 2000; Loyal Women, 2000; No Jam in the Astrid, 2002; The Divine Peter, 2002; On Baker's Level, 2002; Selected Long Poems, 2003; Desert Voices, 2003; The Ruffian on the Stairs, 2005; Going for God, 2005; Islandia, 2005; Unfinished Business, 2006. Contributions to: Anthologies and journals. Honour: Baron. Royal Order of the Bohemian Crown, 1995. Address: 7 The Towers, Stevenage, Hertfordshire SG1 1HE, England.

RATHER Dan, b. 31 October 1931, Wharton, Texas, USA. Broadcaster; Journalist. m. Jean Goebel, 1 son, 1 daughter. Education: BA, Journalism, Sam Houston State College, Huntsville, Texas, 1953; University of Houston; South Texas School of Law. Appointments: Staff, United Press International, Houston Chronicle, KTRH Radio, Houston; KHOU-TV, Houston; White House Correspondent, 1964-65, 1966-74, Chief, London Bureau, 1965-66, CBS-TV; Anchorman-Correspondent, CBS Reports, 1974-75; Co-Editor, 60 Minutes, CBS-TV, 1975-81; Anchorman, Dan Rather Reporting, CBS Radio, 1977-; Anchorman and Managing Editor, 1981-2005, co-anchorman, 1993-2005, CBS Evening News with Dan Rather; CBS News special programmes; Dan Rather Reports, 2006. Publications: The Palace Guard (with Gary Gates), 1974; The Camera Never Blinks Twice (with Mickey Herskowitz), 1977; Memoirs: I Remember (with Peter Wyden), 1991; The Camera Never Blinks Twice: The Further Adventures of a Television Journalist, 1994; Deadlines and Datelines: Essays at the Turn of the Century, 1999. Honours: Many Emmy Awards; Dan Rather Communications Building named in his honour, Sam Houston State University, Huntsville, Texas; Honorary Doctor of Humane Letters, Siena College, New York, 2007. Address: c/o CBS News, 524 West 57th Street, New York, NY 10019, USA.

RATNAVEL Ravi, b. 14 August 1964, Colombo, Ceylon. Consultant Dermatologist. m. Pami, 1 son, 1 daughter. Education: MA (Oxon), DM (Oxon), Trinity College, Oxford; King's College, London; MBBS (Lond); FRCP (UK). Appointment: Consultant Dermatologist to Buckinghamshire Hospitals. Membership: Fellow, Royal College of Physicians; Fellow, Royal Society of Medicine. Address: PO Box 684, Amersham, Buckinghamshire, HP6 5SA, England. E-mail: ratnavel@talk.21.com

RATTLE Sir Simon, b. 19 January 1955, Liverpool, England. Conductor. m. (1) Elise Ross, 2 sons, (2) Candace Allen, 1996. Education: Royal Academy of Music. Career: Has conducted orchestras including: Bournemouth Symphony, Northern Sinfonia, London Philharmonic, London Sinfonietta, Berlin Philharmonic, Los Angeles Philharmonic, Stockholm Philharmonic, Vienna Philharmonic, Philadelphia Orchestra, Boston Symphony; Début: Queen Elizabeth Hall, 1974; Royal Festival Hall, 1976, Royal Albert Hall, 1976, Assistant Conductor, BBC Symphony Orchestra, 1977; Associate Conductor, Royal Liverpool Philharmonic Society, 1977-80; Glyndebourne début, 1977, Royal Opera, Covent Garden, 1990; Artistic Director London Choral Society, 1979-84; Principal Conductor and Artistic Advisor, City of Birmingham Symphony Orchestra (CBSO), 1980-90, Music Director, 1990-98; Artistic Director, South Bank Summer Music, 1981-83; Joint Artistic Director, Aldeburgh Festival, 1982-93; Principal Guest Conductor, Los Angeles Philharmonic, 1981-94, Rotterdam Philharmonic, 1981-84; Principal Guest Conductor, Orchestra of the Age of Enlightenment, 1992-; Chief Conductor and Artistic Director, Berlin Philharmonic Orchestra, 2002-. Publications: Over 30 recordings with CBSO. Honours: Edison Award, 1987; Grand Prix du Disque, 1988; Grand Prix Caecilia, 1988; Gramophone Record of the Year Award, 1988; Gramophone Opera Award, 1989; International Record Critics' Award, 1990; Grand Prix de l'Academy Charles Cros, 1990; Gramophone Artist of Year, 1993; Montblanc de la Culture Award, 1993; Officier des Arts et des Lettres, 1995; Toepfer Foundation Shakespeare Prize, 1996; Gramophone Award for Best Concerto recording, Albert Medal (RSA), 1997; Choc de l'Année Award, 1998; Gramophone Award for Best Opera Recording, 2000; Gramophone Awards for Best Orchestral Recording and Record of the Year, 2000; Comenius Prize, Germany, 2004; Classical BRIT Award, 2004. Address: c/o Askonas Holt Ltd, Lonsdale Chambers, 27 Chancery Lane, London, WC2A 1PF, England.

RAVERTY Aaron (Thomas Donald), b. 13 March 1950, Stillwater, Minnesota, USA. Benedictine Monk; Anthropologist; Editor. Education: BA, Anthropology, 1972, MA, Anthropology, 1979, PhD, Sociocultural Anthropology, 1990, University of Minnesota, Minneapolis; MA, Systematic Theology, St John's University, Collegeville, Minnesota, 1979. Appointments: Preparatory School Instructor, St John's Preparatory School, Collegeville, Minnesota, 1975-76; University Instructor, St John's University, Collegeville, 1975-90; Editor, The Liturgical Press, Collegeville, 1991-; General Editor, Worship Magazine, 1993-94; Book Review Editor, Monastic Interreligious Dialogue Bulletin. Publications: Contributions to newsletters and journals; Editor, The Modern Catholic Encyclopedia, 1994, 2004; The Encyclopedia of American Catholic History, 1997; Professional papers presented at universities and colleges within America. Honours: Certificate of Merit, St John's University, 1987; Fellowship Status in the American Anthropological Association, 1993; Choice Editorial Award, The Encyclopedia of American Catholic History, 1998; Listed in Who's Who publications and biographical dictionaries. Memberships: American Benedictine Academy; Fellow, American Anthropological Association; Board Member, Monastic Interreligious Dialogue; International Graphoanalysis Society, 1996-; American Men's Studies Association 2003-;. Address: PO Box 2015, St John's Abbey, Collegeville, MN 56321-2015, USA.

RAWNSLEY Andrew Nicholas James, FRSA (Fellow of the Royal Society of Arts) b. 5 January 1962, Leeds, England. Journalist; Broadcaster; Author. m. Jane Hall, 1990, 3 daughters. Education: Sidney Sussex College, Cambridge; MA, History, Cambridge. Appointments: BBC, 1983-85; Reporter, Feature Writer, 1985-87, Political Columnist, 1987-93, The Guardian; Writer, Presenter, A Week in Politics, 1989-97, Bye Bye Blues, 1997, Blair's Year, 1998, Channel 4 series; Associate Editor, Chief Political Commentator, The Observer, 1993-; Writer, Presenter, The Agenda, ITV series, 1996, The Westminster Hour, Radio 4 series, 1998-2006; The Unauthorised Biography of the United Kingdom, 1999; The Sunday Edition (with Andrea Catherwood), 2006. Publication: Servants of the People: The Inside Story of New Labour, 2000. Honours: Student Journalist of the Year, 1983; Young Journalist of the Year, 1987; Columnist of the Year, What the Papers Say Awards, 2000; Book of the Year, Channel 4/House Magazine Political Awards, 2001; Journalist of the year, Channel 4 Awards, 2003. Address: The Observer, 119 Farringdon Road, London EC1R 3ER, England. E-mail: andrew.rawnsley@observer.co.uk

RAY Asim Kumar, b. 6 October 1937. Teacher; Researcher. m. Parul Basu, 1 daughter. Education: BSc (honours), Physics, University of Calcutta, 1956; MSc, Physics, University of Calcutta, 1958; PhD, Particle Physics, Carnegie Mellon University, 1969. Appointments: Trainee, Atomic Energy Establishment, Trombay, Bombay, 1959-60; Research Associate, Tata Institute of Fundamental Research, Bombay, 1960-63; Lecturer, 1969-76, Reader, 1976-84, Professor, 1984-, Head of Department of Physics, 1981-87, Dean of Faculty of Science, 1990-92, Professor in Charge, Computer Centre, 1991-97, Registrar, 1992-93, Retired, 2002, Visva-Bharati University, India; Visiting Scientist, USA, Japan and Italy, 1980-95; Senior Associate, IUCAA, Pune, India, 1994-97; Currently Visiting Faculty, S N Bose National Centre for Basic Sciences, Salt Lake Sector III, Kolkata, India. Publications: Editor and co-editor, Dirac and Feynman, Pioneers in Quantum Mechanics; Editor and co-editor, Proceedings of XI DAE Symposium on High Energy Physics; Over 40 professional research papers. Honours: Fulbright Scholar. Memberships: Indian Physics Association; Indian Physical Society; Indian Association of Cultivation Science; Indian Association of General Relativity and Gravitation. Address: Uttaran, Purva Palli (North), Santiniketan 731235, India. E-mail: asimkray@yahoo.co.in

RAYNER Claire Berenice, (Sheila Brandon, Ann Lynton, Ruth Martin), b. 22 January 1931, London, England. Writer; Broadcaster. m. Desmond Rayner, 23 June 1957, 2 sons, 1 daughter. Education: State Registered Nurse, Gold Medal, Royal Northern Hospital, London, 1954; Midwifery, Guy's Hospital. Publications: Over 90 books, ranging from medical to fiction, 1961-97; Autobiography, How Did I Get Here from There? 2003. Contributions to: Professional journals, newspapers, radio, and television. Honours: Freeman, City

of London, 1981; Medical Journalists Association Award, 1987; Honorary Fellow, University of North London, 1988; Best Specialist Consumer Columnist Award, 1988; Order of the British Empire, 1996; Honorary Doctorate from Oxford Books' University, 2000; Honorary Doctorate, Middlesex University, 2002; Honorary Associate, National Secular Society. Memberships: Royal Society of Medicine, fellow; Society of Authors; President, Patients Association; President, Gingerbread; Vice-President, British Humanist Society; Council member, Charter 88; Video Appeals Committee, British Board of Film Classification. Address: Holly Wood House, Roxborough Avenue, Harrow-on-the-Hill, Middlesex HA1 3BU, England.

RAYNER Desmond, b. 31 October 1928, London, England. Artist; Writer; Actor. m. Claire Rayner, 2 sons, 1 daughter. Education: Certificate in Acting, LGSM, Guildhall School of Music and Drama, 1950-51. Career: RAF, 1946-49; Numerous advertising and public relations posts, 1957-; Agent and manager to wife Claire Rayner. Creative works: Designed productions: Heaven and Charing Cross Road; A Murder Has Been Arranged; The Boy With A Cart; Lady Windermere's Fan; Numerous art exhibitions, 1975-2002, including Art Deco in Egypt, New York – Another Perspective, London – Another Perspective; and many others; Private collections in Australia, Canada, USA and UK. Publications: Novels: The Dawlish Season, 1984; The Husband, 1992; Encore. Memberships: Equity; Royal Academy of Fine Art; Actors Centre. Address: Holly Wood House, Roxborough Avenue, Harrow-on-the-Hill, Middlesex, HA1 3BU, England.

RAYNER Heather Eirene Hope, b. 17 September 1945, Barton-on-Sea, Hampshire, England. Translator. Education: BA (Hons), Hull University, England, 1967; Translator's diploma, Interpreters' School, Geneva University, Switzerland, 1972; German Diploma, Italian General Certificate, Institute of Linguists, London, England, 1998. Appointments: English Teacher, language schools in France, Spain, Germany and UK, 1967-70; Interpreter/Translator, Inter-Parliamentary Union, Geneva, 1972-74; Translator/Editor, Battelle Scientific Research Centre, Geneva, 1974-78; Translator/Reviser, Permanent Mission of Germany to the UN, Geneva, 1978-82; Translator/Editor, International Committee of the Red Cross, Geneva, 1982-83; Research Executive, Gira UK, London, 1984-89; Assistant Manager, Seda UK, London, 1989-91; Senior Translator, Willis Faber & Dumas, London, 1991-98; Research Editor, Reuters, London, 1999-2002; Translator, Swiss Federal Chancellery, Bern, 2002-. Memberships: Institute of Linguists, London (Fellow, 1995); Institute of Translation and Interpreting, London; London Tourist Board Driver-Guide, London; International Association of Conference Translators, Geneva. Address: Hochfeldstr 53, 3012 Bern, Switzerland. E-mail: heather.rayner@bk.admin.ch

RÉ Paul Bartlett, b. 18 April 1950, Albuquerque, New Mexico, USA. Artist; Writer; Poet; Peace Worker. Education: BSc, Physics (with Top Honours), California Institute of Technology, Pasadena, California, 1972. Career: Artist, Writer, Poet, 1972-; Artist Advisory Board (Access to Art), Museum of American Folk Art, 1987-94; Director, the Paul Ré Collection and Archives, 1994-; Advisor, Paul Bartlett Ré Peace Prize Committee, University of New Mexico, 2007; Exhibit "Touchable Art: An Exhibit for the Blind and Sighted" shown 18 times in USA and Canada, 1981-; 22 solo exhibitions in 13 states. Publications: Books: Touchable Art: A Book for the Blind and the Sighted (embossings with text), 1983; The Dance of the Pencil: Serene Art by Paul Ré (drawings, essays, poetry), 1993; Articles in: Journal of Visual Impairment and Blindness, 1983; Leonardo Art Journal, 1980-82; New America; Design Journal; SCETV TV documentary, Touchable Art, 1990; Chapter in Spirit of Enterprise: The 1990 Rolex Awards; 7 covers and poems, Spirit Magazine; 4 books in progress (Réograms (hybrid hand-digital prints), humour, essays and poetry). Honours: First Place in Physics, International Science Fair, 1967 and 1968; Wurlitzer Foundation Residencies, 1982, 1984; The Dance of the Pencil cited as one of the outstanding art books of the year, Journal of the Print World; World Lifetime Achievement Award, American Biographical Institute, 2004; Legion of Honor, United Cultural Convention, 2005; 21st Century Award for Achievement, IBC, 2005; Who's Who in America, 2005; Genius Laureate of the United States, ABI, 2005; 500 Greatest Geniuses of the 21st Century, ABI, 2006; Listed in Who's Who publications and biographical encyclopaedias; The Paul Bartlett Ré Peace Prize and the Paul Ré Collection and Sculpture Garden, University of New Mexico, Albuquerque; IBC Hall of Fame, 2006; Sovereign Ambassador, Order of American Ambassadors, 2006; Da Vinci Diamond, IBC, 2006; World's Most Respected Expert, ABI, 2006; IBC Roll of Honour, 2007; Works highly regarded by Raymond Jonson, Georgia O'Keeffe, Nobel Laureates, College Presidents and other notables; Acclaimed by art critics as "a virtuoso of the pencil" and for his art of "quiet greatness and noble simplicity", it's aim is to harmonise the world. Memberships: Life Member, CALTECH Alumni Association; Life Member, The Nature Conservancy. Address: 10533 Sierra Bonita Avenue NE, Albuquerque, NM 87111, USA. Website: www.unm.edu/~jonsong/paul%20re

READ Anthony, b. 21 April 1935, Staffordshire, England. Writer; Dramatist. m. Rosemary E Kirby, 29 March 1958, 2 daughters. Education: Queen Mary's Grammar School, Walsall, 1945-52, Central School of Speech and Drama, London, 1952-54. Publications: The Theatre, 1964; Operation Lucy (with David Fisher), 1980; Colonel Z (with David Fisher), 1984; The Deadly Embrace (with David Fisher), 1988; Kristallnacht (with David Fisher), 1989; Conspirator (with Ray Bearse), 1991; The Fall of Berlin (with David Fisher), 1992; Berlin: The Biography of a City (with David Fisher), 1994; The Proudest Day: India's Long Road to Independence (with David Fisher), 1997; The Devil's Disciples, 2003; The Baker Street Boys: The Case of the Disappearing Detective, 2005; The Baker Street Boys: The Case of the Captive Clairvoyant, 2006; The Baker Street Boys: The Case of the Ranjipur Ruby, 2006; Baker Street Boys: The Case of the Limehouse Laundry, 2007; The World on Fire, 2008; Other: Over 200 television films, plays, series and serials. Honours: Pye Colour TV Award, 1983; Wingate Literary Prize, 1989. Membership: Trustee, Past Chairman, Writers Guild of Great Britain. Address: 7 Cedar Chase, Taplow, Buckinghamshire, England.

READE John Brian, b. 4 July 1938, Wolverhampton, England. University Lecturer. m. Suzanne, 3 sons, 2 daughters. Education: LRAM, 1956; 1st Class Honours (Wrangler), 1961, Part III Distinction, 1962, PhD, 1962-65, Trinity College, Cambridge. Appointments: Lecturer in Mathematics, Birmingham University, 1965-67; Lecturer in Mathematics, University of Manchester, 1967-2003. Publications: Books: Introduction to Mathematical Analysis, 1986; Calculus with Complex Numbers, 2003; Various research papers on mathematics. Honours: MA, PhD, Cambridge University. Memberships: London Mathematical Society; Cambridge Philosophical Society. Address: 123 Andover Avenue, Middleton, Manchester M24 1JQ, England. E-mail: sue.reade@virgin.net

REAGAN Nancy Davis (Anne Francis Robbins), b. 6 July 1921, New York, USA. Former American First Lady. m. Ronald Reagan, 1952, deceased 2004, 1 son, 1 daughter, 1 stepson, 1 stepdaughter. Education: BA, Smith College, Massachusetts, USA. Appointments: Contract actress, Metro-Goldwyn-Mayer, 1949-56; Former author, syndicated column on prisoners-of-war and soldiers missing in action; Civic worker active on behalf of Vietnam War veterans, senior citizens, disabled children and drug victims; Member, Board of Directors, Revlon Group Inc, 1989-; Honorary National Chairman, Aid to Adoption of Special Kids, 1977; Actress in films including: The Next Voice You Hear, 1950; Donovan's Brain, 1953; Hellcats of the Navy, 1957. Publications: Nancy, 1980; To Love a Child (with Jane Wilkie); My Turn (memoirs), 1989. Honours: One of Ten Most Admired American Women, Good Housekeeping Magazine, 1977; Woman of Year, Los Angeles Times, 1977; Permanent member, Hall of Fame of Ten Best Dressed Women in US, Lifetime Achievement Award, Council of Fashion Designers of USA, 1988. Address: 2121 Avenue of the Stars, 34th Floor, Los Angeles, CA 90067, USA.

REAMSBOTTOM Barry, b. 4 April 1949, Nairn, Scotland. A Senior Secretary to Speaker of the House of Commons. Education: St Peter's Roman Catholic Secondary School, Aberdeen, 1959-64; Aberdeen Academy, 1964-66. Appointments: Scientific Assistant, Isaac Spencer & Co, Aberdeen, Scotland, 1966-69; Social Security Officer, DHSS, Aberdeen, 1969-76; Area Officer, National Union of Public Employees, Edinburgh, 1976-79; Head of Education Department, 1979-87, Press Officer, Journal Editor, 1987-92, General Secretary, 1992-2002, Civil and Public Services Association, London, then Public and Commercial Services Union; Currently, a Senior Secretary to the Speaker of the House of Commons. Honour: Fellow, Centre for American Studies, Salzburg, Austria. Memberships: Amnesty International; Labour Party. Address: 156 Bedford Hill, London SW12 9HW, England. E-mail: reamsy156@lycos.co.uk

REARDON Raymond (Ray), b. 8 October 1932, Tredegar, Wales. Snooker Player. m. (1) Susan Carter, divorced, 1 son, 1 daughter. (2) Carol Lovington, 1987. Career: Welsh Amateur Champion, 1950-55; English Amateur Champion, 1965; Turned professional, 1967; Six times World Snooker Champion, 1970-78; Benson & Hedges Masters Champion, 1976; Welsh Champion, 1977, 1981, 1983; Professional Players Champion, 1982; Retired, 1992; Active in running World Professional Billiards and Snooker Association; Occasional TV appearances. Publications: Classic Snooker, 1974; Ray Reardon (autobiography), 1982. Honour: MBE.

REDDA Tsehay, b. 27 June 1962, Ethiopia. Deputy Chief. m. 3 daughters. Education: BSc, Animal Science, Alemaya University of Agriculture, Ethiopia, 1981; MSc, Grassland Science, University of Reading, England, 1989; Rural Dairy Processing/Dairy Technology, Animal Feeds & Nutrition, Computer Science, Business Development, Dairy Products Marketing, General Management & Staff Administration; Home Economics. Appointments: Team Leader, Southern Regions Agricultural Development Bureau, Ketena, 1983-87; Project Co-ordinator, Small-scale Dairy Development Pilot Project, 1990-94; Smallholder Dairy Development Project Manager & Head, Livestock & Fisheries Resources Development and Regulatory Department, Ministry of Agriculture, 1995-2000; Head, Federal Dairy Development Program, 2000-02; Technical Advisor, Integrated Livestock Development Project, Austria Development Co-operation, 2002-04; Deputy Chief of Party, Land O'Lakes Inc, 2005-.

Publications: Numerous articles in professional journals. Memberships: Ethiopian Society of Animal Production; National Veterinary Institute. Address: PO Box 3431, Addis Ababa, Ethiopia. E-mail: tsehayredda@yahoo.com

REDFORD Robert, b. 18 August 1936, Santa Monica, California, USA. Actor. m. Lola Van Wegenen, divorced, 4 children. Education: University of Colorado. Creative Works: Films include, War Hunt, 1961; Situation Hopeless But Not Serious, 1965; Inside Daisy Clover, 1965; The Chase, 1965; This Property is Condemned, 1966; Barefoot in the Park, 1967; Tell Them Willie Boy is Here, 1969; Butch Cassidy and the Sundance Kid, 1969; Downhill Racer, 1969; Little Fauss and Big Halsy, 1970; Jeremiah Johnson, 1972; The Candidate, 1972; How to Seal a Diamond in Four Uneasy Lessons, 1972; The Way We Were, 1973; The Sting, 1973; The Great Gatsby, 1974; The Great Waldo Pepper, 1974; Three Days of the Condor, 1975; All the President's Men, 1976; A Bridge Too Far, 1977; The Electric Horseman, 1980; Brubaker, 1980; The Natural, 1984; Out of Africa, 1985; Legal Eagles, 1986; Havana, 1991; Indecent Proposal, 1993; The Clearing, Sacred Planet, 2004, Director, Ordinary People, 1980; Milagro Beanfield War (also producer), 1988; Promised Land (executive producer), 1988; Sneakers, 1992; A River Runs Through it (also director), 1992; Quiz Show (director), 1994; The River Wild, 1995; Up Close and Personal, 1996; The Horse Whisperer, 1997; The Legend of Bagger Vance, (also director, producer), How to Kill Your Neighbour's Dog (executive producer), 2000; The Last Castle, 2001; Spy Game, 2001; The Motorcycle Diaries, 2004; The Clearing, 2004; An Unfinished Life, 2005; Charlotte's Web (voice), 2006; Lions for Lambs, 2007. Honours: Academy Award, Golden Globe Award, Best Director, 1981; Audubon Medal, 1989; Dartmouth Film Society Award, 1990; Screen Actors' Guild Award for Lifetime Achievement, 1996; Honorary Academy Award, 2002. Address: c/o Creative Artists Agency, 9830 Wilshire Boulevard, Beverly Hills, CA 90212, USA.

REDGRAVE Lynn, b. 8 March 1943. Actress; Playwright. m. John Clark, 1967-2000, divorced, 1 son, 2 daughters. Education: Central School of Speech and Drama. Career: Films include: Girl With The Green Eyes; Tom Jones; Georgy Girl; Smashing Time; The Virgin Soldiers; The Deadly Affair; The National Health; Every Little Crook and Nanny; The Happy Hooker; Sunday Lovers; Getting It Right; Morgan Stewart's Coming Home; Everything You Always Wanted to Know About Sex; The Big Bus; Midnight; Shine; Strike; The Simian Line; Touched; The Annihilation of Fish; The Next Best Thing, 2000; My Kingdom, 2001; Spider, 2002; Unconditional Love, 2002; The Wild Thornberrys Movie (voice), 2002; Hansel & Gretel,2002; Anita and Me, 2002; Charlie's War, 2003; Peter Pan, 2003; Kinsey, 2004; The White Countess, 2005; The Jane Austen Book Club, 2007; My Dog Tulip, 2008. TV includes: Pygmalion; Egg on the Face of the Tiger; The Bad Seed; Whatever Happened to Baby Jane; Gauguin the Savage; White Lies; Gods and Monsters; Rude Awakening; My Sister's Keeper; Me, Eloise; Nurses. Stage work includes: Hamlet; Much Ado About Nothing; Andorra; Hay Fever; Slag; My Fat Friend; Shakespeare for My Father; California Suite; Saint Joan; Les Liaisons Dangereuses; The Cherry Orchard; Mrs Warren's Profession; Don Juan in Hell; Notebook of Trigorin; Moon Over Buffalo, 1996; The Mandrake Root, 2001; Noises Off, 2001; Radio includes: As You Like It; Vile Bodies; Tales for Halloween. Honours include: Sarah Siddons, Chicago and Jefferson Awards (Misalliance). Publications: This is Living, 1991; Named President of the Players, 1994. Address: c/o John Clark, PO Box 1207, Topanga, CA 90290, USA,

REDGRAVE Sir Steve (Steven Geoffrey), b. 23 March 1962, Marlow, England. Former Oarsman. m. Ann, 1 son, 2 daughters. Education: Doctor Civil Law, honoris causa. Appointments: Represented, UK at Junior World Championships, 1979; Silver medal, 1980; Stroke, British Coxed 4, Gold Medal Winners, Los Angeles Olympic Games, 1984; Gold Medals, Single Scull, Coxless Pair (with Andy Holmes) and Coxed 4, Commonwealth Games, 1986; Coxed Pair (with Holmes), World Championships, 1986; Coxless Pair Gold Medal and Coxed Pair Silver Medal (with Holmes), World Championships, 1987; Gold Medal (with Holmes), Coxless Pair and Bronze Medal, Coxed Pair, Olympic Games, Seoul, 1988; Silver Medal (with Simon Berrisford), Coxless Pairs, World Championships, 1989; Bronze Medal, Coxless Pair (with Matthew Pinsent), World Championships, Tasmania, 1990; Gold Medal, Coxless Pair (with Pinsent), World Championships, Vienna, 1991; Gold Medal, Olympic Games, Barcelona, 1992; Gold Medals at World Championships, Czech Republic, 1993; USA, 1994, Finland, 1995; Gold Medal, Olympic Games, Atlanta, 1996; Winners of World Cup, Gold Medal, Coxless 4, France, (with Pinsent, Foster, Cracknell), 1997; Gold Medal Winners, Coxless 4, World Championships, Cologne, 1998; Gold Medal Winners, Coxless 4, St Catherines (with Pinsent, Coode, Cracknell), 1999; Gold Medal, Olympic Games, Sydney, 2000. Publications: Steven Redgrave's Complete Book of Rowing, 1992; A Golden Age (autobiography), 2000; You Can Win At Life, 2005. Honours: MBE, 1987; CBE, 1997; Sports Personality of the Year, 2000; British Sports Writers; Association Sportsman of the Year, 2000; Laurens Lifetime Achievement Award, 2001; Honorary DSc (Buckingham, Hull), 2001; Knighted, 2001; BBC Golden Sports Personality, 2003. Address: c/o British International Rowing Office, 6 Lower Mall, London W6 9DJ, England.

REDGRAVE Vanessa, b. 30 January 1937, England. Actress. m. Tony Richardson, 1962, divorced 1967, deceased 1991, 2 daughters, m. Franco Nero, 2006, 1 child. Education: Central School of Speech and Drama. Career: Films include: Morgan – A Suitable Case for Treatment; Sailor from Gibraltar, 1965; Charge of the Light Brigade; The Seagull; Isadora Duncan, 1968; The Devils, 1970; Mary Queen of Scots, 1971; Murder on the Orient Express, 1974; Julia, 1977; Playing for Time, 1980; Wetherby, 1984; Howard's End, 1992; Breath of Life, The Wall, Sparrow, They, The House of the Spirits, Crime and Punishment, Mother's Boys, Little Odessa, A Month by the Lake, 1996; Mission Impossible, 1996; Looking for Richard, 1997; Wilde, 1997; Mrs Dalloway, 1997; Bella Mafia (TV), 1997; Deep Impact, 1998; Cradle Will Rock, 2000; The House of the Spirits; Crime and Punishment; Little Odessa; The 3 Kings, 2000; A Rumor of Angels, 2000; The Pledge, 2001; Crime and Punishment, 2002; Good Boy (voice), 2003; The Fever, 2004; Short Order, 2005; The White Countess, 2005; The Thief Lord, 2006; The Riddle, 2007; How About You, 2007; Evening, 2007; Atonement, 2007. Produced and narrated documentary film The Palestinians, 1977; Theatre includes: A Midsummer Night's Dream, 1959; The Prime of Miss Jean Brodie, 1966; Cato Street, 1971; Threepenny Opera, 1972; Macbeth, 1975; Ghosts, 1986; A Madhouse in Goa, 1989; Heartbreak House, 1992; Antony and Cleopatra, Houston, Texas (also directed), 1996; John Gabriel Borkman, 1996; Song at Twilight, 1999; The Cherry Orchard, 2000; The Tempest, 2000; Lady Windermere's Fan, 2002. Publications include: An Autobiography, 1991. Honours: Variety Club Award; Evening Standard Award for Best Actress, 1961; Cannes Film Festival Best Actress (Morgan-A Suitable Case for Treatment, 1966); UK Film Critic's Guild and National Society of Film Critics Leading Actress Award (Isadora

Duncan,) 1969; Academy Award Best Supporting Actress (Julia, 1978); TV Award for Best Actress (Playing for Time, 1981); Laurence Olivier Award, 1984; Dr hc, Massachusetts, 1990. Memberships: Co-Founder Moving Theatre, 1974; Workers' Revolutionary Party (Candidate for Moss Side, 1979); Fellow, BFI, 1988.

REDMAN Christopher Willard George, b. 30 November 1941, Pretoria, South Africa. Clinical Professor of Obstetric Medicine. m. Corinna Susan Page, 4 sons, 1 daughter. Education: MB BChir, Cambridge University, 1967; MRCP, London, 1972; FRCP, London, 1981. Appointments: Training in Baltimore, USA, Oxford and Sheffield UK, 1967-70; Lecturer in Medicine, Oxford University, 1970-76; University Lecturer , 1976-89, Clinical Reader, 1989-92, Clinical Professor, 1992-, Obstetric Medicine, University of Oxford. Publications: More than 200 research and review articles on pre-eclampsia and medical disorders of pregnancy, 1973-. Honours: Chesley Award, International Society for the Study of Hypertension in Pregnancy; Barnes Award, International Society of Obstetric Medicine. Memberships: Fellow of the Royal College of Physicians, London; Fellow of Lady Margaret Hall, Oxford. Address: Nuffield Department of Obstetrics and Gynaecology, John Radcliffe Hospital, Oxford OX3 9DU, England.

REDTENBACHER Andreas Gottlieb, b. 8 May 1953, Vienna, Austria. Roman Catholic Priest. Education: Mag Theol, University of Vienna, Austria, 1977; Lic Theol, 1979, Dr Theol, 1983, Gregorian University, Rome; Postgraduate Student for Habilitation, University of Trier, Germany, 2002-. Appointments: Ordained Priest, 1978; Religions Professor and Rector for Students, 1979; University Assistant in Liturgy and Lecturer in Liturgy, University of Vienna, Austria, 1981; Parish Priest in St Vitus, 1990; Nominated President, Committee for Liturgy in the Episcopal-Vikariat of the City of Vienna, Austria, 1981; Nominated President of the Conference of Liturgists in the Austrian Roman Catholic Church, 1995. Publications: Presbyter und Presbyterium, 1980; Zukunft aus den Erbe, 1984, second edition, 2006: Wo Sich Wege Kreuzen, 1985; Liturgie und Leben, 2002; Reihe: Pius – Parsch-Studien, bisher Bd I-VI; Die Zukunft der Liturgie, 2004; Kultur der Liturgie, 2006; Many published articles. Honour: Archiepiscopal Konsistorialrat. Memberships: International Societas Liturgica; Editorial Board, Heiliger Dienst; Corresponding Member, Editorial Board, Bibel und Liturgie. Address: Stiftplatz 1, A-3400 Klosterneuburg, Austria. E-mail: a.redtenbacher@stift-klosterneuburg.at

REDWOOD John Alan (Rt Hon), b. 15 June 1951, Dover, England. Member of Parliament. Divorced, 1 son, 1 daughter. Education: BA, Honours 1971, MA, DPhil, 1975, Oxford University. Appointments: Fellow, All Souls College, Oxford, 1972-86, 2003-2005; Manager, then Director, NM Rothschild & Sons, 1977-89; Chairman Norcros Plc, 1987-89; MP for Wokingham, 1987-; Minister, UK Government, 1989-95; Shadow President, Board of Trade, 1997-99; Shadow Front Bench Spokesman on the Environment, 1999-2000; Head, Parliamentary Campaigns Unit, 2000; Shadow Secretary of State for Deregulation, 2004-; Chair, Murray Financial Corporation, 2002-04; Chairman Concentric plc, 2003-. Publications: Reason, Ridicule and Religion, 1976; Public Enterprise in Crisis, 1980; Co-author, Value for Money Audits, 1981; Co-author, Controlling Public Industries, 1982; Going for Broke, 1984; Equity for Everyman, 1986; Popular Capitalism, 1989; Global Marketplace, 1994; The Single European Currency, with others, 1996; Our Currency, Our Country, 1997; The Death of Britain? 1999; Stars and

Strife, 2001; Just Say No, 2001; Third Way – Which Way, 2002; Singing the Blues, 2004; Superpower Struggles, 2005. Honours: Parliamentarian of the Year Awards, 1987, 1995, 1997. Address: House of Commons, London, SW1A 0AA, England.

REED Lou, b. 2 March 1942, Brooklyn, New York, USA. Musician. m. Sylvia Morales, 1980. Education: BA, Syracuse University. Songwriter and recording artist, 1965-; Founder member, Velvet Underground band, 1966-70; Toured with Andy Warhol's The Exploding Plastic Inevitable; Poet; Film actor. Publications: Recordings, solo albums include: Lou Reed, 1972; Rock'n'Roll Animal, 1972; Berlin, 1973; Sally Can't Dance, 1974; Metal Machine Music, 1975; Lou Reed Live, 1975; Coney Island Baby, 1976; Walk on the Wild Side; Street Hassle, 1978; Live, Take No Prisoners, 1978; Vicious, 1979; The Bells, 1979; Growing Up in Public, 1980; Rock 'n' Roll Diary, 1967-80; Blue Mask, Legendary Hearts, 1983; New York, 1989; Songs for Drella (with John Cale), 1990; Magic and Loss, 1992; Set the Twilight Reeling, 1996; Perfect Night Live in London, 1998; Ecstasy, 2000; American Poet, 2001; Extended Versions, 2003; The Raven, 2003; Animal Serenade, 2004; Le Bataclan '72, 2004; Hudson River Wind Meditations, 2007; Several albums with Velvet Underground. Publication: Between Thought and Expression (selected lyrics), 1991; Pass Thru Fire, 2000. Honour: Rock and Roll Hall of Fame, 1996. Address: c/o Sister Ray Enterprises, 584 Broadway, Room 609, New York, NY 10012, USA.

REED Peter Kirby, b. 27 July 1981, Seattle, USA. Rower. Education: Officer Training, Royal Navy (BRNC Dartmouth); Mechanical Engineering Degree at University of the West of England; MEng, Oxford University. Appointments: Lieutenant in the Royal Navy; Member of the Great Britain Coxless Four. Honours: Member of the Winning Oxford University Boat Race Crew, 2005; World Champion in Coxless Four in 2005, 2006; Combined Armed Services Sportsperson of the year, 2005; Senior Pairs Trial Winner, 2005-08. Memberships: Leander Club; Oxford University Boat Club; Bosporus Boat Club; Coldharbour Boat Club; The Royal Navy.

REES David Benjamin, b. 1 August 1937, Wales. Minister of Religion; Lecturer; Author. m. 31 July 1963, 2 sons. Education: BA, BD, MSc, University of Wales; MA, University of Liverpool; PhD, University of Salford; FRHisS. Appointments: Minister, Presbyterian Church of Wales, Cynon Valley, 1962-68, Heathfield Road, Liverpool, 1968-; Part-time Lecturer, University of Liverpool, 1970-99; Editor, Angor, Liverpool, 1979-; Professor, Ecclesiastical History, North West University, South Africa, 1999-; Editor, Peace and Reconciliation Magazine, 2000-02. Publications: Chapels in the Valley: Sociology of Welsh Non-Conformity, 1975; Wales: A Cultural History, 1980; Preparation for a Crisis: Adult Education in England and Wales 1945-1980, 1981; Liverpool, Welsh and Their Religion, 1984; Owen Thomas: A Welsh Preacher in Liverpool, 1991; The Welsh of Merseyside, 1997; Local and Parliamentary Politics in Liverpool from 1800 to 1911, 1999; Mr Evan Roberts: The Revivalist in Anglesey 1905, 2005. Contributions to: Magazines and newspapers such as Independent and Guardian. Honour: Ellis Griffith Prize, 1979; Paul Harris Fellow, Rotary International, 2005; Vice President, Liverpool Welsh Choral Union; Listed in Who's Who publications and biographical dictionaries. Memberships: Cymmrodorion Society; Welsh Academy; Wales and the World; University of Wales, Aberystwyth Court of Governors, 2003-; Chairman and Founder Member of Merseyside Welsh Heritage Society, 1999-2007. Address: 32 Garth Drive, Liverpool L18 6HW, England. E-mail: ben@garthdrive.fsnet.co.uk

REES David William Alan, b. 12 March 1947, Ruislip, Middlesex, England. Engineering Educator; Author; Researcher. Education: Student Apprentice, Black & Decker Ltd, Harmondsworth and Maidenhead, England; National Diploma and Engineering Institutions examinations, Southall Technical College, Middlesex, 1963-68; Postgraduate Student, Applied Mechanics, Imperial College, London, 1969-70; PhD, Research, Kingston University, 1973-76. Appointments: Engineering Apprentice, 1963-68, Engineering Designer, 1968-69, Black & Decker Ltd; Postgraduate Student, 1969-70, Experimental Officer, 1970-71, Imperial College, London; Research Assistant, 1971-72, Lecturer, 1972-77, Kingston University; Lecturer, Trinity College, Dublin, 1977-84; Lecturer, Surrey University, 1984-85, Lecturer, 1985-95, Senior Lecturer, 1995-2006, Brunel University; Visiting Fellow, Joint Research Centre, Petten, 1982; National Physical Laboratory, 1983, 1985; Regional Fellow, Royal Society of Medicine, London, 2007. Publications: Books: The Mechanics of Solids and Structures, 1990; Basic Solid Mechanics, 1997, Mechanics of Solids & Structures, 2000; Basic Engineering Plasticity, 2006; Recent articles: Nutting creep in mono- and bi-layer polymers, 2002; Anisotropy in thin canning sheet metals, 2003; Autofrettage of thick-walled pipe bends, 2004; Simulation of advanced sheet metals under stretch forming, 2006; Errors in r-value when based upon total strain measurements, 2006; Forming properties of four high strength sheet steels, 2006; Descriptions of reversed yielding in bending, 2007; Creep behaviour of fibre-reinforced polymer mat composites, 2007. Honours: National Diploma Prize, 1968; MSc/DIC, Imperial College, 1970; PhD, Kingston University, 1976; Honorary MA, Trinity College, Dublin, 1981; DSc, Brunel University, 2004; Best Paper, Fylde Prize, Strain, 1993; Best Paper, CEGB Prize, Journal of Strain Analysis, 1998; Listed in international biographical dictionaries. Memberships: Institution of Mechanical Engineers; Council of Engineering Institutions; Royal Society of Medicine. Address: Brunel University, School of Engineering and Design, Kingston Lane, Uxbridge, Middlesex UB8 3PH, England. E-mail: david.rees@brunel.ac.uk

REES Peter Wynford Innes (Baron of Goytre in the County of Gwent), b. 9 December 1926. Life Peer; Barrister; Politician. m. Anthea Peronelle Wendell. Education: Christ Church, Oxford. Appointments: Served in Scots Guards, 1945-48; Called to the Bar, Inner Temple, 1953; Bencher; Practised Oxford circuit; Contested, as a Conservative, Abertillery, 1964, 1965, Liverpool, West Derby, 1966; Elected MP (Conservative), Dover, 1970-74, Dover and Deal, 1974-83, Dover, 1983-87; PPS to Solicitor General, 1972; Minister of State, HM Treasury, 1979-81; Minister of Trade, 1981-83; Chief Secretary to the Treasury and Member of Cabinet, 1983-85. Honours: QC, 1969; PC, 1983. Memberships: Former Member, Court and Council, Museum of Wales, Museum and Galleries Commission; Liveryman, Worshipful Company of Clockmakers. Address: Goytre Hall, Abergavenny, Monmouthshire NP7 9DL, Wales.

REES-MOGG Lord William, Baron Rees-Mogg of Hinton Blewitt, b. 14 July 1928, Bristol, England; Journalist; Writer. m. Gillian Shakespeare Morris, 1962, 2 sons, 3 daughters. Education: Balliol College, Oxford. Appointments: Staff, The Financial Times, 1952-60; The Sunday Times, City Editor, 1960-61, Political and Economic Editor, 1961-63, Deputy Editor, 1964-67, Times; Editor, 1967-81, Columnist, 1992-,

The Times; Columnist, The Mail on Sunday, 2004-; Director, Times Newspapers Ltd, 1978-81, GEC, 1981-97, EFG Private Bank, 1993-2005, Value Realisation Trust, 1996-99; Vice-Chairman, Board of Governors, BBC, 1981-86; Chairman, Arts Council of Great Britain, 1982-89, Pickering and Chatto Ltd, 1983-, Sidgwick and Jackson, 1985-88, Broadcasting Standards Council, 1988-93, International Business Communications plc, 1993-98; Chairman, Fleet Street Publications, 1995-. Publications: The Reigning Error: The Crisis of World Inflation, 1974; An Humbler Heaven, 1977; How to Buy Rare Books, 1985; Blood in the Streets (with James Dale Davidson), 1987; The Great Reckoning (with James Dale Davidson), 1991; Picnics on Vesuvius: Steps Toward the Millennium, 1992; The Sovereign Individual: How to Survive and Thrive During the Collapse of the Welfare State (with James Dale Davidson), 1997. Honours: Honorary LLD, University of Bath, 1977; Knighted, 1981; Life Peerage, 1988. Address: 17 Pall Mall, London SW1Y 5LU, England.

REEVE Jonathan, b. 5 January 1943, Pembury, Kent, England. Physician. m. Caroline, 2 sons, 3 daughters. Education: Oriel College, Oxford and Guy's Hospital, London, 1961-68, 1965-68; MA, BM, BCh, 1976; DM, 1976; FRCP (Lond), 1983; DSc (Oxon), 1984. Appointments: MRC Clinical Research Fellow, Clinical Research Centre, Harrow, 1973-76; Fogarty-NIH International Travelling Fellow, Massachusetts General Hospital, 1976-77; MRC Clinical Scientific Staff, CRC, Harrow, 1977-93, (Head Bone Research, 1985-93); MRC ESS and Consultant Physician, Addenbrooke's Hospital, Cambridge, 1994-. Publications: 220 peer reviewed articles in scientific literature, principally concerning diseases of the skeleton; 117 other articles including reviews and book chapters. Honours: André Lichtwitz Prize for Research on Calcified Tissues, INSERM, France, 1984; Kohn Award for Excellence in Osteoporosis, National Osteoporosis Society, 2001. Memberships: Academy of Medical Sciences; Royal College of Physicians, London; Association of Physicians; Bone and Tooth Society; American Society of Bone and Mineral Research. Address: Box 157, Department of Medicine, Addenbrooke's Hospital, Cambridge CB2 2QQ, England.

REEVES John Drummond, b. 8 December 1914, Troy, New York, USA. College Teacher. m. Mary Moore, 1951. Education: BA, Williams College, 1937; MA, Columbia University, 1941. Appointments: Teacher, English, Irving School, Tarrytown, New York, 1937-40; Teacher, English, Horace Mann School, Riverdale, New York, 1940, 1946; Active duty, Lieutenant USNR, Pacific Theater of Operations, 1941-45; Instructor, Latin and English, Whitman College, Walla Walla, Washington, 1956-62; Assistant Professor, English, Millikin University, Decatur, Illinois, 1962-65; Professor, English, Hofstra University, Hempstead, New York, 1965-73; Retired, 1973. Publications: Author, Windows on Melville, 2001; Contributor to professional journals including: Thomas Middleton and Lily's Grammar: Some Parallels, 1952; A Supposed Indebtedness of Shakespeare to Peele, 1952; The Judgment of Paris as a Device of Tudor Flattery, 1954; The Cause of the Trojan War, According to Peele, 1955; Perseus and the Flying Horse in Peele and Heywood, 1955; Two Perplexities in Peele's "Edward the First", 1956; The Cause of the Trojan War: A Forgotten Myth Revived, 1966; The Cause of the Trojan War: Addendum, 1967; Motivations in Literary Forgery, 1967. Memberships: American Association of University Professors; College English Association; American Council of Learned Societies; Walla Walla Archaeological Association; Masons. Address: 20 Devonwood Drive, Apt 161, Farmington, CT 06032, USA.

REEVES Keanu, b. 2 September 1964, Beirut, Lebanon. Actor. Education: Toronto High School for Performing Arts; Training at Second City Workshop. Career: Stage appearances include: Wolf Boy; For Adults Only; Romeo and Juliet; with rock band Dogstar, 1996-; TV films: Letting Go, 1985; Act of Vengeance, 1986; Babes in Toyland, 1986; Under the Influence, 1986; Brotherhood of Justice, 1986; Save the Planet (TV special), 1990; Films: Prodigal, Flying, 1986; Youngblood, 1986; River's Edge, 1987; Permanent Record, 1988; The Night Before, 1988; The Prince of Pennsylvania, 1988; Dangerous Liaisons, 1988; I Love You to Death, 1990; Tune in Tomorrow, 1990; Bill and Ted's Bogus Journey, 1991; Point Break, 1991; My Own Private Idaho, 1991; Bram Stoker's Dracula, 1992; Much Ado About Nothing, 1993; Even Cowgirls Get the Blues, Little Buddha, 1993; Speed, 1994; Johnny Mnemonic, 1995; A Walk in the Clouds, 1995; Chain Reaction, Feeling Minnesota, The Devil's Advocate, 1996; The Last Time I Committed Suicide, 1997; The Matrix, 1998; The Replacements, 2000; The Watcher, 2000; The Gift, 2000; Sweet November, 2001; The Matrix: Reloaded, 2003; The Matrix: Revolutions, 2003; Something's Gotta Give, 2003; Constantine, 2005; A Scanner Darkly, 2006; The Lake House, 2006; The Night Watchman, 2008. Honour: Star on Hollywood Walk of Fame, 2005. Address: c/o Kevin Houvane, 9830 Wilshire Boulevard, Beverly Hills, CA 90212, USA.

REEVES Saskia, b. 1962, London, England. Actress. Education: Guildhall School of Music and Drama, London. Career: Toured South America, India and Europe, Cheek By Jowl Theatre Company; Stage appearances include: Metamorphosis; Who's Afraid of Virginia Woolf?; Measure for Measure; Separation; Smelling A Rat; Ice Cream; The Darker Face of the Earth; TV includes: In My Defence; A Woman of Substance, 1983; Children Crossing, 1990; Cruel Train, 1995; Plotlands, 1997; A Christmas Carol, 1999; Dune, 2000; Suspicion, 2003; Waking the Dead, 2003; Island at War, 2004; A Line in the Sand, 2004; The Commander: Virus, 2005; Afterlife, 2005; The Inspector Lynley Mysteries, 2006; Spooks, 2006; Bodies, 2006; Films: December Bride, 1990; Antonia and Jane, 1991; Close My Eyes, 1991; In the Border Country, 1991; The Bridge, 1992; Traps, 1994; ID, 1995; The Butterfly Kiss, 1995; Different for Girls, 1996; Much Ado About Nothing, 1998; LA Without a Map, 1998; Heart, 1999; Ticks, 1999; Bubbles, 2001; The Tesseract, 2003; The Knickerman, 2004; Fast Learners, 2006. Address: Markham & Froggat Ltd, 4 Windmill Street, London W1P 1HF, England.

REGIS John, b. 13 October 1966, Lewisham, London, England. Athlete. Career: Winner, UK 200m (tie), 1985; 100m, 1988, Amateur Athletics Association 200m, 1986-87; UK record for 200m, Silver Medal, Olympic Games Seoul, 1988; 300m indoor record holder Commonwealth Games, 1990; Silver Medal 200m, 1991; Gold medal 4 x 100m relay, 1991; Gold Medal 200m 4 x 400m relay, 4 x 400m relay, 1993; Gold Medal World Cup, 1994; Member, British team Olympic Games, Atlanta, 1996; Retired, 2000; Member, Great Britain bobsleigh training team, 2000-; Founder, Stellar Athletes Ltd, 2001; Coach, UK Athletics sprint relay team, 2001-. Address: c/o Belgrave Harriers Athletic Club, Batley Croft, 58 Harvest Road, Englefield Green, Surrey, England.

REGNARD Thomy Maxime Christian, b. 7 October 1958, Curepipe, Mauritius. Company Managing Director. m. M A Alexandra Pitot, 3 sons. Education: SC; HSC. Appointments: Marketing Manager, Ferney Textiles, 1983-89; Managing Director, Associated Textiles, 1989-. Honours: Certificate of Award Department Management, 1980; Certificate of Merit, 1980; Certificate in Marketing Management, 1980; Diploma

in Marketing Management, 1981. Memberships: Mauritius Turf Club; Dodo Club; Institute of Marketing Management, South Africa. Address: Bois Cheri Road, Moka, Mauritius.

REID Derek Donald, b. 30 November 1944, Aberdeen, Scotland. Businessman. m. Janice Anne, 1 son, 1 daughter. Education: Inverurie Academy; Aberdeen University; Robert Gordon's University. Appointments: Divisional Director of Cadbury-Schweppes Ltd; Founding Director/Shareholder of Premier Brands Ltd; CEO of Scottish Tourist Board; Visiting Professor of Tourism at Abertay University; Advisor/Consultant to several community/national bodies; Director of several small businesses e.g. Harris Tweed Textiles Ltd. Honours: Honorary Doctorate at Robert Gordon's University. Membership: Fellow of George Thomas Society; Fellow of the Institute of Contemporary Scotland Royal Society of Arts; Blairgowrie, Royal Perth, St Andrews, Hamilton, New Zealand, Mill Brook, Queenstown, New Zealand, Golf Clubs. Address: Broomhill, Kinclaven, Stanley, Perth, PH1 4QL. E-mail: dd.reid30@btinternet.com

REID Graham Charles, b. 29 August 1945, Finchley, England. Chartered Accountant. m. Gaye, 1 son. Education: Kings College, London University, 1963-66. Appointments: Articled Clerk, Legg London & Co, 1966-69; Chartered Accountant, Grant Thornton (formerly Thornton Baker), London Office, 1970-77, Manager, Founded Ipswich Office, 1977-79, Partner, Ipswich Office, 1979-2002; Retired, Tax Planning Consultant, 2002-. Memberships: Treasurer, Suffolk Branch of the Institute of Directors; Retired Chairman, Suffolk Board, The Prince's Trust; Retired Member, Eastern Regional Council, The Prince's Trust. Address: Mitchery Farmhouse, Rattlesden, Bury St Edmunds, Suffolk, IP30 0SS, England. E-mail: grahamcreid@msn.com

REID John, b. 8 May 1947, Bellshill, Lanarkshire, Scotland. Politician. m. (1) Cathie, deceased 1998, 2 sons, (2) Carine Adler 2002. Education: PhD, History, Stirling University; PC, 1998. Appointments include: Research Officer, Labour Party in Scotland, 1979-83; Political Adviser to Labour Leader, Neil Kinnock, 1983-85; Scottish Organiser, Trade Unionists for Labour, 1986-87; Member of Parliament representing Motherwell North and then Hamilton North and Bellshill for the past 17 years; Parliamentary Posts: Opposition Spokesman on Children, 1989-90; Opposition Spokesman in Defence, 1990-97; Minister of Defence, 1997-98; Minister for Transport, 1989-99; Secretary of State for Scotland, 1999-2001; Secretary of State for Northern Ireland, 2001-2002; Party Chair and Minister without Portfolio, 2002-2003; Leader of the House of Commons, 2003; Secretary of State for Health, 2003-05; for Defence, 2005-2006; Home Sectretary, 2006-2007; Chairman, Celtic F.C., 2007-. Address: House of Commons, London, SW1A 0AA, England.

REID SCOTT David Alexander Carroll, b. 5 June 1947, Ireland. Company Chairman. m. (1) 3 daughters, (3) Clare Straker, 1 son. Education: MA, Lincoln College, Oxford. Appointments: Vice-President, White Weld & Co, 1969-77; Seconded Senior Advisor, Saudi Arabian Monetary Agency, 1978-83; Managing Director, Merrill Lynch & Co, 1983-84; Managing Director, DLJ Phoenix Securities Ltd, 1984-98; Vice Chairman, Donaldson Lufkin & Jenrette, 1998-2000; Vice-Chairman, CSFB, 2000-2001; Chairman, Hawkpoint Partners, 2001-. Honours: BA, MA, Modern History. Memberships: Whites Club; Marks Club; Turf Club; Kildare Street Club, Dublin; Irish Georgian Society; Lloyd's of London; Advisor to the Board, The Cabo Delgado Biodiversity and Tourism Project, Mozambique; Governor, The Ditchley

Foundation; Chairman, Newbridge Capital; Rector's Council, Lincoln College. Address: 2 Cottesmore Gardens, London W8 5PR, England. E-mail: david.reidscott@hawkpoint.com

REIF Stefan Clive, b. 21 January 1944, Edinburgh, Scotland. Professor; Writer. m. Shulamit Stekel, 19 September 1967, 1 son, 1 daughter. Education: BA, Honours, 1964, PhD, 1969, University of London; MA, 1976, LittD, 2002, University of Cambridge, England. Appointments: Emeritus Professor of Medieval Hebrew Studies and Founder Director of Genizah Research Unit, University of Cambridge; Editor, Cambridge University Library's Genizah Series, 1978-. Publications: Shabbethai Sofer and his Prayer-book, 1979; Interpreting the Hebrew Bible, 1982; Published Material from the Cambridge Genizah Collections, 1988; Genizah Research after Ninety Years, 1992; Judaism and Hebrew Prayer, 1993; Hebrew Manuscripts at Cambridge University Library, 1997; A Jewish Archive from Old Cairo, 2000; Why Medieval Hebrew Studies, 2001; The Cambridge Genizah Collections, 2002; Problems with Prayers, 2006. Contributions to: Over 300 articles in Hebrew and Jewish studies. Memberships: Fellow, Royal Asiatic Society; Jewish Historical Society of England, ex-president, 1991-92; Honorary Fellow, Mekize Nirdamim Society, Jerusalem; British Association for Jewish Studies, ex-president, 1992; Society for Old Testament Study; Theological Society, Cambridge, ex-president, 2002-04. Address: Cambridge University Library, West Road, Cambridge CB3 9DR, England.

REINER Rob, b. 6 March 1947, New York, USA. Actor; Writer; Director. (1) Penny Marshall, 1971, divorced, (2) Michele Singer, 1989, 3 children. Education; University of California at Los Angeles. Career: Appeared with comic improvisation groups: The Session; The Committee; Scriptwriter for Enter Laughing, 1967; Halls of Anger, 1970; Where's Poppa, 1970; Summertree, 1971; Fire Sale, 1977; How Come Nobody's on Our Side, 1977; TV appearances: All in the Family, 1971-78; Free Country, 1978; Thursday's Game, 1974; More Than Friends, 1978; Million Dollar Infield, 1972; Director, This is Spinal Tap, 1984; The Sure Thing, 1985; Stand By Me, 1986; The Princess Bride, 1987; Misery, 1990; Co-producer, director, When Harry Met Sally, 1989; A Few Good Men, 1992; North, The American President, 1995; Ghosts of the Mississippi, 1996; The Story of Us, 1999; Alex and Emma, 2003; Rumor Has It ..., 2005; Everyone's Hero (voice), 2006; The Bucket List, 2007. Address: c/o Castle Rock Entertainment, 335 North Maple Drive, Suite 135, Beverly Hills, CA 90212, USA.

REITMAN Ivan, b. 27 October 1946, Komarno, Czechoslovakia. Film Director and Producer. m. Genevieve Robert, 1 son, 2 daughter. Education: MusB, McMaster University. Career: Producer, stage shows: The Magic Show, 1974; The National Lampoon Show, 1975; Merlin (also director), 1983; Director and Executive Producer, films: Cannibal Girls, 1973; They Came From Within, 1975; Death Weekend, 1977; Blackout, 1978; National Lampoon's Animal House, 1978; Heavy Metal, 1981; Stop! Or My Mom Will Shoot, 1992; Space Jam, 1996; Private Parts, 1996; Producer and Director: Foxy Lady, 1971; Meatballs, 1979; Stripes, 1981; Ghostbusters, 1984; Legal Eagles, 1986; Twins, 1988; Ghostbusters II, 1989; Kindergarten Cop, 1990; Dave, 1993; Junior, 1994; Executive Producer: Rabid, 1976; Spacehunter: Adventures in the Forbidden Zone, 1983; Big Shots, 1987; Casual Sex?, 1988; Feds, 1988; Beethoven, 1992; Beethoven's 2nd, 1993; Commandments, 1996; Road Trip, 2000; Evolution, 2001; Killing Me Softly, 2002; Old School, 2003; Eurotrip, 2004; Trailer Park Boys: The Movie, 2006;

Disturbia, 2007. Producer and director, TV series: The Late Shift, 1996; Father's Day, 1997. Membership: Director's Guild of America. Address: c/o CAA, 9830 Wilshire Boulevard, Beverly Hills, CA 90212, USA.

REMNICK David J, b. 29 October 1958, Hackensack, New Jersey, USA. Journalist; Writer. m. Esther B Fein, 2 sons, 1 daughter. Education: AB, Princeton University, 1981. Appointments: Reporter, Washington Post, 1982-91; Staff writer, 1992-, Editor-in-Chief, 1998-, The New Yorker. Publications: Lenin's Tomb: The Last Days of the Soviet Empire, 1993; The Devil Problem (and Other True Stories), 1996; Resurrection: The Struggle for a New Russia, 1997; King of the World: Muhammad Ali and the Rise of an American Hero, 1998; Life Stories: Profiles from The New Yorker (editor), 1999; Wonderful Town: Stories from The New Yorker (editor), 1999; Reporting: Writings from the New Yorker, 2006; Contributions to: Newspapers and periodicals. Honours: Livingston Award, 1991; Pulitzer Prize for General Non-Fiction, 1993; Helen Bernstein Award, New York Public Library, 1994; George Polk Award, 1994; Editor of the Year, 1999. Address: The New Yorker, Four Times Square, New York, NY 10036, USA.

RENDELL Ruth Barbara (Baroness Rendell of Babergh), (Barbara Vine), b. 17 February 1930, England. Writer. m. Donald Rendell, 1950, divorced 1975, 1 son, remarried Donald Rendell, 1977, deceased 1999. Publications: From Doon with Death, 1964; To Fear a Painted Devil, 1965; Vanity Dies Hard, 1966; A New Lease of Death, 1967; Wolf to the Slaughter, 1967 (televised 1987); The Secret House of Death, 1968; The Best Man to Die, 1969; A Guilty Thing Surprised, 1970; One Across Two Down, 1971; No More Dying Then, 1971; Murder Being Once Done, 1972; Some Lie and Some Die, 1973; The Face of Trespass, 1974 (televised as An Affair in Mind, 1988); Shake Hands for Ever, 1975; A Demon in My View, 1976 (film 1991); A Judgement in Stone, 1977; A Sleeping Life, 1978; Make Death Love Me, 1979; The Lake of Darkness, 1980 (televised as Dead Lucky, 1988); Put on by Cunning, 1981; Master of the Moor, 1982 (televised 1994); The Speaker of Mandarin, 1983; The Killing Doll, 1984; The Tree of Hands, 1984 (film 1989); An Unkindness of Ravens, 1985; Live Flesh, 1986; Heartstones, 1987; Talking to Strange Men, 1987; A Warning to the Curious: The Ghost Stories of M R James (editor), 1987; The Veiled One, 1988 (televised 1989); The Bridesmaid, 1989; Ruth Rendell's Suffolk, 1989; Going Wrong, 1990; Kissing the Gunner's Daughter, 1992; The Crocodile Bird, 1993; Simisola, 1994; The Reason Why (editor), 1995; Road Rage, 1997; A Sight for Sore Eyes, 1999; Harm Done, 1999; The Babes in the Wood, 2002; The Rottweiler, 2003; Thirteen Steps Down, 2004; End in Tears, 2005; The Water's Lovely, 2006; Not in the Flesh, 2007. As Barbara Vine: A Dark-Adapted Eye, 1986 (televised 1994); A Fatal Inversion, 1987 (televised 1992); The House of Stairs, 1988; Gallowglass, 1990; King Solomon's Carpet, 1981; Asta's Book, 1993; The Children of Men, 1994; No Night is Too Long, 1994; The Keys to the Street, 1997; The Brimstone Wedding, 1996; The Chimney Sweeper's Boy, 1998; Grasshopper, 2000; The Blood Doctor, 2002; The Minotaur, 2005; The Thief, 2006; The Birthday Present, 2008; Short Stories: The Fallen Curtain, 1976; Means of Evil, 1979; The Fever Tree, 1982; The New Girl Friend, 1985; Collected Short Stories, 1987; Undermining the Central Line (with Colin Ward), 1989; The Copper Peacock, 1991; Blood Lines, 1995; Piranha to Scurfy and Other Stories, 2000. Honours: Arts Council National Book Award for Genre Fiction, 1981; Royal Society of Literature, Fellow, 1988; Sunday Times Award for Literary Excellence, 1990; Cartier Diamond Dagger Award,

Crime Writers Association, 1991; Commander of the Order of the British Empire, 1996; Life Peerage, 1997. Memberships: Royal Society of Literature, Fellow. Address: 26 Cornwall Terrace Mews, London, NW1 5LL, England.

RENFREW (Andrew) Colin (Baron Renfrew of Kaimsthorn), b. 25 July 1937, Stockton-on-Tees, England. Educator; Archaeologist; Author. m. Jane M Ewbank, 1965, 2 sons, 1 daughter. Education: St John's College, Cambridge; BA Honours, 1962, MA, 1964, PhD, 1965, ScD, 1976, Cambridge University; British School of Archaeology, Athens. Appointments: Lecturer, 1965-70, Senior Lecturer in Prehistory and Archaeology, 1970-72, Reader, 1972, University of Sheffield; Head of Department, Professor of Archaeology, University of Southampton, 1972-81; Head of Department, Disney Professor of Archaeology, University of Cambridge, 1981-2004; Master, 1986-97, Professor Fellow, 1997-2004, Emeritus Fellow, 2004-, Jesus College, Cambridge; Director, 1990-2004, Fellow, 2004-, McDonald Institute for Archaeological Research; Guest Lecturer, universities, colleges; Narrator, television films, radio programmes, British Broadcasting Corporation. Publications include: The Emergence of Civilisation: The Cyclades and the Aegean in the Third Millennium BC, 1972; Before Civilisation: The Radiocarbon Revolution and Prehistoric Europe, 1973; Problems in European Prehistory, 1979; Approaches to Social Archaeology, 1984; The Archaeology of Cult: The Sanctuary at Phylakopi, 1985; Archaeology and Language: The Puzzle of Indo-European Origins, 1988; The Idea of Prehistory, co-author, 1988; Archaeology: Theories, Methods, and Practice, co-author, 1991, 2nd edition, 1996; The Cycladic Spirit: Masterpieces from the Nicholas P Goulandris Collection, 1991; The Ancient Mind: Elements of Cognitive Archaeology, co-editor, 1994; Loot, Legitimacy and Ownership, 2000; Archaeogenetics (editor), 2000; Contributor to: Journals including Archaeology; Scientific American. Honours: Rivers Memorial Medal, Royal Anthropological Institute, 1979; Fellow, St John's College, Cambridge, 1981-86; Sir Joseph Larmor Award, 1981; DLitt, Sheffield University, 1987; Huxley Memorial Medal and Life Peerage, 1991; Honorary Degree, University of Athens, 1991; DLitt, University of Southampton, 1995; Foreign Associate, National Academy of Sciences, USA, 1997; Fyssen Prize, 1997; Language and Culture Prize, University of Umeå, Sweden, 1998; Rivers Memorial Medal, European Science Foundation Latsis Prize, 2003; Bolzan Prize, 2004. Memberships include: Fellow, British Academy; Ancient Monuments Board for England, 1974-84; Royal Commission on Historical Monuments, 1977-87; Historic Buildings and Monuments Commission for England, 1984-86; Ancient Monuments Advisory Committee, 1984-; British National Commission for UNESCO, 1984-86; Trustee, British Museum, 1991-. Address: McDonald Institute for Archaeological Research, Downing Street, Cambridge, CB2 3ER, England.

RENO Janet, b. 21 July 1938, Miami, Florida, USA. Lawyer. Education: BA, Cornell University; LLB, Harvard University. Appointments: Florida Bar, 1963; Associate, Brigham & Brigham, 1963-67; Partner, Lewis & Reno, 1971-72; Administrative Assistant State Attorney, 11th Judicial Circuit Florida, Miami, 1973-76, State Attorney, 1978-93; Partner, Steel, Hector & Davis, Miami, 1976-78; US Attorney-General, 1993-2001. Memberships: American Bar Association; American Law Institute; American Judicature Society. Honours: Women First Award, YWCA, 1993; National Women's Hall of Fame, 2000. Address: Department of Justice, 10th Street and Constitution Avenue, NW Washington, DC 20530, USA.

RENO Jean, b. 30 July 1948, Casablanca, Morocco. Actor. m. (1) divorced, 1 son, 1 daughter, (2) Nathalie Dyszkiewicz, 1996-200, (divorced) 1 son, 1 daughter; (3) Zofia Borucka, 2006. Career: Films: Clair de Femme, 1979; Le Dernier Combat, 1983; Signes Extérieurs de Richesse, 1983; Notre Histoire, 1984; Subway, 1985; I Love You, 1986; The Big Blue, 1988; L'Homme au Masque d'Or, 1990; La Femme Nikita, 1991; L'Operation Corned Beef, 1991; Loulou Graffitti, 1991; The Visitors (also wrote screenplay), 1993; Leon, 1994; French Kiss, 1995; Roseanna's Grave, 1997; Les Couloirs du Temps, 1998; Godzilla, 1998; Les Rivieres pourpres, 2000; Just Visiting, 2001; Wasabi, 2001; Decalage horaire, 2002; Rollerball, 2002; Tais-toi, 2003; Les Rivieres pourpres 2 – Les anges de l'apocalypse, 2004; Onimusha 3, 2004; L'Enquête corse, 2004; Hotel Rwanda, 2004; L'Empire des loups, 2005; The Pink Panther, 2005; The Tiger and the Snow, 2005; The Da Vinci Code, 2006; Flyboys, 2006; Flushed Away (voice), 2006; Margaret, 2007; Cash, 2008. Honours: National Order of Merit (France), 2003. Address: Chez Les Films du Dauphin, 25 rue Yves-Toudic, 75010 Paris, France.

RESENDE Marcelo, b. 26 August 1963, Rio de Janeiro, Brazil. Researcher; Lecturer. Education: BA, Economics, 1985, BS, Psychology, 1990, State University of Rio de Janeiro; MSc, Pontifical Catholic University, 1989; MA, Economics, University of Pennsylvania, 1993; DPhil, Economics, University of Oxford, 1997. Appointments: Lecturer, Pontifical Catholic University, 1987-89; Assistant Professor, State University of Rio de Janeiro, 1990; Assistant Professor, 1990-98, Associate Professor, 1998-, Federal University of Rio de Janeiro; Visiting Fellow, European University Institute, Italy, 2005-06. Publications: Several articles in professional journals. Honours include: Listed in Who's Who and biographical publications; Scholarships, Ministry of Science and Technology and Ministry of Education, Brazil. Membership: Brazilian Society of Econometrics. Address: Av Pasteur 250, URCA, 22290-240 Rio de Janeiro, Brazil. Email: mresende@ie.ufrj.br

RESIN Vladimir Iosifovich, b. 21 February 1936, Minsk, Belarus. Government Official. m. Marta Yakovlevna Chadayeva, 1 daughter. Education: Graduate, Moscow Mining Institute, 1958. Appointments: USSR Ministry of the Coal Industry and USSR Ministry of Assembly and Special Construction, 1958; Construction sites in the regions of Murmansk, Kaluga and Smolensk; Deputy Head, Glavmosinzhstroi (Main Moscow Engineering Construction Administration), 1974-85; Chairman, Moscow Construction Committee, 1989-91; Vice Chairman, Moscow Municipal Executive Committee, 1989-91; Vice Premier, Moscow Government, 1991-92; First Vice Premier, Moscow Government and Head, Prospective Development Complex (later Complex of Architecture, Construction, Development & Reconstruction of the City – CACDR, 1999-), 1992-; First Deputy Mayor, Government of Moscow City and Head of the Complex (CACDR), 2000-; Doctor of Economic Sciences, Professor and Head of the Chair, Plekhanov Russian Academy of Economics; Honorary Professor, Moscow State Lomonosov University and Moscow International University; Academician, Russian Academy of Architecture and Construction Sciences; Actual Fellow, 13 Russian and International specialised academies. Publications: 90 scientific articles; 12 books and monographs; 33 inventions. Honours: 22 USSR and Russian Federation State Prizes including the Rank III Order for Service to the Fatherland; 4 Russian Orthodox Church orders; 59 awards of different public organisations; Distinguished Builder of the Russian Federation; Honored Builder of the Russian Federation; Honored Builder of Russia and Moscow; Renowned Engineer of Russia; Laureate of the USSR State Prize; Twice Laureate of the Russian Federation Prize; Winner of the USSR Council of Ministers' Prize; Winner of the Russian Federation President's Prize; Laureate of the Russian Federation Government Prize; Several large gold and silver medals of the International Engineering Academy; V G Shukhov Gold Medal; Memorable Medal, International Scientific Academy; 6 gold and 5 silver medals, URRS VDNKh (Exhibition of Economic Achievements) and All-Russia Exhibition Center. Memberships: Board Member, Russian Employers' and Industrials Union; Presidium of Academy of Architecture and Construction Sciences; Chairman, Moscow Division of the Russian Community of Civil Engineers. Address: c/o Complex of Architecture, Construction, Development & Reconstruction of the City, Government of Moscow, Nikitsky per 5, R-103009 Moscow, Russia.

RETNEV Vladimir Mikhailovich, b. 4 May 1926, Yaroslavl, Russia. Professor, Occupational Medicine. m. Retneva Elena Nickolaevna, 1 son, 1 daughter. Education: Doctor of Medicine, 1965. Appointments: Doctor, Occupational Medicine, 1950-51; Postgraduate Course, 1951-54; Assistant, 1954-59, Lecturer, 1963-68, Professor, 1968-74, Head, 1974-94, Professor, 1994-, Occupational Health Department, Saint Petersburg Medical Academy of Postgraduate Education; Deputy Director of Research, Scientific Research Institute of Industrial Hygiene and Occupational Diseases, 1959-63; St Petersburg Medical Academy of Postgraduate Studies, 1965-76. Publications: About 600 articles, including 18 monographs and guidelines. Honours: Professor; Honoured Scientist; Numerous orders and medals of Russia. Memberships: Academician, International Academy of Sciences in Ecology and Safe Lifestyle; Academician, Russian Academy of Natural Sciences. Address: 195027, PO Box N10, Saint Petersburg, Russia.

REYMOND Claude Jean-Marie, b. 21 November 1923, Yverdon, Switzerland. Professor of Law. m. Claire, deceased 1995, 2 sons, 1 daughter. Education: Diploma, State Classical College, Lausanne, Switzerland 1941; Dr en droit (LLM), 1948; State Bar Examination, 1950. Appointments: Partner, 1952-76, Senior Partner, 1979-96, of Counsel, 1996-2002, Baudat et Reymond, Barristers and Solicitors; Professor, Lausanne University School of Economics, 1965-82; Associate Professor, Geneva University School of Law, 1971-89; Professor Emeritus, Lausanne University, 1982. Publications: Essai sur l'acte fiduciaire, 1948; Le trust et le droit suisse, 1955; Co-author, Swiss National and International Arbitration Law, 1989; Numerous articles on commercial law and the law of arbitration. Honours: Holder of Paul Foriers Chair, Free University of Brussels, School of Law, 1983; Correspondant de L'Institut de France, Académie des Sciences morales et politiques, 2001; Prix de l'Université de Lausanne, 2002. Memberships include: Vaud and Swiss Lawyers Associations; International Law Association; Comité français de droit international privé; Chartered Institute of Arbitrators, London. Address: 15 chemin de Passiaux, CH-1008 Prilly, Switzerland. E-mail: reymond@grand-chene.ch

REYNDERS Didier, b. 4 August 1958, Liège, France. Deputy Prime Minister; Minister of Finance. m. Bernadette Prignon, 2 sons, 2 daughters. Education: Degree in Law, University of Liège, 1981. Appointments: Director General, Local Authorities Department of the Ministry of the Walloon Region, 1985-88; Chief of Staff of the Deputy Prime Minister, Minister of Justice and of Institutional reforms, Mr Jean Gol, 1987-88; Chairman, Societe Nationale des Chemin de fer belges (SNCB-NMBS), 1986-91; Member, Liège Town Council, 1988; Leader, PRL group, Provincial Council of Liège, 1991; Chairman, National Society of Airways, 1991-93; Chairman, Board of Directors of the SEFB Record Bank, 1992-99; Deputy Chairman, PRL, 1992; Member of Parliament, 1992; Chairman of the group PRL-FDF group, 1995; Leader, PRL group, Liège, 1995-; Chairman, Provincial and District PRL Federation (later the MR), 1995; Minister of Finance, 1999-; Chair, Euro group and Ecofin, 2001; Chair, G10, 2002-; Deputy Prime Minister, 2004-; President, Mouvement Réformateur, 2004-.

REYNOLDS Albert, b. 3 November 1935, Rooskey, County Roscommon, Ireland. Politician; Company Director. m. Kathleen Coén, 2 sons, 5 daughters. Education: Notre Dame University; Stoney Hill College, Boston; National University of Ireland; University of Philadelphia, Jesuits; University of Melbourne; University of Aberdeen. Appointments include: Company Director, own family business: C&D Foods, Edgeworthstown, Co Longford, Ireland; Director, many Irish and international companies; Political Career: Entered national politics, 1977, Elected to Dáil; Minister for Posts and Telegraphs and Transport, 1979-81; Minister for Industry and Energy, 1982; Minister for Industry and Commerce, 1987-88; Minister for Finance and Public Service, 1988-89; Minister of Finance, 1989-91; Vice-President, 1983-92, President, 1992-94, Fianna Fáil Party; Elected Taoiseach (PM), 1992-94; Chair, Bula Resources, 1999-2002, Longford Recreational Devt Centre. Memberships: Board of Governors: European Investment Bank; World Bank International Monetary Fund. Honour: Hon LLD (University College, Dublin), 1995. Address: Leinster House, Dáil Éirann, Kildare Street, Dublin 2, Ireland.

REYNOLDS Graham, b. 10 January 1914, Highgate, London, England. Writer; Art Historian. Education: BA, Honours, Queens' College, Cambridge. Publications: Nicholas Hilliard and Isaac Oliver, 1947, 2nd edition, 1971; English Portrait Miniatures, 1952, revised edition, 1988; Painters of the Victorian Scene, 1953; Catalogue of the Constable Collection, Victoria and Albert Museum, 1960, revised edition, 1973; Constable, The Natural Painter, 1965; Victorian Painting, 1966, revised edition, 1987; Turner, 1969; Concise History of Watercolour Painting, 1972; Catalogue of Portrait Miniatures, Wallace Collection, 1980; The Later Paintings and Drawings of John Constable, 2 volumes, 1984; English Watercolours, 1988; The Earlier Paintings of John Constable, 2 volumes, 1996; Catalogue of European Portrait Miniatures, Metropolitan Museum of Art, New York, 1996; The Miniatures in the Collection of H.M. the Queen, The Sixteenth and Seventeenth Centuries, 1999. Contributions to: Times Literary Supplement; Burlington Magazine; Apollo; New Departures. Honours: Mitchell Prize, 1984; Officer of the Order of the British Empire, 1984; Commander of the Victorian Order, 2000; British Academy, Fellow, 1993; Honorary Keeper of Miniatures, Fitzwilliam Museum, Cambridge, 1994. Address: The Old Manse, Bradfield St George, Bury St Edmunds, Suffolk IP30 0AZ, England.

REYNOLDS Keith Ronald, (Kev Reynolds), b. 7 December 1943, Ingatestone, Essex, England. Author; Photojournalist; Lecturer. m. Linda Sylvia Dodsworth, 23 September 1967, 2 daughters. Publications: Walks and Climbs in the Pyrenees, 1978, 3rd edition, 1993; Mountains of the Pyrenees, 1982; The Weald Way and Vanguard Way, 1987; Walks in the Engadine, 1988; The Valais, 1988; Walking in Kent, 1988; Classic Walks in the Pyrenees, 1989; Classic Walks in Southern England, 1989; The Jura, 1989; South Downs Way, 1989; Eye on the

Hurricane, 1989; The Mountains of Europe, 1990; Visitors Guide to Kent, 1990; The Cotswold Way, 1990; Alpine Pass Route, 1990; Classic Walks in the Alps, 1991; Chamonix to Zermatt, 1991; The Bernese Alps, 1992; Walking in Ticino, 1992; Central Switzerland, 1993; Annapurna, A Trekkers' Guide, 1993; Walking in Kent, Vol II, 1994; Everest, A Trekkers' Guide, 1995; Langtang: A Trekkers Guide, 1996; Tour of the Vanoise, 1996; Walking in the Alps, 1998; Kangchenjunga: A Trekkers' Guide, 1999; Walking in Sussex, 2000; 100 Hut Walks in the Alps, 2000; Manaslu: A Trekkers' Guide, 2000; Tour of Mont Blanc, 2002; Alpine Points of View, 2004; The Pyrenees, 2004; Tour of The Jungfrau Region, 2006. Contributions to: The Great Outdoors; Climber and Hill Walker; Environment Now; Trail Walker; Country Walking; High. Membership: Outdoor Writers' Guild. Address: Little Court Cottage, Froghole, Crockham Hill, Edenbridge, Kent TN8 6TD, England.

REYNOLDS Vernon, b. 14 December 1935, Berlin, Germany. Professor Emeritus, Oxford University. m. Frances Glover, 5 November 1960, 1 son, 1 daughter. Education: BA, PhD, London University; MA, Oxford University. Publications: Budongo: A Forest and its Chimpanzees, 1965; The Apes, 1967; The Biology of Human Action, 1976, 2nd edition, 1980; The Biology of Religion (with R Tanner), 1983; Primate Behaviour: Information, Social Knowledge and the Evolution of Culture (with D Quiatt), 1993; The Chimpanzees of the Budongo Forest, 2005. Address: Orchard House, West Street, Alfriston, East Sussex BN26 5UX, England.

REZNIK Nadezhda I, b. 26 September 1945, Svobodny, Russia. Physicist; Methodologist. m. Alexander Reznik, 2 sons, 2 daughters. Education: Graduate, Physics, Far East State University, 1969; PhD, Candidate, State Pedagogical University, Chelyabinsk, 1989, Moscow, 1990; Docent, Radioelectronics, State Education Committee, Moscow, 1992; Certificate, International Association of Humanistic Psychology, San Francisco, CA/Moscow, Russia, 1994; Doctor of Pedagogical Science, State Higher Attestation Committee, Moscow, 1997; Professor of Radioelectronics, Ministry of General Education, Moscow, Russian Federation, 1998. Appointments: Engineer, 1969-70, Lecturer, 1970-90, Assistant Professor, 1990-97, Professor, 1997-99, Department of Radio Electronics, Pacific Higher Naval Academy, Vladivostok, Russia; Consultant Professor, Institute of New Forms of Education, Tel Aviv Branch, Israel, 1999-2001; Scientific Research Worker, Ben Gurion University of the Negev, Israel, 2001-. Publications: Over 70 publications in pedagogy and psychology of education, methodology and methods of education, among which: 2 monographs, 2 manuals; Invariant Basis of Intersubject and Innersubject Connections: Methodological and Methodical Aspects (monograph), 1998; Co-ordination of educational systems: Psychological aspects (journal article), 2003. Honours: Award for Excellence in the field of higher education, Moscow, 1991; Grant and Bonus as a best teacher on behalf of the Governor, Primorsk Region, 1997. Memberships: Editorial Council of the Science, Culture, Education Journal, Ministry of Higher Education; Science Council on Doctoral Theses, Far East Technical University; Maslan Women's Support Centre; Israel Crisis Centre; Fund for Needy Immigrants, Israel. Address: Lui Pikard Street 38/9, Be'er Sheva, Israel 84710. E-mail: nadreznik@hotmail.com

RHEE Chang Kyu, b. 21 June 1960, Seoul, Korea. Researcher. m. Soo Kyung Kim, 1 son, 1 daughter. Education: BS, Hanyang University, Seoul, 1983; MS, 1985, PhD, 1992, Korea Advanced Institute of Science and Technology,

Daejeon. Appointments: Head, Nuclear Nano Materials Development Laboratory, Korean Atomic Energy Research Institute, 1985-; Researcher, University of British Columbia, Canada, 1995-97. Publications: 286 articles in international and domestic journals; 28 research reports; 17 patents. Honours: Patented Tech Prize, Korea Intellectual Properties Office. Memberships: Korea Nuclear Society; Korea Institute of Metals and Materials; Korea Powder Metallurgy Institute; Korea institute of Military Science and Technology; Listed in national and international biographical dictionaries. Address: 150 Dukjin, Yusong, Daejeon 305-353, Korea. E-mail: ckrhee@kaeri.re.kr

RHODES Richard (Lee), b. 4 July 1937, Kansas City, Kansas, USA. Writer. m. Ginger Untrif, 1993, 2 children by previous marriage. Education: BA, cum laude, Yale University, 1959. Publications: Non-Fiction: The Inland Ground, 1970; The Ozarks, 1974; Looking for America, 1979; The Making of the Atomic Bomb, 1988; A Hole in the World, 1990; Making Love, 1992; Dark Sun, 1995; How to Write, 1995; Deadly Feasts, 1997; Trying to get some Dignity (with Ginger Rhodes), 1996; Visions of Technology, 1999; Why They Kill, 1999; Masters of Death, 2001; John James Audobon, 2004; Arsenals of Folly: The making of the nuclear arms race, 2007; Fiction: The Ungodly, 1973; Holy Secrets, 1978; The Last Safari, 1980; Sons of Earth, 1981. Contributions to: Numerous journals and magazines. Honours: National Book Award in Non-Fiction, 1987; National Book Critics Circle Award in Non-Fiction, 1987; Pulitzer Prize in Non-Fiction, 1988. Membership: Authors Guild. Address: c/o Janklow and Nesbit Associates, 455 Park Avenue, New York, NY 10021, USA.

RHODES Zandra Lindsey, b. 19 September 1940. Fashion Designer. Education: Royal College of Art. Career: Designer (textile, 1964-); Print Factory/Studio with A McIntyre, 1965; Fashion Industry, 1966-; Produced dresses from own prints in partnership with S Ayton, shop on Fulham Rd, 1967-68; US solo collection, 1969; annual fantasy shows in US, founded Zandra Rhodes (UK) Ltd; with A Knight & R Stirling, 1975-86; now world-wide, currently works in: interior furnishings, fine art with various collections in US and England, Speaker. Publications: The Art of Zandra Rhodes, 1984; The Zandra Rhodes Collection by Brother, 1988. Honours include: English Designer of the Year, 1972; Emmy for Best Costume (Romeo and Juliet, US, 1984); Lifetime Achievement at the British Fashion Awards, 1995; CBE, 1997. Address: 79-85 Bermondsey Street, London, SE1 3XF, England.

RHYS David Garel, b. 28 February 1940, Swansea, Wales. Economist. m. Charlotte Mavis, 1 son, 2 daughters. Education: University of Wales, Swansea; University of Birmingham. Appointments: Lecturer and Assistant Lecturer, University of Hull; Lecturer and Senior Lecturer, University College, Cardiff; Professor of Motor Industry Economics and Director of the Centre for Automotive Research, Cardiff University Business School; Emeritus Professor, Cardiff University, 2005; Chairman, Welsh Automotive Forum; Chairman, Economic Research Advisory Panel of the Welsh Assembly Government. Publications: The Motor Industry: An Economic Survey, 1972; The Motor Industry in the European Community, 1989; Contributions to: Journal of Industrial Economics; Journal of Transport History; Journal of Transport Economics; Bulletin of Economic Research; Scottish Journal of Political Economy; Journal of Economic Studies; Journal of Accounting and Business Research; World Economics. Honours: OBE, 1989; Castrol – IMI Gold Medal, 1989; Welsh Communicator of the Year, 1993; Neath Port Talbot Business

Award, 1999; Motortrader Outstanding Achievement in the Motor Trade, 2001; Honorary Fellow, University of Wales Swansea Institute, 2003. Memberships: Royal Automobile Club, Pall Mall; Fellow, Royal Society for Arts Commerce and Manufacture; Fellow, Institute of Transport Administration; President, Institute of the Motor Industry; Freeman of the City of London and Liveryman, Carmen's Company, C.B.E. 2007, Listed in biographical dictionaries. Address: Cardiff University Business School, Aberconway Building, Colum Drive, Cardiff CF10 3EU, Wales. E-mail: rhysg@cardiff.ac.uk

RHYS Sylvia Marjorie, b. 1 August 1932, Wellingborough, England. University Course Tutor; Counsellor. Divorced, 1 son. Education: BA (Hons), Geography, London School of Economics, 1953; Postgraduate Diploma in Social Sciences, 1965, MSc (Econ.), Social Research: Theory and Method, 1983, University of Wales; Diploma in Counselling, Gwent College of Higher Education, 1984. Appointments: Secretary to Administrator, Joseph Lucas Research Laboratories, 1954-55; Technical Writer, British Thomson-Houston Co Ltd, 1955-57; Tutorial Assistant, Cardiff University, 1965-72; Research Officer, University of Wales, Swansea, 1983-85; Course Tutor and Counsellor, Open University, 1972-. Publications: Articles: The Process of Marking Tutor-Marked Assignments: The Tutor in Action, 1975; Interaction in Tutorials: Tutorial Styles and Tutor Assumptions (with C Lambert), 1983; Study Skills and Personal Development, 1988; Book: Guidance and Counselling in Adult and Continuing Education (with R Woolfe and S Murgatroyd), 1987; Book Chapters: Mastery and Sympathy in Nursing, in Progress in Reversal Theory (editors: M J Apter, J H Kerr, M P Cowles), 1988; Training Student Health Visitors in Helping Skills, in Experiential Training (editor T Hobbs), 1992; Dilemmas? Focus on some potentially contending forces underlying the process of improving the quality of student learning, in Improving Student Learning: Theory and Practice (editor G Gibbs), 1994. Memberships: Society for Research into Higher Education; British Association for Counselling and Psychotherapy.

RIBBANS William John, b. 28 November 1954, Northampton, England. Orthopaedic Surgeon. m. Sian Williams, 3 daughters. Education: BSc, 1977, MB BS, 1980, Royal Free Hospital School of Medicine; MChOrth, University of Liverpool, 1990; FRCSEd, 1985; FRCSOrth, 1990; PhD, 2003; FFSEM (UK), 2006. Appointments: Orthopaedic Consultant, Royal Free Hospital, London, 1991-96; Northampton General Hospital, 1996-. Honour: Professor of School of Health, The University of Northampton. Address: Department of Orthopaedic Surgery, Northampton General Hospital, Northampton NN1 5BD, England. E-mail: wjribbans@uk-consultants.co.uk

RICCI Cristina, b. 12 February 1980, Santa Monica, California, USA. Film Actress. Career: Actor in commercials then in films: Mermaids, 1990; The Hard Way, 1991; The Addams Family, 1991; The Cemetery Club, 1993; Addams Family Values, 1993; Casper, 1995; Now and Then, 1995; Gold Diggers: The Secret of Bear Mountain, 1995; That Darn Cat, 1996; Last of the High Kings, 1996; Bastard Out of Carolina, 1996; Ice Storm, 1997; Little Red Riding Hood, 1997; Fear and Loathing in Las Vegas, 1998; Desert Blue, 1998; Buffalo 66, 1998; The Opposite Sex, 1998; Small Soldiers, 1998; Pecker, 1999; 200 Cigarettes, 1999; Sleepy Hollow, 1999; The Man Who Cried, 2000; Monster, 2003; Cursed, 2005; Penelope, 2006; Black Snake Moan, 2006; Home of the Brave, 2006; Speed Racer, 2008. Address: c/o ICM, 8942 Wilshire Boulevard, Beverly Hills, CA 90211, USA.

RICE Condoleezza, b. 14 November 1954, Birmingham, Alabama, USA. Government Official; Academic. Education: University of Denver; University of Notre Dame. Appointments: Teacher, 1981-2001, Provost, 1993-99; Currently Hoover Senior Fellow and Professor of Political Science, Stanford University, California; Special Assistant to Director of Joint Chiefs of Staff, 1986; Director, then Senior Director, Soviet and East European Affairs, National Security Council, 1989-91; Special Assistant to President for National Security Affairs, 1989-91; Primary Foreign Policy Adviser to Presidential Candidate, George W Bush, 1999-2000; Assistant to President for National Security Affairs and National Security Advisor, 2001-04; Secretary of State, 2004-. Publications: Uncertain Allegiance: The Soviet Union and the Czechoslovak Army, 1984; The Gorbachev Era (co-author), 1986; Germany Unified and Europe Transformed (co-author), 1995; numerous articles on Soviet and East European foreign and defence policy. Honours: Dr hc (Morehouse College) 1991, (University of Alabama) 1994, (University of Notre Dame) 1995, (Mississippi College School of Law) 2003, (University of Louisville) 2004. Memberships: Board of Directors: Chevron Corporation; Charles Schwab Corporation; William and Flora Hewlett Foundation; numerous other boards; Senior Fellow, Institute for International Studies, Stanford; Fellow, American Academy of Arts and Sciences. Address: Department of State, 2201 C Street, NW, Washington, DC 20520, USA. Website: www.state.gov

RICE Susan Ilene, b. 7 March 1946, Providence, Rhode Island, USA. Banker. m. C Duncan Rice, 2 sons, 1 daughter. Education: BA, Wellesley College; M Litt, Aberdeen University. Appointments: Medical Researcher, Yale University Medical School, 1970-73; Dean of Saybrook College, Yale University, 1973-79; Staff Aide to the President, Hamilton College, 1980-81; Dean of Students, Colgate University, 1981-86; Senior Vice President, NatWest Bancorp, 1986-96; Head of Branch Banking, then Managing Director, Personal Banking, Bank of Scotland, 1997-2000; Chief Executive, Lloyds TSB, Scotland, 2000-; Member, HM Treasury Policy Action Team on Access to Financial Services, 1997-2000; Member, Aberdeen Common Purpose Advisory Board, 1999-2006; Member, Foresight Sub-Committee on Retail Financial Services, 2000; Trustee, David Hume Institute, 2000-05; Member, Scottish Advisory Task Force on the New Deal, 2000-05; Chair, Edinburgh International Book Festival, 2001-; Treasurer, The March Dialogue, 2001-04; Director, Scottish Business in the Community, 2001-; Director, UK Charity Bank, 2001-08; Chair, Advisory Committee of the Scottish Centre for Research on Social Justice, 2002-; Member, BP Scottish Advisory Board, 2002-2003; Director, Scottish and Southern Energy plc, 2003-; Member, HMT Financial Inclusion Taskforce, 2005-; Director, Scotland's Futures Forum, 2005-; Director, Bank of England, 2007-; Chair, Edinburgh Festivals Forum, 2008-. Publications: Articles on banking, insurance, business, marketing, diversity, corporate responsibility and financial exclusion published in The Scotsman, The Herald, Scotland on Sunday, Insurance Day, New Statesman, Finance Ethics Quarterly, Scottish Banker, Scottish Homes, Business AM, Holyrood Magazine, Business Insider Magazine, Being Scottish and in the proceedings of several conferences; Co-author of several articles published in medical journals, early 1970's. Honours: CBE; Chartered Banker; FCIBS; CCMI; FRSA; FRSE; Spirit of Scotland Annual Business Award, 2002; Corporate Elite Business Award, 2002; Logica Business Leadership Award, Scotland, 2007; HRH Ambassador for Corporate Responsibility in Scotland, 2005-2006; President, cdfa, 2007-; DBA (Hon), The Robert Gordon University; Dr honoris causa, Edinburgh University;

DLitt (Hon), Heriot Watt University; DUniv (Hon), Paisley University; DUniv (Hon), Glasgow University; DUniv (Hon), Queen Margaret University. Address: Lloyds TSB Scotland, Henry Duncan House, 120 George Street, Edinburgh EH2 4TS, Scotland. E-mail: susan.rice@lloydstsb.co.uk

RICE Tim (Sir) (Miles Bindon), b. 10 November 1944, Amersham, Buckinghamshire, England. Songwriter; Broadcaster. m. Jane Artereta McIntosh, 1974, 1 son, 1 daughter. Education: Lancing College. Career: EMI Records, 1966-68; Norrie Paramor Organisation, 1968-69; Founder, Director, GRRR Books Ltd, 1978-, Pavilion Books Ltd, 1981-97. Appearances on TV and radio including Just A Minute, Radio 4; Creative Works: Lyrics for stage musicals (with Andrew Lloyd Webber): Joseph and the Amazing Technicolor Dreamcoat, 1968; Jesus Christ Superstar, 1970; Evita, 1976; Cricket, 1986; Other musicals: Blondel, with Stephen Oliver, 1983; Chess, with Benny Andersson and Bjorn Ulvaeus, 1984; Tycoon, with Michel Berger, 1992; Selection of songs, Beauty and the Beast, with Alan Menken, 1994; Heathcliff, with John Farrar, 1996; King David, with Alan Menken, 1997; Aida, with Elton John, 1998; Lyrics for musical films: Aladdin, with Alan Menken, 1992; The Lion King, with Elton John, 1994, theatre version, 1997; Aida, with Elton John, 1998; El Dorado, with Elton John, 1999; Lyrics for songs with other composers including Paul McCartney, Mike Batt, Freddie Mercury, Graham Gouldman, Marvin Hamlisch, Rick Wakeman, John Barry. Publications: Songbooks from musicals; Co-author of over 20 books in the series Guinness Book of British Hit Singles, Albums, etc; Fill Your Soul, 1994; Cricket Writer, National Newspapers and Cricket Magazines; Treasures of Lords, 1989; Oh, What a Circus, autobiography, 1995. Honours: Oscar, Golden Globe, Best New Song, A Whole New World, 1992, for Can You Feel The Love Tonight, with Elton John, 1994, and for You Must Love Me with Andrew Lloyd Webber, 1996; Gold and platinum records in numerous countries; 11 Ivor Novello Awards; 2 Tony Awards; 5 Grammy Awards; Kt, 1994. Memberships: Chairman, Stars Organisation for Spastics, 1983-85; Shaftesbury Avenue Centenary Committee, 1984-86; President, Lords Taverners, 1988-90; Dramatists' Saints and Sinners, Chairman, 1990; Cricket Writers; Foundation for Sport and the Arts, 1991-; Garrick Club; Groucho Club; Main Committee, 1992-94, 1995-, President, 2002-03, MCC. Address: c/o Lewis & Golden, 40 Queen Anne Street, London, W1M 0EL, England.

RICH Adrienne (Cecile), b. 16 May 1929, Baltimore, Maryland, USA. Poet; Writer. m. Alfred H Conrad, 1953, deceased 1970, 3 sons. Education: AB, Radcliffe College, 1951. Appointments: Visiting Poet, Swarthmore College, 1966-68; Adjunct Professor, Columbia University, 1967-69; Lecturer, 1968-70, Instructor, 1970-71, Assistant Professor, 1971-72, Professor, 1974-75, City College of New York; Fannie Hurst Visiting Professor, Brandeis University, 1972-73; Professor of English, Douglass College, New Brunswick, New Jersey, 1976-78; A D White Professor-at-Large, Cornell University, 1981-85; Clark Lecturer and Distinguished Visiting Professor, Scripps College, Claremont, California, 1983; Visiting Professor, San Jose State University, California, 1985-86; Burgess Lecturer, Pacific Oaks College, Pasadena, California, 1986; Professor of English and Feminist Studies, Stanford University, 1986-94; Board of Chancellors, Academy of American Poets, 1989-91; Clark Lecturer, Trinity College, Cambridge, 2002. Publications: Poetry: A Change of World, 1951; (Poems), 1952; The Diamond Cutters and Other Poems, 1955; Snapshots of a Daughter-in-Law: Poems 1954-1962, 1963; Necessities of Life: Poems 1962-1965,

1966; Selected Poems, 1967; Leaflets: Poems 1965-1968, 1969; The Will to Change: Poems 1968-1970, 1971; Diving into the Wreck: Poems 1971-1972, 1973; Poems Selected and New, 1975; Twenty-One Love Poems, 1976; The Dream of a Common Language: Poems 1974-1977, 1978; A Wild Patience Has Taken Me This Far: Poems 1978-1981, 1981; Sources, 1983; The Fact of a Doorframe: Poems Selected and New 1950-1984, 1984; Your Native Land, Your Life, 1986; Time's Power: Poems 1985-1988, 1989; An Atlas of the Difficult World: Poems 1988-1991, 1991; Collected Early Poems 1950-1970, 1993; Dark Fields of the Republic: Poems 1991-95, 1995; Midnight Salvage: Poems 1995-1998, 1999; Arts of the Possible: Essays and Conversations, 2001; Fox: Poems 1998-2000, 2001; The Fact of a Doorframe: Poems 1950-2000, 2002; The School Among the Ruins: Poems, 2000-04, 2004; Poetry and Commitment, 2007; Telephone Ringing in the Labyrinth, 2007. Other: Of Woman Born: Motherhood as Experience and Institution, 1976; On Lies, Secrets and Silence: Selected Prose 1966-1978, 1979; Blood, Bread and Poetry: Selected Prose 1979-1985, 1986; What Is Found There: Notebooks on Poetry and Politics, 1993, revised 2003; Arts of the Possible: Essays and Conversations, 2001. Honours: Yale Series of Younger Poets Award, 1951; Guggenheim Fellowships, 1952, 1961; American Academy of Arts and Letters Award, 1961; Bess Hokin Prize, 1963; Eunice Tietjens Memorial Prize, 1968; National Endowment for the Arts Grant, 1970; Shelley Memorial Award, 1971; Ingram Merrill Foundation Grant, 1973; National Book Award, 1974; Fund for Human Dignity Award, 1981; Ruth Lilly Prize, 1986; Brandeis University Creative Arts Award, 1987; Elmer Holmes Bobst Award, 1989; Commonwealth Award in Literature, 1991; Frost Silver Medal, Poetry Society of America, 1992; Los Angeles Times Book Award, 1992; Lenore Marshall/ Nation Award, 1992; William Whitehead Award, 1992; Lambda Book Award, 1992; Harriet Monroe Prize, 1994; John D and Catharine T MacArthur Foundation Fellowship, 1994; Academy of American Poets Dorothea Tanning Award, 1996; Lannan Foundation Lifetime Achievement Award, 1999; Bollingen Prize for Poetry, 2003; Editor, Muriel Rukeyser, Selected Poems, 2004; National Book Critics Circle Award, 2005; Honorary doctorates. Address: c/o W W Norton & Co, 500 Fifth Avenue, New York, NY 10110, USA.

RICH Frank Hart, b. 2 June 1949, Washington, District of Columbia, USA. Journalist. m. (1) Gail Winston, 1976, 2 sons, (2) Alexandra Rachelle Witchel, 1991. Education: BA, Harvard University, 1971. Appointments: Co-Editor, Richmond Mercury, Virginia, 1972-73; Senior Editor and Film Critic, New York Times Magazine, 1973-75; Film Critic, New York Post, 1975-77; Film and Television Critic, Time Magazine, 1977-80; Chief Drama Critic, 1980-93, Op-Ed Columnist, 1994-, New York Times; Columnist, New York Times Sunday Magazine, 1993. Publications: The Theatre Art of Boris Aronson (with others), 1987; Hot Seat: Theater Criticism for the New York Times 1980-93, 1998; Ghost Light, 2000. Contributions to: Newspapers and periodicals. Address: c/o The New York Times, 229 West 43rd Street, New York, NY 10036, USA.

RICHARD Cliff (Harry Webb) (Sir), b. 14 October 1940, Lucknow, India. Singer. Appointments: Leader, Cliff Richard and The Shadows; Solo Artist; International Concert Tours, 1958-; Own TV Show; Numerous TV and radio appearances. Creative Works: Films: The Young Ones; Expresso Bongo; Summer Holiday; Wonderful Life; Musicals: Time, 1986-87; Heathcliff, 1996-97; Albums include: 21 Today, 1961; The Young Ones, 1961; Summer Holiday, 1963; 40 Golden Greats, 1977; Love Songs, 1981; Private Collection, 1988;

The Album, 1993; Real as I Wanna Be; Something's Goin' On, 2004; Over 120 singles. Publications: Questions, 1970; The Way I See It, 1972; The Way I See It Now, 1975; Which One's Cliff, 1977; Happy Christmas from Cliff, 1980; You, Me and Jesus, 1983; Mine to Share, 1984; Jesus, Me and You, 1985; Single-Minded, 1988; Mine Forever, 1989; My Story: A Celebration of 40 Years in Showbusiness, 1998. Honours: OBE, 1980; Knighted, 1995; Numerous music awards. Membership: Equity. Address: c/o PO Box 46C, Esher, Surrey KT10 0RB, England.

RICHARDS Isaac Vivian Alexander (Sir) (Viv), b. 7 March 1952, St John's, Antigua. Cricketer. m. Miriam Lewis, 1 son, 1 daughter. Career: Right-hand batsman, off-break bowler; Played for Leeward Islands, 1971-91 (Captain 1981-91), Somerset, 1974-86, Queensland, 1976-77, Glamorgan, 1990-93; 121 tests for West Indies, 1974-91, 50 as Captain, scoring 8,540 runs (average 50.2) including 24 hundreds and holding 122 catches; Scored 36, 212 first-class runs (114 hundreds, only West Indian to score 100 hundreds); Toured England, 1976, 1979 (World Cup), 1980, 1983 (World Cup), 1984, 1988 (as Captain), 1991 (as Captain); 187 limited-overs internationals scoring 6, 721 runs (11 hundreds including then record 189 not out v England at Old Trafford, 1984; Chair, Selectors, West Indies Cricket Board, 2002-. Publication: Co-author, Viv Richards (autobiography); Hitting Across the Line (autobiography), 1991; Sir Vivian, 2000. Honour: Wisden Cricketer of the Year, 1977; One of Wisden's Five Cricketers of the Century, 2000; Cricket Hall of Fame, 2001; Dr hc (Exeter), 1986. Address: West Indies Cricket Board, PO Box 616, St John's, Antigua.

RICHARDS Keith, (Keith Richard), b. 18 December 1943, Dartford, Kent, England. Musician; Vocalist; Songwriter. m. (1) Anita Pallenberg, 1 son, 1 daughter, (2) Patti Hansen, 1983, 2 daughters. Education: Sidcup Art School. Career: Member, The Rolling Stones, 1962-; Co-Writer (with Mick Jagger) numerous songs and albums, 1964-. Creative Works: Albums: The Rolling Stones, 1964; The Rolling Stones No 2, 1965; Out of Our Heads, 1965; Aftermath, 1966; Between the Buttons, 1967; Their Satanic Majesties Request, 1967; Beggar's Banquet, 1968; Let it Bleed, 1969; Get Yer Ya-Ya's Out, 1969; Sticky Fingers, 1971; Exile on Main Street, 1972; Goat's Head Soup, 1973; It's Only Rock'n'Roll, 1974; Black and Blue, 1976; Some Girls, 1978; Emotional Rescue, 1980; Still Life, 1982; Steel Wheels, 1989; Flashpoint, 1991; Voodoo Lounge, 1994; Stripped, 1995; Bridges to Babylon, 1997; No Security, 1999; Forty Licks, 2002; Live Licks, 2004; Singles: It's All Over Now; Little Red Rooster; (I Can't Get No) Satisfaction; Jumping Jack Flash; Honky Tonk Women; Harlem Shuffle; Start Me Up; Paint It Black; Angie; Going to a Go-Go; It's Only Rock'n'Roll; Let's Spend the Night Together; Brown Sugar; Miss You; Emotional Rescue; She's So Cold; Undercover of the Night; Highwire, 1991; Love Is Strong, 1994; Out of Tears, 1994; I Go Wild, 1995; Like A Rolling Stone, 1995; Wild Horses, 1996; Anybody Seen My Baby, 1997; Saint of Me, 1998; Out of Control, 1998; Don't Stop, 2002; Films: Sympathy for the Devil, 1970; Gimme Shelter, 1970; Ladies and Gentlemen, the Rolling Stones, 1974; Let's Spend the Night Together, 1983; Hail Hail Rock'n'Roll, 1987; Flashpoint, 1991. Honours: Grammy, Lifetime Achievement Award, 1986; Rock'n'Roll Hall of Fame, 1989; Q Award, Best Live Act, 1990; Ivor Novello Award, Outstanding Contribution to British Music, 1991; Songwriters Hall of Fame, 1993. Address: c/o Jane Rose, Raindrop Services, 1776 Broadway, Suite 507, New York, NY 10019, USA.

RICHARDS Philip Brian, b. 3 August 1946, Nottingham, England. Circuit Judge. m. Julia Jones, 1 step son, 3 daughters. Education: Cardiff High School; Bristol University. Appointments: Assistant Recorder, 1995; Recorder, 2000; Circuit Judge, 2001. Publications: Government of Wales Bill (joint), 1996; Judicial Training in Welsh Language, 2002. Memberships: Cardiff and County Club; Patron, Mountain Ash RFC. Address: Cardiff Crown Court, Cathays Park, Cardiff, CF10 3PG, Wales. E-mail: prichards@cymrul.net

RICHARDS Rex Edward (Sir), b. 28 October 1922, Colyton, Devon, England. Academic. m. Eva Vago, 2 daughters. Education: BA (Oxon), 1945; FRS, 1959, DSc (Oxon), 1970; FRIC, 1970; FRSC, FBA (Hon), 1990; Hon FRCP, 1987; Hon FRAM 1991. Appointments: Fellow of Lincoln College, Oxford, 1947-1964; Dr Lee's Professor of Chemistry, Oxford, 1964-70; Warden of Merton College, Oxford, 1969-84; Vice-Chancellor, Oxford University, 1977-81; Chairman, Oxford Enzyme Group, 1969-1983; Chancellor, University of Exeter, 1982-98; Commissioner, Royal Commission for Exhibition of 1851, 1984-1997; Director, The Leverhulme Trust, 1984-94; Chairman, British Postgraduate Medical Federation, 1986-93; President, Royal Society of Chemistry, 1990-92; Retired, 1994. Publications: Numerous in scientific journals. Honours: Corday-Morgan, Chemical Society, 1954; Fellow of the Royal Society, 1959; Tilden Lecturer, Chemical Society, 1962; Davy Medal, The Royal Society, 1976; Theoretical Chemistry and Spectroscopy, Chemical Society, 1977; Knight Bachelor, 1977; EPIC, 1982; Medal of Honour, University of Bonn, 1983; Royal Medal, The Royal Society, 1986; President's Medal, Society of Chemical Industry, 1991; Associé étranger, Académie des Sciences, Institut de France, 1995; Honorary degrees: East Anglia, 1971; Exeter, 1975; Dundee, 1977; Leicester, 1978; Salford, 1979; Edinburgh, 1981; Leeds, 1984; Kent, 1987; Cambridge, 1987; Thames Polytechnic (University of Greenwich) Centenary Fellow, 1990; Birmingham, 1993; London, 1994; Oxford Brookes, 1998; Warwick, 1999. Memberships: Trustee: National Heritage Memorial Fund, 1980-84, Tate Gallery, 1982-88, 1991-93, National Gallery, 1982-88, 1989-93; National Gallery Trust, 1996-, Chairman, 1996-99; National Gallery Trust Foundation, 1997-, (Chairman, 1997-1999); Henry Moore Foundation 1989-, (Chairman, 1994-2001). Address: 13 Woodstock Close, Oxford, OX2 8DB, England. E-mail: rex.richards@merton.oxford.ac.uk

RICHARDSON Joely, b. 9 January 1965, Lancashire, England. Actress. m. Tim Bevan, divorced, 1 daughter. Education: The Thacher School, Ojai, California; Royal Academy of Dramatic Art. Career: London stage debut in Steel Magnolias, 1989; TV appearances include: Body Contact, Behaving Badly, 1989; Heading Home, Lady Chatterly's Lover, 1993; The Tribe, 1998; Echo, 1998; Nip/Tuck, 2003-2007; Fallen Angel, 2003; Lies My Mother Told Me, 2005; Wallis & Edward, 2005; Fatel Contact: Bird Flu in America, 2006; Freezing, 2007. Films: Wetherby, 1985; Drowning by Numbers, 1988; Shining Through, 1991; Rebecca's Daughters, 1992; Lochness, 1994; Sister, My Sister, 1995; 101 Dalmatians, 1995; Believe Me, 1995; Hollow Reed, 1996; Event Horizon, 1996; Wrestling with Alligators, Under Heaven, The Patriot, Maybe Baby, Return to Me, 2000; The Affair of the Necklace, 2001; Shoreditch, 2003; The Fever, 2004; The Last Mimzy, 2007; The Christmas Miracle of Jonathan Toomey, 2007. Address: c/o ICM, Oxford House, 76 Oxford Street, London, W1N 0AX, England.

RICHARDSON Miranda, b. 3 March 1958, Southport, England. Actress. Education: Old Vic Theatre School, Bristol. Career: Theatre appearances include: Moving, 1980-81; All My Sons; Who's Afraid of Virginia Woolf?; The Life of Einstein; A Lie of the Mind, 1987; The Changeling; Mountain Language, 1988; Etta Jenks; The Designated Mourner, 1996; Aunt Dan and Lemon, 1999; Film appearances: Dance With a Stranger, 1985; The Innocent; Empire of the Sun; The Mad Monkey; Eat the Rich; Twisted Obsession; The Bachelor, Enchanted April, The Crying Game, 1992; Damage, 1993; Tom and Viv, La Nuit et Le Moment, 1994; Kansas City; Swann, 1995; Evening Star, The Designated Mourner, Apostle, 1996; All for Love; Jacob Two Two and the Hooded Fang; The Big Brass Ring, 1998; Sleepy Hollow, 1998-99; Get Carter, 1999; Snow White, The Hours, Spider, Rage on Placid Lake, 2001; The Actors, Falling Angels, 2002; The Prince and Me, Phantom of the Opera, 2003; Wah-Wah, Harry Potter and the Goblet of Fire, 2004; Provoked, 2005; Paris I Love You, Southland Tales, 2006; Puffball, Spinning Into Butter, Fred Claus, 2007. TV appearances include: The Hard Word; Sorrel and Son; A Woman of Substance; After Pilkington; Underworld; Death of the Heart; Blackadder II and III; Die Kinder (mini series), 1990; Sweet as You Are; Fatherland; Saint X, 1995; Magic Animals; Dance to the Music of Time, 1997; The Scold's Bridle; Merlin, 1997; Alice, 1998; Ted and Ralph, 1998; The Miracle Maker (voice), 2000; Snow White, 2001; The Lost Prince, 2003; Gideon's Daughter, 2005; Merlin's Apprentice, 2006; The Life and Times of Vivienne Vyle, 2007. Honours: Golden Globe Award for Best Comedy Actress, 1993; BAFTA Award for Best Supporting Actress, 1993; Golden Globe Award, 1995; Royal TV Society's Best Actress. Address: c/o ICM, 76 Oxford Street, London, W1N 0AX, England.

RICHARDSON Natasha Jane, b. 11 May 1963. Actress. (1) Robert Fox, 1990, divorced, 1994, (2) Liam Neeson, 1994, 2 sons. Education: Central School of Speech and Drama. Career: Theatre includes: A Midsummer Night's Dream; Hamlet; The Seagull, 1985; China, High Society, 1986; Anna Christie, 1990, 1992; Cabaret, 1998; Closer, 1999; The Lady from the Sea, 2003; A Streetcar Named Desire, 2005; Film appearances include: Every Picture Tells a Story, 1985; Gothic, A Month in the Country, 1987; Patty Hearst, 1988; Fat Man and a Little Boy, 1989; The Handmaid's Tale, The Comfort of Strangers, 1990; The Favour, The Watch and the Very Big Fish, 1992; Past Midnight, Widows Peak, Nell, 1994; The Parent Trap, 1998; Blow Dry, Waking up in Reno, 2000; Maid in Manhattan, 2003; Asylum, The White Countess, 2005; Evening, 2007; Wild Child, 2008. TV includes: In a Secret State, 1985; Ghosts, 1986; Hostages, 1992; Suddenly Last Summer, Zelda, 1993; Tales From the Crypt, 1996; Haven, 2000; The Mastersons of Manhattan, 2007. Honours: Most Promising Newcomer Award, 1986; Plays and Players Award, 1986, 1990; Best Actress, Evening Stand Film Awards, 1990; London Theatre Critics Award, 1990; Tony Award, 1998. Address: c/o ICM, Oxford House, 76 Oxford Street, London, W1D 1BS, England. Website: icmtalent.com

RICHIE Lionel, b. 20 June 1949, Tuskegee, Alabama, USA. Singer; Songwriter; Musician (piano); Actor; Record Producer. m. Diane Alexander, 1996. Education: BS, Econs, Tuskegee University, 1971. Career: Member, the Commodores, 1968-82; Support tours with The Jackson 5, 1973; The Rolling Stones, 1975; The O'Jays, 1976; Numerous other concerts; Solo artiste, 1982-; Concerts include: Closing ceremony, Olympic Games, Los Angeles, 1984; Live Aid, Philadelphia, 1985. Compositions: Hits songs with the Commodores: Sweet Love, 1975; Just To Be Close To You, 1976; Easy, 1977; Three Times A Lady (Number 1, US and UK), 1979; Sail On, 1980;

Still (Number 1, US), 1980; Oh No, 1981; for Kenny Rogers: Lady (Number 1, US), 1981; for Diana Ross: Missing You, 1984; Solo hits: Endless Love, film theme duet with Diana Ross (Number 1, US), 1981; Truly (Number 1, US), 1982; All Night Long (Number 1, US), 1983; Running With The Night, 1984; Hello (Number 1, US and UK), 1984; Stuck On You, 1984; Penny Lover (co-writer with Brenda Harvey), 1984; Say You Say Me (Number 1, US), 1986; Dancing On The Ceiling, 1987; Love Will Conquer All, 1987; Ballerina Girl, 1987; My Destiny, 1992; Don't Wanna Lose You, 1996; Contributor, We Are The World (co-writer with Michael Jackson), USA for Africa (Number 1 worldwide), 1985; Recordings: Albums with the Commodores: Machine Gun, 1974; Caught In The Act, 1975; Movin' On, 1975; Hot On The Tracks, 1976; Commodores, 1977; Commodores Live!, 1977; Natural High 1978; Greatest Hits, 1978; Midnight Magic, 1979; Heroes, 1980; In The Pocket, 1981; Solo albums: Lionel Richie, 1982; Can't Slow Down, 1983; Dancing On The Ceiling, 1986; Back To Front, 1992; Louder Than Words, 1996; Time, 1998; Renaissance, 2000; Encore, 2002; Just For You, 2004; Coming Home, 2006. Solo singles: All Night Long, 1985; Do It To Me, 1992; My Destiny, 1992; Ordinary Girl, 1996; Don't Wanna Lose You, 1996. Honours include: ASCAP Songwriter Awards, 1979, 1984-96; Numerous American Music Awards, 1979-; Grammy Awards: Best Pop Vocal Performance, 1982; Album Of The Year, 1985; Producer Of The Year (shared), 1986; Lionel Richie Day, Los Angeles, 1983; 2 NAACP Image Awards, 1983; NAACP Entertainer of the Year, 1987; Oscar, Best Song, 1986; Golden Globe, Best Song, 1986. Current Management: John Reid. Address: 505 S Beverly Drive, Ste 1192, Beverly Hills, CA 90212, USA.

RICHMOND Douglas, b. 21 February 1946, Walla Walla, Washington, USA. History Professor. m. Belinda González, 1 daughter. Education: BA, 1968, MA, 1971, PhD, 1976, University of Washington. Appointments: Assistant Professor, 1976-82, Associate Professor, 1982-92, Professor of History, 1992-, Department of History, University of Texas, Arlington. Publications: Venustiano Carranza's Nationalist Struggle, 1983; Carlos Pellegrini and the Crisis of the Argentine Elites, 1880-1916, 1989; The Mexican Nation: Historical Continuity and Modern Change, 2001. Honour: Harvey P Johnson Award, 1985, 2004 and 2006; Capitán Alonso de Léon Medalla, 2004. Memberships: Southwest Council on Latin American Studies; Conference on Latin American History. Address: Department of History, Box 19529, University of Texas, Arlington, TX 76019-0529, USA.

RICHMOND, LENNOX AND GORDON, Duke of, Charles Henry Gordon Lennox, b. 19 September 1929. London, England. Chartered Accountant. m. Susan Monica Grenville-Grey, 1 son, 4 daughters. Education: Eton, 1944-48; William Temple College, Rugby, 1956-58; Chartered Accountant, 1956. Appointments: 2nd Lieutenant, KRRC (60th Rifles), 1949-50; Lieutenant, Queen's Westminsters (KRRC) TA, 1951-54; Financial Controllers Department, Courtaulds Ltd, Coventry, 1959-64; Director of Industrial Studies, William Temple College, 1964-68; Member, West Midlands Regional Economic Planning Council, 1965-68; Member, West Sussex Economic Forum Steering Group, 1996-2002; Chairman, Rugby Council of Social Service, 1961-68; Chairman, Goodwood Group of Companies, 1969-, Dexam International (Holdings) Ltd, 1965-, Trustees of Sussex Heritage Trust, 1978-2001; Sussex Rural Housing Partnership, Action in rural Sussex, 1993-2005, Wiley Europe Limited, 1993-98; Boxgrove Priory Trust, 1994-2008, and Member, Boxgrove Almshouses Trust, 1955-; Chairman, Chichester Cathedral Development Trust, 1985-1991;

Chairman, West Sussex Coastal Strip Enterprise Gateway, 2000-05; Member, 1960-80, Chairman, Board for Mission and Unity of the General Synod, 1969-78, Church of England General Synod/Church Assembly; Church Commissioner, 1963-76; Member, Central and Executive Committees, World Council of Churches, 1968-75; Chairman, Christian Organisations Research and Advisory Trust, 1965-87; Lay Chairman, Chichester Diocesan Synod, 1976-79; Vice-Chairman, Archbishops' Commission on Church and State, 1966-70; Treasurer, 1979-82, Chancellor, 1985-98, University of Sussex; Deputy Lieutenant, 1975-1990, Lord Lieutenant, 1990-94, West Sussex. Honours: Honorary LLD Sussex University, 1986; Medal of Honour, British Equestrian Federation, 1983; Winner, FT Arts and Business Award for Individuals, 2000. Memberships: Institute of Chartered Accountants, 1956-; Companion, Institute of Management, 1982-; Honorary Treasurer, 1975-82, Deputy President, 1982-86, Chairman South East Region, 1975-78, Historic Houses Association; Chairman, Bognor Regis Regeneration and Vision Group, 2002-07; Member, Joint Steering Group on Bognor Regis Regeneration, 2002-07; President: Sussex Rural Community Council (Action in rural Sussex), 1973-2005; Chichester Festivities, 1975-; South East England Tourist Board, 1990-2004; Sussex County Cricket Club, 1994-2000, Patron, 2000-; President, British Horse Society, 1976-78; African Medical and Research Foundation UK, 1996-; Chairman, Sussex Community Foundation, 2006-08; Freedom of the City of Chichester, 2008; Lifetime Achievement Award, Chichester Observer Business Awards, 2008. Address: Molecomb, Goodwood, Chichester, West Sussex PO18 0PZ, England. E-mail: richmond@goodwood.co.uk

RICKMAN Alan, 21 February, 1946, Actor. Education: Chelsea College of Art; Royal College of Art; Royal Academy of Dramatic Art (RADA). Career: 2 seasons with Royal Shakespeare Company, Stratford; Stage Appearances include: Bush Theatre, Hampstead and Royal Court Theatre; Les Liasons Dangereuses; The Lucky Chance; The Seagull; Tango at the End of Winter, 1991; Hamlet, 1992; Director, The Winter Guest, 1997; Antony and Cleopatra, 1998; Private Lives, 2001-02; TV appearances include: Obadiah Slope, The Barchester Chronicles, 1982; Pity in History, 1984; Revolutionary Witness, Spirit of Man, 1989; Rasputin (USA), 1995; Films include: The January Man; Close My Eyes; Truly Madly Deeply; Die Hard; Robin Hood: Prince of Thieves; Bob Roberts, 1992; Mesmer, 1993; An Awfully Big Adventure, 1994; Sense and Sensibility, 1995; Michael Collins, 1996; Rasputin, 1996; Mesmer; Dark Harbour, 1997; The Judas Kiss, 1997; Dogma, 1998; Galaxy Quest, 1999; Blow Dry, 1999; Play, 2000; The Search for John Gissing, 2000; Harry Potter and the Philosopher's Stone, 2001; Harry Potter and the Chamber of Secrets, 2002; Love Actually, 2003; Harry Potter and the Prisoner of Azkaban, 2004; Something the Lord Made, 2004; Harry Potter and the Goblet of Fire, 2005; Snow Cake, 2006; Perfume: The Story of a Murderer, 2006; Nobel Son, 2007; Harry Potter and the Order of the Pheonix, 2007; Sweeney Todd: The Demon Barber of Fleet Street, 2007; Bottle Shock, 2008. Honours: Time Out Award, 1991; Evening Standard Film Actor of the Year, 1991; BAFTA Award, 1991; Golden Globe Award, 1996; Emmy Award, 1996; Variety Club Award, 2002. Address: c/o ICM, Oxford House, 76 Oxford Street, London, W1N 0AX, England.

RICKS Christopher (Bruce), b. 18 September 1933, London, England. Professor of the Humanities; Writer; Editor. m. (1) Kirsten Jensen, 1956, divorced 1975, 2 sons, 2 daughters, (2) Judith Aronson, 1977, 1 son, 2 daughters. Education: BA, 1956, BLitt, 1958, MA, 1960, Balliol College,

Oxford. Appointments: Lecturer, University of Oxford, 1958-68; Visiting Professor, Stanford University, 1965, University of California at Berkeley, 1965, Smith College, 1967, Harvard University, 1971, Wesleyan University, 1974, Brandeis University, 1977, 1981, 1984; Professor of English, University of Bristol, 1968-75, University of Cambridge, 1975-86; Professor of the Humanities, Boston University, 1986-; Co-Director, Editorial Institute, 1999-; Andrew W Mellon Distinguished Achievement Award, 2004-07. Publications: Milton's Grand Style, 1963; Tennyson, 1972, revised edition, 1987; Keats and Embarrassment, 1974; The Force of Poetry, 1984; Eliot and Prejudice, 1988; Beckett's Dying Words, 1993; Essays in Appreciation, 1996; Reviewery, 2002; Allusion to the Poets, 2002; Decisions and Revisions in T S Eliot, 2003; Dylan's Visions of Sin, 2003. Editor: Poems and Critics: An Anthology of Poetry and Criticism from Shakespeare to Hardy, 1966; A E Housman: A Collection of Critical Essays, 1968; Alfred Tennyson: Poems, 1842, 1968; John Milton: Paradise Lost and Paradise Regained, 1968; The Poems of Tennyson, 1969, revised edition, 1987; The Brownings: Letters and Poetry, 1970; English Poetry and Prose, 1540-1674, 1970; English Drama to 1710, 1971; Selected Criticism of Matthew Arnold, 1972; The State of the Language (with Leonard Michaels), 1980, new edition, 1990; The New Oxford Book of Victorian Verse, 1987; Inventions of the March Hare: Poems 1909-1917 by T S Eliot, 1996; Oxford Book of English Verse, 1999; Selected Poems of James Henry (editor), 2002; Reviewery, 2003; Dylan's Visions of Sin, 2003; Decisions and Revisions In, T S Eliot, 2003; Samuel Menashe: Selected Poems, 2005. Contributions to: Professional journals. Honour: Honorary DLitt, Oxford, 1998; Honorary D Litt, Bristol, 2002. Memberships: American Academy of Arts and Sciences, fellow; British Academy, fellow; Tennyson Society, vice-president; Housman Society, vice-president. Address: 39 Martin Street, Cambridge, MA 02138, USA.

RIDLEY Brian Kidd, b. 2 March 1931, Newcastle upon Tyne, England. Physicist. m. Sylvia Jean Nicholls, 1 son, 1 daughter. Education: BSc 1st Class Honours, Physics, 1953, PhD, 1957, University of Durham. Appointments: The Mullard Research Laboratory, Redhill, 196-64; Lecturer, 1964-67, Senior Lecturer, 1967-71, Reader, 1971-84, Professor, 1984-90, Research Professor, 1990-2008, Professor Emeritus, Department of Physics, University of Essex, Colchester; Visiting appointments: Distinguished Visiting Professor, 1967, Research Fellow, 1976, 1990-; Visiting Professorships: Stanford, 1967, Danish Technical University, 1969, Princeton, 1973, Lund, 1977, Santa Barbara, 1981, Eindhoven Technical University, 1983, Hong Kong University of Science and Technology, 1997, 1999, Cornell, 3 months annually, 1990-2004; Consultancies: UK Ministry of Defence, Great Malvern; British Telecom (now Corning), Office of Naval Research. Member: Programme Committee International Conference on Hot Carriers, 1986-89; Honorary Editorial Board, Solid State Electronics, 1990-95; Advisory Editorial Board of Journal of Physics Condensed Matter, 1996-2000; Executive Board, Journal of Physics, 2000-2003; Physics College of Engineering and Physical Sciences Research Council of the UK. Publications: Over 200 research papers; Books include: Time, Space and Things, 1976, 3rd edition, 1995, reprinted 2000; The Physical Environment, 1979; Quantum processes in Semiconductors, 1982, 4th edition, 1999; Electrons and Phonons in Semiconductor Multilayers, 1997, 2nd edition, 2008; On Science, 2002; 7 book chapters. Honours: Fellow of the Royal Society; Paul Dirac Medal and Prize; Fellow of the Institute of Physics. Membership:

American Physical Society. Address: Department of Electronic Systems Engineering, University of Essex, Colchester, Essex CO4 3SQ, England.

RIDPATH Ian (William), b. 1 May 1947, Ilford, Essex, England. Writer; Broadcaster. Publications: Over 30 books, including: Worlds Beyond, 1975; Encyclopedia of Astronomy and Space (editor), 1976; Messages From the Stars, 1978; Stars and Planets, 1978; Young Astronomer's Handbook, 1981; Hamlyn Encyclopedia of Space, 1981; Life Off Earth, 1983; Collins Guide to Stars and Planets, 1984-2007; Gem Guide to the Night Sky, 1985; Secrets of the Sky, 1985; A Comet Called Halley, 1985; Longman Illustrated Dictionary of Astronomy and Astronautics, 1987; Monthly Sky Guide, 1987-2006; Star Tales, 1989; Norton's Star Atlas (editor), 1989-2003; Book of the Universe, 1991; Atlas of Stars and Planets, 1992-2004; Oxford Dictionary of Astronomy (editor), 1997-2007; Eyewitness Handbook of Stars and Planets, 1998; Gem Stars, 1999; Times Space, 2002; Times Universe, 2004. Membership: Fellow, Royal Astronomical Society; Member, Society of Authors, Association of British Science Writers. Address: 48 Otho Court, Brentford Dock, Brentford, Middlesex TW8 8PY, England. Website: www.ianridpath.com

RIEGER Gebhard, b. 10 March 1940, Vienna, Austria. Researcher; Medical Educator. m. Irmgard Strasser, 3 sons, 1 daughter. Education: Degree, Secondary School in Linz, 1959; Med Dr, Medical School University, Vienna, 1966; Assistant, I U Eye Clinic, Vienna, 1966-72; Eye Specialist, 1972. Appointments: Emeritus Head, Department of Ophthalmology, Paracelsus Institute, Bad Hall, Austria, 1972; Lecturer, 1998, Professor, 2003, University Eye Clinic, Innsbruck, Austria. Publications: Over 75 papers on dry eye syndrome and balneological themes. Honours: Grantee, Dr Heinz and Helen Adam, Frankfurt, 1990; Gold Medal, Upper Austrian country, 2007. Memberships: Austrian Ophthalmology Society; Vienna Ophthalmology Society; German Ophthalmology Society; New York Academy of Sciences; Society of Free Radical Research; Austrian Society of Balneology and Medical Climatology; Association of Austria Cure Physicians; Paracelsus Society of Balneology and Iodine Research; Medical Society of Upper Austria; Van Swieten Society, Vienna. Address: Paracelsus Society, Kurpromenade 1, A-4540 Bad Hall, Upper Austria.

RIESENHUBER Klaus, b. 29 July 1938, Frankfurt am Main, Germany. Professor of Philosophy; Jesuit Priest. Education: Study of Philosophy, St Georgen, Frankfurt, 1957-58; Study of Philosophy, Berchmanskolleg Pullach, 1960-62; Lic Phil, 1962; Study of Philosophy, Universität München, 1962-67; Dr Phil, 1967; Study of Japanese Culture, Kamakura, Japan, 1967-69; Study of Theology, Sophia University, 1969-72; Master of Theology, 1972; Dr of Theology, 1989. Appointments: Lecturer, Philosophy, Sophia University, 1969; Assistant Professor, 1974; Director, Institute of Medieval Thought, Sophia University, 1974-2004; Professor, 1981-; Director, Zen-Hall Shinmeikutsu, Tokyo, 1990-; Part time Guest Professor: Tokyo University; Kyushu University; Tohoku University; Japanese Broadcast University; Keio University; Waseda University; Tokyo Metropolitan University. Publications: Die Transzendenz der Freiheit zum Guten, 1971; Existenzerfahrung und Religion, 1968 (Portuguese translation, 1972); Freedom and Transcendence in the Middle Ages (in Japanese), 1988; History of Ancient and Medieval Philosophy (in Japanese), 1991; Fundamental Streams of Medieval Philosophy (in Japanese), 1995; Internal Life (in Japanese), 1995; History of Medieval Thought (in Japanese), 2002; Man and Transcendence (in Japanese),

2004; Faith Searching for Understanding (in Japanese), 2004; Editor and co-editor of 72 books in Japanese; Co-editor of Nishida Kitaro Collected Works (24 volumes, in Japanese, in progress). Memberships: Japanese Society of Medieval Philosophy; Japanese Society of Philosophy; Japanese Fichte Society; 5 other philosophical associations. Address: S J House, Sophia University, 7-1 Kioicho, Chiyoda-ku, Tokyo 102-8571, Japan.

RIFKIND Linda, b. Glasgow, Scotland. Actress; Singer; Writer; Teacher; Broadcaster. m. Nathaniel Rifkind, October 1958, deceased. Education: Diploma SD, DSD, Royal Scottish Academy of Music and Drama, Glasgow. Appointments: Numerous appearances on TV including Tutti Frutti; Charles Rennie MacIntosh; Naked Video; The Campbells; Taggart; The Justice Game; More than Just a Disease; City Lights; Winners & Losers; The Gift; Scotch and Wry; Rab C Nesbitt; The Advocates; Triple Scotch and Wry; A Time to Dance; Broadcast own stories for 3 years; Theatre: Female Lead, Fiddler on the Roof; Major Part, Anne of Green Gables; One Women shows; Female Lead, Inherit the Wind; Female Lead, A Streetcar Named Desire; Female Lead, Taming of the Shrew; Dubbed Video, 4 Female Leads, the Beginning of the Bible; Role Play, Communications Skills to Medics, Glasgow University and in Spotlight, for actresses and Equity's CD Rom, Glasgow University for BBC Glasgow, 2001-; Served on Equity Task Force and Negotiating Team, Guild House, London, 2004-05; Organiser, Compere, in fundraising activities including all-star cast variety shows to raise money for artistes and good causes in Scotland including a hospice for terminally ill children; Negotiated the Pavilion Theatre, Glasgow as The Scottish National Theatre of Variety, 2007. Honours: Gold Medal for the Arts, 1988; Certificate of Merit, Distinguished Services, IBC; Listed in international biographical dictionaries. Memberships include: First Secretary, Scottish Variety Branch, 1991-2008; Equity Variety Advisory Committee, London; Campaign, Negotiating Variety taskforce, Scottish National Committee Actors; The Variety Club of Great Britain; Research Board of Advisors, 1998-2004; Past Councillor, Equity; Listed in numerous biographical publications. Address: c/o British Actors' Equity Association, 114 Union Street, Glasgow G1 3QQ, Scotland.

RIGG (Enid) Diana (Elizabeth) (Dame), b. 20 July 1938, Doncaster, England. Actress. m. (1) Manahem Gueffen, 1973, divorced 1976, (2) Archibald Hugh Stirling, 1982, divorced 1993, 1 daughter. Education: RADA. Career: Professional début as Natella Abashwilli, The Caucasian Chalk Circle, York Festival, 1957; Repertory Chesterfield and Scarborough 1958; Films include: A Midsummer Night's Dream, 1969; On Her Majesty's Secret Service, 1969; Julius Caesar, 1970; The Hospital, 1971; Theatre of Blood, 1973; A Little Night Music, 1977; The Great Muppet Caper, 1981; Evil Under the Sun, 1982; A Good Man in Africa, 1993; Parting Shots, 1999; Heidi, 2005; The Painted Veil, 2006. TV appearances include: Emma Peel in the Avengers, 1965-67; Women Beware Women, 1965; Married Alive, 1970; Diana (USA), 1973; In This House of Brede, 1975; Three Piece Suite, 1977; The Serpent Son, 1979; The Marquise, 1980; Hedda Gabler, 1981; Rita Allmers in Little Eyolf, 1982; Reagan in King Lear, 1983; Witness for the Prosecution, 1983; Bleak House, 1984; Host Held in Trust, A Hazard of Hearts, 1987; Worst Witch, 1987; Unexplained Laughter, 1989; Mother Love, 1989; Host Mystery! (USA), 1989; Running Delilah, 1994; Zoya, 1995; The Haunting of Helen Walker, 1995; The Fortunes and Misfortunes of Moll Flanders, 1996; Samson and Delilah, 1996; Rebecca, 1997; The Mrs Bradley Mysteries, 1998-99; In the Beginning, 2000; The American, 2001; The 100 Greatest TV Characters (Mrs

Peel), 2001; Victoria & Albert, 2001; Charles II: The Power and the Passion, 2003; Many leading roles with RSC and with theatres in UK and USA. Publications: No Turn Unstoned, 1982; So To The Land, 1994; Honours include: Plays and Players Award for Best Actress, 1975, 1978; Honorary doctorates, Stirling University, 1988; Leeds, 1991, South Bank, 1996; BAFTA Award, Best Actress, 1990; Evening Stand Award, 1993, 1996, 1996; Tony Award, Best Actress, 1994; Emmy, Best Supporting Actress, 1997; BAFTA, 2000; Theatregoers' Award for Best Actress, 2005. Memberships include: Vice-President, Baby Life Support Systems (BLISS), 1984-; Chancellor, University of Stirling, 1997-.

RILEY Patrick Anthony, b. 22 March 1935, Neuilly-Sur-Seine, France. Pathologist. m. Christine E Morris, 1 son, 2 daughters. Education: MB, BS (Lond), 1960; PhD (Lond), 1965; DSc (Lond), 1990; FRCPath, 1985; FIBiol, 1976. Appointments: Rockefeller Scholar, 1962-63; MRC Junior Clinical Research Fellow, 1963-66; Beit Memorial Research Fellow, 1966-68; Wellcome Research Fellow, 1968-70; Lecturer in Clinical Pathology, University College Hospital Medical School, London, 1970-73; Senior Lecturer in Biochemical Pathology, 1974-76, Reader in Cell Pathology, 1976-84, Professor of Cell Pathology, 1984-2000, Emeritus Professor, 2000-, University College, London; Currently, Director, Totteridge Institute for Advanced Studies and Honorary Research Associate, Gray Cancer Institute. Publications: Reviews and chapters in books; Dictionary of Medicine; More than 250 substantive research contributions to learned journals. Honours: Myron Gordon Award, 1993; Centenary Medal, Charles University, Prague, Czech Republic, 1996. Memberships include: Linnean Club; Athenaeum Club; Royal Society of Medicine; NCUP. Address: 2 The Grange, Grange Avenue, London N20 8AB, England.

RIMAN Joseph Vavrinec Prokop, b. 30 January 1925, Horni Sucha, Silesia. Biochemist; Scientist. m. Vera Tomek. Education: MD, Charles University, Prague, 1950; PhD, Chemistry, CS Academy of Science, 1955; DSc, Chemistry, 1967; Associate Professor, Habil Doc, Medical Faculty, Charles University, 1967; Full Professor, Biochemistry, Science Faculty, 1984; DSc, Biology h c, Purkynje University, 1987. Appointments: Research Physician, 1st Clinic Pediatrics, Medical Faculty, Charles University, Prague, 1950-51; Scientist, Senior Scientist, Institute of Organic Chemistry and Biochemistry, CS Academy of Sciences, Prague, 1951-74; Founder, Director, Institute of Molecular Genetics, 1975-91. Publications: Published in various international journals; 128 original experimental papers, Biochemistry of retroviruses and growing vertebrate cells. Honours include: Laureate of the State Prize for Science of Czechoslovakia, 1969 and 1977, and Soviet Union, 1978; Gold Plaque of J G Mendel, Czechoslovak Academy of Science, 1980; Silver Medal, Charles University, 1985; Gold Einstein-Russel Pugwash Medal, 1987; Skrjabin's Medal, 1987; J E Fogarty NIH Medal, 1987; Hippocrates Medal, Kyoto University Medical School, 1988; Gold Lomonosov Medal, 1986; Gold Medal, Slovak Academy of Science for Merits, 1989; Gold Medal, Meidji University, Nagoya, 1990; K Yagis Gold Memorial Medal, 1990; Gold Plaque for Merits for Science and Mankind; Gold Pin, G W Leibniz Society; Listed in national and international biographical dictionaries. Memberships include: Honorary Member, Hungarian Academy of Science; Foreign Member, Bulgarian Academy; Foreign Member, Russian Academy of Science; Foreign Fellow, Indian National Science Academy; Foreign Member G W Leibniz Society, Germany; Foreign Member German Society of Biological Chemistry; Full Member Central European Academy of Science and Art, 1997-; Science Secretary, 1977-, Vice-President Biological

Sciences, 1982-, President, 1986-90, Czechoslovak Academy of Sciences. Address: Nehrovská Street 18, Praha 6, 160 00, Czech Republic.

RIMINGTON Dame Stella, b. 1935. Civil Servant. m. John Rimington, 1963, 2 daughters. Education: Edinburgh University. Career: Director-General, Security Service, 1992-96; Non Executive Director, Marks and Spencer, 1997-2004, BG PLC, 1997-2000, BG Group, 2000-, GKR Group (now Whitehead Mann), 1997-2001; Chair, Institute of Cancer Research, 1997-2001. Publications: Open Secret, 2001; At Risk (novel), 2004. Honours: Honorary Air Commodore 7006 (VR) Squadron Royal Auxiliary Air Force, 1997-2001; Hon LLB (Nottingham) 1995, (Exeter) 1996, (London Metropolitan University) 2004; DCB, 1996. Address: PO Box 1604, London SW1P 1XB, England.

RINGLESBACH Dorothy, b. 14 August 1925, Fort Wayne, Indiana, USA. RN Retired. m. John Ringlesbach, 2 sons, 3 daughters. Education: Wisherd Memorial Hospital School of Nursing, 1947. Appointments: Interpreter, Colonial Williamsburg; Registered Nurse, now retired. Publications: Many essays in local and national journals; Book, OSS: Stories that can now be told. Honours: President, The Woman's Auxiliary to the Indiana State Medical Association. Memberships: Lutheran Church; Carpet Baggers Newsletter; OSS Newsletter; Member, The Women's Memorial. Address: 303 Farmville Lane, Williamsburg, VA 23188, USA. E-mail: esp22693@widomaker.com

RIPPON Angela, b. 12 October 1944, Plymouth, Devon, England. Television and Radio Presenter; Writer. m. Christopher Dare, 1967, divorced. Education: Grammar School, Plymouth, England. Appointments: Presenter, Reporter, BBC TV Plymouth, 1966-69; Editor, Presenter, Producer, Westward Television, 1967-73; Reporter, BBC TV National News, 1973-75, Newsreader, 1975-81; Founder, Presenter, TV-am, 1983; Arts Correspondent, WNETV (CBS), Boston, 1983; Reporter, Presenter, BBC and ITV, 1984; TV appearances: Angela Rippon Meets...; Antiques Roadshow; In the Country; Compere, Eurovision Song Contest, 1976; The Morecombe and Wise Christmas Show, 1976, 1977; Royal Wedding, 1981; Masterteam, 1985, 1986, 1987; Come Dancing, 1988-; What's My Line? 1988-; Healthcheck; Holiday Programme; Simply Money, 2001-; Channel 5 News, 2003-; Cash in the Attic, 2007; Radio: Angela Rippon's Morning Report for LBC, 1992; Angela Rippon's Drive Time Show, LBC, 1993; The Health Show, BBC Radio 4; Friday Night with Angela Rippon, BBC Radio 2; LBC Arts Programme, 2003-. Publications: Riding, 1980; In the Country, 1980; Mark Phillips: The Man and His Horses, 1982; Angela Rippon's West Country, 1982; Victoria Plum, 1983; Badminton: A Celebration, 1987; Many recordings. Honours: Dr hc, American International University, 1994; New York Film Festival Silver Medal, 1973; Newsreader of the Year, Radio and Television Industries Awards, 1976, 1977, 1978; Television Personality of the Year, 1977; Emmy Award, 1984; Sony Radio Award, 1990; New York Radio Silver Medal, 1992; Royal TV Society Hall of Fame, 1996; European Woman of Achievement, 2002; OBE, 2004. Memberships: Vice-President, International Club for Women in Television; British Red Cross; NCH Action for Children; Riding for the Disabled Association; Director, Nirex, 1986-; Chair, English National Ballet, 2000-. Address: Knight Ayton, 114 St Martin's Lane, London, WC2N 4AZ, England.

RITBLAT Lady Jillian Rosemary (Jill), b. 14 December, 1942, United Kingdom. Barrister. m. (1), 1 son, 1 daughter, (2) Sir John Ritblat. Education: BA, Westfield College, London. Appointments: Called to the Bar, Gray's Inn, 1964; Pupillage to Robin Simpson, QC, Victor Durand and Jeremy Hutchinson's Chambers, 1964-65; Alternate Delegate for International Council of Jewish Women, UN, Geneva, 1977-79; Patrons of New Art Tate Gallery; Events Organiser, 1984-87; Chairman, 1987-90; Member Acquisitions Sub-Committee, 1992-93; International Council Member, 1995-; Member, 1995-; Vice-Chairman, 1996-2001; Member, Steering Group, 1995-2001; Co-Curator: The Curate's Egg, Anthony Reynolds Gallery, 1994; One Woman's Wardrobe, Victoria and Albert, 1998-99; Executive Producer, Normal Conservative Rebels: Gilbert & George in China, Edinburgh Film Festival, 1996; Member, Arts Council Appraisal for West Midlands Arts, 1994; Board Member: British Telecom New Contemporaries, 1991-, Vice-Chair, 1991-; Jerusalem Music Centre, 1991; Design Trustee, Public Art Commissioners Agency, 1996-99; Jury Member: Painting in the Eighties, 1987; Turner Prize, 1988; British Airways New Artist Award, 1990; Swiss Bank Corporation Euro Art Competition, 1994, 1995; NatWest 90's Prize for Art 1995, 1995; Financial Times Arts and Business Awards, 2000, 2001; Board member RIBA Trust, 2005. Honours: V&A Catalogue Design and Art Direction Silver Award for Graphic Design, 1999; Gold Medal, Chicago Film Festival, 1996. Memberships: Member, 1986-, Council Member, 1993-, Association of Museum of Modern Art, Oxford; International Council, Jerusalem Museum, 1987; Advisory Council Friends of the Tate Gallery, 1990; Special Events Committee, National Art Collections Fund, 1991-92; William Townsend Memorial Lectureship Committee, 1991-; Patron, National Alliance for Art, Architecture and Design, 1994-; Royal Academy of Music Development Committee, 2002-. Address: Lansdowne House, Berkeley Square, London W1J 6ER, England.

RITCHIE Guy, b. 10 September 1968, Hatfield, Hertfordshire, England. Film Director. m. Madonna Ciccone, 2000, 1 son, 1 adopted son, 1 step-daughter. Education: Standbridge Earls. Career: Directed numerous 1980s pop videos; Films: The Hard Case, 1995; Lock, Stock and Two Smoking Barrels, 1998; Snatch, 2000; What it Feels Like for a Girl (video), 2001; The Hire: Star, 2001; Swept Away, 2002; Mean Machine (supervising producer), 2002; Revolver, 2005; Suspect, 2007. TV: The Hard Case, 1995; Lock, Stock and Two Smoking Barrels (series executive producer), 2000. Honours: British Industry Film Award, 1998; London Film Critics' Circle Award, 1999.

RITCHIE Ian Carl, b. 26 June 1947, Hove, England. Architect. 1 son. Education: Diploma with Distinction, University of Westminster, 1972; Registered Architect ARB, 1979; Royal Institute of British Architects, 1979; Membre de l'Ordre des Architectes Francais, 1981; Member, Society of Industrial Artists and Designers, 1982; Registered German Architect, 1993; Fellow, Royal Society of Arts, 1987; Royal Academician, 1998. Appointments: Teacher, Oita University, Japan, 1970; Project Architect, Foster Associates, 1972-76; Lecturer, University of Westminster, London, 1973; Private Practice, France, 1976-78; Unit Tutor, Architectural Association, London, 1978-81; Co-Founder Partner, Chrysalis Architects, 1979-81; Independent Consultant, UK, 1979-81; Co-Founder Director, 1981-89, Consultant, 1989-91, Rice Francis Ritchie, Paris; Ian Ritchie Architects, London, 1981-; Member, British Steel Corporation Teaching project, 1987-89; Visiting Professor, Moscow Institute of Architecture, 1992; Visiting Professor, Technical University,

Vienna, 1994, 1995; Special Professor, Leeds University School of Civil Engineering, 2001-04. Publications: 9 books; Numerous articles in professional journals; Contributions to books, book reviews, films and critical reviews; TV and radio interviews; Guest lectures. Honours: Many awards including most recently: CDA Innovation in Copper, 2003; RIBA Award & Stirling Prize shortlist, 2004; Best New Building & Overall Abercrombie Architectural Design Award, 2005; Shortlisted for Mies van der Rohe Prize, 2005; West Midlands Architects of the Year, 2006; RIBA National Award & Stirling Prize shortlist, 2007. Memberships: Royal Academy of Arts; RSC International Council; GLA Design Board; RIBA Stirling Prize Jury. Address: Ian Ritchie Architects Ltd, 110 Threecolt Street, London, E14 8AZ, England. E-mail: mail@ianritchiearchitects.co.uk

RITCHIE Lewis Duthie, b. 26 June 1952, Fraserburgh, Scotland. Academic General Practitioner. m. Heather Skelton. Education: BSc, Chemistry, 1978, MBChB, Commendation, 1978, University of Aberdeen; MSc, Community Medicine, University of Edinburgh, 1982; MD, University of Aberdeen, 1993; Vocational Training in General Practice, 1979-82; Specialist Training in Public Health Medicine, 1982-87. Appointments: General Practice Principal, Peterhead Health Centre, 1984-; Consultant in Public Health Medicine, Grampian Health Board, 1987-92; Honorary Consultant in Public Health Medicine, Grampian Health Board, 1993-; Sir James Mackenzie Professor of General Practice, University of Aberdeen, 1993-; Membership of a number of national medical advisory committees on behalf of the Scottish Executive Health Department and the Department of Health England, 1989-. Publications: Book: Computers in Primary Care, 1986; Over 130 publications on computing, cardiovascular prevention, lipids, hypertension, immunisation, oncology, intermediate care, community hospitals, and fishermen's health. Honours: Munday and Venn Prize, University of Aberdeen, 1977; John Watt Prize, University of Aberdeen, 1977; Kincardine Prize, North East Faculty, Royal College of General Practitioners, 1978; John Perry Prize, British Computer Society, 1991; Ian Stokoe Memorial Award, Royal College of General Practitioners, 1992; Blackwell Prize, University of Aberdeen, 1995; OBE, 2001; Eric Elder Medal, Royal New Zealand College of General Practitioners, 2007. Memberships: Diploma of the Royal College of Obstetricians and Gynaecologists, 1980; British Computer Society, 1985; Fellow, Royal Society of Medicine, 1987; Member Royal Environmental Health Institute for Scotland, 1991; Fellow, Faculty of Public Health Medicine, 1993; Fellow Royal College of General Practitioners, 1994; Fellow, Royal College of Physicians of Edinburgh, 1995; Fellow, British Computer Society, 2004; Chartered Computer Engineer, 1993; Fellow, Royal Society of the Arts, 2001; Founding Fellow of the Institute of Contemporary Scotland, 2001; Chartered Information Technology Professional, 2004. Address: Department of General Practice and Primary Care, University of Aberdeen, Foresterhill Health Centre, Westburn Road, Aberdeen AB25 2AY, Scotland. E-mail: l.d.ritchie@abdn.ac.uk

RITTER Mary Alice, Pro-Rector. m. Roger Morris, 3 sons. Education: BA (Hons), Zoology, Class 2I, 1966, Diploma in Human Biology (Distinction), 1967, D Phil, 1971, MA, 1971, University of Oxford. Appointments: Postdoctoral Research Fellow, Department of Zoology, University of Oxford, 1971-76; Research Associate, Department of Pathology, University of Connecticut Health Centre, USA, 1976-78; Research Fellow, Imperial Cancer Research Fund, London, 1978-82; Lecturer, 1982-86, Senior Lecturer, 1986-88, Reader, 1988-91, Professor, 1991-, Immunology, Vice Dean

(Education), 1992-97, Royal Postgraduate Medical School; Assistant Vice Principal (Postgraduate Medicine), Imperial College School of Medicine, 1997-2000, Director, Graduate School of Life Sciences and Medicine, 2000-06, Chairman, Department of Immunology, Faculty of Medicine, 2004-06, Imperial College London. Publications: Numerous articles in professional journals. Memberships: Royal College of Pathologists; City and Guilds Institute; Royal Society of Arts; Higher Education Academy. Address: Level 4, Faculty Building, South Kensington Campus, London SW7 2AZ, England. E-mail: m.ritter@imperial.ac.uk

RITTERMAN Janet, b. 1 December 1941, Sydney, Australia. Education: DSCM, Piano, New South Wales State Conservatorium of Music, 1962; FTCL, Piano, 1966; BMus, University of Durham, England, 1971; MMus, 1977, PhD, 1985, University of London. Appointments: Head of Music, Strathfield Girls' High School, Sydney, 1963-66; Music Teacher, Cheltenham Girls' High School, Sydney, 1967-68; Music Teacher, Swaffield JMI School, London, 1969; Music Teacher, Watford Grammar School for Girls, 1970-75; Senior Lecturer in Music, Middlesex Polytechnic, 1975-79; Senior Lecturer in Music, University of London, Goldsmiths College, 1980-87; Head of Music, 1987-90, Dean (Academic Affairs), 1988-90, Principal, 1990-93, Dartington College of Arts; Visiting Professor, Music Education, University of Plymouth, 1993-2005; Director, Royal College of Music, London, 1993-2005. Publications: Articles and chapters in books; Reports. Honours: Hon RAM, Royal Academy of Music, 1995; D Univ, University of Central England in Birmingham, 1996; Fellow, Royal Northern College of Music, 1996; Fellow, University College, Northampton, 1997; Fellow, Dartington College of Arts, 1997; Hon GSMD, Guildhall School of Music & Drama, 2000; Dame Commander of the British Empire, 2002; Senior Fellow, Royal College of Art, 2004; HonDLitt, University of Ulster, 2004; DUniv, Middlesex University, 2005. Listed in biographical dictionaries. Memberships: Fellow, Higher Education Academy; Royal Musical Association; Royal Society of Musicians of Great Britain; Nuffield Foundation Education Advisory Committee; Governing Body, Middlesex University; Governing Body, Dartington College of Arts; Member of Court, Worshipful Company of Musicians; Advisory Board, The Institute for Advanced Studies in the Humanities, University of Edinburgh; Board of Directors, Anglo-Austrian Society; Board of Directors, The Voices Foundation; Advisory Council, Institute of Germanic and Romance Studies and Institute of Musical Research, University of London; Trustee, Plymouth Chamber Music Trust, Mitglied des Wissenschaftsrates, Bundesministerium für Bildung, Wissenschaft und Kultur, Austria; Trustee, The Countess of Munster Musical Trust.

RIVERS Ann, b. 26 January 1939, Texas, USA. Poet. Education: BA, 1959. Appointments: Editor-Publisher, SHY, 1974-79; Guest Editor, As-Sharq, 1979; Contributing Editor, Ocarina, 1979-82. Publication: Samos Wine, 1987; A World of Difference, 1995; Pilgrimage and Early Poems, 2000; Pluto Probe, 2003. Contributions to: Ore; Iotà; Orbis; Poetry Nottingham; Pennine Platform. Address: Hydra, GR 180 40 Greece.

ROBBINS Tim, b. 16 October 1958, New York, USA. Actor; Director; Screen Writer. 2 sons with Susan Sarandon. Education: University College of Los Angeles. Career: Member, Theatre for the New City; Founder, Artistic Director, The Actor's Gang, 1981-; Theatre includes: As actor: Ubu Roi, 1981; As director, A Midsummer Night's Dream, 1984; The Good Woman of Setzuan, 1990; As writer: (with

Adam Simon): Alagazam; After the Dog Wars; Violence; The Misadventures of Spike Spangle; Farmer; Carnage – A Comedy (Represented USA at Edinburgh International Festival, Scotland); As writer: Embedded, 2004; Films: As actor: No Small Affair, Toy Soldiers, 1984; The Sure Thing, Fraternity Vacation, 1985; Top Gun, Howard the Duck, 1986; Five Corners, 1987; Bull Durham, Tapeheads, 1988; Miss Firecracker, Eric the Viking, 1989; Cadillac Man, Twister, Jacob's Ladder, 1990; Jungle Fever, 1991; The Player, Bob Roberts, Amazing Stories: Book Four, 1992; Short Cuts, 1993; The Hudsucker Proxy, The Shawshank Redemption, Prêt-à-Porter, IQ, 1994; Nothing to Lose, 1997; Arlington Road, The Cradle Will Rock, Austin Powers: The Spy Who Shagged Me, 1999; Mission to Mars, High Fidelity, 2000; Antitrust, Human Nature, 2001; The Truth About Charlie, 2002; The Day My God Died, Mystic River, Code 46, 2003; The Secret Life of Words, Zathura: A Space Adventure, 2005; Catch a Fire, Tenacious D in The Pick of Destiny, 2006; Noise, The Lucky Ones, 2007. As writer/director: Bob Roberts, 1992; Dead Man Walking, 1995; Cradle Will Rock, 1999. Honours: Golden Globe, Best Supporting Actor, 2004; Critics' Choice Award, Best Supporting Actor, 2004; Screen Actors Guild, Best Supporting Actor Award, 2004; Academy Award, Best Supporting Actor, 2004. Address: c/o Elaine Goldsmith Thomas, ICM, 40 West 57th Street, New York, NY 10019, USA.

ROBERT Leslie (Ladislas), b. 24 October 1924, Budapest, Hungary. Biochemist. m. Jacqueline Labat, 3 daughters. Education: MD, Paris, 1953; PhD, Lille, 1977; Postdoctoral Training, Department of Biochemistry, University of Illinois, Chicago; Columbia University, New York; Honorary Research Director, French National Research Center (CNRS), 1994-. Appointment: Research Director, Department of Ophthalmic Research, Hotel Dieu Hospital, Paris, France. Publications: 7 books on ageing biology; 1 book on time-regulations in biology; 12 books on connective tissues; 980 publications in international journals. Honours: Honorary doctorate, Semmelweis Medical University, Budapest, 1972; Verzar Medal for Gerontology Research, University of Vienna, 1994; Novartis Prize, International Gerontological Association, 1997. Memberships: Academy of Sciences of Hungary and Germany (Nordrhein-Westfalen); French and International Biochemical Societies; Past president, French Society for Connective Tissue Research; Past president, French Society of Atherosclerosis. Address: 7 Rue J B Lully, 94440 Santeny, France. E-mail: lrobert5@wanadoo.fr

ROBERTS Brian, b. 19 March 1930, London, England. Writer. Education: Teacher's Certificate, St Mary's College, Twickenham, 1955; Diploma in Sociology, University of London, 1958. Appointments: Teacher of English and History, 1955-65. Publications: Ladies in the Veld, 1965; Cecil Rhodes and the Princess, 1969; Churchills in Africa, 1970; The Diamond Magnates, 1972; The Zulu Kings, 1974; Kimberley: Turbulent City, 1976; The Mad Bad Line: The Family of Lord Alfred Douglas, 1981; Randolph: A Study of Churchill's Son, 1984; Cecil Rhodes: Flawed Colossus, 1987; Those Bloody Women: Three Heroines of the Boer War, 1991. Address: 7 The Blue House, Market Place, Frome, Somerset, BA11 1AP, England.

ROBERTS Denys Tudor Emil, b. 19 January 1923, London, England. Judge. m. Fiona Alexander, 10 February 1985, 1 son. Education: MA, Wadham College, Oxford 1948; BCL, 1949; Bar, London, 1950. Appointments: Crown Counsel, Nyasaland, 1953-59; Attorney General, Gibraltar, 1960-62; Solicitor General, Hong Kong, 1962-66; Attorney General,

Hong Kong, 1966-73; Chief Secretary, Hong Kong, 1973-78; Chief Justice, Hong Kong, 1979-88; Chief Justice, Brunei Darussalam, 1979-2001; President, Court of Appeal, Bermuda, 1988-94; Member, Hong Kong Court of Final Appeal, 1997-2003; President, Court of Appeal, Brunei Darussalam, 2002-03. Publications: Books: Smuggler's Circuit, 1954; Beds and Roses, 1956; The Elwood Wager, 1958; The Bones of the Wajingas, 1960; How to Dispense with Lawyers, 1964; I'll Do Better Next Time, 1995; Yes Sir, But, 2000; Another Disaster, 2006. Honours: OBE, 1960; CBE, 1970; KBE, 1975; SPMB, Brunei, 1984. Memberships: Honorary Fellow, Wadham College, Oxford; Honorary Bencher, Lincoln's Inn; President, MCC, 1989-90. Address: The Grange, North Green Road, Pulham St Mary, Norfolk IP21 4QZ, England.

ROBERTS Dorothy (Elizabeth), b. Brisbane, Queensland, Australia. Concert Pianist; Abstract Artist. Divorced, 1 son. Education: Studies at Sydney Conservatorium of Music, including Piano, Harmony, History of Music, Form of Music, Chamber Music; Clara Schumann technique with Adelina de Lara, London. Career: Music concerts at Balliol College, Oxford, Purcell Room, South Bank, London; Performed Liszt's Piano Concerto in E Flat with London Symphony Orchestra at Royal Albert Hall, London; Other concerto performances with the Hallé Orchestra, Northern Sinfonia Orchestra and London Bach Players; Recitals in London, UK provinces, Glasgow, Germany, Australia, France, Netherlands, Canada; TV appearance with the Hallé Orchestra; Other TV appearances with Richard Bonynge, 2 pianos, including playing with the BBC Orchestra; Many one man shows as abstract painter including London, Provinces, New York; Works in collections in UK, Europe, Canada, USA and Australia as Dorothy Lee Roberts. Honours: AMusA; LMus; Honorary DLit, Bradford University, 1995; Recently confirmed as the only Grand Pupil of the Clara Schumann piano-playing tradition; Winner, 95 Art International, New York. Address: Alveley House, 17 Lindum Road, Lincoln LN2 1NS, England.

ROBERTS John Hughes, b. 6 July 1932, Gravesend, Kent, England. Theoretician. m. Diana, 1 son, 1 daughter, deceased. Education: Gravesend County Grammar School, 1940-51; BSc, Mathematics, Reading University, 1954. Appointments: 40 years in Maths Departments of GEC, Plessey, Siemens; Retired 1993. Publications: Numerous authored and co-authored papers in Electronics Literature; Author, Angle Modulation, No 5 in the IEE Telecommunications series, 1977. Honours: Awarded Premiums by the IEE for published papers 3 times. Membership: Fellow, Institute of Mathematics and Its Applications. Address: 61 Pine Crescent, Chandler's Ford, Hampshire, SO53 1LN, England.

ROBERTS Mary Belle, b. 27 September 1923, Akron, Ohio, USA. Social Worker. Education: Bachelor of Psychology, University of Michigan, 1948; MSW, 1950; New York School of Social Work, Third Year Social Work, 1953-54. Appointments: Instructor of Alabama Medical School, Department of Psychiatry, 1951-53; ALA, Department of Public Health, Division of Mental Hygiene, 1950-53; Bur MH, Div Com Serv, Pennsylvania Department of Public Welfare, 1954-55; DHEW, PHS, NIMH, Com Services, 1955-64; Private practice, 1964-68; Family Counseling Service of Miami and prior organisations, 1968-90; Private practice, 1990-; Apogee, 1994-96. Publications: JPSW Effective Mental Health by Activation of Community's Potential; Edit the Vocational Rehabilitation of the Mentally Ill; Leadership Training for Mental Health Promotion; Editorials, Alabama Mental Health Bulletin. Honours: Phi Kappa Phi; Licensed MD and Fl; Life Fellow, Royal Society Health; Diplomate,

NASW; AAUW named gifts, 1978 and 1981. Memberships: NASW; ACSW; Royal Society of Health; ABECSW; DAR; USD of 1812; AAUW; YWCA; IBC; ABI; University of Michigan Alumni Association; Smithsonian; AARP. Address: 8126 SW, 105th Place, Ocala, FL 34481-9132, USA.

ROBERTS Michael Victor, b. 23 September 1941, High Wycombe, England. Librarian. m. Jane Margaret, deceased, 1 son, 1 daughter. Education: Bachelor of Arts, Clare College, Cambridge, 1960-63; Loughborough Technical College, 1963-64; Master of Arts, 1966. Appointments: Various junior professional posts in Loughborough, Leeds and City of London, 1964-70; Principal Cataloguer, 1970-73, Keeper of Enquiry Services, 1973-82, Guildhall Library, City of London; Deputy Director, City of London Libraries and Art Galleries, 1982-95. Publications: Numerous articles in professional and academic journals; Editor, Guildhall Studies in London History, 1973-82; Editor, Branch Journal of the Library Association Local Studies Group, 1996-98; Editor, Archives and the Metropolis, 1998; Editor, Framlingham Historical Society, 1997-. Honours: Associate of the Library Association, 1967; Chartered Librarian, 1967; Member, Chartered Institute of Library and Information Professionals, 2002. Memberships: Governor, 1996-, Deputy Chairman, 1999-2002, 2005-, Chairman, 2002-05, Bishopsgate Foundation; Member, Council of British Records Association, 1987-; Member, East of England Regional Archives Council, 1999-; Member, Shadow East of England Museums, Libraries and Archives Council, 2001-02; Trustee, Housing the Homeless Central Fund, 1997-; Officer/Trustee of various local societies and charities. Address: 43 College Road, Framlingham, Suffolk IP13 9ER, England.

ROBERTS Robert (James), b. 11 January 1931, Penrith, Cumbria, England. Retired Headmaster; Poet. m. Patricia Mary Milbourne, 8 August 1959, 1 son, deceased, 1 daughter. Education: MA, Pembroke College, Cambridge, 1951-55. Appointments: Assistant Master, Fettes, 1955-75; Housemaster, 1970-75; Headmaster, Worksop, 1975-86. Publications: Amphibious Landings, 1990; First Selection, 1994; Genius Loci, 1995; Second Selection, 1995; Worm's Eye View, 1995; Third Selection, 1996; Fourth Selection, 1997; Fifth Selection, 1998; Sixth Selection , 1999; Flying Buttresses, 1999. Seventh Selection, 2000; Lest We Forget, 2001; Midwinter Power Cut, 2004; Precarious Footholds, 2005; Under the Hammer, 2006; Garnerings, 2007. Contributions to: Spectator; Countryman; Poetry Review; Acumen; Envoi; Orbis; Outposts; Poetry Nottingham; Staple; Westwords; Iota; Literary Review; Poetry Wales; Seam. Honours: Many awards; Listed in international biographical dictionaries. Address: Ellon House, Harpford, Sidmouth, Devon EX10 0NH, England.

ROBERTSON George Islay McNeill (Lord Robertson of Port Ellen), b. 12 April 1946. Politician. m. Sandra Wallace, 1970, 2 sons, 1 daughter. Education: MA honours, Economics, University of Dundee, 1968. Appointments: Research Assistant Tayside Study, 1968-69; Scottish Organiser, General and Municipal Workers Union, 1969-78; MP for Hamilton, 1978-97, for Hamilton South, 1997-99; Parliamentary Private Secretary to Secretary of State for Social Services, 1979; Opposition Spokesman on Scottish Affairs, 1979-80, on Defence, 1980-81, On Foreign and Commonwealth Affairs, 1981; Principal Spokesman for Scotland, 1994-97; Secretary of State for Defence, 1997-99; Secretary General, NATO, 1999-2003; Executive Deputy Chair, Cable & Wireless, 2003-; Non-Executive Director, Smiths Group, 2004-, Weir, 2004-. Honours: Grand Cross; Order of Merit (Germany,

Hungary, Italy, Luxembourg, etc); Joint Parliamentarian of the Year, 1993; Received life peerage, 1999; Grand Cross of the Order of the Star of Romania, 2000; Knight, Order of the Thistle, UK, 2004; Knight Grand Cross, Order of St Michael and St George, UK, 2004; Honorary Regimental Colonel of the London Scottish Volunteers; Honorary Doctorates: University of Dundee, St Andrews; University of Bradford; Cranfield University-Royal Military College of Science; Baku State University, Azerbaijan; The French University, Yerevan, Armenia; Academy of Sciences, Azerbaijan and Kirgyz Republic; National School of Politics and Administration Studies, Bucharest. Memberships: Vice-Chairman, Board British Council, 1985-94; Governor, Ditchley Foundation, 1989-; Member, Her Majesty's Privy Council, 1997; President, Royal Institute of International Affairs, 2001-; Elder Brother, Trinity House, 2002-; President, Hamilton Burns Club, 2002-. Address: House of Lords, London SW1A 0PW, England. Website: www.cwplc.com

ROBERTSON George Wilber, b. 20 December 1914, Alberta, Canada. Agrometeorologist. m. Lucille Eileen Davis, 1 son, 1 daughter. Education: BSc, Mathematics and Physics, University of Alberta, 1939; MA, Physics and Meteorology, University of Toronto, 1948. Appointments: Meteorological Assistant, Meteorological Service of Canada, 1938; Officer in Charge, Meteorological Section, No 2 Air Observer School, British Commonwealth Air Training Plan, Edmonton, 1940; Meteorologist, MSC Meteorological Office, Edmonton Airport, 1945; Meteorologist, Central Meteorological Analysis Office of MSC, Ottawa, 1950; Agrometeorologist, Field Husbandry, Soils and Agricultural Engineering Division of Experimental Farms Service, Canada Department of Agriculture, Ottawa, 1951; Expert in Agrometeorology and Climatology, World Meteorological Organization, Philippines, 1969; Senior Scientist, Head of Environment Section, Research Station, Swift Current, Saskatchewan, 1971; Consultant, Food and Agriculture Organisation, Rome, Italy, 1972; Retired from Government Service, 1973; Consultant, Canadian Wheat Board, Winnipeg, 1973; Consultant, WMO, Geneva, 1974; Project Manager, FAO/UNDP Technical Assistance Project with Malaysia Federal Land Development Authority, 1975; Private Consultant in Agrometeorology, several short term projects in developing countries with various international agencies, 1977-98. Publications: Numerous scientific papers, technical reports, feasibility studies and press articles. Honours: Literary A Pin, University of Alberta, 1938; President's Award, 1951, Darton's Prize, 1953, Canadian Branch, Royal Meteorological Society; Accredited as Consulting Meteorologist, Canadian Meteorological and Oceanographic Society, 1987; Elected Fellow, Canadian Society of Agrometeorology, 1987; John Patterson Medal, Atmospheric Environmental Service, Canada, 1992; Honouree, Baier & Robertson Symposium on Modeling and Measurement of Soil Water Content, 1995. Memberships: American Meteorological Society; Fellow, Royal Meteorological Society, London; Agricultural Institute of Canada; Canadian Society of Agronomy; Ontario Institute of Professional Agrologists; Canadian Meteorological and Oceanographic Society; American Association for the Advancement of Science; The New York Academy of Sciences; Canadian Society of Agrometeorology. Address: 1604-3105 Carling Avenue, Ottawa, ON K2H 5A6, Canada. E-mail: georger400@aol.com

ROBERTSON Thomas John McMeel, b. 10 January 1928, Nagpur, India. Chartered Engineer. m. Maureen Enca, 12 June 1954, 2 sons. Education: BSc, Mechanical Engineering, Glasgow University, 1952; Member, Institute of Mechanical

Engineers, 1961; European Engineer, 1988; Member, Institute of Patentees & Inventors, 1988. Appointments: Royal Air Force, Engineering Officer, English Electric Test & Design Engineer; Cowley Concrete - Works Manager, Sir W G Armstrong Whitworth Equipment Co, Development Engineer, UKAEA, Reactor Operations & Project Engineer. Publications: Anthologies: Crime Against the Planet, 1994; To You With Love, 1997; A Variety of Verse, 1997; Timeless Exposures, 1998; Isis Valley Verses, 1999; National Poetry Anthology, 2002; National Poetry Anthology, 2003. Contribution to: Creative Writing (Pamphlet), 1996. Membership: Sinodun Writing Group. Address: The Poplars, School Lane, Milton, Abingdon, Oxon OX14 4EH, England.

ROBERTSON-PEARCE Anthony Brian, b. 3 April 1932, Lyndhurst, Hampshire, England. Anthropologist. m. Ingrid Christina Nystrom, 18 May 1956, divorced 1974, 1 son, 2 daughters. Education: Study in Munich, 1952; Diploma, French, Alliance, Française, Paris, 1959; Anthropology, Archaeology, Cambridge, 1963; Diploma, Archaeological Photography, University of Stockholm, 1965. Appointments: Supervisor, Photographer, Excavations, Moyta, Sicily on behalf of Leeds-London-Farleigh Dickinson Universities; Special programme for British School of Archaeology under Professor Sir Max Mallowan, Baghdad, Iraq, 1966; Archaeological Supervisor, Medical Officer, on behalf of University of Pennsylvania, Excavations at Tall-A-Rmah, Northern Iraq, 1967; Photographer, Medical Officer, British Excavations, Tawilan, Wadi Musa, Maan, Jordan, 1968; Field Archaeological Photographer, 1969, Publishing Department, 1972, Editor, Head, Publishing Department, 1974-79, Central Board of National Antiquaries, Stockholm, Sweden; PR Officer, Sollentuna Kommun, Stockholm, 1983-; Film debut: Commodore in Swedish Royal Navy, Swedish TV film The Inquiry, 1989; Retired 1995, continue to give lectures in History, Archaeology and Anthropology at Uppsala and Stockholm. Publications: Doctor James Robertson 1566-1652, Court Physician to King Gustavus Adolphus II of Sweden, biography, 1972; The Prehistoric Enclosure of Ekornavallen Sweden, 1974; The Ruins of Kronoberg Castle, 1974; Kaseberg Ship-setting, 1975; Klasro School 1804-1881, 1984; Rotebro and Rotsunda, The Battle of Rotebro 1497, 1985; Living Science Volume 001(author of Introduction on Iraq), 2003 Contributions to 100s of archaeological reports. Honours include: Knight, Military and Hospitaller Order of St Lazarus of Jerusalem, 1980; Malta GC; Commander, Ordre Souverain des Chevaliers du Saint-Sepulchre, 1987; Honorary DH, London, 1991; Knight of Justice, Sovereign Order of St John of Jerusalem, 1997; Lifetime Ambassador General, United Cultural Convention, USA, 2006. Memberships include: Duine Uasail of Clan Dhonnachaidh (Robertson Clan), Scotland; Fellow, Royal Anthropological Institute of Great Britain; International Commission on Monuments and Sites, Paris; Deputy Member, International Parliament for Safety and Peace, UN; Gentleman of the Bodyguard Balgouie Castle, Fife, Scotland; Country Gentlemen's Association; Several other professional and civic organizations. Address: Nybrogatan 54, S-11440, Stockholm, Sweden.

ROBINSON (Alfred) Christopher, b. 18 November 1930, York, England. Soldier; Charity Worker. m. Amanda Boggis-Rolfe, dissolved, 2 sons, 2 daughters. Education: Royal Military Academy, Sandhurst. Appointments: Major, 16th/5th The Queen's Royal Lancers, 1951-65; Trade Indemnity Company Ltd. 1066-70; Glanvill Enthoren Ltd, 1970-73; The Spastic's Society, now Scope, 1973-91; Ferriers Barn Centre for Young Disabled People, 1973-, President, 1987; The Little Foundation, 199-, Chairman, 1996; The Mother & Child

Foundation, 1994-, Chairman, 2001. Memberships: Institute of Fundraising, Welfare Committee Chairman, Royal British Legion, Bures Branch; Executive Committee, Dedham Vale Society; Vice-Chairman, Colne Stow Countryside Association; Fundraising Committee Chairman, British Red Cross, Suffolk Branch; Lay Chairman, Sudbury Deanery Synod; Member, St Edmundsbury and Ipswich Diocesan Synod. Address: Water Lane Cottage, Bures, Suffolk CO8 4DE, England.

ROBINSON Anne Josephine, b. 26 September 1944, Crosby, Liverpool, England. Journalist; Broadcaster. m. John Penrose, 1 daughter. Education: Farnborough Hill Convent, Hampshire; Les Ambassadrices, Paris. Appointments: Reporter, Daily Mail 1967-68; Reporter, Sunday Times, 1968-77; Women's Editor, 1979-80, Assistant Editor, 1980-93, Columnist, 1983-93, Daily Mirror; Columnist, Today, 1993-95; Columnist, The Sun, 1995-97; Columnist, The Express 1997-98; Columnist, The Times, 1998-2001; Columnist, Daily Telegraph, 2003-; Television: Afternoon Plus, Thames TV, 1986; Breakfast Time, BBC TV, 1987; Presenter and Writer, Points of View, BBC TV, 1988-98; Presenter and Editor, The Write Stuff, Thames TV, 1990; Presenter, Questions, TVS, 1991; Presenter, Watchdog, BBC TV, 1993-2001; Presenter, Going for a Song, BBC TV, 2000; Presenter, The Weakest Link, BBC TV, 2000-; Presenter, The Weakest Link, NBC Television, 2001-2002; Presenter, Test the Nation, BBC TV, 2002- Presenter, Guess Who's Coming to Dinner, BBC TV, 2003; Presenter, Out Take TV, BBC TV, 2003-; Travels with My Unfit Mother, 2004; Radio: Presenter, The Anne Robinson Show, BBC Radio 2, 1988-93. Honour: Honorary Fellow, Liverpool John Moores University, 1996. Membership: Vice-President Alzheimer's Society. Address: c/o Drury House, 34-43 Russell Street, London WC2B 5HA, London. E-mail: tracey.chapman@css-stellar.com

ROBINSON Derek, (Dirk Robson), b. 12 April 1932, Bristol, England. Writer. m. Sheila Collins, 29 April 1968. Education: MA, Downing College, Cambridge, England. Publications: Goshawk Squadron, 1971; Rotten With Honour, 1973; Kramer's War, 1977; The Eldorado Network, 1979; Piece of Cake, 1983; War Story, 1987; Artillery of Lies, 1991; A Good Clean Fight, 1993; Hornet's Sting, 1999; Kentucky Blues, 2002; Damned Good Show, 2002; Invasion, 1940, 2005; Red Rag Blues, 2006. Honour: Shortlisted for Booker Prize, 1971; Listed in biographical dictionaries. Address: Shapland House, Somerset Street, Kingsdown, Bristol BS2 8LZ, England.

ROBINSON Ivor, b. 28 October 1924, Bournemouth, England. Artist-Bookbinder. m. Olive Trask, 14 April 1952, 1 son, 1 daughter. Education: Southern College of Art, Bournemouth 1939-42. Appointments: Royal Navy, 1942-45; Lecturer, Bookbinding, Salisbury School of Art, 1946-53; Lecturer, Bookbinding, London School of Printing and Graphic Arts, 1953-58; Lecturer, Bookbinding, Bookworks and Visual Studies, Oxford Polytechnic, 1959-89; External Examiner, Ecole National Superieur D'Architecture et des Arts Visuels, Brussels, 1979; Adviser, Banbury School of Art, 1995-96. Publications: Introducing Bookbinding, 1st edition, 1969, 2nd edition, 1984; Contributor to the annual publication The New Bookbinder, 1981-. Creative Works: One-Man Exhibitions: Hantverket, Stockholm, Sweden, 1963; Galleria Del Bel Libro, Ascona, Switzerland, 1969; The Prescote Gallery, Cropredy, Oxfordshire, 1981; Contributor to 106 group exhibitions, 1951-2002; Work represented in collections of: The British Library; The Victoria & Albert Museum; The Bodleian Library, Oxford; Crafts Council Collection; The Keatley Trust, UK; The Rhösska Museum, Gothenburg, Sweden; The Royal Library, Copenhagen, Denmark; The

Royal Library, Stockholm, Sweden; The Royal Library, The Hague; British Royal Collections and major public and private collections in Great Britain and overseas. Honours: MBE; Honorary Fellow, Oxford Brookes University; Honorary Fellow, Designer Bookbinders; Honorary Fellow Meister Der Einbandkunst, Germany; Triple Medallist, Priz Paul Bonet, Ascona, Switzerland, 1971. Membership: Fellow, Designer Bookbinders, 1955-2003, President, 1968-73. Address: Trindles, Holton, Oxford, OX33 1PZ, England.

ROBINSON James William, b. 12 July 1923, England. Professor Emeritus. m. Winifred, 1 son, 2 daughters. Education: BSc (Hons), 1949, PhD, 1952, Chemistry, DSc, 1978, University of Birmingham; Fellow, Royal Chemical Society, 1979. Appointments: Senior Scientific Officer, British Civil Service, 1952-55; Research Associate, Louisiana State University, 1955-56; Senior Chemist, Esso Research Laboratories, 1956-63; Technical Advisor, Ethyl Research Laboratories, 1963-64; Associate Professor of Chemistry, 1964-66, Professor of Chemistry, 1966-93, Professor Emeritus (active in research), 1993-, Louisiana State University. Publications: Over 200 articles in professional journals; Textbook, Undergraduate Instrumental Analysis, 2006; 20 invited chapters in books. Honours: Guggenheim Fellowship, 1975; Honor Scroll, American Institute of Chemistry, 1980; Visiting Distinguished Professor, University of Sydney, Australia, 1983; Gold Medal Award, New York Section, Society of Applied Spectroscopy, 2000. Address: Department of Chemistry, Louisiana State University, Baton Rouge, LA 70803, USA. E-mail: jrobi24@1su.edu

ROBINSON Karen, b. 15 August 1958, New Brunswick, New Jersey, USA. Dietician. m. Richard A Robinson. Education: BS, Home Economics, Montclair State College, New Jersey, 1980; Certified Food Services Sanitation Manager, New Jersey, 1984; Dietetic Internship, Veterans Affairs Medical Center, Virginia, 1991; Masters Degree, Health Sciences, Dietetics, James Madison University, Virginia, 1992. Appointments: Temporary Sales Secretary, Banquet preparation Staff, Boar's Head Inn, Charlottesville, Virginia, 1986-88; Head Diet Counsellor, Diet Center, Charlottesville, Virginia, 1986-90; Public Health Nutritionist, Central Shenandoah Health District, Waynesboro, Virginia, Health Department, 1993-97; Dietetic Intern Mentor, 1993-97; Consulting Dietician, Hebrew Hospital Home, Bronx, New York, 1998; Food Service Manager, Sodexho Marriot Services, Morningside House Nursing Home, Bronx, New York, 1998-99; Clinical Dietician, Yonkers General Hospital, Yonkers New York, 1999-2001; Community Services Instructor, Westchester Community College, Valhalla, New York, 2001; Inpatient/Outpatient Dietician, Park Care Pavilion (formerly Yonkers General Hospital, 2001-); Clinical Dietician, St John's Riverside Hospital, Yonkers, New York, 2002-; Outpatient Dietician, St John's Riverside, Valentine Lane Family Practice, Yonkers, 2005 and 2007. Publications: Abstract as co-author: The psychological predictors of successful weight loss, 1992; Contributed articles to local newspapers and journals. Honours: Recipient, New York State Dietetic Association Grant. Listed in Who's Who publications and biographical dictionaries. Memberships: American Dietetics Association; Nutrition Entrepreneurs; Dieticians in Nutrition Support; Healthy Aging; Consultant Dieticians in Health Care Facilities; Westchester Rockland Dietetic Association; Virginia Dietetics Association, 1993-97; Virginia Public Health Association, 1995-97. Address: 10-02 Hunter Lane, Ossining, NY 10562, USA.

DICTIONARY OF INTERNATIONAL BIOGRAPHY

ROBINSON Sir Kenneth (Ken), b. 4 March 1950, Liverpool, England. Educator. m. Marie Thérése, 1 son, 1 daughter. Education: B Ed (with Honours), English and Drama, University of Leeds, 1972; Certificate of Education (with Distinction); Doctor of Philosophy, University of London, 1980. Appointments: Co-ordinator, Drama 10-16, National Development Project , Schools Council of England and Wales, 1974-77; Freelance lecturer, writer, 1977-79; Director, Calouste Gulbenkian Foundation National Committee of Inquiry on The Arts in Schools, 1979-81; Director, Gulbenkian Foundation/Leverhulme Inquiry: The Arts and Higher Education, 1981-82; Director, Calouste Gulbenkian Foundation, Arts Education Development Programme, 1981-83; Publisher, Managing Editor, Arts Express, monthly magazine, 1983-85; Director, National Curriculum Council's, Arts in Schools Project, 1985-89; Professor of Arts Education, 1989-2001, Professor Emeritus, 2001-, University of Warwick; Currently, Senior Adviser, J Paul Getty Trust, Los Angeles, California, USA. Publications: 18 books and monographs; 17 book chapters and journal papers; Numerous newspaper features and interviews and appearances on radio and television. Honours: Knighted for services to the arts, June 2003. Memberships include: Member of Board and Chairman, Education Committee, Birmingham Royal Ballet; Education Adviser, Chairman Education Policy Group, Arts Council of Great Britain; Education Advisory Council, Independent Television Commission; Director, British Theatre Institute; Adviser to Outreach Programme, The Royal Academy. Address: J Paul Getty Trust, 1200 Getty Center Drive, Los Angeles, 90049, USA.

ROBINSON Mary, b. 21 May 1944, Ballina, County Mayo, Ireland. International Civil Servant; Former Head of State. m. Nicholas Robinson, 1970, 2 sons, 1 daughter. Education: Trinity College, Dublin; King's Inns, Dublin; Harvard University, USA. Appointments: Barrister, 1967, Senior Counsel, 1980; Called to English Bar (Middle Temple), 1973; Reid Professor of Constitutional and Criminal Law, Trinity College, Dublin, 1969-75; Lecturer, European Community Law, 1975-90; Founder, Director, Irish Centre for European Law, 1988-90; Senator, 1969-89; President, Ireland, 1990-97; UN High Commissioner for Human Rights, 1997-2002; Chancellor, Dublin University, 1998-; Professor of Practice, Columbia University School of International and Public Affairs, New York, 2004-; The Elders, 2007. Honours include: LLD honoris causa (National University of Ireland; Cambridge; Brown; Liverpool; Dublin; Montpellier; St Andrews; Melbourne; Columbia; National University of Wales; Poznan; Toronto; Fordham; Queens University, Belfast); Dr honoris causa Public Services (Northeastern University); Honorary Docteur en Sciences Humaines (Rennes), 1996; Honorary LLD (Coventry), 1996; Berkeley Medal, University of California; Medal of Honour, University of Coimbra; Medal of Honour, Ordem dos Advogados, Portugal; Gold Medal of Honour, University of Salamanca; Andrés Bello Medal, University of Chile; New Zealand Suffrage Centennial Medal; Freedom Prize, Max Schmidheiny Foundation (Switzerland); UNIFEM Award, Noel Foundation, Los Angeles; Marisa Bellisario Prize, Italy, 1991; European Media Prize, The Netherlands, 1991; Special Humanitarian Award, CARE, Washington DC, 1993; International Human Rights Award, International League of Human Rights, New York, 1993; Liberal International Prize for Freedom, 1993; Stephen P Duggan Award (USA), 1994; Freedom of the City of Cork; Honorary AO; Council of Europe North South Prize, Portugal, 1997; Collar of Hussein Bin Ali, Jordan, 1997; F D Roosevelt Four Freedoms Medal, 1998; Erasmus Prize, Netherlands, 1999; Fulbright Prize, USA, 1999; Garrigues Walker Prize, Spain, 2000; William

Butler Prize, USA, 2000; Indira Gandhi Peace Prize, India, 2000; Sydney Peace Prize, 2002. Memberships include: Royal Irish Academy; Honorary Bencher Kings Inns, Dublin, Middle Temple, London. Address: Columbia University School of International and Public Affairs, 420 West 118th Street, New York, NY 10027, USA. Website: www.sipa.columbia.edu

ROBINSON Tony, b. 15 August 1946, London, England. Actor; Writer; TV Presenter. 1 son, 1 daughter. Education: Central School of Speech and Drama. Career: Theatre: Numerous appearances as a child actor including the original stage version of the musical Oliver!; Several years in repertory theatre; Theatre director, 2 years, then Chichester Festival Theatre, Royal Shakespeare Company and National Theatre; Touring in 1 man show, Tony Robinson's Cunning Night Out, 2005; Television: Ernie Roberts in Horizon's Joey; Baldrick in Black Adder (4 series, BBC); Sheriff of Nottingham in Maid Marian and Her Merry Men (also writer, 4 series); Alan in My Wonderful Life (3 series, Granada); Leading role in Channel 4 series, Who Dares Wins; As presenter: Points of View; Stay Tooned; Time Team (Channel 4,); Social history series: The Worst Jobs in History, 2004; Historical Documentaries for Channel 4 on: The Peasants Revolt, the Roman Emperors, Macbeth, Robin Hood, the Holy Grail. Publications: Children's television programmes include: 30 episodes of Central TV's Fat Tulips Garden; 13 part BBC series based on Homer's Iliad and Odyssey: Odysseus – The Greatest Hero of Them All; 26 episodes of the Old Testament series Blood and Honey; Mrs Caldicot's Cabbage War, 2000; Tales from the Madhouse, 2000; Spider Plant Man, 2005; Hogfather, 2006; 17 children's books include: Tony Robinson's Kings and Queens; Adult books include most recently: The Worst Jobs in History; Archaeology is Rubbish – A Beginners Guide (with Professor Mick Aston); In Search of British Heroes; Currently putting the entire works of Terry Pratchett onto audio tape. Honours: 2 Royal Television Society Awards; BAFTA Award; International Prix Jeunesse; Honorary MA: Bristol University, 1999, University of East London, 2002; Honorary Doctorate: University of Exeter, 2005; Open University, 2005. Memberships: British Actors Equity, Vice-President, 1996-2000; President, Young Archaeology Club; National Executive Committee, Labour Party, 2000-2004. Address: c/o Jeremy Hicks Associates, 114-115 Tottenham Court Road, London W1T 5AH, England.

ROBINSON William Peter, Professor Emeritus; Social Psychology. Education: MA, D Phil (Oxon); Fellow, Australian and British Psychological Societies; Chartered Psychologist; CSCE Qualified Interpreter in Russian. Appointments: Academic positions at Universities of Hull, London, Southampton; Chairs of Education at Macquarie and Bristol Universities; Chair of Social Psychology, Bristol University; Currently, University and Leverhulme Senior Research Fellow and Professor Emeritus, Bristol University; Trustee: College of St Paul and St Mary, Cheltenham; Chair, Deaf Studies Trust; Chair and Vice-Chair, The Red Maid's School, Bristol; Bristol Municipal Charities. Publications: 6 authored books; 2 technical reports; 6 edited books; 4 edited series; More than 100 journal articles and chapters; Including most recently: Books: The New Handbook of Language and Social Psychology (co-editor), 2001; Language in Social Worlds, 2003; Arguing To Better Conclusions, 2006. Honours include: DSIR (ESRC) Postgraduate Award; Honorary Professor, Instituto Superior de Psicologia Aplicada, Lisbon; Visiting Professor, Monash University, Cheltenham CHE; Fellow, Japanese Society for the Promotion of Science; Visiting Scholar, Wolfson College, Oxford; JV Smyth Memorial Lecturer, Melbourne; Centenary Lecturer,

University of Hanover; 13 funded research projects; listed in national and international biographies. Memberships: Various committees, SSRC/ESRC; Chair and Committee Member Social Psychology Section, Member of Council, British Psychological Society; Co-founder and Foundation President, International Association of Language and Social Psychology; Research Committee, International Communication Association; Co-founder triennial international conferences on language and social psychology, 1979-. Address: Holmbury, Thorncliffe Drive, Cheltenham, GL51 6PY, England.

ROBISON Victor James, b. 29 April 1920, Youngstown, Ohio, USA. Retired US Naval Officer. Education: BS, 1942, MA, 1948, Case Western Reserve University, Cleveland , Ohio; Continued studies in American Culture at Sorbonne University, Paris, 1949-50, and Philosophy, Columbia University, New York City, 1950-51. Appointments: Communications Officer, USS Taylor (DD468), Pacific, 1943-46; Training Officer, US Naval Reserve Training Center, Baltimore, Maryland, 1952-55; Assistant Operations Officer, USS Worcester (CL144), 1956-57; US Naval Attaché and Naval Attaché for Air, American Embassy, Warsaw, Poland, 1957-58; Officer-in-Charge, Naval Liaison Group and Chief, Plant Engineering and Maintenance Division, Alternative Joint Communication Agency, Ft Richie, Maryland, 1958-61; US Naval Attaché and Naval Attaché for Air, American Embassy, Brussels, Belgium, 1962-66; Assistant Curator for the US Navy, Washington DC, 1967-69; Appraiser of Naval Memorabilia and Artefacts, 1970-76. Honours: Awarded Naval Unit Commendation and Asian-Pacific Medal with 13 Battle Stars and other medals for service during WWII from Taylor; Decorated Order of Leopold II, Belgian Minister of Defence, 1966. Memberships: Beta Theta Pi Fraternity; Veterans of Foreign Wars; American Legion; Smithsonian Institution; Navy League. Address: 423 Seventh St SE, Washington DC 20003, USA.

ROBSON Sir Bobby (Robert William), b. 18 February 1933, Sacriston, Co Durham, England. Professional Football Manager; Former Football Player. m. Elsie Mary Gray, 1955, 3 sons. Education: Waterhouses Secondary Modern, Co Durham. Career: Player: Fulham, 1950-56, 1962-67, West Bromwich Albion, 1956-62; 20 caps for England; Manager, Vancouver FC, 1967-68, Fulham, 1968-69, Ipswich Town, 1969-82 (won FA Cup, 1978, UEFA Cup, 1981), England national team, 1982-90; PSV Eindhoven, 1990-92, 1998 (won Dutch title twice), Sporting Lisbon, 1993, Porto, 1994-96 (won Portuguese title twice), Barcelona, 1997-98 (won Spanish Cup, European Cup Winner's Cup), Newcastle United, 1999-2004; Republic of Ireland national team, International Football Consultant. Publications: Time on the Grass (autobiography), 1982; So Near and Yet So Far: Bobby Robson's World Cup Diary, 1986; Against the Odds, 1990; Living the Game, 2004; My Autobiography: An Englishman Abroad, 1998; Farewell but not Goodbye, 2005. Honours: CBE, 1990; Hon MA (University of East Anglia) 1997; Freedom of Ipswich, 2002; Knighted, 2002; Hon DCL (Newcastle University) 2003; English Football Hall of Fame, 2003. Address: c/o Newcastle United FC, St James' Park, Newcastle Upon Tyne, NE1 4ST, England.

ROBSON Bryan, b. 11 January 1957, Chester-le-Street, England. Professor Football Manager; Former Professional Football Player. m. Denise, 1979, 1 son, 2 daughters. Education: Birtley Lord Lawson Comprehensive. Career: Player with: West Bromwich Albion, 1974-81; Manchester United (FA Cup winners) 1983, 1985, 1990; Euro Cup Winners' Cup, 1991; Winner, League Championship, 1992-93,

1993-94; 90 caps (65 as captain), scoring 26 international goals; Player, Manager, Middlesborough FC, 1994-2001, Bradford City, 2003-04, West Bromwich Albion, 2004-2006; Sheffield United, 2007-; Formed Robson Lloyd Consultancy Ltd, 2007. Assistant Coach, national team, 1994. Publications: Autobiography: Robbo, 2006. Honours: OBE; Hon MA (Salford), 1992, (Manchester), 1992; English Football Hall of Fame, 2002. Address: West Bromwich Albion, The Hawthorns, West Bromwich, West Midlands B71 4LF, England. Website: www.wba.co.uk

ROCCA Costantino, b. 4 December 1956, Bergamo, Italy. Golfer. m. 1 son, 1 daughter. Career: Former factory worker and caddie; Turned professional, 1981; Qualified for PGA European Tour through 1989 Challenge Tour; Won Open V33 Da Grand Lyon and Peugeot Open de France; First Italian Golfer to be member European Ryder Cup team, 1993; Member, winning European Ryder Cup team, 1995; AIB Irish Seniors Open, 2007.

ROCHA John, b. 23 August 1953, Hong Kong. Fashion Designer. Education: London College of Fashion. Career: Founder, own fashion design company, 1980, menswear line, 1993, jeans line, 1997; Regular collections at all major international fashion shows; Designed interiors for hotels and office blocks including: The Morrison Hotel, Dublin; Designed glassware for Waterford Crystal; Runs own brand labels for Debenhams. Honours: British Designer of the Year, 1993. Address: John Rocha, 12-13 Temple Lane, Dublin 2, Ireland.

ROCHA-PEREIRA Maria Helena, b. 3 September 1925, Oporto, Portugal. Professor Emeritus. Education: MA, Classics, University of Coimbra, Portugal, 1947; Student, University of Oxford, England, 1950-51, 1954, 1959; DLitt, University of Coimbra, 1956. Appointments: Lecturer, Latin and Greek, Centre for Humanistic Studies attached to the University of Oporto, 1948-57; Lecturer, 1951-56, Senior Lecturer, 1956-62, Reader, 1962-64, Professor, 1964-95, Professor Emeritus, 1995-, University of Coimbra; Visiting Professor, Federal University of Minas Gerais, Brazil, 1980; Lectures and Seminars, Federal University of Minas Gerais and Federal University of Rio de Janeiro, 1987, 96; Vice-Chancellor, University of Coimbra, 1970-71; President, Scientific Council, Coimbra Faculty of Arts, 1977-89. Publications: Greek Vases in Portugal, 1967; Estudos de Historia da Cultura Classica, Vol 1, 10th edition, 2006; Vol 2, 3rd edition, 2002; Novos Ensaios sobre Temas Classicos na Poesia Portuguesa, 1988; Pausanias (critical edition) 3 volumes, 2nd edition, 1989-90; Helade, 9th edition, 2005; Romana, 5th edition, 2005; Paysage réel et paysage spitituel de la Grèce chez quelques poètes portugais contemporains (paper presented to Congress in Zagreb, 2000). Honours: Essay Prize, Portuguese Ministry of education, 1966; Essay prize, PEN Club, 1988; Woman of the Year, American Biographical Institute, 1994; Great Cross of the Order of St Jacob-of-the-Sword, Portugal, 2004; Essay Prize, Center for Iberian Studies, 2004; International Educator of the Year, IBC, 2004; Essay Prize, International Association of Literary Critics, 2006; University of Coimbra Prize, 2006; The Plato Award, IBC, 2006; Latinity Prize, Union Latine, 2006; Golden Medal of the City of Oporto, 2007. Memberships: National Council for University Education; Scientific Council for the Humanities of the National Institute for Scientific Research; President, National Committee for the Evaluation of Portuguese State Universities, Classical and Modern Languages and Literatures; Representative of the Lisbon Academy of Sciences in the Standing Committee for the Humanities of the European Science Foundation, 1988-98;

Representative of Portugal in the Scientific Council of the Lexicon Iconographicum Mythologiae Classicae; Honorary member of the Foundation for Hellenic Culture, Athens. Address: 1 Praceta Dias da Silva, 3000 Coimbra, Portugal. E-mail: classic@ci.uc.pt

ROCHE DE COPPENS Peter G, b. 24 May 1938, Vevey, Switzerland. Professor, Author. m. Maria Teresa Crivelli. Education: BS, Columbia University, New York, 1965; MA, 1966, PhD, 1972, Fordham University, New York. Appointments: Professor of Sociology/Anthropology, East Stroudsburg University of Pennsylvania, 1970-; Created TV program: Soul Sculpture, East Stroudsburg University, 1991-; Consultant, United Nations, PNUCID, 1997; Adjunct Professor, Department of Culture and Values in Education, McGill University, Montreal, 1998. Publications: Divine Light and Fire and Divine Light and Love, 1992, 1994; L'Alternance Instinctive and La Voie Initiatique de l'An 2000 (Louise Courteau); Prayer: the Royal Path of the Spiritual Tradition, 2003; True and Great Love Stories, 2005; The Spiritual family in the 21st Century, 2005. Medicine and Spirituality with 13 vols. Of which 9 are published: Medicina e Spiritualita 2003; La Preghiera, Strumento di Guarigione. La Thea Flora 2004; Il Perdono, Il Destino 2005; Religion, Spirituality and Healthcare, 2007. Honours: Phi Beta Kappa; Woodrow Wilson Fellow; Knight Commander of Malta; American Biographical Institute's Commemorative Medal of Honor; Listed in national and international biographical dictionaries. Memberships: American Sociological Association; American Orthopsychiatric Association; New York Academy of Sciences; American Association for the Advancement of Science. Address: 124 S Kistler Street, East Stroudsburg, PA 18301 2604, USA.

ROCK David Annison, b. 27 May 1929, Sunderland, England. Architect. m. (1) Daphne Elizabeth Richards, 3 sons, 2 daughters, (2) Lesley Patricia Murray. Education: B Arch Hons (Dunelm), School of Architecture, Kings College, University of Durham, 1947-52; Cert TP (Dunelm), Department of Town Planning, Kings College, University of Durham, 1950-52; School of Town Planning, University of London, 1952-53. Appointments: 2nd Lieutenant, Royal Engineers, 1953-55; Basil Spence & Partners, 1952-53, 1955-59; David Rock Architect, 1958-59; Partner, Building Design Partnership, 1959-71; Chairman, Managing Director, Rock Townsend, 1971-92; Head, Lottery Architecture Unit, Arts Council of England, 1995-99; Partner, Camp 5, 1992-; Chairman, 5 Dryden Street, 1971-80; Chairman, Barley Mow Workspace, 1973-92; Lottery Awards Panel, Sports Council of England, 1995-97; Vice-President, 1987-88, 1995-97, President, 1997-99, Royal Institute of British Architects; Vice-President, 2000, President, 1997-99, 2002-, Architects Benevolent Society; Trustee, Montgomery Sculpture Trust, 2000-2004; Trustee, South Norfolk Building Preservation Trust, 2002-2005; Finance Director, Huguenot Court Limited, 2003-05, 2006-. Publications: Books: Vivat Ware! 1974; The Grassroots Developers, 1980; Numerous articles in building press, 1960-. Honours: Department of the Environment Housing Medals, RIBA Architecture Awards, Civic Trust Awards, 1965-92; Glover Medal, 1949; HB Saint Award, 1950; Crown Prize, 1951; Soane Medallion, 1954; Owen Jones Studentship, 1960; RIBA/Building Industry Trust Fellow, 1979; President's Medal, AIA, 1998; Honorary Fellow, American Institute of Architects, 1998. Memberships: Past President, RIBA; Fellow, Chartered Society of Designers. Address: The Beeches, 13 London Road, Harleston, Norfolk IP20 9BH, England. E-mail: david.rock1@btinternet.com

RODAHL Kaare, b. 17 August 1917, Rodal, Norway. Retired. m. Joan Hunter, 1 son, 1 daughter. Education: MD, 1948, DSc, 1950, Oslo University; USA Medical Degree, 1957. Appointments: Special Consultant, US Air Force, 1949; Chief, Department of Physiology, Arctic Aeromedical Laboratory, Fairbanks, Alaska, 1950-52; Assistant Professor of Physiology, Oslo University, 1952-54; Director of Research, Arctic Aeromedical Laboratory, Fairbanks, Alaska, 1954-57; Director of Research, Lankenau Hospital, Philadelphia, 1957-65; Director, Institute of Work Physiology, Oslo, Norway, 1965-87; Professor, Norwegian College of Physical Education, Oslo, Norway, 1966-87; Retired. Publications include: Textbook of Work Physiology, 4th edition, 2003; The Physiology of Work, 1989; Stress Monitoring in the Workplace, 1994. Honours include: Honorary member, staff and faculty, US Army Command and General Staff College, Fort Leavenworth, Kansas, 1960; Knight of the Royal Norwegian Order of St Olav, 1988. Memberships: American Physiological Society; Norwegian Medical Association. Address: Maaltrostveien 40, Oslo 0786, Norway.

RODMAN Dennis Keith, b. 13 May 1961, Trenton, New Jersey, USA. Basketball Player. Education: Cooke County Junior College; Southeastern Oklahoma State University. Career: West Detroit Pistons, 1986-93; Forward San Antonio Spurs, 1993-95, Chicago Bulls, 1995-99; L A Lakers, 1999; Dallas Mavericks, 2000; Retired, 2000; Resumed career with Long Beach Jam (American Basketball Association), 2003; Orange County Crush, 2004-. Honours: NBA Defensive Player of Year, 1990, 1991; NBA Championship Team, 1989-90, 1996; All-Defensive First Team, 1989-93, All-Defense Second Team, 1994; All Star Team, 1990, 1992. Film appearances: Cutaway; Simon Sez; Double Team. Publications: Bad as I Wanna Be, 1997; Walk on the Wild Side, 1997; Words from the Worm: An Unauthorised Trip Through the Mind of Dennis Rodman, 1997; I Should Be Dead By Now, 2005. Address: L A Lakers, 3900 West Manchester Boulevard, Inglewood, CA 90306, USA.

RODRIGUEZ DELGADO Aldo, b. 8 July 1955, Havana, Cuba. Guitarist. m. Victoria Diaz de Villegas Rozhkova, 1 son, 2 daughters. Education: National School of Arts, 1968-73; Studies under Professors Issac Nicola and Martha Cuervo, Instituto Superior de Arte de la Habana, 1976-81; Postgraduate studies in counterpoint, harmony, history of music, musical analysis, guitar. Career: Guitar Professor, Basic Music School of Holguin, 1973-76; Guitar Professor, Escuela Nacional de Arte, La Habana, Cuba, 1976-78; Guitar Professor, Escuela de Bellas Artes, Cartagena, Colombia, 1997; Teacher at numerous master classes; Participant in International Music Festivals: Varna, Bulgaria, Morelia, Mexico, Moscow, Russia, Mendoza, Argentina, Rostock, Germany, Ankara, Turkey; International Guitar Festivals: Volos, Greece, Esztergom, Hungary, Havana, Cuba, Tychi, Poland, Istanbul, Turkey, Laredo, Spain, Gotze-Delchev, Bulgaria; Performances with orchestras including: National Symphony Orchestra de Cuba and Matanzas, Cuba; Symphony and Philharmonic Orchestra of Bogota, Colombia; Radio and Television Symphonic Orchestra, Bulgaria; Symphonic Orchestra of Matanzas, Camaguey y Santiago de Cuba; Philharmonic Orchestra of Istanbul, Turkey; Philharmonic Orchestra of Wrocklaw, Poland; Porto Symphony Orchestra, Portugal. Publications: Una Vida a Contramano (book about the life of Maria Luisa Anido); Isaac Nicola: Maestro de Maestros (book about the teacher's life); Metodo de Guitarra (study manual). Compositions include: Cancion y Fuga en Son (2 guitars); La Leyenda del Juglar; Cancion y Danza; Retrato de Mujer; Aire Brasilero. Recordings: Latin American Concert;

Album "Rodrigo-Brouwer; Masterly Concert (live); Album "Bach-Vivaldi". Honours include: 1st prize, International Guitar Contest, Esztergom, Hungary, 1979; 3rd Prize, International Guitar Contest, Alirio Diaz, Caracas, Venezuela, 1979; 1st Prize, Chamber Music Contest, Higher Institute of Arts of Havana, 1981; 3rd Prize, International Guitar Contest of Havana, Cuba, 1982; Laureate, International Guitar Contest, Francisco Tarrega Benicasim, Spain, 1982; 3rd and Special Prize given by La banca de San Paolo di Torino, Italy, Alessandria, 1983; Diploma of Honour, Contest "Maria Canals", Barcelona, Spain, 1985; Egrem Prize for the Most Sold Classical Music Disc, 1987; Egrem Prize for the Greatest Cultural Contribution Disc, 1991. Address: Calle 13, No 108, Apartamento 74 e/ L y M Vedado, La Habana, Cuba. E-mail: aldor@cubarte.cult.cu

RODRIGUEZ Alfredo E, b. 3 October 1950, Cordoba, Argentina. Interventional Cardiology. m. Marta Biagioni, 3 sons, 3 daughters. Education: Medical Doctor, Cordoba National University, School of Medicine, 1973; PhD, Cordoba Catholic University, 1984; Specialist in Hemodynamics and Angiography, Argentine Collegium of Hemodynamics, 1985. Appointments: Intern, Internal Medicine, Air Force Hospital, Cordoba, 1974; Resident, 1975-78, Chief of Residents, 1979, Cardiology Department, Staff Member, 1980-85, Assistant Director, 1985-88, Interventional Cardiology Service, Hospital Privado Sanatorio Guemes, Favaloro Foundation, Buenos Aires, Argentina; Intern, Interventional Cardiology Service, San Francisco Heath Institute, San Francisco, USA, 1981; Chief , Interventional Cardiology Service, Praxis Medica, Buenos Aires, 1988-92; Chief, Interventional Cardiology Service, 1988-99, Co-Director, Teaching Unit, 1991-98, Sanatorio Anchorena, Buenos Aires; Consultant, Interventional Cardiology Service, Cosme Argerich Hospital, Buenos Aires, 1991; Consultant, Interventional Cardiology Service, Spanish Hospital, Mendoza, 1992-; Founder and President, Center for Investigations in Interventional Cardiology, 1993-; Chief, Interventional Cardiology Service, Otamendi Hospital, Buenos Aires, 1993-; Consultant, Interventional Cardiology, Spanish Hospital, Bahia Blanca, 1993-; Associate Professor, Intervential Cardiology, School of Medicine, Barcelo University, 1998-2000; Chief, Interventional Cardiology Service, Adrogue Medical Institute, Adrogue-Buenos Aires, 1998-; Director, Post Graduate Medical School, Buenos Aires University School of Medicine, 2001, 2002; Chief, Interventional Cardiology Service, Las Lomas Institute, Buenos Aires, 2003-. Publications: More than 400 articles in professional journals. Honours: Rafael Bullrich Award, National Academy of Medicine, 1981; Dr Luis Sivori Award, 1990; Argentine Foundation of Cardiology Award, 1993; Argentine Society of Cardiology Award, 1993; Argentine Journal of Cardiology, 1994; Roberto Villavicencio Foundation Aard, 1995; Solaci Award, 1996; Nominee, Ethica Award, 1997; USCAS Award, 2000; Geronimo H Alvarez National Academy of Medicine, 2001; Alejandro Spinetta Award, 2001; Best Abstract Presentation, European Society of Cardiology Congress, 2005. Memberships: Argentine Society of Cardiology; Bolivian Society of Cardiology; Argentine Collegium of Hemodynamics. Address: Av Callao 1441-4 Floor, B (1024), Buenos Aires, Argentina.

RODRIGUEZ Roberto Miguel, b. 18 February 1944, Cuba. Company President. m. Lourdes Maria, 1 son, 1 daughter. Education: Doctor en Psicologia, 1961, Doctor en Sico-Pedagogia, 1962, Universidad Latino Americana de la Habana, Cuba; Doctor of Philosophy, University of Minnesota, 1998; Juris Doctor, Northwestern California School of Law, 2006. Appointments: Owner and CEO: AHR Properties Inc; AHR Construction Inc; Shoreview Investments LLC; Blaine Investments Incorporated; RMR Estate Company. Publications: Cuba must discover Democracy, 1996; Purchasing properties in foreclosure, 1997; What do we know about creativity? 2007. Honours: National Award Winner, US Achievement Academy; Capps Capozzolo Award in Academic Excellence, University of Southern Colorado. Memberships: Institute of Management Accountants; Southern Poverty Law Center; Christian Solidarity International; Academy of Political Sciences. Address: 11916 Davenport Court NE, Blaine, MN 55449, USA. E-mail: rbrtrod@earthlink.net

RODRIGUEZ SALVADOR Marisela, b. 6 January 1969, Mexico City, Mexico. Science Educator. Education: Degree (Hon), Food Engineering, Universidad Auto Noma Metropolitan, Mexico City, 1991; PhD (Hon), Universidad Politecnica de Cataluna, Barcelona, 1999. Appointments: Design of Competitive and Technical Intelligence Systems; Management of Innovation and Technology; Competitive and Technical Intelligence, Iberoamerica Pioneering; Competitive and Technical Intelligence, Centro de Calidad y Manufactura. Publications: Numerous articles in prestigious journals including Revista de Giencia y Techologia, Brazil: Economia Industrial, Spain; Puzzle Revista Hispana de la Inteligencia Competitiva, Spain; Competitive Intelligence Review, USA; Escuela de Economia y Necocios, Argentina; Research Evaluation, UK; International Journal of Technology, Intelligence and Planning, Switzerland. Honours: Mexican Representative, World Intellectual Property and World Trade Organization, 2004. Memberships: National Research System of Mexico. E-mail: marisrod@itesm.mx Website: http://inteligenciacompetitiva.mty.itesm.mx

RODWELL (His Honour) Daniel Alfred Hunter, b. 3 January 1936, Bombay, India. Lawyer. m. Veronica Cecil, 2 sons, 1 daughter. Education: Munro College, Jamaica; Worcester College, Oxford. Appointments: National Service, 1954-56: 2nd Lieutenant, The West Yorkshire Regiment, 1955; Captain and Adjutant, 3rd Battalion, Prince of Wales Own Regiment of Yorkshire, 1962-66; Called to Bar, Inner Temple, 1960; Assistant Recorder, 1976; Recorder, 1980; Queen's Counsel, 1982; Circuit Judge, 1986-2002; Resident Judge, Luton Crown Court, 1993-2000; Resident Judge, Aylesbury Crown Court, 1999-2002; Deputy Circuit Judge, 2002-05. Publications: Journal article: Applications for Third Party Material Where Public Interest Immunity is Likely to be Claimed, 1998; Problems with the Sexual Offences Act, 2003. Honour: Queen's Counsel 1982. Memberships: Royal Institution of Great Britain; Bar Yacht Club; Pegasus Club; Inner Temple. Address: Roddimore House, Winslow Road, Great Horwood, MK17 0NY, England. E-mail: dan.rodwell@btinternet.com

RÖHLING Horst Rudolf, b. 28 October 1929, Zwickau/Sa, Germany. Retired Librarian; Lecturer in Eastern Churches History. Education: University final examination, 1953; Doctor's Degree, 1956; Librarian Examination, 1963. Appointments: University Assistant, 1955-58; Collaborator in University and Library, 1958-61; Librarian, 1963-94. Publications: Studien zur Geschichte der balkanslavischen Volkspoesie, 1975; Slavica-Bibliotheca-Ecclesia Orientalis, 1981; Drei Bulgaro-Germanica, 1983; Publikationsformen als verbindendes Element, 1992; Numerous publications on slavistics, eastern churches and library science. Honours: Fellow, American Biographical Institute. Memberships: Wolfenbütteler Arbeitkreis für Bibliotheks-, Buch- und Mediengeschichte; Deutsche Gesellschaft für die Erforschung des 18 Jahrhunderts; Study Group on 18th Century Russia;

Südosteuropa-Gesellschaft; Honorary Member, ABDOS; 4C's Club; Honorary Member Deutsch-Bulgarische Gesellschaft; Verein der Freunde der Ratsschulbibliothek Zwickau; Gesellschaft der Freunde und Förderer der Sächsischen Landesbibliothek Dresden; Gesellschaft Anna Amalia Bibliothek Weimar; Internationale Buchwissenschaftliche Gesellschaft. Address: Unterkrone 37, D-58455 Witten, Germany.

ROGOZKIN Victor, b. 23 February 1928, Leningrad, Russia. Biochemist. m. Komkova Antonina. Education: AB, Military Institute of Physical Culture, Leningrad, 1953; State University, Leningrad, 1958; BD (Hon) State University, Leningrad, 1960; DSc, Institute of Physiology, Leningrad, 1966. Appointments: Researcher, Research Institute of Physical Culture, Leningrad, 1959-65; Professor of Biochemistry, 1966-70; Director of the Institute, 1970-2003. Publications: Current Research in Sport Science, 1996; Co-editor: Nutrition, Physical Fitness and Health, 1978; Author: Physical Activity in Disease Prevention and Treatment, 1985; Metabolism of Anabolic Andorgenic Steroids, 1991; Over 360 papers; Current major research interests relate to exercise biochemistry and sports nutrition. Honours: Honoured Scientist of Russian Federation, 1989; Award, United States Sports Academy, 1991. Memberships: Research Group on Biochemistry of Exercise UNESCO; Editorial Board, International Journal Sport Nutrition. Address: Research Institute of Physical Culture, Dynamo Ave 2, 197110 St Petersburg, Russia.

ROH Moo-hyun, b. 6 August 1946, Gimhae, Gyeongsangnam-do, Korea. President of the Republic of Korea. m. Kwon Yang-sook, 1 son, 1 daughter. Education: Graduate, Busan Commercial High School, 1966; Passed 17th National Bar Examination, 1975. Appointments: Judge, Daejeon District Court, 1977; Practising Attorney, 1978-; Human Rights Lawyer, 1981-; Chairman and Director, Busan Headquarters, Citizens' Movement for a Democratic Constitution, 1987; One of Leaders of June Democratisation Struggles, 1987; Elected to 13th National Assembly in Busan's Eastern District, 1988; Member, Special Committee to Investigate Political Corruption during the Fifth Republic, 1988; Spokesman, 1991, Senior Member, Central Committee, 1993, United Democratic Party; Director, Research Centre for Local Autonomy, 1993; Standing Committee Member, Committee for the Promotion of National Reconciliation and Unity, 1996; Vice-President, National Congress for New Politics, 1997; Elected to 15th National Assembly, 1998; Minister of Maritime Affairs and Fisheries, 2000-2001; Advisor and Senior Member, Central Committee, Millennium Democratic Party, 2000; Elected President of the Republic of Korea, 2002; Sworn in as President for a 5 year term of office, 2003; Stripped of constitutional powers following impeachment vote, then later returned to office after Constitutional Court overturned impeachment, 2004. Publications: Honey, Please Help Me! 1994; Roh Moo-hyun Meets Lincoln, 2001; Thoughts on Leadership, 2002. Address: Office of the President, Chong Wa Dae (The Blue House), 1 Sejong-no, Jongno-gu, Seoul. Website: www.bluehouse.go.kr

ROHATGI Pradip Krishna (Roy), b. 10 November 1939, Calcutta, India. Professor; Consultant. m. Pauline Mary Rohatgi. Education: Bachelor of Commerce, Calcutta University, 1960; Bachelor of Science, Economics, University of London, 1964; Associate Examinations of the Institute of Taxation (UK), 1967; Associate Member, 1969, Fellow, 1974, Institute of Chartered Accountants of England and Wales; Fellow, Institute of Chartered Accountants of India, 1980. Appointments: Senior Economist and Statistician in industrial

market research, London, 1963-66; Articled and qualified as a Chartered Accountant, Mann Judd & Co, London, 1966-70; Arthur Andersen Worldwide Organisation, 1970-94, London Office Manager, 1974, Partner 1980, Head of Accounting and Audit Division for Gulf Countries, Dubai Office, 1980-84, Managing Partner for South Asia, Mumbai, India, 1980-89; Senior Partner and Consultant, London, 1990-94, retired as Partner, 1994; International Taxation and Strategy Advisor, 1994-2004; Conference Director, Annual International Taxation Conference, Mumbai, India, 1995-; Visiting Professor in International Taxation, RAU University, South Africa, 1996; Advisor to the Mauritius Offshore Business Activities Authority (subsequently Financial Services Promotion Agency) and Ministry of Economic Affairs, Financial Service and Corporate Affairs, 2000-05; Professor of International Tax Planning, St Thomas University School of Law, Miami, USA, 2002-06; Visiting Professor, Vienna University of Economics and Business Administration, Austria, 2007-. Publications: Book: Basic International Taxation, 2001, 2nd edition, 2005; More than 300 articles and over 1,000 presentations. Memberships: International Fiscal Association; International Tax Planning Association. Address: Olympus Apartments 512, Altamount Road, Mumbai 400026, India. E-mail: royrohatgi@gmail.com

ROHEN Edward, (Bruton Connors), b. 10 February 1931, Dowlais, South Wales. Poet; Writer; Artist. m. Elizabeth Jarrett, 4 April 1961, 1 daughter. Education: ATD, Cardiff College of Art, 1952. Appointments: Art Teacher, Ladysmith High, British Columbia, Canada, 1956-57; Head of Art, St Bonaventures, London, 1958-73; Ilford County High for Boys, Essex, 1973-82. Publications: Nightpriest, 1965; Bruised Concourse, 1973; Old Drunk Eyes Haiku, 1974; Scorpio Broadside 15, 1975; Poems/Poemas, 1976; A 109 Haiku and One Seppuku for Maria, 1987; Sonnets for Maria Marriage, 1988; Sonnets: Second Sequence for Maria, 1989. Contributions to: Poetry Wales; Anglo-Welsh Review; Irish Press; Mabon; Tribune; Argot; Edge; Little Word Machine; Second Aeon; Planet; Carcanet; Poetry Nippon; Riverside Quarterly; Littack; Wormwood Review; Twentieth Century Magazine. Memberships: Korean War Veterans Writers and Arts Society; Academician, Centro Cultural Literario e Artistico de o Jornal de Felgeiras, Portugal; Welsh Academy; Poet's Society of Japan. Address: 57 Kinfauns Road, Goodmayes, Ilford, Essex IG3 9QH, England.

RÖHSER Günter, b. 27 July 1956, Rothenburg ob der Tauber, Germany. m. Hedwig Röhser, 3 sons. University Professor. Education: Studies in Protestant Theology in Erlangen, Heidelberg and Neuendettelsau, 1975-81; Doctor of Theology, 1986; Habilitation in New Testament Theology, 1993. Appointments: Director of Studies, Ecumenical Institute, University of Heidelberg, 1982; Pastor, Lutheran Church, Bavaria, 1987; Associate Professor, University/GHS Siegen, 1994; Professor for Bible Studies, RWTH Aachen, 1997; Professor for the New Testament, University of Bonn, 2003. Publications: Metaphorik und Personifikation der Sünde, 1987; Prädestination und Verstockung, 1994; Stellvertretung im Neuen Testament, 2002. Memberships: Studiorum Novi Testamenti Societas; Academic Society for Theology; Society for Protestant Theology; Society of Biblical Literature; International Society for the Study of Deuterocanonical and Cognate Literature; Centre for Religion and Society, University of Bonn. Address: Faculty of Protestant Theology, Section for the New Testament, University of Bonn, Am Hof 1, D-53113 Bonn, Germany. E-mail: g.roehser@ev-theol.uni-bonn.de

ROMAN Cristian, b. 26 September 1957, Bucharest, Romania. Technical Construction Consultant. m. Mihaela Ramona, 1 son, 1 daughter. Education: Licence Diploma of Construct Engineering Degree, Technical University of Construction, Bucharest, 1982; Faculty of Law, Hyperion University, Bucharest, 1997-98; Management and Marketing courses, Pro Management Institute, Bucharest, 1999; Faculty of European Studies, Babes-Balyai University, Cluj-Napoca, 2000-01; Executive Master of Business Administration, National Conservatory of Arts and Trade, Paris, France, 2002. Appointments: Trainee Engineer, Project Manager, Site Inspector, Workroom Chief, Commercial Manager, General Consultant, Appraiser/Supervisor, Councillor/Project Manager, Quality Controller & Managerial Consultant, most recently: Consultant and Quality Controller, Tosun Group Construct, Bucharest, 2007-; Quality Controller, Sariden Construct, Bucharest, 2007; Managerial Consultant, Hispano Construct, Bucharest, 2007-08; Managerial Consultant, Kingdom Constructii, Bucharest, 2008; Managerial Consultant & Quality Controller, Edrasis Construct Group, Bucharest, 2008-; Senior Project Manager, South Pacific Group, Bucharest, 2008-. Honours: European Engineer, European Federation of National Engineering. Memberships include: Eco-Ethics International Union; General Association of the Engineers in Romania; National Registry of Experts; European Economic Association; Bioinformatics Organization; Swiss Engineering UTS; Fulbright Academy of Science and Technology. Address: 36 Dumbrava Noua str, Bl P 25, Ap 34, Bucharest 5, 051154, Romania. E-mail: cris@europe.com

RONALDINHO GAÚCHO (Ronaldo de Assis Moreira), b. 21 March 1980, Pôrto Alegre, Brazil. Footballer. 1 son. Career: Player: Gremio de Pôrto Alegre, 1998-2001, Paris St Germain, France, 2001-03; FC Barcelona, Spain, 2003-; 42 caps for Brazil, won Copa America, 1999 (scoring 4 goals), won World Cup, 2002. Honours: Won World Youth Cup with Brazil Under 17 team; EFE Trophy, 2004; FIFA World Footballer of the Year, 2004. Address: c/o Futbol Club Barcelona, Avenida Arístides Maillol, 08028 Barcelona, Spain. Website: www.fcbarcelona.com

RONALDO, b. 22 September 1976, Bento Ribero, Rio de Janeiro, Brazil. Professional Football Player. Career: Player: Social Ramos, Rio (12 games, 8 goals), Sao Cristovao, Rio Second Division (54 games, 36 goals), Cruzeiro, Brazil (60 games, 58 goals), PSV Eindhoven, Netherlands (58 games, 54 goals), Barcelona, Spain (49 games, 47 goals), Inter Milan, 1997-2002 (90 games, 53 goals); Real Madrid, 2002-2007; Brazilian National Team, 1994- (67 international caps, 47 goals); A C Milan, 2007-. Honours: Winning team, World Cup, 1994, 2002 and Copa America, 1997; Spanish Cup and European Cup Winners' Cup, 1997; World Soccer Magazine World Player of the Year, 1996; FIFA World Footballer of the Year, 1996, 1997, 2002; European Footballer of the Year, 1997, 2002. Address: c/o FC Real Madrid, Estadio Santiago Bernabeu, Paseo de la Castellana 104, Madrid, Spain. Website: www.realmadrid.com

RONAY Egon, b. Pozony, Hungary (UK citizen). Publisher; Journalist. m. (1) 2 daughters, (2) Barbara Greenslade, 1967, 1 son. Education: LLD, University of Budapest; Academy of Commerce, Budapest; Trained in kitchens of five family restaurants and abroad. Appointments: Manager, 5 restaurants within family firm; Emigrated from Hungary, 1946; General Manager, 2 restaurant complexes in London before opening his Marquee Restaurant, 1952-55; Founder, The Egon Ronay Guides, 1957, Publisher, 1957-85; Gastronomic and good living weekly columnist, Sunday Times, 1986-91, Sunday Express, 1991. Publications: The Unforgettable Dishes of My Life, 1989; Weekly columnist on eating out, food, wine and tourism, Daily Telegraph and later Sunday Telegraph, 1954-60; Weekly column, the Evening News, 1968-74; Editor-in-Chief, Egon Ronay Recommends (Heathrow Airport Magazine), 1992-94. Honours: Médaille de la Ville de Paris, 1983; Chevalier de l'Ordre du Mérite Agricole, 1987. Memberships: Academie des Gastronomes (France), 1979 Founding Vice-President, International Academy of Gastronomy; Founder, President, British Academy of Gastronomes. Address: 37 Walton Street, London SW3 2HT, England.

ROOKE Denis Eric, b. 2 April 1924, London, England. Chemical and Mechanical Engineer. m. Elizabeth Brenda, 1 daughter. Education: Westminster City School; Addey and Stanhope School; BSc (Eng) Diploma, Mech Eng and Chem Eng, University College, London; Chancellor, Loughborough University, 1989-2003. Appointments: Military Service, REME UK and India, 1944-49; Staff of South Eastern Gas Board on Coal Tar By Products, 1949; Deputy Manager, Tar Works, 1954; Seconded to North Thames Gas Board for work on LNG, 1957; Member, Technical Team on Methane Pioneer, world's first demonstration of LNG transfer across ocean; Development Engineer, South Eastern Gas Board, 1959; Development Engineer, Gas Council, 1960; Member, Production and Supplies, Gas Council, 1966-71; Deputy Chairman, British Gas Corporation, 1972-76; Chairman, British Gas, 1976-89. Publications: Papers to Institution of Gas Engineers, World Power Conference and World Petroleum Conference. Honours: Prince Philip Medal, Royal Academy of Engineering, 1992; Rumford Medal, Royal Society, 1986; CBE, 1970; Knight Bachelor, 1977; Order of Merit, 1997; Numerous honorary degrees. Memberships: Former Fellowship of Engineering, 1977-, President, 1986-91, Royal Academy of Engineering; Royal Society, 1978-; Penultimate Line-Commissioner, 1984, Chairman, 1987-2001, Royal Commission for Exhibition of 1851. Address: 23 Hardy Road, Blackheath, London SE3 7NS, England.

ROONEY Mickey (Joe Yule Jr), b. 23 September 1920, Brooklyn, USA. Actor. m. (1) Ava Gardner, (2) Betty J Rase, 2 sons, (3) Martha Vickers, (4) Elaine Mahnken, (5) Barbara Thomason, 4 children, (6) Margie Lang, (7) Carolyn Hockett, 2 sons, (8) Jan Chamberlin, 2 stepsons. Education: Pacific Military Academy. Career: Served AUS, World War II; TV programmes including series: The Mickey Rooney Show; Films include: Judge Hardy's Children; Hold That Kiss; Lord Jeff; Love Finds Andy Hardy; Boys Town; Stablemates; Out West With the Hardys; Huckleberry Finn; Andy Hardy Gets Spring Fever; Babes in Arms; Young Tom Edison; Judge Hardy and Son; Andy Hardy Meets Debutante; Strike up the Band; Andy Hardy's Private Secretary; Men of Boystown; Life Begins for Andy Hardy; Babes on Broadway; A Yank at Eton; The Human Comedy; Andy Hardy's Blonde Trouble; Girl Crazy; Thousands Cheer; National Velvet; Ziegfeld Follies; The Strip; Sound Off; Off Limits; All Ashore; Light Case of Larceny; Drive a Crooked Road; Bridges at Toko-Ri; The Bold and the Brave; Eddie; Private Lives of Adam and Eve; Comedian; The Grabbers; St Joseph Plays the Horses; Breakfast at Tiffany's; Somebody's Waiting; Requiem for a Heavyweight; Richard; Pulp; It's a Mad Mad Mad Mad World; Everything's Ducky; The Secret Invasion; The Extraordinary Invasion; The Comic; The Cockeyed Cowboys of Calico Country; Skidoo; BJ Presents; That's Entertainment; The Domino Principle; Pete's Dragon; The Magic of Lassie; Black Stallion; Arabian Adventure; Erik the Viking; My Heroes Have Always Been Cowboys, 1991; Little Nimo: Adventures in Slumberland (Voice), 1992; Silent Deadly Night 5; The

Toymaker; The Milky Life; Revenge of the Baron; That's Entertainment II; The Legend of OB Taggart, 1995; Kings of the Court, 1997; Killing Midnight, 1997; Boys Will Be Boys, 1997; Animals, 1997; Sinbad: The Battle of the Dark Knights, 1998; Babe: Pig in the City, 1998; The Face on the Barroom Floor, 1998; The First of May, 1998; Holy Hollywood, 1999; Internet Love, 2000; Lady and the Tramp II: Scamp's Adventure, 2001; Topa Topa Bluffs, 2002; Paradise, 2003; Strike the Tent, 2004; The Happy Elf (voice), 2005; Night at the Museum, 2006; The Yesterday Pool, 2007; A Christmas Too Many, 2007; Bamboo Shark, 2007; Lost Stallions: The Journey Home, 2007; Wreck the Halls, 2008. Address: PO Box 3186, Thousand Oaks, CA 91359, USA.

ROONEY Wayne, b. 24 October 1985, Croxeth, Liverpool, England. Footballer. Teams: Everton, 2002-04; England, 2003-; Manchester United, 2004-. Sponsers: Coca-Cola; Nike. Shirt Numbers: 8; 9; 18; 21; 23. Awards: October Goal Of The Month, ITV, 2002; Young Sports Personality of the Year, 2002; PFA Fans Player of the Month, 2004; Golden Boy, Best Young Player in Europe, 2004; Match of the Day's Goal of the Season, 2004-05, 2006-07; FIFPro Young Player Award, 2005; PFA Fans' Player of the Year (Premiership), 2006.

ROSE, Rt Hon Sir Christopher Dudley Roger, b. 10 February 1937, Hyde, England. Chief Surveillance Commissioner. m. Judith, 1 son, 1 daughter. Education: Morecambe Grammar School, Repton; LLB, Hughes Prize, Leeds University, 1954-57; BCL, 1959, Eldon Scholar, 1959, Wadham College, Oxford. Appointments: Law Lecturer, Wadham College Oxford, 1959-60; Teaching Fellow, University of Chicago, 1960-61; Called to Bar, Middle Temple, 1960; Practised, Northern Circuit, 1961-85; Queen's Counsel, 1974; High Court Judge (QBD), 1985-92; Presiding Judge, Northern Circuit, 1987-90; Lord Justice of Appeal, 1992-2006; Chairman, Criminal Justice Consultative Council, 1994-2000; Vice-President, Court of Appeal (Criminal Division), 1997-2006; Chief Surveillance Commissioner 2006-. Honours: Middle Temple, Bencher, 1983, Treasurer, 2002; Kt, 1985; Privy Counsellor, 1992.

ROSE Sir Clive Martin, b. 15 September 1921, Banstead, Surrey, England. British Diplomatist (retired). m. Elisabeth MacKenzie Lewis, 1946, deceased 2006, 2 sons, 3 daughters. Education: Marlborough College; Christ Church, Oxford. Appointments: Rifle Brigade (rank of Major, mentioned in despatches), Europe, India, Iraq, 1941-46; Commonwealth Relations Office, 1948; High Commission, Madras, 1948-49; Foreign Office, 1950; Served in Bonn, Montevideo, Paris, Washington and London, 1950-73; Imperial Defence College, 1968; Ambassador and Head of UK Delegation to Mutual and Balanced Force Reduction talks, Vienna, 1973-76; Deputy Secretary to Cabinet Office, 1976-79; UK Permanent Representative on North Atlantic Council, 1979-82; Consultant to Control Risks Group Ltd, 1983-95; Director, 1986-93, Chair, 1991-93, Control Risks Information Services Ltd. Publications: Campaigns Against Western Defence: NATO's Adversaries and Critics, 1985; The Soviet Propaganda Network: a Directory of Organisations Serving Soviet Foreign Policy, 1988; The Unending Quest: A Search for Ancestors, 1996; Alice Owen: the life, marriages and times of a Tudor Lady, 2006; Contributor, Détente, Diplomacy and MBFR, 2002. Memberships: President, Emergency Planning Association, 1987-93; Member, Advisory Board, Royal College for Defence Studies, 1985-92; Chair, 1983-86, Vice President, 1986-93, Vice Patron, 1993-2001, Council, Royal

United Services Institute; Chair, 1985-88, Vice President, 1988-, Suffolk Preservation Society. Address: Chimney House, Lavenham, Suffolk CO10 9QT, England.

ROSEANNE (Roseanne Barr), b. 3 November 1952, Salt Lake City, USA. Actress. m. (1) Bill Pentland, 3 children, (2) Tom Arnold, divorced 1994, (3) Ben Thomas, 1994-2002 (divorced) 1 son. Appointments: Former window dresser, cocktail waitress; Comic in bars and church coffee-house, Denver; Producer, forum for women performers Take Back the Mike, University of Boulder, Colorado; Performer, The Comedy Store, Los Angeles; Featured, TV special Funny and The Tonight Show; TV special, On Location: The Roseanne Barr Show, 1987; Star, TV series, Roseanne ABC, 1988-97; Host, Roseanne Show, 1998-; Actress in films: She Devil, 1989; Freddy's Dead, 1991; Even Cowgirls Get the Blues, 1994; Blue in the Face, 1995; Unzipped, 1995; Meet Wally Sparks, 1997; Home on the Range (voice), 2004. Publications: My Life as a Woman, 1989; Roseanne: My Lives, 1994. Honours: Emmy Award, Outstanding Actress in a Comedy Series, 1993. Address: c/o Full Moon and High Tide Productions, 4024 Radford Avenue, Dressing Room 916, Studio City, CA 91604, USA.

ROSEN Michael, b. 17 October 1927, Dundee, Scotland. Medical Practitioner. m. Sally Cohen, 2 sons, 1 daughter. Education: MB ChB, St Andrew's University, 1949; FFARCS, 1957. Appointments: House appointments, Bolton, Portsmouth, Bradford, 1949-53; RAMC, 1953-55; Registrar, Anaesthesia, Royal Victoria Infirmary, Newcastle upon Tyne, 1954-57; Senior Registrar, Cardiff, 1957-60; Fellow, Case Western University, Ohio, USA, 1960-61; Consultant Anaesthetist, Cardiff Hospitals, 1961-94; Honorary Professor in Anaesthetics, 1986; Member, GMC, 1989-92. Publications: Percutaneous Cannulation of Great Veins, 1981, 2nd edition, 1991; Obstetric Anaesthesia Safe Practice, 1982; Patient-Controlled Analgesia, 1984; Tracheal Intubation, 1985; Awareness and Pain in General Anaesthesia, 1987; Ambulatory Anaesthesia, 1991; Quality Measures Emergency, 2001. Honours: CBE, 1990; Honorary Member, French and Australian Societies of Anaesthesia; Honorary FFARCSI, 1990; Honorary Fellow, Academy of Medicine, Malaysia; Honorary LLD, Dundee, 1996; FRCOG, 1989; FRCS, 1994. Memberships: President, Association of Anaesthetists, 1986-88; President, Royal College of Anaesthetists, 1988-91. Address: 45 Hollybush Road, Cardiff CF 23 6TZ, Wales. E-mail: rosen@mrosen.plus.com

ROSEN Norma, b. 11 August 1925, New York, New York, USA. Writer; Teacher. m. Robert S Rosen, 1960, 1 son, 1 daughter. Education: BA, Mt Holyoke College, 1946; MA, Columbia University, 1953. Appointments: Teacher, Creative Writing, New School for Social Research, New York City, 1965-69, University of Pennsylvania, 1969, Harvard University, 1971, Yale University, 1984, New York University, 1987-95. Publications: Joy to Levine! 1962; Green, 1967; Touching Evil, 1969; At the Center, 1982; John and Anzia: An American Romance, 1989; Accidents of Influence: Writing as a Woman and a Jew in America (essays), 1992; Biblical Women Unbound: Counter-Tales (narratives), 1996; The Lovemaking of I B Singer, 1996; Elixir, 1998; My Son, the Novelist, 1999; Desperately Seeking Siblings, 1999; Orphan Lovers, 2000; Writers' Gift, Writers' Grudge, 2001; The Greatest Challenge Ever Told, 2002; What Goes Down Must Go Up, 2003; Of Need and Guilt, 2004; Deconstructing Jacques, 2005; The Writers Among Us, 2006; Betrayal: A Name Change, 2007; Contributions to: Anthologies and other publications; Commentary, New York Times Book Review &

Magazine, MS, Raritan, etc. Honours: Saxton; CAPS; Bunting Institute; Listed in national biographies. Memberships: PEN; Authors Guild; Phi Beta Kappa.

ROSS Amanda, b. 4 August 1962, Rochford, England. Joint Managing Director. m. Simon Ross. Education: BA (Hons), Drama and Theatre Arts, University of Birmingham. Appointments: Joint Managing Director (with Simon Ross), Cactus TV, 1994. Publications: Richard & Judy's Wine Guide, 2005; Saturday Kitchen Cookbook, 2007; Saturday Kitchen Best Bites Cookbook, 2008. Honours: Named Most Important Person in Publishing by many British newspapers; British Book Award for inspiring further reading, 2005; Best Read Bookseller Award for expanding the retail market, 2006; Summer Read Bookseller Award for expanding the retail market, 2007. Memberships: British Academy of Film and Television; Royal Television Society; Trustee, Kidscape.

ROSS Diana, b. 26 March 1944, Detroit, Michigan, USA. Singer; Entertainer; Actress; Fashion Designer. m. (1) Robert Ellis Silberstein, 1971, 3 daughters; (2) Arne Ness, 1985, divorced 2002, 1 son. Career: Backing singer, the Temptations, Marvin Gaye, Mary Wells; Lead singer, Diana Ross and The Supremes; Solo artiste, 1969-; Appearances include: Opening ceremonies, Football World Cup, USA, 1994; Rugby World Cup, South Africa, 1995; Film appearances: Lady Sings The Blues, 1972; Mahogany, 1975; The Wiz, 1978; Television specials: An Evening With Diana Ross, 1977; Diana, 1980; Christmas In Vienna, 1992; Business ventures: Diana Ross Enterprises Inc; Anaid Film Productions; RTM Management Corp; Chondee Inc. Recordings: Albums include: Diana Ross, 1970; Lady Sings The Blues, 1972; Touch Me In The Morning, 1973; The Boss, 1979; Why Do Fools Fall In Love?, 1981; Eaten Alive, 1984; Silk Electric, 1982; Chain Reaction, 1986; Ain't No Mountain High Enough, 1989; The Force Behind The Power, 1991; Motown's Greatest Hits, 1992; Live...Stolen Moments, 1993; One Woman - The Ultimate Collection, 1993; The Remixes, 1994; Take Me Higher, 1995; Very Special Christmas, 1998; Every Day is a New Day, 1999; Voice of Love, 2000; Gift of Love, 2000. Publication: Secrets Of A Sparrow (autobiography), 1993. Honours include: Citations: Vice-President Humphrey; Mrs Martin Luther King, Rev Abernathy; Billboard award: Record World award, World's Outstanding Singer; Grammy Award, 1970; Female Entertainer Of The Year, NAACP, 1970; Golden Globe, 1972; Antoinette Perry Award, 1977; Nominated Rock and Roll Hall Of Fame, 1988; BET Lifetime Achievement Award, 2007; Kennedy Center Honors Award, 2007. Address: RTC Management, PO Box 1683, New York, NY 10185, USA.

ROSS Donald Nixon, b. 4 October 1922, Kimberley, South Africa. Surgeon. m. Barbara Cork, 1 daughter. Education: BSc, 1942, MB Ch B, First Class Honours, University of Cape Town, 1946; FRCS Eng., 1949; FACS, 1966; FACC, 1982; FRCS Hon Ireland, 1984; FRCS Hon Thailand, 1989; FACS Hon USA, 1993. Appointments: Senior Registrar, Thoracic Surgery, Bristol, 1952; Research Fellow, 1953, Senior Thoracic Registrar 1954, Guy's Hospital; Consultant Thoracic Surgeon, 1958, Senior Surgeon, 1967, National Heart Hospital; Director, Department of Surgery, Institute of Cardiology, 1970; Consultant Surgeon, Middlesex Hospital, 1978. Publications: More than 250 publications include: Books: A Surgeon's Guide to Cardiac Diagnosis. Part I. The Diagnostic Approach, 1962; A Surgeon's Guide to Cardiac Diagnosis. Part II. The Clinical Picture, 1967; Medical and Surgical Cardiology (co-author), 1969; Surgery and Your Heart (with Barbara Hyams), 1982; Cardiac Valve Allografts (co-editor), 1988; Principles of Cardiac Diagnosis and

Treatment (with Terence English and Roxanne McKay), 1992. Honours include: University Gold Medal, University of Cape Town, 1946; National Heart Hospital Lecturer, 1971; St Cyres Lecturer, 1974; Order of Cedars of Lebanon, 1975; Order of Merit, Federal Republic of Germany, 1975; Guest Lecturer, Association of Thoracic Surgeons, USA, 1980; Honorary DSc, Council for National Academic Awards, Guildhall, London, 1982; Clement Price Thomas Award, Royal College of Surgeons, 1983; Guest Lecturer, Southern Thoracic Surgeons, USA, 1984; Denton Cooley Award, 1984; Thomas Burford Lecturer, St Louis, USA, 1986; Tudor Edwards Lecturer, Royal College of Surgeons, 1988; John Kirkland Lecturer, Mayo Clinic, 1992; Visiting Professor, Cleveland Clinic, 1992; Order of Thailand, 1994; Honorary Fellow, Royal Society of Medicine, 1995; Lifetime Achievement Award, Heart Research UK and Society for Cardiothoracic Surgery, Great Britain and Ireland, 2008. Memberships include: Thoracic Surgical Societies of: India, Australasia, Thailand, Greece, Chile, Spain, Florida, Pennsylvania; Fellow, Royal Society of Medicine; Past President, Society of Thoracic Surgeons of Great Britain and Ireland; Honorary Fellow, Society of Thoracic Surgeons of America and the American Association of Thoracic Surgery. Address: 25 Upper Wimpole Street, London W1G 6NF, England. E-mail: donald.ross@ukonline.co.uk

ROSS James Magnus, b. 3 March 1972, United Kingdom. Orchestra Conductor. Education: MA, History, 1993, MST, Music, 1994, D Phil, Music, 1998, Christ Church, Oxford University. Appointments: Music Director: Christ Church Festival Orchestra, 1993-, Chorus and Orchestra, Royal College of Paediatricians, 1994-, Northampton University Orchestra, 2001-, Welwyn Garden City Music Society, 2000-, St Albans Symphony Orchestra, 2001-; Oxford Unib Sinfonietta, 2005-; Guest Conductor: Sarajevo Philharmonic Orchestra, Bosnia, 1998, 1999, Oxford University Philharmonia, UK, 1999, Camden Chamber Orchestra, UK, 1999, Oxford Opera Society, UK, 1999; Bologna University Chamber Choir, Italy, 2002, Harbin Symphony Orchestra, China, 2002; Nis Symphony Orchestra, Serbia, 2002, Symphony Orchestra of Sri Lanka, Sri Lanka, 2001, 2003, 2005. Publications: Book chapters: Music in the French Salon in French Music since Berlioz (eds. C Potter and R Langham Smith), 2005; Republican Patriotism in the Third Republic Opera in Nationalism and Identity in Third Republic France (ed. B Kelly), 2005; Vincent d'Indy l'interpreté in Vincent d'Indy et son temps, 2005; Articles and reviews in professional journals include: D'Indy's Fervaal: Reconstructing French Identity at the Fin de Siècle, 2003. Honours include: British Academy Studentship, 1993-97; Osgood Award, 1996; Sir Donald Tovey Memorial Prize, 1998. Memberships: Performers and Composers Section, Incorporated Society of Musicians, UK; Conductors Guild, USA. E-mail: conductor@saso.org.uk Website: www.james-ross.com

ROSS Nicholas David (Nick), b. 7 August 1947, London, England. Broadcaster. m. Sarah Patricia Ann Caplin, 3 sons. Education: BA (Hons), Psychology, Queen's University Belfast. Appointments: Broadcaster and Moderator; Freelance 1971-; Television: Northern Ireland's main news, 1971-72; Man Alive, BBC2, 1976-83; Out of Court, BBC2, 1981-84; Breakfast Time & Sixty Minutes, BBC1, 1983-85; Crimewatch UK, BBC1 1984-2007; A Week in Politics, Channel 4, 1985-87; Star Memories, BBC1, 1985; Crimewatch File, BBC1, 1986-2007; Watchdog, BBC1, 1985-86; Crime Limited, BBC1, 1992-95; Westminster with Nick Ross, BBC2, 1994-97; Party Conferences live coverage, BBC2, 1997; Election Campaign, BBC2, 1997; Trail of Guilt, BBC1,

1999; Nick Ross, BBC2, 1999; Destination Nightmares, BBC1, 1999-2000; Storm Alert, BBC1, 1999; The Syndicate, BBC1, 2000; The Search, BBC1, 1999-2000; British Bravery Awards, BBC1, 2000; So You Think You Know How to Drive, BBC1, 1999-2002; Radio: Call Nick Ross, 1986-97; The Commission, 1998-. Publications: Various newspaper and magazine articles. Honours: Radio Broadcaster of the Year, Broadcasting Press Guild Awards, 1996; Winner, Best TV Documentary, Celtic Film Festival, 1999; Winner, Best Factual Programme, TV Quick Awards, 2001; Honorary Doctorate, Queen's University, Belfast. Memberships: Fellow, Royal Society of Arts, Fellow Royal Society of Medicine; Ambassador World Wildlife Fund; Chairman, Jill Dando Institute of Crime Science, University College London; Nuffield Council of Bioethics; Royal College of Physicians Committee on Medical Ethics; Academy of Medical Sciences Study on the Use of Non-Human Primates; President, Healthwatch; Advisory Board, Victim Support; Director, UK Stem Cell Foundation; Patron: Saneline, National Missing Persons Helpline, Apex Trust, National Depression Campaign, Prisoners Abroad, Simon Community Northern Ireland; Reynaud & Scleroderma Association; Tacade; Myasthenia Gravis Association; Animal Care Trust; British Wireless for the Blind Fund. Address: PO Box 999, London W2 4XT, England. E-mail: nickross@lineone.net

ROSSE 7 Earl of, Sir Brendan Parsons, 10th Bart, also: Baron Ballybritt and Oxmantown. Lord of the Manors of Womersley and Woodhall in England and Parsonstown, Newtown and Roscomroe in Ireland, b. 21 October 1936 (Irish National). Director. m. Alison Cooke-Hurle, 2 sons, 1 daughter. Education: Grenoble University; MA, Christ Church, Oxford University. Appointments: United Nations Official, 1963-80; Successively, UNDP and UNESCO Representative, UN Volunteer Field Director, Iran; UN Disaster Relief Co-Ordinator, Bangladesh; Director, Historic Irish Houses and Gardens Association, 1980-91; Director, Agency for Personal Service Overseas, 1981-89; Appointed to Irish Government's Advisory Council in Development Co-Operation, 1983-88; Founding Director, Birr Scientific and Heritage Foundation, responsible for Ireland's Historic Science Centre. Honours: LLD, Honoris causa, Dublin; Honorary FIEI; Honorary Life Member, RDS. Memberships: RAS; RNS; Royal Society for Asian Affairs. Address: Birr Castle, Co. Offaly, Ireland.

ROSSELLINI Isabella, b. 18 June 1956, Rome, Italy (US citizen). Actress; Model. m. (1) M Scorsese, 1979, divorced 1982, (2) J Wiedemann, divorced, 1 daughter. Education: Rome Academy of Fashion and Costume; New York School for Social Research. Career: Costume Designer for Roberto Rossellini (father), New York, 1972; Journalist for Italian TV; Vogue Cover Girl, 1980; Contracted to Lancome Cosmetics, 1982-95; Vice President, Marketing Department, Lancaster Cosmetics GPs, 1995-; As Actress: Films include: A Matter of Time, 1976; Blue Velvet, 1986; Cousins, 1989; Wild at Heart, 1990; Death Becomes Her, 1994; Immortal Beloved, 1994; Wyatt Earp, 1994; The Innocent, 1995; The Funeral, 1996; Big Night, 1996; Crime of the Century, 1996; Left Luggage, 1998; The Imposters, 1998; The Real Blonde, 1998; Don Quixote, 2000; Il Cielo cade, 2000; Empire, 2002; Roger Dodger, 2002; The Tulse Luper Suitcases, Part 1: The Moab Story, 2003; The Saddest Music in the World, 2003; The Tulse Luper Suitcases, Part 2: Vaux to the Sea, 2004; King of the Corner, 2004; Heights, 2005; La Fiesta del chivo, 2005; TV: Ivory Hunters, 1990; Lies of the Twins, 1991; The Gift, 1994; Crime of the Century, 1996; The Odyssey, 1997; Don Quixote, 2000; Napoleon, 2002; Monte Walsh, 2003; Legend of Earthsea, 2004; The Architect, 2006; Infamous, 2006; Brand Upon the

Brain!, 2006; The Accidental Husband, 2008; My Dog Tulip, 2008. Address: c/o United Talent Agency, 9560 Wilshire Boulevard, Floor 5, Beverly Hill, CA 90212, USA.

ROSSWICK Robert Paul, b. 1 June 1932. Consultant, General and Endocrine Surgery. Education: MB BS (Lond) The London Hospital Medical College, 1955; D Obst, RCOG, 1957; FRCS (Eng), 1961; MS (Surgery), Illinois, 1963; MAE, 1997. Appointments: House Surgeon, Poplar Hospital, London, England, 1955-1956; House Physician, Swindon Hospital, Wiltshire, 1956; Obstetric SHO, Greenwich Hospital, London, 1957; Lecturer in Anatomy, Kings College, London, 1957-59; Surgical SHO, 1959-1960, Locum SHO, 1963, The London Hospital; Surgical Registrar, St Andrew's, Bow, London, 1961-62; Surgical Registrar, Harold Wood Hospital, Essex, 1963-64; Surgical Registrar, 1964-66, Senior Registrar, 1966-70, St George's Hospital, London; Senior Registrar, Winchester and Royal Marsden Hospital, 1966-1970; Consultant-in-Charge, Accident and Emergency Department, 1970-74, Consultant Surgeon, 1970-93, Honorary Senior Lecturer in Surgery, St George's Hospital Medical School, 1970-93, St George's Hospital, London; Surgeon, The Royal Masonic Hospital, 1975-1993; Examiner in Surgery: The University of London; The Society of Apothecaries; PLAB. Publications: Numerous papers on abdominal surgery, thyroid surgery; Letters in medical journals; Addresses to medical societies; Presidential address, The Medical Society of London, a review of 1000 thyroidectomies, 1990. Honours: Robertson-Exchange Fellow in Surgery, Rush-Presbyterian-St Luke's Hospital, Chicago, USA, 1962-63; Past member of Council, Section of Surgery, Royal Society of Medicine; Chairman, Wandsworth Division, 1984-87, Delgate, ARM, etc, British Medical Association; Councillor, Hunterian Society, 1987-1995; Editor, 1984-1989, President, 1990-1991, Treasurer and Trustee, 1994-, The Medical Society of London. Memberships: Fellow: The Association of Surgeons; The British Association of Endocrine Surgeons; The CRC Multiple Endocrine Neoplasia Group; The British Society of Gastroenterology; The Collegium Internationale of Chirurgicae Digestiva; The Chelsea Clinical Society; Liveryman: The Worshipful Society of Apothecaries, Treasurer, Livery Committee, 1992-96; Member: Independent Doctors Forum; Medical Appeals Tribunals, Independent Tribunal Service; The Academy of Experts; UK Register of Expert Witnesses. Address: 5 Staffordshire House, 50 Broughton Avenue, London N3 3EG, England.

ROTENBERG Vadim, b. 5 August 1941, Kirov, USSR. Physician; Scientist. m. Samarovich Nataly, 2 daughters. Education: MD, 1st Moscow Medical Institute, 1964; Postgraduate Student, Academy of Sciences, USSR, 1966-69; PhD, 1970; DSc, 1979. Appointments: Junior Doctor, City Hospital, Moscow, 1964-66; Junior Scientist, 1st Moscow Medical Institute, 1969-78, Senior Scientist, 1978-88, Head of Laboratory, 1988-90; Emigration to Israel, 1990; Head Laboratory Abarbanel Mental Health Centre Bat-Iam, Israel, 1992-2001; Senior Lecturer, Tel Aviv University, 1995-; Head Psychologic Project Zionist Forum, 1996-2002. Publications: Over 150 scientific articles in professional journals; Books: The Adaptive Function of Sleep, 1982; Search Activity and Adaption, 1984; Self Image and Behaviour, 2001; Dreams, Hypnosis and Brain Activity, 2001. Honours: Best Annual Science Publication, Moscow Medical Institute, 1982, 1984; Wolfsson Grant for Outstanding Scientists, Tel-Aviv, 1992; Listed in Who's Who publications. Memberships: European Society Sleep Research; International Psychophysiological Society; New York Academy of Sciences. Address: Abarbanel Mental Health Centre, Keren Kayemet 15, Bat-Yam, Israel.

ROTH Andrew, b. 23 April 1919, New York, New York, USA. Political Correspondent. m. (1) Mathilda Anna Friederich, 1949, divorced 1984, 1 son, 1 daughter (2) Antoinette Putnam, 2004. Education: BSS, City College of New York, 1939; MA, Columbia University, 1940; Harvard University; Honorary PhD, Open University, 1992. Appointments: Reader, City College, 1939; Research Associate, Institute of Pacific Relations, 1940; Editorial Writer, The Nation, 1945-46; Foreign Correspondent, Toronto Star Weekly, 1946-50; London Correspondent, France Observateur, Sekai, Singapore Standard, 1950-60; Director, Parliamentary Profiles, 1955-; Political Correspondent, Manchester Evening News, 1972-84; New Statesman, 1984-96; Obituarist, Guardian, 1996-. Publications: Japan Strikes South, 1941; French Interests and Policies in the Far East, 1942; Dilemma in Japan, 1945; The Business Background of MPs, 1959, 7th edition, 1980; The MPs Chart, 1967, 6th edition, 1987; Enoch Powell: Tory Tribune, 1970; Can Parliament Decide..., 1971; Heath and the Heathmen, 1972; Lord on the Board, 1972; Sir Harold Wilson: Yorkshire Walter Mitty, 1977; Parliamentary Profiles, Vols I-IV, 1984-85, 2nd edition, 1988-90, 4th edition, 1998, 5th edition, 2004; New MPs of '92, 1992; Mr Nice Guy and His Chums, 1993; New MPs of '97, 1997; New MPs of '01, 2001, 2001. Address: 34 Somali Road, London NW2 3RL, England.

ROTH Tim, b. 14 May 1961, Dulwich, England. Actor. Education: Brixton and Camberwell College of Art. m. Nikki Butler, 1993, 2 sons (1 son from previous relationship). Career: Fringe groups including: Glasgow Citizens Theatre, The Oval House and the Royal Court; Appeared on London stage in Metamorphis; Numerous TV appearances; Films: The Hit; A World Apart; The Cook, The Thief, His Wife and Her Lover; Vincent and Theo; Rosencrantz and Guildenstern are Dead; Jumpin at the Boneyard; Resevoir Dogs; Bodies Rest and Motion; Pulp Fiction; Little Odessa; Rob Roy; Captives; Four Rooms; Hoodlums; Everyone Says I Love You; Liar; The War Zone (director); The Legend of 1900, Vatel; Lucky Numbers; Planet of the Apes; Invincible; The Musketeer; Emmett's Mark; Whatever We Do; To Kill A King; With It, 2004; The Beautiful Country, 2004; Silver City, 2004; New France, 2004; The Last Sign, 2004; Don't Come Knockin', 2005; Dark Water, 2005; Jump Shot, 2005; Even Money, 2006; Youth Without Youth, 2007; Funny Game U.S., 2007; Virgin Territory, 2007. Address: Ilene Feldman Agency, 8730 West Sunset Boulevard, Suite 490, Los Angeles, CA 90069, USA.

ROTHSCHILD Evelyn de (Sir), b. 29 August 1931. Banker. m. (1) Victoria Schott, 1972, dissolved 2000, 2 sons, 1 daughter, (2) Lynn Forester, 2000. Education: Trinity College, Cambridge. Appointments: Chairman, Economist Newspaper, 1972-89, United Racecourses Ltd, 1977-94, British Merchant Banking and Securities Houses Association (formerly Accepting Houses Committee), 1985-89; Chairman, N M Rothschild and Sons Ltd, 1976-. Address: N M Rothschild & Sons Ltd, New Court, St Swithin's Lane, London, EC 4, England.

ROTTE Karl Heinz, b. 18 October 1933, Pasewalk, Germany. Retired Radiologist. m. Ursula Kambach, 1 son. Education: Studies at Humboldt University, Berlin, Germany, 1953-58; MD, 1958; Resident, General Hospital Prenzlau, Germany, 1959-62. Appointments: Specialisation in Diagnostic Radiology, Robert-Rössle Cancer Research Institute, Berlin-Buch, 1962-77; Habilitation, 1974; Chairman, Department Diagnostic Radiology, Lung Research Institute Berlin-Buch, 1977-80; Chairman, Department of Computed Tomography and Department of Diagnostic Radiology, Cancer Research Institute, Berlin-Buch, 1980-96; Interim Chairman, Department of Diagnostic Radiology, Kuwait Cancer Control Centre, 1984-86; Professor of Diagnostic Radiology, Academy of Sciences, Berlin, 1987. Publications: 2 monographs: Computer aided diagnosis of peripheral bronchial cancer, 1977; Computed tomography in oncology, 1989; 200 publications in scientific journals and book contributions. Honours: Leibnitz Medal, Academy of Sciences, Berlin, 1974; W-Friedrich Award, Society of Radiology of Germany, 1976. Memberships: German Roentgen Society; Roentgen Society of Berlin. Address: Grabbe-Allee 14, D-13156 Berlin, Germany. E-mail: krotte5025@aol.com

ROURKE Mickey Philip Andre, b. 1956, New York, USA, Actor; Boxer. m. (1) Debra Fuer, (2) Carre Otis, divorced. Education: Actor's Studio, New York, USA. Career: Film appearances include: Fade to Black, 1941, 1979; Heaven's Gate, 1980; Body Heat, 1981; Diner, 1982; Eureka, 1983; Rumblefish, 1983; Rusty James, 1983; The Pope of Greenwich Village, 1984; 9½ Weeks, 1984; Year of the Dragon, 1985; Angel Heart, 1986; A Prayer for the Dying, 1986; Barfly, 1987; Johnny Handsome, 1989; Homeboy, 1989; Francesco, 1989; The Crew, 1989; The Desperate Hours, 1990; Wild Orchid, 1990; On the Sport, 1990; Harley Davidson and the Marlboro Man, 1991; White Sands, 1992; FTW; Fall Time; Double Time; Another 9½ Weeks; The Rainmaker, 1997; Love in Paris, 1997; Double Team, 1997; Buffalo '66, 1997; Thursday, 1998; Shergar, 1999; Shades, 1999; Out in Fifty, 1999; The Animal Factory, 2000; Get Carter, 2000; The Pledge, 2001; The Hire: Follow, 2001; Picture Claire, 2001; They Crawl, 2001; Spun, 2002; Masked and Anonymous, 2003; Once Upon A Time in Mexico, 2003; Driv3r (voice), 2004; Man on Fire, 2004; Domino, 2005; Stormbreaker, 2006; Killshot, 2008.

ROUX Albert Henri, b. 8 October 1935, Smur-en-Broinnais, France. Chef; Restaurateur. m. Monique Merle, 1959, 1 son, 1 daughter. Appointments: Military service, Algeria; Founder (with brother Michel Roux), Le Gavroche Restaurant, London (now co-owner with son Michel J), 1967-; The Waterside Inn, Bray (now sole owner), 1972-; Opened 47 Park Street Hotel, 1981; Opened Le Poulbot, le gamin, Gavvers, Les Trois Plats and Rouxl Britannia (all as part of Roux Restaurants Ltd), 1969-87; Began consultant practice, 1989. Publications: (with Michel Roux) New Classic Cuisine, 1983; The Roux Brothers on Pâtisserie, 1986; The Roux Brothers on French Country Cooking, 1989; Cooking for Two, 1991. Honours: Maître Cuisinier de France, 1968; Honorary Professor, Bournemouth University, 1995-; Chevalier du Mérite Agricole; Honorary DSc (Council for National Academic Awards), 1987. Memberships: Founder Member, Academy Culinaire de Grande Bretagne. Address: Le Gavroche, 43 Upper Brook Street, London, W1Y 1PF, England.

ROUX Michel André, b. 19 April 1941. Chef; Restaurateur. m. (1) Francoise Marcelle Becquet, divorced 1979, 1 son, 2 daughters. (2) Robyn Margaret Joyce, 1984. Appointments: Commis Patissier and Cuisinier, British Embassy, Paris, 1955-57; Commis Cook to Cécile de Rothschild, 1957-59, Chef, 1962-67; Military Service, 1960-62; Proprietor: Le Gavroche, 1967, The Waterside Inn, 1972, Le Gavroche Mayfair, 1981. Publications: New Classic Cuisine, 1983; Roux Brothers on Patisserie, 1986; At Home With the Roux Brothers, 1987; French Country Cooking, 1989; Cooking for Two, 1991; Desserts, A Lifelong Passion, 1994; Sauces, 1996; Life is a Menu, autobiography, 2000; Only the Best, 2002; Eggs, 2005. Honours: Numerous Culinary Awards including: Gold Medal,

Cuisiniers Français, Paris, 1972; Laureate Restaurateur of the Year, 1985; Chevalier, Ordre National du Mérite, 1987; Ordre des Arts et des Lettres, 1990; Honorary OBE, 2002; Chevalier de la légion d'Honneur, 2004; Numerous other awards and decorations. Memberships: Academician, Culinaire de France, English Branch; Association Relais et Desserts; Association Relais et Chateaux. Address: The Waterside Inn, Ferry Road, Berkshire SL6 2AT, England.

ROWE John Richard, b. 1 August 1942, Woodford, Essex. Film and Television Producer and Director. m. Rosa Mary Balls. Education: Royal Society of the Arts Education Certificate in English Literature. Appointments: Cutting Rooms and Film Library, 20th Century Fox, 1958-61; Film Researcher, Associated Redifusion, 1962-65; Film Researcher first major ITV documentary series, The Life and Times of Lord Mountbatten, 1965-69; Film Researcher, Thames Television, 1965-69; Principal Film Researcher, The World at War, 1971-74; Head of Production Research, Thames Television, 1972-82; Head of Programming, Sky Television, 1982-84; Head of Production, British Sky Broadcasting, 1984-93; Executive Producer and set up television side of QVC, The Shopping Channel, 1993-95; Producer and Director TV commercials for various clients, 1995-96; Producer, Director for Screeners, 13 half hour shows on the cinema, 1997; Producer, Director, children's series, Blue's Clues, 1997-2002; Producer, Director, children's comedy show, Havakazoo, 65 half hour shows, 2001; Director, Documentary on Anthony Quinn, Reflections in the Eye, 2001; Director, Monkey Makes, 2003; Director, Big Cook Little Cook, 2004, 2005; Writer/Director, stage production for Nickelodeon Jump Up Live Event, 2005, 2006; Currently, Chief Executive John Rowe Productions. Publications: In depth interview, Televisual, 1983; Contributor to: Satellite Wars, Channel 4, 1993. Honour: Part of the Emmy Award winning team for The World at War. Address: 24 Long Hill, Mere, Warminster, Wiltshire, BA12 6LR, England.

ROWLANDS Robert Trevor, b. 15 September 1949, London, England. Scientific Consultant. Education: BSc (Honours), Biological Science, University of Leicester, England, 1971; PhD, Microbial Genetics, University of Bristol, England, 1974. Appointments: Beit Memorial Medical Research Fellow, University of London, England, post held at Department of Bacteriology, University of Bristol Medical School, 1974-77; Section Head, Genetics and Screening Sections, Glaxo Operations, Ulverston, Cumbria, England, 1977-81; Senior Section Head, Strain Improvement Section, Beecham Pharmaceuticals, Worthing, England, 1981-84; Director, Biotechnology Services, Panlabs Inc, Cardiff, Wales, 1984-98; Self-employed Consultant under the name of Dragon Associates, 1998-. Publications: Over 30 publications in scientific journals and presented at conferences as author and co-author include most recently: The future of the fermentation industry. The shift to developing economic areas of the world, 1999; Rapid and sensitive quantitation of antibiotics in fermentations by electrospray mass spectrometry, 2001; Fermentation yield improvement – Part I. Strain improvement by traditional methods, Part II. Strain improvement by rational screening, Part III. Scale up for selected mutant strains, 2003. Honour; Honorary Lecturer in Applied Microbiology, University of Wales, Cardiff, 1996-2009. Membership: Society for General Microbiology. Address: 22 Adventurers Quay, Cardiff, CF10 4NP. E-mail: dragonassociates@aol.com

ROWLEY Rosemarie (Rose Mary, Rosemary) Teresa, b. 7 October 1942, Dublin, Ireland. 1 son. Writer; Poet; Essayist. Education: BA, 1969, MLitt, 1984, Trinity College, Dublin, Ireland; Dip Psych, National University of Ireland, 1996. Career: Green Activist, 1983-87; Poet and Essayist. Publications: The Broken Pledge, 1985; The Sea of Affliction, 1987; Betrayal into Origin, 1987, revised 1996; The Wake of Wonder, 1987, revised 1996; Freedom & Censorship – why not have both?, 1987, reprinted 1996; Flight into Reality, 1989, issued on cassette tape 1996; The Puzzle Factory, 2001; Hot Cinquefoil Star, 2002; Seeing the Wood and the Trees, co-editor, 2003; In Memory of Her, 2008. Honours: Image/ Maxwell House Award, 1988; Scottish International Open Poetry Competition, Long Poem Award, 1996, 1997, 2001, 2004. Memberships: MENSA, UK and Ireland; President, Irish Byron Society at United Arts Club; Trinity College Dublin Alumni; Long Poem Group, UK. Address: Booterstown, Co Dublin, Ireland. E-mail: rowleyrosie@yahoo.ie

ROWLING J(oanne) K(athleen), b. 1965, Bristol, England. Writer. (1) divorced, 1 daughter, (2) Neil Murray, 2001, 1 son, 1 daughter. Education: Graduated, University of Exeter, 1986. Publications: Harry Potter and the Philosopher's Stone, 1997; Harry Potter and the Chamber of Secrets, 1998; Harry Potter and the Prisoner of Azkaban, 1999; Harry Potter and the Goblet of Fire, 2000; Quidditch Through the Ages, 2001; Fantastic Beasts and Where to Find Them, 2001; Harry Potter and the Order of the Phoenix, 2003; Harry Potter and the Half-Blood Prince, 2005; Harry Potter and the Dealthy Hallows, 2007. Honours: British Book Award Children's Book of the Year, 1997; Rowntree Nestle Smarties Prizes, 1997, 1998; Officer of the Order of the British Empire, 2000; Premio Príncipe de Asturias, 2003; WHSmith People's Choice fiction prize, 2004; Variety UK Entertainment Personality Award, British Industry Film Awards, 2004; LLD, University of Aberdeen, 2006; Pride of Britain Award, 2007; Order of the Forest, Markets Initiative, 2007. Address: c/o Christopher Little Literary Agency, Ten Eel Brook Studios, 125 Moore Park Road, London SW6 4PS, England. Website: www.jkrowling.com

ROWSELL Joyce (Joyce Gwyther), b. 20 November 1928, Mardy, Glamorgan, South Wales. Artist. m. Geoffrey Norman Rowsell, 2 sons. Education: BA, University of London, History of Art, 1988. Career: Draughtswoman, British Telecom, 1947-60; Freelance Illustrator; Self Employed artist exhibiting in UK and abroad; Miniaturist, USA and UK; Permanent Collections: Miniature Artists of America; The Dutch Foundation of Miniature Art; The Hilliard Collection; Miniature Art Society of Florida. Publications: Somerset Magazine, 2001; The Artist (UK), 2001; West Country Life, 2001; Countryman, 2005. Honours: 66 awards for miniature painting; Title, Miniature Artist of America. Memberships: Founder Member, Hilliard Society; Miniature Art Society, Florida; Miniature Painters, Sculptors and Gravers Society of Washington DC; Royal Society of Miniature Painters, Sculptors and Gravers; Cider Painters of America; Roswell Fine Art Society, NM. Address: Spring Grove Farm, Milverton, Somerset, TA4 1NW, England. E-mail: joyce@rowsell.net Website: www.joycerowsell.com

ROXMAN (Pia) Susanna (Ellinor), b. 29 August 1946, Stockholm, Sweden. Poet; Critic. Education: King's College, London University; BA, hons, Comparative Literature, Philosophy, Lund University, 1973; PhD, Comparative Literature, Gothenburg University, 1984. Appointments: Visiting Lecturer, Lund University and elsewhere, 1976-2004; Critic on Swedish National Newspapers and the National Radio, Sweden, 1977-; Head, Centre of Classical Mythology,

Lund University, 1996-2005. Publications: Written in English: Guilt and Glory: Studies in Margaret Drabble's Novels 1963-80, 1984; Goodbye to the Berlin Wall, 1991; Broken Angels, 1996; Emblems of Classical Deities in Ancient and Modern Pictorial Arts, 2003; Imagining Seals, 2006; Several books written in Swedish; Numerous English poems in Cimarron Review, USA, Crab Orchard Review, USA, The Fiddlehead, Canada, Grain, Canada, Magma, UK, Imago, Australia, New Contrast, South Africa, Orbis, UK, Poetry Kanto, Japan, Poetry Salzburg Review, Austria, Prairie Schooner, USA, Room of One's Own, Canada, The Spoon River Poetry Review, USA, Stand, UK, Staple, UK, Wascana Review, Canada, Windsor Review, Canada and many other magazines world-wide; and English poetry contributed to websites such as Greek Mythology Link and Verse Daily; Also more than a couple of thousand arts articles world-wide and scholarly contributions to academic journals, anthologies and encyclopaedias. Honours: Arts Award, County Council of Malmo, Sweden, 1984; Swedish Balzac Prize, 1990; Editor's Choice Prize, Marjorie Lees Linn Poetry Award, USA, 1994, 1995; Arts Award, City of Lund, for Broken Angels, 1996; Second Prize, for short story, Vigil in Berlin, New Fiction Award Contest, New York, 2001; Susanna Roxman, although, or because, Anglophone, is one of the internationally best known Scandinavian poets. Memberships: Authors' Centre South, Sweden; Conservatory of American Letters. Address: Lagerbrings Vag 5B, SE-224 60 Lund, Sweden. E-mail: susanna.roxman@telia.com

ROY Arundhati, b. 1961, Bengal, India. Writer. m. (1) Gerard da Cunha, divorced, (2) Pradeep Krishen. Education: Delhi School of Architecture. Appointments: Artist; Actress; Film and Television Writer. Publications: The God of Small Things, 1997; The End of Imagination, essay, 1998; The Great Common Good, essay, 1999; The Cost of Living, collected essays, 2002; The Algebra of Infinite Justice, collected essays, 2002; Power Politics, 2002; The Ordinary Person's Guide to Empire, 2004; Public Power in the Age of Empire, 2004; The Checkbook and the Cruise Missile: Conversations with Arundhati Roy, 2004. Screenplays: In Which Annie Gives It Those Ones, 1988; Electric Moon, 1992; DAM/AGE, 2002. Contributions to: Periodicals. Honour: Booker Prize, 1997; Lannan Prize for Cultural Freedom, 2002. Address: c/o India Ink Publishing Co Pvt Ltd, C-1, Soami Nagar, New Delhi 110 017, India.

ROY Michael Presley-Roy, b. 20 April 1928, London, England. Artist (Drawing and Painting). Education: Oxford School Certificate, 1944; Newland Park College, Bucks, 1967-70; Teacher's Certificate, Art Advanced Level, Distinction, Reading University; Hornsey College of Art, Postgraduate Department, Diploma in Art Education, London University, 1973-76. Appointments: From 1950, various teaching and commercial positions including: Head of Art Department, Orchard School, Slough; Art Lecturer, Langley College, Berkshire; Semi-retirement, 1984-; The State Apartments, Windsor Castle, 1985-88; A professional artist in multi-media (landscapes, religious themes, figurations, flower-pieces and abstract/fantasy idiomatic motifs); Originator of "Art Lark" monoprint series from original works by Michael Roy; Group exhibitions at Wessex Biennial and exhibitions curated by/at Southampton Civic AG (viz: Aquarium, Le Coq dans la Boîte, The Artist's Chair, Art From Words – Self Portrait, 2001, Pattern, 2006). Publications: Author: The Rôle of the Art Teacher, 1976; The Art Lark, 1992; Featured in: British Contemporary Art, 1993; International Panorama of Contemporary Art, 1998; Ahoy Clausentum, 1994; Outstanding Artists and Designers of the

20th Century, 2001; Who's Who in Art, 2008; Cambridge Blue Book, 2008; Sotheby's charity auction catalogues. Commissions and Creative Works: In various private and public collections in UK and abroad including: Flight of the Holy Family, Allington Castle, Kent, 1958; Mary Magdalene, Crowmarsh Church, Oxon, 1959; Carisbrooke Halt, Trustees, Carisbrooke Castle Museum, Isle of Wight, 1957; Calvary, Windsor Parish Church, Berks, 1967; Flamingo Dancers, Red Swans, Reading AG, Berks, 1980; Quarr Abbey from the South, Quarr Abbey, Isle of Wight 1970; Oil painting, Sailing into the Millennium 2000, presented by Gosport Borough Council, Hants, 2005 to Holy Trinity Church, Gosport, Hants (www.holytrinitygosport.co.uk); Holy Trinity Church, Crucifixion, Madonna and Child Jesus, 1970. Honours: Los Peroquitos (Diploma Award, international section, visual poetry Biennial) Mexico City, 1996; Bronze Medal, Best Poetry of 1996, International Society of Poetry, Maryland, USA, 1996. Address: La Palette, 110 Anns Hill Road, Gosport, Hants, PO12 3JZ, England.

ROZGONYI Ferenc, b. 21 September 1938, Tarcal, Hungary. MD; Professor for Medical Microbiology. m. (1) Gertrúd Mária Szécsi (deceased), (2) Katalin Szitha. Education: Medical Doctor, summa cum laude, Medical University of Debrecen, 1963; Diploma, Specialist for Laboratory Medicine, 1967; Diploma, Specialist for Medical Microbiology, 1979; Medical Microbiology Expert in Forensic Medicine, 1999-. Appointments: USA Scholarship, Department of Pharmacology, Faculty of Medicine, University of Kentucky, Lexington, USA, 1969-70; PhD, 1978; Dr Med Sciences, 1988; Visiting Professor, Department of Bacteriology and Epizootology, Swedish University of Agricultural Science and Department of Biochemistry, University of Uppsala, 1984-85; Department of Bacteriology, Royal Infirmary, University of Glasgow, 1994; Dr Med/ Habil, Debrecen, 1995; University Professor in Debrecen, 1995; Chief, Central Bacterial Diagnostic Laboratory, Medical University, Debrecen, 1993-96; Director, Chairman, Institute of Medical Microbiology, Semmelweis University, Budapest, 1996-2003 (retired from this position); University Professor, 2003-. Publications: Over 160 articles and other publications on antibiotic resistance and pathogenicity of bacteria; About 400 lectures and posters presented in national and international conferences; Author: (manual) Rapid Microbiology Diagnostic Methods for General Practitioners, 1994; Clinical Microbiology Fast Diagnostics, 2006. Honours: Eminent Student Medal, Ministry of Education, 1957; Doubly awarded by Hungarian Academy of Sciences, 1972, 1985; Honoured twice for excellent teaching, Ministry of Public Health, 1980, Ministry of Welfare, 1991; L Batthyány – Strattmann Award, Minister of Public Health, Welfare and Family Affairs of Hungary, 2003, in recognition of his outstanding professional activity and achievement of several decades; Recipient, Doctoral School Medal, Semmelweis University, 2000; Honourable Certification, Hungarian Association for Innovation, 2003; Gold Seal-Ring, Ignác Semmelweis plaquette, Semmelweis University, 2003; Rezső Manninger plaquette, Hungarian Society for Microbiology, 2003. Memberships: Chairman, Curators Board for the Foundation of Struggle for Health, Hungary, 1990-; Executive Board, 1991-2007, Secretary, 1997-2007, Hungarian Society of Chemotherapy; Hungaria Helvetia Association, Debrecen, 1991-2004; Editorial Boards: J Chemotherapy, 1993-96; Zbl Bakt, Ab I, 1994-97; Acta Microbiologica et Immunologica Hungarica, 1996-; Hungarian Venerology Archive, 1998-; Board of Advisors, Focus Medicinae, 1999-; Member, Hungarian Medical Chamber, 1992-; European Society for Clinical Microbiology and Infectious Diseases,

1992-, Hungarian Representative at its European Council, 2001-05; New York Academy of Science, 1997-; World-wide Hungarian Medical Academy, 1999-; American Association for the Advancement of Science, 2002-; ECDC Roster of Scientists, 2005-. Address: Institute of Medical Microbiology, Faculty of Medicine, Semmelweis University, Nagyvárad tér 4, Budapest, H-1089, Hungary. E-mail: rozfer@net.sote.hu

RUBINSTEIN Shimon, b. 21 January 1941, Berlad, Romania. Historian. m. Gretty Rotman-Rubinstein, deceased, 1 son. Education: BA General Modern History and Political Sciences, 1965, Secondary School Teacher's Certificate, 1966, Certified Historical Archivist, 1968, Hebrew University of Jerusalem. Appointments: High School Teacher of History, Dimona, Israel, 1966-68; Director, Historical Archives of Yad Ben-Zvi Institute, Jerusalem, 1970-2001. Publications include: At a Close Perspective: Reflections on the Centenary of David Ben-Gurion, 1986; German Atrocity or British Propaganda: The Seventieth Anniversary of a Scandal – German Corpse Utilisation Establishments in WW1, 1987; The Negev – The Great Zionist Blunder 1919-1929, 4 volumes, 1988; Crisis and Change, Petah-Tikva in the Transition Period from Turkish to British Rule, 5 volumes, 1988-90; German-Turkish Endeavours in the Field of Engineering, Water Exploration and Agriculture in the Sinai and the Negev during WW1 and the Part Played Therein by the (Jewish) Yishuv, 1989; At the Height of Expectations: The Land Policy of the Zionist Commission in 1918, 1993; From Berlad to the Maabarah of Rosh Pina: The First Years of an Immigrant Family in the Galilee 1950-1956, 1993; Coinage, Measures and Weights in Eretz-Israel from the Beginning of the 19th Century to the Period of Transition from Ottoman to British Rule, 1997; A Personal Exchange of Letters with a Hebrew Patriot [Abraam Thomi], in the Diaspora 1985-1991, 2 volumes, 1999; Personal Tragedies as a Reflection to a Great Tragedy Called Struma, 2003; Annotated Bibliography on the Transition Period from Turkish to British Rule in Eretz-Israel, 3 volumes, 2004; The Monetary Crisis in Eretz-Israel during WWI, 2006. Honours: Shulamit and Professor Kalugai Award, Institute for Eretz-Israel Research of Yad Ben-Zvi, 1980. Memberships: Israel Association of Graduates in the Social Sciences; World Union of Jewish Studies; Israel Genealogical Society. Address: Haavtaha St 14, P O Box 7360, Jerusalem 91072, Israel.

RUBINSZTEIN David Chaim, b. 14 March 1963, Cape Town, South Africa. Medical Scientist. m. Judy, 1 son, 2 daughters. Education: MB ChB, 1981-86; BSc (Med) Hons, 1988; PhD, 1993; DipRCPath, 1996; MRCPath, 1997; FRCPath, 2005. Appointments: Senior Registrar, Genetic Pathology, Addenbrooke's Hospital, Cambridge, 1993-98; Glaxo Wellcome Research Fellow, Honorary Consultant in Medical Genetics, 1998-2002, Wellcome Trust Senior Research Fellow, Honorary Consultant in Medical Genetics, 2002-, Reader in Molecular Neurogenetics, 2003-2005, Professor in Molecular Neurogenetics, 2005-, University of Cambridge. Publications: More than 140 research papers in international journals including: Nature Genetics; Nature Medicine; Proceedings of the National Academy of Science, USA; American Journal of Human Genetics; Human Molecular Genetics. Honours: GA Reynolds Scholarship, 1981-86; MRC Post-Intern Award, Guy Elliott Fellowship, 1988; MRC Post-graduate Bursary, Marion Beatrice Waddell Award, University of Cape Town Research Associateship, Stella and Paul Loewenstein Research Scholarship, 1989-93; Glaxo Wellcome Research Fellowship, 1998; Wellcome Trust Senior Clinical Fellowship, 2002; Fellow of the Academy of Medical Sciences, 2004. Memberships: Clinical Genetics Society; British Society for Human Genetics; World Federation of Neurology Research Group on Huntington's Disease. Address: Cambridge Institute for Medical Research, Addenbrooke's Hospital, Hills Road, Cambridge CB2 0XY, England. E-mail: dcr1000@hermes.cam.ac.uk

RUCKMAN Robert Julian Stanley, b. 11 May 1939, Uxbridge, Middlesex, England. Chartered Engineer; Civil Servant. m. Josephine Margaret Trentham, 1 son, deceased 31 January 2005, 1 daughter. Education: ONC, Electrical Engineering, 1957-60, HNC, Electrical and Electronic Engineering, 1960-62; IERE Endorsements, 1963, Harrow Technical College; MSc Transport Studies, Cranfield Institute of Technology, 1974-75. Appointments: Computer Testing and Commissioning, Elliott Bros Ltd, Borehamwood, Hertfordshire, 1961-64; Logic and Systems Designer, Serck Controls, Leamington Spa, Warwickshire, 1964-66; Technical Staff, System Sciences Corporation, Falls Church, USA, 1966-67; Transitron Electronic Corporation, Boston, USA, 1967-68; J Langham Thompson Ltd, Luton, Bedfordshire, 1968-70; Ministry of Transport, 1970-74; Birmingham Regional Office, Department of Transport, 1975-78; Cost Benefit Analyst, Computer Analyst, Department of Transport Road construction Unit, 1978-87; Computer Manager (Senior Professional Technical Officer), Department of Transport, West Midlands Region, Birmingham, 1987-95; Assessor, British Computer Society Professional Review Panel. Publications: Articles in scientific journals include: A Data Logger Scaler and Alarm Limit Comparator, 1967; Alarm Detection Using Delay Line Storage, 1966; Integral Alarms for Data Loggers, 1967; The Effects of Trip Characteristics on Interurban Model Choice, 1975; Guide for WMRO Geographical Information System, 1991. Honours: Department of Transport Award in recognition of work for development of Accident Analysis Geographical Information System, 1991; UCC International Peace Prize, ABI, 2005; Man of the Year, 2004-2007; World Lifetime Achievement Award, 2005; Fellow, ABI; Lifetime Deputy Governor, ABI; Hall of Fame, ABI, 2005-06; Research Fellow, ABI. Memberships: Member of the Institution of Electrical Engineers; Member of The British Computer Society; Fellow, Institution of Analysts and Programmers; Member, Institute of Logistics and Transport; Chartered Engineer (C.Eng); European Engineer (Eur-Ing); Cranfield Society. Address: 13 Alexander Avenue, Droitwich Spa, Worcestershire WR9 8NH, England. E-mail: robert_ruckman@tinyworld.co.uk

RUDKIN James David, b. 29 June 1936, London, England. Dramatist. m. Alexandra Margaret Thompson, 3 May 1967, 2 sons, 1 deceased, 2 daughters. Education: MA, St Catherine's College, Oxford, 1957-61. Appointment: Judith E Wilson Fellow, University of Cambridge, 1984; Visiting Professor, University of Middlesex, 2004-; Honorary Professor, University of Wales, 2006-. Publications: Afore Night Come (stage play), 1964; Schoenberg's Moses und Aron (translation for Royal Opera), 1965; Ashes (stage play), 1974; Cries From Casement as His Bones are Brought to Dublin (radio play), 1974; Penda's Fen (TV film), 1975; Hippolytus (translation from Euripides), 1980; The Sons of Light (stage play), 1981; The Triumph of Death (stage play), 1981; Peer Gynt (translation from Ibsen), 1983; The Saxon Shore (stage play), 1986; Rosmersholm (translation from Ibsen), 1990; When We Dead Waken (translation from Ibsen), 1990. Opera Libretti: The Grace of Todd, music by Gordon Crosse, 1969; Inquest of Love, music by Jonathan Harvey, 1993; Broken Strings, music by Param Vir, 1994. Book: Dreyer's Vampyr (monograph), 2005. Contributions to: Drama; Tempo; Encounter; Theatre Research Journal. Honours: Evening Standard Most Promising Dramatist Award, 1962; John

Whiting Drama Award, 1974; Obie Award, New York, 1977; New York Film Festival Gold Medal for Screenplay, 1987; European Film Festival Special Award, 1989; Sony Silver Radio Drama Award, 1994. Memberships: Hellenic Society. Address: c/o Casarotto Ramsay Ltd, Waverley House, 7-12 Noel Street, London W1F 8GQ, England.

RUDOLF (Ian) Anthony, b. 6 September 1942, London, England. Literary Critic; Poet; Translator; Publisher. Divorced, 1 son, 1 daughter. Education: BA (Modern Languages Tripos, Part One; Social Anthropology Part Two) Trinity College, Cambridge, 1964; Diploma, British Institute, Paris, 1961. Appointments: Co-Founder and Editor, Menard Press, London, 1969; Adam Lecturer, Kings' College, London, 1990; Pierre Rouve Memorial Lecturer, University of Sofia, 2001; Visiting Lecturer, Arts and Humanities, London Metropolitan University, 2001-2003; Royal Literary Fund Fellow, University of Hertfordshire, 2003-2004, 2004-2005; Royal Literary Fund Fellow, University of Westminster, 2005-2008. Publications: The Same River Twice, 1976; After the Dream: Poems 1964-79, 1980; Primo Levi's War Against Oblivion (literary criticism), 1990; Mandorla (poetry), 1999 and 2007; The Arithmetic of Memory (autobiography), 1999; Kafka's Doll, 2007; Engraved in Flesh, 2007; Translations include: Yesterday's Wilderness Kingdom (poetry) by Yves Bonnefoy, 2001; Blood from the Sky (novel) by Piotr Rawicz, 2004; Contributions to periodicals. Honours: Chevalier de l'Ordre des Arts et des Lettres, 2004; Fellow, Royal Society of Literature, 2005. Address: 8 The Oaks, Woodside Avenue, London N12 8AR, England. E-mail: anthony.rudolf@virgin.net

RUDY Dorothy L, b. 27 June 1924, Ohio, USA. Professor of English and Creative Writing; Poet. m. Willis Rudy, 31 January 1948, 1 son, 2 daughters. Education: BA, Queens College, 1945; MA, Philosophy, Columbia University, 1948. Appointments: Professor of English and Creative Writing, Montclair State University, 1964-88; Lecturer, Fairleigh Dickinson University, 1988-90, 1996-2002, Bergen Community College, 1991-96, YMHA Wayne, Humanities Scholar of the Arts, 1993-. Publications: Quality of Small and Other Poems, 1971; Psyche Afoot and Other Poems, 1978; Grace Notes to the Measure of the Heart, 1979; Voices Through Time and Distant Places, 1993. Contributions to: Passaic Herald News; Letters; Poem; Laurel Review; Just Pulp; Composers; Authors and Artists Quarterly; Scimiter and Song; Bitterroot; Cellar Door; Pet Gazette; Black Buzzard Press. Honour: American Poets Fellowship, 1971; New Jersey Literary Society Hall of Fame, 1994; Certificate of Achievement in the Arts, Literature, Contemporary Women's Club of Bergenfield, 1997; Listed in Who's Who publications and biographical dictionaries. Memberships: Composers, Authors and Artists of America; PEN Women; Bergen Poets; New York Poetry Forum; Browning Society; New England Small Press Association, Women's Board; Scambi International. Address: 161 West Clinton Avenue, Tenafly, NJ 07670, USA.

RUI Mu, b. 14 July 1908, Wuxing county, Zhejiang Province, P R China. Law. Education: BA, Aurora Univ, Shanghai, China, 1930; LLM, University of Paris, France, 1932; PhD, Law, University of Frankfurt, Germany, 1935. Appointments: Honorary Chairman, Standing Committee of Chinese Law, Europe-China Law Association; Advisor to China Law Society; Vice Chairman, Chinese Society of Economic Law; Vice Chairman, Chinese Society of International Law; Vice Chairman, China International Economic and Trade Arbitration Commission; Secretary General, Study Centre for Economic Laws and Regulations, State Council; Committee

for Drafting the Basic Law of the Hong Kong Special Administrative Region; Commission of Legislative Affairs, National People's Congress; Associate Director, Institute of Law, Chinese Academy of Social Sciences; Director, International Economic Law Institute, Peking University; Director, Economic Law Institute, Peking University; Associate Dean, Peking University Law Department; Law Professor, Chongqing Central University, National Southwest Associated University, Beijing College of Political Science and Law, Law Institute of Chinese Academy of Social Sciences; Law Professor, Peking University. Publications: Numerous books and articles in professional journals. Memberships: Commission of Legislative Affairs, National People's Congress; Committee for Drafting the Basic Law of the Hong Kong Special Administrative Region; China International Economic and Trade Arbitration Commission; Chinese Society of International Law; Chinese Society of Economic Law; China Law Society. Address: 65#, Yannan Garden, Peking University, Beijing 100871, China.

RUKIEH Mohamad, b. 1 June 1951, Tartous, Syria. Geologist; Director General. m. Amal Ibrahim, 2 sons, 3 daughters. Education: Bachelor, Geological Sciences, Damascus University, 1973; Diploma, Mining Geological Engineering, 1977; PhD, Geology and Mineralogy, Moscow Geological Prospecting Institute. Appointments: Director of Prospecting, General Establishment of Geology and Mineral Resources, Ministry of Petroleum, 1980-86; General Supervisor of Marble Quarries, Marble Company; Director of Field Studies, 1986-, Director General, 2002-, General Organisation of Remote Sensing; Exploration of sites of hydrothermal iron accompanied with Sulphid of minerals (copper, lead and zinc) in Sirghaya area, Syria, Oolitic iron in Addmeir area, Syria; Important sites to the deep xenoliths in the volcanic rocks in Aldqadmous area, Syria; Most recent areas of research include: New data about the Features of the Geological Structure of the Coastal Ridge and Levant Transform Fault in Misyat Area by Interpretation of Space Images; Methodology for Determining the Sanitary Landfill and Solid Waste dump sites by Using Remote Sensing Techniques and Geographic Information System; The Topographic and Tectonic Features of the Arab Rift and Its Water Influences; New Data about the Tectonic Structure of the Arabian Plate by the Interpretation of Space Images; Physiographic analysis and littology mapping from space images (case study from Syria). Publications: 2 books: Water and Life, 2004; The Annular structures in Space Images and their Importance in Subsurface Resources Exploration in the Arabian Plate, 2006; More than 45 researches, articles, and scientific papers in professional technical journals include most recently: The Tectonic Position, Mineralogical Composition and Geochemical Characteristics for Iron and Sulphid Deposits Discovered in AlKota, Dahr Alkhanzeer and Toufahta Sites in Sirghaya Area, Syria, 2003; Quaternary and Ancient Man in Palmyra Area, Syria, 2003; Studying the Rift Tectonics and Volcanism phenomena in the South of the Coastal Range Using Remote Sensing Techniques, 2004; New Data about the Tectonic Activity in Wadi Al-Meyah in Syria by Interpretation of Space Images, 2004. Honours: Man of the Year, ABI, 2003; Man of Achievements, 2005. Memberships include: Academy of Engineering Sciences of the Russian Federation; Syrian Geological Society; Syrian Scientific Society for Information; Editor, Remote Sensing Journal; Editorial Board, Syrian Journal of Geology; Editor-in-Chief, Geological Sciences Review; Member of Scientific Committees in many International Conferences Address: PO Box 93, Barzeh, Damascus, Syria. E-mail: m-rukieh@scs-net.org Website: www.gors-sy.r.org

RUMANE Abdul Razzak, b. 8 June 1948, Chandve, India. Electrical Engineer; Consultant. m. Noor Jehan, 1 son, 1 daughter. Education: BE, (Electrical), Government College of Engineering, Marathwada University, Aurangabad, India, 1972; Diploma in Modern Management, British Career Training College, 1981; Diploma in International Trade, British Management Association, 1982; MS, General Engineering, Kennedy-Western University, USA, 2002; PhD, Kennedy Western University, USA, 2005. Appointments: Trainee Engineer, Electro Sales Corporation, 1972-73; Assistant Officer, Ruttonsha Electronics, 1973-76; Assistant Engineer, Mandovi Pellets Ltd, 1976-79; Staff Engineer, Crompton Greaves Ltd, 1979-80; Officer, Dynacraft Machine Co, Ltd, 1981-83; Officer/Engineer, Toyo Engineering, India, Ltd, 1981-83; Electrical Engineer, Mansour Al Subaie Est, Kuwait, 1983-84; Electrical Engineer, Abdullah Al Otaibi Est. Kuwait, 1984-86; Electrical Engineer, Jassim Shaban and Sons Co. Kuwait, 1986-90; Electrical Engineer, Al Othman Centre for Architectural and Engineering Design, Al Khobar, Saudi Arabia, 1991; Senior Electrical Engineer, Pan Arab Consulting Engineers, Bahrain and Kuwait, 1991-99; Senior Electrical Engineer, Dar Al Handasah (Shair and Partners), Kuwait, 1999-2004; Senior Electrical Engineer, Pan Arab Consulting Engineers, Kuwait, 2004-. Publications: Numerous papers and articles in technical journals and newsletters. Honours: Listed in numerous international biographical directories, Deputy Director-General, International Order of Merit, Lifetime Achievement Award, IBC; Continental Governor, American Order of Excellence, ABI; Global Award of Accomplishment, Who's Who Institute, USA: The World Order of Science-Education-Culture with title of "Cavalier", European Academy of Informatisation; Medal of Science and Peace, Albert Schweitzer International University Foundation; Bharat Gaurav Award, Gem of India Award, India International Friendship Society; ASIF Gold Medal, Albert Schweizer International Foundation; Meritorious Service Bronze Medal, The Sovereign Order of the Knights of Justice. Memberships: Associate Member, American Society of Civil Engineers; Fellow, ABI; Patron, IBA; Fellow, The Institution of Engineers, India; Senior Member, Institute of Electrical and Electronics Engineers (USA); American Society for Quality; Save International (The Value Society); Kuwait Society of Engineers; Chartered Engineer, IEI; Honorary Fellowship, Chartered Management Association, Hong Kong; MEW Kuwait Registration (Supervisor First Class); Member, National Geographic Society; Member, London Diplomatic Academy; Member, Board of Governors; Honorary Vice Governor, International Benevolent Research Forum; Honorary Fellow, Chartered Management Association (HK). Address: PO Chandve, Talk – Mahad District, Raigad, Maharashtra, India, 402301. E-mail: rarazak@yahoo.com

RUNAYKER Irene, b. Whitechapel, London, England. Painter. Education: NDD Painting, Camberwell School of Arts & Crafts, London, 1958; Postgraduate Life Drawing, with Merlyn Evans, Central School of Art, London, 2 years; Modern & Contemporary Art, I & KK, Tate Gallery; Exhibition Creation & Creation, curatorial course, Birkbeck Summer School, London; Language & Literacy, Reading Development, Open University; Professional Development Programme, Creative Routes II, University of Creative Arts. Career: Visiting Lecturer, BA Honours Degree Course, Anglia University, Cambridge, 1990-93; Public exhibitions of work in Scotland, East Sussex, numerous galleries throughout London, France, Germany and New York; Work held in public collections in: London Borough of Camden Permanent Collection; In-Search Language Unit of University of Technology, Sydney, Australia; Our Lady of Dolours, London;

Hallfield School, London; Work held in private collections in: Australia, Barbados, Canada, Mexico, USA and throughout Europe. Publications: Appears in: Camberwell School of Art, It's Tutors and Students 1943-60, 1995; Femmes Artistes Internationales interview with Laurence Morechand, Paris; Education Through Art brochure, University of Brighton, UK; East Magazine interview with Adam Lloyd-Monaghan, Eastbourne; Vido, Artwave, 1998; Listed in national and international biographical publications. Memberships: International Artists Association; Foundation for Womens Art; INIVA; DACS. Address: Flat 1, 68 Terminus Road, Eastbourne, BN21 3LX, England.

RUNDMO Torbjörn, b. 7 February 1955, Tromsö, Norway. Professor. Education: Cand Mag, Sociology & Social Sciences; Cand Psychol, Psychology; Certified Psychologist; Dr Philos. Appointments: Senior Lecturer, Social Psychology, 1992-93, Senior Lecturer, Health Psychology, 1993-98, Professor, Organisational Psychology, 1998-99, Professor of Community Psychology, 1998-, Norwegian University of Science and Technology, Trondheim, Norway; Research Scientist, 1986-91, SINTEF, Trondheim; Research Scientist, Institute of Transport Economics, Oslo, Norway, 1991-92. Publications: 260 publications, book chapters, granted research reports, mainly within risk and safety research, health and community psychology. Honours: Philosophy Doctor of Honour (Dr Phil hc), Stockholm School of Economics, 2005. Memberships: Appointed Member, Academy of the Royal Norwegian Society of Science & Letters, 2005-. Address: Grim Saxeviks vei 18, 7562 Hundhamaren, Norway. E-mail: torbjorn.rundmo@svt.ntnu Website: http://www.svt.ntnu.no/psy/torbjorn.rundmo

RUPP Gary Alvin, b. 9 July 1948, St Cloud, Minnesota, USA. Educational Consultant. Education: BSc, University of Minnesota at St Cloud, 1970; M Ed, Administration, New England University, Australia, 1981; Ed D, Trinity University, Spain, 1996. Appointments: Teacher, Administrator and Educational Consultant in USA, Australia, Philippines, Papua New Guinea, Thailand, Mexico, Venezuela and Oman, 1970-2007; Educational Consultant, CECNEDUCONSULT. Publications: Innovative Work Education Program. Memberships: MENSA. E-mail: garyet4419@hotmail.com

RUSH Geoffrey, b. 6 July 1951, Toowoomba, Queensland, Australia. Actor. m. Jane Menelaus, 1988, 1 son, 1 daughter. Education: Jacques Lecoq of Mime, Paris. Career: Began with Queensland Theatre Company; Films include: The Wedding, 1980; Starstruck, 1982; Twelfth Night, 1986; Midday Crisis, 1994; Dad and Dave on our Selection, 1995; Shine; Children of the Revolution, 1996; Elizabeth, 1998; Shakespeare in Love, 1998; The Magic Pudding, 1999; Mystery Men, 1999; House on Haunted Hill, 1999; Quills, 1999; The Tailor of Panama, 2000; Lantana, 2001; Frida, 2002; The Banger Sisters, 2002; Swimming Upstream, 2003; Ned Kelly, 2003; Finding Nemo (voice), 2003; Pirates of the Caribbean: The Curse of the Black Pearl, 2003; Intolerable Cruelty, 2003; Harvie Krumpet (voice), 2003; The Life and Death of Peter Sellers (TV), 2004; Munich, 2005; Candy, 2006; Pirates of the Caribbean: At World's End, 2007; Elizabeth: The Golden Age, 2007. Theatre includes: Hamlet; The Alchemist; The Marriage of Figaro; The Small Poppies; TV includes: Menotti, 1980-81; The Burning Piano, 1992; Mercury, 1995; Bonus Mileage, 1996. Honours: Academy and BAFTA Awards, Australian Film Institute Award, Golden Globe Award for Shine; BAFTA Award for Best Supporting Actor, 1998; Golden Globe, Best

Actor in a Miniseries or TV Movie, 2005; Screen Actors Guild Awards, 2005. Address: C/o Shanahan Management, PO Box 478, Kings Cross, NSW 2011, Australia.

RUSHDIE (Ahmed) Salman, Sir, b. 19 June 1947, Bombay, India. Writer. m. (1) Clarissa Luard, 1976, dissolved 1987, died 1999, 1 son, (2) Marianne Wiggins, 1988, divorced 1993, 1 stepdaughter, (3) Elizabeth West, 1997, divorced, 1 son, (4) Padma Lakshmi, 2004, separated. Education: MA, King's College, Cambridge. Appointments: Actor, Fringe Theatre, London, 1968-69; Advertising Copywriter, 1969-73; Part-time Copywriter, 1976-80. Publications: Grimus, 1975; Midnight's Children, 1981; Shame, 1983; The Jaguar Smile: A Nicaraguan Journey, 1987; The Satanic Verses, 1988; Haroun and The Sea of Stories, 1990; Imaginary Homelands (essays), 1991; The Wizard of Oz, 1992; The Ground Beneath Her Feet, 1999; Fury, 2001; Step Across the Line: Collected Non-Fiction 1992-2002, 2002; Telling Tales (anthology), 2004; Shalimar the Clown, 2005; The Enchantress of Florence, 2008. TV Films: The Painter and The Pest, 1985; The Riddle of Midnight, 1988; Contributions to professional journals. Honours: Booker McConnell Prize for Fiction, 1981; Arts Council Literary Bursary, 1981; English Speaking Union Literary Award, 1981; James Tait Black Memorial Book Prize, 1981; Prix du Meilleur Livre Etranger, 1984; Nominated for Whitbread Prize, 1988; Booker Prize, 1993; Commander of the Order of Arts and Letters of France, 1999, Knighted, 2007. Memberships: PEN; Production Board, British Film Institute; Advisory Board, Institute of Contemporary Arts; FRSL; Executive, Camden Committee for Community Relations, 1975-82. Address: c/o Aitken & Stone Ltd, 29 Fernshaw Road, London SW10 0TG, England.

RUSHMAN Geoffrey Boswall, b. 20 August 1939, Northampton, England. Medical Practitioner. m. Gillian Mary, 3 daughters. Education: MB BS, St Bartholomew's Hospital, 1957-62; Conjoint Diploma (MRCS LRCP), 1962; Royal College of Anaesthetists (FFARCS), 1970. Appointments: Trainee Anaesthetist, St Bartholomew's Hospital, 1968-73; Consultant Anaesthetist, Southend Hospital, 1974-99; Examiner Royal College of Anaesthetists, 1991-99; Council Member, 1985-88, Secretary, 1991-92, President, 1999-2000, Section of Anaesthetics, Royal Society of Medicine; Council Member, Royal Society of Medicine, 2001-2005; Licensed Lay Minister, Diocese of Oxford. Publications: Parenteral Nutrition for the Surgical Patient (jointly), 1971; Synopsis of Anaesthesia (jointly), 8th, 9th, 10th, 11th and 12th editions, 1977, 1982, 1987,1993, 1999 (with Greek, Polish, Spanish, Italian and German Editions); Short History of Anaesthesia (jointly), 1996; Short Answer Questions in Anaesthesia, 1997. Honours: Hichens Prize (jointly), 1962; Police Award for Bravery, 1969; Association of Anaesthetists Prize for contributions to anaesthesia (jointly), 1971. Address: Aylesbury Road, Thame, Oxon, England.

RUSPOLI Francesco, b. 11 December 1958, Paris, France. Artist; Painter. Education: MA, Set and Costume design, Central St Martin, England, 1995. Career: Abstract figurative painter and colourist; Theatre designer of set and costumes; Exhibitions: Numerous exhibitions in UK and abroad 1983- include most recently: Group shows: Galiere d'Art, Nice, 2000; Agora Gallery, New York, 2000, 2001; Llewellyn Alexander Gallery, London, 2000, 2001; Hay's Gallery, London, 2001; Royal Free Hampstead Hospital, London, 2001; Nobleart Gallery, Cambridge, 2001; Salon des Arts, London, 2002; Plus One Plus Two Galleries, London, 2002; Artlands, Norfolk, 2002; DACS, London, 2002; Colouris, London, 2003; One man shows: Sylvia White Gallery, New York, 2000; Ministere des Finances, Paris, 2000; Mayfair Festival, London, 2000, 2003; Hay's Gallery, London, 2001; Artlands, London, 2003, 2004; Set and Costume Design: Shakespeare's Universe, Barbican, 1994; Loves Labours Lost, Cochrane Theatre, 1994; Triangle, Cochrane Theatre, 1995; Commercial, CTVC Studios, 1995; Snuff, London Film Festival, 1995; The May, Barons Court Theatre, 1997; Mind the Gap, Canal Café Theatre, 1999; Commissions: Painting, The Rating and Evaluation Association, London; Painting, Temple, Barristers, London; Mural, Le Cigale Restaurant, London; Mural, Insurance MGA, Nice, France; Painting, Hotel Grau Roig, Andorra; Private collections and museums: Robert Hardy; Dame Felicity Lott; Decia De Pauw; Gauguin Museum, Tahiti; Works in private collections in London, Paris, Tel-Aviv, Barcelona, Rome, Milan, Glasgow, Deauville, Cannes, Nice, Lille, Lyon, New York. Publications: Works featured in Exhibit A Magazine; Observer Magazine. Honours: Silver Medal, Grand Prix of Rome, 1985; Bronze Medal, Biennial, Villeneuve-Loubet, 1985; Golden Painting, 1986, Silver Medal, 1986, Gold Medal, 1988, Institute of French Culture; Eugene Frometin, Federation Latin, France, 1987; Bronze Medal, Mairie 17e Arrond Paris, France, 1991; Academician, 1994, Knight of the Art, 1998, Academy Geci-Marino, Italy. Address: 54 Chestnut Grove, Balham, London SW12 8JJ, England. E-mail: francesco.ruspoli@virgin.net Website: www.francesco-ruspoli.com

RUSSELL Anthony Patrick, b. 11 April 1951, Wirral, England. Senior Circuit Judge. Education: MA, Pembroke College, Oxford. Appointments: Called to the Bar, 1974; Queen's Counsel, 1999; Circuit Judge, 2004-06; Senior Circuit Judge and Resident Judge of Preston Crown Court, 2006-; Honorary Recorder of Preston, 2006-. Honours: Listed in national and international biographical directories. Membership: Honorary Fellow, 2002, Vice-President, 2004, Guild of Church Musicians. Address: The Law Courts, Openshaw Place, Ring Way, Preston PR1 2LL, England.

RUSSELL Bruce John, b. 16 July 1946, London, England. Artist; Professor. Education: Chelsea School of Art, 1964-69; Cheltenham Fellowship, 1969-70. Appointments: Founder, Co-Director, Polytechnic Gallery, Newcastle, 1975-78; Founder, Director, Stanley Picker Gallery, Kingston University, 1997-2002; Lecturer, York School of Art, 1971-74; Senior Lecturer, Painting, Newcastle Polytechnic, 1975-78; Senior Lecturer, Painting, St Martin's School of Art (Central St Martin's), 1979-87; Professor of Fine Art, Head of School of Fine Art, Kingston University, London, 1987-2006; 25 solo exhibitions in public and commercial galleries, 1971-; Included in major group and survey shows internationally; Work in public, corporate and private collections around the world; Co-director, Frari Books, UK. Publications: Various international and national reviews and catalogues; Glyphs, Morphs and Tropes, 1999; Circles & Diamonds, 2006; Squares, 2007. Honours: Arts Council Major Award, 1976; Fellow, Royal Society of Arts, 2000-; Professor of Fine Art, 1993-; Emeritus Professor, 2006-; Visiting Professor, Cambridge School of Art, 2007-, Represented by Beardsmore Gallery, London, Leinster Gallery, Dublin. Memberships: Chelsea Arts Club, 1993-; FRSA, 2006-. Address: The Laurels, Farnham Road, West Liss, Hampshire GU33 6JU, England. E-mail: bruce@llauri.plus.com Website: www.brucestudio.co.uk

RUSSELL John, b. 22 January 1919, Fleet, England. Art Critic; Writer. Education: MA, Magdalen College, Oxford, 1940. Appointments: Honorary Attaché, Tate Gallery, 1940-41; Staff, Ministry of Information, 1941-43, Naval Intelligence Division, Admiralty, London, 1943-46; Contributor, 1945-49,

DICTIONARY OF INTERNATIONAL BIOGRAPHY

Art Critic, 1949-74, The Sunday Times; Art Critic, 1974-82, Chief Art Critic, 1982-91, The New York Times. Publications: Shakespeare's Country, 1942; British Portrait Painters, 1945; Switzerland, 1950; Logan Pearsall Smith, 1950; Erich Kleiber, 1956; Paris, 1960, 2nd edition, 1983; Seurat, Private View (with Bryan Robertson and Lord Snowdon), 1965; Max Ernst, 1967; Henry Moore, 1968; Ben Nicholson, 1969; Pop Art Redefined (with Suzi Gablik), 1969; The World of Matisse, 1970; Francis Bacon, 1971; Édouard Vuillard, 1971; The Meanings of Modern Art, 1981, new and enlarged edition, 1990; Reading Russell, 1989; London, 1994; Matisse: Father and Son, 1999. Contributions to: Various publications including New York Review of Books, 1999-2000. Honour: Honorary Member, Century Association, New York, 2000. Membership: American Academy of Arts and Letters, 1966; Guggenheim Fellow, 2000-2001. Address: 166 East 61st Street, New York, NY 10021, USA.

RUSSELL Ken, b. 3 July 1927, Southampton, England. Film Director. m. (1) Shirley Kingdam, divorced 1978, 4 sons, 1 daughter, (2) Vivian Jolly, 1984, 1 son, 1 daughter, (3) Hetty Baines, 1992, divorced 1997, 1 son, (4) Lisi Tribble, 2001. Education: Nautical College, Pangbourne, England. Career: Former actor, freelance magazine photographer; Director, numerous TV documentaries for BBC, shown all over world; Documentaries include: Elgar; Bartok; Debussy; Hebri Rousseau; Isadora Duncan; Delius; Richard Strauss; Clouds of Glory; The Mystery of Dr Martini; The Secret Life of Arnold Bax; TV series: Lady Chatterly's Lover; Director, films: French Dressing, 1964; Billion Dollar Brain, 1967; Women in Love, 1969; The Music Lovers, 1970; The Devils, 1971; The Boyfriend, 1971; Savage Messiah, 1972; Mahler, 1973; Tommy, 1974; Lisztomania, 1975; Valentino, 1977; Altered States, 1981; Gothic, 1986; Aria (segment), 1987; Salome's Last Dance, 1988; The Lair of the White Worm, 1988; The Rainbow, 189; Whore, 1990; Prisoners of Honour, 1991; Lion's Mouth, 2000; The Fall of the Louse of Usher, 2002; Revenge of the Elephant Man, 2004; Trapped Ashes, 2006. Actor, film: The Russia House, 1990; The Rake's Progress (Stravinsky), 1982; Die Soldaten (Zimmerman), 1983; Opera: Princess Ida, 1992; Salome, Bonn, 1993. Publications: A British Picture: An Autobiography, 1989; Altered States: The Autobiography of Ken Russell, 1991; Fire Over England, 1993; Mike and Gaby's Space Gospel, 1999. Address: c/o Peter Rawley, ICM, 8942 Wilshire Boulevard, Beverly Hills, CA 90021, USA.

RUSSELL Kurt von Vogel, b. 17 March 1951, Springfield, Massachusetts, USA. Actor. m. Season Hubley, 1979, divorced, 1 son, 1 son with Goldie Hawn. Career: Child actor, Disney shows and films; Professional baseball player, 1971-73; Films include: It Happened at the World's Fair, 1963; Unlawful Entry, 1992; Captain Ron, 1992; Tombstone, 1993; Stargate, 1994; Executive Decision, 1996; Escape from LA, 1996; Breakdown, 1997; Soldier, 1998; Vanilla Sky, 2001; Interstate 60, 2002; Dark Blue, 2002; Miracle, 2004; Sky High, 2005; Dreamer: Inspired by a True Story, 2005; Poseidon, 2006; Grindhouse, 2007; Death Proof, 2007; Cutlass, 2007. TV series include: lead role in Travels With Jamie McPheeters, 1963-64; The New Land, 1974; The Quest, 1976; TV films include: Search For the Gods, 1975; The Deadly Tower, 1975; Christmas Miracle in Caulfield USA, 1977; Elvis, 1979; Amber Waves, 1988; Numerous guest appearances. Honours: 5 acting awards; 10 baseball awards; 1 golf championship. Memberships: Professional Baseball Players' Association; Stuntman's Association. Address: Creative Artists' Agency, 9830 Wilshire Boulevard, Beverly Hills, CA 90212-1825, USA.

RUSSELL Martin James, b. 25 September 1934, Bromley, Kent, England. Writer. Publications: No Through Road, 1965; The Client, 1975; Mr T, 1977; Death Fuse, 1980; Backlash, 1981; The Search for Sara, 1983; A Domestic Affair, 1984; The Darker Side of Death, 1985; Prime Target, 1985; Dead Heat, 1986; The Second Time is Easy, 1987; House Arrest, 1988; Dummy Run, 1989; Mystery Lady, 1992; Leisure Pursuit, 1993. Memberships: Crime Writers' Association; Detection Club. Address: 15 Breckonmead, Wanstead Road, Bromley, Kent BR1 3BW, England.

RUSSELL Norman Atkinson, b. 7 August 1943, Belfast, Northern Ireland. Anglican Priest. m. Victoria Christine Jasinska, 2 sons. Education: MA, Churchill College, Cambridge; BD, London. Appointments: Articled Clerk, Cooper Brothers & Company, London, 1966-67; Curate, Christ Church with Emmanuel, Clifton, Bristol, 1970-74; Curate, Christ Church, Cockfosters, London and Anglican Chaplain, Middlesex Polytechnic, 1974-77; Rector of Harwell with Chilton, 1977-84; Priest in Charge of Gerrrards Cross, 1984-88 and Fulmer, 1985-88; Rector of Gerrards Cross and Fulmer, 1988-98; Archdeacon of Berkshire, 1998-. Honour: Honorary Canon, Christ Church, Oxford, 1995-98. Address: Foxglove House, Love Lane, Donnington, Newbury, Berkshire RG14 2JG, England. E-mail: archdber@oxford.anglican.org

RUSSELL Willy, (William Martin Russell), b. 23 August 1947, Liverpool, England. Dramatist; Writer. m. Ann Seagroatt, 1969, 1 son, 2 daughters. Education: Certificate of Education, St Katherine's College of Education, Liverpool. Appointments: Teacher, 1973-74; Fellow, Creative Writing, Manchester Polytechnic, 1977-78. Publications: Theatre: Blind Scouse, 1971-72; When the Reds (adaptation) 1972; John, Paul, George, Ringo and Bert (musical), 1974; Breezeblock Park, 1975; One for the Road, 1976; Stags and Hens, 1978; Educating Rita, 1979; Blood Brothers (musical), 1983; Our Day Out (musical), 1983; Shirley Valentine, 1986; The Wrong Boy (novel), 2000; Films: Dancin' Tru the Dark, 1990; Terraces, 1993. Songs and poetry; Hoovering The Moon (Album), 2003. Television Plays: King of the Castle, 1972; Death of a Young Young Man, 1972; Break In (for schools), 1974; Our Day Out, 1976; Lies (for schools), 1977; Daughter of Albion, 1978; Boy With Transistor Radio (for schools), 1979; One Summer (series), 1980. Radio Play: I Read the News Today (for schools), 1979. Screenplays: Band on the Run, 1979; Educating Rita, 1981. Honours: Honorary MA, Open University; Honorary Director, Liverpool Playhouse. Address: c/o Margaret Ramsay Ltd, 14A Goodwin's Court, St Martin's Lane, London WC2, England.

RUSSELL BEALE Simon, b. 12 January 1961, Penang, Malaya. Actor. Education: Gonville & Caius College, Cambridge; Associate Artist, RSC, 1986; Theatre: Traverse Theatre, Edinburgh; Lyceum, Edinburgh; Royal Court, London; Royal National Theatre; Donmar Warehouse, London; Almeida, London; RSC Productions: The Winter's Tale; The Art of Success; Everyman in his Humour; The Fair Maid of the West; The Storm; Speculators; The Constant Couple; The Man of Mode; Restoration; Mary and Lizzie; Some Americans Abroad; Playing with Trains; Troilus and Cressida; Edward II; Love's Labours Lost; The Seagull; Richard III; The Tempest; King Lear; Ghosts; Othello; Films: Orlando, 1992; Persuasion, 1995; Hamlet, 1996; The Temptation of Franz Shubert, 1997; An Ideal Husband, 1999; Blackadder Back & Forth, 1999; The Gathering, 2002; TV: A Very Peculiar Practice; Downtown Lagos, 1992; The Mushroom Picker, 1993; A Dance to the Music of Time, 1997; The Temptation of Franz Schubert, 1997; Alice in Wonderland, 1999; The Young

Visiters, 2003; Dunkirk, 2004. Honours: Royal TV Society Award for Best Actor, 1997; BAFTA Award for Best Actor, 1998; Olivier Award, Best Actor, 2003.

RUSSO Carlo Ferdinando, b. 15 May 1922, Naples, Italy. University Professor. m. Adele Plotkin. Education: Degree in Filologia antica, University of Pisa, 1943; Diploma, Scuola Normale, Pisa, 1945. Appointments: Assistant Editor, 1946-62, Managing Editor, 1962-, Belfagor journal; Instructor, University of Florence, Italy, 1946-48; Instructor, University of Cologne, Germany, 1948-50; Libero Docente, Greek and Latin Philology, Rome, 1951; Professor, University Bari, Italy, 1950-62; Professor tenure, 1962-97; Professor Emeritus, 1999. Publications: Senecae, Apocolocyntosis, 1948, 6th edition, 1985; Hesiodi, Scutum, 1950, 3rd edition, 1968; La Coppa di Nestore di Pitecusa-Ischia, (Monumenti Antichi, Accademia dei Lincei), 1955-92; Aristofane Autore di Teatro, 1962, 3rd edition, 1992, English edition, 1994, paperback, 1997; Die Gestalt einer archaischen Handschrift und einer kyklischen Ilias, 1983; Omero e il Disco di Festo, 1995; Omero nasce con le Olimpiadi (Olimpiade seconda), 1999; L'anno poetico XXXVI, 2003; I dolori di Omero omicida, 2005; Curator of works by H Fränkel, G Pasquali and E Fraenkel, 1969-83, 1992, 1994. Address: Casa ed Olschki, Casella post 66, 50100 Florence, Italy. E-mail: cf.russo@lgxserve.ciseca.uniba.it

RUSSO René, b. 17 February 1954, California, USA. Actress. m. Dan Gilroy, 1992, 1 daughter. Career: Formerly model Eileen Ford Agency; Film appearances include: Major League, 1989; Mr Destiny; One Good Cop; Freejack; Lethal Weapon 3; In the Line of Fire; Outbreak; Get Shorty; Tin Cup; Ransom; Buddy; Lethal Weapon 4, 1998; The Adventures of Rocky and Bullwinkle, 1999; The Thomas Crown Affair, 1999; Showtime, 2002; Big Trouble, 2002; 2 for the Money, 2005; Yours, Mine and Ours, 2005. TV appearance: Sable (series). Address: c/o Progressive Artists Agency, 400 South Beverly Drive, Suite 216, Beverly Hills, CA 90212, USA.

RUSTAN Peter Agne, b. 21 February 1941, Köping, Västmanland, Sweden. Mining Engineer. m. Brita Järvhammar, divorced 2002, 1 son, 3 daughters. Education: Mining Engineer, 1965; Technical Licentiate, 1973; Technical Dr, Mining, 1995; Associate Professor, Mining, 1995. Appointments: Stockholm Assistant in Mining, Royal Institute of Technology, 1965-70; Mine Planning Engineer, Luossavaara-Kirunavaara, Malmberget, Sweden, 1971-74; Researcher and Teacher, Lulea University of Technology, Lulea, Sweden, 1974-98; Consultant, 1998-. Secretary-General, International Society of Explosives Engineers – Flagblast Section and the International Organizing Committee for Rock Fragmentation by Blasling Symposia. Publications: Co-author, Underground Ventilation, Stiftelsen Bergteknisk Forskning, Sweden, 1984; Editor-in-Chief, Rock Blasting Terms and Symbols; A A Balkenna, Rotterdam, 1998. Memberships: International Society of Explosives Engineers, USA. Address: Lagmansvagen 20, SE-954 32 Gammelstad, Sweden. E-mail: agne.rustan@spray.se

RUTTER Michael Llewellyn, b. 15 August 1933, Brummanna, Lebanon. Professor of Developmental Psychiatry; Writer. m. Marjorie Heys, 27 December 1958, 1 son, 2 daughters. Education: MB ChB, 1950-55, MD, 1963, University of Birmingham; DPM, University of London, 1961. Appointments: Professor of Developmental Psychopathology, University of London; Social, Genetic and Developmental Psychiatry Research Centre. Publications: Depression in Young People: Development and Clinical Perspectives (co-editor), 1986; Language Development and

Disorders (co-editor), 1987; Treatment of Autistic Children (co-editor), 1987; Parenting Breakdown: The Making and Breaking of Intergenerational Links (co-author), 1988; Assessment and Diagnosis in Child Psychopathology, 1988; Straight and Devious Pathways From Childhood to Adulthood, 1990; Biological Risk Factors for Psychosocial Disorders, 1991; Developing Minds: Challenge and Continuity Across the Lifespan, 1993; Stress, Risk and Resilience in Children and Adolescents, Processes, Mechanisms and Interventions (co-editor), 1994; Child and Adolescent Psychiatry: Modern Approaches (co-editor), 3rd edition, 1994; Development Through Life: A Handbook for Clinicians (co-editor), 1994; Psychosocial Disorders in Young People: Time Trends and their Causes (co-editor), 1995; Behavioural Genetics (co-author), 3rd edition, 1997; Antisocial Behaviour by Young People (co-author), 1998. Contributions to: Numerous professional journals. Honours: 10 honorary doctorates; Knight Baronet, 1992; American Psychological Association Distinguished Scientific Contribution Award, 1995; Castilla del Pino Prize for Achievement in Psychiatry, Cordoba, Spain, 1995; Royal Society of Medicine, honorary fellow, 1996; Royal College of Paediatrics and Child Health, honorary founding fellow, 1996; Society for Research in Child Development, president elect, 1997. Memberships: American Academy of Arts and Sciences, honorary foreign member; Royal College of Psychiatrists, fellow; Royal College of Physicians, fellow; Fellow, Royal Society, 1997-; President, Society for Research into Child Development, 1999-. Address: SGDP Research Centre, Institute of Psychiatry, De Crespigny Park, Denmark Hill, London SE5 8AF, England.

RÜTTGERS Jürgen, b. 26 June 1951, Cologne, West Germany. Minister-President, State of Northrhine-Westphalia. m. 3 children. Education: Law and History studies at university. Appointments: State Chairman, Christian Democratic Union's youth wing, Junge Union, 1980-86; Erftkreis County Chairman, CDU, 1985-99; Chairman, Parliamentary Technology Assessment Commission, 1987-89; Member, Bundestag, 1987-2000; CDU/CSU Party Whip, Bundestag, 1989-90; Chief Whip, CDU/CSU Parliamentary Party, 1990-94; Deputy Chairman, 1993-99, Chairman, 1999-, CDU's North Rhine-Westphalia state branch; Federal Minister for Education, Research and Technology, 1994-98; Deputy Leader, CDU/CSU Parliamentary Party, Bundestag, 1998-2000; Deputy Chairman, Federal CDU, 2000-; Member, Landtag, 2000-; Leader, CDU/CSU Parliamentary Party, Landtag, 2000-05; State Premier, North Rhine-Westphalia, 2005-. Address: Staatskanzlei Nordrhein-Westfalen, 40190 Düsseldorf, Germany. E-mail: juergen.ruettgers@stk.nrw.de

RUTTY Jane Elizabeth, b. 6 January 1964, Watford, England. Registered Nurse; Academic. m. Guy Nathan Rutty. Education: Registered General Nurse, Hedgecock School of Nursing, Barking Hospital, 1988; Intensive Care Nursing, SE Thames College of Nursing, The Brook Hospital, 1990; Diploma in Professional Studies in Nursing, University of Westminster, 1992; BSc (Hons) Education Studies (Nursing, University of Wolverhampton, 1994; MSc, Nursing, Royal College of Nursing Institute, London, 1998; PhD, University of Bradford, ongoing, 1998-. Appointments: Staff Nurse, Medicine, King George Hospital Ilford, 1988; Staff Nurse, Intensive Care and Coronary Care Unit, The Brook Hospital, Woolwich, 1988-89; Research Nurse, Thrombosis Research Unit, Medical School, King's College Hospital, London, 2089-90; Post Registration Student Nurse, SE Thames College of Nursing, The Brook Hospital, 1990; Staff Nurse, Intensive Care, Coronary Care and Theatre Recovery Unit, Northwick Park Hospital, Harrow, 1990-92; Staff Nurse, Intensive Care

Unit, Groby Road Hospital, Leicester, 1992-93; Nurse Tutor Student,1993-94, Senior Lecturer, 1994-96, University of Wolverhampton; Lecturer, 1996-2000, Senior Academic Lecturer, Nursing, 2000-2002, University of Bradford; Principal Lecturer, Nursing, DeMontfort University, Leicester, 2002-. Publications: 15 articles as author and co-author on professional journals; 6 abstracts in journals; 4 book chapters. Honours: Medici Fellowship, 2004-2005; Member, Higher Education Academy; Member, Global Advisory Board for the Journal of Forensic Nursing. Memberships: International Association of Forensic Nursing; National Clinical Skills Network; Qualitative Research Network; British Association of Critical Care Nursing; Royal College of Nursing: Critical Care Forum, Research Society, Education Forum, Ethics Forum, History of Nursing Society; Founder and President, European Association of Forensic Nurse Practitioners. Address: School of Nursing and Midwifery, De Montfort University, 266 London Road, Leicester LE2 1RQ, England. E-mail: jrutty@dmu.ac.uk

RUZICKA Marek Captain, b. 29 August 1960, Sobeslav, Czech Republic. Naturalist. m. Magdalena Zhofova, 2 sons. Education: MSc, Environmental Engineering, 1984; Postgraduate course, Enzyme Engineering, 1988; Postgraduate studies, Applied Mathematics, 1987; PhD, Chemical Engineering, 1990; Partial study of Physics, Charles University, Prague, 1990-94. Appointments: Scientist, Institute of Chemical Process Fundamentals, Academy of Sciences, Prague, Czech Republic, 1990-; Associate Professor of Chemical Engineering Prague Institute of Chemical Technology, Prague, Czech Republic 2005-. Publications: Over 20 articles in professional scientific journals. Honours: British Chevening Scholarship, University of Birmingham, 1994-95; Honorary Research Fellow, University of Birmingham. Memberships: Union of Czech Mathematicians and Physicists; Euromech. Address: Institute of Chemical Process Fundamentals, Rozvojova 135, 16502 Prague, Czech Republic. E-mail: ruzicka@icpf.cas.cz

RYAN Meg, b. 19 November 1961, Fairfield, Connecticut, USA. Actress. m. Dennis Quaid, 1991, divorced, 1 son. Education: New York University. Career: Formerly in TV commercials; TV appearances: As The World Turns; One of the Boys; Amy and the Angel; The Wild Side; Charles in Charge; Owner, Prufrock Pictures; Films: Rich and Famous, 1981; Amytyville III-D; Top Gun; Armed and Dangerous; Innerspace; DOA; Promised Land; The Presidio; When Harry Met Sally; Joe Versus the Volcano; The Doors; Prelude to a Kiss; Sleepless in Seattle; Flesh and Bone; Significant Other; When a Man Loves a Woman; IQ; Paris Match; Restoration; French Kiss, 1995; Two for the Road, 1996; Courage Under Fire, 1996; Addicted to Love, 1997; City of Angels, 1998; You've Got Mail, 1998; Hanging Up, 1999; Lost Souls, 1999; Proof of Life, 2000; Kate & Leopold, 2001; In the Cut, 2003; Against the Ropes, 2004; In the Land of Women, 2007; My Mom's New Boyfriend, 2008; The Deal, 2008; The Women, 2008. Address: c/o ICM, 8942 Wilshire Boulevard, Beverly Hills, CA 90211, USA.

RYDER Winona, b. 29 October 1971, Minnesota, USA. Actress. Education: American Conservatory Theatre, San Francisco. Career: Films include: Lucas, 1986; Beetlejuice, 1988; Great Balls of Fire; Heathers, 1989; Edward Scissorhands, 1990; Bram Stoker's Dracula, 1992; Age of Innocence, 1993; Little Women; How to Make an American Quilt; The Crucible; Looking for Richard; Boys; Alien Resurrection; Girl Interrupted, 1999; Lost Souls, 1999; Autumn in New York, 1999; Mr Deeds, 2002; S1m0ne, 2002;

The Day My God Died, voice, 2003; The Heart is Deceitful Above All Things, 2004; The Darwin Awards, 2006; A Scanner Darkly, 2006; The Ten, 2007; Sex and Death 101, 2007; Welcome, 2007; The Last Word, 2008. Honours: Golden Globe Best Supporting Actress, 1994. Address: 10345 W Olympic Boulevard, Los Angeles, CA 90064, USA.

RYDYGIER Edward, b. 17 November 1953, Warsaw, Poland. Physicist; Financial Analyst; Teacher. m. Hanna Rydygier. Education: Master of Science in Physics, Warsaw University, 1978; Postgraduate Studies, Statistical Methods Diploma, 1992, Computer Science Diploma, Polish Academy of Sciences, Mathematical Institute, 1992; Cand. for PhD, Technical Sciences,Kazimierz Pulaski University of Technology, Radom, Poland, 2005; Postgraduate Studies, Insurance and Banking Diploma, 2001, Warsaw Technical University. Appointments: Physicist, Institute of Nuclear Research, Otwock, Poland, 1978-82; Adjunct Lecturer, Institute for Nuclear Studies, Otwock, Poland, 1983-99; Inspector Warsaw District Labour Office, Warsaw, Poland, 2000; Consultant of the World Bank with the Ministry of the State Treasury, Warsaw, Poland, 2000; Lecturer, Education Centre, Vocational Studies of Business and Economics, Warsaw, Poland, 2001-; Inspector, Archive of Municipal Office of Warsaw, 2002-; Lecturer, University of Economics and Technology in Legionowo, Poland, 2004-2006. Publications: 90 scientific publications including 50 conference articles presented at international scientific conferences and workshops, Honours: European Vocational Title, European Physicist, conferred by President of European Physical Society on behalf of European Commission of EU, 1997; Listed in national and international biographical dictionaries. Member, Research Board of Advisors of the American Biographical Institute, 2001-. Memberships: Polish Physical Society; Founder Member, Polish Nuclear Society; Member General Revision Committee Polish Society of Universalism. Address: ul Narbutta 60 m. 8, 02-541 Warsaw, Poland. E-mail: erydygier@targowek.waw.pl

RYU Dae Hyun, b. 6 August 1960, Busan, Republic of Korea. Professor. m. Myung-Hee Jung, 1 son, 1 daughter. Education: BA, 1983, MA, 1985, PhD, 1997, Busan National University, Republic of Korea. Appointments: Researcher, Goldstar Co Ltd (now LG Electronics), 1985-86; Senior Researcher, Electronics and Telecommunications Research Institute, 1987-98; Professor, Division of IT, Hansei University, 1998-; CEO, XecureNexus Co Ltd, 2000-03. Memberships: Regular Member, IEEE; IEEK (Korea); KIISC; KIPS; KIMICS. E-mail: dhryu@hansei.ac.kr

RYU Si-Wook, b. 16 September 1970, Kyungsangbuk-do, South Korea. Professor. m. Eun-ju Kwon, 2 sons. Education: PhD, Industrial Engineering, Pusan National University, 2004; Postdoctoral Course, Institute of Electronic Commerce, Dongguk University, 2005. Appointments: Visiting Researcher, Institute of Electronic Commerce, 2001-05, Adjunct Professor, 2004-05, Dongguk University; Team Manager, LeachEI Corporation, 2002-04; Research Professor, Safety Research Center, Hanzhong University, 2006-. Publications: Book, Electronic Commerce @ e-business, 2nd edition, 2005; Articles: International Journal of Production Economics; International Journal of Industrial Engineering; The Korean Journal of Operations Research and Management Science Society. Honours: Who's Who in the World, 23rd Edition. Memberships: International Symposium on Inventory Research, Korean Operations Research and Management

Science Society. Address: 627-1 Bugok 2 dong, Kumjung-ku, Busan, South Korea. E-mail: swryu@pusan.ac.kr/ swkryu@hanzhong.ac.kr

RZEDOWSKI Jerzy, b. 27 December 1926, Lwów, Poland. Botanist. m. Graciela Calderón, 3 daughters. Education: Biology, National School of Biological Sciences, National Polytechnic Institute, Mexico, 1954; Doctor of Biology, Faculty of Science, National University of Mexico, 1961. Appointments: Professor, San Luis Potosí University, 1954; Professor, Researcher, Postgraduate College, 1959; Professor, National School of Biological Sciences, National Polytechnic Institute, 1961; Researcher, Institute of Ecology, 1984-. Publications: 120 articles in scientific journals; 26 fascicles; 45 book chapters; 6 books. Honours: Diploma al mérito botánico; Ordre des palmes académiques; Doctorado honoris causa, Universidad Autónoma Chapingo; Doctorado honoris causa, Universidad Michoacana de San Nicolás de Hidalgo; Premio al mérito ecologico; Asa Gray Award; Botany Millennium Award; José Cuatrecasas Medal for Excellence in Tropical Botany. Memberships: Botanical Society of America; American Society of Plant Taxonomists; Sociedad Argentina de Botánica; International Association of Plant Taxonomy; Sociedad Botánica de México. Address: Apartado postal 386, 61600 Pátzcuaro, Michoacán, Mexico. E-mail: jerzy.rzedowski@inecol.edu.mx

S

SA Tongmin, b. 21 March 1960, Seoul, Korea. Professor. m. Eunkyung Bae, 1 son, 1 daughter. Education: BS, 1984, MS, 1986, Seoul National University; PhD, North Carolina State University, USA, 1990. Appointments: Researcher, Agricultural Biotechnology; Professor, Sun Moon University; Professor, Chungbuk National University. Publications: Over 60 scientific articles. Memberships: Sigma Xi. Address: Department of Agricultural Chemistry, Chungbuk National University, Cheongju, Chungbuk, Korea. E-mail: tomsa@chungbuk.ac.kr

SAAD Akram Saad, b. 19 December 1956, Cairo, Egypt. Civil Engineer. m. Hanan, 1 son, 1 daughter. Education: BSc, Civil Engineering, Cairo University, 1979; MBA, Project Management, Missouri University, 2002; Certified Senior Corrosion Technologist & Protective Coating Specialist, NACE International, USA; Certified by IBM in MS project advanced. Appointments: Project Manager, Lahmeyer International; Resident Engineer, Hyder Consultants; Project and Follow-up Engineer, SPECO; Project Manager, RAMW; Project Manager; Project Manager, Al SaLama; Site Manager, TEKSIS; Site Engineer, Arab Swiss Engineering; Site Engineer, Cementation; Site Engineer, Aarding BV; Site Engineer. Publications: Report in Concrete Repair by the use of SFRS; Use of bonding Agent in Concrete Rehabilitation, Case Study. Honours: Coating Inspector, NACE International. Memberships: ASCE; NACE; SEI; GROHE; Egyptian Engineering Syndicate; Project Management Institute (PMI). Address: Lahmeyer International, Abu Dhabi 2413, United Arab Emirates. E-mail: akram.saad@gmail.com

SAAIMAN Nolan, b. 21 December 1960, Pretoria, South Africa. Internal Auditor. m. Anita, 2 sons. Education: B Comm, Accounting Sciences, 1982; B Comm, Honours, Accounting, 1988; Diploma, Datametrics, 1992; Certified Information Systems Auditor, 1992; Certified Financial Services Auditor, 1996; Computer Professional Qualifying Examination of the Computer Society of South Africa, 1996; Certified Internal Auditor, 1998; Certified Financial Consultant, 2001; Certified Business Manager, 2001. Appointments: Senior Internal Auditor, South African Post Office, 1985-88; Accountant Van Wyk and Louw, 1988-89; Manager's Assistant, Information Systems Audit Department, First National Bank, 1990-92; Manager, Computer Audit Services, SA Eagle, 1992-94; IT Audit Manager, SA Housing Trust, 1995-97; Audit Manager, Senior Auditor, Daimler Chrysler, South Africa, 1997-. Publications: Articles about computer audit, membership matters and internal audit, in Newsletter of the Institute of Internal Auditors, South Africa, 1995-96; Article on internal audit in Institute of Directors Directorship Magazine, 1997. Honours: Completed Comrades Marathon (90kms), 1984, 1986; Served on Board of Institute of Internal Auditors, South Africa, 1996-97; 21st Century Award for Achievement, IBC, 2001; Listed in Who's Who Publications and biographical dictionaries. Memberships: Information Systems Audit and Control Association; Institute of Directors; Institute of Internal Auditors; Computer Society of South Africa; Institute of Financial Consultants, The Association of Professionals in Business Management, USA. Address: 26 Retha Court, Veglaer Street, Pierre Van Ryneveld Park, 0157 South Africa. E-mail: nolan.saaiman@daimlerchrysler.com

SÄÄKSLAHTI Arja Kaarina, b. 24 September 1966, Lapua, Finland. Senior Department Researcher. m. Erkki Emil, 2 sons, 1 daughter. Education: Master of Science, 1993; PhD, 2005. Appointments: Infant Swimming Instructor and Educator, -1987; Physical Education Teacher, Kindergarten Teacher Training School, 1992-93; Researcher, University of Turku, Finland, 1993; Teacher of Didactics, 1994; Researcher, Department of Physical Education, 1994-2000, Physical Education Teacher, Researcher in Teacher Training School, -2000, Senior Lecturer, 2006, Senior Assistant, 2007-, University of Jyväskylä, Finland; Writer of books, -1997; Scriptwriter for TV programmes, 1998, 1999, 2006; Member, Editorial Board, Finnish Sport and Science. Publications: 3 articles in professional journals; Books: Physical Education Curriculum for Preschool, Grade 1 and 2; One, Two and Dive – Theory and Practice in Infant Swimming; Baby Swimming; Numerous articles as a part of different books. Honours: Best Abstract in Sport Pedagogy in Olympic Congress, 1996; The Award of Finnish Association of Life Saving and Teaching Swimming, 1996, 2005; 2nd Prize, Poster Presentation, AIESEP World Congress, 2008. Memberships: The Finnish Association of Life Saving and Teaching Swimming; NUORI SUOMI; The Finnish Society for Research in Sport and Physical Education; International Association for Physical Education in Higher Education. Address: Vahverontie 16-18 B18, 40640 Jyväskylä, Finland.

SAATCHI Charles, b. 9 June 1943. Advertising Executive. m. (1) Doris Lockhart, (2) Kay, 1990, divorced 2001, 1 daughter; (3) Nigella Lawson. Education: Christ's College, Finchley, London, England. Appointments: Former junior copywriter, Benton and Bowles (US advertising agency), London; Associate Director, Collett Dickinson Pearce, 1966-68; with Ross Cramer formed freelance consultancy, Cramer Saatchi, Director, 1968-70; Co-founder (with Maurice Saatchi) of Saatchi and Saatchi (advertising agency), 1970, Saatchi & Saatchi PLC, 1984, Director, 1970-93, President, 1993-95; Co-founder, Partner, M&C Saatchi Agency, 1995-; Founder, The Saatchi Gallery, 2003-. Address: 36 Golden Square, London, W1R 4EE, England.

SAATCHI Baron (Life Peer) Maurice, b. 21 June 1946. Advertising Executive. m. Josephine Hart, 1984, 1 son, 1 stepson. Education: BSc, London School of Economics. Appointments: Co-Founder, Saatchi & Saatchi Company, 1970; Chairman, Saatchi & Saatchi Company PLC, 1984-94; Director, 1994; Co-founder, Partner, M&C Saatchi Agency, 1995-; Chairman, Megalomedia PLC, 1995-; Director (non-executive) Loot, 1998-; Shadow Cabinet Office Minister, 2001-03; Co-Chair, Conservative Party, 2003-. Publications: The Science of Politics, 2001. Memberships: Governor, LSE; Council, Royal College of Art, 1997-; Trustee, Victoria & Albert Museum, 1988-. Address: 36 Golden Square, London, W1R 4EE, England.

SABAH Muna, b. 27 June 1970, Damascus, Syria. Consultant Pathologist. m. Hasan Mahayni, 1 son, 1 daughter. Education: MD (Hons), Damascus University, 1994; M Med Sc (Hons), University College, Dublin, 1995; MRC Path, 2001; FF Path (RCPI), 2005; MD (RCSI), 2005; FRC Path, 2008. Appointments: SHO, 1996-97, Registrar, 1998-99, Cork University Hospital; SHO, Waterford Regional Hospital, 1997-98; Lecturer, SpR, 1999-2004, Consultant Histopathologist, Senior Lecturer, 2004-07, Department of Pathology, Royal College of Surgeons in Ireland and Beaumont Hospital; Consultant Histopathologist, Department of Pathology, Connolly Hospital, Blanchardstown, Dublin, 2007-. Publications: Numerous articles in professional journals. Honours: MD (1st class honours), 1994; M Med Sc (Pathology) (1st class honours), 1995; Listed in international biographical dictionaries. Memberships: Fellow, Royal College of Pathologists; Fellow, Faculty of Pathology, Royal

College of Physicians in Ireland. Address: Department of Pathology, Connolly Hospital, Blanchardstown, Dublin 15, Ireland. E-mail: munsabah@gmail.com

SABAYO Muhammand Ramzan, Senior Professor; Dean. m. Asmat Khatoon, 4 daughters. Education: BE, Mechanical engineering, University of Sindh, Pakistan, 1968; MSc, 1974, PhD, 1977, University of Manchester, England; DSc, Energy Sciences, World University, Arizona, USA, 1990. Appointments: Visiting Scientist, University of Miami Clean Energy Institute of Science, 1980, and Dechema, Frankfurt, Germany, 1982-, Royal Society of London, England, 1985; Founder and Chairman, Department of Metallurgical Engineering, 1977-84, Founder and Chairman, Mining Engineering Department, 1977-81, Chairman, Library Committee, 1979-85, Senior Professor, Metallurgical Department, 1981-, Founder and Director, Industrial Liaison, 1984-87, Director of Postgraduate Studies, 1988-94, Director of Continuing Education, 1996-2001, Senior Professor, Department of Metallurgy and Materials Engineering, 2001-, Dean, Faculty of Science, Technology & Humanities, Mehran University, Jamshoro, Pakistan; Executive Committee Member, and Member of Accreditation Committee, Pakistan Engineering Council, 1985-87. Publications: 90 papers and articles in professional journals. Honours: Pride of Performance, Mehran University Alumni Association, 1997; Honoured Meritorious Award of Appreciation in field of Materials Science and Technology, 1998; Best University Teacher Award, 2000; Professor Meritorious Grade 21, 2001-; Agha Hassan Abedi Foundation Gold Medal in Engineering & Technology, 2001; Listed in international biographical dictionaries. Memberships: Research Board of Advisors, ABI; Advisory Board Member, IAHE, Florida; Council Member, ICF Sandia, Japan; Member, Advanced Studies and Research Board, Mehran University; Chartered Engineer, Engineering Council, London; Fellow, Institute of Materials, Minerals and Mining, London. Address: Mehran University of Engineering & Technology, Jamshoro, Sindh, Pakistan. E-mail: sabayo@muet.edu.pk

SACHDEV Perminder Singh, b. 27 July 1956, Ludhiana, India. Neuropsychiatrist. m. Jagdeep, 1986, 2 daughters. Education: MBBS, 1978, MD, 1981, AIIMS; FRANZCP, 1985; PhD, University of New South Wales, 1991. Appointments: Junior Resident, 1979-81, Senior Research Officer, Senior Resident, 1982, Department of Psychiatry, AIIMS; Psychiatric Registrar, Auckland Hospital Board, New Zealand, 1983-85; Consultant Psychiatrist, Otago Hospital Board, Dunedin, New Zealand, 1985-87; Clinical Lecturer, Department of Psychological Medicine, University of Otago Medical School, Dunedin, 1986; Senior Lecturer in Psychiatry, 1987-93, Associate Professor of Neuropsychiatry, 1993-98, Professor of Neuropsychiatry, 1999-, University of New South Wales; Clinical Director, Neuropsychiatric Institute, Prince of Wales Hospital, Australia. Publications: Numerous articles in professional medical journals; Editorial or author contributions to several respected psychiatric books. Honour: Sita Ram Jindal Gold Medal, 1972; Panjab University Gold Medal, 1973; Delhi Medical Association Diamond Jubilee Award, 1977; National Scholarship, 1972-78; Organon Senior Research Award, 1995; President Lecture, 5th Annual International Neuropsychiatry Congress, 2004; IAPA Outstanding Academician Award, 2004; Novartis Oration Award, 2004; Inaugural INA India Lecture Award, 2005. Memberships: Australian Society for Psychiatric Research; Australian Society for Biological Psychiatry; Tourette Syndrome Association; Tourette Syndrome Association of Australia; Movement Disorders Society; Sydney Movement

Disorders Society; Alzheimer's Association; International Neuropsychiatric Association; International College of Geriatric Psychopharmacology; Society of Biological Psychiatry. Address: NPI, Prince of Wales Hospital, Randwick, NSW 2031, Australia.

SACHS Horst, b. 27 March 1927, Magdeburg, Germany. Mathematician; University Teacher. m. Barbara Nowak. Education: Diploma, 1953, Dr rer nat, 1958, Dr rer nat habil, 1963, Martin-Luther-University, Halle-Wittenberg, Halle (Saale), Germany. Appointments: Science Assistant, University Halle-Wittenberg, Germany, 1953-63; Professor of Mathematics, Technical University of Ilmenau, Ilmenau, Germany, 1963-92; Retired, 1992. Publications: Textbooks on graph theory, 1970-72; Monograph: Co-author, Spectra of Graphs, 1980, 1982, 1995; Scientific articles mainly of graph theory, 1956-2005. Honour: Founding Fellow, Institute of Combinatorics and its Applications, TICA, Winnipeg, 1991; Euler Medal, 2000; Honorary Fellow, International Academy of Mathematical Chemistry, 2005. Memberships: TICA; Deutsche Mathematiker-Vereinigung; Mathematische Gesellschaft in Hamburg. Address: Grenzhammer 65, D-98693 Ilmenau, Germany. E-mail: horst.sachs@tu-Ilmenau.de

SACHS Leo, b. 14 October 1924, Leipzig, Germany. Scientist. m. Pnina Salkind, 1 son, 3 daughters. Education: BSc, University of Wales, Bangor, 1948; PhD, Trinity College, Cambridge University, England, 1951. Appointments: Research Scientist, Genetics, John Innes Institute, England, 1951-52; Research Scientist, 1952-, Founder, Department of Genetics and Virology, 1960, Professor, 1962, Head, Department of Genetics, 1962-89, Dean, Faculty of Biology, 1974-79, Otto Meyerhof Professor of Biology, Weizmann Institute of Science, Rehovot, Israel. Publications: Science papers in professional journals. Honours: Israel Prize, Natural Sciences, 1972; Fogarty International Scholar, National Institutes of Health, Bethesda, 1972; Harvey Lecture, Rockefeller University, New York, 1972; Rothschild Prize, Biological Sciences, 1977; Wolf Prize, Medicine, 1980; Bristol-Myers Award, Distinguished Achievement in Cancer Research, New York, 1983; Doctor Honoris Causa, Bordeaux University, France, 1985; Royal Society Wellcome Foundation Prize, London, 1986; Alfred P Sloan Prize, General Motors Cancer Research Foundation, New York, 1989; Warren Alpert Foundation Prize, Harvard Medical School, Boston, 1997; Doctor of Medicine Honoris Causa, Lund University, Sweden, 1997; Honorary Fellow, University of Wales, Bangor, 1999; Emet Prize for Life Sciences, 2002. Memberships: European Molecular Biology Organization; Israel Academy of Sciences and Humanities; Foreign Associate USA National Academy of Sciences; Fellow, Royal Society, London; Foreign Member, Academia Europaea; Honorary Life Member, International Cytokine Society. Address: Weizmann Institute of Science, Department of Molecular Genetics, Rehovot, Israel.

SACKS Jonathan Henry, b. 8 March 1948, London, England. Rabbi. m. Elaine Taylor, 1970, 1 son, 2 daughters. Education: Christ's College, Finchley; Gonville and Caius College, Cambridge; New College, Oxford; London University; Jews' College, London; Yeshivat Etz Hayyim, London. Appointments: Lecturer, Middlesex Polytechnic, 1971-73, Jew's College, London, 1973-76, 1976-82; Rabbi, Golders Green Synagogue, London, 1978-82, Marble Arch Synagogue, London, 1983-90; Chief Rabbi Lord Jakobvits Professor (1st incumbent), Modern Jewish Thought, 1982-; Director, Rabbinic Faculty, 1983-90, Principal, 1984-90, Chief Rabbi, 1991-, United Hebrew Congregations of the Commonwealth; Editor, Le'ela (journal), 1985-90; Presentation Fellow, King's

College, London, 1993; Association President, Conference of European Rabbis, 2000-; Visiting Professor of Philosophy, Hebrew University, Jerusalem and of Theology and Religious Studies, King's College, London. Publications: Torah Studies, 1986; Tradition and Transition, 1986; Traditional Alternatives, 1989; Traditional in an Untraditional Age, 1990; The Persistence of Faith, 1991; Orthodoxy Confronts Modernity (Editor), 1991; Crisis and Covenant, 1992; One People? Tradition, Modernity and Jewish Unity, 1993; Will We Have Jewish Grandchildren? 1994; Faith in the Future, 1995; Community of Faith, 1995; The Politics of Hope, 1997; Morals and Markets, 1999; Celebrating Life, 2000; Radical Then Radical Now, 2001; The Dignity of Difference: How To Avoid the Clash of Civilizations, 2002; The Chief Rabbi's Haggadah, 2003; From Optimism to Hope, 2004; To Heal a Fractured World, 2005. Honours: Honorary degrees from the Universities of: Bar Ilan, Cambridge, Glasgow, Haifa, Middlesex, Yeshiva University New York, University of Liverpool, St Andrews University and Leeds Metropolitan University; Honorary Fellow, Gonville and Caius College, Cambridge, 1993; Kings College; Jerusalem Prize, 1995; Awarded Doctorate of Divinity by Archbishop of Canterbury, 2001; Knighted, Queen's Birthday Honours, 2005. Address: 735 High Road, London, N12 0US, England.

SAFFACHE Pascal Marie, b. 5 August 1971, Fort-de-France, Martinique. Senior Lecturer; Dean. Education: Master's degree, 1995, PhD, 1998, Physical Geography, Université des Antilles et de la Guyane, Martinique. Appointments: Assistant, 1997-2000, Senior Lecturer, 2001-, Director, Department of Geography and Physical Planning, 2002-05, Dean, Faculty of Human Sciences and Letters, 2005-, Université des Antilles et de la Guyane. Publications: Contributions to: Glossary of Geomorphology, 2003; Simplified Dictionary of Geography, 2003; West Indian Coastlines at Stake: From land settlement to sustainable development, 2005. Honours: Local Development Prize, 1998; National TOYP Prize, 2005; Blue Ribbon Trophy of Ecology, 2006. Memberships: European Interdisciplinary Academy of Sciences; French Geographical Society. Address: 46 Residence les Charmeures, Batiment B, Porte 3, Ravine Vilaine, 97200 Fort-de-France, Martinque, French West Indies. E-mail: pascal.saffache@martinque.univ-ag.fr

SAFIRE William, b. 17 December 1929, New York, New York, USA. Columnist; Writer. m. Helene Belmar Julius, 16 December 1962, 1 son, 1 daughter. Education: Syracuse University, 1947-49. Appointments: Reporter, New York Herald-Tribune Syndicate, 1949-51; Correspondent, Europe and the Middle East, WNBC-WNBT, 1951; Radio-TV Producer, WMBC, New York City, 1954-55; Vice-President, Tex McCrary Inc, 1955-60; President, Safire Public Relations, 1960-68; Special Assistant to President Richard M Nixon, 1969-73; Columnist, The New York Times, 1973-. Publications: The Relations Explosion, 1963; Plunging into Politics, 1964; Safire's Political Dictionary, 1968, 3rd edition, 1978, new edition as Safire's New Political Dictionary, 1993; Before the Fall, 1975; Full Disclosure, 1977; Safire's Washington, 1980; On Language, 1980; What's the Good Word?, 1982; Good Advice on Writing (with Leonard Safire), 1982, new edition, 1992; I Stand Corrected, 1984; Take My Word for It, 1986; You Could Look It Up, 1988; Language Maven Strikes Again, 1990; Leadership (with Leonard Safire), 1990; Fumblerules, 1990; The First Dissident, 1992; Lend Me Your Ears, 1992; Quoth the Maven, 1993; In Love with Norma Loquendi, 1994; Sleeper Spy, 1995; Watching My Language, 1997; Spread the Word, 1999; Scandalmonger, 2000; Let A Smile Be Your Umbrella, 2002. Contributions to: Newspapers and magazines. Honour: Pulitzer Prize for Distinguished Commentary, 1978.

Membership: Pulitzer, Board, 1995-; Chairman, The Charles A Dana Foundation. Address: c/o The Dana Foundation, 900 15th St NW, Washington, DC 20005, USA.

SAH Bindeshwar Prasad, b. 3 September 1946, Chak Kusiyari, Bidupur R.S., Bihar, India. Lecturer; Teacher. m. Smt Sumitra, 3 sons. Education: BA, Honours, English, 1967; MA, English, 1969; LLB, 1971; MA, Hindi, Gold Medal; Bachelor of Teaching (BT); Master of Education (MEd); Diploma in Distance Education from IGNOU; PhD, English, English and Hindi Drama. Appointments: Postgraduate Teacher, 1972; Lecturer in English, 1981; Counsellor and Assistant Co-ordinator, IGNOU, 1987-94; Senior Lecturer in English, 1986; Reader in English, 1994; Guest Lecturer, Arunachal University, 1999; Co-ordinator, College Steering Committee for National Assessment and Accreditation Council; Co-ordinator, Internal Quality Assurance Cell and Quality Assurance Committee; Chairman, Managing Director, Global Guidance and Educational Services, Sakarpur, Delhi. Publications: Poems in English and Hindi, 1962-; Articles in English and Hindi; Self-Study Report of the College, 2003-05; Booklets on spoken English and English grammar, 2004-06; Editor, 12 books; Institutional magazines; Presented research papers in professional seminars and workshops. Honours: Nehru Academic Award, 1964; National Merit Scholarship, 1964; University Topper in English Honours Exam, 1967; International Man of the Year, IBC, 1999-2000; Man of the Year, ABI, 1999; International Distinguished Leadership Award, ABI, 2000. Memberships: Life Member, ASRC, Hyderabad; The Quest, Ranchi; Board of Studies, English, of Arunachal Varsity; Secretary, Ar Pr College Teachers' Association; Fellow of the United Writers' Association of India, Chennai; Member, Research Board of Advisers, ABI, 2000-; Deputy Governor, ABI; Deputy Director General, IBC, England. Address: C/o Dr Hari Bhajan Sah, N.H. Clinic, AT & P.O. Bidupur Rly. Stn., District – Vaishali, Bihar-844502, India.

SAHA Manoranjan, b. 8 January 1952, Manikganj, Dhaka, Bangladesh. Professor of Applied Chemistry and Chemical Technology. m. Kabita, 1 son, 1 daughter. Education: BS (Hons), Chemistry, Dhaka University, 1974; MS, Chemical Engineering, Azerbaijan Institute of Petroleum and Chemistry, Baku, USSR, 1977; PhD, Petroleum and Petrochemicals, 1982; Postdoctoral Studies, Indian Institute of Science, Bangalore, 1995, Indian Institute of Petroleum, Dehradun, 1996. Appointments: Assistant Professor, 1983-90, Associate Professor, 1990-94, Professor, 1994-, Chairman, Department of Applied Chemistry and Chemical Technology, 1998-2001, Dhaka University, Dhaka, Bangladesh. Publications: 135 publications in national and international journals. Honours: Listed in Who's Who publications and biographical dictionaries. Memberships: Asiatic Society Bangladesh; Bangladesh Association for the Advancement of Science; Bangladesh Chemical Society; Bangladesh Association of Scientists and Scientific Professions. Address: Department of Applied Chemistry and Chemical Technology, University of Dhaka, Dhaka-1000, Bangladesh. E-mail: msaha@udhaka.net

SAHABDEEN Desamanya Abdul Majeed Mohamed, b. 19 May 1926, Gampola, Sri Lanka. Former Administrator; Entrepreneur. m. Ruchia Halida, 1959, 1 son, 1 daughter. Education: BA (Hons), PhD, University of Ceylon. Appointments: Founder Chairman, Majeedsons Group of Companies, 1973-; Former Administrator, Civil Service; Member, Public Service Commission; Member, Presidential Commissions on Finance and Banking, Industrialisation,

Taxation, and Delimitation of Electoral Districts; Founder Chairman, AMM Sahabdeen Trust Foundation, 1991 incorporated by Act of Parliament No 03 of 1991; Established: The Mohamed Sahabdeen Institute for Advanced Studies and Research, Pahamune, 1997; Mohamed Sahabdeen International Awards for Science, Literature and Human Development; Pahamune House Rehabilitation Centre for Children in Need; Scholar; Writer. Publications: Several articles and books on philosophy and allied subjects including Sufi Doctrin in Tamil Literature, 1986; God and the Universe, 1995; The Circle of Life, 2001. Honours: Received Desamanya - highest Civil honour – 1992; Listed in Who's Who publications and biographical dictionaries. Memberships: President, Ceylon Muslim Scholarship Fund; Vice Patron, Sri Lanka-India Friendship Society. Address: 30/12 Bagatelle Road, Colombo 03, Sri Lanka. E-mail: ammstrust@gmail.com

SAHNI Gurudutt, b. 26 May 1974, Punjab, India. Engineer. Education: BE (Hons), Mechanical Engineering, Gurunanak Dev Engineering College; DME (Hons), Mechanical Engineering, Mehr Chand Polytechnic; NDT Level II Certified, American Society of Non Destructive Testing; NDT Level II Certified, DP Testing, Indian Society of Non Destructive Testing; MBA, IGNOU; MS, Mechanical Engineering, UOD; Doctor of Philosophy, Mechanical Engineering, CWU, Texas, USA. Appointments: AE, Assembly & Sub Assembly Section, 1995-97; Production Head, JP Steels Inds, 2000; Senior Engineer, Production Planning and Executive Department, 2001-03; Manager, 2005, Production Planning and Executive Department and Assembly Department, Head of Department and Manager, Production Planning and Executive Department and Assembly Department, Deputy Management Representative, Leader Valves Ltd. Publications: Papers and articles in professional engineering journals. Honours: Best Project Award, Punjab State Council of Science & Technology; Award of Merit (1st) in all semesters in Diploma in Mechanical Engineering; Best Technical Editor Award; Best Mess Member Awards, GNDEC, LDH(PB); Member, NSS Unit during academics. Memberships: International Association of Engineers; Institution of Engineering and Technology, UK; Indian Society of Mechanical Engineering; International Society of Technical Education; Institution of Engineers, India; Society of Automobile Engineers; Indian Institute of Metals; Indian Institute of Welding. Address: 154 Kapurthala Road, Nr Patel Chowk, Jalandharcity – 144008, Punjab, India. E-mail: guru_sahni@rediffmail.com

SAINT Dora Jessie, (Miss Read), b. 17 April 1913, Surrey, England. Novelist; Short Story Writer. Education: Homerton College, 1931-33. Publications: Village School, 1955; Village Diary, 1957; Storm in the Village, 1958; Hobby Horse Cottage, 1958; Thrush Green, 1959; Fresh From the Country, 1960; Winter in Thrush Green, 1961; Miss Clare Remembers, 1962; The Market Square, 1966; The Howards of Caxley, 1967; Country Cooking, 1969; News from Thrush Green, 1970; Tyler's Row, 1972; Christmas Mouse, 1973; Battles at Thrush Green, 1975; No Holly for Miss Quinn, 1976; Village Affairs, 1977; Return to Thrush Green, 1978; The White Robin, 1979; Village Centenary, 1980; Gossip From Thrush Green, 1981; A Fortunate Grandchild, 1982; Affairs at Thrush Green, 1983; Summer at Fairacre, 1984; At Home in Thrush Green, 1985; Time Remembered, 1986; The School at Thrush Green, 1987; The World at Thrush Green, 1988; Mrs Pringle, 1989; Friends at Thrush Green, 1990; Changes at Fairacre, 1991; Celebrations at Thrush Green, 1992; Farewell to Fairacre, 1993; Tales From a Village School, 1994; The Year at Thrush Green, 1995; A Peaceful Retirement, 1996; Chronicles of Fairacre, 2005; Village School, 2005; Village Diary, 2005; Storm in the Village, 2005; Christmas at Fairacre, 2005. Honour: Member of the Order of the British Empire, 1998. Membership: Society of Authors. Address: c/o Michael Joseph, Penguin Books Ltd, 80 Strand, London WC2R 0RL, England.

SAITO Hisashi, b. 8 December 1930, Niigata City, Japan. Physician. m. Sachiko, 1 son. Education: MD, Niigata University, 1962. Appointments: Chief, Nuttari Clinic, Niigata City, 1964-76; Director, Kido Hospital, 1976-93, Director, Health Care Center of Kido Hospital, 1993-2004, Honorary Director, 2004-, Kido Hospital, Niigata City. Publications: Niigata Minamata Disease (in Japanese), 1996; Prenatal and postnatal methyl mercury exposure in Niigata Japan: adult outcomes, 2004; Congenital Minamata disease: a description of two cases in Niigata, 2004. Honours: Tajiri Prize, Citizen Concerning Pollution, 1992; Kubo Medical and Culture Prize, 2005. Memberships: Niigata Medical Cooperative Society. Address: 2-19-16 Ohmi, Niigata City, 950-0971, Japan. E-mail: hisasaito@y.dion.ne.jp

SAITO Makoto, b. 30 August 1940, Japan. Professor of Economics. Education: BA, Commerce, Waseda University, Tokyo, 1967; MA, Economics, 1972; ABD, Economics, Keio University, Tokyo, 1976. Appointments: Lecturer, Daito Bunka University, Tokyo, 1977-81; Associate Professor, 1981-90; Professor, Economics, 1990-. Publications: A Unification of European Currencies and Development; Adjustment of Incomes and Prices in the Process of General Equilibrium, 1999; An Introduction to Monetary Economics, 2005. Honour: Short-Term Visiting Scholar, University of Cambridge, England, 1994; Listed in international biographical dictionaries. Membership: Japan Association of Monetary Economics. Address: 3-27-A-1202 Nakadai, Itabashi-Ku, Tokyo, Japan.

SAITO Yoshihiro, b. 22 October 1954, Sapporo, Japan. Ophthalmologist. m. Motomi Saito, 2 sons, 1 daughter. Education: BS, University of Kyoto, Japan, 1977; MD, Osaka University, Japan, 1982; PhD, Osaka University, 1991; Postdoctoral Felloeship, Yale University, USA, 1994. Appointments: Assistant Professor, Department of Ophthalmology, Osaka, 1989-95; Postdoctoral Research Associate, Department of Ophthalmology and Visual Science, Yale University, 1992-94; Associate Professor, Department of Ophthalmology, Osaka University, 1995-98; Director, Department of Ophthalmology, Hyogo Prefecture Hospital, 1998-2001; Clinical Associate Professor, Osaka University, 1998-; Chairman of Ophthalmology, Osaka National Hospital. Publications: Numerous articles in professional journals. Memberships: Societas Ophthalmologica Japonica; American Academy of Ophthalmology; Japan Diabetes Society; Association for Research Vision and Ophthalmology; Japanese Society of Ophthalmic Surgeons. Address: Saito Eye Centre, 2-6-32-4F, Sakane, Kawanishi, Hyogo 666-0021, Japan.

SAIZESCU Geo, b. 14 November 1932, Prisaceaua, Mehedinti, Romania. Professor; Doctor; Actor; Writer; Director. m. Angela, 1 son, 1 daughter. Education: Philosophy Studies, University of Bucharest; Upper Music Studies, Music Conservatory, Bucharest; Film Direction, Institute of Theatre, Art & Cinema, il Caragiale of Bucharest; Studies at Cinecitta movie studios, Rome, 1967-68, and Hollywood movie studios, USA, 1974. Appointments: Director, 5 TV soap operas, 10 TV films, and over 100 documentary films including: A Smile in the Middle of Summer, 1963; Love at 0 Degrees, 1964; At the Gates of the Earth, 1965; Saturday

Night Ball, 1967; Tonight We Dance in Family, 1972; Pacala, and Pacala Returns, 1973; Actor, over 50 films and over 25 theatre plays including: The Millionaire, 1966; These Sad Angels, 1970; A Doubting Family, 1970; The Travesti Homer, 1978; Playing Vacation, 1981; Meeting or Rendezvous at Senlis, 1993; Red Pain, 2003; Life of an Actor, 2003. Publications: Numerous articles in professional journals including: Youth and the Film; Minor and Major Problems in the Modern Film; Through the Desert of the Comedy; Author: The Journal of an Old Cinema Wolf, 2004; The Film, an Aesthetic Belief and an Artistic Profession, 2004; Tonight We Dance with ... Bachus. Honours: Excellence Diploma and Trophy, IONESCO, Slatina, Craiova, 1997; Medal of the State of Israel, 1998; Mihai Eminescu, 2000; Jean Negulesco, 2000; Honour Citizen of the City of Craiova; Diploma and Medal, Magna Cum Laudae, National University of Theatre and Film; The Golden Earth Trophy and the Prize of Excellence of the National Centre of Cinema, Ministry of Culture; Cultural Merit and National Order for the Faith Service at the level of Cavalier; Diploma of Excellence, and Golden Claquette prize, Union of Authors and Film Directors; Honour Diploma and Crystal Globe Prize, Independent Cinema Society; Honour Diploma and Magister Magne title, Cinema Society of Moldova; Citizen of Honour, City of Turnu Severin, 2005. Memberships: Cinema Association of Romania; Film Society of Romania; Cultural European Institute for Communication and Education through Image; Hyperion International Theatre and Film Student Festival; Pacala Humouristic Society; Romanian Hellenic Cultural Ligue for Art, Science, Philosophy and Religion; Friendship Association of Romania-Belgium; Friendship Association of Romania-Portugal; Association of Romania-Tunisia; Association of Romania-Israel; Association of Romania-France; National Foundation of Some Romanians. Address: Str Dionisie Lupu, 74, Sect 1, 010459 Bucharest, Romania. E-mail: saizescugeo@yahoo.com

SAJIENĖ Valiulytė Antanina, b. 28 February 1931, Pakalniškiai, Šiauliai District, Lithuania. Primary Education Teacher. m. Kazimieras Sajus, 2 daughters. Education: Primary Education Pedagogics and Methods, Telšiai Pedagogical School, 1953-55; Masters Degree, Special School Teacher and Speech Therapy, Šiauliai Pedagogical Institute, Faculty of Defectology, 1969-76. Appointments: Teacher, Mickiškė Primary School, 1951-52; Head, Patausalė Primary School, 1952-53; Head, Vaitkaičiai Primary School, 1955-69; Teacher, Šiauliai 5th Secondary School, 1969-91; Teacher-Administrator, Šiauliai Catholic Primary School, 1991-93; Primary Education Teacher, Šiauliai Didždvaris Gymnasium, 1993-2001; Lecturer on quality evaluation of primary education changes, The Centre of Pedagogues' Professional Development of the Republic of Lithuania; Lecturer, Šiauliai University In-Service Training Institute for raising teachers' qualifications; lecturer, Centre of School Development of the Republic of Lithuania. Publications: Co-author, Integrated Education and Self-education in First Grade, 1997; Created a system of criterion evaluation by ideographic principle of individual advance and 1st-2nd and 3rd –4th year pupils' Achievement Books applied to this system, 1998; Created first level (primary) daybook suitable for ideographic evaluation that is used currently in Lithuania as an official document, 1999; Prepared and published, Integrated Education and Self-education in the Second Grade, 2002; Gives consultations in periodicals; Co-author, Aims and Contents of Primary Education and Self-Education, 2006. Honours: The Remembrance Medal of the International Festival of Songs and Dances, 1960; The Seal of Work Veteran, 1973; Title of Primary Education Teacher Supervisor, 1996; The 2nd Degree Medal of Grand

Duke of Lithuania Gediminas by the President of Lithuania, 1997; Jubilee Medal of Lithuanian School 1397-1997, 1997; Teacher of the Year 1999 and awarded a National Premium; Title, Primary Education Teacher, Expert. Membership: Lithuanian Association of Primary Education Pedagogues. Address: Dariaus ir Girėno 14-68, Šiauliai, LT-78249, Lithuania. E-mail: seltinis@takas.lt

SAKAI Masahiro, b. 1 April 1959, Sumoto, Hyogo, Japan. Professor. m. Takami Shimokawa, 1 son, 1 daughter. Education: BS, 1981, MS, 1983, Miyasaki University; PhD, University of Tokyo. 1992. Appointments: Assistant Professor, 1986-92, Associate Professor, 1993-94, Kitasato University; Associate Professor, 1995-2003, Professor and Chair, 2004-, Miyasaki University. Publications: More than 150 articles in scientific journals including: Journal of Fish Diseases; Applied and Environmental Microbiology; Fish Pathology; Fish and Shellfish Immunology; Journal of Endocrinology; Vaccine; Gene; Developmental and Comparative Immunology; Molecular Immunology. Honours: Scientific Promoing Award, Japanese Society of Fish Pathology, 2004; Miyazaki Bunko Syou, Miyasaki Prefectural Government, 2004. Memberships: Japanese Society of Fish Pathology; Japanese Society of Fisheries Sciences; American Society for Microbiology. Address: University of Miyasaki, Gakuenkibanadi nishi, 1-1 Miyazaki City, Miyazaki 8892192, Japan. E-mail: m.sakai@cc.miyasaki-u.ac.jp

SAKAMOTO Yoshikazu, b. 16 September 1927, Los Angeles, California, USA. Political Scientist. m. Kikuko Ono, 2 daughters. Education: Hogakushi, Faculty of Law, University of Tokyo, 1951. Appointments: Associate Professor, Faculty of Law, 1954, Professor of International Politics, Faculty of Law, 1964-88, Professor Emeritus, 1988-, University of Tokyo; Professor, Meiji-Gakuin University, 1988-93; Senior Research Fellow, International Christian University, 1993-96. Publications: Editor: Asia: Militarization and Regional Conflict, 1988; Global Transformation, 1994; Author, The Age of Relativization, 1997; Nuclearism and Humanity, 2 volumes (editor), 1999; Selected Works, 6 Volumes, 2004-2005. Honours: Rockefeller Fellow, 1956-57; Eisenhower Fellow, 1964; Special Fellow, United Nations Institute for Research and Training; Mainichi National Book Award, 1976. Memberships: Secretary-General, International Peace Research Association, 1979-83; American Political Science Association; Japanese Political Science Association. Address: 8-29-19 Shakujii-machi, Nerimaku, Tokyo 177-0044, Japan.

SAKURADA Yutaka, b. 1 January 1933, Kyoto, Japan. Company President. m. Keiko, 2 sons. Education: BS, Petro-chemicals, 1956, MS, Polymer Chemistry, 1958, PhD, Polymer Chemistry, 1966, Kyoto University, Japan. Appointments: Research Fellow, Kuraray Company Ltd, 1958-62; International Fellow, Stanford Research Institute, 1962-64; General Manager Medical Products, Kuraray Company Ltd, 1977-88; General Manager, Corporate R&D, 1988-89; Managing Director, Kuraray Plastics, 1989-91; President, Haemonetics, Japan, 1991-2001, Chairman and Chief Executive Officer, Haemonetics, Japan, 2003-2005; Chairman, Haemonetics Japan/Asia, 2005-06. Publication: Book chapter, Impact of Medical Technology Utilizing Macromolecules on Society, in Macromolecular Concept and Strategy for Humanity in Science Technology and Industry (editors Okamura, Ranby, Ito), 1996. Honours: Chemical Technology Award, Japan Society of Polymer, 1984; Chemical Technology Award, Japanese Chemical Society, 1985; Distinguished Fellows Award, International Center for

Artificial Organs and Transplantation, 1993. Memberships: Japanese Chemical Society; Japanese Society of Polymer; International Society for Artificial Organs. Address: GM Ebisunomori 1304, 23-6, 4-Chome, Ebisu, Shibuya-ku, Tokyo, Japan 150-0013. E-mail: ysakurada@star.ocn.ne.jp

SALA PARCERISAS Robert, b. 8 September 1949, Torà, Spain. Physician. Education: Student, University of Barcelona, 1966-75; Physician, 1976; Professional Degree, 1977; Master in Tropical Medicine, 1992, Medical Doctor, 1995, University of Barcelona. Appointments: Adjunct Physician, Residència Sanitària, Hospital Arnau de Vilanova, Lleida, 1976; Clinical Physician: FERS (Spain), Mbini, Guinea Ecuatorial, 1997; Medicus Mundi Asturias (Spain), Ntita, Burundi, 1994; Médicos sin Fronteras (Spain), N'Giva, Angola, 1992; Ministério da Saúde, Tete and Quelimane, Moçambique, 1982-84; JOSPICE (United Kingdom), Morazán, Honduras, 1978; Assistant, Unitat d'Eritropatologia (Eritropathology Unity), Hospital Clínic i Provincial of Barcelona, Spain, 2003-. Publications: Functional Aspects of Granulocytic Leukocytes, Mainly Neutrophils, Related With Effects of the Heroin (doctoral thesis), 1995; Oxygen-derived germicide metabolites and ultraviolet radiation in the neutrophilic leukocyte phagosome, 1998; Concomitant factors influencing a measles epidemic in Ondgiva, 1998; Annotation concerning the initial energy in the phagosome oxidative burst of the segmented neutrophil, 1999; A Perspective on the Oxidative Burst in the Phagosome of the Leukocyte and its Neoplastic Transformation, 2002. Honours: Scholar, Sociedad Española de Patología del Aparato Respiratorio, 1989-90; Member, Research Board of Advisors, ABI, 2006. Address: Plaça del Pati nº5 2n 4a, 25750 Torà (Lleida), Spain. E-mail: r.sala@antics.ub.edu

SALAM Gazi, b. 21 February 1968, Jessore, Bangladesh. Journalist. m. Lubna Borsa, 1 son, 2 daughters. Education: Graduate. Appointments: Journalist and Author, Chanchra, Bangladesh. Publications: Moulobad and Bornobad; Bivrantir Verajale Islam; Shomorpan (novel). Honours: National and local awards. Memberships: Jessore Press Club; Local Organisation. Address: Vill: Chanchramor, PO Chanchra, PS Kotwali, Dist: Jessore, Bangladesh.

SALIM Muhammad Khurram, b. 23 June 1967, Dhaka, Bangladesh. m. Fateha Begum, 1994. Education: BA, English and European Studies, Phillips University, 1989; Diplomas in Journalism, London School of Journalism; Diploma, Business and Office Skills, Lewisham College, 2001; Certificate, ECDL, British Computer Society, 2004. Appointments: Administration Assistant, Bon Marche Ltd, 2001-. Publications: Bangladesh Observer; Asian Times; Phillips University Publication; Buckingham University Publication; United Press; Poetry Now anthologies. Address: 116 Ewhurst Road, Crofton Park, London SE4 1SD, England.

SALINGER J(erome) D(avid), b. 1 January 1919, New York, USA. Author. m. Claire Douglas, divorced, 1 son, 1 daughter. Education: Military college. Career: Travelled in Europe, 1937-38; Army service with 4th Infantry Division (Staff Sergeant), 1942-46. Publications include: Novels: The Catcher in the Rye, 1951; Franny and Zooey; Raise High the Roof Beam; Carpenter and Seymour - An Introduction, 1963; Stories: For Esme with Love and Squalor, 1953; Numerous stories, mostly in the New Yorker, 1948-; Hapworth 16, 1924, 1997. Address: c/o Harold Ober Associates Inc, 425 Madison Avenue, New York, NY 10017, USA.

SALISBURY-JONES Raymond Arthur, b. 31 July 1933, Camberley, England. Director of Music. Education: MA (Hons), Modern History, Christ Church, Oxford, 1953-56. Appointments: Executive, Rolls Royce Ltd/Rolls Royce Motors Ltd, 1956-75; Director, Rolls Royce International, 1973-75; Chairman, Hambledon Vineyards Ltd, 1974-85; Managing Director, RSJ Aviation International Ltd, 1976-91; Non-executive Director Daniel Thwaites plc, 1974-98; Senior Consultant, Middle East Consultants Ltd, 1995-98; Consultant to mi2g Ltd (Internet Security Specialists), 1997-2000; Organist, St Mark's, Islington, 2002-. Honours: Rowe Piano Competition, 1948; Harford Lloyd Organ Prize, 1950; MA (Hons), Oxon. Memberships: Royal College of Organists. Address: The Charterhouse, Charterhouse Square, London EC1M 6AN, England. E-mail: rsj100@talk21.com

SALTZMAN Kurt, b. 28 June 1981, Roseburg, Oregon, USA. Scientific Technician. m. Megan. Education: Law and Justice Major, Economics and Environmental Studies, Central Washington University. Publications: Articles in professional journals; Does special mean young, white and female? Deconstructing the meaning of "special" in Law & Order: Special Victims Unit, forthcoming. Memberships: Delta Epsilon; Alpha Phi Sigma. Address: 403 East 7th Street, Ellensburg, WA 98926, USA. E-mail: kurtsaltzman@gmail.com

SAMADDAR Shivaprasad, b. 23 December 1926, Nathullabad, Barisal, Bangladesh. Retired Civil Servant; Education Consultant; Editor; Literateur. m. Shivani, 2 daughters. Education: AIISc, Chemical Engineering, DII Sc, Indian Institute of Science, Bangalore, 1950; National Defence College, New Delhi, 1962; Fellow, India Society of Engineers, Kolkata, 1974; Fellow Institute of Engineers of India, 1990; PhD, Economics, Calcutta University. Appointments: IAS, 1950; Acting Deputy High Commissioner for India in East Pakistan, 1960; Managing Director, West Bengal Industrial Development Corporation, 1971; Chairman, Calcutta Metropolitan Water and Sanitation Authority, 1973; Government appointed Mayor of Calcutta, 1974; Additional Chief Secretary, West Bengal, 1980; Secretary, Ministry of Steel and Mines, Government of India, 1980; Member, UPSC, 1982; Honorary Co-Chairman, Assessment Centre for Defence Scientists, Government of India. Publications: Regular contributor in urban, ecological, training, employment and management periodicals in English and Bengali; Editor, Educational Technology, 1990; Contributed to Yojana Planning Commission and Nagarlok (IIPA Urban Studies) journals; Editor, anthologies of Koltaka poems in Bengali, Hindi and English; Approximately 25 books. Honours: External Examiner, Asiatic Society, 1970 and Indian Institute of Technology Kharagpur, 1989; Cited in Encyclopaedia Britannica for book "Calcutta Is", 1986. Memberships: Lions Club of Central Calcutta; India International Centre, Delhi; President, 1993, Institute of Modern Management, Koltaka; Consultant to Royal Institute of Management, Thimphu, Bhutan; Resource Person to Visra Bharati University, Santiniketen for Human Rights Education. Address: K-1997 Chittaranjan Park, New Delhi 110019, India.

SAMBROOK Richard Jeremy, b. 24 April 1956, Canterbury, England. Journalist; Broadcasting Executive. m. Susan Jane Fisher, 1 son, 1 daughter. Education: BA (Hons) Reading University; MSc, Birkbeck College, London University. Appointments: Trainee Journalist, Thomson Regional Papers, 1977-80; BBC Radio News, 1980-84; BBC TV News, 1984-92; News Editor, 1992; Head of Newsgathering, 1996-2000;

Deputy Director, BBC News, 2000-2001; Director, BBC News, 2001-2004; Director, World Service and Global News, 2004-; Vice President, European Broadcasting Union, 2006-. Honours: Fellow, RTS; Fellow, RSA. Address: BBC, Bush House, The Aldwych, London WC2B 4PM, England.

SAMEDOV Victor, b. 30 November 1945, Baku, USSR. Professor of Physics. Education: Engineer-Physicist, 1968, Candidate of Science, PhD, 1972, Doctor of Science, 1987, Moscow Engineering Physics Institute. Appointments: Researcher, 1968-69, Postgraduate, 1968-69, Assistant, 1972-74, Assistant Professor, 1974-76, Associate Professor, 1976-88, Scientific Head of Department, Vidhuk Scientific Research Centre, 1987-95, Professor, 1988-, Professor, Institute of International Relations, 1999-, Moscow Engineering Physics Institute. Publications: History of Science and Technique, 2002; Quantum Concepts in Modern Science and Technique, 2003; Numerous articles in professional journals. Honours: Veteran, Moscow Engineering Physics Institute, 1994; Medal, Commemoration of 850th Anniversary of Moscow, 1997; Veteran of Labour, Government of Russian Federation, 1998; International Professional of the Year, IBC, 2006; Decree of Excellence, IBC, 2007; Outstanding Educators Worldwide, IBC, 2007; Veteran, Atomic Power Engineering and Industry, Rosatom of Russian Federation, 2008. Address: Moscow Engineering Physics Institute, 31 Kashirskoye Shosse, Moscow 115409, Russia. E-mail: y-samedov@yandex.ru

SAMPRAS Pete, b. 12 August 1971, Washington DC, USA. Tennis Player. m. Brigette Wilson, 2 sons. Career: US Open Champion, 1990, 1993, 1995, 1996; Grand Slam Cup Winner, 1990; IBM/ATP Tour World Championship - Frankfurt Winner, 1991; Member, US Davis Cup Team, 1991, 1995; US Pro-Indoor Winner, 1992; Wimbledon Singles Champion, 1993, 1994, 1995, 1997, 1998, 1999, 2000; European Community Championships Winner, 1993, 1994; Ranked No 1, 1993; Winner, Australian Open, 1994; RCA Championships, 1996, ATP Tour World Championships, 1996, Australian Open, 1997; Winner, San José Open, 1997; Philadelphia Open, 1997; Cincinnati Open, 1997; Munich Open, 1997; Paris Open, 1997; Hanover Open, 1997; Advanta Championship, 1998; Winner of 63 WTA Tour singles titles and 2 doubles; Investor, Partner and Special Consultant, Tennis Magazine, 2003-. Retired, 2006. Honours: International Tennis Hall of Fame, 2007. Address: ATP Tour, 420 West 45th Street, New York, NY 10036, USA. Website: www.petesampras.com

SAMRA Jorge José H, b. 25 November 1920, Republic of Lebanon. Naturalised Argentinean. Mechanical and Electrical Engineer; Investigator. Education: Graduated as Mechanical and Electrical Engineer, La Plata National University, Argentina. Appointments: Positions in leading companies, more than 30 years, including Chief Engineer, Pilkington PLC subsidiary, 22 years; About 22 European and US visits regarding projects. Publications: Papers: Astronomical Contributions on the Solar System; Cosmic Rays Velocities Exceed Considerably the Speed of Light: Firm evidence of the Newtonian constancy of Length, Time and Mass. Honours: Best Graduate, High School (at the University entrance year); 1 of Best Graduates, La Plata National University; Letter of Congratulation for paper on Astronomical contributions to the solar system, National Research Council, Canada, 1992. Membership: COSPAR Associate. Address: Universidad Nacional de La Plata, Suipacha 1274, 1011 Buenos Aires, Argentina.

SANCHEZ-VICARIO Arantxa, b. 18 December 1971, Barcelona, Spain. Tennis Player. Career: Coached Juan Nunez; Winner, 1st professional title at Brussels, 1988; Winner, French Open Women's title, 1989, 1994, 1998; International Championships of Spain, 1989, 1990, Virginia Slims Tournaments, Newport, 1991, Washington, 1991; Winner, Canadian Open, 1992, Australian Open, 1992, 1993, US Open, 1994, named International Tennis Federation World Champion, 1994; Silver Medal, doubles, Bronze Medal, singles, Olympics, 1992; Silver Medal, singles, Bronze Medal, doubles, Olympics, 1996; Spanish Federal Cup team, 1986-98, 2000-01; winner of 14 Grand Slam titles, 96 WTA Tour titles and over 16 million dollars in prize money at retirement November 2002. Honours: Infiniti Commitment to Excellence Award, 1992; Tennis Magazine Comeback Player of the Year, 1998; Principe de Asturiasi Award, Spain, 1998; International Tennis Federation Award of Excellence, 2001; International Tennis Hall of Fame, 2007. Memberships: Spanish Olympic Committee, 2001. Addresss: International Management Group, 1 Erieview Plaza, Suite 1300, Cleveland, OH 4414, USA.

SANCTUARY Gerald P, b. 22 November 1930, Bridport, Dorset, England. Solicitor. 3 sons, 2 daughters. Education: Law Society's School of Law London, 1949-53; Royal Air Force, qualified as pilot on jets (Vampire Mark V), awarded Wings, 1955. Appointments: Assistant Solicitor, Sherrards, Kingston-on -Thames, 1955-57; Partner, Hasties Solicitors, Lincoln's Inn Fields, London, 1957-63; Field Secretary, National Marriage Guidance Council, 1963-65; National Secretary, National Marriage Guidance Council, 1965-68; Executive Director, Sex Information and Education Council of the United States (SIECUS), 1969-71; Secretary, Professional and Public Relations, The Law Society, 1971-78; Executive Director, International Bar Association, London, 1978-79; Legal Adviser and Senior HQ Co-ordinator for regional and Local Affairs, MENCAP (Royal Society for Mentally Handicapped Children and Adults), London, 1979-84; Secretary, NUJ Provident Fund, London, 1985-95; Retired, 1995. Publications: Marriage Under Stress, 1968; Divorce - and After, 1970; Before You See a Solicitor, 1973; After I'm Gone - What Will Happen to my Handicapped Child? 1984, second edition, 1991; The Romans in St Albans, The Monastery at St Albans, Tudor St Albans, Fishpool Street St Albans, historical booklets, 1984, 1985, 1986; Shakespeare's Globe Theatre, 1992; Running a Marriage Guidance Council; Local Society Handbook; Editor, 12 titles in the series: It's Your Law, 1973-78; Numerous articles in professional journals and newspapers and magazines. Memberships: The Law Society; The Guild of Air Pilots and Air Navigators of the City of London, Past Honorary Treasurer; The Institute of Public Relations. Address: 99 Beechwood Avenue, St Albans, Hertfordshire AL1 4XU, England.

SANDER Louis Wilson, b. 31 July 1918, San Francisco, California, USA. Professor of Psychiatry. m. Betty Thorpe, 2 sons, 1 daughter. Education: AB, 1939, MD, Medical School, 1942, University of California; Intern, University of California Hospital, 1942-43. Appointments: 2nd Lieutenant to Major, USAAF Medical Corps, 1943-46; Resident in Psychiatry to Professor of Psychiatry, School of Medicine, 1947-68, Principal Investigator, Longitudinal Study in Early Personality Development, 1963-87, Professor of Psychiatry, School of Medicine, 1968-78, Boston University; Professor of Psychiatry, Senior Scholar, School of Medicine, University of Colorado, 1978-87. Publications: Contributor, over 50 articles, book chapters; reviews to professional publications, 1962-2002; Living Systems, Evolving Consciousness, The

Emerging Person, 2007. Honours: Recipient, Research Career Development Award, US Public Health Service, 1963-68; Research Scientist Awards, US Public Health Service, 1968-78; Research Grantee, US Public Health Service, March of Dimes, W Grant Foundation; MacArthur Foundation, Spencer Foundation, National Council on Alcoholism; other organisations; Honorary Membership Award, American Psychoanalytic Association, 2001. Memberships: American Medical Association; American Psychiatric Association; American College of Psychoanalysts; Boston Psychoanalytic Society; American Association for the Advancement of Science; Society for Research in Child Development; American Academy of Child Psychiatry; World Association for Infant Mental Health; Boston Change Process Study Group, 1995-; San Francisco Psychoanalytic Society and Institute. Address: 2525 Madrona Ave, St Helena, CA 94574-2300, USA.

SANDER Peter, b. 9 September 1933, Budapest, Hungary. Composer; Arranger; Lecturer. Divorced, 2 sons, 1 daughter. Education: BA, History, University of Budapest, 1951-55; Music Academy, Budapest, 1955-56; LGSM, Piano and Theory, Guildhall School of Music and Drama, 1959; College of Music, Debrecen, Hungary; Trinity College of Music, London; MMus, 1987, PhD, 1992, Composition, University of London, Goldsmiths College. Appointments: Teacher of Composition, City Literary Institute, 1974-98; Composer of film, commercial, jazz and concert music Currently retired but teaching piano and composition and composing. Compositions include: String Quartet Nos 1 and 2; Wind Quintet Nos 1 and 2; Brass Quintet No 1; Exploration, for guitar; Anecdotes, Light Orchestral and Vocal Piece; Piano Pieces; Cause Cèlebre (opera), 1991. Recordings: String Quartet No 1; Wind Quintet No 1; Intarsii, for orchestra; Essay Nos 1 and 2, for orchestra; Exploration; String Trio; Piano Trio; Wind Trio. Publications: String Quartet No 1, Wind Quintet No 1, Brass Quintet, Exploration, Duolith, Anecdotes, Piano Pieces. Contributions to: Melody Maker; Music Maker; Into Jazz. Honour: 1st Mention, French Radio and TV International Composition Competition, 1974. Memberships: British Academy of Composers and Songwriters; PRS; MCPS. Address: 73 The Avenue, London NW6 7NS, England.

SANDERS Christopher Daniel Stephen, b. 29 May 1958, Plymouth, England. Vice President of Joint Venture Purchasing. m. Sandra Christine, 2 sons, 1 daughter. Education: City and Guilds 501, 705/ 1 and 2, 706/ 1 and 2, Cambourne Technical College; Two national culinary diplomas in live competitions. Appointments: Executive Chef for Bass Leisure and Milton Keynes Entertainment Company, 1980-83; Director of International Purchasing for United Cinemas International, 1983-93; Director of Group Purchasing for Warner Bros. International Theatres, 1993-2000; Vice-President of Joint Procurement for Warner Bros. International Cinemas and United Cinemas, 2000-. Publications: Articles in professional journals including: Supply Chain Management Magazine; The Caterer; Screen International; Speaker at the industry forums in the United Kingdom, Amsterdam, Brussels, United States, Hong Kong, Thailand; Speaker on training forums for Mars, Weavers International, Pepsi and Coca Cola. Honours: Board Member, National Association of Concessionaires; Advisory Board, Catering Forum 2005; 2005 Who's Who Historical Society for Professional Achievements. Memberships: Chartered Institute of Purchasing; Chartered Institute of Directors; National Association of Concessionaires. Address: c/o UCI, Lee House, 90 Great Bridgewater Street, Manchester M1 5JW, England. E-mail: sanders.chris@btopenworld.com

SANDERS Jeremy Keith Morris, b. 3 May 1948, London, England. Chemist. m. Louise Sanders, 1 son, 1 daughter. Education: BSc, Chemistry, Imperial College, London; PhD, Chemistry, 1972, MA, 1974, ScD, 2001, University of Cambridge; FRSC, C Chem, 1978. Appointments: Research Associate, Pharmacology, Stanford University, USA, 1972-73; Demonstrator, then Lecturer, then Reader in Chemistry, 1973-96, Professor of Chemistry, 1996-, Head, Department of Chemistry, 2000-2006, Deputy Vice-Chancellor, 2006-; University of Cambridge; Chair, Chemistry sub-panel, 2008 UK Research Assessment Exercise, 2004-. Publications: Book: Modern NMR Spectroscopy (with B K Hunter), 1987, 1992; Over 250 research papers on aspects of organic, inorganic and biological chemistry. Honours: Meldola Medal, Royal Institute of Chemistry, 1975; Hickinbottom Award, Royal Society of Chemistry, 1981; Pfizer Academic Award for work on nuclear Overhauser effect, 1984; Pfizer Academic Award for work on in vivo NMR, 1988; Josef Loschmidt Prize, Royal Society of Chemistry, 1994; Elected FRS, 1995; Elected FRSA, 1997; Pedler Medal and Prize, Royal Society of Chemistry, 1996; Visiting Fellow, Japan Society for the Promotion of Science, 2002; Izatt-Christensen Award in Macrocyclic Chemistry, USA, 2003. Membership: The Athenaeum. Address: University Chemical Laboratory, Lensfield Road, Cambridge CB2 1EW, England. E-mail: jkms@cam.ac.uk Website: www-sanders.ch.cam.ac.uk/

SANDERS Roy, b. 20 August 1937, England. Honorary Professor in Plastic Surgery; Honorary Consultant Plastic Surgeon. Education: BSc Honours, Anatomy, 1959, MB, BS, 1962, University of London; FRCS England, 1967. Appointments: Gunner, 1957-62, Regimental Medical Officer, 1963-75; Member, Company of Pikemen & Musketeers, Honourable Artillery Company, 1981-2004; OC Light Cavalry, Honourable Artillery Company, 1996-2004; Senior Lecturer, Institute of Orthopaedics, University of London, 1973-76; Honorary Consultant and Director, Regional Burns Centre, 1973-76, Trustee, Mount Vernon Hospital Reconstructive Plastic Surgery Trust, 1973-97, Member, Executive Board (or predecessor), 1986-98, Clinical Director and Consultant Plastic Surgeon, 1986-98, Trustee, Restoration and Appearance Function Trust (RAFT) 1989-92, Advisor to the Board of Trustees of RAFT, 1992-98, Director of RAFT Institute and Consultant Plastic Surgeon, 1998-2004; Honorary Professor in Plastic Surgery, University College, London; Founder and Convenor of the European Conference of Scientists and Plastic Surgeons, 1997-2003. Publications: Numerous articles in medical journals. Memberships: Royal College of Surgeons of England; British Association of Plastic Surgeons; Academy of Experts; Vice-president, Honourable Artillery Company, 2004-2006. Address: 77 Harley Street, London W1G 8AN, England. E-mail: docact@btopenworld.com

SANDERSON Teresa (Tessa) Ione, b. 14 March 1956. Athlete. Career: Represented Britain in javelin, 1974-; Commonwealth Games Gold Medallist, 1978, 1986, 1990; European Championship Gold Medallist, 1978; Olympic Games Gold Medallist, Olympic Record, 1984; World Cup Gold Medallist, 1992; Other achievements: Fourth Place at Barcelona Olympics, 1992; Several records including: UK Javelin record, 1976; Presenter, Sky News Sports, 1989-92; Involvement with various charities. Publications: My Life in Athletics, 1985. Honours: British Athletics Writers Association Female Athlete of the Year, 1977, 1978, 1984; Honorary BSc University of Birmingham; MBE, 1985; OBE, 1998, CBE, 2004. Memberships: Board member,

English Sports Council, 1998-. Address: c/o Derek Evans, 68 Meadowbank Road, Kingsbury, London NW9, England. E-mail: tessa@tprmplus.freeserve.co.uk

SĂNDESCU Felicia, b. 4 December 1943, Bacău, Romania. Chemical Engineer. m. Nicolae Săndescu, deceased, 1 son. Education: Graduate, 1966, PhD, 1981, Industrial Chemical University of Iassy, Romania; Fellowship, Osterreichische Chemifasern-Institut, Austria; Fellowship, Shirley Institute, UK. Appointments: Technologist Engineer, Synthetic Fibers Works, Săvinești, Romania, 1966-70; Researcher and Quality Control Engineer, 1970-75, Head of Research and Control Laboratory, 1970-2002, Acrylic Fibers Works, Săvinești, Romania; Retired, 2002-. Publications: 23 original patents in field of Acrylic Fibers, Polymers and Textile Auxiliaries; Books: Surfactants as Textile Auxiliaries; Applied Researches on Acrylic Polymer & Fibers; Advances in the Chemistry & Technology of Polymers; The Etylene Carbonate; Acrylic Fibers, Technology, Structure & Properties; 30 original articles published in Romanian & international journals. Honours: Original patents at Romanian Invention-Salons; Listed in national and international biographical directories. Memberships: Academy of the Romanian Scientists. Address: Str Privighetorii, nr 5, bl B3/18, PC 610139, Piatra-Neamț, Romania.

SANDLER Adam, b. 9 September 1966, Brooklyn, New York, USA. Actor; Screenwriter. m. Jackie Titone, 2003, 1 child. Education: New York University. Career: Actor, films include: Shakes the Clown; Coneheads; Mixed Nuts; Airheads; Billy Madison; Happy Gilmore; Bullet Proof; Guy Gets Kid, 1998; The Wedding Singer, 1998; The Water Boy, 1998; Big Daddy, 1999; Little Nicky, 2000; Punch-Drunk Love, 2002; Mr Deeds, 2002; Anger Management, 2003; Fifty First Dates, 2004; Spanglish, 2004; Longest Yard, 2005; Click, 2006; Reign Over Me, 2007; I Now Pronounce You Chuck and Larry, 2007. Actor, writer, Saturday Night Live; TV appearances include: Saturday Night Live Mother's Day Special, 1992; MTV Music Video Awards, 1994; Saturday Night Live Presents President Bill Clinton's All-Time Favourites, 1994; 37th Annual Grammy Awards, 1995; ESPY Awards, 1996. Publications: Co-writer: Billy Madison; Happy Gilmore; The Water Boy; Recordings: Album: Stan and Judy's Kid; They're All Gonna Laugh at You! 1993. Honours: Peoples Choice Award, 2000. Address: c/o Ballstein-Grey, 9150 Wilshire Boulevard, Suite 350, Beverly Hills, CA 90212, USA.

SANDRA Ferry, b. 11 March 1973, Pekanbaru, Indonesia. Scientist. m. Lia Cintya Devianti, 1 daughter. Education: DDS, 1996; PhD, 2001. Appointments: Postdoctoral Fellow, 2001-02, Scientist, 2003-05, Kyushu University; Postdoctoral Fellow, Harvard Medical School, 2002-03; Head, IHVCB-UI, 2005-06; Director, Stem Cell & Cancer Institute, 2006-; Research Senior Advisor, Pt Kalbe Farma, 2006-. Publications: Keynote or invited speaker at over 40 international or national conferences; Over 20 international peer-reviewed journals/magazines; Over 10 national peer-reviewed journals/magazines. Honours: Monbusho Scholarship, 1997; Grant-in-Aid for Scientific Research, JSPS, 2003; Eminent Awards, 43rd Congress of Korean Association of Maxillofacial Plastic and Reconstructive Surgeons, 2004. Memberships: International Society of Stem Cell ; Human Proteome Organisation; Indonesian Stem Cell Association; Asia Pacific Biosafety Association; Japanese Society for Bone and Mineral Research; Japanese Biochemical Society; Japanese Society of Oral and Maxillofacial Surgery. E-mail: ferrysandra@yahoo.com Website: www.sci-indonesia.org

SANDS Roger Blakemore, b. 6 May 1942, London, England. Clerk of the House of Commons, now retired. m. Jennifer Ann Cattell, 2 daughters, 1 deceased. Education: University College School, Hampstead; MA, Oriel College, Oxford, 1965. Appointments: Secretary to the House of Commons Commission, 1985-87; Clerk of the Overseas Office, 1987-91; Registrar of Members Interests, 1991-94; Clerk of Public Bills, 1994-97; Clerk of Legislation, 1998-2001; Clerk Assistant, 2001-02; Clerk of the House and Chief Executive, House Commons 2003-06; Independent Chairman, Standards Committee, Mid-Sussex DC, 2007-; Publications: Articles in various parliamentary publications. Honours: KCB, 2006. Membership: Commonwealth Club; Holtye Golf Club. Address: 4 Woodbury House, Lewes Road, East Grinstead, West Sussex RH19 3UD. E-mail: rjsxrandjsands.demon.co.uk

SANT CASSIA Louis Joseph, b. 19 September 1946, St Paul's Bay, Malta. Obstetrician & Gynaecologist. m. Antoinette Ferro, 1 son, 1 daughter. Education: Lyceum, Malta; MD, Royal University of Malta, 1973; DM, University of Nottingham, 1986. Appointments: Consultant Obstetrician & Gynaecologist, 1987-; Coventry District Tutor, RCOG, 1988-94; Chairman, Division of Obstetrics & Gynaecology, 1989-93; Visiting Clinical Lecturer, University of Warwick, 1993-2002; Chairman, Coventry Research Ethics Committee, 1993-2004; Chairman, Medical Advisory Committee, Warwickshire Nuffield Hospital, 1995-2000; Leading Clinician Gynaecological Oncology, Coventry, 1997-; Honorary Lecturer, University of Malta, 1998-; Examiner Diploma, 1999-2001, Examiner, MRCOG, Royal College of Obstetricians & Gynaecologists; Lead Gynaecological Surgeon, Arden Network (Warwickshire Oncology), 1999-; Chairman, Senior Hospital Medical Staff Committee, University Hospital Coventry & Warwickshire, 2004-; Examiner, Warwick Medical School, 2006-; Examiner, MBBS 1985, 1992, 2003, Birmingham Medical School. Publications: Numerous articles in professional journals. Memberships: Founder Member, Malta College of Obstetrics & Gynaecology; British Society for Colposcopy and Cervical Pathology; British Gynae Cancer Society. Address: Four Winds, Stoneleigh Road, Blackdown, Leamington Spa, Warwickshire CV32 6QR, England. E-mail: ljsantcassia@hotmail.co.uk

SANTER Jacques, b. 18 May 1937, Wasserbilig. Politician. m. Danièle Binot, 2 sons. Education: Athenée de Luxembourg; University of Paris; University of Strasbourg; Inst d'Etudes Politiques, Paris. Appointments: Advocate, Luxembourg Court of Appeal, 1961-65; Attaché, Officer of Minister of Labour and Social Security, 1963-65; Govt attaché, 1965-66; Parliament Secretary Parti Chrétien-Social, 1966-72, Secretary-General, 1972-74, President, 1974-82; Secretary of State for Cultural and Social Affairs, 1972-74; Member, Chamber of Deputies, 1974-79; Member, European Parliament, 1975-79, VP, 1975-77; Municipal Magistrate, City of Luxembourg, 1976-79; Minister of Finance of Labour and of Social Security, 1979-84; Prime Minister, Minister of State and Minister of Finance, 1984-89, Prime Minister, Minister of State, of Cultural Affairs and the Treasury and Financial Affairs, 1989-94; President, European Committee, 1994-99; Member, European Parliament, 1999-2004. Honour: Hon LLD (Wales), 1998. Address: 69 rue J-P Huberty, 1742 Luxembourg.

SANTOS Nunos C, b. 17 July 1972, Lisbon, Portugal. Biochemist; Researcher; Professor. m. Elisabete Santos, 2 sons. Education: Degree in Biochemistry, 1995; PhD, Biochemistry, 1999, University of Lisbon. Appointments:

Researcher, Technical University of Lisbon, 1994-99; Teaching Assistant, 1999-2000, Assistant Professor, 2000-, University of Lisbon (Lisbon Medical School); Head of Unit, Institute of Molecular Medicine, 2008-. Publications: Author of more than 40 scientific articles and book chapters on molecular biophysics and biomembranes. Honour: Calouste Gulbenkian Foundation Award, 2001; Jose Luis Champalimaud Award (Basic Sciences, ex-aequo), 2004, (Applied Research and Technologies), 2005. Membership: Biophysical Society, USA. Address: Instituto de Medicina Molecular, Faculdade de Medicina da Universidade de Lisboa, Av Prof Egas Moniz, 1649-028 Lisbon, Portugal. E-mail: nsantos@fm.ul.pt

SARAMAGO José, b. 16 November 1922, Azinhaga, Portugal. Author; Poet; Dramatist. Education: Principally self-educated. Publications: Fiction: Manual de Pintura e Caligrafia, 1977, English translation as Manual of Painting and Calligraphy, 1994; Objecto Quase (short stories), 1978, English translation as Quasi Object, 1995; Levantado do Chao (Raised from the Ground), 1980; Memorial do Convento, 1982, English translation as Baltasar and Blimunda, 1987; A Jangada de Pedra, 1986, English translation as The Stone Raft, 1994; O Ano da Morte de Ricardo Reis, 1984, English translation as The Year of the Death of Ricardo Reis, 1991; Historia do Cerco de Lisboa (The History of the Siege of Lisbon), 1989; O Evangelho segundo Jesus Cristo, 1991, English translation as The Gospel According to Jesus Christ, 1994; Ensaio Sobre A Cegueira, 1996, English translation as Blindness; All the Names, 1999; The Tale of the Unknown Island, 1999; The Cave, 2002; The Double, 2004; Seeing, 2006. Other: Poems, plays, diaries, etc. Contributions to: Various publications. Honours: Several literary awards and prizes, including the Nobel Prize for Literature, 1998. Address: c/o Harcourt Brace & Co, 6277 Sea Harbor Drive, Orlando, FL 32887, USA.

SARANDON Susan Abigail, b. 4 October 1946, New York, USA. Actress. m. Chris Sarandon, divorced, 1 daughter, 1 daughter with Franco Amurri, 2 sons with Tim Robbins. Education: Catholic University of America. Career: Stage appearances include: A Coupla of White Chicks Sittin' Around Talkin'; An Evening with Richard Nixon; A Stroll in the Air; Albert's Bridge; Private Ear, Public Eye; Extremities; numerous TV appearances; Actor, films include: Joe, 1970; Lady Liberty, 1971; The Rocky Horror Picture Show, Lovin' Molly, 1974; The Great Waldo Pepper, 1975; The Front Page, Dragon Fly, 1976; Walk Away Madden; The Other Side of Midnight, The Last of the Cowboys, 1977; Pretty Baby, King of the Gypsies, 1978; Loving Couples, 1980; Atlantic City, 1981; Tempest, 1982; The Hunger, 1983; Buddy System, 1984; Compromising Positions, 1985; The Witches of Eastwick, 1987; Bull Durham, Sweet Hearts Dance, 1988; Married to the Mob; A Dry White Season, The January Man, 1989; White Palace; Thelma and Louise, Light Sleeper, 1991; Lorenzo's Oil; The Client; Little Women, Safe Passage, 1995; Dead Man Walking, James and the Giant Peach, 1996; Illuminate, Twilight, 1998; Stepmom, Anywhere But Here, Cradle Will Rock, 1999; Rugrats in Paris, Joe Gould's Secret, 2000; Cats and Dogs, 2001; Igby Goes Down, 2002; The Banger Sisters, The Nazi Officer's Wife, Last Party 2000, 2003; Noel, Shall We Dance? Alfie, 2004; Elizabethtown, Romance & Cigarettes, 2005; Irresistible, 2006; In the Valley of Elah, Mr Woodcock, Emotional Arithmetic, Bernard and Doris, Enchanted, 2007; Middle of Nowhere, Speed Racer, 2008. Honour: Academy Award for Best Actress, 1996. Address: c/o ICM, Martha Luttrell, 8942 Wilshire Boulevard, Beverly Hills, CA 90211, USA.

SARBU Ioan, b. 31 August 1951, Timisoara, Romania. Civil Engineer; Professor. m. Eleonora Sarbu, 1 daughter. Education: Hydrotechnics, Technical University of Timisoara, 1970-75; PhD, Civil Engineering, Technical University, 1993; License in Laboratory Testing of Building Equipment, Ministry of Public Works, 2001; European Engineer, European Federation of National Engineering Associations, 2001. Appointments: Design Engineer, Water Resources Management Company, Timisoara, 1975-79; Assistant Professor, Technical University, 1979-88; Lecturer, 1988-94, Associate Professor, 1994-98, Professor, 1998-, Politechnica University; Doctoral Degree Advisor, 2004-; Head of Building Equipment Department, 2000-; Head of National Building Equipment Laboratory, 2001-; Expert Reviewer, National Board of Scientific Research for Higher Education, Bucharest, 1999-; VP, National Board of Certified Energetical Auditors Buildings, Bucharest, 2003-; Co-ordination, International Academic Research Gnomon Project, Global Gnomon Co, Madrid, 2003-; Scientific Advisor, Science Bulletin of Politechnica University, Timisoara, 2004-; Reviewer of Journal of Hydraulic Research, 2007-. Publications: Books (author): Hydraulics of town constructions and installations, 1989; Numerical and optimizing methods in building equipment design, 1994; Computer utility in installation engineering, 1996; Energetical optimization of water distribution systems, 1997; Refrigerating systems, 1998; Computer aided design of building equipment, 2000; Energetical optimization of buildings, 2002; Thermal building equipments, 2007; Editor: Building equipment and ambiental comfort, 2007; Thermal Building Equipment, 2007; Contributor of up to 200 articles in professional journals; Author of up to 20 computer programmes; Author of 5 patent certificates. Honours: Distinguished Professor, Ministry of Education, 1986; Award, Romanian General Association of Engineers, 1997; Excellency Diploma, Association of Building Equipment Engineer, 2001; Plaque, Great Minds of the 21st Century, ABI, 2005; Diploma, Outstanding Scientist of the 21st Century, IBC, 2005; World Medal of Freedom, ABI, 2006; Diploma, Outstanding Intellectuals of the 21st Century, IBC, 2007; Diploma, 21st Century Award for Achievement, IBC, 2007; Plaque, Gold Medal for Romania, ABI, 2007; Listed in Who's Who publications and biographical dictionaries. Memberships: International Association of Hydraulic Engineering and Research; American Society of Heating, Refrigerating and Air-Conditioning Engineers; Science Academy; Society for Computer Aided Engineering; Research Board of Advisors, ABI, 2005. Address: Piata Bisericii, No 4A, Ap 3, 300233 Timisoara, Romania. E-mail: ioan.sarbu@ct.upt.ro

SARGENT John Richard, b. 22 March 1925, Birmingham, England. Economist. m. Hester, deceased 2004, 1 son, 2 daughters. Education: BA, First Class, Christ Church, Oxford, 1948. Appointments: Fellow and Lecturer in Economics, Worcester College, Oxford, 1951-62; Economic Consultant, H M Treasury, 1963-65; Professor of Economics, Founder Member of Department of Economics, 1965-73, Pro-Vice-Chancellor, 1970-72, University of Warwick; Group Economic Advisor, Midland Bank, 1974-84; Houblon-Norman Research Fellow, Bank of England. Publications: Numerous articles in economic journals include most recently: Roads to Full Employment, 1995; Towards a New Economy? Recent Inflation and Unemployment in the UK, 2002; Book, British Transport Policy, 1958. Honours: Rockefeller Fellow, USA, 1959-60; Honorary Professor of Economics, University of Warwick, 1974-81; Visiting Professor, London School of Economics, 1981-82. Memberships: Reform Club, 1965-; Member of Council, Royal Economic Society, 1969-74; Member, Doctors and Dentists Pay Review Body, 1972-75;

Member, Armed Forces Pay Review Body, 1972-85; Member, Economic and Social Research Council, 1980-85. Address: 38 The Leys, Chipping Norton, Oxfordshire OX7 5HH, England.

SARKISSIAN Yuri Levon, b. 9 February 1941, Yerevan, Armenia. Academic. m. Margarit Suren Petrossyan, 1 daughter. Education: Mechanical Engineer's Diploma, Yerevan Polytechnic Institute, 1962; Candidate of Technical Sciences (PhD), Moscow Chemical Machinery Institute, 1967; IREX Exchange Program, Stanford University, USA, 1971-72; Doctor of Technical Sciences, Moscow Machine Science Institute, 1975. Appointments: Assistant, Associate, Full Professor, 1962-88, Chairman, 1975-, Theory of Mechanisms and Machines, President/Rector, 1988-2006, Professor, Department of Mechanics and Machine Science, 2006-, State Engineering University of Armenia; Visiting Professor, Stanford University, University of Illinois, Chicago, USA, 1977; Vice President, National Academy of Sciences, Armenia, 1994. Publications: Over 150 articles in professional journals, books, monographs, patents, conference papers and keynote lectures. Honours: ASME Best Paper Award, 1978; Proctor & Gamble Prize, 1978; Lifetime Achievement Award, Armenian Educaitonal Foundation, 2003; RA Order, Mesrop Mashtots, 2003; IBC Top 100 Educators, 2006. Memberships: National Academy of Sciences, Armenia; International Engineering Academy. Address: State Engineering University of Armenia, 105 Teryan Street, Yerevan, 375009, Armenia. E-mail: yusarg@seua.am

SASAKI Naruo, b. 16 June 1967, Suginami-Ku, Tokyo, Japan. Physicist; Professor. Education: BSc, 1992, MSc, 1994, PhD, 1997, University of Tokyo, Japan. Appointments: Research Fellow, Japan Society for the Promotion of Science, 1997-2000; CREST Researcher, 2000-01, PRESTO Researcher, 2001-02, Japan Science and Technology Agency; Instructor, Department of Applied Physics, Seikei University, Japan, 2002-03; Associate Professor, Seikei University, Japan, 2003-06; Professor, Department of Materials and Life Science, Seikei University, Japan, 2006-; Part-time Instructor, Osaka University, Japan, 2007-. Publications: Papers and articles in professional scientific journals. Honours: Young Scientist Award, JSAP, 2001; Young Scientist Award, Ministry of Education, Culture, Sports, Science and Technology, 2005; Academic Award, Seikei Alumni Association, 2005; Contribution to Academic Research Award, Seikei Institute, 2006; SSSJ Paper of the Year, Gold Medal, 2006; UBS Special Award, Nanotechnology Division, 2006; Paper Award, Surface Science Society, Japan, 2006; Paper Award, Japan Society of Tribology, 2007; Who's Who in the World, 2007. Memberships: American Physical Society; Surface Science Society, Japan; Japan Society of Tribology; Physical Society of Japan; Japan Society of Applied Physics; Chemical Society of Japan. Address: Department of Materials and Life Science, Faculty of Science and Technology, Seikei University, 3-3-1 Kichijoji-Kitamachi, Musashino-Shi, Tokyo 180-8633, Japan. E-mail: naru@st.seikei.ac.jp Website: www.ap.seikei.ac.jp/ntechlab

SASEANU Andreea Simona, b. 26 August 1974, Ploiesti, Romania. Lecturer. Education: Bachelor's degree, Academy of Economics Studies, Faculty of Commerce, 1998; 3 month training course, University of Orleans, France, 2002; MSc, Business Administration, 2003; Doctor of Economics, 2005. Appointments: Economist, SC Grup Romet SA, Bucharest, 1999-2000; Tutor, 2000-02, Assistant Lecturer, 2002, Hyperion University; Assistant Lecturer, 2002-05, PhD Lecturer, 2005-, Faculty of Commerce, Academy of Economic Studies, Bucharest. Publications: Commercial Economics, Tests, Applications and Case Studies, 2003; Company Economics – Concepts, Resources, Strategies, 2004; Sectorial and Company Strategies in the Bakery Industry; Business Negotiation and Communication Techniques, 2005. Honours: Doctor of Economics, Praise Certificate for Young Researchers, Bucharest, 2005, 2006. Memberships: AROMAR, 2006. Address: Bl 15B, ScA, Et8, Ap44, 104 Dristor Street, Bucharest, Romania. E-mail: saseanu@yahoo.com

SASSOON Vidal, b. 17 January 1928, London, England. Hair Stylist. m. divorced 1980, 2 sons, 2 daughters. Education: New York University. Career: Served with Palmach Israeli Army; Creator, hairdressing style based on Bahaus and geometric forms; Founder, Chairman, Vidal Sassoon Inc; President, Vidal Sassoon Foundation; Founder, Vidal Sassoon Centre for the Study of Anti-Semitism and Related Bigotries at Hebrew University, Jerusalem. Publications: A Year of Beauty and Health. Honours: Awards include: French Ministry of Culture Award; Award for services rendered, Harvard Business School; Intercoiffure Award, Cartier, London, 1978; Fellow, Hair Artists International.

SATO Kazuhiko, b. 14 September 1959, Natori, Japan. Assistant Professor. Education: BA, Tohoku Gakuin University, 1982; MA, English Linguistics, University of Northern Iowa, 1991. Appointments: Teacher, Tohoku Gakuin Junior and Senior High School, Sendai, Japan, 1982-89; Instructor, 1994-99, Assistant Professor, 1999-, Miyagi National College of Technology, Natori, Japan. Publications: Several articles and research reports. Memberships: Teachers of English to Speakers of Other Languages; Linguistic Society of America; Linguistic Association of Great Britain; Cognitive Science Society. Address: 18-12 Aza Naganumashita, Sakamoto, Yamamoto-cho, Watari-gun, Miyagi 989-2111, Japan.

SATO Manabu, b. 30 May 1951, Hiroshima, Japan. Professor. m. Yukiyo, 1 daughter. Education: BA, Tokyo University of Education; M Ed, PhD, Graduate School of Education, The University of Tokyo. Appointments: Associated Professor, Mei University, 1982; Associated Professor, 1988, Professor, 1996, Dean, Graduate School of Education, 2002-03, The University of Tokyo. Publications: Criticism of Curriculum, 1996; Aporia of Teaching Professor, 1997; Designing Educational Reform, 1999; Pleasure of Learning, 2001; Challenging Teachers, 2004; Challenging Schools, 2005. Honours: Award, Association of Educational Science, 1998. Memberships: President, Japanese Educational Research Association; National Academy of Education, USA; Japan Council of Sciences. Address: 2-14-8 Jakuencho, Higashikurume, Tokyo 203-0021, Japan. E-mail: manabusato101@aol.com

SATYAMURTI Carole, b. 13 August 1939, Bromley, Kent, England. Poet; Writer; Lecturer. Education: BA, Honours, London University, 1960; Diploma in Social Work, University of Birmingham, 1965; MA, University of Illinois, 1967; PhD, University of London, 1979. Appointments: Lecturer, Principal Lecturer, University of East London, 1968-2004. Publications: Occupational Survival, 1981; Broken Moon (poems), 1987; Changing the Subject (poems), 1990; Striking Distance (poems), 1994; Selected Poems, 1998; Love and Variations (poems), 2000; Acquainted with the Night: Psychoanalysis and the Poetic Imagination (co-edited with Hamish Canham), 2003; Stitching the Dark: New and Selected Poems, 2005. Honours: 1st Prize, National Poetry Competition, 1986; Arts

Council of Great Britain Writers Award, 1988; Cholmondeley Award, 2000. Address: 15 Gladwell Road, London N8 9AA, England.

SAUNDERS Ann Loreille, (Ann Cox-Johnson), b. 23 May 1930, London, England. Historian. m. Bruce Kemp Saunders, 4 June 1960, 1 son, 1 daughter, deceased. Education: Plumptre Scholar, Queen's College, London, 1946-48; BA Honours, University College, London, 1951; PhD, Leicester University, 1965. Appointments: Deputy Librarian, Lambeth Palace, 1952-55; Archivist, Marylebone Public Library, London, 1956-63; Honorary Editor, Costume Society, 1967-; London Topographical Society, 1975-. Publications: London, City and Westminster, 1975; Art and Architecture of London, 1984; St Martin-in-the-Fields, 1989; The Royal Exchange, monograph, 1991; The Royal Exchange, editor and co-author, 1997; St Paul's: the Story of the Cathedral, 2001; The History of the Merchant Taylors' Company (with Matthew Davies), 2004; Victorian London: photographs form the Howarth-Loomes Collection, forthcoming. Contributions to: Magazines. Honours: Prize for Best Specialist Guide Book of the Year, British Tourist Board, 1984; Fellow, University College, London, 1992; MBE, 2002. Memberships: Society of Antiquaries, Fellow; Costume Society; London Topographical Society. Address: 3 Meadway Gate, London NW11 7LA, England.

SAUNDERS Jennifer, b. 6 July 1958, England. Actress; Writer. m. Adrian Edmondson, 3 daughters. Education: Central School of Speech and Drama, London. Career: Theatre: An Evening with French and Saunders (tour), 1989; Me and Mamie O'Rourke, 1993; French and Saunders Live in 2000 (tour), 2000; TV: The Comic Strip Presents …, 1990; Girls on Top; French and Saunders (5 series); Absolutely Fabulous, 1993, 1994, 995, 2001; Ab Fab The Last Shout, 1996; Let Them Eat Cake, 1999; Mirrorball, 2000; Jam & Jerusalem, 2006; A Bucker o' French & Saunders, 2007; The Life and Times of Vivienne Vyle, 2007. Films: The Supergrass, 1984; Muppet Treasure Island, 1996; Spice World the Movie; Maybe Baby, 2000; Shrek 2 (voice), 2004; L'Entente cordiale, 2006; Coraline (voice), 2008. Publications: A Feast of French and Saunders, 1992; Absolutely Fabulous: The Scripts, 1993; Absolutely Fabulous Continuity, 2001. Honours: Emmy Award, 1993; OBE, 2001; Honorary Rose, Montreux, 2002. Address: c/o Peters, Fraser & Dunlop, Drury House, 34-43 Russell Street, London, WC2B 5HA, England.

SAVKOVIC-STEVANOVIC Jelenka, 21 January 1946, Markovica, Serbia. Professor of Chemical Engineering. m. Miroljub Stevanovic. Education: BS, Degree, 1970; MSc, Degree, 1975, Department of Chemical Engineering, University of Belgrade; PhD, Degree, Institut für Thermodynamik und Anlegentechnik, Technische Universität, West Berlin and Department of Chemical Engineering, University of Belgrade, 1981. Appointments: Researcher, Department of Chemical Catalysis, Institute for Chemical Technology and Metallurgy, Belgrade, 1970; Assistant, 1972, Assistant Professor, 1982, Associate Professor, 1988, Full Professor, 1993, Department of Chemical Engineering Faculty of Technology and Metallurgy, University of Belgrade, Yugoslavia. Publications: Author and co-author: Books: Stochastic Models in Process Analysis and Optimization, 1982; Information Systems in the Process Techniques, 1987; Artificial Intelligence in Chemistry and Chemical Engineering, 1989; Process Modeling and Simulation, 1995; Process Engineering Intelligent Systems, 1999; Informatics, 2001, 2nd edition 2007; Over 800 articles to professional journals, patentee in field. Honours: First Prize from Belgrade City for Bachelor of Science Thesis,

1970; DAAD Prize for Research Work, 1980; 2nd Prize TI, St Petersburg, 1989; The Gold Medal, Nikola Tesla, 1993, 2004, 2006; The Silver Medals, Nikola Tesla, 2003, 2004, 2005; The Bronze Medals, 2003, 2005; Listed in Who's Who publications and biographical dictionaries. Memberships: European Federation of Chemical Engineering; Computer Aided Process Engineering; The Institute of Chemical Engineers; The Society of Computer Simulation; The Association of Chemists and Chemical Engineers of Serbia; Modelling, Simulation and Informatics; European Simulation, The Technical Committee Qualitative Simulation. Address: Faculty of Technology and Metallurgy, University of Belgrade, Karnegijeva, 4, 11000 Belgrade, Serbia. Website: www.tmf.bg.ac.yu

SAWADA Edward A, b. 20 April 1920, Agaña, Guam, USA. Physician; Obstetrician and Gynaecologist. m. Joan Carole Macbeth, deceased, 1 son, 2 daughters. Education: BS, Biological Sciences (Pre-Medicine), Georgetown University, Washington DC; MD, University of Virginia School of Medicine, Charlottesville, Virginia; Master of Public Health, Johns Hopkins School of Hygiene and Public Health, Baltimore, Maryland, USA. Appointments: Internship in Medicine, University of Virginia Hospital; Residency in Obstetrics and Gynaecology, University of Virginia Hospital, Maryland General Hospital, Naval Hospital, St Albans, New York; Fellowship, Gynaecological Malignancy, State University of New York; Residency in Preventive Medicine, Johns Hopkins School of Hygiene and Public Health; Flight Surgeon Training, Fort Rucker Alabama; Physician Consultant, State of Maryland Colposcopy Clinics County Health Department; Supervising Physician, Clinical Faculty, Communicable Diseases, Baltimore City Health Department, Union Memorial Hospital, Baltimore; Chief, Division of Cancer Control, Maryland Department of Health and Mental Hygiene; Private Practice of Medicine, Glen Cove, Long Island, New York; Associate Director, Maternity Programs and Physician Consultant in Obstetrics, Nassau County Health Department, Mineola, Long Island, New York; Teaching Appointments: Delegate, People to People Ambassador Program to Mainland China; Faculty, Sexually Transmitted Disease Training Center, Baltimore; Assistant Instructor and Instructor, Gynaecological Malignancy Service, Department of Obstetrics and Gynaecology, State University of New York, Brooklyn. Publications: Numerous papers in medical journals and presented at conferences. Memberships include: American Cancer Society; Lung Association of Maryland; Japanese American Fellowship of Baltimore; Japanese American Citizen League; Guam Society of America. Address: PO Box 9814, Towson, MD 21284-9814, USA. .

SAWYER Roger Martyn, b. 15 December 1931, Gloucester, England. Historian. m. Daisy Harte, 30 August 1952, 2 sons. Education: BA Honours, T G James Prize in Education, Diploma in Education, University of Wales, 1958; PhD, History, University of Southampton, 1979. Appointments: Housemaster, Blue Coat School, Edgbaston, 1958-60; Deputy Head, Headmaster, Bembridge Preparatory School, 1960-83. Publications: Casement: The Flawed Hero, 1984; Slavery in the Twentieth Century, 1986; Children Enslaved, 1988; The Island from Within (editor), 1990; 'We are but Women': Women in Ireland's History, 1993; Roger Casement's Diaries 1910: The Black and The White (editor), 1997. Contributions to: Anti-Slavery Reporter; BBC History; Immigrants and Minorities; South, UN Development Forum. Honour: Airey Neave Award, 1985. Memberships: Anti-Slavery International, council member, 1984-98; Governor, Wycliffe College; Research Fellow, Airey Neave Trust; Fellow, Royal Geographical Society; Bembridge Sailing Club; Old

Wycliffian Society; Incorporated Association of Preparatory Schools. Address: Ducie House, Darts Lane, Bembridge, Isle of Wight PO35 5YH, England.

SAYERS Bruce McArthur, b. 6 February 1928, Hampstead, London England. Emeritus Professor of Computing Applied to Medicine. m. Ruth Woolls Humphery. Education: BSc, MSc, University of Melbourne, Australia, 1944-48; PhD, DIC, DSc, University of London. Appointments: Biophysicist/ Electronic Engineer, Baker Medical Research Institute and Clinical Research Unit, Alfred Hospital Melbourne, 1949-54; Philips Electrical Limited Research Fellow in Human Auditory Communication, DSIR Research Assistant in Psychoacoustics, Telecommunications Section, 1954-58, Lecturer, Electrical Engineering, 1958-62, Senior Lecturer, Medical Electronics, 1962-65, Reader, 1965-68, Professor of Electrical Engineering Applied to Medicine, 1968-84, Head of Department of Electrical Engineering, 1979-84, Professor of Computing Applied to Medicine, 1984-90, Head of Department of Computing, 1984-89, Dean of City and Guilds College, 1984-85, 1985-88, 1991-93, Kobler Professor of the Management of Information Technology, 1990-93, Director, Centre for Cognitive Systems, 1990-98, Emeritus Professor of Computing Applied to Medicine, 1993-, Imperial College, London; Temporary Advisor, 1970-87, 1995-96, Member of Expert Panel on Health Research, 1988-2000, Member, 1988-94, Vice-Chairman, 1997-2000, Global Advisory Committee on Health Research, WHO. Publications: Publications on: Speech and hearing, Audiology and neuro-otology, biomedical signal and systems analysis, cardio-respiratory physiology, circulation and cardiology, epidemiological modelling, health technology, public health and health assessment, knowledge based health indicators; Co-editor and contributor, Understanding the Global Dimensions of Health, 2004. Honours: Travelling Lecturer, Nuffield Foundation and National Research Council of Canada, 1970-71; President, Section of Measurement in Medicine, Royal Society of Medicine, 1971-72; Visiting Professor, Birmingham, Alabama, McGill, Melbourne, Rio de Janeiro, Toronto; Freeman City of London, 1986; Liveryman, Worshipful Company of Scientific Instrument Makers, 1985; Honorary Foreign Member, Societa Medica Chirurgia di Bologna, 1965; Honorary Member: WHO Medical Society, 1974, Eta Kappa Nu, 1984; Honorary Fellow, World Innovation Foundation, 2002; Vice-President, International Commission on theme: Health and Medical Sciences, UNESCO Encyclopaedia of Life Support Systems, 2004-. Memberships: FIEE, 1980, FCGI, 1983, FREng, 1990, FIC, 1996. Address: Lot's Cottage, Compton Abbas, Shaftesbury, Dorset SP7 0NQ, England.

SCACCHI Greta, b. 18 February 1960, Milan, Italy. Actress. 1 son, 1 daughter. Education: Bristol Old Vic Drama School. Career: Films include: Second Sight; Heat and Dust; Defence of the Realm; The Cocoa-Cola Kid; A Man in Love; Good Morning Babylon; White Mischief; Paura e Amore (Three Sisters); La Donna dell Luna (Woman in the Moon); Schoolmates; Presumed Innocent; Shattered; Fires Within; Turtle Beach; Salt on Our Skins; The Browning Version; Jefferson in Paris, 1994; Country Life, 1995; Emma, 1996; Cosi; The Serpent's Kiss, 1997; The Red Violin, Cotton Mary, 1998; Ladies Room, The Manor, 1999; Tom's Midnight Garden, Looking for Anbrandi, One of the Hollywood Ten, 2000; Festival in Cannes, 2001; Baltic Storm, Il Ronzio delle mosche, 2003; Sotto falso nome, Beyond the Sea, 2004; Flightplan, 2005; Nightmares and Dreamscapes: From the Stories of Stephen King, The Book of Revelations, The Handyman, Icicle Melt, 2006; Amour cache' L', The

Trojan Horse, 2007; Shoot on Sight, Brideshead Revisited, 2008.Theatre includes: Cider with Rosie; In Times Like These; Airbase; Uncle Vanya; The Guardsman; TV includes: The Ebony Tower; Dr Fischer of Geneva; Waterfront (series); Rasputin; The Odyssey (series), 1996; Macbeth, 1998; Christmas Glory, 2000; Jeffrey Archer: The Truth, 2002; Maigret: L'ombra cinese, 2004; Marple: By the Pricking of My Thumbs, 2006; Broken Trail, 2006; Miss Austen Regrets, 2007. Honours: Emmy Award, 1996. Address: Susan Smith Associates, 121 San Vincente Boulevard, Beverly Hills, CA 90211, USA.

SCALES Prunella M R West, 22nd June, 1932. Actress. m. Timothy West, 1963, 2 sons. Education: Old Vic Theatre School, London; Herbert Berghof Studio, New York, USA; Repertory in Bristol Old Vic, Oxford, Salisbury, England; Chichester and Stratford, 1967-68; London Theatre Appearances include: The Promise, 1967; The Wolf, 1975; An Evening with Queen Victoria, 1979-99; Quartermaine's Terms, 1981; When We Are Married, 1986; Single Spies, National Theatre, 1988; School for Scandal, National Theatre, 1990; Long Day's Journey Into Night, National Theatre, 1991; At Leeds: Happy Days, 1993; The Birthday Party, 1999; The Cherry Orchard, 2000; The External, 2001; Too Far to Walk (King's Head), 2002; A Woman of No Importance, 2003; TV includes: Fawlty Towers, 1975, 1978; Mapp and Lucia (series), 1985-86; What the Butler Saw, 1987; After Henry, 1988-92; Signs and Wonders, 1995; Breaking the Code, 1997; Emma, 1997; Midsommer Murders, 1999; Silent Witness, 2000; Queen Victoria, 2003; Station Jim, 2001; A Day in the Death of Joe Egg, 2002; Looking for Victoria, 2003; Essential Poems for Christmas, 2004; The Shell Seekers, 2006. Films: An Awfully Big Adventure, 1994; Stiff Upper Lips, 1997; An Ideal Husband, 1998; The Ghost of Greville Lodge, 2000; Brank Spanking (voice), 2004; Helix, 2006. Numerous other areas of work including: Radio; Directing (Leeds, South Australia, National Theatre Studio, Nottingham Playhouse). Honours: CBE; Honorary DLitt, Bradford; Honorary DLitt, University of East Anglia. Address: c/o Conway Van Gelder, 18-21 Jermyn Street, London SW1Y 6HP, England.

SCANLON Mary Elizabeth, b. 25 May 1947, Dundee, Scotland. Member of Scottish Parliament. 1 son, 1 daughter. Education: MA, Economics, Political Science, University of Dundee; Fellow of the Institute of Professional Development. Appointments: Secretarial and administrative posts in civil service and private sector, 1962-73; Full-time Mother (Part-time Evening Class Lecturer); Student, University of Dundee, 1979-83; Lecturer, Economics, Abertay University, Dundee and Perth College, 1983-94; Lecturer in Economics and Business Management, Inverness College (University of the Highlands and Islands Network), 1994-99; Member of the Scottish Parliament, Highlands and Islands, 1999-2006, 2007-; Scottish Conservative Spokesman on Communities; Convenor of the Scottish Parliament Cross Party Group on Funerals and Bereavements; Vice Convenor of Cross Party Group on Kidney Disease. Address: (Constituency): 37 Ardconnel Terrace, Inverness IV2 3AE, Scotland. E-mail: mary.scanlon.msp@scottish.parliament.uk

SCARFE Gerald A, b. 1 June 1936, London, England. Cartoonist. m. Jane Asher, 2 sons, 1 daughter. Career: Contributor, cartoons to Punch, 1960-, Private Eye, 1961-, Daily Mail, 1966-, Sunday Times, 1967-, Time, 1967-; Animator and film director, BBC, 1969-; Group exhibitions at Grosvenor Gallery, 1969, 1970, Pavilion d'Humour, Montreal, 1969, Expo, 1970, Osaka, 1970; Solo exhibitions: Waddell Gallery, New York, 1968, 1970, Vincent Price Gallery,

Chicago, 1969, Grosvenor Gallery, 1969, National Portrait Gallery, 1971, Royal Festival Hall, 1983, Langton Gallery, 1986, Chris Beetles Gallery, 1989, National Portrait Gallery, 1989-99; Comic Art Gallery, Melbourne; Gerald Scarfe in Southwark, 2000; Consultant designer and character designer for film: Hercules, 1997; Theatre design: Ubu Roi, Traverse Theatre, 1957; What the Butler Saw, Oxford Playhouse, 1980; No End of Blame, Royal Court, London, 1981; Orpheus in the Underworld, English National Opera, Coliseum, 1985; Who's A Lucky Boy, Royal Exchange, Manchester, 1985; Born Again, 1990; The Magic Flute, Los Angeles Opera, 1992; An Absolute Turkey, 1993; Mind Millie for Me, Haymarket, 1996; Fantastic Mr Fox, Los Angeles Opera, 1998; Peter and the Wolf, Holiday on Ice, Paris and world tour; Television: Director and presenter: Scarfe on Art; Scarfe on Sex; Scarfe on Class; Scarfe in Paradise; Subject of Scarfe and His Work with Disney, South Bank Special. Publications: Gerald Scarfe's People, 1966; Indecent Exposure, 1973; Expletive Deleted: The Life and Times of Richard Nixon, 1974; Gerald Scarfe, 1982; Father Kissmas and Mother Claus, 1985; Scarfe by Scarfe (autobiography), 1986; Gerald Scarfe's Seven Deadly Sins, 1987; Line of Attack, 1988; Scarfeland, 1989; Scarfe on Stage, 1992; Scarfe Face, 1993; Hades: the truth at last, 1997. Honours: Zagreb Prize for BBC film, Long Drawn Out Trip, 1973; CBE, 2008. Address: c/o ICM, Oxford House, 76 Oxford Street, London W1N 0AX, England.

SCARFE Norman, b. 1 May 1923, Felixstowe, England. Writer. Education: King's School, Canterbury, Senior King's Scholar, 1940; 3rd Infantry Division Artillery (from landing on Sword Beach, in front of Caen early on D-Day, to the surrender of Bremen); MA, Honours, History, Oxford, 1949. Appointments: Lecturer in History, Leicester University, 1949-63; Chairman, Centre of East Anglia Studies, University of East Anglia, 1989-96; Founder, Honorary General Editor, Suffolk Records Society, 1958-92. Publications: Assault Division: The 3rd British Infantry Division from D-Day to VE Day, 1947, new edition with foreword by Sir Michael Howard, 2004; Suffolk: A Shell Guide, 1960, retitled Suffolk Guide, 5th edition, 2007; The Suffolk Landscape, 1972, 2nd edition, 1987, new edition, 2002; Shell Guide to Essex, 1968; Shell Guide to Cambridgeshire, 1983; Suffolk in the Middle Ages, 1986; A Frenchman's Year in Suffolk (1784), 1988; Innocent Espionage: The La Rochefoucauld Brothers' Tour of England in 1785, 1995; Jocelin of Brakelond, 1997; To the Highlands in 1786: The inquisitive journey of a young French aristocrat, 2001, (the 3rd book in the La Rochefoucauld Brothers in Britain trilogy); Contributions to: Proceedings, Suffolk Institute of Archaeology; Aldeburgh Festival Annual Programme Book; Country Life; The Book Collector; Dictionary of National Biography. Honours: Fellow, Society of Antiquaries, 1964; Honorary Litt D, University of East Anglia, 1989; Member of the Order of the British Empire, 1994; Citoyen d'Honneur, Colleville Montgomery, Basse-Normandie, 1994; East Anglia's History: Studies in Honour of Norman Scarfe, 2002; President, Suffolk Institute of Archaeology and History; President, Suffolk Records Society. Memberships: International PEN; Suffolk Book League, founder chairman, 1982. Address: The Garden Cottage, 3 Burkitt Road, Woodbridge, Suffolk IP12 4JJ, England.

SCARGILL Arthur, b. 11 January 1938, Worsborough, Yorkshire, England. Trade Unionist. m. Anne Harper, 1961, 1 daughter. Education: White Cross Secondary School. Appointments: Former factory employee; Worked at Wolley Colliery, 1955; Member, Barnsley Young Communist League, 1955-62; Member, National Union of Minewrokers (NUM), 1955-; NUM Branch Committee, 1960; Branch delegate to NUM Yorkshire Area Council, 1964; Member, NUM National Executive, 1972-, President, Yorkshire NUM, 1972-82, President, NUM, 1981-2002, Honorary President and Consultant, 2002-; Chairman, NUM International Committee; President, International Miners Organisation, 1985-; Member, Labour Party, 1966-95; Member, TUC General Council, 1986-88; Founder, Socialist Labour Party, 1996, General Secretary, 1996-, Leader, 2006-; Contested Newport East seat, 1997, Hartlepool, 2001. Address: National Union of Mineworkers, 2 Huddersfield Road, Barnsley, S Yorks, S70 2LS England. Website: www.socialist-labour-party.org.uk

SCATENA Lorraine Borba, b. 18 February 1924, San Rafael, California, USA. Farmer-Rancher; Women's Rights Advocate. m. Louis G Scatena, 14 February 1960, deceased 1 November 1995, 1 son, 1 daughter. Education: BA, Dominican College, San Rafael, 1945; California Elementary Teacher Certificate, 1946; California School of Fine Arts, 1948; University California, Berkeley, 1956-57. Appointments: Teacher of mentally handicapped, San Anselmo, California School District, 1946; Teacher, Fairfax Elementary School, California, 1946-53; Assistant to Mayor Fairfax City Recreation, 1948-53; Teacher, Librarian, US Dependent Schools, Mainz am Rhine, Germany, 1953-56; Translator, Portugal Travel Tours, Lisbon, 1954; Bonding Secretary, American Fore Insurance Group, San Francisco, 1958-60; Rancher, Farmer, Yerington, Nevada, 1960-98; Member, Nevada State Legislative Commission, 1975; Co-ordinator, Nevadans for Equal Rights Amendment, 1975-78; Testifier, Nevada State Senate and Assembly, 1975, 1977; Member, Advisory Committee, Fleischmann College of Agriculture, University of Nevada, 1977-80, 1981-84; Speaker, Grants and Research Projects, Bishop, California, 1977, Choices for Tomorrow's Women, Fallon, Nevada, 1989; Trustee Wassuk College Hawthorne, Nevada, 1984-87; Travelled to AAUW South Pacific Conferences in Hawaii, to address women of Arizona, California, Hawaii and Nevada on women's study and action projects through networking and coalition, continued tour to Washington DC where she led discussion groups for AAUW presidents of North Dakota, Louisiana, Maine and Montana, states where women share the same problems of transportation, communication, employment and medical care, 1982; Attended and assisted with leadership meetings with AAUW elected officers from 16 states in Denver, Colorado, 1982. Honours include: AAUW Nevada State Humanities Award, 1975; Invitation to first all-women delegation to USA from People's Republic of China, US House of Representatives, 1979; AAUW branch travelship, Discovering Women in US History, Radcliffe College, 1981; NRTA State Outstanding Service Award, 1981; AAUW Future Fund National Award, 1983; Soroptimist International Women Helping Women Award, 1983; Fellow World Literary Academy, 1993; AAUW, Lorraine Scatena Endowment Gift named in her honour for significant contributions to AAUW National Educational Foundation, 1997. Memberships include: Marin Society of Artists, 1948-53; American Association of University Women, 1968-, Nevada State Convention General Chairman, 1976, 1987; Lyon County Museum Society, 1978-; Lyon County Retired Teachers' Association, Unit President, 1979-80, 1984-86; State Convention General Chairman, 1985; Participated in public panel with solo presentation, Shakespeare's Treatment of Women Characters, Nevada Theatre for the Arts hosting Ashland, Oregon Shakespearean actors local performance, 1987; Rural American Women Inc; AAUW, Branch President, 1972-74, 1974-76; President, AAUW, Nevada State, 1981-83; Nevada Representative for First White House Conference for Rural American Women, Washington, 1980; Italian Catholic Federation, Branch President, 1986-88; Charter Member,

Eleanor Roosevelt Education Fund for Women and Girls, 1990, sustaining member, 1992-; Member, Nevada Women's History Project, University Nevada, 1996-; Poetry presenter, World Congress on Arts and Communication, Lisbon, Portugal, 1999; Washington, 2000; Cambridge University, St John's College, 2001; Vancouver, Canada, 2002; Dominican University of California, President's Circle, 1997-; American Association of University Women, Leaders Circle, 1998-; The National Museum of Women in the Arts, Washington DC, charter member, 1987, council member, 1999-; University of California, Berkeley, Bancroft, Librarian's Council, 2002. Address: PO Box 247, Yerington, NV 89447-0247, USA.

SCHAEFER Henry, b. 8 June 1944, Grand Rapids, Michigan, USA. Education: BS, Chemical Physics, Massachusetts Institute of Technology, 1966; Fellow, National Defense Education Act, 1969; PhD, Chemical Physics, Stanford University, 1969. Appointments include: Assistant Professor of Chemistry, 1969-74, Associate Professor of Chemistry, 1974-78, Professor of Chemistry, 1978-87, University of California at Berkeley; Director, Institute for Theoretical Chemistry, University of Texas, 1979-80; Wilfred T Doherty Professor of Chemistry, University of Texas, 1979-80; Director, Centre for Computational Chemistry, University of Georgia, 1987-; Graham Perdue Professor of Chemistry, University of Georgia, 1987-; Visiting Professor, Australia, Switzerland, Argentina and France; Professor of Chemistry Emeritus, University of California at Berkeley, 2004-. Publications: 1,150 journal articles; Book chapters; Books; Conference proceedings. Honours include: American Chemical Society Award in Pure Chemistry, 1979; Leo Hendrik Baekeland Award, 1983; Schrodinger Medal, World Association of Theoretical and Computational Chemists, 1990; Centenary Medal, Royal Society of Chemistry, 1992; Lamar Dodd Award, University of Georgia, 1995; Professor Honoris Causa, St Petersburg State University, 1996; Doctor Honoris Causa, University of Plovdiv, 1998; Doctor Honoris Causa, Beijing Institute of Technology, 1999; Doctor Honoris Causa, University of Sofia, 1999; Professor Honoris Causa, Beijing Normal University, 1999; Gold Medal, Comenius University, 2000; Professor Honoris Causa, Fudan University, 2001; Professor Honoris Causa, Chinese Academy of Sciences, Shanghai, 2001; Doctor Honoris Causa, Huntington College, 2002; Professor Honoris Causa, Yunnan University, Kunming, 2002; Professor Honoris Causa, Guangxi Normal University, Guilin, China, 2003; Professor Honoris Causa, Chengdu University, Chengdu, China, 2003; American Chemical Society Award in Theoretical Chemistry, 2003; Ira M Remsen Award, American Chemical Society, 2003; Professor Honoris Causa, Xinjiang University, Urumqi, China, 2004; Joseph O Hirschfelder Prize, University of Wisconsin, 2005; Professor Honoris Causa, Sichuan University, China, 2005; Professor Honoris Causa, Lanzhou University, Lanzhou, China, 2006; Guest lecturer at numerous universities, conferences and symposia; Several grants and research funding. Memberships include: Fellow, American Academy of Arts and Sciences; Fellow, American Physical Society; Fellow, American Association for the Advancement of Science; Fellow, Alfred P Sloan Foundation; Fellow, John S. Guggenheim Foundation; Member, Editorial Board, Chemical Physics Letters; Member, Editorial Board, Advances in Quantum Chemistry; Fellow, American Scientific Affiliation; Fellow, American Institute of Chemists; Member, Editorial Board, Journal of Molecular Structure; Editor in Chief, Molecular Physics; President, World Association of Theoretical and Computational Chemists; Fellow, Royal Society of Chemistry (London), 2005; Member, International Academy of Quantum Molecular Sciences. Address: Centre for Computational and Quantum Chemistry,

University of Georgia, Room 505 Computational Chemistry Building, 1004 Cedar Street, Athens, GA 30602-2525, USA. E-mail: hfs@uga.edu Website: www.ccqc.uga.edu/group/Dr.Schaefer.html

SCHAFFER Sandra Sue, b. 12 January 1947, Kansas City, Missouri, USA. Artist; Educator. m. Larry Alan Schaffer, 1 son, 1 daughter. Education: BA, Psychology, University of Missouri, Columbia; MSc, Learning Disabilities (Diagnostic Testing), Central Missouri State University, Warrensburg, Missouri. Appointments: Learning Disabilities Teacher, Blue Springs School District, 1980-90; Professional watercolour artist, 1997-; Director, Special Education, The Plaza Academy, Kansas City, 2000-. Publications: Today's Best Painters, 2002; Best of America watercolour, 2007; Splash 10, 2008; Listed in international biographical dictionaries. Honours: Numerous honours and awards including: Induction into Watercolor Honor Society, 2005; Silver Award, Montana Watercolor Society National Show, 2006; Purple SF Sage Signature Status, Texas Watercolor Society, 2006; Watercolor USA, Museum Cash Award, 2007; Distinction, Missouri Watercolor Society National Show, 2007; Jack Richeson, Daniel Smith and Artist and Craftsman Awards, Brown-Forman Patron Purchase, Kentucky Watercolor Society National Show, 2007. Memberships: Board of Directors, Watercolor Honor Society; Board of Directors, Missouri Watercolor Society; Purple Sage Society; Texas Watercolor Society; Watercolor Honor Society; Kansas Watercolor Society; Kentucky Watercolor Society; Pennsylvania Watercolor Society; Academic Artists Association; Northeast Watercolor Society; Eastern Washington Watercolor Society; Watercolor West Watercolor Society; Texas Watercolor Society; WAS-Houston Watercolor Society; Missouri Watercolor Society; Mississippi Watercolor Society; Louisiana Watercolor Society; Western CO Watercolor Society; Red River Watercolor Society; San Diego Watercolor Society; Address: 12700 East 64th Ct, Kansas City, Missouri 64133, USA.

SCHAMA Simon Michael, b. 13 February 1945, London, England. Historian; Academic; Writer; Art Critic. m. Virginia Papaioannou, 1983, 1 son, 1 daughter. Education: Christ's College, Cambridge. Career: Fellow and Director of Studies in History, Christ's College, Cambridge, 1966-76; Fellow and Tutor in Modern History, Brasenose College, Oxford, 1976-80; Professor of History (Mellon Professor of the Social Sciences), Harvard University, 1980; University Professor, Columbia University, 1997-; Art Critic, New Yorker, 1995-; Vice President, Poetry Society; TV: Rembrandt: The Public Eye and the Private Gaze (film), BBC, 1992; A History of Britain (series), 2000-01. Publications: Patriots and Liberators: Revolution in the Netherlands 1780-1813, 1977; Two Rothschilds and the Land of Israel, 1979; The Embarrassment of Riches: An Interpretation of Dutch Culture in the Golden Age, 1987; Citizens: A Chronicle of the French Revolution, 1989; Dead Certainties (Unwarranted Speculations), 1991; Landscape and Memory, 1995; Rembrandt's Eyes, 1999; A History of Britain Vol 1: At the Edge of the World? 3000 BC-AD 1603, 2000, Vol 2: The British Wars 1603-1776, 2001, Vol 3: The Fate of Empire 1776-2001, 2002; Hang-Ups: Essays on Painting, 2004; Rough Crossings, 2005; The Power of Art, 2006. Honours: Wolfson Prize, 1977; Leo Gershoy Prize (American Historical Association), 1978; National Cash Register Book Prize for Non-Fiction (for Citizens), 1990. Address: Department of History, 522 Fayerweather Hall, Columbia University, New York, NY 10027, USA. Website: www.columbia.edu/cu.history

SCHELLIN Thomas Erling, b. 31 July 1939, Hamburg, Germany. Marine Engineer. m. Andrea Bielfeldt, 11 April 1984, 1 step son, 1 step daughter. Education: BS, Rensselaer Polytechnic Institute, Troy, New York, USA, 1962; MS, Massachusetts Institute of Technology, Cambridge, Massachusetts, USA 1964; PhD, Mechanical Engineering, Rice University, 1971. Appointments: Teaching Assistant, Department of Naval Architecture Massachusetts Institute of Technology, 1962-64; Mechanical Engineer, Shell Development Co, Houston, Texas, USA 1964-68; Research Assistant, Rice University, Houston, Texas, USA, 1968-71; Design Engineer, The Offshore Co, Houston, Texas, USA 1971-72; Research Scientist, GKSS, Geesthacht, Germany, 1972-75; Naval Architect, Germanischer Lloyd, Hamburg, 1976-2004; Visiting (Adjunct) Professor, Virginia Technical University, Department of Aerospace and Ocean Engineering, Blacksburg, Virginia, USA, Fall, 2004; Naval Architect (part-time after retirement in 2004), Germanischer Lloyd, Hamburg, Germany, 2005-; Lecturer, Berlin Technical University, Department of Naval Architecture and Ocean Engineering, Berlin, Germany, Spring 2005, 2006, 2007 and 2008. Publications include most recently as co-author: Validation of Numerical Tools to Predict Parametric Rolling, 2006; CFD and FE Methods to Predict Wave Loads and Ship Structural Response, 2006; Wave Load and Structural Analysis for a Jack-Up Platform in Freak Waves, 2007; Simulation of Sloshing in LNG-Tanks, 2007; Numerical Prediction of Impact-Related Wave Loads on Ships, 2007; Dynamics of Single Point Mooring Configurations, 2007. Honours: Achievement Award, 1993, Fellow, 2007-, American Society of Mechanical Engineers; Listed in Who's Who publications and biographical dictionaries. Memberships include: American Society of Mechanical Engineers; Society of Naval Architects and Marine Engineers; Schiffbautechnische Gesellschaft. Address: Abteistrasse 23, 20149 Hamburg, Germany. E-mail: thomas.schellin@gl-group.com

SCHIFFER Claudia, b. 25 August 1970, Düsseldorf, Germany. Model. m. Matthew Vaughn, 2002, 1 son, 1 daughter. Career: Worked for Karl Lagerfeld, 1990; Revlon Contract, 1992-; Appearances on magazine covers, calendars, TV; Released own exercise video; Appeared in films: Ritchie Rich; The Blackout, 1997; Desperate But Not Serious, 1999; The Sound of Claudia Schiffer, 2000; Black and White, 2000; Chain of Fools, 2000; In Pursuit, 2000; Life Without Dick, 2001; Love Actually, 2003; Retired from modelling, 1998; Owns share in Fashion Café. Publication: Memories. Memberships: US Committee, UNICEF, 1995-98. Address: c/o Elite Model Management, 40 Parker Street, London WC2B 5BH, England.

SCHILD Rudolph Ernst, b. 10 January 1940, Chicago, Illinois, USA. Astrophysicist. m. Jane Struss. Education: BS, 1962, MS, 1963, PhD, 1967, University of Chicago. Appointments: Research Fellow, Postdoctorate, California Institute of Technology, 1967-69; Scientist, Smithsonian Astrophysical Observatory, 1969-; Lecturer, Harvard University, 1977-82. Publications: Over 200 scientific papers in refereed journals; The Electronic Sky: Digital Images of the Cosmos, 1985; Voyage to the Stars, CD Rom, 1994; 2 patents. Honours: Discovered gravitational lens time delay, 1986; Discovered nature of missing mass, 1997; Discovered luminous quasar structure, 2006. Memberships: American Astronomical Society, 1967-; International Astronomical Union, 1969-. Address: Centre for Astrophysics, 60 Garden Street, Cambridge, MA 02138, USA. E-mail: rschild@cfa.harvard.edu

SCHILLING (Karl Friedrich) Guenther, b. 16 August 1930, Leipzig, Germany. Agricultural Chemistry Educator. m. Gudrun Linschmann, 2 sons. Education: Studies in Agricultural Sciences and Chemistry, Friedrich-Schiller-University, Jena, Germany, 1951-56; Diploma in Agricultural Sciences, 1954, in Chemistry, 1956; Dr agr, 1957; Training in Radio Chemistry, Moscow, USSR, 1958; Dr agr habilitatus, 1960. Appointments: Lecturer, Plant Nutrition, 1960-61, Full Professor, Plant Nutrition and Soil Science, Director, Institute of Agricultural Chemistry, 1961-70, Friedrich-Schiller-University Jena, Germany; Full Professor, Physiology and Nutrition of Crop Plants, Martin-Luther-University Halle-Wittenberg, Germany, 1970-95; Professor Emeritus, 1995; Dean of Agricultural Faculty, 1983-90; Rector of Martin-Luther-University Halle-Wittenberg, 1990-93; Vice President, Rector's Conference of the Federal Republic of Germany, 1991-95. Publications: 230 contributions to scientific journals and books; 1 monograph; 1 handbook contribution; Author and editor, Pflanzenernährung und Düngung, university textbook, revised edition, 2000. Honours include: Medal and Diploma, 8th International Fertiliser Congress, Moscow, 1976; National Prize for Science and Technology, Berlin, 1982; Dr Heinrich Baur Prize, Munich, 1994; Golden Sprengel-Liebig-Medal, Leipzig, 1997. Listed in national and international biographical dictionaries. Memberships: Deutsche Akademie der Naturforscher Leopoldina; Matica Srbska; Verband Deutscher Landwirtschaftlicher Untersuchungs-und Forschungsanstalten, Vice-President, 1993-96. Address: Institute of Agricultural and Nutritional Sciences of the Martin-Luther-University Halle-Wittenberg, Julius-Kuehn-Str 31, 06112 Halle (Saale), Germany. E-mail: schilling@landw.uni-halle.de

SCHLECHTE Gunter B, b. 1 June 1951, Hannover, Germany. Plant Pathologist and Mycologist. m. Ute Schlechte, 2 sons, 1 daughter. Education: Diploma in Horticulture, 1974, PhD, Horticulture, 1978, University of Hannover; Certificate in Phytomedicine, DPG Giessen, 1983. Appointments: Research Assistant, University of Hannover, 1975-78; Research Associate and Project Leader, University of Hannover/University of Göttingen, 1979-83; Assistant Professor, University of Göttingen, 1984-88; Research Associate, Institute of Industrial Microbiology and Biotechnology, Grosshansdorf, 1990-96; Visiting Lecturer, Heinz Sielmann Foundation, Duderstadt, 1998-2000; Commissary of Nature Conservancy, 1989-; Consultant, Growing Media Industry, Germany, 1994-; Business Owner, Expert and Research Office of Applied Microbiology, Bockenem, 1997-. Publications: Books: Wood-inhabiting Fungi, 1986; Structure of the Basidiomycete Flora in Polluted Forests, 1991; Soil Basidiomycete Communities and Air Pollution, 1996. Numerous papers and articles in scientific journals. Honours: Scholarship, German Research Community, Bonn, 1989; Honorary Professor, Yorkshire University, 2003. Memberships: German Phytomedical Society (DPG); Society of Mycology and Lichenology in Germany (GML). Address: Tillyschanze 9, 31167 Bockenem, Germany.

SCHLOTTERBACK Edward Earl, b. 11 February 1952, Garrett, Indiana, USA. Developmental Tester. 1 son, 2 daughters. Education: AAS degree, Air Conditioning/Refrigeration, Los Angeles Metropolitan College, Los Angeles, California, 1979; AS degree, Vocational Technical Education, State Technical Institute, Memphis, Tennessee, 1979; BS degree, Industrial Technology, Southern Illinois University, Carbondale, Illinois, 1984; AAS degree, Electronics Technology, Ivy Tech State College, Fort Wayne, Indiana, 1998. Appointments: Communication Navigation Technician,

Electronics Instructor, US Marine Corps, Washington, DC, 1970-79; Associate Electrical Engineer, King-Seeley Thermos Co, Kendallville, Indiana, 1979-82; Senior Metrologist, VDO North America (QS9000 Certified), Auburn, Indiana, 1982-2001; Adjunct Faculty Instructor, Ivy Tech State College, Fort Wayne, Indiana, 2002-04; Developmental Tester, General Electric Advanced Manufacturing Lab (UL & CSA Certified), Fort Wayne, Indiana, 2003-. Publications: (Poems) Once Upon A Winters Day, Best Poems of 1998; Planets Peril; Whispers at Dusk. Memberships: Senior Member, Chairman, Chapter 56 Society of Manufacturing Engineers; Senior Member, American Society for Quality Section 0905; American Legion Post #86; Board of Directors, Ivy Tech Alumni Association; Board of Advisors, Four County Area Vocational Co-operative Industrial Maintenance Program; Board of Advisors, Anthis Career Center Aviation Program. Address: 9812N 1000E, Kendallville, IN 46755, USA. E-mail: eschlotterback@yahoo.com

SCHMEIDLER Felix, b. 20 October 1920, Leipzig, Germany. m. Marion Pampe, 1 son, 1 daughter. Education: Universität München, Studium der Astronomie, 1938-41; Dr rer nat, Universität München, 1941; Habilitation für Astronomie an Universität München, 1950. Appointments: Assistant der Universitätssternwarte München, 1943; Professor für Astronomie an Universität München, 1957; Assistant Director, Universitätssternwarte, München, 1979-86; University Observatory Cambridge, England, 1950-51; Mt Stromlo Observatory, Canberra, Australia, 1954-55. Publications: More than 100 articles in scientific journals; Books: Alte und moderne Kosmologie, 1961; Nikolaus Copernicus, Serie Große Naturforscher, 1970; Edition, Works of the Astronomers Hevelius, 1969, Regionmontanus, 1972; Kommentar zu "De revolutionibus, 1998. Honours: Silberne Medaille der Universität Helsinki, 1968; Kulturpreis der Landsmannschaft Westpreußen, Münster, 1973; Honorary Citizen der Stadt Königsberg in Bayern, 1982; Ehrenschild Deutschordensland der Ost- und Westpreußenstiftung in Bayern, 1997; Minor planet 1992ST17 named Schmeidler by International Astronomical Union, 2006. Memberships: Royal Astronomical Society London, 1951; International Astronomical Union, 1955; Altpreußische Gesellschaft für Wissenschaft, Kunst und Literatur, 1981. Address: Mauerkircher Strasse 17, D81679 München, Germany.

SCHMIDKUNZ Heinz, b. 3 October 1929, Graslitz, Czech Republic. Professor of Chemistry. m. Liselotte, 1 daughter. Education: Diploma, Master of Chemistry, 1959; PhD, Physical Chemistry, 1963; Professor of Chemistry, 1980. Appointments: Assistant, Physical Chemistry, University of Frankfurt/M, Germany, 1959; University Lecturer for Teacher Education at University, 1963-80; Professor of Chemistry, University of Dortmund, Germany, 1980-. Publications: 11 books; 200 articles in journals. Honour: Heinrich-Roessler-Award, German Chemical Society, 1989; Literary Award, Austrian Society of Chemistry Teachers, 2004; Honorary Member, German Chemical Society, 2005. Memberships: German Chemical Society; Austrian Society of Teachers in Chemistry. Address: Obermarkstr. 125, D-44267 Dortmund, Germany. E-mail: heinz.schmidkunz@uni-dortmund.de

SCHMITZ Nicole Marie Renée, b. 6 October 1962, Luxembourg City, Luxembourg. Cancer Research Scientist. Education: Certificat d'Etudes Scientifiques, University of Luxembourg, 1984; Diplomvorprüfung Biology, University of Karlsruhe, Germany, 1985; Diploma, Molecular Biology, University of Zurich, Switzerland, 1990; PhD, Swiss Institute for Experimental Cancer Research & University of Lausanne, Switzerland, 1994. Appointments: Postdoctoral Fellow, Institute of Biochemistry and Molecular Biology, 1994-96, Postdoctoral Research Associate, Department of Clinical Research, 1997-2004, Coproject Leader, 2000-04, University of Bern, Switzerland; Visiting Scientist, Institute of Microbiology, Swiss Federal Institute of Technology, Zurich, 2004-05; Research Fellow, Cancer Research UK Institute for Cancer Studies, Division of Cancer Studies, The University of Birmingham, England, 2006. Achievements: RB phosphorylation by CDK2 & CDK4 in childhood acute lymphoblastic leukemia (ALL), and CD34+ hemopoietic progenitor cells; Serine 612 Phosphorylation by CDK4 in Acute Lymphoblastic Leukemia; Cyclin D1 expression in ALL; Detection of The MCM4/RB/NF-I complex in NALM-6 cells; CAF20: An inhibitor of translation initiation. Effects of vertebrate p34 CDC2 upon cell cycle progression in the fission yeast; Articles in scientific journals including: EMBO Journal, 1997; Molecular and General Genetics, 1999; Hematology, 2001; The Pezcoller Foundation Journal, 2003; Biochemical and Biophysical Research Communications, 2004; Leukemia, 2005; Stem Cells, 2005; American Journal of Pathology, 2006; Licencing Factor MCM4 AM493756, 2007. Honours: Scolar Subsidies, ARBED Foundation, Luxembourg, 1985; Study Grant, Luxembourg's Ministry for National Education, 1990/91; Fellowship, Luxembourg's Ministry for Cultural Affairs and Higher Education, 1992; Congress Travel Grant, Union of the Swiss Societies for Experimental Cell Biology and Swiss Institute for Experimental Cancer Research, Epalinges/Lausanne, 1993; Honour Fellow Travel Grant, British Society for Cell Biology, 1993, 1994; Study Grant, Paul Eyschen Foundation, Luxembourg, 1994; Congress Travel Grant, Institute of Biochemistry and Molecular Biology, University of Bern, Switzerland, 1994; Congress Travel Grants, Foundation for Clinical and Experimental Cancer Research Bern, Switzerland, 1997, 2000, 2001; Research Grant, Swiss National Science Foundation, 2000; Research Grant, Foundation for Bone Marrow Transplantation, University Children's Hospital, Bern, Switzerland, 2000; Miles Award, Free Flights, Swiss Travel Club, 2001, 2002; Certificate of Participation, CNIO CC 2002, Spanish National Cancer Centre, Madrid; American Medal of Honor, American Biographical Institute, 2004; Fellow, International Biographical Association, England, 2004; International Peace Prize, The United Cultural Convention, USA, 2005; Leading Scientists of the World, International Biographical Centre, 2005; Crystal Globe, Marquis Who's Who, USA, 2005; Top 100 Scientists 2005 Wall Plaque, IBC; Scientific Adviser to the Director General, IBC, 2005; Presidential Seal of Honor Plate, ABI, USA, 2005; Tiffany & Co framed biography, Marquis Who's Who, USA, 2005; Fellow, ABI, 2005; Senator of the World Nations Congress, ABI, 2006; World Medal of Freedom, ABI, 2006; Founding Member, American Order of Excellence, ABI, 2006; IBC's Salute to Greatness Award, 2006; Ambassador of the Inaugural World Forum, Oxford University, 2006; Archimedes Medal of Honor, IBC, 2006; Honorary Director General Europe, IBC, 2006; Mahogany Wall Plaque, 2007; Marquis Who's Who, USA; Publication Awards, Santa Cruz Biotechnology Inc, USA, 1999, 2001, 2007. Memberships: American Association for Cancer Research; British Society for Cell Biology; European Association for Cancer Research; Union of Swiss Societies for Experimental Biology; FASEB; International Society for Computational Biology; New York Academy of Science. Website: www.nicole-mr-schmitz.info

SCHNEEWEISS Ulrich, b. 25 March 1923, Potsdam, Germany. Doctor; Medical Microbiologist. m. Sigrid Schmilinsky, 1 son, 2 daughters. Education: Student, 1946-52,

Dr med, 1952, Dr med habil, 1960. Appointments: Scientific Assistant, 1952-55, Head Assistant, 1956-63, Department of Serology, University Lectureship, Medical Microbiology, Immunology, Epidemiology, 1961-68, Humboldt University, Berlin; Scientific Assistant, 1963-68, Professor, Head of Department of Diagnostic Research, 1968-88, German Academy of Sciences, Institute for Cancer Research, Robert Roessle Clinic. Publications: 90 research papers, textbooks, monographs: Reihenuntersuchung auf Syphilis..., 1963; Grundriss der Impfpraxis, 1964-68; Allgemeine/ Spezielle Mikrobiologie, 1968; Transplantations- und Tumorimmunologie, 1973; Tumorforschung am biologischen Modell, 1980; Penicillin – eine medizinhistorische Perspektive, 1999. Honour: Robert Koch Medal, German Academy of Sciences, 1982. Honours: European Association for Cancer Research, 1982; German Academy of Scientists LEOPOLDINA, Halle (Saale), 1986. Address: Boenkestrasse 55, D-13125 Berlin, Germany.

SCHÖN Wilhelm, b. 12 October 1951, Linz, Danube, Austria. Civilisation Critic; Novelist; Environmentalist; Amateur Cosmologist. Education: Studies in Philology, History and Philosophy, University of Vienna, 1972-76; Private studies, Frankfurt, Main and Zurich, Switzerland, 1976-77; Employment Instructions in plastics industry, 1978-79; Private forestry planning, early 1980s; Characterisation curriculum, Computer PC for MS/DOS Microsoft, 1994. Appointments: Adjunct in the physics laboratory of Dr Kofler, Foliplast in Tyrol and Chemielaborant at Chemo-Phos, 1980-84; Private projects, 1984; First book published, 1985. Publications: Sturmvögel ziehen nach Nirgendwo, novel, 1985; Im Schatten des Drachenflugs der Macht, documentary, 1986; Meine Nation heißt Würde, 1987; Urlaub vom Wort Zwei: Collected Papers, 1994; Articles: Systemterrorismus, 1986; The Ecological Manifesto, 1988; Charta des Analytischen Naturalismus, 1991; Dissidenten-Chronologie, 1994; Kinderfänger, 1999; Rudi and Wilhelm Schön: Teufel Emerich, 2002. Honours: Silver Needle HK Klbg; Medal, 2000 Outstanding Intellectuals of the 21st Century, 2007. Memberships: Amnesty International, 1983-95; Friends of the Earth, 1989-94; IGAA, 1991-2000; IGoöA, 1991-2001; IASCP and the International Society for Environmental Ethics, early 1990's; NPG and Argus, 1994-; THWA, 1998-2000; ODV, 1998-; PRO GS. Address: orb Zentrum, Abensbergstr 51, A-4061 Pasching, Austria.

SCHOENHAGEN Paul, b. 27 January 1964, Koblenz, Germany. Physician; Cardiovascular Imaging Specialist. m. Noelle Schoenhagen, 2 sons, 1 daughter. Education: Medical School Marburg, Germany, 1985-91, Tuebingen, Germany, 1991-92; MD, 1992; Doctoral Thesis, Cardiovascular Medicine, Marburg, Germany, 1995. Appointments: Residency, Internal Medicine and Radiology, Stuttgart, Germany, 1992-96; Residency, Internal Medicine, 1996-99, Fellowship, Cardiovascular Medicine, 1999-2002; Fellowship, Cardiovascular Tomography, 2002-2003; Staff, Department of Diagnostic Radiology and Cardiovascular Medicine, 2003-, The Cleveland Clinic Foundation, Cleveland, Ohio, USA. Publications: Articles in scientific journals include most recently: Extent and Direction of Arterial Remodeling in Stable versus Unstable Coronary Syndromes: An Intravascular Ultrasound Study, 2002; Relation of matrix-metalloproteinase 3 found in coronary lesion samples retrieved by directional coronary atherectomy to intrvascular ultasound observations on coronary remodeling, 2002; Coronary Plaque Morphology and Frequency of Ulceration Distant from Culprit Lesions in Patients with Unstable and Stable Presentation, 2003; Atlas and Manual of Cardiovascular Computed Tomography. Honours: Postdoctoral Fellowship Grant, Ohio Valley, American Heart Association, 2001-2003; 2nd James E Muller Vulnerable Plaque Award, 2002. Memberships: European Society of Cardiology; Fellow American Heart Association; Radiologic Society of North America. Address: The Cleveland Clinic Foundation, Radiology H6-6, 9500 Euclid Avenue, Cleveland, OH 44195, USA. E-mail: schoenp1@ccf.org

SCHÖNFELDER Volker, b. 5 October 1939, Barmstedt, Germany. Professor of Physics. m. Bärbel Schönfelder, 3 sons. Education: Diploma in Physics, 1966; Dr.rer.nat., 1970; Dr. rer. nat. habil., 1979; Professor of Physics, 1995. Appointment: Head, Gamma Ray Astronomy Group, Max-Planck-Institut für Extraterrestrische Physik, until October 2004. Publications: About 400 publications in scientific journals; Editor of the book: The Universe in Gamma Rays, 2001. Honours: NASA Exceptional Scientific Achievement Award, 1993; Deutscher Philip Morris Forschungspreis, 1997. Memberships: Deutsche Physikalische Gesellschaft; Astronomische Gesellschaft. Address: Max-Planck-Institut für Extraterrestrische Physik, Postfach 1603, 85740 Garching, Germany. E-mail: vos@mpe.mpg.de

SCHROEDER Gerhard Fritz Kurt, b. 7 April 1944, Mossenberg, Germany. Politician. m. Doris Koepf, 2 children. Education: Degree in Law, Goettingen University, 1971. Appointments: Lawyer, Hanover, Germany, 1978-90; Chairman, Young Social Democrats, 1978-80; Legislator, German Bundestag, 1980-86; Leader of the Opposition, State Parliament of Lower Saxony, 1986-90; Prime Minister, Lower Saxony, 1990-98; Chancellor, Government of Germany, 1998-2005. Publications: Contributor of articles to numerous professional publications.

SCHUCK Otto, b. 26 August 1926, Prague, Czech Republic. Nephrologist. m. L Cizkova, 16 August 1950. Education: MD, 1950, DSc, 1966, Charles University, Prague; Research Fellow, Medical Clinic, University of Manchester, 1966-67. Appointments: Research Fellow, First Medical Clinic, Prague, 1950-51; Assistant Director, Institute for Experimental Therapy, Prague, 1962-65; Director, Clinic of Nephrology, Prague, 1967-85; Head, Department of Nephrology, Postgraduate Medical School, Prague, 1976-92; Researcher, Institute for Clinical Experimental Medicine, Prague, 1985-; Researcher, Internal Clinic, Charles University, 2006-. Publications include: Nephrologie für den praktischen Artzt, 1968; Examination of Kidney Function, 1984; Clinical nephrology, 1995, 2006; Scientific papers in international journals dealing with kidney diseases. Honours: Bruno Watschinger Award, Danube Symposia, 1962, 1987; Jan Brod Award, 1966; Cilag Foundation Award, 1996; Purkynje Award, 1996; Honorary President, Czech Society of Nephrology; Honorary Member, Slovak Nephrology Society; Rector's award, Charles University, 1997. Listed in national and international biographical dictionaries. Memberships: Gesellschaft für Nephrologie; New York Academy of Sciences; Czech Society of Nephrology; Slovak Society of Nephrology; European Society of Internal Medicine; Editorial Boar, International Journal Clinical Pharmacology and Therapeutics. Address: Kratochvilova 4, 162 00 Prague 6, Czech Republic.

SCHULBERG Budd, b. 27 March 1914, New York, New York, USA. Author. m. (1) Virginia Ray, 23 July 1936, divorced 1942, 1 daughter, (2) Victoria Anderson, 17 February 1943, divorced 1964, 2 sons, (3) Geraldine Brooks, 12 July 1964, deceased 1977, (4) Betsy Anne Langman, 9 July 1979, 1 son, 1 daughter. Education: AB cum laude, Dartmouth College, 1936. Appointments: Founder-President, Schulberg Productions; Founder-Director, Watts Writers Workshop,

Los Angeles, 1965-; Founder-Chairman, Frederick Douglass Creative Arts Center, New York City, 1971-. Publications: What Makes Sammy Run?, 1941; The Harder They Fall, 1947; The Disenchanted, 1950; Some Faces in the Crowd, 1953; Waterfront, 1955; Sanctuary V, 1969; The Four Seasons of Success, 1972; Loser and Still Champion: Muhammad Ali, 1972; Swan Watch, 1975; Everything That Moves, 1980; Moving Pictures: Memories of a Hollywood Prince, 1981; Love, Action, Laughter and Other Sad Tales, 1990; Sparring with Hemingway and Other Legends of the Fight Game, 1995. Editor: From the Ashes: Voices of Watts, 1967. Screenplays: Little Orphan Annie (with Samuel Ornitz), 1938; Winter Carnival (with F Scott Fitzgerald), 1939; Weekend for Three (with Dorothy Parker), 1941; City Without Men (with Martin Berkeley), 1943; Government Girl, 1943; On the Waterfront, 1954; A Face in the Crowd, 1957; Wind Across the Everglades, 1958. Contributions to: Leading magazines. Honours: Academy Award, 1954; New York Critics Circle Award, 1954; Screen Writers Guild Award, 1954; Venice Film Festival Award, 1954; Christopher Award, 1955; German Film Critics Award, 1957; B'hai Human Rights Award, 1968; Prix Literaire, Deauville Festival, 1989; Westhampton Writers Lifetime Achievement Award, 1989; World Boxing Association Living Legend Award, 1990; Southampton Cultural Center 1st Annual Literature Award, 1992. Memberships: American Civil Liberties Union; American Society of Composers, Authors and Publishers; Authors Guild; Dramatists Guild; Players' Club, founder member; PEN; Phi Beta Kappa; Writers Guild East. Address: c/o Miriam Altschuler Literary Agency, RR1, Box 5, Old Post Road, Red Hook, NY 12571, USA.

SCHULER Robert Jordan, b. 25 June 1939, California, USA. Professor of English; Poet. m. Carol Forbis, 7 September 1963, 2 sons, 1 daughter. Education: BA, Honours, Political Science, Stanford University, 1961; MA, Comparative Literature, University of California, Berkeley, 1965; PhD, English, University of Minnesota, 1989. Appointments: Instructor in English, Menlo College, 1965-67; Instructor in Humanities, Shimer College, 1967-77; Professor of English, University of Wisconsin, 1978-. Publications: Axle of the Oak, 1978; Seasonings, 1978; Where is Dancers' Hill?, 1979; Morning Raga, 1980; Red Cedar Scroll, 1981; Floating Out of Stone, 1982; Music for Monet, 1984; Grace: A Book of Days, 1995; Journeys Toward the Original Mind, 1995; Red Cedar Suite, 1999; In search of "Green Dolphin Street", 2004; Dance into Heaven, 2005; Songs of Love, 2006; Collection, 2007; Blueline Anthology; Contributions to: Caliban; Northeast; Tar River Poetry; Longhouse; Dacotah Territory; Wisconsin Academy Review; Wisconsin Review; North Stone Review; Wisconsin Poetry 1991 Transactions; Hummingbird; Abraxas; Lake Street Review; Inheriting the Earth; Mississippi Valley Review; Coal City Review; Gypsy; Imagining Home, 1995. Honours: Danforth Fellow, Yale, 1969-70; Wisconsin Arts Board Fellowship for Poetry, 1997; Awards from Wisconsin Humanities Council; Illinois Arts Council; NEA; Listed in Who's Who publications and biographical dictionaries. Membership: Phi Kappa Phi; Land Commissioner, Land Use Planner, Dunn County, Menomonie Township. Address: E4549 479th Avenue, Menomonie, WI 54751, USA. E-mail: Schulerr@uw.stout.edu

SCHULLER Gunther (Alexander), b. 22 November 1925, New York, New York, USA. Composer; Conductor; Music Educator; Publisher. m. Marjorie Black, 8 June 1948, deceased 1992, 2 sons. Education: St Thomas Choir School, New York City, 1937-40. Appointments: Teacher, Manhattan School of Music, New York City, 1950-63; Teacher, 1963-84, Artistic Co-Director, 1969-74, Director, 1974-84, Berkshire Music

Center, Tanglewood, Massachusetts; Faculty, Yale School of Music, 1964-67; President, New England Conservatory of Music, Boston, 1967-77; Music Publisher, 1975-2000; Artistic Director, Festival at Sandpoint, 1985-2000. Publications: Horn Technique, 1962, 2nd edition, 1992; Early Jazz: Its Roots and Musical Development, 2 volumes, 1968-1988; Musings, 1985. Contributions to: Various publications. Honours: Guggenheim Fellowship, 1962-63; ASCAP-Deems Taylor Award, 1970; Rodgers and Hammerstein Award, 1971; William Schuman Award, Columbia University, 1989; John D and Catharine T MacArthur Foundation Fellowship, 1991; Pulitzer Prize in Music, 1994; Honorary doctorates. Memberships: American Academy of Arts and Sciences; American Academy of Arts and Letters. Address: 167 Dudley Road, Newton Centre, MA 02159, USA.

SCHUMACHER Joel, b. 29 August 1939, New York, USA. Film Director. Education: Parson School of Design, New York. Appointments: Work in fashion industry aged 15; Owner boutique Paraphernalia; Costume designer, Revlon, 1970s; Set and production design; Writer, director for TV; Films include: The Incredible Shrinking Woman; DC Cab (also screenplay); St Elmo's Fire (also screenplay); The Lost Boys; Cousins; Flatliners; Dying Young; Falling Down; The Client; Batman Forever; A Time to Kill; Batman and Robin; Eight Millimeter; Flawless (also screenplay and producer); Gossip; Tigerland; Phone Booth; Bad Company; Veronica Guerin, 2003; The Phantom of the Opera, 2004; The Number 23, 2007; Town Creek, 2008. Publications: (screenplays) Sparkle; Car Wash; The Wiz. Address: Joel Schumacher Productions, 400 Warner Boulevard, Burbank, CA 91522, USA.

SCHUMACHER Michael, b. 3 January 1969. Motor Racing Driver. m. Corinna Betsch, 1995, 2 children. Appointments: Began Professional Career, 1983; 2nd Place, International German Formula 3 Championship, 1989; Driver for Mercedes, 1990; International German Champion Formula 3 Championship, 1990; European Formula 3 Champion, 1990; World Champion, Formula 3, Macau and Fiji, 1990; Formula 1 Contestant, 1991-; 1st Formula One Victory, Belgium, 1992; Other Grand Prix wins: Argentina, 1998, American, 2000, Australian, 2000, 2001, 2002, 2004, Austrian, 2002, 2003, Bahrain, 2004, Belgium, 1992, 1995, 1996, 1997, 2001, 2002, 2004, Brazil, 1994, 1995, 2000, 2002, Britain, 1998, 2002, 2004, Canadian, 1994, 1998, 2000, 2002, 2003, 2004, European, 1994, 1995, 2000, 2001, 2004, French, 1994, 1997, 1998, 2001, 2002, 2004, Germany, 1995, 2002, 2004, Hungarian, 1994, 1998, 2001, 2004, Italian, 1996, 1998, 2000, 2003, Japanese, 1995, 1997, 2000, 2001, 2002, 2004, Malaysian, 2000, 2001, 2004, Monaco, 1994, 1995, 1999, 2001, Pacific, 1994, 1995, Portuguese, 1993, San Marino, 1994, 2000, 2002, 2003, 2004, Spanish, 1995, 2001, 2002, 2003, 2004, USA, 2000, 2003, 2004; Third Place, World Motor Racing Championship, 1992, Fourth Place, 1993; Formula One World Champion, 1994, 1995, 2000, 2001, 2002, 2003, 2004. Retired, 2006; Ferrari's advisor and Jean Todt's assistant. 2007. Ambassador for UNESCO. Publication: Formula for Success (with Derick Allsop), 1996; Michael Schumacher (biography with Christopher Hilton), 2000. Address: c/o Weber Management GmbH, 70173 Stuttgart, Hirschstrasse 36, Germany. Website: www.mschumacher.com

SCHUNK Werner (Walter), b. 12 January 1938, Sundhausen/ Gotha, Germany. Doctor; University Teacher. m. Christine Margarete Seyfert, 1 daughter. Education: Study of Medicine, Humboldt University, Berlin and Medical Academy in Erfurt; Doctor of Medicine, 1963; Dr Habilitatus, University of Halle, 1974; Specialist in Occupational Medicine. Appointments:

Chief Doctor, Company Outpatients Department Gotha, 1968-72; Director of Occupational Medicine, 1972-92, Professor of Medicine, 1976, Pro-Rector, 1976-81 Medical Academy of Erfurt; Director of Institute of Science (Private), 1992-; Private Practice; Specialist in Toxicology and Internal Medicine; Research work in Medical Schools including: London, Birmingham, Paris, Karolinska Institute, Stockholm. Publications: Author: Schadstoffe in der Gummiindustrie, 1995, 1996, 1998, 2000; Arbeits und Gewerhetoxikologie, 1997, 1998, 1999, 2000, 2004; Eco-med edition: Stoffkataster für das Backgewerbe, 2002, 2003, 2004, CD and book, 2005; 65 patents in the field of biomaterials: new polymers and your toxicology. Honours: Title: Medizinalrat; Science Prize of Academy in Germany, 1978, 1983. Membership: Gesellschaft of Arbeits und Unweltmedizin. Address: Gallettistrasse 2, 99867 Gotha/Thür. Germany. E-mail: werner.schunk@web.de Website: www.werner-schunk.de

SCHUPP Ronald Irving, b. 10 December 1951, Syracuse, New York, USA. Civil and Human Rights Leader; Retired Clergyman. Education: Ordained Ministry, The Old Country Church, 1972; Ordained Baptist Ministry, 1976; Certificates, Moody Bible Institute, 1986, 1988; Advanced Certificate, Evangelical Training Association, 1992; Certificates, Emmaus Bible College, 1996, 1997; Certificate, Centre for Biblical Counseling, 2001; Certificates, Henry George School of Social Science, Chicago, Illinois, 2002, 2003; Certificate, Radio Emergency Associated Communications Teams International, 2003. Appointments: Missionary, Assistant Pastor, 1972-76, The Old Country Church, Chicago; Nite Pastor, Chicago, 1972-78; Southern Culture Exchange Center, 1973-76; Assistant Director, Uptown Community Organisation, Chicago, 1974-76; Alternative Christian Training School, Chicago, 1974-78; Chicago Area Conference on Hunger and Malnutrition, 1974-78; Field Organiser and Staff Person, The Great American Coffeehouse, Chicago, 1976-78; Missionary, Solid Rock Baptist Church, Chicago, 1976-89; Director, Chicago Action Centre, 1978-80; Chicago Clergy and Laity Concerned, 1981-87; Representative, Chicago Welfare Rights Organization, 1986-88; Missionary, Marble Rock Missionary Baptist Church, Chicago, 1990-2007. Publications: Contributor of songs and poems to periodicals. Honours: Recipient, Letter of Commendation, Chicago Fire Department, 1983; Appreciation Award, People United to Serve Humanity, 1990; Appreciation Award, West Englewood United Organisation/ Clara's House Shelter, Chicago, 1992; Recipient of Support Statements from Coretta Scott King (1992), Nelson Mandela (1993), Archbishop Desmond Tutu (1993), 14th Dalai Lama, The Gandhi Foundation and Cesar Chaves; Named Wa-Kin-Ya-Wicha-Ho Thunder Voice by Traditional Lakota Elders, 1993; Named Kiyuyakki Northern Lights by Inuit Elder Etok, 1994; Appreciation Award, Nuclear Energy Information Service, 2000; Numerous proclamations, resolutions and congressional record statements. Memberships: Founding Member, National Campaign for Tolerance, 2000; American Association of Christian Counselors, 2001-; American Indian Center, Chicago, 2004-07; Life Member: American Association of Retired Persons; The National Association for the Advancement of Colored People; The Southern Christian Leadership Conference. Address: 4541 North Sheridan Road, Apartment 409, Chicago, Illinois 60640, USA.

SCHWABIK Stefan, b. 15 March 1941, Gelnica, Slovakia. Mathematician. m. Ludmila Vodičková, 1 son, 1 daughter. Education: RNDR, Charles University, 1968; PhD, Academy of Science, Prague, 1977; DRSC, Academy of Science, Prague, 1990; Full Professor, Czech Republic, 2000. Appointments: Senior Researcher, 1964-2008, Emeritus, 2008-, Academy of Science, Czech Republic, Institute of Mathematics. Publications: Differential and Integral Equations, 1979; Generalized Ordinary Differential Equations, 1992; Topic in Banach Space Integration, 2005; Over 70 scientific papers. Honours: Prize, Academy of Science, Czechoslovakia, 1987; Honorary Member, Union of Czech Mathematicians and Physicists. Memberships: European Mathematical Society; American Mathematical Society; Union of Czech Mathematicians and Physicists. Address: Batelovska 1207/7, Praha 4, Czech Republic. E-mail: schwabik@math.cas.cz Website: www.math.cas.cz/~schwabik

SCHWARZ Berthold Eric, b. 20 October 1924, Jersey City, USA. Physician. m. 22 January 1955, 1 son, 1 daughter. Education: AB, Dartmouth College, 1945; Certificate, Dartmouth Medical School, 1945; MD, New York University College of Medicine, 1950; MS, Mayo Graduate School of Medicine, 1957. Appointments: Intern, Mary Hitchcock Memorial Hospital, Hanover, New Hampshire, 1950-51; Fellowship, Psychiatry, Mayo Foundation, Rochester, Minnesota, 1951-55; Private Practice, Montclair, New Jersey, 1955-82; Consultant, Essex County Medical Centre, Cedar Grove, New Jersey, 1965-82; Private Practice, Vero Beach, Florida, 1982-2001; Research into parapsychiatry and ufology, 2001-. Publications include: Co-author, with B A Ruggieri, Parent Child Tensions; You Can Raise Decent Children; Author: Psychic Dynamics; The Jacques Romano Story; Parent Child Telepathy; Psychic Nexus; UFO Dynamics; Into the Crystal; Psychiatric and Paranormal Aspects of Ufology; More than 175 articles. Honours: Listed in national and international biographical dictionaries. Memberships: American Medical Association; American Psychiatric Association; American Association for the Advancement of Science; American Society for Psychical Research; Parapsychlogical Association; Academy of Spirituality and Paranormal Studies. Address: 642 Azalea Lane, Vero Beach, FL 32963, USA. E-mail: ardisps@aol.com

SCHWARZENEGGER Arnold Alois, b. 30 July 1947, Graz, Austria (US citizen, 1963). Actor; Author; Businessman; Former Bodybuilder; US Governor of California. m. Maria Owings Shriver, 1985, 2 sons, 2 daughters. Education: University of Wisconsin-Superior. Appointment: Elected Governor of California, 2003. Career: Film appearances include: Stay Hungry, 1976; Pumping Iron, 1977; The Jayne Mansfield Story, 1980; Conan the Barbarian, 1982; The Destroyer, 1983; The Terminator, 1984; Commando, 1985; Raw Deal, 1986; Predator, 1987; Running Man, 1987; Red Heat, 1988; Twins, 1989; Total Recall, 1990; Kindergarten Cop, 1990; Terminator II, 1991; Last Action Hero, 1993; Dave (cameo), 1993; True Lies, 1994; Junior, 1994; Eraser, 1996; Single All the Way, 1996; Batman and Robin, 1997; With Wings with Eagles, 1997; End of Days, 1999; The Sixth Day, 2001; Collateral Damage, 2002; Terminator 3: Rise of the Machines, 2003; The Rundown, 2003; Around the World in 80 Days, 2004; The Kid & I, 2005. Publications: Arnold: The Education of a Bodybuilder, 1977; Arnold's Bodyshaping for Women, 1979; Arnold's Bodybuilding for Men, 1981; Arnold's Encyclopedia of Modern Bodybuilding, 1985; Arnold's Fitness for Kids (jointly), 1993. Honours: National Weight Training Coach Special Olympics; Bodybuilding Champion, 1965-80; Junior Mr Europe, 1965; Best Built Man of Europe, 1966; Mr Europe, 1966; Mr International, 1968; Mr Universe (amateur), 1969. Memberships: Volunteer, prison rehabilitation programmes; Chairman, President's Council on Physical Fitness and Sport, 1990. Address: PMK, Suite 200, 955 South Carillo Drive, Los Angeles, CA 90048, USA.

SCHWARZKOPF H Norman, 22 August 1934, Trenton, New Jersey, USA. Army Officer (retired). m. Brenda Holsinger, 1968, 1 son, 2 daughters. Education: Bordentown Military Institute; Valley Forge Military Academy; US Military Academy, West Point; MME, University of Southern California, 1964. Appointments: 2nd Lieutenant, Infantry & Airborne Training, Ft Benning, Georgia; 101st Airborne Division, Ft Campbell, Kentucky; Teacher, Military Academy, West Point, 1964, 1966-68; Task Force Advisor, South Vietnamese Airborne Division, 1965; Commander, 1st Battalion, 6th Infantry, 198th Infantry Brigade, Armored Division, 1969-73; Deputy Commander, 172nd Infantry Brigade, Ft Richardson, Arkansas, 1974-76; Commander, 1st Brigade, 9th Infantry Division, Ft Lewis, Washington, 1976-78; Deputy Director of Plans, US Pacific Commander, Camp Smith, Hawaii, 1978-80; Assistant Division Commander, 8th Mechanized Infantry Division, West Germany, 1980-82; Director, Military Personnel Management Office of Deputy Chief of Staff for Personnel, Washington DC, 1982-83; Commander, 24th Mechanized Infantry Division, Ft Stewart, Georgia, 1983-85; Commander, US Ground Forces & Deputy Chief for Operations & Plans, Washington DC, 1987-88. Publication: It Doesn't Take a Hero (autobiography with Peter Petre), 1992. Honours: DSM with Oak Leaf Cluster; DFC; Silver Star with 2 Oak Leaf Clusters; Bronze Star with 3 Oak Leaf Clusters; Purple Heart with Oak Leaf Cluster. Address: 40 West 57th Street, New York, NY 10019-4001, USA.

SCHWIMMER David, b. 12 November 1966, New York, USA. Actor; Writer; Director. Education: Beverly Hills High School; Northwestern University, Chicago. Career: Co-founder, Lookingglass Theater Co, Chicago, 1988; Actor: Theatre: West; The Odessey; Of One Blood; In the Eye of the Beholder; The Master and Margarita; Some Girl(s), 2005; Films: Flight of the Intruder, 1990; Crossing the Bridge, 1992; Twenty Bucks, 1993; The Waiter, 1993; Wolf, 1994; The Pallbearer, 1996; Shooting the Moon (executive producer), 1996; Apt Pupil, 1998; Kissing a Fool (executive producer), 1998; Six Days Seven Nights, 1998; The Thin Pink Line, 1998; All the Rage, 1999; Picking Up the Pieces, 2000; Hotel, 2001; Dogwater (also director); Duane Hopwood, 2005; Madagascar (voice), 2005; Big Nothing, 2006; TV: The Wonder Years, 1988; Monty, 1993; NYPD Blue, 1993; Friends, 1994-2004; LA Law; The Single Guy; Happy Birthday Elizabeth: A Celebration of Life, 1997; Breast Men, 1997; Since You've Been Gone, 1998; Band of Brothers, 2001; Uprising, 2001; Director: Theatre: The Jungle; The Serpent; Alice in Wonderland. Honours: Six Joseph Jefferson Awards. Memberships: Board of Directors, Rape Foundation for Rape Treatment Center of Santa Monica. Address: c/o The Gersh Agency, PO Box 5617, Beverly Hills, CA 90210, USA.

SCORSESE Martin, b. 17 November 1942, Flushing, New York, USA. Film Director; Writer. m. (1) Laraine Marie Brennan, 1965, 1 daughter. (2) Julia Cameron, divorced, 1 daughter. (3) Isabella Rossellini, 1979, divorced 1983. (4) Barbara DeFina, 1985. Education: New York University. Appointments: Faculty Assistant, Instructor, Film Department, New York University, 1963-66; Instructor, 1968-70; Director, Writer of Films, including: What's a Nice Girl Like You Doing in a Place Like This?, 1963; It's Not Just You, Murray, 1964; Who's That Knocking At My Door?, 1968; The Big Shave, 1968; Director, Play, The Act, 1977-78; Director, Writer of Documentaries; Supervisor Editor, Assistant Director, Woodstock, 1970; Associate Producer, Post-Production Supervisor, Medicine Ball Caravan, 1971, Box Car Bertha, 1972; Director, Films: Mean Streets, 1973; Alice Doesn't Live Here Any More, 1974; Taxi Driver, 1976; New York, New

York, 1977; King of Comedy, 1981; Actor, Director, The Last Waltz, 1978; Director, Raging Bull, 1980, After Hours, 1985, The Color of Money, 1986; Director, The Last Temptation of Christ, 1988, Goodfellas, 1989, Cape Fear, 1991, The Age of Innocence, 1993, Clockers, 1994, Casino, 1995; Kundun, 1997; Bringing Out the Dead, 1999; The Muse, 1999; The Gangs of New York, 2002; The Aviator, 2004; No Direction Home: Bob Dylan, 2005; Shine a Light, 2008; The Departed, 2006; Executive Producer, The Crew, 1989; Producer, The Grifters, 1989; Co-Producer, Mad Dog and Glory, 1993; Producer, Clockers, 1995; Executive Producer, You Can Count on Me, 2000; Executive Producer, Something to Believe in, 2004; Executive Producer, Lymelife, 2008; Producer, The Young Victoria, 2008. Publications: Scorsese on Scorsese, 1989; The Age of Innocence: The Shooting Script (with Jay Cocks), 1996; Casino (with Nicholas Pileggi), 1996; Kundun, 1997; Bringing Out the Dead, 1999; The Muse, 1999; Gangs of New York, 2002; The Aviator, 2004. Honours: Edward J Kingsley Foundation Award, 1963, 1964; 1st Prize, Rosenthal Foundation Awards of Society of Cinematologists, 1964; 1st Prize, Screen Producers Guild, 1965, Brown University Film Festival, 1965, Shared Rosellini Prize, 1990; Named Best Director, Cannes Film Festival, 1986; Courage in Filmmaking Award, Los Angeles Film Teachers Association, 1989; Award, American Museum of the Moving Image, 1996; Award for Preservation, International Federation of Film Wards, 2001; Golden Globe for Best Director, 2003; Oscar, Best Director, The Departed, 2006. Address: c/o United Artists, 10202 West Washington Blvd, Culver City, CA 90230, USA.

SCOTT James, (Dr) b. 8 December 1954, Croxdale Hall, Croxdale, Durham, England. Cleric. Education: New College, Durham, 1971-75; Certificate, 1993, Diploma, 1994, Christian Studies, Westminster College, Oxford; BA, Theology, 1999, MA, Theology (Dogma and Church History), 2002; Greenwich School of Theology; Doctor of Letters (Church Ministry), Trinity College, 1998; PhD, Theology (Dogma and Church History), Greenwich School of Theology, 2006. Appointments: Durham County Treasury, 1973-76; Novitiate, Third Order of Franciscans (Church of England), 1976; Scargill House Community, 1977-79; Life Profession, Third Order of Franciscans (Church of England), 1979; Personal Assistant to the Prior of GCA, 1979; Disabled due to the effects of a spinal cord tumour, 1978-; Pastoral Assistant, Church of England, 1980-93; Received into the Catholic Church and Life Profession, transferred to Roman Catholic Franciscan Third Order, 1993; Personal Tutor, Greenwich School of Theology, 2002-; Personal Mentor for students at Brookes, Oxford and Westminster, Oxford, 2005-. Publications: The Problem of Evil for the Religious Believer (monograph), 1997; The Meaning of the Concept of Covenant in the Holy Scriptures (BA thesis), 1998; The Life of St Francis of Assisi: Is Franciscanism Relevant Today? (MA thesis), An Evaluation of the Doctrine of Miraculous Healing, Within the Roman Catholic Tradition (PhD thesis), 2006. Honours: Serving Brother, Order of St John, 1986; Mensa Certificate of Merit, 1995; Knight of St Columba, 1995; Officer, Order of St John, 1996; Awarded Richardson Salver for exceptional service to the community in the face of great personal adversity, St John Ambulance, 1998. Memberships: St John Ambulance, 1971-2001: Divisional President, 1987-93, Area Vice-President, 1993-96, Northumbria County Vice-President, 1996-2001; Knights of St Columba, 1995-: Deputy Grand Knight, Council 549, 1996, Grand Knight, Council 549, 1997-99, Northumbrian Provincial Action Convenor, 1995, Deputy Grand Knight, Council 142, 2001-2004; Alumni:

Westminster College, Oxford, 1994-, Greenwich School of Theology, 1998-, Brookes, Oxford, 2001-. Address: Wear Lodge, Manor Lane, Aisthorpe, Lincoln, LN1 2SG, England.

SCOTT Paul Henderson, b. 7 November 1920, Edinburgh, Scotland. Essayist; Historian; Critic; Former Diplomat. Education: MA, MLitt, University of Edinburgh. Publications: 1707: The Union of Scotland and England, 1979; Walter Scott and Scotland, 1981; John Galt, 1985; Towards Independence: Essays on Scotland, 1991; Scotland in Europe, 1992; Andrew Fletcher and the Treaty of Union, 1992; Scotland: A Concise Cultural History (editor), 1993; Defoe in Edinburgh, 1994; Scotland: An Unwon Cause, 1997; Still in Bed with an Elephant, 1998; The Boasted Advantages, 1999; A Twentieth Century Life, 2002; Scotland Resurgent, 2003; The Union of 1707: Why and How, 2006; The Age of Liberation, 2007. Contributions to: Newspapers and journals. Honours: Andrew Fletcher Award, 1993; Oliver Brown Award, 2000. Memberships: International PEN, former president, Scottish Centre; Saltire Society; Association for Scottish Literary Studies; Scottish National Party. Address: 33 Drumsheugh Gardens, Edinburgh EH3 7RN, Scotland.

SCOTT Philip John, b. 26 June 1931, Auckland, New Zealand. Medicine; Medical Science. m. (1) Elizabeth Jane MacMillan, deceased 2001, 1 son, 3 daughters, (2) Margaret Fernie Wann, deceased 2007. Education: B Med, Science, 1952, MB ChB, 1955, University of Otago, New Zealand; MD (DM), University of Birmingham, England, 1962. Appointments: Resident/Registrar posts, Auckland, New Zealand, 1956-58, London and Birmingham, England, 1959-62; Research Fellow, University of Birmingham, 1961-62; Research Fellow, Auckland, New Zealand, 1962-69; Senior Lecturer, University of Otago, 1969-72; Honorary Senior Lecturer, University of Auckland, 1970-72; Associate Professor of Medicine, 1972-75, Professor of Medicine, Personal Chair, 1975-96, Emeritus Professor, 1996-, University of Auckland; Head, Department of Medicine, Auckland, 1994-97; Head, Department of Clinical Sciences, South Auckland, 1993-97. Publications: Over 200 papers and articles in professional journals. Honours: Fellow, 1987-, President, 1998-2008, Royal Society of New Zealand; President, New Zealand Medical Association, 1998-99; College Medal, RACP, 1992; Knight Commander of the British Empire (KBE), 1987. Memberships: Medical Research Society, London, -1988; Cardiac Society of Australia; Nutrition Society of New Zealand; International Physicians for Prevention of Nuclear War; Australia & New Zealand Society of History of Medicine. Address: 64 Temple St, Meadowbank, Auckland 1072, New Zealand.

SCOTT Sir Ridley, b. 30 November 1937, South Shields, England. Film Director. Education: Royal College of Art. Career: Director, numerous award-winning TV commercials, 1970-; Début as feature film director with The Duellists, 1978; Other films include: Alien, 1979; Blade Runner, 1982; Legend, 1985; Someone to Watch Over Me, 1987; Black Rain, 1989; Thelma and Louise, 1991; 1492: Conquest of Paradise, 1992; Monkey Trouble, 1994; The Browning Version, 1994; White Squall, 1996; G I Jane, 1997; Clay Pigeons, 1998; Where the Money Is, 2000; Gladiator, 2000; Hannibal, 2001; Black Hawk Down, 2001; Six Bullets from Now, 2002; The Hire: Hostage, 2002; The Hire: Beat the Devil, 2002; The Hire: Ticker, 2002; Matchstick Men, 2003; Kingdom of Heaven, 2005; In Her Shoes, 2005; Domino, 2005; Tristan & Isolde, 2006; TV: Z Cars, 1962; The Troubleshooters, 1965; Adam Adamant Lives! 1966; The Informer, 1966; Robert, 1967; The Hunger, 1997; RKO 281, 1999; The Last Debate, 2000; AFP: American Fighter Pilot, 2002; The Gathering Storm, 2002;

Numb3rs, 2005; Tristan & Isolde, 2006; A Good year, 2006; Law Dogs, 2007; The Company, 2007; The Assassination of Jesse James by the Coward Robert Ford, 2007; Churchill at War, 2008. Honour: Honorary D Litt, Sunderland; Academy Award, Best Motion Picture, 2000; TV Emmy for Best Made-for-TV Film, 2002. Address: William Morris Agency, One William Morris Place, Beverly Hills, CA 90212, USA. Website: www.wma.com

SCOTT Tony, b. 21 June 1944, Newcastle upon Tyne, England. Film Director. Education: Sunderland College of Art; Leeds College of Art; Royal College of Art Film and TV Department. Career: Assistant Director, Dream Weaver, 1967; The Movement Movement, 1967; Cameraman: The Visit; Untitled; Compromise; Milian; Fat Man; Worked for Derrick Knight & Alan King Associates; Visual Director and Cameraman, pop promotional films, Now Films Ltd; TV cameraman, Seven Sisters, 1968; Co-producer, actor, Don't Walk; Assistant Director, Gulliver; Writer, Director, Editor, Loving Memory, 1969-70; Visual Director, Cameraman, publicity film for Joe Egg; Director, One of the Missing, 1989; Other films include: Revenge; Top Gun; Beverly Hills Cop II; Days of Thunder; The Last Boy Scout; True Romance; Crimson Tide; The Fan; Enemy of the State; Spy Game; Man on Fire; Domino; Déjà vu; Tristan & Isolde; Churchill at War; Director, Scott Free Enterprises Ltd; Director, TV and cinema commercials for Ridley Scott and Associates. Honours: Grand Prix, Mar del Plata Festival, Argentina; Prix de la TV Suisse, Nyon; 2nd Prize, Esquire Film Festival, USA; Diploma of Merit, Melbourne. Address: Totem Productions, 8009 Santa Monica Boulevard, Los Angeles, CA 90046, USA.

SCOTT-THOMAS Kristin, b. Redruth, England. Actress. m. François Oliviennes, 1 son, 1 daughter. Education: Central School of Speech and Drama; Ecole National des Arts et Technique de Théâtre, Paris. Career: Resident in France from age of 18; Stage appearances include: La Terre Etrangère; Naive Hirondelles and Yves Peut-Etre; Appearances on TV in France, Germany, Australia, USA, Britain include: L'Ami d'Enfance de Maigret; Blockhaus; Chameleon La Tricheuse; Sentimental Journey; The Tenth Man; Endless Game; Framed; Titmuss Regained; Look at it This Way; Body and Soul; Actress in films: Djamel et Juliette; L'Agent Troubé; La Méridienne; Under the Cherry Moon; A Handful of Dust; Force Majeure; Bille en tête; The Bachelor; Bitter Moon; Four Weddings and a Funeral; Angels and Insects; Richard III; The English Patient; Amour et Confusions; The Horse Whisperer; Random Hearts; Up at the Villa; Gosford Park; Life As a House; Petites Coupures, 2003; Résistantes, 2004; The Three Ages of the Crime, 2004; Arsène Lupin, 2004; Man to Man, 2005 Chromophobia, 2005; Kepping Mum, 2005; La Doublure, 2006; Ne le dis à personne, 2006; Mauvaise pente, 2007; The Walker, 2007; The Other Boleyn Girl, 2008; Il y a longtemps que je t'aime, 2008. Honours include: BAFTA Award; Evening Stand Film Award; Chevalier, Legion d'honneur, 2005. Address: c/o PMK 85600 Wilshire Blvd, #700, Beverly Hills, CA 90211-3105, USA.

SCOWCROFT Philip Lloyd, b. 8 June 1933, Sheffield, England. Retired Solicitor. m (Elsie) Mary Robinson, deceased, 2 daughters. Education: MA, LLM Cantab., Trinity Hall, Cambridge, 1953-56; Admitted Solicitor, 1959. Appointments: Solicitor to successive Doncaster Local Authorities, 1959-93; Retired 1993. Publications include: Cricket in Doncaster and District, 1985; Lines to Doncaster, 1986; Singing for Pleasure: A Centenary History of Doncaster Choral Society, 1988; British Light Music, 1997; Railways in British Crime Fiction, 2004; Numerous articles on music, transport, crime fiction, military history and sport for many different periodical publications and for Grove's Dictionary, 2001 edition and various Oxford Companions. Memberships: Many societies to do with music, transport, crime fiction, military history and sport including: Committee member: Spohr Society of Great Britain, Railway and Canal Historical Society, Dorothy L Sayers Society; Chairman, Doncaster Arts and Museum Society, 1968-; Chairman, William Appleby Trust Awards; President, Doncaster Choral Society, 1992-; President, Railway and Canal Historical Society, 2008-10. Address: 8 Rowan Mount, Doncaster DN2 5PJ, England.

SCUDAMORE Jeremy Paul, b. 27 April 1947, Bristol, England. Company Director. m. Ruth, 1 son, 1 daughter. Education: Birkenhead School; BA (Hons), Nottingham University; INSEAD. Appointments: ICI Group, 1971-84; Division General Manager, ICI Brazil, Sao Paulo, 1984-88; Various General Manager jobs in ICI and Zeneca, 1988-94; Managing Director, Zeneca Seeds, Business Director, Zeneca Agrochemicals, and Zeneca Group Regional Executive, Eastern Europe, 1994-97; Chief Executive Officer, Zeneca Specialties, Chairman of Zeneca Manufacturing Partnership, 1997-99; Chief Executive Officer, 1999-2005, Chairman and Chief Executive Officer, 2005-06, Avecia Group.

SCUDAMORE Peter, b. 13 June 1958, Hereford, England. Jockey. m. Marilyn, 1980, 2 sons. Career: Former point-to-point and amateur jockey; Estate agency; Professional National Hunt Jockey, 1979-93; 1,677 winners; 7 times champion National Hunt Jockey, record 221 winners, 1988-89; Retired as Jockey, 1993; Director, Chasing Promotions, 1989-; Racing Journalist, Daily Mail, 1993-; Partner with Trainer Nigel Twiston-Davis. Publications: A Share of Success (co-author), 1983; Scudamore on Steeplechasing (co-author); Scu: The Autobiography of a Champion, 1993. Membership: Joint President, Jockeys Association.

SEAGAL Steven, b. 10 April 1951, Lansing, Michigan, USA. Actor; Martial Arts Expert. m. (1) Miyako Fujitoni, 1 son, 1 daughter, (2) Kelly Le Brock, 1 son, 2 daughters. Career: Established martial arts academies (dojo) in Japan and LA; Chief Executive Officer, Steamroller Productions; Actor in films: Above the Law, 1988; Hard to Kill, Marked for Death, 1990; Out for Justice; Under Siege/On Deadly Ground, 1994; Under Seige 2, 1995; The Glimmer Man; Executive Decision; Fire Down Below; The Patriot (also producer), 1998; Ticker, Exit Wounds, 2001; Half Past Dead, 2002; The Foreigner, Out for a Kill, Belly of the Beast, 2003; Clementine, Out of Reach, 2004; Into the Sun, Today You Die, Black Dawn, 2005; Shadow Man, Attack Force, 2006; Flight of Fury, Urban Justice, The Onion Movie, 2007; Pistol Whipped, 2008. Address: c/o ICM, 8942 Wilshire Blvd, Beverly Hills, CA 90211-1934, USA. Website: www.stevenseagal.com

SEAGER (OLSON-STOKES) Dauna Gayle, b. 22 September 1925, Logan, Cache Co, Utah, USA. Audiologist; Speech Pathologist. m. (1) Arch J Stokes, deceased 1970, 2 sons, 1 daughter, (2) Floyd W Seager, deceased 1996. Education: AS, Weber State University, 1964; BS, Utah State University, 1968; MS, Utah State University, 1969. Appointments: Clinic Supervisor, USU Speech/Hearing Clinic, 1966-69; Speech Pathologist, Weber County Schools and Davis County Schools, 1969-71; Speech Pathologist, St Benedict's Hospital, 1970; Homecare, St Benedict's and Mokay-Dee Hospitals, 1970-96. Publications: Articles in newspapers and magazines including 150 Years of Ogden, a sesquicentennial book of Ogden's history. Honours: Ogden Business and Professional Women's Woman of the Achievement Award, 1982; Ogden

Business and Professional Women's Woman of the Year, 1984; Utah Governor's Silver Bowl Award, 1990; President George Bush's Point of Light Award, 1990; Utah State Paint of Light #101, 2003; Book of Golden Deeds award, Ogden Chapter of National Exchange Club. Memberships: Ogden Business and Professional Women's Organisation; Altrusa International; Daughters of Utah Pioneers; Daughters of the American Revolution; Womanise Legislative Council; Weber County Republican Women; Aglaia Charitable Club; Child Culture Club. Address: 4046 South 895 East, Ogden, Utah 84403-2416, USA.

SEAGROVE Jennifer (Jenny) Ann, b. Kuala Lumpur, Malaysia. Actress. Education: Bristol Old Vic Theatre School. Career: Theatre includes: Title role in Jane Eyre, Chichester Festival Theatre; Ilona in the Guardsman, Theatr Clwyd; Bett in King Lear in New York, Chichester Festival Theatre; Opposite Tom Conti in Present Laughter in the West End; Annie Sullivan in The Miracle Worker, UK tour and West End; Dead Guilty with Hayley Mills by Richard Harris, on tour and West End; The Dark Side, Thorndike Theatre, Leatherhead and on tour; Canaries Sometime Sing, Vertigo and Dead Certain, Theatre Royal, Windsor; Gertrude in Hamlet, Ludlow; Brief Encounter at the Apollo; The Female Odd Couple, Windsor and West End; Title role in The Constant Wife, Lyric Theatre, Shaftesbury Avenue; David Hare's The Secret Rapture, Lyric Theatre, Shaftesbury Avenue. Television includes: Emma Harte in A Woman of Substance; Paula in Hold the Dream; The title roles in Diana and Lucy Walker; Laura Fairlie in The Woman in White; The heroines of The Hitch-Hiker Killer and In Like Flynn; Leading roles in The Betrothed with Burt Lancaster, Magic Moments, Some Other Spring, The Eye of the Beholder, Incident at Victoria Falls, Deadly Games; Judge John Deed, 2001-. Films: To Hell and Back in Time for Breakfast; A Shocking Incident (Oscar for Best Film); Tattoo; Moonlighting; Sherlock Holmes' The Sign of Four; Savage Islands; Local Hero; Appointment with Death; A Chorus of Disapproval; The Guardian; Miss Beatty's Children; Don't Go Breaking My Heart; Zoe. Honour: The Michael Eliott Fellowship Award, 2004. Memberships: Equity; SAG. Address: c/o ICM, Oxford House, 76 Oxford Street, London W1N 0AX, England.

SEARLE Ronald, b. 3 March 1920, Cambridge, England. Artist; Writer. m. (1) Kaye Webb, divorced 1967, deceased 1996, 1 son, 1 daughter, (2) Monica Koenig, 1967. Education: Central School, Cambridge; Cambridge School of Art, 1939. Career: First drawings published 1935-39; Served with Royal Engineers, 1939-46; Prisoner-of-war in Japanese camps, 1942-45; Contributor to national publications, 1946; Member, Punch 'Table', 1956; Special Features Artist, Life magazine, 1955, Holiday, 1957, The New Yorker, 1966-, Le Monde, 1995-; Designer of medals for the French Mint, 1974-, British Art Medal Society, 1983-; Work represented in Victoria and Albert Museum, Imperial War Museum and British Museum (London), Bibliotheque Nationale, Paris and several German and American museums; Designer of several films; Exhibitions of work in UK, USA and Europe. Publications: Forty Drawings, 1946; Le Nouveau Ballet Anglais, 1947; Hurrah for St Trinian's, 1948; The Female Approach, 1949; Back to the Slaughterhouse, 1951; Souls in Torment, 1953; Rake's Progress, 1955; Merry England, 1956; Which Way Did He Go?, 1961; Searle in the Sixties, 1965; From Frozen North to Filthy Louvre, 1964; Pardong M'sieur, 1965; Searle' Cats, 1969; Hommage à Toulouse Lautrec, 1969; Secret Sketchbook, 1970; The Addict, 1971; More Cats, 1975; Drawings From Gilbert and Sullivan, 1975; The Zoodiac, 1977; Ronald Searle, 1978; The King of Beasts,

DICTIONARY OF INTERNATIONAL BIOGRAPHY

1980; The Big Fat Cat Book, 1982; Winespeak, 1983; Ronald Searle in Perspective, 1984; Ronald Searle's Golden Oldies, 1985; To the Kwai - and Back, 1986; Something in the Cellar, 1986. Ah Yes I Remember it Well: Paris 1961-1975, 1987; The Non-Sexist Dictionary, 1988; Slightly Foxed - but still desirable, 1989; The Curse of St Trinian's, 1993; Marquis de Sade meets Goody Two Shoes, 1994; Ronald Searle dans le Monde, 1998. Honour: Royal Designer for Industry, 1988; Several film festival awards; LA Art Directors' Club Medal, 1959; Philadelphia Art Directors' Club Medal, 1959; National Cartoonists' Society Award, 1959, 1960; Gold Medal, III Biennale, Tolentino, Italy, 1965; Prix de la Critique Belge, 1968; Grand Prix de l'Humour noir, France, 1971; Prix d'Humour, Festival d'Avignon, 1971; Medal of French Circus, 1971; Prix International 'Charles Huard', 1972; La Monnaie de Paris Medal, 1974; Bundesrechtsanwaltskammer Award, Germany, 1998. Address: The Sayle Literary Agency, Bickerton House, 25-27 Bickerton Road, London N19 5JT, England. Website: www.sayleliteraryagency.com

SEBASTIAN Phylis Sue (Ingram), b. 24 January 1945, Childersburg, Alabama, USA. Real Estate Broker; Real Estate Appraiser; Fine Art Appraiser. m. (1) Robert E Martin, 1965, divorced 1978, 2 sons, 2 daughters, (2) Thomas Haskell Sebastian III, 1985, 1 stepson, 3 stepdaughters. Education: BS, Accounting and Business Administration, 1988; Real Estate Broker, Career Education Systems, 1988; Real Estate Appraisal Certificate, PREA, CIMA, International College of Real Estate Appraisal, Nashville, Tennessee; Computer Specialist, 1999. Appointments: Hostess, radio show, St Louis, Missouri, 1970s; Numerous feature articles published in St Louis Globe Democrat and Post Dispatch Newspapers, 1970s; Owner, Astrology Consultants, 1970-2003; Licensed Real Estate Broker, Owner, Broker Phylis Sebastian Real Estate, Farmington, Missouri, 1989-2003; US Auto Sales, Park Hills, Missouri, 1993-97; Owner, Business & Legal Services, Park Hills, 1993-2003; Partner La Femme Fine Antique Auction Service, Ironton, Missouri, Arcadia Valley Auction Co Inc, 1997-2003; Ordained minister, Progressive Universal Life Church, 2002; Numerous appearances on TV, St Louis. Publications: 5 books including: Marriages in Madison County Missouri for 1848-1868, 1998; 1910 Census for Madison County Missouri, 1998; Published poet; Many articles in various newspapers. Memberships: 1st Treasurer, Co-founder, Astrological Association of St Louis, 1976-77; Co-founder, Missouri Mental Health Consumer Network, Mineral Area Chapter, 1989-93; Member, National Gardening Club; Library of Congress; Smithsonian; National Historic Society; Founder, Genealogy Society of Madison County Missouri. Address: Arcadia Valley Auction Co Inc & Real Estate, 315 West Russell Street, Ironton, Missouri 63650-1316, USA. E-mail: phylis@phylissebastian.com

SEDAGHATIAN Mohamad Reza, b. 11 February 1938, Shiraz, Iran. Consultant Neonatologist. m. Nezhat Khalili, 3 sons, 1 daughter. Education: MD, Shiraz medical School, Iran, 1964; American Board of Pediatrics, USA, 1972; American Sub-Board of Neonatal and Perinatal Medicine, 1991, 1998, 2005. Appointments: Professor of Paediatrics, Shiraz Medical School, Shiraz, Iran, 1973-84; Senior Consultant, Head, Neonatal Department, 1985-, Acting Medical Director, 2003, Deputy Medical Director, 2003, Chairman, Department of Paediatrics, 2005, Mafraq Hospital, Abu Dhabi, United Arab Emirates; Professor of Paediatrics, Gulf Medical College, 2005. Publications: More than 40 articles in different medical journals. Honour: Physician Recognition Award, American Medical Association, 1998-2000. Membership: President, Emirates Perinatal Society; President, Emirates Neonatal

Society; Emirate Medical Association; American Academy of Pediatrics; American Academy of Perinatal Medicine. Address: PO Box 2851, Abu Dhabi, United Arab Emirates. E-mail: reza@sedaghatian.net

SEDAKA Neil, b. 13 March 1939. Singer; Songwriter. m. Leba Margaret Strassberg, 11 September 1962, 1 son, 1 daughter. Musical Education: Graduate, Juilliard School of Music. Career: Solo performer, worldwide, 1959-; Television appearances include: NBC-TV Special, 1976. Compositions include: Breaking Up Is Hard To Do; Stupid Cupid; Calendar Girl; Oh! Carol; Stairway To Heaven; Happy Birthday Sweet Sixteen; Laughter In The Rain; Bad Blood; Love Will Keep Us Together; Solitaire; The Hungry Years; Lonely Night (Angel Face). Recordings: Albums include: In The Pocket; Sedaka's Back; The Hungry Years; Steppin' Out; A Song; All You Need Is The Music; Come See About Me; Greatest Hits, 1988; Oh! Carol And Other Hits, 1990; Timeless, 1992; Calendar Girl, 1993; Tuneweaver, 1995; The Immaculate, 1997; Tales Of Love, 1999; The Singer and His Songs, 2000; The Very Best of Neil Sedaka: The Show Goes On, 2006; The Miracle of Christmas, 2006; Neil Sedaka: The Definitive Collection, 2007. Honours: Songwriters' Hall Of Fame, 1980; Platinum album, Timeless, 1992; Numerous Gold records; Various industry awards. Memberships: AGVA; AFofM; AFTRA. Address: c/o Neil Sedaka Music, 201 East 66th Street, Suite 3N, New York, NY 10021, USA.

SEDEJ Maksim Jr, b. 6 November 1935, Ljubljana, Slovenia. Painter. m. Anka. Education: Basic art education with Professor Maksim Sedej Sr. Appointments: Status of Artist, Nacional Art Commission, 1964; Chairman, Oder 57 theatre, 1964-65; Secretary, Slovenian Professional Association of the Fine Arts, 1968-72; Chairman, Professional Association of Fine Artists, Ljubljana, 1985-88; Founder and Editor, Likovne Besede (professional periodical for fine artists), 1986-89. Publication: The Four Faces of the Soul, 2000. Honours: Redemption Award, Grado, Italy, 1968; Župancic Award, 1989; Grand Prix, II Biennale Middle European Art, Sežana, 1993; National Reconciliation in Slovenia award, Slovenian Cardinal Msg Dr Franc Rode, 2004. Membership: Slovenian Artists Society, Ljubljana, Slovenia. Address: Rožna Dolina C II/22, 1000 Ljubljana, Republic of Slovenia.

SEFERTA Joseph, b. 18 November 1938, Baghdad, Iraq. Retired Teacher. m. Widad, 1 son, 2 daughters. Education: BA, 1962, MA, Philosophy, 1963, BD, 1968, Boston College, USA; MA, Islamic Studies, American University of Beirut, Lebanon, 1970; PhD, Comparative Religion, Birmingham University, England, 1984. Appointments: Teacher of Religion, English & Mathematics, Baghdad High School, Iraq, 1963-66; Teacher, Arabic & English, various language institutes, 1970-72; Teacher of Religion, St Thomas of Canterbury Secondary, Birmingham, 1972-75; Head of RE Department, 1975-93; Senior Teacher, 1993-98, St Edmond Campion, Birmingham Comprehensive. Publications: Numerous articles in academic and popular journals. Honours: Teacher of the Year Award, 1997. Memberships: Birmingham Council of Faiths; Archdiocesan Commission for Inter-Religious Dialogue; Birmingham Catholic Inter-Faith Network. Address: 4 Turchill Drive, Walmley, Sutton Coldfield, West Midlands B76 1YQ, England. E-mail: joeseferta@hotmail.com

SEHERR-THOSS Hans Christoph, b. 13 October 1918, Potsdam, Nr Berlin, Germany. Mechanical Engineer; Historian; Biographer. m. Therese Kunath. Appointments: Design Work, ZF Friedrichshafen, 1947-49; Librarian, German Automobile Club, 1954-83; Vice President, FIA

- 947 -

Historical Commission, 1983-98; Consulting Engineer; Registrar; Author, Independence, 1984-. Publications: Die Entwicklung der Zahnradtechnik, 1965; Die deutsche Automobilindustrie, 1974, 1979; FIA - Automobile World Records, 1988; Oldtimer, 1965; 75 Years ADAC, 1978; FIA, Dictionary of Famous Personalities in the Automobile World, 2000, 2002; Co-author: Sport – Ueberblick, 1951; Forum der Technik, 1966; 50 Years of BMW, 1966, 1972; 170 Biographies in NDB; Raederwerk, 1989; Yearbook Presse u Sport, 1958; H Buessing, 1986; MAN Nutzfahrzeugbau, 1991; Universal Joints and Driveshafts, 1992, 2006; Editor: Zwei Maenner – ein Stern, 1984. Memberships: German Units: ADAC; German Archivists Association (VdW); FIA Historical Commission, 1983-, Chairman Personalities, 1988-2007. Address: Habichtstrasse 39, Unterhaching, 82008, Germany.

SEINFELD Jerry, b. 29 April 1955, Brooklyn, USA. Comedian. m. Jessica Sklar, 1999, 2 sons, 1 daughter. Education: Queens College, New York. Career: Former Salesman; Stand-up Comedian, 1976-; Joke-writer, Benson (TV series), 1980; Actor, Seinfeld (TV series), 1989-97, also co-writer, producer; The Ratings Game, film, 1984; The Seinfeld Chronicles, 1990; I'm Telling You for the Last Time, 1999; Co-writer and Voice, Bee Movie, 2007. Publication: Sein Language, 1993. Honours: 2 American Comedy Awards; Emmy Award for Outstanding Comedy Series (Seinfeld), 1993. Address: c/o Lori Jonas Public Relations, 417 South Beverly Drive, Suite 201, Beverly Hills, CA 90212, USA.

SEK Danuta, b. 8 December 1935, Katowice, Poland. Chemist; Scientist. m. Mieczyslaw Sek, 1 son. Education: MS, 1958; PhD, 1967; DSc, 1983; Professor, 1999. Appointments: Head of Laboratory, Cefarm, Katowice, 1958-64; Assistant, Technical University, Gliwice, 1964-67; Head of Laboratory, 1967-74, Deputy Director, 1974-1998, Director, 1998-2002, Head of Department, 2002-, Institute of Polymer Chemistry, Zabrze. Publications: Over 120 articles in scientific journals. Honours: Award, Scientific and Technical Committee, Warsaw, 1967; Award, Scientific Secretary, Polish Academy of Sciences, 1973. Memberships: New York Academy of Sciences; International Eurasian Academy of Sciences. Address: Centre of Polymer Chemistry, Polish Academy of Sciences, 34 M Curie-Sklodowska Street, PO Box 20, 41-819 Zabrze, Poland.

SELEŠ Monica, b. 2 December 1973, Novi Sad, Yugoslavia (US Citizen, 1994). Tennis Player. Career: Winner of: Sport Goofy Singles, 1984; Singles and Doubles, 1985; French Open, 1990, 1991, 1992; Virginia Slims Championships, 1990, 1991, 1992; Australian Open, 1991, 1992, 1993, 1996; US Open, 1991, 1992; Canadian Open, 1995, 1996, 1997; Los Angeles Open, 1997; Tokyo Open, 1997; Semi-finalist at: French Open, 1989; Quarter-finalist at: Wimbledon, 1990; Member, winning US Federal Cup team, 1996, 1999, 2000; 59 WTA Tour titles, 9 Grand Slam titles and over $14million in prize money, -2002; Played exhibition match Australia, 2005. Publication: Monica: From Fear to Victory, 1996. Honours: Named youngest No 1 ranked player in tennis history for women and men, at 17 years, 3 months and 9 days; Ted Tinling Diamond Award, 1990; Associated Press Athlete of the Year 1990-91; Tennis Magazine Comeback Player of the Year, 1995; Flo Hyman Award, 2000. Address: IMG, 1 Erieview Plaza, Cleveland, OH 44114, USA.

SELF Will, b. 26 September 1961. Author; Cartoonist. m. (1) Katherine Sylvia Anthony Chancellor, 1989, divorced 1996, 1 son, 1 daughter, (2) Deborah Jane Orr, 1997, 2 sons. Education: Christ's College; Exeter College, Oxford. Appointments: Cartoon illustrator, New Statesman, City Limits; Columnist: The Observer, 1995-97; The Times, 1997-; Independent on Sunday, 2000-. Publications: Collected cartoons, 1985; Junk Mail (selected journalism), 1995; Sore Sites, collected journalism; Short stories: Quantity Theory of Insanity, 1991; Grey Area, 1994; Tough Tough Toys and Tough Tough Boys, 1998; Dr Mukti and Other Tales of Woe, 2003; Novellas: Cock and Bull, 1992; The Sweet Smell of Psychosis, 1996; Dr Mukti, 2004; The Undivided Self: Selected Stories, 2008; Novels: My Idea of Fun, 1993; Great Apes, 1997; How the Dead Live, 2000; Perfidious Man, 2000; Feeding Frenzy, 2001; Dorian, 2002; The Book of Dave, 2006; Psychogeography, 2007. Address: The Wylie Agency, 17 Bedford Square, London WC1B 3BA, England.

SELISHCHEV Vladimir, b. 1 August 1949, Moscow, Russia. Engineer. m. 1 son, 1 daughter. Education: PhD, 1977. Appointments: Researcher, Moscow Higher Technical School (Bauman University), 1972; Director General, CEL, 2000; Assistant of Professor, Institute of the In-Plant Training of Specialists of Education, 2000-. Publications: Nearly 100 articles on concentration of energy devices, biological energy, control systems, theory of causality. Honours: PhD; Senior Staff Scientist; Diploma de Chevalier, Brussels, 2006; Diploma de Officier, Brussels, 2008; Many gold medals and awards in innovation exhibitions, 2005-08. Memberships: International Association of Specialists on Work in Causality; Scientist School of Causality. Address: 11-2-73 Pronskaja str, Moscow 109145, Russia.

SELKIRK OF DOUGLAS, Baron of Cramond in the City of Edinburgh, James Alexander Douglas Hamilton, b. 31 July 1942, United Kingdom. Life Peer. m. Priscilla Susan (Susie) Buchan, 4 sons. Education: MA, Balliol College, Oxford; LLB, University of Edinburgh. Appointments: Officer TA 6/7 Battalion Cameronians Scottish Rifles, 1961-66, TAVR, 1971-74, Captain, 2nd Battalion Lowland Volunteers; Advocate, 1968-76; MP, Conservative, Edinburgh West, 1974-97; Scottish Conservative Whip, 1977; A Lord Commissioner of the Treasury, 1979-81; Parliamentary Private Secretary to Malcolm Rifkind MP, as Foreign Office Minister, 1983-86, as Secretary of State for Scotland, 1986-87; Parliamentary Under Secretary of State for Home Affairs and Environment, 1987-92 (including, local government at the Scottish Office, 1987-89, additional responsibility for local government finance, 1989-90 and for the arts in Scotland, 1990-92); Parliamentary Secretary of State for Education and Housing, Scottish Office, 1992-95; Disclaimed Earldom of Selkirk, 1994 (prior to succession being determined, 1996) Heir to Earldom of Selkirk (son), John Andrew Douglas-Hamilton, Master of Selkirk); Minister of State for Home Affairs and Health (with responsibility for roads and transport and construction) Scottish Office, 1995-97; Scottish Parliament: Business Manager and Chief Whip, Conservative Group, 1999-2000, Spokesman on Home Affairs, 2001-2003, on Education, 2003-2007. Publications: Motive for a Mission: The Story Behind Hess's Flight to Britain, 1971; The Air Battle for Malta: the Diaries of a Fighter Pilot; Roof of the World: Man's First Flight Over Everest, 1983; The Truth About Rudolf Hess, 1993. Honours: Oxford Boxing Blue, 1961; President, Oxford Union, 1964; Privy Counsellor, 1996; QC (Scotland), 1996; Life Peer, 1997. Memberships: Honorary President, Scottish Amateur Boxing Association, 1975-98; President, Royal Commonwealth Society Scotland, 1979-87, Scottish National Council, UN Association, 1981-87, International Rescue Corps, 1995; Royal Company of Archers (Queen's Body Guard for Scotland); Honorary Air Commodore No 2

(City of Edinburgh) Maritime HQ Unit, 1994-99; 603 (City of Edinburgh) Squadron RAAF, 1999-; Life Member, National Trust for Scotland; Patron, Hope and Homes for Children, 2002-; President, Scottish Veterans Garden City Association Inc, 2003-. Address: c/o House of Lords, London SW1A 0PW, England.

SELLECK Tom, b. 29 January 1945, Detroit, Michigan, USA, Actor. Education: University of Southern California. m. (1) Jackie Ray, 1 step son, (2) Jillie Mack, 1 daughter. Career: Actor, films include: Myra Beckinridge; Midway; Coma; Seven Minutes; High Road to China; Runaway; Lassiter; Three Men and a Baby; Her Alibi, 1988; Quigley Down Under; An Innocent Man, 1989; Three Men and a Lady, Folks, Mr Baseball, 1991; Christopher Columbus: The Discovery, Folks!, 1992; Mr Baseball, In and Out; The Love Letter, 1999; Meet the Robinsons (voice), 2007; TV includes: Returning Home; Bracken's World; The Young and the Restless; The Rockford Files; The Sacketts; Role of Thomas Magnum in Magnum PI; Divorce Wars; Countdown at the Super Bowl; Gypsy Warriors; Boston and Kilbride; The Concrete Cowboys; Murder She Wrote; The Silver Fox; The Closer (series), 1998; Last Stand at Saber River; Friends, 1996, 2000; Ruby Jean and Joe; Broken Trust, 1995; Washington Slept Here, Louis l'Amour's Crossroads Trail, Running Mates, 2000; Monte Walsh, 12 Mile Road, 2003; Reversible Errors (TV), Ike; Countdown to D Day, 2004; Stone Cold, 2005; Jess Stone: Night Passage, Jesse Stone: Death in Paradise, Boston Legal, America's Top Sleuths, 2006; Jesse Stone: Sea Change, Las Vegas, 2007. Honours: Hon LLD, Pepperdine University, 2004; Distinguished American Award, Horatio Alger Association, 2004. Address: c/o Esme Chandlee, 2967 Hollyridge Drive, Los Angeles, CA 90068, USA.

SELTZER Gilbert L, b. 11 October 1914, Toronto, Ontario, Canada. Architect. m. Molly, deceased, 1 son, 1 daughter. Education: B Arch, University of Toronto, Canada, 1937. Appointments: Partner, Gehron & Seltzer, New York, New York, 1952-58; Sole Proprietor, Gilbert L Seltzer Associates, New York, New York and West Orange, New Jersey, specialising in governmental and institutional projects, 1958-; Representative work includes: Projects at US Military Academy, US Merchant Marine Academy, Denison University, City College of New York, Rutgers University, William Paterson University, New Jersey City University, Kean University, University of Medicine and Dentistry of New Jersey, Utica Memorial Auditorium, Veterans Administration Medical Centers. Publications: Numerous articles in Architectural Journals. Honours: Numerous awards including: Henry Hering Medal of National Sculpture Society. Memberships: American Institute of Architects; New Jersey Society of Architects. Address: 80 Main Street, West Orange, NJ 07052, USA.

SEN Amartya Kumar, b. 3 November 1933, Santiniketan, India. Professor of Economics and Philosophy; Writer. m. (1) Nabaneeta Dev, 1960, divorced 1974, 2 daughters, (2) Eva Colorni, 1977, deceased 1985, 1 son, 1 daughter, (3) Emma Rothschild, 1991. Education: BA, Presidency College, Calcutta, 1953; BA, 1955, MA, PhD, 1959, Trinity College, Cambridge. Appointments: Professor of Economics, Jadavpur University, Calcutta, 1956-58; Fellow, Trinity College, Cambridge, 1957-63, All Souls College, Oxford, 1980-88; Professor of Economics, Delhi University, 1963-71, London School of Economics and Political Science, 1971-77; Professor of Economics, 1977-80, Drummond Professor of Political Economy, 1980-88, University of Oxford; Andrew D White Professor at Large, Cornell University, 1978-85;

Lamont University Professor and Professor of Economics and Philosophy, 1988-98, 2004-, Professor Emeritus, 2004-, Harvard University; Master Trinity College, Cambridge, 1998-2004. Publications: Choice of Techniques, 1960; Collective Choice and Welfare, 1970; Guidelines for Project Evaluation (with P Dasgupta and Stephen Marglin), 1972; On Economic Inequality, 1973; Employment, Technology and Development, 1975; Poverty and Famines: An Essay on Entitlement and Deprivation, 1981; Choice, Welfare and Measurement, 1982; Resources, Values and Development, 1984; Commodities and Capabilities, 1985; On Ethics and Economics, 1987; The Standard of Living (with others), 1987; Hunger and Public Action (with Jean Dreze), 1989; Jibanayatra o arthaniti, 1990; The Political Economy of Hunger (editor with Jean Dreze), 3 volumes, 1990-91; Money and Value: On the Ethics and Economics of Finance/Denaro e valore: Etica ed economia della finanza, 1991; Inequality Reexamined, 1992; The Quality of Life (editor with Martha Nussbaum), 1993; Economic Development and Social Opportunity (with Jean Dreze), 1995; Development as Freedom, 1999. Contributions to: Professional journals. Honours: Mahalanobis Prize, 1976; Honorary Doctor of Literature, University of Saskatchewan, 1979; Nobel Prize in Economic Science, 1998; Honorary CH, 2000; Grand Cross, Order of Scientific Merit, Brazil, 2000. Memberships: American Academy of Arts and Sciences; American Economic Association, president, 1994-; British Academy, fellow; Development Studies Association; Econometric Society, fellow; Indian Economic Association; International Economic Association, president, 1986-88, honorary president, 1988-; Royal Economic Society. Address: c/o Trinity College, Cambridge CB2 1TQ, England.

SEN Tapas Kumar, b. 1 March 1933, Calcutta, India. Teacher; Manager. m. Sondra Kotzin Sen, 1 son, 1 daughter. Education: MSc, Applied Psychology, Calcutta University, 1954; PhD, Psychology, Johns Hopkins University, 1963. Appointments: Member, Technical Staff, Bell Laboratories, 1963-72; Human Resources Director, AT&T, 1973-96; Executive Director, Workforce Development, Rutgers University, New Brunswick, New Jersey, USA, 1999-; Executive Committee Member, Governor's State Employment and Training Commission, New Jersey, 2000-; Chair, Governance Committee, State Employment and Training Commission, 2004-05. Publications: 15 papers in professional publications include: Building the Workplace of the Future in A Blueprint for Managing Change, A Conference Board Report; Advisory Editor, Work in America Encyclopedia, 2003. Honours: The Mayflower Group Leadership Award, 1985; Toastmasters International, Area Governor of the Year, public speaking, 1970. Memberships: Fellow, Human Factors and Ergonomics Society; American Psychological Association; The Dearborn Group. Address: 29 Arden Road, Mountain Lakes, NJ 07046, USA. E-mail: tsitsi@optonline.net

SENDO Takeshi, b. 5 August 1915, Japan. Educator; Researcher; Author. m. Hide, 16 April 1945, 2 sons, 1 daughter. Education: BE, Tokyo University, Japan. Appointments: Professor, Mechanical Engineering, 1959-90, Honorary Professor, 1990-, Curator of Library, Meijo University, Nagoya, 1975-80. Publications: Treatise of High Speed Deformation of Metal, 1993, 2nd Edition, 1994; Papers About Behaviour of AL Column by Drop Hammer Test, 1959-90; Over 60 collected papers to professional journals. Honours: Honour Professor; Listed in Who's Who publications and biographical dictionaries Memberships: Fellow, Japan Society of Mechanical Engineering; Fellow, Japan Society of Precision Engineering. Address: 21-8, Choei, Moriyama-ku, Nagoya 463, Japan.

SEO Dong Cheol, b. 3 July 1974, Sacheon, Gyeongsangnam-do, Republic of Korea. Environmental Chemist; Researcher. Education: BSc, 2000, MSc, 2002, PhD, 2005, Gyeongsang National University, Republic of Korea; Postdoctoral Researcher, Louisiana State University, USA, 2006-08. Appointments: Instructor, Jinju National University, Republic of Korea, 2003-06; Researcher, Institute of Agriculture and Life Sciences, Gyeongsang National University, 2005-06; Postdoctoral Researcher, Wetland Biogeochemistry Institute, Louisiana State University, 2006-08. Publications: Numerous articles in professional journals. Honours: Best Presentation Prize, College of Agriculture and Life Science, Gyeongsang National University, 1998; Best Presentation Award, 2002, Promising Scientist Award, 2006, Korean Society of Agriculture and Environment. Memberships: Korean Society of Agriculture and Environment; Korean Society for Applied Biological Chemistry; Korean Society of Soil Science and Fertilizer. Address: Wetland Biogeochemistry Institute, Louisiana State University, Baton Rouge, LA 70803, USA. E-mail: dseo@lsu.edu

SEO Sung Il, b. 17 July 1962, Seoul, South Korea. Researcher. m. Baek Ran Choe, 1 son, 1 daughter. Education: BS, 1984, MA, 1986, PhD, 1994, Department of Naval Architecture, Seoul National University. Appointments: Senior Research Engineer, Hanjin Heavy Industries Co Ltd, 1986-2002; Principal Researcher, Korea Railroad Research Institute, 2002-. Publications: A study on the prediction of deformations of welded structures, 1999; Optimum structural design of naval vessels, 2003; Fatigue strength evaluation of the aluminium carbody of urban transit unit by large scale dynamic load test, 2005; TTX is coming, 2006; A study on fluctuating pressure load on high speed train passing through tunnels, 2006. Honours: Best Paper Awards, Korean Federation of Science and Technology Societies, 2005; Best Paper Awards, Society of Naval Architects of Korea, 1998; Research Awards, Ministry of Construction and Transportation, 2006. Memberships: Society of Naval Architects of Korea; Korean Society of Mechanical Engineers; Korean Society for Railway. E-mail: siseo@krri.re.kr

SEOK Chang Sung, b. 24 March 1957, Seoul, Korea. University Professor. m. Sun Hee Tu, 1 son, 1 daughter. Education: B Eng, 1981, M Eng, 1983, Mechanical Engineering, PhD, Fracture Mechanics, 1990, Sungkyunkwan University, Korea. Appointments: Employee, Daewoo Motor Company, Incheon, Korea, 1984-85; Assistant Professor, 1993-97, Head, 1997-98, 2005-, Associate Professor, 1997-2002, Professor, 2002-, School of Mechanical Engineering, Sungkyunkwan University; Visiting Professor, North Carolina State University, 1998-99. Publications: 39 articles in professional scientific journals. Honours: Yoo-Dam Award, Korean Society of Mechanical Engineers, 1999. Memberships: Korean Society of Precision Engineering; Korean Society of Mechanical Engineers. Address: School of Mechanical Engineering, Sungkyunkwan University, 300 Cheonchoen-Dong, Jangan-Gu, Suwon, 440-746, Korea. E-mail: seok@skku.edu

SEONG Seung-Hwan, b. 16 January 1965, Busan, Republic of Korea. Researcher. m. Young-Shin Sonn, 1 son, 1 daughter. Education: BS, 1987, MS, 1989, PhD, 1995, Nuclear Engineering, Seoul National University. Appointments: Senior Researcher, Korea Atomic Energy Research Institute, Daejon, 1995-. Publications: Development of fast-running simulation methodology using neural networks for load follow operation, 2002; Diagnostic Algorithm for check valve with spectral estimations and Neural network models using

acoustic signal, 2005; Establishment of Design requirements for flow blockage detection system through LES analysis of temperature fluctuation in Upper plenum, 2006. Honours: Listed in international biographical directories. Memberships: Korea Nuclear Society. Address: 112-705 Clover Apt, Dunsan-dong, Seo-Gu, Daejon, Republic of Korea, 302-120. E-mail: shseong@kaeri.re.kr

SEREBRIER José, b. 3 December 1938, Montevideo, Uruguay. Musician; Conductor. m. Carole Farley, 29 March 1969, 1 daughter. Education: Diploma, National Conservatory, Montevideo, 1956; Curtis Institute of Music, 1958; BA, University of Minnesota, 1960; Studied with Aaron Copland, Antal Dorati, Pierre Monteux. Career: Debut, Carnegie Hall; Independent Composer and Conductor, 1955-; Apprentice Conductor, Minnesota Orchestra, 1958-60; Associate Conductor, American Symphony Orchestra, New York, 1962-66; Musical Director, American Shakespeare Festival, 1966; Composer-in-Residence, Cleveland Orchestra, 1968-71; Artistic Director, International Festival of Americas, Miami, 1984-; Opera Conductor, United Kingdom, USA, Australia and Mexico; Guest Conductor, numerous orchestras; International tours in USA, Latin America, Australia and New Zealand. Compositions: Published over 100 works; Variations on a Theme from Childhood, for chamber orchestra; Symphony for Percussion; Concerto for Violin and Orchestra; Concerto for Harp and Orchestra; Symphonie Mystique, 2003; Orchestration and recording of George Gershwin's Three Piano Preludes and the Lullaby; Also works for chorus, voice, keyboard; Over 250 recordings for major labels with orchestras from United Kingdom, Germany, Oslo, Spain, Italy, Sicily, Belgium, Czechoslovakia and Australia. Honours: Ford Foundation Conductors Award; Alice M Ditson Award, 1976; Deutsche Schallplatten Critics Award; Music Retailers Association Award; Guggenheim Fellow, 1958-60; 2 Guggenheim awards; Rockefeller Foundation Grants; Commissions, National Endowment for the Arts and Harvard Musical Association; BMI Award; Koussevitzky Foundation Award; 28 Grammy Nominations, 1975-2004; Subject of book by Michel Faure, 2002; 5 Grammy Nominations in 2004, including Best New Composition for 3rd symphony, Symphonie Mystique; Winner, Latin Grammy for Best Classical Album for recording of Carmen Symphony by Bizet-Serebrier with Barcelona Symphony Orchestra, 2004. Memberships: American Symphony Orchestra League; American Music Center; American Federation of Musicians. Address: 270 Riverside Drive, New York, NY 10025, USA.

SERIU Masafumi, b. 23 September 1964, Kyoto, Japan. Theoretical Physicist. Education: BS, 1987, MSc, 1989, DSc, 1992, Kyoto University. Appointments: Research Fellow, Department of Physics, Kyoto University, 1992-93; Postdoctoral Fellow, Inter-University Centre for Astronomy and Astrophysics, Pune, 1993-95; Yukawa Memorial Fellow, Yukawa Institute for Theoretical Physics, Kyoto University, 1996; Research Fellow, Japan Society for Promotion of Sciences, 1996; Associate Professor, Fukui University, 1996-; Visiting Research Associate, Institute of Cosmology, Tufts, University, USA, 1999-2000. Publications: Several articles in professional journals. Honours: Prize, Silver Jubilee Essay Competition, Indian Association for Research Award, 1993; Honda Heihachiro Memorial Scholarship, Japan Association for Mathematical Sciences, 1994, 1995; Yukawa Memorial Fellowship, 1995; Research Fellowship, Japan Society for the Promotion of Sciences, 1996; Grant-in-Aid, Inamori Foundation, 1998. Memberships: Japan Physical Society; Japan Astronomical Society; Seiwa Scholars Society. Address: Fukui University, Bunkyo 3-9-1, Fukui 910-8507, Japan.

SERNICKI Jan Kazimierz, b. 7 April 1943, Warsaw, Poland. Electronic Engineer - Nuclear Electronics. m. Krystyna Elzbieta Łysakowska-Sernicka. Education: Master's degree, 1969, Postgraduate training, 1971-75, Doctor of Engineering, 1976, Warsaw Technical University. Appointments: Electronic Engineer, 1969-71, Research Engineer, 1976-78, Institute of Nuclear Research, Świerk; Scientific Worker, Joint Institute of Nuclear Research, Dubna, Russia, 1978-81; Specialist, Department of Nuclear Spectroscopy and Technique, The Andrzej Soltan Institute for Nuclear Studies, Świerk, 1981-. Publications: Author, papers in Progress in Medical Physics, 2 in 1977, 3 in 1978; Co-author, paper in Nukleonika, 1981; Author, papers in Nuclear Instruments and Methods in Physics Research A, 1983, 2 in 1985, 1986, 2 in 1988, 1990, 1997, 2007 in Nukleonika, 1995, 2000. Address: Saska 99-4, 03-914 Warsaw, Poland.

SERVADEI Annette, b. 16 October 1945, Durban, Natal, South Africa. Pianist. m. 1972-1981, 1 son, 1 daughter. Education: Began studies with concert pianist mother, 1949; Also Violin and Organ studies, diploma level; 1964-1972: Further piano studies in Milan, Detmold, Salzburg, Positano, with Ilonka Deckers, Klaus Schilde, Carlo Zecchi, Wilhelm Kempff; LTCL (T), 1964; LRSM (P), 1965; UPLM, 1965; FTCL, 1970; BMus, 1979; Fine Arts Diploma KIAD, 2000; HND in Sound Production, UKC, 2003; BA (Hons) in Fine Art, University of Kent, 2005. Debut: Wigmore Hall, London, 1972. Career: Radio broadcast at age 10, concerto debut with Durban Symphony Orchestra at 12, began performing career; Performed recitals and concertos, also on radio and TV in Southern Africa, UK, Western Europe, USA; Wide repertoire University Senior Piano Tutor; Lecture recitals, Masterclasses; Eisteddfod Adjudicator; Outstanding performer of Liszt, Ravel and 20th century American music. World premieres: Palintropos (John Tavener), London, 1980; Perpetual Angelus (Gordon Kerry) London, 1991; Severe health problems interrupted career in 1997; Used enforced sabbatical to study Mozart, Fine Art and Electronic Sound production; Resumed concerts, specialising in Mozart, 2003-. Recordings: Britten and Khachaturian Piano Concertos with London Philharmonic Orchestra; Mendelssohn, Schumann and Brahms piano pieces; Complete piano music of Sibelius, 5 CDs; 2 CDs Dohnanyi piano music. Honours: Scholarships, Oppenheimer Trust and UNISA, 1965-70; UNISA, 1974; Letter from Wilhelm Kempff for Beethoven interpretation, 1974; Artist of the Year, UK Sibelius Society, 1993. Membership: Incorporated Society of Musicians. Address: 3 Bournemouth Drive, Herne Bay, Kent CT6 8HH, England. E-mail: annetteservadei@tiscali.co.uk Website: www.annetteservadei.co.uk

SESÉ Luis M, b. 18 September 1955, Madrid, Spain. Chemistry Educator; Researcher. m. Mercedes Mejias, 1 son. Education: BS, University Complutense Madrid, 1976; MSc, honours, 1978; PhD, 1983. Appointments: Ayudante, 1978-80, Encargado, 1980-81, University Complutense; Encargado, 1981-82, Colaborador, 1982-84, Titular, 1985-87, Titular Numerario, 1987-, University National Educational Distance, Madrid. Publications: Research papers in professional journals; Books; Educational Video: Fifteen minutes in the life of the electron, 2002. Honours: Premio Extraordinario de Licenciatura, University Complutense, 1979; 3rd Prize, X Bienal Internacional de Cine y Video Científico, Spain, 2001; 2nd Prize, XXII Bienal Internacional de Cine Científico, Spain, 2002; 2nd Prize, Fisica en Acción 3 (RSEF), Spain, 2002; Scientific Radio Shows; Listed in several Who's Who and biographical publications. Memberships: New York Academy of Sciences; Planetary Society; Spanish Royal Society of Physics, 2002-; Einsteinian Chair of Science, World Academy of Letters; American Association for the Advancement of Science; American Chemical Society. Address: Facultad de Ciencias, University National Educational Distance, Senda del Rey 9, 28040 Madrid, Spain.

SEWARD George Chester, b. 4 August 1910, Omaha, Nebraska, USA. Lawyer. m. Carroll Frances McKay, 2 sons, 2 daughters. Education: Louisville, Kentucky Male HS with honours, 1929; BA, 1933, LLB, 1936, University of Virginia. Appointments: Director, 1952-66, President, 1964-66, Witherbee Sherman Corp; Director, Howmet Corp, 1955-75; Director, Chas P Young Co, 1965-72; Director, Howmedica Inc, 1970-72; Director, Benson Mines Inc, 1980-85; Trustee, Benson Iron Ore Trust, 1969-80; Lawyer, Seward & Kissel LLP, New York, USA. Publications: Author: Basic Corporate Practice, 1977; Seward and Related Families, 1994; Co-author: Model Business Corporation Act Annotated, 1960; We Remember Carroll, 1992. Memberships: Trustee, 1983-93, President, 1991-93, Arts and Sciences Council, University of Virginia; Trustee, Edwin Gould Foundation for Children, 1955-96; Trustee, Nature Conservancy of Ea L I, 1969-80; Trustee, New York Genealogy and Biographical Society, 1990-2006; Downtown Association, New York City; Athenaeum Literary Association; Greencroft Club of Charlottesville, Virginia; University Club of Chicago; Metropolitan Club of Washington, DC; Bohemian Club of San Francisco, California; Gardiner's Bay Country Club; NY Yacht Club; Shelter Island Yacht Club; Knickerbocker Club of New York City; Delta Sigma Rho; Theta Chi; Phi Beta Kappa; President, Phi Beta Kappa Fellows; Order of Coif; Raven Society; Cum Laude Society. Honours: American Bar Association Chairman Section on Business Law, 1958-59; ABA House of Delegates, 1963-74; American Law Institute; Honorary Life President, International Bar Association; IBA, George Seward Lectures by heads of state, New Delhi, 1988, Lisbon, 1992, Budapest, 1993; Named to Louisville Male HS Alumni Association Hall of Fame, 1991; Commissioned Kentucky Colonel, 1993; Fellow, New York State Bar Foundation; Fellow, American Bar Foundation. Address: Seward & Kissel LLP, One Battery Pk Plaza, New York City, NYC 10004, USA.

SEWELL Brian, Art historian; Art critic. Career: Art Critic, Evening Standard newspaper. Publications: South from Ephesus, 1988; The Review that Caused the Rumpus, 1994; An Alphabet of Villains, 1995. Honours: British Press Awards Critic of the Year, 1988; Arts Journalist of the Year, 1994; Hawthornden Prize for Art Criticism, 1995; Foreign Press Association Arts Writer of the Year, 2000; The Orwell Prize, 2003; Critic of the Year, British Press Awards, 2004. Address: The Evening Standard, Northcliffe House, 2 Derry Street, London W8 5EE, England.

SEWELL Geoffrey Leon, b. 27 January 1927, Leeds, England. Mathematical Physicist. m. Robina. Education: Mathematics, University College, Oxford; PhD, King's College, London. Appointments: Held posts at the Universities of Liverpool, Aberdeen and Hull; Professor of Mathematical Physics, Queen Mary, University of London. Publications: Quantum Theory of Collective Phenomena, 1986; Quantum Mechanics and its Emergent Macrophysics, 2002; Numerous articles on mathematical physics, quantum physics, and condensed matter physics. Membership: International Association of Mathematical Physicists. Address: Department of Physics, Queen Mary, University of London, Mile End Rd., London E1 4NS, England. E-mail: g.l.sewell@qmul.ac.uk

SEWELL Rufus Frederick, b. 29 October 1967. Actor. m. Yasmin Abdallah, 1999, 1 son with Amy Gardner. Career: Actor; Films include: Twenty-One; Dirty Weekend; A Man of No Importance; Carrington; Victory; Hamlet; The Woodlanders; The Honest Courtesan; Martha Meet Frank; Daniel and Laurence; Illuminata; Dark City; Bless The Child; A Knight's Tale; The Extremists; Tristan and Isolde; The Illusionist, 2006; Amazing Grace, 2006; The Holiday, 2006; Downloading Nancy, 2008; Vinyan, 2008; TV appearances include: The Last Romantics; Gone To Seed; Middlemarch; Dirty Something; Citizen Locke; Cold Comfort Farm; Henry IV; Charles II: The Power and the Passion; Helen of Troy; Shakespeare Retold: The Taming of the Shrew; Stage appearances include: Royal Hunt of the Sun; Comedians; The Last Domain; Peter and the Captain; Pride and Prejudice; The Government Inspector; The Seagull; As You Like It; Making it Better; Arcadia; Translations; Rat in the Skull; Macbeth; Luther; Taste. Honours: London Critics' Circle Best Newcomer, 1992; Broadway Theatre World Award, 1995. Address: c/o Julian Belfrage Associates, 46 Albermarle Street, London, W1X 4PP, England.

SEYMOUR David, b. 24 January 1951, Surrey, England. Lawyer. m. Elisabeth, 1 son, 2 daughters. Education: MA, Jurisprudence, The Queen's College, Oxford, 1969-72; LLB, Fitzwilliam College, Cambridge, 1973-74; Gray's Inn, Called to the Bar, 1975. Appointments: Law Clerk, Rosenfeld, Meyer & Susman (Attorneys), Beverly Hills, California, 1972-73; Legal Adviser's Branch, Home Office, 1975-97; Legal Secretary to the Attorney General, 1997-2000; Legal Adviser, Home Office and Northern Ireland Office, 2000-. Honours: Open Exhibition, The Queen's College, Oxford, 1969-72; Holt Scholar, Gray's Inn, 1974; Elected Bencher, Gray's Inn, 2001; CB, New Year Honours List, 2005. Address: Home Office, 2 Marsham Street, London SW1P 4DF, England. E-mail: david.seymour@homeoffice.gov.uk

SHABALIN Igor Logan, b. 26 August 1950, Kamensk-Uralskii, Russia. Materials Scientist; Chemist; Engineer. m. Svetlana Astakhova, 1 son. Education: MSc, Engineering, 1973, PhD, 1977, Senior Research Fellow, 1982, Ural State Technical University. Appointments: Laboratory Assistant, 1970-73, Research Engineer, 1973-74, PhD Student/Junior Research Fellow, 1974-77, Assistant Professor,/Junior Research Fellow, 1977-78, Senior Research Fellow (jointly Associate Dean in Research), 1978-84, Department of Less-Common Metals, Ural State Technical University, Yekaterinburg, Russia; Lecturer, Department of Metallurgy, Ural College of Mining and Metallurgy, 1978-82; Expert, Powder Metallurgy Group, All-Russian Institute for Scientific and Technical Information, Moscow, 1978-83; Consultant, Perm Higher Military Engineering Academy for Strategic Rocket Force, 1988-91; Head, National Branch Scientific Research Laboratory ONIL-123, USSR Aerospace Industry Ministry, 1985-93; Director, Eastern Scientific Research Institute of Refractory Materials, Yekaterinburg, 1994-99; Professor, Applied Economics & Engineering, Ural State Forestry Technical University, Yekaterinburg, 2000-01; Professor, Applied Economics & Engineering, Russian State Vocational & Pedagogical University, Yekaterinburg, 2001-03; Teacher Trainee, Chemistry Sessions, Manchester College of Art and Technology, Manchester, England, 2004-05; Researching Professor, Institute for Materials Research, University of Salford, Greater Manchester, England, 2005-. Publications: Numerous articles, scientific research and technical reports in professional journals. Honours: Lenin Research Scholarship, 1970-73; Silver and Bronze Medals, 1980, Gold Medal, 1981, Grand Prix Award, 1982, All-USSR

National Achievement Exhibition; Honorary Member, All-Russian Society of Inventors and Innovators, 1990; Listed in international biographical dictionaries. Memberships: All-Russian Society of Inventors and Innovators; Supreme Panel, All-Russian Commission for Implementation of Universities Achievements in Industry; Structural Ceramics Network; Materials Knowledge Tranfer Network; Ceramics Society. E-mail: i.shabalin@salford.ac.uk

SHAFAEDDIN Mehdi, b. 21 July 1945, Iran. Development Economist; Educator. m. Shahnaz, 28 August 1970, 2 daughters. Education: BA, Economics, Tehran University, 1969; MA, Economics, Tehran University, 1971; DPhil, Economic Development, Oxford, 1980. Currently freelance consultant on trade, industrial policy, competitiveness and WTO issues; Affiliated to the Institute of Economic Research, University of Neuchatel, Switzerland. Appointments: Former Head, Macroeconomic and Development Polices Branch, UNCTAD; Senior Economist, Co-ordinator, Economic Co-operation Among Developing Countries; Chief, Enterprise Development Strategy; Chief, Policy Development; Senior Adviser, Trade Policy; Lecturer, Webster University, Geneva; Editor, UNCTAD Bulletin; Assistant Professor, University of Abureyhan, Tehran; Acting Chief, Industrial Research and Programmes, Institute of Standards and Industrial Research, Tehran. Publications: Trade Policy at the Crossroads, 2005 and many articles in professional journals. Honours: Scholarship, British Counsel for B Lit, Oxford; Scholarship, Tehran University, D Phil and BA; Listed in National and International Biographical Who's Who Publications. Memberships: Development Study Association, UK; International Development Economics Association; International Development Economics Association; European Trade Study Group. E-mail: m.shafaeddin@gmail.com

SHAFFER Peter (Levin), b. 15 May 1926, Liverpool, England. Dramatist. Education: BA, Trinity College, Cambridge, 1950. Appointments: Literary Critic, Truth, 1956-57; Music Critic, Time and Tide, 1961-62; Cameron Mackintosh Visiting Professor of Contemporary Theatre and Fellow, St Catherine's College, Oxford, 1994. Publications: Plays: Five Finger Exericse, 1958; The Private Ear, 1962; The Public Eye, 1962; The Merry Roosters Panto (with Joan Littlewood), 1963; The Royal Hunt of the Sun, 1964; Black Comedy, 1965; White Lies, 1967; The White Liars, 1968; The Battle of Shrivings, 1970; Amadeus, 1979; Yonadab, 1985; Lettice and Lovage, 1987; The Gift of Gorgon, 1992. Contributions to: Radio and television. Honours: Evening Standard Drama Awards, 1958, 1979, 1988; New York Drama Critics Cricle Awards, 1959, 1976; London Theatre Critics Award, 1979; Plays and Players Award, 1979; Tony Awards, 1979, 1980; Drama Desk Award, 1980; Academy Award, 1985; Golden Globe Award, 1985; Los Angeles Film Critics Association Award, 1985; Premi David di Donatello, 1985; Commander of the Order of the British Empire, 1987; Shakespeare Prize, Hamburg, 1989; William Inge Award for Distinguished Achievement in the American Theatre, 1992. Membership: Royal Society of Literature, fellow. Address: c/o McNaughton-Lowe Representation, 200 Fulham Road, London SW10 9PN, England.

SHAFIK Ahmed, b. 10 May 1933, Shebin-el-Kom, Menoufia Governorate, Egypt. Surgeon. m. Olfat Elsibai, 2 sons. Education: Undergraduate studies, 1951-57, MD, 1962, Cairo University Faculty of Medicine. Appointments at Cairo University Faculty of Medicine, Kasr el Aini Teaching Hospital: House Officer, 1957-58; Lecturer of Surgery, 1962-70; Assistant Professor of Surgery, 1970-75; Full Professor of

Surgery, 1975; Head, Emergency Division, 1980-84; Head, Surgical Divisions 27 and 29, 1984-90; Chairman, Department of Surgery and Experimental Research, 1990-. Publications: Over 950 contributions to medical research, introducing new anatomical, physiological, pathological and therapeutical findings in coloproctology, gastroenterology, urology, andrology, gynaecology and others, describing amongst other entities over 80 hitherto unknown reflexes there by enhancing the understanding of mechanisms that regulate and co-ordinate anal and vesical continence and evacuation, or are responsible for deglutition or control genital functions and sexual performance including coitus in both sexes; Also created an immunostimulating antiviral drug, MM1, which has proved very successful in the combat of AIDS. Honours: State Award for Science and Arts, 1st Class, 1977; Nomination for Nobel Prize in Medicine, 1981. Memberships include: International Society of University Colon and Rectal Surgeons; The American Society of Colon and Rectal Surgeons; American Association of Anatomists; New York Academy of Sciences; Society of Experimental Biology and Medicine; Academy of Surgical Research; International Pelvic Floor Dysfunction Society; Mediterranean Society of Pelvic Floor Disorders; Mediterranean Society of Coloproctology. Address: 2 Talaat Harb Street, Cairo, Egypt. E-mail: shafik@ahmedshafik.com

SHAH Shirish, b. 24 May 1942. Professor. Education: BSc, St Xavier's College, Gujarat University, India, 1962; Graduate School, Cornell University, USA, 1962-63; PhD Physical Chemistry, University of Delaware, Newark, 1968; Additional Studies: Virginia Poly Institute, University of Minnesota, George Washington University, Community College of Baltimore, University of Virginia, Georgia State University, Georgia Tech University, North East University, Central Arkansas University, University of Millersville. Appointments: Research Fellow, University of Delaware, 1964-67; Assistant Professor, Washington College, Chestertown, 1967-68; Director, Quality Control, Vita Foods Inc, 1968-72; Assistant Professor, Science, 1968-72, Coord, Vocational Program, 1974-76, Associate Professor, Science, Administrator, Marine Science and Food, Scientific Projects, Chesapeake College, Maryland, 1972-76; Associate Professor, 1976-79, Coord Science and Technology, 1976-79, Chair, Tech Studies, 1979-82, Educational Administrator, CETA Electronics Communications Project, 1980-81, Consultant for Joint Apprenticeship Committee, Baltimore City, 1982-91, Chairperson, Computer Systems and Engineering Technology, Professor, Science, 1979-91 (Retired 1991), Community College of Baltimore; Urban Transportation Project, 1981-82; Water & Waste Water Education Project, 1982-89; Prison Programs, Patuxent Institute, 1982-91; Telecommunications Project, 1985-89; Associate Professor of Chemistry, College of Notre Dame, Maryland, 1991-2002 (Retired); FYE Advisor, 1998-, Lecturer of Chemistry, 2005-, Towson University; Lecturer of Chemistry, Morgan State University, 1999-2006; Coppin State University Physical Science, 1996-98; Villa Julie College, Physical Science, 2002-05. Publications: Radiation Chemistry of Nitroso Compounds in Aqueous Solutions, 1968; Various articles in professional journals. Honours: Nominated Outstanding Educator, or Faculty, or Faculty Member Most Likely to Succeed in Administration, 1972, 1977, 1979, 1981; Regional III Leadership Award, National Association of Industrial Technology, 1990-91; Public Relations Award, 1996, Public Science Policy (Govt Relations Award), 2000, American Chemical Society; Phoenix Award for National Chemistry Week, 1998; Salute to Excellence, 2004; Outstanding Co-ordinator, Chemagination Project, American Chemical Society, 2005; Chair, The Mentoring and the Success of Undergraduate and Graduate Students in

Interdisciplinary Research in Fields Such as Material Science, Environment Chemistry, Biochemistry, Medicinal Chemistry, and Forensic Chemistry, EAS Final Program, 2005; Recipient, various grants, others; Listed in: First Five Hundred; International Register of Profiles; Men of Achievement; Men and Women of Distinction; Who's Who in the World, 2006-07; Who's Who is Science & Engineering, 2006-07; Who's Who in Medicine & Healthcare, 2006-07; Who's Who in Finance & Industry, 2007. Memberships: Board Member, American Lung Association of Maryland, 1971-80; Chair, Mid Atlantic States of Higher Education Evaluation Teams, 1987-2007; National Science Teachers Association; President, MD Association of Community and Junior Colleges, 1979-91; Chair, MD, 1996-98, Chair, Public Relations, 1996-2007, Chair, Government Relations, 1996-2007, Maryland Section of American Chemical Society; President, Industrial Hygiene Association (Chesapeake Section), 2003-04; American Vocational Association; Life Member, American Technical Education Association; Life Patron, American Biographical Institute; Sigma Xi; Iota Lambda Nu; Republican Senatorial Committee; Data Processing Management Association; IEEE; Life Fellow, International Biographical Association. Address: 5605 Purlington Way, Baltimore, MD 21212, USA. Website: http://pages.towson.edu/sshah

SHAHEEN Rashed, b. 18 June 1964, Manama, Bahrain. Engineer. Education: Bachelor of Computer Science, 1987; MSc, Management of Information Technology, 2000; Certified Project Management Professional, 2005. Appointments: Head, Information Technology, Bahrain Telecommunications Company, 1990-96; Independent IT & Strategic Planning Advisor, 1996-2007; Chief Executive, The International Consortium (ICON), 2007-. Honours: Listed in international biographical dictionaries. Memberships: Institute of Electrical and Electronic Engineering; Association for Computing Machinery; British Computer Society; Project Management Institute; Law Specialist Group (UK and USA); Project Management Specialist Group (UK and USA); Information System Methodologies Specialist Group, USA; IEEE Computer Society, USA; Information Systems Specialist Group, USA. Address: PO Box 20030, Manama, Kingdom of Bahrain. E-mail: rashaheen@acm.org

SHAKHOVSKY Victor Ivanovich, b. 9 January 1939, Nikolaevsk, Volgograd Region, Russia. Teacher of English; Linguist. 1 daughter. Education: Graduate, Volgograd Pedagogical University, 1963; Doctor of Linguistics; Full Professor. Appointments: Chair of SLT, 1974-85; Professor and Chair of Linguistics, Head, Laboratory "Language and Personality", Volgograd State Pedagogical University, Russia, 1988-. Publications: 290 publications on language and emotions; 12 books include: Categorization of emotions by lexico-semantic system of the language; Text and its Cognitivo-emotive transformations; Emotions in Business Communication. Honour: Honoured Scientist of the Russian Federation. Address: Titov Street 32, Apt 8, Volgograd 400123, Russia. E-mail: shakhovsky@inbox.ru

SHAMS Hoda Zaky, b. 26 January 1943, Cairo, Egypt. Professor of Organic Chemistry. m. Kadry Youssef Dimian, 2 sons. Education: BSc, Chemistry, 1963, MSc, Organic Chemistry, 1970, PhD, Organic Chemistry, Cairo University, 1977. Appointments: Demonstrator & Lecturer, 1963; Lecturer, 1971; Associate Professor, 1986; Professor, Organic & Applied Chemistry, Helwan University, Helwan, Cairo, Egypt, 1993-; Examiner, Cairo University; Visitor Researcher, Rutgers University, USA; Participator, NIH, 1990; Director, PhD and MSc students, Helwan and Cairo

Universities. Publications: Pigment and Resin Technology; Phosphorus, Sulfur and Silicon; Numerous articles in scientific journals, Design, synthesis and structure elucidation of fused and pendant heterocyclic systems; Applications as pharmaceuticals and as dyes and pigments for dyeing and printing; Formulation of photopolymers. Honours: Nominated as International Educator; Nominated as a Leading Scientist of the World; Listed in several Who's Who and biographical dictionaries. Memberships: Literati Club; MCB University, Bradford, UK. Address: Department of Chemistry, Faculty of Science, Helwan University, Helwan, Cairo, Egypt. E-mail: shamshodaz@yahoo.com

SHAND William Stewart, b. 12 October 1936, Derby, England. Surgeon. m. Caroline, deceased 2005, 2 sons, 1 stepson, 2 stepdaughters. Education: Repton School; St Johns College, Cambridge; The Medical College of St Bartholomew's Hospital London; MA, 1962; MD Cantab, 1970; FRCS, 1969; FRCS Ed, 1970. Appointments include: Consultant Surgeon, King Edward VII's Hospital for Officers, London; Honorary Consultant Surgeon, St Mark's Hospital for Diseases of the Colon and Rectum, London; Consultant Surgeon to Hackney and Homerton Hospitals, London; Honorary Consultant, St Luke's Hospital for the Clergy, London; Penrose May Tutor, Royal College of Surgeons of England, London, 1980-85; Governor of the Medical College of St Bartholomew's Hospital; Governor of the British Postgraduate Medical Federation; Member of the Court of Examiners of the Royal College of Surgeons of England, 1985-91; Consultant Surgeon, St Bartholomew's Hospital London, 1973-96; Currently: Penrose May Teacher, Royal College of Surgeons of England, London, 1985-; Governor of Sutton's Hospital in Charterhouse, 1989-; Trustee, 1995-2000, Vice President, 2001-, Phyllis Tuckwell Hospice, Farnham, Surrey; Member, Honorary Medical Panel of the Artists' General Benevolent Institution, 1979-; Honorary Consulting Surgeon to St Bartholomew's Hospital and the Royal London Hospital, London. Publications: Articles in various journals and contributions to books on surgery, colorectal disease, chronic inflammatory bowel disease in children and oncology; Book: The Art of Dying – The Story of Two Sculptors' Residency in a Hospice (co-author), 1989. Honour: National Art Collections Fund Award, 1992. Memberships: Member of the Court of Assistants of the Worshipful Society of Apothecaries of London, Master, 2004-2005; Member of the Court of Assistants of the Worshipful Company of Barbers of London, Master, 2001-2002; Travelling Surgical Society of Great Britain and Northern Ireland, President, 1994-97; Fellow, Association of Surgeons of Great Britain and Ireland; Fellow, Hunterian Society; Fellow, Harveian Society of London; Chairman, Homerton Hospital Artwork Committee, 1985-92; Honorary Curator of Ceramics, Royal College of Surgeons, England, 1980-. Address: Fenel Cottage, 25 Station Road, Nassington, Peterborough, PE8 6QB, England.

SHANGGUAN Dongkai, b. 12 December 1963, Henan Province, China. Materials Scientist. m. Guilian Gao, 2 sons. Education: BSc, Tsinghua University, China, 1984; DPhil, University of Oxford, England, 1989; MBA, San Jose State University, 2003. Appointments: Postdoctoral Visiting Fellow, University of Cambridge, England, 1989; Postdoctoral Research Fellow, The University of Alabama, USA, 1989-91; Manufacturing Engineer, Technical Specialist, Senior Technical Specialist, Supervisor, Ford Motor Co, USA, 1991-2001; Vice-President of Advanced Technology, Flextronics, 2001-. Publications: Book, Cellular Growth of Crystals; Book, Lead-Free Solder Interconnect Reliability; Over 200 technical papers; 20 US and international patents.

Honours: St Edmund Hall Brockhues Graduate Awards, Oxford University, 1986, 1987; Outstanding Young Manufacturing Engineer Award, Society of Manufacturing Engineers, 1998; Soldertec Lead-Free Soldering Award, 2002; Total Excellence in Electronics Manufacturing Award, SME, 2005; President's Award, IPC, 2006. Memberships: Board of Review, Metallurgical and Materials Transactions; Board of Advisors, Association of Forming and Fabricating Technologies - Society of Manufacturing Engineers; SAE Transactions Review Committee; Senior Member, SME; Board of Governors, IEEE CPMT Society. E-mail: dshangguan@yahoo.com

SHANKAR Ravi, b. 7 April 1920, Varansi, India. Musician (sitar); Composer. m. Sukanya, 23 January 1989, 1 son, 2 daughters. Musical Education: Studied under Ustad Allaudin Khan of Maihar. Career: International career as solo sitarist; Former director of music, All-India Radio; Founded National Orchestra, All India Radio; Founder, Director, Kinnara School of Music, Bombay, 1962, Los Angeles, 1967; Currently Regents professor, University of California; Concerts worldwide (except East and South Africa); Major festivals include: Edinburgh; Woodstock; Monterey. Compositions include: 2 Concertos, sitar and orchestra, 1971, 1981; Swagathan Su Swagathan, 1982; Arpan (in honour of George Harrison); Film scores: Pather Panchali; Charlie; Chappaqua; Ghandhi; Music for television production, Alice In Wonderland; Opera-ballet, Ghanashayam, 1989. Recordings: Over 50 albums include: Concertos 1 and 2 for Sitar and Orchestra, Raga Jageshwari, 1981; Homage To Mahatma Ghandhi, 1981; West Meets East (with Yehudi Menuhin and others); Chants of India; Full Circle: Carnegie Hall 2000. Publications: My Music My Life (autobiography), 1968; From India, 1997; Mantram: Chant of India, 1997; Raga Jogeshwari, 1998; In London [live], 1999; Concerto for Sitar and Orchestra, 1999; Full Circle: Carnegie Hall, 2001; Flowers of India, 2007. Honours: Fellow, Sangeet Natak Academy, 1976; Padma Vibushan, 1981; Elected to Rajya Sabha (Indian Upper House), 1986; Magisaysay; Grand Prize, Fukuoka, Japan; Praemium Imperiale Arts Award; Juliet Hollister Award; The Polar Music Prize, given by the King of Sweden; Bharat Ratna The Jewel of India; Commandeur de la Legion d'Honneur, France; Honorary Knight Commander of the Order of the British Empire, 2001; 12 honorary doctorates worldwide. Address: The Ravi Shankar Foundation, 132 N El Camino Real, Suite 316, Encinitas, CA 92024, USA.

SHARIF Omar (Michael Chalhoub), b. 10 April 1932, Cairo, Egypt. Actor. m. (1) Faten Hamama, 1 son, (2) 1973. Education: Victoria College, Cairo. Career: Salesman, lumber-import firm; 24 Egyptian films and 2 French co-production films; Films include: Lawrence of Arabia; The Fall of the Roman Empire; Behold a Pale Horse; Genghis Khan; The Yellow Rolls Royce; Doctor Zhivago; Night of the Generals; Mackenna's Gold; Funny Girl; Cinderella-Italian Style; Mayerling; The Appointment; Che; The Last Valley; The Horseman; The Burglars; The Island; The Tamarind Seed; Juggernaut; Funny Lady; Ace Up My Sleeve; Crime and Passion; Bloodline; Green Ice; Top Secret; Peter the Great (TV); The Possessed; Mountains of the Moon; Michaelangelo and Me; Drums of Fire; Le Guignol; The Puppet; The Rainbow Thief; 558 rue Paradis; Gulliver's Travels (TV); Heaven Before I Die; The 13th Warrior; The Parole Officer; Shaka Zulu: The Citadel (TV); Monsieur Ibrahim et les fleurs de Coran; Soyez prudents… (TV); Urban Myth Chillers (TV); Hidalgo; Benji: Off the Leash! 2004; The Search for External Egypt, 2005; The Ten Commandments, 2006; Kronprinz Rudolf, 2006; One Night with the King, 2006; 10,000 B.C. (narrator), 2008; Theatre: The Sleeping Prince, England,

1983. Publications: The Eternal Male (autobiography), 1978. Address: c/o William Morris Agency, 151 El Camino Drive, Beverly Hills, CA 90212, USA.

SHARMA Ram, b. 11 June 1974, India. Lecturer. Education: BA, TDC, 1993; MA, English, 1995; M Phil, English, 1996; PhD, English, 2005. Appointments: Temporary Lecturer, SSV (PG) College, Hapur, Ghaziabad, 1997-98; Temporary Lecturer, NAS (PG) College, Meerut, 1998-99; Permanent Lecturer, UP Higher Service Commission (UPHSC), Janta Vedic College, Baraut, 2000-. Publications: Numerous articles in professional journals and several books. Address: Department of English, Janta Vedic College, Baraut, Baghpat, UP 250611, India.

SHARMA Renduchintala Raghavendra Kumar, b. 12 January 1959, Khamgaon, Maharastra State, India. Professor. m. R Sheela Sharma, 2 sons. Education: BE, Mechanical Engineering, Visvesvaraya Regional College, Nagpur, India, 1980; Fellow, Indian Institute of Management, Ahmedabad, India, 1988. Appointments: Graduate Engineer Trainee, TATA Motors, 1980-82; Sales Executive, TVS Suzuki, India, 1988-89; Faculty, 1989, Professor, 2001-, Department of Industrial and Management Engineering, Indian Institute of Technology, Kanpur, India. Publications: 13 book chapters; 21 journal articles in national and international journals; 5 international conference proceedings; 1 book; Several papers in national and international conferences. Honours: Vijay Shree Award, India; Glory of India Gold Medal, India. Memberships: TIMS; ORSA; ORSI India. Address: Department of Industrial and Management Engineering, Indian Institute of Technology, Kanpur 208016, India. E-mail: rrks@iitk.ac.in

SHARMA Sanjeev, b. 25 October 1963, Shyangja, Nepal. Researcher; Engineer. m. Anupama Panta, 1 daughter. Education: MS, Aeroelectrical Engineering, Kiev Institute of Civil Aviation Engrs, USSR, 1991; PhD, University of Newcastle, Australia, 2001. Appointments: Airworthiness Engineer, Department of Civil Aviation, Nepal, 1991-96; Part-time Lecturer, Staff member, University of Newcastle, Australia, 1996-99; Human Factors Specialist, Tenix Defense Aerospace Division, Melbourne, Australia; Lead Human Factors Engineering Specialist, BAE Systems, Australia, 2004-. Publications: Articles in professional journals; 2 seminal papers, 1 accepted in international peer-reviewed scientific journals. Honours: World's first to employ nonlinear dynamical system theory in human factors research (empirical); Listed in international biographical dictionaries. Memberships: Founder, Society for Nonlinear Dynamics in Human Factor; Member, Human Factos & Ergonomics Society, USA. Address: 8 Declivity St, Highbury, Adelaide, SA 5089, Australia. E-mail: sanjeev.sharma@baesystems.com

SHARON Ariel, b. 1928. Politician; Army Officer - retired. m. 2 sons. Education: Studies at Hebrew University, 1952-53; Studies Staff College, Camberley UK, 1957-58. Appointments: Active in Hagana since early youth; Instructor Jewish Police units, 1947; Platoon Commander Alexandroni Brigade; Regimental Intelligence Officer, 1948; Company Commander, 1949; Commander Brigade Reconnaissance Unit, 1949-50; Intelligence Officer Central Command and Northern Command, 1951-52; In charge of Unit 101 on numerous reprisal operations until 1957; Commander Paratroopers Brigade Sinai Campaign, 1956; Training Commander General Staff, 1958; Commander Infantry School, 1958-69; Commander Armoured Brigade, 1962; Head of Staff Northern Command, 1964; Head Training Department of Defence Forces, 1966; Head Brigade Group during Six-Day War, 1967; Resigned from Army, July

1973; Recalled as Commander Central Section of Sinai Front during Yom Kippur War, October1973; Forged bridgehead across Suez Canal; Adviser to Prime Minister, 1975-77; Minister of Agriculture in charge of Settlements, 1977-81; Minister of Defence, 1981-83; Minister without Portfolio, 1990-92; Minister of Trade and Industry, 1984-90; Minister of Construction and Housing, 1990-92; Minister of National Infrastructure, 1996-99; Chairman Cabinet Committee to oversee Jewish immigration from USSR, 1991-96; Prime Minister of Israel, 2001-; Since January 2006, has been totally incapacitated by the effects of a massive hemorrhagic stroke, day-to-day governance of Israel is now exercised by acting Prime Minister, Ehud Olmert. Publication: Warrior (autobiography), 1989. Memberships: Founder Member Likud Front, 1973; Member Knesset - Parliament - 1973-74, 1977-; Member Ministerial Defence Committee, 1990-92. Address: Ministry of National Infrastructure, P O Box 13106, 234 Jaffa Street, Jerusalem 91130, Israel.

SHARP Dennis Charles, b. 30 November 1933, Flitwick, Bedford, England. Architect. m. Yasmin A Shariff, 1 son, 1 daughter. Education: Luton School of Art, 1951-54; AA Dipl., AA School, London; MA, Leverhulme Fellow, School of Architecture, Liverpool University, 1960-63; Registered Architect (ARB); Chartered Architect (RIBA). Appointments: Architect with British Rail Modernisation Group; Bedfordshire County Architect's Department, 1958-60; Architect and Research Officer, Civic Trust for the North West, 1963-64; Lecturer, University of Manchester, 1964-68; Senior Lecturer, AA School, and AA General Editor, London, 1968-82; Dennis Sharp Architects, London and Hertford, 1982-. Publications: Modern Architecture and Expressionism, 1966; The Picture Palace, 1968; The Rationalists, 1978, new edition, 2000; Santiago Calatrava, 1992, 1995; 20th Century Architecture, 1994, 3rd edition, 2001; The Bauhaus, 1994; Connell, Ward & Lucas, 1995, 2007. Honours: Professor, International Academy of Architecture, 1987; Medaille D'Argent, Academie d'Architecture, Paris, 1991; UIA Jean Tschumi Award, 1993; Various Architecture Research Awards including: RIBA, AA, RSA. Memberships: Director, CKA: International Architectural Critics Committee; Co-Chair, Docomomo UK; Architectural Association; RIBA; FBUA; Architecture Club; Society of Authors. Address: 1 Woodcock Lodge, Epping Green, Hertford SG13 8ND, England. E-mail: dsharp@sharparchitects.co.uk

SHARPE David Thomas, b. 14 January 1946, Kent, England. Consultant Plastic Surgeon. m. (1) Patricia Lilian Meredith, 1971, dissolved 2002, 1 son, 2 daughters, (2) Tracey Louise Bowman, 2004. Education: Grammar School for Boys, Gravesend; MA, Downing College, Cambridge; MB BChir, Clinical Medical School, Oxford; FRCS, 1975; House Surgeon, Radcliffe Infirmary, Oxford, 1970-71; Senior House Officer, Plastic Surgery, Churchill Hospital, Oxford, 1971-72; Accident Service, Radcliffe Infirmary, 1972; Pathology, Radcliffe Infirmary, 1972-73; General Surgery, Royal United Hospital, Bath, 1973-75; Plastic Surgery, Welsh Plastic Surgery Unit, Chepstow, 1976. Appointments: Registrar, Plastic Surgery, Chepstow, 1976-81; Canniesburn Hospital, Glasgow, 1978-80; Senior Registrar, Plastic Surgery, Leeds and Bradford, 1980-84; Visiting Consultant Plastic Surgeon, Yorkshire Clinic, Bradford, 1985-; BUPA Hospital Elland, West Yorkshire, 1985-; Cromwell Hospital, London, 1985-; Chairman, Breast Special Interest GP, British Association of Plastic Surgeons, 1997-; President, British Association of Aesthetic Plastic Surgeons, 1997-99; Chairman, Yorkshire Air Ambulance, 2001-03; Inventor and Designer of medical equipment and surgical instruments and devices; Exhibitor,

Design Council, London, 1987. Publications: Chapters, leading articles and papers on plastic surgery topics, major burn disaster management , tissue expansion and breast reconstruction. Honours: OBE, 1986; British Design Award, 1988; Prince of Wales Award for Innovation & Production, 1988. Memberships: British Association of Plastic Surgeons; British Association of Aesthetic Plastic Surgeons; Fellow, Royal College of Surgeons of England; International Society of Aesthetic Plastic Surgeons. Address: Hazelbrae, Calverley Lane, Calverley, Leeds LS28 5QQ, England. E-mail: profsharpe@hotmail.com

SHARPE Errol, b. 2 February 1940, Summerside, Canada. Publisher. Education: BA, University of Prince Edward Island; MA, St Mary's University. Appointments: Publisher, Fernwood Publishing Co Ltd; Past President, Atlantic Publishers Marketing Association. Publications: A People's History of Prince Edward Island. Memberships: Canadian Association of Sociology and Anthropology; Society for Socialist Studies; Council of Canadians; Canadian Centre for Policy Alternatives. Address: Site 2A, Box 5, 32 Oceanvista Lane, Black Point, NS B0J 1B0, Canada.

SHARPE Tom (Thomas Ridley), b. 30 March 1928, London, England. Novelist. m. Nancy Anne Looper, 1969, 3 daughters. Education: Pembroke College, University of Cambridge. Appointments: Social Worker, 1952; Teacher, 1952-56; Photographer, 1956-61; Lecturer in History at Cambridge College of Arts and Technology, 1963-71; Full-time novelist, 1971-. Publications: Riotous Assembly, 1971; Indecent Exposure, 1973; Porterhouse Blue, 1974; Blott on the Landscape, 1975; Wilt, 1976; The Great Pursuit, 1977; The Throwback, 1978; The Wilt Alternative, 1979; Ancestral Vices, 1980; Vintage Stuff, 1982; Wilt on High, 1984; Grantchester Grind, 1995; The Midden, 1996; Wilt in Nowhere, 2005. Address: 38 Tunwells Lane, Great Shelford, Cambridge, CB2 5LJ, England.

SHATNER William, b. 22 March 1931, Montreal, Quebec, Canada. Actor. m. (1) Gloria Rosenberg, 1956, divorced 1969, 3 children, (2) Marcy Lafferty, 1973, divorced 1996, (3) Nerine Kidd, 1997, deceased 1999, (4) Elizabeth Anderson, 2001. Education: BA, McGill University. Career: Appeared, Montreal Playhouse, 1952, 1953; Juvenile roles, Canadian Repertory Theatre, Ottawa, 1952-53, 1953-54; Shakespeare Festival, Stratford, Ontario, 1954-56; Broadway appearances include: Tamburlaine the Great, 1956; The World of Suzie Wong, 1958; A Shot in the Dark, 1961; Numerous TV appearances; Films include: The Brothers Karamazov, 1958, The Explosive Generation, 1961, Judgement at Nuremberg, 1961, The Intruder, 1962, The Outrage, 1964, Dead of Night, 1974, The Devil's Rain, 1975, Star Trek, 1979, The Kidnapping of the President, 1979, Star Trek: The Wrath of Khan, 1982, Star Trek III, The Search for Spock, 1984, Star Trek IV: The Voyage Home, 1986, Star Trek V: The Final Frontier, 1989, Star Trek VI: The Undiscovered Country, 1991, National Lampoon's Loaded Weapon, 1993; Star Trek: Generations, 1994; Ashes of Eden, 1995; Star Trek: Avenger, 1997; Tek Net, 1997; Free Enterprise, 1999; Miss Congeniality, 2000; Groom Lake (also director and co-writer), 2002; Dodgeball, 2004; Miss Congeniality 2: Armed and Fabulous, 2005; The Wild (voice), 2006; Over the Hedge (voice), 2006. Publications: Ashes of Eden; Star Trek: Avenger, 1997; Step into Chaos, 1999; Get a Life, 1999; The Preserver, 2000; Spectre, 2000; Albums: The Transformed Man, 1968, Has Been, 2004. Honours: Emmy Award for Outstanding Guest Actor in a Drama Series, 2004; Best Supporting Actor in a

Series, Miniseries or TV Movie, Golden Globe Awards, 2005. Address: c/o Melis Productions, 760 North La Cienega Boulevard, Los Angeles, CA 90069, USA.

SHAW Fiona, b. 10 July 1958, Cork, Ireland. Actress. Education: University College, Cork; Royal Academy of Dramatic Art. Career: Stage appearances include: The Rivals; Howard Brenton's Bloody Poetry; With RSC: As You Like It; Gorky's Philistines; Les Liaisons Dangereuses; Much Ado About Nothing; The Merchant of Venice; The Taming of the Shrew; James Shirley's Hyde Park; Sophocles's Electra; Brecht's The Good Person of Sichuan; Hedda Gabler; Beckett's Footfalls; Richard II; The Waste Land, 1996; The Prime of Miss Jean Brodie, 1998; Widower's Houses, 1999; Medea, 2000, 2001; The Power Book, 2002; Films include: My Left Foot; Mountains of the Moon; Three Men and a Little Lady, 1990; Super Mario Brothers, 1992; Undercover Blues, 1993; The Waste Land, 1995; Persuasion, 1995; Jane Eyre, 1996; The Avengers, 1997; The Butcher's Boy, 1997; Anna Karenina, 1997; The Last September, 1999; The Triumph of Love, 2000; Harry Potter and The Philosopher's Stone, 2001; Doctor Sleep, 2001; Harry Potter and The Chamber of Secrets, 2002; Harry Potter and the Prisoner of Azkaban, 2004; The Black Dahlia, 2006; Catch and Release, 2006; Fracture, 2007; Harry Potter and the Order of the Phoenix, 2007; Many radio and TV appearances. Honours: Tree Prize, RADA, 1982; Ronson Award, RADA, 1982; Olivier Award for Best Actress, 1990; London Critics' Award for Best Actress, 1990; London Critics' Award, 1992; Olivier Award, Evening Standard Award for Machinal, 1995; Hon LLD, National University of Ireland, 1998; Honorary Professor of Drama, Trinity College, Dublin; Officier des Arts et des Lettres, 2001; Honorary OBE, 2002; Hon DUniv, Open University, 1999; Hon DLitt, Trinity College, Dublin, 2001; Evening Standard Award for Best Actress, 2001; Bancroft Gold Medal, RADA. Address: ICM, Oxford House, 76 Oxford Street, London W1N 0AX, England.

SHAW Sen-Yen, b. 26 March 1945, Taiwan. Professor of Mathematics. m. Tsui Yueh Chen, 2 daughters. Education: BS, Fu-Jen University, 1967; MA, 1972, PhD, 1977, University of Illinois, Chicago. Appointments: Associate Professor, National Central University, Chung-Li, Taiwan, 1977-82; Professor, 1982-2003, Head, Department of Mathematics, 1987-90; Professor, Lunghwa University of Science and Technology, 2003-. Publications: Over 90 papers in professional mathematical journals or books. Honour: Sun Yat-Sen Prize, 1985. Memberships: American Mathematical Society; Mathematical Society of Taiwan. Address: F20, 295, Wenhua Road Sec 2, Banchiao City, Taiwan.

SHE Jin-Hua, b. 23 May 1963, Jinshi, Hunan, China. University Professor. m. Yoko Miyamoto. 1 son. Education: Masters Degree, 1990, PhD, 1993, Tokyo Institute of Technology, Japan. Appointments: Lecturer, 1993-2001, Associate Professor, 2001-, Tokyo University of Technology, Japan; Guest Lecturer, Toyota Technical Development Corporation, Japan, 2001-; Guest Professor, Central South University, China, 2002-. Publications: Articles in scientific journals including: IEEE Transactions on Automatic Control, Automatica, Systems and Control Letters, Transactions of ASME; Control Engineering Practice; Engineering Application of Artificial Intelligence; IEE Proceedings. Honour: Prize Paper Award, International Federation of Automatic Control, 1999. Memberships: IEEE; Institute of Electrical Engineers of Japan; Society of Instrument and Control Engineers. Address: School of Bionics, Tokyo University of Technology,

1404-1 Katakura, Hachioji, Tokyo 192-0982, Japan. E-mail: she@cc.teu.ac.jp Website: www.teu.ac.jp/kougi/hp037/She.htm

SHEARER Alan, b. 13 August 1970, Gosforth, Newcastle upon Tyne, England. Footballer. Career: Coached as child at Wallsend Boys' Club; Striker; Striker, played for Southampton, 1987-92, Blackburn Rovers, 1992-96; Signed by Newcastle United for world record transfer of £15 million (Captain), 1996; First played for England, 1992-2000 (63 caps, 30 goals), Captain 1996-2000; Premiership all-time leading scorer; First player to score 200 Premiership goals and first to score 100 League goals for two different clubs; Scored 400th career goal, January 2005; Pundit, Match of the Day. Address: Newcastle United Football Club, St James Park, Newcastle Upon Tyne, NE1 4ST, England. Website: www.nufc.co.uk

SHEEN Charlie, b. 3 September 1965, New York, USA. Actor. m. (1) Donna Peele, 1995, divorced 1996, (2) Denise Richards, 2003, 2 children, divorced 2006; 1 child with Paula Profit. Actor, TV films include: Silence of the Heart; The Boys Next Door; Sugar Hill, 1999; Spin City, 2000-02; Two and A Half Men, 2003-2007; Films include: Apocalypse Now; Grizzly II; The Predator; The Red Dawn; Lucas; Platoon; The Wraith; Day Off; Young Guns; Wall Street; Eight Men Out; Major League; Backtrack; Men at Work; Courage Mountain; Navy Seals; The Rookie; Stockade (director); Secret Society; Hot Shots; Dead Fall; The Three Musketeers; The Chase; Major League II, 1994; Terminal Velocity, 1994; The Shadow Conspiracy, 1995; Shockwave, 1995; All Dogs Go to Heaven (voice), The Arrival, 1996; Money Talks, 1997; No Code of Conduct, 1998; Free Money, 1998; Letter From Death Row, 1998; Being John Malkovich, 1999; Cared X; Good Advice, 2000; Lisa Picard is Famous, 2001; Scary Movie 3, 2003; Deeper Than Deep, 2003; The Big Bounce, 2004; Foodfight, 2008. Honours: Golden Globe for Best Actor, 2002. Address: c/o Jeffrey Ballard Public Relations, 4814 Lemara Avenue, Sherman Oaks, CA 91403, USA.

SHEEN Martin (Ramon Estevez), b. 3 August 1940, Dayton, Ohio, USA. Actor. m. Janet Templeton, 1961, 3 sons, 1 daughter. Career: Actor, films include: The Incident; Catch 22; Rage; Badlands; Apocalypse Now; Enigma; Gandhi; The King of Prussia; The Championship Season; Man, Woman and Child; The Dead Zone; Final Countdown; Loophole; Wall Street; Night Beaker; Da, 1988; Personal Choice, 1989; Cadence (also director), 1990; Judgement in Berlin, 1990; Limited Time; The Maid, 1990; Cadence (also director), 1990; Hear No Evil; Hot Shots part Deux (cameo); Gettysburg, 1993; Trigger Fast; Hit!; Fortunes of War; Sacred Cargo; The Break; Dillinger and Capone; Captain Nuke and the Bomber Boys; Ghost Brigade; The Cradle Will Rock; Dead Presidents; Dorothy Day; Gospa; The American President; The War At Home; Spawn; Storm, Monument Avenue, Free Money; Lost & Found, 1999; Apocalypse New Redux, 2001; Catch Me If You Can, 2003; Milost mora, 2003; The Commission, 2003; Jerusalemski sindrom, 2004; Bordertown, 2006; Bobby, 2006; The Departed, 2006; Flatland: The Movie, 2007; Talk to Me, 2007; TV appearances include: The Defenders; East Side/West Side; My Three Sons; Mod Squad; Cannon; That Certain Summer; Missiles of October; The Last Survivors; Blind Ambition; Shattered Spirits; Nightbreaker; The Last POW?; Roswell; The West Wing, 1999-; Stage appearances: The Connection (New York and European tours); Never Live Over A Pretzel Factory; The Subject was Roses; The Crucible. Honours include: Honorary Mayor of Malibu, 1989-; Golden

Satellite Award, 2000; Golden Globe Award, 2000. Address: c/o Jeff Ballard, 4814 Lemara Avenue, Sherman Oaks, CA 91403, USA.

SHEESLEY Mary Frank, b. 1 August 1947, Minnesota, USA. Art Education Instructor. 2 sons. Education: Child Development Associate Credential, CDA Consortium, Washington DC, 1976; Associate of Arts Degree (summa cum laude), Art Education, Chipola Junior College, Florida, 1983; BSc (magna cum laude), Elementary Education, Troy State University, Alabama, 1986; MSc, Art Education, Florida State University, Panama City, Florida, 1991; PhD, Art Education, Florida State University, Tallahassee, Florida, 2000. Appointments: Social Service Co-ordinator, Head Start Teacher, Region 6E Head Start, Cosmos, Minnesota, 1975-79; Adult Community Education Instructor, Washington-Holmes Area Vo-Tech, Chipley, Florida, 1982; Art Instructor, Tyndall Elementary School, Panama City, 1986-91; Teaching Assistant, Florida State University, Tallahassee, 1991-92; Adjunct Instructor, University of West Florida, 1992; Art Instructor, Smith Elementary School, Panama City, 1992-95, 1996-2003, 2005-; Art Instructor, Frankfurt International School, Oberursel, Germany, 1995-96; Adjunct Instructor, Gulf Coast Community College, Panama City, 2002; Assistant Professor of Art Education, University of West Georgia, Carrollton, 2003-05; Numerous presentations and exhibitions throughout career. Honours: Returning Women Scholarship, 1982-83; Art Scholarship, 1983-84; Academic Scholarship, 1984-86; Arrowmount Scholarship, 1988; State Chairperson, Instructional Art Materials Committee, 1993-94; Fulbright Memorial Teacher Scholarship, Japan, 1997; $5,000 Artful Truth Grant, 1998; Listed in international biographical dictionaries. Memberships: Founder, Global Art Exchange Program; International Society for Education through Art; National Art Education Association; Florida Art Education Association; Bay County Art Teachers Association; Visual Arts Center; Florida League of Art Teachers. E-mail: sheesmf@bay.k12.fl.us

SHEINWALD Sir Nigel (Elton), b. 26 June 1953, London, England. Her Majesty's Diplomatic Service. m. Julia Dunne, 3 sons. Education: Harrow County Grammar School; BA, Classics, Balliol College, Oxford, 1976. Appointments: Joined HM Diplomatic Service, 1976, Japan Desk, 1976-77; British Embassy, Moscow, 1978-79; Rhodesia, Zimbabwe Dept, 1979-81; Head, FCO Anglo-Soviet Section, 1981-83; Political Section of British Embassy in Washington, 1983-87; Deputy Head, FCO's Policy Planning Staff, 1987-89; Deputy Head, FCO's European Union (Internal) Department, 1989-92; Head, UK Representation's Political and Institutional Section, Brussels, 1993-95; Head, FCO News Department, 1995-98; Europe Director, FCO, 1998-2000; Ambassador and UK Permanent Representative to European Union, Brussels, 2000-03; Foreign Policy Adviser to the Prime Minister and Head of Cabinet Office, Defence and Overseas Secretariat, 2003-; British Ambassador to the United States, 2007-. Honours: CMG, 1999; KCMG, 2001. Address: 10 Downing Street, London, SW1A 2AA, England.

SHENG Hui Zhen, b. 28 June 1953, Shanghai, China. Medical Researcher. m. Tiegian Lu, 1 son. Education: MD, Shanghai Second Medical University (now Shanghai Jiao Tong University School of Medicine), 1976; PhD, La Trobe University, Victoria, Australia, 1988. Appointments: Visiting Fellow, Visiting Associate, Senior Staff Fellow, Staff Scientist (permanent position), National Institutes of Health, Bethesda, Maryland, USA, 1989-2000; Professor and Head, Shanghai Laboratory of Developmental Biology, Shanghai Jiao Tong

University School of Medicine, 2000-. Publications: Over 30 papers and articles in professional journals including: Multistep control of pituitary organogenesis, 1997; Early steps in pituitary organogenesis, 1999; Embryonic stem cells generated by nuclear transfer of human somatic nuclei into rabbit oocytes, 2003; Nuclear reprogramming: the strategy used in normal development is also used in somatic cell nuclear transfer and parthenogenesis, 2007; Nuclear reprogramming: the zygotic transcription program is established through an "erase-and-rebuild" strategy, 2007. Honours: NIH Merit Award, USA; Chang-Jiang Scholar Award, China. Memberships: International Society for Stem Cell Research.

SHEPARD Sam, (Samuel Shepard Rogers), b. 5 November 1943, Fort Sheridan, Illinois, USA. Dramatist; Actor. m. O-Lan Johnson Dark, 9 November 1969, divorced, 1 son; 1 son, 1 daughter with Jessica Lange. Education: Mount San Antonio Junior College, Walnut, California, 1961-62. Career: Plays: Cowboys, Rock Garden, 1964; 4-H Club, Up to Thursday, Rocking Chair, Chicago, Icarus's Mother, 1965; Fourteen Hundred Thousand, Red Cross, Melodrama Play, 1966; La Turista, Cowboys #2, Forensic and the Navigators, 1967; The Holy Ghostly, The Unseen Hand, 1969; Operation Sidewinder, Shaved Splits, 1970; Mad Dog Blues, Terminal, Cowboy Mouth (with Patti Smith), Black Bog Beast Bait, 1971; The Tooth of Crime, 1972; Blue Bitch, Nightwalk (with Megan Terry and Jean-Claude van Itallie), 1973; Geography of a Horse Dreamer, Little Ocean, Action, Killer's Head, 1974; Suicide in B-Flat, Angel City, 1976; Curse of the Starving Class, 1977; Buried Child, 1978; Tongues, Savage/Love, Seduced, 1979; True West, 1981; Fool for Love, Superstitions, The Sad Lament of Pecos Bill on the Eve of Killing his Wife, 1983; A Lie of the Mind, 1985; States of Shock, 1991; Simpatico, 1993; TV: Lily Dale, 1996; Purgatory, 1999; Hamlet, 2000; Films: Days of Heaven; Frances; The Right Stuff; Country; Crimes of the Heart; Baby Boom; Defenceless, 1989; Voyager; Thunderheart, 1992; The Pelican Brief, 1994; Safe Passage, The Good Old Boys, 1995; Curtain Call, The Only Thrill, 1997; Snow Falling on Cedars, 1999; One Kill, 2000; Shot in the Heart, Swordfish, The Pledge, 2001; The Notebook, 2004; Don't Come Knockin', Stealth, 2005; Walker Payne, Bandidas, The Return, Charlotte's Web (narrator), 2006; Ruffian, The Assassination of Jesse James by the Coward Robert Ford, 2007; The Accidental Husband, 2008. Publications: A Murder of Crows, novel, Cruising Paradise, short stories, 1996; Great Dream of Heaven, short stories, 2002; The Rolling Thunder Logbook, 2005. Honours: Obie Awards, 1966, 1966, 1966, 1968, 1973, 1975, 1977, 1979, 1984; Rockefeller Foundation Grant, 1967; Guggenheim Fellowships, 1968, 1971; National Institute and American Academy of Arts and Letters Award, 1974; Creative Arts Award, Brandeis University, 1975; Pulitzer Prize in Drama, 1979; New York Drama Critics' Circle Award, 1986. Memberships: American Academy of Arts and Letters; Theater Hall of Fame. Address: c/o International Creative Management, 8942 Wilshire Boulevard, Beverly Hills, CA 90211, USA.

SHEPHARD Gillian Patricia (Rt Hon), b. 22 January 1940, England. Politician. m. Thomas Shephard, 1975, 2 stepsons. Education: St Hilda's College, Oxford. Appointments: Schools Inspector and Education Officer, 1963-75; Cambridge University Extra Mural Board Lecturer, 1965-87; Norfolk County Council, 1977-89; For Norfolk County Council: Chair of Social Services Committee, 1978-83; Education Committee, 1983-85; Chair, West Norfolk and Wisbech Health Authority, 1981-85; Norwich Health Authority, 1985-87; Conservative MP South West Norfolk, 1987-97, Norfolk South West, 1997-;

Parliamentary Private Secretary to Economic Secretary to the Treasury, 1988-89; Parliamentary Under Secretary of State, Department of Social Security, 1989-90; Treasury Minister of State, 1990-92; Employment Secretary of State, 1992-93, for Agriculture, Fisheries and Food, 1993-94, for Education, 1995, for Education and Employment, 1995-97; Women's National Commission Co-Chair, 1990-91; Shadow Leader of the House of Commons and Shadow Chancellor of Duchy of Lancaster, 1997-99; Opposition Spokesman on Environment, Transport and the Reginos, 1998-99; Deputy Chair, Conservative Party, 1991-92, 2002-03; Vice President, Hansard Society, 1997-2003. Publication: The Future of Local Government, 1991; Shephard's Watch, 2000. Memberships: Council Member, University of Oxford, 2000-. Honour: Honorary Fellow, St Hilda's College, Oxford, 1991. Address: House of Commons, London SW1A 0AA, England.

SHEPHERD Cybill, b. 18 February 1950, Memphis, Tennessee, USA. Actress. m. (1) David Ford, 1978, divorced, 1 daughter, (2) Bruce Oppenheim, 1987, divorced 1990, 1 son, 1 daughter. Career: Former magazine cover girl; Commercials for L'Oreal Preference, 8 years; Film include: The Last Picture Show, 1971; The Heartbreak Kid, 1973; Daisy Miller, 1974; At Long Last Love, 1975; Taxi Driver, 1976; Special Delivery, 1976; Silver Bears, 1977; The Lady Vanishes, 1978; Earthquake, 1980; The Return, 1986; Chances Are, 1988; Texasville, 1990; Alice, 1990; Once Upon a Crime, 1992; Married to It, 1993; The Last Word, 1995; Due East, 2003; Open Window, 2006; Hard Luck, 2006; numerous TV films; Plays include: A Shot in the Dark, 1977; Vanities, 1981; The Muse, 1999; Marine Life, 2000; TV includes: The Yellow Rose, 1983-84; Moonlighting, 1985-89; Cybill, 1994-98; Martha Behind Bars, 2005; Detective, 2005; The L Word, 2007-08. Publication: Cybill Disobedience, 2000. Honours: Emmy Award, 1985. Website: www.cybill.com

SHEPHERD John Alan (Sir), b. 27 April 1943, Edinburgh, Scotland. m. Jessica Nichols, 1 daughter. Education: MA, Selwyn College, Cambridge, 1961-64; MA, Stanford, 1964-65. Appointments: HM Diplomatic Service, 1965-2003 including: Ambassador, Bahrain, 1988-91; Minister, Bonn, 1991-95; Director, Middle East, Foreign and Commonwealth Office, 1996-97; Deputy Under Secretary, Foreign and Commonwealth Office, Member of Boards of Foreign and Commonwealth Office, BOTB later BTI, 1997-2000; Member, Review Committee of Government Export Promotion Services, 1998-99; Ambassador to Italy, 2000-2003; Currently: Secretary-General, Global Leadership Foundation; Chairman, Norbert Brainin Foundation; Deputy-Chairman, Trustees of Prince's School for Traditional Arts. Publication: Rhine Tasting in Motor Boat and Yachting, 1996. Honours: CMG, 1988; KCVO, 2000. Membership: Oxford and Cambridge Club. Address: GLF, 14 Curzon Street, London W1J 5HN, England.

SHER Sir Antony, b. 14 June 1949, Cape Town, South Africa. Actor; Artist; Author. Career: Films: Shadey; the Young Poisoner's Handbook; Alive and Kicking; Mrs Brown; Shakespeare in Love; TV appearances include: The History Man; Collision Course; The Land of Dreams; Genghis Cohn; The Moon Stone; Plays include: John, Paul, Ringo and Bert; Teeth n' Smiles; Cloud Nine; A Prayer for My Daughter; Goosepimples; King Lear; Tartuffe; Richard II; Merchant of Venice; The Revenger's Tragedy; Hello and Goodbye; Singer; Tamburlaine the Great; Travesties; Cyrano de Bergerac; The Winter's Tale; Torch Song Trilogy; True West; Arturo Ui; Uncle Vanya; Titus Andronicus; Stanley; Mahler's Conversion; ID, 2003; The Malcontent; Primo, 2005; Kean, 2007. Publications:

Year of the King, 1986; Middlepost, 1988; Characters, 1989; Changing Steps (Screenplay), 1989; The Indoor Boy, 1991; Cheap Drives, 1995; Woza Shakespeare! (co-author), 1996; The Feast, 1998; Beside Myself (autobiography), 2001; Primo, 2005; Primo Time, 2005. Honours: Best Actor Awards, Drama Magazine, London Standard Awards, 1985; Olivier Award for Best Actor, Society of West End Theatres, 1985, 1997; Best Actor Award, Martini TMA Awards, 1996; Peter Sellers Evening Standard Film Award, 1998; Honorary D Litt (Liverpool) 1998, (Exeter) 2003; KBE, 2000. Address: c/o ICM, Oxford House, 76 Oxford Street, London W1N 0AX, England.

SHER Emmanuil Moiseyevich, b. 29 March 1929, Port Khorly, Ukraine. Physicist Researcher. m. Elena, 1 son. Education: BS, Moscow State University, 1951; Physicist, St Petersburg State University, 1952; PhD, Physical Electronics, 1967; DSc, Physics of Semiconductors and Dielectrics, 1983. Appointments: Senior Engineer, Vacuum Technology, 1952-59; Researcher, Senior Scientific Researcher, Leading Scientific Researcher, Physics of Thermoelectricity, Electron Emission, High Temperature Superconductors and Thin Solid Films, 1959-. Publications: 100 articles, 21 patents, scientific editor of 2 books. Honours: Bronze Medal, 1963, Silver Medal, 1983; Honorary Academician, International Academy of Refrigeration, 1999. Memberships: AF Ioffe Physico-Technical Institute, Russian Academy of Sciences, 1959-; International Thermoelectric Society, 1991; New York Academy of Sciences, 1996. Address: 20 Orbely Str, apt 73, 194223 St Petersburg, Russia. E-mail: em.sher@mail.ioffe.ru

SHERBET Gajanan Venkatramanaya, b. 25 March 1935, Bantval, Karnataka, India. Pathologist; Cell Biologist; Research Scientist. m. Madurai Subramanyam Lakshmi. Education: BSc, 1956, MSc, 1958, PhD, 1962, University of Pune, India; MSc, 1967, DSc, 1978, University of London. Appointments: Research Scientist, Chester Beatty Research Institute, London, 1964-69; Research Fellow, Harvard University, USA, 1966; Research Scientist, University College Hospital Medical School, University of London, 1970-77; Research Scientist, Cancer Research Unit, 1977-81; Acting Director, Cancer Research Unit, 1988-89, Deputy Director, 1981-2000, Reader in Experimental Oncology, Cancer Research Unit, 1988-2000, Member of Communication and Signal Processing Research Group, School of Electrical, Electronic & Computer Engineering, 2001-, University of Newcastle upon Tyne; Adjunct Professor, Institute for Molecular Medicine, Huntington Beach, California, USA, 1999-; Associate Editorships: Anticancer Research, 1998-; Cancer Genomics and Proteomics, 2004-; Editorial Board, Current Cancer Therapy Review, 2005-; The Open Cancer Journal. Publications: Books: The Biophysical and Biochemical Characterisation of Cell Surface, 1977; The Biology of Tumour Malignancy, 1982; The Metastic Spread of Cancer, 1987; The Genetics of Cancer: Genes Associated with Cancer Invasion, Metastasis and Cell Proliferation, 1997; Calcium Signalling in Cancer, 2001; Genetic Recombination in Cancer, 2003; Editor of 4 books; Numerous articles to professional journals. Honours: The Lord Dowding Fund Award, London University, 1969-73; Beit Memorial and Williams Fellow, London University, 1969-3; Felix Wankel and Ernst Hutzenlaub Prize, 1977; Cancer Research Campaign Fellow, University of Newcastle upon Tyne, 1985-2000. Memberships: Fellow, Royal College of Pathologists; Fellow Royal Society of Chemistry; American Association for Cancer Research; British Neuro-Oncology Group; Life Member, Indian Association for Cancer Research. Address: School of

Electrical, Electronic and Computer Engineering, University of Newcastle upon Tyne, Merz Court, Newcastle upon Tyne NE1 7RU, England. E-mail: gajanan.sherbet@ncl.ac.uk

SHERIFF Bat-Sheva, b. 28 June 1937, Tel-Aviv, Israel. Professor, Chairman, Israel Postal and Philatelic Museum. m. Mordechai Manfred Segal, 1962, 2 sons. Education: Teacher's Diploma, University of Tel Aviv; Graduated, Philosophy and Literature, Hebrew University, Jerusalem. Appointments: Teacher, Secondary School, 1956-71; Director, Cultural Project for Underprivileged Youth in Development Areas, 1971-86; Editor, Monthly Journal for Inspectors; Inspector, Ministry of Education and Culture. Publications: Poems, 1956; Not All the Rivers, 1964; Love Poems, 1972; Persuasive Words, 1974; Man That is Honour – Psalm 49, 1978; Festive Poems, 1981; Ashes Instead of Bread, 1982; By Necessity and By Right, 1986; Letters to Bat-Sheva, 1990; Ancient People, 2002; The Soul is the Matter, 2003; Wilderness of the Eagle-Owl, 2004; Moments in Time-Sea of Galilee-Jerusalem, 2006. Numerous videos; Contributions to newspapers and periodicals, radio and television broadcasts. Memberships: Executive Committee, Hebrew Writers' Association; Press Council of Israel; PEN Israel; Israeli Council of Arts and Culture; Society of Authors, Composers and Music Publishers; International Confederation of Societies of Authors and Composers. Address: 10 Emek Rafaim, PO Box 7353, Jerusalem 91072, Israel.

SHESHTAWY Adel, b. 1 February 1946, Egypt. Petroleum Engineer. m. Valentina Tasseva, 2 sons, 1 daughter. Education: BS, MS, PhD, Petroleum Engineering. Appointments: Senior Engineer, Phillips Petroleum; Lead Drilling Engineer, Mobil Oil Co; Drilling Superintendent, Amaco Oil Co; Associate Professor, Petroleum Engineering, University of Oklahoma, USA; Chairman, Chief Executive Officer, Tri-Max Industries. Publications: Oil Wells Blow Out Prevention Methods and Practice; New Batton Holes Assembly for Slinder Wells Drilling; Numerous other articles for professional journals. Honours: IR 100 for Best Product Developed, 1979; Best Invention, 1980. Memberships: Society of Petroleum Engineers; IADD. E-mail: trimax@trimax-inds.com

SHEU Maw-Shyong, b. 18 November 1939, Chia-Yi, Taiwan. Professor. m. Yu-I Tsai, 1 son, 2 daughters. Education: BS in Civil Engineering, National Cheng-Kung University, Taiwan, 1962; MS in Civil Engineering, National Taiwan University, Taiwan, 1965; PhD of Civil Engineering, University of Washington, Seattle, USA, 1975. Appointments: Lecturer, 1965-75, Associate Professor, 1975-78, Department Chairman, 1978-81, Professor, 1978-2004, Professor Emeritus, 2004-, Department of Architecture, National Cheng-Kung University, Taiwan; President, Evergreen Consulting Engineering, Taipei, Taiwan, 1976-86; Division Head, Disaster Mitigation of Earthquake Engineering, National Science Council, Taiwan, 1982-92. Publications: Architectural Structural Systems, 1999; Around 100 technical papers on structural engineering in journals and at conferences. Honours: Outstanding Teaching Professor, Ministry of Education, Taiwan, 1989, 1994; Outstanding Paper Awards: Institute of Engineers, Taiwan, 1990, 2003; Institute of Civil and Hydraulic Engineering, 1979, 1980, 1990, 2003; Institute of Architecture, Taiwan, 1998, 2003, 2004; Institute of Structural Engineering, Taiwan, 1997; Tsuboi Prize, International Association of Shell and Spatial Structures, 2004. Memberships: Institute of Engineers, Taiwan; Institute of Architecture, Taiwan; Institute of Structural Engineering, Taiwan; Institute of Civil and Hydraulic Engineering, Taiwan. Address: Department of Architecture, National Cheng-Kung University, Tainan, Taiwan 70101, Taiwan. E-mail: mssheu@mail.ncku.edu.tw

SHI Xiangguo, b. 20 July 1974, Changchun City, Jilin Province, China. Chemist. m. Lei Ci. Education: BSc, 1998, PhD, 2003, Shenyang Pharmaceutical University. Appointments: Research Fellow, Division of Supramolecular Biology, Yokohama City University, Japan, 2004-06; Research Fellow, Rowland Institute at Harvard, Harvard University, USA, 2006-. Publications: More than 30 papers in peer-reviewed scientific journals in English, Japanese and Chinese; 1 book chapter; Numerous international conference papers. Honours: Excellent presentation award, 53rd Annual Conference on Mass Spectrometry of Japan, 2005. Memberships: American Association of Pharmaceutical Scientists; American Society for Mass Spectrometry; American Chemical Society; Sigma Xi. Address: Rowland Institute at Harvard, Harvard University, 100 Edwin H Land Blvd, Cambridge, MA 02142, USA. E-mail: shi@rowland.harvard.edu

SHIBAKAWA Rinya, b. 15 February 1934, Hokkaido, Japan. Professor. m. Sachiko, 2 daughters. Education: Master Degree, Graduate School of Commerce and Management of Hitotsubashi University, 1958; PhD, Economics, Kyushu University, 1980. Appointments: Professor, Aoyama Gakuin University, 1966; Dean and Professor, Graduate School of Tsukuba University, 1979; Professor, Graduate School of Hitotsubashi University, 1990-97; Emeritus Professor, Hitotsubashi University, 1997-; Dean and Professor, Graduate School of Business, Jobu University, 2007-. Publications: Financial Characteristics of Japanese Corporations, 1990; Corporate Governance, Cost of Capital and Financial Distress, 1994. Honours: Nikkei Economics Award, 1969. Memberships: Japanese Finance Association; Japan Society of Business Administration. Address: 2-18-14, Umezono, Tsukuba City, Ibaraki, 305-0045, Japan. E-mail: rinya@kde.biglobe.ne.jp

SHIBATA Tokushi, b. 19 November 1941, Tokyo, Japan. Scientific Consultant, Japan Atomic Energy Agency; Professor Emeritus. m. Tomoe, 1 son, 1 daughter. Education: BA, Chiba University, 1965; MA, 1967, PhD, 1975, Nuclear Physics, Osaka University. Appointments: Research Associate, 1970-77, Lecturer, 1977-80, Associate Professor, 1980—87, Faculty of Science, Osaka University; Professor, 1987-97, Professor Emeritus, Institute of Nuclear Study, University of Tokyo; Professor, 1997-2005, Professor Emeritus, High Energy Accelerator Research Organisation, Head of Radiation Science Center; Professor Emeriuts, Graduate University for Advanced Studies; Member, Board of Directors, Japan Radioisotope Association. Publications: Measurements of Radiation; Radiation Physics. Memberships: Science Council of Japan, 1997-2005. Address: 2-8-18 Shibakubo, Nishi-Tokyo, Tokyo 188-0014, Japan. E-mail: tokushi.shibata@kek.jp

SHIEH Wung Yang, b. 22 September 1956, Taipei, Taiwan. Professor. m. Jiin Jiun Leu, 2 sons, 1 daughter. Education: Master's Degree, University of Tokyo, 1986; Doctor's Degree, 1989. Appointments: Associate Professor, 1989-94, Professor, 1994- Institute of Oceanography, National Taiwan University, Taipei. Publications: Contribution of articles to professional journals including International Journal of Systemic and Evolutionary Microbiology and Canadian Journal of Microbiology. Memberships: The Japanese Society of Microbial Ecology; The Taiwanese Society of Microbiology. Address: Institute of Oceanography, National Taiwan University, PO Box 23-13, Taipei, Taiwan. E-mail: winyang@ntu.edu.tw.

SHIEL Derek Alexander George, b. 18 April 1939, Dublin, Ireland. Painter; Writer; Sculptor; Landscape Designer; Lecturer; Curator; Psychotherapist; Film Director. Education:

Fettes College, Edinburgh; Edinburgh College of Art, 1956-61; Diploma of Art, 1960; Travelling Scholarship to USA, 1961-62. Appointments: Art Tutor, Berkshire College of Art, 1963-65; Art Tutor, West Sussex College of Art, 1964-69; Lecturer in Art Appreciation and Art Tutor, The City Literary Institute, London, 1965-77; Gardening: Landscape Gardener/Designer, 1978-98. Theatre: Writer and Director, 1980-2005; wrote stage adaptation of Gogol's The Overcoat; wrote and directed, Which One of Me?, performed in 5 European countries; wrote and directed, Landing Site; directed puppet play, The Way to St Bernard; co-directed improvised production of Bluebeard; Director and Actor/Puppeteer for Hilary Pepler Celebration, Ditchling Museum, East Sussex; Director and Actor in Celebration of Writers of Little Venice. Exhibitions: exhibitions of paintings, sound sculpture, works in theatre, landscape design, colour structures with living plants, held in Britain and Europe. Music: Originator/Percussionist with other musicians in Shiel's ensemble, Sculpted Sound, performing at museums, art galleries, theatres, festivals and for UK radio and television broadcasts; Twenty composers have so far written for Shiel's sound sculptures; Painter/Performer with Composer Julia Usher in their duo, SoundPaint, performances at art and music festivals, universities, conferences. Psychotherapy: Psychotherapist and participant in The Men's Movement; articles in magazines, Wingspan (USA), Achilles Heel (UK); Founder of The Men's Databank. Publications: essay in Fathers and Sons, 1995; Co-author, David Jones: The Maker Unmade, 1995 (second edition, 2003); Editor, David Jones: Ten Letters, 1996; essay in The Chesterton Review, David Jones Special Issue, 1997; essay in Diversity in Unity, 2000; Editor and essay in David Jones in Ditchling, 2003; Author, Arthur Giardelli, Paintings, Constructions, Relief Sculptures, Conversations with Derek Shiel, 2001; Film: Director, In Search of David Jones, Artist, Soldier, Poet, 2007. Curator of exhibitions: Arthur Giardelli, National Library of Wales, 2002; David Jones in Ditchling, Ditchling Museum, 2003 (co-curator); Art Exhibition, Little Venice Music Festival, 2004. Lecturer: lectures at art galleries, museums, universities and art societies on David Jones, Arthur Giardelli or Sound Sculptures. Honour: First Artist-in-Residence, Estorick Collection of Modern Italian Art, London, 2000. Membership: PEN. Address: 25 Randolph Crescent, London W9 1DP, England.

SHIH Hong, b. 2 December 1945, Qingdao, P R China. Materials Science. m. Linda Chen, 1 daughter. Education: BS, Chemistry, Peking University, China, 1970; MS, Electrochemistry, China, 1981; Research Assistant Professor, USC, 1987-90; PhD, Metallurgy, The Pennsylvania State University (Materials Science and Engineering), USA, 1986; Post doctor, University of Southern California (Materials Science and Engineering), USA, 1986-87. Appointments: Post Doctor & Research Professor, University of Southern California, 1986-90; Senior Research Scientist, GM Research Center, USA, 1990-91; Member, Technical Staff, FMC Corporate Technology Center, 1991-92; Technical Consultant, 1992-94; Senior Engineer, Member of Technical Staff, Senior Technical Staff, Technical Director, Applied Materials Inc, 1994-2002; Technical Director, Lam Research Corp, USA, 2002-. Publications: Over 100 articles in referred journals and books; Over 150 consultant reports in national and international presentations; Over 1,000 technical reports in semiconductor technology, Applied Materials & Lam Research; 86 US & international patents applied and 40 awarded. Honours: 1st place, NACE Student Post Competition, 1984; Wesley W Horner Award, ACEA, 1993; Pennsylvania State University McFarland Award, 2004; Vista Award, Lam Research Corp,

2007. Memberships: Electrochemical Society; National Association of Corrosion Engineers. Address: 2187 Bray Ave, Santa Clara, CA 95050, USA. E-mail: hong.shih@lamrc.com

SHIH Neng-Hui, b. 26 June 1963, ZhangHua County, Taiwan. Associate Professor. m. Dong-Ling Wang, 2 sons. Education: Bachelor's degree, Department of Applied Mathematics, Feng Chia University, Taiwan, 1988; Master's degree, Department of Mathematical Sciences, National Chengchi University, Taiwan, 1990; PhD, Industrial Engineering, National Tsing Hua University, Taiwan, 1994. Appointments: Chairman, Department of Business Administration, 1991-2001, Founder, Department of Marketing and Logisitics Management, and Department of Commerce Automation and Management, 2001, Founder, Graduate School in Marketing and Logistics Management, 2002, National Pingtung Institute of Commerce, Taiwan; Director, Business Modernization Academy, Taiwan, 2003-05; Senior Principle Investigator, Research Project supported by National Science Council, Taiwan, 1995-. Publications: Simulation of Maximum Flow in Multistate Networks, 2002; Economic optimization of off-line inspection with inspection errors, 2003; Impact of Inspection errors on the lot size problem, 2004; Estimating the completion-time distribution in stochastic activity networks, 2005; On the project scheduling under resource constraints, 2006. Honours: First Grade Research Award, National Science Council, Taiwan, 1995-98; Listed in international biographical dictionaries. Memberships: Business Modernization Academy, Taiwan. Address: 51 Min Shen E Road, Pingtung 900, Taiwan, ROC.

SHIH Tso-Min, b. 4 April 1935, Ying-Cheng, Shantung, China. Mining Engineering Educator. m. Ching-Ch'i Hsia Shih, 1 June 1961, 1 son, 2 daughters. Education: BSc, National Cheng-Kung University, Taiwan, 1958; MSc, McGill University, Montreal, Canada, 1965. Appointments: Research Assistant, Nova Scotia Technical College, Halifax, Canada, 1965-66; Lecturer, 1968-72, Associate Professor, 1972-74, Professor, Department Chairman, 1974-80, Professor, 1980-2000, Part time Professor, 2000, Retired, 2000, National Cheng-Kung University, Tainan, Taiwan, China; Director, Chinese Institute of Mining and Metal Engineering, 1976-78; Director, Mining Association of China, 1988-96; Director, Tainan Tai-Chi and Ba-Kiua-Chang Society, 2001-2003; Full Professor, 2003-06, Retired, 2006, Diwan University, Tainan County. Publications: Diamond, book (in Chinese), 1996; The Exploitation and Utilization of Graphite, book (in Chinese); More than 50 publications in journals and conference proceedings. Honours: Chinese Institute of Mining and Metal Engineering, Taipei, 1972, 1991; Pi Epsilon Tau National Petroleum Engineering Honor Society, Los Angeles, 1989; Department of Reconstructions, Taiwan Provincial Government, 1993; Mining Association of China, 1996. Memberships: Chinese Institute of Engineers. Address: No 74 Fl 1 Tung-Ning Road, Tainan, Taiwan, 701, China.

SHIHABI Samir S, b. 27 May 1925, Jerusalem, Palestine. Diplomat. m. Widad K Shihabi, 1 son, 1 daughter. Education: BA, American University, Cairo, 1947; Yale Law School, USA, 1947; Fitzwilliam College, Cambridge, England, 1948-49; MA, New York University, 1987; Honorary LLD, American University in Cairo. Appointments: Ambassador to Turkey, 1964-73; Ambassador to Somalia, 1974; Ambassador to Pakistan, 1980-83; Ambassador and Permanent Representative to United Nations, New York, 1983-91; President of the General Assembly of the UN, 1991-92; Ambassador to Switzerland, 1994-98. Publications: Many articles on diplomacy and politics. Honours: King Abdulaziz

Distinguished Order, Saudi Arabia, 1973; Sitara Pakistan, President of Pakistan, 1982. Memberships: Honorary Life President, International Association of Permanent Representatives to the UN; Chairman, Council of Presidents of the General Assembly of the UN. Address: PO Box 119, Jedda 21411, Saudi Arabia.

SHIKHMURZAEV Yulii Damir, b. 12 September 1957, Ryazan, USSR. Mathematician. m. Zimfira Gallyamova, 1 daughter. Education: MSc, Applied Mathematics and Mechanics, 1980, PhD, Physics and Mathematics, 1985, Moscow State University. Appointments: Junior Research Scientist, 1984-88, Research Scientist, 1989-92, Senior Research Scientist, 1992-96, Moscow State University; Lecturer, University of Leeds, UK, 1996-98; Senior Lecturer, 1999-2001, Reader, 2001-2006, Professor 2006-, School of Mathematics, University of Birmingham, UK; Visiting Researcher, University of Naples, Italy, 1988-89; Visiting Professor, University of Pierre and Marie Curie, France, 2002, University of South Australia, 2006; Associate Editor, Continuum Mechanics & Thermodynamics, 2005-. Publications: More than 40 articles; 2 patents. Memberships: International Society of Coating Science and Technology; European Mechanics Society; German Society for Applied Mathematics and Mechanics; London Mathematical Society. Address: School of Mathematics, University of Birmingham, Edgbaston, Birmingham B15 2TT, England. E-mail: yulii@for.mat.bham.ac.uk

SHIM Chan Shik, b. 11 March 1962, Seoul, South Korea. Medical Doctor. m. In-kyung Shin, 1 son, 1 daughter. Education: MD, 1987; MA, 1994; PhD, 2003; Board Certified, Korean Board of Neurological Surgery, 1996. Appointments: Vice-President, Medical Affairs, Wooridul Spine Hospital, Seoul, Korea, 2002-2003; Visiting Professor, Department of Neurosurgery, Kyung-Hee University, College of Medicine, Seoul, Korea, 2000-; Vice-President, Academic Affairs, Wooridul Spine Hospital, Seoul, Korea, 2005-. Publications: Articles in medical journals include: Partial disc replacement with PDN prosthetic disc nucleus device: Early clinical results, 2003; Fluoroscopically assisted percutaneous translaminar facet screw fixation following anterior lumbar interbody fusion: Technical report, 2005; Vertical split fracture of the vertebral body following total disc replacement using ProDisc: Report of 2 cases, 2005; Early and radiological outcomes of cervical arthroplasty with Bryan Cervical Disc Prosthesis, 2006; CHARITÉ vs ProDisc: A comparative study of a minimum 3-year follow-up, 2007; Posterior avulsion fracture at the adjacent vertebral body during cervical disc replacement with ProDisc-C: A case report, 2007; Soft stabilization with an artificial ligament in Grade 1 degenerative spondylolisthesis: Comparison with instrumented posterior lumbar intebody fusion, 2007. Honour: The SAS Leon Wiltse Award for Best Overall Paper, Montreal, Canada, 2006. Memberships: Spine Arthroplasty Society; Korean Neurosurgical Society; International Society of Minimal Intervention for Spine Surgery; North American Spine Society. Address: 47-4 Chungdam-Dong, Kangnam-Gu, Seoul, South Korea 135-100. E-mail: shimcs@wooridul.co.kr

SHIM Kwan-Shik, b. 24 August 1965, Gwangju, Republic of Korea. Electronics Engineer; Researcher. m. Eun-Hee Park, 1996, 3 children. Education: BS, 1991, MS, 1993, PhD, 1997, Chonnam National University; Registered Professional Engineer, Korea Electrical Engineering Association, 2006. Appointments: Sargeant, Korean Army, 1985-88; Assistant Professor, Seonam University, Namwon, Republic of Korea, 1997-2004; Chair, Department of Electical Engineering, Asan

Campus, 2003-04; Senior Researcher, Research Institute of Industrial Technology, Chonnam National University, 2004-; Technical Director, Seo Electronics Co Ltd, Gwangju, 2004-; Representative, Cosmos Energy Research, Gwangju, 2006-. Publications: Numerous articles in professional journals. Memberships: IEEE; Korean Institute of Electrical Engineers. Address: Cosmos Energy Research, 996-3 Moon Heung-Dong, Buk-Gu, Gwangju Metropolitan, Chonnam 500-110, Republic of Korea. E-mail: simgong@ieee.org

SHIMADA Yasuyuki, b. 12 May 1960, Kyoto, Japan. Medical Doctor. Education: MD, 1985, PhD, 1996, Kyoto Prefectural University of Medicine. Appointments: Research Fellow, Rayne Institute, St Thomas Hospital, London, England, 1993-95; Registrar, Cardiothoracic Surgery, St George Hospital, Australia, 1996-98; Senior Lecturer, Kyoto Prefectural University of Medicine, 1999-2002; Director, Cardiovascular Surgery, Saiseikai Suota Hospital, 2003-2004; Director, Cardiovascular Surgery, Yuri Kumiai General Hospital, 2005-; Fellowship, Japanese Association for Thoracic Surgery, 2000; Active Member of the International Society for Cardiovascular Surgery, 2002-; Board Certified Surgeon, The Japanese Board of Cardiovascular Surgery, 2004-. Memberships: International Fellow, American Heart Association; American Stroke Association. American Chemical Society, 2007. Address: Cardiovascular Surgery, Yuri Kumiai General Hospital, 38 Ieno-ushiro Aza, Kawaguchi, Honjo, Akita 015-8511, Japan. E-mail: yasuyuki.shimada@ma8.seikyou.ne.jp

SHIN Byeong Rog, b. 28 June 1959, Chung-Nam, Korea. Professor. m. Chong-Hee Park, 1 son. Education: Bachelor of Mechanical Engineering, Hanyang University, Seoul, Korea, 1981; Master of Engineering, Yonsei University, Seoul, 1983; PhD of Engineering, Tohoku University, Sendai, Japan, 1991. Appointments: Research Associate, 1991-93, Associate Professor, 1997-2003, Tohoku University, Sendai, Japan; Professor (Brain Pool), Chungnam National University, Korea, 1993-95; Research Engineer, Hitachi Co Ltd, Hitachi, Japan, 1995-97; Associate Professor, Changwon National University, Changwon, Korea, 2003-; Visiting Scholar, Princeton University, USA, 2006-07. Publications: Textbook, Fundamentals of Computational Fluid Dynamics, 1994. Honours: Best Paper Award, Turbomachinery Society of Japan, 2001; National Prize of Korea, The Prime Minister's Commendation, 2002. Memberships: Senior Member, AIAA; Director, KSCFE; KFMA; Regional Editor, CFD Journal; JSME; JSFM; KSME; JSMF; TSJ; KSEAJ; JSAS. Address: Department of Mechanical Engineering, Changwon National University, Sarim-dong, Changwon, Geongnam 641-773, Korea. E-mail: brshin@changwon.ac.kr

SHIN Dong-Keun, b. 13 June 1959, Incheon, South Korea. Independent Researcher in Computer Science. m. Helen Chang, 2 sons. Education: UC Berkeley, USA; George Washington University, USA. Publications: A Comparative Study of Hash Functions for a New Hash-Based Relational Join Algorithm, 1991; A Sorting Method by Dong-Keun Shin, 1998; Writing letters to the world's academic communities, Dr Dong-Keun Shin has challenged to be the greatest computer scientist in the world since 1997. Address: Hwa Shin Building, Suite 701, 705-22 Yuksam-dong, Kangnam-gu, Seoul 135-080, Korea. Website: www.dkshin.com

SHIN Jeong-Hoon, b. 21 July 1969, Daegu Si, Korea. Professor. m. Yoon-Young Ahn, 1 son, 1 daughter. Education: BS, 1992, MS, 1994, PhD, 2005, Sungkyunkwan University, Republic of Korea. Appointments: Researcher, SKC R&D Center, Daejeon Si, 1994; Chief Researcher, DACOM R&D Center, Daejeon Si, 1995-2001; Affiliated Professor, Induk College, Seoul Si, 2002-05; Professor, Catholic University of Daegu, Daegu Si, 2006-. Publications: Keypad gloves: glove-based text input device and input method for wearable computers, 2005; Implementation and Performance Evaluation of Glove-based HCI methods: Gesture Recognition Systems Using Fuzzy Algorithm and Neural Network for the Wearable PC, 2005; Performance Evaluation of Gesture Recognition System using Fuzzy Algorithm and Neural Network for Post PC platform, 2005; An Improved HCI Method and Information Input Device Using Gloves for Wearable Computers, 2005; Design and Implementation of Enhanced Real Time News Service using RSS and Voice XML, 2007; Implementation of a 3-Dimensional motion detectable Game for Developing Balanced Brain-Wave, 2007. Honours: Listed in international biographical dictionaries. Memberships: Institute of Electronics Engineers of Korea; Korean Institute of Signal Processing and Systems; Korea Information Processing Society. Address: Catholic University of Daegu, 330 Geumnak 1-ri, Hayang-eup, Gyeongsan-si, Gyeongbuk, 712-702, Republic of Korea. E-mail: only4you@cu.ac.kr Website: http://hci.cu.ac.kr

SHIN Jong-Dug, b. 25 January 1958, Seoul, Republic of Korea. Professor. m. Young-Mi Lee, 1 son. Education: BS, Yonsei University, Seoul, 1981; MS, University of Texas at Austin, USA, 1987; PhD, Texas A&M University, USA, 1991. Appointments: Member, Technical Staff, Huneed Technology Inc, Gyunggi-Do, Republic of Korea, 1980-83; Senior Research Engineer, ETRI, Daejeon, Republic of Korea, 1991-95; Professor, 1995-, Head, 2003-05, School of Electronic Engineering, Associate Dean, College of Information Technology, 2006-07, Soongsil University, Seoul; Visiting Professor, Alcatel USA, Plano, Texas, 2001-02; Programme Manager, Korea Research Foundation, Seoul, 2006. Honours: Listed in international biographical dictionaries. Memberships: IEEE Lasers and Electro-Optic Society; Communications Society. Address: School of Electronic Engineering, Soongsil University, 511 Sangdo-Dong, Dongjak-Gu, Seoul 156-743, Republic of Korea. E-mail: jdshin@ssu.ac.kr

SHIN Joong-Rin, b. 10 September 1949, Seoul, Korea. Professor. m. Myung-Hee Jun, 2 sons. Education: BS, 1979, MS, 1984, PhD, 1989, Electrical Engineering, Seoul National University, Seoul. Appointments: Chairman, Electricity Policy Research Korea, Korean Institute of Electrical Engineering; Chief, Research Centre for Innovative Electricity Market Technology, Chief Representative, Korea Power Engineering Professor Forum, 2000-03; Professor, Electrical Engineering, 2003-, Dean, Graduate School of Engineering, 2004-06, Dean, College of Engineering, 2006-2007, Vice President, 2007-, Konkuk University, Seoul. Publications: Co-author, Theory and Practice of Power Transmission Tariff, 2003; Editorial Supervisor, Trend of Foreign Power Industry, 2005. Honours: Academic Achievement Award in Engineering, Konkuk University, 2003; Academic Achievement Award, KIEE, 2004; Fellowship, 20 Leading Persons of the 21st Century in the Korean Electrical Community. Memberships: Senior Member, IEEE PES; Member (Trustee), KIEE; Member (Steering Director), Society for Electricity Industry Studies, Korea.

SHIN Kwang-Ho, b. 21 January 1970, Daegu, Korea. Electronic Engineer. m. Jeongmin Lee, 1 daughter. Education: BS, 1993, MS, 1995, Electrical Engineering, Dong-A University, Korea; PhD, Research Institute of Electrical Communication, Tohoku University, 1999. Appointments:

Researcher, Pharmaceuticals and Medical Devices Agency, Tokyo, Japan, 1999-2000; Member, Technical Staff, Samsung Advanced Institute of Technology, Suwon, Korea, 2000; Associate Professor, Kyungsung University, Pusan, Korea, 2000-; Chief of Researchers, CNK Co, Jinju, Korea, 2002-03; Director, Research Center, NRDtech Co, Pusan, Korea, 2004-05; Associate Professor, Toyohashi University of Technology, Toyohashi, Japan, 2006-07. Publications: Over 62 technical papers published in professional journals in the field of electronic devices and functional materials; Patents for magnetic sensors, signal conditioning of magnetic sensors, strain sensors, vibrating sample magnetometers, RFID sensors, and magneto-static wave devices. Honours: Best Presentation Award, 1997, Best Presentation Award, 1998, Institute of Electrical Engineers of Japan; Takei Award, Magnetics Society, Japan, 1999; Best Paper Award, Korean Magnetics Society, Korea, 2004. Memberships: Institute of Electrical and Electronic Engineers; Korean Institute of Electrical and Electronic Materials; Korean Sensors Society; Korean Magnetics Society; KIEE; MSJ. Address: 102-1003 Metrocity APT, Yong-ho-dong, Nam-gu, Pusan 608-776, Korea. E-mail: khshin@star.ks.ac.kr

SHINAWATRA Thaksin, b. 26 July 1949, Chiangmai Province, Thailand. Prime Minister of Thailand. m. Khunying Potjaman Shinawatra, 1 son, 2 daughters. Education: Graduate, Police Academy, Thailand, 1973; Master Degree in Criminal Justice, Eastern Kentucky University, USA, 1975; Doctorate Degree in Criminal Justice, Sam Houston State University, USA, 1978. Appointments: Royal Thai Police Department, 1973-87; Founder, Shinawatra Computer and Communications Group, 1987-94; Founder, THAICOM Foundation, long distance satellite education programme, 1993; Established Thai Rak Thai Party and Leader of Thai Rak Tai Party, 1998-; 23rd Prime Minister of Thailand, 2001-2006. Honours: Royal Decorations: Knight Grand Cordon (Special Class) of the Most Noble Order of the Crown of Thailand, 1995; Knight Grand Cordon (Special Class), Most Exalted Order of the White Elephant, 1996; Knight Grand Cross (First Class), Most Admirable Order of the Direkgunabhorn, 2001; Knight Grand Commander, Most Illustrious Order of Chula Chom Klao, 2002; Foreign Decorations: The Royal Order of Sahametrei (Grand Cross), Kingdom of Cambodia, 2001; Ahmed Al Fateh, Kingdom of Bahrain, 2002; The Most Blessed Order of Setia Negara Brunei (First Class), Brunei Darussalam, 2002; Commander Grand Cross of the Royal Order of the Polar Star of the Kingdom of Sweden, 2003; Numerous other awards include: Honorary Doctorate, Thammasat University, 1994; Sam Houston Humanitarian Award, Sam Houston State University, USA, 2002; Honorary Doctorate, Tokyo Institute of Technology, Japan, 2003. Memberships: President, Northerners Association of Thailand, 1998-. Address: Office of the Prime Minister, Government House, Thanon Nakhon Pathem, Bangkok 10300, Thailand.

SHIPLEY Rt Hon Jennifer Mary (Jenny), b. 1952, New Zealand. Politician. m. Burton, 1 son, 1 daughter. Appointments: Former School Teacher; Farmer, 1973-88; Joined National Party, 1975; Former Malvern County Councillor; MP for Ashburton (now Rakaia), 1987-; Minister of Social Welfare, 1990-93, Womens Affairs, 1990-98, Health, 1993-96, State Services, 1996-97, State Owned Enterprises, Transport, Accident Rehabilitation and Compensation Insurance; Minister Responsible for Radio New Zealand; Minister in Charge of New Zealand Security Intelligence Services, 1997-; Prime Minister of New Zealand,

1997-99; Leader of the Opposition, 2000-2001. Address: Parliament Buildings, Wellington, New Zealand. E-mail: hq@national.org.nz Website: www.national.org.nz

SHIRLEY Dame (Vera) Stephanie, (Steve), b. 16 September 1933, Dortmund, Germany. Philanthropist. m. Derek George Millington Shirley, 1 son, deceased. Education: BSc (Spec.), Sir John Cass College, London, 1956; FBCS, 1971; CEng, 1990; CITP; CIMgt. Appointments: PO Research Station, Dollis Hill, 1951-59; CDL, Subsidiary of ICL, 1959-62; Founder and Chief Executive, 1962-87, Director, 1962-93, Life President, 1993-, Xansa Plc (now part of Steria); Director, Tandem Computers Inc, 1992-97; Director, AEA Technology Plc, 1992-2000; Director, John Lewis Partnership, 1999-2001; European Advisory Board, Korn/Ferry International, 2001-2004; CSR Advisory Board, Steria, 2008-. Publication: The Art of Prior's Court School, 2002. Honours: DBE, 2000; OBE, 1980; CCMI (CBIM, 1984); FREng, 2001; Honorary FCGI, 1989; Honorary Fellow: Manchester Metropolitan University, 1989, Staffordshire University, 1991, Sheffield Hallam University, 1992, IMBC, 1999, Birkbeck, 2002, New Hall, Cambridge, 2002; Foundation Fellow, Balliol College, Oxford, 2001; Honorary DSc: Buckingham, 1991, Aston, 1993, Nottingham Trent, 1994, Solent, 1994, Southampton, 2003, Brunel, 2005; Honorary DTech: Loughborough, 19991, Kingston, 1995; DUniv: Leeds Metropolitan, 1993, Derby, 1997, London Guildhall, 1998, Stirling, 2000; Honorary DLitt, de Montfort, 1993; Honorary DBA: West of England, 1995, City, 2000; Honorary Dr, Edinburgh, 2003; Honorary D Laws, Leicester, 2005; Bath, 2006; Recognition of Information Technology Achievement Award, 1985; Gold Medal Chartered Management Institute, 1991; Mountbatten Medal, IEE, 1999; Beacon Award for Start-ups, 2003; British Computer Society Lifetime Achievement Award, 2004; US National Woman's Hall of Fame, 1995. Memberships include: Council, Industrial Society, 1984-90; NCVQ, 1986-89; President, British Computer Society, 1989-90; Vice-President, C&G, 2000-05; Member, Council, Duke of Edinburgh's Seventh Commonwealth Study Conference, 1991-92; British-North American Committee, 1992-2001; Chairman, Women of Influence, 1993; Trustee, Help the Aged, 1987-90; Patron: Disablement Income Group, 1989-2001; Centre for Tomorrow's Co, 1997-; Honours Subcommittee, Economy, 2005-; Member, Oxford University Court of Benefactors; Cambridge Guild of Benefactors; Founder: The Kingwood Trust, 1993, The Shirley Foundation, 1996, Prior's Court Foundation, 1998, Autism Cymru, 2001; Trustee and UK Chair, National Alliance for Autism Research, 2004-06; UK Chair, Autism Speaks, 2006-; Master, Information Technologists Company, 1992, Liveryman, 1992; Freeman, City of London, 1987. Address: 47 Thames House, Phyllis Court Drive, Henley on Thames, Oxfordshire RG9 2NA, England. E-mail: steve@steveshirley.com

SHITTU Gaffar Mola, b. 24 June 1948, Kano, Nigeria. Consultant Paediatrician. m. Gabriella Hulicsko, 3 sons. Education: MD, Medical University of Debrecen, Hungary, 1970-76; Paediatric Institute, 1980-82; Member Hungarian College of Paediatricians. Appointments: Medical Officer, National Stadium, Surulere, Lagos, 1976-77; FIFA Registers Sports Medicine Doctor, 1977; Health Services Management Board, Kano, 1977-80; Medical Officer Grade I, Asmau Memorial Hospital, Kano, 1982-84; Consultant Paediatrician. Honours: National Treasurer, then Social Secretary, Guild of Medical Directors; President, Rotary Club of Bompai, Kano, Nigeria; Chairman, Kano Chapter, GM Directors and Nigerian Medical Association; Listed in numerous Who's Who publications. Memberships: Hungarian College of

Paediatricians; Nigerian Paediatric Association; Guild of Medical Directors; District Chairman, Polio Plus; Chairman, Publicity and Ethics Committee, Nigerian Medical Association. Address: Classic Clinics Ltd, 1A Abbas Road, Arakan Avenue, PO Box 244, Kano, Nigeria. E-mail: piu1948@yahoo.co

SHNITKA Theodor Khyam, b. 21 November 1927, Calgary, Alberta, Canada. Physician; Pathologist. m. Toby Garfin. Education: BSc. 1948, MSc, 1952, MD, 1953, University of Alberta, Edmonton; Resident in Pathology, University of Alberta Hospital, Edmonton, 1954-58; Speciality Certification, Royal College of Physicians and Surgeons of Canada, 1958; Postdoctoral Fellow in Surgery, Histochemistry, Johns Hopkins University School of Medicine, USA, 1959-60; Fellow, Royal College of Physicians and Surgeons of Canada, 1972. Appointments: Lecturer, 1958-59, Assistant Professor, 1959-62, Associate Professor, 1962-67, Professor, 1967-87, Chairman, Department of Pathology, 1980-87, Professor Emeritus of Pathology, 1987-, Faculty of Medicine, University of Alberta, Edmonton, Canada; Director, Diagnostic Electron Microscopy Laboratory, Department of Pathology, University of Alberta, 1975-87. Publications: Enzymatic histochemistry of gastrointestinal mucous membrane, 1960; Co-author, Macroscopic identification of early myocardial infarcts, by alterations in dehydrogenase activity, 1963; Co-editor, International Symposium "Gastric Secretion - Mechanisms and Control" 1967; Author, co-author of 45 other scientific articles and 7 book chapters on diagnostic pathology and electron microscopy, cell biology and pathobiology of lysosomes and peroxisomes, and neurobiology of reactive astrocytes. Honours: Annual Outstanding Achievement Award, Medical Alumni Association, University of Alberta, Edmonton, 1983; Honorary Affiliate Membership, Canadian Society of Laboratory Technologists, 1988; Outstanding Physician Award, Edmonton Academy of Medicine, 1988. Memberships: Life Member: New York Academy of Sciences; Alberta and Canadian Medical Associations; Emeritus Member: Microscopy Society of America; Histochemical Society Inc; Canadian Association of Pathologists; American Society for Cell Biology; Active, Microscopical Society of Canada, Alpha Omega Alpha Honour Medical Society. Address: 12010 87th Avenue NW, Edmonton, Alberta, T6G 0Y7, Canada.

SHOKIN Yurii, b. 9 July 1943, Kansk, Russia. Mathematician. m. Eleonora N Lozhkina, 2 daughters. Education: Novosibirsk State University, 1966; DSc, 1981. Appointments: Head of Laboratory, Institute of Theoretical and Applied Mathematics, Novosibirsk, 1976-83; Director, Computing Centre SD RAS, Krasnoyarsk, 1983-90; Director, Institute of Computational Technologies, Novosibirsk, 1990-; General Science Secretary, Russian Academy of Science, Siberian Branch, Novosibirsk, 1991-97; Director, Technopark Novosibirsk, 1998-. Publications: Author: Interval Analysis, 1981; Method of Differential Approximation, 1983; Co-author: Numerical Experiment in Tsunami Problem, 1989; Numerical Simulation of the Fluid Flows with Surface Waves, 2001. Honours: Order of Merit, 1982; Order of Friendship, 1999; Order of Honour, 2004. Memberships: International Commission on Numerical Methods in Fluid Dynamics; Working Group on International Organisation Information Processes; Society of Computer Modelling; Russian Academy of Science. Address: Lavrentyeva ave 6, 630090 Novosibirsk, Russia. E-mail: shokin@ict.nsc.ru

SHON Yoon, b. 14 May 1953, Seoul, Korea. Professor. m. Ae Kyung Mun, 1 son. Education: BS, 1978, PhD, 1993, Physics, Dongguk University; MS, Physics, Pusan National University, 1982. Appointments: Staff, Korea Atomic Energy Research Institute, 1978; Researcher, Quantum Functional Semiconductor Research Centre, 1999, Professor, 2000, Dongguk University. Publications: Papers and articles in professional scientific journals. Honours: Honor Prize, Dongguk University, 2003. Memberships: Fellow, Korean Physical Society. Address: #101-1103 Samsung Apt, 354-2 ChangAn3-Dong, DongDae Mun-Gu, Seoul 130-718, South Korea. E-mail: son-yun@hanmail.net

SHORT Rt Hon Clare, b. 15 February 1946, Birmingham, England. Politician. m. (1) 1964, divorced 1974, (2) A Lyon, 1981, deceased 1993, 1 son. Education: BA Honours, Political Science, Universities of Leeds and Keele. Appointments: Civil Service, Home Office, 1970-75; Director, All Faith for One Race, 1976-78; Youthaid, 1979-83; Labour MP, Birmingham Ladywood, 1983-; Shadow Employment Spokesperson, 1985-89, Social Security Spokesperson, 1989-91, Environmental Protection Spokesperson, 1992-93; Spokesperson for Women, 1993-95; Shadow Secretary of State for Transport, 1995-96, for Overseas Development, 1996-97; Secretary of State for International Development, 1997-2003; Select Committee Home Affairs, 1983-85; Chair, All Party Group on Race Relations, 1985-86; NEC, 1988-98; Vice-President, Socialist International Women, 1992-96; Chair, Women's Committee National Executive Committee, 1993-97; Chair, NEC International Committee, 1996-98; Party Representative, Social International Congress, 1996. Publication: An Honourable Deception? New Labour, Iraq and the Misuse of Power, 2005. Membership: UNISON. Address: House of Commons, London SW1A 0AA, England.

SHORT Nigel, b. 1 June 1965, Leigh, Lancashire, England. Chess Player. m. Rea Karageorgiou, 1987, 1 daughter. Appointments: At age of 12 beat Jonathan Penrose in British Championships; International Master, 1980; Grand Master, 1984; British Champion, 1984, 1987; English Champion, 1991; President, Grand Masters Association, 1992; Defeated Anatoly Karpov, 1992; Defeated by Kasparov, 1993; Ranked 7th Player in World; Chess Columnist, The Daily Telegraph, 1991; Stripped of International Ratings by World Chess Foundation, 1993, reinstated, 1994; Resigned from FIDE and formed Professional Chess Association with Gary Kasparov, 1993, left PCA, 1995; Ranked 17th in the world by FIDE, January 2003; Commonwealth Champion, 2004. Publications: Learn Chess with Nigel Short, 1993. Honours: Honorary Fellow, Bolton Institute, 1993-; Honorary MBE, 1999. Address: c/o The Daily Telegraph, 1 Canada Square, London, E14 5DT, England. E-mail: ndshort@hotmail.com

SHORTER John, b. 14 June 1926, Redhill, Surrey, England. Chemist. m. Mary Patricia Steer, 28 July 1951, 2 sons, 1 daughter. Education: BA, 1947, BSc, 1948, DPhil, 1950, Exeter College, Oxford. Appointments: Assistant Lecturer, 1950-52, Lecturer in Chemistry, 1952-54, University College, Hull; Lecturer in Chemistry, 1954-63, Senior Lecturer, 1963-72, Reader, Physical Organic Chemistry, 1972-82, Emeritus Reader in Chemistry, 1982-, University of Hull; RT French Visiting Professor, University of Rochester, New York, USA, 1966-67. Publications include: Correlation Analysis in Organic Chemistry, 1973; Correlation Analysis of Organic Reactivity, 1982; Co-editor: Advances in Linear Free Energy Relationships, 1972; Correlation Analysis in Chemistry, 1978; Similarity Models in Organic Chemistry, Biochemistry and Related Fields, 1991. Honour: 75th Anniversary Medal, Polish Chemical Society, 2001. Memberships: Fellow, Royal Society of Chemistry; Secretary, International Group for Correlation Analysis in Chemistry (formerly organic chemistry), 1982-2004; International Union of Pure and Applied Chemistry. Address: 29A Meadowfields, Whitby, North Yorkshire YO21 1QF, England.

SHORTHOUSE Andrew J, Consultant Colorectal Surgeon; Honorary Professor. Education: BSc; MBBS; MS; FRCS. Appointments: Research Fellow, Institute of Cancer Research, 2 years; Consultant Colorectal Surgeon and Honorary Professor, Sheffield Teaching Hospital NHS Foundation Trust. Publications: 76 peer-reviewed papers; 101 other publications; 8 book chapters; 4 videos; Referee, 6 cited journals. Honours: Honorary Professor, Sheffield Hallam University; Honorary Senior Lecturer, University of Sheffield. Memberships: President, Association of Coloproctology of Great Britain and Ireland, 2005-06; President, European Society of Coloproctology, 2007-08; President, Section of Coloproctology, Royal Society of Medicine, 2009-10. Address: Department of Colorectal Surgery, Northern General Hospital, Herries Road, Sheffield S5 7AU, England. E-mail: shorthouse@doctor.org.uk

SHU Hung-Yee, b. 18 February 1963, Taipei, Taiwan. Environmental Engineering Faculty. m. Ming-Chin Chang, 1 daughter. Education: MS, Environmental Science, 1990, PhD, Chemical Engineering, 1993, New Jersey Institute of Technology, Newark, New Jersey, USA. Appointments: Chairman, Department of Environmental Engineering, 1997-2000, Dean of Extension Education, 2000-02, Dean of Academic Affairs, 2002-03, Hung Kuang University. Publications: 26 papers and articles in professional journals. Honours: Listed in international biographical directories. Memberships: International Water Association; Chinese Institute of Environmental Engineering. Address: 34 Chung-Chie Road, Shalu, Taichung 433, Taiwan. E-mail: hyshu@sunrise.hk.edu.tw

SHU Su-Frang, b. 21 November 1965, Kaohsiung, Taiwan. Education. Education: BS, Electrical Engineering, 1987, MA, 1994, PhD, 2003, Electro-optical Engineering, NCTU. Appointments: Assistant Church Preacher, Taipei, 1987-91; Software Network Administrator, Hsin-Shing Professional School, 1994-99; Adjunct Lecturer, National Open University, Taipei, 2002; Adjunct Lecturer, 2003-04, Assistant Professor, 2004-, Ching-Yun University. Publications: Numerous articles in professional journals. Honours: Leader, National Science Council projects; Leader, Ministry of Education projects. Memberships: OSA; SPIE. Address: Ching-Yun University, 229 Chien-Hsin Rd, Jung-Li, Taiwan, ROC. E-mail: sfshu@cyu.edu.tw

SHUBIK Martin, b. 24 March 1926, Manhattan, New York, USA. Economics Educator. m. Julia Kahn, 1 daughter. Education: BA, 1947, MA, 1949, University of Toronto, Canada; AM, Political Economy, 1951, PhD, 1953, Princeton University, New Jersey, USA. Appointments: Part-time Demonstrator, Physics, University of Toronto, 1948-49; Part-time Research Assistant, 1950-51, Research Assistant, 1951-53, Research Associate, 1953-55, Economics Research Project, Princeton University; Fellow, Center for Advanced Study in Behavioural Sciences, Palo Alto, California, 1955-56; Consultant, Management Consultation Services, General Electric Company, 1956-60; Adjunct Research Professor, Pennsylvania State University, 1957-59; Visiting Professor of Economics, Yale University, 1960-61; Staff, T J Watson Research Laboratories, IBM, 1961-63; Professor of Economics of Organization, Yale University, 1963-75; Visiting Professor, Escuela de Estudios Economicos, University of Chile, 1965; Institute for Advanced Studies, Vienna, Austria,

1970; Consultant, RAND Corporation, California, 1970-71; Visiting Professor, Department of Economics, University of Melbourne, Australia, 1973; Director, Cowles Foundation for Research in Economics, 1973-76, Seymour H Knox Professor of Mathematical Institutional Economics, 1975-, Yale University. Publications: Books include: Readings in Game Theory and Political Behaviour, 1954; Strategy and Market Structure, 1959; Editor, Essays in Mathematical Economics in Honour of Oskar Morgenstern, 1967; Uses and Methods of Gaming, 1975; The War Game, co-author, 1979; The Mathematics of Conflict, 1983; The Theory of Money and Financial Institutions, Volumes I and II, 1999; Numerous articles in professional journals. Honours: Lanchester Prize, 1984; Koopman Prize, Military Application Section, INFORMS, 1995; International Insurance Society Shin Research Excellence Award, 1999; Numerous scholarships. Memberships include: Fellow, Center for Advanced Study in the Behavioural Sciences, 1955; Fellow, Econometric Society, 1971; Fellow, World Academy of Arts and Sciences, 1975; Fellow, American Academy of Arts and Sciences, 1985; Fellow, Connecticut Academy of Arts and Sciences, 1993; Science Board, Santa Fe Institute, 1997-2003. Address: Cowles Foundation for Research in Economics, Yale University, PO Box 208281, New Haven, CT 06520, USA.

SHUCKBURGH Julian John Evelyn, b. 30 July 1940, Ottawa, Canada. Publisher. 2 sons, 3 daughters. Education: Law Tripos, Peterhouse, Cambridge, 1958-61. Appointments: Editor, Methuen & Co, 1961-65; Senior Editor, Weidenfeld & Nicolson Ltd, 1965-72; Editorial Director, W H Allen Ltd, 1972-75; Publishing Director and Managing Director, Pitkin Pictorials Ltd, Garrod & Lofthouse (Printers), 1975-78; Managing Director and Founder, Shuckburgh Reynolds Ltd, 1978-87; Publishing Director, Condé Nast Books, 1992-97; Associate Publisher, Ebury Press, 1992-2000; Managing Director, Barrie & Jenkins Ltd, 1987-2000. Publications: The Bedside Book, 1979; The Second Bedside Book, 1981; London Revealed, 2003; Spectacular London, 2006. Memberships: The Garrick Club; The Bach Choir. Address: 22 Ellingham Road, London W12 9PR, England. E-mail: julianshuckburgh@22ellingham.com

SHUREY Richard, b. 22 September 1951, Wales. Factory Worker. m. Christine, 6 May 1972, 2 sons, 1 daughter. Educations: Pentre Grammar School. Publications: Jewels of the Imagination, 1997; By the Light of the Moon, 1997; On Reflection, 1997; Never Forget, 1998; From the Hand of a Poet, 1999; Open Minds, 1999. Contributions to: South Wales Echo; Celtic Press; Rhondda Leader. Honours: Editor's Choice Award for Outstanding Achievement in Poetry, International Library of Poetry, 1997. Memberships: Poetry Guild. Address: 107 Tylacelyn Road, Penygraig, Tonypandy, Rhondda-Cynon-Taff CF40 1JR, South Wales.

SHVANYOVA Irina, b. 4 October 1959, Lipetsk City, Russia. Psychologist. m. Leonid Davydov, 2 daughters. Education: Master of Pedagogy, Moscow External University of the Humanities, 1999; PhD, Psychology, The Russian Academy of Natural Sciences, Moscow, Russia, 2003. Appointments: Research Officer, Senior Research Officer, Dnepropetrovsk Medical Academy, Ukraine, 1996-99; Head of Psychology Department, Russian Academy of Natural Sciences, Moscow, Russia, 1999-. Publications: The Typological Classification of Personality Based on the Function of Integrated Potential, 2001; The Integral Approach in Psychology, 2001; The Psychology of Noospheric Development; Patent: The Diagnostic Method of Psychological States and Individual Characteristics (Ukraine); 2 fiction books; 1 poetry book;

Author of music and songs. Honours: Woman of the Year 2003, ABI; Medal "For Contribution to Development of Medicine and Health Care," Russian Academy of Natural Sciences; Laureate of International Festivals of Creative Works, Ukraine. Memberships: Russian Academy of Natural Sciences; Union of Russian, Belorussian and Ukrainian Writers. Address: Lermontova Street 3, Fl 72, Dzerzhinsky City, Moscow region 140090, Russia. E-mail: leoniya@monnet.ru

SICHIK Vasily, b. 14 June 1937, Bereza, Belarus. Professor. 2 sons. Education: Higher Education, Radio Electronics Faculty, Odessa Polytechnical Institute; Postgraduate Course, Institute of Solid-State Physics and Semiconductors, National Academy of Sciences, Republic of Belarus; Candidate of Technical Sciences; Assistant Professor; Doctor of Technical Sciences; Professor; Academician. Appointments: Assistant Professor, Belarussian Polytechnical Institute; Professor, Head of Department, Belarussian State Polytechnical Academy; Co-Chairman, Committee on Renewable Energy Sources, National Academy of Sciences, Republic of Belarus; Vice-President, International Academy on Information Technologies. Publications: 8 manuals, 40 patents in Russia and the Republic of Belarus, 60 inventions, 160 published papers, abstracts and reports at international conferences; papers in national and international research journals include: An experimental substantiation of magnetodynamics forces, 1989; Measuring converters of ionizing radiation on the basis at semiconductor instrument structures, 1991; Computer simulation of dialectic spectrum of GaASm 1998; Electronic phonedoscope, 2000; Effective control of electrostatic fields, 2002; Contactless control of constant voltage over high voltage circuits, 2002; Electric models of active components of sensing measuring device, 2003; Principles of construction of simulator on instrument structures of measuring converters, 2004. Honours: Honoured Scientist of the International Academy of Information Technologies; Medal, USSR Inventor; Medal, International Academy of Information technologies for high achievement in the field of science. Memberships: Academician, International Academy of Information Technologies; Academician of the Belarussian Engineering Academy; Member of 3 Scientific Boards/Committees on the Defence of Doctor's Theses. Address: 49-18 Pr Rokossovskogo, Minsk 220094, Republic of Belarus.

SIDIBE El Hassane, b. 12 May 1951, Thilene, Dagana, Saint Louis, Senegal. Doctor of Medicine; Teacher; Researcher. m. Amsatou Sow, 2 sons, 2 daughters. Education: Threefold Excellence Prize and Sevenfold registered in Honor Table, Bachelor of Science, Lycee Charles de Gaulle, St Louis, 1970; Medical Doctor, Dakar University, 1984; Internship, Dakar, 1977; Medical Assistant, Paris, 1984; Resident, Paris, 1986; Registered candidate in Academie Nationale de Medecine, 2000. Appointments: Assistant, Endocrinology Faculty of Medicine, Dakar, 1986-98; Certificate in Internal Medicine and Endocrinology, Metabolism and Nutrition, 1994; Aggregate Professor in Endocrinology, Metabolism, Nutrition, 1998; Master of Medical Sciences, 2000, Proposed Emeritus Professor, 2005, Paris VII University. Publications: African Diabetic microangiopathy, 1979; Primary hypothyroidism in Senegal, 1984; Major diabetes mellitus complications in Africa, 2000; Sheehan disease African experience, 2000; Pheochromocytoma in Africa, 2001. Honours: LS Senghor Foundation Grant, 1984; Medal, Societe Medicale des Hopitaux de Paris 150th Birthday, 1999; Chevalier des Palmes Academiques Françaises, 2001. Memberships: New York Academy of Sciences, 1995; SMHP; SNFMI; ALFEDIAM; SFE; Endocrine Society; Panafrican Diabetes Study Group;

MDSG; SPE; ADA; ARCOL; Societé Québecoise de l'HTA; SNFBMN; Member, European Academy of Sciences; Art and Humanities Candidate in Academie des Sciences; Full Member, Academie Française, Paris. Address: Villa 2A, Rue 1xC Point E, BP 5062, Fann, Dakar, Senegal.

SIEFKEN Hinrich Gerhard, b. 21 April 1939, Cologne, Germany. University Teacher. m. Marcia Corinne Birch, 1 son, 1 daughter. Education: German and English, University of Tübingen (Vienna and Newcastle); Dr Phil, magna cum laude, 1964; Staatsexamen, 1964. Appointments: Tutor, University of Tübingen, 1962-65; Lektor, University College of North Wales, Bangor, 1965-66; Wissenschaftlicher Assistent, University of Tübingen, 1966-67; Lecturer, Senior Lecturer, German, Saint David's University College, Lampeter, 1969-79; Professor of German, Head of Department, 1979-97, Head of School of Modern Languages, 1986-88, Dean of Faculty of Arts, 1988-91, Director, Institute of German, Austrian and Swiss Affairs, 1991-93, University of Nottingham. Publications: Books include: Kafka. Ungeduld und Lässigkeit, 1997; Thomas Mann – Goethe "Ideal der Deutschheit", 1981; Die Weisse Rose und ihre Flugblätter (editor), 1994; Theodor Haecker, Leben und Werk (co-editor), 1995; Experiencing Tradition: Essays of Discovery. For Keith Spalding, with A Bushell, 2003; Numerous articles in academic journals. Honours: D Litt, University of Nottingham, 1990; Ehrengabe zum Theodor Haecker-Preis der Stadt Esslingen, 1995; Emeritus Professor, University of Nottingham, 1997; Honorary Professor of Modern Languages, University of Wales Bangor, 1999. Address: 6 Mountsorrel Drive, West Bridgford, Nottingham NG2 6LJ, England. E-mail: hinrichsiefken@hotmail.com

SIEGEL Robert (Harold), b. 18 August 1939, Oak Park, Illinois, USA. Professor of English. m. Roberta Ann Hill, 19 August 1961, 3 daughters. Education: BA, Wheaton College, 1961; MA, Johns Hopkins University, 1962; PhD, Harvard University, 1968. Appointments: Assistant Professor, Dartmouth College, 1968-75; Visiting Lecturer in Creative Writing, Princeton University, 1975-76; Poet-in-Residence, McManes Visiting Professor, Wheaton College, 1976; Visiting Professor, J W v Goethe Universitat, Frankfurt, 1985; Coordinator, Graduate Program in Creative Writing, University of Wisconsin-Milwaukee, 1977-80 and 1992-94; Professor of English, University of Wisconsin-Milwaukee, 1983-. Publications: Poetry: The Beasts and The Elders, 1973; In A Pig's Eye, 1980; The Waters Under the Earth, 2005; A Pentecost of Finches: New and selected Poems, 2006. Fiction: Alpha Centauri, 1980; Whalesong, 1981; The Kingdom of Wundle, 1982; White Whale, 1991; The Ice At the End of the World, 1994. Contributions to: Anthologies and journals. Honours: Honorable Mention, Merit Awards, Atlantic Monthly College Poetry Contest, 1960; Margaret O'Loughlin Foley Award, 1970; The Cliff Dwellers' Arts Foundation Award, 1974; Chicago Poetry Prize, Society of Midland Authors, 1974; Prairie Schooner Poetry Prize, 1977; Poetry Magazine's Jacob Glatstein Memorial Prize, 1977; Ingram Merrill Award, 1979; National Endowment for the Arts Fellowship, 1980; ECPA Gold Medalion, 1981; Book of the Year Award, Campus Life Magazine, 1981; 1st Prize for Juvenile Fiction, Council for Wisconsin Writers, 1981; 1st Prize for Poetry, Society of Midland Authors, 1981; Matson Award, 1982; Golden Archer Award, 1986; Pushcart Prize Nominations, 1990, 1995; Milton Center Poetry Prize, 1994; EPA Poetry Prize, 2003. Memberships: Author's Guild; Association of Literary Scholars and Critics. Address: English Department, University of Wisconsin, PO Box 413, Milwaukee, WI 53201, USA. E-mail: siegelrh@uwm.edu

SIGLER-BOWEN Jeanne Michelle, b. 23 November 1958. Health Information Management. m. William Bowen, 2 daughters. Education: Associate of Science, Wabash Valley College, 1978; Bachelor of Science, Illinois State University, Normal, Illinois, USA, 1980; Registration Examination, RHIA, 1980; Assistant Director, Health Information Department, Des Moines, Iowa, 1982-86. Appointments: Health Information Manager for Dr William Bowen; Business Consultant for long-term care facilities; Involved in other civic and local business operations. Honours: NRCC Business Woman of the Year, 2004; Congressional Order of Merit, 2004, 2005; Republican Honor Roll, 2005; Presidents Club, 2004, 2005, 2006, 2007; Honor Roll, National Republican Senatorial Committee, 2006; Member, Republican Inner Circle, 2007-2008; Champion of Republican Party, 2005; Woman of the Year, 2007; International Peace Prize, UCC, 2007; Republican Senatorial American Spirit Medal, 2007; Outstanding Intellectuals of the 21st Century; Listed in international biographical dictionaries. E-mail: truegritindy@aol.com

SIKDAR Malay Kanti, b. 1 January 1948, Brahmachal, Bangladesh. Writer; Scientist; Scholar; Manager. m. Susmita, 1 daughter. Education: BSc (Physics with honours), Calcutta University; MBB, Agartala College, 1969; MSc (Physics), 1971, PhD (Physics), Kalyani University. Appointments: UGC Junior, Senior Fellow, 1973-77, CSIR Senior/PD Fellow, 1977-79; District Manager, Food Corporation of India, 24-Parganas, Howrah, Kolkata. Publications: Many research papers and articles in scientific journals include: Tables of Clebsch Gordan Co-efficients of Magnetic groups, 1976; Tables of Magnetic Double Point group, 1977; Group Theoretical Analysis of second order phase transitions in Magnetic Structures, 1979; Rach co-efficients for Crystalline solids, 1980; Higher Order of Lives in the Universe, 2002; Holy Bath in the Ocean of Brahman, 2007; 1 novel: Kalinga Judher Prantare, 1983 and short stories: Ghare Baire Pathe Prantare, 1989; Swarga Martya Jiban Mrityu, 2006; More publications forthcoming. Honours: Bal Sahayog Award, 2000; Bharat Excellency Award with Gold Medal, 2001; Secular India Harmony Award, 2001; UWA Lifetime Achievement Award, 2002; Indian Growing Personalities Award with Gold Medal, 2002; Man of the Year, 2002; American Medal of Honor, 2003; ABI World Lifetime Achievement Award, 2003; International Peace Prize, 2003; Eminent Personality of India, International Biographical Research Foundation, Nagpur, India, 2003; Great Indian Achievement Award Gold Medal, 2004; FFI Lifetime Achievement Award and Gold Medal, 2004; Bright Indian Citizen Award and Gold Medal, 2004; Human Excellence Award and Gold Medal, 2004; Da Vinci Diamond Award, IBC, 2004; FFI Udyog Gaurav Award, 2005; Bharat Yogyta Award, 2005; Rashtray Jyoti Award; IIFS Vijoy Rattan Award, 2005; IBC Leading Educators of the World, 2005; IISA Glory of India Award, 2006; IIFS Vijoy Shree Award, 2006; IPH Best Citizen of India Award, 2006; FFI Glory of India International Award, 2006; ABI Eminent Fellow for Magnificent and Distinguished Deed, 2006; IIEM Life Time Achievment Gold Award, 2006; ISC Jewel of India Award, 2006; IPH Best Citizen of India Award, 2006; IIEM Eminent Citizen of India Award, 2007; IBC Mother India Excellence Award, 2007; FFI Arch of Excellence Award, 2007; FFI Indian Golden Achiever Award, 2007. Memberships: Indian Association for the Cultivation of SC; Indian Science Congress, Nikhi; Bharat Banga Sahitya Sanmelan; Institute of Commercial Management, UK. Address: C/27, Navadarsha Co-operative Housing Society Ltd, Birati, Kolkata 700134, India.

SIKI Bela, b. 21 February 1923, Budapest, Hungary. Pianist; Professor. m. Yolande Oltramare, 1 son, 1 daughter. Education: Franz Liszt Academy, Budapest, 1945; Prix De Virtuosite Avec Distinction, Geneva, 1948. Appointments: Adjunct Professor, Geneve, 1951-53; Professor, University of Washington, Seattle, 1965-93; Professor, University of Cincinnati, 1980-85. Publications: Piano Repertoire, 1981; Worldwide concert tours, numerous recordings. Honour: Concours International D'Execution Musicale. Address: 5424 Elleray Lane NE, Seattle, WA 98105, USA.

SILBERSTON (Zangwill) Aubrey, b. 26 January 1922, London, England. Economist. m. Michèle Ledic, 1 son. Education: London School of Economics; Jesus College Cambridge. Appointments: War Service, Royal Fusiliers, Iraq, Egypt, Italy, 1941-45; Economist, Courtaulds Limited, 1946-50; Research Fellow, St Catharine's College, Cambridge, 1950-53; Lecturer in Economics, University of Cambridge, 1951-71; Fellow, St John's College, Cambridge, 1958-71; Chairman, Faculty Board of Economics and Politics, University of Cambridge, 1966-70; Official Fellow in Economics, 1971-78, Dean, 1972-78, Nuffield College, Oxford; Professor of Economics, Imperial College London, 1978-87; Senior Research Fellow, Tanaka Business School, Imperial College, 1987-2005; Professor Emeritus of Economics, University of London, 1987-. Publications: Education and training for industrial management, 1955; The motor industry (jointly), 1959; The patent system (jointly), 1967; The economic impact of the patent system (jointly), 1973; The future of the multi-fibre arrangement (with Michèle Ledic), 1989; Environmental economics,(editor), 1995; The changing industrial map of Europe (jointly), 1996; Anti-dumping and Countervailing Action (jointly), 2007; Articles in academic journals. Honours: Rockefeller Fellow, University of California, Berkeley, 1959-60; CBE, 1987. Memberships: Royal Economic Society; Council of Experts, Intellectual Property Institute, London. Address: Rue Jules Lejeune 2, B-1050, Brussels. E-mail: asilberston@yahoo.co.uk

SILLITOE Alan, b. 4 March 1928, Nottingham, England. Writer; Poet; Dramatist. m. Ruth Fainlight, 19 November 1959, 1 son, 1 daughter (adopted). Education: Principally self-taught. Appointments: Writer, 1948-. Publications: Without Beer or Bread (poems), 1957; Saturday Night and Sunday Morning (novel), 1958; The General (novel), 1960; The Rats and Other Poems, 1960; Key to the Door (novel), 1961; Road to Volgograd (travel), 1964; A Falling Out of Love and Other Poems, 1964; The Death of William Posters (novel), 1965; A Tree on Fire (novel), 1967; A Start in Life (novel), 1967; Shaman and Other Poems, 1968; Love in the Environs of Voronezh and Other Poems, 1968; Travel in Nihilon (novel), 1971; Raw Material (memoir), 1972; The Flame of Life (novel), 1974; Storm and Other Poems, 1974; Barbarians and Other Poems, 1974; Mountains and Caverns: Selected Essays, 1975; The Widower's Son (novel), 1976; The Storyteller (novel), 1979; Snow on the North Side of Lucifer (poems), 1979; Her Victory (novel), 1982; The Lost Flying Boat (novel), 1983; Down from the Hill (novel), 1984; Sun Before Departure (poems), 1984; Life Goes On (novel), 1985; Tides and Stone Walls (poems), 1986; Out of the Whirlpool (novel), 1987; The Open Door (novel), 1989; Lost Loves (novel), 1990; Leonard's War, 1991; Snowstop, 1993; Collected Poems, 1994; Collected Stories, 1995; Leading the Blind (travel), 1995; Life Without Armour (autobiography), 1995; Alligator Playground (stories), 1997; Collected Stories, 1997; The Broken Chariot (novel) 1998; The German Numbers Woman (novel), 1999; Birthday, novel, 2001; Flight of Arrows, essays, 2003; A Man of His Time, novel, 2004. Other: Short stories; Plays. Honours: Author's Club Prize, 1958; Hawthornden Prize, 1960; Honorary Fellow, Manchester Polytechnic, 1977; Honorary Degrees, Nottingham Polytechnic, 1990, Nottingham University, 1994; Visiting Professor, Honorary Doctorate, 1998, De Montfort University, Leicester. Memberships: Royal Geographical Society, fellow; Society of Authors; Writers Action Group. Address: 14 Ladbroke Terrace, London W11 3PG, England.

SILVA Christopher P, 17 March 1960, Fortuna, California, USA. Electrical Engineer. Education: BSc, Electrical Engineering, 1982, MSc, Electrical Engineering, 1985, PhD, Engineering, 1993, University of California at Berkeley. Appointments: Member of Technical Staff, 1989, Senior Member of the Technical Staff, 1995, Engineering Specialist, 1999, Senior Engineering Specialist, 2003-, The Aerospace Corporation, El Segundo, California. Publications: Technical conference and professional journal papers, book contributions, and technical presentations in various professional, academic and industrial venues; Co-organiser of technical conference workshops. Honours: BSEE with highest honours distinction, UC Alumni Scholar, National Science Foundation Fellowship; Lockheed Leadership Fellowship; Fellowship, Institute for Electrical and Electronic Engineers; Senior Membership, American Institute of Aeronautics and Astronautics; Corporate Division Team and Individual Achievement Awards; Corporate President's Award; Listed in numerous biographical publications. Memberships include: American Association for the Advancement of Science; American Mathematical Society; Society of Industrial and Applied Mathematics; Eta Kappa Nu; Phi Beta Kappa; Tau Beta Pi. Address: 26766 Menominee Place, Rancho Palos Verdes, CA 90275, USA. E-mail: chris.p.silva@aero.org

SILVA Paulo Burlamaqui da , b. 28 January 1942, Brazil. Medicine; Education; Project Manager. m. Mathilde Andery B Silva, 1 son. Education: MD, University of Federal Ceara, 1967; MA, Informatics, Pontifical Catholic University of Campinas, 2000. Appointments: Medical Officer, R Maria da Conceição Franco de Andrade, 621; Resident, Pediatrics, Union Workers Hospital and Downstate University, New York, USA; Fellow of Neonatology, Tufts University, Massachusetts University, Hospital Administration at St Camilo Health Facility; Project Management Professional (PMP), Project Management Institute, USA. Publications: Author, several professional publications; A Guide for the Management of Medical Projects, 2005. Honours: Physicians Recognition Award. Memberships: Pediatric Society Rio; American Medical Association; American Management Association; New York Academy of Science; American Association for the Advancement of Science; Project Management Institute. Address: PO Box 661, Campinas, SP 13 012-970, Campinos, Brazil.

SILVER Peter John, b. 8 September 1949, Birmingham, England. Chartered Accountant. m. Marylyn Anne, 2 sons, 1 daughter. Education: Solihull School, Solihull, 1958-68; Lanchester Polytechnic (now University of Coventry), 1968-69. Appointments: Articled Clerk, Whinney Murray & Co (now Ernst & Young), 1968-73; Senior, Vincent Vale & Co (now BDO Stoy Hayward), 1973-74; Senior, Tranter Lowe & Co, 1974-78; Partner, Holyoak Southgate & Co, 1978-89; Partner, Silver & Co, 1989-; Director, Broad Oaks Investments Ltd, 1999-; Director, Sastak Ltd, 2001-; Director, Dudley and West Midlands Zoological Society Ltd, 2003-. Honours: Fellow, Institute of Chartered Accountants; Fellow, Royal Society of Arts. Memberships: Federation of Small Business; Talyllyn Railway Society; Severn Valley Railway Company; Great Western Railway Society; Shropshire Chamber of Agriculture; National Farmers Union. Address: The Hollies, 16 St John Street, Bridgworth, Shropshire WV15 6AV, England.

SILVERMAN Hirsch Lazaar, b. 19 June 1915, New York City, USA. Psychologist; Educator; Administrator. m. Mildred Friedlander, 1942, 2 sons, 1 daughter. Education: BS, CCNY, 1936; MS, CUNY, 1938; MA, NYU, 1947; PhD, Yeshiva University, 1951; MA, Seton Hall University, 1957; DSc, Lane College, Jackson, Tennessee, 1962; LLD (hon), Florida Memorial College, 1965; Doctor of Humane Letters, Ohio College of Pediatric Medicine, 1972; Diplomate: Clinical Psychology; Forensic Psychology; Neuropsychology; Behavioural Medicine; Psychotherapy; American Board of Professional Psychologists; American Board of Forensic Psychologists; American Board of Behavioural Medicine. Appointments: Assistant Professor, Mohawk College, Utica, New York, 1946-48; Educational Vocation Consultant, Stevens Institute of Technology, Hoboken, New Jersey, 1948-49; Assistant Professor, Psychology, Rutgers University, New Brunswick, New Jersey, 1948-53; Private practice Psychologist, Newark, West Orange, New Jersey, 1951-; Assistant Superintendent, Nutley (NJ) Board of Education, 1953-59; Professor, Chairman, Educational Psychology, Yeshiva University, New York City, 1959-65; Professor, Chairman, Educational Administration, Seton Hall University, South Orange, New Jersey, 1965-80; Expert Witness, Consultant, Superior Court of New Jersey; Professor Emeritus, Seton Hall University, 1980-; Research Clinical Psychologist, Columbus Hospital, St Vincent's Hospital, New York Medical College; Visiting Professor, Lane College and Florida Memorial College. Publications: Author, 28 books; Over 270 articles to professional journals. Honours: Townsend Harris Medal, CCNY, 1976; Distinguished Practitioner in Psychology National Academies of Practice. Memberships: Fellow, APHA; Fellow, APA; College of Preceptors; Association for Advancement of Psychotherapy; Society for Adolescent Medicine; Royal Society of Medicine; Royal Society of Health; World Academy of Arts and Sciences; American Association of Clinical Counsellors; Academy of Psychologists in Marital Therapy; Philosophical Society of Enquiry; New Jersey Association of Marriage and Family Therapists; Phi Beta Kappa; Sigma Xi; Psi Chi; Phi Sigma Tau; Kappa Delta Pi. Address: 123 Gregory Ave, West Orange, NJ 07052-4740, USA.

SILVERSTONE Alicia, b. 4 October 1976, California, USA. Actress. m. Christopher Jarecki, 2005. Appointments: Stage Debut in Play, Carol's Eve, Metropolitan Theatre, Los Angeles; Stared in 3 Aerosmith Videos including: Cryin; Formed own production company, First Kiss Productions; Films: The Crush, 1993; The Babysitter, 1995; True Crime, 1995; Le Nouveau Monde, 1995; Hideaway, 1995; Clueless, 1995; Batman and Robin, 1997; Excess Baggage (also Producer), 1997; Free Money, 1998; Blast from the Past, 1999; Love's Labour Lost, 2000; Scorched, 2002; Global Heresy, 2002; Scooby Doo: Monsters Unleashed, 2004; Beauty Shop, 2005; Silence Becomes You, 2005; Stormbreaker, 2006; TV: Torch Song, 1993; Shattered Dreams, 1993; The Cool and the Crazy, 1994; The Wonder Years, 1997: Miss Match, 2003-2005; Pink Collar, 2006; Candles on Bay Street, 2006; The Singles Table, 2007. Address: c/o Premiere Artists Agency, Suite 510, 8899 Beverly Boulevard, Los Angeles, CA 90048, USA.

SIM Yoon Sub, b. Korea. Manager. Education: BSc, Seoul National University, 1978; MS, 1979, PhD, 1983, University of Michigan, Ann Arbor, USA. Appointments: Head, Nuclear

Core Thermal Hydraulic Design Department, Korea Atomic Energy Research Institute, 1987-90; Manager, Nuclear Steam Supply System Department, 1989-97; Manager, Liquid Metal Reactor Fluid System Design Technology Development Project, 1997-2002; Manager, High Temperature Gas Cooled Reactor Cavity Cooling System Improvement Project, Korea Atomic Energy Research Institute, 2005-. Publications: Numerous articles in professional journals; Various patents on liquid metal reactor designs for technical innovation. Honours: Distinguished Service Award, KAERI, 1989; Listed in international biographical dictionaries. Memberships: Korean Society of Mechanical Engineers; Korean Nuclear Society. Address: Korea Atomic Energy Research Institute, 150 Duckjindong, Daejeon 305-503, Republic of Korea. E-mail: yoon92ia@paran.com

SIMCHERA Vasily, b. 26 February 1940, Transkarpatia, Ukraine. Scientist. m. Nina N, 1 son, 1 daughter. Education: Statistics, Languages, Mathematical Lvov's Trade and Economic Institute, 1961; Moscow Institute of Foreign Languages, 1976; Economic Division, Russian Academy of Sciences, 1964. Appointments: Full Professor, Russian Economic and Financial Institute; Director, Russian Statistical Research Institute; Vice President, Russian Academy of Economic Sciences. Publications: More than 50 books and over 500 other publications including most recently: Introduction to financial and actuarial calculations, 2003; Arrangement of public statistics in Russian Federation, 2004; Statistics, 2005; Techniques of multivariate analysis of statistical data, 2006; Moral economy, 2006; Russia: 100 years of economic growth (1900-2000). Historical series, trends of centuries, institutional cycles, 2006. Honours: Honoured Person of the Science of Russia; Knight of St Nikolay Chudotrosets; Nobleman. Memberships: Russian Academy of Economic Science; International Academy of Management and Engineering; many others. Address: 113-70, p2 Vernadskoho, 119571 Moscow, Russia. E-mail: vms@senator.ru

SIMIC Charles, b. 9 May 1938, Belgrade, Yugoslavia (US citizen, 1971). Associate Professor of English; Poet; Writer. m. Helen Dubin, 1964, 1 son, 1 daughter. Education: University of Chicago, 1956-59; BA, New York University, 1967. Appointments: Faculty, California State College, Hayward, 1970-73; Associate Professor of English, University of New Hampshire, 1973-. Publications: Poetry: What the Grass Says, 1967; Somewhere Among Us a Stone is Taking Notes, 1969; Dismantling the Silence, 1971; White, 1972, revised edition, 1980; Return to a Place Lit by a Glass of Milk, 1974; Biography and a Lament, 1976; Charon's Cosmology, 1977; Brooms: Selected Poems, 1978; School for Dark Thoughts, 1978; Classic Ballroom Dances, 1980; Shaving at Night, 1982; Austerities, 1982; Weather Forecast for Utopia and Vicinity: Poems: 1967-1982, 1983; The Chicken Without a Head, 1983; Selected Poems 1963-1983, 1985, revised edition, 1990; Unending Blues, 1986; The World Doesn't End: Prose Poems, 1989; In the Room We Share, 1990; The Book of Gods and Devils, 1990; Hotel Insomnia, 1992; A Wedding in Hell, 1994; Walking the Black Cat, 1996; Jackstraws, 1999; Night Picnic, 2001; The Voice at 3:00am, 2003; Selected Poems 1963-2003, 2005; My Noiseless Entourage: Poems, 2005; Monkey Around, 2006; Sixty Poems, 2008; That Little Something: Poems, 2008; Monster Loves His Labyrinth, 2008. Other: The Uncertain Certainty: Interviews, Essays and Notes on Poetry, 1985; Wonderful Words, Silent Truth, 1990; Dimestore Alchemy, 1992; Unemployed Fortune Teller, 1994; Orphan Factory, 1998; A Fly in the Soup, 2000. Editor: Another Republic: 17 European and South American Writers (with Mark Strand), 1976; The Essential Campion, 1988.

Translator: 12 books, 1970-92. Honours: PEN Awards, 1970, 1980; Guggenheim Fellowship, 1972; National Endowment for the Arts Fellowships, 1974, 1979; Edgar Allan Poe Award, 1975; American Academy of Arts and Letters Award, 1976; Harriet Monroe Poetry Award, 1980; Fulbright Fellowship, 1982; Ingram Merrill Foundation Fellowship, 1983; John D and Catharine T MacArthur Foundation Fellowship, 1984; Pulitzer Prize in Poetry, 1990; Academy of American Poets Fellowship, 1998; Poet Laureate Consultant in Poetry to the Library of Congress, 2007. Address: c/o Department of English, University of New Hampshire, Durham, NH 03824, USA. Website: www.unh.edu/english

SIMM Robert James (Bob), b. 2 March 1948, Manchester, England. Art Consultant. m. (1) Sally Elizabeth, 1977, dissolved 1995, 2 sons, 1 daughter; Partner, Helen Anna Potter. Education: Languages, Spanish, French and Japanese. Appointments: Various positions rising to Head of Training & Management Development, Marks & Spencer, 1971-77; Management consultant rising to Head of Human Resources Consulting Practice, Price Waterhouse, 1977-84; Leader of Global Human Resources Practice rising to UK Chairman and member of KPMG UK board, KPMG Consulting, 1984-95; Independent Art Consultant, 1995-; Non-executive directorships. Publications: Cabinet Office Performance Appraisal Techniques; Books: Leadership Skills; Art & Business – How They Meet; John Bratby & Other Artists; Numerous articles in many publications including: Lancaster University; London Business School; Oxford Templeton College; INSEAD; IMEDE; The Times. Honours: BA (Hons); MATA; FBIM; FIMC; ACIEW, (Affiliate); PhD; G10; FRSA; Man of the Year, ABI; Great Minds of the 21st Century; International Peace Prize, United Cultural Convention; Research Board of Advisors, ABI; Gold Medal, IBC; Gold Medal, ABI. Address: 77 Greenhill, Prince Arthur Road, Hampstead, London NW3 5TZ, England.

SIMMONS Michael, b. 17 October 1935, Watford, England. Writer. m. Angela Thomson, 20 April 1963, 2 sons. Education: BA, Honours, Russian, Manchester University, 1960; Birkbeck College, 1998-. Appointments: Parliamentary Correspondent, Glasgow Herald, 1964-67; East Europe Correspondent, Financial Times, 1968-72; Deputy Editor, Society, East Europe Correspondent, Third World Editor, The Guardian, 1977-97; Freelance Writer and Editor, 1997-. Publications: Berlin: The Dispossessed City, 1988; The Unloved Country; A Portrait of the GDR, 1989; The Reluctant President, A Life of Vaclav Havel, 1992; Landscapes of Poverty, 1997; On the Edge, 2001; Essays on: Church and Community, 2000; Getting a Life, 2002. Membership: Trinity Cricket Club. Address: 24 Rodney Road, New Malden, Surrey KT3 5AB, England. E-mail: micsimmo@compuserve.com

SIMON Josette, Actress. Education: Central School of Speech Training and Dramatic Art. m. Mark Padmore, 1996, 1 child. Career: TV: Blake's 7; Kavanagh QC; Silent Witness; Dalziel and Pascoe; The Last Detective' Poirot; Midsomers Murders; Casualty, 2006; The Whistleblowers, 2007; Lewis, 2007; The Bill, 2008; Stage: with RSC: Measure for Measure, 1988; Arthur Miller's After the Fall; The White Devil; Ibsen's The Lady From the Sea; The Taming of the Shrew, 1995; The Maids, 1997; A Midsummer Night's Dream, 1999; several concert performances; Films: Cry Freedom; Milk and Honey; A Child from the South; Bitter Harvest; Bridge of Time. Honours: Best Actress Atlantic Film Festival, 1988; Paris Film Festival, 1990; Hon MA (Leicester), 1995. Address: Conway van Gelder Ltd, 18-21 Jermyn Street, London SW1Y 6HP, England.

SIMON Neil, b. 4 July 1927, New York, USA. Playwright. m. (1) Joan Baim, 1953, deceased, 2 daughters, (2) Marsha Mason, 1973, divorced, (3) Diane Lander, 1987, 1 daughter. Education: New York University. Appointments: Wrote for various TV programmes including: The Tallulah Bankhead Show, 1951; The Phil Silvers Show, 1958-59; NBC Special; The Trouble with People, 1972; Plays: Come Blow your Horn, 1961; Little Me (musical), 1962; Barefoot in the Park, 1963; The Odd Couple, 1965; Sweet Charity (musical), 1966; The Star-Spangled Girl, 1966; Plaza Suite, 1968; Promises, Promises (musical), 1968; Last of the Red Hot Lovers, 1969; The Gingerbread Lady, 1970; The Prisoner of Second Avenue, 1971; The Sunshine Boys, 1972; The Good Doctor, 1973; God's Favourite, 1974; California Suite, 1976; Chapter Two, 1977; They're Playing Our Song, 1979; I Ought to be in Pictures, 1980; Fools, 1981; Little Me (revised version), 1982; Brighton Beach Memoirs, 1983; Biloxi Blues, 1985; The Odd Couple Female Version, 1985; Broadway Bound, 1986; Rumors, 1988; Lost in Yonkers, 1991; Jake's Women, 1992; The Goodbye Girl (musical), 1993; Laughter on the 23rd Floor, 1993; London Suite, 1995; Proposals, 1997; The Dinner Party, 2000; 45 Seconds from Broadway, 2001; Rose's Dilemma, 2003; Screenplays include: After the Fox, 1966; Barefoot in the Park, 1967; The Odd Couple, 1968; The Out of Towners, 1970; Plaza Suite, 1971; The Last of the Red Hot Lovers, 1972; The Heartbreak Kid, 1973; The Prisoner of Second Avenue, 1975; The Sunshine Boys, 1975; Murder by Death, 1976; The Goodbye Girl, 1977; The Cheap Detective, 1978; California Suite, 1978. Honours: Many awards and nominations include: Emmy Award; Antoinette Perry (Tony) Awards for The Odd Couple; Writers Guild Screen Award for the Odd Couple, 1969; American Comedy Award for Lifetime Achievement, 1989; Pulitzer Prize, 1991. Publication: Rewrites: A Memoir, 1996; Individual Plays. Address: c/o A DaSilva, 502 Park Avenue, New York, NY 10022, USA.

SIMON Norma, b. 24 December 1927, New York City, USA. Children's Book Author. m. Edward Simon, 7 June 1951, 1 son, 2 daughters. Education: BA, Economics, Brooklyn College, 1943-47; MA, Early Childhood Education, Bank St College of Education, 1968; Graduate Work, New School of Social Research. Appointments: Clerical Worker, Frances I duPont & Co, New York City, 1943-46; Teacher, Vassar Summer Institute, Poughkeepsie, New York, Department of Welfare, Brooklyn, New York, 1948-49; Downtown Community School, New York City, 1949-52, Thomas School, Rowayton, Connecticut, 1952-53; Founder, Director, Teacher, Norwalk Community Cooperative Nursery School, Rowayton, Connecticut, 1953-54; Teacher, Norwalk Public Schools, Connecticut, 1962-63; Group Therapist, Greater Bridgeport Child Guidance Center, Connecticut, 1965-67; Special Teacher, Mid-Fairfield Child Guidance Center, Connecticut, 1967-69; Consultant, Stamford Pre-School Program, Connecticut, 1965-69; Consultant, School Division, Macmillan Publishing Co, Inc, New York City, 1968-70; Consultant to Publishing Division, Bank Street College of Education, 1967-74, Follow-Through Program, 1971-72; Consultant, Davidson Films Inc, 1969-74, Aesop Films, 1975-79, San Francisco, California; Consultant, Children's Advertising, Dancer-Fitzgerald-Sampler Inc, New York City, 1969-79; Volunteer, Wellfleet Elementary School, 1972-2000; Consultant, Fisher-Price Toys, East Aurora, New York, 1978. Publications include: Firefighters, 1995; The Baby House, 1995; Wet World, 1995; The Story of Hanukkah, 1997; The Story of Passover, 1997; Looking Back at Wellfleet, 1997; All Kinds of Children, 1999; All Families are Special, 2003. Honours include: Jeremiah Cahir Friend of Education Award, Barnstable County Education Association, 1987; Parents'

Council on Books Choice, 1998. Memberships: Authors Guild; Delta Kappa Gamma; AAUW. Address: PO Box 428, South Wellfleet, MA 02663-0428, USA.

SIMON Paul, b. 13 October 1941, Newark, New Jersey, USA. Singer; Composer. m. (1) Peggy Harper (divorced), 1 son, (2) Carrie Fisher (divorced), (3) Edie Brickell, 30 May 1992, 2 sons, 1 daughter. Education: BA, Queens College; Postgraduate, Brooklyn Law School. Career: Duo, Simon And Garfunkel, with Art Garfunkel, 1964-71; Appearances with Garfunkel include: Monterey Festival, 1967; Royal Albert Hall, 1968; Reunion concerts: Central Park, New York, 1981; US, European tours; Solo artiste, 1972-; Apperances include: Anti-war Festival, Shea Stadium, New York, 1970; Farm Aid V, 1992; Hurricane Relief concert, Miami, 1992; Born At The Right Time Tour; Tour, Europe and Russia; Television includes: Paul Simon Special, 1977; Paul Simon's Graceland - The African Concert, 1987; Paul Simon - Born At The Right Time, 1992; Film appearances: Monterey Pop, 1968; Annie Hall, 1977; All You Need Is Cash, 1978; One Trick Pony, 1980; Steve Martin Live, 1985. Compositions include: The Sound Of Silence; Homeward Bound; I Am A Rock; Mrs Robinson; The Boxer; Bridge Over Troubled Water; Cecilia; Slip Slidin' Away; Late In The Evening; You Can Call Me Al; The Boy In The Bubble; Graceland; Paul Simon - Songs From The Capeman, 1997. Albums: with Art Garfunkel: Wednesday Morning 3AM, 1964; Sounds Of Silence, 1965; Parsley Sage Rosemary And Thyme, 1967; The Graduate (film soundtrack), 1967; Bookends, 1968; Bridge Over Troubled Water, 1970; Simon and Garfunkel's Greatest Hits, 1972; Breakaway, 1975; Watermark, 1978; Collected Works, 1981; The Concert In Central Park, 1982; Various compilation albums; Solo albums: Paul Simon, 1972; There Goes Rhymin' Simon, 1973; Live Rhymin': Paul Simon In Concert, 1974; Still Crazy After All These Years, 1975; Greatest Hits Etc, 1977; One-Trick Pony, 1980; Hearts And Bones, 1983; Graceland, 1986; Negotiations and Love Songs, 1988; Rhythm Of The Saints, 1990; Paul Simon's Concert In The Park, 1991; Paul Simon 1964-1993, 1993; Paul Simon - Songs From The Capeman, 1997; You're the One, 2000; Surprise, 2006; The Essential Paul Simon, 2007. Publications: The Songs of Paul Simon, 1972; New Songs, 1975; One-Trick Pony (screenplay), 1980; At The Zoo (for children), 1991. Honours include: Grammy awards: two for The Graduate soundtrack, 1968, six for Bridge Over Troubled Water, 1970, two for Still Crazy After All These Years, 1986, one for Graceland, 1987; Emmy Award, Paul Simon Special, NBC-TV, 1977; Inducted into Rock And Roll Hall Of Fame, with Art Garfunkel, 1990; Antoinette Perry Award, The Capeman, Best Original Score Written For The Theatre 1997-98; Honorary Doctorate of Music, Berkelee College of Music, 1986, Yale University, 1996, Queens College, 1997; Numerous Grammy Awards. Address: Paul Simon Music, 1619 Broadway, Suite 500, New York, NY 10019, USA.

SIMONENKO Sergey Victorovich, b. 2 July 1959, Uglekamensk, USSR. Engineer; Physicist. 2 daughters. Education: Engineer-Physicist diploma, Moscow Physical-Technical Institute, 1984; Post-graduate studies, Pacific Oceanological Institute, Vladivostok, 1987-92; PhD, Physical-Mathematical Sciences, USSR, Moscow, 1993. Appointments: Engineer, 1984-87, Junior Research Associate, 1992-94, Research Associate, 1994-96, Senior Scientist, 1996-2000, Pacific Oceanological Institute, Far Eastern Branch of Russian Academy of Sciences, Vladivostok; Leading Scientist, 2000-08, V I Il'ichev Pacific Oceanological Institute, Far Eastern Branch of Russian Academy of Sciences, Vladivostok; Associate Professor,

Interchangeability and Quality Control, 2002-08, Pacific State University of Economics, Vladivostok. Publications: Articles: The macroscopic non-equilibrium kinetic energies of a small fluid particle, 2004; Generalization of the classical special formulation of the law of large numbers, 2005; Statistical thermohydrodynamics of irreversible strike-slip-rotational processes, 2007; Monographs: Non-equilibrium Statistical Thermohydrodynamics, Vol II. Towards the foundation of the theory of the non-equilibrium dissipative small-scale turbulence and the tolerance theory related with the quality control, 2005; Non-equilibrium statistical thermohydrodynamics of turbulence, 2006; Non-equilibrium Statistical Thermodynamics, Foundation of the theory of the small-scale turbulence and the tolerances theory, 2006; Thermohydrogravidynamics of the Solar System, 2007; Thermohydrogravidynamic evolution of the planets and the tolerances theory, 2008. Honours: Diploma, Moscow Physical-Technical Institute, 1975; Award, Presidium of the Far Eastern Branch of Russian Academy of Sciences, 1989. Memberships: Fiztech Club, Moscow Physical-Technical Institute. Address: V I Il'ichev Pacific Oceanological Institute, Far Eastern Branch of Russian Academy of Sciences, 43 Baltiyskaya St, Vladivostok, 690041, Russia. E-mail: sergeysimonenko@mail.ru

SIMONS Peter Murray, b. 23 March 1950, Westminster, London, England. Professor. m. Susan Jane Walker, 1 son, 1 daughter. Education: BSc (Hons), Mathematics, 1971, MA, Philosophy, 1973, PhD, Philosophy, 1975, University of Manchester, Manchester, England. Appointments: Assistant Librarian, University of Manchester, 1975-77; Lecturer in Philosophy, Bolton Institute of Technology, Bolton, England, 1977-80; Lecturer in Philosophy, University of Salzburg, Austria, 1980-95; Professor of Philosophy, University of Leeds, Leeds, England, 1995-. Publications include: Parts 1987, 2000; Philosophy and Logic in Central Europe from Bolzano to Tarski, 1992; About 200 articles. Honours: Cultural Prize, City of Salzburg, 1986; Habilitation, University of Salzburg, 1986; Honorary Professor of Philosophy, University of Salzburg, 1996; Fellow of the British Academy, 2004; Member, Academia Europaea, 2006. Memberships include: American Philosophical Association; British Philosophical Association; Aristotelian Society; MIND Association; Gesellschaft für Analytische Philosophie; Internationale Bernard Bolzano Gesellschaft. Address: Department of Philosophy, University of Leeds, Leeds, LS2 9JT, England. E-mail: p.m.simons@leeds.ac.uk

SIMPSON John Cody Fidler-, b. 9 August 1944, Cleveleys, England. Broadcaster; Writer. m. (1) Diane Jean Petteys, 1965, divorced 1995, 2 daughters, (2) Adèle Krüger, 1996. Education: MA, Magdalene College, Cambridge. Appointments: Various positions, BBC, 1966-82; BBC Diplomatic Editor, 1982-88, Foreign, later World Affairs Editor, 1988-; Associate Editor, The Spectator, 1991-95; Columnist, The Sunday Telegraph, 1995-. Publications: The Best of Granta (editor), 1966; Moscow Requiem, 1981; A Fine and Private Place, 1983; The Disappeared: Voices From a Secret War, 1985; Behind Iranian Lines, 1988; Despatches From the Barricades, 1990; From the House of War: Baghdad and the Gulf, 1991; The Darkness Crumbles: The Death of Communism, 1992; In the Forests of the Night: Drug-Running and Terrorism in Peru, 1993; The Oxford Book of Exile (editor), 1995; Lifting the Veil: Life in Revolutionary Iran, 1995; Strange Places, Questionable People (autobiography), 1998; A Mad World, My Masters, 2000; News from No Man's Land: Reporting the World, 2002; The Wars Against Saddam: Taking the Hard Road to Baghdad, 2004; Days From a Different World: A Memoir of Childhood,

2005; Not Quite World's End: A Traveller's Tales, 2007; Twenty Tales from The War Zone, 2007. Honours: Fellow, Royal Geographical Society, 1990; Commander of the Order of the British Empire, 1991; BAFTA Reporter of the Year, 1991, 2001; RTS Richard Dimbleby Award, 1991; Columnist of the Year, National Magazine Awards, 1993; Honorary DLitt, De Montfort University, 1995; RTS Foreign Report Award, 1997; Peabody Award, USA, 1997; Dr hc, Nottingham, 2000; Emmy Award, 2002; Bayeux War Correspondents' Prize, 2002; International Emmy Award, New York, 2002. Address: c/o BBC Television Centre, Wood Lane, London W12 7RJ, England.

SIMPSON O J (Orenthal James), b. 9 July 1947, San Francisco, USA. Former Professional Football Player; Actor; Sports Commentator. m. (1) Marguerite Whitley, 1967, divorced, 1 son, 1 daughter, (2) Nicole Brown, 1985, divorced 1992, deceased 1994, 2 sons. Education: University of Southern California; City College, San Francisco. Appointments: Member, World Record 440 yard relay team (38.6 sec), 1967; Downtown Athletic Club, 1968; Halfback, Buffalo Bills, 1969-75; San Francisco 49'ers, 1978-79; American Football League All-Star team, 1970; ProBowl Team, 1972-76; Sports Commentator, ABC Sports, 1979-86; Analyst, ABC Monday Night Football Broadcasts, 1984-85; co-host, NFL Live on NBC, 1990; Has appeared in several TV films; Acquitted of two charges of murder, 1995; Found responsible for the deaths of Nicole Brown Simpson and Ronald Goldman by civil jury, 1997; Films include: The Towering Inferno, 1974; Killer Force, 1976; The Cassandra Crossing, 1977; Capricorn One, 1978; Firepower, 1979; Hambone and Hillie, 1984; The Naked Gun, 1988; The Naked Gun 2 ½: The Smell of Fear, 1991; The Naked Gun 33 1/3: The Final Insult. Publication: I Want to Tell You, 1995. Honours: Recipient of various football awards.

SINCLAIR Adrian Ivan, b. 6 January 1948, Guildford, Surrey, England. Company Secretary. m. Patricia Evelyn, 2 sons, 2 daughters. Education: St Peters, Guildford. Appointments: Financial Analyst/Advisor to the Chairman, AIBC Financial Corp, Florida, USA, 1988-89; Vice President and General Manager, Beddows Commodities Inc, Florida, 1989-91; Director/Company Secretary, Sinclair & Associates Ltd, Gibraltar, 1992-95; Company Secretary, Tucker Accounting & Business Services Ltd & Noronha Advogados (Attorneys), 1996-97; Director/Company Secretary, Tax Consultants International Ltd, 1997-2001; Chief Executive, Orinda Registrars Ltd, 2001-; Associate Lecturer, South East Essex College, 2002-05; Chief Executive, Global Strategy & Development Ltd, 2004-; Chief Executive, Association of Lawyers for Animal Rights, 2005-. Address: 58 Torquay Drive, Leigh-on-Sea, Essex SS9 1SE, England. E-mail: sinclair@justice.com

SINCLAIR Andrew Annandale, b. 21 January 1935, Oxford, England. Writer; Historian. m. Sonia Melchett, 25 July 1984, 2 sons. Education: Major Scholar, BA, PhD, Trinity College, Cambridge, 1955-59; Harkness Fellow, Harvard University,1959-61; American Council of Learned Societies Fellow, Stanford University, 1964-65. Appointments: Founding Fellow, Churchill College, 1961-63; Lecturer, University College, London, 1965-67; Publisher, Lorrimer Publishing, 1968-89; Managing Director, Timon Films Limited, 1968-2007; Films: Under Milk Wood, Dylan on Dylan, Sundance Festival, 2003. Publications: The Breaking of Bumbo, 1959; My Friend Judas, 1959; Prohibition: The Era of Excess, 1961; Gog, 1967; Magog, 1972; Jack: A Biography of Jack London, 1977; The Other Victoria, 1981;

King Ludd, 1988; War Like a Wasp, 1989; The War Decade: An Anthology of the 1940's, 1989; The Need to Give, 1990; The Far Corners of the Earth, 1991; The Naked Savage, 1991; The Strength of the Hills, 1991; The Sword and the Grail, 1992; Francis Bacon: His Life and Violent Times, 1993; In Love and Anger, 1994; Jerusalem: The Endless Crusade, 1995; Arts and Cultures: The History of the 50 Years of the Arts Council of Great Britain, 1995; The Discovery of the Grail, 1998; Death by Fame: A Life of Elisabeth, Empress of Austria, 1998; Guevara, 1998; Dylan the Bard: A Life of Dylan Thomas, 1999; The Secret Scroll, 2001; Blood and Kin, 2002; An Anatomy of Terror, 2003; Rosslyn, 2005; Viva Che!, 2005; The Grail: The Quest for a Legend, 2007; The Reivers' Trail, 2007; Contributions to: Sunday Times; Times; New York Times; Atlantic Monthly. Honours: Somerset Maugham Prize, 1967; Venice Film Festival Award for Under Milk Wood, 1971; Listed in national and international biographical dictionaries. Memberships: Society of American Historians, fellow 1970; Royal Society of Literature, fellow 1968; Royal Society of Arts, fellow, 2007. Address: Flat 20, Millennium House, 132 Grosvenor Road, London SW1V 3JY, England.

SINCLAIR Sir Clive Marles, b. 30 July 1940, London, England. Inventor; Business Executive. m. Ann Trevor-Briscoe, 1962, divorced 1985, 2 sons, 1 daughter. Education: St George's College, Weybridge. Appointments: Editor, Bernards Publishers Ltd, 1958-61; Chair, Sinclair Radionics Ltd, 1962-79, Sinclair Research Ltd, 1979-, Sinclair Browne Ltd, 1981-85, Cambridge Computer, 1986-90; Chair, 1980-98, Honorary President, 2001-, British Mensa; Visiting Fellow, Robinson College, Cambridge, 1982-85; Visiting Professor, Imperial College, London, 1984-92; Director, Shaye Communications Ltd, 1986-91, Anamartic Ltd. Publications: Practical Transistor Receivers, 1959; British Semiconductor Survey, 1963. Honours: Hon Fellow, Imperial College, London, 1984; Hon DSc (Bath) 1983, (Warwick, Heriot Watt), 1983, (UMIST) 1984; Royal Society Mullard Award, 1984. Address: Sinclair Research Ltd, Flat A, 1-3 Spring Gardens, Trafalgar Square, London SW1A 2BB, England. Website: www.sinclair-research.co.uk

SINCLAIR Olga Ellen, (Ellen Clare, Olga Daniels), b. 23 January 1923, Norfolk, England. Writer. m. Stanley George Sinclair, 1 April 1945, 3 sons. Publications: Gypsies, 1967; Hearts By the Tower, 1968; Bitter Sweet Summer, 1970; Dancing in Britain, 1970; Children's Games, 1972; Toys, 1974; My Dear Fugitive, 1976; Never Fall in Love, 1977; Master of Melthorpe, 1979; Gypsy Girl, 1981; Ripening Vine, 1981; When Wherries Sailed By, 1987; Gretna Green: A Romantic History, 1989; as Olga Daniels: Lord of Leet Castle, 1984; The Gretna Bride, 1995; The Bride From Faraway, 1987; The Untamed Bride, 1988; The Arrogant Cavalier, 1991; A Royal Engagement, 1999; An Heir for Ashingby, 2004; The Countess and the Miner, 2005. Memberships; Society of Authors; Romantic Novelists Association; Society of Women and Journalists; Norwich Writer's Circle, president. Address: Sycamore, Norwich Road, Lingwood, Norfolk NR13 4BH, England.

SINDEN Sir Donald, b. 9 October 1923, Plymouth, Devon, England. Actor; Writer. m. Diana Mahony, 1948, deceased 2004, 2 sons. Appointments: Professional Actor, 1942-; Films for the Rank Organisation, 1952-60; Associate Artist, Royal Shakespeare Company, 1967-. Publications: A Touch of the Memoirs, 1982; Laughter in the Second Act, 1985; Everyman Book of Theatrical Anecdotes (editor), 1987; The English Country Church, 1988; Famous Last Words (editor), 1994. Honour: Drama Desk Award, 1974; Variety Club of

Great Britain, Stage Actor of 1976; Evening Standard Drama Award, Best Actor, 1977; Commander of the Order of the British Empire, 1979; Knighted, 1997; D Litt (Leics), 2005. Memberships: Council of British Actors Equity, 1966-77, trustee, 1988-2004; Arts Council, Drama Panel, 1973-77, Advisory Board, 1982-86 Federation of Playgoers' Societies, president, 1968-93; Royal Theatrical Fund, president, 1983-; Royal Society of Arts, fellow, 1966-; Green Room Benevolent Fund, president, 1998-2004. Address: Rats Castle, TN30 7HX, England.

SINGER Nicky Margaret, b. 22 July 1956, Chalfont-St-Peter, England. Novelist. m. James King-Smith, 2 sons, 1 daughter. Education: University of Bristol. Appointments: Associate Director of Talks, ICA, 1981-83; Programme Consultant, Enigma Television, 1984-85; Chair, Brighton Festival Literature Committee, 1988-93; Member of Ace Literary Magazines Group, 1993-96; Co-Founder, Co-Director, Performing Arts Labs, 1987-96; Board Member, Printer's Devil, 1993-97; Presenter, BBC2's Labours of Eve, 1994-95; Board Member, South East Arts, 2000-03. Publications: Novels: To Still the Child, 1992; To Have and To Hold, 1993; What She Wanted, 1996; My Mother's Daughter, 1998. Non-Fiction: The Tiny Book of Time (with Kim Pickin), 1999; The Little Book of the Millennium (with Jackie Singer), 1999; Children's Fiction: Feather Boy, 2002, adapted for TV, 2004, adapted as a musical, National Theatre, 2006; Doll, 2003; The Innocent's Story, 2005; GemX, 2006; The Knight Crew, 2008. Honours: Winner, Blue Peter Book of the Year Award (Feather Boy), 2002; Winner, BAFTA Best Drama (Feather Boy), 2004); Shortlisted, Book Trust Teenage Prize (Doll), 2003. Address: c/o Conville and Walsh, 2 Ganton Street, London WIF 7QL, England.

SINGH Harmeet, b. 22 November 1974, Rohtak, India. Radiation Oncologist. m. Savita Verma, 1 son. Education: MB BS, MD (Radiotherapy). Appointments: Senior Resident, 2003-06, Assistant Professor, 2006-, Department of Radiotherapy, Post Graduate Institute of Medical Sciences, Rohtak 124001, India. Publications: 12 articles in national and international journals. Memberships: Life Member, Association of Radiation Oncologists of India; Corresponding Member, American Society for Therapeutic Radiology and Oncology; Member, European Society for Therapeutic Radiology and Oncology; Member, American Brachytherapy Society. Address: 67-L, Model Town, Rohtak 124001, India.

SINGH Hazara, b. 30 November 1922, Sheikhupura, India (now Pakistan). Retired University Teacher; Writer. m. Phool Kaur, 1949, 2 sons, 2 daughters. Education: BA, Punjab University, Lahore, 1945; MA, 1950, LLB, 1955, Punjab University, Chandigarh. Appointments: Lecturer of English, Khalsa College, Amritsar, 1950-53; Assistant Professor of English, Government Agricultural College, Ludhiana, 1954-66; Associate Professor of English, 1966-84, Head, Department of Languages and Journalism, 1977-82, Punjab Agricultural University, Ludhiana; Secretary to Vice-Chancellor, Guru Nanak Dev University, Amritsar, 1985-88; Versatile writer in English, Urdu and Punjabi; Participated in freedom struggle against Imperialism, jailed three times, scholarship confiscated and medal withdrawn; Migrated to India. Publications: Contributions to professional journals; Manuals for Researchers; Books in English: Poetry: Aspirations, 1980; Yearnings, 1987; Expectations, 1999; Destination, 2007; Prose: Sikhism and it's Impact on Indian Society, 1969, 1999; Lala Lajpat Rai – An Appraisal, 2003; Happy Meaningful Life, 2004; Freedom Struggle against Imperialism, 2007; Apostle of Non-Violence, 2007. Honours:

Rattigan Gold Medal, Khalsa College, Amritsar, 1945; Tamra Patra for meritorious contribution to freedom struggle, during Silver Jubilee of Independence 1972, Government of India. Memberships: Indian Society of Authors; Punjabi Sahitya Academy, Ludhiana. Address: 3-C Udham Singh Nagar, Ludhiana 141001, India. Website: www.hazarasingh.com

SINGH Malvinder, b. 11 December 1951, Roorkee, Uttrakhand, India. Engineer. m. Manjeet Kaur, 1 son. Education: Master of Engineering, Mechanical Engineering, University of Roorkee, 1980. Appointments: Junior Executive, 1978-81, Engineer, 1981-85, Sr Engineer, 1985-89, Quality Control, Deputy Manager, 1989-92, Manager, 1992-97, Senior Manager, 1997-99, Deputy General Manager, 2007-, Quality Assurance, Heavy Electrical Equipment Plant, Bharat Heavy Electrical Ltd (BHEL), Haridwar – 249403, Uttrakhand, India. Publications: Numerous articles in professional journals. Honours: Chartered Engineer, Institution of Engineers, India; Man of Achievement Award, 2000; Millennium Achiever Award, 2001; Bharat Excellence Award; Rashtriya Gaurav Award; Jewel of India Award; Listed in international biographical dictionaries. Memberships: Institution of Engineers, India; Indian Institute of Welding Kolkata, India; American Welding Society, USA; Institute of Directors, New Delhi, India; National Centre for Quality Management Mumbai, India; All India Management Association, New Delhi, India. Address: Heep Bhel, Haridwar – 249403, Uttrakhand, India. E-mail: malvin@bhelwr.co.in

SINGH Raj Kumar Prasad, b. 2 July 1947, Sheotar, Bihar, India. Metallurgical Engineer. m. Chintamani, 1 son, 1 daughter. Education: BSc, Engineering, Bihar Institute of Technology, Sindri, 1970; M Tech, Indian Institute of Technology, Bombay, 1975; PhD, Indian Institute of Technology, Madras, 1994. Appointments: Deputy Manager, Bokard Steel Plant, SAIL, 1972-79; Assistant General Manager, Research and Development Centre for Iron and Steel, Steel Authority of India, 1980-94; General Manager, Quality Control, Research and Development, Lloyds Steel Industries Ltd, 1994-99; Professor, VNIT, Nagpur, 2000-2003; Director General, Institute for Steel Development and Growth, 2003-. Publications: Over 50 national and international publications, including, EDD Quality Steels Al-Deoxidation Techniques; Sulphide Shape Control in HSLA Steels; Combined Blowing of Converters; Failure Analysis. Honours: Listed in several international biographical directories. Memberships: Life Fellow, Indian Institute of Metals; Life Member, Indian Society of Non-Destructive Testing. Address: Ispat Niketan, 1st Floor, 52/1A Ballygunge Circular Road, Kolkata 700 019, India. E-mail: rkpsingh@hotmail.com

SINGLETON Valerie, b. 9 April 1937, England. Education: Arts Educational School London, RADA. Appointments: Broadcast Personality and Writer; Bromley Rep, 1956-57, subsequently, No 1 Tour, Cambridge Arts Theatre, Theatre work, TV appearances, Compact and Emergency Ward 10 and others, top voice over commentator for TV commercials and advertising magazines; BBC 1: Continuity Announcer, 1962-64, Presenter, Blue Peter, 1962-72, Nationwide, 1972-78, Val Meets the VIPs (3 series), Blue Peter Special Assignment (4 series), Blue Peter Royal Safari with HRH The Princess Anne, Tonight and Tonight in Town, 1978-79, Blue Peter Special Assignments Rivers Yukon and Niagara, 1980; BBC 2: Echoes of Holocaust, 1979, The Migrant Workers of Europe, 1980, The Money Programme, 1980-88; Radio 4: PM 1981-93, several appearances Midweek; Freelance Broadcaster and Travel Writer, 1993-; Channel 4: Presenter, Back-Date (daily quiz programme), 1996; Playback, History

Channel, 1998, second series, 1999; Numerous appearances in TV advertising. Honour: OBE. Membership: Equity. Address: c/o Arlington Enterprises, 1-3 Charlotte Street, London W1, England.

SINHA Neeti, b. 29 June 1970, Lucknow, India. Scientist (Biophysics). m. 1 daughter. Education: PhD/DPhil, University of Oxford England, 1998; Post-doctoral Research, National Institutes of Health, USA, 5 years. Appointments: Associate Research Scientist, Johns Hopkins University, Baltimore, USA, 2003-; Assistant Director, Computational Biophysics, CDRI, India, 2004. Publications: Book on Mind & Psychology; 14 research articles on protein structure and thermodynamics in top rated scientific journals. Honours: Felix Scholarship Award for D Phil at Oxford; Radhakrishnan Bequest at Oxford; Post-doctoral Visiting Fellowship, NIH, USA; Outstanding Scientist Category in USA; JR Fellowship and Lectureship, CSIR, India; Delivered course on Biophysical approaches and supervised training in Protein Thermodynamics; Listed in Who's Who publications and biographical dictionaries. Memberships: Invited Editorial Board Member, CPPS; Invited Editorial Board Member, PPS; Invited Member, Medical Science Monitor International Reviewers Panel. Address: 106 Mudd Hall, Johns Hopkins University, 3400 N Charles Street, Baltimore, MD 21218, USA. E-mail: nsinha@jhu.edu

SINHA Ritesh Kumar, b. 13 December 1976, Birmingham, England. Doctor of Medicine. Education: MD cum laude (with honours), General Medicine, 2003; PhD (magna cum laude), Pharmacology, 2003; PhD (magna cum laude), Family Medicine, 2006; Postgraduate diplomas in: General Medicine, General Surgery, Geriatric Medicine, Obstetrics & Gynaecology, Minor Surgery, Medical Ethics, Occupational Medicine, Public Health, Cardiology, and Medical Education, 2006; Postgraduate Certificate, Electrocardiography, 2006. Appointments: Customer Service Professional (part time), Advisor (part time), 1996-97, Assistant Manager, 1997-99, General Manager, 1999-2004, Nirvana Health Spa; Resident, General Medicine, 2003; Chief Executive Officer, Global Recruitment Agency UK (part time), 2003-; Resident, General Surgery, 2004; Resident, Geriatric Medicine, 2004; Resident, Obstetrics & Gynaecology, 2005; Senior Resident, Family Medicine, 2005-06. Honours: Employee of the Year, 1997, Manager of the Year, 2002, Nirvana Health Spa; SRU, Certificate of Achievement, Dean's List of High Academic Achievement, 2003; SRU, Highest Academic Award Designation of Valedictorian, 2003. Memberships: General Medical Council; Latvian Medical Association; Fellow, Royal Society of Medicine; Fellow, Royal Society of Tropical Medicine and Hygiene; Fellow, Royal Society for the Promotion of Health; Member, American College of Clinical Pharmacology; Member Associate, Family Doctor's Association of Latvia; Member, Migraine in Primary Care Advisors; Member, Primary Care Cardiovascular Society; Member, British Medical Association. Address: Saroswati, 15 Margaret Road, Blundellsands, Liverpool, Merseyside L23 6TR, England. E-mail: dr_rks@hotmail.com

SINNOTT Jan Dynda, b. 14 June 1942, Cleveland, Ohio. Psychologist. 2 sons, 2 daughters. Education: BS, St Louis University, 1964; MA, 1973, PhD, 1975, Catholic University of America. Appointments: Workshop Lecturer, 1971-; Social Rehabilitation Services Research Trainee, 1971-74; Research Assistant, 1971-72, Teaching Assistant, 1973, Catholic University of America; Research Associate, Human Sciences Research, Virginia, 1975; Lecturer, 1975-77, Research Associate, 1975-77, Catholic University of America; Founder and Director, Human Development Research, 1977-80; Principal Investigator, Centre on Ageing, University of Maryland, 1977-80; Guest Scientist, Gerontology Research Centre, National Institute on Ageing, NIH, 1980-89; Director, Centre for Study of Adult Development and Ageing, 1989-91, Associate Director, Institute for Cognition and Teaching, 2001-, Tenured Professor of Psychology, 1978-, Towson University, Maryland. Publications: The Development in Logic in Adulthood: Postformal Thought and Its Application; Plus numerous other reviews, books, articles, book chapters and papers. Honours: Towson University Faculty Excellence Award; Listed in Who's Who publications and biographical dictionaries. Memberships: Fellow, American Psychological Association; Fellow, Gerontological Society of America; Fellow, American Psychological Society; many others. Address: 9923 Cottrell Terrace, Silver Spring, Maryland 20903, USA. E-mail: jsinnott@towson.edu

SINYAGIN Yury, b. 22 June 1954, Ulyanovsk, Russia. Psychology. m. Natalia, 1 son, 1 daughter. Education: PhD, Moscow State University, 1981; Visiting Scholar, Junior Faculty Development Programme Global Affairs Institute, Syracuse University, USA, 1994-95; Doctoral Degree, Russian Academy of State Service, 1997; International Training Programme Human Resource Development, UK, 2001. Appointments: Vice President, Department of Psychology and Acmeology of Professional Activity, 1998-, Director, Center for Assessment and Evaluation, 2000-, Russian Academy of State Service. Publications: More than 100 articles; 14 books including: Psychology of interorganisational relations, 1995; Psychological techniques in forming management team, 2005; Child suicide: Psychological view, 2006; Acmeological Assessment, 2007. Honours: Multiple government and industrial awards; Prize of the President of Russian Federation Exceptional Achievements in the Educational Sphere. Memberships: International Acmeological Academy; Academy of Security, Protection and Law Enforcement Problems. Address: Apt 167, Azovskaya st, 24-2, 117452, Russia, Moscow. E-mail: yvsin@yandex.ru Website: www.potentiales.ru

SIRIK Yury, b. 13 May 1946, Dnepropetrovsk, Ukraine. Aerospace Engineer. m. Tatiana Sirik, 1 son, 1 daughter. Education: Hydroaerodynamics, Mechanical Mathematical Faculty, State University of Dnepropetrovsk, Ukraine, 1965-70; Scientific Research Energy Institute, Moscow, Russia, 1969; Increased Qualification Course, Central Scientific Research Institute Machine-building, Kaliningrad, Russia, 1979; Theory of Design, State Design Office "Yuzshnoe", Dnepropetrovsk, Ukraine, 1980. Appointments: Engineer, Research Institute of Machine-building Technology, Zlatoust, Russia, 1970-73; Engineer, Design Office Mechanical Engineering, Miass, Russia, 1973-80; Engineer, State Design Office "Yuzshnoe", Pavlograd, Ukraine, 1980-; Senior Investigator, Physical-Technical Group, Pavlograd, Ukraine, 1991-. Publications: More than 10 research reports; 11 articles; 5 patents. Address: Balashovskaya Street 14, 33, Pavlograd, Dnepropetrovsk oblast, 51413, Ukraine.

SISSONS Peter George, b. 17 July 1942. Television Presenter. m. Sylvia Bennett, 1965, 2 sons, 1 daughter. Education: University College Oxford. Appointments: Graduate Trainee, ITN, 1964, General Reporter, 1967, Industrial Correspondent, 1970, Industrial Editor, 1972-78, Presenter, News at One, 1978-82; Presenter, Channel 4 News, 1982-89; Presenter, 6 O'Clock News, 1989-93, 9 O'Clock News, 1994-2000, 10 O'Clock News, 2000-03, News 24, 2003-, BBC TV News; Chair, BBC TV Question Time, 1989-93. Honours:

Broadcasting Press Guild Award, 1984; Royal TV Society Judges' Award, 1988; Honorary Fellow, Liverpool John Moores University, 1997; Hon LLD, University of Liverpool, 2002. Address: BBC Television Centre, Wood Lane, London, W12 7RJ, England.

SJÖRS Hugo M, b. 1 August 1915, Stora Skedvi, Sweden. Emeritus Professor. m. Gunnel Thelander, 1 son, 2 daughters. Education: Fil Mag, 1942, Fil Lic, 1945, Fil Dr, 1948, Uppsala University. Appointments: Docent, 1948, Professor of Ecological Botany, 1962-80, Emeritus, 1980, Uppsala University; Deputy Assistant Professor, Lund University, 1952-55; Assistant Professor, School of Forestry, Stockholm, 1955-62. Publications: 2 Textbooks: Nordic Plant Geography, Ecological Botany (both in Swedish); About 200 papers on Plant Ecology and Peatlands. Honours: Linnaeus Gold Medal, Royal Physiographic Society, Lund; Nature Conservation Prize, Species Data Bank, Swedish Agricultural University. Memberships: Royal Swedish Academy of Sciences; Foreign Member, Finnish Academy of Sciences; Honorary Member, British Ecological Society; Honorary Member, Swedish Botanical Society. Address: Stenbrohultsvägen 103, 75758 Uppsala, Sweden.

SKARD Torild, b. 29 November 1936, Oslo, Norway. Senior Researcher. m. Kåre Ø Hansen. Education: BA, 1962, MA, 1965, University of Oslo; Norwegian Certificate as Psychologist, 1975. Appointments: School Psychologist, Municipal Psychiatric Clinic for Children and Youth, and Youth Club Worker, Oslo, 1965-67; Lecturer, Norwegian Teachers' Training College for Special Education, Baerum, 1965-72; First Lecturer, Institute of Social Sciences, University of Tromso, 1972-73; Member, Norwegian Parliament, First Woman President of Lagting (Upper Chamber) and Vice President of Judiciary Committee, 1973-77; Researcher, Work Research Institutes, Oslo, 1978-84; Director for the Status of Women, UNESCO, Paris, 1984-86; Director General and Assistant Secretary General, Norwegian Ministry for Development Co-operation/Ministry of Foreign Affairs, Oslo, 1986-94; Regional Director, West and Central Africa, UNICEF, Abidjan, 1994-98; Senior Advisor, Norwegian Ministry of Foreign Affairs, Oslo, 1999-2003; Senior Researcher, Norwegian Institute of International Affairs, Oslo, 2003-. Publications: Numerous articles and books including most recently: You have to Pay a Price to be a Tough Guy – Particularly if You are a Woman: Women Journalists in Norway, 1984; Equality between the Sexes – Myth or Reality in Norden? 1984; Norwegian Municipal Councils – a Place for Women? 1985; Continent of Mothers, Continent of Hope, Understanding and Promoting Development in Africa Today, 2001; Development Thinking and Practice: Reflections on Future Contributions of the United Nations System, 2005; Breaking the glass ceiling? Women Heads of State and Government 1945-2006, 2006. Honours: Commander, National Lion Order, Senegal, 1998; Women of the Year, ABI, 1997. Memberships: Norwegian Women's Rights Association. Address: Norwegian Institute of International Affairs, Postbox 8159 Dep, 0033 Oslo, Norway. E-mail: toriskar@online.no

SKÁRMETA Antonio, b. 7 November 1940, Antofagasta, Chile. Writer. Education: Graduated, University of Chile, 1963; MA, Columbia University, 1966. Appointments: Ambassador to Germany, 2000-01. Publications: El entusiasmo, 1967; Desnudo en el tejado, 1969; El ciclista del San Cristóbal, 1973; Tiro libre, 1973; Soñé que la nieve ardía, 1975, English translation as I Dreamt the Snow Was Burning, 1985; Novios y solitarios, 1975; La insurrección, 1980, English translation as The Insurrection, 1983; No pasó nada, 1980; Ardiente paciencia, 1985, English translation as Burning Patience, 1987; Match Ball, 1989; Watch Where the Wolf is Going, 1991; La boda del trombón, 2001; El baile de la victoria, 2003. Contributions to: Periodicals. Honours: Premio Casa de las Américas, 1969; Guggenheim Fellowship, 1986; Academy Award Nomination, 1996. Address: Chilean Embassy, 53173 Bonn, Kronprinzenstr 20, Germany.

SKARSGÅRD J Stellan, b. 13 June 1951, Goteborg, Sweden. Actor. m. My Gunther, 1976, 5 sons, 1 daughter. Appointments: With Royal Dramatic Theatre, Stockholm, 1972-87; Films Include: Simple Minded Murderer, 1982; Serpent's Way, 1986; Hip Hip Hurrah, 1987; The Unbearable Lightness of Being, 1988; Good Evening Mr Wallenberg, 1990; The Ox, Wind, 1992; The Slingshot, 1993; Zero Kelvin, 1994; Breaking the Waves, 1995; Insomnia, Amistad, Good Will Hunting, 1997; Ronin, Deep Blue Sea, 1998; Passion of Mind, 1999; Kiss Kiss (Bang Bang), Signs & Wonders, Timecode, Dancer in the Dark, Aberdeen (also associate producer), 2000; The Hire: Powder Keg, Taking Sides, 2001; The House on Turk Street, City of Ghosts, 2002; Dogville, 2003; King Arthur, Eiffeltornet, Exorcist: The Beginning, 2004; Torte Bluma, 3 & 3, 2005; Pirates of the Caribbean: Dead Man's Chest, Goya's Ghosts, 2006; Pirates of the Caribbean: At World's End, 2007; Boogie Woogie, God on Trial, Mamma Mia, 2008; For TV, Hamlet, 1984; Harlan County War, 2000; Helen of Troy, 2003. Honours: Best Actor, Berlin Film Festival, 1982; Twice Best Film Actor in Sweden; Best Actor, Rouen Film Festival, 1988, 1992; Best Actor, Chicago Film Festival, 1991; Jury's Special Prize, San Sebastian Film Festival, 1995; European Film Award.

SKEHEL Sir John James, b. 27 February 1941, Blackburn, Lancashire, England. Research Scientist. m. Anita Varley, 2 sons. Education: PhD, University of Manchester, 1966. Appointments: Postdoctoral Fellow: University of Aberdeen; Department of Biological Chemistry and Duke University Medical Centre, North Carolina, Department of Microbiology and Immunology, 1965-69; MRC National Institute for Medical Research, Mill Hill, London Division of Virology, 1969-; Member, Medical Research Council Scientific Staff, 1971-; Director, WHO Collaborating Centre for Reference and Research on Influenza, 1975-93; Head, Division of Virology, 1990-2001; Head, Infections and Immunity Group, 1985-; Director, MRC National Institute for Medical Research, 1987-. Publications: Numerous articles in scientific journals. Honours: Member, EMBO, 1983; Fellow, Royal Society, 1984; Wilhelm Feldberg Prize, 1986; Robert Koch Prize, 1987; Louis Jeantet Prix de Medecine, 1988; Honorary DSc, CNAA, 1990; Leeuwenhoek Lecture of Royal Society, 1990; Member, Academia Europaea, 1992; ICN International Prize in Virology, 1992; Knight Bachelor, Queen's Birthday Honours List, 1996; Visiting Professorship, University of Glasgow, 1997-2003; Fellow, Academy of Medical Sciences, 1998; Vice President, Academy of Medical Sciences, 2001-07; The Royal Society Royal Medal, 2003; Honorary Professor, University College London, Division of Virology, 2003; Ernst Chain Prize, 2004; Honorary DSc, University College, London, 2004; Honorary Fellow, The University of Wales, 2004; Honorary Member, Society of General Microbiology, 2005; Le Grand Prix de Fondation Louis D, Institut de France, 2007. Address: MRC National Institute for Medical Research, The Ridgeway, Mill Hill, London NW7 1AA, England.

SKIFF Warner Mason, b. 11 December 1955, Oxnard, California, USA. Physical Chemist. Education: BA, Chemistry, 1977, PhD, Chemistry, 1985, Arizona State University. Appointments: Research Associate, Centre for Solid State Science, Arizona State University, 1985-88; Senior Research Chemist, Shell Oil Company, Houston, Texas, 1988-99; Assistant Professor, University of Alaska, Fairbanks, 1999-2004; Vice President, General Molecular Inc, Fort Collins, Colorado, USA, 1999-. Publications: About a dozen articles; Research contributions: Electron energy loss spectroscopy, force field development and application, theoretical catalysis. Honours: Burton Medal, Microscopy Society of America; Visiting Scientist, Shell Research and Technology Centre, Amsterdam, The Netherlands. Address: P O Box 271, Dillingham, Alaska 99576, USA.

SKOPINSKY Vadim Nikolaevich, b. 3 May 1946, Moscow. Higher School Professor. m. Elena, 2 sons. Education: Graduate, 1970; Post Graduate, 1970-73; Candidate of Technical Sciences, 1974; Doctor of Technical Sciences, Moscow Engineer Construction Institute, 1989. Appointments: Research Worker, 1973-76; Associate Professor, 1976-89; Professor, 1989-90; Head of Material Strength Chair, 1990-. Publications: Articles to professional journals and proceedings at conferences. Honours: Science Grantee, Academy of Transport Sciences, Moscow; Fundamental Research Grantee, Russian State Commission in Higher Education, 1996. Memberships: Member Academic Board; Member, Research Board of Advisors, ABI, USA; Member, Special Science Council, Institute of Technology and Mechanical Engineering; Member, Science Council, Moscow. Address: Alleya Zhemchugovoy 1-1-127, 111402 Moscow, Russia.

SKOROBOGATOV German, b. 10 January 1937, Datsan Cheata Region, Siberia. Physics-Chemistry Educator. m. Eugeniaja Nadeoshkeana, 3 daughters. Education: Magister, 1959, PhD, 1967, Department of Chemistry, Leningrad State University; Professor of Chemistry, St Petersburg State University, 1996. Appointments: Researcher, Institute of Silicate Chemistry, 1960-61; Researcher, Department of Physics, 1966-67, Chief of Photochemistry Laboratory, Department of Chemistry, 1968-2007, Professor, Department of Chemistry, 1984-2007, St Petersburg (Leningrad) State University. Publications: Co-author, book: Radiochemistry and Chemistry of Nuclear Reactions, 1960; Orthodoxical and Paradoxical Chemistry, 1985; Theoretical Chemistry, 2000, 2nd edition, 2005; Take Care! Tap Water!, 2003; Foundations of Theoretical Chemistry, 2003; Articles in professional journals. Honours: Research Fellow, Coin, ABI, Bronze edition, 1993, Silver edition, 1996; Listed in national and international biographical dictionaries. Memberships: Mendeleev's Chemical Society (Moscow), 1975-2007; American Mathematical Society, 1988-98; Planetary Society, 1992-99. Address: Department of Chemistry, St Petersburg State University, Universitetskii prosp 26, 198504 St Petersburg, Russia. E-mail: 2gera.skor@pobox.spbu.ru Website: www.red.antiglobalism.ru

SKRZYPCZYNSKA Małgorzata Cecylia, b. 26 December 1940, Wadowice, Poland. Professor. m. Andrzej, 1 daughter. Education: MA, Faculty of Biology and Earth Science, Jagiellonian University, Kraków, 1958-63; Dr of Forest Sciences, 1971, Dr Sc, 1979, Professor Dr Sc, Forest Entomology, 1994, Agricultural University of Kraków. Appointments: Assistant, 1964-71, Adjunct Professor, 1971-79, Assistant Professor, 1979-94, Professor, 1994-, Agricultural University of Kraków. Publications include: 302 publications including 165 monographs, studies and dissertations; 2 Books, 1 with Professor J Křistek; Numerous articles in magazines and journals dealing with forest entomology with particular reference to seed insect pests of conifers and zoocecidology/ plant galls. Honours: Stypendist, Czechoslovak Academy of Science, 1974; Stipendist, University of Bodenkultur, Vienna, Austria, 1979, 1981; Złoty Krzyż Zasługi, 1986; Krzyż Kawalerski Orderu Odrodzenia Polski, 2000; Medal Komisji Edukacji Narodowej, 2006; Diploma of the Polish Academy of Sciences, 2004. Memberships: Deputy, Working Party IUFRO, 1992-; Polish Entomological Society; Polish Forest Society. Address: Agricultural University of Kraków, Department of Forest Entomology, 31-425 Kraków, Al 29 Listopada 46, Poland. E-mail: rlbozek@cyf-kr.edu.pl

ŠLAPAL Josef, b. 21 December 1955, Brno, Czech Republic. Mathematician. m. Ivana Rybárová, 2 daughters. Education: MA Pure Mathematics, 1975-80, PhD Algebra, 1989-92, Masaryk University, Brno. Appointments: Lecturer, 1981-82, Senior Lecturer, 1982-86, Technical University of Ostrava; Senior Lecturer, 1986-94, Associate Professor, 1994-2000, Professor, 2000-, Head of Department, 2003-, Technical University of Brno. Publications: Over 60 research papers in renowned mathematical journals. Honours: German Academy of Sciences Fellowship, 1994; DAAD Fellowship, Germany, 1998; Dr Jiri Nehnevajsa Memorial Award, University of Pittsburgh, 1999; NATO-CNR Outreach Fellowship, Italy, 2002. Memberships: American Mathematical Society; New York Academy of Sciences; Union of Czech Mathematicians and Physicists; National Geographic Society. Address: Department of Mathematics, Technical University of Brno, 616 69 Brno, Czech Republic. E-mail: slapal@fme.vutbr.cz Website: http://at.yorku.ca/h/a/a/a/10.htm

SLATER Christian, b. 18 August 1969, New York, USA. Actor. Appointments: Appeared at age of seven in TV series One Life to Live; Professional stage debut at age of nine in touring production of The Music Man. Stage appearances include: Macbeth; David Copperfield; Merlin; Landscape of the Body; Side Man; One Flew Over the Cuckoo's Nest, 2004-05; The Glass Menagerie, 2005; TV: Sherlock Holmes, 1981; Living Proof: The Hank Williams Jr Story, The Haunted Mansion Mystery, 1983; Ryan's Hope, 1985; Secrets, 1986; Desperate for Love, 1989; Merry Christmas, George Bailey, 1997; Prehistoric Planet, 2002; The West Wing, 2003, 2004; A Light Knight's Odyssey, 2004. Films: The Legend of Billie Jean, 1985; The Name of the Rose, Twisted, 1986; Tucker: The Man and his Dream, 1988; Gleaming the Cube, Heathers, Beyond the Stars, The Wizard, 1989; Tales from the Darkside: The Movie; Young Guns II: Blaze of Glory, Pump Up the Volume, 1990; Robin Hood: Prince of Thieves, Star Trek: The Undiscovered Country, 1991; Kuffs, Ferngully: The Last Rainforest, Where the Day Takes You, 1992; Untamed Heart, True Romance, 1993; Jimmy Hollywood, Interview with a Vampire, 1994; Murder in the First, 1995; Bed of Roses, Broken Arrow, 1996; Austin Powers: International Man of Mystery, Julian Po, 1997; Hard Rain (also producer), Basil (also co-producer), Very Bad Things (producer), 1998; Love Stinks, 1999; The Contender, 2000; 3000 Miles to Graceland, Who is Cletis Tout? 2001; Run for the Money, Windtalkers, 2002; Masked and Anonymous, 2003; The Good Shepherd, Mindhunters, Churchill: The Hollywood Years, Pursued, 2004; Alone in the Dark, The Deal, 2005; Bobby, 2006; Slipstream, He Was a Quiet Man, 2007; Love Lies Bleeding, 2008. Honours: Theatregoers' Choice Award for Best Actor, 2005. Address: c/o CAA, 9830 Wilshire Boulevard, Beverly Hills, CA 90212, USA.

SLATER Edward Charles, b. 16 January 1917, Melbourne, Australia. Biochemist. m. Marion Winifred Hutley, 1 daughter. Education: MSc, University of Melbourne, 1935-39; PhD, DSc, Cambridge University, England, 1946-48. Appointments: Biochemist, Australian Institute of Anatomy, Canberra, Australia, 1939-46; Research Fellow, Molteno Institute, Cambridge University, 1946-55; Professor of Biochemistry, University of Amsterdam, 1955-85; Honorary Professor, Southampton University, 1985-90. Publications: About 450 articles in scientific journals and books; 1 monograph: The Story of a Biochemical Journal, 1986; Co-editor several publications. Honours include: Dixon Scholarship, Major James Cuming Memorial Scholarship in Chemistry, University of Melbourne, 1937; British Council Scholarship, 1946; Rockefeller Foundation Fellowship, 1949; University of Brussels Medal, 1956; Gold Medal, University of Bari, Italy, 1965; Medal of the Societe de Chimi Biologiqie, France, 1966; Keilin Medal, Biochemical Society, 1974; Knighthood in the Order of the Netherlands Lion, 1984; Honorary DSc, University of Southampton, 1993; Honorary D Biol. Sci., University of Bari, 1997. Memberships: Royal Netherlands Academy of Science, 1964; Dutch Company of Science, 1970; Corresponding Member, National Academy of science of Argentina, 1973; Honorary Member, Japanese Biochemical Society, 1973; Fellow of the Royal Society, 1975; Honorary Member, Biochemical Society, 1987; Fellow World Innovation Foundation, 2001. Address: 9 Oaklands, Lymington, Hants SO41 3TH, England. E-mail: ecslater@btinternet.com

SLATER Paul Bernard, b. 23 February 1940, Brooklyn, New York, USA. Physicist. 2 sons. Education: BS, Mathematics, Massachusetts Institute of Technology, 1961; Harvard Law School, 1961-63; PhD, Regional Science, University of Pennsylvania, 1972. Appointments: Postdoctoral Researcher, University of Pennsylvania, 1972-73; Assistant Professor, West Virginia University, 1973-79; Research Analyst, University of California, Santa Barbara, 1979-84; Research Physicist, Kavli Institute of Theoretical Physics, University of California, Santa Barbara, 1985-. Publications: Spatial and temporal effects in residential sales prices, 1973; Disaggregated Spatial-temporal analyses of residential sales prices, 1974; Qubit-Qutrit separability probability ratios, 2005; Dyson Indices and Hilbert-Schmidt separability functions and probabilities, 2007; Two-qubit separability probabilities and beta functions, 2007. Honours: National Science Foundation Grant, 1975; National Institute of Health Grant, 1983-84; Fulbright Award, Florence, Italy, 1985. Memberships: American Statistical Association; Regional Science Association. Address: 522 N Alisos St, Santa Barbara, CA 93103, USA.

SLAVIK Zdenek, b. 2 June 1957, Prague, Czech Republic. Paediatric Cardiologist. Education: Doctor of Medicine, Charles University, Prague, 1982; Doctor of Medicine (Postgraduate degree), University of Southampton, England, 1998. Appointments: Consultant Paediatric Intensivist, Glenfield Hospital, Leicester, England, 1995-97; Consultant Paediatric Cardiologist/Intensivist, Harefield Hospital, 1997-2001; Consultant Paediatric Cardiologist/Intensivist, 2001-06, Consultant Paediatric Cardiologist, 2006-, Royal Brompton Hospital. Honours: Visiting Professorship in Paediatrics, Medical School, Pilsen, and Charles University, Czech Republic. Memberships: Fellow, Royal College of Paediatrics and Child Health, UK. Address: Royal Brompton Hospital, Sydney Street, London SW3 6NP, England. E-mail: z.slavik@rbht.nhs.uk

SLAVITT David R(ytman), (David Benjamin, Henry Lazarus, Lynn Meyer, Henry Sutton), b. 23 March 1935, White Plains, New York, USA. Novelist; Poet; Translator; Lecturer. m. (1) Lynn Nita Meyer, 27 August 1956, divorced 1977, 2 sons, 1 daughter, (2) Janet Lee Abrahm, 16 April 1978. Education: BA, magna cum laude, Yale University, 1956; MA, Columbia University, 1957. Appointments:

Instructor in English, Georgia Institute of Technology, Atlanta, 1957-58; Staff, Newsweek magazine, 1958-65; Assistant Professor, University of Maryland, College Park, 1977; Associate Professor of English, Temple University, Philadelphia, 1978-80; Lecturer in English and Comparative Literature, Columbia University, 1985-86; Lecturer, Rutgers University, 1987-; Lecturer in English and Classics, University of Pennsylvania, 1991-97; Faculty Member, Bennington College, 2000-; Visiting Professorships; Many university and college poetry readings. Publications: Novels: Rochelle, or Virtue Rewarded, 1966; Anagrams, 1970; ABCD, 1972; The Outer Mongolian, 1973; The Killing of the King, 1974; King of Hearts, 1976; Jo Stern, 1978; Cold Comfort, 1980; Alice at 80, 1984; The Agent, 1986; The Hussar, 1987; Salazar Blinks, 1988; Lives of the Saints, 1989; Turkish Delights, 1993; The Cliff, 1994; Get Thee to a Nunnery: Two Divertimentos from Shakespeare, 1999. Henry Sutton: The Exhibitionist, 1967; The Voyeur, 1969; Vector, 1970; The Liberated, 1973; The Sacrifice: A Novel of the Occult, 1978; The Proposal, 1980. As Lynn Meyer: Paperback Thriller, 1975. As Henry Lazarus: That Golden Woman, 1976. As David Benjamin: The Idol, 1979. Non-Fiction: Understanding Social Life: An Introduction to Social Psychology (with Paul F Secord and Carl W Backman), 1976; Physicians Observed, 1987; Virgil, 1991; The Persians of Aeschylus, 1998; Three Amusements of Ausonius, 1998; Re-Verse: Essays on Poets and Poetry, 2005. Other: Editor: Adrien Stoutenburg: Land of Superior Mirages: New and Selected Poems, 1986; Short Stories Are Not Real Life: Short Fiction, 1991; Crossroads, 1994; A Gift, 1996; Epigram and Epic: Two Elizabethan Entertainments, 1997; A New Pleade: Seven American Poets, 1998. Translator: The Eclogues of Virgil, 1971; The Eclogues and the Georgics of Virgil, 1972; The Tristia of Ovid, 1985; Ovid's Poetry of Exile, 1990; Seneca: The Tragedies, 1992; The Fables of Avianus, 1993; The Metamorphoses of Ovid, 1994; The Twelve Minor Prophets, 1999; The Voyage of the Argo of Valerius Flaccus, 1999; Sonnets of Love and Death of Jean de Spande, 2001; The Elegies of Propertius, 2001; The Poetry of Manuel Bandeira, 2002; The Regrets of Joachim du Bellay, 2004; The Phoenix and Other Translations, 2004; Contributions to: Various other books as well as periodicals. Honours: Pennsylvania Council on the Arts Award, 1985; National Endowment for the Arts Fellowship, 1988; American Academy and Institute of Arts and Letters Award, 1989; Rockefeller Foundation Artist's Residence, 1989. Address: 523 South 41st Street, Philadelphia, PA 19104, USA.

SLAVOV Zdravko, b. 27 October 1955, Yambol, Bulgaria. Mathematician; Economist. m. Blaga, 2 daughters. Education: BS and MS, Mathematics, University of Sofia, 1975-80; BS and MS, Economics, University of Economics, Varna, 1984-91; PhD, Mathematics, Institute of Mathematics, Sofia, 1999-2004. Appointments: Cybernetic Research Fellow, National Bank, 1981-85; Assistant Professor, Shumen University, 1986-98; Assistant Professor, 1999-2004, Associate Professor, 2005-, Varna Free University. Publications: Author of textbooks: Statistics, 2006; Mathematics, Informatics and Education, 2007; Numerous articles in professional journals. Honours: Awards for High Science Achievements, 2005 and 2006. Memberships: Senior Member, Member of Board, Union of Bulgarian Mathematicians Professional Association. Address: 18 Ljuben Karavelov str, Varna 9002, Bulgaria. E-mail: slavovibz@yahoo.com

SLEEP Wayne, b. 17 July 1948, Plymouth, England. Dancer; Actor; Choreographer. Education: Royal Ballet School (Leverhulme Scholar). Appointments: Joined Royal Ballet, 1966; Soloist, 1970; Principal, 1973; Roles in: Giselle;

Dancers at a Gathering; The Nutcracker; Romeo and Juliet; The Grand Tour; Elite Syncopations; Swan Lake; The Four Seasons; Les Patineurs; Petroushka (title role); Cinderella; The Dream; Pineapple Poll; Mam'zelle Angot; 4th Symphony; La Fille Mal Gardee; A Month in the Country; A Good Night's Sleep; Coppelia; Also roles in operas: A Midsummer Nights Dream; Aida; Theatre Roles: Ariel in the Tempest; title role in Pinocchio; Genie in Aladdin; Soldier in The Soldiers Tale; Truffaldino in the Servant of Two Masters; Mr Mistoffelees in Cats; Choreography and lead role, The Point; co-starred in Song and Dance, 1982, 1990; Cabaret, 1986; formed own company, DASH, 1980; Dancer and Joint Choreographer, Bits and Pieces, 1989; Film: The Virgin Soldiers; The First Great Train Robbery; The Tales of Beatrix Potter; Numerous TV appearances include: Series, The Hot Summer Show, 1983; I'm a Celebrity Get Me Out of Here! 2003; Ant and Dec's Saturday Night Takeaway, 2008. Publications: Variations on Wayne Sleep, 1983; Precious Little Sleep, 1996. Honours: Show Business Personality of the Year, 1983. Address: c/o Nick Thomas Artists, Event House, Queen Margaret's Road, Scarborough, YO11 2SA, England.

SLOANE J P, b. 1942, Hollywood, California, USA. Biblical Scholar; Lecturer; Author. Education: Certificate in TV Production, Purdue University, 1981; Graduate of Oral Roberts University Institute of Charismatic Studies, Tulsa, Oklahoma, 1985; Institute of Jewish-Christian Studies, Dallas, Texas, 1992; Moody Bible Institute, Chicago, Illinois, 1998; IBEX Campus, Abu Gosh, Israel, 2001; Graduate, BA, Summa Cum Laude, 2003, Master in Nouthetic Counseling, The Masters College, Los Angeles, California; Doctorate of Theology, Trinity Theology Seminary, Newburg, Indiana, in progress; Studied: Religions of the Middle East, Jewish Thought and Culture, Physical Geography of Israel and Archeology. Appointments: In addition to lectures around the USA, Christian TV appearances include The PTL Club; Lester Sumrall Today; Richard Roberts Live; The 700 Club; LeSea Broadcasting's World Harvest and Trinity Broadcasting's Praise The Lord. Publications: Contributor to Focus on the Family's; Adventures in Odyssey; Alexander Scourby's Dramatized Version of the Bible; Word, Inc; Co-author (with daughter, Shannon), You Can Be A Virgin Again, 2006, Winner of the excellence in Media 2007, Angel Award; The Christian Counselors Guide to Restoring Virginity, 2006. Honours: Featured in the 1998-99, 1999-2000 publications of The National Dean's List, representing only the top ½ of 1% of the United States college students; The National Scholars Honor Society (Life), 2005; Appeared in the Smithsonian and Who's Who in the World, Millennium edition, also current editions of Who's Who in the World and Who's Who in America, Providence, New Jersey; Dictionary of International Biography and 2000 Outstanding Intellectuals of the 21st Century, Cambridge, England; recipient of four international Angel awards; Medal of Merit, President Ronald Reagan; Keys to the Cities of New Orleans, Louisiana; Nashville, Tennessee; Monticello, Indiana; Governor's Commendation and appointment as Honorary Lieutenant Governor for the State of Indiana; Honorary Kentucky Colonel; Honorary Colonel and Aide-de-Camp of Governor Treen and Governor Edwards and, State of Louisiana; Honorary Sheriff of Los Angeles County. Address: Ste 407, 2219 East Thousand Oaks Blvd, Thousand Oaks, CA 91362-2930, USA. Website: www.jpsloane.com

SMELLIE Jean McIldowie, b. 14 May 1927, Liverpool, England. Paediatrician. m. Ian Colin Stuart Normand, 1 son, 2 daughters. Education: Huyton College, Liverpool; St Hugh's College, Oxford; University College Hospital,

London; Degrees and Diplomas: BA Hons Physiology Oxon, 1947; BM Oxon, 1950; DCH England, 1953; MRCP London, 1954; MA Oxon, 1957; FRCP London, 1975; DM Oxon, 1981. Appointments include: House appointments, 1951-54; Paediatric Registrar, 1955-56, Paediatric First Assistant, 1956-60, University College Hospital, London; Lecturer, Infant Nutrition and Dietetics, Queen Elizabeth College, University of London, 1957-60; Lecturer, Paediatrics, Nuffield Department of Medicine, Oxford, 1960-61; Fellow in Pathology, Johns Hopkins Hospital, Baltimore, USA, 1964-65; Locum Consultant Paediatrician, 1961-63 and 1968-69, Honorary Consultant Paediatrician (part-time), 1970-93, University College Hospital, London; Part-time appointments: Senior Lecturer, Paediatrics, Department of Clinical Sciences, University College, London, 1976-93; Senior Clinical Medical Officer, Southampton and SW Hampshire District, 1977-92; Honorary Senior Clinical Lecturer, University of Southampton, 1987-93; Honorary Consultant Paediatric Nephrologist, Guy's Hospital, London, 1984-93, Honorary Consultant Paediatric Nephrologist, Hospital for Sick Children, Great Ormond Street, London, 1984-; Emeritus Consultant Paediatrician, University College Hospitals, 1993-; Scientific Adviser, International Reflux Study in Children (Europe and USA), 1974-2006; Member, Medical Advisory Committee, Sir Jules Thorn Charitable Trust, 1987-97. Publications: More than 120 original articles, approximately 56 in peer reviewed journals, on urinary tract infections, vesico-ureteric reflux, renal scarring, neonatal, general and metabolic paediatric conditions; 16-18 book chapters. Honours: Open Scholarship, St Hugh's College, Oxford, 1944-48; Honorary Member: European Society for Paediatric Urology, 1993; British Paediatric Association, 1995; British Association for Paediatric Nephrology, 1995; American Urological Association, 1998; Honorary Fellow, Royal College of Paediatrics and Child Health, 1996. Memberships: European Society of Paediatric Nephrology; Renal Association; International Paediatric Nephrology Association; Founder Member: British Association for Paediatric Nephrology; Neonatal Society. Address: 23 St Thomas Street, Winchester, Hampshire SO23 9HJ, England. E-mail: icsn@icsnormand.freeserve.co.uk

SMENDZIANKA Regina, b. 9 October 1924, Toruń, Poland. Pianist; Teacher. Education: MA, (Diploma with Highest Distinction) Academy of Music in Cracow, Poland, 1948. Appointments: Concert-pianist debut with Cracow Philharmonic Orchestra, 1947; Numerous concert tours in Poland and 33 countries of Europe, Asia and the Americas as recitalist and as soloist with orchestras, 1947-; Numerous gramophone records in Poland, Japan, Holland, Italy, Germany; Numerous radio and TV records, films in Poland and abroad; Large repertoire from 16th century to contemporary music; Teacher, Cracow Academy of Music, 1964; Assistant Professor, 1967; Rector, 1972, 1973; Head of Chair of Piano, 1972-96, Professor, 1977-96, Honorary Member of Chair of Piano, 1996-, Honorary Professor, 1997-, Doctor honoris causa, 2002, F Chopin Academy of Music, Warsaw; Numerous courses of interpretation, lectures and concert lectures in Poland, Denmark, Germany, Finland, Japan, France, Venezuela and Mexico; Member of Piano Competition Juries in Poland, Japan, Russia, Finland, Germany, Italy and Sweden. Publications: Editor, music publications and records; Articles on music in Poland, USA and Japan; Papers on scientific issues of Warsaw F Chopin Academy of Music; Introductions and articles to concert-programmes; Book, How to Play Chopin – an attempt to answer, 2000, vol 2, 2005. Honours include: Prize winner, IV International F Chopin Competition, Warsaw, 1949; Composers Association

Medal, 1971; Badge of Merit Culture Worker, 1971 Minister of Culture Prizes, 1955, 1959, 1965, 1977, 1987, 1994; Chevalier Cross, 1959, Officer Cross, 1964, Commander Cross with Star, 2004, Polonia Restituta Order; Primate Gold Medal: Ecclesiae Populoque Servitium Praestanti, 2005; Tadj Order, Shah of Iran, 1968, Banner of the Labour Order II class, 1975, I class, 1985; Aguilla de Tlatelolco Medal of the Foreign Affaires Minister of Mexico, 1978; Minister of Culture Team Prize, 1979; Excellentia International Order of Merit, IBC Cambridge, 1990; Listed in numerous Who's Who publications and biographical dictionaries. Memberships include: F Chopin Society, Warsaw, 1947-; Polish Musicians Association (SPAM), 1958-; Member Correspondent, Mexico Institute of Culture, 1978-; Iberian Culture Society, Warsaw, 1978-; President of own Foundation (Regina Smendzianka Foundation) in support of Polish music culture and young Polish pianists, 1988-; Honorary Vice-President of EPTA Society (Polish section of European Pianist Teachers Association in London), 1991; Honorary Friend of PTNA (Piano Teachers National Association of Japan), 1999-. Address: 02-529 Warszawa, Narbutta 76/10, Poland.

SMETANA Karel, b. 28 October 1930, Prague, Czech Republic. Physician; Scientist. m. Vlasta Smetanova, 24 October 1953, 1 son. Education: MUDr (MD), Charles University, Prague, Czech Republic, 1955; CSc, (PhD), 1962; DrSc (DSc), 1967. Appointments: Lecturer, Dept of Histology, Charles University, Prague, 1955-62; Scientific Officer, Head, Senior Scientific Officer, Department of Blood Cytology, Laboratory of Ultrastruct Research, Czechoslovak Academy of Science, 1962-84; Research Fellow, Department of Pharmacology, Baylor College of Medicine, Houston, Texas, USA, 1962; Visiting Associate Professor, 1963; Professor, 1970; Director, Institute of Hematology and Blood Transfusion, Prague, 1984-90; Senior Scientific Officer, 1990-, Head of Laboratory, Cytology and Electron Microscopy, 1990-2000; Head, Chair of Hematology and Transfusion Service, 1985-93; Lecturer, Hematology and Transfusion Service, Institute of Postgraduate Medical Study, Prague, 1993-; Chairman, Board of Postgraduate Scientific Studies in Cell Biology and Pathology, Charles University, Prague, 1994-. Publications: 280 articles on cell nucleus, nucleolus, malignant cells; 1 monograph with H Busch, The nucleolus; 6 Monographic Chapters in various science monographs; Chapters in 7 textbooks. Honours: State Prize; Scientific Prize, Minister of Health; State Purkynje Medal; Purkynje Medal; Honorary Medals; Wilhelm Bernhard's Medal; Honorary Membership, Czech Hematological Society, Czech and Slovak Biological Society; Czech Histochemical Society; Science Prize; Many others. Memberships: Czech Histochemical Society; Czech Hematological Society; Czech Histochemical Society; Society of Clinical Cytology. Address: Prague 4, Puchovska 2, Czech Republic 141 00.

SMEU Grigore, b. 26 October 1928, Baltisoara Village, Gorj County, Romania. Scientific Researcher in Aesthetics. m. Georgeta, 1 son. Education: Graduate, 1953, PhD in Philosophy, branch of Aesthetics, 1971, Faculty of Philosophy, University of Bucharest. Appointments: Scientific Researcher, 1950-95, Retired as Principal Scientific Researcher, Head of Aesthetics Department, 1967-89, Deputy Director, 1979-89, Institute of Philosophy of the Romanian Academy. Publications: Books (in Romanian): Senses of beauty in Romanian Aesthetics, 1969; Predictable and Unpredictable in Epics, 1972; Aesthetic Marks in the Romanian Village, 1973; The Inclined Garden (novel), 1974; Pilgrimage (poetry), 1974; The Relation Social-Autonomous on Art, 1976; Introduction in Amateurs' Art Aesthetics, 1980; The Romanian Aesthetic

Sensitivity, 1983; Aesthetics (main co-ordinator), 1983; The Interdependence of Values in Literature, 1987; The Daily Aesthetic in Today's World, 1992; Marin Preda – a Philosophy of Nature, 1994; The Ceremonies of Shadows (poetry), 1996; The Artistic Freedom in Romanian Literature, 2005; Vocation Transplant, 2007; Over 200 published studies, articles, essays and communications in proceedings and various journals. Honour: Romanian Academy Prize for 2 papers on Industrial Aesthetics (first of the kind in Romania), 1966. Memberships: Writers' Union in Romania; Organising Committee, 7th International Aesthetics Congress, Bucharest, 1972. Address: Apt 111, Stage 3, Bock 1, Section D, "Ion Mihalache" Boulevard 168, Bucharest 011214, Romania. E-mail: emil_smeu@physics.pub.ro

SMITH Andrew Benjamin, b. 6 February 1954, Dunoon, Scotland. Palaeontologist. m. Mary Patricia Cumming Simpson, 2 daughters. Education: BSc, Geology, 1st Class Honours, University of Edinburgh, 1976; PhD, Biological Sciences, University of Exeter, 1979; DSc, University of Edinburgh, 1989. Appointments: Lecturer, Department of Geology, University of Liverpool, 1981-82; Research Scientist, Department of Palaeontology, The Natural History Museum, London, 1982-. Publications: More than 200 monographs and scientific papers. Honours: Linnean Society Bicentenial Medal, 1993; Geological Society Bigsby Medal, 1995; Geological Society Lyell Medal, 2002; Elected Fellow of the Royal Society of Edinburgh, 1996; Elected Fellow of the Royal Society, 2002; Linnean Medal for Zoology, 2005. Memberships: Fellow of the Linnean Society; Fellow of the Geological Society; Fellow of the Royal Society of Edinburgh; Fellow of the Royal Society. Address: Department of Palaeontology, The Natural History Museum, Cromwell Road, London SW7 5BD, England. E-mail: a.smith@nhm.ac.uk

SMITH C Philip, b. 10 June 1928, Southport, Lancashire, England. Book Artist; Binder; Inventor; Author. m. Dorothy Mary Weighill, 3 sons. Education: Southport School of Art, 1949-51; Royal College of Art, London, (Roger Powell), 1951-54, ARCA (1st Class), 1954. Career: MDE (Meister der Einbandkunst), 1970; Fellow, Designer Bookbinders, President, 1977-79; Editor, The New Bookbinder, 1980-95; Teacher of Drawing, Modelling (sculpture), Bookbinding at Malvern School of Art, 1955-57; Assistant to Sydney Cockerell (Bookbinder), 1957-61; Own studio, 1961-; British Museum team for Florence Flood Disaster, 1966-67; Bindings in many public and private collections world-wide include: Victoria and Albert Museum, British Library, Royal Collection, Royal Library, Holland, New York Public Library, HRHRC, Texas, The Lilly Library, Indiana, USA; 14 Lecture Tours in USA since 1975 and 9 Lectures in Europe and other countries; 150 book arts exhibitions, Major Retrospective Exhibition, Portland, Oregon of works collected in USA & Canada, 2007, several painting exhibitions include: John Moores, RBA. Publications: The Lord of the Rings and Other Bookbindings of Philip Smith, 1970; New Directions in Bookbinding, 1974; The Book: Art & Object, 1982; A Book Art: Concept & Making in preparation; Numerous articles, reviews, exhibition catalogues internationally. Honours: Gold Medal, 2nd International Biennale, Sao Paulo, 1972; Presidium of Honour, Czechoslovakia, 1989; Silver Medal, Paris International Bookbinding Art, 1992; Gold Medal EEC Bookbinding Prize, 1993; Patents for Maril, 1971; Lap-Back Book- structure, UK and USA, 1994; 1st Prize, Bookbinding, Czech Republic, 2004; MBE for Services to Art, 2000; Silver Medal, International Exhibition of Books as Art, Italy, 2000, 2002; British Library National Sound Archive: National Life Story Collection, 2004; Listed in international biographical dictionaries. Memberships: Society for the Study of Normal Psychology, 1957-; Designer Bookbinders; Meister der Einbandkunst, Germany; Canadian B and B Artists Guild (CBBAG); Society of Bookbinders, UK; Centre for Book Arts, New York. Address: The Book House, Yatton Keynell, Chippenham, Wiltshire SN14 7BH, England.

SMITH Charles F Jr, b. 5 January 1933, Cleveland, Ohio, USA. Educator; Education Professor Emeritus. m. Lois Anna Thompson, 1 son, 1 daughter. Education: BS Ed, Bowling Green State University, 1960; EdM, Kent State University, 1963; CAS, Harvard University Graduate School of Education, 1965; EdD, Michigan State University, 1969. Appointments: Staff Sergeant United States Army Medical Corps, Active Duty, Austria and Italy, 1954-56, Inactive Duty, Ohio, 1956-62; Elementary School Teacher, 5th Grade, Lorain, Ohio, 1960-62; Academics Director, Peace Corps Field/ Center Training Camp, Puerto Rico, 1962-63; Peace Corps, Special Assistant Washington DC, 1963; Teaching Fellow, Harvard University School of Education, 1963-65; Assistant Director of Elementary Education, Flint, Michigan, 1965-66; Education Instructor, 1966-68, Michigan State University; Education Professor, 1968-96, Education Professor Emeritus, Boston College, 1996-; Founder and President, The Charles F Smith Jr Educational Foundation; Numerous humanitarian goodwill mission fellowships representing the United States: Jamaica, 1953, West Germany, 1954, Austria, 1954, Canada, 1957, French Cameroon, 1958, Nigeria, 1960; Participated in educational goodwill tours of Egypt, 1993, Russia, 1995, People's Republic of China, 1996, Australia, 1997, New Zealand, 1997, Fiji Islands, 1997. Honours: Danforth Associate, 1974; Visiting Scholar, University of Michigan, 1990, Atlanta University, 1993, Yale University, 1995; Phi Delta Kappa Emeritus, 1998; Recommendation, Nobel Peace Prize for Outstanding Achievement and Contributions to Humanity, 2002; Secretary-General of United Cultural Convention of ABI, 2004; Man of the Year, ABI, 2005; Listed in Who's Who publications and biographical dictionaries. Memberships: Board of Directors, National Council for the Social Studies Supervisors Association and Massachusetts Council for the Social Studies; American Association of University Professors; American Association of College Teachers; American Association of School Administrators; Association for Supervision and Curriculum Development; Department of Elementary School Principals; National Council for Social Studies; Phi Delta Kappa; Chairman, Newton, Massachusetts Area Welfare Board; Vice-Chairman, Black Citizens of Newton, Massachusetts; Founder and Chairman of the Council of Black Faculty, Staff and Administrators of Boston College. Address: 194 Parker Street, Newton Centre, MA 02459, USA. E-mail: charles.smith.1@bc.edu

SMITH Chris(topher) Robert (Rt Hon) (Lord Smith of Finsbury), b. 24 July 1951. Politician. Education: Pembroke College, Cambridge; Harvard University (Kennedy Scholar 1975-76). Appointments: Development Secretary, Shaftesbury Society Housing Association, 1977-80; Development Co-ordinator, Society for Co-operative Dwellings, 1980-83; Councillor, London Borough of Islington, 1978-83; Chief Whip, 1978-79; Chair, Housing Committee, 1981-83; Labour, MP for Islington South and Finsbury, 1983-2005; Opposition Spokesman on Treasury and Economic Affairs, 1987-92; Principal Opposition Spokesman on Environmental Protection, 1992-94; National Heritage, 1994-95; Social Security, 1995-96; Health, 1996-97; Secretary of State for Culture, Media and Sport, 1997-2001; Chairman, Millennium Commission, 1997-2001; Created Life Peer, 2005; Member, Committee on Standards in Public Life, 2001-05; Chairman,

Classic FM Consumer Panel, 2001-; Senior Adviser to The Walt Disney Company Ltd on UK film and television work; Visiting Professor in Culture and Creative Industries, University of the Arts, London, 2002-; Member of Board of Royal National Theatre; Chairman, Donmar Warehouse; Chairman of Wordsworth Trust; Member of Advisory Council of London Symphony Orchestra; Senior Associate of Judge Institute in Management Studies, Cambridge University; Honorary Fellow, Pembroke College, Cambridge, 2004-; Director of Clore Leadership Programme, 2003-; Chairman of Judges, Man Booker Prize, 2004; Chair, London Cultural Consortium, 2004-; Formerly: Chair, Labour Campaign for Criminal Justice, 1985-88; Tribune Group of MP's, 1988-89; President, Socialist Environmental and Resources Association, 1992-; Member, Executive of the Fabian Society, 1990-97 (Chair, 1996-97); Member of the Board of Shelter, 1986-92; Has held positions in several other organisations. Publication: Creative Britain, 1998. Address: House of Lords, London, SW1A 0PW, England.

SMITH David John, b. 10 October 1948, Melbourne, Australia. Physicist; Educator. m. Gwenneth Bland, 1971, divorced 1992, 2 daughters. Education: BSc, Honours, University Melbourne, 1970; PhD, University Melbourne, 1978; DSc, University Melbourne, 1988. Appointments: Postdoctoral Scholar, University Cambridge, England, 1976-78; Senior Research Associate, 1979-84; Associate Professor, 1984-87, Arizona State University; Professor, 1987-, Regents' Professor, 2000-. Publications: Author, 20 book chapters, 425 professional journal articles; Editor, 20 conference proceedings. Honours: Fellow, Institute of Physics, England, 1981; Charles Vernon Boys Prize, Institute Physics, England, 1985; Faculty Achievement Award, Burlington Resources Foundation, 1990; Director, Cambridge University High Resolution Electron Microscope, 1979-84; NSF Center for High Resolution Electron Microscopy, 1991-96; ASU Centre for High Resolution Electron Microscopy, 1996-2006; Director, Center for Solid State Science, Arizona State University, 2001-2004; Fellow, American Physical Society, 2002; President-Elect, Microscopy Society of America, 2008. Memberships: American Physical Society; Microscopy Society of America; Material Research Society; Institute of Physics, UK. Address: Department of Physics, Arizona State University, Tempe, AZ 85287-1504, USA.

SMITH David Lawrence, b. 3 December 1963, London, England. Historian. Education: Eastbourne College, 1972-81; BA 1st Class Hons, 1985, MA, 1989, PhD, 1990, Selwyn College, Cambridge. Appointments: Fellow, 1988-, Director of Studies in History, 1992-, Admissions Tutor, 1992-2003, Praelector, 1996-2006, Tutor for Graduate Students, 2004-, Selwyn College, Cambridge; Affiliated Lecturer in History, 1995-, University of Cambridge; Visiting Assistant Professor, University of Chicago, 1991; Visiting Professor, Kyungpook National University, South Korea, 2004. Publications: Books: Oliver Cromwell, 1991; Louis XIV, 1992; Constitutional Royalism and the Search for Settlement, 1994; The Theatrical City (with R Strier and D Bevington), 1995; A History of the Modern British Isles, 1603-1707: The Double Crown, 1998; The Stuart Parliaments, 1603-1689, 1999; The Early Stuart Kings (with G Seel), 2001; Crown and Parliaments (with G Seel), 2001; Cromwell and the Interregnum (editor), 2003; Contributions to Oxford Dictionary of National Biography, 2004, also contributions to academic journals. Honours: Alexander Prize, Royal Historical Society, 1991; Thirlwall Prize, University of Cambridge, 1991. Membership: Fellow,

Royal Historical Society, 1992; President, Cambridge History Forum, 1997-. Address: Selwyn College, Cambridge CB3 9DQ, England. E-mail: dls10@cam.ac.uk

SMITH Deirdre Armes, b. 29 September 1922, England. Retired Teacher; Poet. m. 1947, 2 sons, 2 daughters. Education: The College, Saffron Walden, Essex. Appointments: Retired head teacher of infant department of primary school. Publications: Cycles to the Moon, 1970; Church Bells on a Wet Sunday, 1985; The Real Thing, 1987; Winter Tennis Courts, 1987; Mother of Wales, 1990; With Untold Care, 1991; Invisibly Lady, 1996; Scorched Paper From a Bonfire, 1998; Home Of the Wind, 1998; Contributions to various publications. Honours: Inclusion in anthologies by Women's Press, 1990; Poetry read on Radio Merseyside, 1991, Poetry Festival, Maryland, USA, 1992; Finalist, Bard of the Year Competition, University of Leicester, 1993, 1994; Silver Salver and Cup, Women Writers Society poetry competition; Readings of own poetry at Manchester Central Library, 1996; Inclusion in anthology by Cussells, 1996. Membership: Society of Women Writers. Address: Talgarth, 21 Parr Fold Avenue, Worley, Manchester M28 4EJ, England.

SMITH Delia, b. 18 June 1941. Cookery Writer; Broadcaster. m. Michael Wynn Jones. Appointments: Several BBC TV Series; Cookery Writer, Evening Standard, (later Standard), 1972-85; Columnist, Radio Times; Director, Norwich City Football Club; Canary Catering. Publications: How to Cheat at Cooking, 1971; Country Fare, 1973; Recipes From Country Inns and Restaurants, 1973; Family Fare, book 1, 1973, book 2, 1974; Evening Standard Cook Book, 1974; Country Recipes From "Look East", 1975; More Country Recipes From "Look East", 1976; Frugal Food, 1976; Book of Cakes, 1977; Recipes From "Look East", 1977; Food For Our Times, 1978; Cookery Course, part 1, 1978, part 2, 1979, part 3, 1981; The Complete Cookery Course, 1982; A Feast For Lent, 1983; A Feast For Advent, 1983; One is Fun, 1985. Editor: Food Aid Cookery Book, 1986, A Journey into God, 1988, Delia Smith's Christmas, 1990, Delia Smith's Summer Collection, 1993; Delia Smith's Winter Collection, 1995; Delia's Red Nose Collection, Comic Relief, 1997; How to Cook, Book 1, 1998; How to Cook Book 2, 1999; How to Cook Book 3, 2001; Delia's Chocolate Collection, Comic Relief, 2001; Delia's Vegetarian Collection, 2002; The Delia Collection: Soup, Chicken, Chocolate, Fish, 2003; The Delia Collection: Italian, Pork, 2004; The Delia Collection – Puddings, 2006; Delia's Kitchen Garden, 2007; How to Cheat at Cooking, 2008. Honours: OBE, 1995; Honorary Degree, Nottingham University, 1996; Fellowship, Royal TV Society, 1996; Honorary Degree, UEA, 1999; Honorary Fellow, Liverpool John Moores, 2000. Address: c/o Deborah Owen Ltd, 78 Narrow Street, London E14 8BP, England.

SMITH Donald Frederick, b. 30 January 1945, Chicago, Illinois, USA. m. Helle B Smith, 2 sons. Education: BSc, Psychology, Duke University, Durham, North Carolina, 1967; MA, Physiology and Psychology, McMaster University, Hamilton, Ontario, Canada, 1968; PhD, Biopsychology, Pritzker School of Medicine, University of Chicago, Illinois, 1971; Dr.med, University of Copenhagen, Denmark, 1980. Appointments: include: Research Assistant, Division of Behavioural Sciences, Department of Psychology, University of Chicago, 1968-71; Senior Lecturer, Health Psychology and Psychobiology, University of East London, Department of Psychology, 1992-93; Consultant, Health Psychology, Committee on Social Health Services, Aarhus Municipality; Psychotherapist, Clinic for Applied Psychology, Private Practice, Arhus, 1986-; Senior Scientist, Center for

Psychiatric Research, Psychiatric Hospital of Aarhus University and PET Centre of Aarhus University Hospital, Denmark; Senior Lecturer, Postgraduate Medical Faculty, Aarhus University, Medical English Writing and Speaking; Member, Danish National University Censor Corps, Medical and Health Psychology. Publications include: Monoaminergic mechanisms in stress-induced analgesia, 1982; Stereoselective effects of tranylcypromine enantiomers on brain serotonin, 1982; Lithium and carbamazepine: Effects on locomotion of planaria, 1983; Role of 5-HT and NA in spinal dopaminergic analgesia, 1983; Handbook of Stereoisomers: Drugs in Psychopharmacology, 1984; Handbook of Stereoisomers: Therapeutic Drugs, 1989; PET neuroimaging of clomipramine challenge in humans: focus on the thalmus, Brain Research, 2001; (N-methyl-11C) Mirtazapine for positron emission tomography of antidepressant actions in humans. Memberships: Several societies and associations. Address: Center for Psychiatric Research, Psychiatric Hospital of Aarhus University, 8240 Risskov, Denmark.

SMITH Frank Neale, b. 6 July 1943, Newcastle-upon-Tyne, England. Materials and Corrosion Engineer. Education: BSc, Chemistry & Physics, Durham University, 1964; MSc, Electrochemistry, Newcastle University, 1965; PhD, Metallurgical Engineering, Queen's University, Ontario, Canada, 1973. Appointments: Senior Metallurgical Engineer, Corporate Engineering Division, DuPont Canada, 1973-79; Manager, Product Development, Granges NYBY Canada, 1979-81; Investigator/Project Leader, Research & Development, Alcan International Ltd, 1981-87; Engineering Specialist/Acting Supervisor, Materials Engineering & Corrosion Control Division, Saudi Arabian Oil Company, 1988-95; Technical Director, Nickel Development Institute, 1995-97; Consultant, 1998-; Adjunct Professor, Department of Mechanical & Materials Engineering, Queen's University, Kingston, Ontario, 1999-. Publications: Numerous articles in professional journals; 3 patents. Honours: P Eng (Professional Engineer, Ontario); Chartered Chemist (C Chem), UK; Listed in international biographical dictionaries. Memberships: National Association of Corrosion Engineers; Royal Society of Chemistry, UK; Professional Engineers, Ontario; ASM International; American Society for Testing & Materials.

SMITH Hamilton Othanel, b. 23 August 1931, New York, New York, USA. Microbiologist. m. Elizabeth Anne Bolton, 1957, 4 sons, 1 daughter. Education: Graduated, Mathematics, University of California at Berkeley, 1952; MD, Johns Hopkins University, 1956. Appointments: Junior Resident Physician, Barnes Hospital, 1956-57; Lieutenant, USNR, Senior Medical Officer, 1957-59; Resident, Henry Ford Hospital, Detroit, 1959-62; Postdoctoral Fellow, Department of Human Genetics, 1962-64, Research Associate, 1964-67, University of Michigan; Assistant Professor, 1967-69, Associate Professor, 1969-73, Professor of Microbiology, 1973-81, Professor of Molecular Biology and Genetics, 1981-, Johns Hopkins University; Sabbatical year with Institut fur Molekular-Biologie, Zurich University, 1975-76. Honour: Guggenheim Fellow, 1975-76; Joint Winner, Nobel Prize for Physiology or Medicine, 1978. Memberships: NAS; AAAS; Institute for Genomic Research, 1998. Address: Department of Molecular Biology, Johns Hopkins University School of Medicine, 720 Rutland Avenue, Baltimore, MD 21205, USA.

SMITH Ivor Ramsey, b. 8 October 1929, Birmingham, England. University Professor. m. Pamela Mary. Education: BSc, 1954, PhD, 1957, DSc, 1973, University of Bristol. Appointments: Design & Development Engineer, GEC, Witton, Birmingham, 1956-59; Lecturer, Senior Lecturer,

Reader, Birmingham University, 1959-74; Professor of Electrical Engineering, 1974-, Head of Department of Electronic & Electrical Engineering, 1980-90, Dean of Engineering, 1983-86, Pro-Vice Chancellor, 1987-91, Loughborough University. Publications: More than 350 articles in learned society journals and at international conference proceedings in his field. Memberships: Fellow, Institution of Electrical Engineers; Fellow, Royal Academy of Engineering. Address: Department of Electronic & Electrical Engineering, Loughborough University, Loughborough, Leicestershire, LE11 3TU, England. E-mail: i.r.smith@lboro.ac.uk

SMITH Jacqueline Mitchell, b. 7 July 1930, Reading, Pennsylvania, USA. Artist. m. Calvin E Smith, 2 sons, 1 daughter. Education: Pennsylvania State University, 1951-52; Art League of Alexandria, Virginia, 1970's-; Bachelor of Arts, Albright College, 1971; Master of Education, Temple University, 1976; Master of Education in Spanish, Millersville University, 1989. Career: Commissioned to paint local historical scenes, seascapes and figurative works, 1950's-; Works exhibited at William Ris Galleries, Stone Harbor, New Jersey, 1993-2006; Numerous exhibitions include most recently: Miniature Art Society of Florida, St Petersburg, Florida, 2005, 2006, 2007; Berks Art Alliance Juried Art Exhibition, Reading Museum, Pennsylvania, 2002-05; The Hilliard Society, Wells, Somerset, England, 2003-06; The Royal Miniature Society, Westminster Gallery, London, England, 2003, 2005; The MPSGS of Washington DC, 1998-2006; Cider Painters of America, Dallas, Pennsylvania, 2004, 2005, 2006; Galerie BelAge, Westhampton Beach, New York, 2005; Stone Harbor Art & Music Festival, Stone Harbor, New Jersey, 2003, 2005, 2006; Berks Art Council, Gallery 20, West Reading, Pennsylvania, 2002-05; Doylestown Art League Exhibition, Doylestown, Pennsylvania, 2001-05; Birdsboro Friends of the Arts, Birdsboro, Pennsylvania, 2004-2006; World Federation of Miniaturists, Smithsonian, Washington DC, 2004; SAMAP France International Exhibition, Chateau de Bernicourt, France, 2004. Publications: Articles about her works include: Berks In Focus, 1977; The Reading Eagle, 2005; The Butler Eagle, 1999; The Derrick, Venango Newspaper, 1999. Honours: Honourable Mention, Doylestown Art League Exhibition, 1999; Second Place in Portraiture Award, The Miniature Painters, Sculptors and Gravers Society of Washington, DC Exhibition, 2003; Best New Exhibitor Award, The Hilliard Society Exhibition, Somerset, England, 2003; 1st Place, Award of Excellence and Purchase Award, Boscov's, Berks Art Alliance Juried Exhibition, Reading, Pennsylvania, 2005; Honourable Mention Art Gallery of Fells Point, Baltimore, Maryland, 2006. Memberships: Miniature Painters, Sculptors and Gravers Society of Washington, DC; World Federation of Miniaturists; Cider Painters of America; Doylestown Art League; Berks Art Alliance; The Hilliard Society. Address: 113 East Penn Avenue, Wernersville, PA 19565-1611, USA. E-mail: jmsces@comcat.com Website: www.jacquelinesmith.net

SMITH Rt Hon Jacqui, b. 3 November 1962, Malvern, Worcestershire, England. Home Secretary; Member of Parliament for Redditch. m. Richard J Timney, 1987, 2 sons. Education: BA, Philosophy, Politics and Economics, Hertford College, Oxford; PGCE, Worcester College of Higher Education. Appointments: Teacher, Economics, Arrow Vale High School, Redditch, 1986-88; Teacher, Worcester Sixth Form College; Head of Economics, GNVQ Co-ordinator, Haybridge High School, Hagley, 1990-97; Elected Member of Parliament for Redditch, Inkberrow, Cookhill and Feckenham, 1997-; Minister of State for the Department for

Trade and Industry; Minister of State for Schools, Department of Education and Skills, 2005-06; Chief Whip, 2006; Home Secretary, 2007-.

SMITH James Cuthbert, b. 31 December 1954, London, England. m. 3 children. Chairman; Professor. Education: First Class honours degree, Natural Sciences (Zoology), Christ's College, Cambridge, England, 1976; PhD, London University, 1979. Appointments: NATO Postdoctoral Fellow, Sidney Farber Cancer Institute and Harvard Medical School, 1979-1981; ICRF Postdoctoral Fellow, 1981-1984; National Institute for Medical Research, 1984-1990; Head, Laboratory of Developmental Biology, 1991, Head Genes and Cellular Controls Group, 1996, NIMR; Member of Zoology Department, Senior Group Leader and Chairman-designate, Wellcome/CRC Institute, Cambridge, 2000; Fellow, Christ's College, Cambridge, 2001; Chairman, Wellcome Trust/Cancer Research UK Institute, Cambridge, 2001-; Humphrey Plummer Professor of Developmental Biology, University of Cambridge, 2001-. Publications: Numerous co-authored papers and articles to professional journals. Honours: Zoological Society's Scientific Medal, 1989; Otto Mangold Prize, German Society for Developmental Biology, 1991; Wellcome Visiting Professor, Basic Medical Sciences, 1991-1992; Elected Member, European Molecular Biology Organisation, 1992; Howard Hughes Medical Institute International Research Scholar, 1993-98; Elected Fellow, Royal Society, 1993; EMBO Medal, 1993; Honorary Senior Research Fellow, Department of Anatomy and Developmental Biology, University College, London, 1994; Jenkinson Lecture, Oxford University, 1997; Marshal R Urist Lecture and Award, 1997; Elected Fellow, Institute of Biology, 1997; Visiting Professor, Queen Mary and Westfield College, University of London, 1997-; Founder Fellow, Academy of Medical Sciences, 1998; Feldberg Foundation Award, 2000; Member, Academia Europaea, 2000; William Bate Hardy Prize, 2001. Memberships: Numerous committees including: HFSPO Review Committee – Molecular Approaches, 1997-2000; Council, Royal Society, 1997-1999; Council, Academy of Medical Sciences; 1998-2001. Address: Wellcome Trust/Cancer Research UK Institute of Cancer and Developmental Biology, University of Cambridge, Tennis Court Road, Cambridge CB2 1QR, England.

SMITH Kenneth George Valentine, b. 11 March 1929, Birmingham, England. Retired Entomologist. m. Alma Vera Thompson, 2 sons. Education: Birmingham Central College of Technology, 1945-47; University of Keele, 1952-54. Appointments: Field Assistant Entomologist, Ministry of Agriculture, Fisheries and Food, 1950-52; Senior Technician, Hope Department of Entomology, Oxford University, 1954-62; Principal Scientific Officer, British Museum (Natural History), 1962-89; Editor in Chief, Entomologist's Monthly Magazine, 1982-. Publications: Over 300 papers on entomology in scientific journals including books: Empididae of South Africa, 1969; Insects and Other Arthropods of Medical Importance, 1973; A Bibliography of the Entomology of the Smaller British Offshore Islands, 1983; Manual of Forensic Entomology, 1986; Darwin's Insects, 1987; An Introduction to the Immature Stages of British Flies, 1989. Memberships: Chartered Biologist; C Biol; F I Biol; FRES; FLS. Address: 31 Calais Dene, Bampton, Oxfordshire OX18 2NR, England.

SMITH Dame Maggie Natalie, b. 28 December 1934, Ilford, Essex, England. Actress. m. (1) Robert Stephens, 1967, divorced 1975, deceased 1995, 2 sons, (2) Beverley Cross, 1975, deceased 1998. Career: Theatre appearances include: With Old Vic Company, 1959-60; Rhinoceros, 1960;

The Private Ear and the Public Eye, 1962; With the National Theatre played in The Recruiting Officer, 1963; Othello, 1964; Much Ado About Nothing 1965; The Beaux' Stratagem, 1970; Private Lives, 1972; 1976, 1977, 1978, 1980 seasons, Stratford Ontario Canada; Lettice and Lovage, London, 1987, New York, 1990; The Importance of Being Earnest, 1993; Three Tall Women, 1994-95; Talking Heads, 1996, Australian tour, 2004; The Lady in the Van, 1999; Films include: The VIP's 1963; The Pumpkin Eater, 1964; Young Cassidy, 1965; Othello, 19666; The Honey Pot, 1967; Hot Millions, 1968; The Prime of Miss Jean Brodie, 1969; Travels with My Aunt, 1972; Love and Pain and the Whole Damn Thing, 1973; Murder by Death, 1975; Death on the Nile, 1978; California Suite, 1978; Quartet, 1980; Clash of the Titans, 1981; Evil Under the Sun, 1982; The Missionary, 1982; A Private Function, 1984; A Room with a View, 1986; The Lonely Passion of Judith Hearn, 1987; Hook, 1991; The Secret Garden, 1993; Richard III, 1995; First Wives Club, 1996; Washington Square, 1998; Tea with Mussolini, 1999; The Last September, 2000; Harry Potter and the Philosopher's Stone, 2001; Gosford Park, 2002; Harry Potter and the Chamber of Secrets, 2002; Harry Potter and the Prisoner of Azkaban, 2004; Ladies in Lavender, 2004; Harry Potter and the Goblet of Fire, 2005; Keeping Mum, 2005; Becoming Jane, 2007; Harry Potter and the Order of the Pheonix, 2007. Honours include: Honorary D Lit, St Andrew's and Leicester Universities, 1982, Cambridge, 1993; Evening Standard Best Actress Award, 1962, 1970, 1982, 1985, 1994; Best Actress Award, Film Critics' Guild, USA, 1969; BAFTA Award, Best Actress,1984, 1987, 1989; BAFTA Award for Lifetime Achievement, 1992; Tony Award, 1990. Address: c/o Write on Cue, 29 Whitcomb Street, London, WC2H 7EP, England.

SMITH Stanley Desmond, b. 3 March 1931, Bristol, England. Physicist. m. Gillian Anne Parish, 1 son, 1 daughter. Education: BSc, Physics Department, University of Bristol, 1949-52, PhD, Physics Department, University of Reading, 1952-56; DSc, University of Bristol, 1966. Appointments: Senior Scientific Officer, Royal Aircraft Establishment, Farnborough, 1956-58; Research Assistant, Department of Meteorology, Imperial College, 1958-59; Research Assistant, Lecturer, Reader, Physics Department, University of Reading, 1959-70; Professor of Physics, Head of Department, Dean of Science Faculty, Heriot-Watt University, Edinburgh, 1970-96; Chairman and Chief Executive Officer, Edinburgh Instruments Ltd, 1996- (previously part-time Chairman and Founder, Director, 1971-). Publications: Books: Infrared physics, 1966; Optoelectronic Devices, 1995; Some 215 scientific papers and review articles on semiconductors, IR spectroscopy, interference filters, tunable lasers, optical computing, satellite meteorology; Chairman, Scottish Optoelectronics Association, 1996-98. Honours: C V Boys Prize, Institute of Physics, 1976; EPIC Award (Education in Partnership with Industry or Commerce) 1st Prize, 1982; TOBIE Award (Technical or Business Innovation in Electronics), Department of Trade and Industry, 1986; James Scott Prize, Royal Society of Edinburgh, 1987; OBE, 1998; Hon DSc, Heriot-Watt University, 2003. Memberships: Fellow, Royal Society of Edinburgh, 1973; Fellow, Royal Society, 1976; Fellow, Institute of Physics, 1976; Advisory Council on Science and Technology, Cabinet Office, 1985-88; Defence Scientific Advisory Council, 1985-91. Address: Treetops, 29D Gillespie Road, Edinburgh EH13 0NW, Scotland. E-mail: des.smith@edinst.com

SMITH Troy Alvin, b. 4 July 1922, Sylvatus, Virginia, USA. Aerospace Research Engineer. m. Grace Marie (Peacock) Dees, 1990. Education: BCE degree, University of Virginia, 1948; MSE degree, University of Michigan,

1952; PhD degree, University of Michigan, 1970; Registered Professional Engineer, Virginia, Alabama. Appointments: US Navy Reserve, Pacific Theatre of Operations, 1942-46; Structural Engineer, Corps of Engineers, US Army, 1948-59; Chief Structural Engineer, Brown Engineering Company Inc, Huntsville, Alabama, 1959-60; Structural Research Engineer, US Army Missile Command, Redstone Arsenal, Alabama, 1960-63; Aerospace Engineer, US Army Missile Command, 1963-80; Aerospace Research Engineer, US Army Missile Command, 1980-96; Aerospace Engineer Emeritus, US Army Aviation and Missile Command, Redstone Arsenal, Alabama, 1996-2003; Aerospace Engineer Emeritus, US Army Research, Development, and Engineering Command, Aviation and Missile Research, Development, and Engineering Center, Redstone Arsenal, Alabama, 2003-. Publications: Numerical Solution for the Dynamic Response of Rotationally Symmetric Shells of Revolution under Transient Loadings, (doctoral dissertation, University of Michigan, 1970); Articles in AIAA Journal and Journal of Sound and Vibration on analysis of shells; 17 major US Army technical reports on analysis of shells and other structures. Honour: Awarded Secretary of the Army Research and Study Fellowship for Graduate Study at the University of Michigan, 1969. Memberships: Sigma Xi; New York Academy of Sciences; Association of US Army. Address: 2202 Yorkshire SE, Decatur, AL 35601-3470, USA.

SMITH Will, (Willard C Smith II), b. 25 September 1968, Philadelphia, Pennsylvania, USA. Singer; Rap Artist; Actor. m. (1) Sheree Zampino, 1 son, (2) Jada Pinkett, 1997, 1 son, 1 daughter. Career: Formed duo, DJ Jazzy Jeff and the Fresh Prince; Star of TV sitcom, The Fresh Prince of Bel Air; Film appearances, Six Degrees of Separation, 1993, Bad Boys, 1995, Independence Day, 1996, Men in Black, 1997, Enemy of the State, 1998; Wild Wild West, 1999; Legend of Bagger Vance, 2000; Men in Black: Alien Attack, 2002; Ali, 2002; Bad Boys II, 2003; Shark Tale (voice), 2004; I, Robot, 2004; Hitch, 2005; The Pursuit of Happyness, 2006; I Am Legend, 2007; Hancock, 2008. Recordings: With DJ Jazzy Jeff: Singles: Parents Just Don't Understand; I Think I Could Beat Mike Tyson; Summertime, 1991; Boom! Shake the Room, 1993; Albums: Rock the House, 1997; He's the DJ, I'm the Rapper, 1988; And In This Corner..., 1989; Homebase, 1991; Code Red, 1993; Greatest Hits, 1998; Solo: Singles: Just Cruisin', 1997; Men in Black, 1997; Gettin' Jiggy With It, 1998; Miami, 1998; Wild Wild West, 1999; Albums: Big Willie Style, 1997; Willennium, 1999; Born to Reign, 2002; Lost and Found, 2005. Honours: Grammy Awards, with DJ Jazzy Jeff, Best Rap Performance, 1988, 1991; Grammy Award, Best Rap Solo Performance, 1998; MTV Music Video Awards, Best Male Video, Best Rap Video, 1998; American Music Awards, Favorite Male Artist, Favorite Album, Favorite Male Soul/R&B Artist, 1999; Cesar d'honneur, 2005. Address: Ken Stovicz, Creative Artists Agency, 9830 Wilshire Boulevard, Beverly Hills, CA 90212, USA.

SMITH Zadie (Sadie Smith), b. 27 October 1975, London, England. Writer; Poet. M. Nick Laird, 2004. Education: King's College, Cambridge. Career: Writer-in-Residence, Institute of Contemporary Arts, London; Radcliffe Fellow, Harvard University. Publications: White Teeth (novel), 2000; Piece of Flesh (editor), 2001; The May Anthologies (editor), 2001; The Autograph Man (novel), 2002; The Burned Children of America (editor), 2003; On Beauty, 2005; Contributions to anthologies and periodicals. Honours: Rylands Prize, King's College, London; Betty Trask Prize, 2001; Guardian First Book Award, 2001; Whitbread First Novel and Book of the Year Awards, 2001; James Tait Memorial Prize for Fiction,

2001; Commonwealth Writers' Best First Book Prize, 2001. Address: A P Watt Ltd, 20 John Street, London WC1N 2DR, England. E-mail: zsmith@literati.net

SMITH OF CLIFTON (Lord), Professor Sir Trevor Arthur Smith, b. 14 June 1937, London, England. Politician. m. Julia, 2 sons, 1 daughter. Education: London School of Economics, 1955-58. Appointments: Lecturer in Politics, University of Exeter, England, 1959-60; Lecturer in Politics, University of Hull, England, 1962-67; Lecturer, Senior Lecturer, Professor of Politics, 1967-91, Deputy Principal, 1985-90, Queen Mary, London; Vice-Chancellor, University of Ulster, 1991-99; Liberal Democrat Front Bench Spokesman on Northern Ireland, 2000-. Publications: The Fixers; The Politics of Corporate Economy; Anti-Politics; Direct Action & Representative Democracy; Town & County Hall; Town Councillors; Training Managers; Numerous articles. Honours: Knighted, 1996; Life Peer, 1997; Honorary LLD, Dublin, Hull, Belfast, National University of Ireland; Honorary DHL, Alabama; Honorary DLitt, Ulster; Honorary Fellow, Queen Mary, London. Memberships: Fellow Royal Historical Society; AcSS; Vice-President, Political Studies Association. Address: House of Lords, London SW1A 0PW, England. E-mail: smitht@parliament.uk

SMITHERS Alan George, b. 20 May 1938, London, England; Professor of Education; Author; Broadcaster. 2 daughters. Education: BSc, First Class Honours, Botany, 1959, PhD, Plant Physiology, 1966 King's College London; MSc, Psychology and Sociology of Education, 1973, PhD, Education, 1974, Bradford; MEd, Manchester, 1981; Chartered Psychologist, 1988. Appointments: Lecturer in Biology, College of St Mark and St John, Chelsea, 1962-64; Lecturer in Botany, Birkbeck College, University of London, 1964-67; Research Fellow in Education, 1967-69, Senior Lecturer in Education, 1969-76, University of Bradford; Professor of Education, University of Manchester, 1977-96; Professor of Policy Research, Brunel University, 1996-98; Sydney Jones Professor of Education, University of Liverpool, 1998-2004; Professor of Education and Director, Centre for Education and Employment Research, University of Buckingham, 2004-; Royal Society Committee on Teacher Supply, 1990-94; National Curriculum Council, 1992-93; Beaumont Committee on National Vocational Qualifications, 1995-96; Special Adviser to House of Commons Education and Skills Committee, 1997-. Publications: Numerous publications include most recently: The Reality of School Staffing, 2003; England's Education, 2004; Five Years On, 2006; The Paradox of Single-Sex and Co-education, 2006; School Headship, 2007; Physics: Bucking the Trend, 2007; Blair's Education, 2007; Over 100 research papers in botany, psychology and education; Columnist, Times Educational Supplement, 1995-97; Columnist, The Independent, 1997-; Panellist, The Times ed forum, 2001-04; Regular broadcaster, speaker and contributor to the print media. Honours: Fellow, Society for Research into Higher Education. Memberships: British Psychological Society; Society for Research into Higher Education; Listed in biographical dictionaries. Address: Centre for Education and Employment Research, Department of Education, University of Buckingham, Buckingham MK18 1EG, England. E-mail: alan.smithers@buckingham.ac.uk

SMITHSON Simon, b. 28 June 1954, London, England. Architect. Education: BA (hons), 1976, Dip Arch, 1979, Corpus Christi College, Cambridge; MA, Urban Design, Harvard University, 1982. Appointments: Architect, George Candelis, Paris, France, 1976-77; Foster Associates, London, 1979-80; Teaching Assistant, Harvard University, 1981-82;

Cambridge Seven Associates, Cambridge, USA, 1982-85; Civitas Inc, Denver, Colorado, USA, 1985-88; Visiting Design Critic, University of Colorado, 1987-88; Nicholas Hare Architects, London, 1989-91; Architect, 1991-, Associate, 1996-, Richard Rogers Partnership, London; Recent lectures include: Leeds Metropolitan University; Madrid University, Spain; University of Utah, USA; University of Valencia, Spain; University of Valladolid, Spain; Director, Richard Rogers SL Spain, 2005. Memberships: London Rowing Club. Address: Richard Rogers Partnership, Thames Wharf, Rainville Road, London W6 9HA, England.

SMITHWICK Peter Alexander, b. 15 February 1937, Kilkenny, Ireland. Judge. m. Deirdre Anne Cooper, 2 daughters. Education: Castleknock College, Dublin; University College, Dublin. Appointments: Judge of the Special Criminal Court and Ex-Officio Judge of the Circuit Court; President of the District Court, 1990-2005; Judge of the District Court, 1988; Solicitor, 1958-88; Sole Member, Tribunal of Inquiry into Allegation of Collusion by Members of An Garda Siochana in the Murders of Two RUC Senior Officers, 2005-. Publications: Several articles in Irish Georgian Society Bulletin, The Old Kilkenny Review. Memberships: Hereditary Freeman of Kilkenny; Kildare Street & University Club, Dublin; Stephen's Green Hibernian Club, Dublin; Royal Irish Automobile Club, Dublin; Casino Maltese, Valletta, Malta. Address: The Old Rectory, Inistioge, County Kilkenny, Ireland. E-mail: judge@smithwicktribunal.ie

SNÆDAL Magnús, b. 17 April 1952, Akureyri, Iceland. Linguist; Philologist; Educator. 1 son. Education: BA, Icelandic Language and Literature, 1978, Cand. mag. Degree, Icelandic Linguistics, 1982, University of Iceland, Reykjavík. Appointments: Language Consultant for the Terminological Committee of the Icelandic Medical Association, 1984-96; Lecturer, General Linguistics, 1989-94, Associate Professor of General Linguistics, 1994-2005; Regular Professor 2005-, University of Iceland, Reykjavík. Publications: Book: A Concordance to Biblical Gothic, Volumes I and II, 1998, 2nd edition, 2005; 22 articles, 9 of them on the Gothic language written in English; Editor of 5 books/dictionaries in the field of Icelandic medical terminology. Address: Ránargata 35a, 101 Reykjavík, Iceland. E-mail: hreinn@hi.is

SNELL Renée, b. 2 July 1945, Paris, Texas, USA. Education. 1 son. Education: (Asian Art Study Scholarship) University of British Columbia, Vancouver, Canada, 1977; (Graduate Research Scholarship Grant), University of British Columbia, Vancouver, Canada, 1978. Appointments: Department of International Studies, Ogaki Women's College, Ogaki-shi, Gifu-ken, Japan; Treasurer and Membership Chair, Elected Office, Japan Association for Language Teaching Bilingualism National Interest Group, 1996-. Publications: (book) The Story of Chiune Sugihara (English consultant for textbook), 1992; (translations) Appreciating Emily Dickinson, 1994; Appreciating English Haiku, 1995; A Selection of Haiku by Francine Porad, 1996; Selected Haiku from the Writing of Anne Mckey, 1997; Translations of poetry with Ikuyo Yoshimura; Research articles; Contributions to journals. Honours: Educational grants, scholarships. Memberships: Japan Association for Language Teaching (JALT) 1989-; Member, English Consultant, Evergreen Haiku Society, 1992-; Elected Officer, Treasurer and Membership Chair, JALT Bilingualism National Interest Group, 1996-; Licence Teacher, Japanese 13-stringed Zither, Japan Todo Musical Association, 1996-; New York Academy of Sciences, 1996-. Address: 917 20th Street SE, Paris, TX 75460-7546, USA.

SNIEDZE Ojars Andrejs, b. 19 January 1930, Latvia. Inventor; Researcher. m. Janet Mary Pearce, 2 sons, 1 daughter. Education 1st Class Certificate in Wireless Telegraphy, 1958; Certificate, Marine Radar, 1959; Part of Dip Tech, Business Administration, 1969; Technical and Further Education Certificate in Occupational Health and Safety. Appointments: Chief Radio Officer, R&K Shipping, New York City, 1959-66; Project Engineer, E&C Engineering, Adelaide, South Australia, 1969-74; Senior Technical Officer, Telecom, Australia, 1987-93; Manager, Research and Development, SA Safety Engineering, Lonsdale, South Australia, 1993-97; Owner Manager, SA Safety Engineering, Tranmere, South Australia, 1997-; Director, Payneham Table Tennis Academy, Firle, South Australia, 2000-; Director, Maid for Mum, Australia Pty Ltd, Tranmere, South Australia, 2006-; CEO, Family Home Support Services Pty Ltd, Tranmere, 2007-. Publications: Various publications on occupational health and safety and on home security for neighbourhood watch schemes; Energy absorbing bollards for protection of outdoor diners, pedestrians and property from out of control vehicles (own invention). Honours: Meritorious Service Award, 1994; Member of Management Committee, Communications Workers Union, Adelaide, South Australia; Various Certificates in Occupational Health and Safety. Memberships: Life Member, IEEE; Ex-Member, Safety Institute of Australia and Ergonomics Society of Australia and New Zealand; Joined Latvian Air Force, Volunteer, October 1944. Address: 47 Hallett Avenue, Tranmere, South Australia 5073. E-mail: sniedze@picknowl.com.au

SNIPES Wesley, b. 31 July 1962, Orlando, USA. Actor. (1) April, 1985, divorced 1990, 1 child, (2) Nikki Park, 2003, 4 children. Education: High School for Performing Arts, New York; State University of New York. Appointments: Telephone Repair Man, New York; Broadway Appearances include Boys of Winter; Execution of Justice; Death and King's Horseman; Waterdance; Appeared in Martin Scorsese's video Bad, 1987; Films Include: Wildcats; Streets of Gold; Major League; Mo Better Blues, 1990; Jungle Fever, 1991; New Jack City; White Men Can't Jump; Demolition Man; Boiling Point; Sugar Hill; Drop Zone; To Wong Foo: Thanks for Everything, Julie Newmar, 1995; The Money Train; Waiting to Exhale; The Fan, 1996; One Night Stand; Murder at 1600; Blade, 1997; The Vampire Slayer, 1997; US Marshals, 1998; Down in the Delta, 1998; The Art of War, 2000; Blade 2, 2002; Undisputed, 2002; Unstoppable, 2004; Blade: Trinity, 2004; Nine Lives, 2004; 7 seconds, 2005; The Marksman, 2005; Chaos, 2005; Gallowwalker, 2009. Co-Founder, Struttin Street Stuff Puppet Theatre, mid 1980's. Honours: ACE Award for Best Actor for Vietnam War Stories, 1989. Address: Amen RA Films, 9460 Wilshire Boulevard, Beverly Hills, CA 90212, USA.

SNODGRASS W D (S S Gardons, Will McConnell, Kozma Prutkov), b. 5 January 1926, Wilkinsburg, Pennsylvania, USA. Poet; Writer; Dramatist; m. (1) Lila Jean Hank, 6 June 1946, divorced December 1953, 1 daughter, (2) Janice Marie Ferguson Wilson, 19 March 1954, divorced August 1966, 1 son, (3) Camille Rykowski, 13 September 1967, divorced 1978, (4) Kathleen Ann Brown, 20 June 1985. Education: Geneva College, 1943-44, 1946-47; BA, 1949, MA, 1951, MFA, 1953, University of Iowa. Appointments: Instructor in English, Cornell University, 1955-57; Instructor, University of Rochester, New York, 1957-58; Assistant Professor of English, Wayne State University, Detroit, 1959-67; Professor of English and Speech, Syracuse University, New York, 1968-77; Visiting Professor, Old Dominion University, Norfolk, Virginia, 1978-79; Distinguished Professor, 1979-80, Distinguished Professor of Creative Writing and Contemporary Poetry,

1980-94, University of Delaware, Newark; Various lectures and poetry readings. Publications: Poetry: Heart's Needle, 1959; After Experience, 1967; As S S Gardons, Remains: A Sequence of Poems, 1970, revised edition, 1985; The Fuehrer Bunker, 1977; If Birds Build With Your Hair, 1979; D D Byrde Calling Jennie Wrenne, 1984; A Colored Poem, 1986; The House the Poet Built, 1986; A Locked House, 1986; The Kinder Capers, 1986; Selected Poems, 1957-87, 1987; W D's Midnight Carnival (with DeLoss McGraw), 1988; The Death of Cock Robin (with DeLoss McGraw), 1989; Each in His Season, 1994; The Fuehrer Bunker: The Complete Cycle, 1995. Essays: In Radical Pursuit, 1975; After-Images, 1999. Play: The Fuehrer Bunker, 1978. Other: Translations of songs; Selected Translations, 1998; Criticism: De/Compositions: 101 Good Poems Gone Wrong, 2001; To Sound Like Yourself: Essays on Poetry (criticism), 2002; Make-Believes: Verses and Visions, 2004. Contributions to: Essays, reviews, poems to many periodicals. Honours: Ingram Merrill Foundation Award, 1958; Longview Foundation Literary Award, 1959; National Institute of Arts and Letters Grant, 1960; Pulitzer Prize in Poetry, 1960; Yaddo Resident Awards, 1960, 1961, 1965; Guinness Poetry Award, 1961; Ford Foundation Grant, 1963-64; National Endowment for the Arts Grant, 1966-67; Guggenheim Fellowship, 1972-73; Government of Romania Centennial Medal, 1977; Honorary Doctorate of Letters, Allegheny College, 1991; Harold Morton Landon Translation Award, Academy of American Poets, 1999; Doctor of Humane Letters, University of Delaware, 2005. Memberships: National Institute of Arts and Letters; Academy of American Arts & Sciences; Poetry Society of America; International PEN. Address: 3061 Hughes Road, Erieville, NY 13061, USA.

SNOW Jon (Jonathan George), b. 28 September 1947. Partner, Madeleine Colvin, 2 daughters. Education: St Edward's School, Oxford; University of Liverpool. Appointments: Voluntary Service Overseas, Uganda, 1967-68; Co-ordinator, 1970-73, Chair, 1986-, New Horizon Youth Centre, London; Journalist, Independent Radio News, LBC, 1973-76; Reporter, 1977-83, Washington Correspondent, 1983-86, Diplomatic Editor, 1986-89, ITN; Presenter, Channel Four News, 1989-; Visiting Professor of Broadcast Journalism, Nottingham Trent University, 1992-2001, University of Stirling, 2002-; Chair, Prison Reform Trust, 1992-96, Media Trust, 1995-, Tate Modern Council, 1999-; Trustee, Noel Buxton Trust, 1992-, National Gallery, 1999; Chancellor, Oxford Brookes University, 2001-. Publications: Atlas of Today, 1987; Sons and Mothers, 1996; Shooting History: A Personal Journey, 2004. Honours: Hon DLitt (Nottingham Trent), 1994; Monte Carlo Golden Nymph Award, 1979; TV Reporter of the Year, Royal Television Society, 1980; Valient for Truth Award, 1982; International Award, RTS, 1982; Home News Aard, RTS, 1989; RTS Presenter of the Year, 1994, 2002; BAFTA Richard Dimbleby Award, 2005. Address: Channel Four News, ITN, 200 Gray's Inn Road, London WC1X 8HB, England. E-mail: jon.snow@itn.co.uk

SNOW Peter John, b. 20 April 1938, Dublin, Ireland. Television Presenter; Reporter; Author. m. (1) Alison Carter, 1964, divorced 1975, 1 son, 1 daughter, (2) Ann Macmillan, 1976, 1 son, 2 daughters. Education: Wellington College and Balliol College, Oxford. Appointments: 2nd Lieutenant, Somerset Light Infantry, 1956-58; Newscaster, Reporter, ITN, 1962-79; Diplomatic and Defence Correspondent, 1966-97; Presenter, BBC Newsnight, 1979-97; Tomorrows World, 1997-2001; BBC Election Programmes, 1983-; BBC Radio 4 Mastermind, 1998-2000; Radio 4 Random Edition, 1998-; Radio 4 Masterteam, 2001; Battlefield Britain, BBC2 (jointly with son, Dan Snow), 2004. Publications: Leila's

Hijack War (co-author), 1970; Hussein: a biography, 1972. Honours: Judges Award, Royal TV Society, 1998. Address: c/o BBC TV Centre, Wood Lane, London W12 7RJ, England. E-mail: peter.snow@bbc.co.uk

SNOWDON Antony Charles Robert Armstrong-Jones (1st Earl of), b. 7 March 1930, London, England. Photographer. m. (1) HRH The Princess Margaret, 1960, divorced 1978, deceased 2002, 1 son, 1 daughter, (2) Lucy Lindsay-Hogg, 1979, 1 daughter, divorced, 2000. 1 son with Melanie Cable-Alexander. Education: Jesus College, Cambridge. Appointments: Consultant, Council of Industrial Design, 1962-89; In charge of design of Investiture of HRH the Prince of Wales, Caernarfon, 1969; Editorial Adviser, Design Magazine, 1961-67; Artistic Adviser to The Sunday Times, Sunday Times Publications Ltd, 1962-90; Photographer, Telegraph Magazine, 1990-96; Constable of Caernarfon Castle, 1963-; President, Civic Trust for Wales, Contemporary Art Society for Wales, Welsh Theatre Company; Vice President, University of Bristol Photographic Society; Senior Fellow, Royal College of Art, 1986; Provost, 1995-; Fellow, Institute of British Photographers, British Institute of Professional Photographers; Chartered Society of Design; Royal Photographic Society; Royal Society of Arts; Manchester College of Art and Design; Member, Faculty Royal Designers for Industry; South Wales Institute of Architects; Chair Snowdon Report on Integrating the Disabled, 1972; Member, Council, National Fund for Research for the Crippled Child; Founder, Snowdon Award Scheme for Disabled Students, 1980; President, International Year of Disabled People, 1981; Patron, British Disabled Water Ski Association; Member, Prince of Wales Advisory Group on Disability, 1983; Metropolitan Union of YMCAs; British Water Skiing Federation; Welsh National Rowing Club; Circle of Guide Dog Owners. Publications: London, 1958; Malta, 1958; Private View, 1965; Assignments, 1972; A View of Venice, 1972; Photographs by Snowdon: A Retrospective, 2000; Many others. Honours include: Honorary Member, North Wales Society of Architects; Dr hc, Bradford, 1989; LLD, Bath, 1989; Dr hc, Portsmouth, 1993; Art Directors Club of New York Certificate of Merit, 1969; Society of Publication Designers Certificate of Merit, 1970; The Wilson Hicks Certificate of Merit for Photocommunication, 1971; Society of Publication Designers Award of Excellence, 1973; Designers and Art Directors Award, 1978; Royal Photographic Society Hood Award, 1979. Address: 22 Launceston Place, London, W8 5RL, England.

SNOWMAN Daniel, b. 4 November 1938, United Kingdom. Writer; Lecturer; Broadcaster. m. Janet Linda Levison, 1 son, 1 daughter. Education: Double First Class Honours in History, University of Cambridge, 1958-61; Fulbright Scholarship, MA in American Government, Cornell University, USA, 1961-63. Appointments include: Lecturer in American Studies and Politics, University of Sussex, 1963-67; Visiting Professor of American History, California State University, 1972-73; Chief Producer, Features, BBC Radio, 1982-95 (joined BBC, 1967); Senior Research Fellow, Institute of Historical Research, London, 2004-2006; Principal BBC radio productions as presenter and/or producer include: A World in Common; The Vatican; Reith Lectures; Northern Lights; Victoria's Children; Spitalfields; Vaughan Williams London; TV: Plácido Domingo's Tales from the Opera, BBC Television and World Wide International Films, 1992-94. Publications: Books: America Since 1920, 1968; Eleanor Roosevelt, 1970; Britain and America: An Interpretation of their Culture, 1977; If I Had Been...Ten Historical Fantasies (editor), 1979; The Amadeus Quartet: The Men and The Music, 1981; The World of Plácido Domingo, 1985; Beyond the Tunnel of History: the 1989 BBC Reith Lectures (with Jacques Darras), 1990; Pole Positions: The Polar Regions and the Future of the Planet, 1993; Plácido Domingo's Tales From the Opera, 1994; Fins de Siècle (with Asa Briggs), 1996; Pastmasters: The Best of "History Today" (editor), 2001; The Hitler Emigres: The Cultural Impact on Britain of Refugees from Nazism, 2002; Historians, 2007. Book chapters articles and reviews. Address: 46 Molyneux Street, London W1H 5JD, England. E-mail: daniel@danielsnowman.org.uk Website: www.danielsnowman.org.uk

SODERBERGH Steven, b. 14 January 1963, Atlanta, USA. Film Director. m. (1) Elizabeth Jeanne Brantley, 1989, divorced 1994, 1 child, (2) Jules Asner, 2003. Education: high school and animation course, Louisiana State University. Appointments: Aged 15 made short film Janitor; Briefly editor, Games People Play (TV show); Made short film Rapid Eye Movement while working as coin-changer in video arcade; Produced video for Showtime for their album 90125; Author, Screenplay for Sex, Lies and Videotape, 1989; Kafka, The Last Ship, 1991; King of the Hill, 1993; The Underneath, Schizopolis, 1996; Out of Sight, 1998; Executive Producer: Suture, 1994; The Daytrippers, 1996; Writer Mimic, 1997; Nightwatch, 1998; The Limey, Erin Brockovich, 1999; Traffic, 2000; Ocean's Eleven, 2001; Solaris, 2002; Ocean's Twelve, Able Edwards, Criminal, Keane, 2004; The Big Empty, The Jacket, Good Night and Good Luck, Syriana, Rumor Has It, 2005; A Scanner Darkly, The Half Life of Timofey Berezin, 2006; Wind Chill, Michael Clayton, I'm Not There, 2007; Guerrilla, The Argentine, 2008. Honours: Academy Award for Best Director, Traffic, 2000. Address: P O Box 2000, Orange, VA 22960, USA.

SODJA Lovro, b. 24 April 1938, Ljubljana. Professor of Flute. m. Ivana, 1 son, 1 daughter. Education: Graduate, Ljubljana Academy of Music; Ballet High School, Ljubljana; Pedagogue Counsellor, Ministry of Education and Sport, Republic of Slovenia, 2002. Appointments: Music Teacher (Flute), 1963-; Manager, Culture Agency LANE, 1992-; Secretary, Slovenian Music Competitions for Youth, 1992-2005; Head, Slovenian Music School, Klagenfurt, Austria, 1986-1997; Professional Singer, Ljubljana Opera Choir, 1963-75; Professional Ballet Dancer, Ljubljana Ballet Theatre, 10 years. Publications: Numerous articles in professional journals; Author, 2 books: My Twenty Musical Years in Carinthia, 2002; Young Slovenian Musicians in Europe, 2006. Honours: Community of Education Prize, Ljubljana, 1973; Award, Ministry of Education, Science and Sport, and Ministry of Culture of Slovenia, 2001; Honorary Golden Badge, Mountaineering Club, 2002; Austrian Cross for Science and Culture, 2005. Memberships: Member of Board, European Union of Music Competitions for Youth, Munich; Managing Board, Society of Slovenian-Austrian Friendship, Ljubljana; Member, Association of Ballet Artists of Slovenia. Address: Cesta dolomitskega odreda 35, 1358 Log pri Brezovici, Slovenija. E-mail: lovro.sodja@guest.arnes.si

SOFIOS Dimitrios, b. 16 January 1947, Potamos, Kithira, Greece. Managing Director. m. Eleni Sofiou, 1 daughter. Education: Academy Business of Tourism, Sydney, Australia, 1969-71; Diploma of Tourism, Operation Management, 1 year; Diploma, Hospitality Management, 1 year; Advance Diploma of Tourism Management, 2 years. Appointments: General Agent, Olympic Airlines for the Greek Islands; Director, CarPlan; Director, VillaPlan; Managing Director, Interdynamic SA DMC/PCO; Managing Director, Unique Luxury Prestigious Cars; Managing Director, The Finest Hotels of the World; Chairman & Founder, Pacific Asia Travel

Association, PATA Greece & Cyprus Chapter; Member, Pacific Asia Travel Association, PATA Board of Directors. Publications: The Finest Hotels of the World – The Best of the Crete; The Finest Hotels of the World – The Best of Greek Islands; The Finest Hotels of the World – The Beach of Greek Mainland; Elounda the Elegant Resorts; The Preferred Greek Conference Centres; The Finest Hotels of the World – The Best of Greece. Honours include: TUV Certification, TUV Austria, 2003; Q Label Certificate for Quality System in Tourism, Swiss Q Quality Label, 2004; Best Greek Brochure of the Year, HATTA, 2004, 2006; CIMPA CIMP Certificate, 2005; International Award for Excellence in Business Management, 2007, Quality and Excellent Service Award, 2008; Touristic Quality Award, 2008, Excellence in Business Management Award, 2008, Actualidad; International Gold Star Award for Quality, World Quality Commitment, 2007; Best Tourism Project 2008 Award, MENA Travel Awards, 2008; ISLQ International Star for Leadership in Quality Award, Platinum Category, World Quality Commitment, 2008. Memberships: GNTO; HATTA; HAPCO; SETE; ACTA; ISES; ICCA; UIA; SITE; ASAE; ITMA; MPI; PATA; ASTA; ETOA; MEA; HCEA; ACE; ACOM; SKAL; UFTAA; ADME; CIMPA; EFAPCO; IFWTO. Address: Idomeneos Street (Interdynamic Building), 71500 Prassa, Crete, Greece.

SOHN Dong-Seok, b. 6 August 1964, Daegu, Republic of Korea. Professor. m. Young-Hee Hwang, 2 sons. Education: DDS, School of Dentistry, Kyungbook National University, 1989; PhD, School of Dentistry, Dankook University, 2001. Appointments: Associate Professor, School of Medicine, Catholic University of Daegu; Chairman, Board of Directors, International Congress of Oral Implantologists. Publications: Immediate Loading with Temporary Implants, 2002; Book, Innovative Implant Dentistry, 2003. Honours: Diplomate, International Congress of Oral Implantologists. Address: Department of Dentistry & Oral and Maxillofacial Surgery, Catholic University Hospital, 3056-6, Daemyung 4-Dong, Nam-Gu, Daegu, Republic of Korea.

SOHN Keun Yong, b. 9 July 1964, Republic of Korea. Professor. m. Kwang-Ok Mi, 1 son, 1 daughter. Education: BS, Korea University, 1985; MSc, Korean Advanced Institute of Science and Technology, 1987; PhD, University of Florida, USA, 1997. Appointments: Researcher, Korea Institute of Science and Technology, 1987-92; Research Assistant, University of Florida, 1993-97; Research Fellow, University of Michigan, USA, 1997-2000; Research Graduate, Ford Motor Co, USA, 1997-2000; Principal Researcher, Korea Institute of Machinery & Materials, 2000-06; Assistant Professor, Inje University School of Nano Engineering, 2006-. Publications: Co-author, The Basic and Application of Magnesium Alloys, 2004; Contributed over 40 articles to professional journals. Honours: Korean Government Scholarship, 1985-87; Excellent Research Scientist, KIST, 1991; Jang Young Sil Prize, 2002. Memberships: Korea Institute of Metals & Materials; Korean Magnetic Society; Korean Foundrymen's Society. Address: Seongju-Dong, Union Village 113-403, ChangWon, GyeongNam 641-939, Republic of Korea. E-mail: ksohn@inje.ac.kr

SOJLI Elvira, b. 2 August 1981, Tirana, Albania. Assistant Professor of Finance. Education: BSc, Accounting and Finance, London School of Economics and Political Science, 2002; MSc (with distinction), Economics and Finance, 2003; PhD, Finance, 2008, Warwick Business School. Appointments: Internships at Norges Bank and Bank of Canada; Research Economist, Research Department, Bank of Albania, 2002-03; Warwick Postgraduate Research Fellow, University of

Warwick, 2005-08; Assistant Professor of Finance, Rotterdam School of Management, Erasmus University, 2008-14. Publications: Financial crises propagation to Albania: a comparison of the Russian and Turkish crises, 2005; Order flow analysis of exchange rates, 2006; Contagion in emerging markets: the Russian debt crisis, 2007; The feeble link between exchange rates and fundamentals: Can we blame the discount factor?, forthcoming. Honours: Solon Foundation scholarship, Switzerland; Warwick Business School scholarship; Overseas research scheme award, ORSAS, UK; AP Scholar with Honour. Memberships: American Finance Association; American Economic Association; European Finance Association; European Economic Association. Address: Department of Financial Management, Rotterdam School of Management, Erasmus University, Postbus 1738, 3000 DR Rotterdam, Netherlands. E-mail: elvira.sojli04@phd.wbs.ac.uk

SOLDOVIERI Francesco, b. 27 March 1966, Cosenza, Italy. Research Scientist. m. Teresa Chiapparrone, 2 sons. Education: Laurea, Ingegneria Elettronica, University of Salerno, 1992; PhD, Federico II University, Naples, 1996. Appointments: Post PhD Research Fellowship, University of Naples, 1996-98; Research Fellowship, Second University of Naples, 1998-2001; Research Scientist, 2001-06, Senior Research Scientist, 2006-07, Institute for Electromagnetic Sensing of Environment, CNR. Publications: 60 international papers in professional journals; More than 120 conference proceedings papers. Honours: H A Wheeler Honorable Mention, IEEE Antennas and Propagation Society. E-mail: soldovieri.f@irea.cnr.it Website: www.irea.cnr.it

SOLIMANDO Dominic A, Jr, b. 4 April, Brooklyn, New York, USA. Pharmacist; Medical Writer; Consultant. Education: BSc Pharmacy, Philadelphia College of Pharmacy and Science, 1976; AMEDD Officer Basic Course, US Army Academy of Health Sciences, Fort Sam, Houston, Texas, 1976; MA, Management and Supervision: Healthcare Administration, Central Michigan University, Mt Pleasant, 1980; AMEDD Officer, Advanced Course, US Army Academy of Health Sciences, Fort Sam, Houston, Texas, 1982; US Army Command and General Staff College, Fort Leavenworth, Kansas, 1985; PhD Candidate, Clinical Pharmacy, Purdue University, West Lafayette, Indiana, 1986-89. Appointments: Staff Pharmacist, Walter Reed Army Medical Centre, Washington, DC, 1977; Chief, Pharmacy Service, Andrew Rader Army Health Clinic, Fort Myer, Virginia, 1977-79; Clinical Pharmacist, Haematology-Oncology Service, Walter Reed Army Medical Centre, 1979-82; Clinical Preceptor, College of Pharmacy, Medical College of Virginia, Virginia Commonwealth University, 1982; Chief, Oncology Pharmacy Section, Tripler Army Medical Centre, Honolulu, Hawaii, 1983-86; Clinical Preceptor, 1983, Adjunct Professor, 1984-86, 1989-90, College of Pharmacy, University of the Pacific; Chief, Haematology-Oncology Pharmacy, Letterman Army Medical Centre, San Francisco, 1989-90, 1991-92; Clinical Preceptor, Oncology, ASHP Residency in Pharmacy Practice, Letterman Army Medical Centre, 1989-90; Chief, Pharmacy Service, Operation Desert Shield/Desert Storm, Saudi Arabia/Iraq, 1990-91; Chief, Haematology-Oncology Pharmacy Section, Walter Reed Army Medical Centre, 1992-96; Clinical Assistant Professor, School of Pharmacy, University of Maryland, 1992-96; Clinical Preceptor, School of Pharmacy and Pharmacal Sciences, Howard University, 1992-96; Clinical Preceptor, Oncology, ASHP Residency in Pharmacy Practice, Walter Reed Army Medical Centre, 1992-96; Programme Director, ASHP Speciality Residency in Oncology Pharmacy, Walter Reed Army Medical Centre, 1992-96, 2001-02; Clinical Associate Professor, School of

Pharmacy, University of Arkansas, 1995, 2001; Oncology Pharmacist, Department of Pharmacy, Thomas Jefferson University Hospital, Philadelphia, 1996-98; Clinical Preceptor (Oncology), ASHP Residency in Pharmacy Practice, Thomas Jefferson University Hospital, Philadelphia, 1996-98; Clinical Preceptor, College of Pharmacy, Temple University, 1998; Clinical Associate Professor, 1998, Clinical Preceptor, 1996-98, Philadelphia College of Pharmacy, University of the Sciences in Philadelphia; Oncology Pharmacy Manager, Lombardi Cancer Centre, Georgetown University Medical Centre, Washington, 1998-99; Director of Oncology Drug Information/Consultant, cancereducation.com, New York, 1999-2000; Oncology Pharmacy Consultant/Medical Writer, Arlington, Virginia, 1999-; Oncology Pharmacist, Department of Pharmacy, Walter Reed Army Medical Centre, 2000-; President, Oncology Pharmacy Services Inc, Arlington,Virginia, 2000-; Assistant Professor, School of Pharmacy, Howard University, Washington, DC, 2003-. Publications: Numerous articles in scientific journals; Drug Information Handbook for Oncology, 1999, 2000, 2003. Honours include: 'A' Proficiency Designator, Office of the Surgeon General, Department of the Army, 1994; WMSHP-Bayer Recognition Award, Washington Metropolitan Area Society of Health System Pharmacists, 2000; Board Certified Oncology Pharmacist, 2000-; Distinguished Achievement Award in Hospital and Institutional Practice, Academy of Pharmacy Practice and Management, American Pharmaceutical Association, 2001. Memberships: American College of Clinical Pharmacy; American Institute of the History of Pharmacy; American Medical Writers Association; American Pharmacists Association; American Society of Health-System Pharmacists; Federation Internationale de Pharmaceutique; International Society of Oncology Pharmacy Practitioners. Address: Oncology Pharmacy Services Inc., 4201 Wilson Boulevard # 110-545, Arlington, VA 22203, USA. E-mail: oncrxsvc@aol.com

SOMEKAWA Mina, Concert Pianist; Piano Teacher. Education: Bachelor of Arts, English, Sophia University, 1981; Postgraduate Musical Studies, University of Missouri-Columbia, 1990-92; Bachelor of Music in Piano Performance, 1993; Master of Music in Piano Performance, 1995, Doctor of Musical Arts in Piano Performance, in progress, University of Illinois at Urbana-Champaign. Appointments: Teaching: Teaching Assistant, University of Illinois at Urbana-Champaign, 1994-96; Faculty, Blue Lake Fine Arts Camp, Twin Lake, Michigan, 1998; Visiting Assistant Professor of Music, Millsaps College, Jackson, Mississippi, 2002; Private piano instructions, various cities in Illinois, 1996-2001, various cities in Mississippi, 2002-; Adjudication: National Federation of Music Clubs, 1998; Mississippi Symphony Orchestra Young Artists' Competition, 2002; Mississippi Music Teachers Association, 2004; Performance Activities: Associate Keyboardist: Civic Orchestra of Chicago, 1995-96; Principal Keyboardist: Sinfonia da Camera, Urbana, Illinois, 1995-2001; Champaign-Urbana Symphony, Illinois, 1996-2004; Illinois Symphony Orchestra, Springfield, Illinois, 1997-2006; Fresno Philharmonic, California, 1998-; Major Solo Piano Recitals: Artist Presentation Society Recital Series, St Louis, 1993; Dame Myra Hess Memorial Concert Series, Chicago, 1998 (live radio broadcast); Concerto Solo on Piano and Harpsichord, University of Illinois Summer Festival Orchestra, 1994; Illinois Chamber Orchestra, 2000, 2003; Fresno Philharmonic, 2004. Publications: Ballet Class I played by Mina Somekawa (cassette tape), 1989; The Snowman, Easy Piano Picture Book Series, 1989; The Snowman, piano reduction score, 1987, translated Japanese editions from Zen-on, reprinted annually. Honours: Numerous prizes in piano competitions, 1991-95; Honour for Highest Academic Performance, Sophia University, 1978; Phi Beta Kappa, 1991; Sigma Alpha Iota/Ruth Melcher Allen Memorial Award, University of Missouri, 1991; Golden Key National Honor Society, 1991; University Fellowship, Music, University of Illinois, 1993-94; Recognition as an Excellent Teaching Assistant, University of Illinois, 1995, 1996, Pi Kappa Lambda, 1996; Listed in Who's Who publications. Memberships: College Music Society; American Federation of Musicians – Local #12, Sacramento, California. Address: 1315 N Jefferson St #214, Jackson, MS 39202, USA. E-mail: msomekaw@msn.com

SOMMARIVA Corrado, b. 5 April 1962, Genoa, Italy. Consultant. 1 son, 1 daughter. Education: PhD, Chemical Engineering, University of Genoa; Diploma in Management, University of Leicester; Ashridge Leadership Course. Appointments: President, European Desalination Society; Director of Water Projects, Ansaldo Energia; Research Director, Middle East Research Center; Head of Desalination Department, Mott MacDonald Ltd; Vice President, International Desalination Association; President, European Desalination Society. Publications: Numerous articles and papers published in professional scientific journals; Book, Desalination Management and Economics. Honours: High Quality Treatise Award, High Quality Essay Award, IDA, 1995; Best Paper Award, 2001, 2002, 2003, Technology Innovation Award, 2003, Mott MacDonald; Milne Award for Innovation, 2005. Memberships: Board of Directors, IDA; Board of Directors, European Desalination Association; Powergen Advisory Board; Waste Water Europe; President, European Desalination Association; Chairman, WHO Committee for Safe Water Supply. Address: Mott MacDonald Ltd, PGB, Victory House, Trafalgar Place, Brighton, East Sussex BN1 4FY, England.

SOMMER Elke, b. 5 November 1940, Berlin, Germany. Actress. m. (1) Joe Hyams (twice), (2) Wolf Walther, 1993. Career: Films include: L'Amico del Giaguaro, 1958; The Prize; The Victors; Shot in the Dark; The Oscar; Himmelsheim; Neat and Tidy; Severed Ties; Own TV show, Painting with Elke, 1985. Honours: Golden Globe Award, 1965; Jefferson Award; Merit of Achievement Award, 1990. Address: 91080 Marloffstein, Germany.

SON Byung Ho, b. 5 April 1967, Pohang, Korea. Medical Doctor. m. Hyun-Hye Choi, 1 son, 1 daughter. Education: MD, College of Medicine, Kyungpook National University, Korea, 1990; MS, Graduate School, Kyemyung University, Korea, 1997; PhD, Graduate School, University of Ulsan, Korea, 2002. Appointments: Diplomate, 1990, Korean Board of Surgery, 1998, Ministry of Health and Welfare, Seoul; Internship, Kyungpook National University Hospital, Taegu, 1993-94; Resident, Surgery, Kyenyung University, Dongson Medical Centre, Taegu, 1994-98; Fellowship, Breast Surgery, 1998-2000, Clinical Director of Breast Division, 2002-03, Assistant Professor, 2003-, Department of Surgery, College of Medicine, University of Ulsan, Asan Medical Centre, Seoul; Chief of Breast Clinic, Department of Surgery, Sung Ae Hospital, Seoul, 2000-02. Publications: Treatment Guide for Breast Cancer Patients, 2005; The Breast, 2005. Honours: Roche's Academic Award, Korean Breast Cancer Society, 2003; Novatis Endocrine Therapy Award, Korean Breast Cancer Society, 2005; Listed in Who's Who publications. Memberships: Korean Surgical Society; Korean Breast Cancer Society; Korean Cancer Society; Korean Association of Endocrine Surgery; American Association of Cancer Research, 2006. Address: Department of Surgery, College of

Medicine, University of Ulsan, Asan Medical Centre, 388-1 Pungnap-dong, Songpa-gu, Seoul 138-736, Korea. E-mail: brdrson@korea.com

SON Moorak, b. 8 June 1968, Youngjoo, South Korea. Government Official. m. Wonkyung Song. Education: BS, Civil Engineering, Hanyang University, Seoul, South Korea, 1993; MS, Hanyang University, 1994-96, University of Illinois, Urbana, USA, 1996-98; PhD, Civil (Geotechnical) Engineering, University of Illinois, 2003. Appointments: Daewoo Engineering Co, Seongnam, Korea, 1993-94; Graduate Research Assistant, Hanyang University, 1994-96; Graduate Research Assistant, University of Illinois, 1997-2003; Senior Researcher, Korean Institute of Construction Technology, Ilsan, 2003-04; Government Official, Korean Intellectuals Property Office, Daejeon, 2004-. Publications: 30 articles and papers; 2 book chapters; 5 research reports; Estimation of building damage due to excavation-induced ground movements, 2005; Ground-liner interaction in rock tunneling, 2006. Honours: Outstanding Young Engineer, Hanyang University, 2007; Listed in international biographical dictionaries. Memberships: Korea Society of Civil Engineers; Korean Geotechnical Society; Korean Tunneling Association. Address: Daewon@101-101, 502-7 Mukzdong, Yangchon, Seoul, 158-807, Korea. E-mail: moorakson@empal.com

SONDHEIM Stephen Joshua, b. 22 March 1930, New York, USA. Composer; Lyricist. Education: BA, Williams College, 1950. Compositions: Incidental Music: The Girls of Summer, 1956; Invitation to a March, 1961; Twigs, 1971; Lyrics: West Side Story, 1957; Gypsy, 1959; Do I Hear A Waltz?, 1965; Candide, (additional lyrics) 1973; Music and Lyrics: A Funny Thing Happened on the Way to the Forum, 1962; Anyone Can Whistle, 1964; Evening Primrose, 1966; Company, 1970; Follies, 1971; A Little Night Music, 1973; The Frogs, 1974; Pacific Overtures, 1976; Sweeney Todd, 1979; Merrily We Roll Along, 1981, 1997; Sunday in the Park With George, 1984; Into the Woods, 1987; Assassins, 1991; Passion, 1994; Bounce, 2003; The Frogs, 2004. Anthologies: Side by Side by Sondheim, 1976; Marry Me A Little, 1980; You're Gonna Love Tomorrow, 1983; Putting It Together, 1992; Company …In Jazz, 1995; A Little Night Music, 1996. Film: Stavisky, 1974; Reds, 1981; Dick Tracy, 1990. Honours: Antoinette Perry Award, 1971, 1972, 1973, 1979; Drama Critics' Award, 1971, 1972, 1973, 1976, 1979; Evening Standard Drama Award, 1996; Grammy Award, 1984, 1986. Memberships: President, Dramatists Guild, 1973-81; American Academy and Institute of Arts and Letters. Address: c/o Flora Roberts, 157 West 57th Street, New York, NY 10019, USA.

SONG Gook-Sup, b. 14 November 1957, Korea. Professor. m. Young-Whee Kang, 1 son, 1 daughter. Education: Bachelor's degree, Department of Architecture, 1979, Master's degree, 1981, Doctor's degree, 1991, Graduate School, Chung Ang University. Appointments: Professor, Bucheon College, 1981-; Chief Editor, The Korean Society of Living Environmental System, 2000; Vice Director, Building Service Division, 2002-03, Vice Director, Environmental Division, 2006-, Architectural Institute of Korea. Publications: Buttock responses to contact with finishing materials over the ONDOL floor heating system, 2005; Changes in the scrotal temperature of subjects in a sedentary posture over a heated floor, 2006. Honours: Scholarship Award, Korean Society of Living Environmental System, 2004. Memberships: Korean Society of Living Environmental System; Architectural Institute of Korea. Address: 424 New Seoul Apt, Songne-Dong, Sosa-Gu, Bucheon-Si, GeongKiDo, 422-730, Korea. E-mail: songsup@bc.ac.kr

SONG Ho-Young, b. 26 January, Seoul, Korea. Engineer. m. Jung-Ae Seo, 1 son, 1 daughter. Education: Doctor, University of Inha, 2004. Appointments: Senior Engineer, R&D of LED, Samsung Electro-Mechanics Co Ltd, 2004-07. Publications: Characteristics of Ir etching using AtKb Indactively coupled plasma; Effect of time-rating axial magnetic shield on phototesist ashing in an ICP; ICP etching of Pt thin film for fabrication of SAW device. Memberships: American Vacuum Society; Fellowship, IMID. Address: Samsung Electro-Mechanics Co Ltd, 314 Maetan 3-Dong, Yeontong-Gu, SuWon, Gyunggi-Do, 443-743, Korea. E-mail: hoyo.song@samsung.com

SONG Il-Keun, b. 3 March 1961, Daejeon, Korea. Principal Researcher. m. Seon Hee Bae, 1 son, 1 daughter. Education: BS, 1984, MS, 1986, PhD, 1997, Soongsil University, Seoul. Appointments: Group Leader, KEPRI, KEPCO, 1985. Publications: Over 67 articles in professional journals; 15 patents for multi stress aging test facility for insulators. Honours: Awards from Minister of Commerce, Industry and Energy, 1999, 2002; Prime Minister's Citation, 2005; Listed in international biographical dictionaries. Memberships: Korean Institute of Electrical Engineers; CIRED, Korea; IEEE. Address: 103-16, Munji-Dong, Daejeon 305-380, Korea. E-mail: iksong@kepri.re.kr

SONG Jin Woo, b. 7 December 1972, Seoul, Korea. Engineer; CTO. m. Hyeyoung Lee, 1 daughter. Education: BS, 1995, MS, 1997, PhD, 2002, Post doctorate Studies, 2002-03, Department of Control and Instrumentation Engineering, Seoul National University, Seoul. Appointments: Postdoctoral Researcher, Seoul National University, 2002-03; Manager, 2003-04, CTO, 2005-, Microinfinity Co Ltd, Seoul; Workgroup Leader, Next-generation PC Standardization Forum, Seoul, 2005-; Organising Committee, IT-SOC 2005 Exhibition, Association of Next Generation PC Industry, Seoul, 2004, 2005; Director, Next-generation PC Forum, Seoul, 2006-; Committee, Telecommunication Technology Association Standardization Committee, Seoul, 2006-; Committee, National Defense Technology Forum, Defense Agency for Technology and Quality, Seoul, 2006-; Editor, ICROS Journal, Seoul, 2007-. Publications: Numerous articles in professional journals; 3 patents. Honours: Best Student Paper Award, NAECON2000, USA, 2000; IEEE, National Aerospace and Electronics Conference, 2000; IT R&D Engineer of the Year – H/W Part, Ministry of Information and Communication, Republic of Korea, 2005; Listed in international biographical dictionaries. Memberships: Korea Institute of Electrical Engineers; Institute of Control, Robotics and Systems; Korea Society for Aeronautical & Space Sciences; Institute of Electrical and Electronics Engineers; Association for Unmanned Vehicle Systems International; Korea Institute of Military Science and Technology. Address: Microinfinity Co Ltd, 8th Hanshin IT Tower II, 60-18 Gasan-dong, Geumcheon-gu, Seoul 153-801, Korea. E-mail: sjw@minfinity.com

SONG Joon-Tae, b. 15 February 1952, Gimje-si, Jeollabuk-do, Korea. Professor. m. Hye Ja Park, 1 son, 2 daughters. Education: BS, 1975, MS, 1977, PhD, 1981, Department of Electrical Engineering, Yonsei University. Appointments: Assistant Professor, 1981-85, Associate Professor, 1985-90, Professor, 1990-, Sungkyunkwan University; Visiting Scholar, Rensselaer Polytechnic Institute, USA, 1985-86; Visiting Professor, Surrey University, England, 1997-98; Visiting Professor, Peking University, China, 2005-06. Publications: 7 books including: Introduction of Electrical Engineering; Electromagnetic Theory; More than 200 professional papers on electrical and electronic engineering. Honours: Best Paper Award, Korean Institute of Electrical Engineers, 1981; Best Paper Award, Korean Institute of Electrical and Electronic Material Engineers, 1995. Address: School of Information and Communication Engineering, Sungkyunkwan University, 200 Cheoncheon-dong, Jangan-gu, Suwon-si, Gyeonggi-do, 440-746, Republic of Korea. E-mail: jtsong@ece.skku.ac.kr Website: http://icc.skku.ac.kr/~edal/

SONNENFELD Barry, b. 1 April 1953, New York. Cinematographer; Film Director. Appointments: Cinematographer, Producer and Director: m. Susan Ringo,1 child. Films: Blood Simple, 1984; Compromision Positions, 1985; Three O'Clock High, 1987; Raising Arizona, 1987; Throw Momma from the Train, 1987; Big, 1988; When Harry Met Sally..., 1989; Miller's Crossing, 1990; Misery, 1990; The Addams Family, 1991; Addams Family Values, 1993; For Love of Money, 1993; Get Shorty, 1995; Men in Black, 1997; Wild Wild West, 1999; Chippendales, 2000; Big Trouble, 2002; Men in Black II, 2002; The Ladykillers, 2004; Lemony Snicket's A Series of Unfortunate Events, 2004; Enchanted, 2007; Space Chimps, 2008.TV: Out of Step, 1984; Fantasy Island, 1998; Secret Agent Man, 2000; The Crew, 2000; The Tick, 2001; Karen Sisco, 2003; Pushing Daisies, 2007. Honours: Emmy Award for best cinematography. Address: Gersh Agency, 232 North Canon Drive, Beverly Hills, CA 90210, USA.

SOPER Michael Courtney, b. 20 September 1941, Bournemouth, England. Researcher; Author. Education: BA (Hons), 1969, MA, 1989, Keele University; InterEurope Certificate, 1988. Appointments: Scientific Assistant, Physics, R R E Malvern, 1961-63; Elect Draughtsman, Heenan, Worcester, 1964-65; Freelance Maths Tutor, 1982-; Tutor, Open University; Lecturer II, Electronics, Oxford Polytechnic, 1984-85; Electronics, Oxford University Res Tech, 1982-84, 1986-88; Freelance Tech Author, 1988-93; PFTN Electroquantics CLB, New Marston, Oxford; Res Director, PFTN Research, Oxford, 1990-2007. Publications: Numerous articles in professional journals. Memberships: CIUFOR Research Organisation, Wheatley, Oxfordshire.

SOROUR Khalid Aly, b. 30 August 1950, Cairo, Egypt. Doctor. m. Soheir Mahmoud Mahfouz, 1 son, 1 daughter. Education: MB BGh, 1973, MS, 1978, MD, 1983, Cardiology, Professor of Cardiology, Cairo University Medical School, Cairo, Egypt. Appointments: Resident, 1975-78, Assistant Lecturer, 1979-83, Lecturer, 1983-87, Assistant Professor, 1987-93, Professor, 1993-, Cardiology, Head of Cardiac Cath Lab, 2004-06, Cairo University; Supervisor, Cardiac Department, Beni Suef University, 2004-. Publications: Balloon Dilatation for Co-Auctation of Aorta in Children and Adults, 1989; Rheumatic Fever & Heart Disease in Garson's Science and Practice of Pediatric Cardiology, 1998. Honours: Graduated with honours, 1973; Best Professor Award, Cairo University, 2005-06. Memberships: Egyptian Societies of Cardiology, Hypertension, Pediatric Cardiologists and Cardiac Surgeons; Pan Arab Congenital Heart Disease Association. Address: No 19, Rd 18, Mandi, 11431, Cairo, Egypt. E-mail: khldsorour@yahoo.com

SORVINO Mira, b. 28 September 1968. Actress. m. Christopher Backus, 2004, 2 children. Education: Harvard University. Career: Film appearances include: Amongst Friends, The Second Greatest Story Ever Told, 1993; Quiz Show, Parallel Lives, Barcelona, 1994; Tarantella, Sweet Nothing, Mighty Aphrodite, The Dutch Master, Blue in the Face, 1995; Beautiful Girls, Norma Jean and Marilyn, Jake's Women, 1996; Romy and Michele's High School Reunion,

The Replacement Killers, Mimic, 1997; Summer of Sam, At First Sight, 1999; Joan of Arc: The Virgin Warrior, 2000; Lisa Picard is Famous, The Great Gatsby, The Triumph of Love, 2001; Wisegirls, The Grey Zone, 2002; Gods and Generals, 2003; The Final Cut, 2004; The Reader, 2005; Reservation Road, Leningrad, 2007; Like Dandelion Dust, The Trouble with Cali, Multiple Sarcasms, 2008. Television: The Great Gatsby, 2000. Honours: Academy Award, Best Supporting Actress, 1995. Address: The William Morris Agency, 1325 Avenue of the Americas, New York, NY 10019, USA.

SOUDAN Jean Pol, (Soudan Lord John's) b. 2 July 1953, Louise-Marie, Belgium. Flemish Artist; Painter. Divorced, 1 son. Education: Academy of Tournai, 1968-70; Academy of London, 1972-73; Academy of Lille, 1973-74; Academy of Brussels, 1974-76. Career to date: Painter, originally inspired by the Ardennes countryside and the North Sea; Later work in more fantastic and symbolic style, oriented towards an austral painting looking for high colours; Puts finishing touches to his paintings by scraping with a palette knife, which is an expression of excellence; Represented in many different museums in Belgium and several other countries; Architect, Industrial Design Draughtsman, concentrated on making projects concerning various ancient and new villas styles or luxury buildings; Involved with projects on Belgian power stations, Brussels Underground system and many building companies in Brussels; Signs paintings under the name of Lord John's. Publications: Featured in many reference publications and other books. Memberships: Royal Association and Royal Foundation of the Professional Belgian Artists Painters; Royal Association and Royal Foundation, Sabam of Belgium; Authors Rights Copyright and Preservations for the Belgian Artists; Member, Accadémia del Verbano. Address: 95 rue de la Lorette, The Old Memphis, Renaix 9600, Belgium. Website: www.artpartnerscenter.com

SOUTHGATE Christopher Charles Benedict, b. 26 September 1953, Exeter, Devon. Writer; Editor. m. Sandra Joyce Mitchell, 23 June 1981, 1 stepson. Education: BA, Honours, Natural Sciences, 1974, MA, PhD, Biochemistry, 1978, Christ's College, University of Cambridge; GMC, South-West Ministerial Training Course, Exeter, 1991. Appointments: Research Associate, Biochemistry, University of North Carolina; Research Officer, Bath University; Pastoral Assistant, University Chaplaincy, 1990-96, Director of Modular Studies, 1997-2001, Honorary University Fellow, School of Classics and Theology, 1999, Exeter University; Staff Tutor, South West Ministry Training Course, 2001; Visiting Scholar, Graduate Theological Union, Berkeley, California, 2005. Publications: Landscape or Land?, 1989; Annotations: Selected Early Poems, 1991; Stonechat-Ten Devon Poets (editor), 1992; A Love and Its Sounding: Explorations of T S Eliot, 1997; God, Humanity and the Cosmos: A companion to the Science-Religion Debate,1990, 2003, 2005, revised and updated edition; Beyond the Bitter Wind: Poems 1982-2000, 2000; God and Evolutionary Evil: Theodicy in the Light of Darwinism, 2002; God, Humanity and the Cosmos, 2nd edition, 2005; Easing the Gravity Field: Poems of Science and Love, 2006. Honours: South West Arts Literature Award, 1985; Iolaire Arts Prize, 1987; Sidmouth Arts Festival Prize, 1991; Southwest Open Poetry Commendation, 1991; Templeton Foundation; Science and Religion Course Award, 1996; Science and Religion Course Development Award, 1999; Hawthornden Fellowship, 1999. Memberships: Committee, Science and Religion Forum; Trustee, Cumberland Lodge, Windsor; The Society of

Authors; Christians in Science; Marylebone Cricket Club; Hawk's Club. Address: Parford Cottage, Chagford, Devon TQ13 8JR, England.

SPACEK Mary Elizabeth (Sissy), b. 25 December 1949, Quitman, Texas, USA. Actress. m. Jack Fisk, 1974, 2 daughters. Education: Lee Strasberg Theater Institute. Career: Films: Prime Cut, Ginger in the Morning, 1972; Badlands, 1974; Carrie, 1976; Three Women, Welcome to LA, 1977; Heart Beat, Coal Miner's Daughter, 1980; Raggedy Man, 1981; Mising, 1982; The river, 1984; Marie, 1985; Violets are Blue, Crimes of the Heart, 'night Mother, 1986; JFK, 1991; The Long Walk Home; The Plastic Nightmare; Hard Promises, 1992; Trading Mom, 1994; The Grass Harp, The Streets of Laredo, 1995; If These Walls Could Talk, 1996; Affliction, 1998; Blast From the Past, 1999; In the Bedroom, 2001; Verna: USO Girl, Tuck Everlasting, 2002; Last Call, 2003; A Home at the End of the World, 2004; The Ring II, Nine Lives, The Ring Two, North Country, An American Haunting, 2005; Summer Running: The Race to Cure Breast Cancer, Gray Matters, 2006; Hot Rod, 2007; Lake City, Four Christmasses, 2008. TV: The Girls of Huntington House, The Migrants, 1973; Katherine, 1975; Verna, USO Girl, 1978; A Private Matter, 1992; A Place for Annie, 1994; The Good Old Boys, 1995. Honours: Best Actress, National Society of Film Critics, 1976; Best Supporting Actress, New York Film Critics, 1977; Best Actress, New York and Los Angeles Film Critics, Foreign Press Association, National Society of Film Critics, 1980; Album of the Year Award, Country Music Association, 1980. Address: c/o Steve Tellez, CAA, 9830 Wilshire Boulevard, Beverly Hills, CA 90212, USA.

SPACEY Kevin, b. 26 July 1959, South Orange, New Jersey, USA. Actor; Theatre Director. Education: Juilliard Drama School, New York. Career: Stage debut in Henry IV, Part 1; Broadway debut in Ghosts, 1982; Other theatre appearances include: Hurlyburly, 1985; Long Day's Journey into Night, London, 1986; Yonkers, New York; The Iceman Cometh, London, 1998; Films: Working Girl, 1988; See No Evil, Hear No Evil, 1989; Dad, 1989; Henry and June, 1990; Glengarry Glen Ross, 1992; Consenting Adults, 1992; Hostile Hostages, 1994; Outbreak, 1995; The Usual Suspects, 1995; Seven, 1995; Looking for Richard, 1996; A Time to Kill, 1996; LA Confidential, 1997; Midnight in the Garden of Good and Evil, 1997; American Beauty, 1999; Ordinary Decent Criminal, 2000; Pay It Forward, 2000; The Shipping News, 2001; The Life of David Gale, 2003; Beyond the Sea, 2004; Edison, 2005; Superman Returns, 2006; Fred Claus, 2007; 21, 2008; Telstar, 2008.Director, Albino Alligator, 1997; Member, Board of Trustees, Old Vic, London, Artistic Director, 2003-. Honours: Tony Award, 1986; Academy Award for Best Actor, 1999. Address: William Morris Agency, One William Morris Place, Beverly Hills, CA 90212, USA. Website: www.wma.com

SPADER James, b. 7 February 1960, Boston, USA. Actor. m. Victoria, 1987, divorced, 2004, 2 children. Education: Phillips Academy. Career: Films: Endless Love, 1981; The New Kids, 1985; Pretty in Pink, 1986; Baby Boom, 1987; Less Than Zero, 1987; Mannequin, 1987; Jack's Back, 1988; The Rachel Papers, 1989; Sex, Lies and Videotape, 1989; Bad Influence, 1990; The Music of Chance, 1993; Dream Lover, 1994; Wolf, 1994; Stargate, 1994; Two Days in the Valley, 1996; Crash, 1997; Keys to Tulsa, 1997; Critical Care, 1997; Curtain Call, 1998; Supernova, 1998; Slow Burn, 1999; Secretary, 2002; I Witness, 2003; Alien Hunter, 2003; Shadow of Fear, 2004; TV: The Pentagon Papers, 2003; The Practice, 2003-04; Boston

Legal, 2004-. Honours: Emmy Award, Outstanding Lead Actor in a Drama, 2004. Address: c/o ICM, 8942 Wilshire Boulevard, Beverly Hills, CA 90211, USA.

SPAGHI Stefano, b. 8 July 1964, Milan, Italy. Economist. Education: Diploma, Economist Ragioneer, 1982; BEcon, Catholic University, Milan, 1986; Diploma, Economist, 1988. Appointments: With Communal Studio, Milan, 1991-99. Publications: Economic Development: Different Ways to Calculate It. Honours: Listed in international biographical dictionaries. Address: Via Martiri Triestini 10, 20148 Milan, Italy. E-mail: stefanospaghi@libero.it

SPALL Timothy, b. 27 February 1957, London, England. Actor. m. Shane, 1981,1 son, 2 daughters. Education: Battersea County Comprehensive, Kingsway and Princeton College of Further Education; Royal Academy of Dramatic Art, London. Career: TV: The Brylcream Boys, 1978; Auf Wiedersehen Pet, 1983, 1985; Roots, 1993; Frank Stubbs Promotes, Outside Edge, 1994, 1995; Neville's Island, Our Mutual Friend, 1997; Shooting the Past, 1999; The Thing About Vince, 2000; Vacuuming Completely Nude in Paradise, Perfect Strangeres, 2001; Auf Wiedersehen Pet (3rd series), 2002; My House in Umbria, 2003; Cherished, Mr Harvey Lights a Candle, 2005; Mysterious Creatures, 2006; A Room with a View, 2007; Gunrush, 2008. Plays: Merry Wives of Windsor; Nicholas Nickleby; The Three Sisters; The Knight of the Burning Pestle, 1978-81; St Joan, 1985; Mandragola, 1985; Le Bourgeois Gentilhomme, 1993; A Midsummer Night's Dream, 1994; This is a Chair, 1996; Films: Quadrophenia, 1978; Gothic, 1986; The Sheltering Sky, 1989; Life is Sweet, 1990; Secrets and Lies, 1996; The Wisdom of Crocodiles, Still Crazy, 1998; Topsy Turvy, Clandestine Marriage, 1999; Love's Labour's Lost, 2000; Intimacy, Lucky Break, Rock Star, Vanilla Sky, 2001; All or Nothing, Nicholas Nickleby, 2002; Gettin' Square, The Last Samurai, 2003; Harry Potter and the Prisoner of Azkaban, Lemony Snicket's A Series of Unfortunate Events, 2004; The Last Hangman, Harry Potter and the Goblet of Fire, 2005; Death Defying Acts, Enchanted, Oliver Twist, Sweeney Todd: The Demon Barber of Fleet Street, 2007; Jackboots on Whitehall, 2008. Address: c/o Markham & Froggatt, 4 Windmill Street, London W1P 1HF, England.

SPEAR Walter Eric, b. 20 January 1921. Physicist. m. Hilda Doris King, 2 daughters. Education: BSc, PhD, DSc, University of London. Appointments: Lecturer then Reader, Physics, University of Leicester, 1953-68; Harris Professor of Physics, 1968-91, Professor Emeritus, 1991-, University of Dundee. Publications: Author of numerous research papers on electronic and transport properties in crystalline solids, liquids and amorphous semi-conductors. Honours: Europhysics Prize, European Physical Society, 1977; Max Born Medal and Prize, Institute of Physics and German Physical Society, 1977; Makdougall-Brisbane Medal, Royal Society of Edinburgh, 1981; Maxwell Premium, Institute of Electrical Engineers, 1981, 1982; Rank Prize for Optoelectronics, 1988; Mott Award, 1989; Rumford Medal, Royal Society, 1990. Memberships: FInstP, 1962; Fellow of the Royal Society of Edinburgh, 1972; Fellow of the Royal Society, 1980. Address: 20 Kelso Place, Dundee DD2 1SL, Scotland.

SPEARING Ruth Lilian, b. 7 January 1952, England. Haematologist. m. Leslie Snape, 1 son, 1 daughter. Education: MB, ChB, University of Bristol, 1977; FRACP, FRCPA (Haematology). Appointments: Intern, Christchurch Hospital (Surgery), New Zealand, and Professor A E Read, Bristol, UK (Medicine), 1977-78; Registrar, Internal Medicine, Christchurch Hospital, 1978-81; Registrar, Internal Medicine (part-time), 1981-82, Haematology (part-time), 1982-83, Dunedin Hospital, New Zealand; Registrar, Haematology (part-time), Plymouth General Hospital, UK, 1983-84; Senior Registrar, Haematology (part-time), Royal Liverpool Hospital, UK, 1984-87; Acting Director, Regional Blood Transfusion Service, Christchurch, 1987-89; Clinical Lecturer, Department of Pathology, University of Otago, 1987-96; Consultant Haematologist, Clinical and Laboratory Haematology, 1989-, Acting Clinical Director, when Clinical Director absent, 1993-98, Clinical Director, Haematology, 1998-2004, Christchurch Hospital; Senior Clinical Lecturer, Department of Pathology, University of Otago, 1996-; Member, 1996-, Chairman, 1996-2000, 2002-06, Ceredase Treatment Panel; Member, NZ Specialist Advisory Committee for Higher Training in Haematology, Royal Australasian College of Physicians, 1998-; Member, New Zealand Cancer Treatment Working Party, 2001-; Member, Haematology Medical Oncology Subcommittee of the NZCTWP, 2001-; Chairman, Senior Medical Staff Association, Christchurch Hospitals, 2003-; Member, IT subcommittee, NZCTWP, 2002-; Chairman, IT subcommittee, NZCTWP, 2003-; Member, Clinical Board, Canterbury District Health Board, 2003-. Publications: Numerous articles in professional scientific journals, abstracts presented as oral presentations at professional meetings, invited presentations at professional meetings and abstracts presented as posters at professional meetings. Honours: Numerous successful grant applications. Memberships: Fellow, Royal Australasian College of Physicians; Fellow, Royal College of Pathologists of Australasia; Member, British Society of Haematology; Member, Haematology Society of New Zealand and Australia; Member, Australian and New Zealand Bone Marrow Transplant Society, Chairman of the New Zealand Joint Specialist Academy Committee in Haematology, 2007-; Member, American Society of Bone Marrow Transplantation; Member, New Zealand Society of Cancer Specialists. Address: Department of Haematology, Christchurch Hospital, Private Bag, Christchurch, New Zealand. E-mail: ruth.spearing@cdhb.govt.nz

SPEARS Britney Jean, b. 2 December 1981, Kentwood, Louisiana, USA. Singer. m. Kevin Federline, 2004, 2 sons, divorced, 2007. Career: Presenter, Mickey Mouse Club; Solo artist, 1998-; Numerous tours, TV and radio appearances; Owner, southern grill restaurant, Nyla; Film: Crossroads, 2002; Recordings: Albums: Baby One More Time, 1999; Oops! I Did It Again, 2000; Britney, 2001; In the Zone, 2003; My Prerogative, 2004; B In The Mix: The Remixes, 2005. Singles: Baby One More Time, 1999; Sometimes, 1999; (You Drive Me) Crazy, 1999; Born to Make You Happy, 2000; From the Bottom of My Broken Heart, 2000; Oops! I Did It Again, 2000; Lucky, 2000; Stronger, 2000; Don't Let Me Be The Last To Know, 2001; I'm A Slave For You, 2001; Overprotected, 2002; I'm Not A Girl Not Yet A Woman, 2002; I Love Rock 'n' Roll, 2002; Toxic, 2004; Blackout, 2007. Honours: MTV Europe Music Awards for Best Female Artist, 1999, 2004; Best Breakthrough Act, 1999; Best Pop Act, 1999; Several MTV Video Music Awards, 1999; Best Female Pop Vocal Performance, 2000; Billboard Music Award, 2000; American Music Award for Favourite New Artist, 2000; Grammy Award for Best Dance Recording, 2005. Address: The Official Britney Spears International Fan Club, CS 9712, Bellingham, WA 98227, USA. Website: www.britneyspears.com

SPEDDING Sir Colin Raymond William, b. 22 March 1925. Emeritus Professor. Widower, 2 children. Education: BSc, Zoology, London, 1951; MSc, Zoology, 1953; PhD, Science, London, 1955; FZS, 1962; DSc (London), 1967; FIBiol, 1967;

CBiol, 1984; FIHort, 1986; FLS, 1995. Appointments: Ilford Ltd Research Laboratory, 1940-43; RNVR, 1943-46; Allen & Hanbury Research Laboratory, 1948-49; Staff Member, later Deputy Director, Head of Ecology Division, Grassland Research Institute, 1949-75; Visiting professor, Part-time Professor, 1970-75, Head, 1975-83, Department of Agriculture and Horticulture, Dean, Faculty of Agriculture and Food, 1983-86, Professor of Agricultural Systems, Department of Agriculture, 1970-90, Director, Centre for Agricultural Strategy, 1981-90, Pro-Vice-Chancellor, 1986-90, Emeritus Professor, 1990-, University of Reading. Publications: Over 200 articles in professional journals; Books include: Fream's Principles of Food and Agriculture, 1992; Agriculture and the Citizen, 1996; Animal Welfare, 2005; The Natural History of a Garden, 2003; The Second Mouse Gets the Cheese: Proverbs and their Uses, 2005. Honours: CBE, 1988; Kt, 1994; Hon Assoc, RCVS, 1994; Hon FIBiol, 1994; Hon DSc (Reading), 1995. Memberships: Family Farmers' Association; Honorary Life Member, British Society of Animal Science; Patron, Land Heritage; Vice President, RSPCA; Special Scientific Adviser, WSPA; Fellow, Royal Agricultural Society of England; Fellow, Royal Agricultural Societies; Fellow, Royal Society of Arts.

SPENCER Aida Besancon, b. 2 January 1947, Santo Domingo, Dominican Republic. Professor; Minister. m. William David Spencer, 1 son. Education: BA, Douglass College, 1968; ThM, MDiv, Princeton Theological Seminary, 1973, 1975; PhD, Southern Baptist Theological Seminary, 1982. Appointments: Community Organiser, 1969-70; Campus Minister, 1973-74; Adjunct Professor, New York Theological Seminary, 1974-76; Academic Dean, Professor, Alpha-Omega Community Theological School, 1976-78; Professor of New Testament, Gordon-Conwell Theological Seminary, 1982-. Publications: God through the Looking Glass: Glimpses from the Arts; Global God; Prayer Life of Jesus; Beyond the Curse: Women Called to Ministry; Paul's Literary Style; Goddess Revival; Joy through the Night; 2 Corinthians; Latino Heritage Bible. Honours: Eternity Book of the Year, 1986; Christianity Today Book Award, 1996. Memberships: Society of Biblical Literature; Evangelical Theological Society; Christians for Biblical Equality; Institute for Biblical Research; Asociacion para la Educacion Teologica Hispana. Address: Gordon-Conwell Theological Seminary, 130 Essex Street, S Hamilton, MA 01982, USA.

SPENCER David A, b. 7 November 1963, Stepney, London, England. Geologist. Education: BSc (Honours), Geology, University of Exeter, UK, 1983-86; Diploma of Imperial College, Structural Geology and Rock Mechanics, Royal School of Mines, Imperial College of Science and Technology, University of London, 1987-88; MSc, Structural Geology and Rock Mechanics, Royal School of Mines, London, 1987-88; Doctor of Natural Sciences, Swiss Federal Institute of Technology (ETH), Zurich, 1989-93. Appointments include: Hydrological Consultant, Partnerscaft Pro Aliminos, Philippines, 1992-94; Accepted as Senior Post-Doctoral Research Fellow (SNSF) at Universities of: Cambridge (UK), Stanford (USA), California (Santa Barbara), Maine (USA), Punjab (Pakistan), Tokyo Institute of Technology, MIT, Boston, USA, 1997-99; Research Assistant Professor, Lecturer in Structural Geology, University of Maine, Orono, USA, 1997-98; Staff Geologist - Structural Geologist, Project Manager, Saga Petroleum ASA, Oslo, Norway, 1998-2000; Senior Reservoir Geologist, Roxar Software Solutions, London, 2003-05; Principal Geologist, BG International Limited, 2005-. Publications: 24 scientific publications, 46 articles, 81 abstracts, 4 theses, 1 consultant report, 22 research

reports, 6 expedition reports. Honours: Many scholarships and awards, also many athletic awards in a variety of sports. Memberships include: Fellow, Royal Geographic Society (with Institute of British Geographers); Fellow, Royal Astronomical Society; Fellow, American Geographical Society; Fellow, Geological Society; Fellow, Geological Association of Canada; Fellow, Geological Society of India; Fellow, Royal Society of Arts; Fellow, Linnean Society of London. Address: PO Box 2827, Reading, Berkshire RG1 9EN, England. E-mail: David@Spencer.name

SPENCER Gillian Bryne White, b. 22 July 1931, London, England. Museum Curator. 1 son. Education: Selhurst Grammar School for Girls, Croydon; BA, History, 1952, MA, 1956, Newnham College, Cambridge; Academic Postgraduate Diploma in Prehistoric Archaeology, Institute of Archaeology, London University, 1954. Appointments: Curator, Saffron Walden Museum, 1958-61; Museums Education Officer, City of Norwich Museums, 1969-74; Director, Wakefield MDC Art Gallery, Museums and Castles, 1974-90; First Chairman, Wakefield Cathedral Fabric Advisory Committee, 1991-96. Publications: A Beaker Burial at Weeke, Winchester; Excavation of the Battle Ditches, Saffron Walden (co-author); Discoveries in Old World Archaeology, Encyclopaedia Britannica Year Book, 1961; Museums in Education: Trends in Education, 1974. Honours: State Scholarship, 1949-52, 1952-54; Fellow of the Museums Association, 1990. Membership: Museums Association. Address: 12 Belgrave Mount, Wakefield, West Yorkshire WF1 3SB, England.

SPICER (William) Michael (Hardy) (Sir), b. 22 January 1943, United Kingdom. Member of Parliament. m. Patricia Ann Hunter, 1 son, 2 daughters. Education: MA, Economics, Emmanuel College, Cambridge. Appointments: Assistant to Editor, The Statist, 1964-66; Conservative Research Department, 1966-68; Director, Conservative Systems Research, 1968-70; Managing Director, Economic Models Ltd, 1970-80; Member of Parliament, South Worcestershire, 1974-97, West Worcestershire, 1997-; PPS, Department of Trade, 1979-81; Parliamentary Under Secretary of State (Minister for Aviation, 1985-87), Department of Transport, 1984-87; Parliamentary Under Secretary of State (Minister for Coal and Power), Department of Energy, 1987-90; Minister of State (Minister for Housing and Planning), Department of the Environment, 1990; Member, Treasury Select Committee, 1997-2001; Chairman, Treasury Sub-Committee, 1999-2001. Publications: A Treaty Too Far, 1992; The Challenge from the East, 1996; Novels: Final Act, 1981; Prime Minister Spy, 1986; Cotswold Manners, 1989; Cotswold Murders, 1990; Cotswold Mistress, 1992; Cotswold Moles, 1993; Contributor, Royal Institution Public Administration. Honour: Knighted, 1996. Memberships: Vice-Chairman, Deputy Chairman, 1983-84, Conservative Party; Chairman: Parliamentary Office of Science and Technology, 1990, Parliamentary and Scientific Committee, 1996-99, European Research Group, 1994-2001, Congress for Democracy, 1998-; President, 1996-, Chairman, 1991-96, Association of Electricity Producers; Governor, Wellington College, 1992-2004; Chairman and Captain, Lords and Commons Tennis Club, 1996-; Member, 1997-99, Chairman, 2001-, 1922 Committee; Member of Board, Conservative Party, 2001. Address: House of Commons, London SW1A 0AA, England.

SPIELBERG Steven, b. 18 December 1947, Cincinnati, Ohio, USA. Film Director; Producer. m. (1) Amy Irving, 1985, divorced 1989, 2 sons, (2) Kate Capshaw, 5 children. Education: California State College, Long Beach. Career: Film Director, Universal Pictures; Founder, Amblin Entertainment;

Co-founder, Dreamworks SKG Inc, 1995-; Founder, Starbright Foundation. Creative Works: As Film Director: Duel (for TV), 1971; Something Evil (for TV), 1972; The Sugarland Express, 1974; Jaws, 1975; Close Encounters of the Third Kind, 1977; 1941, 1979; Raiders of the Lost Ark, 1981; E.T. (The Extra Terrestrial), 1982; Twilight Zone - The Movie, 1983; Indiana Jones and the Temple of Doom, 1984; The Color Purple (also producer), 1985; Empire of the Sun, 1988; Always, 1989; Hook, 1991; Jurassic Park, 1992; Schindler's List, 1993; Some Mother's Son, 1996; The Lost World, 1997; As Producer: I Wanna Hold Your Hand, 1978; Poltergeist (also co-writer), 1982; Gremlins, 1984; Young Sherlock Holmes (executive producer), 1985; Back to the Future (co-executive producer), 1986; The Goonies (writer, executive producer), 1986; Batteries Not Included (executive producer), 1986; The Money Pit (co-producer), 1986; An American Tail (co-executive producer), 1986; Who Framed Roger Rabbit, 1988; Gremlins II (executive producer), 1991; Joe Versus the Volcano (executive producer), 1991; Dad (executive producer) 1991; Cape Fear (co-executive producer), 1992; The Flintstones, 1994; Casper, 1995; Twister (executive producer), 1996; Men in Black, 1997; The Lost World: Jurassic Park, 1997; Amistad, 1997; Deep Impact, 1998; Saving Private Ryan, 1998; The Last Days (documentary), 1999; AI; Artificial Intelligence, 2001; Minority Report, 2002; Catch Me If You Can, 2002; The Terminal, 2004; The Legend of Zorro, 2005; Memoirs of a Geisha, 2005; Director, TV episodes, including Columbo; E.R; Band of Brothers, 2000; Semper Fi, 2000; Taken, 2002; Munich, 2005; Monster House, 2006; Spell Your Name, 2006; Flags of Our Fathers, 2006; Letters from Iwo Jima, 2006; Transformers, 2007. Publication: Close Encounters of the Third Kind (with Patrick Mann). Honours include: Directors Guild of America Award Fellowship, 1986; BAFTA Awards; Irving G Thalberg Award, 1987; Golden Lion Award, Venice Film Festival, 1993; Academy Awards; John Huston Award, 1995; Dr hc, University of Southern California, 1994; Lifetime Achievement Award, Directors' Guild of America, 1999; Britannia Award, 2000; Grosses Bundesverdienstkreuz, 1998; Hon KBE. Address: CAA, 9830 Wilshire Boulevard, Beverly Hills, CA 90212, USA.

SPOONER David Eugene, b. 1 September 1941, West Kirby, Wirral, England. Writer; Naturalist. m. Marion O'Neil, 9 March 1986, 1 daughter. Education: BA, hons, University of Leeds, 1963; Diploma in Drama, University of Manchester, 1964; PhD, University of Bristol, 1968. Appointments: Lecturer, University of Kent, 1968-73; Visiting Professor, Pennsylvania State University, 1973-74; Lecturer, Manchester Polytechnic, 1974-75; Head of Publishing Borderline Press, 1976-85; Director, Butterfly Conservation, East Scotland; Academic Board, London Diplomatic Academy, 2001-. Publications: Unmakings, 1977; The Angelic Fly: The Butterfly in Art, 1992; The Metaphysics of Insect Life, 1995; Creatures of Air: Poetry 1976-98, 1998; Insect into Poem: 20th Century Hispanic Poetry, 1999, 2001; Thoreau's Insects, 2002; The Insect-Populated Mind: how insects have influenced the evolution of consciousness, 2005; Karl Spitteler: Imago, translation, 2006. Contributions to: Iron; Interactions; Tandem; Weighbauk; Revue de Littérature Comparée; Bestia (Fable Society of America); Margin; Corbie Press; Butterfly Conservation News; Butterfly News; Field Studies. Honours: American Medal of Honor for Natural History; Admitted to American Hall of Fame; Congressional Medal of Achievement in Literature. Memberships: The Welsh Academy Associate; Association Benjamin Constant; Thoreau Society; Nabokov Society; Authors Guild. Address: 96 Halbeath Road, Dunfermline, Fife KY12 7LR, Scotland.

SPRINGMAN Sarah Marcella, b. 26 December 1956. Professor. Education: BA, Engineering Sciences, 1978, MA, Engineering Sciences, MPhil, 1984, PhD, 1989, Soil Mechanics, Cambridge University. Appointments: Trainee, Sir Alexander Gibb & Partners, 1975-79; Engineer, Gibb Australia, Adelaide, Australia, 1979; Sir Alexander Gibb & Partners, Reading, England, 1980-83; Graduate Engineer, Gibb Australia, Fiji, 1981-82; Research Assistant, Cambridge University, 1983-89; Research Associate, 1988, Research Fellow, 1988-90, Assistant Lecturer, 1991-93, Lecturer, 1993-96, Cambridge University & Magdalene College; Professor, ETH Zurich, Switzerland, 1997-. Publications: Numerous articles in professional journals. Honours: Woman of Achievement Award, Cosmopolitan-Clairol, 1991; Global Young Leader, World Economic Forum, Geneva, 1993-96; Officer of the Order of British Empire, 1997; Life Fellow, Royal Society of Arts. Memberships: EPSRC Peer Review College; Fellow, Institution of Civil Engineers; Chair, Technical Committee on Physical Modelling; International Society of Soil Mechanics and Geotechnical Engineering; Chair, ETHZ Natural Hazards Group; Member, ETH Zurich Competence Centre for Environmental Sustainability; Swiss Platform for Natural Hazards; President, 2007-, British Triathlon Federation; Member, National Olympic Committee of Great Britain. Address: ETH Zurich, Institute for Geotechnical Engineering, Department of Civil, Environmental and Geomatic Engineering, 8093 Zurich, Switzerland. E-mail: sarah.springman@igt.baug.ethz.ch

SPRINGSTEEN Bruce, b. 23 September 1949, New Jersey, USA. Singer; Songwriter; Musician. m. (1) Julianne Phillips, divorced, (2) Patti Scialfa, 1 son, 1 daughter. Appointments: Recording Artist, 1972-; Founder, The E-Street Band, 1974; Numerous national and worldwide tours. Creative Works: Albums: Greetings From Ashbury Park, 1973; The Wild The Innocent and The E Street Shuffle, 1973; Born to Run, 1975; Darkness on the Edge of Town, 1978; The River, 1980; Nebraska, 1982; Born in the USA, 1984; Live 1975-85, 1986; Tunnel of Love, 1987; Human Touch, 1992; Lucky Town, 1992; In Concert - MTV Plugged, 1993; Greatest Hits, 1995; The Ghost of Tom Joad, 1995; Bruce Springsteen Plugged, 1997; 18 Tracks, 1998; The Rising, 2002; Roll of the Dice, 2003; Devils & Dust, 2005; We Shall Overcome: The Seeger Sessions, 2006; Magic, 2007. Honours: 3 Grammy Awards, 1984, 1987, 2003; Brit Award, Best International Solo Artist, 1986; Rock'n'Roll Hall of Fame, 1988; Numerous Platinum and Gold Discs; Oscar, Best Original Song, 1994. Address: c/o Premier Talent Agency, 3 East 54th Street, New York, NY 10022, USA.

SPROT Aidan Mark, b. 17 June 1919, Lilliesleaf, Scotland. Soldier; Farmer. Education: Stowe School, Buckinghamshire. Appointments: Commissioned Scots Greys, 1940; Served in Palestine, Egypt, Libya, Italy, France, Belgium, Holland, Germany, WWII; Served Libya, Egypt, Jordan, Germany, retired as Lieutenant Colonel, 1962; Adjutant of Regiment, 1945-46, Commanding Officer, 1959-62; Inherited Haystoun Estate in Peeblesshire, 1965; Farmed 3 farms (hill sheep and cattle); Retired, 2003; County Councillor, Peeblesshire, 1963-75; County Director, 1966-74, Patron, 1983-, Peeblesshire Red Cross; County Commissioner, 1968-73, President, 1973-99, Peeblesshire Scout Association. Publication: Swifter than Eagles, War Memoirs 1939-45, 1998. Honours: Military Cross, 1944; Scout Association Medal of Merit, 1973; British Red Cross Association Badge of Honour, 1998; JP, Peeblesshire, 1966-; Deputy Lieutenant, Peeblesshire, 1966-80; Lord Lieutenant, Tweeddale (formerly Peeblesshire), 1980-94; Honorary Freeman, County of

Tweeddale, 1994-. Memberships: Queen's Bodyguard for Scotland, Royal Company of Archers, 1950-; Member, 1970-89, President, 1986-89, Lowlands of Scotland TA and VRA; Service Chaplains' Committee, Church of Scotland, 1974-82, 1985-92; Member, 1947-, Secretary, 1964-74, Royal Caledonian Hunt; President, 1988-96, Lothian Federation of Boys Clubs; Trustee, 1989-98, currently Honorary Vice-President, Royal Scottish Agricultural Benevolent Institution; Honorary Member, Rotary Club of Peebles, 1986-; Honorary President, 1990-, Peebles Branch, Royal British Legion; Honorary President, 1994-, Tweeddale Society. Address: Crookston, by Peebles EH45 9JQ, Scotland.

SPURWAY Marcus John, b. 28 October 1938, Surrey, England. Retired Insurance Broker and Director. m. Christine Kate Townshend, 2 sons. Appointments: National Service, 4 Regiment, Royal Horse Artillery; Insurance Broker, Director, Morgan Reid & Sharman, Ltd (Lloyd's Brokers, formerly B&C Aviation Insurance Brokers); Specialist in Aviation Insurance; Retired 1999. Publications: Aviation Insurance Abbreviations, Organisations and Institutions, 1983; Aviation Insurance. The Market and Underwriting Practice, 1991; Aviation Law and Claims, 1992. Address: Lomeer, Common Road, Sissinghurst, Kent TN17 2JR, England.

SPYROPOULOS Christos-Christopher, b. 11 December 1937, Rododafni Aegiou, Greece (American citizen, 1975). Orchestra Conductor; University Professor. m. Georgia Meintanas, 1971, 1 son, 3 daughters. Education: Theological School, Corinth, 1949-54; Theology and Philosophy, University of Athens, 1954-58; Byzantine Music, Advanced Theory in Classical Music, Athens Conservatory, 1953-60; Instrumentation and Orchestra Conducting with Professor Hans Swarowski, Academy of Music, Vienna, 1962-64; Advanced Training in International Law, University of Vienna, 1962-64; Special Tutorship with Professor A Votto and T Serafin (Italian Opera Repertory), Santa Cecilia Music Academy, Rome, Italy. Appointments: NATO Alliances Officer, Greek Royal Airforce, 1957-60; Reserve (current rank of Brig General), USAF, 1964; Professor of Music, National Academy of Music, Athens, Greece, 1960-62, 1979-85; Professor, ORFIO Conservatory of Music, Athens, 1960-62; Education Director, Professor, The Hellenic-American Schools, New York City, USA, 1963-66; Full and Part time Air Line Pilot, Braniff International Airways (Central and South America Division), also Trans World Airlines (Trans Atlantic Division), 1966-71; Inspector, US Civil Aviation (FAA), 1972-74; Advisor to President Richard M Nixon, Washington DC, 1971-74; Chairman Examining Committee, American Federation of Musicians (Local 802), New York City, 1973-77; Marketing Advisor, ARAMCO, Saudi Arabia and Nigeria, 1987-89; Professor of International Law, Worcester University, Massachusetts, USA, 1989-91; Marketing Director, Olympic Airways, Boston, 1989-91; Guest Conductor with symphony orchestras in Vienna, Salzburg, Moscow, Paris, Geneva (Grand Theater Opera House), Sydney, Minneapolis, Philadelphia, Los Angeles, Chicago, 1964-2002. Publications: The Philosophical Approach of Leadership, Leaders toward Government, Organizations and Business Establishments, 1975; Sociological Approach to an interpretation of Religious Phenomena, 1976. Honours: Award in Flight Safety, 1970; Beethoven Medal of Honor, and title of Great Conductor, and Great Musician (in memory of the 200th anniversary of Beethoven's birth), The Opera Society in Vienna, 1970; Distinction (Flag) for 200 years of American Independence, US Government, 1976; Award, Greek Literature Association, 1995; Award for achievements in literature and the arts, USA, 2005; International Musician of the Year, 2005, One

of 2000 Outstanding Intellectuals if the 21st Century, 2005, IBC; International Peace Prize, United Cultural Convention, 2006; American Medal of Honor, USA, 2006; Nominated International Professional of the Year, 2006; World Medal of Freedom, 2006; Man of the Year, USA, 2006; Master Diploma in Literature, World Academy of Letters, USA, 2007; Recognition from great conductors and music critics including: I Stravinsky, B Walter, M Cross, L Stokovsky, G Solti, F Reiner, F Cleva, H V Karajan, L Bernstein, C Boehm and others; Listed in international biographical dictionaries. Memberships: International Musicians Association of America, President, 1973; The Air Line Pilots Association International, 1968; The Greek-American Organization (AHEPA), 1966; The Greek-American Professors Union in USA; Greek Literature Association. Address: 32 Rododafnis Str, Glyka Nera of Attica, 15344, Athens, Greece.

SRIVASTAVA Chandra Mani, b. 10 January 1932, Ballia (UP), India. Physics Educator. m. Leela, 3 sons. Education: BS, Banaras Hindu University, Varanasi, 1950; MS, 1952; D Phil, London University, England, 1957. Appointments: Lecturer, Physics, Banaras Hindu University, 1957-58; Lecturer, 1958-62, Assistant Professor, 1962-69, Associate Professor, 1969-72, Head, Department of Physics, 1971-73, Professor, 1972-92, Head, Advanced Centre for Research in Electronics, 1976-92, Head, Materials Science Centre, 1976-92, Professor Emeritus, 1995-, Indian Institute of Technology, Bombay. Publications: Contributed articles to professional journals; Author, Introduction to Special Theory of Relativity, 1972; Co-author, Science of Engineering Materials, 1987, 2nd edition, 1972; Editor, Recent Advances in Materials Research, 1984; Advances in Ferrites Vol 1 & 2, 1989. Honours: Fellow, National Academy of Sciences and Indian National Science Academy; Life Member, IEEE. Address: 604 Prerana, opp IIT Main Gate, Powai, Mumbai 400 076, India. E-mail: cms_604@yahoo.co.in

SRIVASTAVA Chandrika Prasad, b. 8 July 1920, Unnao, India. Retired Diplomat. m. Nirmala Salve, 2 daughters. Education: BA, First Class, 1940, BA, First Class Honours, 1941, MA, First Class, 1942, Bachelor of Laws First Class, 1944, Lucknow, India. Appointments include: Officer on Special Duty, 1946-48, Under Secretary, 1948-49, Ministry of Commerce, Government of India; City Magistrate, Lucknow, 1950; Additional District Magistrate, Meerut, 1951-52; Officer on Special Duty, Directorate General of Shipping, 1953; Deputy Director-General of Shipping, 1954-57; Deputy Secretary, Ministry of Transport, Private Secretary to the Minister of Transport and Communications/Minister of Commerce and Industry, 1958; Senior Deputy Director-General of Shipping; Managing Director, Shipping Corporation of India Limited, Bombay, 1961-64; Joint Secretary to the Prime Minister of India, 1964-66; Chairman of the Board of Directors and Managing Director, Shipping Corporation of India Ltd, 1966-73; Chairman, Board of Directors, Mogul Line Limited, 1967-73; Secretary General, 1974-89, Secretary General Emeritus, 1990-, International Maritime Organisation, United Nations; Chancellor, 1983-91, Founding Chancellor Emeritus, 1991-, World Maritime University; Specialisation in national and international maritime affairs. Publications: Lal Bahadur Shashtri Prime Minister of India 1964-66, 1995; Corruption: India's Enemy Within, 2001; World Maritime University – First Twenty Years, 2003. Honours: Over 30 world-wide decorations and honours include: Honorary Member, The Honourable Company of Master Mariners, UK, 1978-89; Commander du Merite Maritime, France, 1982; Order of Prince Henry, the Navigator (Commander), Portugal, 1983; Commander's

Cross of the Order of Merit, Poland, 1986; Seatrade Award for Achievement, Seatrade Organisation, 1989; Honorary Knight Commander of the Most Distinguished Order of St Michael and St George, UK, 1990; Similar decorations and honours from India, Italy, Germany, Norway, Spain, Sweden and several other countries; International Maritime Prize, IMO, United Nations, 1992; Doctor of Laws, Honoris Causa: Bhopal University, 1984, University of Wales, 1987. University of Malta, 1988. Memberships: Life Governor, The Maritime Society, UK; Life Member, Board of Governors, World Maritime University; Anglo-Belgian Club, London; India International Centre, New Delhi; Willingdon Club, Mumbai; Poona Club, Pune, India. Address: Prastishthan, NDA Road, Post Box No 2, Pune 411023, India.

SRIVASTAVA Jitendra Kumar, b. 28 February 1946, Gonda, Uttar Pradesh, India. Senior Scientist. m. Sudha, 2 sons. Education: BSc, Maharani Lal Kunwari Degree College, 1963; MSc, University of Gorakhpur, 1965; PhD, University of Bombay, 1977. Appointments: Research Training in Physics, Atomic Energy Establishment Trombay, 1965-66; Research Associate (C), 1966-73, Fellow (D), 1973-86, Reader (E), 1986-90, Associate Professor (F), 1990-2001, Professor (G), 2001-, Tata Institute of Fundamental Research; Honorary Consultant, Crystec, Mumbai, 1997-99. Publications: 3 books; 9 book chapters; 140 refereed scientific papers. Honours: Invited speaker at national and international symposia, conferences and meetings. Memberships: Indian Physics Association; Indian Mossbauer Society; Council of Scientific and Industrial Research. Address: N S Group, Tata Institute of Fundamental Research, Homi Bhabha Road, Colaba, Mumbai 400005, India. E-mail: jks@tifr.res.in

SRIVASTAVA Radhey Shyam, b. 7 June 1931, Bahadurganj (UP), India. Scientist. m. Vijay Laxmi, 1 son, 2 daughters. Education: BSc, 1951, MSc, 1953, PhD, 1963, Lucknow University; Certificate in Proficiency in French, 1957. Appointments: Research Fellow, Lecturer, 1954-58, Lucknow University; Junior Scientific Officer, 1958-61, Senior Scientific Officer, 1961-71, Principal Scientific Officer, 1971-80, Deputy Chief Scientific Officer, 1980-91, Defence Science Centre, New Delhi, India. Publications: Books: Turbulence (pipe Flows), 1977; Interaction of Shock Waves, 1994; Research papers and reports. Honours: Postdoctoral Royal Society Research Fellow, Imperial College of Science and Technology, London, 1965-67; Visiting Scientist: Institute for Aerospace Studies, University of Toronto, 1980-81; Materials Research Laboratories, Melbourne, 1983; Chiba University, Japan, 1991; Visiting Professor, Ernst Mach Institute, Freiburg, Germany, 1995; Visiting Professor, Chiba University, Japan 2000; Visiting Professor, Tohoku University, Japan, 2000; Visiting Professor, Tokyo Denki University, Japan, 2001; Visiting Professor, Aachen University, Germany, 2002; 2000 Millennium Medal of Honor, ABI, USA, 2000; Great Minds of the 21st Century, ABI, 2003; 20th Century Award for Achievement, 1998; Vijay Rattan Award, India, 2005; Rajiv Gandhi Excellence Award, 2006; Rising Personalities of India Award, 2006; Bharat Jyoti Award, India, 2008; Rashtriya Samman Puraskarand Gold Medal, India, 2008. Listed in national and international biographical dictionaries. Memberships: Fellow, National Academy of Science, India; Life Member, Bharat Ganita Parishad, India; Indian Science Congress; Kothari Centre for Science, Ethics and Education (KCSEE); Fellow, United Writers' Association of India. Address: A-3/260, Janakpuri, New Delhi 110058, India.

ST CLEMENT Pamela, b. 11 May 1942. Actress; Presenter. m. Andrew Louis Gordon, 1970, divorced 1979. Education: The Warren, Worthing; Rolle College, Devon; Rose Bruford College of Drama, Kent. Career: Television appearances include: Wild at Heart; BBC Animal Awards: Zoo Chronicles; Adopt-a-Wild-Animal; BBC Eastenders, 1986-; Whipsnade, (2, 13 part wildlife series); Not for the Likes of Us (Play for Today); The Tripods; Cats Eyes; Partners in Crime; Shoestring; Emmerdale Farm; Horseman Riding By (BBC series); Shall I See You Now (BBC play); Within these Walls (2 series); Theatre includes: Joan Littlewood's Theatre Royal, Stratford; Royal Shakespeare Company; Prospect Theatre Company (Strindberg and Chekov); Thorndike Theatre (Macbeth); Yvonne Arnaud Theatre (I am a Camera); Leeds Playhouse (Once a Catholic); Victoria Theatre/Dome Brighton (The Music from Chicago); Films include: Hedda; Dangerous Davies; The Bunker; Scrubbers. Honour: Presented Duke of Edinburgh Awards, St James' Palace, 2000. Memberships: President, West Herts RSPCA; Vice-President, Scottish Terrier Emergency Care Scheme; Patron: London Animal Day; Tusk Trust; Africat (UK); Pets as Therapy; Leicester Animal Aid Association; Ridgeway Trust for Endangered Cats; Pro-Dogs; Other charities involved with: PDSA; Blue Cross; National Animal Welfare Trust; Battersea Dogs Home; Environmental Investigation Agency; Hearing Dogs for Deaf People; International League for the Protection of Horses; Kennel Club Good Citizens Dog Scheme; Project Life Line; Earth Kind; WSPA; Humane Education Trust; Member, Institute of Advanced Motorists. Address: c/o Saraband Associates, 265 Liverpool Road, London N1 1LX, England.

STAČIOKAS Stasys, b. 25 August 1937, Alytus, Lithuania. Doctor of Social Sciences; Associate Professor; Judge. m. (1) Irena, 1959 deceased 2000, 2 sons, (2) m. Marija Nijolė, 2001. Education: Faculty of Law, Vilnius University. Appointments: Lecturer, Senior Lecturer, Associate Professor, Vice Dean, Faculty of Law, 1960-93; Director, Institute of Research in Forensic Examination, 1973-90; Judge, Constitutional Court of the Republic of Lithuania, 1993-96, 1999-; Chairman, Committee for Legal Affairs, 1996-99; Member, Committee for European Affairs, the Seimas of the Republic of Lithuania; Member, Committee on Legal Affairs and Human Rights of the Parliamentary Assembly of the Council of Europe; Participant, international scientific conferences in Lithuania, Norway, USA, Belgium, Portugal, Italy, Malta, Greece, Netherlands, Russia, Chile and others. Publications: Author, over 100 studies on constitutional, land law, law research and theory of law; Journal articles in Lithuania and abroad. Honour: Freedom Defenders' Commemorative Medal, 2003; Lithuanian Grand Duke Gediminas 3rd Degree Order Bearer; Participated in drafting Lithuanian Republic laws and constitution. Memberships: European Legislation Association; Lithuanian Lawyers Association. Address: L R Konstitucinis Teismas, Gedimino pr 36, LT-01104 Vilnius, Lithuania. E-mail: s.staciokas@lrkt.lt

STACK Steven, b. 20 December 1947, Providence, Rhode Island, USA. College Professor. 3 sons. Education: Assistant Professor of Sociology, Alma College, 1976-79; Assistant Professor of Sociology, Indiana University, 1979-81; Associate Professor of Sociology, Penn State University, 1981-85; Associate, Full Professor, Sociology, Auburn University, 1985-90; Full Professor of Criminal Justice, Wayne State University, 1990-. Publications include: 175 articles in professional journals; 33 book chapters; 249 papers read in professional meetings. Honours: Grant, National Institute of Mental Health; grants, Henry Frank Guggenheim Foundation; Edwin Shneidman Award, American Association of Suicidology; Louis Dublin Award, American Association of Suicidology; Donal McNamara Award, Academy of Criminal Justice Sciences, 2008. Memberships: American Association of Suicidology; American Sociological Association; National Council on Family Relations; American Society of Criminology; Academy of Criminal Justice Sciences. Address: Department of Criminal Justice, Wayne State University, Detroit, MI 48292, USA. E-mail: aa1051@wayne.edu

STADELMAN William Ralph, b. 18 July 1919, Ontario, Canada. Professional Engineer. m. Jean MacLaren, 1 daughter. Education: BASc, University of Toronto, 1941; MBA, Wharton School of Finance & Economics, University of Pennsylvania, 1949. Appointments: Chief Process Engineer, Canadian Synthetic Rubber Ltd, 1943-47; Lecturer, Marketing, University of Pennsylvania, 1948-49; Assistant to Manager, Pennsylvania Salt Manufacturing Co, 1950; Secretary-Treasurer, 1950-64, President, 1964-84, Ontario Research Foundation, Mississauga; President, WRS Associates, Toronto, 1984-; Director, Senior Executive, Institute of Chemical Science and Technology, 1985-89. Honours: Canada Medal, 1967. Memberships: Committee of Directors of Research Associations in Great Britain; Board of Trade of Metropolitan Toronto; Innovation Management Association of Canada; Club of Rome; Fellow, World Academy of Art and Science. Address: 1055 Don Mills Road, Ste 504, Toronto, ON M3C 1W8, Canada.

STAFFORD Francis Melfort William Fitzherbert (Lord), b. 13 March 1954, Rhynie, Scotland. Landowner. m. Katharine, 2 sons, 2 daughters. Education: Reading University, England; RAC, Cirencester, England. Appointments: Non Executive Director, Tarmac Industrial Products, 1985-94; Chair, Governor, Swynnerton School, 1986-; Non Executive Director, NHS Foundation Trust, 1990-99; Vice Chairman, Harper Adams University College, 1990-; Vice Chairman, Hanley Economic Building Society, 1993-; Pro Chancellor, Keele University, 1993-; Landowner. Honours: Deputy Lieutenant, 1994-; High Sheriff of Staffordshire, 2005. Memberships: Army and Navy Club; Lord's Taverners; Sunningdale Golf Club; Patron and President various organisations mainly in Staffordshire. Address: Swynnerton Park, Stone, Staffordshire, ST15 0QE, England. E-mail: ls@lordstafford.demon.co.uk

STAFFORD-CLARK Max, b. 17 March 1941. Theatre Director. m. (1) Carole Hayman, 1971, (2) Ann Pennington, 1981, 1 daughter. Education: Trinity College, Dublin. Appointments: Artistic Director, Traverse Theatre, Edinburgh, 1968-70; Director, Traverse Workshop Company, 1970-74; Artistic Director, Joint Stock, 1974-79; English Stage Company, Royal Court Theatre, 1979-93; Out of Joint, 1993-; Visiting Professor, Royal Holloway and Bedford College, University of London, 1993-94; Maisie Glass Professor, University of Sheffield, 1995-96; Visiting Professor, University of Hertfordshire, 1999-; Visiting Professor, University of York, 2003-; Principal Productions: Fanshen; Top Girls; Tom and Viv; Rat in the Skull; Serious Money; Our Country's Good; The Libertine; The Steward of Christendom; Shopping and Fucking; Blue Heart; Drummers; Some Explicit Polaroids; Rita, Sue and Bob Too/A State Affair; A Laughing Matter; The Permanent Way; Macbeth. Publication: Letters to George 1989; The Overwhelming, 2007. Honours: Hon Fellow, Rose Bruford College, 1996; Hon DLitt, Oxford Brookes, 2000; Hon DLitt, Hertfordshire, 2000; Special Award, Evening Standard Theatre Awards, 2004. Address: Out of Joint, 7 Thane Works, Thane Villas, London N7 7PH, England.

STAHL Alexander Hans Joachim, b. 27 April 1938, Netzschkau, Vogtland. Official. m. Bärbel Schultheis, 2 sons. Education: Diploma in Politics, Free University, Berlin, 1965. Appointments: Adviser in informal education for the young at the Arbeitskreis deutscher Bildungsstätten, Bonn, 1965-67; Lecturer, Political Education, Jugenhof Vlotho, 1967-69; Youth Officer, Land Youth Office Westfalen-Lippe, Landschaftsverband Westfalen-Lippe, 1972-; Deputy-in-Chief, board of film censors, (Freiwillige Selbstkontrolle der Filmwirtschaft) Wiesbaden, 1989-. Publications: Editor, journal: Mitteilungen des Landesjugendamtes Westfalen-Lippe, Landschaftsverband Westfalen-Lippe, Landeshaus Münster, 1969-; Honour: Councillor, Stadt Münster, 1975-79; Honorary Member, Bavarian Association of Youth Officers. Address: Von-Humboldt-Str 33, D48159 Münster, Germany.

STALLONE Sylvester Enzio, b. 6 July 1946, New York, USA. Actor; Film Director. m. (1) Sasha Czach, 1974, divorced, 2 sons, (2) Brigitte Nielsen, 1985, divorced 1987, (3) Jennifer Flavin, 1997, 3 Children. Education: American College of Switzerland; University of Miami. Appointments: Has had many jobs including: Usher; Bouncer; Horse Trainer; Store Detective; Physical Education Teacher; Now Actor, Producer, Director of own films; Founder, White Eagle Company; Director, Carolco Pictures Inc, 1987-; Film appearances include: Lords of Flatbush, 1973; Capone, 1974; Rocky, 1976; FIST, Paradise Alley, 1978; Rocky II, 1979; Nighthawks, Escape to Victory, 1980; Rocky III, 1981; First Blood; Rambo, 1984; Rocky IV, 1985; Cobra, Over the Top, Rambo II, 1986; Rambo III, 1988; Set Up, Tango and Cash, Rocky V, 1990; Isobar, Stop or My Mom Will Shot, Oscar, 1991; Cliffhanger, 1992; Demolition Man, 1993; Judge Dredd, The Specialist, 1994; Assassins, 1995; Firestorm, Daylight, 1996; Cop Land, 1997; An Alan Smithee Film: Burn Hollywood Burn, 1998; Get Carter, 2000; Driven, 2001; D-Tox, Avenging Angelo, 2002; Shade, Spy Kids 3-D: Game Over, 2003; Rocky Balboa, 2006; Rambo, 2008; Producer, Director, Staying Alive, 1983. Publications: Paradise Alley, 1977; The Rocky Scrapbook, 1997. Honours: Oscar for best film, 1976; Golden Circle Award for best film, 1976; Donatello Award, 1976; Christopher Religious Award, 1976; Honorary Member, Stuntmans' Association; Officier Ordre des Arts et des Lettres. Memberships: Screen Actors' Guild; Writers' Guild; Directors' Guild. Address: William Morris Agency, 151 El Camino Drive, Beverly Hills, CA 90212, USA.

STAMP Terence, b. 22 July 1938, London. Actor. m. Elizabeth O Rourke, 2002. Career: Theatre work before film debut in Billy Budd, 1962; Other films include: Term of Trial, 1962; The Collector, 1965; Modesty Blaise, 1966; Far From the Madding Crowd, Poor Cow, 1967; Blue, Theorem, Tales of Mystery, 1968; The Mind of Mr Soames, 1969; A Season in Hell, 1971; Hu-man, 1975; The Divine Creature, 1976; Striptease, 1977; Meetings With Remarkable Men, Superman, 1978; Superman II, 1979; Death in the Vatican, 1980; The Bloody Chamber, 1982; The Hit, 1984; Link, 1985; Legal Eagles, The Sicilian, 1986; Wall Street, Alien Nation, Young Guns, 1988; Prince of Shadows, 1991; The Real McCoy, 1992; The Adventures of Priscilla Queen of the Desert, 1994; Bliss, Limited Edition, 1995; Mindbender; Love Walked In, 1996; Kiss the Sky, 1997; The Limey, Bow Finger, 1999; Red Planet, 2000; My Wife is an Actress, 2002; My Boss's Daughter, 2003; The Haunted Mansion, Dead Fish, 2004; Elektra, 2005; September Dawn, These Foolish Things, 9/11: The Twin Towers, 2006 (voice); Get Smart, Wanted, Valkyrie, Yes Man, 2008; Theatre: Dracula; The Lady from the Sea. Publications: Stamp Album, Coming Attractions, 1988; Double Feature, 1989; The Night, 1992; Stamp Collection,

1997. Honours: Hon Dr of Arts, University of East London, 1993. Address: c/o Markham and Froggatt, 4 Windmill Street, London, W1P 1HF, England.

STANCHEVA Magdalina Mihailova, b. 8 September 1924, Sofia, Bulgaria. Archaeologist, Philologist. m. (1) Teophil Ivanov, divorced 1950, (2) Stancho Stanchev, divorced 1967. Has sons and daughters. Education: MA, Classical Philology, 1948. Appointments: Assistant Curator, Curator, Head of Archaeology, Scientific Researcher, Senior Scientific Researcher, Museum of Sofia's History, 1952-85; Part-time Assistant Professor in Museology, Academy of Fine Arts 1979-90, University of Sofia, 1979-, New Bulgarian University 1994; President, National Council of Cultural Monuments, Bulgarian Delegation to World Heritage Committee, 1979-91; Now retired. Publications: Bulgaria: Three Ancient Capitals, 1981; Archaeological Sites in Modern Bulgarian Towns, 1982; The Bulgarian Contribution to the World Heritage (ed), 1993; Nine Bulgarian Wonders, 1993; The Equestrian of Madara, 1996; Sofia in Times Far Back, 1999; Sofia from Antiquity to the End of the Middle Ages, Sofia from Antiquity to Modern Times, 1999; 150 scientific and 300 popular scientific articles. Honours: Order of Cyril and Methodius (First and Second Class); Austrian Order of Merit with Silver Cross; Bulgarian Silver Medal of Labour; Awarded two medals to celebrate 1300th Anniversary since the Founding of the Bulgarian State. Membership: International Red Cross Organisation, Union of the Scientific Workers of Bulgaria. Address: Mladost 1, bl. 5, vh. V, app. 55, 1784 Sofia, Bulgaria. E-mail: magdalinast@abv.bg

STANKIEWICZ Anna, b. 11 September 1958, Szczecinek, Poland. Educating Engineering. Education: PhD in Agricultural Engineering, Agricultural Academy, Lublin, Poland, 2007; MSc, Computer Science and Control Systems, Institute of Engineering Cybernetics, Technical University of Wroclaw, Poland. Appointments: Assistant in the Institute of Engineering Cybernetics, Technical University of Wroclaw, Poland, 1983-85; Assistant Professor, Technical University of Lublin, Department of Automation, Poland, 1988-94; Lecturer, Institute of Technical Sciences, Agricultural Academy of Lublin, Poland, 1996-; Assistant Professor, University of Life Sciences in Lublin, Department of Technical Sciences, 2007-. Publications: Over 45 articles and papers in specialist scientific journals. Honours: Award of the Polish Academy of Sciences, 1981, 1982; Award from the Rector of Wroclaw Technical University, 1985; 1986; Award of the Rectors of Polish Agricultural Universities, 2005; Award of the Rector of Agriculture University of Lublin, 2007; Award of the Rector of University of Life Sciences, Lublin, 2008. Listed in Who's Who publications and biographical dictionaries. Memberships: Institute of Electrical and Electronics Engineers, Control Systems Society, 1999-; Polish Society of Agrophysics, 2008-. Address: University of Life Sciences in Lublin, Department of Technical Sciences, Doswiadczalna 50A 20-282 Lublin, Poland. E-mail: anna.stankiewicz@ar.lublin.p

STAŃSKI Mieczysław, b. 7 November 1925, Osuchów, Poland. Historian. m. Maria, 1 daughter. Education: History, University of Wrocław; Archives studies, University of Toruń; MA, History, University of Poznań; PhD, History, Institute of History, PAN (Polish Academy of Science); World Health Organization Scholarship, 1970-71; Professor of Arts, 1996; Tutor and Promotor of 34 PhD papers by MDs. Appointments: State Archives, Poznań, Poland, 1958; Department of the History of Poland, PAN (Polish Academy of Science); Lecturer in Philosophy, Chair of the History of Medicine (Lecturer), Head, Department of Philosophy, 1959-72, Chair of Social Studies (Head), University of Medical Sciences, Poznań, 1972-96; Professor Emeritus, 1996-. Publications: 57 monographs and studies; 34 research papers and reports; 4 handbooks; 5 compilations of bibliographies or materials; 30 reviews; 52 biographical entries in dictionaries and encyclopaedias. Honours: Individual award for special achievements in research on humanistic approach in medicine, Polish Ministry of Health and Welfare; Individual awards for special achievements in research and teaching. Memberships: Polish Society of the History of Medicine; Poznań Society of the Science Friends, Committee of the History and Philosophy of Medicine; Institute of the Philosophy and Sociology of Medicine, Polish Academy of Science, Section of the Sociology of Medicine. E-mail: estansk@am.poznan.pl

STAPLETON Katharine H, b. 29 October 1919, Kansas City, Missouri, USA. Retired Food Journalist; Philanthropist. 2 sons, 1 daughter. Education: Barstow School for Girls, Kansas City; Vassar College, AB, Poughkeepsie, New York. Appointments: Retired Food Journalist; Live radio broadcasts, CBS-KOA radio, 15 years; Involved in local, national and international charities for over 60 years; Lone woman (among 16) on board to celebrate Colorado Centennial. Honours: Etoile Noire, French Government; Founder and First Chairman, Denver Debutante Ball, 1959; Girl Scout Award, 2007. Memberships: Denver Country Club; Commandeur, Chevalier du Tastevin; Christ Episcopal Church, Denver. Address: Eight Village Road, Cherry Hills Village, Colorado 80113, USA.

STARK Ian David, b. 22 February 1954, Galashiels, Scotland. Equestrian. m. Jenny, 1 son, 1 daughter. Education: Galashiels Academy. Career: 4 Olympic Silver Medals, 1984, 1988, 1992, 1996, 2000; 3 times winner, Badminton, 1986, 1988, 1999; Team Gold, World Championships, 1986; 6 team Gold Medals, European Championships; Individual Gold Medal, European Championships, 1991. Publications: Flying Scot, 1988; Glenburnie & Murphy Himself, 1992; Stark Approach, 1998; Walking a Cross Country Course, 1999; Stark Reality, 2000. Honours: MBE, 1989; OBE, 2001; Fellow, British Horse Society, 2005. Memberships: British Horse Society; British Eventing; British Show Jumping Association. Address: Haughhead, Ashkirk, Selkirk, TD7 4NS, Scotland. E-mail: haughhead@yahoo.co.uk

STARKEY Lawrence Harry, b. 10 July 1919, Minneapolis, Minnesota, USA. Synoptic Philosopher. m. (1) 1 son, 2 daughters, (2) Hallie Jean Hughes. Education: BA, honours, University of Louisville, 1942; MDiv, Southern Baptist Theological Seminary, 1945; MA, 1951, PhD, 1960, University of Southern California. Appointments: Engineering Draftsman, Electromotive Division, General Motors, 1937-39; Instructor, Assistant Professor, Registrar, Los Angeles Baptist College and Seminary, 1945-51; Science Film Writer, Moody Institute of Science, 1955-57; Associate Professor, Bethel College, St Paul, 1958-62; Associate Professor, Department Chair, Linfield College, 1962-63; Engineering Writer, Convair Division, General Dynamics, 1963-66; Associate Professor, Alma College, 1966-68; Associate Editor, Principal Editor, Philosophy, Encyclopaedia Britannica, 1968-72; Associate Professor, Department Chair, Jamestown College, 1973-75; Part-time Lecturer, Program Co-ordinator, Television Producer, North Dakota State University, 1976-79; Draftsman, Machine Designer, Concord Inc, North Dakota, 1977-85; Instructor, Moorhead State University, 1985-86; Lecturer, University of Missouri, Rolla, 1986-88; Adjunct Instructor, Marian College, 2005. Publications: Red River of Life (film); Several articles in professional journals, a children's encyclopaedia, the World Congress of Philosophy

Web Site, in Abstracts of the Particles Conference, Sweden, in The Vorträge of the Leibniz-Kongress, Germany. Honours: Speed Junior Scholarship; University Graduate Scholarship; Citizen Ambassador to Russia, Hungary. Memberships include: American Philosophical Association; Section President, American Scientific Affiliation, 1954, 1970, 1971; Metaphysical Society of America. Address: 2312 North 71st Street, Apt 2, Wauwatosa, WI 53213, USA.

STARR Kenneth Winston, b. 21 July 1946, Vernon, Texas, USA. Lawyer. m. Alice J Mendell, 1970, 1 son, 2 daughters. Education: George Washington University; Brown University; Duke University. Appointments: Law Clerk, Court of Appeals, Miami, 1973-74; Supreme Court, 1975-77; Associate, Gibson, Dunn and Crutcher, Los Angeles, 1974-75; Associate Partner, 1977-81; Counsellor to Attorney General, Justice Department, Washington, DC, 1981-83; Solicitor General, 1989-93; Judge, Court of Appeals, 1983; Partner, Kirkland and Ellis, Washington, DC, 1993-94; Independent Counsel for Whitewater Investigations as well as any collateral matters arising out of any investigation of such matters including obstruction of justice or false statements, 1994-; Professor and Dean, Pepperdine University School of Law, 2004-. Publications: Contributor, articles to legal journals. Memberships: Several law organisations. Address: Pepperdine University School of Law, 24255 Pacific Coast Highway, Malibu, CA 90263, USA. Website: www.law.pepperdine.edu

STARR Ringo (Richard Starkey), b. 7 July 1940, Dingle, Liverpool, England. Musician. m. (1) Maureen Cox, 1965, divorced, 2 sons, 1 daughter, (2) Barbara Bach, 1981. Career: Member, Rory Storm and The Hurricanes; Member, The Beatles, 1962-70; Worldwide tours, 1963-; Attended Transcendental Meditation Course, Maharishi's Academy, Rishkesh, India, 1968; Co-Founder, Apple Corps Ltd, 1968; Solo Artiste, 1969-; Narrator, Thomas The Tank Engine, (children's TV). Creative Works: Recordings by the Beatles include: Please, Please Me, 1963; With the Beatles, 1963; A Hard Day's Night, 1964; Beatles for Sale, 1965; Help!, 1965; Rubber Soul, 1966; Revolver, 1966; Sergeant Pepper's Lonely Hearts Club Band, 1967; The Beatles (White Album), 1968; Yellow Submarine, 1969; Abbey Road, 1969; Let it Be, 1970; Films by the Beatles: A Hard Day's Night, 1964; Help! 1965; Yellow Submarine (animated colour cartoon film), 1968; Let it Be, 1970; Solo: Sentimental Journey, 1969; Beaucoups of Blues, 1970; Ringo, 1973; Goodnight Vienna, 1974; Blasts From Your Past, 1975; Ringo's Rotogravure, 1976; Ringo the 4th, 1977; Bad Boy, 1977; Stop and Smell the Roses, 1981; Old Wave, 1983; All-Starr Band, 1990; Time Takes Time, 1992; Live From Montreaux, 1994; Vertical Man, 1998; I Wanna Be Santa Clause, 1999; Ringo Starr & His All-Star Band: The Anthology, 2001; King Biscuit Flower Hour, 2002; Ringorama, 2003; Anthology ... So Far, 2004; Choose Love, 2005; Individual appearance in films: Candy, 1968; The Magic Christian, 1969; 200 Motels, 1971; Blindman, 1971; That'll Be the Day, 1973; Born to Boogie (also directed and produced), 1974; Son of Dracula (also produced), 1975; Lisztomania, 1975; Ringo Stars, 1976; Caveman, 1981; The Cooler, 1982; Give My Regards to Broad Street, 1984. Honours: BPI Awards; Rock'n'Roll Hall of Fame, 1988; Percussive Hall of Fame, 2002. Address: Primary Talent International, Fifth Floor, 2-12 Pentonville Road, London N1 9PL, England. Website: www.ringostarranthology.com

STARY Frank E, b. 3 January 1941, St Paul, Minnesota, USA. Professor. m. Education: BChem, University of Minnesota, 1963; PhD, Inorganic Chemistry, University of Cincinnati, 1969; Appointments: Undergraduate Research,

University of Minnesota, 1960-63; Graduate Research, University of Cincinnati, 1964-68; Postdoctoral Research, University of California Irvine, 1968-72; Research Associate, University of Missouri-St Louis, 1972-74; Assistant Professor, Professor, Maryville University-St Louis, Missouri, 1974-. Publications: 15 articles. Honours: Distinguished Teaching Award, 1981. Memberships: American Chemical Society; Phi Lambda Upsilon, Sigma Xi. Address: Maryville University, 650 Maryville University Drive, St Louis, MO 63141-7299, USA. E-mail: fstary@maryville.edu

STAUNTON Imelda Mary Philomena Bernadette, b. 9 January 1956. Actress. m. Jim Carter, 1983, 1 daughter. Appointments: Repertory Exeter, Nottingham, York, 1976-81; Stage appearances include: Guys and Dolls, 1982, 1996; Beggar's Opera, She Stoops to Conquer; Chorus of Disapproval, The Corn is Green, 1985; Fair Maid of the West, Wizard of Oz, 1986; Comrades, 1987; Uncle Vanya, 1988; Into the Woods, Phoenix, 1990; Life x 3, 2000; TV appearances include: The Singing Detective, 1986; Yellowbacks, Sleeping Life, Roots, Up the Garden Path, 1990; Antonia and Jane; David Copperfield, 1999; Victoria Wood Xmas Special, 2000; Murder, 2001; Cambridge Spies, Strange, 2002; Film appearances include: Peter's Friends, 1992; Much Ado About Nothing, 1993; Deadly Advice, 1994; Sense and Sensibility; Twelfth Night; Remember Me, 1996; Shakespeare in Love, 1998; Another Life, Rat, 1999; Crush, 2000; Bright Young Things, Virgin of Liverpool, Blackball, Family Business, 2002; Vera Drake, 2004; Nanny McPhee, 3 & 3, 2005; Freedom Writers, How About You, Harry Potter and the Order of the Phoenix, Where Have I Been All Your Life, 2007; Three and Out, 2008. Honours: Oliver Award, Best Supporting Actress, 1985; Oliver Award, Best Actress in a Musical, 1990; Best Performance by an Actress, British Industry Film Awards, 2005; Best Actress, European Film Awards, 2005; Los Angeles Film Critics' Association, 2005; New York Film Critics' Circle, 2005; Evening Standard British Film Awards, 2005; Best Actress in a Leading Role, BAFTA Awards, 2005; OBE, 2006. Address: c/o ARG, 4 Great Portland Street, London W1W 4PA, England.

STAVANS Ilan, b. 7 April 1961, Mexico. Critic; Writer; Professor. m. Alison Sparks, 1988, 2 sons. Education: BA, Universidad Autónoma Metropolitana, 1984; MA, The Jewish Theological Seminary, 1987; MA, 1988, MPhil, 1989, PhD, 1990, Columbia University. Appointments: Series Editor, Jewish-Latin America; Series Editor, Latino Voices; Lewis-Sebring Professor in Latin American and Latino Culture, Amherst College, Department of Spanish, 1993-; 5-College 40th Anniversary Professor, 2005-2008; Research Fellow, Institute of Latin American Studies, University of London, 1998-99; Host of television show La Plaza: Conversations with Ilan Stavans, 2001-. Publications include: The Hispanic Condition; Art and Anger; The Riddle of Cantinflas; The One-handed Pianist; Mutual Impressions; The Oxford Book of Jewish Stories; The Essential Ilan Stavans; Latino USA: A Cartoon History; The Inveterate Dreamer: Essays and Conversations on Jewish Literature; On Borrowed Words: A Memoir of Language; The Schocken Book of Modern Sephardic Literature. Octavio Paz: A Meditation; The Poetry of Pablo Neruda; Spanglish: The Making of a New American Language; Isaac Barhevis Singer: Collected Stories (3 vols), Encyclopedia Latina (4 vols), Dictionary Days; Ruben Dario: Selected Writings; Conversations with Ilan Stavans; Collins Q&A: Latino History and Culture; I Explain a Few Things; Love and Language; An Organizer's Tale; The Disappearance. Honours include: National Endowment for the Humanities, 1991-92; Latino Literature Prize, 1992; Bernard M Baruch

Excellence in Scholarship Award, 1993; Nomination to the Nona Balakian Excellence in Reviewing Award, National Book Critics Circle, 1994; Guggenheim Fellowship, 1998-99; Chile's Presidential Medal; Emmy Nomination; Antonia Pantoja Award; Latino Hall of Fame, 2001; Commonwealth Humanities Scholar, 2005; National Jewish Book Award, 2005; Latino Prize, 2006; Latino Health Institute Award, 2007. Address: Department of Spanish, Amherst College, Amherst, MA 01002, USA.

STEAD C(hristian) K(arlson), b. 17 October 1932, Auckland, New Zealand. Poet; Writer; Critic; Editor; Professor of English Emeritus. m. Kathleen Elizabeth Roberts, 8 January 1955, 1 son, 2 daughters. Education: BA, 1954, MA, 1955, University of New Zealand; PhD, University of Bristol, 1961; DLitt, University of Auckland, 1982. Appointments: Lecturer in English, University of New England, Australia, 1956-57; Lecturer, 1960-61, Senior Lecturer, 1962-64, Associate Professor, 1964-67, Professor of English, 1967-86, Professor Emeritus, 1986-, University of Auckland; Chairman, New Zealand Literary Fund Advisory Committee, 1972-75, New Zealand Authors' Fund Committee, 1989-91. Publications: Poetry: Whether the Will is Free, 1964; Crossing the Bar, 1972; Quesada: Poems 1972-74, 1975; Walking Westward, 1979; Geographies, 1982; Poems of a Decade, 1983; Paris, 1984; Between, 1988; Voices, 1990; Straw Into Gold: Poems New and Selected, 1997; The Right Thing, 2000; Dog: Poems, 2002; The Red Tram, 2004. Fiction: Smith's Dream, 1971; Five for the Symbol, 1981; All Visitors Ashore, 1984; The Death of the Body, 1986; Sister Hollywood, 1989; The End of the Century at the End of the World, 1992; The Singing Whakapapa, 1994; Villa Vittoria, 1997; The Blind Blonde with Candles in her Hair (stories), 1998; Talking about O'Dwyer, 2000; The Secret History of Modernism, 2002; Mansfield, 2004; Non-fiction: The New Poetic: Yeats to Eliot, 1964, revised, 1987, 2005; In the Glass Case: Essays on New Zealand Literature, 1981; Pound, Yeats, Eliot and the Modernist Movement, 1986; Answering to the Language: Essays on Modern Writers, 1990; The Writer at Work, 2000; Kin of Place: Essays on Twenty New Zealand Writers, 2002; Mansfield, 2004; My Name Was Judas, 2006; The Black River, 2007. Editor: World's Classics: New Zealand Short Stories, 1966, 2nd edition, 1975; Measure for Measure: A Casebook, 1971, revised edition, 1973; Letters and Journals of Katherine Mansfield, 1977, 2004; Collected Stories of Maurice Duggan, 1981; The New Gramophone Room: Poetry and Fiction (with Elizabeth Smither and Kendrick Smithyman), 1985; The Faber Book of Contemporary South Pacific Stories, 1994; Werner Forman, New Zealand, 1994. Contributions to: Poetry, fiction and criticism to various anthologies and periodicals. Honours: Katherine Mansfield Prize, 1960; Nuffield Travelling Fellowship, 1965; Katherine Mansfield Menton Fellowship, 1972; Jessie Mackay Award for Poetry, 1972; New Zealand Book Award for Poetry, 1975; Honorary Research Fellow, University College, London, 1977; Commander of the Order of the British Empire, 1984; New Zealand Book Award for Fiction, 1985 and 1995; Queen Elizabeth II Arts Council Scholarship in Letters, 1988-89; Queen's Medal for services to New Zealand literature, 1990; Fellow, Royal Society of Literature, 1995; Senior Visiting Fellow, St John's College, Oxford, 1996-97; Hon DLitt, University of Bristol, 2001; Fellow, English Association, 2004; Order of New Zealand, 2007. Membership: New Zealand PEN, chairman, Auckland branch, 1986-89, national vice president, 1988-90. Address: 37 Tohunga Crescent, Auckland 1, New Zealand.

STEADMAN Alison, b. 26 August 1946, Liverpool, England. Actress. m. Mike Leigh, divorced 2002, 2 sons. Education: Drama School, Loughton, Essex. Appointments: Began career in repertory theatre, Lincoln, Bolton, Liverpool Worcester and Nottingham; Stage appearances include: Sandy in the Prime of Miss Jean Brodie; Beverley in Abigail's Party; Mae-Sister Woman in Cat on a Hot Tin Roof, National Theatre; Mari Hoff in The Rise and Fall of Little Voice; David Edgar's Maydays, Royal Shakespeare Company, Joking Apart; Kafka's Dick, Royal Court; Marvin's Room, 1993; The Plotters of Cabbage Patch Corner; The Provoked Wife, 1997; When We Are Married; The Memory of Water; Entertaining Mr Sloane; The Woman Who Cooked Her Husband; Radio: Cousin Bette; TV Appearances: Z Cars; Hard Labour; Abigail's Party; Nuts in May; The Singing Detective; Virtuoso; Newshounds; The Short and Curlies; Gone to Seed; Selling Hitler; Pride and Prejudice; The Wimbledon Poisoner; Karaoke; No Bananas; The Missing Postman; Let Them Eat Cake; Fat Friends; Adrian Mole: The Cappuccino Years; Dalziel and Pascoe; Fat Friends (series 3); The Worst Week of My Life; Bosom Pals; Gavin & Stacey. Films: Champions; Wilt; Shirley Valentine; Life is Sweet; Blame it on the Bellboy; Topsy Turvy; Happy Now; Chunky Monkey; DIY Hard; The Life and Death of Peter Sellers; The Housewife; Confetti; Dead Rich, 2006. Honours: Honorary MA, University of East London; Evening Standard Best Actress Award, 1977; Olivier Award for Best Actress, 1993; Dr hc (Essex), 2003. Address: PFD, Drury House, 34-43 Russell Street, London WC2B 5HA, England.

STEEL Danielle, b. 14 August 1947, New York, USA. Writer. m. (2) Bill Toth, 1977; (3) John A Traina Jr, 1981-1996, 5 children (4) Thomas J Perkins, 1998, separated. Education: Lycee Francais; Parsons School of Design, New York; University of New York. Appointments: Public Relations and, Advertising Executive, Manhattan, New York; Published first novel, 1973, then wrote advertising copy and poems for women's magazines; Wrote first bestseller, The Promise, 1979. Publications: Going Home, 1973; Passion's Promise, 1977; Now and Forever, Seasons of Passion, 1978; The Promise, 1979; Summer's End, 1980; The Love Again, Palomino, Loving, Rememberance, 1981; A Perfect Stranger, Once in a Lifetime, Crossings, 1982; Thurston House, 1983; Full Circle, Having a Baby, 1984; Family Album, 1985; Wanderlust, 1986; Fine Things, Kaleidoscope, 1987; Zoya, 1988; Star, Daddy, 1989; Heartbeat, Message from Nam, No Greater Love, 1991; Jewels, Mixed Blessings, 1992; Vanished, 1993; Accident, The Gift, 1994; Wings, Lightning, Five Days in Paris, Malice, 1995; Silent Honor, The Ranch, 1996; The Ghost, Special Delivery, 1997; The Ranch, The Long Road Home, The Klone and I, Mirror Image, 1998; Bittersweet, 1999; The Wedding, The House on Hope Street, Journey, 2000; Lone Eagle, 2001; Answered Prayers, 2002; Dating Game, Johnny Angel, Safe Harbour, 2003; Ransom, Second Chance, Echoes, 2004; Impossible, Miracle, Toxic Bachelors, 2005; The House, Coming Out, H.R.H. 2006; Sisters, Amazing Grace, 2007; Honour Thyself, 2008; Bungalow Two, 2008; Rogue, 2008. Eight Children's Books; One Book of Poetry. Address: c/o Dell Publishing, 1745 Broadway, New York, NY 10019, USA.

STEEL OF AIKWOOD David Martin Scott Steel (Baron) (Life Peer), b. 31 March 1938, Kirkcaldy, Scotland. Politician; Journalist; Broadcaster. m. Judith Mary MacGregor, 1962, 2 sons, 1 daughter. Education: Prince of Wales School, Nairobi, Kenya; George Watson's College; Edinburgh University. Appointments: President, Edinburgh University, Liberals, 1959; Member, Students Representative Council, 1960; Assistant Secretary, Scottish Liberal Party, 1962-64; Member of Parliament for Roxburgh, Selkirk and Peebles, 1965-83; for Tweeddale, Ettrick and Lauderdale, 1983-97; Scottish Liberal Whip, 1967-70; Liberal Chief Whip, 1970-75; Leader, Liberal Party, 1976-88; Co-Founder Social and Liberal Democrats, 1988; President, Liberal International, 1994-96; Member of Parliament delegate to UN General Assembly, 1967; Former Liberal Spokesman on Commonwealth Affairs: Sponsor, Private Member's Bill to Reform law on abortion, 1966-67; President, Anti-Apartheid Movement of UK, 1966-69; Chair, Shelter, Scotland, 1969-73; Countryside Movement, 1995-97; BBC TV Interviewer in Scotland, 1964-65; Presenter of Weekly Religious Programmes for Scottish TV, 1966-67; for Granada, 1969; for BBC, 1971-76; Director, Border TV, 1991-98; Rector, University of Edinburgh, 1982-85; Chubb Fellow, Yale University, USA, 1987; D L Ettrick and Lauderdale and Roxburghshire. Publications: Boost for the Borders, 1964; No Entry, 1969; A House Divided, 1980; Border Country, 1985; Partners in One Nation, 1985; The Time Has Come, 1987; Mary Stuart's Scotland, 1987; Against Goliath, autobiography, 1989. Honours: Freedom of Tweeddale, 1989; KBE, 1990; Ettrick and Lauderdale, 1990; Hon Dr, Stirling, 1991; German Grand Cross, 1992; Hon D Litt: Buckinghamshire, 1994, Heriot Watt, 1996; Hon LLD: Edinburgh, 1997, Strathclyde, 2000, Aberdeen, 2001; Bronze Medal, London-Cape Town Rally, 1998; D Univ, Open University, 2001; LL D (St Andrews) 2003, (Glasgow Caledonian) 2004; Legion d'Honneur, 2003; KT, 2004; LL D, Glasgow-Caledonian, 2004. Address: House of Lords, London, SW1A 0PW, England.

STEELE Tommy (Thomas Hicks), b. 17 December 1936, Bermondsey, London, England. Actor; Singer. m. Ann Donoghue, 1960, 1 daughter. Career: First stage appearance, Empire Theatre, Sunderland, 1956; First London appearance, Dominion Theatre, 1957; Major roles include: Buttons, Rodgers and Hammerstein's Cinderella, 1958; Tony Lumpkin, She Stoops To Conquer, 1960; Arthur Kipps, Half A Sixpence, 1963-64; The Same, 1965; Truffaldino, The Servant Of Two Masters, Queen's, 1969; Dick Whittington, 1969; Meet Me In London, 1971; Jack Point, The Yeoman Of The Guard, City Of London Festival, 1978; The Tommy Steele Show, 1973; Hans Andersen, 1974, 1977; One-man show, Prince of Wales, 1979; Singing In The Rain (also director), 1983; Some Like It Hot, 1992; What A Show, 1995; Tommy Steele in Concert, 1998; Scrooge, 2003-04; Film appearances: Kill Me Tomorrow, 1956; The Tommy Steele Story; The Duke Wore Jeans; Tommy The Toreador; Light Up The Sky; It's All Happening; The Happiest Millionaire; Half A Sixpence; Finian's Rainbow; Where's Jack?; Television: Writer, actor, Quincy's Quest, 1979. Compositions: Composed, recorded, My Life My Song, 1974; A Portrait Of Pablo, 1985. Publications: Quincy, 1981; The Final Run, 1983; Rock Suite - An Elderly Person's Guide To Rock, 1987. Honour: OBE, 1979. Address: Laurie Mansfield, International Artistes, 4th Floor, 193-197 High Holborn, London WC1V 7BD, England.

STEENBURGEN Mary, b. 8 February 1953, Newport, Arizona, USA. Film Actress. m. (1) Malcolm McDowell, 1980, divorced, 1 son, 1 daughter, (2) Ted Danson, 1995. Education: Neighborhood Playhouse. Appointments: Films include: Goin' South, 1978; Time After Time, 1979; Melvin and Howard, 1980; Ragtime, 1981; A Midsummers Night's Sex Comedy, 1982; Romantic Comedy, Cross Creek, 1983; Sanford Meidner - Theatre's Best Kept Secret, 1984; One Magic Christmas, 1985; Dead of Winter, End of the Line, The Whales of August, 1987; The Attic: The Hiding of Anne Frank, 1988; Parenthood, Back to the Future Part III, Miss Firecracker, 1989; The Long Walk Home, 1990; The Butcher's Wife, 1991; What's Eating Gilbert Grape, Philadelphia, 1993; Pontiac Moon, Clifford, It Runs in the Family, 1994; Pontiac Moon; My Family; Powder; The Grass Harp; Nixon; Gulliver's Travels, 1996; About Sarah, 1998; Trumpet of the Swan, Nobody's Baby, I Am Sam, Life as a House, The Trumpet of the Swan (voice), 2001; Sunshine State, Wish You Were Dead, 2002; Hope Springs, Casa de los babys, Elf, 2003; Marilyn Hotchkiss' Ballroom Dancing and Charm School, 2005; Inland Empire, The Dead Girl, 2006; Elvis and Anabelle, Nobel Son, Numb, The Brave One, Honeydipper, 2007; In the Electric Mist, Step Brothers, Four Christmases, 2008. Theatre appearances include: Holiday, 1987; Candida, 1993. Address: c/o Ames Cushing, William Morris Agency Inc, 151 El Camino Drive, Beverly Hills, CA 90212, USA.

STEIN Peter Gonville, b. 29 May 1926, Liverpool, England. Professor of Law; Writer. m. (1) Divorced, 3 daughters, (2) Anne M Howard, 1978. Education: BA, 1949, LLB, 1950, Gonville and Caius College, Cambridge; Admitted as Solicitor, 1951; University of Pavia, 1951-52. Appointments: Professor of Jurisprudence, University of Aberdeen, 1956-68; Regius Professor of Civil Law, University of Cambridge, 1968-93. Publications: Regulae Iuris: From Juristic Rules to Legal Maxims, 1966; Legal Values in Western Society (with J Shand), 1974; Legal Evolution: The Story of an Idea, 1980; Legal Institutions: The Development of Dispute Settlement, 1984; The Character and Influence of the Roman Civil Law, 1988; The Teaching of Roman Law in England Around 1200 (with F de Zulueta), 1990; Roman Law in European History (translated into 6 languages), 1999. Contributions to: Professional journals. Honours: Honorary Dr Iuris, University of Göttingen, 1980; Honorary Dott Giur, University of Ferrara, 1991; Honorary QC, 1993; Honorary Fellow, Gonville and Caius College, 1999; Honorary LLD, University of Aberdeen, 2000; Hon Dr, University of Perugia, 2001; Hon Dr, University of Paris II, 2001. Memberships: British Academy, fellow; Belgian National Academy; Italian National Academy, foreign fellow; Selden Society, vice-president, 1984-87; Society of Public Teachers of Law, president, 1980-81. Address: Queens' College, Cambridge CB3 9ET, England.

STEIN Robert A, b. 5 August 1933, Duluth, Minnesota, USA. Writer; Educator. m. Betty L Pavlik, 1955, 3 sons. Education: BSc, Industrial Management, 1956, University of Iowa; US Air Force Squadron Officers' School, 1960; US Air Force Command and Staff College, 1966; Air Force Academic Instructor School, with Honors, 1966; Permanent Professional Counselling/Teaching Certificate, Iowa Board of Public Instruction, 1968; MA, Counselling/Education, 1968; Industrial College of the Armed Forces, with Honors, 1973; MA, Writing, 1986. Appointments: Officer and Pilot, USAF, 1956-77, Retired as Colonel; Assistant Professor of Aerospace Studies, 1964-66, University of Iowa; Associate Professor, 1966-68; Professor, 1975-77; Member, Faculty Division of Writing, Kirkwood Community College, Iowa City and Cedar Rapids, Iowa, 1984-89; Instructor, Creative Writing Program, Iowa City/Johnson County Senior Center, 1994-. Publications: Novels: Apollyon: A Novel, 1985; The Chase, 1988; The Black Samaritan, 1997, 2nd edition, 2000; The Vengeance Equation, 2000, 2nd edition, 2001, Screenplay, 2001; Fiction: Death Defied, 1988; Non-Fiction: Statistical Correlations, 1967; Engineers Vs. Other Students: Is There A Difference?, 1967; WhatEVER Happened to Moe Bushkin?, 1967; Quest for Viability: One Way!, 1976; Threat of Emergency, 1988. Honours: 5 Wartime Decorations, 9 Merit Awards; All-American Swimming, 1950; Outstanding Faculty Award, University of Iowa, 1967-68; Iowa Authors' Collection, 1985; Minnesota Authors' Collection, 1987;

International Literary Award, 1988; Lifetime Achievement Award, University of Iowa, 1999; Entered in Iowa Athletics Hall of Fame, 2002; Listed in Who's Who publications and biographical dictionaries. Memberships: The Authors Guild; The Authors League of America; Alumni Association, University of Iowa; Presidents Club, University of Iowa; Daedalians; Air Force Association; Rotary International, Paul Harris Fellow; National "I" Lettermen's Club, Past President, 1978-79; National Iowa Varsity Club Hall of Fame; National Iowa Varsity (Letterwinners) Club, National Board of Directors, 1998-2005, 2006-09, Past President 2002-03.

STEINBACH Manfred, b. 4 May 1937, Dessau (Anhalt), Germany. Engineer. m. Helga Steinbach, 1 son, 3 daughters. Education: Dipl.-Ing. (Academically Qualified Engineer), 1960; Dr.-Ing.(Doctor of Engineering Science), 1965. Appointments: Scientific Assistant, Technical University Ilmenau, Thuringia, 1959-61; Scientific Associate, Carl Zeiss Jena Factory, 1961-88; Design Engineer, Krupp Factory, Duisburg, 1989-90; Professor for Engineering Design and Precision Mechanics, University for Applied Sciences Lübeck, 1990-2000; Owner of a designing firm for precision mechanics and instruments, 1997-. Publications: Approximately 100 on precision instruments, engineering design and accurate length measurement; Most recent articles in: Jenaer Jahrbuch zur Technik und Industriegeschichte. Honours: German National Award, 1967, 1979; Membership: Chairman, Association for Technical History. Address: Wildenbruchstrasse 15, D-07745 Jena, Germany. E-mail: stb@ingenieurbuero-steinbach.de

STENGAARD Erik, b. 18 June 1947, Skive, Denmark. Headmaster. m. Sonja Stengaard, 1 daughter. Education: Cand mag (Master's Degree), History and English, Copenhagen University, 1975. Appointments: Teacher, Rosborg Gymnasium and HF, 1975-84; Vice-President, Member of Executive Committee, in charge of salary negotiations and educational affairs, Trade Union for Danish Teachers at Upper Secondary Level (GL), 1979-84; Headmaster, Haslev Gymnasium and HF, Upper Secondary School, Grammar, Sixth Form, 1985-86, 1988-; President, Trade Union Centre for the Academic Professions in Denmark (AC), 1986-87; Chairman, Educational Committee within Radical Left Party in Denmark (liberal-social), 1989-2004. Publications: Co-author, History of Haslev Gymnasium, 1989; The Mural Paintings of Queen Agnes in the Church of Sct Bendts, 1995; A Fair Salary Policy, contribution to the History of The Trade Union Centre for the Academic Professions in Denmark, 1997. Honour: Knight of the Order of Dannebrog. Membership: The Sandbjerg Group of Danish Headmasters Address: Tofteagervej 20, DK 4690 Haslev, Denmark. E-mail: erik.stengaard@stofanet.dk

STEPHENS Jack, b. 1 December 1936, Huntington Park, California, USA. Writer; Photographer. m. Kristi Kellogg Stephens. Education: BA, Journalism, Washington State University, 1962. Appointments: Editor-Reporter, Ferndale Record, 1961; Reporter Maui News, 1963-67; Reporter, Pacific Business News, 1969-72; Journalism Instructor, Maunaolu College, 1967-73; Owner, Aquarius Enterprises, 1968-. Publications: Contributions to a variety of magazines. Honours: Bay League Long Jump Champion, 1953-54; Southern California Long Jump Champion, 1954; Martin Relays Long Jump Champion, 1960. Memberships: Society of Professional Journalists, 1959-; Maui's Maunaolu College Journalism Instructor and Publications Director, 1967-73. Address: 3-3400 Kuhio Highway A-103, Lihue, HI 96766-1051, USA.

STEPHENS William Peter, b. 16 May 1934, Penzance, Cornwall, England. Methodist Minister; Professor of Church History (Emeritus). Education: Clare College, Cambridge, 1952-57; Wesley House, Cambridge, 1955-57; University of Lund, Sweden, 1957-58; Universities of Strasbourg, France and Münster, Germany, 1965-67; MA BD (Cantab) Docteur ès Sciences Religieuses (Strasbourg). Appointments: Assistant Tutor, Hartley Victoria College, Manchester, 1958-61; Ordained as Methodist Minister, 1960; Minister and University Chaplain, Nottingham West Circuit, 1961-65; Minister, Croydon (South Norwood) Circuit, 1967-71; Ranmoor Chair of Church History, Hartley Victoria College, Manchester, 1971-73; Randles Chair of Historical and Systematic Theology, Wesley College, Bristol, 1973-80; Research Fellow, 1980-81, Lecturer, Church History, 1981-86, The Queen's College, Birmingham; Professor, Church History, 1986-99, Dean, 1987-89, Provost, 1989-90, Faculty of Divinity, University of Aberdeen; President, Methodist Conference, 1998-99; Superintendent Minister, Plymouth Methodist Mission Circuit, 1999-2000; Minister of the Mint, Exeter and Methodist Chaplain, University of Exeter, 2000-02; Superintendent Minister, Liskeard and Looe Circuit, 2002-03; Chairman and General Superintendent, Methodist Church, The Gambia, 2003-04; Minister, Mid-Sussex Circuit, 2004-06; Minister, Camborne Circuit, 2006-. Publications: Books, papers and articles in professional and popular press. Honours: Max Geilinger Prize, 1997; Visiting Professor, University of Exeter, 2001-04; Honorary Research Fellow, University of Exeter, 2004-. Address: Trewavas House, Polwithen Road, Penzance, Cornwall TR18 4JS, England.

STEPHENSON Timothy Congreve, b. 7 March 1940, London, England. Executive Search Consultant. m. Diana-Margaret Soltmann, 5 sons, 2 daughters. Education: Harrow; London Business School. Appointments: Regular Commission, Welsh Guards, 1958-65; Gallaher Ltd, 1965-76; Managing Director, Grafton Ltd, 1980-86; Managing Director, Stephenson Cobbold Ltd, 1987-95; Chairman, Stephenson and Co, 1996-. Memberships: Clubs: Brooks's; Beefsteak; Pratts; City of London; MCC. E-mail: tcs@stephensonandco.com

STEVEN Stewart Gustav, b. 30 October 1935, Hamburg, Germany. Journalist. m. Inka Sobieniewska, 1 son. Education: Mayfield College, Sussex. Appointments: Political Reporter, Central Press Features, 1961-63; Political Correspondent, Western Daily Press, 1963-64; Political Reporter, 1964-65, Diplomatic Correspondent, 1965-67, Foreign Editor, 1967-72, Daily Express; Assistant Editor, 1972-74, Associate Editor, 1974-82, Daily Mail; Editor, 1982-92, Columnist, 1996-, Mail on Sunday; Director, Associated Newspapers Holdings Ltd, 1989-95; Editor, Evening Standard, 1992-95. Publications: Operation Splinter Factor, 1974; The Spymasters of Israel, 1976; The Poles, 1982. Memberships: Chair, Liberty Publishing and Media Ltd, 1996-97; Chair, Equity Theatre Commission 1995-96; National Campaign for the Arts, 1996-; Member, Board for Better English Campaign, 1995-97; Thames Advisory Group, 1995-97; London Film Commission, 1996-; Honorary Perpetual Student, Bart's Hospital, 1993. Address: 29 Priory Avenue, Chiswick, London, W4 1TZ, England.

STEVENS Barbara Christine, b. 4 September 1939, Guildford, Surrey, England. Clinical Psychologist. m. John Ridsdale, 1974, deceased. Education: BA Honours, Sociology, London School of Economics, 1961; BA Honours, Psychology, University College London, 1962; PhD, Institute of Psychiatry, London, 1967; Academic Postgraduate Diploma, Clinical Psychology, British Psychology Society, 1982. Appointments: Medical Research Council

Social Psychiatry Unit, 1962-72; Research Staff, Institute Psychiatry, 1972-77; Senior Psychologist, HM Prison Service, 1977-83; Senior Psychologist, 1983-85, Consultant Forensic Psychologist, 1985-2002, Runwell Hospital, Wickford, Essex. Publications: Marriage and Fertility of Women Suffering from Schizophrenia and Affective Disorders, 1969; Dependence of Schizophrenic Patients on Elderly Relatives, 1972; The Role of Fluphenazine Decanoate in Lessening the Burden of Chronic Schizophrenics in the Community, 1973; Numerous other scientific papers. Honours: Mapother Research Fellowship, 1962-66; Member, Medical Research Council Scientific Staff, 1962-72. Memberships: Associate Fellow, British Psychology Society, Member Criminological and Clinical Divisions, 1982; Elected, Academy of Experts, Grays Inn, London, 1996; Member of Royal Society for the Prevention of Cruelty to Animals, The Dog's Trust, Peoples Dispensary for Sick Animals, World Wildlife Fund; World Society for Protection of Animals. Address: 14 Devonshire Place, London W1G 6HX, England.

STEVENS Geoffrey, b. 4 June 1942, West Bromwich, England. Chemist; Poet. m. (1) Barbara C Smith, 1965, 1 daughter, (2) Geraldine M Wall, 1996. Education: HNC, Chemistry, Wolverhampton Polytechnic. Appointments: Director of Industrial Archaeology, Black Country Society; Editor, Purple Patch Poetry Magazine, 1976-. Publications: Ecstasy, 1992; Field Manual for Poetry Lovers, 1992; A Comparison of Myself With Ivan Blatny, 1992; The Surreal Mind Paints Poetry, 1993; The Complacency of the English, 1995; Skin Print, 1995; For Reference Only, 1999; The Phrenology of Anaglypta, 2003; A Keelhauling Through Ireland, 2005; The All Night Cafe, 2006; Reality is Not Achievable, 2006; Contributions to: Magazines and periodicals. Honour: Award for Service to Poetry, Hastings Poetry Festival, 1997. Address: 25 Griffiths Road, West Bromwich B71 2EH, England.

STEVENS Jocelyn Edward Greville (Sir), b. 14 February 1932, London, England. Publisher. m. Jane Armyne Sheffield, 1956, dissolved 1979, 1 son, deceased, 2 daughters. Education: Cambridge University. Appointments: Military Service, Rifle Brigade, 1950-52; Journalist, Hulton Press, 1955-56; Chair and Managing Director, Stevens Press Ltd, Editor, Queen Magazine, 1957-58; Personal Assistant to Chair, 1968, Director, 1971-81, Managing Director, 1974-77, Beaverbrook Newspapers; Managing Director, Evening Standard Co Ltd, 1969-72; Managing Director, Daily Express, 1972-74; Deputy Chair and Managing Director, Express Newspapers, 1974-81; Editor and Publisher, The Magazine, 1982-84; Director, Centaur Communications, 1982-84; Governor, Imperial College of Science, Technology and Medicine, 1985-92; Governor, Winchester School of Art, 1986-89; Rector and Vice Provost, RCA, 1984-92; Chair, The Silver Trust, 1990-93; English Heritage, 1992-2000; Deputy Chair, Independent TV Commission, 1991-96; Non Executive Director, The TV Corporation, 1996, Asprey & Co, 2002, Garrad & Co, 2002; President, The Cheyne Walk Trust, 1989-93; Trustee, Eureka! Children's Museum, 1990-2000; Chair, The Phoenix Trust; Director, The Prince's Foundation, 2000. Honours: Hon D Litt, Loughborough, 1989, Buckingham, 1998; Hon FCSD, 1990; Senior Fellow, RCA, 1990. Address: 14 Cheyne Walk, London, SW3 5RA, England.

STEVENS Shakin' (Michael Barratt), b. 4 March 1948, Ely, Cardiff, South Wales. Singer; Songwriter. Career: Enjoyed much success touring for many years with his band, the Sunsets; Starred in the multi-award-winning West End musical, Elvis, which ran for 19 months from 1977; Signed as solo artist with Epic Records world-wide in 1978; First

UK Top 30 single, Hot Dog, charted in 1980; First European chart entry, Marie Marie, in 1980; First UK Number 1, later a major international hit, This Ole House, 1981; 38 hit singles, 36 of which were consecutive, throughout the 1980s and 1990s; UK hits: Four No.1s, three No.2s, 12 Top 5 hits, 15 Top 10 hits, 25 Top 20 hits, 30 Top 30 hits and 32 Top 40 hits; Musical collaborations include Bonnie Tyler, Roger Taylor, Hank Marvin and Albert Lee; Tours, personal appearances and television performances world-wide; Headlining to an audience of 200,000 in Vienna in 2003; Most successful hit-maker of the 1980s in the UK, with more weeks in the charts (254 in the 80's alone) than any other international recording artist; His work has been covered by many artists including Eddie Raven (A Letter To You) and Sylvia (Cry Just A Little Bit), No 1 and No 9 in the Nashville charts, and Barry Manilow (Oh Julie), US hit in 1982. Recordings: Hit singles, albums and songs have sold millions of copies, earning numerous honours and awards, including many Gold and Platinum discs world-wide; Hit albums include (UK): Shakin' Stevens Take One!; This Ole House; Shakin' Stevens; Give Me Your Heart Tonight; The Bop Won't Stop; Greatest Hits; Lipstick, Powder and Paint; Let's Boogie; A Whole Lotta Shaky; There's Two Kinds Of Music - Rock'n'Roll; The Epic Years; The Collection; UK hit singles include: Hot Dog; Marie Marie; This Ole House; You Drive Me Crazy; Green Door; It's Raining; Oh Julie; Shirley; I'll Be Satisfied; The Shakin' Stevens EP; It's Late; Cry Just A Little Bit; A Rockin' Good Way (To Mess Around And Fall In Love), duet with Bonnie Tyler; A Love Worth Waiting For; A Letter To You; Teardrops; Breaking Up My Heart; Lipstick Powder And Paint; Merry Christmas Everyone; Turning Away; Because I Love You; A Little Boogie Woogie (In The Back Of My Mind); What Do You Want To Make Those Eyes At Me For?; Love Attack; I Might; The Best Christmas Of Them All; Radio. Honours include: 30 Top 30 hits in a decade, unsurpassed by any other artist; Best singer/performer, MIDEM; Chartmaker Award for 4 simultaneous singles in the German chart; Gold and Platinum discs world-wide; First double platinum single ever to an international artist, Sweden; Most weeks in UK charts for international recording artist; Gold Badge Award from the British Academy of Composers and Song Writers; Number One Gold Award from The Guinness Book of British Hit Singles; In 2004 ranked as the 16th highest selling artist in the UK ever. Address: c/o Sue Davies, The HEC Organisation, PO Box 184, West End, Woking, Surrey GU24 9YY, England. E-mail: suedavies@shakinstevens.com

STEVENS Stuart Standish, b. 30 April 1947, Ferozepore, India. Barrister. 4 sons, 1 daughter. Education: St Josephs E H School, Bangalore; Acton County Grammar School; Royal Holloway College, London University; Inns of Court School of Law; London School of Economics, London University. Appointments: Called to the Bar, 1970; Head of Chambers, 3 Kings Bench Walk Temple, EC4, 1982; Head of Chambers, Holborn Chambers, 1994. Honours: Freeman of the City of London, 1991; Specialist in White Collar Fraud and Substantial Criminal Matters. Address: Holborn Chambers, The Chambers of Stuart Stevens, 6 Gate Street, Lincolns Inn Fields, London WC2A 3HP, England. E-mail: stevens@holbornchambers.co.uk

STEVENSON Juliet, b. 30 October 1956, England. Actress. 1 son, 1 daughter, 2 stepsons. Education: Hurst Lodge School, Berkshire; St Catherine's School, Surrey; Royal Academy of Dramatic Arts. Appointments: Plays include: Midsummer Night's Dream; Measure for Measure; As You Like It; Troilus and Cressida; Les Liaisons Dangereuses; No I; Footfalls; Other Worlds; Death and the Maiden; Duchess of Malfi;

Hedder Gabler; The Caucasian Chalk Circle; Private Lives; A Little Night Music; Films include: Drowning by Numbers; Ladder of Swords; Truly Madly Deeply; The Trial; The Secret Rapture; Emma; The Search for John Gissing; Who Dealt?; Beckett's Play; Bend It Like Beckham; Food of Love; Nicholas Nickleby; Mona Lisa Smile; Being Julia; A Previous Engagement, 2005; Red Mercury, 2005; The Last Hangman, 2005; Infamous, 2006; Breaking and Entering, 2006; And When Did You Last See Your Father, 2007; The Secret of Moonacre, 2008; Several TV roles include: The Politician's Wife; Cider with Rosie; The Politician's Wife; A Doll's House; Life Story; Antigone; The March; Maybury; Thomas and Ruth; Aimée; The Mallens; Living With Dinosaurs; The Snow Queen, 2005; Marple: Ordeal by Innocence, 2007; 10 Days to War, 2008; Wrote and fronted BBC documentary Great Journeys; Radio includes: To the Lighthouse; Volcano; Albertina; House of Correction; Hang Up; Cigarettes and Chocolate; A Little Like Drowning; Victory; The Pallisers; Mary Poppins; The Lovers of Viorne. Publications: Clamourous Voices, 1988; Shall I See You Again?; Players of Shakespeare. Honours: Bancroft Gold Medal, Royal Academy of Dramatic Arts, 1977; Time Out Award for Best Actress, 1991; Evening Standard Film Award for Best Actress, 1992; Lawrence Olivier Theatre Award for Best Actress, 1992. Address: c/o Markham and Froggatt Ltd, Julian House, 4 Windmill Street, London, W1P 1HF, England.

STEWART Alec James, b. 8 April 1963, Merton, London, England. Cricketer. m. Lynn, 1 son, 1 daughter. Education: Tiffin Boys' School, Kingston Upon Thames. Appointments: Right-hand opening Batsman; Wicket Keeper; Surrey, 1981-2003 (Captain 1992-97); 126 Tests for England, 1989-90 to 2 Jan 2003, 14 as Captain, scoring 8187 runs (average 40.13) including 15 hundreds; Scored 25,438 first class runs (48 hundreds) to end of 2002; Held 11 catches, equaling world first-class record, for Surrey v Leicestershire, Leicester, 19-22 August, 1989; Toured Australia, 1990-91, 1994-95 and 1998-99 (captain); Overtook record (118) of Graham Gooch to become England's most-capped cricketer, Lords July 2002; 161 limited-overs internationals to 7 January 2003; Retired, 2003; Director of Business, Surrey County Cricket Club, 2003-. Publications: Alec Stewart: A Captain's Diary, 1999; Playing for Keeps, 2003. Honour: Wisden Cricketer of the Year, 1993; OBE, 2003. Address: c/o Surrey Cricket Club, Kennington Oval, London, SE11 5SS, England.

STEWART Dave, b. 9 September 1952, Sunderland, Tyne and Wear, England. Musician (guitar, keyboards); Songwriter; Composer. m. Siobhan Fahey, 1 August 1987, divorced, 1 son. Career: Musician, Harrison and Stewart (with Brian Harrison); Longdancer; The Catch, 1977; Renamed The Tourists, 1979-80; Formed Eurythmics with Annie Lennox, 1980-89; Worldwide concerts include Nelson Mandela's 70th Birthday Tribute, Wembley, 1988; As solo artiste: Nelson Mandela Tribute concert, Wembley, 1990; Amnesty International Big 30 concert, 1991; Founder, Spiritual Cowboys, 1990-92; Vegas, with Terry Hall, 1992-93; Founder, own record label Anxious Records, 1988; Owner, The Church recording studio, 1992; Producer, session musician, for artistes including Bob Dylan; Mick Jagger; Tom Petty; Daryl Hall; Bob Geldof; Boris Grebenshikov; Sinead O'Connor; Feargal Sharkey. Compositions for film and TV: Rooftops, 1989; De Kassiere (with Candy Dulfer), 1989; Jute City, BBC1, 1991; GFI (TV series with Gerry Anderson), 1992; Inside Victor Lewis-Smith (TV series), 1993; No Worries, 1993; The Ref, 1994; Showgirls, 1995; Beautiful Girls, 1996; Crimetime, 1996; TV Offal (TV series title theme), 1997; Cookie's Fortune, 1999; Honest (director), 2000; Le Pont de trieur, 2000; Chaos, 2002;

Around the World in 80 Days, 2004; Alfie, 2004. Recordings: Albums: with The Tourists: The Tourists, 1979; Reality Affect, 1979; Luminous Basement, 1980; with Eurythmics: In The Garden, 1982; Sweet Dreams, 1983; Touch, 1984; Be Yourself Tonight, 1985; Revenge, 1986; Savage, 1988; We Too Are One, 1989; Eurythmics Live 1983-89, 1992; Peace, 1999; with the Spiritual Cowboys: Dave Stewart And The Spiritual Cowboys, 1990; with Vegas: Vegas, 1992; Solo: Greetings From The Gutter, 1994; Hit singles include: with the Tourists: I Only Want To Be With You, 1979; So Good To Be Back Home, 1979; with Eurythmics: Sweet Dreams, Love Is A Stranger, Who's That Girl?, Right By Your Side, 1983; Here Comes The Rain Again, Sex Crime (1984), 1984; Would I Lie To You?, There Must Be An Angel, Sisters Are Doin' It For Themselves, 1985; It's Alright, When Tomorrow Comes, Thorn In My Side, The Miracle of Love, Missionary Man, 1986; Beethoven, Shame, 1987; I Need A Man, You Have Placed A Chill In My Heart, 1988; Revival, Don't Ask Me Why, 1989; King and Queen of America, Angel, 1990; Love Is a Stranger, Sweet Dreams, 1991; I Saved the World, 17 Again, 1999; Solo: Old Habits Die Hard (with Mick Jagger), 2004. Honours: MTV Music Awards, Best New Artist Video, 1984; 3 BRIT Awards, Best Producer, 1986, 1987, 1990; Grammy, Best Rock Performance, 1987; 2 Ivor Novello Awards, Songwriters of the Year (with Annie Lennox), 1984, 1987; Hon DMus (Westminster) 1998; BRIT Award, Outstanding Contribution, 1999; Golden Globe Award, Best Original Song, 2005. Address: 19 Management Ltd, Unit 33, Ransomes Dock, 35-37 Park Gate Road, London SW11 4NP, England. Website: www.davestewart.com

STEWART Gordon Thallon, b. 5 February 1919, Paisley, Scotland. Physician; University Professor. m. (1) Joan Kego, deceased (2) Georgina Walker, 2 sons, 2 daughters. Education: BSc, 1939, MB, ChB, 1942., MD 1949, University of Glasgow; DTM and H, University of Liverpool, 1947. Appointments: House Surgeon then House Physician, Glasgow, Scotland, 1942-43; Medical Officer, Royal Navy (Surgeon Lieutenant, RNVR), 1943-46; Hospital and research appointments in UK (Aberdeen, Liverpool, London), 1947-63; Professor of Epidemiology, Schools of Medicine and Public Health, University of North Carolina at Chapel Hill, USA, 1963-68; Watkins Professor and Head, Department of Epidemiology and Professor of Medicine, Tulane University, New Orleans Louisiana, USA, 1968-72; Consultant Physician, Epidemiology and Preventive Medicine, National Health Service, UK and Mechan Professor of Public Health, University of Glasgow, 1972-84; Emeritus Professor, 1984-. Publications: Books: Chemotherapy of Fungal Infection (with R W Riddell), 1955; Penicillin Group of Drugs, 1965; Penicillin Allergy (with J McGovern), 1970; Editor: Trends in Epidemiology, 1972; Chapters on epidemiology, control of infectious diseases and education in other books; Articles on same and on drug abuse and public health subjects in mainline medical journals, articles on liquid crystals and ordered structures in biology and medicine. Honours: High Commendation for MD Thesis, University of Glasgow, 1949; WHO Visiting Professor, Dow Medical College, Karachi, Pakistan, 1953; Senior Visiting Foreign Fellow, US National Science Foundation, 1963-64; Visiting Professor, Cornell University Medical College, New York, USA, 1971; Emeritus Fellow, Infectious Diseases Society of America; Visiting Lecturer and Consultant at various hospitals and colleges in Europe, Canada, America, India, Pakistan, Middle East, Africa; Consultant WHO; New York City Health Department; US Navy (Camp Lejeune, North Carolina). Memberships: Fellow: Royal College of Physicians, Glasgow; Royal College of Pathology, London; Faculty of Public Health of the Royal College of Physicians;

Royal Statistical Society; Medical Society of London; Royal Society of Medicine. Address: 29/8 Inverleith Place, Edinburgh EH3 5QD, Scotland.

STEWART Ian, b. 28 August 1950, Blantyre, Scotland. Member of Parliament. m. 2 sons, 1 daughter. Education: Stretford Technical College; Manchester University. Appointments: Regional Office, Transport and General Workers Union, 1978-97; Member of Parliament for Eccles, 1997-; Fellow, Industry and Parliament Trust; Member, Deregulation Select Committee, 1998-2001; Member, Information Select Committee, 1998-2001; Backbench PLP Groups: Education and Employment, 1997-, Trade and Industry, 1997-, Foreign Affairs, 1997-2001; Treasury, 2001-; All Party Groups: Chemical Industry Group, Retail Industry Group, Regeneration Group. Occupational Health & Safety Group, Parliamentary Information Technology Committee (executive member); United Nations Association, Commonwealth Parliamentary Association, Vice-Chair, All Party China Group; Vice Chair, APPG on Kazakhstan; Chair, Group for Vaccine Damaged Children; Chair, All Party Community Media Group; Parliamentary Private Secretary to Brian Wilson MP, Minister for Industry and Energy (Stephen Timms), 2001-; PPS at DTI, 2005. Address: London Parliamentary Office, House of Commons, London SW1A 0AA, England. E-mail: ianstewartmp@parliament.uk

STEWART Jan E J, b. 28 February 1948, Los Angeles, USA. Professor. m. Misa, 1 son, 1 daughter. Education: BA, University of California, Santa Barbara, 1974; MA, Claremont Graduate School, 1977. Appointments: Professor, Chikushi Women's University; Lecturer, Riyadh College of Health Sciences. Publications: Changes, 1987; English for Health Care Professionals, 1996; A Dewdrop on a Bamboo Leaf, 2002; The War of Mirrors, 2006; The Lyre Birds, 2008. Honours: International Educator of the Year, 2005. Memberships: Modern Language Association; Japan Association of College English Teachers. E-mail: jan-stewart@jcom.home.ne.jp

STEWART Martha Kostyra, b. Jersey City, New Jersey, USA. Editor; Author; Business Executive. m. Andy Stewart, 1961, divorced 1990, 1 son. Education: Barnard University. Career: Former model, stockbroker, caterer; Owner, Editor-in-Chief, Martha Stewart Living magazine, 1990-; Chair, CEO, 1997-2003, Member of Board, -2004, Founding Editorial Director (non-executive), 2004-, Martha Steward Living Omnimedia; Appears in cooking feature, Today Show; Member of Board, NY Stock Exchange, 2002; Member of Board, Revlon Inc, -2004; Under investigation for alleged insider trading, 2002-; Found guilty of conspiracy, making false statements and obstruction of justice, 2004. Publications: (with Elizabeth Hawes): Entertaining, 1982; Weddings, 1987; (as sole author): Martha Stewart's Hors d'Oeuvres: The Creation and Presentation of Fabulous Finger Food, 1984; Martha Stewart's Pies and Tarts, 1985; Martha Stewart's Quick Cook Menus, 1988; The Wedding Planner, 1988; Martha Stewart's Gardening: Month by Month, 1991; Martha Stewart's New Old House: Restoration, Renovation, Decoration, 1992; Martha Stewart's Christmas, 1993; Martha Stewart's Menus for Entertaining, 1994; Holidays, 1994; The Martha Rules, 2005; Martha Stewart Baking Handbook, 2005; Martha Stewart's Homekeeping Handbook, 2006. Address: Martha Stewart Living Omnimedia, 11 West 42nd Street, 25th Floor, New York, NY 10036, USA. Website: www.marthastewart.com

STEWART Lady Mary Florence Elinor, b. 17 September 1916, Sunderland, England. Writer; Poet .m. Frederick Henry Stewart, 24 September 1945. Education: BA, 1938, DipEd, 1939, MA, 1941, University of Durham. Publications: Madam, Will You Talk?, 1955; Wildfire at Midnight, 1956; Thunder on the Right, 1957; Nine Coaches Waiting, 1958; My Brother Michael, 1960; The Ivy Tree, 1961; The Moonspinners, 1962; This Rough Magic, 1964; Airs Above the Ground, 1965; The Gabriel Hounds, 1967; The Wind Off the Small Isles, 1968; The Crystal Cave, 1970; The Little Broomstick, 1971; The Hollow Hills, 1973; Ludo and the Star Horse, 1974; Touch Not the Cat, 1976; The Last Enchantment, 1979; A Walk in Wolf Wood, 1980; The Wicked Day, 1983; Thornyhold, 1988; Frost on the Window and Other Poems, 1990; Stormy Petrel, 1991; The Prince and the Pilgrim, 1995; Rose Cottage, 1997. Contributions to: Magazines. Honours: Frederick Niven Prize; Scottish Arts Council Award; Honorary Fellow, Newnham College, Cambridge. Memberships: PEN. Address: House of Letterawe, Loch Awe, Dalmally, Argyll PA33 1AH, Scotland.

STEWART Patrick, b. 13 July 1940, Mirfield, Yorkshire, England. Actor. m. (1) Sheila Falconer, 1966, 1 son, 1 daughter, (2) Wendy Neuss, 2002. Education: Bristol Old Vic Theatre School. Career: Junior Reporter, local newspaper; Actor, various repertory companies; Actor, 1966, Associate Artist, 1967-87, Royal Shakespeare Company; Founding Director, ACTER; Director, Flying Freehold Productions, Paramount Studios, LA, 1998-; Films: Hedda: Excalibur; Dune; Lady Jane; Gunmen; Robin Hood – Men in Tights; LA Story; Jeffrey; Star Trek: First Contact; Conspiracy Theory; Dad Savage; Masterminds; Star Trek: Insurrection, 1999; X-Men, 2000; Moby Dick; Star Trek: Nemesis, 2002; X-Men: X2, 2003; Boo, Zino and the Snurks (voice), 2004; Chicken Little (voice), 2005; The Game of Their Lives, 2005; X-Men: The Last Stand, 2006; TMNT (voice), 2007; Theatre: Antony and Cleopatra, 1979; Henry IV, 1984; Who's Afraid of Virginia Woolf?, 1987; A Christmas Carol, 1988-96; The Tempest, 1995; Othello, 1997; The Ride Down Mount Morgan, 1998; The Master Builder, 2003; TV: Star Trek: The Next Generation; The Mozart Inquest; Maybury; I Claudius; Tinker, Tailor, Soldier, Spy; Smiley's People; The Lion in Winter, 2003; Mysterious Island, 2005; The Snow Queen, 2005; Eleventh House, 2006; Family Guy, 2005-07; American Dad, 2005-07; Music: narrative to Peter and the Wolf, 1996. Olivier Award, Society of West End Theatre Awards, 1979; London Fringe Award, 1987; Drama Desk Award, 1992; Olivier Award, 1992; Grammy Award, 1996. Address: International Creative Management Inc, 8942 Wilshire Boulevard, Beverly Hills, CA 90211, USA.

STEWART Paul, b. 4 June 1955, London, England. Author. m. Julie, 1 son, 1 daughter. Education: BA in English, 1st class honours, Lancaster University, 1974-77; MA in Creative Writing with Malcolm Bradbury, UEA, 1978-79; German, University of Heidelberg, 1980-82. Appointments: EFL Teacher, Germany, 1980-82; EFL Teacher, Sri Lanka, 1982-83; EFL Teacher, Brighton, 1984-90; Writer, Child Carer (of own children), 1990-. Publications include: Stormchaser, 1999; The Birthday Presents, 1999; The Blobheads, series of 8 books, 2000; Midnight Over Sanctaphrax, 2000; Rabbit's Wish, 2001; The Curse of the Gloamglozer, 2001; The Were-pig, 2001; Muddle Earth, 2003, VOX, 2003; Freeglader, 2004; Fergus Crane, 2004. Honours: Gold Medal; Winner of Smarties Prize; Corby Flood, Honours Silver Medal, Nestle Book Prize, 2005, 2006; Hugo Pepper, 2006.

STEWART Rod (Roderick David), b. 10 January 1945, Highgate, North London, England. Singer. 1 daughter with Susannah Boffey, m. (1) Alana Collins, 1 son, 1 daughter, 1 daughter with Kelly Emberg, (2) Rachel Hunter, 1990, divorced 2006, 1 son, 1 daughter, (3) Penny Lancaster, 2007, 1 son. Career: Singer with: Steampacket; Shotgun Express; Jeff Beck Group, 1967-69; Concerts include: UK tour with Roy Orbison, 1967; US tours, 1967, 1968; The Faces, 1969-75; Appearances include: Reading Festival, 1972; UK, US tours, 1972; Solo artiste, 1971-; Solo appearances include: Rock In Rio, Brazil, 1985; Vagabond Heart Tour, 1991-92. Recordings: Singles include: Reason To Believe; Maggie May; (I Know) I'm Losing You; Handbags And Gladrags; You Wear It Well; Angel; Farewell; Sailing; This Old Heart Of Mine; Tonight's The Night (Gonna Be All Right); The Killing Of Georgie (Parts 1 and 2); Get Back; The First Cut Is The Deepest; I Don't Want To Talk About It; You're In My Heart; Hot Legs; D'Ya Think I'm Sexy?; Passion; Young Turks; Tonight I'm Yours; Baby Jane; What Am I Gonna Do; Infatuation; Some Guys Have All The Luck; Love Touch; Every Beat Of My Heart; Downtown Train; Rhythm Of My Heart; This Old Heart Of Mine; Have I Told You Lately; Reason To Believe; Ruby Tuesday; You're The Star; Albums include: 2 with Jeff Beck; 4 with the Faces; Solo albums: Every Picture Tells A Story, 1971; Never A Dull Moment, 1972; Atlantic Crossing, 1975; A Night On The Town, 1976; Foot Loose And Fancy Free, 1977; Blondes Have More Fun, 1978; Foolish Behaviour, 1980; Tonight I'm Yours, 1981; Camouflage, 1984; Love Touch, 1986; Out Of Order, 1988; The Best Of, 1989; Downtown Train, 1990; Vagabond Heart, 1991; Lead Vocalist, 1992; Unplugged... And Seated, 1993; A Spanner In The Works, 1995; When We Were the New Boys, 1998; It Had To Be You: The Great American Songbook, 2002; Stardust: The Great American Songbook 3, 2004; Still the Same: Great Rock Classics of our Time, 2006; Numerous compilations. Honours include: First artist to top US and UK singles and album charts simultaneously, 1971; BRIT Awards, Lifetime Achievement Award, 1993; UK Music Hall of Fame, 2006. Address: c/o Warner Music, 28 Kensington Church Street, London, W8 4EP, England.

STEWART William Gladstone, b. 15 July 1933, Lancaster, England. Television Producer; Presenter; Writer. m. Laura Calland Stewart, 2 daughters, 3 other children. Education: Shooters Hill Grammar School, London, 1945-50; Woolwich Polytechnic, 1951-52. Appointments: Royal Army Educational Corps, 1952-55; Served with Kings African Rifles in Kenya; Worked with BBC, 1958-67; Independent and Freelance, Producer, Director, 1967-; Productions include: Eric Sykes, Bless this House with Sid James; Father Dear Father with Patrick Cargill; Father Dear Father, feature film, 1972; Entertainment Series and one off "specials" with Max Bygraves, Tommy Cooper, Frankie Howerd, Bruce Forsyth; Leslie Crowther; Harry Worth; Reg Varney; Chris Evans; Major long-running series with David Frost, The Frost Programme, David Frost Live from London; With Johnny Speight, Lady is a Tramp, 'Till Death, The 19th Hole; Major drama series for Channel 4, Tickets for the Titanic; Georgian Giants, Radio 4, 2005; Co-Founder (with Colin Frewin), Sunset and Vine Productions, 1976; Founder, Regent Productions, 1980-; Presenter Channel 4 programme, Fifteen-to-One, 1988-2003. Publications: Regular contributor of articles on media matters to national newspapers and journals including, Independent, RTS Journal, Broadcast, The Listener, The Producer, Televisual, Evening Standard, Impact; Lectures on the return of cultural artefacts, especially the Parthenon Marbles to Athens, at The European Parliament in Strasbourg, UNESCO in Paris, The Smithsonian in Washington, in Athens, London and New York; Institute of Art and Law Annual Lecture, 2000; 5 city lecture tour across USA and Canada, 2003. Memberships: Fellow, Royal Television Society; British Academy Film and Television Arts; Royal Horticultural Society; Hall of Fame of the Royal Television Society; President, The Media Society 2003-2005. Address: PO Box 429, New Malden KT3 9AW, England. E-mail: putneycommon@aol.com

STEWARTBY Baron, Sir (Bernard Harold) Ian (Halley) Stewart, b. 10 August 1935, United Kingdom. m. Deborah Charlotte Buchan, 1 son, 2 daughters. Education: MA, Jesus College Cambridge, 1956-59; D Litt, University of Cambridge, 1978. Appointments include: National Service: Sub-Lieutenant, RNVR, 1954-56, later Lieutenant Commander, RNR; Brown Shipley & Co Ltd, Merchant Bankers, 1960-82, Director, 1971-83; MP, Conservative, North Hertfordshire (Hitchin), 1974-92; Parliamentary Private Secretary to Chancellor of the Exchequer, 1979-83; Parliamentary Under-Secretary of State for Defence Procurement, 1983; Economic Secretary to the Treasury, 1983-87; Minister of State for the Armed Forces, 1987-88; Minister of State, Northern Ireland, 1988-89; Non-Executive Director, 1990-93, Deputy Chairman, 1993-2004, Standard Chartered plc; Non-Executive Director, Diploma plc, 1990-2007; Chairman, The Throgmorton Trust PLC, 1990-2005; Member, Financial Service Authority, 1993-97; Deputy Chairman, Amlin plc, 1995-2006; Non-Executive Director, Portman Building Society, 1995-2002; Chairman, Brazilian Smaller Companies Investment Trust PLC, 1998; President, Sir Halley Stewart Trust, 2000-. Publications: The Scottish Coinage, 1955, 2nd edition, 1967; Coinage in Tenth Century England (joint author), 1989. Honours: RD, 1972; FBA, 1981; FRSE, 1986; PC, 1989; Kt, 1991; Baron, 1992; K St J, 1992; Sanford Saltus Gold Medal, British Numismatic Society, 1971; Medallist, Royal Numismatic Society, 1996. Memberships: Director, British Numismatic Society, 1965-75; County Vice-President, St John Ambulance, Hertfordshire, 1978-; British Academy Committee for Sylloge of Coins of the British Isles, 1967-, Chairman, 1993-2003; Member of Council, Haileybury, 1980-95; Chairman, Treasure Valuation Committee, 1996-2001. Address: House of Lords, Westminster, London SW1A 0AA, England.

STEYER Rolf, b. 1 December 1950, Fulda, Germany. m. Anna-Maria, 1 son, 1 daughter. Education: Military Service, Bundesgrenzschutz border police, 1969-71; Diploma in Psychology, Göttingen, 1977; PhD, Psychology, Frankfurt am Main, 1982; Habilitation, Psychology, University of Trier, 1989. Appointments: Research Assistant, University of Göttingen, 1977; Assistant, University of Frankfurt am Main, 1977-82; Assistant Professor, University of Trier, 1982-94; Director of Methodology Research, ZUMA, Mannheim, 1994; Associate Professor, Methodology and Assessment, University of Magdeburg, 1995; Full Professor, Methodology and Evaluation Research, University of Jena, 1996-; General Secretary, European Association of Psychological Assessment, 1996-99; Co-Editor in Chief, European Journal of Psychological Assessment, 1999-2003; Prorektor, University of Jena, 2002-04; President, Center for Human Resources, Research, Development and Training, 2002-04; President, European Association of Methodology, 2004-2008. Publications: Theory of causal regression models, 1992; Measuring and Testing, co-author, 1993; Probability and Regression, author, 2002; Editor of several newsletters. Memberships: German Society for Psychology; European Association of Methodolgy; European Association of Personality Psychology; European Mathematical Psychology Group; European Association of Psychological Assessment;

Psychometric Society. Address: Institute of Psychology, Am Steiger 3, Haus 1, D-07743 Jena, Germany. E-mail: rolf.steyer@uni-jena.de

STICH Michael, b. 18 October 1968, Pinneberg, Germany. Former Professional Tennis Player; Business Executive. m. Jessica Stockmann, 1992, divorced 2003. Appointments: National Junior Champion, 1986; Turned professional, 1988; Semi-finalist, French Open, 1990; Member, West German Davis Cup Team, 1990; Won first professional title, Memphis, 1990; Winner, Men's Singles Championship, Wimbledon, 1991; Men's Doubles (with John McEnroe), 1992; Won ATP World Championship, 1993; Retired, 1997; Won 28 professional titles; UN Ambassador, 1999-; German Davis Cup team Captain, 2001-2002. Address: Magdalenstr 64B, 22148 Hamburg, Germany.

STIGWOOD Robert Colin, b. 16 April 1934, Adelaide, Australia. Business Executive. Education: Sacred Heart College, Adelaide. Appointments: Established Robert Stigwood Organisation (RSO), 1967; Formed RSO Records, 1973; Founder, Music for UNICEF; Producer of films: Jesus Christ Superstar; Bugsy Malone; Gallipoli; Tommy; Saturday Night Fever; Grease; Sergeant Pepper's Lonely Hearts Club Band; Moment by Moment; Times Square; The Fan; Grease 2; Staying Alive; Evita; Gallipoli; Producer of stage musicals: Hair; Oh! Calcutta; The Dirtiest Show in Town; Pippin; Jesus Christ Superstar; Evita; Grease, 1993; Saturday Night Fever; TV producer in England and USA: The Entertainer; The Prime of Miss Jean Brodie; Chair of Board, Stigwood Group of Companies. Honours: Key to City of Los Angeles; Tony Award, 1980, for Evita; International Producer of the Year, ABC Interstate Inc. Address: c/o Robert Stigwood Organization, Barton Manor, Wippingham, East Cowes, Isle of Wight, PO32 6LB, England.

STILES Frank, b. 2 April 1924, Chiswick, London, England. Composer; Conductor; Violist. m. (1) Estelle Zitnitsky, 1969, 4 daughters, (2) Elizabeth Horwood, 1988. Education: BSc, Imperial College, 1949; BMus, Durham University, 1952; Postgraduate studies, Paris Conservatoire, 1955; LGSM; AGSM. Appointments: War Service Fleet Air Arm, 1942-46; Composer; Conductor Violist; Principal Conductor, Priory Concertante of London; Director, Holland Music School, 1982-92; Composer in Residence, Protoangel Visions Festival, Normandy by Spital, Lincolnshire. Publications: 5 symphonies; Dramatic Cantata Masada; Song Cycle for Tenor and Orchestra and for Baritone and Piano Mans 4 Seasons; 7 Concertos for violin, viola (2), guitar, clarinet, cello, piano; 6 string quartets; Trios; Duos; 2 violin and piano sonatas; 2 viola and piano sonatas; among others. Honours: City of London Award for Composition, 1955; ABI Medal of Honour, 2000; ABI Stature of Universal Accomplishment, 2001; ABI Man of the Year 2005; Listed in national and international biographical dictionaries. Memberships: Composers' Guild of Great Britain; Chairman, Association of British Music; Incorporated Society of Musicians; British Academy of Composers and Songwriters; Musicians Union; PRS; MCPS; Royal Society of Musicians. Address: 43 Beech Road, Branston, Lincoln LN4 1PP, England. E-mail: frankstiles@callnetuk.com Website: www.impulse.music.co.uk/stiles.htm

STILINOVIC Damir, b. 20 September 1968, Zagreb, Croatia. Electrical Engineer. m. Hrvatska. Education: Mr Sc, Electrical Engineering, Faculty of Electrical Engineering and Computing, University of Zagreb, Croatia, 1988-93; CCNP, CCNA, Network Security Courses, CISCO Networking Academy, Carnet, Zagreb, 2001-04. Appointments: Mobile Network Support Engineer, Croatian Post and Telecommunications, Zagreb, 1993-95; Systems Engineer, Privredna Bank, Zagreb, 1995-2003; Network Support Engineer, Financial Agency, Zagreb, 2003-05; Network Engineer, Coting, 2005-06; Senior Network Engineer, T-HT, Zagreb, 2006-; CISCO Academy Instructor, Polytechnic of Zagreb, 2006-; Network Consultant, Kripton, Karcovac, 2006. Honours: Listed in international biographical dictionaries. Memberships: IEEE; IEEE Communications Society. Address: Dubovacka 49, 10110 Zagreb, Croatia.

STILLER Ben, b. 30 November 1965, New York, USA. Actor; Film Director. m. Christine Taylor, 2000, 2 children. Education: University of California at Los Angeles. Career: Films: Empire of the Sun, 1988; Reality Bites (also director), 1994; Happy Gilmore, Flirting with Disaster, The Cable Guy (also director), 1996; Zero Effect, Your Friends and Neighbors, There's Something About Mary, Permanent Midnight, 1998; Mystery Men, Black and White, 1999; Meet the Parents, Keeping the Faith, 2000; Zoolander (also director), The Royal Tenenbaums, 2001; Duplex, Nobody Knows Anything, 2003; Along Came Polly, Starsky & Hutch, Envy, Dodgeball, Meet the Fockers, Madagascar (voice), 2004; School for Scoundrels, Night at the Museum, 2006; The Heartbreak Kid, 2007; The Marc Pease Experience, Tropic Thunder, Madagascar: Escape 2 Africa, 2008; TV: The Ben Stiller Show, 1990-93. Honours: Emmy Award, 1990. Address: United Talent Agency, 9560 Wilshire Boulevard, Suite 500, Beverly Hills, CA 90212, USA.

STING (Gordon Matthew Sumner), 2 October 1951, Wallsend, Newcastle-Upon-Tyne, England. Singer; Musician (bass); Actor. m. (1) Frances Tomelty, 1 May 1976, divorced 1984, 1 son, 1 daughter; (2) Trudie Styler, 1992, 2 sons, 2 daughters. Career: School teacher, Newcastle, 1975-77; Singer, songwriter, bass player, The Police, 1977-86; Solo artiste, 1985-; Numerous worldwide tours, television and radio, with the Police and solo; actor in films: Quadrophenia, 1980; Secret Policeman's Other Ball, 1982; Brimstone And Treacle, 1982; Dune, 1984; The Bride, 1985; Plenty, 1985; Julia And Julia, 1988; Stormy Monday, 1988; The Adventures Of Baron Munchausen, 1989; Stormy Monday, 1989; Rosencrantz and Guildenstern are Dead; Resident Alien; The Music Tells You; The Grotesque; Mercury Falling, 1996; Lock, Stock and Two Smoking Barrels, 1998; The Tulse Luper Suitcases: The Moab Story, 2003; Broadway Performance: Threepenny Opera, 1989. Recordings: Hit singles include: Walking On The Moon; Message In A Bottle; So Lonely; Roxanne; De Do Do Do, De Da Da Da; Every Little Thing She Does; Every Breath You Take; Invisible Sun; Can't Stand Losing You; Don't Stand So Close To Me; If You Love Somebody; Englishman In New York; If I Ever Lose My Faith In You; Fields Of Gold; Love Is Stronger Than Justice; Cowboy Song (with Pato Banton); Let The Soul Be Your Pilot; Roxanne 97; Brand New Day; After the Rain has Fallen, 2000; Whenever I Say Your Name (with Mary J Blige), 2003; Stolen Car (Take Me Dancing), 2004; Taking the Inside Rail, 2005; Always on Your Side (with Sheryl Crow), 2006; Albums: with the Police: Outlandos D'Armour, 1977; Regatta De Blanc, 1979; Zenyatta Mondatta, 1980; Ghost In The Machine, 1981; Synchronisity, 1983; Bring On The Night, 1986; Solo albums: The Dream Of The Blue Turtles, 1985; Nothing Like The Sun, 1987; The Soul Cages, 1991; Ten Sumner's Tales, 1994; Mercury Falling, 1996; Brand New Day, 1999; After the Rain has Gone, 2000; Sacred Love, 2003; Songs from the Labyrinth, 2006; Contributor, Tower Of Song (Leonard Cohen tribute), 1995. Publications: Jungle Stories: The Fight for the Amazon, 1989; Escape Artist (memoir), 2003. Honours include: 14 Grammy

Awards (with Police and solo); Ivor Novello Award for Best Song They Dance Alone, 1989; Q Award, Best Album, 1994; BRIT Award, Best Male Artist, 1994; 4 songwriting awards (BMI), 1998; Brit Award for Outstanding Contribution to Music, 2002; Emmy Award for Best Performance (Sting in Tuscany.... All This Time), 2002; MusiCares Foundation Person of the Year, 2003; Billboard Music Century Award for Creative Achievement, 2003; Grammy Award, Best Pop Collaboration with Vocals, 2004. Membership: PRS. Address: Kathryn Shenker Associates, 12th Floor, 1775 Broadway, New York, NY 10019, USA.

STIPE Michael, b. 1960, Decatur, Georgia, USA. Rock Musician. Education: University of Georgia. Appointments: Lead singer and song writer with REM band, 1980-; Owner OO (film co). Albums include: (for IRS): Murmur, 1982-83, Document; (for Warner): Green, 1988; Out of Time, 1991; Automatic for the People, 1992; Monster, 1994; New Adventures in Hi-Fi, 1996; Up, 1998; Reveal, 2001; Bad Day Pt 1 and 1, 2003; Glastonbury 1999, 2003; Around the Sun, 2004. Honours: Numerous MTV Music Video Awards; Earth Day Award, 1990; Billboard Award, Best Modern Rock Artist, 1991; BRIT Awards, Best International Group, 1992, 1993, 1995; Grammy Awards, Best Pop Performance, Best Music Video, 1992; Atlanta Music Awards, Video of the Year, 1992; IRMA Award, International Band of the Year, 1993; Rolling Stone Critics Award, Best Band, 1993. Address: REM/Athens Ltd, 250 W Clayton Street, Athens, GA 30601, USA. Website: www.remhq.com

STIRES Midge, b. 10 April 1943, Orange, New Jersey, USA. Painter. m. Peter D Schnore, 2 sons. Education: Bachelor of Fine Art, Syracuse University, USA. Honours: Pollock and Krasner Foundation Grant; Elizabeth Foundation for the Arts Grant; Artists for the Environment Residency Grant. Publications: Painting Panoramas, The Artists Magazine, 1990. Memberships: National Association of Painters in Casein and Acrylic. Address: 144 Red Oak Dr, Boyertown, PA 19512 8963, USA.

STOJKOV Sava, b. 29 March 1925, Sombor, Serbia. Painter. m. Barbara, 2 sons. Education: Self-educated naïve painter. Appointments: Over 300 individual exhibitions and over 500 group exhibitions worldwide. Honours: 1st Prize, Magistrate Circolo Artistico, Naples, 1974; 1st Prize, San Remo, 1974; Golden Prize, Tabor, 1980; Grande Premio IV Bienale, Milan, 1980; Premio Internazionale, Varena, 1984; Prize, Space Gallery, Wonsodung/Seoul, Korea, 1989; Prize, Europa Haus, Klagenfurt, 1991; Prize for Life Achievement, Serbia, 1993; Masaryk Prize, Arts Academy, Praha, Czech Republic, 1996. Memberships: ULUS Beograd; IBC, England; Inter Tabor of Painters, Trebnje, Slovenia. Address: Čitaoničla br 22, 25000 Sombor, Serbia.

STOLL David (Michael), b. 29 December 1948, London, England. Composer. Education: Worcester College, Oxford, 1967-70; BA (hons), MA (Oxon); Royal Academy of Music, London, 1970-71. Career: Music Director, Greenwich Young People's Theatre, 1971-75; Freelance Composer and Music Producer working in concert music, theatre and media. Publications: Books: Building Music, 2005; Key Stage 2 Composing, 2006; Concert works include: Piano Quartet, 1987; Sonata for 2 Pianos, 1990; Piano Sonata, 1991; String Trio, 1992; Fanfares and Reflections (wind sextet), 1992; String Quartet no 1, 1994; The Bowl of Nous (cantata), 1996; The Shakespeare Suite, 1997; Motet in Memoriam, 1998; Midwinter Spring (symphonic poem), 1998; String Quartet no 2, 1999; Cello Concerto, 2000; Octave Variations (tuba

quartet), 2001; The Path to the River, octet, 2001; Cello Sonata, 2001; Fools by Heavenly Compulsion (String Quartet no 3), 2002; Sonnet (string orchestra), 2002; Theatre Dreams (brass quintet), 2003; A Colchester Suite (pipes), 2003; String Quartet no 4, 2005; Gallions Concerto, 2006; Many works recorded for commercial release; Stage works include False Relations (opera), 1997 and Gulliver, 2007, scores of several theatre productions (RSC, A&BC etc); Consultant in Music & Creativity in education; Seminar Leader, In Tune In Europe (DCMS/EU, 1998); Project Leader, Building Music (DfES, 2004). Honours: Hadow Open Scholarship in Composition to Worcester College, Oxford, 1967; Associate, Royal Academy of Music, 2002; Fellow, Royal Society of Arts. Memberships: British Academy of Composers and Songwriters (former Chairman). Address: 26 Belgrave Heights, Belgrave Road, Wanstead, London E11 3RE, England. E-mail: davidstoll@btconnect.com

STONE Oliver William, b. 15 September 1946, New York, USA. Screenwriter; Director. m. (1) Najwa Sarkis, 1971-77, divorced, (2) Elizabeth Stone, 1981-93, divorced, 2 children, (3) Sun-jung Jung, 1996. Education: BFA, Yale University; New York University Film School. Appointments include: Teacher, Cholon, Vietnam, 1965-66; US Merchant Marine, 1966; Served, US Army, Vietnam, 1967-68; Taxi Driver, New York City, 1971; Screenwriter, Seizure, 1973, Midnight Express, 1978, The Hand, 1981, Conan the Barbarian, with J Milius, 1982, Scarface, 1983, Year of the Dragon, with M Cimino, 1985, 8 Million Ways to Die, with D L Henry, 1986, Salvador, with R Boyle, 1986; Writer, Director, Platoon, 1986; Co-writer and Director: Wall Street, 1987; Talk Radio, 1988; The Doors, 1991; Screenwriter, Producer and Director: Born on the Fourth of July, 1989; JFK, 1991; Heaven and Earth, 1993; Natural Born Killers, 1994; Nixon, 1995; Director, U-Turn, 1997; Co-Writer, Evita, 1996; Producer: South Central, 1992; Zebrahead, 1992; The Joy Luck Club, 1993; Wild Palms, TV mini-series, 1993; New Age, 1994; Freeway, 1995; The People vs Larry Flynt, 1996; Any Given Sunday, 2000; Comandante (documentary), 2003; Alexander, 2004; Executive Producer: Killer: A Journal of Murder, 1995; (HBO)Indictment: The McMartin Preschool, 1995; The Corrupter, 1999; Any Given Sunday, 1999. Honours: Winner of numerous awards including: 2 Academy Awards for Platoon and Born of the Fourth of July; BAFTA Award, Directors Guild of America Award, for Platoon; Purple Heart with Oak Leaf Cluster; Bronze Star. Memberships: Writers' Guild of America; Directors' Guild of America; Academy Motion Pictures Arts and Sciences. Address: Ixtlan, 201 Santa Monica Boulevard, 6th Floor, Santa Monica, CA 90401, USA.

STONE Peter Talbot, b. 7 November 1925, London, England. University Teacher. m. Evelyn Jean Ballantyne (deceased), 1 son, 1 stepson. Education: Intermediate BSc, Chemistry, Physiology and Zoology, Chelsea Polytechnic, London University, 1947-49; Certificate in Social Science, London School of Economics, London University, 1949-51; BSc (Hons), Psychology, Birkbeck College, London University, 1951-55. Appointments: Sick Berth Branch, Royal Navy, 1944-46; Biochemistry Technician, Wellcome Physiological Research Laboratories, Beckenham, Kent, 1946-48; Social Worker, Audiology Unit, Royal National Throat, Nose & Ear Hospital, London, 1952-56; Senior Psychologist, CEPRE, Ministry of Supply, Farnborough, Hants, 1956-60; Lecturer, Senior Lecturer, Loughborough College of Technology (later Loughborough University), 1960-79; Reader in Vision and Lighting, Loughborough University, 1979-84; Consultant in Vision and Lighting, Stone Consultants, 1984-95; Retired, 1995-. Publications: Numerous articles and papers including: Discomfort glare and visual performance; Light and the eyes at work; Proposals for a practical method for evaluating complaints of eye discomfort arising from clerical work; Lighting and visual work in industry (in Textbook of Occupational Medicine); Lighting for the partially sighted; Fluorescent lighting and health. Honours: Walsh-Weston Award, The Illuminating Engineering Society, London, 1968; Owen-Aves Memorial Lecture, Yorkshire Optical Society, 1979; Honorary Fellow, Ergonomics Society, 1995. Memberships: Associate Fellow, The British Psychological Society; Fellow, The Chartered Institution of Building Services Engineers; Fellow, The Society of Light and Lighting; Fellow, The Ergonomics Society. Address: 47 Loughborough Road, Quorn, Loughborough, Leicestershire LE12 8DU, England.

STONE Sharon, b. 10 March 1958, Meadville, USA. Actress. m. (1) Michael Greenburg, 1984, divorced 1987, (2) Phil Bronstein, 1998, divorced 2004, 3 adopted sons. Education: Edinboro College. Career: Films include: Star Dust Memories (debut); Above the Law; Action Jackson; King Solomon's Mines; Allan Quatermain and the Lost City of Gold; Irreconcilable Differences; Deadly Blessing; Personal Choice; Basic Instinct; Dairy of a hit Man; Where Sleeping Dogs Lie; Sliver; Intersection; The Specialist; The Quick and the Dead; Casino; Last Dance; Diabolique, 1996; Sphere; The Might, 1999; The Muse, 1999; Simpatico, 1999; Gloria, 1999; Beautiful Joe, 2000; Cold Creek Manor, 2003; A Different Loyalty, 2004; Catwoman, 2004; Jiminy Glick in La La Wood, 2004; Alpha Dog, 2006; Basic Instinct 2, 2006; Bobby, 2006; If I Had Known I Was a Genius, 2007; When a Man Falls in the Forest, 2007; Democrazy, 2007; The Year of Getting in Know Us, 2008; Five Dollars a Day, 2008; TV includes: Tears in the Rain; War and Remembrance; Calendar Girl Murders; The Vegas Strip Wars. Honour: Chevalier, Ordre des Arts et des Lettres. Address: c/o Guy McElwaine, PO Box 7304, North Hollywood, CA 91603, USA.

STOPPARD Tom (Sir), (Thomas Straussler), b. 3 July 1937, Zin, Czechoslovakia (British citizen). Dramatist; Screenwriter. m. (1) Jose Ingle, 1965, divorced 1972, 2 sons, (2) Dr Miriam Moore-Robinson, 1972, divorced 1992, 2 sons. Publications: Plays: Rosencrantz and Guildenstern are Dead, 1967; The Real Inspector Hound, 1968; Albert's Bridge, 1968; Enter a Free Man, 1968; After Magritte, 1971; Jumpers, 1972; Artists Descending a Staircase, and, Where Are They Now?, 1973; Travesties, 1975; Dirty Linen, and New-Found-Land, 1976; Every Good Boy Deserves Favour, 1978; Professional Foul, 1978; Night and Day, 1978; Undiscovered Country, 1980; Dogg's Hamlet, Cahoot's Macbeth, 1980; On the Razzle, 1982; The Real Thing, 1983; The Dog It Was That Died, 1983; Squaring the Circle, 1984; Four Plays for Radio, 1984; Rough Crossing, 1984; Dalliance and Undiscovered Country, 1986; Largo Desolato, by Vaclav Havel (translator), 1987; Hapgood, 1988; In the Native State, 1991; Arcadia, 1993; Indian Ink, 1995; The Invention of Love, 1997; The Seagul, 1997; The Coast of Utopia: Ttrilogy: Part One: Voyage, Part Two: Shipwreck, Part Three: Salvage, 2002; The Television Plays 1965-1984, 1993. Fiction: Introduction 2, 1964; Lord Malquist and Mr Moon, 1965. Other: 8 screenplays; Various unpublished state, radio, and television plays. Honours: John Whiting Award, Arts Council, 1967; New York Drama Critics Award, 1968; Italia Prize, 1968; Tony Awards, 1968, 1976, 1984; Evening Standard Awards, 1968, 1972, 1974, 1978, 1993, 1997; Olivier Award, 1993; Knighted, 1997; Order of Merit, 2000.

STOREY David (Malcolm), b. 13 July 1933, Wakefield, England. Writer; Dramatist; Screenwriter; Poet. m. Barbara Rudd Hamilton, 1956, 2 sons, 2 daughters. Education: Diploma, Slade School of Art, 1956. Publications: This Sporting Life, 1960; Flight into Camden, 1960; Radcliffe, 1963; Pasmore, 1972; A Temporary Life, 1973; Edward, 1973; Saville, 1976; A Prodigal Child, 1982; Present Times, 1984; Storey's Lives: Poems 1951-1991, 1992; A Serious Man, 1998; As it Happened, 2002. Honours: Macmillan Fiction Award, 1960; John Llewellyn Memorial Prize, 1960; Somerset Maugham Award, 1960; Evening Standard Awards, 1967, 1970; Los Angeles Drama Critics Award, 1969; Writer of the Year Award, Variety Club of Great Britain, 1969; New York Drama Critics Award, 1969, 1970, 1971; Geoffrey Faber Memorial Prize, 1973; Fellow, University College, London, 1974; Booker Prize, 1976. Address: c/o Jonathan Cape Ltd, Random Century House, 20 Vauxhall Bridge Road, London SW1V 2SA, England.

STRANGE Curtis, b. 30 January 1955, Norfolk, Virginia, USA. Professional Golfer. m. Sarah Jones, 2 sons. Education: Wake Forest University. Career: Professional, 1976-; First joined PGA tour, 1977; Won Pensacola Open, 1979; Won Sammy Davis Jr Greater Hartford Open, 1983; Won LaJel Classic, 1984; Won Honda Classic, Panasonic-Las Vegas International, 1985; Won Canadian Open, 1985; Won Houston Open, 1986; Won Canadian Open, Federal Express – St Jude Classic, NEC Series of Golf, 1987; Won Sandway Cove Classic, Australia, 1988; Won Industry Insurance Agent Open, Memorial Tournament, US Open, Nabisco Championships, 1988; Won US Open, Palm Meadows Cup, Australia, 1989; Won Holden Classic, Australia, 1993. Memberships: Member, PGA Tour Charity Team, Michelob Championship, Kingsmill, 1996. Honours: Captain US Ryder Cup Team after playing on five Ryder Cup Teams, 2002; Golf Analyst, ABC Sports, 1997-; Golfer of the Year, 1986, 1987. Address: c/o IMG, 1 Erieview Plaza, Suite 1300, Cleveland, OH 44114, USA.

STRAUSS Botho, b. 2 December 1944, Naumberg-an-der-Saale, Germany. Author; Poet; Dramatist. Education: German Language and Literature, Drama, Sociology, Cologne and Munich. Publications: Bekannte Gesichter, gemischte Gefühle (with T Bernhard and F Kroetz), 1974; Trilogie des Wiedersehens, 1976; Gross und Klein, 1978; Rumor, 1980; Kalldeway Farce, 1981; Paare, Passanten, 1981; Der Park, 1983; Der junge Mann, 1984; Diese Erinnerung an einen, der nur einen Tag zu Gast War, 1985; Die Fremdenführerin, 1986; Niemand anderes, 1987; Besucher, 1988; Kongress: Die Kette der Demütigungen, 1989; Theaterstücke in zwei Banden, 1994; Wohnen Dammern Lügen, 1994. Honours: Dramatists' Prize, Hannover, 1975; Schiller Prize, Baden-Württemberg, 1977; Literary Prize, Bavarian Academy of Fine Arts, Munich, 1981; Jean Paul Prize, 1987; Georg Büchner Prize, 1989. Membership: PEN. Address: Keithstrasse 8, D-17877, Berlin, Germany.

STRAW Jack (John Whitaker Straw) (Rt Hon), b. 3 August 1946, Buckhurst Hill, Essex, England. Politician; Lawyer. m. (1) Anthea L Watson, 1968, divorced 1978, 1 daughter, deceased, (2) Alice E Perkins, 1978, 1 son, 1 daughter. Education: University of Leeds. Appointments: President, National Union of Students, 1969-71; Member, Islington Borough Council, 1971-78; Inner London Education Authority, 1971-74; Deputy Leader, 1973-74; Called to bar, Inner Temple, 1972; Bencher, 1997; Practised as Bar, 1972-74; Special Adviser to Secretary of State for Social Services, 1974-76; To Secretary of State for Environment, 1976-77; On Staff of Granada TV (World in Action), 1977-79;

Member of Parliament for Blackburn, 1979-; Opposition Treasury Spokesman, 1980-83; Local Government Spokesman, 1982-87; Member of Parliament, Committee of Labour Party (Shadow Cabinet), 1987-97; Shadow Secretary of State for Education, 1987-92; For the Environment (Local Government), 1992-94; Shadow Home Secretary, 1994-97; Home Secretary, 1997-2001; Secretary of State for Foreign and Commonweath Affairs, 2001-; Lord Chancellor, Secretary of State for Justice, 2007-; Member, Council Institute for Fiscal Studies, 1983-2000; Lancaster University, 1988-92; Vice President, Association of District Councils; Visiting Fellow, Nuffield College, Oxford, 1990-98; Governor, Blackburn College, 1990-; Pimlico School, 1994-2000 (Chair 1995-98); Fellow, Royal Statistics Society, 1995-; Labour; Hon LLD, 1999; Labour Publications: Contributions to pamphlets, newspaper articles, Policy and Ideology, 1993. Address: House of Commons, London, SW1A 0AA, England.

STREEP Meryl (Mary Louise), b. 22 June 1949, Summit, New Jersey, USA. Actress. m. Donald Gummer, 1978, 1 son, 3 daughters. Education: Singing Studies with Estelle Liebling; Studied Drama, Vassar; Yale School of Drama. Appointments: Stage debut, New York, Trelawny of the Wells; 27 Wagons Full of Cotton, New York; New York Shakespeare Festival, 1976 in Henry V and Measure for Measure; Also in Happy End (musical); The Taming of the Shrew; Wonderland (musical); Taken in Marriage; Numerous other plays; Films include: Julia, 1976; The Deer Hunter, 1978; Manhattan, 1979; The Seduction of Joe Tynan, 1979; The Senator, 1979; Kramer vs Kramer, 1979; Still of the Night, 1982; Silkwood, 1983; Plenty, 1984; Falling in Love, 1984; Ironweed, 1987; A Cry in the Dark, 1988; The Lives and Loves of a She Devil, 1989; Hollywood and Me, 1989; Postcards from the Edge, 1991; Defending Your Life, 1991; Death Becomes Her, 1992; The House of the Spirits; The River Wild, 1994; The Bridges of Madison County, 1995; Before and After; Marvin's Room; One True Thing, 1998; Dancing at Lughnasa, 1999; Music of the Heart, 1999; The Hours, 2002; Adaptation, 2003; The Manchurian Candidate, 2004; Lemony Snicket's A Series of Unfortunate Events, 2004; Prime, 2005; A Prairie Home Companion, 2006; The Music of Regret, 2006; The Devil Wears Prada, 2006; The Ant Bully, (voice), 2006; Dark Matter, 2007; Evening, 2007; Rendition, 2007; Lions for Lambs, 2007; Mamma Mia! 2008; Doubt, 2008; TV appearances include: The Deadliest Season; Uncommon Women; Holocaust; Velveteen Rabbit; First Do No Harm, 1997; Angels in America, 2003; Many others. Honours: Academy Award for Best Supporting Actress for Kramer vs Kramer, 1980; Best Supporting Actress Awards from National Society of Film Critics for the Deer Hunter; New York Film Critics Circle for Kramer vs Kramer, The Seduction of Joe Tynan and Sophie's Choice; Emmy Award for Holocaust; British Academy Award, 1982; Academy Award for Best Actress for Sophie's Choice, 1982; Hon Dr, Yale, 1983; Dartmouth, 1981; Lafayette, 1985; Bette Davis Lifetime Achievement Award, 1998; Special Award Berlin International Film Festival, 1999; Golden Globe for Best Supporting Actress, 2003; Commander, Ordre des Arts et des Lettres, 2003; Golden Globe, Best Actress in a Miniseries or TV Movie, 2004; Screen Actors Guild Award, Best Actress in a Miniseries, 2004; Emmy Award, Outstanding Lead Actress in a Miniseries or Movie, 2004. Address: c/o Creative Artists Agency, 9830 Wilshire Boulevard, Beverly Hills, CA 90212, USA.

STREET Brian Vincent, b. 24 October 1943, Manchester, England. Professor. 1 son, 2 daughters. Education: BA, Hons, London, 1966; Dip Soc Anth, 1967, D Phil, Oxon, 1970, Institute of Social Anthropology, Oxford. Appointments; Lecturer

in English Language and Literature, University of Mashad, Iran, 1970-71; Lecturer in Social Anthropology, University of Sussex, 1974; Visiting Associate Professor, Graduate School of Education, University of Pennsylvania, 1988; Senior Lecturer in Social Anthropology, University of Sussex, 1989-96; Adjunct Professor of Education, Graduate School of Education, University of Pennsylvania, 1993-; Professor of Language Education, School of Education, King's College, London University, 1996-. Publications: Various books and articles on literacy and anthropology published worldwide include: The Savage in Literature, 1975; Literacy in Theory and Practice, 1984; Social Literacies: Critical Approaches to Literacy in Education, Development and Ethnography, 1995. Honours: David S Russell Award for Distinguished Research, NCTE, 1995; Shortlisted for the BAAL Annual Book Prize, 1993 and 2002; Awarded numerous grants in Europe and America. Memberships: Fellow of the British Institute of Persian Studies, Iran, 1969-70; Fellow, Royal Anthropological Institute, 1974-; Association of Social Anthropologists, 1974-; British Educational Research Association, 1996-; American Educational Research Association, 1996-; British Association for Applied Language Studies, 1992-. Address: Department of Education and Professional Studies, Franklin Wilkins Building, Waterloo Bridge Annex, 120 Stamford Street, London, SE1 9NN, England. E-mail: brian.street@kcl.ac.uk

STREET-PORTER Janet, b. 27 December 1946, England. Journalist; TV Presenter; Producer; Editor. m. (1) Tim Street-Porter, 1967, divorced 1975, (2) A M M Elliot, 1976, divorced 1978, (3) Frank Cvitanovich, divorced 1988, deceased 1995. Education: Architectural Association. Career: Petticoat Magazine Fashion Writer and Columnist, 1968; Daily Mail, 1969-71; Evening Standard, 1971-73; Own Show, LBC Radio Programme, 1973; Presenter, London Weekend Show, London Weekend Television (LWT), 1975; Producer, presenter, Saturday Night People (with Clive James and Russell Harty), The Six O'Clock Show (with Michael Aspel), Around Midnight, 1975-85; Network 7 for Channel 4, 1986-; BBC Youth and Entertainment Features Head, 1988-94; Head, Independent Production for Entertainment, 1994; Managing Director, Live TV, Mirror Group plc, 1994-95; TV Presenter, Design Awards, Travels with Pevsner, Coast to Coast, The Midnight Hour, 1996-98, As the Crow Flies (series), 1999; Cathedral Calls, 2000; J'Accuse, Internet, 1996; Janet Save the Monarchy, 2005; So You Think You Can Teach, 2004; Editor, The Independent on Sunday, 1999-2001; Editor-at-Large, 2001-; Contestant, I'm a Celebrity.... Get Me Out of Here!; The F-Word, 2006; Deadline, 2007. Publications: Scandal, 1980; The British Teapot, 1981; Coast to Coast, 1998; As the Crow Flies, 1999; Baggage, 2004. Honours: Prix Italia for the Vampyr, 1992; BAFTA award for originality for Network 7, 1998. Memberships: Vice President, Ramblers' Association; President, Globetrotters Club, 2003-; Fellow, Royal Television Society. Address: c/o Emma Hardy, Princess Television, Princess Studios, Whiteley, 151 Queensway, London WC2 4SB, England. E-mail: emma.hardy@princesstv.com

STREETEN Paul Patrick, b. 18 July 1917, Vienna, Austria. Retired Professor. m. Ann H Higgins, 9 June 1951, 1 stepson, 2 daughters. Education: MA, University of Aberdeen, 1944; BA, 1947 MA, 1952, Oxon; DLitt, 1976. Appointment: Chairman of the Board of World Development, 1972-2003. Publications: Economic Integration, 1961, 2nd edition, 1964; Frontiers of Development Studies, 1972; Development Perspectives, 1981; First Things First, 1981; What Price Food?, 1987; Mobilizing Human Potential, 1989; Thinking About Development, 1995, paperback, 1997; Globalisation: Threat or Opportunity, 2001. Contributions to: Magazines, journals and books. Honours:

Honorary Fellow, Institute of Development Studies, 1980; Honorary Fellow, Balliol College, 1986; Essays in Honour of Paul Streeten: Theory and Reality in Development, (edited by Sanjaya Lall and Frances Stewart), 1986; Development Prize, Justus Liebig University, 1987; Honorary LLD, University of Aberdeen, 1980; Honorary DLitt, University of Malta, 1992; Silver Sign of Honour for Services to the Land of Vienna; Wassily Leontief Award, Tufts University. Memberships: Royal Economic Society; American Economic Association; Society for International Development Address: Box 92, Spencertown, NY 12165, USA.

STREHLOW Kathleen Stuart, b. 10 April 1936. Research Director. Education: Teachers Certificate, Claremont Teachers College of Washington; BA, University of Adelaide, 1977; Edith Cowan University, an Alumna, 1999; MA, University of Toronto, 2000; Hon PhD. Appointments: Teaching posts, 1955-64; Research, University of Adelaide, 1964-75; Research Director, The Strehlow Research Foundation, 1975-; Invited Visiting Professor, University of Prince Edward Island, 1984-85; Invited Visiting Professor, Ansted University, 2000; Invited for Conferment of Honorary Degree, Ansted University, 2000. Publications: Aboriginal Central Australia, Map in Songs of Central Australia, 1971; Aboriginal Land Ownership in Central Australia; Aboriginal Women ... in Central Australia with Special Reference to their Land Ownership, 1986;The Operation of Fear in Traditional Aboriginal Society in Central Australia, 1991; Symbolism in Aboriginal Art, 1992; Mythical Origins, 1998; Editor, The Land of Altjira, 1995; Editor, Agencies of Social Control in Central Australia, 1995; Editor, Aranda Regular and Irregular Marriages, 1995. Honours: Bursary to Claremont Teachers College, 1952; Commonwealth Scholarship to University of Adelaide and Washington, 1968, 1953; Founding Member, The Bradman Legacy. Memberships: Fellow, Fellowship of Australian Writers; Foundation Member, Australian Stockman's Hall of Fame and Outback Heritage Centre; Australian Society of Writers; Life Fellow, IBA; John McDouall Stuart Society Inc; Member, Australian Society of Authors; Member, International Committee for Urgent Anthropological and Ethnological Research, Vienna. Listed in: Dictionary of International Biography; The World Who's Who of Women; International Authors and Writers Who's Who; International Who's Who of Intellectuals; Honours List, Dictionary of International Biography for Outstanding Contribution to Education. Address: The Strehlow Research Foundation, 30 Da Costa Avenue, Prospect, SA 5082, Australia.

STREISAND Barbra Joan, b. 24 April 1942, Brooklyn, New York, USA. Singer; Actress; Director; Producer; Writer; Composer; Philanthropist. m. (1) Elliott Gould, 1963, divorced 1971, 1 son, (2) James Brolin, 1998. Education: Erasmus Hall High School. Career: Began recording career with Columbia records, 1963; Appeared in musical play Funny Girl, New York, 1964, London, 1966; TV programme My Name is Barbra shown in England, Holland, Australia, Sweden, Bermuda and the Philippines; Films: Funny Girl, 1968; Hello Dolly, 1969; On a Clear Day You Can See Forever, 1969; The Owl and the Pussycat, 1971; What's Up Doc?, 1972; Up the Sandbox, 1973; The Way We Were, 1973; For Pete's Sake, 1974; Funny Lady, 1975; A Star is Born, 1977; The Main Event, 1979; All Night Long, 1981; Yentl, 1934; Nuts, 1987; Sing 1989; The Prince of Tides, 1990; The Mirror Has Two Faces, 1996; Meet the Fockers, 2004; Numerous albums, singles, TV and concert appearances. Honours: New York Critics Best Supporting Actress Award, 1962; Grammy Awards for Best Female Pop Vocalist, 1963, 64, 65, 77, 86; GB Variety Poll Award, Best

For Actress, 1966; Golden Globe Academy Award, 1968; Special Tony Award, 1970; Golden Globe, Best Picture, Best Director, 1984; 5 Emmy Awards; Peabody Award; 3 Cable Ace Awards; 37 Gold and 21 Platinum Albums. Address: c/o Jeff Berg, ICM, 8942 Wilshire Boulevard, Beverly Hills, CA 90211, USA.

STRITCH Elaine, b. 2 February 1926, Detroit, USA. Actress; Singer. m. John Bay, 1973, deceased 1982. Education: Sacred Heart Convent, Detroit; Drama Workshop; New School for Social Research. Career: Stage: Loco, 1946; Three Indelicate Ladies, 1947; Yes M'Lord, 1949; Pal Joey, 1952; Bus Stop, 1955; Sail Away, 1961, 1962; Who's Afraid of Virginia Woolf?1962, 1965; Company, 1970, 1971; Love Letters, 1990; Elaine Stritch At Liberty, 2002; Film: The Scarlet Hour, 1956; Three Violent People, 1956; A Farewell to Arms, 1957; The Perfect Furlough, 1958; Who Killed Teddy Bear, 1965; Pigeons, 1971; September, 1988; Cocoon: The Return; Cadillac Man, 1990; Out to Sea, 1997; Screwed, 2000; Small Time Crooks, 2000; Autumn in New York, 2001; Monster-in-Law, 2005; Romance & Cigarettes, 2005; TV: My Sister Eileen, 1962; Two's Company, 1975-76, 1979; Stranded, 1986; Elaine Stritch: At Liberty, 2004; Paradise, 2004; 30 Rock, 2007. Publications: Am I Blue? – Living with Diabetes and, Dammit, Having Fun, 1984. Honours: Emmy Award, Outstanding Individual Performance in a Variety or Music Programme, 2004.

STRONG Sir Roy (Colin), b. 23 August 1935, London, England. Writer; Historian; Lecturer. m. Julia Trevelyan Oman, 1971, deceased, 2003. Education: Queen Mary College, London; Warburg Institute, London. Appointments: Assistant Keeper, 1959, Director, Keeper and Secretary, 1967-73, National Portrait Gallery, London; Ferens Professor of Fine Art, University of Hull, 1972; Walls Lecturer, J Pierpoint Morgan Library, New York, 1974; Director, Victoria and Albert Museum, London, 1974-87; Director, Oman Publications Ltd; Andrew Carnduff Ritchie Lecturer, University of Yale, 1999; Host TV Series, The Diets That Time Forgot, 2008. Publications: Portraits of Queen Elizabeth I, 1963; Holbein and Henry the VIII, 1967; The English Icon: Elizabethan and Jacobean Portraiture, 1969; Tudor and Jacobean Portraits, 1969; Van Dyck: Charles I on Horseback, 1972; Splendour at Court: Renaissance Spectacle and the Theatre of Power, 1973; Nicholas Hilliard, 1975; The Renaissance Garden in England, 1979; Britannia Triumphans: Inigo Jones, Rubens and Whitehall Palace, 1980; Henry, Prince of Wales and England's Lost Renaissance, 1986; Creating Small Gardens, 1986; Gloriana: Portraits of Queen Elizabeth I, 1987; A Small Garden Designer's Handbook, 1987; Cecil Beaton: The Royal Portraits, 1988; Creating Small Formal Gardens, 1989; Lost Treasures of Britain, 1990; A Celebration of Gardens (editor) 1991; The Garden Trellis, 1991; Small Period Gardens, 1992; Royal Gardens, 1992; A Country Life, 1994; Successful Small Gardens, 1994; William Larkin: Vanitù giacobite, Italy, 1994; The English Vision: Country Life 1897-1997; The Story of Britain, 1996; The Tudor and Stuart Monarchy, 3 volumes, 1995-97; The Story of Britain, 1996; The English Vision: Country Life 1897-1997, 1997; The Roy Strong Diaries 1967-1987, 1997; The Spirit of Britain. A Narrative History of the Arts, 1999, re-issued as The Arts in Britain, 2004; Garden Party, 2000; The Artist and the Garden, 2000; Ornament in the Small Garden, 2001; Feast – A History of Grand Eating, 2002; The Laskett – The Story of a Garden, 2003; Passions Past & Present, 2005; Coronation: A History of Kingshill and the British Monarchy, 2005; A Little History of the English Country Church, 2007. Co-Author: Leicester's Triumph, 1964; Elizabeth R, 1971; Mary Queen of Scots,

1972; Inigo Jones: The Theatre of the Stuart Court, 1973; An Early Victorian Album: The Hill-Adamson Collection, 1974; The English Miniature, 1981; The English Year, 1982; Artists of the Tudor Court, 1983; The Diary of John Evelyn, 2006. Honours: Fellow, Queen Mary College, 1976; Knighted, 1982; Senior Fellow, Royal College of Arts, 1983; High Bailiff and Searcher of the Sanctuary of Westminster Abbey, 2000; Honorary doctorates: Leeds 1983; Keele, 1984; Worcester, 2004; Honorary Fellow, Royal Society of Literature, 1999; President of the Royal Photographic Society's Award, 2003. Memberships: Arts Council of Great Britain, chairman, arts panel, 1983-87; British Council, Fine Arts Advisory Committee, 1974-87; Royal College of Arts Council, 1979-87; Westminster Abbey Architectural Panel, 1975-89; President, Garden History Society, 2000-. Address: The Laskett, Much Birch, Herefordshire HR2 8HZ, England.

STRUTHERS Allan David, b. 14 August 1952, Medical Professor. m. Julia, 1 son, 1 daughter. Education: Hutchesons Boys School, Glasgow; Glasgow University, 1969-77. Appointments: Senior Registrar, Royal Postgraduate Medical School, Glasgow, 1982-85; Senior Lecturer/Reader, 1985-92, Professor of Cardiovascular Medicine & Therapeutics, 1992-, Dundee University. Publications: Spironolactone increases nitric oxide bioactivity improves endothelial vasodilator dysfunction and suppresses vascular angiotension I/II conversion in patients with chronic heart failure, 2000; Gradual reactivation over time of vascular tissue angiotensin I to angiotensin II conversion during chronic lisinopril therapy in chronic heart failure, 2002; Allopurinol improves endothelial dysfunction in chronic heart failure, 2002; High dose allopurinol improves endothelial function by profoundly reducing oxidativ stress and not by lowering uric acid, 2006. Honours: SKB Prize; Menarini Academy Research Award; Australian Visiting Lecturer of British Pharmacological Society. Memberships: Fellow, European Society of Cardiology; Fellow, British Pharmacological Society; Fellow, Royal College of Physicians, London. Address: Division of Medicine & Therapeutics, Ninewells Hospital & Medical School, Dundee DD1 9SY, Scotland. E-mail: a.d.struthers@dundee.ac.uk

STUART Jessica Jane, b. 20 August 1942, Ashland, Kentucky, USA. Retired; Teacher; Poet; Writer. Divorced, 2 sons. Education: AB, Western Reserve University, Cleveland, Ohio, 1964; MA, 1967, MA, 1969, PhD, 1971, Indiana University, Bloomington, Indiana. Appointments: Teaching, University of Florida, 1986-88, Santa Fe Community College, Gainesville, Florida, 1986-88; Flagler College and St Johns River Community College, St Augustine, Florida, 1989-90. Publications: Eyes of the Mole, 1968; White Barn, 1971; A Year's Harvest, 1956; Transparencies (with prose), 1986; Novels: Yellowhank, 1973; Passerman's Hollow, 1974; Land of the Fox, 1975; A Peaceful Evening Wind, 2002; Short stories: Gideon's Children, 1976; Chapbooks: Finding Tents, 2002; Celestial Moon, 2003; Spanish Moss, 2003; Mardi Gras, 2004; The Turning Year, 2005; Along the River's Shore, 2004; Haiku, 2004; Violets, 2006; A November Moon, 2006, Pretending (a mini chap book), 2007; Spring Moon, 2007. Honours: Grand Prix, KSPS Kentucky State Poetry Society, 1993; Cameo Chapbook Contest Award (Poetry), 1998; State Poetry Contests Award; Mississippi Poetry Society First Place, 2002. Memberships: MPS (Mississippi); CSPS California State Poetry Society; APS (Arizona); KSPS (Kentucky State Poetry Society). Address:225 Stuart Lane, Greenup, KY 41144, USA.

STUBBS Imogen Mary, b. 20 February 1961, Rothbury, England. Actress. m. Trevor Nunn, 1994, 1 son, 1 daughter. Education: Exeter College, Oxford; Royal Academy of Dramatic Arts. Appointments: Appeared with RSC in The Rover; Two Noble Kinsmen; Richard II, 1987-88; Othello, 1991; Heartbreak House, 1992; St Joan, 1994; Twelfth Night, 1996; Blast from the Past, 1998; Betrayal, 1998; The Relapse, 2001; Three Sisters, 2002; TV appearances include: The Rainbow; Anna Lee; After the Dance; Mothertime, 1997; Blind Ambition, 2000; Big Kids, 2000; Casualty, 2005; Marple: The Moving Finger, 2006; Brief Encounters, 2006; Films include: Nanon; A Summer Story; Erik the Viking; True Colours; A Pin for the Butterfly; Fellow Traveller; Sandra c'est la vie; Jack and Sarah; Sense and Sensibility, 1995; Twelfth Night, 1996; Collusion, 2003; Dead Cool, 2004; Stories of Lost Souls, 2006. Honours: Gold Medal, Chicago Film Festival. Address: c/o Nick Hern Books Ltd, The Glasshouse, 49a Goldhawk Road, London W12 8QP, England.

STUBBS Jean, b. 23 October 1926, Denton, Lancashire, England. Author. m. (1) Peter Stubbs, 1948, 1 son, 1 daughter, (2) Roy Oliver, 1980. Education: Manchester School of Art, 1944-47; Diploma, Loreburn Secretarial College, Manchester, 1947. Appointments: Copywriter, Henry Melland, 1964-66; Reviewer, Books and Bookmen, 1965-76; Writer-in-Residence for Avon, 1984. Publications: The Rose Grower, 1962; The Travellers, 1963; Hanrahan's Colony, 1964; The Straw Crown, 1966; My Grand Enemy, 1967; The Passing Star, 1970; The Case of Kitty Ogilvie, 1970; An Unknown Welshman, 1972; Dear Laura, 1973; The Painted Face, 1974; The Golden Crucible, 1976; Kit's Hill,1979; The Ironmaster, 1981; The Vivian Inheritance, 1982; The Northern Correspondent, 1984; 100 Years Around the Lizard, 1985; Great Houses of Cornwall,1987; A Lasting Spring, 1987; Like We Used To Be, 1989; Summer Secrets, 1990; Kelly Park, 1992; Charades, 1994; The Witching Time, 1998; I'm a Stranger Here Myself, 2004. Contributions to: Anthologies and magazines. Honours: Tom Gallon Trust Award, 1964; Daughter of Mark Twain, 1973. Memberships: PEN; Society of Women Writers and Journalists; Detection Club; Lancashire Writers Association; West Country Writers; Society of Authors. Address: Trewin, Nancegollan, Helston, Cornwall TR13 0AJ, England.

STUCHEBNIKOV Vladimir Mikhailovich, b. 25 February 1942, Ryazan, Russia. Physicist. m. Tatyana, 1 son, 2 daughters. Education: Degree in Physics, Moscow State University, 1965; Masters degree in Physics, 1967; Doctor Degree in Technical Science, 1987. Appointments: Researcher, Physics, Moscow State University, 1963-71; Department Chief, Institute of Instrumentation Technique, Korolyev, 1971-75; Laboratory Chief, Research Development Institute Teplopribor, Mechanical Instrumentation, Moscow, 1975-88; Professor, Ulyanovsk State University, 1988-; Vice Director, Integrated Sensors Institute, Ulyanovsk, 1988-91; General Director, Joint Stock Co Microelectronic Sensors and Devices, Ulyanovsk, 1991-; Vice Director, Ulyanovsk Centre for Microelectronics, 1992-. Publications: Over 150 articles in professional magazines; 30 patents. Gold and Silver Medals of Russian State Exhibitions; Star of Russian Management, Russian Industrial Trade Forum, 2005. Memberships: Russian Metrological Academy; IEEE; AAAS; New York Academy of Sciences. E-mail: mida@mv.ru Website: www.midaus.com

STUDER Gerald C, b. 31 January 1927, Smithville, Ohio, USA. Christian Minister. m. Marilyn Ruth Kreider, 2 daughters. Education: BA, Goshen College, 1947; ThB, Goshen Biblical Seminary, 1949; BD GBS, 1957, MDiv, GBS, 1971. Appointments: Pastor, Smithville (Ohio) Mennonite

Church, 1947-61; Scottdale (PA) Mennonite Church, 1961-73; Plains Mennonite Church, Lansdale, Pennsylvania,1973-90; Conference Minister, Atlantic Coast Mennonite Conference, 1990-94. Publications: Numerous articles in magazines; Books: Christopher Dock: Colonial Schoolmaster, 1967; After Death, What?, 1976. Memberships: First President of the North American Mennonite Youth Fellowship, 1947-50; Mennonite Publication Board, 1956-59, 1965-68, 1993-01; General Mennonite Board, 1971-73; Mennonite Historical and Research Committee, 1960-71; International Society of Bible Collectors, 1965-, President, 1988-2002. Address: 207 W Summit St, Apt A-150, Souderton, PA 18964-2063, USA.

STUMMER Peter Olaf, b. 1 June 1942, Jauernig, Czech Republic. Senior Lecturer. m. Anne Stummer-Schwegmann. Education: English, Romance Philology, Philosophy, 1961-66; Teacher's Diploma, 1966; PhD, 1969; 2nd Teacher's Diploma, 1970. Appointments: Tutor Students' Hall of Residence, 1965-70; Tutor, English Department, Munich, 1967-69; Secondary School Teacher and University Lectureship, 1969-71; Assistant Professor, University of Cologne, 1971-74; Assistant Professor, 1974-78, Lecturer (tenured), 1978-, Senior Lecturer, Literatures Written in English, 1980-, University of Munich. Publications: Author and editor of several books; Author of over 30 articles on various aspects of diverse literatures written in English, especially from Africa, India and Australia; Conference Convenor; Originator of Postgraduate Programme on English Speaking Countries. Honours: German Studies Association, University of Aberdeen; Visiting Professor, University of Trento; Lectureship, University of Passau. Memberships: One-time Vice President, ASNEL; EACLALS; ACLALS; EASA; ASAL; BASA; German Association for Australian Studies. Address: Edelweiss-strasse 115, D-82178 Puchheim, Germany. E-mail: peter.stummer@lmu.de

SU Chun-Lien, b. 18 December 1971, Taiwan. Power Engineering. m. Ching-Fang Lin, 1 daughter. Education: Diploma, Electrical Engineering, National Kaohsiung Institute of Technology, Taiwan; MS, 1997, PhD, 2001, Electrical Engineering, National Sun Yat-Sen University, Taiwan. Appointments: Associate Professor, Marine Engineering Department, National Kaohsiung Marine University, 2002-. Publications: Over 50 technical papers in IEEE journals and Power Engineering Conference; Co-author, Electrical Power Systems Quality. Honours: Outstanding Young Researcher Award, Taiwan National Science Council, 2006; Outstanding Paper Award, MATLAB & SIMULINK Tech Forum Expo, 2006; Listed in international biographical dictionaries. Memberships: IEEE; IASTED; Taiwan Association for Hydrogen Energy and Fuel Cell; Power, Electronic, Solar and New Energy; Cogeneration; Naval Architects and Marine Engineers. Address: Department of Marine Engineering, National Kaohsiung Marine University, No 482, Jhungjou 3rd Road, Chijin-Chiu, Kaohsiung 805, Taiwan. E-mail: cls@mail.nkmu.edu.tw

SU Sunyu, b. 8 April 1955, Jinjiang, Fujian, China. MRI Scientist. m. Rong Luo, 2 sons. Education: MSc, University of New Brunswick, Fredericton, New Brunswick, Canada, 1986; PhD, University of Toronto, Toronto, Ontario, Canada, 1991. Appointments: Postdoctoral Fellow, University of Toronto, 1991-93; Research Associate, Institute for Biodiagnostics, National Research Council Canada, Winnipeg, 1993-96; MRI Scientist, Toshiba America MRI Inc, South San Francisco, USA, 1996-2000; RF Coils Program Manager, GE Healthcare Coils – USA Instruments Inc, Aurora, USA, 2000-. Publications: 15 papers in professional journals; 17

conference papers and presentations; 10 patents. Honours: Connaught Doctoral Scholarship Award, 1986, U of T Open Fellowship Award, 1987, E F Burton Fellowship Award, 1989, University of Toronto; Management Award, CEO Award, GE Healthcare Coils, 2006; Listed in international biographical directories. Memberships: International Society of Magnetic Resonance in Medicine. E-mail: sunyu.su@med.ge.com

SUBASIC Marko, b. 13 April 1976, Zagreb, Croatia. Electrical Engineer. Education: BSc, Electrical Engineering, 1994-99; MSc, Electrical Engineering, 1999-2003, Faculty of Electrical Engineering and Computing, University of Zagreb. Appointments: Junior Research Fellow, Faculty of Electrical Engineering and Computing, University of Zagreb, 1999. Publications: 1 journal paper; 1 book chapter; 12 refereed conference papers. Memberships: IEEE; Croatian Nuclear Society. E-mail: msubasic@hotmail.com

SUCHET David Courtney, b. 2 May 1946, London, England. Actor. m. Sheila Ferris, June 1976, 1 son, 1 daughter. Appointments: Former Member, National Youth Theatre, Chester Repertory Company; RSC, 1973, Associate Artist. Creative Works: Roles includes: Tybalt in Romeo and Juliet, Orlando in As You Like It, Tranio in Taming of the Shrew, 1973; Zamislov in Summerfolk, The Fool in King Lear, 1974, 1975; Pisanio in Cymbeline, Wilmer in Comrades, 1974; Hubert in King John, Ferdinand King of Navarre in Love's Labour's Lost, 1975; Shylock in The Merchant of Venice, Gruio in Taming of the Shrew, Sir Nathaniel in Love's Labour's Lost, Glougauer in Once in a Lifetime, Caliban in The Tempest, Shylock in The Merchant of Venice, Sextus Pompey in Antony and Cleopatra, 1978; Angelo in Measure for Measure, 1979; Oleanna, 1993; What a Performance, 1994; Who's Afraid of Virginia Woolf?, 1997; Saturday, Sunday and Monday, 1998; Amadeus, 1998-2000; Man & Boy, 2004-05; Once in a Lifetime, 2005-06. Films include: Big Foot & The Hendersons, 1986; Crime of Honour, The Last Innocent Man, 1987; A World Apart, To Kill a Priest (also known as Popielusko), 1988; The Lucona Affair, When the Whales Came, 1990; Executive Decision, Deadly Voyage, 1995; Sunday, 1996; A Perfect Murder, Wing Commander, 1998; RKO, Sabotage, 1999; Live From Baghdad, The Wedding Party, Foolproof, 2002; The Flood, 2006; The Bank Job, Act of God, 2008; Numerous TV appearances including: Master of the Game, Reilly – Ace of Spies, 1984; Mussolini: The Untold Story, 1985; The Life of Agatha Christie, Hercule Poirot in Agatha Christie's Poirot, 8 Series including 100th Anniversary Special: The Mysterious Affair at Styles, 1990-; Days of Majesty, 1994; The Cruel Train, Moses, 1995; Solomon, Seesaw, 1997; The Way We Live Now, 2001; National Crime Squad, 2001-02; The First Lady, Henry VIII, 2003; A Bear Named Winnie, 2004; Maxwell, 2007; Several radio drama roles, audio recordings and voice overs. Publications: Author of essays in Players of Shakespeare, 1985. Honours: Brown Belt in Aikido; 1st Master of Japanese Samurai; Best Radio Actor of the Year, 1979; Best Actor, Marseilles Film Festival, 1983; Best Actor, British Industry/Science Film Association, 1986; Best Actor, Royal TV Society Performance Awards, 1986; Best Actor, Variety Club Award, 1998; 1994; Several BAFTA, SWET, Oliver and other nominations; Critics' Circle Award for Best Actor, 1997; Best Actor, Backstage Theatre Award, LA, 2000; Best Actor, TV, Radio and Industry, Royal Television Society, Broadcasting Press Guild, 2002; OBE. Memberships: Fellow, Royal Society of Arts; Governor, Royal Shakespeare Company; Fight Directors Association; Garrick Club, London; St James's Club, London. Address: c/o Ken McReddie, 36-40 Glasshouse Street, London W1B 5DL, England.

SUDELEY, 7th Baron, Merlin Charles Sainthill Hanbury-Tracy, b. 17 June 1939, London, England. Lecturer and Author. m (1) Elizabeth Villiers (2) Margarita Kellett. Education: History, Worcester College, Oxford, 1960-63. Appointments: Fellow of the Society of Antiquaries; Chairman, Conservative Monday Club; Lay Patron, Prayer Book Society; Patron, Bankruptcy Association; Vice-Chancellor, Monarchist League; Chairman, Constitutional Monarchy Association; Introduced debates in the House of Lords on: Export of manuscripts, 1973; Cathedral finance, 1980; Teaching and use of the Prayer Book in theological colleges, 1987; Cleared the Prayer Book (Protection) Bill on second reading in the House of Lords, 1981; Lecture tours to the USA, 1983, 1996; Occasional Lecturer, Extra-Mural Department, University of Bristol; Appearances on radio and television, 1960-. Publications: Book: The Sudeleys – Lords of Toddington (joint author), 1987; Contributor to: Contemporary Review; Family History; London Magazine; Monday World; Quarterly Review; Vogue; The Universe; John Pudney's Pick of Today's Short Stories; Montgomeryshire Collections; Salisbury Review; Transactions of the Bristol and Gloucester Archaeological Society. Honour: FSA, 1989. Address: 25 Melcombe Court, Dorset Square, London NW1 6EP, England.

SUG Hyontai, b. 5 October 1960, Busan, Republic of Korea. Professor. m. Aee-Ran Eum, 1 son, 2 daughters. Education: Bachelor of Science, Pusan National University, 1983; Master of Science, Hankuk University of Foreign Studies, 1986; PhD, University of Florida, USA, 1998. Appointments: Researcher, Agency for Defense Development, Chinhae, 1986-92; Full-time Lecturer, Pusan University of Foreign Studies, Busan, 1999-2001; Associate Professor, Dongseo University, Busan, 2001-. Publications: Reducing on the Number of Testing Items in the Branches of Decision Trees, 2004; A Comprehensively Sized Decision Tree Generation Method for Interactive Data Mining of Very Large Databases, 2005; Using Reliable Short Rules to Avoid Unnecessary Tests in Decision Trees, 2006. Honours: Knight of Justice, The Sovereign Order of the Knights of Justice, 2007; Best Software Development Award, Chinhae Machine Depot, 1990, 1991; Best Professor Award, Dongseo University, 2007; Adviser to the Director General, IBC, 2006; Deputy Director General, IBC, 2006; Diploma of Achievement Award, IBC, 2005/06, 2006/07; The Order of International Fellowship, IBC, 2006; The International Order of Merit, IBC, 2006; International Educator of the Year, IBC, 2006; 21st Century Award for Achievement, IBC, 2006, 2007; Meritorious Decoration Certificate, IBC, 2006; International Medal of Honor, IBC, 2006; Leading Scientists of the World, IBC, 2006; Leading Educators of the World, IBC, 2006; The Da Vinci Diamond, IBC, 2006; Salute to Greatness Award, IBC, 2006; Hall of Fame, IBC, 2006; The IBC Top 100 Scientists, 2007; Vice President, World Congress of Arts, Sciences and Communications, 2007; The Universal Award of Accomplishment, ABI, 2006; Outstanding Professional Award, ABI, 2006; Man of the Year, ABI, 2006; International Commendation of Success, ABI, 2006; International Medal of Vision, ABI, 2006; American Hall of Fame, ABI, 2007; Master Diploma with Honors, World Academy of Letters, 2007; International Cultural Diploma of Honor, ABI, 2007; International Peace Prize, United Cultural Convention, 2007; American Medal of Honor, ABI, 2007; World Lifetime Achievement Award, ABI, 2007; Listed in national and international biographical dictionaries including: Marquis Who's Who in the World, 2006, 2007; Marquis Who's Who in Science and Engineering, 2006-07; Marquis Who's Who in Asia, 2007; The Great Minds of the 21st Century (One of the Greatest Minds), ABI, 2007; 2000 Outstanding Intellectuals of the 21st Century (dedication entry), IBC, 2007; The Cambridge Blue Book, IBC, 2007. Memberships: Director, The Korea Institute of Signal Processing and Systems; The Korea Information Science Society; The Korea Contents Association. Address: Division of Computer and Information Engineering, Dongseo University, Joo-Rye-2-dong, San 69-1, Sa-Sang-gu, Busan 617-716, Republic of Korea. E-mail: hyontai@yahoo.com

SUGAR Alan, b. 24 March 1947, London, England. Business Executive. m. Ann Simons, 1968, 2 sons, 1 daughter. Education: Brooke House School, London. Appointments: Chair and Managing Director, 1968-97, CEO, -1993, Chair, 1997-2001, Chair and CEO, 2001-, Amstrad plc; Chair, Owner, Tottenham Hotspur plc, 1991-2001; Chair, Viglen plc, 1997-; The Apprentice, 2005-. Honours: Hon Fellow, City and Guilds of London Institute; Hon DSc (City University), 1988. Address: Amstrad plc, 169 King's Road, Brentwood, Essex CM14 4EF, England. Website: www.amstrad.com

SUGIMOTO Maki, b. 15 January 1971, Tokyo, Japan. Surgeon; Educator. Education: MD, Teikyo University School of Medicine, Tokyo, 1996; PhD, Teikyo University Graduated School, Tokyo, 2004. Appointments: Teikyo University Hospital, Tokyo, 1994-96; Teikyo University, Chiba Medical Center, 1998-2004; National Tokyo Medical Center, Tokyo, 1996-98, 2004-07. Publications: Numerous articles in professional journals. Honours: JDDW Excellent Presenter Award, 2005; JSES Karl Storz Award, 2005, 2006; ICS Young Investigator Award, 2006; JHPBS Congress Chairman Award, 2006; EAES Video Award, 2007. Memberships: International Society of Surgery; International College of Surgeons; Radiological Society of North America; Listed in international biographical dictionaries; Numerous grants. Address: #299-0111, Department of Surgery, Teikyo University, 3426-3 Anesaki Ichihara, Chiba, Japan.

SUH Keun Tae, b. 5 May 1939, Ulsan, Republic of Korea. Professor. m. Kyong Nam Park, 2 sons. Education: BA, 1963, MA, 1966, Economics, Pusan National University; PhD, Economics, Pusan National Fisheries University, Korea, 1982. Appointments: Professor, International Trade, 1969-2004, Honorary Professor, 2004-, Pusan National University; Visiting Professor, Seoul National University, 1978-79; Visiting Professor, University of California in Berkeley, 1983-84; President, Korean Trade Research Association, 1991-92; Visiting Professor, Waseda University, Japan, 1995-96; President, Ulsan Development Institute, 2001-. Publications: Principle of International Trade, 1989; International Economics, 1995; Theory of International Commerce, 1999. Honours: Research Grant, Korean Government, 1986; Research Fellowship, Korea-Japan Foundation, 1988-89; National Service Merit of Green Stripes, Korean Government, 2004. Memberships: Senior Member, Korean Trade Research Association; Senior Member, Korean Economic Association. Address: 967-3 Ilsan-Dong, Dong-Gu, Ulsan 682-050, Republic of Korea.

SUKHAREV Mikhail, b. 6 May 1937, Groznyi, USSR. Applied Mathematics. m. Neonila Bogazkaja, 3 sons. Education: Moscow State University, 1954-59; Candidate of Science, Institute of Natural Gases, Moscow, 1966; Doctor of Science, Oil and Gas State University, Moscow, 1973. Appointments: Researcher, Institute of Natural Gases, Moscow, 1959-70; Lecturer, Oil and Gas State University, Moscow, 1970-; Researcher, Promgaz Company, Moscow, 1995-. Publications: Calculation of Gas Transport Systems, 1971; Reliability of Gas and Oil Supplies, 1994; Book,

Principles of Computer Imitation, 2000. Honours: Honoured Scientist, 1997. Memberships: Fellow, International Academy of Ecology and Safety Science. E-mail: mgsukharev@mail.ru

SUKUL Diwaker, b. 5 April 1965, Delhi, India. Clinical Psychologist. m. Rakhi, 1 daughter. Education: BA (Honours); MA, Clinical Psychology; PhD (Psychology); MD (Alternative Medicine); Diploma in Addictive Behaviour; Diploma in E. Hypnotherapy, Psychotherapy, NLP. Appointments: Director, Turning Point Alcohol Project, 1991-97; Founder, Director, Kamkus group of clinics in Harley Street, London, Birmingham, Dubai, India, 1997-; Dean, Kamkus Institute of Integrated Medicine, 2004-. Publications: Addiction; Alcohol Report – Complementary Therapy for the Treatment of Addiction; Several papers in international conferences on Addiction, Eastern Psychotherapy, Panchkarma Therapy (in publication). Honours: MD, Alternative Medicine; Listed in Who's Who publications and biographical dictionaries. Memberships include: Addiction Forum; Alcohol Concern; Hypnotherapy Register; Fellow of Royal Society of Medicine (FRSM), British Compementary Association (BCMA), Though Field Therapy (BTFTA). Address: The Kamkus Clinic, 97 Harley Street, London W1, England. E-mail: dsukul@usa.net Website: www.kamkushealthcare.co.uk

SULEIMAN Michael Wadie, b. 26 February 1934, Tiberias, Palestine. University Professor. m. Penelope Ann Powers, 1 son, 1 daughter. Education: BA, Bradley University, 1960; MSc, 1962, PhD, 1965, University of Wisconsin-Madison, Wisconsin. Appointments: Assistant Professor, 1965-68, Associate Professor, 1968-72, Professor, 1972-90, University Distinguished Professor, 1990-, Kansas State University. Publications: Books, monographs and edited works include: Political Parties in Lebanon: The Challenge of a Fragmented Political Culture, 1967; American Images of Middle East Peoples: Impact of the High School, 1977; The Arabs in the Mind of America, 1988; Arab Americans: Continuity and Change (Co-editor, co-author), 1989; US Policy on Palestine from Wilson to Clinton, (editor and co-author), 1995; (Arabic translation) US Policy on Palestine from Wilson to Clinton, 1996; Arabs in America: Building a New Future (editor and co-author), 1999; The Arab-American Experience in the United States and Canada: A Classified, Annotated Bibliography, 2006; Numerous journal articles, essays, papers. Honours: Ford Faculty Research Fellowship, 1969-70; American Research Centre in Egypt Fellowship, 1972-73; Center for International Exchange of Scholars (CIES) Islamic Civilisation Grant, 1985; National Endowment for the Humanities (NEH) Grant, 1989-91; University Distinguished Professor, Kansas State University, 1990-; Faculty Research Abroad Program (Fulbright-Hayes) Fellowship, 1983-84, summers, 1991, 1993, 1994, 2004; Institute for Advanced Study Fellowship, Princeton, NJ, 1994-95; Fellow, Woodrow Wilson International Center for Scholars, 2005. Address: Department of Political Science, Kansas State University, 226 Waters Hall, Manhattan, KS 66506-4030, USA. E-mail: suleiman@ksu.edu

SULLIVAN John William, Teacher; Professor. m. Jean Salkeld, 3 sons, 1 daughter. Education: Westcliff High School; BA, Hull University, 1970; PGCE, Liverpool University, 1971; Dip Theol, Christ's College, Liverpool, 1974; Dip Ed, London, 1977; M Litt, Lancaster University, 1981; PhD, London University, 1998. Appointments: Catholic Secondary School Teacher, 1971-83; Deputy Head, Douay Martyrs Comprehensive School, 1983-85; Vice Principal, St Francis Xavier Sixth Form College, 1985-89; Head, Professional Development & Deputy Chief Inspector/Acting Chief Inspector, Wandsworth Education Authority, 1989-93; Headteacher, Christ's School, Richmond, 1993-94; Education Management Consultant, Reader in Catholic Education, St Mary's University College, Twickenham, 1994-2002; Professor of Christian Education, Liverpool Hope University, 2002-. Publications: Catholic Schools in Contention, 2000; Catholic Education: Distinctive and Inclusive, 2001; The Idea of a Christian University, 2005; Dancing on the Edge: Chaplaincy Church & Higher Education, 2007; Over 60 further chapters and articles on religion and education in books and journals in UK, Ireland, Europe, Australia and USA. Honours: Outstanding Contribution to Catholic Teacher Formation and Development, National Catholic Educational Association, 2001. Memberships: Catholic Theological Society of Great Britain; Fellow, Higher Education Academy; Association des Amis de Maurice Blondel. Address: Holly Tree Cottage, Elmcroft Lane, Hightown, Liverpool, L38 3RW, England. E-mail: sullivj@hope.ac.uk

SULLIVAN Wendy, b. 18 May 1938, London, England. Painter; Poet. Education: Notre Dame High School, London. Career: Exhibitions: Brixton Gallery, 1981-97; Royal Academy Summer Shows, 1989,1990, 1997, 1998; South Bank Picture Show, 1990; Dagmar Gallerie, East Dulwich, 1990-92; Cooltan Arts, Brixton and Camden, 1992-95; Brixton Gallery, Retrospective, 1995; 2 Solo Shows, West Norwood Library, 1997, 1999; 2 Solo Shows Ritzy Cinema, 2000, 2001, Solo Show, Brixton Library, 2000; Artist in Residence, ASC Studios, Brixton, 2000-01; Solo Show, Jacaranda Restaurant, Brixton, 2002-04; Solo Show, The Village Hall, Brixton, 2002; Brixton Open, 2003; Solo Show, Bettie Moreton Gallery, Brixton, 2004; 1st Annual Dulwich Art Fair, 2004; Works in collections: St Mark's Centre, Deptford; Lambeth Archives; St John's Church, Brixton; Breast Scanning Clinic, Camberwell; Dagmar Gallerie (now private), France; Movement for Justice. Publications: Contributions to poetry magazines for 40 years. Honours: Winner Brixton Open, 2003; Listed in Who's Who publications and biographical dictionaries. Address: 127 Crescent Lane, London SW4 8EA, England.

SUMANU HRM Oba Jerome Ojo Oloruntobi, b. 14 September 1941, Ogidi-Ijumu, Nigeria. Retired Teacher; Paramount Ruler. m. (1) Lucy Abike, deceased, (2) Tabitha Mowa, deceased, 3 sons, 2 daughters. Education: Teacher's Grade Three, Teachers' College, Our Lady of Schools College, Anyigba, 1957-59; Teachers' Certificate Grade Two, Teachers' College, St Enda's College, Zaria, 1961-62; Nigeria Certificate in Education, Advanced Teachers' College, Zaria, 1965-66, 1967-68; BA (Special Honours), History, Ahmadu Bello University, Zaria, 1973-74, 1975-76; MA, History, University of Ilorin, Ilorin, 1990-91. Appointments: Tutor, Our Lady of Schools College, Anyigba, 1964-65; Teacher of History/English, 1964-65, 1968-73, Principal, 1982-83, St Augustine's College, Kabba; History Teacher/English, Omuaran High School, 1976-77; Vice Principal, 1977-78, Principal, 1979-82, St Monica's College, Kabba; Principal, St Kizito's College, Isanlu, Nigeria, 1984-92; Assistant Director of Education, Monitoring; Deputy Director of Education, Teaching Service Commission; Paramount Ruler of Ijumu Kingdom, Kogi State, Nigeria, 1994-. Publications: The History of the Relations of the Yoruba-speaking People of Kabba Division with the Nupe up to the 1920s, 1976; Evaluation of the Place of Islamic Historian in the History of West Africa, 1991; Political Institutions and Organisations Among the Benin and Edo People, 1991; Archaeological Sources: Methods of Collection, Techniques, Usefulness and Limitations, 1991; Nation-building in Nigeria before the Introduction of the Richard's Consitution of 1946, 1991.

Honours: Certificate of Honour, Boy Scouts of Nigeria, 1998; Special Award, 1998, Certficate of Merit, 1999, Catholic Youth Organisation of Nigeria; General Custodian of the Ijumu Tradition, 1999; Honorary Award, Best Christian Royal Father, Igbala Apostolic Church of Christ, 1999; Certificate of Merit, Ijumu Students' Union, 2001; Distinguished Merit Award of Excellence, 2001; Certificiate of Training, Nigeria Peace Corps, 2002; Certificate of Participation, Ahmadu Bello University College of Agriculture, 2003; Certificate of Merit, Kabba Deanery of Catholic Women Organisation of Nigeria, 2003; Honorary Award of Fellowship Doctor in Communication Arts and Public Administration, California Christian University, USA, 2004; Grand Commander of NYSC Ijumu, 2005; Award of Excellence, Paragon of Okunland, 2006; Award of Recognition, Ijumu NYSC, 2006. Memberships: History Teachers' Association, Nigeria; Craft Council of Nigeria. Address: PO Box 9, Kabba, Kogi State, Nigeria.

SUMIYOSHI Tomiki, b. 18 December 1964, Tokyo, Japan. Psychiatrist; Researcher. m. Sawako Suemasa. Education: MB, 1989, MD, 1989, PhD, 1993, Kanazawa University School of Medicine; Diplomate, National Medical Board of Japan, 1989. Appointments: Resident, Fukui Prefectural Psychiatric Hospital, Japan, 1990; Ward Administrator, Kanazawa University Hospital, Japan, 1991-93; Research Associate, Department of Psychiatry, Case Western Reserve University, Cleveland, 1993-95; Assistant Professor, Department of Psychiatry, Saitama Medical School, Japan, 1995-96; Assistant Professor, Department of Neuropsychiatry, Director, Neurochemistry Research, Toyama Medical and Pharmaceutical University, 1996-2000; Appointed Psychiatrist, Health and Welfare Ministry, Japan, 1996-; Associate Professor, Department of Neuropsychiatry, University of Toyama School of Medicine, Japan, 2000-; Visiting Professor, Department of Psychiatry, Vanderbilt University School of Medicine, Nashville, USA, 2000-2002. Publications: Numerous articles as author and co-author in medical journals in English include most recently: Serotonin 1A receptors in memory function, 2004; Plasma glycine and serine levels in schizophrenia compared to normal controls and major depression: Relation to negative symptoms, 2004; Prediction of changes in memory performance by plasma homovanillic acid levels in clozapine-treated patients with schizophrenia, 2004; Disorganization of semantic memory underlies alogia in schizophrenia: An Analysis of verbal fluency performance in Japanese subjects, 2005; Verbal memory deficits in a preadolescent case of lesions of the left parahippocampal gyrus associated with a benign tumour, 2006; 12 book chapters in English, French and Japanese. Honours: Research Award, Saburo Matsubara Memorial Fund for Psychiatric Research, 1993; Rotary Ambassadorial Scholarship, Rotary International, 1994-95; Young Investigator Award, National Alliance for Research on Schizophrenia and Depression, Chicago, 1995, New York, 2001; Society Award, Japanese Society of Biological Psychiatry, 1996; Japan Education and Science Ministry Fellowship for Long-term Research in Foreign Countries, 2000-2002; ACNP Memorial Travel Award, American College of Neuropsychopharmacology, 2001. Memberships: World Federation of Societies of Biological Psychiatry; Society for Neuroscience; Collegium Internationale Neuro-Psychopharmacologicum; Schizophrenia International Research Society; New York Academy of Sciences. Japanese Society of: Biological Psychiatry, Neuropsychopharmacology, Clinical Neuropsychopharmacology, Psychiatry and Neurology, Prevention of Psychiatric Disorders, Brain Sciences, Psychiatric Diagnosis, Clinical Neurophysiology, Schizophrenia Research. Address: Department of Neuropsychiatry, University of Toyama School of Medicine, 2630 Sugitani, Toyama, 930-0194 Japan. E-mail: sumiyo@med.u-toyama.ac.jp

SUMMER Donna, b. 31 December 1948, Boston, USA. Singer; Actress. m. (1) Helmut Sommer, divorced, 1 daughter, (2) Bruce Sudano, 1 son, 1 daughter. Appointments: Singer, 1967-; Appeared in German stage production, Hair, in Europe, 1967-75; Appearing in Vienna Folk productions of Porgy and Bess; German production of The Me Nobody Knows; Has sold over 20 million records; Albums: The Wanderer; Star Collection; Love to Love You Baby; Love Trilogy; Four Seasons of Love; I Remember Yesterday; The Deep; Shut Out; Once Upon a Time; Bad Girls; On the radio; Walk Away; She Works Hard for the Money; Cats without Claws; All Systems Go, 1988; Another Time and Place, 1989; Mistaken Identity, 1991; Endless Summer, 1994; I'm a Rainbow, 1996; Live & More Encore, 1999. Honours: Best Rhythm and Blues Female Vocalist, National Academy of Recording Arts and Sciences, 1978; Best Female Vocalist, 1879; Favourite Female Pop Vocalist, American Music Awards, 1979; Favourite Female Vocalist of Soul Music, 1979; Ampex Golden Reel Award for single and album On the radio, 1979; Album Bad Girls, Soul Artist of Year, Rolling Stone Magazine, 1979; Best Rock Performance; Best of Las Vegas Jimmy Award, 1980; Grammy Award for Best Inspirational Performance, 1984; Several Awards for Best Selling Records. Address: 2401 Main Street, Santa Monica, CA 90405, USA.

SUN Jie, 21 April 1946, Qingdao, China. Professor. Education: MS, Chinese Academy of Science, People's Republic of China, 1981; MS, 1983, PhD, 1986, University of Washington, USA. Appointments: Assistant Professor, Northwestern University of USA, 1986-92; Senior Lecturer, 1993-97, Associate Professor, 1998-2001, Professor, 2002-, National University of Singapore. Publication: Advances in Optimisation and Approximation, 1994. Honour: Outstanding University Researcher, 1999. Membership: Mathematical Programming Society: Board Member, Pacific Optimisation Activity Group; Member of 4 editorial boards. Address: Department of Decision Sciences, National University of Singapore, Republic of Singapore 119260. E-mail: jsun@nus.edu.sg

SUN Ron, b. 8 October 1960, Shanghai, China. Cognitive Scientist; Computer Scientist. Education: BSc in Computer Information Science, Fudan University, 1983; MSc in Mathematics and Computer Science, Clarkson University, USA, 1986; PhD in Computer Science, Brandeis University, 1991. Appointments: Assistant Professor of Computer Science and Psychology, 1992-98, Associate Professor of Computer Science and Psychology, 1998-99, Departments of Computer Science and Psychology, University of Alabama at Tuscaloosa; Adjunct Professor of Psychology, University of Alabama at Birmingham, 1998-2000; Visiting Scientist, NEC Research Institute, Princeton, New Jersey, 1998-2003; Associate Professor of Computer Engineering and Computer Science, Department of Computer Engineering and Computer Science, University of Missouri-Columbia, Columbia, 1999-2002; Full Professor and James C Dowell Endowed Professor of CECS, Department of CECS, University of Missouri, Columbia, 2002-2003; Full Professor, Department of Cognitive Science, Rensselaer Polytechnic Institute, 2003-. Publications: Author, Integrating Rules and Connectionism for Robust Commonsense Reasoning, 1994; Duality of the Mind, 2002; Editor: Cognition and Multi-Agent Interaction, 2006; Editor, The Cambridge Handbook of Computational Psychology, 2008; Co-editor: Computational Architectures Integrating

Neural and Symbolic Processes, 1994; Connectionist Symbolic Integration, 1997; Hybrid Neural Systems, 2000; Sequence Learning: Paradigms, Algorithms, and Applications, 2001; Numerous book chapters, papers and articles in the field, especially in human and machine learning, reasoning and representation in neural networks, hybrid models, autonomous agents and multi-agent systems. Honours include: Graduate Fellowship and Scholarship in Computer Science, Brandeis University, 1988-91; David Marr Award in Cognitive Science, Cognitive Science Society, 1991; Senior Member, Institute of Electrical and Electronics Engineers, 1998; Member, European Academy of Science, 2002; Member, Governing Board of International Neural Networks Society; Member, Governing Board of Cognitive Science Society; Hebb Award, International Neural Networks Society, 2008. Memberships: Institute of Electrical and Electronics Engineers; Cognitive Science Society; Life Member, American Association for Artificial Intelligence; International Neural Network Society; Upsilon Pi Epsilon. Address: Cognitive Science Department, Rensselaer Polytechnic Institute, 110 8th Street, Troy, NY 12180, USA.

SUNG Baek Ju, b. 5 September 1966, Sang Ju-Gun, Gyung Buk, Korea. Researcher. m. Hyun-Soon Park, 2 sons. Education: Bachelor, 1990, Master, 1992, Busan National University; PhD, Chung Nam National University, 2006. Appointments: Assistant Teacher, Busan National University, 1990-92; Researcher, Korea Institute of Machinery & Materials, 1992-. Publications: Numerous articles in professional journals. Honours: Listed in international biographical dictionaries. Memberships: Korean Institute of Electrical Engineers; Korean Society of Automotive Engineers. Address: 305-343 KIMM, 171, Jang-Dong, Yusung-Gu, Dae Jeon City, Korea. E-mail: sbj682@kimm.re.kr

SUNG Dae Dong, b. 17 June 1945, Sichunmyun, Kyung Nam, Korea. Educator; Professor. m. Byung Hee Yoon Sung, 1 son, 1 daughter. Education: BA, 1969, MS, 1975, DSc, 1981, Department of Chemistry, Dong-A University, Korea. Appointments: Postdoctoral Researcher, Princeton University, USA, 1981-83; Assistant Professor, Associate Professor, Professor, 1983-2005, Dean of College of Natural Sciences, 1997-99, Dong-A University, Korea; Royal Society Fellow Researcher, Liverpool University, England, 1989-90; Visiting Professor, Mie University, Mie, Japan, 1991. Publications: 283 articles in scientific journals, 1975-2006, including most recently: Organic Biomolecular Chemistry, 2004; Journal of Physical Organic Chemistry, 2004; Collective Czech Chemical Communications, 2004; Dalton Transactions, 2005; Journal of Physical Chemistry A, 2005; Journal of Organic Chemistry, 2005. Honours: Prominent Scientific Researcher Prize, President of Dong-A University, 1993; Teacher's Day Prize, Prime Minister of Republic of Korea, 2000. Memberships: American Chemical Society; Korean Chemical Society; Photoscience; New York Academy of Science. Address: Department of Chemistry, Division of Chemistry and Biology, College of Natural Sciences, Dong-A University, Saha-Gu, Busan 604-714, Korea. E-mail: ddsung@daunet.donga.ac.kr

SUNG Sang Kyung, b. 11 February 1973, Seoul, Korea. System Engineer. m. So Youn Kim. Education: BS, 1996, MS, 1998, PhD, Electrical Engineering, 2003, Seoul National University. Appointments: Researcher of Automatic Control Research Center, Seoul National University, 1996-2002; Voting Member, IEEE WLAN WG, 2003-04; Korean Delegate for ISO TC204 WG 14/WG 15, 2003-04; Delegate for OMA POC/PAG WG, 2004-; Senior Standard Engineer, Samsung Electronics Co Ltd; International Journal Reviewer, IEEE

Transactions on Circuits and Systems; Journal Reviewer, Telecommunication Review. Publications: Development and test of MEMS accelerometer with self-sustained oscillation loop; Design and Performance Test of an oscillation loop for a MEMS Resonant Accelerometer; 3 more journal papers; 40 more international patents. Honours: Best Student Paper Award, IEEE NAECON, 2000; Bronze Medal, Samsung R&D Contest, 2005; Best Patent Award, Samsung TN Business; Listed in Who's Who in the World, 2006; Invited Speaker, Korean Internet Conference, 2005; Invited Speaker, KWISA Workshop, 2005; Invited Speaker, Korea VoIP Forum, 2006. Memberships: Associate Member, IEEE; Member, TTA, Korea; Member, Korean Institute of Communication and Sciences. Address: 107-1205, Woosung Apt, Bangbae 2 dong, Seocho, Seoul, Korea. E-mail: sksung@konkuk.ac.kr Website: www.samsung.com

SUNG Wen-Tsai, b. 20 February 1969, Keelung, Taiwan. Professor; Educator. m. Tusi-Hwa Chen, 1 son, 1 daughter. Education: Bachelor's degree, Industrial Education Department, National Taiwan Normal University, 1994; Master's degree, 2000, PhD, 2007, Electrical Engineering Department, National Central University. Appointments: Lecturer, Information Department, Taipei Da-An Vocational High School, 1993-2006; Assistant Professor, Electrical Engineering Department, National Chin-Yi University of Technology, 2006-07. Publications: Numerous articles in professional journals. Honours: Phi Tau Phi; Development of Bioinformatics Technology and System Science; Dragon Thesis Award, Acer, 2000. Memberships: IEEE; Chinese Engineering Society. E-mail: songchen@mslo.hinet.net

SUNKLODAS Jonas Kazys, b. 28 September 1945, Užpaliai Town, Utena District, Lithuania. Mathematician, m. Janina Survilaitè, 1 son, 3 daughters. Education: Mathematics major, Vilnius University, 1963-68; Postgraduate studies, Institute of Physics and Mathematics, Lithuanian Academy of Sciences, 1972-74; Doctors degree, Mathematics, Vilnius University, 1979; Habilitated Doctors degree of Physical Sciences, Mathematics, Institute of Mathematics and Informatics, 1999; Title of Professor, Vilnius Gediminas Technical University, 2004. Appointments: Junior Research Fellow, Institute of Physics and Mathematics, Lithuanian Academy of Sciences, 1970-71; Instructor, Faculty of Mathematics and Mechanics, Vilnius University, 1973-78; Junior Research Fellow, 1975-81, Senior Research Fellow, 1982-2002, Chief Research Fellow, 2003-, Institute of Mathematics and Informatics, Lithuanian Academy of Sciences; Associate Professor, 1997-99, Professor, 1999-, Faculty of Fundamental Sciences, Vilnius Gediminas Technical University. Publications: Articles in science publications on probability theory; Author, over 60 scientific publications. Memberships: Lithuanian Mathematicians' Society. Address: Institute of Mathematics and Informatics, Akademijos 4, 220 cab, LT-08663 Vilnius, Lithuania.

SUPANVANIJ Janikan, b. 6 August 1971, Bangkok, Thailand. University Professor. Education: BBA, Finance, Thammasat University, 1993; MFN, Finance, 1995, MBA, Finance and Economics, 1997, PhD, Finance, 2003, Saint Louis University, USA. Appointments: Foreign Exchange Dealer, The Thai Military Bank Ltd, International Banking Facility, Department of Treasury Investment Banking, Bangkok, Thailand, 1993; Instructor, Finance and International Financial Management, Saint Louis University, 1997-2003; Assistant Professor, 2003-06, Associate Professor, 2006-, Managerial Finance, Financial Institutions and International Finance, St Cloud State University. Publications: Articles in professional journals and presented at conferences as author and co-author include: Consumer Perception of Country-of-Origin Effect and Brand Effect, 1999; The Determinants of Productivity, 1999; Evolution of the US Banking System: From Glass-Steagall to Universal Banking, 2000; Executive Compensation and Degree of International Involvement, 2004; The Impact of Hedging Gain on Management Compensation (abstract), 2005; Derivative Gain/Loss, Currency Hedging and Management Compensation, 2005; Does the Composition of CEO Compensation Influence the Firm's Advertising Budgeting? 2005. Honours: Beta Gamma Sigma, Alpha Epsilon Lambda, Saint Louis University Outstanding Teaching Assistant, St Louis University, 2002; Best Paper Award Certificate for Executive Compensation and Degree of International Involvement, Association of Global Business, 2004; Faculty of the Year Nominee, 2004-05, 2005-06, Research Collaboration Award, 2000-05, Distinguished Research Award, 2000-05; Listed in Who's Who publications and biographical dictionaries. Memberships: American Finance Association; Financial Management Association; Midwest Finance Association. Address: St Cloud State University, G R Herberger College of Business, Department of Finance, Insurance and Real Estate, 720 Fourth Avenue South, St Cloud, MN 56301, USA. E-mail: jsupanvanij@stcloudstate.edu

SUTCLIFFE Serena Gillian, b. 21 May 1945, England. Expert on Wine; Author; Consultant. m. David Peppercorn. Education: England and Switzerland; Master of Wine Examination, 1976. Appointments: Translator, UNESCO; Director, Peppercorn and Sutcliffe, 1988-91; Senior Director, Member European Board, Head, International Wine Department, Sotheby's London, 1991-; Chairman, Institute of Wine, 1994-95. Publications: Books: Wines of the World; Great Vineyards and Winemakers; The Wine Drinker's Handbook; A Celebration of Champagne; Bollinger, 1994; The Wines of Burgundy, new edition, 2005; Contributor of articles to: The World of Fine Wine; Decanter; Quarterly Review of Wines; Planet Vins et Spiritueux. Honours: Chevalier Dans l'Ordre des Arts et des Lettres; New York Institute of Technology's Professional Excellence Award; Lifetime Achievement Award, American Society of Bacchus; Book of the Year Award for A Celebration of Champagne, Decanter; Chevalier Dans L'Ordre National De La Légion D'Honneur. Memberships: Institute of Masters of Wine; Académie Internationale du Vin. Address: c/o Sotheby's, 34-35 New Bond Street, London W1A 2AA, England. E-mail: serena.sutcliffe@sothebys.com

SUTHERLAND Donald McNichol, b. 17 July 1935, St John, Canada. Actor. m. (1) Lois May Hardwick, 1959; m. (2) Shirley Jean Douglas, 1966, divorced, 1 son, 1 daughter, (3) Francine Racette, 1971, 3 sons. Education: University of Toronto. Appointments: Appeared on TV (BBC and ITV) in Hamlet; Man in the Suitcase; The Saint; Gideon's Way; The Avengers; Flight into Danger; Rose Tattoo; March to the Sea; Lee Harvey Oswald; Court Martial; Death of Bessie Smith; Max Dugan Returns; Crackers; Louis Malle; The Disappearance; Commander in Chief; Dirty Sexy Money; Films include: The World Ten Times Over, 1963; Castle of the Living Dead, 1964; Dr Terror's House of Horrors; Fanatic, 1965; Act of the Heart, M*A*S*H*, Kelly's Heroes, Little Murders, 1970; Don't Look Now, 1973; The Day of the Locust, 1975; 1900, 1976; The Eagle Has Landed, 1977; The Great Train Robbery, 1978; Lock Up, Apprentice to Murder, Los Angeles, 1989; The Railway Station Man, Scream from Stone, Faithful, JFK, 1991; Backdraft; Agaguk; Buffy the Vampire Slayer; Shadow of the Wolf, Benefit of the Doubt; Younger and Younger, Six Degrees of Separation, 1993; The Puppet Masters; Disclosure; Outbreak; Hollow Point; The

Shadow Conspiracy; A Time To Kill; Virus, Instinct, Toscano, 1999; The Art of War, Panic, Space Cowboys, 2000; Uprising, The Big Herst, Final Fantasy: The Spirits Within, Big Shot's Funeral, 2001; Five Moons Plaza, Italian Job, Baltic Storm, Cold Mountain, 2003; Aurora Borealis, Fierce People, Pride & Prejudice, American Hun, An American Haunting, 2005; Land of the Blind, Ask the Dust, 2006; Sleepwalkers, Reign Over Me, Puffball, 2007; Fool's Gold, 2008; Plays: Lolita, 1981; Enigmatic Variations, 2000; President, McNichol Pictures Inc. Honours: TV Hallmark Hall of Fame; Officer, Ordre des Lettres; Order of Canada; Hon PhD; Golden Globe for Best Supporting Actor in a TV series or TV Movie, 2003. Address: 760 N La Cienega Boulevard, Los Angeles, CA 90069, USA.

SUTHERLAND Kiefer, b. 21 December 1966, London, England. Actor. m. (1) Camelia Kath, 1987, divorced 1990, 2 daughters, (2) Kelly Winn, 1996-2004, divorced, 2 stepsons. Career: Debut, LA Odyssey Theatre, aged 9 years; Films: Max Dugan Returns, 1983; The Bay Boy, 1984; At Close Range, Crazy Moon, Stand By Me, 1986; The Lost Boys, The Killing Time, Promised Land, 1987; Bright Lights, Big City, Young Guns, 1988; Renegades, 1989; Chicago Joe and the Showgirl, Flashback, Flatliners, The Nutcracker Prince (voice), Young Guns II, 1990; Article 99, 1991; Twin Peaks: Fire Walk with Me, A Few Good Men, 1992; The Vanishing, 1993; The Three Musketeers; The Cowboy Way; Teresa's Tattoo; Eye for an Eye; A Time to Kill, 1996; Truth or Consequences NM (also director), Dark City, 1997; Ground Control, The Breakup, 1998; Woman Wanted, The Red Dove, Hearts and Bones, 1999; Beat, Picking up the Pieces, The Right Temptation, 2000; Cowboy Up, To End All Wars, 2001; Desert Saints, Dead Heat, Behind the Red Door, Phone Booth, 2002; Paradise Found, 2003; Taking Lives, Jiminy Glick in La La Wood, 2004; River Queen, 2005; The Wild (voice), 2006; Mirrors, 2008; TV: Amazing Stories; Trapped in Silence; Brotherhood of Justice; Last Light (also director); 24, 2001-. Honours: Golden Globe, Best Actor in a TV Series, 2002; Screen Actors Guild, Best Actor in a Drama Series Award, 2004. Address: International Creative Management, 8942 Wilshire Boulevard, Beverly Hills, CA 90211, USA.

SUTHERLAND Peter Denis, b. 25 April 1946, Dublin, Ireland. Lawyer. m. Maria Del Pilar Cabria Valcarcel, 2 sons, 1 daughter. Education: Gonzaga College; University College, Dublin; The King's Inns; BCL. Appointments: Called to Bar, King's Inns, 1968; Middle Temple, 1976; Bencher, 1981; Attorney of New York Bar, 1981; Attorney and Counsellor of Supreme Court of USA, 1986; Tutor in Law, University College, Dublin, 1969-71; Practising Member, Irish Bar, 1969-81, 1981-82; Senior Counsel, 1980; Attorney General of Ireland, 1981-82, 1982-84; Member, Council of State, 1981-82, 1982-84; Commissioner for Competition and Commissioner for Social Affairs and Education, EEC, 1985-86, for Competition and Relations with European Parliament, 1986-89; Chairman, Allied Irish Banks, 1989-93; Director, GPA, 1989-93; Director, CRH plc, 1989-93; Director, James Crean plc, 1989-93; Chairman, Board of Governors, European Institute of Public Administration, 1991-96; Director, Delta Air Lines Inc, 1992-93; Director General, GATT, later WTO, 1993-95; Honorary Bencher, King's Inns, Dublin, 1995; Director, Investor, 1995-2005; Chairman, Goldman Sachs International, 1995-; Director, Telefonaktiebolaget LM Ericsson, 1996-2004; Goodwill Ambassador to the United Nations Industrial Development Organisation; Chairman, BP plc, 1997-; Director, Royal Bank of Scotland Group plc, 2001-; Chairman (Europe), Special Representative of the DG of the UN for Migration and Development, 2006-, Trilateral

Commission, 2001-; The Federal Trust, President; Member, Royal Irish Academy. Publications: Premier Janvier 1993 ce qui va changer en Europe, 1989; Numerous articles in law journals. Honours include: Honorary LLD: St Louis, 1986; NUI, 1990; Dublin City, 1991; Holy Cross, Massachusetts, 1994; Bath, 1995; Suffolk, USA, 1995; TCD, 1996; Reading, 1997; Nottingham, 1999; Exeter, 2000; Queens University Belfast, 2003; Koc University, Turkey, 2004; University of Notre Dame, 2004; DUniv, Open, 1995; Gold Medal, European Parliament, 1988; The First European Law Prize, Paris, 1988; Grand Cross: King Leopold II, Belgium, 1989; Grand Cross of Civil Merit, Spain, 1989; New Zealand Commemorative Medal, 1990; Chevalier, Legion d'Honneur, France, 1993; Commander, Order of Ouissam Alaouite, Morocco, 1994; Order of Rio Branco, Brazil, 1996; Order of Infante Dom Henrique, Portugal, 1998; The David Rockefeller International Leadership Award, 1998; UCD Foundation Day Medal; Honorary KCMG, 2004. Memberships: The Stephen's Green Hibernian Club, Dublin; Fitzwilliam Lawn Tennis, Dublin; Lansdowne FC, Dublin; The Athenaeum, London; Marks Club, London. Address: Goldman Sachs International, Peterborough Court, 133 Fleet Street, London, EC4A 2BB, England.

SUZMAN Janet, b. 9 February 1939, Johannesburg, South Africa. Actress; Director. m. Trevor Nunn, 1969, divorced 1986, 1 son. Education: BA, University of Wittwatersrand; Graduate, London Academy of Music and Dramatic Arts, 1962. Career: For the RSC: The Wars of the Roses; Portia, Ophelia, Celia, Rosalind, Katherina; The Relapse; The Greeks, 1980; London Theatre includes: The Birthday Party; Three Sisters; Hedda Gabler; The Duchess of Malfi; Andromache; The Retreat from Moscow; Television includes: The Family Reunion; St Joan; Macbeth; Twelfth Night, Hedda Gabler; Three Men in a Boat; Clayhanger (serial), 1975-76; Mountbatten-Last Viceroy of India, 1985; The Singing Detective, 1986; The Miser, 1987; Revolutionary Witness, 1989; Masterclass on Shakespearean Comedy, 1990; Masterclass from Haymarket Theatre (Sky TV), 2001; White Clouds (BBC), 2002; Films include: A Day in the Death of Joe Egg, 1970; Nicholas & Alexandra, 1971; Nijinsky, 1978; The House on Garibaldi Street; The Priest of Love, 1981; The Black Windmill; Nuns on the Run, 1990; Leon the pig-Farmer, 1992; Max, 2001; Fairy Story, 2002; Numerous performances in South Africa; Wrote and Directed The Free State – a South African response to the Cherry Orchard, performed at the Birmingham Repertory Theatre, 1997 (revived for UK tour, 2000); The Guardsman, 2000; Television: Othello, 1988, Measure for Measure, 2004; Trial & Retribution: Sins of the Father, 2006; Lectures include: The Spencer Memorial Lecture, Harvard University, USA, 1987; The Tanner Lectures, Brasenose College, Oxford, 1995; The Judith E Wilson Annual Lecture, Trinity Hall, Cambridge, 1996; The Draper's Lecture, Queen Mary and Westfield College, University of London. 1997. Publications: Hedda Gabler: The Play in Performance, 1980; Acting with Shakespeare – Three Comedies, 1996; The Free State, 2000; A Textual Commentary on Anthony and Cleopatra, 2001. Honours: Honorary Degrees: MA, Open University; D Lit, Warwick University; D Lit, Leicester University; D Lit, Queen Mary and Westfield College, London University; D Lit, University of Southampton, 2002; Vice-President of London Academy of Music and Dramatic Arts. Address: c/o Steve Kenis & Co, Royalty House, 72-74 Dean Street, London W1D 3SG, England. E-mail: sk@sknco.com

SUZUKI Fujio, b. 17 February 1933, Toyonaka, Osaka, Japan. Professor Emeritus. m. Yuriko Nagai, 2 sons, 1 daughter. Education: BA, Department of Chemistry, Faculty

of Science, 1955, PhD, Department of Bioorganic Chemistry, Graduate School of Science, 1960, Osaka University. Appointments: Instructor, 1960-61, 1964-65, Assistant Professor, 1965-66, Associate Professor, 1966-77, Professor, 1977-96, Councilor, 1979-81, Advisor, 1980-81, Director, Life Science Library, 1989-93, Professor Emeritus, 1996-, Department of Biochemistry, Faculty of Dentistry, Osaka University, Japan; Assistant Research Biochemist, University of California, Berkeley, 1961-64; Visiting Professor, SUNY Upstate Medical Center, 1974-75; Professor Emeritus, Norman Bethune Medical University, Changchun, China, 1993; Editor-in Chief , 1994-, Editor Emeritus, 2006-, Journal Bone and Mineral Metabolism. Publications: Regulation of cartilage differentiation and metabolism, 1994; Cartilage-derived growth factor and anti-tumour factor. Past, present and future studies. Breakthroughs and views, 1999. Honours: Fulbright Fellow, 1961-64; Young Investigators Award, Japan Biochemical Society, 1970; Award Asahi Press, 1984; Award, 1996, Special Award, 2006, Japanese Society for Bone and Mineral Research; Kroc Foundation Lectureship, 1996. Memberships: Japan Biochemistry Society; Japan Society for Bone and Mineral Research; Japan Medical Library Association; New York Academy of Sciences; Japan Society for Connective Tissue Research; Japan Society for Cartilage Metabolism. Address: 2-13-11 Nakasakurazuka, Toyonaka, Osaka 561-0881, Japan. E-mail: fsuzuki@oak.ocn.ne.jp

SVALASTOG Borgny Farstad, b. 18 July 1943, Nesset, Norway. Artist. m. Sondre Svalastog, 2 sons, 1 daughter. Education: Completed studies at Bergen Art Academy, Bergen. Appointments: Group Exhibitions: Winterland, Olympic Art Exhibition, 1994; Heritage International Peace Centre, Bethlehem, 2000; Solo Exhibitions: Trondheim Art Association, 1991; Bergen Art Association, 1995; Travana, Slovakia, 1996; The Hedmark Museum, Hamar, Norway, 1999; Kreuzkirche, Dresden, 2003; Meissendom, Meissen, 2003; Centre for the Study of the Cultural Heritage of Mediaeval Ritual, University of Copenhagen, Denmark, 2004; Hamsun Festival, Hamaroy, Norway, and Hamaland Museum, Vreden, Germany, 2004; Museo das Peregrinacion, Spain, 2006; Nordens Hus, Iceland, 2006; Kunstbanken Hedmark Art Centre, Norway, 2007; The Archbishop's Palace, Trondheim, 2007; Art Centre, Silkeborg Bad, Silkeborg, Denmark, 2007. Publications: Between Fullness and Emptiness. On the Art of Borgny Svalastog, 2001; Borgny Svalastog's Episcopal Cops of Agder, 2006; 14 + 1 Stations. Exercises in Touching, 2006; Numerous catalogues. Honours: Guaranteed minimum income for artists, Norway; Scholarships: Oppland County; Norwegian Art Council; City of Lillehammer; Ministry of Foreign Affairs, Oslo; Norwegian Church Council; OCA, Oslo; Cultural Prize, The Valley of Gudbrandsdalen, 2003. Memberships: Association of Norwegian Visual Artists. Address: Erlends vei 26, N-2618 Lillehammer, Norway. E-mail: sondre.svalastog@hil.no

ŠVEC Jan G, b. 22 November 1966, Olomouc, Czech Republic. Voice Scientist. m. Hana Švecová. Education: MSc, Fine Mechanics and Optics, 1990, PhD, Biophysics, Palacký University, Olomouc, Czech Republic, 1996; PhD, Medical Sciences, University of Groningen, The Netherlands, 2000. Appointments: Assistant Professor, Institute of Postgraduate Medical Education, Department of Phoniatrics and Audiology, Prague, Czech Republic, 1995-99; Research Scientist, Centre for Communication Disorders, Medical Healthcom Ltd, Prague, Czech Republic, 1995-; Visiting Research Scientist, National Center for Voice and Speech, Denver Center for the Performing Arts, Denver, Colorado, USA, 2001-04; Research Scientist, Groningen Voice Research Laboratory, Department of Biomedical Engineering, University of Groningen, The Netherlands, 2004-. Publications: Over 100 scientific papers, over 30 as first author in journals and proceedings; over 200 presentations, approx 100 personally presented at scientific congresses, symposia and seminars in Europe, North America, Africa and Australia; Video Programme: Introduction to Videokymography, 1997. Honours: Fulbright Commission Award, 1995; Silver Medal for Best Scientific Video, AVEC World Video Festival of the XVI World ORL Congress, Sydney Australia, 1997; Best Publication Award, Czech ORL Society, 2000; International Scientist of the Year 2002, International Biographical Centre; Best Publication Award, Institute of Thermomechanics, Academy of Sciences of the Czech Republic, 2003; Distinguished Alumnus, Palacký University, Czech Republic, 2006. Memberships: Czech Acoustical Society, 1992-2001; International Association of Logopedics and Phoniatrics, Voice Committee, Chair, 2004-2007; The Voice Foundation, Associate; Acoustical Society of America, Associate; International Biographical Centre Research Council, 2003-2005; Research Board of Advisors, American Biographical Institute, 2003-2004; Deputy Editor-in-Chief, Logopedics, Phoniatrics, Vocology. Address: UMCG, Sector F, Groningen Voice Research Laboratory, Department of Biomedical Engineering, University of Groningen, P.O. Box 196, NL9700 AD Groningen, The Netherlands. E-mail: svecjan@vol.cz Website: http://www.ncvs.org

SVENSSON Charles Robert Wilhelm, b. 11 September 1947, Göteburg, Sweden. Associate Professor; Scientist. Education: Associates Degree, Electronics, 1969; BSc, Physics, 1983, MSc, Physics, 1991, PhD, Thermionic Energy Converter Concept, 1994, Göteburg University. Appointments: Design Engineer, electronic temperature meters and heart beat monitors, -1981; Part-time teacher, 1981-83, Full-time Teacher, 1983-87, College of Applied Engineering and Maritime Studies, Chalmers University of Technology; Graduate Student, Department of Physical Chemistry, Göteburg University and Chalmers University of Technology, 1987-94; Assistant Professor, Chalmers University of Technology, 1995-96; Associate Professor, Chalmers University of Technology, 1996-; Visiting Research Professor, West Virginia University, USA, 2004, 2005, 2006, 2007. Publications: Numerous articles and papers; 2 patents. Memberships: American Institute of Aeronautics and Astronautics. Address: Dörravägen 1, SE-43893 Landvetter, Sweden. E-mail: term@chalmers.sc Website: www.chl.chalmers.se/~term

SVICHENSKAYA Oksana, b. 6 April 1966, Moscow, Russia. Director; Teacher of Music; Psychologist; Investigator. m. Nick Chulkov, 2 sons. Education: Musician (piano), Music College, 1986; Musician, Teacher of Music, Musical Pedagogical Institute, 1993; Candidate of Biological Sciences, International Academy of Energetic-Information Sciences, 2001; Psychologist, Pedagogical Institute, 2002. Appointments: Teacher of Music and Musician (piano), 1986; Master of Work in the Cause, Candidate of Biological Sciences, 2001; Psychologist, Director and Head of Council, Centre of Cause-Consequence Study "Star of the Morning", 2002-. Publications: 24 articles; 3 patents; 2 author's methodics. Honours include: Silver Medal, Eurika, Belgium, 2001; Gran-Pri Golden and Silver Medals, Archimed, Moscow, 2002; Woman Inventor's Diploma and Prize, Romania, 2004; Silver Medal, New Time, Ukraine, 2005; Silver Medal, Moscow, 2005; Order of Glory of the Spirit, Scientific School of Causality, Ukraine; Diploma of Great Work in National Medicine, 2005; Medal for Ecological Clear Technology, Moscow, 2006; Great Woman of the 21st Century, USA, 2006.

Memberships: International Association of Specialists of the Work in the Cause; Member, International Innovational Club, Archimed. Address: Flat 209, House 5, Vorontsovskie prydi, Moscow 117630, Russia. E-mail: zvezdaytrennia@nm.ru

SVIRIDOV Andrei Valentinovitsh, b. 22 December 1946, Moscow, Russia. Entomologist. Education: Moscow Lomonosov State University, 1965-70. Appointments: Senior Laboratory Assistant, 1970-71, Junior Researcher, 1971-86, Researcher, 1987-92, Senior Researcher, 1992-, Moscow Lomonosov State University; Scientific degree, Candidate of Biological Sciences (Dr), 1984; Academic Studies, Senior Researcher, 1995. Publications: 327 scientific publications, 1970-, include books: Types of the Biodiagnostic Keys and Their Applications, 1994; Biodiagnostical Keys: Theory and Practice, 1994; Key to the insects of Russian Far East, Vol 5, Part 4, 2003. Memberships: Russian Entolomological Society; Moscow Society Naturalists; Society Europea Lepidopterology; Systematic Zoology/Biology; Hist-Genealogy Society, Moscow; Descendents Council of the Great War of 1812-1814 Vets; Commission of Red Book of Russia; Commission of Red Book of CIS. Honours: Listed in Who's Who publications and biographical dictionaries. Address: Dr A V Sviridov, Zoological Museum, Moscow State Lomonosov University, Bolshaya Nikitskaya St 6, 125009 Moscow, Russia.

SWAMINATHAN Monkombu Sambasivan, b. 7 August 1925, Tamil Nadu, India. Director. Education: BSc, Travancore University, 1944; BSc, Agriculture, Coimbatore Agricultural College, Madras University, 1947; Associateship, Indian Agricultural Research Institute, New Delhi, 1949; UNESCO Fellow, Agricultural University, Wageningen, The Netherlands, 1949-50; PhD, School of Agriculture, University of Cambridge, England, 1952; Research Associate, Genetics, University of Wisconsin, USA, 1952-53. Appointments: Teacher, Researcher, Research Administrator, Central Rice Research Institute, Cuttack, Indian Agricultural Research Institute, New Delhi, 1954-72; Director General, Indian Council of Agricultural Research, Secretary, Government of India, Department of Agricultural Research and Education, 1972-80; Secretary, Government of India, Ministry of Agriculture and Irrigation, 1979-80; Acting Deputy Chairman, Planning Commission, Government of India, 1980; Member, Planning Commission, Government of India, 1980-82; Director General, International Rice Research Institute, Los Banos, Philippines, 1982-88; Honorary Director, Centre for Research on Sustainable Agricultural and Rural Development, Madras, 1989-; UNESCO Chair in Ecotechnology and President, Pugwash Conferences on Science and World Affairs, 1994-; Chairman, National Commission on Farmers, Government of India, 2004-06. Publications: Numerous articles in professional journals. Honours include: Raja Rammohan Roy Purasakar, 2005; The Crop Science Society of America Presidential Award, 2005; Commander of the Agricol Merit, 2006; Sahametrei Medal, Royal Government of Cambodia, 2006; Life Time Achievement Award, All India Management Association, 2007; Distinguished Global Thinker Award, 2007; 53 honorary doctorates from numerous universities world wide. Address: M S Swaminathan Research Foundation, 3rd Cross Street, Taramani Institutional Area, Chennai (Madras) 600 113, India.

SWANK Hilary, b. 30 July 1974, Bellingham, Washington, USA. Actress. m. Chad Lowe, 1997. Career: Films: Buffy the Vampire Slayer, 1992; The Next Karate Kid, 1994; Sometimes They Came Back ...Again, 1996; Heartwood, 1997; Boys Don't Cry, 1999; The Gift, 2000; Affair of the Necklace, 2000;

Insomnia, 2002; The Core, 2003; 11:44, 2003; Red Dust, 2004; Million Dollar Baby, 2004; The Black Dahlia, 2006; Freedom Writers, 2007; The Reaping, 2007; P.S. I Love You, 2007; Birds of America, 2008; Iron Man, 2008; TV: Terror in the Family, 1996; Leaving LA, 1997. Academy Awards, Best Actress, 1999; Golden Globe Awards, Best Dramatic Actress, 2005; Screen Actors Guild Awards, 2005. Address: c/o Metropolitan Talent Agency, 4526 Wilshire Boulevard, Los Angeles, CA 90010, USA.

SWAYZE Patrick, b. 18 August 1954. Actor; Dancer. m. Lisa Niemi, 1976. Education: Harkness and Joffrey Ballet Schools. Appointments: Began as dancer in Disney on Parade on tour as Prince Charming; Appeared on Broadway as dancer in Goodtime Charley Grease; TV appearances in North and South: Books I and II; The New Season; Pigs vs Freaks; The Comeback Kid; The Return of the Rebels; The Renegades. Films include: Skatetown USA, 1979; The Outsiders; Uncommon Valor; Red Dawn; Grandview USA - also choreographer; Dirty Dancing - co-wrote song and sings She's Like the Wind; Steel Dawn; Tiger Warsaw; Road House; Next of Kin; Ghost; Point Break; City of Joy; Father Hood; Tall Tales; To Wong Foo - Thanks for Everything - Julie Newmar; Three Wishes; Letters from a Killer, 1997; Vanished, 1998; Black Dog, 1998; Without a Word, 1999; The Winddrinker, 2000; Forever Lulu, 2000; Donnie Darko, 2001; Waking Up in Reno, 2002; One Last Dance, 2003; Dirty Dancing: Havana Nights, 2004; George and the Dragon, 2004; Keeping Mum, 2005; Jump! 2007; Christmas in Wonderland, 2007; Powder Blue, 2008. Address: c/o William Morris Agency, 151 South El Camino, Beverly Hills, CA 90212, USA.

SWEENEY Ronald Terence, b. 1 September 1932, Hull, England. Journalist; Company Director. m. Amy, 1 daughter. Education: Diplomate in Architectural Studies, Hull College (now University of Humberside); Institute of Practitioners in Advertising Postgraduate in Race Relations and Social Analysis, University of Bradford, 1987; Postgraduate, Church and Social Studies, Napier University, Edinburgh, 2000. Appointments: Journalist; Editor; Director of Marketing, PR Company, Leeds, Manchester, London; Head of Marketing and Communications, Bradford University College; Lecturer at several universities in western-eastern Europe; Managing Director, International Travel and Conferences. Publications: Editor of Education News; Many articles in newspapers and trade professional press. Honours: Nationally Accredited Lay Preacher; Several awards for educational publications and public speaking. Memberships: Life Member, National Union of Journalists; International Federation of Journalists (Brussels); Several Travel/Conference Related Organisations. Address: "Tirconnell", 11 Endor Crescent, Burley-in-Wharfdale, West Yorkshire LS29 7QH, England.

SWETCHARNIK Sara Morris, b. 21 May 1955, Shelby, NC, USA. Artist; Sculptor; Painter; Writer. m. William Norton Swetcharnik, 2 August 1981. Education: The Art Students League of New York, 1979-81; Postgraduate, Schuler School of Fine Art, Baltimore, Maryland, 1973-78; Private Study, Melvin Gerhold Studio, Frederick, Maryland, 1970-73. Appointments: Instructor, Frederick Academy for the Arts, Frederick, Maryland, 1981-82; Workshop Instructor, Landon School, Washington DC, 1991-96; Invitational Lecturer, Arts Task Force, Fulbright Conference, 2000, 2001; Guest Lecturer, The Institute, Mount Saint Mary's College, Emmitsburg, Maryland, 2001; Juror at several national and international exhibitions. Creative Works: Solo Exhibitions including: Catepetl Gallery, Frederick, Maryland, 1977; Holly Hills Country Club, Frederick, Maryland, 1991; Landon

School Gallery, Washington DC, 1992; Frederick Community College Art Gallery, Maryland, 1993; Showcase of Terra-cotta Animal Sculpture, Weinberg Center for the Arts, Frederick, Maryland, 1994; Komodo Dragon Yearling and other Animal Sculptures, Reptile Discovery Center, National Zoological Park, Washington DC, 1995-2001; Jungle Tails: Narratives and Sculptures of Animals, http://www.marrder.com/htw/special/jungletails; Several group and two person exhibitions; Publications include: Glass Lizard, 1998; Marked for Life, 1998; Birthday Burro, 1998; Alfredo's Tigrillo, 1998. Honours include: IIE Fulbright Fellowship, Sculpture, Spain, 1987-88, 1988-89; Artist in Residence Fellowship, American Numismatic Association Conference, 1994; Fellowship, Virginia Center for the Creative Arts. Memberships: Delaplaine Visual Art Centre, Frederick, Maryland; Fulbright Association. Address: Swetcharnik, National Capitol Post Office Station, PO Box 77794, Washington, DC 20013, USA. E-mail: saraswetcharnik@fulbrightweb.org Website: www.swetcharnik.com

SWIFT Graham Colin, b. 4 May 1949, London, England. Writer. Education: Dulwich College; Queens' College, Cambridge; University of York. Publications: The Sweet Shop Owner, 1980; Shuttlecock, 1981; Waterland, 1983; Out of This World, 1988; Ever After, 1992; Last Orders, 1996; The Light of Day, 2003; Tomorrow, 2007; Short Stories: Learning to Swim and Other Stories, 1982; The Magic Wheel, 1986. Honours: Geoffrey Fabor Memorial Prize; Guardian Fiction Prize; Royal Society of Literature Winifred Holtby Award, 1983; Premio Grinzane Cavour, Italy, 1987; Prix du Meilleur livre etranger, France, 1994; Booker Prize, James Tait Black Memorial Prize, 1996; Hon LittD, East Anglia, 1998; Hon DUniv, York, 1998. Address: c/o A P Watt, 20 John Street, London, WC1N 2DR, England.

SWIFT Peter George Furmston, b. 22 January 1943, Shrewsbury, England. Consultant Paediatrician (retired). m. Heather, 3 daughters. Education: Wyggeston Boys Grammar School, 1953-62; BA (Nat Sci), 1965, MA (Cantab), 1969, Downing College, Cambridge; MBBChir, 1968, Guy's Hospital, London. Appointments: Paediatric Registrar, Sheffield Children's Hospital, 1972-74; Senior Registrar, Paediatrics, Royal Hospital for Children, Bristol, 1974-77; Senior Registrar, Paediatrics, Exeter Hospital, 1977-78; Consultant Paediatrician, University Hospitals, Leicester, 1979-2006. Publications: Articles on Paediatric Diabetes and Paediatric Endocrinology; Editor in Chief of Consensus Guidelines on Childhood and Adolescent Diabetes, 2000. Honours: Lestradet Prize for Education and Advocacy, 2006, International Society, Pediatric and Adolescent Diabetes. Memberships: Diabetes UK; British Society Paediatric Endocrinol and Diabetes; ISPAD; MRCP (UK), FRCP (UK), FRCPCH. Address: 21 Westminster Road, Stoneygate, Leicester LE2 2EH, England.

SWIFT Thomas, b. 17 November 1930, Oldham, England. Aeronautical Engineer. m. Irene, 1 daughter. Education: Full Technological City and Guilds of London Institute, 1950, Higher National, Mechanical Engineering, 1956, Grad I Mech E, 1957, Oldham College of Science and Technology, UK; Postgraduate Studies, Advanced Aero Structures and Metallurgy, Manchester University, UK, 1960-62; Postgraduate Studies, Theory of Elasticity, Advanced Aero Structures, Advanced Differential Equations, Newark College of Engineering, New Jersey, USA, 1962-65; Postgraduate Studies, Advanced Mathematics, Partial Differential Equations, Vector Analysis and Complex Variables, Stevens Institute of Technology, New Jersey, 1965-66; Upgrade to BSc, 1966-68, MSc, 1973, Mechanical Engineering, California State University, Long Beach, California, USA. Appointments: Engineering Apprenticeship Training, Oldham, 1947-51; Deputy Works Manager, Mellows and Co Ltd, Oldham, 1951-55; Design Engineer, Engineering Development Department, 1955-57, Stress Engineer, 1959-62, A V Roe and Co Ltd, Manchester; Stress Engineer, AVRO Aircraft, Malton, Ontario, Canada, 1957-59; Member of Technical Staff, RCA Missile Electronics and Controls, Burlington, Massachusetts, 1959; Project Engineer, Structural Analysis, X-19 VTOL Aircraft, Curtiss Wright Corp, Caldwell, New Jersey, 1962-66; Supervisor, Fuselage Fatigue, Fail-Safe Analysis and Structural Test Group, 1967-72, Stress Analysis, 1966-67, Chief, Fatigue and Fracture Mechanics Group, 1972-80, Chief Technology Engineer (Chief of Stress), C-17 Structural Analysis, 1986-87, McDonnell Douglas Corp, Long Beach, California; Lecturer, Fatigue and Damage Tolerance Technology, UCLA, 1975-; FAA National Resource Specialist, 1980-86, 1987-89, FAA Chief Scientific/Technical Advisor, 1989-97, Fracture Mechanics/Metallurgy; Aeronautical Consultant, Visiting Professor, Cranfield University, England, 1997-. Publications: Over 40 papers, articles and technical publications. Honours: John Platt Memorial Award, 1953-56; Engineer of the Month Award, Douglas Aircraft, Long Beach, California, USA, 1969; Plantema Medal, International Committee on Aeronautical Fatigue, 1987; John W Lincoln Medal, US Air Force, 1998; Wakefield Gold Medal, Royal Aeronautical Society, UK, 1999; Listed in international biographical dictionaries. Memberships: Fellow, Institution of Mechanical Engineers, UK; Chartered Engineer (C Eng), UK; Member, Council of Engineering Institutions, UK; Registered Member of Professional Engineers, Ontario, Canada; Retired Member of Fatigue Committee, Engineering Sciences Data Unit (ESDU); Retired Member, MIL-HDBK 5 Industry Co-ordinating Committee; Retired Member, FAA Technical Oversight Group-Aging Aircraft; Past Member, NASA Aeronautics Advisory Committee. Address: 3 Blencathra Gardens, Kendal, Cumbria LA9 7HL, England. E-mail: tomswiftken@aol.com

SWINBURNE Richard Granville, b. 26 December 1934, Smethwick, Staffordshire, England. Professor of Philosophy; Author. m. Monica Holmstrom, 1960, separated 1985, 2 daughters. Education: BA, 1957, BPhil, 1959, Dip Theol, 1960, MA, 1961, University of Oxford. Appointments: Fereday Fellow, St John's College, Oxford, 1958-61; Leverhulme Research Fellow in the History and Philosophy of Science, University of Leeds, 1961-63; Lecturer to Senior Lecturer in Philosophy, University of Hull, 1963-72; Visiting Associate Professor of Philosophy, University of Maryland, 1969-70; Professor of Philosophy, University of Keele, 1972-84; Distinguished Visiting Scholar, University of Adelaide, 1982; Nolloth Professor of the Philosophy of the Christian Religion, 1985-2002, Emeritus Nolloth Professor, 2002-, University of Oxford; Visiting Professor of Philosophy, Syracuse University, 1987; Visiting Lecturer, Indian Council for Philosophical Research, 1992; Visiting Professor of Philosophy, University of Rome, 2002; Visiting Professor of Philosophy, Catholic University of Lublin, 2002; Visiting Professor of Divinity, Yale University, 2003; Visiting (Collins) Professor of Philosophy, St Louis University, USA, 2003. Publications include: Space and Time, 1968, 2nd edition, 1981; The Concept of Miracle, 1971; An Introduction to Confirmation Theory, 1973; The Coherence of Theism, 1977, revised edition, 1993; The Existence of God, 1979, 2nd edition, 2004; Faith and Reason, 1981, 2nd edition, 2005; Personal Identity (with S Shoemaker), 1984; The Evolution of the Soul, 1986, revised edition, 1997; Responsibility and

Atonement, 1989; Revelation, 1992, 2nd edition, 2007; The Christian God, 1994; Is There a God?, 1996; Providence and the Problem of Evil, 1998; Epistemic Justification, 2001; The Resurrection of God Incarnate, 2003. Honour: Fellow, British Academy, 1992. Address: 50 Butler Close, Oxford OX2 6JG, England. E-mail: richard.swinburne@oriel.ox.ac.uk

SYAL Meera, b. 27 June 1963, Wolverhampton, England. Writer; Actress. m. (1) 1989, 1 daughter, (2) Sanjeev Bhaskar, 2005. Education: Queen Mary's High School for Girls, Walsall; University of Manchester. Career: One-woman comedy, One of US; Former actress, Royal Court Theatre, London; Writer of screenplays and novels; Actress and comedienne in theatre, film and on TV; Contributions to The Guardian newspaper; Plays include: Serious Money, 1987; Stitch, 1990; Peer Gynt, 1990; Bombay Dreams, 2001; Radio: Legal Affairs, 1996; Goodness Gracious Me, 1996-98; The World as We Know It, 1999; Films: Samme and Rosie Get Laid, 1987; A Nice Arrangement (also writer); It's Not Unusual; Beautiful Thing, 1996; Girls' Night, 1997; Mad Sad & Bad, 2008; TV: The Real McCoy (5 series), 1990-95; My Sister Wife (also writer), 1992; Have I Got News For You, 1992, 1993, 1999; Sean's Show, 1993; The Brain Drain, 1993; Absolutely Fabulous, 1995; Soldier Soldier, 1995; Degrees of Error, 1995; Band of Gold, 1995; Drop the Dead Donkey, 1996; Ruby, 1997; Keeping Mum, 1997-98; The Book Quiz, 1998; Goodness Gracious Me (co-writer), 1998-2000; Room 101, 1999; The Kumars at No 42, 2002-; The All Star Comedy Show, 2004; Bad Girls, 2004; M.I.T: Murder Investigation Team, 2005; The Amazing Mrs Pritchard, 2006; Kingdom, 2007; Jekyll, 2007; Written work: Bhaji on the Beach (film), 1994; Anita and Me (novel and TV adaption), 1996; Life Isn't All Ha Ha Hee Hee (novel), 1999. Honours: National Student Drama Award; Scottish Critics Award for Most Promising Performer, 1984; Best TV Drama Award, Commission for Racial Equality; Awards for Best Actress and Best Screenplay, Asian Film Academy, 1993; Woman of the Year in Performing Arts, Cosmopolitan Magazine, 1994; Betty Trask Award, 1996; Chair's Award, Asian Women of Achievement Awards, 2002. Address: Rochelle Stevens, 2 Terretts Place, Islington, London N1 1QZ, England.

SYAMALA M, b. 30 May 1966, Kolavennu, Krishna District, India. Chemist; Researcher. m. Mandali Harikrishna. Education: BSc, Sri Venkateswara University, Tirupathi, 1986; MSc, National Institute of Technology, Warangal, 1988; PhD, Osmania University, Hyderabad, 2000. Appointments: Research Professional in Chemistry, Indian Institute of Chemical Technology, Hyderabad, 1989-. Publications: Contributed articles to reputed international professional journals; Articles include: A decade of advances in three-component reactions: A review. Honours: Elected Fellow, International Biographical Association, UK; Listed in international biographical dictionaries; Best performance award, CSIR Foundation Day, 1999. Memberships: Life Member, Chemical Research Society of India; Life Member, Indian Women Scientists Association; Life Member, Indian Society for Analytical Scientists. Address: Flat #104, Acropolis Villa, Street #6, Habsiguda, Hyderabad, Andhra Pradesh 500 007, India. E-mail: syamala_frs@yahoo.co.in

SYDOW Max Von, b. 10 April 1929, Lund, Sweden. Actor. m. (1) Kerstin Olin, 1951, divorced 1979, 2 sons, (2) Catherine Brelet, 1997, 2 sons. Education: Royal Dramatic Theatre School, Stockholm; Norrköping-Linköping Theatre, 1951-53; Hälsingborg Theatre, 1953-55; Malmo Theatre, 1955-60; Royal Dramatic Theatre, Stockholm, 1960-74, 1988-94; Plays: Peer Gynt; Henry IV; The Tempest; Le misanthrope;

Faust; Ett Drömspel; La valse des toréadors; Les sequestrés d'Altona; After the Fall; The Wild Duck; The Night of the Tribades, 1977; Duet for One, 1981; The Tempest, 1988; Swedenhielms, 1990; And Give US the Shadows, 1991; The Ghost Sonata, 1994; Films: Bara en mor, 1949; Miss Julie, 1950; The Seventh Seal, 1957; The Face, 1958; The Virgin Spring, 1960; Through a Glass Darkly, 1961; Winter Light, 1963; The Greatest Story Ever Told, 1963; 4x4, 1965; Hawaii, 1965; Quiller Memorandum, 1966; The Hour of the Wolf, 1966; The Shame, 1967; A Passion, 1968; The Emigrants, 1969; The New Land, 1969; The Exorcist, 1973; Steppenwolf, 1973; Heart of a Dog, 1975; Three Days of the Condor, 1975; The Voyage of the Damned, 1976; The Desert of the Tartars, 1976; Cadaveri Eccelenti, 1976; Deathwatch, 1979; Flash Gordon, 1979; Victory, 1980; The Flight of the Eagle, 1981; Hannah and Her Sisters, 1985; Duet for One, 1986; Pelle the Conqueror, 1986; Father, 1989; Until the End of the World, 1990; The Silent Touch, 1991; Time is Money, 1993; Needful Things, 1994; Judge Dredd; Hamsun, 1996; What Dreams May Come, 1997; Snow Falling on Cedars, 1999; Non ho sonno, 2000; Intacto, 2000; Minority Report, 2002; Kingdom in Twilight, 2004; Heidi, 2005; Rush Hour 3, 2007; Emotional Arithmetic, 2007; Director, Katinka, 1989; TV: The Last Civilian; Christopher Columbus; The Last Place on Earth, 1984; The Belarus File, 1984; Gosta Berling's Saga, 1985; The Wisdom and the Dream, 1989; Red King White Knight; Hiroshima Out of the Ashes, 1990; Best Intentions, 1991; Radetzky March, 1994; Citizen X, 1995; Confessions, 1996; Solomon, 1997. Publicatinos: Loppcirkus (with Elizabeth Sörenson), 1989. Honours: Best Actor, European Film Award, Berlin, 1988. Address: London Management, 2-4 Noel Street, London W1V 3RB, England.

SYKES Alfred Geoffrey, b. 12 January 1934. Professor Emeritus of Chemistry. m. Elizabeth Blakey, 2 sons, 1 daughter. Education: Huddersfield College; BSc, PhD, 1958, DSc, 1973, University of Manchester; CChem, FRSC, 1972. Appointments: Postdoctoral studies, Princeton University, 1958-59, Adelaide University, 1959-60; Lecturer, 1961-70, Reader, 1970-80, University of Leeds; Professor of Inorganic Chemistry, University of Newcastle upon Tyne, 1980-99, Professor Emeritus, 1999-; Visiting Scientist, Argonne National Laboratories, USA, 1968; Visitor or Visiting Professor: Heidelberg University, 1975; Northwestern University, USA, 1978; University of Berne, 1980; University of Sydney, 1984; University of Kuwait, 1989; Universities of Adelaide and Melbourne, 1992; University of Newfoundland, 1995; Universities of the West Indies, 1997; University of Lausanne, 1998; University of Stellenbosch, Cape Town and Bloemfontein, 1999, University of La Laguna, Spain, 2000, City University of Hong Kong, 2001/2; Denmark Technical University, 2002; Troisième Cycle Lecturer, Les Rasses, 1971, Les Diablerets, 1987 Champéry, 2000, French-speaking Swiss Universities. Publications: Editor: Advances in Inorganic and Bio-inorganic Mechanisms, volumes 1-4, 1982-86; Advances in Inorganic Chemistry, volumes 32-53, 1988-2002; Book: Kinetics of Inorganic Reactions, 1966; Over 470 papers and reviews in scientific journals. Honours: Tilden Lecturer, Medal and Prize, RSC, 1984; Fellow, Japanese Society for the Promotion of Science, 1986; Fellow, Royal Society, 1999; Royal Society, Kan Tong Po Fellow, Hong Kong, 2002; Honorary DSc, Free State University, South Africa, 2003. Address: 73 Beech Court, Darras Hall, Newcastle upon Tyne, NE20 9NE, England. E-mail: a.g.sykes@ncl.ac.uk

SYKES Eric, b. 4 May 1923, England. Actor; Writer; Director. m. Edith Eleanor Milbradt, 1 son, 3 daughters. Education: Ward St School, Oldham. Appointments: Long running TV comedy show Sykes (with Hattie Jacques); Many other TV appearances; Films include: actor: Orders are Orders; Watch Your Stern; Very Important Person; Heavens Above; Shalako; Those Magnificent Men in Their Flying Machines; Monte Carlo or Bust!; The Boys in Blue; Absolute Beginners; The Others, 2000; Mavis and the Mermaid, 2004; Harry Potter and the Goblet of Fire, 2005; Son of Rambow, 2007; Plays include: Big Bad Mouse, 1977-78; A Hatful of Sykes, 1977-78; Run for your Wife, 1992; The 19th Hole, 1992; Two of a Kind, 1995; Fools Rush In, 1996; The School for Wives, 1997; Kafka's Dick, 1998-99; Caught in the Net, 2001-02; Three Sisters, 2003; As You Like It, 2003; Radio includes: (as writer) Educating Archie; The Goon Show, Co-wrote 24 episodes with Spike Milligan including 2 specials; The Frankie Howerd Show. Publications: The Great Crime of Grapplewick, 1996; UFO's Are Coming Wednesday, 1995; Smelling of Roses, 1997; Sykes of Sebastopol Terrace, 2000; Eric Sykes' Comedy Heroes, 2003; If I Don't Write It, Nobody Else Will (autobiography), 2005. Honours: OBE, 1986; Freeman City of London, 1988; Lifetime Achievement Award, Writer's Guild, 1992; CBE, 2005. Address: 9 Orme Court, London, W2 4RL, England.

SYKES Richard N, b. 11 January 1942, Charlotte, North Carolina, USA. History Professor; Department Chair (retired). Education: AB, History and English, Southern Wesleyan University, 1964; MA, Social Science and Reading Specialisation, Appalachian State University, 1965; PhD, History, Greenwich University, 2001. Appointments: Instructor, History and Political Science, Gordon College, 1965-67; Assistant Professor of History and Reading, Gardner-Webb College, 1967-69; Instructor of History and Reading, Central Piedmont Community College, 1969-70; Co-ordinator, Secondary Reading, Chester County, 1971-73; Reading Specialist, Williamsburg County, 1973-74; Reading Diagnostician, Chesterfield County, 1974-79; Teacher, Reading Specialist, Lancaster County, 1979-90, South Carolina Schools; Professor of History, 1990-2005, Department Chair, 2001-05, Retired, 2006, Aiken Technical College. Publications: Saint Anselm's Life, Archbishopric and Theology: Their Contribution to Church and Society. Honours: AB summa cum laude; Faculty Member of the Year, Aiken Technical College, 1999; Educator of the Year, Aiken Technical College, 1991-92; Medal, Institute for Staff and Organisational Development, 2000; Governor's Distinguished Professor Award for Aiken Technical College, South Carolina Commission on Higher Education, 2000. Memberships: Certified Educator, North Carolina and South Carolina Public Schools; South Carolina Technical Education Association; South Carolina State Employees Association; National Geographic Society; Smithsonian Institution. Address: 838 Osbon Drive, Aiken, SC 29801-4154, USA.

SYME Paul David, b. 28 November 1957, Broxburn, Scotland. Doctor of Medicine. m. Sarah, 1 son, 1 daughter. Education: Bathgate Academy; BSc (Hons), MBChB, MD, FRCP Edin, University of Edinburgh. Appointments: SHO, Manchester and Edinburgh hospitals; Registrar, Hammersmith Hospital; Senior Registrar, MRC Clinical Scientist, University of Oxford; Part-time Senior Lecturer, University of Edinburgh; Lead Stroke Physician, Head of Clinical Service, DME; Consultant Physician, NHS Borders. Publications: Over 30 articles in professional journals; International patents for the treatment of stroke and multiple sclerosis using transcranial doppler ultrasound; Chair of sign guideline on the management of patients with stroke or TIA: Assessment Investigation, Immediate Management and Secondard Prevention. Honours: John Newlands Bursary; Glaxo Junior

Research Fellowship,Green College, Oxford; Hoechst Young Investigator of the Year, British Hypertension Society; MRC Travelling Fellowship; Twice Finalist, Life Sciences Award for Best Innovation, NHS. Memberships: Fellow, Royal College of Physicians; QIS Advisor, Stroke Services National Panel, Stroke Standards. E-mail: p.d.syme@btinternet.com

SYMS Sylvia, b. 6 January 1934, London, England. Actress; Director. m. Alan Edney, 1957, divorced 1989, 1 son, 1 daughter. Education: Royal Academy of Dramatic Art. Appointments: Founder Member, Artistic Director, Arbela Production Company; Numerous lectures include: Dodo White McLarty Memorial Lecture, 1986; Member, The Actors' Centre, 1986-91; Films include: Ice Cold in Alex, 1953; The Birthday Present, 1956; The World of Suzie Wong, 1961; Run Wild Run Free, 1969; The Tamarind Seed, 1974; Chorus of Disapproval, 1988; Shirley Valentine, 1989; Shining Through, 1991; Dirty Weekend, 1992; Staggered, 1994; Food for Love, 1996; Mavis and the Mermaid, 1999; The Queen, 2006; Is There Anybody There? 2008; TV includes: Love Story, 1964; The Saint, 1967; My Good Woman, 1972-73; Nancy Astor, 1982; Ruth Rendell Mysteries, 1989; Dr Who, 1989-90; May to December, 1989-90; The Last Days of Margaret Thatcher, 1991; Natural Lies; Mulberry; Peak Practice; Ruth Rendell Mysteries, 1993, 1997-98; Ghost Hour, 1995; Heartbeat, 1998; At Home with the Braithwaites, 2000-03; The Jury, 2002; Where the Heart Is, 2003; Born and Bred, 2003; Child of Mine, 2005; Judge John Deed, 2006; Dalziel and Pascoe, 2006; Doctors, 2004-06; Casualty, 2007; Eastenders, 2007; Theatre includes: Dance of Death; Much Ado About Nothing; An Ideal Husband; Ghosts; Entertaining Mr Sloane, 1985; Who's Afraid of Virginia Woolf?, 1989; The Floating Lightbulb, 1990; Antony and Cleopatra, 1991; For Services Rendered, 1993; Funny Money,1996; Ugly Rumours, 1998; Radio includes: Little Dorrit; Danger in the Village; Post Mortems; Joe Orton; Love Story; The Change, 2001, 2003; Plays and TV Director: Better in My Dreams, 1988; The Price, 1991; Natural Lies, 1991-92. Honours: Variety Club Best Actress in Films Award, 1958; Ondas Award for Most Popular Foreign Actress, Spain, 1966. Address: c/o Barry Brown and Partners, 47 West Square, London, SE11 4SP, England.

SYNEK Miroslav, b. 18 September 1930, Czechoslovakia. Physicist; Chemist; World Affairs Independent Consultant. 1 son, 1 daughter. Education: Certificate, Industrial Chemistry Technical School, Prague, 1946-50; Analytical Chemist, Industrial Medicine Institute, 1950-51; Certificate in Liberal Arts, 1951; MS, Physics with distinction, Charles University, 1956; PhD, University of Chicago, 1963. Appointments: Research Physicist, Academy of Sciences, Prague, 1956-58; Assistant to Associate Professor, De Paul University of Chicago, 1962-67; Professor, Texas Christian University, Fort Worth, 1967-71; Lecturer, Researcher, University of Texas, Austin, 1971-75; Faculty tenure, University of Texas San Antonio, 1975-95; Scientific advisor to various institutions and organisations. Publications: Articles in numerous scientific journals, abstracts to presentations; Reviewer for several professional publications. Honours: Fellow, American Association for the Advancement of Science; Texas Academy of Science; American Institute of Chemists; Life Fellow, American Physical Society; Judge and grand award judge at many science competitions; Listed in a number of Who's Who and biographical publications. Memberships include: American Association of University Professors; National Education Association; Texas State Teachers Association; Emeritus Member, The American Association of Physics Teachers; American Chemical Society; American Museum of Natural History; Distinguished Member, International Society

of Poets; Diplomat Member, World Affairs Council, SA; Astronomical Association, SA. Address: PO Box 5937, San Antonio, TX 78201-0937, USA. E-mail: m.synek@juno.com

SYRISTOVA Eva, b. 7 November 1928, Prague. Professor Emeritus of Psychopathology and Psychotherapy. m. Syriste Jaroslav MD, 1 son. Education: PhD, 1951, C Scientiarum in Psychopathology and Psychotherapy, Charles University, 1962. Appointments: Editor, SPN Publications, Prague, 1951-53; Clinical Psychologist, Institute of Psychiatry, Prague, 1953-57; Lecturer, 1957-67, Professor 1967-94, Prodean for Scientific Research, 1992-94, Professor Emeritus, 1994-, Psychopathology, Psychotherapy, Charles University, Prague; Pioneer of psychotherapy and art-therapy of schizophrenic psychosis in the Czech Republic. Publications: The Possibilities and Limitations of the Psychotherapy of Schizophrenic Diseases, 1965; The Imaginary World, 1973; Normality of the Personality, 1973; The Cracked Time, 1988; The Group Psychotherapy of Psychoses, 1989; Man in Crisis, 1994; The Poem as a Home in the Homelessness of Paul Celan, 1994. Honours: Honorary Appreciation Czech Medical Society for contribution to Czech Sciences, 1978; Honorary Prize for Translation of Celan's Poetry, 1983. Memberships: IAAP; IBRO; World Phenomenology Institute, International Association of Phenomenology and Sciences of Life; New York Academy of Sciences; Czech Medical, Psychiatric and Artistic Association; Director, White Rawen for Non-professional Art in Prague. Address: Sluknovska 316, 190 00 Prague 9, Czech Republic.

SYRKIN Alexander, b. 16 August 1930, Ivanovo, USSR. Philologist; Professor Emeritus. Education: Graduate (MA), Moscow State University, 1953; Candidate of History (PhD), 1962; Doctor of Philology, 1971. Appointments: Junior Research Associate, Institute of History, Academy of Science of USSR, Moscow, 1955-61; Junior Research Associate, 1961-71, Senior Research Associate, 1971-77, Institute of Oriental Studies, Academy of Science of USSR, Moscow; Research Fellow, Associate Professor, Institute of Asian and African Studies, 1978-98, Professor Emeritus, 1998-, Hebrew University, Jerusalem. Publications: Books, articles, commented translations of classical texts, essays on subjects including: Indology, Byzantine Studies, Russian Literature, etc; Examples include: Poem about Digenes Akritas, Moscow, 1964; Certain Problems Regarding the Study of the Upanishads, Moscow, 1971; To Descend in Order to Rise, Jerusalem, 1993; Upon Re-reading the Classics, Jerusalem, 2000; The Path of the Personage and the Author, Jerusalem, 2001; Upanishads, 3rd edition, Moscow, 2003. Former Memberships include: FRAS of Great Britain and Ireland; International Association of Buddhist Studies; International Association of Semiotic Studies. Address: Dov Gruner Str 236, Apt 17, Talpiot Mizrah, Jerusalem 91291 (POB 29278), Israel.

SZABÓ István, b. 18 February 1938, Budapest, Hungary. Film Director. m. Vera Gyürey. Education: Graduate, Academy of the Art of Theatre and Film, Budapest, 1961. Appointments: Film Director; Guest Professor at various film schools; University Professor, DLA. Publications: Short films: Concert, 1961; Variations upon a Theme, 1963; You, 1963; Piety, 1967; Budapest, I Love You, 1971; City Map, 1977; Feature films: The Age of Daydreaming, 1964; Father, 1966; Love Film, 1970; 25 Fireman's Street, 1973; Premiere (TV play), 1974; Budapest Tales, 1976; Confidence, 1979; The Green Bird (TV play), 1979; Mephisto, 1981; Catsplay (TV play), 1982; Bali (TV play), 1983; Colonel Redl, 1985; Hanussen, 1988; Meeting Venus, 1991; Sweet Emma, Dear Böbe (sketches and nudes), 1991; Offenbach's Secret, 1995;

Steadying the Boat (TV), 1996; Sunshine, 1998; Taking Sides, 2000; Being Julia, 2004; Relatives, 2006; Director of several operas and theatre plays including: Boris Godunov, Opera Leipzig, 1993; Il Trovatore, Vienna State Opera, 1993; Chekov's Three Sisters, Staatstheater Kassel, and opera version by Péter Eötvös, Kassel Opera House, 2002. Honours include: American Academy Award; British Academy Award; David Donatello Award; Visconti Award; Silver Bear, Berlin; Fellini Award, Italy, 2002; Four times nominated for Oscar, 1981, 1983, 1986, 1989; Twice nominated for Golden Globe, 1986, 1998. Memberships: AMPAS; EFA.

SZABÓ Zoltán, b. 18 March 1957, Tirgu-Mures, Romania. Anaesthesiologist. m. Márta Harangi, 1 son, 2 daughters. Education: MD, Institutul de Medicina si Farmacie, Tirgu-Mures, Romania. 1983; Specialist in Anaesthesia and Intensive Care, Hungarian Board of Anaesthesia, Hungary, 1988; PhD, Thoracic and Cardiovascular Anaesthesia, Linköping, Sweden, 2001. Appointments: Resident, Sitalul Clinic, Judetean Mures, Romania, 1983-86; Resident 2, Sebészeti Klinika, 1986-88, Specialist in Anaesthesia, 1988-95, Debrecen University, Hungary; Doctor and Specialist in Anaesthesia, 1995-2001, Consultant Anaesthetist, 2001-, University Hospital, Linköping Heart Centre. Publications: Articles in scientific journals as co-author include most recently: Neurological injury after surgery for ischemic heart disease: risk factors, outcome and role of metabolic interventions, 2001; Early postoperative outcome and medium term survival in 540 diabetic and 2239 nondiabetic patients undergoing coronary artery bypass grafting, 2002; Simple intra operative method to rapidly pass a pulmonary artery flotation catheter into the pulmonary artery, 2003; High Dose Glucose-Insulin-potassium after cardiac surgery: a retrospective analysis of clinical safety issues, 2003. Honour: First Prize for Best Poster, Congress of Cardiac Anaesthesia, Budapest, EACTA, 1990. First Prize for the best Thoracic Anesthesiological Oral presentation at the Thoracic Meeting, Linköping, 2006. Memberships: EACTA; SFTAI; Founding Member, Rotary, Debrecen; EASD; DCRA; SSRCTS; SFAI; SSAI. Address: Department of Cardiothoracic and Vascular Anaesthesia, Östergötlands Heart Centre, S-58185 Linköping, Sweden.

SZCZERBAKOW Andrzej, b. 28 September 1943, Wojslawice, Poland. Materials Engineer; Researcher. m. Barbara Gertler, 2 sons. Education: MSc, Chemical Technology, Technical University, Wroclaw, 1969; PhD, Crystallography, Humboldt University, Berlin, 1983; DSc, Electronics, Institute of Electron Technology, Warsaw, 2005. Appointments: Engineer, Military Technical Academy, Warsaw, 1969-74; Engineer, later Researcher, Institute of Physics, Polish Academy of Science, Warsaw, 1974-90; Chief Specialist, Materials Engineering, Infrared Detector Laboratory, VIGO Ltd, Warsaw, 1990-92; Researcher, Institute of Physics, Polish Academy of Science, Warsaw, 1993-. Publications: Monocrystalline ZnS sphalerite films grown by atomic layer epitaxy in a gas flow system, 1998; Model of the temperature field in tube furnaces and its application to a system of "contactless" crystal growth from the vapour, 2003; Self-selecting vapour growth of bulk crystals – Principles and applicability progress in crystal growth and characterization of materials, 2005; Numerous articles in professional journals. Honours: Commemorative Medal, Interkosmos Scientific Council, 1979; Awards, Scientific Secretary, Polish Academy of Sciences, 1979, 1987. Address: ul. Lukowa 7 m 60, Warsaw, 02-767, Poland. E-mail: a.szczerb@wp.pl Website: http://szczerbakow.info

T

TAATONG Patsaraaporn, b. 14 December 1978, Bangkok, Thailand. English Teacher. Education: BA, English, 2000; MA, Business English for International Communication, 2006. Appointments: Part time English Teacher, Demonstration School of Ramkamhaeng University, Bangkok, 2001-02; Part time English Teacher, Rajamangala University of Technology, Bangkok, 2002-03; Full time English Teacher, Don Bosco Technical School, Bangkok, 2003-. Publications: An Analysis of Rhetorical Figures used in Magazine Headlines in Print Facial Skin Care Advertisements from 2001-2005. Honours: Best readers for Wat Sungwet Secondary School Library, 1994; Outstanding Student for Social and Thai Subjects in Wat Sungwet Secondary School, 1994; Good Practicer for Buddhism Student in Wat Sungwet Secondary School, 1995; Many scholarships during studies. Memberships: Teachers Council of Thailand, Ministry of Education, 2005-2010; Srinakharinwirot University Alumni Association for English Major Students; Don Bosco Technical School Teachers, Students and Parents Association. Address: 171/1975 Paholyothin Road, Saimai, Bangkok 10220, Thailand. E-mail: starlit_night19@hotmail.com

TADESSE Solomon, b. 12 September 1958, Harar, Ethiopia. Economic Geologist. m. Etsehiwet Geneti, 1 son, 1 daughter. Education: BSc, Geology, AAU, 1980; MSc, Mineral Exploration, 1986, PhD, Economic Geology, 1989, University of Cagliari, Italy. Appointments: Assistant Professor, 1991-95; Associate Professor, 1996-2004; Professor, 2005-. Publications: 25 articles; 2 books. Honours: Listed in international biographical dictionaries. Memberships: Geological Society of Africa. Address: Bole Administration Region, Kebele 08/09, House No 290, PO Box 6912, Addis Ababa, Ethiopia. E-mail: solotade@geol.aau.edu.et

TAEL Kaja, b. 24 July 1960, Tallinn, Estonia. Diplomat. Education: Estonian Language and Literature, Tartu University, 1978-83; PhD, Institute for Language and Literature of the Academy of Sciences of Tallinn, 1989. Appointments: Researcher, Department of Grammar, Institute for Language and Literature, Academy of Sciences, Tallinn, 1984-89; Guest Scholar, Chair of Finno-Ugric Languages, Uppsala University Sweden, 1990-91; Director, Estonian Institute Tallinn (non-governmental institution for informational and cultural exchange in co-operation with the Foreign Ministry), 1991-95; Lecturer, Chair of Nordic Languages, Tallinn Pedagogical University, 1995-2000; Foreign Policy Advisor to the President of Estonia, Mr Lennart Meri, 1995-98; Joined the Estonian Foreign Ministry, 1998; Executive Secretary of the Estonian-Russian Intergovernmental Commission, 1998-99; Director General, Policy Planning Department, Estonian Ministry of Foreign Affairs, 1999-2001; Ambassador Extraordinary and Plenipotentiary of the Republic of Estonia at the Court of St James, London, 2001. Publications: Computer Analysis of the Estonian Word Order (PhD thesis), 1989; An Approach to Word Order Problems in Estonian, 1990; Book chapter in The scientific Grammar of the Estonian Language, 1993, 1996; Articles on information structure and word order; Translations into Estonian: John Stuart Mill "On Liberty", 1996; Henry Kissinger "Diplomacy", 2000; Eric Hobsbawm "The Age of Extremes", 2002. Honours: Swedish Polar Star, 1995; Finnish Lion, 1995; Mexican Aguila Azteca, 1996; Estonian Order of the White Star, 2000. Memberships: Chairman of the Board, Estonian Institute; Farmers Club, London. Address: The Estonian Embassy, 16 Hyde Park Gate, London SW7 5DG, London.

TAHA Mohamed, b. 29 August 1978, Egypt. Director of Planning & Evaluation. Education: BSc, Chemistry, 1999, MSc, Analytical Chemistry, 2005, Cairo University, Beni-Suef Branch, Egypt. Appointments: Occupational Safety & Health Inspector, Egypt, 3 years; Chemistry Instructor, Industrial Education College, Egypt, 1 year; Director of Planning & Evaluation in Arabian Fire Safety Academy, Kingdom of Saudi Arabia, 2005-. Publications: Equilibrium Studies of the Binary and Ternary Complexes Involving Tricine and Some Selected Amino Acids, 2004; Thermodynamic Study of the Second-stage Dissociation of N,N- bis-2-hydroxyethyl)glycine (Bicine) in Water at Different Ionic Strength and Different Solvent Mixtures, 2004); Thermodynamic of the Second-stage Dissociation of 2-[N-(2-hydroxyethyl)-N-methylaminomethyl]- propenoic Acid(HEMPA) in Water at Different Ionic Strength and Different Solvent Mixtures, 2005; Mixed Ligand Complex Formation Equilibria of Cobalt-, Nickel- ,and N,N-Bis(2-hy droxyethyl)glycine Copper(II) with Bicine and some Amino Acids, 2005; Buffers For The Physiological Ph Range: Acidic Dissociation Constants Of Zwitterionic Compound In Various Hydroorganic Media, 2005; Metal Ion-Buffer Interactions. Complex Formation of [N,N-bis- (2-hydroxyethyl)glycine] (Bicine) with Various Biologically Relevant Ligands, 2005; Mixed Ligand Complexes in Solution: Metal Ions-Salicylhydroxamic Acid-Benzohydroxamic Acid Systems, 2006; Metal Ions Complexation of Some Zwittrerionic Buffers in NaNO3 Solutions in Water and in Mixtures of Water and Dioxane, in press; Potentiometric and Thermodynamic Studies of the Protonation Equilibria and Thermodynamic Studies on Complexation of Divalent Transition Metal Ions With Some Zwitterionic Buffers for Biochemical and Physiological Research, 2007. Honours: Listed in international biographical dictionaries. Memberships: Active Member, American Chemical Society. Address: Qai, Ehnasia, Beni-Suef, EGYPT. E-mail: mtaha@yahoo.com

TAHERZADEH Mohammad J, b. 22 March 1965, Isfahan, Iran. Biotechnologist. m. Arezoo Keivandarian, 2 sons. Education: BSc, Chemical Engineering, 1989; MSc, Chemical Engineering, 1991; PhD, Biochemical Engineering, 1999. Appointments: Vice Director, Jahad Daneshgahi, Isfahan University of Technology, Iran, 1988-91; Lecturer, Chemical Engineering, Isfahan University of Technology, 1992-94; Assistant Professor, Chemical Reaction Engineering, Chalmers University of Technology, Sweden, 1999-2001; Assistant Professor, Chemical Engineering, Lund University of Technology, Sweden, 1999-2001; Associate Professor, Chemical Reaction Engineering, Sweden, 2002-04; Professor, School of Engineering, University of Boras, Sweden, 2004-. Honours: Prize for the Excellent Rank among the Graduated MSc students by Iran's President; Listed in biographical publications. Address: School of Engineering, University of Boras, 50190 Boras, Sweden.

TAHIR Mustapha, b. 12 September 1960, Sokoto, Nigeria. General Practitioner. m. Clare, 1 son. Education: MBBS, University of Benin, Nigeria, 1986; DFFP, Royal College of Obstetricians & Gynaecologists, London, 2000; Joint Committee Certificate Postgraduate Training in General Practice, Wessex Deanery, 2000; Currently long-distance training in Masters in Medical Law & Ethics, De Montfort University, Leicester. Appointments: House Officer, SHO rotations, University of Benin, 1985-90; SHO, Redruth & Royal Cornwall Hospital, and Hammersmith Hospital, London, 1990-93; Research Fellow, Registrar, Obstetrics & Gynaecology, Southmead Hospital, and St Michael's Hospital, Bristol, 1993-97; SHO, GP VTS, Swindon Princess Margaret

Hospital, 1997-99; GP Registrar, Old Town Surgery, Swindon, 1999-2000; Full time GP, Riverview Park Surgery, Gravesend, 2003-; Trustee, Royal Society of Medicine, London, 2005-09; Kent County Appointed School Governor, 2006-08; Press Secretary, BMA Dartford, Medway & Cravesham branch; Chairman Elect, BMA Dartford, Medway & Cravesham, 2009-. Publications: Numerous articles in professional journals. Honours: Division I Distinction, West African School Certificate, 1979; Resident Doctor Annual Prize, University Teaching Hospital, Benin City, 1986; Royal College of Obstetricians & Gynaecologists Prize, 1994. Memberships: BMA; MDU; GMC; Royal Society of Medicine; De Montfort University Law School. Address: Riverview Park Surgery, No 1 Whin Fell Way, Gravesend, Kent, DA 11 7NL, England. E-mail: drmmtahir@hotmail.com

TAI Li-Ming, b. 30 October 1951, Taipei, Taiwan. Assistant Professor; Consultant. m. Timothy Tai-Sheng Wei, 1 son. Education: BA, 1974, MA, 1976, Education, National Cheng-chi University, Taipei; MEd, 1989, PhD, 1998, University of California at Los Angeles, USA. Appointments: School Supervisor, Bureau of Education, Taipei County Government, 1977-80; Director, Extension and Public Relations, Kaohsiung City Public Library, Taiwan, 1980-82; Senior Supervisor, Bureau of Education, Kaohsiung City Government, Kaohsiung, Taiwan, 1982-84; Principal, Kaohsiung Municipal Shih-Chia Junior High School, Kaohsiung, 1984-95; Principal, National Experimental High School, Science-based Industrial Park, Hsin-Chu, 1995-2003; Principal, National Hsin-Chu Commercial Vocational High School, Hsin-Chu, Taiwan, 2003-04; Secretary General, Yu-Da College of Business, Miao-Li, Taiwan, 2004-05; Assistant professor, Department of Early Childhood Education and Care, Yu-Da College of Business, Miao-Li, 2004-06; Assistant Professor, Center for Teacher Education, Yuan Ze University, Tao-Yuan, 2006-. Publications: Many articles in professional journals; Several book chapters. Honours: Outstanding Alumna, Graduate School of Education, National Cheng-chi University, Taiwan, 1987; National Best School Educator of the Year, 1987, Model Government Employee of the Year, 1989, Kaohsiung City Government; Listed in international biographical dictionaries. Memberships: Board Director, Chung-Hwa School of Arts, Kaohsiung. Address: 135 Yuan-Tung Road, Chung-Li, Tao Yuan, 320, Taiwan.

TAIT Andrew, b. 4 November 1958, Wallsend, nr Newcastle upon Tyne, England. Poet; Music Teacher. Education: Science A Levels, Tynemouth Sixth Form College, 1975-77; French Horn, Guildhall School of Music and Drama, 1977-81. Publications: Poetry Collections: On the Sea I Spied Him, 21 Pre-Metaphysical Poems, 2005; I've Seen Where She's Bound For, 2007; Songs: 12 albums of songs released via the music page of Viz magazine including: Songs From The Heart of the Primal Goat, 1989; Why Do Hamsters Look At You Like That? 1994; My Love is Like a Whirling Elephant, 1997; Back Off! There's a Lobster Loose! 2001; Autobiography: Me and Peter Beardsley; Poetry in periodicals: The Sunday Times, The Independent, The Big Issue, Other Poetry, Morden Tower Poets; Interviews: Features in many publications, including The Sunday Times Magazine, Time Out, Get Rhythm, Viz, The Independent, Poetry Now; Poems: Going Back Over The Wasteland; Everyone's a Fruit and Nutcase; Damson in Distress; Robert's Oriental Tea Garden; The Little Leafy Lane Off To The Left; Metaphysical Experiences; Thursdays; Suspense Account; Television and radio appearances. Honours: Winner, Bloodaxe Poetry Competition; Winner, Iron Press

30th Anniversary Haiku Competition. Memberships: Morden Tower Poetry Society. Address: PO Box 1041, Newcastle Upon Tyne, NE99 2TY, England.

TAIT Marion Hooper, b. 7 October 1950, Barnet, Hertfordshire, England. Ballet Mistress. m. David Morse. Education: Royal Academy of Dance; Graduate, Royal Ballet School, 1968. Appointments: Dancer, 1968-, Principal Dancer, 1974-95, Ballet Mistress, 1995-, Royal Ballet Touring Company (later known as Sadlers Wells Royal Ballet and now Birmingham Royal Ballet). Honours: OBE, 1992; Evening Standard Ballet Award for Outstanding Performance and named Dancer of the Year, 1994; CBE, 2003; Twice nominated for Olivier Awards. Address: c/o Birmingham Royal Ballet, Birmingham Hippodrome, Thorp Street, Birmingham B5 4AU, England.

TAKAGI Shinjiro, b. 6 September 1935. Attorney at Law. Education: LLB, Chuo University, 1960; Graduate, Legal Training Research Institute, 1963; Admitted to Bar in Japan, 1963; PhD, Doctor of Law, Toyo University, 2002. Appointments: Private practice mainly in re-organisation and bankruptcy, 1963-87; Lecturer in Law, Hosei University, 1987-95; Judge, Tokyo District Court, 1988-94; President & Chief Judge, Yamagata District & Family Court, 1995-96; President & Chief Judge, Nigata District Court, 1997; Judge, Tokyo High Court (Court of Appeal), 1998-2000; Professor of Law, Dokkyo University, 2000-03; Professor, Chuo University Law School, 2003-06; Chair, IRC Commission, Industrial Revitalization Corporation, 2003-07; Advisor, Nomura Security Ltd. Publications: Numerous books and articles in professional journals. Honours: Outstanding Service and Contribution to International Insolvency, International Insolvency Institute, 2005; The Order of Rising Sun, Gold Star and Silver Star, Japanese Emperor, 2007. Memberships: Tokyo Bar Association; Japan Federation of Bar Associations; Tokyo Bar Association; American College of Bankruptcy; Japan Association of Business Recovery; National Network of Bankruptcy Lawyers; Japanese Association of Turnaround Professionals; Education Center for Restructuring Advisors; Japanese Federation of Insolvency Professionals; International Insolvency Institute. Address: 3-8-6, Kugahara, Ota-ku, Tokyo 146-0085, Japan. E-mail: stakagi@dance.plala.or.jp

TAKAGI Yoichi, b. 29 November 1940, Kamikatsucho, Tokushima prefecture, Japan. Engineer. m. Masako Hakozaki, 2 sons. Education: Yamanashi University. Appointments: Hitachi Ltd, 1959-95; Hitachi Process Computer Engineering Inc, 1995-2000. Publications: Application of image recognition and flow technologies automated sewing systems, 1993; Developing of a non-contact liquid level measuring system image processing, 1997, 1998, 2001. Honours: Japanese Electric Encouragement Prize, 1991, 1999; Listed in international biographical dictionaries. Memberships: Institution of Professional Engineers, Japan. Address: 14-9 Kanesawacho 6-chome, Hitachi-City, 316-0015, Japan. E-mail: takagiyo@green.ocn.ne.jp

TAKAMI Sachi, b. 10 February 1970, Osaka, Japan. Researcher; Teacher. m. S Takami. Education: BA, Osaka City University, 1993; MEd, Kyoto University, Japan, 2004. Appointments: Teacher, Taisho Nishi Junior High School, 1993-2004; Teacher, Junior High School, Osaka, 2004-; Researcher, Osaka City Com English, Osaka, 1996-; Researcher, Com Zero Tolerance, Osaka, 2006-; Member, Ministry of Education Com, Tokyo, 2007; Member, Osaka City Education Center, 2008-. Publications: Contributing Author: Zero Tolerance, 2006; Regarding the New Student

Discipline Policy, 2008; School Law, 2008. Honours: Bounty, Ministry of Education, 2008. Memberships: Vice President, Institution for the Promotion of Youth.

TAKAMURA Seishi, b. 29 June 1968, Nagoya, Japan. m. Sawako Takamura, 1 son, 1 daughter. Education: BS, Engineering, 1991, MS, Engineering, Graduate School, 1993, PhD, Engineering, Graduate School, 1996, Faculty of Engineering, Electronic Engineering, University of Tokyo. Appointments: Chief Research Engineer, 1998-2004, Senior Research Engineer, 2004-; Human Interface Laboratories, Visual Communication Laboratory, Video Coding Group (currently NTT Cyberspace Laboratories, Image Media Communication project, Video Coding Group), Nippon Telegraph and Telephone Corporation; ITSCJ Technical Committee SC29/WG11/VIDEO Subcommittee Member, 1998-2006, SC29/WG11/MEPEG-4 Subcommittee Member, 1998-2006; Research Fellow, NICT Natural Vision Project, 2000-2006; Referee, ITE Paper Publication Committee, 2002-; OB Referee, 2004-07; Board Member, IEICE Image Engineering Technical Group: PCSJ/IMPS Organisation Committee, 2002-; Board Member, IPSJ Audio Visual and multimedia information processing, 2003-2005; PCM Program Committee Member, 2004-2007; ITE Senator, 2004-2006; Visiting Scholar, Stanford University, California, 2005-2006; Publications: 28 international conference papers; 55 domestic conference papers, 10 journal papers, 4 books, 17 commentaries, 60 patent applications (13 patened), domestic and international; 16 ISO/IEC JTC 1/SC 29 WG (MPEG) and ITU-T VCEG/JVT Standardisation contributions; Associate Editor, IEEE Transactions on Circuits and Systems for Video Technology (CSVT), 2006-. Honours include: Pre-Business Award, Director of NTT Human Interface Laboratories, 1999; Research Promotion Award, Institute of Image Electronics Engineers of Japan, 2001; Niwa-Takayanagi Memorial Award (Best Paper Award), Institute of Image Information and Television Engineers, 2002; Pest Poster Award, 2002, 2003, Frontier Award, 2004, Picture Coding Symposium of Japan; Telecom System Technology Award, Telecommunication Advancement Foundation, 2004; Nagao Special Researcher Award, Information Processing Society of Japan, 2006; Yamashita SIG Research Award, Information Processing Society of Japan, 2007; Listed in national and international biographical dictionaries. Memberships: Institute of Image Electronics Engineers of Japan; Institute of Image Information and Television Engineers, Information Processing Society of Japan; Institute of Electronics, Information and Communication Engineers (IEICE); IEEE Senior Member. Address: 1-9-20 Yuigahama, Kamakura, Kanagawa 248-0014, Japan.

TAKAOKA Akinori, b. 29 July 1967, Japan. Professor. Education: PhD, 1996, MD, 1996, Internal Medicine, Sapporo University, Japan; Postdoctoral, Immunology, University of Tokyo, Japan, 1996-97. Appointments: Research Associate, 1997-2000, Assistant Professor, 2000-2002, Lecturer, 2002-, Department of Immunology, Graduate School of Medicine and Faculty of Medicine, University of Tokyo. Publications: Articles in scientific journals as co-author include: Cross talk between interferon γ and $\alpha\beta$ signalling components in caveolar membrane domains, 2000; Integration of IFN-$\tilde{\alpha}\beta$ signalling to p53 responses in tumor suppression and antiviral defense, 2003; Integral role of IRF-5 in the gene induction programme activated by Toll-like receptors, 2005; DAI (DLM-1/ZBP1) is a cytosolic DNA sensor and an activator of innate immune response, 2007. Honours: Ohno Award, Sapporo Medical University, 1992; Young Investigator Award, International Cytokine Society, 2000; Research

Award, Japanese, Cancer Association, 2001; Milstein Young Investigator Award, International Society for Interferon and Cytokine Research, 2003; The Princess Takamatsu Cancer Research Fund, 2003; Mitsubishi Chemical Award, 2005. Memberships: International Society for Interferon and Cytokine Research; Japanese Cancer Association; Japanese Society for Immunology; Japanese Society of Internal Medicine; Japanese Society of Gastroenterology; Japan Gastroenterological Endoscopy Society; Molecular Biology Society of Japan. Address: Division of Signalling in Cancer and Immunology, Institute of Genetic Medicine, Hokkaido University, Kita-15, Nishi-7, Kita-ku, Sapporo 060-0815, Japan. E-mail: takaoka9@m.u-tokyo.ac.jp

TAKAYAMA Hiroaki, b. 1 January 1933, Kyoto, Japan. Advisor. m. Mieko, 2 daughters. Education: Faculty of Pharmaceutical Sciences, Chiba University, 1957; Master, Graduate School of Pharmaceutical Sciences, 1960, Doctor of Pharmaceutical Sciences, 1964, Tokyo University. Appointments: professor, Faculty of Pharmaceutical Sciences, Teikyo University, 1977-2003; Emeritus Professor, Teikyo University, Director, Japan Industrial Research Center, 2003-. Publications: Creation of Functional Organic Compounds and their Applications, 2002. Honours: Award for Scientific Contribution to Pharmaceutical Society of Japan, 2001. Memberships: Pharmaceutical Society of Japan; Vitamin Society of Japan. Address: 2-6-12 Hatagaya, Shibuya-ku, Tokyo 151-0072, Japan. E-mail: htakayam@abox23.so-net.ne.jp

TAKEMURA Hiroshi, b. 23 June 1962, Komagane, Nagano, Japan. Anaesthesiologist. m. Yoshiko Takemura, 1 son, 1 daughter. Education: MD, 1988, PhD, 1998, Showa University School of Medicine, Shinagawa-ku, Tokyo, Japan. Appointments: Resident, Department of Anaesthesiology, Showa University Hospital, Shinagawa-ku, 1988-90; Medical Staff, Sempo Tokyo Takanawa Hospital, Minato-ku, 1990-91; Assistant, Department of Anaesthesiology, Showa University Toyosu Hospital, Koutou-ku, 1991-93, Showa University Hospital, Shinagawa-ku, 1993; Medical Expert (Technical Co-operation), Cairo University Paediatric Hospital, Cairo, 1993-94; Assistant, Department of Anaesthesiology, Showa University Hospital, Shinagawa-ku, 1994-2003; Medical Practitioner, Pain Management Office TA, Yokohama, Japan, 2003-. Publications: Articles in medical journals: Correlation of cleft type with incidence of perioperative respiratory complications in infants with cleft lip and palate (clinical investigation, author), 2002; Mandibular nerve block treatment for trismus associated with hypoxic-ischemic encephalopathy (case report, author), 2002. Memberships: American Society of Regional Anesthesia and Pain Medicine; Japan Society of Pain Clinicians; Japanese Society of Anesthesiologists. Address: Pain Management Office TA, 13-74 Kakinokidai Aoba-ku, Yokohama, 227-0048 Japan. E-mail: hy-take@msd.biglobe.ne.jp

TALSTAD Ingebrigt, b. 23 January 1927, Fraena, Romsdal, Norway. Doctor of Medicine. m. Hjortnaes Talstad Turid, 2 sons, 1 daughter. Education: Cand Med, 1953, Doctor of Medicine, 1973, University of Bergen; Speciality in Internal Medicine, 1962, Speciality in Blood Disorders, 1982; Research Fellow, The Norwegian Research Council, 1965-69. Appointments: Resident, 1954-58, Assistent, 1962-65, Overlege, 1974-94, Medical Department B, Haukeland Hospital; Assistent, Medical Department, Namdal Hospital, 1958-59; Reservelege, Molde, 1958-62; Reservelege, Medical Department A, Rikshospitalet, 1970-73; Professor, Haematology, University of Bergen, 1974-94; Overlege, Fürst Medical Laboratory, 1994-2003. Publications: Numerous articles and papers in professional journals. Honours: His Majesty's the King's Gold Medal, University of Oslo, 1974; Fellow, International Society of Haematology. Memberships: International Society of Haematology. Address: Torjusbk 19B, 0378 Oslo, Norway. E-mail: ingebrigt.talstad@chello.no

TAM Bit-Shun, b. 21 February, 1951. Professor; Mathematician. Education: BA, Mathematics, 1973, PhD, Mathematics, 1977, University of Hong Kong. Appointments: Teaching Assistant, University of Hong Kong, 1973-78; Postdoctoral Fellow, University of Waterloo, Canada, 1978-79; Instructor, Auburn University, Alabama, USA, 1979-81; Associate Professor, 1981-84, Professor, 1984-, Research Professor, 1995-2003, Tamkang University, Taiwan, Lady Davis Visiting Professor, 2004, Technion, Israel. Publications: About 50 research papers in international mathematical journals. Honours: Editor, Tamkang Journal of Mathematics, 1982-; Associate Editor, Linear Algebra and Its Applications, 1991-2005; Associate Editor, Applied Mathematics E-Notes, 2001-; Associate Editor, Electronic Journal of Linear Algebra, 2002-. Memberships: American Mathematical Society; Mathematical Society of Republic of China; International Linear Algebra Society; Chinese Linear Algebra Society, Vice-President, 1996-. Address: Department of Mathematics, Tamkang University, Tamsui, Taiwan 251, Republic of China. E-mail: bsm01@mail.tku.edu.tw

TAN Amy, b. 19 February 1952, Oakland, California, USA. Writer. m. Lou DeMattei, 6 April 1974. Education; BA, 1973, MA, 1974, San Jose State College; Postgraduate studies, University of California at Berkeley, 1974-76. Publications: The Joy Luck Club, novel, 1989, film, 1993; The Kitchen God's Wife, novel, 1992; The Moon Lady, children's book, 1992; The Chinese Siamese Cat, children's book, 1994; The Hundred Secret Senses, novel, 1995; The Bonesetter's Daughter, 2000; Saving Fish from Drowning, 2005; Numerous short stories and essays. Contributions to: Various periodicals. Honours: Commonwealth Club Gold Award for Fiction, San Francisco, 1989; Booklist Editor's Choice, 1991; Marian McFadden Memorial Lecturer, Indianapolis-Marion County Public Library, 1996. Address: c/o Ballantine Publications Publicity, 201 East 50th Street, New York, NY 10022, USA.

TAN Kok Kiong, b. 25 August 1967, Singapore. Lecturer. m. Po Lean Chee, 1 son, 1 daughter. Education: Bachelor of Engineering (1st Class), 1992; PhD, Electrical Engineering, 1995. Appointments: Research Fellow, Singapore Institute of Manufacturing Technology, 1995-96; Lecturer, 1996-2000, Associate Professor, 2000-, Department of Electrical and Computer Engineering, National University of Singapore. Publications: More than 100 journal article; 6 books; 10 book chapters. Honours: Shortlisted for Young Scientist Award, 2000; Shortlisted for Singapore Youth Award, 2001. Memberships: IEEE; ISA; SME. Address: Department of Electrical and Computer Engineering, 4 Engineering Drive 3, National University of Singapore, Singapore 117576, Singapore. E-mail: eletankk@nus.edu.sg

TAN Man Ho, b. 6 February 1953, Kluang, Malaysia. Professor. m. Lee Kwai Fah, 2 sons, 2 daughters. Education: Advance Production Engineering Certificate; Teaching Certificate; Bachelor of Arts in Business Administration; Master of Business Administration; Doctor of Letters in Psychophilosophy. Appointments: Government School Teacher; Lecturer, RIMA College; Lecturer, Southern College; Principal, Institute KTC Megah Kluang; CEO, Kolej Tebrau; Professor, St Clements University; Assistant to Vice Minister, International Parliament for Safety & Peace

(IPSP), Department of South East Asia; Director, J B City View Hotel, Sdn Bhd; Executive Director, Holistic Touch, Sdn Bhd. Publications: Real World Series, Vols 1-22; The Fourthway ManHo E-Journal Volumes 1-12; A Philosophy of Material-Reflection; An Inquiry into the Nature and Process of Recent Privatization and Economic Reforms; On the Possibility of Transforming the Captive Communication and Behavioural Styles in a Manager; More than 40 other consultancy and project papers. Honours: Great Minds of the 21st Century; Man of the Year 2005; 500 Geniuses of the 21st Century; Genius Laureate; Research Board of Advisors, ABI. Memberships: Doctor member, Institute of Professional Financial Managers, UK; Member, Malaysian Society for Complementary Therapies; Member, Thai Traditional Medical Services Society; Affiliate, St Clements University. Address: 55 Jalan Damai, 9 Taman Damai, 81400 Senai, Johor, Malaysia. E-mail: tanmanho@hotmail.com Website: http://www.geocities.com/tanmanho

TAN Sinforosa, b. 7 July 1943, Lugait, Misamis Oriental, Philippines. College Professor. m. William H P Kaung. Education: BS, Chemical Engineering, University of San Carlos, Philippines, 1965; MST, Mathematics, Cornell University, USA, 1970; PhD, Curriculum Development, Syracuse University, USA, 1975. Appointments: Teacher, Iligan Capitol College, 1965-68; Mathematics Chairperson, 1967-68; Counsellor, Advanced Placement Programme, Cornell University, summer 1970; Resident Assistant, Crouse-Irving Memorial Hospital School of Nursing, 1970-73; Graduate Assistant, Syracuse University, 1973-75; Math Consultant, Mount Vernon Board of Education, 1975-76; Director, Metric Programme, Bronx Community College, 1976-77; Adjunct Mathematics Faculty, Mercy College, 1976-78; Teacher, Westchester Community College, 1977-; Professor, Mathematics, 1991-; Sophia and Joseph C Abeles Distinguished Professorial Chair in Mathematics. Publications: Revitalising Mathematics with problem solving, collaborative learning and the TI graphing calculators; Implementing the crossroads in mathematics as a pilot programme; Transforming the teaching of mathematics, technology recharging faculty, and reforming the mathematics curriculum; Calculators in education: A survey of calculator technology in the Westchester and Putnam high schools; Implementing Reform Methods of Teaching Mathematics in a Traditional and Conservative Department; many others. Honours: New York State Mathematics Association of Two Year Colleges, Outstanding Contributions to Mathematics Education Award; Pi Lambda Theta, Region 1 Outstanding Educator Award for Teaching Excellence; State University of New York, Chancellor's Excellence in Teaching Award; University of San Carlos Most Outstanding Alumnus; Outstanding Contributor Award, Westchester Community College Student Senate, 1999; Outstanding Achievement Award in Education, Philippine Chinese Association of America (Northeast), Inc, 2001; Outstanding Achievement Award in the field of Education, YWCA of White Plains and Central Westchester, 2002; Center for Faculty Technology Incentive Award and Fellowship for Distance Learning, 2003; Installed in YWCA Academy of Honorees of the 75th Anniversary Gala, YWCA White Plains and Central Westchester, 2004; Spring for Scholarships Award for outstanding support for scholarships, 2006; Organisation of Chinese Americans, Westchester Hudson Valley Chapter, Dynamic Achiever Award, 2006; Numerous other outstanding service awards. Memberships: Pi Lambda Theta International Honour and Professional Association in Education; American Mathematical Association of Two Year Colleges; New York State Mathematical Association of two Year Colleges; National Council of Teachers of Mathematics; Association of Filipino Teachers of America; Numerous others. Address: Mathematics Department, Westchester Community College, 75 Grasslands Road, Valhalla, NY 10595-1636, USA.

TAN Xincai, b. 24 October 1956, Haikou, Hainan, China. Engineer. m. Xiangyue Lu, 1 daughter. Education: B Eng (Hons), University of Science and Technology, Beijing, China, 1978-82; M Eng (Hons), Anshan University of Science and Technology, China, 1985-88; PhD, Technical University of Denmark, Denmark, 1996-99. Appointments: Teacher, Teaching and Administration, Changdong Elementary School, 1975-78; Engineer, Engineering Management and Innovations, Changsha Steel Plant, 1982-85; Senior Engineer, Leader of Projects, Research and Development in Alloy Products, Changsha Research Institute of Mining and Metallurgy, 1988-93; Assistant Professor (PhD Research Staff), Modelling and Testing in Metals Cold Bonding, Central South University, 1993-96; PhD Research Staff, Modelling and Testing in Metal Forming and Tribology, Technical University of Denmark, 1996-99; Research Associate, Modelling and Testing in Materials Properties and Laser Welding, Loughborough University, 1999-2001; Research Associate, Modelling and Testing in Textile Composite Cellular Materials, Manchester University (former UMIST), 2001-03; Research Fellow, Project Co-ordinator, Engineering Design and Materials Engineering, University of Strathclyde, 2003-06; Research Fellow, Systems Engineering, Cost Engineering and Materials Engineering, Queen's University, Belfast, 2007-. Publications: 35 articles in professional scientific journals. Honours: Listed in international biographical dictionaries. Memberships: China Materials Association. Address: 78 Gorse Crescent, Stretford, Manchester, M32 0UQ, England. E-mail: xincai_tan@hotmail.com

TANAKA Masami, b. 22 August 1965, Saitama, Japan. Physician. m. Sachie Murata, 1 son. Education: MD, Tohoku University School of Medicine, Sendai, Japan, 1991. Appointments: Doctor, 1995, Resident, 1991-93, Clinical Instructor, 1996, Attending Physician, 1993-96, Clinical Instructor, 1998-99, Department of Medicine, Institute of Clinical Endocrinology, Tokyo Women's Medical College; Research Associate, Department of Biochemistry, Vanderbilt University, Nashville, USA, 1996-98; Attending Physician, 1999-2003, Vice Director, 2003-06, Department of Internal Medicine, Misato Kenwa Hospital, Saitama, Japan; Clinical Instructor, Attending Physician, Department of Endocrinology, Tenri Hospital, Nara, Japan, 2006-. Memberships: Fellow, Japan Diabetes Society; Member, Japanese Endocrine Society; Japanese Society of Internal Medicine. Address: Tenri Hospital, Department of Endocrinology, 200 Mishimacho, Tenri Nara, 632 8552, Japan. E-mail: tana176k@sepia.ocn.ne.jp

TANAKA Shuhei, b. 10 May 1949, Kiyo, Abu-cho, Yamaguchi, Japan. Professor. m. Yukiko, 1983, 2 daughters. Education: Bachelor of Agriculture, 1972, Master of Agriculture, 1974, PhD, Microbiology, 1989, Yamaguch University. Appointments: Assistant Professor, 1977, Associate Professor, 1989, Professor, 2006, Plant Pathology, Yamaguchi University. Publications: Occurrence and distribution of clubroot disease on two cruciferous weeds, Cardamine flexuosa and C scutata, in Japan, 1993; Detection of Cymbidium mosaic potexvirus and Odontoglossum ringspot tobamovirus from Thai orchids by rapid immunofilter paper assay, 1997; Biological mode of action of the fungicide, flusulfamide, against Plasmodiophora brassicae (clubroot), 1999; Electron microscopy of primary zoozporogenesis in Plasmodiophora brassicae, 2001; Distribution of clubroot disease of a cruciferous weed, Cardamine flexuosa, in major isolated

islands, Hokkaido and Okinawa, in Japan, 2006; Colonization by two isolates of Plasmodiophora brassicae with differing pathogenicity on a clubroot-resistant cultivar of Chinese cabbage (Brassica rapa L subsp pekinensis), 2006. Honours: 7th Asia Pacific Orchid Conference Academic Encouragement Prize, 2001. Memberships: The Plant Pathological Society of Japan; The Mycological Society of Japan; Japanese Society of Microscopy; American Phytopathological Society; Japanese Society for Bacteriology; Japanese Society of Soil Microbiology. Address: Yoshiki 1440-16, Yamaguchi 753-0811, Japan. E-mail: stanaka@yamaguch-u.ac.jp

TANAKA-AZUMA Yukimasa, b. 7 March 1964, Sakai, Japan. Pharmacologist; Biochemist; Researcher. m. Hiromi Tanaka, 31 March 1991, 1 son, 1 daughter. Education: BSc, Biology, 1982-86, MSc, Biology, 1986-88, Konan University, Kobe, Japan; PhD, Pharmacology, Okayama University, Okayama, Japan, 2000. Appointments: Central Research Institute, Nissin Food Products Co Ltd, 1988-2002; Research Student, Japan Collection of Microorganisms, RIKEN, Wako, Japan, 1999-2000; Food Safety Research Institute, Nissin Food Products Co Ltd, 2002-. Publications: 19 papers in scientific journals include: Cholesterol-lowering effects of NTE-122, a novel acyl-CoA: cholesterol acyltransferase (ACAT) inhibitor, on cholesterol diet-fed rats and rabbits, 1998; Effects of NTE-122, a novel acyl-CoA: cholesterol acyltransferase inhibitor, on cholesterol esterification and secretions of apoliprotein B-containing lipoprotein and bile acids in HepG2, 1999; Effects of NTE-122, a novel acyl-CoA: cholesterol acyltransferase inhibitor, on cholesterol esterification and high-density lipoprotein-induced cholesterol efflux in macrophages, 1999; Effects of NTE-122, an acyl-CoA: cholesterol acyltransferase inhibitor, on cholesterol esterification and lipid secretion from CaCo-2, and cholesterol absorption in rats, 1999; Biological evaluation of styrene oligomers for endocrine-disrupting effects (II), 2000; Effects of NTE-122, an acyl-CoA: cholesterol acyltransferase inhibitor, prevents the progression of atherogenesis in cholesterol-fed rabbits, 2001; Lactobacillus casei NY1301 increases the adhesion of Lactobacillus gasseri NY0509 to human intestinal Caco-2 cells, 2001. Honours: Listed in Who's Who publications and biographical dictionaries. Memberships: Member, Scientific Council, The Japanese Pharmacological Society; Member, The Japanese Society for Food Science and Technology. Address: Food Safety Research Institute, Nissin Food Products Co Ltd, 2247 Noji, Kusatsu, Shiga 525-0055, Japan. E-mail: y-azuma@mb1.nissinfoods.co.jp

TANDALE Tukaram, b. 1 June 1949, Kolhapur, India. Engineering Geologist. m. Meghna Hawal, 1 son, 1 daughter. Education: BSc, 1972; MSc, 1974; PhD, 1986. Appointment: Geological Unit Pune, Koyana Project, Jalsampatti Bhavan Kothrud, Pune, Maharashtra, India, 1991-. Publications: Over 35 research papers in engineering geology, conjunctive use of groundwater and surface water, Laterites and Laterite profiles, coastal studies, Maharashtra, Laterites, Quaternary geology, remote sensing. Memberships: Geological Society; Indian Society for Rock Mechanics and Tunnelling Technology. Address: 13 Mayur Complex, R S No 39, Kothrud, Pune 411029, Maharashtra, India.

TANDBERG Erik, b. 19 October 1932, Oslo, Norway. Consultant; Writer. Divorced, 1986, 1 son, 1 daughter. Education. BSME, University of Santa Clara, California, 1957; MS, Metallurgy, Stanford University, California, 1959; Postgraduate Studies, Rocket Propulsion, Princeton University, New Jersey, 1965. Appointments: Royal Norwegian Air Force, 1959-71, Major, 1966; Consultant, Hartmark & Co, 1972-74;

Chief Engineer, Director, Norconsult, 1974-80. Publications: 5 Books; Numerous articles in professional journals on Space related matters; Several TV and radio programs. Honours: Gold Medal, Norwegian Society of Chartered Technical and Scientific Professionals, 2005; Officer of The Royal Norwegian Order of St Olav, 2007. Memberships: Oslo City Council, 1971-90; American Institute of Aeronautics and Astronautics; Fellow, British Interplanetary Society; Norwegian Association for Chartered Engineers. Address: PO Box 5267 Majorstuen, 0303 Oslo, Norway.

TANIKAWA Hisashi, b. 21 June 1929, Tokyo, Japan. Professor of Law. m. Keiko Hoshino, deceased 2006, 1 son, 1 daughter. Education: LLB, 1953, LLM, 1955, PhD in Law, 1958, University of Tokyo. Appointments: Associate Professor, Osaka City University, 1958-66; Professor, 1966-98, Emeritus Professor, 1998-, Seikei University, Tokyo; Corporate Auditor, Nippon Steel Corporation, 1999-; Managing Director, Japan Energy Law Institute, Tokyo, 2001-; President, International commercial Law Institute, Tokyo, 2006-. Publications: System and Characteristics of Maritime Private Law, 1958; Sales of Goods, 1964; Commentary on the Security Law on Compensation for Oil Pollution Damage, 1979. Honours: Medal with Blue Ribbon, Japanese Government, 1984; Gold and Silver Star, Order of Rising Sun, 2001. Memberships: Honorary President, International Nuclear Law Association, 1992-; Honorary Vice President, International Maritime Committee, 2001-. Address: c/o Japan Energy Law Institute, Tanakayama Bldg 7F, 4-1-20 Toranomon, Minato-ku, Tokyo 105-0001, Japan.

TANN Rosa Lee Burnham, b. 4 May 1948, Norfolk County, Norfolk, Virginia, USA. Educator; Teacher. 2 sons, 1 daughter. Education: NA, Holmes School of Nurses Aid, 1974; Child Development Associate Credential, Bank Street College, Washington DC, 1982; BS, Early Childhood/ Elementary, 1986, MA, Severe and Profound Handicaps, Norfolk State University, Virginia; DD, Annie B Campbell School of Ministry College, San Diego, California, 2006. Appointments: Administrator, Teacher, Harvestime Christian Academy, San Diego; Director, Teacher, Rosa Tann Family Child Care, San Diego; Instructor, Annie B Campbell School of Ministry College, San Diego. Publications: An Usher Manuel Handbook, 1985. Honours: Chesapeake Bureau of Social Services Foster Parent Certificate, 1974; CDA Child Development Association Credential, 1982; Parent Involvement Certificate, 1984. Memberships: Tidewater Child Development Association, 1979; National Education Association, 1980; Council for Exceptional Children, 1986; Church of God in Christ, 1960-. Address: 6019 Brooklyn Avenue, San Diego, CA 92114-2421, USA.

TARAKANOV Boris Vasiljevich, b. 19 April 1933, Wichuga, Russia. Microbiologist. m. Ludmilla Isaeva, 23 May 1959, 2 daughters. Education: DVM, Agricultural Institute, Ivanovo, 1956; D in Biological Sciences, All Russian Research Institute of Animal Physiology, Biochemistry and Nutrition, 1985; Professor, 1996. Appointments: Veterinarian, Sovkhoz, Chitinsky, Russia, 1956-62; From Aspirant to Chief, Department of Biotechnology of Micro-organisms, All Russian Research Institute of Animal Physiology, Biochemistry and Nutrition, Borovsk, Russia, 1962-; Chairman, Council, Agricultural Science, Scientific Centre, Kaluga, Russia, 1993-97; Assessor, Australian Research Council, Canberra, 1996-. Publications: Study of the Microflora in Forestomachs of Ruminants, 1977; Microbiology of the Digestion of Ruminants, 1982; Methods of Study of the Digestive Tract Microflora in Farm Animals and Poultry, 1998, 2006; Using

of Probiotics in Animal Husbandry, 1998; Perspectives of Creation of New Probiotics on the Base of Recombinant Strains of Bacteria Expressing Eucaryotic Genes, 2002; Chapter in Reference Book: Normal the Microflora of the Forestomachs of Ruminants, 2002; Phenomenon of Bacteriophagy in the Rumen of Ruminants, 2006; Methods of Study of the Digestive Tract Microflora in Farm animals and Poultry, 2006; Phenomenon of Bacteriophagy in the Rumen of Ruminants, 2006. Honours: Meritorious Scientific Worker, Russian Federation, 1995; Gold Medal, All Russian Exhibition Centre, 1997; Medal, 2000 Outstanding Scientists of the 21st Century, 2002; Premium of K E Tsiolkovsky, 2006; Listed in national and international biographical dictionaries. Memberships: Russian Society of Microbiology; Russian Society of Physiology. Address: All Russian Research Institute of Animal Physiology, Biochemistry and Nutrition, 249013, Borovsk, Russia.

TARANTINO Quentin, b. 1963, Los Angeles, USA. Film Director. Appointments: Worked in Video Archives, Manhattan Beach; Actor; Producer; Director; Films: My Best Friend's Wedding, 1987; Reservoir Dogs, Past Midnight, 1992; Siunin Wong Fei-hung tsi titmalau, Eddie Presley, 1993; Sleep With Me, Killing Zoe, Somebody to Love, Pulp Fiction, 1994; Destiny Tunes on the Radio, Desperado, Four Rooms, Red Rain, 1995; Girl 6, From Dusk Till Dawn, Curdled, 1996; Jackie Brown, 1997; God Said 'Ha!', 1998; 40 Lashes, Little Nicky, 2000; Kill Bill: Vol 1, 2003; Kill Bill: Vol 2, 2004; Freedom's Fury, Daltry Calhoun, 2005; Freedom's Fury, 2006; Grindhouse, Hostel: Part 11; Planet Terror, 2007; Hell Ride, 2008; TV: ER episode, 1994; Alias episode, 2004; CSI: Crime Scene Investigation episode, 2005. Honours: Golden Palm, Cannes Film Festival, 1994; Officier, Ordre des Arts et des Lettres; Empire Film Award for icon of the decade, 2005. Address: WMA, 151 El Camino Drive, Beverly Hills, CA 90212, USA.

TASHLYKOVA-BUSHKEVICH Iya Igorevna, b. 31 May 1975, Minsk, Belarus. Physicist; Educator. m. Alexey Vladimirovich Bushkevich, 1 daughter. Education: Diploma, 1997, PhD, 2000, Physics, Belarusian State University. Appointments: Junior Scientific Collaborator, 2000-01, Head of Research Project, 2000-02, Belarusian State University, Minsk; Associate Professor, 2001-, Head of Research Project, 2003-05, Belarusian State University of Informatics and Radioelectronics, Minsk. Publications: Author of textbook, Physics: Part I: Mechanics, Molecular Physics and Thermodynamics, Electricity and Magnetism (in Russian), 2006; Contributed articles to professional journals, 1997-. Honours: Winner of the Monetary Premium of special Fund of the President of Belarus on social support of the gifted pupils and students, 1998; Belarus President's Grant to the talented young scientists, 2002-03; International Soros Science Education Program, 1995, 1996; Grantee, Government of Belarus Grant for postgraduate students, 1999, 2000. Memberships: Belarusian Physical Society. Address: Gikalo 6, Ap 57, Minsk 220005, Belarus. E-mail: lya_tb@mail.ru

TASTRA I Ketut, b. 28 March 1954, Singaraja, Indonesia. Agricultural Mechanization Researcher. m. Ni Nyoman Sariati, 1985, 1 daughter. Education: MS, Bogor Agricultural University, Indonesia, 1983. Appointments: Head of System Analysis Section, Sukarami Research Institute for Food Crops, Western Sumatra, Indonesia, 1986-88; Head of Post Harvest and Mechanization Section, Indonesian Legume and Tuber Crops Research Institute, Malang, Indonesia; Lecturer, Undergraduate Student Advisor, Brawijaya University, Malang, 1999-. Publications: Patents for maize power sheller. Memberships: American Society of Agricultural Engineers; Indonesian Society for Agricultural Engineers; Asian Association for Agricultural Engineering. Address: Indonesian Legume and Tuber Crops Research Institute, Jl Raya Kendalpayak, Malang 65101, Indonesia. E-mail: iktastra@yahoo.com

TATAI-BALTĂ Cornel, b. 5 April 1944, Sibiu, Transylvania, Romania. Professor. m. Ana, 1 daughter. Education: Iacob Mureşianu High School, Blaj, 1961; Faculty of History and Philosophy, History of Arts, 1967, PhD History of Fine Arts, 1992, Babeş-Bolyai University, Cluj-Napoca, Romania. Appointments: Head Master, History Museum, Blaj, 1967-1992; Lecturer, 1992, Senior Lecturer, 1999, Professor, 2004, December 1st 1918 University of Alba Iulia. Publications: Aspects of the Fine Arts in Blaj (18th-20th Centuries), 1993; Wood Engravers from Blaj (1750-1830), 1995; Pages of Romanian Art, 1998; On the Art and Culture of Blaj, 2000; Images of Blaj, 2002, European Culture and Artistic Interferences, 2003; Iuliu Moga (1906-1976), 2004; Writing about Art, 2005; International Art Camp Ioan Inocenţiu Micu-Klein from Blaj, 2007, Cultural and Artistic Hypostases, 2007 and 80 scientific works (in Romania and abroad); Editor of the reviews 'Christian Culture', 'The Astra of Blaj' and 'Romanian Thought'. Honours: Prize for History awarded by ASTRA, Timotei Cipariu Department, Blaj, 2000; Citizen of Honour of the Municipality of Blaj, 2003. Memberships: Ars Transsilvaniae Society; Member of Honour of ASTRA Society, Timotei Cipariu Department, Blaj. Address: Str. Petru Maior, nr 23, Blaj, Jud Alba, Romania. E-mail: ctataibalta@yahoo.com

TATCHELL Peter Gary, b. 25 January 1952, Melbourne, Australia. Gay Rights and Human Rights Campaigner; Journalist. Education: Mount Waverley High School, Melbourne, 1964-68; West London College, 1972-74; BSc (Hons) Sociology, Polytechnic of North London, 1977. Appointments: Secretary, Christians for Peace, 1970-71; Executive, Vietnam Moratorium Campaign, 1971; Activist, Gay Liberation Front, London, 1971-73; Student, 1972-77; Author and Freelance Journalist, 1978-; Secretary, Southwark & Bermondsey Labour Party, 1980-85; Labour candidate, Bermondsey by-election, 1983; Activist, UK AIDS Vigil Organisation, 1987-89; Activist, Green & Socialist Conferences, 1987-89; Activist, ACT UP, London, 1989-91; Organiser, OutRage! 1990-; Independent Green Left candidate, London Assembly, 2000; Green Party candidate, Oxford East; Green Party Human Rights Spokesperson, 2007-. Publications: The Battle for Bermondsey, 1983; Democratic Defense – A Non-Nuclear Alternative, 1985; AIDS: A Guide to Survival, 1986, 1987, 1990; Europe in the Pink – Lesbian & Gay Equality in the New Europe, 1992; Safer Sexy – The Guide to Gay Sex Safely, 1994; We Don't Want to March Straight – Masculinity, Queers and the Military, 1995; Numerous articles in magazines and journals. Memberships: Labour Party, 1978-2000; National Union of Journalists; Republic; Green Party. E-mail: peter@petertatchell.net Website: www.petertatchell.net

TAUR Der-Ren, b. 26 July 1949, Canton City, China. Aerospace Engineer. m. Mei-Yu Fang, 2 sons. Education: Bachelor, Physics, National Taiwan Normal University, 1971; Master, Physics, National Tsing Hua University, 1974; PhD, Aeronautical and Astronautical Engineering, University of Illinois, USA, 1989. Appointments: Instructor, Physics, Dong-High University, Tai-Chung, Taiwan, 1974-75; Research Assistant, 1976-84, Associate Scientist, 1985-2001, Senior Scientist, 2002-07, Chung-Shan Institute of Science

and Technology, Lung-Tan, Taiwan. Publications: Over 40 papers on missile guidance in national and international professional journals and conferences. Honours: Member, Phi Kappa Phi Honor Society, 1989; Academic Achievement Award, Defense Department, Taiwan Government, 1989. Memberships: Senior Member, American Institute of Aeronautics and Astronautics. Address: No 8-4, Alley 12, Lane 75, Chian-Kuo Road, Lung-Tan, Taoyuan, 325, Taiwan, ROC. E-mail: taur.taur@msa.hinet.net

TAYLER Graham, b. 27 March 1946, Tuatapere, New Zealand. Academic/Management Consultant. Education: Fellow, Inst Securities, Banking and Finance, Australasia, 1973; MBA, Keele, England, 1994; PhD, Accounting and Finance, Manchester, England, 2001. Appointments: Securities Officer, Bank NSW, Chief Managers Office, Wellington, New Zealand, 1969-72; Finance Executive Southland Development Cooperation, Invercargill, New Zealand, 1974-80; Chief Accountant/Secretary, Southland Building Society, Invercargill, New Zealand, 1980-85; Graham Management Associates, Huddersfield, UK, 1986-. Publications: Evidence and Disclosure of Confidential Information by Bank Journal of Bankers, Institute of Australasia, Vol 86(9), 1973; UK Building Society Demutualisation Motives, Business Ethics: A European Review, Vol 12(4), 2003; Strategy Theory and Application – The Case of the UK Building Societies, 2004; UK Building Societies: Deregulation Change Myths, Service Industries Journal, Vol 25(6). Address: 13A Park Drive, Huddersfield, HD1 4EB, England. E-mail: tayler@onetel.com

TAYLOR Alison, b. 20 April 1944, Stockport, Cheshire, England. Author; Journalist. 1 son, 1 daughter. Education: Certificate of Qualification in Social Work; Diploma in Social Work. Appointments: Psychiatric social work and probation; Senior childcare posts, Gwynedd County Council, 1976-86; Claim for unfair dismissal settled, 1989; Author; Journalist; Conference guest speaker. Publications: 5 novels: Simeon's Bride; In Guilty Night; The House of Women; Unsafe Convictions; Child's Play; Papers on child care, ethics and social issues; Lectured and written on 18th and 19th century Welsh and German literature, music and poetry. Honours: Community Care Readers Award, 1996; Campaign for Freedom of Information Award, 1996; Pride of Britain Award, 2000. Memberships: Elected, Welsh Academy, 2001; Elected Fellow, Royal Society of Arts, 2003; Member, American Beethoven Society. Address: c/o Larinia Trevor Literary Agency, 7 The Glasshouse, 49a Goldhawk Road, London W12 8QP, England.

TAYLOR Anna, b. 14 July 1943, Preston, Lancashire, England. Teacher; Writer; Artist; Translator. m. John E Coombes, 22 December 1967, divorced 1982, 1 son. Education: BA (Honours), German and English, University of Bristol, 1965; CertEd, University of York, 1967; MA, Modern German Literature (incomplete) Manchester University, 1967-68; MA, Sociology of Literature, University of Essex, 1980. Career: Intermittent Teacher, 1964-94; Artistic Collaborator to French Sculptor, Michael Serraz, Paris, 1969-90; Since 1984, published writer of poetry, also several theatre credits; Published reviews and essays in diverse publications. Publications: Poetry: FAUSTA, 1984; Cut Some Cords, 1988; Both And: A Triptych, 1995; Out of the Blues, 1997; INTER-, 1998; Bound-un-bound, 2003; Novella: Pro Patria: a private suite, 1987; Poems selected for many anthologies. Honours: Scholarship to Manchester University, 1967; RedBeck Press Short Collection, Joint 1st Prize, 1995; 1st prize for Poem: Chthonia, Second Light Poetry Competition, 2002; 2nd, 3rd prizes and several short-listings in poetry competitions since 1980. Membership: Writers Guild of Great Britain; Founder Member, Yorkshire Playwrights. Address: 82 Blackhouse Road, Fartown, Huddersfield, West Yorkshire HD2 1AR, England.

TAYLOR Harris C, b. 30 April 1940, Brooklyn, New York, USA. Physician; Endocrinologist. m. Diana Kahn Taylor, 1 son, 1 daughter. Education: BS, Queens College, City University of New York, 1961; MD, University of Chicago School of Medicine, 1965. Appointments: Director, Endocrinology Laboratory, 1978-96, Director, Internal Medicine Residency, 1985-94, Lutheran Hospital, Cleveland, Ohio; Currently Clinical Professor of Medicine-Endocrinology, Case Western Reserve University School of Medicine, Cleveland; Principal Investigator, National Institutes of Health, ACCORD study. Publications: 34 papers in peer reviewed journals; 5 book chapters. Honours include: Phi Beta Kappa; Best Doctors in America, 1998, 2001-02, 2003-04; Master Teacher Award, American College of Physicians, 2001. Memberships: Fellow, American College of Physicians; Fellow, American College of Endocrinology; Endocrine Society; President, Diabetes Association of Cleveland, 1982-84. Address: Division of Clinical & Molecular Endocrinology, Case Western Reserve University, Biomedical Research Building, Cleveland, OH 44106, USA.

TAYLOR John, b. 22 August 1925, Atherton, Lancashire, England. Retired University Reader. Education: Scholar, MA, Balliol College, Oxford, 1943-44, 1947-50. Appointments: Lecturer and Senior Lecturer, 1950-70, Reader in Medieval History, 1970-90, Chairman School of History, 1979-82, Leeds University; Visiting Associate Professor, Princeton University, USA, 1961-62; President, Yorkshire Archaeological Society, 1984-89; President, Leeds Philosophical and Literary Society, 1972-74. Publications include: English Historical Literature in the Fourteenth Century, 1987; Rymes of Robin Hood (co-author), 3rd edition, 1997; The St Albans Chronicle 1376-94 (co-author), 2003; Many articles. Honours: Leverhulme Research Fellow, 1982-83; FRHistSoc. Memberships: Royal Historical Society; Yorkshire Archaeological Society. Address: Storey Cottage, Main Street, Kirkby Overblow, Harrogate, North Yorkshire HG3 1HD, England. E-mail: storeycottage@tesco.net

TAYLOR John C, b. 22 July 1914. Dentist; Missionary; Teacher; Writer; Political Advisor and Counsellor. m. Adah, 2 sons, 5 daughters. Education: BS, Muskingum College, 1937; BD Reformed Presbyterian Seminary, Ordained 1939; Certificate, Landour Language School, India, 1941, Hindi; Certificate, Henry Martin School of Islamics, India, 1941, Urdu; Medical College of Virginia School of Dentistry, 1945-46; DDS, University of Pittsburgh School of Dentistry, 1949; Diploma, Northwestern School of Taxidermy, 1952; Diploma, Academy of General Dentistry, 1975. Career includes: Pastor, 5 Churches in Pennsylvania; Appointed Missionary (serving under several denominational boards and authorities); Served in India, Nepal, Liberia Africa, Shell Equador and Mexico; Teacher/Lecturer/Clinical, Schools, Clubs, Churches, Seminars; Registered General Dentist, 7 Different Practices; Artist/Photographer; Superintendent, Presbyterian Home Mission Board, 1947-52; Director of Dental Clinic, Methodist Mission Hospital, Bariely, India, 1954-55; Founder and Director, Landour Community Hospital Dental Department 1955-59. Publications: Books: Wildlife in India's Tiger Kingdom; Face the Devil's Roar; God's Kingdom Helps Animal Kingdoms. Honours: Athlete of the Year Award, Woodstock High School, 1931; 4-Letter Man, Muskingum College, 1933-37; Past President, Diamond-Studded Medallion, Mt. Union Rotary Club, 1965; Lecturer's Award for Serving 7th District Rotary Club; Listed in numerous national and international biographical directories. Memberships: American Dental Association; Academy of General Dentistry; Rotary Club; Lions Club; Sportsmen's Club; Life Fellow, International Biographical Association; Global Outreach Mission. Address: 166 Arrowhead Lane, Irwin, PA 15642, USA. E-mail: tgrtlr@juno.com

TAYLOR John Mark, b. 19 August 1941, Great Britain. Solicitor. Education: Solicitors Intermediate Examination, 1962, Secretary, Birmingham Law Students Society, 1964, Solicitors Final Qualifying Examination, 1965, College of Law; Admitted to Supreme Court of England and Wales, 1966. Appointments: Various positions in private practice; Elected member, Solihull County Borough Council, 1971-74; Co-founder, Solihull Duty Solicitor Scheme, 1973; Co-founder, Shirley Citizens Advice Bureau, Solihull, 1973; Elected member, West Midlands Metropolitan County Council, 1973-86; Leader, Opposition on WMCC, 1975-77; Leader, WMCC, 1977-79; Directly Elected Member, European Parliament, 1979-84; Conservative Budget Spokesman in the European Parliament, 1979-81; Deputy Leader, Conservative Group in the European Parliament, 1982-83; Member of Parliament for Solihull, 1983-2005; Member, Environment Select Committee, 1983-87; Government Whip, latterly as Vice-Chamberlain of Her Majesty's Household, 1988-92; First ever Junior Minister to the Lord Chancellor, 1992-95; Minister for Consumer Affairs, Investigations, Insider Trading, Prosecution and matters relating to Companies House, Dti, 1995-97; Various Opposition duties, 1997-2005. Address: Apartment 8, Blossomfield Gardens, 34 Blossomfield Road, Solihul, West Midlands B91 1NZ, England. E-mail: jmt@blossomfield.net

TAYLOR Judy, (Julia Marie Hough), b. 12 August 1932, Murton, Swansea, Wales. Writer. m. Richard Hough, 1980. Appointments: Bodley Head Publishers, 1951-81; Director, Bodley Head Ltd, 1967-84, Chatto, Bodley Head and Jonathan Cape Ltd, 1973-80, Chatto, Bodley Head & Jonathan Cape Australia Pty Ltd, 1977-80; Consultant to Penguin, Beatrix Potter, 1981-87, 1989-92. Publications: Sophie and Jack, 1982; My First Year: A Beatrix Potter Baby Book, 1983; Sophie and Jack in the Snow, 1984; Dudley and the Monster, 1986; Dudley Goes Flying, 1986; Dudley in a Jam, 1986; Dudley and the Strawberry Shake, 1986; That Naughty Rabbit: Beatrix Potter and Peter Rabbit, 1987; Beatrix Potter 1866-1943, 1989; Beatrix Potter's Letters: A Selection, 1989; So I Shall Tell You a Story, 1993. Play: Beatrix (with Patrick Garland), 1996; Edward Ardizzone's Sketches for Friends: A Selection, 2000. Contributions to: Numerous professional journals. Honour: Member of the Order of the British Empire, 1971. Memberships: Publishers Association Council; Book Development Council; UNICEF International Art Committee; UK UNICEF Greetings Card Committee; Beatrix Potter Society; Royal Society of Arts, fellow. Address: 31 Meadowbank, Primrose Hill Road, London NW3 3AY, England.

TEBBIT, Baron of Chingford in the London Borough of Waltham, Norman Beresford Tebbit, b. 29 March 1931, Enfield, England. Politician. m. Margaret Elizabeth Daines, 1956, 2 sons, 1 daughter. Education: Edmonton County Grammar School. Appointments: RAF Officer, 1949-51; Commercial Pilot and holder of various posts, British Air Line Pilots' Association, 1953-70; Member of Parliament for Epping, 1970-74; Chingford, 1974-92; Parliamentary

Private Secretary, Department of Employment, 1972-73; Under Secretary of State, Department of Trade, 1979-81; Ministry of State, Department of Industry, 1981; Secretary of State for Employment, 1981-83; Trade and Industry, 1983-85; Chancellor of the Duchy of Lancaster, 1985-87; Chairman, Conservative Party, 1985-87; Director, BET Plc, 1987-96; British Telecom Plc, 1987-96; Sears PLC, 1987-99; Spectator Ltd, 1989-2005; Advisor, JCB Excavators, 1991-; Co-Presenter, Target, Sky TV, 1989-97; Columnist, The Sun, 1995-97; Columnist, Mail on Sunday, 1997-2001. Publications: Upwardly Mobile, 1988; Unfinished Business, 1991; Weekly Columnist, The Sun, 1995-97 and The Mail on Sunday, 1997-2001; Numerous political booklets, newspapers and magazine articles. Honours: Life Peer, Baron Tebbit of Chingford; Companion of Honour. Memberships: Association of Conservative Peers; Liveryman of the Guild of Air Pilots and Navigators; Council Member of the Air League; Companion of the Royal Aeronautical Society; Chairman, Nuffield Orthopaedic Centre Appeal, 1990-2005; Chairman, Battle of Britain London Monument Appeal, 2003-. Address: House of Lords, Westminster, London, SW1A 0PW, England.

TEBBS Margaret Cecilia, b. 5 September 1948, Hillingdon, Middlesex, England. Botanical Illustrator. Education: Manor School, Ruislip, Middlesex. Appointments: Curator and Botanist, Department of Botany, Natural History Museum, London, 1967-91; Freelance Botanical Illustrator; Commissions mostly from staff and visitors to the Herbarium, Royal Botanic Gardens, Kew, England. Publications: Illustrator of books including most recently: Airplants – a study of the genus Tillandsia. New Plantsman vol 2 by A Rodriguez, 1995; Flora of Egypt, vols 1-4, by L Boulos, 1999-2005; Blepharis, a taxonomic study by K Vollesen, 2000; The Leguminosae of Madagascar by D Du Puy et al, 2002; Studies in the genus Hypericum by NKB Robson, 2002. Honours: Margaret Flockton Award, 2nd prize, 2006. Address: 2 Furzey Corner, Shipton Lane, Burton Bradstock, Dorset DT6 4NQ, England. E-mail: tebbsatfurzey@aol.com

TEICHMANN Mare, b. 1 March 1954, Estonia. Professor. m. Marco Teichmann, 1 son. Education: Graduate, Industrial Psychology, Tartu University, Estonia, 1979; PhD, Medical Psychology, Bekhterev Psychoneurological Research Institute, St Petersburg, Russia, 1987. Appointments: Engineer, Institute Kommunaalprojekt, Tallinn, 1979-80; Researcher, Estonian Institute of Experimental and Clinical Medicine, Department of Occupational Pathology, Tallinn, 1980-88; Senior Lecturer, 1987-92, Professor of Psychology, 1992-, Tallinn University of Technology, Tallinn; Founder and Director, PE Consult Ltd, Tallinn, 1996-. Publications include: Work and family: An international comparative study of work-family stress and occupational strain, 2005; Spiritual Needs and Quality of Life in Estonia, 2006; Work Locus of Control – Eastern European Managers versus Western Managers: Ten years later, 2007; Integrated Contact- and E-learning Course in Managerial Psychology for Engineering Students, 2007; Engineers' Occupational Stress and Stress Prevention System: E-psycho-diagnostics and E-learning, 2007; Students' Self-management: E-course, E-tutoring and Online Support System, 2007. Honours: 7 certificates of innovation proposals, Popov Association of Creators and Innovators. Memberships: WHO Quality of Life Centres Network; WHO Estonian Quality of Life Centre, Tallin; Collaborative International Study of Managerial Stress, Manchester; European Network of Work and Organisational Psychologists, Paris. Address: Künni 10A, Tallinn 10918, Estonia. E-mail: mare@pekonsult.ee

TEJASWI Diwakar, b. 18 August 1968, Patna, India. Medical Doctor. m. Dipika Tejaswi, 1 daughter. Education: MBBS; MCH; FCCP; PhD. Appointments: Head of Department and Assistant Dean, Faculty of Health Sciences, Alemaya University, Ethiopia; Medical Director, Regional Aids Training Centre and Network in India, International Health Organisation, USA. Publications: Conference papers: RNTPL and DOTS strategy in curing tuberculosis patients, International Conference of American Academy of family Physicians, Orlando, Florida, 2004; Issues related to people living with HIV AIDS, Special Session, International AIDS Conference: AIDS in Culture II, Papantla, Mexico, 2005; Technical Review Panel, Red Ribbon Award, International AIDS Conference, Mexico City, 2008. Honours: University Gold Medal in MBBS, 1992; Vishisth Chikitsa Medal, 1996; Health Professional of the Year 2005, IBC, England. Memberships: American Academy of Family Physicians; Royal College of General Practitioners, UK; American Public Health Association; Association of Physicians of India. Address: MIG-161, Lohianagar, Kankarbagh, Patna-800 020, India. E-mail: diwakartejaswi@yahoo.com

TEKELIOGLU Bilge Kaan, b. 31 March 1971, Ankara, Turkey. Researcher; Lecturer. m. Larissa, 2 sons. Education: Adana Anadolu Lisesi, Faculty of Veterinary Medicine, University of Istanbul, 1990-96; PhD, Microbiology, Institute of Health Science, 1997-2002. Appointments: First Aid, Basic Life Support and AED (Automated External Defibrillator) Provider, Course Director, Course Organiser and Instructor certified by Turkish Ministry of Health, European Resuscitation Council, and American Hearth Association for Adult, Child and Infant; Guest Researcher, Japan Racing Association, Epizootic Research Station, Equine Research Institute, Tochigi, Japan, 2000; Lifeguard, Turkish Scuba & Lifeguard Federation, 2003; CRM Instructor, Turkish Civil Aviation Authority, 2004; Dangerous Goods Regulations Instructor, International Air Transport Association, 2006; Volunteer, Search and Rescuer approved by Turkish Republic, Mayor of Istanbul, 2007; Instructor, Aviation Security by Green Light, IATA approved degree, 2008. Publications: Reproduction of Rainbow trout by photoperiod culture possibilities in subtropic region, 1995; Affects of different stocking rate on the growth of pilthead seabream (Sparus aurata L 1758) fry, 1997; Detection of Equine Herpes Virus 1 (EHV-1) and Equine Herpes Virus 4 (EHV-4) infections in race horses using PCR, 2003; A serological and clinical investigation on the Leishmaniasis in Turkish Dogs, 2003; Detection of Equine Herpes Virus Type 1 (EHV-2) DNA in Organs of Neonatal Dead Foals in Turkey, 2005. Honours: First detection of EHV-1 and EHV-4 viruses by PCR in Turkey. Memberships: European Resuscitation Council; American Health Association; Fenerbahce Sports Club; Turkish Microbiology Society. Address: Turkish Airlines Inc, Flight Training Centre, Besyol Birlik Cad Polis Egitim, Merkezi Arkasi, Florya, Istanbul 34295, Turkey. E-mail: ktekelioglu@gmail.com

TEMPEST Henry Roger, b. 2 April 1924, London, England. Retired. m. Janet Evelyn Mary Longton, 2 sons, 3 daughters. Education: Christ Church, Oxford. Appointments: Scots Guards, 1943-47, served North West Europe (wounded 1945); Appointed to Q Staff HQ Guards Division, 1945; Staff Captain, 1946; Britannia Rubber Co Ltd, 1947-51; Emigrated to Lusaka, Northern Rhodesia, 1952; Incorporated Cost Accountant (AACWA), South Africa, 1961; Returned to UK, 1961; Financial Officer, University of Oxford Department of Nuclear Physics, 1962-72; Inherited Broughton Hall Estate, 1970; Lord of the Manors of Broughton, Coleby, Burnsall and Thorpe, and of Coleby, Lincolnshire. Honours: Knight of Malta, 1949; A Deputy Lieutenant of North Yorkshire, 1981. Memberships: North Yorkshire County Council, 1974-85; Skipton Rural District Council, 1973-74; Executive Committee, Country Landowners Association, Yorkshire, 1973-87; Council, Order of St John, North Yorkshire, 1977-97; President Skipton Branch Royal British Legion, 1974-91; Governor: Craven College of Further Education, 1974-85, Skipton Girls' High School, 1976-85; Member, Pendle Forest and Craven Harriers Hunt Committee, 1973-98; ACIS, 1958; FCIS, 1971; Member, British Computer Society, 1973-; Clubs: Lansdowne; Pratt's. Address: Broughton Hall, Skipton, N Yorks BD23 3AE, England. E-mail: henrytempest@hormail.com

TEPFERS Ralejs, b. 28 December 1933, Rezekne, Latvia. Professor Emeritus. m. Ira Majors, 1 son, 2 daughters. Education: Civ Eng (MSc), 1958, Tekn lic degree, 1966, Tekn dr, 1973, Docent, Reinforced Concrete Structures, 1973, Chalmers University of Technology, Göteborg; Dr ing hc, Latvian Academy of Sciences, 1996. Appointments: Worked on building sites, Sweden and Switzerland; Military service, 1959; Assistant, Department of Building Technology, 1960, Development of Structural Laboratory, 1967-69, Associate Professor, Building Materials and House Building Techniques, 1969, Professor, Building Technology, 1995, Professor Emeritus, 2001-, Chalmers University of Technology. Publications: Numerous articles in professional journals. Honours: JSPS Fellowship, Tohoku University, Sendai, Japan, 1988. Memberships: Swedish Concrete Association; Latvian Concrete Association; Nordic Concrete Federation; Life Honorary Membership, Comité Euro-Internationale du Béton-fédération internationale du béton; RILEM Committee; American Concrete Institute. Address: Department of Civil & Environmental Engineering, Structural Engineering and Concrete Structures, Chalmers University of Technology, SE-412 96 Goteborg, Sweden. E-mail: ralejs.tepfers@chalmers.se Website: www.chalmers.se

TERAJIMA Katsuyuki, b. 5 January 1968, Tokyo, Japan. Anesthesiologist. m. Nagano Kuniko, 1 son, 1 daughter. Education: MD, 1993; PhD, 2000. Appointments: Associate Professor, Department of Anesthesiology, Nippon Medical School, Tokyo; Editor, Journal of Artificial Blood. Publications: Hemodynamic effects of volume resustation by hypertonic saline-dextran (HSD) in porcine acute cardiac tamponade, 2004; Fluid resustation with hemoglobin vesicles in a rabbit model of acute hemorragic shock, 2006. Honours: Listed in international biographical dictionaries. Memberships: Japanese Society of Anesthesiologists; Japanese Society of Intensive Care Medicine; Japan Society of Pain Clinicians. Address: 1-1-5 Sendagi, Bunkyo-ku, Tokyo 113-8603, Japan. E-mail: terajima.katsuyuki@nifty.com

TERNYIK Stephen, b. 29 July 1960. Economist; Educator. m. Lisa Steven, 1988, 2 sons, 1 daughter. Education: MA, Technical University of Berlin, 1986; Postgraduate Studies, SUNY, 1997; Diploma, Jerusalem Institute of Biblical Polemics, 2000; Entrepreneurship Certificate, German Open University. Appointments: Expert, Advisor in Human Development & Monetary Learning, 1986-; Ternyik Research & Development Techno-Logos Inc. Publications: Contributor of poems to professional publications, essays, reports and abstracts; author, Social Learning Processes, 1989. Honours: Visiting Research Fellow, Tokyo University, 1993; International Order of Merit; Pioneer Award; Deputy Governor, ABI. Memberships: Indian Sociological Society; American Consultants League; Club of Budapest; Tikkun Community. Society for Humanistic Judaism. Listed in national and international biographical

dictionaries. Address: POB 201, D-82043 Munich/Pullach, Germany. E-mail: e.ternyik@kjr-muenchen-land.de. Website: www.marquiswhoswho.net/ternyik.

TERPSTRA Vern, b. 20 August 1927, Wayland, Michigan, USA. Emeritus Professor. m. Bonnie Fuller, 1 son, 1 daughter. Education: BBA, 1950, MBA, 1951, PhD, 1965, University of Michigan. Appointments: Director, Normal School, Belgian Congo, 1953-61; Professor, Wharton School, University of Pennsylvania, 1964-66; Professor, University of Michigan, 1966-92; Professor Emeritus, 1992-. Publications: Books: International Marketing, 8th edition; International Marketing, 9th edition; Cultural Environment of International Business, 3rd edition; International Dimensions of Marketing, 4th edition; American Marketing in Common Market; International Marketing, 2006; Global Environment of Business, 2006; Over 75 articles in professional journals. Honours: President, 1971-72, Fellow, 1976, Academy of International Business; Global Marketing Award, American Marketing Association, 2004; Listed in Who's Who publications and biographical dictionaries. Memberships: Academy of International Business; American Marketing Association. Address: Business School, University of Michigan, Ann Arbor, MI 48109, USA. E-mail: vterp@umich.edu

TETA João Sebastião, b. 5 December 1956, Vige, Angola. IT Engineer. m. Malgorzata, 1 son, 4 daughters. Education: Medium Course of Electronics, Romania, 1973-77; Bachelor and Master degree, Information Technology, Faculty of Information Technology and Management, Technical University of Wroclaw, Poland, 1981; Master Degree, IT Engineering, 1986; PhD, Faculty of Electrotechnics, Automatization and Electronics, Academy of Mining and Metallurgy, Crocavia Academy, Poland, 1991. Appointments: Trainee Assistant and Assistant, Department of IT, Faculty of Information Technology and Management, Technical University of Wroclaw, 1989-90; Assistant Professor, IT, Electronics and Electrotechnics Department, 1992, Dean, 1993, Head of Operative Systems 1 and 2, 1993, Head of Semantic of Languages and Compilers, 1993, Head of Database and System Analysis, 1993, Faculty of Engineering, Associated Professor, 1995, Senior Professor, 2000, Rector and Chancellor, 2002-, Agostinho Neto University. Publications: Deficiency of Traditional Database Logical Models; Overview on database research; L'informatique dans le Secteur Public en Republique d'Angola; Development strategy of engineering training in Angola; Computing society and its importance for Angolan scientific development; and others. Memberships: Institute of Electrical and Electronics Engineers Inc; National Télématiques Committee; Inter-Ministerial Committee Y2K. Address: Bairro Miramar, Rua Companhia de Jesus, Nrs 12-14, PO Box 815, Luanda, Angola.

TETANGCO Amando M Jr, b. 14 November 1952, Pampanga, Philippines. Central Bank Governor. m. Elvira Ma Plana, 1 son, 2 daughters. Education: MA, Public Policy and Administration (Development Economics), University of Wisconsin, Wisconsin, USA; AB, Economics, Ateneo de Manila University, Manila, Philippines. Appointments: Governor, Bangko Sentral ng Pilipinas, 2005-; Deputy Governor, 1999-2006; Managing Director, 1991-99; Director, 1986-91; Alternate Executive Director, International Monetary Fund, 1992-94. Honours: Top Six Central Bank Chiefs 2006, Global Finance Magazine. Address: Bangko Sentral ng Pilipinas, A Mabini corner P Ocampo Sts, Malate, Manila, Philippines 1004. E-mail: atetangco@bsp.gov.ph

TEWARI Brij Bhushan, b. 15 July 1959, Jaunpur, UP, India. Teaching; Research. m. Jai Devi, 1 son. Education: High School, 1975, Intermediate, 1977, UP Board, India; BSc, 1979, MSc, 1981, D Phil, 1985, Allahabad Central University, India; Certificate in Russian Language, Indian Institute of Technology, Roorkee, India, 1995. Appointments: Teaching/Research at: Allahabad Central University, India; Meerut University, India; IIT, Roorkee, India; Hebei University, China; Inra Montpellier, France; South Dakota Uiniv, USA; FIT, Florida, USA; Visiting Professor offers: University of California Santa Barbara, USA; University of Alaska, Fairbank, USA; Professor, Chemistry, University of Guyana, 2004-. Publications: 84 articles in international journals; 93 conference/seminars attended/papers presented, 1998-; Book on chemical evolution under preparation. Honours: MRSC, 2004; Listed in international biographical dictionaries. Memberships: Fellow, Indian Chemical Society; Member, American Chemical Society; Vice Chairman, CAS. Address: Faculty of Natural Sciences, University of Guyana, PO Box 101110, Georgetown, Guyana, South America. E-mail: brijtew@yahoo.com

THABIT JONES Peter, b. 18 May 1951, Swansea, Wales. Poet; Writer. m. Hilary, 4 sons, 2 daughters. Education: Diploma in Higher Education, University of Wales; Diploma in Office Studies; Higher National Certificate in Leisure/Conservation Management; Degree, Postgraduate Certificate in Education (Further and Higher Education). Appointment: Editor, SWAG Magazine, 1995-99; Chairman and Treasurer, Swansea Writers and Artists Group, 1996-99; Tutor, Part-time Degree Programme, University of Wales, Swansea. Publications: Tacky Brow, 1974; The Apprenticeship, 1977; Clocks Tick Differently, 1980; Visitors, 1986; The Cold Cold Corner 1995; Ballad of Kilvey Hill, 1999; The Lizard Catchers (USA), 2006; The Newspaper Birds, a bilingual collection, 2007. Contributions to: 2Plus2; Poetry Wales; Poetry Review; Anglo-Welsh Review; Planet; Outposts Poetry Quarterly; Poetry Nottingham; NER/BLQ; Urbane Gorilla; Docks; Cambrensis; Orbis; White Rose; Exile; Iota; Krax; Weyfarers; Western Mail; South Wales Evening Post; Momentum; Asp; Children's poetry included in many anthologies; Work translated into Russian and published throughout Russia in a British Council Moscow schools project. Honours: Eric Gregory Award for Poetry, 1979; Grants, Royal Literary Fund, 1987, Society of Authors, 1987, Welsh Arts Council, 1990; Commendations, National Poetry Competition, 1983, 1988, Bridport Arts Festival, 1984, Welsh Arts Council (prose), 1986, (poetry), 1987; Outposts Competition Winner, 1988; Workshop Writer, St Thomas School Workshop for Prince Charles, Swansea, 1995; Invited to attend conference in Serbia by Serbian Writers' Association, 2006 and 2007; Poem incorporated into a stained glass window in New Community School, Eastside Swansea; Poem used in Secondary Schools Curriculum Exams, UK, 2006; Poetry reading tour of America with Dylan Thomas's daughter, Aeronwy Thomas, 2008. Memberships: Poetry Society, London; Swansea Writers and Artists Group, Chairman and Treasurer, 1995-99; The Welsh Academy, full member, 1995-; Founder and Editor, The Seventh Quarry, Swansea poetry magazine, 2005. Address: Dan y Bryn, 74 Cwm Level Road, Brynhyfryd, Swansea SA5 9DY, Wales.

THAMBIRATNAM David Pathmaseelan, b. 12 August 1943, Sri Lanka. Professor of Structural Engineering. m. Sulogini Vethanayagam, 2 sons, 1 daughter. Education: BSc (Engin) First Class Honours, 1968; MSc (Struct), 1975; PhD (Struct), 1978. Appointments include: District, Construction Engineer, Department of Buildings and PWD, Government

of Sri Lanka, 1968-73; Chief Construction Engineer, (Colombo South) Department of Buildings, Government of Sri-Lanka, 1978-79; Senior Structural Engineer, Department of Buildings, Government of Sri Lanka, 1979-80; Lecturer, 1980-81, Senior Lecturer 1981-87, 1988-90; Department of Civil Engineering, National University of Singapore; Lecturer, 1990-91, Senior Lecturer, 1991-93, Associate Professor, 1993-96, Professor, 1996-, Structural Engineering, School of Civil Engineering/School of Urban Development, Queensland University of Technology; Major research areas: Structural dynamics, disaster mitigation and impact attenuation of structural systems, dynamics of flexible structures and health monitoring of bridges. Publications: 180 articles in international journals and conference proceedings. Honours: Canadian Commonwealth Scholarship, 1973-78; Graduate Fellowship, University of Manitoba, 1975-78; Commendation by Prime Minister of Sri Lanka, 1979; Listed in Who's Who publications. Memberships: Fellow, American Society of Civil Engineers; Fellow, Institution of Engineers, Australia; Fellow, Institution of Civil Engineers, UK. Address: School of Urban Development Faculty of Built Environment and Engineering, Queensland University of Technology, GPO Box 2434, Brisbane, QLD 4001, Australia.

THAO Vo Dang, b. 8 March 1941, Saigon, Vietnam. Educator. m. Le Luu Ka, 2 sons. Education: Bachelor, Mathematics, Hanoi University, 1965; Dr rer nat, Complex Analysis, Humboldt University, Berlin, 1974. Appointments: Lecturer, Mathematics, Hanoi University of Technology, 1966-69; Head, Department of Mathematics, Ho Chi Minh City University of Technology, 1976-87, 1996-98; Associate Professor, Department of Mathematics, National University of Ho Chi Minh City, 1999-. Publications: Behaviour of Schlicht Conformal Mappings of Domains Laying in Circular Rings, 1976; Estimates for Quasiconformal Mappings of Plane Domains, 1993; Estimates of Quasiconformal Mappings onto Canonical Domains, 2002. Honours: National Medal for Achievements in Education, 1995; Listed in international biographical dictionaries. Memberships: Vietnamese Mathematical Society. Address: G1 To Hien Thanh, P14, Q10, Ho Chi Minh City, Vietnam.

THATCHER, Baroness of Kesteven in the County of Lincolnshire, Margaret Hilda Thatcher, b. 13 October 1925, Grantham, England. Barrister; Politician; Former Prime Minister. m. Dennis Thatcher, 1951, deceased 2003, 1 son, 1 daughter. Education: Somerville College, Oxford. Appointments: Research Chemist, 1947-51; Entered Bar, Lincoln's Inn, 1953; Conservative Member of Parliament, Barnet, Finchley, 1959-92; Minister of Pensions and National Insurance Parliamentary Secretary, 1961-64; Opposition Spokesperson for Education, 1969-70; Secretary of State for Education and Science, 1970-74; Leader of Her Majesty's Opposition, 1975-79; First Lord of the Treasury and Minister for Civil Service, 1979-90; Conservative Party Leader, 1975-90; Prime Minister, 1979-90; Retired from public life, 2002. Publications: In Defence of Freedom, 1986; The Downing Street Years, 1979-90, 1993; The Path to Power, 1995; The Collected Speeches of Margaret Thatcher, 1997; Statecraft, 2002. Honours: Honorary Fellow, Royal Institute of Chemistry, Freedom of the Royal Borough of Kensington and Chelsea, 1979; Freedom of the London Borough of Barnet, 1980; Freedom of the Falkland Islands, Honorary Master of the Bench at Gray's Inn, 1983; Freedom of the City of London, 1989; Freedom of The City of Westminster, 1990; Hon LLD, Buckingham, 1986; Dr hc, Rand Afrikaans, 1991; Presidential Medal of Freedom, USA, 1991; Order of Good Hope, South Africa, 1991; Dr hc, Weizman Institute of Science, 1992; MacArthur Foundation Fellowship, 1992; Hon Citizen of Gorasde, 1993; Dr hc, Mendeleyev, 1993; Hilal-i-Imitaz, 1996; LG; OM; PC; FRS; Life Peer, created 1992. Memberships: Honorary Bencher, Gray's Inn, 1975; No Turning Back Group President, 1990-; Bruges Group Honorary President, 1991-; International Advisory Board, British American Chamber of Commerce; Worshipful Company of Glovers (Member); Chancellor, University of Buckingham, 1993-; Advisory Board Chair University of London Institute of US Studies, 1994-; Royal Society of St George Vice President, 1999-; Conservative Companion of Guild of Cambridge Benefactors, 1999-. Address: The House of Lords, Westminster, London SW1A 0PW, England.

THEOBALD-HICKS Barry John Frederick, b. 25 October 1945, Lockington Hall, Castle Donnington, Derbyshire. Company Director; Administrator; Amateur Historian; Genealogist; Archivist; 19th Lord of the Manor of Danbury with Bretton, County of Essex. m. Sharon Ann Friend. Education: Morely College, London, 1960-65; London College of Art and Printing, 1963-66; University of London, 1986-88; Certificate of Safety Management, British Institute of Management, 1992. Appointments: Served with RAMC/v – 217 London General Hospital (City of London) Detachment, HAC, 1970-75; Deputy Manager to Lady Tara Heffler, Catalogue Department, Manager, Printing and Stationary, Fire, Health and Safety Manager (UK), Sotheby's Auctioneers, Mayfair, London, 1978-93; Served with The Legion of Frontiersmen (Canadian Division) Captain (Staff), c 1989; Currently serving with The Earl Kitcheners Own (UK Command – VCF) Major (Staff), 2005, Lt Col (Staff) 2006, Chief of Staff – GHQ, 2006; Senior Museum Assistant, Leighton House Museum and Art Gallery, Royal Borough of Kensington and Chelsea, 1993-96; Director, Parke Morrison Construction Ltd, 1994-98; Director, Consolidated Land Ltd, 1995-98; Managing Director, Theobald-Hicks, Morris & Gifford Ltd, 1999-; Facilities Management, University of Greenwich, 2000-07; Director, The St Stanislas Trust (UK), 2004. Publications: History of the Lords of the Manor of Danbury in Essex (unpublished); History of Heather Parish Church, Leicestershire, 1986; Now I Know Where You Are Granddad, 1998; Contributor to: The Millennium Book of All Saints Church, Kent, 2000; A Theobald History (The Faversham Connection), 2004; Newsletter of the St John Historical Society. Honours include: St John Ambulance Long Service Medal, 1975 with 4 bars, 1980, 1985, 2002, 2007; Silver Medal of Merit, Sovereign Order of Malta, 1988; Freeman, City of London, 1985; Officer, The Venerable Order of St John of Jerusalem, 1988; Commander, Orthodox Order of Hospitallers, 1989; Officer, 1992, Commander, 1995, Knight of Justice, 2000, Knight Commander, 2002, Officer, Companionate of Merit, 2001, Order of St Lazarus; Knight Grand Cross of Justice, Order of St Stanislas, 2000; Knight Commander, Order of St Gregory the Great, 2004; Knight of Justice, Knight Commander, 2002, Order of the Collar of St Agatha of Paterno, 1997; Liveryman of the Worshipful Company of Scriveners. Memberships include: Fellow: Royal Microscopical Society, Royal Society of Art, Society of Antiquaries of Scotland; Member, British Institute of Management, Institute of Administrative Management; Museums Association, Associate, Ambulance Service Institute; President, St John Historical Society, 1994-96; Deputy Chairman, Royal Army Medical Corps Association (City of London) Branch, 2000-06; President, The Royal British Legion (Sidcup & Foots Cray Branch), 2005-07; Victory Club. Address: 3 Leechcroft Avenue, Blackfen, Kent DA15 8RR, England.

THEODOROU Stavroula, b. 6 March 1973, Ioannina, Greece. Physician; Radiologist. Education: MD, University of Ioannina School of Medicine, Ioannina, Greece, 1997; Speciality in Radiology, University of Ioannina Medical Centre, 1998-2003; Clinical duties and research in Musculoskeletal Imaging and Quantitative Bone Densitometry, University of California San Diego Medical Center, San Diego, California, USA, 1999, 2000-2001. Appointments: Department of Radiology, University of Ioannina Medical Centre, Ioannina, Greece, 1998-2003; Department of Radiology, University of California, San Diego, California, USA, 1999, 2000-2001; Department of Radiology, Thornton Hospital, University of California San Diego, California, USA, 1999; Department of Clinical Radiology and Bone Densitometry, University of Manchester, England, 2004-06. Publications: 50 original articles; Co-author, 7 books. Honours: Award of Excellence in University Studies, Greek National Scholarship Foundation, 1992, 1994; Award of Excellence in Pathology, University of Ioannina Medical Centre, 1996; Support in Research, Veterans Affairs, San Diego Medical Center Grant, California, USA; Certificate of Merit for Educational Exhibit, Radiological Society of North America, 1999, 2000; Certificate of Merit for Educational Exhibit, American Roentgen Ray Society, Washington DC, 2000; Best Scientific Exhibit, American Society of Spine Radiology, Florida, 2001. Memberships: American College of Radiology, Radiological Society of North America; Society for Clinical Densitometry; American Society for Bone Mineral Research; Los Angeles Radiological Society; National Osteoporosis Foundation. Address: 13 Papadopoulos Street, Ioannina 45444, Greece. E-mail: rjtheodorou@hotmail.com

THEOTOKOGLOU Efstathios E, b. 19 January 1956, Athens, Greece. Associate Professor. Education: MSc, 1979, PhD, 1984, National Technical University of Athens. Appointments: Research and Teaching Associate, 1979-88, Lecturer, 1988-92, Assistant Professor, 1992-99, Associate Professor, 1999-, National Technical University of Athens. Publications: Numerous articles in professional journals. Honours: Postdoctoral Fellowship, NTH-Department of Marine Structures, Trondheim, Norway, 1989-91. Memberships: Technical Chamber of Greece; International Association of Computational Mechanics. E-mail: stathis@central.ntua.gr

THERON Charlize, b. 7 August 1975, South Africa. Actress. Education: Trained as a ballet dancer. Appointments: Model, Milan, 1991; Actress, Los Angeles, 1992-; Films include: Children of the Corn III, 1994; Two Days in the Valley, That Thing You Do! 1996; Trial and Error, Hollywood Confidential, Devil's Advocate, Cop Lane/The Yards, 1997; Might Joe Young, Celebrity, 1998; The Cider House Rules, The Astronaut's Wife, 1999; The Yards, Reindeer Games, Men of Honour, The Legend of Bagger Vance, Navy Diver, 2000; Sweet November, The Curse of the Jade Scorpion, 15 Minutes, 2001; The Yards/Nightwatch, Waking Up in Reno, Trapped, 24 Hours, Executive Producer, Sweet Home Alabama, 2002; The Italian Job, Monster, 2003; The Life and Death of Peter Sellers, Head in the Clouds, 2004; North Country, Æon Flux, 2005; In the Valley of Elah, Battle in Seattle, Sleepwalking, 2007; Hancock, 2008. Honours: Golden Globe Award, Best Dramatic Actress, 2004; Critics' Choice Award, Best Actress, 2004; Screen Actors Guild, Best Actress Award, 2004; Academy Award, Best Actress, 2004. Address: c/o Spanky Taylor, 3727 West Magnolia, Burbank, CA 91505, USA.

THEROUX Paul Edward, b. 10 April 1941, Medford, Massachusetts, USA. Writer. m. (1) Anne Castle, 4 December 1967, divorced 1993, 2 sons, (2) Sheila Donnelly, 18

November 1995. Education: BA, University of Massachusetts. Appointments: Lecturer, University of Urbino, Italy, 1963, Soche Hill College, Malawi, 1963-65; Faculty, Department of English, Makerere University, Uganda, 1965-68, University of Singapore, 1968-71; Visiting Lecturer, University of Virginia, 1972-73. Publications: Fiction: Waldo, 1967; Fong and the Indians, 1968; Girls at Play, 1969; Murder in Mount Holly, 1969; Jungle Lovers, 1971; Sinning with Annie, 1972; Saint Jack, 1973; The Black House, 1974; The Family Arsenal, 1976; The Consul's File, 1977; Picture Palace, 1978; A Christmas Card, 1978; London Snow, 1980; World's End, 1980; The Mosquito Coast, 1981; The London Embassy, 1982; Half Moon Street, 1984; O-Zone, 1986; My Secret History, 1988; Chicago Loop, 1990; Millroy the Magician, 1993; My Other Life, 1996; Kowloon Tong, 1997; Collected Stories, 1997; Hotel Honolulu, 2000; Telling Tales (anthology), 2004; Blinding Light, 2006; The Elephanta Suite, 2007; Non-Fiction: V S Naipaul, 1973; The Great Patagonian Express, 1979; The Kingdom by the Sea, 1983; Sailing Through China, 1983; Sunrise with Sea Monsters, 1985; The White Man's Burden, 1987; Riding the Iron Rooster, 1988; The Happy Isles of Oceania, 1992; The Pillars of Hercules, 1995; Sir Vidia's Shadow: A Friendship Across Five Continents, 1998; Fresh Air Fiend, 2000; Nurse Wolf and Dr Sacks, 2001; Dark Star Safari, 2002. Honours: Editorial Awards, Playboy magazine, 1972, 1976, 1977, 1979; Whitbread Award, 1978; James Tait Black Award, 1982; Yorkshire Post Best Novel Award, 1982; Thomas Cook Travel Prize, 1989; Honorary doctorates. Memberships: Royal Geographical Society; Royal Society of Literature, fellow; American Academy of Arts and Letters. Address: Hamish Hamilton Ltd, 80 Strand, London WC2, England.

THEWLIS David, b. 20 March 1963. Actor. m. Sara Jocelyn Sugarman, 1992. Education: Highfield High School, Blackpool; St Anne's College of Further Education; Guildhall School of Music and Drama, London. Career: Theatre: Buddy Holly at the Regal; Ice Cream; Lady and the Clarinet; The Sea; TV: Dandelion Dead; Valentine Park; Road; The Singing Detective; Bit of a Do; Skulduggery; Journey to Knock; Filipina; Dreamgirls; Frank Stubbs Promotes; Prime Suspect 3; Dinotopia (voice), 2002; The Street, 2007; Films include: Short and Curlies, 1987; Vroom, 1988; Resurrected, 1989; Afraid of the Dark, 1991; Life is Sweet, 1990; Damage, 1992; The Trial, 1993; Naked, 1993; Black Beauty, 1994; Dragonheart, 1996; Seven Year in Tibet, 1997; Divorcing Jack, 1998; The Big Lebowski, 1998; The Miracle Maker (voice), 2000; DIY Hard, 2002; Cheeky, 2003; Timeline, 2003; Harry Potter and the Prisoner of Azkaban, 2004; Kingdom of Heaven, 2005; All the Invisible Children, 2005; The New World, 2005; Basic Instinct 2, The Omen, 2006; The Inner Life of Martin Frost, 2007; Harry Potter and the Order of the Phoenix, 2007; The Boy in Striped Pyjamas, 2008. Honours: Edinburgh Fringe First: Best Actor, Rheims Film Festival, 1992; Best Actor, Cannes Film Festival, 1993.

THILL Georges Emile André, b. 30 November 1935, Bullange, Belgium. University Emeritus Professor. Education: Mathematics, Belgian Licence and Agrégation enseignement secondaire, University of Louvain, Philosophy, BA; Doctorate, Theological Sciences, Paris; Postgraduate Studies, High Energy Physics. Appointments: Researcher, Laboratoire de Physique Nucléaire, Collège de France, Paris, 1966-67 and Institut Interuniversitaire belge des sciences nucléaires, Laboratoire des Hautes Energies, Brussels, 1967-73; Scholar, University of Namur, Belgium, 1973-2001; Director of the interdisciplinary Department for Sciences, Philosophies, Societies, Faculty of Natural Science, Namur, 1976-88; Member of the Executive Committee, Course Director in the Field, Science Technology Society, Inter-University Centre of Postgraduate Studies, Dubrovnik, 1986-94; Senior Fellow, EC Programme Monitor/FAST, Science Research Development, Brussels, 1991-94; Chair Professor, Professeur Ordinaire, 1986-2001, Emeritus Professor, University of Namur, 2001-; Emeritus Professor, Faculty of Human Sciences, State University of Haïti, Port-au-Prince, Haïti, 2002-; Visiting or Invited Professor in different universities: Dakar, Louvain, Brussels, Copenhagen, Donetsk National Technical University and others; Director of the Scientific Co-ordination, PRELUDE, International Networking Programme of Research and Liaison between Universities for Development, Research and Educational Network for sustainable co-development, NGO of UNESCO Collective Consultation on Higher Education implemented on the five continents (72 countries), 1985-; Responsible for the UNESCO-PRELUDE Chair of Sustainable Development, 2001-05. Publications: 26 books including: La fête scientifique, 1973; Technologies et sociétés, 1980; Plaidoyer pour des universités citoyennes et responsables, 1998; Le dialogue des savoirs, 2001; L'eau, patrimoine commun mondial, 2002; Femmes et Developpements Durables et Solidaires, Savoirs Sciences et Entrepreneuriat, 2007. Over 100 scientific articles. Honours: Director of the Scientific Co-ordination of PRELUDE; Scientific Director, UNESCO Unitwin-PRELUDE Chair; President, Institut Interuniversitaire Belge de la Vie, Sciences et Qualité de Vie, Brussels; 2003 International Peace Prize, United Cultural Convention, USA; Ambassador General, United Cultural Convention, USA. Memberships: Notably Scientific Society of Brussels; Steering Committee, International Network on the Role of the Universities for Developing Areas; Deontological Committee, Service Public Fédéral (SPF) de Belgique, Santé Publique, Sécurité de la Chaîne Alimentaire et Environment Division Bien-Être Animal et CITES; Joint Committee of Bioéthics of the Centre d'études et de recherches vétérinaires et agronomiques (CERVA), Institut Pasteur, Institut Scientifique de Santé Publique (ISP), Brussels; Editing Board, La Revue Nouvelle, PRELUDE Review and Newsletter. Address: 65, Rue Saint-Quentin, B-1000, Brussels, Belgium.

THILLAINAYAGAM Chinnamanur Veluchamy, b. 10 June 1925, Chinnamanur, Tamilnadu, India. Retired Director of Public Libraries, Government of Tamilnadu. m. Gomathy, 1 son, 1 daughter. Education: Bachelor of Arts, Economics, History and Politics, 1948, Diploma in Librarianship, 1950, Madras University; Master of Arts, Economics, Nagpur University, 1955; Certificate in German, Annamalai University, 1957; Bachelor of Teaching, Madras University, 1958; Master of Library Science, Delhi University, 1962. Appointments: Non-Gazetted Librarian, Directorate of Public Libraries, 1949-62, Gazetted Librarian of Connemara (State Central) Public Library, 1962-72, Director of Public Libraries, 1972-82, Government of Tamilnadu; Chairman, Tamilnadu Library Improvement Committee, 1998-; Consulting Editor, The Contemporary Who's Who, ABI, 2002-2003. Publications: Over 21 books including: Narmarintha Ranganathan Valmai (biography), 1994; Ranganathan – Kaula Gold Medal Awardee, 1994, Vethi, 1995; Nulaga Vithagar Seventy (Vethi), 1995; New Dimensions of Library Scenario in India, 1997; S R Ranganathan and Madras Public Libraries Act, 1997; Nenchil Nirkindravargal (Life Sketches), 1998; Nulaga Padalgal (poems on library services), 2002; 654 published papers. Honours include: Madras UNESCO Mandram Awards for teaching Library Science in Tamil, 1970; Awards, Government of Tamilnadu, 1971, 1975, 1978; Honorary Doctorate, World University, 1982; Thanjavur Tamil University Award, 1989; Dr C D Sharma Award, Indian Library Association, 1994;

Ranganathan-Kaula Gold Medal, 1994; Indian Library Association Abburi-Shiyali Research Award, 2001; Puravalar Mani, Mukkudai Monthly of Madras Jain Youth Forum, 2001; Tamil Pani Semmal Award, International Tamil Integration Society of Madras, 2002; Aanmiga Rathna Award, Tiruvannamalai Ashrama, 2003; Honoree of Contemporary Who's Who 2002-03 for Significant Achievement and Contributions to Society, 2004; Madurai Humanity, Tamil Monthly Award for Contributions, 2004, 2005; Vethiana, 2005; Listed in International Biographical Dictionaries. Memberships include: Fellow, Nagpur International Biographical Association, 2002; Foundation for Information and Communication, Madras, 2002; Fellow, Madras United Writers Association, 2003; Research Board of Advisors, ABI, 2004; Life Member: Indian Library Association; Tamilnadu Library Association; Madras Library Association; Tamilnadu Pensioners Associations at Ambasamuthram, Cumbum, Madras, Madurai and Uthamapalayam. Address: Director of Public Libraries (Retired), 48 VOC Square, Cumbum, Tamil Nadu 625 516, India.

THISTLETHWAYTE (John) Robin, b. 8 December 1935, London, England. Land Owner; Chartered Surveyor. m. Mary Katharine Grasett, 2 sons, 1 daughter. Education: Royal Agricultural College, Cirencester. Appointments: Partner, Savills, 1961-86; Consultant to Savills plc, 1986-96; Mayor of Chipping Norton, 1964, 1965; Justice of the Peace; Chairman, Chipping Norton Petty Sessional Division, 1985, 1985; Chairman North Oxfordshire and Chipping Norton Petty Sessional Division, 1989-91. Memberships: Fellow of the Royal Institution of Chartered Surveyors; Clubs: Boodle's, St James's. Address: Sorbrook Manor, Adderbury, Oxfordshire OX17 3EG, England.

THOMAS Donald Michael, b. 27 January 1935, Redruth, Cornwall, England. Poet; Writer; Translator. 2 sons, 1 daughter. Education: BA, 1st Class Honours, English, MA, New College, Oxford. Appointment: English teacher, Teignmouth, Devon, 1959-63; Lecturer, Hereford College of Education, 1963-78; Full-time author, 1978-. Publications: Poetry: Penguin Modern Poets 11, 1968; Two Voices, 1968; Logan Stone, 1971; Love and Other Deaths, 1975; The Honeymoon Voyage, 1978; Dreaming in Bronze, 1981; Selected Poems, 1983; Puberty Tree, 1992. Fiction: The Flute Player, 1979; Birthstone, 1980; The White Hotel, 1981; Ararat, 1983; Swallow, 1984; Sphinx, 1986; Summit, 1987; Lying Together, 1990; Flying into Love, 1992; Pictures at an Exhibition, 1993; Eating Pavlova, 1994; Lady With a Laptop, 1996; Alexander Solzhenitsyn, 1998; Charlotte, 2000. Translator: Requiem, and Poem Without a Hero, by Akhmatova, 1976; Way of All the Earth, by Akhmatova, 1979; The Bronze Horseman, by Pushkin, 1982. Honours: Gollancz/Pan Fantasy Prize; Pen Fiction Prize; Cheltenham Prize; Los Angeles Times Fiction Prize. Address: The Coach House, Rashleigh Vale, Tregolis Road, Truro TR1 1TJ, England. E-mail: dmthomas@btconnect.com

THOMAS Iwan, b. 5 January 1974, Farnborough, Hampshire. Athlete. Education: Brunel University. Appointments: Fourth-ranked BMX rider, Europe, 1988; Fifth Olympic Games 400m, 1996; Silver Medal, 4 x 400m relay; Gold Medal Amateur Athletics Association, Championships 400m, 1997, British records, 44.36 seconds, 1998; Silver Medal World Championships 4 x 400m relay, 1997; Gold Medal European Championships 400m, 1998; Gold Medal, World Cup 400m, 1998; Gold Medal Commonwealth Games 400m, 1998; Contestant on and winner of reality show Deadline. Honours: British Athletics Writers Male Athlete of the Year, 1998; Patron Norwich Union Startract Scheme. Address:

c/o UK Athletics, Athletics House, 10 Harbourne Road, Edgbaston, Birmingham, B15 3AA, England. Website: www.iwanthomas.com

THOMAS Kenneth G, b. 25 June 1944, Llanelli, Wales. Managing Director. m. Beth, 2 daughters. Education: BSc Honours, Metallurgy, University College, Cardiff, Wales, 1970; MSc and DIC, Management Sciences, Imperial College, University of London, 1971; PhD, Technical Sciences, Delft University of Technology, Delft, The Netherlands, 1994; Chartered Engineer, UK. Appointments: Mill Superintendent, Giant Yellowknife Mines Limited, Gold Producer, Northwest Territories, Canada, 1985-87; Vice-President, Metallurgy, 1987, Vice-President, Metallurgy and Construction, 1989, Senior Vice-President, Metallurgy and Construction, 1990, Senior Vice-President, Technical Services, 1995, Barrick Gold Corporation, Gold Producer, Ontario, Canada, 1987-2001; Global Managing Director, Mining and Mineral Processing, 2001, Managing Director, Western Australia, 2002-2003; Hatch, Consulting Engineers and Construction Managers, Mississauga, Ontario, Canada; Executive Vice President, Operations and Chief Operating Officer, Crystallex International Corporation, International Gold Company, Toronto, Canada, 2003-05; Managing Director, Hatch, Consulting Engineers and Construction Managers, Mississauga, Ontario, Canada, 2005-. Publications: Numerous technical and management papers internationally. Book: Research, Engineering Design and Operation of a Pressure Hydrometallurgical Facility for Gold Extraction. Honours: Mill Man of the Year Award, 1991, Airey Award, 1999, Selwyn G Blaylock Medal, 2001, Canadian Institute of Mining, Metallurgy and Petroleum. Memberships: Association of Professional Engineers of Ontario, Canada; Fellow, Institute of Mining, Metallurgy and Mining, UK; Fellow, Canadian Institute of Mining, Metallurgy and Petroleum; Fellow, Canadian Academy of Engineering. Address: 2005, Heartwood Court, Mississauga, Ontario L5C 4P7, Canada.

THOMAS Lindsey Kay Jr, b. 16 April 1931, Salt Lake City, Utah, USA. Research Ecologist Emeritus; Consultant; Educator. m. Nancy Ruth Van Dyke, 2 sons, 2 daughters. Education: BS, Utah State Agricultural College, Logan, Utah, 1953; MS, Brigham Young University, Provo, Utah, 1958; PhD, Duke University, Durham, North Carolina, 1974. Appointments: Park Naturalist, National Capital Parks, National Park Service, 1957-62; Wildlife Consultant for Girl Scouts of America Camp 1958; Park Naturalist (Research), Region 6, 1962-63; Research Park Naturalist, National Capital Region, 1963-66; Instructor, Department of Agriculture Graduate School, 1964-66; Research Biologist for Southeast Temperate Forests, 1966-71; Aquatic Ecology Consultant for Fairfax County (Va) Federation of Citizen Associations 1970-71; Research Biologist, National Capital Parks, 1971-74; Research Biologist, National Capital Region, 1974-93; Guest Lecturer, Washington Technical Institute (University of the District of Columbia), 1976; Adjunct Professor, George Mason University, 1988-; Adjunct Professor, George Washington University, 1992-98; Research Biologist, National Biological Service, 1993-96; Resource Management Specialist, Baltimore-Washington Parkway, National Park Service, 1996, National Capital Parks East, 1996-98; Member, Board of Directors, Prince William County (Virginia) Service Authority, 1996-2004; Ecological and Resource Management Consultant, National Capital Region, 1998-; Preservation and Management Consultant for McAteean Magnolia Bogs in Charles County, Maryland, 2002-2006; Consultant for Natural Resources Division, Arlington County, Va, 2004-. Publications: Numerous articles in professional journals.

Honours include: Boy Scouts of America Training Award, Superior Performance Award for Conduct and Progress in the Exotic Plant Management Research Programme; Incentive Award for Safety Feature at Overlook; Incentive Award for Interpretive Information to be placed on C&O Canal Location Map. Listed in Who's Who publications and biographical dictionaries. Memberships: American Association for the Advancement of Science; Botanical Society of Washington; Ecological Society of America; George Wright Society; The Nature Conservancy; Society for Early Historic Archaeology; Sigma Xi the Scientific Research Society; Southern Appalachian Botanical Society; Washington Biologists' Field Club; National Trust for Historic Preservation; Maryland Native Plant Society. Address: 13854 Delaney Road, Woodbridge, VA 22193-4654, USA.

THOMAS Neil Philip, b. 29 April 1950, London, England. Consultant Surgeon. m. Julia, 1 son, 2 daughters. Education: Stowe School, 1963-67; BSc (Hons) 1971, MBBS, 1974, Middlesex Hospital Medical School, London University; FRCS, 1978. Appointments: H P Professorial Medical Unit, Middlesex Hospital, UCH/Westminster Orthopaedic Training Rotation, 1980-86; Consultant Orthopaedic Surgeon, North Hampshire Hospital, Hampshire Clinic; Founder, Wessex Knee Unit; Visiting Professor, Perugia University, 2005; Godfather to ESSKA/AOSSM Travelling Fellows, 2005. Publications: Clinical Challenges in Orthopaedics: The Knee; Numerous articles in peer reviewed scientific journals: JBJS, The Knee, AJSM; Editorial Board Member, The Knee, JBJS (B) and KSSTA journals. Honours: Fitton Prize, Herbert Seddon Prize and Medal; BASK President's Medal. Memberships: ISAKOS; Secretary, 1993-96, President, 2002-04, British Association of Surgery of the Knee (BASK); Council Member, 1998-2002, British Orthopaedic Association; President, ESSKA 2000 (European Society of Sports Traumatology Knee Surgery and Arthroscopy); Secretary to the Council and Editorial Board Member, JBJS; Club: The Athenaeum. Address: Little Bullington, Sutton Scotney, Winchester, Hampshire SO21 3QQ, England. E-mail: neilthomas@wessexknee.co.uk

THOMAS Zdenek, b. 11 May 1929, Opava, Czechoslovakia. Civil Engineer. m. Jitka Kadlecova, 1 son. Education: Civil Engineer, 1954; PhD, 1967; Doctor of Sciences, 1992. Appointments: Water Research Institute, Prague, 1954-91; Delft Hydraulic Laboratory, The Netherlands, 1968-69; Institute for Water Structures, University of Stuttgart, Germany, 1989; Institute of Hydrodynamics, Czech Academy of Sciences, 1992; Engineering Institute, Mexican National Autonomous University, 1996-97; Mexican Petroleum Institute, 1999-2004. Publications: 32 scientific papers including 3 monographs. Honours: Listed in Who's Who publications and biographical dictionaries. Memberships: Scientific-Technical Society, Prague; Union of Czech Mathematicians and Physicists; Czech Association for Chemical Technology. Address: Kladenska 19, 16000 Prague 6, Czech Republic. E-mail: ZThomas@seznam.cz

THOMPSON Daley, b. 30 July 1958, Notting Hill, London, England. Athlete. m. Tisha Quinlan, 1987, 1 child. Appointments: Sussex Schools 200m title, 1974; First competitive decathlon, Welsh Open Championship, 1975; European Junior Decathlon Champion, 1977; European Decathlon Silver Medallist, 1978; Gold Medallist, 1982, 1986; Commonwealth Decathlon Gold Medallist, 1978, 1982, 1986; Olympic Decathlon Gold Medallist, Moscow, 1980, LA, 1984; World Decathlon Champion, 1983; Established new world record for decathlon (at Olympic games, LA); Set four world records and was undefeated between 1978 and 1987;

Retired, July 1992; Invited to run leg of the Olympic Torch relay at the opening of Sydney Olympic Games, 2000; Played football for Mansfield Town and Wimbledon. Publications: Going for Gold, 1987; The Greatest, 1996. Honours: MBE, 1982; OBE, 1986; BBC Sports Personality of the Year, 1982; Britain's Athlete of the Century, 1999; CBE, 2000. Address: Church Row, Wandsworth Plain, London, SW18, England.

THOMPSON David Morgan, b. 9 July 1929, Ryde, Isle of Wight, England. Art Critic. m. Freda Dowie. Education: BA, Corpus Christi, Oxford. Appointments: Art Critic, The Times, 1956-64; Founder, Director, Stage Sixty theatre company, Theatre Royal, Stratford East, 1964-66; Director, Institute of Contemporary Arts, London, 1969-72. Publications: Scripted 10 BBC TV art programmes, 1980-86; Monograph, Becker, 2003. Honours: Council of Europe Award; Blue Ribbon Award, New York Film Festival; BAFTA Best Specialist Film Award. Memberships: British Council Fine Art Committee; Arts Council Exhibitions Committee; Hayward Gallery Advisory Committee; Greater London Arts Association; Lloyd Committee for a National Film School. Address: Hollies, Love Lane, Westleton, Nr Saxmundham, Suffolk IP17 3BA, England.

THOMPSON Emma, b. 15 April 1959, England. Actress. m. (1) Kenneth Brannagh, 1989, divorced, (2) Greg Wise, 1 daughter. Education: Newnham College, Cambridge, England. Career: Cambridge Footlights while at University; Films include: Henry V, 1989; Howards End, Dead Again, 1991; Cheers, 1992; Peter's Friends, 1992; Much Ado About Nothing; In the Name of the Father, Remains of the Day, 1993; My Father the Hero, 1994; Junior, 1994; Sense and Sensibility, wrote screenplay and acted, 1996; The Winter Guest, 1997; Primary Colors, 1997; Judas Kiss, 1997; Imagining Argentina, 2002; Love Actually, 2003; Harry Potter and the Prisoner of Azkaban, 2004; Nanny McPhee, 2005; Stranger Than Fiction, 2006; Harry Potter and the Order of the Phoenix, 2007; I Am Legend, 2007; TV includes: Carrott's Lib; Saturday Night Live; Tutti Frutti; Fortunes of War; Thompson; Knuckle; The Winslow Boy; Look Back in Anger; Blue Boy; Ellen; Wit; Angels in America, 2002; Stage appearances include: Me and My Girl, 1984-85; Look Back in Anger, 1989; A Midsummer Night's Dream, 1990; King Lea, 1990. Honours: Best TV Actress Awards: Tutti Frutti and Fortunes of War; Evening Standard Awards: Howards End, 1992; Remains of the Day, 1994; Academy Awards: Howards End, 1994, Sense and Sensibility, 1996; BAFTA Award: Howards End, 1994. Address: Hamilton Hodell Ltd, 1st Floor, 24 Hanway Street, London W1T 1UH, England.

THOMPSON Richard Paul Hepworth, b. 14 April 1940, Esher, Surrey, England. Medicine. m. Eleanor Mary Hughes. Education: Epsom College, 1954-58; Worcester College, Oxford University, 1958-62; St Thomas' Hospital Medical School, 1962-64. Appointments: Consultant Physician, 1972-2005, Emeritus Consultant Physician, 2005-, Guy's & St Thomas' Hospitals; Management Committee, 1985-97, Chairman, Grants Committee, 1989-97, King Edward VII's Hospital Fund for London; Physician to HM the Queen, 1993-2005; Trustee of THRIVE, 2000-; Visiting Professor, King's College London, 2001-; Vice Chairman of Council, British Heart Foundation, 2001-; Treasurer, Royal College of Physicians, 2003-; Council, Royal Medical Foundation of Epsom College, 2003-; Independent Monitoring Board, Feltham Young Offenders Institute, 2005-. Publications: 2 medical textbooks; 250 medical and scientific publications in journals. Honours: DM, Oxon; FRCP; KCVO. Address: 36 Dealtry Road, London, SW15 6NL, England. E-mail: richard@rpht.co.uk

THOMPSON Terence, b. 19 January 1928, Staffordshire, England. Composer; Teacher; Clarinettist; Saxophonist. Education: ABSM, performer and teacher; ABSM, (T T D), Birmingham School of Music, after Military Service in the South Staffordshire Regiment. Career: Music Master, West Bromwich Technical High School, 1950-59; Part-Time Clarinet Tutor, Birmingham School of Music, 1954-55; Head of Music, March End School, Wednesfield, 1960-66; Part-Time Lecturer, West Midlands College of Higher Education, 1965-89; Senior Teacher, Wolverhampton Music School, 1968-93. Compositions: Boogie and Blues; Suite Chalumeau Swing; Suite City Scenes; Back to Bach; Two syncopated dances; Something Blue; Romance in Sepia; 36 other arranged works published; 17 other compositions self published; 37 other arranged works self published. Recordings: London Saxophone Quartet in digital; Two Light Pieces, 1999; A Cumbrian Voluntary, 2000 Music for a While; Music for the New Millennium; Variations on The Young May Moon; Summertime. Memberships: Performing Right Society; British Academy of Composers and Songwriters; The Light Music Society; National Union of Teachers; Mechanical-Copyright Protection Society; Birmingham Conservatoire Association; British Association of Symphonic Bands and Wind Ensembles. Address: 58 Willenhall Road, Bilston, West Midlands WV14 6NW, England.

THOMPSON-CAGER-STRAND Chezia Brenda, Poet; Director; Artist; Educator. Education: BA, 1973, MA, 1975, Washington University; Doctorate of Arts, Carnegie-Mellon University, 1984. Appointments: Assistant Professor of English, Clarion State College, 1980-82; Site Reviewer, National Endowment for the Arts Expansion Arts Program, 1984; Assistant Professor, Afro-American Studies, University of Maryland, Baltimore, 1982-85; Associate Professor, Theater/African–American Studies, Mendenhall Center for the Performing Arts, Smith College, 1985-88; Artist in Residence, Theater Department, University of Pennsylvania; Consultant, African American Newspaper Archives and Research Center, 1989-92; Artist in Residence, Albany (Georgia) State College, 1994; Consultant, Baltimore City Public Schools Multicultural Initiative, 1992-94; Professor of Language and Literature, 1994-, Director, Spectrum of Poetic Fire Reading Series, 1999-, Maryland Institute College of Art; Poet Scholar in Residence, Towson University 2006-2007. Publications: 2 books; 3 poetry chapbooks; When Divas Laugh, poetry, 2002; Teaching Jean Toomer's 1923 Cane, 2006; When Divas Dance, poetry, 2006; Regional Poetry CD, The Road Less Taken: The Saint Valentine Sunday Poetry Marathon, 2001; Contributor of poems, reviews and articles in professional and public journals. Honours include: Distinguished Black Marylander Award in the Arts, Towson University, 2000; Maryland State Arts Council Individual Artist Award in Poetry, 1999, 2001; Lucus Grant in Teaching, MICA, 2001; Associate Fellowship in Poetry, Atlantic Center for the Arts, 2002; Tuition Grant in Poetry, Bread Loaf, 2002; Finalist in 2002 Naomi Madgett Long Poetry Competition for Lotus Press; Finalist, River Styx International Poetry Contest, 2004; Legacy Award from Poetry for the People Association, 2005. Memberships: Board of Directors, LINK: A Journal of the Arts in Baltimore and the World; Modern Language Association; Poetry Society of America; Academy of American Poets; National Council of Teachers of English; College Language

Association. Address: 1300 Mount Royal Avenue, Baltimore, MD 21217, USA. E-mail: spectrum@mica.edu Website: www.spectrumofpoeticfire.com.

THOMSON John Ansel Armstrong, b. 23 November 1911, Detroit, Michigan, USA. Maufacturing Biochemist. m. June Anna Mae Hummel, deceased, 1 son, 2 daughters. Education: AA, Pasadena City College, 1935; AB (cum laude), USC, 1957; BGS (Honorary), Cal State Polytech University, 1961; MA, PhD, Columbia Pacific University, 1978-79; DA, International Institute of Advanced Studies, Clayton, Missouri, 1979; Certified Secondary Teacher, California. Appointments: Chemist, J A Thomson Bio-Organic Chemist, LA, 1938; Founder/President, Vitamin Institute (formerly J A Thomson Bio-Organic Chemist), LA and North Hollywood, California, 1939-; Vocational Education Instructor, US War Manpower Commission, 1943-44. Publications: Author of booklets: Whose Are the Myths? 1949; Non-toxic Vitamins-Hormones Answers to Environmental Public Problems, 1972; Minimization of Toxics in Agriculture, 1991; Support of Pressures to Homeostasis, Normality, 1990; Need for Recognition and Reversal of Rapid Decline of Heritage of American and World Children, 1995, 1996; Contributor of articles to journals. Honours: Science and Industry Gold Medal, Golden Gate International Exposition, 1940; Many other awards. Memberships: Listed in international biographical dictionaries. Address: 12610 Saticoy Street South, North Hollywood, CA 91605, USA. Website: www.superthrive.com

THOMSON Wendy, b. 28 October 1953, Montreal, Canada. University Professor. 1 adopted daughter, 2 step sons. Education: Diploma Collegial Studies, Bachelor of Social Work, Master of Social Work, McGill University, Canada; PhD, Bristol University. Appointments: Executive Director, Head and Hands, Montreal, 1976-80, West Island Association for People with Learning Disabilities, Quebec, 1981-82; Senior Programmes Officer, Greater London Council, 1985-86; Head of Finance and Programmes, London Strategic Policy Unit, 1986-87; Assistant Chief Executive, Islington Council, 1987-93; Chief Executive, Turning Point Charity, 1993-96; Chief Executive, London Borough of Newham, 1996-99; Director of Inspection, Audit Commission, 1999-2001; Chief Executive, Office of Public Service Reform, Cabinet Office, 2001-05; Professor and Director, McGill School of Social Work, 2005-; Former Member, Government's Urban Task Force and Better Regulation Task Force; Board Member, Agence de Santé et Services Sociaux de Montréal. Publications: Books: Bureaucracy and Community (contributor), 1990; Citizen's Rights in a Modern Welfare System (contributor), 1992; Management for Quality in Local Government (contributor), 1992; Fitness for Purpose: Shaping New Patterns for Organisations and Management (co-author), 1993; Articles: Local Leadership for Global Times, 2007; Labour's Record on Social Exclusion, 2007; Blair's Social Legacy, 2007; Contributor to other publications and author of numerous conference papers. Honours: Board Member, McGill University Health Centre, Quebec, 2006; Expert Panel, UN Expert Committee, Global Forum on Reinventing Government. Memberships: CASSW; Centre for Research on Children & Families. Address: 3506 University, Rm 301, Montreal, Quebec, H3A 2A7, Canada.

THÖRNQVIST Christer, b. 11 August 1961, Tibro, Sweden. Researcher; Academic Teacher. Divorced. Education: BA, Cultural Science, 1986, PhD, History, 1994, University of Gothenburg. Appointments: Researcher, The Network Arbetslivi, Vastsverige, 1998-99; Researcher and Academic Teacher, Department of Work Science, 2000-02,

Researcher and Academic Teacher, 2005-08, University of Gothenburg; Visiting Researcher, University College, Trollhattan-Uddevalla, 2003-04; Visiting Professor, Yale University, New Haven, Connecticut, 2008-09. Publications: Listed in international biographical dictionaries. Honours: Docent (Associate Professor), University of Gothenburg, 2004; McMillan Center Visiting Professor, Yale University, New Haven, 2008-09. Memberships: International Industrial Relations Association. Address: Department of Work Science, University of Gothenburg, PO Box 705, SE 405 30 Gothenburg, Sweden. E-mail: christer.thornqvist@av.gu.se Website: www.av.gu.se

THORNTON Billy Bob, b. 4 August 1955, Hot Springs, Arizona, USA. Actor; Writer; Director. m. (1) Melissa Lee Gatlin, divorced 1980, 1 daughter, (2) Toni Lawrence, divorced 1988, (3) Cynda Williams, divorced 1992, (4) Pietra Dawn Chernak, divorced 1997, 2 sons, (5) Angelina Jolie, 2000, divorced 2003, 1 adopted son, 1 daughter with Connie Angland. Appointments: Films include: Sling Blade, 1996; U-Turn, 1997; A Thousand Miles, 1997; The Apostle, 1997; A Gun a Car a Blonde, 1997; Primary Colours, 1997; Homegrown, 1998; Armageddon, 1998; A Simple Plan, 1998; Pushing Tin, 1998; The Man Who Wasn't There, 2001; Bandits, 2001; Monster's Ball, 2001; Love Actually, 2003; Intolerable Cruelty, 2003; Bad Santa, 2003; The Alamo, 2004; Friday Night Lights, 2004; The Ice Harvest, 2005; Bad News Bears, 2005; School for Scoundrels, 2006; Mr Woodcock, 2007; The Astronaut Farmer, 2007; TV: The 1,000 Chains; Don't Look Back; The Outsiders; Hearts Afire. Honours: Academy Award for Best Actor; Independent Spirit Awards. Address: c/o Miramax, 7966 Beverly Boulevard, Los Angeles, CA 90048, USA.

THORNTON Frank (Frank Thornton Ball), b. 15 January 1921, Dulwich, London. Actor. m. Beryl Jane Margaret Evans. 1 daughter. Education: Alleyn's School, Dulwich; London School of Dramatic Art, Scholarship, 1938-39; Qualified as Navigator, RAFVR, 1944; Demobbed as Flying Officer, 1947. Appointments: Council Actors' Benevolent Fund, Vice-President, 1982-90; Actor; Theatre includes: Laertes, Bassanio, Lysander, Catesby, Bardolph, Mosca in Jonson's Volpone, Donald Wolfit's Shakespeare Company, Strand and St James's Theatres, 1941-42; John Gielgud's Macbeth, Piccadilly Theatre, 1942; Flare Path, Apollo Theatre, 1942-43; Post-war several tours and repertory; Meals on Wheels, Royal Court, 1965; Alibi for a Judge, Savoy, 1966-67; The Young Visiters, Piccadilly, 1969; When We are Married, Strand, 1970; Eeyore in Winnie-the-Pooh, Phoenix, 1971-72; Aguecheek in Twelfth Night, Duncan in Macbeth, RSC, Stratford and Aldwych, 1974-75; Sir Patrick Cullen in The Doctor's Dilemma, Mermaid; The Chairs, Royal Exchange, Manchester, 1980; Sir John Tremayne in Me and My Girl, Adelphi, 1984-85; John of Gaunt in Richard II, Ludlow Festival, 1987; The Tutor, Old Vic, 1988; Ivanov and Much Ado About Nothing, Strand, 1989; George Bernard Shaw in The Best of Friends, 1990 and 1991; The Major General in The Pirates of Penzance, London Palladium, 1990; It Runs in the Family, Playhouse, 1993; Harvey, Shaftesbury, 1995; Hobson in Hobson's Choice, Lyric, 1995-96; Cash on Delivery, Whitehall, 1996-97; The Jermyn Street Revue, J S Theatre, 2000; Television: Many dramas and situation comedies include: It's a Square World; The World of Beachcomber; HMS Paradise; Scott on....; The Taming of the Shrew; Captain Peacock in Are You Being Served?, 1972-84; Truly in Last of the Summer Wine, 1997-; Films include: The Bed-Sitting Room; A Funny Thing Happened on the Way to the Forum; A Flea in her Ear; Great Expectations; The Old Curiosity Shop; Gosford Park; Back

in Business; Radio includes: Propaganda broadcasts, 1942-43; The Embassy Lark; The Big Business Lark; Mind Your Own Business. Membership: The Garrick Club. Address: David Daly Personal Management, 68 Old Brompton Road, London SW7 3LQ, England.

THORNTON Leslie Tillotson, b. 26 May 1925, Skipton, North Yorkshire, England. Sculptor; Principal Art Lecturer (Retired). m. Constance Helen Billows, 1 son, 1 daughter. Education: Keighley Art School, 1940-42; Conscripted for Mines, 1943-45; National Diploma of Art and Design, Leeds College of Art, 1945-48; Sculpture School, Royal College of Art, 1948-51; Associate of RCA. Appointments: Part-time Lecturer in London Art Colleges: Bromley, Hammersmith and Central School, 1951-65; Senior Lecturer in Charge of Sculpture, University of Sunderland, 1965-70; Principal Lecturer in Charge of Sculpture, University of Stafford, 1970-89; Exhibitions include: Arts Council Contemporary British Sculpture, 1957/58; 10 Young British Sculptors, IV Sao Paulo Biennale, Brazil, 1957; CAS Religious Theme Exhibition, Tate Gallery, 1958; 10 Young British Sculptors, British Council Touring Exhibition, Rio de Janeiro, Montevideo, Santiago, Lima, Caracas, 1958; 5th and 10th International Biennale Middleheim Park, Antwerp, 1959, 1969; British Artists Craftsmen Exhibition touring America, 1960; English Painters and Sculptors, Zurich, 1963; Art Sacre, Museum of Modern Art, Paris, 1965; Northern Sculptors Exhibition, Newcastle, 1967; One man Exhibitions, Gimpel Fils Gallery, London, 1957, 1960, 1969; Sion House, London, 1970; Royal Academy, London, 1974/76, 1978/79; Solihull Annual Exhibition, 1979; Retrospective Exhibition, Holden Gallery, Manchester, 1981; Royal Academy, 1987; 100 Years of Sculpture, Moore Institute, Leeds, 2004; Commissions: Daily Mirror Building, London, 1961; Crucifix, St Louis Priory, Missouri, 1965; Crucifix, St Ignatious College, Enfield, 1968; Works in collections including: Museum of Modern Art, New York; Peggy Guggenheim Collection, Venice; Arts Council of Great Britain; Victoria and Albert Museum; Leeds City Art Gallery; National Gallery of Scotland; Private collections in UK North and South America, Sweden and Belgium. Publications: Works reviewed in books and journals including: 20th Century Steel Sculptures US, 2002; Handbook of 20th Century British Sculpture, 2004. Honours: Panel Member, Council for National Academic Awards; Fellow, Royal Society of Arts; Associate, Royal Society of British Sculptors. Address: Stable Cottage, 45 Chatsworth Place, Harrogate HG1 5HR, England.

THORPE David Richard, b. 12 March 1943, Huddersfield, England. Political Biographer. Education: Fettes College, Edinburgh; BA Honours, 1965, MA, 1969, Selwyn College, Cambridge. Appointment: Appointed Official Biographer of Lord Home of the Hirsel, 1990; New Authorised Biographer of Sir Anthony Eden, 1996. Publications: The Uncrowned Prime Ministers: A Study of Sir Austen Chamberlain, Lord Curzon and Lord Butler, 1980; Selwyn Lloyd, 1989; Alec Douglas-Home, 1996; Eden: The Life and Times of Anthony Eden, 1st Earl of Avon 1897-1977, 2003. Contributions to: The Blackwell Biographical Dictionary of British Political Life in the 20th Century, 1990; Telling Lives: From WB Yeats to Bruce Chatwin (edited by Alistair Horne), 2000; The Oxford Dictionary of National Biography, 2004; and on-line updates, 2006. Memberships: Johnson Club; Oxford and Cambridge Club; Archive Fellow, Churchill College, Cambridge, 1986; St Antony's College, Oxford, Alistair Horne Fellow, 1997-98; Brasenose College, Oxford, Senior Member, 1998-. Address: Brasenose College, Oxford OX1 4AJ, England.

THRUSH Brian Arthur, b. 23 July 1928, Hendon, England. Retired University Professor. m. Rosemary Catherine Terry, 1 son, 1 daughter. Education: BA, MA, PhD, ScD, Emmanuel College, Cambridge. Appointments: Lecturer, Assistant Director of Research, Demonstrator in Physical Chemistry, 1953-69, Reader in Physical Chemistry, 1969-78, Professor of Physical Chemistry, 1978-95, Professor Emeritus, 1995-, University of Cambridge; Fellow, 1960, Vice Master, 1986-90, Emmanuel College, Cambridge: Visiting Professor of Chinese Academy of Sciences, 1980-90. Publications: Many original papers in learned scientific journals. Honours: Tilden Lecturer, Chemical Society , 1965; Michael Polanyi Medallist, Royal Society of Chemistry, 1986; Rank Prize for Opto-Electronics, 1992. Memberships: Fellow Royal Society, 1976, Council Member, 1990-92; Fellow, Royal Society of Chemistry, 1977; Lawes Trust Committee, 1979-89; National Environment Research Council, 1985-90; Member, Academia Europaea, 1990, Council Member, 1992-98. Address: Brook Cottage, Pemberton Terrace, Cambridge, CB2 1JA, England.

THUBRON Colin Gerald Dryden, b. 14 June 1939, London, England. Writer. Publications: Mirror to Damascus, 1967; The Hills of Adonis: A Quest in Lebanon, 1968; Jerusalem, 1969; Journey Into Cyprus, 1975; The God in the Mountain (novel), 1977; Emperor (novel), 1978; The Venetians, 1980; The Ancient Mariners, 1981; The Royal Opera House Covent Garden, 1982; Among the Russians, 1983; A Cruel Madness, 1984; Behind the Wall: A Journey Through China, 1987; Falling, 1989; Turning Back the Sun, 1991; The Lost Heart of Asia, 1994; Distance (novel), 1996; In Siberia, 1999; To the Last City (novel), 2002; Shadow of the Silk Road, 2006. Contributions to: Times; Times Literary Supplement; Independent; Sunday Times; Sunday Telegraph; New York Times; Granta. Honours: Fellow, Royal Society of Literature, 1969; Silver Pen Award, 1985; Thomas Cook Award, 1988; Hawthornden Prize, 1989; RSGS Mungo Park Medal, 2000; RSAA Lawrence of Arabia Memorial Medal, 2001; Vice-President, Royal Society of Literature, 2003; C.B.E., 2007. Membership: PEN. Address: 28 Upper Addison Gardens, London W14 8AJ, England.

THURLOW, 8th Baron (Francis Edward Hovell-Thurlow-Cumming-Bruce), The Rt Hon the Lord Thurlow, b. 9 March 1912. m. Yvonne Diana, 1949, deceased 1990, 2 sons, 2 daughters. Education: Shrewsbury; MA, Trinity College, Cambridge. Appointments: Department of Agriculture for Scotland, 1935-37; Joined HM Diplomatic Service: Secretary, New Zealand, 1939-44; Secretary, Canada, 1944-45; Private Secretary to Secretary of State for Commonwealth Relations, 1947-49; Counsellor, New Delhi, 1949-52; Adviser to Governor of Gold Coast, 1955; Deputy High Commissioner, Ghana, 1957; Deputy High Commissioner, Canada, 1958; High Commissioner, New Zealand, 1959-63; High Commissioner, Nigeria, 1963-66; Deputy Under Secretary, FCO, 1964; Governor and Commander-in-Chief of Bahamas, 1968-72. Honours: KCMG, 1959; Knight of St John. Memberships: Travellers. Address: 102 Leith Mansions, Grantully Road, London W9 1LJ, England. E-mail: thurlow@btinternet.com

THURMAN Uma, b. 29 April 1970. Actress. m. (1) Gary Oldman, 1990, divorced 1992, (2) Ethan Hawke, 1998, divorced 2004, 1 son, 1 daughter. Appointments: Model; Actress; Films: The Adventures of Baron Munchhausen; Dangerous Liaisons; Even Cowgirls Get the Blues; Final Analysis; Where the Heart Is; Henry and June; Mad Dog and Glory; Pulp Fiction; Robin Hood; Dylan; A Month by the Lake; The Truth About Cats and Dogs; Batman and Robin;

Gattaca; Les Miserables; Sweet and Lowdown; Vatel; The Golden Bowl; Tape; Chelsea Walls; Kill Bill Vol 1, 2003; Paycheck; Kill Bill Vol 2, 2004; Be Cool, 2005; Prime, 2005; The Producers, 2005; My Super Ex-Girlfriend, 2006; The Life Before Her Eyes, 2007; The Accidental Husband, 2008; TV: Hysterical Blindness, 2002. Honours: Golden Globe, Best Actress in a Miniseries or TV movie, 2003. Address: c/o CAA, 9830 Wilshire Boulevard, Beverly Hills, CA 90212, USA.

THURSBY Peter Lionel, b. 23 December 1930, Salisbury, Wiltshire. Sculptor. m. Maureen Aspden. Education: West of England College of Art; Exeter College of Art; ATD, Bristol University. Appointments: Head of Art, Hele's Grammar School, Exeter, 1960-71; Head of School of Art and Design, Exeter College, 1971-89. Publications: Art Education for New Society, 1968; Turning Bronzes, 1975; Painting and Sculpture in Britain, 1976; Open Air Sculpture in Britain, 1984; Peter Thursby, by Vivienne Light & Simon Olding, 2007. Honours: Silver Medal, Royal Society of British Sculptors, 1986; Hon D'Art, University of the West of England, Bristol, 1995; President, Royal West of England Academy, Bristol, 1995-2000. Memberships: Royal West of England Academy; Fellow, Royal Society of British Sculptors; Fellow, Royal Society of Arts; Member, Art and Architecture Association; Chelsea Arts Club. Address: Oakley House, 28 Oakley Close, Pinhoe, Exeter EX1 3SB, England. E-mail: thursby.sculpture@virgin.net

THURSBY-PELHAM Vaughan Brian George, b. 27 December 1934, Wimbledon, London, England. Retired Chartered Accountant. m. Brigid Kathleen Doherty, 2 sons, 3 daughters. Education: Beaumont College, Old Windsor, Berkshire. Appointments: Trained with Peat Marwick Mitchell (now KPMG); Previously Board Secretary/Financial Director of various public companies; Board Secretary/Financial Controller, Engineering Construction Industry Training Board, 1990-97. Memberships: Fellow, Institute of Chartered Accountants in England & Wales; Member, Catenian Association, formerly Provincial Counsellor. Address: Two Woodlands Avenue, New Malden, Surrey KT3 3UN, England.

THWAITE Ann, b. 4 October 1932, London, England. Writer. m. Anthony Thwaite, 4 August 1955, 4 daughters. Education: MA, Dlitt, Oxford University (St Hilda's College). Appointments: Visiting Professor, Tokyo Women's University; Contributing Editor, Editorial Board, Cricket Magazine (US). Publications: Waiting for the Party: A Life of Frances Hodgson Burnett (reissued as Frances Hodgson Burnett: Beyond the Secret Garden); Edmund Gosse: A Literary Landscape; A A Milne: His Life; Emily Tennyson: The Poet's Wife; Glimpses of the Wonderful, The Life of Philip Henry Gosse. Honours: Duff Cooper Prize, 1985; Whitbread Biography Award, 1990. Memberships: Fellow, Royal Society of Literature; Society of Authors; PEN. Address The Mill House, Low Tharston, Norwich NR15 2YN, England.

THWAITE Anthony Simon, b. 23 June 1930, Chester, Cheshire, England. Poet; Critic; Writer; Editor. m. Ann Barbara Harrop, 4 August 1955, 4 daughters. Education: BA, 1955, MA, 1959, Christ Church, Oxford. Appointments: Visiting Lecturer in English, 1955-57, Japan Foundation Fellow, 1985-86, University of Tokyo; Producer, BBC, 1957-62; Literary Editor, The Listener, 1962-65, New Statesman, 1968-72; Assistant Professor of English, University of Libya, 1965-67; Henfield Writing Fellow, University of East Anglia, 1972; Co-Editor, Encounter, 1973-85; Visiting Professor, Kuwait University, 1974, Chairman of the Judges, Booker

Prize, 1986; Director, 1986-92, Editorial Consultant, 1992-95, André Deutsch, Ltd; Poet-in-Residence, Vanderbilt University, 1992. Publications: Poetry: Home Truths, 1957; The Owl in the Tree, 1963; The Stones of Emptiness, 1967; Inscriptions, 1973; New Confessions, 1974; A Portion for Foxes, 1977; Victorian Voices, 1980; Poems 1953-1983, 1984, enlarged edition as Poems 1953-1988, 1989; Letter from Tokyo, 1987; The Dust of the World, 1994; Selected Poems, 1956-1996, 1997; A Different Country, 2000. Other: Contemporary English Poetry, 1959; Japan (with Roloff Beny), 1968; The Deserts of Hesperides, 1969; Poetry Today, 1973, 3rd edition, revised and expanded, 1996; In Italy (with Roloff Beny and Peter Porter), 1974; Twentieth Century English Poetry, 1978; Odyssey: Mirror of the Mediterranean (with Roloff Beny), 1981; Six Centuries of Verse, 1984. Editor: The Penguin Book of Japanese Verse (with Geoffrey Bownas), 1964 revised and expanded, 1998; The English Poets (with Peter Porter), 1974; New Poetry 4 (with Fleur Adcock), 1978; Larkin at Sixty, 1982; Poetry 1945 to 1980 (with John Mole), 1983; Collected Poems of Philip Larkin, 1988; Selected Letters of Philip Larkin, 1992; Further requirements: Philip Larkin, 2001; A Move in the Weather, 2003; The Ruins of Time (Poetry of Place) (editor), 2006; Collected Poems, 2007. Honours: Richard Hillary Memorial Prize, 1968; Fellow, Royal Society of Literature, 1978; Cholmondeley Prize, 1983; Officer of the Order of the British Empire, 1990. Address: The Mill House, Low Tharston, Norfolk NR15 2YN, England.

TIJARDOVIĆ Ivica, b. 1 September 1960, Šibenik, Croatia. Shipmaster. 1 daughter. Education: Officer Certificate, Slovenia, 1980; Bachelor of Science, Navigation, Croatia, 1983; Master Mariner Certificate, Croatia, 1986; Master of Science, Technology of Transport, Croatia, 1989; Instructor for ARPA and Bridge Team Training, Norway, 1990; PhD (youngest with Shipmaster experience), Navigation, Naval Academy, Gdynia, Poland, 1994. Appointments: Sea experience: Cadet, 1979; Officer, 1981, Captain (youngest with MSc degree), 1990; Since 1998 has been sailing again as Captain (only Shipmaster with PhD); Supervisor of Commercial and Technical Management for vessels with the Shipbuilding Company of Split, Croatia, 1986-87; Assistant of Navigation, 1987, Lecturer in Navigation, 1990-98, Maritime Faculty, Split, Croatia; Assistant Professor of Navigation, 2000; Specialist for GPS and AIS receiver application in practice; Expert in Ship Stability, visited more than 200 vessels and met more than 350 Captains and Officers. Publications: More than 40 articles (over 100 pages) in Brown's Nautical Almanac (www.skipper.co.uk); Articles in Journal of Navigation (www.rin.org.uk); Articles in: Safety at Sea International, Solutions, Shiptalk.com, Fairplay, etc; The Simplest and Fastest Star Finder; Articles on the commercial and technical management of ships; 12 books for students in Croatia; 3 books for International Market: Draft Survey Book, Book of Differences in GPS Rhumbline Distances and Practical Ship Stability Book (www.iims.org.uk); Fully corrected the leading books of navigation and ship stability (over 4,000 pages). Honours: One of 3 captains nominated for Shipmaster of the Year 2004, Lloyd's List and Institute of Navigation, UK; Nominated again for Shipmaster of the Year 2005; IBC Awards: 2000 Outstanding Intellectuals of the 21st Century for 2005 (Honours List); International Professional for 2005; Lifetime Achievement Award; Honorary and Deputy Director General; Adviser to the Director General; The Da Vinci Diamond; The IBC Hall of Fame; Decree of Excellence; Great Lives of the 21st Century; The Excellence Award; Member, Order of International Fellowship; Member, International Order of Merit; Life Fellow, IBA; Lifetime Achievement Award and Vice President of the World

Congress of Arts, Sciences and Communications; Order of American Ambassadors, ABI; Marquis Who's Who in the World, 2007; According to USA Notice to Mariners, the Observer No 1 with the most acknowledged reports for Safety of Navigation, 1998-2003; Recognition for contributions to navigation from HRH The Duke of Edinburgh KG KT, 2004 (www.jadranbrod.com). Memberships: Fellow, Royal Institute of Navigation; Member, Nautical Institute, UK; Singer, 1st Tenor in Split, Croatia. E-mail: ivica.tijardovic@st.t-com.hr

TILAAR Henry Alexis Rudolf, b. 16 June 1932, Tondano, Indonesia. Professor. m. Martha, 2 sons, 2 daughters. Education: Diploma in Education A and B, Bandung, 1957, 1959; Master in Education, cum laude, University of Indonesia, 1961; Master of Science, 1966, Doctor of Education, 1969, Indiana University, USA. Appointments: Primary School Teacher, Secondary School Teacher, University Lecturer, 1952-64; Staff, National Planning Office, 1970-86; Assistant Minister for Human Resources Development, 1986-93; Professor of Education, Graduate School, State of University of Jakarta, 1986-. Publications: 200 articles on education and related science; 10 books. Honours: Medal of Grand Merit, Republic of Indonesia, 1998. Memberships: National Society for the Advancement of Social Sciences; Indonesian Educationalists Association; Indonesian National Research Council. Address: Jl Patra Kuningan Utara, Blok L-VII No 4, Jakarta Selatan 12950, Indonesia. Email: hartilaar@marthatilaar.net

TILAHUN Nega, b. 21 June 1975, Addis Ababa, Ethiopia. Agricultural Economics. m. Firewoini Mehari, 1 son. Education: BSc, Agricultural Economics, 1999; Postgraduate Diploma, Marketing of Services, 2003. Appointments: Development of local community in Ethiopia. Publications: Improving the marketing activities of youth persons towards effective livelihood; Simulators of general farm management in Excel spreadsheet; Study on the financial performance of dairy cows under improved management practices; Study on the economic performances of forage crops against crop production; Study on the procedures of micro financial institutions towards lending to the dairy sector. Memberships: Ethiopian Economic Association; Ethiopian Society of Animal Production. Address: PO Box 2803, Addis Ababa, Ethiopia.

TILLEKERATNE Herbert Walter, b. 5 March 1932, Kadugannawa, Sri Lanka. Educator. m. Elizabeth de S Gunasekera, 2 sons. Education: Specialist Science Trained Certificate, 1959; Advanced Science Trained Certificate, 1961; BSc, 1980; YMCA Secretarial Training Certificate, 1985; Asia YMCA Advanced Studies Certificate, 1985; Diploma in Business Management and Administration, 1988; MIPM, 1988; PhD, 2003. Appointments: Science Teacher, 1959; Science Lecturer, Teacher Training College, 1970; National Training Secretary, 1984; Admission to Sri Lanka Education Administrative Service, 1982; Vice-Principal, 1986, Acting Principal, 1988; Manager, Scientific Enterprise, 1989; Senior Consultant, Tertiary and Vocational Education Commission, 1991; Honorary Positions: Secretary, 1971, Vice-President, 1973, Sri Lanka Training Colleges Tutorial Staffs Union; Vice-President, Jathika Adyapana Sevaka Sangamaya, 1983; Vice-President, Colombo District Schools Football Association, 1987; Board Member, Mount Lavinia YMCA Board of Management, 1989; Director, Dehiwela YMCA, 1998; Chairman, Leadership Development Committee of the National Y, 1994; President, Sri Lanka Fellowship of YMCA Retirees, 1999; Secretary-Treasurer, South Asia Fellowship of YMCAR, 2000; President, SAFYR, 2001; Vice-Chairperson for South-SE Asia of the World Fellowship of YMCAR, 2003. Publications: Towards the Challenge of YMCA Mission (editor); Editor News Bulletins: Sapphire, Concern; Article: Sri Lanka Environment and Development. Honours: 21st Century Award for Achievement, International Illuminated Diploma of Honour, IBC, England; International Peace Prize, UCC, USA; Outstanding Intellectual of the 21st Century, IBC, England. Memberships: Membership and Extension Committee, NC/YMCAs, 1994; Development, Education and Projects Committee, 1994; Child Development Committee, 1994; Environment Concerns Committee, 1994; Personal and Conferences Committee, 1994. Address: 72/6 Chakkindarama Road, Ratmalana, Sri Lanka.

TIMPA FEWEL Vicki, b. 20 August 1955, Houston, Texas, USA. Registered Nurse. m. John Fewel, 1 son, 1 daughter. Education: BSc, Nursing, Texas Womans University, 1977; MSc, 1990; Nurse Practitioner Certificate, Board of Nursing Examiners, State of Texas, 1993. Appointments: Nurse, Registered Nurse, Research, ER and ICU, 1977-1990; Manager of Education, two Methodist Hospitals in Texas, 1993; Patient Education Co-ordinator and Continuing Medical Education Co-ordinator Nurse, 1994-. Publications: Small Calipher Bypass Grafts and LP, 1993; Plain Language, 1997. Honours: National lecture to VHA leaders and physicians, 1997; Great 100 Nurse, 1997; Contributed documented facts for US congressional legislation, 2003; Plank Award, 2003-05; Grant for Public Health VHA, 2007-08. Memberships: Sigma Theta Tau International Honor Society. Address: 1307 High Ridge Dr, Duncanville, TX 75137, USA. E-mail: vickiern7@netzero.net

TINDLE David, b. 29 April 1932, Huddersfield, Yorkshire, England. Education: Coventry School of Art. Career: Artist: Designed and painted set for Iolanta (Tchaikovsky), Aldeburgh Festival, 1988; Visiting Tutor, 1973-83, Fellow, 1981, Honorary Fellow, 1984, Royal College of Art; Ruskin Master of Drawing, St Edmund Hall, Oxford, 1985-87; Now lives and works in Italy; Numerous exhibitions in London and the provinces, 1952-, include: First one-man exhibition, London, 1953; regular one-man shows, Piccadilly Gallery, 1954-83; Hamburg Gallerie XX, 1974-85; Los Angeles and San Francisco, 1964; Bologna and Milan, 1968; One-man show, Fischer Fine Art, 1985, 1989, 1992; Redfern Gallery, London, 1994, 1996, 1998-99, 2000, 2001, 2003, 2005, 2007; St Edmund Hall, Oxford, 1994; The Shire Hall Gallery, Stafford, 1994; Numerous group exhibitions and international biennales in Europe; Works in many public and private collections including the Tate Gallery, National Portrait Gallery. Honours: Elected Associate of the Royal Academy (ARA), 1973; Elected Full Royal Academician (RA), 1979; Honorary Fellow, St Edmund Hall, Oxford, 1988-; Honorary Member, Birmingham Society of Artists; Honorary MA, St Edmund Hall, Oxford, 1985; RA Johnson Wax Award, 1983; Listed in Who's Who publications and biographical dictionaries. Address: Via C Barsotti 194, S. Maria del Giudice, 55058 Lucca, Italy.

TINDLE Lily Elizabeth (née Baker), b. 31 March 1939, Hebburn-on-Tyne, Co Durham, England. Psychologist. m. Robert William Tindle, 1 son, 1 daughter. Education: Eastbourne Training College, University of London, Institute of Education, 1957-59; University of South Australia, Diploma of Teaching, University of Adelaide, 1964-75; Bachelor of Arts, Postgraduate Diploma in Applied Psychology, Queensland University of Technology, 1993-99; Doctor of Education. Appointments: PE and Geography Teacher, Coates Endowed Secondary School, Northumberland, 1959-63; Sport and PE Teacher, Woodville High School, 1963-70; Counsellor, Education Department,

SA, 1970-75; Counselling Psychologist, Adelaide University, South Australia, 1975-76; Research Assistant, Charles Darwin Research Station, Galapagos Islands, 1976-79; Research Officer/Lecturer, Paisley University, Scotland; Counselling Psychologist, South Dorset Technical College, 1983-85; Lecturer, Crawley College of Technology, 1985-87; Research Officer, Griffith University, 1988-89; Tutor, Faculty of Education, University of Queensland, 1987-89; Psychologist, Queensland University of Technology, 1989-. Publications: Many articles and papers in professional journals. Honours: Associate Fellow, British Psychological Society; Fellow, Australian Psychological Society; Evaluator of Supervision; Psychologists' Registration Board; Chair, APS College of Counselling Psychologists; Queensland Office on the Status of Women; Trailblazer Award, 1999. Memberships: British Psychological Society; Australian Psychological Society; APS College of Counselling Psychologists; British Association of Behavioural and Cognitive BABCP Psychotherapists; Australian Association of Clinical Psychologists; Registered Psychologist, Queensland Health Board; Registered Teacher. Address: 14 Cranwood Street, Kenmore, Queensland, 4069, Australia. E-mail: e.tindle@qut.com

TINSLEY Pauline, b. 27 March 1928, Wigan, England. Singer (Soprano). m. George M Neighbour, 1 son, 1 daughter. Education: Northern School of Music, Manchester, LRAM, 1949; Opera School, London; Further study with Eva Turner and Eduardo Asquez. Career: Professional engagements in the United Kingdom from 1961 include: London debut as Desdemona in Rossini's Otello; Leading roles in Verdi's I Masnadieri, Ernani, Il Corsaro and Bellini's Il Pirata; Welsh National Opera from 1962 as: Susanna, Elsa, Lady Macbeth, Sinaide (Rossini's Moses), Abigaille, Aida, Tosca, Turandot, Kostelnicka (Jenufa), Elektra and Dyer's Wife (Frau Ohne Schatten), 1981; Sadler's Wells/English National Opera from 1963 as: Gilda, Elvira (Ernani), Fiordiligi, Queen of Night, Countess, Donna Elvira (Don Giovanni), Beethoven's Leonore and Fidelio, Leonora (Force of Destiny), Elizabeth (Mary Stuart), 1973; Mother/Witch (Hansel and Gretel), 1987, Kabanicha (Katya Kabanova), 1989; Covent Garden from 1965 as: Overseer (Elektra), Amelia (Ballo in Maschera), 1971, Helmwige and 3rd Norn (The Ring), Santuzza, 1976; Mere Marie (Carmelites), 1983; Lady Billows (Albert Herring), 1989; Various roles with Scottish Opera including Kostelnicka and with Opera North (Fata Morgana in Love for 3 Oranges) and with Handel Opera Society; From 1966 performed abroad in Germany, Netherlands, Italy, USA, Canada, Sweden, Czechoslovakia, Spain, Belgium and Ireland (including The Witch in Humperdinck's Königskinder and Lady Jowler in Nicholas Maw's The Rising of the Moon); Latest performances include: Lady Billows at Garsington, 1996, Mrs Grose in Britten's The Turn of the Screw, Cincinnati, 1999 and Grandmother Burya in Jenufa for Opera North, 1995 and 2002 and for Netherlands Opera, 1997 and 2001; Many concerts, recitals, broadcasts and television operas. Recordings include: Elektra in Mozart's Idomeneo.

TIRIMO Martino, b. 19 December 1942, Larnaca, Cyprus. Concert Pianist; Conductor. m. Mione J Teakle, 1973, 1 son, 1 daughter. Education: Royal Academy of Music, London; Vienna State Academy. Debut: Recital, Cyprus, 1949. Career: Conducted La Traviata 7 times at Italian Opera Festival, Cyprus, 1955; London debut, 1965; Concerto performances with most major orchestras, and recitals, TV and radio appearances in Britain, Europe, USA, Canada, South Africa and the Far East from 1965; Gave public premiére of complete Schubert Sonatas, London, 1975, 1985; Public premiére of Beethoven concertos directing from the keyboard, Dresden and London, 1985, 1986; Gave several premiéres of Tippett Piano concerto since 1986; Four series of performances of complete Beethoven piano sonatas, 2000; Two series devoted to the major piano works of Robert and Clara Schumann, 2001; Six-concert series devoted to the major piano works of Chopin, 2002; Founded Rosamunde Trio 2002; Professor, Trinity College of Music, 2003-; Performed at special Athens Festival during Olympic period with Vienna Philharmonic in 2004; Mozart complete solo piano works in 8 concerts, London's Cadogan Hall, 2006. Compositions include: film score for the Odyssey in 8 episodes for Channel 4 TV, 1998. Recordings: Brahms Piano Concertos; Chopin Concertos; Tippett Piano Concerto (with composer conducting); Rachmaninov Concertos; Complete Mozart piano works; Complete Debussy piano works; Complete Janacek piano works; Complete Schubert Piano Sonatas; Various other solo recordings with mixed repertoire. Publications: Schubert: The Complete Piano Sonatas, 3 volumes, edited for Wiener Unitext Edition (with own completions to the unfinished movements), 1997-99. Honours: Gold Medal, Associated Board of the Royal Schools of Music; Liszt Scholarship, Royal Academy of Music; 11 other Prizes at Royal Academy of Music including Macfarren Medal; Boise Foundation Scholarship, 1965; Gulbenkian Foundation Scholarship, 1967-69; Joint Winner, Munich International Competition, 1971; Winner, Geneva International Competition, 1972; ARAM, 1968; FRAM, 1979; FRSAMD, 2005; Silver Disc, 1988; Gold Disc, 1994; Ran with the Olympic Torch, 2004. Memberships: ISM, 2005. Address: 1 Romeyn Road, London SW16 2NU, England. E-mail: martino@tirimo.fslife.co.uk

TISCH Johannes Hermann, b. 11 December 1929, Austria. (Swiss and Australian citizen). University Professor; Educator; Justice of the Peace. m. Regula B C Wackernagel, 12 April 1957, 2 sons, 2 daughters. Education: University of Basle, Switzerland, 1949-53; University of Oxford, England, 1953-54; First Recipient of J Fenimore Cooper Fellowship; University of Göttingen, Germany, 1954-55; MA, PhD, University of Basle, 1961. Appointments include: Lecturer, German, University of Oxford, England, 1957-60; Lecturer, Australian National University, 1961-63; Senior Lecturer, Deputy Head, University of Sydney, 1964-65; Foundation Professor, Joint Head, Modern Languages Department, University of Tasmania, 1966-92; Visiting Professor, University of Pittsburgh, USA, 1970; Comparative Literature School, La Nouvelle Sorbonne, Paris, France, 1973-74; Professor Emeritus; Honorary Research Associate, 1993-98; Honorary Consul for Switzerland, 1966-99; Dean, Consular Corps, 1981-84. Publications include: Over 100 articles in professional journals; Books include: Andrean Gryphius: Leo Arminius, 1968; Renaissance and Rococo, 1973; The Italian Novella and German Humanism, 1984; The Red Cross and Modern Switzerland, 1987; Hrafnkels Saga - A Reappraisal, 1995; Samson Agonistes and Milton's Ideas of Worldly and Religious Immortality, 1984; Essays in Comparative Literature, 2003; Advisory Contributor, Kindlers Literatur/Lexikon, Munich. Honours include: Knight of Order of St Lazarus; PhD, Marquis Giuseppe Scicluna International University Foundation, USA; DSc (HC), Peace Studies, Albert Einstein Academy with Bronze Medal for Peace; Ambassador at Large, Honorary Deputy Governor, ABI; Honorary Deputy Director General, IBC, Cambridge; G Marconi Medal, Civic Merit; American Medal of Honor, ABI; Medal of Honour, IBC; Commander of Merit, former Herald, now Archivist, Order of St Lazarus of Jerusalem. Memberships include: Australian College of Education; Life Patron, IBA; Life Member, Royal Commonwealth Society and University Staff Club; Board, Hutchins Foundation; Committee, Australian Institute of

Directors; Tasmanian Director of NAATI; Level IV Advisor; Life Member, University Staff Club; Inaugural Member of Tasmanian Ministerial Advisory Council on Multicultural and Ethnic Affairs, 1992-95; Life Fellow, World Literary Academy; Baden Powell Society; Life Member, Modern Language Association of America; Research Committee, ILCA, 1970-80; Hobart City Mission; Partnership Member, St John Ambulance, Australia; Faculty Member, Australian Roundtable Fellowship Inc; Friends of Christian Medical College and Hospital, Vellore. Address: 1 Cedar Court, Sandy Bay, Hobart, Tas 7005, Australia.

TITCHMARSH Alan Fred, b. 2 May 1949, Ilkley, England. Gardener; Writer; Broadcaster. m. Alison Margaret Needs, 1975, 2 daughters. Education: Shipley Art and Technical Institute, 1964-68; National Certificate in Horticulture, Hertfordshire College of Agriculture and Horticulture, 1968-69; Diploma in Horticulture, Royal Botanic Gardens, Kew, 1969-1972. Appointments include: Apprentice Gardener, Parks Department, Ilkley, Urban District Council, 1964-68; Supervisor, Staff Training, Royal Botanic Gardens, Kew, 1972-74; Assistant Gardening Editor, Hamlyn Publishing, 1974-76; Assistant then Deputy Editor, Amateur Gardening, 1976-79; Freelance Writer and Broadcaster, 1979-; Contributor to: Daily Express; Sunday Express; Radio Times; BBC Gardeners' World Magazine; Many radio and television programmes including: Breakfast Time, Songs of Praise; Points of View; Pebble Mill; Gardeners' World; Ground Force; BBC Proms; British Isles, a Natural History; How to Be a Gardener; Royal Gardeners; 20th Century Roadshow; Vice-President, Wessex Cancer Trust, 1988-; Patron, Vice Patron, President and Vice President of numerous charitable organisations; Ambassador, The Prince's Trust; Honorary Patron of the Friends, Castle of Mey; Trustee, National Maritime Museum. Publications: More than 40 books including: Mr MacGregor (novel), 1998; The Last Lighthouse Keeper (novel), 1999; Animal Instincts (novel), 2000; Only Dad (novel), 2001; How to Be a Gardener, 2002; Trowel and Error (memoirs), 2002; Royal Gardeners, 2003; Rosie (novel), 2004; Fill My Stocking (Christmas anthology), 2005; The Gardener's Year, 2005. Honours: Freeman, City of London; RHS Gold Medal, Chelsea Flower Show, 1985; Yorkshire Man of Year, 1997; Hon DSc, Bradford, 1999; Hon DUniv, Essex, 1999, Leeds Metropolitan, 2003; Variety Club Television Personality of the Year, 1999; MBE, 2000. Deputy Lieutenant, Hampshire, 2001; Victoria Medal of Honour, Royal Horticultural Society, 2004. Memberships: Royal Horticultural Society; Garden Writers Guild; Fellow, Institute of Horticulture; Fellow, City & Guilds of London Institute; Worshipful Company of Gardeners; Royal London Yacht Club; Lord's Taverners. Address: c/o Caroline Mitchell, Colt Hill House, Colt Hill, Odiham, Hampshire RG29 1AL, England.

TITORENKO Vladimir Efimovich, b. 6 August 1958, Moscow, Russia. Diplomat. m. Irina, 2 sons, 1 daughter. Education: Foreign Affairs, Moscow State Institute of Foreign Relations. Appointments: Minister-Counsellor, Russian Embassy in Iraq, 1994-99; Deputy Director, MFA of Russia, 1999-2002; Ambassador of Russia in Iraq, 2002-03; Ambassador at Large, MFA of Russia, 2003-04; Ambassador of Russia in Algeria, 2004-. Publications: Monograph, Foreign Relations of Egypt after Nasser (1970-1993), 1994; More than 40 articles and publications on peace process in the Middle East, Islamic Fundamentalism, Arab Gulf, Egypt, Iraq, etc. Honours: Order of Courage; Order of St Nickolas (for military merits); Honorary Executive, MFA of Russia. Address: 7 Chemin du Prince d'Annam, El-Biar, Algiers, Algeria. E-mail: ambrussie@yandex.ru

TJHIN Wei Foen Dorcas, b. 30 June 1951, Bandung, Indonesia. Voice Educator; Choral Conductor. m. Benny Soenarjo, 3 sons. Education: Certificate, Department of Economics, Parahyangan Catholic University, Bandung, 1978; Certified Choral Conductor, Toronto Children's Chorus, 4th International, Canada, 1997; Certificate of Achievement, Des Moines International Choral, 1999; Grade 5 Theory of Music, Grade 8 Singing, ABRSM; Singapore Bible College, Department of Church Music, 2003. Publications: Voice Building Series (Beginner, Intermediate and Advanced); Before You Start a Children's Choir. Honours: Listed in international biographical dictionaries; Who's Who in the World, 2007. Memberships: World Association of Chinese Youth Choir; American Choral Directors Association; International Federation for Choral Music; Choristers Guild. Address: Setra Duta Lestari 33, Block E2/21, Bandung 40151, West Java, Indonesia. E-mail: benjo@bdg.centrin.net.id

TLÁSKAL Tomáš, b. 2 April 1950, Prague, Czech Republic. Paediatric Cardiac Surgeon. m. Květa Laurinová, 1 daughter. Education: MD, Charles University, Prague, 1974; General Surgery Diploma, 1978, Cardiac Surgery Diploma, 1984, Institute for Postgraduate Medical Education, Prague; CSc, PhD, Medicine, 1991, Associated Professor of Surgery Diploma, 1997, Professor of Surgery Diploma, 2007, Charles University, Prague; Fellow, European Board of Thoracic and Cardiovascular Surgery Diploma, 1998. Appointments: Senior House Officer, Hospital Novy Bydzov, 1974-76; Senior House Officer, 1976-1978, Senior Registrar, 1979-84, Staff Cardiac Surgeon, 1985-90, Consultant Paediatric Cardiac Surgeon and Deputy Chief, 1991-2004, Kardiocentrum, University Hospital Motol, Prague; Consultant Paediatric Cardiac Surgeon, Cardiocentro, Hospital W Soller, Havana, Cuba, 1987-88; Teacher, 2nd School of Medicine, Charles University, 1992-; Associate Professor of Surgery, 1997-, Professor of Surgery, 2007-, Charles University, Prague; Associate Professor of Surgery, 1999-, Professor of Surgery, 2007, Institute of Postgraduate Education in Medicine; Consultant, Institute for Mother and Child Care, 1998-; Head of Department of Paediatric Cardiac Surgery, Kardiocentrum, University Hospital Motol, Prague and Charles University, 2nd School of Medicine, Prague, 2004-; Professor of Surgery, Charles University, Prague, 2007-. Publications: Over 100 articles published in professional journals. Honour: Fellow of the Research Board, American Biographical Institute, Raleigh, USA. Memberships: Association for European Paediatric Cardiology; European Association for Cardio-Thoracic Surgery; Czech Medical Society; Czech Society of Cardiology; Czech Society of Cardiovascular Surgery; Czech Paediatric Society; Czech Society of Paediatric Surgery; Czech Society of Surgery; Movement for Life (Czech Republic); International Society of Cardio-Thoracic Surgeons; CTS Net; World Society for Pediatric and Congenital Heart Surgery. Address: Nad Palatou 3, 150 00 Prague 5, Czech Republic. E-mail: tomas.tlaskal@lfmotol.cuni.cz Websites: www.ctsnet.org/home/ttlaskal; www.myprofile.cos.com/ttlaskal.

TOBACH Ethel, b. 7 November 1921, Miaskovka, USSR (moved to USA 1923). Psychologist; Curator Emerita. m. Charles Tobach, deceased 1969. Education: Hunter College; New York University. Appointments: Research Fellow, 1958-61, Associate Curator, 1964-69, Curator, 1969-87, Curator Emerita, 1990-, American Museum of Natural History; Research Fellow, New York University, 1961-64; Professor of Psychology, CUNY, 1964-. Publications: Co-Editor, Genes and Gender series, 1978-96; Editor, International Journal of Comparative Psychology, 1987-93; Books: Challenging Racism and Sexism, 1994; Behavior

Development – Concept of Integrative Levels, 1995; Book chapters: Understanding Rape, in Evolution, Gender and Rape, 2003; Studying Animals in Zoos and Aquariums, in Encylopedia of Animal Behavior, 2004. Memberships: Fellow, American Psychology Association; International Society of Comparative Psychology; New York Academy of Sciences; Eastern Psychology Association. Address: American Museum of Natural History, Central Parkway at 79th Street, New York, NY 10024-5192, USA.

TOBIAS Edward Spencer, b. 13 December 1965, Paisley, Scotland. Clinician; Scientist. m. Ruth Tobias. Education: BSc (1st Class Honours), Molecular Biology, 1987; MBChB with Commendation, 1990; MRCP UK (Royal College of Physicians UK), 1993; PhD, Biochemistry and Molecular Biology, 1997, University of Glasgow; CCST in Medical Genetics, 2001; FRCP, Royal College of Physicians and Surgeons, Glasgow, 2004. Appointments include: Senior House Officer, Glasgow Western/Gartnavel Hospitals General Medical Rotation, 1991-93; MRC Training Fellow, Division of Biochemistry and Molecular Biology, University of Glasgow, 1993-96; Clinical Research Scientist, Cancer Genetics Laboratory, Beatson Institute for Cancer Research, 1996-97; Specialist Registrar in Medical Genetics, Duncan Guthrie Institute of Medical Genetics, Yorkhill Hospital, Glasgow, 1997-2001; GlaxoSmithKline Clinical Research Fellow, University of Glasgow, 2001-07; Currently: Clinical Senior Lecturer, University of Glasgow; Honorary Consultant in Medical Genetics, Yorkhill Hospital, Glasgow; Discovered the TES gene on human chromosome 7. Publications: Articles in medical journals as first author and co-author include most recently: Gastric carcinoid: germline and somatic mutation of the neurofibromatosis type 1 gene, 2007; COL2A1-related skeletal dysplasias with predominant metaphyseal involvement, 2007; The M531 mutation in CDKN2A is a founder mutation that predominates in melanoma patients with Scottish ancestry, 2007; Selected book chapter: The Molecular Biology of Cancer, 2006, in Principles and Practice of Medical Genetics, 5th Edition. Honours: MRC Training Fellowship, 1993; Glaxo Wellcome Clinical Research Fellowship, 2001. Memberships: British Society for Human Genetics; Cancer Genetics Group (UK); British Association for Cancer Research; European Association for Cancer Research; Glasgow Southern Medical Society; Royal Medico-Chirurgical Society of Glasgow; British Medical Association; The Royal Philosophical Society of Glasgow. Address: Section of Medical Genetics, Division of Developmental Medicine, University of Glasgow, Yorkhill Hospital, Glasgow G3 8SJ, Scotland. E-mail: gbcv55@udcf.gla.ac.uk

TOBIAS Phillip Vallentine, b. 14 October 1925, Durban, Natal, South Africa. Retired University Professor. Education: BSc, 1946, BSc Hons, 1947, MBBCh, 1950, PhD, 1953, DSc, 1967, University of Witwatersrand, Johannesburg. Appointments: Lecturer, 1951-52, Senior Lecturer, 1953-58, Professor, 1959-93, Head of Department, 1959-90, Dean of Faculty of Medicine, 1980-82, Member of Council, 1971-74, 1975-84, Professor Emeritus, 1994-; Honorary Professorial Research Fellow, 1994-, School of Anatomical Sciences, University of Witwatersrand; Past Chairman, Kalahari Research Committee; Past Director, Palaeo-Anthropology Research Unit; Past Director, Sterkfontein Research Unit; Past President, International Association of Human Biologists; Former President, Royal Society of South Africa; Founder and Sometime President, Institute for the Study of Mankind in Africa, Anatomical Society of Southern Africa, South African Society for Quaternary Research; Former President, South African Science Writers Association. Publications: Over 1160 including 40 books, 90 chapters in books; Notable works Chromosomes, sex cells and evolution in a mammal, 1956; Australopithecus boisei, 1967; The Bushmen, San Hunters and Herders of the Kalahari, 1978; Hominid Evolution Past Present and Future, 1985; The Brain in Hominid Evolution, 1971; Man's Anatomy, 1963-88; The Meaning of Race, 1961-72; Homo habilis, 1991; Humanity from African Naissance to Coming Millennia, 2001; Into the Past, 2005. Honours: Rivers Memorial Medal, 1978; Balzan Prize, 1987; LSB Leakey Prize, 1991; Carmel Award of Merit, 1992; Order of Meritorious Service of South Africa, 1992; Fellow of the Royal Society London, 1996; Charles Darwin Lifetime Achievement Award, 1997; Commander of the National Order of Merit of France, 1998; Order of the Southern Cross of South Africa, 1999; Hrdlicka Medal, 1999; Commander of the Order of Merit of Italy, 2000; UNESCO Medal, 2001; ISMS Medal, 2001; Honorary Cross for Science and Arts, First Class, Austrian Federal Government, 2002; Fellowship Art and Science of Medicine Gold Medal, 2007; Walter Sisulu Special Award, City of Johannesburg, 2007. Memberships: Academy of Science of South Africa; Royal Society, London; Royal Society of South Africa; South African Medical Association; South African Archaeological Society; American Association of Physical Anthropologists; National Academy of Sciences, USA; American Philosophical Society; American Academy of Arts and Sciences; American Anthropological Association; Royal Anthropological Institute of Great Britain and Ireland; Royal College of Physicians, London; Linnean Society, London; South African Institute of Race Relations; Anatomical Society of Southern Africa; Anatomical Societies (hon) of USA, Great Britain and Ireland, Canada, Israel; South African Dental Association (hon). Address: School of Anatomical Sciences, University of the Witwatersrand Medical School, 7 York Road, Parktown, Wits 2050, Johannesburg, South Africa. E-mail: phillip.tobias@wits.ac.za

TOMALIN Claire, b. 20 June 1933, London, England. Author. m. (1) Nicholas Osborne Tomalin, deceased 1973, 2 sons (1 deceased), 3 daughters (1 deceased), (2) Michael Frayn, 1993. Education: MA, Newnham College, Cambridge, 1954. Appointment: Literary Editor, New Statesman, 1974-77; Literary Editor, The Sunday Times, London, 1979-86. Publications: The Life and Death of Mary Wollstonecroft, 1974; Shelley and His World, 1980; Parents and Children, 1981; Katherine Mansfield: A Secret Life, 1987; The Invisible Woman: The Story of Nelly Teran and Charles Dickens, 1990; The Winter Wife, 1991; Mrs Jordan's Professions, 1994; Jane Austin: A Life, 1997; Maurice by Mary Shelley, 1998; Several Strangers: writing from three decades, 1999; Samuel Pepys: The Unequalled Self, 2002; Thomas Hardy: The Time-Torn Man, 2006; Exhibitions: Mrs Jordan, English Heritage Kenwood, 1995; Hyenas in Petticoats: Mary Wollstonecraft and Mary Shelley, Wordsworth Trust and National Portrait Gallery, 1997-98; Play: The Winter Wife, 1991. Honours: Whitbread First Book Prize, 1974; James Tait Black Memorial Prize, 1990; Hawthornden Prize, 1991; NCR Prize, 1991; Los Angeles Times Book Prize, 2002; Whitbread Biography Award, 2002; Whitbread Book of the Year, 2002; British Book Awards Biography of the Year (shortlist), 2003; Samuel Pepys Award, 2003; British Book Awards Biography of the Year (shortlist), 2007. Membership: PEN, Vice-president, 1998; Member, London Library Committee, 1997-2000; Advisory Committee for the Arts, Humanities and Social Sciences, British Library, 1997-; Council, Royal Society of Literature, 1997-2000. Address: 57 Gloucester Crescent, London NW1 7EG, England. E-mail: clairetomalin@dial.pipex.com

TOMESCU Ioan, b. 5 November 1942, Ploieşti, Romania. Professor of Computer Science. m. Marioara Tomescu, 1 son, 1 daughter. Education: BA (Hons), Computer Science and Mathematics, 1965, PhD, Computer Science, 1971, Bucharest University, Romania. Appointments: Assistant Professor, 1965-72, Senior Lecturer, 1972-90, Professor, 1990-, Department of Computer Science, Bucharest University, Romania; Visiting Professor: The University of Tirana, Albania, 1974, Auckland University, New Zealand, 1995; School of Mathematical Sciences, G C University, Lahore, Pakistan, 2005-08; Visiting Senior Research Fellow, National University of Singapore, 2002. Publications: About 125 research papers in combinatorics and graph theory published in scientific journals including: Discrete Mathematics; Journal of Combinatorial Theory (B); Combinatorica; Journal of Graph Theory; Theoretical Computer Science (A); Introduction to Combinatorics; Colette's, London and Wellingborough; Problems in Combinatorics and Graph Theory, J Wiley, New York. Honours: Prize for Applied Mathematics, First Balkan Mathematics Competition for Young Researchers, Bucharest, 1971; Gheorghe Tzitzeica Mathematics Prize, Romanian Academy, 1975. Memberships: American Mathematical Society; Honorary President, Romanian Mathematical Society; Corresponding Member, Romanian Academy. Address: Sos Colentina nr 4, Sc B, Ap. 64, 021173 Bucharest, Romania. E-mail: ioan@fmi.unibuc.ro

TOMLINSON, Hon Mr Justice, Hon Sir Stephen Miles, b. 29 March 1952, Wolverhampton, England. Justice of the High Court. m. Joanna Greig, 1 son, 1 daughter. Education: Scholar, Worcester College, Oxford; Eldon Law Scholar, MA; Called to the Bar, Inner Temple, 1974. Appointments: Barrister in practice, 1975-2000; QC, 1988; A Recorder of the Crown Court, 1995-2000; Judge of the High Court of Justice, 2000. Honour: Knighted, 2000. Address: Royal Courts of Justice, Strand, London WC1A 2LL, England.

TONKOVICH Teresa Zenovia Maria, b. 30 July 1952, Toronto, Canada. Institutional Administrator. m. John Tonkovich, deceased, 2 sons, 2 daughters. Education: BA, Psychology and Sociology, University of Toronto, Ontario; Certified Administrator, Homes for the Aged, McMaster University, Hamilton, Ontario. Appointments: Executive Administrator, Ivan Franko Home (Ukrainian Home for the Aged), Mississauga, Ontario. Honours: 2000 Notable American Women; Personalities of the Americas; International Leaders in Achievement; Community Leaders in Achievement; Personalities of America; Directory of Distinguished Americans; 5000 Personalities of the World; International Book of Honour; Community Leader of America; Canadian Merit Award; Outstanding Young Woman of '78; International Who's Who of Business Women; Lifetime Deputy Governor, ABI. Memberships: Ontario Gerontological Association; Canadian Association of Gerontology; Ukrainian Pensioners' Club. Address: 3584 Cherrington Cres, Mississauga, Ontario L5L 5C5, Canada. E-mail: tzmtonkovich@hotmail.com

TOOVEY Stephen, b. 29 November 1953, London, England. Physician. m. Linda, 1 daughter. Education: MB BCh, University of the Witwatersrand, 1978; Certified in Clinical Tropical Medicine and Travellers' Health, American Association of Tropical Medicine and Hygiene; PhD, University of Ghent, 2006. Appointments: Clinical Consultant, Tropix Healthcare Ltd; Tutor, Royal Free Medical School, London; Managing Director, SAA-Netcare Travel Clinics; Managing Director, British Airways Travel Clinics, South Africa; International Medical Leader for avian and pandemic influenza, F Hoffman–La Roche, Switzerland. Publications: 89 articles in professional journals. Honours: Kurt Gilles Memorial Award in Psychiatry; Roche Gold Olympian Award. Memberships: Fellow, Australasian College of Tropical Medicine; Fellow, Faculty of Travel Medicine; American Society of Tropical Medicine and Hygiene; International Society of Travel Medicine. Address: Burggartenstrasse 32, Bottmingen, CH-4103, Switzerland.

TOPOLSKI Daniel, b. 4 June 1945, London, England. Freelance Writer; Broadcaster; Photojournalist. m. Susan Gilbert, 1 son, 2 daughters. Education: Lycée Français, London; Westminster School; BA, Geography, 1967, DipSoc, Anthropology, 1968, MA, 1970, New College, Oxford. Appointments: Writer and TV broadcaster on travel and sport; BBC TV Researcher and Producer, 1969-73; TV and Radio Presenter and Commentator, 1982-; Expeditions: Brazil, 1963; Iran (Marco Polo), 1973-74; Travel in Africa, North and South America, India, Himalayas, China, Middle East, SE Asia, and Australia. Publications: Muzungu: One Man's Africa, 1976; Travels with my Father: Journey through South America, 1983; Boat Race, 1985; True Blue (made into feature film, 1996), 1989; Henley: the Regatta, 1989; Numerous articles in professional and popular journals. Honours: Rowing Competitor: Boat Race, Oxford, 1967, 1968; World Championships, 1969-78 (Gold Medal, 1977); 4 victories, Henley Regatta; Rowing Coach of Oxford Boat Race Crew, 1973-87 (12 victories, record 10 in a row); Coached World Championships and Olympics, 1979, 1982, 1984; Churchill Fellow, 1980; Sports Book of the Year (True Blue), 1991; Radio Travel Programme of the Year Award for Topolski's Travels, 1993. Memberships: Churchill Fellow; Henley Steward; Leander Club; London RC. Address: 69 Randolph Avenue, London W9 1DW, England.

TOPORKOV Victor Vasilievich, b. 24 September 1956, Lepel, Vitebsk, Belarus. Computer Scientist. m. Anna S Anikushina. Education: Graduate, 1979, PhD, 1985, Doctor of Technical Sciences, 2000, Moscow Power Engineering Institute. Appointments: Researcher, Moscow Power Engineering Institute, 1979-1987; Head of Laboratory, Ministry of Aviation Industry, Moscow, 1987-96; Head of Computer Science Department, Moscow Power Engineering Institute, 1996-; Federal Expert, Ministry of Education and Science, Russia, 2005-. Publications: Books: Behavioural Synthesis of Systems, 2001; Models of Distributed Computations, 2004; Models of Distributed Congratulations, 2004; Choice of a Target Architecture and Strategies for Resource Allocation in Computer Systems, 2004; Articles to professional journals including: Journal of Computer and Systems Sciences International; Programming and Computer Software; Automation and Remote Control; Automatic Control and Computer Sciences. Honours: Senior Researcher, High Attestation Commission, 1990-; Professor, Ministry of Education, Russia, 2001-. Membership: Russian Academy of Electrotechnical Sciences. Address: Moscow Power Engineering Institute, ul. Krasnokazarmennaya 14, Moscow, 111250, Russia. E-mail: toporkovvv@mpei.ru Website: http://www.mpei.ru/vt.mpei.ac.ru

TORAN Felix, b. 6 March 1973, Valencia, Spain. Engineer. m. Silvia Bernabeu, 1 daughter. Education: MSc, 1999, European PhD, 2007, Electrical Engineering, University of Valencia, Spain. Appointments: IT Engineer, AIMME (Metal-Mechanics Institute), Spain, 1999; Software Engineer, European Feder Projects, ATSA, Spain, 1999; Electrical Engineer, ITE (Electrical Technology Institute), Spain, 2000; System Engineer, European Space Agency, Toulouse,

France, 2000-. Publications: Over 100 technical publications; 10 book chapters of international book, EGNOS – A Cornerstone to Galileo. Honours: European Space Agency Award for Outstanding Performance, 2002; Salva I Campillo Telecommunications International Award for Most Original Project, 2004; US Institute of Navigation Best Presentation Award, 2001, 2006; Listed in international biographical dictionaries. Memberships: IEEE; ION; Rotary International (President Elect, Rotary E-Club of Latinoamerica). E-mail: ftoran@esa.int

TORO-HARDY Alfredo, b. 22 May 1950, Caracas, Venezuela. Ambassador. m. (1) 2 sons, 1 daughter, (2) Gabriela Gaxiola. Education: Lawyer, Central University of Venezuela, Caracas, 1973; Diploma in Public Administration, Institut International d'Administration Publique (Ecole National d'Administration), Paris, France, 1974; Attestation in Comparative Petroleum Law, University of Paris II, Institute of Comparative Law, Paris, France, 1974; Magister Scientiarum, International Trade Law, Central University of Venezuela, 1977; Legum Magister, Corporate Law, University of Pennsylvania Law School – Wharton School, Philadelphia, USA, 1979. Appointments include: Assistant to the Director of Petroleum Energy, Ministry of Energy and Mines, Caracas, 1975-76; Joint Legal Advisor, International Trade Institute, Caracas, 1976-77; Director, Centre for North American Studies and Co-ordinator of Institute for Higher Latin American Studies, Simon Bolivar University, Caracas, 1989-91; Director, "Pedro Gual" Institute for Higher Diplomatic Studies, Foreign Affairs Ministry, 1992-94; Ambassador to Brazil, 1994-97; Ambassador to Chile, 1997-99; Non-resident Ambassador to the Commonwealth of the Bahamas, 2000-2001; Ambassador to the White House, Washington DC, 1999-2001; Ambassador to the Court of St James's, London, 2001-; Concurrently, Non Resident Ambassador to the Republic of Ireland, 2002-. Publications: Author of 16 books including: The Age of Villages: The small village vs the global village, 2002; Irak y la Reconfiguración del Orden Mundial, 2003; Tiene Futuro América Latina, 2004; Hegemonia e Imperio, 2007; Co-author of 11 books; Numerous articles in academic magazines including: Cambridge Review of International Affairs (UK); Politica Externa (Brazil); Revista del Parliamento Latinoamericano (Latin America). Honours: Several Venezuelan and foreign decorations. Memberships include: Royal Institute for International Affairs, UK; Windsor Energy Group, UK; The Chairmans Club, UK; Global Dimensions, UK; Comisión Interamericana de Justicia y Paz, Chile; Fundación de Estudios del Futuro, Caracas, Venezuela; Asociación Política Internacional, Caracas, Venezuela. E-mail: alfredotorohardy@hotmail.com

TORPHICHEN The Rt Hon Lady (Pamela Mary), b. 11 July 1926, Middlesex, England. Musician; Composer. m. (1) Thomas Philip Hodson Pressinger, deceased 1961, 1 son, 1 daughter, (2) James Bruce Sandilands, 14th Lord Torphichen, deceased 1975. Education: Old Palace Convent, Mayfield; LRAM, Royal College of Music, London, 1940-43. Appointments: Nurse, The Red Cross & VAD, Royal Navy, 1944-46; elected Borough Councillor for Hampstead, Conservative Party, 1949-52; Honorary Secretary, The Catholic Prisoners Aid Society, 1961-65; Honorary Secretary, The Wiseman Society, 1965-75; President, The Ladies of Charity of St Vincent de Paul, Westminster, 1975-. Publications: Various musical compositions for piano, 1976-2000. Honours: Catholic Woman of the Year, 1996; Companion of the Sovereign Military Order of Malta, Delegation of Scotland, 1990. Memberships: Catholic Union of Great Britain; Latin Mass Society; The Ladies of Charity of St Vincent de Paul;

The European-Atlantic Group, Ladies Committee; The Turf Club, Lady Associate Member; Aid to the Church in Need; British Academy of Composers & Songwriters. Address: 69 Cornwall Gardens, London SW7, England.

TORRANCE Sam, b. 24 August 1953, Largs, Scotland. Golfer. m. Suzanne, 1 son, 2 daughters. Appointments: Professional Golfer, 1970-; Has played in 8 Ryder Cups and represented Scotland on numerous occasions; Winner, Scottish PGA Championship, 1978, 1980, 1985, 1991, 1993; Member, Dunhill Cup Team (8 times); World Cup Team (11 times); Hennessy Cognac Cup Team (5 times); Double Diamond Team (3 times); Captain, European Team in Ashai Glass Four Tours Championships, Adelaide, 1991; Captain, Ryder Cup Team, 2001; Winner of 28 tournaments world-wide since 1972 including: Italian Open, 1987; Germany Masters, 1990; Hersey Open, 1991; Kronenbourg Open, 1993; Catalan Open, 1993; Honda Open, 1993; Hamburg Open, 1993; British Masters, 1995; French Open, 1998; Played US Senior Tour, 2003-04; Returned to European Senior Tour, 2004-. Publications: Sam: The Autobiography of Sam Torrance, 2003. Honours: OBE, 2003. Address: c/o Parallel Murray Management, 56 Ennismore Gardens, Knightsbridge, London SW7 1AJ, England. Website: www.samtorrance.com

TORRANCE Thomas F(orsyth), b. 30 August 1913, Chengdu, China. Minister of Religion; Professor of Theology. m. Margaret Edith Spear, 2 October 1946, 2 sons, 1 daughter. Education: MA, 1934; BD, 1937; DrTheol, 1946; DLitt, 1971. Appointments: Founder-Editor, Scottish Journal of Theology, 1948-88; Moderator, General Assembly, Church of Scotland, 1976-77. Publications: The Doctrine of Grace, 1949; Calvin's Doctrine of Man, 1949; Kingdom and Church, 1956; Conflict and Agreement in the Church, 2 volumes, 1959-60; Theology in Reconstruction, 1965; Theological Science, 1969; God and Rationality, 1971; Theology in Reconciliation, 1975; Space, Time and Resurrection, 1976; Space, Time and Incarnation, 1979; The Ground and Grammar of Theology, 1980; Christian Theology and Scientific Culture, 1980; Divine and Contingent Order, 1981; Reality and Scientific Theology, 1984; The Hermeneutics of John Calvin, 1987; The Trinitarian Faith, 1988; The Christian Frame of Mind, Reason, Order and Openness in Theology and Natural Science, 1989; Karl Barth, Biblical and Evangelical Theological Theologian, 1990; Senso del divino e scienza mnoderna, 1992; Theological Dialogue between Orthodox and Reformed Churches (editor), 1993; Royal Priesthood, 1993; Divine Meaning: Studies in Patristic Hermeneutics, 1994; Trinitarian Perspectives: Toward Doctrinal Agreement, 1994; The Christian Doctrine of God, One Being Three Persons, 1996; Scottish Theology: From John Knox to John McLeod Campbell, 1996. Contributions to: Numerous publications. Honours: Honorary doctorates; Honorary DD, Edinburgh, 1996. Memberships: British Academy; International Academy of Religious Sciences, president, 1972-81; International Academy of the Philosophy of Sciences; Center of Theological Inquiry, Princeton, New Jersey; Royal Society of Edinburgh. Address: 37 Braid Farm Road, Edinburgh EH10 6LE, Scotland. E-mail: ttorr@globalnet.co.uk

TORVILL Jayne, b. 7 October 1957, England. Ice Skater. m. Philip Christensen, 1990. Career: British Pair Skating Champion with M Hutchinson, 1971; Insurance Clerk, 1974-80; With Christopher Dean: British Ice Dance Champion, 1978-83, 1994; European Ice Dance Champion, 1981-82, 1984, 1994; World Ice Dance Champion, 1981-84; World Professional Ice Dance Champion, 1984, 1985, 1990, 1995, 1996; Olympic Ice Dance Champion, 1984; Olympic

Ice Dance Bronze Medal, 1994; Tours include: Australia and New Zealand, 1984; Royal Variety Performance, London, 1984; World tour with own company of international skaters, 1985; Guest artists with IceCapades, 1987; World tour with company of skaters from Soviet Union, 1988; Guest of South Australian Government, 1991; Great Britain tour with company of Ukraine skaters, 1992; Torvill & Dean, Face the Music, World Tour, UK, Australia and North America, 1994; Stars on Ice Tour, USA and Canada, 1997-98; Torvill and Dean Ice Adventures, UK, 1997-98; Television: Path of Perfection, 1984; Fire & Ice, 1986; World Tour (video), 1988; Bladerunners (documentary), 1991; Great Britain Tour (TV special and video), 1992; The Artistry of Torvill and Dean, 1994; Face the Music (video), 1995; Torvill and Dean: The Story So Far (video), 1996; Bach Cello Suite (with Yo-Yo Ma), 1996; Dancing on Ice, 2006- Publications: with Christopher Dean: Torvill and Dean: Autobiography, 1984; Torvill and Dean: Facing the Music, 1995. Honours: MBE, 1981; BBC Sports Personality of the Year with Christopher Dean, 1983-84; Olympic Ice Dance Gold Medal, 1984; Figure Skating Hall of Fame with Christopher Dean, 1989; Olympic Ice Dance Bronze Medal, 1994; Hon MA, Nottingham Trent University, 1994; OBE, 2000. Address: c/o Sue Young, PO Box 32, Heathfield, East Sussex TN21 0BW, England.

TOTH Gabor, b. 31 July 1969, Szeged, Hungary. Educator; Researcher; Speech Pathology Services Professional. m. Naeko Sugaya, 2 daughters. Education: BSc, summa cum laude, Barczi Gusztav College of Special Education, Budapest, 1995; MSc, magna cum laude, Department of Education, Graduate School of Liberal Arts & Human Sciences, Eotvos Lorand University of Sciences, Budapest, 1997; MEd, Department of Special Education, Graduate School of Education, Yokohama National University, Yokohama, 2002; PhD, Medicine, Department of Biology and Function in the Head and Neck, Graduate School of Medicine, Yokohama City University, Yokohama, 2006. Appointments: Special Education Teacher & Speech Language Pathologist, Metropolitan Institute of Speech and Language Therapy, Budapest, Hungary, 1995-96; Full time Clinical Instructor and Speech-language Pathologist, Institute of Speech and Language Therapy, National Resource Centre for Special Educational Support Services, Eotvos Lorand University of Sciences, Budapest, 1996-2006; Teaching Assistant, Graduate School of Education Science, Yokohama National University, Yokohama, 2001-02; Visiting Associate Professor, Department of Biology and Function in the Head and Neck, Graduate School of Medicine, Yokohama City University, Yokohama, 2006-. Publications: Numerous articles in professional journals. Honours: Frecot Andrea Award, 1995; Early Career Investigator Award, 1996; SPIO Award of Merit, 2004, 2005. Memberships: International Reading Association; Hungarian Association of Special Education; Hungarian Phonetic, Phoniatric and Logopedics Society; International Association for the Scientific Study of Intellectual Disabilities; International Society for Quality of Life Research; Oto-Rhino-Laryngological Society of Japan; Japanese Society of Logopedics and Phoniatrics; Japanese Association of Special Education; American Association on Intellectual and Developmental Disabilities. Address: YCU ORL 3-9 Fukuura, Kanazawa-ku, Yokohama-shi, 236-0004, Japan. E-mail: gabor@med.yokohama-cu.ac.jp

TOTTERDELL Michael S, b. 21 September 1950, Woodford, Essex. Academic; Educationalist; Researcher. m. Rebecca Helen Burdge. Education: BA (Hons), Theology & Philosophy, 1982, PGCE, 1983, MA (Distinction), Education, 1988, University of London; MID, Historical Policy Studies, University of Strasbourg, 1998. Appointments: Military

Service, HM Armed Forces, The Parachute Regiment, 1970-79; Religious Studies Teacher, Dr Challoner's Grammar School, Buckinghamshire, 1983; Religious Education Teacher, Cheshunt School, Hertfordshire, 1983-88; Senior Teacher, Henrietta Barnett School, London, 1988-90; Lecturer in Education, 1991-93; PGCE Course Director, 1993-99, Assistant Dean of Teacher Education, 1999-2001, Dean of Teacher Education, 2001-03, Institute of Education, University of London; Professor & Director, later Dean & Pro-Vice Chancellor Designate, Institute of Education, Manchester Metropolitan University, 2004-07; Professor & Dean of Education, University of Plymouth, 2007-. Publications: 19 articles in professional journals. Honours: Mentioned in Dispatches, UN Peacekeeping Force, Cyprus, 2004. Memberships: American Educational Research Association; British Educational Research Association; European Educational Research Association; Churchill Fellow, 1992; Fellow, Institute of Administrative Management; Executive Board Member, Leading Aspect Award; International Fellow at Large, Phi Delta Kappa; Fellow, Royal Society for the encouragement of the Arts, Manufactures and Commerce. Address: The Rectory, Bockings, Walkern, Hertfordshire, SG2 7PB, England. E-mail: m.totterdell@btinternet.com

TOURIÑÁN LOPEZ José Manuel, b. 29 October 1951, A Coruña, Spain. Professor. m. Teresa Morandeira, 2 daughters. Education: BA, Primary School Teacher, School of Teacher Education, A Coruña, 1969; Graduate Magister Pedagogy, 1974, Scholar Assistant, and Fellow Doctoral Studies, 1975-77, PhD, Pedagogy, 1978, University of Complutense. Appointments: Assistant Lecturer, Complutense University, 1974-80; Head, Department of Systematic Pedagogy, 1980-82, Assistant Professor, 1981-88, Secretary, Faculty of Sciences, 1982-83, Full Professor, 1988-, Head, Department of Theory and History of Education, 1986-88, Head, Research Group, 1998-, University of Santiago de Compostela, A Coruña, Spain; General Director, Universities' Management and Police Research, Galicia, 1990-93; General Director, Universities and Research, Galicia, 1994-97; Advisor of Science and Technology Office, Department of Government Presidency, Madrid, 1998-99; Member, Spanish Chapter of ATEI, Madrid, 1999-; General Manager, Caixa Galicia Foundation, Caixa Galicia Enterprise, A Coruña, Spain, 1999-2002; Member, National Commission of Education, Ministry of Education, Madrid, 2003-06; Head, Co-ordinator, Pan-American project on Values in education, ATEI, 2006-. Publications: Numerous articles in professional journals; Author, many books in the field of education including most recently: Education in Values, Interculturalism and Pacific Coexistence, 2007; Education on Values, Civil Society and Civil Development, 2008; Education on Values, Intercultural Education and Education for Peaceful Coexistence, 2009. Honours: Prize, 1974, National Prize, 1976, Ministry of Education and Science; BA Award, 1975, PhD Award, 1979, Complutense University; National Prize, Spanish Foundation for Vocation, Barcelona, 1975; San Jose de Calasanz of Pedagogical Research Prize, 1976; Honours, UNED Chrysler Associate Center, 1975-80; Honorary Professor, University of Buenos Aires, 1993; Golden Insignia of the University of Santiago de Compostela, 1998; Silver Medal of Galicia, 1998; Golden Insignia, A Coruña University, 2000; many other honours and awards. Memberships: National Society of Pedagogues, Spain; AERA; CREAD; SID; EUCEN; Member of editorial advisory board of several journals. Address: University of Santiago de Compostela, Faculty of Sciences of Education, Santiago de Compostela, A Coruña 15782, Spain. E-mail: hejmtl@usc.es

TOWNES Charles Hard, b. 28 July 1915, Greenville, South Carolina, USA. Physicist. m. Frances Brown, 4 daughters. Education: BA, BS, Furman University, 1935; MA, Duke University, 1937; PhD, California Institute of Technology, 1939. Appointments: Bell Telephone Laboratories, 1939-47; Associate Professor, 1948-50, Professor, 1950-61, Chairman, Department of Physics, 1952-55, Columbia University; Executive Director, Columbia Radiation Laboratory, 1950-52; Vice-President, Director of Research, Institute for Defense Analyses, 1959-61; Provost, Professor of Physics, 1961-66, Institute Professor, 1966-67, Massachusetts Institute of Technology; University Professor, 1967-86, Emeritus Professor, 1986-94, Professor, Graduate School, 1994-, University of California, Berkeley. Publications: Books: Microwave Spectroscopy, 1955; Making Waves, 1995; How the Laser Happened. Adventures of a Scientist, 1999. Honours: Thomas Young Medal and Prize, Institute of Physics and The Physical Society, England, 1963; Nobel Prize for Physics, 1964; Medal of Honour, Institute of Electrical and Electronics Engineers, 1966; Wilhelm Exner Award, Austria, 1970; Niels Bohr International Gold Medal, 1979; Officier de la Légion d'Honneur, France, 1990; Rabindranath Tagore Birth Centenary Plaque of the Asiatic Society, 1999; Founders Award of the National Academy of Engineering, 2000; Lomonosov Gold Medal of the Russian Academy of Science, 2001; Templeton Prize, 2005; Vannevar Bush Award, 2006; 29 honorary doctorates, US and abroad; Numerous prizes, awards, lectureships, other honours. Memberships: Fellow, American Physical Society, Council, 1959-62, 1965-71, President, 1967; Life Fellow, Institute of Electrical and Electronics Engineers; National Academy of Sciences; American Philosophical Society; Royal Society of London; National Academy of Engineering; Many more. Address: Department of Physics, University of California, Berkeley, CA 94720, USA. E-mail: cht@ssl.berkeley.edu

TOWNSEND Sue, b. 2 April 1946, Leicester, England. Author. Publications: The Secret Diary of Adrian Mole Aged Thirteen and Three-Quarters, 1982; The Growing Pains of Adrian Mole, 1984; The Diaries of Adrian Mole, 1986; Bazaar and Rummage, Groping for Words, Womberang: Three Plays, 1984; True Confessions of Adrian Albert Mole; Mr Bevan's Dream, 1989; Ten Tiny Fingers, Nine Tiny Toes, play, 1989; Adrian Mole From Minor to Major, 1991; The Queen and I, 1992; Adrian Mole – The Wilderness Years, 1993; Plays, 1996; Ghost Children, 1997; Adrian Mole: The Cappuccino Years, 1999; Number Ten, 2002; Adrian Mole and the Weapons of Mass Destruction, 2004; The Queen in Hell Close (chapbook), 2005; Queen Camilla, 2006. Honours: Playwright Award for Womberang, 1981; Frink Award, 2003; 2 Honorary Doctorates, University of Leicester, and Loughborough University, 2007; James Joyce Award, 2007. Memberships: Writers Guild; PEN. Address: Reed Books, Michelin House, 81 Fulham Road, London, SW3 6RB, England.

TOWNSHEND Peter Dennis Blandford, b. 19 May 1945, Isleworth, London. Composer; Performer of Rock Music; Author. m. Karen Astley, 1968, 1 son, 2 daughters. Education: Acton County Grammar School; Ealing Art College. Appointments: Contracted as member of The Who to Fontana Records, 1964; MCA Records, 1965; WEA Records, 1979; Retired from the Who, 1984; Contracted as solo artist to Atco Records, USA, 1979; To Virgin Records, 1986; Owner, Eel Pie Recording Ltd, 1972-83; Established, Eel Pie (bookshops and publishing co), 1976-83; Established Meher Baba Oceanic (UK archival library), 1976-81; Editor, Faber and Faber (publishers), 1983; Final tour with The Who, 1989; Recordings include: Albums with The Who:

My Generation, 1965; A Quick One, 1966; Happy Jack, 1967; The Who Sell Out, 1967; Magic Bus, 1968; Tommy, 1969; Live At Leeds, 1970; Who's Next, 1971; Meaty Beefy Big and Bouncy, 1971; Quadrophenia, 1973; The Who By Numbers, 1975; The Story of The Who, 1976; Who Are You, 1978; The Kids Are Alright (live), 1979; Face Dances, 1981; Hooligans, 1982; It's Hard, 1982; Rarities Vols 1 and 2, 1983; Who's Last (live), 1984; Two's Missing, 1987; Join Together (live), 1990; Live at the Isle of Wight Festival 1970, 1996; The BBC Sessions, 2000; Moonlighting, 2005; Solo: Who Came First, 1972; Rough Mix, 1977; Empty Glass, 1980; All The Best Cowboys Have Chinese Eyes, 1982; Scoop, 1983; White City: A Novel, 1985; Another Scoop, 1987; Iron Man: A Musical, 1989; Psychoderelict, 1993; Pete Townsend Live, 1999; Lifehouse Chronicles, 2000; The Oceanic Concerts, 2001; Live: La Jolla, 2001; Live: Sadler's Wells, 2001; Films: Tommy, 1975; Quadrophenia, 1979; The Kids Are Alright, 1979. Publications: The Story of Tommy (with Richard Barnes); Horse's Neck, 1985; Tommy: The Musical, 1995; London, 1996. Honours: Ivor Novello Award, 1981; British Phonographic Industry Award, 1983; Rock and Roll Hall of Fame, 1990; Oliver Award, 1997; Q Award for Lifetime Achievement, 1997; Ivor Novello Lifetime Achievement Award, 2001; PRS Awards for CSI and CSI Miami, 2004; BMI TV Music Awards, 2004; Silver Clef, 30th Anniversary Award for The Who, 2005. Address: PO Box 305, Twickenham, TW1 1TT, England. Website: www.eelpie.com

TRALDI Lorenzo, b. 22 May 1955, Rome, Italy. Mathematician. m. Sharon Richter, 3 sons, 1 daughter. Education: BA, Queens College, City University of New York, 1976; PhD, Yale University, 1980. Appointments: Assistant Professor, 1980, Associate Professor, 1986, Professor, 1994, Marshall R Metzgar Professor of Mathematics, 2001-, Lafayette College, Easton. Publications: Numerous articles in professional journals. Memberships: American Mathematical Society; Institute for Combinatorics and its Applications; Institute of Electrical and Electronics Engineers. Address: Department of Mathematics, Lafayette College, Easton, PA 18042, USA. E-mail: traldil@lafayette.edu

TRAN Nghiep Dai, b. 20 July 1942, Lynham, Hanam, Vietnam. Physicist; Researcher. m. Thi Nam Pham, 1 son, 1 daughter. Education: Bachelor's degree, Belorussian University, 1967; Doctor's degree, Institute of Physics, Hanoi, 1986. Appointments: Director, Centre of Nuclear Technique, 1998-2001; Vice Director, Institute of Nuclear Science and Technique, 2001-03; Vice President, World Council of Nuclear Workers, Paris, France, 2003-; Editor of international journals, Low Radiation and Nuclear Energy, Science and Technology, 2004-; Co-Chairman, Low Radiation Committee, Paris, 2006-. Publications: Books: Radiation Safety; Radiation Technology; Articles: Energy Transfer Model in Dosimetry; Extended Energy Transfer Model in Astrophysics; Cyclical Model of Cosmos; Continuous Kinetic Function Method in Nuclear Decay; Non-Exponential Deviation in Nuclear Decay. Memberships: Vietnamese Society of Nuclear Physics. Address: 12, 294/30 Kim Ma, Hanoi 10103, Vietnam. E-mail: dainghiep_tran@yahoo.com

TRATTNER Carola-Lotty, b. 29 May 1925, Braila, Romania. Senior University Lecturer. m. Egon, 1 son. Education: Certificate, Philology Branch, Onescu College, Bucharest, Romania, 1943-44; MA, Language and Literature, Faculty of Philology, University of Bucharest, 1944-47; Certificate, Postgraduate Pedagogical Seminar, Bucharest, 1947-48; Certificate, Second Pedagogical Seminar, Tel Aviv, Israel, 1974. Appointments: English Assistant, Faculty of Philology,

University of Bucharest, 1949-52; English Assistant, Reader, Senior Lecturer, Teacher Trainer and Examiner, Institute of International Relations, Bucharest, 1952-56; English Senior Lecturer, Teacher Trainer and Examiner, Academy of Economic Studies, Bucharest, 1956-73; English Teacher for New Immigrants, Academic Recycling Institute, Ramat Gan, Israel, 1974-77; Lecturer for Communication English, French, Business French, Tel Aviv-Jaffa People's University, Tel Aviv, 1974-86; Teacher, Head of English Department, Teacher Trainer and Examiner, Shazar High School, Bat Yam, Israel, 1976-89; Recycling courses Lecturer, Organiser and Examiner for potential English Teachers, Ministry of Education and Culture, 1989-90; Senior Lecturer, Organiser, Examiner for the Tel Aviv-Jaffa Chamber of Commerce, Ministry of Labour, 1978-2002; Senior Lecturer, Academic College, Holon, 1990-2006; International interpreter (simultaneous translation) for English, French, Romanian, German (more than 100 conventions for the United Nations, FAO, governmental bodies, law/medicine/agriculture/various technical branches/journalism/youth/women, etc from Oxford to China). Publications: Over 20 books in English, French, Romanian and Hebrew, 1952-2005, among them monolingual and bilingual Dictionaries, general and specific (English-Hebrew, Hebrew-English, Juridical and Economic; English-Romanian and English-Hebrew; Glossaries for foreign trade, banking, diplomatic activities, the textile industry, motor-car technology) and University specialised textbooks; Translation into English of 10th grade World Geography textbook; Collections of texts for translation. Memberships: English Teachers' Association in Israel. Address: 52 Eilat St, 58364 Holon, Israel. E-mail: trattner@post.com

TRATTNER Egon, b. 8 September 1923, Brasov, Romania. Economist. m. Carola Klekner, 1 son. Education: MSc, Economic, Financial and Social Studies, Academy of High Commercial and Industrial Studies, Cluj-Brasov, Romania, 1948; PhD, Economic Sciences, Academy of Economic Studies, Bucharest, Romania, 1962. Appointments: Laboratory Worker, Vacuum Oil Co, Oil Refinery, Brasov Romania, 1940-41; Forced Labourer, Romanian Army, Romania, 1941-44; Secretary, Indumin Sugar Factories, Tg-Mures & Bod, Romania, 1945-49; Section Chief, Ministry of Food Industry, Bucharest, 1950-51; Economist, Institute for Food Industry Projects, Bucharest, 1951-52; Planning Co-ordinator, Department Chief, Ministry of Consumer Goods Industry, Bucharest, 1952-1956; Head Economic Research Division, Food Technological Research Institute, Bucharest, 1956-72; Expert Instructor, Food Industry Postgraduate Study Centre, 1972-73; Senior Research Fellow, Tel-Aviv University Centre for Interdisciplinary Forecasting, Tel-Aviv, Israel, 1974-76; Project Leader, Israeli Productivity Institute, Tel-Aviv, 1976-79; Senior Researcher, Institute for Development Studies, Rechovot, Israel, 1979-88. Publications: Over 100 articles published internationally on forecasting and planning, siting and sizing industrial units, measurement of labour productivity, economics of the food industry, philosophy of science. Honour: Medal of Labour, 1953; Listed in Who's Who publications. Memberships: Central Board of Statistics, Scientific Methodological Council, Bucharest, 1952-57; Food Technological Research Institute, Scientific council Bucharest, 1956-72; Cybernetics Centre, Scientific Council, Bucharest, 1967-73; Israeli Association of Graduates in the Social Sciences and Humanities, Israel; Israel's Economic Association; Emeritus Member, New York Academy of Sciences; World Future Studies Federation. Address: 52 Eilat St, Holon 58364, Israel. E-mail: trattner@POBoxes.com

TRAVOLTA John, b. 18 February 1954, Englewood, New Jersey, USA. Actor. m. Kelly Preston, 1991, 1 son. Appointments: Films: Carrie, The Boy in the Plastic Bubble (for TV), 1976; Saturday Night Fever, 1977; Grease, Moment by Moment, 1978; Urban Cowboy, 1980; Blow Out, 1981; Staying Alive, Two of a Kind, 1983; Perfect, 1985; The Experts, 1988; Chains of Gold, Look Who's Talking, 1989; Look Who's Talking Now, 1990; The Tender, All Shook Up, 1991; Look Who's Talking 3, Pulp Fiction, 1994; White Man's Burden, Get Shorty, 1995; Broken Arrow, Phenomenon, 1996; Michael, Face Off, She's So Lovely, 1997; Primary Colors, A Civil Action, 1998; The General's Daughter, 1999; Battlefield Earth, Lucky Numbers, 2000; Swordfish, Domestic Disturbance, 2001; Austin Powers in Goldmember, 2002; Basic, 2003; The Punisher, A Love Song for Bobby Long, Ladder 49, 2004; Be Cool, Magnificent Desolation: Walking on the Moon (voice), 2005; Lonely Hearts, 2006; Wild Hogs, Hairspray, 2007; TV Series: Welcome Back Kotter, 1975-77; l.p. records, 1976, 1977. Publication: Staying Fit, 1984. Honours: Billboard Magazine Best New Male Vocalist Award, 1976; Best Actor Award, National Board of Review, 1978; Male Star of the Year, National Association of Theatre Owners, 1983; Alan J Pakula Prize, 1998.

TREANOR Frances, b. Penzance, Cornwall. Artist; Author. Divorced, 1 daughter. Education: Fine Art, Goldsmiths College, London University; Postgraduate Studies, Middlesex University, 1966-67; ATC (Lon); Diploma in Geriatric Art Teaching, London University, 1972; Certificate in Psychotherapy Counselling. Appointments: Taught and lectured on art and design appreciation in various ILEA and adult establishments including: Erith College of Technology; American Intercontinental University; Blackheath Conservatoire of Music and the Arts; Twice Vice Chair, Blackheath Art Society; Freelance sponsored workshops; Private and corporate commissions; Artist in Residence, Royal Greenwich Park, 2005-06; Exhibitions include: The Pastel Society, Centenary Exhibition at FBA, 2000; English Heritage, Rangers House, Greenwich Artists Group, 2000; St Alphege Church, Open Studios Exhibition, 2000; Greenwich and Docklands, International Festival Open Studios, 2002, 2003, 2004; London Chamber of Commerce and Industry, selected artist, 2002; The Stephen Lawrence Gallery, University of Greenwich, mixed show, 2004. Honours: The Royal Drawing Society's Exhibit Prize, The Children's Royal Academy, London; Major County Scholarship, 1962; Twice winner, Law Society Art Group Special Prize, 1972, 1973; Dip d'Honneur, Salon d'Antony, Paris, 1975; Winner, L'Artiste Assoiffe Award, 1980; Exhibitor, The Lord Mayor's Award Exhibition, Guildhall, 1975, 1977; Represented Greenwich at twin town of Maribor, Yugoslavia, 1980; Lewisham art representative, Reinickendorf, Berlin, Germany, 1982; The George Rowney Pastel Award, Birmingham, 1982; The Frank Herring Award for Merit, 1984; Conte (UK) Award, 1986; Willi Hoffmann-Guth Award, 1988; Nominated Woman of the Year, 2006, Governing Board of Editors, ABI. Membership: London Press Club. Address: 121 Royal Hill, Greenwich, London SE10 8SS, England. E-mail: francestreanor@btinternet.com Website: www.francestreanor.com

TREBY Ivor Charles, b. Devonport, England. Poet. Education: MA, Honours, Biochemistry, Oxford. Publications: Poem Cards, 1984; Warm Bodies, 1988; Foreign Parts, 1989; Woman with Camellias, 1995; The Michael Field Catalogue: A Book of Lists, 1998; Translations From the Human, 1998; A Shorter Shīrazād, 101 poems of Michael Field chosen and annotated by Ivor C Treby, 1999; Awareness of the Sea, selected poems 1970-1995, 2000; Music and Silence, The Gamut of

Michael Field, chosen and annotated by Ivor C Treby, 2000; Uncertain Rain, Sundry Spells of Michael Field chosen and annotated by Ivor C Treby, 2002; Binary Star, Leaves from the Journal and Letters of Michael Field 1846-1914, chosen and annotated by Ivor C Treby, 2006; Blanche's Last Fling, 2006. Contributions to: Windmill Book of Poetry; Bete Noire; Poetry Review; Staple; Anglo-Welsh Review; Contemporary Review; Honest Ulsterman; Literary Review; Rialto. Address: Parapets, 69 Redcliffe Close, RB Kensington and Chelsea, London SW5 9HZ, England.

TREVELYAN (Walter) Raleigh, b. 6 July 1923, Port Blair, Andaman Islands. Author. Education: Winchester. Appointment: Rifle Brigade, World War II; Publisher, 1948-88. Publications: The Fortress, 1956; A Hermit Disclosed, 1960; Italian Short Stories: Penguin Parallel Texts (editor), 1965; The Big Tomato, 1966; Princes Under the Volcano, 1972; The Shadow of Vesuvius, 1976; A Pre-Raphaelite Circle, 1978; Rome '44, 1982; Shades of the Alhambra, 1984; The Golden Oriole, 1987; La Storia dei Whitaker, 1989; Grand Dukes and Diamonds, 1991; A Clear Premonition, 1995; The Companion Guide to Sicily, 1996; Sir Walter Raleigh, 2002. Contributions to: Newspapers and journals. Honours: John Florio Prize for Translation, The Outlaws by Luigi Meneghello, 1967. Memberships: Anglo-Italian Society for the Protection of Animals, President; English PEN, a vice-president; Royal Society of Literature, fellow. Address: 18 Hertford Street, London W1J 7RT, England.

TRICHET Jean-Claude, b. 20 December 1942, Lyon, France. President of the European Central Bank. Education: Ingénieur civil des Mines, Ecole nationale supérieure des Mines de Nancy, 1964; Economics, University of Paris, 1966; Graduate, Institut d'études politiques de Paris, 1966; Graduate, Ecole nationale d'administration, 1969-71. Appointments: Engineer in the competitive sector, 1966-68; Inspecteur adjoint de Finances, 1971; Assigned to the General Inspectorate of Finance, 1974; Assigned to the Treasury Department, 1975; Secretary General, Interministerial Committee for Improving Industrial Structures, 1976; Adviser to the Minister of Economic Affairs, 1978; Adviser to the President of the Republic on Industry, Energy and Research, 1978; Head, Development Aid Office, Deputy Director of Bilateral Affairs, 1981, Head, International Affairs, 1985, Chairman of the Paris Club - sovereign debt rescheduling (1985-93), Director, 1987, Treasury Department; Director, Private Office of the Minister for Economic Affairs, Finance and Privatisation, 1986; Alternate Governor, International Monetary Fund, -1993; Alternate Governor, World Bank, 1987; Censor, Banque de France, 1987; Chairman, European Monetary Committee, 1992-93; Governor, Banque de France, 1993; Member, Board of Directors of the Bank for International Settlements, 1993; Governor, World Bank, 1993-95; Chairman, Monetary Policy Council, Banque de France, 1994; Member, Council of the European Monetary Institute, 1994; Alternate Governor, International Monetary Fund, 1995-2003; Member, Governing Council of the European Central Bank, 1998; Governor of the Banque de France, 1999; Chairman, Group of Ten Governors, 2003; President, European Central Bank, 2003-. Honours: Officier de l'Ordre national de la Légion d'honneur, France; Officer de l'Ordre national du Mérite, France; Commander or Grand Officer, National Orders of Merit in Argentina, Austria, Belgium, Brazil, Ecuador, Germany, Ivory Coast and Yugoslavia; Policy Maker of the Year, The International Economy magazine, 1991; Prize, Zerilli Marimo, Academie des Sciences morales et politiques, 1999; International Prize, Pico della Mirandola, 2002. Address: European Central Bank, Postfach 16 03 19, D-60066 Frankfurt am Main, Germany.

TRIMBLE W David (Baron Trimble of Lisnagarvey), b. 15 October 1944. Politician. m. (1) Heather McComb, divorced, (2) Daphne Elizabeth Orr, 1978, 2 sons, 2 daughters. Education: LLB, 1st class, Queens University, 1968. Appointments: Bar at Law, 1969, Lecturer, Law, Senior Lecturer, 1977, Head of Department, Commercial and Property Law, 1981-89; Convention Member, South Belfast, 1975-76; Joined Ulster Unionist Party, 1977; Vice Chairman, Lagan Valley Unionist Association, 1983-85; Chairman, 1985, 1990-96, Honorary Secretary, Ulster Unionist Council; Chairman, UUP Legal Committee, 1989-95; Member of Parliament, Upper Bann, 1990-2005; Chairman, UUP Constitutional Development Committee, 1995; Leader, Ulster Unionist Party, 1995-2005; Member of the New Northern Ireland Assembly, Upper Bann Constituency, 1998-2002; First Minister until Assembly suspended, 2002; Joined House of Lords, 2006; Joined Conservative Party, 2007. Honours: Shared Nobel Peace Prize, 1998; Honorary LLD, Queen's, 1999, New Brunswick, 2000, Wales, 2002; Life Peer, 2006. Memberships: Devolution Group, 1979-84; Founder, Chairman, Ulster Society, 1985-90; Chairman, Lisburn Ulster Club, 1985-86.

TRIVEDI Nikunj, b. 18 June 1959. Consultant Homeopath. Education: DHMS, Gold Medallist. Appointments: Honorary Lecturer, R K Medical College, Anand, Gujarat, India, 1982; External Examiner, Council of Homeopathic Medicine, Gynaecology and Obstetrics, 1984-85; Honorary Consultant and Team Leader assisting socially deprived women in a village in Central Gujarat; Charitable work with Red Cross in Anand, Gujarat; Work with socially underprivileged during Gujarat Earthquake, 2000; Consultant Homeopath in private practice. Publications: Launched website, www.articlinic.co.uk, 1998; Article presented, 5th International Conference of Homeopathy & Complimentary Medicine, 1999; Article presented, 5th Gujarat Millennium Seminar, 2000; Article presented, 6th International Conference of Homeopathy & Complimentary Medicine, Malaysia, 2002; Article published, Homeopathy to the XXI Century at OMSK, North Siberia, Russia, 2003. Memberships: Fellow, British Institute of Homeopathy; Life Member, HMAI, India; Life Member, GHMA, Anand. Address: 91 Jacklin Drive, Rusheymead, Leicester LE4 7SU, England.

TROFIMOV Boris Alexandrovich, b. 2 October 1938, Tchita, Eastern Siberia, Russia. Chemist. m. Nina Ivanovna Vodyannikova, 1 son. Education: Graduate, 1961, PhD equivalent, 1964, Irkutsk State University; DSc Degree, St Petersburg (Leningrad) University, 1970. Appointments: Head of Laboratory, 1970, Professor, 1974, Vice-Director, 1990, Irkutsk Institute of Organic Chemistry, SB, USSR Academy of Sciences; Director, A E Favorsky Irkutsk Institute of Chemistry, SB, Russian Academy of Sciences, 1994. Publications: More than 2,350 publications include: 15 monographs, 1,000 major papers, more than 500 Russian and foreign patents; Promoter of 62 PhD students, 24 D Sci (habilitations). Honours: Basic Research in Siberian Chemical Science, 1984, 1990; Applied Research in Siberian Chemical Science, 1985; Gold, 1979, Silver, 1987 and 2 Bronze Medals, 1972, 1978, Russian Exhibition for Economic Achievements; Orders: Sign of Honour, 1986, Friendship, 1999; Butlerov Prize, Russian Academy of Sciences, 1997; Medal and Diploma of Mendeleev Reader, St Petersburg, 2003. Memberships: Academician, Russian Academy of Science; Editorial Board Member: Zh.Organ.Khim (Russia), Sulfur Letters, Sulfur Reports (UK); Presidium, Irkutsk Scientific Centre, Russian Academy of Sciences; Presidium, East Siberian Scientific Centre, Russian Academy of Medical Science; Asia-Pacific Academy of Materials; Council of Experts of the Supreme Commission on Scientific Qualification; National Committee of Russian Chemists; Interdepartmental Scientific Council on Chemical and Biological Weapon Convention at the Russian Academy of Sciences and Russian Agency of Ammunition; International Council for Main Group Chemistry, The Netherlands; Honorary Fellow, Florida Center for Heterocyclic Compounds; Bureau of Scientific Council on Organic and Elemento-Organic Chemistry, Russian Academy of Sciences; Council of the section "Organic Chemistry", D I Mendeleev Russian Chemical Society; Scientific Council, Research Centre of Energy Infrastructure "Asia-Energy". Address: A E Favorsky Irkutsk Institute of Chemistry SB RAS, 1, Favorsky Str, Irkutsk 664033, Russia. Website: www.inchemistry.irk.ru

TROLLOPE Joanna, b. 9 December 1943. Author. m. (1) David Potter, 1966, 2 daughters, (2) Ian Curteis, 1985, divorced 2001, 2 step-sons. Education: MA, St Hugh's College, Oxford, 1972. Appointments: Information and Research Department, Foreign Office, 1965-67; Various teaching posts, 1967-79; Chair, Advisory Committee on National Reading Initiative, Department of National Heritage, 1996; Member, Advisory Committee on National Year of Reading, Department of Education, 1998; Trustee and Member, Joanna Trollope Charitable Trust, 1995-; Patron County of Gloucestershire Community Foundation, 1994-. Publications: Eliza Stanhope, 1978; Parson Harding's Daughter, 1979; Leaves from the Valley, 1980; The City of Gems, 1981; The Steps of the Sun, 1983; Britannia's Daughter: A Study of Women in the British Empire, 1983; The Taverner's Place, 1986; The Choir, 1988; A Village Affair, 1989; A Passionate Man, 1990; The Rector's Wife, 1991; The Men and the Girls, 1992; A Spanish Lover, 1993; The Country Habit, 1993; The Best of Friends, 1995; Next of Kin, 1996; Faith, 1996; Other People's Children, 1998; Marrying the Mistress, 2000; Girl From the South, 2002; Brother and Sister, 2004; Second Honeymoon, 2006; The Book Boy, 2006; As Caroline Harvey: Legacy of Love, 1980; A Second Legacy, 1993; A Castle in Italy, 1993; Parson Harding's Daughter, 1996; The Steps of the Sun, 1996; The Brass Dolphin, 1997; City of Gems, 1999; The Taverner's Place, 2000; Leaves from the Valley; Contributions to newspapers and magazines. Honours: Romantic Novelist of the Year, 1980; OBE, 1996; Deputy Lieutenant for the County of Gloucestershire, 2002; Memberships: Vice-President, Trollope Society; Council Member, Society of Authors; Council Member, West Country Writers Association. Address: c/o Peters Fraser and Dunlop, Drury House, 34-43 Russell Street, London, WC2B 5HA, England. Website: www.joannatrollope.net

TROYAN Volodymyr, Physician. Education: Training at the Institute for Cardiovascular Surgery, Ukraine, 1988; Training at the Bakulev Institute for Cardiovascular Surgery, Russia, 1976; Kharkiv Medical Institute, Ukraine, 1965-1971. Appointments: Surgeon, SI Institute of General and Urgent Surgery of Ukraine, 1971-1976; Vascular Surgeon, SI Institute of General and Urgent Surgery of the AMS of Ukraine, 1976-1983; Senior Research Associate, SI Institute of General and Urgent Surgery of the AMS of Ukraine, 1983-2007; Senior Research Associate, Kharkiv Center for Cardiovascular Surgery, Ukraine, 1992-2002. Publications: Author, 25 scientific papers in various professional journals. Memberships: Ukrainian Society for Cardiovascular Surgery; European Society for Vascular Surgery; French Society for Angiology. Address: 63 Ilynskaya Street, Apt 11, Kharkiv, Ukraine 61093. E-mail: cardiovasc@ukr.net

TRUBETSKOY Kliment Nikolayevich, b. 3 July 1933, Moscow, USSR. Mining Engineer. m. 2 sons. Education: Moscow Institute of Non-Ferrous Metals and Gold, 1961; Doctor of Technical Sciences, 1981; Professor, 1982; Academician, RAS. Appointments: Manager of Mines, 1953-56; Associate, Mining Institute A A Skochinskii, 1961-67; Senior Associate, Institute of Earth Physics, 1967-77; Head of Laboratory, 1977, Deputy Director, 1987, Director, 1987-2003, Institute of Complex Exploitation of Mineral Resources; Member of the Presidium, RAS, 1996-2001; Adviser of the Presidium, Russian Academy of Sciences, 2001; Vice-President, Academy of Mining Sciences; Head of Chair, Russian State Geological Prospecting University, 2003. Publications: 690 publications; 34 monographs; Art for Encyclopaedia of Life Support Systems, 2002; 8 learned books; 75 patents. Honours: USSR and Russian State Prizes; Prize of the President of Russian Federation; 2nd Prize of the Government of Russian Federation for the field of science, technics and education; N Melnikov Gold Medal and Prize, 1989, 2004; B Krupinsky Medal, WMC; 300 Years of German-Russian Friendship in Mining Medal. Memberships: Academician, Russian Academy of Sciences; Foreign Member, Academy of Engineering Sciences of Serbia and Montenegro. Address: Kryukovski Tupik 4, Moscow 111020, Russia. E-mail: trubetsk@ipkonran.ru

TRUELSEN Hans Henrik Land, b. 11 May 1945, Nykobing F, Denmark. Medical Doctor; General Practitioner. 4 sons, 1 daughter. Education: MD, University of Copenhagen, 1972; Passed American MD, 1974; Specialist in Disorders of School Children, 1976; Swedish Social Laws, University of Lund, 1980; Advanced Level of Traditional Chinese Medicine, University of Kunming, 2007. Appointments: Specialist in General Medicine, 1982-; Own practice, Amager, Copenhagen, 1982-. Publications: Upper Airway Allergy in Children, 1971; Gastric Ulcers in Manic-Depressive Illness, 1979; Depressive Disorders in Copenhagen 1977-78, A Survey, 1979; A Malignant Hypertermia-like Reaction as a Possible Cause of SIDS; Sudden Infant Death in Denmark 1973-74, 1982; Articles on historic medical objects; Poetry, 1994-2007; 3 unpublished novels; Correspondence in Ugeskr Läg, 1972-2000; Heparin in the treatment of tenosynovitis; Medico-historical objects, eg, Hygiea; Short texts, eg, poetry. Honours: Man of the Year, 2007; Peace Medal, 2007; International Health Professional of the Year, 2007. Memberships: Copenhagen Medical Society; Nordic Society of Medical Humour; Medica Etnic Society. Address: Hostrups Have 14, 4, DK-1954 Frederiksberg, Denmark. E-mail: hhlt@dadlnet.dk

TRUETT Philip Arthur, b. 14 October 1942, Croydon, Surrey. m. Juliet Macadam, 2 daughters. Education: Cranleigh School; Grenoble University. Appointments: Lloyd's, 1961, Member of Lloyd's, 1973-; Directorships: Furness-Houlder (Reinsurance) Ltd, Furness-Houlder (Overseas Insurance Services) Ltd, 1971-80; MWE Underwriting Agencies Ltd, 1980-83; Fenchurch Underwriting Agencies Ltd, 1983-93; Minories Ltd, 1993-97; Aberdeen Underwriting Agencies Ltd, 1997-99; Hampden Private Capital Ltd, 1999-; Chairman, Lloyd's Benevolent Fund, 2005. Publications: Heather and Heaven – Walton Heath Golf Club (Chief Research Assistant); Chapters in: Aspects of Collecting Golf Books, 1996 - Yearbooks and Annuals; Hazards, 1993 - To Rake or Not to Rake Bunkers. Honour: Heather and Heaven winner of USGA International Book Award, 2003. Memberships: Royal and Ancient Golf Club; Walton Heath Golf Club, Captain, 1993, Director, 1992-93, 1999-2000; Rye Golf Club; Royal Cinque Ports Golf Club; Clapham Common Golf Club, Lloyd's Golf

Club, Honorary Secretary, 1985-95, Captain, 1996, President, 2000; British Golf Collectors Society, One of 5 Founding Members, Captain, 1992-93, Honorary Life Member, 2007; Old Cranleighan Golf Society, Honorary Secretary, 1968-73, Captain, 1982; South Eastern Junior Golf Society, Captain, 1968, Vice-President, 1975, President, 1991-; Golf Collectors Society (US), Board, 1997-2003; Senior Golfers' Society; Kadahar Ski Club; Ephemera Society; Private Libraries Association; Committee, Annual National Service for Seafarers; Walton-on-the-Hill and District Local History Society, President, 1998-; United States Golf Association, Museum and Library Committee, 2006. Address: Woodbine House, 12 Spencer Road, South Croydon, Surrey CR2 7EH, England. E-mail: philip@truett.co.uk

TRUMP Donald John, b. 14 June 1946, New York, USA. Property Developer. m. (1) Ivana Zelnicek, 1977, divorced 1991, 2 sons, 1 daughter, (2) Marla Maples, 1993, 1 daughter, (3) Melania Knauss, 2005, 1 son. Education: Fordham University; University of Pennsylvania. Appointments: President, Trump Organisation; Board of Directors, Police Athletic League; Advisory Board, Lenox Hill Hospital and United Cerebral Palsy; Director, Fred C Trump Foundation; Founder Member, Committee to complete construction of Cathedral of St John the Divine and Wharton Real Estate Centre; Former Co-Chair, New York Vietnam Veterans Memorial Fund; Radio: Clear Channel Radio broadcasts, 2004; TV: The Apprentice, 2004. Publications: Trump: The Art of the Deal, 1987; Trump: Surviving at the Top, 1990; The Art of the Comeback, 1997; The America We Deserve, 2000; How to Get Rich, 2004; Think Like a Billionaire, 2004; The Way to the Top, 2004; Trump World Magazine, 2004; Trump: Think Like a Billionaire, 2004; Trump: The Best Golf Advice I Ever Received, 2005; Trump: The Best Real Estate Advice I Ever Received, 2007; Trump 101: The Way to Success, 2007; Trump Never Give Up, 2008. Honours: Hotel and Real Estate Visionary of the Century, UJA Federation, 2000. Address: Trump Organization, 725 Fifth Avenue, New York, NY 10022, USA.

TRUTER Ilse, b. 5 May 1964, Port Elizabeth, South Africa. Pharmacist; University Professor. Education: BCom, 1985, BCom Hons, 1987, MCom, 1988, DCom, 1993, BPharm, 1993, MSc, 1994, University of Port Elizabeth; PhD, Potchefstroom University for Christian Higher Education, 2000. Appointments: Temporary Lecturer, Department of Business Economics, University of Port Elizabeth, 1988; Pharmacist Intern, Westway Pharmacy, Port Elizabeth, 1993-94; Temporary Lecturer, Pharmacy Practice, Department of Pharmacy, 1993, Temporary part-time Lecturer, Pharmacy Practice, Department of Pharmacy, 1994-95, Researcher, Drug Utilisation Research Unit, 1994-, Permanent full-time Lecturer, Pharmacy Practice, Department of Pharmacy, 1995-97, Permanent full-time Senior Lecturer, Department of Pharmacy, 1998-2000, University of Port Elizabeth; Associate Professor, Department of Pharmacy, 2001-2004, Associate Professor, Department of Pharmacy, 2005-, Nelson Mandela Metropolitan University. Publications: Author, over 185 research publications; Author of 207 publications; Author and co-author of 251 presentations at conferences and symposia; Author, 18 radio talks. Honours: Runner-up, 1985, Winner, 1986; AIESEC-Barclays National Essay Competition; Alfred Radis Memorial Award and Medal, 1990; Gencor S_2A_3 Bronze Medal, Best Masters study, 1994; Pharmacia and Upjohn Achievement Award winner, 1996, 1997; Euro Durg EACPT Poster Prize, Germany, 1998; ISPE Poster Prize, USA, 1999; Recipient of the Roche Best Publication Award, in conjunction with The Academy of Pharmaceutical

Sciences in 2001 for the best publication in Pharmacy Practice in South Africa in 2000; Wellness Excellence Award, South African National Wellness Conference, University of Port Elizabeth, 2003; Pharmacy Teacher of the Year Award, South Africa, 2003; Excellence in Teaching Award, University of Port Elizabeth, 2004; Listed in national and international biographical publications. Memberships: South African Pharmacy Council; Pharmaceutical Society of South Africa; South African Academy of Pharmaceutical Sciences; South African Association of Hospital and Institutional Pharmacists; International Society for Pharmacoepidemiology; Pharmacological Society of South Africa; Public Health Association of South Africa; Southern African Institute for Management Scientists. Address: Department of Pharmacy, Nelson Mandela Metropolitan University, PO Box 77000, Port Elizabeth 6031, South Africa. E-mail: ilse.truter@nmmu.ac.za

TSAO Vivian J Y, b. 24 April 1950, Taipei, Taiwan (American Citizen). Artist; Art Professor; Author. m. Raymond Clyde Coreil. Education: BA, Fine Arts, National Taiwan Normal University, Taiwan, 1973; Master of Fine Arts in Painting, Carnegie Mellon University, Pittsburgh, Pennsylvania, USA, 1976. Appointments: Assistant Editor, Children's Art Page, Central Daily News, Taiwan, 1971-74; Art Instructor, National Taipei Teachers College, Taiwan, 1972-74; Worked on consignments for: Kingpitcher Gallery, Pittsburgh, Pennsylvania, USA, 1976-77; Nardin Galleries, New York City, USA, 1979-80; The Art Collaborative, New York City, USA, 1985-87; Correspondent, Hsiung Shih Art Monthly, Taiwan, 1980-96; Programme Auditor, Free-lance Reviewer of Exhibitions, 1990-96; Juror on Panel, 1996-99, New York State Council on the Arts, New York City; Adjunct Assistant Professor of Drawing and Design, Department of Fine Arts, Pace University, New York City, 1990-; Contributing writer in the USA, United Daily News, Literary Page, Taiwan; 14 solo and 51 group exhibitions include: American Academy of Arts and Letters; The Brooklyn Museum; Taipei Fine Arts Museum; Ceres Gallery; Biddington's Internet Gallery. Publications: Book: The Mark of Time: Dialogues with Vivian Tsao on Art in New York, 2003; Article: A Holistic Approach to Art Criticism: An Interview with Art Critic Michael Brenson, 1988; Black Velvet at Dusk (essay), 2000; Essay: Boy on the Rocking Horse: An Introduction to the Art and Life of Eugene Speicher, 2005; Paintings published in book "100 New York Painters" by Cynthia Dantzic, 2006. Honours: Artist-in-Residence, New York State Council on the Arts; Certificate of Merit, Pastel Society of America; Scholarship Grant, Carnegie Mellon University. Memberships: Inducted Fellow, Society of Fellows, Dyson College, Pace University; Elected Full Member, Pastel Society of America; College Art Association of America. Address: 17 Fuller Place, Brooklyn, NY 11215-6006, USA. E-mail: viviantsao@earthlink.net

TSAY Jyh-Shen, b. 25 October 1969, Kinmen, Taiwan. Professor. Education: BSc, 1992, PhD, 1997, National Taiwan Normal University. Appointments: Postdoctoral Research Fellow, Academia Sinica, 1997-99; Visiting Research Fellow, Institute for Physical and Theoretical Chemistry, Bonn University, 1999-2000; Assistant Professor, Tunghai University, 2000-04; Associate Professor, National Chung-Cheng University, 2004-06; Associate Professor, 2006-2007, Professor, 2007-, National Taiwan Normal University. Publications: 60 articles in scientific journals. Honours: Best Dissertation Award, Physical Society of Republic of China, 1998; Research Award, Taiwan Association for Magnetic Technology, 2003; Best Poster Award, Physical Society, Republic of China, 1997. Address:

Department of Physics, National Taiwan Normal University, 88 Sec 4, Ting-Chou Road, Taipei 116, Taiwan, ROC. E-mail: jstsay@phy.ntnu.edu.tw

TSIFRINOVICH Vladimir, b. December 1950, Sverdlovsk, Russia. Physicist. m. Tatyana, 1 son, 1 daughter. Education: MS, Physics, Krasnoyarsk University, 1972; PhD, Physics, 1977, Dr of Sciences, Physics, 1992, Institute of Physics, Russian Academy of Sciences, Krasnoyarsk. Appointments: Senior Research Scientist, Leading Research Scientist, 1987-93, Institute of Physics, Russian Academy of Sciences; Adjunct Professor, 1994-98, Instructor of Physics, 1999-2002, Lecturer of Physics, 2002-, Polytechnic University, New York. Publications: Introduction to Quantum Computers, 1998; Modern Physics and Technology for Undergraduates, 2003; Perturbation Theory for Solid-State Quantum Computation with Many Quantum Bits, 2005; Magnetic Resonance Force Microscopy and a Single-Spin Measurement, 2006. Honours: Listed in international biographical directories. Memberships: American Physics Society. Address: Department of Physics, Polytechnic University, 6 MetroTech Center, Brooklyn, NY 11201, USA.

TSITVERBLIT Naftali Anatol, b. 29 October 1963, Kiev, Ukraine. Researcher. Education: MSc, Faculty of Mechanical and Power Engineering, Kiev Polytechnic Institute, 1987; PhD, Faculty of Mechanical Engineering, Tel-Aviv University, 1995. Appointments: Engineer, Scientific Research Institute of Robotics, Kiev, USSR, 1985-87; Teaching Assistant, Instructor, Tel-Aviv University, 1988-94; Visiting Scientist, Cornell University, 1994; Postdoctoral Research Fellow, Lamont-Doherty Earth Observatory of Columbia University, 1995-97; Postdoctoral Fellow, Geophysical Fluid Dynamics Summer Program, Woods Hole Oceanographic Institution, 1996; Visiting Scientist, Department of Fluid Mechanics and Heat Transfer of Tel-Aviv University, 1997-. Publications: In scientific journals, books and conference proceedings; Finite-Amplitude double-component convection due to different boundary conditions for two compensating horizontal gradients, 2000; Mechanism of finite-amplitude double-component convection due to different boundary conditions, 2004; Double-component convection due to different boundary conditions in an infinite slot diversely oriented to the gravity, 2007. Memberships: American Physical Society, 1995-2003; American Geophysical Union, 1995-; New York Academy of Science, 1995-2002; American Association for the Advancement of Science, 1999-2003. Address: 1 Yanosh Korchak Street, Apt 6, Kiryat Nordau, Netanya 42495, Israel. E-mail: naftali@eng.tau.ac.il

TSUJIMOTO Tatsuhiro, b. 11 December 1967, Kashihara, Nara, Japan. Gastroenterologist; Researcher. m. Kazuko Hiasa, 1999, 2 daughters. Education: MD, Nara Medical University, Graduate School, 2001. Appointments: Senior Staff, Department of Gastroenterology, Ishinkai Yao General Hospital, Yao, Osaka, 2000-05; Assistant Professor, Department of Endoscopy and Ultrasound, Nara Medical University, Kashikara, Nara, 2005-. Publications: Numerous articles in professional journals including: Pancreatitis Research Advances, 2008. Honours: 8th Japan Society of Ultrasonics in Medicine Award. Memberships: Japan Gastroenterological Endoscopy Society; Japanese Society of Gastroenterology; International Endotoxin and Innate Immunity Society; Asian Pacific Association for the Study of the Liver. Address: Nara Medical University, 840 Shigo-cho, Kashihara, Nara 634-8522, Japan. E-mail: tat-tyan@xa2.so-net.ne.jp

TSUJINO Yoshio, b. 5 May 1963, Tokyo, Japan. Physician. Education: BS, 1991, PhD, 2003, Shimane Medical University. Appointments: Associate Professor, 1992, 1998; Head Physician, Unnan Municipal General Hospital, 1996; Associate Professor, Shimane University School of Medicine, 2003. Publications: 10 articles in professional journals. Memberships: Japanese Dermatological Association; Japanese Society of Legal Medicine; Japanese Association of Forensic Toxicology; The International Association of Forensic Toxicologists. Address: 89-1 Enya, Izumo, Shimane 693-8501, Japan. E-mail: ytsujino@med.shimane-u.ac.jp

TSURUMOTO Toshiyuki, b. 21 November 1957, Kitakyushu, Japan. Orthpaedic Doctor. m. Misako, 2 sons, 1 daughter. Education: MD, School of Medicine, 1984, PhD, Graduate School of Medicine, 1990, Nagasaki University. Appointments: Assistant Professor, School of Medicine, 1999, Associate Professor, Graduate School of Biomedical Science, 2007, Nagasaki University. Publications: Nanbacteria-like particles in human arthritic synovial fluids. Memberships: Japanese Orthopaedic Association. E-mail: tsurumot@nagasaki-u.ac.jp

TSUTSUI Toshinori, b. 14 March 1952, Shiota, Saga, Japan. Anaesthesiologist. m. Kimiko Takeda. Education: Master of Science, 1978, Doctor of Medicine, 1986, Yamaguchi University, Japan. Appointments: Assistant Lecturer, Yamaguchi University, 1980-84; Senior Lecturer, Osaka City University, 1986-88; Chief Anaesthesiologist, Shimonoseki Welfare Hospital, 1988-96; Chief Anaesthesiologist, Saga National Hospital, 1996-2004. Memberships: Fellow, Japanese Society of Anaesthesiologists, 1978-; Fellow, Biomedical Fuzzy Systems Association, 1988-. Address: Tsutsui Clinic, 4-12-35, Kohno-Nishi, Saga, Saga, 840-0805 Japan. E-mail: tsutsui@av6.mopera.ne.jp

TSVELIKH Alexander, b. 16 February 1960, Moscow, Russia. Mathematics Software Development Researcher; Engineer. m. Olga Axenenko. Education: B Eng (with distinction), Radioelectronics, 1983, PhD, Computational Mathematics, 1987, Moscow Institute of Electronic Machine Construction. Appointments: Engineer, Junior Research Fellow, Moscow Institute of Electronic Machine Construction, 1983-85; Lecturer, Research Fellow, Moscow Machine Tool Institute, 1985-93; Research Engineer, Swinburne University of Technology, Melbourne, Australia, 1993-96; Mathematical Software Development Specialist, University of Melbourne, Australia, 1996-97; Principal Scientist/Managing Director, Computational Mechanics Australia Pty Ltd, Melbourne, 1998-. Publications: Variety of articles in areas of finite element analysis and computational geometry. Honours: Who's Who in the World, 2006, 2007; Who's Who in Science and Engineering, 2006, 2008. Address: PO Box 736, Camberwell South, VIC 3124, Australia. E-mail: comecau@bigpond.com Website: http://www.comecau.com

TSVETKOV Oleg Boris, b. 7 September 1939, Leningrad, USSR. Professor of Thermophysical Properties of Fluids. m. Marianna Konstantin Utkina, 2 daughters. Education: Diploma in Engineering, Technological Institute of Refrigeration (TIR), Leningrad, 1961; PhD, TIR, 1965; DSc, TIR, 1983; Postgraduate, Northwestern University, Evanston, Illinois, USA, 1979-80; TIR, Leningrad, 1980-83; University of Maryland, Washington DC, 1987-88. Appointments: Research Assistant Professor, TIR, 1964-68; Associate Professor, Royal University, Phnom-Penh, Cambodia, 1968-70; Acting Director, Research Department, TIR, 1970-79; Pro Rector of Research, State Academy of Refrigeration and Food Technology

(SARFT former TIR), St Petersburg, Russia, 1983-98, Head of Department, State University of Refrigeration and Food Engineering (formerly SARFT), St Petersburg, 1991-. Publications: Numerous articles in professional journals. Honours include: Vice Chairman, 14th World Congress of Refrigeration, Moscow, 1975; Vice-President Com B1, International Institute of Refrigeration, 1972-75, 1995-; Medal, USSR Ministry of Higher Education, Moscow, 1981; President, Science and Technology Society of Food Industry, St Petersburg, 1990-98; Recipient, Excellence in Teaching and Research, 1993; Vice-President, International Academy of Refrigeration, 1998; Research Grantee, International Science Foundation, 1994; Medal, Fifty Years of Victory in Second World War, 1995; Deputy editor-in-chief Proc. of the International Academy of Refrigeration, 1997; Research Grantee, EU Contract, 1998-2002; Professor Emeritus, 1999; Medal, 300 Years of St Petersburg, 2003; Vice President, Programm Committee of XI Russian Thermophysical Properties Conference, 2004; Medal, 60 Years of the Liberation of Leningrad from the Blockade, 2004; Medal, Sixty Years of Victory in Second World War, 2005; Medal, 100 Years of Russian Trade Unions, 2006; Laureat 2007 of State Russia prize. Memberships: International Academy of Sciences in Higher Education, 1992-; Member, Editorial Board, Kholodilnaya Teknika, Moscow, 1992-; Member, International Academy of Refrigeration, 1993; Member, International Union of Pure and Applied Chemistry, 1994-; Member, Editorial Board, Refrigeration Business, 1995-; Member, National Committee on Thermophysics, Russian Academy of Sciences, 1997-. Address: 31 Moika Embankment, Apt 54, 191186 St Petersburg, Russia. E-mail: obereg@softrex.com

TUCKER Eva Marie, b. 18 April 1929, Berlin, Germany. Writer. m. 11 March 1950 (widowed 1987), 3 daughters. Education: BA, Honours, German, English, University of London. Appointments: C Day-Lewis Writing Fellow, Vauxhall Manor School, London, 1978-79; Hawthornden Writing Fellowship, 1991. Publications: Contact (novel), 1966; Drowning (novel), 1969; Berlin Mosaic (novel), 2005; Radetzkymarch by Joseph Roth (translator), 1974. Contributions to: BBC Radio 3 and 4; Encounter; London Magazine; Woman's Journal; Vogue; Harper's; Spectator; Listener; Times Literary Supplement; PEN International. Memberships: English PEN; Society of Authors; Dorothy Richardson Society. Address: 63B Belsize Park Gardens, London NW3 4JN, England.

TUCKER Helen, b. 1 November 1926, Raleigh, North Carolina, USA. Writer. m. William Beckwith. Education: BA, Wake Forest University, 1946; Graduate Studies, Columbia University, 1957-58. Appointments: Newspaper Reporter and Writer for radio, 1946-57; Editorial Department, Columbia University Press, 1959-60; Director, Publications and Publicity, North Carolina Museum of Art, 1967-70. Publications: The Sound of Summer Voices, 1969; The Guilt of August Fielding, 1971; No Need of Glory, 1972; The Virgin of Lontano, 1973; A Strange and Ill-Starred Marriage, 1978; A Reason for Rivalry, 1979; A Mistress to the Regent: An Infamous Attachment, 1980; The Halverton Scandal, 1980; A Wedding Day Deception, 1981; The Double Dealers, 1982; Season of Dishonor, 1982; Ardent Vows, 1983; Bound by Honor, 1984; The Lady's Fancy, 1991; Bold Impostor, 1991. Contributions to: Lady's Circle; Ellery Queen Mystery Magazine; Alfred Hitchcock Mystery Magazine; Ladies Home Journal; Crecent Review; Montevallo Review; Redbook Magazine. Honours: Distinguished Alumni Award, Wake Forest University, 1971;

Franklin County Artist of the Year Award, 1992. Memberships: Mystery Writers of America; Carolina Crime Writers. Address: 2930 Hostetler Street, Raleigh, NC 27609, USA.

TUDAWE Ajith Erandan, b. 9 June 1953, Colombo, Sri Lanka. Chartered Accountant. m. Rohini Lasitha Fernando, 2 sons. Education: Bachelor of Arts, Accounting, CNAA, England. Appointments: Group Director, Tudawe Brothers Ltd, its subsidiaries and associate companies, 1983-; Chairman and Chief Executive, Ceylon Hospitals Ltd, (Durdans Hospital), 1994-; Chairman, Healthcare Group, 2003-. Publications: Accounting and management articles. Memberships: Institute of Chartered Accountants in England and Wales; Institute of Chartered Accountants of New Zealand; Fellow, CPA Australia; Fellow, Association of Chartered Certified Accountants of the UK; Fellow, Chartered Institute of Marketing in the UK; Past President, ACCA Sri Lanka. Address: 175/2 Havelock Road, Colombo 5, Sri Lanka. E-mail: ajithtudawe@durdans.com

TUDOR-CRAIG Pamela Wynn (Pamela, Lady Wedgwood), b. 26 June 1928, London, England. Art Historian; Writer. m. (1) Algernon James Riccarton Tudor-Craig, 27 July 1956, deceased 1969, 1 daughter, (2) Sir John Wedgwood, 1 May 1982, deceased 1989. Education: 1st Class Honours degree, 1949, PhD, 1952, Courtauld Institute of Art, University of London. Appointments; Teacher, several US Colleges; Presenter, The Secret Life of Paintings television series, 1986; Publications: Richard III, 1973; Co-author, The Secret Life of Paintings, 1986; Bells Guide to Westminster Abbey (co-author), 1986; Contributor, Exeter Cathedral, 1991; Anglo-Saxon Wall Paintings, 1991; The Regal Image of Richard II and the Wilton Diptych, 1997; King Arthur's Round Table, 2000; Old St Paul's 1616, 2004. Many contributions to the Church Times, History Today, and learned Journals. Founder of Harlaxton Symposium of English Medieval Studies and Cambridgeshire Historic Churches Trust. Honour: Honorary Doctor of Humanities, William Jewell College, 1983. Memberships: Cathedrals Advisory Commission, 1975-90; Architectural Advisory Panel, Westminster Abbey, 1979-98; Cultural Affairs Committee, English Speaking Union, 1990-98; Society of Antiquaries, fellow, 1958-; council member, 1989-92; Founder of Harlaxton Symposium of English Medieval Studies and Cambridgeshire Historic Churches Trust. Address: 9 St Anne's Crescent, Lewes, East Sussex BN7 1SB, England.

TUKE Diana Rosemary, b. 5 July 1932, Weymouth, Dorset, England. Lecturer; Freelance Journalist; Writer; Author. Education: British Horse Society Preliminary Instructor's Certificate, Porlock Vale Riding School, 1954. Appointments: Picture Editor, The Encyclopaedia of the Horse, 1973; Lectured, updated Equine Feeding Section of Instruction Manual, Metropolitan Police, 1986. Publications: A Long Road to Harringay, 1960; Bit-by-Bit, 1965; Riding Cavalcade, contributor, 1967; Tomorrow, short story, 1968; Stitch-by-Stitch, 1970; Horse-by-Horse, 1973; The Complete Book of the Horse (contributor), 1973; The Encyclopaedia of the Horse (contributor), 1973; Getting Your Horse Fit, 1977; The Rider's Handbook, 1977; Feeding Your Horse, 1980; Cottage Craft Guide to Aintree Bits, 1982; Horse Tack - The Complete Equipment Guide for Riding and Driving (contributor), 1982; The Country Life Book of Saddlery and Equipment (contributor), 1982; Clipping Your Horse, 1984; Feeding Your Horse and Pony, 2nd edition, 1988; Horse Trials Review No 2 - Feeding for Fitness, video, 1990; Clipping, Trimming and Plaiting Your Horse, 2nd edition, 1992; Nursing Your Horse, 1999, 2nd edition, 2002; Novels: Ravensworth, 2000, 2nd edition, 2005; When the Rivers

Roared, 2000, 2nd edition, 2005; Away in the Mountains, 2001, 2nd edition, 2005; The Lonely Shore, 2001, 2nd edition, 2005; The Old Mill, 2004; Contributions to: Riding; Horse and Hound; The Daily Telegraph; The Field; The Cronical of the Horse, USA; Others. Honours: Trophies for sale of books: Bit-by-Bit, 25,000 copies, 1995; Getting Your Horse Fit, 25,000 copies, 1995; Clipping, Trimming and Plaiting Your Horse, 10,000 copies, 1998. Membership: British Equestrian Writer's Association. Address: Gallery House, Duddenhoe End, Saffron Walden, Essex CB11 4UU, England.

TULASIEWICZ Witold, b. Berlin, Germany. Part time Professor of Language Education; Researcher. Appointments: Fellow, Wolfson College Cambridge; Former Full-time University Teacher, University of Cambridge; Director and Co-director of several national and international projects including: Education as Dialogue, Europe East and West; Intercultural Education in a multicultural and multilingual context; Currently researching and practising the application of a language awareness approach to the study of language and intercultural education; Visiting Chairs in Calgary and Montreal, Canada, Warsaw and Bialystok, Poland, Canton and Hong Kong, China, Mainz, Germany. Publications include: Index Verborum zur deutschen Kaiserchronik (author); Teaching the Mother Tongue in a Multilingual Europe (co-author); Education in a Single Europe (co-author). Memberships: Comparative Education Society in Europe; Association of Language Awareness; Committee for Russian and East European Studies in Cambridge; Polish Academy of Sciences Abroad; Belarus Academy of Educational Studies; Corresponding Member, Brandenburg Berlin Academy; Consultant to EU Committee of the Regions. Address: Wolfson College, Barton Road, Cambridge CB3 9BB, England. E-mail: wft20@cam.ac.uk

TULEEV Aman Gumirovich, b. 13 May 1944, Krasnovodsk, Turkmenian Republic. Politician. m. Elvira Solovyeva, 2 sons, 1 deceased. Education: Novosibirsk Institute of Railway Engineering, 1973; Academy of Social Studies, 1989. Appointments: Assistant Station Master, 1964-69, Station Master, 1969-73, Railway Station, Moundebash; Station Master, Railway Station, Mezhdurechensk, 1973-78; Head, Novokuznetsk Line, Kemerovo Railway, 1978-85; Head, Transport Department, Kemorovo's Regional Committee of the CPSU, 1985-88; Head, Kemerovo Railway, 1988-90; Chairman, Kemerovo's Regional Council of People's Deputies, People's Deputy of RSFSR, 1991; Peoples' Deputy of Russian Federation, 1990-93; Candidate for Presidency, 1991, 1996, 2000; Supported coup d'etat attempt, 1991; Member, CP of Russian Federation, 1993-2003; Yedinaya Rossiya party, 2003-; Chair, Legislative Assembly, Kemerovo Region, 1994-96; Minister of Co-operation with CIS, 1996-97; Governor, Kemerovo Region, 1997-; Member, Council of Federation, 1993-95, 1997-2001; Candidate, Russian presidential elections, 2000; Supported Putin's regional party, 2003; Joined United Russia, 2005. Publications: Author of more than 100 articles and books including: Power in hands of a man and man in hands of the power, 1993; State power in region: personal factor, social contacts, 1998; To remain yourself, 1999; Political leader and political leadership in regional conflicts, 1999; We have the only Russia, 1999; Political leadership in modern Russia, 2000. Honours: Medal for Labour Valour, 1976; Medal, Labour Veteran of USSR, 1992; Medal, 300th Anniversary of Russian Navy, 1998; The Order of Honor, 1999; The Order of the North Star; Peter the Great International Award, 2002; International Millennium Award for Service to Humanity, 2003; Order for Outstanding Country Service IV degree, 2003; Andrey

Pervozvanny International Award for Faith and Loyalty, 2003. Memberships: Honorary Railwayman; Freeman of Kemerovo and Novokuznetsk; Honorary Doctor of Sciences, Ulan-Bator University of Mongolian Academy of Sciences; Full Member, International Academy of Informatization; Full Member, International Engineering Academy. Address: pr Sovetskiy, 62, 650099 Kemerovo, Russia. Website: www.mediakuzbass.ru

TULLY (Sir) (William) Mark, b. 24 October 1935, Calcutta, India. Journalist; Broadcaster. m. Margaret Frances Butler, 13 August 1960, 2 sons, 2 daughters. Education: Marlborough College; MA, Trinity Hall, Cambridge, 1959. Appointments: Regional Director, Abbeyfield Society, 1960-64; Assistant, Appointments Department, 1964-65, Assistant, later Acting Representative, New Delhi, 1955-69, Programme Organiser and Talks Writer, Eastern Service, 1969-71, Chief of Bureau, Delhi, 1972-93, South Asia Correspondent, 1993-94, BBC; Freelance writer, broadcaster, journalist, 1994-. Publications: Amritsar: Mrs Gandhi's Last Battle (with Satish Jacob), 1985; From Raj to Rajiv (with Z Masani), 1988; No Full Stops in India, 1991; The Heart of India, 1995; The Lives of Jesus, 1996; India in Slow Motion (with Gillian Wright), 2002; No Full Stops in India; The Heart of India; Divide and Quit; India – 50 years of Independence; India's Unending Journey; The Lives of Jesus, BBC TV series; Four Faces: A Journey in Search of Jesus the Divine, the Jew, the Rebel, the Sage. Honours: Officer of the Order of the British Empire, 1985; Padma Shri, India, 1992; Honorary Fellow, Trinity Hall, Cambridge, 1994; Honorary Doctor of Letters, University of Strathclyde, 1997; Padma Bhushan, 2005. Address: 1 Nizamuddin East, New Delhi 110 013, India. E-mail: tulwri@ndf.vsnl.net.in

TURCAN Robert Alain, b. 22 June 1929, Paris, France. Professor. m. Marie Deleani, 1 son, 2 daughters. Education: Bachelor's degree in Arts, 1953; Diploma of Higher Studies, 1954; Aggregation of Letters, 1955; D Litt, Paris, Sorbonne, 1966. Appointments: Ecole Normale Supérieure, Paris-Ulm, 1952-55; Ecole Française de Rome, 1955-57; Assistant, 1957-63, Master of Conferences, 1963-69, Professor, University of Lyon, 1969-87, University of Paris-Sorbonne, 1988-94; Member, Institute of France, 1990-. Publications: Numerous books, papers and articles in professional journals. Honours: Prix Jeanbernat, 1958; Prix Th Reinach, 1967; Prix Saintour, 1981; Chevalier de la Légion d'Honneur; Officier des Arts et des Lettres; Commandeur des Palmes Académiques. Memberships: Académie des Inscriptions et Belles-Lettres, Institut de France; Académie Centrale Européene de Science et Art; Institut Archéologique de Berlin. Address: 3 residence du Tourillon, F-69290 Craponne, France.

TURCOTTE Paul-André Gaëtan, b. 10 July 1943, Saint-Cuthbert, Canada. Professor; Researcher. Education: Baccalaureate of Arts, Collège de Joliette, 1964; Baccalaureate in Education, Laval University, Quebec, 1970; Licence and Master in Theology, University of Montreal, 1970; Doctorate in Sociology, École des Hautes Études en Sciences Sociales, 1979; Doctorate in Theology, Institut Catholique de Paris, 1987. Appointments: Professor, University of Haiti, 1971-75; Associate Researcher, French National Research Centre, 1977-; Professor, Saint-Paul's University, Ottawa, 1980-98; Professor, University of Montreal, 1984; Visiting Researcher, IRESCO, Paris, 1986-87; Fellow, School of Graduate Studies and Research, University of Ottawa, 1987-2000; Professor of Sociology, Institut Catholique de Paris, 1993-2008; Visiting Researcher, Instituto de Investigacion en Ciencias Socialis (INCIS), Valencia, Spain, 1996-2002; Visiting Professor, UCAC, Yaoundé, Cameroon, 2000-2005; University of Roma Tre, 2003, 2006; University St Joseph, Beirut, Lebanon,

2003, 2006; University of Valencia, Valencia, Spain, 2005. Publications: Réconciliation et Libération, 1972; L'Éclatement d'un monde, 1981; Les Chemins de la différence, 1985; L'Enseignement secondaire public des frères éducateurs, 1988; Intransigeance ou Compromis, 1994; Sociologie du Christianisme, 1996; La Religion dans la modernité, 1997; Compromis religieux et mutation du croire, 1998; Sociologia e Storia della Vita Consecrata, 2000; Le Phénomène des sectes, 2002; Handbook of Early Christianity, 2002; Médiation et Compromis, 2006; Editor of 8 collective works and 17 issues of Social Compass, Retm Le Supplément, Pastoral Sciences, Claretianum; Over 250 papers and articles in 25 different journals or chapters of collective works. Honours: Prize of the Provincial Bank, Faculty of Theology, University of Montreal, 1970; Cafe-Best Publication, Canadian Society for the Study of Education, 1989; IBC Top 100 Educators, 2005; Man of the Year, 2005; Genius Laureate of France, 2006. Memberships: Confrontations, Paris, 1994-; International Council of Museums, UNESCO, 1998-; Association of Canadian Studies, 1998-. Address: 170 Blvd du Montparnasse, 75014 Paris, France.

TURK Austin Theodore, b. 28 May 1934, Gainesville, Georgia, USA. Sociologist; Criminologist. m. Ruth-Ellen Marie Grimes. Education: BA, cum laude, University of Georgia, 1956; MA, University of Kentucky, 1959; PhD, University of Wisconsin, 1962. Appointments: Instructor, to Professor, Indiana University, 1962-74; Professor of Sociology, University of Toronto, 1974-88; Professor of Sociology, 1988-, Chair, 1989-94, University of California at Riverside. Publications: Criminality and Legal Order, 1969; Political Criminality: The Defiance and Defense of Authority, 1982. Honours: President, American Society of Criminology, 1984-85; Fellow, American Society of Criminology, 1978. Memberships: American Society of Criminology; American Sociological Association; Academy of Criminal Justice Sciences; Law and Society Association. Address: Department of Sociology, University of California, Riverside, CA 92521, USA.

TURNER Amédée Edward, b. 26 March 1929, London, England. Queens Counsel. m. Deborah Dudley Owen, 1 son, 1 daughter. Education: BA, 1951, MA, 1953, Christ Church, Oxford. Appointments: Practised at Patent Bar, Inner Temple, London, 1954-57; Counsel at Kenyon & Kenyon (Patent Attorneys) New York, USA, 1957-60; Practice at Patent Bar, London, 1960-; Contested General Elections (Conservative) Norwich North, 1964, 1966, 1970; Appointed Queens Counsel, 1976-; Elected to European Parliament for Suffolk and Harwich and Suffolk and Cambridgeshire (Conservative), European Democratic Group, European People's Party, 1979-94; Chief Whip, 1989-2002, Chairman, 2002-04, Civil Liberties Committee; Counsel, Oppenheimer Wolff & Donnelly, Brussels, 1994-2001; Senior Counsel, Apco Europe, 1995-98; Member Executive Committee European League for Economic Co-operation, 1996-; Director, CJA Consultants, 2001-, Chairman, 2005-; Phare Advisor to Macedonian Parliament on approximation of EU legislation, 2001-2002; Member, Advisory Council to the Anglican Observer to UN, 2002-. Publications: The Law of Trade Secrets, 1964; The Law of the New European Patent, 1979; Reports for the European Commission including Intellectual Property Law and the Single Market, 1997; Manuals for the Macedonian Parliament on the Approximation of EU Laws and on Democratic Procedures, 2002; Numerous political articles on behalf of the Conservative Party; Numerous studies for the European Commission. Honours: Queens Counsel, 1976; Honorary Member of the European Parliament, 1994. Memberships:

Carlton Club; The European Network; Conservative Group for Europe; Tory Reform Group; Kenya Society; African Society; International Association for the Protection of Industrial Property; Bar Association for Commerce and Industry. Address: Penthouse 7, Bickenhall Mansions, London W1U 6BS, England. E-mail: amedee.turner@btinternet.com

TURNER (Jonathan) Adair, b. 5 October 1955, Ipswich, England. Business Executive, Public Policy Specialist. m Orna ni Chionna, 2 daughters. Education: Degree, Economics and History, Cambridge University, 1974-78. Appointments: McKinsey and Company, 1982-95; Director-General, Confederation of British Industry, 1995-99; Director, United Business Media, 2000-; Chairman UK Low Pay Commission, 2003-06; Chairman, UK Pension Commission, 2003-06; Vice-Chairman, Merrill Lynch Europe, 2000-06. Director, Standard Chartered plc 2006-; Director, Patemoster Ltd 2006-; Director Siemens plc 2006-; Chairman Economic and Social Research Council, 2007. Publication: Just Capital, The Liberal Economy, 2002. Honours: Non Party Peerage, UK House of Lords, Lord Turner of Ecchinswell, 2005; Honorary Doctorate, City University, 2004. Memberships: Trustee of the World-Wide Fund for Nature, WWF, UK; Trustee, Save The Children, UK.

TURNER Kathleen, b. 19 June 1954, Springfield, Missouri, USA. Actress. m. (1) David Guc, divorced 1982, (2) Jay Weiss, 1984, divorced, 1 daughter. Education: Central School of Speech and Drama, London; SW Missouri State University; University of Maryland. Career: Theatre: various roles including: Gemini, 1978; The Graduate, London, 2000; TV includes: The Doctors, 1977; Leslie's Folly, 1995; Style and Substance, 1996; Legalese, 1998; Films: Body Heat, 1981; The Man With Two Brains, 1983; Crimes of Passion, 1984; Romancing the Stone, 1984; Prizzi's Honour, 1985; The Jewel of the Nile, 1985; Peggy Sue Got Married, 1986; Julia and Julia, 1988; Switching Channels, 1988; The Accidental Tourist, 1989; The War of the Roses, 1990; V I Warzhawski, 1991; House of Cards; Undercover Blues, 1993; Serial Mom, 1994; Naked in New York, 1994; Moonlight and Valentino, 1995; A Simple Wish, 1997; The Real Blonde, 1997; The Virgin Suicides, 1999; Love and Action in Chicago, 1999; Baby Geniuses, 1999; Prince of Central Park, 2000; Beautiful, 2000; Without Love, 2004; Monster House, 2006; TV includes: Cinderella; King of the Hill; Friends; Law & Order; Nip/Tuck. Address: c/o Chris Andrews, ICM, 8942 Wilshire Boulevard, Beverly Hills, CA 90211, USA.

TURNER Lynette, b. 28 May 1945, London, England. Graphic Artist. Education: BSc (Hons) Zoology, Manchester University, 1965-68; Etching, City and Guilds Art School, 1968-69; HNDD, Graphic Design, Manchester Polytechnic, 1970-71. Career: Set up etching workshop at home at the Oval in London and sold prints at Heal's and Liberty's, 1975-94; Moved to Cornwall 1994-; Exhibitions: Century Gallery, Henley, 1976; Margaret Fisher Gallery, 1976; RA, 1977; SE London Art Group, YMCA, Great Russell Street, 1983; RA Summer Show, 1987; Etchings and watercolours, The Crypt of St Martin-in-the-Fields, 1989. Publications: Works featured in the Observer, 1989; Currently working on comic strip adventures. Honour: 2nd Prize for Etching, City and Guilds Art School. Membership: Royal Cornwall Polytechnic Society. Address: Pendynas, Minnie Place, Falmouth, Cornwall TR11 3NN, England.

TURNER Neil Clifford, b. 13 March 1940, Preston, England. Research Scientist. m. Jennifer Gibson, 3 sons. Education: BSc (Hons), 1962; PhD, 1968; DSc, 1983. Appointments:

Plant Physiologist, CT Agricultural Experimental Station, New Haven, USA, 1967-74; Senior Research Scientist, 1974-84, Research Leader, 1984-93, Chief Research Scientist, 1993-2005, CSIRO Plant Industry, Canberra and Perth, Australia; Adjunct Professor, University of Western Australia, Perth, Australia, 1998-2006; Director, Centre for Legumes in Mediterranean Agriculture, The University of Western Australia, Perth, 2006-07. Publications: Adaption of Plants to Water and High Temperature Stress, 1980; Plant Growth, Drought and Salinity, 1986; Crop Production on Duplex Soils, 1992; The Role of Agroforestry and Perennial Pasture in Mitigating Waterlogging and Secondary Salinity, Special Issue, Agricultural Water Management, 2002; Water Scarcity: Challenges and Opportunities for Crop Science, Special Issue, Agricultural Water Management, 2006. Honours: Fellow, American Society of Agronomy, 1982; Fellow, Crop Science Society of America, 1985; Fellow, Australian Academy of Technology Sciences and Engineering, 1992; Medallist, 1993, Fellow, 1995, Australian Institute of Agricultural Science and Technology; Institute for Scientific Information Australian Citation Laureate, 2001; Foreign Fellow, Indian Academy of Agricultural Sciences, 2003; Centenary Medal, Australia, 2003. Memberships: Australian Academy of Technology Sciences and Engineering; Australian Institute of Agricultural Science and Technology, ACT President, 1978-79. Address: Centre for Legumes in Mediterranean Agriculture, M080, The University of Western Australia, 35 Stirling Highway, Crawley, Western Australia 6009, Australia.

TURNER R Chip, b. 18 January 1948, Shreveport, Louisiana, USA. Television Network Executive. m. Sandra Aymond Turner, 2 sons. Education: BA, Communications, Louisiana College, 1970; Baptist Theological Seminary, New Orleans, 1973; Accredited in Public Relations (APR-PRSA), 1995. Appointments: State Director, ACTS Television Network, State Media Director, Louisiana Baptist Convention, 1981-85; Assistant Director of Development, Coordinator of Telecommunications, Northwestern State University, 1995-97; National Director of Local Programming, Odyssey Cable Network, 1997-99; Vice-President for Marketing and Distribution, Family Net Television, Fort Worth, Texas, 1999-; Senior Director for Corporate Relations, Family Net Television and Radio, 2006-; National President of the Association of Baptists for Scouting, 2005-. Publications: The Church Video Answer Book; The Church and Video; Why Not Baptist? A History of the Association of Baptists for Scouting; Managing Editor and Contributor, 75 Glorious Years, A History of Calvary Baptist Church; Author of articles in over 35 magazines. Honours: National Distinguished Eagle Scout Award; Named Senior Practitioner for Southern Public Relations Federation; National Outstanding Youth Leadership Award for Religious Heritage of America; 50 year Veteran Recognition, Boy Scouts of America, 2006; Silver Good Shepherd Recognition, Association of Baptists for Scouting, 2006. Memberships: Public Relations Society of America; Baptist Communicators Council; National Cable Telecommunications Association; National Religious Broadcasters; National Board of Directors – Christians in Cable. Address: Family Net, 6350 West Freeway, Fort Worth, TX 76116, USA. E-mail: cturner@familynet.com

TURNER Simon Paul, b. 21 March 1959, Richmond, Surrey, England. Educator; Manager; Consultant. Education: Academic and professional qualifications in the fields of: Health & Safety; Electrical; Engineering (Electronic & Mechanical); Computing; Science; Life/Key Skills; Teaching and Learning; Management; and others. Appointments: Junior Technician, 1980-84, Corporal, 1984-85, RAF General

Technician Electrical, Royal Air Force West Raynham; Flying Officer, RAF Engineering Officer, Royal Military College of Science, Swindon, and RAF (Cranwell, Chivenor, Marham and Cottesmore) 1985-89; Sole Proprietor, Eastern Office Equipment, Norfolk, 1989-93; Part time Private Tuition, Norfolk Home Tutor Agency, 1991-93; Part time Lecturer, Adult Education Centre, Litcham, Norfolk, 1992-93; Lecturer, 1993-95, Head of Section Engineering, 1995-99, Head of Technology (Construction, IT and Engineering), 1999-2001, Deputy Head of Faculty (Design & Technology), 2001-03, Director of Operations, 2003-06, Isle College, Wisbech, Cambridgeshire; Part time Electrical & Electronic Private Work, Kings Lynn, Norfolk, 1993-98; Part time External Verifier, City and Guilds, 2005-; Part time Educational Consultant, Huntingdonshire Regional College, 2006-. Publications: Introduction of Foundation Provision for Vocational Programmes. Honours: RAF Certificate of Merit; Norfolk Circle Electrical Prize; Royal Military College of Science College Prize; Listed in international biographical dictionaries. Memberships: Institute of Electrical Engineers; Institution of Engineering and Technology; Institute of Incorporated Engineers; Institute for Learning; Institute of Motor Industries; Institute of Physics; Institute of Leadership and Management; British Astronomical Association; City & Guilds Association; Association of College Managers; Association of External Verifiers; Uganda Association for the Promotion of Science; Graduate, City and Guilds Institute; Engineering Council registered Incorporated Engineer; Institute of Assessors and Verifiers; City & Guilds Institute; Affiliate Member, Computer Society. Address: 2 Wesley Avenue, Terrington St Clement, Kings Lynn, Norfolk, PE34 4NJ, England.

TURNER Ted (Robert Edward II), b. 19 November 1938. American Broadcasting Executive; Yachtsman. m. (1) Judy Nye, divorced, 1 son, 1 daughter, (2) Jane S Smith, 1965, divorced 1988, 1 son, 2 daughters, (3) Jane Fonda, 1991, divorced 2001. Education: Brown University. Appointments: General Manager, Turner Advertising, Macon, Georgia, 1960-63; President, CEO, various Turner companies, Atlanta, 1963-70; Chair of Board, President, Turner Broadcasting System Inc, 1970-96; Established Cable News Network (CNN), 1980, Headline News Network, 1992, CNN International, 1985; Chair, Better World Society, Washington, DC, 1985-90; Acquired MGM library of film and TV properties, 1986; Founder, Turner Foundation Inc, 1991; Launched Cartoon Network, 1992; TBS merged with New Line Cinema, 1994; Vice Chair, Time Warner Inc (after TBS merger with Time Warner Inc), 1996-2001; Founder, UN Foundation, 1997; Founder, Nuclear Threat Initiative, 2001; Vice Chair, AOL Time Warner (after Time Warner Inc merger with AOL), 2001-03; Founder, Ted Turner Pictures and Ted Turner Documentaries, 2001; Founder, Ted's Montana Grill restaurant chain, 2002; Former owner and President, Atlanta Braves professional baseball team; Former owner and Chair of Board, Atlanta Hawks professional basketball team; Director, Martin Luther King Center, Atlanta. Publication: The Racing Edge, 1979. Honours: Fastnet Trophy, 1979; Man of the Year, Time Magazine, 1991; Cable and Broadcasting's Man of the Century, 1999; Cable TV Hall of Fame, 1999; U Thant Peace Award, 1999; World Ecology Award, University of Missouri, 2000; Named Yachtsman of the Year 4 times. Address: c/o Ted's Montana Grill, 133 Luckie Street, NW, Atlanta, GA 30303, USA. Website: www.tedturner.com

TURNER Tina (Annie Mae Bullock), b. 26 November 1939, Brownsville, Tennessee, USA. Singer. Songwriter. m. Ike Turner, 1958, divorced 1978. Career: Member, Ike

& Tina Turner, 1958-78; Worldwide tours include: Support to Rolling Stones, UK tour, 1966, US tour, 1969; European tour, 1971; Newport Festival, 1969; Solo artiste, 1978-; US tour, 1981; Support to Lionel Richie, UK tour, 1984; Rock In Rio Festival, Brazil, 1985; Live Aid, Philadelphia, 1985; European tour, 1985; Prince's Trust Gala, London, 1986; World tours, 1987, 1990; Record 182,000 audience attend concert, Rio De Janeiro, 1988; First woman to play Palace of Versailles, France, 1990; Film appearances: Tommy, 1974; Mad Max - Beyond Thunderdome, 1985; Life story documented in film What's Love Got To Do With It?, 1992. Compositions include: Nutbush City Limits; Recordings: Albums with Ike Turner: Live! The Ike And Tina Turner Show, 1965; River Deep, Mountain High, 1966; Outa Season, 1969; The Hunter, 1969; Come Together, 1970; Workin' Together, 1971; Live At Carnegie Hall, 1971; 'Nuff Said, 1971; Feel Good, 1972; Nutbush City Limits, 1974; Solo albums: The Acid Queen, 1975; Private Dancer; Mad Max - Beyond The Thunderdome, 1985; Break Every Rule (Number 1 in nine countries), 1986; Live In Europe, 1988; Foreign Affair (Number 1, UK), 1989; Simply The Best, 1991; What's Love Got To With It (film soundtrack), 1993; Wildest Dreams, 1996; Dues Paid, 1999; Twenty Four Seven, 1999; Hit singles include: with Ike Turner: It's Gonna Work Out Fine, 1961; Poor Fool, 1962; River Deep, Mountain High, 1966; I Want To Take You Higher, 1970; Proud Mary, 1971; Nutbush City Limits, 1973; Solo: Let's Stay Together, 1983; What's Love Got To Do With It? (Number 1, US), 1984; Better Be Good To Me, 1984; Private Dancer, 1984; We Don't Need Another Hero, theme for film Thunderdome (Number 2, US), 1985; One Of The Living, 1985; It's Only Love, with Bryan Adams, 1985; Typical Male (Number 2, US), 1986; The Best, 1989; I Don't Wanna Lose You, 1989; Be Tender With Me Baby, 1990; It Takes Two, duet with Rod Stewart, 1990; Way Of The World, 1991; I Don't Wanna Fight, 1993; Goldeneye (film theme), 1995; Missing You, 1996; In Your Wildest Dreams, 1996; When the Heartache is Over, 1999; Whatever You Need, 2000; Contributor, We Are The World, USA For Africa, 1985. Publications: I Tina (autobiography). Honours include: Grammy Awards: Record of the Year; Song of the Year; Best Female Vocal Performance; Best Female Rock Vocal, 1985; American Music Awards: Favourite Soul/R&B Female Artist, and Video Artist, 1985; Best Female Pop/Rock Artist, 1986; MTV Music Video award, 1985; Star on Hollywood Walk of Fame, 1986; Rock And Roll Hall Of Fame, with Ike Turner, 1991; World Music Award, Outstanding Contribution To The Music Industry, 1993; Kennedy Center Honors, 2005. Address: c/o Roger Davies Management, 15030 Ventura Blvd, Suite 772, Sherman Oaks, CA 91403, USA.

TURNER-WARWICK Margaret, b. 19 November 1924, London. Physician. m. Richard Turner-Warwick, 2 daughters. Education: MA, BM, BCh, Oxford University, 1950, MRCP, 1952, DM, 1956; PhD, London University, 1961; Clinical Training, University College Hospital, Brompton Hospital, 1950-61; FRCP, 1969; Consultant Physician: Elizabeth Garrett Anderson Hospital, 1961-67, Brompton and London Chest Hospitals, 1967-72; Professor of Medicine, Brompton and Cardiothoracic Institute, London, 1972-87; Dean, Cardiothoracic Institute, London, 1984-87; President, Royal College of Physicians, 1989-92; Chairman, Royal Devon Exeter Healthcare Trust, 1992-95. Publication: Book: Immunology of Lung, 1979. Honours: Dame Commander of the British Empire; Osler Medal, Oxford, 1996; Presidential Award, European Respiratory Society, 1997; President's Medal, British Thoracic Society, 1999; Honorary DSc: New York University, 1985, Exeter University, 1990, University of London, 1990, Hull University, 1991, University of Sussex,

1992, University of Oxford, 1992, University of Cambridge, 1993, University of Leicester, 1997; Fellowships: ACP (Hon); Royal College of Radiology; Fellow, Academy of Medical Science, 1998; Royal College of Physicians, Ireland; Royal College of Physicians and Surgeons, Glasgow; University College, London; Faculty of Public Health Medicine; Faculty of Occupational Medicine; Royal Australian College of Physicians; Bencher, Middle Temple (Hon); Royal College of Physicians and Surgeons, Canada (Hon); Royal College of Anaesthetists (Hon); College of Medicine of South Africa (Hon); Royal College of Pathologists (Hon); Imperial College London (Hon); Royal College of General Practitioners (ad eundum); Royal College of Physicians of Edinburgh; Royal College of General Practitioners; Green College, Oxford (Hon); Lady Margaret Hall, Oxford (Hon); Girton College, Cambridge (Hon). Memberships: British Thoracic Society, President, 1982; Academy of Malaysia; South German and Australasian Thoracic Societies (Hon); Association of Physicians of Great Britain and Ireland (Hon); Alpha Omega Alpha. Address: Pynes House, Thorverton, Nr Exeter, Devon EX5 5LT, England.

TURNHAM ELVINS Mark Anthony Lawrence, b. 26 November 1939. Warden Greyfriars Hall, Oxford. Education: Dover College; St Stephen's House, Oxford; Beda College, Rome; MA, Heythrop College, University of London; GradDipSip, Milltown Institute, Dublin; Ordained, Easter Sunday, 1973. Appointments: Sandhurst Entry, 1958; Ruskin School of Drawing, 1960; Assistant Manager, St James's Gallery, Jermyn Street, London, 1961-62; Assistant Editor, Debrett's Peerage (and Assisting at College of Arms), 1962-64; St Stephen's House, Oxford, 1964; Founder, Simon House for the Homeless, 1964; Ordained Anglican, 1967; Allen Hall, 1969; Beda College, 1970; Ordained Catholic Priest, 1973; Curate, Arundel; Founder, Association for English Worship; Curate, Brighton, 1980; Founder, St Thomas Fund for the Homeless); Parish Priest, Henfield, 1991; Entered Order of Friars Minor Capuchin, Definator and Retreat Director, 1995-. Publications: Old Catholic England, 1979; Arundel Priory 1380-1980, 1981; The Church's Response to the Homeless, 1985; Cardinals and Heraldry, 1989; Catholic Trivia, 1992; Towards a People's Liturgy, 1993; Gospel Chivalry 2006, A Eucharistic Vision, 2006; CTS pamphlets and articles in Catholic Press. Honours: Chaplain of Magistral Grace, Sovereign Military Order of Malta, 1981; Ecclesiastical Knight of Grace of the Constantinian Order of St George, 1982; Gold Medal of Merit, 2003; Warden, Greyfriars Hall, Oxford, Chaplain to the University of Central Lancs, 2006-07. Memberships: Life Member, Heraldry Society; Life Member, Kent Archaeological Society; Fellow, Ancient Monument Society; Veteran Member, Honourable Artillery Company. Address: Greyfriar's Hall, Iffley Road, Oxford, OX4 1SB, England.

TURTURRO John, b. 28 February 1957, Brooklyn, USA. Actor. m. Katherine Borowitz, 1 son. Education: State University of New York at New Paltz; Yale Drama School. Career: Former labourer; Films: Raging Bull; Desperately Seeking Susan; Exterminator III; The Flamingo Kid; To Live and Die in LA; Hannah and Her Sisters; Gung Ho; Offbeat; The Color of Money; The Italian Five Corners; Do the Right Thing; Miller's Crossing; Men of Respect; Mo' Better Blues; Jungle Fever; Barton Fink; Brain Doctors; Mac; Being Human; Quiz Show; Fearless; Clockers; Search and Destroy; Unstrung Heroes; Sugartime; Grace of My Heart; Box of Moonlight; The Truce; The Big Lebowski, 1997; Animals, 1997; Lesser Prophets, 1998; Rounders, 1998; Illuminata, 1998; The Source, 1999; The Cradle Will Rock, 1999; Company Men,

1999; Two Thousand and None, 1999; Oh Brother, Where Art Thou?, 1999; The Man Who Cried, 1999; The Luzhin Defense, 1999; Thirteen Conversations About One Thing, 2000; Collateral Damage, 2001; Mr Deeds, 2002; Fear X, 2003; Anger Management, 2003; 2B Perfectly Honest, 2004; Secret Passage, 2004; Secret Window, 2004; She Hate Me, 2004; The Moon and the Son: An Imagined Conversation (voice), 2005; Romance & Cigarettes, 2005; Quelques jours en Septembre, 2006; The Good Shepherd, 2006; Slipstream, 2007; Transformers, 2007; Margot at the Wedding, 2007; Joulutarina (voice), 2007; What Just Happened? 2008. Address: c/o ICM, 40 West 57th Street, New York, NY 10019, USA.

TUTSSEL Mark Christopher, b. 1958, Cardiff, Wales. Advertising Creative Director. m. Julie Elizabeth Tutssel, 1 son. Education: Cardiff College of Art and Design, 1976-80; Harrison Cowley Advertising Fellowship, 1979-80. Appointments: Junior Art Director, Saatchi & Saatchi, 1980-81; Art Director, MWK Advertising, 1981-86; Art Director, 1986-90, Creative Director, 1990-99, Executive Creative Director, 1999-2002, Leo Burnett, London; Vice-Chairman and Deputy Chief Creative Officer, Leo Burnett USA, 2002-2004; Vice-Chairman and Regional Chief Creative Officer, Leo Burnett North America, 2004-06; Worldwide Chief Creative Officer, Leo Burnett, 2006-. Publications: Work appears in various books including: Design and Art Direction; The One Show; Eurobest; Communication Arts, USA; The Andy's; The Art Directors' Club of Europe; The Art Directors' Club of New York; Cannes Awards; The British Television Awards. Honours: Numerous advertising awards including: The Cannes Grand Prix; 10 Cannes Gold Lions; 2 Eurobest Grand Prix; 30 Eurobest Golds; 5 D&AD Silver Pencils; The Clio Grand Prix; The Andy Grand Prix, 20 Andy Awards; Former Welsh Schoolboys Champion, Football and Basketball; Most Awarded Advertising Creative Director in the World, 2001; Listed in biographical dictionaries. Memberships: Design and Art Direction; The One Club, New York; Fellow, Royal Society of Arts; Soho House, London and New York; East Bank Club, Chicago; Chicago Creative Club; London Welsh Rugby Club, London; Art Directors' Club of New York. Address: Leo Burnett, 35 West Wacker Drive, Chicago, IL 60601, USA. E-mail: mark.tutssel@leoburnett.com

TUTT Leslie William Godfrey, b. London, England. Mathematical Statistician and Actuary. Education: MSc, PhD, London University. Appointments: Lecturer on financial, business statistical and actuarial topics to professional bodies and universities in UK, USA and throughout central and eastern Europe, 1970-; Consultant to a number of British companies, 1981-. Publications: Many research papers and technical articles on finance, pensions and insurance, modelling of mortality and morbidity trends, application of stochastic simulation to decision making, social policy issues associated with genetics, for UK and overseas actuarial, statistical and financial journals; Author, joint author of 17 books including: Private Pension Scheme Finance, 1970; Pension Scheme Investment, Communications and Overseas Aspects, 1977; Financial Advisers Competence Test, 1985; Financial Services Marketing and Investor Protection, 1988; Taxation and Trusts, 1989; Private Investment Planning, Corporate Investment Planning, 1990; Pensions and Insurance Administration, 1992; Personal Financial Planning, 1995; Pension Law and Taxation, 2002. Honour: Lectureship Diploma, Department of Mathematics, Moscow State University, Russia, 1995. Memberships: Fellow, Past Chairman, Institute of Statisticians of Royal Statistical Society; Fellow, Faculty of Actuaries, Member of Council, 1975-78, Board of Examiners,

1980-90; Associate, Society of Actuaries, USA, Fellow Society of Actuaries of Ireland, 1977; Chartered Insurance Institute, Examinations Assessor, 1980-2000; Fellow, Pensions Management Institute, 1976; Founder Member, Pensions Research Accountants Group, Member of Executive Committee, 1976-85; National Association of Pension Funds, Member of Council, 1979-83. Address: 21 Sandilands, Croydon, Surrey CR0 5DF, England.

TUTT Sylvia Irene Maud, b. London, England. Chartered Secretary and Administrator. Appointments: Chartered Secretary and Administrator in private practice; Writer; Senior Examiner, Chartered Insurance Institute, 1975-2004; Examiner, Society of Financial Advisers, 1992-2004. Publications: Author of numerous technical articles in professional and financial journals; Author or joint author of the following books: Private Pension Scheme Finance, 1970; Pensions and Employee Benefits, 1973; Pension Law and Taxation, 1981; Financial Aspects of Pension Business, 1985; Financial Aspects of Life Business, 1987; A Mastership of a Livery Company, 1988; Financial Aspects of Long Term Business, 1991; Pension Law and Administration, 2002. Memberships: Fellow and Past Member of Council, The Publications and Public Relations Committee, Education Committee, Benevolent Management Committee and Crossways Trust, Past President of its Women's Society and Past Chairman of London Branch, Institute of Chartered Secretaries and Administrators; Fellow Royal Statistical Society; Fellow Royal Society of Arts; Member of Court of City University London; Past President, Soroptimist International of Central London; Past President, United Wards Club of the City of London; Past President, Farringdon Ward Club, London; President, City Livery Club, London, 2001-2002; Past Chairman and currently Vice-President, Royal Society of St George, City of London Branch; Master, The Scriveners Company, 2007; Master, 1983-84, Worshipful Company of Chartered Secretaries and Administrators, Member of its Finance and General Purposes Committee, Managing Trustee of its Charitable Trust, 1978-; Freeman, Guild of Freemen of the City of London. Address: 21 Sandilands, Croydon, Surrey CR0 5DF, England.

TUTU Desmond Mpilo, (Most Rev), b. 7 October 1931, Klerksdorp, South Africa. Archbishop Emeritus. m. Leah Nomalizo Tutu, 1955, 1 son, 3 daughters. Education: Bantu Normal College; University of South Africa; St Peter's Theological College, Rosettenville; King's College, University of London; LTh; MTh. Appointments: Schoolmaster, 1954-57; Parish priest, 1960-; Theology Seminary Lecturer, 1967-69; University Lecturer, 1970-71; Associate Director, Theology Education Fund, World Council of Churches, 1972-75; Dean of Johannesburg, 1975-76; Bishop of Lesotho, 1977-78; Bishop of Johannesburg, 1984-86; Archbishop of Cape Town, Metropolitan of the Church of the Province of Southern Africa, 1986-96; Chancellor, University of Western Cape, 1988-; President, All Africa Conference of Churches, 1987-; Secretary-General, South Africa Council of Churches, 1979-84; Visiting Professor, Anglican Studies, New York General Theology Seminary, 1984; Elected to Harvard University Board of Overseers, 1989; Director, Coca Cola, 1986-; Visiting Professor, Emory University, Atlanta, 1996-; Leader, Truth and Reconciliation Commission, 1995-; Archbishop Emeritus, Cape Town, 1996-; Robert R Woodruff Visiting Distinguished Professor, Candler School of Theology, 1998-99; William R Cannon Distinguished Visiting Professor, Emory University, 1999-2000; Visiting Professor, King's College, London, 2004. Publications: Crying in the Wilderness, 1982; Hope and Suffering, 1983;

The Rainbow People of God, 1994; An African Prayer Book, 1996; The Essential Desmond Tutu, 1997; No Future without Forgiveness, 1999. Honours include: Numerous Honorary Degrees; Nobel Peace Prize, 1984; Carter-Menil; Human Rights Prize, 1986; Martin Luther King Junior Peace Award, 1986; Third World Prize, 1989; Order of Jamaica; Freedom of Borough of Merthyr Tydfil, Wales; Order of Meritorious Service, South Africa, 1996; Order of Grand Cross, Germany; Nelson Mandela Award for Health and Human Rights, Florida, USA, 1998; Monismanien Prize, Uppsala University Sweden, 1999; MESB Service Award, Medical Education for South African Blacks, 1999; Athenagoras Award for Human Rights, 2000. Memberships: Third Order of Society of St Francis; President, All Africa Conference of Churches; Council for National Orders, Republic of South Africa. Address: c/o Truth and Reconciliation Commission, PO Box 3162, Cape Town 8000, South Africa.

TVEDT Terje Walter, Professor. m. Anne Marie Groth, 2 sons, 2 daughters. Education: Cand polit, History, 1984, Dr Philos, Faculty of Social Sciences, 1993, University of Bergen. Appointments: Programme Officer, Juba, Sudan, UN High Commissioner for Refugees, 1984-85; Researcher, UN High Commissioner for Refugees, Geneva, 1985; Research Fellow, Christian Michelsen Institute, 1986-89; Research Fellow, 1989-93, Senior Researcher, 1994-98, Professor/Research Director, Faculty of Social Sciences, Centre for Development Studies, 1998-2004, Professor, Department of Geography, 2004-, Research Director, Nile Basin Research Program, 2007, University of Bergen; Professor II, Department of Political Science, University of Oslo, 2007-; Group Leader, Centre for Advanced Studies, Norwegian Academy of Science and Letters, 2008-09. Publications: Numerous articles in professional journals and books including: Images of 'the other'. About the Developing Countries in the Era of Development Aid, 1990, 1991, 2002; Angels of Mercy or Development Diplomats, NGOs and Foreign Aid, 1998; World Views and Self Images. A Humanitarian Power's Intellectual History, 2002; Development Aid, Foreign Policies and Power. The Norwegian Model, 2003; Southern Sudan. An Annotated Bibliography (2 vols), 2004; Main Editor, A History of Water, 2005-08 (4 volumes); The River Nile in the Age of the British. Political Ecology & the Quest for Economic Power, 2006; Bibliography on the River Nile 1850-2000 (vol I), Bibliography on the River Nile 2000-2006 (vol II) and Bibliography on the River Nile: Plans and Reports (vol III), 2008; TV documentaries: A Journey in the History of Water (4 episodes), 1997; A Journey in the Future of Water (3 episodes), 2008. Honours: Jubilee Prize, Melzer-fund and Bergen University fund, 1998; Grand Prix, 17th Festival International du Film d'Environment, 1999; Vannviten Prize, Norwegian Hydrological Society and Norwegian Water Associations, 2000; Popularization Prize, Norwegian Research Council, 2005; Norwegian Freedom of Expression Foundation's Award, 2007. Address: Ullevålsveien 48F, 0454 Oslo, Norway. E-mail: terje.tvedt@global.uib.no

TWAIN Shania, b. 28 August 1965, Windsor, Toronto, Canada. Country Singer; Songwriter. m. Robert John Lange, 1 son. Appointments: Several TV performances on CMT and TNN; Songwriter with husband. Creative Works: Albums: Shania Twain, 1993; The Woman in Me, 1995; Come On Over, 1997; On The Way, 1999; Beginnings 1989-90, 1999; Wild and Wicked, 2000; Complete Limelight Sessions, 2001; Up! 2002; Greatest Hits, 2004; Singles: What Made You Say That, 1993; Dance With The One That Brought You, 1993; You Lay A Whole Lotta Love On Me, 1993; Whose Bed Have Your Boots Been Under, 1995; Any Man of Mine, 1995; Woman

In Me, 1995; You Win My Love, 1996; God Bless The Child, 1996; I'm Outta Here, 1996; Love Gets Me Every Time, 1997; Don't Be Stupid, 1997; You're Still The One, 1998; From This Moment On, 1998; When, 1998; That Don't Impress Me Much, 1998; Man, I Feel Like a Woman, 1999; You've Got A Way, 1999; Don't Be Stupid (You Know I Love You), 2000; I'm Gonna Get You Good, 2002; Ka-Ching! 2003; Up, 2003; Forever & Always, 2003; Thank You Baby For Making Someday Come So Soon, 2003; When You Kiss Me, 2003; Party For Two, 2005; Don't! 2005; I Ain't No Quitter, 2005; Shoes, 2005. Honours: CMT Europe, Rising Video Star Of The Year, 1993; Entertainer of the Year, Academy of Country Music and Country Music Association, 1999; 5 Grammy Awards including Best Female Country Vocal Performance, 2000 and Best Country Song, 2000; 27 BMI Songwriter Awards; First non-US citizen to win the CMA award; Canada's Walk of Fame, 2003; Officer in the Order of Canada, 2005. Address: Mercury Nashville, 54 Music Square E, Nashville, TN 37203, USA. Website: www.shaniatwain.com

TWEED Jill, b. 7 December 1931, UK. Artist, Sculptor. m. Philip Hicks, 1 son, 1 daughter. Education: MA, Slade School of Art. Appointments: Professional Sculptor and Draughtsman; Large Public Sculptures commissioned including 11 in UK and 1 in France; Exhibits at Messums Gallery, London. Memberships: Fellow of Royal British Society of Sculptors. Address: Royal British Society of Sculptors, 108 Old Brompton Road, London, SW7 3RA, England.

TYLER Anne, b. 25 October 1941, Minneapolis, Minnesota, USA. Writer. m. Taghi M Modaressi, 3 May 1963, 2 children. Education: BA, Duke University, 1961; Postgraduate Studies, Columbia University, 1962. Publications: If Morning Ever Comes, 1964; The Tin Can Tree, 1965; A Slipping Down Life, 1970; The Clock Winder, 1972; Celestial Navigation, 1974; Searching for Caleb, 1976; Earthly Possessions, 1977; Morgan's Passing, 1980; Dinner at the Homesick Restaurant, 1982; The Best American Short Stories, 1983 (editor with Shannon Ravenel), 1983; The Accidental Tourist, 1985; Breathing Lessons, 1988; Saint Maybe, 1991; Tumble Tower (juvenile), 1993; Ladder of Years, 1995; A Patchwork Planet, 1998; Back When We Were Grown-ups, 2001; The Amateur Marriage, 2004; Digging to America, 2006; Short stories in magazines. Honours: PEN/Faulkner Prize for Fiction, 1983; National Book Critics Circle Award for Fiction, 1985; Pulitzer Prize for Fiction, 1989; Orange Broadband Prize for Fiction, 1996, 2007. Memberships: American Academy of Arts and Letters; American Academy of Arts and Sciences. Address: 222 Tunbridge Road, Baltimore, MD 21212, USA. E-mail: atmBaltimore@aol.com

TYLER Liv, b. 1 July 1977, Portland, Maine, USA. Actress. m. Royston Langdon, 2003, 1 son. Career: Film appearances include: Silent Fall; Empire Records; Heavy; Stealing Beauty; That Thing You Do!; Inventing the Abbotts; Plunkett and Macleane, 1999; Armageddon, 1998; Cookie's Fortune, 1999; Onegin, 1999; The Little Black Book, 1999; Dr T and the Women, 2000; The Lord of the Rings: The Fellowship of the Ring, 2001; One Night at McCool's, 2001; The Lord of the Rings: The Two Towers, 2002; The Lord of the Rings: The Return of the King, 2003; Jersey Girl, 2004; Lonesome Jim, 2004; Reign Over Me, 2007; Smother, 2007; The Strangers, 2008. Address: c/o CAA, 9830 Wilshire Boulevard, Beverly Hills, CA 90212, USA.

TYMAN John Henry Paul, b. 9 November 1923, London. Retired Academic. m. Barbara Eveline Hood Phillips, 2 sons. Education: BSc, Chemistry, Maths, University of London,

1943; PhD, 1960; FRSC, 1969; DSc, 1982. Appointments: Works and Development Chemist, May and Baker Ltd, Rhone, Poulenc, 1943-45; Research Scientist, Senior Scientist, Unilever Ltd, 1945-56; Research and Development Manager, Proprietary Perfumes, now Quest International, 1956-62; Lecturer, Reader, Chemistry, Brunel University, 1963-89. Publications: Numerous academic papers to learned societies, educational videos, patents and contributions to international symposia on chemistry totalling 200 topics; 5 books. Honours: Several research grants. Memberships: Royal Society of Chemistry, 1944-; Society of Chemical Industry, 1951-. Address: 150 Palewell Park, East Sheen, London, SW14 8JH, England. E-mail: jhptyman@hotmail.com

TYSON Mike G, b. 30 June 1966, New York, USA. Boxer. m. (1) Robin Givens, 1988, divorced 1989, (2) Monica Turner, 1997, divorced 2003, 2 children. Appointments: Defeated Trevor Berbick to win WBC Heavyweight Title, 1986; Winner WBA Heavyweight Title, 1987; IBF Heavyweight Title, 1987; Former Undefeated World Champion, winner all 32 bouts, lost to James Buster Douglas, 1990; Defeated Donovan Ruddock, 1991; Sentenced to 6 years imprisonment for rape and two counts of deviant sexual practice, 1992; Appealed against sentence; Appeal rejected by US Supreme Court, 1994; released, 1995; Regained title of Heavyweight World Champion after defeating Frank Bruno, 1996; Lost to Evander Holyfield, 1996; License revoked by Nevada State Athletics Commission after disqualification from rematch against Holyfield, 1996; reinstated on appeal 1998; Sentenced to a years imprisonment for assault, 1999; released on probation, 1999; Fought Lennox Lewis, 2002 for the WBC and IBF titles, knocked out in eighth round; Defeated Clifford Etienne, 2003; Lost to Danny Williams, 2004; Retired, 2005. Honours: Honorary Chair Cystic Fibrosis Association, 1987; Young Adult Institute, 1987. Address: Don King Productions, 501 Fairway Drive, Deerfield Beach, FL 33441, USA.

TYUMENEVA Elena, b. 27 February 1971, Elektrougli, Russia. Poetess. m. Andrey Tyumenev. Education: Applied Mathematics, Moscow Energy Institute; Study of the Method of Work in Cause © by V P Hoch, New Runic Language. Appointments: Editor, Hebo literary anthology, International Scientific School of Causality; Editor, New Runic Collection; Director, author's literary-musical theatre, ELKO; Art Director, textile painting, VALEL studio; Programmer. Publications: Poems in The Selected Works of School, 1998-2001; Poems and fairytales: The Rise, 1999, The New Fairytales of the New Time, 2001; Poems and prose, The Life of Life, 2002; Co-author, The New Word, 2004; Poems in professional journals and magazines. Honours: In a Glory of Spirit symbol of distinction, International Scientific School of Causality, 2006. Memberships: Russian Union of Writers; International Association of Specialists in the Work in Cause. Address: Pionerskaya 2-46, Elektrougli, 142455, Russia.

U

UBAIDULLOEV Mahmadsaid, b. 1 February 1952, Tajikistan. Politician; Electrical Engineer. m. R Karimova, 2 sons, 1 daughter. Education: Tajik Polytechnic Institute, Dashanbe, Tajikistan; Kharkov Polytechnic Institute, Kharkov, Ukraine. Appointments: Senior Engineer, 1974-75, Main Engineer, 1975-76, Director, Computation Center, 1976-79, Department of Statistics, Kulob; Instructor, 1979-81, Department Head, 1981-83, Organising Department, Department Head, Department of Industry, Transport and Food, 1986-88, Communist Party Committee, Kulob; Listener, Tashkent Higher CPSU School, Uzbekistan, 1983-85; Deputy Head, Central Department of Statistics, Dushanbe, Soviet Socialist Republic of Tajikistan, 1985-86; Head, Khatlon Regional Department of Statistics, Kurghon-Teppa, 1988-90; Deputy Chairman, Executive Committee, Kulob Regional People's Deputy Council, Kulob, 1990-92; Deputy Chairman, Council of Ministers, Dushanbe, Republic of Tajikistan, 1992-94; First Deputy of the Prime Minister, Dushanbe, Republic of Tajikistan, 1994-96; Chairman (Mayor), Dushanbe, 1996-; Chairman, Majlisi milli Majlisi Oli (National Assembly), Republic of Tajikistan, 2000-. Publications: Editor: The Foundation of Newest Statehood, 2002; History of Dushanbe city (from ancient time till our days), 2004; Co-author, Dushanbe – city of Peace, 2004. Honours: Order of the Dusti (Friendship), 1998; Order of the Ismoili Somoni, 1999; 21st Century Achievement Award, 2001; International Honour Diploma, 2001; Order of the Ismoili Somoni I degree, 2006; Diploma, UN-HABITAT, World HABITAT Day, 2006. E-mail: dushanbe80@yahoo.com

UBUKATA Yuu, b. 18 January 1945, Gumma, Japan. Professor. m. Yohko Ida, 2 sons, 1 daughter. Education: Master of Engineering, 1969, Doctor of Science, 1996, Tokyo Metropolitan University. Appointment: Department of Civil Engineering, Tokyo Metropolitan University, 1969-. Publications: Physiology of Phosphate-removing Bacteria; Fundamental Mechanisms in Biological Wastewater Treatment; Contributions to professional journals. Honours: IBC Leading Engineers of the World, 2006; ABI Man of the Year, 2006; AAS 2nd International Conference Paper Award; Listed in Who's Who publications and biographical dictionaries. Memberships: New York Academy of Sciences; International Water Association. Address: Tokyo Metropolitan University, Department of Civil & Environmental Engineering, 1-1 Minami-ohsawa, Hachiohji, Tokyo 192-0397, Japan. E-mail: ubukata@ecomp.metro-u.ac.jp

UCHIYAMA Shoichi, b. 1 August 1927, Tokyo, Japan. Mechanical Engineer. m. Teruko Shimizu, 2 sons. Education: BS, Chiba University, 1953; MS, UCLA, 1957; PhD, 1963. Appointments: Assistant Research Engineer, UCLA, 1957-63; Project Engineer, Aerospace Research Associates Inc, W Covina, California, 1963-65; Member, Technical Staff, North America Rockwell, Downey, California, 1965-71; General Manager, NKK, Japan, 1971-86; Technical Counselor, NKTEKS, Tokyo, 1986-93; Technical Advisor, Kawana International Patent Office, Tokyo, 1993-96; Lecturer, Musashi Institute of Technology, Tokyo, 1987-2002; Lecturer, Toin University, Yokohama, 1990-95. Honours: Listed in international biographical dictionaries. Memberships: AIAA, USA. Address: 5-9-2, Hiyoshidai, Toganeshi, Chiba-ken, Japan.

UDEH Kenneth Ogbonna, b. 26 May 1959, Naze-Owerri, Nigeria. Food Biotechnologist. m. Zofia Urszula Udeh, 1 April 1989, 2 daughters. Education: Diploma, Cold Storage Technology, College of Food Technology, Sandomierz, Poland, 1981; MSc, Lublin Agriculture University, 1986; PhD, Lublin Agriculture University, 1996; PhD in Food Biotechnology. Appointments: Doctoral Student, 1991-96, Research Fellow, 1996, Reader, 2001- Department of Biotechnology, Human Nutrition and Food Quality Sciences, Lublin Agriculture University; Deputy Director General, IBC, England, 1999. Publications: Several articles in professional journals; Patentee in field. Honours: International Man of the Year, IBC, 1998-99, 1999-2000; Listed in several biographical publications. Memberships: New York Academy of Sciences; Polish Food Technology Society. Address: Przy Stawie Street 4/3, Lublin 20-067, Poland.

UEDA Hiromasa, b. 27 January 1942, Nara, Japan. University Professor. m. Tomoko, 2 sons, 1 daughter. Education: BS, 1964, MS, 1966, PhD, 1969, Chemical Engineering, Kyoto University. Appointments: Research Associate, 1969, Lecturer, 1971, Department of Chemical Engineering, Kyoto University; Section Head, National Institute for Environmental Studies, 1976; Professor, Section of Atmospheric Physics, Disaster Prevention Research Institute and Advanced School of Kyoto University, 1997-; Director General, Acid Deposition and Oxidant Research Center, Network Center for EANET, 2005. Publications: Numerous articles in professional journals. Honours: Science Award, Society of Atmospheric Environment, Japan, 1995; Award, Society of Chemical Engineers, Japan, 2002. Memberships: Society of Chemical Engineers, Japan; Japanese Society of Fluid Mechanics; Heat Transfer Society of Japan; Japan Association of Aerosol Science and Technology; Meteorological Society of Japan; Society of Atmospheric Environment, Japan; Society of Environmental Science, Japan. Address: Minami-aoyama 6-7-5-504, Minami-ku, 107-0062 Tokyo, Japan. E-mail: ueda@adorc.gr.jp

UÉDA Kenji, b. 1 December 1952, Osaka, Japan. Senior Research Scientist. Education: BSc, Physiology and Biochemistry, 1976, MSc, Physiology, 1978, University of Osaka; PhD, Biophysics, University of Kyoto, 1988. Appointments: Research Scientist, Toray Industry Inc, Kamakura, 1981-85; Research Fellow, National Institute of Genetics, Mishima, 1985-87; Visiting Scholar, 1987-91, Assistant Research Neuroscientist, 1991-93, Department of Neurosciences, School of Medicine, University of California, San Diego, USA; Senior Research Scientist, Department of Molecular Biology, 1993-96, Senior Research Scientist, Department of Neurochemistry, 1996-2001, Senior Research Scientist, Department of Neural Plasticity, 2001-05, Senior Research Scientist, Division of Psychobiology, 2005-, Tokyo Institute of Psychiatry; Visiting Research Professor, 1995-96, Visiting Research Scientist, 1996-99, Department of Biochemistry, The Tokyo Metropolitan University; Visiting Professor, Capital University of Medical Sciences (CUMS), Beijing, China, 2001-; Co-Director, Sino-Japan Joint Laboratory for Neurodegenerative Diseases, Xuanwu Hospital, CUMS, Beijing, 2001-; Achievements include discovery of human Alpha-Synuclein/NACP, the mutations of which cause Parkinson's disease and dementia with Lewy bodies. Publications: Numerous articles and papers in professional scientific journals; Invited presentations and professional services. Honours: Principal Investigator of many Grant-in-Aid for Scientific Research, 1994-. Memberships: Society for Neuroscience; Japanese Society for Neurochemistry; Molecular Biology Society of Japan; Japanese Society of Dementia Research. Address: Division of Psychobiology, Tokyo Institute of Psychiatry, Setagaya, Tokyo 156-8585, Japan. E-mail: kenueda@prit.go.jp Website: www.prit.go.jp

UEJIMA Kazuo, b. 27 January 1956, Japan. General Physician. m. Yumi, 1 son, 1 daughter. Education: Graduate, Kasugaoka High School, 1974; Qualified Medical Doctor, Kawasaki Medical College, 1981. Appointments: Junior Resident, Izumisano Municipal Hospital, 1981-83; Junior Resident, 2nd Internal Medicine Department, Osaka University Hospital, 1983-84; Intern, Kawanishi Municipal Hospital, 1984; Intern, Esaka Hospital, 1985; Intern, Izumisano Municipal Hospital, 1985; General Physician, Clinical Office, 1996-. Publications: Extramedullary Plasmacytoma Producing Biclonal Gammapathy, 1993. Honours: Man of the Year, ABI, 2006; Key of Success Award, ABI. Memberships: Japanese Society of Internal Medicine; International Society of Hematology; Senri Rotary Club. Address: 169-6-501 Jyoroku Higashi Sakai, 599-8122 Japan.

UESUGI Takamichi, b. 15 September 1935, Kyoto Prefecture, Japan. Professor. m. Mitsuyo, 3 daughters. Education: MA, Graduate School, Kyoto University, 1961. Appointments: Associate Professor, Nara Women's University, 1973; Associate Professor, 1978, Professor, 1987, Emeritus Professor, 1999, Kyoto University; Professor, Ryukoku University, 1999; Professor, Kio University, 2006. Publications: Modern Culture and Education (Kobundo-Shuppansha), 1989; Development of Community Education (Shorai-Sha), 1993. Memberships: Director, Japan Society for the Study of Education: Director, Japan Society for the Study of Adult and Community Education. Address: 2-38-10 Yuyamadai, Kawanishi, Hyogo, Japan. E-mail: uesugi15@bea.hi-ho.ne.jp

UGAJIN Ryuichi, b. 17 June 1963, Tokyo, Japan. Physicist. Education: PhB, University of Tokyo, 1988; MS, 1990; PhD, 1997. Appointments: Research Scientist, Sony Research Centre, 1990-99; Frontier Science Laboratories, Sony Corporation, 1998-2002-; Fusion Domain Laboratory, Sony Corporation, 2002-2006; Senior Research Scientist, Head, Bio/Complex Area Laboratory, 2000; Leader Biomorphic Materials Initiative, 2001-2002; Editorial Board, J Nanosci Nanotechnology, 2001-. Publications: Physical Review Letters; Applied Physics Letters; Articles in various journals. Memberships: Physical Society of Japan. Address: 4-1-1 Hon-machi, Shibuya-ku, Tokyo 151-0071, Japan. E-mail: ads17386@nifty.com

UGUR Mehmet, b. 3 April 1954, Hatay, Turkey. Academic. m. Sema, 1 son, 1 daughter. Education: BSc, Economics, METU, Turkey, 1978; MSc, Economics, 1988, PhD, IR/Economics, 1996, London School of Economics. Appointments: Lecturer, Economics, 1990-97, Senior Lecturer, Economics, 1997-2003, Reader, Economics, 2003-, Programme Leader, MA/MSc Business and Financial Economics, 2005-, University of Greenwich. Publications: 6 monographs and edited books; 19 refereed journal articles; 16 articles in edited books; 7 invited/commissioned articles. Honours: Jean Monnet Honorary Chair, European Political Economy, 1997-2005. Memberships: University Association of Contemporary European Studies; European Union Studies Association; European Corporate Governance Institute. Address: University of Greenwich, Business School, Old Royal Naval College, Park Row, London SE10 9LS, England. E-mail: m.ugur@gre.ac.uk

ULLMAN Susanne, b. 15 May 1938, Copenhagen, Denmark. Physician; Professor of Dermatology; Doctor of Medical Science. Education: Medical Degree, University of Copenhagen, 1965; Postgraduate Training in Dermatology, Rigshospital, University of Copenhagen. Appointments: Visiting Professor, University of Minnesota, Minneapolis, USA, 1974-76; Professor of Dermatology, Rigshospital, University of Copenhagen, 1979; Visiting Professor, King Faisal University, Dahran, Saudi Arabia, 1981; Visiting Professor, Hunan Medical University, Changsa, Hunan, China, 1989; Professor of Dermatology, Bispebjerg Hospital and Rigshospital, University of Copenhagen, 1996; Co-ordinator, Education of Dermatologists in Denmark, 1983-90; Member, National Board of Health's Advisory Group on AIDS, 1984-89; Member, National Board of Health's Advisory Group on Sexually Transmitted Diseases, 1987-1996; Member, Committee for The Robert J Gorlin Conference on Dysmorphology, Minneapolis, 1996-. Publications: Author and Co-author, 105 publications in international and Danish journals. Memberships: Listed in Who's Who publications and biographical dictionaries. Address: Bispebjerg Hospital, Department of Dermatology, DK 2400, Copenhagen, Denmark.

ULMANIS Guntis, b. 13 September 1939, Riga, Latvia. Economist. m. Aina, 1 son, 1 daughter. Education: Diploma of Highest Education in Economy, The State University of Latvia, 1963. Appointments: Riga Public Transportation Board, 1965-71; Various positions and eventually Manager of Riga's Municipal Services, 1971-92; Member of the Board of the Bank of Latvia, 1992-93; Member of Parliament, 1993; President of Latvia, 1993-99; Director General of 2006 IIHF World Championship Organising Committee, 2002-2006. Publication: Autobiographical book: No tevis Jau Neprasa Daudz (subsequently translated into Russian). Honours: 14 Highest Decorations of various states, Honorary Doctor of Charleston University, USA and Latvia University; East-West Studies Institutes, 1996 Award; Ceeli 1997 award; Anti-Defamation League award, 1998, etc. Membership: National Library of Latvia Support Foundation. Address: President's Chancery, Pils Laukums 3, Riga LV-1900, Latvia. E-mail: eva@president.lv

UMEZULIKE Augustine Chibuzor, b. 7 January 1960, Enugu, Nigeria. Medical Doctor. m. Clara Duchi, 1 son, 2 daughters. Education: School of Medicine, University of Benin, Benin City, Nigeria, 1980-86; University of Nigeria Teaching Hospital, Enugu, Nigeria, 1992-98; Chaim Sheba Medical Center, Tel Aviv University, Israel, 2003-2004. Appointments: House Officer, University of Nigeria Teaching Hospital, 1986-87; Youth Corps Doctor, Enugu Local Government Health Services, 1987-88; Doctor-in-Charge, Anambra State Prison Medical Service, 1988-92; Senior House Officer, Registrar, Senior Registrar, University of Nigeria Teaching Hospital, Enugu, 1992-98; Consultant Obstetrician and Gynaecologist, National Hospital Abuja, 1999-2006; Senior Obstetrician and Gynaecologist, 2006-; Editor of the Archives of Nigerian Medical and Medical Sciences. Publications: 20 published articles or publications in both local and international journals in various aspects of obstetrics and gynaecology. Honours: Best Student in Medical Microbiology Examination, 1984; Ministerial Commendation for the First Surgical Operation in Enugu Prison, 1988; Rotaract Award for Selfless Services to Humanity, 1994; National Hospital Management Commendation for initiating and co-ordinating most successfully the First International Gynaecological Edoscopic Surgery Workshop in Nigeria, 2005; Listed in Who's Who publications and biographical dictionaries, 2004-05. Memberships: Nigerian Medical Association; Society of Gynaecologists and Obstetricians of Nigeria; Founder and Co-ordinator of "Women Health

Issues" an NGO that surgically repairs VVF free of charge to patients; Medical Co-ordinator, Zarephat Foundation, an NGO working on HIV/AIDS, Rural Surgical Practice; Affiliated to Israeli Training Endoscopic Center. Address: Department of Obstetrics and Gynaecology, National Hospital Abuja, C/o PO Box 4509, Garki, Abuja, Nigeria. E-mail: acumezulike@yahoo.com

UMORU Mahmoud Salihu, b. 6 October 1934. Industrialist. Education: Baking, Zaria College of Science and Technology, 1957; Association of International Accountants, Cost and Works Accountants, School of Accountancy, Glasgow, Scotland, 1960; Marketing Management, Harvard University, USA, 1965. Appointments include: Assistant Accountant, British and French Bank Ltd, 1959-62; Financial Coordinator, Mobil Oil (Nig) Ltd. Lagos, 1962-67; Banking Manager Central Bank of Nigeria, Lagos 1968-72; General Manager, Bagauda Textile Mill Ltd, Kano, 1972-76; Chairman, Nigerian Engineering Manufacturing Co Ltd, Kano, 1974-76; Managing Director, Business International (Nig) Ltd, Kana, 1976-80; Currently, Chairman, Board of Directors, Business International (Nig) Ltd; Karkara Rapid Development Ltd, Kano; Mineral Exploitation Co Ltd, Kano; Umoro Investment Holdings Ltd, Kano; Agbede Agricultural Project Ltd; Executive Chairman, Board of Directors, Ceramic Manufacturers, Nigeria Ltd. Publications: Various papers at seminars and conferences; Supervisors Manual, 1973; The Manager's Guide, 1988. Honours include: Honorary DBA, World University Roand table, USA; Honorary LLD, Newport Universiy; Grand Ambassador of Achievement, ABI. Memberships include: Fellow, Institute of Certified Bookkeepers and Related Data Processing; Association of International Accountants; Association of Cost and Works Accountants; Academy of International Business; Nigerian Institute of Management; Institute of Management Consultants; Governing Council, Kaura Namoda Federal Government Polytechnic; Chief Daudu of Ayele Lane, 1986. Listed in: International Who's Who of Intellectuals; 500 Notable Personalities of the World. Address: Umoru Investment Holding Ltd, 2nd floor, Ap Plaza, Wuse II, Abuja FCT, Nigeria.

UNDERWOOD Kerry, b. 4 June 1956, South Ruislip, England. Solicitor. Education: College of Law; Nottingham Trent University; Chartered Institute of Arbitrators. Appointments: London Borough Councillor, 1978-82; Senior Partner, Underwoods Solicitors, 1991-; Senior Partner, Underwoods, South Africa; Employment Judge (part time), 1993-2000; Consultant and Adviser to various Commonwealth countries. Publications: Books: No Win No Fee No Worries; Fixed Costs; Editor and contributing author; Butterworths Personal Injury Litigation Service; Contributing Author, Workplace Law Handbook; Regular appearances on TV and radio; Numerous articles in professional journals. Honours: Knight Commander of the Order of St John; Fellow, Chartered Institute of Arbitrators. Memberships: The Lord's Taverners; Fellow, Chartered Institute of Arbitrators; Law Society; Bovingdon Cricket Club; Toynbee Hall. Address: 79 Marlowes, Hemel Hempstead, Hertfordshire, HP1 1LF, England. E-mail: kerry@kerryunderwood.co.uk

UNSWORTH Barry (Forster), b. 10 August 1930, Durham, England. Novelist. m. (1) Valerie Moor, 15 May 1959, divorced, 1991, 3 daughters, (2) Aira Pohjanvaara-Buffa, 1992. Education: BA, University of Manchester, 1951. Appointments: Lectureships in English; Writer-in-Residence, University of Liverpool, 1984-85, University of Lund, Sweden, 1988. Publications: The Partnership, 1966; The Greeks Have a Word for It, 1967; The Hide, 1970; Mooncrankers Gift,

1973; The Big Day, 1976; Pascalis Island, 1980, US edition as The Idol Hunter, 1980; The Rage of the Vulture, 1982; Stone Virgin, 1985; Sugar and Rum, 1988; Sacred Hunger, 1992; Morality Play, 1995; After Hannibal, 1996; Losing Nelson, 1999; The Songs of the Kings, 2002; The Ruby in her Navel, 2006. Honours: Heinemann Award, Royal Society of Literature, 1974; Arts Council Creative Writing Fellowship, 1978-79; Literary Fellow, University of Durham and University of Newcastle upon Tyne, 1983-84; Co-Winner, Booker Prize, 1992; Hon LittD, Manchester, 1998. Address: c/o Hamish Hamilton, 22 Wrights Lane, London W8 5TZ, England.

UPDIKE John (Hoyer), b. 18 March 1932, Shillington, Pennsylvania, USA. Author; Poet. m. (1) Mary Entwistle Pennington, 26 June 1953, divorced 1977, 2 sons, 2 daughters, (2) Martha Ruggles Bernhard, 30 September 1977, 3 stepchildren. Education: AB, Harvard University, 1954; Ruskin School of Drawing and Fine Art, Oxford, 1954-55. Publications: The Poorhouse Fair, 1959; Rabbit, Run, 1960; The Centaur, 1963; Of the Farm, 1965; Couples, 1968; Bech, a Book, 1970; Rabbit Redux, 1971; Buchanan Dying (play), 1974; A Month of Sundays, 1975; Marry Me, 1977; The Coup, 1978; Rabbit is Rich, 1981; Bech is Back, 1982; The Witches of Eastwick, 1984; Roger's Version, 1986; S, 1988; Rabbit at Rest, 1990; Memories of the Ford Administration, 1992; Brazil, 1994; In the Beauty of the Lilies, 1996; Toward the End of Time, 1997; Bech at Bay, 1998; Gertrude and Claudius, 2000; Rabbit Remembered, 2001; Seek My Face, 2002; Villages, 2004; Terrorist, 2006; The Widows of Eastwick, 2008; Short story collections; Poetry; Non-fiction essays and criticism. Honours: Guggenheim Fellowship, 1959; National Book Award for Fiction, 1966; Prix Medicis Etranger, 1966; O Henry Awards for Fiction, 1966, 1991; MacDowell Medal for Literature, 1981; Pulitzer Prizes in Fiction, 1982, 1991; National Book Critics Circle Awards for Fiction, 1982, 1991, and for Criticism, 1984; PEN/Malamud Memorial Prize, 1988; National Medal of Arts, 1989; Scanno Prize, 1991; Harvard Arts Medal, 1998; National Book Foundation Award, Lifetime Achievement, 1999; PEN/Faulkner Award, 2004. Memberships: American Academy of Arts and Letters; American Academy of Arts and Sciences. Address: Beverly Farms, MA 01915, USA.

UPPER OSSORY & CASTLETOWN, Earl of, Horace Fitzpatrick, b. 1934, Louisville, Kentucky, USA (British National). University Research Professor; Musician. Education: BA, 1956, MMus, 1958, Yale University; Diploma (1st Honours), State Academy of Music and Drama, Vienna, 1959; Studied horn with Reginald Morley-Pegge, London, Philip Farkas, Chicago, John Barrows, Yale, Gottfried v. Freiberg, Vienna; Teenage conducting studies with uncle, Glenn Welty, leading free-lance conductor, Chicago Radio; Later with Paul Hindemith (Yale), Hans Swarowsky (Vienna), and Robert Heger (Munich); Doctor of Philosophy, Oxford University, 1965. Career includes: Various orchestral posts as principal horn, 1958-66, including: Metropolitan Opera, Radio Symphony of the Air (New York under Leonard Bernstein), Vienna Philharmonic and State Opera (deputy); Orchestra da Camera di Palazzo Pitti, Florence; Cairo State Opera; Hamburg Kammerorchester; Royal Opera House Covent Garden; London Mozart Players; Deputy Curator, Yale Collection of Musical Instruments, 1956-58; First ever Lecturer in European Music, American University, Cairo, 1959-60; First ever solo recording on 18th century horn, Golden Crest Records, 1959; Solo Debut on Natural Horn, Wigmore Hall, London, 1964; International appearances as Soloist on Natural Horn including, Salzburg, City of London,

Flanders (Bruges), Edinburgh and Vienna Festivals, 1964-88; Tutoring in Music History, Wadham College, Oxford University, 1961-64; Stipendiary Lecturer, St Catherine's College, Oxford University, Member of Faculty of Music, History of Instruments, 1963-71; Pioneering research into use of music (mainly Classical period 1740-1830), according to Greek philosophical principles, as a form of healing support, 1966-; Director, International Summer Academy for Historic Performance, Austria, 1971-80; Secured Philip Bate Collection for Oxford University, set up Oxford Foundation for Historic Musical Instruments, 1964-71; Established Atelier for Historic Wind Instruments, Oxford, 1971; Professor of Natural Horn, Guildhall School of Music and Drama, 1972-79; Founded Hanover Band, 1974 and the Florilegium, 1975; Leverhulme Visiting Professor, Johannes Gutenberg-Universität, Mainz, 1981-86; Leverhulme Visiting Research Professor, Music University "Mozarteum", Salzburg, 1985-; Research Unit and Laboratory Orchestra (historic instruments) at Salzburg in dialogue with the Royal Swedish Academy of Music and the Royal Technical Institute, Stockholm, 1985-; Chairman, Aula Classica, a research, education and performance network to study the music of the Mozartean Era through its related disciplines, 1988-; Patronage of the Secretary General of the Council of Europe, 1989; Professorial Research Fellow, Institute of Musicology, University of Vienna, 1994-2000. Publications include: The Horn and Horn-Playing and the Austro-Bohemian Tradition 1680-1830, 1970; Telemann, 1973; 17 articles in The New Grove; Articles in German, French and Spanish music encyclopaedias; Concert and book reviews for The Times, Times Literary Supplement and Oxford Mail. Honours: Numerous research grants and scholarships; Medaglia d'Oro per la Cultura, Italy, 1959; Order of St Martin, Austria, 1977; Listed in biographical dictionaries. Memberships: Athenaeum, 1981-97; Founding Member, Country Club UK. Address: c/o Wadham College, Oxford OX1 3PN, England.

UPTON Graham, b. 30 April 1944, Birmingham, England. Educationalist. m. (1) Jennifer Clark, 1 son, 1 daughter, (2) Bebe Speed. Education: BA, 1966, Dip Ed, 1966, MA, 1979, University of Sydney, Australia; M Ed, University of New South Wales, 1973; PhD, University of Wales, 1978. Appointments: Schoolteacher, New South Wales Department of Education, Australia, 1966-70; Lecturer in Education, Sydney Teachers' College, Australia, 1971; Temporary Lecturer in Education, Chester College of Education, 1972; Lecturer in Special Education, Leeds Polytechnic, 1972-74; Variously Lecturer, Senior Lecturer and Reader in Education, Head of Department of Education, Dean of Collegiate Faculty of Education and Dean of Faculty of Education and Related Professional Studies, University College, Cardiff, 1974-88; Professor, Educational Psychology and Special Educational Needs and Head, School of Education, 1988-93, Pro Vice-Chancellor, 1993-97, University of Birmingham; Vice Chancellor, 1997-2007, Emeritus Professor, Oxford Brookes University; Chairman, Oxford Playhouse Board of Directors; Educational Consultant, Ministry of Education, Brunei. Publications: Over 100 books, chapters in books and articles in learned and professional journals; Key publications: Special Educational Needs, 1992; Emotional and Behavioural Difficulties in Schools: From Theory to Practice, 1994; The Voice of the Child: A Handbook for Professionals, 1996; Effective Schooling for Children with Emotional and Behavioural Difficulties, 1998. Memberships: Chartered Psychologist; Fellow, British Psychological Society; Fellow, Royal Society of Arts; Academician, Learned Society for the Social Sciences; Honorary Fellow, Birmingham College of Food, Tourism and Leisure. Address: Brock Leys, Pullens Lane, Oxford OX3 0BX, England. E-mail: grahamupton@aol.com

URCH David Selway, b. 10 February 1933, London, England. University Reader Emeritus. m. Patricia Maria Erszebet Hair, 4 sons, 1 daughter. Education: Drapers' Company's Scholar, 1951; BSc, 1st Class Honours, Chemistry, 1954, PhD, 1957, Queen Mary College, University of London. Appointments: Research Fellow, Yale University, USA, 1957-59; Lecturer, Birmingham University, England, 1960; Lecturer, Reader, Chemistry, Queen Mary and Westfield College, University of London, 1961-98; Senior Lecturer, Chemistry, Brunel University, 1998-2000; Chemistry Lecturer, New York University in London, 2000-. Publications: Over 200 papers in scientific literature; Book: Orbitals and Symmetry, 1970, revised, 1979. Honours: Fellow Royal Society of Chemistry; Chartered Chemist. Memberships: Royal Society of Chemistry; American Chemical Society; Association of University Teachers; Catenian Association. Address: 56 Mount Ararat Road, Richmond, Surrey TW10 6PJ, England. E-mail: du3@nyu.edu

UYKAN Zekeriya, b. 10 November 1971, Istanbul, Turkey. Electrical Engineer. Education: BSc, Electronics and Communications Engineering, 1993, MSc, Control and Computer Engineering, 1996, Istanbul Technical University; Licentiate of Technology, 1998, PhD, 2001, Helsinki University of Technology, Finland. Appointments: Research and Teaching Assistant, Istanbul Technical University, 1994-96; Research Scientist, Helsinki University of Technology, 1996-2001; Visiting Researcher, Sabanci University, Turkey, 2000; Research Engineer, Nokia Research Center, 2000-07; Nokia Siemens Networks, Finland, 2007-; Visiting Scholar, Electrical Engineering, Stanford University, California, 2002. Publications: Author and co-author, over 20 journal and conference papers. Honours: Awards from Academy of Finland Graduate School, GETA, 1999, 2000, 2002; Center for International Mobility, CIMO, 1996, 1997; Imatran Voiman Found, 1999; Telia Sonera, 1999; Elisa, 2000; Listed in Who's Who in the World, 2006 and Who's Who in Science and Engineering, 2006-07. Memberships: Istanbul Technical University Alumni Foundation, 1993-; Finnish Association of Graduate Engineers, TEK, 1999-; IEEE Member; Life Fellow, International Biographical Association. Address: Nokia Siemens Networks, Espoo, Finland. E-mail: zekeriya.uykan@nsn.com

UZUNIDIS Dimitri Nicolas, b. 24 May 1960, Alexandropolis, Greece. Professor; Economist. m. Sophie Boutillier, 1 son, 1 daughter. Education: Diploma, Journalism, Athens, Greece, 1979; Master in Sociology, 1985, PhD, Economics, 1987, University of Paris 10. Appointments: Associate Professor, Institute of Political Studies, Lille, France, 1991-96; Professor, University of Littoral, Dunkirque, France, 1992-; Professor, Postgraduate School, University of Littoral, Invited Professor, Institute of Social Management, Paris, 2002-; Director, Research Unit: Industry and Innovation, 1994-; Editor: Innovations, L'esprit economique. Publications: Le Travail brade, 1997; La Legende de l'entrepreneur, 1999; Mondialisation et Citoyennete, 1999; L'histoire des entrepreneurs, 2002; L'innovation et l'economie contemporaine, 2004: Firm Power In "Contemporary Post-Keynsian Analysis", 2005; John Kenneth Galbraith and the Future of Economics; Innovation, Evolution and Economic Change; Cluster of Entrepreneurs; The Capitalism. Honours: Ministry of Industry, Athens, Greece, 1989; Ministry of National Education, Paris, 1999; Palmes Academiques, 2004. Memberships: French Council of Universities; Association of French Economists; The Society of Advancement of Socio-Economics; Observatory of Globalization; Vice-President, European Citizenship Association; Resp of Research on Innovation Network (Paris, Seattle). Address: MRSH-Lab RII, 21 Quai de la Citadelle, F-59140 Dunkirque, France. E-mail: Uzunidis@univ-littoral.fr Website: rii.uni-littoral.fr

V

VAGNORIUS Gediminas, b. 10 June 1957, Plunge District, Lithuania. Politician. m. Nijole Vagnorienė, 1 son, 1 daughter. Education: D Econ Science, Institute of Engineering and Construction, Vilnius, Lithuania. Appointments: Engineer-Economist, Junior Researcher, Researcher, Institute of Economics, Lithuanian Academy of Sciences, 1989-90; Deputy to Lithuanian Supreme Soviet, Member, Presidium, 1990-91; Prime Minister of Lithuania, 1991-92, 1996-99; Member of Parliament, 1992-; Chair, Council of Ministers of Lithuania, 1991-92, 1996-99; Chair, Board, Homeland Union/ Lithuanian Conservative Party, 1993-2000; Chair, Moderate Conservative Union, 2000-; Chair, Christian Conservative Social Union (CCSU). Address: CCSU, Odminiu Str 5, 01122 Vilnius, Lithuania. E-mail: sekretoriatas@nks.lt

VAGUNDA Vaclav, b. 16 December 1959, Uherske Hradiste, Czech Republic. Medical Doctor; Pathologist; Researcher. m. Marcela, 1 son, 1 daughter. Education: MD (General Medicine), Faculty of Medicine, Purkyne University, Brno, 1985; Pathology, degree I, 1988, Pathology, degree II, 1992, Institute for Postgraduate Study in Health Care, Prague; PhD (Oncology), Faculty of Medicine, Masaryk University, Brno, 2004. Appointments: Resident, 2nd Institute of Pathology, Faculty Children Hospital, Brno, 1985-88; Medical Researcher, Pathology Department, Research Institute of Clinical and Experimental Oncology, Brno, 1988-93; Consultant Pathologist, 1993-95, 1st Institute of Pathology, Faculty Hospital, Brno, 1993-95; Lecturer, Faculty of Medicine, Masaryk University, Brno, 1993-2004; Head, Department of Pathology, Masaryk Memorial Cancer Institute, Brno, 1995-2003; Cytopathologist, Department of Cytology, 2004; Sanatorium Helios Ltd, Brno; Head, CEDELAB Ltd, Laboratory of Pathology and Clinical Cytology, Hospital St Zdislava, Velke Mezirici, Czech Republic, 2005-. Publications: 13 articles in professional journals. Honours: International Scientist of the Year, IBC, 2003. Memberships: The Czech Medical Society, Society of Pathologists, 1986; Founding President, Vice-Chairman, League Against Cancer, Brno, 1990; Pathology Group, Organisation of European Cancer Institutes, 1995; The Czech Medical Society, Society of Clinical Cytology, 1996; International Academy of Pathology, Czech section, 1996; WHO, Melanoma Programme, 1997; European Society of Pathology, 2003; Society for Melanoma Research, 2004. Address: CEDELAB Ltd, Laboratory of Pathology & Cytology, Hosp St Zdislava, Mostiste 105, 594 01 Velke Mezirici, Czech Republic. E-mail: vagunda@cedelab.cz Website: www.cedelab.cz

VAIDYA Udaychandra, Astrologer. Education: PhD, Astrology. Appointments: Jain Gospel Astrologer of Vedic K.P. Astrology. Honours: Numerous honours and awards including: MahaMahopadhyay, Gold Medallist, Sri Lanka; Jyotish Maharshi, Gold Medallist; Jyotish Chakravarty; Jyotish Vishwa Vidyacharya; Jyotish Mahasagar, Gold Medallist; Jyotish Bharat Bhushan; Jyotish Acharya; Jyotish Samrat; Jyotish Ratna; International Award in Astrology, Sri Lanka, 2002; James Silver International Award, USA, 2002; Man of the Year, ABI, 2004; Honorary Research Advisor, ABI, USA; International Professional of the Year, IBC, 2005; An Outstanding Intellectual of the 21st Century, IBC; 21st Century Award for Achievement, IBC; The Cambridge Blue Book Man of the Year, IBC, 2005; Honorary Research Associate, IBC; Man of the Year, ABI, 2006; Honorary Research Advisor, ABI; World's Most Respected Expert in Vedic K.P. Astrology, ABI, 2007. Memberships: MAIAS (USA); FMAFA (USA); PMIFA (Sri Lanka); MARP (CAL).

Address: Om Astro Research Center, #494 Kulkarni Galli, Belgaum – 590 002, Karnataka, India. E-mail: drudaychandra_ vaidya@yahoo.com

VAIOU Maria, b. Greece. Byzantinist. Education: Diploma (Hons), Greece, 1988; Diploma (Hons), 1992, Master, (distinction), 1994, Late Antique and Byzantine Studies, King's College, University of London, England; PhD, Byzantine Studies, University of Oxford, England, 2002. Appointments: Assistant to Archbishop Gregorios of Thyateira and Great Britain, London, 1990-94; Teacher of Greek, 1995-99; Research Fellow, Sabançi University, Istanbul, Turkey, 2005-06; Presentations at seminars. Publications: Numerous articles in learned journals; Books: 'Theophanes' [entry], in Christian-Muslim Relations: A Bibliographical History Vol I: seventh to tenth century, 2007; Diplomacy in the Early Islamic World. A tenth century treatise on Byzantine-Arab relations: Ibn al-Farra's Book of Messengers of Kings, 2008; The Byzantine Churches of Constantinople: A bibligraphical, chronological and photographical survey, 2008; The diplomatic relations between the Abbasid Caliphate and the Byzantine Empire, 2008; Dictionary of the Byzantine-Muslim diplomacy, 2008; Selections of Sources for the History of Muslim-Byzantine Relations, 2008; Byzantium and the Muslim World: a preliminary bibliographical guide, 2008. Honours: Many awards from: A G Leventis Foundation, 1991-95; Hellenic Foundation, 1993-94; Stavros Costopoulos Foundation, 1998-99; Oxford Centre of Islamic Studies, 1999; British Academy, 2002. Memberships: Oxford University Society; The Society for Libyan Studies, Association of Middle East Medievalists; Commission on History of Science and Technology in Islamic Civilization.

VAJPAYEE Atal Bihari, b. 25 December 1924, Gwalior, Madhya Pradesh, India. 11th Prime Minister of India; Poet. Education: Student of political science and law. Career: Journalist; Joined Bharatiya Jana Sangh, now Bharatiya Janata Party, 1951-; Elected to the Lok Sabha, House of the People, 9 times; Elected to the Rajya Sabha, House of the States, twice; Foreign Minister; Leader of the Opposition; Prime Minister of India, 1996, 1998-2004; Minister of Health and Family Welfare, Atomic Energy and Agriculture, 1998-2004; Chair, National Security Council, 1998-2004; Senior Leader, Bharatjiya Janata Party; Retired from politics, 2005. Publications: New Dimensions of India's Foreign Policy; Jan Sangh Aur Musalmans; Three Decades in Parliament; collections of poems and numerous articles. Honours: Hon PhD, Kanpur University, 1993; Padma Vibhushan; Best Parliamentarian, 1994. Memberships: Chair, National Security Council, 1998-; Member, National Integration Council, 1961-. Address: 7 Race Course Road, New Delhi 110011, India.

VAKARIN Sergey, b. 25 May 1952, Chita, Russia. Physicist. Education: Student studies, Physics Department, Urals State University, 1970-75; PhD, Physics and Mathematics, High-Temperature Electrochemistry Institute, Russian Academy of Sciences, 1997. Appointments: Research Scientist, 1991-2007, Junior Research Scientist, 1983-91, Engineer, 1975-83, Senior Technician, 1975, High-Temperature Electrochemistry Institute, Russian Academy of Sciences. Publications: 1 monograph; 28 articles; 12 inventions; 11 scientific reports. Honours: Inventor of the USSR Medal, 1991; Veteran of Work, 2001; Archimedes Award, 2006; Vernadsky Medal (Russian Academy of Natural History), 2006; Listed in international biographical dictionaries. Memberships: Corresponding Member, International Personnel Academy, Council of Europe/UNESCO; Professor of Russian Academy of Natural History; An Active Working Partnership, European

Academy of Natural History. Address: Aviatorov Street 7, Apartment 21, Ekaterinburg 620910, Russia. E-mail: s.vakarin@ihte.uran.ru

VALLANCE-OWEN John, b. 31 October 1920, Ealing, London, England. Physician. m. Reneé Thornton, 2 sons, 2 daughters. Education: Friars School, Bangor, 1930-36; Epsom College, 1936-39; St John's College Cambridge, 1939-43; MA, MB BChir Cantab, 1946, London Hospital, 1943-46; MD, Cantab, 1951; FRCP, 1962; FRCPath, 1971; FRCPI, 1973. Appointments include: Pathology Assistant and Medical First Assistant to Sir Horace Evans, London Hospital, 1946-51; Medical Tutor, Royal Postgraduate Medical School, Hammersmith Hospital, 1952-55, 1956-58; Consultant Physician and Lecturer in Medicine, King's College, University of Durham, 1958-64; Consultant Physician, Royal Victoria Infirmary and Reader in Medicine, University of Newcastle upon Tyne, 1964-66; Professor of Medicine, Queen's University, Belfast, 1966-82; Consultant Physician, Royal Victoria Hospital, Belfast, 1966-82, Belfast City Hospital, 1966-82, Foster Green Hospital, 1975-82; Foundation Professor and Chairman, Department of Medicine, 1983-88, Assistant Dean, 1984-88, The Chinese University of Hong Kong; Consultant in Medicine to Hong Kong Government, 1984-88, to British Army in Hong Kong, 1985-88; Medical Adviser on Clinical Complaints, North East Thames Regional Health Authority, 1989-96, Thames Regional Health Authority, 1995-96; Visiting Professor, Imperial College of Science Technology and Medicine, Hammersmith Hospital, 1989-; Consultant Physician, London Independent Hospitals, 1989-99 and Wellington Hospital, 1999-2003. Publications: Essentials of Cardiology, 1961, 2nd edition, 1968; Diabetes: Its Physiological and Biochemical Basis, 1976; Numerous papers in biochemical, medical and scientific journals. Honours: Rockefeller Fellowship, 1955-56; Oliver Sharpey Prize, Royal College of Physicians, 1976. Memberships: Life Member, Royal Society of Medicine; East India; United Services Recreation, Hong Kong. Address: 10 Spinney Drive, Great Shelford, Cambs, CB22 5LY, England.

VAMVUKA Despina, b. 20 June 1958, Hania, Greece. Chemical Engineer. m. Theodore Kaloumenos, 2 sons. Education: Diploma in Chemical Engineering, 1982; MSc, Organic Chemical Technology, 1982; MSc, Advanced Chemical Engineering, 1983; PhD, Chemical Engineering, 1988. Appointments: Research Assistant, UMIST, UK, 1984-88; Postdoctoral, University of Patras, Greece, 1989-91; Associate Teaching Scientist, 1991-92, Professor, 1993-, Technical University of Crete. Publications: Book: Clean Use of Coals; University publications for students; About 65 articles in international scientific journals and conference proceedings. Honours: Invited Lecturer in universities and workshops; Member of Organising and Scientific Committees in conferences; Referee of international journals and research programmes. Memberships: Greek Association of Chemical Engineers; Greek Chamber of Technology; Board of Directors, Combustion Institute (Greek); ACS. Address: Department of Mineral Resources Engineering, Technical University of Crete, Hania 73100, Greece.

VAN DAMME Jean-Claude, b. 18 October 1961, Brussels, Belgium. Actor. m. (1) Maria Rodriguez, 1980, divorced 1984, (2) Cynthia Derderian, 1985, divorced 1986, (3) Gladys Portugues, 1987, divorced 1992, re-married 1999, 1 son, 1 daughter, (4) Darcy LaPier, 1994, divorced 1997, 1 son. Career: Former European Professional Karate Association Middleweight Champion; Films: Bloodsport; Death Warrant; Kickboxer; Cyborg; AWOL; Universal Soldier; No Retreat;

No Surrender; Nowhere to Run; Monaco Forever; Hard Target; Streetfighter; Time Cop; Sudden Death; The Quest; Maximum Risk; Double Team; Universal Soldier: The Return, 1999; The Order, 2001; Replicant, 2001; Derailed, 2002; The Savage, 2003; In Hell, 2003; Narco, 2004; Wake of Death, 2004; Kumite, 2005; Second in Command, 2006; The Hard Corps, 2006; Sinave, 2006; Until Death, 2007; The Shepherd: Border Patrol, 2008. Address: United Talent Agency, Suite 500, 9560 Wilshire Boulevard, Beverly Hills, CA 90212, USA.

VAN DER BANK Christiena Maria, b. 9 April 1957, Thabazimbi, South Africa. Professor in Law. m. David Cornelius, 1 son, 1 daughter. Education: BA (cum laude), PU, 1976; B Proc, 1981, LLB, 1998, LLM, 1999, UNISA; LLC, PU for CHE, 2001. Appointments: CEO, SANCA; Lecturer, 1996-2001, Principal Lecturer, 2001-05, Executive Dean, Human Sciences, 2005-. Publications: 9 international papers; 2 international papers; 2 chapters in books; Article in European Journal of Social Sciences; 10 textbooks. Honours: Researcher of the Year, 2006; Best Student in B Proc; Editorial Board, Institutional Journal. Memberships: Patent Examination Board, Academy of World Business, Marketing and Management Development; Advocate of the High Court. Address: PO Box 3929, Vanderbijlpark, 1900, South Africa. E-mail: riana@vut.ac.za

VAN DUYN Mona (Jane), b. 9 May 1921, Waterloo, Iowa, USA. Poet; Writer; Critic; Editor; Reviewer; Lecturer. m. Jarvis A Thurston, 31 August 1943. Education: BA, Iowa State Teachers College, 1942; MA, State University of Iowa, 1943. Appointments: Reviewer, Poetry magazine, 1944-70; Instructor in English, State University of Iowa, 1945, University of Louisville, 1946-50; Founder-Editor (with Jarvis A Thurston), Perspective: A Quarterly of Literature, 1947-67; Lecturer in English, 1950-67, Adjunct Porfessor, 1983, Visiting Hurst Professor, 1987, Washington University, St Louis; Poetry Advisor, College English, 1955-57; Lecturer, Salzburg Seminar in American Studies, 1973; Poet-in-Residence, Bread Loaf Writing Conferences, 1974, 1976; Poet Laureate of the USA, 1992-93; Numerous poetry readings. Publications: Valentines to the Wide World: Poems, 1959; A Time of Bees, 1964; To See, To Take, 1970; Bedtime Stories, 1972; Merciful Disguises: Poems Published and Unpublished, 1973; Letters From a Father and Other Poems, 1982; Near Changes: Poems, 1990; Lives and Deaths of the Poets and Non-Poets, 1991; If It Be Not I: Collected Poems, 1992; Firefall, 1993; Selected Poems, 2002. Contributions to: Many anthologies; Poems, criticism, reviews, and short stories in various periodicals. Honours: Eunice Tietjens Memorial Prize, 1956; National Endowment for the Arts Grants, 1966-67, 1985; Harriet Monroe Memorial Prize, 1968; Hart Crane Memorial Award, 1968; 1st Prize, Borestone Mountain Awards, 1968; Bollingen Prize, 1970; National Book Award for Poetry, 1971; Guggenheim Fellowship, 1972-73; Loines Prize, National Institute of Arts and Letters, 1976; Fellow, Academy of American Poets, 1981; Sandburg Prize, Cornell College, 1982; Shelley Memorial Award, Poetry Society of America, 1987; Ruth Lilly Prize, 1989; Pulitzer Prize in Poetry, 1991. Memberships: Academy of American Poets, chancellor, 1985; National Institute of Arts and Letters. Address: 7505 Teasdale Avenue, St Louis, MO 63130, USA.

VAN MEERTEN Reinier Jan, b. 2 July 1919, Kediri, Java. Retired Academic. m. Ans Van der Heide. Education: MSc, Biology and Chemistry, University of Wageningen, 1947; PhD, Physics, University of Nijmegen, 1966. Appointments: Chemistry Teacher for 13 years; Head of Lung Function Laboratory for 20 years. Publications: Computer Guided

Diagnosis, 1971; Book: Creation (Evolution bears continuous Creation, sustaining Evolution with $E=2mc^2$), 2007; Structures of photon, pion, muon, electron, neutron, proton, neutrinos, Kinetic $E=mv^2$ Nm ($v<<c$); Seven Secrets of Saturn's Rings; Decipherment of the First Seals of Knossos. Honour: Summary of his book "Creation" featured in "Update", New York Academy of Sciences, 2005; Einstein's Man of the Year, ABI, 2005. Membership: Darwin Benefactor, New York Academy of Sciences. Address: De Vyvers 12, 7991 BW, Dwingeloo, The Netherlands.

VAN SANT Gus Jr, b. 1952, Louisville, Kentucky, USA. Film Director; Screenwriter. Education: Rhode Island School of Design. Appointments: Former Production Assistant to Ken Shapiro. Films include: Mala Noche; Drugstore Cowboy, 1989; My Own Private Idaho, 1991; Even Cowgirls Get the Blues, 1993; To Die For, 1995; Kids, 1995; Ballad of the Skeletons, 1996; Good Will Hunting, 1997; Psycho, 1998; Finding Forrester, 2000; Gerry, 2002; Elephant, 2003; Red Hot Chili Peppers: Greatest Videos, 2003; Last Days, 2005; Paris, j t'aime, 2006; To Each His Cinema, 2007; Paranoid Park, 2007. Publications: 108 Portraits, 1995; Pink, 1997. Honours: National Society of Film Critics Awards for Best Director and Screenplay, 1990; New York Film Critics and Los Angeles Film Critics Award for Best Screenplay, 1989; PEN Literary Award for Best Screenplay Adaptation, 1989; American Civil Liberties Union of Oregon, Freedom of Expression Award, 1992; Palme d'Or and Best Director, Cannes Film Festival, 2003. Address: c/o William Morris Agency Inc, 151 South El Camino Drive, Beverly Hills, CA 90212, USA. Website: www.wma.com

VAN ZANTEN David Theodore, Professor of Art History. Education: Visiting Student, Courtauld Institute of Art, University of London, England, 1963-64, BA, Princeton University, 1965; MA, 1966, PhD, 1970, Harvard University. Appointments: Assistant Professor, McGill University, Canada, 1970-71; Assistant Professor, promoted to Associate Professor, University of Pennsylvania, 1971-79; Associate Professor promoted to Professor, Northwestern University, 1979-; Visiting Professor: Cornell University, 1976, University of California, Berkeley, 1979, Columbia University (Mathews Lectures), 1980. Publications include: The Architecture of the Ecole des Beaux Arts (contributor), 1977; The Architectural Polychromy of the 1930's, 1977; The Beaux-Arts Tradition in French Architecture (editor), 1982; Louis Sullivan: The Function of Ornament (contributor), 1986; Designing Paris: The Architecture of Duban, Labrouste, Vaudoyer and Duc, 1987; Building Paris: Architectural Institutions and the Transformation of the French Capital, 1830-1870, 1995; Sullivan's City: The Meaning of Ornament for Louis Sullivan, 2000. Honours: Fulbright Fellowship, Paris, 1968-69; Prix Bernier, Académie des Beaux-Arts, Paris; Alice Davis Hitchcock Award (best book in architectural history that year), 1988; NEH Senior Fellowship, 1989-90, 1997-98; Named Chevalier of the Ordre des Arts et des Lettres, Minister of Culture, Republic of France, 1995; Guggenheim Fellowship, 2001-2002; Institut National d'Histoire de l'Ael, 2006; Ecole des Hautes Etudes eu Sciences Sociales, 2008. Address: Department of Art History, Northwestern University, Evanston, IL 60208-2208, USA. E-mail: d-van@northwestern.edu

VANDERHAEGEN Frédéric Bernard Michel, b. Lille, France. Professor. 1 son, 1 daughter. Education: Diploma in Computer Science, University of Lille, France, 1986; Degree in Industrial Automation, 1987, Master's Degree, Industrial Automation, 1988, Postgraduate Diploma, Industrial Automation, 1989, Doctorate Diploma, Industrial and Human Automation, 1993, Habilitation to manage research on Industrial and Human Automation, 2003, University of Valenciennes, France. Appointments: Postdoctoral Researcher, Joint Research Centre of the European Commission, Ispra, Italy, 1994-95; Researcher, Engineering Department, Researcher and Scientific Project Co-ordinator, Laboratory of Automated, Mechanical and Computer Science Studies integrating Industrial and Human Aspects (LAMIH), CNRS, 1995-2005; Professor, University of Valenciennes and Head, Human-Machine System Group of the LAMIH, 2005-. Publications: Book: Analysis and Control of Human Error; Articles in scientific journals including: IEEE Transactions on Reliability; International Journal on Human-Computer Interaction; Interacting with Computers; Reliability and System Safety; Le Travail Humain; Control Engineering Practice; Safety Science. Honour: Third Prize for the best doctoral thesis on Automation between 1993 and 1994, AFCET, CNRS and MESR, 1995. Memberships include: Regional Research Group on Transport; Regional Research Group on Integrated Automation and Human-Machine System; National Research Group on Modelling, Analysis and Control of Systems; Civil Activity Organiser, Eclaireuses et Eclaireurs de France, 1984-93, 1995-98; Co-Chairman, Fretttt Production Association to promote the regional music group Tante Adèle et La Famille, 1996-. Address: 36 rue Claudin Le Jeune, 59300 Valenciennes, France. E-mail: frederic.vanderhaegen@univ-valeniennes.fr

VANGELIS (Evangelos Papathanassiou), b. 29 March 1943, Volos, Greece. Musician (keyboards); Composer. Education: Academy of Fine Arts, Athens. Musical Education: Studied Classical music with Aristotelis Coudourof. Career: Member, Formynx, 1960s; Member, Aphrodite's Child, with Demis Roussos; Composer, Paris, 1972; Built Nemo recording studio, London, 1974; Partnership with Jon Anderson as Jon & Vangelis, 1980-1984. Compositions: Music scores for French wildlife films, 1972; Heaven and Hell, Third Movement, theme for Carl Sagan's TV series Cosmos, BBC1, 1981; Film scores: Chariots Of Fire; Blade Runner; Missing; Mutiny On The Bounty; City; 1492 - Conquest Of Paradise; De Nuremberg a Nuremberg, 1994; Rangeela, 1995; Kavafis, 1996; I Hope, 2001; Alexander, 2004; Blade Runner Trilogy: 25th Anniversary, 2007; All tracks on solo albums self-composed, played and produced. Recordings: Albums: with Aphrodite's Child: Aphrodite's Child, 1968; Rain & Tears, 1968; End of the World, 1969; It's Five O'Clock, 1970; 666, 1972; Solo albums: Terra, Dragon, 1971; L'Apocalypse des animaux, 1972; Earth, 1972; Heaven And Hell, 1975; Albedo 0.39, 1976; The Vangelis Radio Special, 1976; Spiral, 1977; Beauborg, 1978; Hypothesis, 1978; China, 1979; Odes, 1979; See You Later, 1980; To The Unknown Man, 1981; Soil Festivities, 1984; Invisible Connections, 1985; Magic Moments, 1985; Mask, 1985; Direct, 1988; The City, 1990; Themes, 1989; Voices, 1995; El Greco, 1995; Oceanic, 1997; Reprise 1990-1999, 2000; Mythodea: Music for the NASA Mission – 2001 Mars Odyssey, 2001; As Jon & Vangelis: Short Stories, 1980; The Friends Of Mr Cairo, 1981; Private Collection, 1983; The Best Of Jon & Vangelis, 1984; Page Of Life, 1991. Honour: Oscar, Best Original Score, Chariots Of Fire, 1982. Address: c/o Sony Classical, 550 Madison Avenue, New York, NY 10022-3211, USA. Website: www.vangelisworld.com

VANYUSHIN Boris, b. 16 February 1935, Tula, Russia. Professor. m. Abrosimova Valeria Ivanovna. Education: MS, Biology Department, Moscow State University, 1957; PhD, Bakh Biochemistry Institute, Academy of Sciences, Moscow, 1961; DSci, Biology Department, Moscow State

University, 1973. Appointments: Junior Research Scientist, Plant Biochemistry Department, 1960-64, Senior Research Scientist, Laboratory of Bio-organic Chemistry, 1965-73, Moscow State University; Postdoctoral Research Fellow, Virus Research Unit ARC, Cambridge, England, 1964-65; Head, Department of Molecular Bases of Ontogenesis, Belozersky Institute, Moscow State University, 1973-; Regent's Lecturer, Department of Biochemistry, University of California at Irvine, USA, 1976; UNESCO Expert in Molecular Biology, Lucknow University, India, 1978; Head, Laboratory of Hormonal Regulation of Plant Ontogenesis, Institute of Agricultural Biotechnology, Moscow, 1985-96; Visiting Professor, University of Catania, Italy, 1990; Visiting Research Fellow, National Centre for Toxicology Research, Arkansas, USA, 1994-95. Publications: Book, Molecular and Genetic Mechanisms of Ageing, 1977; Author of more than 400 papers in various journals. Honours: Award, Lomonosov Prize, 2002; Belozersky Prize, 2004; Grants, International Science Foundation, 1994-95; Russian Foundation of Fundamental Research, 1993-95, 1996-98, 1999-. Memberships: Russian Biochemical Society; Russian Society of Plant Physiologists; DNA Methylation Society; Corresponding Member, Russian Academy of Sciences. Address: Belozersky Institute of Physico-Chemical Biology, Moscow State University, 119992 Moscow, Russia. E-mail: vanyush@belozersky.msu.ru

VAOS George, b. 8 October 1950, Lamia, Fthiotida, Greece. Paediatric Surgeon. m. Vassilia Demetroulaki, 1 daughter. Education: MD, 1974, PhD, 1988, Athens University Medical School; Fellowship in General Surgery (Medical), 1982, Fellowship in Paediatric Surgery (Medical), 1986, Ministry of Health, Athens; European Board in Paediatric Surgery (Medical), European Union of Medical Specialities, Brussels, 1997. Appointments: Paediatric Surgical Registrar and Research Fellow, University of Liverpool, Royal Liverpool Children's Hospital, Alder Hey, Liverpool, England, 1983-86; Consultant Paediatric Surgeon, P and A Kyriakou Children's Hospital, Athens, 1986-2001; Director, Senior Paediatric Surgeon, 2001-, Medical Director, 2004-, Penteli General Children's Hospital, Athens; Professor, Department of Paediatric Surgery, Alexandroupolis University Hospital, Democritus University of Thrace, Alexandroupolis, 2007-. Publications: Chapters in medical books; Articles in international medical journals. Honours: Award, Scholarship, Neonatal Surgery, State Scholarship Foundation, Athens, 1982; Award, Junior Staff Short Paper Award, University of Liverpool, 1986; Award, Intestinal Neuronal Abnormalities, Greek Association of Paediatric Surgeons, 1988; Award, Experimental Surgery, Greek Surgical Association, 1988. Memberships: Greek Association of Paediatric Surgeons; Greek Surgical Association; European Paediatric Surgeons Association; British Association of Paediatric Surgeons. Address: 16 Gardenias Street, 14569 Anoixis, Athens, Greece. E-mail: gvaos@hotmail.com

VARALLO Francis "Bob" V, b. 28 June 1935, Chicago, Illinois, USA. US Army Colonel (Retired). 1 son, 2 daughters. Education: BSH, Loyola University, Chicago, 1958; US Army Command and General Staff College, 1971; National Security Management, National War College, 1972. Appointments: From Second Lieutenant to Colonel, US Army, 1958-88, Deputy Director for Intelligence Collection, Vietnam, 1967-68; Deputy Corps Advisor, Vietnam, 1971-72, G-2, 8th Infantry Division, 1972-74; US Army Attaché, 1974-75; Plans and Policy Intelligence Officer, 1975-78, Installation Commander, 1978-79, Duty Director for Intelligence, 1979-81, Defense Intelligence Agency; J-2, (Senior US Military Intelligence Officer) United States Forces, Japan,

1981-84; Director of Intelligence and Security, Defense Nuclear Agency, 1985-88; Regional Security Manager, Unisys Corporation, Salt Lake City, Utah, 1988-90; President, Nevada Association of Manufactured Home Owners Inc, 1997-. Honours: NRCC Nevada Businessman of the Year, 2002, 2003, 2004, 2005, 2006; The Ronald Reagan Gold Medal, 2004, 2005, 2006; Congressional Order of Merit, 2004, 2005, 2006, 2007; 2000 Outstanding Intellectuals of the 21st Century, 2005; International Professional of the Year, 2005; Nevada Republican of the Year, 2006; Congressional Medal of Distinction, 2006; The Speaker's Citizen Task force, 2006; The Presidential Business Commission, 2006; Man of the Year, ABI, 2006, 2007; The Order of American Ambassadors, ABI, 2006; United Cultural Convention's International Peace Prize, 2005, 2006, 2007; United Cultural Convention's Lifetime Achievement Award, 2006; Gold Medal for the United States, ABI, 2007; Listed in Who's Who publications and biographical dictionaries. Memberships include: American Council for Immigration Reform; American Policy Foundation; Association of Former Intelligence Officers; American Civil Rights Union; Army Historical Foundation; The American Air Museum; The Conservative Caucus; US Border Security Council; Center for Individual Freedom; National Trust for Historic Preservation; The National Museum of the US Army; United States Justice Foundation; Federation for American Immigration Reform; World War II Veterans Committee; The National Police Defense Foundation; American Conservative Union; US Veterans Hospice Foundation; World Trade Center Memorial Foundation; The Naval Institute Foundation; Gettysburg National Battlefield Museum Foundation. Address: 2900 S Valley View Blvd, Suite 251, Las Vegas, NV 89102, USA.

VARGAS-HERNÁNDEZ José Guadalupe, b. 8 November 1951, Zapotiltic, Jalisco, México. Economist. m. Maria Elba González, 6 May 1976, 3 sons. Education: MBA, 1980; PhD, Economics, 1992; PhD, Public Management, 1998. Appointments: Professor, Instituto Tecnológico de Cd Guzmán, 1974-94; Director, Mass Media Communication, Presidencia Municipal Cd Guzmán, Jalisco, 1985-1990; Director, Patronato Instituto Tecnológico de Cd Guzmán, 1983-93; General Manager, Consejo de Colaboración Ciudadana, Cd Guzman, 1992-94; CEO, Novacal, 1994-95; Independent Consultant, 1980-2000; Research Professor, Instituto Tecnológico de Colima, 1994-2000; Research Professor, Universidad de Colima, 1994-2000; Research Professor, Instituto Tecnológico de Cd Guzmán, 2000-; Research Professor, Centro Universitario del Sur, Universidad de Guadalajara, 2000-; Research Professor, Doctorate in Management Studies, UASLP; Research Assistant, University of California at Berkeley. Publications: Over 300 essays and articles in professional scientific journals and reviews in the field of organisational economics; Books A Challenge to the Quest for Leadership and Managerial Effectiveness, 1980; La Culturocracia en México;. Honours include: Sommer Al Mérito; CONACYT Award; PSU Award; British Council Award, 1982. Memberships: Academy of Management; British Academy of Management; Eastern Region of Organisation of Public Administrators. Address: Cerrada Petronilo López 31, Cd Guzmán, Jalisco 49000, México. E-mail: jvargas@cusur.udg.mx

VASILENKO Tatyana F, b. 18 July 1952, Atamanovo, Russia. Physiologist; Researcher. m. V Muravyev, 2 daughters. Education: Doctor in Biology, State University, St Petersburg, 1980. Appointments: Junior Researcher, Institute of Biology, Komi Department, Academy of Sciences of USSR, Syktyvkar, Russia, 1981-86; Researcher, 1986-91, Senior Researcher,

1991-98, Senior Researcher, 1998-2004, Head of Laboratory of Physiology of Ruminant Animals, 2004-, Institute of Physiology, Komi Science Centre, Ural Division, Russian Academy of Sciences, Syktyvkar, Russia. Articles in scientific journals including: ALCES, 1999, 2001; Integrative Zoology, 2006; Zoological Journal of the Russian Academy of Sciences, 2000, 2002; Doklady Biological Sciences, Russia, 2008; 12 patents. Membership: Physiological Society named after J P Pavlov, Russian Academy of Sciences. Address: Institute of Physiology, Pervomayskaya St 50, Komi Republic, Syktyvkar 167982, Russia. E-mail: vasilenko@physiol.komisc.ru

VASILJEV Alexander V, b. 21 June 1955, Kuragata, Kazakhstan. Economist; Metallurgy Engineer. m. Marina G Tuzovskaya, 31 December 1985, 2 daughters. Education: Diploma, Engineering, Metallurgy Institute, 1977; Candidate, Technical Sciences, Moscow, 1982; Top (Doctorant) Scholar Institute, Economic Industry NAS, Ukraine, Donetsk, 1991-93; High Science Employee, Sociology, Academy of Management, Moscow, 1992; PhD, Economics, Academy of Management, Moscow, 1993; Top Scholar (Doctorant), Institute Economical Industry, NAS, Ukraine, 1991-93; Probationer, Institute IBMER, Poland, 2000-2001. Appointments: Junior then Senior scientific employee, Institute Mariupol, Ukraine, 1980-84; Manager, Research Laboratory, Metallurgy Institute, Manager, Institute of Labour of Ukraine, Manager, Institute of Economic-Law Research, NAS, Ukraine, 1985-98; Chairman, Sectory Science Council, Institute Olga W Wasilievoy-Catholic of Economic and Social/ Cultural Research, Mariupol, 1989-; Lecturer, Donetsk University, Donetsk, 1990-91; Lecturer, Donetsk University, Donetsk, 1990-91; Professor, PriAzov State Technical University, Mariupol, 1993-98; Professor, Mariupol Humanitary Institute, Donetsk University, Mariupol, 1994-95; Professor, Mariupol Humanitary Institute, Donetsk University, Mariupol, 1994-95; Organiser, Mariupol branch, Institute of Economic-Law Research, NAS, Ukraine, Mariupol, 1995-97; Professor, Taganrog's Institute of Management and Economics, 2001-02; Vice-Chairman, Civil International Committee, 2001-; Chief Branch of Management of Mariupol's Department of Academy of Management Staff, 2002-2003; Professor, Department of Inter-regional Academy of Control of Staff, Mariupol, 2003-2004; Professor, Odessa I I Mechnikov National University, Odessa, 2004-06; Lecturer, Odessa Branch of University Ukraine, Odessa, 2005-06; Chief Branch of Economics and Entrepreneurship, Carpatskiy Institute of Entrepreneurship, University Ukraine, Khust, 2006-. Publications include: Problems of maintenance of reproduction of a labour in conditions of intensive development of integration processes, 2005; Keyns's ideas in Ukrainian monetarizme of first fourth of XXI century: the way of the realization of the Law of Preservation of labour in the fiscal policy, 2006; Contributed articles to professional journals. Honours: Recipient, Certificate, Fredrick P Furth Foundation, 1990; Medal "Met Gotey & Cafa, St Ignatia", 1999; Certificate For Good Work to 140 years Odessa I I Mechnikov National University, 2005; Honorary Member, Academy of Economic Sciences and Entrepreneurship. Memberships: New York Academy of Sciences; 1817 Heritage Society, New York Academy of Sciences; American Association for the Advancement of Sciences; Research Board of American Biographical Institute; Union of Economists of Ukraine. Address: Fl 519, Dovzgenko 9B St, 65058 Odessa, Ukraine. E-mail: vasiljev@cic-wsc.org Website: www.cic-wsc.org

VASSOU Vassoulla, b. 25 December 1974, Cyprus. Asset Management Consultant. m. Salman Rashid. Education: HND, Civil Engineering, Higher Technical Institute, Nicosia, Cyprus, 1992-95; B Eng (Hons), Civil Engineering,

MBA, Master's of Business Administration, University of Glamorgan, Wales, 1995-98; PhD, Civil Engineering, Aston University, England, 1998-2003. Appointments: Materials Engineer, Aston Services Ltd, Birmingham, 1998-2002; Research Associate, Aston University, 1998-2002; Graduate Engineer, Faber Maunsell Ltd, Birmingham, 2002-03; Senior Engineer, 2003-05, Assistant Group Engineer, 2005-06, Asset Management Consultant, 2006-, Atkins Consultants Ltd, Birmingham. Publications: 4 refereed papers in primary journals; 3 articles and short papers; Contributions to symposia and compiled volumes. Honours: Represented Cyprus in N Ireland as an exchange student, IAESTE; Best performance in Civil Engineering Subjects, Best performance in Building Construction Subjects, Best project in Civil Engineering Works, Best aggregate performance in all subjects studied in Civil Engineering, Higher Technical Institute, 1992-95; 2 bursaries, University of Glamorgan, 1995-98; Model Analysis Award, Institution of Structural Engineers, 1997; Studentship, Aston University, 1998-2003; Travel Scholarship, The British Institute of Non-Destructive Testing, 2005; International Travel Grant, The Royal Academy of Engineering, 2005; QUEST Travel Award, Institution of Civil Engineers, 2005; Listed in international biographical dictionaries. Memberships: Fédération Europpéne d'Associations Nationales d'Ingénieurs; Chartered Member, Institution of Civil Engineers; Chartered Member, British Institute of Non-Destructive Testing; Member, Cyprus Professional Engineers' Association; Member, Technical Chambers of Cyprus. E-mail: vicky.vassou@atkinsglobal.com

VASUDEV Kadaba Srinath, b. 5 May 1943, Mysore, India. Retired Doctor. m. Pratibha, 2 sons, 1 daughter. Education: MBBS, Bangalore University; FRCPATH, The Royal College of Pathologists, England. Appointments: Senior House Officer, 1969-70, Registrar, Histopathology, 1970-72, Withington Hospital, Manchester, England; Senior Registrar, Histopathology, Manchester Group of Hospitals, 1972-77; Consultant Histopathologist, Blackpool, Fylde and Wyre NHS Trust, 1977-2005. Publications: Papers on breast and gastro-intestinal pathology. Honours: Deputy Lieutenant for the County of Lancashire. Memberships: Rotary Club of Blackpool Palatine; Lodge Amounderness No 7105; Life Education Centres for Lancashire; Bharatiya Vidya Bhauan, Manchester. Address: 10 Silverdale Road, St Annes, Lancashire FY8 3RE, England. E-mail: vasudev@globalnet.co.uk

VASYLIEV Oleksii, b. 12 April 1959, Taganrog, Russia. Information Professional. m. Choch, 1 son, 1 daughter. Education: Master's degree (Magister), Computer Science, Kyiv Politechical Institute (now National Technical University, Kyiv Politechica Institute), 1982; PhD, Energy Saving Problem Institute, National Academy of Science of Ukraine, 1991. Appointments: STN International, Regional Representation in Ukraine, 1994-2000; IRC Co-ordinator, Information Resource Center, US Embassy, Kiev, Ukraine, 2000-05; Director, Information Consortium Association, 2002-; Director, Information Computer Centre, National University Kyiv Mohyla Academy, 2005-. Publications: 63 publications including: 2 monographs; 10 print reports; 24 journal articles; 22 conference papers. Honours: Listed in Who's Who publications and biographical dictionaries. Memberships: IEEE; ACM. Address: Ap 55, Build 1, Sviatoshynska Sq, Kyiv, UA03115, Ukraine. E-mail: ovasylyev@gmail.com

VAUGHAN Dindy Belinda, b. 26 December 1938, Kogarah, New South Wales, Australia. Consultant in Arts Education and Environment. 1 daughter. Education: BA (honours), University of Sydney, Australia, 1967; MA, Flinders University, South Australia, 1970. Appointments: Tertiary Lecturer, Royal Melbourne Institute of Technology and Footscray Institute (now Victoria University of Technology); Academic Assessor, Deakin University; Community Arts Officer; Frequent contracts and commissions for music composition; Consultant in arts, education and environment; Established Gallery Without Walls; Instigated and co-ordinated Focus on Water; Composed music for Lake Bolac Eel Festival; World premiere, Violin Sonata, Burrinja, Upwey, Victoria. Publications: By-line Correspondent for local paper, 1979-81; CD, Up the Creek, 2005; www.gallerywithoutwalls.com.au; Books and articles on environment and the arts; Musical composition scores including tutoring books. Honours: University of Sydney Alumni Association Award for achievements in community service; Finalist, Australian Classical Music Awards, 2006; Listed in several biographical dictionaries. Memberships: Life Member, University of Sydney Alumni Association; Life Member, Sydney University Arts Association; Melbourne Composer's League; Australian Geographic; Candlebark Community Nursery; Life Member, Croydon Conservation Society; Life Member, Dandenong Ranges Community and Cultural Centre; Greenpeace; Australian Conservation Foundation; Initiator and Chief Co-ordinator for Focus on Water, Victoria, 2005; Member, Australian Performing Rights Association. Address: PO 668 Ringwood, VIC 3134, Australia. E-mail: gallerywithoutwalls@bigpond.com.au

VEERAKYATHIAH V D, b. 25 June 1926, Vaddagere, India. Retired. m. V Rajamma, 25 June 1955, 2 sons. Education: BSc, Agriculture. Appointments: Village Level Worker, 1954-55; Agricultural Extension Officer, 1955-57; Block Development Officer, 1957-65; Principal, State Level Young Farmers Training Centre, 1 year; Instructor, Orientation and Study Centre, Government of India, Poona, 1 year; Assistant Development Commissioner, 1967-71; Assistant Director, Land Army, 1971-72; Principal, Rural Development Training Centre, Mandya, Karnataka, 1972-75; Secretary, Chief Executive Officer, State Khadi and Village Industries Board, Bangalore, 1976-77; Project Director, SFDA, Government of Karnataka, 1977-80; Selected for Indian Administrative Service, Government of India; Director, Special Economic Programmes, IRDP, Government of Karnataka, 1980-82; Director, Backward Classes and Other Weaker Sections, 1982-84. Publications: 3 professional papers in the Indian Science Congress Sessions. Memberships: Honorary Director, Asian Institute for Urban Development; Advisor, Ganga Rural Development Trust; Bangalore Zilla Aadhar Member, Age Foundation, Ministry of Social Welfare, Government of India; Honorary President, Vaddagere Temple Development Committee; Founder-President, Akhila Kunchitigara Mahal Mardal, Bangalore. Address: 596 IInd Stage 1 E Block, Rajajinagar, Bangalore 560010, India.

VELINOV Milen T, b. 29 July 1959, Bulgaria. Physician; Researcher. m. Milena Velinova, 1 son, 1 daughter. Education: MD, Higher Medical Institute, Sofia, 1986; PhD, Biomedical Institute, Sofia, 1995. Appointments: Postdoctoral Fellow, University of Connecticut Health Centre, USA, 1991-95; Resident in Paediatrics, New York Methodist Hospital, 1995-98; Staff Research Scientist, New York State Institute for Basic Research, Staten Island, 1998-; Fellow in Clinical Genetics, Maimonides Medical Centre, 1999-2003; Assistant Professor of Paediatrics, State University of New York, College of Medicine, 2004; Program Director, Comprehensive Genetic Services, Assistant Director, Speciality Clinical Laboratories, 2004-, NYS Institute for Basic Research; Assistant Professor, State University of New York, 2004-06; Assistant Professor,

Department of Human Genetics, Mount Sinai Medical Center, 2006-. Publications: Co-author: Connective Tissue Research, 29:13, 1993; American Journal of Medical Genetics, 47:294, 1993; Nature Genetics, 6(3):314, 1994; Molecular Genetics and Metabolism, 69:81, 2000. Honours: Fellow's Clinical Research Award, Society for Paediatric Research, 1994; Resident Research Grant, American Academy of Paediatrics, 1997. Memberships: American Society of Human Genetics; American Academy of Paediatrics; American College of Medical Genetics. Address: New York State Institute for Basic Research, 1050 Forest Hill Road, Staten Island, NY 10314, USA. E-mail: velinovm@aol.com

VENABLES Terry Frederick, b. 6 January 1943. Professional Football Manager; Commentator. m. Yvette, 2 daughters. Education: Dagenham High School. Career: Professional Footballer, Chelsea, 1958-66 (Captain, 1962), Tottenham Hotspur, 1966-68 (FA Cup winners, 1967), Queens Park Rangers, 1968-73; Coach, Crystal Palace, 1973-76, Manchester, 1976-80; Manager, Queens Park Rangers, 1980-84; Manager, Barcelona, 1984-87 (winners, Spanish Championship, 1984, European Cup finalists, 1985); Manager, Tottenham Hotspur, 1987-91 (FA Cup winners, 1991); Chief Executive, Tottenham Hotspur plc, 1991-93; Coach, England National Team, 1994-96; Director of Football, Portsmouth Football Club, 1996-98; Coach, Australian National Team, 1996-98; Head Coach, Crystal Palace, 1998; Coach, Middlesborough, 2001; Manager, Leeds United, 2002-03; Assistant to Manager Steve McClaren, England, 2006-07; Only player to have represented England at all levels. Publications: They Used to Play on Grass, 1971; Terry Venables: The Autobiography, 1994; The Best Game in the World, 1996; Venables' England – The Making of the Team, 1996. Honours: Honorary Fellow, University of Wolverhampton; English Football Hall of Fame, 2007. Address: Terry Venables Holdings Ltd, 213 Putney Bridge Road, London, SW15 2NY, England.

VENDLER Helen, (Helen Hennessy), b. 30 April 1933, Boston, Massachusetts, USA. Professor; Poetry Critic. 1 son. Education: AB, Emmanuel College, 1954; PhD, Harvard University, 1960. Appointments: Instructor, Cornell University, 1960-63; Lecturer, Swarthmore College and Haverford College, Pennsylvania, 1963-64; Associate Professor, 1966-68, Professor, 1968-85, Boston University; Fulbright Lecturer, University of Bordeaux, 1968-69; Poetry Critic, The New Yorker, 1978-99; Overseas Fellow, Churchill College, Cambridge, 1980; Senior Fellow, Harvard Society of Fellows, 1981-93; Visiting Professor, 1981-85, Kenan Professor, 1985-90, Associate Academic Dean, 1987-92, Porter University Professor, 1990-, Harvard University; Charles Stewart Parnell Fellow, 1996, Honorary Fellow, 1996-, Magdalene College, Cambridge. Publications: Yeats's Vision and the Later Plays, 1963; On Extended Wings: Wallace Stevens' Longer Poems, 1969; The Poetry of George Herbert, 1975; Part of Nature, Part of Us: Modern American Poets, 1980; The Odes of John Keats, 1983; Wallace Stevens: Words Chosen Out of Desire, 1984; The Harvard Book of Contemporary American Poetry (editor), 1985; Voices and Visions: The Poet in America, 1987; The Music of What Happens, 1988; Soul Says, 1995; The Given and the Made, 1995; The Breaking of Style, 1995; Poems, Poets, Poetry, 1995; The Art of Shakespeare's Sonnets, 1997; Seamus Heaney, 1998; Coming of Age as a Poet, 2003; Poets Thinking, 2004; Invisible Listeners, 2005; Our Secret Discipline, 2007. Contributions to: Professional journals. Honours: Lowell Prize, 1969; Guggenheim Fellowship, 1971-72; American Council of Learned Societies Fellow, 1971-72; National Institute of Arts and Letters Award, 1975; Radcliffe College Graduate

Society Medal, 1978; National Book Critics Award, 1980; National Endowment for the Humanities Fellowships, 1980, 1985, 1994, 2005; Keats-Shelley Association Award, 1994; Truman Capote Award, 1996; Jefferson Medal, American Philosophical Society, 2002; Jefferson Lecturer, NEH, 2004; Many honorary doctorates; Phi Beta Kappa. Memberships: American Academy of Arts and Letters; American Academy of Arts and Sciences, vice-president, 1992-95; American Philosophical Society; English Institute; Modern Language Association, president, 1980. Address: Harvard University, Department of English, Barker Center, Cambridge, MA 02138, USA.

VENGATESAN Balasubramanian, b. 4 June 1962, Villupuram, India. Materials Scientist. m. Kusuma, 1 son, 1 daughter. Education: BSc, 1982; MSc, 1984; PhD, 1990. Appointments: Researcher, 1984-89; Lecturer, Anna University, 1989-93; Research and Development Manager, 1993-2002, Deputy Director, NanoTech Laboratory, 2002-05, Director, 2005-, Canare Electric Co Ltd, Japan. Publications: Several research papers in international reputed journals. Honours: Visiting Professor, University of Madras, India, 2007-; Distinguished Professor, Nanotechnology, Anna University, India, 2008-; Numerous national and international awards. Memberships: IEEE, USA; IET, UK. Address: Canare Electric Co Ltd, NanoTech Laboratory, 2888-1 Rikka, Kumabari, Nagakute-cho, Aichi-gun, Aichi-ken, 480-1101, Japan. E-mail: cbsvenki@canare.co.jp

VENIAMIN Christodoulos, b. September 1922, Katomoni, Cyprus. Law. Education: Barrister at Law, Middle Temple. Appointments: Served in administrative offices in various capital cities up to 1960; Director General, Ministry of Foreign Office, 1968-75; Minister of Interior and Defence, 1975-88; Minister of Interior, 1988-93; Member of Parliament, 1995-99. Address: 5 Kleanthi Lerodiaconou, 2431 Engomi, Nicosia, Cyprus.

VENN George Andrew Fyfe, b. 12 October 1943, Tacoma, Washington, USA. Professor; Writer; Editor; Poet; Critic. m. Elizabeth Cheney, divorced, 1 son, 1 daughter. Education: BA, College of Idaho, 1967; MFA, Creative Writing, University of Montana, 1970; Central University, Quito, Ecuador; University of Salamanca, Spain; City Literary Institute, London. Appointments: Writer-on-Tour, Western States Arts Foundation, 1977; Foreign Expert, Changsha Railway University, Hunan, China, 1981-82; General Editor, Oregon Literature Series, 1989-94; Writer-in-Residence, Eastern Oregon University. Publications: Sunday Afternoon: Grande Ronde, 1975; Off the Main Road, 1978; Marking the Magic Circle, 1988; Oregon Literature Series, 1992-94; West of Paradise: New Poems, 1999; Soldier to Advocate: CES Wood's 1877 Legacy, 2006. Many other poems, essays and stories. Contributions to: Oregon Humanities; Writer's Northwest Handbook; North West Review; Northwest Reprint Series; Poetry Northwest; Willow Springs; Clearwater Journal; Oregon East; Portland Review; Worldviews and the American West (book). Honours: Pushcart Prize, 1980; Oregon Book Award, 1988; Stewart Holbrook Award, 1994; Andres Berger Poetry Prize, Northwest Writers, 1995; Listed in Who's Who publications and biographical dictionaries. Memberships: Fishtrap Gathering; Authors Guild, Western Writers of America. Address: Department of English, Eastern Oregon University, La Grande, OR 97850, USA. E-mail: gvenn@eou.Edu Website: www.georgevenn.com

VENSON Lily Pagratis, b. 24 October 1924, Chicago, Illinois, USA. Journalist; Lecturer. m. George John Venson, 1 son, 1 daughter. Education: Associate of Arts Degree, Wright College, Chicago, Illinois, 1943; Further studies, University of Chicago, Illinois, 1944. Appointments: Reporter, editorial writer, picture page editor, feature writer, Lerner Newspapers, Chicago, 1963-73; Chief, Public Information Officer and Editor of two newsletters, Health and Hospitals Governing Commission of Cook County, Illinois, operator of three Chicago public hospitals, 1973-77; Public Information Officer and Cook County Editor, Hotline News magazine, Illinois Department of Children and Family Services, 1980-91; Journalism Lecturer, Columbia College, Chicago, 1997-. Publications: 10 years of articles as reporter and staff writer, Lerner Newspapers, 1963-73; 100+ Lerner articles on successful 7-year crusade to save land for public park (100 acres), Chicago, 1966-72; Series of three articles on politics of Greece, Congressional Record, Washington, DC, (originally published in Lerner Newspapers, Chicago), 1968; First Place Award-winning articles, Hotline Magazine; Illinois Women's Press Association, 1989, 1990, 1991; Poetry author, International Library of Poetry, 2001. Honours: Nominee, Pulitzer Prize Community Service Award, Columbia University, 1973; Illinois Traffic Safety Editors, Community Service, 1965; Civil Rights Brotherhood Award, National Conference of Christians and Jews, 1965; 1st Place, Community Service Award, American Newspaper Guild, Chicago Chapter, 1970; Community Service Award, Northtown Community Council, 1970; Outstanding Reporting Award, Illinois Governor, 1972; National Writing Award, National Federation of Press Women, 1990. Memberships: Society of Professional Journalists; Chicago Headline Club; Illinois Woman's Press Association; National Federation of Press Women; Fellowship of Reconciliation Peace Activists; Statue of Liberty - Ellis Island Foundation; St Andrew's Greek Orthodox Church Philoptochos Society (Friends of the Poor); Hellenic Museum and Cultural Center; Illinois Commission on the Status of Women, Courts and Corrections Committee, -1968. Address: 3180 N Lake Shore 5D, Chicago, IL 60657, USA. E-mail: 102424@msn.com

VENTER Andre, b. 7 November, Pretoria, South Africa. Education: Afrikaans Medium High School, Lyttelton; Distinction Aggregate and Distinctions in Biology, Science and Mathematics, 1971; MB CHB, University of Pretoria, 1977; Diploma in Child Health, 1980, FCP (Paed), 1984, College of Medicine of South Africa; Registered as Paediatrician, South African Medical and Dental Council, 1986; MMED (Paediatrics), University of Witwatersrand, 1988; PhD, Medical Sciences (Paediatrics), University of Alberta, Canada, 1991; Developmental Paediatrics, South African Medical and Dental Council, 1998. Appointments: Intern, Boksburg-Benoni Hospital, 1978; National Service, Medical Officer, Paediatric Department at 1 Military Hospital, Voortrekkerhoogte, 1979-80; Senior Medical Officer, Department of Paediatrics, Boksburg-Benoni Hospital, 1981-82; Registrar, Paediatrics, University of the Witwatersrand, Johannesburg Hospital and Baragwanath Hospital, 1982-84; Research Registrar, Department of Paediatrics and MRC Research Unit for Paediatric Mineral Metabolism, 1984-86; Paediatrician, Department of Paediatrics, University of the Witwatersrand and Baragwanath Hospital, 1986-89; Kathleen Swallow Clinical Fellow, Neurodevelopmental Medicine, Department of Paediatrics, University of Alberta, Canada, 1988-91; Senior Specialist, Department of Paediatrics, Baragwanath Hospital and the University of the Witwatersrand, 1989-93; Senior Specialist, 1993-95, Principal Specialist, 1995-96, Department of Paediatrics, Coronation Hospital and the

University of the Witwatersrand; Chief Specialist, Professor and Academic Head, Department of Paediatrics and Child Health, Universitas Hospital and the University of the Orange Free State, 1996-. Publications: Numerous articles in refereed journals; 3 books and chapters. Honours: Protea Prize, Pretoria University, 1977; Wellcome Award for Excellence in Research, Alberta, 1991; MSC Excellence Award, 1996; Long Service Certificate, 1997; Golden Ventricle Award, 2002; Van Der Riet Medal, University of Free State, 2005; International Nestle Nutrition Research Prize (Africa), 2005. Memberships: American Academy for Cerebral Palsy and Developmental Medicine; Advisory Board of the South African Institute for Sensory Integration; Paediatric Neurology and Development Association of Southern Africa; International Child Neurology Association; International Paediatric Chairs Association; South African Paediatric Association; Faculty of Paediatrics of the College of Medicine; ADHD Support Group; International Advisory Panel for ADHD. Address: PO Box 339 (g69), Bloemfontein, South Africa. E-mail: gnpdav.md@mail.uovs.ac.za

VERDY Violette, b. 1 December 1933, Pont L'Abbé, France. Ballet Teacher; Coach; Choreographer. Education: Trained with Carlotta Zambelli, Rousane Sarkissian and Victor Gsovsky. Appointments: Principal Dancer: Roland Petit's companies, 1945-56; London Festival Ballet, 1954-55; American Ballet Theatre, 1957-58; New York City Ballet, 1958-76; Guest Artist with most companies around the world; Guest Teacher at many ballet companies and schools including: New York City Ballet, The Royal Ballet, The Paris Opera, The Australian Ballet Company, The Royal Danish and The Bolchoi Ballet Company; Artistic Director, Paris Opera Ballet and Boston Ballet; Artistic Advisor, Rock School of Dance Education, Philadelphia, Pennsylvania. Publications: Giselle, or the Wilis, 1970; Ballerina, biography, 1976; Of Swans, Sugar Plums and Satin Slippers, 1991. Honours: Mademoiselle Award, 1958; Dance Magazine Award, 1968; Chevalier dans l'Ordre des Arts et Lettres, 1971; Doctor of Humane Letters, Skidmore College, 1971; Doctor of Arts, Goucher College, 1987; Doctor of Arts, Boston Conservatory, 1997; Distinguished Professor of Ballet, Indiana University Jacobs School of Music. Address: 3809 St Remy Dr, Bloomington, IN 47401, USA. E-mail: viverdy@indiana.edu

VERE HODGE (Richard) Anthony, b. 27 December 1943, Burnham-on-Sea, England. Biochemist. m. 1 son, 2 daughters. Education: BA, Trinity College, Dublin, Ireland, 1962-66; D Phil, Worcester College, Oxford, England, 1966-69. Appointments: Employee, 1969-96, Beecham Pharmaceuticals (then SmithKline Beecham Pharmaceuticals, now GlaxoSmithKline), 1969-96; (Project Manager, Interferon Inducers, Human Interferon, 1974-76; Chief Biochemist, Antiviral Chemotherapy Project which discovered penciclovir, 1983, famciclovir, 1985, 1981-92; Seconded as Expert on famciclovir, 1993-94, Associate Director, Anti-Infectives Section, World-wide Strategic Product Development, 1995-96); Director, Vere Hodge Antivirals Ltd, 1996-; Consultant to Pharmasset Inc, Atlanta, Georgia, USA, 2000-05; Reviews Editor, Antiviral Chemistry & Chemotherapy (AVCC), 2005-. Publications in professional journals include: Selection of an oral prodrug (BRL 42810; famciclovir) for the antiherpesvirus agent BRL 39123 [9-(4-hydroxy-3-hydroxymethylbut-1-yl)guanine; penciclovir], 1989; Mode of action of 9-(4-Hydroxy-3-Hydroxymethylbut-1-yl)Guanine (BRL 39123) against herpes simplex virus in MRC-5 cells, 1989; Famiciclovir and penciclovir. The mode of action of famciclovir including its conversion to penciclovir, 1993;

Chirality presents a challenge: Famciclovir – a case study, 1995; Telbivudine/Torcitabine, 2004; Book Chapter, Famciclovir: Discovery and development of a novel antiherpesvirus agent, 1998; Numerous papers presented at international conferences. Memberships: Royal Society of Chemistry, 1968; The Chromatographic Society, 1989; International Society for Antiviral Research, 1990; American Society for Microbiology, 1997. Address: Old Denshott, Leigh, Reigate, Surrey RH2 8RD, England. E-mail: averehodge@aol.com

VEREKER John (Michael Medlicott) (Sir), b. 9 August 1944, UK. Governor of Bermuda. m. Judith Diane Rowen, 1 son, 1 daughter. Education: BA (Hons), University of Keele, 1967. Appointments: World Bank, Washington, 1970-72; Principal, Ministry of Overseas Development, 1972; Private Secretary to successive Ministers of Overseas Development, 1977-78; Prime Minister's Office, 1980-83; Under Secretary, 1983-88, Principal Finance Officer, 1986-88, Overseas Development Administration, Foreign and Commonwealth Office; Deputy Secretary, Department for Education, 1988-93; Permanent Secretary, Department for International Development, 1994-2002; Governor and Commander-in-Chief of Bermuda, 2002-07. Publication: Blazing the Trail (Journal of Development Studies), 2002. Honours: CB, 1992; CIMgt, 1995; Hon D Litt, University of Keele; KCB, 1999; FRSA, 1999, KStJ, 2001. Memberships: Chairman, Student Loans Co Ltd, 1989-91; Board Member, British Council, 1994-2001; Board Member, Institute of Development Studies, 1994-2000. Address: Government House, Hamilton, Bermuda.

VERNAGLIONE Luigi, b. 14 October 1968, Taranto, Italy. Physician (Nephrologist). m. Maria La Gioia, 1998. Education: Medical Degree, 1993, Postgraduate Diploma of Hypertension Specialist, 1997, Nephrology Specialist Diploma, 1997, University of Bari, Italy. Master on Healthcare Units Managing – Milan (Italy) 2006-. Appointments: Internship and Fellowship, 2nd Internal Medicine Institute, 1991-94, Fellowship, Postgraduate School of Nephrology, 1994-97, University of Bari; Resident, Nephrology and Dialysis Unit, Hospital of Martina Franca, Italy, 1997-98; Attending Nephrologist, Nephrology and Dialysis Unit, Hospital of Manduria, Italy, 1998-; Clinical Research Fellowship, Department of Nephrology, Keck School of Medicine, Los Angeles, California, USA, 2003-05. Publications: Scientific papers in professional journals. Honours: Congress Best Poster Award, 1998; Master in Hypertension, Charité Humboldt University, Berlin, 2002; Master in Peritoneal Dialysis, Sheffield Hospital, England, 2002; Congress Best Poster Award, 2003; Grantee, Italian Society of Nephrology, 2003-04; Many other papers published on Professional Journals. Memberships: Italian Society of Nephrology; European Society of Nephrology; American Society of Nephrology; Italian Society of Hypertension. Address: Nephrology Unit, M Giannuzzi Hospital, via Mandonion 1, Taranto, Manduria, 74024, Italy. E-mail: vernalu@libero.it

VERNICKAITĖ Ruslana, b. 22 September 1934, Minsk, Belarus. Physician; Obstetrician-gynaecologist. Education: Doctor's Assistant-Obstetrician, Kaunas Paramedical and Obstetrical School, 1950-54; Diploma, 1954; Physician, Kaunas Medical Institute, 1960-67, Diploma, 1967; Candidate in Science degree, Diploma, 1984; DSc, Medicine, Vilnius, Lithuania, 1993. Appointments: Physician Obstetrician-Gynaecologist, Kretinga Maternity Clinic, 1967-68; Obstetrician-Gynaecologist and Chief Consultant, Obstetrical Department, Klaipėda City Hospital, 1968-89; Obstetrician-Gynaecologist, Women's Consultation No 3, Klaipėda City Hospital, 1989-97; Obstetrician-Gynaecologist,

Unit No 2, Klaipėda City Primary Health Care Centre, 1997-. Publications: Monograph, SOS to the Life on Earth: The effect of environmental factors and atmospheric chemical pollutants on the human organism at certain periods of its ontogenesis, 1999; 95 scientific works on obstetrics, perinatology, chronomedicina, chronopharmacology, cytochemistry, clinical pathophysiology, human ontogenesis and ecology, published in Europe, Japan, USA, Canada, China, Denmark, Finland, Slovenia, Slovakia, Bulgaria, Ukraine, Russia; 1 invention. Honours: Fellow of the American Biographical Institute with Gold Medallion, International Cultural Diploma of Honour, 1996; Greatest and Great Minds of the 21st Century, ABI, USA, 2002; 2000 Outstanding Scientists of the 20th Century, IBC, 1999, The IBC Millennium Time Capsule, 1999, Gold Medal and Scroll, Living Legends, IBC, 2004, International Scientist of the Year, IBC, Gold Medal, 2001, IBC, England; Torch of Global Inspiration, ABI, 2000, Scientific Excellence Gold Medal, USA, 2001; The World Order Science – Education – Culture, The European Academy of Informatisation, Brussels, Belgium, 2002; Diploma, Greatest and Great Minds of the 21st Century, USA, 2002; Diploma, Ambassador of Grand Eminence, USA, 2002; Great Minds of the 21st Century Gold Medal, USA, 2002; Da Vinci Diamond, IBC, 2004; Albert Schweitzer International University Medal for Science and Peace, Spain, 2004; American Medal of Honor, 2004; World Medal of Freedom, ABI, 2004; 21st Century Genius Laureate Title and Gold Medal, 2006; The Marie Curie Award, IBC, 2006; Proclamation: The Genius Elite (Documented in Leading Intellectuals of the World, ABI, USA), 2004; Living Legends, IBC, 2004; World Medal of Freedom, ABI, 2004; 21st Century Genius of Distinction, 21st Century Medal, ABI, 2005. Memberships: International Association of Biometeorology, Calgary, 1993; LFIBA, DDG, 1995; IBA, 1995; ABI Board of Governors, 1996; ABIRA, 1996; Secretary General, United Cultural Convention, USA, 2001; Founder Diplomatic Counsellor, London Diplomatic Academy, England, 2000; International Diplomatic Academy, London, 2002; Honourable Member, Bulgarian Association of Clinical and Experimental Pathophysiology, Sofia, 1997; Member of the Assembly of the International Diplomatic Academy, Geneva, 2002. Address: Rambyno 7-5, LT-93173 Klaipėda, Lithuania.

VERSACE Donatella, b. 2 May 1955, Reggio Calabria, Italy. Vice-President and Chief Designer of the Versace Group. m. Paul Beck, 1 son, 1 daughter. Appointments: Joined Versace, 1978; Formerly overseer of advertising and public relations, accessories designer, children's collection designer, solo designer, Versus and Isante Lines; Creative Director, Gianni Versace Group, 1997-; Launched own fragrance, Versace Woman, 2001. Address: c/o Keeble Cavaco and Duka Inc, 450 West 15th Street, Suite 604, New York, NY 10011, USA. Website: ww.versace.com

VETTATH Murali, b. 2 January 1960, Kerala, India. Cardiac Surgeon. m. Suja Murali, 2 daughters. Education: MBBS, DNB, General Surgery; MCh, Cardiothoracic and Vascular Surgery. Appointments: Senior Registrar, Department of Cardiothoracic Surgery, Royal Adelaide Hospital, 1996-98; Clinical Director and Chief Cardiac Surgeon, Z H Sikder Cardiac Care and Research Centre, Dhaka, 1999-2001; Currently, Senior Consultant and Chief Cardiac Surgeon and Director, MIMS, Kozhikode, Kerala, India. Publications: Inventions: Vettath's anastamotic obturator – a simple proximal anastamotic device; Development of aortocoronary shunt for beating heart surgery; Indigenous stabiliser for beating heart surgery, off pump coronary artery bypass. Honours: Title "Sarvashri" and Gold Medal in Cardiac Surgery, 2004; Title of

"Sir" and Gold Medal in Cardiac Surgery, 2005; Melvin Jones Fellow, Lions Club International, 2007; Glory of India Award, India International Friendship Society, 2008. Memberships: Fellow, Australasian Society of Cardiac Surgery; Fellow, Asian Society of Cardiovascular Surgery; Fellow, International Society of Minimally Invasive Cardiac Surgeons; Member, Rotary; Member, Lions. Address: Malabar Institute of Medical Science, Mini Bypass Road, Govindapuram, Kerala State, Kozhikode 673016, India. E-mail: mvettathcts@hotmail.com Website: www.mvettathcts.com

VICAR Jan, b. 5 May 1949, Olomouc, Czech Republic. Musicologist; Composer. m. (1) Anna Betkova, 2 sons, (2) Eva Slavickova, 1 son, 1 daughter. Education: MA, Palacky University Olomouc, 1972; Conservatory in Ostrava, 1972; PhD, 1974; MA, Academy of Music and Performing Arts, Prague, 1981; CSc, 1985. Appointments: Teacher, Department of Musicology, Palacky University, 1973-; Chair, 1990-98, 2000-2003; 2007-; Teacher, Department of Music Theory and History, Academy of Music and Performing Arts, Prague, 1980-; Editor in Chief, Hudebni Rozhledy, 1986-89; Professor, Theory and History of Music, Prague, 1998-; Professor, Composition, Birmingham Southern College, Alabama, USA, 2005. Publications: The Accordion and its Musical Use; Vaclav Trojan; Music Criticism and Popularization of Music; Music Aesthetics; Imprints: Essays on Czech Music and Aesthetics; Compositions: String Quartet; Nonet; The Cry; Japanese Year; Preludes/Phantasms; Choruses and Songs for Children; Three Marches for Dr Kabyl; Vivat Universitas!; Towards the Mountains. Honours: Fulbright Scholar, 1998-99, USA. Memberships: Czechoslovak Society of Arts and Sciences. Address: Malostranske namesti 13, 118 00 Praha 1, Czech Republic.

VIDAL Gore, (Edgar Box), b. 3 October 1925, West Point, New York, USA. Writer. Education: Graduate, Phillips Exeter Academy, 1943. Publications: Novels: Williwaw, 1946; In a Yellow Wood, 1947; The City and the Pillar, 1948; The Season of Comfort, 1949; A Search for the King, 1950; Dark Green, Bright Red, 1950; The Judgment of Paris, 1952; Messiah, 1954; Julian, 1964; Washington, DC, 1967; Myra Breckinridge, 1968; Two Sisters, 1970; Burr, 1973; Myron, 1974; Kalki, 1978; Creation, 1981; Duluth, 1983; Lincoln, 1984; Empire, 1987; The Smithsonian Institution, 1998; The Golden Age, 2000; Clouds and Eclipses: The Collected Short Stories, 2006; Stories: A Thirsty Evil, 1956; Play: Visit to a Small Planet, 1957. Television and Broadway productions: The Best Man, 1960; Romulus, 1966; Weekend, 1968; An Evening with Richard Nixon, 1972; Gore Vidal's Lincoln, 1988; On the March to the Sea, 2005; Non fiction: Rocking the Boat, 1962; Reflections upon a Sinking Ship, 1969; Homage to Daniel Shays, 1973; Matters of Fact and of Fiction, 1977; The Second American Revolution, 1982; Armageddon?, 1987; At Home: Essays 1982-88, 1988; A View from the Diners Club: Essays 1987-91, 1991; Screening History (memoir), 1992; United States: Essays 1952-1992, 1993; Palimpest (memoir), 1995; Virgin Islands: A Dependency of United States Essays 1992-97, 1997; The Last Empire: Essays 1992-2000, 2001; Perpetrual War for Perpetual Peace: How We Go So Hated, 2002; Inventing a Nation: Washington, Adams, Jefferson, 2003; Imperial America, 2004; Point to Point Navigation: A Memoir, 2007. Teleplays: The Death of Billy the Kid, 1958; Dress Gray, 1986; Criticism in Partisan Review; The Nation; New York Review of Books; Times Literary Supplement. Honour: National Book Award, 1993. Membership: American Academy of Arts and Letters; Honorary Associate, National Secular Society. Address: c/o Random House, 201 E 50th Street, New York, NY 10022, USA.

VIENS Louis, (Nathaniel Thorne), b. 15 February 1957, Montréal, Québéc, Canada. Author. Education: Diploma, Human Sciences (History), Collège de Maisonneuve, Montréal, Québéc, Canada, 1980. Publications: Le Dernier virage ou un chrétien en colère, 1994; D'une catacombe l'autre, 1995. Contributions to: Journal Voir. Memberships: French-Speaking Writers of America, 1992; Union des écrivains Québécois, 1995. Address: 1607 av Letourneux, Montréal, Quebec, Canada H1V 2M6. E-mail: nathaniel@distributel.net Website: http://lederneirvirage.iquebec.com

VIERTL Reinhard, b. 25 March 1946, Hall in Tirol, Austria. Professor of Applied Statistics. m. Dorothea, 2 sons. Education: Dipl Ing, 1972; Dr techn. 1974. Appointments: Assistant, 1972-79; University Docent, 1979-80; Research Fellow, University of California, Berkeley, 1980-81; Visiting Docent, University of Klagenfurt, 1981-82; Full Professor, Vienna University of Technology, 1982-; Visiting Professor, University of Innsbruck, 1991-93; Seasonal Instructor, University of Calgary, summer 2003. Publications: 10 books, including Statistical Methods for Non-Precise Data, 1996; Over 100 scientific papers in mathematics, probability theory, life testing, regional statistics, Bayesian statistics, and statistics with non-precise data. Honours: Max Kade Fellow, 1980. Memberships: Royal Statistical Society, London; Austrian Statistical Society; International Statistical Institute; German Statistical Society; New York Academy of Sciences; Austrian Mathematical Society. Address: Department of Statistics, Vienna University of Technology, Wiedner Hauptstr 8/107, A-1040 Vienna, Austria. E-mail: r.viertl@tuwien.ac.at

VIJAYARATNAM Kanapathipillai, b. 10 May 1948, Analaitivu, Ceylon (Sri Lanka). Chartered Civil, Water, Environmental Engineer and Manager; Consultant; Educator. m. Sakuntala Mylvaganam, 1979. Education: BSc, Engineering (Honours), 1971; MEng, 1977; MSc, Eng (London), 1982; DIC (London), 1982; DSc (Eng), 2004; Certificate, Sustainable Business, World Business Council on Sustainable Development, 1999. Appointments include: Instructor, Civil Engineering, University of Ceylon, 1972; Civil Engineer, Mahaveli (River) Development Board, 1972-75; Civil Engineer, Renardet Engineering, Singapore, 1977-80; Engineer, Chanton Engineering Ltd, Middlesex, England, 1984-85; Engineer, S P Collins & Associates, Consulting Engineers, Cambridge, 1985-86; Consulting Engineer, 1986-88; Senior Engineer, Neilcot Construction, 1988-90; Engineer, Clean Water Department, Binnie & Partners Consulting Engineers, 1990-94; Senior Engineer, Gr I, SMHB, Consulting Engineers, KL Malaysia, 1995-96; Principal Engineer (Deputy Project Manager), Resident Engineer, SSP Consulting Engineers, Malaysia, 1996-97; Engineering Consultant, England, 1998; Director, Rosebury Consulting Ltd, Engineering Consultants, 1999-; Executive Director, AITA – NET (Europe) Ltd, 2001-04; Founder, Executive President and Dean, London Engineering School, 2004-; Founder and Dean, Faculty of Engineering Management and Environment, Irish International University, 2004-05; Adjunct Faculty, Professor and Dean, School of Engineering Management, Sustainable Development and Public Policy, American University of London, 2003-; Pioneer of multidisciplinary Faculty of Engineering Management and Environment, 2004; President, Founder & Director General, World Academy of Engineering (www.waeng.org), 2006-. Publications: Contributions to international conferences on Engineering, 1977-; Vijayaratnam's Technical Contribution on www.mit.edu, 2000-; Wide-ranging Engineering, Water, Environment and public policy forums on www.bbc.co.uk, 2001-. Honours: Awarded several medals, prizes and accolades for pioneering contribution to Sustainable Engineering Environment; Listed in numerous world, USA & UK biographical publications. Memberships: CEng, MICE, 1977; MCIWEM, 1979; MASCE, 1986; MIWRA, 1992; MIAHR, 1993; MIWA, 1993; MIHA, 1998; Member, Association of Environmental Engineering and Science Professors, 2005; Member, United Nations International Centre for Engineering Education, Australia, 1999-; Member, Royal Institution, London, 2000-; Member, Cambridge Network, 2005-; Top Mentor and London Engineering School are listed in Worldwide Education, 2005- (www.worldwide.edu). Address: 1 Ashcroft Rise, Coulsdon, Surrey CR5 2SS, England. E-mail: president@waeng.org Website: www.vijayaratnam.com

VIKBERG Veli Valtteri, b. 2 November 1936, Pyhäjärvi, Ul, Finland. Retired Physician; Amateur Entomologist. m. Marjatta Kurkela, 1 son, 3 daughters. Education: Licenciate of Medicine, 1961, Specialising in medical microbiology, 1967, University of Helsinki. Appointments: Senior Physician, Laboratory Department, Central Hospital of North Karelia, Joensuu, 1967-74; Senior Physician, Laboratory Department, 1974-87, Senior Physician, Department of Clinical Microbiology, 1988-95, Central Hospital of Kanta-Häme, Hämeenlinna; Retired, 1995. Publications: Numerous articles in scientific journals, 1960-2007. Honours: Silvery Saalas-medal, The Entomological Society of Finland, 2007. Memberships: The Entomological Society of Finland, 1959; The International Society of Hymenopterists, 1991. Address: Liinalammintie 11 as. 6, FI-14200 Turenki, Finland.

VILLAS-BOAS Jose Manuel, b. 23 February 1931, Porto, Portugal. Diplomat; Professor. m. Maria. Education: Faculty of Law, University of Lisbon. Appointments: Ambassador to NATO, Brussels, 1979-84; Ambassador to South Africa, 1984-88; Ambassador to China, 1989-93; Ambassador to Russia, 1993-96; Professor of Political Science and International Relations, University of Minho, Braga, Portugal, 1997-; Member, Strategic Council of University of Minho, 2005. Publications: Orthodoxy and Political Power in Russia, 1998; Caderno de Memorias, 2003; many articles. Honours: KCMG (UK); Commander, Legion d'Honneur, France; Grand Cross, Order of Merit, Portugal; Cruzeiro do Sul, Brazil; Order Merito Civil, Spain; Order of Saint Olav, Norway; many others. Memberships: Turf Club, Lisbon. Address: Casa de Esteiro, Vilarelho, 4910 Caminha, Portugal.

VILLENEUVE Jacques, b. 9 April 1971, Canada. Racing Car Driver. Appointments: Started racing in Italian Touring Car Championship Italian Formula 3, 1989, 1990; With Reynaud and Alfa Romeo, 1992; Japanese Formula 3, 1993; Formula Atlantic, 1993; IndyCar Driver, 1994-95; IndyCar Racing Champion, 1995; Drove Formula One Cars with Williams Renault Team, then British American Racing team, now with BAR-Honda; Grand Prix Winner, Britain, 1996, 1997, Brazil, 1997; Argentina, 1997; Spain, 1997; Hungary, 1997, Austria, 1997; Luxembourg, 1997; Formula One Champion, 1997; Owns restaurant/bar, Newtown in Montreal; Guest driver, Renault, last three races, 2004; Driver, Formula 1 with Sauber team, 2005-06; Driver, Peugot, 2007; Driver, NASCAR, 2007; Driver, Speedcar, 2008. Publications: Album, Private Paradise. Website: www.jv-world.com

VINCENT John James, b. 29 December 1929, Sunderland, England. Writer; Community Activist; Broadcaster; Methodist Minister. m. Grace Johnston Stafford, 4 December 1958, 2 sons, 1 daughter. Education: BD, Richmond College, London University, 1954; STM, Drew University, 1955; DTheol, Basel University, 1960. Appointments: Ordained Minister,

Methodist Church, 1956; Leader, Ashram Community, 1967-; Founder and Director, Urban Theology Unit, 1969-97; Director Emeritus 1997-; Adjunct Professor, New York Theological Seminary, 1979-87; President, Methodist Church of Great Britain, 1989-90; Honorary Lecturer, Sheffield University, 1990-, Birmingham University, 2003-; Centenary Award, Sheffield University, 2005. Publications: Christ and Methodism, 1964; Here I Stand, 1967; Secular Christ, 1968; The Race Race, 1970; The Jesus Thing, 1973; Stirrings, Essays Christian and Radical, 1975; Alternative Church, 1976; Disciple and Lord, 1976; Starting all over Again, 1981; Into the City, 1982; OK Let's Be Methodists, 1984; Radical Jesus, 1986; Mark at Work, 1986; Britain in the 90's, 1989; Liberation Theology from the Inner City, 1992; A Petition of Distress from the Cities, 1993; A British Liberation Theology, bi-annual volumes, editor,1995-; The Cities: A Methodist Report, 1997; Hope from the City, 2000; Faithfulness in the City, 2003; Methodist and Radical, 2004; Mark: Gospel of Action, 2006; A Lifestyle of Sharing, 2007. Memberships: Studiorum Novi Testamenti Societas; Alliance of Radical Methodists; Urban Theologians International, Joint Chair, 1995-. Address: 178 Abbeyfield Road, Sheffield S4 7AY, England.

VINE Jeremy, b. 17 May 1965, Epsom, Surrey, England. Broadcaster. m. Rachel Schofield, 2 daughters. Education: Epsom College; First Class honours degree, English, University of Durham. Appointments: Journalist, Coventry Evening Telegraph, 1986-87; New Trainee, 1987-89, Programme Reporter, Today, 1989-93, Political Correspondent, 1993-97, Africa Correspondent, 1997-99, Presenter, Newsnight, 1996-2002 (full-time 1999-2002), BBC; Presenter, The Jeremy Vine Show, BBC Radio 2, 2003-. Honours: Best Speech Broadcaster, Sony Radio Academy Award, 2005. Address: c/o Room G680, BBC Television Centre, Wood Lane, London W12 7RJ, England. Website: www.bbc.co.uk

VINGT-TROIS André, b. 7 November 1942, Paris, France. Cardinal. Education: Bachelor's degree, Theology, Institut Catholique of Paris, 1962; Military Service, Germany, 1964-65; Ordination for the Archdiocese of Paris, 1969. Appointments: Assistant Pastor, St Jeanne de Chantal's Parish, Paris, 1969-74; Director, St Sulpice Seminary of Issy-les-Moulineaux, Professor of Sacramental and Moral Theology, 1974-81; Vicar General, Archdiocese of Paris, 1981-99; Auxiliary Bishop of Paris, ordained, 1988; Metropolitan Archbishop of Tours, 1999; Appointed to succeed Jean-Marie Cardinal Lustiger as Archbishop of Paris and Ordinary of Oriental Rite Catholics in France, 2005; Created Cardinal with the see of St Louis of the French in Rome, 2007; President, French Bishops' Conference, 2007-10. Publications: Numerous articles in professional journals. Honours: Knight of the Legion of Honor; Officer of the National Order of Merit. Memberships: Presidency Committee, Pontifical Council for the Family and of the Congregation for Bishops.

VINTROVA Ruzena, b. 16 December 1929, Nekor, Czech Republic. Researcher. m. Josef Vinter (deceased), 2 sons. Education: University of Economics, Prague, 1948-51; Ing, University of Economics and Finance, Petersbourg, 1955; PhD, Institute of Central Planning, Prague, 1967; Dr Sc, Academy of Sciences, Moscow, 1979. Appointments: Officer, 1955-58, Head of Department, 1958-68, National Accounts Department, Statistical Office, Czechoslovakia, Prague; Leading Researcher, Academy of Sciences Economic Institute, 1968-84; Deputy Director, Academy of Sciences Institute of Economic Forecasting, 1984-93; Researcher, Institute of Economic Policy, Ministry of Economics and Trade, 1993-95;

Leading Economic Analyst, Czech Statistical Office, 1995-98; Adviser, Prime Minister's Office, 1998-2004; Researcher, Centrum of Economic Studies, University of Economics and Management (UEM), Prague, 2005-. Publications: Stability Before Growth? 1996; The Macroeconomics of Structural Transformation, 1999; The CEE Countries on the Way into the EU, 2005. Memberships: Czech Economic Association. Address: Konevova 161, Prague 3, 13000, Czech Republic. E-mail: vintrova.ruzena@seznam.cz Website: www.cesvsem.cz

VISNJIC Goran, b. 9 September 1972, Sibenik, Croatia. Actor. m. Ivana Vrdoljak, 1999, 1 adopted son, 1 daughter with Mirela Rupic. Education: Academy of Dramatic Arts, Zagreb. Career: Films: Braca Po Materi, 1988; Welcome to Sarajevo, 1997; The Peacemaker, 1997; Rounders, 1998; Practical Magic, 1998; Committed, 2000; The Deep End, 2001; Ice Age (voice), 2002; Doctor Sleep, 2002; Duga mracna noc, 2004; Elektra, 2005; TV: ER, 1999-2008; Spartacus, 2004. Honours: Best Croatian Actor, 2004; Vladimir Nazor Award for Best Realization of a Theatrical Performance – Film, 2005.

VITART Frederic Pol, b. 7 July 1966, Brest, France. Research Scientist. m. Siew Tin Lim, 2 sons. Education: PhD, Atmospheric and Oceanic Sciences, Princeton University, USA, 1999. Appointments: Visiting Scientist, Los Alamos National Laboratory, USA, 1990-92; Research Scientist, CEA, France, 1992-94; Research Scientist, ECMWF, 1999-. Publications: Papers and articles in professional journals including: Dynamical Seasonal Forecasts of Tropical Storms Statistics, Hurricanes and Typhoons Past, Present and Future, 2004; Seasonal Forecast of Tropical Storm Frequency Using a Multi-Model Ensemble, 2005. Memberships: Royal Meteorological Society. Address: 44 Lakeside, Early, Reading RG6 7PQ, England. E-mail: fpv07@yahoo.com

VITHARANA Vini, b. 2 June 1928, Tangalla, Sri Lanka. Professor Emeritus. m. Tilaka Abeysiriwardana, 1 son, 1 daughter. Education: BA, 1956, BA (Hons), 1958, MA, 1959, PhD, 1968, University of London, England; PhD, University of Ceylon, Sri Lanka, 1966. Appointments: Assistant Teacher, Mahinda College, Galle, Sri Lanka, 1949-53; Assistant Teacher, St Thomas' College, Mt Lavinia, Sri Lanka, 1954-57; Assistant Editor, Sinhala Encyclopaedia, Ministry of Cultural Affairs, 1957-60; Lecturer, Senior Lecturer, Associate Professor of Sinhala, Vidyodaya (later Jayawardenepura) University, Nugegoda, Sri Lanka, 1960-81; Professor of Sinhala, Ruhuna University, Matara, Sri Lanka, 1981-93; Visiting Professor: University of Kelaniya, 1993-, Buddhist & Pali University, 1996-97, University of Sri Jayawardenepura University, 1996-2006, University of Sabaragamuva, 1997-98; Editor in Chief, Sinhala Dictionary, 2001-04; Discipline Specialist, Maritime Archaeology, Central Cultural Fund. Publications: Dictionary of Geography, 1961; Eight Essays on the History of Sinhala Literature, 1975; Totagamuva, 1986; The Curative Dance Ritual, 1992; The Oru and the Yatra, 1992; Sun and Moon in Sinhala Culture, 1993; Common Errors & Literary Composition, 1993, revised 2007; Sri Lankan-Maldivian Cultural Affinities, 1997; Sri Lanka – the Geographical Vision, 1999; Numerous articles in learned journals; Translation into Sinhala Verse: Godamanela (a few English poems), 1978; Light of Asia, 2000; Rubaiyat, 2002; Gitanjali, 2004; Translation into Sinhala Prose: Light of Asia, 1955; Translation of Sinhala Classical Works into English: Muvadevdavata & Sasadavata (12th century poems); Saddharmaratnavaliya (13th century prose work); Mayūra Sandesa (14th century poem) Sinhala poetry: Megharagaya, 1978. Honours: UNESCO Award for Sinhala Literature,

1962; Sri Lanka Sahitya Mandala Award, 1978; Kala Kirti National Presidential Award, 1993; All Ceylon Buddhist Congress Award, 1997; Sinhala Institute of Culture Award, 2001; Rohana Ransilu Award, Southern Provincial Council, 2004; Sarvodaya Trust Award for Research, 2002; Sri Lanka Kala Mandala Award for Best Translation, 2003; Sri Lanka Arts Society Award, 2005. Memberships: Vice President, Royal Asiatic Society of Sri Lanka; Sri Lanka Archaeological Society; Mahinda College Old Boys' Association; President, Sri Lanka Archaeological Society, 2007-. Address: 67/1 Samudrasanna Road, Mt Lavinia and Lilavasa, Pangalla, Sri Lanka.

VIZINCZEY Stephen, b. 1933, Kaloz, Hungary. Writer. m. September 1963, 3 daughters. Education: University of Budapest, 1949-50; Academy of Theatre Arts, Budapest, 1951-56. Appointments: Editor, Exchange Magazine, 1960-61; Producer, Canadian Broadcasting Corporation, 1962-65. Publications: In Praise of Older Women, 1965; The Rules of Chaos, 1969; An Innocent Millionaire, 1983; Truth and Lies in Literature, 1986; The Man with the Magic Touch, 1994; Be Faithful unto Death (translation), 1995; Wishes, 2005. Contributions to: Currently; The Los Angeles Times Book Review. Memberships: PEN; Society of Authors; ALCS; Award, Premio Letterario Isola d'Elba R Brignetti, 2004. Address: 70 Coleherne Court, Old Brompton Road, London SW5 0EF, England.

VODICKA Mark Andrew John, b. 1959, Melbourne, Australia. Legal Author; Independent Counsel; Barrister; Head, Median Chambers. Education: St John's School Hawthorn, Camberwell High School, HSC Taylors' College, Melbourne, 1978; BA, Art History and Russian, Australian National University, 1982; LLB, University of Sydney, 1986; LLM, by dissertation, University of New South Wales, 1990; Languages: Czech, Russian and French. Appointments: Para-Legal, Allen, Allen & Hemsley, Sydney, 1985; Clerk, Department of the Attorney-General for NSW, 1986; Voluntary Barrister, Redfern Legal Centre, 1986-91; Research Academic, University of Sydney, 1987; Law Lecturer, University of Western Sydney, 1988-89; Legal Advisor, Australian Stock Exchange, Sydney, 1990-91; Legal Consultant, Prague, Czechoslovakia, 1992-94; Independent Counsel, and Barrister, Melbourne, Australia, 1995-. Publications: Article, The Extraterritorial Operation of Australian Securities Laws, Company and Securities Law Journal, Sydney, 1991; Textbook, International Securities Trading, Legal Books/Longman International (Penguin), 1992. Memberships: Australian Bar Association; International Bar Association; Hawthorn FC. Address: Median Chambers, PO Box 13357, Law Courts, Melbourne, VIC 8010, Australia. Website: www.markvodicka.com

VOHRALIK Martin, b. 22 May 1977, Pardubice, Czech Republic. Mathematician; Consultant; Educator. Education: Master degree (honours), Mathematical Modeling, Faculty of Nuclear Sciences and Physical Engineering, Czech Technical University in Prague, 2000; PhD, 2004, Czech Technical University in Prague and University of Paris-South, France. Appointments: Part-time Research and Teaching Assistant, Czech Technical University in Prague, 2001; Part-time Research Assistant, Technical University of Liberec, Czech Republic, 2002-06; Society HydroExpert, Paris, France, 2002-04; Postdoctoral Fellow, University of Paris-South, French National Center for Scientific Research, 2005-06; Associate Professor, Jacques-Louis Lions Laboratory, Pierre and Marie Curie (Paris 6) University, France, 2006-. Publications: Numerous articles in professional journals. Honours: Vice President, 1996-99, Student Union, Faculty of

Nuclear Sciences and Physical Engineering, Czech Technical University in Prague; President, 1997-98, Student Union, Czech Technical University in Prague; Rector's Award for Excellent Achievements, 1998, 1999; Honorary Prize, Foundation of Marie, Zdenka and Josef Hlavka, 2000; Siemens Main Prize for Research, 2000; Scholar, French Government, 2001-04; Fellow, French National Center for Scientific Research, 2005-06. Memberships: French Society for Industrial and Applied Mathematics. E-mail: vohralik@ann.jussieu.fr Website: www.ann.jussieu.fr/~vohralik

VOIGHT Jon, b. 29 December 1938, Yonkers, New York, USA. Actor. m. (1) Lauri Peters, 1962, divorced 1967, (2) Marcheline Bertrand, 1971, divorced, 1 son, 1 daughter. Education: Catholic University. Career: Theatre: A View From The Bridge; That Summer That Fall, 1966; San Diego Shakespeare Festival; A Streetcar Named Desire, 1973; Hamlet, 1975; Films: Hour of the Gun, 1967; Fearless Frank, 1968; Out of It, 1969; Midnight Cowboy, 1969; The Revolutionary, 1970; The All-American Boy, 1970; Catch 22, 1970; Deliverance, 1972; Conrack, 1974; The Odessa File, 1974; Coming Home, 1978; The Champ, 1979; Lookin' to Get Out, 1982; Table for Five, 1983; Runaway Train, 1985; Desert Bloom, 1986; Eternity; Heat; Rosewood; Mission Impossible, 1996; U-Turn, 1997; The Rainmaker, 1997; Varsity Blues, 1998; The General, 1998; Enemy of the State, 1998; Dog of Flanders, 1999; Lara Croft: Tomb Raider, 2001; Pearl Harbour, 2001; Ali, 2001; Zoolander, 2002; Holes, 2003; Superbabies, 2003; Karate Dog, 2003; The Manchurian Candidate, 2004; National Treasure, 2004; Superbabies: Baby Geniuses 2; TV: End of the Game, 1976; Gunsmoke and Cimarron Strip; Chernobyl: The Final Warning, 1991; The Last of His Tribe, 1992; The Tin Soldier; Convict Cowboy, 1995; The Fixer, 1998; Noah's Ark, 1999; Second String, 2000; Jasper Texas, 2003; The Five People You Meet in Heaven, 2004; September Dawn, 2006; Glory Road, 2006; The Legend of Simon Conjurer, 2006; Transformers, 2007; Bratz, 2007; National Treasure: Book of Secrets, 2007. Honours: Academy Award, Best Actor, 1979; Best Actor Awards, 1969, 1979; Cannes International Film Festival, Golden Globe Award, Best Actor, 1979. Address: c/o Martin Baum and Patrick Whitesell, CAA 9830 Wilshire Boulevard, Beverly Hills, CA 90212, USA.

VOLLMAR James Anthony, b. 8 January 1952, Wellingborough, Northamptonshire, England. Writer; Poet; Playwright. Education: Queen Mary College, University of London, 1970-72. Appointment: Founder, Editor, Greylag Press, 1977-. Publications: Circles and Spaces; Orkney Poems; Hoy: The Seven Postcards; Warming the Stones; Explorers Log Book; Notes from Café Bizarre; Play, Clearing the Colours; Contributions to: Agenda; Iron; Oasis; Joe Soaps Canoe; Ally; Pacific Quarterly; Ambit. Memberships: Writers' Guild of Great Britain. Address: c/o The Sharland Organisation, The Manor House, Raunds, Northamptonshire NN9 6JW, England.

VON BLÜCHER HSH Prince Dennis Wilhelm, b. 21 August 1944, Rostock, Germany. International Diplomat. Education: Bachelors degree, Theatre Arts, Royal Academy of Dramatic Arts; Doctorate, Homeopathy, London College of Homeopathy; Masters degree, International Relations, Vienna Diplomatic Academy; Doctorate, International Diplomatic Relations, Belford University. Appointments: Contract Player, Universal Studios, Hollywood, USA, 1974-84; Instructor/ Director, Pasadena Playhouse, 1984-88; Head of Production, D W Productions Inc, California, 1988-92; Established Homeopathic Practitioners Clinic, Palm Springs, 1992-99; Consultant & Executive Vice President, In-Home Assistance

Service, 2000-01; Honorary Ambassador at Large/International Consultant, Grant Orient of Monarchy, Afghanistan, 2001-03; Consultant to the Sovereign Nation of the Kingdom of Hawai'i, 2004-; Consultant to the Council of the European Union, 2004-. Honours include: International Professional of the Year 2006; Chevalier of Malta St John of Jerusalem; Chevalier Grand Cross of Justice; Chevalier of the Order of Victory; Chevalier Grand Cross of the Imperial Order of St Constantine the Great; Chevalier of the Order of San Firminus de Gabales, Grand Cross of Justice; Order of Merit, Outstanding Service to the Diplomatic Community; Outstanding Contribution to Special Olympics, Kennedy Foundation; City of Hope Award; United Way Award; Hollywood Heritage Award; Men & Women of Distinction, Diploma of Distinction Permanent Roll of Honour; Outstanding Achievement and Leadership; Humanitarian of the Year, Southern California Motion Picture Council. Memberships: World Affairs Council; English Speaking Union of the Desert; Austrian-American Council West; Traditions und Leben, German Monarchist Society; The Prince's Council on Cultural Preservation; International Monarchist League; Order of the Golden Fleece; Fellow of the Augustan Society, First Class; Associate Member, Charles F Menninger Society; Member, Royal Society of North America; Chevalier of Malta St John of Jerusalem; Chevalier of the Order of Victory; Chevalier of the Order of San Firminus de Gabales, Grand Cross of Justice; Chevalier of the Order of Santa Maria of Buenos Aires (also Ambassador/Prior); Order of Merit – Outstanding Service to the Diplomatic Community; Order of the Prussian Crown, First Class; Member of Students' Council, Belford University; Organiser of Summer Party for the Jubilee Celebration of Queen Elizabeth II and participant of same; Member, Freelance Consulting Team of Diplomaticnet.com; Southwest Blue Book, Society Register of Southern California; Regent/Member of International Fraternity of Nobles of Titled Houses; Listed in the Imperial College of Princes and Counts of the Holy Roman Empire. Address: 331 S Sunrise Way, Palm Springs, CA 92262, USA. E-mail: dvblucher@juno.com

VON WRIGHT Moira Johanna, b. 23 December 1957, Helsinki, Finland. Professor of Education. m. Erik Van Mansvelt, 1 son. Education: Class teacher, 1982; BA, 1982; MA, 1988; Phil Licent, 1997; PhD, 2000; Docent, 2003; Professor, 2007; Research Associate, VHI, St Edmund's College, Cambridge, 2007; Guest Professor of Philosophy of Education, Oslo University, 2007-09. Appointments: Teacher, 1981-92, Helsinki & Inio, Finland; Lecturer, Education, 1994-96, Senior Lecturer, 1997-2002, Associate Dean of Academic Affairs, 2002-03, Associate Professor, 2003, Stockholm Institute of Education, Sweden; Reader/Docent, Helsinki University, 2003-; Professor of Education, 2007, Deputy Vice Chancellor, 2008, Orebro University, Sweden. Publications: A Night in the Library, 1970; Inio koket, 1986; Gender & Text, 1999; What or Who? 2000; Going Visiting, 2001; Narr Imagination & Taking Perspective of Others, 2002; The Punctual Fallacy of Participation, 2006; Where am I When I am at Ease? 2007; Goodness as an Orientation in Education, 2008. Honours: Quality Award for Successful Research & Development Project, 2006. Memberships: NERA; AERA; PESGB; INPE; NeoMeadian Society. E-mail: moira.vonwright@oru.se

VORACEK Michal, b. 26 October 1958, Prague, Czech Republic. Consultant; Entrepreneur. 3 daughters. Education: Diploma of Engineer, 1981, PhD, 1987, University of Economics, Prague. Appointments: Publisher, Director & Editor-in-Chief, Czechoslovak Profit; Management Board Chairman & General Director, Ringier CR; Supervisory Board Chairman, TV NOVA, TV Prima; Supervisory Board Member, Medea (Media Agency); Supervisory Board Member, AC Sparta Praha football; Supervisory Board Chairman, E-Centrum. E-mail: office.center@ibc.cz

VORONENKOVA Galina, b. 30 January 1947, Kostroma Region, Russia. Professor of Journalism. M. Mikhail Voronenkov, 1 daughter. Education: Lomonosov Moscow State University, 1969-74; Leipzig University, Germany, 1979-80; Dortmund University, Germany, 1999-2000. Appointments: Literary Contributor to local paper, Kostroma Region, 1965-67; Staff member, Journalism Department, MSU, 1974-81; Teacher, Russian language, House of Soviet Science and Culture, and Business Management Journalists' Club, Berlin, Germany, 1987-90; Reporter, Soviet Women, Germany, 1990-92; Professor, Faculty of Journalism, MSU, 1992-; Director, Free Russian-German Institute for Publishing, 1994-; Corresponding Member, Academy of Information and Communication; Participant, St Petersburg Dialog, 2001-07; Election Observer, Federal Chancellor Elections; Participant and Moderator of international and bilateral Russian-German conferences: Berlin, Bonn, Maastricht, Frankfurt on Main, Karlsruhe, Leipzig, Moscow, Saint-Petersburg, Rostov on Don, and others. Publications: Author, monographs, text books and collected volumes. Honours: Federal Council of Russian Award, 1995, 1996; A Karelskij Prize Winner, Academy Civil Society and Foreign Literature magazine; Order of St Apostolic Princess Olga from His Holiness the Patriarch of Moscow and all Russia, 2004; Bundesverdienstkreuz der I Klasse, 2004. Memberships: Free Russian-German Institute for Publishing; Academy of Information and Communication; International Academy for Sustainable Development and Technologies, Karlsruhe. Address: MSU, Faculty of Journalism, Mochovaja ul 9, Apt 235, 125009 Moscow, Russia. E-mail: frdip-mgu@yandex.ru

VRANA Ivan, b. 12 June 1941, Myjava, Czech Republic. University Professor. m. Hana, 1 son, 1 daughter. Education: MSc, Radioelectronics, 1963; PhD, Radioelectronics, 1973; Dr Sc, Radioelectronics, 1990, Associate Professor, Radioelectronics, 1991. Full Professor, Informatics, 1992. Appointments: Senior Research Fellow, 1974; Principal Research Fellow, 1990; Head, Department of Informatics, 1991; Vice Rector, 1993; Head, Department of Information Engineering, 1997. Publications: On a Direct Method of Analysis of the SPRT, 1982; Optimum Statistical Estimates in Conditions of Ambiguity, 1993; 3 books. Honours: Master of Sports, 1987; President, EUNIS-CZ, 1997; General Secretary, EUNIS, 1999. Memberships: IEEE; ACM; ECAR; EUNIS. Address: Czech University of Life Sciences, Prague 16521, Czech Republic. E-mail: vrana@pef.czu.cz

W

WADDINGTON David James, b. 27 May 1932, Edgware, Middlesex, England. University Professor. m. Isobel Hesketh, 2 sons, 1 daughter. Education: BSc, ARCS, DIC, PhD, Imperial College, University of London. Appointments: Senior Lecturer, 1965-78, Professor of Chemical Education, 1978-2000, Pro-Vice Chancellor, 1985-91, Professor Emeritus, 2000-, University of York; Visiting Professor, Institut für Pedagogik der Naturwissenschaften (IPN), University of Kiel, Germany, 2000-. Publications: Organic Chemistry, 1962; Organic Chemistry Through Experiment (with H S Finlay), 1965; Modern Organic Chemistry (with R O C Norman), 1972; Chemical Education in the Seventies (with A Kornhauser and C N R Rao), 1980; Teaching School Chemistry (editor), 1985; Education, Industry and Technology (jointly), 1987; Chemistry: the Salters Approach (jointly), 1990; Salters Advanced Chemistry (jointly), 1994, 2nd edition 2000; Science for Understanding Tomorrow's World (jointly), 1995; Partners in Chemical Education (with J N Laxonby), 1996; Salters Higher Chemistry (jointly), 1999; Essential Chemical Industry (jointly), 1999; Evaluation as a tool for improving science education (jointly), 2005; Context based learning of Science (jointly), 2005. Honours: Nyholm Medal, Royal Society of Chemistry, 1985; Brasted Award, American Chemical Society, 1988; National Order of Scientific Merit, Brazil, 1997; Honorary Professor, University of Chemical Technology, Moscow, 1998. Memberships: President, Education Committee, Royal Society of Chemistry, 1981-83; Chairman, Committee of Teaching of Chemistry, IUPAC, 1981-86; Chairman, Committee of Teaching of Science, ICSU, 1990-94; Liveryman, Salters Company, 2001-. Address: University of York, York YO10 5DD, England. E-mail: djw1@york.ac.uk

WADE (Sarah) Virginia, b. 10 July 1945, Bournemouth, England. Tennis Player. Education: University of Sussex. Appointments: Amateur player, 1962-68, professional, 1968-; British Hard Court Champion, 1967, 1968, 1973, 1974; USA Champion, 1968 (singles) 1973, 1975 (doubles); Italian Champion, 1971; Australian Champion, 1972; Wimbledon Ladies Champion, 1977; Played Wightman Cup for Great Britain, 1965-81, Captain 1973-80; Played Federation Cup for Great Britain, 1967-81, Captain, 1973-81; Commentator, BBC, 1980-. Publications: Courting Triumph (with Mary Lou Mellace), 1978; Ladies of the Court, 1984. Honours include: LLD, Sussex, 1985; International Tennis Hall of Fame, 1989; Federation Cup Award of Excellence, 2002. Membership: Committee, All England Lawn Tennis Club, 1983-91. Address: c/o International Management Group, Pier House, Strand on the Green, London W4 3NN, England.

WAGNER Robert, b. 10 February 1930, Detroit, Michigan, USA. Actor. m. (1) Natalie Wood, 1957, divorced 1962, re-married 1972, deceased 1981, 1 daughter, 1 stepdaughter, (2) Marion Marshall Donen, 1 daughter, (3) Jill St John, 1991. Career: Films: Halls of Montezuma, The Frogmen, Let's Make It Legal, 1951; With a Song in My Heart, What Price Glory? Stars and Strips Forever, 1952; The Silver Whip, Titantic, Star of Tomorrow: Beneath the 12-Mile Reef, 1953; Prince Valiant, Broken Lance, 1954; White Feather, 1955; A Kiss Before Dying, The Mountain, 1956; The True Story of Jesse James, Stopover Tokyo, 1957; The Hunters, In Love and War, Mardi Gras, 1958; Say One For Me, 1959; Between Heaven and Hell; All the Fine Young Cannibals, 1960; Sail a Crooked Ship, 1961; The Longest Day, The War Lover, The Condemned of Altona, 1962; The Pink Panther, 1963; Harper, 1966; Banning, 1967; The Biggest Bundle of Them

All, Don't Just Stand There! 1968; Winning, 1969; Madame Sin, Journey Through Rosebud, 1972; The Towering Inferno, 1974; Midway, 1976; The Concorde: Airport '79, 1979; The Curse of the Pink Panther, 1983; Dragon: The Bruce Lee Story, 1993; Overdrive, Austin Powers: International Man of Mystery, 1997; Wild Things, Something to Believe In, 1998; The Kidnapping of Chris Burden, Dill Scallion, Crazy in Alabama, No Vacancy, Love and Fear; Austin Powers: The Spy Who Shagged Me, Play It to the Bone, 1999; Forever Fabulous, The Mercury Project, 2000; The Retrievers, Sol Goode, Jungle Juice, 2001; Nancy and Frank – A Manhattan Love Story, Austin Powers in Goldmember, The Calling, 2002; El Padrino, 2004; Little Victim, 2005; The Wild Stallion, Hoot, 2006; Man in the Chair, Netherbeast Incorporated, 2007; TV: numerous TV series including Hart to Hart, 1979-. Honours: 6 Golden Globes. Address: c/o William Morris Agency, One William Morris Place, Beverly Hills, CA 90212, USA. Website: www.robert-wagner.com

WAGONER David (Russell), b. 5 June 1926, Massillon, Ohio, USA. Professor of English; Poet; Author. m. (1) Patricia Parrott, 1961, divorced 1982, (2) Robin Heather Seyfried, 1982, 2 daughters. Education: BA, Pennsylvania State University, 1947; MA, Indiana University, 1949. Appointments: Instructor, DePauw University, 1949-50, Pennsylvania State University, 1950-53; Assistant Professor, 1954-57, Associate Professor, 1958-66, Professor of English, 1966-, University of Washington, Seattle; Editor, Poetry Northwest, 1966-; Elliston Professor of Poetry, University of Cincinnati, 1968. Publications: Poetry: Dry Sun, Dry Wind, 1953; A Place to Stand, 1958; Poems, 1959; The Nesting Ground, 1963; Staying Alive, 1966; New and Selected Poems, 1969; Working Against Time, 1970; Riverbed, 1972; Sleeping in the Woods, 1974; A Guide to Dungeness Spit, 1975; Travelling Light, 1976; Collected Poems, 1956-1976, 1976; Who Shall be the Sun?: Poems Based on the Love, Legends, and Myths of Northwest Coast and Plateau Indians, 1978; In Broken Country, 1979; Landfall, 1981; First Light, 1983; Through the Forest: New and Selected Poems, 1977-1987, 1987; Traveling Light: Collected and New Poems, 1999. Fiction: The Man in the Middle, 1954; Money, Money, Money, 1955; Rock, 1958; The Escape Artist, 1965; Baby, Come on Inside, 1968; Where Is My Wandering Boy Tonight?, 1970; The Road to Many a Wonder, 1974; Tracker, 1975; Whole Hog, 1976; The Hanging Garden, 1980. Editor: Straw for the Fire: From the Notebooks of Theodore Roethke 1943-1963, 1972. Honours: Guggenheim Fellowship, 1956; Ford Foundation Fellowship, 1964; American Academy of Arts and Letters Grant, 1967; National Endowment for the Arts Grant, 1969; Morton Dauwen Zabel Prize, 1967; Oscar Blumenthal Prize, 1974; Fels Prize, 1975; Eunice Tietjens Memorial Prize, 1977; English-Speaking Union Prize, 1980; Sherwood Anderson Prize, 1980; Pacific Northwest Booksellers Award, 2000. Membership: Academy of American Poets, chancellor, 1978. Address: University of Washington, 4045 Brooklyn Avenue NE, Seattle, WA 98105, USA.

WAHLBERG Mark, b. 5 June 1971, Dorchester, Massachusetts, USA. Actor. Partner, Rhea Durham, 1 son, 1 daughter. Career: Films: Renaissance man, 1994; The Basketball Diaries, 1995; Fear, 1996; Traveller, 1997; Boogie Nights, 1997; The Big Hit, 1998; The Corruptor, 1999; Three Kings, 1999; The Yards, 2000; The Perfect Storm, 2000; Metal God, 2000; Planet of the Apes, 2001; Rock Star, 2001; The Truth About Charlie, 2003; The Italian Job, 2003; I Heart Huckabees, 2004; Four Brothers, 2005; Invincible, 2006; The Departed, 2006; Shooter, 2007; We Own the Night, 2007; TV: Teen Vid II, 1991; The Substitute, 1993. Recordings:

Albums: Music for the People, 1991; You Gotta Believe, 1992. Address: c/o United Talent Agency, 9560 Wilshire Boulevard, Suite 500, Beverly Hills, CA 90212, USA. Website: www.markwahlberg.com

WAINWRIGHT Geoffrey, b. 16 July 1939, Yorkshire, England. Professor of Systematic Theology; Methodist Minister. m. Margaret Wiles, 20 April 1965, 1 son, 2 daughters. Education: BA, 1960, MA, 1964, BD, 1972, DD, 1987, University of Cambridge; DrThéol, University of Geneva, 1969. Appointments: Editor, Studia Liturgica, 1974-87; Professor of Systematic Theology, The Divinity School, Duke University, Durham, North Carolina, 1983-. Publications: Christian Initiation, 1969; Eucharist and Eschatology, 1971, 2nd edition, 1981; The Study of Liturgy (co-editor), 1978, 2nd edition, 1992; Doxology, 1980; The Ecumenical Moment, 1983; The Study of Spirituality (co-editor), 1986; On Wesley and Calvin, 1987; Keeping the Faith: Essays to Mark the Centenary of Lux Mundi (editor), 1989; The Dictionary of the Ecumenical Movement (co-editor), 1991; Methodists in Dialogue, 1995; Worship With One Accord, 1997; For Our Salvation, 1997; Is the Reformation Over? Catholics and Protestants at the Turn of the Millennia, 2000; Lesslie Newbigin: A Theological Life, 2000; The Oxford History of Christian Worship (co-editor), 2006; Embracing Purpose: Essays on God, the World and the Church, 2007. Contributions to: Reference books and theological journals. Honours: Numerous named lectureships world-wide; Berakah Award, North American Academy of Liturgy, 1999; Received a Festschrift: Ecumenical Theology in Worship, Doctrine, and Life: Essays Presented to Geoffrey Wainwright on his 60th Birthday, 1999; Outstanding Ecumenist Award, Washington Theological Consortium, 2003; Johannes Quasten Medal, 2005. Memberships: American Theological Society, secretary, 1988-95, president, 1996-97; International Dialogue Between the World Methodist Council and the Roman Catholic Church, chairman; Societas Liturgica, president, 1983-85; World Council of Churches Faith and Order Commission, 1976-91. Address: The Divinity School, Duke University, Durham, NC 27708, USA.

WAITE Terence Hardy, b. 31 May 1939, Bollington, England. Writer and Broadcaster. m. Helen Frances Watters, 1964, 1 son, 3 daughters. Education: Church Army College, London. Appointments: Lay Training Advisor to Bishop and Diocese of Bristol, 1964-68; Advisor to Archbishop of Uganda, Rwanda and Burundi, 1968-71; International Consultant with Roman Catholic Church, 1972-79; Advisor, Archbishop of Canterbury on Anglican Communion Affairs, 1980-92; Iranian Hostages Mission, 1981; Libyan Hostages Mission, 1985; Kidnapped in Beirut, 1987, Released, 1991. Publications: Taken on Trust, 1993; Footfalls in Memory, 1995; Travels with a Primate, 2000. Honours include: Hon DCL, Kent, 1986, City of London, Durham, 1992; Hon DLL, Liverpool; Hon LLD, Sussex, 1992; Hon LHD, Wittenberg University, 1992; Hon Dr International Law, Florida Southern University, 1992; Dr hc, Yale University Divinity School, 1992; Roosevelt Freedom Medal, 1992; Man of the Year, England, 1985; Freeman, City of Canterbury, 1992, Borough of Lewisham, 1992; Hon DPhil, Anglia Polytechnic, 2001; Hon DLitt, Nottingham Trent, 2001. Memberships: Church of England National Association, 1966-68; Co-ordinator, Southern Sudan Relief Project, 1969-71; Butler Trust, Prison Officers Award Programme; President, Y-Care International (YMCA International Development Committee); President, Emmaus UK (for the Homeless), 1996-; Founder Chair, Friends of Victim Support, 1992-; Patron, Strode Park Foundation for the Disabled; Rainbow Trust; Fellow Commoner, Trinity Hall,

Cambridge, 1992-; Honorary Chancellor, Florida Southern University, 1992; Chairman, Prison Video Trust; Trustee Freeplay Foundation. Address: Trinity Hall, Cambridge, CB2 1TJ, England.

WAITS Tom, b. 7 December 1949, Pomona, California, USA. Singer; Songwriter; Musician (piano, accordion); Actor. m. Kathleen Brennan, 31 December 1981, 1 son, 1 daughter. Career: Recording artist, 1973-; Concerts include: Ronnie Scott's jazz club, 1976; London Palladium, 1979; The Black and White Night - Roy Orbison And Friends, 1987; Actor, films including: Paradise Alley, 1978; Wolfen, 1981; Stone Boy; One From The Heart, 1982; The Outsiders, 1983; Rumblefish, 1983; The Cotton Club, 1984; Down By Law, 1986; Cold Feet, 1989; The Fisher King, 1991; At Play In The Fields Of The Lord, 1991; Queen's Logic, 1991; Bram Stoker's Dracula, 1992; Short Cuts, 1993; Mystery Men, 1999; Coffee And Cigarettes, 2003; Domino. Compositions include: Ol' 55, The Eagles, 1974; Angel Wings, Rickie Lee Jones, 1983; Downtown Train, Rod Stewart, 1990; The Long Way Home, Norah Jones, 2004; Temptatino, Diana Krall, 2004; Jersey Girl, Bruce Springsteen. One From The Heart (film soundtrack), 1981; Co-writer (with wife), musical Frank's Wild Years, 1986; Score, Alice In Wonderland, Hamburg, 1992. Recordings: Albums: Closing Time, 1973; The Heart Of Saturday Night, 1974; Nighthawks At The Diner, 1975; Small Change, 1976; Foreign Affairs, 1977; Blue Valentine, 1978; Heartattack And Vine, 1980; One From The Heart, 1982; The Asylum Years - Bounced Check, 1983; Anthology, 1983; Swordfishtrombones, 1983; Raindogs, 1985; Frank's Wild Years, 1987; Big Time, 1988; Stay Awake, 1988; Bone Machine, 1992; Black Rider, 1993; Mule Variations, 1999; Used Songs 1973-80, 2001; Alice, 2002; Blood Money, 2002; Real Gone, 2004; The Orphans Tour, 2006; Contributor, compilation albums: Lost In The Stars, 1984; Stay Awake, 1988; Contributor, Night On Earth (film soundtrack), 1992. Honours: Oscar Nomination, One From The Heart, 1982; Grammy Award, Best Alternative Music, Bone Machine, 1993. Address: c/o Anti-Inc, 2798 Sunset Blvd, Los Angeles, CA 90026, USA.

WAKEHAM John (Baron Wakeham of Maldon), b. 1932. Chartered Accountant; Politician. m. (1) Roberta, deceased 1984, 2 sons, (2) Alison Ward, 1985, 1 son. Appointments: Chartered Accountant with own practice; Retired from business, 1977; Elected Conservative Member of Parliament for Maldon and Rochford, 1974, South Colchester and Maldon, 1983; Ministerial Appointments: Assistant Government Whip, 1979; Lord Commissioner of the Treasury, 1981; Parliamentary Under Secretary of State, Department of Industry, 1981; Minister of State, Treasury, 1982; Government Chief Whip, 1983; Appointed Member of the Privy Council, Lord Privy Seal and Leader of the House of Commons, 1987; Lord President of the Council and Leader of the House of Commons, 1988; Secretary of State for Energy, 1989; Lord Privy Seal and Leader of the House of Lords, 1992; Retired from Government, 1994; 6 Non-Executive Directorships; Chairman, Cothill House, 1998; Chairman, Alexandra Rose Day, 1998; Chairman, Vosper Thorneycroft Holdings Plc, 1995; Chairman, Press Complaints Commission, 1995-2002; Non-Executive Director, Enron Corporation, 1994-2002; Bristol and West PLC, 1995-2002; NM Rothschild & Sons Ltd, 1995-2002; Chairman, Royal Commission on House of Lords Reform, 1999-2000; Chairman, Michael Page International Plc, 2001-02. Honours: JP; DL; FLA; Honorary PhD; Honorary D Univ. Memberships: Director, National Association for Gambling Care, Educational Resources and Training; Trustee and Committee of Management, RNLI;

Trustee, HMS Warrior 1860; Clubs: Garrick, Carlton, Royal Yacht Squadron, Royal Southern Yacht Club. Address: House of Lords, London SW1, England.

WAKELEY Amanda, b. 15 September 1962, England. Fashion Designer. m. Neil David Gillon, 1992. Appointments: Fashion industry, New York, 1983-85; Designing, private clients, England, 1986; Launched own label, 1990; Retail, wholesale world-wide, bridal, high street brand Amanda Wakeley for Principles and corporate-wear consultancy; Co-chair of Fashion Targets Breast Cancer Campaign and raised over £5 million for Breakthrough in 1996, 1998, 2000, 2002 and 2004. Honours: Glamour Award, British Fashion Awards, 1992, 1993, 1996. Membership: Co-Chair, Fashion Targets Breast Cancer Campaign, 1996, 1998, 2000, 2002. Address: Amanda Wakeley Ltd, 26-28 Conway Street, London W1T 6BQ, England. Website: www.amandawakeley.com

WAKOSKI Diane, b. 3 August 1937, Whittier, California, USA. Poet; Professor of English. m. Robert J Turney, 14 February 1982. Education: BA, English, University of California at Berkeley, 1960. Appointments: Poet-in-Residence, Professor of English, 1975-, University Distinguished Professor, 1990-, Michigan State University; Many visiting writer-in-residencies. Publications: Poetry: Coins and Coffins, 1962; Discrepancies and Apparitions, 1966; The George Washington Poems, 1967; Inside the Blood Factory, 1968; The Magellanic Clouds, 1970; The Motorcycle Betrayal Poems, 1971; Smudging, 1972; Dancing on the Grave of a Son of a Bitch, 1973; Virtuoso Literature for Two and Four Hands, 1975; Waiting for the King of Spain, 1976; The Man Who Shook Hands, 1978; Cap of Darkness, 1980; The Magician's Feastletters, 1982; The Collected Greed, 1984; The Rings of Saturn, 1986; Emerald Ice: Selected Poems 1962-1987, 1988; Medea the Sorceress, 1991; Jason the Sailor, 1993; The Emerald City of Las Vegas, 1995; Argonaut Rose, 1998; The Butcher's Apron: New and Selected Poems, 2000. Criticism: Towards a New Poetry, 1980. Contributions to: Anthologies and other publications. Honours: Cassandra Foundation Grant, 1970; Guggenheim Fellowship, 1972; National Endowment for the Arts Grant, 1973; CAPS Grant, 1988, New York State, 1974; Writer's Fulbright Award, 1984; Michigan Arts Council Grant, 1988; William Carlos Williams Prize, 1989; Distinguished Artist Award, Michigan Arts Foundation, 1989; Michigan Library Association Author of the Year, 2004. Memberships: Author's Guild; PEN; Poetry Society of America. Address: 607 Division Street, East Lansing, MI 48823, USA.

WALCOTT Derek (Alton), b. 23 January 1930, Castries, St Lucia, West Indies. Poet; Dramatist; Visiting Professor. m. (1) Fay Moyston, 1954, divorced 1959, 1 son, (2) Margaret Ruth Maillard, 1962, divorced, 2 daughters, (3) Norline Metivier, 1982, divorced 1993. Education: St Mary's College, Castries, 1941-47; BA, University College of the West Indies, Mona, Jamaica, 1953. Appointments: Teacher, St Mary's College, Castries, 1947-50, 1954, Grenada Boy's Secondary School, St George's, 1953-54, Jamaica College, Kingston, 1955; Feature Writer, Public Opinion, Kingston, 1956-57; Founder-Director, Little Carib Theatre Workshop, later Trinidad Theatre Workshop, 1959-76; Feature Writer, 1960-62, Drama Critic, 1963-68, Trinidad Guardian, Port-of-Spain; Visiting Professor, Columbia University, 1981, Harvard University, 1982, 1987; Assistant Professor of Creative Writing, 1981, Visiting Professor, 1985-, Brown University. Publications: Poetry: 25 Poems, 1948; Epitaph for the Young: XII Cantos, 1949; Poems, 1951; In a Green Night: Poems 1948-1960, 1962; Selected Poems, 1964; The Castaway and Other Poems,

1965; The Gulf and Other Poems, 1969; Another Life, 1973; Sea Grapes, 1976; The Star-Apple Kingdom, 1979; Selected Poems, 1981; The Fortunate Traveller, 1981; The Caribbean Poetry of Derek Walcott and the Art of Romare Bearden, 1983; Midsummer, 1984; Collected Poems 1948-1984, 1986; The Arkansas Testament, 1987; Omeros, 1989; Collected Poems, 1990; Poems 1965-1980, 1992; Derek Walcott: Selected Poems, 1993. Plays: Cry for a Leader, 1950; Senza Alcun Sospetto or Paolo and Francesca, 1950; Henri Christophe: A Chronicle, 1950; Robin and Andrea or Bim, 1950; Three Assassins, 1951; The Price of Mercy, 1951; Harry Dernier, 1952; The Sea at Dauphin, 1954; Crossroads, 1954; The Charlatan, 1954, 4th version, 1977; The Wine of the Country, 1956; The Golden Lions, 1956; Ione: A Play with Music, 1957; Ti-Jean and His Brothers, 1957; Drums and Colours, 1958; Malcochon, or, The Six in the Rain, 1959; Jourmard, or, A Comedy till the Last Minute, 1959; Batai, 1965; Dream on Monkey Mountain, 1967; Franklin: A Tale of the Islands, 1969, 2nd version, 1973; In a Fine Castle, 1970; The Joker of Seville, 1974; O Babylon!, 1976; Remembrance, 1977; The Snow Queen, 1977; Pantomime, 1978; Marie Laveau, 1979; The Isle is Full of Noises, 1982; Beef, No Chicken, 1982; The Odyssey: A Stage Version, 1993; Tiepolo's Hound, 2000; The Prodigal: A Poem, 2005; Selected Poems, 2007. Non-Fiction: The Antilles: Fragments of Epic Memory: The Nobel Lecture, 1993; What the Twilight Says (essays), 1998. Honours: Rockefeller Foundation Grants, 1957, 1966, and Fellowship, 1958; Arts Advisory Council of Jamaica Prize, 1960; Guinness Award, 1961; Ingram Merrill Foundation Grant, 1962; Borestone Mountain Awards, 1964, 1977; Heinemann Awards, Royal Society of Literature, 1966, 1983; Cholmondeley Award, 1969; Eugene O'Neill Foundation Fellowship, 1969; Gold Hummingbird Medal, Trinidad, 1969; Obie Award, 1971; Officer of the Order of the British Empire, 1972; Guggenheim Fellowship, 1977; Welsh Arts Council International Writers Prize, 1980; John D and Catharine T MacArthur Foundation Fellowship, 1981; Los Angeles Times Book Prize, 1986; Queen's Gold Medal for Poetry, 1988; Nobel Prize for Literature, 1992. Memberships: American Academy of Arts and Letters, honorary member; Royal Society of Literature, fellow. Address: c/o Faber & Faber, 3 Queen Square, London, WC1N 3AU, England.

WAŁĘSA Lech, b. 29 September 1943, Popowo, Poland. Former Politician; Trade Union Activist. m. Danuta, 1969, 4 sons, 4 daughters. Appointments: Electrician, Lenin Shipyard, Gdańsk, 1966-76, 1983-; Chair, Strike Committee in Lenin Shipyard, 1970; Employed Zremb and Elektromontaz, 1976-80; Chair, Inter-institutional Strike Committee, Gdańsk, 1980; Co-Founder and Chair, Solidarity Industry Trade Union, 1980-90; Chair, National Executive Committee of Solidarity, 1987-90; Interned, 1981-82; Founder, Civic Committee attached to Chair of Solidarity, 1988-90; Participant and Co-chair, Round Table debates, 1989; President, Polish Republic, 1990-95; Chair, Country Defence Committee, 1990-95; Supreme Commander of Armed Forces of Polish Republic for Wartime, 1990-95; Founder, Lech Wałęsa Institute Foundation, 1995; Founder, Christian Democratic Party of the Third Republic, 1997; Appointed President, 1998, Chair, -2000, Honorary Chair, 2000-; Retired from politics. Publications: Autobiographies: A Path of Hope, 1987; The Road to Freedom, 1991; The Struggle and the Triumph, 1992; Everything I Do, I Do for Poland, 1995. Honours include: Order of the Bath, 1991; Grand Cross of Legion d'honneur, 1991; Grand Order of Merit (Italy), 1991; Order of Merit (FRG), 1991; Great Order of the White Lion, 1999; Orden Heraldica do Cristobal Colon, 2001; 100 honorary doctorates; Man of the Year, Financial Times, 1980, The Observer, 1980,

Die Welt, 1980, Die Zeit, 1981, L'Express, 1981, Le Soir, 1981, Time, 1981, Le Point, 1981; Let Us Live in Peace Prize of Swedish journal, Arbetet, 1981; Love International Award (Athens), 1981; Freedom Medal (Philadelphia), 1981; Medal of Merit (Polish American Congress), 1981; Free World Prize (Norway), 1982; International Democracy Award, 1982; Social Justice Award, 1983; Nobel Peace Prize, 1983; Humanitarian Public Service Medal, 1984; International Integrity Award, 1986; Phila Liberty Medal, 1989; Human Rights Prize, Council of Europe, 1989; White Eagle Order (Poland), 1989; US Medal of Freedom, 1989; Meeting-90 Award (Rimini), 1990; Path for Peace Award, Apostolic Nuncio to the UN, 1996; Freedom Medal of National Endowment for Democracy (Washington, USA), 1999; International Freedom Award (Memphis, USA). Address: Lech Wałęsa Institute Foundation, Al Jerozolimskie 11/19, 00 508 Warsaw, Poland. Website: www.ilw.org.pl

WALKEN Christopher, b. 31 March 1943, Astoria, New York, USA. Actor. m. Georgianne, 1969. Education: Hofstra University. Career: Films: Me and My Brother, 1969; The Anderson Tapes, 1971; The Happiness Cage, 1972; Next Stop Greenwich Village, 1976; Roseland, The Sentinel, Annie Hall, 1977; The Deer Hunter, 1978; Last Embrace, 1979; Heaven's Gate, 1980; Shoot the Sun Down, The Dogs of War, Pennies From Heaven, 1981; The Dead Zone, Brainstorm, 1983; A View to a Kill, 1984; At Close Range, 1986; Deadline, 1987; The Milagro Beanfield War, Biloxi Blues, Homeboy, 1988; Communion, The Comfort of Strangers, 1989; King of New York, 1990; McBain, 1991; Mistress, Batman Returns, Day of Atonement, 1992; True Romance, Wayne's World II, 1993; A Business Affair, Scam, Pulp Fiction, 1994; Wild Side, Search and Destroy, Things to do in Denver when You're Dead, The Prophecy, The Addiction, Nick of Time, 1995; Celluloide, Basquiat, The Funeral, Last Man Standing, 1996; Touch, Excess Baggage, Suicide Kings, Mousehunt, 1997; Illuminata, New Rose Hotel, Trance, Antz (voice), 1998; Blast from the Past, Sleepy Hollow, Kiss Toledo Goodbye, 1999; The Opportunists, 2000; Jungle Juice, Scotland, Pa, Joe Dirt, America's Sweethearts, The Affairs of the Necklace, Popcorn Shrimp, 2001; Poolhall Junkies, The Country Bears, Plots with a View, 2002; Catch Me If You Can, Kangaroo Jack, Gigli, The Rundown, 2003; Man on Fire, Envoy, The Stepford Wives, Around the Bend, 2004; Romance & Cigarettes, Domino, 2005; Click, Fade to Black, Man of the Year, 2006; Hairspray, Balls of Fury, 2007; Theatre: West Side Story; Macbeth; The Lion in Winter; The Night Thoreau Spent in Jail, 1970-71; Cinders, 1984; A Bill of Divorcement, 1985; The Seagull, 2001. Honours: Clarence Derwent Award, 1966; Joseph Jefferson Award, 1970; New York Film Critics and Academy Awards, Best Supporting Actor, 1978; Oscar, 1979; BAFTA Award for Best Supporting Actor, 2003; Montreal World Film Festival, Best Actor, 2004; Hollywood Film Award, Ensemble of the Year, 2007. Address: William Morris Agency, 151 El Camino Drive, Beverly Hills, CA 90212, USA.

WALKER Alice (Malsenior), b. 9 February 1944, Eatonton, Georgia, USA. Author; Poet. m. Melvyn R Leventhal, 17 March 1967, divorced 1976, 1 daughter. Education: BA, Sarah Lawrence College, 1966. Appointments: Writer-in-Residence and Teacher of Black Studies, Jackson State College, 1968-69, Tougaloo College, 1970-71; Lecturer in Literature, Wellesley College, 1972-73, University of Massachusetts at Boston, 1972-73; Distinguished Writer, Afro-American Studies Department, University of California at Berkeley, 1982; Fannie Hurst Professor of Literature, Brandeis University, 1982; Co-Founder and Publisher, Wild Trees Press, Navarro, California, 1984-88. Publications: Once, 1968; The Third Life of Grange Copeland, 1970; Five Poems, 1972; Revolutionary

Petunias and Other Poems, 1973; In Love and Trouble, 1973; Langston Hughes: American Poet, 1973; Meridian, 1976; Goodnight, Willie Lee, I'll See You in the Morning, 1979; I Love Myself When I'm Laughing..., 1979; You Can't Keep a Good Woman Down, 1981; The Color Purple, 1982; In Search of Our Mother's Gardens, 1983; Horses Make a Landscape Look More Beautiful, 1984; To Hell With Dying, 1988; Living by the Word: Selected Writings, 1973-1987, 1988; The Temple of My Familiar, 1989; Her Blue Body Everything We Know: Earthling Poems, 1965-1990, 1991; Finding the Green Stone, 1991; Possessing the Secret of Joy, 1992; Warrior Marks (with Pratibha Parmar), 1993; Double Stitch: Black Women Write About Mothers and Daughters (with others), 1993; Everyday Use, 1994; By the Light of My Father's Smile, 1998; The Way Forward is with a Broken Heart, 2000; A Long Walk of Freedom, 2001; Sent By Earth: A Message from the Grandmother Spirit After the Bombing of the World Trade Center and Pentagon, 2001; Woman; Absolute Trust in the Goodness of the Earth: New Poems, 2003; The Third Life of Grange Copeland, 2003; A Poem Traveled Down My Arm: Poems And Drawings, 2003; Now is the Time to Open Your Heart, 2004; Collected Poems, 2005; We Are the Ones We Have Been Waiting For, 2006; Mississippi Winter IV. Honours: Bread Loaf Writer's Conference Scholar, 1966; Ingram Merrill Foundation Fellowship, 1967; McDowell Colony Fellowships, 1967, 1977-78; National Endowment for the Arts Grants, 1969, 1977; Richard and Hinda Rosenthal Pound Award, American Academy and Institute of Arts and Letters, 1974; Guggenheim Fellowship, 1977-78; Pulitzer Prize for Fiction, 1983; American Book Award, 1983; O Henry Award, 1986; Nora Astorga Leadership Award, 1989; Freedom to Write Award, PEN Center, West, 1990; Honorary doctorates. Address: c/o Random House, 201 E 50th Street, New York, NY 10022, USA.

WALKER Catherine, b. 27 June 1945, Pas de Calais, France. Couturier. m. John Walker, deceased, 2 daughters. Education: University of Lille; University of Aix-en-Provence. Appointments: Director, Film Department, French Institute, London, 1970; Lecturer, French Embassy, London, 1971, The Chelsea Design Company Ltd, 1978-; Founder Sponsor, Honorary Member of Board, Gilda's Club; Founder Sponsor, Haven Trust. Publication: Catherine Walker, an Autobiography by the Private Couturier to Diana Princess of Wales, 1998; Catherine Walker, Twenty Five Years 1977-2002. Honours: Designer of the Year for British Couture, 1990-91; Designer of the Year for Glamour Award, 1991-92. Address: 65 Sydney Street, Chelsea, London SW3 6PX, England.

WALKER Jeffery Tandy, b. 27 January 1962, Mena, Arkansas, USA. Professor of Criminology. m. Diane Elizabeth Burns, 1 son, 1 daughter. Education: BSBA, Personnel Management and Computer Science, University of Arkansas, Fayetteville, 1984; MA, Criminal Justice, University of Arkansas, Little Rock, 1988; PhD, Sam Houston State University, Huntsville, Texas, 1992. Appointments: Researcher, Arkansas Governor's Commission on Crime Control, 1988-89; Assistant Professor, 1990-94, Associate Professor, 1994-99, Graduate Co-ordinator, 1997-, Professor, 1999-, Department of Criminal Justice, University of Arkansas at Little Rock; Criminal Justice Track Co-ordinator (Joint Appointment), Public Policy PhD, University of Arkansas, Fayetteville, 2001-; Professor (Joint Appointment), Department of Health Policy and Management, University of Arkansas for Medical Sciences, 2002-. Publications: Numerous papers and articles in professional journals. Honours: Winner, Student Paper Competition, Southwestern Association of Criminal Justice, 1988; Outstanding Criminal

Justice Graduate, University of Arkansas at Little Rock, 1988; Jesse H Gibbs, Houston Endowment Doctoral Fellowship, College of Criminal Justice, Sam Houston State University, 1988-90; Faculty Electee, Phi Kappa Phi Honor Society, 1995; Frederick M Thrasher Award, National Gang Crime Research Center, 1995; Faculty Excellence Award for Research, College of Professional Studies, University of Arkansas at Little Rock, 1997; Mentor of the Year, American Society of Criminology, 2001; Invited Lecturer, Alpha Phi Sigma Annual Lecturer Series, University of South Carolina, 2004; Faculty Excellence Award for Research, College of Professional Studies, University of Arkansas at Little Rock, 2006. Memberships: Academy of Criminal Justice Sciences; American Society of Criminology; Southwestern Association of Criminal Justice; Arkansas Criminal Justice Association. E-mail: jtwalker@ualr.edu

WALKER Miles Rawstron, b. 13 November 1940, Colby, Isle of Man. Politician; Company Director. m. Mary L Cowell, 11 October 1966, 1 son, 1 daughter. Education: Shropshire College of Agriculture, 1959-60. Appointments: Member and Chairman, Arbory Parish Commissioners, 1970-76; Member of House of Keys, Isle of Man Government, 1976-; Elected to Chief Ministry, 1986-96, Member of Treasury, 1996-, Isle of Man Government. Publications: Isle of Man Government Policy Documents, 1987-96. Honours: CBE, 1991; Awarded LLD, Liverpool University, 1994; KB, 1997. Memberships: Member, Isle of Man Treasury, 1996-2000; Chair, Isle of Man Swimming Association; President, Rotary Club, 2000-01; Port St Mary Rifle Club. Address: Magher Feailley, Main Road, Colby, IM9 4AD, Isle of Man. E-mail: miles.walker@talk21.com

WALKER OF WORCESTER, Baron of Abbots Morton in the County of Hereford and Worcester, Peter Edward Walker, b. 25 March 1932, Harrow, Middlesex, England. Businessman; Politician. m. Tessa Joan Pout, 3 sons, 2 daughters. Education: Latymer Upper School, 1944-48. Appointments: Member, Conservative Party National Executive Committee, 1956; National Chairman, Young Conservatives, 1958-60; Parliamentary Candidate, Dartford, 1955, 1959; Member of Parliament, Worcester, 1961-92; Youngest Member of Shadow Cabinet, 1965; Youngest Member of the Cabinet, 1970; Member of all Conservative Cabinets, 1970-90; Minister for Housing and Local Government, 1970; Secretary of State for the Environment, 1970-72, for Trade and Industry, 1972-74; Opposition Spokesman on Trade and Industry and Consumer Affairs, 1974, Defence, 1975-75; Minister for Agriculture, Fisheries and Food, 1979-83; Secretary of State for Energy, 1983-87; Secretary of State for Wales, 1987-90; Non-Executive Director: British Gas plc, 1990-96, Dalgety plc, 1990-96, Tate & Lyle plc, 1990-2001; Caparo Group Limited, 1995-; LIFFE, 1995-; ITM Power plce, 2004-; Chairman, Allianz Cornhill Insurance plc (formerly Cornhill Insurance), 1992-2006; Chairman, Kleinwort Benson Group plc, 1996-98; Vice-Chairman, Dresdner Kleinwort (formerly Dresdner Kleinwort Benson, later Dresdner Kleinwort Wasserstein); Former Chairman, English Partnerships; Former Advisor on disposal of state owned assests in former Eastern Germany, Treuhand, Germany. Publications: The Ascent of Britain, 1976; Trust the People, 1987; Staying Power (autobiography), 1991. Honours: MBE, 1960; PC, 1970; Venezuelan Order of Miranda, 1971; Commander's Cross of the Order of Merit of the Federal Republic of Germany, 1994; Chilean Order of Bernardo O'Higgins, Degree Gran Official, 1995; Rank of Grand Officer of the Order of May of the Argentine Republic, 2002; Freedom of the City of Worcester, 2003. Memberships: UK-China Forum; British-Mexican Business Network;

President, 1999-2002, Current Vice-President, German-British Chamber of Industry and Commerce; Chairman, Carlton Club, 1998-2004; Worcestershire County Cricket Club. Address: Abbots Morton Manor, Gooms Hill, Abbots Morton, Worcester WR7 4LT, England.

WALL Charles Terence Clegg, b. 14 December 1936, Bristol, England. Mathematician. m. Alexandra Joy Hearnshaw, 2 sons, 2 daughters. Education: BA, 1957, PhD, 1960, Trinity College, Cambridge. Appointments: Fellow, Trinity College Cambridge, 1959-64; Harkness Fellow, IAS Princeton, 1960-61; Lecturer, Cambridge University, 1961-64; Reader, Oxford University, Fellow St Catherine's College, 1964-65; Professor of Pure Mathematics, 1965-99, Senior Fellow, 1999-2003, Emeritus Professor, 1999-, University of Liverpool; Royal Society Leverhulme Visiting Professor, Mexico, 1967; SERC Senior Fellow, 1983-88; JSPS Fellow, Tokyo Institute of Technology, 1987; Invited speaker at numerous international conferences. Publications: Books: Surgery on compact manifolds, 1970; A geometric introduction to topology, 1972; The geometry of topological stability (with A A du Plessis), 1995; Singular points of plane curves, 2004; About 160 papers in scientific journals. Honours: Numerous academic awards at school and university; Junior Berwick Prize, 1965, Whitehead Prize, 1976, Polya Prize, 1988, London Mathematical Society; Sylvester Medal, Royal Society, 1988. Memberships: Cambridge Philosophical Society; American Mathematical Society; London Mathematical Society; Fellow of the Royal Society, Council, 1974-76; Foreign Member, Royal Danish Academy; Honorary Member, Irish Mathematical Society. Address: 5 Kirby Park, West Kirby, Wirral, Merseyside CH48 2HA, England. E-mail: terry6.wall@which.net

WALLACE-CRABBE Chris(topher Keith), b. 6 May 1934, Richmond, Victoria, Australia. Poet; Writer. m. (1) Helen Margaret Wiltshire, 1957, 1 son, 1 daughter, (2) Marianne Sophie Feil, 2 sons. Education: BA, 1956, MA, 1964, University of Melbourne; Reader in English, 1976-87, Professor of English, 1987-, Personal Chair, 1987-97, Professor Emeritus, 1998-, University of Melbourne; Visiting Chair in Australian Studies, Harvard University, 1987-88, USA. Publications: Poetry: No Glass Houses, 1956; The Music of Division, 1959; Eight Metropolitan Poems, 1962; In Light and Darkness, 1964; The Rebel General, 1967; Where the Wind Came, 1971; Act in the Noon, 1974; The Shapes of Gallipoli, 1975; The Foundations of Joy, 1976; The Emotions Are Not Skilled Workers, 1979; The Amorous Cannibal and Other Poems, 1985; I'm Deadly Serious, 1988; For Crying out Loud, 1990; Falling into Language, 1990; From the Republic of Conscience, 1992; Rungs of Time, 1993; Whirling, 1998; By and Large, 2001; Next, 2004; The Universe Looks Down, 2005; Then, 2006; Selected Poems 1956-1994, 1995. Novel: Splinters, 1981. Other: Melbourne or the Bush: Essays on Australian Literature and Society, 1973; Falling into Language, 1990; Author! Author!, 1999. Editor: Volumes of Australian poetry and criticism. Honour: Masefield Prize for Poetry, 1957; Farmer's Poetry Prize, 1964; Grace Leven Prize, 1986; Dublin Prize, 1987; Christopher Brennan Award, 1990; Age Book of the Year Prize, 1995; Philip Hodgins Memorial Medal, 2002; Centenary Medal, 2003. Address: c/o The Australian Centre, University of Melbourne, Melbourne, Victoria 3010, Australia.

WALLIAMS David, b. 20 August 1971, Surrey, England. Comedian; Actor. Education: Reigate Grammar School, Surrey; Drama, Bristol University; National Youth Theatre. Career: TV: Rock Profile, 1999; Sir Bernard's Stately Homes, 1999; Coming Soon, 1999; The Web of Caves, 1999; The

Pitch of Fear, 1999; The Kidnappers, 1999; Attachents, 2000; Ted and Alice, 2002; Cruise of the Gods, 2002; Little Britain, 2003; Comic Relief 2003: The Big Hair Do, 2003; The All Star Comedy Show, 2004; Marple: The Body in the Library, 2004; My Life with James Bond, 2006; Capturing Mary, 2007; Rather You Than Me, 2008; Film: Plunkett & Macleane, 1999; Tristram Shandy: A Cock and Bull Story, 2005; Decameron: Angels & Virgins, 2006; Virgin Territory, forthcoming. Publications: Yeah but No But: The Biography of Matt Lucas and David Walliams, 2006; Inside Little Britain, 2006. Honours: The Mirror's Pride of Britain Award for the Most Influential Public Figure, 2006.

WALTER Hugo, b. 12 March 1959, Philadelphia, Pennsylvania, USA. Professor. Education: BA, Princeton University, 1981; PhD, Literature, Yale University, 1985; MA, Humanities, Old Dominion University, 1989; PhD, Humanities, Drew University, 1996. Appointments: Assistant Professor, Washington and Jefferson College, 1989-92; Assistant Professor, Fairleigh Dickinson University, 1992-96; Assistant Professor, Humanities, Kettering University, 1996-99; Associate Professor, Humanities, Berkeley College, 1999-. Publications: The Apostrophic Moment in 19th and 20th Century Lyric Poetry, 1988; Evening Shadows, 1990; Golden Thorns of Light and Sterling Silhouettes, 1990; Waiting for Babel Prophesies of Sunflower Dreams, 1992; Along the Maroon Prismed Threshold of Bronze Pealing Eternity, 1992; The Light of the Dance is the Music of Eternity, 1993; Dusk, Gloaming Mirrors and Castle Winding Dreams, 1994; Amaranth Sage Epiphanies of Dusk Weaving Paradise, 1995; Amaranth Sage Epiphanies of Dusk Weaving Paradise, 1996; Space and Time on the Magic Mountain: Studies in European Literature, 1999; A Purple-Golden Renascence of Eden-Exalting Rainbows, 2001. Honours: Outstanding Achievement in Poetry, 1992, 1993, 1994, 1995, 1996, 1997; Faculty of the Year Award for Outstanding Teaching in Berkeley College's Online Program. Listed in Who's Who publications and biographical dictionaries. Memberships: International Society of Poets; American Poetry Association. Address: 157 Loomis Court, Princeton, NJ 08540, USA.

WALTERS Barbara, b. 25 September 1931, Brookline, Massachusetts, USA. Television Broadcaster. m. (1) Lee Guber, 1963, divorced 1976, 1 adopted daughter, (2) Merv Adelson, 1986, divorced 1993. Education: Sarah Lawrence College, New York. Appointments: Writer, Producer, WNBC TV, Station WPIX, CBS TV Morning Broadcasts; Producer, NBC TV; Writer, Today Programme, NBC TV, 1961, Reporter, Panel Member, 1963-74, Co-Host, 1974-76; Moderator, Not for Women Only, 5 years; Correspondent, ABC News, Co-Anchor, Evening News Programme, 1976-78, Co-Host, 20/20, 1979-2004; Co-Executive Producer, The View ABC, New York, 1997-. Publications: How to Talk with Practically Anybody About Practically Anything, 1970; Contributor to several magazines. Honours include: Silver Satellite Award, American Women in Radio and TV, 1985; Named One of the 100 Most Important Women of the Century, Good Housekeeping, 1985; President Award, Overseas Press Club, 1988; Lowell Thomas Award for Journalism, 1990, 1994; Lifetime Achievement Award, International Women's Media Foundation, 1992. Address: 20/20 147 Columbus Avenue, 10th Floor, New York, NY 10023, USA.

WALTERS Julie, b. 22 February 1950, Birmingham, England. Actress. m. Grant Roffey, 1998, 1 daughter. Education: Manchester Polytechnic; School Governor, Open University. Creative Works: Films include: Educating Rita, 1983; She'll Be Wearing Pink Pyjamas, 1984; Personal Services, 1986;

Prick Up Your Ears, 1986; Buster, 1987; Mack the Knife, 1988; Killing Dad, 1989; Stepping Out, 1991; Just Like a Woman, 1992; Sister My Sister, 1994; Intimate Relations, 1996; Titanic Town, 1997; Girls Night, 1997; All Forgotten, 1999; Dancer, 1999; Billy Elliot, 2000; Harry Potter and the Philosopher's Stone, 2001; Before You Go, 2002; Harry Potter and the Chamber of Secrets, 2002; Calendar Girls, 2003; Harry Potter and the Prisoner of Azkaban, 2004; Mickybo and Me, 2004; Wah-Wah, 2005; Driving Lessons, 2006; Becoming Jane, 2007; Harry Potter and the Order of the Phoenix, 2007; TV includes: Talent, 1980; Wood and Walters, 1981; Boys From the Blackstuff, 1982; Say Something Happened, 1982; Victoria Wood as Seen on TV, 1984, 1986, 1987; The Birthday Party, 1986; Her Big Chance, 1987; GBH, 1991; Stepping Out, 1991; Julie Walters and Friends, 1991; Clothes in the Wardrobe, 1992; Wide Eyed and Legless, 1993; Bambino Mio, 1993; Pat and Margaret, 1994; Jake's Progress, 1995; Little Red Riding Hood, 1995; Intimate Relations, 1996; Julie Walters in an Alien, 1997; Dinner Ladies, 1998-99; Jack and the Beanstalk, 1998; Oliver Twist, 1999; My Beautiful Son, 2001; Murder, 2002; The Canterbury Tales, mini-series, 2003; The Return, 2003; Ahead of the Class, 2005; The Ruby in the Smoke, 2006; Several stage appearances; Acorn Antiques: The Musical, 2006. Publication: Baby Talk, 1990; Julie Walters: Seriously Funny, 2003. Honours: Variety Club Best Newcomer Award, 1980; Best Actress Award, 1984; British Academy Award for Best Actress, 1984; Golden Globe Award, 1984; Variety Club Award for Best Actress, 1991; Olivier Award, 2001; CBE, 2008. Address: c/o ICM, 76 Oxford Street, London W1N 0AX, England.

WALTERS Sherwood George, b. 9 May 1926, Detroit, Michigan, USA. Professor; Consultant. m. Alexandra Sielcken, 4 September 1952, 1 son, 3 daughters. Education: BA cum laude, Economics, History and Political Science, Western Maryland College, 1949; MS, International Trade, History, Columbia University, 1950; MBA with distinction, Columbia University Graduate School of Business, 1953; PhD honours scholar, New York University, 1960; Certificate Area Studies Specialist in Latin American Affairs, Institute of Public Affairs and Regional Studies, Government Department, New York University, 1960. Appointments: Private through 1st Lieutenant, Infantry/Quartermaster Corps, service in the European Theatre of Operations, 1944-47; Instructor through Associate Professor of Economics, Sociology and Marketing, College of Business Economics, Lehigh University, Bethlehem, Pennsylvania, 1950-60; Fellow, EI DuPont de Nemours, Wilmington, DE, summer 1951; President, Director, S G Walters Associates, management consultant firm, 1952-; Producer, Director and Co-presenter with wife, Breakfast with the Walters, commercially sponsored half-hour daily commentary/interview radio programme, WEST/NBC, Easton, Pennsylvania, 1953-57; Director Research Committee, US Council for Small Business Development, Co-Director, EI DuPont de Nemours Interdisciplinary Research Team and Ford Foundation Special Studies Scholar at Harvard University Business School, Cambridge, MA, summer 1956; Project Director, US Small Business Administration, Export potential for US small business in Latin America; Executive Vice President, Director of Mobil Centers Inc, Retail Planning Manager, Development Projects Manager, Mobil Oil, New York City, 1960-65; Executive Officer, Marketing Director, General Tire and Rubber International Plastics Co, Manager, Commercial Marketing, Chemical Plastics Division, Akron, Ohio, 1965-70; Professor, Rutgers Business School, New Jersey, 1970-93; Professor Emeritus, Management Studies, Rutgers University, 1993-; Founding Director, Interfunctional Management Program, Rutgers University Business School,

1970-88; Founding Director, PhD Management Program; Chairman, Organization and Operations Management Department, Rutgers Graduate School of Business Administration; Director, various international programmes in management, banking and science in Romania, Puerto Rico, Sweden, France and Northern Ireland, for International Labor Organization (ILO), United Nations Industrial Development Organization (UNIDO), US State Department, National Science Foundation (NSF), 1971-2004; Evaluator/Emissary, US National Science Foundation Industry University Co-operative Research Centers Program, 1980-2004; Helped establish and sustain many Industry/University Co-operative Research Centers and International Tie Research Programs whilst working with National Science Foudnation and the New Jersey Commission for Science and Technology at Rutgers University. Publications: Co-author, 7 books; 186 articles and government reports; 3 seminal books: Marketing Management Viewpoints Commentary and Readings, 2nd edition, 1970; Mandatory Housing Finance Programs, A Comparative International Analysis, 1975; Managing the Industry, University Co-operative Research Centres: A Guide for Directors and Other Stakeholders, 1998. Honours: World War II Victory Medal, Army of Occupation Medal, Germany; President, Economics Society, Western Maryland College, 1948-49; Member, Aragonaut Honors Society, Western Maryland College, 1949; Founders Day Award, New York University, 1960; Professor of the Year (student selected), Rutgers Graduate School of Business, 1976; Christian R & Mary F Lindback Award for Excellence in Teaching, Rutgers University, 24 May 1983; Republican Presidential Legion of Merit, 11 February 1994; National Science Foundation Excellence Award for many years of dedicated service and significant contributions to the Nation and the NSF Industry University Co-operative Research Centers Program, 2004; Board of Trustees Alumni Award, McDaniel College (formerly Western Maryland College), 2005; Beta Gamma Sigma Honorary Society, Columbia University, 1953-; Secretary, Treasurer, President, Lehigh Chapter, 1953-60; Secretary, Treasurer, President, Rutgers Chapter, 1970-88; Presented to HRH Prince Charles, 6 May 1997 at Queen's University, Belfast, Northern Ireland to comment on the accomplishments of Industry University Co-operative Research Centres in the United Kingdom and the United States; Businessman of the Year Award Winner from North Carolina, Business Advisory Council of the National Republican Congressional Committee, 2003, 2004, 2005; Listed in national and international biographical dictionaries; Sons of the Revolution; Sons of the American Revolution; Appointed to New Jersey Governor's Commission Task Force on Energy; Judicial Committee on Energy Safety Standards; Committee on Liquefied Natural Gas; Chairman, Sub-Committee, Forecasting Demand and Supply for Liquefied Natural Gas, 1975, 1976. Memberships: Chairman, University/Industrial Partnerships, John Von Neumann Center, Princeton University, Princeton, New Jersey, 1986; Director, Co-Director, Moderator, Advisor, Speaker, NSF/IUCRC Semi-Annual Evaluators Conference, Washington DC, Arlington Virginia, 1983-2004; New Jersey Research and Development Council, 1984-93; Newcomen Society; Advisor, US Agency for International Development on Research Project Measurement and Management Decision Making, Washington DC, 1991; Fellow, Academy of Political Science, 2006; Adviser, National Republican Congressional Commission on Tax Reform, 2001; Honorary Chairman, Business Advisory Council, National Republican Congressional Committee, 2003-04; Elder, Trustee, Co-Director Christian Education Committee, Topsail Presbyterian Church, Hampstead, North Carolina. Address: 110 Topsail Watch Lane, Hampstead, NC 28443-2728, USA.

WALTON James Stephen, b. 27 November 1946, Kingston upon Thames, Surrey, England. Research Scientist. m. Dorcas Ann Graham, 1 son, 1 daughter. Education: Diploma in Physical Education, 1968, Certificate of Education, 1968, Carnegie College of Physical Education, Leeds, England; MA, Education, Michigan State University, USA, 1970; MS, Applied Mechanics, Stanford University, California, USA, 1976; PhD, Physical Education, Biomechanics, Pennsylvania State University, USA, 1981. Appointments: Graduate Teaching Assistant, Michigan State University, 1968-69; Teacher, Gaynesford High School, Carshalton, Surrey, England, 1969-70; Graduate Teaching and Research Assistant, Pennsylvania State University, 1970-74; Graduate Teaching Assistant, Stanford University, California, 1974-76; Director of Engineering, Computerised Biomechanical Analysis, Amherst, Massachusetts, 1979; Associate Senior Research Scientist, 1979-81, Senior Research Scientist, 1981-85, Biomedical Science Department, General Motors Research Laboratories; Vice-President Applications Engineering, Motion Analysis Corporation, 1987-88; President/Owner, 4D Video, Sebastopol, California, 1988-; US National Delegate to the International Congress on High-Speed Photography and Photonics, 2005-2011. Publications: Numerous papers in scientific journals and presented at conferences including: Image-Based Motion Measurement: The Camera as a Transducer, 1997; Image-Based Motion Measurement: An Introduction to the Elements of the Technology, 1998; Calibration and Processing of Images as an After Thought, 2000; A High-Speed Video Tracking System for Generic Applications, 2000; The Camera as a Transducer, 2000. Honours: Fellow, Society of Photo-optical Instrumentation Engineers (SPIE) Honorary Fellow, British Association for Physical Training. Memberships include: American Association for the Advancement of Science; American Society for Photogrammetry and Remote Sensing; New York Academy of Sciences; Sigma Xi; Society of Photo-Optical Instrumentation Engineers Address: 4D Video, 825 Gravenstein Highway North, Suite #4, Sebastopol, California 95472-2844, USA.

WANAMAKER Zoë, b. 13 May 1949, New York, USA (British citizen, 2000). Actress. m. Gawn Grainger, 1994, 1 stepson, 1 stepdaughter. Education: Hornsey College of Art; Central School of Speech and Drama. Appointments: Actor; Theatre: A Midsummer Night's Dream, 1970; Guys and Dolls, 1972; The Cherry Orchard, 1970-71; Dick Whittington, 1971-72; Tom Thumb, Much Ado About Nothing, 1974; A Streetcar Named Desire, Pygmalion, The Beggar's Opera, Trumpets and Drums, 1975-76; Wild Oats, 1977; Once in a Lifetime, 1970-80; The Devil's Disciple; Wild Oats; Ivanov; The Taming of the Shrew; Captain Swing; Piaf; A Comedy of Errors, Twelfth Night and The Time of Your Life, 1983-85; Mother Courage; Othello; The Importance of Being Earnest 1982-83; The Bay at Nice and Wrecked Eggs, 1986-87; Mrs Klein; The Crucible; Twelfth Night, 1973-74; Cabaret, 1974; Kiss Me Kate, 1974; The Taming of the Shrew, 1975; Loot; Made in Bangkok, 1988; The Last Yankee, 1993; Dead Funny, 1994; The Glass Menagerie; Sylvia, 1996; Electra, 1997; The Old Neighbourhood, 1998; Electra, New York, 1998; Battle Royal, 1999; Boston Marriage, Donmar Warehouse, 2001; Boston Marriage, New Ambassadors, 2002; Hildy in His Girl Friday, National Theatre, 2003; TV: Sally for Keeps, 1970; The Eagle Has Landed, 1972; Between the Wars, 1973; The Silver Mask, 1973; Lorna and Ted, 1973; The Confederacy of Wives, 1974; The Village Hall, 1975; Danton's Death, 1977; Beaux Stratagem, 1977; The Devil's Crown, 1978-79; Strike, 1981; Baal, 1981; All the World's A Stage, 1982; Richard III, 1982; Enemies of the State, 1982; Edge of Darkness, 1985;

Paradise Postponed, 1985; Poor Little Rich Girl, 1987; Once in a Lifetime, 1987; The Dog It Was That Died, 1988; Ball Trap on the Cote Sauvage, 1989; Othello, 1989; Prime Suspect, 1990; Love Hurts, 1991-93; Dance to the Music of Time, 1997; Gormenghast, Leprechauns, David Copperfield, 1999; Adrian Mole, The Cappuccino Years, 2001; My Family, BBC Series 1-5, 2000-04; Miss Marple: A Murder is Announced, 2004; Commentary, Someone to Watch Over Me, 2004; Dr Who: The End of the World, 2005; Film: Harry Potter and the Philosopher's Stone, 2001; Five Children & It, 2003; Radio including: The Golden Bowl, Plenty, 1979; Bay at Nice, 1987; A February Morning, 1990; Carol, book reading, 1990; Such Rotten Luck, 1991, series I and TV films: The Blackheath Poisonings, Central, 1991; Memento Mori, BBC, 1991; Countess Alice, BBC, 1991; The English Wife, 1994; The Widowing of Mrs Holroyd, BBC, 1995; Wilde; Swept in By the Sea. Honours: SWET Award, 1979; Numerous Tony nominations; Drama Award, Mother Courage, 1985; Honorary DLitt, Southbank University, 1995; Variety Club of Great Britain Award, Best Actress, Electra, 1997; Olivier Awards including Best Actress for Electra, 1997; Calaway Award, New York, Best Actress, Electra; Best Actress, BAFTA for Love Hurts, Prime Suspects and Wilde; Honorary Doctorate Richmond American University of London; CBE; Boston Marriage, Oliver Nomination, Best Actress, 2002; Patron, Prisoners of Conscience; UK TV Mummies' Favourite UK TV Mum, 2004; Award for Excellence in the Arts, DePaul University, Chicago, 2004; Rose d'Or, Best Comedy Actress, My Family, 2005. Membership: Honorary Member, Voluntary Euthanasia Society; Trustee, Honorary President, Shakespeare's Globe. Address: c/o Conway Van Gelder, 18/21 Jermyn Street, London SW1Y 6HP, England. Website: www.geocities.com/zwsite

WANG Cheng-Xiang, b. 23 May 1975, Shandong, P R China. Lecturer. m. Qi Yao, 2000. Education: BSc, 1997, M Eng, 2000, Shandong University; PhD, Aalborg University, Denmark, 2004. Appointments: Research Assistant, Department of Communication Networks, Technical University of Hamburg-Harburg, Germany, 2000-01; Visiting Researcher, Baseband Algorithms & Standardization Laboratory, Seimens AG – Mobile Phones, Munich, Germany, 2004; Research Fellow, Department of Information and Communication Technology, University of Agder, Norway, 2001-05; Lecturer, Heriot-Watt University, Edinburgh, UK, 2005-. Publications: 31 refereed journals; 66 refereed conference papers; 1 invited keynote speech; 2 reports. Honours: Excellent Paper Award, 1999; Siemens Scholarship, 2000; Scientific Improvements Award, 2000; Excellent Master Thesis Award, 2001; Research Grant Award, Germany, 2005-07; International Exchange Programme Grant Award, 2007; Research Grant Awards, 2007-10; Honorary Fellowship, University of Edinburgh, 2006-; Adjunct Professor, Guilin University of Electronic Technology, 2006-; Guest Researcher, Xidian University, 2007-; Listed in international biographical dictionaries; Editor, 4 international journals. Memberships: Higher Education Academy, UK; Institution of Engineering and Technology; Institute of Electrical and Electronics Engineers. Address: Electrical, Electronic and Computer Engineering, School of Engineering & Physical Sciences, Heriot-Watt University, Edinburgh EH14 4AS, United Kingdom. E-mail: cheng-xiang.wang@hw.ac.uk

WANG Chun-Hsiang, b. 19 September 1958, Taiwan. Physician. m. Tsui-Chen Chang, 1 son, 2 daughters. Education: Bachelor of Medicine, Chung Shan Medical University, 1979-80; MSc, Green College, Oxford University, 1990-91. Appointments: Gastroenterologist, Tainan

Municipal Hospital, 1992-; Instructor, Chung Jung University. Publications: A Survival Model in Patients Undergoing Radical Resection of Ampullary Adenocarcinoma, 2004; Does Type and Duration of Antiretroviral Therapy Attenuate Liver Fibrosis in HIV/HCV Coinfected Patients?, 2006. Honours: Listed in international biographical dictionaries. Memberships: American Gastroenterological Association; New York Academy of Science; American Association for the Advancement of Science. Address: 670 Chongde Road, Tainan, Taiwan. E-mail: chunhsiang@gmail.com

WANG Chung-Jing, b. 18 September 1958, Taiwan. Urologist. m. Shiu-Dan Yen, 1 son, 1 daughter. Education: MD, National Taiwan University; EMBA, National Chiayi University. Appointments: Vice Superintendent, St Marting de Parres Hospital, Chia-Yi; Chairman, Chia-Yi Medical Association; Associate Professor. Publications: Efficacy of α-L Blocker in Expulsive Therapy of the Lower Ureteral Stones, 2008. Honours: 1st Prize in Memory of Professor Hsieh Yo-Ho for paper context. Memberships: Farmason Medical Association; Taiwan Urological Association; Taiwan Surgical Association; The American Urological Association. E-mail: jing@stm.org.tw

WANG Haibo, b. 28 June 1962, Guangdong, China. Anaesthesiologist; Microbiologist; Tropical Medicine Specialist. m. Chaoyin Han, 1 son, 1 daughter. Education: MD, Zhanjiang Medical College, China, 1984; Master in Medicine, Jinan University School of Medicine, China, 1987; PhD, Microbiology, Medical College of Virginia, USA, 1996. Appointments: Lecturer, Jinan School of Medicine, China, 1987-91; House Officer and Fellow, 1996-2001, Assistant Professor, 2001- Louisiana State University School of Medicine, Shreveport, USA. Publications: As co-author, Phlebotomine sandflies in Zhejiang Province with the description of a new species sergentomyia zhongi, 1991; Cyclin dependent kinases in plasmodium falciparum, 1993; Cell cycle and regulation in Plasmodium falciparum (PhD Dissertation), 1996. Honours: ABA Diplomas. Memberships: AMA; ASA. Address: Department of Anesthesiology, Louisiana State University Health Science Center, Shreveport, LA 71130, USA. E-mail: hwang2@lsuhsc.edu

WANG Jennie (Lin Jian), b. 19 March 1952, Shanghai, China. Literature Educator. Education: BA, cum laude, San Francisco State University, California, USA, 1983; MA, English, Stanford University, California, USA, 1984; PhD, English, State University of New York at Buffalo, Buffalo, New York, USA, 1992. Appointments: Instructor of English, Department of Foreign Languages, Shanghai Jiao-Tong University, Shanghai, China, 1977-79; Teaching Fellow, Department of English, State University of New York at Buffalo, Buffalo, New York, 1987-91; Preceptor, Expository Writing Program, Harvard University, Cambridge, Massachusetts, 1992-93; Research Associate, Department of Ethnic Studies, University of California at Berkeley, Summer 1996; Assistant Professor, 1993-98, Associate Professor, 1998-, Department of English Language and Literature, University of Northern Iowa, Cedar Falls, Iowa; Visiting Scholar, Department of English, University of California at Berkeley, 2000-01, 2003-04; Full Professor of Comparative Literature, PhD Dissertation Director, Department of Chinese Language and Literature, Fudan University, Shanghai, China, 2004-. Publications: Author: Novelistic Love in the Platonic Tradition: Fielding, Faulkner and the Postmodernists, 1997; Chinese Translator, Smiles on Washington Square: A Love Story of Sorts by Raymond Federman, 1999; The Iron Curtain of Language: Maxine Hong Kingston and American

Orientalism, 2006; Editor, Querying the Genealogy: Comparative and Transnational Studies in Chinese American Literature, 2006; Numerous articles on Post-modern fiction and American Orientalism in literary journals and books. E-mail: linjian@fudan.edu.cn

WANNER Sonia Viktoria, b. 15 March 1931, Gothenburg, Sweden. Artist in Fine Arts. m. Sigvard Ulf, 2 sons. Appointments: Chalmers University of Technology and Architecture, Gothenburg, 1976-94; More than 100 exhibitions in Sweden, Norway, Geneva, Innsbruck, New York, Los Angeles, Paris, Vienna, Rome, Florence, Beirut, Seoul, Milan, London, Plymouth, Utrecht, Sahlsburg, Brussels, Millais Gallery, Southampton Institute in the Museum, Southampton; Craig Atkinsson Museum, Southport; Best known for marine oils of rough seas, also acclaimed for well-balanced landscapes and still life paintings. Publications: Author and editor: "Oceans" Sonia Wanner Art (book). Honours: Scholarship, Eva Ljungqvist's Scholarship Fund, 1992; Hall of Fame for Outstanding Achievements in the field of Fine Arts, USA, 2000; Toile D'Or de L'Année, Fédération Nationale de la Culture Française, France, 2001; Art-atlas of the World: 1001 Reasons to Love the Earth, World Art Collection, Netherlands, 2001; Medaille D'Argent, Arts-Science-Lettres, Paris, 2005; Medaille D'Argent, Société Accademique Française, Paris, 2005; Oscar Della Cultura, Florence, 2005; Medaille D'Argent, Accademia, Milano, 2005; Arts and Humanities Advisor to the Director General, International Biographical Centre, England, (AdVAh); Picture of painting included in Artists from the 15th-21st Century, France, 2006; Woman of the Year, ABI, 2006; Premio la Dea Alata, 2006; Diploma d'Onore per la Classe Pittura, Accademia Centro Storico, Florence, 2006; Gold Medal, Trophy and Diploma, 1° Premio Europa Arte Stranieri per la Pittura Tema Libero, Academia Internazionale Santaria, Torino; Premio Internazionale Donatello, 2006; Accademia Il Marzocco di Firenze, 2006; Award Diploma Academic Master with Silver Medal, Del Sever Centra Culturale Internazionale d'Arte Sever, Florence, 2006; Great Women of the 21st Century; Listed in numerous biographical publications. Memberships: Chamber of Commerce and Industry, Gothenburg; Regional Resource Centre for Women's Work and Development in Western Sweden, Gothenburg; Women's Art Library, London; National Museum of Women in the Arts, Washington; Metropolitan Museum of Arts, New York; Linos School, New York and Verona; Société Academique Arts-Science-Lettres, Paris France; Academia Nacional De Artes Plasticas, Brazil; Salão Internacional De Pintura, ANAP, Brazil; Culturale Internazionale d'Arte Sever; Associazione Galleria Centro Storico, Florence, Italy; Accademia Severiade Milan, Italy; Accademia Internazionale "Greci-Marino", Accademia del Verbano di Lettere, Arti, Scienze, Italy; Accademia Internazionale Santarita, Arti, Cultura, Scienze, Religioni, Turin, Italy; Federation Nationale de la Culture Française, Paris; European Art Group. Address: Haljerod 620, 442 96 Kode, Sweden. Website: www.wanner.net

WANSELL (Stephen) Geoffrey, b. 9 July 1945, Greenock, Scotland. Author; Journalist. Divorced, 1 son, 1 daughter. Education: BSc, Econ, London School of Economics, 1962-66; MA Student and Tutorial Assistant, University of Sheffield, 1966-67. Appointments: Reporter, Columnist, News Editor, Times Educational Supplement, 1967-70; Reporter, Feature Writer, The Times, 1970-73; Programme Controller, London Broadcasting Company and Independent Radio News, 1973-75; Pendennis Columnist, The Observer, 1977-78; Columnist, Now! Magazine, 1979-81; Columnist, Sunday Telegraph Magazine, 1981-85; Executive Producer,

Motion Picture, When The Whales Came, 1989; Columnist, Sunday Express, 1993; Feature Writer, Daily Mail, 1999-2008. Publications: Author of 8 books. Honour: Shortlisted for the Whitbread Book of the Year, 1995. Membership: Garrick Club; Society of Authors. Address: 28B Bedford Place, London WC1B 5JH, England. E-mail: geoffreywansell@aol.com

WARD Simon, b. 19 October 1941, Beckenham, England. Actor. m. Alexandra Malcolm, 3 daughters. Education: Royal Academy of Dramatic Art. Creative Works: Stage appearances include: Konstantin in The Seagull, Birmingham Repertory, 1964; Abel Drugger in The Alchemist and Hippolytus in Phèdre, Playhouse, Oxford, 1965-66; Dennis in Loot, Jeannetta Cochrane and Criterion, 1966; The Unknown Soldier in the Unknown Soldier and His Wife, Ferdinand in The Tempest and Henry in The Skin of Our Teen, Chichester Festival, 1968; Donald in Spoiled, Haymarket, 1971; Romeo in Romeo and Juliet, Shaw, 1972; Troilus in Troilus and Cressida, Young Vic; Films include: I Start Counting, 1970; Young Winston, 1971; Hitler - The Last Ten Days, 1972; The Three Musketeers, 1973; The Four Musketeers, Deadly Strangers, All Creatures Great and Small, 1974-75; Aces High, 1975; Battle Flag, 1976; The Four Feathers, 1978; Zulu Dawn, 1979; Supergirl, Around the World in 80 Days, Double X, 1992; Wuthering Heights, 1992; Ghost Writers; TV includes: The Black Tulip; The Roads to Freedom; Holocaust (serial). Address: c/o Shepherd & Ford Associates Ltd, 13 Radner Walk, London SW3 4BP, England.

WARFIELD John N(elson), b. 21 November 1925, Sullivan, Missouri, USA. Researcher. m. Rosamond Howe, 2 sons, 1 daughter. Education: BA, Mathematics, 1948, BSc, Electrical Engineering, 1948, MSc, Electrical Engineering, 1949, University of Missouri; Army Specialised Training Program, 1944-46, Graduate Study, 1949-51, Pennsylvania State University; PhD, Electrical Engineering, Purdue University, 1952. Appointments: Instructor, Electrical Engineering, University of Missouri, 1949; Instructor, 1949-51, Assistant Professor, 1952-53, Associate Professor, 1953-55, Electrical Engineering, Pennsylvania State University; Assistant Professor, 1955-56, Associate Professor, 1956-57, University of Illinois, Urbana; Associate Professor, Associate Director of Computer Laboratory, Purdue University, Indiana, 1957-58; Associate Professor, 1958-59, Professor, 1959-66, University of Kansas; Visiting Professor, University of Colorado at Boulder, 1965; Adjunct Professor of Electrical Engineering, Ohio State University, Columbus, 1966-73; Senior Research Leader, Battelle Memorial Institute, 1966-74; Chairman, Department of Electrical Engineering, 1974-78, Harry Douglas Forsyth Professor of Electrical Engineering, 1974-83, Director, Centre for Interactive Management, 1980-81, University of Virginia at Charlottesville; Visiting Professor of Management, University of Northern Iowa, 1980-81; University Professor, 1984-2000, Emeritus, 2000-, George Mason University, Fairfax, Virginia. Publications: Co-translator, Synthesis of Linear Communications Networks; Introduction to Electronic Analog Computers, 1959; Principles of Logic Design, 1963; Societal Systems: Planning, Policy and Complexity, 1976; A Science of Generic Design: Managing Complexity Through Systems Design, 1994; Co-author, A Handbook of Interactive Management, 1994; Understanding Complexity: Thought and Behaviour, 2002; The Mathematics of Structure, 2003; Discovering Systems Science, 2003; An Introduction to Systems Science, 2006; Numerous articles in professional journals. Honours include: Western Electric Fund Award for Excellence in Instruction of Students, 1966; Eminent Scholar, University of Virginia, 1974-83, George Mason University, 1984-; Outstanding Contribution Award, IEEE Systems, Man and Cybernetics Society, 1977; Centennial Medal, IEEE, 1984; Peace Pipe Award, Americans for Indian Opportunity, 1987; Mayor's Certificate, City of Austin, Texas, 1993; Plaque of Recognition, Minister of Social Development, Governor of Guanajuato, 1994; Third Millennium Medal, IEEE, 2000; Laureate, George Mason University, 2002; J G Wohl Career Achievement Award, IEEE Systems, Man and Cybernetics Society, 2006; Pioneer Award, International Council of Systems Engineering, 2007. Memberships include: IEEE; Association for Integrative Studies; Charles S Peirce Society; Society for Design and Process Science; Tau Beta Pi; Eta Kappa Nu; Sigma Xi; Panetics Society; Board of Advisers, Magic Circle Chamber Opera Company, New York; President, Integrative Sciences, Inc, 2001; President, AJAR Publishing Company, 2002. Address: 100 Willow Bend Court, Sheffield, AL 35660-7252, USA. E-mail: jnwarfield@aol.com Website: http://jnwarfield.com

WARNE Shane Keith, b. 13 September 1969, Ferntree Gully, Melbourne, Australia. Cricketer. m. Simone, 1 son, 2 daughters. Appointments: Leg-Break and Googly Bowler; Right-Hand Lower-Order Batsman; 183 first-class matches for Hampshire took 70 wickets (average 23.1), 2000; Highest ever Australian wicket taker in Tests; 107 Tests for Australia, 1991-92 to 2002, taking 491 wickets (average 25.71) and scoring 2,238 runs, took hat-trick v England, Melbourne, 1994; Took 850 wickets and scored 4,103 runs in 1st class cricket, to 2003; Toured England, 1993, 1997, 2001; 191 limited-overs internationals (11 as Captain), to 2003; Captain Victoria Sheffield Shield Team (Bushrangers), 1996-99; received 12 month ban for testing positive for a banned substance, 2003; Captain of Hampshire, 2004-; Retirement from limited-overs internationals, 2004. Publications: Shane Warne: The Autobiography, 2001. Honours: Wisden Cricketer of the Year, 1994; Selected as one of five Wisden Cricketers of the Century, 2000. Address: c/o Victorian Cricket Association, 86 Jolimont Street, Victoria 3002, Australia.

WARNER Joshua Wayne, b. 4 January 1974, Colorado Springs, USA. Law Enforcement Officer; Educator; Volunteer Firefighter. m. Kimberley Kay Pierce, 1 son, 1 daughter. Education: BA, Political Science, Mesa State College, Grand Junction, Colorado, 1998-2002; Graduate Certificate, University of Washington, 2004-05; MSc, University of Cincinnati, 2003-05. Appointments: Appliance Repair/Sales, Bob's Appliance and Repair, Craig, Colorado, 1986-93; Explorer, Craig Police Department Explorer Post 2196, Craig, 1988-92; Aircrew, Wild West Radio, Craig, 1991-92; General Labor, Black Nugget Motel, Craig, 1991; Cadet, US Coast Guard, New London, Connecticut, 1992-93; NCE Aircrew, KDUR Radio, Durango, Colorado, 1993; Missionary, Church of Jesus Christ of Latter-Day Saints, Mitcham, Surrey, England, 1993-95; Reserve Police Officer, Craig Police Department, Craig, 1996; Lead Instructor, Rocky Mountain Institute of Transportation Safety, Colorado State University, Denver, Colorado, 1998-2005; Volunteer Firefighter/EMS Provider, Lower Valley Fire Protection District, Fruita, Colorado, 2002-; Law Enforcement Academy Instructor, Colorado Northwestern Community College, Rangely, Colorado, 2002-; Patrol Deputy, 1996-2000, Patrol Deputy III, 2000-05, Corporal, 2005, Sergeant, 2005-, Mesa County Sheriff's Office, Grand Junction, Colorado. Honours: Numerous awards and recognition including: Excellence Award, Recruiting, Retention & Retirement Committee Service, 2006; Excellence Award, Formation of and service in Peer Support Team, 2006; Medal of Merit, Pursuit of high-risk fugitive, 2006. Memberships: American Criminal Justice Association; American Sniper Association; American

Society of Criminology; Colorado Law Enforcement Officers Association; Colorado Police Protective Association; Emergency Medical Services Association of Colorado; Rocky Mountain Tactical Team Association; International Association of Chiefs of Police; International Tactical Emergency Medical Services Association; Mesa County Deputy Sheriffs Association; National Association of Field Training Officers; National Tactical Officers Association; Pi Sigma Alpha Honor Society of Political Science.

WARNER Margaret Anne (Megan), b. 4 September 1943, Epsom, Surrey, England. Educator. Education includes: Teacher's Certificate, Mathematics, Froebel Educational Institute, London, 1964; Diploma, English as a Second Language, 1976, Diploma, School Management Studies, 1979, College of Preceptors; Master's Degree, Educational Studies, University of Surrey at Roehampton, 1990; OFSTED Registered Inspector, 1996; Performance Management Consultant, DfES/NPQH/Consortium, 2000. Appointments include: Assistant Teacher various schools, ILEA and Australia, 1964-72; Deputy Headteacher, Church of England Primary School, Oxfordshire, 1973-79; Headteacher, Church of England Primary School, ILEA, 1979-89; Teaching Practice Supervisor, primary and nursery classes, London Boroughs, 1990-91; SEN Co-ordinator, Mathematics Teacher, Girls' High School, Merton, 1991-92; Assistant Teacher, Merton Middle School, 1992-93; Head of Religious Education Departments, Wandsworth, 1993, 1994-95, i/c Pupils with Statements, 1994, Wandsworth Comprehensive School; Team Inspector, Primary, Secondary, Special, 1994-2005; Registered Primary Inspector, 1996-2005; DfES Trained Performance Management Consultant, 2000-; Assessor of HLTAs, 2005-; International Teacher Trainer, Qatar and India, 2006-07; Sole Trader trading as MAW Education, 1999-; Life Coach, 2007-. Publications: Headteachers' perceptions of their role in spiritual education (book chapter, editor R Best), 1996; Reflections on Inspection (book chapter, editor R Best), 2000; 81 Ofsted Inspection Reports, 1996-2004. Honours: Professional of the Year in Education, Empire Who's Who, 2005-2006; International Peace Prize, United Cultural Convention, USA, 2005; Featured Member, Madison Who's Who, 2005-2006; Woman of the Year 2005 and 2006, American Biographical Institute; Marquis Who's Who, 2006; Deputy Governor, Research Board of Advisors, ABI, 2006; Legion of Honor, United Cultural Convention, 2006; World Lifetime Achievement Award, ABI, 2006; Professional of the Year representing Education: Consulting and Training, Cambridge Who's Who Registry of Executives, Professionals and Entrepreneurs, 2006-07. Memberships: Association of Professionals in Education and Children's Trusts; Council for Education in the Commonwealth; Association for Supervision and Curriculum Development; Royal Commonwealth Society; Associate, College of Preceptors; Business: nrg Business Networks UK. Address: 27 Old Gloucester Street, London WC1N 3XX, England. E-mail: maweducation@easynet.co.uk

WARNER Marina (Sarah), b. 9 November 1946, London, England. Author; Critic. m. (1) William Shawcross, 1971, divorced 1980, 1 son, (2) John Dewe Mathews, 1981, divorced 1998. Education: MA, Modern Languages, French and Italian, Lady Margaret Hall, Oxford. Appointments: Getty Scholar, Getty Centre for the History of Art and the Humanities, California, 1987-88; Tinbergen Professor, Erasmus University, Rotterdam, 1991; Visiting Fellow, British Film Institute, 1992; Visiting Professor, University of Ulster, 1995, Queen Mary and Westfield College, London, 1995-, University of York, 1996-2000; Reith Lecturer, 1994; Whitney J Oakes Fellow, Princeton University, 1996; Mellon Professor, University of

Pittsburgh, 1997; Visiting Fellow Commoner, Trinity College, Cambridge, 1998; Tanner Lecturer, 1999; Visiting Professor, University of Stanford, California, USA, 2000; Clarendon Lecturer, Oxford, 2001; Visiting Fellow, All Souls' College, Oxford, 2001; Visiting Fellow, Italian Academy, Columbia University, New York, 2003; Professor, Department of Literature, Film and Theatre Studies, University of Essex, 2004-; Robb Lecturer, University of Auckland, 2004; Senior Fellow, Remarque Institute, New York University, 2006; Janina Tammes Professor (Visiting), University of Groningen, 2007. Publications: The Dragon Empress, 1972; Alone of All Her Sex: The Myth and the Cult of the Virgin Mary, 1976; Queen Victoria's Sketchbook, 1980; Joan of Arc: The Image of Female Heroism, 1981; Monuments and Maidens: The Allegory of the Female Form, 1985; L'Atalante, 1993; Managing Monsters: Six Myths of Our Time, 1994; From the Beast to the Blonde: On Fairy Tales and Their Tellers, 1994; No Go the Bogeyman: Scaring, Lulling and Making Mock, 1998; Fantastic Metamorphoses, Other Worlds, 2002; Signs and Wonders: Essays on Literature and Culture, 2003; Phantasmagoria: Spirit Visions, Metaphors, and Media, 2006. Fiction: In a Dark Wood, 1977; The Skating Party, 1983; The Lost Father, 1988; Indigo, 1992; The Mermaids in the Basement, 1993; Wonder Tales (editor), 1994; The Leto Bundle, 2001; Murderers I Have Known, 2004; Cancellanda, 2004; Libretti: The Legs of the Queen of Sheba, 1991; In the House of Crossed Desires 1996. Other: Children's and juvenile books; Contributions to various publications, artists' catalogues, radio and television; Exhibitions (curator): The Inner Eye, South Bank Touring, Manchester, Swansea, Dulwich, 1996; Metamorphing, Wellcome Trust, Science Museum, London, 2002-03; Eyes, Lies & Illusions (curatorial advisor), Hayward Gallery, London, 2005; Only Make-Believe: Ways of Playing, Compton Verney, 2005. Honours: Fellow, Royal Society of Literature, 1985; Honorary D Litt, University of Exeter, 1995; Hon Dr, Sheffield Hallam University, 1995; Hon D Litt, University of York, 1997; Hon D Litt, University of St Andrew's, 1998; Hon Dr, Tavistock Institute, University of East London, 1999; Katharine Briggs Award, 1999; Rosemary Crawshay Prize, British Academy, 2000; Fellow, British Academy, 2005; Hon D Litt, University of Kent; Hon D Litt, University of Oxford, 2006; Hon D Litt, University of Leicester, 2006. Memberships: Arts Council, literature panel, 1992-97; British Library, advisory council, 1992-97; Charter 88, council member, 1990-97; PEN; Trustee, Artangel; Chevalier des Arts et des Lettres, 2000; Stella di Solidareità dell'Ordine delle Arti e Lettere, 2005. Address: c/o Rogers, Coleridge and White, 20 Powis Mews, London W11 1NJ, England. Website: www.marinawarner.com

WARNOCK Helen Mary, (Baroness), b. 14 April 1924, England. Philosopher; Writer. m. Sir Geoffrey Warnock, 1949, deceased 1995, 2 sons, 3 daughters. Education: MA, BPhil, Lady Margaret Hall, Oxford. Appointments: Fellow and Tutor in Philosophy, 1949-66, Senior Research Fellow, 1976-84, St Hugh's College, Oxford; Headmistress, Oxford High School, 1966-72; Talbot Research Fellow, Lady Margaret Hall, Oxford, 1972-76; Mistress, Girton College, Cambridge, 1985-91; Visiting Professor of Rhetoric, Gresham College, 2000-2001; Several visiting lectureships. Publications: Ethics Since 1900, 1960, 3rd edition, 1978; J-P Sartre, 1963; Existentialist Ethics, 1966; Existentialism, 1970; Imagination, 1976; Schools of Thought, 1977; What Must We Teach? (with T Devlin), 1977; Education: A Way Forward, 1979; A Question of Life, 1985; Teacher Teach Thyself, 1985; Memory, 1987; A Common Policy for Education, 1988; Universities: Knowing Our Minds, 1989; The Uses of Philosophy, 1992; Imagination and Time, 1994; Women Philosophers (editor), 1996; An Intelligent Person's Guide to Ethics, 1998; A Memoir: People and Places, 2000; Making Babies, 2002; Nature and Mortality, 2003; Utilitarianism (editor), 2003. Honours: 15 honorary doctorates; Honorary Fellow, Lady Margaret Hall, Oxford, 1984, St Hugh's College, Oxford, 1985, Hertford College, Oxford, 1997; Dame Commander of the Order of the British Empire, 1984; Life Peer, 1985; Albert Medal, RSA; Honorary Fellowship, British Academy, 2000. Address: 60 Church Street, Great Bedwyn, Wiltshire SN8 3PF, England.

WARWICK Kevin, b. 9 February 1954, Coventry, England. University Professor. m. Irena Voračkova, 1 son, 1 daughter. Education: BSc (1st), Electrical and Electronic Engineering, Aston University, 1979; PhD, DIC, 1982, DSc, 1993, Computer Control, Imperial College, London; DrSc, Technical Cybernetics, Czech Academy of Science, Prague, 1994. Appointments: Telecomms Engineer, BT, 1970-76; Lecturer, University of Newcastle on Tyne, 1982-85; Research Lecturer, Oxford University, 1985-87; Senior Lecturer, Warwick University, 1987-88; Professor of Cybernetics, University of Reading, 1988-. Publications: March of the Machines, 1997; QI: the Quest for Intelligence, 2000; I Cyborg, 2002. Honours: Honorary Member, Academy of Science, St Petersburg, 1999; Future of Health Technology Award, MIT, 200; IEE (IET) Achievement Award, 2004. Memberships: Chartered Engineer (C Eng); Fellow, Institute of Engineering & Technology (FIET); Fellow, City & Guilds of London Institute (FCGI).

WARWICK (Marie) Dionne, b. 12 December 1940, East Orange, New Jersey, USA. Singer. m. Bill Elliott, divorced 1975, 2 sons. Education: Hartt College of Music, Hartford, Connecticut; Masters Degree, Music. Appointments: Singer, Gospel Groups, The Drinkard Singers, The Gospelaires; Solo Singer, 1962-; Numerous concerts, tours and benefit shows worldwide. Creative Works: Singles: Anyone Who Had A Heart, 1964; Walk On By, 1964; A Message To Michael, 1966; Alfie, 1967; I Say A Little Prayer, 1967; Do You Know The Way To San José, 1968; This Girl's In Love With You, 1969; I'll Never Fall In Love Again, 1970; Then Came You, 1974; I'll Never Love This Way Again, 1979; Heartbreaker, 1982; All The Love In The World, 1983; That's What Friends Are For (AIDS charity record), 1985; Albums include: Greatest Hits, 1990; Dionne Warwick Sings Cole Porter, 1990; Hidden Gems: The Best of Dionne Warwick, Volume 2, 1992; Friends Can Be Lovers, with Whitney Houston, 1993; Dionne Warwick and Placido Domingo, 1994; Aquarela do Brasil, 1994; From the Vaults, 1995; Dionne Sings Dionne, 1998; I Say a Little Prayer For You, 2000. Honours: Top Selling Female Artist, NARM, 1964; Best Female Pop Vocal Performance, 1969, 1970, 1980; Best Contemporary Vocal Performance, 1971; Best Female R&B Vocal Performance, 1980; Best Pop Performance, Duo or Group, 1987; Song of the Year, 1987; Star on Hollywood's Walk of Fame, 1985; NAACP Key of Life Award, 1990; CORE Humanitarian Award, 1992; Nosotros Golden Eagle Humanitarian Award, 1992; City of New York Award, Contribution to AIDS Research, 1987; DIVA Award, 1992; Platinum and Gold Discs. Address: c/o Arista Records Inc, 6 West 57th Street, New York, NY 10019, USA.

WASHINGTON Denzel, b. 28 December 1954, Mount Vernon, New York, USA. Film Actor. m. Pauletta Pearson, 1983, 2 sons, 2 daughters. Education: Fordham University; American Conservatory Theatre, San Francisco. Creative Works: Off-Broadway appearances include: Ceremonies in Dark Old Men; When the Chickens Come Home to Roost; A Soldier's Play; Films include: A Soldier's Story, 1984; The Mighty Quinn, 1987; Cry Freedom, 1987; Heart Condition, 1989; Glory, 1990; Love Supreme, 1990; Mo' Better Blues,

1990; Ricochet, 1991; Mississippi Masala, 1991; Much Ado About Nothing, 1992; Malcolm X, 1992; The Pelican Brief, 1993; Philadelphia, 1993; Devil in a Blue Dress, 1995; Courage Under Fire, 1996; The Preachers Wife, 1996; Fallen, 1997; He Got Game, 1998; The Siege, 1998; The Bone Collector, 1999; The Hurricane, 1999; Remember the Titans, 2001; Training Day, 2001; John Q, 2002; Antwone Fisher, 2002; Out of Time, 2003; Man on Fire, 2004; Manchurian Candidate, 2004; Inside Man, 2006; Déjà vu, 2006; American Gangster, 2007; The Great Debaters, 2007. Honours include: Academy Award, Best Supporting Actor, 1990; Awards for Best Actor, Supporting Actor and Director, National Association for the Advancement of Colored People Awards, 2003. Address: c/o ICM, 8942 Wilshire Boulevard, Beverly Hills, CA 90211, USA.

WASTERLAIN Claude, b. 15 April 1935, Courcelles, Belgium. Neurologist. m. Anne Thomsin, 1 son. Education: CSc, 1957, MD, 1961, University of Liege; LSc, Molecular Biology, Free University of Brussels, 1969. Appointments: Resident, 1964-66, Chief Resident, 1966-67, Medical College, New York City; Assistant Professor, Cornell University, 1970-75; Associate Professor, Cornell University Medical College, 1975-76; Associate Professor, 1976-79, Professor of Neurology, 1979-, University of California, Los Angeles School of Medicine; Chair, VA Greater Los Angeles Health Care System, 1997-. Publications: Over 400 articles; Many books and book chapters; Status Epilepticus (book), 1984; Neonated Seizures (book). Honours: Milken Award for Basic Research in Epilepsy, American Epilepsy Association, 1992; Golden Hammer Teaching Award, University of California, Los Angeles. Memberships include: American Neurological Association; Fellow, American Academy of Neurology; American Epilepsy Society; American and International Societies for Neurochemistry. Address: Neurology Department (127), VA Medical Center, 11301 Wilshire Boulevard, West Los Angeles, CA 90073, USA.

WATANABE Toru, b. 2 May 1960, Niigata, Japan. Medical Doctor; Paediatrician. m. Chieko Hoshi, 2 sons, 2 daughters. Education: MD, Niigata University, 1985; PhD, Niigata University Graduate School of Medicine and Dental Science, 2002. Appointments: Resident, 1985-90, Staff, 1991-, Department of Paediatrics, Niigata City General Hospital. Publications: 76 articles in medical journals including: Pediatric Nephrology; Nephron; Clinical Nephrology; Journal of Clinical Endocrinology and Metabolism; Pediatrics International; Pediatrics; European Journal of Pediatrics. Honours: Plenary Presentation Award, 1994, Best Clinical Research Award, 1999, Japanese Society for Pediatric Nephrology; Top 100 Health Professionals Pinnacle of Achievement Award, 2005, Salute to Greatness, 2005, Leading Health Professionals of the World, 2005, Diploma of Achievement in Medicine and Healthcare Award, 2005, International Biographical Centre; American Medal of Honor, 2005, American Biographical Association; Listed in Who's Who publications and biographical dictionaries. Memberships: Japanese Society for Paediatric Nephrology; International Pediatric Nephrology Association; Editorial Board of Pediatric Nephrology; Japan Pediatric Society; Japanese Society of Nephrology. Address: Department of Paediatrics, Niigata City General Hospital, 463-7 Shumoku, Chuoku, Niigata 950-1197, Japan. E-mail: twata@hosp.niigata.niigata.jp

WATELAIN Eric, b. 18 October 1971, France. Senior Lecturer. m. Laure de Thierry de Faletans, 1 son, 2 daughters. Education: Master, University of Lille, 1995; Certificate, Lifesavers France National Degree, 1996;

PhD, Lille University, France, 1999; Research Habilitation Direction Degree, 2006. Appointments: Temporary Assistant Teaching and Research, 1999-2000, Senior Lecturer, Human Movement Analysis, Specialist in Adapted Physical Activity and Locomotion, 2000-, University of Valenciennes, France; Assistant Physician, Medicine, Central Hospital, Lille, France, 2002-. Publications: Articles on the evaluation and control of human locomotion in scientific medical journals including: Gait and Posture; Clinical Biomechanics; Archives of Physical Medicine and Rehabilitation. Memberships: French Association of Research in Physical Activity and Sport; Biomechanics Society, France; International Society of Gait and Posture Research. Address: LAMIH, University of Valenciennes le Mont Houy, 59313 Valenciennes, Cedex 9, France. E-mail: eric.watelain@university-valenciennes.fr

WATERS General Sir (Charles) John, b. 2 September 1935, Rangoon, Burma. Retired Army Officer. m. Hilary Doyle Nettleton, 3 sons. Education: Oundle; Royal Military Academy, Sandhurst; Army Staff College, Camberley, 1967; Royal College of Defence Studies, 1982. Appointments: Commissioned into Gloucestershire Regiment, 1955; Instructor Army Staff College, 1973-75; Commanding Officer, 1 Battalion The Gloucestershire Regiment, 1975-77; Colonel General Staff, 1 Armoured Division, 1977-79; Commanded 3 Infantry Brigade, 1979-81; Royal College of Defence Studies, 1982; Deputy Commander, Land Forces, Falklands, 1982; Commander 4 Armoured Division, 1983-85; Commandant, Staff College, Camberley, 1986-88; General Officer Commanding and Director of Operations, Northern Ireland, 1988-90 (dispatches 1990); Colonel, The Gloucestershire Regiment, 1985-91; Colonel Commandant, Prince of Wales Division, 1988-92; Commander-in-Chief, United Kingdom Land Forces, 1990-93; Deputy Supreme Allied Commander Europe, 1993-94; ADC General to HM The Queen, 1992-94; Magistrate 1998-2006. Honours: OBE, 1977; CBE, 1981; KCB, 1988; GCB, 1995; Honorary Colonel, Royal Devon Yeomanry, 1991-97, Wessex Yeomanry, 1991-97; Kermit Roosevelt Lecturer, 1992; Deputy Lieutenant, Devon, 2001-. Memberships: Advisory Council, Victory Memorial Museum, Arlon, Belgium, 1988-97; Chairman of the Council, National Army Museum, 2002-05; President, Officers' Association, 1997-2006; County President, Devon Royal British Legion, 1997-2002; Admiral: Army Sailing Association, 1990-93, Infantry Sailing Association, 1990-93; Member of the Council, Cheltenham College, 1990-97; Governor, Colyton Primary School, 1996-2002; President, Honiton and District Agricultural Society, 2004; Patron, Royal Albert Memorial Museum, 2006-. Address: c/o Lloyds Bank, Colyton, Devon EX23 6JS, England.

WATERS Brian Richard Anthony, b. 27 March 1944, Liverpool, England. Architect. m. Myriam Leiva Arenas. Education: City of London School, 1958-63; Degree and Diploma in Architecture, St Johns, Cambridge, 1963-68; PCL Diploma in Town Planning, 1969-71; RIBA, 1972; MRTPI, 1973. Appointments: City Corporation Planning Department, 1968-70; Greater London Council Architects Department, 1969-70; Shankland Cox & Associates, 1970-72; Founder, The Boisot Waters Cohen Partnership, 1972; Director of Planning, HTA, 2007-. Publications: Joint Publishing Editor, Planning in London; International Building Press Award; 4 commendations for articles in Architect's Journal, Building, RIBA Journal; Winner, Magazine of the Year, Planning in London, 2007; Current Planning correspondent of Architects' Journal. Honours: Master, Worshipful Company of Chartered Architects, 2002-03; Highly Commended, Best Personal Contribution, London Planning Awards, 2007. Memberships:

RIBA Council; President, 2007-09, Association of Consultant Architects; London Planning & Development Forum; Society of Architect Artists; Old Citizens' Association; City of London School Alumni. Address: 17 Lexham Mews, London W8 6JW, England. E-mail: brian@bwcp.co.uk

WATERTON-ANDERSON David Alexander Richard, b. 16 May 1944, Hazlewood Castle, Yorkshire, England. m. Elizabeth McLauchlan. Education: Kelvinside Academy, Glasgow; St Andrew's College, Bradfield, Reading; BA (hons), Fine Art and History, University of Leeds; Certificate of Medical & Orthopaedic Technologies, University of Dundee. Appointments: Various business ventures (restaurant/retail); 3M Health Care; Rank Organisation; De la Rue Security Express. Publications: Tartan as Armorial Ensign (thesis), 1966; Anderson Heraldry, 1994; Heraldic Legacy of Gilling Castle, 2007; Author/presenter, 14 nostalgia videos on Scottish cities, towns and districts, 1996-2000. Honours: Venerable Order of St John, Air Ambulance Wing, Service Medal, 1979; Order of Malta 'Lourdes' Medal, 1994; Companion of the Order of Malta, 1994; Jerusalem Pilgrim's Cross of Honour, (Bronze) 1997, (Silver) 1999; Knight of St Gregory the Great (Civil Division), 2006. Memberships: Life Member: Royal Celtic Society; Scottish Tartans Society; Scottish Tartans Authority; National Trust for Scotland; Chairman/Editor, Anderson Association; Member: English Heritage; St John's Historical Society; Society of Scottish Presidents; The Heraldry Society of Scotland; President, The Friends of Pontefract Castle; Pipe Major, Clan Lachlan Pipe Band; Personal Piper to the Duke of Hamilton & Brandon; Apostalship of the Sea, Leeds Diocese Representative. Address: Stapleton Lodge, High Street, Carlton-juxta-Snaith, North Yorkshire DN14 9LU, England.

WATSON Emily, b. 14 January 1967, London, England. Actress. m. Jack Waters, 1 daughter. Creative Works: Films: Breaking the Waves; Mill on the Floss; Metroland; The Boxer; Hilary and Jackie; Angela's Ashes, 199l; The Cradle Will Rock; Trixie; The Luzhin Defense; Gosford Park, 2001; Equilibrium, 2002; Red Dragon, 2002; Punch-Drunk Love, 2002; Blossoms and Blood, 2003; Life and Death of Peter Sellers, 2004; Separate Lies, 2004; Wah Wah, 2005; The Proposition, 2005; Corpse Bride, 2005; Crusade in Jean, 2005; Miss Potter, 2006; The Water Horse: Legend of the Deep, 2007; Fireflies in the Garden, 2008; Theatre includes: Uncle Vanya; Twelfth Night. Honours include: New York Society of Film Critics Award; National Society of Film Critics Award. Address: c/o ICM Ltd, Oxford House, 76 Oxford Street, London W1N 0AX, England.

WATSON James Dewey, b. 6 April 1928, Chicago, Illinois, USA. m. Elizabeth Lewis, 1968, 2 sons. Education: Graduated, Zoology, University of Chicago, 1947; Postgraduate Research, University of Indiana, PhD, 1950. Appointments: Research into viruses, University of Copenhagen, 1950; Cavendish Laboratory, Cambridge University, 1951; Senior Research Fellow, Biology, California Institute of Technology, 1953-55; Several positions, Department of Biology, Harvard University; Assistant Professor, 1955-58, Associate Professor, 1958-61, Professor, 1961-68; Director, 1968, President, 1994-, Quantitative Biology, Cold Spring Harbor Laboratory; Associate Director, NIH (USA), 1988-89; Director, National Center for Human Genome Research, NIH, 1989-92; Newton Abraham Visiting Professor, Oxford University, England, 1994; Research to help determine the structure of DNA. Publications: Molecular Biology of the Gene, 1965, 1970, 1976; The Double Helix, 1968; The DNA Story, 1981; Recombinant DNA: A Short Course, 1983; The Molecular Biology of the Cell, 1986; Recombinant DNA, 1992; Avoid Boring People: Lessons from a Life in Science; Papers on the structure of DNA, on protein synthesis and on the induction of cancer by viruses. Honours: Joint Winner, Nobel Prize for Physiology or Medicine, 1962; John J Carty Gold Medal, 1971; Medal of Freedom, 1977; Gold Medal Award, National Institute of Social Sciences, 1984; Kaul Foundation Award for Excellence, 1992; Capley Medal of Royal Society, 1993; National Biotechnology Venture Award, 1993; Lomosonov Medal, 1994; National Medal of Science, 1997; Liberty Medal Award, 2000; Benjamin Franklin Medal, 2001; Gairdner Award, 2002; Lotos Club Medal of Merit, 2004; Othmer Gold Medal, Chemical Heritage Foundation, 2005. Address: Cold Spring Harbor Laboratory, PO Box 100, Cold Spring Harbor, New York NY 11724, USA.

WATSON Thomas Sturges (Tom), b. 4 September 1949, Kansas City, USA. Golfer. m. Linda Tova Rubin, 1973, 1 son, 1 daughter. Education: Stanford University. Appointments: Professional, 1971-; British Open Champion, 1975, 1977, 1980, 1982, 1983; Record low aggregate for British Open of 268, record two single round scores of 65, lowest final 36-hole score of 130, Turnberry, 1977; Won US Masters Title, 1977, 1981; Won US Open, 1982; Won World Series, 1975, 1977, 1980; Winner, numerous other open championships, 1974-; First player ever to win in excess of $500,000 in prize money in one season, 1980; Ryder Cup Player, Captain, 1993-; Senior Tour victories: 1999 Bank One Championship; 2000 IR Senior Tour Championship; 2001 Senior PGA Championship; 2002 Senior Tour Championship; Senior British Open 2003. Publication: Getting Back into Basics (jointly), 1992; Tom Watson's Strategic Golf. Honours include: Top Money Winner on US PGA Circuit, 1977, 1978, 1979, 1980; US PGA Player of the Year, 1977, 1978, 1979, 1980, 1982; PGA World Golf Hall of Fame, 1988; Payne Stewart Award, 2003. Address: PGA America, PO Box 109801, 100 Avenue of the Champions, Palm Beach Gardens, FL 33410, USA.

WATTS Charlie (Charles Robert), b. 2 June 1941, England. Musician. m. Shirley Anne Shepherd, 1964, 1 daughter. Appointments: Drummer, Rolling Stones, 1963-. Creative Works: Albums with The Rolling Stones include: The Rolling Stones, 1964; The Rolling Stones No 2, 1965; Out of Our Heads, 1965; Aftermath, 1966; Big Hits, 1966; Got LIVE if You Want It!, 1967; Between the Buttons, 1967; Their Satanic Majesties Request, 1967; Beggars Banquet, 1968; Let it Bleed, 1969; Get Yer Ya-Ya's Out!, 1970; Stone Age, 1971; Sticky Fingers, 1971; Goats Head Soup, 1973; It's Only Rock 'N' Roll, 1974; Black and Blue, 1976; Love You Live, 1977; Some Girls, 1978; Emotional Rescue, 1980; Tattoo You, 1981; Still Life, 1981; Dirty Work, 1986; Steel Wheels, 1989; Flashpoint, 1991; Voodoo Lounge, 1994; Stripped, 1995; Bridges to Babylon, 1997; Forty Licks, 2002; Live Licks, 2004; Solo albums include: Charlie Watts Orchestra - Live at Fulham Town Hall, 1986; From One Charlie, 1992; Warm and Tender, 1993; From One Charlie, 1995; Long Ago and Far Away, 1996; Anybody Seen My Baby, 1997; Saint of Me, 1998; Out of Control, 1998; Don't Stop, 2002. Films include: Sympathy For the Devil, 1969; Gimme Shelter, 1970; Ladies and Gentlemen, The Rolling Stones, 1977; Let's Spend the Night Together, 1983; Flashpoint, 1991. Publication: Ode to a High Flying Bird, 1965; According to the Rolling Stones (joint autobiography), 2003. Address: c/o Munro Sounds, 5 Church Row, Wandsworth Plain, London SW18 1ES, England.

WAX Ruby, b. 19 April 1953, Illinois, USA. Comedienne; Actress. m. Edward Richard Morison Bye, 1988, 1 son, 2 daughters. Education: Berkeley University; Royal Scottish

Academy of Music and Drama. Appointments: With Crucible Theatre, 1976, Royal Shakespeare Company, 1978-82. Creative Works: TV includes: Not the Nine O'Clock News, 1982-83; Girls on Top, 1983-85; Don't Miss Wax, 1985-87; Hit and Run, 1988; Full Wax, 1987-92; Ruby Wax Meets..., 1996, 1997, 1998; Ruby, 1997, 1998, 1999; Ruby's American Pie, 1999, 2000; Hot Wax, 2001; The Waiting Game, 2001, 2002; Ruby, 2002; Films include: Miami Memoirs, 1987; East Meets Wax, 1988; Class of '69; Ruby Takes a Trip, 1992; Tara Road, 2005; Ruby Wax with ..., 2003; Popetown (series), 2003; Plays include: Wax Acts (one woman show), 1992; Stressed (one woman show), 2000. Publication: How Do You Want Me? (autobiography), 2002. Honours: Performer of the Year, British Comedy Awards, 1993. Address: c/o ICM, Oxford House, 76 Oxford Street, London W1N 0AY, England.

WAY Danny, b. 15 April 1974, Portland, Oregon, USA. Professional Skateboarder. m. Kari Way, 2 sons. Career: Started skateboarding 1988, Turned professional for Alein Workshop 1989. Film appearances include: The DC video, 2002; Alien Workshop – mosaic, 2003. TV appearances include: Legends or the Extreme, 2003. Honours: MTV Sports and Music Festival 1st Place in highest air, 1999; Holds the Guinness Book of World Records highest air on a skateboard at 18'+, and longest air on a skateboard at 79'; Thrasher Magazine Skater of the Year, 1992 and 2004; Big Air Gold Medal, 2004, 2005; First person to jump the Great Wall of China on a skateboard or any other non-motorized vehicle, 2005. Address: Carlsbad, California, USA.

WEAVER Sigourney, b. 8 October 1949, New York, USA. Actress. m. James Simpson, 1984, 1 daughter. Creative Works: Films include: Annie Hall, 1977; Tribute to a Madman, 1977; Camp 708, 1978; Alien, 1979; Eyewitness, 1981; The Year of Living Dangerously, 1982; Deal of the Century, 1983; Ghostbusters, 1984; Une Femme ou Deux, 1985; Half Moon Street, 1986; Aliens, 1986; Gorillas in the Mist, 1988; Ghostbusters II, 1989; Aliens 3, 1992; 1492: Conquest of Paradise, 1993; Dave, 1993; Death and the Maiden, 1994; Jeffrey, 1995; Copycat, 1996; Snow White in the Black Forest, 1996; Ice Storm, 1996; Alien Resurrection, 1997; A Map of the World, 1999; Galaxy Quest, 1999; Get Bruce, 1999; Company Man, 1999; Airframe, 1999; Heartbreakers, 2001; Tadpole, 2002; The Guys, 2002; Holes, 2003; The Village, 2004; Snow Cake, 2006; The TV Set, 2006; Infamous, 2006; Happily N'Ever Afater, 2006; The Girl in the Park, 2007; Be Kind Rewind, 2008; Vantage Point, 2008. Honours include: Golden Globe Best Actress Award, 1988; Best Supporting Actress Golden Globe Award, 1988. Address: c/o ICM, 8942 Wilshire Boulevard, Beverly Hills, CA 90211, USA.

WEBB David John, b. 1 September 1953. Professor. m. Margaret Jane Cullen, 1984, 3 sons. Education: MB BS, 1977, MD, 1990, University of London; DSc, University of Edinburgh, 2000. Appointments: House Officer Posts, Royal London Hospital scheme, 1977-78; Senior House Officer, Chelmsford Hospitals, 1978-79; Senior House Officer, Stoke Mandeville Hospital, 1979-80; Registrar, Royal London Hospital, 1980-82; Registrar, 1982-85, MRC Clinical Scientist, MRC BP Unit, 1982-85, Western Infirmary, Glasgow; Lecturer, Clinical Pharmacology, St George's Medical School, 1985-89; Senior Registrar in Medicine, St George's Hospital, London, 1985-89; Consultant Physician, Lothian University Hospitals NHS Trust, 1990-; Senior Lecturer, Medicine, 1990-95, Christison Professor of Therapeutics and Clinical Pharmacology, 1995-, Director, Clinical Research Centre, 1990-96, Head, University Department of Medicine, 1997-98,

Head, Department of Medical Sciences, 1998-2001, Wellcome Trust Research Leave Fellowship, and Leader, Wellcome Trust Cardiovascular Research Initiative, 1998-2001, Convenor, Cardiovascular Interdisciplinary Group, 1999-2000, Head, Centre for Cardiovascular Science, 2000-04, University of Edinburgh; Director, Education Programme, Wellcome Trust Clinical Research Facility, Edinburgh, 1998-; Chairman, New Drugs Committee, 2001-05, Chairman, 2005-, Scottish Medicines Consortium. Publications: The Molecular Biology & Pharmacology of the Endothelins, 1995; The Endothelium in Hypertension, 1996; Vascular Endothelium in Human Physiology and Pathophysiology, 1999; The Year in Therapeutics Vol 1, 2005. Memberships: Royal College of Physicians Edinburgh; British Hypertension Society; British Pharmacological Society; High Blood Pressure Foundation; International Union for Pharmacology. Address: Queen's Medical Research Institute, Centre for Cardiovascular Science, University of Edinburgh, E3 22, 47 Little France Crescent, Edinburgh, EH16 4TJ, Scotland. E-mail: d.j.webb@ed.ac.uk

WEBB Robert Gravem, 18 February 1927, Long Beach, California, USA. Retired Professor of Biological Sciences. m. Patricia A (Peden) Webb, 1 son. Education: BS, 1950, MS, 1952, University of Oklahoma; PhD, University of Kansas, 1960. Appointments: University of Texas at El Paso, 1962-93; Retired, 1993. Publications: 1 book: Reptiles of Oklahoma, 135 publications dealing with amphibians and reptiles. Honours: Faculty Research Award, University of Texas at El Paso, 1978; President, Society for the Study of Amphibians and Reptiles, 1980. Memberships: Herpetologists' League; American Society of Ichthyologists and Herpetologists; Society for the Study of Amphibians and Reptiles; Societas Europeae Herpetologica; Southwestern Association of Naturalists. Address: Department of Biological Sciences, University of Texas at El Paso, El Paso, TX 79968-0519, USA. E-mail: rgwebb@utep.edu

WEBSTER Henry de Forest, b. 22 April 1927, New York, USA. Neuroscientist. m. Marion Havas Webster, 4 sons, 1 daughter. Education: BA, Chemistry (cum laude), Amherst College, Massachusetts, 1948; MD, Harvard Medical School, Boston, Massachusetts, 1952. Appointments: Postgraduate training, Internal Medicine, Neurology, Neuropathology, 1952-59, Instructor, Neurology to Assistant Professor, Neuropathology, Harvard Medical School, 1959-66; Associate Professor, Professor, Neurology, University of Miami Medical School, 1966-69; Head, Section Cell Neuropathology, 1969-97, Chief, Laboratory of Experimental Neuropathology, 1984-97, Emeritus Scientist, 1997-, NINDS, National Institute of Health, Bethesda, Maryland, USA. Publications: Co-author of book: Fine Structure of the Nervous System, 1970, 1976, 1991; Author of book: Cellular Neuroscience: Projects and Images 1957-1997, 2006; Book chapters, reviews and scientific articles. Honours: Weil Award, American Association of Neuropathologists, 1960; Superior Service Award, US Public Health Service, 1977; Alexander von Humboldt Foundation (Germany) Senior US Scientist Award, 1985; Honorary Professor, Norman Bethune University Medical Science, 1991; Scientific Award, Peripheral Neuropathy Association, 1994; Award for Meritorious Contributions to Neuropathology; American Association of Neuropathologists, 2001. Memberships: American Association of Neuropathologists, President, 1978-79; International Society of Neuropathology, President, 1986-90; Honorary Member, International Society of Neuropathology and Japanese Society of Neuropathology; Fellow, Royal College of Medicine. Address: National Institutes of Health, Bldg 10, Rm 5B-16, Bethesda, MD 20892-1400, USA. E-mail: websterh@ninds.nih.gov

WEBSTER John Barron, (Jack Webster), b. 8 July 1931, Maud, Aberdeenshire, Scotland. Journalist. m. Eden Keith, 17 February 1956, 3 sons. Education: Maud School; Peterhead Academy; Robert Gordon's College, Aberdeen. Publications: The Dons, 1978; A Grain of Truth, 1981; Gordon Strachan, 1984; Another Grain of Truth, 1988; Alistair MacLean: A Life, 1991; Famous Ships of the Clyde, 1993; The Flying Scots, 1994; The Express Years, 1994; In the Driving Seat, 1996; The Herald Years, 1996; Webster's World (1997); From Dali to Burrell (1997); Reo Stakis Story (1999); The Auld Hoose (2005). Television Films: The Webster Trilogy, 1992; John Brown: The Man Who Drew a Legend, 1994. Honours: Bank of Scotland Awards, Columnist of the Year, 1996; UK Speaker of the Year, 1996. Address: 58 Netherhill Avenue, Glasgow G44 3XG, Scotland.

WEBSTER Richard, b. 6 May 1933, Derby, England. Scientist. m. Mary Buxton, 1 son, 2 daughters. Education: BSc, Chemistry, University of Sheffield, 1954; D Phil, Oxford University, 1966; DSc, Sheffield University, 1983. Appointments: Soil Chemist, Northern Rhodesia (Zambia) Government, 1957-61; Research Associate, Oxford University, 1961-68; Senior Scientific Officer, 1968-71, Principal Scientific Officer, 1971-79, Soil Survey of England and Wales; Senior Research Scientist, CSIRO Division of Soils, Australia, 1973-74; Senior Principal Scientific Officer, Soils Department, Rothamsted Experimental Station, 1979-90; Maître de Recherche, Ecole Nationale Supérieure des Mines de Paris, 1990; Chief Editor of Catena, 1990-95; Directeur de Recherche, Institut National de la Recherche Agronomique, France, 1990-91; Visiting Scientist, Rothamsted Experimental Station, 1991-92, 1993-94; Guest Professor, Swiss Federal Institute of Technology, 1992-94; Professor, Eidgenössische Forschungsanstalt für Wald, Schnee und Landschaft (WSL), Switzerland, 1994-95; Editor-in Chief, European Journal of Soil Science, 1995-2003; Visiting Professor in Soil Science, University of Reading, 1997-; Currently Deputy Editor, European Journal of Soil Science; Senior Research Fellow, Rothamsted, 2003-; Visiting Professor, Universidad Nacional Autónoma de México, 2006-. Publications: Author of more than 200 papers in scientific journals, conference proceedings and other collected works; 3 text books; 3 atlases; 20 technical reports. Honour: Docteur Honoris Causa, Louvain, 1995. Membership: British Society of Soil Science. Address: Rothamsted Research, Harpenden, Hertfordshire AL5 2JQ, England. E-mail: richard.webster@bbsrc.ac.uk

WEBSTER Sue Lynn, b. 9 September 1967, Leicester, England. Artist. Education: Foundation Course, Cheltenham Art College, 1985-86; BA (Hons), Fine Art, Nottingham Trent University, 1986-89; Artist in Residence, Dean Clough, Halifax, West Yorkshire, 1989-92. Career: Solo Exhibitions: British Rubbish, IAS, London, 1996; Home Chance, 20 Rivington Street, London, 1997; WOW, Modern Art, London, 1998; The New Barbarians, Chisenhale Gallery, London, 1999; I ♥ YOU, Deitch Projects, New York, 2000; British Wildlife, Modern Art, London, 2000; Masters of the Universe, Deste Foundation, Athens, 2000; Instant Gratification, Gagosian Gallery, Beverly Hills, 2001; Ghastly Arrangements, Milton Keynes Gallery, 2002; Tim Noble & Sue Webster, P S 1 MoMA, New York, 2003; Modern Art is Dead, Modern Art, London, 2004; Tim Noble & Sue Webster, Museum of Fine Arts, Boston, 2004; The Joy of Sex, Kukje Gallery, Seoul, 2005; The Glory Hole, Bortolami Dayan, New York, 2005; Polymorphous Perverse, The Freud Museum, London, 2006; Group Exhibitions: Lift, Atlantis Basement, Brick Lane, London, 1993; Hijack, New York, London, Berlin, 1994; The Fete Worse Than Death, Hoxton Square, London, 1994; Absolut Art, RCA, London, 1994; The Hanging Picnic, Hoxton Square, London, 1995; Sex and the British, Galerie Thaddaeus Ropac, Salzburg, Paris, 2000; Apocalypse – Beauty and Horror in Contemporary Art, RAA, London, 2000; Form Follows Fiction, Castello di Rivoli Museo – d'Arte Contemporanea, Turin, 2002; 2001 A Space Oddity, The Colony Room Club Artists' Show, London, 2001; State of Play, The Serpentine Gallery, London, 2004; New Blood, Saatchi Gallery, London, 2004; Monument To Now, Dakis Joannou Collection, Athens, 2004. Honours: BA (Hons) Degree in Fine Art. Memberships: The Colony Room Club. E-mail: info@scumbags.org.uk

WEERAPERUMA Claudia Valentine, b. 1 April 1961, Berne, Switzerland. Writer; Poet; Painter; Book Illustrator. m. Susunaga Weeraperuma. Education: Ecole des Beaux-Arts, Toulouse; Feusi Rüedi Schulen, Berne; Kunstgewerbeschule, Berne; Neue Mädchenschule, Berne; Licentiate, University of Berne; PhD, Comparative Religion, Somerset University. Publications: Contemplative Prayer in Christianity and Islam; Ocean of Compassion, poems; Hunt of Hera, novella; Jiddu Krishnamurti: Begegnungen und Gespräche, translation. Memberships: The Theosophical Society. Address: Villa Claudia, 338 Chemin du Colombier, 83460 Les Arcs sur Argens, France.

WEERAPERUMA Susunaga, b. 19 May 1934, Galle, Sri Lanka. Author. m. Claudia Valentine Weeraperuma. Education: Mahinda College, Galle; Ananda College, Colombo; MSc (Economics), London University; D Litt; Associate of the Library Association. Appointments: Senior Librarian, British Library; Senior Librarian, Parliamentary Library of South Australia. Publications: Religion and Philosophy: Major Religions of India; Divine Messengers of Our Time; Homage to Yogaswami; The Pure in Heart; Miraculous Waters of Lourdes; Servant of God: Sayings of a Self-Realised Sage Swami Ramdas; My Philosophy of Life; Autobiographical Writings: So You Want to Emigrate to England, Mohandas; Memoirs of an Oriental Philosopher; Library Science: Staff Exchanges in Librarianship; In-Service Training in Librarianship; The Role of Conferences in the Further Education of Librarians; Drama: The Pleasures of Life; Short Stories: The Holy Guru and Other Stories; The Stranger and Other Stories; Mysterious Stories of Sri Lanka; The Homeless Life and Other Stories; J Krishnamurti: J Krishnamurti As I Knew Him; Living and Dying from Moment to Moment; That Pathless Land; Bliss of Reality; Sayings of J Krishnamurti; A Bibliography of the Life and Teachings of Jiddu Krishnamurti; Jiddu Krishnamurti: A Bibliographical Guide; Buddhism: New Insights into Buddhism; Nirvana the Highest Happiness; The First and Best Buddhist Teachings. Memberships: Life Member, Vegetarian Society of the UK; Life Member, Indian Vegetarian Congress; Member, The Theosophical Society. Address: Villa Claudia, 338 chemin du Colombier, 83460 Les Arcs-sur-Argens, France.

WEIDNER Stanislaw Marian, b. 22 March 1947, Wrzesnia. Biochemist; Plant Physiologist. Educator. m. Maria Minakowska, 1 son, 1 daughter. Education: Master, Olsztyn University of Agricultural Technology, Poland, 1971; Doctor, 1980; Teaching: Biochemistry, Enzymology, Proteomics. Appointments: Assistant, 1971-80, Adjunct, 1980-89, Assistant Professor, 1989-92, Associate Professor, 1992-2001, Olsztyn University of Agricultural Technology; Visiting Professor, Okayama University, 1998-99; Professor, 2001-, Head of Department of Biochemistry, 2005-, University of Warmia and Mazury, Olsztyn; Achievements include research in possible involvement of cytoskeleton in regulation of cereal caryopses dormancy and germination. Publications: 65 refereed journal publications; 70 conference papers; Co-Editor, Biochemistry of Vertebrates, 1998, 2005 and 2007. Honours: Silver and Gold Cross for Achievements in Science and Educational Fields, President of Poland, 1994, 2003; Awards of the Minister of Education: 1990, 1999, 2006; State Commission for Scientific Research Grantee, 1993-96, 1997-01, 2004-07; COST project European Co-op, 1996-2001, 2008-09, 2007-2011; Recipient of several research fellowships. Memberships: Federation of European Biochemical Societies; Federation of European Societies of Plant Biology; International Society for Seed Science; Polish Society for Experimental Biology; Polish Botanical Society; Editorial Council, Acta Physiologiae Plantarum, 2000-. Address: Iwaszkiewicza Street 41/3, PL-10089 Olsztyn, Poland. E-mail: weidner@uwm.edu.pl Website: www.geocities.com/stanislawweidner/

WEINBERG Steven, b. 3 May 1933, New York, New York, USA. Professor of Science; Author. m. Louise Goldwasser, 6 July 1954, 1 daughter. Education: BA, Cornell University, 1954; Postgraduate Studies, Copenhagen Institute of Theoretical Physics, 1954-55; PhD, Princeton University, 1957. Appointments: Research Associate and Instructor, Columbia University, 1957-59; Research Physicist, Lawrence Radiation Laboratory, Berkeley, 1959-60; Faculty, 1960-64, Professor of Physics, 1964-69, University of California at Berkeley; Visiting Professor, 1967-69, Professor of Physics, 1979-83, Massachusetts Institute of Technology; Higgins Professor of Physics, Harvard University, 1973-83; Senior Scientist, Smithsonian Astrophysics Laboratory, 1973-83; Josey Professor of Science, University of Texas at Austin, 1982-; Senior Consultant, Smithsonian Astrophysics Observatory, 1983-; Various visiting professorships and lectureships. Publications: Gravitation and Cosmology: Principles and Application of the General Theory of Relativity, 1972; The First Three Minutes: A Modern View of the Origin of the Universe, 1977; The Discovery of Subatomic Particles, 1982; Elementary Particles and the Laws of Physics (with R Feynman), 1987; Dreams of a Final Theory, 1992; The Quantum Theory of Fields, Vol I, Foundations, 1995, Vol II, Modern Applications, 1996, Vol III, Supersymmetry, 2000; Facing Up, 2001; Glory and Terror, 2004. Contributions to: Books, periodicals and professional journals. Honours: 16 honorary doctoral degrees; J Robert Oppenheimer Memorial Prize, 1973; Dannie Heineman Prize in Mathematical Physics, 1977; American Institute of Physics-US Steel Foundation Science Writing Award, 1977; Nobel Prize in Physics, 1979; Elliott Cresson Medal, Franklin Institute, 1979; Madison Medal, Princeton University, 1991; National Medal of Science, National Science Foundation, 1991; Andrew Gemant Prize, American Institute of Physics, 1997; Piazzi Prize, Governments of Sicily and Palermo, 1998; Lewis Thomas Prize for the Scientist as Poet, Rockefeller University, 1999; Benjamin Franklin Medal of American Philosophical Society, 2004. Memberships: American Academy of Arts and Sciences; American Mediaeval Academy; American Philosophical Society; American Physical Society; Council on Foreign Relations; History of Science Society; International Astronomical Union; National Academy of Science; Phi Beta Kappa; Philosophical Society of Texas, president, 1994; Royal Society; Texas Institute of Letters. Address: c/o Department of Physics, University of Texas at Austin, Austin, TX 78712, USA.

WEINSTEIN Harvey, b. USA. Film Company Executive. Appointment: Co-Chair, Miramax Films Corporation, New York. Creative Works: Films produced jointly include: Playing for Keeps, 1986; Scandal, 1989; Strike it Rich, Hardware,

1990; A Rage in Harlem, 1991; The Crying Game, 1992; The Night We Never Met, Benefit of the Doubt, True Romance, 1993; Mother's Boys, Like Water for Chocolate, Pulp Fiction, Pret-A-Porter, 1994; Smoke, A Month by the Lake, The Crossing Guard, The Journey of August King, Things To Do In Denver When You're Dead, The Englishman Who Went Up A Hill But Came Down A Mountain, Blue in the Face, Restoration, 1995; Scream, The Pallbearer, The Last of the High Kings, Jane Eyre, Flirting with Disaster, The English Patient, Emma, The Crow; City of Angels, Beautiful Girls, 1996; Addicted to Love, 1997; Shakespeare in Love, 1998; Allied Forces, She's All That, My Life So Far, The Yards, 1999; Bounce, Scary Movie, Boys and Girls, Love's Labour Lost, Scream 3, About Adam, Chocolat, 2000; Spy Kids, Scary Movie 2, The Others, Lord of the Rings: The Fellowship of the Ring, Iris, 2001; Halloween: Resurrection, Spy Kids 2: Island of Lost Dreams, Lord of the Rings: The Two Towers, Gangs of New York, Chicago, 2002; Spy Kids 3-D: Game Over, Kill Bill: Vol 1, Scary Movie 3, Lord of the Rings: Return of The King, Cold Mountain, 2003; Kill Bill: Vol 2, Paper Clips, Fahrenheit 9/11, Shall We Dance, Cursed, The Aviator, 2004; Cursed, Sin City, The Adventures of Sharkboy and Lavagirl 3-D, Dracula III: Legacy, The Great Raid, An Unfinished Life, The Brothers Grimm, Underclassman, Proof, The Prophecy: Forsaken, Venom, Feast, Curandero, Derailed, 2005; Project Jay, Scary Movie 4, Clerks II, Pulse, Breaking and Entering, School for Scoundrels, Factory Girl, 2006; Grindhouse, The Last Legion, Sicko, Killshot, Death Proof, 1408, Planet Terror, Who's Your Caddy? The Nanny Diaries, Halloween, Rogue, The Mist, Awake, 2007; Hell Ride, Rambo, The Promotion, The No 1 Ladies' Detective Agency, Superhero Movie, 2008. Honour: Fellow, British Film Institute. Address: Miramax Films Corporation, 375 Greenwich Street, New York, NY 10013, USA.

WEINSTEIN Robert, b. 1954, USA. Film Producer; Executive. Appointment: Co-Chair, Miramax Films Corporation. Creative Works: Films produced include: Playing for Keeps (with Alan Brewer), 1986; Scandal (with Joe Boyd and Nik Powell), 1989; Strike it Rich, Hardware (with Nik Powell, Stephen Wooley, Trix Worrell), 1990; A Rage in Harlem (with Terry Glinwood, William Horberg, Nik Powell), 1991; The Night We Never Met (with Sidney Kimmel), Benefit of the Doubt, True Romance (with Gary Barber, Stanley Margolis, James G Robinson), 1993; Mother's Boys (with Randall Poster), Pulp Fiction (with Richard N Gladstein), Pret-A-Porter (with Ian Jessel), 1994; Smoke (with Satoru Iseki), A Month By the Lake (with Donna Gigliotti), The Crossing Guard (with Richard N Gladstein), The Journey of August King, Things To Do in Denver When You're Dead (with Marie Cantin), The Englishman Who Went Up a Hill But Came Down a Mountain (with Sally Hibbin, Robert Jones), Blue in the Face (with Harvey Keitel), Restoration (with Donna Gigliotti), 1995; Velvet Goldmine, Shakespeare in Love, 1998; Allied Forces, My Life So Far, The Yards, Music of the Heart, The Cider House Rules, 1999; Down To You, Boys and Girls, Scream 3, Love's Labour's Lost, Scary Movie, Chocolat, 2000; Spy Kids, Scary Movie 2, The Others, Lord of the Rings: The Fellowship of the Ring, Iris, 2001; Halloween: Resurrection, Spy Kids 2: Island of Lost Dreams, Lord of the Rings: The Two Towers, Gangs of New York, Chicago, 2002; Spy Kids 3-D: Game Over, Kill Bill: Vol 1, Scary Movie 2, Lord of the Rings: Return of the King, Cold Mountain, 2003; Kill Bill: Vol 2, Paper Clips, Fahrenheit 9/11, Shall We Dance, Cursed, The Aviator, 2004; Cursed, Sin City, The Adventures of Sharkboy and Lavagirl 3-D, Dracula III: Legacy, The Great Raid, An Unfinished Life, The Brothers Grimm, Underclassman, Proof, The Prophecy: Forsaken,

Venom, Feast, Curandero, Derailed, 2005; Project Jay, Scary Movie 4, Clerks II, Pulse, 2006; Breaking and Entering, School for Scoundrels, Factory Girl, 2006; Grindhouse, Sicko, Killshot, Death Proof, 1408, Planet Terror, Who's Your Caddy? The Nanny Diaries, Halloween, Rogue, The Mist, Awake, 2007; Hell Ride, Rambo, The Promotion, Superhero Movie, 2008. Honour: Fellow, British Film Institute. Address: Miramax Films Corporation, 375 Greenwich Street, New York, NY 10013, USA.

WEIR Kenneth Ross, b. 23 May 1938, Perthshire, Scotland. Piano Performer. Education: BA, Classical Greek, English, Music, 1960, B Mus (Hons), 1961, Otago University, New Zealand. MM, Piano Performance, Indiana University, USA, 1972; AMusD, Organ and Piano Performance, University of Michigan, Ann Arbor, USA, 1979. Appointments: Associate Instructor (part-time), Piano, Indiana University, 1970-72; Lecturer in Piano, Canterbury University, New Zealand, 1973-75; Part-time Tutor in Piano, University of Melbourne, Australia, 1981-83; Lecturer in Piano, West Australian Academy of Performing Arts, 1984-87; Head of Keyboard Studies, 1987-95, Visiting Specialist Teacher, Piano, 1995-, Sherborne School, Dorset, England; Concerts in the UK, Europe, USA, Asia, Australia and New Zealand including recitals with international soloists and ensembles; Broadcaster on ABC (Australia), Radio New Zealand and BBC. Publication: Research paper: Aspects of Rhythm in the Organ and Piano Music of Jehan Alain, 1986. Recordings: Choir and Organ, with Peter Godfrey, Conductor, New Zealand, 1970; Organ Music by Clérambault, Messiaen, Alain, New Zealand, 1975; Ginastera, Debussy, Granados, Haydn, 1992; Rachmaninoff, Debussy, Franck, 2001. Honours: James Clark Prize in Greek, Otago, 1959; Evans Travelling Scholarship in Music, Otago, 1963-65; International Prize, St Albans Organ Festival, 1967; Highest Distinction Award in Piano, Indiana University, 1972; Rackham Research Travel Grant, University of Michigan, 1978; International Peace Prize, UCC, 2006; Man of the Year Award, ABI, 2006; American Medal of Honor, 2006; Listed in international biographical dictionaries. Address: 28 Herrison House, Charlton Down, Dorchester, Dorset DT2 9XA, England. E-mail: info@kennethweir.com Website: www.kennethweir.com

WEIR Peter Lindsay, b. 21 August 1944, Sydney, Australia. Film Director. m. Wendy Stites, 1966, 1 son, 1 daughter. Education: Sydney University. Appointments: Real Estate, 1965; Stagehand, TV, Sydney, 1967; Director, Film Sequences, Variety Show, 1968; Director, Amateur University Reviews, 1967-69; Director, Film Australia, 1969-73; Made Own Short Films, 1969-73; Independent Feature-Film Director, Writer, 1973-. Creative Works: Films: Cars That Ate Paris, 1973; Picnic at Hanging Rock, 1975; The Last Wave, 1977; The Plumber (TV), 1978; Gallipoli, 1980; The Year of Living Dangerously, 1982; Witness, 1985; The Mosquito Coast, 1986; The Dead Poets Society, 1989; Green Card, 1991; Fearless, 1994; The Truman Show, 1997; Master and Commander: The Far Side of the World, 2003. Honours include: BAFTA Award, Best Director, 1997; BAFTA Award, Best Director, 2004. Address: Salt Pan Films Pty Ltd, PO Box 29, Palm Beach, NSW 2108, Australia.

WEISMAN Malcolm, Barrister, Minister of Religion. m. Rosalie Spiro, 2 sons. Education: Parminter's School; HarrogateGrammar; London School of Economics; MA, St Catherine's College, Oxford. Appointments: Jewish Chaplain, RAF, 1956; Honorary Chaplain, University of Oxford, 1971-; Senior Chaplain, HM Forces, 1972-; Secretary General, 1980-92, Honorary President, 1993-, Allied Air Forces Chief of Chaplains Committee; Secretary, Former Chiefs of Air Forces Chaplains Association, 1994; Called to the Bar, Middle Temple, 1961; Assistant Commissioner, Parliamentary Boundaries, 1976-88; Recorder of the Crown Court, 1980; Head of Chambers, 1982-90; Special Immigration Adjudicator, 1998; Member, Bar Disciplinary Tribunal; Editor, Menorah Magazine; Adviser to small Jewish communities and Hillel Counsellor to Oxford and Cambridge Universities. Honours: Blackstone Pupillage Award, 1961; Man of the Year Award, 1980; Chief Rabbi's Award for Excellence, 1993; Honorary Chaplain to: Mayor of Westminster, 1992-93, Mayor of Barnet, 1994-95; OBE, 1997; Chaplain to Mayor of Redbridge, 2005-06; USA Military Chaplaincy Award for Outstanding Service, 1998; Gold Medal, International Council of Christians and Jews, 2002; Rabbinical Council Award for Service, 2005; United Synagogue Award, 2005; United Synagogue Outstanding Leadership, 2005; Fellowship, University of Lancaster, 2006. Memberships: MOD Advisory Committee on Military Chaplaincy; Cabinet of Chief Rabbi of Commonwealth; Member of Courts of Universities of: East Anglia, Sussex, Kent, Lancaster, Essex, Warwick; Member Senior Common Room Universities of: Kent, East Anglia, Lancaster; Fellow, University of Essex Centre for the Study of Theology; Governor and Trustee, Parmiter's School; Trustee, Multi-Faith and International Multi-Faith Chaplaincy Centre, University of Derby; Trustee, Jewish Music Heritage Trust; Patron, Jewish National Fund; Fellow, Lancaster University, 2006. Address: 1 Gray's Inn Square, London WC1R 5AA, England.

WEISS Richard J, b. 14 December 1923, New York City, New York, USA. Physicist. m. Daphne Watson, 1 son, 2 daughters. Education: BS, City University of New York, 1944; Ensign, US Naval Academy, Annapolis, Maryland, 1944; MA, University of California, 1947; PhD, New York University, 1950. Appointments: Physicist, Materials Laboratory, Watertown, MA, 1949-79; Research Assistant, Cavendish Laboratories, Cambridge, England, 1956-57; Research Scientist, Imperial College, London, 1962-63; Professor of Physics, King's College, London, 1979-89; Editor, World Scientific Series in Popular Science, 1985-; Secretary, Fakebusters (scientific detection of fakery in art). Publications: Books: Solid State Physics for Metallurgists, 1962; X-Ray Determination of Electron Distributions, 1966; X-Ray Diffraction, 1972; Compton Effect, 1976; Magic of Physics, 1987; A Brief History of Light, 1990; Fakebusters I, 1999; Fakebusters II, 2001; A Physicist Remembers, 2007. Honour: Rockefeller Public Service Award, 1956. Address: 4 Lawson Street, Avon, MA 02322, USA. E-mail: rjwboug@aol.com

WEISS Simona, b. 8 September 1929, Brooklyn, New York, USA. Retired Paralegal. Divorced, 1 son, 1 daughter. Education: Columbia University, New York, 1968-70; BA (cum laude), Fairleigh Dickinson University, Teaneck, New Jersey, 1974; Postgraduate, New York University, New York City; Graduate School of Public Administration, 1974-76; Certified Paralegal, Upsala College, East Orange, New Jersey, 1980; William Patterson University, Wayne, New Jersey, Graduate School of Art and Communication, 2003. Appointments: Vice President of Fundraising, Haworth (New Jersey) Home and School Association, 1967-69; Financial and Corresponding Secretary, Temple Beth El, Closter (New Jersey), 1968-72; Program and Publicity Chairman, 1st Bergen County Women's Center, Teaneck (New Jersey), 1972-74; Chairman, Haworth (New Jersey) Parks & Playgrounds Committee, 1972-78; Candidate, Non-Partisan Bergen County (New Jersey) Charter Study Commission, 1973-74; County Committee

DICTIONARY OF INTERNATIONAL BIOGRAPHY

Municipal Chairman, Haworth (New Jersey) Republican Organization, 1973-79; Primary Candidate, Bergen County (New Jersey) Board of Chosen Freeholders, 1977; Paralegal: Witco Chemical Corp, 1980-81; Pitney, Hardin, Kipp & Szuch, 1982; Willkie Farr & Gallagher, 1983-84; Robinson Silverman Pearce Aronsohn & Berman, 1984-90; Freddie Mac, 1991; The Prudential Insurance Company of America, 1992-94; Cleary, Gottlieb, Steen & Hamilton, 1994-96; Hannoch Weisman, 1996-98; Unilever Bestfoods, 1998-2002; Temple Sholom, 2007. Publications: Numerous articles in professional journals. Honours: Mayor's Certificate, Borough of Haworth, 1979; Scholar, Fairleigh Dickinson University, 1971-74; Phi Omega Epsilon Honor Society. Memberships: Legal Assistant Management Association; National Paralegal Association; Industrial Commercial Real Estate Women; Association of Real Estate Women; National Council of Jewish Women; Dazzling Damsels; Dizzy Dames; Mingle and Meet; National Network of Commercial Real Estate Women. Address: 2000 Linwood Ave, Apt 19U, Fort Lee, NJ 07024, USA. E-mail: simona_wei@msn.com

WEISZ Rachel, b. 7 March 1971, London, England. Actress. 1 son. Education: English, Cambridge University. Career: Model, age 14; Formed theatre company, Talking Tongues, 1991; Theatre: Design for Living, 1994; Face of Revlon, 2005-; Acted on stage, film and television; Films include: Stealing Beauty, 1996; Bent, 1997; The Land Girls, 1998; The Mummy, 1999; The Mummy Returns, 2001; Enemy at the Gates, 2001; About a Boy, 2002; The Shape of Things, 2003; Confidence, 2003; Runaway Jury, 2003; Envy, 2004; Constantine, 2005; The Constant Gardener, 2005; The Fountain, 2006; Eragon (voice), 2006; My Blueberry Nights, 2007; Fred Claus, 2007; Definitely, Maybe, 2008. Honours: Guardian Award, Edinburgh Festival; Most Promising Newcomer, London Critics' Circle, 1994; Named as one of European films' Shooting Stars, European Film Promotion Board, 1998; Oscar, Best Supporting Actress, 2006. Memberships: Patron, The X Appeal, Royal College of Radiologists.

WEITZMAN Sarah Brown, b. 6 February 1935, Port Washington, New York, USA. Poet; Retired Educator. m. Arthur H Weitzman, 1965, divorced 1989. Education: BS, 1956, MA, 1957, English Literature, New York University, New York. Appointments: Instructor in English, New York University; Teacher of English, Sewardpark High School, 1957-63; Instructor in English, New York University, 1963-67; Editor, Curriculum Writer, NYC Board of Education, New York City, 1968-72; Teacher of English, various secondary schools in New York City, 1972-85; Director, on-site teacher training and staff development program, UFT/NYC Board of Education/NY State Department of Education, 1985-91; Retired, 1991-. Publications: Eve and Other Blasphemy (poems), 1984; The Forbidden (chapbook poems), 2004; Never Far From Flesh (poems), 2005; Over 200 poems published in numerous journals. Honours: National Endowment for the Arts Award, 1984; Finalist, AWP Poetry Award, 1981; Finalist, Walt Whitman First Book Award, Academy of American Poets, 1981, 1982; Finalist, Puddinghouse Chapbook Contest, 2004; Finalist, Foley Prize, America Magazine, 2003; Director at Large, University Club, Florida Atlantic University, 2005; Director on Board of Directors, Torch Club, 2005-07. Memberships: Poetry Society of America; Academy of American Poets; International Torch Club; FAU University Club; Palm Beach Round Table; The Forum Club; The Economic Forum; Boca Raton Round Table; The Palm Beach Symphony Society; The English Speaking Union; NYU Alumni; The World Affairs Council of the Palm Beaches; The Coudert Institute; The Palm Beach Preservation

Society; The Palm Beach Historical Society; The St George's Society of Palm Beach; National Croquet Club; English Speaking Union of Palm Beach. Address: 555 SE 6th Avenue, Apt 2B, Delray Beach, FL 33483, USA.

WEIZSÄCKER Carl Friedrich von, b. 28 June 1912, Kiel, Germany. Theoretical Physicist. Education: PhD, University of Leipzig, 1933. Appointments: Assistant, Institute of Theoretical Physics, University of Leipzig, 1934-36; Kaiser Wilhelm Institute of Physics, Berlin-Dahlem; Lecturer, University of Berlin, 1936-42; Chair, University of Strasbourg, 1942; Kaiser Wilhelm Institute, 1944; Member of German research team investigating feasibility of nuclear weapons, but feared that such weapons may be used by the Nazi government; Director, Department, Max Planck Institute of Physics, Göttingen, 1946, with Honorary Professorship; Professor of Philosophy, University of Hamburg, 1957-69; Honorary Chair, University of Munich, 1969; Director, Max Planck Institute, 1970; Investigated the way in which energy is generated in the centre of stars; Devised theory on the origin of the solar system. Publications include: Bedingungen der Freiheit, 1990; Der Mensch in seiner Geschichte, 1991; Zeit und Wissen, 1992; Der bedrohte Friede-heute, 1994; Wohin gehen wir?, 1997. Address: Alpenstrasse 15, 82319 Starnberg, Germany.

WELCH Raquel, b. 5 September 1940, Chicago, Illinois, USA. Actress. m. (1) James Westley Welch, 1959, divorced, 1 son, 1 daughter, (2) Patrick Curtis, divorced, (3) Andre Weinfeld, 1980, divorced, (4) Richard Palmer, 1999, divorced 2003. Career: Former model for Neiman-Marcus stores; Films include: Fantastic Voyage, 1966; One Million Years BC, 1967; Fathom, 1967; The Biggest Bundle of Them All, 1968; Magic Christian, 1970; Myra Breckinridge, 1970; Fuzz, 1972; Bluebeard, 1972; Hannie Caulder, 1972; Kansas City Bomber, 1972; The Last of Sheila, 1973; The Three Musketeers, 1974; The Wild Party, 1975; The Four Musketeers, 1975; Mother, Jugs and Speed, 1976; Crossed Swords, 1978; L'Animal, 1979; Right to Die, 1987; Scandal in a Small Town, 1988; Trouble in Paradise, 1989; Naked Gun 33 1/3, 1993; Folle d'Elle, 1998; Chairman of the Board, 1998; The Complete Musketeers, 1999; Tortilla Soup, 2001; Legally Blonde, 2001; Plays include: Woman of the Year, 1982; Torch Song, 1993; Videos: Raquel: Total Beauty and Fitness, 1984; A Week with Raquel, 1987; Raquel: Lose 10lbs in 3 Weeks, 1989. Publication: The Raquel Welch Total Beauty and Fitness Program, 1984. Address: Innovative Artists, 1999 Avenue of the Stars, Suite 2850, Los Angeles, CA 90067, USA.

WELD Tuesday Ker, b. 27 August 1943, New York City, USA. Actress. m. (1) Claude Harz, 1965, divorced 1971, 1 daughter, (2) Dudley Moore, 1975, divorced, 1 son, (3) Pinchas Zukerman, 1985. Education: Hollywood Professional School. Career: Fashion and catalogue model, aged 3 years; Magazine cover-girl and in child roles on TV by age 12; Numerous TV programmes and TV films including: The Many Loves of Dobie Gillis, 1959; Cimarron Strip; Playhouse 90; Climax; Ozzie and Harriet; 77 Sunset Strip; The Millionaire; Tab Hunter Show; Dick Powell Theatre; Adventures in Paradise; Naked City; The Greatest Show on Earth; Mr Broadway; Fugitive; Films include: Rock Rock, 1956; Serial; Rally Round the Flag Boys; The Five Pennies; The Private Lives of Adam and Eve; Return to Peyton Place; Wild in the Country; Bachelor Flat; Lord Love a Duck; Pretty Poison; I Walk The Line; A Safe Place; Play It As It Lays; Because They're Young; High Time; Sex Kittens Go To College; The Cincinnati Kid; Soldier in the Rain; Looking for Mr Goodbar; Thief; Author!; Once

Upon A Time in America; Heartbreak Hotel; Falling Down; Feeling Minnesota, 1996; Chelsea Walls, 2001; Investigating Sex, 2001.

WELDON Fay, b. 22 September 1931, Alvechurch, Worcestershire, England. Writer. m. (1) Ron Weldon, 12 June 1961, 4 daughters, (2) Nick Fox, 1994. Education: MA, St Andrews University, 1952; CBE. Career: Numerous theatre plays and over 30 television plays, dramatizations and radio plays. Publications: Fat Woman's Joke, 1968; Down Among the Women, 1971; Female Friends, 1975; Remember Me, 1976; Praxis, 1978; Puffball, 1980; The President's Child, 1982; Letters to Alice, 1984; Life and Loves of a She Devil, 1984; Rebecca West, 1985; The Shrapnel Academy, 1986; The Hearts and Lives of Men, 1987; Leader of the Band, 1988; Wolf of the Mechanical Dog, 1989; The Cloning of Joanna May, 1989; Party Puddle, 1989; Moon Over Minneapolis or Why She Couldn't Stay, (short stories), 1991; Life Force, 1992; Growing Rich, 1992; Affliction, 1994; Splitting, 1995; Worst Fears, 1996; Wicked Women, (short stories), 1996; Big Women, 1998; A Hard Time to be a Father (short stories), 1998; Rhode Island Blues, 2000; Godless in Eden (essays), 2000; Nothing to Wear, Nowhere to Hide, 2002; Auto-da-Fay (autobiography), 2002; Mantrapped, 2004; She May Not Leave, 2005; What Makes Women Happy, 2006; The Spa Decameron, 2007; Contributor to numerous journals and magazines. Honours: DLitt, Universities of Bath, 1989 and St Andrews, 1992; PEN/Macmillan Silver Pen Award, 1996: Women in Publishing, Pandora Award, 1997; CBE, 2001. Memberships: Royal Society of Authors. Address: c/o Curtis Brown, 5th Floor, Haymarket House, 28-29 Haymarket, London SW1Y 4SP, England.

WELLER Elizabeth Boghossian, b. 7 August 1949, Beirut, Lebanon. Psychiatrist; Physician. m. Ronald A Weller, 1 son, 1 daughter. Education: BSc, 1971, MD, 1975; Resident in Psychiatry, Washington University, 1978; Fellow, Child Psychiatry, University of Kansas, 1979. Appointments: University of Kansas, 1979-85; OSU, 1985-96; Professor of Psychiatry and Pediatrics, University of Pennsylvania, 1996- Publications: Papers in refereed journals. Honours include: Alpha Omega Alpha, 1975; American Academy, Clinical Psychiatry Research Award, 1982, 1984, 1988; Outstanding Young Woman in Psychiatry, 1985; Professor of Year, Department of Psychiatry, 1990; Distinguished Award, Program Chair, American Academy of Clinical Psychiatry, 1992; Outstanding Mentor Award, presented at annual meeting, American Academy of Child and Adolescent Psychiatry, Toronto, Canada, 1997. Memberships: Fellow, Academy of Child and Adolescent Psychiatry; President, Society of Biological Psychiatry, 1995; American College of Psychiatrists, 1995; Director, American Board of Psychiatry and Neurology, 1996-; President, American Board of Psychiatry and Neurology, 2004. Address: 3440 Market Street, Department of Child and Adolescent Psychiatry, Suite 200, Philadelphia, PA 19104, USA.

WELLER Paul, b. 25 May 1958, Woking, Surrey, England. Singer; Songwriter; Musician (guitar, piano). m. Dee C Lee, December 1986. Career: Founder, singer, guitarist, The Jam, 1976-1982; Concerts include: Reading Festival, 1978; Great British Music Festival, 1978; Pink Pop Festival, 1980; Loch Lomond Festival, 1980; Founder, The Style Council, 1983-89; Appearances include: Miners benefit concert, Royal Albert Hall, London, 1984; Live Aid, Wembley Arena, 1985; Film: JerUSAlem, 1987; Founder, The Paul Weller Movement, 1990; Solo artiste, 1990-; UK and international tours; Phoenix Festival, 1995; T In The Park Festival, Glasgow, 1995; Own

record label, Freedom High. Creative works: Compositions include: My Ever Changing Moods; Shout To The Top; The Walls Come Tumbling Down; Have You Ever Had It Blue, for film Absolute Beginners; It Didn't Matter; Wanted; Sunflower; Wild Wood; The Weaver; Recordings: Albums: with The Jam: In The City, 1977; This Is The Modern World, 1977; All Mod Cons, 1978; Setting Sons, 1979; Sound Affects, 1980; The Gift, 1982; Dig The New Breed, 1982; Snap!, 1983; Greatest Hits, 1991; Extras, 1992; Live Jam, 1993; The Singles: Box Set, 2001; The Sound of The Jam, 2002; The Jam at the BBC, 2002; with Style Council: Introducing The Style Council, 1983; Café Bleu, 1984; Our Favourite Shop, 1985; Home And Abroad, 1986; The Cost Of Loving, 1987; Confessions Of A Pop Group, 1988; The Singular Adventures Of The Style Council, 1989; Here's Some That Got Away, 1993; Solo albums: Paul Weller, 1992; Wild Wood, 1993; Live Wood, 1994; Stanley Road, 1995; Heavy Soul, 1997; Modern Classics, 1998; Heliocentric, 2000; Illumination, 2002; Fly on the Wall: B-Sides and Rarities, 2003; Studio 150, 2004; Singles: with The Jam: In the City, 1977; This is the Modern World, 1977; David Watts/A Bomb in Wardour Street, 1978; Down In The Tube Station at Midnight, 1978; Strange Town, 1979; Eton Rifles, 1979; Going Underground/Dreams of Children, 1980; Start! 1980; That's Entertainment, 1981; Funeral Pyre, 1981; Absolute Beginners, 1981; Town Called Malice/Precious, 1982; Just Who Is The 5 O'Clock Hero, 1982; The Bitterest Pill, 1982; Best Surrender, 1982; with the Style Council: Speak Like a Child, 1983; Money Go Round, 1983; Long Hot Summer, 1983; A Solid Bond In Your Heart, 1983; My Ever Changing Moods, 1984; You're The Best Thing, 1984; Shout to the Top, 1984; Walls Come Tumbling Down, 1985; The Lodgers, 1986; Have You Ever Had It Blue, 1986; It Didn't Matter, 1987; Wanted, 1987; Promised Land, 1989; Solo: Into Tomorrow, 1991; Uh Huh Oh Yeh, 1992; Sunflower, 1993; Wild Wood, 1993; The Weaver, 1993; Hung Up, 1994; Out Of The Sinking, 1994; The Changing Man, 1995; You Do Something To Me, 1995; Broken Stones, 1995; Peacock Suit, 1996; Brushed, 1997; Friday Street, 1997; Mermaids, 1997; Brand New Start, 1998; Wild Wood, 1999; Hung Up, 1999; Sweet Pea, My Sweet Pea, 2000. Honours include: Ivor Novello Award; BRIT Awards, 1995, 1996. Address: c/o Go'Discs Ltd, 72 Black Lion Lane, Hammersmith, London W6 9BE, England. Website: www.paulweller.com

WELLS Martin John, b. 24 August 1928, London, England. Zoologist; Educator. m. Joyce Finlay, 8 September 1953, 2 sons. Education: BA, 1952; MA, 1956; ScD, 1966. Publications: Brain and Behaviour in Cephalopods, 1962; You, Me and the Animal World, 1964; Lower Animals, 1968; Octopus: Physiology and Behaviour of an Advanced Invertebrate, 1978; Civilization and the Limpet, 1998. Contributions to: Several journals. Honours: Silver Medal, Zoological Society, 1968; Fellow, Churchill College, Cambridge. Memberships: Philosophical Society; Cambridge Drawing Society; Royal Highland Yacht Club. Address: The Bury Home End, Fulbourn, Cambridge, England.

WELLS Peter George, b. 27 April 1925, Sheffield, England. Medical Doctor. m. Finola Fidelma Ginty, deceased 2000, 1 son, 1 daughter. Education: University of Sheffield Medical School; Numerous Postgraduate Institutes from 1955-1970. Appointments: Sub-Lieutenant RNVR, Royal Navy, 1943-46; House Physician, Royal Postgraduate Medical School, Hammersmith Hospital; London Chest Hospital; Resident Medical Officer, Maida Vale Hospital for Nervous Diseases; RMO, National Heart Hospital; Registrar, General Medical Unit, West Middlesex Hospital; General Practice, West Kirby, Cheshire; Registrar, 1963, Senior Registrar, 1966-69,

Deva Hospital, Chester; Senior Registrar, United Liverpool Hospitals; Senior Registrar, Walton Hospital, Tavistock Clinic, London; Consultant, Adolescent Psychiatry, Mersey and NWRHA's, 1970-1992; Seconded to create a brief for services for disturbed adolescents in the Hunter Valley, New South Wales, Australia, 1980-81; Locum Consultant, Isle of Wight, 1992, 1993; Psychiatric Adviser to Visyon, 1994-Founder five mental after-care clubs and mental after-care home in Chester. Publications: Numerous articles in medical journals including: Are Adolescent Units Satisfactory, 1982; Cut Price Adolescent units that Meet All Needs and None?, 1986; Whatever Happened to the Nursing Process?, 1986; Another Big Bang, 1986; Management of The Disturbed Adolescent, 1987; Why admit to a bed? Disposal of 1000 referrals to a Regional Adolescent Service, 1989; Survival in a cold climate, 1992; Inpatient treatment of 165 adolescents with emotional and conduct disorders – a study of outcome, 1993; Henbury: History of a Village, 2003; Co-author, Two Lost Water Corn Mills, 2004; Henbury Deeds, 2004; Poetry in various poetry journals; 4 Psychiatric Films. Honours: BMA Silver Medal for film, 1969; Fellow, Royal College of Psychiatrists, 1979; Fellow, Royal Australian and New Zealand College, 1983; 'C' Merit Award, 1979; Cheadle Royal Prize for Research Paper, 1992. Memberships: British Medical Association; Association for Professionals in Service for Adolescents; Poetry Society. Address: High Trees, Dark Lane, Henbury, Macclesfield, SK11 9PE.

WENDT Albert, b. 27 October 1939, Apia, Western Samoa. Professor of English; Writer; Poet; Dramatist. 1 son, 2 daughters. Education: MA, History, Victoria University, Wellington, 1964. Appointments: Professor of Pacific Literature, University of the South Pacific, Suva, Fiji, 1982-87; Professor of English, University of Auckland, 1988-; Visiting Professor of Asian and Pacific Studies, University of Hawaii, 1999. Publications: Comes the Revolution, 1972; The Contract, 1972; Sons for the Return Home, 1973; Flying-Fox in a Freedom Tree, 1974; Inside Us the Dead: Poems 1961-74, 1975; Pouliuli, 1977; Leaves of the Banyan Tree, 1979; Shaman of Visions, 1984; The Birth and Death of the Miracle Man, 1986; Ola, 1990; Black Rainbow, 1992; Photographs, 1995; The Best of Albert Wendt's Short Stories, 1999; The Book of the Black Star, 2002; Whetu Moana: A Collection of Pacific Poems, 2002; The Mango's Kiss: a Novel, 2003; The Songmaker's Chair, 2004. Honours: Landfall Prize, 1963; Wattie Award, 1980; Commonwealth Book Prize, South East Asia and the Pacific, 1991; Companion of the New Zealand Order of Merit, 2001. Address: c/o Department of English, University of Auckland, Private Bag 92019, Auckland 1, New Zealand. Website: www.auckland.ac.nz

WENG Yueh-Sheng, b. 1 July 1932, Chaiyi, Taiwan. Professor of Law. m. Chuan Shu-Chen, 3 daughters. Education: LLB, National Taiwan University, 1960; Dr Jur, Heidelberg University, Germany, 1966. Appointments: Associate Professor of Law, 1966-70, Professor of Law, 1970-72, National Taiwan University; Commissioner of the Legal Commission, Executive Yuan, 1971-72; Commissioner of Research, Development and Evaluation Commission, Executive Yuan, 1972; Justice, Council of the Grand Justices, Judicial Yuan, 1972-99; Commissioner & Convenor of Administrative Procedure Act Research Commission, Judicial Yuan, 1981-92; Member, 1988-99, Standing Member, 1996-99, Council of Academic Reviewal Evaluation, Ministry of Education; Visiting Professor, School of Law, University of Washington, Seattle, 1991; Commissioner of Academic Consultation Commission, 1991-2001, Convenor, 1998-2001, Sun Yat-Sen Institute of Social Sciences and Philosophy,

Academica Sinica; Presiding Justice of the Constitutional Court, 1992-99; President, Judicial Yuan & Chairman, Council of the Grand Justices, 1999-2003; Chief Justice of Constitutional Court & President of Judicial Yuan, 2003-07; Professor of Law, National Chengchi University, College of Law. Publications: Die Stellung der Justiz im Verfassungsrecht der Republik China, 1970; Administrative Law and Rule of Law, 1976; Administrative Law and Judiciary in a State Under the Rule of Law, 1994; Administrative Law I and II, 2000; Annotation of Administrative Procedure Act, 2003. Honours: Judicial Medal of the First Grade, Merit and Achievement Medal of the First Grade, Judicial Yuan, Republic of China, 1994; President, 1999-2004, Honorary President, 2004-, Chinese Society of Constitutional Law, Republic of China; President, 1998-2004, Honorary President, 2004-07, Taiwan Administrative Law Association, Republic of China; Golden Medal of the Distinguished Justice, Supreme Court of the Republic of Guatemala, 2000; Order of Propitious Clouds with Special Grand Cordon, President of the Republic of China, 2000; Chung-Cheng Medal of Honour, President of the Republic of China, 2007; Honorary President, German Academic Exchange Service, Republic of China, 2003-07; Honorary President, Taiwan Jurist Association, Republic of China, 2003-06. Memberships: Director, Chiang Ching-kuo Foundation for International Scholarly Exchange, Taiwan, 2001-2010; Society of Comparative Law, Germany; Public Law Association, Japan; International Association of Constitutional Law, South Africa; East Asia Administrative Law Association. Address: 19 Alley 9, Lane 143, Jun-Gong Road, Taipei 11655, Taiwan.

WEPPEN Wolfgang von der, b. 6 September 1943, Znojmo, Czechoslovakia. Freelance Author. m. Brigitte Vongehr, 3 daughters. Education: Philosophy, German Language and Literature; History; Politics; Psychology; History of the Arts, Universities of Vienna, Austria and Wuerzburg, Bavaria, Germany; Master of Arts, 1971; High School Teacher, 1971; Dr phil, 1983. Appointments: Assistant, Philosophy, University of Wuerzburg; University Expert of the Bavarian High School Association; High School Head Master; Freelance Author; Member of the Executive Committee of the Humboldt-Gesellschaft; Chairman, Socratic Society. Publications: Philosophy: Die existentielle Situation und die Rede; Articles to: Philosophy of Language and Philosophy of Culture; Ethics: W. von Humboldt, Wittgenstein, Karl Mannheim, Josef Pieper, Franz Vonessen; Philosophical Essays: Der Spaziergänger, Das verlorene Individuum; Lyrics (amongst other one: Metaphysische Gedichte) and narrative prose: Viktorsberg (novel); Tales; Sokrates-Studien Bd VI, 2006: Sokrates im Gang der Zeitan (Editor together withj B. Zimmermann). Listed in national and international biographical dictionaries. Honours: Preis des Kuratoriums der Unterfraenk. Gedenkjahrstiftung, University of Wuerzburg, 1984; Great Minds of the 21st Century, ABI, USA, 2004. Memberships: Sokratische Gesellschaft; Humboldt Gesellschaft; Gesellschaft für wissenschaftliche Phänomenologie; Forschungskreis für Metaphysik; Société Européene de Culture, Venice; Member, Research Board of Advisors, ABI, 2005; Life Fellowship, IBA, 2005. Address: Pfeffingerweg 33, D-83512 Wasserburg, Germany. E-mail: wolfgangvdweppen@gmx.de Website: www.sokratische-gesellschaft.de

WESKER Arnold, b. 24 May 1932, London, England. Dramatist; Playwright; Director. m. Dusty Bicker, 2 sons, 2 daughters. Appointments: Founder-Director, Centre Fortytwo, 1961-70. Publications: Chicken Soup with Barley, 1959; Roots, 1959; I'm Talking About Jerusalem, 1960; The Wesker Trilogy, 1960; The Kitchen, 1961; Chips with Everything,

1962; The Four Seasons, 1966; Their Very Own and Golden City, 1966; The Friends, 1970; Fears of Fragmentation (essays), 1971; Six Sundays in January (stories), 1971; The Old Ones, 1972; The Journalists, 1974; Love Letters on Blue Paper (stories), 1974, 2nd edition, 1990; Say Goodbye!: You May Never See Them Again (with John Allin), 1974; Words--As Definitions of Experience, 1976; The Wedding Feast, 1977; Journey Into Journalism, 1977; Said the Old Man to the Young Man (stories), 1978; The Merchant (renamed Shylock), 1978; Fatlips, 1978; The Journalists: A Triptych, 1979; Caritas, 1981; Distinctions (essays), 1985; Yardsale, 1987; Whatever Happened to Betty Lemon, 1987; Little Old Lady, 1988; Shoeshine, 1989; Collected Plays, 7 volumes, 1989-97; As Much As I Dare (autobiography), 1994; Circles of Perception, 1996; Break, My Heart, 1997; Denial, 1997; The Birth of Shylock and the Death of Zero Mostel (diaries), 1997; The King's Daughters (stories), 1998; Barabbas (play for TV), 2000; Groupie (play for radio), 2001; The Wesker Trilogy, 2001; One Woman Plays, 2001; Longitude, 2002; Letter to Myself, 2004; Contributions to: Stage, film, radio and television. Honours: Fellow, Royal Society of Literature, 1985; Honorary DLitt, University of East Anglia, 1989; Honorary Fellow, Queen Mary and Westfield College, London, 1995; Honorary DHL, Denison University, Ohio, 1997; Evening Standard Award, Most Promising Playwright, 1959; Premio Marzotto Drama Prize, 1964; Gold Medal, Premios el Espectador y la Critica, 1973, 1979; The Goldie Award, 1986; Last Frontier Award for Lifetime Achievement, Valdez, Alaska, 1999; Annual pension and award for lifetime achievement, Royal Literary Fund, 2003. Memberships: International Playwrights Committee, president, 1979-83; International Theatre Institute, chairman, British Centre, 1978-82. Address: Hay on Wye, Hereford HR3 5RJ, England. Website: www.arnoldwesker.com

WESSEX HRH The Earl of Wessex; Viscount Severn, Prince Edward Antony Richard Louis, b. 10 March 1964. m. Sophie Rhys-Jones, 1999, 1 son, 1 daughter. Education: BA, History, Jesus College, Cambridge, 1986. Appointments: Second Lieutenant, Royal Marines; Theatre production, Really Useful Group; Founder, Ardent Productions Ltd, 1993; Opened Commonwealth Games, Auckland and Malaysia, 1998; President, Commonwealth Games Federation; UK and International Trustee, The Duke of Edinburgh's Award; Chair, International Council, The Duke of Edinburgh's Award International Association; Patron, National Youth Music Theatre, National Youth Theatre, Royal Exchange Theatre Co, Manchester; Haddo Arts Trust; National Youth Orchestras of Scotland, City of Birmingham Symphony Orchestra and Chorus; London Mozart Players; Cheetham School of Music; Orpheus Trust; State Management Association; Scottish Badminton; Globe Theatre, Saskatchewan, Canada; Friends of Wanganui Opera House, New Zealand; British Ski and Snowboard Federation; Central Caribbean Marine Institute. Publications: Crown and Country, 1999. Honours: Queen Elizabeth II Silver Jubilee Medal, 1977; Commander of the Royal Victorian Order, 1989; Commemorative Medal (150th anniversary of Treaty of Waitangi), 1990; Honorary Degree, University of Victoria, Canada, 1994; Queen Elizabeth II Golden Jubilee Medal, 2002; Knight Commander of the Royal Victorian Order, 2003; Personal Aide-de-Camp to the Queen, 2004; Honorary Member, Saskatchewan Order of Merit, 2005; Commemorative Medal, Centennial of Saskatchewan, 2005; Knight of the Garter, 2006; Honorary Degree, University of Prince Edward Island, 2007; Royal Honorary Colonel, the Royal Wessex Yeomanry; Royal Colonel, of the 2nd Battalion, The Rifles; Commodore-in-Chief, Royal Fleet Auxiliary;

Colonel-in-Chief, The Hastings and Prince Edward Regiment; Colonel-in-Chief, The Prince Edward Island Regiment; Colonel-in-Chief, Saskatchewan Dragons.

WEST Ben, b. 30 November 1963, Greenwich, London, England. Writer; Journalist. m. Bryony Imogen Menzies Clack, 2 sons, 1 daughter. Education: Addey & Stanhope School, London. Appointments: Contributions to: Guardian, Times, Independent, Telegraph, Mail, Express, Mirror, Star, Evening Standard, Vogue, Reader's Digest and others; Films: Gertrude, 2004; Emily, 2004; Maureen, 2005; Stage: Gertrude's Secret, various venues including Minerva Theatre, Chichester and Greenwich Theatre, London, 2006-. Publications: Books: London for Free, 1996; Buying a Home, 2003; Buying a Property Abroad, 2004; Cameroon, 2004; and others. Address: 37 Vanbrugh Park, London, SE3 7AA, England. E-mail: ben@benwest.info

WEST Peter Christopher, b. 4 December 1951, Kent, England. Professor. m. Susan Amanda, 1 son, 1 daughter. Education: BSc, ARCS, Theoretical Physics, 1973, PhD, 1976, Imperial College. Appointments: Academic Visitor, 1976-77, Visiting Professor, 1999, Ecole Normale Superieure, Paris, France; Postdoctoral Fellowship, Imperial College, 1977-78; Lecturer, 1978-85, Professor, 1986, King's College, London; Visiting Associate, Theoretical Physics, California Institute of Technology, Pasadena, California, 1984-85; Paid Scientific Associate, CERN, Geneva, Switzerland, 1985, 1986-89, 2000; Chalmers 150th Anniversary Professor, The Chalmers Institute of Technology, Goteborg, Sweden, 1992, 1993; Programme Organiser, Newton Institute, Cambridge University, 1997; PPARC Senior Research Fellow, 2003-06. Publications: Numerous articles in professional journals. Honours: Imperial College Scholarship, 1971-74; Governors Prize, 1973; Granville Scholarship, London University, 1973-74. Memberships: Royal Society; Fellow, Institute of Physics; Fellow, King's College, London. Address: Department of Mathematics, King's College, Strand, London WC2R 2LS, England. E-mail: peter.west@kcl.ac.uk

WEST Timothy Lancaster, b. 20 October 1934. Actor; Director. m. (1) Jacqueline Boyer, 1956, dissolved, 1 daughter, (2) Prunella Scales, 1963, 2 sons. Education: Regent Street Polytechnic, London, 1951-52. Appointments: Freelance Actor and Director, 1956-, Member, various times, Royal Shakespeare Company, National Theatre, Old Vic Company and Prospect Theatre Company; Artistic Director, Billingham Theatre Company, 1974-76, Old Vic Company, 1980-82; Director in Residence, University of Washington, 1982; Associate Director, Bristol Old Vic, 1991-; Theatre: The External King Lear, Edinburgh Festival, 1971; The Merchant of Venice, Royal Flemish Theatre Brussels, 1981; King Lear, English Touring Theatre Company, 2003; Coriolanus, Royal Shakespeare Company, Stratford-upon-Avon, 2007; Opening of St Pancras railway station as William Henry Barlow, 2007; Film appearances include: The Looking Glass War; The Day of the Jackal; Oliver Twist; Cry Freedom; 102 Dalmatians; The Fourth Angel; Villa des Roses; Iris; Beyond Borders; TV appearances include: Why Lockerbie?; Framed; Smokescreen; Reith to the Nation; Eleven Men Against Eleven; Cuts; Place of the Dear; Midsomer Murders; Murder in Mind; Bedtime; Dickens; The Alan Clark Diaries; The Inspector Lynley Mysteries; Essential Poems for Christmas; Waking the Dead; Bleak House; Numerous theatre appearances. Publications: I'm Here I Think, Where Are You? 1997; A Moment Towards the End of the Play, 2001; Various articles in national newspapers, National Trust magazine, Times Literary Supplement. Honours: CBE, 1984; Honorary DUniv,

Bradford, 1993; Honorary DLitt, West of England, 1994; East Anglia, 1995; Honorary DLitt, University of Westminster, 1999. Memberships: FRSA, 1992-; Chairman, London Academy of Music and Dramatic Art, 1992-; Chairman, All Change Arts, 1986-99; At various times, member of Arts Council Drama and Touring Panels, various Theatre Boards; Director, National Student Drama Festival; President, Society for Theatrical Research.

WESTBROOK Clinton Howard, b. 1 March 1919, Brooklyn, New York, USA. m. Catherine Wetzel, 1942, deceased 2006, 4 sons (2 deceased), 1 daughter. Education: Graduated high school, 1940; 1½ Community College; Various Navy schools, 1940-67; Various Civil Defense courses, 1967-72; Various VA/County Service Officer courses, 1967-84. Appointments: US Navy Peace/WWII, 1940-46; X-ray Equipment Service Engineer, NY area, 1946-50; Recalled to Active Duty, Korean War, 1950-52; Field Engineer, large training devices for US Air Force, 1952-55; Re-entered Active Duty, 1955-67; Emergency Director, Seminole County, Florida, 1967-74; County Service Officer, 1967-84; State of Florida County Service Officer of the Year, 1984; Retired (2nd time), 1984; Lecturer, Seminole County Schools, 1984-2007. Publications: Various interviews, media and TV; TV documentaries; Included in book on USS Arizona; Listed in international biographical dictionaries. Honours: Purple Heart, 1941; Presidential Unit Award, 1943; Good Conduct, 5 stars; Liberation of Philippines, 4 stars; South Pacific Theatre Ribbon, 22 stars; Pearl Harbor Bar; 2 Congressional Bronze Medals; Peace Time, 1940; American Defense Bar with Fleet Clasp; American Theatre Ribbon and European/Africa/Asia Theatre Ribbon and South Pacific/Asian, 1942-45; Victory Ribbon; Occupation Ribbon, Japan; 3 Cold War Ribbons; Honoured by Honorary Chairman, Golden Age Games, Sanford, Florida, 2002; Appearance in 6 Memorial Day Parades and Grand Marshall in one, 2001-07; Threw out first ball and had game named in his honour at ball game of Active Duty Travelling military team versus local Summer League players, 2007; Appearance in 5 Veteran's Day Parades and Grand Marshall in one, 2002-07; Special VIP, tribute to all military personnel street festival, Sanford, 2007; Clinton Westbrook Day, 10 November 2007, City of Sanford, Seminole County; Florida & Key to the City of Sanford, 2007. Memberships: Life Member, USS Arizona Reunion Association; Life Member, Tin Can Sailor; Member of Reunions for USS Maddox DD168, USS Conyngham DD391, USS Taylor DD468, and USS Waldron DD699. Address: 283 Raintree Drive, Altoona, FL 32702, USA.

WESTBROOK Roger, b. 26 May 1941, Surrey, England. Retired Diplomat. Education: MA, Modern History, Hertford College, Oxford. Appointments: Foreign Office, 1964: Assistant Private Secretary to the Chancellor of the Duchy of Lancaster and Minister of State, Foreign Office, 1965; Yaoundé, 1967; Rio de Janeiro, 1971; Brasilia, 1972; Private Secretary to Minister of State, Foreign Office, 1975; Head of Chancery, Lisbon, 1977; Deputy Head, News Department, 1980, Deputy Head, Falkland Islands Department, 1982, Overseas Inspectorate, Foreign and Commonwealth Office, 1984; High Commissioner, Brunei, 1986-91; Ambassador to Zaire, 1991-92; High Commissioner, Tanzania, 1992-95; Ambassador to Portugal, 1995-99, UK Commissioner, Expo 98, Lisbon; Chairman, Spencer House, 2000-06; Chairman,2000-03, Vice President, 2006-, Anglo Portuguese Society; Council, Book Aid International, 2002-; Chairman, Foreign and Commonwealth Office Association, 2003-; Chief Honorary Steward, Westminster Abbey, 2006-. Honour: CMG, 1990. Address: 33 Marsham Court, Marsham Street, London, SW1P 7JY, England.

WESTERBERG Siv, b. 11 June 1932, Borås, Sweden. Lawyer. m. Per Westerberg, 2 sons, 1 daughter. Education: Medicine Kandidat, 1954, Medicine Licentiat, 1960, University Uppsala; Juris kandidat, 1982, University of Lund. Appointments: Hospital Doctor, University Clinics in Gothenburg, Sweden, 1960-63; GP, Gothenburg, 1964-79; Lawyer, Gothenburg, 1982-; Specialised in medical and sociomedical cases; Tried and won several cases in the European Court of Human Rights. Publication: Books, To be a Physician, 1977; Punishment Without Crime, 2004. Address: Skårsgatan 45, SE-412 69, Göteborg, Sweden.

WESTERDAHL John, b. 3 December 1954, Tucson, Arizona, USA. Nutritionist; Health Educator. m. Doris Mui Lian Tan, 1 daughter. Education: BS, Pacific Union College, 1979; MPH, Loma Linda University, 1981; PhD, Pacific Western University, 2001; Registered Dietitian; Certified Nutrition Specialist. Appointments: Director, Health Promotion, Castle Medical Center, Kailua, Hawaii, 1981-89; Senior Nutritionist, Shaklee Corporation, San Francisco, California, 1990-96; Director of Nutrition, Dr McDougall's Right Foods Inc, South San Francisco, California, 1996-98; Director, Wellness and Lifestyle Medicine, Castle Medical Center, Kailua, Hawaii, 1998-2006; Director, Murad Inclusive Health Center, Murad Inc, El Segundo, California, 2006-07; Director, Bragg Health Foundation, Director of Health Science, Bragg Live Food Products, Santa Barbara, California, 2007-. Publications: Books: Medicinal Herbs: A Vital Reference Guide, 1997; The Millennium Cookbook: Extraordinary Vegetarian Cuisine, 1998; Magazine column: Nutritionally Speaking, in Veggie Life Magazine. Honours: Listed in Who's Who publications and biographical dictionaries. Memberships: American Academy of Anti-Aging Medicine; American Association for the Advancement of Science; American College of Nutrition; American Dietetic Association; American Society of Pharmacognosy; American College of Lifestyle Medicine. Address: Bragg Health Foundation, 199 Winchester Canyon Road, Santa Barbara, CA 93117, USA.

WESTERLUND Elaine M, b. 19 November 1945, Boston, Massachusetts, USA. m. Joseph F Doherty, 1 son. Education: BSc, Northeastern University, 1980; EdM, 1982, EdD, 1987, Boston University. Appointments: Founder, 1980, Peer Counsellor, Group Facilitator, 1980-82, Psychotherapist, 1982-88, Director, 1988-, Incest Resources Inc, 1st organisation in the country and world for survivors of childhood sexual abuse, 1980; Psychology Trainee, Solomon Carter Fuller Mental Health Centre, Roxbury, Massachusetts, 1981-82, Laboure Centre Mental Health Clinic, South Boston, Massachusetts, 1982-83; Psychology Intern, South Shore Mental Health Centre, Quincy, Massachusetts, 1983-84; Psychologist in private practice, Cambridge, Massachusetts, 1988-; Consultant, Guest Lecturer in field; Pioneer of survivor self-help movement in USA; Developed original programmes and treatment models for survivors. Publications: Author: Responding to Incest: In Memory of Nancy, 1987; Women's Sexuality After Childhood Incest, 1992; Articles including Thinking About Incest, Deafness and Counseling, 1993. Honours: Dean's Citation, Northeastern University, 1980; Teaching Fellowship, 1982-83, Practitioner-Teacher Award, 1982-83, School of Education Award, 1983-84, Boston University; Counselling Award and Academy Award, US Achievement Academy, 1987; Diplomate, American Board of Psychological Specialties, 1999; Diplomate, American Psychotherapy Association, 1999; Outstanding Alumni Award for Health Sciences, Northeastern University, 1999; Psi Chi; Pi Lambda Theta; Sigma Epsilon Rho. Memberships: Massachusetts Psychological Association; American College of Forensic Examiners; American Psychotherapy Association; Massachusetts State Association of the Deaf; Founding Member, Deaf Women's Counselling Project, 1986. Address: One Arnold Circle, Cambridge, MA 02139-2250, USA.

WESTMINSTER, Archbishop of (RC), His Eminence Cardinal Cormac Murphy-O'Connor, b. 24 August 1932, Reading Berkshire, England. Education: The Venerable English College Rome; PhL, STL, Gregorian University, Rome. Appointments: Ordained Priest, 1956; Assistant Priest, Corpus Christi Parish, Portsmouth, 1956-63, Sacred Heart Parish, Fareham, 1963-66; Private Secretary, Chaplain to Bishop of Portsmouth, 1966-70; Parish Priest, Parish of the Immaculate Conception, Southampton, 1970-71; Rector, The Venerable English College, Rome, 1971-77; Bishop of Arundel and Brighton, West Sussex, 1977-2000; Archbishop of Westminster, 2000-; Created Cardinal Priest of the title Santa Maria sopra Minerva, 2001; Chairman: Bishops' Committee for Europe, 1978-83; Committee for Christian Unity, 1983-2000; Department for Mission and Unity Bishops' Conference of England and Wales, 1993-; Joint Chairman, ARCIC-II, 1983-2000; President, Catholic Bishops' Conference of England and Wales, 2000-; Vice-President, Council of the Episcopal Conferences of Europe, 2001-. Publications: The Family of the Church, 1984; At the Heart of the World, 2004. Honours: Honorary DD, Lambeth, 1999; Freeman of the City of London, 2001; Honorary Bencher of the Inner Temple, 2001; Bailiff Grand Cross of Sovereign Military Order of Malta, 2002; Prior of British and Irish Delegation of Constantine Order, 2002. Memberships: Presidential Committee of the Pontifical Council for the Family, 2001-; Congregation for Divine Worship and the Discipline of the Sacraments, 2001-; Administration of the Patrimony of the Holy See, 2001; Pontifical Council for Culture, 2002-; Pontifical Commission for the Cultural Heritage of the Church, 2002-; Pontifical Council for Promoting Christian Unity, 2002. Address: Archbishop's House, Westminster, London SW1P 1QJ, England. E-mail: archbishop@rcdow.org.uk Website: www.rcdow.org.uk/archbishop.

WESTWOOD Vivienne Isabel, b. 8 April 1941, England. Fashion Designer. 2 sons. Career: Developed Punk fashion in partnership with Malcolm McLaren, Chelsea, London, 1970-83; Work produced for musicians including: Boy George; The Sex Pistols; Bananarama; Adam and the Ants; Bow Wow Wow; Solo avant-garde designer, 1984-; Also worked with S Galeotti, Italy, 1984; Launched Mini Crini, 1985; Produced collection featuring Harris tweed suits and princess coats; Pagan 5, 1989; Opened own shop in Mayfair, London, 1990; Launch of debut fragrance, Boudoir, 1998; Launch of Red Label, USA, 1999; First shop in New York, 1999; Vivienne Westwood: the Collection of Romilly McAlpine exhibition, Museum of London, 2000; Launch of second fragrance, Libertine, Europe, 2000; Shop opens in Hong Kong, 2002; Shop opens in Milan, 2003; Shop opens in Liverpool, 2003; Vivienne Westwood retrospective, Victoria and Albert Museum, London, 2004; Numerous fashion shows including: London; Paris Tokyo; New York. Honours: Professor of Fashion, Academy of Applied Arts, Vienna, 1989-91; Hochschule der Künste, Berlin, 1993-; Senior FRCA, 1992; British Designer of the Year, 1990, 1991; OBE, 1992; Queen's Award for Export, 1998; Moët & Chandon Fashion Tribute, V&A, 2001; UK fashion Export Award for Design, 2003. Address: Westwood Studios, 9-15 Elcho Street, London SW11 4AU, England.

WHALING Frank, b. 5 February 1934, Pontefract, Yorkshire, England. Professor of the Study of Religion; Methodist Minister. 1 son, 1 daughter. Education: BA History, 1957, BA, Theology, 1959, MA, 1961, PhD, 1990, Cambridge University; ThD, Comparative Religion, Harvard University, 1973. Appointments: Methodist Minister, Birmingham, England, 1960-62; Methodist Minister and College Manager, Faizabad and Banaras, India, 1962-66; Methodist Minister, Eastbourne, England, 1966-69; Teaching Fellow, Harvard University, 1971-72; Lecturer to Professor of the Study of Religion, Edinburgh University, Scotland, 1973-99; Visiting Professor, Chinese Academy of Social Sciences, Beijing, Dartmouth College, USA, Indiana University, USA, Witwatersrand University, Johannesburg, South Africa, Washington DC Wesley Seminary, UTC Bangalore, India, 1973-; Consultant for 26 volume series World Spirituality: An Encyclopaedic History of the Religious Quest for Crossroad Publishers, New York, 1981-89; Consultant for publishers T & T Clark (Edinburgh), Edinburgh University Press, Routledge, One World, Harper-Collins, 1985-; Consultant for Radio Clyde, Radio Forth, BBC Radio, BBC and ITV Television, 1988-; General Editor of 9 volume series on Understanding Religion for Dunedin Academic Press Edinburgh, 2000-; Consultant on Religious Studies for Church of Scotland and Methodist Church, 1986-. Publications: Written or edited: An Approach to Dialogue: Hinduism and Christianity, 1966; The Rise of the Religious Significance of Rama, 1980; John and Charles Wesley in the Classics of Western Spirituality, 1981; The World's Religious Traditions: Current Perspectives in Religious Studies, 1984; Contemporary Approaches to the Study of Religion: The Humanities, 1984; Contemporary Approaches to the Study of Religion: The Social Sciences, 1985; Christian Theology and World Religions: A Global Approach, 1986; Religion in Today's World, 1987; Compassion Through Understanding, 1990; Dictionary of Beliefs and Religions, 1992; The World: How It Came into Being and Our Responsibility for It, 1994; Theory and Method in Religious Studies, 1995; A Book of Christian Prayer, 2002; Over 100 articles and papers and over 250 reviews in various journals. Honours: Fellow, Royal Asiatic Society; International Biographical Association; World Literary Academy; American Biographical Institute; Institute of Contemporary Scotland; World Institute of Achievement; Scottish Academy of Merit; Peregrine Maitland Award in Comparative Religion, Cambridge; John E Theyer Honor Award, Harvard; Cook Trust Award, Farmington Trust Award; British Council Awards; Carnegie Awards; Commonwealth Foundation Award; British Academy Awards; Spalding Award; Moray Award, Pollock Award; Fulbright Award; Honorary Life Member: British Association for the Study of Religion. Memberships: British Labour Party; British Society of Authors; Institute of Contemporary Scotland; International Association of Buddhist Studies; International Inter-Faith Centre; Scottish Council for Moral and Religious Education: Scotland/China Association. Address: 21 Gillespie Road, Edinburgh EH13 0NW, Scotland.

WHALLEY Joanne, b. 25 August 1964, Salford, England. Actress. m. Val Kilmer, 1988, divorced 1996, 1 son, 1 daughter. Career: Stage: Began acting during teenage years; Season of Edward Bond plays, Royal Court Theatre, London; The Three Sisters; What the Butler Saw; Lulu; TV includes: The Singing Detective; A Kind of Loving; A Quiet Life; The Gentle Touch; Bergerac; Reilly; Edge of Darkness; A Christmas Carol; Save Your Kisses; Will You Love Me Tomorrow?; Scarlett; 40, 2003; Criminal Minds, 2005; Child of Mine, 2005; The Virgin Queen, 2005; Far from Home, 2006; Justice League, 2006; Life Line, 2007; Films: Pink Floyd – The Wall; Dance

With a Stranger; No Surrender; The Good Father; To Kill A Priest; Willow; Scandal; Kill Me Again; The Big Man; Navy Seals; Miss Helen; Shattered; Crossing the Line; Storyville; Mother's Boys; A Good Man in Africa; Trial By Jury; The Man Who Knew Too Little; The Guilty, 1999; Run the Wild Fields, 2000; Jacqueline Kennedy Onassis: A Life, 2000; Virginia's Run, 2001; Before You Go, 2002; The Californians, 2005; Played, 2006; Flood, 2007. Address: Creative Artists Agency, 9830 Wilshire Boulevard, Beverly Hills, CA 90212, USA.

WHATELY Kevin, b. 6 February 1951, Northumberland, England. Actor. m. Madelaine Newton, 1 son, 1 daughter. Education: Newcastle Polytechnic; The Central School of Speech and Drama, 1972-75. Career: Extensive television work including: Neville Hope in Auf Wiedersehen Pet, 1982-2004; Sergeant Lewis in Inspector Morse, 1986-2001; Steve in B & B, 1992; Dr Jack Kerruish in Peak Practice, 1992-95; Skallagrig, 1994; Trip Trap (BBC), 1996; Gobble, 1996; Jimmy Griffin in the Broker's Man, 1997-98; Pure Wickedness (BBC), 1999; What Katy Did (Tetra), 1999; Plain Jane (Carlton), 2001; Nightmare Neighbour (BBC), 2001; Hurst in Promoted to Glory, 2003; Dad, 2005; Belonging, ITV 2005; Footprints in the Snow, 2005; Lewis, 2006-; New Tricks, 2006; Dogtown, 2006; Who Gets the Dog? 2007; The Children, 2008; Theatre includes: Prince Hal in Henry IV Part 1 (Newcastle), 1981; Andy in Accounts (Edinburgh and London), 1982; Title Role in Billy Liar (national tour), 1983; John Proctor in The Crucible (Leicester), 1989; Daines in Our Own Kind (Bush), 1991; Twelve Angry Men (Comedy), 1996; Snake in the Grass (Pert Hall Co, Old Vic), 1997; How I Learned to Drive (Donmar), 1998; Film: The English Patient, 1996; Paranoid, 1999; Purely Belter, 2000; Silent Cry, 2001; The Legend of the Tamworth Two, 2003. Honours: Pye Comedy Performance of the Year Award, 1983; Variety Club Northern Personality of the Year, 1990; Honorary Doctor of Civil Law, Northumbria University. Memberships: Ambassador for the Prince's Trust; Ambassador for Newcastle and Gateshead; Ambassador for Sunderland; Vice-President, NCH; Patron, SPARKS; Patron, The Rose at Kingston Theatre; Patron, Oesophageal Patients Association. Address: c/o CDA, 125 Gloucester Road, London SW7 4TE, England.

WHEALIN Alice Marie, b. 1956, Germantown, Philadelphia, Pennsylvania, USA, Visual Fine Artist. Education: BA, Art, Rowan University, Glassboro, New Jersey, 1974-78; Certification in Structures, The Johnson Atelier Technical Institute for Sculpture, Princeton, New Jersey, 1978-80; MA, Tufts University, Medford Massachusetts and MA, MFA program, The Museum School, Boston, Massachusetts, 1981-84. Appointments: Teaching Assistant, The School of the Museum of Fine Arts, Boston, 1981; Museum Assistant, 1985-87, Docent, 1985-86, Museum Supervisor, 1987-95, Senior Museum Supervisor, 1995-, The Phillips Collection, Washington DC; Board Member, Arts and Space Inc, Arlington, Virginia, 1997-; Selected exhibitions include: New Jersey Craftsmen, Gallery 401, Magnolia, New Jersey, 1980; The School of the Museum of Fine Arts, Boston, Massachusetts, 1983; McCrillis Gallery Bethesda, Maryland, 1990; Robert Brown Gallery, Washington DC, 1992; International Monetary Fund, Washington, DC, 1994; United Nations 4th World Conference on Women, Beijing, China, 1995-96; Ellipse Art Center, Arlington, Virginia, 1996; Addison Ripley Gallery, Washington DC, 1998; Staff Exhibit, The Phillips collection, Washington DC, 1999; Contemporary Museum, Baltimore, Maryland, 2000; George Mason University, Arlington, Virginia, 2001, 2002; Fraternity Federal Bank, Baltimore, Maryland, 2003; Boulder Museum of Contemporary Art,

Boulder, Colorado, 2004; Delaplaine Visual Arts Education Center, Frederick, Maryland, 2004; Kathleen Ewing Gallery, Washington, DC, 2005; Montgomery College, Rockville, Maryland, 2005; Arlington Art Center, Arlington, Virginia, 2006. Honours: Review, The Washington Post, 1992; Article in the Northern Virginia Sun, 1995; Listed in biographical dictionaries. Memberships: Arlington Art Center; Childreach; The Nature Conservancy; Organized Women Voters of Arlington, VA; VA Verified Voting.org. Commissions and Creative works: Rowan University, Glassboro, New Jersey, commissioned set design, 1978; Bio-Dynamics, Millstone, New Jersey, commissioned sculpture, 1980; The Phillips Collection, Archives Collection, Washington DC, 1993; National Museum of Women in the Arts, Archives Collection, Washington DC, 1995. Address: Reeb Hall Studios, Studio #9, 4451 First Place, South, Arlington, VA 22204, USA. E-mail: alicewhealin@yahoo.com Website: www.alicewhealin.com

WHEATER Roger John, b. 24 November 1933, Brighton, Sussex, England. Conservationist. m. Jean Ord Troup, 1 son, 1 daughter. Education: Brighton, Hove & Sussex Grammar School, 1945-50; Brighton Technical College, 1950-51. Appointments: Assistant Superintendent of Police, Uganda, 1956-61; Chief Warden, Murchison Falls National Park, 1961-70; Director, Uganda National Parks, 1970-72; Director, Royal Zoological Society of Scotland, 1972-98; Chairman: Federation of Zoological Gardens of Great Britain & Ireland, 1993-96; Anthropoid Ape Advisory Panel, 1977-91; Editorial Board, World Zoo Conservation Strategy, 1991-93; European Association of Zoos & Aquaria, 1994-97; Access Forum, 1996-2000; Tourism and Environment Forum, 1999-2003; National Trust for Scotland, 2000-05; Heather Trust, 1999-2003; Deputy Chairman, Scottish Natural Heritage, 1997-99; President: Association of British Wild Animal Keepers, 1984-99; International Union of Zoo Directors (now World Association of Zoos and Aquaria), 1988-91; Cockburn Trout Angling Club, 1997-. Publications: Wide range of publications on national park management, environmental education, captive breeding, animal welfare, access to countryside, National Trust for Scotland Properties, etc. Honours: OBE, 1991; Honorary Professor, Edinburgh University, 1993; Honorary Doctorate, DUniv, 2004; Honorary Fellow, RSGS, 1995; Honorary Fellow, RZSS, 1999; Awards for outstanding achievement, World Association of Zoos and Aquaria, 2001; National Federation of Zoos in Great Britain and Ireland, 1998; European Association of Zoos and Aquaria, 2004. Memberships: Fellow: Royal Society, Edinburgh, 1985-; Royal Society of Arts, 1991-, Institute of Biology, 1987-; Trustee: The Gorilla Organisation, 1993-; Dynamic Earth, Edinburgh, 1998-; President, Scottish Wildlife Trust, 2006-; Trustee, Tweed Foundation, 2007-. Address: 17 Kirklands, Innerleithen, Peeblesshire, EH44 6NA, Scotland. E-mail: roger.wheater@btinternet.com

WHEELER Charles Selwyn, b. 26 March 1923, Bremen, Germany. Journalist. m. Dip Singh, 2 daughters. Education: Tynemouth School; Cranbrook School. Appointments: Journalist, Daily Sketch, 1940-41; BBC News, 1946-50; BBC German Service correspondent, Berlin, 1950-53; Producer, Panorama, 1956-58; Staff correspondent, Berlin, 1959-65; Panorama, 1965-73; South Asia, USA and Europe, 1959-75; Presenter, Panorama, 1975-76, BBC; Freelance journalist, 1977-; Newsnight correspondent; Documentaries for BBC, Channel 4 TV and BBC Radio 4. Honours: KB; CMG; Hon Dr of Letters, University of Sussex; Hon Dr of the Open University; KB 2007; Listed in national and international biographical dictionaries. Membership: Patron, Reprieve. Address: 10A Portland Road, London W11 4LA, England.

WHEELER (Henry) Neil George (Sir), b. 8 July 1917, Plymouth, Devon, England. Air Chief Marshal. m. Alice Elizabeth Weightman, 2 sons, 1 daughter. Education: RAF College Cranwell, 1935-37. Appointments: Royal Air Force, 1935-76; Retired as Air Chief Marshal; Director Rolls Royce Ltd, 1977-82; Director Flight Refuelling Ltd, 1977-85. Publications: Numerous articles on aeronautical matters mostly connected with operations during the 1939-45 war. Honours: DFC, 1941; Bar to DFC, 1943; DSO, 1943, OBE, 1949; AFC, 1954; CBE, 1957; ADC to H M The Queen, 1957-61; CB, 1967, KCB, 1969, GCB, 1975. Memberships: Fellow of the Royal Aeronautical Society; Companion of the British Institute of Management; Vice-President of the Air League; Past Master of the Guild of Air Pilots and Air Navigators. Address: Boundary Hall, Cooksbridge, Lewes, East Sussex BN8 4PT, England.

WHELAN Peter, b. 3 October 1931, Newcastle-under-Lyme, England. Playwright. Education: BA (Hons), University of Keele, Staffordshire, 1955. Appointments: Director, Garland Compton Ltd Advertising Agency, 1977; Director, Reeves Robertshaw Ltd, 1982; Associate Writer, Royal Shakespeare Company, 1990-. Plays produced and published: Double Edge (co-author), 1975; Captain Swing, RSC, 1978; The Accrington Pals, RSC, 1981; Clay, RSC, 1982; The Bright and Bold Design, RSC, 1992; The School of Night, RSC, 1993; Shakespeare Country, BT/Little Theatre Guild, 1993; The Tinderbox, New Vic, Newcastle, 1994; Divine Right, Birmingham Rep, 1996; The Herbal Bed, RSC, Sydney and New York, 1997; Overture, New Vic, Newcastle, 1997; A Russian In The Woods, RSC, 2001; The Earthly Paradise, Almeida Theatre, 2005. Honours: Writers Guild Best Play Nominations; Lloyds Private Banking Playwright of the Year, 1996; TMA Regional Theatre Awards, Best New Play, 1996; Nomination Best Play, Olivier Awards, 1997. Address: c/o The Agency, 24 Pottery Lane, Holland Park, London W11 4LZ, England.

WHELAN Ruth, b. 26 February 1956, Tullow, Co Carlow, Republic of Ireland. Education: BA, Trinity College, Dublin, 1977; Higher Diploma in Education, Trinity College, Dublin, 1978; MA, 1981; Diplôme d'études approfondies, University of Paris X, Nanterre, 1982; PhD, Trinity College, Dublin, 1984. Appointments: French language teacher, Rathdown School, Dublin, 1977-78; Instructor in English as a foreign language, Ecole d'Été de Dublin, 1978; Academic tutor, Department of French, Trinity College, Dublin, 1979-81; Instructor in English as a foreign language, École Normale Supérieure, Paris, 1981-82; Instructor in English as a foreign language, École Nationale Supérieure de la Statistique et des Affaires Économiques, Paris, 1983-84; Student Mentor, 1991-97, Lecturer in French, 1984-96, Senior Lecturer in French, 1996-97, Trinity College, Dublin; Editorial Board, Correspondance de Pierre Bayle, Voltaire Foundation, Oxford, 1988-98; Editorial Board of the Oxford Encyclopaedia of the Enlightenment, New York, 1996-2003; Professor of French and Head of Department, National University of Ireland, Maynooth, 1997-2007; Board of the National Museum, Ireland, 2005-; Research Associate, University of Nantes, 2005-; Senior Research Fellow, Archbishop Marsh's Library, Dublin, 2007-08. Publications: 10 books; Over 60 articles and essays; 7 translations. Honours: Irish Government Scholarship, 1973-78; Dr Hely-Hutchinson Stewart Literary Scholarship, Trinity College, Dublin, 1977-79; Graduate Studentship, Research Award, Trinity College, Dublin, 1978-81; Visiting Studentship, École Normale Supérieure, Paris, 1981-84; French Government Scholarship, 1981-82; Research Fellowship, Collège de France, Paris and The

Winifred Cullis Grant, The International Federation of University Women, Geneva, 1982-83; Arts (Letters) Faculty Research and Travel Award, 1987; Visiting Fellow, Herzog August Bibliothek, Wolfenbuttel, Germany, and Research Award, Faculty of Arts and Social Sciences Benefaction Fund, Trinity College, Dublin, 1988; Elected Fellow, Trinity College, Dublin, 1990; Senior Visitor, Linacre College, and the Voltaire Foundation, Oxford, 1992; Research Award, Provost's Fund, Trinity College, Dublin, and Research Award, Faculty of Arts and Social Sciences Benefaction Fund, Trinity College, Dublin, 1995; Elected Member, Royal Irish Academy, 2000; Research Professorship, NUI Maynooth, 2004-05; Post doctoral Fellow, Irish Council for the Humanities and Social Sciences, 2005-06; Publication grants, National University of Ireland and NUI Maynooth; Chevalier dans l'Ordre des Palmes Académiques; Listed in international biographical dictionaries. Memberships: Friends of the Library, Trinity College, Dublin; The Huguenot Society of Great Britain and Ireland; Society for French Studies, Great Britain and Ireland; Founding Member, Association Pierre Bayle, Paris. Address: Department of French, National University of Ireland, Maynooth, Co Kildare, Ireland. E-mail: ruth.whelan@nuim.ie

WHICKER Alan Donald, b. 2 August 1925. Television Broadcaster; Journalist; Author. Education: Haberdasher's Aske's School. Career: Director, Army Film and Photo Unit, 8th Army and US 5th Army; War Correspondent, Korea; Foreign Correspondent, Exchange Telegraph, 1947-57, BBC TV, 1957-68; Founder Member, Yorkshire TV, 1968; TV appearances include: Whicker's World, 1959-60; Whicker Down Under, 1961; Whicker in Sweden, 1963; Whicker's World, 1965-67; 122 documentaries for Yorkshire TV; Whicker's World - The First Million Miles! 1982; Whicker's World, A Fast Boat to China, 1983; Whicker! 1984; Whicker's World - Living with Uncle Sam, 1985; Whicker's World - Living with Waltzing Matilda, 1988; Whicker's World - Hong Kong, 1990; Whicker's World - A Taste of Spain, 1992; Around Whicker's World, 1992; Whicker's World - The Sultan of Brunei, 1992; South Africa: Whicker's Miss World and Whicker's World - The Sun King, 1993; South-East Asia: Whicker's World Aboard the Real Orient Express, Whicker's World - Pavarotti in Paradise, 1994; Travel Channel, 1996; Whicker's Week, BBC Choice, 1999; Travel Ambassador on the Internet for AOL, 2000; One on One, 2002; Whicker's War Series, 2004; Radio includes: Whicker's Wireless World, 1983; Around Whicker's World, 1998; Whicker's New World, 1999; Whicker's World Down Under, 2000; Fabulous Fifties, 2000; It'll Never Last - The History of Television, 2001; Fifty Royal Years; Around Whicker's World, 2002. Publications: Some Rise by Sin, 1949; Away - with Alan Whicker, 1963; Best of Everything, 1980; Within Whicker's World (autobiography), 1982; Whicker's Business Travellers Guide, 1983; Whicker's New World, 1985; Whicker's World Down Under, 1988; Whicker's World - Take 2! 2000; Whicker's War, 2005. Honours: Various awards including: Guild of TV Producers and Directors; Personality of the Year, 1964; Silver Medal, Royal TV Society; Dimbleby Award, BAFTA, 1978; TV Times Special Award, 1978; First inductee, Royal TV Society's Hall of Fame, 1993; Travel Writers' Special Award, 1998; BAFTA Grierson Documentary Tribute Award, 2001; National Film Theatre tribute; 6th TV Festival, 2002. Address: Trinity, Jersey, JE3 5BA, Channel Islands.

WHITAKER (Baroness of Beeston in the County of Nottinghamshire); Janet Alison Whitaker, Life Peer; Member of the House of Lords. Education: Major Scholar BA, Girton College, Cambridge; Farley Graduate Scholar,

MA, Brynmawr College, USA; Radcliffe Fellow, Harvard, USA. Appointments: Commissioning Editor, André Deutsch Ltd, 1961-66; Speechwriter to Chairman of the Health and Safety Commission, 1976; Head of Gas Safety, Health and Safety Executive, 1983-86, Head of Nuclear Safety Administration, 1986-88; Head of Health and Safety, Department of Employment, 1988-92; Head of Sex Equality, 1992-96; Member, Employment Tribunals, 1995-2000; Consultant, CRE and Commonwealth Secretariat, 1996-99; Member: Immigration Complaints Audit Committee, 1998-99, European Union Select Committee Sub-Committee on Education, Social Affairs and Home Affairs, 1999-2003, Joint Committee on Human Rights, 2000-03, Joint Parliamentary Committee on the Draft Corruption Bill, 2003-, Friends Provident Committee of Reference; Chair, Camden Racial Equality Council, 1999; Chair, Working Men's College, 1998-2001; Non Executive Director, Tavistock and Portman NHS Trust, 1997-2001; Deputy Chair, Independent Television Commission, 2001-2003; Vice President, British Humanist Association, One World Trust; Trustee: UNICEF; Patron, British Stammering Association; SoS Sahel; Runnymede Trust. Memberships: Overseas Development Institute Council; Opportunity International; Advisory Council, Transparency International (UK); Interact Worldwide; Reform Club. Address: The House of Lords, London SW1A 0PW, England.

WHITBREAD Fatima, b. 3 March 1961, Stoke Newington, England. Athlete. m. Andrew Norman, 1997, 1 son. Appointments: UK International Debut as Javelin Thrower, 1977; European Junior Champion, 1979; European Cup Champion, 1983; European Cup Silver Medallist, 1985; European Champion, 1986; Commonwealth Games Bronze Medallist, 1982, Silver Medallist, 1986; Olympic Games Bronze Medallist, 1984, Silver Medallist, 1988; World Championships Silver Medallist, 1983; World Record Holder, 1986; World Champion, 1987; Retired, 1990; Founder Member, President, Chafford Hundred A.C; Marketing Consultant. Honours include: BBC Sports Personality of the Year, 1987; British Sports Writers Sportswoman of the Year, 1986, 1987; British Athletic Writers Woman Athlete of the Year, 1986, 1987. Memberships include: Voluntary Service Overseas Ambassador, 1992-93; President, Thurrock Harriers Athletic Club, 1993-; Governor, King Edward Grammer School, Chelmsford, 2000-02. Address: Chafford Hundred Information Centre, Elizabeth Road, Chafford Hundred, Grays, Essex RM16 6QZ, England. E-mail: champinternational@tinyworld.co.uk

WHITE Edmund (Valentine III), b. 13 January 1940, Cincinnati, Ohio, USA. Writer. Education: BA, University of Michigan, 1962. Appointments: Writer, Time-Life Books, New York City, 1962-70; Senior Editor, Saturday Review, New York City, 1972-73; Assistant Professor of Writing Seminars, Johns Hopkins University, 1977-79; Adjunct Professor, Columbia University School of the Arts, 1981-83; Executive Director, New York Institute for the Humanities, 1982-83; Professor, Brown University, 1990-92; Professor of Humanities, Princeton University, 1999-. Publications: Fiction: Forgetting Elena, 1973; Nocturnes for the King of Naples, 1978; A Boy's Own Story, 1982; Aphrodisiac (with others), stories, 1984; Caracole, 1985; The Darker Proof: Stories from a Crisis (with Adam Mars-Jones), 1987; The Beautiful Room is Empty, 1988; Skinned Alive, stories, 1995; The Farewell Symphony, 1997; The Married Man, 2000; Fanny: A Fiction, 2003; Chaos: A Novella and Stories, 2007; Hotel de Dream, 2007; Non-Fiction: The Joy of Gay Sex: An Intimate Guide for Gay Men to the Pleasures of a Gay Lifestyle (with Charles Silverstein), 1977; States of Desire: Travels in Gay America,

1980; The Faber Book of Gay Short Fiction (editor), 1991; Genet: A Biography, 1993; The Selected Writings of Jean Genet (editor), 1993; The Burning Library, essays, 1994; Our Paris, 1995; Proust, 1998; The Flâneur: A Stroll Through the Paradoxes of Paris, 2000; Arts and Letters, 2004; Plays: Terre Haute, 2006; Contributions to: Many periodicals. Honours: Ingram Merrill Foundation Grants, 1973, 1978; Guggenheim Fellowship, 1983; American Academy and Institute of Arts and Letters Award, 1983; Chevalier de l'ordre des arts et lettres, France, 1993; Officier Ordre des Arts et des Lettres, 1999. Memberships: American Academy of Arts and Letters; American Academy of Arts and Sciences. Address: c/o Amanda Urban, International Creative Management, 40 West 57th Street, New York, NY 10019, USA.

WHITE Elvina, b. 29 January 1966, Petersfield, Hampshire, England. Care Pathways Co-ordinator. m. Kevin Dunk, 2 sons. Education: BSc Biology, University of Sussex, England, 1987. Appointments: Research Assistant, Liverpool Congenital Malformations Registry, University of Liverpool, 1988-91; Medical Audit Administrator, St Helens & Knowsley Health Authority, 1991-92; Medical Audit Facilitator, Wigan & Bolton Health Authority, 1992-2000; Evaluation Co-ordinator, Department of Health Secondment, Bolton Community Healthcare NHS Trust, 1996-97; Care Pathways Co-ordinator, Royal Liverpool Children's NHS Trust, Alder Hey, 2000-. Publications: Using Integrated Care Pathways as an Effective Tool to Implement Guidelines, 2002; An Integrated Care Pathway for Burns, 2003. Address: Royal Liverpool Children's NHS Trust, Alder Hey Hospital, Eaton Road, Liverpool L12 2AP, England. E-mail: elvina.white@rlc.nhs.uk

WHITE George Edward, b. 19 March 1941, Northampton, Massachusetts, USA. Professor. m. Susan Davis White, 2 daughters. Education: BA, Amherst College, 1963; MA, PhD, Yale University, 1967; JD, Harvard Law School, 1970. Appointments: Law Clerk, Chief Justice Earl Warren, Supreme Court of United States, 1971-72; Assistant Professor of Law, University of Virginia Law School, 1972-74; Associate Professor, 1974-77; Professor, 1977-86; John B Minor Professor of Law and History, 1986-2003; University Professor, 1992-2003; David and Mary Harrison Distinguished Professor of Law, 2003-. Publications: The Eastern Establishment and the Western Experience, 1968; The American Judicial Tradition, 1976; Patterns of American Legal Thought, 1978; Tort Law in America, 1980; Earl Warren: A Public Life, 1982; The Marshall Court and Cultural Change, 1987; Justice Oliver Wendell Holmes: Law and the Inner Self, 1993; Intervention and Detachment: Essays in Legal History and Jurisprudence, 1994; Creating the National Pastime, 1996; The Constitution and the New Deal, 2000; Alger Hiss's Looking-Glass Wars, 2004; Oliver Wendell Holmes Jr, 2006; History and the Constitution: Collected Essays, 2006. Honours: Fellow, National Endowment for the Humanities, 1977-78, 1982-83; Fellow, Guggenheim Foundation, 1982-83; Triennial Award for Distinguished Scholarship, Association of American Law Schools, 1996. Memberships: Phi Beta Kappa; American Academy of Arts and Sciences; Society of American Historians; American Law Institute. Address: School of Law, University of Virginia, 580 Massie Road, Charlottesville, VA 22903, USA.

WHITE Marco Pierre, b. 11 December 1961, Leeds, England. Chef; Restaurateur. m. (1) Alexandra McArthur, 1988, divorced 1990, 1 daughter, (2) Lisa Butcher, 1992, divorced 1994, (3) Matilda Conejero-Caldera, 2000, divorced 2007, 2 sons, 1 daughter. Appointments: Commis Chef, The Box Tree, Ilkley, 1978; Commis Chef de Partie, Le

Gavroche, 1981, Tante Claire, 1983; Sous Chef, Le Manoir aux Quat' Saisons, 1984; Chef, Proprietor, Harveys, 1987-, The Restaurant, 1993-; Co-Owner, The Canteen, 1992-96; Founder, Criterion Restaurant with Sir Rocco Forte, 1995-; Re-opened Quo Vadis, 1996-; Oak Room, Le Meridien, 1997-99; MPW Canary Wharf, 1997-; Café Royal Grill Room, 1997-; Mirabelle Restaurant, Curzon Street, 1998-; L'Escargot Belvedere, 1999; Wheeler of St James, 2002; Head Chef, Hell's Kitchen, ITV, 2007; Publications: White Heat, 1990; White Heat II, 1994; Wild Food From Land and Sea, 1994; Canteen Cuisine, 1995; The Mirabelle Cookbook, 1999. Honours include: Restaurant of the Year, Egon Ronay (for The Restaurant), 1997. Address: Mirabelle Restaurant, 56 Curson Street, London W1Y 7PF, England.

WHITE Susan Dorothea, b. 10 August 1941, Adelaide, South Australia. Visual Artist; Painter; Sculptor; Printmaker; Author. m. Brian Freeman, 2 sons, 1 daughter. Education: Full-time studies, South Australian School of Art, Adelaide, 1959-60; Full-time studies, Julian Ashton Art School, Sydney, 1960-61; Additional studies in sculpture, 1959-61, 1985-89 and printmaking, 1972, 1975, 1978. Career: Solo exhibitions, Australia, Europe, USA, 1962-98; Group exhibitions, Australia, Europe, USA, Asia, South America, 1959-2008; Author and Illustrator, Draw Like Da Vinci, 2006; Dessiner à la manière de Léonard de Vinci, 2007. Collections held in: Buhl Collection, New York; International Arts & Artists - Hechinger Collection, Washington DC; National Gallery of Australia, Canberra; Dr Ulla Mitzdorf Collection, Munich; Museum of International Contemporary Graphic Art, Norway; FMK Gallery, Budapest; Gallery of Modern Art, Lublin; Mornington Peninsula Regional Gallery, Victoria; Westmead Centre, Sydney. Publications: Artwork appears in numerous publications; Significant artwork: The First Supper, 1988; The Seven Deadly Isms, 1992; The Seven Deadly Sins of Modern Times, 1993; It Cuts Both Ways, 1998; Next-Door Neighbours, 2000; Menopausal Me in a Saucepan Lid, Warts 'n All, with Everything, including the Kitchen Sink, 2001; Lost for Words, 2003; Stretching the Imagination, 2005. Memberships: Viscopy; National Association for the Visual Arts. Address: 278 Annandale St, Annandale (Sydney), NSW 2038, Australia. Website: www.susandwhite.com.au

WHITNEY Stewart Bowman, b. 15 November 1938, Buffalo, New York, USA. Professor Emeritus; Expedition Leader. m. Joan Noel Conti, 2 sons, 4 daughters. Education: BA, University of Buffalo, 1961; MA, 1965, PhD, 1972, SUNY, Buffalo. Appointments: Study Director, School of Medicine, SUNY, Buffalo, 1962-65; Assistant Professor, Ithaca College, 1965-69; Assistant Professor, Antioch College, 1970-73; Professor, Niagara University, 1973-2006; Director, Niagara Research Institute, 2006-. Publications: Several book and numerous articles in professional journals. Honours: Outstanding Achievement, International Wildlife; CFLE, National Council on Family Relations; FAACS, American Board of Sexology; Alpha Kappa Delta. Memberships: National Council on Family Relations; American Board of Sexology; American Sociological Association; World Future Society; Society for Scientific Study of Sexuality. Address: Niagara Research Institute, 73 Niagara Falls Blvd, Buffalo, NY 14214, USA.

WHITTINGDALE John, b. 1959. Member of Parliament. m. Ancilla, 2 children. Education: Economics Degree, University College, London. Appointments: Head, Political Section, Conservative Research Department, 1982-84; Special Advisor to three consecutive Secretaries of State for Trade and Industry, 1984-85; Political Secretary to the

Prime Minister, 1988-90; Private Secretary to Baroness Thatcher, 1990-92; Elected Member of Parliament for South Colchester and Maldon, 1992; Member, House of Commons Select Committee on Health, 1993-97; Parliamentary Private Secretary to the Minister of State for Education and Employment, 1994-96; Elected Member of Parliament for Maldon and East Chelmsford, 1997; Opposition Whip, 1997; Frontbench Treasury Spokesman, 1998; Parliamentary Private Secretary to the Leader of the Opposition, 1999; Shadow Secretary of State for Trade and Industry, 2001; Shadow Secretary of State for Culture, Media and Sport, 2002, 2004-05; Shadow Secretary of State for Agriculture, Fisheries and Food, 2003-04; Chairman of the House of Commons Culture, Media and Sport Select Committee, 2005-; Parliamentary representative, Board of the Conservative Party, 2006; Vice Chairman, Conservative Parliamentary Party 1922 Committee, 2006. Memberships: President, Maldon District Chamber of Commerce; Patron, Dawn Sailing Barge Trust; Patron, Home-Start, Maldon; Vice-Patron, Helen Rollason Cancer Care Centre Appeal; President, Maldon Branch, Parkinson's Disease Society; Patron, Friends of St Lawrence Newland Church Trust; Honorary 'Friend of Swans', SWANS, Maldon (Sometimes We All Need Support); Patron, East Coast Sail Trust; Patron, Victoria County History of Essex Appeal Fund; Patron, Friends of St Mary's Church, Burnham. Address: House of Commons, London SW1A 0AA, England. E-mail: jwhittingdale.mp@tory.org.uk

WHITTINGTON Ralph Edward, b. 13 January 1945, Washington, DC, USA. Retired Curator. Divorced, 1 daughter. Education: High school, Surrattsville, Clinton, Maryland, 1963. Appointments: Curator, Library of Congress, retired. Publications: The Library of Sexual Congress, Washington City Paper, 1997; The Daily Show with John Steward Comedy Central (Cable TV), 1999; The Librarian of Sexual Congress, Spin Magazine, 1999; Extra TV, 1999; The King of Porn: The World's Foremost Collector of Fine Tart, Penthouse.com, 2000; TV2, Hungary, 2002; King of Porn Empties out his Castle, Washington Post, 2002; The Librarian of Sleaze, Details magazine, 2002; As It Happens (radio), Canadian Broadcast Corporation, 2002; World's Largest Professionally Catalogued Collection of Pornography, Time Magazine, 2002. Honours: Who's Who in America, 2004-2008; Who's Who in the World, 2008. Memberships: Consultant, The Museum of Sex in New York. Address: 9204 Greenfield Lane, Clinton, MD 20735, USA.

WIDDECOMBE Rt Hon Ann Noreen, b. 4 October 1947, Bath, Somerset, England. Member of Parliament. Education: BA (Hons) Latin, University of Birmingham, 1966-69; BA (Hons) Politics, Philosophy and Economics, University of Oxford, Lady Margaret Hall, 1976. Appointments: Marketing, Unilever, 1973-75; Senior Administrator, London University, 1975-87; Member of Parliament, Maidstone and The Weald, 1987-2007; Parliamentary Under Secretary (1) Social Security (2) Employment, 1990-94; Minister of State, Employment, 1994-95; Minister of State, Home Office, 1995-97; Shadow Health Secretary, 1998-99; Shadow Home Secretary, 1999-2001. Publications: The Clematis Tree, 2000; An Act of Treachery, 2002; Father Figure, 2005; An Act of Peace, 2005. Honour: Privy Counsellor, 1997. Address: House of Commons, London SW1, England.

WIDDICOMBE (Mary Josephine) Catherine, b. 22 May 1928, Montreux, Switzerland. Educator; Consultant. Education: Certificate of Education, St Mary's College, Newcastle upon Tyne, 1948; Community Development and Extension Course, 1970, Diploma in Education, 1978; Master of Philosophy, 1984, Institute of Education, University of London. Appointments: Teacher, St Benedict's Boys School, Ealing, London, 1948-49; Various posts including: Sales and Publicity for Grail Publications, Grail Youth Movement, Ecumenical Centre Work in London, Training Officer - as a Member of the Grail Society (a Roman Catholic lay community), 1949-69; Project 70-75 (action research), 1970-76; Co-Founder and Associate Director, Avec (a service agency for church and Christian community work based in Chelsea, work with church and community organisation leaders in UK and Ireland and people from overseas), 1976-92; Freelance Consultant, Trainer and Facilitator in church and community development, Researcher and Writer, Work in UK, Ireland, Italy and Nigeria, 1992-; President of the Grail Society, 1993-96; Co-Founder, Avec Resources (resources for people working and consulting in church and community), 1993-. Publications: Churches and Communities: An Approach to Development in the Local Church (co-author with George Lovell), 1978, reprinted, 1986; Meetings that Work: A Practical Guide to Teamworking in Groups, 1994, 2000; Small Communities in Religious Life: Making Them Work, 2001; Book chapter: Practicalities of Creative Collaborative Community Living in "Creating Harmony: Conflict Resolution in Community" (ed. Hilda Jackson), 1999; Many articles in In Touch, the magazine of the Grail. Honour: Awarded the Cross of St Augustine by Rowan William, Archbishop of Canterbury for advancing friendly relations between various Christian communities and churches, 2006. Memberships: The Grail Society; Pinner Association of Churches; Christians for a New Awareness; Confraternity of St James; The Bede Griffiths Sangha; London Society of Jews and Christians; The Three Faiths Dialogue, Pinner; The Church's Community Work Alliance; Living Spirituality Network; World Community of Christian Meditation. Address: 125 Waxwell Lane, Pinner, Middlesex HA5 3ER, England. E-mail: jcwiddicombe@tiscali.co.uk

WIDMER Winifred Ruth, b. 25 January 1921, Herkimer, New York, USA. Law and Educational Research Administration. m. Francis E Downey, 1 step-son, 2 step-daughters. Education: LLB, cum laude, Albany Law School, Union University, 1954; BA, History and Government, Russell Sage College, 1958; JD, Albany Law School, 2003. Appointments: Admitted to practice, New York State Bar, 1954, United States Supreme Court, 1958; Officer, Assistant Director for Administration, Corporate Secretary, The Research Foundation of State University of New York, a non-profit educational corporation administering research and educational funds for the State University of New York, 1954-80; Retired, 1988. Honours: Honorary Juris Doctor, Albany Law School, Union University, 2003; Kate Stoneman Award, Albany Law School, 2003; Member, Justinian Society honorary legal society. Memberships: Former Member, Council on Governmental Relations, subcommittee of NACUBO, representing the Research Foundation; Former member, New York State Bar Association; Board of Trustees, Capital District Genealogical Society; The Essex Society for Family History; National Curtis/Curtiss Society. Address: 3 Colonial Avenue, Albany, New York 12203-2009, USA. E-mail: fnwdowney@worldnet.att.net

WIEMANN Marion R Jnr, b. 7 September 1929, Chesterton, Indiana, USA. Biologist; Microscopist. 1 daughter. Education: BSc, Biological Sciences, Indiana University, Bloomington, 1959; Certificates and Formal Training in Microscopy, McCrone Research Institute, Chicago, 1967-71; ScD Hons, The London Institute of Applied Research, 1994; ScD Hons, World Academy, Germany, 1995; Professor of Science,

Australian Institute for Co-ordinated Research, Australia, 1995. Appointments: Histological Research Technician, 1959, Research Assistant, 1959-62, Research Technician, 1962-64, 1965-67, Senior Research Technician, 1967-70, Research Technologist, 1970-79, University of Chicago; Science Teacher, Westchester Township School Corporation, Chesterton, Indiana, 1964-66; Principal, Marion Wiemann and Associates, Consulting, Research and Development, Chesterton, Indiana, 1979-89; Ambassador General, American Embassy, Indiana, 2007-. Publications: Tooth Decay, Its Cause and Prevention Through Controlled Soil Composition and Soil pH, 1985. Honours: Scholarships; Various awards of merit; Recipient, Scouter's Key, 1968, Arrowhead Honour, 1968, Boy Scouts of America; Henri Dunant Silver Medal with Silver Bars, 1995; Albert Einstein Silver Medal, Huguenin, Le Locke, Switzerland, 1995; Listed in national and international biographical dictionaries. Memberships: ABI Research Association; Field Museum of Natural History; Life Patron, IBA and ABI; Life Member, World Institute of Achievement; Life Fellow, World Literary Academy; Vice President, 1967-70, President, 1970-71, State Microscopal Society of Illinois; World Explorers Club; Enobled, Royal College Heraldry, Australia, 1991; National Weather Service. Address: PO Box 1016, Chesterton, IN 46304, USA.

WIENER Marvin S, b. 16 March 1925, New York City, USA. Rabbi; Editor; Executive. m. Sylvia Bodek, 1 son, 1 daughter. Education: BS, 1944; MS, 1945; BHL, 1947; MHL and Ordination, 1951; DD (Hon), 1977. Appointments: Registrar, Rabbinical School, Jewish Theological Seminary of America, 1951-57; Consultant, Frontiers of Faith, television series, NBC, 1951-57; Director, Instructor Liturgy, Cantors Institute-Seminary College Jewish Music, Jewish Theological Seminary of America, 1954-58; Faculty Co-ordinator, Seminary School and Womens Institute, 1958-64; Director, National Academy for Adult Jewish Studies, United Synagogue, New York City, 1958-78; Editor, Burning Bush Press, 1958-78, United Synagogue Review, 1978-86; Director, Committee on Congregational Standards, United Synagogue, 1976-86; Consultant, Community Relations and Social Action, 1981-82, Editor, Executive, Joint Retirement Board, 1986-. Publications: Editor of numerous volumes of Judaica; Author of articles in professional journals. Memberships include: American Academy of Jewish Research; Association of Jewish Studies; Rabbinical Assembly, New York Board of Rabbis. Address: 67-66 108th Street, Apt D-46, Forest Hills, NY 11375-2974, USA.

WIESEL Elie(zer), b. 30 September 1928, Sighet, Romania (US citizen, 1963). Author; Professor in the Humanities Religion and Philosophy. m. Marion Erster Rose, 1969, 1 son. Education: Sorbonne, University of Paris, 1948-51. Appointments: Distinguished Professor, City College of the City University of New York, 1972-76; Andrew W Mellon Professor in the Humanities, 1976-, Professor of Philosophy, 1988-, Boston University; Distinguished Visiting Professor of Literature and Philosophy, Florida International University, Miami, 1982; Henry Luce Visiting Scholar in the Humanities and Social Thought, Yale University, 1982-83. Publications include: La Nuit (Night), 1958; Le Mendiant de Jerusalem (A beggar in Jerusalem), 1968; Célébration Hassidique (Souls on Fire), 1972; Célébration Biblique (Messengers of God: Biblical Portraits and Legends), 1976; Le Mal et l'Exil (Evil and Exile), 1988; L'Oublié (The Forgotten), 1989. Honours: Numerous, including: Prix Medicis, 1969; Prix Bordin, 1972; US Congressional Gold Medal, 1985; Nobel Prize for Peace, 1986; US Presidential Medal of Freedom, 1992; Grand-Croix of the French Legion of Honor, 2001.

Memberships: American Academy of Arts and Sciences; Amnesty International; Author's Guild; European Academy of Arts and Sciences; Foreign Press Association, honorary lifetime member; Jewish Academy of Arts and Sciences; PEN; Writers Guild of America; The Royal Norwegian Society of Sciences and Letters; Founding President, Universal Academy of Cultures, Paris, 1993-; PEN New England Council, 1993-; Fellow, American Academy of Arts and Letters, Department of Literature, 1996-; Honorary Fellow, Modern Language Association of America, 1998; Honorary Member, Romanian Academy, 2001. Address: Boston University, 147 Bay State Road, Boston, MA 02215, USA.

WIGGINS Christopher David, b. 1 February 1956, Leamington Spa, England. Composer; Music Teacher. m. Karin Czok, 1985, divorced 1995. Education: University of Liverpool, 1974-77, Postgraduate, 1978-79; Bretton Hall College, University of Leeds, 1977-78; Goldsmiths College, London (part-time), 1980-82; University of Surrey (part-time), 1991-97; BA honours, Music, 1977, BMus, 1979, Liverpool University; PGCE, Bretton Hall, University of Leeds, 1978; MMus, London, 1982; FTCL, Composition, 1986; MPhil, Surrey, 1997. Career: Teacher of Music, Putteridge High School, Icknield High School, Luton Sixth Form College, Luton, 1979-95; GCSE Examiner, Music, 1989-95; Conducted various concerts by Central Music School String Orchestra, Tallinn, Estonia, 1990-93; Education Director, Classical Music Show, London, 1993-94; A Level Examiner, Music, 1995-; Head of Music and Examinations Co-ordinator, International School, Berlin-Potsdam, 1995-98; Co-founder and Vice Principal, Erasmus International School, Potsdam, 1999-2003; Co-ordinator, with Berliner Landesmusikakademie, visit to Berlin by string ensemble from University of Surrey, 2001; Member of Senior Management Team, Schiller Academy, Potsdam, Germany, 2003-2004; Teacher of Music and English, Neues Gymnasium Potsdam, 2004; Inspector for Examination Centres, 2004-; I B Music Examiner, 2005-; IGCSE Music Examiner, 2006-; Major Compositions: About 150 compositions, over 110 performed including St-Johannes Passion, op 145, Concerto for 4 horns, op 93, Kleine Freiburger Messe, op 111, Triple Concerto, op 134; Over 90 published in total in USA, Netherlands, Germany, Sweden and UK, including music for strings, horn ensemble and choir. Recordings include: Missa Brevis op 69,Germany; Ave Maria op 70, Germany; Soliloquy IX op 94 no 9; In Einem Kripplein Lag Ein Kind op 72, Germany; Elegy op 83, Estonia; Five Miniatures for 4 horns op 85, USA; Fanfare for Quedre, op 139, USA. Honours: Allsop Prize, Composition, Liverpool, 1977; Wangford Composers' Prize, 1991. Memberships: International Horn Society; British Horn Society; Schools Music Association; PRS; MCPS; ESTA, UK; ABCD, Member of Convocation, University of London. Address: c/o Tilsdown Lodge, Dursley, Gloucestershire GL11 5QQ, England.

WILBUR Richard (Purdy), b. 1 March 1921, New York, New York, USA. Poet; Writer; Translator; Editor; Professor. m. Mary Charlotte Hayes Ward, 20 June 1942, 3 sons, 1 daughter. Education: AB, Amherst College, 1942; AM, Harvard University, 1947. Appointments: Assistant Professor of English, Harvard University, 1950-54; Associate Professor of English, Wellesley College, 1955-57; Professor of English, Wesleyan University, 1957-77; Writer-in-Residence, Smith College, 1977-86; Poet Laureate of the USA, 1987-88; Visiting Lecturer at various colleges and universities. Publications: Poetry: The Beautiful Changes and Other Poems, 1947; Ceremony and Other Poems, 1950; Things of This World, 1956; Poems, 1943-1956, 1957; Advice to a Prophet and

Other Poems, 1961; The Poems of Richard Wilbur, 1963; Walking to Sleep: New Poems and Translations, 1969; Digging to China, 1970; Seed Leaves: Homage to R F, 1974; The Mind-Reader: New Poems, 1976; Seven Poems, 1981; New and Collected Poems, 1988; Bone Key and other poems, 1998; Mayflies: New Poems and Translations, 2000; Collected Poems, 1943—2004, 2004; For Children: Loudmouse, 1963; Opposites, 1973; More Opposites, 1991; A Game of Catch, 1994; Runaway Opposites, 1995; Opposites, More Opposites and Some Differences, 2000; The Pig in the Spigot, 2000. Non-Fiction: Anniversary Lectures (with Robert Hillyer and Cleanth Brooks), 1959; Emily Dickinson: Three Views (with Louise Bogan and Archibald MacLeish), 1960; Responses: Prose Pieces, 1953-1976, 1976. Editor: Modern American and Modern British Poetry (with Louis Untermeyer and Karl Shapiro), 1955; A Bestiary, 1955; Poe: Complete Poems, 1959; Shakespeare: Poems (with Alfred Harbage), 1966, revised edition, 1974; Poe: The Narrative of Arthur Gordon Pym, 1974; Witter Bynner: Selected Poems, 1978. Translator: Molière: The Misanthrope, 1955; Molière: Tartuffe, 1963; Molière: The School for Wives, 1971; Molière: The Learned Ladies, 1978; Racine: Andromache, 1982; Racine: Phaedra, 1986; Molière: The School for Husbands, 1992; Molière: The Imaginary Cuckold, 1993; Molière: Amphitryon, 1995; Molière: Don Juan, 2000; Molière: The Bungler, 2000. Honours include: Edna St Vincent Millay Memorial Award, 1957; Pulitzer Prizes in Poetry, 1957, 1989; National Book Award for Poetry, 1957; Ford Foundation Fellowship, 1960; Bollingen Prizes, 1963, 1971; Chevalier, Ordre des Palmes Academiques, 1983; 2nd US Poet Laureate; Ruth Lilly Poetry Prize, 2006. Memberships: Academy of American Poets, chancellor; American Academy of Arts and Letters, president, 1974-76, chancellor, 1976-78, 1980-81; American Academy of Arts and Sciences; American Society of Composers, Authors and Publishers; Authors League of America; Dramatists Guild; Modern Language Association, honorary fellow. Address: 87 Dodwells Road, Cummington, MA 01206, USA.

WILBY Basil Leslie, (Gareth Knight), b. 1930, Colchester, England. Writer. Education: BA, Hons, French, Royal Holloway College, University of London, 2000; Postgraduate Diploma, Imperialism and Culture, Sheffield Hallam University, 2002. Publications: A Practical Guide to Qabalistic Symbolism, 1965; The New Dimensions Red Book, 1968; The Practice of Ritual Magic, 1969; Occult Exercises and Practices, 1969; Meeting the Occult, 1973; Experience of the Inner Worlds, 1975; The Occult: An Introduction, 1975; A History of White Magic, 1978; The Secret Tradition in Arthurian Legend, 1983; The Rose Cross and the Goddess, 1985; The Treasure House of Images, 1986; The Magical World of the Inklings, 1990; The Magical World of the Tarot, 1991; Magic and the Western Mind, 1991; Tarot and Magic, 1991; Evoking the Goddess, 1993; Dion Fortune's Magical Battle of Britain, 1993; Introduction to Ritual Magic (with Dion Fortune), 1997; The Circuit of Force (with Dion Fortune) 1998; Magical Images and the Magical Imagination, 1998; Principles of Hermetic Philosophy (with Dion Fortune), 1999; Merlin and the Grail Tradition, 1999; Dion Fortune and the Inner Light, 2000; Spiritualism and Occultism (with Dion Fortune), 2000; Pythoness, the Life and Work of Margaret Lumley Brown, 2000; Dion Fortune and the Threefold Way, 2002; The Wells of Vision, 2002; The Abbey papers, 2002; Granny's Magic Cards, 2004; Dion Fortune and the Lost Secrets of the West, 2005; The Occult Fiction of Dion Fortune, 2007; The Arthurian Formula (with Dian Fortune & Margaret Lumley Brown), 2007; Magic and the Power of the Goddess, 2008; Contributions to: Inner Light Journal, 1993-2008. Address: c/o 38 Steeles Road, London NW3 4RG, England.

WILBY David Christopher, b. 14 June 1952, Leeds, England. Barrister at Law; Queen's Counsel. m. Susan Christine, 1 son, 3 daughters. Education: Roundhay School, Leeds; BA (Hons), MA, Downing College, Cambridge. Appointments: Called to the Bar, Inner Temple, 1974; Chairman, Criminal Injuries Appeal Panel, 2007; Bencher, 2002; Silk, 1998; Recorder, 2000; Recorder in Civil, 2001. Publications: Editor, Professor Negligence and Liability Law Reports, 1996-; Professional Negligence Key Cases, 1996; Author, The Law of Damages, Butterworths Common Law Series, 2002, 2007 (online); Editor, Atkins Court Forms, Health and Safety, 2001, 2006; Munkman Employer's Liability, 2006. Honours: Member, Bar Council, 1997-99; Executive Committee, PNBA, 1995-; Chairman, North America Bar Council, 1998-2000; Chairman, Millennium Bar Conference, 2000; Judicial Studies Board Civil Committee, 2005. Memberships: Royal Overseas League; Pannal Golf Club; American Bar Association; International Association of Defense Counsel, USA. Address: 4 Dickens Mews, Britton Street, Clerkenwell, London EC1M 5SZ, England.

WILCHEK Meir, b. 17 October 1935, Warsaw, Poland. Biochemist. m. Esther Edlis, 1 son, 2 daughters. Education: BS, Bar-Ilan University, Ramat Gan, Israel, 1960; PhD, Weizmann Institute of Science, Rehovot, 1965. Appointments: Chief Chemist, Yeda Co, Rehovot, Israel, 1960-62; Chief Consultant, Miles-Yeda (Bio Makor), Rehovot, 1960-87; Research Associate, Department of Biophysics, 1965-66, Senior Scientist, 1968-71, Associate Professor, 1971-74, Professor, 1974-, Department Head, 1977-78, 1983-87, Dean of Biochemistry, 1995-99, Weizmann Institute of Science, Rehovot; Visiting Fellow, 1966-67, Research Associate, 1967-68, Visiting Scientist, 1972, 1974-75, Fogarty Scholar, 1981-82, National Institutes of Health, USA. Publications: 400 articles in professional journals. Honours: Rothschild Prize for Chemistry, Israel, 1984; Wolf Prize for Medicine, Israel, 1987; Pierce Prize, Rockford, Illinois, USA, 1987; Honorary DSc, University of Waterloo, Canada, 1989; Israel Prize in Biotechnology, Israeli Government, 1990; Sarstedt Prize for Analytical Biochemistry, 1990; Honorary PhD, Bar-Ilan University, Ramat Gan, 1995; Distinguished Clinical Chemist Award, International Federation of Clinical Chemistry, 1996; Honorary PhD, University of Jyvaskyla, Finland, 2000; Honorary PhD, Ben-Gurion University, Beer-Sheva, Israel, 2000; Anfinsen Award, Protein Society, USA, 2004; Wilhem-Exner-Medal, Austria, 2004; EMET Prize for Chemistry, Israel, 2005; Listed in several Who's Who and biographical publications. Memberships: Honorary Member, American Society of Biological Chemists; American Chemical Society; Foreign Associate, Institute of Medicine, National Academy of Sciences, USA; European Molecular Biology Organisation; Israel Biochemistry Society; Israel Chemical Society; Israel Immunological Society; Israeli Academy of Sciences. Address: Ha-Avoda St 3Bm Rehovot, Israel.

WILDER Gene, b. 11 June 1935, Milwaukee, Wisconsin, USA. Film Actor; Director; Producer. m. (1) Mary Joan Schutz, 1967, divorced 1974, 1 daughter, (2) Gilda Radner, 1984, deceased, (3) Karen Boyer, 1991. Education: University of Iowa; Bristol Old Vic Theatre School. Appointment: US Army, 1956-58. Creative Works: Films include: Bonnie and Clyde, 1966; The Producers, 1967; Start the Revolution Without Me, 1968; Quackser Fortune Has a Cousin in the Bronx, 1970; Willy Wonka and the Chocolate Factory, 1970; The Scarecrow, 1972; Everything You Always Wanted to Know About Sex, But Were Afraid to Ask, 1971; Rhinoceros, 1972; Blazing Saddles, 1973; Young Frankenstein, 1974; The

Little Prince, 1974; Thursday's Game, 1974; The Adventure of Sherlock Holmes's Smarter Brother, 1975; Silver Streak, 1976; The World's Greatest Lover, 1977; The Frisco Kid, 1979; Stir Crazy, 1980; Sunday Lovers, 1980; Hanky Panky, 1982; The Woman in Red, 1984; Haunted Honeymoon, 1986; See No Evil, Hear No Evil, 1989; Funny About Love, 1990; Another You, 1991; Stuart Little (voice), 1999; Murder in a Small Town, 1999; Instant Karma, 2005; Will & Grace, 2002-03; TV appearances include: The Scarecrow, 1972; The Trouble With People, 1973; Marlo Thomas Special, 1973; Thursday's Games, 1973; Something Wilder, 1994-; Alice in Wonderland (film), 1999; The Lady in Question (film), 1999. Publications: Kiss Me Like a Stranger: My Search for Love and Art, 2005; My French Whore, 2007. Address: Ames Cushing, William Morris Agency, 151 El Camino Drive, Beverly Hills, CA 90212, USA.

WILDGOOSE Jane, b. 22 August 1954, England. Artist; Designer; Writer; Researcher. 1 daughter. Education: BA (Hons) Fashion and Textiles, Winchester School of Art, 1977. Appointments: Freelance costume and production designer for stage and film, 1979-2000; Visiting Lecturer, Winchester School of Art, 1994-; Founder, Keeper, The Wildgoose Memorial Library, 2003-; Co-devisor, On One Lost Hair, BBC Radio 4, with Gregory Whitehead and Neil McCarthy, 2004; Artists' Mentor, Commissions East, Cambridge, 2004-2006; Exhibitions in Manchester, Maidstone, London, Bexhill, Eastbourne and Oxford. Publications: Articles in professional and popular journals. Honours: Arts Council Year of the Artist Award with Sally Hampson, Upstream, 2000-01; Arts Council Year of the Artist Award with Mary Hooper, A Rose Flowering by the Sea, 2000-01; Wellcome Sciart Research Award with consultant gastroenterologist Dr Peter Isaacs and opera director Philip Parr, Viewing the Instruments, 2000-01; Victoria Rashbone Award, Manchester Letherium Ideas Competition, 2005; NESTA Dream Time Fellowship, 2005-06. Memberships: Costume Society; Trustee, Willis Fleming Historical Trust, 2005-. Address: 21A Topsfield Parade, London N8 8PP, England. E-mail: wildgoose@janewildgoose.co.uk

WILFORD John Noble, b. 4 October 1933, Murray, Kentucky, USA. Journalist; Writer. m. Nancy Watts Paschall, 25 December 1966, 1 daughter. Education: BS, Journalism, University of Tennessee, 1955; MA, Political Science, Syracuse University, 1956; International Reporting Fellow, Columbia University, 1961-62. Appointments: Science Reporter, 1965-73, 1979-, Assistant National Editor, 1973-75, Director of Science News, 1975-79, Science Correspondent, 1979-, New York Times, New York City; McGraw Distinguished Lecturer in Writing, Princeton University, 1985; Professor of Science Journalism, University of Tennessee, 1989-90. Publications: We Reach the Moon, 1969; The Mapmakers, 1981; The Riddle of the Dinosaur, 1985; Mars Beckons, 1990; The Mysterious History of Columbus, 1991; Cosmic Dispatches, 2000. Contributions to: Nature; Wilson Quarterly; New York Times Magazine; Science Digest; Popular Science; National Geographic. Honours: Westinghouse-American Association for the Advancement of Science Writing Award, 1983; Pulitzer Prizes for National Reporting, 1984, shared 1987; DHL (Hons) Rhode Island College, 1987; DSc (Hons) Middleburg College, 1991; Ralph Coats Roe Medal, American Society of Mechanical Engineers, 1995; American Academy of Arts and Sciences, fellow, 1998; Listed in Who's Who publications and biographical dictionaries. Memberships: Century Club, New York City; National Association of

Science Writers; American Geographical Society, council member, 1994-. Address: New York Times, 229 West 43rd Street, New York, NY 10036, USA.

WILHELMI Cynthia Joy, b. 12 September 1946, Marshaltown, Iowa, USA. Information Technology Consultant. 1 son, 1 daughter. Education: BA, Art, University of Iowa, 1969; BA, Equivalent Degree in Journalism, 1993, MA, Communication, 1996, University of Nebraska. Appointments include: Editor, Publisher, Contributing Author, Salaam, Omaha, Nebraska, 1985-86; Master Artist-in-Residence, Nebraska Arts Council, 1985-91; Graduate Teaching Assistant, University of Nebraska, 1993-95; Program Co-ordinator, Family Friends of Eastern Nebraska, Visiting Nurse Association, 1996-97; College Instructor, Midland Lutheran College, Fremont, 1997-99; Information Technology Consultant, Inacom Headquarters, Omaha, 1998; Information Technology Consultant, Bass and Associates, Omaha, 1999-2000; Information Technology Consultant, RHI Consulting, Omaha, 2000; Information Technology Consultant, TEKsystems, Omaha, 2000-03; IT Business Analyst, Alegent Health, Omaha; Test Engineer, Regression Test Development, Project Leader, IT Consultant, Ameritrade (Securities Trading); Senior Test Engineer, Third Party Vendor Interface Management, Lincoln Benefit Life Insurance Company, Lincoln, Nebraska; Senior Test Engineer, Ameritas Life Insurance Corporation, Omaha, Nebraska; US Airforce Data Manager (Contractor), ESC (Secret Clearance), Bellvue Airforce Base, Nebraska; Farmer, 2001-; Proposal Co-ordinator, Raytheon Systems, Bellevue, Nebraska, 2003-2004; Senior Business Systems Analyst, Wells Fargo Home Mortgage, West Des Moines, Iowa, 2005; Senior QA/ Senior Test Engineer; Consultant for Nationwide Agribusiness Insurance, Des Moines, Iowa, 2006; Senior Project Manager (IT), Wells Fargo Corporate Headquarters, Des Moines, Iowa, 2006; Project Manager, MSI Solution Integrators, Des Moines, 2006-. Publications: Numerous articles in professional journals. Honours: Outstanding Graduate Teaching Assistant Award, University of Nebraska at Omaha, 1995; Admiral in the Great Navy of Nebraska; Honorary Member, Society of Collegiate Journalists; Nebraska Republican Gubernatorial Re-election Campaign Committee; One Thousand Great Scientists, Cambridge Blue Book, 2000 Outstanding Intellectuals of the 21st Century, IBC, Cambridge, England; FABI; Listed in Who's Who publications and Biographical Dictionaries. Memberships: Delta Phi Gamma; Nebraska Admirals' Association; American Association of University Women; Advisory Council, Foster Grandparents; Society for Technical Communication; Board of Directors for Friends of Art, University of Nebraska; Mensa (Nebraska-Western Iowa Executive Committee, National Nominating Committee, S1GHT Co-ordinator); Central Iowa Mensa, National Nominating Committee; American Meteorological Society. Address: 1201 Office Park Road, #306, West Des Moines, IA 50265-2404, USA. E-mail: cwi813@earthlink.net

WILKES Maurice Vincent (Sir), b. 26 June 1913, England. Mathematician. Education: Graduated, Mathematics, St John's College, Cambridge. Appointments: University Demonstrator, 1937; Radar and Operational Research, World War II; Lecturer, Acting Director, Mathematical Laboratory, Cambridge University, 1945, Director of Laboratory, 1946-70; Head, Computer Laboratory, 1970; Professor of Computer Technology, University of Cambridge, 1965-80; Staff Consultant, Digital Equipment Corporation, 1980-86; Adjunct Professor, MIT, 1981-85; Research Strategy, Olivetti Research Board, 1986-96; Adviser on Research Strategy, Olivetti and Oracle Research Laboratory, 1996-99; Staff

Consultant, AT&T Laboratories, Cambridge, 1999-2002; Emeritus Professor, Computer Laboratory, University of Cambridge, 2002. Publications: Oscillations of the Earth's Atmosphere, 1949; Preparation of Programs for an Electronic Digital Computer, 1951, 1957; Automatic Digital Computers, 1956; A Short Introduction to Numerical Analysis, 1966; Time-Sharing Computer Systems, 1968; The Cambridge CAP Computer and its Operating System, 1979; Memoirs of a Computer Pioneer, 1985; Computing Perspectives, 1995. Honours: 9 honorary degrees; Harry Goode Memorial Award, 1968; Eckert-Mauchly Award, 1980; McDowell Award, 1981; Faraday Medal, 1981; Pender Award, 1982; C and C Prize, 1988; Italgas Prize, 1991; Kyoto Prize, 1992; John von Neumann Medal, 1997; Mountbatten Medal, 1997. Memberships include: Fellow, St John's College, Cambridge, 1950; Fellow, Royal Society, 1956; First President, British Computer Society, 1957; American Academy of Arts and Sciences; US National Academy of Engineering; Fellow, Association for Computing Machinery; Knighted, New Years Honours List, 2000. Address: Computer Laboratory, University of Cambridge, William Gates Building, J J Thomson Road, Cambridge, CB3 0FD, England.

WILKINSON Jonny Peter, b. 25 May 1979, Surrey, England. Rugby Player. Education: Lord Wandsworth College. Career: Selected for English under-16 team, 1995; Selected for English under 18 team tour of Australia, 1997; Player, Newcastle Falcons; Selected to play for England; International debut, 1998; British Lions Tour, 2001; Player, Rugby World Cup, 2003; Irish Lions Tour, 2005. Publications: Lions and Falcons: My Diary of a Remarkable Year, 2002; My World, 2004; How to Play Rugby My Way, 2005; DVDs: Jonny Wilkinson: The Perfect 10; Jonny Wilkinson - The Real Story. Honours: MBE, 2003; International Rugby Board, International Player of the Year, 2003; BBC Sports Personality of the Year, 2003; OBE, 2004; Honorary Doctorate in Civil Law, Northumbria University, 2005.

WILLAMOWSKI Michael, b. 23 November 1939, Brno, Czech Republic. Academic Librarian. m. Sibylle Zwirner-Willamowski, 2 sons, 1 daughter. Education: Degree in Physics, 1972; Doctor rerum naturalium, 1975. Appointments: Captain, German Airforce, 1961-62; Teacher, Hamburg, Germany, 1966-70; Information Broker, Librarian, Helmut-Schmidt-Universität/Universität der Bundeswehr, Hamburg, 1976-2004. Honours: Research Board of Advisors, ABI, 2004-; Listed in national and international biographical directories. Publications: Achievements include: Invention of semipermeable membranes for reverse osmosis. Memberships: Deutsche Gesellschaft für Schiffahrt-und Marinegeschichte; Verband der Elekrotechnik; Patriotische Gesellschaft von 1765. Address: Grüner Bogen 10, D-22113 Oststeinbek, Germany. E-mail: tuscade@hotmail.com Website: www.topsurfen.de/

WILLCOCKS Michael (Sir), b. 27 July 1944, Kent, England. Lieutenant General Retired; Gentleman Usher of the Black Rod. m. Jean, 1 son, 2 daughters. Education: Royal Military Academy, Sandhurst, 1962-64; BSc (Hons) London University, 1965-68; Army Staff College, 1975-76; Higher Command and Staff Course, 1988; Royal College of Defence Studies, 1991. Appointments: Regimental and Staff Appointments, 1965-83; Commanding Officer, 1st Regiment Royal Horse Artillery, 1983-85; Staff Posts, UK, 1985-89; Commander, Royal Artillery 4th Armoured Division, 1989-90; Chief of Staff, Land Operations, Gulf War, 1991; Director, Army Plans and Programme, 1991-93; Director General, Land Warfare, 1993-94; Chief of Staff,

Allied Command Europe Rapid Reaction Corps, 1994-96; Chief of Staff, Land Component Implementation Force, Bosnia-Herzegovina, 1995-96; Assistant Chief, UK Army, 1996-99; Deputy Commander (Operations) Stabilisation Force, Bosnia-Herzegovina, 1999-2000; UK Military Representative to NATO, the EU and WEU, 2000-2001; Retired 2001; Gentleman Usher of the Black Rod, Secretary to the Lord Great Chamberlain and Serjeant at Arms of the House of Lords, 2001-. Publication: Airmobility and the Armoured Experience, 1989. Honours: Meritorious Service Medal (USA), 1996, 2000; CB (Companion Order of Bath), 1997; KCB (Knight Commander Order of Bath), 2000. Memberships: Pilgrims; European Atlantic Group; Honourable Artillery Company; Honorary Colonel 1st Regiment Royal Horse Artillery; Colonel Commandant Royal Artillery; Commissioner, Royal Hospital Chelsea, 1996-99; Clubs: National Liberal, Pitt. Address: House of Lords, London SW1A 0PW, England. E-mail: willcocksm@parliament.uk

WILLIAM SCOTT Seann, b. 3 October 1976, Cottage Grove, Minnesota, USA. Actor. Films include: Born into Exile, 1997; American Pie, 1999; Final Destination, Road Trip, Dude, where's my car?, 2000; Evolution, American Pie 2, Jay and Silent Bob Strike Back; 2001; Stark Raving Mad, 2002; Old School, Bulletproof Monk, American Wedding, The Rundown, 2003; The Dukes of Hazzard, 2005; Ice Age 2: The Meltdown, Southland Tales, Lost Historical Films on the Ice Age Period, 2006; Trainwreck: My Life as an Idiot, Mr Woodcock, 2007; Ball's Out: The Gary Houseman Story, The Promotion, 2008; TV Appearances include: Unhappily Ever After, 1996; Something So Right, 1998; The Big Breakfast, 2001; The Tonight Show with Jay Leno, 2001; Diary, 2003. Honours: MTV Movie Award, 2002; MTV Movie Award, 2004.

WILLIAMS C(harles) K(enneth), b. 4 November 1936, Newark, New Jersey, USA. Poet; Professor. m. (1) Sarah Dean Jones, 1966, divorced 1975, 1 daughter, (2) Catherine Justine Mauger, April 1975, 1 son. Education: BA, University of Pennsylvania, 1959. Appointments: Visiting Professor, Franklin and Marshall College, Lancaster, Pennsylvania, 1977, University of California at Irvine, 1978, Boston University, 1979-80; Professor of English, George Mason University, 1982; Visiting Professor, Brooklyn College, 1982-83; Lecturer, Columbia University, 1982-85; Holloway Lecturer, University of California at Berkeley, 1986; Professor, Princeton University, 1996-. Publications: A Day for Anne Frank, 1968; Lies, 1969; I Am the Bitter Name, 1972; With Ignorance, 1977; The Women of Trachis (co-translator), 1978; The Lark, the Thrush, the Starling, 1983; Tar, 1983; Flesh and Blood, 1987; Poems 1963-1983, 1988; The Bacchae of Euripides (translator), 1990; A Dream of Mind, 1992; Selected Poems, 1994; The Vigil, 1997; Poetry and Consciousness (selected essays), 1998; Repair (poems), 1999; Misgivings, A Memoir, 2000; Love About Love, 2001; The Singing, 2003; Collected Poems, 2006; Contributions to: Akzent; Atlantic; Carleton Miscellany; Crazyhorse; Grand Street; Iowa Review; Madison Review; New England Review; New Yorker; Seneca Review; Transpacific Review; TriQuarterly; Yale Review; Threepenny Review. Honours; Guggenheim Fellowship; Pushcart Press Prizes, 1982, 1983, 1987; National Book Critics Circle Award, 1983; National Endowment for the Arts Fellowship, 1985; Morton Dawen Zabel Prize, 1988; Lila Wallace Writers Award, 1993; Berlin Prize Fellowship, 1998; PEN Voelker Prize, 1998; Pulitzer Prize, 2000; Los Angeles Times Book Prize, 2000; National Book Award, 2003; Ruth

Lilly Prize, 2005. Memberships: PEN; American Academy of Arts and Science. Address: 245 Moore St, Princeton, NJ 08540, USA.

WILLIAMS Christopher Maxwell John, b. 25 September 1948, Sydney, Australia. Agricultural Scientist. m. Judith Barbara Spall, 1 daughter. Education: BScAgric Hons, Agriculture, University of Sydney 1970; PhD, Agronomy, University of Adelaide, 1978. Appointments: Senior Research Officer, South Australia Department of Agriculture, Naracoorte, South Australia 1975-79; Senior Lecturer, Massey University, Palmerston North, New Zealand 1979-81; Senior Agronomist, Department of Agriculture, Walpeup, Victoria, Australia 1981-82; Senior Research Scientist, Water Resources and Irrigated Crops, Sustainable Systems, South Australian Research and Development Institute, Adelaide, 1982-, including Convenor, Potatoes, 2000, Australian Potato Research and Development conference in Adelaide July 2000. Publications: Author or co-author of over 100 articles on potato, horticulture and viticulture crop agronomy; Potato Varieties for South Australia. Honours: Recipient, Howard Memorial Trust Scholarship, 1977; Best Paper Award, Australian Potato Industry Conference, 1990; Research Team first to show Molybdenum deficiency can be a major cause of yield loss in grapevines and can be a major cause of the world-wide problem of millerandage or seedless tiny berries at harvest in wine grapes. Also devised remedial Mo foliar spray strategies; Listed in Who's Who publications. Memberships: Australian Institute of Agricultural Science and Technology; International and Australian Societies for Horticultural Science. Address: South Australian Research and Development Institute, Waite Precinct, GPO Box 397, Adelaide, SA 5001, Australia. E-mail: williams.chrism@saugov.sa.gov.au

WILLIAMS Cynthia Ann, b. 8 December 1959, Portsmouth, Virginia, USA. Nurse. 2 sons, 2 daughters. Education: Medical Specialist Diploma, 1982; Primary Leadership Development Diploma, 1984; Licensed Practical Nurse Diploma, 1986; Basic Non-Commissioned Officers Course Diploma, 1993; Associate Arts Degree, 1994; Bachelor of Arts in Theology Degree, 2004. Appointments: United States Army, 1981-2001; LPN, Home Health Care Pediatrics; Equal Opportunities Representative, 1996; Ordained Minister, Victory New Testament Fellowship, 2001-; Independent Advertiser, World's Greatest Vitamin; President, It's a New Day Productions; Entrepreneur, NSE Enterprises; Global Domain International Independent Affiliate. Publications: Marriage – Not Just a Simple "I Do" (commentary), 1999; One of Those Women (book), 2001; Monthly articles, Freewill Fellowship Ministry On-line, 2000-2001; Relationships On-line Producer Romauld Wells. Honours: 21st Century Universal Award of Achievement for Theology and Spiritual Healing, 2004; 2004 Female Executive Award for Theology and Spiritual Healing; Lifetime Achievement Award for Spiritual Healing and Theology; 2007 Woman of the Year in the field of Theology and Spiritual Healing. Memberships: Living Christian Fellowship, Presidential Prayer Team; Concerned Women of America; Hampton Reads Medical Reserve Corp; Non-Commissioned Officers Association; Partner, Aaron's Army, Paula White Ministries, KCM Ministries, BELL Ministries; Life Member, IBA; Fellow, ABI; Member, Veterans of Foreign Wars; Deputy Director General, IBC. Address: 87 Deer Run Trail, Newport News, VA 23602, USA. E-mail: oneofthosewomen@yahoo.com

WILLIAMS Herbert Lloyd, b. 8 September 1932, Aberystwyth, Wales. Writer; Poet; Novelist; Biographer; Novelist. m. Dorothy Maud Edwards, 1954, 4 sons, 1

daughter. Publications: The Trophy, 1967; A Lethal Kind of Love, 1968; Battles in Wales, 1975; Come Out Wherever You Are, 1976, new edition 2004; Stage Coaches in Wales, 1977; The Welsh Quiz Book, 1978; Railways in Wales, 1981; The Pembrokeshire Coast National Park, 1987; Stories of King Arthur, 1990; Ghost Country, 1991; Davies the Ocean, 1991; The Stars in Their Courses, 1992; John Cowper Powys, 1997; Looking Through Time, 1998; A Severe Case of Dandruff, 1999; Voices of Wales, 1999; The Woman in Back Row, 2000; Punters, 2002; Wrestling in Mud, 2007. Television Dramas and Documentaries: Taff Acre, 1981; A Solitary Mister, 1983; Alone in a Crowd, 1984; Calvert in Camera, 1990; The Great Powys, 1994; Arouse All Wales, 1996. Radio Dramas: Doing the Bard, 1986; Bodyline, 1991; Adaptations: A Child's Christmas in Wales, 1994; The Citadel, 1997. Contributions to: Reviews and journals. Honours: Welsh Arts Council Short Story Prize, 1972, and Bursary, 1988; Aberystwyth Open Poetry Competition, 1990; Hawthornden Poetry Fellowship, 1992; Rhys Davies Short Story Award, 1995; Cinnamon Press Novella Award, 2007. Memberships: Welsh Academy, fellow; The Society of Authors. Address: 63 Bwlch Road, Fairwater, Cardiff CF5 3BX, Wales

WILLIAMS Hermine Weigel, b. 4 February 1933, Sellersville, Pennsylvania, USA. College Teacher; Writer and Editor. Performing Musician. m. Jay Gomer Williams, 2 sons, 2 daughters. Education: AB, 1954, MA, 1956, Vassar College; PhD, Musicology, Columbia University, 1964. Appointments: Teacher of Music History: Vassar College, 1954-59; Hamilton College, 1964-65; Teacher, Religion and Arts, Hamilton College, 1972-93; Scholar in Residence, Hamilton College, 1994-; Assistant to Donald Jay Grout, The Operas of Scarlatti, 1980-87; Member, international editorial board for complete works edition of G B Pergolesi; Professional accompanist, organist, choral director, area churches; Organ soloist with Utica Symphony; Solo and ensemble recitals; Freelance writer and editor. Publications: The Operas of Scarlatti, vol 6, 1980; The Symphony 1720-1840, series B, 1983; Co-author, A Short History of Opera, 3rd edition, 1988, 4th edition (greatly expanded and revised), 2003; Co-author, Giovanni Battista Pergolesi: A Guide to Research, 1989; Sibelius and His Masonic Music, 1998; Francesco Bartolomeo Conti: His Life and Music, 1999; Thomas Hastings: An Introduction To His Life and Music, 2005; Contributor to music books and journals. Honours: Maarston Fellowship; Theodore Presser Award, Composition; Commission from San Francisco Opera, 1982; Fulbright Lecturer in Musicology; Council of International Exchange of Scholars, New Zealand, 1987; Dewitt Clinton Masonic Award for Community Service. Memberships: American Musicological Society; Fulbright Association; Member, Board of Directors for the William Lincer Foundation, 1999-. Address: 7153 College Hill Road, Clinton, New York 13323, USA.

WILLIAMS Robbie (Robert Peter), b. 13 February 1974, Stoke-on-Trent, Staffordshire, England. Singer. Career: Member, UK all-male vocal group Take That, 1990-95; Solo artiste, 1995-; Television includes: Take That And Party, C4, Take That Away documentary, BBC2, 1993; Take That In Berlin, 1994. Recordings: Albums: Take That And Party, 1992; Everything Changes, 1993; Greatest Hits, 1996; Solo album: Life Thru A Lens, 1997; I've Been Expecting You, 1998; The Ego Has Landed, 1999; Sing When You're Winning, 2000; Swing When You're Winning, 2001; Escapology, 2002; Live at Knebworth, Greatest Hits, 2004; Intensive Care, 2005; Rudebox, 2006; Hit singles: with Take That: It Only Takes A Minute, I Found Heaven, A Million Love Songs, 1992; Could It Be Magic, Why Can't I Wake Up With You, Pray, Relight

My Fire (with Lulu), Babe, 1993; Everything Changes, Sure, Love Ain't Here Anymore, 1994; Never Forget, Back For Good, 1995; Solo hit singles: Freedom, 1996; Old Before I Die, Lazy Days, South of the Border, Angels, 1997; I've Been Expecting You, Millennium, Let Me Entertain You, 1998; No Regrets, She's The One/It's Only Us, Strong, 1999; Rock DJ, Kids, with Kylie Minogue, Supreme, 2000; Let Love Be Your Energy, Eternity/Road To Mandalay, Better Man, Somethin' Stupid (with Nicole Kirman), 2001; Feel, My Culture, 2002; Come Undone, Something Beautiful, Sexed Up, 2003. Publications: F for English, 2000; Numerous videos, books, magazines. Honours include: 7 Smash Hit Awards, 1992; 1 Smash Hit Award, 1996; BRIT Awards: Best Male Artist, Best Single, Best Video, 1998; MTV Award, Best Male, 1998; Smash Hits, Best Male, 1998; Nordoff-Robbins Music Therapy Original Talen Award, 1998; BRIT Awards: Best Video, Best Single, 1999; Echo Award, Best International Male Rock and Pop Artist, Germany, 2005. Memberships: Equity; Musicians' Union; MCPS; PRS; ADAMI; GVC; AURA. Address: c/o IE Music Ltd, 59 A Chesson Road, London, W14 9QS, England. Website: www.robbiewilliams.com

WILLIAMS Robert Joseph Paton, b. 25 February 1926, Wallasey, Cheshire, England. Scientist; Academic. m. Jelly Klara Büchli, 2 sons. Education: BA, 1948, DPhil, 1951, Chemistry, Merton College, Oxford University. Appointments: Junior Research Fellow, Merton College, Oxford, 1951-55; Tutor, Chemistry, Wadham College, Oxford, 1955-68; Lecturer, Chemistry, Oxford University, 1955-72; Commonwealth Fellow, Harvard Medical School, USA, 1965-66; Tutor, Biochemistry, Wadham College Oxford, 1966-72; Reader, Chemistry, 1972-74; Royal Society Napier Research Professor, 1974-91; Senior Research Fellow, 1991-93, Emeritus Fellow, 1993-, Wadham College, Oxford; Visiting Professor, Royal Free Hospital, London University, 1991-95. Publications: Books: Inorganic Chemistry (with C S G Phillips) volume 1 and 2, 1966; The Natural Selection of the Chemical Elements (with J R R Fràusto da Silva), 1996; Bringing Chemistry to Life (with J R R Fràusto da Silva), 1999; The Biological Chemistry of the Elements (with J R R Fràusto da Silva), 2nd edition, 2001; Editor of several books; Over 600 articles in chemical and biological journals. Honours include: Fellow of the Royal Society, 1972; Twice Medallist of the Biochemical Society; Twice Medallist of the Royal Society; Three times Medallist of the Royal Chemical Society; Twice Medallist of the European Biochemical Societies and the International Union of Biochemistry; Named Lecturer at Numerous colleges and universities in the UK, USA and Europe; Honorary Doctorates: Universities of Leicester, Keele, East Anglia and Lisbon. Memberships: Fellow Royal Society of Chemistry; Honorary Member, British Biophysics Society, Society for Biological Inorganic Chemistry, Society for the Study of Calcium Proteins; Member, Biochemical Society; Editor of several journals; Foreign Member, Academies of Belgium, Sweden, Portugal and Czechoslovakia. Address: Inorganic Chemistry Laboratory, Oxford University, South Parks Road, Oxford, OX1 3QR, England. E-mail: bob.williams@chem.ox.ac.uk

WILLIAMS Robin, b. 21 July 1951, Chicago, USA. Actor; Comedian. m. (1) Valerie Velardi, 1978, 1 son, (2) Marsha Garces, 1989, 1 son, 1 daughter. Education: Juillard School, New York. Creative Works: TV appearances include: Laugh-In; The Richard Pryor Show; America 2-Night; Happy Days; Mork and Mindy, 1978-82; Carol and Carl and Whoopi and Robin; Stage appearances include: Waiting for Godot; Films include: Popeye, 1980; The World According to Garp, 1982; The Survivors, 1983; Moscow on the Hudson, 1984;

Club Paradise, 1986; Good Morning Vietnam, 1987; Dead Poets' Society, 1989; Awakenings, 1990; The Fisher King, Hook, Dead Again, 1991; Toys, 1992; Being Human, Aladdin (voice), Mrs Doubtfire, 1993; Jumanji, The Birdcage, Jack, Hamlet, Joseph Conrad's The Secret Agent, 1996; Good Will Hunting, Flubber, 1997; What Dreams May Come, Patch Adams, 1998; Jakob the Liar, Bicentennial Man, Get Bruce, 1999; One Hour Photo, 2001; Insomnia, Death to Smoochy, 2002; The Final Cut, House of D, Noel, 2004; Robots, The Big White, 2005; The Night Listener, RV, Everyone's Hero, Man of the Year, Happy Feet, Night at the Museum, 2006; License to Wed, August Rush, 2007. Recordings: Reality, What a Concept, 1979; Throbbing Python of Love; A Night at the Met. Honours include: Several Emmy Awards; Several Grammy Awards; Golden Globe Award, 1988, 1991; Academy Award, 1998; Cecil B DeMille Award, Golden Globe Awards, 2005. Address: CAA, Creative Artists Agency, 9830 Wilshire Boulevard, Beverly Hills, CA 90212, USA.

WILLIAMS Roger Stanley, b. 28 August 1931, Beckenham, Kent, England. Physician. m. (1) Lindsay Mary Elliot, 2 sons, 3 daughters, (2) Stephanie de Laszlo, 1 son, 2 daughters. Education: London Hospital Medical School, University of London; MRCS, LRCP, MBBS (Honours), 1953; MRCP (London, 1957; MD (London), 1960; FRCP, 1966. Appointments: Junior Medical Specialist, Queen Alexandra Hospital, Millbank, 1956-58; Medical Registrar and Tutor, Royal Postgraduate Medical School, 1958-59; Lecturer in Medicine, Royal Free Hospital, 1958-65; Consultant Physician, Royal South Hants and Southampton General Hospital, 1965-66; Director Institute of Liver Studies and Consultant Physician, King's College Hospital and Medical School, 1966-96; Professor of Hepatology, King's College London, 1994-96; Director, The Institute of Hepatology, University College London, and Honorary Consultant Physician, University College London Hospitals, 1996-; Member Scientific Group on Viral Hepatitis, WHO Geneva, 1972; Consultant, Liver Research Unit Trust, 1974-; Member, Advisory Group on Hepatitis, DHSS, 1980-96; Member, Clinical Standards Advisory Committee, Department of Health, 1994-; Medical Director, Foundation for Liver Research; Director, International Office, Royal College of Physicians, 2003-, Director, The Liver Unit, The London Clinic, 2006-. Publications: Author and co-author of approximately 2,500 papers articles, chapters and books. Honours: Honorary Fellowships: FRCPI, FRCP, FRCS, FRCPEd, FRACP, F MedSci; Nightingale Prize, International Federation of Medical and Biochemical Engineering (jointly), 1980; Gold Medal, Canadian Liver Foundation, 1992; Hospital Doctor of the Year Award for Gastoenterology, 1994; British Association for the Study of the Liver Lifetime Achievement Award, 2003; Wyeth Senior Achievement Award in Clinical Transplantation, American Society of Transplantation, 2004; Numerous named and invited lectures. Memberships include: Royal Society of Medicine; European Association for the Study of the Liver; President, 1989-90, British Society of Gastroenterology; Freeman City of London; Liveryman, Worshipful Society of Apothecaries. Address: Institute of Hepatology, Royal Free and University College Medical School, University College, London, 69-75 Chenies Mews, London WC1E 6HX, England. E-mail: roger.williams@ucl.ac.uk

WILLIAMS Rowan Douglas (Most Reverend and Right Honourable the Lord Archbishop of Canterbury), b. 14 June 1950, Swansea, Wales. Archbishop. m. Jane Paul, 1 son, 1 daughter. Education: BA, 1971, MA, 1975, Christ's College, Cambridge; D Phil, Wadham College, Oxford, 1975; College of the Resurrection, Mirfield, 1975; Deacon,

1977, Priest, 1978; DD, 1989. Appointments: Tutor, Westcott House, Cambridge, 1977-80; Honorary Curate, Chesterton St George, Ely, 1980-83; Lecturer in Divinity, Cambridge, 1980-86; Dean and Chaplain, Clare College, Cambridge, 1984-86; Canon Theologian, Leicester Cathedral, 1981-82; Canon Residentiary, Christ Church, Oxford, 1986-92; Lady Margaret Professor of Divinity, Oxford, 1986-92; Enthroned as Bishop of Monmouth, 1992; Enthroned as Archbishop of Wales, 2000; Enthroned as Archbishop of Canterbury, 2003. Publications: The Wound of Knowledge, 1979; Resurrection, 1982; The Truce of God, 1983; Arius, Heresy and Tradition, 1987, 2nd edition, 2001; Teresa of Avila, 1991; Open to Judgement (sermons), 1994; After Silent Centuries (poetry), 1994; On Christian Theology (essays), 2000; Lost Icons: Reflections on Cultural Bereavement, 2000; Christ on Trial, 2000; Remembering Jerusalem (poetry) 2001; Ponder These Things, 2002; Writing in the Dust, 2002; The Dwelling of the Light: praying with icons of Christ, 2003; Silence and Honey Cakes, 2003; Anglican Identities, 2004; Christian Imagination in Poetry and Polity, 2004; Grace and Necessity, 2005; Why Study the Past? 2005; The Worlds We Live In: dialogues with Rowan Williams on global economics and politics, 2005; Tokens of Trust: An Introduction to Christian Belief, 2007; Wrestling with Angels: Conversations in Modern Theology, 2007; Dostoevsky: Language, Faith and Fiction, forthcoming. Membership: Fellow of the British Academy. Address: Lambeth Palace, London SE1 7JU, England.

WILLIAMS Serena, b. 26 September 1981, Saginaw, Michigan, USA. Professional Tennis Player. Education: Coached by father, Richard Williams. Career: Turned professional, 1994; Won mixed doubles (with Max Mirnyi), Wimbledon and US Open, 1998; Doubles winner (with Venus Williams), Oklahoma City, 1998, French Open, 1999, Hanover, 1999, Wimbledon, 2000, 2002, Australian Open, 2001, 2003; Single semi-finalist, Sydney Open, 1997, Chicago, 1998; Singles finalist, Wimbledon, 2000; Winner, US Open, 1999, 2002, Paris Indoors, 1999, 2003, Indian Wells, 1999, 2001, LA, 1999, 2000, Grand Slam Cup, 1999; Hanover, 2000, Tokyo, 2000, Canadian Open, 2001, French Open, 2002, Wimbledon, 2002, 2003, Australian Open, 2003, 2005, Miami, 2003; US Federation Cup Team, 1999; US Olympic Team (won doubles gold medal with Venus Williams), 2000; Ranked world No 1 in 2002; 25 WTA Tour singles titles (including 7 Grand Slam titles) and US $14,789,661 prize money; Debuted The Serena Williams Collection designed by Nike, 2005; Numerous appearances on TV. Honours: Sanex WTA Tour Most Impressive Newcomer Award, 1998; Most Improved Player, 1999; Teen Awards Achievement Award (shared with Venus Williams), 2000; Associated Press Female Athlete of the Year, 2002. Address: c/o William Morris Agency, One William Morris Place, Beverly Hills, CA 90212, USA. Website: www.serenawilliams.com

WILLIAMS Venus Ebone Starr, b. 17 June 1980, Lynwood, California, USA. Professional Tennis Player. Education: Associate Degree in Fashion Design, Art Institute of Fort Lauderdale, 2007. Career: Professional debut, Bank of West Classic, Oakland, California, 1994; Bausch & Lomb Championships, 1996; Winner, numerous singles titles (WTA Tour) including Oklahoma City, 1998, Lipton, 1998, 1999, Hamburg, 1999, Italian Open, 1999; Grand Slam Cup, 1998; 5 Grand Slam doubles titles (with Serena Williams): French Open, 1999, US Open, 1999, Wimbledon, 2000, 2002, Australian Open, 2001, 2003; Singles finalist, Wimbledon, 2000, 2001, 2005, 2007, US Open, 2000, 2001, French Open, 2002, Australian Open, 2003; with Serena Williams, first sisters in tennis history to have each won a Grand Slam singles title; First sisters to win Olympic Gold Medal in doubles, 2000;

Olympic Gold Medal in doubles, 2000; Olympic Gold Medal in singles, 2000; only sisters in 20th Century to win a Grand Slam doubles title together; US Federation Cup Team, 1995, 1999; Awarded largest-ever endorsement contract for a female athlete by Reebok, 2002; Founder, V Starr Interiors, 2002; Launched fashion line, EleVen, 2007. Honours: Sports Image Foundation Award, 1995; Tennis Magazine Most Impressive Newcomer, 1997; Most Improved Player, 1998; Sanex WTA Tour Player of the Year and Doubles Team of the Year (with Serena Williams), 2000; Women's Sports Foundation Athlete of the Year, 2000; ESPY Awards for Best Female Athlete and Best Female Tennis Player of 2001, 2002, Certificate of Achievement Howard University, 2002. Address: V Starr Interiors, 1102 West Indiantown Road, Suite 11, Jupiter, FL 33458, USA. Website: www.venuswilliams.com

WILLIS Bruce Walter, b. 19 March 1955, Germany. Actor; Singer. m. Demi Moore, divorced 2000, 3 daughters. Education: Montclair State College; Moved to USA, 1957; Studied with Stella Adler. Creative Works: Stage appearances: (off Broadway): Heaven and Earth, 1977; Fool for Love, 1984; The Bullpen; The Bayside Boys; The Ballad of Railroad William; Films: Prince of the City, 1981; The Verdict, 1982; Blind Date, 1987; Sunset, Die Hard, 1988; In Country, 1989; Die Hard 2: Die Harder, Bonfire of the Vanities, 1990; Hudson Hawk, The Last Boy Scout, 1991; Death Becomes Her, Distance, Color of Night, North, Nobody's Fool, Pulp Fiction, 1994; Die Hard with a Vengeance, 12 Monkeys, 1995; Four Rooms, Last Man Standing, 1996; The Jackal, The Fifth Element, 1997; Mercury Rising, Armageddon, Breakfast of Champions, 1998; The Story of US, The Sixth Sense, 1999; Unbreakable, Disneys' The Kid, 2000; Bandits, 2001; Hart's War, Grand Champion, True West, 2002; Tears of the Sun, Rugrats Go Wild! (voice), Charlie's Angels: Full Throttle, 2003; The Whole Ten Yards, 2004; Hostage, Sin City, 2005; Alpha Dog, Lucky Number Slevin, 16 Blocks, Over the Hedge, Fast Food Nation, The Astronaut Farmer, Hammy's Boomerang Adventure, 2006; Grindhouse, Perfect Stranger, Die Hard 4.0, Nancy Drew, Planet Terror, 2007; Assassination of a High School President, 2008; TV: Trackdown (film); Miami Vice (series); The Twilight Zone (series); Moonlighting (series), 1985-89; Friends (guest), 2000; That '70s Show, 2005; Recordings: The Return of Bruno, 1987; If It Don't Kill You, It Just Makes You Stronger, 1989. Honours include: People's Choice Award, 1986; Emmy Award, 1987; Golden Globe Award, 1987.

WILLMOT William Clarence, b. 26 June 1925, Elizabeth, New Jersey, USA. Technical Writer; Editor. m. Florence C Veverka, 22 May 1948. Education: LLB, Blackstone School of Law, 1958; BGS, Rollins College, Florida, 1967; MS, Florida Institute of Technology, 1970; MEd, Stetson University, Florida, 1972; PhD, Hawaii University, Hawaii, 1997; PhD, Chapel Christian University, 1998. Appointments: US Army, World War II, 1943-46; Small Arms Disassembler, Small Arms Assembler, Small Arms Inspector, Weapons Specialist, Technical Writer, Systems Improvement Officer, Chief, Program Management Office, Raritan Arsenal, Metuchen, New Jersey, 1947-61; Technical Writer, Ordnance, Picatinny Arsenal, Dover, New Jersey, 1961-62; Technical Writer, Supervisory Technical Editor, Program Management Specialist, Emergency Preparedness Officer, John F Kennedy Space Center, 1962-79; Technical Editor, Pan Am World Services, Florida, 1983-88; Technical Editor, Computer Sciences Raytheon (CSR), Florida, 1988-95; Communication Consultant, Merritt Island, Florida, 1995-; Adjunct Instructor, Brevard Community College, Cocoa, Florida, 1988-2001; Adjunct Instructor, University Central Florida, 1998-2001.

Honours: Bronze Star Medal, US Army, New Guinea Campaign, World War II, 1944; Superior Achievement Award, NASA, 1970; Group Achievement Award, NASA, 1972; Distinguished Service Medal, State of New Jersey, Trenton, 1994; International Man of Year Award, IBC, 1997-98; Man of Year Award, ABI, 1998. Memberships: Fellow, ABI, Radio Club of America; Life Member, Society of Wireless Pioneers, Quarter Century Wireless Association, US Army Signal Corps Association; Psi Chi; Board of Directors, Chapel Christian University; Member, Board of Directors, Military Society of the Blue Badge. Address: 1630 Venus Street, Merritt Island, FL 32953-3162, USA.

WILLSIE Sandra K, b. 18 August 1953, Parsons, Kansas, USA. Physician. m. Thomas Syverson. Education: BS, Pittsburg State University, Pittsburg, Kansas, USA, 1975; Doctor of Osteopathic Medicine, Kansas City University of Medicine and Biosciences, College of Osteopathic Medicine, Kansas City, Missouri, 1983; Rotating Internship, 1983-84; Internal Medicine Internship, 1984-85; Internal Medicine Residency, 1985-87; Fellowship, Pulmonary Diseases and Critical Care Medicine, 1987-89. Appointments include: Assistant Professor of Medicine, 1989-94, Associate Professor of Medicine, 1994-99, Interim Chair, Department of Medicine, 1998-2000, Professor of Medicine, 1999-2000, UMKC School of Medicine, Kansas City Missouri; Professor of Medicine, 2000-, Vice-Dean of Academic Affairs, Administration and Medical Affairs, 2000-2002, Vice-President for Academic Affairs/Dean, 2002-, Kansas City University of Medicine and Biosciences, Kansas City, Missouri; Medical Director, Pulmonary Clinic, Truman Medical Center, 1991-2000; Medical Director, Kansas City Public Health Department Tuberculosis Clinic, 1996-2000; Pulmonologist, Affiliated with University Family Medical Care Center, Medical Center of Independence, Independence, Missouri, 2000-. Publications: Numerous articles as author and co-author in medical journals include most recently: Improved strategies and new treatment options for allegic rhinitis, 2001; Tumor necrosis alpha's role in lung injury following ischemia and reperfusion: model studies, 2003; Helicobacter pylori-related immunoglobulins in Sarcoidosis, 2004; 5 book chapters; Numerous published abstracts. Honours include: Numerous Research Grants; UMKC Chancellor's Teaching Enhancement Award, 1990; AMA, Physician Recognition Award, 1991, 2004; Young Investigator Award, American College of Chest Physicians, 1992; Harvard University's Macy Institute's Physician Educator Program, 2001, participated as invited "Returning Faculty", 2002, 2003, 2004, 2005, 2006. Memberships include: Fellow: American College of Physicians, American College of Chest Physicians; American Thoracic Society; Society of Critical Care Medicine; American Osteopathic Association; Greater Kansas City Bioterrorism Medical Advisory Panel; Medical Group Management Association. Address: Kansas City University of Medicine and Biosciences, 1750 Independence Avenue, Kansas City, MO 64106, USA. E-mail: sandra.willsie@gmail.com

WILSON Andrew Bray Cameron (Hon), b. 3 June 1936, Adelaide, South Australia. Former Justice of the High Court of Fiji. m. Julie Elizabeth Pearce, 11 April 1987. 2 sons, 6 daughters. Education: LLB, University of Adelaide, 1959. Appointments: Barrister and Solicitor, 1960-72; Judge, Adelaide Juvenile Court, 1972-76; Judge District Court of South Australia, 1972-99; Acting Justice of the Supreme Court of Papua New Guinea, 1973; Lecturer, Criminology, University of Adelaide, 1973; Justice of the National and Supreme Courts, Papua New Guinea, 1978-80; Justice of the Supreme Court of Samoa, 1999-2000; Justice of the High Court of Fiji,

2002-03; Auxiliary Judge, District Court of South Australia, 2003-; Consultant to People's Courts of Lao PDR, 2003-04; Adjunct Professor, RMIT University, Melbourne, 2005-. Honours: Churchill Fellowship, 1972; AM, 1998; Listed in Who's Who publications. Memberships: Member, Council, Law Society, South Australia, 1961-72; Chairman, Prisoners Aid Association, South Australia, 1966-73; Member, Social Welfare Advisory Council, 1970-72; Member, Australia and New Zealand Society of Criminology, 1971-; Member, Law Reform Committee, South Australia, 1972; Member Law Asia, 1977-; Vice-President, 1973-77, 1991-93, President, 1993-95, Australian Crime Prevention Council; Member Coalition Against Crime, 1990-94; Chairman, McDouall Stuart Board, Burra Art Gallery, South Australia, 1995-97; President, Offenders Aid and Rehabilitation Services, South Australia, 1997-99. Address: 114 Allinga Avenue, Glenunga, SA 5064, Australia.

WILSON A(ndrew) N(orman), b. 27 October 1950, England. Author. m. (1) Katherine Duncan-Jones, 2 daughters, (2) Ruth Alexander Guilding, 1991, 1 daughter. Education: MA, New College, Oxford. Appointments: Lecturer, St Hugh's College and New College, Oxford, 1976-81; Literary Editor, The Spectator, 1981-83. Publications: The Sweets of Pimlico (novel), 1977; Unguarded Hours (novel), 1978; Kindly Light (novel), 1979; The Laird of Abbotsford, 1980; The Healing Art (novel), 1980; Who Was Oswald Fish (novel), 1981; Wise Virgin (novel), 1982; A Life of John Milton, 1983; Scandal (novel), 1983; Hilaire Belloc, 1984; Gentlemen in England (novel), 1985; Love Unknown (novel), 1986; The Church in Crisis (co-author), 1986; Stray (novel), 1987; Landscape in France, 1987; Incline Our Hearts (novel), 1987; Penfriends from Porlock: Essays and Reviews, 1977-86, 1988; Tolstoy: A Biography, 1988; Eminent Victorians, 1989; C S Lewis: A Biography, 1990; A Bottle in the Smoke (novel), 1990; Against Religion, 1991; Daughters of Albion (novel), 1991; Jesus, 1992; The Vicar of Sorrows (novel), 1993; The Faber Book of Church and Clergy, 1992; The Rise and Fall of the House of Windsor, 1993; The Faber Book of London (editor), 1993; Hearing Voices (novel), 1995; Paul: The Mind of the Apostle, 1997; Dream Children (novel), 1998; God's Funeral, 1999; The Victorians, 2002; Beautiful Shadow: A Life of Patricia Highsmith, 2003; My Name is Legion, 2004; Iris Murdoch as I Knew Her, 2004; London: A Short History, 2004; A Jealous Ghost, 2005; After the Victorians, 2005; Betjeman, 2006; Winnie and Wolf, 2007; Columnist for London Evening Standard; Occasional contributor to Daily Mail, Times Literary Supplement; New Statesman, The Spectator and The Observer. Honours: Royal Society of Literature, fellow, 1981; Whitbread Biography Award, 1988. Address: 5 Regent's Park Terrace, London, NW1 7EE, England.

WILSON Brian, b. 20 June 1942, Inglewood, California, USA. Musician (bass, keyboards); Singer; Composer. Founder member, the Beach Boys, 1961-; Retired from live performance, to concentrate on composing and recording, 1964-; Appearances include: Australian tour, 1964; Headlines Million Dollar Party, Honolulu, 1964; US tour, 1964; Established Brother Records label, 1967; Concert at International Center, Honolulu, 1967; Plays with Beach Boys, Whiskey-A-Go-Go, Los Angeles, 1970; Filmed for NBC Special, 1976; Presenter, Don Kirshner's Second Annual Rock Music Awards, Hollywood, 1976; 15th Anniversary Beach Boys show, 1976; Rejoins band for US concerts, 1989; Solo appearance, China Club, Hollywood, 1991; Documentaries include: Prime Time Live, ABC, 1991; I Just Wasn't Made For These Times, BBC, 1995; Performed at Live 8, Germany, 2005; Debut of That Lucky Old Sun (Narrative), Royal Festival Hall, London, 2007; Free concert, Sydney Festival, Australia, 2008. Compositions: Many hit songs include: Caroline No; Co-writer, California Girls; Good Vibrations; Fun Fun Fun. Recordings: Albums include: Surfin' Safari, 1962; Surfer Girl, 1963; Little Deuce Coupe, 1963; Shut Down Vol 2, 1964; All Summer Long, 1964; Surfin' USA 1965; Beach Boys Party, 1966; Pet Sounds, 1966; Beach Boys Today!, 1966; Smile, 1967; Surfer Girl, 1967; Smiley Smile, 1967; Wild Honey, 1968; 15 Big Ones, 1976; The Beach Boys Love You, 1977; Solo albums: Brian Wilson, 1988; I Just Wasn't Made For These Times, 1995; Imagination, 1998; Gettin' in Over My Head, 2004; SMiLE, 2004; What I Really Want for Christmas, 2005; Contributor, vocals for film soundtrack Shell Life; Singles include: Surfin' USA; Surfer Girl; Little Deuce Coupe; In My Room; I Get Around; When I Grow Up To Be A Man; Dance Dance Dance; Producer: Help Me Rhonda; Barbara Ann; Caroline No; Sloop John B; God Only Knows; Good Vibrations; Wouldn't It Be Nice; Friends; Do It Again; I Can Hear Music; Brian Wilson, 1988; Sweet Insanity, 1990; I Just Wasn't Made for These Times, 1995; Orange Crate Art, 1995. Honours include: Rock And Roll Hall Of Fame, 1988; Special Award Of Merit, 1988; Grammy Award, Best Rock Instrumental Performance, 2005; UK Hall of Fame, 2006; Lifetime of Contributions to American culture through the performing arts in music, Kennedy Center Honors, 2007. Current Management: Elliott Lott, Boulder Creek Entertainment Corp, 4860 San Jacinto Circle West, Fallbrook, CA 92028, USA.

WILSON Colin Henry, b. 26 July 1931, Leicester, England. Author. m. (1) Dorothy Betty Troop, 1 son, (2) Joy Stewart, 2 sons, 1 daughter. Appointments: Visiting Professor, Hollins College, Virginia, 1966-67, University of Washington, Seattle, 1967, Dowling College, Majorca, 1969, Rutgers University, New Jersey, 1974. Publications: The Outsider, 1956; Religion and the Rebel, 1957; The Age of Defeat, 1959; Ritual in the Dark, 1960; The Strength to Dream, 1962; Origins of the Sexual Impulse, 1963; Necessary Doubt, 1964; Eagle and the Earwig, 1965; The Glass Cage, 1966; Sex and the Intelligent Teenager, 1966; Voyage to a Beginning, 1969; Hermann Hesse, 1973; Strange Powers, 1973; The Space Vampires, 1976; Mysteries, 1978; Starseekers, 1980; Access to Inner Worlds, 1982; Psychic Detectives, 1983; The Essential Colin Wilson, 1984; Rudolf Steiner: The Man and His Work, 1985; An Encyclopedia of Scandal (with Donald Seaman), 1986; Spider World: The Tower, 1987; Aleister Crowley - The Man and the Myth, 1987; An Encyclopedia of Unsolved Mysteries (with Damon Wilson), 1987; Marx Refuted, 1987; Written in Blood (with Donald Seaman), 1989; The Misfits - A Study of Sexual Outsiders, 1988; Beyond the Occult, 1988; The Serial Killers, 1990; Spiderworld: The Magician, 1991; The Strange Life of P D Ouspensky, 1993; Unsolved Mysteries Past and Present (with Damon Wilson), 1993; Atlas of Holy Places and Sacred Sites, 1996; From Atlantis to the Sphinx, 1996; Alien Dawn, 1998; The Devil's Party, 2000; Atlantis Blueprint (with Rand Fle'math), 2000; Spiderworld: Shadowland, 2003; Autobiography Dreaming to some Purpose, 2004; Atlantis and the Kingdom of the Neanderthals, 2006; Crimes of Passion: The Thin Line Between Love and Hate, 2006; The Rise and Fall of the Angry Young Men, 2007; Serial Killer Investigations, 2007. Contributions to: The Times; Daily Mail. Membership: Society of Authors. Address: Tetherdown, Trewallock Lane, Gorran Haven, Cornwall, PL26 6NT, England.

WILSON OF TILLYORN, Baron (Life Peer) of Finzean in the District of Kincardine and Deeside and of Fanling in Hong Kong, Sir David Clive Wilson, b. 14 February 1935. m. Natasha Helen Mary Alexander, 2 sons. Education:

Scholar, MA, Keble College, Oxford; University of Hong Kong; Visiting Scholar, Columbia University New York, USA; PhD, University of London. Appointments: HM Diplomatic Service: Joined SE Asia Department, Foreign Office, 1958; Third Secretary, Vientiane, 1959-60; Language Student, Hong Kong, 1960-62; Third then Second Secretary, Peking, 1963-65; First Secretary, Far Eastern Department, 1965-68, resigned 1968; Editor, The China Quarterly, Contemporary China Institute SOAS, University of London, 1968-74; Rejoined HM Diplomatic Service, 1974; Cabinet Office, 1974-77; Political Adviser, Hong Kong, 1977-81; Head, Southern European Department, Foreign and Commonwealth Office 1981-84; Assistant Under Secretary of State responsible for Asia and the Pacific, Foreign and Commonwealth Office, 1984-87; Governor and Commander in Chief of Hong Kong, 1987-92; Member of the Board, British Council, 1993-2002, Chairman, Scottish Committee, 1993-2002; Council, CBI Scotland, 1993-92; Prime Minister's Advisory Committee on Business Appointments, 2000-; Chairman, Scottish and Southern Energy (formerly Scottish Hydro-Electric), 1993-2000; Director, Martin Currie Pacific Trust plc, 1993-2003; Chancellor, University of Aberdeen, 1997-; Master, Peterhouse, Cambridge, 2002-. Honours: CMG, 1985; KCMG, 1987; GCMG, 1991; Life Peer, 1992; KT, 2000; Honorary Fellow, Keble College, Oxford, 1987; KStJ, 1987; Honorary LLD, University of Aberdeen, 1990, University of Abertay Dundee, 1995, Chinese University of Hong Kong, 1996; Honorary DLitt, University of Sydney, 1991; FRSE, 2000; Burgess, Guild of City of Aberdeen, 2004; Honorary degree, University on Hong Kong, 2006. Memberships: President: Bhutan Society of the UK, 1993-, Hong Kong Society, 1994-, Hong Kong Association, 1994-; Vice-President, RSGS, 1996; Chairman of Trustees, National Museums of Scotland, 2002-; Chairman, Council of Glenalmond College, 2000-05, Scottish Peers' Association, 2000-2002; Member, Carnegie Trust for the Universities of Scotland, 2000-; Registrar, Order of St Michael and St George, 2001-. Address: House of Lords, London SW1A 0PW, England or The Master's Lodge, Peterhouse, Cambridge, CB2 1QY, England.

WILSON David Geoffrey, b. 30 April 1933, Urmston, Lancashire, England. Retired Banker. m. Dianne. Education: Leeds Grammar School, 1944-46; Hulme Grammar School for Boys, 1947-50; Honorary MA, Manchester University, 1983; Honorary MA, Salford University, 1996. Appointments: Williams Deacon's Bank Ltd, 1952-70, Company Secretary, 1965-70; Merger into Williams & Glyn's Bank Ltd, 1970-86, Company Secretary, 1970-72, Manager (Mosley Street, Manchester), 1973-77, Superintendent of Branches, 1977-78, Area Director, 1978-82; Seconded as Regional Director, National Enterprise Board for North West, Yorkshire & Humberside (British Technology Group), 1982-85; Regional Director based in Manchester, British Linen Bank, 1985-91; Retired, 1991; High Sheriff of Greater Manchester, 1991-92; Chairman, North Manchester Health Authority and North Manchester NHS Healthcare Trust, 1991-97; Chairman, Manchester Business Link, 1993-2001; Chairman, Business Link Network Ltd, 1998-2001. Honours: Honorary Consul for Iceland, 1981-; Deputy Lieutenant, Greater Manchester, 1985; OBE, 1986; Vice Lord-Lieutenant of Greater Manchester, 2003-; OBE; DL. Memberships: Army & Navy Club, London; Lancashire County Cricket Club, Manchester. Address: 28 Macclesfield Road, Wilmslow, Cheshire SK9 2AF, England. E-mail: wilsondg@talk21.com

WILSON Francis Xavier, b. 8 January 1964, Derby, England. Chemist. m. Fiona, 1 son, 1 daughter. Education: Nottingham High School, 1975-82; MA, 1987, DPhil, 1990, Keble College, Oxford. Appointments: Team Leader, later Project Leader, Roche Discovery, Welwyn, 1990-2001; Departmental Manager, Medicinal Chemistry, 2001-02, Head of Chemistry, 2003, Xenova; Associate Director, 2003-04, Director, 2005-07, Chemistry, Cellzome; Director, Chemistry, Summit plc, 2007-. Publications: 28 articles in professional scientific journals; 2 posters; 16 patents. Memberships: Royal Society of Chemistry; Society of Chemistry and Industry; Society of Medicines Research. E-mail: francis.wilson@summitplc.com

WILSON Jim C, b. 16 July 1948, Edinburgh, Scotland. Writer; Poet. m. Mik Kerr, 21 August 1971. Education: MA, Honours, English Language and Literature, University of Edinburgh, 1971. Appointments: Lecturer, English Telford College, Edinburgh, 1972-81; Writer-in-Residence, Stirling District, 1989-91; Creative Writing Tutor, University of Edinburgh, 1994-; Royal Literary Fund Fellow, 2001-. Publications: The Loutra Hotel, 1988; Six Twentieth Century Poets; Cellos in Hell, 1993; A Book of Scottish Verse, 2001; Poems in The Edinburgh Book of Twentieth-Century Scottish Poetry, 2005; Contributions to: Scotsman; The Herald; Chapman; Lines Review; Radical Scotland; Times Educational Supplement; Cencrastus; Outposts; Orbis; Acumen; Rialto; Poetry Canada Review; Envoi; 2 Plus 2; Poet's Voice; Iron; Stand; Encounter; Literary Review; Imago (Australia). Honours: Scottish Arts Council Writer's Bursary, 1987, 1994; 1st Prize Scottish International Open Poetry Competition, 1997, 2005; Award, 1987; 1st Prize, Swanage Arts Festival Literary Competition, 1988, 1989, 1997; Hugh MacDiarmid Trophy for Poetry, 1997, 2005; 1st Prize, Scottish National Galleries Competition, 2006. Memberships: Scottish PEN; Edinburgh's Shore Poets. Address: 25 Muirfield Park, Gullane, East Lothian EH31 2DY, Scotland.

WILSON Lela May, b. 31 October 1910, Thornhill (now Toronto), Canada. Curator; Author. m. Ronald York Wilson (deceased). Appointments: Co-founder, Annual York Wilson Endowment Award, 1998-; Co-founder, Women's Volunteer Committee, Art Gallery of Ontario; Founder, Director, Art Gallery of Ontario Gift Shop. Publications: Author, York Wilson, His Life and Work, 1997; Art Columnist, Atencion", San Miguel de Allende, Mexico, 1970s and 1980s; Contributor to various other works. Honours: Order of Ontario, 2003. Memberships: Women's Committee of The Toronto Symphony Orchestra; The Arts and Letters Club; Heliconian Club; University of Toronto Women's Club. Address: 41 Alcina Avenue, Toronto, Ontario M6G 2E7, Canada.

WILSON Robert Woodrow, b. 10 January 1936, USA. Radioastronomer. m. Elizabeth Rhoads Sawin, 1958, 2 sons, 1 daughter. Education: Bachelor's Degree, Rice University, 1957; PhD, California Institute of Technology, 1962. Appointments: Technical Staff, Bell Telephone Laboratory, Holmdel, New Jersey, 1963, Head, Radiophysics Department, 1976-94; Senior Scientist, Harvard-Smithsonian Center for Astrophysics, 1994-; Detected cosmic microwave background radiation, supposedly a residue of the Big Bang. Publications: Numerous articles in scientific journals. Memberships: NAS; American Astronomical Society; American Physical Society; International Astronomical Union. Honours: Henry Draper Award, National Academy of Sciences, 1977; Herschel Award, Royal Astronomical Society, 1977; Joint Winner, Nobel Prize for Physics, 1978. Address: Harvard-Smithsonian Center for Astrophysics, 60 Garden Street #42, Cambridge, MA 02138, USA.

WINCH Donald Norman, b. 15 April 1935, London, England. Professor of the History of Economics. m. Doreen Lidster, 5 August 1983. Education: BSc, London School of Economics and Political Science, 1956; PhD, Princeton University, 1960. Appointments: Visiting Lecturer, University of California, Berkeley, 1959-60; Lecturer in Economics, University of Edinburgh, 1960-63; Lecturer, 1963-66, Reader, 1966-69, Dean, School of Social Sciences, 1968-74, Professor of the History of Economics, 1969-, Pro-Vice-Chancellor, Arts and Social Studies, 1986-89, University of Sussex; Publications Secretary, Royal Economic Society, 1971-; Visiting Fellow, Institute for Advanced Study, Princeton, New Jersey, 1974-75; King's College, Cambridge, 1983, Australian National University, 1983, St Catharine's College, Cambridge, 1989, All Souls College, Oxford, 1994; Review Editor, Economic Journal, 1976-83; British Council Distinguished Visiting Fellow, Kyoto University, 1992; Carlyle Lecturer, University of Oxford, 1995. Publications: Classical Political Economy and Colonies, 1965; James Mill: Selected Economic Writings (editor), 1966; Economics and Policy, 1969; The Economic Advisory Council 1930-1939 (with S K Howson), 1976; Adam Smith's Politics, 1978; That Noble Science of Politics (with S Collini and J W Burrow), 1983; Malthus, 1987; Riches and Poverty, 1996. Contributions to: Many learned journals. Honours: British Academy, fellow, 1986-, vice president, 1993-94; Royal Historical Society, fellow, 1987-. Address: c/o Arts B, University of Sussex, Brighton BN1 9QN, England.

WINEGARTEN Renee, b. 23 June 1922, London, England. Literary Critic; Author. m. Asher Winegarten, deceased, 1946. Education: BA, 1943, PhD, 1950, Girton College, Cambridge. Publications: French Lyric Poetry in the Age of Malherbe, 1954; Writers and Revolution, 1974; The Double Life of George Sand, 1978; Madame de Staël, 1985; Simone de Beauvoir: A Critical View, 1988; Accursed Politics: Some French Women Writers and Political Life 1715-1850, 2003 Contributions to: Journals. Memberships: George Sand Association; Society of Authors; Authors Guild. Address: 12 Heather Walk, Edgware, Middlesex HA8 9TS, England.

WINFREY Oprah, b. 29 January 1954, Missouri, USA. Talk Show Host; Actress. Education: Tennessee State University. Career: Radio WVOL while at University in Tennessee, then on TV Stations: WTVF-TV Nashville as Reporter and Anchor, WJZ-TV Balt News, Co-anchor, 1976; People are Talking, Co-host, 1978; AM Chicago, Host, show re-named The Oprah Winfrey Show, 1985-; formed Harpo Productions, Owner/Producer, 1986; Founder, Editing Director, The Oprah Magazines, 2000-; Partner, Oxygen Media, 2000-; Producer of several TV films; Actress: The Color Purple, 1985; Native Son, 1986; The Woman of Brewster Place, TV, 1989; Throw Momma From the Train, 1988; Listen Up: The Lives of Quincy Jones, 1990; Beloved, 1998; Their Eyes Were Watching God, 2005; Charlotte's Web (voice), 2006; Bee Movie (voice), 2007. Publications: Oprah, 1993; In the Kitchen with Rosie, 1996; Make the Connection, 1996. Honours: Numerous awards including: International Radio and Television Society's Broadcaster of the Year Award, 1988; Lifetime Achievement Award, National Academy of TV Arts and Sciences, 1998. Address: Harpo Productions, 110 N Carpenter Street, Chicago, IL 60607, USA.

WING Robert Farquhar, b. 31 October 1939, New Haven, Connecticut, USA. Astronomer. m. Ingrid McCowen Wing, deceased, 2 sons, 1 daughter. Education: BS, Yale University, 1961; Attended Cambridge University, 1961-62; PhD, University of California, Berkeley, 1967. Appointments: Assistant Professor, 1967-71, Associate Professor, 1971-76, Professor, 1976-2002, Professor Emeritus, 2002-, Astronomy Department, Ohio State University. Publications: Approximately 150 research articles in journals of astronomy and astrophysics; The Carbon Star Phenomenon (editor), 2000. Honours: Various research grants from the NSF and NASA. Memberships: International Astronomical Union; Royal Astronomical Society; American Astronomical Society; Astronomical Society of the Pacific; American Association of Variable Star Observers; International Amateur-Professional Photoelectric Photometry Association; International Dark Sky Association. Address: 400 Lenappe Drive, Columbus, OH 43214, USA. E-mail: wing@astronomy.ohio-state.edu

WINGER Debra, b. 16 May 1955, Cleveland, USA. Actress. m. (1) Timothy Hutton, 1986, divorced 1990, 1 son, (2) Arliss Howard, 1996, 1 son. Education: California University, Northridge. Appointments: Served, Israel Army, 1972; First Professional Appearance, Wonder Woman, tv series, 1976-77. Creative Works: Films include: Thank God Its Friday, 1978; French Postcards, 1979; Urban Cowboy, 1980; Cannery Row, 1982; An Officer and a Gentleman, 1982; Terms of Endearment, 1983; Mike's Murder, 1984; Legal Eagles, 1986; Black Widow, 1987; Made in Heaven, 1987; Betrayed, 1988; The Sheltering Sky, 1990; Everybody Wins, 1990; Leap of Faith, 1992; Shadowlands, 1993; A Dangerous Woman, 1993; Forget Paris, 1995; Big Bad Love, 2002; Radio, 2003; Eulogy, 2004; TV includes: Dawn Anna, 2005; Sometimes in April, 2005. Address: c/o CAA, 9830 Wilshire Boulevard, Beverly Hills, CA 90212, USA.

WINIARCZYK Marek, b. 30 June 1947, Wrocław, Poland. Historian. Education: MA, 1970, PhD, 1976, Doctor habilitatus, 1982, Department of Classics, University of Wrocław, Poland. Appointments: Librarian, 1970-73, Lecturer, Department of Foreign Languages, 1973-83, Associate Professor of Classical Languages, 1983-93, Professor of Ancient History, 1993-, University of Wrocław. Publications: Diagorae Melii et Theodori Cyrenaei reliquiae, 1981; Euhemeri Messenii reliquiae, 1991; Bibliographie zum antiken Atheismus, 1994; Co-editor: Abkürzungen aus Personalschriften des XVI bis XVIII Jahrhunderts, 1993 (second edition, 2002); Author, dictionary: Sigla Latina in libris impressis occurrentia, 1995; Euhemeros von Messene. Leben, Werk und Nachwirkung, 2002. Honours: Listed in Who's Who publications and biographical dictionaries. Memberships: Wrocławskie Towarzystwo Naukowe; Polskie Towarzystwo Filologiczne; Polskie Towarzystwo Historyczne; American School of Classical Studies at Athens, 1995. Address: Mianowskiego 25/2, 51-605, Wrocław, Poland.

WINKEL Wolfgang, b. 15 June 1941, Danzig, Germany. Zoologist. m. Doris Laux, 1 daughter. Education: Graduation (Dr rer nat), University Brunswick, 1968. Scientific Assistant, Institute of Avian Research, Wilhelmshaven, Germany, 1970-77; Head, working group population ecology of Vogelwarte Helgoland, Brunswick, 1978-2006. Publications: Over 150 in scientific journals; Co-author, Eco-ornithological Glossary, 1983; Co-author, Die Vogelfamilien der Westpaläarktis, 1995; Editor-in-Chief, Die Vogelwelt, 1971-87; Co-editor, Die Vogelwarte, 1972-2004. Honours: Silberne Ehrennadel, Deutscher Bund für Vogelschutz, 1984; Förderpreis der Werner-Sunkel-Stiftung, Deutsche Ornithologen-Gesellschaft, 2001. Memberships: Deutsche Ornithologen-Gesellschaft; British Ornithologists' Union; American Ornithologists' Union. Address: Bauernstr 14/15, D-38162 Cremlingen-Weddel, Germany.

WINKELMAN Joseph William, b. 20 September 1941, Keokuk, Iowa, USA. Artist; Printmaker. m. Harriet Lowell Belin, 2 daughters. Education: BA, English, University of the South, Sewanee, Tennessee, 1964; CFA, University of Oxford, 1971. Appointments: President, Royal Society of Painter-Printmakers, 1989-95; Artist-in-Residence, St John's College, Oxford, 2004. Honours: Honorary Member: Royal Watercolour Society, Oxford Art Society, Printmaker's Council of Great Britain. Memberships: Royal Society of Painter-Printmakers. Address: The Hermitage, 69 Old High Street, Headington, Oxford OX3 9HT, England.

WINNER Michael Robert, b. 30 October 1935, London, England. Producer; Director; Writer. Education: Downing College, Cambridge University. Appointments: Film Critic and Fleet Street Journalist; Contributor to: The Spectator, Daily Express, London Evening Standard; Columnist, The Sunday Times, The News of the World; Panellist on Any Questions, BBC Radio; Presenter, Michael Winner's True Crimes; Entered motion pictures, 1956 as Screen Writer, Assistant Director, Editor; Member of the Council and Trustee, Director's Guild of Great Britain, 1983-; Founder and Chairman, The Police Memorial Trust, 1984; Director, Scimitar Films Ltd. Films include: Play it Cool, The Cool Mikado, 1962; West Eleven, The System, 1963; You Must Be Joking, 1965; The Jokers, 1966; I'll Never Forget What's 'isname, 1967; Hannibal Brooks, 1968; The Games, 1969; Lawman, 1970; The Nightcomers, Chato's Land, 1971; The Mechanic, Scorpio, 1972; The Stone Killer, 1973; Death Wish, 1974; Won Ton Ton The Dog That Saved Hollywood, 1975; The Sentinel, 1976; The Big Sleep, 1977; Firepower, 1978; Death Wish Two, 1981; The Wicked Lady 1982; Scream for Help, 1984; Death Wish Three, 1985; Appointment with Death, 1988; A Chorus of Disapproval, 1989; Bullseye!, 1990; Dirty Weekend, 1993; Parting Shots, 1997; Actor: For the Greater Good, 1990; Decadence, 1993; Radio Play: The Flump, 2000; Theatre Productions: The Tempest, Wyndhams, 1974; A Day in Hollywood A Night in Ukraine, 1978; TV: Starring in and/or directing commercials including: Esure Insurance; Kenco, Doritos, Books for Schools. Publications: Winner's Dinners, 1999, revised edition, 2000; Winner Guide, 2002; Biography, Winner Takes All: a Life of Sorts, 2004. Honour: MA (Cantab). Address: 219 Kensington High Street, London W8 6BD, England. E-mail: winner@ftech.co.uk

WINSLET Kate, b. October 1975, Reading, England. Actress. m. (1) Jim Threapleton, 1998, divorced 2001, 1 daughter, (2) Sam Mendes, 2003, 1 son. Education: Theatre School, Maidenhead. Creative Works: TV appearances: Get Back; Casualty; Anglo-Saxon Attitudes; Films: A Kid in King Arthur's Court; Heavenly Creatures, 1994; Sense and Sensibility, 1996; Jude, 1996; Hamlet, 1996; Titanic, 1997; Hideous Kinky, 1997; Holy Smoke, 1998; Quills, 1999; Enigma, 2000; Iris, 2001; The Life of David Gale, 2002; Plunge: The Movie, 2003; Eternal Sunshine of the Spotless Mind, 2004; Finding Neverland, 2004; Pride (voice), 2004: Romance & Cigarettes, 2005; All the King's Men, 2005; Flushed Away (voice), 2006; The Holiday, 2006. Honours include: BAFTA Award; 5 Golden Globes; Best European Actress, European Film Academy, 1998; Film Actress of the Year, Variety Club of Great Britain, 1998.

WINTERTON Rosie, b. 10 August 1958, Leicester, England. Member of Parliament. Education: BA (Hons) History, University of Hull, England, 1979. Appointments: Assistant to John Prescott MP, 1980-86; Parliamentary Officer, London Borough of Southwark, 1986-88; Parliamentary Officer, Royal College of Nursing, 1988-90; Managing Director, Connect Public Affairs, 1990-94; Head of Private office of John Prescott MP, Deputy Leader of the Labour Party; Entered Parliament as MP for Doncaster Central, 1997-; Elected representative of Parliamentary Labour Party on the National Policy Forum of the Labour Party, 1997-2001; Chair of Transport and General Worker's Parliamentary Group, 1998-99; Leader of Leadership Campaign Team, 1998-99; Member on Standing Committee of Transport Bill, 2000; Intelligence and Security Committee, 2000; Member on Standing Committee of Finance Bill, 2000; Standing Committee of the Local Government Finance (Supplementary Credit Approvals) Bill and the Regional Development Agencies Bill; Member of the Labour Party Strategic Campaign; Parliamentary Secretary at the Lord Chancellor's Department, 2001-03; Minister of State, Department of Health, 2003-07; Minister of State for Transport, 2007-. Address: Guildhall Advice Centre, Old Guildhall Yard, Doncaster, South Yorkshire, DN1 1OW, England.

WINWOOD Stephen Lawrence, Birmingham, England. Musician; Composer. m. Eugenia Crafton, 1987, 1 son, 3 daughters. Career: Singer, Musician, Spencer Davis Group, 1964-67, Traffic, 1967-74, Blind Faith, 1970; Solo Artist, 1974-; Director, F S Ltd. Creative Works: Albums (with Traffic): Mr Fantasy, 1967; Traffic, 1968; Last Exit, 1969; John Barleycorn Must Die, 1970; Welcome to the Canteen, 1971; The Low Spark of High Heeled Boys, 1971; Shoot Out at the Fantasy Factory, 1973; On the Road, 1973; When the Eagle Flies, 1974; Far from Home, 1994; The Last Great Traffic Jam, 2005; (with Blind Faith): Blind Faith, 1969; (with Go): Go, 1976; Go Life from Paris, 1976; (solo): Steve Winwood, 1977; Arc of a Diver, 1980; Talking Back to the Night, 1982; Back in the High Life, 1986; Roll with It, 1988; Refugees of the Heart, 1990; Junction Seven, 1997; About Time, 2003; Nine Lives, 2008. Honours: 14 Gold Records; 4 Platinum Record Awards; 2 Grammy Awards. Address: c/o Trinity Cottage, Tirley, Gloucs GL19 4EU, England.

WISDOM Sir Norman, b. 4 February 1915. Actor; Comedian. m. 1947, divorced, 1969. Career: Films: Trouble in Store, 1953; One Good Turn, 1954; There Was a Crooked Man, 1960; The Girl on the Boat, 1962; On the Beat, 1962; A Stitch in Time, 1963; Double X: The Name of the Game, 1992; Cosmic Brainsuckers, 2000; Five Children and It, 2004. Plays: Walking Happy; The Legendary Norman Wisdom, 1982-96; Norman Wisdom and Friends; numerous Royal Variety Performances and pantomimes. Radio: Robin Hood (series); TV: numerous TV series; TV plays: Going Gently, 1981; Between the Sheets, 2003; Appeared in: Bergerac, 1982; Casualty, 1986; The Last of the Summer Wine, 1995; Dalziel and Pasce, 2002; The Last Detective, 2003; Coronation Street, 2004. Publications: Trouble in Store, 1991; Don't Laugh At Me (autobiography), 1992; Cos I'm A Fool, 1996; My Turn, 2002. Honours: Best Newcomer Academy Award, 1953; 2 Broadway Awards; Lifetime Achievement Award British Comedy Awards, 1991; Freeman of Tirana, Albania, 1995, City of London, 1995, Douglas (Isle of Man); Special Achievement Award, London Film Critics Circle, 1996; Knighthood, 2002. Address: c/o Johnny Mans Productions Ltd, PO Box 196, Hoddesdon, Hertfordshire EN10 7WG, England.

WISZNIEWSKI Leslaw, b. 6 February 1936. Professor; Colonel CAF (USA) (Retired). m. (1) 1 son, (2) Kathleen Margaret, 1982. Education: Xaverian College, Manchester; Saltley College of St Peter, Birmingham; Studied Psychology at universities of Manchester, Birmingham and Somerset, Louisiana. Appointments: Retired from Junior Secondary and Special Education, 1985; Instructor, Lecturer, Technical

Advisor with several police forces; Writer. Publications: The Martial Arts Instructor, 1975; Practical Psychology, 1980; Evasion Techniques, 1980; Dynamic Baton Techniques, 1980; Practical Hypnosis, 1981; Control of Self: Sequences and Situation; Spiritual Aspects of Kung Fu, 1987; Practical Hypnosis, 1988; Fic-Choy-Sau (Self Defence), 1989; Psychology: The Subtle Approach, 1997; A Thought and other Poems, 1998; End of Century Reflections, 1999; The Spider's World, 1999; New Poems for a New Millennium, 2000; We, The Rats, 2000; From My Memoirs, 2000; The Gorilla and The Snail, 2001; The Way, 2001; In Vino Veritas, 2002; The Gift, 2003; A Book of Selected Verse, 2004; Several publications in Polish. Honours: CF Medal, Ministry of Defence, 1983; Police Award for Services Rendered, 2004. Memberships: Fellow, College of Preceptors; Fellow, Institute of Linguists; Numerous sports organisations of Oriental derivation; President, Self Defence Society; Chief advisor to several organisations. Address: 7 Ambleside Court, Congleton, Cheshire CW12 4HZ, England.

WITHERSPOON Reese, b. 22 March 1976, Baton Rouge, Louisiana, USA. Actress. m. Ryan Phillippe, 1999, divorced 2007, 1 son, 1 daughter. Education: English Literature, Stanford University. Career: Model, age 7; Appeared in TV commercials; First place in Ten-State Talent Fair, age 11; Own production company, Type A Films; Films include: The Man in the Moon, 1991; Jack the Bear, 1993; A Far Off Place, 1993; Fear, 1996; Freeway, 1996; Pleasantville, 1998; Election, 1999; Cruel Intentions, 1999; Legally Blonde, 2001; Sweet Home Alabama, 2002; The Importance of Being Earnest, 2002; Legally Blonde 2: Red, White & Blonde, 2003; Vanity Fair, 2004; Walk the Line, 2005; Just Like Heaven, 2005; Penelope, 2006; Rendition, 2007. Membership: Gamma Phi Beta Sorority. Honours: Best Actress, Oscars, 2006.

WITTFOHT Hans, b. 26 November 1924, Wittingen, Germany. Structural Engineer. Education: Dipl-Ing, 1951, Dr-Ing, 1963, Technical Hochschule, Karlsruhe; Dr-Ing Eh (honoris causa), Technical University of Stuttgart, 1979. Appointments: Masoner (professional employment); Deputy Director, Chief of Prestressed Concrete Department, 1952; Director, Head of Technical Department, 1959; Managing Director, Partner, President, Polensky & Zöllner Gesellschaft mbH & Co, with special responsibility for the technical development and overseas activity; Presidential Member, 1969-, President, 1985-91, German Concrete Association. Publications: Contributor, many articles to professional journals; Author: Kreisfoermig gekruemmte Trager, 1964; Triumph der Spannweiten, 1972; Printed puentes, ejemples internacionales, 1975; Building Bridges, 1984; Bridgebuilder from Passion: mosaics from the life of an entrepreneur (contractor), 2005. Honours: Iron Cross I for service in the German Army 1942-45; National Ehrenzichen des, VDI, 1977; Medal of Honour, 1978, 1994; Emil-Mörsh Denkmünze des Deutschen Beton-Vereins award, 1981; Board member, 1969-, President between 1985-91; Board member, First President of BDI-Civil Engineers, 1968-72; Golden Medaille, Gustave Magnel, 1984; German Society of Structural Engineers, 1986; Honorary Fellow, Institute of Structural Engineers, London, 1986; Silver medal, Ville de Paris, 1987; Kerensky Medal, 1988; International Award of Merit, Structural Engineers in Association with American Society of Civil Engineers and IABSE, 1989; Freyssinet Medal of FIP, 1994; Numerous other awards for bridge construction in national and international competitions. Memberships: Vice President, Research Association for Underground Transport Facilities; President, 1984-88, Honorary President, 1988-, Federation Internationale Prècontrainte; President of Technical Committee, Vice President, International Association of Bridge and Structural Engineering (IABSE); German Concrete Society; German Engineers Society; VDI – Civil Engineers. Address: 20 Am Kiekeberg, 22587 Hamburg, Germany.

WOGAN Terry (Michael Terence), b. 3 August 1938, Ireland. Broadcaster. m. Helen Joyce, 1965, 2 sons, 1 daughter. Education: Crescent College, Limerick; Belvedere College, Dublin. Appointments: Announcer, RTE, 1963, Senior Announcer, 1964-66; Various programmes for BBC Radio, 1965-67; Late Night Extra, BBC Radio, 1967-69; The Terry Wogan Show, BBC Radio 1, 1969-72, BBC Radio 2, 1972-84; Wake Up to Wogan, BBC Radio 2, 1993-. Creative Works: TV shows include: Lunchtime with Wogan, ATV; BBC: Come Dancing; Song for Europe; The Eurovision Song Contest; Children in Need; Wogan's Guide to the BBC; Blankety Blank; Wogan; Terry Wogan's Friday Night; Auntie's Bloomers; Wogan's Web; Points of View, 2000-01. Publications: Banjaxed, 1979; The Day Job, 1981; To Horse, To Horse, 1982; Wogan on Wogan, 1987; Wogan's Ireland, 1988; Bumper Book of Togs, 1995; Is It Me?, autobiography, 2000. Honours include: Radio Award, 1980; Radio Industry Award, 1982, 1985, 1987; Carl Alan Award, 3 times; Variety Club of Great Britain Special Award, 1982; Showbusiness Personality, 1984; Radio Personality of Last 21 years, Daily Mail National Radio Awards, 1988; Sony Radio Award, Barcelona Olympics, 1993; Sony Radio Award, Best Breakfast Show, 1994; Honorary OBE, 1997 New Year's Honours List; Radio Broadcaster of the Year, Broadcasting Press Guild Awards, 2005; Honorary Knighthood, 2005. Address: c/o Jo Gurnett, 2 New Kings Road, London SW6 4SA, England.

WOHLLEBEN Rudolf, b. 4 June 1936, Bad Kreuznach, Germany. Retired Telecommunications and Antenna Engineer; Writer. m. Rosemarie, 2 sons, 1 stepson, 1 stepdaughter. Education: BSEE, University of Karlsruhe, 1957; MSEE, Dipl-Ing, Technical University, Munich; Dr Ing, 1969; RWTH, Aachen. Appointments: Lecturer, Radar, Antennas, Radioastronomy, Microwaves, University of Kaiserslautern, Germany, 1980-2006; Forschungsinst f HF-Physik, Rolandseck, 1961-64; Institut f Techn Elektronik, RWTH Aachen, 1964-70; Writer, 1968-; Max-Planck Institute fuer Radioastronomie, Electronics Division, Bonn, 1971-99; Retired, 1999-; Archiver, WSC-Sammlung, Institut fuer Hochschul Kunde, University Library of Wuerzburg, Germany, 2003-. Publications: 70 articles in professional journals; 8 books, including Interferometry in Radioastronomy and Radar Techniques, 1991; Fruehe Spaetlese, poems, 1997; (The Poet) Stefan George, for enthusiasts and scholars (in German), 2004; Co-author (with K E Wild and A P Faust), Literatur-Geschichte des Nahelands u Hunsruecks, 2009. Honours: Sport Medal, town of Bonn, 2002; Theodor Heuss Medal, FDP, 1990. Listed in national and international biographical dictionaries. Memberships include: Informationstechnische Gesellschaft, Germany; Verband deutscher Schriftsteller, Stefan-George-Gesellschaft/Bingen, 4 WSC-Corps; Chairman, Verein für corpsstudent. Geschichtsforschung; Vice Chairman, Verein d Freunde u Foerderer d Wachenburg b Weinheim. Address: Kurhausstr 1A, D-55543 Bad Kreuznach, Germany. E-mail: r.wohlleben@freenet.de

WOLFE John Henry Nicholas, b. 4 June 1947, Cardiff, Wales. Vascular Surgeon. m. Dorothy, 3 sons, 2 daughters. Education: St Thomas's Hospital Medical School; London University. Appointments: Senior House Officer, St James's Hospital, Balham; Surgical Registrar, Salisbury Infirmary; Lecturer in Surgery, St Thomas's Hospital; Research Fellow, Brigham and Women's Hospital, Harvard Medical School;

Senior Surgical Registrar, St Thomas's Hospital; Honorary Senior Lecturer, Imperial College School of Medicine; Honorary Consultant Vascular Surgeon, Royal Brompton Hospital; Honorary Consultant Vascular Surgeon, Edward VII Hospital for Officers; Consultant Vascular Surgeon, St Mary's Hospital; Honorary Vascular Surgeon, Great Ormond Street Hospital for Children. Publications: 300 articles in professional journals; Associate Editor, Rutherfords Vascular Surgery, 1984; Editor, Author, ABC Vascular Disease, 1992; Associate Editor, Year Book of Vascular Surgery, 2001. Honours: Hunterian Professor, Royal College of Surgeons of England, 1982; Moynihan Fellow, Association of Surgeons of Great Britain and Ireland; Honorary Member, Society of Vascular Technologists; Honorary Member, Vascular Society of India; Editorial Board, European Journal of Vascular and Endovascular Surgery; Chairman, CME Committee for Vascular Surgery in UEMS; Vice President, Division of Vascular Surgery, UEMS; President, Board of Vascular Surgery, UEMS; Chairman, Vascular Advisory Committee of the Association of Surgeons of Great Britain and Ireland; Council of the Association of Surgeons of Great Britain and Ireland; Trustee, British Vascular Foundation. Memberships: Surgical Research Society; Association of Great Britain and Ireland; Past President, 2006-07, Vascular Society of Great Britain and Ireland; European Cardio-Vascular Society and European Chapter of the International Cardiovascular Society; President, 2007-08, European Vascular Society; Honorary Corresponding of the Society of Vascular Surgery; Fellow, Royal Geographic Society; Member, Medical Arts Society; Member, Royal Ocean Racing Club. Address: Emmanuel Raye House, 37a Devonshire Street, London W1G 6QA, England.

WOLFE Tom, (Thomas Kennerly Wolfe Jr), b. 2 March 1930, Richmond, Virginia, USA. Writer; Journalist; Artist. m. Sheila Berger, 1 son, 1 daughter. Education: AB, Washington and Lee University, 1951; PhD, American Studies, Yale University, 1957. Appointments: Reporter, Springfield Union, Massachusetts, 1956-59; Reporter and Latin American Correspondent, Washington Post, 1959-62; Writer, New York Sunday Magazine, 1962-66; City Reporter, New York Herald Tribune, 1962-66; Magazine Writer, New York World Journal Tribune, 1966-67; Contributing Editor, New York magazine, 1968-76, Esquire magazine, 1977-; Contributing Artist, Harper's magazine, 1978-81. Publications: The Kandy-Kolored Tangerine-Flake Streamline Baby, 1965; The Electric Kool-Aid Acid Test, 1968; The Pump House Gang, 1968; Radical Chic and Mau-mauing the Flak Catchers, 1970; The Painted Word, 1975; Mauve Gloves and Madmen, Clutter and Vine, 1976; The Right Stuff, 1979; In Our Time, 1980; From Bauhaus to Our House, 1981; The Purple Decades: A Reader, 1982; The Bonfire of the Vanities, 1987; A Man in Full, 1998; Hooking Up, 2000; I am Charlotte Simmons, 2004. Contributions to: Newspapers and magazines. Honours: Various honorary doctorates; American Book Award, 1980; Harold D Vursell Memorial Award, American Academy of Arts and Letters, 1980; John Dos Passos Award, 1984; Theodore Roosevelt Medal, Theodore Roosevelt Association, 1990; St Louis Literary Award, 1990. Membership: American Academy of Arts and Letters. Address: c/o Janklow & Nesbit Associates, 445 Park Avenue, New York, NY 10022, USA.

WOLFF Tobias J A, b. 19 June 1945, Birmingham, USA. Writer. m. Catherine Dolores Spohn, 1975, 2 sons, 1 daughter. Education: BA, Oxford University, 1972; MA, Stanford University, 1975; LHD (hon), Santa Clara University, 1996. Appointments: US Army, 1964-68; Reporter, Washington Post, 1972; Writing Fellow, Stanford University, 1975-78; Writer-in-Residence, Arizona State University, 1978-80,

Syracuse University, 1980-97, Stanford University, 1997-; Director, creative writing programme, 2000-02. Publications: Hunters in the Snow, 1981; The Barracks Thief, 1984; Back in the World, 1985; This Boy's Life, 1989; In Pharaoh's Army: Memories of a Lost War, 1994; The Vintage Book of Contemporary American Short Stories, 1994; The Best American Short Stories, 1994; The Night in Question, 1996; Old School, 2003; Our Story Begins: New and Selected Stories, 2008. Honours include: O Henry Award, 1981, 1982, 1985; Guggenheim Fellow, 1983; National Endowment Fellow, 1978, 1984; PEN/Faulkner Award for Fiction, 1985; Rea Award, 1989; Whiting Foundation Award, 1989; Los Angeles Times Book Prize, 1989; Ambassador Book Award, 1990; Lila Wallace/Readers Digest Award, 1993; Esquire-Volvo-Waterstone Award for Non-Fiction, 1994; Exceptional Achievement Award, American Academy of Arts and Letters, 2001; Fairfax Prize for Literature, 2003; PEN/Faulkner Award for Fiction nominee, 2004. Address: English Department, Stanford University, CA 94305-2087, USA.

WON Dongho, b. 23 September 1949, Seoul, Republic of Korea. Educator; Professor. m. Yoon Sook Han, 1 son, 1 daughter. Education: BS, 1976, MS, 1978, PhD, 1988, Electronic Engineering, Sungkyunkwan, Suwon, Korea. Appointments: Research Scientist, Electronics & Telecommunications Research Institute, Seoul, 1978-80; Professor, School of Information & Communication Engineering, 1982-, Director, Computer Center, 1992-94, Dean, Division of Student & Academic Affairs, 1995-97, Director, Information & Communication Technology Research Lab, 1997-99, Dean, Graduate School of Information & Communication, 1999-2001, Dean, Divison of Research & Development Affairs, 2002-04, Director, Authentication Technology Research Center, 2004-, Sungkyunkwan University, Suwon; Research Scientist, Department of Electrical & Electronic Engineering, Tokyo Institute of Technology, Japan, 1985-86; Visiting Professor, Department of Computer Science, University of California at Irvine, California, USA, 2004-05. Publications: Numerous articles in professional journals. Honours: Honor Award for Outstanding Achievement; National Intelligence Service of Korea, 2000; Honor Award for Outstanding Achievement, Korea Minister of Information and Communication, 2001; Sungkyun Academic Award, The Association of Sungkyunkwan University CEO Alumni, 2007. Memberships: Regular Member, Institute of Electronics, Information & Communication Engineers; Member, Institute of Electrical & Electronics Engineers; Member, Korea Institute of Information Security & Cryptology; Member, Institute of Electronics Engineers of Korea. Address: 903, Sinbanpo 17th Apt 334, Jamwon-dong, Seocho-gu, Seoul 137-951, South Korea. E-mail: dhwon@security.re.kr

WONDER Stevie (Steveland Morris), b. 13 May 1950, Saginaw, Michigan, USA. Singer; Musician; Composer. m. Syreeta Wright, 1970, divorced 1972, (2) Yolanda Simmons, 3 children, (3) Kai Milla, 2001, 2 sons. Education: Michigan School for the Blind, 1963-68; Self-taught, harmonica and piano. Appointments: Motown Recording Artist, 1963-70; Founder, President, Black Bull Music Inc; Founder, Wonderdirection Records Inc and Taurus Productions; Numerous concerts worldwide. Creative Works: Fingertips Part 2, 1963; Uptight (Everything's Alright), 1966; I Was Made to Love Her, 1967; For Once in My Life, 1968; My Cherie Amour, Yester-Me, Yester-You, Yesterday, 1969; Signed Sealed Delivered I'm Yours, 1970; Superstition, You Are the Sunshine of My Life, 1973; Higher Ground, Living For the City, You Haven't Done Nothin', 1974; Boogie On Reggae Woman, 1975; I Wish, Sir Duke, 1977; Master

Blaster, 1980; Lately, Happy Birthday, 1981; Ebony and Ivory, 1982; I Just Called To Say I Love You, 1984; Part-Time Lover, Don't Drive Drunk, 1985; Albums include: Music of My Mind, 1972; Innervisions, 1973; Songs in the Key of Life, 1976; Journey Through the Secret Life of Plants, 1979; Hotter than July, 1980; Original Musiquarium, 1981; Woman in Red, 1984; In Square Circle, 1986; Characters, 1987; Jungle Fever, 1991; Inner Peace, Motown Legends, 1995; Conversation Peace, 1995; A Time to Love, 2005. Honours: Edison Award, 1973; Songwriters Hall of Fame, 1983; Numerous American Music Awards; Oscar, Best Song, 1984; Gold Ticket, Madison Square Garden, 1986; Soul Train Heritage Award, 1987; Rock'n'Roll Hall of Fame, 1989; Songwriters Hall of Fame; Nelson Mandella Courage Award, 1991; IAAAM Diamond Award for Excellence, 1991; Lifetime Achievement Award, National Academy of Songwriters, 1992; NAACP Image Award, 1992; Numerous Grammy, Charity and Civil Rights Awards; Polar Music Prize, 1999; Kennedy Center Honour, 1999; George and Ira Gershwin Lifetime Achievement Award, 2002; Billboard Music Award, Century Award, 2004; Michigan Walk of Fame, 2004. Address: c/o Steveland Morris Music, 4616 W Magnolia Blvd, Burbank, CA 91505, USA.

WONG Albert Wing Kuen, b. 17 June 1951, Hong Kong. Certified Financial Planner. m. Titania, 1 son, 1 daughter. Education: B Com, Clayton, USA; MBA, Tasmania, South Australia; PhD, Business Administration, Sussex, England; PhD, Banking and Finance, Wisconsin, USA; Advance Diploma, China Commercial Law, Shenzhen University, China; Advance Certificate in Meditation, Chinese University; Certificate of Completion, Directors' College of Executive Program by Stanford Law School, USA. Appointments: Group Financial Controller of Man Sang International Ltd, Hong Kong; Chief Executive Officer, Ming Hua International Holdings Ltd, USA; Managing Director and Chairman, Charise Financial Planning Ltd; Corporate Finance and Planning Advisor, KND & Co CPA Ltd; Independent Non-Executive Director, APAC Resources Ltd. Publications: Cash Flow Management; Financial Planning Important for Corporation and Individual. Honours: Honorary Associate of Baptist University, Hong Kong; Honorary Advisor, Ying Tak Educational Bureau, China. Memberships include: American Institute of Certified Public Accountants; Institute of Certified Public Accountants in Ireland; Fellow, Association of International Accountants; Fellow, Chartered Management Institute, UK; Fellow, National Institute of Accountants, Australia; Fellow, Society of Registered Financial Planners Ltd, Hong Kong; many others. Address: 14th Floor, West Wing, Sincere Insurance Building, 4-6 Hennessy Road, Wan Chai, Hong Kong. E-mail: cpa5106@yahoo.com.hk

WONG Po-Keung, b. 17 August 1954, Hong Kong. Professor. m. Lai-hor Lee, 1 son, 2 daughters. Education: BSc, Honours, Biology, 1977, M Phil, Biology and Microbiology, 1979, The Chinese University of Hong Kong; PhD, Microbiology, University of California, Davis, USA, 1983. Appointments: Lecturer, 1986-94, Senior Lecturer, 1994-96, Associate Professor, 1996-97, Professor, 1997-, The Chinese University of Hong Kong. Publications: More than 200 articles in journals of environmental science, technology, microbiology and ecotoxicology. Honours: Member, ISO 1400 Technical Committee, Hong Kong; Editor-in-Chief, Journal of Environmental Sciences; Editorial Board Member, Ecotoxicology and Environmental Safety. Memberships: Chartered Institution of Water and Environmental Management; American Chemical Society; International Water Association;

Society of Toxicology. Address: Department of Biology, The Chinese University of Hong Kong, Shatin, NT, Hong Kong SAR, China. E-mail: pkwong@cuhk.edu.hk

WONG Vincent, b. 2 July 1961, Penang. Financier; Lawyer; Businessman; Arbitrator. Education: Blackpool and Clyde College of Further Education; Diploma in Commodity Futures Trading, University of Sarasota; Bachelor in Business Administration (Hons), Master in Business Administration (cum laude), State University California; PhD (Jurisprudence), Cosmopolitan University, 2006. Appointments: Trader, frank Commodities, 1985; Treasury Manager, International Investment Research Centre, 1985-87; General Manager, Interventure Investments Management Pty Ltd, 1987-88; Director, United Asia-Pacific Securities Plc, 1988-1990; Financier, Muhamad Ali Islamic Foundation; Founder and Owner, Wong International Research Centre Inc and Vincent Wong & Partners. Publications: The Future for Venture Capital in South East Asia; The Development of Offshore Centres in the Asia Pacific Region; Foreign investments in Indonesia; The Financial Deregulations of Indonesia; India: Food Supplies; The Management and Operations of a Hunger Foundation. Honours: Honorary Consul to the Republic of Maldives. Memberships: Founder Member, Western Australian Chinese Chamber of Commerce, Institute of Directors, England; Society of Senior Executives, Australia; Bankers Club of Malaysia; International Bar Association; Commonwealth Lawyers Association; London Court of International Arbitration; American Bar Association; Inter-Pacific Bar Association; Institute of Chartered Arbitrators; Malaysian Institute of Arbitrators; Society for Construction Law; National Association for Criminal Defense Lawyers. Address: PO Box 6636, Kampong Tunku, 47300 Petaling Jaya, Selangor, Malaysia. E-mail: vincentwong939@yahoo.com

WOO John, b. 1948, Guangzhou, China. Film Director. m. Annie Woo Ngau Chun-lung, 3 children. Education: Matteo Ricci College, Hong Kong. Appointments: Production Assistant, Assistant Director, Cathay Film Co, 1971; Assistant Director to Zhang Che, Shaw Bros. Creative Works: Films: The Young Dragons, 1973; The Dragon Tamers; Countdown in Kung Fu; Princess Chang Ping; From Riches to Rags; Money Crazy; Follow the Star; Last Hurrah for Chivalry; To Hell with the Devil; Laughing Times; Plain Jane to the Rescue; Sunset Warriors (Heroes Shed No Tears); The Time You Need a Friend; Run Tiger Run; A Better Tomorrow; A Better Tomorrow II; Just Heroes; The Killer; Bullet in the Head; Once a Thief; Hard Boiled; Hard Target; Broken Arrow; Face/Off; Kings Ransom; Mission Impossible II; The Last Word; Windtalkers, 2000; The Hire: Hostage, 2002; Red Skies (producer), 2002; Paycheck, 2003; Bullet Proof Monk, 2003; All the Invisible Children, 2005; Appleseed Ex Machina, 2007; Stranglehold, 2007; Red Cliff, 2008. Address: c/o MGM Studios Inc, 2500 Broadway Street, Santa Monica, CA 90404, USA.

WOO Sam Yong, b. 15 March 1960, Young Joo, Korea. Scientist. m. Okja Son, 2 sons. Education: BS, Mechanical Engineering, Seoul National University, Korea, 1981; MS, 1992, PhD, 1998, Mechanical Engineering, ChungNam National University, Korea. Appointments: Researcher, Daewoo Heavy Industry, 1984-86; Principal Research Scientist, Group Leader, Division of Physical Metrology, Korea Research Institute of Standards and Science, 1986-. Publications: Numerous articles in professional scientific journals. Honours: Best Paper Prize, KRISS, 2004. Memberships: American Vacuum Society; Institute of Physics;

Korea Physics Society; Korea Vaccum Society. Address: KRISS, 1 Dayong-Dong, Yuseong-Gu, Daejeon 305-340, Korea. E-mail: sywoo@kriss.re.kr

WOOD David Bernard, b. 21 February 1944, Sutton, England. Playwright; Director; Actor; Magician. m. Jacqueline Stanbury, 2 daughters. Education: Chichester High School for Boys; BA (Hons) in English, Worcester College, Oxford, 1963-66. Appointments: Freelance actor, playwright, director, magician, children's book author. Publications: Many plays; Children's books. Honours: OBE, 2004; Honorary MA, University of Chichester, 2005. Memberships: Society of Authors; British Actors' Equity; The Magic Circle (MIMC); International Brotherhood of Magicians; Chair, Action for Children's Arts. Address: c/o Casarotto Ramsay Ltd, Waverley House, 7-12 Noel Street, London, W1F 8GQ, England. E-mail: agents@casarotto.uk.com

WOOD Elijah, b. 28 January 1981, Ceder Rapids, Iowa, USA. Actor. Education: Avent Studios, Modelling school. Films include: Back to the Future Part II, 1989; Internal Affairs, 1990; The Adventures of Huck Finn, 1993; The War, 1994; The Ice Storm, 1997; Oliver Twist, 1997; Deep Impact, 1998; The Faculty, 1998; Chains of Fools, 2000; The Lord of the Rings: The Fellowship of the Ring, 2001; The Adventures of Tom Thumb and Thumbelina, 2002; The Lord of the Rings: The Two Towers, 2002; The Lord of the Rings: The Return of the King, 2003; Eternal Sunshine of the Spotless Mind, 2004; Christmas on Mars, 2005; Hooligans, 2005; Sin City, 2005; Everything is Illuminated, 2005; Paris, je t'aime, 2006; Bobby, 2006; Happy Feet (voice), 2006; Day Zero, 2007; Legend of Spyro: The Eternal Night (voice), 2007; The Oxford Murders, 2008. TV Appearances include: Frasier, 1994; Adventures from the Book of Virtues, 1996; SM:TV Live, 2001; The Osbournes, 2002; The Buzz, 2002; Player$, 2002; The Tonight Show with Jay Leno, 2003; Saturday Night Live, 2003; NY Graham Norton, 2004; King of the Hill (voice), 2004; Robot Chicken (voice), 2006; American Dad, 2006. Honours: Young Artist Award, 1991; Saturn Award, 1994; Young Star Award, 1998; Empire Award, 2002; Young Hollywood Award, 2002; MTV Movie Award, 2003; National Board of Review, USA, 2003; Saturn Award, 2004; Broadcast Film Critics Association Award, 2004; Screen Actors Guild Award, 2004; Visual Effects Society Awards, 2003. Address: c/o Nicole David 151 S El Camino Drive, Beverly Hills, CA 90212-2775, USA.

WOOD James Albert, b. 9 November 1949, Enterprise, Oregon, USA. Professor. m. Maritza Alvarez, 1 daughter. Education: BS, David Lipscomb University, 1975; BA, MA, Southern Oregon University, 1979; EdD, Texas A&M University, 1986; Postgraduate Studies, University of Tennessee and Sul Ross State University Rio Grande College. Appointments: Graduate Teaching Assistant, Texas A&M University at Kingsville, and University of Tennessee; Spanish ESL Teacher, Sheldon ISD, Texas, Galena Park, ISD, Texas, Rice Consolidated ISD, Texas, Jefferson Co ISD, Madras, Oregon; Senior Program Development Specialist, University of Oklahoma; Full Professor, Sul Ross State University Rio Grande College. Publications: Co-author, Teaching Latino Students: Effetive Strategies for Educating America's Minorities, 2005; 41 articles in refereed journals. Honour: Dean's Grant, Bilingual Fellowship; Listed in national and international biographical dictionaries. Memberships: National Association for Bilingual Education; Texas Association for Bilingual Education; TESOL; ASCD; TTE; Life Member,

Non-Commissioned Officers Association; American Legion; Life Member, VFW; Masonic Lodge 472. Address: PO Box 1415, Uvalde, TX 78802, USA. E-mail: jawood@sulross.edu

WOOD Mark William, b. 28 March 1952. Chief Executive. m. Helen Lanzer, 1 son, 1 daughter. Education: BA (Honours), University of Leeds; MA, Warwick University; Certificate of Education, Oxford University. Appointments: Correspondent (Vienna, East Berlin, Moscow), 1977-85, Chief Correspondent (West Germany), 1985-87, Editor (Europe), 1987-89, Editor-in-Chief, 1989-2000, Head, Strategic Media Investments and Alliances, 2000-02, Reuters; Director, Reuters Holdings, 1990-96; Chairman, Reuters Television, 1992-2002; Director, 1993-, Chairman, 1998-, Chief Executive, 2003-, Independent Television News. Memberships: Member, 1995-2000, Vice Chairman, 1998-99, Chairman, 1999-2000, Library and Information Commission; Commonwealth Press Union, 1996-2000; Rathenau Gesellschaft, Germany, 1999-; Board Member, 2000-, Chairman, 2003-, MLA, Council for Museums, Archives and Libraries. Address: ITN, 200 Grays Inn Road, London WC1X 8XZ, England. Website: www.itn.co.uk

WOOD Ronnie (Ronald), b. 1 June 1947, England. Musician. m. (1) Krissy Findlay, 1971, divorced 1978, 1 son, (2) Jo Howard, 1985, 1 son, 1 stepson, 1 daughter. Appointments: Guitarist, Jeff Beck Group, 1968-69, The Faces, 1969-75, The Rolling Stones, 1975-. Creative Works: Albums (with Jeff Beck Group): Truth, 1968; Beck-Ola, 1969; with The Faces: First Step, 1970; Long Player, 1971; A Nod's As Good As A Wink...To A Blind Horse, 1971; Ooh La La, 1973; Coast to Coast Overtures and Beginners, 1974; (with The Rolling Stones): Black and Blue, 1976; Love You Live, 1977; Some Girls, 1978; Emotional Rescue, 1980; Tattoo You, 1981; Still Life, 1981; Undercover, 1983; Rewind 1971-1984, 1984; Dirty Work, 1986; Steel Wheels, 1989; Flashpoint, 1991; Voodoo Lounge, 1994; Bridges to Babylon, 1997; A Bigger Bang, 2005; Solo albums include: Slide on This, 1992; Not for Beginners, 2001; Ronnie Wood Anthology: The Essential Crossexion, 2006; Buried Alive: Live in Maryland, 2006; The First Barbarians: Live from Kilburn, 2007. Films include: Let's Spend the Night Together, 1983; Flashpoint, 1991; Also played with Bo Diddley, Rod Stewart, Jerry Lee Lewis. Address: c/o Monroe Sounds, 5 Church Row, Wandsworth Plain, London SW18 1ES, England. Website: www.ronniewood.com

WOODHAMS Reiko, b. 9 December 1970, Nagoya, Aichi, Japan. Radiologist. m. Dale Woodhams. Education: Medical Doctor, Kumamoto University School of Medicine, Kumamoto, 1995; PhD, Kitasato University School of Medicine, Kanagawa, 2006. Appointments: Instructor, Department of Emergency Medicine, Tokyo Women's Medical University, 1997-99; Instructor, 1999-2005, Research Associate, 2005-07, Department of Radiology, Kitasato University School of Medicine; Visiting Scientist, Brigham and Women's Hospital, 2007-. Publications: Diffusion-Weighted Imaging of Malignant Breast Tumors: The Usefulness of Apparent Diffusion Coefficient (ADC) Value and ADC Map for the Direction of Malignant Breast Tumors and Evaluation of Cancer Extension, 2005; ADC Mapping of Benign and Malignant Breast Tumors, 2005. Address: 1-15-1 Kitasato, Sagamihara, Kanagawa, 229-0012, Japan. E-mail: reiko99@db3.so-net.ne.jp

WOODRING Carl, b. 29 August 1919, Terrell, Texas, USA. Educator. m. Mary Frances Ellis, 24 December 1942, deceased 2003. Education: BA, 1940, MA, 1942, Rice University; AM, 1947, PhD, 1949, Harvard University. Publications:

Victorian Samplers, 1952; Virginia Woolf, 1966; Wordsworth, 1965, revised edition, 1968; Politics in English Romantic Poetry, 1970; Nature into Art, 1989; Table Talk of Samuel Taylor Coleridge (editor), 1990; Columbia History of British Poetry (editor), 1993; Columbia Anthology of British Poetry (co-editor), 1995; Literature: An Embattled Profession, 1999; Lucky Thirteen: USS Hopkins, DD 249, DMS 13 (co-author), 2000. Contributions to: Western Review; Virginia Quarterly Review; PMLA; Keats-Shelley Journal; Comparative Drama. Honours: Guggenheim Fellowship, 1955; American Council of Learned Societies, Fellow, 1965; Phi Beta Kappa Gauss Prize, 1971; PKB Visiting Scholar, 1974-75; Senior Mellon Fellow, 1987-88. Memberships: American Academy of Arts and Sciences; International Association of University Professors of English; Grolier Club. Address: 1034 Liberty Park Drive, Austin, TX 78746, USA.

WOODS Philip Wells, b. 2 November 1931, Springfield, Massachusetts, USA. Musician (Alto Saxophone, Clarinet); Composer. m. Jill Goodwin, 20 December 1985, 1 son, 2 daughters. Education: Lessons with Harvey Larose, Springfield; Manhattan School, New York, 1948; Juilliard Conservatory, 1948-52. Career: Appearances with Benny Goodman, Buddy Rich, Quincy Jones, Thelonious Monk, Michel Legrand, Dizzy Gillespie and others; Appearing with own bands, Phil Woods Quintet, Phil Woods Little Big Band, Phil Woods Big Band; Featured, soundtracks of films including It's My Turn; Bandleader, Composer, Arranger and Soloist. Compositions include: Three Improvisations for Saxophone Quartet; Sonata for Alto and Piano; Rights of Swing; The Sun Suite; Fill the Woods with Light; I Remember; Deer Head Sketches. Recordings include: Images, with Michel Legrand, 1976; I Remember, Phil Woods Quartet, 1979; Dizzy Gillespie Meets Phil Woods Quintet; Evolution, Phil Woods Little Big Band; An Affair to Remember, Phil Woods Quintet; The Rev & I, with Johnny Griffin; Elsa, 1998; Porgy and Bess, 1999; Phil Woods in Italy, 2000; Giants at Play, 2001; The Thrill is Gone, 2002; Big Encounter at Umbria, 2003; Woodlands, 2004; Blues for New Orleans, 2005; American Songbook II, 2006. Honours: Down Beat Magazine New Star Award, 1956, Critics' Poll Winner, alto saxophone, 1975-79, 1981-90, 1992, Readers' Poll Winner, alto saxophone, 1976-95; Grammy Award, Images with Michel Legrand, 1976, for More Live, Phil Woods Quartet, 1982, 1983; National Association of Jazz Educators Poll Winner, alto saxophone, 1987, Phil Woods Quintet, 1987; East Stroudsburg University Honorary Degree, 1994; Induction into American Jazz Hall of Fame, 1994; Officier des Arts et des Lettres; Beacon in Jazz Award, 2001; Swing Journal Readers' Poll, 2004; Jazz Times Readers' Poll, 2004-2006; Alto Saxophonist of the Year, Jazz Journalists Association Jazz Awards, 2005-06; National Endowment for the Arts Jazz Master Fellowship, 2007; President's Merit Award from the Grammy Foundation, 2007; Kennedy Center Living Legends in Jazz Award, 2007. Memberships: Delaware Water Gap Celebration of the Arts; Board of Directors, Al Cohn Memorial Jazz Collection; American Federation of Musicians; International Association of Jazz Educators. Address: Box 278, Delaware Water Gap, PA 18327, USA.

WOODS Tiger (Eldrick), b. 30 December 1975, Cypress, California, USA. Golfer. Education: Stanford University. Career: 11 amateur wins; 64 official PGA Tour wins; 7 European Tour wins; 22 individual professional titles; 2 team titles, two-man WGC World Cup; Winner, inaugural FedEx Cup playoffs; Successfully defended a title 21 times on PGA Tour; Member, US Team World Amateur Team Championship, 1994; Member, US Walker Cup Team, 1995; Member, Ryder Cup 1997, 1999, 2002, 2004; Winner, The Masters, 1997,

2001, 2002, 2005; Winner, PGA Championship, 1999, 2000, 2006, 2007; Winner, US Open, 2000, 2002; Winner, The Open Championship, 2000, 2005, 2006; Winner, WGC American Express Championship, 2006; Winner, Buick International, 2007; Winner, Arnold Palmer Invitational, 2008. Publications: Columnist, Golf Digest, 2001-; Book, How I Play Golf. Honours include: 9 times, PGA Player of the Year; 8 times, PGA Tour Money Leader; 7 times, Vardon Trophy winner; 8 times, Byron Nelson Award; One of five players (and youngest) to have won all four professional major championships in his career; Associated Press Male Athlete of the Year, 1997, 1999, 2000, 2006; Sports Illustrated Sportsman of the Year, 2000; World Sportsman of the Year, 2001, 2002; California Hall of Fame, 2006; California Museum for History, Women and the Arts, 2007. Address: PGA, PO Box 109601, 100 Avenue of the Champions, Palm Beach Gardens, FL 33418, USA.

WOODWARD Edward, b. 1 June 1930, Croydon, Surrey, England. Actor; Singer. m. (1) Venetia Mary Collett, 1952, 2 sons, 1 daughter, (2) Michele Dotrice, 1987, 1 daughter. Education: Kingston College; Royal Academy of Dramatic Art. Creative Works: Stage appearances include: Mercutio in Romeo and Juliet, Laertes in Hamlet, Stratford, 1958; Rattle of a Simple Man, Garrick, 1962; Two Cities (musical), 1968, Cyrano in Cyrano de Bergerac; Flamineo in The White Devil, National Theatre Company, 1971; The Wolf, Apollo, 1973; Male of the Species, Piccadilly, 1975; On Approval, Theatre Royal, Haymarket, 1976; The Dark Horse, Comedy, 1978; Beggar's Opera, 1980; The Assassin, 1982; Richard III, 1982; The Dead Secret, 1992; 3 productions, New York; Films include: Becket, 1966; The File on the Golden Goose, 1968; Hunted, 1973; Sitting Target, 1974; Young Winston, 1974; The Wicker Man, 1974; Stand Up Virgin Soldiers, 1977; Breaker Morant, 1980; The Appointment, 1981; Comeback, 1982; Merlin and the Sword, 1982; Champions, 1983; A Christmas Carol, 1984; King David, 1984; Uncle Tom's Cabin, 1989; Mister Johnson, 1990; Deadly Advice, 1993; A Christmas Reunion, 1994; Gulliver's Travels, 1995-96; The Abduction Club, 2002; Hot Fuzz, 2007; Over 2000 TV productions including title role in Callan, 1966-71; The New Professionals, 1998-99; Night Flight, 2002; Murder in Suburbia, 2004; Where the Heart Is, 2005; Five Days, 2007; First Landing, 2007; 12 LP records as singer, 3 as poetry; 14 talking book recordings. Honours: Numerous international and national acting awards.

WOODWARD Rt Hon Shaun, b. 26 October 1958, Bristol, England. Member of Parliament for St Helen's South; Secretary of State for Northern Ireland. m. Camilla Davan Sainsbury, 1 son, 3 daughters. Education: Bristol Grammar School; Double First, English Literature, Jesus College, Cambridge University. Appointments: Parliamentary Lobbyist, National Consumer Council, 1981-82; Researcher and Producer, BBC TV News and Current Affairs programmes, 1982-90; Director of Communications for the Conservative Party, 1991-92; Conservative Member of Parliament for Witney, 1997-99; Labour Member of Parliament for St Helens South, 2001-; Parliamentary Under Secretary of State at the Northern Ireland Office, 2005-06; Parliamentary Under Secretary of State at the Department for Culture, Media and Sport, 2006-07; Secretary of State for Northern Ireland, 2007. Publications: Co-author: Ben: Story of Ben Hardwick, 1985; Drugwatch: Just Say No! 1986; Death by Television, 1999.

WOOLFSON Michael Mark, b. 9 January 1927, London, England. Emeritus Professor. m. Margaret Frohlich, 2 sons, 1 daughter. Education: Jesus College, Oxford, 1944-47; UMIST, 1949-52; MA (Oxon), 1951; PhD (Man), 1952; DSc

(Man), 1961. Appointments: 2nd Lieutenant, Royal Engineers, National Service, 1947-49; Research Fellow, Cambridge, 1952-54; ICI Fellow, Cambridge, 1954-55; Lecturer, 1955-61, Reader, 1961-65, UMIST; Professor of Theoretical Physics, York, 1964-94, Emeritus Professor, 1994-. Publications: Direct Methods in Crystallography, 1960; An Introduction to X-ray Crystallography, 1970, 2nd edition, 1997; The Origin of the Solar System: The Capture Theory, 1989; Physical and non-physical methods of solving crystal structures, 1995; An introduction to computer simulation, 1999; The origin and evolution of the Solar System, 2000; Planetary Science, 2002; Mathematics for Physics, 2007; Articles in learned journals. Honours: C.Phys, 1961; FRAS, 1966; FRS, 1984; Hughes Medal, Royal Society, 1986; Patterson Award, American Crystallographic Association, 1990; Gregori Aminoff Medal, Royal Swedish Academy, 1992; Dorothy Hodgkin Prize, British Crystallographic Association, 1997; Honorary Fellow, Jesus College, Oxford, 2001; Ewald Prize, International Union of Crystallography, 2002. Memberships: Institute of Physics; Royal Astronomical Society; Royal Society; Yorkshire Philosophical Society, President, 1985-99. Address: Physics Department, University of York, York YO10 5DD, England. E-mail: mmw1@york.ac.uk

WOOSNAM Ian Harold, b. 2 March 1958, England. Golfer. m. Glendryth Pugh, 1983, 1 son, 2 daughters. Education: St Martin's Modern School. Appointments: Professional Golfer, 1976-. Creative Works: Tournament Victories: News of the World Under-23 Matchplay, 1979; Cacharel Under-25 Championship, 1982; Swiss Open, 1982; Silk Cut Masters, 1983; Scandinavian Enterprise Open, 1984; Zambian Open, 1985; Lawrence Batley TPC, 1986; 555 Kenya Open, 1986; Hong Kong Open, 1987; Jersey Open, 1987; Cepsa Madrid Open, 1987; Bell's Scottish Open, 1987, 1990; Lancome Trophy, 1987; Suntory World Match-Play Championship, 1987, 1990; Volvo PGA Championship, 1988; Million Dollar Challenge, 1988; Carrolls Irish Open, 1988, 1989; Panasonic Euro Open, 1988; Welsh Pro Championship, 1988; American Express Mediterranean Open, 1990; Torras Monte Carlo Open, 1990; Epson Grand Prix, 1990; World Cup Team and Individual Winner, 1987; World Cup Individual Winner, 1991; US Masters, 1991; USF+G Lassic, 1991; PGA Grand Slam, 1991; Fujitsu Mediterranean Open, 1991; Torras Monte Carlo Open, 1991; European Monte Carlo Open, 1992; Lancome Trophy, 1993; Murphy's English Open, 1993; British Masters, 1994; Cannes Open, 1994; Heineken Classic, 1996; Scottish Open, 1996; German Open, 1996; Johnnie Walker Classic, 1996; Volvo PGA Championships, 1997; Hyundai Motor Masters, 1997; Ryder Cup Member, 1983, 1985, 1987, 1989, 1991, 1993, 1995, 1997; European Ryder Cup Team Captain, 2006; Numerous team events. Publications: Ian Woosnam's Golf Masterpieces (with Peter Grosvenor), 1991; Golf Made Simple: The Woosie Way, 1997. Membership: President, World Snooker Associate, 2000-. Address: cc/o IMG, McCormack House, Burlington Lane, London W4 2TH, England. Website: www.woosie.com

WORKMAN Robert Peter, b. 27 January 1961, Chicago, Illinois, USA. Artist; Author. Education: Art Institute of Chicago; Doctoral, Ecole Du Louvre; Docteur, Faculte De Medecine Clermont Ferrand, France. Appointments: Maitre de Conferences, Paris; Adjunct Lecturer, University Arizona; Graphic Artist, Cartoonist, Columnist, Village View Publications, Oak Lawn, 1983-98; Founder, Librarian, Kennedy Park Library, Chicago; Professor, Histoire de l'Art, Speialité, Archeologie Egyptienne, France. Publications: 10 children's books under Sesqui-Squirrel; Angels of Doom (graphic novel); Contribution, Journey to Infinity. Honours:

Resolution, City Council of Chicago, 1992, Illinois House of Representatives, 1994; Pulitzer Prize Nomination, 1983; First American artist accepted into collection of Musee de Louvre for 21st Century; Youngest artist accepted into Musee de Louvre, 2001. Memberships: Knights of Columbus; Mensa; Alumni School, Art Institute of Chicago; Working Press of Chicago; Registration with General Medical Council, England; Listed in several biographical publications. Address: 2509 W 111th Street, Apt #1E, Chicago, IL 60655, USA.

WORRICKER Julian Gordon, b. 6 January 1963, Woking, Surrey, England. Journalist; Broadcaster. Education: Epsom College, Epsom, Surrey, 1976-81; BA (Hons), English, Leicester University, 1981-84; Diploma in Radio Journalism, Cornwall College, Falmouth, 1984-85. Appointments: BBC Radio Leicester; BBC Midlands Today; Presenter, Five Aside, Radio Five, 1991-94; Presenter, Weekend Breakfast, Five Live, 1994-97; Presenter, Nationwide, Radio Five Live, 1997-98; Presenter, Breakfast, Radio Five Live, 1998-2003; Presenter, Worricker on Sunday, BBC Radio Five Live; Presenter, BBC News 24; Occasional Presenter, The World Tonight, Radio Four and Newshour, BBC World Service. Publications: Articles on media and travel published in Independent and Guardian newspapers. Honours: 3 Sony Gold Radio Awards for programmes on BBC Radio Five Live; 1 TRIC (TV & Radio Industry Club Award) for Five Live Breakfast. E-mail: jgwo@aol.com

WORSLEY Sir (William) Marcus John, 5th Baronet, b. 6 April 1925, Hovingham, Yorkshire, England. Retired Landowner. m. Bridget Assheton, deceased 2004, 3 sons, 1 daughter. Education: New College Oxford. Appointments: JP, 1957-90 (Chairman, Malton Bench 1983-90); Member of Parliament for Keighley, 1959-64; Member of Parliament for Chelsea, 1966-74; Second Church Estates Commissioner, 1970-74; Church Commissioner, 1976-84; Deputy Chairman, National Trust, 1986-92; High Sheriff, North Yorkshire, 1982; Lord Lieutenant, North Yorkshire,1987-99. Address: Park House, Hovingham, York, YO62 4JZ, England.

WORSLEY William Ralph, 12 September 1956, York, England. Chartered Surveyor. m. Marie-Noelle Dreesmann, 1 son, 2 daughters. Education: Royal Agricultural College. Appointments: Chairman, Hovingham Estates; Vice-Chairman, Scarborough Building Society; Director, The Brunner Investment Trust plc; Member, Executive Committee, Country Land and Business Association; Member, Forestry Commission's Advisory Panel; Vice-Chairman, Howardian Hills AONB JAC. Honour: Fellow, Royal Institution of Chartered Surveyors. Address: Hovingham Hall, York, England. E-mail: office@hovingham.co.uk.

WORSTHORNE Sir Peregrine (Gerard), b. 22 December 1923, London, England. Journalist; Editor; Writer. m. (1) Claudie Bertrand de Colasse, 1950, deceased 1990, 1 daughter, (2) Lady Lucinda Lambton, 1991. Education: BA, Peterhouse, Cambridge; Magdalen College, Oxford. Appointments: Sub-editor, Glasgow Herald, 1946; Editorial Staff, The Times, 1948-53; Daily Telegraph, 1953-61; Deputy Editor, 1961-76, Associate Editor, 1976-86, Editor, 1986-89, Editor, Comment Section, 1989-91, Sunday Telegraph. Publications: The Socialist Myth, 1972; Peregrinations: Selected Pieces, 1980; By the Right, 1987; Tricks of Memory (autobiography), 1993; In Defence of Aristocracy, 2004. Contributions to: Newspapers and journals. Honours: Granada Columnist of the Year, 1980; Knighted, 1991. Address: The Old Rectory, Hedgerley, Buckinghamshire SL2 3VY, England.

WÓRUM Ferenc, b. 15 March 1936, Hungary. Professor of Medicine; Cardiologist. m. Erzsébet Mészáros, 2 sons. Education: MD, University Medical School of Debrecen, 1960; Specialist of Internal Diseases, 1965; Specialist of Cardiac Diseases, 1988; PhD, Hungarian Academy of Sciences, 1980; Széchenyi Professorial Scholarship, 1998. Appointments: Assistant Professor, Lecturer, Associate Professor, 1960-92, Professor, 1992-, Departments of Internal Medicine, Medical and Health Science Centre, University of Debrecen; Pioneer of Clinical Cardiac Electrophysiology and modern Arrhythmology in Hungary (His-Bundle ECG, Programmed Electro-stimulation); Head of the Research Working Group of Cardiac Arrhythmias, Cardiac Electrophysiology, Pacemaker and Implantable Defibrillator Therapy; Developed several new cardiologic instruments and methods; Reader of 4 medical journals. Publications: 186 publications (45 passages in books); 231 lectures in 18 countries; 69 European, World and International Congresses, 10 in USA, Canada, Australia and Hong Kong. Honours: 3 Governmental Awards: Award for Sporting Activity, 1976; Awards for University Teaching, 1980, 1986; Listed in national and international biographical dictionaries. Memberships: Hungarian Society of Internal Medicine, 1965-; Hungarian Society of Cardiology, 1975-; European Society of Cardiology, 1975-; Board, Hungarian Society of Cardiology, 1990-98; Board, Hungarian Arrhythmia's and Pacemaker Working Group, 1990-98; Fellow of European Society of Cardiology, 2008. Address: 1st Department of Medicine, Medical and Health Science Centre, University of Debrecen, Nagyerdei krt. 98, PO Box 19, H-4012 Debrecen, Hungary. E-mail: worum@internal.med.unideb.hu

WOSZCZAK Daniel, b. 16 October 1959, New York, USA. Banking; Global Custody. Education: Graduate, Academy of Aeronautics (now Vaughn College of Aeronautics and Technology), New York, 1983; FAA Licensed, FAA Mechanic, A&P. Appointments: Employee, Captron Headwear, 1977; Methods Engineer, Eagle Electric Manufacturing Company, New York, 1984; Employee, Manufactures Hanover Trust Company, 1987; Employee, 1998, Assistant Treasurer, 1999, Assistant Vice President, 2004, The Bank of New York. Honours: Chase Manhattan Bank Spot Award for Innovation, 1997; Listed in international biographical dictionaries. Memberships: Lifetime Alumni Member, Vaughn College of Aeronautics and Technology; Member, National Aeronautic Association. Address: The Bank of New York, Mellon, One Wall Street, New York, NY 10286, USA. E-mail: daniel.woszczak@bnymellon.com

WRIGHT George T(haddeus), b. 17 December 1925, New York, New York, USA. Professor Emeritus; Author; Poet. m. Jerry Honeywell, 28 April 1955. Education: BA, Columbia College, 1946; MA, Columbia University, 1947; University of Geneva, 1947-48; PhD, University of California, 1957. Appointments: Teaching Assistant, 1954-55, Lecturer, 1956-57, University of California; Visiting Assistant Professor, New Mexico Highlands University, 1957; Instructor, Assistant Professor, University of Kentucky, 1957-60; Assistant Professor, San Francisco State College, 1960-61; Associate Professor, University of Tennessee, 1961-68; Fulbright Lecturer, University of Aix-Marseilles, 1964-66, University of Thessaloniki, 1977-78; Visiting Lecturer, University of Nice, 1965; Professor, 1968-89, Chairman, English Department, 1974-77, Regents' Professor, 1989-93, Regents' Professor Emeritus, 1993-, University of Minnesota. Publications: The Poet in the Poem: The Personae of Eliot, Yeats and Pound, 1960; W H Auden, 1969, revised edition, 1981; Shakespeare's Metrical Art, 1988; Aimless Life: Poems 1961-1995, 1999; Hearing the Measures: Shakespearean and Other Inflections,

2002. Editor: Seven American Literary Stylists from Poe to Mailer: An Introduction, 1973. Contributions to: Articles, reviews, poems and translations in many periodicals and books. Honours: William Riley Parker Prize, Modern Language Association, 1974, 1981; Guggenheim Fellowship, 1981-82; National Endowment for the Humanities Fellowship, 1984-85; Robert Fitzgerald Prosody Award, 2003. Memberships: Minnesota Humanities Commission, 1985-88; Modern Language Association; Shakespeare Association of America; Phi Kappa Phi. Address: 2617 West Crown King Drive, Tucson, AZ 85741, USA.

WRIGHT John Robert, b. 20 October 1936, Carbondale, Illinois, USA. Priest; Professor. Education: BA optime merens, University of the South, Sewanee, Tennessee, 1958; MA Honours, Mediaeval History, Emory University, Atlanta, Georgia, 1959; MDiv cum laude, General Theological Seminary, New York City, 1963; DPhil, Oxford University, England, 1967. Appointments: Ordained, 1963; Instructor in Church History, Episcopal Divinity School, Cambridge, Massachusetts, 1966-68; Assistant Professor of Church History, 1968-71, Professor of Church History, 1971-, St Mark's Professor of Ecclesiastical History, 1974-, General Theological Seminary, New York City; Several visiting positions including Visiting Professor, St George's College, Jerusalem, 1982, 1992, 1995, 1996; Provost's Visiting Professor in Divinity, Trinity College, University of Toronto, 1989. Publications: Author, co-author, editor, co-author, 16 books including: Episcopalians and Roman Catholics: Can They Ever Get Together?, 1972; Handbook of American Orthodoxy, 1972; A Communion of Communions: One Eucharistic Fellowship, 1979; The Church and the English Crown, 1305-1334: A Study based on the Register of Archbishop Walter Reynolds, 1980; Called to Full Unity: Documents on Anglican-Roman Catholic Relations 1966-1983, 1986; Prayer Book Spirituality, 1989; Readings for the Daily Office from the Early Church, 1991; The Anglican Tradition: A Handbook of Sources, 1991; On Being a Bishop: Papers on Episcopacy from the Moscow Consultation 1992, 1993; Saint Thomas Church Firth Avenue, 2001; Russo-Greek papers 1863-1874, 2002; Ancient Christian Commentary on Scripture: Proverbs, Ecclesiastes, and Song of Solomon, 2005; A Companion to Bede, 2008; Forthcoming: Anglican Commentaries on the 39 Articles; The Privilege of England 1231-1530; 3 booklets; 169 papers and articles. Honours include: Phi Beta Kappa, Pi Gamma Mu and Omicron Delta Kappa, 1958; Life Fellow, Royal Historical Society, London, 1981-; DD hc, Episcopal Theological Seminary of the Southwest, Austin, Texas, 1983; Honorary Canon Theologian to Bishop of New York, 1990-; DD hc, Trinity Lutheran Seminary, 1991; DCnL hc, University of the South, 1996; Dr Theol hc, University of Bern (Switzerland), 2000; Holy Crosses of the Orthodox Patriarchs of Constantinople, Jerusalem, Antioch and Moscow; Historiographer of the Episcopal Church, 2000-; Life Fellow, Society of Antiquaries, London, 2001; One Lord, One Faith, One Baptism: Studies in Christian Ecclesiality and Ecumenism in Honor of J Robert Wright, 2006; Cross of St Augustine of Canterbury, 2007. Memberships include: The Anglican Society, President, 1994-; North American Academy of Ecumenists, President, 1989-91; Conference of Anglican Church Historians, Convenor, 1995-; American Catholic Historical Association; American Society of Church History; Medieval Academy of America. Address: c/o General Theological Seminary, 175 Ninth Avenue, New York, NY 10011, USA. E-mail: wright@gts.edu

WRIGHT Michael, b. 24 May 1949. Vice Chancellor. m. Pamela, 2 sons, 1 daughter. Education: Bearsden Academy, Glasgow; LLB, University of Birmingham, 1969; LLM, Distinction in Common Law, 1970. Appointments: Lecturer, Principal Lecturer in Law, University of West England, 1970-79; Head, Department of Law and Public Administration, Glasgow Caledonian University, 1980-83; Dean of Business School, Assistant Principal, 1983-87, Assistant Principal, 1987-92, Deputy Vice Chancellor, 1992-97, Napier University, Edinburgh; Vice Chancellor, Canterbury Christ Church University, 1997-. Memberships: General Synod Board of Education HE & FE Committee; Council of Church Colleges & Universities; Governing Body of Thanet College; Commissioner, Duke of York's Royal Military School; Lay Canon of Canterbury Cathedral, 2004-; Deputy Lieutenant of Kent. E-mail: michael.wright@canterbury.ac.uk

WRIGHT Robert Alfred (Air Marshal Sir), b. 10 June 1947, Hamble, Hampshire, England. Military Representative. m. Margaret, 1 son, 1 daughter. Education: Graduate, Royal Air Force Staff College, 1982. Appointments: Operational Requirements Division, Ministry of Defence, 1982-84; Directing Staff, Royal Air Force Staff College, 1984-87; Officer Commanding IX Squadron, RAF Brueggen, 1987-89; Personal Staff Officer to Chief of Air Staff, 1989-91; Station Commander, RAF Brueggen, 1992-94; Assistant Chief of Staff, Policy & Plans, NATO HQ, High Wycombe, 1994-95; Air Commander, Operations Headquarters Strike Command, 1995-97; Promoted to Air Vice Marshal, 1997; Military Advisor to High Representative, Sarajevo, 1997-98; Chief of Staff to Air Member for Personnel and Deputy Commander-in-Chief, Personnel & Training Command, RAF Innsworth, 1998-2000; Assistant Chief of Staff, Policy & Requirements, Supreme Headquarters Allied Powers Europe, 2000-02; Promoted to Air Marshal, 2002; UK Military Representative to NATO and EU Military Committees, 2002-. Honours: Air Force Cross, 1982; KBE, 2004. Memberships: Fellow, Royal Aeronautical Society; President: Combined Services Winter Sports Association; RAF Winter Sports Federation; RAF Athletics Association; Naval 8/208 Squadron Association. Address: UKMILREP, HQ NATO, Boulevard Leopold III, 1110 Brussels, Belgium.

WRIGHT Theodore Paul Jr, b. 12 April 1926, Port Washington, New York, USA. Professor. m. Susan J Standfast, 1 son, 2 daughters. Education: BA, Swarthmore College, 1949; MA, 1951, PhD, 1957, Yale University. Appointments: Instructor to Associate Professor, Bates College, Lewiston, Maine, USA, 1955-65; Associate Professor, Professor, Graduate School of Public Affairs, State University of New York at Albany, Albany, New York, 1965-95; Emeritus Professor, 1995-. Publications: American Support of Free Elections Abroad, 1963; 78 articles and chapters in books on Muslim politics, India and Pakistan, 1963-2007. Honours: Phi Beta Kappa, 1949; BA with high honours, Swarthmore College; Fulbright Awards to India, 1961, 1963-64, to Pakistan, 1983, 1990; SSRC/ACLS to London, 1974-75; AIIS to India, 1969-70. Memberships: Association for Asian Studies; Board Member, American Council for the Study of Islamic Societies; Past President, now Newsletter Editor, South Asian Muslim Studies Association; Columbia University Faculty Seminar on South Asia, 1967-; Past President, New York Conference on Asian Studies; European Conference on Modern South Asian Studies, 1974-; Board Member, New Netherland Institute; Past President, The Dutch Society of Albany; Member, Dutch Settlers' Society of Albany. Address: 17 Wellington Way, Niskayuna, NY 12309, USA. E-mail: wright15@Juno.com

WRONG Dennis Hume, b. 22 November 1923, Toronto, Ontario, Canada. Emeritus Professor of Sociology. Education: BA, University of Toronto, 1945; PhD, Columbia University, New York City, 1956. Appointments: Instructor, Department of Economics and Social Institutions, Princeton University, 1949-50; Instructor in Sociology, The Newark Colleges, Rutgers University, Newark, New Jersey, 1950-51; Research Associate and Lecturer, Department of Political Economy, University of Toronto, 1954-56; Assistant Professor and Associate Professor, Department of Sociology, Brown University, 1956-61; Associate Professor of Sociology, Graduate Faculty, The New School for Social Research, 1961-63; Professor and Chairman, Department of Sociology, University College, New York University, 1963-65; Professor of Sociology, University of Nevada, Reno, 1965-66; Professor of Sociology, 1966-94, Emeritus Professor of Sociology, 1994-, New York University. Publications: Author and editor: 12 books; Numerous articles in professional, intellectual and political journals. Honours: Visiting Fellow, Nuffield College, Oxford University, 1978; Guggenheim Fellow, 1984-85; Visiting Fellow, European University Institute, Florence, Italy, 1996-97. Listed in Who's Who publications and biographical dictionaries. Memberships: Pre-doctoral Fellow, Canadian Social Science Research Council; Fellow, Woodrow Wilson International Center for Scholars, Washington DC, 1991-92. Address: 144 Drakes Corner Road, Princeton, NJ 08540, USA.

WU Chung-Hsin, b. 23 March 1969, Tainan, Taiwan. Environmental Engineering Educator. m. Chao-Yin Kuo, 1 son, 1 daughter. Education: BS, Department of Environmental Engineering, 1993, MS, Graduate Institute of Environmental Engineering, 1995, National Chung-Hsing University, Taichung, Taiwan; PhD, Graduate Institute of Environmental Engineering, National Taiwan University, Taipei, Taiwan, 1999. Appointments: Assistant Professor, Yuanpei University of Science and Technology, Hsinchu, Taiwan, 2001-04; Part-time Associate Professor, National Yunlin University of Science and Technology, Yunlin, Taiwan, 2005-; Associate Professor, Da-Yeh University, Chung-Hua, Taiwan, 2005-. Honours: Outstanding Academic Paper Award, Chinese Institute of Environmental Engineering, 2003; Excellent Academic Paper Award, 2003; Excellent Academic Paper Award, 2005; Who's Who in the World, 2006. Memberships: The Chinese Institute of Environmental Engineering; Chinese Environmental Analytical Society; The Formosa Association of Resource Recycling; Major Industrial Accident Prevention Association. Address: Da-Yeh University, 112 Shan-Jiau Road, Da-Tsuen, Chang-Hua 515, Taiwan. E-mail: chunghsinwu@yahoo.com.tw

WU Guofa Felix, b. 19 October 1945, Nanchang, China. Information Technologist; Computer Scientist and Engineer. m. (1) Youming Zhong, 1 son, (2) Juan Liu, 1 daughter. Education: BS, Physics, 1965-70, M Eng, Computer Science and Engineering, 1984, Tsinghua University, China; MS, Industrial Engineering, USA, 1992; PhD, Computer Information Systems, USA, 1995. Appointments: Technician and Business Administrator, Sichuan Province, China, 1970-80; Computer Engineer, Central Iron and Steel Research Institute, China, 1980-88; Consultant, Director, Vice-President, Compaq/HP, Computer Science Corporation, American Management Systems, Boston Consulting Group, etc., USA, 1989-97; Manager and Technology Specialist, Volpe National Transportation Systems Center of US Department of Transportation, 1997-99; President, Global Internet Corporation, USA, 1999-; Adjunct Professor, Boston University, USA, 2001; President, North American Society of Experts and Entrepreneurs, USA, 2001-; Guest Professor, Xi'an Jiaotong University, China, 2001-; Guest Professor, Harbin Institute of Technology, China, 2002-; Member of Presidential Business Commission for President George W Bush, USA, 2002-08; President, Pacific Review Monthly (magazine), Hong Kong, 2005-06. Publications: 80 academic papers in English and Chinese journals and at national and international symposia and conferences. Honours include: Prize for Achievement in Science and Technology, Ministry of Metallurgical Industry, China, 1988; Award for Excellent Academic Paper, International Symposium of Regression Analysis, Montreal, Canada, 1990; Advisor in Science and Technology, Panzhihua City Government, China, 2001-; Advisor in Economics, Nanching City Government, China, 2002-; Honorary Chairman, US Business Advisory Council, 2002-; National Leadership Award, 2002, Business Man of the Year, 2003, US Business Advisory Council; Advisor, Association of Chinese Entrepreneurs in Europe, 2003-; Honorary Chairman, US House Majority Trust, 2004-06; International Professional of the Year 2005, International Biographical Centre, England, 2005; Platinum Member of the President Club, 2005. Memberships: Fellow, North American Society of Experts and Entrepreneurs; American Management Association; American Association for the Advancement of Science. Address: 36 Parsons Street Boston, MA 02135, USA. E-mail: gf.wu@yahoo.com

WU Ming-Lu, b. 3 March 1963, Nanzhao County, Henan Province, China. Management Consultant. m. Chung Shing, 1 son, 1 daughter. Education: BEng, Applied Mathematics, Jihin University of Technology, Changchun, China, 1983; MSc, Operations Research and Cybernetics, 1986, PhD, Probability and Mathematical Statistics, 1994, Academia Sinica, Beijing, China. Appointments: Assistant Professor, 1986-91, Associate Professor, 1994-95, National Research Centre for Science and Technology for Development, Beijing; Research Fellow, Department of Management Sciences, City University of Hong Kong, 1995-. Publications: 15 recent papers in internationally refereed journals; Co-authored 2 books: China's Economic Development and Some Related Factors' Analysis, 1991; International Competitiveness, 1992. Address: Department of Management Sciences, City University of Hong Kong, 83 Tat Chee Avenue, Kowloon, Hong Kong. E-mail: msminglu@cityu.edu.hk

WULSTAN David, b. 18 January 1937, Birmingham, England. Research Professor. m. Susan Graham, 1 son. Education: Royal Masonic School, Bushey; BSc (Lond), College of Technology, Birmingham; MA, Magdalen College, Oxford; Studied under Egon Wellesz and Bernard Rose, also Lennox Berkeley and Peter Wishart (composition), Clarence Raybould and Sir Adrian Boult (conducting). Appointments: Fellow and Lecturer, Magdalen College, Oxford, 1964-78 (pupils include Professors David Hiley, John Deathridge, Jan Smaczny, Nicola le Fanu, also Jane Glover, Geoffrey Skidmore, Harry Christophers & Peter Philips); Visiting Professor, Department of N E Studies, Berkeley, USA, 1979; Statutory Lecturer and Professor of Music, University College, Cork (pupils include Mary O'Neill, Professors Desmond Hunter & Noel O'Regan), 1979-83; Gregynog Professor of Music, University of Wales, Aberystwyth, 1983-90; Research Professor, 1990-; Director, The Clerkes of Oxenford (founded 1961). Publications: Tudor Music, 1985; Editions of Gibbons & Sheppard; The Emperor's Old Clothes, 2001; The Poetic and Musical Legacy of Heloise and Abelard, 2003; The Play of Daniel (new edition), 2007; Music from the Paraclete, 2008; Appearances at BBC Proms and many festivals in Britain and Europe; Broadcasts and TV appearances. Honours: Honorary Fellow,

St Peter's College, Oxford, 2006. Memberships: Member of Council, Plainsong & Mediæval Music Society; Consulting Editor, Spanish Academic Press; Fellow, Royal Society of Musicians; Musical Consultant, Centre for the Study of the Cantigas de Santa Maria, Oxford; Instructor, British Aikido Federation. Address: Hillview Croft, Lon Tyllwyd, Llanfarian, Aberystwyth, Cardiganshire, SY23 4UH, Wales.

WUU Shou-Gwo, b. 25 May 1958, Tainan, Taiwan. Deputy Director. m. Wen-Ying Ma, 1 son, 3 daughters. Education: Bachelor's degree, Master's degree, Tsing-Hua University, Hsinchu, Taiwan, 1977-83; Dr Ing, Hamburg Technology University, Germany, 1988-92. Appointments: Researcher, Hamburg Technology University, 1992; Technical Manager, TFT SRAM project, 1992-98, SRAM Program Manager, 1998-2000, Deputy Director, CMOS Image Sensor Program, RD, 2000-06, Deputy Director, Embedded ORAM Program, RD, 2002-04, Deputy Director, Mature Technology Development Division, 2006-07, TSMC. Publications: Numerous articles in professional journals. Honours: Subcommittee Chair, International Electron Device Meeting, 2004; Member, Subcommittee on Display, Sensor and MEMS, IEDM, 2002-03; Member, Technology Program Committee, IEEE, International Image Sensor Workshop, 2003-07. Memberships: IEEE. Address: No 116, Ln 486, Min-Hu Rd, Hsinchu City, 300, Taiwan. E-mail: skwu@tsmc.com

WYATT Sheri Brown, b. 22 November 1968. Model; Artist; Poet; Educator. m. Gene Arthur Wyatt Jr. Education: Diploma, Bluefield High School, Bluefield, West Virginia, 1987; BA degree, Commercial Art & Advertising, Concord College, Athens, West Virginia, 1992-. Appointments: Author, numerous poems in anthologies; Owner, T J Cool Advertising, 1992-; Writer, Hill Top Records, Hollywood, California, USA, 2001; Model for Magic Mart Stores Inc, 2005. Publications: Poems published with: The International Library of Poetry; National Library of Poetry; Poetry.com; Hill Top Records; The Poetry Guild. Honours: International Library of Poetry Editor's Choice Award, 1987; BHS Senior Art Award, Honour Roll, Band. Memberships: Scott Street Baptist Church; House of Prayer; International Society of Poets; Concord Adv Club; Bluefield High School Art Club; Bible Club; Band; Church Choir; Co Drum Majorette-Blfd, 1983-84; Junior High School Band; University of Tennessee Honours Band. Address: 120 Russell Terrace, Bluefield, WV 24701, USA.

WYMAN Bill (William George), b. 24 October 1941, London, England. Musician. m. (1) Diane Cory, 1959, divorced 1968, 1 son, (2) Mandy Smith, 1989, divorced 1991, (3) Suzanne Accosta, 1993, 3 daughters. Career: Bass-Player, The Rolling Stones, 1962-93; Owner, Ripple Records, Ripple Music, Ripple Publications, Ripple Productions; Bill Wyman Enterprises; Formed new band, The Rhythm Kings, 1997-. Creative Works: Albums include: 12 x 5, 1964; New, 1965; Big Hits, 1966; Got Live If You Want It, 1967; Flowers, 1967; Sucking in the 70's, 1981; Still Life, 1981; Rewind, Dirty Work, 1986; Emotional Rescue, 1988; Steel Wheels, 1989; Flashpoint, 1991; Voodoo Lounge, 1994; Solo recordings include: Stone Alone, 1976; Monkey Grip, 1974; Bill Wyman, 1981; Willie & the Poor Boys, 1985; Stuff, 1993; Struttin' Our Stuff, 1997; Anyway the Wind Blows, 1998; Groovin', 2000; Double Bill, 2001; Blues Odyssey, 2001; Just for a Thrill, 2004; Single: (Si Si) Je Suis Un Rock Star; Films: Sympathy for the Devil, 1970; Gimme Shelter, 1970; Ladies and Gentlemen the Rolling Stones, 1974; Let's Spend the Night Together, 1982; Digital Dreams, 1983; Filmscore: Green Ice, 1981. Publications: Stone Alone: The Story of a Rock and Roll Band (with Ray Coleman), 1990;

Wyman Shoots Chagall, 2000; Bill Wyman's Blues Odyssey (with Richard Havers), 2001; Rolling With The Stones (with Richard Havers), 2002; Bill Wyman's Treasure Islands, 2005. Honours include: Prince's Trust Award, 1991; Ivor Novello Award for Outstanding Contribution to British Music, 1991; Blues Foundation, Memphis Literary Award, 2002. Address: c/o Ripple Productions Ltd, 344 Kings Road, London SW3 5UR, England.

WYNNE-PARKER Michael, b. 20 November 1945, Willersley Castle, Derbyshire, England. Author; PR Consultant. m. (1) divorced, 1991, 2 daughters, (2) Mandana Farzaneh, 1995. Education: Lady Manners School. Appointments: Founder and Chairman, English Speaking Union of Sri Lanka, 1983-; Founder and President, English Speaking Union of South Asia, 1985-; Consultant to Public and Private Companies in 26 countries, also to governments, charities and individuals; Founder and President, Introcom International, 1989-; Chairman, Guild of Travel and Tourism, 1999-; Trustee, A Heart for Russia, 2005-. Publications: Healing and the Wholeness of Man, 1972; Bridge Over Troubled Water, 1989, 1998; The Mandana Poems, 1998; Impressions of Orthodoxy in Estonia, 2004; Reflections in Middle Years, 2005; Fifty Estonia Recipes, 2005 and others. Honours: Papal Medal, Pope Paul VI, 1971; Miembro de Honor, Union Monarquica Espanola, 1974; Grand Cordon, Order of the Crown of Yemen, 1977; Knight Commander, Military and Hospitaller Order of St Lazarus of Jerusalem, 1980; Harpers and Queen Award for Excellence, Philanthropist of the Year, Runner-up to HRH Prince Charles, 1988; Patron, St George Foundation, Estonia, 2006-. Memberships: Founder Patron, Pensthorpe Waterfowl Trust; Former Chairman, Council for the Advancement of Arab-British Understanding, Eastern Region, UK; Chairman, 1999 British Forces Foundation Ball; Co-Founder, Mencap City Foundation; Life Member, Royal Society of St George; Founder Member, Sri Lanka Friendship Association; Life Member, Norfolk Naturalists Trust. Address: Guild of Travel and Tourism, Suite 193, Temple Chambers, Temple Avenue, London EC4Y 0DB, England. E-mail: info@introcominternational.com

X

XIA Jisong, b. 15 May 1925. Professor in Modern Philosophy. m. 1 April 1956, 1 son, 1 daughter. Education: Bachelor in Politics, National Central University, Nanjing, 1943-48; MPhil, People's University of China, Beijing, 1952-54. Appointments: Assistant Lecturer, Department of Politics, National Central University, 1948-52; Lecturer, Department of Politics, Nanjing University, 1954-78; Associate Professor and Deputy Head of Department, Department of Philosophy, Nanjing University, 1978-82; Professor and Head of Department, Department of Philosophy, Nanjing University, 1982-90; Professor, Department of Philosophy, Hangzhou University and Zhejiang University, Hangzhou, 1990-. Publications: More than 10 books including: Course of the Modern Philosophy in the West, 1985; Mathematics Philosophy in the West, 1986; Review on Existentialism, 1987; Philosophy of Science in the West. Honour: Honorary Head of the Philosophy Department, Nanjing University. Memberships: Philosophy Division of the State Council's Academic Degree Committee in China; Vice Chairman, Society of Modern Foreign Philosophy Study in China; Chairman of the Society of Foreign Philosophy Study in East China. Address: Department of Philosophy, College of Humanities, Zhejiang University, Hangzhou 310028, China.

XIAO Lingzhi, b. 6 January 1964, Guangzhou, China. Chief Research Scientist. m. Huiqiang Lu, 1 son, 1 daughter. Education: BSc, Guangzhou University, 1985; MSc, 1995, PhD, 1998, Graduate School of Science and Engineering, Saitama University, Japan; Diploma of the Primary Course of Chinese Medicine, 2000, Diploma of the 15th Chinese Medicine Special Course, 2001, Diploma of the 16th Chinese Medicine Special Course, 2003, Japanese Chinese Medicine Society. Appointments: Executive Manager, Huang Pu Education Bureau, Guangzhou, China, 1985-90; Research Scientist, 2001-02, Chief Research Scientist & Manager, 2002-07, Research & Development Division, Precision System Science Co Ltd, Chiba, Japan; Research Scholar Scientist, National Institute of Neurological Disorders and Stroke, National Institute of Health, Bethesda, USA, 2004-05; Research Scholar Scientist, Department of Oncology, Georgetown University Medical Center, Washington DC, USA, 2006-07. Publications: 19 papers and articles in professional scientific journals including: Presentation and Demonstration of Bio-Strand Microarray Technology and Magtration Technology, 2004; Presentation and Demonstration of Handy Bio-Strand Microarray Technology and its application for detection of metabolic disease, particularly for Gaucher disease, 2005; Analysis of the global gene expression profile in mammalian cells derived from patients with Gaucher diseases, 2006. Honours: Patent application, Precision System Science Co Ltd, 2005; NIH (US Government) patent application, 2005; Title, Making her own scientific invention achievement more valuable, The SinoAmerican Times, 2006. Memberships: Society for Neuroscience. Address: 12125 Village Square Ter 202, Rockville, MD 20852, USA. E-mail: reishi.syou@pss.co.jp

Y

YABLANSKI Tsanko, b. 9 September 1944, Biala Slatina, Bulgaria. Geneticist. m. Liliana, 1 son, 1 daughter. Education: Agronomist Bachelor, 1969, PhD, Animal Genetics, 1975, University of Agriculture, Sofia; Dr Sc, Animal Genetics and Breeding, Trakia University, Stara Zagora, 1988. Appointments: Assistant Professor, 1975-83, Associate Professor, 1983-90, Vice President of University, 1990-95, Full Professor, Head of Department of Genetics, 2003-, Trakia University; Editor-in-chief of Bulgarian Journal of Animal Science, 1990-95; Mayor of the City of Stara Zagora, 1995-99; Ambassador of the Republic of Bulgaria to State of Israel, 1999-2003. Publications: Over 60 articles and books in the field of genetics and animal breeding. Honours: Honorary Member, Union of Scientists in Bulgaria, 1997; Honorary Citizen, City of Durham, NK, USA, 1998; Outstanding Friend of Strasburg Medal, 1998; Listed in Who's Who publications and international biographical dictionaries. Memberships: Union of Scientists in Bulgaria; European Association for Animal Production, International Society for Animal Genetics; Rotary Club Stara Zagora. Address: bul Ruski 56, ap 11, 6000 Stara Zagora, Bulgaria. E-mail: ts_yablanski@yahoo.co.uk

YADLIN Aharon, b. 17 April 1926, Ben Shemen, Tel Aviv, Israel. Chairman. m. Ada Hacohen, 1950, deceased 1998, 3 sons. Education: Graduate, Reali High School, Haifa, 1944; BA, 1954, MA, 1964, Hebrew University of Jerusalem. Appointments: National Leader, Boy Scout Movement, 1945-46; Founder Member, Kibbutz Hatzerim, 1946-; Educational Attache, Palmach (Hagana Forces), 1948-49; Member, Executive Council of the Histadrut (Israel Federation of Labour), 1950-52; Lecturer, Director, Beit Berl, 1955-57; Member, Israeli Parliament (Knesset), 1959-79; Deputy Minister of Education, Chairman of Public Council on Youth, Chairman of Zionist Council in Israel, Chairman of the Board of Directors of Beit Berl, 1964-72; Secretary, Israeli Labour Party, 1972-74; Minister of Educatino and Culture, 1974-77; Chairman, Educational and Cultural Committee, Israeli Parliament, 1977-79; Chairman, Scientific Council of the Ben Gurion Institute and Archives, 1979-85; Chairman, Beer Sheva Theatre, 1980-82; Chairman, Beit Berl, College of Education, 1981-82; Member, Faculty of Efal College and of Yad Tabenkin Institute for Kibbutz Studies, 1981-84; Visiting Scholar, Jewish Studies, Harvard University, Boston, USA, 1982; General Secretary, United Kibbutz Movement, 1985-89; Chairman, Bialik Institute, 1990-; Chairman, World Labour Zionist Movement, 1992-2002; Chairman, Efal College and Yad Tabenkin Research Center, 2002-; Deputy Chairman, Executive Council of Ben Gurion University of the Negev, 1990-; Chairman, Beit Yatziv Educational Center, Beer Sheva, 1992-. Publications: Understanding the Social System, 1957; The Aim and the Movement, On Humanistic Socialism/Articles of Israeli Sociology, the Labour Movement, Education, Youth Problems and Kibbutz issues, 1979. Honours: Doctor of Philosophy Honouris Causa, Ben Gurion University of the Negev, 1988. Address: Kibbutz Hatzerim, M P Hanegev 85420, Israel.

YAKOVLEV Valery Petrovitch, b. 28 September 1940, Volgograd, Russia. Physicist. m. Margarita Yakovleva, 2 daughters. Education: MS, Distinction, 1963, PhD, 1967, DSc, 1987, Moscow Engineering Physics Institute. Appointments: Assistant Professor, 1967-69, Senior Lecturer, 1969-75, Associate Professor, 1975-88, Full Professor, 1988-, Moscow Engineering Physics Institute; Heraeus Professor, Universität Ulm, Germany, 1994-1996. Publications: Over 170 scientific papers on quantum electrodynamics of strong fields, physics of semiconductors, interferometry of atomic states and matter waves, subrecoil laser cooling and atom optics and strange kinetics; Monograph, Mechanical Action of Light on Atoms, 1990. Address: Theoretical Nuclear Physics Department, Moscow Engineering Physics Institute, Kashirskoe shosse 31, 115409 Moscow, Russia. E-mail: yakovlev@theor.mephi.ru

YALOW Rosalyn, b. 19 July 1921, New York, New York, USA. Medical Physicist. m. Aaron Yalow, 1943, 1 son, 1 daughter. Education: Graduated, Physics, Hunter College, New York, 1941; PhD, Experimental Nuclear Physics, University of Illinois, 1945. Appointments: Assistant in Physics, University of Illinois, 1941-43; Instructor, 1944-45; Lecturer and temporary Assistant Professor in Physics, Hunter College, New York, 1946-50; Physicist and Assistant Chief, 1950-70, Acting Chief, 1968-70, Chief Radioimmunoassay Reference Laboratory, 1969, Chief Nuclear Medicine Service, 1970-80, Senior Medical Investigator, 1972-92, Senior Medical Investigator Emeritus, 1992-, Director, Solomon A Berson Research Laboratory, Veterans Administration Medical Center, 1973-92, Radioisotope Service, Veterans Administration Hospital, Bronx, New York; Research Professor, 1968-74, Distinguished Service Professor, 1974-79, Department of Medicine, Mount Sinai School of Medicine, New York; Distinguished Professor at Large, 1979-85, Professor Emeritus, 1985-, Albert Einstein College of Medicine, Yeshiva University; Chair, Department of Clinical Sciences, Montefiore Hospital, Bronx, 1980-85; Solomon A Berson Distinguished Professor at Large, Mt Sinai School of Medicine, New York, 1986-; Harvey Lecturer, 1966; American Gastroenterology Association Memorial Lecturer, 1972; Joslyn Lecturer, New England Diabetes Association, 1972; Franklin I Harris Memorial Lecturer, 1973; 1st Hagedorn Memorial Lecturer, Acta Endocrinologia Congress, 1973; President, Endocrine Society, 1978-79; Honours: Over 60 honorary doctorates; Joint Winner, Nobel Prize for Physiology or Medicine, 1977; More than 30 other awards. Memberships: NAS; American Physics Society; Radiation Research Society; American Association of Physicists in Medicine; Biophysics Society; American Academy of Arts and Sciences; American Physiology Society; Foreign Associate, French Academy of Medicine; Fellow, New York Academy of Science; Radiation Research Society; American Association of Physicists in Medicine; Associate Fellow in Physics, American College of Radiology; American Diabetes Association; Endocrine Society; Society of Nuclear Medicine. Address: Veterans Administration Medical Center, 130 West Kingsbridge Road, Bronx, New York, NY 10468, USA.

YAMADA Toshiro, b. 29 January 1949, Kanazawa, Ishikawa, Japan. Professor. m. Kazuko Ohara, 1 son, 1 daughter. Education: ME, 1973, PhD, 1989, Kanazawa University. Appointments: Research Co-ordinator to Chief Researcher, Toyobo Co Ltd, 1988; Professor, 1995, Chairman, Invention Committee, Kanazawa University; Director, Kureha Scholarship Association Foundation, 1988-; Inspector, Kansai Branch, 2000-, Chair, Executive for Autumn Meeting, 2003, Senator, 2004-, Japan Society for Polymer Processing. Publications: 101 refereed papers; 9 technical books; 83 international and 146 domestic conference proceedings; 70 patents. Honours: Best Paper Award, Japan Society for Polymer Processing; Award for Excellence, 8th International Symposium on Polymers for Advanced Technologies, 2005; Who's Who in the World, 2006, 2007; Who's Who in Asia, 2007; Who's Who in Science and Engineering, 2006-2007. Memberships: The Japan Society of Polymer Processing; Polymer Processing Society; The Society of Polymer Science, Japan; The Society of Chemical Engineers, Japan; The Japan

DICTIONARY OF INTERNATIONAL BIOGRAPHY

Society for Precision Engineering; Materials Science Society of Japan. Address: 10-15, Teraji 2-chome, Kanazawa, Ishikawa, 921-8178, Japan. E-mail: tyamada@t.kanazawa-u.ac.jp

YAMAGATA Toshio, b. 25 March 1948, Utsunomiya City, Japan. Physical Oceanographer. m. Yoko Yamagata, 1 son, 1 daughter. Education: Bachelor of Science, 1971, Master of Science, 1973, Doctor of Science, 1977, University of Tokyo. Appointments: Associate Professor, Research Institute for Applied Mechanics, Kyushu University, 1979; Associate Professor, 1991, Professor, 1995-, Graduate School of Science, University of Tokyo. Publications: About 100 publications in professional scientific journals including: Philosophical Transactions, Royal Society London, 1989; Bulletin of the American Meteorological Society, 1997; Nature, 1999. Honours: Okada Prize and Society Prize, Japan Oceanographic Society; Society Prize, Japan Meteorological Society; Burr Steinbach Scholar of Woods Hole Oceanographic Institution; The Sverdrup Gold Medal, American Meteorological Society; Medal with Purple Ribbon, The Emperor of Japan. Memberships: Japan Oceanographic Society; Japan Meteorological Society; American Geophysical Union; American Meteorological Society, (Fellow); The Oceanographic Society of the United States of America. Address: Department of Earth and Planetary Science, Graduate School of Science, The University of Tokyo, Tokyo 113-0033, Japan. Website: http://www-aos/eps.s.u-tokyo.ac.jp/~yamagata/indexj.html

YAMAGUCHI Masashi, b. 1 September 1948, Yamagata, Japan. Associate Professor. m. Naoko Terakawa, 2 sons, 1 daughter. Education: BS, Yamagata University, Yamagata, Japan, 1971; MS, Tokyo Metropolitan University, Tokyo, Japan, 1974; DSc, 1978. Appointments: Visiting Research Fellow, Memorial Sloan-Kettering Cancer Center, New York, USA 1979; Associate Researcher, 1980; Staff Scientist, Monell Chemical Senses Center, Philadelphia, USA, 1980-81; Research Associate, The Jikei University School of Medicine, Tokyo, Japan, 1981-88; Lecturer, 1988-96; Associate Professor, 1996-, Chiba University, Chiba, Japan. Publications: Articles in medical journals include: Dynamics of hepatitis B virus core antigen in a transformed yeast cell, 1994; The spindle pole body duplicates in early G1 phase in a pathogenic yeast Exophiala dermatitidis, 2002; Structome of Exophiala yeast cells determined by freeze-substitution and serial ultrathin sectioning electron microscopy, 2006; Guide Book for Electron Microscopy (in Japanese), 2004. Honours: Best Paper Award, Japanese Society of Electron Microscopy, 1996; Best Paper Award, Japanese Society of Microscopy, 2005. Memberships: Japanese Society of Microscopy; Japanese Society of Medical Mycology; Mycological Society of Japan. Address: Medical Mycology Research Centre, Chiba University, 1-8-1 Inohana, Chuo-ku, Chiba 260-8673, Japan. Website: http://www.pf.chiba-u.ac.jp/

YAMAGUCHI Masayoshi, b. 15 June 1947, Atami, Japan. Professor. m. Eiko Yamaguchi, 1 son, 1 daughter. Education: Bachelor, 1971, Master, 1973, PhD, 1976, Pharmaceutical Sciences, Shizuoka College of Pharmacy. Appointments: Research Associate, 1973-86, Assistant Professor, 1986-87, Shizuoka College of Pharmacy; Visiting Lecturer, University of Pennsylvania, 1981; Visiting Assistant Professor, Texas Tech University, 1985-86; Visiting Assistant Professor, University of Texas, 1988-89; Faculty, 1987-91, Associate Professor, 1991-93, Professor, 1993-2007, Life and Health Sciences, University of Shizuoka; Scientific Advisor, Kemin Health L C, 2005-; Visiting Professor, Emory University School of Medicine, 2007-; President, Institute of Bone Health and

Nutrition, 2007-; Scientific Advisor, Primus Pharmaceuticals Inc, 2007. Publications: Over 500 original scientific papers; Calcium and Life; Biometals; Prevention of Osteoporosis and Nutrition; Discoverer of regucalcin as a regulatory protein in intercellular signalling and a novel protein RGPR-p117 as transcription factor; 55 reviews and books; 8 international and 15 national patents. Honours include: Bounty from Yamanouchi Foundation for Research in Metabolic Disorders, Japan, 2004; International Scientist of the Year, International Biographical Centre, 2004; Lifetime Achievement Award, IBC, 2004; International Order of Merit, IBC, 2004; Hall of Fame, IBC, 2004; Outstanding Professional Award, American Biographical Institute, 2004; American Hall of Fame, ABI, 2004; World Lifetime Achievement Award, ABI, 2004; International Peace Prize, United Cultural Convention, 2004; Lifetime Achievement Award, United Cultural Convention, USA, 2005; Lifetime Achievement Award, World Congress of Arts, Sciences and Communications, 2005; American Order of Excellence, ABI, 2005; Senji Miyata Foundation Award, Japan, 2006; Salute to Greatness Award, IBC, 2006; American Medal of Honour, ABI, 2006; Distinguished Service to Science Award, IBC, 2007; Award, Japan Society for Biomedical Research on Trace Elements, 2007; Gold Medal for Japan, ABI, 2008. Memberships: New York Academy of Sciences; American Society of Cell Biology; American Society for Bone and Mineral Research; International Society for Bone and Mineral; American Society for Biochemistry and Molecular Biology; Japan Society of Biochemistry (councillor); The Japan Endocrine Society (councillor); Japanese Society for Bone and Mineral Research (councillor); Japan Society of Pharmacology (councillor); Japan Society for Biomedical Research on Trace Elements (councillor); Japan Society for Osteoporosis (councillor); Editor, Biomedical Research on Trace Elements, Japan; Editorial Academy Member of the International Journal of Molecular Medicine; Deputy Director General, IBC; Research Board Advisor, ABI; Deputy Governor, ABI; Listed in international biographical dictionaries. Address: Senagawa 1-chome, 15-5, Aoi-ku, Shizuoka City 420-0913, Japan. E-mail: yamamasa1155@yahoo.co.jp

YAMAMOTO Irwin Toraki, b. 5 April 1955, Wailuku, Maui, Hawaii. Editor; Publisher. Education: YB, Business Administration, Marketing, Chaminade University, 1977. Appointments: President, Editor, Publisher, The Yamamoto Forecast, Kahului, Hawaii, 1977-. Publications: Book: Profit Making in the Stock Market, 1983; Columnist, The Hawaii Herald, 1978-. Honours: Named: Top Market Timer; Top Gold Timer; Top Bond Timer; Timer Digest Honor Roll, Timer Digest; Also honors by: Select Information Exchange; Rating the Stock Selectors. Address: PO Box 573, Kahului, HI 96733-7073, USA.

YAMAMOTO Kentaro, b. 12 November 1969, Yokohama, Japan. Researcher. Education: Bachelor of Engineering, 1993, Master of Engineering, 1995, Doctor of Engineering, 1998, Kumamoto University, Japan. Appointments: Consulting Engineer, Kokusai Kogyo Co, Amagasaki, Japan, 1990-91; Research Associate, Kagoshima University, Kagoshima, Japan, 1998-; Assistant Professor, Kagoshima University, Kagoshima, Japan, 2007-. Publications: Articles in scientific journals including: Geotextiles and Geomembranes; Soils and Foundations. Honours: Listed in Who's Who publications and biographical dictionaries. Memberships: Japan Society of Civil Engineers; Japanese Geotechnical Society; International Society for Soil Mechanics and Geotechnical Engineering. Address: Department of Ocean Civil Engineering, 1-21-40, Korimoto, Kagoshima, 890-0065 Japan. E-mail: yamaken@oce.kagoshima-u.ac.jp

YANG Cheng-Hong, b. 8 May 1957, Taiwan. Professor. m. Li-Yeh Chuang, 2 daughters. Education: MS, 1988, PhD, 1991, Department of Computer Science, MS, Department of Statistics, 1992, NDSU, USA. Appointments: Professor, 1999-, Director, Computer Center, 2003-, NKU of Applied Science, Taiwan; Director, Computer Center, Ministry of Education, Taiwan, 2006-. Publications: Odds Ratio-based Genetic Algorithms for Generating SNP Barcode of Genotypes to Predict Disease Susceptibility. Honours: Senior Member, IEEE; Excellent Award, Teaching Media Competition, Ministry of Education. E-mail: chyang@cc.kuas.edu.tw

YANG Chih-Hung, b. 5 October 1953, Taipei, Taiwan. Professor. Education: BL, Sociology, Soo-Chow University, 1977; MA, Journalism, National Chen-Chi University, 1980; PhD, Mass Communication, National Chen-Chi University, 1992. Appointments: Managing Director, Young Generation Foundation; Vice Chair, Committee of ETTV News; President, Media News; Trustee, Center News Agency; Board Member, Taiwan Television Enterprise; Board Member, Eastern Broadcasting Co Ltd; President, Communications Management Association of Taiwan; Dean of School of Communication, Director of Graduate School of Communications Management, Ming-Chuan University. Publications: The analysis of conglomerization of Broadcasting Media in China; User's evaluation of News Website content and technological functions; Profile of Mass Media: a media worker's observation; The Research on the Media Choice of Internet Advertisement. Honours: Prime Teacher Award, Academy of Taiwan, ROC Education Industry, 1998; IBC Leading Educators of the World, 2005. Memberships: Academic Journalism; Mid Power FM Broadcasting Association; Institution Education for Mass Communication. Address: School of Communication, Ming-Chuan University, No 250, Sec 5, Chung-Shan N Rd, Taipei 251, Taiwan. E-mail: echyang@gmail.com

YANG Dal Mo, b. 7 April 1963, Sang Ju, Republic of Korea. Radiologist. m. Gum-Hee Lee, 2 daughters. Education: MD, Kyung-Hee University, Seoul, Korea, 1988; National Medical Licence, Ministry of Health and Welfare of Korea, 1988; Korean Board of Diagnostic Radiology, Ministry of Health and Welfare of Korea, 1992; PhD, Kangwon National University, Chuncheon, Korea. Appointments: Radiology Residency, Kyung-Hee University Hospital, Seoul, Korea, 1989-92; Director of Diagnostic Radiology, Gil Medical Centre, Incheon, Korea, 1992-99; Assistant Professor of Diagnostic Radiology, 1999-2001, Associate Professor of Diagnostic Radiology, 2001-05, Gachon Medical School Gil Medical Centre; Professor of Diagnostic Radiology, Kyung Hee University East-West Neo Medical Center, Seoul, 2006-. Publications: 20 articles in medical journals as author and co-author include most recently: Imaging findings of hepatic sinusoidal dilation, 2004; Acute necrotizing encephalopathy in Korean infants and children: imaging findings and diverse clinical outcome, 2004; Unusual causes of tubo-ovarian abscess: CT and MR imaging findings, 2004; Cystic lesions in the posterosuperior portion of the humeral head on MR arthography: correlations with gross and histologic findings in cadavers, 2005; Tailgut cyst: MRI evaluation, 2005; Torsted appendix testis: gray scale and color Doppler sonographic findings compared with normal appendix testis, 2005; Borderline serious surface papillary tumor of the ovary; MRI characteristics, 2005; Anomaly of the portal vein with total ramification of the intrahepatic portal branches from the right umbilical portion, 2005; Computed tomography and sonographic findings of hepatic mestases from gastrointestinal stromal tumors after chemotherapy, 2005; MR arthrography in the differential diagnosis of type

II superior labral anteroposterior lesion and sublabral recess, 2006; Diagnostic values of sonography for assessment of sternal fractures compared with conventional radiography and bone scans, 2006; 64 multidetector-row computed tomography for preoperative evaluation of gastric cancer: historic correlation. Honours: Cum Laude Award, Radiological Society of North America, 2003; Certificate of Merit Award, American Roentgen Ray Society, 2003; Cum Laude Award European Congress of Radiology, 2004. Memberships: Korean Radiological Society; Korean Society of Abdominal Radiology. Address: Kyung Hee University East-West Neo Medical Center, 149 Sangil-Dong, Gangdong-Gu, Seoul 134-090, Korea. E-mail: dmy2988@paran.com

YANG Po-Chun, b. 17 January 1987, Taipei, Taiwan. Researcher. Education: Research into communication application of Solar Global Position System, Department of Communication Engineering, National Central University, 2004-. Publications: Multifunction Soft Communication Centre. Honours: Patent of Solar Cell Array, 2007. Memberships: Student Member, IEEE. Address: IOF-4 V86 Keelung Rd Sec 1, Taipei, Taiwan. E-mail: sophia@joytel.com.tw

YANG Tae Young, b. 25 May 1962, Kyungbuk, Korea. Professor. m. 2 sons. Education: BS, Mathematics, Korea University, Seoul, 1985; MS, Statistics, University of Vermont, Burlington, USA, 1987; PhD, Statistics, University of Connecticut, Storrs, USA, 1994. Appointments: Visiting Scholar, Department of Statistics, Stanford University, 1994-95; Visiting Assistant Professor, Department of Statistics, University of Missouri at Columbia, 1994-96; Assistant Professor, 1996-2000, Associate Professor, 2000-04, Professor, 2005-, Head, 2005-, Department of Mathematics, Myongji University, Korea; Associate Editor, Pakistan Journal of Statistics, 1997-99; Visiting Scholar, Department of Statistics and Actuarial Science, Simon Fraser University, 2002-04. Publications: Numerous articles in professional journals. Honours: Noether Awardee, Statistics Department, University of Connecticut, 1991; Grant, Korea Science and Engineering Foundation. Memberships: American Statistical Association. Address: Department of Mathematics, Myongji University, Yougin, Kyonggi, 449-728, Korea. E-mail: tyang@mju.ac.kr

YANG Victor Ting Hsun, b. 9 April 1931, Peikang, Taiwan. Physician. Education: MB, National Taiwan University, Taipei, 1957. Appointments: Intern, 1959, Resident, 1959-63, Fellow, Gastroenterology, 1963-66, Staff Physician, 1966-92, Department of Medicine, National Taiwan University Hospital, Taipei; Instructor, Medicine, National Taiwan University College of Medicine, 1969-92; Fellow, Gastroenterology, Department of Medicine, University of Pennsylvania School of Medicine, 1971-72; Retired, 1992.

YANG Xinjian (Sam), b. 15 November 1954, Hunan, China. Environmental Engineer. m. Bing Shui, 1 son. Education: Bachelor of Engineering, Xiangtan University, China, 1982; Master of Science, University of Cincinnati, Cincinnati, Ohio, 1991. Appointments: Lecturer, Xiangtan University, China, 1982-86; Research Scholar, University of Cambridge, England, 1987-88; Research Assistant, Graduate Student, University of Cincinnati, part-time USEPA Contractor, Cincinnati, 1988-91; Senior Engineer, Process and Development, Preussag Noell Inc, Long Beach, California, 1991-97; Senior Engineer: Mitsubishi, 1997-2000, ABB-Alstan Inc, 2000-2001, ERM Inc, 2004-05, City of Los Angeles, 2005-. Publications: Many published papers in China, England and United States authorised textbooks;

Invented 7 patent applications and one privately owned patent. Honours: Chinese Education Committee Scholarship; Honorary Fellowship, Salford University; Visiting Scholar, University of Cambridge, England; Listed in national and international biographical dictionaries. Memberships: Air and Waste Management Association, USA; Chinese Science and Technology Association, China. Address: 12001 Cherry Street, Los Alamitos, CA 90720, USA.

YANG Youxin, b. 11 September 1963, Xuzhou, China. Specialist in Cancer Medicine. Education: MD, 1986, MSc, 1991, Nanjing Railway Medical College, China; PhD, Paris University VI, France, 2000. Appointments: Director, Art Exploration, 1993-97; Director, CREST, 1998-2000; Founding Member, President, Science Art Society, 2001-. Honours: Young Scientist Award, France, 2000; Top (Platinum) Remi Award, USA, 2004; Accolade Award, USA, 2004; Aegis Award, USA, 2004; Communicator Award, USA, 2004; Book: Youxin Yang MD PhD. An Artist and Scientist, by Espace Richelieu; Over 20 review articles in world-wide journals including World Journal, Europe Journal, European Times about her accomplishments in both scientific and artistic fields; Listed in Who's Who publications and biographical dictionaries. Membership: American Association for Cancer Research. Address: 350 Third Street, Unit 901, Cambridge, MA 02142, USA. E-mail: yyang@bidmc.harvard.edu

YAO Kui, b. 14 October 1967, Huainan, China. Senior Scientist. Education: BEng, Xi'an Jiaotong University, China, 1989; MS, Xidian University, China, 1992; PhD, Xi'an Jiaotong University, China, 1995. Appointments: Post Doctoral Fellow, 1995-97, Research Fellow, assigned to Institute of Materials Research and Engineering, 1997-98, Nanyang Technological University, Singapore; Research Associate, Pennsylvania State University, USA, 1998-99; Research Fellow, 1997-2001, Senior Research Fellow, 2002-2003, Senior Scientist, 2003-, Institute of Materials Research and Engineering (IMRE), Singapore. Publications: Invention patents, technical services and publications on functional materials and devices, including ferroelectric, piezoelectric, photovoltaic and chemical sensor materials and their applications. Memberships: Senior member, IEEE; MRS. Address: Institute of Materials Research and Engineering, 3 Research Link, Singapore 117602, Singapore.

YAP Yee Guan, b. 19 December 1967, Malaysia. Cardiologist; Physician; Scientist. m. Wendy, 3 sons. Education: B Med Sci Hons (Nottm), 1990, MBBS (Nottm), 1992, University of Nottingham Medical School, England; MCRP (UK), 1996; MD (London), 2005; UK Postgraduate Medical Education & Training Board Certified Cardiologist & General Physician, European Board for the Speciality of Cardiology Certified Cardiologist. Appointments include: Junior House Officer, General Surgery, Gynaecology, University Hospital, Nottingham, 1992-93; Junior House Officer, General Medicine, Gastroenterology, Southampton General Hospital, 1993; Senior House Officer, Cardiology, CCU and Chest Medicine, The Cardiothoracic Centre, Liverpool, 1993-94; Senior House Officer, General Medicine, Cardiology, Neurology, Diabetes and Endocrinology, Ashford Hospital, Middlesex, 1994-95; Senior House Officer, Neurology, Atkinson Moreley Hospital, London, 1995-96; Senior house Officer, Gastroenterology and General Medicine, St George's, 1996; British Heart Foundation Research Fellow in Cardiology and Honorary Registrar in Cardiology, St George's Hospital Medical School, London and Mayday University Hospital, Croydon, 1997-2000; Specialist Registrar, Cardiology, General Internal Medicine, St Peter's Hospital, Chertsey,

Surrey, 2000-2001; Frimley Park Hospital, Camberley, Surrey, 2001-2002; Specialist Registrar in Cardiology, Mayday University Hospital, Thornton Heath, Surrey, 2002-2003; Senior Specialist Registrar in Cardiology & Senior Interventional Fellow, St George's Hospital, Tooting, London, 2003-05; Associate Professor and Head of Department of Medicine & Section of Cardiology, Department of Medicine, Faculty of Medicine & Health Sciences, University Putra Malaysia, and Consultant Cardiologist and interventionist, Serdang Hospital, Selangor, Malaysia, 2005-; Consultant Interventional Cardiologist, Prince Court Medical Centre, Kuala Lumpur, Malaysia. Publications: Books as co-author: Drug-induced Long QT Syndrome. Clinical Approaches to Tachyarrhythmias, 2002; Acquired Long QT Syndrome, 2004; Handbook of Atrial Fibrillation; 11 book chapters; 13 review articles; 16 original scientific papers; 90 abstracts; 1 editorial. Honours: Vale of Trent Faculty of the Royal College of General Practitioners Student Audit Prize, 1992; British Heart Foundation Research Fellowship, 1997-99, Project Grants, 1998-99, 2000-2001; Listed in Who's Who publications and biographical dictionaries. Memberships: Fellowships: Royal College of Physicians of Edinburgh; Royal College of Physicians of Glasgow; European Society of Cardiologists; Society of Cardiovascular Angiography & Interventions, USA; American Heart Association; Academy of Medicine of Singapore. Address: Department of Medicine, Faculty of Medicine & Health Sciences, University Putra Malaysia, No 72, 10B Floor, Grand Seasons Avenue, Jalan Pahang, 53000 Kuala Lumpur, Malaysia. E-mail: ygyap@aol.com

YASUFUKU Sachio, b. 11 November 1929, Qingdao, China. Electrical Engineer. m. Yoko Kikutani, 16 December 1958. Education: BSc, 1952, DEng, 1979, Nagoya University. Appointments: Engineer, Furukawa Electric Co Ltd, Japan, 1952-72; Senior and Chief Specialists, Toshiba Corporation, Japan, 1972-89; Adjunct Professor, Tokyo Denki University, 1989-2005. Publications: 13 papers, on IEEE Transactions Electrical Insulation; 10 papers on IEEE Electrical Insulation Magazine; 13 papers on IEEE DEIS Sponsored Conference Proceedings; Altogether over 60 papers published; Over 10 patents (including US patents). Honours: National Award Invention, Japan, 1963; 23rd National Award for JEMA, about Progress of Electric Machinery, 1974; IEEE Fellow Award, 1993; Distinguished Service Award, IEEE DEIS, 1997; IEEE Life Fellow, 2001. Memberships: Society Polymer Science, Japan, 1952; IEEE, 1972; IEEJ, 1974. Address: 603, 2-5 2-chome, Katase, Fujisawa City, 251-0032 Japan.

YATUSEVICH Anton Ivanovich, b. 2 January 1947, Brest Region, Belarus. Veterinary Surgeon. m. Valentina P Yatusevich, 1 son, 1 daughter. Education: Zoo-Vet, Technical School, Pinsk, 1967; Veterinarian, 1972; Vitebsk State Veterinary Medicine Institute, 1972; PhD, Veterinary Science, 1978; Doctor of Veterinary Medicine, 1989; Associate Professor, 1980; Professor, 1990. Appointments: Farm Veterinary Surgeon, 1972-73; Assistant, 1973-80, Associate Professor, 1980-84, Pro-rector for Academic Affairs, 1984-89, Parasitology Department, Vitebsk Veterinary Medicine Academy; Head, Parasitology Department, 1990-; Rector, Vitebsk Veterinary Medicine Academy, 1998-; Chief Editor, Veterinarnaya Gazeta, 1995-99; Chief Editor, Veterinary Medicine, 2001-; Scientific Editor, Veterinarnaya Encyclopedia; Editor, Vestnik VSAVM. Publications: 34 textbooks and monographs; 30 invention patents; 590 articles. Honours: Honorary Badge, Inventor of the USSR; Silver Medal of the Exhibition of National Economic Achievements of the USSR; Letters of Honour, Vitebsk Region Executive Committee; Letters of Honour, the Ministry of Agriculture;

Honourary Scientist of Belarus; Memorable Medal, Christianity 2000; Memorable Medal, 60 Years to the Victory in the Great Patriotic War 1941-1945; Honourary Badge, Leader in Education. Memberships: Petrovskaya Academy of Sciences and Arts; Russian Agrarian Education Academy; Russian Academy of Agri-Sci; International Parasitocenologists Association; Belarusian Society of Protozoologists. Address: Dovatora Street 7/11, Vitebsk 210026, Republic of Belarus. E-mail: vetlib@vitebsk.by

YE Minglu, b. 13 April 1936, Fujian Province, China. Professor of Chemistry. m. Jingjuan Tang, 1 son, 1 daughter. Education: Graduated, Chemistry Department, Fudan University, Shanghai, China, 1958. Appointments: Worked in Department of Nuclear Science, 1958-96, then Department of Environmental Science and Engineering, 1996-98, Fudan University, Shanghai, 1958-98; Professor and Director of the Nuclear Chemistry Section, Fudan University; Lectures, Nuclear Chemistry and Application of Nuclear Technology and completed many science research projects; Visiting Scholar, Freie Universitat Berlin (Free University, Berlin), West Germany, 1984-85; Visiting Researcher, Japan Atomic Energy Research Institute, 1994; Retired, 1998. Publications: 5 books include: Radiochemistry Experiments, 1991; Introduction of Environmental Chemistry, 1997; 62 scientific papers. Honours: 5 science and technology prizes awarded by Shanghai Science Commission and Ministry of Nuclear Industry of China, 1984-96; Biography listed in several national and international biographical publications. Memberships: Council Member: Isotope Society of China, 1985-98, Nuclear and Radiochemistry Society of China, 1991-98; President, 2001-03, Honourable President, 2003-, Australia Alumni Association of Fudan University. Address: 14 Sydney Road, Lindfield, NSW 2070, Australia. E-mail: mingluye@yahoo.com.au

YEGHIAZARYAR Vladimir Sahak, b. 20 May 1955, Altay region, Russia. Computer Science. m. Kazine Hakobyan, 2 daughters. Education: Applied Mathematics, Yereyan State University, 1977; Lomonosov Fellowship, Moscow State University, 1981-84; Docent degree, Computer Science. Appointments: Dean, Faculty of Information and Applied Mathematics, 1994-2000, Docent, Chair of Programme, 2000-02, Yereyan State University; Dean, Faculty of Applied Mathematics and Informatics, 2002-, Head of Chair, System Programming, 2004-, RAU. Publications: More than 50 scientific publications. Honours: Gold and Silver Medals, Yereyan State University, 1998, 2005; F Nansen Gold Medal, 2005; Reward, Ministry of Science and Education, 2005. Memberships: Editorial Board of Journal, Bnaget; Editorial Board of Journal, Vestnik, RAU. Address: Lomonosov St 37, 375008 Yerevan, Armenia. E-mail: pmi@rau.am

YEH Peter Shue-Yen, b. 20 April 1966, Chang-Hua, Taiwan. Obstetrician. Education: Cambridge University, England; Imperial College London, England. Appointments: Specialist Registrar in Obstetrics and Gynaecology, Addenbrookes Hospital, Cambridge, England. Membership: Member of the Royal College of Obstetricians and Gynaecologists. Address: 19 Playsteds Lane, Great Cambourne, Cambridge, CB23 6GA, England.

YEKEH YAZDANDOOST Kamya, b. 16 February 1964, Abadan, Iran. Research Scientist. m. Aigul Kulnazarova, 1 son. Education: BE, Electronics, Toosi University, Tehran, Iran, 1988; MSc, 1996, PhD, 2000, Electronic Science, Pune University, India. Appointments: Researcher, Nagoya University, Japan, 2001-03; Expert Researcher, NICT,

Japan, 2003-. Publications: More than 30 papers and articles in refereed journals and conferences. Honours: Japan Association for Education; Japan Society for Promotion of Science. Memberships: IEEE; European Microwave Association. Address: Medical ICT Institute, National Institute of Information and Communications Technology (NICT), New Generation Wireless Communications Research Centre, 3-4 Hikanino-oka, Yokosuka 239-0847, Japan. E-mail: yazdandoost@nict.go.jp

YELTON Michael Paul, b. 21 April 1950, Birkenhead, England. Circuit Judge. m. Judith Sara, 2 sons, 1 daughter. Education: Colchester Royal Grammar School; BA, 1971, MA, 1974, Corpus Christi College, Cambridge. Appointments: Fellow of Corpus Christi College, Cambridge, 1977-81; Barrister in Practice, 1973-98; Circuit Judge, 1998-. Publications: Fatal Accidents: A Practical Guide to Compensation, 1998; Martin Travers (1886-1948): An Appreciation, written with Rodney Warrener, 2003; Trams Trolleybuses Buses and the Law, 2004; Peter Anson, Monk, Writer and Artist, 2005; Anglican Papalism 1900-1960, 2005 and 2008; Alfred Hope Patten and the Shrine of Our Lady of Walsingham, 2006; Empty Tabernacles: Twelve Lost Churches of London, 2006; Anglican Churchbuilding in London 1915-45, written with John Salmon, 2007; Alfred Hope Patten: His Life and Times in Pictures, 2007. Address: Cambridge County Court, 197 East Road, Cambridge, CB1 1BA, England.

YENTOB Alan, b. 11 March 1947, England. Television Administrator. 1 son, 1 daughter, by Philippa Walker. Education: University of Grenoble, France; University of Leeds. Appointments: BBC General Trainee, 1968; Producer, Director, 1970-, Head of Music & Arts, 1985-88, BBC TV; Controller, BBC 2, 1988-93, BBC 1, 1993-96; BBC Director of Programmes, 1997-2000, Director of Drama, Entertainment and Children's Programmes, 2002-, Creative Director, 2004-, BBC Television; Presenter, Imagine, arts series, BBC1, 2003-. Honours: Honorary Fellow, RCA; RIBA; Royal TV Society. Memberships: Board of Directors, Riverside Studios, 1984-88, British Film Institute Production Board, 1985-93; British Screen Advisory Council; Advisory Committee, Institute of Contemporary Arts; Council, Royal Court Theatre; Governor, National Film School, 1998-; South Bank Board, International Academy of Television Arts and Sciences, 1999-. Timebank, 2001-. Address: BBC Television, Television Centre, Wood Lane, London W12 7RJ, England.

YEO Kiam Beng, b. 11 February 1962, Singapore. Director; Associate Professor. m. 3 sons, 1 daughter. Education: ACGI Diploma in Aeronautical Engineering, 1989, B Eng, Aeronautical Engineering, 1989, PhD, Mechanical Engineering, 1993, DIC, Engineering Adhesive, 1993, Imperial College of Science, Technology and Medicine, University of London, England. Appointments: Research Technician, 1989, Tutor for Laboratory Experiment, 1991-92, Research Engineer, 1989-93, Imperial College of Science, Technology and Medicine, University of London; Part time Teacher, Bartley Secondary School, Singapore, 1995; Engineering Lecturer, International Islamic University, Malaysia, 1995-97; Chairman, Mechanical Engineering Program, 1997-2001, Postgraduate Studies and R&D, 2001-03, Senior Lecturer, 2003-05, Visiting Lecturer, 2005-06, Mechanical Engineering, Director, Centre of Materials & Minerals Research Centre, 2006-, School of Engineering & Information Technology, Universiti Malaysia Sabah. Publications: 3 books; Numerous papers and articles in professional scientific journals. Honours: Scholarship, British Ministry of Defense, Royal Admiral Research

Center, 1989-92; Excellent Professional Award in Academics for the Year 2002, 2004; Excellent Professional Award in Academics for the Year 2003, 2004; Excellent Professional Award in Academics for the Year 2004, 2006. Memberships: Associate, City & Guilds of London Institute; Incorporated Royal Charter of Aeronautical Engineering. Address: Hse 38, Lorong Kingfisher Sulaman 2, TMN Kingfisher Sulaman Fasa 2A, JLN Sulaman, Menggatal, 88450, Kota Kinabalu, Sabah, Malaysia. E-mail: nooryeo@yahoo.com

YERRA Rama Mohan Rao, b. 24 September 1961, Bhimavaram, Andhra Pradesh, India. Principal. m. Y V M Lakshmi, 1 son, 2 daughters. Education: BE (Civil); ME (Environmental Engineering); PhD (Environmental Engineering). Appointments: Lecturer, 1985; Senior Lecturer, 1992; Principal, 2003-. Publications: 42 articles in national and international journals. Honours: Best Citizens of India, International Publishing House, New Delhi, 2001; Listed in international biographical dictionaries. Memberships: Indian Waterworks Association; Institution of Engineers; Indian Society for Technical Education; Indian Association of Environmental Management. Address: Dr Pauls Engineering College, Vanur Taluk, Villupuram District, 605 109, India. E-mail: profmrao1@yahoo.com

YI Jeong Hyun, b. 27 November 1969, Seoul, Korea. Computer Scientist. m. Soyeon Kim, 1 son, 1 daughter. Education: BS, 1993, MS, 1995, Computer Science, Soong-Sil University, Seoul; PhD, Information and Computer Science, University of California, Irvine, USA, 2005. Appointments: Member of Research Staff, Electronics and Telecommunications Research Institute, 1995-2001; Guest Researcher, National Institute of Standards and Technology, 2000-01; Graduate Student Researcher, University of California, Irvine, 2001-05; Principal Researcher, Samsung Advanced Institute of Technology, Korea, 2005-. Publications: 1 book chapter; Numerous refereed journal publications, conferences papers and other articles; 1 patent. Honours: Best Project Award, Secure EDI Systems, KT Telecom, Seoul, 1998; Best Project Award, PKI Systems, 2001, IT National Scholarship, 2001-05, Ministry of Information and Communications, Korea Government; Graduate Researcher Fellowship, University of California, 2001-02; Cal (IT)^2 Fellowship, California Institute for Telecommunications and Information Technology, 2002; Talented Alumnus Scholarship, Soong-Sil University, Seoul, 2004-05; UCI Regents' Dissertation Fellowship, University of California, Irvine, 2005; Listed in international biographical dictionaries. Memberships: ACM; IEEE Computer Society; Korea Institute of Information Security and Cryptology; Korean Information Science Society. Address: 33-23 Sambu Apt, Taepyong-dong, Joong-gu, Daejon 301-150, Republic of Korea. E-mail: jeong.yi@samsung.com

YI Jung Hyuk, b. 30 January 1960, Seoul, South Korea. Engineering Manager. m. Mi Young Kim, 2 sons. Education: BA, Metallurgy, Yonsei University, Korea, 1985; PhD, Materials Science & Engineering, Monash University, Australia, 1992. Appointments: Engineering Manager, Gas Turbine Repair Service Centre, Korea Plant Service and Engineering, 1993-.

YILDIZHAN Ahmet, b. 24 February 1956, Ladik-Samsun, Turkey. Neurosurgeon; Educator. m. Zeynep Sema Ugur, 4 children. Education: MD, Ankara University, Turkey, 1980; Certificate, Neurosurgeon, Ministry of Health, 1986. Appointments: Resident, Faculty of Medicine, Erciyes University, Kayseri, Turkey, 1981-86; Founder, Department of Neurosurgery, SSK Hospital, Kayseri, Turkey, 1986-88;

Associate Professor, Vakif Gureba Hospital, Istanbul, 1989-94; Associate Professor, Merter Vatan Hospital and Istanbul Vatan Hospital, Universal Hospitals Group, 1994-; Advisory Board, Turkish Journal of Medicine, Ankara, 1994-2004; Principal Owner, Education and Science Magazine, Istanbul, 1998-; Visiting Researcher, Harvard University, Cambridge, Massachusetts, 1992; Neurosurgeon, Gulhane Military Medical Academy, Ankara, 1990-91; Associate Professor, Faculty of Medicine, Yeditepe University, Istanbul, 2003-. Publications: Author, Bel Fitigi ve Korunma Yollari, 1997, 14th edition 2006; Author, Lumbar Disc Herniation and Its Prevention (100 Recommendations for Low Back Health), 2005, 2nd edition 2006 (English publication of "Bel Fitigi ve Korunma Yollari"); Author, Bilim Egitim ve Kultur Yazilari – Kuresel Problemler Nasil Cozulur?, 2007 (Science Education and Cultural Essays – How are Global Problems Resolved?); Author, Mutululugun Denklemi (Evren-Insan-Ruh ve Olumsuzluk), 2007 (Equation of Happiness/The Universe-The Human Being-The Soul and Immortality); Author, Evrensel Bahceye (Didaktik Siirler), 2007 (Didactic Poems for the Universal Garden); 53 scientific papers in the field of Neurosurgery; Over 50 additional articles on health related and other topics. Honours: International Publication Award, 1989, 1990, 1992. Memberships: Member, American Association of Neurological Surgeons (AANS); Member, Society for Neuro-Oncology; Member, Turkish Neurosurgical Society; Member, Istanbul Chamber of Medicine; Member, National Geographic Society; Member, Yesilay, Istanbul; Lifetime Volunteer Member, TEMA; Supporter, NREF; Supporter, Provision of Clean Water for Africa; Supporter, Handicapped and Their Friends Club; Supporter, Campaign for the Education of Girls in Antolia. Address: Yildizhan Saglik Ltd, Valikonagi Caddesi 85/4, 34371 Nisantasi, Istanbul, Turkey. E-mail: ayildizhan@e-kolay.net Website: www.belfitigi.com

YIM Soo-Jae, b. 27 September 1961, Seoul, Korea. Medical Doctor. m. Mi-Yeom Lee, 1 son, 2 daughters. Education: MD, Medical College, SoomChumHyang University, Seoul, 1981-87; Master Degree, Postgraduate School, SoomChumHyang Medical School, 1990-92; Degree of Doctor of Philosophy in Medicine, 1994-97. Appointments: Professor, Department of Orthopaedic Surgery, SoomChumHyang Medical School, 1995-; Clinical Adult Reconstructive Surgery Fellowship, Department of Orthopaedic Surgery, Princess Elizabeth Orthopaedic Centre and Exeter & Devon Hospital, Exeter, England, 1997-98. Publications: Impaction allograft with cement for the revision of the femoral component – A minimum 39-month follow-up study with the Exeter stem in Asian hips, 2006. Honours: Korean Orthopaedic Association Scholarship, 1999; Great Minds of the 21st Century, 2006. Orthopaedic Surgery Specialist; Sports Medicine Specialist. E-mail: yimsj@chol.com

YOELI Pinhas (Günther Aptekmann), b. 1 July 1920, Bayreuth, Germany. Professor. m. Agi Izsakova, 2 sons. Education: Eidgenoessische Technische Hochschule, Switzerland, 1956. Appointments: Senior Lecturer, Technion, Israel, 1957-64; Associate Professor, 1964-68; Professor, Tel Aviv University, 1968-91; Professor Emeritus, 1991-. Publications: Cartographic Drawing with Computers, author, 1982; Contributions to articles in professional journals. Honours: Honorary Fellowship of the International Cartographic Association. Memberships: Israel Surveyors Association; Association of Engineers and Architects; Israel Cartographic Association, president, 1988-91. Listed in national and international biographical dictionaries. Address: Tel Aviv University, Ramat Aviv, Tel Aviv, Israel. E-mail: yoeli@post.tau.ac.il

YOO Chang-Hak, b. 4 July 1963, Busan, Korea. Surgeon; Associate Professor. m. Sung-Hee Hahn, 2 sons. Education: MD, College of Medicine, Yonsei University, 1988; Master's degree, Postgraduate School of Medicine, 2002; PhD, Postgraduate School of Medicine, Korea University, 2006. Appointments: Internship, 1988-89, Resident, 1989-92, Severance Hospital, Yonsei University; Captain, Military Medical Service, 1993-95; Fellow, Department of Surgery, Yonsei University College of Medicine, 1996-98; Assistant, Associate Professor, Department of Surgery, Kangbuk Samsung Hospital, Sungkyunkwan University School of Medicine, 1999-2007; Research Fellow, Medial University of South Carolina, USA, 2004-05. Publications: Numerous articles in professional journals. Memberships: International Gastric Cancer Congress; Korean Surgical Society; Korean Gastric Cancer Society. Address: Kangbuk Samsung Hospital, Sungkyunkwan University, 108 Pyung-dong, Jongro-ku, Seoul 110-102, Republic of Korea.

YOO Hee-Young, b. 26 August 1940, South Chungchong Province, Korea. Museum Director. Education: BA, College of Fine Art, Seoul National University, 1962. Appointments: Professor, 1984-2005, Dean, 1995-99, College of Arts & Design, Ewha Womans University; Chairman, Federation of the Asian International Artists Korea Committee, 1995-; Member, National Academy of Arts, Korea, 2006-; Director, Seoul Museum of Art, Korea, 2007-. Publications: Ryu Hee-Young's Color Field Paintings as Windows on Mentality, 2003. Honours: Twice winner, Minister of Culture and Public Information Prize, 1969, 1971; Presidential Prize, National Art Exhibition, 1973; Recommended Artist's Prize, National Art Exhibition, 1979; Selected Solo Exhibitions: Hyundai Art Gallery, Seoul, 1991; Galerie Etienne De Causans, Paris, 1994; Gallery Hyundai, Seoul, 1998, 2003; Walter Wickiser Gallery, New York, 1999, 2006; Selected Group Exhibitions: Cannes International Art Festival, Cannes, France, 1995; MANIF, Seoul Arts Center, Seoul, 1995, 1996, 2000; SIAF, Korea Trade Center, Seoul, 1997; Asia International Art Exhibition, Fukuoka Metropolitan Museum of Art, Japan, 1993; Four Korean Contemporary Artists' Exhibition, Neptuno Gallery, Madrid, Spain, 1995; International Exhibition of Seven Korean Contemporary Artists, Denis Rene Gallery, Paris, 1996. Memberships: National Academy of Arts, Korea. Address: Museum of Art-gil 28, Seosomun-dong 37, Jung-gu, Seoul 100-813, Korea.

YOO Kee Young, b. 23 October 1952, Daegu, Korea. Professor. m. Sook Hyang Kwon, 1 son, 2 daughters. Education: BS, Mathematics, Kyungpook National University, 1976; MS, Computer Science, Korea Advanced Institute of Science and Technology, 1978; PhD, Computer Science, Rennselaer Polytechnic Institute, 1992. Appointments: Assistant Professor, Department of Electrical Engineering, 1978-86, Professor, Department of Computer Engineering, 1986-, Chair, Computer Center, 2000-02, Kyungpook National University; Branch Chair, 1997-98, Board of Directors, 1999-2002, 2004-, Korea Information Security Society. Publications: 8 books; 54 domestic journal papers; 105 domestic conference papers; 95 international conference papers; 130 international journal papers. Honours: Award, Ministry of Information and Communication, 2006. Address: Department of Computer Engineering, Kyungpook National University, Daegu 702-701, Korea. E-mail: yook@knu.ac.kr

YOO Kwang Soo, b. 15 January 1957, Gangwon-do, Korea. Professor. m. Hyun Sim Cho, 2 sons. Education: BS, Hanyang University, Seoul, 1981; MS, Seoul National University, Seoul, 1983; PhD, Arizona State University, Tempe, Arizona, USA,

1991. Appointments: Staff, Hyundai Electronics Industry Ltd, Seoul, 1983-84; Research Scientist, 1984-87, Senior Research Scientist, 1991-95, Korea Institute of Science and Technology, Seoul; Professor, University of Seoul, 1995-; Deputy Dean, Academic Affairs, 2001-03, Director, 2005-07, Institute of Industrial Technology; Dean, College of Engineering, 2007-. Publications: 86 research papers; 5 books; 16 patents. Honours: 12th Award for Excellent Science and Technology papers, Federation of Korea Science and Technology, 2002; Research Award, Korean Ceramic Society, 2003. Memberships: Korean Sensors Society; Korean Ceramic Society. Address: Department of Materials Science & Engineering, University of Seoul, 90 Jeonnong-dong, Dongdaemun-gu, Seoul 130-743, Korea. E-mail: ksyoo@uos.ac.kr

YOO Seung-Eul, b. 9 October 1960, Seoul, Republic of Korea. Materials Scientist. m. Hye-Ryun Park, 2 daughters. BS, Yonsei University, 1984; MS, 1987, PhD, 1990, Tokyo Institute of Technology, Japan. Appointments: Researcher, 1984-85, Research Assistant, Laboratory for Advanced Ceramics, 1987-88, Visiting Researcher, The Research Laboratory of Engineering Materials, 1990, Tokyo Institute of Technology, Japan; Director, Korea Automotive Technology Institute, Korea, 1991-. Publications: Patents: Double Oxide Thin Film; High Wear Resistance Aluminium Brake Disc Rotor Treated by a Plasma Transferred Arc Welding and Method for Manufacturing Thereof; Bipolar Plate for Fuel Cell; Numerous articles in professional journals. Honours: Excellent Paper Presentation Award, Korean Electrochemical Society, 2004; Superior Prize, Newtech Korea, 2004. Memberships: Korean Ceramic Society; Ceramic Society of Japan; Society of Automotive Engineers; Korean Society of Automotive Engineers; Society of Automotive Engineers of Japan; Korean Electrochemical Society; Korea Society of Industrial and Engineering Chemistry; Korea Society for New and Renewable Energy; Korean Institute of Resources Recycling. Address: Ssangyong Apt 5-808, Daechi-Dong, Gangnam-Gu, Seoul 135-776, Korea. E-mail: seyoo@katech.re.kr

YOO Vak Yeong, b. 28 June 1947, Seoul. Physician. Education: EWHA Women's Medical University, 1968-74. Appointments: Director of Hospital, Cheongvak Primebeyond Hospital; YVY-QOL Meno-Osteoporosis Group President. Publications: Quality of Midbeyonds Women's Life; Phytoestrogen; How to Manage a Menopause Clinic; Aging and Gender Specific Quality of Life; Journal of the Korean Geriatrics Society; Journal YVY-QOL Meno/Osteoporosis. Memberships: North American Menopause Society; The Endocrine Society; International Menopause Society; American Society of Bone Mineral Research; National Osteoporosis Foundation Professional Partner Network. Address: 582 Shinsa Dong Kangnam Ku Seoul 135-892, Korea.

YOON Byung-Koo, b. 16 September 1957, Seoul, Korea. Medical Doctor. m. Eun-Kyung Zong, 2 sons. Education: Premedical Course, Seoul National University, College of Liberal Arts and Science, 1978; MD, 1982, Master of Medical Science, 1986, PhD, Medical Science, 1992, Seoul National University, College of Medicine. Appointments: Intern, 1982-83, Resident, 1983-86, Clinical Fellow, Division of Reproductive Endocrinology and Infertility, 1989-91, Department of Obstetrics and Gynaecology, Seoul National University Hospital; Military Physician, Korean Army, 1986-89; Research Fellow, Endocrine Research Unit, Mayo Clinic, 1991-93; Research Fellow, Division of Reproductive Endocrinology and Infertility, Department of

Obstetrics and Gynaecology, Beth Israel Hospital Boston, Harvard Medical School, 1993-94; Clinical Staff, Director of Menopause Research, Department of Obstetrics and Gynaecology, Samsung Medical Centre, 1994-; Associate Professor, 1997-2002, Professor, 2002-, Department of Obstetrics and Gynaecology, Sungkyunkwan University School of Medicine. Publications: 4 articles in professional medical journals. Honours: Best Paper Award, 1999, MSD Scientific Award, 2001, Korean Menopause Society; Academic Award, Korean Society of Endocrinology, 2002. Memberships: Korean Society of Obstetrics & Gynaecology; Korean Society of Endocrinology; Korean Menopause Society; Korean Society of Bone and Mineral Research; Korean Society of Medical Biochemistry and Molecular Biology; Korean Society of Circulation; Korean Society of Lipidology and Atherosclerosis; North American Menopause Society; International Menopause Society; American Heart Association: Arteriosclerosis, Thrombosis & Vascular Biology Council. Address: Department of Obstetrics & Gynaecology, Samsung Medical Centre, Sungkyunkwan University School of Medicine, 50, Ilwon-Dong, Kangnam-Ku, Seoul 135-710, Korea. E-mail: bkyoon@smc.samsung.co.kr

YOON Eun-Jun, b. 28 December 1971, Daegu, South Korea. Professor. m. Bok-Hee, 1 son, 1 daughter. Education: BS, School of Textile and Fashion Technology, 1995, MS, Computer Engineering, 2003, Kyung Il University; PhD, Computer Engineering/Information Security Laboratory, Department of Computer Engineering, Kyungpook National University, 2007. Appointments: Teacher, Siji Computer Academy, Daegu, Korea, 1998-2004; Part time Lecturer, School of Computer Information, Keimyung College, Daegu, Korea, 2003-04; Part time Lecturer, Department of Computer Engineering, 2004-06, Part time Lecturer, School of Computer Information, 2004-06, Yeungjin Cyber College, Daegu; Visiting Professor, Department of Computer Engineering, Kung Il University, 2006-07; Full time Lecturer, Faculty of Computer Information, Daegu Polytechnic College, 2007-. Publications: 97 papers including 57 papers in Science Citation Index Expanded International Journals and 5 papers in Science Citation Index International Journals. Honours: Distinguished Leadership Award, ABI, 2006; Man of the Year, ABI, 2006. Address: 9 Sawol-Dong, Suseong-Gu, Daegu 706-160, South Korea. E-mail: y7777@daum.net

YOON Hyun Joong, b. 19 December 1973, Seoul, Republic of Korea. Senior Engineer. m. Ye-Won. Education: BS, Yonsei University, Seoul, 1997; MS, 1999, PhD, 2004, Korean Advanced Institute of Science and Technology, Daejeon. Appointments: Post Doctorate, Integrated Manufacturing Technologies Institute, National Research Council, Canada, 2004-05; Senior Engineer, Mechatronics Center, Corporate Technology Operations, Samsung Electronics Co Ltd, 2005-. Publications: Deadlock-Free Scheduling of Photo-Lithgraphy Equipment in Semiconductor Manufacturing, 2004; On-Line Scheduling of Integrated Single-Wafer Processing Tools with Temporal Constraints, 2005. Memberships: Institute of Electrical and Electronics Engineering; INFORMS. Address: Posco the Sharp, 103-1004, Seocho-Dong, Seocho-Gu, Seoul 137-721, Republic of Korea. E-mail: yunkii@kaist.ac.kr

YOON Kyung-Chul, b. 4 December 1971, Gwang-Ju, South Korea. Professor; Doctor. m. Jin Choi, 1 son, 1 daughter. Education: Bachelor's degree, Chonnam National University Medical School, 1994; Master's degree, 1997, Doctor's degree, 2003, Chonnam National University Graduate School. Appointments: Intern, Chonnam National University Hospital, 1994-95; Resident, Chonnam National University Hospital,

1995-99, Yonsei University Severence Hospital, 1998; Clinical Instructor, 2003-04, Full time Instructor, 2004-05, Assistant Professor, 2006-, Department of Ophthalmology, Chonnam National University Medical School and Hospital; Director, Korean Society of Cataract and Refractive Surgery, 2004-05; Director, Korean Society of External Eye Diseases, 2006-. Publications: Book, Refractive Surgery, 2006; 100 papers in national and international journals; 160 domestic and international presentations. Honours: Best Poster Award, Asia Pacific Academy of Ophthalmology, 2006. Memberships: Korean Ophthalmological Society; American Academy of Ophthalmology; American Society of Cataract and Refractive Surgery; European Society of Cataract and Refractive Surgery; Association for Research in Vision and Ophthalmology. Address: Department of Ophthalmology, Chonnam National University Medical School and Hospital, 8 Hak-Dong, Dong-Gu, Gwangju, 501-757, South Korea. E-mail: kcyoon@choonam.ac.kr

YOON Seokhyun, b. 1 December 1966, Seoul, Korea. Professor; Electrical & Computer Engineer. m. Yunjeong Lee, 1 daughter. Education: BS, 1992, MS, 1996, Electronics Engineering, Sung Kyun Kwan University, Suwon, Korea; PhD, Electrical & Computer Engineering, New Jersey Institute of Technology, Newark, USA, 2003. Appointments: Technical Staff Member, Electronics & Telecom Research Institute, Daejeon, Korea, 1999; Senior Technical Staff Member, Telecom R&D Center, Samsung Electronics, Suwon, Korea, 2003-05; Assistant Professor, Department of ECE, Dankook University, Seoul, Korea, 2005-. Publications: Performance analysis of linear multiuser detectors for randomly spread CDMA using Gaussian approximation, 2002; A parallel algorithm for low latency turbo decoding, 2002; Packet data communication over coded CDMA Part II: Throughput bound of CDMA unslotted ALOHA with Type II Hybrid ARQ, 2004. Honours: Hashimoto Prize for academic excellence, NJIT, 2003. Memberships: Institute of Electrical & Electronics Engineers; Institute of Electronics, Information and Communication Engineers. Address: Department of ECE, Dankook University, Suji-gu, Jukjeon-dong San 44-1, Kyunggi-do, Korea. E-mail: syoon@dku.edu

YOON Won Ku, b. 1 January 1960, Seoul, Republic of Korea. Orthopaedic Surgeon. m. Eun Kyung Shim, 1 son. Education: Medical Doctor, Hanyang University College of Medicine, 1984; Orthopaedic Surgeon, Hanyang University Hospital, 1989; Spine Surgeon, Hanyang University Hospital and Asahikawa Medical College, Japan, 1995; Advanced Healthcare Management Program, Seoul National University, 2007. Appointments: Director, Orthopaedic Department, 1990-94, Vice President, 1995-2001, Jecheon Seoul General Hospital; Fellowship, Spine Surgery Hanyang University Hospital, 1994-95; Technical Consultant, LG Life Science, 1996-2008; Lecturer, Department of Oriental Medicine, Semyung University, 1997-2001; Consulting Doctor, Samsung Insurance Company, 2000-01; Chairman, Dr Yoon's Orthopaedic Clinic, 2001-; Clinical Professor, Samsung Medical Center (Sungkyunkwan), 2005-; Clinical Professor, Hanyang University Medical College, 2007-; President, Jecheon Medical Association, 2008-. Publications: 10 articles in professional journals. Honours: Best Graduate Award, Advanced Healthcare Management Program, Seoul National University Hospital, 2007. Memberships: Lifetime Member, Korea Orthopaedic Association; Lifetime Member, Korea Association of Spine Surgery; Active Member, GICD; Active Member, SICOT; Lifetime Member, Korea Academy of Primary Care; Member, Health Industry CEO Summit.

Address: 25-1, Joongangro 2ga, Jecheon, Chungbuk, 390-012, Republic of Korea. E-mail: spinekr@gmail.com Website: www.dryoonos.co.kr

YORK HRH The Duke of York, Earl of Inverness and Baron Killyleagh, Prince Andrew Albert Christian Edward, b. 19 February 1960, London, England. m. Sarah Ferguson, 1986, divorced 1996, 2 daughters. Education: Lakefield College School, Ontario, Canada; Britannia Royal Naval College, Dartmouth. Appointments: Seaman Officer, Pilot, 1979, Royal Navy; Flying training with RAF Leeming, Yorkshire; Helicopter training at Royal Naval Air Station Culdrose, Cornwall; Received Wings, 1981; Front-line unit 820 Naval Air Squadron, Anti-Submarine Warfare Carrier HMS Invincible; Participated in Falklands conflict; Rank of Lieutenant, 1984; Personal ADC to HM The Queen, 1984; Flight Pilot in NAS, Type 22 Frigate HMS Brazen, 1984-86; Helicopter Warfare Instructor, 702 NAS, 1987; Officer of the Watch, Type 42 Destroyer HMS Edinburgh, 1988-89; Formed HMS Campbeltown Flight, RNAS Portland; Flight Commander, 829 NAS, 1989-91; Army Command and Staff Course, Staff College, Camberley, 1992; Rank of Lt Commander, 1992; Commanded Hunt Class Minehunter HMS Cottesmore, 1993-94; Senior Pilot, 815 NAS, RNAS Portland, 1995-96; Staff Officer, Ministry of Defence, London, Directorate of Naval Operations, 1997-99; Rank of Commander, Diplomacy Section of Naval Staff, London, 1999-2001; Special Representative for International Trade and Investment, 2001-; Admiral of the Sea Cadet Corps, 1992-; Colonel-in-Chief, Staffordshire Regiment, 1989-; Royal Irish Regiment, 1992-; Royal New Zealand Army Logistic Regiment, Small Arms School Corps, Royal Highland Fusiliers (Princess Margaret's Own and Ayrshire Regiment), 9th/12th Royal Lancers (Prince of Wales's); Honorary Air Commodore RAF Lossiemouth, Morayshire; Patron of over 90 organisations including: Greenwich Hospital, Fight for Sight, Defeating Deafness, Jubilee Sailing Trust, Royal Aero Club; Trustee, National Maritime Museum, Greenwich; Chair, Trustees Outward Bound Trust; Captain, Royal and Ancient Golf Club of St Andrews; Member, Advisory Board of Governors, Lakefield College School; Commodore Royal Thames Yacht Club; Elder Brother, Trinity House.

YORK Michael (Michael York-Johnson), b. 27 March 1942, Fulmer, England. Actor. m. Patricia McCallum, 1968. Education: University College, Oxford. Appointments: Dundee Repertory Co, 1964, National Theatre Company, 1965; Guest Lecturer, Chair, CA Youth Theatre. Creative Works: TV appearances include: The Forsyte Saga; Rebel in the Grave; True Patriot; Much Ado About Nothing; Jesus of Nazareth; A Man Called Intrepid; For Those I Loved; The Weather in The Streets; The Master of Ballantrae; Space; The Far Country; Are You My Mother, 1986; Ponce de Leon, Knot's Landing, 1987; The Four Minute Mile, The Lady and the Highwayman, The Heat of the Day, 1988; A Duel of Love, The Road to Avonlea, 1990; Teklab, 1994; September, A Young Connecticut Yankee in King Arthur's Court, Not of This Earth, 1995; The Ring, True Women, 1996; The Haunting of Hall House, 2000; The Lot, 2001; Founding Fathers, Founding Brothers; La Femme Musketeer, 2004; Radio: Jane Eyre, Alice in Wonderland, 2002; The Trial of Walter Raleigh, 2003; Films include: The Return of the Musketeers, 1988; Till We Meet Again, The Heat of the Day, 1989; The Night of the Fox, Eline Vere, Duel of Hearts, 1990; The Wanderer, The Long Shadow, Wide Sargasso Sea, Rochade, 1991; Discretion Assured, 1993; The Shadow of a Kiss, Fall From Grace, 1994; Gospa, 1995; Goodbye America, Austin Powers, Dark Planet, 1996; The Ripper, 1997; A Knight in Camelot, Perfect Little

Angels, Wrongfully Accused, One Hell of a Guy, 1998; The Omega Code, 1999; Borstal Boy, 2000; Megiddo, 2001; Austin Powers in Goldmember, 2002; Moscow Heat, 2004; Scarface: The World is Yours (voice), 2006; Flatland: The Movie, 2007; Numerous TV appearances; Music: Christopher Columbus: A Musical Journey, 2002; Enoch Arden, 2003. Publications: The Courage of Conviction, 1986; Voices of Survival, 1987; Travelling Player (autobiography), 1991; Accidentally on Purpose (autobiography), 1992; A Shakespearian Actor Prepares, 2000; Dispatches From Armageddon, 2002. Honours: Numerous. Address: c/o Andrew Manson, 288 Munster Road, London SW6 6BQ, England. Website: www.michaelyork.net

YORK Susannah, b. 9 January 1942, London, England. Actress. m. Michael Wells, 1960, divorced 1976, 1 son, 1 daughter. Education: Royal Academy of Dramatic Art. Creative Works: Films include: Tunes of Glory, 1960; The Greengage Summer, 1961; Freud, 1962; Tom Jones, 1963; The Seventh Dawn, 1964; Act One Scene Nun, 1964; Sands of the Kalahari, 1965; Scruggs, 1966; Kaleidoscope, 1966; A Man for All Seasons, 1966; Sebastian, 1967; The Killing of Sister George, 1968; Duffy, 1968; Lock Up Your Daughters, 1969; They Shoot Horses, Don't They?, 1969; Country Dance, 1970; Jane Eyre, 1970; Zee and Co, 1971; Happy Birthday Wanda June, 1971; Images, 1972; The Maids, Gold, 1974; Conduct Unbecoming, 1974; That Lucky Touch, 1975; Skyriders, 1976; Eliza Fraser, 1976; The Shout, 1977; The Silent Partner, Superman II, 1980; Yellowbeard, Fatal Attraction, 1985; A Summer Story, 1987; Melancholia, 1988; Just Ask for Diamond, 1988; Princess, 1993; Loop, 1997; So This Is Romance?, 1998; Jean, 2000; The Book of Eve, 2002; Visitors, 2003; The Gigolos, 2006; Maude, 2007; TV appearances: The Crucible; Fallen Angels; Second Chance; We'll Meet Again; The Other Side of Me; Macho; Trainer; Devices and Desires; Ruth Rendell Mysteries; St Patrick, The Irish Legend; Holby City; Casualty; Numerous stage appearances. Publications: Childrens books: In Search of Unicorns; Larks Castle. Honours include: Best Actress Award, Cannes Film Festival.

YORKE Margaret, (Margaret Beda Nicholson), b. 30 January 1924, Surrey, England. Writer. 1 son, 1 daughter. Appointments: Assistant Librarian, St Hilda's College, Oxford, 1959-60; Library Assistant, Christ Church, Oxford, 1963-65; Chairman, Crime Writers Association, 1979-80. Publications: Summer Flight, 1957; Pray Love Remember, 1958; Christopher, 1959; Deceiving Mirror, 1960; The China Doll, 1961; Once a Stranger, 1962; The Birthday, 1963; Full Circle, 1965; No Fury, 1967; The Apricot Bed, 1968; The Limbo Ladies, 1969; Dead in the Morning, 1970; Silent Witness, 1972; Grave Matters, 1973; No Medals for the Major, 1974; Mortal Remains, 1974; The Small Hours of the Morning, 1975; Cast for Death, 1976; The Cost of Silence, 1977; The Point of Murder, 1978; Death on Account, 1979; The Scent of Fear, 1980; The Hand of Death, 1981; Devil's Work, 1982; Find Me a Villain, 1983; The Smooth Face of Evil, 1984; Intimate Kill, 1985; Safely to the Grave, 1986; Evidence to Destroy, 1987; Speak for the Dead, 1988; Crime in Question, 1989; Admit to Murder, 1990; A Small Deceit, 1991; Criminal Damage, 1992; Dangerous to Know, 1993; Almost the Truth, 1994; Pieces of Justice, 1994; Serious Intent, 1995; A Question of Belief, 1996; Act of Violence, 1997; False Pretences, 1998; The Price of Guilt, 1999; A Case to Answer, 2000; Cause for Concern, 2001. Honours: Swedish Academy of Detection, 1982; Cartier Diamond Dagger, Crime Writers Association, 1999 Address: c/o Curtis Brown Ltd, Haymarket House, 28/29 Haymarket, London SW1Y 4SP, England.

YOSHIDA Fumitake, b. 20 March 1913, Saitama, Japan. Professor Emeritus, Kyoto University. m. Kazuko, deceased, 1 son, 1 daughter. Education: BEng, 1937, Dr Eng, 1951, Kyoto University. Appointments: Chemical Engineer, Hitachi Ltd, 1937-45; Assistant Professor, 1945-51, Professor, 1951-76, Professor Emeritus, 1976-, Kyoto University; Visiting Fellow, Yale University, 1952; Research Fellow, University of Wisconsin, 1959; Visiting Professor, University of California, Berkeley, 1963; Visiting Professor, University of Pennsylvania, 1970; Guest Professor, University of Dortmund, 1987. Publications: Around 60 research papers; Book: Chemical Engineering and Artificial Organs, with Sakai, in Japanese, 1993. Honours: Distinguished Service Citation, University Wisconsin, 1988; Honorary Dr Ing, University of Dortmund, 1992. Memberships: National Academy of Engineering, USA; American Institute of Chemical Engineers; American Chemical Society; Society Chemical Engineers, Japan; Japanese Society of Artificial Organs. Address: 2 Matsugasaki-Yobikaeshi, Sakyo-ku, Kyoto 606-0912, Japan.

YOSHIDA Hiroshi, b. 5 August 1962, Sasebo, Nagasaki, Japan. Doctor; Educator; Scientist. m. Mayumi Watanabe, 1 son. Education: MD, 1987, PhD, 1999, National Defence Medical College; Medical Diplomate, Japan, 1987. Appointments: Lieutenant Colonel, Medical Department, Ground Staff Office, Japan Defence Agency, 2000-2001; Instructor, 2001-2003, Assistant Professor, 2003-, Department of Internal Medicine, Chief Physician of General Medicine, 2003-, Associate Professor, Director, 2007-, Department of Laboratory Medicine, Jikei University School of Medicine. Publications: Articles as first author and co-author in medical journals including: ATVB, 1997, 1998; Biochemical Journal, 1998; Atherosclerosis, 1998, 2005; Biochemical Pharmacology, 1999; Current Opinion in Lipidology, 2003; Journal of Lipid Research, 2003; Clinical Science, 2005; Clinica Chimica Acta, 2004, 2005. Honours: Award for Outstanding Publication Article, National Defence Medical Society, 2000; Encouragement Prize, Japanese Society of Laboratory Medicine, 2004. Memberships: Fellow, Japanese Society of Internal Medicine, 1993-; Fellow Japanese Circulation Society, 1994-; Councillor, Japan Atherosclerosis Society; American College of Physicians; Fellow, American Heart Association, 2006; Fellow, American College of Physicians, 2007. Address: Division of General Medicine, Department of Internal Medicine, Kashiwa Hospital, Jikei University School of Medicine, 163-1 Kashiwashita, Kashiwa, Chiba, 277-8567 Japan. E-mail: hyoshida@jikei.ac.jp

YOSHIDA Tsuguo, b. 12 September 1952, Yokosuka City, Japan. Physician; Professor. m. Shizue Komori, 1 son, 2 daughters. Education: Bachelor of Science, Tokyo University of Education, Tokyo, 1971-76; Doctor of Medicine, University of Tsukuba, Tsukuba City, 1979-86; MS in Education, Meisei University, Tokyo, 2004-2006. Appointments: Systems Engineer, IBM, Tokyo, Japan, 1976-79; Physician Tsukuba University Hospital, 1986-92; Part-time Radiologist, Tsukuba Municipal Hospital Tsukuba City, 1986-2006; Associate Professor, Tsukuba College of Technology, Tsukuba City, 1992-2004; Professor, Tsukuba University of Technology, Ibaraki Prefecture, Japan, 2005-. Publications: Articles in medical journals conference proceedings include: Evaluation on Surface and Deep Temperature of Phantom Irradiated by Pulsed or Continuous Microwaves, 1997; Mental health of the visually and hearing impaired students from the viewpoint of University Personality Inventory, 1998; Making Tactile Charts on a Personal Computer for Blind Students in the Allied Health Professions, 2002; MRI of Testicular

Epidermoid Cyst, 2004. Honours: Life Science Foundation, 1992, The Telecommunication Advancement Foundation, 1999. Memberships: MENSA International, London; Consultant, Tsukuba City Office, Tsukuba City, Ibaraki Prefecture, Japan, 2001-2006, Address: 2-15-30 Higashi, Tsukuba City, Ibaraki Prefecture, Japan 305-0046. E-mail: tyoshida@k.tsukuba-tech.ac.jp

YOSHIOKA Shoichi, b. 3 November 1962, Okayama, Japan. Geophysicist. m. Masako Kunita. Education: BSc, Kobe University, Japan, 1985; MSc, 1987, PhD, 1990, Kyoto University, Japan. Appointments: Postdoctoral Fellow, Kyoto University, Japan, 1990-91; Postdoctoral Fellow, University of Tokyo, 1991-92; Postdoctoral Fellow, Utrecht University, The Netherlands, 1992-94; Assistant Professor, Ehime University, Matsuyama, Japan, 1994-97; Associate Professor, Kyushu University, 1997-. Publications: Contributor of numerous articles to professional journals. Memberships: American Geophysical Union; Seismological Society of Japan. Address: Aquitaine 203, Maimatsubara 5-12-5, Higashi Ward, Fukuoka 813-0042, Japan.

YOUNG Allan Edward, b. 21 June 1939, Brooklyn, New York, USA. University Professor. 1 son, 2 daughters. Education: BA, SUNY, New York, 1961; MBA, 1963, PhD, 1967, Columbia University. Appointments: Professor, Syracuse University; Research Professor, Curtin University. Publications: 10 books; Over 100 articles. Honours: Fulbright Awards, 1991-92, 2005. Memberships: Financial Management Association. Address: 27 Ely Drive, Fayetteville, NY 13066, USA. E-mail: aeyoung@som.syr.edu

YOUNG Gordon, b. 25 April 1928, Macclesfield, Cheshire, England. Architect (Lecturer). m. Hélène Regina, 2 daughters. Education: Articled pupil in office of Dobson Chapman & Associates, 1944-47; Architectural Student, Victoria University, Manchester School of Architecture, 1944-49; Professional Diploma, Architecture, 1950; Postgraduate Diploma, French government, 1960. Appointments: Architectural Assistant, R A Riseley, Architect, Macclesfield, Cheshire, England, 1950-56; Assistant Design Architect, Architect-in-Chief's Department, Adelaide, Australia, 1956-59; Postgraduate Research Scholar, French Ministry of Construction, 1959-60; Lecturer, 1960-70, Lecturer in charge, second year Architectural Studio, 1970-83, Senior Lecturer in charge, second year Design and Environmental Studies, 1979-83, Senior Lecturer in charge, fifth year Architecture Design and Environmental Studies, 1983-87, Retired, 1987-, Architecture and Building, School of Architecture, SAIT; Design Architect, Housing Research and Development Section, Department of Architecture and Civic Design, Greater London Council, England, 1969-70; Visiting Fellow and Lecturer, School of Humanities, Flinders University, South Australia, 1987-93; Founder, Director, South Australian Centre for Settlement Studies. Publications: Numerous conference papers and journal articles; Books include: Design of Doctors Surgeries handbook, 1984; Part-author, Discover the Barossa, 2000-03. Memberships: Elected Associate, Royal Institute of British Architects; Elected Fellow, Royal Institute of Australian Architects.

YOUNG Henry E, b. 5 December 1951, Dayton, Ohio, USA. m. Valerie, 1976, 1 daughter. Education: BS, Biology, Ohio State University, 1974; MS, Zoology, University of Arkansas, 1977; PhD, Anatomy, Texas Tech University, 1983; Postdoctoral Fellow, Glycoconjugate Biochemistry, Case Western Reserve University, 1983-87. Appointments: Graduate Student Teaching Assistant, University of

Arkansas, 1975-77; Graduate Student Teaching Assistant, Texas Tech University Health Sciences Center, 1978-83; Postdoctoral Fellow, Muscular Dystrophy Association of America, 1983-85; Postdoctoral Fellow, NIH Fellowship in Developmental Biology, Case Western Reserve University, 1985-87; Instructor, Rush-Presbyterian-St Luke's Medical Center, Chicago, 1987-88; Assistant Professor of Anatomy, 1988-95, Director of Embryology, 1988-, Co-Director of Histology, 1988-93, Associate Professor of Anatomy, 1995-, Full Professor of Anatomy (with tenure), 2004-, Division of Basic Medical Science, Adjunct Assistant Professor of Surgery, 1988-94, Interim Director of Surgical Research, 1988-89, Assistant Director of Surgical Research, 1989-94, Department of Surgery, Adjunct Associate Professor of Pediatrics, 1995-, Adjunct Full Professor of Pediatrics, 2004-, Department of Pediatrics, Mercer University School of Medicine, Macon, Georgia. Publications: Over 50 articles in professional scientific journals; 4 US patents. Honours include: Hooding Award, 1993, 1994, Gender Equity Award, 1997, Mercer University School of Medicine; Humanism in Medicine Award, Arnold P Gold Foundation, 2005; Inductee, Gold Humanism Honor Society, 2005; Numerous invited presentations and seminars. Memberships: American Association of Anatomists; American Society for Cell Biology; Federation of American Societies for Experimental Biology; Society for In Vitro Biology; The Wound Healing Society; Society for Experimental Biology and Medicine; Society of Regenerative Medicine and Stem Cell Biology; Gold Humanism Honor Society. Address: Mercer University School of Medicine, 1550 College Street, Macon, GA 31207, USA. E-mail: young_he@mercer.edu

YOUNG Ian George, b. 5 January 1945, London, England. Poet; Writer; Editor. Appointments: Director, Catalyst Press, 1969-80, Director, TMW Communications, 1990-. Publications: Poetry: White Garland, 1969; Year of the Quiet Sun, 1969; Double Exposure, 1970; Cool Fire, 1970; Lions in the Stream, 1971; Some Green Moths, 1972; The Male Muse, 1973; Invisible Words, 1974; Common-or-Garden Gods, 1976; The Son of the Male Muse, 1983; Sex Magick, 1986. Fiction: On the Line, 1981. Non-Fiction: The Male Homosexual in Literature, 1975, 2nd edition, 1982; Overlooked and Underrated, 1981; Gay Resistance, 1985; The AIDS Dissidents, 1993; The Stonewall Experiment, 1995; The Aids Cult, 1997; The Beginnings of Gay Liberation in Canada, 2005; Out in Paperback, 2007. Honours: Several Canada Council and Ontario Arts Council Awards. Membership: International Psychohistory Association. Address: 2483 Gerrard Street East, Scarborough, Ontario M1N 1W7, Canada.

YU Chang Yeon, b. 10 November 1956, HoengSong, Gangwondo, Korea. Professor. m. Jung Mi Cho, 1 son. Education: BS, Kangwon National University, Chunchon, Korea, 1982; MS, Seoul National University, Korea, 1984; PhD, University of Illinois, Urbana-Champaign, USA, 1991. Appointments: Committee, Biogreen 21 Project, RDA, Korea, 2002-04; Director, Bioherb Research Institute, 2004-, Dean, Agricultural Education & Training, 2005-, Kangwon National University; Vice President, Korean Medical Crop Science, 2005-; Editor in Chief, Korean Society of Medicinal Crop Science, 2005-. Publications: Comparison of resveratrol, SOD activity, phenokc compounds and free amino acids in R glutinosa under temperature and water stress; Resveratrol synthase transgene expression and accumulation of Resveratrol glycocide. Honours: Excellent Scientist Award, Korean Society for Medicinal Crop Science, 1999; Excellent Science Paper Award, Korean Federation of Science and Technology, 2003. Memberships: Korean Society for Medicinal Crop

Science; Korean Breeding Society; Plant Resources Society, Korea. Address: Division of Applied Plant Science, Kangwon National University, Chunchon 200-701, Korea. E-mail: cyyu@kangwon.ac.kr

YU Kwang-Won, b. 7 July 1964, Geumsan, Chungnam, Korea. Professor. m. Kyu-Sun Lee, 1 son, 1 daughter. Education: BSc, Department of Food Engineering, Korea University, 1987; MSc, Department of Food Engineering, Korea University, 1989; PhD, Department of Life Science, Graduate School of Korea University, 2000. Appointments: Food Researcher, The Central Research Center, Daihan Sugar Co Ltd, 1989-94; Foreign Researcher, The Oriental Medicine Research Center, Kitasato Institute, Japan, 1996-98; Assistant Professor, Department of Kimchi and Food Science, College of Cheongju National Science and Technology, 2001-06; Vice Professor, Division of Food and Biotechnology, Chungju National University, 2006-. Publications: Numerous articles in professional journals. Honours: Listed in Who's Who in the World 2008 and American Biographical Institute, 2008. Memberships: Korean Society of Food Science and Technology; Korean Society of Food and Nutrition. Address: Division of Food and Biotechnology, Chungju National University, Jeungpyueong-eup Yonggang-ri 24, Jeungpyeong-gun, Chungbuk 368-701, Republic of Korea. E-mail: kwyu@cjnu.ac.kr

YUSHINA Ludmila Dmitrievna, b. 14 October 1929, Kazan, Tatarstan, USSR. Physico-Chemist. m. Brajnin Semion Abramovich, 1 son. Education: Diploma with distinction, Ural State University, 1947-52; Diploma of the Candidate of Chemical Sciences, 1958; Diploma of Doctor Chemical Sciences, 1984; Diploma of Corresponding Member, 2004, Diploma of Academician, 2006, Russian Academy of Natural History. Appointments: Scientific Counsellor, Institute of High Temperature Electrochemistry, 1986-; Master of Shop at Optical Plant, 1952-53, Scientific Worker, Institute of Electrochemistry, 1953-, Russian Academy of Sciences, Ural Division. Publications: Author, over 170 publications in different scientific journals; 1 monograph; 14 inventions. Honours: Medal, 1970; Medal, 1979; Veteran of Labour medal, 1984; Over 40 diplomas, 1960-; Daughter of Russia medal, 2002; Medal of Order for merit in front of native land, 2005. Memberships: International Society for Solid State Ionics; New York Academy of Sciences; Academician, Russian Academy of Natural History; European Academy of Natural History. Address: Institute of High Temperature Electrochemistry, Ural Division, Russian Academy of Sciences, St S Kovaleskoj 20, Ekaterinburg 620219, Russia.

Z

ZABUSKY Norman J, b. 4 January 1929, New York, USA. Visiting Professor. m. Charlotte Fox Zabusky, 1 son, 2 daughters. Education: BEE, Magna cum Laude, College of the City of New York, 1947-51; MS, Electrical Engineering, Massachusetts Institute of Technology, 1951-53; PhD, Physics, California Institute of Technology, 1955-59. Appointments: Visiting Research Associate in Physics, Princeton University Plasma Physics Research, 1960-61; Member of Technical Staff, Supervisor of Plasma Physics, Department Head of Computational Physics Research Department, Bell Laboratories, 1971-76; Professor of Mathematics, University of Pittsburgh, 1976-88; State of New Jersey Professor of Computational Fluid Dynamics, Department of Mechanical and Aerospace Engineering, Rutgers University, 1988-2006; Visiting Professor, Weizmann Institute of Science, Physics of Complex Systems, 2006-; Consultant and Scientific Visitor: Naval Research Laboratory, Washington DC, 1976-91, Los Alamos Scientific Laboratory, 1983-94, Institute of Laser Engineering, Osaka, Japan, 2001; Director, ScArt4 (Science and Art International Symposium), New Brunswick, New Jersey, 2005. Publications: Book: Topics in Non-Linear Physics (editor), 1966; Over 300 publications in refereed journals and conference proceedings, including: Interaction of "Solitons" in a Collisionless Plasma and the Recurrence of Initial States, 1965; Scientific computing visualization – a new venue in the arts, 2000. Honours: Howard Hughes Fellow, 1955-57; Standard Oil Company of California Fellow, 1958-59; National Science Foundation Postdoctoral, 1959-60; Fellow, American Physical Society, 1970-; J S Guggenheim Memorial Foundation Fellowship, 1971-72; Howard N Potts Medal, Franklin Institute (shared), 1986; Kiev Non-Linear Medal, 1989; Jacobs Professor of Applied Physics, Rutgers University, 2000-2003; Otto LaPorte Award, American Physical Society, Division of Fluid Dynamics, 2003. Membership: Fellow, American Physical Society. Address: Weizmann Institute of Science, Physics of Complex Systems, 76100 Rehovot, Israel. E-mail: norman.zabusky@gmail.com

ZACHARIASSON Toini Maria, b. 14 March 1943, Hedenaeset, Sweden. Director; Business Owner. Education: Computer Degree, Scandinavian School, Gothenburg, Sweden, 1974; Degree, Philosophy, Stockholm University, Sweden, 1980. Appointments: Clerk, Executive, The Defence Office, Stockholm, 1962-64; Secretary of Business, Eriksson, Stockholm, 1964-79; Secretary of Parliament, 1979-82; Director of Business, Hedenaeset, Norrbotten, Sweden, 1982-88, 1988-; Taxation Professional, The Central Party, Stockholm, 1977-88. Memberships: Volunteer, Marine Defence, Sweden; Member, The Central Party. Address: Lasarettsgatan 55B, S-98234 Gallivare, Norrbotten, Sweden.

ZACHARY Stefan Hedley, b. 30 June 1948, Leeds, England. Designer. m. Patricia, 2 sons, 1 daughter. Education: Pre-Diploma, Harrogate School of Art, 1966-67; BA (Hons), 3-D Design, Leeds College of Art, 1967-70; Passed Joint First Cadet, Royal Military College, Sandhurst, 1975. Appointments: Designer, Conran Design Group, 1970-71; Chief Interior Designer, Duport Group, 1971-; Associate Partner, Howard Sant Architects, 1971-77; Group Managing Director, McColl Group plc, 1977-92; Managing Partner, Zachary Design, 1992-. Publications: Chartered Society of Designers (CSD) Works Agreement, 1983, 1989; CSD Works Agreement Guide, 1983; CSD Code of Conduct, 1990. Honours: Founder and Life Honorary Joint President, Design Business Association, 1989; Liveryman, Painter-Stainers, 1989; Freeman City of London, 1989. Memberships:

Past President, Chartered Society of Designers; Fellow, Royal Society of Arts; Fellow, British Institute of Interior Design, 1982; British Council of Shopping Centres, 1995. Address: Little Moseley House, Naphill, Bucks HP14 4RE, England. E-mail: zacharydesign@btconnect.com Website: www.zacharydesign.com

ZAHARIE Gabriela Corina, b. 18 September 1966, Cluj Napoca, Romania. Physician. m. Toader, 2 sons. Education: MD, 1990, PhD, 2000, Master in Clinical Pharmacology, University of Medicine & Pharmacy, Cluj Napoca. Appointments: Physician, Clinical Hospital of Adulh Cluj, 1990-92; Resident in Medicine-Paediatrics, Childrens Hospital of Cluj Napoca, 1992-95; Assistant Professor, 1993-2001, Associate Professor, Department of Neonatology, 2001-, Puericulture Department of University of Medicine & Pharmacy, Cluj Napoca. Publications: 45 articles; 2 books: Cresterea Copilului, 2001; Puericulture, 2003. Memberships: L'union Medicale Balcanique; Societatea Romana de Perinatologie; Asociatia Romana Neonatologie. Address: Str Decebal 96, Cluj Napoca, 400205, Romania. E-mail: gabriela_zaharie@yahoo.com

ZAID Shakir Tor Ishaq, b. 6 June 1961, Oakland, California, USA. Pastor; Chief Executive Officer; Founder. m. Nette Pierce, 5 sons, 2 daughters. Education: Doctor of Divinity, Master in Theology, Speaker Association (Toast Master); Motivational Speakers School. Appointments: Pastor, Founder and Teacher, Rapture International Ministries; Chief Executive Officer, Marceau Nicyia Investment, Zaid Inc, Zaid Films, Movies, Books, Internet, Motivational Speaker, Mentor, TV Talk Show Host "Ask Shak". Honours: Honorary Director General, IBC; Man of the Year, 2006; Doctor of Divinity; Master of Theology; Listed in Who's Who publications and biographical dictionaries. Address: 1271 Washington Ave, San Leandro, California 94577, USA. E-mail: drshakirzaid@minister.com

ZAK Vladimir, b. 13 December 1929, Moscow, former USSR. Musicologist. m. Maya Korsunskaya, 1 son. Education: BA, Music Composition, 1947, MA, Summa Cum Laude, Musicology, 1952, Moscow Conservatory; Doctorate, Musicology, 1979, Post-doctoral Degree, Music Theory, 1989, National Institute for the Study of Arts under the Ministry of Culture of the USSR. Appointments: Participant in documentary music films, 1959-; Composer of music for theatre and TV shows, 1959-; Lecturer on own original music analysis theory at dozens of scientific musicology seminars in the former USSR as well as 23 international music symposiums in many countries, 1962-; Deputy Chairman, 1962-86, Chairman, 1986-91, Musicology Commission of the USSR Union of Composers; Lecturer in America, Jewish organisations, Holocaust Survivor's centres, radio, TV, City University of New York Graduate Center, 1991-; Advisor, International Émigré Association of Arts and Sciences, New York, 1993-; Consultant, MusicaRussia Foundation, New York, 2003-; Board Advisor, "Russian Music. Past and Present", 2005-. Publications: Author of 5 books on classical and contemporary music; Monographs include: Melodics of the Popular Song, 1979; Laws of Song Melodics, 1990; Schostakovich and the Jews, 1997; More than 200 articles include: Asafiev's theory of intonation and the analysis of popular song, 1982; The Wondrous World of Popular Intonation, 1985; O Melodike Josepha Haydna, 1982; Chaikovsky's Melodies, 1990; Shostakovich's Idioms, 1998; Remembering, 2000; Jüdisches und Nicht-Jüdisches bei Schostakovich, 2003; Die Hoffnung Bleibt, 2003; Dmitri Shostakovich and

Children? 2003. Honours: First Prize Winner, B Asafiev's Competition of Musicologists of the USSR, 1982; State Order of Honour, USSR, 1986; Certificate of Appreciation, Council of Jewish Émigré Community Organizations and International Émigré Association of Arts and Sciences, 2003; Silver Medal of Honour, International Biographical Association, 2004. Memberships: Russian Union of Composers, 1962-; Association of Eastern European Jews, 1993-; International Émigré Association of Arts and Sciences, 1993-; MusicaRussia Foundation, 2003-; Russian-American Cultural Heritage Center. Address: 731 West 183rd Street, Apt 3L, New York, NY 10033, USA. E-mail: a_zak@hotmail.com

ZAKHARCHENKO Irina, b. 19 July 1946, Rostov-on-Don, Russia. X-ray Physicist. m. Krivitskii V V, 2 sons. Education: Graduate, Department of Physics,1969; PhD, Physics and Mathematics, 1978, Rostov State University. Appointments: Junior Researcher, 1969-77; Senior Researcher, 1978-92; Leading Researcher, Laboratory of Ferroelectric Thin Films, Institute of Physics, Rostov State University, 1993-. Publications: Several articles for professional journals. Memberships: International Union of Crystallography. Address: Institute of Physics, Rostov State University, Pr Stachky 194, Rostov-on-Don 344090, Russia. E-mail: zinik@ip.rsu.zu

ZAMANI Adil, b. 5 May 1960, Alma-Ata, Kazakhstan. Professor of Medicine. m. Ayse Gül, 2 sons. Education: MD, Sechenov First Moscow Medical Institute, Moscow, 1986. Appointments: Research Fellow, Department of Chest Diseases and TB, Ankara University Hospital, Ankara, Turkey, 1987-91; Visiting Research Fellow, Department of Respiratory Medicine, University of Edinburgh, 1991; Assistant Professor, 1993-96, Assistant Head Physician, 1997-98, Associate Professor, 1996-2002, Professor, 2002-, Department of Chest Diseases, Selçuk University Hospital, Konya, Turkey; Visiting Research Fellow, Department of Thoracic Medicine, London Chest Hospital, 1993-94; Associate Professor, Lieutenant, Department of Chest Diseases, Gülhane Military Academy, Ankara, Turkey, 1998-2000. Publications: Numerous articles on pulmonology in Turkish and foreign medical journals, conference proceedings, book chapters; Music Albums for Classical Guitar; Compositions; Classical Guitar Magazine, England; Soundboard Magazine (GFA), USA. Honours: The Living Composers List, USA; Classical Guitar Composers List, USA; Guitar Reference (editor V Pocci), Italy; Listed in Who's Who publications and biographical dictionaries. Membership: President, Working Group of Diagnostic Methods, Turkish Thoracic Society, 2003-06. Address: Nalcaci Cad., Saglik Apt, 5/5, 42060 Konya, Turkey. E-mail: adzamani@hotmail.com

ZAMBARAS Vassilis, b. 1 May 1944, Revmatia, Messenias, Greece. Teacher of English as a Second Language; Poet. m. Eleni Nezi, October 1980, 1 son, 1 daughter. Education: BA, English, 1970, MA, English, 1972, University of Washington, Seattle. Publications: Sentences, 1976; Aural, 1984. Contributions to: How the Net is Gripped: Selection of Contemporary American Poetry, 1992; Chiron Review; CLWN WR; First Intensity; Kater Murr's Press; Maverick Magazine; NOON: journal of the short poem; Poetry Salzburg Review; The London Magazine; The Salt River Review; Tattoo Highway; Fine-Words.com; Poetry Northwest; Madrona; West Coast Review; Wisconsin Review; Assay; Edge; Text; Smoot Drive Press; Rialto; Shearsman; Southeastern Review; Southern Poetry Review; Longhouse; Intermedio; Workshop; Falcon; Klinamen; Apopeira, Poetry Greece; Möbius, Arabesques Review. Honours: Harcourt, Brace and

Jovanovich Poetry Fellowship to the University of Colorado, Boulder, 1970; University of Washington Poetry Prizewinner, 1972. Address: 21K Fotopoulou, Meligalas 24002, Messenias, Greece.

ZANE Billy, b. 24 February 1966, Chicago, Illinois, USA. m. Lisa Collins, 1988, divorced 1995. Education: American School, Switzerland. Career: Stage: American Music, New York; The Boys in the Backroom, Chicago; Films: Back to the Future, 1985; Critters, 1986; Dead Calm, Back to the Future Part II, 1989; Megaville, Memphis Belle, 1990; Blood and Concrete: A Love Story, Millions, Femme Fatale, 1991; Posse, Orlando, Sniper, Flashfire; Tombstone, 1993; The Silence of the Hams, Cyborg Agent; Only You, 1994; Tales from the Crypt Presents: Demon Knight, Reflections in the Dark; Danger Zone, 1995; The Phantom, This World – Then the Fireworks, Head Above Water, 1996; Titanic, 1998; Taxman, Morgan's Ferry, Cleopatra, 1999; Hendrix, 2000; Invincible, The Diamond of Jeru, The Believer, 2001; Sea Devils, 2002; Vlad, Imaginary Grace, 2003; Silver City, Three, Dead Fish, Big Kiss, Kingdom Hearts: Chain of Memories, 2004; The Pleasure Drivers, The Last Drop, BloodRayne, Three, 2005; Valley of the Wolves, Memory, 2006; The Mad, Alien Agent, Fishtales, 2007; Perfect Hideout, 2008; TV: Twin Peaks; Cleopatra; Brotherhood of Justice; The Case of the Hillside Stranglers, 1989; Lake Consequence; Running Delilah; The Set Up. Address: Creative Artist Agency, 9830 Wilshire Boulevard, Beverly Hills, CA 90212, USA.

ZAPF Hermann, b. 8 November 1918, Nuremberg, Germany. Designer. m. Gudrun Zapf von Hesse, 1 son. Education: D in Fine Arts (Hon), University of Illinois, USA. Appointments: Freelance designer, 1938-; Type Director, D Stempel AG, type foundry, Frankfurt, 1947-56; Design Consultant, Mergenthaler Linotype Co, New York and Frankfurt, 1957-74; Consultant, Hallmark International, Kansas City, Missouri, 1966-73; Vice President, Design Processing International Inc, New York, 1977-86; Professor, typographic computer programs, Rochester Institute of Technology, New York, 1977-87; Chairman, Zapf, Burns and Co, New York City, 1987-91; Instructor, Lettering Werkkunstschule, Offenbach, Germany, 1948-50; Professor, Graphic Design, Carnegie Institute of Technology, 1960; Instructor, Typography Technische Hochschule, Darmstadt, Germany, 1972-81. Publications: Author: William Morris, 1948; Pen and Graver, 1952; Manuale Typographicum, 1954, 1968; About Alphabets, 1960, 1970; Typographic Variations, 1964; Orbis Typographicus, 1980; Hora fugit/Carpe diem, 1984; Hermann Zapf and His Design Philosophy, 1987; ABC-XYZapf, 1989; Poetry Through Typography, 1993; August Rosenberger, 1996; CD-ROM, The World of Alphabets, 2001; Alphabet Stories, A Chronicle of technical Developments by Hermann Zapf, 2007. Film, The Art of Hermann Zapf; Designer of over 180 typefaces. Honours: Honorary President, Edward Johnston Foundation, England; Honorary Curator, Computer Museum, Boston; Silver Medal, Brussels, 1962; 1st Prize Typography Biennale, Brno, Czechoslovakia, 1966; Gold Medal, Type Directors Club, New York; Frederic W Goudy Award, Institute of Technology, Rochester, 1969; Silver Medal, International Book Exhibition, Leipzig, 1971; Gold Medal, 1989; Johannes Gutenberg Prize, Mainz, Germany, 1974; Gold Medal, Museo Bodoniano, Parma, Italy, 1975; J H Merck Award, Darmstadt, 1978; Robert Hunter Middleton Award, 1987; Euro Design Award, 1994; Wadim Lazursky Award, Academy of Graphic Arts, Moscow, 1996; Named Honorary Citizen, State of Texas, 1970; Honorary Royal Designer for Industry, 1985; Listed in national and international biographical dictionaries. Memberships: Royal Society of Arts; American

Mathematical Society; Alliance Graphique Internationale; Bund Deutscher Grafik Designer; International Gutenberg Gessellschaft; Honorary Member, Type Directors Club, New York City; Sociéte Typographique de France, Paris; Society of Typographic Arts, Chicago; Double Crown Club, London; Letter Exchange, London; Society of Scribes and Illuminators, London; Friends of Calligraphy, San Francisco; Society of Printers, Boston; Society of Graphic Designers, Canada; Bund Deutscher Buchkünstler; Grafiska Institute, Stockholm; Typophiles, New York; Alpha Beta Club, Hong Kong; Society of Calligraphy, Los Angeles; Wynkyn de Worde Society, London; Monterey Calligrapher's Guild; Washington Calligraphers Guild; Eesti Kalligraafide Koondis, Tallinn, Estonia; Chicago Calligraphers Guild; Caxton Club, Chicago; Typographers International Association; Art Directors Club, Kansas City; Alcuin Society, Vancouver; Goudy International Centre; Brno Biennale Association; Society of Scribes, New York; Dante e V, German TEX Group, Heidelberg; Gamma Epsilon Tau. Address: D-64287 Darmstadt, Seitersweg 35, Germany.

ZARATHUSTRA Azsacra, b. 7 October 1960, Magnitogorsk, Chelyabinsk region, Russia. Professional Writer; Philosopher; Poet. 2 daughters. Education: 4 courses, Department of Literature and Russian Language, Magnitogorskiy State Pedagogical Institute. Appointments: Co-editor, Harvests of New Millennium, India. Publications: The Lotuses of Evil, 2007; America: Invasion of the Heart, 2008; Tao Kampf, 2008. Honours: Azsacra International Poetry Award, Taj Mahal, India. Memberships: The Academy of American Poets; The Haiku Society of America; The Poetry Society of Britain; World Haiku Association; International Group of the Authors Taj Mahal Review. Address: Flat 22, House 11, Voroshilova str, Magnitogorsk, Chelyabinsk region, 455048, Russia. E-mail: dragon@azsacra-zarathustra.ru Website: www.azsacra-zarathustra.ru

ZARDARI Asif Ali, b. 26 July 1955, Karachi, Pakistan. President of Pakistan. Widower of Benazir Bhutto, 1 son. Education: Graduate, Cadet College Petaro, Dadu, 1972; Business & Economics, Pedinton School, London, 1976. Appointments: Director of M/s Zardari Group (Pvt.) Ltd; Member, National Assembly, 1990-93; Member, National Assembly, 1993-96; Federal Minister, 1993; Federal Minister, 1995-96; Senator, 1997-99; President of Pakistan, 2008-.

ZAREMBKA Paul, b. 17 April 1942, St Louis, Missouri, USA. Economist. m. Beata Banas, 1 daughter. Education: BS, Mathematics, Purdue University, 1964; MS, PhD, Economics, 1967, University of Wisconsin. Appointments: Assistant Professor, Department of Economics, University of California, Berkeley, 1967-72; Visiting Professorships: Heidelberg University, 1970-71; Goettingen University, 1971-72; Associate Professor, then Professor, Department of Economics, State University of New York at Buffalo, 1973-; Senior Research Officer, World Employment Program, International Labor Office, Geneva, Switzerland, 1974-77; Researcher, Group for Research on Science, Louis Pasteur University, Strasbourg, 1978-79. Publications: Author, Toward a Theory of Economic Development, 1972; Editor, Frontiers in Econometrics, 1974; Co-editor with M Brown and K Sato, Essays in Modern Capital Theory, 1976; General Editor, Research in Political Economy, to date, 23 volumes, 1977-, including "The Hidden History of 9-11-2001", 2006, and Transitions in Latin America, Poland and Syria, 2007; Numerous articles and book chapters. Honours: Fulbright-Hayes Lecturer, Poznan, Poland, 1979; Listed in numerous biographical dictionaries. Address: Department of Economics, 415 Fronczak Hall,

State University of New York at Buffalo, Buffalo, New York 14260, USA. E-mail: zarembka@buffalo.edu. Website: http://ourworld.compuserve.com/homepages/PZarembka

ŽARSKIENE-ŠIMONYTE Ruta, b. 6 January 1964, Vilnius, Lithuania. Ethnomusicologist. 2 sons. Education: Master of Ethnomusicology, 1992, PhD, History of Art, Field Ethnomusicology, 1999, Lithuanian Academy of Music and Theatre. Appointments: Institute of Lithuanian Literature and Folklore, 1991-, Assistant, 1992-99, Research Fellow, 1999-2002, Elder Research Fellow and Head of Department of Folklore Archives, 2002-. Publications: Monographs: Music Making with Multi-Pipe Whistles in Northeastern Europe, 2003; Skudučiai and its Relations: Comparative Studies, 1993; 4 ontologies, joint author from series "Phonograph records of 1935-1941"; "Songs and Music from Suvalkijà", 2003; "Songs, Sutartinès and Instrumental Music from Aukštaitija", 2004; "Songs and Music from Žemaitija", 2005, "Songs and Music from Dzūkija", 2005; 25 scientific articles in periodicals in Lithuania, Germany, Hungary, Sweden, 1993-2006. Memberships: ICTM, 2000-; ESEM, 2002-. Address: Antakalnio str 6, LT-10308 Vilnius, Lithuania. E-mail: ruta@llti.lt

ZAVATI Constantin C, b. 7 July 1923, Bacau, Romania. Teacher. m. Iulia Bucur, 1 daughter. Education: Scoala de Baieti No 2, Bacau; Scholarship, Stefan Cel Mare Military Boarding College; Baccalauréat, Distinction, 1942; Private Merit Regiment 10; Chemistry Faculty, University Alexandru Ioan Cuza, 1947-51; MSc, honours, 1951. Appointments: Various Military Positions; Assistant Lecturer, University Alexandru Ioan Cuza and Academy Iasi, Romania; High school teacher, Chemistry and Physics, Ferdinand I Boarding College, Bacau; High school teacher, Chemistry and Physics, Head of Chemistry, Vasile Alecsandri Boarding College, Bacau; Schools Inspector for Chemistry, county/City of Bacau. Publications: Numerous scientific papers at various national conferences; Many scientific articles in newspapers and magazines under the pen name, A Tom; Co-author, 1 book on applied sciences; Organised the first modern school science laboratories in the county/City of Bacau. Honours: Citation for great bravery during the Second World War; Several Orders and Medals for Bravery in Battle; Professor Fruntas, 1964; Professor Grade 1, 1972; Advanced Captain, Major and Colonel in the Army Reserves. Memberships: Societatea de Stiinte Fizice Si Chimice; Societatea Stiintelor Medicale; First President, Radio Club, Bacau. Address: c/o Mariana Zavati Gardner, 14 Andrew Goodall Close, East Dereham, Norfolk, NR19 1SR, England.

ZAVATI Iulia Bucur, b. 19 July 1921, Racova-Bacau, Romania. Pharmacist. m. Constantin C Zavati, 26 January 1947, 1 daughter. Education: Baccalauréat with Distinct; MSc, Pharmacy, 1st class honours, University of Bucharest, Romania. Appointments: Opened own pharmacy at Valea Rea-Târgu Ocna, Romania; Pharmacist, State Pharmacy in Bacau, Romania; Appointed Principal Pharmacist; Deputy Director, Director, Oficiul Farmaceutic, City and Region Judet of Bacau-Romania; Directed, re-organised and modernised all pharmacies in Bacau; Established links with western pharmacy companies; Lecturer, Scoala Sanitara for nurses and pharmacy assistants in Bacau. Honours: Medals and Orders for modernising and re-organising pharmacies in Bacau. Membership: Romanian Society of Pharmacists. Address: c/o Andrew Goodall Close, East Dereham, Norfolk NR19 1SR, England.

ZAYRATIYANTS Oleg Vadimovich, b. 24 September 1958, Moscow, Russia. Pathologist. m. Tatiana G Barsanova, 1 son. Education: Physician, Moscow State University of Medicine and Dentistry, 1981; Pathologist, 1982, Candidate of Medical Sciences, 1987, MD, Doctor of Medical Sciences, 1993, Moscow I M Sechenov Medical Academy; Professor, Russian Medical Academy of Postgraduate Education, 1997. Appointments: Pathologist, Moscow Clinical Hospital 61, 1981-87; Assistant, Docent, Department of Pathology, Moscow I M Sechenov Medical Academy, 1987-94; Professor, Department of Pathology, Russian Medical Academy of Postgraduate Education, 1994-95; Chief Pathologist, Department of Health Care of Moscow, Russia, 1995-; Chief, Moscow City Centre of Pathological Academy, A A Ostroumovsky Moscow Clinical Hospital 33, 1995-; Chief, Department of Pathology, Moscow State University of Medicine and Dentistry, 2002-. Publications: 6 books; 215 articles. Honours: Diploma, Moscow I M Sechenov Medical Academy, 1998; Diploma, Moscow Health Care Department, 1996; Medal of Moscow Government 850 years of Moscow, 1997; Diploma, Moscow State University of Medicine and Dentistry, 2004; World Medal of Freedom, 2007. Memberships: Moscow Society of Pathologists; Russian Society of Pathology; European Society of Pathology; International Academy of Pathology. E-mail: ovzair@mail.ru

ZEČEVIĆ Miodrag Dj, b. 4 September 1930, Topola, Serbia. University Professor Emeritus. m. Ljubica, 1 son, 1 daughter. Education: BA, Faculty of Law, 1956, BA, Faculty of Philosophy, 1961, MA, Faculty of Political Science, 1967, PhD, Faculty of Law, 1970, University of Belgrade. Appointments: Federal Secretariat for Internal Affairs and Institute of Social Sciences in Belgrade; Secretary, Political Council of the Serbian Assembly, 1960; Teacher, University of Belgrade Law School, 1961-70; President, Legislative and Juridical Committee of Parliament, Republic of Serbia, 1969-74; Professor, University of Belgrade's Faculty of Political Science, 1973-97; President, Legislative and Juridical Committee of Parliament, SFR Yugoslavia, 1974-82; High Official, Parliament of Yugoslavia, 1982-85; Federal Counsellor, Government of Federal Republic of Yugoslavia, 1985-87; Director, Archives of Yugoslavia, 1987-95. Publications: 20 books and numerous articles and studies in the field of history and law; Constitutional Law, 1975; Creation of General Enactments, 1978: Joint Interests in the Federation, 1984; The Contradictions of the Yugoslav Law, 1987; Yugoslavia 1918-1992, 1994; The Beginning of The End of the SFR Yugoslavia, 1998; Documents from Ravna Gora Trial, 2001; Hunting in Yugoslavia, Serbia and Montenegro from 1818 to 2000 – Laws, Politics and Ethics, 2002. Memberships: General Secretary, 1997-2003, President, 2004-, Yugoslav War Veterans Organisation; Former President, Yugoslav Ecology Organisation; Former President, Scientific Association of Science and Society; Member, Association for Constitutional Law; Member, Association for Political Sciences; Secretary General, Yugoslav Hunting Organisation. Address: Njegoševa 56, 11000 Belgrade, Serbia.

ZEFFIRELLI G Franco, b. 12 February 1923, Florence, Italy. Opera & Film Producer; Designer. Education: Liceo Artistico, Florence; School of Agriculture, Florence. Appointments: Designer, University Productions, Florence; Actor, Morelli Stoppa Co; Collaborated with Salvador Dali on sets for As You Like It, 1948; Designed sets for A Streetcar Named Desire, Troilus, Cressida, Three Sisters; Producer, Designer, numerous operas. Creative Works: Operas: Lucia di Lammermoor,1959, 1973; Falstaff, 1961; L'elisir d'amore, 1961; Don Giovanni, 1962, 1972, 1990; Tosca, 1964, 1966,

1973, 1985, 2000; Otello, 1972, 1976; Antony and Cleopatra, 1973; La Bohème, 1981, 2003; Turandot, 1983, 1985, 1987; Don Carlos, 1992; Carmen, 1996, 2003; Aida, 1997, 2000, 2002; La Traviata, 1998; Il Trovatore, 2001; I Pagliacci, 2003, 2005; Madame Butterfly, 2004; Theatre: Romeo and Juliet, 1960; Othello, 1961; Amleto, 1964; After the Fall, 1964; Who's Afraid of Virginia Woolf, 1964, 1965; Much Ado About Nothing, 1966; Black Comedy, 1967; A Delicate Balance, 1967; Saturday, Sunday, Monday, 1973; Filumena, 1977; Six Characters in Search of an Author, 1992; Absolutely Perhaps! 2002; Films: The Taming of the Shrew, 1966; Florence, Days of Destruction, 1966; Romeo and Juliet, 1967; Brother Sun and Sister Moon, 1973; Jesus of Nazareth, 1977; The Champ, 1979; Endless Love, 1981; La Traviata, 1983; Cavalleria Rusticana, 1983; Otello, 1986; The Young Toscanini, 1987; Hamlet, 1990; Sparrow, 1994; Jane Eyre, 1995; Tea With Mussolini, 1998; Callas Forever, 2002; Ballet: Swan Lake, 1985; Producer, Beethoven's Missa Solemnis, San Pietro, Rome, 1971. Publication: Zeffirelli by Zeffirelli (autobiog), 1986. Honours: Prix des Nations, 1976; Senator Forza Italia, 1994-2002, Cultural Collaborator, 1976, Italian Ministry of Culture and Arts; Honorary KBE, 2005. Address: Via Lucio Volumnio 45, 00178 Rome, Italy.

ZEGVELD Liesbeth, b. 1970, Ridderkerk, Netherlands. Lawyer; Professor. m. A Nollkaemper, 2 daughters. Education: Atheneum A, Rijksscholengemeenschap, Middelharnis, 1988; Study leave, Faculty of Law, University of Orleans, France, 1993; Certificate, Course on International Humanitarian Law, International Committee of the Red Cross, 1995; Degree in Law, Faculty of Law, University of Utrecht, 1995; PhD International Law, cum laude, 2000; Professor, International Humanitarian Law, in particular the Rights of Women and Children, Leiden University, 2006. Appointments: Lecturer, Public International Law, Legal Proficiency, University of Utrecht, 1994; Apprenticeship, Dutch Ministry of Foreign Affairs, Directorate Political United Nations Affairs, 1995; Visiting Researcher, Inter-American Commission on Human Rights, Washington, USA, 1998; Visiting Scholar, School of Law, New York University, New York, and American University, Washington, 1998; Guest Lecturer, European Master's Programme in Human Rights and Democratization, Venice, 1998; Lecturer and Research Associate, Erasmus University, Rotterdam, 1999; Lawyer in International Law and International Criminal Law, Amsterdam, 2000-; Guest Lecturer, Advanced Course International Refugee Law, TMC Asser Institute, The Hague, 2001; Guest Lecturer, International Refugee Law, International Responsibility, Amsterdam Center of International Law, 2002-, Guest Lecturer, Advanced International Public Law, Executive Masters in International and European Relations & Management, 2003-, University of Amsterdam; Lawyer, International Law and Human Rights Law, 2000-, Partner, 2005-, Böhler Franken Koppe Wyngaarden law firm, Amsterdam; Professor, International Humanitarian Law, Leiden University, 2006. Publications: 3 books; Numerous articles, contributions to books and book reviews. Honours: Premium Onderwijsrecht for thesis; Fulbright Grant; Cum laude doctorate; Netherlands Human Rights Award, 2000; J C Baak Award, 2002; Moddermanprijs, 2005. Memberships: Netherlands Society of International Law; International Law Association; International Law Association's Committee for Compensation for War Victims. Address: Keizersgracht 560-562, 1071 EM Amsterdam, Netherlands.

ZEHEL Wendell E, b. 6 March 1934, Brownsville, Pennsylvania, USA. Surgeon. m. Joan, 1 son, 1 daughter. Education: Pre-medical Studies, Washington and Jefferson

College; BA, Mathematics, 1956; MD, University of Pittsburgh Medical School, 1960. Appointments: Internship, Shadyside Hospital; Military Service, discharged with honour, USAF, 1961-63; Surgical Residency, University of Pittsburgh, Veterans Administration Hospital; Wilmington Medical Center, Delaware; Established own practice, Pittsburgh; Postgraduate, Carnegie-Mellon University, advanced studies in bio-engineering and computer technology. Publications: Medical Instrumentation, 1983; Novel, The Long Silk Line, 1997; Biotechnology: Physiologic and Medical Applications, 1999; Novel, Life Lines, 1999. Memberships: American College of Surgeons; American Medical Association; New York Academy of Sciences; Charles Darwin Associates; Association for the Advancement for Medical Instrumentation; American Association for the Advancement of Science. Address: 110 Fort Couch Road, 3rd Floor, Pittsburgh, PA 15241, USA.

ZELLWEGER Renée, b. 25 April 1969, Katy, Texas, USA. Actress. m. Kenny Chesney, 9 May 2005, annulled December 2005. Education: University of Texas at Austin. Appointments: Films: Dazed and Confused, 1993; Reality Bites, Love and a .45, 8 Seconds, 1994; The Low Life, Empire Records, 1995; The Whole Wide World, Jerry Maguire, 1996; Texas Chainsaw Massacre: The Next Generation, Deceiver, 1997; One True Thing, Back to the Future II, A Price Above Rubies, 1998; The Bachelor, 1999; Me, Myself and Irene, Nurse Betty, 2000; Bridget Jones' Diary, 2001; Chicago, 2002; Down With Love, Cold Mountain, 2003; Bridget Jones: The Edge of Reason, 2004; Cinderella Man, 2005; Miss Potter, 2006; Bee Movie (voice), 2007; Leatherheads, 2008; TV: Shake, Rattle and Rock Movie, 1993; Murder in the Heartland, 1994. Honours: Golden Globe Best Comedy Film Actress Award for Nurse Betty, 2001; Golden Globe Best Actress in a Musical for Chicago, 2003; Screen Actors Guild Award for Best Actress for Chicago, 2003; BAFTA Award for Best Supporting Actress, 2004; Best Supporting Actress Oscar for Cold Mountain, 2004.

ZEMECKIS Robert, b. May 1952, Chicago, USA. Film Director; Producer; Writer. m. Mary Ellen Trainor, 1980, divorced 2000, 1 son, (2) Lesley Harter, 2001-. Education: University South California. Creative Works: Films: The Life, 1972; Field of Honor, 1973; I Wanna Hold Your Hand, 1978; Used Cars, 1980; Romancing the Stone, 1984; Back to the Future, 1985; Who Framed Roger Rabbit, 1988; Back to the Future II, 1989; Back to the Future III, 1990; Death Becomes Her, 1992; Forrest Gump, 1994; Bordello of Blood, 1996; Contact, 1997; The House on Haunted Hill, 1999; What Lies Beneath, 2000; Cast Away, 2000; 13 Ghosts, 2001; Ghost Ship, 2002; Matchstick Men, 2003; Gothika, 2003; Clink Inc, 2003; Polar Express, 2004; House of Wax, 2005; Monster House, 2006; Beowulf, 2007; TV: Tales from the Crypt, 1989; Two-Fisted Tales, 1991; Johnny Bago, 1993; WEIRD World, 1995; Perversions of Science, 1997. Honours: Academy Award for Best Director, 1995. Address: c/o CAA, 9830 Wilshire Boulevard, Beverly Hills, CA 90212, USA.

ZERI Aferdita, b. 2 February 1962, Berat, Albania. Textile Engineer; Lawyer. m. Tahir Numani, 1 son, 2 daughters. Education: Textile Engineer, 1986, Laywer, 1997, Tirana University; Master on Public Administration, 2005; Doctor of Science, 2006. Appointments: Various positions in the textile industry, 1986-92; Member of Parliament, 1992-96; Various position in Public Administration, 1996-99; Executive Director, Women for Global Action, 1999-2005; Juridical Consulent and General Secretary, MND, 2005-. Publications: Numerous articles in professional journals. Honours: Science Doctor; Women Can Do It, OSCE;

Women in Politics, Parliament of California; Many other certificates and diplomas for contribution and participation in different activities. Memberships: General Secretary, MND; Coordinator, Network for a Developed Society without Arms; Board Member and Executive Director, Women for Global Action Association; Member, Role of Women in Politics Network; 3 times Candidate for Parliament; CE; OSCE; UNDP; World Bank; ILO; Oxfam; DFID; NPA; USAID; CO-PLAIN. Address: Rr Don Bosko, Pal 43, Shk 1 Ap 10, Tirana, Albania.

ZHANG Ho-Yeol, b. 19 January 1963, Busan, Korea. Medical Doctor. m. Seung-Eun Lee, 2 sons. Education: Diploma, Yonsei Medical College, 1987; Master, 1992, PhD, 2000, Yonsei University College of Medicine; Postdoctoral Researcher, Stanford University College of Medicine, 2003-04. Appointments: Internship, 1987, Resident, Department of Neurosurgery, 1988-92, Severance Hospital, Yonsei University; Captain, Republic of Korea Army, 1992-95; Assistant Professor, 1995-2002, Clinical Professor, 2003-, Department of Neurosurgery, Yonsei University College of Medicine; Chief, Department of Neurosurgery, National Health Insurance Corporation, Ilsan Hospital, 2003-. Publications: Many articles in professional journals; 10 book chapters in 3 books. Memberships: Korean Neurosurgical Society; Korean Society of Thermology; Korean Spinal Neurosurgery Society. Address: Department of Neurosurgery, National Health Insurance Corporation, Ilsan Hospital, 1232 Baeksokdong, Ilsangu, Koyang, Kyonggido, 410-719, Korea. E-mail: hyzhang@nhimc.or.kr

ZHANG Jingguo, b. 7 October 1940, Shanghai, China. Materials Scientist; Engineer. m. Ninghua Zhu, 1 son. Education: Graduate, Department of Physical Metallurgy, University of Science and Technology, Beijing, China, 1964. Appointments: Research Assistant, 1964-74, Research Engineer, 1974-80, 1980-1982 in USA, Director of Testing Centre, 1983-84, Deputy Director of Institute, Senior Engineer, 1984-87, Vice-President, Academic Committee, Associate Chief Engineer, Professor of Materials Science and Engineering, 1987-2000, Shanghai Iron and Steel Research Institute; Senior Specialist, Professor of Materials Science and Engineering, Shanghai Bao Steel Research Institute, 2000-2003; Visiting Professor, Tongji University, 2004-; Visiting Scholar, Columbia University, USA, 1980; Assistant Professor, University of Connecticut, USA, 1980-82; Senior Expert on Materials, Science & Engineering, Shanghai Society of Metals, Shanghai, China, 2005-. Publications: 38 and 48 papers published in scientific and engineering journals in English and Chinese respectively; Co-author 2 books in Chinese; Recently published papers: Structure of Amorphous Fe-Zr-B powders obtained by chemical reduction, 2002; Microstructure and CCT Thermograms of Spray Formed G Cr15 Steel, 2002; Superplastic Ultra-high Carbon Steels Processed by Spray Forming, 2003; Microstructure and Mechanical Properties of Spray Formed Ultrahigh-Carbon Steels, 2004; Co-author "Recent New Development of Spray Formed Ultrahigh-Carbon Steels", 2005. Honours: Honours and Prize for distinct achievements and contribution in engineering, The State Council of China, 1993; Li Xun Prize, Acta Metallurgica Sinica, 1993; Special Prize for Scientists in the fields of applied basic research, Science and Technology Commission of Shanghai Municipality, 1994-95, 1998-99. Memberships: Institute of Materials Science, University of Connecticut, USA, 1980-82; SAMPE, Japan, 1993-95; Board of Directors: Chinese Society of Metals, 1991-94, Chinese

Materials Research Society, 1991-2003, Chinese Stereology Society, 1991-2004. Address: Room 2603, No 12, Lane 300, Wu Ning Road, Shanghai 200063, PR China.

ZHANG Rong Ye, b. 28 December 1938, Guan Dong, China. Professor. m. Xiu Zhu Chen, 1 son, 1 daughter. Education: Graduate, Mathematics Department, Fu Dan University, Shanghai, China, 1965. Appointment: Researcher into Mathematics and Mechanics, Institute of Mathematics, Chinese Academy of Science. Publications include: RRG approximation and its estimate of the two points boundary value problem; Approximation to the solution of First Order Linear Implicit Differential-Operational Equation in Hilbert Spaces; Cauchy Problem of some Second Order Linear Differential-Operational Equation in Hilbert Spaces and its Approximate Solution; The approximate computation of the Bounded Linear Functional on Hilbert Spaces; Newtonian Mechanics on Kähler Manifold; Lagrangian vector field on Kähler Manifold; Dynamics in Newtonian Remannian Space-time; Lagrange Mechanics on Kähler Manifolds; Hamilton Mechanics on Kähler Manifolds. Membership: Academician of the Chinese Academy of Computing Mathematics. Address: Room 403, Building 906, Zhong guan cun, Beijing 100086, China. E-mail: zry@math.ac.cn

ZHAO Gong Yun, b. 5 March 1955, China. Associate Professor. m. Zhi-Qian Wan, 1 son. Education: PhD, Würzburg University, Germany, 1991. Appointments: Teaching Fellow, Lecturer, Senior Lecturer, Associate Professor, National University of Singapore, 1992-. Publications: More than 30 articles published in journals including: Mathematical Programming; Mathematics of Operations Research; SIAM Journal on Optimization. Honour: Award of Commonwealth Fellowship, 2000-2001. Membership: International Advisory Committee, 15th International Symposium on Mathematical Programming. Address: Department of Mathematics, National University of Singapore, Republic of Singapore. E-mail: matzgy@nus.edu.sg Website: www.math.nus.edu.sg/~matzgy

ZHOU Yuming, b. 23 June 1934, Hebei, China. Senior Translator. m. Shuying Li, 2 sons. Education: Graduate, Faculty of Foreign Languages and Literature, University of Central China, 1956. Appointments: Assistant Professor, University of Central China, 1956; English Translator, Chinese Ministry of the Petroleum Industry, 1974; Senior Translator, China National Offshore Oil Corporation, 1984; Retired 1994; Senior Translator, Enron Oil and Gas China Ltd, 1994-1999; Retired from Enron Oil and Gas, China, 1999. Publications: Books of modern lyrics: Flowing Bunch of Flowers; Kiss of Wings; Love of Dolphin; The Tenderly Grown Green; Selected Poems of Yuming; Earth Newborn; Selected Verses by Yuming; Books of long epic poems: Liang Shanbo and Zhu Yingtai – Chinese Romeo and Juliet; Love Between a Human Being and a Serpentine Being; Far Away Off the Milky Way (extracts in book: Eternal Motherlove, 2005); Two Verse Dramas ("Moses" and "Salem"); Verse Dramas: Wordless Longing and Wedding Date. Honours: Gold Prize of the Chinese Long "Dragon" Culture; Award, International Poet of Merit, International Society of Poets, America; Honorary Doctor of Literature of the World Academy of Arts and Culture; Distinguished Leadership Award, American Biographical Institute; Man of the Year 2002, ABI; The Founders Award, IBC; Universal Award of Accomplishment; American Medal of Honor; ABI World Laureate of China; Worldwide Honours List, IBC; First Class Award for Far Away Off the Milky Way, Chinese Ministry of Culture, 2005. Memberships: China Poetry Association; Member and Membership Director, World

Congress of Poets; Distinguished Member, International Society of Poets. Address: 233, Building 7, Ruyili, Western District, Beijing 100035, China.

ZHOU Zhi-Hua, b. 20 November 1973, Guangzhou, China. Professor. m. Yuan Jiang. Education: BSc, 1996, MSc, 1998, PhD, 2000, Computer Science, Nanjing University, Nanjing China. Appointments: Lecturer, 2000-2002, Associate Professor, 2002-2003, Professor, 2003-, Department of Computer Science and Technology, Nanjing University, Nanjing, China. Publications: Widely published in the fields of artificial intelligence, machine learning, data mining, pattern recognition. Honours: National Excellent Doctoral Dissertation Award of China, 2003; Award of National Science Fund for Distinguished Young Scholars of China, 2003; Matopma; Science & Technology Award for Young Scholars of China, 2006. Memberships: Associate Editor, Knowledge and Information Systems; Editorial Board Member: Artificial Intelligence in Medicine, International Journal of Data Warehousing and Mining, Journal of Computer Science and Technology; Journal of Software. Address: National Laboratory for Noval Software Technology, Nanjing University, Nanjing 210093, China. Website: http://cs.nju.edu.cn/people/zhouzh

ZIA Mohammad Ramin, b. 17 February 1964, Iran. Education: First Honour Diploma, Calligraphy, Iran Calligraphers Association, Tehran, Iran; Certificate, Executive Management, Industrial Management Institute, Tehran, Iran; BA, TV Production (Graphic), Islamic Republic of Iran Broadcasting, Tehran, Iran; MA, Graphic Design, Doctor of Fine Arts (Aesthetics and Sacred Arts), and Doctor of Philosophy, Complementary Health Studies (Holistic Psychotherapy), MA-Master of Arts (Counselling Psychology), and Professorship (Fine Arts), Calamus International University (CIU), British West Indies; Certificate, Holistic Health Practitioner, American Association of Drugless Practitioners; Post-Doctorate, Holistic Sciences, Universal University, USA/Panama; Doctor of Science (Clinical Psychotherapy), Post-Doctorate, Visual Arts (Education and Programming), Grand Doctor of Philosophy in Non-Traditional and Alternative Medicine (Specializing Holisticology), and Professorships (Visual Arts, and Holisticology), International University of Fundamental Studies (IUFS), Saint Petersburg, Russia; Qualifications: A) Visual Arts: Photography, Calligraphy and Typography, Sacred Arts and Aesthetics, Graphic Designing and Advertising, Arts Management; B) Holistic Sciences: Complementary Health and Healing, Yoga and Meditation, Psychotherapy and Counselling, Art Therapy, Metaphysics and Spirituality; C) Education: Multi-national and Integrated Educational Programming, Higher-Education Leadership, Course Creating, Research Proposal, and Curriculum Development. Appointments: Chairman of the Board (Founder, Principal and Academic Dean), Lotus Educational Institute FZ-LLC, Professional Training Centre, Dubai Knowledge Village, United Arab Emirates. Publications: Compiler/lecturer, editor in chief/writer of several books and articles/manuscripts and research proposals, course syllabuses, and educational programmes. Honours: Listed in international biographical dictionaries: Man of the Year 2006 in the fields of Education, Arts, Counselling, and Healing, International Commendation of Success in the profession of Higher-Education Leadership, 2007 Gold Medal for the UAE, Great Minds of the 21st Century for Founding Holisticology, and Outstanding Intellectuals of the 21st Century 2007 in the fields of Visual Arts, Holisticology, and Education. Memberships: American Association of Drugless Practitioners, IUFS (MVAK- IHEC) International Higher Examination Council and International Council of Secondary Education (ICSE); International

Advisory Boards and Exclusive Authorized Representative of CIU and IUFS. Address: PO Box 500016, DXB, United Arab Emirates. E-mail: DrZia@lotus.ae Website: www.lotus.ae

ZIMET Lloyd, b. Brooklyn, New York, USA. Health Psychologist; Educator. m. Jeanne. Education: BA, Whittier College, 1973; MA, College of Health & Human Performance, 1983, PhD, 1984, University of Maryland; Master of Public Health, New York University, 1989. Appointments: Postdoctoral Researcher, NYU School of Nursing, New York University AIDS Regional Training Center, 1988-89; Director of Prevention/Education, AIDS Center of Queens County, 1989-90; Camp Director, World of Discovery Day Camp, 1998-2000; Consultant, International Community and Occupational Health, 1984-; Prevention Specialist, Division of Health Services, Hillsborough County Public Schools, Florida, 2004-08. Publications: Numerous articles in professional journals. Honours: Keynote Speaker, US Public Health Service, 1991; Listed in international biographical dictionaries. Memberships: American Psychological Association; American Public Health Association; American Alliance for Health, Physical Education, Recreation and Dance.

ZLOCHEVSKAYA Alla, b. 10 November 1951, Moscow, Russia. Literary Critic; Researcher. Education: MA, Philology, Moscow State University; Defended and published 2 literary research theses: PhD equivalent, 1982 and 2002. Appointments: Research Worker, 1985-2000, Senior Researcher, 2000-, Department of Philology, Moscow State University, Russia. Publications: Published more than 80 research articles concerning Russian literature of XIX-XX centuries and Czech and Slovak Rusistik; In-depth study of F Dostoyevsky, V Nabokov, M Bulgakov; Monograph: Artistic World of V Nabokov and Russian Literature of XIX Century, 2002. Membership: F M Dostoyevsky Society, Moscow. Address: Olympic Village 8, Flat 153, Mitchurinsky Pr. Moscow 119602, Russia. E-mail: zlocevskaya@mail.ru

ZOLBERG Vera L, b. 22 September 1932, Vienna, Austria. Sociology Professor. m. Aristide R Zolberg, 1 son, 1 daughter. Education: AB, Hunter College, 1953; MA, Boston University, 1956; PhD, University of Chicago, 1974. Appointments: Edgewood College, Madison, Wisconsin, 1962-64; St Xavier College, Chicago, 1964-67; Purdue University, 1974-84; Professor, New School for Social Research, 1984-. Publications include: After Bourdieu: Influence, Critique, Elaboration; Outsider Art: Contested Boundaries in Contemporary Culture; The Happy Few-en Masse: Franco-American Comparisons in Cultural Democratization; Constructing a Sociology of the Arts. Honours: Rockefeller Humanities Fellowship; ACLS Fellowship; Many travel grants; Listed in Who's Who publications and biographical dictionaries. Memberships: American Sociological Association; Society for Social Theory, Politics and the Arts; International Sociological Association; Association Internationale des Sociologues de Langue Francaise; Eastern Sociological Society. Address: New School for Social Research, 65 5th Avenue, New York City, NY 10003, USA.

ZUBRITSKY Alexander, b. 14 March 1949, Severo-Kurilsk, Sakhalin Region, Russia. Pathologist. 2 sons. Education: Curative and Preventative Faculty, Sverdlovsk Medical Institute, 1968-74; 1 year specialism in Pathological Anatomy, Sverdlovsk Regional Clinical Hospital No 1, 1975; Advanced Training Course for Pathological Anatomy, Kharkov, Ukraine Institute of Advanced Medical Studies, 1977; Advanced Training Course for Perinatal Pathology, Moscow Institute for

Postgraduate Medical Training, 1986; PhD, 1991; Advanced Training Course for Cytology, Moscow Regional Research Clinical Institute, 1994; Pathological Anatomy, Russian Medical Academy for Postgraduate Training, 2000, 2006; Advanced Training Course for Histological Diagnostics of Endometrium Scrape, Research Centre of Obstetrics, Gynaecology and Perinatology, Russian Academy of Medical Sciences, 2004; Advanced Training Course for Diagnostics of Soft Tissue Tumors, 2008. Appointments: Hospital Attendant, Department of Pathology, City Hospital No 21, Sverdlovsk, 1965-67; Hospital Attendant, Medico-Legal Morgue No 1, Sverdlovsk, 1967-68; Chief of Pathology Department, Central Regional Hospital in Neviyansk, Sverdlovsk Region, 1975-76; Chief of Pathology Department, Head Pathologist, Sverdlovsk Road, 1976-83; Lecturer, Pathological Anatomy, Medical School of Sverdlovsk Road, 1976-77; Chief of Department of Pathology, Municipal Institution, Taldom Central Regional Hospital, Taldom, Moscow Region, 1983-; Pathologist, Pathology Department, City Clinical Hospital No 81, Moscow, 2004. Publications: 4 rationalisation proposals; 180 published works as sole author. Honours: Certificate, A Finalist, Marvin I Dunn Award, Best Poster Presentation in Cardiology, American College of Chest Physicians, 1990; Pathology Research Practice Award for the Expert Quiz, Innsbruck, MD Taldom, 1993; International Man of the Year, 1994-95; Certificate, Researcher of the Year, ABI, 2001; International Peace Prize Winner, UCC, 2003; 21st Century Award for Achievement (Bronze Medal), IBC, 2003; Gold Medal International Scientist of the Year 2004, IBC; The World Medal of Freedom for significant accomplishments in the field of Pathological Anatomy, ABI, 2005; 2005 Man of Achievement Award for Outstanding Contributions to Pathological Anatomy of Cor Pulmonale, ABI, 2005; The Best People of Russia Medal, 2006; Gold Medal for Russia, ABI, 2007. Memberships: European Society of Pathology, 1989; International Union Against Tuberculosis and Lung Disease, 1990; European Section, International Society for Heart Research, 1992; International Society on Diagnostic Quantitative Pathology, 1994; New York Academy of Sciences, 1995; Research Board of Advisors, ABI, 2000; Honorary Member, IBC Advisory Council, 2000; American Association for the Advancement of Science, 2003; Research Fellow, ABI, 2005; Atlantic-Euro-Mediterranean Academy of Medical Sciences, 2006; Academic Board , Atlantic-Euro-Mediterranean Academy of Medical Sciences, 2008. Address: Prospekt Mira 101B/79, Moscow 129085, Russia. E-mail: alex_26zubr@yahoo.com

ZUCCONI Paolo, b. 4 December 1950, Trieste, Italy. Neuro Psychotherapist. m. 2 daughters. Education: Psychologist Degree, specialisation in cognitive and behavioural psychotherapy; European Certificate of Psychotherapy; Postgraduate of: Communication, addiction, forensic psychology, neuropsychology, Clinical sexology, hypnosis; Master in clinical nutrition, Phytotherapy and Clinical Sexology. Appointments: Assistant Professor, Triest University; Teacher of General Psychology; Psychotherapist in hospital; Adjunct Professor of Clinical Methodology. Honours: Associate Fellow of Albert Ellis Institute for Rational Emotive Behaviour Therapy, New York; Diplomate in Behavioural Medicine, International Academy of Behavioural Medicine, Counselling and Psychotherapy Inc; Decree of Merit, Outstanding Scientist of the 21st Century, IBC; European Certificate of Psychotherapy, EAP; Knight of the Order of Merit of the Italian Republic; World Certificate for Psychotherapy; European Certificate of Hypnosis. Memberships: International Society of Hypnosis; Certified Hypnotherapist of National Guild of Hypnotists;

European Association for Behaviour and Cognitive Therapy. Address: Casella Postale 183, 33100 Udine, Italy. Website: www.dr-zucconi.it

ZUCHA Rudolf O, b. 14 October 1940, Vienna, Austria. Psychologist; Editor. 1 son. Education: PhD, Psychology, Anthropology, Philosophy, University of Vienna, 1970; Postdoctoral studies in Psychotherapy and Social Sciences. Appointments: Editor in Chief, Zeitschrift fuer Sozialpsychologie und Gruppendynamik; Expert Witness, Organizational Psychology; Speaker, Consultant; Author; Senior Lecturer, University of Vienna. Publications: Articles in professional journals. Honours: Recipient, Forderungspreis fuer Erwachsenenbildung, City of Vienna, 1979; Professor, Government of Austria, 1999. Memberships: Verein fuer Psychologie, Padagogie und Psychotherapie; Osterreich-Amerikanische Gesellschaft. Address: Fraungrubergasse, 5/4/13, A-1120 Wien, Austria. E-mail: rudolf.zucha@blackbox.at

ZUCKER-FRANKLIN Dorothea, b. 9 August 1930, Berlin, Germany. Physician, Scientist. m. Edward C Franklin, deceased, 1 daughter. Education: BA, Hunter College, New York, 1952; MD, New York Medical College, New York, 1956; Post-Doctoral Fellowships: Department of Hematology, Montefiore Hospital, Bronx, 1959-61; Department of Anatomy, New York University School of Medicine, 1961-63. Appointments include: Assistant Professor of Medicine 1963-68, Associate Professor of Medicine 1968-74, Professor of Medicine 1974-, Department of Medicine, New York University School of Medicine. Publications include: Numerous articles in professional journals. Honours include: Phi Beta Kappa; AOA; Henry Moses Prize for Research, 1973, 1985; Elected member, Institute of Medicine of the National Academy of Sciences, 1995; Woman of the Year Award, American Women in Science, 1996; Fellow, American Association for the Advancement of Science, 1997; Doctor of Science, honoris causa, City University of New York, 1996; Elected, American Academy of Arts and Sciences, 2001; Listed in several biographical dictionaries. Memberships include: Numerous scientific societies including: FASEB, 1966-; American Society of Clinical Investigations, 1973; American Association of Physicians, 1974; American Association of Immunologists, 1979-; Greater New York Blood Program Ad Hoc committee for donor notification, criteria and protocols AIDS study, 1982-84; IV International Symposium on Amyloid-Organizing Committee, 1983-84; VA AIDS Center Grant Review Panel, 1988 and 1989; Member of Board of Directors, Henry M and Lillian Stratton Foundation Inc, 1987-95; Many other Ad Hoc NIH and academic committees at various institutions; Institute of Medicine, National Academy of Science, 1995; President, American Society of Hematology, 1995. Address: New York University School of Medicine, Department of Medicine, 550 First Avenue. New York, NY 10016, USA.

ZUCKERMAN Jane Nicola, b. London, England. Medical Practitioner. m. Education: MB BS, 1987, MD, 1996, University of London; CBiol MIBiol, 2000; MFPM (by distinction), 2000, FFPM (by distinction), 2002, FFPHM (by distinction), 2005, Royal College of Physicians; FRCPath (by distinction), Royal College of Pathologists, 2003; FIBiol, 2003; ILTM, Higher Education Academy, 2005; FFTM, Royal College of Physicians & Surgeons, Glasgow, 2006. Appointments: House Physician, Cardiology and General Medicine, 1987-88, Senior House Officer & Registrar, Accident & Emergency and Intensive Care Unit, 1989-91, Royal Free Hospital; House Surgeon, General Surgery and

Orthopaedics, Northwick Park Hospital, 1988; Senior House Officer, Medical Rotation, Harefield Hospital & Regional Unit, Mt Vernon Hospital, 1988-89; Clinical Research Fellow & Acting Senior Registrar, Occupational Medicine, Royal Free Hospital School of Medicine & Royal Free Hampstead NHS Trust, 1991-95; Senior Clinical Research Fellow & Honorary Consultant, Academic Unit of Travel Medicine and Vaccines, Royal Free Hospital School of Medicine, 1995-97; Medical Director, Royal Free Clinical Trials Centre, Royal Free & University College Medical School & Royal Free Hampstead NHS Trust, 1995-2004; Medical Consultant, Royal Free Hospital School of Medicine British Airways Travel Clinic jointly with the Hampstead Group Practice, London, 1995-98; Senior Lecturer & Honorary Consultant (1998), Academic Centre for Travel Medicine & Vaccines, WHO Collaborating Centre for Travel Medicine & Department of Immunology & Infectious Diseases, Royal Free & University College Medical School & Royal Free Hampstead NHS Trust, 1997-; Medical Director, Royal Free Travel Health Centre, Royal Free & University College Medical School, 1999-. Publications: Numerous articles and papers in professional medical and scientific journals. Honours: Special Achievement Award for European Clinical Research, 1999; UK Hospital Doctor of the Year 2001 Award, 2001; UK Hospital Doctor Innovation Award for 2001; Listed as one of 82 Pioneers in patient care: NHS consultants leading change, 2001; Listed as one of the Women of the Year, 2002. Memberships: British Association of Pharmaceutical Physicians; British Association of Research Quality Assurance; Institute of Clinical Research; Society of Pharmaceutical Medicine; International Society of Travel Medicine; Forum for Hepatitis B and Travellers; British Infection Society; Medical Research Society; United Kingdom Paediatric Vaccine Group; London Infectious Disease Research Network Collaborative Research – Viral Hepatitis. Address: The Academic Centre for Travel Medicine & Vaccines, WHO Collaborating Centre for Reference, Research & Training in Travel Medicine, Royal Free and University College Medical School, Royal Free Campus, Rowland Hill Street, London NW3 2PF, England. E-mail: j.zuckerman@medsch.ucl.ac.uk

ZUK Gerald, b. 25 October 1929, Chicago, Illinois, USA. Psychologist. m. Carmen Zuk, 2 daughters. Education: PhD, Psychology, University of Chicago, 1955. Appointments: Full Professor and Associate Director in Psychiatric Institutes and Medical Colleges, 1956-86; Currently semi-retired doing clinical research, writing and consulting with colleagues. Publications: Nearly 100 publications include: Books: Family Therapy : a Triadic-Based Approach, 2nd edition, 1981; Process and Practice in Family Therapy, 2nd edition, 1986; The Psychology of Delusion, 2005; Articles in professional journals. Honours: Fellow, American Psychological Association; Listed in Who's Who publications and biographical dictionaries. Membership: American Psychological Association. Address: 7620 Hollister Avenue, #219, Goleta, CA 93117, USA.

ZUK Carmen Veiga, b. 5 March 1939, Buenos Aires, Argentina. Child Psychiatry. m. Gerald H Zuk, 2 daughters. Education: MD, University of Buenos Aires; Residency, Medical College of Pennsylvania, USA. Appointments: Part-time worker in psychiatric clinics in several California counties, Los Angeles, Ventura, Santa Barbara, USA; Partner, Kaiser-Permanente, Southern California, USA; Private practice, Buenos Aires, Argentina. Publications: Co-author, articles in Contemporary Family Therapy; Co-author, articles in Argentine psychiatric journals; Co-author, Psychology of Delusion. Honours: Diplomate, American Board of Psychiatry and Neurology; Listed in international biographical dictionaries. Memberships: American Medical Association;

International Society for Adolescent Psychiatry. Address: 7620, No 219, Hollister Ave, Goleta, CA 93117, USA. E-mail: carmenzuk@msn.com

ZWIERZCHOWSKI Henryk, b. 24 October 1926, Lódź, Poland. Orthopaedic Surgeon. m. Danuta Anna Zuchowicz, 2 sons. Education: MD, Medical University, Lódź, 1952; PhD, 1964; DSc, 1974; Specialist of Orthopaedics and Traumatology, 1957. Appointments: From Assistant to Senior Assistant, 1952-63, Consultant, Outpatient Clinic, 1958-74, Orthopaedic Hospital, Lódź; From Lecturer to Assistant Professor, Orthopaedic Clinic, 1964-78, Head of Orthopaedic Clinic, 1979-83, Associate Professor, 1984-91, Professor, 1991-, Head of Orthopaedic Department, 1984-97, Medical University, Lódź; Active Member, Scientific Council of the Surgical Institute, Lódź, 1976-87; Member of Editorial Committee, Chirurgia Narządów Ruchu i Ortopedia Polska (Journal of the Polish Society of Orthopaedics and Traumatology, 1984-; Regional Consultant, Orthopaedics and Traumatology, Lódź, 1995-98. Publications: Author or co-author of 176 research articles, clinical reviews and research reports published in various scientific periodicals as well as 5 books all related to the area of orthopaedics, traumatology and rehabilitation of the motor system; patentee prosthese of crutiate ligament, 1993. Honours: Cavalier Cross of the Order Polonia Restituta, 1984; Golden Badge, Polish Society for Fight with Cripleness Award, 1984; Ministers Award, 1985, 1987, 1995; Honorary Member, Polish Orthopaedics and Traumatology Society, 1996; Consulting Editor, Contemporary Who's Who, ABI, 2003. Memberships: Polish Society for Fight with Cripleness, 1964-90; Polish Orthopaedics and Traumatology Society, 1952-, Vice-President, 1982-86, Chairman Lódź Branch, 1979-82, 1987-90. Address: Zachodnia 12, Apt 63, 91-058 Lódź, Poland.

ZYAZIKOV Murat Magometovich, b. 10 September 1957, Osh, Kirgizstan. Politician. m. Rukiyat, 3 sons. Education: Diploma in History, Checheno-Ingushetian State University, 1980; KGB of the USSR Supreme Courses, 1984; Diploma in Law, South-Russian Humanitarian Institute, 2002; Doctor of Philosophical Science, 2003. Appointments: Official, State Security Committee, CHIASSR, 1984-92; Deputy Head, Federal Security Services, Russian Federation on the Republic of Ingushetia, Secretary of Security Council of the Republic of Ingushetia, 1992-96; Deputy Head, Department of the Federal Security Serivces, Russian Federation on Astrakhan region, 1996-2002; Deputy, Plenipotentiary Representative of the President of Russia, Southern Federal district, 2002; President of the Republic of Ingushetia, and Member of the State Council of the Russian Federation, 2002-. Publications: 4 books; More than 100 scientific papers including: A Traditional Ingush Culture: History and Contemporaneity, 2004; Ethnoconcepts of the Culture of the Ingush Nation, 2004. Honours: Numerous national and international honours and awards; Rank of General-Lieutenant of the Federal Secuity Services of the Russian Federation. Address: Magas, Republic of Ingushetia, prospectus Idrisa Zyazikova, 14, Administration of the President of the Republic of Ingushetia, 386000, Russia. E-mail: ingpress@yandex.ru

20th CENTURY HONOURS LIST

NAME: Dr Farid A Akasheh LFIBA

ADDRESS: PO Box 2173
Amman
Jordan

OCCUPATION: Doctor (Consultant Obstetrician and Gynaecologist)

YEAR OF ENTRY: 1986

CITATION: For your Outstanding Contribution to Medicine

- -

NAME: Abdullatif A R Al-Bahar

ADDRESS: PO Box 89
Safat
13001 Kuwait City
Kuwait

OCCUPATION: Director General, Office of H H The Crown Prince &
Prime Minister - Kuwait

YEAR OF ENTRY: 1989

CITATION: For you Outstanding Contribution to his present position
within the field of Political & Economics Institutions

- - - - - - - - - - - - - - - - - - - -

NAME: Ahmad Mohamad Ali

ADDRESS: Islamic Development Bank
PO Box 5925
Jeddah 21432
Saudi Arabia

OCCUPATION: President, Islamic Development Bank

YEAR OF ENTRY: 1990

CITATION: For your Outstanding Contribution to the Banking
Business

- - - - - - - - - - - - - - - - - - - -

NAME: Jacob Oladele Amao DDG LFIBA

ADDRESS: PO Box 51722
Ikoyi
Lagos
Nigeria

OCCUPATION: Company President – Executive

YEAR OF ENTRY: 1990

CITATION: For your Outstanding Contribution to the Banking
Business

- - - - - - - - - - - - - - - - - - -

NAME: Professor Basile Angelopoulos MD PhD LPIBA

HonDG

ADDRESS: Ipsilamtou Str 37
Athens 106-76
Greece

OCCUPATION: Professor in Pathologic Physiology

YEAR OF ENTRY: 1986

CITATION: For your Outstanding Contribution to Medicine

- - - - - - - - - - - - - - - - - - -

NAME: Kathlyn Ballard LPIBA

ADDRESS: 40 Mont Victor Road
Kew
3101 Melbourne
Australia

OCCUPATION: Artist

YEAR OF ENTRY: 1986

CITATION: For your Outstanding Contribution to Art

- - - - - - - - - - - - - - - - - - -

NAME: Abdul Rahman Batal LPIBA LFWLA DDG

 AdVBus

ADDRESS: Chairman, Hannibal Tourism & Transport Co
 PO Box 4088
 Damascus
 Syria

OCCUPATION: Company Chairman

YEAR OF ENTRY: 1986

CITATION: For your Outstanding Contribution to Tourism and
 Transport

- - - - - - - - - - - - - - - - - - -

NAME: Shauna D Boulton LFIBA DDG

ADDRESS: 1516 Glen Arbor
 Salt Lake City
 UT 84105
 USA

OCCUPATION: Educator

YEAR OF ENTRY: 1986

CITATION: For your Outstanding Contribution to Education

- - - - - - - - - - - - - - - - - - -

NAME: Richard E Butler LFIBA

ADDRESS: 40 Barrington Avenue
 Kew
 Victoria 3101
 Australia

OCCUPATION: International Official

YEAR OF ENTRY: 1990

CITATION: For your Outstanding Contribution to International
 Cooperation and to World-wide Telecommunication
 Development

- - - - - - - - - - - - - - - - - - -

NAME: Professor Chen Jian Hong

ADDRESS: Gansu University of Tech
Lanzhou
Gansu
China

OCCUPATION: President, Professor

YEAR OF ENTRY: 1989

CITATION: For your Outstanding Contribution to the Science and Education of China

- - - - - - - - - - - - - - - - - - -

NAME: Thomas J Cleary

ADDRESS: 933 Kiowa
Burkburnett
TX 76354
USA

OCCUPATION: Clinical Social Worker, Teaching Assistant, Graduate Student US History MSU

YEAR OF ENTRY: 1989

CITATION: For your Outstanding Contribution to Social Work Service

- - - - - - - - - - - - - - - - - - -

NAME: The Hon Dame Dr Joy Beaudette Cripps N.H DGC DCMSS IOM LFWLA MOIF LDAF

ADDRESS: 3 Mill Street
Aspendale
Victoria 3195
Australia

OCCUPATION: Publisher, Poet, Photographer

YEAR OF ENTRY: 1988

CITATION: For your Outstanding Contribution to Literature

- - - - - - - - - - - - - - - - - - -

NAME: Basil V Damálas

ADDRESS: Parission 171
Athens 112 52
Greece

OCCUPATION: Publicist and Economist

YEAR OF ENTRY: 1986

CITATION: For your Outstanding Contribution to Economics

- - - - - - - - - - - - - - - - - - - -

NAME: Dr J Edward Dealy MS PhD

ADDRESS: 1040 W Rio Guaymas
Green Valley
AZ 85614-4026
USA

OCCUPATION: Forestry

YEAR OF ENTRY: 1986

CITATION: For your Outstanding Contribution to Forestry

- - - - - - - - - - - - - - - - - - - -

NAME: Thaneswari De Silva LPIBA

ADDRESS: 148/2A Kynsey Road
Colombo 8
Sri Lanka

OCCUPATION: Estate Proprietoress and Directress 'Leighton Park'
Montessori and Junior School

YEAR OF ENTRY: 1986

CITATION: For your Outstanding Contribution as Montessori and
Junior School Directress

- - - - - - - - - - - - - - - - - - - -

NAME:	Howard M Dupuy Jr BA LLP
ADDRESS:	465 NE 181st Avenue = 110
	Portland
	OR 97230
	USA
OCCUPATION:	Lawyer
YEAR OF ENTRY:	1986
CITATION:	For your Outstanding Contribution to The Law

- - - - - - - - - - - - - - - - - - - -

NAME:	Chris Economides
ADDRESS:	6 Dositheos
	PO Box 1632
	Nicosia
	Cyprus
OCCUPATION:	Director
YEAR OF ENTRY:	1988
CITATION:	For your Outstanding Contribution to Economics

- - - - - - - - - - - - - - - - - - - -

NAME:	Professor M Gembicki MD
ADDRESS:	Department of Endocrinology
	University School of Medicine in Poznan
	Al Przybyszewskiego 49
	PL-60 355, Poland
OCCUPATION:	Doctor
YEAR OF ENTRY:	1986
CITATION:	For your Outstanding Contribution to Medicine

- - - - - - - - - - - - - - - - - - - -

NAME: Dr Richard Sherwin Gothard

ADDRESS: Gothard House
Henley-on-Thames
Oxon RE9 1AJ
England

OCCUPATION: Information Scientist

YEAR OF ENTRY: 1986

CITATION: For your Outstanding Contribution to Information
Science

- - - - - - - - - - - - - - - - - - - -

NAME: Violet Edna Hobbs Hain

ADDRESS: 3530 Raymoor Road
Kensington
MD 20895
USA

OCCUPATION: Artist

YEAR OF ENTRY: 1986

CITATION: For your Outstanding Contribution to Art

- - - - - - - - - - - - - - - - - - - -

NAME: Dr Kazuyuki Hatada DDG LFIBA IOM

ADDRESS: Department of Mathematics
Faculty of Education, Gifu University
1-1 Yanagido, Gifu City
Gifu Prefecture 501-1193, Japan

OCCUPATION: Mathematician

YEAR OF ENTRY: 1990

CITATION: For your Outstanding Contribution to Pure
Mathematics, especially to the Theory of Modular
Forms

- - - - - - - - - - - - - - - - - - - -

NAME: Professor Zuey-Shin Hsu MD LFIBA DDG IOM MOIF

ADDRESS: Department of Physiology
Kaohsiung Medical College
No 100 Shih-Chuan 1st Road, Kaohsiung
Taiwan

OCCUPATION: Professor of Physiology

YEAR OF ENTRY: 1989

CITATION: For your Outstanding Contribution to Medical Science and the Teaching Profession

- - - - - - - - - - - - - - - - - - - -

NAME: Dr Drago Ikic LFIBA

ADDRESS: Croation Academy of Sciences and Arts
Gunduliceva 24/11
Zagreb 10000
Croatia

OCCUPATION: Doctor

YEAR OF ENTRY: 1986

CITATION: For your Outstanding Contribution to Medicine

- - - - - - - - - - - - - - - - - - - -

NAME: Kristjan G Kjartansson

ADDRESS: Einimelur 7
107 Reykjavik
Iceland

OCCUPATION: Company Vice President

YEAR OF ENTRY: 1986

CITATION: For your Outstanding Contribution to Commerce

- - - - - - - - - - - - - - - - - - - -

NAME: Professor Lidia Agnes Kozubek

ADDRESS: ul J Dabrowskiego 77m.9
02-503 Warsaw
Poland

OCCUPATION: Pianist, Educator and Musicologist

YEAR OF ENTRY: 1986

CITATION: For your Outstanding Contribution to Music

- - - - - - - - - - - - - - - - - - - -

NAME: Dato Dr Sip Hon Lew

ADDRESS: 15 Jalan 12
Taman Tun Abdul Razak
Ampang Jaya
Selangor, Malaysia

OCCUPATION: Company Director, Retired Ambassador

YEAR OF ENTRY: 1988

CITATION: For your Outstanding Contribution to the economic,
political and cultural life of Malaysia and to your role in
the larger world community

- - - - - - - - - - - - - - - - - - -

NAME: Konstantin Mandic IOM

ADDRESS: PO Box 672
Gaborone
Botswana
Africa

OCCUPATION: Architect

YEAR OF ENTRY: 1989

CITATION: For your Outstanding Contribution to Architecture

- - - - - - - - - - - - - - - - - - -

NAME: Professor Dr Mitsuo Masai

ADDRESS: Faculty of Engineering
Kobe University
Rokkadai-Cho, Nada-Ku
Kobe 657
Japan

OCCUPATION: University Professor

YEAR OF ENTRY: 1986

CITATION: For your Outstanding Contribution to Catalysis

- - - - - - - - - - - - - - - - - -

NAME: Emeritus Professor Junji Matsumoto LFIBA IOM

ADDRESS: 2-3-14 Asukano Minami
Ikoma City
630-01 Japan

OCCUPATION: Neuroscientist

YEAR OF ENTRY: 1988

CITATION: For your Outstanding Contribution to Science

- - - - - - - - - - - - - - - - - -

NAME: Professor Seiichi Matsumoto

ADDRESS: Yuigahama 1-11-17
Kamakura 248-0014
Japan

OCCUPATION: Director and Professor

YEAR OF ENTRY: 1986

CITATION: For your Outstanding Contribution to Medicine

- - - - - - - - - - - - - - - - - -

NAME: Ralph E Montijo DDG IOM LPIBA

ADDRESS: 7811 E Edison St
Tucson
AZ 85715-4255

OCCUPATION: Company President, Executive

YEAR OF ENTRY: 1987

CITATION: For your Outstanding Contribution to Business

- - - - - - - - - - - - - - - - - - - -

NAME: Peggy Jean Mueller IOM

ADDRESS: PO Box 5868
Austin
TX 78763
USA

OCCUPATION: Dance Teacher/Choreographer

YEAR OF ENTRY: 1990

CITATION: For your Outstanding Contribution to Dancing,
Ranching and Trail Riding

- - - - - - - - - - - - - - - - - - - -

NAME: Hassenally Nanuck LFIBA

ADDRESS: PO Box 40346
Gaborone
Botswana

OCCUPATION: Auto Body Mechanic and Panel Beater

YEAR OF ENTRY: 1992

CITATION: For your Outstanding Contribution to Auto Body
Mechanics and Panel Beating

- - - - - - - - - - - - - - - - - - - -

NAME: Dr Wilson Reid Ogg LPIBA LFWLA DDG MOIF

ADDRESS: Pinebrook at Bret Harte Way
1104 Keith Avenue
Berkeley
CA 94708
USA

OCCUPATION: Poet, Graphic Illustrator, Publisher, Retired Lawyer
and Educator

YEAR OF ENTRY: 1991

CITATION: For your Outstanding Contribution to the Legal
Profession

- - - - - - - - - - - - - - - - - - - -

NAME: Masa Aki Oka DDG

ADDRESS: 3-24-15-401
Tsurumaki
Setagaya-ku
Tokyo 154
Japan

OCCUPATION: Businessman

YEAR OF ENTRY: 1991

CITATION: For your Outstaniding Contribution to Finance and
Banking

- - - - - - - - - - - - - - - - - - - -

NAME: Dr Irene M K Ovenstone LFIBA

ADDRESS: 10 Moor Road
Calverton
Nottingham
NG14 6FW
England

OCCUPATION: Consultant Psychiatrist

YEAR OF ENTRY: 1986

CITATION: For your Outstanding Contribution to Psychiatry

- - - - - - - - - - - - - - - - - - - -

NAME: Dr Pritam Singh Panesar LFIBA DDG

ADDRESS: PO Box 46235
Nairobi
Kenya

OCCUPATION: Engineer and Pilot

YEAR OF ENTRY: 1986

CITATION: For your Outstanding Contribution to Engineering

- - - - - - - - - - - - - - - - - - - -

NAME: Dr Lucy T Parker LPIBA DDG IOM

ADDRESS: 205 Harbor Drive
Sitka
AK 99835-7552
USA

OCCUPATION: Director, The Parker Academy

YEAR OF ENTRY: 1986

CITATION: For your Outstanding Contribution to Education

- - - - - - - - - - - - - - - - - - - -

NAME: Robert Al Serlippens LPIBA IOM

ADDRESS: c/o Vanderbeck
2 Chemin Coparty Bte 5
B1400 Nivelles
Belgium

OCCUPATION: Attorney at Law

YEAR OF ENTRY: 1986

CITATION: For your Outstanding Contribution to The Law

- - - - - - - - - - - - - - - - - - - -

NAME: Dr Isadore Shapiro BChE PhD DDG IOM

ADDRESS: PO Box 16737
Beverly Hills
CA 90209
USA

OCCUPATION: Material Scientist

YEAR OF ENTRY: 1990

CITATION: For your Outstanding Contribution to Science

- - - - - - - - - - - - - - - - - - - -

NAME: Carolyn Juanita Shearer LFIBA

ADDRESS: 205 South Tucson Circle
Aurora
CO 80012
USA

OCCUPATION: Educator

YEAR OF ENTRY: 1990

CITATION: For your Outstanding Contribution to Education

- - - - - - - - - - - - - - - - - - - -

NAME: Dr Muhammad M Mukram Sheikh PhD HLFIBA
DDG

ADDRESS: PO Box 1974
Gaborone
Botswana

OCCUPATION: Government Official, Marketing Executive, Public
Relations Specialist

YEAR OF ENTRY: 1992

CITATION: For your Outstanding Contribution to Trade Journalism

- - - - - - - - - - - - - - - - - - - -

NAME: Daphne Marjorie Sheldrick

ADDRESS: David Sheldrick Wildlife Trust
Box 15555
Nairobi
Kenya

OCCUPATION: Authoress and Wildlife Specialist

YEAR OF ENTRY: 1989

CITATION: For your Outstanding Contribution to Wildlife
Conservation

- - - - - - - - - - - - - - - - - - - -

NAME: Professor Koki Shimoji MD DDG LFIBA

ADDRESS: 45-304 Yarai-Cho
Shinjuku-Ku
Tokyo 162-0805
Japan

OCCUPATION: Professor and Chairman

YEAR OF ENTRY: 1986

CITATION: For your Outstanding Contribution to Medicine

- - - - - - - - - - - - - - - - - - - -

NAME: Kathleen Stuart Strehlow LFIBA

ADDRESS: 30 Da Costa Avenue
Prospect
SA 5082
Australia

OCCUPATION: Research Director

YEAR OF ENTRY: 1986

CITATION: For your Outstanding Contribution to Education

- - - - - - - - - - - - - - - - - - - -

NAME: Dr Srikanta M N Swamy LFIBA DDG IOM

ADDRESS: H961-49
Concordia University, Montreal
Quebec H3G 1M8
Canada

OCCUPATION: Electrical Engineer

YEAR OF ENTRY: 1986

CITATION: For your Outstanding Contribution to Engineering

- - - - - - - - - - - - - - - - - -

NAME: M R Wiemann LPIBA LFWLA DDG IOM MOIF

ADDRESS: 418 South 9th Street
PO Box 1016
Chesterton
IN 46304
USA

OCCUPATION: Biologist, Microscopist

YEAR OF ENTRY: 1991

CITATION: For your Outstanding Contribution to Theoretical and
Applied Biology

- - - - - - - - - - - - - - - - - -

NAME: Dr Azi Wolfenson U PhD LPIBA DDG

ADDRESS: 3781 NE 208 Terr
N Miami Beach
FL 33180
USA

OCCUPATION: Engineer

YEAR OF ENTRY: 1986

CITATION: For your Outstanding Contribution to Engineering and
Development

- - - - - - - - - - - - - - - - - -

NAME: Professor Dr Ken-ichi Yoshihara LPIBA DDG IOM MOIF AdVAh

ADDRESS: 2-9-26 Yamanone
Zushi
Kanagawa 249-0002
Japan

OCCUPATION: Professor of Engineering

YEAR OF ENTRY: 1988

CITATION: For your Outstanding Contribution to Mathematical Statistics

- - - - - - - - - - - - - - - - - - - -

NAME: Professor Zhang Shi-ding LFIBA IOM

ADDRESS: 1911-43-401 Caobao Road
Shanghai 201101
China

OCCUPATION: Teacher

YEAR OF ENTRY: 1991

CITATION: For your Outstanding Contribution to Education

21st CENTURY HONOURS LIST

NAME: Dorothy W. Bertine

ADDRESS: PO Box 2965
Denton
TX 76202
USA

OCCUPATION: Artist, Writer and Teacher

YEAR OF ENTRY: 2005

CITATION: For your Outstanding Contribution to Art and Teaching

- -

NAME: Dr John Julius Biesele

ADDRESS: 2500 Great Oats Parkway
Austin
TX 78756-2908
USA

OCCUPATION: Professor Emeritus

YEAR OF ENTRY: 2008

CITATION: For your Outstanding Contribution to Cell Biology

- -

NAME: Lady of Soul Eleonore Hajdar Bregu

ADDRESS: Holy Mission Eleonore
Ru. "Komuna e Parisit" #4
PO Box 7435
Tirana
Albania

OCCUPATION: Missionary

YEAR OF ENTRY: 2006

CITATION: For your Outstanding Contribution to Improving Life

- -

NAME: Daniel D Brunda DDG LPIBA MOIF IOM
AdVSci DO

ADDRESS: 106 West Upper Ferry Road
Ewing
NJ 08628
USA

OCCUPATION: Consultant: Mechanical/Electromagnetic Powerline
Radiation/Engineer/Scientist

YEAR OF ENTRY: 2002

CITATION: For your Outstanding Contribution to the Design and
Control of Electrical Transmission, Distribution and
Service Lines

- -

NAME: Dr Barry Lloyd Chapman

ADDRESS: 31 Elbrook Drive
Rankin Park
NSW 2287
Australia

OCCUPATION: Consultant Cardiologist (Retired)

YEAR OF ENTRY: 2006

CITATION: For your Outstanding Contribution to Medical
Research, Teaching and Treatment

- -

NAME: Dr C Juliana Ching LPIBA DDG IOM MOIF
AdVBus DO HonDG

ADDRESS: 4 Mount Butler Drive
Jardine's Lookout
Hong Kong

OCCUPATION: Businesswoman

YEAR OF ENTRY: 2000

CITATION: For your Outstanding Contribution to Business &
Medicine

- -

NAME: Christodoulos Christodoulou

ADDRESS: Central Bank of Cyprus
80 Kennedy Avenue
1076 Nicosia
Cyprus

OCCUPATION: Governor of Central Bank of Cyprus

YEAR OF ENTRY: 2006

CITATION: For your Outstanding Contribution to Central Banking

- -

NAME: Dr Miss Sara Ciampi

ADDRESS: Via San Fruttuoso 7/4
16143 Genova
Italy

OCCUPATION: Writer

YEAR OF ENTRY: 2006

CITATION: For your Outstanding Contribution to Literature and
Philosophy

- -

NAME: Donald Mercer Cormie LLM. Q.C. IOM

ADDRESS: 9369 Rockwood Drive
Scottsdale
AZ 85255-9255
USA

OCCUPATION: Barrister

YEAR OF ENTRY: 2001

CITATION: For your Outstanding Contribution to Law

- -

NAME: Sandra Lynn Daves LFIBA

ADDRESS: 6825 Susanna Ct
Citrus Hts
CA 95621
USA

OCCUPATION: Poet Laureate and Lyricist

YEAR OF ENTRY: 2006

CITATION: For your Outstanding Contribution to Poetry and Music

- -

NAME: Dr Tarun Kumar De, Scientific (H) VECC DAE

ADDRESS: 22a Motilal Nehru Road
Calcutta
700029
India

OCCUPATION: Scientist, Engineer & Researcher

YEAR OF ENTRY: 2000

CITATION: For your Outstanding Contribution to Engineering
Research

- -

NAME: Joan E Hirsh Emma

ADDRESS: 23 Pheasant Lane
E Setauket
NY 11733
USA

OCCUPATION: Teacher, Writer

YEAR OF ENTRY: 2000

CITATION: For your Outstanding Contribution to College Teaching
and Manuscript Development

- -

NAME: Professor Dr James M Fragomeni Ph.D. LFIBA
MOIF AdVSci HonDG IOM

ADDRESS: 25105 Biarritz Circle, #C
Oak Park
MI 48237-4021
USA

OCCUPATION: Educator and Researcher

YEAR OF ENTRY: 2006

CITATION: For your Outstanding Contribution to Mechanical
Engineering and Engineering Education

- -

NAME: Bruce Alan Grindley LFIBA

ADDRESS: Tenerife Property Shop S.L.
117 Puerto Colon
Playa De Las Americas, Adeje, Tenerife
Canary Islands
Spain

OCCUPATION: Estate Agent

YEAR OF ENTRY: 2001

CITATION: For your Outstanding Contribution to International
Business Integrity in Property Conveyancing

- -

NAME: Rev Dr Prof Tzu-Yang Hwang LPIBA AdVAh AIOM

ADDRESS: 11768 Roseglen Street
El Monte
CA 91732
USA

OCCUPATION: Supreme Grand Master; Chair; CEO; Chancellor

YEAR OF ENTRY: 2008

CITATION: For your Outstanding Contribution to Multi-Religio-
Philo-Cultu-Theo-Arts-Educa

- -

NAME: Neil Herman Jacoby Jr LPIBA IOM AdVSci CH
DO DDG

ADDRESS: 1434 Midvale Avenue
Los Angeles
CA 90024
USA

OCCUPATION: Astrodynamic Scientist

YEAR OF ENTRY: 2000

CITATION: For your Outstanding Contribution to Astrodynamics

- - - - - - - - - - - - - - - - - - - -

NAME: Dr Tien-Ming Jen MD

ADDRESS: Clinical Mycology Study
No 24-5 3rd Floor
Lane 24 Kinmen Road
Taipei 100-17
Taiwan ROC

OCCUPATION: Educator, Consultant and Physician

YEAR OF ENTRY: 2002

CITATION: For your Outstanding Contribution to Medical Research

- - - - - - - - - - - - - - - - - - - -

NAME: Dr Nella Kacergiene MOIF DDG FIBA

ADDRESS: Virsuliskiu 89-22
Vilnius
LT-2056
Lithuania

OCCUPATION: Physician, Paediatrician

YEAR OF ENTRY: 2000

CITATION: For your Outstanding Contribution to Paediatrics and
Human Ecology

- - - - - - - - - - - - - - - - - - - -

NAME: Tetsuo Kaneko LPIBA DDG AdVSci IOM

ADDRESS: Kogane Kazusacho 16-1
Matsudo-shi
270-0015
Japan

OCCUPATION: Physicist

YEAR OF ENTRY: 2000

CITATION: For your Outstanding Contribution to Scientific
Research

- -

NAME: Dr Khoo Boo-Chai AdVMed DDG IOM MOIF

ADDRESS: Parkway Parade Medical Centre # 05-12
80 Marine Parade
Singapore 449269

OCCUPATION: Medical Doctor

YEAR OF ENTRY: 2001

CITATION: For your Outstanding Contribution to Reconstructive
Plastic Surgery

- -

NAME: Prof Kwang Seog Kim LFIBA MOIF HonDG

ADDRESS: Dept of Plastic & Recon. Surgery
Chonnam Nat Univ Medical School
8 Hak-dong
Dong-gu Gwangju
501-757 Korea

OCCUPATION: Plastic and Reconstructive Surgeon, Biomedical
Researcher and Educator

YEAR OF ENTRY: 2005

CITATION: For your Outstanding Contribution to Plastic Reconstructive
Surgery, Biomedical Research and Education

- -

NAME: Dr Kyoung Soo Kim LPIBA IOM MOIF HonDG
DDG AdVSci

ADDRESS: Chirogenix Co Ltd
801 Kowoon Inst of Tech Innovation, Suwon Univ
Whasung City, Kyunggi-do 445-743
Korea

OCCUPATION: Researcher, CEO

YEAR OF ENTRY: 2006

CITATION: For your Outstanding Contribution to Medicinal Chemistry

- -

NAME: Professor Pill Soo Kim LPIBA DDG IOM AdVSci CH

ADDRESS: Dept of Automotive Engineering
Daelim College
526-9 Bisan-dong, Dongan-ku
Anyang-si. Kyunggi-do
431-715 Korea

OCCUPATION: Professor

YEAR OF ENTRY: 2001

CITATION: For your Outstanding Contribution to Engineering

- -

NAME: Mr Masashi Kimura MOIF DDG IOM DO HonDG
AdVSci

ADDRESS: Dept of Molecular Pathobiochemistry
Gifu University School of Medicine
Yanagido 1-1
Gifu 501-1194
Japan

OCCUPATION: Researcher

YEAR OF ENTRY: 2005

CITATION: For your Outstanding Contribution to Cell Biology

- -

NAME:	Professor Eliezer I Klainman LPIBA IOM AdVMed DDG
ADDRESS:	86 Pardess-Meshutaf St Raanana Israel 43350
OCCUPATION:	Cardiologist
YEAR OF ENTRY:	2000
CITATION:	For your Outstanding Contribution to Cardiology

- -

NAME:	Dr Vladimir Kozlovskiy
ADDRESS:	14478 Potsdam Saarmunder Str. 85 Germany
OCCUPATION:	Technical Physics
YEAR OF ENTRY:	2008
CITATION:	For your Outstanding Contribution to Physics of Dielectric Crystals

- -

NAME:	Professor Distinguished Soji Kurimoto IOM AdVMed DDG
ADDRESS:	Asthma Institute 1-17 Tamondori-2 chome Chuoku, Kobe 650 Japan
OCCUPATION:	Physician
YEAR OF ENTRY:	2000
CITATION:	For your Outstanding Contribution to Education and Professional Training in Medicine

- -

NAME: Professor Chul Lee IOM

ADDRESS: Department of Chemistry
Hanyang University
133-791 Seoul
Korea

OCCUPATION: Professor

YEAR OF ENTRY: 2000

CITATION: For your Outstanding Contribution to Chemistry

- -

NAME: Dr.-Ing. Paul Ih-Fei Liu

ADDRESS: 1715 Oak Street
Santa Monica
CA 90405
USA

OCCUPATION: Engineer, Educator and Writer

YEAR OF ENTRY: 2006

CITATION: For your Outstanding Contribution to Engineering
Education

- -

NAME: Associate Professor Cornelis A Los

ADDRESS: Block B Nanyang Avenue
10-04 Singapore
639611
Singapore

OCCUPATION: Economist

YEAR OF ENTRY: 2000

CITATION: For your Outstanding Contribution to Financial
Economics

- -

NAME: The Revd Prof. John Warwick Montgomery, Ph.D., D.Théol., LL.D.

ADDRESS: 55 rue de Rountzenheim
67620 Soufflenheim
France

OCCUPATION: Christian Apologetics

YEAR OF ENTRY: 2006

CITATION: For your Outstanding Contribution to The International Law of Human Rights

- -

NAME: Dr Ivka Maria Munda AdVSci DDG

ADDRESS: Centre for Scientific Research
Slovene Academy of Science & Arts
Novi trg 2
1000 Ljubljana
Slovenia

OCCUPATION: Marine Biologist, Phycologist

YEAR OF ENTRY: 2002

CITATION: For your Outstanding Contribution to Marine Biology

- -

NAME: Dr Tadeusz K Murawski DDG MOIF LFIBA IOM

ADDRESS: ul. Szkoly Orlat 4
Apt 59
03-984 Warsaw
Poland

OCCUPATION: Economist

YEAR OF ENTRY: 2001

CITATION: For your Outstanding Contribution to Environmental Economics

- -

NAME: Dr Shoichi Nakakuki

ADDRESS: 281-2 Oosonoki
Shimotsuma-city
Ibaraki
304-0801
Japan

OCCUPATION: Researcher and Educator

YEAR OF ENTRY: 2006

CITATION: For your Outstanding Contribution to Comparative
Anatomy and Veterinary Medicine

- -

NAME: Professor Shiro Nii, MD, PhD

ADDRESS: Famir Okayama 206
Hama 372-1
Okayama 703-8256
Japan

OCCUPATION: Researcher and Educator

YEAR OF ENTRY: 2005

CITATION: For your Outstanding Contribution to Research and
Education

- -

NAME: Dr Tanya Niyamapa

ADDRESS: Agricultural Machinery & Management
Dept of Agricultural Eng
Kasetsart Univ Kampaeng Saen
Campus Nakornpathom 73140
Thailand

OCCUPATION: Agricultural Engineer

YEAR OF ENTRY: 2000

CITATION: For your Outstanding Contribution to Agricultural
Engineering

- -

NAME:	Dr Takashi Oguchi DDG IOM DO HonDG AdVSci MOIF
ADDRESS:	Center for Spatial Info Science Univ of Tokyo 5-1-5 Kashiwanoha Kashiwa 277-8568 Japan
OCCUPATION:	Scientist and Educator
YEAR OF ENTRY:	2006
CITATION:	For your Outstanding Contribution to Geomorphology and Geography

- -

NAME:	Joyce A. Oliver IOM
ADDRESS:	904 Silver Spur Rd Suite 449 Rolling Hills Estate CA 90274 USA
OCCUPATION:	Author/Journalist
YEAR OF ENTRY:	2001
CITATION:	For your Outstanding Contribution to Commercial Journalism

- -

NAME:	Eugene T Ouzts LFIBA
ADDRESS:	739E Cottonwood Road Duncan AZ 85534-8108 USA
OCCUPATION:	Minister
YEAR OF ENTRY:	2001
CITATION:	For your Outstanding Contribution to Education and Religion

- -

NAME: Dr Roland Peter

ADDRESS: Schwesternweg 11/74
A-5020 Salzburg
Austria

OCCUPATION: Biologist, Educator

YEAR OF ENTRY: 2001

CITATION: For your Outstanding Contribution to Biology, Science and Education

- -

NAME: Thresia Pierce LFIBA DDG AdVAh

ADDRESS: 1600 So. Valley View Blvd
Bldg 6, Apt 1106
Las Vegas
NV 89102
USA

OCCUPATION: Teacher

YEAR OF ENTRY: 2001

CITATION: For your Outstanding Contribution to Teaching and Writing

- -

NAME: Professor Dr Desider A Pragay FIBA IOM

ADDRESS: C/O Dr G Roland
Hauzenberger Strasse 13
D 80687 Munchen
Germany

OCCUPATION: Scientist

YEAR OF ENTRY: 2001

CITATION: For your Outstanding Contribution to Biochemistry and Education

- -

NAME: Professor Naseem Rahman

ADDRESS: Department of Chemistry
University of Trieste
Via Giorgieri No 1
34100 Trieste
Italy

OCCUPATION: Professor

YEAR OF ENTRY: 2001

CITATION: For your Outstanding Contribution to Chemistry

- - - - - - - - - - - - - - - - - - - -

NAME: Luis B Rosario MD, FESC

ADDRESS: R Quinta Grande 8 r/c
2780-156 Oeiras
Portugal

OCCUPATION: Physician

YEAR OF ENTRY: 2001

CITATION: For your Outstanding Contribution to Cardiology

- - - - - - - - - - - - - - - - - - - -

NAME: Honorable Dr Kazuo Sato DDG

ADDRESS: 3-11-21 Yabe
Sagamihara-shi
Kanagawa-ken 229-0032
Japan

OCCUPATION: University Professor

YEAR OF ENTRY: 2001

CITATION: For your Outstanding Contribution to Engineering

- - - - - - - - - - - - - - - - - - - -

NAME: Dr Mika Sato-Ilic

ADDRESS: Institute of Policy & Planning Sciences
University of Tsukuba
Tenodai 1-1-1
Tsukuba, Ibaraki 305-8573
Japan

OCCUPATION: Assistant Professor

YEAR OF ENTRY: 2000

CITATION: For your Outstanding Contribution to Engineering

- - - - - - - - - - - - - - - - - -

NAME: Count Hans C von Seherr-Thoss LFIBA AdVSci DO

ADDRESS: Habichtstr 39
D 82008 Unterhaching
Germany

OCCUPATION: Mechanical Engineer

YEAR OF ENTRY: 2000

CITATION: For your Outstanding Contribution to Mechanical
Engineering

- - - - - - - - - - - - - - - - - - - -

NAME: Dr Ingeborg Hildegard Solbrig

ADDRESS: 1126 Pine Street
Iowa City
IA 52240
USA

OCCUPATION: Educator

YEAR OF ENTRY: 2004

CITATION: For your Outstanding Contribution to Writing,
Education and Research

- - - - - - - - - - - - - - - - - - -

NAME: Mary Goldacre Spencer

ADDRESS: Tenerife Property Shop SL
117 Puerto Colon
Playas De Las Americas
Adeje Tenerife
Canary Islands, Spain

OCCUPATION: Real Estate Agent

YEAR OF ENTRY: 2001

CITATION: For your Outstanding Contribution to International
Business Integrity

- -

NAME: Professor Dr Andy Sun IOM MOIF LPIBA DDG
CH AdVMed HonDG

ADDRESS: National Taiwan University Hospital
Taipei
Taiwan
Republic of China

OCCUPATION: Immunologist

YEAR OF ENTRY: 2001

CITATION: For your Outstanding Contribution to Immunology and
Medical Science

- -

NAME: Dr Manfred Thiel IOM LPIBA DDG MOIF
AAAS CH DO

ADDRESS: Rohrbacherstr 20
69115 Heidelberg
Germany

OCCUPATION: Philosopher, Poet

YEAR OF ENTRY: 2000

CITATION: For your Outstanding Contribution to Philosophy and
Poetry

- -

NAME: Captain Dr Ivica Tijardović DDG LFIBA MOIF IOM HonDG AdVSci

ADDRESS: Nazorov Prilaz 37
Split 21000
Croatia

OCCUPATION: Shipmaster and Scientist

YEAR OF ENTRY: 2006

CITATION: For your Outstanding Contribution to Maritime Navigation

- -

NAME: J E Vander Naald LFIBA DDG IOM

ADDRESS: 44 Darby Creek Ct.
Bluffton
SC 29909-6222
USA

OCCUPATION: Educator

YEAR OF ENTRY: 2000

CITATION: For your Outstanding Contribution to Education

- -

NAME: Dr Ruslana Vernickaite DDG LFIBA IOM

ADDRESS: Rambyno 7-5
LT-93173 Klaipeda
Lithuania

OCCUPATION: Physician, Obstetrician-Gynaeologist

YEAR OF ENTRY: 2000

CITATION: For your Outstanding Contribution to Obstetrics, Gynaecology and Ecology

- -

NAME: Dr Veniamin Volkov MD

ADDRESS: Rileeva Str. 11/3
St. Petersburg 191014
Russia

OCCUPATION: Ophthalmosurgeon

YEAR OF ENTRY: 2006

CITATION: For your Outstanding Contribution to Ophthalmology

- -

NAME: Professor Hugo Walter

ADDRESS: 157 Loomis Court
Princeton
NJ 08540
USA

OCCUPATION: College Professor

YEAR OF ENTRY: 2000

CITATION: For your Outstanding Contribution to Humanities and
Poetry

- -

NAME: Lt Gen John MacNair Wright, Jr

ADDRESS: 21227 George Brown Avenue
Riverside
CA 92518-2881
USA

OCCUPATION: Lieutenant General, U.S.Army (Retired)

YEAR OF ENTRY: 2002

CITATION: For your Outstanding Contribution to the Military

- -

NAME: Dr Xiaoping Xiong

ADDRESS: 5322 McKans Cove
Memphis
TN 38120
USA

OCCUPATION: Researcher and Statistician

YEAR OF ENTRY: 2006

CITATION: For your Outstanding Contribution to Research in
Statistics and it's Applications

- -

NAME: Professor Masayoshi Yamaguchi IOM DDG

ADDRESS: Senagawa 1-chome 15-5, Aoi-ku
Shizuoka City 420-0913
Japan

OCCUPATION: University Professor

YEAR OF ENTRY: 2005

CITATION: For your Outstanding Contribution to Life Sciences

- -

NAME: Professor Michiru Yasuhara LFIBA IOM AdVSci

ADDRESS: 34-18 Neura Iwasaki
Nissin-city
Aichi 470-0131
Japan

OCCUPATION: Professor

YEAR OF ENTRY: 2000

CITATION: For your Outstanding Contribution to Education

- -

NAME: Dr Vak Yeong Yoo MOIF DDG LPIBA AdVMed
IOM DO HonDG

ADDRESS: Cheong-Vak Antiaging Hospital
582 Shinsa Dong Kangnam Gu
Seoul 135-892
Korea

OCCUPATION: Physician

YEAR OF ENTRY: 2001

CITATION: For your Outstanding Contribution to Medicine

- -

NAME.

ADDRESS.

OCCUPATION.

YEAR OF ENTRY.

CITATION.

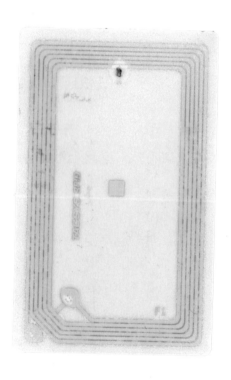